| High Performance |
| Elegance |
| Simplicity |
| Expandability |

GREAT SOUND WITH STYLE AND SIMPLICITY: BOSE® LIFESTYLE

Integrated System Design

At Bose®, we believe in building complete systems – playback, amplification and speakers, all designed to work together beautifully. Only by doing this can we give you home entertainment systems that perform to the peak of their ability with the minimum of effort from you, look elegant everywhere from traditional homes to hi-tech lofts, and offer you the opportunity to expand and develop them to suit your growing entertainment needs.

It's called Integrated System Design. Whilst some audio enthusiasts spend time and effort choosing separate components to give optimum performance, often ending up with systems that lack visual appeal and sacrificing ease of use, we build our systems to work harmoniously delivering total home entertainment. What's more they do so without filling your home with equipment or requiring a training course to operate them: even our range-topping systems comprise just a slim, elegant control centre and a package of speakers so compact that it all but vanishes in your room.

But this doesn't mean sacrificing quality or upgradability: we design our products to work together. We know how our loudspeakers perform, so can build playback and control electronics to make the most of them. And whether you want some extra speakers in another room or a complete integrated whole-house entertainment system, we have the technology to give you just what you want.

Better sound through research®

Music the way you want it where you want it

WHETHER YOU WANT TO BE CALMED DOWN OR ENERGISED, uMusic™ LEARNS THE WAY YOU WANT TO LISTEN, AND SELECTS THE MUSIC FOR YOUR MOOD

uMusic™: the intelligent storage system that thinks like you do

The idea of the music server has taken home entertainment by storm, allowing you to store your entire CD collection in one place, ready for instant playback. Bose® takes this idea one step further with uMusic™, available on the flagship Bose® LIFESTYLE® 38 and 48 DVD Home Entertainment systems: an intelligent playback concept that learns the way you listen, and adjusts the music choice accordingly.

It's like having your own radio station, playing exactly what you want to hear, on hand all day, every day. The system can store up to 350 CDs on a hard disc in its media centre, creating a library you can access by album, by composer, or even by genre. Fancy an evening of opera or chamber music? You select the category, and the system delivers.

But then the really clever stuff begins. When you play music from the system, you're not the only one listening. uMusic™ is

monitoring your selections too, learning the sequences of music you enjoy, even checking what you choose at different times of day, so that when you just want to relax and listen to a selection from your library, it's ready to put together a programme to suit your mood. And it can do the same for several users.

What's more, uMusic™ keeps on learning: it will suggest pieces you may not have listened to for a while, allowing you to tell it whether or not you agree with its choices, and further refining the sequences of music it presents. And it learns the music you like to listen to most, building that into its repertoire.

uMusic™ is exclusive to Bose®, and will create a music library that's unique to you: listening to your CD collection may never be the same again.

The latest Bose® systems go beyond simply playing music and DVDs: now they can program your music collection to suit your mood, and deliver it wherever you want to listen

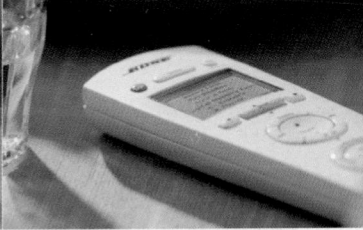

Bose® link: your music, where you want it

We don't listen to music in one room: most households have radios or secondary systems scattered around the place to provide entertainment where it's needed. With Bose® link, available on all of our LIFESTYLE® systems and the latest Wave and 3•2•1 models, you can connect up your whole home, allowing you to access the music and entertainment you want, where you want it. What's more, you're not limited to the same music everywhere in the house: two 'zones' or groups of rooms can be programmed, and each can receive something different. That means you could be listening to CD in the main room while the radio plays in the kitchen or bathroom or wherever; and with one of the uMusic™ equipped systems you can access different music from the hard drive server in each zone.

At its simplest, Bose® link comprises an amplifier and a pair of speakers in a second room, connected using a special cable and 'driven' using a system remote handset. This lets you access your main system from the second zone, and you can add to it to extend the system.

Beyond that, Bose® systems can be linked together using Bose® link, so you could have a LIFESTYLE® 38 or 48 in your main room and a 3•2•1 or WAVE® system in other rooms, using the smaller systems to access all the content stored on the main system. Suddenly you have a complete integrated system around the home – you can even have Bose® Environmental Speakers out in the garden for long summer evenings.

Bose® link is so simple that you can easily install and configure it yourself, adding to it as your budget allows and your requirements change. Or of course your local Bose authorised dealer will be able to advise you.

Better sound through research.

The new WAVE® in home entertainment

The brand new WAVE® Music System and WAVE® Radio II: now with Bose® link and even better sound

The WAVE® range of products have long been some of the most iconic Bose® models, defying the idea that you need a big, cumbersome system with separate speakers to enjoy fine stereo sound. Now the latest WAVE® models – the new-generation WAVE® Radio and WAVE® Music System – are even better, with an enhanced version of the proprietary technology that allows them to create a big, rich sound from a compact enclosure, and Bose® link to allow them to integrate with a home-wide Bose® system to access your music wherever you want.

The original WAVE® Radio has been refined, making it the perfect choice for bedrooms, kitchens – in fact anywhere you need great sound from the radio in a compact package. With FM/AM reception, alarm facilities and a simple credit card remote control, it's easy to use, and that WAVE® technology, using folded chambers behind the loudspeakers to enhance the bass, means you get a big, powerful sound from a unit just 36cm wide and a little over 10cm tall. In fact, the latest WAVE® Radio has half an octave more bass extension than the original model, and the provision of Bose® link technology means you could even use it to listen to music stored on your main LIFESTYLE® system. Imagine being able to take your entire music collection to bed with you!

But the real star is the new WAVE® Music System: it's the same size as the WAVE® Radio II, but it adds CD playback – even handling CDs you burn with MP3 files stored on your computer or downloaded from the internet – and an auxiliary input, for example allowing you to improve the sound of your kitchen or study TV set with the Bose® 'WAVE® guide' speaker technology. Just as in the WAVE® Radio, here the improved version of this proprietary

design gives even greater bass extension – it's hard to believe such a big sound is coming from so small a unit – while further Bose® technology expands the sense of stereo the system develops.

The CD player has slot-loading to keep things compact, there are six presets each for FM and AM radio, a gentle ramp up of sound levels to wake you up without the nasty shocks, and Bose® link to let the WAVE® Music System integrate with the rest of your entertainment set-up.

And best of all the system is simplicity itself to use: the main unit has no controls whatsoever, and everything's to hand with that compact credit card remote handset. With the original WAVE® Radio, Bose® redefined the way we thought about compact music systems; the latest WAVE® models take that thinking to a new level.

GREAT MUSIC AT THE TOUCH OF A BUTTON, AND A BIG SOUND FROM A VERY COMPACT ENCLOSURE: THE NEW WAVE® MUSIC SYSTEM AND RADIO FROM BOSE

Better sound through research.

Music for the individual

DOCK YOUR POD FOR A BIG, RICH SOUND: THE NEW SoundDock™ TURNS THE APPLE iPOD INTO A COMPLETE HOME MUSIC SYSTEM – AND IT'LL EVEN CHARGE YOUR PLAYER!

SoundDock™: Making the most of today's digital music systems

The way we listen has undergone a massive revolution with the arrival of the iPod® and MP3-based music devices. Now you can pack your entire music collection onto one easily portable device, or download new music from the internet for playback on your home computer or when you're out and about.

Bose® has long been a leader in technology, so it's no surprise that it's leading the way when it comes to making the most of these new music formats. From headphones to let you listen to your music at its best, even in noisy environments, to computer and personal music speaker systems, it has something to appeal to everyone. Now, with the arrival of the SoundDock™ digital music system for the Apple® iPod® range, Bose is able to offer you the simplest way to turn personal music into music you can share with your friends.

The SoundDock™ is easy: as the name suggests, you just dock your iPod® or iPod® Mini into the slot provided on the front, and it's then connected to the speakers built into the unit, recharging as you play your music. There's a 'credit card' infrared remote control to control the sound and basic functions of the iPod®, and of course the SoundDock™ uses proprietary Bose® amplification and speaker technology to make the most of your music.

Active electronic equalisation combines with optimised bass reflex port design to give a big, powerful stereo sound from a unit that stands just 16cm tall and a little over 30cm wide, while digital signal processing automatically adjusts the bass and treble to give a vibrant sound whether you're playing at low volumes or making the most of the high levels the SoundDock™ can deliver, while avoiding compression effects even when you're playing it loud.

Perfect Companions™
for computer music

And if you don't have an iPod®, or if you just want to listen to music stored on your computer? That's where the Bose® Companion speakers come in, offering a choice of solutions for connection to your home computer, or even to the audio output of other personal players.

The Companion™ 2 is a conventional-looking stereo multimedia speaker system that packs a mighty punch, thanks to ported cabinets and unified development of speaker drive units and amplification. The mains-powered speakers combine active electronic equalisation and digital signal processing to make the most of the sound, while proprietary TrueSpace™ processing creates an open, expansive stereo sound even when the speakers are used either side of a computer monitor. Oh, and the speakers are magnetically shielded so you can use them close to your computer without affecting the monitor!

One step beyond the Companion 2, the Companion 3 system offers the perfect solution for music from the computer, or for boosting the sound from personal music players. It uses the same signal processing as the Companion 2, but splits the speakers into a pair of truly tiny satellites, under 9cm tall and just over 6.5cm wide, and a powerful subwoofer module using the famous Bose® Acoustimass® bass technology. If you want a big, big sound, this is the perfect choice.

Your personal music player or computer output plugs into a sleek circular controller – just turn its outer ring to change the volume, or push to mute it – and with just that and the little satellites on your desk, with the Acoustimass module hidden away, you have a truly magical music system that takes up minimal space and yet delivers maximum performance.

Better Sound everywhere

WANT TO SHUT OUT THE
WORLD? BOSE TRIPORT®
HEADPHONES BRING YOU
THE FINEST SOUND

Perfect Performance
wherever you choose to listen

There's much more to Bose® than just speakers and systems for home use, but the company's continuous investment in research and development in one field often finds applications in another. That's why you'll find Bose® headphones in use by airline pilots, Bose® speakers in use in sound reinforcement systems in concert halls, arenas, clubs and other locations around the world, and Bose® systems offered either as standard or a premium option in some of the most luxurious cars on the road.

From the company's innovative WAVE® Radio and CD players, designed to give big-system sound from a compact table top product through clever use of bass-enhancing Wave® guide labyrinths within their casework, right through to whole-house music systems and PA speakers, Bose® technology is everywhere.

Slip behind the wheel of a top Audi, Cadillac or Mercedes, or splash out on vehicles as diverse as the Porsche 911 Turbo or the massive Hummer SUV, and the chances are you'll be listening to a Bose® sound system, fitted at the factory as standard equipment.

And you can even enjoy the fruits of Bose® research for your personal listening: the company's QuietComfort headphones draw on the technology developed for pilots' noise cancelling headsets – vital for safety – to ensure those down the back of the plane can enjoy their music or movie soundtracks in peace, too.

Using Acoustic Noise Cancelling®, the QuietComfort® headphones monitor the noise inside the headphone enclosure with microphones, then apply electronic processing to correct the difference between the input signal and what's being heard. This combines with the company's Tri-Port® design, a further passive system to reduce the intrusion of external noise, to create a design that can block aircraft engines or the rumble of a train. And being battery powered, the QuietComfort® headphones can be used with a personal music player as easily as they can be plugged into an airliner's entertainment system.

That's just another example of Bose® design and technology in action – and it's all about bringing you the best possible sound, wherever you are.

BOSE

Better sound through research.

INTRODUCTION

O ur partners, once again, in publishing *The Gramophone Classical Good CD & DVD Guide* are Bose, whose dedication to producing fine audio equipment closely matches the ideals of *Gramophone* itself: the nourishment of expertise based on experience, consistency and an awareness of the needs of the enthusiast for great music and great sound.

The Gramophone Classical Good CD & DVD Guide is designed to eliminate the confusion of record-buying and unite you, quickly and painlessly, with the best in classical music on disc. Drawing on the expertise of the magazine's own 1000-issue-long history and an unequalled panel of critics, *The Classical Good CD & DVD Guide* will, we are sure, become a trusted friend as you build your music collection.

Published by haymarket consumer

**38-42 Hampton Road
Teddington
Middlesex TW11 0JE
Great Britain**

EDITOR	David Roberts
EDITORIAL CONSULTANT	James Jolly
PRODUCTION EDITOR	John Bryant
ART EDITOR	Susana de Dios
DESIGNER	Sharon O'Connor
PRODUCTION MANAGER	Yuki Haly
PUBLISHING DIRECTOR	Nicole LeVesconte
PUBLISHER	Simon Temlett
PUBLISHING MANAGER	Madeleine Milne
CIRCULATION CO-ORDINATOR	Sandy Davies
COMMERCIAL MANAGER	John Burke
FINANCE DIRECTOR	Brian Freeman
GROUP DESIGN DIRECTOR	Paul Harpin
GROUP EDITORIAL DIRECTOR	Mel Nichols
MANAGING DIRECTOR	Kevin Costello
GROUP CHAIRMAN	Eric Verdon-Roe

© **haymarket consumer 2005**
ISBN 0-860-24972-7 (UK)
GG20060 (USA)

ACKNOWLEDGEMENT

Material from **GROVE**music reproduced from
The Concise Grove Dictionary of Music
under licence from Oxford
University Press, New York, USA

SALES AND DISTRIBUTION

North America
Music Sales Corporation
257 Park Avenue South
New York, NY 10010 USA
Telephone (212) 254 2100 **Fax** (212) 254 2013

UK and Rest of World
haymarket consumer
38-42 Hampton Road
Teddington, Middlesex TW 11 0JE
Great Britain
Telephone +44 (0)20 8267 5140 **Fax** +44 (0)20 8267 5844
e-mail goodcdguide@haynet.com

Printed in England by
William Clowes Limited, Beccles, Suffolk

CONTRIBUTORS

Andrew Achenbach
Nicholas Anderson
Mary Berry
Alan Blyth
Joan Chissell
Robert Cowan
Peter Dickinson
Duncan Druce
John Duarte
Adrian Edwards
Richard T Fairman
David Fallows
David J Fanning
Andrew Farach-Colton
Iain Fenlon
Hilary Finch
Fabrice Fitch
Jonathan Freeman-Attwood
Edward Greenfield
David S Gutman
Martyn Harry
Stephen Johnson
James Jolly
Lindsay Kemp
Tess Knighton
Andrew Lamb
Richard Lawrence
Robert Layton
Ivan March
Ivan Moody
Bryce Morrison
Patrick O'Connor
Michael Oliver
Richard Osborne
Tim Parry
Stephen Plaistow
Peter Quantrill
Nicholas Rast
Guy Rickards
Marc Rochester
Julie-Anne Sadie
Stanley Sadie
Lionel Salter
Alan Sanders
Michael Scott Rohan
Edward Seckerson
Robert Seeley
John Steane
Michael Stewart
Jonathan Swain
David Vickers
John Warrack
Richard Whitehouse
Arnold Whittall
Richard Wigmore
Barry Witherden
William Yeoman

CONTENTS

THE CLASSICAL
GOOD
CD & DVD
GUIDE
2006

FOREWORD

By James Jolly, Editor of *The Gramophone*

The year 2006 sees a number of major anniversaries: it's 100 years since the birth of Dmitri Shostakovich, arguably the 20th century's greatest symphonist, and it's 150 years since the death of Robert Schumann, one of the 19th century's archetypical Romantic composers. But the anniversary that will inevitably garner the most column inches, new recordings and festival themes is the 250th anniversary of the birth of Wolfgang Amadeus Mozart. Along with Johann Sebastian Bach and Ludwig van Beethoven, he forms a triumvirate of extraordinary creativity and sheer unrivalled genius. That he died a few months short of his 36th birthday is even more amazing – he left a legacy across more genres than either Bach (who wrote no operas) or Beethoven (who wrote one opera to Mozart's 21, five piano concertos to Mozart's 29, or two Masses to Mozart's 17). But this is not a contest: Mozart is Mozart and will be celebrated for his unique contribution to Western civilisation in a way that is sure to enrich anyone who encounters his music. This year, to mark Mozart Year, we asked David Vickers to respond to the question 'Why Mozart matters' and, in the company of Sir Charles Mackerras, Sir Colin Davis, Christopher Hogwood, Sir John Eliot Gardiner and Sir Roger Norrington, he makes a strong case for this remarkable man.

But classical music is a whole lot more than Mozart – or indeed Bach and Beethoven – and this edition of *The Classical Good CD & DVD Guide* makes that point dramatically. In its 1472 pages we recommend recording from seven centuries and across just about every style ever attempted. If it's 15th-century polyphony you're after, read on; if it's 19th-century Italian opera, this is the place to start; or if it's the best of today's music, we're here to help. And to give you some guidance we've five essays that tell the story of classical music across those seven centuries – and we recommended some key recordings of music from those periods to complete the story.

Classical music is something we at *The Gramophone* have been passionate about since 1923 when the vision of one man, the writer and broadcaster Compton Mackenzie, brought into existence a publication that has guided generations of music lovers to great recordings of fine music but also has been a companion in many a journey of discovery in the vast and often life-changing world of classical music.

The horizon has changed in ways that Mackenzie could never have imagined, but the last few years have seen its greatest transformation. The strength of the independent sector has seen works brought to disc that would never have seemed possible, but those small and tremendously dedicated companies have also introduced numerous musicians to a wider public, musicians whose careers have subsequently taken them around the world and into the leading concert halls and opera houses on every continent.

The interpretation of music is something that fascinates us at *The Gramophone*. How can two musicians approach the same piece of music, with the same score, and yet produce performances that sound so different? What do these different interpretations tell us about the music? Indeed, what do our individual responses tell us about ourselves? Following the recorded history of a particular work forms a regular feature of the magazine and here we distil those deliberations and hours of listening and comparison to give you, the record enthusiast, our considered opinions on what version(s) you should consider. We've attempted where possible to offer you a few alternatives, versions to suit different pockets or different expectations. Are you building a classical music collection on a tight budget, or are you intrigued and excited by what the musicians of a past Golden Age had to say? We hope we have identified and offered a recording to suit every taste and requirement.

The Gramophone's annual awards have become one of the barometers of the health of the classical record industry; an occasion awaited by record executives, musicians and music-lovers alike. Throughout the *Guide* we draw attention to those recordings that have won *Gramophone* Awards or gathered critical opinion down the years. We've introduced a Gramophone Star to draw attention to this group of outstanding recordings. On page XIV, we list those discs which have been awarded the ultimate accolade, the *Gramophone* Record of the Year Award, discs that invariably go on to achieve classic status – icons of the classical catalogue.

The classical music world is a place of tremendous energy and creativity, and generations of A&R executives and their artists have managed to fuse the often very different requirements of art and commerce. Great A&R means record sales, and record sales mean profits. It's a complex balancing act but one that leaves us – classical music lovers – as the beneficiaries. *The Classical Good CD & DVD Guide*, too, has a secondary role to play: as it catalogues nearly a century's worth of great music-making, it charts the trends and idiosyncracies of different musical approaches, but above all it celebrates the vast riches of the repertoire.

We are at the dawn of a new way of consuming music, downloaded to our PCs: to whet your appetite or simply to offer some beginner's guidance, we consider downloading on page VIII. However you acquire your music, I hope this guide will help you begin or continue to build a collection of outstanding recordings that will give you the pleasure it has given us at *The Gramophone* in auditioning them for you.

ARTISTS OF THE YEAR

Each year we ask the readers of The Gramophone to vote for our Artist
of the Year, which is presented as part of the Gramophone Awards.
For the Awards 2005 we proposed six artists who have all had an outstanding
musical year: here's that list with our suggested CD recommendations

Susan Graham
Mezzo-soprano

Whether it's Octavian in *Der Rosenkavalier* at the
Met, Idamante in *Idomeneo* in Houston, Sesto in
La clemenza di Tito in Paris or Donna Elvira in
Don Giovanni in Chicago, Susan Graham has
been entrancing audiences with her glorious
voice and winning personality the world over.
On DVD her Dido, in an outstanding performance of *Les troyens* under Sir John Eliot
Gardiner, captured many hearts, while a mixed
French collection – Chausson's heady *Poème de
l'amour et de la mer*, Ravel's *Shéhérazade* and four
of Debussy's Baudelaire settings in ravishing
orchestrations by John Adams – offered some of
the most sensuous singing for many months.
Susan Graham is a mezzo in her prime and an
artist of tremendous style.

Essential recordings
Berlioz Les nuits d'été *ROHO / Nelson*
Sony Classical – see page 154
Berlioz Les Troyens *Gardiner*
BBC Opus Arte – see page 1298
Chausson Poème de l'amour et de la mer
Ravel Shéhérazade *BBC SO / Tortelier*
Warner Classics – see page 272
Purcell Dido and Aeneas *Le Concert d'Astrée /
Haïm* Virgin Classics – see page 768
French operetta arias *CBSO / Abel*
Erato – see page 768

Marc-André Hamelin
Pianist

Is there nothing this man can't play? Another
busy series of Hyperion sessions leaves us with
a handful of pianistic riches. As a late entry for
the Ives anniversary, Hamelin gave us a splendid coupling of the fiendish *Concord* Sonata
and Barber's single Piano Sonata – and, despite
some magnificent interpretations of both
works already in the catalogue, neither of these
newcomers is to be overlooked. Then, a couple
of months ago, he sprung a wonderful surprise
– a two-disc set of Albéniz's kaleidoscopic

series of musical portraits of his native Spain,
Ibéria. As with everything Hamelin does, the
virtuoso demands were swept imperiously
aside but the poetry, the colour, the scents and
sounds of this amazing music emerged with
astounding richness and vibrancy.

Essential recordings
Albéniz Ibéria Hyperion – see page 10
Bernstein Symphony No 2, 'Age of Anxiety'
Bolcom Piano Concerto *Ulster Orchestra /
Sitkovetsky* Hyperion – see page 159
Busoni Piano Concerto *CBSO / Elder – see
page 252*
Godowsky 53 Studies on Chopin's Etudes
Hyperion – see page 406
Grainger Piano works Hyperion – see page
416
Barber. Ives Piano Sonatas Hyperion – see
page 518
Kapustin Piano Sonata etc Hyperion – see
page 530
Medtner Piano sonatas Hyperion – see page 619
Scriabin Piano sonatas Hyperion – see page 917

René Jacobs
Conductor

The 2005 Record of the Year, an astonishing
stripping away of years of varnish from
Mozart's *The Marriage of Figaro*, confirmed
René Jacobs's genius in 18th-century
dramatic literature. That was followed
this year by two equally revelatory discs of
Haydn: two symphonies and the powerful
Scena di Berenice with the glorious mezzo
Bernarda Fink, and a set of *The Seasons* that
brought Haydn's late masterpiece to life as
rarely before. Jacobs, whose early career
as a countertenor clearly gave him an uncommon sympathy for the vocal repertoire, has
that rare ability to galvanise his musicians to
performances of both individual virtuosity and
ensemble work of quite sublime unanimity. A
true musicians' musician, Jacobs has had a
truly magnificent year.

Essential recordings
Monteverdi Madrigals Book 8 *Concerto Vocale*
Harmonia Mundi – see page 644
Monteverdi Il ritorno d'Ulisse in Patria *Concerto Vocale* Harmonia Mundi – see page 646
Mozart La nozze di Figaro *Concerto Köln*
Harmonia Mundi – see page 686
Purcell Dido and Aeneas *Orchestra of the Age of Enlightenment* Harmonia Mundi – see page 767
A Scarlatti La Griselda *Akademie für Alte Musik, Berlin* Harmonia Mundi – see page 846
Telemann Orpheus *Akademie für Alte Musik, Berlin* Harmonia Mundi – see page 1041

Anne-Sophie Mutter
Violinist
Anne-Sophie Mutter made the transition from teenage prodigy to fully fledged virtuoso as effortlessly as she tosses off a Kreisler cadenza or a world premiere of fearsome complexity. This year found her coupling two Romantic violin concertos – the Korngold and the Tchaikovsky – with her husband André Previn once again proving a near-perfect accompanist. There is nothing predictable in anything Mutter does – each bar, each note has been minutely considered but in concert there is a winning spontaneity that willingly translates to disc. And then, earlier this year, came a recording of a new work, one that she has been waiting for since her teens – *Sur le même accord* by Henri Dutilleux. The range of volume and colour she draws from her violin are breathtaking.

Essential recordings
Berg Violin Concerto **Rihm** Gesungene Zeit
Chicago SO / Levine DG – see page 140
Bernstein Serenade **Previn** Violin Concerto
LSO, Boston SO / Previn DG – see page 739
Dutilleux Sur le même accord **Bartók** Violin Concerto No 1 **Stravinsky** Violin Concerto
FNO / Masur DG

Michael Tilson Thomas
Conductor, pianist & composer
Music-making on the US's West Coast has become something those on the East Coast must look at with envy. Michael Tilson Thomas joined the San Francsco Symphony as its music director back in 1995 and in the decade since has gathered around him a loyal audience who are prepared to be challenged and who respond to his inspired programming

policy. In the concert hall, MTT has been working his way through the Mahler symphonies, a journey that has been faithfully documented on the SFS's own record label. The results have been impressive indeed, revealing performances of intensity and, above all, exquisite orchestral work. The lasting impression of his recent Mahler Ninth is, in AF-C's words, one of 'lyrical radiance'.

Essential recordings
Copland Appalachian Spring. Billy the Kid. Rodeo *SFSO* RCA – see page 293
Mahler Symphony No 6 *SFSO* SFS Media – see page 593
Shostakovich Cello Concertos *Maisky; LSO* DG – see page 921
Stravinsky Circus Polka. Ode. Scherzo à la russe. Agon. Scènes de ballet *SFSO* RCA – see page 989
Stravinsky Firebird. The Rite of Spring. Perséphone *SFSO* SFS Media – see page 991
Villa-Lobos Bachianas brasileiras Nos 4, 5-7 & 9. Chôros No 10 *Fleming; New World SO* RCA – see page 1094
Bernstein. Gershwin. Hindemith. Milhaud. Rakson Les nuits d'été *New World SO* RCA – see page 1167

Rolando Villazón
Tenor
When we asked a handful of opera experts who they would put money on as a possible successor – impossible task – to Plácido Domingo (see page 27), the name that cropped up more than all others was Rolando Villazón. His debut disc of Italian arias was one of the most acclaimed first recordings by any young singer and the follow-up, a skilfully chosen collection of French arias, made a comparable impact. Clearly Villazón – like Domingo – is one of the more intellectual tenors around: the intelligence he brings to his singing goes well beyond the musical – he engages totally with the drama. He has had an impressive year onstage with, high on his list of successes, a run of *Roméo et Juliettes* in LA made an impact way beyond the States and a *Rigoletto* and *Bohème* charmed Covent Garden audiences.

Essential recordings
Gounod. Massenet Opera arias *Pidò* Virgin Classics – see page 611
Italian opera arias *Viotti* Virgin Classics – see page 1254

DOWNLOADING

By James Jolly

Look around you on the bus, the train or simply in the street: every other person seems to be sporting those natty little white headphones, a sure sign that they're wired up to an iPod. Music on the move is nothing new – the cassette Walkman saw to that – but where the digital revolution has taken over is in the sheer quantity of music people are able to keep in a small MP3 player about the same size as a packet of cigarettes. Of course, to embrace the world of downloading you don't have to shell out for an iPod or any of the other types of MP3 player on the market. You can keep all your music on the hard-drive of your computer and listen through speakers attached to the PC – or if you're into wiring up your house, by linking your PC to your hi-fi. What defines downloading is the ability to acquire your music via the internet.

So what's out there?

Though the download revolution has been shaped and steered by pop and rock music – with a staggering proportion of the music flying through cyberspace of dubious legality (copyright is a concept that many young music-lovers have little time for) – there's a lot of classical music available for download; and during the life of this guide, many more sites will no doubt be unveiled.

Apple's own digital download site, iTunes – launched to stimulate sales of iPods, no doubt, but certainly none the worse for that – offers an impressive cross-section of music of all genres. And classical music certainly has not been neglected – it is the website that Universal Classics (Decca, DG and Philips) has focused on, offering exclusive additional tracks for many albums. Apart from downloading the iTunes Jukebox (see below) it's well worth checking out iTunes for the wealth of legal music on offer.

There are other Digital Service Providers (DSPs), among which Napster has the highest profile. As with traditional record stores, go and have a browse and see which suits your style. And don't neglect the record companies themselves: Chandos, the large UK independent, has a substantial MP3 offering on its site and is well priced and easy to use.

How?

Step 1 Go to **apple.com/itunes** and download the iTunes Jukebox (there are many alternatives but this is a classy bit of software that works in the intuitive way that characterises Apple products). There are versions for Mac and PC, so everyone is

catered for. Once installed, the set-up process is very easy: you simply follow the instructions on the screen.

Step 2 If you are going to buy music online you will have to set up an account. Again, it's very easy and iTunes is scrupulous in e-mailing receipts within 24 hours.

Step 3 I suggest you try ripping a few of your favourite CDs simply to get a feel for the quality you are happy with. On a PC go to 'Edit', then 'Preferences', click on 'Importing' and you will be offered a number of file-format options. I would recommend experimenting with AAC and MP3 at various bit-rates; and if these don't impress, try Apple Lossless (but remember the higher the quality, the more space it will consume on your hard disc). For Mac users you can access these options via the iTunes menu.

Now you are set up to download. To offer some guidance in this new world, we've introduced a download feature to *The Gramophone*'s website (**www.gramophone. co.uk**) where you can find a selection of the discs that feature in this Guide that are also offered on the UK iTunes site (readers from abroad, unless they hold a UK-based credit card, should go direct to their local iTunes). You can also download the iTunes Jukebox from our site. Since Naxos discs are among the best priced on iTunes (as they are in the stores); why not spend £4.74 and download something that takes your fancy? I promise you will be impressed at the ease of the transaction – and that all the disc information comes across with the music.

Storing your music

You will be amazed at how quickly you can build a substantial collection of music on your PC (usually through a combination of ripping CDs and downloading) so it's a good idea to create a 'house style' for cataloguing the music. The information that accompanies a music file – whether acquired automatically on the web using a service like Gracenote or as supplied by the DSP – can arrive in a variety of styles. Decide early on how you are likely to sort though your music when you are looking for something to listen to.

If you listen to both classical and other genres (pop, rock, jazz, world and so on), the chances are that you will sort your classical music initially by composer and your non-classical music by artist or album. For the eclectic music consumer I would recommend that you remove composer details from all kinds of music other than classical: this makes searching far quicker; and besides, the chances are that you've never heard of half the people who compose pop tunes.

Simplicity is the key note: pare the details down to the minimum.

Ludwig van Beethoven
Symphony No 3 in C minor, Op 55, 'Eroica'
Allegro con brio
Berlin Philharmonic Orchestra /
Herbert von Karajan

may satisfy the completist (or the librarian), but that's an awful lot of information to contain in the small window of an iPod (which actually has a larger window than many MP3 players). Why not settle for:

Beethoven
Symphony No 3
I (or first movt)
BPO / Karajan

It says exactly what is playing and gets the message across with economy and clarity. The best advice is to experiment and decide how much information you need to find your music quickly and efficiently.

Another decision that needs to be taken is whether to keep your music in its original album form (do you want the Bruch Violin Concerto always to deliver the Mendelssohn as well?) or to store your music as individual pieces. There are strong arguments to be made for both approaches: on a purely practical level you'd be amazed how quickly you seem to be re-programming your iPod if you have broken up albums into individual pieces (though you

can easily make a special playlist that includes all your favourite violin concertos, so you can have a feast of Maxim Vengerov in great concertos if you want).

Podcasting

Though still in its infancy at the time this Guide went to press, Podcasting is set to become an important new media tool. A Podcast is, in essence, a radio programme that is available to download and, if it is part of a series, will automatically download to your PC whenever a new instalment is available. Once rights issues are resolved (and currently they deter quite a lot of creative programming), this could prove a really dynamic new format for talking about and listening to music. Check out the Podcasting section of iTunes and keep an eye out for individual record companies creating their own Podcasts.

To the future

Don't expect the CD to disappear overnight – there are far too many vested interests – but do expect certain recordings to cease to appear in physical format. What better way for a major company to store its historic back-catalogue than as an archive of MP3 files available for anyone to access and purchase at their will? And what more perfect a format for young, up-and-coming talent to be showcased than as a download? You've no restriction on length and you can get feedback from your audience at the click of a mouse. These are exciting times: let's hope the classical music world embraces the opportunities with imagination and speed!

100 Great Recordings

Bach Goldberg Variations
Glenn Gould pf
(Sony Classical, rec 1981)
Reviewed on page 47

Bach Cello Suites
Pablo Casals vc (EMI, rec 1936-39)
Reviewed on page 36

Bach St Matthew Passion
John Eliot Gardiner cond
(Archiv, rec 1989)
Reviewed on page 68

Bax Complete symphonies
Vernon Handley cond
(Chandos, rec 2003)
Reviewed on page 89

Bartók Concerto for Orchestra
Fritz Reiner cond (RCA, rec 1955)
Reviewed on page 83

Beethoven Fidelio
Christa Ludwig sop etc
Otto Klemperer cond
(EMI, rec 1962)
Reviewed on page 133

Beethoven Piano Sonatas
Artur Schnabel pf (EMI, rec 1932-35)
Reviewed on page 123

Beethoven
Violin Concerto
Itzhak Perlman pf
Carlo Maria Giulini cond
(EMI, rec 1953)
Reviewed on page 101

Beethoven Symphony No 3, Eroica
Otto Klemperer cond
(EMI, rec 1954)
Reviewed on page 108

Beethoven
Symphonies Nos 5 and 7
Carlos Kleiber cond
(DG, rec 1974 & 1976)
Reviewed on page 109

Beethoven Symphony No 6, Pastoral
Karl Böhm cond (DG, rec 1971)
Reviewed on page 110

Beethoven Symphony No 9, Choral
Wilhelm Furtwängler cond
(EMI, rec 1951)
Reviewed on page 111

Beethoven String Quartets
Quartetto Italiano
(Philips, rec 1967-69)
Reviewed on page 112

Beethoven Missa solemnis
John Eliot Gardiner cond
(Archiv, rec 1989)
Reviewed on page 131

Berlioz Les Troyens
Jon Vickers ten etc
Colin Davis cond (Philips, rec 1969)
Reviewed on page 157

Boulez Répons
Pierre Boulez cond (DG, rec 1996)
Reviewed on page 188

Brahms
Ein deutsches Requiem
Elisabeth Schwarzkopf sop etc
Otto Klemperer cond
(EMI, rec 1961)
Reviewed on page 212

Brahms
Piano Concerto Nos 1 and 2
Emil Gilels pf
Eugen Jochum cond (DG, rec 1972)
Reviewed on page 193

Brahms Piano Concerto No 1
Clifford Curzon pf
George Szell cond (Decca, rec 1955)
Reviewed on page 194

Brahms Symphony No 4
Carlos Kleiber cond (DG, rec 1980)
Reviewed on page 203

Britten Peter Grimes
Peter Pears ten etc
Benjamin Britten cond
(Decca, rec 1958)
Reviewed on page 233

Britten War Requiem
Philip Langridge ten etc
Richard Hickox cond
(Chandos, rec 1991)
Reviewed on page 225

Bruckner Symphony No 4
Karl Böhm cond (Decca, rec 1973)
Reviewed on page 243

Bruckner Symphony No 8
Herbert von Karajan cond
(DG, rec 1988)
Reviewed on page 245

Bruckner Masses
Edith Mathis sop etc
Eugen Jochum cond
(DG, rec 1962, 1971-72)
Reviewed on page 248

Chopin Piano Concerto No 1
Maurizio Pollini pf
Paul Kletzki cond (EMI, rec 1960)
Reviewed on page 276

Chopin and **Grieg**
Piano Concertos
Dinu Lipatti pf
Otto Ackermann, Alceo Galliera conds
(EMI, rec 1950, 1947)
Reviewed on page 422

Mozart Piano Concertos
Murray Perahia pf/cond
(Sony Classical, rec 1975-84)
Reviewed on page 653

Mozart String Quintets
Grumiaux Ensemble
(Philips, rec 1973)
Reviewed on page 667

Mozart Die Zauberflöte
Tiana Lemnitz sop etc
Sir Thomas Beecham cond
(EMI, Naxos, Pearl, rec 1937-38)
Reviewed on page 688

Mozart Don Giovanni
Eberhard Waechter bar etc
Carlo Maria Giulini cond
(EMI, rec 1959)
Reviewed on page 680

Mozart Le nozze di Figaro
Cesare Siepi bass etc
Erich Kleiber cond (Decca, rec 1955)
Reviewed on page 685

Mozart Idomeneo
Anthony Rolfe Johnson ten etc
John Eliot Gardiner cond
(Archiv, rec 1990)
Reviewed on page 683

Prokofiev
Symphony No 5
Hebert von Karajan cond
(DG, rec 1968)
Reviewed on page 744

Puccini La bohème
Jussi Björling ten etc
Sir Thomas Beecham cond
(EMI, rec 1956)
Reviewed on page 754

Puccini Tosca
Maria Callas sop etc **Victor de Sabata** cond (EMI, rec 1953)
Reviewed on page 761

Rachmaninov
Piano Concerto No 3
Martha Argerich pf
Berlin RSO / Chailly
(Philips, rec 1982)
Reviewed on page 774

Ravel and **Rachmaninov**
Piano Concertos
Arturo Benedetti Michelangeli pf
Ettore Gracis cond (EMI, rec 1957)
Reviewed on page 775

Ravel
Daphnis et Chloé
Pierre Monteux cond
(Decca, rec 1959)
Reviewed on page 792

Rossini
Opera arias
Cecilia Bartoli sop
(Decca, rec 1991)
Reviewed on page 818

Schoenberg Verklärte Nacht
Herbert von Karajan cond
(DG, rec 1973-73)
Reviewed on page 855

Schubert
Symphonies Nos 3, 5 and 6
Sir Thomas Beecham cond
(EMI, rec 1955-59)
Reviewed on page 862

Schubert
String Quintet
Isaac Stern, Alexander Schneider vns
Milton Katims va **Paul Tortelier,
Pablo Casals** vcs
(Sony Classical, rec 1952)
Reviewed on page 865

Schubert
Wandererfantasie
Maurizio Pollini pf
(DG, rec 1973)
Reviewed on page 876

Schubert Winterreise
Dietrich Fischer-Dieskau bar
Jörg Demus pf
(DG, rec 1965)
Reviewed on page 890

Schumann Fantasie etc
Sviatoslav Richter pf
(EMI, rec 1961-62)
Reviewed on page 905

Schumann String Quartets Nos 1 & 3
Zehetmair Quartet
(ECM, rec 2002)
Reviewed on page 899

Shostakovich
String Quartets
Fitzwilliam Quartet
(Decca, rec 1975-77)
Reviewed on page 932

Sibelius
Symphonies Nos 3 and 5
Robert Kajanus cond
(Koch, rec 1932-33)
Reviewed on page 941

Sibelius and **Nielsen**
Violin Concertos **Cho-Liang Lin** vn
Esa-Pekka Salonen cond
(Sony Classical, rec 1989)
Reviewed on page 937

Smetana Má vlast
Václav Talich cond
(Supraphon, rec 1954)
Reviewed on page 958

R Strauss Orchestral works
Rudolf Kempe cond
(EMI, rec 1971-74)
Reviewed on page 974

R Strauss Ein Heldenleben.
Also sprach Zarathustra
Fritz Reiner cond (RCA, rec 1954)
Reviewed on page 973

R Strauss Four Last Songs
Elisabeth Schwarzkopf .sop
George Szell cond (EMI, rec 1964)
Reviewed on page 977

R Strauss Salome
Birgit Nilsson sop etc
Sir Georg Solti cond
(Decca, rec 1961)
Reviewed on page 985

R Strauss Der Rosenkavalier
Elisabeth Schwarzkopf sop etc
Herbert von Karajan cond
(EMI, rec 1956)
Reviewed on page 983

Stravinsky
Stravinsky Edition
Stravinsky cond
(Sony Classical, rec 1930s-60s)
Reviewed on page 988

Tchaikovsky Francesca da Rimini
Leopold Stokowski cond
(dell'Arte, rec 1958)
Reviewed on page 1029

Tchaikovsky Symphony No 5
Mariss Jansons cond
(Chandos, rec 1884)
Reviewed on page 1026

Tchaikovsky
Symphonies Nos 4-6
Evgeny Mravinsky cond
(DG, rec 1960)
Reviewed on page 1025

Tchaikovsky Symphony No 6, Pathétique
Mikhail Pletnev cond
(Virgin Classics, rec 1991)
Reviewed on page 1026

Verdi Aida
Montserrat Caballé sop etc
Riccardo Muti cond (EMI, rec 1974)
Reviewed on page 1074

Verdi Otello
Ramon Vinay ten etc
Arturo Toscanini cond
(RCA, rec 1947)
Reviewed on page 1082

Verdi Falstaff
Giuseppe Valdengo bar etc
Arturo Toscanini cond
(RCA, rec 1950)
Reviewed on page 1077

Verdi La traviata
Maria Callas sop
Carlo Maria Giulini cond
(EMI, rec 1955)
Reviewed on page 1088

Wagner Tristan und Isolde
Kirsten Flagstad sop etc
Wilhelm Furtwängler cond
(EMI, rec 1952)
Reviewed on page 1131

Wagner Der Ring des Nibelungen
George London bass-bar **Hans Hotter** bass-bar
Régine Crespin sop **Wolfgang Windgassen** ten
Birgit Nilsson sop etc
Sir Georg Solti cond
(Decca, rec 1958-65)
Reviewed on page 1125

Wagner Parsifal
Peter Hoffmann ten etc
Herbert von Karajan cond
(DG, rec 1979-80)
Reviewed on page 1132

Walton Violin and Viola Concertos
Nigel Kennedy vn/va
André Previn cond
(EMI, rec 1987)
Reviewed on page 1144

Webern Opp 1 and 2
Pierre Boulez cond
(Sony Classical, rec 1969-70)
Reviewed on page 1144

Martha Argerich pf
Début Album (DG, rec 1960 & 1971)
Reviewed on page 1178

David Munrow var instrs/cond
The Art of The Netherlands
(EMI, rec 1975)
Reviewed on page 1273

Maurizio Pollini pf
20th-century piano music
(DG, rec 1971 & 1986)
Reviewed on page 1190

Joan Sutherland sop
Art of the Prima Donna
(Decca, rec 1960)
Reviewed on page 1250

RECORDS OF THE YEAR

The annual *Gramophone* Awards celebrate the best in recorded music –
listed below are the best of the best, the winners of the Records of the Year

1977 (Opera)
Janáček
Kát'a Kabanová
**Vienna State Opera Chorus; Vienna Philharmonic
Orchestra / Sir Charles Mackerras**
Decca ② 421 852-2DH2   *Reviewed page 523*

1978 (Opera)
Puccini
La fanciulla del West
**Soloists; Royal Opera House Chorus and
Orchestra, Covent Garden / Zubin Mehta**
DG ② 419 640-2GH2   *Reviewed page 756*

1979 (Chamber)
Haydn
Piano Trios
Beaux Arts Trio
Philips ⑨ 432 061-2PM9

1980 (Opera)
Janáček
From the House of the Dead
**Soloists; Vienna State Opera Chorus; Vienna
Philharmonic Orchestra / Sir Charles Mackerras**
Decca 430 375-2DH2   *Reviewed page 523*

1981 (Opera)
Wagner
Parsifal
**Soloists; Chorus of the Deutsche Oper, Berlin;
Berlin Philharmonic Orchestra / Herbert von Karajan**
DG ④ 413 347-2GH4   *Reviewed page 1123*

1982-83 (Concerto)
Tippett
Triple Concerto
**György Pauk; Nobuko Imai; Ralph Kirshbaum;
London Symphony Orchestra / Sir Colin Davis**
Decca 470 196-2

1984 (Orchestral)
Mahler
Symphony No 9
**Berlin Philharmonic Orchestra /
Herbert von Karajan**
DG ②-474 537-2   *Reviewed page 596*

1985 (Concerto)
Elgar
Violin Concerto
Nigel Kennedy *vn* **London Philharmonic
Orchestra / Vernon Handley**
EMI Red Line 573750-2
HMV Classics HMV5 72483-2   *Reviewed page 355*

1986 (Opera)
Rossini
Il viaggio a Reims
**Soloists; Prague Philharmonic Chorus;
Chamber Orchestra of Europe /
Claudio Abbado**
DG ② 415 498-2GH2

1987 (Early music)
Josquin Desprez
Masses – Pange lingua; La sol fa re mi
The Tallis Scholars / Peter Phillips
Gimell CDGIM009   *Reviewed page 526*

1988 (Orchestral)
Mahler
Symphony No 2, 'Resurrection'
**Soloists; City of Birmingham Symphony
Orchestra and Chorus / Sir Simon Rattle**
EMI ② 747962-8   *Reviewed page 589*

1989 (Chamber)
Bartók
String Quartets Nos 1-6
Emerson Quartet
DG ② 423 657-2GH2   *Reviewed page 84*

1990 (Opera)
Prokofiev
The Love for Three Oranges
**Soloists; Chorus and Orchestra of Lyon Opéra /
Kent Nagano**
Virgin Classics (no longer available)

1991 (Choral)
Beethoven
Mass in D, 'Missa solemnis'
**Soloists; Monteverdi Choir; English Baroque
Soloists / Sir John Eliot Gardiner**
Archiv Produktion 429 779-2AH *Reviewed page 131*

1992 (Orchestral)
Beethoven
Symphonies Nos 1-9
**Chamber Orchestra of Europe /
Nikolaus Harnoncourt**
Teldec ⑤ 0927 49768-2   *Reviewed page 104*

1993 (Solo vocal)
Grieg
Songs
Anne Sofie von Otter *mez* **Bengt Forsberg** *pf*
DG 476 1815   *Reviewed page 426*

1994 (Instrumental)
Debussy
Préludes
Krystian Zimerman *pf*
DG ② 435 773-2GH2   *Reviewed page 308*

1995 (Concerto)
Prokofiev Violin Concerto No 1*
Shostakovich Violin Concerto No 1**
Maxim Vengerov *vn*
**London Symphony Orchestra / Mstislav
Rostropovich**
*Warner Elatus 0927 49567-2, **Warner Elatus
0927 46742-2   *Reviewed pages 742 & 922*

1996 (Concerto)
Sauer. Scharwenka
Piano Concertos
Stephen Hough *pf* **City of Birmingham Symphony
Orchestra / Lawrence Foster**
Hyperion CDA66790   *Reviewed page 849*

1997 (Opera)
Puccini
La rondine
**Soloists; London Voices; London Symphony
Orchestra / Antonio Pappano**
EMI ② 556338-2   *Reviewed page 759*

1998 (Choral)
Martin
Mass for Double Choir. Passacaille.
Pizzetti Messa di Requiem. De Profundis
Westminster Cathedral Choir / James O'Donnell
Hyperion CDA67017   *Reviewed page 605*

1999 (Opera)
Dvořák
Rusalka
**Soloists; Kühn Mixed Choir; Czech Philharmonic
Orchestra / Sir Charles Mackerras**
Decca ③ 460 568-2DHO3   *Reviewed page 351*

2000 (Orchestral)
Mahler
Symphony No 10 (ed Cooke)
Berlin Philharmonic Orchestra / Sir Simon Rattle
EMI 556972-2   *Reviewed page 597*

2001 (Orchestral)
Vaughan Williams
A London Symphony (original 1913 version)
Butterworth
The Banks of Green Willow
London Symphony Orchestra / Richard Hickox
Chandos CHAN9902; SACD CHSA5501
                             Reviewed page 1057

2002 (Concerto)
Saint-Saëns
Piano Concertos Nos 1-5. Wedding Cake.
Rapsodie d'Auvergne. Africa
Stephen Hough *pf* **City of Birmingham Symphony
Orchestra / Sakari Oramo**
Hyperion ② CDA67331/2   *Reviewed page 835*

2003 (Chamber)
Schumann
String Quartets Nos 1 and 3
Zehetmair Quartet
ECM 472 169-2   *Reviewed page 899*

2004 (Opera)
Mozart
Le nozze di Figaro
**Collegium Vocale; Concerto Köln /
René Jacobs**
Harmonia Mundi HMC90 1818/20
                             Reviewed page 686

SUGGESTED BASIC LIBRARY

ORCHESTRAL

Bach Brandenburg Concertos
Bach Concerto for two violins
Bach Orchestral Suites
Barber Adagio for strings
Barber Violin Concerto
Bartók Concerto for Orchestra
Bartók The Miraculous Mandarin
Bartók Violin Concerto No 2
Beethoven Complete symphonies
Beethoven Piano Concertos Nos 4 and 5
Beethoven Violin Concerto
Berg Violin Concerto
Berlioz Symphonie fantastique
Brahms Complete symphonies
Brahms Piano Concerto No 1
Brahms Violin Concerto
Britten Young Person's Guide to the Orchestra
Bruch Violin Concerto No 1
Bruckner Symphonies Nos 4, 5, 8 and 9
Chopin Piano Concertos
Copland Appalachian Spring
Copland Fanfare for the Common Man
Corelli 12 Concerti grossi, Op 6
Delibes Coppélia
Debussy Jeux
Debussy La mer
Debussy Prélude à l'après-midi d'un faune
Dvořák Cello Concerto
Dvořák Symphony No 9, New World
Elgar Cello Concerto
Elgar Enigma Variations
Elgar String music
Elgar Symphonies Nos 1 and 2
Elgar Violin Concerto
Falla Noches en los jardines de España
Gershwin Rhapsody in Blue
Górecki Symphony No 3
Grieg Peer Gynt Suite
Grieg Piano Concerto
Handel Fireworks Music
Handel Water Music
Haydn Cello Concerto in C
Haydn London Symphonies
Haydn Trumpet Concerto
Holst The Planets
Ives Three Places in New England
Mahler Symphonies Nos 5 and 9
Mendelssohn A Midsummer Night's Dream
Mendelssohn Hebrides Overture
Mendelssohn Symphony No 4 , 'Italian'
Mendelssohn Violin Concerto
Messiaen Turangalîla Symphony
Mozart Clarinet Concerto
Mozart Horn Concerto No 4
Mozart Piano Concertos Nos 20-27
Mozart Serenade for 13 Winds
Mozart Symphonies Nos 40 and 41
Mussorgsky Pictures at an Exhibition
Pärt Tabula rasa
Prokofiev Lieutenant Kijé
Prokofiev Peter and the Wolf
Prokofiev Piano Concerto No 3
Prokofiev Romeo and Juliet

Prokofiev Symphonies Nos 1 and 5
Rachmaninov Paganini Rhapsody
Rachmaninov Piano Concertos Nos 2 and 3
Rachmaninov Symphony No 2
Ravel Boléro
Ravel Daphnis et Chloé
Ravel Piano Concerto in G
Respighi Roman Trilogy
Rimsky-Korsakov Scheherazade
Rodrigo Concierto de Aranjuez
Rossini Overtures
Saint-Saëns Le carnaval des animaux
Saint-Saëns Piano Concerto No 2
Saint-Saëns Symphony No 3
Schoenberg Five Orchestral Pieces, Op 16
Schoenberg Variations for Orchestra, Op 31
Schubert Symphony No 8, 'Unfinished'
Schumann Piano Concerto
Shostakovich Cello Concerto No 1
Shostakovich Piano Concerto No 2
Shostakovich Symphonies Nos 5 and 10
Sibelius Finlandia
Sibelius Symphonies Nos 2 and 5
Sibelius Tapiola
Sibelius Violin Concerto
Smetana Má vlast
Strauss J II Waltzes
Strauss R Alpine Symphony
Strauss R Also sprach Zarathustra
Strauss R Till Eulenspiegel
Stravinsky Agon
Stravinsky The Rite of Spring
Stravinsky The Firebird
Tchaikovsky Romeo and Juliet
Tchaikovsky 1812 Overture
Tchaikovsky Ballets – The Nutcracker,
  Sleeping Beauty and Swan Lake
Tchaikovsky Piano Concerto No 1
Tchaikovsky Symphonies Nos 4-6
Tchaikovsky Violin Concerto
Vaughan Williams Symphony No 2, 'London'
Vaughan Williams Symphony No 5
Vaughan Williams Tallis Fantasia
Vaughan Williams The Lark Ascending
Vivaldi The Four Seasons
Walton Violin and Viola Concertos

CHAMBER

Bartók String Quartets
Beethoven Piano Trio in B flat, Op 97, 'Archduke'
Beethoven String Quartets [late]
Beethoven Violin Sonatas
Borodin String Quartet No 2
Brahms Clarinet Quintet
Debussy Sonata for Flute, Viola and Harp
Debussy String Quartet
Dvořák String Quartet No 12
Franck Violin Sonata
Haydn String Quartets, Opp 20 and 76
Mendelssohn Octet
Mozart Clarinet Quintet
Mozart String Quartet in C, K465, 'Dissonance'
Mozart String Quintet in G minor, K516
Ravel String Quartet

Reich Different Trains
Schubert Piano Quintet, 'Trout'
Schubert Piano Trios
Schubert Arpeggione Sonata in A minor, D821
Schubert String Quartet No 14
Schubert String Quintet
Shostakovich String Quartet No 8

INSTRUMENTAL

Bach Cello Suites
Bach Das wohltemperierte Klavier
Bach Goldberg Variations
Bach Solo Violin Sonatas and Partitas
Beethoven Complete piano sonatas
Beethoven Diabelli Variations
Biber Mystery Sonatas
Brahms Variations on a Theme of Paganini
Chopin Nocturnes
Chopin Piano Sonata No 2
Chopin Preludes
Debussy Children's Corner Suite
Debussy Préludes
Grieg Lyric Pieces
Haydn Piano Sonata E flat major, HobXVI/52
Liszt Piano Sonata
Mozart Piano Sonata No 11 in A, K331
Paganini 24 Caprices
Prokofiev Piano Sonata No 7
Ravel Gaspard de la nuit
Satie Piano works
Schubert Impromptus
Schubert Piano Sonata in B flat, D960
Schubert Wandererfantasie
Schumann Carnaval
Schumann Kinderszenen
Schumann Kreisleriana

VOCAL

Allegri Miserere
Bach Cantatas – No 82 'Ich habe genug' and
    140 'Wachet auf'
Bach Magnificat
Bach Mass in B minor
Bach St Matthew Passion
Beethoven Missa solemnis
Berlioz Grande messe des morts
Berlioz L'enfance du Christ
Berlioz Les nuits d'été
Bernstein West Side Story
Brahms Ein deutsches Requiem
Britten Serenade
Britten War Requiem
Bruckner Motets
Byrd Masses for 3, 4 and 5 voices
Canteloube Chants d'Auvergne
Duruflé Requiem
Elgar The Dream of Gerontius
Fauré Requiem
Handel Coronation Anthems
Handel Dixit Dominus
Handel Messiah
Haydn Nelson Mass
Haydn The Creation
Howells Hymnus Paradisi

Mahler Das Lied von der Erde
Mahler Kindertotenlieder
Mendelssohn Elijah
Monteverdi 1610 Vespers
Monteverdi Madrigals, Book 8
Mozart Mass in C minor
Mozart Requiem
Orff Carmina burana
Palestrina Missa Papae Marcelli
R Strauss Four Last Songs
Rachmaninov Vespers
Ravel Schéhérazade
Schubert Winterreise
Schumann Dichterliebe
Tallis Spem in alium
Vaughan Williams Serenade to Music
Verdi Requiem
Victoria Requiem
Vivaldi Gloria in D, RV589
Walton Belshazzar's Feast

OPERA, OPERETTA & STAGE WORKS

Bartók Duke Bluebeard's Castle
Beethoven Fidelio
Bellini Norma
Berg Wozzeck
Bizet Carmen
Bizet Les pêcheurs de perles
Britten Peter Grimes
Britten Turn of the Screw
Debussy Pelléas et Mélisande
Gershwin Porgy and Bess
Gluck Orfeo ed Euridice
Handel Alcina
Handel Giulio Cesare
Handel Rinaldo
Janáček The Cunning Little Vixen
Lehár Die lustige Witwe
Leoncavallo Pagliacci
Mascagni Cavalleria rusticana
Monteverdi L'Orfeo
Mozart Die Zauberflöte
Mozart Don Giovanni
Mozart Le nozze di Figaro
Mussorgsky Boris Godunov
Puccini La bohème
Puccini Madama Butterfly
Puccini Tosca
Puccini Turandot
R Strauss Der Rosenkavalier
Rossini Il barbiere di Siviglia
Strauss J II Die Fledermaus
Sullivan The Pirates of Penzance
Tchaikovsky Eugene Onegin
Verdi Aida
Verdi Il trovatore
Verdi La traviata
Verdi Otello
Verdi Rigoletto
Wagner Der Ring des Nibelungen
Wagner Tristan und Isolde
Weber Der Freischütz

WHY MOZART MATTERS

In the 250th anniversary year of Mozart's birth, **David Vickers** examines

our perception of the composer and talks to Sir Colin Davis,

Sir John Eliot Gardiner, Christopher Hogwood, Sir Charles Mackerras,

Sir Neville Marriner and Sir Roger Norrington

'I believe that without Mozart any classical musician's life would be decimated.'
Sir Neville Marriner

January 27, 2006 is the 250th anniversary of the birth of Johann Chrysostom Wolfgang Amadeus (or Gottlieb) Mozart. He and his sister Maria Anna (Nannerl) were taught music by their father Leopold, a respected theorist, composer and violinist at the Salzburg court. It seems likely that Leopold was responsible for their entire education, including mathematics, languages, literature and religious training. The child prodigies were taken on exhausting concert tours all over Europe. Mozart's skill as a composer benefited enormously from his experiences in Italy, Germany, France and England. After such an itinerant life at many of the most important royal courts and musical cities in Europe, it is little wonder that after reaching adulthood Mozart could not settle at Salzburg, which he considered to be a provincial backwater. He spent the last ten years of his life in Vienna, moving house frequently according to his economic circumstances. He died of a severe rheumatic fever on December 5, 1791, a few weeks short of his 36th birthday.

The average layman's perception of Mozart has been moulded by legends. Consequently, each generation reinvents Mozart for itself. This is evident in the numerous scholarly or popular biographies of Mozart to have been published in the last 50 years, which reveal a trend moving from myth-based stories to academic reconstructions of his career and musical achievements, and more recently examinations of the Mozart family's dysfunctional life.

The most influential and widespread impression of Mozart was created in Milos Forman's 1984 film *Amadeus*, which was advertised with the mendacious slogan 'Everything you have heard is true!' Adapted from a play by Peter Shaffer, *Amadeus* introduced legions of cinemagoers and video renters to the exuberant perfection of Mozart's musical genius. It firmly convinced its audience that the under-appreciated Mozart was buried in an unmarked pauper's grave, after being driven to a miserable premature death by his jealous enemy Salieri. The real truth makes for less entertaining melodrama. Mozart had sufficient

reason to be optimistic about the immediate future until his final illness. Salieri was among the few mourners at the funeral organised by Baron Gottfried van Swieten at St Stephen's Cathedral. Mozart's burial outside the city in a communal grave was in accordance with the prevalent custom of the time, influenced by Emperor Joseph II's reforms about simple economical and hygienic burials proposed in 1784. Furthermore, a group of Mozart's friends gathered for a memorial service at St Michael's Church organised by Emanuel Schikaneder (librettist of *Die Zauberflöte* and the first Papageno), at which members of the court orchestra and choir performed part of Mozart's unfinished Requiem.

Yet there was some truth in *Amadeus*: Mozart did not enjoy an easy relationship with his father, nor with his Salzburg patron Archbishop Colloredo; it seems he was not prepared to accept Joseph II's alleged criticism that *Die Entführung aus dem Serail* contained far too many notes; he did not shirk from controversy in setting Lorenzo Da Ponte's libretto *Le nozze di Figaro*, based on a play by Beaumarchais that had been banned by Joseph II for its seditious content (although Joseph fully accepted the operatic version). Mozart's letters reveal an unpredictable man capable of every characteristic ranging from childish pranks, vulgar humour, artistic passion, emotional yearning, melancholy, intellectual solemnity and emotional depth. The most important truth communicated in *Amadeus* was that these elements abound in Mozart's music. They continue to resonate strongly with us.

The soundtrack was recorded by the Academy of St Martin in the Fields and Sir Neville Marriner at Abbey Road before any of the footage had been filmed. Marriner observes that 'Peter Shaffer always said "this is not a documentary, this is a fantasy"'. Although I'm sure he has received many rebukes for the way he portrayed Mozart, he still thinks of it as a fantasy. The actual impact of the music was extraordinary because it really identified the vitality and the attitude of the man, and I think we were all surprised that the film had such success with young people – normally you expect the film audience for that sort of topic to be the same as in your concert halls. But I think the character of the music, portrayed in a youthful and brilliant way, made it a popular success. Subsequent to that we were invited to play everywhere in the world, to perform music we had used in the film. As long as we were able to keep Mozart as Mozart, and not as a soundtrack to a Hollywood film, we were all very happy.'

Symphonies

Mozart's earliest known public performance was as a dancer in a play at Salzburg University in September 1761. His earliest known composition dates from around this time (a miniature *Andante and Allegro*, K1*a* and K1*b*). Most of the young Mozart's compositions contain significant traces of collaboration with his father. A few orchestral compositions once thought to be among Mozart's earliest symphonies are now attributed to Leopold, and others composed before 1767 were transparently modelled on JC Bach's style and other examples the boy Mozart encountered during his 'Grand Tour'. The young Mozart composed symphonies for London, Vienna, Rome, Bologna and Milan, and for Salzburg he provided a flurry of 22 brightly assured symphonies composed there between 1772 and 1776. Mozart's symphonic production rate slowed dramatically after 1775, and during his years in Vienna he only composed six, including three intended for performance elsewhere. His last three symphonies (Nos 39-41) composed in the space of about three months during summer 1788. Mozart scholar Cliff Eisen described as 'the pinnacle of his symphonic achievement and among the most important and influential symphonies composed during the 18th century'.

These symphonies have persistently been at the forefront of the Mozart discography. Sir Neville Marriner's pioneering recordings for Philips were significant contributions. As Marriner points out, The Academy of St Martin in the Fields 'was very accommodating when the big surge of companies recording everything anybody had ever written began. We were there at the right time when LPs began, and in order to make the catalogue complete record companies were looking for orchestras of the right size and scale to play Mozart. By that time symphony orchestras were already not considered the ideal vehicle, so we were lucky that the Academy had the reputation of being ideal for 18th-century music.'

Marriner notes the practical and artistic advantages that the project brought to his orchestra. 'It allowed us to stay in London instead of having to chase a living touring and becoming unsettled. When we started performing classical repertoire one of the cloudy issues was that you often could not see the wood for the trees, but we tried really hard to seek out the bones of the music and then added the colours, which I think really helped.

Every member of the Academy wanted to achieve clarity and to be an important part of the structure.'

Christopher Hogwood agrees that 'one of the biggest revolutions that occurred in the last half of the 20th century was to hear chamber orchestras playing Mozart, people like Sir Neville Marriner, who showed the musical public that a really serious classical symphony could be played by only 25 people instead of more than 75. The alteration in size also affected balance, with the woodwind becoming more prominent, revealing so much more of Mozart's colours.' This philosophy certainly informed Hogwood's own series of Mozart's symphonies with the Academy of Ancient Music, which commenced in the late 1970s. In addition to what was then considered to be the radical use of period instruments, Hogwood enlisted the support of Neal Zaslaw, who had been running a project at Cornell University for many years delving into the chronology and performance practice of Mozart's symphonies. Hogwood explains 'at first we turned to him for the last word on which works were actually by Mozart, to work out those attributed to him which are either by his father or lesser-known contemporaries. It grew bigger than that because in some instances we were working without the benefit of a *Neue Mozart-Ausgabe* published edition. When we started this recording series the earliest symphony available in the *NMA* was K133, and Neal Zaslaw had to do the musical groundwork and help to prepare an urtext for any earlier symphonies, but it soon became clear we also needed his help in correcting some things in later symphonies.'

In addition to establishing the authenticity of early symphonies and problems with adequate performance material, Hogwood gives enormous credit to Zaslaw for enhancing the project's sense of musical geography. Zaslaw 'pointed out that one peculiarity was the way Mozart could adapt so quickly to the taste and requirements of the places he was visiting. So we made sure that symphonies written for Italy were played by an orchestra that matched such an ensemble as you might have found in Milan, Paris, Salzburg or Vienna – and how each of these places had very different orchestral traditions, varying in size, balance with woodwind or brass sections, and the varying distribution of lower strings.'

Piano concertos

Christopher Hogwood undertook a comparably experimental series of recordings of Mozart's concertos with fortepianist Robert Levin. Mozart composed 27 piano concertos. The earliest of them was composed at Salzburg in December 1773, but most were composed during his final decade in Vienna. Robert Levin has written that it is Mozart's solo concertos, not his symphonies, 'that reveal the evolution in

Mozart's orchestral writing in the Vienna years'. Mozart composed most of these concertos for his own concert performances in which he performed the solo piano part. Hogwood observes that in this repertoire 'the important issues are not about the accurate transmission of text, but about performance and presentation. It had got to the point where even though performances of Mozart's piano concertos were lovely, the result could seem static, frozen and fixed. But in our series of performances and recordings Robert Levin always played a different instrument to keep things fresh, and played continuo in the tuttis – creating a sense of social interaction with the orchestra that made it feel more like a jazz band.' Robert Levin also improvised cadenzas that were different in each performance, restoring 'an element which produced unique events that could not be repeated, and a sense of freshness and spontaneity lost from many modern concerto performances'.

Sir Charles Mackerras recognizes the importance of Mozart's role as the soloist. 'In those works he played himself, the piano part is only a skeleton and it has to be embellished a lot. But in fact there are quite a few with the piano solo parts written for other people, and in those you can see how Mozart expects the line to be embellished. For example, K246, K271 and K453 have everything written out for you.'

Sir John Eliot Gardiner undertook an enterprising survey of Mozart's piano concertos for DG Archiv during the mid-1980s. Gardiner 'found them hugely challenging and stimulating, partly because I had studied the piano concertos very closely when I was a student of Nadia Boulanger in Paris in 1967, but also because of working alongside such a scrupulous stylist as Malcolm Bilson. The textural changes and reorientation caused by using the smaller fortepiano – its variable strength, its stronger bass and lighter upper register, and the way it interacts so naturally in conversation with the woodwind – was a big revelation. As Gardiner's exploration of the piano concertos continued, including a marvellous 1989 performance of the Concerto for Three Pianos (K242) featuring Bilson alongside Robert Levin and Melvyn Tan, Gardiner reveals that 'I grew to feel that one element in their composition owes something to the fact that Mozart was seeking a new way of expressing things that he would have liked to have expressed in operas, but the dramatist in him had started to check and rein in the length and proportions of his arias. After the almost profligate richness and length of arias in *Idomeneo*, he then moved to Vienna and turned to much more concise ways of writing individual arias, especially in the Da Ponte cycle. There is a sense in which that energy he had put into the earlier opera writing found a new outlet in the slow movements of piano concertos, themselves retaining the flavour of arias.'

Church music

Mozart's earliest known sacred music is a *Kyrie* composed at Paris when he was 10 years old (K33), but almost all of his 16 complete Mass settings were composed and performed at Salzburg during the 1770s. Apart from the *Coronation* Mass (K317) and 'Laudate dominum' from *Vesperae solennes de confessore* (K339), most of this music is still comparatively unknown. It is peculiar that Mozart is beloved by choirs all over the world when his fame as a composer of choral music rests squarely on two unfinished works, dating from each end of his years in Vienna.

Mozart commenced work on his great C minor Mass sometime between his marriage to Constanze Weber at St Stephen's Cathedral on August 4, 1782 and writing to his father on January 4, 1783 that 'there is the score of half a Mass, which is lying on my desk in the best of hopes.' Georg Nikolaus Nissen (Constanze's second husband) claimed in his biography of Mozart that the Mass was composed to celebrate the safe delivery of their first child in June 1783. HC Robbins Landon suggested Mozart might also have intended it to be a celebration of his marriage to Constanze, 'which had been contracted in the face of considerable opposition and difficulties.' Despite the incomplete state of the composition, Mozart organized a performance at St Peter's Abbey on October 26, 1783 during a visit home to Salzburg with his new wife, who sang the first soprano part.

It was unusual for Mozart to commence work on a composition without a practical economic motive. Like any sensible 18th-century composer, he did not often work solely for his own amusement. Certainly the ornate blend of Italianate opera solos and Handelian fugues in the C minor Mass were contrary to Joseph II's restrictions on musical performances in Viennese church. Mozart probably abandoned work on it when he realized it would never be performed in Vienna, although much of the music was recycled with Italian words in the oratorio *Davidde Penitente*. We may regret that the Emperor's preference for simplicity in liturgy prevented Mozart from completing any large-scale church music during his finest years. His next sacred composition, the short motet *Ave verum corpus* (K618), was not composed until 17 June 1791.

Mozart's lack of opportunities to compose ambitious choral works is probably one of the reasons he accepted an anonymous commission to compose a Requiem Mass. Scholars have established that the commission came from Count Walsegg-Stuppach, a fellow-freemason whose wife had died on February 14, 1791. Before embarking on the Requiem, Mozart had to complete *Die Zauberflöte* and was further distracted by an invitation to compose *La clemenza di Tito* to celebrate the coronation of Emperor Leopold II as King of Bohemia, in Prague. In late November 1791 Mozart's final illness set in, and after his death his widow Constanze enlisted the help of Joseph Eybler to fulfil Walsegg's commission. Eybler could not complete the task, so it was entrusted to Xaver Süssmayr. Some musicians and scholars have criticized Süssmayr's contribution as inferior to what Mozart might have created.

There have in fact been several attempts to complete the C minor Mass and to re-complete the Requiem, in the hope that musicologists may be able to present a more convincingly Mozartian solution. Of course, it is impossible to pretend that any solution is identical to what Mozart would have written, but Richard Maunder's performance editions of both works are among the most persuasive solutions. These were recorded by Christopher Hogwood, who insists 'there is an issue about how to deal with unfinished works. I don't think there is anything radical in making a performance version of a piece that is unfinished. The Requiem is one of over 100 pieces that are unfinished, and people get a bit over-upset and sentimental about it. It is healthy for each generation to reconsider what to do with it, just as the French retranslate Shakespeare for every generation. I like to use different editions and versions, and hopefully people will remain interested in hearing different solutions. The pieces were only finished in Mozart's head, so we can only do the second best. There will never be a definitive solution.'

The newest solution is Robert Levin's reconstruction of the *Great* C minor Mass published by Carus-Verlag, which at the time of writing has not yet been recorded. One of its champions in 2006 will be Sir John Eliot Gardiner, who chose to commemorate the bicentenary of Mozart's death in 1991 with a concert that featured both the *Great* C minor Mass and the Requiem. Gardiner is fascinated by both incomplete torsos because 'they represent the two opposite poles of his church music – the quasi-Masonic and the neo-Baroque. The moods of the two pieces are very distinct. In regard to the orchestral textures and even in the writing for chorus, the C minor Mass is conceived on a far grander scale. I am tempted to say it is a bigger loss that Mozart did not complete the C minor Mass than the Requiem being unfinished at his death.'

Gardiner praises 'the diversity of texture and the monumental quality' of the C minor Mass. But it was the same diversity and monumental quality that Joseph II would have found too elaborate and unashamedly secular. However, Mozart's letters occasionally reveal a deeply religious character. Gardiner suggests that 'if you want to discover the religious side of Mozart's genius, you would look for it more in

his operas and in some instrumental works - for example the *Adagio* of the *Gran Partita* for 12 wind instruments and double bass, the G minor String Quintet, or in numerous slow movements in piano concertos – than in his church music. In moments such as the Countess's pardon in Act 4 of *Le nozze di Figaro*, the quartet in *Idomeneo*, the burning of the Capitol in *La clemenza di Tito*, Pamina's aria and the two armed men in *Die Zauberflöte*, you get as close to deeply religious music as he ever wrote, and to what one could call the "religious experience".'

Operas

Mozart was only 11 years old when he composed his first opera *Apollo et Hyacinthus* (in Latin) for Salzburg's Benedictine University in 1767. His first serious opera *Mitridate* was performed at Milan three years later. During the 1770s Mozart acquired mastery in a variety of operatic styles. It is unfortunate that the stature of later operas prevents unbridled appreciation of imaginative and delightful works composed during his late teens and early 20s, particularly *La finta giardiniera* (Munich) and *Il rè pastore* (Salzburg), both performed in 1775. Mozart's first mature attempt at singspiel, *Zaide*, was composed between autumn 1779 and mid-1780, but it was considered too serious for Vienna, and lay unperformed until 1866.

It is generally considered that Mozart composed seven great operas: the serious opera *Idomeneo* (Munich, 1781); the singspiel *Die Entführung aus dem Serail* (Vienna, 1782); the 'Da Ponte trilogy' of comedies *Le nozze di Figaro* (Vienna, 1786), *Don Giovanni* (Prague, 1787) and *Così fan tutte* (Vienna, 1790); the serious opera *La clemenza di Tito* (Prague, September 1791) and the singspiel *Die Zauberflöte* (Vienna, also September 1791).

Sir John Eliot Gardiner recorded all seven for DG Archiv during the 1990s, and believes that each opera possesses its own character and personality. 'When we staged and recorded each of the operas in turn, it was a great opportunity to spend an entire year living with a single Mozart opera, to get to know its tonal world and to become closely familiar with its aesthetic and dramatic characteristics. I imagine it would be almost impossible to extrapolate an aria from any one of the big seven mature operas and reallocate them to another without one sensing an uncomfortable big crashing of gears or of mixed metaphor. But I have to say that whatever Mozart opera one is doing at any one time is always the one you currently think is the best! Even if one is aware of minor blemishes in structure, it is impossible to ever say which one is my favourite. Basically all seven are unsurpassed masterpieces. Opera was never quite the same ever afterwards.' Gardiner also praises their stage-worthiness. 'Mozart's operas have an intrinsic theatricality that does not require stage directors to "reinvent" them every few years in order for them to reach their dramatic potential. A great deal of daft stage business that modern stage directors concoct isn't needed in Mozart because the essentials are already there, written in the score – but you do need to be able to read them! It so happens that most opera directors with whom I've collaborated on Mozart use a CD booklet, a printed libretto or, at best, a vocal score in order to tell them how to manage the stage action. But the theatrical information is all in the orchestra: it is the orchestra that tells you not just what is going on at any given point - who is hiding or lurking, who is telling porky pies - but what should be happening on stage, and what each member of the cast is thinking or feeling.'

Sir Colin Davis praises the relevance of Mozart's operas to modern audiences. 'They teach us to forgive ourselves for our own sins, in the most beguiling way possible. Except *Don Giovanni*, they are all about reconciliation: all the quarrels are resolved in the end. One also gets the feeling that Mozart loves all his characters, good or bad – it doesn't make any difference.' The most under-appreciated of the great seven operas is *La clemenza di Tito*, although Christopher Hogwood admires it. 'You don't judge it in the same way as one of the Da Ponte operas. The real point of reference is not *Così fan tutte* or *Die Zauberflöte*. The concept and debate that goes on in *La clemenza di Tito* was important to people who lived in Vienna and Prague who saw a real Emperor at work.' Hogwood concedes that such circumstances might not always resonate with 21st-century audiences, but describes how the opera 'made absolute sense in the theatre for me on one occasion when I attended a performance, shortly after Gorbachev had returned to Moscow after a failed coup and was having to decide how to deal with his enemies. So that night the plot of the opera reflected real-life headlines. With the context of what was going on in Russia, the audience that night was on the edge of its seats because the opera asks a question that remains important: when in a position of power over your enemies, do you show justice or clemency?'

If issues of relevance truly matter, that also raises questions about whether Mozart's operas should be sung in their original languages or in colloquial translations. Sir Charles Mackerras is an exponent of both approaches, as evidenced by his recent recording of *The Magic Flute* for Chandos and his comparably fine Telarc version of *Die Zauberflöte*. Mackerras pragmatically observes that the language in which a performance should be sung 'depends on the circumstances. The original language is always the best, but of course Mozart had no particular prejudices about it. Still in his lifetime, *Don Giovanni* was done in German, probably with all the *secco* recitatives cut and replaced by dialogue.'

Interpreting Mozart

Interpreting Mozart's music is not a responsibility conductors dare to take lightly. Sir Colin Davis exclaims 'Mozart is the God of Music, so I have to serve him extra specially well!' When asked what aspects of Mozart's music he seeks to bring out in performance, Davis enthusiastically responds: 'Everything I can find!' Sir Neville Marriner ponders the question for a moment, and decides 'I'm interested in textures, so when I perform Mozart I'm really trying to bring out the same things I look for in nearly all composers, certainly those until the end of the 19th century.'

Sir Roger Norrington holds a slightly different view. 'I'm fascinated with trying to find out how to play Mozart in a suitable manner, in a way that comes from Handel and Bach rather than from Wagner and Brahms. I've always tried to perform his pieces so that if Mozart came into the room and stood at the back, he might like what he heard – and that he would have recognized it!' In order to achieve this, Norrington emphasises the importance of tempo markings. 'It is essential to really try to pin it down, to research what such markings really meant in the 18th century - and you can to a considerable extent. I like the challenge of trying to make a Mozart *Andante* move along, just like it has to in Handel. It is like discovering the secret world of Mozart when you hear the real pulse of an *Alla breve*, and when you realize the fact that he never really wrote a slow movement, at least not in the way that Mahler would have understood the term.' Norrington cites his pioneering EMI recordings of *Don Giovanni* and *Die Zauberflöte* as an example of how 'we realised the fundamental importance of dance rhythms and forms in Mozart's music, which all came from the baroque. There weren't many recordings of his operas that had tried to seriously address these issues.' Sir John Eliot Gardiner agrees. 'Mozart is the culmination of all the music I study and cherish from the 17th and 18th centuries. I see him very much in that light, rather than as the precursor of the more glamorous music of the 19th century.'

A stimulating blend of the modern- and period-instrument worlds has been developed by Sir Charles Mackerras, who acknowledges that 'with the period instrument movement becoming so important, it has been very revealing to me how the instruments that Mozart knew affect the tempo. Also the lengths of notes – this can often make huge difference, with shorter notes fading much quicker with period instruments. Even when holding out a long note, it still dies much quicker. Both of those things have really affected my view of how Mozart should be played.' Mackerras often uses period trumpets, horns and timpani when performing Mozart with modern-instrument groups. 'I used to notice that during Mozart and Beethoven performances the trumpets always sounded too loud or too soft. If they played with sufficient bite they overpowered everything, but if played softer then they lacked the particular energy that was needed. I immediately noticed when I started working with period instruments that natural trumpets can play as loud as they can to get the energy but it doesn't overpower everything else.' Where once upon a time the modern-instrument world regarded the early music movement with suspicion, Mackerras reports that 'nowadays players in symphony orchestras with whom I do Mozart are all most willing to try using natural trumpets. A player of a modern trumpet has no difficulty changing over for the relatively easier natural trumpet parts written by Mozart, Haydn, Beethoven and even Schubert. They don't have the sort of technical challenges that makes switching over to natural trumpet much harder in Bach and Handel.'

Why Mozart matters

It seems that in 2006 ideas about performance practice using period instruments, stylish interpretation on modern instruments, and a critical perspective of Mozart chronology and biography are flourishing. A healthy variety of decisions about how to play Mozart's music has given the repertoire fresh impetus and enriched the discography. But neither historical curiosity nor merely wishing to make a good tune sound attractively packaged satisfactorily explain why such devoted attention has been lavished upon Mozart. Nor can it explain why such devotion is likely to continue and reinvent itself again in the future.

Christopher Hogwood refers to the anecdote about Joseph II's criticism that *Die Entführung aus dem Serail* contained 'too many notes'. 'I think Mozart expressed it perfectly when he insisted that "there are just the right number, no more or less than I desire". Mozart matters to me as an interpreter because of this sense that every note is consequential. There is very little padding, and there is always a meaning to be found. Because of that you are encouraged to take an extra awareness of what he wrote, how he wrote it, and what the historical precedents are for the way you

deliver it. You could say that matters just as much with Brahms or Tchaikovsky, but with Mozart I do have a heightened sense that all the surplus fat is trimmed off.'

Sir John Eliot Gardiner evaluates that 'what matters to me is the incomparable humanity and probing psychology that Mozart's music displays. At its sublime best Mozart's music contains a feeling of purity that remains an object of utter wonder. More than any composer, he can capture the paradoxical emotional impressions of innocence and complexity.' Sir Neville Marriner makes a similar point. 'Mozart is the composer who provides the most sophisticated human emotional experience. For example, the score of *Die Zauberflöte* is bewildering in the diversity of emotions and styles: the academic treatment of popular Viennese songs for Papageno, the flashy operatic arias of the Queen of Night, solemn music for Sarastro, the comic melodrama of Monostatos. But the church music, symphonies, quartets, concertos, all of the many idioms – they all have that.'

Sir Charles Mackerras regards Mozart as 'simply the greatest of all composers, but the wonderful thing is that no other composer could excel so tremendously in so many different branches of composition: religious music, songs, quartets, quintets, symphonies, and operas – everything that you can think of.' Sir Roger Norrington remarks that 'people talk as if Mozart was some sort of child composer, like his portrayal in *Amadeus*, but in his music he can change from one thing to another so extraordinarily quickly. For example, the *Dissonance* Quartet is remarkably sophisticated music. Mozart is so intensely personal.'

When asked why Mozart still matters, Sir Colin Davis responds with a simple yet profound answer: 'Why do the most complex products of the finest brains mean anything at all? If you look back, European culture was built up from the best brains Europe produced. If that matters, then Mozart was one of the greatest. Some people might not think culture matters anymore, but I think it matters, and to me Mozart represents what it means to be civilised.'

TEN ESSENTIAL MOZART RECORDINGS

UNDERSTANDING EARLY MUSIC

Performing and recording Early Music poses unique problems. **Fabrice Fitch** outlines the challenges and traces the development of Western music from plainchant to the glories of the high Renaissance

Music composed before 1600 makes special demands of performer and listener alike. This is because many notions that we take for granted in Western art-music were only established towards the end of this period, or had not yet been fixed by convention. Some of these notions go to the heart of musical performance, of what we mean when we speak of 'a piece of music': the assignment of specific lines to specific instruments; the precise notation of pitches by means of sharps and flats; indications for tempos and tempo relationships; or the use of written and unwritten ornaments. Often, we have lost the inside knowledge (born of practice) that musicians of the period would have taken for granted. These questions therefore devolve to the performer, who must interpret not only the notation, but also the information that gives clues as to possible solutions. So every performance is necessarily conjectural. Of course, what musical notation 'means' is a valid question for any period; but in pre-tonal music it poses itself more starkly, and the diversity of possible answers – or the degree of conjecture informing different interpretations of one and the same piece – is inevitably more startling.

But the challenges facing us when we confront 'early music' do not end with the way the music sounds. The notion of art for art's sake, of absolute music, would probably have seemed quite strange to medieval composers, no matter how experimental their music sometimes appears to us. The perception of composers as individual creative personalities, conscious of their own worth, is difficult to trace until **Guillaume de Machaut**, the first polyphonist to take effective (and successful) steps for the preservation of his work for posterity. Even then, the status of the composer as a skilled craftsman took a long time to take root: although there is ample documentation of patrons' commissions to painters, illuminators or sculptors throughout the medieval period, the first recorded instances of musicians being paid to compose date from the turn of the 16th century. The fact is that music was mostly improvised and rarely written down, while polyphony (that is, composed music involving more than one line simultaneously) was rarer still. Again, in our own time the notion of originality is still central to our ideas about art; but in pre-tonal music, composers often based their works upon pre-existent material, either plainchant or other polyphony. Finally, and perhaps most crucially: performers and scholars are dependent for their interpretations on the pieces and the information that happens to survive; and that must be a tiny fraction of what once existed. Theoretical treatises and letters mention many lost works by the very greatest composers, and countless documents have disappeared which would have given us more precise indications on the manner of their performance. But on the positive side, it only takes the discovery of a new work or a new document – or a fresh look at a well-known one – to reveal unforeseen perspectives, new ways of understanding and performing the music of the past. Many of the recordings in the following pages are the fruit of such discoveries.

Performance in practice

Many questions confront the performer of early repertories, the most basic being the intended performing forces appropriate to a given work. Music carrying a text is obviously meant to be sung, but does not exclude instrumental participation; conversely, the absence of text does not automatically imply the presence of instruments. These were ubiquitous in the medieval and Renaissance periods, but most of their music was either improvised or else memorised, and is therefore lost to us. (Another loss concerns the instruments themselves: no original medieval instruments survive, so we rely on copies recreated through descriptions from contemporary documents, illustrations drawn from painting and sculpture, and guesswork.) A distinction was traditionally made between 'high' instruments (typically winds and brass), used in outdoor or ceremonial contexts, and 'low' instruments (plucked or bowed strings and soft winds, such as recorders), used indoors: lutes and plucked keyboards became especially popular in courtly circles when musical proficiency became fashionable. From the late middle ages, instruments were also arranged into 'consorts' or families involving several sizes of the same sort of instrument, or of closely related ones (crumhorns, for example – nowadays the string quartet represents a rare survival of this practice). Although one should be wary of generalisations (since performance traditions undoubtedly varied from place to place, from region to region), it does seem that instrumental families had specific functions and carried distinct associations. Similarly, the mix of voices and instruments, familiar from many recordings of medieval and Renaissance music, may not have been as widespread as was once believed.

Even if we assume that a given piece called for exclusively vocal performance, how many singers were involved? Vocal polyphony required specialised singers; until the 15th century it appears to have been performed by small ensembles, with seldom more than one singer on each line. As regards sacred music, many churches banned the use of instruments within their walls (in some, like Cambrai Cathedral, there is no evidence even of an organ), making all-vocal performance the only option. Gradually these ensembles grew in size according to the wealth of the institutions that supported them. In Italy, wealthy magnates like the Dukes of Ferrara and Milan vied with each other for the best singers in their greatest possible number. As with other forms of artistic patronage, they emulated the more established courts like those of France and Burgundy, whose rosters of singer-composers included the best musicians of the period. The 1400s also saw an increase in the use of boy trebles whose training, education and maintenance was often the direct responsibility of the choirmaster. In England, the two great surviving polyphonic manuscripts of the 15th century (the **Old Hall Manuscript**, copied *c*1415, and the **Eton Choirbook** of *c*1500) show a similar shift from adult male ensembles to those including a substantial number of boys. The role of women in musical performances is by no means clear, though it would have been restricted to the secular field. One of the best known instances dates from 16th-century Ferrara, where composers including **Luca Marenzio** (1553/54-99) and **Luzzascho Luzzaschi** (?1545-1607) wrote for a group of ladies, known as the *Concerto delle donne*, who regularly performed for the duke and his entourage.

But even when the performing forces for a given work can be established as precisely as this, there is no room for dogmatism. A piece might be disseminated hundreds of miles from its place of origin to an area whose performance traditions might be very different. There was no fixed pitch-standard even in the Baroque period: each region, town or parish had its own. So the notion of a single authentic manner of performance is a chimera. Besides, contemporary documents tell us very little of sound quality, tone production, and other vital matters. We may be told that the music performed at a given ceremony sounded like the voice of angels, for example, or that singers 'sang very sweetly'; but such descriptions might refer to sounds very different to those with which we might associate them. Medieval representations of singers often show them

ESSENTIAL LISTENING I		
Dufay	Missa San Jacobi etc **The Binchois Consort / Kirkman** Hyperion CDA66997 (7/98)	Ⓕ
Machaut	Messe de Nostre Dame **Oxford Camerata / Summerly** Naxos 8 553833 (2/97)	Ⓢ
Ockeghem	Missa De plus en plus etc **Orlando Consort** Archiv 453 419-2AH (8/97)	Ⓕ
Perotin	Viderunt omnes etc **Hilliard Ensemble / Hillier** ECM New Series 837 751-2 (2/90)	Ⓕ
Various	'The Marriage of Heaven and Hell' **Gothic Voices / Page** Hyperion CDA66423 (12/90)	Ⓕ
Various	'The Spirits of England and France' Volume 2 **Gothic Voices / Page** Hyperion CDA66773 (8/95)	Ⓕ

pulling quite extraordinary faces (think of Van Eyck's singing angels, for instance). Are the artists indulging in caricature, or perhaps mocking singers' vanity? Or did their methods of tone-production vary significantly from those of today's singers? Would we have recognised their performances, or they ours?

In order to help readers find their way around the listed recordings, there follows a brief summary of musical developments during the medieval and Renaissance periods. Naturally, it is only the briefest of sketches; much detail has been omitted, and not just detail. The insert-notes of individual recordings usually provide sufficient information as to specific works and performances. The aim here is to provide a broader context within which to understand them.

Monody

The earliest notated music in the West is known as plainchant or plainsong. As with literacy in general, musical notation was basically the preserve of the church: even the most powerful lay figures tended to be illiterate. Music notation seems originally to have been devised as an aid to memory: the first examples have no musical staves, and indicate only the relative of pitches' positions (higher or lower). Over time it became more specific, but its interpretation remains a matter of conjecture. Chant traditions proliferated across different parts of Europe, and over the centuries several attempts were made to impose some sort of uniformity across a broad region. The last and most successful of these was the Council of Trent (1545-63), which set down the Roman rite as the standard throughout the Catholic church. By this time polyphony had been established for centuries, but it is important to bear in mind that throughout the middle ages and Renaissance periods, plainchant was the norm in church, with polyphony being reserved for special occasions. In the 19th century the monks of Solesmes (France) gathered together and published the corpus of plainchant, and promoted a certain style of performance, which has since been firmly established in the public imagination. More recently, scholars and singers have conducted research into performance traditions based not on the Solesmes style but on historical descriptions from different periods, using original chant manuscripts in preference to modern editions.

Monody was equally important in the secular domain. Certain forms were actually hybrids of the sacred and secular, for example the musical religious dramas devised to make biblical stories come alive for the largely illiterate faithful (a well known example being the **Play of Daniel**). One is set down in a manuscript copied at a Benedictine monastery at Benediktbeuren (Bavaria), a collection that also contains burlesque parodies of scripture (the famous **Carmina Burana**) for use on days when the monks' usually strict rule was relaxed. But perhaps the most famous repertory of secular monody is that of the troubadours (southern French) and trouvères (northern French), who endure in popular lore through the image of the 'wandering minstrel'. Like many such images it is a misleading one, for often these were noblemen who did not wander at all but welcomed musicians and poets into their courts, and practised the arts themselves. Their main theme was the idealised woman whom knights vowed to serve in what has come to be termed 'courtly love' (though we know that such relationships were not always platonic, and that trouvères also sang of physical passion). The tradition of poet-composers reached its apex in the person of **Guillaume de Machaut** (c1300-77), who was equally renowned in both fields (and remains so today) and wrote both monophonic and polyphonic songs; and it extended into the next century with the Burgundian court musicians Gilles de Binche (called **Binchois**, c1400-60) and **Antoine Busnois** (c1430-92).

Sacred polyphony

It is thought that the earliest polyphony arose out of improvisation: singers extemporised new musical parts to existing plainchant. The earliest notated examples date from the 11th century. As with early plainchant, the interpretation of this notation is a matter of conjecture, and is further limited by the small number of surviving sources. The culmination of these early styles is known as the Notre-Dame School which coincided with the foundation of Paris's famous cathedral (1163).

Its leading figures are the first named composers of polyphony: **Leoninus** and **Perotinus**. Perotinus was the first composer of four-voice music in the organum style, in which three free voices weave elaborate, repeating patterns around a slow-moving cantus firmus (fragment of plainchant). The idea of basing new works on pre-existing music (usually plainchant, but later polyphony as well) persists, in different forms, throughout sacred music up to and beyond 1600.

Another enduring thread is the mixture of the sacred and the worldly. One of the earliest examples combining both trends is the 13th-century French motet (a term derived from the French for 'word'). Typically this had different texts in each voice: those in the upper voices were in French or Latin and were often related by their subject-matter (the one commenting upon the other – a typical subject being love, requited or otherwise); the lower voice, called tenor (from the french 'tenir', 'to hold', because the long notes hold the music together) was either performed by instruments or else vocalised (that is, sung to a single vowel). It consisted of a few notes drawn from plainchant, frequently set to a recurring rhythmic pattern. Most often, the words of the chosen plainchant had some sort of bearing upon the subject matter in the upper parts. The motet continued to flourish in the next century, when the notational system was revised to take account of new rhythmic possibilities. This is the period known as **Ars Nova**, led by **Philippe de Vitry** (1291-1361) and Guillaume de Machaut, one of the outstanding figures of medieval culture. While Machaut was primarily concerned with secular music, he also wrote motets, and his *Messe de Nostre Dame* is famously the first complete setting of the Mass Ordinary in the hand of a single named composer.

Before Machaut's Mass, there appear to have been very few pieces in this genre; but by the turn of the 15th century musicians became interested in relating two or more Mass movements by basing them on the same cantus firmus. Early instances of this stem from the English composers **Leonel Power** (*d*1445) and **John Dunstaple** (*c*1390-1453). Their style, remarkable for its emphasis on triadic sonorities, had a considerable impact on younger continental composers like **Guillaume Dufay** (*c*1397-1474) and his younger contemporary **Johannes Ockeghem** (*c*1420-97). Over the course of the 15th century, the Mass came to replace the motet as the pre-eminent form of sacred composition. It absorbed the idea of cantus firmus, and soon composers began using secular songs as well as plainchant as the basis for Mass compositions. At the same time the motet changed its character: the constructivist principles referred to earlier were jettisoned, and the term itself came to denote a polyphonic sacred

piece with a liturgical or paraliturgical text. The first examples of this new breed of motet are found in the **Old Hall Manuscript**. In the 16th century it in turn superseded the Mass as the favoured form of sacred composition, thanks in part to the influence of the late motets of the great **Josquin Desprez** (*c*1455-1521). By the time of Josquin's death, however, motets tended to be freely composed, with no pre-existing material. This marks a general trend through the latter part of the 16th century, which set increasing store in the creation of freely invented pieces: the notion of originality, thereafter one of the hallmarks of creative genius, was coming to the fore. Henceforth the Mass, which persisted in the use of pre-existing material, came to be seen as a rather conservative form. **Orlande de Lassus** (1532-94), perhaps the greatest composer of the high Renaissance, wrote over 600 motets but only 50-odd Masses; yet his great Roman contemporary **Giovanni Pierluigi da Palestrina** (1525/26-94) was still able to write over 100 Masses, many of them very elaborate.

Secular polyphony

From its origins, composers of polyphony tended to write music for both sacred and worldly purposes. This is partly because singing (and by extension, composing) polyphony was a skilled craft, and the same lords who kept private chapels also required music for their entertainment; and because in any medieval town, the cathedral, the market square and the dwellings of the wealthy were in close proximity. Traditionally, singers were members of the minor clergy, earning their living from ecclesiastical benefices (often held without the obligation of residency) negotiated for them by the lords who employed them.

The history of secular polyphony is bound up with the poetic forms that were set to music. These forms were highly conventionalised in their organisation. Thus, in the trouvère repertory mentioned above, the *grant chant* had its own rhyme-scheme and verse-structure, its subject matter being the idealised, unattainable Lady; while lighter genres like the *pastourelle* were more simply organised, and involved the more down-to-earth amorous pursuits of shepherds and shepherdesses (the latter sometimes also pursued by knights!). With the Ars nova, polyphony was concentrated on a few poetic forms known collectively as *formes fixes*: the *rondeau*, the *virelai* (sometimes known in its abbreviated form as the *bergerette*) and the most popular and courtly form of the 14th century, the *ballade*. The rhythmic and chromatic sophistication of the Ars nova reached a climax after the death of Machaut in the style known variously as the Avignon school (after the Papal court that was set up there) or **Ars subtilior** ('the subtler art'), whose notational complexity was unsurpassed until the mid-20th century. The next century saw the *rondeau* eclipse the *ballade* in popularity, and the advent of a more direct, tuneful style typified by Guillaume Dufay, though the *formes fixes'* courtly sophistication endured in the songs of Binchois and Busnois at the court of Burgundy, and with Ockeghem at the court of France.

But by 1500 the *formes fixes* were on the wane, replaced in France by simpler verse/refrain and strophic structures, and a lighter melodic style increasingly centered on the top voice. These new songs were widely circulated in print, bringing a host of composers to the fore, including **Claudin de Sermisy** (*c*1490-1562) and **Clément Janequin** (*c*1485-1558), whose descriptive songs enjoyed a wide vogue. At the same time in Italy a new genre came into being which would have far-reaching influences: this was the madrigal. Many of its first great practitioners were not native Italians, but Franco-Flemish (among them **Philippe Verdelot** and **Jacques Arcadelt**, both active in Florence; and **Adrian Willaert**, master of the music at St Mark's in Venice, and his pupil and successor, known by his Italian name **Cipriano da Rore** (1515/16-65). Soon, the madrigal was established as the predominant secular form of its time: it was exported to England, and on the continent the publication of a book of madrigals for one's opus 1 became a rite of passage for aspiring young composers working in Italy. By this time the madrigal had transcended its popular origins and had become an experimental vehicle for every sort of innovation: think of the chromaticism of **Carlo Gesualdo** (*c*1561-1613), or the blending of voices and specific instruments and the introduction of the basso continuo in the fifth madrigal book of **Claudio Monteverdi** (1567-1643). These innovations had far-reaching implications, for instance to do with the rise of opera in Italy; abroad, the solo madrigal (scored for a single voice with bass accompaniment) found its counterparts in the French air de cour and the English lute song. In this sense, the development of the madrigal marks the transition from the Renaissance to the Baroque.

Instrumental music

In music before 1500 it can be difficult to distinguish between a musical line that happens not to carry a text and one specifically intended for instruments (many variations in performance practice arise from this ambiguity). As mentioned earlier, even when instrumental performance of a given part is possible, it is not always possible to tell whether a specific instrument was intended. Yet a few specifically instrumental forms survive, one of the earliest being the 13th-century *estampie*.

ESSENTIAL LISTENING II		
Byrd	Masses for 3, 4 and 5 voices **The Cardinall's Musick / Carwood** ASV Gaudeamus ASVGAU206 (A/00)	Ⓕ
Josquin	Missa Pange lingua etc Ensemble Clément Janequin; **Ensemble Organum / Pérès** Harmonia Mundi HMC90 1239 (11/86R)	Ⓕ
Lassus	Lagrime di San Pietro etc **Ensemble Vocal Européen / Herreweghe** Harmonia Mundi HMC90 1483 (8/94)	Ⓕ
Palestrina	Missa Assumpta est Maria; **Missa Papae Marcelli etc Pro Cantione Antiqua / Brown** Regis Recordings RRC1025	Ⓑ
Various	'Canciones y Ensaladas' **Ensemble Clément Janequin / Visse** Harmonia Mundi HMC90 1627 (4/98)	Ⓕ
Various	'Music from the Sistine Chapel' **Taverner Consort and Choir / Parrott** HMV Classics HMV5 74371-2 (8/87R)	Ⓑ

And the best instrumentalists achieved renown and made good careers for themselves. Indeed, from the 15th century onwards compositions are increasingly ascribed to named individuals, among them the organist **Conrad Paumann** (*c*1410-73), the lutenists **Francesco Spinacino** (*fl*1507), **Vincenzo Capirola** (1474-after 1548) and **Francesco da Milano** (1497-1543). From the early 15th century come the first manuscripts containing sizeable instrumental repertories: often these were embellished arrangements of pre-existing polyphonic compositions. Typically, specific types of notation called tablature were devised for the different instruments: those for organ, keyboard and lute were the most common. Gradually pieces were written specifically for given instruments: the toccata (from the Italian toccare, 'to touch') was a short, prelude-like piece of an improvisatory, virtuoso character; the fantasia and the ricercar (together with its Spanish counterpart, the *tiento*) were more abstract, polyphonic pieces, forerunners of the fugue; and there were pieces based on ground basses and popular tunes. The lute was the most popular instrument owing to its size and flexibility: it could accompany or play complex polyphony on its own. Music printing (which began at the turn of the 16th century) soon cashed in on this market in a variety of ways; but one has to wait for the early Baroque to find examples of what we call 'scoring', that is, the assignment of specific lines to specific instruments.

Old wine, new bottles

It is not only performers and scholars who reinterpret the music of the past: composers of every stripe have sought inspiration in early music, and continue to do so. This is nothing new: Beethoven regarded Handel as the greatest composer ever, and Brahms was a subscriber to the complete edition of Schütz's works. What is surprising today is the breadth of early music's appeal, the way it cuts across aesthetic positions and stylistic boundaries. Figures as diverse as Pärt, Reich, Schnittke, Andriessen, Ligeti, Kagel, Birtwistle, Maxwell Davies and Ferneyhough (to name only these) have engaged with pre-tonal idioms and procedures at various times in their careers. In some cases (for example in the case of minimalist composers) the link between old and new is clearly audible and overt: thus with much of **Pärt**'s vocal and choral music, or in pieces like **Andriessen**'s *Hocketus*; but equally, composers of what used to be called the avant-garde have adopted and adapted procedures derived from the *modus operandi* of pre-tonal musics: examples include the use of canon in certain movements of **Ligeti**'s *Requiem* and in his *Lux aeterna*; of hocket and isorhythm in much of **Birtwistle**'s music. Other examples include the 'transcriptions' by Michael Finnissy in *Obrecht Motetten* of pieces by the great Flemish composer (*ca*1457-1505); the quotations from Lassus in Schnittke's String Quartet No 3; Kagel's self-explanatorily named *Music for Renaissance Instruments*, in which the soundworld of the period is invoked at its most physical level. Even **Boulez**, that most resolute of modernists, has named some recent works after plainchant forms in recognition of their antiphonal structures: *Répons* and *Anthèmes*.

How can we explain the fascination pre-tonal music holds for present-day composers? It is striking that many of today's tonal composers (for example, Pärt in his *St John Passion*) do not adhere to the tonal system as such, but use elements of its language, most notably its harmonies; similarly, the music of composers like Perotinus or Dunstable has unmistakable whiffs of tonality, because it uses chords which tonal music subsequently took over and used in a very different way. This mixture of the familiar and the foreign connects Pärt and like-minded composers with earlier music. At the same time, the speculative side of much pre-tonal music – its interest in number, in abstract, speculative compositional procedures, or in the intricacies of notation – can be discerned in music whose connection with early music is not immediately audible. Hence the examples mentioned earlier, of Birtwistle, Finnissy and the like. In this opposition between sound and structure, there is of course an element of over-simplification; one might simplify further by saying that early music offers something for everyone. A related point was made earlier: the amount of interpretation and conjecture that is needed to recreate pre-tonal music in sound. The less we know, the more we have to make up, and the creative licence granted to performers applies also to composers, who focus on whichever aspect of the music happens to suit their turn. Finally, today's composer is faced with a superabundance of riches: the whole of Western art music (and much else besides), immediately accessible in both printed and recorded forms. What this means for the future is anyone's guess, but it is a situation that today's composers are forced to confront one way or another.

REPERTOIRE EXPLORATION II

Cornysh — Magnificat; Stabat mater; etc
The Tallis Scholars / Phillips
Gimell CDGIM014 (4/89) Ⓕ
The musical equivalent of perpendicular Gothic architecture: dazzling and intricate, and a performance to match.

Gombert — Credo. Qui colis Ausoniam; etc
Henry's VIII / Brown
Hyperion CDA66828 (10/96) Ⓕ
This is dense, rich polyphony for the court of Hapsburg Emperor Charles V.

Josquin — Missa L'Homme armé sexti toni; Missa L'Homme armé super voces musicales etc
A Sei Voci / Fabre-Garrus
Astrée Naïve E8809 (9/01) Ⓕ
A superlative recording of two of Josquin's most consummate Mass settings.

Various — 'Consonanze Stravaganti'
Stembridge org/hpd
Ars musici AM1207-2 Ⓕ
Keyboard music from late 16th century Naples, which inspired composers such as Frescobaldi.

Various — 'The Art of the Netherlands'
Early Music Consort of London / Munrow
Virgin Veritas VED5 61334-2 (11/97) Ⓜ
An idiosyncratic overview of the 15th century; perhaps David Munrow's finest recording.

THE BAROQUE ERA

The Baroque era is dominated by the output of a handful of
musical giants. **Nicholas Anderson**'s whistlestop tour takes in both
the great and the forgotten

The closing decades of the 16th century were crucial to the forming of many styles which affected music, painting, architecture, and literature. It was a period in which ideas were evolved and forms developed to expand musical vocabulary and to accommodate the expression of an ever-widening range of emotions. The enormous variety of these ideas and forms was developed throughout the 17th and early 18th centuries, gradually became governed by a common musical syntax. Yet, in spite of regularisation, the music of this period has preserved a novelty and an unpredictability capable of evincing passionate responses in us. Since the end of the 19th century we have gathered these multifaceted and multicoloured forms under the umbrella-title of 'Baroque' to provide us with the convenience of an all-embracing stylistic concept.

One of the most intense aspirations of the Baroque period was to find new and more powerful means of strengthening the effect of the spoken word. It led to the creation of opera and the development of song. Italy was the fountain-head from which these new ideas emerged, and it was Italian musicians who played a key role in disseminating ideas in other parts of Europe. The leading composers in this early stage of baroque music were **Caccini, Cavalieri, Peri** and, above all **Monteverdi**. Caccini's songs embrace the new monodic style, underpinned by the essence of Baroque texture – the basso continuo, whose figured shorthand represents the harmonies and intervals to be played above the bass. Caccini's music has more than mere historic significance, though, and his songs have a simple, melodic appeal which engage our emotional responses, just as the composer intended. Monteverdi's nine collections of madrigals, published between 1585 and 1651, reflect an astonishing range of emotions expressed with intensity and psychological insight. The variety of moods and textual sensibility of which Monteverdi was capable is present in each collection, but is strikingly apparent in the Eighth Book (1638) containing 'Il ballo delle ingrate' and the 'Combattimento di Tancredi e Clorinda'.

Monteverdi's first opera, *Orfeo* (1607) was written and performed at Mantua and followed earlier experimental dramas by Orazio Vecchi, Emilio de' Cavalieri and Jacopo Peri. A conspicuous feature of this work is its ample instrumental requirements signposting a path for the future development of the orchestra.

Monteverdi's superior dramatic gifts are even more evident in his two remaining complete operas, *Il ritorno d'Ulisse in patria* (1641), and *L'incoronazione di Poppea* (1642). Here he proves himself a master in handling human relationships and in vivid characterisation. Both operas were written for Venice, where his gifted pupil **Cavalli** produced many successful works during the middle decades of the 17th century. Among these are *Ormindo, Giasone* and *Calisto*. Monteverdi's sacred vocal music is collected mainly in two publications, that of 1610 containing the popularly termed Monteverdi *Vespers*, and another of 1641, *Selva morale e spirituale*.

By the middle of the 17th century new forms were beginning to take shape in Italy which were to influence the direction of music during the early 18th century and, in some cases, far beyond. The most important of these were oratorio, cantata, sonata and instrumental concerto. Oratorio, as a musical form, originated in Rome where those of **Carissimi** provide fine examples. His dramatic flair is apparent in Latin oratorios such as *Jephte* where a rich harmonic vocabulary enhances the Old Testament story. Later in the century another Roman composer, **Stradella**, further developed oratorio, introducing an important instrumental dimension. His best-known oratorio is *San Giovanni Battista*, in which the relationships between Herod and John the Baptist and between Herod and his daughter are handled with insight.

After opera and oratorio, the chamber cantata was the most important vocal form in 17th-century Italy. Early pioneers were Luigi Rossi, Cesti and Carissimi but it was **Alessandro Scarlatti** who, more than any composer, standardised an alternating pattern of recitative-aria-recitative-aria which remained more or less in place until the end of the Baroque period. Scarlatti wrote about 600 chamber cantatas as well as longer *serenatas*, which occupy ground somewhere between cantata and opera.

During the later decades of the century the instrumental forms of sonata and concerto were given definition. Sonatas generally fell into two categories, the more serious *sonata da chiesa* (church sonata) in four movements, and the dance-oriented *sonata da camera*, often suite-like and beginning with a prelude. Legrenzi and Vitali were important composers in the early history of the sonata but it was **Corelli** who consolidated forms, drawing on a wealth of ideas for his trio sonatas. These in turn played a significant part in his 12 *Concerti grossi* (Op 6). Here

Corelli alternated the trio sonata texture of two violins and cello (*concertino*) with a fuller orchestral sound (*grosso*). But, at the beginning of the 18th century the scene shifted from Rome to Venice for the final development of the Baroque concerto.

Alongside new ideas in vocal music, composers were also experimenting with instrumental forms. One of the leading pioneers, above all in keyboard music, was **Frescobaldi**. He introduced a striking virtuosity to his pieces while attaching importance to the emotional involvement entered into by an individual player. Contributions to the development of the violin and members of the violin family were also to have far-reaching consequences for Baroque music. Among the early 17th-century pioneers were composers such as **Marini**, **Fontana**, **Merula** and **Uccellini**. They established new forms, expanded instrumental technique and widened expressive possibilities.

The opening of public opera houses in Rome and Venice during the 1630s, quickly followed by others, established the future of sung dramatic entertainment both in Italy and further afield. At the French court of the Bourbons dance and ballet reigned supreme during the early decades of the 17th century; but, in the 1640s Italian opera was introduced to the court of Louis XIV by his Italian prime minister, Cardinal Mazarin. Cavalli's *Egisto* and Luigi Rossi's *Orfeo* were both performed there, followed by others. The French love of dancing was amply catered for by the inclusion of ballets which followed each act.

The arrival of Lully

All this was to change with the rise to fame and influence of Italian-born Lully, one of the most astute operators in the entire history of music. In the early part of his career Lully mainly composed ballets for the court, earning for himself the almost undying approval of Louis XIV, whom he was to serve throughout his life. During the 1660s a partnership with the great comic playwright, Molière, resulted in a succession of highly original *comédies-ballets*, culminating in the greatest of them, *Le bourgeois gentilhomme*. At about the same time experiments were taking place in creating an indigenous French opera, based on Italian models, but using French texts rather than Italian ones. Lully was at first dismissive but then, sensing that he might be upstaged, turned matters to his advantage. By means of politically adroit moves he eventually held a monopoly for performing virtually all kinds of large-scale dramatic music in France. Between 1673 and his death in 1687 Lully produced a steady flow of operas, among them *Alceste* (1674), *Atys* (1676) and *Armide* (1686). Only after Lully's death and a return to the free opera market was another French composer, **Marc-Antoine Charpentier** able to reveal

dramatic talents equal to, even superior to those of his rival. His fine tragédie-lyrique *Médée* was staged in Paris in 1693. Some other dramatic pieces by Charpentier such as *Actéon* and *Les Arts Florissants* are on a much smaller scale though another major stage work, *David et Jonathas* (1688), a religious drama, was commissioned for private performance by the Jesuits.

Lully and Charpentier were both skilled in the sphere of sacred vocal music. Lully's *Te Deum* and *Miserere*, strongly contrasting pieces, reveal the composer's sensibility to psalm and canticle texts. These follow the layout and scale of the grand motet, calling for solo voices, choir and instruments. *Petits motets* on the other hand, usually involved two or three voices with basso continuo. Charpentier was a master of both forms, though some of his pieces are better understood as dramatic motets in which

---

ESSENTIAL LISTENING I

Cavalli Calisto
Concerto Vocale / Jacobs
Harmonia Mundi HMC90 1515/7 (F)

Charpentier Missa Assumpta Maria
Les Arts Florissants / Christie
Harmonia Mundi
HMC90 1298 (F)

Corelli Concerti grossi, Op 6
The English Concert / Pinnock
Archiv ② 459 451-2ATA2 (M)

Lully Le bourgeois gentilhomme
Tolz Boys' Choir; La Petite Bande / Leonhardt
DHM GD77059 (F)

Monteverdi Madrigals – Book 8
Concerto Italiano / Alessandrini
Opus 111 OPS30-187 (F)

Monteverdi 1610 Vespers
Taverner Consort; Taverner Choir; Taverner Players / Parrott
Virgin Classics ② VBD5 61662-2 (B)

Purcell Dido and Aeneas
Soloists; Academy of Ancient Music Chorus & Orchestra / Hogwood
L'Oiseau-Lyre
436 992-2OHO (F)

Schütz Musicalisches Exequien
Monteverdi Choir; English Baroque Sols; His Majesty's Sagbutts and Cornetts / Gardiner
Archiv 423 405-2AH (F)

Biblical stories are presented both in commentary and in direct speech. *Le reniement de St Pierre* (*St Peter's Denial*) for soloists, chorus and continuo is a masterpiece of the form, whose anguished harmonic progression and grief-stricken inflexions are affecting. Charpentier was unusually gifted in the art of poignant writing, as we can see in his many tenebrae-settings (*Leçons de ténèbres*), but it is in his 11 Masses that he most effectively blends this aspect of his style with more extrovert ceremonial gestures. His last setting of the Mass, *Assumpta est Maria*, is perhaps, the most satisfying of them. It was in the hands of **Lalande**, that the *grand motet* reached one of its high water-marks. Sixty-four of them have survived, of which *De Profundis* provides an outstandingly expressive example.

The Italian influence widens

The influence of Italian music had reached Germany by the early years of the 17th century. But political and religious tensions, and the consequent Thirty Years' War (1618-48) caused such protracted brutality, bitterness and turmoil that artistic endeavour was fragmented. Among the earliest composers to embrace Italian ideas were **Praetorius, Schein** and **Scheidt**. They drew upon newly acquired Italian polychoral techniques in the setting of hymns, Biblical texts and in the deployment of instruments. The leading composer of the early to mid-German Baroque was **Heinrich Schütz** whose rich stylistic vocabulary reflects both a prodigious talent and an unusually long life. Schütz was sent to Venice in 1609 where he studied with Giovanni Gabrieli. He returned to Germany four years later, eventually becoming Kapellmeister at the Dresden court, a post which he held for almost half a century. Schütz visited Venice again in 1628, and this time met Monteverdi while also catching up with new developments in music which had taken place since his previous visit. Schütz's music spans half a century and more and embraces old and evolving compositional styles. By introducing Italian ideas into Germany he laid the foundations of 18th century German sacred music. Among his most impressive achievements are the *Psalms of David*, published in 1619, and *Cantiones sacrae* (1625), both of which reveal Schütz's masterly rapprochement between Italian techniques and Lutheran tradition. The strikingly organised *Musicalisches Exequien* (1636), *Geistliche Chor-Music* (1648), and the emotionally charged *Die sieben Worte unsers lieben Erlösers und Seeligmachers Jesu Christi* (The Seven Last Words of Christ on the Cross) are further examples of Schütz's inspirational gifts in setting sacred texts.

Though Schütz's talent remains unrivalled in early- to mid-17th-century Germany, there were other composers who made enduring contributions to Protestant sacred music. A unique phenomenon was the emergence of a dynasty of musicians, eventually crowned with the genius of its most illustrious member, Johann Sebastian Bach. **Johann Hans Bach**, a younger contemporary of Schütz, contributed a motet of great poignancy, *Unser Leben ist ein Schatten* (Our life is but a shadow), while **Johann Christoph Bach** and **Johann Michael Bach** were also accomplished composers of sacred vocal music. **Franz Tunder, Johann Schelle**, Schütz's pupil **Matthias Weckmann** and, further south, **Johann Erasmus Kindermann** encompassed many of the vocal and instrumental forms of the time and some of these are, at last being explored in recordings.

The leading keyboard composer in Germany during the first half of the 17th century was **Johann Jacob Froberger**. He was influenced by Italian ideas in his toccatas, canzonas and ricercares, while his harpsichord suites incline more toward French idioms. Froberger's puissant and individually expressive powers can be found in his elaborate *Lamentation faite sur la mort très douloureuse de Sa Majesté Impériale, Ferdinand le troisième*.

Among the most important German 17th century composers in the sphere of solo violin and instrumental chamber music were **Rosenmüller, Schmelzer** and **Biber**. Rosenmüller spent much of his active musical life in Italy but returned to Germany towards the end of his life. His compositions provided a fertile channel for the flow of Italian stylistic traits into north and central Germany. Austrian Schmelzer and Bohemian Biber enriched the violin repertoire with music which not only radiated the sounds and colours of central European folk music, but also extended the technique of the instrument itself. Schmelzer's collection, *Sacroprofanus concentus musicus* (1662), his *Fechtschule* and Biber's *Battalia* afford lively examples of their art. But it is Biber's 16 *Mystery Sonatas*, linked to the Catholic devotion of the Rosary, which strike an altogether profounder note, evoking a wide range of emotions, exuberant, contemplative and poignant, in turn.

Though the Low Countries had enjoyed a brilliant indigenous musical culture during the 15th and 16th centuries, the 17th century was less innovative. Musical life continued to thrive but there were fewer leading musicians, apart from Sweelinck whose life embraced the latter decades of the 16th and first two decades of the 17th centuries. **Sweelinck** wrote a small quantity of vocal music but his greater skill lay in instrumental forms, above all those connected with the keyboard. Another gifted composer from the Low Countries at this time was **Jacob van Eyck**, whose recorder music is imaginative and often virtuosic.

English music during the 17th century was receptive to continental developments, the most important stimuli coming from Italy and France. But England was also a favoured destination for foreign musicians, above all Italians, and they in turn may well have responded to stubbornly preserved indigenous musical ideas. In the first quarter of the century madrigals and songs with lute accompaniment were the most popular forms of secular vocal music, with composers such as Dowland, Gibbons, Morley and Weelkes leading a strong and well-populated field. Opera was slow to catch on in England and it was the masque, with its elements of dance, mime and allegory, and plays with music which kept the new Italian entertainment at bay. Masques remained popular up to the mid-century, with composers such as William and Henry Lawes and playwrights like Ben Jonson lending the form real distinction. Among the most gifted composers writing for the Anglican Church were **Thomas Tomkins, Orlando Gibbons** and **Thomas Weelkes**, whose anthems and services are intimately expressive and suitable for wide use. Though instrumental music took second place to music for voices in pre-Restoration England it was a period that none the less sustained a thriving tradition of keyboard and consort music. Among the great keyboard composers were **John Bull** and **Peter Philips**, both of whom were on friendly terms with Sweelinck. Their pieces in variation form are complex and technically brilliant. **Gibbons**, **William Lawes** and **John Jenkins** were all accomplished instrumental composers who made fine, sometimes idiosyncratic contributions to the consort repertoire for viols and/or members of the violin family.

After the Restoration of the monarchy in 1660 musical life in England received a new impetus from the enthusiasm of the king himself. Further experiments were made with opera, the favoured form being semi-opera consisting of music and spoken dialogue. The great master of semi-opera, as of all other musical forms in the last decades of the century was **Purcell**, whose *King Arthur* and *The Fairy Queen* contain music of great originality and charm. Purcell's single true operatic venture, *Dido and Aeneas*, with its wide range of emotions, strikingly imaginative Second Act and its celebrated lament, is musically rewarding at every turn and is one of the great dramatic masterpieces of the Baroque period. A delightful precursor of *Dido and Aeneas* was composed by **John Blow**, whose intimate and fervently expressive *Venus and Adonis* is sung throughout. Purcell was equally at home with instrumental music. As well as trio sonatas he produced a smaller quantity of solo keyboard music – suites and miscellaneous pieces – and 13 subtly expressive fantasias with two *In nomines* for viol consorts. Purcell, along with Pelham Humfrey, Blow and others also enriched Anglican worship with anthems, services, chants and hymns.

The high Baroque

The late Baroque period is dominated by the towering figures of Bach and Handel, yet there were other composers, too, of outstanding and exceptional talent, of whom Vivaldi in Italy, Rameau in France, and Telemann in Germany were the leading lights. The early decades of the 18th century witnessed the crystallisation and stylistic maturity of forms developed in the previous century: opera, oratorio, cantata, sonata, concerto and suite. In Venice, **Albinoni** contributed to the sophistication of the instrumental concerto. His writing for one and two oboes lends distinction to his finest sets of concertos, Opp 7 and 9. But it was another Venetian, **Vivaldi**, whose imagination and organisational skill brought the solo concerto to a definitive peak. Like Albinoni – whose comic intermezzo *Pimpinone* (1708) was one of the earliest of its kind – the Marcello brothers and other Venetians, too, Vivaldi was a skilled composer for the voice. Many of his operas have survived and are receiving growing attention, and it is this sphere of vocal accomplishment that often provided the melodic inspiration for his concertos, especially in slow movements. Sometimes, though, the self-borrowing might occur in reverse. As well as the celebrated printed collections of violin concertos, *L'estro armonico*, *La stravaganza*, *Il cimento dell'armonia e dell'inventione* and *La cetra*, Vivaldi catered generously for the oboe, flute, bassoon and cello and there are few if any dull pieces among them. Vivaldi further demonstrates a lively sense of instrumental colour in concertos for assorted wind and strings while his concertos *a quattro*, for ripieno strings, reveal meticulous craftsmanship, sometimes foreshadowing the idiom of the early symphonists. **Tartini** and **Locatelli** were among the leading composers for the violin in the later years of our period.

Opera continued to thrive in 18th-century Italy, though important structural changes took place. They were influenced by the ideas and texts of Metastasio (1698-1782). He gradually dispensed with the comic elements and other distractions of 17th-century opera to create texts with well-structured plots which were so widely admired that they were set by virtually all the leading *opera seria* composers of the time. Comedy, instead, was concentrated in the intermezzos performed between the acts of serious opera. Naples fostered a lively intermezzo tradition with **Pergolesi**'s *La serva padrona* providing the most celebrated example. Comic scenes and various types of full-length comic opera (*opera buffa*) were also developed in Naples by **Pergolesi, Leonardo Leo, Leonardo Vinci** and Alessandro Scarlatti.

In Spain and the Iberian peninsula, the rapprochement that existed between foreign and indigenous styles is demonstrated by the prolonged stay of Alessandro Scarlatti's son, **Domenico Scarlatti**, by other foreign, mainly Italian composers and by the great castrato Farinelli. Many of Scarlatti's harpsichord sonatas, of which over 500 are known, evoke the colours, moods and rhythms which we think

ESSENTIAL LISTENING II

JS Bach — Brandenburg Concertos
Vienna Concentus Musicus /
Harnoncourt
Teldec Ultima ② 0630-18944-2   Ⓜ

JS Bach — Magnificat
Collegium Musicum 90 Chorus
and Orchestra / Hickox
Chandos Chaconne CHAN0518   Ⓕ

Handel — Concerto grossi, Op 6
Collegium Musicum 90 /
Standage vn
Chandos Chaconne
CHAN0600/16/22   Ⓕ

Handel — Messiah
Gabrieli Consort and Players /
McCreesh
Archiv ② 453 464-2AH2   Ⓕ

Handel — Giulio Cesare
Concerto Cologne / Jacobs
Harmonia Mundi HMC90 1385/7   Ⓕ

Vivaldi — L'Estro Armonico, Op 3
The English Concert / Pinnock
Archiv ⑤ 471 317-2AB5   Ⓑ

of as local to Spain and Portugal. The variety which Scarlatti achieves with a single-movement form is as astonishing as the quantity is prodigious. Among the prominent Spanish composers of this period are: **Torrejón y Velasco**, whose opera *La púrpura de la rosa* (1701) was first performed in Peru in 1701; **Antonio Literes** whose zarzuela (music with spoken dialogue) *Azis y Galatea* was first performed at the Spanish court in 1708; **Carlos de Seixas**, who composed mainly for the keyboard, of which he was a virtuoso; and Italian-born **Domenico Zipoli**, who worked in Argentina where he proselytised on behalf of the Jesuits.

After Lully's death, French opera changed little over a period of almost half a century. Features of the Italian style ever-increasingly attracted French composers, among whom **Campra, Marais, Montéclair** and **Destouches** made original contributions to the *tragédie-lyrique* tradition. Campra, moreover, was an effective pioneer of lighter *opéra-ballet*, in which dance and lavish spectacle assumed greater importance. But it was Rameau's début on the operatic scene, at the age of 50, in 1733, that contributed most of all to a rejuvenation and development of music drama in France. His *tragédies-lyriques* include *Hippolyte et Aricie* (1733), *Castor et Pollux* (1737) and *Les Boréades* (1760), while in a lighter vein *Les Indes galantes* (1735), *Les fêtes d'Hébé* (1739) and a comedy, *Platée* (1745), delighted audiences over an extended period of time. **Leclair** and **Mondonville** also wrote operas of distinction.

On a more intimate level, French chamber cantatas enjoyed enormous popularity during the first three decades or so of the 18th century. **Clérambault** was highly esteemed for his skill in this subtly expressive form, but others like **Campra, Nicolas Bernier, Montéclair** and **Rameau** have left us charming examples. Sacred music continued to thrive in the form of the *grand motet*, with Campra, once again providing many effective pieces for voices and instruments. In the mid-century the *grand motet* reached a summit in a small number of vividly expressive pieces by Mondonville.

Though French composers were late in taking the Italian forms of the sonata and concerto to heart, more expressively home-grown chamber music flourished. Solo harpsichord music was crowned with the 27 *ordres* (suites) of **François Couperin** and by the much smaller but high quality legacy of Rameau. Rewards can also be found in the harpsichord pieces of **Daquin, Dandrieu, Duphly** and **Balbastre**, while the violin and flute sonatas of Leclair, with their pleasing blend of French delicacy and Italian virtuosity, are among the most sophisticated and technically challenging pieces of their kind in the French Baroque repertoire. These fine sonatas may be considered alongside another, more indigenous tradition, that of the bass viol whose music reached unparalleled heights in the masterly suites of **Marais**.

While France had an artistic focal point, first at the Bourbon court then increasingly in Paris, Germany had no centralised culture during the early 18th century. It was both politically fragmented, and also divided in its faith between the Protestant north and Catholic south. North and South were, however, at one in the welcome they gave to French and Italian artists of all kinds. In music this contributed towards an unusually rich stylistic blend, influencing the work of Bach, Fux, Telemann and their contemporaries. In church music the multi-sectional cantata began to take precedence over the motet and vocal concerto. Varied cantata techniques before Bach were imaginatively applied by **Buxtehude, Bruhns, Kuhnau, Zachow, Schelle** and others. Bach's cantatas drew upon these to a varying extent but increasingly embraced Italian virtuosity while at the same time preserving with breathtaking originality the Lutheran chorale tradition. **Bach**'s two great *Passions*, the St John (1724) and the *St Matthew* (1727) follow an earlier tradition established in Leipzig by his predecessor, **Kuhnau**.

The earliest concertos by German composers were based on the Corellian *concerto grosso* concept. But soon the Venetian concertos, above all those of Vivaldi, with their greater emphasis on solo virtuosity were providing rival models. Bach's concertos owe much to Vivaldian organisation but in his most celebrated collection of *Brandenburg*s the music is sometimes blended with French ingredients. But it is in the *ouverture-suites* of German composers that the

French style is most wholeheartedly embraced. Bach, Handel and Telemann excelled in a form that was avidly taken up by **Fasch, Graupner, Stölzel** and others.

The solo instrument, par excellence, in Germany was the organ. Following a tradition established in the 17th century, organ composition and performing virtuosity was brought to a peak by **Buxtehude, Pachelbel, Reincken** and above all Bach, whose music for the instrument has remained unparalleled. Late Baroque German solo and trio sonatas abound, Bach's Sonatas and Partitas for Unaccompanied Violin presented performers with new and demanding challenges, while his Sonatas for Violin and Harpsichord were highly rated during and after his lifetime. **Telemann** was a prolific and rewarding composer of trio sonatas but also pioneered the quartet medium for which he was praised both in Germany and in France. Telemann, ever questing for new means of expression left hardly a musical form untried. Some of his late vocal music is of particular interest, the oratorio *Der Tag des Gerichts* (1762) and the dramatic cantata *Ino* (1765) being of especial merit.

Telemann was also a successful opera composer, but it was his compatriot and friend Handel who achieved international renown with a brilliant succession of Italian operas for the London stage. **Handel** left Germany for Italy in his early twenties, arriving in London first in 1710 then, to settle, in 1712. London was a flourishing centre for music during the first half of the century and a veritable honeypot for foreign musicians, several of whom settled there. Italian opera was the mainstay of musical entertainment until the mid-1730s, Handel contributing most of them, including *Rinaldo* (1711), *Giulio Cesare* (1724), *Tamerlano* (1724), *Rodelinda* (1725), *Orlando* (1733), *Ariodante* (1735), and *Alcina* (1735). By the late 1730s Handel was increasingly directing his talents towards English oratorio, a concept of his own which embraced elements of opera and of English sacred choral music. Among these are *Saul* (1739), *Messiah* (1742), *Semele*, which may justly be considered an English opera (1744), and *Belshazzar* (1745). His English masque *Acis and Galatea* (1718), and the English ode, *L'Allegro, il penseroso ed il moderato* (1740) belong on the same creative level. As well as dramatic music Handel wrote anthems, and celebratory canticles for the church, *concerti grossi*, organ concertos and two splendid occasional pieces,

---

REPERTOIRE EXPLORATION

F Couperin Trois leçons de ténèbres
Les Arts Florissants / Christie
Erato 0630-17067-2 (F)
All three lessons represent Couperin at his most heart-rendingly intense and William Christie is on fine form.

Leclair Violin Sonatas
Fernandez vn Hantaï hpd
Pierlot va da gamba
Auvidis Astrée E8662 (F)
Leclair's technically demanding violin sonatas were hugely popular in his own time and they deserve greater attention from record collectors.

Marais Pièces de viole
Pandolfo bass viol Meyerson hpd
Boysen theorbo/gtr
Glossa GCD920404 (F)
Thrilling and individual performances of some of Marais' wonderful viol music. Don't miss this.

Pergolesi La serva padrona
Soloists; La Petite Bande / Kuijken vn
Accent ACC96123D (F)
A lively performance of Pergolesi's influential mini-masterpiece.

Telemann Musique de Table
Orchestra of the Golden Age
Naxos 8 553732 (S)
Recommendable bargain recordings of some of Telemann's finest music.

---

the *Water Music* and *Music for the Royal Fireworks*. Among the English composers of vocal and instrumental works who lent distinction to London's musical life were **Thomas Arne** and **William Boyce**, whose eight symphonys have long enjoyed popularity with audiences. **Charles Avison** and **John Stanley** wrote exclusively for instruments, their pleasingly crafted concertos affording proof of the excellent health of indigenous talent at the time.

THE CLASSICAL ERA

Richard Wigmore charts the music of the classical era

and explains how the main cultural developments of the time

shaped composers' creativity

The period stretching roughly from the death of Bach in 1750 to the death of Beethoven in 1827 is usefully, if rather loosely, termed the Viennese classical age. Though its three chief protagonists, Haydn, Mozart and Beethoven, would not have recognised themselves as 'classicists' – indeed, in Beethoven's lifetime the German writer ETA Hoffmann characterised all three composers as 'Romantic' – the word does suggest certain dominant ideals of balance, proportion and reconciliation of contrasts central to the art of the Viennese triumvirate and their lesser contemporaries.

At the heart of the so-called Viennese classical style was the sonata principle (the term 'sonata form' was a fabrication of the later 19th century), which evolved from the binary dance movements of the baroque. But whereas a minuet or *courante* by Bach or Handel typically emphasised continuity of texture, a seamless melodic flow and a single emotion, or *Affekt*, the new sonata structures presented a dynamic, dramatic argument based on the contrast of keys and distinct, sharply articulated events, their working-out and their final resolution in the home key. Such was the power and influence of the sonata style by the 1780s and 1790s, when Haydn and Mozart were at their zenith, that it infiltrated all musical forms and genres. In the Act 3 Sextet from *The Marriage of Figaro*, for instance, the sonata design is a perfect musical equivalent of the stage action as the initial situation spawns confusion, discord and eventual reconciliation.

Compare a movement from a concerto or suite by Handel or Bach with an early example of the new sonata style – say, a symphony by **GB Sammartini** (1700/01-75) **or Johann (Jan) Stamitz** (1717-57), or a sonata by **Galuppi** (1706-85), and you are immediately struck by the radical simplification of texture, phrasing and harmony. Gone are the polyphonic textures and often irregular phrasing of the baroque movements. In their place we have, typically, a series of short, rhythmically defined melodic cells, arranged in two- and four-bar phrases, with frequent cadences. The interest is almost exclusively concentrated on the movement of the top line: accompaniments are thinly textured, with chains of repeated notes, harmonies diatonic and slow-changing. Everything is geared towards elegance, 'naturalness' and easy comprehensibility.

This early classical style, the so-called 'style galant', is a counterpart to rococo (the word comes from the French *rocaille*, meaning shellwork) art – typified by the *scènes galantes* of Watteau – and architecture, with their emphasis on airy lightness, graceful, sinuous lines and delicate wit. The 'style galant' found its finest musical expression in the works of JS Bach's youngest son, **Johann Christian Bach** ('The London Bach', 1735-82), with his rare gift for polished, sensuous melody, and of **Luigi Boccherini** (1743-1805), whose string quartets and quintets (with two cellos) composed for the Spanish court combine colourful, often florid textures and a strain of exoticism and a Mediterranean warmth and *morbidezza*. The 'style galant' also pervades many works of Mozart's boyhood and adolescence: indeed, such pieces as the A major Symphony, No 29, and the last three violin concertos raise it to a supreme level – music that, in the words of Mozart's recent biographer Maynard Solomon, 'transforms loveliness into ecstasy, grace into sublimity'.

The Enlightenment

In its emphasis on simplicity and naturalness, the 'style galant' reflected some of the ideals of the Enlightenment, an intellectual movement which had its origins in the 17th-century English empirical philosophers (Locke and Hume), and the work of Isaac Newton and René Descartes. The crucible of Enlightenment thought was France, where church and monarchy had long held absolute sway. A group of *philosophes*, including men such as Montesquieu, Diderot (editor of the seminal *Encyclopédie*) and Voltaire vigorously – and in Voltaire's case vitriolically – opposed the old superstitions and assumptions, including the divine right of kings and the inherited privileges of the aristocracy. In their place they proposed a view of the world centred on man rather than God, and founded on scientific knowledge, reason, social justice and humanitarianism. Another key figure was Jean-Jacques Rousseau, the champion of the common man, 'primitive' virtues and unaffected feeling whose battle cry was 'Back to Nature'.

The ideals of egalitarianism in Enlightenment thought – and which in France were to have their logical culmination in the Revolution – went hand in hand with a new emphasis on education and moral betterment. This was the period when the rapidly burgeoning middle class began to challenge the social and cultural hegemony of the aristocracy. Aristocratic patronage – witness **Haydn** at Eszterháza and **Mozart** at Salzburg – was still crucial to a musician in the late 18th century. But there was also an ever-growing demand for music from the newly powerful bourgeoisie. This was reflected in the rise of the more 'democratic' genres of *opera buffa* and *Singspiel*, which gradually eclipsed the old aristocratic *opera seria*, and the development of public concerts. Another consequence was the expansion of music publishing. For the first time, domestic music-making created a voracious market for sheet music; and composers, Haydn and Mozart among them, supplied for home consumption reams of sonatas, duos (usually with flute or violin), trios and songs, carefully tailored to limited amateur techniques – Mozart's *galant*, 'easy' C major sonata, K545, is a well-known case in point.

The writings of the *philosophes*, their advocacy of nature and simplicity at the expense of artifice, had a crucial effect on the development of opera, especially in France. Factionalism and pamphleteering were favourite sports in mid-18th-century Paris, as they were in London. And the 1750s saw the celebrated – and much satirised – 'Querelle des Bouffons', with the traditionalist adherents of Lully and Rameau, led by Louis XV, vociferously ranged against those who aligned themselves with Rousseau and the Queen in support of the new Italian *opera buffa*, exemplified by Pergolesi's *La serva padrona*. Rousseau, who fancied himself as a composer, produced an opera of his own dealing with ordinary people, the pastoral intermezzo *Le devin du village* (1752), a work of embarrassing naivety and thinness of invention. But the Rousseau faction, and their propagation of Enlightenment values, did succeed in broadening French operatic taste, and helped pave the way for Gluck's triumphs in Paris in the 1770s.

Gluck and opera reform

In Gluck's famous Viennese reform operas of the 1760s, *Orfeo* and *Alceste*, he had sought to eliminate what he dubbed the 'abuses' of Italian *opera seria* – byzantine, often unmotivated plots, endless repetition of words, the artificial divisions into recitative and aria, vacuous ornamentation in deference to singers' vanity – in favour of dramatic truth, a more continuous texture and simple plots drawn from classical mythology. This use of classical subject matter reflects a new interest in the art of ancient Greece and Rome among historians, painters and architects of the time, crucially influenced by the findings of the German archaeologist Johann Winckelmann, whose *History of the Art of the Ancient World* was published in 1764. In his works written for Paris, culminating in *Iphigénie en Tauride* (1779), Gluck created an individual synthesis

SEMINAL WORKS

CPE Bach	Sinfonias H648, H653 and H654. Harpsichord Concerto, H423. Cello Concerto, H432. **Alpermann** *hpd* **Bruns** *vc* **Akademie für Alte Musik, Berlin** Harmonia Mundi HMC90 1711 (6/00)	Ⓕ
Beethoven	Symphony No 3 in E flat, 'Eroica' **Philharmonia Orch / Klemperer** EMI mono CDM7 63855-2	Ⓜ
	String Quartet, Op 131 **Végh Quartet** Auvidis Valois V4408 (6/87)	Ⓕ
	Piano Sonata No 32, Op 111 **Brendel** *pf* Philips 446 701-2PH (12/96)	Ⓕ
	Fidelio **Nielsen** Leonore **Winbergh** Florestan **Hungarian Radio Chor; Nicolaus Esterházy Sinfonia / Halász** Naxos ② 8 660070/1 (12/99)	Ⓢ
Gluck	Orfeo ed Euridice **Ragin** Orfeo **McNair** Euridice **Sieden** Amore; **Monteverdi Choir; English Baroque Soloists / Gardiner** Philips ② 434 093-2PH2 (2/94)	Ⓕ
Haydn	String Quartets, Op 20 **Quatuor Mosaïques** Auvidis Astrée E8785 (5/93)	Ⓕ
	The Creation **Soloists; Monteverdi Choir; English Baroque Soloists / Gardiner** Archiv ② 449 217-2AH2 (4/97)	Ⓕ
Mozart	Piano Concerto No 25 in C, K503 **Schiff** *pf* **Salzburg Mozarteum Camerata Academica / Végh** Decca 425 791-2DH (7/91)	Ⓕ
	String Quintet in G minor, K516 **Grumiaux, Gérecz** *vns* **Janzer, Lesueur** *vas*, **Czako** *vc* Philips 422 511-2PME3 (9/91)	Ⓜ
	Don Giovanni **Waechter** Don Giovanni **Sutherland** Donna Anna **Philharmonia Chor & Orch / Giulini** EMI ② CDS5 56232-2 (12/87R)	Ⓕ

of French *tragédie lyrique*, with its lavish use of spectacle, chorus and ballet, and his own brand of 'beautiful simplicity' and emotional directness. *Iphigénie en Tauride* was to leave its mark on Mozart's first operatic masterpiece *Idomeneo*. But if Gluck was the greatest operatic reformer in the 1760s and 1770s, he was by no means alone: the Italians **Nicolò Jommelli** (1714-74) and **Tommaso Traetta** (1727-79) – above all in his masterpiece, *Antigone* (1772) – were equally concerned to put dramatic truth before singers' egos and purge *opera seria* of its superfluous display and its mechanical sequence of *da capo* arias.

The cult of sensibility

Together with the German poet Klopstock and the Irish writer Laurence Sterne, Rousseau was also a key influence on the German aesthetic of *Empfindsamkeit*, or 'heightened sensibility', above all through his novel of unhappy love, jealousy and soulful melancholy, *La nouvelle Héloïse*. In German literature *Empfindsamkeit* manifested itself in such works as the 'bourgeois tragedies' of Lessing and, most famously, Goethe's novel of thwarted love and suicide, *The Sorrows of Young Werther* – later in life Goethe came to disown the novel's 'pitiable self-torment'. In music this aesthetic was cultivated by a group of North German composers, including **CH Graun**, whose cloyingly sentimental oratorio *Tod Jesu* (1755) became a monument to *Empfindsamkeit*. A far more imaginative and enduring figure, though, was JS Bach's second son, **Carl Philipp Emanuel Bach** (1714-88), whose keyboard fantasias, rondos and sonatas reject the elegant frivolities of the 'style galant' and often distil a very personal vein of brooding introspection, with deceptive and *outré* harmonies and strange discontinuities of rhythm and texture.

This aesthetic of 'heightened sensibility', a reaction to the 'rational' strain in Enlightenment thinking, is closely related to the proto-Romantic movement commonly known as *Sturm und Drang* (Storm and Stress), after Maximilian Klinger's blood-and-thunder drama on the American Revolution (1776). The literature of *Sturm und Drang*, exemplified by such plays as Goethe's *Götz von Berlichingen* and Schiller's *Die Räuber*, stressed violent, irrational emotion and a defiance of political and social convention. Its musical manifestations – the unbridled symphonies and concertos of CPE Bach, Gluck's revolutionary ballet *Don Juan* and the turbulent minor-keyed symphonies of Haydn, the Bohemian **JB Vaňhal**, the teenage Mozart (the 'little' G minor, K183) and others – actually predate the official literary movement. But the fashion for the sombre, the primitive and the terrifying in European art was already being set in the 1760s by James Macpherson's 'Ossian' poems (the greatest literary fraud of the century),

Bishop Percy's *Reliques* and Horace Walpole's Gothic fantasy *The Castle of Otranto*. Such literature was an expression of what the philosopher Edmund Burke termed 'the sublime', which embraced grandeur and terror – inspired by natural phenomena as graveyards, oceans and wild mountains – in contrast to 'the beautiful', which Burke associated with clarity, reason and classical proportion. 'The sublime', as propounded by Burke, became a key concept in late-18th-century aesthetics; and in music it was to be supremely manifested in works such as Mozart's *Don Giovanni*, Haydn's *The Creation* and Beethoven's *Eroica* and Fifth symphonies.

Haydn and the popular style

Goethe renounced the excesses of *Sturm und Drang* with his serene classical drama *Iphigenie auf Tauris* (begun in 1779 – coincidentally the year of Gluck's opera on the same subject), which softens the cruelty of the Euripides original in keeping with the humane values of the Enlightenment. Schiller, too, turned to a loftier, more philosophical manner after the *succès de scandale* of *Die Räuber* in 1782. In Haydn's impassioned, sometimes bizarre symphonies and quartets from around 1770 – in the major as well as the minor mode – intensification of expression does not lead, as it sometimes does in the music of CPE Bach, to the brink of incoherence: a work such as the 'Farewell' symphony (No 45) already shows a formidable power of organisation and cyclic integration. Yet from around 1775 onwards, Haydn tended to abjure violent extremes. Instead he presented an amiable, often jocular face to the world, refining and deepening the language of the comedy of manners, as practised in *opera buffa*, into a supreme vehicle for subtle, civilised discourse. With occasional exceptions, from the mid-1770s onwards Haydn resolves the discordant tensions of the minor key into the major, either in the recapitulation of the opening movement or in the finale: less a question of Haydn's legendary 'cheerfulness' – this was only one aspect of his complex artistic persona – than an acknowledgement of the classical ideal of reconciliation.

In Haydn's hands the sonata style, originally a vehicle for *galant* fripperies, became an infinitely flexible medium, capable of expressing wit, irony, pathos and high drama. In each of his works, whether symphony, string quartet (a genre he evolved almost single-handedly), piano trio or sonata, the material itself dictated the form: and as Tovey pointed out three-quarters of a century ago, no two mature sonata movements by Haydn are identical in design. In his ripest works, from the Op 33 Quartets of 1781 and the 'Paris' symphonies of 1785-86 onwards, Haydn achieved a consummation of the Viennese popular style, in which catchy, folk-like tunes (occasionally, as in the *Drum-Roll* Symphony, No 103, actual folk tunes) formed the basis of immensely complex structures. Haydn's unique combination of intellectual sophistication and popular appeal was infused with 'the sublime' in the two great oratorios and the slow movements of the late quartets and symphonies: indeed, no music of the late 18th century is more exalted or visionary than the 'Chaos' prelude to the *Creation*, whose deeply un-classical effect is, paradoxically, achieved with Haydn's supreme classical control. Both *The Creation* and its equally inspired successor, *The Seasons*, are two of the greatest monuments to the Enlightenment belief in a benign, rationally ordered world and the perfectability of man. More, perhaps, than any music before or since, Haydn's late symphonies, quartets and oratorios appealed to *Kenner* – connoisseurs – and *Liebhaber* – amateurs – alike. They encapsulated and flattered their listeners' 'taste' (an 18th-century buzzword) and understanding while simultaneously expanding and challenging them.

Mozart: a difficult composer?

Mozart also appealed directly to Viennese popular taste in works such as *Die Entführung aus dem Serail* and *Die Zauberflöte*, two of the greatest successes during his lifetime. We can also see him cultivating a calculatedly popular, *faux-naif* style, *à la* Haydn, in the romanze-style slow movements of some of the late piano concertos (most famously, the *Larghetto* of the last concerto, in B flat, K595) and the *Andante* of the String Quintet in E flat, K614. But while it would be a gross exaggeration to portray Mozart as a misunderstood (and impoverished) Romantic figure, out of step with his age, his mature music was often considered 'difficult' to contemporaries in a way Haydn's was not.

Emperor Joseph II's famous royal critique of *Die Entführung* ('Too many notes, my dear Mozart, and too beautiful for our ears') may be apocryphal, but it does point to a recurrent problem in Mozart's music for 18th-century listeners: his language was simply too rich and intricate. Reviewing the first edition of the string quartets Mozart dedicated to Haydn – among his most 'learned' and esoteric works – one writer complained that they were too 'highly seasoned'. The publisher Hoffmeister rejected Mozart's two piano quartets because of their complexity. Mozart's sensuous, even voluptuous, richness of texture and chromatic harmony, which so delights us today, was bewildering to many listeners in his own time. So was the 'demonic' element in his music, as evinced in such works as the piano concertos in D minor and C minor, the great G minor string quintet and symphony, and *Don Giovanni*, a triumph in Prague but a mixed success in Vienna, which preferred the breezy, undemanding *opere buffe* of such

Goethe's famous remark that the string quartet is a 'conversation between four intelligent people' neatly characterises an essential aspect of the medium around 1800, the time of Haydn's last and Beethoven's first quartets. The perfection of the string quartet as a subtle, often witty discourse between four nominally equal players was one of the supreme musical achievements of the Age of the Enlightenment, and a reflection of the 18th century's cultivation of the art of civilised conversation.

Mozart contributed his own brand of sensuality and textural richness to the string quartet in his six works dedicated to Haydn, while Beethoven imbued the medium with a new rhetorical force and symphonic amplitude in the three 'Razumovsky' Quartets, Op 59. But it was Haydn who, on his own admission, stumbled on the string quartet 'by accident' in the late 1750s, who played the crucial role in its evolution. Before him there had been spasmodic examples of divertimentos for two solo violins, viola and cello by Viennese composers such as Ignaz Holzbauer and CG Wagenseil. But these older composers showed no interest in exploring the potential of the quartet as a flexible, conversational medium. And it fell to Haydn, in his sets of quartets from Op 20 (1772) to Op 77 (1799), to raise the genre from its humble beginnings in the outdoor serenade to a vehicle for the most sophisticate and challenging musical discussion.

composers as **Paisiello** (1740-1816), **Martín y Soler** (1754-1806) and **Cimarosa** (1749-1801). This demonic strain, first identified as such by ETA Hoffmann, appealed strongly to 19th-century Romantics, at a time when most of his music was either patronised for its supposed Dresden-china prettiness, or (by the likes of Tchaikovsky) nostalgically idealised as the emblem of a lost Eden.

Mozart, of course, draws freely on the Italian operatic *lingua franca* of the day; on Viennese popular song, too, in *Die Zauberflöte*. But his mature operas far transcend the elegant frivolities of Soler and Cimarosa, in their musical density and complexity, their long-range structural mastery (shown most obviously in the extended act-finales) and their penetrative human understanding. All of his operatic masterpieces, from *Idomeneo* to *La clemenza di Tito* – a late example of Enlightenment *opera seria* – and the uniquely heterogeneous *Zauberflöte*, are touched by a Shakespearean wisdom, compassion and tolerance; in true Enlightenment spirit, forgiveness and reconciliation lie at the heart of each of these works, sometimes expressed in music of transfigured stillness: the reflections on forgiveness in the two finales of *Die*

Entführung; the Countess's pardon of her errant husband near the end of *Figaro*; or the final union of Tamino and Pamina in the second finale of *Die Zauberflöte*. Even in the outwardly cynical, worldly *Così fan tutte*, such numbers as the 'farewell' Quintet and Trio in Act 1 transform the ridiculous into moments of transcendent beauty. The characters may seem self-centred and absurd, but through Mozart's music they are ennobled and redeemed.

Unlike Haydn, Mozart was both a born theatre animal and a supreme keyboard virtuoso. In the first part of the 18th century star performers were almost invariably singers. But with the growing prestige of instrumental music and the rise of public concerts, from the mid-century onwards a new breed of instrumental virtuosos touted their wares around the salons and concert halls of Europe. In Mozart's generation the composer-pianists **Muzio Clementi** (1752-1832) and **JL Dussek** (1760-1812) were influential in the development of the keyboard, both through their flamboyant playing and through their taxing and often prophetic piano sonatas. Their most gifted successors in the next generation were **JN Hummel** (1778-1837) and **John Field** (1782-1837), both of whom had a crucial influence on Chopin. Outside the opera house, Mozart had his greatest professional and financial successes performing his piano concertos at his own Viennese subscription concerts. And the great series of concertos he wrote between 1782 and 1786 represent a unique amalgam of operatic characterisation, chamber musical refinement (above all in the miraculous wind writing), virtuoso display and elaborate symphonic organisation.

Beethoven: firebrand and visionary

It was as a keyboard lion that the young Ludwig van Beethoven announced himself in Vienna in the early 1790s. And within a few years the *sans culotte* from provincial Bonn had improbably become the darling of Viennese salons, admired by aristocratic connoisseurs both for his playing and his brilliant, daring keyboard compositions. Some of Beethoven's early works – the Quintet for Piano and Wind, Op 16, is a case in point – are deliberately cautious, paying homage to Mozart, whose stock was rapidly rising in the years after his death. But in the Op 1 piano trios and many of the early piano sonatas, a new sense of dialectical urgency often goes hand in hand with a subversive vehemence. The classical proportions of Haydn and Mozart are observed. But works like the *Pathétique* Sonata and the finale of the *Moonlight* reveal a composer hell-bent on confronting his audience and imposing his will on them. The language of the classical comedy of manners as perfected by Haydn and Mozart has become

---

REPERTOIRE EXPLORATION

Boccherini String Quintets
Europa Galante
Virgin Veritas VC5 45421-2   Ⓕ
Irresistible music performed by players of the highest calibre and sensitivity. An absolute must.

Cherubini Medea
Sass Medea **Luchetti** Jason
Budapest SO; Hungarian Radio and Television Chor / Gardelli
Hungaraton ② HCD11904/5 (4/87)Ⓕ
A moving, strongly concentrated opera, akin in inventiveness and spirit to Beethoven and Berlioz.

Clementi Keyboard sonatas
Staier fp
Teldec 3984 26731-2 (10/00)   Ⓕ
Expressive and often powerful music in superlative performances.

Dussek Keyboard sonatas – Op 4, No 3 (C39); Op 10 No 2 (C61); Op 35 No 3 (C151); Op 61 (C211)
Marvin pf
Dorian Discovery DIS80125 (7/95) Ⓕ
Op 4 No 3's second-movement Minuet anticipates Schubert with its gentle, reflective mood and subtly coloured major/minor opposition, while Op 35 No 3's opening movement can stand comparison with Beethoven's *Pathétique*.

Hummel Piano Concertos Nos 2 and 3
Hough pf
Chandos CHAN8507 (4/87)   Ⓕ
Exciting and inventive music and superb performances. This disc is a real must.

Traetta Antigona
Bayo Antigona **Anna Maria Panzarella** Ismene;
Accentus Chamber Chor;
Les Talens Lyriques / Rousset
L'Oiseau-Lyre
② 460 204-2OHO2 (3/01)   Ⓕ
Compelling performance of a seminal 18th-century opera worthy to be ranked alongside Gluck's reform operas.

Vaňhal Symphonies
Various artists
Teldec 0630 13141-2
High-voltage readings of four inventive, often impassioned symphonies by one of Haydn's most gifted contemporaries.

trenchant and strenuous, even melodramatic. And already, in pieces such as the C minor Trio from Op 1 or the F major String Quartet Op 18 No 1, Beethoven conceives the recapitulation in a sonata-form movement not merely as a homecoming but as a triumphant apotheosis.

After the turn of the new century, the trauma of encroaching deafness and the artistic credo expounded in the Heiligenstadt Testament unleashed a spate of compositions inspired by the notion of heroic struggle. 'I shall seize Fate by the throat; it shall never wholly subdue me', he wrote – words unthinkable from the pen of Haydn or Mozart. For Beethoven heroism was associated with an ethical idealism, inspired by the theory, if not the reality, of the French Revolution – a striving for liberty, fraternity and a just, enlightened social order. It was this sense of growth through mighty, heroic endeavour to ultimate triumph that lay behind works like the unprecedentedly vast *Eroica* – a tribute less to Napoleon, the original dedicatee, than to Beethoven-as-hero – and the fanatically concentrated Fifth Symphony. Not surprisingly, many found such works initially disturbing, even repellent. But for an ever-growing number of listeners, Beethoven's dynamic, ethically charged vision communicated itself with an unprecedented directness and force.

Beyond the ideals of the Revolution itself, the grandiose, massively scored Revolutionary music of composers like **Méhul** (1763-1817) and **Gossec** (1734-1829) was certainly an influence on Beethoven's famously 'noisy' orchestral style, though in Beethoven's hands the overtly political is transcended and personalised. Similarly, his only opera *Fidelio* transcends the genre of the Revolutionary rescue opera – and the tradition of French *opéra comique* embodied most powerfully by the works of **Cherubini** (1760-1842) –

and becomes a universal hymn to freedom from tyranny and to ideal womanhood: a sort of post-Revolutionary *Zauberflöte* minus the magic and the Freemasonry. The revised version of *Fidelio*, premièred in 1814, marked the zenith of Beethoven's popular acclaim. With a few notable exceptions, like the titanic *Hammerklavier* Sonata, the *Missa solemnis* and the Ninth Symphony, that mighty late affirmation of Enlightenment ideals, his music now abandons the monumental, heroic vision for a more private, introspective questing – though it should be emphasised that Beethoven did not withdraw from the world to compose his last quartets: they were written to order, like so much of Haydn's and Mozart's music. For all their structural and harmonic innovations, the late piano sonatas and quartets still depend on the classical sonata principle he had used with such far-seeing mastery all his life. And it is this, together with his magnificent sanity and control, even *in extremis*, that confirms Beethoven as an essentially classical artist in an age of burgeoning subjective Romanticism. Yet in these sublime late works the sonata ideal is imbued with a new concentration and clarity, while being expanded as never before to embrace fugue, variations, operatic aria (in, for instance, the A flat Sonata, Op 110) and a serene, rarefied lyricism. The lyrical intimacy of much of Beethoven's middle-period music – in, say, the F sharp major Sonata, Op 78, or the E flat Trio Op 70 No 2 – has tended to be overshadowed by the more public, heroic works. But such movements as the final variations of the E major Sonata, Op 109, and the C minor, Op 111, attain a visionary ecstasy that had never been heard in music before. Beethoven's spiritual struggles here find their consummation in music of timeless, transcendental peace.

THE ROMANTIC ERA

Romanticism wasn't merely a matter of expression or sentiment, but gave a new primacy to the individual voice, as **Simon Trezise** explains

Before we can talk about Romanticism in music and its approximate temporal boundaries, the expression has to be defined. The word itself came from the French *lingua romana* and from related literatures, especially romances. As time went on the freedom of the medieval romance was compared unfavourably with the perceived straightjacket of classical tradition, which was thought to be besotted with rules and formalism. So it was that a breach between spontaneous and hidebound art came under philosophical scrutiny towards the end of the 18th century through the writings of Friedrich and August Schlegel and others. In shifting awareness, the influence of Rousseau was immense, for it was he who declared that 'man is born free and everywhere he is in chains'. He proclaimed the nobility of the savage and adumbrated the Romantics' acute interest in the countryside and untrammelled nature, which often found expression in the cultivation of folksong (as in many works of Haydn). Goethe in *The Sorrows of Young Werther* gave birth to the archetypal Romantic hero and set the scene for the individualism of much Romantic literature and music.

Add to this already extremely rich mixture the French Revolution and all the attendant upheaval in society, which overset the old orders of the Age of Enlightenment, destroyed many of the symbols of faith (in the destruction of windows, statues, etc in French churches), and new forces were released into society that were more questioning and more likely to spur deeper emotions than had hitherto been encouraged in individual expression. Whereas baroque composers had access to a range of musical 'topics' (or 'affects') to express generalised emotions according to a well-sorted set of criteria, Mozart, Beethoven, and their successors could depict complex and often contradictory emotions within a short time span, as in Mozart's Symphony No 40.

All of which raises the question of when musical Romanticism actually started. While some would have it in the late 1790s, exemplified by fascinating figures like **Grétry**, others choose to see Beethoven as the last great exponent of the old classical order (challenging and setting many Romantic agendas as he went) and therefore place the start in the 1820s or so. It continued, some would argue, into the early 20th century when it was supplanted by realism, symbolism (Debussy) and modernism (Schoenberg). The musicologist Carl Dahlhaus, however, sees the 1860s onwards as neo-Romanticism, a period in which the ideals and spontaneity of the early period became stereotyped.

Another, rather attractive possibility is to see classicism and Romanticism in music as conjoined streams that needed to coexist, so one finds in Beethoven the formalist Fourth Symphony composed alongside the extremely dramatic, and to many ears, Romantic Fifth. To make Romanticism depend on expression alone is a nonsense, however, for music of all centuries can be highly expressive: witness Bach's chorale preludes, Haydn's *Sturm und Drang* symphonies and so on. Some of Mozart's later works are surely Romantic in every sense in which we have defined the term, and they were claimed as such by the 19th century, especially the minor-key works and *Don Giovanni* (suitably shorn of its thoroughly classical concluding sextet!).

The early Romantics

Allowing for two streams running right through the 19th century, we can at last start to understand **Schubert**, whose early symphonies obediently imitate Mozart and Haydn. While he was writing them he also brought an old form to a new level of expressiveness and versatility, the Lied. His songs among the earliest distinctive fruits of a new spirit in music, and songs such as *Erlkönig* and *Gretchen am Spinnrade* influenced generations of composers from Schumann, through Wagner and beyond. They created a new tonal style strongly contrasted with the structures of the 18th century, and their 'rhetoric' stocked the expressive resources of the new age. Schubert incorporated many of his discoveries into piano sonatas, symphonies, and chamber music, of which his String Quintet is perhaps the most striking fusion of classical forms and Romantic expression.

At the same time as Schubert was bringing his all-too short career to a climax, **Weber** was creating his own revolution in Dresden. His *Singspiel Der Freischütz* is the first unequivocal operatic masterpiece of German Romanticism; it became the bread and butter of every aspiring German composer, performer, conductor and music lover for the rest of the century and beyond. Its mixture of diabolical magical elements (the 'guided' bullets), the redemptive powers of womanly love, folklore and countryside were an irresistible cocktail for the Romantics and led straight to Wagner's early works.

The first generation after these giants – the one that best represents German Romanticism – comprises **Mendelssohn** and **Schumann**, plus a highly distinguished 'guest' from

Poland, Chopin. Schumann's piano cycles, including *Carnaval*, display the public and private faces of the composer, represented by the colourful literary tags Florestan and Eusebius. In addition, numerous allusions are delicately encoded into the music by means of musical ciphers, many of which refer to his initially forbidden love for Clara Wieck. In *Davidsbündlertänze* Schumann invites us to a masked ball, where fleeting meetings, intimacies and dances pass in quick succession, influenced by the important novelist Jean Paul. The musical language is highly expressive and the forms are often radical in their epigrammatic style. On the other hand, this most Romantic of Romantic masters also wrote sonatas and, later, symphonies, which build on the example of Beethoven. After his marriage to Clara he took the Lied further in several magnificent song cycles, including *Dichterliebe*, which perfectly enshrines the agony of Romantic love.

Although closely identified with Schumann through geography, shared interests, and friendship, Mendelssohn was quite a different composer. He was less personal in his expressive aims and spent many of his early years pursuing musical studies that would have been perfectly comprehensible to Mozart (similarly Schumann later made an intense study of counterpoint). No surprise then that the early symphonies, mainly written for strings and played at domestic gatherings of his wealthy family, are closely related to those of Haydn. On the other hand, the exquisite 'Scottish' breathes the air of high Romanticism as it celebrates a strange and distant land and whips up a storm in the first movement. His Fifth Symphony, 'Reformation', celebrates Germany's distant past and looks forward to the nostalgia coursing through the veins of Wagner's *Die Meistersinger*.

Mendelssohn and Schumann set definitive examples for the Romantic concerto in their respective Violin Concerto and Piano Concerto. Gone was the long classical orchestral opening (*tutti* or ritornello), to be replaced by a reciprocal exchange of ideas between soloist and orchestra. Both concertos were much imitated. Their symphonies were similarly adaptive of classical forms: Mendelssohn joined up movements in the *Scottish* and Schumann not only makes his Fourth Symphony (in its second version) flow without a break, he also produces one of the most striking modifications of sonata form in the first movement by basing the recapitulation on a new motive introduced in the development. Sonata form itself, as we also discover in Chopin's sonatas, became less concerned with the contrast of keys in the exposition than with the contrast of themes, so reflecting prevailing dualist ideas in philosophy derived from Hegel. From now on the assertive first subject and more delicate, 'feminine' second subject became commonplace, though not ubiquitous, as Schumann demonstrates.

SEMINAL WORKS

Beethoven	Symphony No 9, 'Choral' **Berlin Philharmonic Orchestra / Karajan** DG Galleria 415 832-2GGA (M)
Berlioz	Symphonie fantastique **London Symphony Orchestra / C Davis** LSO Live LSO0007CD (S)
Chopin	Nocturnes, Op 27 **Pires** pf DG 447 096-2GH2 (F)
Liszt	Piano Sonata in B minor **Argerich** pf DG The Originals 447 430-2GOR (M)
Mendelssohn	A Midsummer Night's Dream **London Philharmonic Orchestra / Litton** Classics for Pleasure CD-CFP4593 (B)
Mussorgsky	Boris Godunov (two versions) **Kirov Chorus & Orchestra / Gergiev** Philips (5) 462 230-2PH5 (M)
Schubert	Erlkönig **Schäfer** sop **Ainsley** ten **George** bass **Johnson** pf Hyperion CDJ33024 (F)
Schumann	Carnaval **Hess** pf Naxos Historical mono 8 110604 (S)
Verdi	La traviata **Callas** Violetta **Kraus** Germont **Lisbon San Carlos National Theatre Orchestra / Ghione** EMI (2) CDS5 56330-2 (11/87R)
Wagner	Tristan und Isolde **Windgassen** Tristan **Nilsson** Isolde **Bayreuth Festival Chorus & Orchestra / Böhm** DG The Originals (3) 449 772-2GOR3 (7/88) (M)
Weber	Der Freischütz **Schreier** Max **Janowitz** Agathe **Leipzig Radio Chor; Staatskapelle Dresden / C Kleiber** DG The Originals (2) 457 736-2GOR2 (11/86R) (F)

ROMANTIC FORMS AND TECHNIQUES

Character piece (lyric piano piece)

Thousands of examples of short, often self-contained pieces, mainly for piano, with names such as *Intermezzo*, *Song without words*, etc, often in simple ternary form (ABA). From Beethoven through Schubert, Brahms, Liszt and Grieg into the 20th century such pieces continued to be written. They epitomise Romantic sensibility.

Cyclic form

The use of a motive or theme (eg *idée fixe*) in all or some movements of a multi-movement work such as the symphony and concerto. ETA Hoffmann detected it in Beethoven's Fifth Symphony, in which the opening 'da-da-da-dum' returns in varied forms in all movements. Berlioz, Saint-Saëns, Tchaikovsky, Elgar and many others employed it in symphonies and chamber music. It generally entailed bringing back an idea from the first movement in subsequent movements, often in an altered form (such as the twisted Witches' Sabbath version of the *idée fixe* in the finale of Berlioz's *Symphonie fantastique*). It satisfied the Romantic desire for explicit unity on the surface, and is closely related to the Lisztian technique of thematic metamorphosis by which an idea changes character but retains its original melodic contour.

Lied

Songs for voice and accompaniment, but differentiated from the 18th century by the independence of the piano part and extensive use of lyric verse inspired and in many instances were written by Goethe and his imitators. When groups of songs are brought together through a shared narrative or, more often, poetic source, the result is the song-cycle, as in Schubert's *Winterreise*.

Leitmotif

Found in operas of 18th- and early 19th-century operas and oratorios, but used most extensively by Wagner in the *Ring*, this is a musical motive or theme (sometimes just a rhythm or chord) used to depict a person, event, mood, or object – Siegmund's sword in *Die Walküre* is represented by a rising arpeggio figure, usually associated with a trumpet.

Symphonic (tone) poem

Liszt invented this genre, which usually comprises a single-movement orchestral piece with a programme of some sort. Sometimes a symphonic poem is more about feelings or impressions than actual events (eg Liszt's *Les préludes*), though in *Don Juan* Richard Strauss graphically depicts the erotic exploits of the old libertine, including an extended wooing sequence that leaves one in no doubt of the outcome.

The greatest instrumental composer of the time alongside Schumann was **Chopin**, whose experiments with form (inspired by Field and others) runs counter to many classical trends. Even so, his works are revered for their classical poise. In Chopin, as in Schubert, Schumann and Mendelssohn, the short character piece became a major purveyor of ideas. He also cultivated national and international dance forms to an astonishing degree in his mazurkas, polonaises and waltzes. In longer works he favoured an episodic solution, like Schumann in his *Fantasie* for piano, Op 17, and the Nocturnes, which lie at the heart of his output, use operatic coloratura (rapid, ornamental passages) to add freedom and eloquence to the singing piano. For many writers trying to some up the Romantic period in music the mixture of melancholy and flights of free fantasy in Chopin are the kernel. They also did much to enhance the status of the pianist as exponent of Romantic alienation from society (the piano was the adored instrument of the century). Curiously, Chopin's magnificent *Etudes* display a classical preoccupation with solving single technical problems (for the keyboard), but their tonal structures build ingeniously upon the foundations laid by Schubert.

Berlioz and Liszt

None of this magical trinity was overly concerned with the demonic or more desperate flights of Romanticism such as we encounter in that quintessential Romantic poet Byron. The adventures of Childe Harold and Don Juan were as congenial to the Romantic palette as the plays of Shakespeare; they figure prominently in the next pair of composers to enter the story, **Berlioz** and **Liszt**. Berlioz's *Symphonie fantastique* is a wonderfully grotesque emanation from post-Revolutionary France with its 'March to the Scaffold' and 'Witches Sabbath'. The symphony is programmatic throughout, depicting the tragic decline of the composer's imagined self as, rejected in love, he takes opium and imagines he has murdered his beloved, hence the scaffold; and then in the finale he enters a gothic world in which reality is supplanted by ghosts, sorcerers and monsters at the Sabbath. This is the very stuff of Romanticism, and yet the symphony wasn't conceived in a Romantic surge of spontaneous creativity: much of it is a compilation of music written for other works – in other words, it is inspired recycling.

The *Symphonie fantastique* was arranged for piano by Liszt and began its triumphant and controversial tour of the world in this form. This was how Schumann encountered it when he was moved to write a famous essay in its defence. Berlioz went on to write more symphonies, including one based on Byron's *Harold* (*Harold en Italie* has a prominent viola part depicting the hero) and operas, not least the imposing grand opera *Les Troyens* in which the classical influence of Gluck is as strong as contemporary Romantic impulses. Goethe enters Berlioz's volcanic output on several occasions, most stirringly in his superb *La damnation de Faust*, a secular oratorio – a genre much favoured in the 19th century.

Liszt was a prolific composer and the most famous pianist of his time. His famous tempo rubato contrasted with the *bel canto* style of Chopin, which leant towards a more metronomic way of playing. He left hundreds of piano works, many of which encapsulate the erotic and spiritual longings of their charismatic creator. The *Liebesträume* are typical, and Romantic interest in exoticism led to the *Hungarian Rhapsodies*, which Liszt mistakenly believed to be based on real Hungarian folksongs (not gypsy melodies based on popular songs as we now know). Even as Liszt wrote character pieces in a single movement in a variety of classical and rhapsodic forms, his classicism burst forth in the one-movement Piano Sonata in B minor. This amazing piece takes over the movements of a classical sonata and fuses them into one movement following the example of Schubert in his *Wandererfantasie*.

Liszt made another major contribution to 19th-century form when he invented the symphonic poem inspired by Beethoven's overtures and Rossini's one-off *William Tell* Overture. Here was a free, usually single-movement form that could satisfy the Romantic preoccupation with literature by basing a musical work on some extra-musical source such as a poem, novel, myth or other source. Dvořák in some of his symphonic poems went as far as basing the very melodies themselves on the rhythm of a specific poem, most famously in *The Golden Spinning-Wheel*. Liszt covered a wide range of topics. *Héroïde funèbre* (1850) responds to revolutionary events in 1848 by recalling the savage quelling of Kossuth's revolt from Hungary's more ancient past. *Hamlet* depicts moods and people rather than narratives from Shakespeare's play. Reflecting the origins of the symphonic poem, *Hamlet* was conceived as an overture to the play before taking on its definitive form. Liszt expanded the horizons of the programmatic symphony and gave vent to his lifelong passion for Goethe's *Faust* by basing a three-movement symphony on it. In this substantial work he followed Berlioz in using a 'cyclic' theme, which depicts the eponymous hero and helps integrate the movements. The use of a cyclic theme or, as in Berlioz, *idée fixe*, was widely imitated and is found in symphonies by Franck, Saint-Saëns, Tchaikovsky and Elgar among many others (it is hinted at in Brahms).

Wagner

Liszt's legacy went beyond formal novelty. He innovated tirelessly in harmony, and his highly chromatic music language – which led to atonality in some late works – found its greatest exponent in one of the really gargantuan figures of the century, **Wagner**. Between Weber and Wagner German opera was active but rarely left a great imprint. With Wagner German opera came to dominate the world and influence virtually every major artistic movement thereafter. Wagner came to opera through diverse French, Italian and German examples, all of which can be heard in the Romantic operas *Der fliegende Holländer*, *Tannhäuser* and *Lohengrin*. In the first two one finds favourite a Wagner theme of a sinning man redeemed through the self-sacrificing love of a woman. These operas still owe something to traditional operatic forms with their use of closed numbers (arias, etc.). From *Der Ring* onwards, starting with *Das Rhinegold*, Wagner embarked on a new chapter in musical expression and based his operatic forms on open-ended structures held together by leitmotifs – musical figures of any length depicting a character, object, emotion or other dramatic event. Wagner called his operas 'music dramas' and held them up as revolutionary *Gesamtkunstwerke* (total works of art – a pompous term for 'theatre' one suspects). *Der Ring*, arguably the most ambitious single work in the history of Western music, comprises four operas lasting in total some 15 hours which present nothing less than the rise and fall of civilisation in a mythical setting, all painted in the most vivid orchestral colours. *Tristan und Isolde* brought the subject of Romantic love to a sumptuous epiphany and erotic explicitness that swept all before it. At around the same time he wrote his loving, nostalgic cry for the artistic soul of the 'old' German nation in the comic opera *Die Mastersinger von Nürnberg*. His last work, *Parsifal*, is also his most difficult. Its religious subject is encrusted with layers of symbolism, and some writers have detected racist overtones, all of which seem transcended by the breathtakingly lovely music so admired by Debussy and countless others.

The age that produced Wagner also produced **Brahms**. A devout classicist he knew the past as well as he knew the present. His works abound in references to the Renaissance, baroque, classical as well as to the present, including Wagner. He was a friend and disciple of Schumann, and his early works are full of the hot-blooded passion of the Romantic movement. As he matured he became more and more entrenched in the classical style. His four concertos even use the Mozartian opening *tutti* (or ritornello) prior to the soloist's entry, long since rejected by the Romantics. And yet commingling with his classicism is a poetic soul and a profound identification with nature and other Romantic ideals. In 1854 this Romantic soul was explicitly bared in the first version of the First Piano Trio, which contains Schumann's Clara themes, but late in life he revised the trio and hid the 'programme'. His symphonies, chamber music, songs, choruses, etc are among the most perfectly formed of all 19th-century works, but it is hardly reasonable that his works should be exalted as emblems of so-called 'absolute' music, which is music with no subject other than music itself.

Italian opera

Crossing the Alps we find a land dominated by opera. Italy was in love with theatre and the human voice. Its classical period had Rossini and its early Romantic composers were **Donizetti** and **Bellini**. *Lucia di Lammermoor*, one of Donizetti's finest operas, represents much of Italian Romanticism. The orchestral sound is fuller, more horn-dominated than Rossini; the harmony has become chromatic, and the subject matter, with its gloomy churchyards and ruins, is taken from one of the most popular literary figures of Romanticism, Sir Walter Scott (*The Bride of Lammermoor*). Donizetti relaxes Rossini's geometric forms, often varying the second verse in the slow part of an aria, and using long scenas with highly varied recitatives now forming a more integrated part of the operatic fabric. The aria in which Lucia loses her reason after murdering her unwanted husband – the Mad Scene – is a classic instance of the triumph of the irrational, in this case triggered by tragic events founded, as is so often the way, on thwarted love.

Bellini's poignant melodies and rich orchestration added another layer to Italian Romantic opera, best heard in *Norma* and *I puritani*, but it was **Verdi** who set the seal on the Italian century. His works blended nationalism and realism with subjects inherited from Romantic poets and novelists to create operas of consummate dramatic power and musical substance. *La traviata* takes the theme of the consumptive courtesan who becomes Romantically involved with a man of good birth (after Dumas's *La dame aux camélias*). Family duty intervenes and she is forced to renounce the love of her life, with heartbreaking consequences. Verdi gradually loosens traditional Italian operatic forms, still using arias and ensembles, but often diluting their formal integrity so that whole scenes or even acts are built in a chain-like way. It is a halfway house between Rossini's closed forms and Wagner's endless melody, and it triumphs in the works of Verdi's old age, especially *Otello* and *Falstaff*. *Don Carlos* is a superlative example of grand historical opera; it uses a vast range of musical devices from conventional arias to vast set pieces; and the orchestra is as important as the voice as a carrier of dramatic truth.

Opera was also the staple diet of Paris, where much of France's musical life flourished. The French liked grand opera *à la* **Meyerbeer**, whose *Les Huguenots* satisfied the taste for

---

KEY CULTURAL INFLUENCES

Goethe, Johann Wolfgang von (1749-1832)
He offered a new, individualistic view of humanity in his poetry, novels, plays and scientific writings which had a profound influence on the Romantic period as well as providing source material for countless operas, symphonic poems, etc, most notably *Faust*.

Hegel, Georg Wilhelm Friedrich (1770-1831)
The most influential philosopher of the time, he produced a philosophy based on the belief that argument, processes, and so on were based upon the opposition of ideas or the conflict of opposites.

Hoffmann, Ernst Theodor Amadeus (1776-1822)
A novelist, critic, composer, Hoffmann did much to establish the beliefs and aspirations of early Romanticism. In particular he was instrumental in establishing Beethoven as the first Romantic composer. One of his greatest works was brought back to life by Offenbach in the opera *The Tales of Hoffmann*.

Nietzsche, Friedrich Wilhelm (1844-1900)
A radical atheistic philosopher who argued that man's great mission is to foster the superman, an individual who can find meaning in a meaningless world and who rejects contemporary materialist aspirations.

Richter, Johann Paul Friedrich (1763-1825)
Pen name Jean Paul, his highly eccentric novels inspired piano works by Schumann, who was doubtless attracted by their quirky, incident-rich content.

Rousseau, Jean-Jacques (1712–78)
He advocated more permissive education for children and voiced more extreme emotions than any other writer of his time; idealised nature and the native.

Schlegel, Friedrich von (1772-1829)
A philosopher and writer on Classical antiquity, he wrote of the inherent dichotomy of Classical and Romantic art.

---

grand scenes, vocal acrobatics, and long ensembles. Berlioz was hard-pressed to compete, as was Wagner on his catastrophic trips to Paris. One composer who did finally succeed in the opera house (albeit in the Opéra-Comique) was **Bizet**, who did not live to see his *Carmen* become one of the favoured vehicles of the new operatic realism (in some ways a post-Romantic phenomenon). As the century wore on the concert life of the salons, the setting for France's instrumental life, extended into newly built concert halls where more and more orchestras sprang up. For most of them Liszt was a hallowed model for form, harmony and motivic development. Inspired by **César Franck** many composers started to write quartets, symphonies, etc: classicism returned to France. The apparently cerebral Franck wrote works of great passion, including a Piano Quintet which takes the Belgian composer out of his beloved organ loft and into the scalding embrace of erotic passion.

Nationalism

It took a while for music in Spain, England, Bohemia, Poland, Hungary, Russia and other countries to develop an individual voice and come forward with major composers. Russia woke up first, in the works of **Glinka**, whose operas used Russian folk music. His example was followed by the 'Five', which comprised Balakirev, Rimsky-Korsakov, Cui, Borodin and **Mussorgsky**. All discovered their roots in Russian folklore and were inspired to base whole works on folksong. Mussorgsky's *Boris Godunov* is probably the greatest product of this movement, but its realism takes us beyond the scope of Romanticism. Alongside these overtly nationalistic composers **Tchaikovsky** was more cosmopolitan. He loved French ballet, hated Wagner, and evidently knew Berlioz and Liszt's music very well (as did the 'Five'). Tchaikovsky's classicism manifested itself in seven symphonies, the later examples of which are among the most original and striking adaptions of the classical, four-movement model. True to the Romantic movement he identified so closely with, his unnumbered symphony is based on Byron's *Manfred* and uses a Berlioz-like *idée fixe*. Tchaikovsky's ballets are considered his greatest achievement, especially *The Sleeping Beauty*; they combine symphonic development in set pieces with strongly characterised shorter numbers, all underpinned by a visceral excitement unique to this composer.

Many countries found themselves awakening to refreshing Romantic air in the nationalist movement. Bohemia boasted Smetana and later **Dvořák**, who worked fluently in both the classical Brahms manner and Romantic prototypes of Liszt (as in his symphonic poems). Dvořák's individuality is best demonstrated in his symphonies, especially the last three, the Cello Concerto, and his highly varied chamber music. His operas are becoming better known thanks to recordings.

Britain and Ireland were less fortunate in the 19th century, though recent excavation has started to uncover some fine Romantic music from Bantock, Parry, Sullivan, Stanford and others. Perhaps the famous renaissance, which started with **Elgar** and **Vaughan Williams**, was not quite so sudden as it sometimes assumed.

The 19th century was a rich, diffuse, multi-layered time for music – far more so than the 18th. Many strands make up the movement loosely referred to as Romanticism. However

one seeks to define it, by 1900 it had largely run its course. Symbolism, modernism, realism and other movements had taken over, in spite of which Romanticism in one form or another continues to play a part in composers as disparate as Barber and Elgar, and a neo-Romantic movement is certainly with us today.

REPERTOIRE EXPLORATION

Albéniz   Iberia
De Larrocha pf
Decca ② 417 887-2DH2 (6/88)   Ⓕ
A treasure trove of Spanish nationalism expressed in glowing keyboard writing.

Alkan   Grande Sonate 'Les Quatre Ages', Op 33
Hamelin pf
Hyperion CDA66794
Alkan's keyboard virtuosity is staggering, as is his fecundity of invention.

Brüll   Piano Concertos No 2, Op 24 Coupling: Piano Concerto No 1, Op 10
Roscoe pf **BBC Scottish Symphony Orchestra / Brabbins**
Hyperion CDA67069 (4/99)   Ⓕ
Little-known riches surface in this brilliantly conceived concerto – a reminder of many hidden Romantic treasures.

Litolff   Concerto symphonique No 4, Op 102 Coupling: Concerto symphonique No 2, Op 22
Donohoe pf **Bournemouth Symphony Orchestra / Litton**
Hyperion CDA66889 (4/97)   Ⓕ
A concerto in the grand tradition with a miraculous *Scherzo* and much to relish in other movements.

Lalo   Namouna – Suites Nos 1 and 2 plus Allegro vivace; Tambourin; La Gitane; Bacchanale
Monte-Carlo Philharmonic Orchestra / Robertson
Auvidis Valois V4677   Ⓕ
Vivid orchestral writing and rhythmic ideas in this ballet so excited the young Debussy that he was evicted from the theatre.

Spohr   Nonet, Op 31 and Octet, Op 32
Gaudier Ensemble
Hyperion CDA66699   Ⓕ
Spohr is an archetypal early Romantic composer, much better known in his own time than ours, but now back in favour.

INTO THE FUTURE

The past century produced a bewildering variety of musical languages,

including plenty of treasures for the adventurous.

Michael Oliver offers guidance

Some of us really looked forward to the end of the 20th century in the hope that we would at long last understand its musical history. Earlier centuries were so much easier, when one could reasonably say that Haydn begat Mozart, who begat Beethoven who begat Schubert and so on. It got a little more complex later on in the 19th century, but by including, so to speak, musical uncles as well as fathers in the chain of heredity we could understand how Wagner and Brahms were if not brothers then fairly close cousins. In the early 20th century it looked as though this pattern might continue, with Richard Strauss audibly the heir of Wagner, and Stravinsky at least for a while audibly the son of Rimsky-Korsakov. But then arrived Schoenberg, and although his descent from Mahler was obvious at first, some other gene soon became dominant. And if there was, even so, a hidden but orderly pattern of descent and influence how on earth did Bartók fit into it? And Hindemith, and Varèse, and Debussy?

There were of course attempts to demonstrate that the 20th century, like the 17th and the 18th, had a central *lingua franca*, and battle lines were drawn between those who thought that it was best represented by Schoenberg and his followers and those who on the contrary saw Stravinsky as the century's crucial figure. Amid the dust of combat faint cries could be heard of 'What about Sibelius, though?', or 'Haven't you forgotten Shostakovich?' or even 'Why do we have to choose one or the other?', but these were on the whole ignored and the controversy degenerated into a war of rival orthodoxies. Partisans of the former camp tended to suggest that the only possible path forward for the art of music was on a line drawn from Wagner through Schoenberg and especially his pupil Anton Webern, and that any composer pursuing any other route was at best an interesting irrelevance, at worst a dangerous saboteur of necessary progress. The followers of Stravinsky were on the whole more tolerant of heterodoxy but most of them were united (since this is why they'd hitched themselves to Stravinsky's bandwagon in the first place) in condemning the serialist tendency.

It is still possible to arouse violent wrath by suggesting that in fact both parties were barking up the wrong tree, but the damage has long since been done. The language of the controversy, and of the attempts to prove either Arnold Schoenberg or Igor Stravinsky the Chosen One was often intemperate and no less frequently phrased in language that most music-lovers found incomprehensible (even those who had taken the trouble to find out what 'sonata form' and 'dominant' and 'canon' meant in the hope of appreciating Beethoven and Haydn the better). The message was unmistakable: most modern music is nasty and difficult, most writing about it is opaque and unhelpful.

Once bitten, twice shy: we have a larger musical public now than at any previous period in history, and the vast majority of them would no sooner go to a concert of contemporary music than they would volunteer for an interesting research project into whether the Black Death was really all that infectious. It isn't so much that they know in advance that the music will be horrid; it's because they know in advance that they won't understand it. Which would be no problem at all if this were true. After all, there's no law compelling anyone to like modern music; and the contemporary music public, minority though it is, is capable with a bit of help from the Arts Council of keeping at least a few living composers above the poverty line. And have not eminent composers themselves suggested (like Elliott Carter) that new music should be subsidised as though it were an educational project, not a form of entertainment, or (like Milton Babbitt) that advanced music inevitably appeals at first only to a few and should be treated therefore as an academic discipline, new works being heard and discussed at closed seminars, not profane concerts?

But it is not true. A great deal of the century's music is exciting, colourful, dramatic, immediately attractive and approachable; a lot of it is tuneful; and you no more need to 'understand' it than you need degrees in geology and botany to enjoy a fine landscape. The trouble is... No: there are two troubles, or rather three. The first is that people have been listening to new music with the wrong expectations, and have inevitably been disappointed. If what you want (at the moment, or in general terms) is a simple melody, simply accompanied, then a Bach fugue will disappoint you just as much as a symphony by Sir Peter Maxwell Davies, and for much the same reason. The second problem is that discussion of modern music has concentrated so much on technicalities that listeners have assumed that if they can't hear those technicalities then the music is above their heads and isn't for them. The most important thing about any piece of music is the way it sounds. If it can only be appreciated by understanding how it was constructed then that piece of music has failed. I think I'd better leave the third problem until later.

The language expands

Musical language expanded during the 20th century. It had done in every previous century, of course, but between 1900 and 2000 the expansion was much more rapid than ever before, and it affected every single aspect of music. Of course people got confused.

Western music, at least since the classical period, has laid great stress on the related areas of harmonic subtlety (which we all hear, whether or not we can describe what we're hearing) and a strong sense of tension between keys (we can all hear that, too); this latter is also important for giving a piece of music a perceived structure or dramatic scenario. In concentrating on these elements Western music rather neglected melodic refinement. We divide the octave into 12 steps, whereas in various non-European musics there are twice as many or more. Most melodies of the classical and romantic periods are either relatively short, spanning an even number of bars (often eight) or, when longer, proceed in closely inter-related phrases, again relatively short and usually of an even number of bars. These successive phrases often aid memorability by repeating a few notes from an earlier phrase. Some modern composers (not all that many) have used divisions of the octave greater than 12 – microtones. Many have written melodies of irregular phrase-length, with few repeated elements or none.

What we take to be a 'tuneless' melody may in fact be amply tuneful, but because it doesn't proceed in eight-bar phrases but is asymmetrical, because its rises and descents aren't those that we half expect and it doesn't repeat itself, it takes a little effort to grasp. The theme of **Schoenberg**'s *Orchestral Variations* Op 31 is often described, accurately but off-puttingly and irrelevantly, as consisting of all four basic versions of a 12-note row (the row itself, the same played backwards, played upside-down and then backwards *and* upside-down). What that description misses, what all such descriptions must miss, is that the theme is unusually long, involving numerous wide leaps of a kind you won't hear in Mozart, but that once you get used to these features it is a melody of great, even romantic beauty and expressiveness. And when you realise that, of course, the variations on that theme are almost as easy to grasp as Brahms. Yet analyses of the piece still tend to concentrate on the technicalities of how it was put together. Remember Bernard Shaw's 'analysis' of Hamlet's 'To be, or not to be' soliloquy?:

SEMINAL WORKS		
Bartók	Piano Concerto No 2	
	Donohoe pf **CBSO / Rattle**	
	EMI CDC7 54871-2	Ⓕ
Berg	Violin Concerto	
	Perlman vn **Boston SO / Ozawa**	
	DG 447 445-2GOR	Ⓜ
Boulez	Le marteau sans maître	
	O de la Martinez	
	Lorelt LNT108	Ⓕ
Britten	The Turn of the Screw	
	Pears / Cross / Britten	
	Decca 425 672-2LH2	Ⓕ
Copland	Piano Variations	
	Hough pf	
	Hyperion CDA67005	Ⓕ
Debussy	La mer	
	BPO / Karajan	
	DG 447 426-2GOR	Ⓜ
Harvey	Mortuos Plango, Vivos Voco	
	Jonathan Harvey	
	Sargasso Records SCD28029	Ⓕ
Ives	Three Places in New England	
	Boston SO / Tilson Thomas	
	DG 423 243-2GC	Ⓜ
Janáček	Sinfonietta	
	VPO / Mackerras	
	Decca 448 255-2DF2	Ⓜ
Ligeti	Atmosphères	
	Ernest Bour	
	Wergo WER60162-50	Ⓕ
Messiaen	Turangalîla-symphonie	
	LSO / Previn	
	EMI CZS5 69752-2	Ⓜ
Schoenberg	Orchestral Variations, Op 31	
	Chicago SO / Boulez	
	Erato 2292 45827-2	Ⓕ
	Five Orchestral Pieces, Op 16	
	Chicago SO / Barenboim	
	Teldec 4509 98256-2	Ⓕ
Shostakovich	Symphony No 10	
	Philadelphia Orch / Jansons	
	EMI CDC5 55232-2	Ⓕ
Stravinsky	Agon	
	Stravinsky	
	Sony Classical SM3K46292	Ⓜ
	Rite of Spring	
	Philharmonia / Markevitch	
	Testament SBT1076	Ⓕ
Xenakis	Metastasis	
	FRNO / M Le Roux	
	Le Chant du Monde	
	LDC278 368	Ⓕ
Varèse	Ionisation and Déserts	
	Riccardo Chailly	
	Decca 460 208-2DH2	Ⓕ

'Shakespear, dispensing with the customary exordium, announces his subject at once in the infinitive, in which mood it is presently repeated after a short connecting passage in which, brief as it is, we recognize the alternative and negative forms on which so much of the significance of repetition depends. Here we reach a colon; and a pointed pository phrase, in which the accent falls decisively on the relative pronoun, brings us to the first full stop.'

A good many composers in the 20th century have expanded their language beyond the conventional perception that music consists of melody, harmony, counterpoint and rhythm. Schoenberg once suggested that it should be possible to make a 'melody' not from notes of different pitches but of different tone-colours, and in the third of his *Five Orchestral Pieces* Op 16 he provided an example. It was originally entitled 'Colours', but he later re-named it 'Summer Morning by a Lake'. It is, in any normal sense, tuneless; to hunt for a melody would be frustrating and pointless. It is a study in shifting and evanescent colour, of the harmonic and instrumental equivalent of sun falling through leaves on to calm water. Provided that you're not vainly searching for a tune it's rather beautiful. And since a lot of modern music explores areas other than melody, harmony, counterpoint and rhythm (though probably including all of those as well), Schoenberg's piece is a useful listening exercise, just as his *Variations* are for exploring what one might call the 20th-century's 'expanded melody'.

SERIALISM

A 19th-century tendency to use notes outside the ostensible key for expressive ends culminated in the Prelude to Tristan und Isolde in which, to evoke unassuageable yearning, Wagner wrote music that can hardly be said to be in a key at all: you cannot sense where the 'Doh' of his scale might be. But the whole Austro-German symphonic tradition depended on a perceptible sense of key and of conflict between keys – this is what gives the great symphonies from Mozart to Mahler their form, their forward movement and their drama. Schoenberg thought that a musie with no sense of key ('atonal' music) was inevitable, but he found that it could only be given structure by sheer imaginative force or by a literary text or programme. He therefore devised a system which would impose a discipline as firm as that governing music under the key system and at the same time guarantee that it would remain atonal. All 12 notes of the Western scale were arranged in a particular order (a 'note-row' or 'tone-row'), which could be played backwards ('retrograde'), upside-down ('inversion') or in retrograde inversion. Any of these could be played at any pitch; any note could be transposed by one or more octaves; parts of the row could be contracted by playing consecutive notes together, as chords; but no note was to be repeated until the other 11 had been heard. The system thus provided an almost limitless range of possibilities, but ensured maximum economy and rigour.

Edgar Varèse's *Ionisation* is another piece, entertaining and striking in itself, which is also valuable for stretching the ears. It's scored for 41 percussion instruments, none of them (until a siren appears towards the end) having a precise pitch. It, too, therefore contains no melody nor harmony in any normal sense. Rhythm, yes, and a rich counterpoint of cross-rhythms. But the palette of tone colours – colours unobtainable from wind, string or keyboard instruments – is still richer, and so is what one can only call the piece's repertoire of textures. You could compare them to passing your fingers over velvet, gravel, brocade, a brush and so on, or to the subtle or dense pen-strokes of an artist, his cross-hatchings and stipplings. Texture is also an area that has been much explored by 20th century composers, and Varèse's piece will open many doors – to the music, to take a single example, of György Ligeti.

Varèse wanted to write a music specifically of the 20th century, responding to and using its technological advances. He had, so to speak, an ambition to write electronic music before anyone got round to inventing the means of doing so. He lived long enough to use the tape recorder, in his astonishing *Déserts*, where an instrumental ensemble alternates with pre-recorded industrial sounds on tape (the 'deserts' of his title include not only wastes of sand and ice, but the inhabited deserts of big cities), and in his last completed work, *Poème électronique*, for stereophonic tape alone.

Younger composers, too, have been excited by the ability of electronic sources to produce either sounds that have never been heard before – and to the composer's precise specification – or to 'play' music with a precision no human performer can match. A classic in this field, and again a work that can open many doors, is **Jonathan Harvey**'s *Mortuos Plango, Vivos Voco*, in which all the sounds are derived, with prodigious technical resource but more importantly with prodigious imagination, from the sounds of a bell (bearing the inscription that gives the work its title: 'I lament the dead, I call the living') and the voice of a child (Harvey's son, then a choirboy). But again it's the sounds that matter, not the process that brought them about. You don't need to be a qualified structural engineer to be moved by the soaring arches of a great cathedral.

Enjoying dissonance

Rhythm took prodigious steps during the 20th century, and it took most of them in a single work, **Stravinsky's** *The Rite of Spring*. Because of the popularity of that piece, and because most people have heard enough jazz to be familiar with off-the-beat syncopation, the rhythmic advances of the century have been easier to absorb than some of the others. The other great advance of *The Rite of Spring* however is its unprecedented level of dissonance. In many other works of the last hundred or so years dissonance can unsettle the listener, who in hearing the music of previous centuries has got used to a good deal of dissonance but always with the expectation that it will eventually resolve to a more 'comfortable' harmony – indeed composers have used the device of teasing the ear with dissonance but sooner or later resolving it as a means of giving a sense of forward movement, structure and drama to their music. Twentieth-century composers have used dissonance as a much more 'normal' element in their music; dissonance has become a sort of expansion of the language of harmony.

Listening to **Charles Ives**'s music is useful here, because it soon becomes obvious that he isn't using dissonance out of the demands of some system or theory, but because he enjoys it. It's fun: in his *Country Band March* you can hear him quite accurately recording how a village bandsman will play a wrong note for the hell of it, or see if a quite different tune will 'go with' the one his colleagues are playing (Ives loved the idea of different musics colliding), and how everyone grins when old George comes in a bar too early. But Ives also relished dissonance as an expressive, almost a pictorial resource. How on earth, he might well have asked, referring to his orchestral *Three Places in New England*, can I describe the varied and simultaneous emotions, sights and sounds of a Sunday morning walk with my wife, not long after our wedding, with 'nice' harmonies? How can I portray a regiment of black soldiers, marching to their deaths in the American Civil War, filled with despair but also with heroic resolve, with only the harmonies that text-books approve of? With Ives it often helps, not to know or understand the techniques and processes he was using, but to understand what he was using them for.

Indeed a major reason for the expansion of musical language in the 20th century was the desire of composers to express or to discuss things that had never been expressed or discussed before; it is one of the prime reasons for any advance in art at any period. Too much has been said of Schoenberg's advances having been made 'necessary' by the threat posed to the conventional major-and-minor key system by Wagner's expressive expansions of that system. The threat was perceived as worrying only by those, like Schoenberg, who felt especially close to that system's Viennese mainstream (Russian composers, who'd been struggling for years to establish a symphonic tradition of their own, independent from the Viennese, weren't bothered by it at all). And although Schoenberg devised his *system* to cope with that situation no composer worthy of the name writes *music* in order to counter a threat to the key system. Schoenberg, like Beethoven, like Wagner, had such powerfully original things to say that he needed to stretch the language of music in order to express them.

After Schoenberg

The idea of the 12-note row, and the techniques that Schoenberg devised for manipulating it, had a powerful influence on many of his juniors, but for a variety of reasons, not just because it offered a way forward from what some saw as a post-Wagnerian impasse. Serialism appealed to many because of its rigorous economy: it provided a means whereby every note in a composition

KEY TERMS	
Aleatory	(From Latin *alea*, 'dice'). Music which allows an element of chance or free improvisation in performance.
Atonal	Music in which little or no sense of key is perceptible.
Bitonal	See 'Polytonal', below.
Cluster	A group of notes, often adjacent ones, played together but which cannot be heard as a chord.
Dodecaphonic	Music using all 12 notes of the chromatic scale; usually used as though synonymous with 'serial'.
Electroacoustic	Music combining electronic and live performance, the former often modifying the latter.
Mode	A scale. Traditional Western music uses two, the major and minor modes, but numerous others exist, found in folk, early or Eastern music, and others still can be devised.
Musique concrète	Music produced by modifying recordings of natural or industrial sounds.
Neoclassical	Literally music which adopts features of the classical style of Haydn and Mozart; Stravinsky, to whom the term is often applied, objected to it, and many of his works in fact refer to such non-classsical composers as Handel and Verdi.
Polytonal	Music in which two or more keys are used simultaneously.
Total serialism	Music in which not only pitch but rhythm, duration, loudness and other factors are determined by the rules of serialism.

REPERTOIRE EXPLORATION

Cage, John 4'33"
Wayne Marshall
Floating Earth FCD004 Ⓕ
Get hold of a kitchen timer, set it
to ring after four minutes and 33
seconds; during that time listen to
and think about every sound. You
have now performed John Cage's
4'33", a 'composition' that contains
no 'music'. Or does it?

Cardew, The Great Learning
Cornelius **Scratch Orchestra**
Cortical Foundation CORTI21 Ⓕ
Leader of the British avant-garde
who writes 'democratic' music for
amateurs and non-musicians: an
oddly impressive, timeless ritual.

Eisler, Hanns Hollywood Songbook
Matthias Görne, Eric Schneider
Decca 460 582-2 Ⓕ
A rebellious Schoenberg pupil,
already skilled at cabaret-style
political propaganda, masters every
style from neo-Schubert to atonality
in nostalgic exile's protest at Nazism.

Harrison, Lou Symphony No 4
California SO / B Jekowsky
Argo 455 590-2ZH Ⓕ
A composer who believes that
'melody is the audience's take-
home pay' and who sees no reason
why a symphony shouldn't end with
someone telling stories.

Nancarrow, Studies for Player Piano
Conlon **C Nancarrow**
Wergo WER6907-2 Ⓕ
Single-minded American pioneer
investigates music of superhuman
velocity, precision and attack.

Thomson, Four Saints in Three Acts
Virgil **Leonard Bernstein**
New York Philharmonic NYP9904Ⓕ
A deceptively simple style rooted in
the American vernacular –
hymn tunes, parlour ballads –
reveals radiant lucidity in
apparently meaningless
text by Gertrude Stein.

('mini-tone-rows', one might call them) since *The Rite of Spring*. For many of the post-Second World War generation, especially those from the German-speaking countries, serialism provided a language that was unsullied by a shameful past that they needed to reject. Schoenberg's method also attracted pedants, of course, and their music was aridly academic and soon forgotten, but other and fiercely independent composers have found aspects of his system invaluable in forming their own styles.

It is unlikely, for example, that either **Elliott Carter** or **Sir Harrison Birtwistle** would have written the sort of music that they have without Schoenberg's example and impetus. But you might find it much more useful to approach each of them with an image in mind rather than a detailed analysis of how their music is put together. With Carter the image might be of a music that can convey an extraordinary effect of space because it is proceeding at several speeds at once – as different elements of the landscape seem to move at different speeds as you rush past them in a train or an aircraft. Something similar happens also in Birtwistle, but here a more useful image might be that of a music on several levels or strata, with a vast something moving at the lowest of them.

Many other composers have stretched musical language, for their own expressive ends, without needing to adopt Schoenberg's system, which was so well adapted to his own needs. **Olivier Messiaen** respected Schoenberg greatly, used his method briefly (and in so doing mastered it so completely that a high proportion of the post-war avant-garde sought him out as a teacher) but what he and Schoenberg wanted to do were vastly different. 'Ornithologist-musician' as he called himself, mystic-musician as he in fact was, he could not transcribe his beloved bird-song into melodies of the major or minor scales because birds seldom use them. This and other considerations led him to explore other scales that had either never been used in Western 'classical' music or had not been used for centuries and which he found invaluable for writing music that expressed his devout religious faith.

Messiaen was the most thorough explorer of this field, but by no means the first. **Debussy** said that he wanted to write music that was 'neither major nor minor' and was excited to discover the quite different scales used in oriental music. **Béla Bartók**, researching the folk music of Hungary, was overwhelmed by the quality of the melodies that he found, and astonished to discover that some of them used a scale, 'neither major nor minor', that Debussy and other 'advanced' modernists were using. Another expansion: no longer only two permissible scales but a range of possibilities. But also: no longer only two permissible father-figures for modern music (Schoenberg or Stravinsky). Composers of the present generation find exciting unfinished business and

earned its place, and was logically related to all the others. There is, for some people, a positive pleasure to be gained from a music of immaculate precision. Stravinsky, for long regarded as Schoenberg's opponent, eventually adopted and adapted his system because in a sense he had been using its essence all along, exhaustively permutating short groups of notes pointers to their own development in Bartók, in Debussy, in Carl Nielsen, Sibelius and others.

And the 20th century, particularly the latter part of it, was also particularly rich in independent figures, who accepted no orthodoxy or party-line but who, from a variety of influences or from none, forged an immediately recognisable personal language. **Benjamin Britten** is an obvious example, in his youth distrusted by the establishment as a too-clever-by-half modernist, in his latter years dismissed by some of his juniors as hopelessly old-fashioned, but now recognized as a major composer, perhaps the greatest of the century's 'one-offs'. And there have been many of them, writing music in a mind-boggling variety of styles. **John Cage**, for many people not a composer at all, in fact a man who listened entranced to the whole world of sound and wanted every musical event to be an unpredictable voyage of discovery. **Iannis Xenakis**, whose work is very often discussed in terms of the mathematical principles which govern it, but whose very first mature composition, *Metastasis*, had its origin in a terrible memory: of how crowds move when threatened by gunfire, of how ordered movement and disciplined chanting becomes disorder. **György Ligeti**, like Xenakis an explorer of fantastically complex textures, but who is open-eared enough to have been interested and influenced by the minimalists, African drumming, that weird but inspired virtuoso of the player-piano Conlon Nancarrow, even Brahms...

And now, of course, comes the third problem that I mentioned earlier. There are so many composers now, writing so many different sorts of music. Even specialists can't keep up with them all; how can the ordinary music-lover manage (who doesn't want to give up Bach, Beethoven and all the others while he or she devotes a year or two to dolefully and dutifully sampling who knows how many living and recent composers)? 'For heaven's sake don't even try' would be my advice. Start with two or three pieces, say one that intrigues but perplexes you (one of those I've mentioned, perhaps), one that lots of people speak highly of and a third that's as different from the other two as possible, perhaps by a young composer. Listen to them with real concentration several times (the way you used to listen to Beethoven when you first discovered him). Maybe one of them will be as perplexing at the end of this process as it was at the beginning – put it aside and forget about it, at least for the time being. But my bet would be that at least one of the others will be starting to make sense, perhaps much more quickly than you expected. More than that: you may well find that the experience of concentratedly listening to that one will unexpectedly open doors to others. And in music the old saying ('When one door opens another shuts') is most certainly not true. One door opens on a corridor of others, all invitingly open.

ABBREVIATIONS

aas	all available separately		**mndl**	mandolin
alto	countertenor/male alto		**narr**	narrator
anon	anonymous		**oas**	only available separately
arr	arranged		**ob**	oboe
attrib	attributed		**Op**	opus
b	born		**orig**	original
bar	baritone		**org**	organ
bass-bar	bass-baritone		**perc**	percussion
bn	bassoon		**pf**	piano
c	circa (about)		**picc**	piccolo
cl	clarinet		**pub**	publisher/published
clav	clavichord		**rec**	recorder
compl	completed		**recons**	reconstructed
cont	continuo		**rev**	revised
contr	contralto		**sax**	saxophone
cor ang	cor anglais		**sngr**	singer
cpsr	composer		**sop**	soprano
cpte(d)	complete(d)		**spkr**	speaker
d	died		**stg**	string
db	double bass		**synth**	synthesizer
dig pf	digital piano		**tbn**	trombone
dir	director		**ten**	tenor
ed	edited (by)/edition		**timp**	timpani
exc	excerpt		**tpt**	trumpet
fl	flute		**trad**	traditional
fl	flourished		**trans**	transcribed
fp	fortepiano		**treb**	treble
gtr	guitar		**va**	viola
harm	harmonium		**va da gamba**	viola da gamba
hn	horn		**vars**	variations
hp	harp		**vc**	cello
hpd	harpsichord		**vib**	vibraphone
keybd	keyboard		**vn**	violin
lte	lute		**voc**	vocal/vocalist
mez	mezzo-soprano		**wds**	words

HOW TO USE THE GUIDE

The presentation and design of this *Guide* is similar to that of its parent publication, *Gramophone*. Reviews of works generally appear in the following sequence: Orchestral, Chamber, Instrumental, Vocal/Choral and Opera.

The title for each review contains the following information: composer(s), work(s), artist(s), record company or label, price range, catalogue number and, where known, the recording date. The circled numeral before the catalogue number indicates the number of discs (if there is more than one), while the timing and mode of recording are given in brackets afterwards. (The abbreviations AAD/ADD/DDD denote analogue or digital stages in the recording/editing or mixing/mastering or transcription processes in CD manufacture.) All other abbreviations used in this *Guide* are given below.

Where three or more composers are represented on a single disc, the review generally appears in the Collections section which starts on page 1158. On page 1293 you will also find a much-expanded DVD section.

The indexes are divided into an artists' index and an index to couplings – an index of works reviewed under other composers. For example, you'll find Prokofiev's Third Piano Concerto with Martha Argerich reviewed under its Bartók Concerto No 3 coupling; to find the page number simply look in the couplings index under Prokofiev.

All recordings are flagged with one or more of the symbols explained below.

KEY TO SYMBOLS

Ⓕ Full price £11 and over
Ⓜ Medium price £7-£10·99
Ⓑ Budget price £5-£6·99
Ⓢ Super-budget price £4·99 and below

🅷 Denotes a Historic recording and generally applies to pre-1960 recordings. It can also be an indication that the recording quality may not be up to the highest standards

🅿 Denotes recordings where period instruments are used

Simply the best
An unrivalled version, a cornerstone of the catalogue. A real star!

●●● **Classic**
Gramophone Award-winners and recordings of legendary status

●● **Outstanding**
Outstanding performance and fine sound/transfer

● **Strongly recommended**
Not a top choice but nonetheless a fine recording

No disc
Recommended
Good performance with the odd reservation

Ⓢ**Value for money**
An exceptional recording at budget price or below

THE CLASSICAL
GOOD
CD & DVD
GUIDE
2006

Adolphe Adam
French 1803-1856

Adam studied at the Paris Conservatoire with Reicha (counterpoint) and Boieldieu (composition). A prolific composer, he wrote more than 80 stage works, some of which, especially those produced for the Opéra-Comique such as Le châlet (1834) and Le postillon de Longjumeau (1836), had considerable and lasting success. Other notable works, showing a natural sense of theatre, fresh invention and graceful melody. include the opera Si j'étais roi (1852) and the well-known ballet Giselle (1841). GROVEmusic

Giselle

Giselle
Royal Opera House Orchestra, Covent Garden / Richard Bonynge
Double Decca ② 452 185-2DF2 (126' · DDD) Recorded 1986 Ⓜ️Ⓞ

Giselle has drawn harsh words from the more superior music critics, but the public has taken it to heart for its atmospheric writing and tender and haunting themes. The text used here is the complete original score; Bonynge's desire to re-record it lies in matters of performance and interpretation. Reviews of his previous version, made with the Monte Carlo Opera Orchestra in 1970, spoke of the limitations of the woodwind and brass, and suggested that a little more rehearsal time might have brought benefits. Here the musicians of the Royal Opera House bring both a confidence of attack and a refinement that aren't quite achieved by the Monte Carlo players. That same extra confidence of attack is displayed by Bonynge himself. Each of the discs of this issue is between one-and-a-half and two minutes longer than the older recording, but the dramatic moments are more vigorously attacked and the slower ones more lovingly caressed – always to considerable effect. Add recorded sound that's warmer and more spacious, and there's no hesitation in acknowledging the superiority of this version over the old. Without a doubt, this represents the first-choice version of Adam's complete score.

Additional recommendation

Giselle
Slovak Radio Symphony Orchestra / Mogrelia
Naxos ② 8 550755/6 (114' · DDD) Recorded 1994 Ⓢ
This has essentially the same text as Bonynge's recording, complete with traditional interpolations. It's a highly enjoyable alternative, with some especially rewarding passages such as the Act 1 'Pas seul'.

Further listening

Le postillon de Lonjumeau
Stuttgart Choristers; Kaiserslautern Radio Symphony Orchestra / Arp
Capriccio ② 60 040-2 (97' · DDD) Ⓕ
Celebrated for the fiendishly difficult tenor solo

'Mes amis, écoutez l'histoire', Adam's opera has a lot of charm. This German language recording must be considered a stop-gap until a French version returns to the catalogue.

John Adams
American b1947

Adams studied at Harvard with Kirchner, Kim, Del Tredici and Sessions, and in 1972 began teaching at the San Francisco Conservatory. He became interested in electronics (Onyx, 1976), then, influenced by Reich, turned to minimalism. His works, in an elegant minimalist style, include Shaker Loops for strings (1978), Harmonium for orchestra with choir (1981), the exuberant, parodistic Grand Pianola Music (1982), the opera Nixon in China (1987) – summary of his musical languages over 10 years – and a violin concerto (1994). His second opera, The Death of Klinghoffer (1991), is again based on recent events; the story unfolds in meditations and narratives, punctuated by choruses, rather than in action. GROVEmusic

Violin Concerto

Violin Concerto[a]. Shaker Loops[b].
Gidon Kremer vn
[a]**London Symphony Orchestra / Kent Nagano;**
[b]**Orchestra of St Luke's / John Adams**
Nonesuch 7559-79360-2 (59' · DDD) Ⓕ Ⓞ

This superb CD displays two very different aspects of Adams's evolving art: *Shaker Loops* dancing to a minimalist pulse, lean, fidgety and cleverly designed (the accelerating 'take-offs' in 'A final shaking' are extremely effective); and the altogether deeper, more intimate Violin Concerto. The latter brings Berg to mind – not his Violin Concerto, but *Wozzeck*, Act 3 Scene 4, where an eerie 'drainage' effect symbolises Wozzeck's drowning beneath a blood-red moon. This aural fluidity is common to both works (the scoring is similar, too), although Adams keeps up the momentum for the whole of his long first movement, shifting colours constantly until a brief solo passage marks a slowing down in preparation for the ensuing Chaconne. Here a quiet chiming suggests parallels with Arvo Pärt, while Adams floats his mysterious textures above a quietly undulating accompaniment. The Sibelius of *Tapiola* seems to hover somewhere around six minutes into the first movement (just as parts of *Shaker Loops* suggest an up-tempo *Lemminkäinen*) and the concerto ends with a fast, dancing toccata. The solo line, which Adams admits is 'almost never ending' includes much double-stopped passagework. In the hands of Gidon Kremer – whose sinewy, lightly bowed tone suits the piece perfectly – it's a compelling monologue.

The earlier *Shaker Loops* started life as a string quartet (*Wavemaker*), then – beyond drastic recomposition – filled out to a septet which, suitably augmented, is how we hear it here. The term 'Shaker' refers to the frenzied dancing of a religious sect, and Adams's four-part structure sets up a varied roster of tempos and textures. There have been other recordings of it, but this is surely the best – agile, precise and extremely well balanced. The sound is excellent.

Chamber Symphony

Chamber Symphony. Grand Pianola Music
London Sinfonietta / John Adams
Nonesuch 7559-79219-2 (53' · DDD) Recorded 1993
Ⓕ◐

A loud bash on an old tin can, and they're off – yelping, tapping, chattering, chasing to and fro, like a barn-yard full of loopy professors. And to think that the prime mover for John Adams's madcap Chamber Symphony (1992) was its 'eponymous predecessor', Schoenberg's Op 9. Even the instrumentation is similar, save that Adams has added synthesizer, jazz-style percussion, trumpet and trombone. It's a raw piece, with the merest suggestion of repose in the central 'Aria with Walking Brass' and a 'Road-runner' finale that includes a manic violin cadenza followed by an ingenious passage where synthesizer, bass clarinet, bassoon and horn crank up for the panic-stricken home straight. It might not be exactly rich in tunes, but it's maddeningly moreish, a high-speed comedy where all the characters are temporarily on holiday from their more serious selves.

In complete contrast, the far gentler *Grand Pianola Music* (1971) provides a relatively 'easy' listen, with its smooth-driving motor rhythms, sensual female voices, warming waves of brass tone and occasional bouts of thumping excitement. Clichés there certainly are, especially the 'big tune' that crowns the third section, 'On the Dominant Divide', which is probably most effective when, towards the end of the work, it slims down to basic harmonic constituents. *Grand Pianola Music* is a sort of aural truck ride, with smooth tarmac, plenty of scenic incident, a glowing sunset on the far horizon and a closing cadence that rather unexpectedly recalls Sibelius. Both performances are fine and the recordings are superb.

El Dorado

Adams El Dorado **Busoni** Berceuse élégiaque, Op 42 (arr Adams)[a] **Liszt** La lugubre gondola, S200 No 1 (arr Adams)[a]
Hallé Orchestra / Kent Nagano; [a]**London Sinfonietta / John Adams**
Nonesuch 7559-79359-2 (47' · DDD) Recorded 1993
Ⓕ◐

El Dorado is a dramatic commentary on irreconcilable opposites: chromaticism versus pure modalities, malignancy versus rude health, and man's destructive impulses versus the unspoiled glory of unpopulated landscapes. Adams claims to have composed the second movement, 'Soledades' – the one 'without man' – in seven

days. Indeed, the whole work appeared to him as a sort of apparition, 'alarmingly complete in its details, even before I wrote down a single sketch'. The first movement, 'A Dream of Gold', opens to sinister held chords, pensive shufflings and rising clouds of string tone. The last section charges forth like some maniacal spectre, racing out of control then stopping dead. By contrast, 'Soledades' weaves a delicate web of sound, at least initially, with unmistakably Sibelian undertones. The ending, however, suggests a tranquil death. Overall, the recording of *El Dorado* reproduces a dynamic sound curve. The performance itself is deft and well paced, very much on a par with Adams's own performances of his Busoni and Liszt arrangements.

The *Berceuse élégiaque* is beautifully realised, while the richly coloured orchestration of Liszt's late *La lugubre gondola* is in total contrast to other, more austere, readings. Winds and solo strings are used to sensitive effect and the playing is uniformly excellent.

Gnarly Buttons

Gnarly Buttons. John's Book of Alleged Dances
Michael Collins cl **Kronos Quartet** (David Harrington, John Sherba vns Hank Dutt va Joan Jeanrenaud vc)
London Sinfonietta / John Adams
Nonesuch 7559-79465-2 (61' · DDD)
Ⓕ◐

John's Book of Alleged Dances (the equivocation in the title refers to dance steps that have yet to be invented) is prime-cut Adams – fidgety, tuneful, teeming with invention and all but tactile in its aural variety; its use of the prepared piano is fascinating. We start by following a streetcar from town to coast and back again, then visit 'Toot Nipple' with 'chainsaw triads on the cello'. There's a raw-edged 'Hoe-Down' for leader David Harrington, a 'Pavane' for cellist Joan Jeanrenaud and a doleful Habanera. 'Hammer & Chisel' are contractor friends who construct to a knotty toccata; a slithery 'Alligator Escalator' employs reptilian harmonics and a chirpy 'Serenade' pays subtle homage to Beethoven and Schubert. These and more are kept on a high flame by the Kronos Quartet, whereas *Gnarly Buttons* calls on the combined talents of Michael Collins and the London Sinfonietta. A more intense piece by far, its dry but colourful demeanour occasionally recalls Schoenberg's similarly spice-flavoured Serenade. The first movement is based on a Protestant shape-note hymn; the second is a 'Mad-Cow' hoe-down; and the third is a warming song of sure-fire hit potential. Collins does Adams proud, and so does the London Sinfonietta. The recordings are first-rate.

Harmonielehre

Harmonielehre. The Chairman Dances. Two Fanfares – Tromba lontana; Short Ride in a Fast Machine
City of Birmingham Symphony Orchestra /

Sir Simon Rattle
EMI 555051-2 (62' · DDD) Recorded 1993 ⓂⓄ

The Chairman Dances and Short Ride in a Fast
Machine are also available on HMV Classics
HMV5 73040-2 Ⓑ

Harmonielehre was inspired by a dream vision of
a massive tanker that suddenly took flight, displaying a 'beautiful brownish-orange oxide on
the bottom part of its hull'; the setting was just
off San Francisco Bay Bridge. 'Those pounding
E minor chords are like a grinding of gears,' says
John Adams of its violent, gunshot opening.
Scored for a huge orchestra and structured in
three contrasted sections, *Harmonielehre* is
probably the nearest thing on offer to a minimalist symphony, and for that reason alone it
could well appeal beyond the élite coterie of
minimalist-fanciers. Rattle's recording has
great heft and dynamic range, an informative
balance and a vivid sense of aural perspective.
The brass components of those opening chords
have enormous weight and presence, and the
ringing marimbas thereafter a bright complex-
ion. Adams's frequent requests for subtle tempo
transitions are subtly honoured by the conductor. In short, Rattle's view of Adams is recommended particularly to those mainstream collectors who aren't yet sold on minimalism.

Naive and Sentimental Music

Naive and Sentimental Music
**Los Angeles Philharmonic Orchestra / Esa-Pekka
Salonen**
Nonesuch 7559-79636-2 (44' · DDD) ⒻⓄⓄ

The title is adapted from *On Naïve and Sentimental Poetry*, a 1795 essay by Schiller, who
regarded the naïve artist as one for whom art is
a natural form of expression, and who creates
without concern for historical significance; the
sentimental artist is all too aware that he and his
art stand apart, and what he creates reflects this
chasm. 'This particular piece,' Adams writes,
'perhaps more than any of my others, attempts
to allow the naïve in me to speak, to let it play
freely.' A symphony in all but name, *Naïve and
Sentimental Music* (1999) is cast in three movements. The first is an 'essay on melody,' built
around an expansive theme that unfolds in long
strands. Adams' harmonic sensitivity and structural control are breathtaking. And the entire
movement unfolds as organically as the melody
that's its *idée fixe*. Adams titled the finale 'Chain
to the Rhythm'. Melody takes a back seat to
what quickly becomes a dazzling and increasingly ominous *moto perpetuo*. *Naïve and Sentimental Music* is dedicated to Esa-Pekka Salonen
and the Los Angeles Philharmonic, who premièred it in February 1999. Though the fiendishly difficult finale could perhaps be played
more tautly, the overall interpretation is very
persuasive indeed.

Road Movies

American Berserk[a]. China Gates[a]. Hallelujah
Junction[ab]. Phrygian Gates[b]. Road Movies[cd]
[a]**Nicolas Hodges**, [b]**Rolf Hind**, [c]**John Novacek** pfs
[d]**Leila Josefowicz** vn
Nonesuch 7559 79699-2 (68' · DDD) ⒻⓄⓄ

John Adams hasn't written much for solo instruments or small ensembles, so this collection is
especially valuable, even if two of the piano
pieces have already been recorded several times.
Certainly the performances here are superb.
Nicolas Hodges plays *China Gates* (1977) with
sublime clarity, registering even the subtlest of
harmonic changes, and giving this brief work a
welcome sense of breadth and wonder. Rolf
Hinds is similarly effective in *Phrygian Gates*
(1977), pacing the long first movement for maximum dramatic effect.

American Berserk (2001), the newest entry,
demonstrates how much Adams's style has
changed over the past quarter-century – and
particularly here, sandwiched between its older
brothers. It's a manic, unabashedly virtuoso creation, comparable in sheer density to Ligeti's
études, though its layers of rhythmically independent ideas also bring Nancarrow to mind.
You might imagine a slightly more unhinged
performance than Hodges gives – but not by
much. Hodges and Hinds join forces for *Hallelujah Junction* (1997), a glorious addition to the
two-piano repertory. The opening, with the
instruments sounding against each other, suggests the joyous pealing of bells, while the central slow movement offers what may be Adams's
most traditionally romantic music yet, with lush
chords riding arpeggiated waves.

Road Movies (1995), for violin and piano, is
more consistent in mood than the mercurial
Hallelujah Junction. Built from motivic fragments that telescope in and out, it features two
spiky, highly caffeinated movements surrounding a spare-textured, folksy meditation that's as
close to Copland's Big Sky Americana as Adams
is likely to get. Leila Josefowicz and John
Novacek negotiate the music's plentiful rhythmic twists and turns with aplomb, and Josefowicz's slightly raw twang in the slow movement
is an imaginative touch. Urgently recommended.

El niño

El niño
Dawn Upshaw sop **Lorraine Hunt Lieberson** mez
Willard White bass **London Voices; Theatre of
Voices; Deutsches Symphony Orchestra, Berlin /
Kent Nagano**
Nonesuch ② 7559 79634-2 (111' · DDD) Text and
translation included Ⓕ

El Niño is an ecstatic celebration of Christ's
birth, at once ethereal and fiercely driven, and
as remote from homely 'Seasonal' images as
Greenland is from Bethlehem. The pain and

alienation of birth is as much a part of Adams's ground plan as the Holy child whose universal significance has kept the legend alive.

Maybe it's coincidence that the score opens like a robust relation of Reich's *The Desert Music*, but given the Biblical setting, the idea of desert isn't exactly inappropriate. Bach is another probable reference point. And yet any influences are absorbed among the pages of a score that, aside from its melodic appeal and considerable rhythmic (ie, quasi-minimalist) vitality, can toy delicately with guitar and harpsichord or breathe fire through trombones and low woodwinds. Adams's facility for musical word-painting at times levels with Benjamin Britten's. Voices and characters intertwine or juxtapose with a skill that only a seasoned opera composer could summon.

Countertenors echo ancient church modes, initially as Gabriel in dialogue with Mary, sweetly sung by Dawn Upshaw, then reporting on the Babe 'that leaped in her womb' and standing by as Joseph (a grainy-voiced Willard White) struggles with the concept of Mary's pregnancy. The choice of texts, many written by Hispanic women, was selected in collaboration with Peter Sellars. The overall aim seems less to tell a consistent story than to create narrative images within a spiritual context. The episodes, whether inwardly lyrical or outwardly aggressive, have an urgency, or relevance, that reaches beyond religious edification. It brings the Christmas story alive. But, be warned – this is no starlit Cosy Encounter. The performance can't be faulted, and the recording achieves a true aural perspective. Very strongly recommended.

The Death of Klinghoffer

The Death of Klinghoffer
Sanford Sylvan bar Leon Klinghoffer **Stephanie Friedman** mez Omar **James Maddalena** bar First Officer **Thomas Hammons** bar First Officer **Thomas Young** sngr Molqui **Eugene Perry** bar Mamoud **Sheila Nadler** mez Marilyn Klinghoffer **London Opera Orchestra Chorus; Lyon Opera Orchestra / Kent Nagano**
Nonesuch ② 7559-79281-2 (135' · DDD) Recorded 1991. Notes and text included ⒡

How many living composers do you suppose would happily watch their scores lead a short life, relevant but finite? Not many; but John Adams might be one. First *Nixon in China*, then *The Death of Klinghoffer*: rarely before has a composer snatched subjects from yesterday's news and made operas out of them. Admittedly, themes of lasting significance lurk beneath this work's immediate surface: conflict between cultures and ideologies, rival claims to ancestral lands, human rights in general. Specifically, however, it takes us back no further than October 1985, when Palestinian terrorists hijacked the Italian cruise liner *Achille Lauro* and murdered wheelchair-bound passenger Leon Klinghoffer. The opera guides us through those

events, albeit in an oblique fashion. Whatever the long-term fate of the opera, Alice Goodman's libretto certainly deserves to be spared from oblivion. It's eloquent and beautiful, compassionate and humanitarian, rich in imagery and spacious in its sentence-structure. If *The Death of Klinghoffer* finally disappoints, it's because the marriage of words and music is so fragile. The opera's musical language is firmly rooted in tradition, but it's doubtful if anyone will come away from it with a memorable lyric moment lodged in the mind. The recording uses the cast of the original production, and contains no weak links. As you expect from Adams, the score has been superbly orchestrated, and it's done full justice by the Lyon Opera Orchestra.

Nixon in China

Nixon in China
Sanford Sylvan bar Chou en-Lai **James Maddaleña** bar Richard Nixon **Thomas Hammons** bar Henry Kissinger **Mari Opatz** mez Nancy T'ang First Secretary to Mao **Stephanie Friedman** mez Second Secretary to Mao **Marion Dry** mez Third Secretary to Mao **John Duykers** ten Mao Tse-Tung **Carolann Page** sop Pat Nixon **Trudy Ellen Craney** sop Chiang Ch'ing **St Luke's Chorus and Orchestra / Edo de Waart**
Nonesuch ② 7559-79177-2 (144' · DDD) Recorded 1987. Notes and text included ⒡

Whatever its weaknesses, there's no denying that *Nixon in China* is striking. Structured curiously, its three acts reduce from three scenes to two, and then to one, and they diminish proportionally in duration from more than an hour in Act 1 to the unbroken 30-minute span of Act 3. This last act played out in the statesmen's bedrooms, is a weary sequence of dialogues and soliloquies, ending in a curious but calculated state of anticlimax. Preceding this, though, is a run of colourful scenes that symbolise the main events without imposing any artificial sense of dramatic shape. By the end of the work, the public faces have given way to private lives; even Nixon and Chairman Mao emerge as mere mortals rather than mythical demi-gods.

The music serves the libretto deftly in fast-moving dialogue but the reflective and rhapsodic portions of text seem to leave Adams baffled, the melodic lines wandering aimlessly, short on intrinsic musical interest and rarely moving the singers to expressive performances. In the handling of spectacle and scene-setting, by contrast, Adams is in his element. He freely avails himself of any idiom, any oblique references or musical quotation that serves as a means to an end. Some passages would be unthinkable without the operas of Philip Glass; elsewhere lie uncanny ghosts of 1930s Stravinsky. Magpie just about sums this score up. The singing is sympathetic, with James Maddalena as an aptly volatile Nixon and Trudy Ellen Craney coping admirably with the coloratura lines of Madam Mao.

Further listening

The Wound-dresser
Coupled with: Fearful symmetries
Sylvan bar **Orchestra of St Luke's / Adams**
Nonesuch 7559-79218-2 (47' · DDD)   Ⓕ

Adams's tender and powerful meditation, to words
by Walt Whitman, on the subject of those lost to
AIDS. Touchingly performed by Sanford Sylvan.

Richard Addinsell   British 1904-1977

After study at the Royal College of Music, London,
and in Vienna, Addinsell visited the USA (1933),
where he wrote for films. Most of his music was for
the theatre and cinema; his popular Warsaw Con-
certo, in the style of Rachmaninov, was used in the
film Dangerous Moonlight (1941). GROVEmusic

Warsaw Concerto

Warsaw Concerto (arr Douglas)[b].The Admirable
Crichton[a] – Polka and Galop; Waltz Sequence
([a]reconstructed by P Lane) The Black Rose – Suite[a].
Blithe Spirit[a] – Prelude; Waltz. Goodbye Mr Chips –
Suite[ac]. Love on the Dole – Suite[a]. Out of the
Clouds – Flame Tango (arr Sharples). Scrooge –
Suite (arr S Bernstein)[c]. Tom Brown's Schooldays –
Overture[a]
[b]**Martin Roscoe** pf [c]**Manchester Cathedral Choir;**
[c]**Chetham's Chamber Choir; BBC Philharmonic**
Orchestra / Rumon Gamba
Chandos CHAN10046 (80' · DDD)   ⒻO

None of the modern versions of the *Warsaw*
Concerto seems to have the freshness, urgency
and lack of self-indulgence of this very fine version. That's a pointer to the high level of playing and interpretation to be found throughout
this ever fascinating and altogether quite
delightful selection of Addinsell's film music.
Though Rachmaninov comes so immediately
and vividly to mind in the most celebrated of
Addinsell's creations, that was strictly for the
purposes of its film context. Elsewhere you're
more likely to be reminded of Vaughan
Williams, Ravel or Eric Coates. Pastiche was an
inevitable part of a film composer's armoury,
but the very real inventive gifts displayed in the
Warsaw Concerto are also evident throughout
this collection.

About half the music has already been
recorded in other Addinsell collections, but not
with the chorus that's especially effective here in
the 'School Song' from *Goodbye Mr Chips*. Of
the new items the sumptuously lyrical finale to
the music for *The Black Rose* is particularly fine
(expertly reconstructed, like much else here, by
Philip Lane), as are the dances from the 1957
film *The Admirable Crichton*.

It's by no means just nostalgia that makes
Addinsell's film music well worth exploring, and
this generously filled CD is undoubtedly the
best single-CD selection available.

Additional recommendation

Warsaw Concerto
Coupled with: **Beaver** Portrait of Isla **Rozsa**
Spellbound Concerto. **Rota** The Legend of the Glass
Mountain **RR Bennett** Murder on the Orient Express
– excs. **Bath** Cornish Rhapsody **Herrmann** Concerto
Macabre **Williams** The Dream of Olwen **Pennario**
Midnight on the Cliffs
Fowke pf RTE **Concert Orchestra / O'Duinn**

Naxos 8 554323 (74' · DDD)   Ⓢ

Fowke plays all the pieces with affection and
panache. If you've always wished that the *Warsaw*
Concerto were longer, this is the disc for you.

Film Music

Blithe Spirit – Prelude; Waltz. Encore – Miniature
Overture. Gaslight – Prelude. Parisienne – 1885.
Southern Rhapsody. Waltz of the Toreadors – March;
The General on Parade; Waltz (all arr. Lane). Fire
over England – Suite (arr. Zalva). Passionate Friends
– Lover's Moon. South Riding – Prelude (both arr
Isaacs). A Christmas Carol – Suite (arr S Bernstein).
WRNS March (arr Douglas)
Robert Gibbs vn **Peter Lawson** pf **Royal Ballet**
Sinfonia / Kenneth Alwyn
ASV White Line CDWHL2115 (68' · DDD)   ⓂO

Nobody should imagine that the *Warsaw Con-*
certo is all that's worth hearing from this fine
composer. Addinsell had a natural feel for richly
tuneful, romantic music in the best tradition of
British light music. The diverse commissions he
fulfilled served to turn these gifts to contrasted
musical styles; these provide a rewardingly varied programme. The most familiar music will
probably be the swaggering march and haunting waltz from the *Waltz of the Toreadors*. Others
will know the prelude and waltz from David
Lean's film of *Blithe Spirit* or the suite from *A*
Christmas Carol. Perennial favourites are the
invigorating *WRNS March*, the delightfully
mysterious prelude to the 1939 film of *Gaslight*
and the waltz from the stage play *Parisienne*.
The last has been given a splendid Glazunovian
orchestration by compiler, producer, arranger
and annotator Philip Lane, who again leaves us
in his debt, as do conductor Kenneth Alwyn and
the admirable Royal Ballet Sinfonia.

Additional recommendation

Film music
Goodbye Mr Chips – exc. Ring around the moon –
exc. Smokey Mountains Concerto. The Isle of
Apples. The Prince and the Showgirl – exc. Tune in
G. Tom Brown's Schooldays – exc. Festival. Journey
to Romance. Fire over England – exc. A Tale of Two
Cities – exc
Martin, Elms pfs **BBC Concert Orchestra / Alwyn**
Marco Polo 8 223732 (68' · DDD)   Ⓕ

A most attractive release. Much of the orchestral
material for this recording was prepared by Philip
Lane, who also provides the informative notes.
Fine performances, too.

Thomas Adès

British b1971

One of the leading lights in contemporary classical music, pianist/conductor/composer Adès's meteoric rise to international musical prominence has been phenomenal. He gained early success as a pianist, winning Second Prize in the 1989 BBC Young Musician of the Year, then read music at King's College, Cambridge (1989-92). Among the works from his student years are his first opus, Five Eliot Landscapes (1990) and the Chamber Symphony (1990) – his first work to receive a professional performance. In 1993 he became Composer in Association to the Hallé Orchestra for whom he wrote The Origin of the Harp (1994) and These Premises Are Alarmed (1996). His most performed work, Living Toys (1993), brought him widespread critical acclaim, though it was the chamber opera Powder Her Face (1995) that earned him an international reputation. In 1998 he became artistic director of the Birmingham Contemporary Music Group and the following year, for his first large-scale orchestral work, Asyla (1997), he received the Ernst von Siemens Prize and the Grawemeyer Award. Also in 1999 he became joint artistic director of the Aldeburgh Festival. Forthcoming commissions include operas for the Royal Opera House, Covent Garden, and Glyndebourne and a Piano Quintet for the Melbourne Festival. Adès's compositions showed exceptional assurance of style and technique from the start, and his success had much to do with the unmistakable presence of a personal accent in music which blends vividness of detail with a clear sense of compelling overall design.   **GROVE**music

Asyla

Asyla[bc]. ... but all shall be well[bd]. Chamber Symphony[ad]. Concerto conciso[ae]. These Premises are Alarmed[bd]
[a]**Birmingham Contemporary Music Group;** [b]**City of Birmingham Symphony Orchestra /** [c]**Sir Simon Rattle,** [d]**Thomas Adès** [e]*pf*
EMI 556818-2 (61' · DDD)   Ⓕ●

This CD includes the *Chamber Symphony*, the work that first aroused interest in Adès's work when he was 18, set alongside *Asyla*, a recent un-chamber symphony and his first work for full orchestra. The progression between them is remarkable: the *Chamber Symphony* has both real invention and real economy, and its use of jazz elements is neither patronising nor culinary. Maybe its last movement adds little of consequence to the preceding three, but *Asyla* genuinely grows from the grave, rather Brittenish horn line that sets it going through the strong drama of the central movements to the almost Sibelian climax of the finale. Adès's own voice is clearly audible throughout, elegant, coolly intelligent but urgent.

These Premises are Alarmed, a sinewy toccata of bright colour and urgent energy, was written for the opening of the Bridgewater Hall, Manchester. In the *Concerto conciso* Adès perhaps takes his pleasure in simple intervals and brief motives a little too far. However, ... *but all shall be well* is something else again. It develops abundant, earnest melody from a pair of simple phrases in an impressively sustained argument that reaches a powerful and satisfying climax. Fine performances, admirably recorded.

Living Toys

Arcadiana, Op 12[a]. The Origin of the Harp, Op 13[b]. Sonata da caccia, Op 11[c]. Living Toys, Op 9[d]. Gefriolsae me, Op 3b[e] [c]**Michael Neisemann** *ob* [c]**Andrew Clark** *hn* [c]**Thomas Adès** *hpd* [a]**Endellion Quartet** (Andrew Watkinson, Ralph de Souza *vns* Garfield Jackson *va* David Waterman *vc*) [e]**King's College Choir, Cambridge / Stephen Cleobury;** [b]**instrumental ensemble / Thomas Adès;** [d]**London Sinfonietta / Markus Stenz**
EMI Debut 572271-2 (64' · DDD) Text and translation included   Ⓑ●○○

The five pieces here suggest a composer as delightedly surprised by his prodigal inventiveness as we are. *Arcadiana*, for example, is a seven-movement string quartet whose central and longest movement (four minutes) contains an extraordinary range of precisely imagined, highly original textures and yet in its penultimate section can settle to a serene and wonderfully beautiful *adagio* whose sound and mood be conveyed only by the adjective 'Beethovenian'. Far more overtly, the engaging *Sonata da caccia* uses elements that are very directly derived from Couperin, but the sensibility is entirely modern, even when you strongly suspect that this or that phrase is a note-for-note quotation. However, as with Adès's first collection, his is an imagination that you can trust. *Living Toys* has a quite Birtwistle-like sense of ritual to it, although more lyrical, quite frequently with a tangible jazz element. *The Origin of the Harp* is a dark, dramatic chamber tone-poem. *Gefriolsae me*, for male voices and organ, is a brief but impressive motet to Middle English words. All five pieces are finely performed. *Arcadiana*, with its exquisite textures and melodic richness, is perhaps Adès's finest achievement so far, a work constantly aware of the musical past but renewing that past with astonishing freshness.

Life story

Catch, Op 4. Darknesse visible. Still sorrowing, Op 7. Under Hamelin Hill, Op 6. Five Eliot Landscapes, Op 1. Traced overhead, Op 15. Life story, Op 8b
Valdine Anderson, Mary Carewe *sops* **Lynsey Marsh** *cl* **Anthony Marwood** *vn* **Louise Hopkins** *vc* **Thomas Adès** *pf/org* **David Goode, Stephen Farr** *orgs*
EMI Debut 569699-2 (77' · DDD) Texts included Ⓑ●○

Adès has the gift of seizing your attention with strange but ravishingly beautiful sonorities and then holding it with entrancingly mysterious inventions that allure the ear. Yet he also has the much rarer quality of inspiring utter confidence. His style can't be defined by simply describing any one of these pieces. Each solves a new problem or investigates a new scenario with such adroitness and completeness that it seems a quite new and delightful adventure. In *Still sorrowing* the starting point is a piano whose central register is muted with a strip of plastic adhesive. The effect on those pitches is obvious: they are dulled to a sort of subdued drumming, but by observing the new light that this casts on the undamped upper and lower registers Adès effectively invents a new and alluring instrument, or rather three of them. And he plays them with poetry and wonder. *Catch* is a game in which a piano trio tempt and tease an off-stage clarinet; he eventually joins them in sober homophony, for this is a game with serious and lyrical substance as well as a jest. A similar but more ambiguous game is played in *Under Hamelin Hill*, where the piping toccata of one organist attracts two others to join him in co-operative apparent improvisation, but he's left alone for a shadowy soliloquy filled with shudders. *Darknesse visible* is a haunting meditation in which the presence of John Dowland is clearest where the music seems least like him; a magical illusion as well as a moving homage. In *Life story* the soprano is asked to imitate the manner of Billie Holiday in her wry reflection on a casual one-night encounter; it's the dark, searching piano that adds pity and bleakness to turn this into a riveting miniature opera. *Traced overhead* is filled with mysterious, glancing references to remembered piano music, but is grippingly coherent. And as if this weren't enough, in the Eliot settings, Op 1, the 17-year-old Adès already proved himself a song-writer of rare talent. The performances are first-rate.

Powder Her Face

Powder Her Face
Jill Gomez sop Duchess **Valdine Anderson** sop
Maid, Confidante, Waitress, Mistress, Society
Journalist, First Rubbernecker **Niall Morris** ten
Electrician, Lounge Lizard, Waiter, Delivery Boy,
Second Rubbernecker **Roger Bryson** bar Hotel
Manager, Duke, Guest, Laundryman, Judge **Almeida
Ensemble / Thomas Adès**
EMI ② 556649-2 (116' · DDD) Text included   Ⓜ️Ⓞ

Powder Her Face was written and had its first performances in 1995, when Adès was 24. It would be remarkable, as his first opera, if it demonstrated the fertility of invention and imaginative resource that erupted from the two discs of his shorter pieces. But it does much more than that. The central character, though referred to in the cast-list simply as 'Duchess', is in fact Margaret, Duchess of Argyll, for many years a prominent figure in London society, who in 1963 was at the centre of a protracted and luridly sensational divorce case: the judge's verdict described her sexual activities as 'dis-

gusting' and 'debased'. Even after the divorce she counted the rich, the famous and the royal among her friends but died, penniless, in 1993.

Adès and librettist Philip Hensher imagine her as 'all cladding – powder, scent, painting, furs – nothing inside': the risk is that she'll appear either as an empty monster for whom we can feel little sympathy or a glittering caricature whom we pity as the subject of the composer and librettist's mockery. Their wit is indeed dazzling. The libretto is outstandingly good and the score is satisfyingly rich, surprising and bizarre. It takes great risks – an aria and a duet sung simultaneously, a musical equivalent of the judge's interminable concluding speech – and they come off brilliantly. Adès alludes to the music that would have furnished the Duchess's glamorous life – the score is pervaded with tangos – but he can use it to convey menace and desolation as well as picturesque period evocation. He draws astonishingly varied sounds and vivid dramaturgy from chamber forces. His highest achievement is his portrayal of the Duchess. From her first appearance, surprising a maid and an electrician sniggering at her grotesque reputation, she has iconic glamour and something like dignity. Although often off-stage she dominates the opera effortlessly, and in the long final scene she achieves not tragic stature, perhaps, but deep and genuine patho.

The opera gains enormously from Jill Gomez's alluring and attention-riveting performance, although all the other singers are very accomplished. The score makes huge demands of the orchestral players, many of them required to be virtuoso soloists. The recording is as vivid as it needs to be. A hugely enjoyable opera.

Alexander Agricola
Franco-Flemish 1446-1506

Agricola's career centred mainly on Italian courts (Milan, Florence, Naples) and the French court – from 1498 until his death he served Philip the Handsome of Burgundy at home and abroad. His travels brought him renown as a singer and composer. His works include eight masses, over 20 motets and other sacred pieces, nearly 50 chansons and c25 instrumental works. His style is predominantly northern, akin to Ockeghem's, using long, rhythmically complex contrapuntal lines built from short, decorative motifs and linked with frequent yet unobtrusive cadences.   **GROVE**music

Fortuna desperata

A la mignonne de fortune. Adieu m'amour.   Ⓟ
Adieu m'amour II. Allez, regretz. Ay je rien fait.
Cecsus non iudicat de coloribus. De tous biens
plaine. De tous biens plaine II. De tous biens
plaine III. Et qui la dira. Fortuna desperata. Guarde vostre
visage. Guarde vostre visage II. Guarde vostre visage

III. J'ay beau huer. S'il vous plaist. Soit loing ou pres.
Sonnes muses melodieusement
Ensemble Unicorn (Bernhard Landauer *counterten*
Johannes Chum *ten* Colin Mason *bass-bar* Marco
Ambrosini *fiddle* Nora Kallai *vihuela d'arco* Thomas
Wimmer *vihuela d'arco/lte* Riccardo Delfino *hp/snare
hp*) / **Michael Posch** *rec*
Naxos 8 553840 (65' · DDD)   Ⓢ**OO**

Agricola was praised by his contemporaries for
the bizarre turn of his inspiration, and his music
likened to quicksilver. By the standards of the
period this is a highly unusual turn of phrase,
but remains spot-on. The Ferrara Ensemble
anthology, the first ever devoted to the composer, focused on the secular music, both
instrumental and vocal, precisely the area covered by Michael Posch and Ensemble Unicorn
in this most satisfying disc. Where there's duplication (surprisingly little, in fact) the performances compare with those of the Ferrara
Ensemble, although the style of singing is very
different. The voices are more up front and less
inflected, perhaps the better to match the high
instruments with which they're sometimes doubled. But the tensile quality of Agricola's lines
comes through none the less, as does the miraculous inventiveness and charm of his music.
Further, much of what's new to the catalogue
really is indispensible, for example Agricola's
most famous song, *Allez, regretz*. Unicorn keeps
its improvisations and excursions to a minimum, and the music is the better for it. This disc
would be indispensable at full price, let alone
super-budget. It really is a must-have.

Kalevi Aho   Finnish b1949

*Aho studied at the Sibelius Academy in Helsinki
under Einojuhani Rautavaara and with Boris
Blacher in West Berlin. He has taught at Helsinki
University and the Sibelius Academy, but since 1993
has been a freelance composer. His extensive output
includes much orchestral music and several operas.*

Orchestral music

Symphony No 11ᵃ. Symphonic Dances
ᵃ**Kroumata Percussion Ensemble** (John Eriksson,
Anders Holdar, Leif Karlsson, Anders Loguin, Ulril
Nilsson, Johan Silvmark *perc*) **Lahti Symphony
Orchestra / Osmo Vänskä**
BIS BIS-CD1336 (61' · DDD)   Ⓕ

Aho's Symphonic Dances (2001) bear the subtitle 'Hommage à Uuno Klami' – and therein
lies the clue to the work's genesis. Klami (1900-
1961), one of the leading Finnish composers of
the last century, had high hopes for his large-
scale, *Kalevala*-inspired ballet *Pyrörteitä*, but by
the time of his death had managed to orchestrate only the second of its three acts. Aho
orchestrated Act 1 in 1988. During 2000 no
material having come to light for the final act,
he embarked on completing Klami's *magnum*

opus, bolstered by the prospect of a production
of the whole score at the Finnish National Ballet. In the event, that belated première never
materialised, and it was left to Osmo Vänskä and
the Lahti SO to champion Aho's 'Third Act' in
the concert hall. A thoroughly approachable,
27-minute creation of exhilarating drive and
colour, its four movements take their names
from Klami's original synopsis. It's stunningly
well served here by artists and production crew
alike.

The Eleventh Symphony is almost as rewarding. It grew out of a commission for an orchestral work involving the Kroumata Percussion
Ensemble, and is cast in three movements, the
last of which distils a wondrous stillness and
inner calm. It also serves as a perfect foil to the
first two movements, both of which demonstrate Aho's comprehensive mastery of rhythm,
timbre and drama. Again, the performance is a
definitive one and BIS's engineering breathtaking in its realism.

Jehan Alain   French 1911-1940

*Alain studied with Dupré and Dukas at the Paris
Conservatoire (1927-39) and was organist of St
Nicolas de Maisons Lafitte in Paris (1935-9); he
was killed in action. He shared Messiaen's enthusiasms for Debussy and Asian music, reflected in the
modalities, rhythmic irregularities and ecstatic ostinatos of his works, which are mostly for the organ or
the Catholic Mass. His organ works include Deux
danses à Agni Yavishtra (1934), two Fantaisies
(1934, 1936), Litanies (1937) and Trois danses
(1937-9).*   **GROVE**music

Organ Works

Suite. Climat. Prélude et Fugue. Choral dorien.
Choral phrygien. Aria. Variations sur 'Lucis créator'.
Berceuse sur deux notes qui cornent. Deux préludes
profanes. Monodie. Ballade en mode phrygien.
Choral cistercian pour une élévation. Variations sur
un thème de Clément Janequin. Le jardin suspendu.
Litanies. Fantasmagorie. Trois danses. Quatre pièces.
Grave. Petite pièce. Intermezzo. Lamento. Première
fantaisie. Deuxième fantaisie. Deux dances à Agni
Yavishta. Cinque pièces faciles – Complainte à la
mode ancienne; Fugue en mode de Fa; Verset-
Choral; Berceuse. Postlude pour l'office de
Complies. Page 21 du huitième cahier de notes de
Jehan Alain
Kevin Bowyer *org*
Nimbus ② NI5551/2 (146' · DDD) Recorded on the
Marcussen Organ, Chapel of St Augustine,
Tonbridge School, Kent 1997   Ⓕ**OOO**

Ⓖ This is the most comprehensive and
impressive recording yet of Alain's
organ music. Bowyer offers nine pieces
not included on Eric Lebrun's two-disc survey
from Naxos. These may not be among the composer's most substantial creations, but Alain
enthusiasts wouldn't like to be without any of

them, least of all the intensely moving page from one of Alain's notebooks setting out his musical reactions to the death, in a mountaineering accident, of his sister, Marie-Odile. Bowyer's performances are thought-provoking, stimulating and often inspired. His tempos aren't especially quick, though he does turn out the fastest performance ever recorded of the *Intermezzo*. Yet even here the choice of speed is symptomatic of his approach; nobody could deny that when played so rapidly the work takes on a new dimension. Nimbus achieves a near-perfect balance between clarity and atmosphere on the new Marcussen in Tonbridge School's rebuilt Chapel. When the disarming dialogue between a single reed and the flutes of the charming *Petite pièce* can be revealed in such detail nobody could realistically ask for a better setting for this magical music. Bowyer proves to be an unusually perceptive and persuasive advocate of Alain's music. It will probably be a long time before a serious contender to this outstanding release comes along.

Litanies. Petite pièce. Le jardin suspendu. Deuxième fantaisie. Variations sur un thème de Clément Janequin. Deux dances à Agni Yavishta. Deux préludes profanes. Choral cistercian pour une élévation. Climat. Monodie. Ballade en mode phrygien. Choral phrygien. Suite
Eric Lebrun *org*
Naxos 8 553632 (64' · DDD) Recorded on the organ of the Church of Saint-Antoine des Quinze-Vingts, Paris 1995   Ⓢ

Trois danses. Intermezzo. Variations sur 'Lucis créator'. Berceuse. Grave. Lamento. Première fantaisie. Prélude et Fugue. Choral dorien. Aria. Postlude pour l'office de Complies
Eric Lebrun *org*
Naxos 8 553633 (66' · DDD) Recorded on the organ of the Church of Saint-Antoine des Quinze-Vingts, Paris 1995   Ⓢ〇

Whether it's the weirdly sombre *Lamento*, the captivating *Intermezzo*, the pseudo-archaic *Variations sur un thème de Clément Janequin* or the dramatically fervent *Litanies*, to have it all brought together under one roof allows us to revel in that magical mix of mysticism, melancholy and modality which makes Alain's voice so distinctive. This splendid Cavaillé-Coll organ, set in a richly atmospheric acoustic, seems the perfect vehicle for Alain's music, with its kaleidoscopic use of subtle colours and effects. It possesses glorious stops and seems fully equipped to deal with everything Alain's music demands of it. What a shame, then, that the recording itself misses the mark. An indistinct focus blurs much of the detail, while there just isn't enough of the church's ambience to compensate for this lack of clarity. There again, Eric Lebrun is guilty of some pretty indistinct articulation himself; that said, much of his playing is outstanding. The best-known works verge on the controversial (*Le jardin suspendu*, for

example, is superficial), but in the rarely heard *Suite* he produces playing of conviction and magnetism. And with a deeply moving account of the *Postlude pour l'office de Complies*, he more than justifies Naxos's faith in him. This deserves a place on the shelves of all organ music devotees.

Isaac Albéniz   Spanish 1860-1909

Albéniz is one of the most important figures in Spanish musical history; he helped create a national idiom and an indigenous school of piano music. He studied at the Brussels Conservatory and with Liszt, Dukas and d'Indy; other important influences were Felipe Pedrell (who inspired him to turn to Spanish folk music), 19th-century salon piano music and impressionist harmony. But he was not simply a follower of the French school and exchanged ideas with Debussy and Ravel in Paris. Most of his many works are for piano solo, the best known being the suite Iberia (1906-8), distinguished by its complex technique, bold harmony and evocative instrumental effects. He also wrote a notable opera, Pepita Jiménez (1896). Albéniz was also a virtuoso pianist with a highly personal style.   **GROVE**music

Guitar Works

Albéniz Mallorca, Op 202. Suite española, Op 47. Cantos de España, Op 232 – Córdoba **Granados** Cuentos de la juventud – Dedicatoria. 15 Tonadillas – El majo olvidado. 12 Danzas españolas, Op 37 – Villanesca; Andaluza (Playera). 7 Valses poéticos
Rodrigo Tres Piezas españolas
Julian Bream *gtr*
RCA Navigator 74321 17903-2 (77' · DDD) Recorded 1982-3   Ⓢ〇〇

This recital offers playing of extraordinary magnetism and an almost total illusion of the great guitarist seated in the room making music just beyond your loudspeakers; this effect is particularly striking in Albéniz's *Córdoba* and the *pianissimo* reprise of the central section of the Granados *Danza española* No 5, which is quite magical. The other works included are all played with comparable spontaneity.

RCA here reissue this disc at super-bargain price on their enterprising Navigator label; moreover, they have added Rodrigo's *Tres Piezas españolas*, recorded a year later. The second of these, a seven-minute 'Passacaglia', is quite masterly, while the final 'Zapateado' brings characteristically chimerical virtuosity from the soloist. It's difficult to identify another recital of Spanish guitar music that surpasses this, and it's now one of the great bargains in the Navigator catalogue.

Piano Works

Iberia. Navarra (compl de Séverac). Suite española, Op 47

Alicia de Larrocha pf
Decca ② 417 887-2DH2 (126' · DDD) Recorded 1986
Ⓕ**OO**

Written during Albéniz's last three years, *Iberia* is his masterwork for the piano. The full extent of the journey he travelled in his all-too-brief life can't be fully appreciated by comparing these 12 richly colourful 'impressions' with the *Suite española*, generally accepted as his earliest serious foray into the nationalist field. Larrocha also gives us the bonus of the exuberant *Navarra* originally intended by the composer (before he rejected it as 'too plebeian') to end *Iberia*. Coming from such a distinguished specialist in the Spanish field, the album is as musically enjoyable as it's musicologically stimulating. Her playing has immediacy, subtlety and charm besides revealing fingers so magically able to conceal Albéniz's sometimes cruel technical demands. Compared to the old LP recording the clarity of colouring is like an old painting newly cleaned. But it isn't just the recording that allows Larrocha's most recent *Iberia* to make a more vivid impact. Everything here carries just that little extra conviction. Every tiny detail in Albéniz's multi-layered textures, every counter-strand, every fleck of colour, is always crystal-clear.

Larrocha's range of colour, and the sensuous beauty of her tone, can only be described as a feast for the ear. She plays the *Suite española* with a spontaneous delight in their tunes, textures and rhythms; she enjoys them as the engaging *morceaux de salon* that, in comparison with what follows in *Iberia*, they undoubtedly are.

Iberia. Navarra. España: Souvenirs. La Vega. Yvonne
en visite! – La révérence!; Joyeuse rencontre et
quelques...
Marc-André Hamelin pf
Hyperion ② CDA67476/7 (126' · DDD)   Ⓕ**OO**

Here's the most immaculate, effortless and refined of all *Iberias*. Where others fight to stay afloat, Marc-André Hamelin rides the crest of every formidable wave with nonchalant ease and poetry. Did Albéniz, as Rubinstein once claimed, need a helping hand in *Iberia*, simplifying textures for greater clarity, brilliance and accessibility? Hamelin's musical grace mocks the very question. His 'Evocación', audaciously free and perfumed, makes you hang on every note, and although characteristically cool, elegant and supple, he's true to the heart of Albéniz's incomparable tapestry of southern Spain. Try 'Almeria' and you'll hear playing of jewelled perfection, a mesmerising dream-world rudely interrupted by 'Lavapiés', where every one of the composer's torrents of notes is made crystal clear.

Again, when has 'Málaga' been played with greater fluency and imaginative delicacy? Perhaps such playing is a compensation for Rubinstein's legendary but never recorded performance. Certainly in its suppleness and trans-

parency it has a Chopinesque rather than Lisztian bias, but Hamelin gives us all the notes and he's recorded in sound as natural and refined as his playing.

After *Iberia* there's *La Vega*, inspired by the plains surrounding Granada, by a 'land of flowers and sapphire skies'. This surely ranks among the greatest recordings of a Spanish piano work. Limpid, haunting and evocative, it resolves every complexity in rapt poetry. For added measure he gives us 'Yvonne en visite', a hilarious imitation of a pianist who stumbles from note to note, tenacious but incompetent. Finally, there is 'Navarra', complete with William Bolcom's coda, a lengthy and witty résumé and cadenza rather than de Sévérac's brief conclusion. Comparison with de Larrocha's benchmark Albéniz is inevitable. But Hamelin's is radically different in both execution and character, and she, for all her magisterial command, is no match for him in musical grace and fluency

Hamelin's Albéniz proudly but nonchalantly, raises a new and astonishing standard.

Henry Clifford

Henry Clifford
Aquiles Machado ten Henry Clifford **Alessandra
Marc** sop Lady Clifford **Carlos Álvarez** bar Sir John
Saint John **Jane Henschel** mez Lady Saint John **Ana
María Martínez** sop Annie Saint John **Christian M
Immler** bar Colin **Ángel Rodriguez** ten Messenger
Pedro Gilabert bar Herald **Madrid Symphony
Chorus and Orchestra / José De Eusebio**
Décca ② 473 937-2DHO2 (140' · DDD)   Ⓕ**O**

The appearance of the colourful Arthurian *Merlin* came as a surprise even to many lovers of Spanish music that Albéniz had written a series of operas to English texts. It was the English banker and philanthropist Francis Burdett Money-Coutts who turned Albéniz in this unexpected direction. He decided that the Spanish composer was just the man to compose an English equivalent to Wagner's *Ring* cycle, to libretti that he would write for him. He gave generous support to Albéniz and his family. *Henry Clifford*, a story of love and conflicting loyalties set at the time of the Wars of the Roses, was the first result, and was staged in Barcelona in Italian translation in 1895.

As with *Merlin*, the big snag is the libretto, for Money-Coutts's talents as a poet were nil. It's amazing how far Albéniz overcomes the burden of the words, for though the story itself is often slow-moving and confused, there are many musical felicities. There are few signs of a Spanish flavour, and the melodies soar engagingly in a fresh, English way, notably in writing for the female characters.

Each act brings its memorable passages, and there are distant echoes of *Tristan und Isolde*, as well as hints of Sullivan and Edward German, quite likely influences when Albéniz was based in London in the early 1890s.

Alessandra Marc as Lady Clifford makes a fine foil for Jane Henschel, and though Ana María Martínez as Annie has some edgy moments, she copes very sweetly with the challengingly high tessitura of the brilliant soprano part. Aquiles Machado sings the title-role with a winningly warm timbre, though Albéniz sets his principal a formidable challenge in writing at the upper extremes of the voice, so he's occasionally taxed to the limit.

Henry Clifford; it will appeal to anyone who enjoys an operatic costume drama in a warm, late-romantic idiom, ripely orchestrated. Though less polished than *Merlin*, it offers a similarly colourful and atmospheric experience, very well recorded in full-bodied sound.

Tomaso Albinoni   Italian 1671-1751

Born of wealthy parents, Albinoni was a dilettante musician, never seeking a church or court post, though he had contact with noble patrons. He concentrated on instrumental and secular vocal music and had early successes with his opera Zenobia (1694, Venice) and 12 trio sonatas Op 1 (1694). His reputation grew, with operas staged in other cities, beginning with Rodrigo in Algeri (1702, Naples); later operas, such as I veri amici (1722, Munich), were staged abroad. In all he wrote over 50 operas, several other stage works and over 40 solo cantatas; few works date from after 1730.

Albinoni's instrumental works, mostly for strings, were especially popular; 10 sets were published in his lifetime. Bach based four keyboard fugues on subjects from the Op 1 sonatas. While Albinoni's concertos were less adventurous and soloistic than Vivaldi's, they were probably the earliest consistently in three movements, and his oboe concertos Op 7 (1715) were the first by an Italian to be published. The sonatas (for one to six instruments with continuo) are mostly in four movements. His music is individual, with a strong melodic character and, especially in the early works, formally well balanced.   **GROVE**music

---

Concerti a cinque, Opp 5, 7 & 9

Op 5 – No 1 in B flat **No 2** in F **No 3** in D **No 4** in G **No 5** in A minor **No 6** in A **No 7** in D minor **No 8** in F **No 9** in E minor **No 10** in A **No 11** in G minor **No 12** in C

Op 7 – No 1 in D **No 2** in C **No 3** in B flat **No 4** in G **No 5** in C **No 6** in D **No 7** in A **No 8** in D **No 9** in F **No 10** in B flat **No 11** in C **No 12** in C

Op 9 – No 1 in B flat **No 2** in D minor **No 3** in F **No 4** in A **No 5** in C **No 6** in G. **No 7** in D **No 8** in G minor **No 9** in C **No 10** in F **No 11** in B flat **No 12** in D

Concerti a cinque Op 5   **P**
Collegium Musicum 90 / Simon Standage vn
Chandos Chaconne CHAN0663 (76' · DDD)   Ⓕ**OO**

Albinoni might be described as a specialist in the medium of the Concerto *a cinque*, of which he composed 54, published at intervals during almost half his productive life. The first six appeared in his Op 2 (1700), together with six sonatas from which they inherited some structural features, and were followed in 1707 by the 12 of Op 5. They were 'halfway houses' on the road to the violin concerto *per se* as we know it – and as Vivaldi established it four years later. Virtuoso passages for a solo violin appear only *en passant* in flanking movements and 'symmetrically' in the *Adagios* of Nos 3, 6, 9 and 12. Each Concerto is in three-movement form and all the finales are fugal, as they are in the Op 2, though in their simplicity they sound rather like rondos.

There was little by way of innovation in Albinoni's concertos, which leant on past examples and stressed some of their most durable features, but the lyricism of the *Adagio* of No 2, 5, 8 and 11 (again symmetrically placed) was indeed new. Their strength is in his gift of melodic invention, their clearly defined form and thematic material, their conciseness – a virtue that didn't survive in some of his later concertos – and their vitality and freshness. The recording and annotation are of the highest standard, and of the performances it might be said that if they're ever bettered in any respect, we and Albinoni will indeed be fortunate.

CHAN0579 – Op 7 Nos 3, 6, 9 & 12.   **P**
Op 9 Nos 2, 5, 8 & 11
CHAN0602 – Op 7 Nos 1, 2, 4 & 5.
Op 9 Nos 1, 3, 4 & 6. Sinfonia in G minor
CHAN0610 – Op 7 Nos 7, 8, 10 & 11.
Op 9 Nos 7, 9, 10 & 12
Anthony Robson, Catherine Latham obs **Collegium Musicum 90 / Simon Standage** vn
Chandos Chaconne CHAN0579/0602/0610 (oas: 72', 63' & 65' · DDD) Recorded 1993, 1996   Ⓕ**O**

Albinoni's Op 7 and Op 9 consist of four concertos *with* (rather than *for*, as the composer insisted) one oboe, four with two oboes and four for strings only. Overall, the last show a strong family resemblance, with vivacious outer movements and suave slow movements that tend to be more chromatic; but the Op 9 string concertos include a solo violin part, at times very elaborate. The first volume contains the works for solo oboe and strings. Albinoni treats the oboe like a voice and the slow movements have tunes that stay in the mind. The second volume contains the string and double-oboe concertos. All are three-movement *da chiesa* works, with cheerful outer movements and slow ones that often remind you that Albinoni wrote a good deal of vocal music. The two oboes 'sing' together for the most part, either in thirds or in unison. The concertos on Vol 3 for two oboes display rather more individuality – the joyous finale of Op 7 No 11 intriguingly sharpens the fourth of the scale, Op 9 No 9 allows the oboes more independence of each other, while in the outer movements of Op 9 No 12 the oboes put up a good pretence at being trumpets.

Anthony Robson and Catherine Latham contribute deftly to the spirit of enjoyment that emanates from the whole of this disc. Collegium Musicum 90 is one of the very best Baroque bands around and here the players are in their element. The recorded balance is just right, keeping soloists and strings in equal perspective. These discs bid strongly for a place on every shelf.

---

8 550739 – 12 Concerti a cinque – Op 9 Nos 2, 3, 5, 8, 9 & 11

8 553002 – Sinfonia in G (arr Camden). 12 Concerti a cinque – Op 7 Nos 1, 2, 3, 8 & 9. Op 9 No 6

8 553035 – 12 Concerti a cinque – Op 7 Nos 4, 5, 6, 11 & 12. Op 9 No 12

Anthony Camden, Julia Girdwood, Alison Alty obs
The London Virtuosi / John Georgiadis
Naxos 8 550739/3002/3035 (oas: 64', 58', 52' · DDD)
Recorded 1992, 1994 Ⓢ⊙

The oboe participates in, rather than dominates, these works in a chamber-music-like fashion. Albinoni wasn't in the business of springing harmonic surprises, but was a fluent writer of engaging tunes, particularly those in the Adagios – each of these works has one – and of elegant discourses between the soloist and the upper strings. Anthony Camden and Julia Girdwood produce liquid sounds from their modern instruments, and are as meltingly expressive in the slow movements as they're light on their feet in the flanking ones. The London Virtuosi performance, also using modern strings, has a nice, clean air about it and gives the music neither more nor less than its due. The recording is bright and well balanced.

Volume 2 begins with a strings-only Sinfonia in G, to which Anthony Camden has added oboe parts; it's thematically related to the Concerto, Op 7 No 4 (given in its original form), but to appreciate this bit of auto-plagiary you'll need Vol 3. The three discs are better sampled than listened to from start to finish – unless you're an oboist or an insatiable 'Baroque person'; there are some delectable pickings to be had, particularly among the slow movements.

The performances and recording quality are of the same order as those of Vol 1, 'couth, kempt and shevelled' – as is the graceful and amiable music itself. As an archive, the complete set is hard to resist at super-bargain price.

Hugo Alfvén   Swedish 1872-1960

Alfvén studied at the Stockholm Conservatory (1887-91) and privately with Lindegren, also training as a painter. Thereafter he worked as a choirmaster and Director Musices at Uppsala University (1910-39). His music is distinguished by orchestral subtlety and a painterly exploitation of harmony and timbre. It is almost all programmatic, often seeking to evoke the landscapes and seascapes of southern Sweden (eg Midsummer Vigil, 1903; Shepherd-girl's Dance, 1923). His main works include five symphonies, much choral music and songs.   **GROVE**music

Swedish Rhapsodies

Swedish Rhapsodies – No 1, Op 19, 'Midsummer Vigil'; No 2, Op 24, 'Upsala-rapsodi'; No 3, 'Dalarapsodi'. A Legend of the Skerries, Op 20. Gustav Adolf II, Op 49 – Elegy
Iceland Symphony Orchestra / Petri Sakari
Chandos CHAN9313 (70' · DDD) Recorded 1993   Ⓕ

Petri Sakari gives us the most natural, unaffected and satisfying *Midsummer Vigil* to be heard on disc. He's light in touch, responsive to each passing mood and every dynamic nuance, self-effacing and completely at the service of the composer. Moreover, in the *Upsala-rapsodi* and its later companion he's fresher and more persuasive than any of his rivals on record. Even the Wagnerian-Straussian echoes from the skerries sound convincing. The only reservation concerns the *Elegy* from the incidental music to Ludwig Nordström's play about Gustav Adolf II, which might have benefited from greater reticence. Unusually for Sakari, he doesn't tell the tale simply or let the music speak for itself. The recorded sound is refreshingly free from analytical point-making; everything is there in the right perspective, although listeners whose first response is to find the recording recessed will find that a higher level of playback than usual will produce impressively natural results on high-grade equipment.

Cantatas

Cantata, 'At the Turn of the Century', Op 12[ac]. Cantata for the 1917 Reformation Festivities in Uppsala, Op 36[bc]. The Bells, Op 13[b]
[a]**Lena Hoel** sop [b]**Karl-Magnus Fredriksson** bar
[c]**Royal Stockholm Philharmonic Choir; Gävle Symphony Orchestra / Stefan Parkman**
Sterling CDS1036-2 (60' · DDD) Texts and translations included   Ⓕ⊙

Cantatas for ceremonial or anniversary occasions have a distinguished tradition in the Nordic countries, as can be seen in the catalogues of Sibelius, Grieg, Nielsen and Holmboe. Hugo Alfvén was as accomplished as any – indeed, comparing the two main works on this new release with Sibelius's 'Conferment' and *Coronation* cantatas, Alfvén was the finer exponent. Listen to the opening movement, 'Life's Empire', of *Vid sekelskiftet* ('At the Turn of the Century'), which has real nobility about it; and if the second and fourth are emptily high-spirited, they still sound fun. Alfvén's style may seem archaic for 1899, but there are sufficient passages – especially in the third movement,

'Väldarnas offer' ('The world's offering', a solo for soprano which can be performed separately) – that reveal the anachronisms to be more calculated than might at first appear. Alfvén's next numbered opus, the ballad *Klockorna* ('The Bells', 1900), was more consistently adventurous in harmony and orchestration, and is an absolute gem, sung beautifully by Karl-Magnus Fredriksson.

Fredriksson also features in the 1917 cantata commemorating the 400th anniversary of Luther nailing his 95 Theses to the chapel door in Wittenberg, thereby setting in motion the Protestant Reformation. The music (built around three Lutheran chorales) is magnificent, particularly in the first two movements, with their deeply affecting nobility of utterance.

Stefan Parkman, who directed several wonderful discs with the Danish National Radio Choir, secures wonderfully full and committed performances from all concerned, and Sterling's recording is warm and clear. A thoroughly estimable project, warmly recommended.

Charles-Valentin Alkan

French 1813-1888

Alkan was a leading piano virtuoso and an unusual composer, remarkable in technique and imagination yet largely ignored by his own and succeeding generations. A child prodigy, he studied at the Paris Conservatoire. Although he held no official appointment and rarely played publicly, he was known for the brilliance of his playing, his wide repertory of earlier music and as a champion of the pedal piano (for which he composed). His complex works include extra-musical elements; he favoured obscure titles and subject matter (often with a satanic, childish or mystical tone), bold tonal structures and unusual metres. He exploited brilliantly the keyboard's resources, often making great demands of technique and stamina, and used scrupulously exact notation. Many of his some 70 opus numbers are organised in long schemes of harmonic studies, such as the 25 Préludes in all the major and minor keys Op 31 (1847) and the 12 Études Op 39 (1857); his most famous and demanding works are his Grande Sonate, Op 33 and the Concerto (for piano solo) from Op 39. He was greatly admired by Liszt and Busoni.
GROVEmusic

Grand duo concertante, Op 21

Grand duo concertante in F sharp minor, Op 21. Sonate de concert in E, Op 47. Trio in G minor, Op 30
Trio Alkan (Kolja Lessing vn Bernhard Schwarz vc Rainer Klaas pf)
Naxos 8 555352 (75' · DDD) Recorded 1991　Ⓢ

As this disc so persuasively reveals, there are a number of Alkan's chamber works that are long overdue for serious consideration. His violin sonata, the *Grand duo concertante*, for instance, is

so thoroughly original and masterly in invention that it should have acquired for itself a prominent place in the French violin sonata repertoire. The somewhat unconventional tonal layout of the bold and memorable first movement suggests, at times, the harmonic world of Berlioz, but perhaps more strikingly looks forward, both here and in the final movement, to the melodic, Gallic charm of the Fauré sonatas.

The *Sonate de concert* for cello and piano is perhaps Alkan's finest and most important contribution to chamber music. Although clearly rooted in the classical tradition, it shouts Alkan from every page. The second movement, in *siciliano* style, is a fine example of Alkan whimsy; in the slow movement, Alkan draws musical inspiration from his Jewish faith to create a serene and somewhat mystical oasis of calm before launching into the helter-skelter activity of the finale. The earlier Piano Trio of 1841 is perhaps even more classical in design and utterance, and is certainly more terse and economical in its use of material. However, it's no easy ride for the performers. The *Scherzo* is strangely prophetic of Tchaikovsky in places and is graced with a fiendishly difficult finale. The performances are quite superb. Klaas copes admirably with all the keyboard pyrotechnics thrown at him, and Lessing and Schwarz provide performances of dedication and great understanding. Recording is full-bodied and close, although not uncomfortably so.

Grande sonate, Op 33

Grande sonate, Op 33, 'Les quatre âges'. Sonatine, Op 61. Barcarolle, Op 65 No 6. Etudes dans les tons mineurs, Op 39 – No 12, 'Le festin d'Esope'.
Marc-André Hamelin pf
Hyperion CDA66794 (70' · DDD) Recorded 1994
Ⓕ**OO**

Les quatre âges is an extraordinary piece in many respects, not least in its rather unconventional layout of four movements, each employing progressively slower tempos. Perhaps for this reason it has never attained a place in the repertoire – the extremely slow finale is hardly the sort of movement to ignite an overwhelming response from an audience at the close of the sonata, despite the feats of hair-raising bravura required in the first two movements. Hamelin's performance is everything you could wish for. The crispness and precision of his finger-work in the dazzling first movement is quite breathtaking and the sometimes superhuman feats of pianism demanded in the Faust-inspired second movement are executed with astounding ease. His reading of the third movement is beautifully poised and charmingly rendered while the tragic, Promethean finale is most effectively and powerfully projected.

The *Sonatine* is an entirely different matter, concise and concentrated in the extreme. Hamelin's direct, finely articulated nonsense reading brings out the clarity and economy of the writing, and he's also quick to underscore the work's more classical stance. A beautifully serene and hypnotic account of the seductive 'Barcarolle' follows, and the disc closes with a stunning display of pianistic gymnastics in the shape of 'Le festin d'Esope' from the Op 39 *Etudes*. Recorded sound is excellent.

12 Etudes, Op 39

12 Etudes dans les tons mineurs, Op 39. Nocturne, Op 22. Etude in F, Op 35 No 5. Assez vivement, Op 38 No 1. Préludes, Op 31 – No 8, La chanson de la folle au bord de la mer; No 12, Le temps qui n'est plus; No 13, J'étais endormie, mais mon coeur veillait. Esquisses, Op 63 – No 2, La staccatissimo; No 4, Les cloches; No 11, Les soupirs; No 48, En songe. Gros temps, Op 74 No 10. First Suite No 2. Barcarolle, Op 65 No 6
Jack Gibbons pf
ASV ② CDDCS227 (155' · DDD)   Ⓕ**OO**

'Comme le vent' ('Like the wind'), the opening *Etude* from Op 39, is a real baptism of fire for the pianist. Marked *prestissimamente*, it's an unrelenting deluge of notes which, if played at Alkan's specified metronome marking, travels at the rate of 160 bars per minute, or to put it another way, traverses 20 densely packed pages in just 4'30". Gibbons throws caution to the wind and completes the whirlwind in a staggering 4'38". On occasion he comes perilously close to tumbling into the abyss, but this ranks among the most exhilarating feats of pianism to be heard on disc. If his credentials as an Alkan pianist aren't sealed in his performance of the first *Etude* then his reading of the following two, 'En rythme molossique' and 'Scherzo diabolico', confirm him as an Alkan interpreter of exceptional authority. These commanding and exceedingly sure-footed performances give the feeling that Gibbons has grown with and nurtured these pieces for some time. The following four *Etudes* make up the *Symphony for Solo Piano*; if anything, he's even more impressive in his reading of this striking work.

There's a wildly romantic reading of *Concerto for Solo Piano* (*Etudes* Nos 8-10). More extraordinary feats of virtuosity await the listener in the 12th *Etude* ('Le festin d'Esope') and the *Allegro barbaro* from the Op 35 *Etudes*, but the delightful selection of miscellaneous pieces that completes the disc shows not only the more introverted side of Alkan's creativity but also allows Gibbons to display a less ostentatious and more directly poetic aspect of his playing. The simple *Nocturne* in B major, with its Chopinesque heartbeat, is beautifully rendered, as are the 'Les soupirs' and 'En songe' from the *Esquisses*, Op 63 and the *Barcarolle*, Op 65 No 6. However, the highlight of these miniatures comes with the sensitive and effective delivery of the potently atmospheric 'La chanson de la folle au bord de la mer' ('Song of the mad woman on the seashore'), one of the most curious piano pieces to emerge from the 19th century.

Highly recommended to Alkan devotees and newcomers alike. Excellent recorded sound.

Three Etudes, Op 76

Alkan Transcription de concert (Beethoven's Piano Concerto No 3 in C minor, Op 37 – first movement). Three Etudes, Op 76 **Busoni** Sonatina No 6 super Carmen (Kammerfantasie) **Chopin/Alkan** Piano Concerto No 1 in E minor, Op 11 – Romanza **Medtner** Danza festiva, Op 38 No 3
Marc-André Hamelin pf
Hyperion CDA66765 (72' · DDD) Recorded live 1994
     Ⓕ**OO**

The solo transcriptions on the first half of this disc aren't intended as substitutes for the real thing but are presented here as supreme examples of the art of piano transcription in the late 19th century. These are superb display pieces, revealing not only the subtleties of the transcriber's art and, in this case, the pianist's ability to render them audible, but also Hamelin's extraordinary ability to make the pieces sound like originals rather than transcriptions. Indeed, in the Alkan transcription of the first movement of Beethoven's Third Piano Concerto, the absence of the orchestra never becomes a concern. The principal glory of the disc, however, is Hamelin's account of Alkan's *Etudes*, Op 76, for the hands separately and reunited, an exceptionally formidable opus which here receives a formidable and awe-inspiring performance. We also have the added *frisson* of knowing that what we hear is a single take before a live audience; listen to the hair-raising final study, a blistering, unbroken five-minute salvo of *prestissimo* semiquavers. The remaining items – a scintillating account of Busoni's *Sonatina* No 6 and Medtner's ebullient *Danza festiva* from Op 38 – provide further evidence of Hamelin's undoubted skill. The recorded sound varies a little from piece to piece but all are excellent in quality.

48 Esquisses, Op 63

48 Esquisses, Op 63
Steven Osborne pf
Hyperion CDA67377 (75' · DDD)   Ⓕ

Here's a superlative record of music to confound the sceptics, including the soloist himself, who, in a witty, concentrated essay, expresses his surprise at discovering Alkan's *Esquisses* and their journey into intimacy rather than gargantuan bravura. Not that these 48 fragments, many of them of a teasing and enigmatic brevity, could be by any other composer. Gnomic, introspective, full of odd twists and turns of phrase and expression, they invariably catch you unawares.

In 'Confidence', a Field-like innocence is countered by enough surprises to declare the composer's identity. 'Les Soupirs' is so much more than a foretaste of Debussyan impressionism. 'Inflexibilité' holds the listener in a vice-like grip and the change from charm ('Petite marche villageoise') to grimness ('Morituri te salutant') is typical of Alkan's volatile yet rigorous command of the widest variety of ideas and pastiches. 'Le frisson', 'Pseudo-Naïveté', 'Délire', 'Fais Dodo', 'L'Homme aux sabots' – the titles predict an eccentricity that's nonetheless qualified by a formidable intellectual focus.

Osborne's performances are of a sensitivity, radiance and finesse rarely encountered from even the finest pianists. He floats the opening of 'La vision' in a magical haze or nimbus of sound, peppers the keyboard with an immaculate virtuosity in 'La staccatissimo', relishes the Norwegien tang of 'Début de quatuor' and brings a wicked *frisson* to 'Les diablotins', where Alkan's little devils are hustled from the field almost as if the composer had lost patience with his own grotesque creation. Misha Donat's notes are as affectionate as they are perceptive, and Hyperion's sound is of demonstration quality. An invaluable disc, particularly for those drawn to music's by-ways.

Gregorio Allegri   Italian c1582-1652

Allegri was a singer and composer at the cathedrals of Fermo and Tivoli and later maestro di cappella of Spirito in Sassia, Rome, and a singer in the papal choir. He composed many of his works for this choir and that of S Maria in Vallicella. His reputation rests on his Miserere, a psalm setting traditionally sung every Holy Week by the papal choir: it is basically a simple five-part chant, transformed by interpolated ornamented passages for a four-part solo choir which reaches top C (rare at that time). These passages were a closely guarded secret for many years; Mozart wrote out the work from memory when he was 14. Allegri was at his best in the a cappella style, as in his five masses; he also published three books of more up-to-date small-scale concertato church music.   GROVEmusic

Miserere mei

Allegri Miserere mei **Palestrina** Motets – Stabat mater a 8. Hodie beata virgo. Senex puerem portabat. Magnificat a 8. Litanie de Beata Virgine Maria I
Roy Goodman treb **King's College Choir, Cambridge / Sir David Willcocks**
Decca Legends 466 373-2DM (56' · ADD) Recorded 1963-4   Ⓜ❍❍❍

It's doubtful if any recording made by the choir of King's College, Cambridge, in the fertile Willcocks era, will prove more enduring than this celebrated performance of Allegri's *Miserere*. Admittedly there are more authentic versions in the catalogue, authentic not only in that they use the original Latin words where Willcocks opts for an English translation, but also in the sense that they search for a style less obviously redolent of choral evensong and the Anglican tradition. At the farthest extreme from King's, other versions strip Allegri's score of its various 18th- and 19th-century accretions – a nice piece of musical archaeology which, ironically, reveals the utter plainness of the *Miserere* when denied its familiar jewels, and sounds like an imposter when dressed up in even more garish baubles. For many the richly communicative singing of King's remains the ideal, however far removed it may be from the orginal intentions of Allegri. The *Miserere* is accompanied here by some classic Palestrina performances, which are still as fresh as when they were recorded in 1964. Some tape hiss intrudes, but otherwise the sound is excellent. A fabulous disc.

Miserere mei (two versions). Missa Vidi turbam magnam. De ore prudentis. Repleti sunt omnes. Cantate domino
A Sei Voci / Bernard Fabre-Garrus with **Dominique Ferran** org
Astrée Naïve E8524 (62' · DDD) Recorded 1994. Texts and translations included   Ⓕ

Allegri's setting of the psalm *Miserere mei* is presented in two versions. The first is sung with ornamentation added by the French musicologist, Jean Lionnet following 17th-century models, while the second presents the Burney-Alfieri version familiar from the classic 1963 Willcocks recording above. A Sei Voci produce a rather varied sound, which is at times somewhat flat and white but at its best is embued with an appropriate Italianate edge. For the most part the embellishments are negotiated with style and verve; just occasionally they're fuzzy or insecure. *Miserere mei* apart, hardly any of Allegri's music is heard either liturgically or in the concert hall. By training a pupil of Nanino, a distinguished follower of Palestrina, his best music is written confidently in the High Renaissance contrapuntal manner. The six-voice *Missa Vidi turbam magnam*, composed on one of his own motets, is a fine work, and shows that the *stile antico*, far from being a mere academic exercise, could still be vividly sonorous and dramatic, qualities which are brought out in this reading. The disc is nicely rounded out with a selection of short continuo motets in the popular new manner, well established in Northern Italy, which was becoming fashionable in Rome.

William Alwyn   · British 1905-1985

Alwyn studied with McEwen at the Royal Academy of Music (1920-23) and later taught there (1926-55); in 1961 he retired to Suffolk to compose. He disowned everything he wrote before the Divertimento for flute (1939), which opened a neo-classical phase, followed in the 1950 by a personal vein of English Romanticism. His music is characterised by precise workmanship. It includes five symphonies (1949, 1953, 1956, 1959, 1973) and two string quartets, opera (Miss Julie, 1976) and songs (often to his own words: he also published poems and essays); he wrote over 60 film scores, too. **GROVE**music

Lyra Angelica

Lyra Angelica. Autumn Legend. Pastoral Fantasia.
Tragic Interlude
Rachel Masters hp **Nicholas Daniel** cor ang
Stephen Tees va **City of London Sinfonia / Richard Hickox**
Chandos CHAN9065 (64' · DDD) Recorded 1991 ⑪○

Alwyn valued his *Lyra Angelica* concerto for harp above all his other music, and indeed it's very beautiful. Alwyn is a master of texture as well as form and the textures here, delicately embroidered by the solo harp, are harmonically rich, and the effect on the listener is very moving. The concerto is played with a real feeling for the music's rapture, and the expansive recorded sound, with rich string timbres and a perfect balance with the solo harp is very fine indeed. The *Pastoral Fantasia* was written in 1939 and looks back nostalgically to a more peaceful England. The music opens like Delius, but the entry of the viola brings an immediate affinity with Vaughan Williams as the solo viola begins in rhapsodic soliloquy. The *Tragic Interlude* dates from 1936, when the composer's foreboding of the imminence of the war brought an eloquent protest at the waste of life. The piece opens passionately and gathers momentum, but after its climax, dissolves into a moving elegiac threnody. *Autumn Legend* is much later (1954). It has a particularly lovely opening, with shafts of sunlight on the strings piercing the clouds, and the music's disconsolate manner has an underlying romantic feeling, rather than conveying pessimism. Yet the dark-hued cor anglais line has a pervading melancholy. It's a fine if ambivalent piece, and Nicholas Daniel, the soloist, captures its mood persuasively, while Richard Hickox shows himself in complete affinity with Alwyn's world. The Chandos recording is outstandingly fine.

Symphonies

Symphonies – No 1 in D; No 4
London Philharmonic Orchestra / William Alwyn
Lyrita SRCD227 (77' · ADD) Recorded 1970s ⑪○

Symphony No 4. Elizabethan Dances. Festival March
London Symphony Orchestra / Richard Hickox
Chandos CHAN8902 (65' · DDD) Recorded 1992 ⑪○

It's interesting to compare Alwyn's own recording with Hickox's version of No 4, an extraordinarily fine work, as the two accounts are remarkably alike. Indeed, when you compare the composer's phrasing of the long and beautiful string cantilena that opens the *Adagio e molto calmato* of the Passacaglia finale, its ebb and flow and dynamic gradations suggest that either Hickox has listened to the composer's LP or has

a remarkable, instinctive feeling for the music (probably both). The *Scherzo* may have a bit more bite with Alwyn, but this is at least partly caused by the more leonine Lyrita sound. The centrepiece of the *Scherzo* brings a glorious blossoming from the violins which is equally thrilling in both performances, while at the very end of the symphony the final brass peroration has great forceful thrust from the composer. However, with the LSO and Hickox the slightly richer, more spacious Chandos recording adds to the weight of sonority. In short, these are both highly compelling performances of a remarkably diverse and well-argued symphony, bursting with lyrical ideas and melodic in the way traditional music is communicative, without being old-fashioned. As to the couplings on Chandos, they're relatively slight. The *Elizabethan Dances* aren't very early Elizabethan, but the languid 'Waltz' (No 2) is rather charming and the 'Poco Allegretto' (No 5) is even more so; the vigorous numbers are more conventional. *The Festival March*, written for the 1951 Festival of Britain, is an agreeable occasional piece, although its big tune isn't as memorable as those of Walton or Elgar. Yet if you want a modern recording of the Fourth Symphony, these are acceptable makeweights. On the other hand, Lyrita offers the Symphony No 1. It's a work teeming with ideas, and quite often reminiscent of Alwyn's film music. With its ample scoring, the composer does go over the top a bit at times and this isn't nearly so cogently argued a piece as the Fourth, although it has a rather appealing *Adagio*. It's splendidly played and the Lyrita recordings have been remastered most skilfully.

Violin Concerto. Symphony No 3
Lydia Mordkovitch vn
London Symphony Orchestra / Richard Hickox
Chandos CHAN9187 (75' · DDD) Recorded 1993 ⑪○

The Violin Concerto, although essentially threnodic and lyrical, opens confidently and the orchestra returns with regular bursts of energy. The end of the movement (the rapt *pianissimo* closing section) is exquisite, reminiscent of Vaughan Williams' *The lark ascending*, although as the second movement *Allegretto* opens, the melodic writing also brings hints of Elgar. The finale is fairly vigorous, but again the lyrical impulse is all important. The work is discursive, yet has moments of great intensity. The performance couldn't be bettered; Mordkovitch's *pianissimo* playing is touchingly beautiful.

The Third Symphony is an outstanding example of Alwyn's earlier symphonic manner and is in three movements. The first combines driving rhythmic agitation with a powerful lyrical thrust. The *Adagio*, introduced by a peaceful horn theme, has an animated, brassy development, then ethereal strings restore the sense of repose, the horns returning glowingly. The finale restores the forward momentum with its rhythmic zest and has a powerful and satisfying resolution. Hickox's reading is truly convincing and the LSO responds committedly to a work that must be rewarding to play.

Piano Concerto No 2. Symphony No 5, 'Hydriotaphia'. Sinfonietta for Strings
Howard Shelley pf
London Symphony Orchestra / Richard Hickox
Chandos CHAN9196 (74' · DDD) Recorded 1993 Ⓕ〇

Piano Concerto No 2 opens heroically and contains a good deal of rhetoric, yet the string writing has a romantic sweep and the *Andante* proves to be the highlight of the piece. Howard Shelley plays with much bravura and an appealing sensitivity. The powerful Fifth Symphony is a cogent argument distilled into one movement with four sub-sections. The energetically kaleidoscopic first movement is sharply contrasted by a melancholy *Andante*. The violent *Scherzo* is followed by a curiously ambivalent finale which provides a moving and compelling, if equivocal, apotheosis for a succinctly argued work. The richly expansive *Sinfonietta for Strings*, almost twice as long as the symphony, is very much in the English tradition of string writing. It's vigorous in the first movement and hauntingly atmospheric in the beautiful but disconsolate *Adagio*. The unpredictable finale begins impulsively before the mood changes completely and becomes altogether more subdued and muted in feeling. The obviously dedicated LSO is particularly responsive in the masterly *Sinfonietta*.

Additional recommendations

Symphony No 1
Coupled with: Piano Concerto No 1
Shelley pf **London Symphony Orchestra / Hickox**
Chandos CHAN9155 (56' · DDD) Ⓕ
A fine modern version of the First Symphony coupled with the eventful First Piano Concerto.

Symphonies Nos 2, 3 and 5
London Philharmonic Orchestra / Alwyn
Lyrita SRCD228 (77' · ADD) Ⓕ
A must if you've caught the Alwyn bug: three very different symphonies given superb performances.

Film Music

The Crimson Pirate – Overture. Green Girdle – excerpts. Take my Life – Aria[a]. A Night to Remember – Main Title. Suite from The Card. Suite from Desert Victory – excerpts. Svengali – Aria: Libera mea[b]. Suite from The Winslow Boy. In Search of the Castaways – excerpts. Suite from State Secret – excerpts.
[a]**Susan Bullock** sop [b]**Canzonetta; BBC Philharmonic Orchestra / Rumon Gamba**
Chandos CHAN9959 (77' · DDD) Ⓕ

With vintage British films of the 1940s and 50s you expected a major orchestral film score. William Alwyn, alongside Malcolm Arnold,

supplied some of the finest examples. His orchestral flair and the ready lyrical flow of his themes brought much that was memorable, and Philip Lane's reconstructions from the original soundtracks continually remind us of his melodic gifts, never more effectively than in the opening *pot-pourri* from *The Crimson Pirate*, which is teeming with lively ideas and nautical colour. In *Take my Life* Alwyn composed a pastiche aria for the operatic heroine, and wrote yet another for *Svengali*, both powerfully sung here by Susan Bullock.

The delectably light-hearted score for *The Card* is a quite perfect, whimsical portrayal of the engagingly resourceful hero (played by Alec Guiness) of one of Arnold Bennett's most endearing lighter novels. It opens, appropriately, with a (human) whistle, but includes both a lively ball sequence and a nice touch of sentimental romantic nostalgia, exquisitely scored; the 'Coachride to Bursley' is a delightful *moto perpetuo scherzando*, and the finale is equally charming and capricious. There's a fine 'Ship's Waltz' and a rumbustious 'Rumba' for *In Search of the Castaways*, while the wartime epic, *Desert Victory*, opens *nobilmente*, and closes in similarly patriotic mood with a grandiloquent march. As shown by the man title for *A Night to Remember* Alwyn wasn't a purveyor of flamboyant Hollywoodian theme tunes, but his music always added much to the background atmosphere, and for the most part stands up very well on its own, especially when it's as superbly played and recorded as it is here.

Miss Julie

Miss Julie
Jill Gomez sop Miss Julie **Benjamin Luxon** bar Jean **Della Jones** mez Kristin **John Mitchinson** ten Ulrik
Philharmonia Orchestra / Vilem Tausky
Lyrita ② SRCD2218 (118' · ADD) Recorded 1983. Notes and text included Ⓕ

In his colourful and confident adaptation of Strindberg's play, Alwyn consistently demonstrates his mastery of atmosphere and timing, bringing out the chilling intensity of this story of Miss Julie's sudden infatuation for her father's man-servant. He adapted the play himself, and understood far more than most librettists the need for economy over text.

The idiom, harmonically rich and warmly lyrical, brings occasional Puccinian echoes which, along with reminiscences of other composers, add to the music's impact. By any reckoning this is a confidently red-blooded opera. Tausky's conducting is strong and forceful, with superb singing from all the principals. Jill Gomez is magnificent in the title-role, producing ravishing sounds. Benjamin Luxon gives a wonderfully swaggering portrait of the unscrupulous manservant, vocally firmer than on almost any of his other recordings. Della Jones is splendidly characterful, relishing her venomous cry of 'Bitch!' when, at the very end of Scene 1, she realises Julie and Jean have gone off together. John Mitchinson is characterful too, in his drunken scene. The recording is excellent.

Louis Andriessen
Dutch 1939

After early training with his father, the composer Hendrik Andriessen, he studied with Kees van Baaren at the Royal Conservatory at The Hague and later with Berio in Milan (1962-3) and Berlin (1964-5). Returning to the Netherlands he established himself as a leading musical figure both through his own compositions and as a performer of his own and others' work. Since 1973 he has taught composition at the Royal Conservatory and since the mid-1980s has been in great demand as a guest lecturer. After a few youthful works influenced by neoclassicism and serialism Andriessen moved away from the postwar European avant garde toward American minimalism, jazz and Stravinsky, developing a musical language that is marked by extremes of ritual and masquerade, of monumentality and intimacy, of formal rigour and intuitive empiricism. The epitome of the Hague School, he is regarded as the most influential Dutch composer of his generation. His most important works include De volharding (1972) De staat (1972-6) De tijd (1980-81) and De materie (1984-9). In the 1990s he collaborated with film director Peter Greenaway on the video M is for Man, Music, Mozart (1991) and the stage works Rosa, A Horse Drama (1994) and Writing to Vermeer (1997-9). **GROVE**music

Rosa: The Death of a Composer

Rosa: The Death of a Composer
Lyndon Terracini *bar* Juan Manuel de Rosa
Miranda van Kralingen *sop* First Singer; Madame de Vries; The Texan Whore; The Investigatrix
Marie Angel *sop* Second Singer; The Blonde Woman; Esmeralda **Christopher Gillett** *ten* / Roger Smeets *bar* Alkan; Lully (The Gigolos); The Cowboys
Phyllis Blanford *spkr* The Index Singer **Schönberg Ensemble; Asko Ensemble / Reinbert de Leeuw**
Nonesuch ② 7559-79559-2 (112' · DDD) Notes and text included Ⓕ**OO**

Rosa: The Death of a Composer, or 'A Horse Drama', gives us blood on the stable floor, dried, ominous and darkly crusted with sexual symbolism. Andriessen's pile-driving score is a musical enactment related by birth to Stravinsky, though it's probably nearer in spirit to rock, jazz and Broadway. *Rosa* has a wonderful lack of compromise, a snorting aggression, especially at 8'45" into the Seventh Scene, where angular rhythms suddenly transform to a wild canter. The mythical Uruguayan composer Juan Manuel de Rosa rides bareback as his hapless fiancée moans of how Juan loves horses more than he loves her. She has already confessed that she 'pretends to be a horse to amuse his lechery'. And if that shocks you, then brace yourself for a feast of debauchery, violence and black humour.

Andriessen's band comprises woodwinds, brass, synthesizers, percussion and a few amplified strings. The style recalls the bold contrasts in, say, *De materie*, with tough-fisted rhythms and stark *fortissimo* chords. The overture is typically confrontational but some of the most powerful music in the score occurs at the end of scene 4 where, in true murder-mystery fashion, a missing clue thwarts the drama's successful resolution. Heavy Blues settle among the opening pages of the fifth scene, and the 11th opens to a Morricone-style solo harmonica, where the hub of the theme reflects another of Andriessen's obsessions. It's a certain Brahms Waltz (from Op 39) that his sister used to hum in their childhood bedroom and that also crops up earlier on in the piece. Who'd have thought sentimentality would figure in such a blatantly bestial context, but there you have it! The last scene is trailed by a raunchy, rock-style 'Index Singer' who opens by defining Abattoir ('The location of the opera…A slaughterhouse', etc) and gets as far as Gas, via the likes of Dump and Envy. She eventually makes an exit, but the printed text takes us all the way from Glass-Haired to Zig-Zag.

Rosa was premièred at the Netherlands Opera in 1994 and the performance under review is superb, though special mention should be made of soprano Marie Angel, a marvellous singer and a formidable vocal actress. Film Director Peter Greenaway's libretto is erotic, often lyrical and profoundly ambiguous. Unusually, the words and synopsis complement each other: you read one, then study the other for further elucidation. But the music is pure Andriessen, blanched in the quieter music, and punch-drunk when the going gets hot. It's a music of extremes. If you're unsure, play a minute or so of the overture and the whole of scene 4. That'll tell you all you need to know … more or less.

George Antheil
American 1900-1959

Antheil studied privately with Sternberg and with Bloch (1920) before moving to Berlin in 1922 to make his name as a modernist. Jazz, noise and ostinato were the means, worked into brutally simple designs in the Airplane Sonata (1922) and Sonata sauvage (1923), these last written after his move from Berlin to Paris. There he wrote the Ballet mécanique (1925) for an ensemble of pianos and percussion including electric bells and propellers. In 1926 he turned to neo-classicism, then to opera: Transatlantic (1930, Frankfurt) was a satire on American political life. In 1936 he settled in Los Angeles, where he wrote symphonies, operas vocal, chamber and piano music along more conventional lines. **GROVE**music

Symphonies

Symphonies – No 1, 'Zingareska'; No 6, 'after Delacroix'. Archipelago

Frankfurt Radio Symphony Orchestra / Hugh
Wolff
CPO CPO999 604-2 (63' · DDD)   Ⓕ Ⓞ

In 1923 Antheil gave a piano recital of his own
music at the Théâtre des Champs-Elysées in
Paris which created the kind of sensation not
seen since *The Rite of Spring* 10 years earlier.
Erik Satie was there and applauded vigorously,
refusing to be deterred by Milhaud. You can see
why. His Symphony No 1, Zingareska (*Gypsy
Song*), comes from the same year as that spectacular piano recital and Antheil was uncertain
about it. The gypsy element perhaps covers his
own unsettled existence between the USA,
Berlin and Paris, but it also symbolises his own
kind of style-modulation long before he could
have heard anything by Ives. We're now starting to enjoy Antheil's bare-faced kleptomania
on its terms. Indeed, there are some lovely
things in this young man's music, often beautifully scored and hovering hazardously between
Petrushka and *Parade*; you never quite know
what's going to happen next. In spite of his
bravado Antheil had soul – take the delicious
opening of the *Doloroso* third movement with
celesta background to the oboe or the melodies
over ostinato patterns in the middle of the final
ragtime – the one which starts at 1'26" gets so
close to the first of Stravinsky's *Five Easy Pieces*
for piano duet as to be actionable.

It's a pity that Symphony No 6 (partly based
on Delacroix's picture *Liberty leading the people*)
duplicates the National Symphony Orchestra of
the Ukraine under Kuchar on Naxos, since both
are strong performances of this substantial piece
from 1948. Antheil pays another debt to Satie
since the *Larghetto* is a slow *Gymnopédie*, an oasis
of calm between patriotic war music. The
riotous *Archipelago*, subtitled 'Rhumba', is in the
tradition of Gottschalk but, via Gershwin's
Cuban Overture, is pure 1930s and ends a most
impressive and enjoyable case for orchestral
Antheil from three different decades.

Symphonies – No 4, '1942'; No 5, 'Joyous'.
Decatur at Algiers
**Frankfurt Radio Symphony Orchestra /
Hugh Wolff**
CPO CPO999 706-2. (63' · DDD)   Ⓕ

Symphony No 4, written in the worst years of
the war, gets an ebullient performance which
has the edge over the Ukranians since the
recorded sound is richer. The music employs
juxtapositions, exactly like cinematic cuts, that
have little to do with symphonic development
and are less dominated by Stravinsky than some
of Antheil's earlier works. The tunes are memorable. The novelty here is *Decatur at Algiers*,
called a nocturne although it's based on Stephen
Decatur conquering the Barbary pirates in the
early 1800s. There's an attractive Arabic flavour
about the spooky principal theme on the oboe.
This release also brings the Fifth Symphony –
first recorded by the Vienna Philharmonia

under Herbert Haefner in 1952 – back into the
catalogue. This is a war symphony too. Antheil
lost his brother in the conflict and dedicated the
symphony to 'the young dead of all countries
who sacrificed everything'.

The first movement is continuously bustling
in an idiom which crosses Stravinsky with jazz:
it works. The *Adagio molto* is an elegiac siciliano,
and the finale is a pot-pourri which raises constant echoes – that's how musical kleptomania
operates. Almost at the start Antheil recalls the
opening of Shostakovich's Fifth in homage to
America's wartime ally. These are all fine performances, well recorded too – another impressive case for later Antheil on his own terms.

Ballet mécanique

Ballet mécanique (rev 1953). Serenade for Strings
No 1. Symphony for Five Instruments.
Concert for Chamber Orchestra
**Philadelphia Virtuosi Chamber Orchestra /
Daniel Spalding**
Naxos 8 559060 (61' · DDD)   Ⓢ

Although *Ballet mécanique* is the inevitable selling point here, the 1953 revision eschews many
of the sonic and rhythmic excesses that give the
work its infamy and, to be honest, its musical
appeal. Spalding secures a zestful performance
from the Philadelphia Virtuosi, less frenetic
than the Ensemble Modern, with the interlocking ostinatos of pianos and percussion readily
invoking *Les noces* in sound if not substance. The
other works give a good overview of Antheil's
changing idiom over the greater part of his
career. From 1948, the *First Serenade* might
seem a continuation of his inter-war neo-classicism, yet the chromatic unease that permeates
the brusque outer movements, and the plaintive
solos and chill *sul ponticelli* of the *Andante* intimate deeper emotions. The Symphony of 1923
offers a statement of stylistic intent to rival
Stravinsky's Octet, though the astringent polytonal writing is more akin to Milhaud's Chamber Symphonies. Nine years on, and the *Concert*
finds the eclipsed composer pursuing understated yet intriguing directions. The succession
of mini-ensembles, linked by a varied *ritornello*
for the whole group, may have its basis in
Stravinsky's *Symphonies of Wind Instruments*, but
Antheil's piece is formally open-ended and
emotionally anything but cathartic. Characterful and well-prepared performances, cleanly
recorded, and informative notes. Probably the
best disc yet in Naxos's American Classics
series.

Thomas Arne   British 1710-1778

*Arne, the son of an upholsterer, was probably encour-
aged in his musical career by his violin teacher
Michael Festing. In 1732-3 he and his sister
Susanna (later Mrs Cibber) were associated with*

19

musicians who aimed to establish an Italian-style English opera. After the success of his masque Dido and Aeneas (1734), Arne was engaged at Drury Lane Theatre, where he was to produce his works until 1775. In 1737 he married the singer Cecilia Young, who appeared in his next production, Comus (1738); influenced by Handel's Acis and Galatea, it was his most individual and successful work. Also popular was the masque Alfred (1740) (including 'Rule, Britannia'). While in Dublin in 1742-4 Arne produced his oratorio The Death of Abel (1744) and music by Handel. His dialogue Colin and Phoebe established him as a leading composer at the London pleasure gardens; during the next 20 years he published annual song collections. Among his next major works were a miniature English opera buffa, Thomas and Sally (1760), the oratorio Judith (1761) and an English opera seria to a metastasio libretto, Artaxerxes (1762), the first and only such work to achieve lasting fame. After his masque The Arcadian Nuptials (1764) Arne's career declined; L'Olimpiade (1765; now lost), his only Italian opera, was a failure. But his last years saw the production of many of his best works, notably Shakespeare Ode (1769), the masque The Fairy Prince (1771) and the afterpiece May-day (1775); he also wrote catches and glees for concerts at Ranelagh House. One of the most significant English composers of his century, Arne wrote over 80 stage works and contributed to some 20 others. His essentially lyrical genius is obvious also in his instrumental music. **GROVE**music

Artaxerxes

Artaxerxes   P
Christopher Robson counterten Artaxerxes
Ian Partridge ten Artabanes **Patricia Spence** mez
Arbaces **Richard Edgar-Wilson** ten Rimenes
Catherine Bott sop Mandane **Philippa Hyde** sop
Semira **The Parley of Instruments / Roy Goodman**
Hyperion ② CDA67051/2 (140' · DDD) Notes and text
included   Ⓕⓞ

This is a work of great historical importance and musically fascinating. Arne, the leading English composer of his time for the theatre, wanted to write serious as well as comic English operas, and decided that Italian *opera seria* should serve, on the literary side, as his model; he chose the most famous of all the Metastasio librettos, *Artaserse*, as the basis for his first (and last) attempt at the genre. It's generally supposed that the translation was his own work. He performed the opera at Covent Garden in 1762 with considerable success, and it remained a favourite for many years. He never followed up that success, and nor, regrettably, did anyone else. English vocal music of this period has quite a distinctive manner, being tuneful, rather short-breathed, often with a faintly 'folky' flavour. It doesn't naturally reflect the exalted emotional manner of an *opera seria* text. Nevertheless, the music is enormously enjoyable, full of good melodies, richly orchestrated, never (unlike Italian operas of the time) long-winded. Several of its numbers became popular

favourites in Arne's time, and for long after.

Much of the best and most deeply felt music goes to Arbaces, very finely and expressively sung by Patricia Spence. She uses more vibrato than anyone else in the cast but her warmth of tone and expressive power are ample justification. Mandane, Arbaces's beloved, composed for Arne's mistress Charlotte Brent, is another rewarding part and is finely sung here by Catherine Bott, who can encompass both the charming English ditties and the more Italianate virtuoso pieces. Christopher Robson makes an excellent Artaxerxes, although this castrato part is bound to be testing for a countertenor and he's often covered by the orchestra. Arne's orchestral style here is very rich, with much prominent wind writing; sometimes the singers don't ride the full textures very comfortably. Roy Goodman's accompaniments aren't generally very subtle. The original score doesn't survive complete, a victim (like so many) of the frequent theatre fires of the time; Peter Holman has done an unobtrusive and stylish job of reconstructing some of the lost recitatives. This recording is recommended warmly to anyone curious about this byway of 18th century opera, and to anyone drawn to Arne's very appealing melodic style.

Sir Malcolm Arnold   British 1921

Arnold studied with Jacob at the Royal College of Music, London, and in 1941 joined the LPO as a trumpeter, leaving in 1948 to devote himself to composition. His most important works are orchestral (nine symphonies, 1951-82; numerous light and serious pieces). His language is diatonic, owing something to Walton and Sibelius, and the scoring is dramatically brilliant, Berlioz being his acknowledged model. A fluent, versatile composer, he has written scores for nearly 100 films. **GROVE**music

Clarinet Concerto No 2

Arnold Clarinet Concerto No 2, Op 115 **Copland**
Concerto for Clarinet and String Orchestra with Harp
and Piano **Hindemith** Clarinet Concerto
Martin Fröst cl **Malmö Symphony Orchestra /**
Lan Shui
BIS CD893 (57' · DDD)   Ⓕⓞⓞ

All three of these concertos were written for Benny Goodman, but, not surprisingly, it's the Arnold work which most fully exploits his dedicatee's jazz background. The first movement is a typical Arnoldian *scherzando*, with an irrepressible *Tam O'Shanter/Beckus the Dandipratt* audacity. Fröst and Lan Shui clearly relish its verve and energy, and then bring a seductive richness to the main theme of the slow movement. Yet they don't miss the plangent emotional ambivalence later, for there are characteristic moments of Arnold-like darkness here too. The outrageous show-stopper finale, with its rooty-tooty clarinet tune and orchestral whoops, also has a surprise up its sleeve in its sudden lyrical interlude; but one and all let their hair down for the boisterous reprise.

At the haunting opening of the Copland concerto, Martin Fröst's clarinet steals in magically on a half-tone. Lan Shui's sympathetic and flexible support contributes to a memorable performance of Copland's masterly first movement, with the coda gently fading into the cadenza. The Hindemith concerto which follows produces a characteristic sinewy lyricism in the first of its four movements, with some nicely touched-in brass and woodwind comments. Again Fröst cajoles the ear with his pliable line and the effect is unexpectedly mellow. With extremely fine recording and marvellous solo playing, this triptych will be hard to surpass.

Symphonies

Symphonies – No 1, Op 22; No 2, Op 40
London Symphony Orchestra / Richard Hickox
Chandos CHAN9335 (61' · DDD) Recorded 1994 (F)O

Here's an entirely appropriate coupling of the first two symphonies, superbly played by the LSO and given demonstration sound in what's surely an ideal acoustic for this music, with striking depth and amplitude and a wholly natural brilliance. The dynamic range is wide but the moments of spectacle – and there are quite a few – bring no discomfort. Richard Hickox shows himself to be thoroughly at home in both symphonies and the readings have a natural flow and urgency, with the two slow movements bringing haunting, atmospheric feeling.

The three-movement First Symphony opens with thrusting confidence on strings and horns, and at its climax, where the strings soar against angry brass ostinatos, the playing generates great intensity; then at the start of the slow movement the purity of the flute solo brings a calm serenity, which returns at the close. The plangent lyrical melancholia of the expansive march theme of the finale is filled out by some superb horn playing, which is enormously compelling. The first movement of Symphony No 2 brings a most winning clarinet solo (Arnold's fund of melodic ideas seems to be inexhaustible). There's an energetic, bustling *Scherzo* to follow, but again it's the slow movement that you remember, for its elegiac opening, its arresting climax and its lovely epilogue-like close. Above all, these are real performances without any of the inhibitions of 'studio' recording.

Symphonies – No 3, Op 63; No 4, Op 71
National Symphony Orchestra of Ireland / Andrew Penny
Naxos 8 553739 (69' · DDD) (S)O

These recordings of two of Arnold's finest symphonies carry the composer's imprimatur (he attended the sessions). Penny is clearly right inside every bar, and the orchestra play with impressive ensemble and feeling, and above all great freshness and spontaneity.

The Naxos recording's concert-hall ambience has been beautifully caught. One of the finest players in Dublin is the principal oboe, whose solos often bring a specially plangent quality, particularly in the slow movement of No 3, where there's a real sense of desolation. The finale then lightens the mood with its kaleidoscope of wind and brass and a wispy string melody that soon becomes more fulsome. Penny's momentum and characterisation here are superb, as is the orchestral response. Similarly the winningly scored opening of the Fourth Symphony flashes with colour: that marvellous tune (2'44") is played with captivating delicacy by the violins. The exquisitely fragile *Scherzo* is etched with gossamer lightness and the slow movement is shaped by Penny with fine lyrical feeling and the most subtle use of light and shade. Its romanticism is heart-warming, yet is also balanced by Arnold's underlying unease. The boisterous fugal finale has some of the best playing of all.

Symphonies – No 5, Op 74; No 6, Op 95
London Symphony Orchestra / Richard Hickox
Chandos CHAN9385 (58' · DDD) (F)O

Arnold's Fifth is one of his most accessible and rewarding works. The inspiration for the work was the early deaths of several of Arnold's friends and colleagues: Dennis Brain, Frederick Thurston, David Paltenghi and Gerard Hoffnung. They are all remembered in the first movement and Hoffnung's spirit pops up in the third and fourth. The Chandos recording is richly resonant and reinforces the impression that in Hickox's hands the *Andante* has an added degree of acceptance in its elegiac close, while the last two movements are colourfully expansive. The Sixth Symphony is nothing like as comfortable as the Fifth, with a bleak unease in the unrelenting energy of the first movement, which becomes even more discomfiting in the desolate start to the *Lento*. This leads to a forlorn suggestion of a funeral march, which then ironically quickens in pace but is suddenly cut down; the drum strokes become menacingly powerful and the despairing mood of the movement's opening returns. Hickox handles this quite superbly and grips the listener in the music's pessimism, which then lifts completely with the energetic syncopated trumpet theme of the rondo finale. Although later there are moments of ambiguity, and dissonant reminders of the earlier music, these are eclipsed by the thrilling life-asserting coda.

Symphonies Nos 7, 8 & 9. Oboe Concerto, Op 39[a]
[a]**Jennifer Galloway** ob **BBC Philharmonic Orchestra / Rumon Gamba**
Chandos ② CHAN9967 (116' · DDD) (M)

In No 7 Gamba takes a more urgent approach than does Andrew Penny in his account for Naxos. With weightier orchestral sound, helped by a full, atmospheric Chandos recording, Gamba is even more compelling, though in that first movement the ragtime march halfway through loses some of its grotesquerie at a faster speed. At a more flowing speed in the slow movement Gamba is warmer than Penny, less chilly. One consistent advantage of Gamba's faster speeds is that the extra challenge to the orchestra brings out an element of daring, almost always an advantage in writing that's surreal in its sharp juxtapositions of ideas and mood, with Mahlerian references to popular music. That's specially true of the *Giubiloso* third movement of No 9. Penny and his Irish players by comparison seem almost too well-behaved, though the transparency of the sound lets you hear the heaviest textures clearly.

The final Mahlerian slow movement of the Ninth is also warmer, weightier and more measured with Gamba than with Penny, though both sustain the slow, spare writing superbly, with Gamba bringing an extra velvety warmth to the final movements of consolation. The Oboe Concerto makes a welcome supplement on that second disc, with Gamba and his excellent soloist, Jennifer Galloway, bringing out the wit and biting jauntiness of earlier Arnold.

Additional recommendations

Symphonies Nos 3 and 4
London Symphony Orchestra / Hickox
Chandos CHAN9290 (74' · DDD)   Ⓕ
  Hickox has the full measure of both symphonies and the Chandos recording is superb.

Symphonies Nos 5 and 6
National Symphony Orchestra of Ireland / Penny
Naxos 8 552000 (57' · DDD)   Ⓢ
  A good bargain alternative worth considering.

Symphonies Nos 1-9
National Symphony Orchestra of Ireland / Penny
Naxos ⑤ 8 505178 (300' · DDD)   Ⓢ Ⓢ
  Penny draws consistently bright-eyed, polished playing from his band. No 1 is perhaps the weakest of the set, though the playing is still powerful and lucid. No 3 is extremely fine, No 4 also a great success and his Nos 5-9 are in almost every way a match for the best. A notable achievement and terrific value for money.

Overtures

Anniversary Overture. Beckus the Dandipratt. The Fair Field. A Flourish for Orchestra. A Grand, Grand Festival Overture. Peterloo. Robert Kett. The Smoke. A Sussex Overture. Tam O'Shanter
BBC Philharmonic Orchestra / Rumon Gamba
Chandos CHAN10293 (76' · DDD)   Ⓕ Ⓞ

Arnold's genius was particularly suited to small-scale orchestral works, and every one of these examples shows his orchestral personality at its exuberant best. *Beckus the Dandipratt* came first, in 1943, a portrait which has the wit of Strauss's *Till* and the harum-scarum quality of Walton's *Scapino*. *Tam O'Shanter*, a brilliantly droll portrayal drawing on the Burns poem, has a spectacular climax bringing an orchestral realisation of bagpipes. The *Grand, Grand Festival Overture*, written for a 1956 Gerard Hoffnung festival, is remembered for including parts for four vacuum cleaners and the floor polisher. But this piece isn't just about high spirits; it has a really good tune, too. There's another memorable tune in the vivid *Peterloo*, which is more of a Lisztian tone-poem. The brief *Anniversary Overture* was for a Hong Kong fireworks spectacular, while *The Smoke* brings a sultry atmosphere in its middle section. *The Fair Field* celebrates the Croydon Concert Hall (with its superb acoustics), *A Sussex Overture* is jauntily characteristic, while the *Orchestral Flourish*, not surprisingly, brings resplendent brass. The lively *Robert Kett* Overture is a recording premiere. The Chandos recording is of the demonstration class.

Dances

Four Cornish Dances, Op 91. English Dances, Op 27; Op 33. Irish Dances, Op 126. Four Scottish Dances, Op 59. Solitaire – Sarabande; Polka
London Philharmonic Orchestra / Sir Malcolm Arnold
Lyrita SRCD201 (61' · ADD/DDD) Recorded 1979-90
                                          Ⓟ Ⓞ Ⓞ

A warm and well-deserved welcome was given to the *English*, *Scottish* and *Cornish Dances*, when these recordings, conducted by the composer, first appeared. Here, with the *Irish Dances* added, as well as the two movements which were written to go with the two sets of *English Dances* as the ballet, *Solitaire*, it's even more of a winner. The analogue sound is given a splendid transfer with plenty of presence and is full and brilliant. The newer items, in digital sound, very well recorded too, bring no feeling of inconsistency. Best known of all is the first of the second set of *English Dances* with its jaunty piccolo theme, but one after another these little jewels first grab and then delight the ear with their brilliant pastiche of folk melodies.

The first of the Irish Dances, written in 1986, opens with a rumbustious movement very much in the style of the earlier sets, with characteristic and attractive syncopations, but the other three dances are both sparer in instrumentation and darker in tone, effectively so. The two movements from Solitaire are equally valuable, particularly the superb, coolly atmospheric 'Sarabande', the longest and most ambitious movement of any here, again made weightier by Arnold's slow speed. Even if you don't want to play all 22 items at one go – and that's no penance at all – this is a wonderful box of delights.

English Dances – Set 1, Op 27; Set 2, Op 33.Four Scottish Dances, Op 59. Four Cornish Dances, Op 91. Four Irish Dances, Op 126. Four Welsh Dances, Op 138
Queensland Symphony Orchestra / Andrew Penny
Naxos 8 553526 (55' · DDD)　Ⓢ Ⓢ●

This set includes the *Four Welsh Dances*, not otherwise available on CD. These were the last to be written, and their mood follows on naturally from the ambivalence of the *Irish Dances*. Penny's tempos are very like Arnold's own in his superb set made with the LPO for Lyrita. Where there's a difference, Penny is slightly faster, but the effect is marginal. The greater character of the LPO under Arnold shows in the very first of the *English Dances*, notably at the reprise, which is more warmly positive. The Queensland Hall is reverberant, and detail is generally less well focused than on the Lyrita disc; yet so vivid is Arnold's scoring that not much is missed. The lovely *Mesto* third *English Dance* is beautifully done in Queensland, and in the second set of *English Dances*, the *Con brio* and *Giubiloso* have all the necessary colour and flair. The Australian orchestra has obviously warmed up for the Scottish set and the inebriated Glaswegian is nicely observed. For some the lyrical third *Scottish Dance* is one of the most beautiful and memorable of all Arnold's many fine tunes. Penny treats it gently; his coda is particularly delicate, but at its appearance on the full strings the composer is that little bit more romantic. However, Penny's closing dance, a Highland fling, is superb in its drunken abandon. In the opening *Cornish Dance* that follows, Penny captures the mysterious evocation of deserted copper mines well, and in the *Irish Dances*, written some 20 years later, he captures the fragile mood of the central *Commodo* and *Piacevole* tenderly. This is altogether an excellent and inexpensive collection.

Ballet music

Homage to the Queen, Op 42*a* – Ballet Suite Rinaldo and Armida, Op 49. Little Suite No 2, Op 78. Organ Concerto, Op 47[a]
[a]**Ulrik Spang-Hanssen** *org* **Royal Aarhus Academy of Music Symphony Orchestra / Douglas Bostock**
Classico CLASSCD424 (65' · DDD)　Ⓕ

No fewer than three first recordings adorn this set, in which some of Denmark's finest young musicians lend spirited advocacy to three appealing Arnold scores from the 1950s.

Bostock's first recording of the 20-minute concert suite from the 1953 Coronation-ballet *Homage to the Queen* is all the more welcome given that Robert Irving's superbly stylish 1954 Philharmonia recording of the complete work is now deleted. Hailed by Dame Ninette de Valois as 'the finest ballet composer since Tchaikovsky', Arnold penned a further three scores for the Royal Ballet. First staged in 1955 and choreographed (like *Homage to the Queen*) by Frederick Ashton, *Rinaldo and Armida* packs a wealth of colourful and touching invention into its tight-knit 22-minute span. Elsewhere, Ulrik Spang-Hanssen is a nimble soloist in the Organ Concerto written in 1954 for Denis Vaughan (the central *Lento* casts quite a spell), and we also get the bright-eyed, impeccably crafted *Little Suite No 2* that Arnold fashioned for the 1963 Farnham Festival.

Nicely prepared, committed performances one and all; reasonably vivid sound. Sir Malcolm's many fans will love this enterprising collection.

Film Music

Trapeze – Suite. No Love for Johnnie – Suite. David Copperfield – Suite. Stolen Face – Ballade or Piano and Orchestra[b]. The Belles of St Trinian's – Comedy Suite[c]. The Captain's Paradise – Postcard from the Med (all arr Lane). You Know What Sailors Are – Scherzetto[a]. The Holly and The Ivy – Fantasy on Christmas Carols (both arr Palmer). The Roots of Heaven – Overture. Symphonic Study, 'Machines', Op 30
[a]**John Bradbury** *cl* [b]**Phillip Dyson**, [c]**Paul Janes** *pfs*
BBC Philharmonic Orchestra / Rumon Gamba
Chandos CHAN9851 (79' · DDD)　Ⓕ●●

Almost all the film music here comes from the 1950s, when memorable ideas were pouring out of Arnold, and his unique orchestral palette was already glowing luminously.

The suite arranged by Philip Lane from *Trapeze* is quite outstanding in the quality of its invention, including a swinging tune for the horns in the Prelude, an engaging blues for saxophone and guitar to follow, an ebullient circus march, and a deliciously lugubrious 'Elephant waltz' for tuba duet, while the closing sequence opens hauntingly and then introduces an accordion to remind us we're in Paris. The suite from *David Copperfield* has a fine lyrical opening sweep, then introduces a delightfully quirky, syncopated *moto perpetuo* representing 'The Micawbers'. This features a solo clarinet, and Christopher Palmer has arranged another witty clarinet *Scherzetto* from an equally winning theme used in *You Know What Sailors Are*.

The *concertante* Ballade for Piano and Orchestra adeptly arranged by Lane from *Stolen Face* is less memorable, but the overture from *The Roots of Heaven* (provided for the film's New York prèmiere) opens with a splendid Hollywood/ Waltonesque flourish, then follows with more catchy syncopation and a lilting waltz tune. Perhaps the most tender, romantic writing comes in *No Love for Johnnie* (after another rousing march). The irrepressible score for *The Belles of St Trinian's* (the composer's favourite film) has something of the audacious sparkle of Ibert's *Divertissement*, and if *The Holly and the Ivy* brings a rather predictable collection of familiar carols, for the most part fully scored and not particularly individual, the jaunty samba from *The Captain's Paradise*, which memorably had Alec

Guinness in the bigamous title-role, makes a splendid finale. The performances have plenty of zest, and the flow of bittersweet lyrical writing is poignantly caught by Rumon Gamba and the excellent BBC Philharmonic in a recording of top Chandos quality. If you enjoy film music, it doesn't come any better than this.

Georges Auric   French 1899-1983

Auric studied at the Paris Conservatoire and with d'Indy at the Schola Cantorum (1914-16), becoming acquainted with Satie, Milhaud and Honegger. He was a member of Les Six, wrote ballets for Diaghilev (Les fâcheux, 1923) and film scores for Cocteau and was also a music critic. In the 1950s and 60s he held administrative posts while maintaining his musical curiosity: some of his later pieces are serial.   **GROVE**music

Film Music

Suites – Caesar and Cleopatra; Dead of night; Father Brown; The Innocents[a]; It always rains on a Sunday; The Lavender Hill Mob; Moulin Rouge[b]; Passport to Pimlico; The Titfield Thunderbolt; Hue and Cry – Overture
BBC Philharmonic Orchestra / Rumon Gamba with [a]**Anthea Kempston**, [b]**Mary Carewe** sops
Chandos CHAN9774 (74' · DDD)   Ⓕ**O**

All the scores here (expertly reconstructed by Philip Lane) are from British films, for which Auric wrote some 30; but he also wrote another 100 or so for French, German, Italian and American movies. It was in fact by a French film – René Clair's delightful satire *A nous la liberté* – that he first won our hearts in 1932; it wasn't until the end of the war that he was taken up by Denham and Ealing. Auric, not one for the 'hit tune' score beloved by commercial exploiters, nevertheless showed in his *Moulin Rouge* waltz that he too could command the popular style. On this disc he's heard running the gamut through the grandiose or the dramatic (*It always rains on a Sunday*, one of his finest pieces), the menacing (the unforgettably scary *Dead of night*) and the atmospheric ('At the Sphinx' in *Caesar and Cleopatra*) to the swirling gaiety of *The Titfield Thunderbolt*, the perky *Passport to Pimlico* and the ebullient high spirits of *Hue and Cry*. From the gusto of the playing throughout, it seems clear that the BBC Philharmonic enjoyed making this disc: understandably so.

Further listening

The Ladykillers
Royal Ballet Sinfonia / Alwyn
Silva Screen FILMCD177 (61' · DDD)   Ⓕ
   A splendid collection of scores for Ealing comedies splayed with lashings of gusto and a great feeling for this now sadly lost idiom. A 1997 *Gramophone* Award winner.

Carl Philipp Emanuel Bach
German 1714-1788

Carl Philipp Emanuel Bach, second son of Johann Sebastian Bach, studied music under his father at the Leipzig Thomasschule and law at university. In 1738 he became harpsichordist to the Prussian crown prince, moving to Berlin when his employer became King Frederick in 1740. There he was accompanist to the royal chamber music, and had the particular task of accompanying the king's flute solos. His most important compositions of this period were his keyboard sonatas; he also wrote his famous Essay on the True Art of Keyboard Playing (1753-62), which established him as the leading keyboard teacher and theorist of his time. He was however discontented in Berlin, because of the poor salary, the want of opportunity and the narrow scope of his duties. In 1767 Frederick reluctantly released him and he then succeeded Telemann as Kantor and music director in Hamburg, with responsibility for teaching, for some 200 performances of music each year at five churches and for ceremonial music on civic occasions. At this time he produced much church music as well as keyboard music, sets of symphonies and concertos.

CPE Bach, the best-known member of his family in his lifetime, was greatly respected for his treatise – which summarised the musical philosophy and the musical practices in north Germany at the middle of the 18th century – as well as for his music. His keyboard sonatas (he composed c150 as well as countless miscellaneous pieces) above all break new ground in their treatment of form and material; he also wrote improvisatory fantasias of intense expressiveness. His symphonies – he wrote c20 – are in the fiery, energetic manner favoured in north Germany, with dramatic breaks, modulations and changes of mood or texture; usually the movements run continuously. There are twice as many concertos (and more concerto-like sonatinas), also vigorous in style; all were written for harpsichord and some were adapted for other instruments. His chamber works are numerous; there are many songs, as well as choral works from his late years, including two fine oratorios (Die Israeliten in der Wüste, Die Auferstehung and Himmelfahrt Jesu), Passion settings and other church works which often include adaptations of his own and other composers' music.   **GROVE**music

Cello Concertos

Cello Concertos – A minor, H432; B flat, H436;   Ⓟ
A, H439
Bach Collegium Japan / Hidemi Suzuki vc
BIS CD807 (68' · DDD)   Ⓕ

Why is it that cellists who bemoan their lack of concerto repertory continue to neglect CPE Bach's three essays in the genre? It's a mystery; they're excellent pieces, full of infectious nervous energy in their outer movements and tender lyricism in central ones. They aren't unknown to the recording catalogues, however, not least because they also exist in alternative versions which the composer made for flute and harpsichord. Though there are times when the low-lying cello has difficulty making itself heard against the orchestra, Suzuki makes light of the matter with performances whose agility, lightness and textural clarity make those of Bylsma and the larger-sounding OAE sound heavy-handed. But while Suzuki – thanks to a generally thinner sound – is the more successful in the way he transmits the surface excitement and energy of the quick movements, he can't match Bylsma's vocal inspiration in the eloquent poetry of the slow movement. Suzuki's, nevertheless, are refreshing, enlivening performances of attractive and substantial music.

Cello Concertos – A minor, H432; B flat, H436; A, H439
Timothy Hugh vc **Bournemouth Sinfonietta / Richard Studt**
Naxos 8 553298 (71' · DDD) ⑤

Timothy Hugh's bow dances in the flanking movements and is matched by those of the Bournemouth Sinfonietta, alert to every nuance and disposed to throw their weight around only as much as is fitting. However, it's the slow movements that are the heart of these works. All are tinged with sadness, but none more than the *Largo* of the A major Concerto, where Hugh's abated vibrato, attenuated lines and resistance to the excessive squeezing of *appoggiaturas* express a sadness that's held within, not spilt in salt tears.

Harpsichord Concertos

Harpsichord Concertos – G minor, H409; **P**
A, H411; D, H421
Miklós Spányi hpd **Concerto Armonico / Péter Szüts**
BIS CD767 (68' · DDD) ⑤

These concertos ademonstrate the emerging inventiveness of CPE's musical personality within the trend towards public concerts in the mid-18th century. In fits and starts there are those sparsely etched landscapes which at their best can captivate us. If decorum is sometimes overworked, Bach's originality is even more remarkable given that the ritornello structure inherited from his father's generation, with its alternating solo and string sections, is less easy to sustain in a relatively uncontrapuntal style. Contrast is therefore a key element, and Bach needs a soloist who can discern how the relationship between the harpsichord and the orchestra can be manipulated to good effect. Miklós Spányi and Concerto Armonico, led by Péter Szüts, givewonderfully lucid, flexible and clearly articulated readings. The shading in the finale of the G minor and middle movement of the D major Concertos is also energised by a naturally discursive balance, a deft textural palette for which artist and engineer can take equal credit. With such eloquent playing, this volume of world première recordings will give

the listener more than just an opportunity to refine his perspective on Bach's achievements. It deserves a welcoming audience.

Keyboard Concertos

Keyboard Concertos – D, H414; E, H417; A, H422 **P**
Concerto Armonico / Miklós Spányi fp
BIS CD785 (74' · DDD) ⑤

With his fifth volume of CPE Bach's complete keyboard concertos, Miklós Spányi comes to three works composed in the mid-1740s, which he plays on a copy of a Silbermann fortepiano of that period. The choice isn't only determined by the existence of such instruments at Frederick the Great's court, where Carl Philipp was employed, but also because the keyboard layout is more suited to the fortepiano than the harpsichord, and because the A major work here – a first recording, like that of the D major – includes the marking *pianissimo*. The present instrument is light and silvery in tone, which makes for some difficulties of proportion in the D major, performed with additional manuscript parts found in Brussels for trumpets and drums. The more embellished version of the A major Concerto is adopted here. The first movement displays some particularly athletic passagework for the piano. The E major Concerto is musically the most inventive and unusual of the three works, and harmonically certainly the most adventurous – a splendid concerto that deserves to be better known. The recording has occasional problems with balance but the performances are praiseworthy.

Keyboard Concertos – E minor, H418; **P**
B flat, H429; G minor, H442
Miklós Spányi fp **Concerto Armonico / Péter Szüts** vn
BIS CD786 (73' · DDD) ⑤

On this recording Miklós Spányi has exchanged his previous harpsichord or fortepiano for a tangent piano: it's like a fortepiano but has the strings struck vertically by tangents (as in the clavichord) rather than at an angle by hammers. Its tone could also be modified by raising the dampers completely or only in the treble, employing only one of each note's two strings (*una corda*), inserting a leather strip ('moderator') between tangents and strings, or creating a harp-like effect by damping the strings with small pieces of cloth. The boldness and unusual style of Emanuel's concertos took his contemporaries aback, and even now they can surprise. The extrovert E minor work, for example, begins with dramatic energy but is interrupted by extraordinary, tentative-sounding broken phrases at the soloist's first entry before being allowed to continue on its way: the *Adagio*, which includes striking chromatic progressions, has imitative interplay between the solo instrument and the violins. The finale of the otherwise more 'normal' *galant* G minor Concerto generates very vehement chordal attacks – or are these being overdone here? Spányi's playing throughout has vitality and neatness, although his lifting of the dampers in running passages inevitably causes them to become blurred.

Sinfonias

CPE Bach Sinfonias, H663-6 – No 1 in D; No 2 in E flat; No 3 in F; No 4 in G **WF Bach** Sinfonia in F
Salzburg Chamber Philharmonic Orchestra / Yoon K Lee
Naxos 8 553289 (52' · DDD) Recorded 1994   ⑤

The exhilarating CPE Bach symphonies presented here aren't the more frequently recorded, surprise-filled string symphonies of 1773 (H657-62), but the set of four for strings, flutes, oboes, bassoons and horns which Bach wrote a couple of years later. They are no less astonishing. Bewildering changes of direction, disorientating rhythmic games and unexpected solos all turn up in this nervous, excitable music, which for originality and life-force could surely only have been matched in its day by that of Haydn. The Salzburg Chamber Philharmonic, under its founder Yoon K Lee, turns in crisp, spirited and (the odd moment of slack tuning apart) disciplined performances which do the music full justice. They aren't timid about making the most of Bach's strong contrasts, although they produce them more by the release of some thunderous *forte* passages than by the pursuit of too many unearthly *pianissimos*. The overall effect is wholly convincing, and only in the symphony by Emanuel's older brother Wilhelm Friedemann – more old-fashioned and less successful as a piece – does the use of modern instruments begin to get in the way of the spirit of music. An undeniably good buy.

___

Additional recommendation

4 Sinfonias, H663-6. Concertos for Flute and Strings – in G, H445; in A minor, H431. Concerto for Harpsichord and Fortepiano in E flat, H479. Concerto for Two Harpsichords, Two Horns and Strings in F, H408
Mathot fp **Hünteler** fl **Amsterdam Baroque Orchestra / Koopman** hp
Warners Ultima ② 8573-88050-2 (DDD)   ⑧
These are top-notch performances of some wonderful, often outlandish works that still have the capacity to astonish; the tart textures of the band really suit the music. Strongly recommended.

Chamber Works

Quartet for Keyboard, Flute, Viola and Continuo   ℗
in D, H538. Viola da gamba Sonata in G minor, Wq88
– Larghetto. Trio Sonatas – Two Violins and Continuo in C minor, H579; Flute, Violin and Continuo in C, H571. Solo Flute Sonata in A minor, H562
Florilegium (Ashley Solomon fl Rachel Podger vn/va Lucy Russell vn Daniel Yeadon vc/va da gamba Neal Peres da Costa hpd/fp)
Channel Classics CCS11197 (59' · DDD)   ℗〇

More than half a century separates the earliest and the latest of the works here. The C major Trio Sonata was one of Bach's earliest compositions, written at the age of 17 more or less under his father's supervision, and the D major Quartet was composed in the last year of his life, while he was Music Director in Hamburg. The remaining items date from his time at the court of Frederick the Great. The C minor Sonata is extraordinary, a programmatic work 'portraying a conversation between a Sanguineus and a Melancholicus' who disagree throughout the first two movements, but the former's outlook prevails in the finale. The talented Florilegium players bring out to the full the bewilderingly diverse character of this sonata.

If the Sonata for unaccompanied flute was written for Frederick, as seems likely, he must have been quite skilled, able to cope with some virtuoso passagework. Ashley Solomon's performance is most persuasive. How far Carl Philipp developed is shown by the late quartet, an attractive composition which, besides promoting the keyboard (fortepiano here) from a mere continuo to prominent solo status, is already in the style of the Viennese classics in form, and links the first two movements. The whole disc is strongly recommended.

Keyboard Sonatas

Keyboard Sonatas – in F sharp minor, H37;
in G minor, H47; in G, H119; in C minor, H121;
in E minor, H281; in D, H286; in A, H135: Andante con tenerezza. Rondos – in A, H276; in C minor, H283; in D minor, H290
Mikhail Pletnev pf
DG 459 614-2GH (79' · DDD)   ℗〇

No one who enjoyed Pletnev's two-disc set of Scarlatti (on Virgin Classics) will be surprised that he has now turned his attention to CPE Bach, whose keyboard music is so important in the transition from the High Baroque to Classical style. Nor is there any need for eyebrow-raising over his use of a modern piano, since it's clear from Bach's notation and from contemporary reports of his playing that he placed a premium on flexibility of tone. In any case, Pletnev's taste, intelligence and virtuosity win the day. It's clear that he's felt free to go his own way with ornamentation and occasionally with rhythm. But he almost always does so in the spirit of the composer. And you can't but admire Pletnev's tasteful rhetoric, his eloquent declamatory flourishes, his pliancy in the Rondos, and his rhythmic alertness and caprice in fast movements, allied to the classiest of fingerwork and the most refined colouristic sense. Given its historical significance, CPE Bach's keyboard music is poorly served on CD. All the more reason to welcome this superbly executed disc. Recording quality is clean but not clinical, with the piano close and always natural-sounding.

Die Auferstehung und Himmelfahrt Jesu

Die Auferstehung und Himmelfahrt Jesu   Ⓟ
Uta Schwabe sop **Christoph Genz** ten **Stephan Genz** bar **Ex Tempore; La Petite Bande / Sigiswald Kuijken**
Hyperion CDA67364 (73' · DDD) Text and translation
included   ⒻⓄ

CPE Bach is much better known for his instrumental works, which are numerous, than his vocal, which are few: but his short oratorio *Die Auferstehung und Himmelfahrt Jesu* ('The Resurrection and Ascension of Jesus'), a late work which was written in the 1770s, has a strong claim to be reckoned among his most original and his finest. It certainly proclaims its originality in its opening bars, a sombre and mysterious passage for cellos and basses alone, and the ensuing chorus at least hints at the grandeur and sense of the momentous that distinguishes his father's great choral works.

The narrative is sung by a tenor in a series of recitatives, mostly starting secco but increasingly coloured by orchestral textures as they gather emotional force. Here they're impressively done by Christoph Genz, with subtle and refined shading of the tone and a quiet intensity of expression. The soprano aria, warmly and touchingly done by Uta Schwabe, with a mournful first part and a joyous second, is a particularly expressive piece, although arguably it's outshone by the duet that follows, with its attractive use of two flutes to accompany the soprano and its typical use of appoggiaturas and the dissonances they create to heighten he expression.

Sigiswald Kuijken's lively but sensitive and thoughtful direction, and his attention to details of the instrumental texture, ensure that the work gets the performance it merits. Compelling and warmly recommended.

Johann Christian Bach
German 1735-1782

Johann Christian Bach, the youngest son of JS Bach, probably studied first under his father, then on his death with his half-brother Carl Philipp Emanuel. in Berlin. In 1754 he left for Italy, where he became Roman Catholic and organist at Milan Cathedral. He also embarked on an operatic career, with operas staged in Turin and Naples. He was then invited to compose for the King's Theatre in London, where he settled in 1762; his operatic career was patchy, but he was soon appointed royal music master and was successful as a teacher. He also promoted and played in a prominent concert series with his friend CF Abel, bringing the newest and best European music to Londoners' notice. (He befriended the boy Mozart on his London visit, 1764-5.) Many of his works were published, including songs written for Vauxhall Pleasure Gardens. In 1772 and 1774 he visited Mannheim for performances of his operas Temistocle and Lucio Silla and in 1779 he wrote Amadis de Gaule for the Paris Opéra, but the success of these works, like that of his London operas, was limited. His popularity faded in the late 1770s, and after financial troubles his health declined; he died at the beginning of 1782, and was soon forgotten.

JC Bach's music blends sound German technique with Italian fluency and grace; hence its appeal to, and influence upon, the young Mozart. His symphonies follow the Italian three-movement pattern: the light, Italian manner of his earlier ones gave way to richer-textured and more fully developed writing by the mid-1760s. The peak of his output comes in the six symphonies of his Op 18, three for double orchestra and exploiting contrasts of space and timbre. His interest in orchestral colour gave rise to several symphonies concertantes, for various soloists and orchestra, suitable material for his London concerts. At these he also played his piano concertos, attractive for their well-developed solo-tutti relationship though still modest in scale. Of his chamber music, the Op 11 quintets are particularly appealing for their charming conversational style and their use of colour. His music is often leisurely in manner, and this must have militated against the operas success as dramatic music. He also composed a quantity of Latin sacred music during his time in Italy. Though sometimes regarded as a decadently hedonistic composer by comparison with his brother CPE, Johann Christian stands firmly as the chief master of the galant, who produced music elegant and apt to its social purpose, infusing it with vigour and refined sensibility.   **GROVE**music

Keyboard concertos

Six Concertos for Keyboard and Strings, Op 7 – Ⓟ
No 1 in C; No 2 in F; No 3 in D; No 4 in B flat;
No 5 in E flat; No 6 in G
Members of the **Hanover Band** (Graham Cracknell, Anna McDonald vns Sebastian Comberti vc) /
Anthony Halstead fp
CPO CPO999 600-2 (73' · DDD)   ⒻⓄ

On Halstead's previous disc of JC Bach's keyboard concertos, he employed nine strings from the Hanover Band; but the present Op 7 concertos, like those of Op 1, call for only two violins and cello. He played the Op 1 work on the harpsichord, as specified on the title-page of the original edition: here he plays a fortepiano on the grounds that not only does the title-page of Op 7 designate 'Harpsichord or Piano Forte', but also that the fortepiano had made considerable headway in London in the seven years since the Op 1 appeared in 1763. The most interesting of these concertos are the last two of the set, each in three movements. No 5 is particularly fine, not merely because of its brilliant keyboard writing (notably in its finale) but because the sturdy initial *Allegro di molto* is more mature in style, with fresh material appearing in the development, and because of its deeply expressive, almost Mozartian, *Andante*. No 6 is distinguished by its central movement's long cantilena lines and for an extraordinary key-move near the end of the finale. Halstead's playing is a model of neatness and crisp rhythmicality: his decorations are in good taste, and in No 5 he adopts the composer's own cadenzas. His string colleagues are excellent. In short, a very pleasing disc.

Harpsichord Concertos – D minor; B flat; F minor Ⓟ
Hanover Band / Anthony Halstead hpd
CPO CPO999 393-2 (57' · DDD) Ⓕ

The works of JC Bach's Berlin years are almost indistinguishable from those of his brother, CPE, and anyone putting on this disc could be excused for thinking the first movement of the D minor Concerto – with its purposeful, energetic scales, its stark textures, its heavily used motifs, its rushing harpsichord writing, its sombre minor key and its total lack of lyricism – to be wholly CPE's work. In fact it's a very accomplished piece for a composer less than 20 years old and there are glimmerings of JC's own voice in the *Adagio affettuoso* that follows; it still sounds like North German music, untouched by Italian softness and sunshine, but the harpsichord cantilena certainly has a more personal expressive character and so does some of the string writing in the ritornellos and accompaniment. The slow movements throughout seem individual and appealing in a sense that CPE's aren't. The quick movements, especially in the B flat Concerto, contain gestures of the abrupt and musically violent kind that CPE so often used. The finale of the D minor has a curious element of fantasy and an imaginative use of pizzicato behind the first solo entry.

Halstead uses a small orchestra, strings only, 3.3.1.1.1, which is quite sufficient and very alert. The solo playing is extremely fluent and indeed brilliant; Halstead plays with ample energy and rhythmic precision and realises the elaborate melodic lines effectively. Some of his cadenzas seem to go harmonically too far afield too quickly and aren't entirely convincing, but this is a small blemish in an admirable disc.

Symphonies concertantes

Symphonies concertantes – F, T287 No 2; Ⓟ
B flat, T287 No 7; D
Anthony Robson ob **Jeremy Ward** bn **Graham Cracknell, Anna McDonald** vns **Sebastian Comberti** vc **Hanover Band / Anthony Halstead**
CPO CPO999 537-2 (52' · DDD) ⒻⓄ

The *symphonie concertante*, predominantly light-hearted, allotted a more prominent role to the solo instruments than did the *concerto grosso*. The earliest of the present three works is that in F, and the JC Bach scholar Ernest Warburton speculates that the choice of a solo oboe and bassoon suggests that it may have been written in 1761 for Naples, where Bach's opera *Catone in Utica* called for outstanding players of just these instruments. It's a cheerfully engaging two-movement work that takes the bassoon up into the tenor register: its first movement is

unorthodox in shape. The D major work, in three movements, likewise ends in a minuet, with a trio in the minor for a change. Overall, the writing places more emphasis on virtuosity for the two soloists, and both in the energetic first movement and the more formal second there's a lengthy cadenza. The most notable *symphonie concertante* here, however, is that in B flat, long considered lost and rediscovered only in 1996: this is its first recording. Probably composed for JC's London concerts in the late 1770s, it allows the orchestra greater say; the initial ritornellos in the first two movements are unusually long. In the *Larghetto* the solo cello drops out, leaving the violin long, sweetly pungent cantilenas – a strikingly fine movement. Halstead secures neat performances of finesse of all three works, which also benefit from skilful soloists and well-balanced recording. Delightful.

Symphonies

Six Symphonies, Op 6 – No 1 in G; No 2 in D; Ⓟ
No 3 in E flat; No 4 in B flat; No 5 in E flat;
No 6 in G minor
Hanover Band / Anthony Halstead
CPO CPO999 298-2 (56' · DDD) Recorded 1994 Ⓕ

In the Op 6 Symphonies the frothy Italianate music of the composer's Italian and early London years was behind him; these pieces, dating from the late 1760s, while still Italian-influenced in their formal clarity and melodic style, are sturdier, more carefully composed, more symphonic. Both the E flat works have something of the solidity and warmth associated with that key, and each has a C minor *Andante*. The G major's first movement has the confident ring and thematic contrasts of his mature music, and the D major contains Mannheim *crescendos* and some delightful textures, with flutes and divided violas, in its charming, slightly playful middle movement. The set ends with Bach's single minor-key symphony in G minor, very similar in spirit to Mozart's No 25; this piece, often recorded before, shows an unfamiliar side to his musical personality. Anthony Halstead and his players convey the music's strength and spirit convincingly. The lively finales all go with a swing, and the opening movements have plenty of energy. The slow movements aren't always quite so persuasive: the third C minor slow movement of the G minor Symphony is a little overly deliberate and becomes detached and modest in expressive impact. Generally, though, these are strong and appealing performances of attractive and unfamiliar music, clearly, slightly drily recorded. Admirers of the London Bach and his music needn't hesitate

---

Symphonies – Op 9: No 1 in B flat; No 2 in E flat; Ⓟ
No 3 in B flat; B flat, Sieber No 1; E flat, Sieber No 2;
E flat (ed Warburton)
Hanover Band / Anthony Halstead
CPO CPO999 487-2 (60' · DDD) ⒻⓄ

This disc offers the Op 9 Symphonies published in The Hague in 1773, two of them in two versions, along with a little-known symphony. Ernest Warburton explains in his notes that the usual texts for these works, with oboes and horns, are in his view arrangements of originals calling for clarinets – still rarities in most European orchestras at the time – and bassoon, in which form one of them was published in Paris. Here, then, Op 9 Nos 1 and 2 are done twice over to allow comparison; and certainly the versions differ markedly in flavour with clarinets and bassoon. The E flat work, No 2, one of Bach's finest and most vigorously argued symphonies, comes out particularly well, with quite a different ring to its tuttis.

The E flat Symphony is an attractive work, with an eloquent violin line in the *Andante*, and a charming final gavotte. Of the works played twice, the B flat is lightish, probably originally an opera overture; the E flat has more substance and notably a C minor slow movement with a melody of a haunting, graceful beauty. The third Op 9 Symphony is a brisk little piece which again started life as an overture. Halstead directs with his usual style and shapeliness.

Overtures

Overtures – Gioas, re di Giuda; Adriano in Siria;   ℙ
Zanaida; Orione. La clemenza di Scipione –
Overture; No 5, March in G; No 22, March in E flat.
Carattaco – Overture; No 20, March in B flat; No 26,
March in G. Symphony in D, Schmitt Op 18 No 1
Hanover Band / Anthony Halstead
CPO CPO999 488-2 (58' · DDD)   Ⓕ●

Small-scale but elegantly fashioned, melodious and pleasurable music: it's no wonder that the London public in the 1760s and 1770s took JC to their hearts. Here we have the overtures to six works of his that were performed at the King's Theatre in the Haymarket – from his first opera there, *Orione* in 1763, to his last, *La clemenza di Scipione* in 1778, and the 1770 oratorio, *Gioas*, plus a symphony which is a *pasticcio* of the *Clemenza* overture with additional trumpets and drums and a revised version of the *Andante* from the overture to his only completed French opera, the 1779 *Amadis de Gaule*.

The most striking feature about all these works, apart from their vigorous openings, is the freedom in the use of wind instruments: *Zanaida* has *soli* clarinets, and the trio of *Orione*'s minuet is for wind band only, as are passages in *Adriano*, the E flat March in *Clemenza* and the brilliant final *Presto* of *Carattaco*.

The Hanover Band's playing is vital and fresh, rhythmically crisp and tonally clean-cut; the recording is first-rate.

Harpsichord Works

Bach and the Möller Manuscript   ℙ
JC Bach Capriccio sopra la lontananza del suo fratello diletissimo, BWV992. Sonata, BWV967. Suite, BWV832. Toccata in D, BWV912 **G Böhm** Capriccio. Suite in D minor **Fabricius** Gigue belle in C minor **Lully** Chaconne **Reincken** Suite **C Ritter** Suite **Zachow** Suite
Carole Cerasi hpd
Metronome METCD1055 (77' · DDD)   Ⓕ●

The young JS Bach absorbed an astonishing range and quantity of music, much of it by way of his older brother Johann Christoph, with whom he lived after the age of nine. Continuing an award-winning trail of engaging recorded recitals, Carole Cerasi explores the world of Bach's early musical influences and the composer's own early attempts. The Möller Manuscript – named after an early owner – is the only surviving Johann Christoph compilation. It reveals the panoply of Teutonising of the French suite by 17th-century masters such as Handel's teacher Zachow, and the *éminences grises*, Böhm and Reincken, whose beautifully argued and flamboyant works are still woefully unrecognised. Cerasi gives an engrossing account of these two masters. The Böhm *Capriccio* is quite simply a gem: no wonder Bach so admired him. This is a compelling recital, dispatched with flair and an acute sensibility.

Johann Sebastian Bach
German 1685-1750

Johann Sebastian was the youngest son of Johann Ambrosius Bach, a town musician, from whom he probably learnt the violin and the rudiments of musical theory. When he was 10 he was orphaned and went to live with his elder brother Johann Christoph, organist at St Michael's Church, Ohrdruf, who gave him lessons in keyboard playing. From 1700-1702 he attended St Michael's School in Lüneburg, where he sang in the church choir and probably came into contact with organist and composer Georg Böhm. He also visited Hamburg to hear JA Reincken at the organ of St Catherine's Church.

After competing unsuccessfully for an organist's post in Sangerhausen in 1702, Bach spent the spring and summer of 1703 as 'lackey' and violinist at the court of Weimar and then took up the post of organist at the Neukirche in Arnstadt. In June 1707 he moved to St Blasius, Mühlhausen, and four months later married his cousin Maria Barbara Bach in nearby Dornheim. Bach was appointed organist and chamber musician to the Duke of Saxe-Weimar in 1708, and in the next nine years he became known as a leading organist and composed many of his finest works for the instrument. During this time he fathered seven children, including Wilhelm Friedemann and Carl Philipp Emanuel. When, in 1717, Bach was appointed Kapellmeister at Cöthen he was at first refused permission to leave Weimar and was allowed to do so only after being held prisoner by the duke for almost a month.

Bach's new employer, Prince Leopold, was a talented musician who loved and understood the art.

Since the court was Calvinist, Bach had no chapel duties and instead concentrated on instrumental composition. From this period date his violin concertos and the six Brandenburg Concertos, as well as numerous sonatas, suites and keyboard works, including several (eg the Inventions and Book I of the '48') intended for instruction. In 1720 Maria Barbara died while Bach was visiting Karlsbad with the prince; in December of the following year Bach married Anna Magdalena Wilcke, daughter of a court trumpeter at Weissenfels. A week later Prince Leopold also married, and his bride's lack of interest in the arts led to a decline in the support given to music at the Cöthen court. In 1722 Bach entered his candidature for the prestigious post of Director musices at Leipzig and Kantor of the Thomasschule there. In April 1723 after the preferred candidates, Telemann and Graupner, had withdrawn, he was offered the post and accepted it.

Bach remained as Thomaskantor in Leipzig for the rest of his life, often in conflict with the authorities, but a happy family man and a proud and caring parent. His duties centred on the Sunday and feast-day services at the city's two main churches, and during his early years in Leipzig he composed prodigious quantities of church music, including four or five cantata cycles, the Magnificat and the St John and St Matthew Passions. He was by this time renowned as a virtuoso organist and in constant demand as a teacher and an expert in organ construction and design. His fame as a composer gradually spread more widely when, from 1726 onwards, he began to bring out published editions of some of his keyboard and organ music.

From about 1729 Bach's interest in composing church music sharply declined, and most of his sacred works after that date including the B minor Mass and the Christmas Oratorio consist mainly of 'parodies' or arrangements of earlier music. At the same time he took over the direction of the collegium musicum that Telemann had founded in Leipzig in 1702 – a mainly amateur society which gave regular public concerts. For these Bach arranged harpsichord concertos and composed several large-scale cantatas, or serenatas, to impress the Elector of Saxony, by whom he was granted the courtesy title of Hofcompositeur in 1736.

Among the 13 children born to Anna Magdalena at Leipzig was Johann Christian, in 1735. In 1744 Bach's second son, Emanuel, was married and in 1747 Bach visited the couple at Potsdam, where Emanuel was employed as harpsichordist by Frederick the Great. At Potsdam Bach improvised on a theme given to him by the king, and this led to the composition of the Musical Offering, a compendium of fugue, canon and sonata based on the royal theme. Contrapuntal artifice predominates in the work of Bach's last decade, during which his membership (from 1747) of Lorenz Mizler's learned Society of Musical Sciences profoundly affected his musical thinking. The Canonic Variations for organ was one of the works Bach presented to the society; the unfinished Art of Fugue may also have been intended for distribution among its members.

Bach's eyesight began to deteriorate during his last year, and in March and April 1750 he was twice operated on by the itinerant English oculist John Taylor. The operations and the treatment that followed them may have hastened Bach's death. He took final communion on 22 July and died six days later. On 31 July he was buried at St John's cemetery. His widow survived him for 10 years, dying in poverty in 1760.

Bach's output embraces practically every musical genre of his time except for the dramatic ones of opera and oratorio (his three 'oratorios' being oratorios only in a special sense). He opened up new dimensions in virtually every department of creative work to which he turned, in format, musical quality and technical demands. As was normal at the time, his creative production was mostly bound up with the external factors of his places of work and his employers, but the density and complexity of his music are such that analysts and commentators have uncovered in it layers of religious and numerological significance rarely to be found in the music of other composers. Many of his contemporaries, notably the critic JA Scheibe, found his music too involved and lacking in immediate melodic appeal, but his chorale harmonisations and fugal works were soon adopted as models for new generations of musicians. The course of Bach's musical development was undeflected (though not entirely uninfluenced) by the changes in musical style taking place around him. Together with his great contemporary Handel (whom chance prevented his ever meeting), Bach was the last great representative of the Baroque era in an age which was already rejecting the Baroque aesthetic in favour of a new, 'enlightened' one. **GROVE**music

Keyboard Concertos

D minor, **BWV1052**; E, **BWV1053**; D, **BWV1054**; A, **BWV1055**; F minor, **BWV1056**; F, **BWV1057**; G minor, **BWV1058**; D minor, **BWV1059**

Harpsichord Concertos – D minor, BWV1052;   **P**
D, BWV1054. Concerto for Flute, Violin, Harpsichord and Strings in A minor, BWV1044. Das wohltemperierte Klavier, BWV846-93 – Preludes and Fugues: F, BWV880; B, BWV892
Le Concert Français / Pierre Hantaï hpd
Astrée Naïve E8837 (70' · DDD) Recorded 1993 Ⓜ●●

The concertos come over well. Ensembles are tautly controlled, and the string playing effectively articulated, although on occasion the first violin is a little too favoured in the recorded balance. However, the string playing is so unanimous in sound and purpose that there's little to worry about in this department. Hantaï himself is impressive for his wonderfully rhythmic playing, the clarity with which he interprets both his own keyboard textures and those which support and punctuate it, and not least for his supple, muscular concept of the music. These are extraordinarily invigorating performances, which draw the listener deep into the harmonic and contrapuntal complexities and conceits of Bach's art. Take for instance the elusive *Adagio* of BWV1052, where careful punctuation and sensitive interaction between solo and *tutti* make for a rewarding coherence. In the A minor

Triple Concerto, Hantaï is joined by his flautist brother, Marc, and François Fernandez the violinist leader of the ensemble. The work is a Leipzig arrangement of movements from earlier pieces not in concerto form. The opening *Allegro* is a little too heavy, but the essentially three-part texture of the middle movement is realised with affection. A stimulating disc.

Keyboard Concertos – D minor, BWV1052;
E, BWV1053; A, BWV1055;
Academy of St Martin in the Fields / Murray Perahia pf
Sony Classical SK89245 (53' · DDD)   Ⓕ**OO**

Soloist-conducted piano concertos can sometimes mean compromise, even chaos…but not in this case. As soloist, Perahia is his usual stylish, discreet and pianistically refined self. He takes the D minor Concerto's opening at a fair lick, a hot-foot sprinter embellishing the line with taste and affecting a little *ritardando*, just as the mood momentarily brightens, *à la* Edwin Fischer. Elsewhere, he's very much his own man, intensifying his tone for rising sequences or softening it to the most rarefied murmur. His command of colour is as striking here as it is on his CD of the *Goldberg* Variations, especially in the *Adagio*, which approaches cantorial heights of intensity.

As for the E major and A major Concertos, elegance is more of the essence than fire, but there too Perahia delivers. He has a way of accenting without jabbing the keys, tracing counterpoint while keeping the top line well to the fore. And how nice to hear the warming tone of a theorbo (bass lute) in the E major Concerto's central Siciliano, a beautiful performance, more ornamental than cantorial, in keeping with the more decorative nature of the music.

Rivals are plentiful, but credible contenders at this level of interpretation are rare. Sviatoslav Richter plays with incredible control while keeping every note alive, but some might find his manner too austere. And while Edwin Fischer is consistently spontaneous, he's rather less elegant than Perahia – and his version of the A major Concerto sounds as if it's 'Busonified'. András Schiff, like Perahia, commands a wide range of colours, though the binding force of Perahia's concentration – always a boon in his latest recordings – leaves the stronger impression. The carefully balanced Sony recordings keep the sound frame tight and lively.

Keyboard Concertos – D, BWV1054; F minor,
BWV1056; F, BWV1057; G minor, BWV1058
Academy of St Martin in the Fields / Murray Perahia pf
Sony Classical SK89690 (54' · DDD)   Ⓕ**OO**

As well as being immensely vital, Perahia's Bach is profoundly pianistic, not in any exhibitionistic sense, but in the way tempo, dynamics and nuance register without undue exaggeration. Perahia's *staccato* never loses quality, even when soft – try the opening movement of the Sixth Concerto. And yet he's just as capable of increasing the pressure as he sees fit: listen out for his brightening tone at 5'16" into the same movement, or the extraordinary dexterity of his finger work from around 1'45" into the finale, a fair match for any fiddler tackling the same passage in the parallel Fourth *Brandenburg* Concerto. The counterpoint-crazy Glenn Gould is the benchmark here, wonderfully absorbing as ever, but this warmer, more discreet and more overtly decorative version is preferable. The sound is beautifully clear (violin desks are antiphonally placed) with impressive richness in the bass. Nothing much more to say except, don't hesitate – life's too short.

Oboe Concertos

Oboe Concertos – F, BWV1053; A, BWV1055;
D minor, BWV1059
Chamber Orchestra of Europe / Douglas Boyd
ob/ob d'amore
DG 429 225-2GH (46' · DDD) Recorded 1989
                                                         Ⓕ**O**

Although Bach isn't known to have written any concertos for the oboe, he entrusted it with some beautiful *obbligato* parts, so he clearly didn't underrate its expressive capacities. He did, however, rearrange many of his works for different instrumental media and there's musicological evidence that original oboe concertos were the (lost) sources from which other works were derived. The Harpsichord Concerto, BWV1055, is believed originally to have been written for the oboe d'amore, while the other two Oboe Concertos have been reassembled from movements found in various cantatas. Whatever the academic reasoning, the results sound very convincing.

Douglas Boyd is a superb oboist, with a clear sound, and a fluency that belies the instrument's technical difficulty. He plays the faster, outer movements with winsome lightness, and with alertness to dynamic nuance; the slow ones, the hearts of these works, are given with sensitivity but without sentimentality – which can easily invade that of BWV1059, taken from Cantata No 156, *Ich steh mit einem Fuss im Grabe*. The Chamber Orchestra of Europe partners him to perfection in this crisp recording.

Violin Concertos, Double Concertos

A minor, **BWV1041**; E, **BWV1042**.
Double Concertos – Two Violins and Strings in D minor, **BWV1043**; Oboe, Violin and Strings in C minor, **BWV1060**

Violin Concertos – BWV1041-2.
Double Concertos – BWV1043; BWV1060[a]
Arthur Grumiaux, Herman Krebbers *vns* **Heinz Holliger** *ob* **Les Solistes Romands; New Philharmonia Orchestra / Arpad Gerecz,** [a]**Edo de Waart**

Philips Silver Line 420 700-2PSL (61' · ADD) Recorded 1970-78 ⓜ○○

In the old days, records of Bach violin concertos were adequately filled by the Concertos in A minor and E major, plus the Double Violin Concerto. On this disc these three works are played strongly by Arthur Grumiaux, who's joined in the Double Concerto by Herman Krebbers. Arpad Gerecz directs Les Solistes Romands and the 1970s recordings are vivid; some may even find it slightly strident. The fourth work (to fill the longer playing time available) is the Concerto for oboe and violin, BWV1060. Heinz Holliger plays beautifully, and Grumiaux is relaxed with the New Philharmonia Orchestra under Edo de Waart in a noticeably warm recording.

Violin Concertos – BWV1041-2.
Double Concertos – BWV1043ᵇ; BWV1060ª
ªAlbrecht Mayer ob ᵇDaniel Stabrawa vn Berlin Philharmonic Orchestra / Nigel Kennedy vn
EMI 557016-2 (59' · DDD) Ⓕ○

Bach isn't a composer you generally associate with Nigel Kennedy, but this recording of the four most popular concertos is far more than a dutiful 250th anniversary offering. Kennedy is nothing if not characterful, taking a positive, often robust view of Bach. It isn't just his breathtakingly fast speeds in finales and in some first movements, too, that will have listeners pricking up their ears, but often a fierceness of manner which can initially take you aback. With brilliant playing not just from the soloist but from the Berlin Philharmonic, the results are certainly exciting. The power of Bach's writing is reinforced thanks also to the rather close recorded balance in the Jesus-Christus Kirche.

However fast Kennedy's speeds in Allegros, he counters any feeling of breathlessness not just in his clean articulation, but in his fine detailing. The Berlin players respond sympathetically, but aren't always quite so adept at springing rhythms at such fast speeds. By contrast, slow movements tend to be taken broadly, but there again Kennedy has thought through his expressive phrasing in detail, consciously pointing rhythms, shading dynamics and colouring tone. Any reservations over Kennedy's readings don't detract their positive strength.

In the Double Concerto Daniel Stabrawa makes a perfectly matched partner, and in the Concerto for oboe and violin there's no question of his seeking to overshadow the fine artistry of the warm-toned Berlin oboist Albrecht Mayer. These are the visions of an exceptional artist, helped by warm, full sound.

Violin Concertos – BWV1041-2ª. Double Ⓟ
Concertos – BWV1043ᵇ; BWV1060 (arr Fischer)ᶜ
ªᵇᶜRyo Terakado, ᵇNatsumi Wakamatsu vns
ᶜMarcel Ponseele ob Bach Collegium Japan / Masaaki Suzuki

BIS CD961 (59' · DDD) Ⓕ○

These aren't just 'authentic' performances, they're also outstandingly musical ones. There's happy animation in the flanking movements – bows are lifted from or stopped on the strings to ensure the cleanest of textures – and a warmth of expression in the slow ones which comes from a deeper source than mere academic study.

The admirable soloist in the A minor and E major Concertos, Ryo Terakado, and his partner in the Double Concerto, Natsumi Wakamatsu, both studied with Sigiswald Kuijken in The Hague and served with various Baroque ensembles in Europe before returning to Japan. It shows in the beautifully 'vocalised' shaping of their lines. Not once do they or their ripieno colleagues jar the ear with acidic sounds, and in the Andante of the A minor Concerto Terakado achieves a pianissimo that's near-miraculous in its quality. Marcel Ponseele, the only European on parade, has a comparably distinguished pedigree. In the reconstructed Concerto BWV1060 his fluency, rounded tone and clean articulation are second to none, and he makes the Adagio one of the serenely lovely high spots of the entire programme. As for the ripieno, you couldn't ask for better, and they're recorded in excellent balance with the soloists. Suzuki directs the whole with sure hands.

Additional recommendation

Violin Concertos – BWV1041-2.
Double Concertos – BWV1043; 1060
Podger vn **Academy of Ancient Music / Manze** vn Ⓟ
Harmonia Mundi HMU90 7155 (57' · DDD) Ⓕ
  Manze projects a highly developed sense of fantasy in his interpretations and, for the most part, it proves immensely effective.

Brandenburg Concertos

No 1 in F, BWV1046; **No 2** in F, BWV1047;
No 3 in G, BWV1048; **No 4** in G, BWV1049;
No 5 in D, BWV1050; **No 6** in B flat, BWV1051

Brandenburg Concertos Nos 1-6 Ⓟ
Tafelmusik / Jeanne Lamon vn
Sony Classical Theta ② SM2K89985 (93' · DDD) Recorded 1993-4 ⓜ○

Tafelmusik's *Brandenburgs* come straight from the heart and as such they're performances that invite repeated listening, and are easy and enjoyable to live with. There are no startling novelties here and nothing which attempts to impede the natural course of musical flow. Tempos are sensibly chosen and, once chosen, consistently adhered to. That isn't to say that there's an absence of affective gesture or a lack of rhetorical awareness. Everything in fact is punctuated in a way that allows the listener to follow the subtly shaded nuances of Bach's dialogue. Some readers may feel that these interpretations lack the stamp of a strong personality but any such fears of interpretative neutrality are largely dispelled by the sensibility of the players and their skill at reaching the heart of the music without the assistance either of pretension or muddled intellectual clutter.

Reservations chiefly concern minutiae of tuning, and to a much lesser extent, ensemble. Neither these weaknesses, nor the occasional blip or thwack, hindering the production of clean notes from oboe, horns or trumpet, spoil enjoyment of Nos 1 and 2. It's a pity that the first movement of No 3 is marred by indifferent tuning and, more disturbingly, by a marked acceleration in speed beginning at bar 84 (3'26"); but the second *Allegro* of the work is so well done that you're inclined to forgive them. Tafelmusik's account of this brilliant binary movement isn't to be missed.

CD80368 – Brandenburg Concertos Nos 1-3 Ⓟ
CD80354 – Brandenburg Concertos Nos 4-6
Boston Baroque / Martin Pearlman hpd
Telarc CD80368/54 (52 & 41' · DDD) Recorded 1994   ⒡Ⓞ

Boston Baroque is a close-knit group of highly accomplished and stylish instrumentalists. On their discs their enthusiasm is clear in the bustling outer movements; it's a wise leader who knows his team, in this case Martin Pearlman, who no doubt set the tempos. In the slow movements there's the breathing-space which is often found lacking. The soloists are first-class (though Friedemann Immer's trumpet trills in Concerto No 2 sound a mite uncomfortable) and the multi-talented Daniel Stepner (violone piccolo in No 2, violin soloist in Nos 4 and 5, and viola soloist in No 6) and Pearlman himself (harpsichord) are especially impressive. However, it's the ensemble, supported by a finely balanced recording, that makes these accounts so outstanding, and those who are allergic to thin or nasal string sounds will find nothing to cringe from in the warmth of tone that characterises these performances. The annotation states (but without explanation) that Concerto No 6 'must remain a chamber piece with one player to a part': whether it must or not, the recording shows it to be wholly effective played in that way. We are also told that 'it includes the transparent sounds of gambas' and so it does, but we're left to guess who their players might be. There can be no clear 'best' in the *Brandenburgs*, but this set is likely to remain among those which will prove to be enduring.

Brandenburg Concertos Nos 1-3   Ⓟ
Oboe Concerto in A, BWV1055. Concerto for Two Violins, Oboe and Orchestra in C minor, BWV1060
David Reichenberg ob **Simon Standage** vn
The English Concert / Trevor Pinnock hpd
Archiv Produktion Blue 471 720-2ABL (71' · DDD) Recorded 1982-4   Ⓜ

BACH BRANDENBURG CONCERTOS – IN BRIEF

New London Consort / Philip Pickett
L'Oiseau-Lyre ② 440 675-2OH2 (95' · DDD)   Ⓕ
A somewhat controversial set built on an elaborate theory expounded by Pickett in the booklet, but don't let that stop you enjoying these lively, imaginative performances.

Orchestra of the Age of Enlightenment
Virgin Classics ② 561552-2 (93' · DDD)   ⒷⓄⓄ
Often taken at quite a lick, these period performances never sound rushed but rather imbued with a spirit of dance.

Tafelmusik / Jeanne Lamon
Sony Classical ② SM2K89985 (93' · DDD)   ⓂⓄ
One of the finest period performances with a broad extrovert flair that occasionally flirts with danger but excites as a result.

Boston Baroque / Martin Pearlman
Telarc CD80368/54 (52' & 41' · DDD)   ⒡Ⓞ
Not quite on the level of their Bach Suites, these are highly enjoyable performances with plenty to marvel at and superbly recorded.

ASMF / Sir Neville Marriner
Philips ② 468 549-2PM2 (98' · ADD)   ⓂⓄ
Middle-of-the-road performances that show the Marriner/ASMF style at its best: *de luxe* soloists add to the allure of the set.

English CO / Benjamin Britten
Decca ② 443 847-2DF2 (128' · ADD)   Ⓑ
A historic set, made in 1968, and one great composer's take on another. Slightly dated in approach but still worth sampling.

Berlin PO / Herbert von Karajan
DG ② 474 287-2GX2 (144' · ADD)   Ⓕ
A set for admirers of Karajan rather than of the composer: there is some impressive solo work but it's all so terribly heavy and leaden.

Brandenburg Consort / Roy Goodman
Hyperion ② CDD22001 (96' · DDD)   Ⓜ
There are sleeker period performances around but few that have as much character or charm.

The English Concert / Trevor Pinnock
DG Blue 471 720-2ABL (Nos 1-3), 474 220-2ABL (Nos 4-6) (99' · DDD)   ⓂⓄ
Something of a modern classic, but only available on two single CDs, Pinnock's period performance interpretations are swift but never rushed and magnificently played.

Concentus Musicus Wien / Nikolaus Harnoncourt
Teldec ② 4509 95980-2 (148' · DDD)   Ⓜ
An imposing set from one of our leading Bachians, full of imaginative detail.

BACH ORCHESTRAL SUITES – IN BRIEF

English Baroque Soloists / Sir John Eliot Gardiner
Erato ② 4509-91800-2 (97' · DDD)   ⒷOO
Gardiner has a wonderful way with Bach and he and his fine players float this music with a real lightness and flair.

The English Concert / Trevor Pinnock
Archiv ② 439 780-2AH2 (121' · DDD)   Ⓜ
A most enjoyable romp through Bach's suites with some delicious solo work and always an engaging rhythmic drive and flair.

ASMF / Sir Neville Marriner
Decca 430 378-2DM (78' · ADD)   ⓂO
A bargain in that all four suites fit onto a single disc. These 1970 performances on modern instruments are stylish and fall freshly on the ear.

Brandenburg Consort / Roy Goodman
Hyperion ② CDD22002 (113' · DDD)   Ⓜ
Sometimes Goodman's players are hard pressed by the speeds he chooses but they cope manfully and deliver the suites with great flair and sparkle.

Amsterdam Baroque Soloists / Ton Koopman
Deutsche Harmonia Mundi RD77864 (79' · DDD)   ⒻOO
An award-winning set of the suites from one of today's most persuasive Bachians and an ensemble of outstanding players.

Philharmonia Orchestra / Otto Klemperer
Testament ② SBT2131 (138' · ADD)   Ⓕ
From 1954, the very grand post-war Bach style is displayed by Klemperer and the great Philharmonia Orchestra. Some stunning solo work but it's all very large scale.

Concert des Nations / Jordi Savall
Naïve Astree ES9958 (61' · DDD)   Ⓜ
A breath of Mediterranean warmth adds an appealing glow to the suites. A fine reminder of one of Spain's leading period ensembles and its charismatic music director.

Brandenburg Concertos Nos 4-6   Ⓟ
Concerto for Flute, Harpsichord and Strings in A minor, BWV1044
Liza Beznosiuk fl **Simon Standage** vn **The English Concert / Trevor Pinnock** hpd
Archiv Produktion Blue 474 220-2ABL (73' · DDD)
Recorded 1982-4   Ⓜ

The chief merits here are the overall zest of the performances, the expressive shaping of slow movements, and the individual contributions of some of the soloists – Pinnock himself brilliant in No 5, Philip Pickett, Lisa Beznosiuk and David Reichenberg admirable on recorder, transverse flute and oboe respectively, and Simon Standage in the violin parts performing prodigies, especially at the breakneck speeds adopted for some of the fast movements (the finale of No 4, for example). This tendency to force the pace makes things uncomfortable for the horns in No 1, and also leads elsewhere to some feelings of instability. Obviously several sessions were needed to record all six concertos, and there are some rather disturbing differences of balance and of ambiance between them. In No 2 the recorder, except when in its high octave, has difficulty in making its part heard, even against only the violin, let alone the oboe and trumpet (though it seems to have been brought in slightly closer for the finale); but in No 4 the internal balance between recorders and violin is quite satisfactory. No 1 is the most cramped acoustically, its larger sonorities needing room to expand; at the other extreme is No 3, which seems too resonant for real clarity; much the best and cleanest sound is achieved in Nos 4 and 5. A somewhat variable level of success, then, though at their best the recordings are highly recommendable.

Brandenburg Concerto No 5 in D, BWV1050[a].
Concerto for Flute, Violin, Harpsichord in A minor, BWV1044[a]. Concerto in the Italian style, 'Italian Concerto', BWV971
[a]**Jaime Martin** fl [a]**Kenneth Sillito** vn [a]**Jakob Lindberg** theo [a]**Academy of St Martin in the Fields / Murray Perahia** pf
Sony Classical SK87326 (55' · DDD)   Ⓕ

Murray Perahia is first among equals in the concertos, and the whole production is infused with a sense of spontaneous musical interplay. The sense of engagement is infectious. The cadenza of the Brandenburg is reminiscent of Alfred Cortot in its bell-like voicing, elegance and, just before the orchestra's return, cumulative excitement.

There are, in a sense, two Perahias at work: the first a non-percussive front-man whose evenly deployed runs are a joy, unlike some who more approximate a hard stick being drawn past iron railings. And then there's the keyboard poet within the orchestra, who even when playing *mezzoforte* or *piano* manages to project a full tone. The presence of a theorbo helps flavour the two concerto slow movements, the Triple

Concerto especially. Superb solo playing, too, flautist Jaime Martin producing a memorably plangent tone.

As on previous Perahia Bach concerto recordings, the overriding impression is of intelligence, sensitivity and drama tempered by humility. The Italian Concerto begs the by-now familiar question as to how one pair of hands can command so many simultaneous dynamic grades without sounding strained or self-conscious. The outer movements are colourful but never prettified, the principal melody of the central *Andante* like a memory of classic *bel canto*.

Even when judged in relation to other top-ranking piano recordings of Bach (among the most recent, Goode, Hewitt, Schiff and Anderszewski) this CD is exceptional. The recorded sound is full and forward.

Trio Sonatas

E flat, **BWV525**; C minor, **BWV526**; D minor, **BWV527**; E minor, **BWV528**; C, **BWV529**; G, **BWV530**

Trio Sonatas – D minor, BWV527; G, BWV530; ℗
A minor, BWV1029; G minor, BWV1030; C, BWV1037
The Rare Fruits Council (Manfredo Kramer *vn*
Pablo Valetti *vn/va* Balàzs Máté *vc* Dirk Boerner *hpd*
Alessandro de Marchi *org*)
Astrée Naïve E8804 (67' · DDD) Ⓕ**OO**

Following recent recordings of, among others, the complete 'true' trio sonatas from Florilegium and the complete organ trios adapted for strings and continuo from the Purcell Quartet, as well as numerous one-off arrangements dropped as fillers into other Bach chamber releases, this one offers a mixed bag of solutions to the irritating little anomaly that the greatest of Baroque instrumental composers wrote hardly any music in one of the Baroque period's most ubiquitous instrumental forms. So, here we get convincing arrangements for various combinations of violins, viola, cello, organ and harpsichord of two of the organ trios, the B minor Sonata for flute and obbligato harpsichord, the C major Sonata genuinely written for two violins and continuo – though not, it seems, by Bach (Goldberg is thought to be the man), and the G minor Sonata for gamba and obbligato harpsichord.

That Bach's music can withstand transcription like nobody else's has been remarked on countless times, but it's nice to be reminded from time to time of another old truth, namely that there's always something new to be found by those with the wit to look for it. That's exactly what's demonstrated here in performances of uncommon energy and imagination that will surely win over the most resistant of transcription sceptics. Genteel and polite they're not; rather, they embrace the music with an inspiriting boisterousness and wholeheartedness. This

is music-making bursting with life.

Most exciting of all, the players revel in Bach's life-enhancing contrapuntal interplay with a joyousness that's almost jazz-like in its freedom and exhilarating spontaneity. Their sound could be described as bold, up-front, occasionally a little coarse, but above all, well, fruity. If you're suffering from Bachian cobwebs, this thoroughly enjoyable release will blow them away.

Additional recommendation

Trio Sonatas, BWV525, 527, 529, 530 ℗
Coupled with: Four Duets, BWV802-5.
14 Verschiedene Canones, BWV1087
Palladian Ensemble
Linn Records CKD036 (75' · DDD) Ⓕ
Refreshingly committed performances which stray from old paths in stimulating ways and show off the corporate style of the Palladian Ensemble.

Solo Cello Suites

No 1 in G, BWV1007; **No 2** in D minor, BWV1008; **No 3** in C, BWV1009; **No 4** in E flat, BWV1010; **No 5** in C minor, BWV1011; **No 6** in D, BWV1012

Solo Cello Suites Nos 1-6
Pierre Fournier *vc*
DG The Originals ② 449 711-2GOR2 (139' · ADD)
Recorded 1961-3 Ⓜ**OOO**

Of all the great cellists, Pierre Fournier came closer to the heart of the music than almost any other. He seems to have possessed all the virtues of his fellow cellists without yielding to any of their self-indulgences. He could be brilliant in execution – his technique was second to none, as he proves throughout this set – profound in utterance, aristocratic in poise and wonderfully coherent in his understanding of Bach's articulation and phrases.

We need look no further than the *Prelude* of the First Suite in G major to find the supreme artistry which characterises each and every moment of these performances. There are very occasionally notes which fail to reach their centre but they're few and far between, and Fournier's intonation compares favourably with that of some of his virtuoso companions. Fournier's rubato is held tightly in rein and when he does apply it, it's in the interests of enlivening aspects of Bach's formal writing. He can sparkle too, as he does in many of the faster dance-orientated movements such as courantes, gavottes and bourrées; in the sarabandes, he invariably strikes a note of grandeur coupled with a concentration amounting at times almost to abstraction. Above all, his Bach playing is crowned with an eloquence, a lyricism and a grasp of the music's formal and stylistic content which will not easily be matched.

It's hardly surprising that these readings seem

BACH CELLO SUITES – IN BRIEF

Mstislav Rostropovich
EMI ② 555363-2 (147' · DDD)　　Ⓕ●

Big-hearted, bold-gestured Bach from one of the greatest cellists of our time. Here is emotion writ large but done with such passion it's hard not to be won·over.

Heinrich Schiff
EMI ② 574179-2 (124' · DDD)　　Ⓑ●●

One of the finest modern-instrument performances that takes academic advances into account, making for a delightfully buoyant set of the suites. Quite a bargain.

Pablo Casals
EMI mono ② 761027-2 (130' · ADD)　　Ⓜ
or Naxos mono ⑧ 8 110915/6 (149 mins)　　Ⓢ●

A historic set from the 1930s which shows off the integrity and artistry of the man who rescued these works for posterity. Warts and all, these have to be heard.

Pierre Fournier
DG ② 449 711-2GOR2 (139' ·: ADD)　　Ⓜ●●●

For many the classic performances: expressive, full-bodied yet never threatening to overwhelm the music. Fournier clearly adores this music and it shows.

Yo-Yo Ma
Sony Classical ② SM2K89754 (143' · DDD)　　Ⓜ●

The first of Ma's two cycles of the suites and at the price well worth considering for this fine cellist's innate musicality.

Pieter Wispelwey
Channel Classics ② CCS12298 (140' · DDD)　　Ⓕ●●

Another cellist with two sets to his name offers a period approach that positively dances with a lightness of touch and songfulness. A real *tour de force*.

Mischa Maisky
DG ② 463 253-2GH2 (155' · DDD)　　Ⓕ

Maisky's return to the Bach suites shows his essentially heart-on-sleeve approach but it's one that threatens the delicacy of much of Bach's writing. Try before you buy…

Paolo Pandolfo
Glossa ② GCD920405 (144' · DDD)　　Ⓕ●●

Pandolfo, one of the finest viola da gamba players of our day, appropriates these suites for his instrument and makes a good case for doing so in the scale and balance of his approach. Pandolfo's artistry cannot be ignored.

Matt Haimowitz
Oxingale ② OX2000 (136' · DDD)　　Ⓕ●

A superb achievement by a young cellist who has taken these works out of the concert hall and into clubs – he really connects with the composer. This is Bach for a new century.

as fresh and as valid today as they did in the 1960s. Out and out purists, poor devils, may not be able to adjust to modern pitch, modern instrument and, in the case of Suites Nos 5 and 6, the wrong instrument, but if that's so they're deserving more of compassion than censure. Fine recorded sound and strongly commended on virtually all counts.

Cello Suites Nos 1-6. English Suite No 6 in D, 　Ⓗ
BWV811 – Gavotte I; Gavotte II (arr Pollain).
Musicalisches Gesangbuch – Komm, süsser Tod,
BWV478 (arr Siloti). Violin Sonata, BWV1003 –
Andante (arr Siloti). Orchestral Suite No 3 in D,
BWV1068 – Air (arr Siloti). Toccata, Adagio and
Fugue in C, BWV564 – Adagio
Pablo Casals vc with **Nikolai Mednikoff, Blas-Net,
Otto Schulf** pfs
Naxos Historical mono ② 8 110915/6 (149' · ADD)
Recorded 1927-39　　　　　　　　　　　　　Ⓢ●

When these recordings first appeared back in the 1930s and 40s, Bach for solo cello was a singular and esoteric concept. Casals had rediscovered the Suites for modern ears and his probing, albeit highly idiosyncratic, playing was a mandatory recommendation. Indeed, in those days it was the only recommendation. Nowadays, with countless period-conscious rivals vying for prominence, Casals the pioneer is viewed as a venerable – if somewhat anachronistic – elder statesman. His achievement is still beyond question, but there will be some listeners who won't like what they hear.

After, say, the elegantly tapered playing of János Starker, Casals can initially sound wilful and ungainly. His bow seems to slice through chords like a meat cleaver. His intonation wanders, and his fingers press down on the strings so forcefully that a note 'pings' even before the bow is drawn. After Starker's rhythmic projection Casals reels and rhapsodises as if blind drunk on expressive freedom.

However, this impression is only transitory. What at first sounds gruff, even off-hand soon registers as boldly assertive. The intonation isn't so much 'faulty' as expressively employed, and as for those pre-echoing 'pings', they soon cease to matter – much as Glenn Gould's mumbling did years later. Time teaches you that the speaking tone, the poetic tenutos, the irresistible lilt in faster dance movements and the varied approach to vibrato were part of a grand musical plan, one that's now cherishable.

Casals makes a singular musical experience out of every movement. Try the Courante and Sarabande of the Fifth Suite – muscular resolve followed by profound self-communing.

Transfer-wise, things could hardly have gone better. True, there's some surface noise, but the sound has considerable realism and the broad contours of Casals's tone are untroubled by excessive filtering. A rival package from Pearl (identical couplings plus a transcription from a Bach-Vivaldi Concerto) reports a fatter cello sound with less well-focused contours. EMI's set offers only the Suites in transfers that, while admirably clear, are rather less natural than Ward Marston's for Naxos.

Solo Cello Suites Nos 1-6
Boris Pergamenschikov *vc*
Hänssler Edition Bachakademie ② 92 120 (128' · DDD)   Ⓕ**OO**

Any worthy recording of Bach's solo cello compositions celebrates the balance of mind and body, prayer and dance, scholarship and unspoiled intuition. One of the most striking features of this set is the lavish way Pergamenschikov ornaments the musical line, usually in a repeat, but always with a convincing sense of style. He's equally adept at charting the precise mood of each movement, making free with the various preludes (usually at a fairly fast tempo), pointing courantes with a lively *staccato*, drawing expressive weight from the sarabandes without obscuring their rhythmic profile and dancing through the various minuets and gigues. His phrasing is supple, flexible and musically varied, his use of vibrato subtly expressive within the boundaries of period style. There's a noticeable lilt to much of the phrasing, and an expressive *legato* that's unhampered by excessive vibrato. Pergamenschikov indulges a genuine sense of play and knows intuitively where to hold back, where to insert a tiny pause, and where to lean on the beginning of the bar. The recordings are excellent. Pergamenschikov should henceforth take his rightful place among the top modern recommendations of this exalted repertoire.

Solo Cello Suites Nos 1-6   Ⓟ
Pieter Wispelwey *vc*
Channel Classics ② CCS12298 (140' · DDD)   Ⓕ**OO**

Netherlands-born cellist Pieter Wispelwey is equally at home on Baroque and modern instruments. These performances are carefully prepared, beautifully executed and most eloquently expressed. The instruments, too, sound well, Wispelwey having chosen an early 18th-century cello by Barak Norman for the first five Suites, and a five-stringed *violoncello piccolo* by an unidentified craftsman for the special requirements of the Sixth.

Wispelwey is an imaginative player with a highly developed sense of fantasy. These qualities are as welcome in his performances of Bach as they're to be treated with circumspection in his almost entirely fanciful written introduction to the music. Preludes come across especially well since it's in these wonderfully varied opening movements, with their rhetorical diversity, that the performer can give rein most freely to his or her most natural conversational inflexions. And he makes the most of that thrilling climax at the peak of a chromatic accent through a full scale and a half. Sarabandes are profound and reflective without being weighty, and allemandes graceful and substantial. The *galanter-*

ies, by contrast, are lightly bowed and redolent of playful and demonstrative gestures. That, to an extent, is true also of the courantes, while the gigues are firmly projected, full-toned and splendidly robust.

Wispelwey's set of Bach's Cello Suites, then, is deserving of praise. If you're familiar with the gruff grandeur of Pablo Casals, or the aristocratic nobility of Fournier, then these performances will throw an entirely different light on the music, more conversational and with airier discourse. You may never want to be without the two earlier sets, but Wispelwey's version sits comfortably on the uppermost range of the period-instrument performance ladder.

Flute Sonatas

B minor, BWV1030; E flat, BWV1031; A, BWV1032;
C, BWV1033; E minor, BWV1034; E, BWV1035

Flute Sonatas – B minor, BWV1030; E flat, 1031;
C, BWV1033; E minor, BWV1034; E, BWV1035.
Violin Sonata in G minor, BWV1020 (arr fl)
James Galway *fl* **Sarah Cunningham** *va da gamba*
Philip Moll *hpd*
RCA Victor Red Seal 09026 62555-2 (75' · DDD)
Recorded 1993   Ⓕ**O**

The basic six flute sonatas, BWV1030-35, can be accommodated on a single disc but Galway plays safe by keeping to what Bach (or someone else) actually wrote, omitting the unfinished A major Sonata, BWV1032, which other players have chosen to present in variously completed forms. From the purist's point of view, there's still a 'risk', since it remains unproven that Bach was the composer of BWV1031, 1033 and 1020. However, their quality justifies their inclusion: if Bach didn't write them you doubt whether he'd have disowned them.

Galway is at his warm, velvet-toned best, phrasing immaculately, caressing the slow movements and fleet of tongue in the quicker ones. His tempos are well chosen and he never allows virtuosity to get the better of his judgement. The 'supporting cast' are no less beyond reproach, but while the flute and viola da gamba are well balanced the harpsichord might profitably have been allowed a rather more equal say in BWV1030 and BWV1031.

Flute Sonatas, BWV1030-35
William Bennett *fl* **George Malcolm** *hpd*
Michael Evans *vc*
ASV Quicksilva CDQS6108 (77' · ADD) Recorded 1978   Ⓢ Ⓢ**OO**

There's something rather special about the flute sonatas, and the more so when they're as well played as they are by William Bennett and George Malcolm. They were obviously written during a happy period in Bach's life for they're amiably inventive pieces, which isn't to imply that they're slight, just very appealing. What matter if the E flat, BWV1031 (which has an engaging *Siciliano* slow movement), and the C major, BWV1033, are probably spurious – they still offer thoroughly worthwhile music. On this reissue, the first three sonatas (BWV1030-32) are played as a simple duet for flute and harpsichord; in the last three (BWV1033-5), written for flute and bass continuo, Michael Evans joins the ensemble and the balance – especially since his isn't a Baroque instrument – is quite perfect. As for that superb flautist Bennett, he too uses a modern instrument, yet is the soul of finesse as well as playing creatively and with consistently beautiful tone. The sound is forward but very convincing; and Malcolm's harpsichord isn't over-amplified but admirably life-size. This is a fine recording indeed and at super-bargain price should not be missed.

Flute Sonatas – B minor, BWV1030;   **P**
C, BWV1033; E minor, BWV1034; E, BWV1035.
Solo Flute Partita in A minor, BWV1013.
Ashley Solomon *fl* **Terence Charlston** *hpd*
Channel Classics CCS15798 (71' · DDD)   Ⓕ**OO**

This is an impressive and enjoyable CD that easily bears repeated listening. There's a soothing quality to the Baroque flute, and its gentle, slightly reedy tone is captured very well here. It's closely recorded in a church acoustic to give a brilliant tone with added depth. Today's makers of the Baroque flute are producing highly refined instruments, exemplified here by the Rod Cameron copy of a Denner, which has a strong, even tone and good balance of register, allowing highly accomplished performers like Ashley Solomon complete technical freedom.

This recording isn't merely music therapy, however, but a genuine musical experience. His performance of the unaccompanied A minor Partita, for example, is nothing short of commanding: the control in articulation and breathing allows the phrasing to be flexible and unfussy. It's the directness of his interpretations that's so telling; there's almost none of that slightly coy *rubato* that some other flautists use to disguise the need to breathe. Rather, Solomon ensures that the phrases are neither choppy nor fragmented. He has an excellent sense of the longer line and the harmonic pull beneath Bach's wonderfully melodic writing. The faster movements are perhaps the most successful, full of buoyancy and energy without seeming rushed or pushed. Try the second movement of the E minor Sonata, for example, or that of the C major. Slow movements are far from inexpressive, but again refreshingly direct: he never wallows (a good example is the introductory movement of the E major Sonata). Solomon is well partnered by Terence Charlston on a rich-toned Ruckers-copy harpsichord. Even if you already have a version of Bach's flute works on CD this can be strongly recommended, and it makes an equally good first-time buy too. Prepare to be uplifted.

Lute Works

Suites – in G minor, **BWV995**; in E minor, **BWV996**; in C minor, **BWV997**; in E, **BWV1006a**
Prelude, Fugue and Allegro in E flat, **BWV998**
Prelude in C minor, **BWV999**
Fugue in G minor, **BWV1000**

Lute Suites – BWV995-7, 1006a. Prelude, Fugue and Allegro in E flat, BWV999. Prelude in C minor, BWV999. Fugue in G minor, BWV1000
Stephan Schmidt *gtr*
Naïve Classique ② V4861 (98' · DDD)   Ⓕ**OOO**

 Whether or not the description of these as 'lute' works is justified has long been a matter for debate, and in their annotation Stephan Schmidt and Claude Chauvel inevitably fail to resolve the matter, though they lean more in the direction of 'yes' than most. In a sense it matters little, for the works have been performed and recorded on a variety of other plucked-string instruments – harpsichord and lute-harpsichord as well as guitar – in exemplary fashion. The 'standard' six-string guitar is a baritone instrument, but its lowest register isn't extended enough to avoid the need for compromises; accordingly guitars with more strings (the extra ones at the bass end) have been in use for over 30 years. Göran Söllscher's DG recordings on an 11-string alto guitar remain as fresh as they were then. Now Schmidt, using 10 strings, sets a new benchmark with this magnificent set. The extra four strings give firmer bass and more resonant bass lines, as did Söllscher's five, and free the player's left hand from the restriction of having to hold many of them down.

Schmidt's touch is happily light in the *galanteries* and in the Loure of BWV1006a, but there's gravity in the unhurried sarabandes – such variations apply not only to pace but to spirit, too. He knows when to embellish (which he does with elegance) and when not. His *rubato* 'bends' a little more than Söllscher's and he's less conservative in his approach to embellishment – but attitudes to such matters have since eased. If there's a better version of these works on any kind of guitar in terms of content and recording quality we have yet to hear it.

Suite in G minor, BWV995. Prelude, Fugue and Allegro in E flat, BWV998. Violin Sonata No 1 in G minor, BWV1001 (arr Stubbs).
Stephen Stubbs *lte*
ATMA Classique ACD22238 (56' · DDD)   Ⓕ

In his booklet notes Stephen Stubbs addresses an age-old question: did Bach intend certain of his works to be played on the lute? Despite doubts surrounding BWV996, 998 and 1006a, he appears confident that the answer is 'yes'. No one seriously believes that Bach played the lute, but he undoubtedly loved the sounds it made: hence his interest in the keyboard Lautenwerck (or lute-harpsichord). It's clear that the works display lute-like textures, but keys such as E major and E minor are far from 'lute-friendly'. These and other doubts cast their shadows on the matter.

The autograph staff-notated manuscript of Suite BWV995 contains a repeated low G that calls for a lute with 14 courses, but that of the contemporary adaptation for the lute is for a 13-course instrument, with the low G raised by an octave. Stubbs bravely uses a 14-course lute.

There's a tablature version of the Fugue from the First Violin Sonata BWV1001 made by Johann Christian Weyrauch, which raises the speculation that he may have considered doing the same for the other movements. Stubbs isn't the first lutenist to have completed what Weyrauch failed to do. Nigel North has even done the same for all six solo violin works and the six Cello Suites; these aren't lute works of Bach but they are lute-friendly and, as such, fair game.

Stubbs's performances are in all respects among the very best in a competitive field. The same may be said of the recording quality and the annotation. Heartily recommended.

Viola da gamba Sonatas

G, **BWV1027**; D, **BWV1028**; G minor, **BWV1029**

Viola da gamba Sonatas, BWV1027-29[a]. □
Harpsichord Capriccios – in B flat, BWV992; in E, BWV993
[a]**Jaap ter Linden** va da gamba **Richard Egarr** hpd
Harmonia Mundi HMU90 7268 (61' · DDD) Ⓕ**O**

Forced to choose just one CD to represent Bach's instrumental chamber music, then among the plethora of transcriptions and double albums there would perhaps be no better group of works to pick than these.

Jaap ter Linden and Richard Egarr enter a largish field which includes a number of modern cellists unable to resist this superb music, but they emerge as serious contenders for a placing. Linden's sound has the smoothness and rich lyricism that you tend to associate with the Baroque cello, while at the same time retaining something of the gamba's pleasing incisiveness of line. Egarr's harpsichord is splendidly sonorous, and while his tautly controlled playing is in many ways the opposite of Linden's, the meeting of instruments and minds is nevertheless a happy one. Egarr, playing an obbligato part, has less opportunity to show off his individualism than he would in an improvised continuo accompaniment but, even if he could have been favoured a little more in the balance, his ability to orchestrate an impressive range of sounds from his instrument is still in evidence, especially in the concerto-like Sonata in G minor. He also dispatches the disc's filler items – two of Bach's early, somewhat old-fashioned solo harpsichord pieces – with vigorous and virtuoso aplomb.

Compared with their recent rivals, then, these are lively performances that steer a middle course between the rich-toned but slightly unimaginative Markku Luolajan-Mikkola and Miklós Spányi and the more intense and inspired but sloppily recorded Jordi Savall and Ton Koopman. Alison Crum and Laurence Cummings suffer too much from a balance unkind to the gamba. It all comes down to taste, but this new recording may just be the one to live with.

Additional recommendation

Viola da gamba Sonatas, BWV1027-9
Coupled with: Trio Sonata in C, BWV529 □
Savall va da gamba **Koopman** hpd
Alia Vox AV9812 (59' · DDD) Ⓕ

A significant Bach gamba release. Savall and Koopman conjure performances whose sheer rightness and creative warmth make the music sound invigoratingly fresh.

Violin Sonatas

No 1 in B minor, BWV1014; **No 2** in A, BWV1015; **No 3** in E, BWV1016; **No 4** in C minor, BWV1017; **No 5** in F, BWV1018; **No 6** in G, BWV1019

Violin Sonatas Nos 1-6, BWV1014-19 □
Sonata for Violin and Continuo in G, BWV1019a[a].
Cantabile, BWV1019a/2. Sonatas for Violin and Continuo[a] – No 2 in G, BWV1021; No 4 in E minor, BWV1023
Rachel Podger vn [a]**Jonathan Manson** va da gamba
Trevor Pinnock hpd
Channel Classics ② CCS14798 (139' · DDD) Ⓜ**OO**

A recording of Bach's violin sonatas that really hits the spot. Rachel Podger has already attracted much praise for her recordings of the solo violin music, but is heard here to even better advantage in the Six Sonatas for Violin and Obbligato Harpsichord, BWV1014-19, for which she's joined by Trevor Pinnock (of whose English Concert she is now the leader).

The two make a fine match. Both are uncomplicated, instinctive musicians with a sure technical command and sound stylistic sense, and in works as robust and complete as these, that's most of the battle already won. But this is also music of great poetry, and, without straining unduly to make their points, Podger and Pinnock bring this out superbly; Pinnock's harpsichord is gently resonant and softly voiced, and Podger coaxes a lyrical flexibility out of her violin, its singing qualities enhanced thanks to a restrained but telling use of vibrato – one which also enables her to play more consistently and blessedly in tune than almost any other Baroque fiddler currently in business.

It's difficult to single out details of this recording for comment; there just seems to be such a tremendous feeling of overall 'rightness' to it.

Maybe the finale of Sonata No 2 seems rather frantic and the wonderful *Adagio ma non tanto* of No 3 a touch lumpy, but there really isn't much else to criticise. And there are true gems to be enjoyed in the opening movement of BWV 1014, where the violin makes an almost imperceptible initial entry, or the warm embrace of BWV1017's *Adagio*, or practically any of the sparkling fast movements, played with invigorating rhythmic drive and clarity.

This recording's most recent period rival, that of Andrew Manze and Richard Egarr, shows a typical wealth of new ideas and inspired moves but is less satisfying as a whole, and suffers from some intonationally hairy moments and a less precisely pointed sound. The only period recording to touch Podger and Pinnock for technical assurance is that of Fabio Biondi and Rinaldo Alessandrini, but in both sound and interpretation it's heavy-handed compared with the spontaneous musicianship and airy texture on display here, and rather meanly it gives the six obbligato sonatas only. Though all the recent recordings of these sonatas have had their merits, this – two discs for the price of one – is, quite simply, the best yet.

Violin Sonatas Nos 1-6, BWV1014-19   Ⓟ
Giuliano Carmignola *vn* **Andrea Marcon** *hpd*
Sony Classical ② S2K89469 (94' · DDD)   Ⓕ**O**

Giuliano Carmignola's reputation as a Baroque violinist has so far rested on his recordings of Vivaldi concertos with the Venice Baroque Orchestra, where his easy virtuosity and sweet sound have made for some highly pleasant, if not always startlingly thought-provoking, listening. With the move to Bach's six supremely eloquent sonatas for violin and obbligato harpsichord, the advantages of his ready technique are equally apparent; this is probably the most consistently in-tune 'Baroque' performance of these pieces currently available, with Bach's exposed and melodically intricate lines giving Carmignola none of the intonation problems which afflict most of his rivals.

With music as well-written and self-supporting as this, he has the battle half-won already, and lovers of these pieces can safely sit back and enjoy an effortlessly classy musical display from both Carmignola and harpsichordist Andrea Marcon. Recorded in a gently glowing church acoustic, and with the harpsichord well represented in the balance but not sounding unnaturally large, there's little more you could wish for. This silky newcomer is, indeed, a strong contender for a top recommendation.

And yet there are some things to be desired, as a visit to a handful of rival recordings will testify: Fabio Biondi (on Opus 111, see below) takes a more muscular and forthright approach in his recording. It's Rachel Podger and Trevor Pinnock (on Channel Classics, reviewed above), however, who offer the best balance, Podger in particular mixing sure technique with typically natural and spontaneous musical personality.

She remains a first choice, though Carmignola gives her a good run for her money and for some listeners Channel Classics' rather less appealing recorded sound may tip the balance the other way. Perhaps this really is one of those cases where the best answer is to have both.

Solo Violin Sonatas & Partitas

Sonatas – **No 1** in G minor, BWV1001; **No 2** in A minor, BWV1003, BWV1005; **No 3** in C. Partitas – **No 1** in B minor, BWV1002; **No 2** in D minor, BWV1004; **No 3** in E, BWV1006

CCS12198: Sonata No 1. Partitas Nos 1 & 2   Ⓟ
CCS14498: Sonatas Nos 2 & 3. Partita No 3
Rachel Podger *vn*
Channel Classics ② CCSSEL2498 (142' · DDD)
Ⓕ**OOO**

Hitherto we have heard Rachel Podger only in early chamber works and as Andrew Manze's partner in Bach double concertos: here now, at last, is an opportunity to hear her on her own. And you couldn't be more on your own than in Bach's mercilessly revealing Solo Sonatas and Partitas, perhaps the ultimate test of technical mastery, expressiveness, structural phrasing and deep musical perception for a violinist. Playing a Baroque instrument, Podger challenges comparison with the much praised and individual reading by Monica Huggett: she has many of the same virtues – flawless intonation, warm tone, expressive nuances, clear understanding of the proper balance of internal strands – but her approach is sometimes markedly different. This is most obvious in the great D minor Chaconne, in which Huggett's rhythmical flexibility worried some people, but in which Podger, here as elsewhere, while fully characterising the varied repetitions of the ground, is intent on building up the cumulative effect. One pleasing general feature of her playing, indeed, is her firm but unassertive rhythmic sense; others are the absence of any suspicion that technical difficulties exist (instead a calm control, as in the G minor's Siciliano), her subtle phrasing (as in the B minor Corrente, with the fleetest of *doubles*), the cross-rhythms of her G minor *Presto* and, most strikingly, the poetic feeling with which she imbues the initial *Adagio* of the G minor Sonata. She touches in chords lightly: though some might have been split downwards rather than upwards so as to preserve the continuity of a lower part (for example, in bar 5 of the B minor Allemande, bar 10 of the Chaconne and in the 18th and 19th bars of its major section). Her D minor Giga is stunning. Altogether a most impressive and rewarding disc.

As a matter of tactics disregarding the printed order of the works, the second disc opens in the most effective way with a joyous performance of the ever-invigorating E major *Preludio*. At once we can recognise Podger's splendid rhythmic and tonal vitality (not merely Bach's marked terraced dynamics but pulsatingly alive gradations within phrases), her extremely subtle accentuations and harmonic awareness (note her change of colour at the move from E to C sharp major in bar 33), are all within total technical assurances. The *Gavotte en Rondeau* is buoyantly dance-like, and in the most natural way she elaborates its final statement (throughout the Partita her ornamentation is stylish and convincing). She takes the *Giga* at a restrained pace that allows of all kinds of tiny rhythmic nuances. Only a rather cut-up performance of the *Loure* detracts.

In the sonatas she shows other sterling qualities. She preserves the shape in the A minor *Grave*'s ornate tangle of notes; she judges to a nicety the balance of the melodic line against the plodding accompanimental quavers of the *Andante*; she imbues the C major's *Adagio* with a hauntingly poetic musing atmosphere, and her lucid part-playing of its *Fuga* could scarcely be bettered. In the *Fuga* of the A minor Sonata, however, she unexpectedly allows herself considerable rhythmic freedom in order to point the structure. The final track is a stunning performance of the C major's closing *Allegro assai* which would bring any audience to its feet.

Sonatas Nos 1-3. Partitas Nos 1-3
Benjamin Schmid *vn*
Arte Nova Classics ② 74321 72113-2 (133' · DDD)
⑤**OO**

Benjamin Schmid counts Harnoncourt, Végh and Heinrich Schiff as significant musical influences. His Bach, like theirs, uses scholarship to fly. In the G minor Sonata's opening *Adagio* his sound ranges from a blanched, unwavering line to judiciously gauged vibrato. His chords are tonally generous (he clearly relishes every note) and his 'softly rolled' *arpeggios* allow the music's rich harmonic drift to register. Articulation is exceptionally clean and the Third Partita's dance movements display a winning rhythmic lilt.

Although the D minor Partita's Chaconne clocks up a fairly swift 12'39" (Végh, for one, is slower by two and a half minutes), Schmid balances courtliness and architecture in ideal proportions. The three sonata fugues work extremely well, the C minor being their crowning glory. Schmid alternates sonorous chords with a chirpy approach to shorter, single note-values, always consistently and with a mastery of tonal colouring. Tempos are generally swifter than the 'traditional' norm (though not dissimilar to various period performances), repeats are played and although some might question the odd slowing here or speeding there, most listeners will find Schmid's readings singularly stimulating and imaginative.

This is remarkable music-making and the silly asking price makes purchase truly mandatory – whether for comparison with better-known alternatives or for a first-time encounter with these magnificent works.

Sonatas Nos 1-3. Partitas Nos 1-3
Itzhak Perlman *vn*
EMI ② 749483-2 (143' · DDD) Recorded 1986-7 Ⓕ**OO**

These works are brutally difficult to play, not least in securing accurate intonation and in minimising the disruptive effect of hacking out the three- and four-note chords but, given today's Olympian standards, technical shortcomings may be tolerated only in performances that are musically relevatory.

Technically Perlman is beyond reproach; chords are traversed deftly and in the *Adagio* of Sonata No 3 skilfully subjugated to the melodic line, and his differentiation between marked *pianos* and *fortes* is very clear. There's brilliance in the faster movements, delicacy in the *galanteries*, and except perhaps for the Allemande of Partita No 2, grave expressiveness in the slower ones; stylistic misfits are far fewer than those of, say, Sándor Végh or Nathan Milstein (1971), and all repeats are offered – usually with some changes of dynamics.

Bach with a fair degree of gloss maybe, but a version by one of today's greatest violinists that's justly popular.

Additional recommendations

Sonatas Nos 1-3. Partitas Nos 1-3 (arr Galbraith)
Galbraith *gtr*
Delos ② DE3232 (119' · DDD)   Ⓕ
Paul Galbraith's embellishments are impeccable. In sum, these thoughtful and majestic performances are strongly recommended, and not only to lovers of the guitar.

Partita No 2 – Chaconne in D minor (arr Busoni)
Coupled with: **Schumann** Kreisleriana **Beethoven** Rondos
Kissin *pf*
RCA Victor 09026 68911-2 (63' · DDD)   Ⓕ
Kissin's Bach/Busoni Chaconne is both grand and thrilling; the instrument is taken to its limits.

English Suites, BWV806-11

Six English Suites, BWV806-11
Glenn Gould *pf*
Sony Classical Glenn Gould Edition ② SM2K52606 (112' · ADD) Recorded 1971-3   Ⓜ**O**

BWV806-808 also available on Glenn Gould Anniversary Edition SMK87765;
BWV809-811 on SMK87766   Ⓜ

There has been no more original genius of the keyboard than Glenn Gould, but this has drawbacks as well as thrilling advantages. He can sacrifice depth of feeling for a relentless and quixotic sense of adventure. Yet love it or deride it, every bar of these lovingly remastered discs tingles with *joie de vivre* and an unequalled force and vitality. Try the opening of the First Suite. Is such freedom glorious or maddening, or is the way the odd note is nonchalantly flicked in the following sustained argument a naughty alternative to Bach's intention? The pizzicato bass in the second Double from the same Suite is perhaps another instance of an idiosyncrasy bordering on whimsy, an enlivenment or rejuvenation that at least remains open to question. But listen to him in virtually any of the sarabandes and you'll find a tranquillity and equilibrium that can silence such criticism. Even at his most piquant and outrageous his playing remains, mysteriously, all of a piece. The fiercely chromatic, labyrinthine argument concluding the Fifth Suite is thrown off with a unique brio, one of those moments when you realise how he can lift Bach out of all possible time-warps and make him one of music's truest modernists.

Toccata in C minor, BWV911. Partita No 2 in C minor, BWV826. English Suite No 2 in A minor, BWV807
Martha Argerich pf
DG The Originals 463 604-2GOR (50' · ADD)
Recorded 1979   Ⓜ︎❂

This recital, first issued in 1980, has an extraordinary authority and panache. Argerich's attack in the C minor Toccata could hardly be bolder or more incisive, a classic instance of virtuosity all the more clear and potent for being so firmly but never rigidly controlled. Here, as elsewhere, her discipline is no less remarkable than her unflagging brio and relish of Bach's glory. Again, in the Second Partita, her playing is quite without those excesses or mannerisms that too often pass for authenticity, and in the *Andante* immediately following the Sinfonie she's expressive yet clear and precise, her following *Allegro* a marvel of high-speed yet always musical bravura. True, some may question her way with the Courante from the Second *English* Suite, finding it hard-driven, even overbearing, yet her eloquence in the following sublime Sarabande creates its own hypnotic authority. The dynamic range of these towering, intensely musical performances has been excellently captured by DG.

French Suites, BWV812-17

Six French Suites, BWV812-17. Sonata in D minor, BWV964. Five Preludes, BWV924-28. Prelude in G minor, BWV930. Six Preludes, BWV933-38. Five Preludes, BWV939-43. Prelude in C minor, BWV999. Prelude and Fugue in A minor, BWV894
Angela Hewitt pf
Hyperion ② CDA67121/2 (151' · DDD)   Ⓕ❂

Even the most out-and-out purists who blench at the thought of Bach on the piano will find it hard not to be won over by Angela Hewitt's artistry. Eschewing all hieratic pretentiousness on the one hand and self-regarding eccentricities on the other, she gives us Bach performances that aren't only admirable in style but marked by poise, and what used to be called a

'quiet hand': 'chaste' might not be too fanciful a term, so long as that does not suggest any lack of vitality. There's intelligence in her carefully thought-out phrasing and subtle variety of articulation: gradations of sound are always alive without their becoming precious. The bulk of this recording is devoted to the *French Suites*. Particularly enjoyable is the lightness of her treatment of the Airs of Nos 2 and 4, the vigour of No 5's Bourrée and the freshness of No 6's Allemande; the extra decorations she adds in repeats everywhere sound properly spontaneous and are in the best of taste; ornaments are always cleanly played and matched up in imitative voices.

Keyboard Partitas, BWV825-30

B flat, BWV825; C minor, BWV826; A minor, BWV827; D, BWV828; G, BWV829; E minor, BWV830

Keyboard Partitas, BWV825-30   Ⓟ
Trevor Pinnock hpd
Hänssler Classic ② 92 115 (149' · DDD)   Ⓜ︎❂❂❂

 The six Partitas are virtually a compendium of Bach's keyboard styles, with toccatas and French overtures, fugues and fantasies and all manner of dances. Trevor Pinnock rises to a new level of mastery in his new recording of them. We all know about the brilliance of his fingerwork and his beautifully sprung, ebullient rhythms; but here he goes further, showing a true grandeur of manner that embraces Bach at his most serious and pensive, his most learned, and – above all – his most vividly rhetorical. Pinnock takes his time over the music: these are measured readings of the partitas, thought through, viewed whole. The natural and spontaneous musicianship of old is still there, but now it's given extra depth and meaning through the carefully judged articulation, the tiny moments of hesitation, all within a fluent larger rhythm, that lend extra point and shape to a phrase, a group of phrases, an entire musical paragraph.

The warm, full, rather resonant recording beautifully captures the rich sound of his fine instrument – a David Way copy from 1983 of a Hemsch original – as well as the detail of his playing. There could hardly have been a happier return to the recording studio for Pinnock than this fine set.

Keyboard Partitas, BWV825-30
Angela Hewitt pf
Hyperion ② CDA67191/2 (143' · DDD)   Ⓕ❂

If Bach is to be played on the piano, this is the kind of way to do it. Inherent in all Hewitt's playing is a rhythmic vitality, always under control, that sweeps you along with its momentum, subtly varied articulation, dynamics that follow the natural rise or fall of phrases without exaggerations, an appreciation of Bach's harmonic tensions, an ability to differentiate between the strength of contrapuntal lines, and an unfailing clarity of texture. This is a sane and sensible interpretation, deeply musicianly and devoid of eccentricity. Her attitude, rather like Toscanini's, is to accept the text *com' è scritto* and then to make legitimate adjustments, so we get double-dotting and assimilation of rhythms. Technically she's immaculate, with the cleanest possible ornaments. In the great E minor Sarabande Hewitt is justifiably emotional, without becoming soggy: only in the first half of the A minor Allemande is there a hint of coyness. No, the whole disc gives unalloyed pleasure.

Keyboard Partitas – in C minor, BWV826; D, BWV828; G, BWV829
Richard Goode *pf*
Nonesuch 7559-79483-2 (72' · DDD)   Ⓕ**OO**

Faced with this level of musicianship, there seems little point in revisiting the 'plucked strings or hammers' debate, save to recall that, yes, the harpsichord's tonal properties have a unique validity in Bach and, yes, a secure knowledge of baroque performing practices is essential for the effective realization of his works. But there's far more to Bach than the performing conventions of his day, and to ignore the many piano recordings of his music is to deny some of the most searching and interpretatively sophisticated playing on disc.

Goode's approach to Bach is to explore expressive implications without recourse to ego-centred gesturing. So much seems new. The opening of the C minor Partita's Sinfonia sounds here like a distant precursor of the opening *Maestoso* from Beethoven's Piano Sonata, Op 111. Not that Goode labours the point: the mobile *Andante* is quietly pointed, the fugue that follows, joyfully, though never aggressively, exuberant. The Courante is urgent but tonally rounded, the Sarabande limpid, the Rondeaux nimble and capricious. The G major Partita works beautifully, but perhaps the finest performance of all is the D major: his skilful handling of the multi-faceted Praeludium shows an impressive mastery of musical transition, and he exhibits a Schnabelian impetuosity in the Courante. The sound is rounded and realistic.

Keyboard Partitas – in B flat, BWV825; A minor, BWV827; E minor, BWV830
Richard Goode *pf*
Nonesuch 7559-79698-2 (65' · DDD)   Ⓕ**OOO**

In this second volume of Richard Goode's complete set of Bach Partitas there's the sense of a distinguished lineage, a tradition of Bach piano playing with a Classical-Romantic bent that reaches back to Harold Samuel via Borowsky, Horszowski, Schnabel and Serkin. Like them (though not

specifically in the Partitas) Goode treats line as paramount, stressing counterpoint only where and when it serves an expressive end, as in the First Partita's Allemande. Like Schnabel, Goode can occasionally accelerate a phrase to focus its place in the larger context. The use of *crescendo* is subtle yet telling (the Corrente) and the way phrases breathe, suggests hours spent focusing on a precise *rubato*.

This is glorious music, and there's barely a second when you aren't aware of that. Everything flows from the logic of the line, and when perspectives do change (at around 46 seconds into the A minor Partita's opening two-part Fantasia, for example, where the lower voice takes the lead) the option seems inevitable.

Everything essential to the spirit is here: dance and reverie, clarity and form, digital brilliance. Goode never forces his tone and although he has a secure sense of rhythm – the faster dances trip along rather than rush – there's no hint of the obsessive drive indulged by the post-Gould school. That, too, can be exciting, but Goode's inner explorations of Bach will probably yield longer-term satisfaction. This is an exceptionally fine set.

Das wohltemperierte Clavier, BWV846-93

48 Preludes and Fugues –
Book 1 BWV846-69; **Book 2** BWV870-93

Das wohltemperierte Clavier, Books 1 & 2   Ⓗ
Rosalyn Tureck *pf*
DG mono ④ 463 305-2GH4 (296' · DDD) Recorded 1954   Ⓕ**OOO**

Here's a performance of a matchless wit, musical grace and eloquence; playing as vivid and life-affirming as any on record, a magical interaction of scholarship and imaginative brio. Tureck can conjure a mystical stillness or a corruscating play of light and shade, of *crescendos* and *decrescendos* that can make the plain-sailing of others seem tentative and inadequate, and much time-honoured wisdom and tradition stale and archaic (try the Third Prelude from Book 1). This is a voice of timeless richness and vitality, one that made Schoenberg declare Bach to be 'the first 12-tone composer'. The devotional flow of the 22nd Prelude in B flat minor is offered with an immaculate and indeed phenomenal pianistic authority and a mastery that allows for a total artistic liberation and unimpeded way to the music's very heart or poetic essence. In each unfailing instance the precise weight and timbre of every polyphonic strand seems to have been sifted and defined a hundred times only to be resolved into a dialogue or continuum as natural as it's piquant and thought-provoking. Early in her career Tureck replaced a highly successful, if more conventional, concert career with a single-minded devotion to a composer who for her makes all others dispensable. Skilfully remastered, such work is beyond price, deserving, in the words of that most august publication *The Record Guide*, 'a heavenful of stars'.

Das wohltemperierte Clavier   Ⓗ
8 110651/2: Book 1
8 110653/4: Book 2
Edwin Fischer pf
Naxos Historical mono ② (107' & 126' · ADD)
Recorded 1933-6   Ⓢ❍❍❍

 Edwin Fischer's recording of the *48* was the first by a pianist of the set, and probably remains the finest of all. Fischer might have agreed with András Schiff that Bach is the 'most romantic of all composers', for his superfine musicianship seems to live and breathe in another world. His sonority is as ravishing as it's apt, never beautiful for its own sake, and graced with a pedal technique so subtle that it results in a light and shade, a subdued sparkle or pointed sense of repartee that eludes lesser artists. No matter what complexity Bach throws at him, Fischer resolves it with a disarming poise and limpidity. All this is a far cry from, say, Glenn Gould's egotism in the *48*. Fischer showed a deep humility before great art, making the singling out of one or another of his performances an impertinence.

In Book 2, you could hardly imagine a more seraphic utterance in No 3, later contrasted with the most skittish *allegro* reply. He possessed a touch with 'the strength and softness of a lion's velvet paw', and there are few recordings from which today's generation of pianists could learn so much; could absorb his way of transforming a supposedly learned tome into a fountain of limitless magic and resource. Here he is, then, at his most sublimely poised and unruffled, at bargain price in beautifully restored sound.

Das wohltemperierte Clavier
CDA67301/2 – Book 1
CDA67303/4 – Book 2
Angela Hewitt pf
Hyperion ② CDA67301/2 and CDA67303/4
(117' & 148' · DDD)   Ⓕ❍❍

Admirers of Canadian pianist Angela Hewitt's lightly articulated and elegantly phrased Bach playing won't be disappointed by this recording. These qualities characterise the playing of each and every one of these profoundly didactic yet sublimely poetic pieces. Her restrained use of the sustaining pedal, her consequently clearly spoken articulation, and the resultant lucidity of musical thought, bring to mind the recorded performances of Edwin Fischer. Hewitt certainly sounds more comfortable in a studio than Fischer ever did, and her technique is more consistently disciplined than his was under these circumstances. Her reflective view of the more inward-looking fugues, such as the lyrical one in

E flat minor, is most attractive. Taut, but with a suppleness that's entirely devoid of stiffness, this is indeed cogent and gracefully beautiful playing of a high order. You may sense, from time to time, an overtly intense element of subjective thought in her understanding of the music, a quality which seems to be endorsed by occasional references in her lively, illuminating and detailed introduction, to Bach's 'sense of inner peace', and so on. However, to conclude on a thoroughly positive and enthusiastic note, these are performances of Book 1 that you'll want to hear many times over. The recording and instrument sound well, too.

Hewitt's Book 2 is a delight to both ear and mind. Everything is in the best taste and free of exhibitionism. There are subtle tonal nuances, natural rises and falls of dynamics, well-defined differentiation of contrapuntal lines and appreciation of the expressive implications of Bach's chromaticisms. Throughout her playing of these preludes and fugues – several longer, more mature and more demanding than those of Book 1 – there's a sense of unhurried poise, with flowing rhythm. The air of tranquillity is underlined by her frequent adoption of very quiet openings, many of which then take on a warmer tone towards the end – even the E major Fugue, which Landowska labelled 'combative', is handled quietly, yet she's able to sound contemplative (as in the E major Fugue) without lapsing into Tureckian reverentiality.

Just occasionally Bach's more intense movements tempt her into emotional rubatos which, though musically affecting, take Bach out of his century, and not everyone will care for the big *allargandos* she makes at the ends of some of the earlier movements. Otherwise these are musicianly and imaginative performances.

Das wohltemperierte Clavier, Book 1   Ⓟ
Kenneth Gilbert hpd
Archiv Produktion Blue ② 474 221-2ABL (110' · DDD)
Recorded 1983   Ⓜ

In Book 1 there are virtually no markings, so the performer carries heavy responsibility for phrasing and articulation. Gilbert's blend of scholarship and technique with artistic sensibility makes for notably convincing, often poetic playing. His interpretation of the D minor Prelude is one of many that haunts the memory. His vital rhythmic sense and love of refinement are qualities that can be strongly felt throughout this vast project. Some may feel he's unadventurous in his registration, but he achieves his contrasts through interpretation, renouncing the facility to emphasise them by more artificial means. In textural clarity he yields nothing to his competitors in this repertoire and arrives at a solution that's refined, lyrical and sometimes dazzlingly virtuoso, as in the Prelude in B flat, BWV866. The acoustic of the Musée de Chartres, where this disc was recorded, is pleasantly resonant. Gilbert plays a 17th-century Flemish harpsichord enlarged first by Blanchet and then by Taskin the following century. A satisfying achievement and an important issue.

Das wohltemperierte Clavier – Book 1
Evgeni Koroliov pf
Tacet ② TACET93 (129' · DDD)   Ⓕ**O**

No music is more impervious to the vagaries of interpretation than Bach's. Play his keyboard music on a piano and it remains obstinately in character. Proponents of the harpsichord may disagree, but musicologist Eva Badura-Skoda has thrown a spanner in the works by arguing that Bach, in his Leipzig years, extensively used fortepianos in an effort to help Silbermann perfect these instruments. So a pianoforte was the next step, after all. Edwin Fischer used it in the first recording of the *48*, but his approach and emendations have their detractors.

What intrigues and impresses is that Koroliov largely ignores the sustaining pedal. He often prefers to let fingers, rather than feet, dictate colour; and his fingers are capable of a variety of touch. They can also project the notes with pinpoint velocity, which, when wrongly applied, turns the G major Fugue into a mechanical exercise. This is a serious miscalculation, but it's the only one. The instrument is closely miked, which can lead to moments of discomfort, for instance in the starkly presented A minor Fugue. But he isn't always uncompromising, and the B flat minor Prelude offers an example of his sensitivity to the changes within a single work, from rigorous beginnings to a resigned ending. He reserves his best for the last pair, for which, unusually, Bach added markings *Andante* and *Largo* respectively. His performance of the Fugue marries tension to an inexorable flow that portrays the structure as an imposing edifice. Purists may quibble at the very slow tempo, but this is a *tour de force*.

Toccatas, BWV910-16

F sharp minor, **BWV910**; C minor, **BWV911**;
D, **BWV912**; D minor, **BWV913**; E minor, **BWV914**;
G minor, **BWV915**; G, **BWV916**

Toccatas, BWV910-16
Angela Hewitt pf
Hyperion CDA67310 (69' · DDD)   Ⓕ**OOO**

As Angela Hewitt tells us in her exemplary accompanying essay, Bach's Toccatas were inspired by Buxtehude's '*stylus fantasticus* – a very unrestrained and free way of composing, using dramatic and extravagant rhetorical gestures'. For Wanda Landowska, they seemed initially 'incoherent and disparate' and it takes an exceptional artist to make such wonders both stand out and unite. Yet Angela Hewitt – always responsive to such a teasing mix of discipline and wildness – presents even the most audacious surprises with a superb and unfaltering sense of balance and perspective. Time and again she shows us that it's possible to be personal and characterful without resorting to self-serving and distorting idiosyncrasy. Everything is delightfully devoid of pedantry or over-emphasis; few pianists have worn their enviable expertise in Bach more lightly. In the F sharp minor Toccata everything is meticulously graded, and in the dazzling D major Toccata, which so fittingly closes her programme, not even Bach's most ebullient virtuosity can induce her to rush; everything emerges with a clarity that never excludes expressive beauty. Her performances could hardly be more stylish or impeccable, more vital or refined; and, as a crowning touch, Hyperion's sound is superb.

Goldberg Variations, BWV988

Goldberg Variations   **P**
Ketil Haugsand hpd
Simax 1192 (71' · DDD)   Ⓕ**OO**

Bach's remarkable set of 30 Variations badly needs a harpsichord performance that projects the various layers of meaning and characterisation in a cohesive whole and, crucially, which makes the harpsichord sound warm, generous and palatable over 70 minutes. Ketil Haugsand has produced just this. He's a player whose rhetorical capabilities and stubbornly musical instincts have found a rightful home in this masterpiece. He starts from a position of sonority. This may seem a vaguely dubious observation but it gains credence when you hear how he allows his measured tempos to enrich the harmonic fabric so that the melodic articulation is completely at one with his idea of abstract beauty of sound. His inventive and poetic personality enables each movement to make its presence felt, as with the infectious jauntiness of Variation 10, the spirited carousel of Variation 14, enhanced by the contrast of resigned pathos from the previous movement, or the clarity of voicing of Variation 23 which is as riotously handled as the halting opening of Variation 19. The great fantasy, Variation 25, is a profound reflection that maintains its shape against all odds; with many harpsichordists, this is where all neuroses emerge in force. The last two variations are joyous and majestic and wonderfully affirm the journey's end.

Haugsand has clearly had his fingers and mind marinading in this music for decades. It's as genial, engaging and mature a musical imagination as any recorded set of *Goldbergs*, especially impressive given that the constraints of performing them on the harpsichord appear even greater by the day, as pianists open up ever-new vistas. This performance throws down the gauntlet, especially with Arne Akselberg's natural and resonant recorded sound. A truly exceptional achievement.

BACH GOLDBERG VARIATIONS – IN BRIEF

Murray Perahia pf
Sony Classical SK89243 (73' · DDD) Ⓕ❍❍❍

☀️ A magnificent achievement combining superb control of the piano with a probing intellect that's also deeply moving. This is an outstanding modern performance.

Angela Hewitt pf
Hyperion CDA67305 (72' · DDD) Ⓕ❍❍

The Bach player of our day brings to the *Goldbergs* every quality that makes her approach to this composer so appealing – a commandingly wide dynamic range and a palette full of colours. A very fine and judiciously subtle achievement.

Glenn Gould pf
Sony Classical ② SM3K87703 (152' · ADD) Ⓜ❍❍

For admirers of the great Canadian pianist, or simply for the curious, this fascinating twin-pack couples Gould's 1955 and 1981 interpretations: structure, voicing, detail and rhythmic complexity are all beautifully attended to. Fascinating stuff.

Wanda Landowska hpd
EMI mono 567200-2 (73' · ADD) Ⓜ❍

A historic document of the woman who put the harpsichord back on the map. Her Pleyel instrument makes a fine sound and she plays with great taste and spirit. It *does* sound its age.

Wilhelm Kempff pf
DG 439 978-2GGA (63' · ADD) Ⓕ❍

A great pianist heard in 1969 in a version that sounds pretty romantic in approach, but which just drips with irresistible musicality and intelligence.

Kenneth Gilbert hpd
Harmonia Mundi HMA195 1240 (77' · DDD) Ⓕ❍❍

A deeply impressive performance from a very serious musician and a very fine harpsichordist: this is not a reading laden with display but it has an honesty and uncluttered feel that's very appealing.

András Schiff pf
ECM New Series 472 185-2 (71' · DDD) Ⓕ❍

A piano version of these boundlessly fruitful variations that has much to say and does so with an appealing style and a greater sense of danger than on his previous set for Decca.

Goldberg Variations
Murray Perahia pf
Sony Classical SK89243 (73' · DDD) Ⓕ❍❍❍

 Murray Perahia's *Goldberg* Variations aren't just colourful, or virtuoso, or thorough in terms of repeats, but profoundly moving as well. Here you sense that what's being played isn't so much 'Bach' as an inevitable musical sequence with a life of its own, music where the themes, harmonies and contrapuntal strands await a mind strong enough to connect them.

Rosalyn Tureck was the first recorded Goldbergian to take the structural route, and her EMI/Philips set remains among the most cogent of older alternatives. And while Glenn Gould achieves formidable levels of concentration, his gargantuan personality does occasionally intrude. Perahia brooks neither distraction nor unwanted mannerism. Yes, there are fine-tipped details and prominent emphases, but the way themes are traced and followed through suggests a performance where the shape of a phrase is dictated mostly by its place in the larger scheme of things. Perahia never strikes a brittle note, yet his control and projection of rhythm are impeccable. He can trace the most exquisite cantabile, even while attending to salient counterpoint, and although clear voicing is a consistent attribute of his performance, so is flexibility. Like Hewitt, he surpasses himself. It's just that in his case the act of surpassing takes him that little bit further. A wonderful CD.

Goldberg Variations
Angela Hewitt pf
Hyperion CDA67305 (72' · DDD) Ⓕ❍❍

Name your leading interpretative preferences in the *Goldberg* Variations, and there's bound to be someone on disc who expresses them. Leaving aside numerous harpsichord versions, the current catalogue is notably rich in colourful piano alternatives. Of the best available options, Rosalyn Tureck holds structure as paramount; Glenn Gould (in his 1981 recording) is strong on rhythmic continuity and contrapuntal clarity and Evgeni Koroliov is distinctive above all for his imaginative handling of repeats. Hewitt's chosen course isn't dissimilar to Koroliov's, at least in principle (they both play all the repeats), but her manner of playing is entirely different. Two things strike you from the start: first, that she can summon many dynamic grades simultaneously; and second, that her variations between repeats aren't restricted to matters of voicing. For example, in Variation 13, she accelerates her phrases as if caught on a spontaneous impulse, then relaxes for the response . When she plays the variation's first half again she significantly modifies her tone and *rubato*, then opts for a more formal approach to the second half. All this in just over four and a half minutes! Her mastery of the keyboard is exemplary. She can launch an elegant *staccato* or allow one voice to weave an ivy-like thread, while others argue above it. Beyond a seamless account of the pivotal 25th Variation, Hewitt rattles off manic trills in 23 and favours a grand, free-wheeling approach for 29. Hewitt makes the subtlest of colourists and has never made a better CD. Strongly recommended.

Goldberg Variations
Glenn Gould pf
Sony Classical Glenn Gould Edition SMK52619 (51' · DDD) Recorded 1981   Ⓜ❍❍❍

Also available coupled with 1955 Variations on Sony SM2K87703   Ⓜ

This astonishing performance was recorded 26 years after Gould's legendary 1955 disc (see below). Gould was not in the habit of re-recording but a growing unease with that earlier performance made him turn once again to a timeless masterpiece and try, via a radically altered outlook, for a more definitive account.

By his own admission he had, during those intervening years, discovered 'slowness' or a meditative quality far removed from flashing fingers and pianistic glory. And it's this 'autumnal repose' that adds such a deeply imaginative dimension to Gould's unimpeded clarity and pin-point definition. The Aria is now mesmerically slow. The tremulous confidences of Variation 13 in the 1955 performance give way to something more forthright, more trenchantly and determinedly voiced, while Var 19's previously light and dancing measures are humorously slow and precise. Var 21 is painted in the boldest of oils, so to speak and, most importantly of all, Var 25 is far less romantically susceptible than before and has an almost confrontational assurance. The Aria's return, too, is overwhelming in its profound sense of solace and resolution. This is surely the finest of Gould's recordings.

Goldberg Variations[a]   Ⓗ
Das wohltemperierte Klavier, Book 2 – No 33 in E; No 38 in F sharp minor
Glenn Gould pf
Sony Glenn Gould Edition mono SMK52594 (46' · ADD) [a]Recorded 1955   Ⓜ❍

Also available coupled with 1981 Variations on Sony SM2K87703   Ⓜ

Gould's pianistic skills have been universally and freely acknowledged, but his musical vision has elicited a range of critical response that has few parallels in this century. The view that Bach was a mere mathematical genius and little more has long passed, but it has its echoes in Gould's approach; he was fascinated by the structure of the music and was supremely skilful in showing the Jacquard-loom patterns woven by its con-

trapuntal threads. Every structural detail is exposed with crystal clarity, but, switching metaphors, what's revealed is a marvellously designed and executed building, inhabited only by a caretaker. An overall time of 38 minutes doesn't seem unreasonable for the *Goldberg Variations* (here shorn of every repeat) but the statistic is misleading: many variations pass at breakneck speeds. As an exposition of the music's mechanism this is a remarkable performance but, despite occasional intrusions of sing-along and sparing use of the pedals (music first, pianism second), it says little of Bach's humanity.

Two Fugues from the *48* extend the playing time to the lower limit of respectability. Neither is hurried and No. 33 proceeds with the solemnity that some others perceived to be its due. The sound quality of the recordings is impressive, but overall this is probably of archival rather than definitive interest.

Goldberg Variations
András Schiff pf
ECM New Series 472 185-2 (71' · DDD)   Ⓕ❍

Whatever your likes or dislikes in the *Goldbergs*, Schiff will surely elicit a positive reaction, more so than with his 1982 Decca recording, which, though similarly felicitous, had little of the daring, imagination and scale of this live remake. After Perahia's probing intellect, Hewitt's sense of fantasy and Tureck's sepulchral *gravitas*, Schiff is the master colourist who, like Gould in his later Sony recording, achieves impressive continuity between variations. Contrasts, too, and never more so than in the sequence of variations Nos 20–22, taking us from brilliantly realised syncopations, to a glowering canon in sevenths, then dipping suddenly for the intimate *stile antico* of the four-part 22nd variation. As for overall style, repeats are often embellished, sometimes radically varied. He has an occasional tendency to spread chords (15), obviously loves to dance (the irresistibly lilting Variation 18), relishes an elegant turn of phrase (13) and has a keen ear for Bach's wit (the tripping exuberance of 23). This is a fascinating, beautiful, deeply pondered and profoundly pianistic account. While not 'authentic' in the scholarly sense, it's appreciative of Baroque manners and ornamentation. It's also beautifully recorded on a mellow, finely tuned Steinway.

Keyboard Works

15 Two-Part Inventions, BWV772-86. 15 Three-Part Inventions, BWV787-801. Chromatic Fantasia and Fugue in D minor, BWV903. Fantasia in C minor, BWV906
Angela Hewitt pf
Hyperion CDA66746 (63' · DDD) Recorded 1994   Ⓕ❍

Angela Hewitt's approach may be gleaned from her refreshingly lucid annotation, or simply by listening to what she does. 'A skilful player can [bring out the different voices] with different colours' and 'To be capable of producing a true *legato* without using the pedal will serve a pianist well in any repertoire.' She puts her fingers where her thoughts are. She never upsets the balance of the lines that it's in the nature of the harpsichord to yield, and her economy with the sustaining pedal helps preserve their clarity.

The two- and three-part *Inventions* are treated as music in their own right, not simply as invaluable exercises; each is given its distinctive character, with a wonderful variety of sensitive touch and shapely rubato that never threatens to become anachronistic. Her readings of the C minor *Fantasia* and the *Chromatic Fantasia and Fugue* are as eloquent and stimulating as any yet recorded by a harpsichordist.

Duets, BWV802-5. French Overture in B minor, BWV831. Italian Concerto in F, BWV971. Capriccios – sopra la lontananza del suo fratello dilettissimo in B flat, BWV992; in E, BWV993
Angela Hewitt pf
Hyperion CDA67306 (69' · DDD)   Ⓕ**OO**

Here is an attractive recital of five varied pieces or suites of pieces, familiar and not so familiar, played with Hewitt's expected intelligence and finish and not a little verve. In her very readable introduction, Hewitt quotes a contemporary review of the *Italian* Concerto describing Bach not only as a great master but as someone 'who has almost alone taken possession of the clavier', and whose compositions are exceedingly difficult to play 'because the efficiency of his own limbs sets his standards'.

They still are, and Hewitt conveys the feeling that the challenges aren't just to be met but should be sensed as integral to successful performance. By giving the quick numbers plenty of pace she makes the music sound difficult in the right way. No question of hustling them along, but rather of touching the core of the rhythmic energy and of making all the lines, throughout the texture, directional and lively. Hewitt's isn't a monumental Bach, rooted to the spot, but one that makes us curious as to what lies around the next corner. The brilliant outer movements of the *Italian* Concerto, the long fugal section of the *French* Overture, the second and fourth of the Duets (those extraordinary studies in two-part writing) are all successes of her musical dynamic and high-stepping style. And the Echo movement of the *French* Overture (track 28) has a positively theatrical allure, like something out of Rameau – wonderful!

What she can't disguise, however, is that some of the movements in this great suite 'in the French style' lie uneasily on the piano, especially when the sonorities characteristic of a two-manual harpsichord are transcribed as if for a piano without sustaining pedal. If only she'd allow herself a dab of it now and then; the music needs to hang in the air a bit, and the 18th-century harpsichord was, after all, an instru-

ment of mass as well as point, richer in colour and weight of sound than Hewitt's pencil-lines and sometimes rather brittle and over-articulated manner suggest.

On the other hand, her characterisation of the two early Capriccios in terms of the modern piano is a tour de force – sparky, fresh, as if improvised. The greatness of the rest of the music here may put them in the shade, a little, but they're delightful. Bach aged 17, trying his hand at programme music? Well, the Capriccio 'on the departure of his beloved brother' remained his only example of it, but it's a reminder too that there was nothing he couldn't do. A stimulating disc, and beautiful sound.

Per cembalo solo...   Ⓟ
Chromatic Fantasia and Fugue in D minor, BWV903. Fantasia and Fugue in A minor, BWV904. Fantasia in C minor, BWV906. Sonata in A minor, BWV965. Concerto in the Italian style in F, 'Italian Concerto', BWV971. Concerto in D, BWV972 (after Vivaldi's Concerto, Op 3 No 9). Concerto in G, BWV973 (after Vivaldi's Concerto, Op 7 No 8).
Richard Egarr hpd
Harmonia Mundi HMU90 7329 (79' · DDD)   Ⓕ**O**

Richard Egarr is the doyen of English harpsichordists at present, displaying uninhibited virtuosity, rhetorical and dramatic sensibilities, and an ear for refinement of sound. This discriminating recital combines the familiar (including a marvellously dapper *Italian* Concerto) with more pragmatic and intimate Bachian creations which are too often lost in the crevices of the expert's discography. The two Vivaldi concertos are idiomatic, thrilling and revealing exposés of Bach's hands-on approach to mastering new styles. Perhaps more diverting still is the Fantasia and Fugue in A minor, where Egarr shrewdly considers the intense coexistence of contrapuntal and textural relationships in the fantasia, before a fugue of extraordinary clarity of interpretative design. This is playing of real stature. The remarkable Sonata in A minor, after Bach's aged spiritual mentor Reinken, might have been arranged as early as 1703; it's a masterful demonstration of a young man in full creative flow. Egarr has the edge on Staier's penetrating but relatively dry execution; here we have a quasi-Toccata and Fugue of dazzling colour and affirmation before an Allemande portrayed with somewhat looser stitching, a highly affecting manipulation of rhythm. This exquisite recital ends with the mature, unfinished Fantasia and Fugue in C minor, with Egarr's own reworking of the fugue.

French Suite No 5 in G, BWV816. Partita No 1   Ⓟ
in B flat, BWV825. Three Minuets, BWV841-43. Clavier-Büchlein for WF Bach – Preludes: C, BWV924; D, BWV925; D minor, BWV926; F, BWV927; F, BWV928; G minor, BWV930. Preludes, BWV939-43. Fugue in C, BWV953. Fughetta in C minor, BWV961. Italian Concerto in F, BWV971. Prelude in C minor,

BWV999. Anna Magdalena Notenbuch – Minuets:
G, BWVAnh114; G minor, BWVAnh115
Richard Egarr hpd
EMI Debut 569700-2 (78' · DDD)   Ⓑ**OO**

Richard Egarr's programme is an attractive one
in which three major solo harpsichord works –
the Partita (BWV825), the *French Suite* (BWV
816), and the *Italian Concerto* (BWV971) – are
interspersed with Preludes, Minuets and two
Fugues from the Kellner Collection, the
Clavier-Büchlein for Wilhelm Friedemann
Bach, 'the son I love, the one who fills me with
joy', and the *Notenbuch* for Bach's second wife,
Anna Magdalena. The character of Egarr's
instrument, a copy by Joel Katzman of a 1638
Ruckers, has been effectively recorded, capturing its warm timbre in an intimate, domestic-
sounding ambience.

Egarr's B flat Partita is an unhurried affair,
reflective in its Prelude and Allemande and
rhythmically supple. Some readers may not at
once respond to the extent to which he leans on
notes, thereby breaking up that strict regularity
of pulse that used to be the order of the day. His
articulation and rhythmic flexibility are both
illuminating and communicative. The music
breathes, and with each breath comes a natural
pause in the declamation allowing for rhetorical
gesture and a feeling for scansion. Just occasionally in the Sarabande phrases are a little too
clipped and skimped over, but such instances,
both here and in the *French Suite*, are both few
and far between. Each of the little Preludes and
Minuets is lovingly shaped and played with a
sense of affection for, and understanding of, the
music's poetry. In short this is an outstanding
disc, both for Egarr's technically accomplished
playing and for his delicacy of feeling.

The Secret Bach   Ⓟ
Partite diverse sopra, 'O Gott, du frommer Gott',
BWV767. Klavierbüchlein für WF Bach – Menuet in
G, BWV841; Menuet in G, BWV843; Allemande in G
minor, BWV836. Chromatic Fantasia and Fugue in D
minor, BWV903a. Adagio in G, BWV968. Fugue in G
minor, BWV1000. Violin Partita No 2 in D minor,
BWV1004 (arr Mortensen)
Christopher Hogwood clav
Metronome METCD1056 (72' · DDD)   Ⓕ

Christopher Hogwood's incisive mind regularly
leads to strong and imaginative concepts: this,
the first of a series of clavichord discs dedicated
to Bach, Handel, Haydn, Mozart and Beethoven, is a perfect example. The clavichord has
a history of domestic usage, the intimate nature
of its utterances seeming both exquisite and
slightly enigmatic. Its main mechanical feature
of stretching strings gives the player the 'touch'
to grade dynamics, alter pitch through vibrating
and other idiomatic colouring. We know that
Bach loved the instrument. Hogwood uses three
clavichords of very particular tonal quality. In
his thoughtful and devotional reading of *O Gott,
du frommer Gott*, he plays a Schmahl copy from

Finchcocks with a lovely cushioned and even
tone. A Bodechtel clavichord provides contrast
for the shorter vignettes, while a larger Hass is
used for the Chromatic Fantasia and the Partita
in A minor (a transcription of the violin Partita
in D minor) – it's as extrovert and bold as you
get with a clavichord. The chaconne, arranged
by Lars Ulrik Mortensen, contains a few questionable harmonic and figurative quirks, but
Hogwood glides through them fluidly and
genially. It leads the mind and ears into revitalised pastures of how this music can be experienced afresh.

The Art of Fugue, BWV1080

The Art of Fugue   Ⓟ
Davitt Moroney hpd
Harmonia Mundi Musique d'Abord ② HMA195
1169/70 (99' · DDD) Recorded 1986   Ⓑ**OOO**

 Bach died before the process of
engraving his last great work had been
completed, thus leaving a number of
performance issues in doubt. Davitt Moroney, a
performer-scholar with a mature understanding
of the complexity of Bach's work; discusses the
problems of presenting it in a lucid essay in the
booklet, and explains his approach to performing it. Moroney has completed Contrapunctus
14 himself, but he also plays the same Contrapunctus in its unfinished state as a fugue on
three subjects. He omits Bach's own reworkings
for two harpsichords of Contrapunctus 13 on
the grounds that they do not play a part in the
composer's logically constructed fugue cycle;
and he omits the Chorale Prelude in G major
(BWV668a) which certainly had nothing to do
with Bach's scheme, but was added in the edition of 1751 so the work shouldn't end in an
incomplete state. Moroney's technique is of a
high order, placing emphasis on the beauty of
the music which he reveals with passionate conviction. Exemplary presentation and an appropriate recorded sound.

The Art of Fugue
Evgeni Koroliov with **Lyupka Haždigeorgieva** pfs
Tacet ② TACET13 (84' · DDD) Recorded 1990   Ⓜ**OO**

Consideration of recordings of *The Art of Fugue*
often raises such issues as whether it was
intended as a theoretical work or for practical
performance, what instrument or instruments it
should be played on, and in what order the
movements are played. For those obsessed with
the last question, the order favoured here is,
after the sixth (French) Contrapunctus, to intersperse the canons with the remainder. Evgeni
Koroliov approaches the first fugue very slowly
and tranquilly, starting and ending quietly but
with increases of tension here and there. Any
fears that this is going to be a bland reading
of the whole are immediately dispelled by
the characterful treatment of the ensuing

movements. Contrapunctus 2 (in dotted rhythm) becomes almost pugnacious, Contrapunctus 4 is taken *presto*, and both it and its immediate successor are played *staccato* without sounding in the least gimmicky. Elsewhere Koroliov employs a judicious variety of dynamics and articulation – *staccato, staccatissimo, legato* and *détaché* – to convey his unfailingly clear linear thinking. The one weakness in this excellent issue is the inadequate presentation material, which doesn't mention, among everything else. *The Art of Fugue* is often made to sound dull and didactic: this performance is absolutely riveting.

preclude expressive articulation; and then to 'Contrapunctus 10', where four-in-a-bar is reflected in a slower pace that also allows more space for a keener, but not overt, subjective response. Indeed, throughout their idiomatically phrased, impressively cohesive and clean-textured exploration of the work, these thoughtful musicians don't italicise anything.

In sum, Fretwork opt for a quiet, controlled intensity that perhaps needs extended listening to be fully appreciated. The recording certainly won't stand in your way. It's expertly balanced, the acoustic giving both ambience and intimacy.

Bach The Art of Fugue – Contrapuncti 1-11; Ⓟ
Fuga **Mozart** Five Fugues, K405. Fugue in G minor, K401/K375e
Phantasm (Laurence Dreyfus, Wendy Gillespie, Jonathan Manson, Markku Luolajan-Mikkola viols)
Simax PSC1135 (65' · DDD) Ⓕⓞ

Seeing that we enjoy Bach and Mozart on a modern piano, should we demur at their music being played on an equally anachronistic consort of viols? Leaving aside the argument advanced in Laurence Dreyfus's note that much viol consort music was fugal in texture anyway, the fact is that the contrapuntal lines here emerge with great clarity and with a subtlety of timbre, articulation and dynamics beyond even the ablest keyboard player, thanks to Phantasm's accomplished and expressive performances. The group offers the first 11 *contrapuncti*, without the canons or mirror fugues, but plus the final uncompleted *chef d'oeuvre* that was to have crowned the project; Phantasm's playing offers new insights into Bach's prodigious mind. In his transcriptions for string quartet of fugues from the *48*, Mozart – who, it's reported, constantly had Bach's volume lying open on his piano – made a few small adjustments to details of rhythm and part-writing; and the process also fired him to write several fugues of his own, including the one in G minor (for piano solo or duet) here. Phantasm, despite a slight tendency to hurry, brings a smile to the lips by its intonation, precision and, above all, musicality.

The Art of Fugue Ⓟ
Fretwork (Richard Boothby, Richard Campbell, Wendy Gillespie, Julia Hodgson, William Hunt, Susanna Pell *viols*)
Harmonia Mundi HMU90 7296 (76' · DDD) Ⓕⓞⓞ

Though *The Art of Fugue* is usually considered a composition for keyboard, the timbre of strings, especially viols played and reproduced this way, does give the music another dimension.

Though there are no tempo directions for the 20 pieces that comprise this work – performers are expected to relate speed to time signatures without other guidance – Fretwork's judgements are difficult to fault. Turn to the 'Canon alla Duodecima', or alternatively 'Contrapunctus 9', where the required swift pulse does not

Organ Trio Sonatas, BWV525-30

No 1 in E flat, BWV525 **No 2** in C minor, BWV526
No 3 in D minor, BWV527 **No 4** in E minor, BWV528
No 5 in C, BWV529 **No 6** in G, , BWV530

Trio Sonatas Nos 1-6
Christopher Herrick *org*
Hyperion CDA66390 (72' · DDD) Recorded on the Metzler organ of St Nikolaus, Bremgarten, Switzerland 1989 Ⓕⓞⓞ

The common assumption is that Bach wrote his Six Trio Sonatas as training studies for his son Wilhelm Friedmann, and young organists still regard the ability to play them as a prerequisite in establishing proper organ technique. But if ever the notion that this is music 'first to practise and secondly to admire' was shown to be false, this stunning disc presents an unanswerable argument. Herrick's performances are immense fun, brimming over with real affection for the music. He allows himself occasional displays of enthusiasm (adding a few exuberant *glissandos* in the last movement of the E flat major Sonata, for example) and he chooses his stops both to enhance the vitality of the quick movements and to underline the beauty of the slower ones. The recording makes this disc a worthwhile buy if only for the glorious sound; the organ speaks into a rich, opulent acoustic which treats each note as a priceless jewel, to be enhanced by its setting but not in any way to be obscured. A disc of rare beauty and a real gem in any collection.

Trio Sonatas Nos 1-6
Kay Johannsen *org*
Hänssler Classic 92 099 (78' · DDD) Recorded on the Metzler organ of the Stadtkirche, Stein am Rhein, Germany 1997 Ⓕⓞⓞ

Kay Johannsen's performance is distinguished by uniformly stylish, immaculately tailored readings of the Trio Sonatas. At the beginning of the 1990s Herrick's Hyperion recording was perceived as the most persuasive, vivid and compelling performances of these sonatas. At last he's met his match. Johannsen has every bit as much verve, spirit and musical persuasiveness, the organ is ideal both for these sparkling performances and the transparency of the musical textures (like Herrick, Johannsen has chosen a glorious Swiss Metzler – this time the 1992 instrument in the municipal church of Stein am Rhein), and Hänssler Classic's recording has exceptional presence and clarity. What many may prefer is Johannsen's avoidance of those *glissandos* and exuberant over-the-top gestures which Herrick favours.

Orgel-Büchlein, BWV599-644

Orgel-Büchlein, BWV599-644
Christopher Herrick *org*
Hyperion CDA66756 (72' · DDD) Recorded on the Metzler organ in the Stadtkirche, Rheinfelden, Switzerland 1994   Ⓕ

With just two manuals and 32 speaking stops, this wonderful organ is relatively small, but still offers sufficient scope for Herrick to find a different registration for each of these 45 Preludes. The softer sounds used for *Herr Jesu Christ, dich zu uns wend* are preferable to the rather coarse *pleno* (*In dir ist Freude*) but it makes an undeniably ravishing sound. The 46 Chorale Preludes of the *Orgel-Büchlein* are so brief that listening to them all in one sitting is the musical equivalent of eating salted peanuts one at a time in quick succession. In an attempt to make it all more palatable Herrick tries two tricks. First, he plays remarkably fast, which some people may not find particularly rewarding. Secondly, he revises the playing order, interspersing those Preludes based on 'general' themes between those for particular times in the church's year, and even mixing up the ones within each group. The booklet deserves paeans of praise. Robin Langley's notes are the perfect match for Herrick's playing: scholarly, erudite, infinitely rewarding and so easily communicative.

Orgel-Büchlein, BWV599-644
Ton Koopman *org*
Teldec Das Alte Werk 3984-24828-2 (70' · DDD) Recorded at Ottobeuren Abbey, Bavaria 1998   ⒻⓄ

These are short pieces, but brevity doesn't necessarily imply inconsequentiality. Koopman is very impressive here, with sensitive, authoritative and perfectly gauged performances, imaginatively registered and stunningly recorded on the 1766 Riepp organ of Ottobeuren Abbey. He never lets the preludes sound short, treating each one as a gem to be lovingly nurtured so that, even when it survives barely 40 seconds, we feel we have lost an old friend as it dies away in the Abbey's ambience. His sense of proportion is flawless, avoiding excessive sentimentality in *O Mensch, bewein' dein' Sünde gross* and creating the perfect balance between liveliness and majesty for *Komm, Gott Schöpfer, Heiliger Geist*. These are distinguished performances indeed, and if in places we hear signs of the instrument's

great age, or its action impinges a little heavily on the ear, that serves only to enhance the sense of authority and stature this admirable release lends to some of Bach's briefest creations.

Schübler Chorales, BWV645-50

Preludes and Fugues – C, BWV545; E flat, BWV552, 'St Anne'. Trio Sonata in E minor, BWV528. Largo in A minor, BWV529. Fantasia in C minor, BWV562. Schübler Chorales, BWV645-50
Piet Kee *org*
Chandos Chaconne CHAN0590 (66' · DDD) Recorded on the Schnitger organ of the Martinikerk, Groningen, The Netherlands 1995   ⒻⓄ

This is playing of heart-warming humanity and spiritual equilibrium, combining deep thought with complete spontaneity. Kee's control of the long, singing line goes hand in hand with a poetic command of Baroque instrumental articulation. Dip anywhere into the Schübler Chorales or to either of the Trio Sonata slow movements and you can hear the separate melodic lines not only given individual character, shape and direction but also combined with ease and gentle authority. Tempos in extrovert movements are unusually moderate, Bach's markings of *Vivace* and *Allegro* being taken by Kee as indications of mood rather than velocity, and yet the musical discourse is involving and full of wit, helped by registrations that are both simple and wise. The disc is crowned by a magnificent performance of the Prelude and Fugue in E flat, one that fully exploits the vivid contrasts of theme and texture and yet binds the work into a structural unity without a hint of haste or stiffness. Rightly, the recording presents this refined, robust organ as heard within its natural acoustic habitat and Kee has subtly absorbed the church's acoustic into his interpretations.

Schübler Chorales. Leipzig Chorales. Kirnberger Chorales, BWV690-91 and BWV694-713
Christopher Herrick *org*
Hyperion ② CDA67071/2 (147' · DDD) Recorded on the Metzler organ of the Jesuitenkirche, Lucerne, Switzerland 1995   Ⓕ

The Schübler Chorales are mostly drawn from cantata movements, the Leipzig, sometimes known as the '18' and sometimes as the 'great' due to their large stature (including in BWV652 the longest chorale prelude Bach wrote), and some miscellaneous chorale preludes which have nothing in common beyond the fact that Johann Philipp Kirnberger, a pupil and admirer of Bach, bundled them all together. Keenly aware of the artificiality of the situation – obviously no organist in Bach's day would have dreamt of playing 44 chorale preludes in one go – Herrick has approached the task with businesslike vigour. *Wachet auf* fizzes like champagne at a wedding – no wonder the sleepers seem so eager to waken with such a riotous wedding feast clearly already in full swing. But such unrelenting bubbliness can also seem misplaced: Schumann's description of *Schmücke dich, o liebe Seele* (BWV654) as 'priceless, deep and full of soul' hardly fits this dancing performance. So perhaps not a recording from which to extract single preludes, but certainly one that can withstand repeated bouts of continuous listening. As ever, not only has Herrick found a simply ravishing Swiss organ which he uses with impeccable good taste (and his invariably sensitive registrations are all detailed in the booklet) but the Hyperion team have come up with a top-notch recording.

Clavier-Übung III, BWV669-89

Clavier-Übung III, BWV669-89. Duets, BWV802-5.
Fugue in E flat, BWV552 No 2
Kay Johannsen org
Hänssler Edition Bachakademie ② 92 101 (100' ·
DDD) Recorded on the Erasmus-Bielfeldt organ,
St Wilhadi, Stade 1998   Ⓕ Ⓞ

These discs transport the listener back to 1736, the date of the Erasmus-Bielfeldt organ recorded here. Three years later Bach published the third part of his *Clavier-Übung*, an academically austere title which disguises one of his most symbolic and liturgically important cycles. He had high hopes for the commercial success of the volume and its successor, the *Goldberg* Variations. The *Clavier-Übung* features the so-called Organ Mass. A Hymn Mass, it uses Lutheran texts and melodies in one major and several minor arrangements.

The two discs open and close with the Prelude and Fugue in E flat, BWV552. From the Prelude's first notes it's clear that Johannsen's playing is of the highest calibre. There's emotional involvement without a superfluity of ornamentation and *rubato*. Here, too, is tenderness, flamboyance, attack and rhythmic drive. In Johannsen's hands the listener is subtly drawn to the core of the music, its complexity simplified through his beautifully balanced registrations. Highlights include the extended prelude on *Vater unser im Himmelreich*, BWV682 and those on *Aus tiefer Not*, BWV686/687. The Four Duets are stylistically related and unified through an ascending key sequence which, as the notes mention, represent the Passion, Easter, Ascension and Pentecost. The superb booklet includes notes on the individual registrations employed. First-rate recording quality .

Chorale Preludes, BWV1090-1120

Chorale Preludes – Neumeister Collection,
BWV1090-1120; Ach Gott und Herr, BWV714;
Der Tag, der ist freudenreich, BWV719; Vater unser
im Himmelreich, BWV737; Ach Herr, mich armen
Sünder, BWV742; Machs mit mir, Gott, nach deiner
Güt, BWV957

Christopher Herrick org
Hyperion CDA67215 (80' · DDD)   Ⓕ

These 38 chorale preludes come from a collection of 83 pieces compiled in the 18th century by Johann Gottfried Neumeister that eventually made its way to Yale University, where it was discovered by the Bach scholar Christoph Wolff. Bach's preludes are early works, and as Wolff so aptly wrote: 'Already there is innovation. There's a degree of originality and sophistication that is really quite remarkable.' Herrick gives clear, attractive performances with rhythmic articulation and lively ornamentation. Some listeners may find his playing too calculated and self-conscious, but these are sprightly readings, free of excessive mannerism. The most enjoyable aspect of the CD is the way Herrick gives each chorale prelude its own distinct sound world, despite having only a nine-stop, one-manual Metzler organ. This instrument is one of the most beautiful organs imaginable, and Herrick achieves a pleasing variety of colour. The organ is well recorded, too, though some may find it a little too closely miked.

Organ Works

Trio Sonata No 1 in E flat, BWV525. Fantasia and
Fugue in G minor, BWV542. Toccata and Fugue in
D minor, BWV565. Pastorale in F, BWV590. Organ
Concerto No 1 in G, BWV592. Erbarm' dich mein,
O Herre Gott, BWV721. Aus tiefer Not schrei ich zu
dir, BWV1099
Kevin Bowyer org
Nimbus NI5280 (67' · DDD) Recorded on the
Marcussen organ of St Hans Kirke, Odense, Denmark
1991   Ⓕ

This disc includes the best-known of all Bach's organ pieces – although some would dispute that it's an organ piece or even that Bach wrote it; Bowyer's account of the *Toccata and Fugue* in D minor is invigorating, exciting and very fast. It sets the scene for a CD of virtuoso performances and sound musicianship. The whole is a well-chosen, self-contained programme which also includes an indisputably 'great' organ work, a Trio Sonata, a transcription Bach made of an effervescent concerto by Ernst, a youthful chorale prelude as well as one from a collection only discovered in 1985 and one real oddity. Much thought has gone into the choice of organ and this instrument serves its purpose admirably; roaring magnificently in the *Fantasia* and emulating the tranquil sounds so characteristic of the *Pastorale*.

Short Preludes and Fugues, BWV553-60. Fantasia
con imitazione in B minor, BWV563. Fugue in
C minor, BWV575. Toccatas – G minor, BWV915;
G, BWV916. Fugues on themes of Albinoni –
A, BWV950; B minor, BWV951
Kevin Bowyer org
Nimbus NI5377 (74' · DDD) Recorded on the

Marcussen organ of St Hans Kirke, Odense, Denmark 1992 Ⓕ

Critical opinion and academic argument may deter others, but Bowyer is content to let the music speak for itself, whether it's 'by JS Bach, JL Krebs or AN Other'. The music here speaks with absolute conviction. A gloriously dramatic rhetoric is brought to the two Toccatas (BWV915 and 916). Harpsichordists may claim these as their own, but who could deny this lovely Odense organ the opportunity to glitter with such flamboyant music? The eight 'short' Preludes and Fugues have a muscular, clean-shaven feel to them underlined by plain and simple registrations. While other recordings of such indefinable pieces seem like scraps from the cutting-room floor, Bowyer sets them firmly in the mainstream of high baroque organ music.

Prelude and Fugue in A minor, BWV551. Trio in C minor, BWV585. Canzona in D minor, BWV588. Wo soll ich fliehen hin, BWV694. Christum wir sollen loben schon, BWV696. Nun komm, der Heiden Heiland, BWV699. Gottes Sohn ist kommen, BWV703. In dich hab' ich gehoffet, BWV712. Fantasia: Jesu, meine Freude, BWV713. Ach Gott und Herr, BWV714. Gelobet seist du, Jesu Christ, BWV723. Lobt Gott, ihr Christen gmein, BWV732. Nun freut euch, lieben Christen g'mein, BWV734. Wie schön leucht' der Morgenstern, BWV739. Ach Gott, vom Himmel sieh' darein, BWV741. Auf meinen lieben Gott, BWV744. Herr Jesu Christ, mein's Lebens Licht, BWV750. O Vater, allmächtiger Gott, BWV758. Vater unser im Himmelreich, BWV762. Wie schön leuchtet der Morgenstern, BWV763. Prelude and Fugue in A minor, BWV894. Toccatas – D, BWV912; D minor, BWV913. Concerto in D minor, BWV974.
Kevin Bowyer org
Nimbus ② NI566970 (199' · DDD) Recorded on the Marcussen Organ at Hanskirche, Odense, Denmark 2000 ⒻⓄ

This is probably by far and away the best release so far in this comprehensive survey of Bach's organ works. What distinguishes it is, first of all, the recorded sound, which has lost that underlying feeling of artificiality in its mix between instrument and acoustic which has occasionally surfaced in previous Nimbus recordings from the Hanskirche in Odense. Most of all, however, the outstanding feature is Bowyer's own playing. Always able to come up with enjoyable and eminently listenable · performances as a result of his phenomenal technique and intense musicianship, his playing here has real authority. There may be stylistic quibbles (Bowyer's ornamentation can be a little too sparing), but few would argue that the playing lacks real understanding of the music's essential spirit. You sense here a level of empathy with the world of Bach which has been missing from earlier releases. The chorale preludes are sweet sounding (as is everything on this splendid Mar-

cussen) but really do sound like the musings of a great master on both the chorale melodies and their texts, while the handful of large-scale display works here seem to look beyond superficial virtuosity and into the mind of a composer for whom every note of music (good or mediocre) was of real intrinsic value. Those not so far tempted to explore this gargantuan series could do a lot worse than invest in this release.

Prelude and Fugue in G, BWV541. Toccata and Fugue in D minor, BWV565. Fugue in G, BWV577. Fugue on a theme by Corelli in B minor, BWV579. Passacaglia and Fugue in C minor, BWV582. Pastorale in F, BWV590. O Mensch, bewein' dein' Sünde gross, BWV622. Wir glauben all' an einen Gott, BWV680. Erbarm' dich mein, O Herre Gott, BWV721. Herzlich tut mich verlangen, BWV727
Peter Hurford org
EMI 5856302 (73' · DDD) Recorded on the Schnitger organ of the Martinikerk, Groningen, The Netherlands 1993 ⓂⓄⓄ

'Peter Hurford playing organs of Bach's Time.' While Bach on 'authentic' instruments is no novelty, we certainly don't hear enough of the wondrous Ahrend organ, which begins this series in such style. Ahrend? Builders of Bach's time? Well, we're obviously going to have to take the title with a hefty pinch of salt. Although it dates back more than 500 years, in its present form the organ dates from only 1984. Bach never played it, and even if he had he certainly wouldn't recognise it now, but it sounds quite wonderful; Henry Mitton and Mark Nations have recorded it magnificently, closely focusing the sound within an aura of spaciousness. Splendid playing by Hurford too. He begins with the ubiquitous Toccata and Fugue in D minor. But what a performance! Everything else is given warmly communicative, unpretentious and immensely appealing performances.

Fantasias and Fugues – C minor, BWV537; G minor, BWV542; C minor, BWV562; G, BWV572. Preludes and Fugues – D, BWV532; F minor, BWV534; A, BWV536; G, BWV541; A minor, BWV543; B minor, BWV544; C, BWV545; C minor, BWV546; C, BWV547; E minor, BWV548, 'Wedge'; E flat, BWV552, 'St Anne'
Christopher Herrick org
Hyperion ② CDA66791/2. (150' · DDD) Recorded on the organ of the Jesuitenkirche, Lucerne, Switzerland 1993 ⒻⓄⓄ

These 15 works are some of the finest and most important music ever written for the organ. They are such mainstays of the repertory that no serious lover of organ music could consider a world without them. Herrick's performances are authoritative, scholarly and perceptive, but if that were all it would merely be putting Bach on a pedestal, making him accessible only to those who already possess the key to the door. Herrick's genius is in bringing the music vividly to life, injecting it with a sense of fun and a

JS Bach Instrumental

directness of appeal without for a moment compromising artistic integrity. Few could fail to be captivated by the wonderfully vibrant and smiling countenance of the great E flat Prelude while those of us who have laboured long and hard just to get our feet round that most ankle-twisting of all fugue subjects must surely surrender in the face of Herrick's effortless fluency in BWV542. The glorious Swiss instrument has been brilliantly recorded, portraying not just the instrument itself but its sumptuous aural setting.

Preludes and Fugues – E minor, BWV533; G minor, BWV535; D minor, BWV539; D minor, BWV549a; G, BWV550. Prelude in A minor, BWV551. Fantasia in A minor, BWV561. Fantasia con imitazione in B minor, BWV563. Toccata and Fugue in E, BWV566. Preludes – in G, BWV568; A minor, BWV569. Fantasia in C, BWV570. Fugues – C minor, BWV575; G, BWV576; G, BWV577, 'Jig Fugue'; G minor, BWV578. Trios – D minor, BWV583; C minor, BWV585; G, BWV586. Aria in F, BWV587. Canzona in D minor, BWV588. Allabreve in D, BWV589. Pastorale in F, BWV590. Four Duets, BWV802-5. Trio Sonata in G, BWV1027a. Musikalisches Opfer, BWV1079 – Ricercar a 3; Ricercar a 6
Christopher Herrick org
Hyperion ② CDA67211/2 (156' · DDD) Recorded on the organ of the Stadtkirche, Rheinfelden, Switzerland 1996 Ⓕ**OO**

Some might be tempted to describe what we have here as the 'scrapings from the barrel', for when you've taken out the chorale-based works, the trio sonatas, the concertos and the big preludes, fantasias, toccatas, passacaglias and fugues this is what's left. However, you could be tempted almost to prefer these crumbs from the table of great genius to those stupendous musical feasts which are everybody's idea of the real JS Bach. And when you have those crumbs seasoned with such loving care, such elegance and such finesse as Christopher Herrick gives to, say, the G minor fugue (BWV578) or the enchanting Trio Sonata (BWV1027a), you realise that here's music every bit as worthy of close attention as anything Bach wrote for the organ. In matters of registration, tempo, articulation and phrasing, Herrick displays immaculate taste. This is playing of the very highest order. The modest two-manual Metzler, built in 1992, makes an enchanting sound, and the recording fully supports the superlative artistry of the playing.

Allein Gott in der Höh sei Ehr: BWV715; BWV717; BWV711; BWV260. Christ lag in Todesbanden: BWV4ᵃ; BWV695. Fugue on a theme by Corelli in B minor, BWV579. Herr Jesu Christ, dich zu uns wend: BWV332ᵃ; BWV655. Jesus Christus unser Heiland: BWV363ᵃ; BWV688. Preludes and Fugues – C minor, BWV549; G, BWV550; E flat, BWV552. Prelude in A minor, BWV569. O Lamm Gottes, unschuldig: BWV401ᵃ; BWV618. Schmücke dich,

o liebe Seele: BWV180ᵃ; BWV654. Trio Sonata No 1 in E flat, BWV525. Valet will ich dir geben: BWV415ᵃ; BWV736
ᵃ**Caroline Magalhaes** mez ᵃ**Philippe Froeliger** ten **Francis Jacob** org
Zig-Zag Territoires ② ZZT001001 (90' · DDD) Recorded on the Aubertin organ of the Parish Church, Saessolsheim, Alsace 2000 ⒻO

This might look like just another organ recital, but in reality it celebrates the remarkable philanthropy of a small Alsatian community who have collectively funded, over nine years, a beautiful organ in Saessolsheim in the north of Alsace. Here it's played by a local son, Francis Jacob, an accomplished young player whose programme is an imaginative cross-section of Bach's organ works. He's not afraid to play a fugue without a prelude if he feels it serves the greater architectural good of the programme. Indeed, his ideals of passing through carefully ordered genres, keys and colourific possibilities are engaging and perceptive.

The performances are striking for the ebullience and vitality of Jacob's fast playing, which is rhythmically assured and with a strong feel for instrumental timbre, not just organ sound – the key to discovering allusions and subtexts as the Bach player must. Lift and immediacy of articulation prevail over endless swathes of *legato*. How refreshing it is to hear such glowing colours in the opening chorale prelude, *Valet will ich dir geben*.

However invigorating Jacob's playing though, there's a tendency to resist the poetic instinct, as if he's mistaking it for indulgence. *Schmücke dich* sounds unyielding, calculated and even wearing. He produces an idiosyncratic equivalent in the middle movement of the Trio Sonata in C major (what possessed him to break this restful melody up into little squares?), and yet all is forgiven in a deeply touching *O Lamm Gottes*, a chorale marvellously disguised as a taut canonic web irradiating ethereal harmonic consequences – this is where the expressive effect of dissonance is more at consonance with the underlying conceit than consonance could ever be! Jacob rattles off *Allein Gott* with supreme dexterity, and the dazzling upper partials are further evident in a compellingly neurotic reading of the A minor Prelude. The programme of two short CDs ends with the E flat *St Anne* Fugue, not as grand or mature in conception as some, but carefully considered and, like most of this recording, it conveys a notably immediate, 'one-off' and animated musical presence.

Sacred Cantatas

No 1 Wie schön leuchtet der Morgenstern; **No 2** Ach Gott, vom Himmel sieh darein; **No 3** Ach Gott, wie manches, Herzeleid; **No 4** Christ lag in Todes Banden; **No 5** Wo soll ich fliehen hin; **No 6** Bleib bei uns; **No 7** Christ unser Herr zum Jordan kam; **No 8** Liebster Gott, wenn werd ich sterben?; **No 9** Es ist das Heil uns kommen her; **No 10** Meine Seel erhebt den Herren; **No 11** Lobet Gott in seinen Reichen (Ascension Oratorio); **No 12** Weinen, Klagen, Sorgen, Zagen; **No 13** Meine Seufzer, meine Tränen; **No 14** Wär Gott nicht mit uns diese Zeit; **No 15** (spurious); **No 16** Herr Gott, dich loben wir; **No 17** Wer Dank opfert, der preiset mich; **No 18** Gleichwie der Regen und Schnee; **No 19** Es erhub sich ein Streit; **No 20** O Ewigket, du Donnerwort

No 21 Ich hatte viel Bekümmernis; **No 22** Jesus nahm zu sich die Zwölfe; **No 23** Du wahrer Gott und Davids Sohn; **No 24** Ein ungefärbt Gemüte; **No 25** Es ist nich Gesundes an meinem Liebe; **No 26** Ach wie flüchtig, ach wie nichtig; **No 27** We weiss, wie nahe mir mein Ende; **No 28** Gottlob! nun gebt das Jahr zu Ende; **No 29** Wir danke dir, Gott; **No 30** Freue dich, erlöste Schar; **No 31** Der Himmel lacht! die Erde jubilieret; **No 32** Liebster Jesu, mein Verlangen; **No 33** Allein zu dir; Herr Jesu Christ; **No 34** O ewiges Feuer, O Ursprung der Liebe; **No 35** Geist und Seele wird verwirret; **No 36** Schwingt freudig euch empor; **No 37** Wer da gläubet und getauft wird; **No 38** Aus tiefer Not schrei ich zu dir; **No 39** Brich dem Hungrigen dein Brot; **No 40** Dazu ist erschienen der Sohn Gottes

No 41 Jesu, nun sei gepreiset; **No 42** Am Abend aber desselbigen Sabbats; **No 43** Gott fähret auf mit Jauchzen; **No 44** Sie werden euch in die Bann tun; **No 45** Es ist dir gesagt, Mensch, was gut ist; **No 46** Schauet doch und sehet; **No 47** Wer sich selbst erhöhet; **No 48** Ich elender Mensch, wer wird mich erlösen; **No 49** Ich geh und suche mit Verlangen; **No 50** Nun ist das Heil und die Kraft; **No 51** Jauchzet Gott in allen Landen!; **No 52** Falsche Welt, dir trau ich nicht; **No 53** (spurious); **No 54** Widerstehe doch der Sünde; **No 55** Ich armer Mensch, ich Sündenknecht; **No 56** Ich will den Kreuzstab gerne tragen; **No 57** Selig ist der Mann; **No 58** Ach Gott, wie manches Herzeleid; **No 59** Wer mich liebet, der wird mein Wort halten **No 60** O Ewigkeit, du Donnerwort

No 61 Nun komm, der Heiden Heiland; **No 62** Nun komm, der Heiden Heiland; **No 63** Christen, ätzet diesen Tag; **No 64** Sehet, welch eine Liebe; **No 65** Sie werden aus Saba alle kommen; **No 66** Erfreut euch, ihr Herzen; **No 67** Halt im Gedächtnis Jesum Christ; **No 68** Also hat Gott die Welt geliebt; **No 69** Lobe den Herrn, meine Seele; **No 70** Wachet! betet! betet! wachtet!; **No 71** Gott ist mein König; **No 72** Alles nur nach Gottes Willen; **No 73** Herr, wie du willt, so schicks mit mir; **No 74** Wie mich liebet, der wird mein Wort halten; **No 75** Die Elenden sollen essen; **No 76** Die Himmel erzählen die Ehre Gottes; **No 77** Du sollt Gott, deinen Herren, lieben; **No 78** Jesu, der du meine Seele; **No 79** Gott der Herr ist Sonn und Schild; **No 80** Ein feste Burg ist unser Gott

No 81 Jesus schläft, was soll ich hoffen?; **No 82** Ich habe genug; **No 83** Erfreute Zeit im neuen Bunde; **No 84** Ich bin vergnügt mit meinem Glücke; **No 85** Ich bin ein guter Hirt; **No 86** Wahrlich, wahrlich, ich sage euch; **No 87** Bisher habt ihr nichts gebeten; **No 88** Siehe, ich will viel Fischer aussenden; **No 89** Was soll ich aus dir machen, Ephraim?; **No 90** Es reisset euch ein schrecklich Ende; **No 91** Gelobet

seist du, Jesu Christ; **No 92** Ich hab in Gottes Herz und Sinn; **No 93** Wer nur den lieben Gott lässt walten; **No 94** Was frag ich nach der Welt; **No 95** Christus, der ist mein Leben; **No 96** Herr Christ, der einge Gottessohn; **No 97** In allen meinene Taten; **No 98** Was Gott tut, das ist wohlgetan; **No 99** Was Gott tut, das ist wohlgetan; **No 100** Was Gott tut, das ist wohlgetan

No 101 Nimm von uns, Herr, du treuer Gott; **No 102** Herr, deine Augen sehen nach dem Glauben; **No 103** Ihr werdet weinen und heulen; **No 104** Du Hirte Israel, höre; **No 105** Herr, gehe nicht ins Gericht; **No 106** Gottes Zeit ist die allerbeste Zeit, 'Actus tragicus'; **No 107** Was willst du dich betrüben; **No 108** Es ist euch gut, dass ich hingehe; **No 109** Ich glaube, lieber Herr, hilf meinem Unglauben!; **No 110** Unser Mund sei voll Lachens; **No 111** Was mein Gott will, das g'scheh allzeit; **No 112** Der Herr ist mein getreuer Hirt; **No 113** Herr Jesu Christ, du höchstes Gut; **No 114** Ach, lieben Christen, seid getrost; **No 115** Mache dich, mein Geist, bereit; **No 116** Du Friedefürst, Herr Jesu Christ; **No 117** Sei Lob und Ehr dem höchsten Gut; **No 118** O Jesu Christ, mein Lebens Licht; **No 119** Preise Jerusalem, den Herrn; **No 120a** Herr Gott, Beherrscher aller Dinge; **No 120b** Gott, man lobet dich in der Stille

No 121 Christum wir sollen loben schon; **No 122** Das neugeborne Kindelein; **No 123** Liebster Immanuel, Herzog der Frommen; **No 124** Meinen Jesum lass ich nicht; **No 125** Mit Fried und Freud ich fahr dahin; **No 126** Erhalt uns, Herr, bei deinem Wort; **No 127** Herr Jesu Christ, wahr' Mensch und Gott; **No 128** Auf Christi Himmelfahrt allein; **No 129** Gelobet sei der Herr, mein Gott; **No 130** Herr Gott, dich loben alle wir; **No 131** Aus der Tiefen rufe ich, Herr, zu dir; **No 132** Bereitet die Wege, bereitet di Bahn!; **No 133** Ich freue mich in dir; **No 134** Ein Herz, das seinen Jesum lebend weiss; **No 135** Ach Herr, mich armen Sünder; **No 136** Erforsche mich, Gott, und erfahre mein Herz; **No 137** Lobe den Herren, den mächtigen König der Ehren; **No 138** Warum berübst du dich, mein Herz?; **No 139** Wohl dem, der sich auf seinen Gott; **No 140** Wachet auf, ruft uns die Stimme

Nos 141-2 (spurious); **No 143** Lobe den Herr, meine Seele; **No 144** Nimm, was dein ist, und gehe hin; **No 145** Ich lebe, mein Herze, zu deinem Ergötzen; **No 146** Wir müssen durch viel Trübsal; **No 147** Herz und Mund und Tat und Leben; **No 148** Bringet dem Herrn Ehre seines Namens; **No 149** Man singet mit Freuden vom Sieg; **No 150** Nach dir, Herr, verlanget mich; **No 151** Süsser Trost, mein Jesus kömmt; **No 152** Tritt auf die Glaubensbahn; **No 153** Schau, lieber Gott, wie meine Feind; **No 154** Mein liebster Jesus ist verloren; **No 155** Mein Gott, wie lang, ach lange; **No 156** Ich steh mit einem Fuss im Grabe; **No 157** Ich lasse dich nicht, du segnest mich denn; **No 158** Der Friede sei mit dir; **No 159** Sehet, wir gehn hinauf gen Jerusalem

No 160 (spurious); **No 161** Komm, du süsse Todesstunde; **No 162** Ach! ich sehe, jetzt, da ich zur Hochzeit gehe; **No 163** Nur jedem das Seine; **No 164** Ihr, die ihr euch von Christo nennet; **No 165**

O heilges Geist- und Wasserbad; **No 166** Wo gehest du hin?; **No 167** Ihr Menschen, rühmet Gottes Liebe; **No 168** Tue Rechnung! Donnerwort; **No 169** Gott soll allein mein Herze haben; **No 170** Vergnügte Ruh', beliebte Seelenlust; **No 171** Gott, wie dein Name, so ist auch dein Ruhm; **No 172** Erschallet, ihr Lieder; **No 173** Erhöhtes Fleisch und Blut; **No 174** Ich liebe den Höchsten von ganzem Gemüte; **No 175** Er rufet seinen Schafen mit Namen; **No 176** Es ist ein trotzig, und verzagt Ding; **No 177** Ich ruf zu dir, Herr Jesu Christ; **No 178** Wo Gott der Herr nicht bei uns hält; **No 179** Siehe zu, dass deine Gottesfurcht; **No 180** Schmücke dich, o liebe Seele

No 181 Leichtgesinnte Flattergeister; **No 182** Himmelskönig, sei willkommen; **No 183** Sie werden euch in den Bann tun; **No 184** Erwünschtes Freudenlicht; **No 185** Barmherziges Herze der ewigen Liebe; **No 186** Ärgre dich, o Seele, nicht; **No 187** Es wartet alles auf dich; **No 188** Ich habe meine Zuversicht; **No 189** (spurious); **No 190** Singet dem Herrn ein neues Lied!; **No 191** Gloria in excelsis Deo; **No 192** Nun danket alle Gott; **No 193** Ihr Tore zu Zion; **No 194** Höchsterwünschtes Freudenfest; **No 195** Dem Gerechten muss das Licht; **No 196** Der Herr denket an uns; **No 197** Gott ist unsre Zuversicht; **No 197a** Ehre sei Gott in der Höhe; **No 198** Laß Fürstin, lass noch einen Strahl, 'Trauer Ode'; **No 199** Mein Herze schwimmt im Blut; **No 200** Bekennen will ich seinen Namen

Volume 1 – Nos 16, 33, 37, 42, 56, 61, 72, 80, 82, 97, 113, 132, 133, 170. **Volume 2** – Nos 22, 23, 44, 54, 57, 85, 86, 92, 98, 111, 114, 135, 155, 159, 165, 167, 188. **Volume 3** – Nos 17, 35, 87, 90, 99, 106, 117, 123, 153, 161, 168, 172, 173, 182, 199. **Volume 4** – Nos 7, 13, 45, 69, 81, 102, 116, 122, 130, 138, 144, 149, 150, 169, 196. **Volume 5** – Nos 6, 26, 27, 46, 55, 94, 96, 107, 115, 139, 156, 163, 164, 178, 179. **Volume 6** – Nos 2, 3, 8, 60, 62, 78, 93, 103, 128, 145, 151, 154, 171, 185, 186, 192. **Volume 7** – Nos 9, 36, 47, 73, 91, 110, 121, 125, 129, 152, 157, 166, 184, 198. **Volume 8** – Nos 18, 30, 40, 49, 79, 84, 88, 89, 100, 108, 136, 140, 176, 187, 194. **Volume 9** – Nos 1, 5, 14, 20, 32, 38, 50, 51, 58, 63, 83, 104, 109, 162, 183, 195. **Volume 10** – Nos 21, 25, 28, 39, 43, 48, 52, 59, 65, 75, 119, 137, 143, 146, 175, 180, 197. **Volume 11** – Nos 4, 10, 12, 64, 70, 71, 74, 76, 95, 101, 105, 124, 127, 131, 134, 158, 177. **Volume 12** – Nos 19, 24, 29, 31, 34, 41, 66, 67, 68, 77, 112, 120, 126, 147, 148, 174, 181 **Ruth Holton, Marjon Strijk** sops **Sytse Buwalda** counterten **Marcel Beekman, Martinus Leusink, Nico van der Meel, Knut Schoch** tens **Bas Ramselaar** bass **Holland Boys Choir; Netherlands Bach Collegium / Pieter Jan Leusink**
Brilliant Boxes ⑤ (12 five-disc sets) 99363/99364/99367/99368/99369/99370/99371/99373/99374/99377-80 (3691' · DDD) Texts included Ⓢ●

Brilliant Classics has, through licensing and creative plundering of old catalogues, has contrived its own Bach Edition. Rather more surprising is that within this patchwork of miscellaneous performances comes a brand new set of the complete cantatas. How on earth can such a project be viable as a realistic competitor to the

meticulously prepared work of leading exponents, or even prudent financially? The answer lies in the spirit of the task, one clearly designed to provide a large audience with the opportunity to experience all these masterworks on period instruments, at an affordable price. A ridiculous price actually. The practice of speed-recording represents quite an art in itself, attempting to engender inspiration while also ensuring acceptable standards of performance and recording – all within an intensive low-budget schedule. Unsurprisingly then, Pieter Jan Leusink's standard-sized Holland Boys Choir and Netherlands Bach Collegium deliver a rather uneven collection of performances with highs and lows in close proximity.

Volumes 1-8: Some readings are simply too indistinct to warrant comparison with more considered and glamorous competition, doubtless in those cases where not enough time has been allowed for the performers to find their interpretative feet beyond merely 'getting it together'. Some, like that of the 'Trauer Ode', miss the point with overt force dispatching fragrant delicacy, while a healthy number constitute refreshing accounts disarmingly caught at the point of discovery. You take the rough with the smooth in this roller-coaster enterprise.

If there's one overriding Achilles heel, it's the unreliability of the solo singing. The tenor contributions, in particular, too often undermine Leusink's generally bright and well-judged conceptions. Volume 5 is a case in point, where Knut Schoch, in the solo tenor cantata, No 55, is simply not up to the task. Judging by the qualities the less ubiquitous Marcel Beekman demonstrates in a beautifully executed No 164, he would have been a better first choice throughout. The most seasoned of the tenors, Nico van der Meel, becomes more authoritative as the set progresses. Soprano Marjon Strijk often finds Bach's taxing melisma a squiggle too far, in marked contrast to the expert if somewhat recessed singing of Ruth Holton and the excellent bass contributions of Bas Ramselaar (they also combine well in their many duets, such as the rollicking No 49). Ramselaar is the best singer on the set and would, for the most part, grace any of the current series; he has the grainy intimacy of Klaus Mertens, and also a burly resonance when it suits him. His reading of 'Ich will den Kreuzstab', No 56, is a commendable achievement by any standards, and there are fine arias in the splendid Ascension works, Nos 37 and 128, as well as in 36, 100 and 108.

Further on the credit side, the boy-led choruses can irradiate a compellingly sure-footed and unmannered perspective of Bach, as in Nos 33 and 97 and in the refreshing and unselfconscious clarity of intent sweetly imparted in Nos 94, 6 and 117; the chorales are also luminously immediate and affecting.

Other cantatas are rather down-played, such as Nos 139 and 62, but are still worthy and enjoyable as honest performances in an unpretentious Kappellmeister mould. If there's a shortage of refinement and blend in No 133 or spit and polish in the rhythmically exacting Nos 26 and 33, bright and energetic declamation is agreeably more the rule than the exception in Leusink's no-airs-and-graces approach. In the general firmament of new cantata recordings, these spontaneous performances stand comparison more in terms of individual movements (many, including several mentioned above, of real conviction and distinction) than complete pieces. Of the handful of cantatas where a special vision of the whole work is unanimously conveyed, with the performers firing on all cylinders, highlights are (in no particular order) Nos 57; 87, 33, 42, 192, 45, 88, 176, 125 and 129. If the choral movements are the best things in these sets, there are still some memorable arias (to counter an abundance of ropey ones) with which Volumes 1, 2, 4, 6, and 8 are particularly well endowed.

Volumes 9-12: Here, Leusink traverses the final peak with far more consistently enduring accounts than the comparative 'hit or miss' of the earlier readings, though unsurprisingly for an enterprise designed around tight rehearse-record schedules, there will always be scrappy moments.

More encouragingly, there's also a striking and rare quality here that shines through more strongly than in most of the earlier volumes, and gives Leusink and his Dutch colleagues genuine credentials. It's the unmannered and straight-forward approach to delivering the essence of the work, the honesty and means to get directly to its heart through real 'performance', often at the point of discovery. In this respect it recalls the earlier recordings from Leonhardt/Harnoncourt, a set that should be increasingly revisited for that very reason. For all the 'al dente' movements here, there are as many refreshingly uninhibited and distinguished readings, notably Nos 119, 43, 74, 197, 127, 104 and 148. There's a keen ear for the fundamental 'conceit' of the music upon which spontaneous music-making happens 'as if live'; unassuming, common sensical and unegotistical, the earthy Kapellmeister approach reminds one of the unspectacular (and occasionally a touch unimaginative) but free-breathing performances by the likes of Karl Ristenpart, Wolfgang Gönnenwein, Fritz Lehmann, Felix Prohaska and Fritz Werner in the 1950s and 60s.

Ears attuned to the refined and homogeneous textures of the top Baroque orchestras will find the grainy and sometimes rather thin violins altogether too disturbing. Others may find this more acceptable and, at times, even liberating, especially when joined by the wonderfully colourful wind playing and robust brass playing; the oboe of Peter Frankenberg, in particular, is one of the set's greatest qualities, though not far behind is the trumpet consort, led by Susan Williams. Notable again is the outstanding bass singing of Bas Ramselaar, whose resonant warmth and musicianly response to text is the most significant vocal strength in the set. Also to be admired are the two main sopranos, Ruth

Holton and Marjon Strijk. Both have a vocal timbre of the effervescent and light variety though they bring much radiance and projection to their music-making, and far more accuracy in matters of tuning than in the earlier boxes. Holton sings splendidly in the two demanding arias in No 75, with breeziness in No 52 and loving understanding in the stunning *cantabile* of No 120 (which Bach used in a later version of the G major Violin Sonata), and with great cultivation in BWV31. She sails through the treacherous No 51 with great élan. Strijk brings considerable fluency to her arias in both Nos 25 and 28.

The alto part is less appealingly taken. Sytse Buwalda should not have been lumbered with the responsibility for all the alto arias, several movements of which represent some of Bach's most treasured examples of reflective ardour (why not use mezzos, contraltos and even boy altos for these parts, rather than the often excellent but over-used countertenor?). Despite Buwalda's unsteadiness, he occasionally delivers something reasonable though, such as in Nos 148 and 83. Exactly the same complaint can be levelled at Knut Schoch, a courageous tenor but one without the capacity for variation of colour in his sound, as you hear and expects from both Paul Agnew for Koopman (Erato) or Gerd Türk for Suzuki on BIS. Too often, the upper tessitura just isn't there or else he can't control it. Luckily, Nico van der Meel is wheeled out for the big ones and he's splendid in both 'Ja, tausendmal tausend' in No 43, as well as No 74. In No 31, he's redolent of the deeply touching singing of Helmut Krebs for Werner. Also used is Marcel Beekman, who shines in No 48 and projects a palpable joie de vivre with Ramselaar in the fine duet, 'Wie will ich mich freuen' from No 146, as does Holton with Ramselaar in the duet of No 32.

The boy-led Holland Choir and 'period' band, Netherlands Bach Collegium, are again central to the success and distinctive essence of this series. The teamwork in the choir is admirably demonstrated in some of the most difficult pieces, such as the large 'da capo' chorus of No 34, the fervent No 197 and infectiously crackling No 70, resulting in white-hot expositions of thrilling proportions. Leusink's success elsewhere comes largely through his admirably well-judged feeling for tempos and a means of accentuation which drives the music forward inexorably. But there's, a fine line here between luminous vitality and panic; the latter afflicts control in some choruses where Bach just can't be learnt in a rush: Nos 65, 48 and 137 are examples where phrases are snatched, or over-sung, to the detriment of both textural cohesion and intonation, as well as general quality of sound.

In sum, these readings deserve to be recognised, primarily for their attractive and well-measured strides, but also for a lack of dogma or self-importance. Hard-driven and intermittently rough in places (especially string intonation), they're nevertheless consistently honest, rarely disastrous, and occasionally illuminating statements. Bachians, old and new, should investigate the series with an eager circumspection, taking the rough with the smooth but relishing the open-hearted spirit of the enterprise. The best performances will bring the listener close to the solar plexus of Bach's 'Kantatenwelt'.

Cantatas Nos 8, 78, 91, 99, 107, 111, 114, 116, 121, 124 & 135 Ⓟ
Lisa Larsson, Sibylla Rubens sops **Annette Markert** contr **Christoph Prégardien** ten **Klaus Mertens** bass **Amsterdam Baroque Choir and Orchestra / Ton Koopman**
Erato ③ 8573-85842-2 (201 minutes: DDD)   Ⓕ

These 11 cantatas represent the absolute kernel of Bach's cantata *oeuvre*, and Koopman's series too, as the great 'chorale' cantatas take fullest flight. Economy of means is one feature of Bach's increasing technical prowess and artistic maturity, but the formal 'straitjacket' of the chorale seems only to have catalysed an even greater imagination.

Koopman's approach is an instinctively musical one, as opposed to one drawn from, say, a reconstructed 'religious' context or any newfangled theory on performance rectitude. This is refreshingly realised in the effervescent and abstracted instrumental quality of No 124 (where the circular thread of oboe d'amore figuration is beautifully articulated) or the thrill of the chase in No 91 (probably not one of Bach's best works in the cycle). Koopman's infectious energy rubs off on the eloquent Christoph Prégardien, whose performances throughout are truly outstanding, from the poetic fluidity of 'Troste mir, Jesu' in No 135, the suspended animation of 'Wo wird in diesem Jammertale' in No 114 and the galant, purring line of 'Drum ich mich ihm' from No 107. His fellow soloists do not fare consistently quite as well. Klaus Mertens exhibits timbral majesty in arguably the best works in the set, Nos 8 and 78, where he's clearly caught up by the music's unstoppable momentum. Yet, there's a discernable line between this and when engagement is limited to merely covering the ground (for instance 'Auf ihn magst' in No 107).

Lisa Larsson, the soprano, is very competent, as she shows in her numerous duets with Annette Markert – who herself has a pleasing if not particularly radiant sound – but this is music whose expressive and colouristic potential deserves better. Sadly, the estimable Sybilla Rubens sings only on the Terzetto of No 116.

However, as mentioned before about this series, you have to count your blessings for distinctly unfussy performances allied to top-class execution – and the Amsterdammers are really top-drawer. Despite the occasional frustration, Nos 99, 124, 111, 78 and 114 can stand alongside the best in the deservedly rich discography of Bach's cantatas.

Cantatas Nos 24, 25, 67, 95, 105, 136, 144, 147, 148, 173, 181 & 184 Ⓟ
Lisa Larsson sop **Bogna Bartosz, Elisabeth von Magnus** mezzos **Gerd Türk** ten **Klaus Mertens** bass **Amsterdam Baroque Choir and Orchestra / Ton Koopman** hpd/org
Erato ③ 3984-23141-2 (214' · DDD) Texts and translations included   Ⓕ

The seventh volume of Ton Koopman's projected complete cantata survey contains pieces which Bach performed at Leipzig in 1723 and 1724. Koopman's line-up of soloists has been taking a while to settle down and, in this volume, the alto solos are shared between Elisabeth von Magnus, one of the greatest strengths of the series so far, and Bogna Bartosz. All the tenor arias are sung by Gerd Türk, and Lisa Larsson and Klaus Mertens provide their stylish and warm-hearted performances as soprano and bass soloists respectively.

As well as containing three superb examples of Bach's genius in the cantata medium – Nos 67, 105 and 147 – Vol 7 contains a handful of rarely heard pieces, of which No 136, with its brilliant opening chorus, is perhaps the most immediately striking. At the opposite end of the affective scale is the sombre, penitential chorus which determines the prevalent character of No 25. This technically ingenious double fugue in E minor is difficult to carry off convincingly in performance but Koopman, with his clearly defined contrapuntal strands and responsive choir, succeeds better than any rival version. The gracefulness and fluency in his direction come together rewardingly in No 95. This highly original cantata, with its syncopations, dissonances, bold key changes, and references to four hymns with their associated melodies, all in the opening chorus, is, quite simply, breathtaking. The music commands our attention at every turn, disturbing and pleasing our senses in equal measure. But perhaps it's the following two movements which most readily capture our imagination and win our hearts. Lisa Larsson sings the former with ingenuous charm while Gerd Türk, in the latter, seems to sustain Bach's mercilessly high vocal range with the greatest of ease.

The overall picture of this set is mainly convincing, with some very fine playing and singing – only the occasionally over-assertive projection of countertenor voices from the choir fails to please. Any disappointment here, though, seems relatively slight beside the many excellent contributions of Koopman's artists. If, on balance, No 105 is a shade lacking in strength of purpose, then such feelings are ameliorated by the wellnigh perfect partnership of Larsson and oboist, Marcel Ponseele, in its poignant soprano aria, certainly one of the highest peaks in a stimulating issue.

Cantatas Nos 50, 50 (recons Kleinbussink), 59, 69, 69a, 75, 76, 104, 179, 186 & 190 Ⓟ
Ruth Ziesak sop **Elisabeth von Magnus** mez **Paul**

Agnew ten Klaus Mertens bass Amsterdam
Baroque Choir and Orchestra / Ton Koopman org
Erato ③ 3984-21629-2 (195' · DDD) Texts and
translations included   Ⓕ🅾

In his sixth volume of Bach's complete cantatas,
Koopman is engaged in the great Leipzig period
from 1723. Bach's inaugural offering was a pair
of substantial bipartite cantatas, Nos 75 and 76.
Koopman gives us the second one initially, *Die
Himmel erzählen die Ehre Gottes*, in a muscular
and assertive performance. The fine opening
chorus, with its swaggering trumpet obbligato,
is zestfully negotiated and appropriately full-
blooded. The same commitment and character
are plentiful in the formidably worked-out contrapuntal edifice of No 75 – a movement passionately declaiming the rewards of seeking
God – and the wonderfully evocative imagery in
No 104, *Du Hirte Israel, höre*. Memorable for
different reasons is *Singet dem Herrn*, No 190, a
cantata whose opening two movements require
major reconstruction. Koopman has completed
the task with a dynamic scoring around the
existing vocal parts. If a somewhat over-elaborate setting, it's nevertheless thrilling, and
employs the sort of fervent Reformation-like
unisons and belting brass which can't fail to stir.

Koopman has found in Ruth Ziesak a soprano
who can get round the notes, sing consistently
in tune (despite one under-par aria in No 186)
and express the meaning of the music with
rhetorical personality. She dances around the
lithe 'Ich nehme mein Leiden' from No 75.
This cantata abounds in arresting arias, none
more so than the delicious 'Mein Jesus soll', a
creation of such ingenious and agreeable
melodic inflexion that Paul Agnew can but relish it devotedly. Both Agnew's and Klaus
Mertens's singing throughout are a joy, a happy
blend of technical security, musicianly shaping
and tonal elegance. Elisabeth von Magnus is the
weak link. Her contribution to the stirring
Part 2 of No 76 isn't especially undistinguished,
but her languid sound is repeatedly enervating,
and too often the pitch dips unacceptably. In all
other respects this is quite a turn-up for the
books after the hits and misses of previous volumes. Bach was clearly intent on impressing his
new employers with the most accomplished
work he could produce; you only have to hear
the richness of these scores (a bonanza here for
those who like trumpets, and brilliantly played
too) to suppose that Koopman has found similar
inspiration at exactly the right time.

Cantatas Nos 18, 143, 152, 155 & 161   Ⓟ
Midori Suzuki, Ingrid Schmithüsen sops Yoshikazu
Mera counterten Makoto Sakurada ten Peter Kooy
bass Bach Collegium Japan / Masaaki Suzuki org
BIS CD841 (78' · DDD) Texts and translations
included   Ⓕ🅾🅾

The fifth volume of Bach's sacred cantatas performed by the Bach Collegium Japan continues
their Weimar survey with five pieces written

between *c*1713 and 1716. It begins with No 18,
performed in its Weimar version – Bach later
revived it for Leipzig, adding two treble
recorders to the purely string texture of the
upper parts of the earlier composition. The
scoring of No 152 is more diverse, featuring in
its opening Sinfonia a viola d'amore, viola da
gamba, oboe and recorder.

A conspicuous feature of No 155 is its melancholy duet for alto and tenor with bassoon
obbligato. While the vocal writing sustains
something of the character of a lament the wonderfully athletic, arpeggiated bassoon solo provides a magical third voice. The accompanying
essay is confused here, emphasising the importance of a solo oboe which in fact has no place at
all in this work. No 161 is a piece of sustained
beauty, scored for a pair of treble recorders,
obbligato organ, strings and continuo. Bach's
authorship of No 143 has sometimes been questioned. Much of it is un-Bach-like, yet at times
it's hard to envisage another composer's hand.

The performances are of unmatched excellence. Suzuki's direction never falters and his
solo vocalists go from strength to strength as the
series progresses. Suzuki makes a richly rewarding contribution with beautifully poised
singing, a crystal-clear voice and an upper range
that only very occasionally sounds at all threatened. Mera and Sakurada sustain a delicately
balanced partnership in the elegiac duet of
No 155, the limpid bassoon-playing completing
this trio of outstanding beauty. Kooy is a tower
of strength, a sympathetic partner to Suzuki in
the dance-like duet between Jesus and the Soul
(No 152), and resonantly affirmative in his aria
from the same cantata. But the highest praise
should go to Mera and Sakurada for their affecting performance in No 161. All the elements of
this superb cantata are understood and deeply
felt by all concerned. The disc is admirably
recorded and, apart from the aforementioned
confusion, painstakingly and informatively documented.

Cantatas Nos 21 & 31   Ⓟ
Monika Frimmer sop Gerd Türk ten Peter Kooy
bass Bach Collegium Japan / Masaaki Suzuki
BIS CD851 (68' · DDD) Texts and translations
included   Ⓕ

Both of these are Weimar compositions, dating
from *c*1713 and 1715 respectively, and both
were later sung at Leipzig. Where No 21 is concerned, the performance history is complex
since Bach, who clearly and understandably set
great store by this extended and profoundly
expressive piece, made no fewer than four versions of it. Following what was probably its
second Weimar performance, in 1714, Bach
produced a new version which he used as a test-
piece in Hamburg's Jacobikirche, when applying for an organist's post there in 1720. It's this
version, for soprano and bass soloists only, in
which the parts are transposed from C minor to
D minor that forms the basis of the present

recording. Suzuki offers listeners an opportunity, by way of an appendix, of hearing Bach's alternative thoughts on certain sections of the cantata. These are meticulously prepared and affectingly declaimed performances. Listen, for instance, to the beautifully articulated and delicately placed bassoon quavers in the poignant opening Sinfonia of No 21. This is most sensitively done and an auspicious beginning to the work. String playing isn't always quite as clean as it could be but the instrumental expertise is impressive. The solo line-up is strong, with Monika Frimmer sustaining several demanding soprano arias with eloquence and tonal warmth. Gerd Türk and Peter Kooy are secure and expressive, and the singing of the 18-voice choir of women's and men's voices is impressive, though tenors sound strained in the first chorus of No 21.

Cantatas Nos 22, 23 & 75   P

Midori Suzuki sop **Yoshikazu Mera** counterten **Gerd Türk** ten **Peter Kooy** bass **Bach Collegium Japan / Masaaki Suzuki** org
BIS CD901 (64' · DDD) Texts and translations included   F**OO**

This eighth volume of Bach Collegium Japan's Bach cantata series bridges the period between Bach's departure from Cöthen and his arrival at Leipzig, early in 1723. *Du wahrer Gott und Davids Sohn* (No 23) was mainly written at Cöthen, while *Jesus nahm zu sich die Zwölfe* (No 22) must have been composed almost immediately on Bach's reaching Leipzig. The remaining cantata, *Die Elenden sollen essen* is on an altogether grander scale, in two parts, each of seven movements. The performances maintain the high standards of singing, playing and scholarship set by the previous issues in this series. There are little insecurities here and there – the oboes, which play a prominent role in each of the three pieces, aren't always perfectly in agreement over tuning – but the careful thought given to the words, their significance and declamation, and the skill with which they're enlivened by the realisation of Bach's expressive musical vocabulary, remain immensely satisfying. The disciplined, perceptively phrased and beautifully sustained singing of the two choral numbers of No 23 illuminate the words at every turn, savouring the seemingly infinite expressive nuances of the music. As for No 75, we can only imagine the astonishment with which Leipzig ears must have attuned to its music. In this absolutely superb piece Bach entertains us with a breathtaking stylistic diversity. Polyphony, fugue, chorale fantasia, *da capo* aria, instrumental sinfonia, varied recitative, wonderful oboe writing and a rhythmic *richesse* all contribute to the special distinction both of this cantata and No 76. Lose no time in becoming acquainted with this one. It reaches, you might say, those parts that other performances do not.

Cantatas Nos 37, 86, 104 & 166   P

Yukari Nonoshita sop **Robin Blaze** counterten **Makoto Sakurada** ten **Stephan MacLeod** bass **Bach Collegium Japan / Masaaki Suzuki**
BIS BIS-CD1261 (64' · DDD) Texts and translations included   F

The first work on this CD is a little-known gem, No 86, *Wahrlich, wahrlich, ich sage euch* ('Verily, I say unto you'). Succinct and imploring, the listener follows the doctrinal and attentive tone set so marvellously by a composer arrested by the intensity of Christ's promise: 'Whatsoever ye shall ask the Father in my name, he will give it you.' Suzuki, as ever, chooses exceptionally well-judged tempi throughout, leaves no stone unturned in his confident preparedness and also introduces a fine new bass to the series, Stephan MacLeod, as the 'vox Christi'.

Of the other three works here, none is particularly long but each contains a central movement of special significance. In No 37 it's the chorale duet of a stanza from 'How brightly shines the morning star', sung with disarming fluency by Yukari Nonoshita and Robin Blaze, and in No 166, the tidy tenor Makoto Sakurada gives a sensitive, if somewhat under-nourished, account of 'Ich will an den Himmel denken'. This cantata also boasts a ravishing and peerless 'Man nehme sich in Acht' from Blaze.

In the great bass aria 'Beglückte Herde', MacLeod gives a gentle and soft-grained performance (very much in the spirit of Suzuki's usual bass, Peter Kooij) as Christ's sheep are offered the rewards of faith. Some will wish for a more involving performance of this highly original work, as Richter provides (from 1973) – with a majestic Fischer-Dieskau – and the radiant spontaneity of Pieter Jan Leusink, which arguably boasts the best bass singing in recent years from Bas Ramselaar.

Suzuki's volume will, however, satisfy many tastes. These are consistently impressive performances, beautifully recorded and Suzuki communicates Bach with unalloyed joy.

Cantatas Nos 40, 60, 70 & 90   P

Yukari Nonoshita sop **Robin Blaze** counterten **Gerd Türk** ten **Peter Kooy** bass **Bach Collegium Japan / Masaaki Suzuki**
BIS BISCD1111 (68' · DDD)   F

Masaaki Sukuki here brings us four more fine cantatas, of which *Wachet! betet! betet! wachet!* (No 70) stands apart as one of Bach's most graphically dramatic and cohesive choral achievements. The first movement is justly celebrated, its tautness, forbidding fanfares and diminished chords representing the coming of Christ and the Last Judgement. The apocalyptic backdrop fascinated early interpreters of Bach in the 1950s and 60s, notably Felix Prohaska with his menacing pacing and sepia-like textures offset against a Viennese elegance.

Suzuki's direction is more pressing and urgent in style; his less theatrical, more meticulous approach allows the filigree in the instrumental writing to emerge in a way too rarely heard. Koopman (Erato) has the edge in conveying a more harrowing perspective to the first movement, but the remainder of the cantata is beautifully crafted by Suzuki, demonstrating the artistic conviction and vocal bravura of Robin Blaze in 'Wenn kommt' (though his soaring tones are heard to even better effect in No 60). The pivotal aria in No 70 is the radiant 'Hebt euer Haupt empor', a succinct piece whose open-heartedness requires something more than Gerd Türk and Suzuki can give. This is where Georg Jelden for Fritz Werner (Erato) sets the gold standard for conveying this gem's utter simplicity of expression.

The most compelling performances on this disc are in the busy counterpoint, such as the opening chorus of No 40, 'Dazu ist erschienen', the vibrant tenor aria 'Christenkinder', which shows off BCJ's exemplary wind section, and (to return to the horror of Judgement) the peerlessly executed bass aria of No 90, where Peter Kooy and the obbligato trumpet of Toshio Shimada find the perfect synergy. But it's in the stirring and decidedly prescient *Sturm und Drang* quality of No 60, 'O Ewigkeit, du Donnerwort', that Suzuki's infectious grasp of pulse, biting accentuation and luminous textures take fullest flight: he entertains no half-measures in the opening chorus. All round, yet another prestigious addition to the series.

Cantatas Nos 48, 89, 109 & 148   **P**
Midori Suzuki *sop* **Robin Blaze** *counterten* **Gerd Türk** *ten* **Chiyuki Urano** *bass* **Bach Collegium Japan / Masaaki Suzuki**
BIS BIS-CD1081 (66' · DDD) Texts and translations included   Ⓕ

Masaaki Suzuki's considered approach to this oeuvre is what marks him out as a distinctive voice in current Bach performance. This volume reveals much of the best in the series so far: consistently good singing, a sustained familiarity with the music (not always to be taken for granted in the studio) beyond mere pristine executancy, and Suzuki's guiding hand which is especially attentive to the textual motivation in Bach's music.

A broader approach seems to win the day for much in this disc, as can be admired in the defining logic of the fine opening fugal chorus of *Bringet dem Herrn* (No 148), whose resplendent contrapuntal bravura takes thrilling flight in the chapel's ringing acoustic. Here, and rather less so in the relatively unpolished Leusink reading, the paragraphs connect in a way which ensures an inexorable momentum and sustained uplift – which was rarely achieved in performances of this work from the early days of Bach cantata recordings. The instrumental and obbligato playing throughout is of a high order (if not perhaps boasting the depth of string quality of Koopman), doubtless inspired by the alto and tenor of Robin Blaze and Gerd Türk respec-

tively – who are the main soloists in all four works. Both sing with delectation and authority. In No 109 Suzuki eschews over-characterisation and instead accentuates the instrumental profile as the means of gathering the disparate melodic ideas. There are many other highlights here. The plangent opening lament-chorus of No 48 is slower than Koopman's, but it's a remarkably controlled, even and luminous creation. If not always emotionally exhaustive, Bach Collegium Japan explore the naked emptiness in this work, leaving you feeling properly wrung out. A notable achievement.

Cantatas Nos 65, 81, 83 & 190   **P**
Robin Blaze *counterten* **James Gilchrist** *ten* **Peter Kooy** *bass* **Bach Collegium Japan / Masaaki Suzuki**
BIS BIS-CD1311 (70' · DDD) Texts and translations included   ⒻⓄ

Another meticulously prepared volume in this distinguished series comprises the late festivities of Christmas 1724 and two Epiphany works from a few weeks later. Taken from the first of Bach's annual cantata cycles, these four works reveal the astonishing variety and textual (and textural) coloration which the composer exercised in this period of free-wheeling creativity from his early months of employment in Leipzig.

While the instrumentation of horns, recorders, oboes da caccia and strings in No 65 captures the spiciness of eastern promise, Suzuki imbues the whole with a relaxed and soft-grained pastoral regality. This is further exemplified in the easy delivery of the aria 'Nimm mich dir zu eigen' in which James Gilchrist performs with supreme awareness, beckoning the listener to inhabit his world: this is exceptionally characterised singing by any standards and Suzuki shouldn't look back.

No less successful is the way Bach Collegium Japan embraces the Christmas message in the incomplete Cantata No 190. Imaginative reconstruction can bring this work to life and Masato Suzuki has found a majestic solution to the opening chorus, which his namesake realises with abandon.

Cantata No 81 is a mesmerisingly compact piece in which St Matthew's account of Jesus calming the storm provides arresting imagery for three fine arias. The middle movement is the set-piece *par excellence*, truly operatic in its posturing bravura and burning focus of conceit. Gilchrist again brings tremendous commitment and open-heartedness with the kind of cultivated vocal *élan* of great Bach tenors in the Helmut Krebs and Anton Dermota mould. Both Robin Blaze and Peter Kooy perform their arias with customary distinction. Altogether, an extremely fine volume, finer than any rival.

Cantatas Nos 71, 106 & 131   **P**
Midori Suzuki, Aki Yanagisawa *sops* **Yoshikazu Mera** *counterten* **Gerd Türk** *ten* **Peter Kooy** *bass*

Bach Collegium Japan / Masaaki Suzuki
BIS CD781 (63' · DDD) Texts and translations
included   Ⓕ

Here these artists are abreast of current thinking concerning Baroque style, yet sometimes
you find yourself longing for a little more
expression and a little less fashionable orthodoxy. The three cantatas included here are
among Bach's earliest essays in the form. Nos
106 and 131 (c1707) belong to the Mühlhausen
period, while No 71 was written in 1708. By and
large, Suzuki has chosen effective tempos,
though there are notable exceptions. One of
these affects the beautiful Sonatina for
recorders and viola da gamba that introduces
the *Actus tragicus* (No 106), a funeral piece of
startling intensity. Suzuki feels too slow here,
adding a full 40 seconds on to performances by
virtually all his rivals. Elsewhere, and above all
in his choice of soloists, Suzuki fields an exceptional team. We can feel this especially in the
effortlessly projected singing of Midori Suzuki
(Nos 71 and 131) and Aki Yanagisawa (No 106),
the uncluttered declamation of Gerd Türk, and
the resonant contributions by Peter Kooy. The
countertenor here lacks either conviction or
consistent aural charm. The Choir is well
drilled and, as with the solo element, the voices
respond urgently to the spirit of the text. Listen
to the thrice supplicatory 'Israel' in the concluding chorus of No 131 for one such example.

Cantatas Nos 105[a], 179 & 186[b]
Miah Persson *sop* [ab]**Robin Blaze** *counterten*
Makoto Sakurada *ten* **Peter Kooy** *bass* **Bach
Collegium Japan / Masaaki Suzuki**
BIS CD951 (63' · DDD) Texts and translations
included   Ⓕⵔ

Bach Collegium Japan's eloquent advance into
the rich repository of cantatas composed during
Bach's first year at Leipzig is distinguished in
Vol 10 by Masaaki Suzuki's remarkable instinct
for the emotional core of each of these three
works. Experiencing *Herr, gehe nicht ins Gericht*
(No 105) reveals a sense of open-hearted fervour and contemplation, never for a minute
cloying or self-regarding at the expense of
vibrant expression. This is a work embued with
a rich discography, yet what Suzuki uniquely
achieves, compelling in the opening chorus, is
an intensity born of subtle contrast in vocal and
instrumental articulation, underpinned by his
uncanny ability to choose a tempo which provides for lyrical intimacy and organic gesture, as
the respective texts demand. Suzuki grasps the
magnificent nobility of the composer's inspired
musical commentary on the human soul in No
105. Miah Persson exhibits sustained control
and delectable purity of tone in the continuo-
less 'Wie zittern und wanken' and 'Liebster
Gott' from No 179. With Peter Kooy's cathartic recitative singing (preparing the spirit of salvation) and the beautifully balanced tenor aria
and final chorale, Herreweghe's elegant and fra-

grant 1990 account, a clear leader until now, has
a companion on the top rung.

The bipartite Trinity cantata, *Ärgre dich, o
Seele, nicht* (No 186), revised from a Weimar
version of 1716, conveys equally Suzuki's assurance and vision. Perhaps the choruses which
frame Part 1 are a touch short on gravitas (and
tuning is intermittently awry in the first) but
here, and in the formidable opening movement
of No 179 rhythmic incision is the order of the
day. This is another first-rate achievement (the
soloists are slightly recessed but the recorded
sound is excellent). Arguably the most complete
and mature offering in the series so far.

Cantatas Nos 119b & 194a   p
[b]**Yoshie Hida,** [a]**Yukari Nonoshita** *sops* [b]**Kirsten
Sollek-Avella** *contr* [a]**Makoto Sakurada** *ten*
[a]**Jochen Kupfer** *bar* [b]**Peter Kooij** *bass* **Bach
Collegium Japan / Masaaki Suzuki**
BIS BISCD1131 (63' · DDD) Texts and translations
included   Ⓕ

Masaaki Suzuki gives No 194 a fittingly airy
charm, heard most infectiously in 'Hilf, Gott'
where an underlying Gavotte (with resonances
of the final movement of the *Wedding* Cantata,
No 202) finds bright-eyed soprano, Yukari
Nonoshita, in confident and beguiling voice.
She's most accomplished throughout and delectably joins the gentle and receptive baritone
Jochen Kupfer in 'O wie wohl' ist uns
geschehn', a bucolic minuet-style duet. This is,
all told, the most persuasive reading on disc, and
supersedes both Rilling's stiff reading and even
Harnoncourt's cultivated (if slightly hit-and-
miss) performance, notable also for the presence of a young Thomas Hampson.

Harnoncourt, however, comes out better in
one of the grandest French-overture cantatas
Bach was to write, 'Preise Jerusalem' (No 119).
Composed to honour the new Leipzig town
council, Bach really pushed the boat out. Suzuki
never quite boasts either the grand sonic cohesion of Philippe Herreweghe's urgent account
or the thrilling characterisation of Harnoncourt. Strongly recommended nevertheless for
Suzuki's superb reading of No 194.

Cantatas Nos 7, 20, 30, 39, 75 & 167
Gillian Keith, Joanne Lunn *sops* **Wilke te
Brummelstroete** *contr* **Paul Agnew** *ten* **Dietrich
Henschel** *bass* **Monteverdi Choir; English Baroque
Soloists / John Eliot Gardiner**
Soli Deo Gloria ② SDG101 (149' · DDD · T/t)   Ⓜ⦿⦿
Recorded live at St Giles Cripplegate, London, 23-6
June 2000

Cantatas Nos 8, 27, 51, 95, 99, 100, 138 & 161
Katharine Fuge, Malin Hartelius *sops* **William
Towers, Robin Tyson** *countertens* **James Gilchrist,
Mark Padmore** *tens* **Thomas Guthrie, Peter
Harvey** *basses* **Monteverdi Choir; English Baroque
Soloists / John Eliot Gardiner**
Soli Deo Gloria ② SDG104 (145' · DDD · T/t)   Ⓜ⦿⦿

Recorded live at the Unser Lieben Frauen, Bremen, Germany, 28 September 2000, and Santo Domingo de Bonaval, Santiago de Compostela, Spain, 7 October 2000

 In 2000 John Eliot Gardiner commemorated the 250th anniversary of Bach's death with the Bach Cantata Pilgrimage, a year-long European tour by the English Baroque Soloists and Monteverdi Choir that presented all of Bach's extant cantatas on the appropriate liturgical feast days. Here are the first two instalments of the complete cycle. Soli Deo Gloria's presentation is first class. The CDs are cased in a handsomely designed hardbound book, complete with texts, translations and Gardiner's extensive, informative notes based on a journal he kept during the pilgrimage.

The interpretations are consistently fine – often superb, in fact – with surprisingly few wrong steps or disappointments, especially given the unusually gruelling performance schedule that produced them. Among the many mind-blowing, beautiful moments is the deliciously syncopated contralto aria from No 30, sung with poise by Wilke te Brummelstroete and graced by playing of magical delicacy from the EBS. And there's the extraordinary opening chorus of No 8, with its seemingly endless melodic tendrils, chiming flute part and plucked strings, sounding like a celestial dance. Special mention must be made of the artistry of tenor Mark Padmore, who maintains his sweet, ringingly clear tone even in the demanding leaps and roulades of his aria in No 95.

It's in delicate or intimate music that Gardiner shines most luminously, and some may find that he unduly emphasises the contemplative. His thoughtful, refined approach is strikingly similar to Suzuki's cycle on BIS, though Gardiner's versions sound just a bit warmer. Although his interpretations offer the finest attributes of period practice – transparency and litheness – there's a long-breathed musicality here that' can be lacking in other accounts.

Cantatas Nos 49, 58 & 82   Ⓟ
Nancy Argenta *sop* **Klaus Mertens** *bass* **La Petite Bande / Sigiswald Kuijken** *vn*
Accent ACC9395 (63' · DDD) Recorded 1993.
Texts and translations included   ⒻⓄⓄ

Few readers will be disappointed either by the music or the performances on this disc. It features one of Bach's very finest cantatas, *Ich habe genug* (No 82) for solo baritone, and two 'Dialogue' cantatas for soprano and bass. Leaving out for the moment such issues as instrumental timbre, Sigiswald Kuijken is among the most thoughtful of present-day practitioners of Baroque music. That isn't to say you'll always like what he does, but that he always has a good reason for doing it, and is prepared to defend it to the end. Here, there are no complaints whatsoever: tempos are beautifully judged, the string

sound is warmer than usual and the overall approach to the music expressive and eloquently shaped. Mertens gives a fine performance of *Ich habe genug*, clearly articulated and resonantly declaimed. Kuijken has opted for the first of several versions of this cantata which Bach made subsequently for various voice pitches and with small instrumental adjustments.

Mertens is joined in the two 'Dialogue' cantatas by Nancy Argenta. Both voices are tonally well focused and project the music in a manner admirably free from needless affectation or contrivance. An expressive peak is reached in Argenta's aria, 'Ich bin herrlich, ich bin schön' (No 49), a ravishing quartet movement with oboe d'amore and a violoncello piccolo beautifully played by Hidemi Suzuki. Add to this a first-rate performance of the organ obbligatos in the opening Sinfonia and final duo of the same cantata and you've a performance of distinction. An outstanding achievement.

Cantatas Nos 51 (arr W F Bach), 202 & 210   Ⓟ
Christine Schäfer *sop* **Musica Antiqua Köln / Reinhard Goebel** *vn*
DG 459 621-2GH (62' · DDD) Texts and translations included   ⒻⓄ

Of the two wedding cantatas, *Weichet nur, betrübte Schatten* (No 202) ranks among Bach's best-loved, but the other, *O holder Tag, erwünschte Zeit* (No 210), is much less heard. To these, Christine Schäfer adds another Bach favourite, *Jauchzet Gott in allen Landen!* (No 51) which, although not specifically for a wedding, confirms propriety in a nuptial context.

The partnership of Schäfer and Reinhard Goebel with his Musica Antiqua Köln is an interesting one, and rewarding more often than not. Schäfer is a spirited singer with a bright tone and an agile technique. Her clearly articulated phrases accord well with Goebel's well-defined instrumental contours and colourfully characterised rhythms – the fourth aria of No 210, in the rhythm of a polonaise, is admirably enlivened in these respects – and her well-controlled vibrato is a pleasure throughout.

If Emma Kirkby's performance of this piece and No 202 is more understated than the present one there's still an underlying expressive subtlety and a warmth of vocal timbre in her singing which may prove the more rewarding and enduring. The opening aria of No 202, a sublime piece of musical imagery, points up some of the essential differences between the two approaches: Schäfer declamatory, demonstrative and bright toned, with an edge to the voice, Kirkby, warm toned, alluring and exercising superb control throughout. On the other hand Schäfer's even technique, with its easier access to the highest notes of the range, often has the edge over Kirkby in more virtuoso movements. And in No 210 Schäfer's vocal brilliance and unfailing security, together with Goebel's lively if on occasion provocative gestures, make one of the most alert and interesting performances of the piece. Schäfer also rises brilliantly to the occasion in No 51. A stimulating and often satisfying release.

Cantatas Nos 63ª, 91, 121 & 133. Magnificat, BWV243ª
Dorothee Mields, ªCarolyn Sampson sops
Ingeborg Danz contr **Mark Padmore** ten **Peter Kooy, ªSebastian Noack** basses **Collegium Vocale, Ghent / Philippe Herreweghe**
Harmonia Mundi ② HMC90 1781/2; SACD 🔊
HMC80 1781/2 (117' · DDD) Texts and translations
included   Ⓕ

Bach composed Christmas music for more than 30 years of his professional life, but none in such a short a space of time as when he arrived at Leipzig in 1723. He used the relatively quiet Advent period to prepare for the onslaught of commitments around Christmas. This recording celebrates his vibrant representation of all the major themes of the season.

The *Magnificat* was his major contribution in his first year, as it was needed for Christmas Day. One his few works in Latin, this grandiloquent 16-movement canticle enabled the new Cantor to make his mark with a supreme exhibition of compositional mastery and acoustical opulence. Today's audiences usually hear the *Magnificat* in D, but it was originally composed in E flat, with four interpolated movements reflecting the special seasonal context. Philippe Herreweghe presents as tailored and tonally refined a reading as you are likely to find, as indeed he did in his more intimate but prosaic account of the D major version from 1990. This new performance also ranks with the best in terms of varied coloration and sonic choral brilliance.

Bach's Christmas cantatas from 1723 and 1724 comprise works of fascinating range. 'Christen, ätzet diesen Tag' (No 63) is another extrovert celebration, with trumpets and drums, originally conceived in Weimar and smartened up for its new surroundings. Most interesting is 'Christen wir sollen', which presents the idea of thanksgiving as coming from within the dark recesses of Advent, preparation and expectation; Collegium Vocale are supreme in austerity, and the distilled *stilo antico*.

Herreweghe can be a touch anodyne, but this is a mild gripe for what is, overall, an outstanding collection of performances to celebrate a Bach Christmas – beyond the great Oratorio.

Cantatas Nos 82 & 199ª   ℗
Concerto for Oboe, Violin and Strings, BWV1060ᵇ
ªEmma Kirkby sop ᵇKatharina Arfken ob **Freiburg Baroque Orchestra / Gottfried von der Goltz** vn
Carus 83 302 (62' · DDD) Texts and translations
included   Ⓕ○○

One of the world's brightest Baroque ensembles performing with one of the world's most admired Baroque sopranos is an enticing propo-

sition. What's more, the solo cantatas on offer here are two of Bach's most moving: No 82, *Ich habe genug*, that serene contemplation of the afterlife; and No 199, *Mein Herze schwimmt im Blut*, a relatively early work with a text that moves from the wallowing self-pity of the sinnner to joyful relief in God's mercy. Each contains music of great humanity and beauty, and each, too, contains an aria of aching breadth and nobility – the justly celebrated 'Schlummert ein' in the case of *Ich habe genug*, and in *Mein Herze* the humble but assured supplication of 'Tief gebückt'.

Both could have been written for Emma Kirkby, who's perhaps at her best in this kind of long-breathed, melodically sublime music, in which pure beauty of vocal sound counts for so much. The support of the Freiburg Baroque Orchestra is total, combining tightness of ensemble with such flexibility and sensitivity to the job of accompaniment that you really feel they're 'playing the words'. The Freiburgers also give one of the most satisfyingly thoroughbred accounts of the Violin and Oboe Concerto on disc. Add a recorded sound which perfectly combines bloom, clarity and internal balance, and you've a CD to treasure.

Cantatas Nos 80 & 147
Ingrid Kertesi sops **Judit Nemeth** mez **Jozsef Mukk** ten **István Gáti** bar **Hungarian Radio Chorus; Failoni Chamber Orchestra, Budapest / Mátyás Antál**
Naxos 8 550642 (54' · DDD) Recorded 1992   Ⓢ

Cantatas Nos 51 & 208
Ingrid Kertesi, Julia Pászthy sops **Judit Nemeth** mez **Jozsef Mukk** ten **István Gáti** bar **Hungarian Radio Chorus; Failoni Chamber Orchestra, Budapest / Mátyás Antál**
Naxos 8 550643 (50' · DDD) Recorded 1992   Ⓢ

Naxos include here four of Bach's most celebrated and accessible cantatas. The performances are far removed in character from the complete Harnoncourt and Leonhardt edition on Teldec; women rather than boys sing all the soprano and alto solos, the Hungarian Radio Chorus is a mixed male and female ensemble and the Failoni Chamber Orchestra of Budapest plays modern rather than period instruments. However, for much of the time this is enjoyable spirited music-making which, in its choice of tempos, its understanding of recitative and its feeling for the lyricism of Bach's writing compares favourably with rival modern instrument versions. The disappointment lies partly in the choice of edition and solution to instrumentation. *Sheep may safely graze* (No 208) is without the treble recorders which Bach specifically asked for and which intensify the pastoral idyll. Here, furthermore the flutes are rather distantly balanced giving them a somewhat irrelevant role which is far from Bach's intention.

More serious is the decision to follow the inflated version of the first and fifth movements of *Ein feste Burg* (No 80) penned by Bach's eldest son, Wilhelm Friedemann shortly after his father's death. Here Friedemann added three trumpets and a kettledrum to the original texture of oboes and strings, and though some may prefer the more overt sense of occasion and the emphasis of the church militant, that this achieves, the scoring of the original is unquestionably effective and in keeping with the piece as a whole. Much else here is sensitively and unsentimentally performed. 'Jesu, joy of man's desiring' (from No 147) is perhaps a shade on the slow side. Most affecting of all though, is the canonic alto/tenor duet from No 80 whose tender writing for oboe da caccia and violin has long been for some one of the purplest of all passages in the entire Bach cantata canon. The soprano Ingrid Kertesi negotiates the many difficulties of *Jauchzet Gott in allen Landen!* fluently and with a youthful zeal and few will be disappointed by her spirited artistry. These are two mainly very enjoyable discs which can be confidently recommended. Clear recorded sound.

Cantatas Nos 82 & 199
Lorraine Hunt Lieberson *mez* **Orchestra of Emmanuel Music / Craig Smith**
Nonesuch 7559 79692-2 (51' · DDD) Texts and
translations included ⓕ**OO**

Lorraine Hunt Lieberson's performances of these two cantatas are like deeply personal, supplicatory confessionals. The American mezzo-soprano has a dark and well-focused sound, and brings words and music to life through a wealth of imaginative detail. The Orchestra of Emmanuel Music (a Boston-based church that incorporates the Bach cantata cycle into its regular liturgy) provides warm-hearted, rich-toned support from eleven strings plus bassoon, and Peggy Pearson shapes the obbligato oboe d'amore parts with exquisite sensitivity. A stunning and remarkably affecting achievement all around.

Cantatas Nos 56, 82 & 158
Thomas Quasthoff *bar* **RIAS Chamber Choir, Berlin; Berlin Baroque Soloists / Rainer Kussmaul** *vn*
DG ⁘ 474 5052GSA (50' · DDD/DSD · T/t) ⓕ**O**

If Bach had heard Thomas Quasthoff he might have considered making his Evangelist a baritone. Such is the telling presence of his interpretations here that one often feels subsumed by the singularly heavy-hearted 'station' of the cross in *Ich will den Kreuzstab* ('I gladly carry the cross') or metaphorically transported to the promised land both here and, by a more gentle route, in both *Ich habe genug* and the aria and chorale which constitutes the body of *Der Friede*.

Just as Fischer-Dieskau brought a pioneering and searing intensity to Cantatas Nos 56 and 82 in 1951 for Karl Ristenpart, Quasthoff renders

these cantatas as deeply personal statements. *Kreuzstab* contains one of the most disarmingly emotional outbursts in Bachian literature, one that resonates with Passion-like inflections in a tantalising search for salvation. The soloist is impressively joined by the Berlin Baroque Soloists whose rich palette (as the most red-blooded of modern-instrument bands with a 'period' conscience) and chamber music sensibilities make for an absorbing experience.

Surround sound provides yet a further fathom of emotional involvement.

Additional recommendation

Cantatas Nos 39, 73, 93, 105, 107, 131
Collegium Vocale, Ghent / Herreweghe
Virgin Veritas ② 562025-2 (120' · DDD)   Ⓜ
This is a veritable treasure trove. The pick of the bunch is No 105, *Herr gehe nicht ins Gericht*, delivered with glowing intensity, led by the shimmering Barbara Schlick. Herreweghe and his beautifully blended ensemble give deeply considered performances.

Secular Cantatas, BWV201-16

No 201 Der Streit zwischen Phoebus und Pan; **No 202** Weichet nur, betrübte Schatten; **No 203** (doubtful); **No 204** Ich bin in mir vergnügt; **No 205** Der zufriedengestellte Äolus; **No 206** Schleicht, spielende Wellen; **No 207** Vereinigte Zwietracht der wechselnden; **No 208** Was mir behagt, ist nur die muntre Jagd; **No 209** Non sa che sia dolore; **No 210** O holder Tag, erwünschte Zeit; **No 211** Schweigt stille, plaudert nicht, 'Coffee'; **No 212** Mer hahn en neue Oberkeet, 'Peasant'; **No 213** Hercules auf dem Scheidewege; **No 214** Tönet, ihr Pauken!; **No 215** Preise dein Glücke, gesegnetes Sachsen; **No 216** Vergnügte Pleissenstadt

---

Cantatas Nos 211 & 212   Ⓟ
Emma Kirkby *sop* **Rogers Covey-Crump** *ten*
David Thomas *bass* **Academy of Ancient Music / Christopher Hogwood**
L'Oiseau-Lyre 417 621-2OH (52' · DDD) Recorded
1984. Texts and translations included ⓕ**O**

These two most delightful of Bach's secular cantatas here receive sparkling performances fully alive to the humour and invention of the music. The *Coffee* Cantata illustrates a family altercation over a current enthusiasm, the drinking of coffee. A narrator tells the story while the soprano and bass soloists confront each other in a series of delightful arias. Thomas brings out the crabby dyspeptic side of Schlendrian's character imaginatively and Kirkby makes a charming minx-like Lieschen. Covey-Crump's sweet light tenor acts as a good foil. The *Peasant* Cantata also takes the form of a dialogue, here between a somewhat dull and simple young man and his sweetheart Mieke, a girl who intends to better herself. Through the 24 short movements Bach conjures up a wonderfully

BACH B MINOR MASS – IN BRIEF

Soloists; Monteverdi Ch; English Baroque Soloists / Sir John Eliot Gardiner
Archiv ② 415 514-2AH2 (106' · DDD)　Ⓕ**OOO**

☀️ Stunning choral singing with fine solo work drawn from the choir. A performance that successfully captures the majesty of the work, but also uncovers its intimacy.

Soloists; Tölz Boys' Choir; The Kings' Consort / Robert King
Hyperion ② CDA67201/2 (110' · DDD)　Ⓕ**OO**

A light-filled, fresh approach to the great Mass, the South German boys blend well with the English men's voices and the whole performance has an uplifting, celebratory feel.

Soloists; Taverner Consort and Players / Andrew Parrott
Virgin Classics ② 561998-2 (103' · DDD)　Ⓜ**O**

A small choir and stylishly swift tempi make this a fleet reading that embraces numerous delights. The period forces perform well and the recording sensitively reflects its scale.

Soloists; Bach Ensemble / Joshua Rifkin
Warner ② 7559 79563-2 (106' · DDD)　Ⓑ**O**

This is the recording which triggered off much of the debate about the size of Bach's choir. It's done one-to-a-part and has a luminosity that's really very convincing.

Soloists; New Philharmonic Choir and Orchestra / Carlo Maria Giulini
BBC Legends BBCL4062-2 (77' · ADD)　Ⓕ

Recorded in St Paul's Cathedral in 1972, this is a performance on a large scale with broad tempi. The soloists and orchestra are superb, though the choir is rather indistinct.

Soloists; BBC Chorus; Boyd Neel Orchestra / Georges Enescu
BBC Legends ② BBCL40087-2 (132' · ADD)　Ⓕ

From 1951, this historic document enshrines Kathleen Ferrier's performance in the piece. The sound is decidedly 'period' but there's a wonderful integrity about this interpretation.

Soloists; Bavarian Radio Chorus and Orchestra / Eugen Jochum
EMI ② 568640-2 (122' · DDD)　Ⓜ**OO**

If you're looking for modern instruments, superb soloists and a conductor totally in sympathy with this piece, Eugen Jochum's 1980 performance is well worth considering.

Soloists; Collegium Vocale / Philippe Herreweghe
Harmonia Mundi ② HMC90 1614/5 (109' · DDD)　Ⓕ**O**

Herreweghe has a very attractive way with Bach, warmer than some North European performances. His excellent choir and orchestra perform with great feeling, and the solo singing is particularly appealing.

rustic picture with some vivid dance numbers and rumbustious ritornellos. The soloists' nicely rounded characterisations emerge with great humour and Hogwood directs with vitality and sprightly rhythmic control. The recording is excellent.

Motets, BWV 225-30

Singet dem Herren, **BWV225**; Der Geist hilft unsrer Schwachheit auf, **BWV226**; Jesu meine Freude, **BWV227**; Fürchte dich nicht, **BWV228**; Komm, Jesu, komm, **BWV229**; Lobet den Herren, **BWV230**

Motets, BWV225-30　Ⓟ
Greta de Reyghere, Katelijne van Laetham sops **Martin van der Zeijst, Sytse Buwalda** countertens **Hans Hermann Jansen** tens **Johannes-Christoph Happel** bar **La Petite Bande Choir; La Petite Bande / Sigiswald Kuijken**
Accent ACC9287 (65' · DDD) Recorded 1992. Texts and translations included　Ⓕ

Motets, BWV225-30
Netherlands Chamber Choir / Ton Koopman
Philips 434 165-2PH (63' · DDD) Recorded 1986-7. Texts and translations included　Ⓕ

These two approaches to Bach's Motets differ strongly from one another. Kuijken directs performances with *colla parte* instrumental support, that's to say, with instruments doubling each of the vocal strands. Koopman, on the other hand, prefers the vocal strands *a cappella* with instruments providing only the basso continuo. The choir in each version is made up of women sopranos and countertenors with the men's voices. Choosing between the versions is difficult and to a large extent must be a matter of which approach you prefer. Kuijken's performances are more relaxed than those of Koopman. He avoids anything in the nature of overdirection and, while neither singing nor playing is always quite as tidy as it might be, there's a lively spontaneity, especially rewarding in the radiant performance of *Singet dem Herren*. Koopman draws more sharply articulated singing than Kuijken from the Netherlands Chamber Choir though sometimes at the expense of natural declamation and spontaneity. But there's greater linear clarity here than in the other and it pays off handsomely in *Komm, Jesu, komm*. It's a pity that Koopman doesn't avail himself of the surviving instrumental parts for *Der Geist hilft* but, in other respects, the strengths and weaknesses of the two performances are fairly evenly distributed and both are highly recommended.

Mass in B minor, BWV232

Mass in B minor
Jenny Hill sop **Dame Janet Baker** contr **Peter Pears** ten **John Shirley-Quirk** bass **New Philharmonia Chorus and Orchestra / Carlo Maria Giulini**

BBC Legends/IMG Artists ② BBCL4062-2
(138' · ADD) Recorded live at St Paul's Cathedral,
London 1972 Ⓜ

In these days of period-instrument hegemony in
the performance of Bach, this 'old-fashioned' B
minor Mass may be considered an anachronism
among younger collectors, but it has its own
validity in terms of Giulini's absolute commitment to the work in hand and in the thorough-
ness of the execution. The downside of the
large-scale approach can be heard in the somewhat lumbering account of 'Qui tollis', its
upside in the grave, measured 'Gratias agimus'
where the successive entries of the same idea are
unerringly propelled. 'Et incarnatus est' and
'Crucifixus' in the *Credo* have a wonderful
inwardness, the 'Sanctus' a power unavailable to
a smaller choir.

When it comes to the soloists this performance wins hands down over authenticity. Janet
Baker, on top form, is warm, vibrant, above all
communicative with her words. Shirley-Quirk,
in both his solos, is confident and bold in his
vocal projection, secure and full in tone. There's
no one to match them today. Jenny Hill sings
purely and with fresh feeling. Only Peter Pears,
already in his sixties, disappoints. The recording
catches both the St Pauls' reverberation and the
sense of a notable occasion.

Lutheran Masses, BWV233-6

F, **BWV233**; A, **BWV234**; G minor, **BWV235**;
G, **BWV236**

Masses,ᵃ BWV233 & 236. Trio Sonata in C, Ⓟ
BWV529 (arr Boothby)
ᵃ**Nancy Argenta** sop ᵃ**Michael Chance** counterten
ᵃ**Mark Padmore** ten ᵃ**Peter Harvey** bass **Purcell
Quartet** (Catherine Mackintosh, Catherine Weiss vns
Richard Boothby vc Robert Woolley org)
Chandos Chaconne CHAN0653 (65' · DDD) Text and
translation included Ⓕ**O**

The absurd prejudice that long deprived us of
adequate recordings of Bach's four Lutheran
Masses (or short Masses, as they're also known
because, in accordance with Lutheran usage,
they set only the *Kyrie* and *Gloria*) seems finally
to have died a death. The Masses' crime has
been to be made up almost entirely of paraphrases of cantata movements from the 1720s,
yet Bach is Bach, whatever the circumstances,
and this is wonderful music which, like the B
minor Mass, offers sober old-style polyphonic
choral movements of impressive cumulative
power alongside choruses of almost physical
excitement and clamour and some first-rate
arias with instrumental obbligato.

As with volume 1, a one-to-a-part approach is
taken, with the four soloists also forming
the choir and the Purcell Quartet being augmented by whatever extra instruments are
needed. The result doesn't sound at all under-

powered, and gains considerably over Herreweghe's typically well-turned but more traditional choral approach in vividness of texture
and harmony, crispness of attack and a madrigalian litheness of expressive response.

The recording allows just the right amount of
bloom without becoming washy. There are
times when the two higher voices sound further
forward than the others, and Michael Chance
occasionally disappears a bit towards the bottom of his range, but in general this release
brings nothing but pleasure both in the music
and in the stylish and lively performances.

Mass in F, BWV233a. Cantatas Nos 65 & 180. Ⓟ
Sanctus in D, BWV238
Ann Monoyios sop **Angus Davidson** counterten
Charles Daniels ten **Peter Harvey** bar **Gabrieli
Consort and Players / Paul McCreesh**
Archiv Produktion ② 457 631-2AH2 (160' · DDD)
Texts and translations included. Includes readings,
congregational hymns and organ works by Bach and
Pachelbel Ⓕ**O**

This two-disc set contains four vocal works by
Bach, set in the context of an Epiphany Mass 'as
it might have been celebrated in St Thomas,
Leipzig *c*1740'. Though several attempts have
been made in the past to re-create the sequence
of events at the two main services where Bach's
cantatas were sung, the *Hauptgottesdienst*, in the
morning, and the Vesper, in the afternoon, this
is the first time that such a project has been
committed to disc. You are very likely to be captivated by much of what Paul McCreesh and his
musicians, with help in liturgical canon from
the scholar, Robin A Leaver, have achieved.

The sacred vocal works which have been cho-
sen for this reconstruction of a *Hauptgottesdienst*
for the 'Feast of the Three Kings' are the
F major Lutheran Mass, the *Sanctus* and two
cantatas, *Sie werden aus Saba alle kommen*, a true
Epiphany piece, and *Schmücke dich, o liebe Seele*
which is foremost a Trinity piece but one that
Bach may well have used on other occasions.
McCreesh did well in securing the services of
Ann Monoyios and Peter Harvey, but all
involved make an impressive showing. The
Missa comes over very well, Monoyios's 'Qui
tollis peccata mundi' outstanding for its warmth
of colour.

The brisk tempo chosen for the superb
chorale fantasy at the start of No 180 fails to
convince. On the other hand, the brilliant tenor
aria with virtuoso flute obbligato that follows
has a well-considered tempo, and is beautifully
articulated by flautist Jed Wentz. But it's
Monoyios who, once more, steals the show with
her affecting account of the lyrical elaboration
with violoncello piccolo of a verse from the
Communion hymn on which the cantata is
based.

Overall, this project is likely to interest all
lovers of Bach's music. The recorded sound,
from Freiburg Cathedral and Brand-Erbisdorf
in Saxony, is excellent.

Magnificat in D, BWV243

Bach Magnificat in D, BWV243　　　　　　　Ⓟ
Vivaldi Ostro picta, RV642. Gloria in D, RV589
Emma Kirkby, Tessa Bonner sops **Michael Chance**
counterten **John Mark Ainsley** ten **Stephen Varcoe**
bar **Collegium Musicum 90 Chorus and Orchestra /
Richard Hickox**
Chandos Chaconne CHAN0518 (64' · DDD)
Recorded 1990. Texts and translations included　Ⓕ Ⓞ

Hickox sets effective tempos in Bach's *Magnificat* and points up the many striking contrasts in colour and texture with which the piece abounds. From among the many successful features of the recording Stephen Varcoe's 'Quia fecit mihi magna' and the 'Et misericordia' sung by Michael Chance and John Mark Ainsley stand out. Vivaldi's *Gloria*, RV589 is the better known of two settings by the composer in D major. In this programme it's prefaced by an introductory motet *Ostro picta*, which may well in fact belong to the *Gloria* and is here sung with warmth and radiance by Emma Kirkby. Hickox's performance of this evergreen vocal masterpiece comes over with conviction. It's gracefully phrased, sensitively sung and affectingly paced with an admirable rapport between vocalists and instrumentalists. The sound is first rate.

Magnificat in D. Cantata No 51　　　　　Ⓟ
Nancy Argenta, Patrizia Kwella, Emma Kirkby sops
Charles Brett counterten **Anthony Rolfe Johnson**
ten **David Thomas** bass **English Baroque Soloists /
Sir John Eliot Gardiner**
Philips 50 Great Recordings 464 672-2PM (41' · DDD)
Texts and translations included　Ⓜ Ⓞ

Bach's *Magnificat* is a work full of contrasts – contrasts of texture, of colour and of temperament – few of which escape the attention of Gardiner, his choir, orchestra and fine group of soloists. The choruses are sung with great vigour and precision; articulation is crisp and diction excellent. The solo singing is of a uniformly high standard with some outstanding contributions from Charles Brett, Anthony Rolfe Johnson and David Thomas. Notable are the 'Quia fecit', in which Thomas is admirably accompanied by a perfectly balanced continuo texture, and the 'Et misericordia' duet for alto and tenor, which is sung with great tenderness and restraint by these artists. Among the obbligato contributions that can be singled out is the oboe d'amore in the 'Quia respexit', which is sensitively played and hauntingly beautiful.

The cantata *Jauchzet Gott in allen Landen!* is one of three for solo soprano which Bach wrote at Leipzig during the 1730s. The spirit of the text, as its title implies, is one of rejoicing. It's a spirit which the soloist, Emma Kirkby, captures well. Her solo partner in the colourful opening movement and in the fugal 'Alleluia' at the close is Crispian Steele-Perkins who manages Bach's exacting trumpet parts with precision. Less

enjoyable is the exaggerated acceleration in tempo for the 'Alleluia' section of the final movement, but it's a dazzling display without a doubt. These are fine performances of two of Bach's best-known church compositions, with admirably clear recordings.

Magnificat in D. Cantata No 21
Greta de Reyghere sop **René Jacobs** counterten
Christoph Prégardien ten **Peter Lika** bass
**Netherlands Chamber Choir; La Petite Bande /
Sigiswald Kuijken**
Virgin Classics The Classics 561833-2 (73' · DDD)
Recorded 1988 Notes, texts and translations
included　　　　　　　　　　　　　　　Ⓑ Ⓞ

The first of this batch of The Classics, coupling performances of Bach's *Magnificat* with Cantata No 21, is in every way recommendable. Indeed Nicholas Anderson's original review commented that in the *Magnificat* Sigiswald Kuijken and La Petite Bande 'reach the heart of Bach's music more convincingly than almost any other [version] currently available'. He went on to comment that he found Kuijken's performance of *Ich hatte viel Bekümmernis* 'profoundly affecting', although he also noticed some instrumental insecurity. Certainly the lovely solo and choral singing in both works, coupled to a superbly atmospheric recording, make this a Bach CD to treasure.

St Matthew Passion, BWV244

St Matthew Passion　　　　　　　　　　Ⓟ
Anthony Rolfe Johnson ten Evangelist **Andreas
Schmidt** bar Jesus **Barbara Bonney, Ann Monoyios**
sops **Anne Sofie von Otter** mez **Michael Chance**
counterten **Howard Crook** ten **Olaf Bär** bar
Cornelius Hauptmann bass **London Oratory Junior
Choir; Monteverdi Choir; English Baroque Soloists
/ Sir John Eliot Gardiner**
Archiv Produktion ③ 427 648-2AH3 (167' · DDD)
Recorded 1989. Text and translation included
　　　　　　　　　　　　　　　　　Ⓕ Ⓞ Ⓞ Ⓞ

What makes Gardiner's *St Matthew Passion* stand out in the face of stiff competition is, more than anything, his vivid sense of theatre. Bach's score is, after all, a sacred drama and Gardiner interprets this aspect of the work with lively and colourful conviction. That in itself isn't sufficient to ensure a fine performance, but here we have a first-rate group of solo voices, immediately responsive choral groups and refined obbligato and orchestral playing. Anthony Rolfe Johnson declaims the Evangelist's role with clarity, authority and the subtle inflexion of an accomplished storyteller. Ann Monoyios, Howard Crook and Olaf Bär also make strong contributions but it's Michael Chance's 'Erbarme dich', tenderly accompanied by the violin obbligato, which sets the seal of distinction on the performance. Singing and playing of this calibre deserve to win many friends and Gardiner's deeply felt account of Bach's great Passion does the music considerable justice. Clear recorded sound.

St Matthew Passion ℗
Christoph Prégardien *ten* Evangelist **Matthias Goerne** *bar* Christus **Christine Schäfer, Dorothea Röschmann** *sops* **Bernarda Fink, Elisabeth von Magnus** *contrs* **Michael Schade, Markus Schäfer** *tens* **Dietrich Henschel, Oliver Widmer** *basses* **Vienna Boys' Choir; Arnold Schoenberg Choir; Concentus Musicus Wien / Nikolaus Harnoncourt**
Teldec ③ 8573 81036-2 (163' · DDD) Includes enhanced CD with full autograph score ⓕ❶❶❶

Harnoncourt waited over 30 years to return to the 'Great Passion', which, but for his live Concertgebouw recording, he last recorded in 1970 when he had completed only a handful of cantatas in Teldec's defining series. Harnoncourt's revisitation presents a unique statement, one that can't fail to make an impression. Recorded in the sumptuous acoustic of the Jesuitenkirche in Vienna, there's a detectable flavour of southern European oratorio, ebulliently theatrical, immediate and free-breathing, and without the austerity of North German rhetoric. What's recognisably perceived as 'spiritual' in the carefully coiffured renderings of Suzuki (BIS) and Herreweghe (Harmonia Mundi) has no place here. Harnoncourt's religiosity isn't imposed but stands rather in a lifetime of musical distillation. This is instantly obvious in the opening chorus, where bridal imagery (in the music's secular, balletic lift) is juxtaposed with the physical imagery of what's at stake (in the broad, enduring bow strokes). While Suzuki's visceral chorale is more spine-tingling, the refinement here of 'Sehet, Wohin?' amid inexorable, paradoxically unquestioning direction, is masterful.

Pacing Part 1 is no easy task, and many a tank has been emptied before reaching what the great Bach scholar Friederich Smend called 'the central message of the work' (encompasssing Nos 46-9). Harnoncourt neither dallies unduly with the chorales nor charges through them; they skilfully counterbalance the remarkably incandescent narrative of Prégardien's Evangelist. The tenor shows a supreme attention to detail (even if his singing is sometimes effortful), and his dialogue with Matthias Goerne's vital Christus is especially compelling. Harnoncourt gives 'Blute nur' a touch of characteristic melodrama, but none can doubt how Dorothea Röschmann and the orchestra, between them, project its expressive core.

The strikingly cultivated crowd scenes of the well-drilled, medium-sized Arnold Schoenberg Choir make a strong contrast with the relatively brazen chorus in Harnoncourt's 1970 version. Unlike the specialists of the pioneering years, Harnoncourt hand-picks his soloists from the widest possible pool. Apart from the excellent Röschmann, Christine Schäfer impresses here far more than in her rather harried solo Bach disc (DG). More relaxed and controlled, she

BACH ST MATTHEW PASSION – IN BRIEF

Soloists; Monteverdi Choir; English Baroque Soloists / Sir John Eliot Gardiner
Archiv ③ 427 648-2AH3 (167' · DDD) ⓕ❶❶❶
A stunning achievement from 1989 projected with powerful conviction. (Also available coupled with the B minor Mass and *St John Passion* – 469 769-2X9: a real bargain.)

Soloists; Arnold Schonberg Choir; Concentus Musicus Wien / Nikolaus Harnoncourt
Teldec ③ 8573 81036-2 (163' · DDD) ⓕ❶❶❶
With its ROM-capabilities offering the full autograph score, and Harnoncourt's long experience and sympathy for the work, this is one of the triumphs of recent times.

Soloists; Gabrieli Players / Paul McCreesh
Archiv ② 474 200-2AH2 (161' · DDD) ⓕ❶❶
There's a brightness and lightness that comes from a one-to-a-part approach, but you must decide whether it sacrifices some of the work's nobility.

Soloists; Choir and Orchestra of the Eighteenth Century / Frans Brüggen
Philips ② 473 263-2PH2 (160' · DDD) ⓕ❶❶
A wonderfully human and humane approach from Brüggen, who eloquently brings out the heart of the work, with its powerful emotional currents.

Soloists; Bach Collegium Japan / Masaaki Suzuki
BIS ③ BIS-CD1000/2 (164' · DDD) ⓕ❶
Suzuki touches the deep spiritual core of this universal drama and inspires his colleagues to scale truly dizzying heights. Beautifully recorded.

Soloists; Philharmonia Chorus and Orchestra / Otto Klemperer
EMI ③ 763058-2 (223' · ADD) Ⓜ❶
Bach on a large canvas from 1962 with fine soloists and the great Philharmonia Chorus. A strong devotional reading with broad tempi – light years away from today's approach.

Soloists; Munich Bach Choir and Orchestra / Karl Richter
Archiv ③ 439 338-2AX3 (197' · ADD) Ⓜ
There are few, if any, finer versions of the *St Matthew Passion* on disc. Richter possesses an extraordinary ability to juxtapose dramatic tension with warmth and dignified composure – a magnificent achievement.

Soloists; Hungarian Festival Choir and State Symphony Orchestra / Géza Oberfrank
Naxos ⑧ 8 550832/4 (163' · DDD) Ⓢ
Don't overlook this fine, modern-instrument set. There are no musical compromises, and these fine Hungarian musicians sing and play with real conviction.

sings with acute coloration and stillness in 'Aus Liebe'. With Bernarda Fink's beguiling 'Erbarme dich' and Michael Schade's resplendent 'Geduld', only Oliver Widmer (who sings 'Gebt mir') gives less than unalloyed pleasure. The pick of the crop is Dietrich Henschel, who sings with great warmth and penetration with a 'Mache dich' to stand alongside (if not to rival) Fischer-Dieskau for Karl Richter. But with even these wonderful contributions, it still takes clarity of vision to graphically propel the drama yet also ponder it reverentially. Again, Harnoncourt leaves his mark with his unerring compassion at most of the critical points.

Finally, mention should be made of Concentus Musicus, grainy and luminous in ensemble, the obbligato wind a far cry from the softer-edged and rounded tonal world of almost all other 'period' groups. In short, this is the most culturally alert reading in years and a truly original and illuminating experience.

St Matthew Passion   Ⓟ
Mark Padmore ten Evangelist **Peter Harvey** bass
Christus **Julia Gooding, Deborah York** sops **Magdalena Kožená, Susan Bickley** mezs **James Gilchrist** ten **Stephan Loges** bass **Gabrieli Players / Paul McCreesh**
Archiv Produktion ② 474 200-2AH2 (161′ · DDD) Text and translation included   ⒻⓄⓄ

In the distinguished performance history of the Great Passion, this is a dynamic and powerful reading. What we have here, primarily, is a compelling directorial vision, a dramatically cohesive whole. The only 'controversial' aspect is the use of single voices in the chorus, thereby applying the research presented in the last two decades by Joshua Rifkin and Andrew Parrott. However, as it happens, Paul McCreesh sees this option as a flexible way of enhancing the rich expressive possibilities of the *St Matthew*, a means to a somewhat greater end, thankfully, than joining the band of zealots who seek world domination in Bach vocal performance. And there can be no denying that McCreesh uses the single voices to great and encouraging effect. The warm intimacy of expression in the chorales is often spell-binding, the lucid realism of the madrigalian commentaries touchingly palpable and the crowd scenes almost crazed, as if you were among the mob. McCreesh's pragmatism also ensures that his quality singers produce a rich tonal body rather than a pushed, squawking consort.

There's some outstandingly characterised singing to be heard here, and a few missed opportunities too. Deborah York sounds somewhat *al dente* in her soprano arias, a limited emotional range partly accentuated by the colour and subtlety of expression of Magdalena Kožená's 'Buss und Reu' as well as the enraptured and troubled 'Ach, nun ist mein Jesus hin!'. Mark Padmore's Evangelist is highly charged and responsive: at times he hovers, regaling the facts of the matter with disarming

poise; at others he becomes agitated, even manic. He seems somehow implicated in Peter's denial in a tableau performed with quite remarkable dramatic power, setting up Kožená's 'Erbarme dich'. Hers is one of the most painfully beautiful performances in years, even if the violin obbligato bulges rather too much.

Of the two basses, the Christus of Peter Harvey conveys neither gilded halo or testosterone-fired ruddiness but he remains an effective and constant companion. Stephan Loges is rhetorically imploring in timbre, unafraid to take risks and a singer you listen to attentively.

There's yet to be a clear leader in *St Matthew Passion* recordings, even if that were desirable. The quality of the production is mainly first-rate, though there are the usual dips and troughs you expect from such a challenging undertaking. 'Können Tränen' is a scrappy and flat affair with a strangely below-par Susan Bickley, and the strings aren't always universally impressive. Overall, if not as culturally resonant as Harnoncourt's remarkably mature and poetic reading, McCreesh's interpretation has an unremitting singularity of purpose, as aesthetically Protestant as Harnoncourt's is Catholic. A memorable and vitally conceived account.

St John Passion, BWV245

St John Passion   Ⓟ
Gerd Türk ten Evangelist **Chiyuki Urano** bass Jesus
Ingrid Schmidthüsen, Yoshie Hida sops **Yoshikazu Mera** counterten **Makoto Sakurada** ten **Peter Kooy** bass **Bach Collegium Japan / Masaaki Suzuki**
BIS ② CD921/2 (110′ · DDD) Text and translation included   ⒻⓄⓄ

Bach seems to have performed his *St John Passion* on four Good Fridays during his tenure as Thomaskantor at Leipzig. However, he continued to make significant revisions right up to the last performance under his direction, on April 4, 1749. Of the four versions, the second, dating from 1725, contains the most distinctive revisions, the first version (1724) and the last bearing close affinity with one another. Masaaki Suzuki and his talented Bach Collegium Japan have chosen Bach's latest version. All has evidently been carefully prepared and deeply considered: what's refreshing about their approach is the importance afforded to the relationship between text and music, to the theological source of Bach's inspiration, and the emotional impact of the story and music on its audience. Some of their thoughts may strike readers as simplistic, even perhaps a shade sentimental, but on the strength of this fervent performance we can hardly question their sincerity.

The role of the Evangelist is sung with clarity and lightness of inflexion by Gerd Türk. His performance is eloquently measured, his phrasing well shaped and his articulation engagingly varied. All this makes him a riveting story-teller. The role of Jesus is taken by Chiyuki Urano, warm-toned and resonant. Ingrid Schmidt-hüsen and Yoshikazu Mera make strongly appealing contributions and Peter Kooy is satisfying and affecting. Excellent, too, are the contributions of the Collegium's choir of women's and men's voices. Choral and instrumental articulation is incisive, propelling the rhythms with energy. The performance draws you in from the start. This is a major recording event, and an eminently satisfying one.

St John Passion

Sir Peter Pears ten Evangelist **Gwynne Howell** bass Jesus **Heather Harper, Jenny Hill** sops **Alfreda Hodgson** contr **Robert Tear, Russell Burgess, John Tobin, Adrian Thompson** tens **John Shirley-Quirk** bar **Wandsworth School Boys' Choir; English Chamber Orchestra / Benjamin Britten**
Double Decca ② 443 859-2DF2 (130' · ADD)
Recorded 1971. Sung in English   Ⓜ**OO**

Britten's recording of the *St John Passion* is very special indeed. Apparently he preferred to perform this Bach choral work because of its natural potential for drama. This account takes over the listener completely. The soloists are all splendid, though Heather Harper must be singled out, and the choral response is inspirational in its moments of fervour. Peter Pears is a superb Evangelist; Britten's direction is urgent and volatile; the Wandsworth School Boys' Choir sings out full-throatedly and the English Chamber Orchestra underpins the whole performance with gloriously rich string textures. The analogue recording offers a demonstration of ambient fullness, vividness of detail and natural balance. In fact, it's as if a live performance at The Maltings, Snape, has been transported to the area just beyond your speakers.

St John Passion   Ⓟ

James Gilchrist ten Evangelist **John Bernays** bass Christus **Eamonn Dougan** bass Pilatus **Joe Littlewood** sop **James Bowman** counterten **Matthew Beale** ten **Colin Baldy** bass **New College Choir, Oxford; Collegium Novum / Edward Higginbottom**
Naxos ② 8 557296/7 (110' · DDD) Text and translation included   Ⓢ

When you hear the ominous first chorus of Bach's *St John Passion* sung and played like this, liturgical ritual and visceral human drama make for an unusually intense experience. The bass line pulsates, the boys articulate the words with supreme clarity and the steady speed provides the movement with just the right length – a consideration too often neglected.

Recorded in New College, Oxford, the resident choristers, choral scholars and lay clerks appear to be entirely at ease with the special juxtaposition of quicksilver action and warm reflection which Bach demands in his choruses and chorales. Edward Higginbottom delivers a palpable sense of narrative, unfussy, as if habit

lies at the root of its being. Just listen to the searing choral chromaticisms as Christ is brought before Caiaphas, the startlingly urgent declamations as the crowd bays for blood or the distraught tenderness of James Bowman in 'Es ist vollbracht'.

The Evangelist is the established tenor James Gilchrist, whose alert and straightforward singing makes his performance wholly believable. Of the current generation of choristers, Joe Littlewood reminds us that English choirboys can sing German music beautifully and convey the emotional essence of the text with maturity and purpose. His 'Ich folge' is a delight.

There's the odd strain in Matthew Beale's testing tenor arias but a pleasing timbre, as indeed there is in John Bernays' proud but unblustering Christus. If there's a general tendency, it's to allow the music to speak in its own time within a relaxed beat. The rest is instinct, experience and letting what will be, be. In such light comes this refreshing and captivating new interpretation.

St John Passion   Ⓟ

Ruth Holton sop **Bogna Bartosz** contr **Markus Brutscher** ten **Thomas Laske** bar **Tom Sol** bass **Cologne Chamber Choir; Collegium Cartusianum / Peter Neumann**
Dabringhaus und Grimm ② MDG332 0983-2 (114' · DDD) Text and translations included   ⒻO

Bach never entirely settled on a single view of the *St John* and there are at least four known versions, from Good Friday 1724 (Bach's first Easter in Leipzig) to a performance the year before he died. Peter Neumann expounds here on the virtues of the second, dating from a year after the first. The differences are neither extensive nor merely cosmetic; such is Bach's skilful pacing of the narrative that the original conception can shift markedly with an ever-so-slight nudge. The most immediate difference is the replacement of the austere, imagery-laden opening chorus, 'Herr, unser Herrscher', with the chorale fantasy 'O Mensch, bewein', later employed to conclude Part 1 of the *St Matthew*.

To the unsuspecting, this is the St John Passion that can have you thinking you're playing the beginning of the second disc of the St Matthew; this and two further movements demonstrate Bach's obsession – as with the cantatas of the period – with employing chorales as integral raw material. Yet perhaps more striking still is the interpolation of new arias, possibly derived from an earlier Passion setting conceived in Weimar. These arias, 'Himmel reisse' and 'Zerschmettert mich', are far more animated and graphic than anything in the earlier version. More remarkable still is 'Zerschmettert', performed with dazzling immediacy by Evangelist and tenor soloist Markus Brutscher. This is a superb piece of theatrical posturing of the sort that Handel and Telemann would have filched for their opera, had they only known. The one casualty in this version is 'Erwäge', a perennial favourite.

Given that the majority of the work remains common to all, this account should not be judged merely on its special properties. Neumann conveys strong musical ideas throughout: the choruses are wonderfully attentive to contrapuntal detail, and mesmerisingly varied in articulation. You can forget how beautifully crafted and selected the chorale tunes are in this work, and Neumann allows the music to breathe so that they represent a kind of caesura in the otherwise intense narrative.

Brutscher is a reliable, if somewhat monochrome Evangelist. His technical ease and superb intonation are noteworthy, but often he chooses to remain studiously uninvolved. Ruth Holton is made for the bright-eyed discipleship of 'Ich folge', but there's more to her Bach than youthful piping, as we can hear in her sensitive account of 'Zerfliesse, mein Herze'. However, the soloists individually aren't what marks out this recording; rather it's Neumann's corporate, controlled and intimate concept. He moves skilfully between incandescence and emotionally charged intensity. This is, then, a persuasive testament to Bach's most radically different version of the St John.

St John Passion   **P**
Caroline Stam sop **Peter de Groot** counterten
Charles Daniels, Gerd Türk tens **Stephan
MacLeod, Bas Ramselaar** basses **Netherlands Bach
Society / Jos van Veldhoven**
Channel Classics ② 🔊 CCSSA22005 (112' · DDD/
DSD · T/t)   Ⓕ●

This is the most beautifully packaged account of the *St John Passion* on the market. The performance is cushioned by informative essays and sharp reproductions of paintings and objects from the Museum Catharijneconvent, Utrecht. Such extras can illuminate an understanding of the music so long as the performance lives up to expectations. Thankfully it does.

Veldhoven brings his distinctive angle to the *St John* by presenting it as a notional 'first version'. Among some judicious tinkering, he ignores Bach's last-minute addition of flutes, made before the premiere in April 1724, and promotes an atmosphere of private devotion where the one-to-a-part ensemble allows for a distilled immediacy in the arias and flexible and varied choral contributions. This is a reading that shows that the argument for size in Bach's chorus – large or small – is better fought on musical grounds than musicological ones.

The Netherlands Bach Society, and Veldhoven especially, are more drawn to rhetorical effect than poetic instinct. The chorales are sometimes over-pointed and even precious, and string articulation rather unyielding, but little detracts from a profoundly luminous sense throughout, led by the supremely clear-sighted Evangelist of Gerd Türk. The other voices, soloists and ripienists alike, make a fine and

colourful impression, especially in the crowd scenes, where Veldhoven presents them as a more questing, equivocal and three-dimensional group than the incessant hectoring of an uncompromising lynch mob.

This *St John* holds a special place in a notable catalogue of which, in their different ways, Gardiner, Fasolis, Higginbottom and Suzuki are all leading lights. Veldhoven is thoughtful and effective, even if he never quite takes flight and allows the music to be expressed on the widest emotional canvas. The Super Audio sound is suitably rich and all-embracing.

St Luke Passion, BWV246 (attrib)

St Luke Passion (attrib)   **P**
Mona Spägele sop **Christiane Iven** contr **Rufus
Müller, Harry van Berne** tens **Stephan
Schreckenberger, Marcus Sandmann** basses
**Alsfeld Vocal Ensemble; Bremen Baroque
Orchestra / Wolfgang Helbich**
CPO ② CPO999 293-2 (106' · DDD) Text and
translation included   Ⓕ●

Though it isn't a genuine Bach work, those who love his music will want to investigate the *St Luke Passion*. In terms of scale, rhetorical intensity, structural and stylistic sophistication, musical invention and artistic ambition generally, it finds no common ground with his two extant passions. But there's much that's intimate and touching about it. The meditative element comes less from contemplative arias than from a continuous and freshly fashioned narrative, although the arias, with their favoured wind obbligato parts, are often skilled and affecting. Wolfgang Helbich and his Bremen forces pitch the dramatic climate just about right throughout. Smoothly articulated, unmannered and technically accomplished, the chorales and *turba* scenes are especially well judged. The Evangelist, Rufus Müller, conveys the Gospel with soft-grained clarity and understated dignity and the other soloists do more than justice to the six arias.

St Mark Passion, BWV247

St Mark Passion (reconstr Koopman)
Sibylla Rubens sop **Bernhard Landauer** counterten
Christoph Prégardien, Paul Agnew tens **Peter
Kooy, Klaus Mertens** basses **Breda Sacraments
Choir; Amsterdam Baroque Choir and Orchestra /
Ton Koopman**
Erato ② 8573-80221-2 (118' · DDD)   Ⓕ●

Not a note of Bach's *St Mark Passion* exists, but we know it did once and that it was a parody work. Koopman makes no bones about the purely speculative nature of this project. He pretends he's a Bach student: 'Here is a libretto; set it to music using anything you find in the works I have written up to now (1731). What you do not find, compose yourself.' He revels in the opportunity to draw on his vast knowledge of Bach's choral music as he matches cantata choruses and quasi-*turbae* to Picander's extant text of Bach's lost Passion. This has been done before, most recently by Andor Gomme and Simon Heighes but using, as the accepted basis of the contemplative texts, the contemporaneous *Trauer* Ode (BWV196) as well as recitatives and choruses from Keiser's *St Mark Passion*. Koopman feels this isn't a satisfying parody, and similarly refuses to raid equivalent music from the *St John Passion* (although he uses 'Zerschmettert mich' from the second version of 1725). In fact, the *St Mark*, as Bach would have recognised, was a different type of proposition from the *St John* or *St Matthew*, and he would have made no attempt to model it on his two previous settings; the libretto here draws more on the austerity of the narrative than the luxuriance of the commentary. Hence there are fewer arias, fewer moments of poetic reflection and a more concentrated gospel narrative.

Koopman's deft sense of the appropriate idiom is reflected in his choice of the opening chorus, taken from BWV25, luminously sung with its well-disguised Passion chorale intensifying the harmonic direction. The arias witness seasoned Bachians in full flow. Paul Agnew conveys 'Falsche Welt' as a graphic declamation, confirming a brilliantly effective transformation taken from BWV179, 'Hypocrites who thus ignore' becoming 'treacherous world, thy flattering kisses are but poison'. This has a more Passion-like bearing than the music from BWV54 used in Gomme and Heighes's reworking. The recitatives, though, just miss being idiomatic. As for the delivery, Christoph Prégardien reveals his best ringing expressivity. The cast is strong, and the chorus and orchestra uniformly fine.

Apart from being the most satisfying account to date, it's a performance that best serves the mystery of the Passion, differently told, as a wonderful narrative for musico-poetic dramatic contours. The only gripe is that Koopman does not list the cantata sources in the booklet.

Christmas Oratorio, BWV248

Christmas Oratorio   Ⓟ
Monika Frimmer sop **Yoshikazu Mera** counterten
Gerd Türk ten **Peter Kooy** bass **Bach Collegium Japan / Masaaki Suzuki**
BIS ② CD941/2 (145' · DDD) Text and translation included   ⒻⓄⓄ

The six cantatas that make up Bach's *Christmas Oratorio* are part of a unified work celebrating not just Christmas itself but also the New Year and Epiphany. Masaaki Suzuki faces plentiful if not invariably stiff competition in this work. In fact, it outstrips most of its rivals, in respect both of vocal and instrumental considerations. A notable quality in Masaaki Suzuki's direction is his feeling for naturally expressive contours, allowing the music to breathe freely. Best of all,

perhaps, is his refusal to pay even lip service to Bach's supposed predilection for fast tempos. Everything here seems to be exceptionally well judged, which isn't to say that the pace of individual movements is necessarily slower than those in competing versions but that it's more interrelated with a concept of each section as a whole, and more textually conscious than some.

The soloists are generally very good indeed. Yoshikazu Mera makes a distinctive contribution and Gerd Türk is a communicative singer whose light articulation suits his partly narrative role. Peter Kooy never puts a foot wrong, while Monika Frimmer makes a favourable impression in her duet with Kooy, 'Herr, dein Mitleid, dein Erbarmen'. A small, well-balanced choir of technical agility and an accomplished quorum of instrumentalists set the seal on an outstanding achievement. The finest all-round performance of the *Christmas Oratorio* on disc.

Christmas Oratorio
Sibylla Rubens sop **Ingeborg Danz** contr **James Taylor, Marcus Ullmann** tens **Hanno Müller-Brachmann** bass **Gächinger Kantorei; Stuttgart Bach Collegium / Helmuth Rilling**
Hänssler Classic ③ 92 076 (144' · DDD) Texts and translations included   ⓂⓄ

Energetic director Helmut Rilling is more fired up than ever here. The choruses crackle with thrilling fervour and a blistering attack and shine to notes which, alongside a forthright Gächinger Kantorei, carry the day persuasively on modern instruments. There will always be those for whom Rilling represents an inflexibility of phrasing and unyielding articulation in Bach, paradoxically more reminiscent of the least alluring elements of period performance than the 'ebb and flow' of mainstream consciousness. This recording doubtless reinforces the odd prejudice, though the habitually hard-edged orchestral textures of the Bach Collegium Stuttgart seem more mollifying and warm hearted in movements such as the pastoral Sinfonia at the beginning of Part 2 and the divinely inspired 'Schlafe, mein Liebster' later in the same cantata (it must be said now, flawed by a tiresomely repeated pull-up before the second phrase).

James Taylor is a natural Evangelist: articulate, discriminating, exacting if not emotionally candid. He also retains focus throughout the events of each tableau and gives clearly etched readings. Yet much of the credit must also go to the outstanding solo singing. Sibylla Rubens and Hanno Müller-Brachmann are stunning in the pivotal duet of Part 3, 'Herr, dein Mitleid', and Ingeborg Danz sings with exquisite and gentle poise in the scene-setting 'Bereite dich, Zion'. If her 'Schlafe' is a touch disappointing, then that reflects the weight of expectation which surrounds this central aria. If you prefer a mezzo to a countertenor, then only Anne Sofie von Otter for Gardiner or Christa Ludwig for Richter can better her largely satisfying contribution. Müller-Brachmann is a fine bass soloist in 'Grosser Herr' and as movingly intimate as Michael George for Philip Pickett in the recitative with chorale, 'Immanuel, O süsses Wort'. Rubens is on really terrific form throughout, and her 'Nur in Wink' in Part 6 is a model of outstanding Bach singing.

There's a spiritual containment which serves its purpose here – there's absolutely no sentimental guff – and yet it perhaps trespasses into the clinical too readily. Rilling, as ever, raises hopes and only intermittently fulfils them, but this is still a distinguished reading.

Wilhelm Friedemann Bach

German 1710-1784

Wilhelm Friedemann, the eldest son of JS Bach, studied under his father at the Leipzig Thomasschule; his father put together a 'Clavier-Büchlein' for him and may have written book 1 of the '48' with him in mind. Friedemann also studied the violin with JG Graun. After university study, he became organist at the Dresden Sophienkirche in 1733; he moved to the Liebfrauenkirche, Halle, in 1746 but his years there were turbulent and he left in 1764. He later lived in Brunswick and then in Berlin, but with his difficult temperament and perhaps dissolute character found no regular employment though his organ playing was admired.

The volatility of his musical style is of a piece with his life. In his early years he wrote mainly for keyboard; at Dresden, for instruments; at Halle, church cantatas and some instrumental music; and in his late years, chiefly chamber and keyboard works. He vacillated in style between old and new, with galant elements alongside conservative Baroque ones, intense north German expressiveness alongside more formal writing. His keyboard music includes fugues and deeply felt polonaises. His gifts are unmistakable here and in such works as the Concerto for two solo harpsichords or the often suite-like Sinfonia in F, but the final impression is of a composer whose potential was never fully realised. **GROVE**music

Cantatas

Cantatas – Lasset uns ablegen die Werke der **P**
Finsternis, F80. Es ist eine Stimme eines Predigers in der Wüste, F89
Barbara Schlick *sop* **Claudia Schubert** *contr*
Wilfried Jochens *ten* **Stephan Schreckenberger** *bass* **Rheinische Kantorei; Das Kleine Konzert /**
Hermann Max
Capriccio 10 425 (54' · DDD) Recorded 1991
Texts and translations included   Ⓕ**O**

This disc makes a valuable contribution towards a fuller understanding of this highly gifted but complex member of the Bach clan. In the mid-1740s Wilhelm Friedemann was appointed Director of Music and organist at the Marienkirche at Halle. He remained in the post for almost 20 years, a period which witnessed the composition and performance of all the cantatas represented here. Among the many delights to be found in this music are those occasioned by Friedemann's disparate, even opposing terms of reference. In other words the stylistic vocabulary is both rich and varied, often harking back to a strong paternal influence – what better one has there ever been? JS Bach's idiom, for instance, is startlingly apparent in the opening chorus of the Advent cantata, F80 ('Let us cast off the works of darkness'). Both the arias of this fine cantata are of high quality, the first, for soprano with obbligato flute ably demonstrating how carefully Friedemann thought out his declamation.

For the most part the performances are excellent. The four soloists are first-rate, Barbara Schlick and Wilfried Jochens in particular; and the singing of the Rheinische Kantorei is effective, though just occasionally its component 16 voices sound under threat from Bach's sometimes exacting requirements.

Imaginative programming and sympathetic performances add to this musical revelation.

Simon Bainbridge

English 1952

Bainbridge studied at the Royal College of Music, London, and Tanglewood; American music, in particular Ives and Reich, has been a formative influence. There is a spatial element in some of his music, which is largely instrumental. Among his most characteristic pieces are the Viola Concerto (1976), Concertante in moto perpetuo (1983) and Fantasia for two orchestras (1984). **GROVE**music

Ad ora incerta

Ad ora incerta (Four orchestral songs from Primo Levi)[a]. Four Primo Levi Settings[b]
Susan Bickley *mez* [a]**Kim Walker** *bn* [b]**Nash Ensemble;** [a]**BBC Symphony Orchestra / Martyn Brabbins**
NMC NMCD059 (54' · DDD) Texts and translations included   Ⓕ**OO**

At the beginning of the fourth Primo Levi setting in *Ad ora incerta* (a depiction of the ghastly chemical factory attached to Auschwitz that Levi miraculously survived) there's a slow orchestral *crescendo*, like the panning of a camera to reveal the full horror of the scene. What follows isn't a shout of protest but sober lyricism, and when that *crescendo* returns it introduces an eloquently poignant melody. Simon Bainbridge is an uncommonly fine musical dramatist. He lets the words speak, and distils his music so as to clarify them. In *Ad ora incerta* the vocalist has a companion, a solo bassoon. Because that fourth poem repeatedly speaks of a dead companion, of course, but also in the way the bassoon shadows or reflects the voice, there's also a subtle and moving suggestion that after Auschwitz Levi lacked and longed for a companion, a fellow survivor who would understand his memories in ways that none of us can. It's scarcely believable that these beautiful but painful poems could be set to music; certainly not with the delicate and imaginative sympathy that Bainbridge shows here.

The four chamber settings are still sparer but no less gravely beautiful. In the seven brief lines of the first of them Levi distils the impossibility of communicating his experiences yet the imperative need to try. Bainbridge's setting conveys that, but adds the most restrained and loving pity. It's a remarkable and a deeply moving achievement. Both performances are fine, that of the chamber settings beyond praise in its quiet intimacy.

Sir Granville Bantock British 1868-1946

Bantock studied with Corder at the Royal Academy of Music (1889-93), then worked as a conductor and teacher (professor at Birmingham, 1908-34). He did much to promote the music of his English contemporaries and produced a large output of orchestral and large-scale choral works, influenced by early Wagner, a taste for the exotic, and Hebridean folksong. Though much performed at the beginning of the century, when he was at his most productive and a prominent figure in the English musical renaissance, his music has all but disappeared from the repertory; the oratorio Omar Khayyám (1906-9), the overture The Pierrot of the Minute (1908), the Hebridean Symphony (1915) and the Pagan Symphony (1928) have been admired for their undemanding lyricism. **GROVE**music

Pagan Symphony

Pagan Symphony. Fifine at the Fair. Two Heroic Ballads
Royal Philharmonic Orchestra / Vernon Handley
Hyperion CDA66630 (80' · DDD) Recorded 1992 (F) ●

This collection confirms Bantock as a composer of real achievement whose music has been undeservedly neglected. He was a superb technician, and his impressively large-scale structures have a real urgency. Or perhaps we should say, a real enjoyment. Despite the potentially tragic undertones of *Fifine at the Fair*, both works are almost untroubled, filled instead with the geniality of a craftsman joyfully exercising a craft of which he's master. The cleverness of the thematic transformations can make you smile with pleasure once you've worked out what he's doing – and then smile again at the realisation that the result of the transformation isn't an arid piece of technique for technique's sake, but another jolly good tune. And it's all very beautifully scored. He was a master of the orchestra. Can he be just a bit too clever, forever finding yet another ingenious and delightful thing to do with a scale-figure? Possibly, but he's never dull. Is real emotional depth lacking, despite hints of it whenever the wronged wife appears in

Fifine? Maybe; possibly he was more given to enjoying than to pondering. The performances are stunning, the recordings most sumptuous. The two *Heroic Ballads*, for all that they're concerned with Cuchullan and his ilk, have not a shred of Irish Sea mist hanging around them: they're bold, colourful and stirring.

Pierrot of the Minute

Christ in the Wilderness – The Wilderness and the Solitary Place[a]; Overture to a Greek Tragedy; Pierrot of the Minute; Three scenes from 'The Song of Songs'[ab]
[ab]**Elizabeth Connell** sop [b]**Kim Begley** ten
RPO / Vernon Handley
Hyperion CDA67395 (78' · DDD) (F)

Written quickly over the summer of 1908 and premièred at that year's Three Choirs Festival in Worcester, Bantock's comedy overture *Pierrot of the Minute* enjoyed much success before the First World War. It's a charming work, and Vernon Handley and the RPO deliver a performance of atmospheric delicacy and wit. Three years later Worcester also played host to the first performance of the *Overture to a Greek Tragedy*, an imposing curtain-raiser. Handley extracts every ounce of drama and lyricism from Bantock's ripely colourful inspiration; the majestically paced reading attains a moving nobility in the radiant, rather Straussian peroration.

From Bantock's two-and-a-half-hour setting of *The Song of Songs* (1912-26) come excerpts from three of the five scenes (or 'Days'). The Second Day and love duet from the Fifth Day are thematically related, and frame a purely orchestral sequence from the Third Day. In their respective roles of the Shulamite and her Shepherd lover, Elizabeth Connell and Kim Begley rise admirably to the wide-ranging vocal challenges. Connell also makes an affectionate showing in 'The Wilderness and the Solitary Place', a pretty, gently exotic six-minute aria from the 1907 oratorio *Christ in the Wilderness*.

Sound of outstanding fidelity and helpful annotation add further lustre to another Bantock/Hyperion gem.

Cello Sonatas

Cello Sonatas[a] – No 1 in B minor; No 2 in F sharp minor. Solo Cello Sonata in G minor. Hamabdil[b]. Pibroch[b]. Elegiac Poem[a]
Andrew Fuller vc with [a]**Michael Dussek** pf [a]**Lucy Wakeford** hp
Dutton Laboratories Epoch CDLX7107 (75' · DDD) (M)

There are some rewarding discoveries here, not least the two sonatas for cello and piano. Both were penned during the first half of the 1940s, though the sketches for the B minor Sonata date back to 1900. The latter is a finely sculpted, generously lyrical creation, boasting a particularly lovely slow movement. For the *scherzo*

Bantock pressed into service his earlier *Fantastic Poem* of 1925, and the whole work ends in a mood of autumnal nostalgia. The impulse for the unaccompanied G minor Sonata appears to have been Kodály's magnificent example in the genre: Bantock had heard Beatrice Harrison give the British première in 1924. Cast in four compact movements, it's an uncommonly well-knit essay and a demanding workout for any aspiring virtuoso (as the giddy *moto perpetuo* of the finale attests). We also get two offerings for cello and harp: particularly striking is *Pibroch*, a wonderfully affecting 'Highland lament' .

Andrew Fuller is an accomplished artist, mellow of tone and technically secure; he enjoys sympathetic support from Michael Dussek. Lucy Wakeford, too, contributes most beautifully. With eminently truthful sound and balance throughout, this enterprising collection deserves a warm welcome.

Violin Sonatas

Violin Sonatas – No 1 in G; No 2 in D. Coronach (Pro Patria Mori). Salve Regina, 'Hail Queen of Heaven'
Lorraine McAslan *vn* **Michael Dussek** *pf*
Dutton Epoch CDLX7119 (64' · DDD)   Ⓜ

Dedicated to that great British violinist Albert Sammons, the first of Bantock's three violin sonatas was penned in 1928-9, and appeared in print a year before its first performance (a BBC broadcast in June 1930, with Sammons accompanied by the composer). It's a work of strong appeal, whose clean-cut, songful demeanour would seem tailor-made for its legendary dedicatee's wonderfully sweet timbre; but somewhat surprisingly, given its lyricism and thematic resourcefulness, it failed to secure a place in the repertoire. The opening movement of its D major successor followed quickly in April 1929, but it was another three years before the two remaining movements were completed. It was finally premièred on the BBC in July 1940, but subsequently sank into oblivion – a great pity in view of its bright-eyed vigour, deftness of touch and impeccable craftsmanship.

Two shorter pieces bring up the rear: originally conceived for strings, organ and harp, *Coronach* (1918) is a wistful elegy in memory of a friend who had perished in the trenches three years previously; the contemplative *Salve Regina* is based on a plainsong melody Bantock had heard in Canada during the summer of 1923.

These interpretations from Lorraine McAslan and Michael Dussek are consistently compelling and sure-footed.

Vocal works

Atalanta in Calydon. Vanity of vanities
BBC Singers / Simon Joly
Albany TROY180 (66' · DDD) Texts included   Ⓕ

In 1911 Bantock embarked on the first of his two unaccompanied 'choral symphonies', a half-hour setting of texts from Swinburne's 1865 verse drama, *Atalanta in Calydon*. Written for the amateur Hallé Choir, it's an extraordinarily ambitious offering. Bantock's luxuriant 20-part writing (the composer envisaged 'not less than 10 voices to each part') exhibits a prodigious technical facility allied to a remarkable fluency and poetic sensibility. By comparison, the 35-minute *Vanity of vanities* (based on Bantock's own selection of verses from the Book of Ecclesiastes) is a model of restraint, being laid out for a mere 12 parts. It was completed in September 1913. Again, the sounds created exhibit a ravishing variety of texture, colour and harmony, further testament to Bantock's fantastically vivid aural imagination. Both works impose great technical demands which are easily surmounted in these incisive, dedicated performances, admirably captured by the recording team.

Samuel Barber   American 1910-1981

Barber studied as a baritone and composer (with Scalero) at the Curtis Institute (1924-32) and while there began to win acclaim with such works as Dover Beach (1931), written for himself to sing with string quartet. His opulent yet unforced Romanticism struck a chord and during the 1930s he was much in demand: his overture The School for Scandal (1933), First Symphony (1936), First Essay (1937) and Adagio (originally the second movement of his String Quartet, 1936) were widely performed, the lyrical, elegiac Adagio remaining a popular classic. In the 1940s he began to include more 'modern' features of harmony and scoring. Of his operas, Vanessa (1958), praised as 'highly charged with emotional meaning', was more successful than Antony and Cleopatra (1966, for the opening of the new Met).
GROVEmusic

Violin Concerto, Op 14

Barber Violin Concerto **Bloch** Baal Shem **Walton**
Violin Concerto in B minor
Joshua Bell *vn* **Baltimore Symphony Orchestra /
David Zinman**
Decca 452 851-2DH (68' · DDD)   Ⓕ**ⱺⱺⱺ**

 Bell's coupling of the Barber Violin Concerto with Walton and Bloch brings together three highly romantic *concertante* works. Bell is placed less forward in the Barber than in the rich-sounding recordings of Gil Shaham and Itzhak Perlman, but if anything the results are even more intense. In the central slow movement the opening oboe solo leads to a magically hushed first entry for the violin, and the balance of the soloist also allows a quicksilver lightness for the rushing triplets in the *moto perpetuo* finale. Shaham may find more humour in that brief movement, but Bell's view is equally valid.

From an American perspective, Walton can well be seen as Barber's British counterpart. The playing of this American orchestra is warmly idiomatic, defying the idea that non-British orchestras find Walton difficult. Bell gives a commanding account – his expansive treatment of the central cadenza of the first movement, making it more deeply reflective – is most appealing. Not just there but in many gentle moments the rapt intensity of his playing is magnetic. Bell's is among the finest versions ever, with Bloch's own 1939 orchestration of *Baal Shem* offering a fine, unusual makeweight.

Barber Violin Concerto, Op 14 **E Meyer** Violin Concerto
Hilary Hahn *vn* **Saint Paul Chamber Orchestra / Hugh Wolff**
Sony Classical SK89029 (50' · DDD)   Ⓕ**OO**

The 19-year-old Hilary Hahn once again shows her natural feeling for the American brand of late Romanticism, bringing out heartfelt emotion without overplaying it. There have been a number of outstanding versions of the Barber Concerto in recent years and Hahn's is among the finest ever. She stands between the urgently, fullbloodedly romantic Shaham and the more meditative Bell. It's partly a question of recording balances. The latter has the advantage of a recording which, setting him a little further back, allows *pianissimos* to be registered in a genuine hush. Hahn, like Shaham, is placed well forward, and it's hardly her fault that dynamic contrasts are reduced. The use of a chamber orchestra also affects the balance. The extra weight in the orchestral sound on the DG and Decca discs is here compensated by the incisiveness of the St Paul Chamber Orchestra under Hugh Wolff, with textures a fraction clearer in detail. Even so, in the long introduction to the *Andante* a smaller body of strings, however refined, can't quite match in ear-catching beauty the bigger string sections of the LSO and Baltimore Symphony. What Hahn and Wolff nicely achieve between them, though, is a distinction between the first two movements, both of them predominantly lyrical. Deceptively, the first is marked *Allegro* (hardly sounding it), but here it's registered as a taut first movement leading to a powerful climax. Speeds in both the first two movements are a fraction broader than with either rival, but Hahn reserves her big coup for the *Presto* finale which is noticeably faster than either rival's, offering quicksilver brilliance and pinpoint articulation.

Meyer's Concerto makes an apt coupling. Unashamedly tonal and freely lyrical, it opens with a yearning folk-like melody that echoes Vaughan Williams, and there's also a folk-like, pentatonic cut to some of the writing in both of the two substantial movements. It's amazing what variety Meyer achieves (a string player himself), considering that conscious limitation of having a sustained drone underlying his argument. Hahn plays with passionate commitment,

amply justifying her choice of so approachable a new piece for this important issue.

Barber Violin Concerto **Korngold** Violin Concerto, Op 35. Much ado about nothing, Op 11 – The maiden in the bridal chamber; Dogberry and Verges; Intermezzo; Hornpipe
Gil Shaham *vn* **London Symphony Orchestra / André Previn** *pf*
DG 439 886-2GH (71' · DDD) Recorded 1993
                Ⓕ**O**

This performance of the Barber, warm and rich with the sound close and immediate, brings out the work's bolder side, allowing moments that aren't too distant from the world of Hollywood music (no disparagement there) and aptly the Korngold emerges as a central work in that genre. There have been subtler readings of Barber's lovely concerto, with the soloist not always helped by the close balance, but it's good to have a sharp distinction drawn between the purposeful lyricism of the first movement, marked *Allegro*, and the tender lyricism of the heavenly *Andante*. In the finale Shaham brings out the fun behind the movement's manic energy, with Previn pointing the Waltonian wit.

In the Korngold, Gil Shaham may not have quite the flair and panache of the dedicatee, Jascha Heifetz, in his incomparable reading (reviewed under Korngold), but he's warm and committed. What emerges again and again is how electric the playing of the LSO is under Previn, rich and full as well as committed. The recording helps, clear and immediate. The suite from Korngold's incidental music to *Much ado about nothing*, dating from his early precocious period in Vienna, provides a delightful and apt filler, with Previn, as pianist, just as understanding and imaginative an accompanist, and Shaham yearningly warm without sentimentality, clean and precise in attack.

Additional recommendations

Violin Concerto
Coupled with: Souvenirs, Op 28. Serenade for Strings, Op 1. Music for a Scene from Shelley, Op 7
Buswell *vn* **Royal Scottish National Orchestra / Alsop**
Naxos 8 559044 (64' · DDD)   Ⓢ
A fine performance, notable for its easy spontaneity and unforced eloquence. If the virtuoso finale lacks the devil-may-care bravado of Hahn, there's ample compensation in the wealth of detail Alsop uncovers.

Symphonies Nos 1 and 2

Symphonies – No 1, Op 9; No 2, Op 19. First Essay for Orchestra, Op 12. The School for Scandal Overture, Op 5
Royal Scottish National Orchestra / Marin Alsop
Naxos 8 559024 (70' · DDD)   Ⓢ**O**

That Marin Alsop is a musician of outstanding gifts is amply reinforced by this all-Barber anthology. In her red-blooded rendering of the wartime Second Symphony, she shows just what a powerfully inspired creation it is, extracting every ounce of sinewy logic from its fraught outer movements, while distilling wonder and atmosphere in the haunting central *Andante, un poco mosso*. No less convincing is her reading of the magnificent First Symphony, always acutely responsive to the music's daring expressive scope and building climaxes of riveting cumulative intensity. In its unhurried authority, big heart and epic thrust, it's the kind of interpretation you could have imagined from Bernstein in his NYPO heyday. Elsewhere, she brings an aptly bardic quality to the outer portions of the *First Essay*, while few could fail to respond to the twinkling affection and gentle wit she lavishes on the irresistible *School for Scandal* Overture. Were the orchestral contribution just a fraction more polished, this would be a world-beater. Zinman's stylish 1991 anthology with the Baltimore SO tends to throw into sharper relief the relative shortcomings of Alsop's hard-working Scots (their fiddles especially lack something in silk-spun refinement and tone when playing above the stave). The expert engineering can't quite disguise the acoustical shortcomings of Glasgow's Henry Wood Hall, but the result is tonally truthful and conveys plenty of impact when required.

Adagio for Strings, Op 11

Adagio for Strings. Symphony No 1, Op 9. First Essay, Op 12. Second Essay, Op 17. Music for a Scene from Shelley, Op 7. The School for Scandal Overture, Op 5
Baltimore Symphony Orchestra / David Zinman
Argo 436 288-2ZH (64' · DDD) Recorded 1991　Ⓕ**OO**

Zinman begins this striking set in quiet understatement with the most challenging of all sustained *legatos* – the *Adagio for Strings*. He and his Baltimore strings are calm, collected, resigned; the grief is contained; no wringing of hands at the climax, rather an intense transfiguration. The first of Barber's bite-size symphonies is rather more demonstrative in its tragedy, working up from the deep-set bass lines of an imposing *Andante sostenuto* to the most public of displays. And then there's the *Second Essay*, Barber rhetoric at its most biblical. The engineering throughout this disc is exceptionally vivid, but nowhere more so than here: the impact of timpani and bass drum is unnervingly realistic, the brass and tam-tam-laden climax comes at you full on. Add to that a pugnacious fugue with Baltimore woodwinds devilishly incisive, and you've an absolute winner.

Zinman's account of the First Symphony is laudably coherent. There's sweep and a strong sense of evolution about its development. The solo oboe and cellos are heart-breakers in the slow movement, the impassioned climax – like everything else here – magnificently inevitable.

The *Music for a Scene from Shelley* is an early piece, but a highly accomplished one. It's an especially beguiling example of Barber's precocious lyric gifts. A sunburst of sound brings on one of Barber's most rapturous melodies, voluptuously scored, and there's an exquisite postlude where two horns briefly ruminate on what has been heard and scented, while the nocturnal murmurings of string and harp quickly evaporate to the barely audible.

Barber Adagio for Strings **Bernstein** Candide – Overture **Copland** Appalachian Spring – ballet **W Schuman** American Festival Overture
Los Angeles Philharmonic Orchestra / Leonard Bernstein
DG Galleria 439 528-2GGA (54' · DDD) Recorded live 1982　ⓂO

This is a beautiful collection of American music, lovingly and brilliantly performed. With Barber's lovely *Adagio* you might fear that Bernstein would 'do a Nimrod' and present it with exaggerated expressiveness. Although the tempo is very slow indeed, the extra hesitations aren't excessive and the Los Angeles strings play with angelic refinement and sweetness, as they do also in the many hushed sequences of the Copland ballet. There the live recording made in San Francisco in a dryish acoustic brings a degree of constriction at heavy *tuttis*, but the advantages of digital recording in this beautiful score are obvious, not least at the climax of the haunting variations on the Shaker hymn, *Simple Gifts*. To the three favourite works here is added William Schuman's brazenly extrovert overture with its virtuoso opening section, its quiet *fugato*, ominously introduced, and a brazen conclusion to match the opening. It's a splendid work, almost as joyously inspired as Bernstein's *Candide* Overture, with the composer here adopting a fairly relaxed speed, though with a wild coda.

Piano Sonata, Op 26

Ballade, Op 46. Excursions, Op 20. Nocturne, Op 33. Piano Sonata, Op 26. Souvenirs, Op 28
Eric Parkin pf
Chandos CHAN9177 (63' · DDD) Recorded 1992　ⒻO

This is the complete published piano music, apart from *Three Sketches*, but there are quite a lot of unpublished pieces. None of this matters when the playing is as polished and sympathetic as Parkin's. He responds wonderfully to the nostalgic melancholia of Barber. The ballet score *Souvenirs* is available in the orchestral and piano-duet versions, but this solo piano treatment is just as engaging. Parkin knows exactly how to present this side of Barber and his treatment of the *Four Excursions* based on different popular idioms is equally convincing. A performer as well versed as Parkin in British post-Romantics such as Ireland and Bax finds home ground again in Barber's *Nocturne* and the late *Ballade*. In Barber's classic, the Sonata, Parkin treats the work lyrically and never forces us to regard the finale, especially, as a hard-hitting block-buster in the way that so many young pianists do. He's transparent in the *Scherzo*, sings in the *Adagio*, and the final fugue subject has exactly the catchy, swinging quality that many players miss. At times there's a lack of brilliance, which the rather dull recording emphasises, but this is a winning anthology of this major American romantic.

Piano Sonata, Op 26. Excursions, Op 20. Nocturne, Op 33, 'Homage to John Field'. Three Sketches. Ballade, Op 46. Interludes – No 1, Intermezzo. Souvenirs, Op 28
Daniel Pollack pf
Naxos 8 550992 (72' · DDD)   Ⓢ

Daniel Pollack studied with (among others) Rosina Lhévinne and Wilhelm Kempf. His playing exudes confidence, especially in the more rhythmic and forthright passages. In his hands the Sonata is powerfully driven and crisply articulated, creating a palpable sense of raw energy and excitement. His full sonorities and sense of shape in the *Interlude* and the *Ballade* are also impressive, and while his tempo in the latter may seem a shade fast, it adds to the essential restlessness of the piece. In the more lyrical works, notably the *Nocturne*, however, Pollack's handling is too brusque, trampling roughshod over the contrast between passion and delicacy. The dance pieces of the *Excursions* and *Souvenirs* are generally more sensitive, and he effectively captures the diversity of distinctive flavours, from the slow blues (*Excursions*) to the Schottische (*Souvenirs*). Horowitz inevitably remains the benchmark in the Sonata, and his virtuoso fire is in a class of its own. Nevertheless, despite the poor recorded sound from Naxos's problematic Santa Rosa studio, this is an enjoyable disc and quite a bargain.

Knoxville: Summer of 1915, Op 24

Knoxville: Summer of 1915, Op 24[a]. Essays for Orchestra – No 2, Op 17; No 3, Op 47. Toccata Festiva, Op 36[b]
[a]**Karina Gauvin** sop [b]**Thomas Trotter** org
Royal Scottish National Orchestra / Marin Alsop
Naxos 8 559134 (57' · DDD) Text included   Ⓢ**OO**

Karina Gauvin and Marin Alsop take a nostalgic view of *Knoxville: Summer of 1915*. Theirs is an adult's bittersweet reminiscence rather than a child's innocent view. The outer sections sway slowly, the phrases longingly caressed as if soprano and orchestra were loath to let them go. Gauvin sings smoothly, generally emphasising song over text, though she's alive to James Agee's fragrant imagery, and varies the colour of her voice appropriately. With deeply expressive playing from the Royal Scottish National

Orchestra, the result is ravishing; this is one of the finest versions of *Knoxville* to date.

Alsop's tautly argued Second Essay is equally satisfying. She resists the temptation to stretch the tempo at climactic moments, creating a strong sense of momentum; you're swept along by the music's powerful current.

Knoxville and the Essays (all recorded in Glasgow's Henry Wood Hall) pack a nice sonic punch. If only Thomas Trotter's brilliant execution of the solo organ part in the *Toccata Festiva* were recorded with greater presence than the acoustic of Paisley Abbey allows. The *Toccata* may not be top-drawer Barber, but it has its moments. Nevertheless, Alsop's ear-opening Barber series reaches a new high-point with this instalment. Strongly recommended.

Additional recommendation

Knoxville: Summer of 1915
Coupled with: works by Menotti, Harbison and Stravinsky
Upshaw sop **Orchestra of St Luke's / Zinman**
Nonesuch 7559-79187-2 (44' · DDD)   Ⓕ
Dawn Upshaw captures the childish innocence of Barber's gorgeous scena in a programme of comparable vocal treats.

Agnus Dei, Op 11

Barber Twelfth Night, Op 42 No 1. To be sung on the water, Op 42 No 2. Reincarnations, Op 16. Agnus Dei, Op 11. Heaven-Haven. Sure on this shining night. The monk and his cat. The Virgin Martyrs, Op 8 No 1. Let down the bars, O Death, Op 8 No 2. God's Grandeur **Schuman** Perceptions. Mail Order Madrigals
Anthony Saunders pf **The Joyful Company of Singers / Peter Broadbent**
ASV CDDCA939 (66' · DDD) Texts included   Ⓕ**O**

Newcomers should make haste to track 6 for a pleasant surprise. Here they will encounter Samuel Barber's indestructible *Adagio* in its alternative and mellifluous 1967 vocal guise, set to the text of the *Agnus Dei*. Peter Broadbent's Joyful Company of Singers acquit themselves extremely well. Also to be particularly relished are the exquisite Op 42 pairing of *Twelfth Night* and *To be sung on the water*, the carefree lilt of *The monk and his cat* and, above all, the majestic, strikingly ambitious 1938 setting of Gerald Manley Hopkins's sonnet, *God's Grandeur* (perhaps the single most impressive achievement on the disc). Further delights are provided by Barber's countryman and contemporary, William Schuman. The concise, beautifully sculpted *Perceptions* (1982) are settings of choice aphorisms from the pen of Walt Whitman, while the *Mail Order Madrigals* (1972) wittily utilise the flowery prose drawn from advertisements contained within a Sears and Roebuck catalogue of 1897. A most attractive issue, in short, excellently produced and engineered.

Vanessa, Op 32

Vanessa
Christine Brewer *sop* Vanessa **Susan Graham** *mez*
Erika **Catherine Wyn-Rogers** *mez* Baroness **William
Burden** *ten* Anatol **Neal Davies** *bass-bar* The Old
Doctor **BBC Singers; BBC Symphony Orchestra /
Leonard Slatkin**
Chandos ② 🔊 CHSA5032 (123' · DDD/DSD ·
S/T/t/N)　　　　　　　　　　　　　　　ⒻO

Gian Carlo Menotti took as his starting-point
for the libretto of *Vanessa* the atmosphere of
Isak Dinesen's *Seven Gothic Tales*. His story is
original, but the ideas that fired him can be
found in the stories. One of Dinesen's heroines
lives a secluded life, and although beautiful,
she's forlorn – 'she knew that she did not exist,
for nobody ever looked at her'. Vanessa, too, has
lived her adult life waiting for the return of her
faithless admirer, Anatol. When he does come,
it's an impostor.

For an opera that's so seldom performed,
Vanessa has been accorded a generous three
complete recordings. This new one, recorded in
London's Barbican after a concert in 2003, has
splendidly vivid sound. Leonard Slatkin draws
full-blooded playing from the BBC Symphony
Orchestra, accentuating Barber's use of yearning, Puccini-inspired melodies, laced with a few
nods to Berg and Strauss. The weirdest music,
that for the ball in Act 3, sounds like some kind
of Western barn dance, even though the setting
is northern Europe.

Excellent though Susan Graham is as Erika,
Christine Brewer is so much in command, and
in such splendid voice, there's no doubt it's
Vanessa's story. One problem is that the three
female voices sound a little similar: Catherine
Wyn-Rogers is a youthful old Baroness.

Anatol, the greatest cad in opera since Pinkerton, is made almost sympathetic by William
Burden. Neal Davies does what he can with the
rather stock figure of the Doctor.

But listening at home one is conscious of an
awful lot of generalised mood music. *Vanessa*
was the last gasp of American *verismo*: its Met
première in 1958 was in the same season as
Bernstein's *West Side Story* on Broadway, and
we all know what that led to.

Additional recommendations

Vanessa

Steber Vanessa **Elias** Erika **Resnik** Baroness **Gedda**
Anatol **Tozzi** Old Doctor **New York Metropolitan
Opera Chorus & Orchestra / Mitropoulos**
RCA Victor Gold Seal ② 2RG 7899 (114' · ADD)　　Ⓜ
The original-cast recording on RCA will always be
irreplaceable. Brilliantly cast, it has the real feel of
theatre. It is also Barber's first version, with four
acts, and includes Vanessa's skating aria.

Chickering Vanessa **Bauwens** Anatol **Matthews**
Erika **Conrad** Old Doctor **Ukrainian National
Capella 'Dumka'; Ukraine National Symphony**

Orchestra / Gil Rose
Naxos ② 8 669140/1 (121' · DDD)　　　　　　Ⓢ
Ellen Chickering is a commanding Vanessa, with
crisp diction, and the other principals are good.
There are moments where the National Symphony Orchestra of Ukraine seems to accentuate
the Russian mood of the music. The sound quality
is clear, the balance between voices and orchestra
excellent. Good value.

Béla Bartók　　　　Hungarian 1881-1945

*Bartók began lessons with his mother, who brought
up the family after his father's death in 1888. In
1894 they settled in Bratislava, where he attended
the Gymnasium (Dohnányi was an elder schoolfel-
low), studied the piano with László Erkel and Anton
Hyrtl, and composed sonatas and quartets. In 1898
he was accepted by the Vienna Conservatory, but following Dohnányi he went to the Budapest Academy
(1899-1903), where he studied the piano with
Liszt's pupil Istvan Thoman and composition with
Janos Koessler. There he deepened his acquaintance
with Wagner, though it was the music of Strauss,
which he met at the Budapest première of Also sprach
Zarathustra in 1902, that had most influence. He
wrote a symphonic poem, Kossuth (1903), using
Strauss's methods with Hungarian elements in
Liszt's manner.*

*In 1904 Kossuth was performed in Budapest and
Manchester; at the same time Bartók began to make
a career as a pianist, writing a Piano Quintet and
two Lisztian virtuoso showpieces (Rhapsody Op 1,
Scherzo Op 2). Also in 1904 he made his first Hungarian folksong transcription. In 1905 he collected
more songs and began his collaboration with Kodály:
their first arrangements were published in 1906.
The next year he was appointed Thoman's successor
at the Budapest Academy, which enabled him to settle in Hungary and continue his folksong collecting,
notably in Transylvania. Meanwhile his music was
beginning to be influenced by this activity and by the
music of Debussy that Kodály had brought back from
Paris: both opened the way to new, modal kinds of
harmony and irregular metre. The 1908 Violin
Concerto is still within the symphonic tradition, but
the many small piano pieces of this period show a
new, authentically Hungarian Bartók emerging,
with the 4ths of Magyar folksong, the rhythms of
peasant dance and the scales he had discovered among
Hungarian, Romanian and Slovak peoples. The
arrival of this new voice is documented in his String
Quartet No 1 (1908), introduced at a Budapest concert of his music in 1910.*

*There followed orchestral pieces and a one-act
opera, Bluebeard's Castle, dedicated to his young
wife. Influenced by Mussorgsky and Debussy but
most directly by Hungarian peasant music (and
Strauss, still, in its orchestral pictures), the work, a
grim fable of human isolation, failed to win the competition in which it was entered. For two years
(1912-14) Bartók practically gave up composition
and devoted himself to the collection, arrangement
and study of folk music, until World War I put an*

end to his expeditions. He returned to creative activity with the String Quartet No 2 (1917) and the fairytale ballet The Wooden Prince, whose production in Budapest in 1917 restored him to public favour. The next year Bluebeard's Castle was staged and he began a second ballet, The Miraculous Mandarin, which was not performed until 1926 (there were problems over the subject, the thwarting and consummation of sexual passion). Rich and graphic in invention, the score is practically an opera without words.

While composing The Miraculous Mandarin Bartók came under the influence of Stravinsky and Schoenberg, and produced some of his most complex music in the two violin sonatas of 1921-2. At the same time he was gaining international esteem: his works were published by Universal Edition and he was invited to play them all over Europe. He was now well established at home, too. He wrote the confident Dance Suite (1923); there was then another lull until the sudden rush of works in 1926 designed for himself to play, including the Piano Concerto No 1, the Piano Sonata and the suite Out of Doors. These exploit the piano as a percussion instrument, using its resonances as well as its xylophonic hardness. The search for new sonorities and driving rhythms was continued in the next two string quartets (1927-8), of which No 4, like the concerto, is in a five-section palindromic pattern (ABCBA).

Similar formal schemes, with intensively worked counterpoint, were used in the Piano Concerto No 2 (1931) and String Quartet No 5 (1934), though now Bartók's harmony was becoming more diatonic. The move from inward chromaticism to a glowing major (though modally tinged) tonality is basic to the Music for Strings, Percussion and Celesta (1936) and the Sonata for Two Pianos and Percussion (1937), both written for performance in Switzerland at a time when the political situation in Hungary was growing unsympathetic.

In 1940 Bartók and his second wife (he had divorced and remarried in 1923) left war-torn Europe to live in New York, which he found alien. They gave concerts and for a while he had a research grant to work on a collection of Yugoslav folksong, but their finances were precarious, as increasingly was his health. It seemed that his last European work, the String Quartet No 6 (1939), might be his pessimistic swansong, but then came the exuberant Concerto for Orchestra (1943) and the involuted Sonata for Solo Violin (1944). Piano Concerto No 3, written to provide his widow with an income, was almost finished when he died, a Viola Concerto left in sketch. **GROVE**music

Piano Concertos

No 1 Sz83; **No 2** Sz95; **No 3** Sz119

Piano Concertos Nos 1-3   🄷
Géza Anda pf **Berlin Radio Symphony Orchestra / Ferenc Fricsay**
DG The Originals 447 399-2GOR (78' · ADD)
Recorded 1959-60   Ⓜ︎⭕

Much as you'd like to tout the new as the best,

there are some older recordings where a very special chemistry spells 'definitive', and that pose an almost impossible challenge to subsequent rivals. Such is this 1959 recording of Bartók's Second Piano Concerto, a tough, playful, pianistically aristocratic performance where dialogue is consistently keen and spontaneity is captured on the wing (even throughout numerous sessions). The first movement is relentless but never tires the ear; the second displays two very different levels of tension, one slow and mysterious, the other hectic but controlled; and although others might have thrown off the finale's octaves with even greater abandon, Anda's performance is the most successful in suggesting savage aggression barely held in check.

The Third Concerto is again beautifully moulded and carefully thought through. Moments such as the loving return from the second movement's chirpy central episode are quite unforgettable, while the finale is both nimble and full toned. The First Concerto was the last to be recorded and is perhaps the least successful of the three: here ensemble is occasionally loose, and characterisation less vivid than with, say, Donohoe and Rattle. Still, it's a fine performance and the current transfer has been lovingly effected.

Piano Concertos Nos 1[a]; 2[b] & 3[c]
[a]**Krystian Zimerman,** [b]**Leif Ove Andsnes,** [c]**Hélène Grimaud** pfs [a]**Chicago Symphony Orchestra;** [b]**Berlin Philharmonic Orchestra;** c**London Symphony Orchestra / Pierre Boulez**
DG 447 5330GH (76' · DDD)   Ⓕ⭕⭕

It's interesting that for Pierre Boulez, Bartók's Third Piano Concerto is 'the Cinderella of the family', and doubly interesting given the recorded evidence, where Boulez and Hélène Grimaud turn prince and princess for the most memorable outing the work has had in years. Grimaud relishes Bartók's solo writing. Then there's the way she can suddenly reduce the volume and body of her tone. The woodwind birdsong at the centre of the Adagio sings out to a keen staccato; the timps and bass drum in the finale are wonderfully vivid.

How different is the Second Concerto, a high-energy production from Berlin. In the first movement the winds yak away while Leif Ove Andsnes approximates an angelic typist tabulating at speed, halfway between Anda's playfulness and Pollini's iron-fisted aggression. The Adagio sections of the second movement are held dead still, with roaring timpani rolls at the centre, while Andsnes's account of the scurrying presto passage is even-fingered and dextrous, the recorded balance allowing for plenty of detail in both the foreground and background. But it's the finale that shows Andsnes and Boulez exhibiting the most power and prowess.

Krystian Zimerman's account of the First Concerto is a refined tour de force, immaculate, controlled, sometimes quite free; Boulez's conducting can be a little stiff-jointed. The sullen waltz at the centre of the second movement builds to a sonorous climax and the finale is feather-light, though Zimerman might have preferred a more playful sparring partner. And the recorded balance makes the piano too close.

Summing up, Grimaud's Third is a winner; the Second with Andsnes has a fabulous finale, and Zimerman's First is brilliant in parts, if not quite a meeting of minds. As to rivals, Peter Donohoe and Simon Rattle give us a cracking First; András Schiff's set with Iván Fischer offers a rather more lyrical slant than the brawny Zoltán Kocsis (also with Fischer); Géza Anda with Ferenc Fricsay evidently loves every moment; and in the first two concertos Pollini and Abbado are bold as brass and just a little brittle.

Bartók Piano Concerto No 3 **Prokofiev** Piano Concertos – No 1 in D flat, Op 10; No 3 in C, Op 26
Martha Argerich pf **Montreal Symphony Orchestra / Charles Dutoit**
EMI 556654-2 (70' · DDD)   Ⓕ**●**

As always with this most mercurial of virtuosos, Martha Argerich's playing is generated by the mood of the moment and many listeners may well be surprised at her relative geniality with Dutoit. Personal and vivacious throughout, she always allows the composer his own voice. This is particularly true in Bartók's Third Concerto where her rich experience in chamber music makes her often *primus inter pares*, a virtuoso who listens to her partners with the greatest care. In the *Adagio religioso* she achieves a poise that has sometimes eluded her in the past and her finale is specially characterful, her stealthy start to the concluding *Presto* allowing the final pages their full glory. Dutoit and the Montreal Symphony achieve a fine unity throughout, a sense of like-minded musicians at work.

All true musicians will recognise performances of a special magic and integrity. In the Prokofiev First Concerto, her opening is arguably more authentically *brioso* than ferocious, her overall view a refreshingly fanciful view of Prokofiev's youthful iconoclasm. The central *Andante assai* is inflected with an improvisatory freedom she probably wouldn't have risked earlier in her career and in the *Allegro scherzando* she trips the light fantastic, reserving a suitably tigerish attack for the final octave bravura display. Her performance of the Third Concerto is less fleet or nimble-fingered than in her early days but is more delectably alive to passing caprice. The recordings are clear and naturally balanced and only those in search of metallic thrills and rushes of blood to the head will feel disappointed.

Viola Concerto, Sz120

Bartók Viola Concerto **Eötvös** Replica **Kurtág** Movement for Viola and Orchestra

Kim Kashkashian va **Netherlands Radio Chamber Orchestra / Peter Eötvös**
ECM New Series 465 420-2 (50' · DDD)   Ⓕ**●**

Kashkashian's superbly engineered recording of the Bartók Viola Concerto bears witness to a total identification between performer and composer. Even the tiny pause bridging the opening and the secondary idea growing out of it, is perfectly judged. Kashkashian makes this music dance, not just in the finale but also in the way that she phrases and articulates the entire piece. Eötvös's conducting offers many parallel insights, not least towards the end of the first movement where a growing sense of agitation throws the succeeding *Adagio religioso* into a particularly favourable light. Eötvös employs Tibor Serly's completion, revising odd details and accommodating a few articulations and phrasings that Kashkashian has herself instigated. If you need convincing that Bartók's Viola Concerto is a great work, then Kashkashian and Eötvos should, between them, do the trick.

Of the other pieces, Eötvös's *Replica* for viola and orchestra is astonishing music in which foggy harmonies hover between startled highs and raucous lows, then mutate into a strange, sickly pulsing. By contrast, György Kurtág's early *Movement for Viola and Orchestra* – two-thirds of a concerto Kurtág completed in 1953-4 – is relatively conventional, with plenty of virtuoso viola writing.

Additional recommendations

Violin Concertos Nos 1 and 2
Coupled with: Piano Concertos
Chung vn **Ashkenazy** pf **Chicago Symphony Orchestra, London Philharmonic Orchestra / Solti**
Decca Double ② 473 271-2DF2 (137' · DDD)   Ⓜ
    Highly extrovert, likeable performances from Chung with Solti a like-minded collaborator. The piano concertos make a great package – Ashkenazy is on superb form.

Violin Concerto No 2
Coupled with: **Bartók** Solo Sonata. **Janáček** Violin Concerto. Violin Sonata. **Weill** Concerto for Violin and Wind Orchestra
Tetzlaff vn **Andsnes** pf **LPO / Gielen; Deutsche Kammerphilharmonie**
Virgin Classics ② 562053-2 (DDD) Recorded 1990-91
    Tetzlaff's playing has great character and   Ⓑ
    technical security; he generates a consistently
    stimulating rapport with Gielen and the LPO.

Concerto for Orchestra, Sz116

Concerto for Orchestra. Kossuth. 5 Village Scenes.
Budapest Festival Orchestra / Iván Fischer
Philips 476 7255 (67' · DDD)   Ⓜ**●●●**

 It is the flavour of this *Concerto for Orchestra* that wins the day. Just sample the subtle *portamento* that spices the

string line at bars 52-3 (2'36'') of the first movement, and the sombre colouring near the end of the movement, at 8'58''. Fischer is a dab hand at shaping and inflecting the musical line, and his characterization of the 'Giuoco delle coppie' – paced, incidentally, at the prescribed crotchet = 94 – is second to none. He invests the 'Elegia' with the maximum respectable quota of passion and the 'Intermezzo interrotto' dances to a few added accents and the finale is a riot of sunshine and swirling skirts, except for the mysterious – and notoriously tricky – *più presto* coda, with its rushing sul ponticello string choirs, which Fischer articulates with great care. One senses that the players are being driven to the very limits of their abilities, which only serves to intensify the excitement.

Additional recommendations

Concerto for Orchestra
Coupled with: Music for Strings, Percussion and
Celesta. Hungarian Sketches

Chicago Symphony Orchestra / Reiner
RCA 09026 61504-2 (767' · ADD) Recorded 1956 Ⓜ**OO**
A classic recording by one of the master Bartók conductors. With staggering playing by the Chicago Symphony and recording that simply dones't sound its age, this is a magnificent achievement. RCA's sound reportage of the *Concerto for Orchestra* has uncanny realism, and if the climaxes are occasionaly reined in, the fervour of Reiner's direction more than compensates. His couplings are excellent: a suave *Music for Strings*… and a stylish *Hungarian Sketches*

The Miraculous Mandarin, Sz73

The Miraculous Mandarin. Hungarian Peasant Songs, Sz100. Hungarian Sketches, Sz97. Romanian Folkdances, Sz68. Transylvanian Dances, Sz96. Romanian Dance, Sz47
Hungarian Radio Chorus; Budapest Festival Orchestra / Iván Fischer
Philips Gramophone Awards Collection 476 1799 (67' · DDD)   Ⓜ**OOO**

 As *Mandarins* go, they don't come more miraculous than this – a vivid, no-holds-barred performance. Everything tells: the flavour is right, the pacing too, and the sound has a toughened, raw-edged quality that's an essential constituent of Bartók's tonal language. Although lurid, even seedy, in narrative detail, this is ultimately a tale of compassion, and Fischer never forgets that. Observable detail, all of it musically significant, occurs virtually by the minute. Delicacy trails bullish aggression, forcefulness alternates with almost graphic suggestiveness: it's all there in the score. Fischer never vulgarises, brutalises or overstates the case; most important, he underlines the quickly flickering, folkish elements in Bartók's

---

BARTÓK'S CONCERTO FOR ORCHESTRA – IN BRIEF

Hungarian Festival Orchestra / Iván Fischer
Philips 476 7255 (67' · DDD)   Ⓜ**OOO**
A tremendous modern performance with lashings of character and some really stunning orchestral work. Fischer negotiates all the changes of tempo and rhythm with his customary panache.

Chicago SO / Fritz Reiner
RCA 09026 61504-2 (76' · ADD)   Ⓜ**OO**
Recorded in 1956, this still sounds stunning and Reiner's interpretation has the idiomatic feel of someone who has really lived with the score. This is Bartók with an iron grip, but thrilling none the less. Coupled with the *Music for strings, percussion and celesta*.

Chicago SO / Sir Georg Solti
Decca ② 470 516-2DF2 (138' · DDD)   Ⓜ
This powerful recording from another great Hungarian conductor comes as part of a most appealing Bartók collection. Rather brightly recorded though!

Concertgebouw Orchestra / Eduard van Beinum
Dutton mono CDK1206 (69' · ADD)   Ⓜ
A wonderfully vital and exciting performance from one of The Netherlands' greatest conductors – the ex-Decca sound is remarkable for the early 1950s.

Boston SO / Serge Koussevitsky
Naxos mono 8 110105 (59' · DDD)   Ⓢ**O**
A radio relay of the first Boston performance under the man who commissioned the work. This has all the energy, excitement and sense of discovery of a creator's recording (it even has the original ending).

Chicago SO / Pierre Boulez
DG 437 826-2GH (60' · DDD)   Ⓕ
A master Bartók conductor with one of the great Bartók orchestras in a reading that shows off both the work's and the players' virtuosity. This is a very exciting modern account of this extraordinary creation.

Berlin PO / Herbert von Karajan
DG 457 890-2GGA (71' · ADD)   Ⓜ
This is one of a number of recordings Karajan made of the work. His quest to seek out the beautiful did somewhat take the pungency out of much of the writing.

musical language that other conductors barely acknowledge.

The strongly individual character of the Budapest Festival Orchestra is delightful. The strings have a biting edge, the woodwinds a gypsy-style reediness, while brass and percussion are forceful and incisive but never raucous. This is Hungarian-grown Bartók that actually *sounds* Hungarian; if only other European orchestras would reclaim parallel levels of individuality.

The Miraculous Mandarin, Sz73[a]. Concerto for Orchestra, Sz116[b]
[a]**Junge Deutsche Philharmonie;** [b]**Gustav Mahler Jugendorchester / Péter Eötvös**
BMC BMCCD058 (70' · DDD) [b]Recorded live 1992
Ⓟ**OO**

This Bartók CD is what recording should be about. There are shortcomings – the odd spot of iffy playing, inconsistent balances and an occasional extraneous noise – but the musical qualities are overwhelming. Of course, it doesn't compare *as a production* with Chailly's imaginatively voluptuous though significantly less intense coupling for Decca. But then you wouldn't expect it to. *The Miraculous Mandarin* in particular has an animalistic impulsiveness, a sense of urgency that drives right to the heart of the drama. The opening sets the atmosphere with precisely the right feeling of panic, the ejection scenes where potential punters are thrown out are positively wild. The chase gains momentum by the second and at the point (soon after) when the tramps decide to kill the Mandarin, Eötvös and his players conjure a series of deathly growls the like of which have surely never been heard this side of Hell! The closing scene has heart-tearing pathos, and the Junge Deutsche Philharmonie play their socks off: they swallow the *Mandarin* whole and take on every insinuating bar with genuine understanding. But then, they're being conducted by a composer, and Eötvös feels his Bartók from the inside.

The *Concerto for Orchestra* (Gustav Mahler Jugendorchester this time) is scarcely less good, though the sound is entirely different – dry and closely balanced to compare with the *Mandarin*'s more airy acoustic. But the performance is a scorcher. The finale generates plenty of fire (Chailly's more pristine performance ' seems cautious by comparison) and chosen tempos are spot-on. Again, the spirit burns away a handful of imperfections that never really mattered in the first place.

Additional recommendations

The Miraculous Mandarin
Coupled with: Two portraits, Op 5
London Symphony Orchestra / Abbado
DG Masters 445 501-2GMA (minutes: DDD)   Ⓜ
Abbado directs an imaginative and atmospheric performance: the climaxes, such as that at the mandarin's entrance, are awe-inspiring.

String Quartets

No 1 Sz40; **No 2** Sz67; **No 3** Sz85; **No 4** Sz91; **No 5** Sz102; **No 6** Sz114

String Quartets Nos 1-6
Takács Quartet (Edward Dusinberre, Károly Schranz *vns* Roger Tapping *va* András Fejér *vc*)
Decca ② 455 297-2DH2 (152' · DDD)   Ⓕ**OOO**

 These performances provide more impressive sampling points than can be enumerated in a single review. The First Quartet's oscillating tempo-shifts work wonderfully well, all with total naturalness. Characterisation is equally strong elsewhere, not least the first movement of the Debussian arpeggios of the Second Quartet, and the second movement where Fejér races back into the rustic opening subject. The nightmare climax in the last movement has rarely sounded more prophetic of the great *Divertimento*'s central movement. The middle quartets work very well, with prominent inner voices in the Third and plenty of swagger in the Fourth. The high spots of No 4 are Fejér's improvisational cello solo in the third movement and a finale where the violent opening is a hefty *legato* to compare with the sharper, more Stravinskian attack of, say, the Tokyo Quartet. Likewise, the sudden dance-like episode in the first movement of the Fifth Quartet, savage music played from the pit of the stomach, while the third movement's bleary-eyed viola melody over teeming violin triplets suggests peasants in caricature.

The Takács are responsive to Bartók's sardonic humour – the 'barrel-organ' episode at the end of the Fifth Quartet, and the corny 'Burletta' in the third movement of the Sixth. The Sixth itself has some of the saddest, wildest and wisest music written in the last 100 years: the opening viola solo recalls Mahler's Tenth and the close fades to a mysterious question. Throughout the cycle, Bartók's metronome markings are treated more as guidelines than literal commands. The playing imparts Bartók's all-embracing humanity. If the greatest string quartets after Beethoven are still unknown to you, this set may well prove the musical journey of a lifetime. The recording has ambient, full-bodied sound that's more reminiscent of the concert hall than the studio.

String Quartets Nos 1-6
Emerson Quartet (Eugene Drucker, Philip Setzer *vns* Lawrence Dutton *va* David Finckel *vc*)
DG ② 423 657-2GH2 (149' · DDD) Recorded 1988
Ⓕ**OOO**

 Any cycle of Bartók quartets has to be special to stand out against the competition. The Emerson Quartet's is, and does: powerful and refined, paying close attention to the letter of the score, and excelling in virtuoso teamwork. The impression is of massive tonal projection and superlative clarity, each textural strand coloured and made audible to a degree possibly unrivalled in the recorded history of these works. DG's close, brightly lit recording quality must share some of the credit for that. Combine this with controlled vehemence, headlong velocity and razor-sharp unanimity (any fast movement from quartets two to five can serve as illustration) and you've a formidable alliance of virtues. Well recorded, when this set first appeared it was hailed as one of the most exciting chamber music recordings for many years.

Additional recommendations

String Quartets 1-6
Juilliard Quartet
Retrospective ③ RET005 (158' · ADD) Recorded 1963
Ⓢ Ⓢ

This legendary set, reissued at bargain price, contains superlative performances in vivid stereo sound. It's a more viscerally exciting reading than the Juilliard's more relaxed 1981 digital remake.

Violin Sonatas, Rhapsodies, Contrasts

Violin Sonatas – No 1 Sz75; **No 2** Sz76
Rhapsodies – No 1 Sz86 **No 2** Sz89
Contrasts Sz111. **Solo Violin Sonata** Sz117

Violin Sonatas Nos 1 & 2. Solo Violin Sonata
Christian Tetzlaff vn **Leif Ove Andsnes** pf
Virgin Classics 545668-2 (79' · DDD)　　Ⓕ❍❍❍

 Would it be too fanciful to divide interpreters of Bartók's violin music into two approximate categories: Szigeti-Végh and Menuhin-Stern? In other words, cerebral-rustic and emotive-universal? Listen to Thomas Zehetmair's Bartók or Isabelle Faust's, Gidon Kremer's or, indeed, Christian Tetzlaff's and the spirit of Végh in particular seems prominent. Whereas Eugene Drucker, György Pauk and Robert Mann (on Bartók Records) are more aligned with Menuhin and Stern.

Tetzlaff's tone is grainy and lightly-brushed, his inward approach most evident in the Solo Sonata, a work he plays with sovereign command – and with greater freedom than on his more straightlaced 1991 recording (Virgin, nla), which veered less towards the Végh axis than this new version does. Here Tetzlaff makes more of the fugue's shifting perspectives and relishes Bartók's bold chord constructions. Other players may at times employ a richer tone palette but few take a more thoughtful interpretative standpoint on what is after all the finest unaccompanied violin sonata since Bach.

The two duo sonatas are also beautifully done. Tetzlaff again proves both focused and expressive, though among modern rivals you might prefer Faust's questing expressiveness, and György Pauk's Naxos coupling offers honest

BARTÓK STRING QUARTETS – IN BRIEF

Emerson Quartet
DG ② 423 657-2GH2 (149' · DDD)　　Ⓑ❍❍❍
 One of the three *Gramophone* Award-winning sets of these seminal 20th-century quartets. High-powered and totally accurate – this is one of the most virtuoso recordings.

Tokyo Quartet
DG ② 476 1833 (159' · ADD)　　Ⓜ❍❍
Recently reissued as part of Universal's *Gramophone* Award series, these are gentler but infinitely subtle performances with great attention to colour and texture.

Takács Quartet
Decca ② 455 297-2DH2 (152' · DDD)　　Ⓑ❍❍❍
The most recent award-winning set and possibly the finest all-round set of the six quartets. The Takács Quartet play every note as if it were their last – the conviction positively crackles from the speakers.

Hagen Quartet
DG ② 463 576-2GH2 (154' · DDD)　　Ⓑ❍❍❍
Adventurous, imaginative performances from one of the younger quartets with a lovely consistency of approach throughout.

Végh Quartet
Auvidis Naïve ② V4870 (155' · ADD)　　Ⓑ❍
From the early 1970s, these wonderful humane performances, warts and all, capture one of the great quartets on top form. They seek out the singing quality of Bartók's writing rather than the power sought by some modern groups.

Juilliard Quartet
Pearl mono ② GEMS0147 (156' · ADD)　　Ⓜ❍
This 1950s set originally from CBS is mightily impressive. As the first cycle to be recorded as a cycle it was something of a milestone, and that quality of novelty and discovery shines through magnificently.

Alban Berg Quartet
EMI ② 747720-8 (150' · DDD)　　Ⓑ
A cycle that should impress more than it does. It's all very well played but it lacks that element of soul and humanity that underpin these amazing works. The ABQ seem to be more interested in technical perfection than in touching the heart.

Keller Quartet
Warner Ultima ② 3984 25594-2 (149' · DDD) Ⓑ❍❍
A fine bargain cycle well worth considering if you're on a tight budget. As Hungarians the Kellers have an innate feel for the idiom, and the digital recording is beautifully handled. At the price you can't go wrong.

musical reportage. But what makes these performances more or less indispensable is the character and control of Leif Ove Andsnes's piano playing, its fastidious deployment of tone and immaculate timing. The clarion alarms in the outer movements of the First Sonata, where tonality is stretched to its limits, ring out without percussive overkill. The Second Sonata's folksy *Allegretto* is strong and tidy but with the unmistakable sense of earth under foot. Andsnes is the stronger personality, Tetzlaff the more confidential, yielding presence (wonderful in the First Sonata's *Adagio*); an ideal anima-animus performing relationship.

This is chamber music playing of the highest order, candid and straightforward enough for a basic library recommendation but also rich enough in subtleties to satisfy even the most discerning connoisseur.

Violin Sonata No 1. Solo Violin Sonata
Isabelle Faust *vn* **Ewa Kupiec** *pf*
Harmonia Mundi Les Nouveaux Interprètes
HMN91 1623 (69' · DDD)   ⑤ ⑧ ○○○

Bartók's First Violin Sonata is notoriously reluctant to yield its secrets yet none is more comprehensively perceptive than this recording by the young violinist Isabelle Faust. Harmonia Mundi counts Faust among the 'cream of the new generation of musicians' and, on this evidence, no one could rightly disagree. Ewa Kupiec provides Faust with motivated support. Faust favours a sensual approach that draws active parallels with the music of Berg. She ventures deep among the first movement's more mysterious episodes. This is empathetic playing, candid, full of temperament and always focused securely on the note's centre. The crescendoing processional that sits at the heart of the second movement is charged with suspense and the steely finale suggests a savage resolve. Faust and Kupiec visit corners in this score that others gloss over, and the recording supports them all the way. The Solo Sonata is virtually as impressive. Here Faust approaches the music from a Bachian axis: her tone is pure, double-stopping immaculate and sense of timing acute. Faust is a persuasive narrator; she and her piano partner break down barriers in the First Sonata that, for some, will mean the difference between approachability and continuing bafflement. Do give them a try.

Violin Sonatas Nos 1 & 2. Contrasts, Sz111
Kálmán Berkes *cl* **György Pauk** *vn* **Jenö Jandó** *pf*
Naxos 8 550749 (75' · DDD) Recorded 1993   ⑤

Readers who habitually fight shy of Bartók's provocatively astringent piano writing might at first find these endlessly fascinating works rather unpalatable, the First Sonata especially. But careful scrutiny reveals manifold beauties which, once absorbed, tend to haunt the memory and prompt repeated listening. Jenö Jandó's

piano playing is fairly forthright yet without the naked agression of, say, Sviatoslav Richter. And it provides an effective foil for György Pauk's warm tone and fluid solo line, especially in the First Sonata, where ungainly tone production could so easily compound the listener's discomfort. Here, however, the interpretation is at once thoughtful and well shaped, and fully appreciative of the mysterious 'night music' that sits at the heart of the *Adagio*.

The Second Sonata is both gentler and more improvisatory, its language and structure – although still pretty formidable – somewhat in the manner of a rhapsody. Pauk and Jandó again hit the target, and the full-bodied recording makes for a homogeneous sound picture. To have a spirited performance of the multi-faceted *Contrasts* (with Kálmán Berkes on clarinet) as a bonus certainly helps promote this well-annotated CD to the front line of competition. A confident mainstream recommendation, then, and superb value for money.

Violin Sonata No 2. Rhapsodies Nos 1 & 2.
Six Romanian Folkdances, Sz56
Isabelle Faust *vn* **Florent Boffard** *pf*
Harmonia Mundi Les Nouveaux Interprètes
HMN91 1702 (46' · DDD)   ⑤ ⑧ ○

The most striking features of Isabelle Faust's first Bartók CD for Harmonia Mundi, which featured the earthen First Sonata, were an empathetic spirit and a fiery temperament. On this recording she exhibits a defining use of nuance and inflection. The two contrasting movements of the tauter, folk-music-derived Second Sonata call for a near-schizoid adaptability to changing moods. In the restless *Molto moderato* first movement Faust suggests feelings of sensual insinuation, though the lacerating attack of her bow at 3'50" has real grit. As the music grows more agitated, she follows suit and her pianist-partner Florent Boffard brooks no compromise in his handling of Bartók's dissonant chordal writing. The Sonata's musical contours have rarely sounded better focused.

Faust offers feisty accounts of the two 1928 *Rhapsodies*, the Second being the more responsive to interpretative innovation. The stamping 'second part' recalls the orchestral *Dance Suite* of five years earlier; she invests it both with delicacy and a palpably rustic edge. The popular *Romanian Folkdances* provide a tuneful encore sequence (again, beautifully played). Despite the short measure, this is a marvellous CD.

Rhapsodies Nos 1 & 2. Contrasts. Solo Violin Sonata.
Six Romanian Folk Dances, Sz56 (arr Székely)
Michael Collins *cl* **Krysia Osostowicz** *vn* **Susan Tomes** *pf*
Helios CDH55149 (72' · DDD) Recorded 1990   ⑨ ○

Unusually for a composer who wrote so much fine chamber music Bartók wasn't himself a string player. But he did enjoy close artistic understanding with a succession of prominent violin virtuosos, including the Hungarians Jelly d'Arányi, Joseph Szigeti and Zoltán Székely, and, towards the end of his life, Yehudi Menuhin. It was Menuhin who commissioned the Sonata for solo violin, but Bartók died before he could hear him play it – Menuhin was unhappy with the occasional passages in quarter-tones and the composer had reserved judgement on his proposal to omit them. It was Menuhin's edition which was later printed and which has been most often played and recorded; but Krysia Osostowicz returns to the original and, more importantly, plays the whole work with intelligence, imaginative flair and consummate skill.

The Sonata is the most substantial work on this disc, but the rest of the programme is no less thoughtfully prepared or idiomatically delivered. There's the additional attraction of an extremely well balanced and natural-sounding recording. As a complement to the string quartets, which are at the very heart of Bartók's output, this is a most recommendable disc.

Violin Duos

Bartók 44 Duos for Two Violins, Sz98 **Kurtág** Ligatura – Message to Frances-Marie, Op 31b **Ligeti** Ballad and Dance
András Keller, János Pilz vns
ECM New Series 465 849-2 (58' · DDD) Ⓕ❍

Hearing top-grade quartet violinists tackle these flavoured educational duos is a delight, though not an original one. (The Emerson's co-leaders Eugene Drucker and Philip Setzer have already done likewise, albeit to quite different effect.) All, or virtually all, is revealed right from the opening 'Transylvanian Dance' where the newcomers' phrasing and rhythm are appropriately unbuttoned, their combined tone full but unforced. (Note: Keller and Pilz actually start at the end with Duo 'No 44'.) Bartók's original plan had been to place the easiest pieces first, then gradually pile on the challenges as the series progressed. However, for concert purposes he sanctioned the idea of not playing them in order.

Their chosen sequence is very well planned. The interpretative axis centres principally on harmony and rhythm, and characterisation is always vivid. In general the slower pieces leave the strongest impression: that's where these players harbour their most personal responses, but then the slowest pieces probably are the best. Though Sándor Végh's accounts with Alberto Lysy are rather more earthy, the advantage of this version is that it seems to have been conceived with continuous listening in mind: the ear never tires.

It would be easy to pigeonhole this set as veering in the general direction of the Végh's Bartók, just as the Keller's Bartók quartet cycle does, then make a parallel observation of Drucker and Setzer as representing the less

stylised manner of their own Emerson Quartet. Which would be fairly accurate and explain a preference for this disc, where an extra shot of interpretative re-creativeness ultimately wins the day. The sound quality is spacious and pleasingly full bodied.

Piano Works

For Children, Sz42. The First Term at the Piano, Sz53. 15 Hungarian Peasant Songs, Sz71. Three Hungarian Folksongs from the Csík District, Sz35a. Hungarian Folktunes, Sz66. Eight Improvisations on Hungarian Peasant Songs, Sz74. Three Rondos on (Slovak) Folk-tunes, Sz84. Romanian Christmas Carols, Sz57. Six Romanian Folkdances, Sz56. Two Romanian Dances, Sz43. Suite, Sz62, with original Andante. Piano Sonata, Sz80. Sonatina, Sz55. 14 Bagatelles, Sz38. Four Dirges, Sz45. Petite Suite, Sz105. Violin Duos, Sz98 (arr Sándor) – No 1, Teasing Song; No 17, Marching Song; No 35, Ruthenian kolomejka; No 42, Arabian Song; No 44, Transylvanian Dance. 10 Easy Pieces, Sz39. Allegro barbaro, Sz49. Out of doors, Sz81. Seven Sketches, Sz44. Two Elegies, Sz41. Three Burlesques, Sz47. Nine Little Pieces, Sz82. Three Studies, Sz72
György Sándor pf
Sony Classical ④ SB4K87949 (287' · DDD) Recorded 1993-5   Ⓑ❍

There can't be many pianists on the current circuit whose fund of experience extends to working with a major 20th-century master; but of those still recording, György Sándor must surely take pride of place. Sándor prepared Bartók's first two piano concertos under the composer's guidance and gave the world premières of the Third Concerto and the piano version of the *Dance Suite*. The present collection is Sándor's second survey of Bartók's piano music and contains all the major works apart from *Mikrokosmos*.

Many of these performances are exceptionally fine, even though the passage of time has witnessed something of a reduction in Sándor's pianistic powers, mostly where maximum stamina and high velocity fingerwork are required (as in the first *Burlesque*). However, you may be astonished at the heft, energy and puckish humour of Sándor's 1994 recording of the Piano Sonata, a more characterful rendition than its predecessor, with a particularly brilliant account of the folkish *Allegro molto* finale. The *Allegro barbaro* is similarly 'on the beam', while Sándor brings a cordial warmth to the various collections of ethnic pieces, the *Romanian Christmas Carols* especially.

His phrasing, rubato, expressive nuancing, attention to counterpoint and command of tone suggest the touch of a master, while his imagination relishes the exploratory nature of the *Improvisations*, *Bagatelles* and *Miraculous Mandarin*-style *Studies*. Sándor connects with all the music's abundant qualities: harmonic or rhythmic innovation, powerful emotion, humour, introspection, ethnic variety and the scope and complexity of Bartók's piano writing in general. Intuitive interpreters, especially those who knew and understand the composers they perform, are becoming a rare breed. In that respect alone, Sándor's Bartók deserves an honoured place in every serious CD collection of 20th-century piano music.

Additional recommendation

Solo piano works etc ☑
Bartók pf
Pearl mono GEMMCD9166 (69' · ADD) Ⓜ
  This Bartók-plays-Bartók compilation offers full-bodied transfers of some fascinating commercial recordings, including the first *Romanian Dances*, *Allegro barbaro* and Liszt's 'Sursum corda'.

Songs

Five Songs, Sz61. Five Songs, Sz63. Hungarian Folk-songs, Sz64 – Black is the earth; My God, my God; Wives, let me be one of your company; So much sorrow; If I climb the rocky mountains. Five Songs, Sz61 (orch Kodály). Five Hungarian Folksongs, Sz101
Júlia Hamari contr **Ilona Prunyi** pf **Hungarian State Orchestra / János Kovács**
Hungaroton HCD31535 (67' · DDD) Recorded 1992. Texts and translations included Ⓕ

Kodály's rose-tinted orchestrations of Bartók's uncompromisingly erotic Op 15 (Sz61) make for pleasant listening, but they sidetrack the real heart of the matter. Bartók had a year-long relationship with the 15-year-old Klára Gombossy, and three of the songs are based on her poetry; the fourth sets a poem by the daughter of Klára's piano teacher, while the remaining 'In Vivid Dreams' is a reworking of another poem by Klára, added later. Heard in its original form for voice and piano, Op 15 is a bold, harmonically far-reaching cycle (countless passages anticipate the harsher Bartók of the 1920s), often angular in design but, within its tough framework, passionately suggestive. Kodály's orchestrations date from 1961 and soften the music's contours in a way that Bartók himself would not have countenanced – at least not in 1915, the year in which the songs were composed. The *Five Songs*, Op 16 consolidate the dark, introspective language of Op 15, while the 10 folk-song settings – Bartók's clearly focused orchestrations (Sz101) and the five for voice and piano (Sz64) – are rather more outgoing and varied.

All this music is so absorbing that you tend temporarily to forget the performers – which wouldn't be possible were they less than good. Júlia Hamari projects a secure, strong body of tone and fully comprehends the potent love images of Op 15, while her accompanist, Ilona Prunyi, etches Bartók's vivid piano writing with a sure hand and much imagination. The orchestral items are patchily dealt with (winds are good, strings not), but the impressionistic nature of the writing (Kodály's especially) res-

ponds better to Kovács's soft-centred approach than, say, the *Village Scenes* would have done. The recordings are perfectly adequate. Recommended to all Bartókians and Lieder *aficionados*.

Duke Bluebeard's Castle

Duke Bluebeard's Castle
Walter Berry bass-bar Bluebeard **Christa Ludwig** mez Judith **London Symphony Orchestra / István Kertész**
Decca Legends 466 377-2DM (59' · ADD) Recorded 1965 Notes, text and translation included
Ⓜ◯

John Tomlinson bass Bluebeard **Anne Sofie von Otter** mez Judith **Sandor Elès** spkr **Berlin Philharmonic Orchestra / Bernard Haitink**
EMI 556162-2 (63' · DDD) Notes, text and translation included
Ⓕ◯◯

Bernard Haitink's poetic axis is vividly anticipated in the rarely recorded spoken prologue where Sandor Elès bids us search beneath the story's surface. Elès's timing and his sensitivity to word-colouring and the rhythmic inflexions of his native language greet the Gothic imagery of Bartók's solemn opening bars. The main characters soon establish very definite personalities, Bluebeard/Tomlinson as commanding, inscrutable and just a little arrogant, von Otter/Judith as profoundly frightened but filled with curiosity. Haitink and the Berlin Philharmonic paint a rich aural backdrop that's neither too slow nor overly lugubrious and that shows due appreciation of Bartók's seamless scoring, especially in terms of the woodwind. The disembodied sighs that greet Judith's violent hammering on the first door mark a momentary retreat from the Philharmonie's ambient acoustic (or so it seems) and in so doing suggest – quite appropriately – a chilling 'world beyond'. Judith's shock as she recoils in horror is conveyed in clipped, halting tones by von Otter (note too how seductively she manipulates Bluebeard into opening the first door).

Beyond the expansive introduction come the doors themselves, and here too Haitink balances the 'outer' and 'inner' aspects of Bartók's score to perfection – whether in the torture chamber, the glowing textures of 'The Secret Garden' or the Brucknerian expanses of the fifth door, 'Bluebeard's Kingdom' (the opera's structural apex), launched here on a series of epic *crescendos*. Von Otter's stunned responses suggest lonely disorientation within a vast space, whereas the sullenness of the 'Lake of Tears' prompts an exquisite blending of instrumental timbres, most particularly between brass and woodwind. Haitink draws an aching curve to the string writing, but when Judith rushes panic-stricken towards the seventh door, fearful of Bluebeard's secret murders, he effects a gradual but cumulatively thrilling *accelerando*. The internment itself is devastating, while Bluebeard's helpless retreat marks a slow journey back to the questioning void. Recording live can have its pitfalls, but here the atmosphere is electric, the grasp of Bartók's sombre tone-painting – whether sung or played – absolute.

EMI's engineering favours a full sound stage rather than picking out specific instrumental details, but the overall effect remains comprehensively satisfying. Kertész, on the other hand, favours a far richer sound stage, with softer contours (his armoury suggests more weight than glinting steel, his torture chamber, anxiety rather than cruelty) and a passionate swell to the string writing. Kertész represents the opera's compassionate core.

When it comes to the husband-and-wife team of Walter Berry and Christa Ludwig, the sense is given more of a woman discovering sinister aspects of the man she loves than an inquisitive shrew intent on plundering Bluebeard's every secret. Judith seems perpetually poised to take Bluebeard's arm and linger lovingly about him, while Berry's assumption of the title-role – which is sung beautifully, if not terribly idiomatically – suggests neither *Angst* nor impatience. Ludwig, too, was in wonderful voice at the time of this recording, and instances of her eloquence are far too numerous to list individually. The transfer is superb, with a thunderous organ beyond the fifth door and merely the odd rogue edit or spot of tape hiss to betray the passing years.

Additional recommendation

Duke Bluebeard's Castle
Troyanos Judith **Nimsgern** Bluebeard
BBC Symphony Orchestra / Boulez
Sony Classical SMK64110 (61' · ADD) Ⓜ

This is the more forceful of Pierre Boulez's two readings (Jessye Norman's soulless Judith mars his later DG set). Tatiana Troyanos's vocally winning Judith and Boulez's ideal pacing put this set among the top recommendations.

Sir Arnold Bax British 1883-1953

Bax studied at the Royal College of Music, London, (1900-1905). After discovering the poetry of Yeats, with which he was deeply impressed, he strongly identified with Irish Celtic culture. Drawing on many sources (Strauss, Debussy, Ravel, Elgar) he created a style of luxuriant chromatic harmony, rich ornament and broad melody, notably deployed in his tone poems The Garden of Fand (1916), November Woods (1917) and Tintagel (1919). Other important works of this period include his First Quartet (1918) and Second Piano Sonata (1919). In the 1920s his music became clearer in outline and more contrapuntal, though without losing its wide range of harmonic resource: Sibelius became an influence. His main works were now symphonies, seven written 1922-39, though he remained a prolific composer in all non-theatrical genres. In 1942 he was made Master of the King's Music, after which he composed little. GROVEmusic

Complete symphonies

Symphonies Nos 1-7. Rogue's Comedy Overture. Tintagel
BBC Philharmonic Orchestra / Vernon Handley
Chandos ⑤ CHAN10122 (5 hours 55' · DDD)
Includes an interview with Vernon Handley by
Andrew McGregor Ⓜ❍❍❍

 This Bax symphony cycle comes under the baton of the composer's doughtiest champion, and superlatives are in order. Even seasoned Baxians will be startled by the propulsive vigour and sinewy strength of these performances.

In its uncompromising thrust and snarling tragedy, Handley's account of the First Symphony packs an almighty punch, but also quarries great detail from Bax's darkly opulent orchestration. In the closing pages the motto theme's sanguine tread is soon snuffed out, as the shredded nerve-ends of this music are exposed as never before.

The wild and brooding Second generates less heady sensuality than either the Thomson or Myer Fredman's pioneering Lyrita version, but there's ample compensation in the chaste beauty and enviable authority of Handley's conception. Scrupulous attention is paid to thematic unity and the many contrapuntal and harmonic felicities that bind together the progress of this extraordinary canvas. The BBC Philharmonic respond with such eager application that it's easy to forgive some slight loss of composure in the build-up to the cataclysmic pinnacle.

There can be no reservations about the Third, an interpretation that's by far the finest since Barbirolli's 1943-4 world première recording with the Hallé. Bax's iridescent textures shimmer and glow, bass lines stalk with reassuring logic and solidity, and these exemplary artists distil all the poetry and mystery in the ravishing slow movement and epilogue. Deeply moving is Handley's tender, unforced handling of the first movement's *Lento moderato* secondary material.

Handley's previous recording of the Fourth is comprehensively outflanked by this bracing remake. If you've ever regarded the Fourth as something of a loose-limbed interloper in the Bax canon, this will make you think again, such is the muscular rigour Handley locates in this lovable creation. At the same time, there's playful affection, rhythmic bite and pagan splendour of both outer movements.

Revelations abound, too, in the Fifth. Handley plots a superbly inevitable course through the first movement. At the start of the slow movement the glinting brilliance and sheen of the orchestral playing take the breath away, as does the richness of the lower strings in the first subject. The finale is stunning, its whirlwind *Allegro* a veritable bevy of cackling demons.

The bass ostinato that launches the Sixth picks up where the epilogue of the Fifth left off. A taut course is steered through this stormy first movement, though in some ways Norman Del Mar's recording got closer still to the essence of

Bax's driven inspiration. The succeeding *Lento* has a gentle radiance that's very affecting. However, it's in the innovatory finale where Handley pulls ahead of the competition, cannily keeping some power in reserve for the clinching return of the introductory material at 11'05", and locating a transcendental wonder in the epilogue.

Handley's Seventh is wonderfully wise and characterful music-making, the first movement in particular sounding for all the world as if it was set down in a single take. There's bags of temperament about the performance, as well as an entrancing freedom, flexibility and purposefulness that proclaim an intimate knowledge of and total trust in the composer's intentions. The BBC Philharmonic respond with unflagging spirit and tremendous body of tone.

A majestic *Tintagel* and rollicking account of the 1936 *Rogue's Comedy Overture* complete the feast. Disc 5 houses an hour-long conversation about Bax the symphonist between the conductor and BBC presenter Andrew McGregor. Stephen Rinker's engineering does fabulous justice to Bax's imaginative and individual orchestration, particularly towards the lower end of the spectrum. The set is magnificent; its insights copious. Chandos's layout is ideal, with none of the symphonies split between discs.

Symphonies – selected

Symphony No 2 in E minor/C. November Woods
Royal Scottish National Orchestra / David Lloyd-Jones
Naxos 8 554093 (57' · DDD) ⑤〇

From the grinding dissonances at the outset through to the inconsolable coda, Lloyd-Jones and his orchestra bring out the unremitting toughness of Bax's uncompromising, breathtakingly scored Second Symphony; even the gorgeous secondary material in the first movement offers an occasional shaft of pale, wintry sunlight. It helps, too, that Lloyd-Jones has clearly thought hard about the task in hand. How lucidly, for example, he expounds the arresting introduction, where the symphony's main building-blocks are laid out before us, and how well he brings out the distinctive tenor of Bax's highly imaginative writing for low wind and brass. The Scottish brass have a field-day.

Lloyd-Jones proves an equally clear-sighted navigator through the storm-buffeted landscape of *November Woods*, for many people, Bax's greatest tone-poem. Thoroughly refreshing in its enthusiasm and exhilarating sense of orchestral spectacle, this recording has a physical impact and emotional involvement that genuinely compel. A veritable blockbuster.

Symphony No 3. The Happy Forest
Royal Scottish National Orchestra / David Lloyd-Jones
Naxos 8 553608 (54' · DDD) ⑤ⓢ〇

Dedicated to Sir Henry Wood, Bax's Symphony No 3 boasts arguably the richest store of memorable melodic invention to be found in any of the composer's cycle of seven, culminating in an inspired epilogue of wondrous, jaw-dropping beauty. David Lloyd-Jones's clear-headed, purposeful conducting of this intoxicating repertoire is the most judiciously paced and satisfyingly cogent Bax Third we've had since Barbirolli's pioneering 1943-4 Hallé account. Moreover, not only does Lloyd-Jones keep a firm hand on the tiller, he also draws some enthusiastic playing from the RSNO, which responds throughout with commendable polish and keen application.

Finely poised, affectingly full-throated solo work from principal horn and trumpet illuminates the progress of the ensuing Lento, whose ravishing landscape Lloyd-Jones surveys in less lingering fashion than either Barbirolli or Thomson. The first half of the finale, too, is a great success, Lloyd-Jones negotiating the fiendish twists and turns dictated by Bax's copious tempo markings with impressive aplomb. Only in the epilogue do you feel a need for a touch more rapt poetry. Tim Handley's excellently balanced recording is rich and refined, though the perspective is perhaps fractionally closer than ideal for The Happy Forest, which receives a performance of bounding vigour, gleeful mischief and muscular fibre; just that last, crucial drop of enchantment remains elusive. No matter, a disc not to be missed.

Symphony No 4. Nympholept.
Overture to a Picaresque Comedy
Royal Scottish National Orchestra / David Lloyd-Jones
Naxos 8 555343 (65' · DDD) ⑤〇

David Lloyd-Jones and the RSNO continue their stimulating championship of Bax with this extremely persuasive account of the Fourth Symphony. It's at once the most exuberantly inventive and most colourful of the cycle (the instrumentation includes six horns and organ). Lloyd-Jones steers a tauter, more athletic course through the eventful first movement than his *Gramophone* Award-winning rival (Bryden Thomson on Chandos), yet there's no want of playful affection, and the orchestral playing satisfyingly combines polish and eagerness. In the gorgeous central *Lento moderato* Lloyd-Jones perceptively evokes a bracing, northerly chill wafting across Bax's dappled seascape. The unashamedly affirmative finale is a great success, its festive pomp and twinkling sense of fun conveyed with personable panache and swagger. If the symphony's jubilant closing pages reverberate in Thomson's version with just that crucial bit of extra weight and splendour in Belfast's Ulster Hall, Tim Handley's expert sound and balance do ample justice to Bax's distinctive scoring and his writing for low woodwind in particular. The *Overture to a Picaresque Comedy* makes an apt and boisterous curtain-raiser, Lloyd-Jones's rip-roaring rendering knocking Thomson's limp LPO version into a cocked hat. *Nympholept* could hardly form a greater contrast: a ravishing nature-poem in Bax's most enchanted Celtic vein. Again, this sensitive account is far preferable to Thomson's curiously laboured conception. Altogether a superb release.

Symphony No 5 in C sharp minor. The Tale the Pine Trees Knew
Royal Scottish National Orchestra / David Lloyd-Jones
Naxos 8 554509 (58' · DDD)   Ⓢ Ⓢ Ⓞ

The Fifth is perhaps the most characteristic of Bax's symphonies. For all the music's powerful range of emotion and its seemingly bewildering profusion of material and countless moments of bewitching beauty, its resourceful symphonic processes aren't easy to assimilate on first hearing. Lloyd-Jones's intelligent and purposeful direction pays handsome dividends, and a well-drilled RSNO responds with sensitivity and enthusiasm. Lloyd-Jones excels in the opening movement's tightly knit canvas, its epic ambition matched by a compelling sense of momentum, architectural grandeur and organic 'wholeness'. In the slow movement Lloyd-Jones paints a chillier, more troubled landscape than does Bryden Thomson (Chandos). The finale's main *Allegro* sets out with gleeful dash and a fine rhythmic snap to its heels. Lloyd-Jones judges that tricky, crisis-ridden transition into the epilogue well, and the apotheosis is a hard-won, grudging victory. The 1931 tone-poem *The Tale the Pine Trees Knew* makes an ideal bedfellow, foreshadowing as it does the bracingly 'northern' (to quote the composer) demeanour of the Fifth. Lloyd-Jones's comparatively extrovert treatment of the work's exultant final climax works perfectly convincingly within the context of his overall conception. Another eminently truthful, judiciously balanced sound picture from producer/engineer Tim Handley.

Symphony No 6. Into the Twilight. Summer Music
Royal Scottish National Orchestra / David Lloyd-Jones
Naxos 8 557144 (58' · DDD)   Ⓢ Ⓞ

David Lloyd-Jones's Bax series goes from strength to strength with this clear-headed interpretation of the exhilarating Sixth Symphony (arguably the last work to show the composer at creative white heat).

Lloyd-Jones rides the tempest of the opening movement with particular success, while still allowing himself plenty of expressive leeway for the ravishing secondary material. In the central *Lento* he paints a bleakly beautiful, snow-flecked landscape. As for the ambitious finale (a *tour de force* of structural innovation and thematic integration), the conductor steers a superbly confident course, and the RSNO respond with

unflagging spirit and no mean skill (there's a wonderfully rapt horn solo at the outset of the sublime epilogue).

As for the competition, Lloyd-Jones's band may not possess the silky sheen of the LPO under Bryden Thomson, but his conception is unquestionably the more satisfyingly taut of the two. Both Lloyd-Jones's fill-ups are sensitively done, although *Into the Twilight* doesn't equal the fragrant beauty and haunting allure of Thomson's intoxicating Ulster version. Unfortunately, the sound, while enormously vivid and wide ranging, is neither quite as natural in timbre nor judiciously blended as on previous instalments (bigger *tutti*s tend towards an aggressive blur). None the less, a firm recommendation.

Additional recommendations

Symphonies – No 1 in E flat; No 7
London Philharmonic Orchestra / [a]Myer Fredman, [b]Raymond Leppard
Lyrita SRCD232 (78' · ADD) Recorded 1970, 1974 Ⓕ Ⓞ Ⓞ

An intelligent and well-contrasted coupling in these classic Lyrita recordings, with exceptionally fine performances and superb digital transfers.

Symphony No 3
Coupled with: Violin Concerto   Ⓗ
Kersey *vn* **Hallé Orchestra / Barbirolli; BBC Symphony Orchestra / Boult**
Dutton Laboratories Epoch CDLX7111 (73' · ADD) Recorded 1943-4   Ⓜ Ⓞ

Barbirolli's recording of Bax's Third was the first of any Bax symphony and is a spellbinding achievement. No account on disc since can match it for authority and depth of feeling. The transfer boasts remarkable body and miraculously quiet surfaces.

Tone Poems

In Memoriam. Concertante for Piano (Left-Hand) and Orchestra[a]. The Bard of the Dimbovitza[b]
[b]Jean Rigby *mez* **[a]Margaret Fingerhut** *pf*
BBC Philharmonic Orchestra / Vernon Handley
Chandos CHAN9715 (77' · DDD)   Ⓕ

The glorious tune that dominates the 1916 tone-poem *In Memoriam* will be familiar to many Bax enthusiasts from its use in his 1948 film score for David Lean's *Oliver Twist*, and to hear it in its original surroundings is both a moving and thrilling experience. It had long been assumed that the 32-year-old composer never got round to scoring this deeply felt elegy so it's pleasing to find that Vernon Handley and the BBC Philharmonic do full justice to its opulent yet iridescent sound world, with its strong echoes of *The Garden of Fand* and *Nympholept*.

The *Concertante* for left-hand piano and orchestra, written for Harriet Cohen after a domestic accident had disabled her right hand, isn't top-drawer Bax, but remains a most appealing creation, with a central *Moderato tranquillo* in the composer's sweetest lyrical vein. Margaret Fingerhut is a deft, sympathetic soloist.

The five orchestral songs that make up *The Bard of the Dimbovitza*, setting poems allegedly based on Romanian folk-songs, contain not a hint of local colour but are purest Bax, the harmonic idiom and overall mood strikingly similar to his *Enchanted Summer*. Jean Rigby vividly characterises the dialogue in the last two songs ('My girdle I hung on a tree-top tall' and 'Spinning Song'), while bringing plenty of drama to the almost operatic scena that's 'The Well of Tears'. Some typically lustrous Chandos engineering adorns this valuable triptych of recorded premières, and the issue as a whole deserves the heartiest of welcomes.

Additional recommendations

November Woods
Coupled with: Northern Ballad No 1. Mediterranean. The Garden of Fand. Tintagel
London Philharmonic Orchestra / Boult
Lyrita SRCD231 (62' · ADD)   Ⓕ
Boult's performance of this tone-poem is masterly and he generates a great deal of tension, atmosphere and drama.

Tintagel
Coupled with: **Vaughan Williams** Symphony No 5
Philharmonia Orchestra; London Symphony Orchestra / Barbirolli
EMI British Composers 5652110-2 (54' · ADD)   Ⓑ
Bax's rugged, wind-swept seascape finds Barbirolli in his element, and his reading is on the whole more passionately involving than either Boult's or Thomson's.

String Quartets

String Quartets – No 1 in G; No 2 in E minor
Maggini Quartet (Laurence Jackson, David Angel *vns* Martin Outram *va* Michal Kaznowski *vc*)
Naxos 8 555282 (54' · DDD)   Ⓢ

Had Dvořák written an *Irish* Quartet to sit alongside his delectable *American*, it might well have sounded like the start of Bax's First String Quartet. Completed in 1918, this is one of Bax's most endearing and approachable scores. The clean-cut opening *Allegretto semplice* positively beams with happiness, and it's succeeded by a wistfully intimate slow movement. The finale begins and finishes in a mood of pagan revelry, though there's time for a ravishing episode in Bax's sweetest lyrical vein, its indelible tune a close cousin to the folksong *The Fair Hills of Ireland*. The Second Quartet of 1924-5 proves an altogether tougher nut to crack. Conceived at the same time as the Second Symphony, it's a knotty, densely plotted creation, as harmonically daring as Bax ever ventured and demanding formidable concentration from performers and listeners alike.

The Maggini Quartet do Bax absolutely proud, their performances striking an ideal balance between urgent expression and purposeful clarity. Both rival readings on Chandos have considerable strengths, but the Maggini's scrupulously dedicated advocacy will captivate both seasoned Baxians and newcomers alike. An outstanding coupling in every way.

String Quartet No 3 in F. Adagio ma non troppo, 'Cathleen-ni-Hoolihan'. Lyrical Interlude for String Quintet[a]
Maggini Quartet (Laurence Jackson, David Angel *vn* Martin Outram *va* Michal Kaznowski *vc*) with [a]**Garfield Jackson** *va*
Naxos 8 555953 (57' · DDD)

Bax composed the last of his three mature string quartets between May and September 1936, inscribing it to the Griller Quartet who gave the first performance on the BBC National Programme the following May. An appealing, cogently structured 37-minute work, it's cast (unusually for Bax) in four movements, the joyous first of which 'was probably influenced by the coming of spring in beautiful Kenmare' (to quote the composer's own descriptive notes in *The Radio Times*). An Irish flavour also permeates the bardic *Poco lento*, while the third movement's 'dreamy, remotely romantic' trio melody is eventually cleverly welded to the 'rather sinister and malicious' *scherzo* material. The vigorous finale builds up a fine head of steam and incorporates a wistful backward glance just before the close that's entirely characteristic of its creator.

The Maggini Quartet forge a well-paced and concentrated interpretation, playing with assurance, infectious rhythmic snap and heartwarming dedication. They are joined by violist Garfield Jackson for the haunting *Lyrical Interlude* from 1922 (a reworking of the slow movement from Bax's ambitious String Quintet of 1908), and there's another rarity in the shape of the lovely *Adagio ma non troppo* centrepiece from the 1903 String Quartet in E major that Bax orchestrated two years later as his first tone-poem, *Cathaleen-ni-Hoolihan*.

Throughout, the sound is faithful in timbre and the balance most musically judged.

Violin Sonatas

Violin Sonatas – No 2 in D; No 3; [No 4] in F
Robert Gibbs *vn* **Mary Mei-Loc Wu** *pf*
ASV CDDCA1098 (72' · DDD)   ⒻⓄ

Robert Gibbs may not command the projection or outsize personality of some of his more illustrious, globe-trotting colleagues, but his neat technique, soft-spoken eloquence and attractively husky tone give enormous pleasure, while Mary Mei-Loc Wu tenders ideally deft support. Theirs is a less 'public', more thoughtfully intimate reading of Bax's turbulent Second Sonata than either of their rivals', an approach well suited to this most autobiographical of Bax's utterances. Their reading of the Third Sonata exhibits similar interpretative and poetic insights. Completed in 1927, it's a two-movement work of strong appeal, comprising a wondrously beautiful *Moderato* in this composer's most wistfully Celtic vein and a dashing *Allegro* whose exuberantly dancing outer portions frame a more poignantly reflective central episode. Gibbs and Wu also do full justice to the F major Sonata, which Bax subsequently recast as his bewitching Nonet. The sound picture is beguilingly warm and the disc as a whole earns the heartiest of welcomes.

Violin Sonatas – in G minor; No 1 in E. Ballad. Legend
Robert Gibbs *vn* **Mary Mei-Loc Wu** *pf*
ASV CDDCA1127 (61' · DDD)   Ⓕ

The First Sonata is a passionate, deeply personal outpouring, essayed here with rapt understanding and tender intimacy. The rival Chandos performance may exhibit rather more in the way of commanding projection and urgent expression, but these newcomers' keen poetic instincts are never in doubt.

Both the *Legend* and *Ballad* date from the First World War years (of the broodingly elegiac *Legend* – much liked by Vaughan Williams, apparently – Bax later recalled to violinist May Harrison that it 'came straight out of the horror of that time'), whereas the single-movement Sonata in G minor is an amiable, confidently argued student effort from November 1901. Again, Gibbs and Wu lend consistently idiomatic and warm-hearted advocacy to this material. A very appealing collection, in short, and a mandatory purchase for confirmed Baxians.

Chamber Works

Nonet. Oboe Quintet. Elegiac Trio. Clarinet Sonata. Harp Quintet
Nash Ensemble (Philippa Davies *fl* Gareth Hulse *ob* Michael Collins *cl* Marcia Crayford, Iris Juda, Elizabeth Wexler *vns* Roger Chase *va* Christopher van Kampen *vc* Duncan McTier *db* Skaila Kanga *hp* Ian Brown *pf*)
Hyperion CDA66807 (73' · DDD)   ⒻOO

A truly first-rate modern recording of Bax's Nonet. What a bewitching creation it is, overflowing with invention and breathtakingly imaginative in its instrumental resource (the sounds created are often almost orchestral). Bax worked on the Nonet at the same time (1929-30) as he was composing his Third Symphony and there are striking similarities between the two. The Nash Ensemble gives a masterly, infinitely subtle reading.

The remainder of the disc brings comparable pleasure. The delightful Oboe Quintet (written for Leon Goossens in 1922) receives immensely

characterful treatment, especially the jaunty, Irish-jig finale (such richly communicative playing). The same is true of the lovely Harp Quintet, essayed here with rapt intensity and delicious poise. In the hands of these stylish artists, the *Elegiac Trio* possesses a delicacy and poignancy that are really quite captivating. That just leaves the engaging Clarinet Sonata, a work that has fared well in the recording studio over the last few years. Suffice to report, Michael Collins and Ian Brown are compelling advocates, and theirs is a performance to set beside (if not supersede) all rivals. Beautiful sound throughout.

Octet. String Quintet. Concerto. Threnody and Scherzo. In Memoriam
Margaret Fingerhut *pf* **Academy of St Martin in the Fields Chamber Ensemble**
Chandos CHAN9602 (72' · DDD)   ⒻO

This is a beautiful and enterprising collection of works by Bax. *In Memoriam* for cor anglais, harp and string quartet probably dates from 1917. It's subtitled 'An Irish Elegy'; like the *Elegiac Trio* from the same period, its poignant mood reflects Bax's despair at the tragic events of the Easter Rising. In the single-movement String Quintet (completed in January 1933) he draws some luscious, almost orchestral sonorities from his chosen forces. Scored for horn, piano and string sextet, the 1934 Octet (labelled 'Serenade' on the short score) is a two-movement work of strong appeal and engaging charm: the magically evocative opening brings echoes of those unforgettable horn solos in the Third Symphony's central *Lento*, while the icy glitter of the piano part from 1'53" in the second-movement *Scherzo* momentarily conjures up the far-Northern landscape of *Winter Legends*.

The *Threnody and Scherzo* for bassoon, harp and string sextet of 1936 is perhaps less immediately striking. The writing is as fluent and accomplished as ever but the melodic material isn't as fresh as might have been wished. By contrast, the Concerto for flute, oboe, harp and string quartet is one of Bax's most likeable chamber offerings. This is a captivating transcription for septet of a Sonata for flute and harp from 1928 and proves an exquisite gem, its deft and joyous outer movements framing a lovely central 'Cavatina'. The sound is warm and transparent.

Elegiac Trio[a]. Fantasy Sonata[b]. Quintet for Harp and Strings[c]. Sonata for Flute and Harp[d]
Mobius ([ad]Lorna McGhee *fl* [c]Kanako Ito, [c]Philippe Honoré *vns* [abc]Ashan Pillai *va* [c]Martin Storey *vc* Alison Nicholls *hp*)
Naxos 8 554507 (65' · DDD)   ⑤⑤OO

Mobius is a gifted young London-based ensemble of seven prize-winning instrumentalists from four different countries, and their scrupulously shaded, fervent playing betokens a very real empathy with this gorgeous repertoire. In both the *Elegiac Trio* and *Harp Quintet* these artists favour a more boldly etched, less delicately evanescent approach than that of the Nash Ensemble (which is perhaps marginally more successful in distilling the poignant heartache of two works indissolubly associated with the tragic events of the 1916 Easter Rising). Especially valuable is the impassioned rendering of the marvellous *Fantasy Sonata* for harp and viola of 1927. Certainly, harpist Alison Nicholls (a beguiling presence throughout) copes heroically with the daunting technical demands of Bax's writing (tailored for the virtuosity of the great Russian harpist, Maria Korchinska); moreover, she's splendidly partnered by violist Ashan Pillai. Likewise, the engagingly relaxed *Sonata for Flute and Harp* that Bax subsequently reworked into his *Concerto for Seven Instruments* (Chandos) emerges with delightful freshness, its plangent central 'Cavatina' as haunting as ever. Sound and balance are just fine. Terrific value and strongly recommended.

Piano Sonatas

Piano Sonatas – No 1 in F sharp minor; No 2 in G. Burlesque. In a Vodka Shop. Nereid. Dream in exile
Ashley Wass pf
Naxos 8 557439 (77' · DDD) Ⓢ ●●●

 Not only does this gifted young pianist possess a rock-solid technique and striking keyboard finesse, his penetrating accounts of both these large-scale, single-movement sonatas make you sit up and listen. So it is that in the bracing First Sonata (written in 1910 during Bax's sojourn in Russia and Ukraine) Ashley Wass finds the balance between epic and introspective. More than that, he brings out the music's brazen Slavic fervour with its echoes of Scriabin and Rachmaninov (the coda's pealing bells toll with magnificent cumulative impact). He paces its turbulent successor of 1919 with cogency and concentration. Even more than the magisterial John McCabe, Wass takes us on a genuine voyage of discovery: the control, sense of colour and dynamic range are remarkable, and his tone never hardens under pressure.

Of the four couplings, *Dream in Exile* stands out. It was written shortly before the 1916 Easter Rising, and again Wass allows Bax's poignant inspiration all the time in the world to cast its spell. He makes the most of the songful *Nereid*, and if it's rollicking fun you're after, the roistering *Burlesque* and *In a Vodka Shop* have it in spadefuls.

The sound throughout is vividly truthful.

Songs

Far in a Western Brookland[b]. The Market Girl[b]. A Milking Sian[a]. The Song in the Twilight[a]. To Eire[b].
The White Peace[b]. A Celtic Song Cycle[a]. The Fairies[b]. Youth[b]. Parting[b]. A Lullaby[a]. Roundel[b]. When I was one and twenty[b]. The Enchanted Fiddle[b]. When We Are Lost[b]
[a]**Jean Rigby** mez [b]**Ian Partridge** ten **Michael Dussek** pf
Dutton Laboratories Epoch CDLX7136 (78' · DDD) Ⓜ

With the exception of *The White Peace* (a favourite of John McCormack), Bax's songs have been largely and undeservedly neglected. Ian Partridge sings with his customary sensitivity and intelligence, responding with particular eloquence to the grateful melodic lines of *To Eire* (1910) and the yearningly ecstatic *Parting*. The latter appeared in the aftermath of the 1916 Easter Uprising, and its haunting strains are heard again in the epilogue of the *Symphonic Variations* completed two years later. Likewise, the opening phrase of the 1914 Chaucer-setting *Roundel* will already be familiar to listeners to the tone-poem *Nympholept*. Jean Rigby works wonders with the youthful *Celtic Song Cycle*, and imparts almost operatic scope to the quietly intense *Song in the Twilight*. She's impressive, too, in *A Lullaby*, a 1910 setting of one of Bax's own poems, conceived in the middle of an unrequited love-affair with a Ukrainian girl, Natalia Skarginska. Michael Dussek's accompaniments are a model of scrupulous musicality.

Amy Beach   American 1867-1944

Amy Marcy Cheney Beach was born in New Hampshire in the United States. Musically precocious, she sang improvised harmony parts at the age of two, composed aged four, and began piano studies with her mother, Clara Imogene Marcy Cheney, at six, giving her first public recitals at seven. In 1885 she made her piano debut with the Boston Symphony. That same year she married Dr Henry Beach, a Harvard professor and amateur musician. In accordance with his wishes, she limited her public appearances and concentrated on composition until after his death in 1910.

Beach compsed works in many genres, including a Mass, a symphony, a piano concerto, and works for chamber ensembles, piano, mixed chorus, and solo voice. Her 30 works for women's chorus, including several cantatas, are well-crafted in a Romantic idiom, always with intelligent text setting.

                                     GROVEmusic

Piano Concerto

Piano Concerto in C sharp minor, Op45[a]. Symphony in E minor, Op 32, 'Gaelic'
[a]**Alan Feinberg** pf **Nashville Symphony Orchestra / Kenneth Schermerhorn**
Naxos 8 559139 (79' · DDD) Ⓢ

Composed in 1898-9, Amy Beach's ambitious, singularly impressive Piano Concerto is at long last coming in from the cold. An expansively rhetorical Allegro moderato launches the work before a playful *perpetuum mobile* Scherzo and moody Largo (described by its creator as a 'dark, tragic lament'); the finale goes with a delightful swing. In fact, it's a rewarding achievement all round, full of brilliantly idiomatic solo writing (Beach was a virtuoso pianist herself and performed the work many times) and lent further autobiographical intrigue by its assimilation of thematic material from three early songs.

Alan Feinberg brings more charisma to bear than Joanne Polk on her rival account for Arabesque, without any loss of delicacy or poetry, and his collaboration with Kenneth Schermerhorn and the Nashville Symphony undoubtedly generates greater thrust and spontaneity. The recording, too, is more pleasingly spacious, if a little lacking in body.

Following the success of her 1889 Mass in E flat, Beach knew that she needed to produce a large-scale symphony to cement her reputation; it was the Boston première of Dvořák's *New World* that finally spurred her into action. Responding to the Czech master's exhortation that American composers should turn to spirituals, plantation songs and minstrel-show music for inspiration, Beach selected four Irish melodies of 'simple, rugged and unpretentious beauty', moulding any additional themes 'in the same idiom and spirit'.

That the *Gaelic* Symphony (1894-6) won golden opinions from the outset comes as no surprise, given its big heart, irresistible charm and confident progress. Happily, Schermerhorn and his eager Nashville band more than hold their own by beside Neeme Järvi and the Detroit SO. Theirs is a convincingly paced, tidy performance with real fire in its belly and plenty of character. A thoroughly enjoyable issue.

Ludwig van Beethoven
German 1770-1827

Beethoven studied first with his father, Johann, a singer and instrumentalist in the service of the Elector of Cologne at Bonn, but mainly with CG Neefe, court organist. At 11 he was able to deputise for Neefe; at 12 he had some music published. In 1787 he went to Vienna, but quickly returned on hearing that his mother was dying. Five years later he went back to Vienna, where he settled.

He studied first with Haydn, though there was some clash of temperaments, and also with Schenk, Albrechtsberger and Salieri. Until 1794 he was supported by the Elector at Bonn, but he found patrons among the music-loving Viennese aristocracy and soon enjoyed success as a piano virtuoso, playing at private houses or palaces rather than in public. His public début was in 1795; about the same time his first important publications appeared, three piano trios Op 1 and three piano sonatas Op 2. As a pianist, it was reported he had fire, brilliance and fantasy as well as depth of feeling. It is naturally in the piano sonatas, writing for his own instrument, that he is at his most original in this period; the Pathétique belongs to 1799, the Moonlight ('Sonata quasi una fantasia') to 1801, and these represent only the most obvious innovations in style and emotional content. These years also saw the composition of his first three piano concertos, first two symphonies and a set of six string quartets Op 18.

1802, however, was a year of crisis for Beethoven, with his realisation that the impaired hearing he had noticed for some time was incurable and sure to worsen. That autumn, at a village outside Vienna, Heiligenstadt, he wrote a will-like document, addressed to his two brothers, describing his bitter unhappiness over his affliction in terms suggesting that he thought death was near. But he came through with his determination strengthened and entered a new creative phase, generally called his 'middle period'. It is characterised by a heroic tone, evident in the 'Eroica' Symphony (No 3, originally to have been dedicated not to a noble patron but to Napoleon), in Symphony No 5, where the sombre mood of the C minor first movement ('Fate knocking on the door') ultimately yields to a triumphant C major finale with piccolo, trombones and percussion added to the orchestra, and in his opera Fidelio. Here the heroic theme is made explicit by the story, in which (in the post-French Revolution 'rescue opera' tradition) a wife saves her imprisoned husband from murder at the hands of his oppressive political enemy. The three string quartets of this period – Op 59, are similarly heroic in scale: the first, lasting some 45 minutes, is conceived with great breadth, and it too embodies a sense of triumph as the intense F minor Adagio gives way to a jubilant finale in the major, embodying (at the request of the dedicatee, Count Razumovsky) a Russian folk melody.

Fidelio, unsuccessful at its première, was twice revised by Beethoven and his librettists and successful in its final version of 1814. Here there is more emphasis on the moral force of the story. It deals not only with freedom and justice, and heroism, but also with married love, and in the character of the heroine Leonore, Beethoven's lofty, idealised image of womanhood is to be seen. He did not find it in real life: he fell in love several times, usually with aristocratic pupils (some of them married), and each time was either rejected or saw that the woman did not match his ideals.

With his powerful and expansive middle-period works, which include the Pastoral Symphony (No 6, conjuring up his feelings about the countryside, which he loved), Symphonies Nos 7 and 8, Piano Concertos Nos 4 (a lyrical work) and 5 (the noble and brilliant 'Emperor') and the Violin Concerto, as well as more chamber works and piano sonatas (such as the 'Waldstein' and the 'Appassionata') Beethoven was firmly established as the greatest composer of his time. His piano-playing career had finished in 1808 (a charity appearance in 1814 was a disaster because of his deafness). That year he had considered leaving Vienna for a secure post in Germany, but three Viennese noblemen had banded together to provide him with a steady income and he remained there, although the plan foundered in the ensuing Napoleonic wars in which his patrons suffered and the value of Austrian money declined.

The years after 1812 were relatively unproductive. He seems to have been seriously depressed, by his deafness and the resulting isolation, by the failure of his marital hopes and (from 1815) by anxieties over the custodianship of the son of his late brother, which involved him in legal actions. But he came out of these trials to write his profoundest music. There are seven piano sonatas in this, his 'late period', including the turbulent 'Hammerklavier' Op 106, with its dynamic writing and its harsh, rebarbative fugue, and Op 110, which also has fugues and much eccentric writing at the instrument's extremes of compass; there is a great Mass and a Choral Symphony, No 9 in D minor, where the extended variation-finale is a setting for soloists and chorus of Schiller's Ode to Joy; and there is a group of string quartets, music on a new plane of spiritual depth, with their exalted ideas, abrupt contrasts and emotional intensity. The traditional four-movement scheme and conventional forms are discarded in favour of designs of six or seven movements, some fugal, some akin to variations (these forms especially attracted him in his late years), some song-like, some martial, one even like a chorale prelude. For Beethoven, the act of composition had always been a struggle, as the tortuous scrawls of his sketchbooks show; in these late works the sense of agonising effort is a part of the music.

Musical taste in Vienna had changed during the first decades of the 19th century; the public were chiefly interested in light Italian opera (especially Rossini) and easygoing chamber music and songs, to suit the prevalent bourgeois taste. Yet the Viennese were conscious of Beethoven's greatness: they applauded the Choral Symphony, even though, understandably, they found it difficult, and though baffled by the late quartets they sensed their extraordinary visionary qualities. His reputation went far beyond Vienna: the late Mass was first heard in St Petersburg, and the initial commission that produced the Choral Symphony had come from the Philharmonic Society of London. When he died 10,000 are said to have attended the funeral. He had become a public figure, as no composer had done before. Unlike composers of the preceding generation, he had never been a purveyor of music to the nobility: he had lived into the age, indeed helped create it, of the artist as hero and the property of mankind at large.

GROVEmusic

Piano Concertos

No 1 in C, Op 15; **No 2** in B flat, Op 19;
No 3 in C minor, Op 37; **No 4** in G, Op 58;
No 5 in E flat, Op 73, 'Emperor'

Complete Piano Concertos

Piano Concertos Nos 1-5
Pierre-Laurent Aimard pf **Chamber Orchestra of Europe / Nikolaus Harnoncourt**
Teldec ③ 0927-47334-2 (184' · DDD)   Ⓜ❶❶❶

 The freshness of this set is remarkable. You do not have to listen far to be swept up by its spirit of renewal and discovery, and in Pierre-Laurent Aimard as soloist Harnoncourt has made an inspired

choice. Theirs aren't eccentric readings of these old warhorses – far from it. But they could be called idiosyncratic – from Harnoncourt would you have expected anything else?

These are modern performances which have acquired richness and some of their focus from curiosity about playing styles and sound production of the past. Harnoncourt favours leaner string textures than the norm and gets his players in the excellent Chamber Orchestra of Europe to command a wide range of expressive weight and accent; this they do with an immediacy of effect that's striking. Yet there's a satisfying body to the string sound, too.

The playing seems to have recourse to eloquence without having to strive for it, and that's characteristic of Aimard's contribution as well. Strong contrasts are explored and big moments encompassed as part of an unforced continuity in which nothing is hurried. The big moments do indeed stand out: one of them is the famous exchange of dramatic gestures between piano and orchestra in the development of the E flat Concerto's (No 5's) first movement; another the equally dramatic but very different exchange when the piano re-enters at the start of the development in the first movement of the G major Concerto (No 4). At these junctures, conductor and pianist allow the gestures to disrupt the rhythmic continuity. Over the top? No, but risky maybe, and if you've strong views about what Beethoven's rubrics permit, or have swallowed a metronome, you may react strongly. For make no mistake, Aimard is as intrepid an explorer here as Harnoncourt – by conviction, not simply by adoption.

Technically he's superbly equipped. This is evident everywhere, but especially in the finales, brimful of spontaneous touches and delight in their eventfulness and in the pleasure of playing them. The finale of the *Emperor* tingles with a continuously vital, constantly modulated dynamic life that it rarely receives; so many players make it merely rousing. And among the first movements, that of the G major Concerto is a quite exceptional achievement for the way Harnoncourt and his soloist find space for the fullest characterisation of the lyricism and diversity of the solo part – Aimard begins almost as if improvising the opening statement, outside time – while integrating these qualities with the larger scheme. It's the most complex movement in the concertos and he manages to make it sound both directional and free as a bird.

The first movement of the E flat Concerto is nearly as good, lacking only the all-seeing vision and authority Brendel brings to it, and perhaps a touch of Brendel's ability to inhabit and define its remoter regions. In general, Aimard imposes himself as a personality less than Brendel. In spite of being different exercises, their distinction touches at several points and is comparable in degree. What Aimard doesn't match is the variety of sound and the amplitude of Brendel's expressiveness in the first two concertos' slow movements. Balances are good, with the piano placed in a concert-hall perspective.

This set balances imagination and rigour, providing much delight and refreshment, and playing that will blow you away.

Piano Concertos Nos 1-5. Choral Fantasia in C minor, Op 80
Daniel Barenboim pf **John Alldis Choir;**
New Philharmonia Orchestra / Otto Klemperer
EMI ③ 763360-2 (211' · ADD) Recorded 1967   Ⓜ❍

Klemperer had done concert cycles, perhaps most memorably in London in the 1950s with Claudio Arrau but his decision to record the piano concertos at the age of 82 came as a result of his admiration for the most precociously talented of all young Beethoven pianists at the time, Daniel Barenboim. Barenboim was 25 and about to embark on what was to be an exceptionally fine cycle of the Beethoven piano sonatas. He was steeped in Beethoven and perhaps peculiarly well suited to the concertos which, we should not forget, are essentially a young man's music. It was a fascinating pairing, Klemperer and Barenboim contrasted in age and to some extent in temperament but at the same time symbiotically at one musically. Had this not been the case, Barenboim would have been swamped, lost in the wash of Klemperer's accompaniments which deliver the orchestral argument and the orchestral detail with an articulacy and authority unique in the history of these works on record.

The performance of the B flat Concerto, the first historically if not numerically, is a typical joy, full of fire and grace and unstoppably vital. Given Klemperer's propensity for taking slow tempos in Beethoven, you might imagine him being taken for a ride by the young Barenboim in the B flat and C major finales. But not a bit of it. It's Klemperer, as much as his youthful soloist, who seems to be the driving force here. Rarely on record has the slow movement of the C major Concerto been played with so natural a sense of concentrated calm, the whole thing profoundly collected on the spiritual plane. One of the joys of the Barenboim/Klemperer cycle is its occasional unpredictability: rock-solid readings that none the less incorporate a sense of 'today we try it this way'.

Ensemble is mostly first rate during the cycle. The tricky coda of the first movement of the C minor Concerto is both rapt and dramatic. But in the coda of the first movement of the G major there's little doubt that Klemperer drags the pulse. And elsewhere there are some occasionally awkward adjustments to be made between soloist and orchestra. At the time of its initial appearance, the *Emperor* performance was generally adjudged a success. Again it's broadly conceived. At first the finale seems a little staid; but later the 6/8 rhythms are made to dance and the performance has a burning energy by the end. So does the account of the *Choral Fantasia*. Given Klemperer's magisterial style and authority, this set could have emerged as five symphonies with piano obbligato. In fact, it's a

set of rare authority and spontaneity, and given the slightly unconventional idea of the soloist as *primus inter pares*, it's probably unique.

Piano Concertos Nos 1-5
Murray Perahia pf **Concertgebouw Orchestra /**
Bernard Haitink
Sony Classical ③ S3K44575 (178' · DDD) Recorded 1983-6. Nos 3-4 won a 1986 *Gramophone* Award
Ⓕ❍❍

Perahia's account of the C minor Concerto (No 3) is a joy from start to finish, wonderfully conceived, executed conducted and recorded. The single issue, coupled with this account of the G major Concerto (No 4), began life by winning the 1986 *Gramophone* Concerto Award. In these two concertos, and in the two earlier ones, Perahia and Haitink are difficult to fault. The First Concerto is especially well done with a quick first movement and the apt and delightful inclusion in the finale of a cadenza that Beethoven sketched in 1800. If Perahia is anywhere slightly below par it's in the *Emperor* Concerto. The reading gives us an emergent view of the work, undiscursive but perhaps at times lacking in a certain largeness of vision and purpose. For that we must return to Kempff or Arrau, which only confirms the pitfalls of buying cycles rather than separate performances. However, the Perahia cycle is one of the most consistently accomplished of those currently available; the recordings are a joy to listen to.

Piano Concertos Nos 1-5
Alfred Brendel pf **Vienna Philharmonic Orchestra /**
Sir Simon Rattle
Philips ③ 462 781-2PH3 (178' · DDD)   Ⓕ❍

Nos 1 & 4 available on Philips 462 782-2PH   Ⓕ
Nos 2 & 3 available on Philips 462 783-2PH   Ⓕ

Happily, Alfred Brendel's fourth recorded cycle of the Beethoven piano concertos shares with the previous three qualities of energy, sensibility, intellectual rigour and high pianistic finish which made the earlier recordings so interesting. Brendel has always played all five slow movements supremely well, drawing the orchestra around him like a celebrant at the communion table and here we have even finer performances than previously.

In the two early concertos the Vienna Philharmonic's playing has a sweetness and allure, in the grander, later works a black-browed power, that's specially its own. Brendel's playing in the early concertos recalls his fine recordings of the early sonatas and the early and late *Bagatelles*, but it's as a private person impatient with the conventions and frock-coated formalities of the concertos as 'public' works. With No 3 we move into a different world. This is a marvellous performance from all three partners, purposeful and robust, the tonic C minor the cue for a reading full of darkness and menace, basses to the fore, drums at the ready. The finale is particularly ominous (relieved only by a lustrous clarinet solo) after an account of the slow movement, full toned yet deeply quiet, the like of which is rarely heard. The C minor Concerto's heroic antitype, the *Emperor* in E flat, fares less well. Not the slow movement or finale, but the first movement which is slower than previously, to no very good effect. Perhaps interpreters nowadays are less happy than their predecessors were with Beethoven's heroic persona. Back in the private world of the Fourth Concerto, soloist, orchestra and conductor are at their inspired best. Brendel's glittering, wonderfully propelled account of the solo part is superbly backed by playing of real fire and sensitivity. The recordings are first rate.

Piano Concertos Nos 1-5
Maurizio Pollini *pf* **Berlin Philharmonic Orchestra /
Claudio Abbado**
DG ③ 439 770-2GH3 (174' · DDD) Recorded live
1992-3   Ⓕ

There may be more individual and idiosyncratic interpreters of the music than Maurizio Pollini but there's none whose command, at best, is sovereign. Concerto No 4 has a keenly felt sense of the evolving drama, and a slow movement where the dialogue between piano and orchestra is spellbinding in its intensity. Maybe he isn't yet entirely reconciled to Beethoven's prankish Concerto No 2. In the outer movements he can seem brusque: ill at ease with the rumbustious, amorous, Hooray Henry mood. By contrast, the performance of No 3 is a joy from start to finish. Abbado and Pollini are hand-in-glove, which gives this cycle a cohesiveness that Pollini's previous set with Jochum and Böhm (for DG) rather obviously lacked, though the Berliners don't play the first movement of the *Emperor* Concerto as commandingly as Böhm and the VPO on the earlier recording. But the slow movement goes well, and the finale is more jovial than before. There are evident musical gains in these live recordings – moments where the tension is palpable in a way that it rarely can be in the recording studio. The sound is full bodied and immediate, with applause, a few squeaks and ill-timed coughs.

Piano Concertos Nos 1ᵃ & 2ᵇ   Ⓗ
Solomon *pf* **Philharmonia Orchestra /** ᵃ**Herbert
Menges,** ᵇ**André Cluytens**
Testament ᵇmono SBT1219 (63' · ADD)   Ⓕ⬤

Piano Concertos Nos 3ᵃ & 4ᵇ   Ⓗ
Solomon *pf* **Philharmonia Orchestra /** ᵃ **Menges,**
ᵇ**Cluytens**
Testament ᵇmono SBT1220 (70' · ADD)   Ⓕ⬤

Beethoven Piano Concerto No 5 **Mozart** Piano   Ⓗ
Sonatas – No 11 in A, K331; No 17 in D, K576
Solomon *pf* **Philharmonia Orchestra / Menges**
Testament mono SBT1221 (74' · ADD) Recorded
1952-6   Ⓕ⬤

Here on three CDs are Solomon's legendary 1952-6 recordings of the Beethoven piano concertos and two Mozart piano sonatas, a felicitous coupling. Time and again Beethoven's exuberant, unpredictable nature is qualified by playing of a supreme poise and equanimity that omits so little of his essential character. It's also one of Solomon's cardinal qualities that he makes it impertinent to single out this or that detail, offering instead a seamless argument as supple and natural as it's understated.

Solomon makes the slow movements the expressive centres of each concerto, and here his ability to sustain an *Adagio* or *Largo* is without equal. This is notably true of the first two concertos, where such writing becomes music to soothe the savage breast rather than awake more immediate emotions. In the outer movements his superfine technique and musicianship make light of every difficulty, and at 6'55" in the Second Concerto, after an impatient if very Beethovenian entry, he re-creates a magical sense of stillness and repose.

In the Third Concerto the *Largo* is impeccably controlled and so, too, is the central *Andante con moto* from the Fourth Concerto. Solomon's momentary lack of control in the first movement at 9'37" is, perhaps, an indication of problems caused by Cluytens' less than vital or stimulating partnership. And yet the finale could hardly be more *vivace*, with all the clarity and grace for which Solomon was celebrated.

In the *Emperor* Concerto Solomon somehow bridges the gap between the Fourth and Fifth Concertos. His immaculate ease and buoyancy in the double-note descent just before the first movement's conclusion, his limpid and serene traversal of the central *Adagio* are pure Solomon, and his finale is among the least opaque on record. Surprises include the shorter cadenza in the First Concerto, Clara Schumann's cadenza in the Third (enterprising if less distinguished than Beethoven's own magnificent offering) and a few teasing elaborations in the two cadenzas from the Fourth.

The recordings come up well (though the sound in the Fifth needs some opening out; it lacks ring and brilliance), and the Mozart sonatas are a delectable bonus. Listening to Solomon's peerless pianism and musicianship, the critic discards pen and paper and listens in awe, wonder and affection.

Piano Concertos – selected

Piano Concertos Nos 1 & 2
Murray Perahia *pf* **Concertgebouw Orchestra /
Bernard Haitink**
Sony Classical SK42177 (70' · DDD) Recorded 1986
                                                    Ⓕ⬤

It's a pleasure here to salute such all-round excellence: a very remarkable soloist, superb orchestral playing and direction, and a recording which gets everything right, offering the kind of sound picture and natural perspective of solo piano with orchestra as we might experience them from a good seat in the Concertgebouw itself, where these performances were recorded.

Precision, clarity of expression, variety of character, beauty of sound: these are the qualities Haitink and Perahia sustain, and through which their readings gain an illuminating force. And it's perhaps in the slow movements that the illumination brings the most distinguished results. Their raptness and distinctive colouring are established from the first notes, and the inward quality of the expression takes breath as if there was nothing to the business of delineating these great set-pieces, so special among the achievements of Beethoven's first maturity, except to sing them through. Perahia has the gift of reducing his voice to the quietest level and still remaining eloquent. The poise of the playing is classical, his authority unblemished by any hint of exaggeration or false emphasis.

Piano Concertos Nos 2 & 3
Martha Argerich pf **Mahler Chamber Orchestra / Claudio Abbado**
DG 477 5026GH (64' · DDD) Recorded live in the Teatro Comunale, Ferrara, 2000, 2004   Ⓕ**OO**

Martha Argerich's two most recent discs have coupled works central to her repertoire with first performances on record. Here her long-awaited recording of Beethoven's Third Concerto appears with the Second, music she's relished over the years. But whether novel or familiar, both performances are of a quality rarely encontered at any time or from any arist.

Characteristically nervous before playing a concerto she had not performed for 20 years, Argerich erased all trepidation with a performance in which every note and phrase seems to spring new-minted from the page. Magisterial, insouciant, scintillating and acute, this greatest of all living pianists resolves every thought and consideration in playing of an enthralling spontaneity. Such unimpeded vitality and indifference to convention may prompt raised eyebrows among die-hards and conservatives; but if such spine-tingling brilliance takes you close to the edge, it's also a reminder that, in the words of Muriel Spark's Jean Brodie, beauty rather than safety comes first. Claudio Abbado, a long-term musical partner, and his youthful Mahler orchestra are entirely at one with their mercurial soloist and the recordings admirably capture both ultra-live occasions.

Piano Concertos Nos 2 & 5
Evgeni Kissin pf **Philharmonia Orchestra / James Levine**
Sony Classical SK62926 (69' · DDD)   Ⓕ

From his very first entry, in the B flat Concerto, Kissin is revealed as a Beethoven player of great articulacy, brilliance and sensitivity after the manner of such pianists as Kempff, Solomon, and Gilels. The playing is vital and fluent, the

technique awesome, not least in the way Kissin is able to refine his tone and taper dynamics in the high-lying coloratura passages where Beethoven's writing is at its most inspired and rarefied. The recitative at the end of the slow movement is predictably beautiful: intense and otherworldly. Levine draws from the Philharmonia playing that's both spirited and engaged. The recorded sound is admirable, too: strong and clean yet appropriately intimate.

The performance of the *Emperor* Concerto is also very fine. If you take the view that this is essentially a symphony with piano obbligato, you may hanker after a grander kind of musical theatre than that provided by Levine. He directs with decision and accompanies superbly. Kissin, too, plays with great flair and technical security. If there's a problem, it's with the articulation of the simple-seeming lyric statements where a degree of self-consciousness occasionally creeps in: where the flow is arrested and music suddenly seems to be walking on stilts. There's an element of this in the slow movement, though Kissin's playing of the bleak, trailing 24-bar-long *diminuendo* close is masterly. This is very much a young man's view of the music, but weighty too, such is the power of his technique.

Piano Concertos Nos 3 & 4
Murray Perahia pf **Concertgebouw Orchestra / Bernard Haitink**
Sony Classical SK39814 (70' · DDD) Recorded 1986   Ⓕ**OOO**

These performances have rightly been described as exceptional. They were directly compared to Alfred Brendel's accounts with James Levine (on Philips) but in the event, there's little to choose between these two distinguished soloists. The first movements are brilliantly and sensitively etched (Perahia uses Beethoven's bigger first cadenza in the first movement of the G major Concerto). Tempos are steady but with a fine degree of forward projection. Once past the daunting opening solo, Perahia plays the C minor's slow movement with great sureness and subtlety of touch; and with Haitink as his partner the exchanges in the G major's slow movement are memorably brought off. Note the superior quality of the Sony recordings and the wonderfully judicious accompaniments prepared for Perahia by the Concertgebouw Orchestra under Haitink. If there's little to choose between Perahia and Brendel as soloists, there's a great gulf between Haitink, who's exemplary, and Levine, who's unexceptional.

Piano Concertos Nos 4 & 5
Emil Gilels pf **Philharmonia Orchestra / Leopold Ludwig**   Ⓗ
Testament SBT1095 (73' · ADD) Recorded 1957 Ⓕ**OO**

This is one of the – perhaps *the* most – perfect accounts of the Fourth Concerto recorded. Poetry and virtuosity are held in perfect poise, with Ludwig and the Philharmonia providing a near-ideal accompaniment. The recording is also very fine, though be sure to gauge the levels correctly by first sampling one of the *tutti*s. If the volume is set too high at the start, you'll miss the stealing magic of Gilels's and the orchestra's initial entries and you'll be further discomfited by tape hiss.

The recording of the *Emperor* Concerto is also pretty good, not quite on a par with that of the Fourth. Ludwig and the orchestra tend to follow Gilels rather than always integrate with him and there are times, too, especially in the slow movement, when Gilels's playing borders on the self-indulgent. This isn't, however, sufficient reason for overlooking this fine and important Testament reissue.

Piano Concertos Nos 4 & 5
Maurizio Pollini pf **Vienna Philharmonic Orchestra / Karl Böhm**
DG Classikon 439 483-2GCL (71' · ADD) Recorded 1976   Ⓑ

This is an outstanding coupling of Pollini's earlier recordings of these works (the complete set of his later recordings with Abbado is reviewed above). The present performances are, arguably, more spontaneous, and the recording (especially of the piano) more natural, with the VPO expanding warmly within the ambience of the Grosser Saal of the Vienna Musikverein. These readings are freshly individual, with poise and poetry nicely balanced in both works, and with Böhm providing admirable accompaniments (the interchange in the slow movement of the G major is memorable). And Pollini is suitably magisterial in the *Emperor*. Most enjoyable, and stimulating too.

Piano Concertos Nos 4 & 5
Murray Perahia pf **Concertgebouw Orchestra / Bernard Haitink**
Sony Classical Theta SMK89711 (73' · DDD) Recorded 1986   Ⓜ❍❍❍

This is a superb bargain, combining Perahia's Gramophone Award-winning Fourth with an excellent *Emperor*, on a level with the best. Comparisons with other pianists, at this level, can be rather futile. It's a splendidly engineered recording, with a natural concert-hall type of balance, and there's good presence to the sound and depth to the perspective. The presentation of the orchestral detail allows you to delight in it, and perhaps to discover new subtleties, without a moment of unease as to whether anything has been forced into the wrong kind of relief. Perahia's performance has the freshness and natural authority we have come to expect of him in Beethoven. His reading might be described as uncomplicated if that didn't risk implying that it's in some way lightweight, or that he plays like a child of nature. The weight is certainly there, in sound

(when he wants it) as in expression.

Perahia himself has spoken of the happy experience of making this Beethoven cycle with Haitink (the other concertos including the complete set are reviewed above). It has indeed been a successful collaboration, and a joyous quality about the music-making communicates itself quite strongly from the beginning.

Piano Concerto No 5
Arturo Benedetti Michelangeli pf **Vienna Symphony Orchestra / Carlo Maria Giulini**
DG 419 249-2GH (42' · ADD) Recorded live 1979   Ⓕ❍

There has, over the years, been mixed reactions to Michelangeli's Beethoven. He was a most perplexing artist, perplexing because he liked to keep his musical personality well hidden – or at any rate mysterious – behind the armour-plated magnificence of his playing; disconcerting too because it's hard to arrive at a reasoned assessment of readings of classical music by someone who evidently isn't a man of balance. To interpret texts of the classical masters in a way which will give them the most vivid life doesn't seem to be his principal concern. There could be an intellectual *froideur* about his playing of Beethoven which verges on the disdainful and which was sometimes more than off-putting.

Not here though. This performance was recorded at a public performance in the Musikverein. He drives the opening flourishes hard, and thereafter responds keenly to Giulini's exposition, grand but always moving forward, matching it with a purpose that seems to derive from just that long-range musical thinking which is so often missing in his accounts of the other concertos. There's spaciousness, and time for everything, and always that rock-like strength of rhythm. The detailing could hardly be bettered but isn't allowed to deflect attention from our perception of the form. The security of the technique is enough to make most other pianists attempting an Olympian view of the concerto seem clumsy; but it doesn't draw attention to itself. Since the depth of his sonority is perfectly matched to the orchestra's, it makes for some especially exciting listening in the finale. Great playing by a great pianist.

Piano Concerto No 5. Triple Concerto in C, Op 56[a]
Leon Fleisher, Eugene Istomin pfs **Isaac Stern** vn **Leonard Rose** vc **Cleveland Orchestra / George Szell;** [a]**Philadelphia Orchestra / Eugene Ormandy**
Sony Classical Essential Classics SBK46549 (74' · ADD) Recorded 1961, [a]1964   Ⓑ❍

Leon Fleisher's recording of the *Emperor* is very powerful indeed. He was relatively young at the time and obviously George Szell had a considerable influence on the reading, but the solo playing is remarkably fresh and its pianistic authority is striking. That great octave passage in the first movement, just before the recapitulation, is enormously commanding, and Fleisher's lyrical playing, in the slow movement especially, has striking poise. Szell keeps the voltage high throughout, but for all its excitement this is by no means a hard-driven, unfeeling interpretation. The recording is bright, bold and forward in the CBS 1960s manner, and the Severance Hall acoustic prevents any ugliness.

A splendid *Emperor*, then, but what makes this disc even more enticing is the inclusion of an equally distinguished version of the TripleConcerto, recorded in Philadelphia Town Hall (a much more successful venue than many used over the years for this great orchestra). The very gentle opening by the orchestra is full of anticipatory tension, and at the beginning of the slow movement Ormandy's preparation for Rose's glorious cello solo demonstrates what a superb accompanist he is. Indeed, this is no mere accompaniment, but a complete partnership. Although Stern's personality dominates marginally, the three soloists play together like a chamber-music team, without in any way submerging their individuality. The sound is very good for its time. This entire disc is a prime example where Sony's sobriquet 'Essential Classics' is justly appended.

Piano Concerto No 5. Choral Fantasia in C minor, Op 80
Alfred Brendel *pf* **London Philharmonic Choir and Orchestra / Bernard Haitink**
Philips Insignia 434 148-2PM (61' · ADD) Recorded 1976-7
Ⓜ︎Ⓞ

Philips achieves consistent success with digital remastering, adding a presence and firmness of focus that seldom produce unwanted edginess. This certainly applies to Alfred Brendel's recording of the Fifth Concerto, coupled with his even more impressive *Choral Fantasia*. This latter is unforgettable, he and Haitink making something especially dazzling of this work. No one plays the big opening cadenza with more power and authority than Brendel and a similar magisterial breadth informs the Emperor; even though the first movement perhaps sounds a little too controlled, this is still a very satisfying performance. The choral contribution to the Fantasia is quite splendid. The recording combines orchestral weight with brilliance, and a most believable piano image.

Violin Concerto in D, Op 61

Violin Concerto
Itzhak Perlman *vn* **Philharmonia Orchestra / Carlo Maria Giulini**
EMI Great Recordings of the Century 566900-2 (44' · DDD) Recorded 1980
Ⓜ︎ⓄⓄⓄ

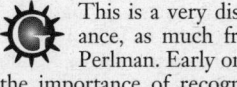 This is a very distinguished performance, as much from Giulini as from Perlman. Early on Giulini makes clear the importance of recognising the difference between *forte* and *fortissimo* in Beethoven – for

BEETHOVEN PIANO CONCERTO NO 5, 'EMPEROR' – IN BRIEF

Murray Perahia; Concertgebouw Orchestra / Bernard Haitink
Sony Classical SMK89711 (73' · DDD)   Ⓜ︎ⓄⓄⓄ

A superb performance of real authority but above all of true poetry. Beautifully accompanied by the great Dutch orchestra. Coupled with an equally fine No 4.

Wilhelm Kempff; Berlin PO / Ferdinand Leitner
DG 447 402-2GOR (70' · ADD)   Ⓜ︎ⓄⓄ
A magnificent, aristocratic interpretation from Kempff's second (stereo) cycle (with No 4). Still sounding very good for its 1962 vintage.

Evgeni Kissin; Philharmonia / James Levine
Sony Classical SK62926 (69' · DDD)   ⒻⓄⓄ
The young Russian pianist reveals himself to be an artist of great articulacy, brilliance and sensitivity. Coupled with a lively No 1.

Emil Gilels; Philharmonia / Leopold Ludwig
Testament SBT1095 (73' · DDD)   Ⓕ
A fine *Emperor* coupled with a superb Fourth. Gilels was a commanding Beethoven interpreter. There is some hiss from the 1957 tape, otherwise fine at reasonable levels.

Maurizio Pollini; Vienna PO / Karl Böhm
DG 439 483-2GCL (71' · ADD)   Ⓑ
A cooler Beethoven than Pollini later gave with Abbado, but certainly spontaneous and fresh sounding (coupled with No 4).

Leon Fleisher; Cleveland Orchestra / George Szell
Sony Classical SBK46549 (74' · DDD)   ⒷⓄ
High-octane Beethoven from Fleisher and Szell: commanding, virtuoso and iron-willed. Not for the faint hearted! Coupled with a fine Triple Concerto.

Solomon; Philharmonia / Herbert Menges
Testament mono SBT1221 (74' · ADD)   ⒻⓄ
A stunning *Emperor* for its classical poise, ease and limpid fingerwork. A reminder of one of the UK's greatest pianists. Coupled with two Mozart piano sonatas.

Robert Levin *fp* **Orchestre Révolutionnaire et Romantique / Sir John Eliot Gardiner**
Archiv 447 771-2AH (71' · DDD)   Ⓕ
A most successful period-instrument *Emperor*: the combination of Levin's fantasy and Gardiner's drama pays dividends. The coupled *Choral Fantasy* with Gardiner's superb Monteverdi Choir is magnificent.

Edwin Fischer; Philharmonia / Wilhelm Furtwängler
EMI mono 574800-2 (78' · ADD)   ⒻⓄⓄ
A great *Emperor* for its sense of grandeur and majesty. A superb collaboration from 1951.

101

example the *ff* of bars 73 and 74 and the which surrounds them; and the marvellous way he gets the Philharmonia to play *sfp* is a pleasure in itself. The liquid smoothness of the winds is another joy.

The slow movement has the utmost calm beauty from both soloist and orchestra, while Perlman plays the finale at an admirably swift speed, yet with all the flexibility it needs, so that it really dances lightly. Contrast Chung on Decca whose finale is almost lethargic in comparison, and Kremer for Philips who takes it at a terrible lick but puts it firmly into a strait-jacket. The clarity of the orchestral texture is outstanding too. The bassoon, for example, sings its solos in the finale easily and without the least forcing, whereas as on the Chung recording it sounds more consciously brought forward. The Decca is no match in general sound either.

Violin Concerto. Romance No 2
Oscar Shumsky vn **Philharmonia Orchestra / Sir Andrew Davis**
ASV Quicksilva CDQS6080 (54' · DDD) Recorded 1988   ⑤Ⓑ**OO**

Oscar Shumsky's recording of the Violin Concerto is one of the finest in the catalogue and was strongly recommended at premium price. In this reissue it's a bargain *par excellence*. The reading is relaxed and assured and has a serene purity of line, notably so in the memorable *Larghetto*, which is quite beautifully played. Andrew Davis provides his soloist with admirable support and the orchestral contribution is highly sympathetic. The sound balance favours the soloist with something of a spotlight, but otherwise the recording is very good: those wanting a bargain-price version of this work could hardly better this, especially as the *Romance* in F major is given as an encore.

Beethoven Violin Concerto. **Bernstein** Serenade
Hilary Hahn vn **Baltimore Symphony Orchestra / David Zinman**
Sony Classical SK60584 (75' · DDD)   Ⓕ**O**

At first glance, this would seem a pretty strange coupling, yet by trailing the most Olympian of classical violin concertos with a semi-concerto based on a Platonic dialogue Hilary Hahn and Sony suggest their own quaint form of programming logic. Hahn employs her sweet-centred tone with utmost finesse and David Zinman's Baltimore accompaniment is smooth, unhurried and clear-sighted. Hahn opts for Kreisler's cadenza and makes a special feature of the simultaneous projection of themes, broadening the pace then re-entering into the movement, as if caught in a trance. Her approach is lyrical and unindulgent, though most definitely post-Romantic. She's an immaculate technician who favours a calculated though richly expressive approach to phrasing. She breathes considerable warmth into the *Larghetto* and offers a

crisp account of the finale. Of its kind, this performance looks unbeatable.

One of Bernstein's most enduring works, the lovable 1954 *Serenade*, draws on ideas from Plato's *The Symposium*, principally those concerning love, and includes a gorgeous three-part song and a finale that looks sideways at *On the Waterfront* and forwards to *West Side Story*. Hahn's tender-hearted rendition lays claim to being the finest interpretation ever, aided and abetted by Zinman's firmly focused conducting. Both works are beautifully recorded.

Violin Concerto. Romances – No 1 in G, Op 40; No 2 in F, Op 50
Gidon Kremer vn **Chamber Orchestra of Europe / Nikolaus Harnoncourt**
Warner Elatus 0927-49773-2 (57' · DDD) Recorded live 1992   Ⓜ**O**

Gidon Kremer offers one of his most commanding performances, both polished and full of flair, magnetically spontaneous from first to last. Rarely do you hear such consistently pure tone in this work and the orchestral writing too is superbly realised. It has become customary to treat the long first movement as expansively as possible but Kremer takes a more urgent view, and after his thoughtful and dedicated, slightly understated reading of the slow movement, he and Harnoncourt round the performance off magically with a finale that skips along the more infectiously thanks to light, clean articulation and textures. Traditional performances seem heavyweight by comparison. The controversial point for some will be the cadenza in the first movement where he uses a transcription of the big cadenza which Beethoven wrote for his piano arrangement of the work. However, this is altogether one of the most refreshing versions of the concerto ever committed to record, backed up by crisp, unsentimental readings of the two *Romances*.

Violin Concerto. Romances – No 1 in G, Op 40;   Ⓟ
No 2 in F, Op 50
Thomas Zehetmair vn **Orchestra of the Eighteenth Century / Frans Brüggen**
Philips 462 123-2PH (54' · DDD)   Ⓕ**OO**

This is a great performance, one that simply has to be heard. The first movement is built on a tug of war between dynamic extremes and, for once, it actually sounds like a concerto, and a brilliant one at that. The more familiar average playing time of around 25 minutes (Zehetmair's lasts a mere 22) tends, for all its beautiful effect, to compromise on forward momentum. Here, the use of period instruments adds extra fibre to the aural mix, and Brüggen's conducting has a pressing urgency about it that, again, intensifies the drama. The *Larghetto* is full of subtle nuances and telling inflexions, and the Rondo has great rhythmic verve.

Two recording venues are used, the excellent

Muziekcentrum at Enschede for the two Romances and the rather cavernous Vredenburg, Utrecht for the concerto. The former yields the more sympathetic acoustic (Zehetmair and Brüggen offer limpidly flowing performances of both pieces), but it's unlikely that the slightly rougher-edged concerto recording will give much cause for complaint. This is one of the recordings of Beethoven's Violin Concerto, and is to be strongly recommended.

Beethoven Violin Concerto[a]   Ⓗ
Mendelssohn Violin Concerto in E minor, Op 64[b]
Yehudi Menuhin vn [a]**Philharmonia Orchestra,**
[b]**Berlin Philharmonic Orchestra / Wilhelm**
Furtwängler
EMI Great Recordings of the Century mono 566975-2
(71' · ADD) Recorded 1952-3   Ⓜ

Furtwängler and Menuhin recorded the Beethoven Concerto on two occasions, and this second version has an extraordinary quality of spirituality and profundity. Furtwängler's conducting of the opening *tutti* has a magnificently arresting, weighty quality, and Menuhin's response, profound and rich in re-creative imagination shows the two great artists in perfect accord. Their account of this movement is on the largest scale, yet they convey Beethoven's vision in a humane, approachable fashion. The slow movement has a highly concentrated yet serene character, with Menuhin's rapt, singing tone achieving rare eloquence, and the finale is superbly balanced, with an affecting sense of a shared, joyful experience. The recording sounds quite similar to the original LP issue, but the quality is quite acceptable.

The Mendelssohn was recorded a year earlier, and here remastering has brought a slight roughening in an orchestral sound which was never very ingratiating, though the defect isn't serious. Menuhin and Furtwängler float the first movement in an unhurriedly serene, elegantly shaped fashion. In the slow movement they achieve a touchingly tender, almost innocent quality and the finale, taken at a moderate tempo, has lightness and an appealingly eager character.

Beethoven Violin Concerto[a]   Ⓗ
Brahms Violin Concerto in D, Op 77[b]
Jascha Heifetz vn [a]**NBC Symphony Orchestra /**
Arturo Toscanini; [b]**Boston Symphony Orchestra /**
Serge Koussevitzky
Naxos Historical mono 8 110936 (77' · AAD) Recorded
[a]1939, [b]1940   Ⓢ Ⓢ ◐◐◐

'An old diamond in the rough' is how Robert C Marsh (*Toscanini and the Art of Orchestra Performance*; London: 1956) recalled the original Victor 78s of this 1940 Heifetz Studio 8-H recording of the Beethoven. Of the LP reissue he wrote: 'On the whole, the recording is so dead and artificial that at times the thin line of violin sound

reminds one of something from the golden age of Thomas Edison's tinfoil cylinder rather than 1940.' Early CD transfers suggested that all wasn't lost but even they barely anticipated the extraordinary fineness of the sound we now have on this transfer by archivist and restorer Mark Obert-Thorn.

The performance itself is one of the most remarkable the gramophone has ever given us. The visionary, high *tessitura* violin writing is realised by Heifetz with a technical surety which is indistinguishable, in the final analysis, from his sense of the work as one of Beethoven's most sublime explorations of that world (in Schiller's phrase) 'above the stars where He must dwell'. Those who would query the 'depth' of Heifetz's reading miss this point entirely. To adapt Oscar Wilde, it is they who are in the gutter, Heifetz who is looking at the stars.

As for Toscanini's contribution – another cue for rancorous comment in the past – it, too, is masterly. Now that we can actually hear the performance, the orchestral *tutti*s seem beautifully balanced both within themselves and *vis-à-vis* the soloist. As for the actual accompaniment, it's discreet and self-effacing, fiery yet refined, and always wondrously subtle.

In the case of the Brahms, it's more reasonable to argue that there are other ways of playing the concerto. Heifetz's isn't a Romantic reading. It's lean, athletic, classical, aristocratic, finely drawn, an approach which wears exceptionally well on record. The Brahms enjoys another impeccable transfer. Musically and technically, this is a real thoroughbred of a release, unignorable at any price.

Beethoven Violin Concerto[a]   Ⓗ
Tchaikovsky Violin Concerto in D, Op 35[b]
Bronislaw Huberman vn [a]**Vienna Philharmonic**
Orchestra / George Szell; [b]**Staatskapelle Berlin /**
William Steinberg
Naxos Historical mono 8 110903 (67' · AAD) Recorded
[a]1934, [b]1928   Ⓢ Ⓢ ◐◐

Virtuoso violinist Bronislaw Huberman was an idealist, an ardent Pan-European and co-founder (with William Steinberg) of the Israel Philharmonic. He was, in a sense, the prototype for such present-day fiddling mavericks as Kremer, Zehetmair, Tetzlaff and Kennedy. Huberman's open letter to the conductor Wilhelm Furtwängler, in which he pledged support of the persecuted, and refused to perform in Nazi Germany, has become famous, and his astringent though frequently dazzling playing translates that steely resolve into musical terms.

This Naxos coupling is very nearly the answer to a prayer. Huberman's interpretation is more in line with, say, Zehetmair and Brüggen than the stately readings of Kreisler, Szigeti, Menuhin or David Oistrakh. His lively speeds and darting inflections spin silver beams where others opt for (for some misplaced) 'Olympian' heights. The luminosity of the reading, its radiance and refusal to dawdle, run counter to the languid sweetness favoured by various of his peers and successors.

The 1929 Tchaikovsky recording is peerless. Huberman's first entry reveals all: elastic phrasing, sweeping *portamentos* and generous *rubato* stamp a giant personality. Thereafter, quick-silver bowing and a steely *spiccato* level with the best of the period. Brahms loved Huberman's playing (he promised the budding youngster a *Fantasy* but never lived to compose it), and no wonder, given the veiled beauty of his tone (*Canzonetta*) and the uninhibited swagger of his bravura style (finale).

You simply have to hear Huberman's recording, and Naxos's give-away price makes it a mandatory purchase. However, the transfer of the Beethoven, although perfectly adequate, is rather spoiled by excessive digital noise reduction. On one occasion in the first movement, the violinist momentarily disappears; in the second movement two chords inadvertently become one. But these technical reservations will likely prove trifling for anyone who has never heard Huberman before. There are no greater violin recordings in existence, and we urge you to buy them.

Triple Concerto in C, Op 56

Beethoven Triple Concerto[a] **Brahms** Double Concerto in A minor, Op 102[b]
David Oistrakh *vn* **Mstislav Rostropovich** *vc*
Sviatoslav Richter *pf* [a]**Berlin Philharmonic Orchestra / Herbert von Karajan;** [b]**Cleveland Orchestra / George Szell**
EMI Great Recordings of the Century mono 566902-2 (70' · ADD) Recorded 1969   Ⓜ ⚫⚫

These are illustrious performances and make a splendid coupling. EMI planned for a long time to assemble this starry line-up of soloists, conductor and orchestra for Beethoven's Triple Concerto, and the artists don't disappoint, bringing sweetness as well as strength to a work which in lesser hands can sound clumsy and long winded. The recording, made in a Berlin church in 1969, is warm, spacious and well balanced, placing the soloists in a gentle spotlight. The account of Brahms's Double Concerto is perhaps the most powerful recorded performance since the days of Heifetz and Feuermann or Thibaud and Casals. The recording has come up extremely well in this remastering: although the sound isn't as smooth as can be achieved nowadays, this is soon forgotten, and you're caught up in the magnificent music-making.

Triple Concerto. Choral Fantasia in C minor, Op 80. Rondo in B flat, WoO6
Pierre-Laurent Aimard *pf* **Thomas Zehetmair** *vn* **Clemens Hagen** *vc* **Arnold Schoenberg Choir; Chamber Orchestra of Europe / Nikolaus Harnoncourt**
Warner Classics 2564 60602-2 (66' · DDD) Recorded live   Ⓕ ⚫⚫

Listening to the opening tutti on this joyful new Triple Concerto, you can just picture Nikolaus Harnoncourt cueing his strings, perched slightly forwards, impatiently waiting for that first, pregnant *forte*. This is a big, affable, blustery Triple, the soloists completing the sound canvas rather than dominating it, a genuine collaborative effort. So beside the Beethovenian strut to this performance there's poetry too. Yet thoughtfulness never spells timidity; Hagen and Thomas Zehetmair throw caution to the winds near the end of the first movement. The Concerto's Largo is simplicity itself, rather like a song without words, but it's the finale that is likely to raise the most smiles, a rumbustious affair, uninhibited without coursing out of control. Harnoncourt and his team go for the burn, always brilliant but, more importantly, full of character and humour.

The fill-ups (like the Concerto, recorded at concerts in Graz) are hardly less engaging. The little B flat Rondo is bubbly from the start, Aimard and the orchestra maintaining a feeling of chamber collaboration. And then the *Choral Fantasia*, so often clunky on disc but here aided by Aimard's sense of style – his arpeggios in the long opening solo have so much colour – and by Harnoncourt's relaxed approach to the music that follows, each variation imaginatively tended within a larger framework. The singing is excellent, the sound both warm and realistic. As 'feel-good' Beethoven programmes go, this is about as enjoyable as it gets, though a high level of musical insight further enhances one's pleasure.

Additional recommendation

Triple Concerto
Coupled with: Choral Fantasia in C minor, Op 80
Perlman *vn* **Ma** *vc* **Chorus of the Deutsche Oper, Berlin; Berlin Philharmonic Orchestra / Barenboim** *pf*
EMI 555516-2 (55' · DDD)   Ⓕ
Superb live performances which grab you with their refreshing spontaneity. Choice between this and Masur's comes down to a preference for crisp co-ordination and the inspiration of the moment.

Symphonies

No 1 in C, Op 21; **No 2** in D, Op 36; **No 3** in E flat, Op 55, 'Eroica'; **No 4** in B flat, Op 60; **No 5** in C minor, Op 67; **No 6** in F, Op 68, 'Pastoral; **No 7** in A, Op 92; **No 8** in F, Op 93; **No 9** in D minor, Op 125, 'Choral'

Complete Symphonies

Symphonies Nos 1-9
Charlotte Margiono *sop* **Birgit Remmert** *mez* **Rudolf Schasching** *ten* **Robert Holl** *bass* **Arnold Schoenberg Choir; Chamber Orchestra of Europe / Nikolaus Harnoncourt**
Warner Elatus ⑤ 0927-49768-2 (358' · DDD) Recorded live 1990-91   Ⓜ ⚫⚫⚫

Symphonies Nos 1 & 2 also available separately on
Warner Elatus 0927 49003-2 Ⓜ
Symphony No 3 (plus Overtures – Die Geschöpfe des
Prometheus, Leonore III) on Warner Elatus
2564 60034-2 Ⓜ
Symphonies Nos 4 & 5 on Warner Elatus
2564 60012-2 Ⓜ
Symphony No 6 (plus Overtures, Leonore II, Coriolan
& Fidelio) on Warner Elatus 0927 49004-2 Ⓜ
Symphonies Nos 7 & 8 (plus Overture, The Ruins of
Athens) available on Warner Elatus 0927 49620-2 Ⓜ
Symphony No 9 on Warner Elatus 0927 46736-2 Ⓜ

Brimful of intrepid character and interpretative incident, this is surely one of the most stimulating Beethoven symphony cycles of recent times. As Harnoncourt himself states in the booklet: 'It has always been my conviction that music is not there to soothe people's nerves...but rather to open their eyes, to give them a good shaking, even to frighten them.' So it transpires that there's a re-creative daring about Harnoncourt's conducting – in essence an embracement of recent scholarly developments and his own pungent sense of characterisation – which is consistently illuminating, thus leaving the listener with the uncanny sensation that he or she is encountering this great music for the first time. In all this Harnoncourt is backed to the hilt by some superbly responsive, miraculously assured playing from the COE: their personable, unforced assimilation of his specific demands, allied to his intimate knowledge of the inner workings of these scores, make for wonderfully fresh, punchy results. In this respect Nos 6-8 in particular prove immensely rewarding, but the Eroica and the Fourth, too, are little short of superb. This is a cycle which excitingly reaffirms the life-enhancing mastery of Beethoven's vision for many years to come.

Symphonies Nos 1-9
Gundula Janowitz sop **Hilde Rössel-Majdan** contr
Waldemar Kmentt ten **Walter Berry** bass
**Vienna Singverein; Berlin Philharmonic Orchestra /
Herbert von Karajan**
DG Collectors Edition ⑤ 463 088-2GB5 (332' · ADD)
Recorded 1961-2. Text and translation included Ⓜ

This was the first set of the Nine to be planned, recorded and sold as an integral cycle. It was also a set that had been extremely carefully positioned from the interpretative point of view. Where Karajan's 1950s Philharmonia cycle had elements in it that owed a certain amount to the old German school of Beethoven interpretation, the new-found virtuosity of the Berliners allowed him to approach more nearly the fierce beauty and lean-toned fiery manner of Toscanini's Beethoven style as Karajan had first encountered it in its halcyon age in the mid-1930s. Nothing demonstrates this better than the 1962 recording of the Fourth Symphony, fiery and radiant as Karajan's reading had not previously been, and never would be again. The

old shibboleth among writers and musicians that the even-numbered symphonies were somehow less dramatic than the odd-numbered ones meant nothing to Karajan. His accounts of the Second, Fourth, Sixth and Eighth Symphonies were every bit as intense as their allegedly sturdier neighbours. Only in the Seventh Symphony's third movement Trio and the Menuetto of the Eighth Symphony – where he continued to follow Wagner's idea of this as an essentially stately dance, a kind of surrogate slow movement – did he deviate significantly from the Toscanini model. And it worked. True, the first movement of the *Pastoral* Symphony was a touch airless, lacking some of the easy wonderment of Karajan's old Philharmonia recording. But, then, Toscanini himself had never managed to replicate the unique charm of his pre-war English recording with the BBC SO.

The original review of the cycle entered a number of caveats, some of which still pertain, though it's the lack of certain repeats and the non-antiphonal dispensation of the violins that may worry some most nowadays. What so enthused us back then was the urgency of the music-making, its vitality and, ultimately, a fierce sense of joy that had its natural point of culmination in a thrillingly played and eloquently sung account of the finale of the Ninth. The playing of the new rejuvenated BPO dazzled throughout, as did Günther Hermanns recordings: clean and clear, and daringly 'lit' with a bright shimmer of reverberation. The recordings have always transferred effortlessly to CD and the present reissue is no exception.

Symphonies Nos 1-9 Ⓟ
Luba Orgonasova sop **Anne Sofie von Otter** mez
Anthony Rolfe Johnson ten **Gilles Cachemaille** bar
**Monteverdi Choir; Orchestre Révolutionnaire et
Romantique / Sir John Eliot Gardiner**
Archiv Produktion ⑤ 439 900-2AH5 (328' · DDD)
Recorded 1993-4 ⒻⓄⓄ

This set is remarkable and many will rate it as Mr Knightley rates Emma Woodhouse 'faultless in spite of her faults'. In his booklet essay, Peter Czorny tells us that the recordings are offered in the hope of transporting the listener back 'to that moment when this music burst forth into a world of heroes, wars and revolution, creating its own world of the sublime and ineffable'. This theme is developed by Gardiner in a robust 20-minute talk on the project that comes free on a sixth CD. Gardiner's opinion that Beethoven wanted his musicians to live dangerously has some peculiar consequences.

Symphony No 1: The opening is superbly judged. Gardiner doesn't overplay the *Adagio molto*, and the *Allegro con brio*, often played with a fatal languor by members of the old German School, is pretty quick. After his absurdly brisk reading of the second movement, Gardiner goes on to conduct dazzlingly successful accounts of the *Scherzo* and finale. Symphony No 2: This is

BEETHOVEN SYMPHONIES – IN BRIEF

CO of Europe / Nikolaus Harnoncourt
Teldec ⑩ 3984 28144-2 (10 hr 40' · DDD)
Ⓑ**○○○**

A ground-breaking set which harnessed fresh ideas, totally committed playing and a *Gramophone* Record of the Year now economically coupled with more Beethoven works. It should be seriously considered.

Zurich Tonhalle / David Zinman
Arte Nova ⑤ 74321 65410-2 (5 hr 36' · DDD)
Ⓢ**○○**

Another set that blends modern instruments and a historically aware approach. There's a freshness and sparkle here that's very hard to resist. Only the Ninth slightly disappoints.

Royal Liverpool PO / Sir Charles Mackerras
CfP ⑤ 575751-2 (5 hr 27' · DDD)   Ⓑ**○○**

Good, honest Beethoven playing under a conductor completely at home with both period and modern instruments. Very inexpensively priced, this is a fine set.

London Classical Players / Sir Roger Norrington
Virgin Classics ⑤ 561943-2 (5 hr 53' · DDD)   Ⓑ**○○**

A fine period-instrument cycle – Nos 2 and 8 won a *Gramophone* Award – with a fine sense of excitement and an intoxicating feeling for the adventure of such a project.

Orchestre Révolutionaire et Romantique / Sir John Eliot Gardiner
Archiv ⑤ 439 900-2AH5 (5 hr 28' · DDD)   Ⓕ**○○**

A superb, carefully considered and very theatrical cycle: this is Beethoven straight off the stage. The playing on period instruments is very fine and the recording nicely handled.

Berlin PO / Herbert von Karajan
DG ⑤ 463 088-2 (5 hr 32' · ADD)   Ⓑ**○○**

Dating from 1961-2, Karajan's second cycle was the first cycle recorded and released as such. It's still fresh and imaginative, boasting a real sense of discovery and excitement.

Vienna PO / Sir Simon Rattle
EMI ⑤ 557445-2 (5 hr 42' · DDD)   Ⓜ

Recorded live, this is a controversial set. Much admired in some quarters, it's lacking in the joy that's so central to this music. Rattle's 'period' approach sits uneasily with the lush, romantic style of the VPO. Sample first…

Berlin PO / Abbado
DG ⑤ 469 000-2GH5 (5 hr 37' · DDD)   Ⓕ**○**

Abbado's second cycle and a total rethink on the VPO cycle: these are light, buoyant readings that make up a most impressive whole. Dramatic and often thrilling.

very fine throughout. By following the written tempo markings and his own musical instincts Gardiner produces a perfomance of the first movement that opens out the drama most compellingly. Symphony No 3: More *révolutionnaire* than *romantique*. A very fast first movement gets within spitting distance of an impossible metronome mark. That and keen texturing make for tremendous dramatic urgency. Unfortunately, there's also too little accommodation *en route* of the rich cargo of ideas that Beethoven has shipped into this movement. In their haste to get to the recapitulation itself, Gardiner and his players are decidedly unpoised. He's superb in the last two movements; but these are considerably less than half the story where the *Eroica* is concerned. Symphony No 4: An unusually quick introductory and brisk *Allegro vivace*. Gardiner treats the pivotal drum entry before the recapitulation atmospherically. Glorious slow movement, impossibly quick finale.

Symphony No 5: Here is the stuff of which revolutions are made. Gardiner plays the piece pretty straight, and at white heat. The orchestra is superb, helped by the Francophone bias of its sound base. That said, the *Scherzo* (with repeat) is surely too fast. It starts briskly and not especially quietly. The pace drops back for the Trio, which is just as well since the strings are hard-pressed to articulate clearly. The finale is also very fast, again ahead of what's generally regarded as a good metronome. There's a grandeur to the Scherzo-cum-finale that could be seen to reflect a vision that transcends the politics of revolution. Still, for its *éclat terrible*, this is unbeatable. The slow movement is also superbly shaped and directed.

Symphony No 6: Despite some lovely playing in the slow movement and an air of brisk efficiency, this is a rather joyless *Pastoral*. Nor is it a spiritually uplifting one. The *Scherzo* – 'A merry gathering of country folk' – is a very high-speed affair. At such a pace the various amusing false entries rather lose their point; to play in this village band you would need to be a virtuoso, and teetotal to boot.

Symphony No 7: A glorious performance. The introduction sets the scene with an ideal blend of weight and anticipation. The *Vivace* has a splendid dance feel and a power that's wholly unforced. *Scherzo* and finale are also superbly paced. The *Allegretto* is eloquent with a sense of barely sublimated grieving. The recording is magnificent. Symphony No 8: In general, the symphony thrives on the Gardiner approach, though in the finale the emphasis is again on high-speed locomotion.

Symphony No 9: The first movement has never been dispatched as rapidly as here. In fact, Gardiner doesn't get the bit between the teeth until bar 51, so the celebrated introduction has room to breathe. But he isn't entirely inflexible, and he and his players show remarkable skill in making busy detail tell. Yet a lot does go by the board. The slow movement is also played very quickly. However, the finale is superb. Tempos are unerringly chosen, the choral singing is beyond criticism, and there's a rare expressive quality to the singing of the solo quartet.

High quality playing from the orchestra and often exceptional Archiv sound. At best, the physical and intellectual vitality of this music-making brings us close to the *Ding an sich'*. It's a best that occurs only intermittently. That it occurs at all is perhaps a sufficient miracle.

Symphonies Nos 1-9
Ruth Ziesak *sop* **Birgit Remmert** *contr* **Steve Davislim** *ten* **Detlef Roth** *bar* **Swiss Chamber Choir; Zurich Tonhalle Orchestra / David Zinman**
Arte Nova Classics ⑤ 74321 65410-2 (336' · DDD)
Ⓢ Ⓢ○○

Also available separately –
74321 63645-2 – Nos 1 & 2 (54')
74321 59214-2 – Nos 3 & 4 (75')
74321 49695-2 – Nos 5 & 6 (74')
74321 56341-2 – Nos 7 & 8 (61')
74321 65411-2 – No 9 (73')

Viewed overall, the performances of Nos 1, 4, 6 and 8 are the best in this set, though there's a certain levelling of dynamics in the Eighth. In the Seventh and the Fifth, the finales might have benefited from a wider curve of dynamics and a little more in the way of tonal weight. On the other hand, Zinman's fleet-footed *Eroica* grows on you, and the Fourth is among the most vivacious accounts available. As to the Ninth, the *Scherzo*'s super-fast Trio makes particular sense at the very end of the movement where Trio and outer section engage in a brief comic tussle. The fast first movement is suitably dangerous and while the finale will no doubt court controversy (primarily for some unusual tempo relations), the *Adagio* sounds matter-of-fact, even a little impatient. Indeed, it's the one movement in this cycle that seems to misfire.

Zinman has used Bärenreiter's new edition of Beethoven's texts, although the extra appoggiaturas and ornaments, invariably sewn along the woodwind lines – were inserted by the conductor, based on sound musicological principles. All repeats are observed, and so are the majority of Beethoven's metronome markings. What matters most is the overall character of Zinman's Beethoven which is swift, lean, exhilarating and transparent. The Tonhalle copes bravely, often with exceptional skill, and the recordings easily compare with their best full-price rivals.

And the best bargain alternatives? Günter Wand's sense of structure (RCA) draws a sympathetic response, while Leinsdorf's solid, strong-arm Beethoven also has much to commend it (RCA). Karajan's 1962 cycle is surely the best of four (see above) and although Mackerras (Classics for Pleasure), like Zinman, sheds revealing beams of light here and there, this Zurich set has the greater impact. Those who favour the darker, weightier, more obviously 'heroic' Beethoven known (wrongly, perhaps) as 'old school' will probably not respond quite so readily, but they should still give Zinman a try.

On balance, his cycle remains the best bargain digital option. Besides, Arte Nova's asking price is so ludicrously cheap that it's worth buying on impulse, if only for the sake of a refreshing change. Just try to have someone else's *Choral* in reserve.

Symphonies Nos 1-9[a]. **Overtures – Coriolan, Op 62; Egmont, Op 84**
Die Geschöpfe des Prometheus, Op 43
[a]**The Schütz Choir of London; London Classical Players / Sir Roger Norrington**
Virgin Classics ⑤ 561943-2 (DDD) Recorded 1986-8
Ⓢ Ⓢ○○

The symphonies in this bargain-price set are also available separately – see the individual symphony entries on the following pages for our review of the set.

Additional recommendations

Symphonies Nos 1-9

Wiens *sop* **Hartwig** *contr* **Lewis** *ten* **Hermann** *bar* **Hamburg State Opera Chorus; North German Radio Chorus; North German RSO / Wand**
RCA Red Seal ⑤ 74321 20277-2　Ⓜ
(356' · DDD) also available separately
　Consistently inspired: Wand's tempos are superbly judged, the orchestral balance ideal, and in the Ninth the soloists make a first-rate team.

NBC Symphony Orchestra / Toscanini　Ⓗ
RCA Red Seal ⑦ 74321 666562/7 (ADD)
also available separately　Ⓢ Ⓜ
　Recorded from 1949 to 1952, these recordings constitute Toscanini's only complete cycle. Strong, lean and direct performances, there isn't a single bar which is unconsidered or routine. Harsh sound but the transfers seem faithful.

Rodgers *sop* **Jones** *mez* **Bronder** *ten* **Terfel** *bass-bar* **Royal Liverpool Philharmonic Choir and Orchestra / Mackerras**
Classics for Pleasure ⑤ 575751-2 (327' · DDD)
Recorded 1991-7　Ⓑ
　A blend of period consciousness and traditional classicism. Mackerras's Fifth and Seventh are particularly fine, and the Liverpool playing rarely less than accomplished. They're at their best in the *Pastoral*, bright and fresh as a spring morning. The soloists in the Ninth are first-rate, though the choral singing is below par.

Symphonies – selected

Symphonies Nos 1 & 4. Egmont Overture, Op 84[a]
Berlin Philharmonic Orchestra / Herbert von Karajan
DG Galleria 419 048-2GGA (64' · ADD) Recorded
[a]1969, 1975-6　Ⓜ○

The opening of the First, perfectly timed and chorded, announces playing of rare pedigree, though the *Allegro* itself, taken at a gently ruminative pace, is a surprise. The autumnal side of

Karajan's make-up is one we don't often see. It's a beautifully shaped reading, with glorious wind playing and a nobly sustained through-rhythm. The mellow *Andante*, like the Minuet and Trio, emerges as a miracle of instrumental ensemble, a reminder of how, summer by summer, Karajan encouraged his players to make chamber music together on vacation. After so gentle a start, the finale seems strangely quick. Orchestrally, it's the finest quick Beethoven playing imaginable and for all the aerial excitement the final *fortissimo* peaks are compelling placed.

Karajan's instinctively dynamic approach to Beethoven is modified in the Fourth by a contrasted but equally strong feel for the German symphonic tradition. The performance strikes deepest at the points of stasis midway through each of the first three movements. Indeed, the sonority of the performance is remarkable throughout, with great use made of bass and cello colourings (something which the BPO had perfected by this time) and a huge dynamic range – implicit in the score from massive *tutti* chords down to the most perfectly regulated quiet drum rolls. It's in such playing, as subtle as it is creatively alive, that the flame of Beethoven's genius can be seen to burn brightly on. The *Egmont* Overture, played superbly and surprisingly swiftly, makes a welcome filler.

Symphonies Nos 2 & 8. Overtures – Coriolan,   **P**
Op 62; Egmont, Op 84
London Classical Players / Sir Roger Norrington
Virgin Veritas 561375-2 (73' · DDD) Recorded 1986
    Ⓜ**OOO**

Norrington's way with Beethoven, which is recognisably Toscaninian in some of its aspects, is, in his own words, his aim of recapturing much of 'the exhilaration and sheer disturbance that his music certainly generated in his day'. Like Toscanini, Erich Kleiber, and others before him, Norrington achieves this not by the imposition on the music of some world view but by taking up its immediate intellectual and physical challenges. He isn't unduly preoccupied by matters of orchestral size but sound interests him a good deal. Throughout, the contributions of horns, trumpets and drums most rivet the attention.

What fascinates Norrington is rhythm and pulse and their determining agencies: 18th-century performing styles, instrumental articulacy (most notably, bowing methods), and Beethoven's own metronome markings. In the Second Symphony Norrington makes the music smile and dance without any significant loss of forward momentum, and he treats the metronome marks more consistently than Karajan (who spins out the symphony's introduction), while sharing with him a belief in a really forward-moving pulse in the *Larghetto* (again an approach to the printed metronome if not the thing itself). The recordings are warm and vivid and generally well balanced.

The *fff* climax of the development of the

Eighth Symphony's first movement is slightly underpowered, which is odd when the horns and trumpets are elsewhere so thrillingly caught; perhaps, in the Eighth, the recording could have been a shade tighter and drier in order better to define the playing of the London Classical Players. None the less, when it first appeared, it was hailed as the most interesting and enjoyable new record of a Beethoven symphony recorded for some considerable time. This reissue also includes vigorous accounts of the *Coriolan* and *Egmont* Overtures.

Symphony No 3. Overtures – Leonore Nos 1 & 2
Philharmonia Orchestra / Otto Klemperer
EMI Great Recordings of the Century mono 567740-2
(76' · ADD) Recorded 1954-5   Ⓜ**OO**

In 1955 the Philharmonia Orchestra was at the peak of its powers. And what cogency there is sustaining and feeding the drama. Where other orchestras and conductors whip themselves into a terrible lather at the start of the finale, Klemperer and the Philharmonia sail majestically on. This is a great performance, steady yet purposeful, with textures that seem hewn out of granite. There's no exposition repeat, and the trumpets blaze out illicitly in the first movement coda, but this is still one of the great *Eroicas* on record. As Karajan announced to Klemperer after flying in to a concert performance around this time: 'I have come only to thank you, and say that I hope I shall live to conduct the Funeral March as well as you have done'. In the *Leonore* Overtures, recorded in 1954, the playing is a bit more rough-edged.

Symphony No 3. Overture – Coriolan, Op 62   **P**
Le Concert des Nations / Jordi Savall
Astrée Naïve ES9959 (52' · DDD) Recorded 1994   Ⓜ

There's a sense of burgeoning excitement at the start of Savall's performance; and the sound of the orchestra conjures up the sense of being transported back to some dusky Viennese concert room *c*1805, where the musicians are as dangerous a crew as the militias roaming the mud-filled streets outside. Yet as the musical arguments begin to multiply and deepen, the performance gets slightly garbled. For all Savall's skill in moulding and modifying the pulse, there's a jauntiness about parts of the first movement development section which muddles and trivialises the music. In the *Marcia funèbre* the performance is astonishing for the mood it conjures. The drum (calf skin head, hard sticks) is fierce and seductive, an instrument of war that suggests also the soft thud of death. Savall's brass are similarly remarkable, at once brazen and mellow sounding. The horn section alone – Thomas Muller, Raul Diaz and Javier Bonet – deserves an award for the way it colours and characterises this astonishing music. There's no disguising the fact that Savall's thinking about tempo is controversial. It's all very modern:

post-modern, even. (After Savall, conductors like Norrington sound distressingly 'safe'.) It's typical of Savall that though he conducts very quick, very earthy, very exciting accounts of the *Eroica*'s *Scherzo* (those horns again!) and finale, he still slows up pretty massively for the finale's oboe-led *Poco andante* at bar 348. It's a performance, none the less, that you'll want for the sonic profile alone. The Auvidis recording is first rate: warm and immediate.

Symphonies Nos 4 & 5
Minnesota Orchestra / Osmo Vänskä
BIS 🔊 BIS-SACD1416 (67' · DDD/DSD) Ⓕ❍❍❍

 It was during Osmo Vänskä's time with the BBC Scottish SO that his Beethoven began winning golden opinions. His reading of the Fourth is fiery but not relentless. Metronome marks are important but not mandatory. Transparent textures and a rigorous way with dynamics also feature. Of particular interest is the skill with which he continuously keeps in view the bass line, and thus the music's harmonic contour, never easy, given the 'open' nature of Beethoven's scoring.

The Minnesota Orchestra are extraordinarily proficient: fleet-footed and articulate, though tonally they have less in reserve than the Berlin or Vienna orchestras. This can be a limitation in the Fifth, where the sound occasionally edges towards coarseness but it makes little or no difference in the Fourth, even in the *Adagio*. What Vänskä sacrifices in lyric poetry he makes up for in justness of rhythm and chasteness of texture. Skilful as BIS's engineers are in dealing with the quietest passages, finding an optimum playback level for the vibrant but *pianissimo*-strewn Fourth takes time and patience.

The performance of the dynamically less problematic Fifth also also bristles with character. Typically, *Scherzo* and finale are bound to one another structurally but not tamed emotionally.

Symphonies Nos 5 & 7
Vienna Philharmonic Orchestra / Carlos Kleiber
DG The Originals 447 400-2GOR (72' · ADD) Recorded 1974 ⓜ❍❍❍

 The recording of the Fifth, always very fine, comes up superbly in this transfer. What, though, of the Seventh, an equally distinguished performance though always perceptibly greyer-sounding on LP, and on CD? Well, it too is superb. What the Original-Image Bit-Processing has done to it, heaven only knows, but the result is a performance of genius that now speaks to us freely and openly for the first time. In some ways this is a more important document than the famous Fifth. Great recordings of the Seventh, greatly played and conducted, but with first and second violins divided left and right, are as rare as gold dust. Freshly refurbished, this Kleiber Seventh would

go right to the top of any short list of recommendable Sevenths. It's wonderful to have these two legendary performances so expertly restored.

Symphonies Nos 5ᵃ & 7ᵇ   Ⓗ
New York Philharmonic Symphony Orchestra / Arturo Toscanini
Naxos Historical mono 8 110840 (77' · ADD)
Recorded at Carnegie Hall, New York ᵇ1936, ᵃlive 1933 Ⓢ❍❍❍

 Toscanini is a near-impossible act to follow. But then in a sense he was fortunate. He didn't have a fat record catalogue full of Rostrum Greats to live up to and he wasn't under pressure to say something new, or at least something different. On the contrary, Toscanini's avowed mission was to clean up where others had indulged in interpretative excess. And he could as well have been cleaning up for the future.

There are numerous Toscanini Fifths in public or private circulation, at least four of them dating from the 1930s. This one is lithe, dynamic and consistently commanding. Comparing it with Toscanini's 1952 NBC recording finds numberless instances where a natural easing of pace helps underline essential transitions, such as the quiet alternation of winds and strings that holds the tension at the centre of the first movement. The glow of the string playing towards the close of the second movement has no parallel with the 1952 version and while the NBC *Scherzo* is better drilled, this finale really blazes. Mark Obert-Thorn has done a first-rate job with the sound, focusing the orchestra's whispered *pianissimos* while keeping surface noise to a minimum.

The commercially released 1936 New York Seventh has already been hailed as a classic. As with the Fifth, Toscanini's ability to gauge pauses to the nth degree – in this case the rests that separate the finale's opening *fortissimo* rallying calls – is truly inimitable. The nobility and the visceral thrill of Toscanini's pre-war version remains unchallenged. The transfer is excellent.

Symphonies Nos 5 & 6   Ⓟ
London Classical Players / Sir Roger Norrington
Virgin Veritas 561377-2 (74' · DDD) Recorded 1988 ⓜ

Norrington conducts an enjoyable, memorable account of the Fifth. He throws off the introduction to the first movement with crisp brilliance, and the *Allegro* conveys enormous underlying energy. His *Andante* is beautifully phrased and flows most delicately; in the bustling double bass theme at the centre of the *Scherzo* the bowing is light, the effect refined and offering easy virtuosity. Norrington's finale is strongly accented, his horns broadly sonorous, partly as a result of the resonant EMI sound.

The *Pastoral* is also a revelation. Norrington

adopts a swift tempo in the joyous first movement but there's no hint of that relentless, driven quality we've sometimes had on record. He's fully up to tempo in the vibrant *tuttis*; elsewhere he's most careful to allow the music to dance and breathe, the transitions always most sensitively moulded. It's also a joy to hear this symphony on period instruments. This *Pastoral* is a real voyage of aural discovery. Sometimes the wind tuning isn't 100 per cent true, at others it's simply a matter of Norrington teasing us with the timing of a trill's release or pointing up dissonances that usually get smoothed over. The sound is wonderfully clear and trenchant.

Beethoven Symphony No 6
Schubert Symphony No 5 in B flat, D485
Vienna Philharmonic Orchestra / Karl Böhm
DG The Originals 447 433-2GOR (74' · ADD)
Recorded 1971, 1979   Ⓜ❍❍❍

Karl Böhm's Beethoven is a compound of earth and fire. His VPO recording of Beethoven's Sixth of 1971 dominated the LP catalogue for over a decade, and has done pretty well on CD on its various appearances. His reading is generally glorious and it remains one of the finest accounts of the work ever recorded. It still sounds well (perhaps the bass is a bit lighter than on LP) and the performance (with the first movement exposition repeat included) has an unfolding naturalness and a balance between form and lyrical impulse that's totally satisfying. The brook flows untroubled and the finale is quite lovely, with a wonderfully expansive climax. The Schubert dates from the end of Böhm's recording career. It's a superb version of this lovely symphony, another work that suited Böhm especially well. The reading is weighty but graceful, with a most beautifully phrased *Andante* (worthy of a Furtwängler), a bold Minuet and a thrilling finale. The recording is splendid. If you admire Böhm this is a worthy way to remember his special gifts.

Symphony No 9
Anna Tomowa-Sintow *sop* **Agnes Baltsa** *mez* **Peter Schreier** *ten* **José van Dam** *bass-bar* **Vienna Singverein; Berlin Philharmonic Orchestra / Herbert von Karajan**
DG Galleria 415 832-2GGA (67' · ADD) Recorded 1976. Text and translation included   Ⓜ❍❍

Symphony No 9 also available coupled with Symphonies Nos 5 & 6 (rec 1977/1976), on DG ② 474 260-2   Ⓜ

All collections need Beethoven's *Choral* Symphony as one of the works at the very core of the 19th-century romantic movement. Within its remarkable span, Beethoven celebrates both the breadth and power of man's conception of his position in relation to the Universe; his sense of spirituality – especially in the great slow move-

ment – and in the finale the essential life-enhancing optimism emerges, which makes human existence philosophically possible against all odds. Karajan lived alongside the Beethoven symphonies throughout his long and very distinguished recording career, and he recorded the Ninth three times in stereo. His 1976 version is the best of the three. The slow movement has great intensity, and the finale brings a surge of incandescent energy and exuberance which is hard to resist. All four soloists are excellent individually and they also make a good team. The reading as a whole has the inevitability of greatness and the recording is vivid, full and clear. At mid-price this is very recommendable indeed.

Symphony No 9   Ⓗ
Aase Nordmo-Løvberg *sop* **Christa Ludwig** *mez* **Waldemar Kmentt** *ten* **Hans Hotter** *bass-bar* **Philharmonia Chorus and Orchestra / Otto Klemperer**
Testament SBT1177 (71' · ADD) Recorded live 1957   Ⓕ❍❍

This is a revelatory live recording by EMI's engineers of Klemperer's performance of the Ninth Symphony at the Royal Festival Hall, immediately before his 1957 EMI recording. Where the studio recording gives us a frontal, ground-level view of the players spread out across the spaces of the Kingsway Hall, this live Festival Hall recording offers us that special Klemperer balance which gave particular prominence to the winds and the timpani. Strings, and in the finale the chorus, are nicely focused; but from where we sit, somewhere above the first oboe, it's winds and timpani that are the centre of interest. No one would have dared balance a studio recording this way, yet this is far closer to what a Klemperer performance really sounded like.

There are a couple of oddities in the finale. In the preliminary orchestral statement of the 'joy' theme, the bassoon descant drowns out the violas and cellos; then, later on, we get a less than clear view of the tenor. (A blessed relief, perhaps, given Kmentt's thin, dried-out sound here.) Interpretatively, the two performances are identical, though the live performance is just that bit more intense. The first movement does not benefit greatly but the Scherzo is transformed; what rather lumbers in the studio is here a thrilling dance of the Titans. The finale is wonderfully performed, thrillingly articulated by the newly founded Philharmonia Chorus and the Philharmonia players. Detail after detail shines out, etched into the imagination by the playing and the persistently enquiring recording.

Symphony No 9   Ⓗ
Elisabeth Schwarzkopf *sop* **Elisabeth Höngen** *mez* **Hans Hopf** *ten* **Otto Edelmann** *bass* **Bayreuth Festival Chorus and Orchestra / Wilhelm Furtwängler**
EMI Great Recordings of the Century mono 566901-2

(75' · ADD) Recorded live 1951 ⓂOO

This performance has become legendary, as much for the occasion as for the music-making itself. The reopening of Wagner's Festival Theatre in Bayreuth in 1951 after the catastrophe of war was nothing if not symbolic. If anything could lay the ghost of Bayreuth's immediate past, the years from 1930 to 1944 when the theatre was run by the English-born, Nazi-worshipping Winifred Wagner, it might be a performance of the Ninth Symphony under the most celebrated of the German conductors who had lived through Nazi rule without being, in any real sense, morally or artistically party to it. Certainly, it isn't difficult to think of the slow movement's second subject, unfolded here in a way that has never been bettered, as an atonement and a benediction.

Not everyone will respond to this vision of the Ninth: as an interpretation it's broadly based, with some slow tempos and some quirky adjustments of pace; though beneath everything – beneath the gear changes and failures in ensemble – a great current massively flows. The solo vocal and choral work in the finale is electric after the *fugato* but is breezily, bumpily Teutonic before that; Hans Hopf is his usual restless, hectic self. The CD transfer provides some added clarity of image for the generally excellent mono recording; and it also provides an all-important continuity. Instrumental bass frequencies are rather wooden but the recording reproduces higher frequency string, wind, and vocal sound more smoothly than was often the case at this time. Many collectors will be looking to a stereo, digital recording of the Ninth as a CD library acquisition; yet this performance has a prior, if not absolute, claim on collectors' attention.

Symphony No 9 Ⓗ
Elisabeth Schwarzkopf *sop* **Elsa Cavelti** *mez* **Ernst Haefliger** *ten* **Otto Edelmann** *bass* **Lucerne Festival Chorus; Philharmonia Orchestra / Wilhelm Furtwängler**
Tahra mono FURT1054/7(78' · ADD) Recorded live 1954 ⒻOOO

 The 40th anniversary of Furtwängler's death on November 30, 1954 brought forth a rich crop of reissues and remasterings, most notably on the French label Tahra, which secured the rights to publish limited editions of some of Furtwängler's most important (and, it must be said, most frequently pirated) live recordings. Some of Furtwängler's finest performances of Beethoven's music were given in the last months of his life, an odd paradox given his failing health, and by November the apparent extinction of his will to live. Yet this Lucerne Ninth is a seismic utterance, the final heroic regrouping of musical and psychic powers that in certain works of the repertory have this gangling figure towering over all his rivals. This is arguably the greatest of all

Furtwängler's recordings of the symphony. Walter Legge wanted to acquire the performance as EMI's official replacement for the momentous 1951 Bayreuth account, but it wasn't to be. Since then, there have been various 'unofficial' editions. The Tahra differs in being 'official', well transferred, and further enhanced by a few introductory remarks made by Furtwängler himself.

Here, the most significant section is that in which Furtwängler sees the problem of interpreting the Ninth as one that effectively postdates the performing culture into which it was born. Furtwängler understood the Ninth as well as any conductor in the 20th century. You can argue this way or that over the pacing of the slow movement (though we defy anyone to say that his performance is anything other than deeply eloquent) or the leisurely speed of the second movement Trio. In the all-important first movement, though, there's no doubt that Beethoven's written tempo markings and frequent subsequent modifications clearly presuppose the kind of uniquely singing, flexible, harmonically searching (but by no means too slow) reading Furtwängler invariably gave us.

Additional recommendation

Symphony No 9
Wiens *sop* **Hartwig** *mez* **Lewis** *ten* **Hermann** *bass* **Hamburg State Opera Chorus; North German Radio Symphony Orchestra and Chorus / Wand**
RCA Red Seal 74321 68005-2 (66' · DDD) ⓈⓈ
A real bargain. Wand's 1986 recording enshrines a wonderfully wise and humane Ninth, unerringly paced and always intensely refreshing in its lean purposefulness, if at times lacking that last ounce of lump-in-the-throat universality.

Septet, Op 20

Beethoven Septet in E flat, Op 20 Ⓗ
Mendelssohn Octet in E flat, Op 20
Members of the **Vienna Octet**
Decca 421 093-2DM (74' · ADD) Recorded 1959, 1972 ⒻO

After its triumphant first performance in 1800, Beethoven's Septet went on to become not only one of the most popular but also one of the most influential chamber works of the period. The composer himself grew to dislike the piece, but it remains one of the most treasured products of the classical era. Curiously, compared to the 1972 Mendelssohn coupling, the 1959 sound in the Septet seems sweeter and more natural, to complement a performance which is an utter delight. Here is that old-fashioned, spontaneous yet relaxed Viennese style, with ample, beautifully shaped phrasing and an engaging, slightly rustic quality in the clarinet tone which, alas, seems to have gone out of fashion.

In the Mendelssohn Octet, the playing has a delicious buoyancy of spirit and an abundance of charm. The *Andante*, in particular, has an affecting, wistful delicacy and there's total clarity in the *fugato* which launches a strongly played finale. The recording is clean and well balanced.

Septet in E flat, Op 20. Piano Quintet in E flat, Op 16.
Sextet in E flat, Op 81b
Ottó Rácz *ob* **József Balogh** *cl* **József Vajda** *bn*
Jenö Keveházi, János Keveházi, Sándor Berki *hns*
Ildikó Hegyi, Péter Popa *vns* **Gyözö Máthé** *va*
Peter Szabó *vc* **István Toth** *db*
Naxos 8 553090 (74' · DDD) Recorded 1994   (S)

These talented Hungarian players offer a fluent, responsive account of the Septet that highlights the music's intimate chamber character – delight in the music's elegance and perfect balance of instrumental forces. In the present instance, vivid recording creates a clear, natural ambience for this alert, sensitively blended ensemble. In the Sextet, horn players, Jenö and János Keveházi play with subtlety and panache as required, their tone spontaneous and free. This excellent, value-for-money Naxos disc also offers an elegant, well-turned performance of Beethoven's E flat Quintet.

Piano Quintet, Op 16

Beethoven Piano Quintet in E flat, Op 16   [H]
Mozart Piano Quintet in E flat, K452. Sinfonia concertante in E flat, K297b
Walter Gieseking *pf* **Philharmonia Wind Quartet**
(Sidney Sutcliffe *ob* Bernard Walton *cl* Dennis Brain *hn* Cecil James *bn*) **Philharmonia Orchestra / Herbert von Karajan**
Testament mono SBT1091 (80' · ADD) Recorded 1955   (F)OO

There have never been any doubts about these performances. The horn playing in the *Sinfonia concertante* is unsurpassable and in the quintets Gieseking's lightness and his clarity and sense of style is simply beyond praise. The tempos are on the slow side in the first movement of the Mozart and the finale of the Beethoven but somehow with Gieseking, slow tempos have a way of seeming to be just about right. Richard Osborne's excellent notes quote a letter from Sidney Sutcliffe of touching modesty. Speaking of their run-through of the Mozart, he says, 'On reaching the *Allegro moderato*, the great man played two bars at an absolutely perfect tempo and then stopped and asked in the most gentle and hesitant manner, "Will that be all right for you?" So it was a most happy occasion although I found it a grave responsibility matching the artistry of my colleagues when Bernard [Walton], Cecil [James] and Dennis [Brain] were producing sounds of breath-taking beauty.' Breathtaking is the right word for all concerned here on one of the great chamber music records of the LP era. Considerable pains have been taken with the transfers, which now sound fresh and full bodied. Thoroughly recommended.

Piano Quartets

Piano Quartets, WoO36 – Nos 1-3. E flat, Op 16 (arr Beethoven)
Raphael Oleg *vn* **Miguel da Silva** *va* **Marc Coppey** *vc*
Philippe Cassard *pf*
Astrée Naïve ② V4715 (88' · DDD) Recorded 1994   (F)

This issue harnesses together the three piano quartets Beethoven completed at the age of 15 but subsequently suppressed, with the 26-year-old composer's piano quartet arrangement of his Op 16 Quintet for piano and wind. Indebted to the still youthful Mozart, the teenage Beethoven may well (and should) have been, as also tempted to entrust too much to the piano But the unpredictability of even immature genius is striking. Never can you for a second foretell what surprise, whether of key, harmony, rhythm or scoring, lies just around the corner. His fluent, confident craftsmanship makes you marvel no less. Even when borrowing the three-movement sequence of Mozart's G major Violin Sonata (K397) for his own E flat major work, Beethoven gives his chromatically intensified opening *Adagio assai*, his stormy minor-key *Allegro* and even the beguiling variations, an unmistakable stamp of his own.

The playing itself contributes to the pleasure, with first praise to Philippe Cassard for never allowing the keyboard to dominate. But all four Paris Conservatoire-trained colleagues are artists of taste and finesse. Their characterisation is most sensitively attuned to the music's own true scale. Never does point-making sound self-consciously inflated. The recording itself has a pleasingly soft-grained intimacy.

String Quartets

Op 18: No 1 in F; **No 2** in G; **No 3** in D; **No 4** in C minor; **No 5** in A; **No 6** in B flat
Op 59 'Rasumovsky': No 1 in F; **No 2** in E minor; **No 3** in C
Op 74 in E flat, 'Harp'; **Op 95** in F minor, 'Serioso'
'Late' Quartets: Op 127 in E flat; **Op 130** in B flat; **Op 131** in C sharp; **Op 132** in A minor; **Op 135** in F
Grosse Fuge in B flat, Op 133

Complete String Quartets

Complete String Quartets. Grosse Fuge
Quartetto Italiano (Paolo Borciani, Elisa Pegreffi *vns* Piero Farulli *va* Franco Rossi *vc*)
Philips ⑩ 454 062-2PB10 (544' · ADD) Recorded 1967-75   (B)OO

The early and middle quartets are also available on Philips Duo:
426 046-2PM (Op 18) and
420 797-2PM3 (Opp 59, 74 & 95)   (B)
The late quartets are also available on Philips Duo:
454 711-2PM2 (Opp 127, 130 & 135; Grosse Fuge) and
454 712-2PM2 (Opp 131 & 12)   (B)
They have also been remastered on a three-disc set:

Philips 50 Great recordings ③ 464 684-2PM3 Ⓜ

It goes without saying that no one ensemble can unlock all the secrets contained in these quartets. The Quartetto Italiano recordings have assumed a variety of formats since their first appearance. The quartets now comprise 10 CDs but Philips wisely offers the performances at a highly competitive price in three separate sets and they should be considered as separate entities. Their claims are strongest in the Op 18 Quartets. The Quartetto Italiano offer eminently civilised, thoughtful and aristocratic readings. Their approach is reticent but they also convey a strong sense of making music in domestic surroundings. Quite frankly, you couldn't do very much better than this set. In the middle-period quartets the Italians are hardly less distinguished, even though there are times when the Végh offer deeper insights, as in the slow movement of Op 59 No 1. Taken in isolation, however, the Quartetto Italiano remain eminently satisfying both musically and as recorded sound. As far as sound quality is concerned, it's rich and warm. In Opp 74 and 95, they more than hold their own against all comers. These are finely proportioned readings, poised and articulate.

The gain in clarity because of the remastering entails a very slight loss of warmth in the middle register, but as recordings the late quartets, made between 1967 and 1969, can hold their own against their modern rivals. Not all of these received universal acclaim at the time of their first release. The opening fugue of Op 131 is too slow at four-in-the-bar and far more *espressivo* than it should be, but, overall, these performances still strike a finely judged balance between beauty and truth, and are ultimately more satisfying and searching than most of their rivals.

Complete String Quartets
Végh Quartet (Sándor Végh, Sándor Zöldy vns Georges Janzer va Paul Szábo vc)
Astrée Naïve ⑧ V4871 (8 hours 46' · ADD) Recorded 1974 Ⓑ**OO**

The Végh's classic accounts of the String Quartets are in a completely different league from any of their rivals: there's no cultivation of surface polish but there's no lack of elegance and finesse. Above all, there's no attempt to glamorise their sound. In Op 18 No 1 they find the *tempo giusto* right at the beginning and they find more depth in the slow movement than anyone else on record. Végh himself floats the melodic line in this movement in a most imaginative way and is wonderfully supported. In the civilised exchanges that open Op18 No 2 the Végh brings alight touch to bear, and has an elegance and wit that's almost unmatched and great refinement of tone. There were complaints of the bottom-heavy recording when it appeared on LP, and it's less transparent and lifelike than more modern recordings.

The *Rasumovsky* set is admirable for its alert-

ness of articulation, rhythmic grasp and flexibility and its subtle range of tone-colour. The effortlessness with which the dialogue proceeds silences criticism. The Végh brings special insights to this inexhaustible music. The style and the quality of perception seem so remarkable and so well sustained here that any deficiencies can be overlooked. There are lapses in tone and intonation, most of them on the part of the leader, yet what a musician he is, and what a remarkable guide to the visionary content of these quartets. Where the music demands most in such matters he's never wanting. These are neither the most 'perfect' nor the most sumptuously recorded accounts available, yet they are the deepest and most searching. When listening to them you're conscious only of Beethoven's own voice. The transfers give a slightly firmer focus and sharper detail, though that slight bottom-heaviness still remains.

String Quartets Op 18

CDDCA1111: String Quartets, Op 18 Nos 1-3
CDDCA1112: String Quartets, Op 18 Nos 4 & 5.
String Quartet in F, H34
CDDCA1113: String Quartet, Op 18 No 6.
String Quintet in C, Op 29ᵃ
The Lindsays (Peter Cropper, Ronald Birks vns Roger Bigley va Bernard Gregor-Smith vc) with ᵃ**Louise Williams** va
ASV CDDCA1111-3 (oas: 78', 66', 58' · DDD) Ⓕ**O**

It's wonderful how the Lindsays, after a career of more than 30 years, can still sound so fresh and spontaneous. From the start of Op 18 No 1 we feel that every phrase is shaped individually, the music felt as it's being played. The dynamics are beautifully differentiated; *pianissimo* always has an altered sound compared with *piano*. Presenting the sense of the music and its emotions is always a priority, which leads to some daring interpretative decisions. The fast and fantastical finale of the Op 29 Quintet, with its scary *tremolos* and wild-sounding *rubato* in the first violin arpeggios is one example of a no-holds-barred approach that gets into the character of the music in a way that a more measured style couldn't. It's a splendid idea to include this neglected quintet as well as Beethoven's brilliant arrangement of the Op 14 No 1 Piano Sonata; the Quintet's rich, often complex, textures are relished, helping us to hear this work as a halfway house between the C major Quintets of Mozart and Schubert.

Despite the air of spontaneity, the Lindsays' interpretations of Op 18 remain very similar to those they offered us 20 years ago. The new recordings are certainly crisper and more immediate than their analogue predecessors, yet the sound has a warmth that enhances the often very atmospheric playing to be found, for instance, in the mysterious *pianissimo* passages at the ends of the slow movements of Nos 3 and 6. The main difference in the playing is that the new performances are generally faster, brighter and rhythmically lighter, with clearer articulation. The earlier version of No 2's highly ornamented *Adagio* has a beautiful sustained sound; in this recording Peter Cropper plays the melody with more fantasy, giving a powerful, rhetorical expression to each phrase. The slight increase in speed of most of the *allegros* brings them more into line with Beethoven's often challenging metronome marks: as a result there's more sparkle and excitement, and the light touch means there's rarely any sense of strain. The two Minuets, in Nos 4 and 5, benefit from being played faster; the passionate C minor character in No 4 is brought out most persuasively. For the *Adagio* of No 6 the Lindsays, in common with most other groups, adopt a more flowing speed than Beethoven's very slow suggestion, and their new recording is noticeably faster than the old. Yet, this is one of the most finely played movements in the set, with soft, sensuous tone, delicate ornamentation, and mysterious, tenuous unisons.

For the *Adagio* of No 1, on the other hand, Beethoven provides what seems a very fast tempo). The Lindsays play it a good deal slower – their earlier version has a particularly impressive, concentrated atmosphere. The 1933 Busch Quartet recording, however, shows how it's possible for the movement to sound even more impressive at a speed close to Beethoven's mark; the fiercely dramatic interruptions lose the somewhat ponderous effect they have when taken more slowly.

With these much-recorded quartets – in their way just as challenging to the performers as the later works – it's impossible to have a single favourite version. The Alban Berg Quartet, as daring in their expressive range as The Lindsays, give an unrivalled spring to the more dance-like movements – No 5's Minuet, the *allegretto* section of No 6's finale. The Emerson Quartet, extraordinarily nimble and precise in the quicker music, impart a fizzy, *opera buffa* quality to No 3's finale. The Quartetto Italiano's 1970s recordings still sound amazingly fine – no daringly fast speeds here, but the most finely blended sound and nobility of expression. Into this Pantheon The Lindsays fit very easily. No group that brings out better the startling range of the youthful Beethoven's imagination.

String Quartets, Op 18
Takács Quartet (Edward Dusinberre, Károly Schranz *vns* Roger Tapping *va* András Fejér *vc*)
Decca ② 470 848-2DH2 (148' · DDD) Ⓕ OO

Robert Simpson disagreed with writers who believed that Beethoven's backward glances to Haydn and Mozart in his Op 18 set were so obvious as to distract attention from his own individuality. The Takács disagree, too. They concede the tradition, but those glances are far from obvious. From the beginning this is Beethoven through and through. The opening bars of Op 18 No 1 are soft yet terse. The answering calls are conciliatory, but the suspense is palpable. And, in a trenchant *Allegro con brio*, every *sforzando* is used to raise the tension, especially in the development. There are no concessions to surface beauty, and the message isn't subdued.

The Takács are particular about dynamics. The *fortissimo* chord near the finish of the slow movement is startling, and the build up from *pianissimo* is as impressive as the drop back to the end. The *Adagio*, though directed to be both impassioned and tender, tends to be fervent, while fine inflections to the line ensure that the fairly swift tempo doesn't appear hurried. Conversely, the *Adagio ma non troppo* of No 6 is compassionately slow, but continuously mobile: these musicians don't overlay textures with fatty tissue. Despite wide separation, ensemble is always close-knit. Just how close may be appreciated in the Scherzos, which are tight and cohesive. That of No 4 has, in addition, precise give and take between the contrapuntal lines. The Takács play them in a way that leads the ear on without ignoring the expressive demands of the unusual marking *Andante scherzoso quasi Allegretto*.

String Quartets, Op 18 Nos 3 & 6
Leipzig Quartet (Andreas Seidel, Tilman Büning *vn* Ivo Bauer *vc* Matthias Moosdorf *vc*)
Dabringhaus und Grimm MDG307 0856-2
(51' · DDD) Ⓕ O

These are performances of exceptional finesse and integrity. Such qualities are immediately apparent at the opening of No 6 where, amid the splendidly vigorous, bustling atmosphere, they manage to give the answering phrases in violin and cello a gentler articulation. The second movement of this Quartet, though marked *Adagio ma non troppo*, has a surprisingly slow metronome mark, which the Leipzigers observe, their fine sense of line allowing the music to flow easily even at this spacious tempo, and they impart an especially chilling aspect to the sinister minor-key middle section.

The D major Quartet starts sweetly and gently, gradually and effortlessly picking up more liveliness as the movement progresses. The *Andante* flows easily, with notably rich, dark-hued tone in the passages in low register, and the third movement winningly combines a lively tempo with a slightly wistful manner.

In short, these must be among the most persuasively played, finely recorded Op 18 performances available. There are places where you might prefer other versions – The Lindsays' spontaneity in the finale of No 6, or the joyful virtuosity of the Emerson in the last movement of No 3 – but, overall, the Leipzig Quartet is as satisfying as any.

String Quartets, Op 18 No 3; Op 59 No 1
Orpheus Quartet (Charles-André Linale, Emilian Piediocuta *vns* Emile Cantor *va* Laurentiu Sbarcea *vc*)

Channel Classics CCS6094 (68' · DDD) Recorded
1993   Ⓕ

The Orpheus Quartet doesn't use this music as
a vehicle for its virtuosity; and they don't draw
attention to their spot-on ensemble, immaculate intonation and tonal finesse, though they
possess all these qualities. Take the *Presto* finale
of Op 18 No 3. The sense of pace is in harmony
with the horse-drawn rather than the jet-driven;
every note speaks, every phrase tells and the
overall effect is all the more exhilarating. Generally speaking, the Orpheus find the *tempo
giusto* throughout. They remain attuned to the
sensibility of the period and relate their pace to
a dance movement in a manner that their rivals
have lost. There's something very natural about
the players' music-making. They're inside these
scores and convey their involvement; no auto
pilot, no *ersatz* feeling, no exaggerated or mech-
anised *sforzatos*. What a relief! The recording is
bright and clean.

String Quartets Op 59, 'Rasumovsky'

String Quartets Op 59 Nos 1-3. String Quartet Op 74
Takács Quartet (Edward Dusinberre, Károly Schranz
vns Roger Tapping *va* András Fejér *vc*)
Decca ② 470 847-2DH2 (144' ·DDD)   Ⓕ❍❍❍

 The Takács do a fine job here: controlled, well paced and impeccably balanced. They manage to balance the
music's vertical and horizontal aspects beautifully, long-breathed contrapuntal lines gliding
serenely above a sharp, occasionally dramatic
accompaniment – masterful playing indeed and
typical of this first lap of the Takács' projected
Beethoven cycle.

The Takács hold both line and rhythm in Op
59 No 1 with imposing control. Their manner
of badinage in the mischievously hocketing second movement is more intense than the rival
account by The Lindsays, and their tempos
consistently swifter. In Op 59 No 3 the Takács
approximate the Busch in a broad, soulful
Andante con moto. And in the fugal finale they're
almost on a par with the Emersons, whose
demonic DG account is one of the most viscier-
ally exciting quartet recordings around. The
finale of Op 59 No 2 is a tautly braced canter
whereas in the *Scherzo* of the *Harp*, Op 74, taken
at a hair-raising lick, the Takács make obsessive
music of the dominating four-note idea – and
there's absolutely no let up in tension for the
cello-led trio. Indeed, the Takács' *Harp* is one of
the finest ever recorded, with fiery reportage of
the first movement's central development and a
delightfully playful account of the finale, the
'tipsy' first variation especially.

The jewel, then, is Op 59 No 2, though you'd
be hard pressed to find a rival digital set of Opp
59 and 74 that's better overall. Andrew Keener's
recording (St George's, Bristol) reports a realistic 'edge' within a sympathetic acoustic. You
won't find a finer quartet recording anywhere.

Late String Quartets

String Quartets, Opp 95, 127, 130, 131, 132 &135.
Grosse Fuge.
Takács Quartet (Edward Dusinberre, Károly Schranz
vns Roger Tapping *va* András Fejér *vc*)
Decca ③ 470 849-2DH3 (3h 40' · DDD)   Ⓕ❍❍❍

 Interpreters of the late quartets have to
convey what at times sounds like a
stream of musical consciousness while
respecting the many written markings. The
Takács do better than most. For openers, they
had access to the new Henle Edition and have
made use of some textual changes – nothing too
drastic but encouraging evidence of a good
musical conscience. In Op 130 they take the
long first-movement exposition repeat, using
the *Grosse Fuge* as the rightful finale (Beethoven's original intention) which, in the context
of their fiery reading of the fugue, works well.
Contemporary incredulity at the sheer scale and
complexity of the fugue caused Beethoven to
offer a simpler alternative finale, in which they
again play the repeat, which helps balance the
'alternative' structure.

The Takács evidently appreciate this music
both as musical argument and as sound. Try
their glassy *sul ponticello* at the end of Op 131's
Scherzo, or the many instances where plucked
and bowed passages are fastidiously balanced.
Attenuated inflections are honoured virtually to
the letter, textures carefully differentiated,
musical pauses intuitively well-timed and inner
voices nearly always transparent.

This set completes one of the best available
Beethoven quartet cycles, possibly the finest in
an already rich digital market, more probing
than the pristine Emersons or Alban Bergs
(live), more refined than the gutsy and persuasive Lindsays, and less consciously stylised than
the Juilliards (and always with the historic
Busch Quartet as an essential reference).

String Quartets, Opp 95 & 127
The Lindsays (Peter Cropper, Ronald Birks *vns* Robin
Ireland *va* Bernard Gregor-Smith *vc*)
ASV CDDCA1116 (59' · DDD)   Ⓕ❍❍❍

 The prospect of actually listening to
Beethoven never loses its appeal. It's
also clear that The Lindsays approach
Beethoven's quartets with undiminished enthusiasm. This is immediately apparent in the physical energy with which they attack the opening
of Op 95. Along with enthusiasm comes a deep
understanding, expressed most strikingly in the
way their fine internal balance is adapted to
allow important subsidiary lines to make their
effect. Nothing as crude as making a decision to
'bring out' an inner part; just the feeling that
each player knows how much pressure is needed
to fulfil a line's potential. Such expressive detail
allied to a lovely *dolce* sound makes a contrapuntal movement like Op 95's *Allegretto* especially
memorable.

BEETHOVEN LATE STRING QUARTETS – IN BRIEF

Quartetto Italiano
Philips ③ 464 684-2PM3 (216' · ADD)   Ⓜ**OO**
'Civilised', 'aristocratic', 'thoughtful' are some of the words often used to describe this great Italian ensemble's approach. Their late quartets were recorded in the late 1960s, and still sound very fine. A notable achievement.

Talich Quartet
Calliope CAL9637/8/9 (213' · DDD)   Ⓕ**O**
A powerfully intimate set which conveys the impression of four outstanding chamber musicians playing for each other – music-making eavesdropped upon, rather than projected to an imagined audience. A fine set.

LaSalle Quartet
DG ③ 453 768-2GCB3 (196' · ADD)   Ⓜ
An intellectually penetrating, at times almost terrifyingly intense set. Technically, the LaSalle Quartet are impeccable, but their approach might feel a little chilly.

Busch Quartet
Pearl mono ③ GEMS0053 (220' · ADD)   Ⓜ**O**
A wonderfully human and humane experience: this is quartet-playing of towering achievement that satisfies at every level. The sound, from the 1930s, is evidently somewhat antique, but the passion and understanding shines down the years.

Lindsay Quartet
ASV ④ CDDCS403 (220' · DDD)   Ⓜ**O**
A *Gramophone* Award-winner back in the 1980s and deservedly so, for this is very impressive quartet playing. The Lindsays have lived long with this music and, though their newer cycle may plumb deeper, this first set is still a notable achievement.

Hollywood Quartet
Testament ③ SBT3082 (193' · ADD)   Ⓕ**O**
A very fine set from the late 1950s featuring the superb Los Angeles-based quartet. Their technical address is considerable and, unlike some American quartets from later generations, they don't overproject this music – it remains appropriately and rightly 'chamber music'.

Takács Quartet
Decca ③ 470 849-2DH3 (3h 40' · DDD)   Ⓕ**OOO**
☀ A staggering achievement to crown a magnificent cycle: the Takács evidently appreciate this music both as musical argument and as sound and it shows in every bar of these beautifully recorded performances.

The Lindsays aren't the smoothest, slickest ensemble to have recorded this music. In the *Scherzo* of Op 95 the Quartetto Italiano's tone is more blemish-free, and the fast coda to this quartet's finale sees the Emerson Quartet create a more brilliant, sparkling impression. But such things only become noticeable with comparative listening; if you stick with The Lindsays what will impress you is the splendid rhythm and drive of the Op 95 *Scherzo*, the magnificent, rich sound, without any sense of aggressiveness or strain, at the start of Op 127, the way the expression is sustained throughout the great *adagio* variations of Op 127, and the delicate, magical atmosphere established at the beginning of this quartet's final section. A hugely compelling set.

String Quartets, Op 59 No 2; Op 130
Talich Quartet (Petr Messiereur, Jan Kvapil *vns* Jan Talich *va* Evzen Rattai *vc*)
Calliope CAL5637 (73' · ADD) Recorded 1977-80   Ⓕ

The advantage of this Talich recording is that it couples a masterpiece from Beethoven's middle period, the great E minor Quartet, Op 59 No 2, with one of the greatest of his last years. The B flat, Op 130, was the third of the late quartets to be composed and at its first performance in 1826 its last movement, the *Grosse Fuge*, baffled his contemporaries. Later that same year, he substituted the present finale. The Talich Quartet has a no less impressive technical command than other ensembles but theirs are essentially private performances, which are a privilege to overhear, rather than the overprojected 'public' accounts that so often appear on record nowadays.

String Quartets, Op 131; Op 135
Végh Quartet (Sándor Végh, Sándor Zöldy *vns* Georges Janzer *va* Paul Szabó *vc*)
Astrée Naïve V4408 (66' · ADD) Recorded 1973 Ⓕ**OO**

Every ensemble brings a different set of insights to this great music so that it isn't possible to hail any single quartet as offering the whole truth – yet these are as near to the whole truth as we're ever likely to come. The Végh give us music-making that has a profundity and spirituality that completely outweigh any tiny blemishes of intonation or ensemble. You don't get the feeling of four professional quartet players performing publicly for an audience, but four thoughtful musicians sharing their thoughts about this music in the privacy of their own home. They bring us closer to this music than do any of their high-powered rivals.

String Quartets, Opp 95; Op 132
Talich Quartet (Petr Messiereur, Jan Kvapil *vns* Jan Talich *va* Evzen Rattai *vc*)
Calliope Approche CAL5639 (68' · ADD) Recorded 1977-9   Ⓜ**O**

After the expansive canvas of the Op 59 quartets and the *Eroica*, Beethoven's F minor Quartet, Op 95, displays musical thinking of the utmost compression. The first movement is a highly concentrated sonata design, which encompasses in its four minutes almost as much drama as a full-scale opera. With it comes one of the greatest masterpieces of his last years, the A minor, Op 132. The isolation wrought first by his deafness and secondly, by the change in fashion of which he complained in the early 1820s, forced Beethoven in on himself. Op 132 with its otherworldly *Heiliger Dankgesang*, written on his recovery from an illness, is music neither of the 1820s nor of Vienna, it belongs to that art which transcends time and place. Though other performances may be technically more perfect, these are interpretations that come closer to the spirit of this great music than any other on CD. The Talich Quartet's readings bring a total dedication to this music: their performances are innocent of artifice and completely selfless. There's no attempt to impress with their own virtuosity or to draw attention to themselves. The recordings are eminently faithful and natural, not overbright but the effect is thoroughly pleasing.

String Quartets, Op 18 No 4; Op 132
Petersen Quartet (Conrad Muck, Gernot Süssmuth *vns* Friedemann Weigle *va* Hans-Jakob Eschenburg *vc*)
Capriccio 10 722 (63' · DDD) Ⓕ❍

The Petersen Quartet possesses impeccable technical address, immaculate ensemble, flawless intonation and tonal finesse. Tempos are judged with real musicianship, and dynamic markings are observed without being exaggerated. The C minor Quartet, Op 18 No 4, has dramatic tension without loss of lyrical fervour and the *Scherzo* has wit. When we move to the first movement of the A minor Quartet the sound world changes as if youth has given way to wisdom and experience. They hardly put a foot wrong here and their *Heiliger Dankgesang* is rapt and inward-looking. They press ahead fractionally in one or two places – on the reprise of the main section in the second movement and when the main theme returns in the finale. But one or two minor reservations apart, theirs is quite simply the most satisfying late Beethoven to have appeared in recent years. Above all the Petersen do not invite you to admire their prowess. They appear to be untouched by the three 'g's (Gloss, Glamour and Glitz) and their concern is with truth rather than beauty.

String Quartets, Opp 132 ; 135
Cleveland Quartet (William Preucil, Peter Salaff *vns* James Dunham *va* Paul Katz *vc*)
Telarc CD80427 (69' · DDD) Ⓕ

The Cleveland Quartet are upholders of tradition, rather than seekers after new truths. One

of this ensemble's most notable characteristics is its rich, warm tone, well captured here. The first movement of the A minor Quartet, Op 132, has a level of emotional commitment that's quite compelling – all the details of this complex music fall into place and contribute to the overall effect.

If the rest isn't quite so outstanding it's still very good, with a lovely swinging rhythm to the second movement, and delightfully sprightly accounts of the *Andante* episodes in the slow movement – absolutely 'feeling new strength', as Beethoven's caption puts it. Their Op 135 is also very impressive. The *Lento* is deeply felt, their rich sound coming into its own. And the finale must be one of the best versions on record – spirited, touching, playful, as the music's mood demands.

Piano Trios

Op 1: No 1 in E flat; **No 2** in G; **No 3** in C minor
Op 11 in B flat
Op 38 in E flat
Op 70: No 1 in D, 'Ghost'; **No 2** in E flat
Op 97 in B flat, 'Archduke'

Complete Piano Trios

Piano Trios. Opp 1, 11, 38, 70, 97; WoO38 & 39. Variations, Opp 44, 121a. Trio in D (after Symphony No 2). Triosatz
Beaux Arts Trio (Isidore Cohen *vn* Bernard Greenhouse *vc* Menahem Pressler *pf*)
Philips ⑤ 468 411-2 (356' · DDD/ADD) Recorded 1980 Ⓜ❍

Growing older doesn't always mean growing wiser, though in the case of the Beaux Arts Trio and Beethoven the passage of some 20-odd years signalled a rare and fruitful broadening of musical vision. In the period between their two recordings of the Beethoven Piano Trios there had been just one personnel change – Daniel Guilet was replaced by ex-Juilliard Quartet second violin Isidore Cohen. The principal route of the Beaux Arts' interpretative development was forged by the pianist, Menahem Pressler, whose increased tonal subtlety and willingness to widen expressive dynamics lent the trio a whole new palette of colours. Just listen to the opening of Op 1 No 2's ineffably deep *Largo con espressione*. Heard superficially, there's not that much in it between the Pressler of the 1960s and of 1980, but labour the comparison and you'll soon hear the benefits of a more variegated touch and a freer approach to phrasing. There are many other plus-points. The *Archduke*, for example, is at once softer-grained and more wistful than its energetic predecessor and you couldn't hope for a happier rendition of the Septet transcription (the E flat Trio, Op 38).

Philips' sound quality is just as good as the original: clear, full-bodied and well balanced. Given the price, the superior sound quality, the comprehensive coverage of repertoire (14 works as opposed to 11 in the 1960s Philips set) and the profundity of the Beaux Art's later interpretative standpoint, this new reissue justifies a front-ranking recommendation. So much is said with so much feeling – and so little fuss – that you're drawn back again and again.

Piano Trios – selected

Piano Trios Op 1 Nos 1 & 2; WoO38
Florestan Trio (Susan Tomes *pf* Anthony Marwood *vn*
Richard Lester *vc*)
Hyperion CDA67393 (72' · DDD)   Ⓕ●

The Florestan Trio seems determined to extract every last ounce of energy, wit and spirit from these early works. Op 1 No 2's finale, for example, fizzes along; all Beethoven's surprising inventions and transformations grab our attention, and the whole piece is evidently as much fun to play as to listen to. The principal vehicle for conveying the music's brightness and verve is Susan Tomes's finger-work, wonderfully precise and rhythmical, though Anthony Marwood and Richard Lester also play with fine spirit and character. The two Op 1 slow movements are taken at flowing speeds, and allow for some relaxation of mood – Marwood's entry at the start of No 2's *Largo* is particularly poetic – but it's the bouncy, extrovert character of the *Allegro*s and *Presto*s that leaves the strongest impression.

Piano Trios – Op 1 No 3; Op 11. Variations in E flat, Op 44
Florestan Trio (Susan Tomes *pf* Anthony Marwood *vn* Richard Lester *vc*)
Hyperion CDA67466 (61' · DDD)   Ⓕ●●

This completes the Florestan Trio's Beethoven series. Their thoughtfulness throughout has been impressive; their overall style avoids heaviness, keeping the textures light and airy, and giving every phrase individual life and character. Occasionally the liveliness can seem relentless, but their bubbling vitality is a natural response to Beethoven's inventiveness. And their care for detail makes the early and not fully characteristic Variations in E flat (Op 44) into an absorbing, thoroughly entertaining piece.

It's interesting to compare Op 1 No 3 with the version by the Kempf Trio, which is finely played but less searching as an interpretation. The contrast is especially noticeable in the *Andante*, treated by Kempf and friends as a poetic, hymn-like slow movement, while the Florestans give us a true 18th-century *Andante*; much faster, and, in places, light and playful.

Op 11 is often more enjoyable in the version with clarinet instead of violin. But this is another Florestan triumph. By modifying the usual robust, jolly character of the outer movements, and introducing more delicate tones, Anthony Marwood can interpret his part in violinistic terms, establishing a close rapport with

the cello, yet, at the start of the finale, proving he can be as bright and perky as any clarinettist.

Piano Trios, Op 70 Nos 1 & 2. Allegretto, WoO39
Florestan Trio (Anthony Marwood *vn* Richard Lester
vc Susan Tomes *pf*)
Hyperion CDA67327 (60' · DDD)   Ⓕ●

Here's a recording that immediately, from the first, impetuous bars of Op 70 No 1, feels just right. In this movement the Florestan makes the long second repeat, but there's such a sense of momentum that no one could find it too extended or repetitious. Indeed, the reiterated chords that precede the lead-back reignite our concentration with their air of tense mystery. And when we reach this point for the second time, the G major harmony at the start of the coda has a wonderful, dense tranquillity. The famous 'Ghost' movement creates a powerful, chilling effect, with stark, *senza vibrato* string tone and the extraordinary writing in the piano's deep bass register exploited by Susan Tomes with superb control and sensitivity.

Op 70 No 2 is something of a Cinderella work, but the Florestan performance helps us to see it as a major achievement of Beethoven's middle period. Although they're a thoughtful, highly controlled group, there's room for moments of the most intense expression. And the finale, one of Beethoven's most prodigiously inventive pieces, has in this performance a feeling of uninhibited enjoyment. The recorded sound and balance are equally fine.

Additional recommendations

Piano Trios, Op 1 Nos 1-3; Op 97
Coupled with: 14 Variations in E flat, Op 44;
Allegrettos – in B flat; in E flat
Barenboim *pf* **Zukerman** *vn* **du Pré** *vc*
EMI Double Forte ② 574831-2 (DDD)   Ⓜ

Piano Trios, Op 70 No 1; WoO38. Piano Trio in E flat (1790/91)
Coupled with: 10 Variations on Müller's song 'Ich bin der Schneider Kakadu'. Cello Sonatas, Op 69; Op 105 No 2
Barenboim *pf* **Zukerman** *vn* **du Pré** *vc*
EMI Double Forte ② 574834-2 (DDD)   Ⓜ
    The players respond beautifully to the raw emotional content of Beethoven's works – listen especially to the moving intensity of the *Ghost*'s slow movement.

String Trios

Op 3 in E flat. **Op 9: No 1** in G; **No 2** in D; **No 3** in C minor

String Trio, Op 3; Serenade in D, Op 8
Leopold String Trio (Marianne Thorsen *vn*
Sarah-Jane Bradley *va* Kate Gould *vc*)
Hyperion CDA67253 (73' · DDD)   Ⓕ●

String Trios Op 9
Leopold String Trio
Hyperion CDA67254 (77' · DDD)　　Ⓕ●

The Leopold String Trio demonstrate the kind of virtues that come from long study together: polished ensemble, excellent intonation and notably consistent and well-conceived interpretations. Just occasionally the viola is swamped by the outer voices, but overall it's a particularly well-balanced and recorded set. They show that a restrained style can bring out the inward aspect to the music. On the fourth track of Op 8, where Beethoven alternates a sombre *Adagio* with a facetiously jolly Scherzo, the stark yet gentle Leopold playing of the slow music expresses more pathos and melancholy than the intensity of other versions. And the Leopold's care and respect for the text also tips the balance in its favour – in Op 3's second Minuet, for example, Marianne Thorsen's beautiful and exact interpretation is winning. In Op 9 No 1's Scherzo, another splendidly poised and spirited reading, there's a special bonus – a second Trio, omitted from most editions. It's an attractive bit of music and gives the movement a new dimension.

Cello Sonatas

No 1 Op 5 No 1 in F; **No 2** Op 5 No 2 in G minor;
No 3 Op 69 in A;
No 4 Op 102 No 1 in C; **No 5** Op 102 No 2 in D

Cello Sonatas, Op 102 Nos 1 & 2. Duo in E flat,
WoO32. Variations on 'See the conqu'ring hero comes'
Maria Kliegel vc **Nina Tichman** pf **Tabea Zimmermann** va
Naxos 8 555787 (59' · DDD)　　Ⓢ

Complete Works for Cello and Piano
Miklós Perényi vc **András Schiff** pf
ECM New Series ② 472 401-2 (151' · DDD)　　Ⓕ●●

Maria Kliegel and Nina Tichman conclude their three-volume Beethoven exploration with fine-toned, vigorous performances of the last two sonatas. Most sets of the cello- and-piano music fit onto two CDs; Naxos's more liberal allowance permits the inclusion of extra items, in this case the Duo, with 'Two Obbligato Eyeglasses', for viola and cello; not, perhaps, one of the young Beethoven's finest achievements, but most imaginatively written for the two instruments. Tabea Zimmermann's spirited playing prompts regret that Beethoven never wrote a *concertante* work for viola.

In the sonatas and variations Tichman and Kliegel make a well-matched pair. They favour firm, rounded tone and strong, expressive projection, and are equally convincing in the passionate A minor *Allegro* that forms the second part of the Fourth Sonata's first movement, and in the preceding *Andante*, where warm sound

and soaring lines perfectly express the music's romantic spirit. What's missing, perhaps, is a range of tone colour that can suggest mystery or solemnity. And in the variations, Kliegel is inclined to phrase in a smooth, somewhat bland way, where a more articulated, 18th-century style would be more in order. The passages in dialogue between the instruments, however, are most beautifully realised.

Turning to András Schiff and Miklós Perényi, the first impression is of a much lighter sound. The piano, indeed, might seem quite brittle, if it weren't for Schiff's beautiful *cantabile* touch and his exceptional ability to balance chords – Beethoven's gruffest harmonies form part of a texture that's richly coloured and always clear. It's the kind of thing we normally only experience with the best period-instrument players.

In contrast to the finely matched pairing of Tichman and Kliegel, Perényi and Schiff appear as distinct, contrasting characters – Perényi suave and elegant, and though demonstrating a wide expressive range, always staying within the boundaries of what is polished and unexaggerated, Schiff much more volatile and extreme. In the high-spirited finales of the first two sonatas you can easily imagine the tempestuous young composer performing before the King of Prussia.

But this contrast of styles doesn't result in unbalanced performances. There are, maybe, one or two places (in the Third Sonata's first movement, for example) where where you might welcome more intensity from Perényi, but overall his playing has all the vigour and commitment one could wish for. And where it's necessary to achieve perfect unity, the two come together in the most inspiring way. The most remarkable instance of this is Op 102's fugal finale, a movement that's often been perceived as impressive rather than attractive, but these two artists match articulation, note-lengths, volume and tone colour in such a way as to make the music seem beautiful as well as uplifting. An outstanding set.

Complete Works for Cello and Piano
Adrian Brendel vc **Alfred Brendel** pf
Philips ② 475 379-2PX2 (148' · DDD)　　Ⓕ●●●

The Brendels, father and son, give us Beethoven's complete works for piano and cello. You'll have to search long and hard to hear performances of a comparable warmth and humanity or joy in music-making. Sumptuously recorded and lavishly presented (including engaging family photographs), the sonatas are offered in a sequence that gives the listener an increased sense of Beethoven's awe-inspiring scope and range.

CD 1 juxtaposes early, middle and late sonatas with a joyous encore in the Variations on Mozart's 'Ein Mädchen oder Weibchen'. CD 2 gives us the Variations on 'See the conqu'ring hero comes' from Handel's *Judas Maccabaeus*, continues with the remaining two sonatas and ends with the other *Magic Flute* Variations, on 'Bei Männern'.

Pianist and cellist are united by a rare unity of purpose and stylistic consistency, whether in strength and exuberance, an enriching sense of complexity or in other-worldly calm (often abruptly terminated). What eloquence they achieve in the opening *Adagio* of the Second Sonata, what musical energy in the following *Allegro molto tanto presto*, instances where Beethoven's volatility is always tempered by the Brendels' seasoned musicianship.

In Op 102 No 2 Beethoven's far-reaching and still bewildering utterance, there is a quiet strength and lucidity; time and again a direction such as *Allegro vivace* is exactly that and not stretched, as in more urgently, even neurotically, propelled performances. Their glowing expressiveness at 10'57" in Sonata No 3 is 'interior' yet never at the expense of impetus, and Adrian Brendel's *ad libitum* lead into the concluding *Allegro* is memorable – improvisatory and relaxed. Both players display rhythmic resilience in the final Rondo from Sonata No 1, and what open-hearted delight and *joie de vivre* there is in the sets of variations.

The Brendels follow hard on Miklós Perényi and András Schiff's highly praised set on ECM New Series. This is indeed distinguished; a marvel of musical energy and finesse. Yet for all their expertise, this team presents a less unified and warmly human front than the Brendels. At the same time both sets are invaluable additions to the recordings of these masterpieces (and ECM includes the Op 17 Sonata for Horn and Piano in Beethoven's cello arrangement).

Additional recommendation

Cello Sonata, Op 69
Coupled with: Sonata in E flat, Op 64; 12 Variations on 'Ein Mädchen oder Weibchen', Op 66
Kliegel vc **Tichman** pf
Naxos 8 555786 (77' · DDD)   Ⓢ

A sound recommendation, both for the rare Op 64 (an arrangement of the Op 3 String Trio) and as an excellent bargain version of the more familiar items. Kliegel and Tichman give highly sympathetic performances; in the A major their playing has a breadth and confidence that easily encompasses the music's great emotional range.

Variations for Cello

12 Variations on Handel's 'See the conqu'ring   Ⓟ
hero comes', WoO45. 12 Variations on Mozart's
'Ein Mädchen oder Weibchen', Op 66. Seven
Variations on Mozart's 'Bei Männern, welche Liebe
fühlen', WoO46. Horn Sonata, Op 17 (arr vc)
Pieter Wispelwey vc **Lois Shapiro** fp
Channel Classics CCS6494 (45' · DDD) Recorded
1994   Ⓕ**O**

There are only 45 minutes of it, but this recital teems with fresh insights in the irresistible serendipity of its playing. Lois Shapiro partners

Wispelwey's 1701 cello on a 1780 Viennese fortepiano whose wiry energies she unleashes in an attention-grabbing opening theme for Handel's *See the conqu'ring hero comes*. Her bright-eyed first variation glints as phrases dart from dynamic shadow to light and back again. Then the cello's lean, slightly astringent voice makes itself felt in no uncertain terms before the keyboard gets its own back in mercurial scale passages. The players' delight in teasing, sparring and debating with each other comes into its own in the variations on *Ein Mädchen oder Weibchen*. The theme itself struts forward cheekily, only to peck its way through the first variation, before the cello makes the most of the wry harmonic subtext of the second. In the seventh, one half of a shared phrase caresses and preens the other; the 10th casts the shadow of Papageno's noose. Each player's imagination and technique is tested to the full in an absorbing account of the more abstracted *Bei Männern* variations. The world of *Singspiel* isn't far away, either, in this performance of the Sonata, Op 17: Wispelwey and Shapiro summon up the nascent world of Marzelline and Jacquino in their quick, ardent responses to the music and to each other.

Violin Sonatas

Op 12: No 1 in D; **No 2** in A; **No 3** in E flat
Op 23 in A minor   **Op 24** in F, 'Spring'
Op 30: No 1 in A; **No 2** in C minor; **No 3** in G
Op 47 in A, 'Kreutzer'   **Op 96** in G

Complete Violin Sonatas
Itzhak Perlman vn **Vladimir Ashkenazy** pf
Decca Ovation ④ 421 453-2DM4 (239' · ADD)
Recorded 1973-5   Ⓜ**OO**

Although Beethoven designated these works as 'for piano and violin', following Mozart's example, it's unlikely that he thought of the piano as leading the proceedings, or the violin either, for that matter: both instruments are equal partners, and in that sense this is true chamber music. Perlman and Ashkenazy are artists of the first rank and there's much pleasure to be derived from their set. Such an imaginative musician as Ashkenazy brings great subtlety to these works composed by a supreme pianist-composer. And the better the pianist is in this music, the better does the violinist play. Discernment is matched by spontaneity and the whole series is remarkably fine, while their celebrated performance of the *Kreutzer* Sonata has quite superb eloquence and vitality.

The recording boasts unusually truthful violin sound capturing all the colour of Perlman's playing.

Complete Violin Sonatas   Ⓗ
Wolfgang Schneiderhan vn **Wilhelm Kempff** pf
DG The Originals ③ 463 605-2GOR3 (236' · ADD)
Recorded 1952   Ⓜ**O**

In the 1950s these recordings would have probably given a very up-to-date impression; the playing is extremely clean – there's never a hint of sentimental violin slides or over-use of the sustaining pedal. But nearly half a century later, perhaps we're more conscious of the old-world virtues – Schneiderhan's beautiful *legato* bowing and gentle vibrato, Kempff's full, unforced tone, and a flexible approach from both artists, with finely graded *ritardandos* and subtle variations of tempo.

Though not regular sonata partners, Kempff and Schneiderhan have an admirable collective sense of rhythm. They favour moderate, poised speeds, and so tend to miss something of the impulsive quality of early Beethoven. And, in the same way, their dedication to pure, well-balanced, unforced tone means that the grotesque element in such a movement as the finale of Op 30 No 2 is underplayed. It's a delight to hear them find so many ways of interpreting Beethoven's frequent *sforzando* markings, from sharp accents to the expressive melodic emphasis they give to the theme of the *Kreutzer* Sonata's variations. But quite often Kempff downgrades or ignores these accents, smoothing away any angular corners, and this tendency towards blandness occasionally leads to disappointingly inexpressive playing, at the start of the *Spring* Sonata, for instance, where Schneiderhan's beautifully lyrical opening doesn't elicit a comparable response from the piano.

If there are a few let-downs, however, there are far more moments where the characteristically moderate, unexaggerated approach bears rich dividends. Schneiderhan's beautiful singing tone is a constant delight: witness the intensely vocal style of Op 24's finale and the luminous sound of his high register in the last of the *Kreutzer* variations. Similarly, Kempff's continual care for clear textures and his finely balanced chordal playing seem to offer glimpses into the essence of Beethoven's thought. The mono sound is beautifully clear and well balanced.

Violin Sonatas, Op 30
Gidon Kremer *vn* **Martha Argerich** *pf*
DG 445 652-2GH (64' · DDD) Recorded 1993　　Ⓕ**O**

Beethoven's Op 30 Violin Sonatas are three irresistibly lively and individual spirits in the hands and imaginations of Martha Argerich and Gidon Kremer. The first, in A major, has that particular quality of blithe and elusive joy reminiscent of the *Spring* Sonata, and created here by the lightest and truest touch on string and key, fused with bright rhythmic clarity. The slow movement is a tremulous song of long-forgotten, far-off things, in which violin and piano find an intimate balance of tone.

The second sonata of the group is here less an heroically clenched C minor fist, more the unfolding of a gripping and tense *Märchen*: a dark children's fairy-tale told through the rapid tapering of a phrase-ending on the violin, the gutsy ebb and flow of a piano *crescendo*, the sudden *pianissimo* picking up after the loud chords of a second theme. At the start of the development, Argerich even seems to be asking if her listeners are sitting comfortably – and rather hoping they aren't.

The G major Sonata's centrepiece is its Minuet and Trio, which Argerich and Kremer cunningly tease and charm into revealing its archaic qualities: a dance glimpsed through a lace veil. It's framed by two fast movements that would identify their performers anywhere, with their high-voltage velocity and wittily imaginative anticipation of each other's every move.

Additional recommendation

Complete Violin Sonatas
Oistrakh *vn* **Oborin** *pf*
Philips ④ 468 406-02PB4 (229' · ADD)　　Ⓕ**O**
The most striking asset of this famous set is Oistrakh's fabulous tone. The other great virtue is the close unity of style and purpose between the pair, both players striving to present a beautifully shaped, unexaggerated picture of the music.

Andante favori

Beethoven Andante favori in F, WoO57 **Chopin** Waltzes, Op 34 – No 2 in A flat; No 3 in A minor; No 4 in F. Scherzo No 2 in B flat minor, Op 31. Barcarolle in F sharp, Op 60 **Debussy** Suite bergamasque. Estampes
Sviatoslav Richter *pf*
Orfeo d'Or C491981B (75' · ADD) Recorded 1977
Ⓜ**OO**

This live Richter recital from Salzburg, unlike some of his other live recordings, is superbly recorded, with plenty of air in the sound and an instrument capable of withstanding fairly imperious *fortissimos* without losing its tonal bloom or firmness of tuning. The *Andante favori* is a gem of a performance, tonally ravishing yet unerringly responsive to the structural flow. In the Chopin group Richter not only displays his customary authority but revels in the music and the occasion. Abandon without indiscipline is the key, and the result is a tremendous sense of *élan*, bordering on exaltation; the applause and bravos between each piece seem only fitting. Debussy's *Suite bergamasque* goes like a dream, with a 'Clair de lune' hypnotically slow yet never in danger of becoming merely prosaic. Richter's concentration wavers a little more in *Estampes*, but what a treasurable recital this is otherwise.

Piano Sonatas

No 1 in F minor, Op 2 No 1 **No 2** in A, Op 2 No 2 **No 3** in C, Op 2 No 3 **No 4** in E flat, Op 7 **No 5** in C, Op 10 No 1 **No 6** in F, Op 10 No 2 **No 7** in D, Op 10 No 3 **No 8** in C minor, Op 13, 'Pathétique' **No 9** in E, Op 14 No 1 **No 10** in G, Op 14 No 2 **No 11** in B flat, Op 22 **No 12** in A flat, Op 26 **No 13** in E flat, Op 27

No 1, 'Quasi una fantasia' **No 14** in C sharp minor,
Op 27 No 2, 'Moonlight' **No 15** in D, Op 28,
'Pastoral' **No 16** in G, Op 31 No 1 **No 17** in D minor,
Op 31 No 2 'Tempest' **No 18** in E flat, Op 31 No 3
No 19 in G minor, Op 49 No 1 **No 20** in G, Op 49
No 2 **No 21** in C minor, Op 53, 'Waldstein' **No 22** in
F, Op 4 **No 23** in F minor, Op 57 'Appassionata'
No 24 in F sharp, Op 78 **No 25** in G, Op 79 **No 26** in
E flat, Op 81a, 'Les adieux' **No 27** in E minor, Op 90
No 28 in A, Op 101 **No 29** in B flat, Op 106,
'Hammerklavier' **No 30** in E, Op 109 **No 31** in A flat,
Op 110 **No 32** in C minor, Op 111

Piano Sonatas Nos 1-32
Alfred Brendel *pf*
Philips ⑩ 446 909-2PH10 (656' · DDD) Recorded
1994-6   Ⓕ**OO**

Also available separately –
442 124-2PH – Nos 1-3 (70')
446 624-2PH – Nos 4, 15 & 20 (65')
446 664-2PH – Nos 5-7 (59')
442 774-2PH – Nos 8-11 (75')
438 863-2PH – Nos 12-14 & 19 (60')
438 134-2PH – Nos 16-18 (72')
438 472-2PH – Nos 21, 22 & 28 (68')
442 787-2PH – Nos 23-25 & 27 (59')
446 093-2PH – Nos 26 & 29 (62')
446 701-2PH – Nos 30-32 (66')

Intensity is very much the order of the day in
this sonata cycle, a throwing open of the gates,
with a far greater use of declamatory effects and
rhetorical tropes than was the case in either of
his two earlier cycles. Nos 4, 15 and 20: Brendel's reading of the Pastoral has changed – and
its status has stratospherically soared – in two
interrelated respects. In the first place, the two
outer movements are both slower than on either
the 1960s Turnabout or 1970s Philips recordings. Some will think the opening movement
too slow, but that would be to ignore the
thrilling way he now opens up the musical argument. What we have here isn't some amiable
musical ramble; rather, it's a multi-layered
music-drama in which the pianist's relish in
debating the issues the music is already asking
itself makes for the most exhilarating kind of listening. Nos 12-14 and 19: Beethoven's description of the two Op 27 sonatas as *quasi una fantasia* may refer primarily to structure, but it's the
element of the fantastic that's most missing: in
No 13 the quirky turns of harmony and texture
in the opening Andante-Allegro or the surprise
return of the Adagio just before the end, in the
'Moonlight' (No 14) the equally surprising
appearance of the light-footed Minuet after the
sad, introverted musing of the opening Adagio.
No, for Op 27 it's in the 1960s cycle that you
find him at his most penetrating.

Nos 16-18: The highlight of Op 31 here is the
Tempest: it's a perceptive reading in which the
thematic threads scattered across the piece are
revealed with great artistry. Nos 21, 22 and 28:
Brendel displays a technical mastery and visionary quality which surpasses his own previous

fine recordings of these three sonatas. In the
Waldstein (No 21), his sense of line and standard
of pianism falls only marginally short of Gilels's
superb 1972 version. Nos 23-5 and 27: Something about the proceedings in these recordings
has resulted in an unwelcome monumental
quality being imparted to the music. It comes
and goes; at its worst it makes you feel Beethoven is being set down on tablets of stone
rather than borne aloft. As to the sound, which
is predominantly neutral, we're quite close to
the instrument – Brendel's sing-along is audible
in the first movement of Op 90 – and the sonorities tend to register as chunky and rather airless.
Yet, in Op 90 Brendel makes the sun come out
magically at the beginning of the second movement, after a true pianissimo at the close of the
first. This performance, along with that of the
Appassionata, is the best here.

Nos 26 and 29: Brendel said that this was the
last recording of the *Hammerklavier* Sonata we
would have from him. He felt that this one,
given in Vienna in the Musikverein, was good
enough to be 'a decent way of leaving the piece'.
There can be no doubt about that for Brendel is
at his very best. The fusion of sound and sense is
thrilling, the pianism marvellous – an object-
lesson in how technique, at this level, is a matter
of knowing what you're doing and of fortune
favouring the brave. Hats off! The recording is
a good one, and the distance from the sound is
just right, with a wide dynamic range defined at
all levels. Brendel in *Les adieux* – less agitated,
warmer and more relaxed than many players – is
very enjoyable, but the gem of these two is the
Hammerklavier.

Nos 30-32: What do you do about a performance so satisfying that, after it, even single well-
honed sentence seems an irrelevance? Retire,
possibly, and devote oneself to a more useful
and benign trade such as growing vegetables. So
much, then, for his Op 109. As for Op 111, a
brute of a thing to interpret, Brendel has always
been one of its most lucid exponents, neither
stalling the introduction, which he plays with a
well-nigh ideal blend of grandeur and impetus,
nor mismanaging the shifting pulses of the subsequent *Allegro con brio ed appassionato*. Brendel
plays the whole of Op 110 superbly too. His
playing is lucidity itself, in a way that seems at
once natural, moving, and true to the letter of
Beethoven's text.

Piano Sonatas Nos 1-32
Richard Goode *pf*
Nonesuch ⑩ 7559-79328-2 (608' · DDD) Recorded
1990s   Ⓜ**OO**

You may have a doubt as to whether all the
playing represents everything Goode is capable
of: sometimes he disappoints, slightly, by
appearing to hold back from the listener the
boldness and fullness of communication the
greatest players achieve. You might say that, for
all their insight and illumination, some of the
performances lack the final leap and a degree of

transcendence. But his playing is so very likeable: the finish, technical and musical, is immaculate, but on top of that he's exciting. His sound always makes you listen. His feeling for it and for fine gradations of sound from one end of his wide dynamic range to the other are those of a virtuoso, and inform everything he does. When he's more obviously on virtuoso territory, he responds to the demands for brilliance and thrilling projection as to the manner born. He's constantly inside the music, and what a lively, cultivated, lucid and stimulating guide he is. There's nothing diffident or half-hearted about the way he makes this cycle of Beethoven resound wonderfully, the earlier sonatas appearing no less masterly as characteristic of their composer than the later. His interpretation of the A major Sonata, Op 101, is one of the finest ever put on record.

Piano Sonatas Nos 1-32   H
Artur Schnabel pf
EMI Références mono ⑧ 763765-2 (605' · ADD)
Recorded 1932-8   Ⓜ OO

Schnabel was almost ideologically committed to extreme tempos; something you might say Beethoven's music thrives on, always provided the interpreter can bring it off. By and large he did. There are some famous gabbles in this sonata cycle, notably at the start of the *Hammerklavier*, with him going for broke. In fact, Schnabel also held that 'It is a mistake to imagine that all notes should be played with equal intensity or even be clearly audible. In order to clarify the music it is often necessary to make certain notes obscure.' If it's true, as some contemporary witnesses aver, that Schnabel was a flawless wizard in the period pre-1930, there's still plenty of wizardry left in these post-1930 Beethoven recordings. They are virtuoso readings that demonstrate a blazing intensity of interpretative vision as well as breathtaking manner of execution. Even when a dazzlingly articulate reading like that of the *Waldstein* is home and dry, the abiding impression in its aftermath is one of Schnabel's (and Beethoven's) astonishing physical and imaginative daring. And if this suggests recklessness, well, in many other instances the facts are quite other, for Schnabel has a great sense of decorum. He can, in many of the smaller sonatas and some of the late ones, be impeccably mannered, stylish and urbane. Equally he can be devilish or coarse. At the other extreme, he's indubitably the master of the genuinely slow movement.
For the recorded sound, there's nothing that can be done about the occasional patch of wow or discoloration but, in general, the old recordings come up very freshly.

Piano Sonatas Nos 1-32   H
Wilhelm Kempff pf
DG Dokumente mono ⑧ 447 966-2GDO8 (511' ·
ADD) Includes bonus disc, 'Wilhelm Kempff – An

All-Round Musician'. Recorded 1951-6   Ⓜ OOO

Wilhelm Kempff was the most inspirational of Beethoven pianists. Those who have cherished his earlier stereo cycle for its magical spontaneity will find Kempff's qualities even more intensely conveyed in this mono set, recorded between 1951 and 1956. Amazingly the sound has more body and warmth than the stereo, with Kempff's unmatched transparency and clarity of articulation even more vividly caught, both in sparkling *Allegros* and in deeply dedicated slow movements. If in places he's even more personal, some might say wilful, regularly surprising you with a new revelation, the magnetism is even more intense, as in the great *Adagio* of the *Hammerklavier* or the final variations of Op 111, at once more rapt and more impulsive, flowing more freely. The bonus disc, entitled 'An All-Round Musician', celebrates Kempff's achievement in words and music, on the organ in Bach, on the piano in Brahms and Chopin as well as in a Bachian improvisation, all sounding exceptionally transparent and lyrical. Fascinatingly, his pre-war recordings of the Beethoven sonatas on 78s are represented too. Here we have his 1936 recording of the *Pathétique*, with the central *Adagio* markedly broader and more heavily pointed than in the mono LP version of 20 years later.

74321-30459-2 – Piano Sonatas Nos 4[b], 13[c], 14[c] & 24[c]
74321-30460-2 – Piano Sonatas Nos 5-7[b] & 26[b]
74321-27762-2 – Piano Sonatas Nos 1-3[a]
74321-27764-2 – Piano Sonatas Nos 8[b], 12[b], 27[b], 28[b]
Alfredo Perl pf
Arte Nova Classics 74321-30459/60-2, 27762/64-2
(oas: 73', 72', 73' & 74' · DDD) Recorded [a]1992-3,
[b]1994, [c]1995   Ⓢ

Alfredo Perl does not follow the sonatas strictly in sequence: this may irritate some collectors, but it does allow each disc to stand as an independent 'recital' while also forming just one part of the complete journey. There's an enormous amount to celebrate in these performances. The rhythmic power of these works is communicated with a genuine sense of enjoyment, and one of the most striking features of Perl's playing is that he never shies away from the *sforzandos* or the *subito pianos* which are so important to Beethoven's style. Indeed, he attacks these dynamic accents and contrasts with such dramatic rigour that certain movements – the finale to the *Moonlight*, for example – are animated with a rare vitality. It's in the more highly charged movements where Perl is most compelling (the outer movements of the *Pathétique*, the opening movement of Op 10 No 1, and the finales of Op 2 No 1 and Op 10 No 2). The A major Sonata, Op 101, receives a tremendous performance, both musically and technically, and the second movement in particular is a marvel of understated virtuosity. In the

BEETHOVEN PIANO SONATAS – IN BRIEF

Richard Goode
Nonesuch ⑩ 7559-79328-2 (10 hr 6' · DDD) Ⓜ**OO**
A very fine set from the 1990s, the result of long and intense encounters with this music. If Goode has a fault, it's his occasional reticence. A wonderful trajectory of genius.

Artur Schnabel
EMI ⑧ 763765-2 (10 hr 5' · ADD) Ⓜ**OO**
From the 1930s – and sounding it – the first traversal of these astonishing works, played with incredible intensity and pianistic wizardry. A classic of the gramophone era.

Wilhelm Kempff
DG ⑧ 447 966-2GDO8 (8 hr 31' · ADD) Ⓜ**OOO**
✵ Kempff's early 1950s cycle is similar to his later stereo set (currently unavailable) but everything is fresher and more vibrant. If his aristocratic style of Beethoven playing appeals – and how can it not – you won't regret the purchase.

Daniel Barenboim
EMI ⑩ 572912-2 (11 hr 27' · ADD) Ⓑ**O**
Like Kempff, Barenboim has made two complete sonata cycles. This early set from the late 1960s, when he was still in his twenties, has a sense of discovery and spontaneity often lacking on the DG set from 15 years later. Some of the extreme tempi may infuriate, but it's a remarkable document from a remarkable man.

Alfred Brendel
Philips ⑩ 446 909-2PH10 (10 hr 56' · DDD) Ⓕ**OO**
A magnificent achivement from a great artist who balances head and heart in readings of probing intensity, but who also cherishes the wit and mercurial side of these works. A wonderful insight into a performer and a composer who seem in total harmony with one another.

Alfredo Perl
Oehms ⑩ OC229 (11 hr 46' · DDD) Ⓑ
A modern cycle from one of the younger generation. He takes quite an extreme view on tempo and some of the movements are either very fast or very slow.

Claudio Arrau
Philips ⑪ 432 301-2PM11 (12 hr 19' · ADD) Ⓜ**O**
Various smaller works take this set up to 11 discs, but each carries majesterial piano playing. Arrau's rigorous style may not be to all tastes, but there's no denying the intellectual rigour at work.

movements of more lyrical simplicity Perl can be less convincing. In the second movement of Op 90, for example, he doesn't make the piano sing, and his tone can occasionally sound a little bland. His *fortes*, too, can be rather hard-edged, although the bright recording doesn't help him here. Perl's tempos have been the cause of some debate: he favours extremes, juxtaposing especially rapid fast movements with protracted slow ones. In Op 101, for example, he follows the march-like second movement, taken dangerously fast, with a particularly drawn-out *Adagio*.

If you wish to sample just one disc from this series to get a flavour of Perl's playing, then try Vol 4 (ranging from the *Pathétique* to Op 101).

SBT1188 – Piano Sonatas – Nos 1; 3; 32 Ⓗ
SBT1189 – Piano Sonatas – Nos 7; 8; 13; 14
SBT1190 – Piano Sonatas – Nos 17; 18; 21; 22
SBT1191 – Piano Sonatas – Nos 26; 27; 29
SBT1192 – Piano Sonatas – Nos 23; 28; 30; 31
Solomon *pf*
Testament mono/ᵉstereo SBT1188-92 (oas: 73', 78', 80', 78' & 79' · ADD) Recorded 1951-6 Ⓕ

By the autumn of 1956, when a stroke ended Solomon's career at the absurdly early age of 54, he'd recorded 18 of the Beethoven piano sonatas, 12 of which had been released. Had his career continued, the cycle would almost certainly have been revised and completed. The immediate rivals would have been the two cycles Wilhelm Kempff recorded for Deutsche Grammophon (mono 1951-6, stereo 1964-5) and the pre-war Schnabel recordings which EMI reissued in its series Great Recordings of the Century in 1963-4. In the event, Solomon's cycle remained incomplete, as did later Emil Gilels's not dissimilar DG cycle.

Some will fret over this but sanguine folk will reflect that all the 'important' sonatas are here in performances that can generally be reckoned 'representative'. Testament's Paul Baily has done a first-rate job on the transfers and the layouts: five CDs, each packed to the gunnels, each logically planned. The only sonata that's significantly out of sequence is Op 111 (No 32), yet curiously, that's the one performance from among the late, great sonatas which isn't entirely up to scratch. Here you might think back to Schnabel. Alongside Schnabel's reading, Solomon's sounds scampered (in the first movement), lacking in depth (in the second), and oddly unspontaneous, as though haunted by the knowledge of the older reading. The rather hollow-sounding 1951 recording doesn't help.

Op 111 is coupled here (SBT1188) with two of the Op 2 sonatas (Nos 1 and 3), the playing by turns fiery and lucid, gracious and gay. If anything's missing, it's its sense of tragic pathos Schnabel finds in the slow movement of the C major Sonata and his radical recklessness of spirit in the two finales.

The second disc contains celebrated readings of the *Moonlight* (No 14) and the *Pathétique*

(No 8). Solomon's reading of the opening movement of the *Moonlight* is famously long-breathed, his reading of the opening movement of the *Pathétique*, and the *Moonlight*'s finale, wonderfully tense and austere.

The remaining three discs are, quite simply, indispensable, Solomon at the peak of his powers as a Beethoven player. In sonata after sonata, we hear virtuosity of the finest and most discriminating kind put at the service of some of the loftiest yet most physically beautiful and physically exciting music known to man. Solomon was famous for the Cistercian clarity of his quick playing (the *Waldstein* – No 21, and *Appassionata* – No 23, sonatas *passim*) and for the concentrated calm of his playing of the great slow movements (this 1952 recording of the *Hammerklavier* – No 29, as fine an example as any). Underpinning both these phenomena is a quality of dynamic control that both gratifies the eye (Beethoven's text lifted off the page with rare precision) and bewitches the ear. It's this latter point which gives Solomon his special ability to define for us that element of unalloyed wonder in Beethoven's writing, those moments when we're brought to what TS Eliot called 'the still point of the turning world'.

There are minor disappointments on each of these three final discs. The 1951 recording of Op 54 (SBT1190) is dowdily recorded and would almost certainly have been remade had circumstances allowed. Both the 1956 Op 90 (SBT1191) and the 1954 Op 101 (SBT1192) are good without being a match for what we have elsewhere on the discs. In the case of Op 90, this is Solomon's legendary elucidation of the *Hammerklavier* Sonata and his well-nigh definitive account of *Les adieux*, a performance, humane and vivid, that's fine almost beyond belief.

Piano Sonatas Nos 2, 14, 31 & 32
Friedrich Gulda pf
Orfeo mono C591021B (80' · AAD) Recorded live
1964   (F)

This succinct, magically fleet recital (Gulda's first at the Salzburg Festival, given in 1964) comes, ironically, from an iconoclast who announced: 'it is not Beethoven that speaks, but jazz…the modern world lives with jazz, not with the glorious dead.' Here, most oddly, is the pianist who journeyed from shock to shock, issued furious diatribes against the Viennese establishment, attempted to give recitals in the nude and finally gave a 'resurrection' recital after he had supposedly died. Yet the finest irony of all is that his actual performances suggest a 'truth that wakes to perish never' and the true re-creation of 'monuments of unaging intellect,' contradicting his increasingly crazed philosophy. His playing is of a near flawless clarity and lucidity and throughout you always sense Gulda's musical sophistication beneath his outwardly plain-speaking surface.

A scrupulously modern pianist, he wore his immense talent lightly, maintaining his individ-

uality yet never allowing anything to obtrude between audience and composer. The finale of Op 2 No 2 may seem fast and metronomic when compared to, say, Kempff's endearing whimsy and idiosyncrasy, but everything is given with an ease and dexterity that will make other pianists weep with envy. The *Adagio* from Op 27 No 2 is supremely natural and unstudied, and in the turbulent finale there's a sudden hush at 4'31" and a gravity to the cadenza just before the final onslaught that are truly breathtaking. Thoroughly recommended.

Beethoven Piano Sonatas Nos 8, 23 & 31.   **H**
Handel Keyboard Suite in D minor, HWV428 –
Prelude; Air and Variations; Presto. Chaconne and
Variations in G, HWV435
Edwin Fischer pf
APR Signature mono APR5502 (72' · AAD) Recorded
1931-8   **M**○○

On this invaluable disc are some of Fischer's finest and most legendary performances. His very first published recording (1931) of the Handel Chaconne, for example, was made at a time when his matchless *leggiero* and radiant tone were unimpeded by obvious blemishes or erratic pianism. Both this performance and that of the pieces from the Suite No 3 are endowed with an improvisatory magic, a strength and grace and supreme assurance. Fischer commences the *Pathétique* with a scrupulous adherence to Beethoven's *fp* marking, a sudden shift of sound that's fascinatingly modernist or prophetic. The *Allegro di molto e con brio* is exactly that, dancing with an irrepressible lightness and urgency; in the slow octave descent just before the final outburst there's a rapt 'all-passion-spent' quality, something that Fischer was able to achieve with supreme naturalness, without even a hint of artifice or calculated effect. All past vicissitudes are finally resolved in Op 110 in a blaze of heroic glory, and time and time again he makes you pause to consider key points and details that have somehow eluded others. There's a richness and humanity here that was uniquely Fischer's.

Piano Sonatas Nos 8, 14, 15, 17, 21, 23 & 26
Alfred Brendel pf
Philips Duo ② 438 730-2PM2 (152' · ADD) Recorded
1970-77   **M**○

The Philips reissue, with seven of Beethoven's most popular sonatas admirably played by Alfred Brendel, is in every way an outstanding bargain, and is well worth obtaining, even if duplication is involved. All the performances are authoritative and offer consistently distinguished playing, while the recording is very realistic indeed. The *Tempest* resonates in the memory and the central movements of the *Pastoral* are most beautifully shaped. The *Pathétique*, *Moonlight* and *Appassionata* all bring deeply satisfying readings that are compellingly conceived and freshly executed. This set can be recommended without any reservations.

Piano Sonatas Nos 8, 14, 17 & 23
Artur Pizarro pf
Linn Records CKD209 (79' · DDD)   (F)

Artur Pizarro gives performances of four Beethoven sonatas sufficiently individual and freshly conceived to make them emerge as new-minted rather than over-familiar. There's always room for another set of established masterpieces when the pianist is has this sort of re-creative energy and exuberance.

The contrast between Beethoven's opening *Grave* and *Allegro di molto e con brio* in the *Pathétique* Sonata is vividly and romantically caught; if the weight at climactic points is punishing, the impetus and momentum are unflagging. Everything is experienced anew: Pizarro presents the central *Adagio* as an uneasy truce between two outer storms (even the finale is fast and urgent; no tame or wistful *Allegretto* anticlimax for him); and in the opening of the *Moonlight* Sonata his free-flowing *Andante* is an entirely valid alternative to, say, the eternally pensive *Adagio* of Solomon fame. The fires of both this and the other Sonatas are raised to fever pitch, conveyed with an unfaltering assurance and musical character. In the *Tempest* he casts a romantic haze across the problematic first-movement recitatives yet still maintains clarity.

Linn's recording, on an uncommonly warm-toned Blüthner, is exceptional.

Piano Sonatas Nos 14-18. Variations on an   H
Original Theme in F, Op 34. Seven Bagatelles, Op 33
Artur Schnabel pf
Pearl mono ② GEMMCDS9123 (141' · AAD)
Recorded 1933   (M)OO

Heavy background hiss is a small price to pay for Schnabel's immediacy and quality, and both of these discs, the original material transferred with a courageous candour and honesty, do much to convince you that Beethoven and Schnabel are, indeed, synonymous. How characteristic is that gruff but musicianly refusal in No 14 of all undue solemnity, all notion of romantic, moonlit effusion. Such robust eloquence will hardly appeal to those who long for a prolonged gaze into the infinite, but the balance of sense and sensibility provides a superbly authoritative alternative. Of course, there are moments when Schnabel's impetuosity, his embattled rather than fluent resolution of purely pianistic problems, can cause momentary confusion. Yet the odd snatched phrase or telescoped rhythm pales into oblivion given Schnabel's overall achievement, his salty brio and the profound eloquence of his slow movements (has anyone played the central *Adagio* of No 17 so directly yet so speculatively?). His technique, while undeniably erratic, was brilliant; and every page pulses with a vividness and rough-

hewn vitality that are somehow pure Schnabel, pure Beethoven.

Time and again he wears his immense learning lightly; in the dazzling wit and repartee of No 16 the dust of ages seems to fall away before your very eyes and ears. The Op 33 *Bagatelles* also prove that Schnabel was as much at home in concentrated aphorism as in lengthy working-out. So, true Beethoven lovers will treasure these discs, even when they turn to a different sort of enlightenment from Wilhelm Kempff, Schnabel's nominated heir. But then Schnabel and Kempff are like North and South Poles of interpretation, and both are indispensable.

Piano Sonatas Nos 21, 23 & 26
Emil Gilels pf
DG 419 162-2GH (68' · ADD)Recorded 1970s   (F)OO

This is one of the most desirable of all Beethoven piano sonata reissues. Perhaps there's something rather chilly and understated about Gilels' reading of the *Waldstein*'s brief slow movement (by contrast, his playing of the slow movement of *Les adieux* is ravishing), but Beethoven must take some of the blame here, too. Throughout these three sonatas Gilels plays with an architect's sense of structure, great technical brilliance, and that uncanny blend of intellectual attack and intellectual distance that give his recordings their peculiar distinction. The transfers are brilliant and true. The opening of *Les adieux* sounds a trifle muted and there's some tape background, but the ear dismisses this as rapidly as it picks it up.

Piano Sonatas Nos 27-32   H
Solomon pf
EMI Références mono/stereo ② 764708-2
(141' · ADD) Recorded 1951-6   (M)OOO

Solomon's 1952 recording of the *Hammerklavier* Sonata is one of the greatest of the century. At the heart of his performance there's as calm and searching an account of the slow movement as you're ever likely to hear. And the outer movements are also wonderfully well done. Music that's so easy to muddle and arrest is here fierily played; Solomon at his lucid, quick-witted best.

The CD transfer is astonishing. It's as though previously we have merely been eavesdropping on the performance; now, decades later, we're finally in the presence of the thing itself. It's all profoundly moving. What's more, EMI has retained the juxtaposition of the 1969 LP reissue: Solomon's glorious account of the A major Sonata, Op 101 as the *Hammerklavier*'s proud harbinger. We must be grateful that Solomon had completed his recording of these six late sonatas before his career was abruptly ended by a stroke in the latter part of 1956.

The Sonatas Opp 90 and 110, were recorded in August 1956. In retrospect the warning signs were already there; yet listening to these edited tapes you'd hardly know anything was amiss. There's the odd fumble in the *Scherzo* of Op 110; but, if anything, the playing has even greater resolve, both in Op 110 and in a songful (but never sentimental) account of Op 90. The recordings of Opp 109 and 111 date from 1951. Sonata Op 109, is very fine; Op 111 is, by Solomon's standards, a shade wooden in places, both as a performance and as a recording.

Still, this is a wonderful set, and very much a collectors' item.

Piano Sonatas Nos 28-32
Maurizio Pollini pf
DG The Originals ② 449 740-2GOR2 (126' · ADD)
Recorded 1975-7 Ⓜ**OOO**

This reissued DG Originals set makes an exceptionally neat package. Consistent praise has been heaped on these recordings since they won the Instrumental Record Award in 1977. One of Pollini's greatest strengths is his ability to stand up to the accumulated momentum of Beethoven's structure, but he can also build on it so as to leave the impression of one huge exhalation of creative breath. In the first movement of the Hammerklavier the astonishing technical assurance has you on the edge of your seat with excitement. His controlled vehemence is without rival in the outer movements, and though he doesn't get right to the bottom of No 29's poetry, his far-sighted phrasing and paragraphing is again remarkable .

In the last three sonatas there are others who stop to peer deeper into some of the psychic chasms, but Pollini's mastery of integration and continuous growth, and his ability to hold potentially conflicting musical demands in balance, are again sources of wonderment.

In terms of the qualities just mentioned, who is Pollini's equal? Other than small touches of pre-echo in Op 111, there's nothing here to distract from the exalted quality of both the music and the playing.

Diabelli Variations, Op 120

Diabelli Variations
Alfred Brendel pf
Philips 426 232-2PH (53' · DDD) Recorded 1988 Ⓕ**O**

Diabelli Variations
Stephen Kovacevich pf
Philips Concert Classics 422 969-2PCC (54' · ADD)
Recorded 1969 Ⓢ Ⓑ**OO**

Here's a treat, indeed; for in Brendel and Kovacevich we have two of the gramophone's finest interpreters of the *Diabelli* Variations. Brendel has now recorded the work three times. His live 1977 recording of the work, made by Philips in collaboration with the BBC, is still something of a landmark. The piano itself may sound a trifle battle-weary by the end, but the performance is a *tour de force*, a finely thought-out reading seemingly improvised into life with astonishing fire and intellectual acumen. By contrast, this 1988 recording is a calmer affair and this relates not so much to tempos but the general mood. We are off the hustings and back in the study. This version is more measured as befits a reading that works its way slightly more circumspectly to the newly poised expressiveness of the final variations, the concluding Minuet now an even more sophisticated essay in sublime gracefulness.

The reissue of Kovacevich's famous recording does, however, present a considerable challenge to Brendel. It's at bargain-price, and though the booklet is bereft of notes, the CD has the full range of cueing points and the sound has almost as much clarity and bloom as the 1988 rival. Kovacevich was a pupil of Dame Myra Hess and his performance has a clarity, poise and vitality that has commended itself to more than one generation of collectors over the past 30 years. It's a performance that avoids other people's mistakes – while teaching us to relish uncomplicated skill. Where the *Diabelli* is concerned, one version can never be enough, but Kovacevich remains the safest recommendation.

Diabelli Variations
Piotr Anderszewski pf
Virgin Classics 545468-2 (63' · DDD) Ⓕ**OO**

This is the most intelligent, searching and delightful account of the *Diabelli Variations* to have reached us since Brendel's. It gives opportunities everywhere to admire a superfine control of every aspect of piano playing, but that isn't the great thing about it, splendid though the finish is. The performance is entirely composer-led, driven by the music, not by ideas *about* the music, and in that sense you hardly notice the means to the end at all. It's an account of the *Diabelli* based on a much closer reading of the text than you usually get, and you've only to hear the theme and the first variation to perceive an exceptional balance of rigour and imagination: rigour in the way Anderszewski has thought about every inflection marked by Beethoven; imagination, evident here and throughout, in the quality with which he has realised them in terms of expression and vividness of character. His rhythm is tremendous. More remarkable still is his feeling for dynamics, so copiously prescribed in this work and yet treated with approximation by so many players. He's not one to play the daredevil, and you could say his tempos in the quick numbers are sometimes surprisingly moderate; but he isn't a sober-sides. He has fingers which are always saying something, a varied and attractive sound, usually built from the bass up, and that rare ability to get from one thing to another with pinpoint accuracy, expressively speaking, as if forging sonority and character with a laser. A fine recording, and the sound is at an apt distance. An outstanding issue.

Piano Variations

32 Variations on an Original Theme in C minor, WoO80. Six Variations on an Original Theme in F, Op 34. Fifteen Variations and a Fugue on an Original Theme in E flat, 'Eroica', Op 35. Six Variations on an Original Theme, 'Die Ruinen von Athen', Op 76. Six Variations on an Original Theme in G, WoO77. Seven Variations in C on 'God save the King', WoO78. Five Variations in D on 'Rule Britannia', WoO79.
Cédric Tiberghien pf
Harmonia Mundi HMC90 1775 (76' · DDD)   ⓕ🔴🔴

Cédric Tiberghien commences the *Eroica* Variations with a meticulous weight and balance of textures and although exceptionally delicate and precise, rarely misses the force and energy underlining one of Beethoven's lithest, most vigorous arguments. He sinks gratefully into reflection in Variation 8 and his musicianship in the richly ornamented *Largo* of Variation 15 is at once individual but unsullied by personal idiosyncrasy. Again, in the *32 Variations* in C minor – that compendium of classical virtuosity – Tiberghien is meticulous but never severe, precisely yet generously registering the mood and character of each brief Variation in a manner that may well have caused Beethoven to alter his unfavourable opinion of his work ('Beethoven, what a fool you have been!'). His *stretto* in Variations 21-2 makes the dark place of Variation 23 sound unusually mysterious while Variations 10-11 show an unfaltering assurance and style.

Tiberghien is no less outstanding in less demanding fare, relishing the explosive whimsy of the *Rule Britannia* and *God save the King* Variations, with their mock solemnity and affectionate digs at British assumptions of superiority. Here, clearly, is a pianist to watch. Harmonia Mundi's sound is excellent, making this an altogether exceptional disc.

Bagatelles

Bagatelles – Op 33; Op 119; Op 126; A minor, WoO59, 'Für Elise'; B flat, WoO60. Rondo in C, Op 51 No 1. Allegretto in C minor, WoO53
Alfred Brendel pf
Philips 456 031-2PH (77' · DDD)   ⓕ🔴

Listening to Beethoven's *Bagatelles* can be like looking over the composer's shoulder as he works. A scrap of a theme, a repeated chord, a formulaic accompanying figure suddenly blossoms into something rich and strange; the one-dimensional turns magically into the three-dimensional. An unassuming little *Andante con moto* tune dissolves into a cadenza, then emerges transfigured in ecstatic counterpoint (Op 126 No 1); an innocent, almost plain folk-melody reappears floating on high, a voice from another world (Op 119 No 11). And so often in the *Bagatelles* humour is at the core. If there's such a thing as profound levity, this is it. Brendel, who has written so effectively about humour in Beet-

hoven, plainly revels in this aspect of the *Bagatelles*. The quirkiness, the delight in pulling the rug from under the listener's feet – he seems to have made it all his own. You could argue with the approach here or there – Op 119 No 5 is perhaps more laboured than *risoluto*; the strange half-pedal at the end of Op 119 No 3 produces a momentarily metallic aura around the notes – but much more often, character and texture are calculated to a nicety. He also conveys a sense of Op 126 as – in Beethoven's own words – a 'cycle of *Bagatelles*', the extraordinary No 11 (a gorgeous *Andante amabile*) making a very thought-provoking finale.

Bagatelles – Op 33; Op 119; C minor, WoO52; C, WoO56. Rondos – Op 51: No 1 in C; No 2 in G; C, WoO48; A, WoO49. Six Minuets, WoO10. Polonaise in C, Op 89. Andante favori in F, WoO57. Variations – Six in F on an Original Theme, Op 34; Nine in C minor on a March by Dressler, WoO63; Six in F on a Swiss Song, WoO64; 24 in D on Righini's 'Venni amore', WoO65; 12 in C on Haibel's 'Menuet à la Viganò', WoO68; Six in G on Paisiello's 'Nel cor più non mi sento', WoO70
Mikhail Pletnev pf
DG ② 457 493-2GH2 (152' · DDD)   ⓕ🔴🔴

From the very first notes of the *Dressler* Variations – Beethoven's first-known composition, dating from 1782 – it's clear that Pletnev is a master of piano texture, and that he's going to use his mastery not only to ravish the ear but to delight the mind. His nuances in the simple Swiss theme and its artless variations are quite delicious. At the opposite extreme, the grand set of 24 Variations on Righini's 'Venni amore' come across as a dry run for later cycles such as the *Eroica* or even the *Diabelli* Variations, both in overall design and in certain idiosyncratic details. Technical *tours de force* abound; Pletnev negotiates them all not only with phenomenal pianistic aplomb but, where appropriate, dry wit. It's a fascinating glimpse into the laboratory of the 20-year-old Beethoven's mind.

In the two early Rondos Pletnev is freer than some might wish with the notated dynamics, phrasing and articulation, and his touch suggests at times that he's thinking more of Scarlatti than of Beethoven. Nevertheless the most startling moments of whimsy in these pieces aren't his but the composer's. By contrast, in the Vienna-period Rondos of Op 51 he seems to be thinking forward to the age of Lisztian rhetoric. But the fact that he's never satisfied with the default response to the surface of the music is much to be welcomed, and almost always his initiatives are stylish and effective. Similarly the bagatelles radiate openness to all sorts of possibilities. In some instances Brendel finds more of a rough-and-tumble edginess; but Pletnev's range of touch and tonal nuance outstrips them both and brings rewards of its own, as in the proto-Schubertian touches of Op 119.

Instrument and recording quality are near to ideal. An outstanding issue.

Additional recommendation

Bagatelles
Buchbinder pf
Warner Apex 0927-49080-2 (60' · AAD)   ⑤Ⓑ⊙

Everything is clear and spruce, and perfectly caught. All the performances are of the most concentrated musical quality and there are fewer finer recorded versions of the *Bagatelles*.

Cantatas

Cantata on the death of the Emperor Joseph II, WoO87. Cantata on the accession of the Emperor Leopold II, WoO88. Opferlied, Op 121b. Meeresstille und glückliche Fahrt, Op 112
Janice Watson, Judith Howarth sops **Jean Rigby** mez **John Mark Ainsley** ten **José van Dam** bass-bar
Corydon Singers and Orchestra / Matthew Best
Hyperion CDA66880 (80' · DDD) Texts and
translations included   Ⓕ

Beethoven was only 19 when he was commissioned to write this 40-minute cantata on the emperor's death. It was never performed, the musicians claiming it was too difficult, and remained buried for almost a century. Arguably Beethoven's first major masterpiece, it was one of his few early unpublished works of which he approved. When he came to write *Fidelio*, he used the soaring theme from the first of the soprano arias here, 'Da stiegen die Menschen an's Licht', for Leonore's sublime moment in the finale, 'O Gott! Welch' ein Augenblick'. The tragic C minor power of the choruses framing the work is equally memorable. Dramatic tension is kept taut through all seven sections, with recitatives indicating the young composer's thirst to write opera. Matthew Best conducts a superb performance, fresh, incisive and deeply moving, with excellent soloists as well as a fine chorus. In this first cantata the solo quartet simply contribute to the opening and closing choruses.

The second cantata, only a little more than half the length of the first, was written soon after, when Leopold II had succeeded as emperor. This second work is less ambitious, expressing less deep emotions, yet it anticipates later masterpieces. Much more specific is the way that the finale of the cantata, 'Heil! Stürzet nieder, Millionen', clearly looks forward to the finale of the Ninth Symphony, a point reinforced by the key of D major. The two shorter pieces, both dating from Beethoven's difficult interim period between middle and late, with Jean Rigby as soloist in the *Opferlied*, make a generous fill-up, performed with equal dedication. With plenty of air round the chorus, the recording has ample weight yet is transparent enough to clarify even the heaviest textures. A revelatory issue.

Songs

Sechs Gellert Lieder, Op 48. Lieder – Op 52: No 3, Das Liedchen von der Ruhe; No 4, Mailied; Op 75: No 2, Neue Liebe, neues Leben; No 3, Aus Goethes Faust; Op 83: No 1, Wonne der Wehmut; No 2, Sehnsucht. Adelaide, Op 46. An die Hoffnung, Op 94. An die ferne Geliebte, Op 98. Klage, WoO113. Der Liebende, WoO139. An die Geliebte, WoO140
Stephan Genz bar **Roger Vignoles** pf
Hyperion CDA67055 (69' · DDD) Texts and
translations included   Ⓕ❍❍❍

The young baritone Stephan Genz is in the first bloom of his youthful prime. Beethoven's setting of Goethe's 'Mailied', with its lightly breathed, springing words, could have been written with Genz in mind. Roger Vignoles, Genz's regular accompanist, contributes an irresistible bounding energy and even a sense of mischief to one of Beethoven's most spontaneous yet subtle settings, 'Neue Liebe, neues Leben'; and an elusive sense of yearning is created as the voice tugs against the piano line in 'Sehnsucht'. The six *Gellert Lieder* form the centrepiece of this recital: Beethoven's song cycle, *An die ferne Geliebte*, its grand finale. The intensity of Genz's cry 'Is there a God?' in *An die Hoffnung*, at the start of the disc, gives some indication of the *gravitas* he brings to his firmly enunciated 'spiritual songs' of Gellert. Genz and Vignoles have here reinstated a number of the original verses omitted by Beethoven in the first printed edition, creating a greater sense of balance and proportion within the set. The concluding song cycle is quite simply one of the best performances currently available. Fresh and bright of tone, awe-filled and beautifully paced and scaled, Genz's singing is modulated exquisitely from song to song by Vignoles's sentient piano accompaniment.

Irish, Welsh and Scottish Songs

Irish Songs, WoO152 – No 1, The Return to Ulster[b]; No 5, On the Massacre of Glencoe[b]; No 6, What shall I do to shew how much I love her[b]; No 8, Come draw we round a cheerful ring[b]; No 9, The Soldier's Dream[c]; No 19, Wife, Children and Friends[abc]; WoO153 – No 4, Since greybeards inform us that youth will decay[b]; No 9, The kiss, dear maid, thy lip has left[c]; WoO154 – No 3, The Farewell Song[b]; No 4, The Pulse of an Irishman[c]. Welsh Songs, WoO155 – No 2, The Monks of Bangor's March[bc]; No 9, To the Aeolian Harp[a]; No 14, The Dream[ab]; No 19, The Vale of Clwyd[a]; No 22, Constancy[bc]; No 25, The Parting Kiss[b]. Scottish Songs, Op 108 – No 5, The sweetest lad was Jamie[a]; No 8, The lovely lass of Inverness[a]; No 11, Oh! thou art the lad of my heart, Willy[a]; No 13, Come fill, fill, my good fellow[abc]; No 20, Faithfu' Johnie[a]; No 24, Again, my Lyre[b]; WoO156 – Womankind[abc]. God save the King!, WoO157[abc]
[a]**Sophie Daneman** sop [b]**Paul Agnew** ten [c]**Peter Harvey** bar **Alessandro Moccia** vn **Alix Verzier** vc **Jérôme Hantaï** fp
Astrée Naïve E8850 (71' · DDD) Notes, texts and
translations included   Ⓕ

Here's an excellent selection of Beethoven's 140

folksong arrangements, performed with all due care and accomplishment, spirit and affection. They're a joy: the songs in themselves, for a start, but more especially Beethoven's work on them. Or put it another way: 'work' is exactly what it does not sound like. It sounds as though he met these tunes (sent him, mostly, by George Thomson of Edinburgh), took to them like magic, found something in each that warmed his heart or set him dancing and, eventually, sorry when the verses had run out, made him add a ritornello or coda like a pat on the back to send each on its way.

Each number is a delight, but among the favourites are *Faithfu' Johnie*, with its deep cello underlining the heart's affections, *The Pulse of an Irishman*, both rumbustious and delicate in its fun, and, unexpectedly, *God save the King*, in which, in spite of its two peremptory calls to attention, Beethoven seems to be doing anything but. A special feature is the use of period instruments, effective in the more dramatic arrangements such as *The Return to Ulster* and the jovial party-pieces, *Come, fill, fill, my good fellows* and *Since greybeards inform us*. All three singers contribute ably, and the occasional collaborations in duet and trio are welcome.

Mass in C, Op 86

Mass in C. Ah! perfido, Op 65.   P
Meeresstille und glückliche Fahrt, Op 112
Charlotte Margiono *sop* **Catherine Robbin** *mez*
William Kendall *ten* **Alastair Miles** *bar* **Monteverdi**
Choir; Orchestre Révolutionnaire et Romantique /
Sir John Eliot Gardiner
Archiv Produktion 435 391-2AH (62' · DDD)
Recorded 1989-91   F OO

Gardiner's genius is in evidence here. The *Kyrie eleison*, is a plea for mercy, but its opening bars speak of comfort: there's almost the simple good faith of a quiet, very Germanic carol about them. Gardiner sets a mood of deliberate seriousness, with lowered period, pitch and a tempo rather slower than that suggested by Beethoven's direction: *Andante con moto, assai vivace, quasi allegretto ma non troppo*. He also appears to have encouraged the soloists, especially the soprano, to shape and shade the phrases, so intensifying the feeling of seriousness and deliberation. Happily, this policy prevails for only a short time, and to some extent the music itself goes out to meet it. As the second *Kyrie* (following the *Christe*) moves towards its climax, the *fortissimo* brings suspensions where the alto part grinds against the soprano, and then come sudden *fortissimos* with intense modulations and momentary discords, all of which are particularly vivid in this performance. What follows has the same exhilarating quality as that which was so applauded in Gardiner's *Missa solemnis* and, just as he did there, Gardiner is constantly illuminating detail while maintaining an apparently easy natural rightness throughout.

Again, an outstanding contribution is made by the Monteverdi Choir. Splendidly athletic, for instance, are the leaps of a seventh in the fugal 'Hosanna'. The tone-painting of *Meeresstille* finds them marvellously alert and vivid in articulation. *Ah! perfido* brings a similar sense of renewal: there isn't even a momentary suspicion of concert routine, but rather as though it's part of an exceptionally intense performance of *Fidelio*. Charlotte Margiono sings the angry passages with the concentration of a Schwarzkopf, and brings to those that are gentler-toned a special beauty of her own. Other soloists in the Mass sing well if without distinction. Distinction is certainly a word to use of the disc as a whole.

Mass in C, Op 86[a]. Meeresstille und glückliche Fahrt, Op 112. Elegischer Gesang, Op 118
[a]**Rebecca Evans** *sop* [a]**Pamela Helen Stephen** *mez*
[a]**Mark Padmore** *ten* [a]**Stephen Varcoe** *bar*
Collegium Musicum 90 / Richard Hickox
Chandos Chaconne CHAN0703 (56' · DDD) Texts and translations included   F

Beethoven's Mass in C, like Haydn's late masterpieces and the Masses of Hummel, was written on commission from Prince Esterházy for the nameday of the Princess. Puzzlingly, Beethoven's 1807 contribution was counted a failure: the prince described the music as 'totally ridiculous'. Beethoven starts his setting more conventionally than Haydn did in his late masses. Where Haydn brilliantly gave his *Kyrie*s a symphonic flavour, Beethoven is devotional in a simpler, more innocent style. That's surely apt in a prayer for mercy, even if you note the Beethovenian modulations and dissonances, individual touches well brought out in Richard Hickox's performance.

Hickox, with an excellent quartet of soloists, gives full-blooded performances that bring out the exuberance of the inspiration. Where Gardiner brings out the work's drama with phenomenally crisp singing and playing, there's an infectious joy to Hickox's reading, in which, with a choir of 24 singers, a closer focus and a marginally more intimate acoustic, the words can be heard more clearly.

Throughout the liturgy one Beethoven took nothing on trust, thinking afresh rather than relying on convention, as when the *Credo*'s first eight bars are quiet before the full outburst of affirmation from the choir, and the setting of 'Et resurrexit' begins with a baritone solo, not with a choral or orchestral outburst. The setting of 'passus' just before it has extraordinary intensity, just it does in the later *Missa*. Hickox brings out such points with clarity, with period forces making the music sound not just more vital but more modern.

The Mass is coupled with the lovely Goethe setting *Meeresstille und glückliche Fahrt*, and the *Elegischer Gesang*, written in a simple, homophonic style to commemorate the passing of a noble friend's wife.

Mass in D, 'Missa solemnis', Op 123

Missa solemnis
Charlotte Margiono sop **Catherine**
Robbin mez **William Kendall** ten **Alastair Miles** bass
Monteverdi Choir; English Baroque Soloists /
Sir John Eliot Gardiner
Archiv Produktion 429 779-2AH (72' · DDD) Recorded
1989. Text and translation included Ⓕ**ⓄⓄⓄ**

The *Missa solemnis* is one of the supreme masterpieces of the 19th century, but attempts to record a genuinely great performance have over many years run into difficulties. Usually the greatness itself is flawed, perhaps in the quality of the solo singers or in passages where the conductor's approach is too idiosyncratic or momentarily not up to the challenge of Beethoven's inspiration. The strain on the choir, especially its sopranos, is notorious; similarly the technical problems of balance by producer and engineers. This performance mixes discipline and spontaneous creativity; the rhythms are magically alive and the intricate texture of sound is made wonderfully clear. The great fugues of the *Gloria* and *Credo* achieve their proper Dionysiac sense of exalted liberation. Gardiner uses a choir of 36 and an orchestra of 60 playing on period instruments, aiming at a 'leaner and fitter' sound. The exceptional clarity of his smaller body of singers and players, their meticulous responsiveness to direction and concentrated attention to detail is impressive; yet you're aware of it *as* a performance. Sometimes, as in the first sounding of drums and trumpets signifying war, Gardiner's additional intensity brings a real gain.

Missa solemnis Ⓟ
Eva Mei sop **Marjana Lipovšek** contr **Anthony**
Rolfe Johnson ten **Robert Holl** bass **Arnold**
Schönberg Choir; Chamber Orchestra of Europe /
Nikolaus Harnoncourt
Teldec ② 9031-74884-2 (81' · DDD) Recorded live
1992. Text and translation included Ⓑ**ⓄⓄ**

There are many marvellous performances in the catalogue of Beethoven's great Mass. Gardiner catches the greatness, rises to it with his uncanny freshness of perception, and secures a performance virtually without fault. Levine, with conventional forces, presents a large-scale performance, not universally liked, but which impresses you almost unequivocally on every hearing. Harnoncourt is very different from either of the others, but brings at least equally the stamp of devotion and high attainment. Choir and orchestra achieve wonderful precision and clarity of articulation; they're sensitive to the needs of shading, to the ever-shifting balance of the parts, and to the purpose of cross-rhythms which at first may look like anarchy.

The soloists, who all meet their immense individual challenges, work intelligently as a quartet. It might be good simply to stop there and say, 'Enjoy it'. But once comparisons start, such

BEETHOVEN'S MISSA SOLEMNIS – IN BRIEF

Margiono; Robbin; Kendall; Miles; Monteverdi Choir; English Baroque Soloists / Sir John Eliot Gardiner
Archiv Produktion 429 779-2AH (72' · DDD) Ⓕ**ⓄⓄⓄ**
Gramophone's 1991 Record of the Year. Magnificent choral singing, four superb soloists and the fervent committed playing of the EBS under Gardiner's incandescent direction. Lean and lithe and terrifically powerful.

Mei; Lipovšek; Rolfe Johnson; Holl; Arnold Schoenberg Choir; CO of Europe / Nikolaus Harnoncourt
Teldec Ultima ② 0630-18945-2 (81' · DDD) Ⓑ**ⓄⓄ**
Period manners and modern instruments combined to great effect: it may lack the dynamism of the Gardiner or the monumental quality of the Levine, but there's binding integrity that makes this a very powerful experience. The soloists are well matched and the COE play their hearts out.

Studer; Norman; Domingo; Moll; Leipzig Radio Chorus; Swedish Radio Choir; Vienna PO / James Levine
DG ② 435 770-2GH2 (83' · DDD) Ⓕ**Ⓞ**
A truly festive performance in memory of Karajan recorded at the Salzburg Festival. This is grand, majestic Beethoven that's mighty impressive and deeply moving.

Orgonasova; Larsson; Trost; Selig; Swiss Chamber Choir; Zurich Tonhalle Orchestra / David Zinman
Arte Nova 74321 87074-2 (66' · DDD) Ⓢ**Ⓞ**
A *Missa solemnis* for the 21st century – the lessons of the period-instrument movement have been well and truly absorbed into this thrillingly vital and low-calorie performance.

Mannion; Remmert; Taylor; Hauptmann; La Chapelle Royale Collegium Vocale; Orchestre des Champs-Elysées / Philippe Herreweghe
Harmonia Mundi ② HMC90 1557 (140' · DDD) Ⓕ
Another successful period-instrument version, recorded live, that captures the questing spirituality at the heart of this great Mass. Four light-voiced, young soloists add to the performance's considerable appeal.

Milanov; Thorborg; von Pataky; Moscona; BBC Choral Society; BBC SO / Arturo Toscanini
BBC Legends ② BBCL4016-2 (145') Ⓕ
Milanov; Castagna; Björling; Kipnis; Westminster Choir; NBC SO / Arturo Toscanini
Istituto Discografico Italiano IDIS6365 (79') Ⓜ**ⓄⓄ**
Beethoven at white heat in 1939 and 1940 with more humanity than the classic RCA set.

simplicity begins to melt. Gardiner's performance is recorded more brightly and sharply.
Returning to Harnoncourt after listening to
that for a few minutes you feel a relative remoteness of contact with the sound. Moving then to
Levine, there's again a more immediate presence in the sound. Yet in this three-way comparison Harnoncourt emerges as a kind of
halfway-house between Gardiner and Levine,
and not quite as colourful as either. You might
opt for Gardiner because his performance is
confined to a single disc. Yet, listening again to
the *Credo*, there's something almost military in
the way his people march along, and, as
Harnoncourt stresses, the whole Mass is above
all 'an appeal for peace'. This is a performance
of great integrity: that is, it's a complete, consistent whole, and all its parts are sound.

Missa Solemnis   H
Zinka Milanov *sop* **Bruna Castagna** *contr* **Jussi
Björling** *ten* **Alexander Kipnis** *bass* **Westminster
Choir; NBC Symphony Orchestra / Arturo
Toscanini**
Istituto Discografico Italiano mono IDIS6365
(79' · ADD) Recorded 1940   Ⓜ️OO

A very fine line separates Toscanini's triumphant 1939 performance from this 1940
reading. On the other hand, John Steane in his
chapter on the work in *Choral Music on Record*
(CUP: 1991) heaped praise on 1940, commenting that 'all elements seem in equilibrium' and
that 'the total effect…is not adequately represented by references to "electricity"'. The two
readings are of such overwhelming conviction
and power that either will come as a revelation
to the newcomer either to the work or the conductor. If the preference is ever so slightly for
the 1940 account, it's because the sound is marginally better, the singing of the Westminster
Choir even more inspired than that of the BBC
Choral Society and the Carnegie Hall soloists
by a small margin superior to their Queen's
Hall counterparts, mainly because of the presence of the irreplaceable Björling and Kipnis.
Zinka Milanov is common to both, but in more
confident form on the later occasion. Listen to
this quartet at 'Et incarnatus' in the *Credo* or in
the whole of the *Benedictus* and you'll hear
singing fit for the gods both in tone and expression, not forgetting the subtle use of *portamento*,
out of fashion today. As for the chorus, hear the
end of the *Gloria* and you must realise why
Toscanini, in this work, is supreme.

Although this Italian issue has fairly primitive
sound, it's worth every penny for anyone wanting to encounter what must be one of the greatest accounts ever of this challenging work..

Additional recommendation

Missa solemnis[a]   H
Coupled with: Symphony No 7
Cherubini Anacréon – Overture. **Mozart** Symphony

No 35 in D, 'Haffner', K385
[a]**Milanov** *sop* [a]**Thorborg** *mez* [a]**Pataky** *ten*
[a]**Moscona** *bass* [a]**BBC Choral Society;
BBC Symphony Orchestra / Toscanini**
BBC Legends/IMG Artists mono ② BBCL4016-2
(145' · ADD) Recorded live 1939   Ⓜ️OO
This is an absolute triumph – a hair's breadth
separates this from the 1940 account reviewed
above; both are equally gripping. The transfer
eschews excessive de-hissing for a quiet sea of
surface noise that soon ceases to matter.

Fidelio

Fidelio
Inga Nielsen *sop* Leonore **Gösta Winbergh** *ten*
Florestan **Alan Titus** *bar* Don Pizarro **Kurt Moll** *bass*
Rocco **Edith Lienbacher** *sop* Marzelline **Herwig
Pecoraro** *ten* Jaquino **Wolfgang Glashof** *bass* Don
Fernando **Péter Pálinkás** *ten* First Prisoner **József
Moldvay** *bass* Second Prisoner **Hungarian Radio
Chorus; Nicolaus Esterházy Sinfonia / Michael
Halász**
Naxos ② 8 660070/1 (114' · DDD) Text included
                            ⓈⓈOO

Naxos has an uncanny knack for choosing the
right artists for its operatic ventures. On this
occasion, four of the singers are among the better known in the field, each judiciously cast.
Halász projects every facet of the score, inspiring his forces to live every moment of the plot in
words and music. This isn't an interpretation in
the romantic, quasi-philosophical mode of Fur-
wängler or Klemperer, rather one that alerts the
mind and ear to the human agony of it all.

In those respects it challenges the hegemony
of Maazel's forceful mid-price set on Decca, the
admired, early stereo Fricsay, also at mid-price
and Mackerras at full price, the last-named
vocally outclassed in almost every case by this
super-bargain Naxos. Nielsen's Leonore is no
projection of subservient femininity but a tormented wife seeking to save her husband, her
plight expressed in every key phrase. She does-
n't provide the heroic sounds of a Nilsson
(Maazel) or all the warmth of Rysanek (Fricsay),
but her slimmer, more compact tone exactly fits
this performance. Winberg is a Florestan equal
to his Leonore in vocal and interpretative assets.
Not even Heppner (Davis) or Seiffert (Harnoncourt), among modern interpreters, sings the
role better. His voice poised between the lyrical
and the heroic, his tone warm, his technique
firm, Florestan's scene can seldom have been so
satisfyingly sung and enacted. As Marzelline,
Edith Lienbacher is something of a discovery,
catching the eagerness, also the sense of nerves
a-jangle predicated by the part.

The dialogue, rather drastically foreshortened, is well spoken by all and intelligently
directed. The orchestral and choral singing
need fear no comparisons, and the recording
has plenty of presence, no tricks. This is a performance that fulfils almost all the demands
made on its principals and at the price should be

eagerly sought after: its most notable predecessors are matched, if not surpassed.

Fidelio

Christa Ludwig mez Leonore **Jon Vickers** ten Florestan **Walter Berry** bass Don Pizarro **Gottlob Frick** bass Rocco **Ingeborg Hallstein** sop Marzelline **Gerhard Unger** ten Jaquino **Franz Crass** bass Don Fernando **Kurt Wehofschitz** ten First Prisoner **Raymond Wolansky** bar Second Prisoner **Philharmonia Chorus and Orchestra / Otto Klemperer**
EMI Great Recordings of the Century ② 567364-2 (128' · ADD) Includes notes, text and translation. Recorded 1962 ⓂOO

If you accept Klemperer's broad, metaphysical view of *Fidelio*, his account of Beethoven's only opera is also a classic. On its own terms it's superb, as are the Philharmonia's playing and the recording, but it lacks the theatrical intensity of some other versions, notably Maazel's (Decca) and Halász's recent Naxos set. That kind of intensity is there in Klemperer's own Budapest recording (in Hungarian on Hungaroton) and in an off-the-air recording of his 1961 Covent Garden production. Legge made the mistake of replacing Jurinac, in this 1962 set, with Ludwig, a wonderful singer but not as natural a Leonore as Jurinac. Similarly, Hotter's raging Pizarro isn't quite matched by Berry's. Vickers' searing, slightly sentimentalised Florestan is common to both. When Klemperer returned to Covent Garden in 1968, Silja was his Leonore, and no one who saw and heard those performances, the conductor's operatic swan-song, will ever forget the occasion – as Richard Osborne says in his perceptive notes. He fails to point out, though – a small but important matter – that Schwarzkopf speaks Marzelline's dialogue for Hallstein.

Fidelio

Charlotte Margiono sop Leonore **Peter Seiffert** ten Florestan **Sergei Leiferkus** bar Pizarro **László Polgár** bass Rocco **Barbara Bonney** sop Marzelline **Deon van der Walt** ten Jaquino **Boje Skovhus** bar Don Fernando **Reinaldo Macias** ten First Prisoner **Robert Florianschütz** bass Second Prisoner **Arnold Schoenberg Choir; Chamber Orchestra of Europe / Nikolaus Harnoncourt**
Teldec ② 4509-94560-2 (119' · DDD) Recorded 1994. Notes, text and translation included ⒻOO
Highlights available on Warner Apex 0927-401374-2 ⓢ

Everything Harnoncourt touches leaves a sense of a country rediscovered: we listen to the piece in hand with new ears. So it is again here. Beethoven's sole but intractable opera has seldom emerged from the recording studio, or indeed the theatre, with such clarity of texture, such promptness of rhythm, such unity of purpose on all sides. This is a reading that gives full play to winds and horns, making you aware, whether it's in the Overture, Pizarro's aria, Leonore's

---

BEETHOVEN'S FIDELIO – IN BRIEF

Inga Nielsen Leonore **Gösta Windbergh** Florestan **Alan Titus** Don Pizarro **Hungarian Radio Chorus, Nicolaus Esterházy Sinfonia / Michael Halász**
Naxos ② 8 660070/1 (114' · ADD) ⓈOO
At bargain price, a good placce to start: a vivid performance with stellar leading singers, and good dramatic conducting.

Christa Ludwig Leonore **Jon Vickers** Florestan **Walter Berry** Don Pizarro **Philharmonia Chorus and Orchestra / Otto Klemperer**
EMI ② 567364-2 (143' · ADD) ⓂOO
Often considered a definitive recording, Klemperer's is a massive, granitic reading harking back to symphonic Beethoven, with a cast of heroic stature. Ludwig is a dark-toned, dramatic soprano Leonora, but Vickers is unforgettable in Florestan's suffering.

Charlotte Margiono Leonore **Peter Seiffert** Florestan **Sergei Leiferkus** Don Pizarro **Arnold Schoenberg Choir, CO of Europe / Nikolaus Harnoncourt**
Teldec ② 4509 94560-2 (119' · ADD) Ⓕ
An attempt at an intimate interpretation, with a lighter-voiced cast in which Seiffert's vigorous Florestan stands out. Harnoncourt's eccentric tempi and the deliberately understated drama won't suit everyone.

Hildegard Behrens Leonore **James King** Florestan **Donald McIntyre** Don Pizarro **Bavarian State Opera Chorus and Orchestra / Karl Böhm**
Orfeo ② C560012I (141' · ADD) ⓂO
A 1978 theatre performance, well recorded but with some resultant noise and stagey dialogue delivery, this is an intense, dramatic reading with a brilliant Leonora in Hildegarde Behrens.

Birgit Nilsson Leonore **James McCracken** Florestan **Tom Krause** Don Pizarro **Vienna State Opera Concert Choir, Vienna PO / Lorin Maazel**
Decca ② 448 104-2DF2 (119' · ADD) ⓂO
Maazel's performance is tautly conducted and well recorded for the 1960s, but chiefly attractive for a steely, heroic Leonore in Birgit Nilsson, McCracken's unconventional but sturdy Florestan, and a decent cast.

Helga Dernesch Leonore **Jon Vickers** Florestan **Zoltan Kélémen** Don Pizarro **Berlin Deutsche Oper Chorus, Berlin PO / Herbert von Karajan**
EMI ② 769290-2 (119' · ADD) Ⓜ
A superb performance at mid-price, with Karajan powerfully eloquent, Vickers again a ringing Florestan and Helga Dernesch one of the most passionate and beautifully sung Leonoras on disc; exceptionally well recorded.

big scena or the Prelude to Act 2, just how important they are to the structure and character of each movement. Where tempos are concerned, Harnoncourt is almost bound to be controversial somewhere. If many speeds are to their advantage just on the measured side of the customary, as in the Dungeon quartet, allowing us for once to hear every strand of the argument, that for 'O namenlose Freude' is uncommonly moderate. At this pace, Leonore and Florestan seem to be conducting a gentle exchange of deeply felt emotions on an interior level rather than allowing their pent-up emotions to burst forth in an explosion of joy, as is more usual.

The dialogue is delivered in an understated fashion. Two vocal interpretations stand out for excellent singing and pungent characterisation. Once Leiferkus's Pizarro takes centre-stage the action lifts on to a new, more tense plane. This vicious little dictator with his incisive diction, spoken and sung, and his biting, vital voice is a commanding presence. But Evil is up against an equally arresting advocate of Good in Margiono's gloriously sung and read Leonore. Hers isn't the quasi-dramatic soprano usually associated with the part, but she never sounds strained in the context of a more lyrical, smaller-scale performance. Seiffert fills Florestan with more refulgent tone than any other tenor on recent recordings – the high tessitura of his aria's close causes him no distress at all – but it must be admitted that there's little of the *Schmerz* in the tone found, quite differently, in the recording of Vickers (Klemperer). In that sense, though, he fits into Harnoncourt's well-ordered scheme of things. The only piece of miscasting is Don Fernando: a role that needs a solid bass with strong low notes has been given to a high baritone who sounds anything but authoritative. Harnoncourt has opted for a professional chamber choir to second the superb Chamber Orchestra of Europe. By the side of the superb Teldec recording, the Klemperer and Maazel sound less than immediate.

Fidelio
Hildegard Behrens *mez* Leonore **James King** *ten* Florestan **Donald McIntyre** *bass-bar* Don Pizarro **Kurt Moll** *bass* Rocco **Lucia Popp** *sop* Marzelline **Norbert Orth** *ten* Jaquino **Nikolaus Hillebrand** *bass* Don Fernando **Friedrich Lenz** *ten* First Prisoner **Hans Wilbrink** *bar* Second Prisoner **Bavarian State Orchestra and Opera Chorus / Karl Böhm** Orfeo d'Or ② C560012I (141' · ADD) Recorded live 1978 Ⓜ**OO**

At 84 this was to be Böhm's last *Fidelio*, and he knew it. Yet absolutely no allowances have to be made for his age in this life-enhancing, dramatically alert reading, quite on a par with his earlier versions of the work on disc. Indeed this now joins those other legendary live performances by great conductors of the past – Böhm himself in 1944 in Vienna, Bruno Walter at the Met in the same year, Toscanini at a concert in

New York in 1945 and Furtwängler at Salzburg in 1950. But, of course, this one is vastly superior in sound. Everyone seems determined to give of their best. None more than Hildegard Behrens, the very epitome of the dedicated, highly strung wife on a rescue mission and singing her heart out at all the important moments, not least in her 'Abscheulicher!'. She far surpasses her performance for Solti on Decca a year later. By her side throughout is the sterling, warm, authoritative Rocco of Kurt Moll in a reading that surpasses his own high standards on other versions. James King, though his voice had dried out a little by 1978, sings a Florestan imbued with anguish. As Pizarro, McIntyre, in powerful voice, is evil personified. For all the vocal glories, Böhm remains the evening's hero. Above all, he makes the opera living drama. Were this *Fidelio* his only work that survived for us to judge him by, it would be enough to clinch his reputation as a great conductor. There's more dialogue than we usually hear either in the theatre or on disc. There's also a deal of stage action. None of that should deter you from hearing such a truthful enactment of this masterpiece, few if any better on CD.

Leonore

Leonore   Ⓟ
Hillevi Martinpelto *sop* Leonore **Kim Begley** *ten* Florestan **Matthew Best** *bass* Pizarro **Franz Hawlata** *bass* Rocco **Christiane Oelze** *sop* Marzelline **Michael Schade** *ten* Jaquino **Alastair Miles** *bass* Don Fernando **Robert Burt** *ten* First Prisoner **Colin Campbell** *bar* Second Prisoner **Monteverdi Choir; Orchestre Révolutionnaire et Romantique / Sir John Eliot Gardiner** Archiv Produktion ② 453 461-2AH2 (138' · DDD) Notes, text and translation included Ⓕ**O**

Romain Rolland described Beethoven's *Leonore* as 'a monument of the anguish of the period, of the oppressed soul and its appeal to liberty'. John Eliot Gardiner, in the first complete recording of *Fidelio*'s predecessor for more than two decades, reveals musically and verbally how the early, more radical opera has worked its spell on him, too. This, he says, is Beethoven struggling to recover the revolutionary fervour of his Bonn years; this is the score where the direct expression of spontaneous emotion, rather than the nobility of philosophical abstraction, is really to be found. The slower musical pace of *Leonore* is counterbalanced by a stronger narrative thrust and the actor, Christoph Bantzer, contributes a sprightly narration which interleaves, deftly and movingly, brief asides from the likes of Wordsworth, Goethe and Hölderlin. And then, of course, there's the music.

The *Leonore* No 2 Overture is distinguished by the telling contrasts Gardiner draws between brooding strata of strings and the pearly light of the woodwind; and a reversal of the first two numbers gives Christiane Oelze a head start as a radiant Marzelline. The Trio which prepares the Quartet 'Mir ist so wunderbar' does tend to impede the momentum, but it has a telling effect on the beat of the work's human heart, and Gardiner's sensitivity to its pulse throughout makes good any shortfall in dramatic impetus. The D major March which introduces Act 2 is here restored to its original place for the first time since the première. With brass and timpani making menacing circumstance out of what can be mere pomp, it makes the entry of Don Pizarro darker still.

Matthew Best is, in articulation if not in range, one of the most blood-curdling Pizarros on disc, just as Alastair Miles is one of the noblest Don Fernandos. 'Komm, Hoffnung' reveals the resilience and steady, gleaming core of Hillevi Martinpelto's Leonore. There are times when you crave a fiercer edge of passion; but, with the equally sharply focused tenor of Kim Begley, it's a joy to hear 'O namenlose Freude' perfectly paced, and really *sung*. This Florestan sings his great aria without *Fidelio*'s vision of an 'Engel Leonore': Begley, no *Heldentenor* after all, is well suited to the constant, dark minor key of this 'Lebens Frühlingstagen', which presages Gardiner's triumphant and often surprising finale.

Vincenzo Bellini   Italian 1801-1835

Bellini was given piano lessons by his father, and could play well when he was five. At six he wrote a Gallus cantavit and began studying composition with his grandfather. After a few years his sacred pieces were being heard in Catania churches and his ariettas and instrumental works in the salons of aristocrats and patricians. In 1819 he went to Naples to study at the conservatory, entering the class of the director, Nicola Zingarelli, in 1822. In 1825 his opera semiseria, Adelson e Salvini, was produced at the conservatory. Its success led to commissions from the Teatro S Carlo and from La Scala, Milan.

Bellini's first opera for Milan, Il pirata (1827), instantly laid the foundation of his career, and with it began his fruitful collaborations with the librettist Felice Romani and the tenor GB Rubini. From 1827 to 1833 Bellini lived mostly in Milan, and during this time his operas, including La sonnambula and Norma, earned him an international reputation, while he himself went through a passionate love affair with Giuditta Cantù, the wife of a landowner and silk manufacturer, Ferdinando Turina. Bellini's amatory entanglements have been romanticised in popular literature but the realities are less creditable.

In 1833 Bellini visited London, where four of his operas were performed with great success at the King's Theatre and Drury Lane. He then proceeded to Paris, where he was commissioned to write I puritani for the Théâtre-Italien and formed a close acquaintance with Rossini and got to know Chopin and other musicians. I puritani enjoyed a genuine

triumph in January 1835, and Bellini was appointed a Chevalier de la Légion d'honneur. He decided to remain in Paris and formulated several projects for his future there, but in August 1835 he fell ill and the following month he died, from 'an acute inflammation of the large intestine, complicated by an abscess of the liver' according to the post-mortem report.

Bellini's importance to posterity is as a composer of opera, especially opera seria; his other works can be ignored without great loss. His first influences were the folksong of Sicily and Naples, the teaching of Zingarelli and, above all, the music of Rossini. The Naples performance of Rossini's Semiramide in 1824 was one of the most decisive musical experiences of his student years, and the novel lyrical style of his early operas represented a sentimentalisation and heightening of Rossinian lyricism, which in Il pirata broadens to include forceful and dramatic emotions. With this opera Bellini became one of Italy's most influential composers; Donizetti and Pacini, Mercadante and Verdi all learnt from him.

The quintessential feature of Bellini's operatic music is its close relationship with the text. He did not look for musical delineation of character, but the content and mood of each scene are given thorough-going musical interpretation and the text is precisely declaimed. His melodic style, of which the famous 'Casta diva' in Norma is a perfect example, is characterised by the building of broad melodic curves from small (usually two-bar) units. While his treatment of rhythm is more conventional, his melodies are supported by some colourful harmony and reticent though effective orchestration. More than any other Italian composer of the years around 1830, Bellini minimised the difference between aria and recitative by introducing a large number of cantabile, aria-like passages into his recitative. His expressive range goes far beyond the delicate, elegiac aspects of his art, which have been frequently overemphasised.

GROVEmusic

I Capuleti ed i Montecchi

I Capuleti ed i Montecchi
Edita Gruberová sop Giulietta **Agnes Baltsa** mez Romeo **Dano Raffanti** ten Tebaldo **Gwynne Howell** bass Capellio **John Tomlinson** bass **Royal Opera House Chorus and Orchestra, Covent Garden / Riccardo Muti**
EMI ② 764846-2 (130' · DDD) Recorded live 1984.
Text and translation included   Ⓜ**O**

Muti and his two principals, caught at white heat on the stage of Covent Garden, offer a rendition of Bellini's supple, eloquent score that gives the work a new definition and standing in the Bellini canon. Away from the limbo of studio recording, the music lives at a heightened level of emotion and the sound reflects a true opera-house balance. Muti persuades his singers and the Royal Opera House players to noble utterance. Baltsa's Romeo has a Callas-like conviction of phrase and diction: here's a Romeo who'll go to his death for the love of his Juliet. Who wouldn't, when that role is sung so delicately and affectingly as by Gruberová, then at the height of her powers, as was Baltsa? Raffanti's open-throated Italian tenor is just right for Tebaldo's bold incursions. Gwynne Howell and John Tomlinson contribute effectively to an engrossing performance.

Norma

Norma
Maria Callas *sop* Norma **Christa Ludwig** *mez* Adalgisa **Franco Corelli** *ten* Pollione **Nicola Zaccaria** *bass* Oroveso **Piero De Palma** *ten* Flavio **Edda Vincenzi** *sop* Clotilde **Chorus and Orchestra of La Scala, Milan / Tullio Serafin**
EMI ③ 5 66428-2 (161' · ADD) Recorded 1960 Notes, text and translation included Ⓜ**OO**

Norma Ⓗ
Maria Callas *sop* Norma **Ebe Stignani** *mez* Adalgisa **Mario Filippeschi** *ten* Pollione **Nicola Rossi-Lemeni** *bass* Oroveso **Paolo Caroli** *ten* Flavio **Rina Cavallari** *sop* Clotilde **Chorus and Orchestra of La Scala, Milan / Tullio Serafin**
EMI Callas Edition mono ③ 556271-2 (160' · ADD) Recorded 1954. Notes, text and translation included Ⓕ**OO**

Norma may be considered the most potent of Bellini's operas, in its subject – the secret love of a Druid priestess for a Roman general – and its musical content. It has some of the most eloquent music written for the soprano voice. The title-role has always been coveted by dramatic sopranos, but there have been few in the history of the opera who have completely fulfilled its considerable vocal and histrionic demands: in recent times the leading exponent has been Maria Callas. Is the 1960 recording better or worse than the 1954 recording? The answer can't be put in a word. But those who heard Callas sing Norma at Covent Garden in 1953-4, and then again, slim, in 1957, will know the difference. The facts are that in 1954 the voice above the stave was fuller, more solid and more certain, but that in 1960 the middle timbres were more beautiful and more expressive; and, further, that an interpretation which was always magnificent had deepened in finesse, flexibility and dramatic poignancy.

The emphasis you give to these facts must be a matter of personal opinion. Certainly Callas's voice lets her down again and again, often when she essays some of her most beautiful effects. The F wobbles when it should crown a heart-rending 'Oh rimembranza'; the G wobbles in an exquisitely conceived 'Son io' – and yet how much more moving it is than the simpler, if steadier *messa di voce* of the earlier set. There are people who have a kind of tone-deafness to the timbres of Callas's later voice, who don't respond to one of the most affecting and eloquent of all sounds. They'll stick to the earlier set. But ardent Callas collectors will probably find that it's the later one to which they will be listening again and again, not unaware of its faults, but still more keenly responsive to its beauties. 'Casta Diva', by the way, is sung in F,

as in 1954 – not in the original G, as in the Covent Garden performances of June 1953. The big duet with Adalgisa is again down a tone, 'Deh! con te' in B flat, 'Mira, o Norma' in E flat, and the change is once again effected in the recitative phrase 'nel romano campo'. Callas doesn't decorate the music. Adalgisa, a soprano role, is as usual taken by a mezzo. Ludwig blends beautifully with Callas in the low-key 'Mira, o Norma' (though her downward scales are as ill-defined as her colleague's). She's no veteran Adalgisa, but youthful and impetuous except when she lets the rhythm get heavy, and Serafin does nothing to correct her.

On the earlier set, Stignani is a worthy partner, while Filippeschi is rough but quite effective. On both sets, Serafin restores the beautiful quiet coda to the 'Guerra' chorus, and on both sets, Callas disappointingly doesn't float over the close of that slow rising *arpeggio*. In the later set, the conducting is spacious, unhurried, elevated and eloquent. Only in his handling of the mounting tension and the two great climaxes and releases of the finale, might you prefer the earlier version. The La Scala playing is superlative, and the recording is excellent.

La sonnambula

La sonnambula Ⓗ
Maria Callas *sop* Amina **Cesare Valletti** *ten* Elvino **Giuseppe Modesti** *bass* Rodolfo **Eugenia Ratti** *sop* Lisa **Gabriella Carturan** *mez* Teresa **Pierluigi Latinucci** *bass* Alessio **Giuseppe Nessi** *ten* Notary **La Scala, Milan Chorus and Orchestra / Leonard Bernstein**
EMI mono ② 567906-2 (141' · ADD) Recorded live at La Scala Theatre, Milan 1955. Notes, text and translation included Ⓜ**OO**

This important historical document comes from live performances at La Scala in the mid-1950s when the diva was at the height of her powers. Callas gives a more vital performance here than on the set recorded in the studio. The only drawback is the intrusive distortion at climactic moments.

It was Callas's particular genius to find exactly the appropriate mode of expression for every role she tackled. Here Callas gives us Amina, the shy, vulnerable sleepwalker. Bernstein and Callas join forces (having performed *Médée* together the previous year) for an utterly charming account of *Sonnambula*. The conductor's feeling for rhythm and colour and Callas's subtle responses to her fragile role are everywhere felt. And it isn't only Callas and Bernstein who make this set so unmissable. Cesare Valletti – a still underrated artist – is as sensitive and involved an Elvino as any on disc – and that's not forgetting Pavarotti – and he duets to perfection with Callas, Bernstein giving them the space to phrase as only they can phrase. And Giuseppe Modesti is a warm Rodolfo. Not to be missed.

La sonnambula
Dame Joan Sutherland sop Amina **Nicola Monti**
ten Elvino **Fernando Corena** bass Count Rodolfo
Margreta Elkins mez Teresa **Sylvia Stahlman** sop
Lisa **Giovanni Foiani** bass Alessio **Angelo Mercuriali**
ten Notary **Chorus and Orchestra of the Maggio
Musicale Fiorentino / Richard Bonynge**
Decca Grand Opera ② 448 966-2DMO2 (136' · ADD)
Recorded 1962. Notes, text and translation included
Ⓜ**OO**

La sonnambula was Bonynge's and Sutherland's
first Bellini recording. Sutherland's Amina in
the early 1960s was sung with extraordinary
freedom and exuberance. It's difficult to
describe her in the role: it's felt. She doesn't
touch a thrilling nerve of passion as Callas can;
but in the final scene – a wonderfully sustained
and imaginative piece of dramatic, as well as delicate and brilliant singing – she's very moving.
Far more so, in fact, than Callas, who overloaded 'Ah! non credea' and made 'Ah non
giunge' too artful. It's no good comparing
Sutherland with Callas at this late stage, though
it's inevitable here, especially as the Elvino,
Nicola Monti, sings the role on both sets. Callas
does superb things in the coloratura of 'Sovra il
sen', Sutherland is full of dramatic fire in the
scene in the inn – the tone, the note-shaping is
simply exquisite. And Bonynge excels in conducting the choruses. A very fine disc.

sources marks most of Benjamin's music from
his early period, though there's always a British
flavour too. This is the *Pastoral Fantasy*'s first
ever recording, and it proves quite a revelation.
Benjamin's imaginative use of the string quartet
involves fascinating and original textures such as
Ravel would have approved of, and the Locrian
players bring out the tender refinement of the
writing.

The Violin Sonatina of 1925 is even more
Ravelian in its first movement, reminding us of
some of the music that Benjamin's friend, Herbert Howells, was writing at that period. Like
the *Pastoral Fantasy*, it suggests a composer feeling his way towards his own individual style.

It's in the *Five Negro Spirituals* of 1929 that
Benjamin emerges as a memorable tunesmith,
using the spirituals most imaginatively in contrasting ways. The *Tune and Variations* was
designed as a simple piece for young students,
but in the hands of Lorraine McAslan it
emerges as a hauntingly beautiful piece in its
own right.

By far the toughest, most ambitious piece is
the Viola Sonata, written during the war when
the composer was in Canada, reflecting the
period's dark mood. It's superbly played by
Philip Dukes. Sophia Rahman is the sensitive
and sympathetic pianist. The sound is vivid and
well-balanced. All round, a thoroughly enjoyable disc.

Arthur Benjamin

Australian-British 1893-1960

*Arthur Benjamin studied at the RCM with Stan-
ford and began teaching there in 1926. Through
travels he came into contact with Caribbean music,
which he used in his Jamaican Rumba (for two
pianos, 1938, later orchestrated) and other light
pieces. His diverse output includes operas, concertante
pieces, songs and chamber music, in a cheerful style;
though the late works (e.g. Concerto quasi una fantasia for piano and orchestra, 1949) are darker. He
was an accomplished pianist who gave several premières.* **GROVE**music

Chamber Works

Five Negro Spirituals[a]. Sonatina[b]. Pastoral Fantasy[c].
Viola Sonata[d]. Three Pieces[e]. A Tune and Variations
for Little People[e]
Locrian Ensemble ([be]Lorraine McAslan,
[c]Rita Manning, [c]Steve Morris vns [cd]Philip Dukes va
[ac]Justin Pearson vc [abd]Sophia Rahman pf)
Dutton Laboratories Epoch CDLX7110 (77' · DDD) Ⓜ

This wide-ranging survey is very welcome
indeed. The enormous popular success of
Jamaican Rumba has tended to obscure the more
substantial, thoughtful works that he wrote.
Four of the six pieces here date from the 1920s,
giving an illuminating outline of his stylistic
development.

The influence of Ravel and other French

George Benjamin

British 1960

*Benjamin studied at the Paris Conservatoire with
Messiaen and at Cambridge with Goehr: Ligeti and
Boulez have been other influences. He first came to
attention with the vividly imagined orchestral piece
Ringed by the Flat Horizon (1980); this was consolidated with A Mind of Winter (1981) for soprano
and small orchestra and At First Light for chamber
ensemble (1982).* **GROVE**music

Antara

Ringed by the flat horizon[a]. A Mind of Winter[b]. At
first light[c]. Panorama[d]. Antara[e]
[b]**Penelope Walmsley-Clark** sop [e]**Sebastian Bell,**
[e]**Richard Blake** fls [c]**Gareth Hulse** ob [b]**Paul
Archibald** tpt [a]**Ross Pople** vc [e]**Pierre-Laurent
Aimard,** [e]**Ichiro Nodaira** pfs [a]**BBC Symphony
Orchestra / Mark Elder,** [bce]**London Sinfonietta /
George Benjamin** [d]electronics
Nimbus NI5643 (71' · DDD) Recorded 1985-6
Text included Ⓕ**OO**

This reissue is a valuable complement to Nimbus's earlier Benjamin CD, which was built
around compositions from the 1990s. But
between March 1979, when *Ringed by the flat
horizon* was begun, and March 1987, when
Antara was completed, foundations of remarkable potential were well and truly laid, and it's
fascinating to be able to trace that process

through four such different works. There are, of course, five items on the disc, but the 2'24" of *Panorama* – a beguiling, all-too-brief indication of Benjamin's work using pre-recorded tape – form a study for *Antara* rather than a wholly independent conception. The overall impression is certainly one of progress, in that the accomplished but in some ways rather stiff procedures to be heard in *Ringed by the flat horizon* led directly to the magnificently fluent setting of Wallace Stevens in *A Mind of Winter*, in which lucid instrumental textures provide the ideal foil for a brilliantly resourceful vocal line. In *At first light*, the stylistic spectrum opens up further, with clear hints of Varèse and even Xenakis. This disc is an essential document of the music of our time.

Sudden Time

Sudden Time[a]. Upon Silence[b]. Upon Silence[c]. Octet[d]. Three Inventions[d]
[bc]**Susan Bickley** *mez* [a]**London Philharmonic Orchestra**, [bd]**London Sinfonietta**, [c]**Fretwork / George Benjamin**
Nimbus NI5505 (65' · DDD) Recorded 1994-6
Texts included   Ⓕ

Sudden Time, originally issued as a CD single, is here reissued in the context of a range of other works which underline its distinctive textural refinement and expressive conviction. *Upon Silence* (1993) is a setting for mezzo-soprano and five viols of a poem by Yeats in which textures of exceptional subtlety reflect a response to the text which is captivating in its blend of spontaneity and stylisation. The alternative version, with the viols replaced by a septet of violas, cellos and double basses is no less imaginative, while obviously lacking the unique quality – old instruments used in an entirely viable modern way – of the original.

Three Inventions (1994) has ear-opening instrumental effects on every page, but these never detract from the essential processes of argument and cogent form-building in music perhaps more urgently expressive (especially in the third piece) than anything else of Benjamin's. With the astonishingly precocious *Octet*, written in 1979, when the composer was 18, and with highly effective recordings of definitive performances, this disc is an outstanding success.

Richard Rodney Bennett

British 1936

Richard Rodney Bennett studied at the Royal Academy of Music (1953-7) and with Boulez in Paris (1957-9), though his public career as a composer had begun before this. At 16 he was writing 12-note music, and the period with Boulez encouraged him towards Darmstadt techniques. But in the 1960s he recovered more conventional aspects to develop a style

of Bergian expressionism (e.g. in his opera The Mines of Sulphur, 1965); his opera Victory was given at Covent Garden in 1970. His subsequent output is large, including many concertos, settings of English poetry, chamber music, and, notably, big Romantic film scores. A musician of great versatility, he has worked as a jazz pianist (several of his scores of the 1960s are in a sophisticated jazz style) and has played and arranged American popular music.
GROVEmusic

Film Music

Murder on the Orient Express – Suite. Far from the Madding Crowd – Suite. Lady Caroline Lamb – Elegy[a]. Tender is the Night – Nicole's Theme. Enchanted April – Suite[b]. Four Weddings and a Funeral – Love Theme
[a]**Philip Dukes** *va* [b]**Cynthia Miller** *ondes martenot*
BBC Philharmonic Orchestra / Rumon Gamba
Chandos Movies CHAN9867 (70' · DDD)   ⒻⓄ

Richard Rodney Bennett possesses a natural flair for composing for both big screen or small. The concept of presenting the music in suites (no credit here for the arrangers) makes the best possible case for it, circumventing the problems encountered on the original soundtracks where fragmentation sometimes marrs enjoyment.

It's a measure of his standing in the film world that all these scores were issued on disc concurrently with the film. The earliest, *Far from the Madding Crowd* (1967), belongs to another era sonically speaking, but on this sumptuously recorded disc you can imagine yourself back in that state-of-the-art Odeon, Marble Arch, as the curtains parted to reveal Hardy's Dorset landscape on its giant curved screen, with Bennett's wistful unaccompanied theme for flute answered by oboe on the soundtrack.

Like that film, *Lady Caroline Lamb* was presented on its initial run as a road-show attraction, with an Overture, Entr'acte and Exit Music on the soundtrack, played respectively before the showing, during the intermission and after the film. The Suite reveals Bennett's fondness for a lyrical line at its most impassioned, with Philip Duke's eloquent viola-playing going to the heart of the story of this aristocratic lady's doomed affair with Byron.

Enchanted April moves us to the sunshine of Italy, where the colours of the percussion and ondes martenot lend a sweet fragrance to the scene. Elgar's *Chanson de matin* makes an unexpected but entrancing appearance.

When concentrating on the music without visual distractions it's easier to note the discreet Love Theme for *Four Weddings and a Funeral*. Beginning on low flute with broken chords on the harp, it subtly underlines the weddings and the funeral where John Hannah reads Auden's poem *Stop all the Clocks*.

From television comes *Tender is the Night – Nicole's Theme*, a popular foxtrot, 20s style, representing Scott Fitzgerald's ill-fated character Nicole Diver, inspired by his wife Zelda. Period dance music plays a part, too, in *Murder on the*

Orient Express, where Yuri Torchinsky, leader of the BBC Philharmonic, catches to a tee that sweet sound so characteristic of Oscar Grasso, leader of Victor Silvester's ballroom orchestra.

Conductor Rumon Gamba knows just how to levitate Bennett's celebrated train waltz theme, and the response of his orchestra throughout this disc suggests that they can turn their hand to the idiom of this music at the flick of a wrist.

Choral Works

Sea Change[a]. Verses. Out of Your Sleep. Puer nobis. A Good-Night. Susanni. A Farewell to Arms[b]. Missa brevis. There is no rose. That younge child. Sweet was the song. Lullay mine liking. What sweeter music
Cambridge Singers / John Rutter with [a]**Charles Fullbrook** bells [b]**Sue Dorey** vc
Collegium Records CSACD901 (75' · DDD · T/t)
Ⓕ❂❂

Hard to believe, but this is the first CD devoted solely to Sir Richard Rodney Bennett's extensive choral output. That it's a richly rewarding body of work is nowhere better exemplified than in the curtain-raiser, *Sea Change* (1984) a marvellously effective, 17-minute cycle to texts by Shakespeare, Andrew Marvell and Edmund Spenser. The Spenser setting thrillingly evokes the terrible monsters encountered by Sir Guyon during a stormy sea voyage by employing a technique akin to *Sprechgesang*, while the concluding 'Full fathom five' is a worthy successor to Vaughan Williams's setting in his *Three Shakespeare Songs*.

Whereas *Sea Change* minimally and subtly deploys tubular bells, *A Farewell to Arms* (2001) memorably incorporates an extensive role for solo cello and sets the same poems by Ralph Knevet and George Peele that Finzi first brought together for his 1945 diptych. It's a tenderly moving creation, as is the part-song 'A Good-Night' (1999) from the sequence *A Garland for Linda*. If Britten's shadow looms large over the *Missa brevis* (1990) for Canterbury Cathedral Choir, it's a no less appealing creation for all that.

Bouquets all round to John Rutter and his Cambridge Singers; theirs is *a cappella* singing of a very high order. Exemplary presentation and admirable sound, tastefully balanced within the comparatively intimate acoustic of LSO St Luke's in the City of London. A delightful anthology.

Alban Berg
Austrian 1885-1935

Berg wrote songs as a youth but had no serious musical education before his lessons with Schoenberg, which began in 1904. Webern was a pupil at the same time, a crucial period in Schoenberg's creative life, when he was moving rapidly towards and into atonality. Berg's Piano Sonata Op 1 (1908) is still tonal, but the Four Songs Op 2 (1910) move away from key and the Op 3 String Quartet (1910) is wholly atonal; it is also remarkable in sustaining, through motivic development, a larger span when the instrumental works of Schoenberg and Webern were comparatively momentary. Berg dedicated it to his wife Helene.

Then came the Five Songs for soprano Op 4 (1912), miniatures setting poetic instants by Peter Altenberg. This was Berg's first orchestral score; and though it shows an awareness of Schoenberg, Mahler and Debussy, it is brilliantly conceived and points towards Wozzeck – and towards 12-note serialism, notably in its final passacaglia. More immediately Berg produced another set of compact statements, the Four Pieces for clarinet and piano Op 5 (1913), then returned to large form with the Three Orchestral Pieces Op 6 (1915), a thematically linked sequence of prelude, dance movement and funeral march. The prelude begins and ends in the quiet noise of percussion; the other two movements show Berg's discovery of how traditional forms and stylistic elements (including tonal harmony) might support big structures.

In May 1914 Berg saw the Vienna première of Büchner's Woyzeck and formed the plan of setting it. He started the opera in 1917, while he was in the Austrian army (1915-18), and finished it in 1922. He made his own selection from the play's fragmentary scenes to furnish a three-act libretto for formal musical setting: the first act is a suite of five character pieces (five scenes showing the simple soldier Wozzeck in different relationships), the second a five-movement symphony (for the disintegration of his liaison with Marie), the third a set of five inventions on different ostinato ideas (for the tragedy's brutally nihilist climax). The close musical structuring, extending to small details of timing, may be seen as an analogue for the mechanical alienness of the universe around Büchner's central characters, though Berg's music crosses all boundaries, from atonal to tonal (there is a Mahlerian interlude in D minor), from speech to song, from café music to sophisticated textures of dissonant counterpoint. Wozzeck had its première in Berlin in 1925 and thereafter was widely produced, bringing Berg financial security.

His next work, the Chamber Concerto for violin, piano and 13 wind (1925), moves decisively towards a more classical style: its three formally complex movements are still more clearly shaped than those of the op.6 set and the scoring suggests a response to Stravinskian objectivity. The work is also threaded through with ciphers and numerical conceits, making it a celebration of the triune partnership of Schoenberg, Berg and Webern.

Then came the Lyric Suite for string quartet (1926), whose long-secret programme connects it with Berg's intimate feelings for Hanna Fuchs-Robettin – feelings also important to him in the composition of his second opera, Lulu (1929-35). The suite, in six movements of increasingly extreme tempo, uses 12-note serial along with other material in projecting a quasi-operatic development towards catastrophe and annulment.

The development of Lulu was twice interrupted by commissioned works, the concert aria Der Wein on poems by Baudelaire (1929) and the Violin Concerto (1935), and it remained unfinished at Berg's death:

his widow placed an embargo on the incomplete third act, which could not be published or performed until 1979. As with Wozzeck, he made his own libretto out of stage material, this time choosing two plays by Wedekind, whom he had long admired for his treatment of sexuality. Dramatically and musically the opera is a huge palindrome, showing Lulu's rise through society in her successive relationships and then her descent into prostitution and eventual death at the hands of Jack the Ripper. Again the score is filled with elaborate formal schemes, around a lyricism unloosed by Berg's individual understanding of 12-note serialism. Something of its threnodic sensuality is continued in the Violin Concerto, designed as a memorial to the teenage daughter of Mahler's widow. GROVEmusic

Violin Concerto

Berg Violin Concerto **Stravinsky** Violin Concerto in D **Ravel** Tzigane[a]
Itzhak Perlman vn **Boston Symphony Orchestra / Seiji Ozawa**; [a]**New York Philharmonic Orchestra / Zubin Mehta**
DG The Originals 447 445-2GOR (57' · ADD/[a]DDD) Recorded 1978 Ⓜ︎**OO**

Perlman's account of the Berg Violin Concerto with the Boston orchestra under Ozawa has long occupied a respected place in the catalogue. The original reviewer in *Gramophone* in March 1980 was completely convinced by Perlman's 'commanding purposefulness'. As to the recording, he wrote that 'though Perlman's violin – beautifully caught – is closer than some will like, there's no question of crude spotlighting'. Twenty years later and in a different competitive climate, his favourable verdict still holds good. Perlman is also a little too close in the *Tzigane*, the recording of which sets him very firmly front-stage again. But this is playing of stature and still among the best available versions. There are, however, more desirable recordings now available of the Stravinsky Concerto.

Berg Violin Concerto **Rihm** Gesungene Zeit
Anne-Sophie Mutter vn **Chicago Symphony Orchestra / James Levine**
DG 437 093-2GH (52' · DDD) Recorded 1992 Ⓕ**O**

One of the very few 12-note pieces to have retained a place in the repertory, Berg's Violin Concerto is a work on many levels. Behind the complex intellectual façade of the construction is a poignant sense of loss, ostensibly for Alma Mahler's daughter, Manon Gropius, but also for Berg's own youth; and behind that's a disconcerting mixture of styles which resists interpretation as straightforward Romantic consolation. Not that performers need to go out of their way to project these layers; given a soloist as comprehensively equipped as Anne-Sophie Mutter and orchestral support as vivid as the Chicago Symphony's they can't fail to register. Their recording makes a fine demonstration-

quality recording alternative to the version of Krasner and Webern.

Violin Concerto. Lyric Suite (original version) Ⓗ
Louis Krasner vn **Galimir Quartet** (Felix Galimir, Adrienne Galimir vns Renee Galimir va Marguerite Galimir vc) **BBC Symphony Orchestra / Anton Webern**
Testament mono SBT1004 (57' · ADD) Recorded 1936 Ⓟ**OOO**

This is an extraordinary issue of more than mere documentary interest. Krasner commissioned the Violin Concerto and had just given the first performance at the 1936 ISCM Festival in Barcelona (with Hermann Scherchen conducting) only three months after Berg's death. Webern was to have conducted, but withdrew at the last moment much to the consternation of the BBC who had booked him for the following month with some misgivings. Fortunately adequate rehearsal time had been allotted, and the players of the BBC Symphony Orchestra proved more expert in coping with the score than their Barcelona colleagues. Webern had appeared on a number of occasions with the orchestra, but no recording of him survives in the BBC Archives. Berg's death had shocked the musical world, though not as much as the death of the 18-year-old Manon Gropius had shaken the composer, who wrote the concerto as a memorial to her.

What's most striking about this performance is its glowing intensity. There's no sense of the bar-line or of the music ever being 'moved on'; time seems to stand still, yet there's also a natural sense of musical pace. The surface noise on this recording, made before an invited audience in the Concert Hall of Broadcasting House, London, can't disguise the care with which the textures are balanced and the finesse of the wind players. This was only the work's second performance, yet the players sound as if they'd lived with the music all their lives. It has all the anguish and poignancy the music demands, and Krasner is an eloquent exponent. The opening bars suffer from some minor audience coughs and the surface noise and moments of distortion call for a tolerance that's well worth extending.

The Galimir Quartet specialised in contemporary music and its playing has commendable ensemble and dedication. Unfortunately its pioneering account of the *Lyric Suite*, recorded shortly before the performance of the Violin Concerto, was hampered by a very dry acoustic that must have deterred many listeners. It was the only version for many years, and in spite of its musical excellence can't have made many new friends for the work. But this shouldn't deter collectors from acquiring this remarkable issue.

Lyric Suite

String Quartet, Op 3. Lyric Suite (original version)

Alban Berg Quartet (Günther Pichler, Gerhard Schulz *vns* Thomas Kakuska *va* Valentin Erben *vc*) EMI 555190-2 (46' · DDD) Recorded 1991-2 Ⓕ

This disc brings into focus Berg's two master-pieces for the medium. EMI offers a broad per-spective, the four players very forward and dis-tinct. Details may at times seem too intrusive for the good of an integrated interpretation, and the concern to make every emotional nuance tell risks spilling the music over into melo-drama. The Berg Quartet probes the extremes of the music determinedly, and their unfailingly bright sound can sometimes seem larger than life. However, there's no doubting the emo-tional power of the recording.

Piano Sonata, Op 1

Berg Piano Sonata, Op 1 **Schoenberg** Drei Klavierstücke, Op 11. Sechs Klavierstücke, Op 19. Fünf Klavierstücke, Op 23. Piano Suite, Op 25. Klavierstücke, Op 33a & Op 33b **Webern** Variations, Op 27
Peter Hill *pf*
Naxos 8 553870 (79' · DDD) Ⓢ ⓈＯＯ

When interviewed by *Gramophone* back in Sep-tember 1989, Peter Hill said he felt he had things to say about the Schoenberg piano works which had not been said on record. Here is the complete vindication of that statement. These are scrupulously prepared performances, with all the polyphonic strands clarified and all the myriad articulation marks respected. In order to accommodate that detail and let it speak musi-cally, Hill takes tempos on the relaxed side of Schoenberg's frequently rather manic metronome indications. The first two of the Op 11 pieces gain a gravity that might have sur-prised the composer, and the fourth piece of Op 23 loses some of the suggested *schwungvoll* char-acter. Yet there's no lack of brilliance and veloc-ity in such pieces as the Gigue from Op 25, and time and again Hill's thoughtfulness and search for expressiveness and beauty of sound justify his spacious approach.

Hill probes with equal subtlety, sympathy and high intelligence in the Webern Variations, while in the Berg Sonata, Hill's unforced lyri-cism, inwardness and flexibility of phrasing are again immensely appealing. Apart from its amazing value for money, Naxos's first-rate recording quality, Peter Hill's own lucid book-let-essay, and what sounds like an ideally regu-lated instrument, all contribute to the outstand-ing success of this issue.

Seven Early Songs

Seven Early Songs. Three Orchestral Pieces, Op 6. Der Wein
Anne Sofie von Otter *mez* **Vienna Philharmonic Orchestra / Claudio Abbado**
DG 445 846-2GH (49' · DDD) Recorded 1992-3. Texts

and translations included Ⓕ Ｏ

Anne Sofie von Otter included the *Seven Early Songs* on a recital disc, a programme glowing in the sunset of German romanticism. Singing with orchestra, von Otter naturally works on a larger scale. The words are more firmly bound into the vocal line; there isn't the detailed give-and-take that's possible with a pianist. But the outline of her interpretation remains that of a true Lieder singer, always lighting upon unex-pected subtleties of colour and emphasis to inflect the poetry. In all this Abbado is an equal partner. Von Otter needs careful accompani-ment in the concert hall if she's to dominate an orchestra and Abbado, in co-operation with DG's technical team, has produced a balance that never drowns her, but still sounds fairly natural. In *Der Wein*, Berg's late concert aria, von Otter and Abbado catch the lilt of the jazz rhythms. In the *Seven Early Songs* are they a touch too cool? Perhaps, but in the final song, 'Sommertage', they throw caution to the winds and end the cycle on a passionate high.

Abbado has recorded the *Three Orchestral Pieces* before and his 1970s recording has long been one of the standard versions of this work. The opportunity to see how his thoughts have developed since then brings more surprises than might have been expected. In short, his outlook is progressing from the Italianate to the Ger-manic. No doubt the influence of the Vienna Philharmonic Orchestra has much to do with this and their marvellously eloquent playing is one of the prime attractions of the disc. In their company Abbado finds more depth and com-plexity in the music than before, although that does mean that the March loses the Bartókian attack and driving rhythms that made his first version so exciting.

Berg Seven Early Songs **Korngold** Liebesbriefchen, Op 9 No 4; Sterbelied, Op 14 No 1; Gefasster Abschied, Op 14 No 4; Drei Lieder, Op 18; Glückwunsch, Op 38 No 1; Alt-spanisch, Op 38 No 3; Sonett für Wien, Op 41 **R Strauss** Wie sollten wir geheim sie halten, Op 19 No 4; Ich trage meine Minne, Op 32 No 1; Der Rosenband, Op 36 No 1; Hat gesagt – bleibt's nicht dabei, Op 36 No 3; Meinem Kinde, Op 37 No 3; Befreit, Op 39 No 4; Die sieben Siegel, Op 46 No 3
Anne Sofie von Otter *mez* **Bengt Forsberg** *pf*
DG 437 515-2GH (64' · DDD) Recorded 1991-3. Texts and translations included Ⓕ ＯＯ

At the centre of this recital are the *Seven Early Songs*. The first, 'Nacht', which is also the longest and most readily memorable, is taken rather more slowly than usual, but gaining in its subtler evocations of the mists and then the sil-vered mountain paths. Draining the voice of all vibrato also helps to create the sense of watchful stillness, just as in the sixth song, 'Liebesode', it makes for an almost other-worldly dreaminess, deepening to a full-bodied passion as the rose scent is borne to the love-bed. Von Otter's

BERG WOZZECK – IN BRIEF

Franz Grundheber *Wozzeck* **Hildegard Behrens**
Wozzeck **VPO / Claudio Abbado**
DG 423587-2GH2   Ⓕ⚫

Still one of the most searing performances of
Wozzeck, with Grundheber excellent at por-
taying the bitterness and humanity. Behrens
offers a magnificently 'full' portrayal of
Marie. Abbado's control is total and superb.

Andrew Shore *Wozzeck* **Josephine Barstow**
Wozzeck **ENO / Paul Daniel**
Chandos CHAN3094   Ⓜ

An English language version with Andrew
Shore a Wozzeck of menace and pathos,
finely sung and superbly characterized.
Opposite him, Josephine Barstow is a Marie
of real intelligence: Stuart Kale's Captain is a
powerful presence. Daniel conducts with real
feeling for the work's drama.

Carl-Johan Falkman *Wozzeck* **Katarina
Dalayman** *Marie* **Swedish Opera / Leif
Segerstam**
Naxos 8 660076/7   Ⓢ

A very impressive super-budget choice for
the work that benefits from Segerstam's
powerful lead of the excellent Swedish Opera
orchestra. Falkman is an impressive Wozzeck
and Dalayman a sympathetic Marie. While
the Captain and Doctor seem somewhat
underplayed, this is none the less a *Wozzeck*
interpretation of real stature.

Eberhard Waechter *Wozzeck* **Anja Silja** *Marie*
VPO / Christoph von Dohnányi
Decca 417 348-2   Ⓕ

A very beautiful performance of Wozzeck
with refined and amazingly accurate playing
by the VPO. Waechter is a sympathetic
Wozzeck and Silja an intelligent, intense
Marie. Generously coupled with *Erwartung*
with Silja on commanding form.

Mack Harrell *Wozzeck* **Eileen Farrell** *Marie*
New York PO / Dimitri Mitropoulos
Sony Classical mono MH2K62759   Ⓜ

Recorded live at Carnegie Hall in 1951, this
is as much a testament to the great Dimitri
Mitropoulos as to his fine cast. With Harrell
and Farrell superb in the main roles, the only
shortcoming is the mono sound.

Franz Grundheber *Wozzeck* **Hildegard Behrens**
Marie **VPO / Claudio Abbado**
DG DVD 100 256   Ⓕ

This is the video version of Abbado's justly
celebrated CD version (see above), and if
anything seeing the anguished and passionate
performances of Grundheber, Behrens and
Zednik only adds to the intensity of the
experience. Adolf Dresen's production is
sensitively handled, and the set, with its
sliding screens, is most effective.

mezzo-soprano voice is always resourcefully
used, able to colour deeply at such points, to
float a pure head-tone in 'Traumgekrönt' or
launch to a simply radiant high A in 'Die
Nachtigall'. The Strauss songs here are gentle
and affectionate, a mood in which von Otter is
often at her best. Not that, having captured a
mood, she's content to let it lie dully over as
much as a verse or a line. For lightness of touch,
the Op 38 songs endear themselves among the
Korngold group: *Glückwunsch* has an unaffected, comfortable way with it, and *Alt-spanisch*
is an absolute charmer.

Lulu

Lulu (Orchestration of Act 3 completed by Friedrich
Cerha)
Teresa Stratas *sop* Lulu **Franz Mazura** *bar*
Dr Schön, Jack **Kenneth Riegel** *ten* Alwa **Yvonne
Minton** *mez* Countess Geschwitz **Robert Tear** *ten*
The Painter, A Negro **Toni Blankenheim** *bar*
Schigolch, Professor of Medicine, The Police Officer
Gerd Nienstedt *bass* An Animal-tamer, Rodrigo
Helmut Pampuch *ten* The Prince, The Manservant,
The Marquis **Jules Bastin** *bass* The Theatre
Manager, The Banker **Hanna Schwarz** *mez*
A Dresser in the theatre, High School Boy, A Groom
Jane Manning *sop* A 15-year-old girl **Ursula Boese**
mez Her Mother **Anna Ringart** *mez* A Lady Artist
Claude Meloni *bar* A Journalist **Pierre-Yves
Le Maigat** *bass* A Manservant **Paris Opéra
Orchestra / Pierre Boulez**
DG Gramophone Awards Collection
③ 476 2524GGR3 (172' · ADD · S/T/t/N) Recorded
1979. Notes, text and translation included   Ⓜ⚫⚫⚫

This is a masterpiece that fulfils all the
requirements for a commercial smash
hit – it's sexy, violent, cunning, sophisticated, hopelessly complicated and emotionally
draining. *Lulu*, Berg's second opera, easily
matches his first, *Wozzeck*, for pathos and dramatic impact. The meaningful but gloriously
over-the-top story-line, after two tragedies by
Frank Wedekind, deserves acknowledgement,
but what matters is that Berg's music is magnificent, Romantic enough to engage the passions
of listeners normally repelled by 12-tone music,
and cerebral enough to keep eggheads fully
employed. It's opulent yet subtle (saxophone
and piano lend the score a hint of jazz-tinted
decadence), with countless telling thematic
inter-relations and much vivid tonal character-
painting. Berg left it incomplete (he orchestrated only 390 of the Third Act's 1326 bars),
but Friedrich Cerha's painstaking reconstruction is a major achievement, especially considering the complicated web of Berg's musical tapestry. This recording first opened our ears to
the 'real' Lulu in 1979, and has transferred
extremely well to CD.

The performance is highly distinguished.
Teresa Stratas is an insinuating yet vulnerable
Lulu, Yvonne Minton a sensuous Gräfin
Geschwitz and Robert Tear an ardent artist. Dr
Schön is tellingly portrayed by Franz Mazura,

Kenneth Riegel is highly creditable as Schön's son and that Boulez himself is both watchful of detail and responsive to the drama, hardly needs saying. It's not an easy listen, but it'll keep you on your toes for a stimulating, even exasperating evening.

Wozzeck

Wozzeck
Franz Grundheber bar Wozzeck **Hildegard Behrens**
sop Marie **Heinz Zednik** ten Captain **Aage
Haugland** bass Doctor **Philip Langridge** ten Andres
Walter Raffeiner ten Drum-Major **Anna Gonda** mez
Margret **Alfred Sramek** bass First Apprentice
Alexander Maly bar Second Apprentice **Peter
Jelosits** ten Idiot **Vienna Boys' Choir; Vienna State
Opera Chorus; Vienna Philharmonic Orchestra /
Claudio Abbado**
DG ② 423 587-2GH2 (89' · DDD) Recorded live 1987.
Notes, text and translation included   ⓕⓞ

A live recording, in every sense of the word. The cast is uniformly excellent, with Grundheber good both at the wretched pathos of Wozzeck's predicament and his helpless bitterness, and Behrens as an outstandingly intelligent and involving Marie, even the occasional touch of strain in her voice heightening her characterisation. The Vienna Philharmonic responds superbly to Abbado's ferociously close-to-the-edge direction. It's a live recording with a bit of a difference, mark you: the perspectives are those of a theatre, not a recording studio. The orchestra is laid out as it would be in an opera-house pit and the movement of singers on stage means that voices are occasionally over-whelmed. The result is effective: the crowded inn-scenes, the arrival and departure of the mil-itary band, the sense of characters actually reacting to each other, not to a microphone, makes for a grippingly theatrical experience. This version has a raw urgency, a sense of bitter protest and angry pity that are quite compelling and uncomfortably eloquent.

Wozzeck
Andrew Shore bar Wozzeck **Dame Josephine
Barstow** sop Marie **Alan Woodrow** ten Drum Major
Peter Bronder ten Andres **Stuart Kale** ten Captain
Clive Bayley bass Doctor **Jean Rigby** contr Margret
Leslie John Flanagan, Iain Paterson bass
Apprentices **John Graham-Hall** ten Idiot **Susan
Singh Choristers; Geoffrey Mitchell Choir;
Philharmonia Orchestra / Paul Daniel**
Chandos/Peter Moores Foundation Opera in English
② CHAN3094 (92' · DDD) Sung in English. Notes
and English libretto included   ⓜ

This is a fine *Wozzeck*; the perfect complement to the outstanding Abbado version (DG) which has been the top recommendation for so long. Abbado's was recorded live at the Vienna Staat-soper, and any studio recording of an opera risks sounding score-bound when compared with a

real, live performance in the theatre. But with *Wozzeck* a studio ambience can bring real advantages, especially if it underlines the kind of claustrophobic intimacy and obsessiveness which theatrical histrionics inevitably broaden and – in some instances – coarsen. Ranting and raving are kept to a minimum in Paul Daniel's interpretation, and the result is intensely mov-ing without in any way underplaying the music's visceral dramatic power.

One result of Daniel's concentrated yet warmly expressive moulding of the score is a strong sense of its late-Romantic background in Strauss and also in Mahler. The Philharmonia play superbly throughout, and the recording successfully balances a spacious orchestral can-vas of the widest dynamic range while placing the voices effectively. Nor are there any weak links in the cast, with three tenors, John Gra-ham-Hall, Stuart Kale and Alan Woodrow, making particularly telling contributions. Josephine Barstow has one or two squally moments in delineating Marie's bewilderment and fear, but her voice remains in remarkably good shape, and the character's conflicting impulses are brilliantly conveyed. Shore is one of the best operatic baritones of our time, and he dominates the drama with an utterly convincing blend of the menacing and the pathetic. More-over, his way with the text is exemplary.

This performance proves that an English *Wozzeck* can easily match the impact of the best German performances. Its virtues are such that it makes as powerful a case for this extraordinary work as any other version.

Additional recommendation

Wozzeck
Falkman Wozzeck **Dalayman** Marie **Qvale** Captain
Swedish Opera Chorus & Orchestra / Segerstam
Naxos ② 8 660076/7 (100' · DDD)   ⑤ⓢ
A few minor quibbles apart – both the Captain and the Doctor are portrayed as being more 'nor-mal' than usual, and the orchestral balance is a lit-tle skewed in places – this is close to being a giant among *Wozzeck* recordings.

Luciano Berio   Italian 1925-2003

Berio studied with his father and grandfather, both organists and composers, and with Ghedini at the Milan Conservatory in the late 1940s. In 1950 he married the American singer Cathy Berberian, and the next year at Tanglewood he met Dallapiccola, who influenced his move towards and beyond 12-note serialism in such works as his Joyce cycle Chamber Music for voice and trio (1953). Further stimulus came from his meetings with Maderna, Pousseur and Stockhausen in Basle in 1954, and he became a central member of the Darmstadt circle. He directed an electronic music studio at the Milan station of Italian radio (1955-61), at the same time producing Sequenza I for flute (1958, the first of a cycle of solo explorations of performing gestures), Circles (1960, a loop of Cummings settings for voice, harp and percussion) and Epifanie (1961, an aleatory set of orchestral and vocal movements designed to show different kinds of vocal behaviour). These established his area of interest: with the means and archetypes of musical communication.

For most of the next decade he was in the USA, teaching and composing, his main works of this period including the Dante-esque Laborintus II for voices and orchestra (1965), the Sinfonia for similar resources (1969, with a central movement whirling quotations round Mahler and Beckett) and Opera (1970), a study of the decline of the genre and of Western bourgeois civilisation. Two more operas, La vera storia (1982) and Un re in ascolto (1984), came out of his collaboration with Calvino. Other works include Coro (1976), a panoply of poster statements and refracted folksongs for chorus and orchestra, and numerous orchestral and chamber pieces.

GROVEmusic

Concerto II, 'Echoing Curves'

Rendering. Concerto II, 'Echoing Curves'. Quattro versioni originali della 'Ritirata notturna di Madrid'
Andrea Lucchesini pf **London Symphony Orchestra / Luciano Berio**
RCA Victor Red Seal 09026 68894-2 (68' · DDD) Ⓕ◐

Reworking takes many different forms with Berio. The simplest kind is to be heard here in the maddeningly repetitive but gloriously witty fusing together of Boccherini's four versions of his successful pot-boiler, *Ritirata notturna di Madrid*. On a much grander scale comes *Rendering*, which works around Berio's orchestration of the sketches for Schubert's 10th Symphony. At 35 minutes this is a big piece – the composer's own reading is phrased throughout with special sensitivity, and relishes the gentle and strange discontinuities between Schubert and Berio with absorbing delicacy. Berio is at his best, and most distinctive, when the composer he reworks is Luciano Berio. *Concerto II, 'Echoing Curves'*, from 1988-9, is a rich, complex elaboration of a work for piano and ensemble called *Points on the curve to find … from 1974. More Boulezian than much Berio in its slow-moving tissue of clusters, trills and tremolandos, its shimmering textures conjure up remarkable density and luminosity, and the music is perfectly shaped to prepare a finely graded 'dying fall'. The performances have absolute authorial conviction, and the 'big hall' sound is plushy without excessive resonance.

Sinfonia

Sinfonia. Eindrücke
Regis Pasquier vn **New Swingle Singers; French National Orchestra / Pierre Boulez**
Warner Apex 8573-89533-2 (45' · DDD) Recorded 1980s Ⓢ◐

This was the first complete recording of Berio's

Sinfonia. Previously this absorbing and bewilderingly complex work was available only in the four-movement version that Berio himself prepared in 1969 for the first performance with the Swingle Singers and the New York Philharmonic Orchestra. Within a few months, he'd completed a fifth and final movement which, though ostensibly an appendix, arguably stands as the apotheosis of the entire work; for it's genuinely a 'sounding together' (sinfonia) of the preceding movements, a rich sequence of reminiscences, just as the celebrated third movement leads us through memories of the standard orchestral repertoire in a kind of stream of subconsciousness. To hear the work in its completed form is a revelation, and for this reason alone Boulez's performance must be said to supersede Berio's own. To complete the disc he chose one of Berio's less-familiar orchestral works, *Eindrücke* ('Impressions', 1973-4). This is a complete contrast: a vast monody, projected by the string orchestra against the stuttering interjections and lingering trills of the wind and percussion, a stark and uncompromising conception. Again, the reading is a powerful one. This is a most important issue, far too good to miss.

Chamber Works

Notturno. Quartetto. Sincronie. Glosse
Arditti Quartet (Irvine Arditti, Graeme Jennings vns Dov Scheindlin va Rohan de Saram vc)
Naïve Montaigne MO782155 (62' · DDD) Ⓕ

Berio's music for string quartet, if hardly central to composing life, contains much that's characteristic and impressive. The two pairs of compositions are separated by a 30-year gap, yet it's fascinating to hear how clearly *Sincronie* (1963-4) anticipates the manner of *Notturno* (1993) in the wide range of its materials, from simple to complex, and the skill with which a large-scale single-movement structure is balanced and sustained. *Sincronie* and *Notturno* give us Berio at his best. Just as *Sincronie* uses its initial perception about the homogeneity of the four string instruments as the starting point for an enthrallingly spontaneous journey which never loses its sense of direction, so *Notturno* ventures well beyond the connotations of tranquil repose into the kind of dark, concentrated volatility which Berio has made his own. *Notturno* was recorded some years ago by the Alban Berg Quartet (EMI), the Arditti's all-Berio programme is more persuasive. These new performances are no less persuasive, bringing the music to fascinating life, with the help of a recording that's well-nigh ideal.

Sequenzas

Sequenzas – I-VIII, IXa, IXb & X-XIII, 'Chanson'
Luisa Castellani sop **Sophie Cherrier** fl **Lazlo Hadady** ob **Alain Damiens** cl **Pascal Gallois** bn

Christian Wirth *alto sax* Gabriele Cassone *tpt*
Benny Sluchin *tbn* Jeanne-Marie Conquer *vn*
Christophe Desjardins *va* Frédérique Cambreling
hp Elliot Fisk *gtr* Florent Boffard *pf* Teodoro
Anzellotti *accordion*
DG ③ 20/21 457 038-2GH3 (158' · DDD) Recorded
1994-7
Ⓕ**OOO**

 Berio's sequence of solo compositions
complements his larger-scale vocal and
orchestral works in various productive
ways. That doesn't make the *Sequenzas* 'miniatures', however: one of the later ones, No 12 for
bassoon (1995), is at 18 minutes also the longest,
and even the shortest, No 1 for flute (1957), at
just over six minutes, offers a distillation which,
for all its elegance, is far from lightweight. The
flexible eloquence with which he imbues some
ordinary avant-garde gestures in No 1 is early
evidence of a distinctive quality of thought was
to mature and intensify in the years ahead. In
No 2 for harp (1963), the instrument's conventionally genteel image is transformed into vivid
confrontations between the seductive and the
aggressive. This formula is developed still more
radically in No 3 for female voice (1965). No 4
(1966) is also highly expressionistic, concentrating on the brittle, dense textures of which the
piano is capable, rather than seeking to spin a
long, connected line. No 5 for trombone (1965),
by contrast, is a haunting exploration of the
instrument's 'voice', as well as of the voice of the
player, the use of long, slow *glissandos* a model
for the more elaborate treatment of the device
in the bassoon *Sequenza* 30 years later.

All the performers on these discs – most are
members of the Ensemble InterContemporain
– are on top of challenging material. They
might not always stick to the letter of dynamic
markings, but the spirit of the music is always
vividly conveyed, and the recordings are good.
Of the later *Sequenzas*, none is finer than the
staggeringly virtuoso No 6 for viola (1967)
charting Berio's complex response to the
Paganinian romantic heritage, and No 8 for violin (1976), where is the model in a piece with
enough of the grandeur and sense of inevitability of Bach's great Chaconne to justify the comparison. With the short No 7 for oboe (1967)
Berio hit on the strategy of placing the instrument's intensely volatile line against a single
sustained tone (off-stage or electronic), and a
comparable effect is used in No 10. Here the
trumpet occasionally plays into an open grand
piano, which catches and transforms the resonance to create ethereal echo-effects. No 9 from
1980 (for clarinet, and also for saxophone) is to
some extent an experiment in constraint, limiting the melodic materials and developing dialogues between varied repetitions, while No 11
(1988) for guitar wittily explores the ways in
which the instrument's own limitations can be
exploited and challenged. With No 12's
superbly long-drawn out but never monotonous
bassoon lament, and No 13 for accordion (also
1995) revealing the instrument's capacity for
delicate and poetic, as well as brusque, even

sinister utterance, it's clear that Berio's interest
in putting single instruments under the spotlight was as strong in the mid-1990s as it had
been nearly 40 years before. These discs are a
definitive document and a wonderful reminder
of why Berio's music matters.

Recital I for Cathy

Berio Recital I for Cathy[a]. 11 Folk Songs[b] Weill (arr
Berio. Sung in English) Die Dreigroschenoper –
Ballade von der sexuellen Hörigkeit. Marie Galante –
Le grand Lustucru. Happy End – Surabaya-Johnny
Cathy Berberian *mez* [a]**London Sinfonietta;**
[b]**Juilliard Ensemble / Luciano Berio**
RCA Victor Gold Seal 09026 62540-2 (65' · ADD)
Recorded 1972. Texts included
Ⓜ**OO**

These are classic recordings that no contemporary music enthusiast or Berberian/Berio
admirer will want to be without. This disc could
be regarded as a fitting tribute to Cathy Berberian and her inimitable vocal genius. As an artist
she was unique. As a champion of contemporary
music (particularly that of Berio, her ex-hus-
band) she was second to none – not only for her
interpretative prowess but also the inspirational
quality of her highly individual style. These
pieces were all composed, or arranged for her,
by Berio. *Recital I for Cathy* makes use of Berberian's dramatic training in a composition in
which the vocalist, frustrated by the non-
appearance of her pianist, struggles through the
programme while sharing a Beckett-like
stream-of-consciousness monologue with her
audience. her performance here is a monumental *tour de force*. Another example of the extraordinary qualities of Berberian's voice can be
found in the celebrated *Folk Songs* of 1964. The
three Weill songs reveal Berberian as a natural
interpreter of his music (perhaps the best since
Lotte Lenya). A wonderful tribute to a phenomenal talent.

Lennox Berkeley   British 1903-1989

*Berkeley studied at Oxford and with Boulanger in
Paris (1927-32), where he met Stravinsky and
became friendly with Poulenc. In 1928 he became a
Roman Catholic. Back in London he worked for the
BBC (1942-5) and taught at the RAM (1946-68).
His official op.1 dates from after he was 30, but
his output is large, including a full-length opera
(Nelson, 1954), three one-acters (including the comedy A Dinner Engagement, 1954), four symphonies,
sacred music (Missa brevis with organ, 1960), songs
(Four Poems of St Teresa of Avila for contralto and
strings, 1947; Five Auden Poems with piano,
1958), chamber and piano music. The earlier music
looks towards Paris, with its suave neo-classicism,
though his acquaintance with the young Britten was
also important. In the 1960s his work became more*

complex and darker, including elements of 12-note serialism. **GROVE**music

Choral music

Missa brevis, Op 57[ae]. A Festival Anthem, Op 21 No 2[cde]. Three Latin Motets, Op 83 No 1. Magnificat and Nunc Dimittis, Op 99[be]. Crux Fidelis, Op 43[d] No 1. Three Pieces, Op 72 – No 1, Toccata[e]. Look up sweet Babe, Op 43 No 2[ce]. The Lord is my Shepherd, Op 91 No 1[be]

[a]Julian Gregory, [b]Benjamin Durrant, [c]James Geidt *trebs* [d]Allan Clayton *ten* [e]Johnny Vaughan *org* St John's College Choir, Cambridge / Christopher Robinson
Naxos 8 557277 (75' · DDD)   ⑤

Lennox Berkeley's church music has now entered the cathedral lists – both Anglican and Roman – to an extent unthinkable even 10 years ago. He was a pious Catholic, and much of his music is rooted in his deep spiritual convictions His personal kind of melody and harmony sounds like nobody else. This is particularly evident in the most familiar of his religious works here – the 1960 *Missa Brevis* for Westminster Cathedral, which Britten much admired, and *The Lord is my shepherd* for Chichester. Just as typical are *Look up sweet babe* and the ecstatic George Herbert setting which forms the central section of the expansive *Festival Anthem*. Once heard, these tunes are difficult to forget.

The Mass for five voices and Three Latin Motets, written for this choir in 1972, are more austere but, like the eloquent sacred works of his friend Poulenc, they clearly come from the same imagination as the composer's other works. And quite late in life Berkeley boldly brings the discoveries of his more advanced later music into the *Magnificat* and *Nunc Dimittis*.

This is an impressive collection which merits repeated hearings. The choir sounds well and boasts fine soloists.

A Dinner Engagement

A Dinner Engagement
Roderick Williams *bar* Earl of Dunmow **Yvonne Kenny** *sop* Countess of Dunmow **Claire Rutter** *sop* Susan **Jean Rigby** *mez* Mrs Kneebone **Anne Collins** *mez* HRH The Grand Duchess of Monteblanco **Robin Leggate** *ten* HRH Prince Philippe **Blake Fischer** *ten* Errand Boy **City of London Sinfonia / Richard Hickox**
Chandos CHAN10219 (60' · DDD) Notes and libretto included   Ⓟ❍

A Dinner Engagement (Aldeburgh, 1954) was written for Britten's English Opera Group, suited their resources and philosophy admirably and was much admired by Britten himself. This jewel of a one-act comic opera has somehow escaped the record catalogue for half a century.

The period is that of British kitchen-sink theatre in the 1950s; however, this kitchen is an aristocratic one. Lord and Lady Dunmow, living in desperately reduced circumstances, have invited the Grand Duchess of Monteblanco to dinner. The Dunmows ardently hope that the Duchess's batchelor son, Prince Philippe, might be interested in their daughter Susan. Paul Dehn's libretto abounds in amusing incidents *en route* to a happy ending. The layout of the opera is an impeccable blend of aria and recitative; the scoring is colourful and effective; and the piece is full of memorable tunes.

Anne Collins as the Duchess is magnificent; Claire Rutter as Susan is enchanting; Robin Leggate makes a mellifluously charming Prince. This is an all-star cast, and the Mozartian ensembles are scintillating. Once again enormous credit to Richard Hickox, whose total understanding of Berkeley's music gives him unrivalled authority in this long-delayed début. Well recorded, too.

Hector Berlioz   French 1803-1869

As a boy Berlioz learnt the flute, guitar and, from treatises alone, harmony (he never studied the piano); his first compositions were romances and small chamber pieces. After two unhappy years as a medical student in Paris (1821-3) he abandoned the career chosen for him by his father and turned decisively to music, attending Le Sueur's composition class at the Conservatoire. He entered for the Prix de Rome four times (1827-30) and finally won. Among the most powerful influences on him were Shakespeare, whose plays were to inspire three major works, and the actress Harriet Smithson, whom he idolised, pursued and, after a bizarre courtship, eventually married (1833). Beethoven's symphonies too made a strong impact, along with Goethe's Faust and the works of Moore, Scott and Byron. The most important product of this time was his startlingly original, five-movement Symphonie fantastique (1830).

Berlioz's 15 months in Italy (1831-2) were significant more for his absorption of warmth, vivacity and local colour than for the official works he wrote there; he moved out of Rome as often as possible and worked on a sequel to the Symphonie fantastique (Le retour à la vie, renamed Lélio in 1855) and overtures to King Lear and Rob Roy, returning to Paris early to promote his music. Although the 1830s and early 1840s saw a flow of major compositions – Harold en Italie, Benvenuto Cellini, Grande messe des morts, Roméo et Juliette, Grande symphonie funèbre et triomphale, Les nuits d'été – his musical career was now essentially a tragic one. He failed to win much recognition, his works were considered eccentric or 'incorrect' and he had reluctantly to rely on journalism for a living; from 1834 he wrote chiefly for the and the Gazette musicale and the Journal des débats .

As the discouragements of Paris increased, however, performances and recognition abroad beckoned: between 1842 and 1863 Berlioz spent most of his time touring, in Germany, Austria, Russia, England and elsewhere. Hailed as an advanced composer, he also became known as a leading modern conductor. He produced literary works (notably the *Mémoires*) and another series of musical masterpieces – *La damnation de Faust*, the *Te Deum*, *L'enfance du Christ*, the vast epic *Les troyens* (1856-8; partly performed, 1863) and *Béatrice et Bénédict* (1860-62) – meanwhile enjoying happy if short-lived relationships with Liszt and Wagner. The loss of his father, his son Louis (1834-67), two wives, two sisters and friends merely accentuated the weary decline of his last years, marked by his spiritual isolation from Parisian taste and the new music of Germany alike.

A lofty idealist with a leaping imagination, Berlioz was subject to violent emotional changes from enthusiasm to misery; only his sharp wit saved him from morbid self-pity over the disappointments in his private and professional life. The intensity of the personality is inextricably woven into the music: all his works reflect something in himself expressed through poetry, literature, religion or drama. Sincere expression is the key – matching means to expressive ends, often to the point of mixing forms and media, ignoring pre-set schemes. In *Les troyens*, his grand opera on Virgil's *Aeneid*, for example, aspects of the monumental and the intimate, the symphonic and the operatic, the decorative and the solemn converge. Similarly his symphonies, from the explicitly dramatic *Symphonie fantastique* with its *idée fixe* (the theme representing his beloved, changed and distorted in line with the work's scenario), to the picturesque *Harold en Italie* with its concerto element, to the operatic choral symphony cum tone poem *Roméo et Juliette*, are all characteristic in their mixture of genres. Of his other orchestral works, the overture *Le carnaval romain* stands out as one of the most extrovert and brilliant. Among the choral works, *Faust* and *L'enfance du Christ* combine dramatic action and philosophic reflection, while the *Requiem* and *Te Deum* exploit to the full Berlioz's most spacious, ceremonial style.

Though Berlioz's compositional style has long been considered idiosyncratic, it can be seen to rely on an abundance of both technique and inspiration. Typical are expansive melodies of irregular phrase length, sometimes with a slight chromatic inflection, and expressive though not tonally adventurous harmonies. Freely contrapuntal textures predominate, used to a variety of fine effects including superimposition of separate themes; a striking boldness in rhythmic articulation gives the music much of its vitality. Berlioz left perhaps his most indelible mark as an orchestrator, finding innumerable and subtle ways to combine and contrast instruments (both on stage and off), effectively emancipating the procedure of orchestration for generations of later composers. As a critic he admired above all Gluck and Beethoven, expressed doubt about Wagner and fought endlessly against the second-rate. **GROVE**music

Symphonie fantastique, Op 14

Symphonie fantastique. Béatrice et Bénédict – Overture
London Symphony Orchestra / Sir Colin Davis
LSO Live LSO0007CD (65' · DDD)   ⑤ⓈⓄⓄ

This LSO performance of the *Symphonie fantastique* is in many ways the subtlest of Davis's four accounts to date, conveying more mystery, with *pianissimo*s of extreme delicacy beautifully caught. There's an overall gain, too, from having a live recording of a work with such an individual structure, with its hesitations and pauses. In overall timings it's marginally longer than earlier versions, maybe also reflecting the conditions of a live performance, even though some of this must have been put together from rehearsal tapes as there's no applause at the end.

The *Béatrice et Bénédict* Overture is taken from the complete recording of the opera on the same label, and makes both a welcome bonus and a tempting sampler. Though the disc comes at super-budget price, it offers splendid notes by David Cairns, author of the definitive, prize-winning biography of the composer.

Symphonie fantastique
Concertgebouw Orchestra / Sir Colin Davis
Philips 50 Great Recordings 464 692-2PM
(55' · ADD) Recorded 1974   ⓂⓄ

Sir Colin Davis's second recording of the *Symphonie fantastique* (an earlier one with the LSO dates from 1963) has remained a first recommendation for a remarkable 27 years. It has acquired excellent rivals in that time but Davis's 1974 reading has withstood all challenges (except possibly for his own – see above).

The *Symphonie fantastique* was in its way as revolutionary a score as Stravinsky's *Rite of Spring*, and the precise ways in which it's so original are apparent throughout this performance. Listen, for example, to the *idée fixe* itself: no one had ever written a melody quite like it before, and Davis's phrasing makes this abundantly clear. The discreet use of the cornet in the second movement makes 'Un bal' a sinister as well as a glittering event, that and Berlioz's way of treating it as though it were a member of the woodwind family; both these are made unassertively obvious. So is the shock, after an apparently tranquil close to the 'Scène aux champs', of the return of the solo oboe, answered now by ominous timpani chords – and Davis makes sure that they're audible as chords, just as he makes you realise how many nervous or spine-chilling quietnesses there are in both the concluding movements. The remastered sound is excellent: indeed, there's nothing that gives away its age.

Symphonie fantastique   Ⓟ
Orchestre Révolutionnaire et Romantique / Sir John Eliot Gardiner
Philips 434 402-2PH (53' · DDD) Recorded 1991   ⒻⓄ

Even if we have here only an approximation to the sounds heard in that first performance, that's a good starting point. Gardiner's reading is in some ways sharper than Norrington's (whose own ground-breaking performance is

BERLIOZ'S SYMPHONIE FANTASTIQUE – IN BRIEF

Lamoureux Orchestra / Igor Markevitch
DG 447 406-2GOR (71' · ADD)   Ⓜ
Of the many recordings with French orchestras, Igor Markevitch's extraordinarily characterful 1961 version with is perhaps the most tangibly idiomatic. A bonus is the remarkably undated sound.

Royal Concertgebouw Orchestra / Sir Colin Davis
Philips 50th 464 692-2PM (56' · ADD)   Ⓜ
Berlioz conducting and playing of abundant pedigree and eloquence from these distinguished artists. Three decades on, this is still a front-runner.

French National Radio Orchestra / Sir Thomas Beecham
EMI 567971-2 (75' · ADD)   Ⓜ
Sir Thomas at his inimitable best: an elegant and exciting interpretation, full of panache. Beecham's thrilling 1958 *Le corsaire* with the RPO provides a cherishable bonus.

Chicago SO / Claudio Abbado
DG 474 165-2GEN (63' · DDD)   Ⓜ
Abbado's imaginative and characterful performance is one of the finest the digital era has yet given us. Stunning orchestral playing; vivid, if not ideally transparent sound.

ORR / Sir John Eliot Gardiner
Philips 434 402-2PH (53' · DDD)   ⒻO
Gardiner brings out the daring originality of Berlioz's visionary inspiration and draws hugely spirited, yet refined playing from his period-instrument band. Exemplary sound and balance, too.

Hallé Orchestra / Sir John Barbirolli
Dutton CDEA5504 (69' · ADD)   Ⓑ
Dating from 1947, a splendidly combustible reading from this magnetic partnership. Barbirolli had a particular affection for this score, and it shows.

London Symphony Orchestra / Sir Colin Davis
LSO Live LSO0007CD (65' · DDD)   ⓈOO
The *Symphonie fantastique* has long been a Davis speciality. Captured live at the Barbican in September 2000, this is Sir Colin's fourth recording of it and arguably his most masterly yet.

available on EMI), and more insistent on detail. This can lead to over-phrasing, though he does almost nothing that can't be justified from Berlioz's intricately, often oddly, marked score. Both performances are of endless fascination and enjoyment. But Gardiner is perhaps more interested in the kind of performance with which Berlioz might have startled his audience that December night in 1830. So the music has an extra emphasis on sudden flicks of phrasing, an extra abruptness in the stamp of a rhythm or the snap of an interrupting chord, a concern for the extreme. Who can tell what the instruments really sounded like? What matters is that we have, to set beside other well-loved performances with a modern orchestra, this one that takes us very close to the sound world out of which Berlioz created a completely new kind of music.

Harold in Italy, Op 16

Harold en Italie. Les troyens – Ballet Music
Tabea Zimmermann va **London Symphony Orchestra / Sir Colin Davis**
LSO Live LSO040 (52' · DDD)   ⓈO

Yet again Sir Colin Davis demonstrates his mastery as a Berlioz interpreter. It's fascinating to compare this latest version of *Harold en Italie* with his 1975 Philips version with Nobuko Imai as soloist, and the 1962 HMV one, no longer available, with Yehudi Menuhin.

Most noticeable is the extra tautness of Davis's interpretation, with speeds consistently faster, sometimes markedly so. The textures are sparer, sharper and lighter, bringing an extra incisiveness all round. The soloist, the magnificent Tabea Zimmermann, is balanced as part of the orchestra instead of being spotlit. The beauty of her tone, with its nut-brown colours on the C-string, is never masked, but at the other end of the spectrum the balance allows *pianissimo*s of a delicacy never achieved by the excellent Nobuko Imai, even though she may well have been playing just as quietly, or by the relaxed and rich-toned Menuhin, who prefers lyrical expansion to urgency.

The fierceness of the *Allegro*s, with their quirky bursts of high dynamic contrasts, is enhanced on the new disc. The first movement, 'Harold in the Mountains', is markedly faster and tauter this time (some 2'30" shorter than with Menuhin), and the more flowing speed for the second movement, 'Pilgrims' March', establishes the feeling of a procession, with the surprisingly gentle dynamic markings meticulously observed. Though the third movement 'Serenade' the skipping rhythms are infectious, with dotted rhythms sparklingly pointed by the oboists at the start, and the 'Brigands' Orgy' of the finale clearly gains in dramatic flair from the extra incisiveness.

The Ballet Music, taken from Davis's prize-winning LSO Live version of *Les troyens* makes an atmospheric bonus. It's marvellous that such wonders can come on a super-budget disc, complete with authoritative notes by David Cairns.

Harold in Italy. Tristia, Op 18   **P**
Gérard Caussé va **Monteverdi Choir; Orchestre Révolutionnaire et Romantique / Sir John Eliot Gardiner**
Philips 446 676-2PH (60' · DDD) Recorded 1994. Text and translation included   ⒻOO

It's to Gardiner's credit that, like Davis, he conveys that element of wildness without ever slackening control. With Gardiner dynamic contrasts are extreme, far more strikingly so than in most period-instrument performances, and some of the *pianissimos* from the ORR strings are ravishing. The central *Canto religioso* of the second movement of the Pilgrims' hymn provides a remarkable instance, with the arpeggios *sul ponticello* of the solo viola far more eerie than usual. Gardiner's soloist, Gérard Caussé, uses vibrato sparingly. Yet for the smooth phrases of Harold's theme, the work's motto, Caussé consciously produces warm tone. It's a fine solo performance, but not so dominant that the lack of a soloist is felt in the last three-quarters of the finale. It's there that Gardiner's reading, intense from the start, reaches white heat, and it's worth noting that there, as in the rest of the performance, his speeds are never excessively fast. Altogether a thrilling performance, highly recommendable to those who would not normally consider a version with period instruments.

Gardiner gives equally refreshing performances in *Tristia*. The epilogue to the 'Hamlet Funeral March', the third of the three movements, is the more chilling and broken in mood for the extreme hush of the *pianissimo*.

Harold in Italy. Le corsaire – Overture.   **H**
King Lear – Overture[a]. Trojan March
Frederick Riddle va **Royal Philharmonic Orchestra;** [a]**BBC Symphony Orchestra / Sir Thomas Beecham**
BBC Legends/IMG Artists mono BBCL4065-2 (72' · ADD) Recorded live [a]1956, [b]1951,[c]1954, [d]1951   ⓂOO

These radio recordings of Beecham in full flight could not be more welcome. The mono sound is limited but beefy and immediate, with fine transfers by Paul Baily, even though the opening *Corsaire* Overture is taken from an acetate disc, not a tape. What above all hits you hard from first to last is that Beecham in such live performances of Berlioz conveyed a manic intensity, a red-blooded thrust that brings out to the full the characterful wildness in this ever-original composer, making almost any rival seem cool.

So, the *Corsaire* Overture has a fierceness and thrust entirely apt to the Byronic subject, culminating in a swaggering climax that verges on the frenetic. It will have you laughing with joy. You find a similar approach in Beecham's studio performances of this overture, but this is even more

uninhibited in its excitement. *King Lear* – with the BBC Symphony Orchestra, not the RPO – surges with warmth in the lyrical first half, before similarly building excitement in the *Allegro*.

Harold in Italy, recorded in 1956 in the dry acoustic of the Usher Hall, Edinburgh, with the dynamic range compressed so as to magnify *pianissimos*, as at the very start, is specially valuable for having as soloist Beecham's chosen leader of his viola section, Frederick Riddle. It was Riddle who made the first recording of the Walton Viola Concerto in 1937 with the composer conducting, arguably still the finest ever interpretation, and here his expressive warmth and responsiveness to Beecham's volatile inspiration make up for the sort of intonation problems that the viola at that period always seemed to invite, even with players of this calibre. The pauseful tenderness of the *Adagio* section just after the start of the finale, is similarly magnetic, thanks to both conductor and soloist, bringing out the parallel in the review of themes with the finale of Beethoven's Ninth. The *Trojan March* makes a swaggering encore, a performance more electrifying for being recorded at the opening concert of the Colston Hall in Bristol in 1951.

Roméo et Juliette, Op 17

Roméo et Juliette
Daniela Barcellona mez **Kenneth Tarver** ten **Orlin Anastassov** bass **London Symphony Chorus and Orchestra / Sir Colin Davis**
LSO Live LSO0003CD (99' · DDD)   ⓈⓈOO

This recording of Berlioz's masterpiece builds in important ways on what Sir Colin has revealed to us in his two previous versions, both for Philips, and preserves what by any reckoning was an electrifying event at the Barbican. The recording was edited from two separate concerts, so ironing out irritating flaws of the moment, while offering the extra dramatic thrust of a live performance. That's most strikingly illustrated in the concluding chorus, a passage that has often been felt to let the rest of the work down, but which here provides an incandescent climax, silencing any doubts. That said, the differences between this live recording and Davis's two studio ones are less a question of interpretation than of recording balance and quality. Davis's view of the work has remained fundamentally unchanged, though his speeds at the Barbican are marginally broader until the concluding sections from Juliet's funeral onwards, which now flow more easily. The live recording may not match in opulence either the 1993 one with the Vienna Philharmonic or the 1968 one with the LSO, for the Barbican acoustic is drier. Yet the refinement of the sound this time, with orchestra and chorus set at a slight distance, brings *pianissimos* of breathtaking delicacy, focused in fine detail. Not only the Love scene but the choral recitatives gain greatly from that, as does the lovely passage before the Love scene where the Capulets return home after the party. The three young soloists are first-rate, characterising strongly. It will be a pity if having this on the LSO Live label, with its limited availability, reduces its circulation, yet everyone will appreciate the benefit of getting such a fine modern recording at so reasonable a price.

Overtures

Overtures – Les francs-juges, Op 3. Waverley, Op 1. King Lear, Op 4. Le carnaval romain, Op 9. Béatrice et Bénédict. Le corsaire, Op 21. Benvenuto Cellini
Staatskapelle Dresden / Sir Colin Davis
RCA Victor Red Seal 09026 68790-2 (74' · DDD)Ⓕ**OO**

Berlioz's seven overtures fit comfortably into an hour and a quarter, in performances that reflect Sir Colin's long absorption with music that remains difficult, original, surprising. The most extrovert, the Ball Scene in *Le carnaval romain*, is exhilaratingly played, but done so without the strenuous attempts after excitement at all costs, through speed and volume, which are all too familiar. The music is more interesting than that, its tensions more dramatic. What are perhaps the two hardest overtures to play successfully, *Waverley* and *King Lear*, benefit from some understatement, especially in the quieter sections when, particularly in *Lear*, a sense of trouble animates the music. As elsewhere, Berlioz's melodies made out of awkward rhythms and uneven metres call for a skilled hand: nowhere is this more evident than at the opening of *Benvenuto Cellini*, whose oddity doesn't immediately strike the listener but whose 'rightness' is proved by its wonderful verve. Davis handles this superbly, as in different vein he does the soft music answering the opening of *Le carnaval romain*, in which he's given some beautiful playing (especially from the cor anglais) by the Dresden orchestra. It responds to his understanding of the different levels of tension and expression, as well as different dynamic levels, at which Berlioz can make his effects, such as at the start of *Les francs-juges*. Sometimes a slight emphasis in the accompaniment, even the touch of warmth on a single note, can illuminate much in the melody. It's all beautifully done.

Benvenuto Cellini – Overture. Le carnaval romain. Le corsaire. Béatrice et Bénédict – Overture. Les Troyens – Chasse royale et orage. Symphonie fantastique. Roméo et Juliette – Queen Mab Scherzo. Les nuits d'été[a]
[a]**Victoria de los Angeles** *sop* **Boston Symphony Orchestra / Charles Munch**
RCA Red Seal Artistes et Répertoires ②
74321 84587-2 (129' · ADD) Recorded 1955-62   Ⓜ

Munch's Berlioz is a set to cherish, less for the *Symphonie fantastique* (fine though that is; prop-

erly volatile), as for the Overtures and shorter pieces, the performances electric with energy, and dispatched with an élan that's at once French in spirit but emphatically transatlantic in execution. Given the mostly fine sound in this set – especially the astonishing width and depth of the image in 'The Royal Hunt and Storm' – it's a shame that stereo tapes do not appear to exist of the 1955 sessions for *Les nuits d'été*. Still, for a marriage of style and content, it remains a benchmark – Victoria de los Angeles with all the vocal range, and variety of expression needed for these songs.

Additional recommendation

Overtures: Le carnaval romain. Le corsaire. Les   Ⓗ
francs-juges. King Lear. Les Troyens – Act 3 Prelude; March. Waverley
Royal Philharmonic Orchestra / Beecham
Sony Classical SMK89807 (69' · ADD) Recorded 1950s
Ⓜ
Astonishing performances. All are played with a wonderful shaping of phrases and with a fiery attack and zest that are utterly satisfying.

Grande messe des morts, Op 5

Grande messe des morts, Op 5[a]. Te Deum, Op 22[b]
[a]**Ronald Dowd,** [b]**Franco Tagliavini** *tens* [b]**Nicolas Kynaston** *org* **Wandsworth School Boys' Choir; London Symphony Chorus and Orchestra / Sir Colin Davis**
Philips 50 Great Recordings ② 464 689-2PM2
(144' · ADD) Recorded 1969. Texts and translations included   Ⓜ**OO**

The similarities between these two great choral works – the monumental style and blend of austerity and brilliance – make them an ideal coupling. Both are tremendous sonic showpieces, and although Sir Colin Davis's Berlioz cycle dates back over 30 years, the performances remain among the front runners.

The key is Davis's ability to concentrate on the inner meaning of the music, rather than its outward effects. In the *Grande messe des morts*, conductors as various as Maazel, Levine and Ozawa have failed to see any more than generalised beauty and grandeur, but Davis is always alive to the specific emotion of the moment, whether it's the pleading of the 'Quaerens me' or the angular pain of the 'Lacrymosa'. His chorus is stretched, especially in the underweight tenor section (Berlioz prescribes 60 tenors, adding helpfully that the numbers may be doubled or tripled if space permits) and Ronald Dowd isn't entirely comfortable in the solo part of the 'Sanctus'. But in all other respects this is a high-quality performance of vision and imagination.

The splendid *Te Deum* is given a performance of comparable virtues, and Philips' natural sound stands up well to recent competition.

Grande messe des morts   Ⓗ
Richard Lewis ten **Royal Philharmonic Chorus and Orchestra / Sir Thomas Beecham**
BBC Music Legends mono BBCL4011-2
(78' · ADD) Recorded live 1959. Text and translation included   Ⓜ︎Ⓞ

Almost 60 years to the day since his first Berlioz performance, Beecham conducted the *Grande messe des morts* in the Albert Hall. Though the *Dies irae* thunders out tremendously, and the 'Lachrymosa' has a wonderful snap on the off-beat chords, it's the quieter movements that characterise what's, after all, a Requiem Mass. Beecham's response to them is with a lifetime's devotion to one of the composers who had been closest to his heart. The 'Quid sum miser' has an enchanting clarity; the long, hushed end of the 'Offertoire', as Berlioz lingers over the gently alternating notes that suffuse the invention, is finely judged; the *Sanctus* is eloquently sung by Lewis and the splendid chorus; the return of the opening 'Te decet hymnus', near the close of the whole work, is sublime. Such things aren't achieved without the attention to detail with which Beecham used to complain people did not credit him. How wrong. His orchestral parts were always covered with powerful blue pencil marks and the signature 'TB', so that it was impossible to mistake intentions which players would then shape for him in rehearsal. Here, the detail is exquisite. Occasionally he takes his own view, not Berlioz's, about phrasing; and the orchestra contains not a whiff of an ophicleide. No matter. This is a recording of a great occasion – full in recording, scarcely bothered by audience noise – but also of a marvellous performance.

Te Deum, Op 22

Te Deum
Roberto Alagna ten **Marie-Claire Alain** org **European Union and Maîtrise d'Antony Childrens Choirs; Orchestre de Paris Chorus; Orchestre de Paris / John Nelson**
Virgin Classics 545449-2 (58' · DDD)   ⒻⓄ

The Berlioz *Te Deum* has been relatively neglected on disc in comparison with his other major works. This latest version has John Nelson as an incisive, understanding conductor of Berlioz, revelling in the weight of choral sound, balancing his forces beautifully. He's helped here by fuller, more detailed digital sound than on previous versions.

The organ sound may be less transparent than it might be, but the authentic French timbre of the Cavaillé-Coll organ of the Madeleine in Paris blends beautifully in the ensemble, and Marie-Claire Alain, as you might expect, is the most idiomatic soloist, making her non-French rivals seem rather square by comparison. It makes for luxury casting, too, to have Roberto Alagna as an imaginative, idiomatic tenor soloist in the prayer, 'Te ergo quaesumus', warmly

persuasive and full of temperament.

An additional plus-point for the new issue, even in relation to Sir Colin Davis's now classic version for Philips (see below), isn't only the fuller, more open recorded sound but the interesting bonus provided. The two extra instrumental movements included here were written by Berlioz expressly for performances celebrating victory, both with military overtones. On CD either can easily be left out, yet Berlioz, even at his most populist, never fails to grab the listener's attention.

Additional recommendation

Coupled with: Grande messe des morts
Dowd, Tagliavini tens **Kynaston** org **Wandsworth School Boys' Choir; London Symphony Chorus and Orchestra / C Davis**
Philips 50 Great Recordings ② 464 689-2PM2
(144' · ADD) Recorded 1969   Ⓜ︎ⓄⓄ
    A classic recording and an ideal coupling: these performances remain among the front-runners, though the chorus sounds rather stretched at times. Philips' natural sound quality stands up well (reviewed above under *Grande messe*).

La damnation de Faust, Op 24

La damnation de Faust
Enkelejda Shkosa mez **Giuseppe Sabbatini** ten **David Wilson-Johnson** bar **Michele Pertusi** bass **London Symphony Orchestra and Chorus / Sir Colin Davis**
LSO Live ② LSO0008CD (132' · DDD) Notes, texts and translations included   ⓈⓈⓄⓄ

This *Damnation de Faust* matches and even outshines previous sets at whatever price, not least in the gripping drama of the performance, the more intense for being recorded live. Even more than in his classic 1973 recording for Philips, Davis involves you in the painful quandry obsessing Faust, never letting tension slip for a moment.

There may be different views over Giuseppe Sabbatini's portrayal of the central character. He's more overtly emotional than any of his immediate rivals. In the heat of the moment he tends to resort to an Italianate style, with the hint of a half-sob or the occasional phrase which is only half vocalised. Purists may resist, yet with his firm, golden, finely shaded tone and his radiant treatment of the highest-lying passages the impact is intensely characterful and involving.

As for Davis, the differences between his reading here and in 1973 are ones of detail and refinement, for there's an extra lightness and resilience in the playing of the current LSO, as in Mephistopheles' Flea song, which is more wittily pointed than before. The little snarling flourishes which herald Mephistopheles' arrival have you sitting up immediately, while the excitement generated in a number such as the Trio at the end of Part 3 leaves you breathless. Michele Pertusi as Mephistopheles matches

Sabbatini in the red-blooded fervour of his singing, weighty yet agile, and Enkelejda Shkosa is a warm, vibrant Marguerite, with a flicker in the voice giving a hint of the heroine's vulnerability. Not just the LSO but the London Symphony Chorus, too, are in searing form, and the recording brings out the detail of Berlioz's orchestration with ideal transparency, though the transfer is at rather a low level, needing fair amplifications for full impact. Davis is given wonderfully refined sound, with any problems from the Barbican acoustic completely eliminated. An astonishing bargain.

La damnation de Faust
Susan Graham sop **Thomas Moser** ten **José van Dam** bass-bar **Frédéric Caton** bass; **Chorus and Orchestra of Opéra de Lyon / Kent Nagano**
Erato ② 0630-10692-2 (122' · DDD) Recorded 1994.
Text and translation included   Ⓜ❶

New versions of *Faust* appear regularly, but one as good this is rare. At its centre is a perception of Berlioz's extraordinary vision, in all its colour and variety and humour and pessimism, and the ability to realise this in a broad downward sweep while setting every detail sharply in place. It's a work about the steady failure of consolations in a romantic world rejecting God, until all Faust's sensations are numbed and Mephistopheles has him trapped in the hell of no feeling. Every stage of the progress is mercilessly depicted here. The chorus is brilliant in all its roles, offering in turn the lively charms of peasant life, raptures of faith in the Easter Hymn, beery roistering in Auerbach's Cellar that grows as foul as a drunken party, cheerful student Latin bawls; later they sing with delicacy as Mephistopheles's spirits of temptation and finally become a vicious pack of demons. Nagano takes the Hungarian March at a pace that grows hectic as the dream of military glory turns hollow. It's all brilliantly realised.

There's the same care for orchestral detail. Nagano seems to be conducting from the New Berlioz Edition score, and he uses his imagination with it. He has an unerring sense of tempo, balancing weight of tone against speed, and he can light upon the telling contrapuntal line, or point a detail of instrumental colour or even a single note (like the snarl in the Ride to the Abyss), elements that give Berlioz's marvellous orchestration its expressive quality. José van Dam is outstanding as Mephistopheles, curling his voice round phrases with hideous elegance, relishing the mock-jollity of the Serenade and the Song of the Flea, taunting Faust with lulling sweetness on the banks of the Elbe, yet also disclosing the sadness of the fallen spirit. Thomas Moser sings gravely and reflectively as he's first discovered on the plains of Hungary, and rises nobly to the challenge of the Invocation to Nature, but is almost at his finest in the many recitative passages as he twists and turns in Mephistopheles's grasp. Susan Graham doesn't match these two superb performances but sings

her two arias simply and well. This version sets Nagano among the outstanding Berlioz conductors of the day.

L'enfance du Christ, Op 25

L'enfance du Christ
Jean Rigby mez **John Aler, Peter Evans** tens **Gerald Finley, Robert Poulton** bars **Alastair Miles, Gwynne Howell** basses **St Paul's Cathedral Choir; Corydon Singers and Orchestra / Matthew Best**
Hyperion ② CDA66991/2 (101' · DDD) Recorded 1994. Text and translation included   Ⓕ❶

Best treats *L'enfance du Christ* as overtly operatic, not so much by cast movements or varied microphone placings as by his pacing of the action and by encouraging his artists to throw themselves wholeheartedly into the emotions of the story. He gets off to a tremendous start with a superb reading by a black-voiced Alastair Miles as a Herod haunted by his dream and startled into belligerent wakefulness by the arrival of Polydorus. Later, there's desperate urgency in the appeals for shelter by Joseph (an otherwise gently lyrical Gerald Finley), harshly rebuffed by the chorus. And, throughout, there are spatial perspectives – the soldiers' patrol advancing (from practically inaudible pizzicatos) to centre-stage and going off again; and a beautifully hushed and atmospheric faraway 'Amen' at the end. Balance in general is excellent.

The clear enunciation (in very good French) of nearly everyone is a plus point. The chorus's response to the mood and meaning of words is always alert and sensitive, matched by the nuanced orchestral playing. The scurrying of the Ishmaelite family to help, played really *pianissimo*, is vividly graphic; and their home entertainment on two flutes and a harp, which can mark a drop in the interest, here has great charm. But overall it's Best's pacing which makes this recording distinctive. This recording stands comparison well with its much-praised predecessors.

Messe solennelle

Messe solennelle (also includes revised version   Ⓟ of Resurrexit)
Donna Brown sop **Jean-Luc Viala** ten **Gilles Cachemaille** bar **Monteverdi Choir; Orchestre Révolutionnaire et Romantique / Sir John Eliot Gardiner**
Philips 464 688-2PM (61' · DDD) Recorded live 1993. Text and translation included   Ⓜ❶❶

The reappearance of Berlioz's lost Mass of 1824 is the most exciting musical discovery of modern times. To an incredulous meeting of the New Berlioz Edition in 1992 the General Editor, Hugh Macdonald, announced that a Belgian choirmaster, Frans Moors, had made contact with news of an improbable find in an

Antwerp organ loft. A few days later, Prof Macdonald reported back from Antwerp that this was indeed the *Messe solennelle* which Berlioz claimed to have burnt after a couple of performances. Gardiner with his Monteverdi Choir and Orchestre Révolutionnaire et Romantique gave performances in Bremen, Vienna, Madrid, Rome and Westminster Cathedral. This is a live recording of that last, thrilling occasion.

Why did Berlioz abandon the work? Only the *Resurrexit* was retained, though it was rewritten: both versions are included here. Some of it, but not much, is dull: the *Offertory* and *Sanctus* sit rather stolidly with the rest. He was unfair on what he denounced in an angry scribble on the MS as an 'execrable' fugue. Some is disconcertingly awkward, and Gardiner tells in the notes to this record of his and the singers' and players' confusion – until they all came together and suddenly the music made sense. The best of the work is superb: among this one may count the *Incarnatus*, the *O Salutaris* and the lovely *Agnus Dei*. The latter was too good to lose, and survives in another form in the *Te Deum*. So do other ideas: it was at first disconcerting to hear the chorus singing 'Laudamus te. Benedicimus te' to the Carnival music from *Benvenuto Cellini*, more so than to hear the slow movement of the *Symphonie fantastique* in the beautiful *Gratias*.

Once these and other associations are overcome, the work coheres remarkably well. Yet perhaps it did not do so well enough for Berlioz, and perhaps he was dissatisfied with the conjunction of some rather academic music with ideas that were too original, indeed too beautiful, to make a satisfying whole. Who knows whether he might have been made to think twice about abandoning the work had he heard a performance such as this? In any case, this is a recording of a great musical event, not to be missed.

Cantatas

Herminie[a]. La mort de Cléopâtre[b]. La mort d'Orphée[c]. La mort de Sardanapale[c]
[a]**Michèle Lagrange** *sop* [b]**Béatrice Uria-Monzon** *mez* [c]**Daniel Galvez Vallejo** *ten* **Choeur Régional Nord, Pas de Calais; Lille National Orchestra / Jean-Claude Casadesus**
Naxos 8 555810 (61' · DDD)   Ⓢ

To have on a single disc Berlioz's four attempts at the Prix de Rome, or at least as much of them as survives, was one of the most enjoyable fruits of the bicentenary year. Together they present a vivid portrait of the composer in his twenties, a Janus figure looking at once back to Gluck and forward to the more highly coloured, Romantic products of the mid-19th century. These four works are all the more extraordinary for being based on a format devised by someone else – something Berlioz preferred to avoid after *Benvenuto Cellini*; even here he couldn't resist adding at times to the texts provided.

He tried to destroy *La mort de Sardanapale*, his

prize-winning cantata of 1830, and only its end has survived by accident. Like its predecessors, it deals with an extreme situation. To that extent they all chimed in with Berlioz's natural propensities for shaking and stirring audiences, even to the point of aural discomfort. It's fascinating to find so many features of the mature Berlioz already in place: the ubiquitous diminished sevenths, the hitching up of tonalities by semitones, the love of descending scales (as in the wonderful line for Cléopâtre's 'Il n'en est plus pour moi que l'éternelle nuit', which could be Dido in *Les troyens* some 30 years later). The poetic Berlioz is also in evidence, notably in the beautiful Nature-music that opens *La mort d'Orphée*, his earliest attempt from 1827.

The contribution of the solo singers on this disc belongs more to the 19th century than to the 18th, which is possibly what Berlioz would have wanted. That's to say, all three voices are dramatic in size and style. There's some spreading at the top of all three above *mezzo forte*, but in giving their all they're merely taking a cue from Berlioz's orchestra, which, under Casadesus's firm direction, miraculously already sounds like the Berlioz we know. In softer passages all three are excellent. Perhaps one of the most astonishing things about this music, for anyone who knows anything about French officialdom, isn't that it should have taken Berlioz four attempts to win the prize but that he should ever have won it at all! Nearly two centuries later, it's still shaking and stirring.

Les nuits d'été, Op 7

Berlioz Les nuits d'été[a] **Ravel** Shéhérazade[a]
Debussy Trois chansons de Bilitis[b] **Poulenc**
Banalités[b] – Chansons d'Orkenise; Hôtel[c]. La courte paille[b] – Le carafon; La reine de coeur[c]. Chansons villageoises[b] – Les gars qui vont à la fête. Deux poèmes de Louis Aragon[b]
Régine Crespin *sop* [b]**John Wustman** *pf* [a]**Suisse Romande Orchestra / Ernest Ansermet**
Decca Legends 460 973-2DM (68' · ADD) Recorded [a]1963, [bc]1967. Texts and translations included

Ⓜ**OOO**

Crespin's *Nuits dété* has always been the interpretation by which others have been assessed and, listening to it again, there's no reason to challenge the verdict. In terms of idiomatic and natural French, languorous tone and understanding of the poetry's and the music's meaning, it stands above all other versions without any question. Even Dame Janet Baker's appreciable reading (now available at bargain price on HMV Classics; also on BBC Legends) sounds a trifle affected in its vocal grammar besides Crespin's, particularly as regards the determinedly bright, jolly tone employed by the British artist in the first and last songs, whose joyous moods Crespin encompasses without resort to contrivance. Crespin's tempos are also ideally chosen.

The only drawback to her version is the some-

BERLIOZ LES NUITS D'ÉTÉ – IN BRIEF

Régine Crespin; SRO / Ernest Ansermet
Decca 460 973-2DM (69' · ADD) Ⓜ❍❍❍
☀ The classic recording in which every nuance has been scrupulously articulated. Gorgeous.

Janet Baker; New Philharmonia / Sir John Barbirolli
EMI 562788-2 (78' · ADD) Ⓜ❍❍❍
☀ The version that for many vies with the Crespin. Baker in 1967 is on top form and her rapport with Barbirolli conjures some moments of breathtaking allure.

Janet Baker; LPO / Carlo Maria Giulini
BBC Legends BBCL4077-2 (75' · ADD) Ⓕ❍❍❍
☀ A live recording from 1975 shines a light on different areas than her earlier version – speeds here tend to be quite slow.

Anne Sofie von Otter; Berlin PO / James Levine
DG 445 823-2GH (63' · DDD) Ⓕ
An early von Otter foray into the French repertoire – it's good, but nowhere as full of the insight she customarily brings to the French repertoire these days.

Susan Graham; ROH Orchestra / John Nelson
Sony Classical SK62730 (61' · DDD) Ⓕ❍❍
A wonderfully imaginative, carefully moulded performance: perhaps the most complete interpretation since the celebrated Régine Crespin version. A modern classic.

Diana Montague; Catherine Robbin; Howard Crook; Gilles Cachemaille; Lyon Opera Orchestra / John Eliot Gardiner
Apex 0927 49583-2 (63' · ADD) Ⓑ❍
The most successful of the multi-voice recordings and a set that showed early on (1989) Gardiner's wonderful way with Berlioz. A real bargain, too.

David Daniels; Ensemble Orchestral de Paris / John Nelson
Virgin Classics 545646-2 (69' · DDD) Ⓕ
A reasonably successful countertenor version, but the mezzos generally find more to say in these magical songs.

Isabel Vernet; Laurent Martin pf
Ligia LIDI0201032 (57' · ADD) Ⓑ
One of the handful of recordings with piano uncovers many subtleties and insights.

Brigitte Balleys; Champs-Elysées Orchestra / Philippe Herreweghe
Harmonia Mundi HMC90 1522 (54' · ADD) Ⓕ❍❍
Fine singing, but Herreweghe's control of his French orchestra is a thing of wonder.

times slack accompanying of Ansermet, not that Barbirolli is ideal in that respect. Crespin's *Shéhérazade* is even more in a class of its own than her account of the Berlioz too. As soon as she launches seductively into 'Asie' we know that singer and music are perfectly matched, and the last two songs are even better. As if this weren't enough, we have Crespin's *Chansons de Bilitis* from a later recital, a performance that wonderfully suggests the distant lassitude of poem and music, and a group of Poulenc songs from the same 1969 record of which the sad, elegiac 'C' (*Deux poèmes*) is the plum. Anyone who thinks that some of Crespin's successors fully understand how to interpret *mélodies* must hear this record.

Les nuits d'été. Herminie
Mireille Delunsch sop **Brigitte Balleys** mez
Orchestre des Champs-Elysées, Paris / Philippe Herreweghe
Harmonia Mundi HMC90 1522 (54' · DDD) Recorded 1994. Texts and translations included Ⓕ❍❍

It isn't fanciful to hear decided pre-echoes in *Herminie* of Cassandra's fateful, searing music (quite apart from the dry-run for the *Symphonie fantastique*'s main motif). This extraordinary work of 1828, almost as arresting as its near-contemporary *Cléopâtre*, receives a grand rendering from Mireille Delunsch, who sings it in a compact, direct manner. Her tone is narrow and focused, her French diction clear. Herreweghe and his orchestra adopt a lean sound, surely close to that of Berlioz's time. Delunsch enters into the inner agony of the distraught, frustrated Herminie with a will. Her interpretation is absorbing from start to finish. The recording imparts a slight glare to her tone as it does to that of Balleys in the much more familiar *Nuits d'été*, but that's hardly enough to detract from an idiomatic, unfussy reading. Her voice doesn't luxuriate in the more sensual moments of the cycle as does Régine Crespin's in her famous version (reviewed below) but it has a clarity of profile and a definition of phrase and, where strength of feeling is called for, Balleys provides it, as in 'Au cimetière' and 'Absence'. This makes a sensible pairing with the cantata. What may also influence your choice is, again, Herreweghe's lean, well-pointed support which often emphasises, rightly, the striking originality of Berlioz's scoring.

Les nuits d'été. Benvenuto Cellini – Tra la la ... Mais qu'ai-je donc?. Les Troyens – Je vais mourir ... Adieu, fière cité. Béatrice et Bénédict – Dieu! Que vien-je d'entendre? ... Il m'en souvient. La damnation de Faust – D'amour l'ardente flamme
Susan Graham mez **Royal Opera House Orchestra, Covent Garden / John Nelson**
Sony Classical SK62730 (61' · DDD) Texts and translations included Ⓕ❍❍

It would be hard to imagine a more inspiriting

and rewarding display of Berlioz singing than this from a singer who has the composer's style in her voice and heart. Graham manages to explore and deliver the soul of each of her chosen pieces, her voice – firm yet vibrant, clear yet warm – responding interpretatively and technically to the appreciable demands placed on it. In *Les nuits d'été*, she faces the greatest challenge from revered favourites and meets it head on, catching in almost every respect the varied moods of each song. Her French pronunciation is excellent and she uses the language to evoke the atmosphere of each song without a hint of exaggeration.

The noble dignity of her account of Dido's farewell, in particular at the recollection of the love duet, is deeply moving, and Béatrice's equivocal thoughts about her lover are another triumph. The fleeter, lighter side of Graham's art is caught in the rapturous cabaletta to Béatrice's aria and in Ascanio's excitable aria from *Benvenuto Cellini*, both dispatched securely. Nelson and the LSO provide idiomatic support, and the recording catches the full colour of the singer's performances.

Berlioz Les nuits d'été, Op 7[a] **Chausson** Poème de l'amour et de la mer, Op 19[b] **Schoenberg** Gurrelieder – Song of the Wood Dove[c]
Dame Janet Baker *mez* [a]London Philharmonic Orchestra / Carlo Maria Giulini; [bc]London Symphony Orchestra / [b]Evgeny Svetlanov, [c]Norman del Mar
BBC Legends/IMG Artists BBCL4077-2 (75' · ADD)
Recorded live [a]1975, [b]1975, [c]1963. Notes but no texts ⓕ❍

These three absorbing interpretations are a welcome addition to the growing discography of Dame Janet in live performances, where the *frisson* of a 'real' occasion adds an extra immediacy to her readings. Dame Janet recorded *Nuits d'étés* some 10 years earlier with Barbirolli, when speeds were on the slow side. Here they're even more deliberate, possibly the longest 'Le spectre de la rose' on disc. The extra time allows the singer to bring an even deeper sense of mystery and longing to the four middle songs. Has 'Absence' ever sounded so sad and eloquent? Her ability to control a wide range of dynamic effects is astonishing. Giulini and the LPO couldn't be more supportive.

All the recordings are a tribute to the BBC's recording expertise, giving more presence to the voice than is often the case today. Apart from one disfiguring cough in the Berlioz, the presence of an audience is hardly intrusive.

Les nuits d'été. La mort de Cléopâtre. Zaïde, Op 19 No 1. La captive, Op 12. La belle voyageuse, Op 2 No 5
Véronique Gens *sop* **Lyon National Opera Orchestra / Louis Langrée**
Virgin Classics 545422-2 (61' · DDD) Notes, texts and translations included ⓕ❍

Berlioz specifically asked for a variety of singers for his orchestral version of *Nuits d'été*; yet – apart from a Colin Davis version (Philips) – record companies seem to prefer, for several obvious reasons, a single soloist. In consequence few provide complete satisfaction. This latest of many has two advantages. It's sung by a native French artist and it avoids the excessive weight of several noted readings in the catalogue. Indeed Gens' interpretation in its simple, uncomplicated way, most closely resembles that of Suzanne Danco, a soprano with similar attributes.

Her fresh yet plaintive tone is perfectly apt for the first and last songs, the most airy ones, and in its unassuming manner often catches the longing and lost love expressed in the reflective pieces. What's missing in such a slight soprano is the ability to cope with emotional overtones of such a key moment as 'J'arrive au paradis' in 'Spectre de la rose', where her tone sometimes comes under undue pressure, or to encompass all the sorrow of 'Sur les lagunes'. In that respect, de los Angeles' glorious, more pointed reading (see below), is to be preferred; every word is savoured and projected, with Munch a superb conductor. Here, the orchestral part is rather underplayed yet, over all, this version has its own justification in a true, natural identification with the cycle's melos. Gens again favours a less subjective approach in *Cleopatra's Death*. If you compare Gens with the similarly voiced Anne Pashely (on Davis's mid-price Decca set, reviewed under *L'enfance du Christ*), it's the older artist who goes to the heart of the matter in conveying Cleopatra's desperation and death. Baker is still better at projecting the heroic-cum-tragic ethos of this still-amazing piece. Gens is at her appreciable best in the three separate songs that complete her programme, where her soft-grained, limpid timbre and feeling for line are of the essence.

Additional recommendation

Les nuits d'été 🄷
Coupled with: Symphonie fantastique. Roméo et Juliette – Queen Mab Scherzo. Overtures – Benvenuto Cellini; Béatrice et Bénédict. Le carnaval romain. Le corsaire. Les Troyens – Chasse royale et orage
De los Angeles *sop* **Boston SO / Munch**
RCA Red Seal Artistes et Répertoires
② 74321 84587-2 (129' · ADD) Ⓜ❍❍
De los Angeles' *Nuits d'été* still remains a benchmark by which all others are judged; she has all the vocal range and variety of expression needed for these songs. It's a shame, though, that no stereo tapes exist for these 1955 sessions. The performances of the overtures are electric.

Songs

Mélodies, Op 19 – No 2, Les champs; No 6, Le Chasseur danois. Mélodies, Op 13 – No 1, Le matin; No 2, Petit oiseau, chant de paysan; No 4, Le Jeune

pâtre breton[c]; No 5, Le Chant des Bretons. Mélodies, 'Irlande', Op 2 – Le coucher du soleil; Chant guerrier[b]; La belle voyageuse; Chanson à boire[b]; Chant sacré[a]; L'origine de la harpe; Adieu Bessy; Elégie en prose. Roméo et Juliette, Op 17 – Premiers transports[d]
Jérôme Corréas bass-bar **Arthur Schoonderwoerd** pf with [a]**Claire Brua**, [a]**Marie-Bénénedicte Souquet** sops [b]**Alain Gabriel**, [a]**Jean-Francois Novelli**, [a]**Jean-Francois Lombard** tens [a]**Vincent Deliau** bar [c]**Claude Maury** hn [d]**Christophe Coin** vc
Alpha ALPHA024 (58' · DDD) Texts and translations included   Ⓕ

It's surprising that Berlioz's songs aren't better known. Anyone who thinks *Les nuits d'été* constitutes a summary of his vocal production need only listen to this disc to be disabused. Jérôme Corréas has so far tended to specialise in Baroque music and his dark, warm bass-baritone is surprisingly flexible in its articulation, with an especially tender *mezza voce*. Berlioz's roots aren't generally thought to extend further back than Gluck, but Corréas's well-focused tone and shapely phrasing is ideal for this music. Certainly Berlioz's vocal lines, asymmetrical and often plain weird, have little to do with Viennese Classicism. Corréas embraces the asymmetry, but is ingenious in finding some logic in the composer's most outlandish effusions, and you can hear every word. Arthur Schoonderwoerd draws wonderful sounds from an 1836 Pleyel and in a song like *Elégie en prose* you can sense Duparc in the making. The other supporting artists are all excellent – a particularl joy is Christophe Coin's cello playing in the marvellous 'Premiers transports'. The spacious church acoustic, with up to a three-second echo, isn't ideal, but then traffic-free venues in Paris are hard to find.

Béatrice et Bénédict

Béatrice et Bénédict
Susan Graham sop Béatrice **Jean-Luc Viala** ten Bénédict **Sylvia McNair** sop Héro **Catherine Robbin** mez Ursule **Gilles Cachemaille** bar Claudio **Gabriel Bacquier** bar Somarone **Vincent Le Texier** bass Don Pedro **Philippe Magnant** spkr Léonato **Lyon Opera Chorus and Orchestra / John Nelson**
Erato MusiFrance ② 2292-45773-2 (111' · DDD) Recorded 1991. Notes, text and translation included   ⒻⓄ

We have to note that the title isn't a French version of *Much Ado about Nothing*. Berlioz takes the two principal characters of Shakespeare's play and constructs an opera around them. The comedy centres on the trick that is played on the pair by their friends, producing love out of apparent antipathy. Much of the charm lies in the more incidental matters of choruses, dances, the magical 'Nocturne' duet for Béatrice and Héro, and the curious addition of the character Somarone, a music-master who rehearses the choir in one of his own compositions. There's also a good deal of spoken dialogue. Perhaps

surprisingly, the extra dialogue is a point in its favour, for it's done very effectively by good French actors and it makes for a cohesive, Shakespearian entertainment. John Nelson secures a well-pointed performance of the score, and with excellent playing by the Lyon Orchestra. Susan Graham and Jean-Luc Viala are attractively vivid and nimble in style, and Sylvia McNair makes a lovely impression in Héro's big solo. The veteran Gabriel Bacquier plays the music-master with genuine panache and without overmuch clownage. There's good work by the supporting cast and the chorus and the recording is finely produced.

Benvenuto Cellini

Benvenuto Cellini
Gregory Kunde ten Benvenuto Cellini **Laurent Naouri** bass Balducci **Jean-François Lapointe** bass Fieramosca **Patrizia Ciofi** sop Teresa **Joyce Di Donato** mez Ascanio **Radio France Chorus; French National Orchestra / John Nelson**
Virgin Classics ③ 545706-2 (3h 8' · DDD · S/T/t/N). Recorded live at the Salle Olivier Messiaen, Paris, November 2003   ⒻⓄ

Thanks to to Hugh Macdonald's brilliant work for the *New Berlioz Edition* the 1838 Paris Opéra version of *Benvenuto Cellini* is once again performable; this adds almost half an hour's music to the Colin Davis recording of 1972 (Philips, nla). It's a splendid achievement. Macdonald's notes are an exemplary guide to the music's youthful genius, and David Cairns's original translation for the Davis recording is augmented by Lisa Hobbs, alongside the French.

Each of the singers responds with a quick understanding to the unexpected, eloquent contours of the recitatives, none more so than Gregory Kunde, who can phrase elegantly Cellini's wistful aria longing for a shepherd's simple life, but also prove an ardent suitor for Teresa, and challenge his adversaries with an heroic, defiant *brio*. Patrizia Ciofi can sound a little timid for him, and for Teresa's light vivacity, though she sings fluently and gracefully. Jean-François Lapointe characterises the devious Fieramosca wittily, and joins the the other two cleverly in the brilliant *tour de force* of their trio. There's a high-spirited performance of Ascanio from Joyce Di Donato that includes witty imitations of the men, and Laurent Naouri vigorously struts his hour on the stage as Teresa's father Balducci.

Berlioz's reckless demands on the orchestra are brilliantly answered. The recording engineers have done extraordinarily well in conveying so much detail even when matters are hurtling full tilt in the Roman Carnival scene and in the final casting of the Perseus. John Nelson steers it all with a sure hand and total conviction. 'Never again will I recapture such verve and vitality,' Berlioz wrote of the opera: here indeed is that verve and vitality.

Les Troyens

Les Troyens
Ben Heppner ten Enée **Michelle DeYoung** mez
Didon **Petra Lang** mez Cassandre **Sara Mingardo**
mez Anna **Peter Mattei** bar Chorèbe **Stephen
Milling** bass Narbal **Kenneth Tarver** ten Iopas **Toby
Spence** ten Hylas **Orlin Annastassov** bass Ghost of
Hector **Tigran Martirossian** bass Panthée **Isabelle
Cals** mez Ascagne **Alan Ewing** bass Priam **Guang
Yang** mez Hécube **Andrew Greenan** bass First
sentry **Roderick Earle** bass Second sentry **Bülent
Bezdüz** ten Hélénus **Leigh Melrose** bass A Trojan
soldier/Mercure **Mark Stone** bar A Greek Chieftain
**London Symphony Chorus and Orchestra /
Sir Colin Davis**
LSO Live ④ LSO0010 (240' · DDD)   💲 ⑤ ❍❍❍

Colin Davis's 1969 recording remains a landmark event, the first time this grand opera of Meyerbeerian length, spectacular *éclat* and Wagnerian artistic ambition had found its way complete onto LP. It effectively changed views about Berlioz the opera composer and orchestral genius and has for many remained the yardstick by which all later performances have been judged. Although studio recorded, it was based on the Covent Garden casting of the day – Jon Vickers' heroic Enée and Josephine Veasey's voluptuous Didon – with a couple of Frenchmen to boost the ranks of lesser Trojans and Carthaginians.

The tantalising glimpses of Régine Crespin's Cassandre and Didon belong to a now lost tradition which none of the singing on the new LSO disc quite emulates – with the possible exception of the delightful young French mezzo Isabelle Cals as Ascagne. Part for part, however, the LSO have assembled a cast which challenges without comprehensively surpassing that of the earlier Davis recording. Some of the *comprimario* singers are without doubt their predecessors' superiors: the handsome-voiced Peter Mattei is a nobler-toned, more youthful and romantic-sounding Chorèbe in his fraught interview with his 'vierge adorée', Cassandre; Sara Mingardo's sumptuous contralto is luxury casting for Didon's sister beside the admirable but plain Heather Begg. And as the Carthaginian court poet, Iopas, Kenneth Tarver's tone catches the microphone just that bit more sweetly than Ian Partridge's.

Any account of *Les Troyens*, however, stands or falls by the casting of the three central characters – Cassandre, Enée and Didon – and this the LSO has done with exceptional results. Michelle DeYoung was originally assigned Cassandre, but was 'promoted' to Didon when Olga Borodina fell ill. Her replacement as Cassandre, the German dramatic mezzo Petra Lang, was a revelation at the Barbican, a passionate prophetess, thrilling in her imprecations against the Greeks and heroic in her suicide as Troy is consumed in flames at the close of Act 2. Her French has a slightly 'thick' Germanic flavour, but she makes every word tell and she has the grand rhetorical manner Berlioz learned from Gluck and Cherubini to the manner born.

It's hard to imagine today – vocally at least –a more musical, more romantic, more impetuous Enée than Ben Heppner who brings real stylish distinction and heroic bravura to bear. Michelle DeYoung's Didon isn't quite so successful. Her big, bright-toned voice is less warm than Veasey's and she has a tendency to 'yowl' on climactic notes. She doesn't really convey Didon's regal bearing either: her imperiousness is that of a bossy housekeeper rather than a great founding Queen. That said, she rises to a magnificent 'Adieu, fier cité' and works herself into a Medea-like rage when she threatens to serve a dismembered Ascagne as her perjured lover's dinner.

What really makes this issue indispensable is Davis's conducting of an LSO on incandescent form. The 'world's greatest Berlioz conductor' seems to become ever more convinced of the greatness of this astonishing score and revels, with greater conviction than ever, in its magical orchestral effects and its grand theatrical rhetoric. For Davis and his orchestra – and the splendid immediacy of the live recording – this account of *Les Troyens* is first choice at any price. This set is a must-buy.

Françoise Pollet sop Dido **Gary Lakes** ten Aeneas
Deborah Voigt sop Cassandra **Gino Quilico** bar
Corebus **Hélène Perraguin** mez Anna **Jean-Philippe
Courtis** bass Narbal **Michel Philippe** bass Pantheus
Catherine Dubosc sop Ascanius **Jean-Luc Maurette**
ten Iopas **René Shirrer** bar Priam's ghost, First
Soldier **Claudine Carlson** mez Hecuba **John Mark
Ainsley** ten Hylas **Marc Belleau** bass Hector's ghost,
Second Soldier, Greek Captain **Gregory Cross** ten
Sinon **Michel Beuachemin** bass Mercury **Montreal
Symphony Chorus and Orchestra / Charles Dutoit**
Decca ④ 443 693-2DH4 (238' · DDD) Recorded
1993. Notes, text and translation included   ⓕ❍❍

Davis's first *Les Troyens* remained unchallenged for a quarter of a century. Then Dutoit and the Montreal Symphony Orchestra established themselves as second to none in the French repertory. Add to that a largely French-speaking cast, on balance even more sensitive and tonally more beautiful than for Davis's 1969 account, and the strengths of this set become clear.

The contrasts between Dutoit's and Davis's interpretations are quickly established. Dutoit launches in at high voltage, more volatile than Davis, conveying exuberance consistently preferring faster speeds. The advantage of his faster speeds comes not just in thrilling *Allegros*, but in flowing *Andantes*. So Cassandra's first solo is more persuasively moulded at a flowing rate, with Deborah Voigt far warmer than Berit Lindholm for Davis, both in her beauty of tone and in her *espressivo* phrasing. In 'La prise de Troie' such a moment as the clash of arms within the Trojan horse comes over more dramatically with Dutoit thanks to his timing, and there's more mystery before the arrival of Hector's ghost at the beginning of Act 2.

The role of Cassandra's lover, Corebus, is taken by Gino Quilico, in rich, firm voice. As Aeneas Gary Lakes is an old hand in this role. His big advantage over Jon Vickers, most of all in the great love scene with Dido in Act 3, is that he shades his voice far more subtly. Though the role of Dido very often goes to a mezzo, here Decca firmly opts for a soprano, Françoise Pollet, who sings consistently with full, even tone, so that, matching Dutoit's expressiveness and the richness of the Montreal sound, she brings out the feminine sensuousness of the role more than a mezzo normally would.

Dutoit's degree of rhythmic freedom throughout intensifies the controlled frenzy behind much of the most dramatic writing, and Dido's hysteria is tellingly conveyed. There's barely a weak link in the rest of the huge cast. As for the chorus, though on balance the Covent Garden Chorus for Davis sings with even crisper ensemble, the passionate commitment of the Montreal Chorus matches the fire of Dutoit's reading. This is a thrilling set, confidently recorded, which will have you marvelling at the electric vitality of Berlioz's inspiration.

Additional recommendation

Ferrer Didon, Cassandre **Giraudeau** Enée   Ⓗ
Cambon Chorèbe, Narba **BBC Theatre Chorus;**
Royal Philharmonic Orchestra / Beecham
Malibran-Music mono ③ CDRG162 (226' · ADD)
Broadcast 1947   Ⓟ❍❍❍

One of the most important documents ever to appear from previously unavailable archives. Beecham is at least Davis's peer here. An arresting, inspiriting performance, which has the benefit of a superb French cast.

Lord Berners   British 1883-1950

English composer, writer and painter Lord Berners was essentially self-taught. He was honorary attaché in Rome (1911-19), where he came to know Stravinsky and Casella. In 1919 he succeeded to the barony, and thereafter was an eccentric English gentleman. His early works are mostly small and ironical (chiefly songs and piano pieces), close to Les Six; later he wrote ballets, including The Triumph of Neptune (1926), Luna Park (1930) and A Wedding Bouquet (1936).   GROVEmusic

Songs / Solo piano works

Polka. Le poisson d'or. Dispute entre le papillon et le crapaud. Trois petites marches funèbres. Fragments psychologiques. March. The expulsion from Paradise. Valse. Lieder Album[a]. Trois chansons[a]. Three English Songs[a]. Dialogue between Tom Filuter and his man by Ned the Dog Stealer[a]. Three Songs[a]. Red Roses and Red Noses[a]. Come on Algernon[a]
[a]**Ian Partridge** ten **Len Vorster** pf

Marco Polo 8 225159 (52' · DDD) Texts and translations included   Ⓕ

The minuscule, dejected, lovelorn *Le poisson d'or*, based on Lord Berners' own poem, has a distant Debussian inheritance, while the *Trois petites marches* and *Fragments psychologiques* are Satie-esque, and not just for their bizarre titles. Yet they, too, have a distinct avant-garde precocity, and 'Un soupir' (the third of the *Fragments*) brings a pensive dolour all its own. Berners' sense of fun erupts in the simulated German *Lieder Album* (the seriousness underpinned with a twinkle), and the French *Trois chansons* are naturally idiomatic, with 'La fiancée du timbalier' engagingly light-hearted. The English songs are most winning. *Tom Filuter*'s dialogue changes mood chimerically, and the *Three Songs* of 1921 are like a re-discovery of the English folksong idiom, while the sentimental *Red Roses and Red Noses* has an endearingly flowing lyrical line. It's followed by the irrepressible *Come on Algernon*, about the insatiable Daisy, who always 'asked for more!', a perfect music-hall number, written for the film *Champagne Charlie*. It makes a delightful pay-off to end the recital. Ian Partridge obviously relishes all the stylistic changes like a vocal chameleon, while Len Vorster backs him up splendidly and is completely at home in the solo piano music. Berners' vignettes ought to be featured more often in recital programmes.

Le carrosse du Saint-Sacrement

Le carrosse du Saint-Sacrement[a]. Fanfare[b] Caprice péruvien[c]
[a]**Ian Caddy** bass Viceroy; [a]**Alexander Oliver** ten Martinez; [a]**John Winfield** ten Balthasar; [a]**Cynthia Buchan** mez La Périchole; [a]**Thomas Lawlor** bar Thomas d'Esquivel; [a]**Anthony Smith** bass Bishop of Lima; [a]**BBC Scottish Symphony Orchestra / Nicholas Cleobury;** [b]**Royal Ballet Sinfonia / Gavin Sutherland;** [c]**RTE Sinfonietta / David Lloyd-Jones**
Marco Polo 8 225155 (79' · DDD) Recorded [a]1983, [c]1995, [b]1999 Notes, text and translation included   Ⓕ

Berners' one-act was neglected after its 1924 Paris première under Ansermet until the BBC Radio 3 revival in 1983, which is issued here for the first time. The libretto is adapted from a short story by Mérimée, also used in Offenbach's *La Périchole*. The attractive score has such Berners fingerprints as the rhythms of his cynical 'Funeral March for a Rich Aunt' and Spanish effects, daringly close to Chabrier, to suit the Peruvian setting. The leading lady, La Périchole, is a young actress carrying on with the jealous, gout-ridden Viceroy. Their extended duet in Scene 4 develops as a fascinating alliance of scoundrels. At the end of it, she prises the Viceroy's brand-new coach out of him so she can parade in it to the cathedral and eclipse her rivals in Lima. After a spectacular ride, including a collision, she upstages everyone by giving the carriage to the church to take the sacrament to the dying. Chris de Souza's excellent radio production used a translation by Adam Pollock of the French libretto. The diction of all the characters is clear: everyone is well cast, especially Cynthia Buchan and Ian Caddy. The *Caprice péruvien* is a later compilation based on music from the opera. Both orchestras are adequate, decently recorded, but above all *Le carrosse* is an enchanting discovery in British comic opera.

Leonard Bernstein   American 1918-1990

Bernstein studied at Harvard and the Curtis Institute and was a protégé of Koussevitzky. In 1944 he made his reputation as a conductor when he stepped in when Bruno Walter was ill; thereafter he was associated particularly with the Israel PO (from 1947), the Boston SO and the New York PO (musical director, 1958-69), soon achieving an international reputation, conducting in Vienna and at La Scala. During his tenure the New York PO flourished as never before. A gifted pianist, he often performed simultaneously as soloist and conductor. At the same time, he pursued a career as a composer, cutting across the boundaries between high and popular culture in his mixing of Mahler and Broadway, Copland and Bach. His theatre works are mostly in the Broadway manner: they include the ballet Fancy Free (1944) and the musicals Candide (1956) and West Side Story (1957). His more ambitious works, many of them couched in a richly chromatic, intense post-Mahlerian idiom, often have a religious inspiration, for example the 'Jeremiah' Symphony with mezzo (1942), 'Kaddish', with soloists and choirs (1963) and the theatre piece Mass (1971).

GROVEmusic

Symphonies

Symphony No 1, 'Jeremiah'[a]. Concerto for Orchestra, 'Jubilee Games'[b]
[a]**Helen Medlyn** *mez* [b]**Nathan Gunn** *bar* **New Zealand Symphony Orchestra / James Judd**
Naxos 8 559100 (55' · DDD)   Ⓢ

In life, Leonard Bernstein ran into criticism for programming his own concert music. Now he's gone, it seems we can't get enough of it – and in a variety of performance styles. Latterday champions such as Michael Tilson Thomas and Marin Alsop still go for the idiomatic jugular. Less extrovert interpreters – David Zinman and Kent Nagano spring to mind – downplay the bravado to discover a fresher transparency. On this disc James Judd, British-born but for many years Florida-based, seems closer to the second camp while remaining remarkably faithful to the composer's own overall timings in both pieces.

Keeping a stiff upper lip isn't an option in the Concerto for Orchestra, one of Bernstein's most exploratory and frankly uneven scores. Some of its music is very beautiful, though it

isn't easy to see what it has to do with the rest. Judd sometimes trumps the composer's own wilder performance with his paler, more neutral tone.

Competition is fiercer in the coupling. The *scherzo* of the *Jeremiah*, rowdy, raw and rhetorical in the composer's New York recording, is brought that much closer to the symphonic mainstream here, the New Zealand winds relatively polite and in tune. The portentous, hieratic tendencies of the last movement may even be less apparent when the singer is an Australasian crossover artist rather than the customary *grande dame*. The sonorities are lighter and the voltage a little lower than you might be used to. A genuine bargain even so, with recorded sound way ahead of the super-budget norm. There are full if not always felicitously expressed notes. Newcomers needn't hesitate.

Bernstein Symphony No 2, 'The Age of Anxiety'
Bolcom Piano Concerto
Marc-André Hamelin *pf* **Ulster Orchestra / Dimitry Sitkovetsky**
Hyperion CDA67170 (59' · DDD)   Ⓕ

After Hamelin's fantastic virtuosity in the outrageously difficult Godowsky *Studies on Chopin's Etudes* (for which he won the *Gramophone* Instrumental Award 2000) these two works for piano and orchestra are – for him – mere bagatelles. But this is an impressive release since it contains the most convincing account of Bernstein's Symphony No 2 (1949) in recent years, benefiting from a richer sound than Kahane under Litton.

The whole piece is Bernstein's obsessive response to Auden's poem *The Age of Anxiety*, published the year before, about four characters struggling to sort themselves out in New York City. Even though Auden apparently disliked it, you can increasingly hear Bernstein's Symphony as saturated with the poem, its ideas and atmosphere. Often programmatic, it represents a particularly original approach to piano and orchestra and is personal in countless ways – the gentleness of the soft opening and its mystical descending scale, the precisely engineered variations, memorable tunes, a splendid jazzy *Scherzo* and so on. Hamelin and the Ulster Orchestra in fine form under Sitkovetsky deliver a well-paced and cogent performance right up to the deliberately inflated, optimistic ending.

Bolcom is one of the most idiosyncratic American composers of the next generation. His 1976 Piano Concerto draws widely on various types of popular music, which he's always performed superbly. The Concerto was written in memory of his teacher, Milhaud, who'd have loved it. The opening movement is captivatingly serene until the blue notes get out of hand; the slow movement is more stable and serious; but the finale comes over as a riotous celebration of Americana. Unfortunately Bolcom intended it to be ironic, as a kind of anti-bicentennial tribute. But tunes like these have a habit of occupying centre-stage on their own terms. Hamelin is again utterly scrupulous and idiomatic, and delivers all the musical styles with supreme confidence – nobody could have mixed them up like Bolcom.

Fancy Free

Candide – Overture. West Side Story – Symphonic Dances. On the Waterfront – Symphonic Suite. Fancy Free
New York Philharmonic Orchestra / Leonard Bernstein
Sony Classical Bernstein Century SMK63085
(69' · ADD) Recorded 1960-63 Ⓜ ⦿⦿

These performances have long been considered definitive. All but *Fancy Free* were taped in New York's Manhattan Center in the early 1960s, a problematic venue in which the original sound engineers sought to reconcile the close-miking of individual sections and sometimes individual players with a substantial reverberation period. The results have a synthetic, larger-than-life quality which suits most of the music here. The exception is the Overture to *Candide*, a more driven sort of reading, the brashness of Broadway insufficiently tempered by the rapid figurations of Rossini, the academicism of Brahms, the *joie de vivre* of Offenbach: subtler details tend to disappear into a fog of resonance. In the Symphonic Dances from *West Side Story*, the players eschew the customary shouts in the 'Mambo' but it's doubtful whether there will ever be a more idiomatic reading of what was then essentially 'new music'. The score, by no means a straightforward 'greatest hits' selection, had only recently been unveiled, with Lukas Foss conducting, at a gala concert intended to raise funds for the New York Philharmonic pension fund. Here certainly was the 'aura of show business' which so irked Harold Schonberg, the influential music critic of the *New York Times*: Bernstein's own recording from March 6th has the quality of an unanswerable rejoinder. *On the Waterfront* is if anything even more intense, its lyrical core dispatched with an overwhelming ardour. Last up is what's almost the best of all possible *Fancy Free*s. It was originally sung in inimitable style by Billie Holiday.

Chichester Psalms

Chichester Psalms[a]. Symphony No 1, 'Jeremiah'[b] Symphony No 2, 'The Age of Anxiety'[c]
[b]**Christa Ludwig** *sop* [c]**Lukas Foss** *pf* [a]**Vienna Jeunesse Choir;** [abc]**Israel Philharmonic Orchestra / Leonard Bernstein**
DG The Originals 457 757-2 (ADD) Recorded 1977.
Texts included Ⓜ

The psalms concerned here are equally part of Jewish and Christian tradition. If elsewhere

Bernstein the prophet may sometimes have been the enemy of Bernstein the composer, then he's no longer here. The burning intensity of the music here finds its natural voice – it's also a marvellously rewarding one. The soloists – piano, soprano, boy treble, speaker – could hardly be bettered; the choral singing is strong; and the recording is of the very best, keeping the diverse forces in excellent balance. In the end only music is the truly universal language; it's one that Bernstein speaks very movingly. The two symphonies form a very useful and equally well-played coupling. Highly recommended, particularly at this price.

Bernstein Chichester Psalms **Barber** Agnus Dei, Op 11 **Copland** In the Beginning. Four Motets – Help us, O Lord; Have mercy on us, O my Lord; Sing ye praises to our King
Dominic Martelli *treb* **Catherine Denley** *mez* **Rachel Masters** *hp* **Gary Kettel** *perc* **Thomas Trotter** *org* **Corydon Singers / Matthew Best**
Hyperion CDA66219 (54 minutes) Recorded 1986.
Texts included Ⓕ

Half of this programme is devoted to unaccompanied choral music by Copland: *In the Beginning*, a striking 15-minute 'Creation' for mixed four-part chorus and solo mezzo (which is eloquently executed by Catherine Denley) written in 1947, and three of four short motets he composed in 1921, while studying with Nadia Boulanger in Paris. The performance of the *Chichester Psalms* recorded here uses Bernstein's own reduced (but very effective) instrumentation of organ, harp and percussion, but follows the composer's New York precedent in employing a mixed chorus – although the illusion of a cathedral choir is persuasively conveyed. It's very impressive.

The singing of the Corydon Singers under Matthew Best is very fine, and the vivid recording, which gives the voices a pleasant bloom while avoiding the resonance of King's College Chapel, reproduces the instrumental accompaniment, notably the percussion, with electrifying impact. Best's soloist is Dominic Martelli, and very sweetly he sings too. The disc is completed by Barber's setting of the *Agnus Dei* from 1967 and is an arrangement of the famous *Adagio for Strings* which made his name when Toscanini performed it in New York in 1938.

This imaginative and enterprising programme is extremely well sung and vividly recorded.

Chichester Psalms[a] On the Waterfront – Symphonic Suite. On the Town – Three Dance Episodes.
[a]**Thomas Kelly** *treb* [a]**Elizabeth Franklin-Kitchen** *sop* [a]**Victoria Nayler** *contr* [a]**Jeremy Budd** *ten* [a]**Paul Charrier** *bass* **Bournemouth Symphony** [a]**Chorus and Orchestra / Marin Alsop**
Naxos 8 559177 (49' · DDD) Ⓢ ⦿⦿

Some years ago Andrew Litton presided over a memorable all-Bernstein concert for Virgin

Classics that showed that the Bournemouth orchestra could swing with the best of them; now it's the turn of new principal conductor Marin Alsop to put them through their paces. Very sassily they strut, too, in the exuberant outer numbers of *On the Town*. It's a similar tale in the symphonic suite from *On the Waterfront*. Alsop displays a special sympathy for this score's intimate undertow, investing softer music with a tingling atmosphere and lyrical poetry that consistently ignite the imagination, and moulding the love theme with a warmth and vulnerability that all but match the composer's NYPO version. Not that there's any lack of red-blooded drama or brazen spectacle, even though Mike Clements's otherwise excitingly dynamic sound-frame exposes some slight thinness of violin tone. The account of the *Chichester Psalms* is polished, communicative and beautifully sprung, attaining eloquent heights in the soothing setting of Psalm 23 for boy treble and mixed choir, as well as the strings' impassioned plea that launches the last movement.

A conspicuous success. The playing-time is comparatively stingy, but, given the superior quality of the music-making and the low Naxos price-tag, not many should complain.

Candide (1988 final version)

Candide
Jerry Hadley *ten* Candide **June Anderson** *sop* Cunegonde **Adolph Green** *ten* Dr Pangloss, Martin **Christa Ludwig** *mez* Old lady **Nicolai Gedda** *ten* Governor, Vanderdendur, Ragotski **Della Jones** *mez* Paquette **Kurt Ollmann** *bar* Maximilian, Captain, Jesuit father **Neil Jenkins** *ten* Merchant, Inquisitor, Prince Charles Edward **Richard Suart** *bass* Junkman, Inquisitor, King Hermann Augustus **John Treleaven** *ten* Alchemist, Inquisitor, Sultan Achmet, Crook **Lindsay Benson** *bar* Doctor, Inquisitor, King Stanislaus **Clive Bayley** *bar* Bear-Keeper, Inquisitor, Tsar Ivan **London Symphony Chorus and Orchestra / Leonard Bernstein**
DG Gramophone Awards Collection ② 474 8572 (112' · DDD) Recorded 1989. Notes and text included Ⓜ️○○○

 Here's musical comedy, grand opera, operetta, satire, melodrama, all rolled into one. We can thank John Mauceri for much of the restoration work: his 1988 Scottish Opera production was the spur for this recording and prompted exhaustive reappraisal. Numbers like 'We Are Women', 'Martin's Laughing Song' and 'Nothing More Than This' have rarely been heard, if at all. The last mentioned, Candide's 'aria of disillusionment', is one of the enduring glories of the score, reinstated where Bernstein always wanted it (but where no producer would have it), near the very end of the show. Bernstein called it his 'Puccini aria', and that it is – bittersweet, long-breathed, supported, enriched and ennobled by its inspiring string counterpoint. And this is but one of many forgotten gems.

It was an inspiration on someone's part (probably Bernstein's) to persuade the great and versatile Christa Ludwig and Nicolai Gedda (in his sixties and still hurling out top Bs) to fill the principal character roles. To say they do so ripely is to do them scant justice. Bernstein's old sparring partner Adolph Green braves the tongue-twisting and many-hatted Dr Pangloss with his own highly individual form of *Sprechstimme*, Jerry Hadley sings the title role most beautifully, *con amore*, and June Anderson has all the notes, and more, for the faithless, airheaded Cunegonde. It's just a pity that someone didn't tell her that discretion is the better part of comedy. 'Glitter and Be Gay' is much funnier for being played straighter, odd as it may sound. Otherwise, the supporting roles are all well taken and the London Symphony Chorus has a field-day in each of its collective guises.

Having waited so long to commit every last note (or thereabouts) of his cherished score to disc, there are moments here where Bernstein seems almost reluctant to move on. His tempos are measured, to say the least, the score fleshier now in every respect: even that raciest of Overtures has now acquired a more deliberate gait, a more opulent tone. But Bernstein would be Bernstein, and there are moments where you're more than grateful for his indulgence: the grandiose chorales, the panoramic orchestra-scapes (sumptuously recorded), and of course, that thrilling finale – the best of all possible Bernstein anthems at the slowest of all possible speeds – and why not (prepare to hold your breath at the choral *a cappella*). You're unlikely to be disappointed by this disc.

West Side Story

West Side Story
Dame Kiri Te Kanawa *sop* Maria (Nina Bernstein) **José Carreras** *ten* Tony (Alexander Bernstein) **Tatiana Troyanos** *mez* Anita **Kurt Ollmann** *bar* Riff **Marilyn Horne** *mez* Off-stage voice **composite chorus and orchestra from 'on and off' Broadway / Leonard Bernstein**
DG 457 199-2GH (77' · DDD) Recorded 1984. Notes and texts included Ⓕ○○

If the job of a 'crossover' record is to shatter preconceptions on both sides of any musical fence, then this is the greatest ever. Not all the aficionados of Broadway musicals are going to warm to de facto operatic treatment of West Side Story: not all opera-lovers or devotees of Bernstein as star conductor are going to rate West Side Story as an equivalent to opera. But any listener who keeps any sort of open mind, forgetting the constriction of barriers, must recognise this historic disc as superb entertainment and great music-making on every level, with an emotional impact closely akin to that of a Puccini opera. That of course is the doing of Leonard Bernstein as conductor as well as composer. It's astonishing that before this recording he had never conducted his most famous work.

Dame Kiri Te Kanawa may not be a soprano

you'd cast as Maria on stage, yet the beauty of the voice, its combination of richness, delicacy and purity, brings out the musical strengths of Bernstein's inspiration. Similarly, with José Carreras as Tony, it's self-evident to point out how such a voice brings out the pure beauty of the big melodies like 'Maria' or 'Tonight', but even a sharp number like his first solo, 'Something's coming', with floated *pianissimos* and subtly graded *crescendos* allied to sharp rhythms, makes it more clearly a question-mark song, full of expectation, more than just a point number. Marilyn Horne is in glorious voice, while Tatiana Troyanos will surprise you as Anita with the way she could switch her naturally beautiful operatic voice into a New York throaty snarl. Troyanos, it appears, was brought up in exactly the area of the West Side, where the story is supposed to be set, which makes her natural affinity with the idiom less surprising. Kurt Ollmann, American too, as Riff equally finds a very confident balance between the traditions of opera and those of the musical. Diction may not always be so clear as with less richtoned singers, but Carreras manages a very passable American accent and Dame Kiri a creditable Spanish-American one. The speed with which the piece moves is astounding, not just as superb entertainment but as a Shakespearean tragedy modernised and intensified.

West Side Story
Tinuke Olafimihan Maria **Paul Manuel** Tony **Caroline O'Connor** Anita **Sally Burgess** Off-stage voice **Nicholas Warnford** Riff **Julie Paton** Rosalia **Elinor Stephenson** Consuela **Nicole Carty** Francisca **Kieran Daniels** Action **Mark Michaels** Diesel **Adrian Sarple** Baby John **Adrian Edmeads** A-rab **Garry Stevens** Snowboy **Nick Ferranti** Bernardo **Chorus and National Symphony Orchestra / John Owen Edwards**
TER ② CDTER2 1197 (101' · DDD) Recorded 1993 Ⓕ

This recording of *West Side Story* is something of an achievement. The set starts with the major advantage of being inspired by a production at the Haymarket, Leicester, so that many of the cast are really inside their roles. They have youth on their side, too. Paul Manuel from that company may not have a large voice, but his sympathetic portrayal of Tony, both in his solos and duets with Maria, makes you feel that he identifies totally with the part. Moreover, the way in which he can float a high note, as at the end of the alternative film version of 'Something's Coming' puts him on a par with Carreras (for Bernstein). His Maria, Tinuke Olafimihan, is a gem. Her ability to interact with him and express the laughter and the tragedy of the heroine is very real. At the heart of the 'Somewhere' ballet, Sally Burgess voices the lovers' plea for peace with a magnificent rendition of its famous soaring tune. Nicholas Warnford as leader of the Jets gives no less than his rival in the tricky 'Cool' sequence and Jet song. John Owen Edwards directs Bernstein's

score as if he believes in every note. He has imparted to his players the very pulse that sets this music ticking.

Wonderful Town

Wonderful Town
Kim Criswell sop Ruth **Audra McDonald** sop Eileen **Thomas Hampson** bar Baker **Brent Barrett** sngr Wreck **Rodney Gilfry** bar Guide, First Editor, Frank **Carl Daymond** bar Second Editor, Chick Clark **Timothy Robinson** ten Lonigan **Michael Dore** bass First Man, Cadet, Third Cop, Villager **Lynton Atkinson** ten Second Man, Second Cop **Simone Sauphanor** sngr First Girl **Melanie Marshall** mez Second Girl **Kimberly Cobb** sngr Violet **Robert Fardell** sngr First Cop **London Voices; Birmingham Contemporary Music Group / Sir Simon Rattle**
EMI 556753-2 (67' · DDD) Notes and text included
Ⓕ❍❍

The Birmingham Contemporary Music Group, with key brass and sax personnel bumped in from the West End, play the Overture with great attitude, trumpets with the throttle full out and a bevy of saxes licking everyone into shape. Check out the Original Cast album (on Sony) and you'll find it's faster, tighter – not much, but enough to sound like NYC in the fast lane; crude and sassy with plenty of grime in the mix. Accept the fact that Rattle's is a pristine *Wonderful Town*, temporarily divorced from its smart book (Joseph Fields and Jerome Chodorov), out of context, and, to some extent, out of its element, and you'll have a good time. No one in the Original Broadway Cast can come within spitting distance of the vocal talent assembled here. Kim Criswell's Ruth has to live with Rosalind Russell's keys – in the bass-baritone range. Where Russell had about three notes in her voice – all dubious – Criswell has them all but doesn't have too much occasion to use them. So she works the lyric of 'One Hundred Easy Ways' a little harder than Russell – a piranha to Russell's shark. Audra McDonald as Sister Eileen uses every part of her versatile voice, wrapping it round a lyric like the two are inseparable, and sings 'A Little Bit in Love' with such contentment that it's as if she's giving herself a big, well-deserved hug. It's a gorgeous voice and the microphone loves her. It loves Hampson, too, and though he will never quite eradicate the 'formality' from his delivery he's rarely sounded quite so unassuming as here imagining his 'Quiet Girl'.

Of the big set-pieces, 'Conversation Piece' sounds as if it could have been lifted from a performance of the show. When the village kids get in on the action that's quite a stretch for Simon Halsey's London Voices. Now and again you catch their English choral tradition, but not long enough for it to get in the way. 'Conga!' sounds sufficiently inebriated and they sound right at home on 'Christopher Street'. You get slightly more *Wonderful Town* for your money with Rattle (a couple of reprises for a start). Don Walker's feisty orchestrations get more of an airing with the addition of 'Conquering New York', a dance number which demonstrates how ready Lenny was to raid his bottom drawer by reusing *Prelude, Fugue and Riffs*.

Franz Adolf Berwald
Swedish 1796-1868

Swedish composer and violinist Berwald is the most individual and commanding musical personality Sweden has produced. He was the son of CFG Berwald (1740-1825), a violinist of German birth who studied with F. Benda and played in the Stockholm court orchestra. Franz was a violinist or violist in the orchestra (1812-28) and probably studied composition with its conductor, JBE Dupuy. He disowned all his early works, which in their bold modulations show Spohr's influence, except a Serenade for tenor and six instruments (1825) and the fine Septet (?1828). He cherished operatic ambitions but failed to stir much interest in any of his works except Estrella de Soria (1841, performed 1862); The Queen of Golconda was not staged until 1968. In fact he was never properly recognised in his own country.

He made his greatest contribution to the repertory in his orchestral compositions of the 1840s, above all the four symphonies: the Sinfonie singulière (1845) is the most original, but all share vigorous freshness, formal originality (he sometimes used cyclic forms) and warm harmony and textures, especially in slow movements. His chamber works (two piano quintets, four piano trios and two string quartets), which occupied his main attention from 1849 to 1859, are often Mendelssohnian in style and show real command of form and idiom. Berwald pursued several business interests (he ran an orthopedic institute, a glassworks and a sawmill) and was active as a polemical writer on social issues from 1856. Although he was made professor of composition at the Swedish Royal Academy in 1867, the discovery of his work was a 20th-century phenomenon. His brother August (1798-1869) was also a violinist and composer, and a granddaughter, Astrid, a leading Swedish pianist.

GROVE*music*

Symphonies

Symphonies – No 1 in G minor, 'Sinfonie sérieuse'; No 2 in D, 'Sinfonie capricieuse'; No 3 in C, 'Sinfonie singulière'; No 4 in E flat. Konzertstück for Bassoon and Orchestra

Christian Davidsson bn **Malmö Symphony Orchestra / Sixten Ehrling**
BIS ② CD795/6 (131' · DDD)   ⓕⱺ

As might be expected, given Sixten Ehrling's excellent account of the *Singulière* and the E flat Symphonies with the LSO for Decca way back in the late 1960s and his no less impressive 1970 Swedish Radio version of the *Sérieuse*, the performances are *echt*-Berwald. Ehrling gives us plenty of space without ever lingering too lovingly. Even apart from the *tempo giusto*, you feel rather more comfortable with Ehrling's

handling of phrasing and balance. He's very attentive to dynamic markings and sometimes, as at the beginning of the *Sinfonie singulière*, *pianissimo* becomes *pianopiano-pianissimo*! The recording reproduces these dynamic extremes flawlessly. The Malmö Concert Hall, where this set was made, has a good acoustic. The recordings are generally excellent, though there seems to be more back-to-front perspective and air around the players in the *Singulière* and E flat Symphonies than in the *Sérieuse*. In short, Ehrling and his fine players bring us closer to the spirit of this music than do any of the current rivals.

Heinrich Biber
Bohemian 1644-1704

Biber is important for his works for the violin, of which he was a virtuoso. In the mid-1660s he entered the service of the Prince-Bishop of Olomouc who maintained an excellent Kapelle at his Kroměříž castle. By 1670 Biber had moved to the Salzburg court Kapelle, becoming Kapellmeister in 1684. His formidable violin technique is best seen in the eight Sonatae violino solo with continuo (1681), where brilliant passage-work (reaching 6th and 7th positions) and multiple stopping abound in the preludes, variations and elaborate finales. Most of the Mystery (or Rosary) Sonatas (c1676, for violin and bass) require scordatura tuning: by linking the open strings to the key the sonority and polyphonic possibilities of the violin were increased. The unaccompanied Passacaglia here, built on 65 repetitions of the descending tetrachord, is the outstanding work of its type before Bach. Besides other violin works (which include a Battalia, with strings and continuo), Biber composed sacred music (in a cappella style as well as large-scale concertato works for solo and ripieno voices), 15 school dramas, three operas (only Chi la dura la vince, 1687, survives) and much instrumental ensemble music (often for unusual combinations including brass). Especially notable are the Requiem in F minor, the Missa Sancti Henrici (1701), the 32-part Vesperae (1693), the motet Laetatus sum (1676), and the Sonata S Polycarpi for eight trumpets and timpani. Biber may have composed the 53-part Missa salisburgensis (1628) formerly attributed to Benevoli.

GROVE*music*

Balletti

Arias a 4 in A. Ballettae a 4 violettae. Balletti a 6 in C. Balletti lamentabili a 4 in E minor. Harmonia Romana. Trombet undt musicalischer Taffeldienst
Ars Antiqua Austria / Gunar Letzbor vn
Symphonia SY95143 (75' · DDD)   ⓕ

The Baroque palace of Kremsier was the summer residence of Prince-Bishop Karl Liechtenstein-Kastelkorn of Olmütz, an ardent music lover. During his rule, 1664-95, the palace library acquired what's a precious collection of manuscripts. This programme features some of the ensemble music by Biber from that source, though the authenticity of the *Harmonia Romana* anthology, some of whose dances are on the disc, hasn't been established. In any case, the sequence put together by violinist and director Gunar Letzbor is entertaining and very well executed. Most is for strings, but there are contributions from variously sized recorders, too, as well as some splendidly gruff, earthy and inebriate interjections from bass, Michael Oman, as the Nightwatchman.

Letzbor has built his programme around an idea of a Carnival feast at the bishop's court: the bishop enters to a fanfare; dance music greets the guests; a nightwatchman passes by; table music during dinner; dancing; the nightwatchman passes by again, this time drunk; peasant dancing; midnight, the end of Carnival and the beginning of Lent. The revelry is concluded by the 12 strokes of midnight sounded on what sounds like a school bell. The notion comes off well, for the scheme allows for a degree of musical contrast, both of sound and mood. Biber's dances are enchanting for the fullness of their character and for their rhythmic bite, and Ars Antiqua bring them to life with vigour, imagination and style. The group offers us well over an hour of first-class entertainment in which only the Bishop's festive board and the contents of his cellar aren't shared with us. The disc is superbly recorded.

Battalia a 10 in D

Biber Battalia a 10 in D[c]. Passacaglia in C minor[a]. ▣
Sonata violino solo representativa in A[c]. Harmonia artificiosa – Partita in C minor[c] **Locke** Canon 4 in 2[c].
The Tempest[c] **Zelenka** Fanfare in D[b]
[a]Luca Pianca *lte* [b]**Innsbruck Trumpet Consort;**
[c]**Il Giardino Armonico / Giovanni Antonini** *rec*
Teldec 3984-21464-2 (68' · DDD)   Ⓕ**OO**

Biber's *Battalia* has arguably become the most celebrated programmatic suite of the 17th century, with its easy Bohemian juxtaposition of poignant airs and almost choreographic stage music. Too often we hear each implicit detail exaggerated to death; here Il Giardino Armonico conveys each movement within the bounds of courtly decorum. The group's leader, Enrico Onofri, provides an effective gimmick in the March, as he walks from right to left and disappears into the distance. His playing in the *Sonata violono solo representativa* is impressive and acutely characterised: the Cuckoo is charming; the Frog leaps in a spontaneous counterpoint of improvised special effects; and the Hen and the Cock display a stirring full-throttled sound and thrilling technical precision. Such qualities are also apparent in the remarkable *Harmonia artificiosa* of 1696, is a beguiling work for two violas d'amore. Il Giardino generates a ringing, almost orchestral palette – darkened by a tenor chalumeau – upon which float these soft-grained violas. Less agreeable is the Allemande, which is fussily handled and never quite allowed to bed down into its natural harmonic

rhythm; in the 'Aria variata' that ends the suite reflective sobriety nonchalantly is sacrificed for Mediterranean effervescence. This is both the strength and weakness of Il Giardino in northern and central European repertoire, exemplified in Locke's music for *The Tempest*, from which a majestic orchestral suite can be wrought. The musical ideas are impressive, but too often miscast with ill-suited outbursts imposed on such temperate dances. Overall though, this is a dynamic and distinctive programme with some brilliant performances.

Violin Sonatas

Eight Sonatas for Violin and Continuo   ▣
(1681). Sonata violino solo representativa in A.
Sonata, 'La Pastorella'. Passacaglia for Solo Lute.
Mystery Sonatas – Passacaglia in G minor
Romanesca (Andrew Manze *vn* Nigel North
lte/theorbo John Toll *hpd/org*)
Harmonia Mundi ② HMX290 7344/45 (127' · DDD)
Recorded 1993-4   Ⓜ**OOO**

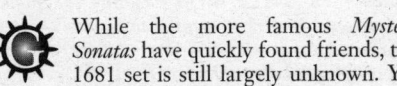

While the more famous *Mystery Sonatas* have quickly found friends, the 1681 set is still largely unknown. Yet what's immediately noticeable from this première recording of the sonatas is that Biber isn't only a legendary virtuoso, probably never bettered in the 17th or 18th centuries, but one of the most inventive composers of his age: bold and exciting, certainly, but also elusive, mercurial and mysterious. Most of the works are preludes, arias and variations of an unregulated nature: improvisatory preludes over naked pedals and lucid arias juxtaposing with eccentric rhetorical conceits are mixed up in an unpredictable phantasm of contrast, and yet at its best it all adds up to a unified structure of considerable potency. Andrew Manze is the player *par excellence* for music that requires a considered response to complement the adventurous spirit of the virtuoso. This is masterful playing in which he doesn't overcharacterise Biber's volatile temperament. The preludes are sweet and restrained, yet there's also a held-back, almost smouldering quality, skilfully pitched against the free-wheeling energy of the fast music.

Eight Sonatas for Violin and Continuo – Nos 3, 4, 6-7
Sonata No 81 in A. Sonata No 84 in E
John Holloway *vn* **Aloysia Assenbaum** *org* **Lars Ulrik Mortensen** *hpd*
ECM New Series 472 084-2 (77' · DDD)   Ⓕ**OOO**

John Holloway has contributed as much as anyone to modern-day recognition of Biber's status as one of the greatest of all violinist-composers. In his notes he draws attention to the difference in character between the sonatas in normal tuning and those that asl for *scordatura* or altered tunings, citing the latter (Nos 4 and 6 from the published set) as 'more intimate, more personal'. But actually this is the side which comes across most strongly in these performances anyway, at the expense of the extrovert maybe, but with no shortage of effective musical moments nevertheless; the point halfway through the Sixth Sonata when the violin re-emerges retuned and with a veiled new sound is managed with ghostly beauty.

With the violin resonating pleasingly through the many double- and triple-stoppings, and Holloway's bowing demonstrating a delicious lightness and freedom, these fundamentally inward, tonally aware performances also seem to have more of the smell of the 17th century about them than their current rivals (including Manze's, reviewed above),which push the violin's sound out a bit more. A respectfully resonant recording is a help here, as is the gentle but effectively unfussy continuo support of harpsichord and organ.

Anyone who already has the Manze need have no qualms about adding this one to their collection.

part string palette – pursuing an exhilarating, intensely wrought and unpredictable musical rhetoric – with quasi-concerted and swaggering trumpets. Unlike some of the other printed collections, which can seem like boxes of tricks, this comprises compelling and accessible music: Sonata IV has a satisfying textural surety and tunefulness; and noble ecclesiastical *alla breve* conclusion Sonata VI is marvellously shaped here.

The secret for performers is to allow the antiquated contrapuntal dance-infused music to unfold as if each contrasted section meant something greater than its mere existence. The emotive, almost physical impact of Biber is lavishly exuded in the Rare Fruits Council's strongly projected account. It takes a glowing, colourful and uncomplicated approach, espousing a textural breadth and rhythmic thrust underpinned by a deep violone, theorbo and harp. The playing is often dazzling – the trumpet sound is peerless, round and coppery – and the total concept unfussy (though this occasionally applies to tuning also).

Violin Sonatas – Nos 2, 3, 5, 7. Nisi Dominus. Ⓟ
Passacaglia[a]
Sonnerie (Monica Huggett *vn/dir* Emilia Benjamin *va da gamba* Gary Cooper *hpd/org* Elizabeth Kenny *theo/gtr*) [a]**Thomas Guthrie** *bass*
ASV Gaudeamus CD GAU 203 (65' · DDD) Ⓕ**OOO**

 Monica Huggett's arrival at these marvels of the 17th-century violin repertoire has the authority of a player to the manner born. She has a strong but fluent technique, and produces from her violin a sweet sound at all times, rarely forcing the tone into stridency (as Manze does, for instance in the clashing dissonances of the Variation of Sonata No 5). Rather, her navigation of what Charles Burney, writing in the 1770s, called the 'most difficult and most fanciful music of any I have seen of the period' is characterised, not by Manze's energetic interpretative gestures, but by her own rather aristocratic brand of easy poise and balance, proving that these sonatas can work as pure music, without the need for urgent drama. It's an alternative view of Biber from that of the fiery virtuoso (though virtuosity is certainly needed to achieve it), and rather a seductive one it is, too. Those who find Manze's fantasies a little over the top may well prefer Huggett's gentler readings; lovers of Biber's music will relish them both.

Sonatae tam aris quam aulis servientes
Rare Fruits Council / Manfredo Kraemer *vn*
Auvidis Astrée E8630 (67' · DDD) Ⓕ

A more radiant and gratifyingly robust collection of Baroque instrumental works would be hard to imagine. These 12 sonatas (which broadly translate as 'sonatas suitable for altar or court') juxtapose pieces for a rich five- or six-

---

Mystery Sonatas Ⓟ
John Holloway *vn* **Davitt Moroney** *org/hpd*
Tragicomedia (Stephen Stubbs *lte/chitarrone* Erin Headley *va da gamba/ lirone* Andrew Lawrence-King *hp/regal*)
Virgin Classics Veritas ② 562062-2 (131' · DDD)
Recorded 1989 Ⓜ**OOO**

Biber's 15 *Mystery Sonatas* with their additional *Passacaglia* for unaccompanied violin were written in about 1678 and dedicated to his employer, the Archbishop of Salzburg. Each Sonata is inspired by a section of the Rosary devotion of the Catholic Church which offered a system of meditation on 15 Mysteries from the lives of Jesus and the Virgin Mary. The music isn't, strictly speaking, programmatic, though often vividly illustrative of events which took place in the life of Christ.

All but two of the 16 pieces require *scordatura* or retuning of the violin strings; in this way Biber not only facilitated some of the fingerings but also achieved sounds otherwise unavailable to him. The Sonatas are disposed into three groups of five: Joyful, Sorrowful and Glorious Mysteries whose contrasting states are affectingly evoked in music ranging from a spirit reflecting South German Baroque exuberance to one of profound contemplation. John Holloway plays with imaginative sensibility. He's supported by a first-rate continuo group whose instruments include Baroque lute, chitarrone, viola da gamba, a 15-string lirone, double harp and regal.

Mystery (Rosary) Sonatas
Les Veilleurs de Nuit (Marianne Muller *va da gamba* Pascal Monteilhet *theo* Elisabeth Geiger *claviorg*) /
Alice Piérot *vn*
Alpha ② ALPHA038 (120' · DDD) Ⓕ

Mystery (Rosary) Sonatas. Includes a reading of the texts that inspired the Composer
Pavlo Beznosiuk *vn* **Richard Tunnicliffe** *va da gamba*
David Roblou *hpd* with **Timothy West** *spkr*
Avieš ② AV0038 (157' · DDD) Ⓕ⬤

Biber was a virtuoso on the violin, and he typically writes extended flourishes over a pedal point, at the start of a piece or approaching a final cadence. The abundant variation movements are always on an unchanging ground bass, with no overlapping of phrases in the violin to add interest and propel the music forward. So listening to all the sonatas at one sitting isn't to be recommended, as they have a sameness that could become wearying.

That there are still many things to enjoy is due to the excellence of Les Veilleurs de Nuit. Alice Piérot dashes off the pyrotechnics with fearsome ease, but she also brings the sensibility of a true musician to the more reflective passages such as the final *Adagio* of the third sonata ('The Nativity'), which is simple and heartfelt. She gives the impression of extemporising in the Praeludium of No 5 ('The 12-year-old Jesus in the Temple'), and the dances skip along like the rams and young sheep of the psalmist.

Elisabeth Geiger plays the claviorganum, a hybrid beast comprising a harpsichord and a two-manual organ. The powerful tones of the latter lend special force to the sonatas reflecting the Agony in the Garden and the Crucifixion, and the occasional use of the four-foot stop on its own makes for a pleasing variety. But the finest piece is the unaccompanied Passacaglia ('The Guardian Angel'), variations over a descending four-note phrase, which Piérot dispatches with a perfect balance between architecture and emotion.

In the Avie recording each sonata is introduced by an exhortation from a Jesuit Rosary psalter, presumably translated from the Latin, read by Timothy West in tones ranging from the measured to the impassioned. The continuo group play in various permutations, one sonata being very effectively accompanied by a double-stopping gamba.

Other differences include a repeat of the sarabandes in two of the sonatas, and decorations from the lute interpolated into the opening phrases of 'The Descent of the Holy Ghost'. Pavlo Beznosiuk is quite the equal of Piérot in virtuosity and musicianship, and in his use of *spiccato* he introduces a positively skittish note to 'The Coronation of Mary'.

Mystery (Rosary) Sonatas
Andrew Manze *vn* **Richard Egarr** *org/hpd* with
Alison McGillivray *vc*
Harmonia Mundi ② HMU90 7321/2 (141' · DDD) Ⓕ⬤⬤
Mystery (Rosary) Sonatas – Nos 1-9
ASV Gaudeamus CDGAU350 (61' · DDD) Ⓕ⬤
Mystery (Rosary) Sonatas – Nos 10-16
ASV Gaudeamus CDGAU351 (57' · DDD) Ⓕ⬤
Sonnerie (Monica Huggett *vn* Emilia Benjamin *va da*

gamba/liro Elizabeth Kenny *alte/theo/bq gtr* Frances Kelly *hp* Matthew Halls *hpd/org*)

Here are two more recordings of the Biber *Mystery* or *Rosary* sonatas to complement the tercentenary offerings from Alice Piérot (Alpha) and Pavlo Beznosiuk (Avie). Arranged in three groups of five, the sonatas, which reflect on episodes in the life of the Virgin Mary from Annunciation to Coronation, were dedicated to Biber's employer, the Archbishop of Salzburg.

In his booklet note, Andrew Manze suggests that a large continuo group is inappropriate for music probably written 'to accompany prayer and provoke meditation'. He is therefore accompanied only by Richard Eggar, the cello appearing in just one sonata; whereas Sonnerie, playing a semitone lower, give us the works.

To say that Manze's playing is thoughtful isn't to imply that no thought has gone into Monica Huggett's interpretation. But Manze is more meditative, and generally takes more time, while Huggett is more extrovert. In No 2 ('The Visitation'), for example, Manze is gentle in the first movement, rapt in the second, where Huggett is positively bullish, though accompanied only by the organ. On the other hand, in Sonnerie's No 14 ('The Assumption'), the cross-rhythm strumming of the guitar, abetted by the harpsichord and supported by the gamba, turns the eight-bar ground bass Aria into an uninhibited stomp at a ceilidh. It's very exhilarating, but for repeated listening you might prefer Manze's gentler approach, and his *pianissimo* at the point where Biber himself essays a spot of syncopation.

There's common ground in No 6 ('The Agony in the Garden'), though Manze takes two minutes longer, even after allowing for a repeat that Huggett doesn't make, and in No 12 ('The Ascension'), with its timpani-like writing for the string bass. In general, though, Huggett's frequent use of *spiccato* invests her playing with a jauntiness largely absent from Manze's account. There's nothing to choose between the performances of the unaccompanied Passacaglia, except that Huggett adds a cadenza. The Manze booklet includes the 16 vignettes from the original manuscript.

Der Türken Anmarsch
Biber Eight Violin Sonatas – No 1 in A; No 2 in D minor (Dorian); No 5 in E minor; No 8 in A **Muffat** Violin Sonata in D **Biber/A Schmelzer** Violin Sonata in A minor 'Victory of the Christians over the Turks'
John Holloway *vn* **Aloysia Assenbaum** *org* **Lars Ulrik Mortensen** *hpd*
ECM New Series 472 432-2 (63' · DDD) Ⓕ

John Holloway plays four sonatas from the set of eight Biber published in 1681 and also dedicated to the archbishop. First, however, comes a curiosity: an adaptation by Andreas Anton Schmelzer (son of the better-known Johann Heinrich) of Biber's 'Crucifixion' sonata, transposed up a tone and retitled as a representation of the siege of Vienna in 1683. It's difficult, though, to detect any difference other than some small changes to the Praeludium and an extra movement at the end.

The 1681 sonatas show Biber's propensity for rhapsodic flights over a pedal point and for variations on a ground bass. In the imitative writing of No 8, the double-stopping is so skilfully done that it's hard to believe that Holloway hasn't cloned himself. In this sonata especially, there's some nicely pointed continuo playing. The Muffat is a *sonata da chiesa*, with a return to the first movement at the end. Here and throughout the disc Holloway plays with a most appealing warmth and a faultless technique.

Missa Bruxellensis

Missa Bruxellensis   ℗
La Capella Reial de Catalunya; Le Concert des Nations / Jordi Savall
Alia Vox AV9808 (52' · DDD) Text included
                          Ⓕ🔾🔾

Modern technology and expert engineering allow us to bask in Biber's magnificent-sounding and spaciously conceived masses, complete with all the glistening attention to detail, the visceral *tutti* impact and the delicate textural contrasts which constitute some of Baroque music's most opulent expressions of earthly potency. Salzburg Cathedral provided exceptional acoustical possibilities. Biber, in his mass, could satisfy the potentate by adorning the unique status of Salzburg as the court with everything. The problem, however, with the *Missa Bruxellensis* – so called since it was discovered in Brussels – is that it appears to serve its purpose more as a professional job than as a vehicle for extended inspiration. Even so, a world première recording of a monumental work by a major composer isn't to be sniffed at, especially when directed by Jordi Savall. He lets Biber's score roll out unassumingly; even if at the expense of fine tuning and exacting ensemble, the final sections of the *Credo* are immensely stylish, and the 'Miserere' from the *Gloria* has the dignity of a spontaneous event rather than a contrived vignette. The recorded sound has a mixed success, taken from sessions held in the original location; there's a natural sense of the cathedral acoustic, though not, happily, at the expense of immediacy in the solo sections. Less satisfactory are the strident upper frequencies, in particular the solo sopranos. Gripes aside, this will delight collectors who relish fortress-like recordings.

Gilles Binchois   French c1400-1460

Binchois was one of the three leading musical figures of the first half of the 15th century (with Dufay and Dunstable). Organist at Ste Waudru, Mons, from 1419, he was granted permission to move to Lille in 1423 and apparently entered the service of William

Pole, Earl of Suffolk, soon after. Later in the 1420s he joined the Burgundian court chapel where he was much honoured and appointed a secretary to the court (c1437). He held prebends in Bruges, Mons, Cassel and Soignies, where he finally retired; there he was appointed provost of the collegiate church of St Vincent (1452), though he continued to receive a pension from the Burgundian court.

Although Binchois name was mentioned in contemporary literature only alongside Dufay's, his works had a more independent reputation and, though less widely circulated than Dufay's, were very popular. Six of his songs survive in keyboard arrangements; tenor lines of two or three were used to make basse danses, and numerous compositions from the mid- and late 15th century, including three mass cycles (Ockeghem's Missa 'De plus en plus', Bedyngham's Missa 'Dueil angoisseux' and the anonymous mass-motet cycle 'Esclave puist il devenir'), were based on his works. The fact that many of his compositions survive in only one source, and that most of those were compiled in southern Europe, far from the Burgundian court, suggests that much of his work may be lost or survive only anonymously. His songs, mostly rondeaux, remain within the conventions of refined courtly tradition. They are nearly all for a single-texted upper voice supported by an untexted tenor in longer notes a fifth lower in range and a contratenor in the same range or a little lower. They are characterised by effortless, graceful melodies, uncomplicated rhythms and carefully balanced phrases. His sacred music tends to be more conservative. No complete mass cycle by him has survived, though some of the mass movements can be paired on the basis of similarity. He wrote only one isorhythmic motet, and many of his smaller sacred works are purely functional.   **GROVE**music

Songs

Triste plaisir et douleureuse joie. Amours merchi de restout mon pooir. Je me recommande humblement. En regardant vostre tres doulx maintiens. Se la belle n'a le voloir. Je vous salue. Adieu mes tres belles amours. De plus en plus. Lune tres belles. Les tres doulx yeux. Amoureux suy et me vient toute joye. Adieu, adieu, mon joieulx souvenir. Jamais tant. Adieu, m'amour et ma maistresse. Dueil angoisseus. Pour prison ne pour maladie. Filles à marier
Ensemble Gilles Binchois / Dominique Vellard ten
Virgin Classics Veritas 545285-2 (60' · DDD) Texts and translations included   Ⓕ🔾

Binchois's songs have rarely appeared in any quantity on CD, yet the booklet-notes to this timely offering set out an objective case for considering Binchois a more significant song composer than his more famous contemporary, Dufay. If you turn to the music, the reasons for Dufay's greater popularity are equally obvious: Binchois's songs yield their secrets more slowly, and operate within a more limited expressive ambit. They demand repeated listening, whereas Dufay's songs tend to make their impact at first hearing. Thus it's all the more important for recordings of Binchois's music to bear repeated listening as well. This one certainly fulfils that requirement, and there's sufficient variety of scoring to sustain interest from song to song. Perhaps the crux of interpreting Binchois is whether to match his fabled restraint in performance, or to coax the songs' expressivity to the surface. Dominique Vellard seems to prefer the former approach, which relies for its effectiveness on the innate vocal qualities of his singers. For the most part, they respond admirably. The special artistry of Lena Susanne Norin is a cause for celebration; Anne-Marie Lablaude's contributions are lighter in tone, but graceful and supple, yet you do wonder whether a more impassioned delivery of the text might not be appropriate – particularly in *Dueil angoisseus*, surely one of the finest poems set to music in the 15th century. And it continues to be puzzling that certain stanzas are shorn of their text to allow for instrumental participation.

The Binchois discography makes up in quality for what it lacks in quantity, and notwithstanding these reservations, this disc sits comfortably in a distinguished niche of the repertory.

Sir Harrison Birtwistle   British 1934

Birtwistle studied at the Royal Manchester College of Music (1952-5), where Davies and Goehr were fellow students, interesting themselves in contemporary and medieval music. He then worked as a clarinettist and schoolteacher for brief periods; in 1975 he was appointed music director at the National Theatre. His works suggest comparison with Stravinsky in their ritual form and style, and sometimes with Varèse in the violence of their imagery (as in the opera Punch and Judy, 1968, a savage enactment of pre-social behaviour). In the 1970s, however, he began to work musical blocks into long, gradual processes of change (The Triumph of Time for orchestra, 1972), then to develop networks of interconnected pulsings beneath such processes (Silbury Air for small orchestra, 1977; agm for voices and orchestral groups, 1979). His biggest work of this period was the opera The Mask of Orpheus (1973-83, performed 1986), a multi-layered treatment of the myth.   GROVEmusic

Earth Dances

Theseus Game[a]. Earth Dances[b]
[a]**Ensemble Modern / Martyn Brabbins, Pierre-André Valade;** [b]**Ensemble Modern Orchestra / Pierre Boulez**
DG 20/21 477 070-2GH (67' · DDD) Recorded live at the [a]Gebläsehalle, Landschaftspark, Duisberg-Nord, 29-20 September 2003; [b]Alte Oper, Frankfurt, 29 October 2001   Ⓕ⊙

In live performance *Theseus Game* (2002-3) offers clear visual contrasts: an ensemble of 30 players has two conductors, and there's a central space at the front of the platform for the succession of soloists who emerge from the ensemble.

This chain of solo melody might represent the magic thread, given to Theseus by Ariadne, which enables him to escape from the Minotaur's labyrinth. Or it might suggest Theseus's heroic determination to survive in an hostile environment, a survival which remains constantly in doubt.

That second interpretation seems the most appropriate to a recording (of the work's first performance) in which distinctions clear to the eye are far less evident to the ear. Here background and foreground, solos and ensemble, converge in a titanic struggle whose rhetoric occasionally strays from drama into melodrama: and while the exuberance of the solo lines might hint at the playful aspects of a game, the atmosphere is too tense, the texture too dense, to suggest anything more athletic than the most strenuous kind of gladiatorial combat. Or perhaps the title indicates that Theseus is 'game' to fight for his survival, whatever the odds?

Earth Dances (1985-6) makes an appropriate coupling. Here, too, there is opposition between a volcanic life force of jagged rhythms and harsh harmonies and aspirations to a gentler, more melodic world of finer human feelings. In this, its third recording, Pierre Boulez leads a measured, alert traversal of the score's labyrinthine highways and byways, and a boldly delineated sound-picture ensures that the music's apocalyptic evolution comes over as devastatingly as ever. Listeners might have been helped by a sequence of timed cues to particular musical events in the notes, at least in relation to what seems like a basic division between the first 17 minutes and the even more implacable remainder. But, with or without such aids to comprehension, *Earth Dances* demands total surrender; as the music unwinds to its end, spasms of the seismic dance stand in the way of any comforting sense of fulfilment, or resolution.

Pulse Shadows

Pulse Shadows
Claron McFadden *sop* **Arditti Quartet** (Irvine Arditti, Graeme Jennings vns Dov Scheindlin va Rohan de Saram vc) **Nash Ensemble / Reinbert de Leeuw**
Teldec 3984-26867-2 (64' · DDD)   Ⓕ❍❍❍

 From Schoenberg's *Pierrot lunaire* to Boulez's *Le marteau sans maître* and Kurtág's *Messages of the late RV Troussova*, modernist composers have used the medium of voice with mixed instrumental ensemble for their most allusive and personal utterances. Birtwistle's *Pulse Shadows* (1991-6) belongs in this company. While not easy listening, it deals with some of the most elemental and profound topics in contemporary culture, and this recording rises to the score's many challenges, both technically and interpretatively. *Pulse Shadows* is subtitled 'Meditations on Paul Celan', acknowledging the poet-author of the texts for the nine vocal movements, and indicating that the nine movements for string quartet with which the vocal movements are interleaved reflect on – shadow – the emotions that setting Celan (mainly in Michael Hamburger's English translations) created in the composer. The poems are oblique rituals, meditations on the state of human consciousness after the Holocaust, and Birtwistle's music links that quality with the kind of innately melancholic, stoical, intensely humane spirit that informs most of his finest works. Claron McFadden proves herself the most mellifluous singer of this music. Together with the precision and empathy of the Arditti Quartet and Reinbert de Leeuw, not to mention the admirable recorded sound, this is a disc to live with, and be haunted by, for years to come.

Five Distances

Birtwistle Five Distances[a]. The Silk House Tattoo[b]. 17 Tate Riffs[c]
[b]**John Wallace,** [b]**Adam Wright** tpts [b]**Sam Walton** perc [a]**Gallimaufry Ensemble**
(Louisa Dennehy fl Holly Fawcett ob Peter Sparks cl Siona Crosdale bn Nicholas Wolmark hn) [c]**Royal Academy of Music Chamber Ensemble**
Royal Academy of Music RAM019 (29' · DDD)   Ⓜ

To coincide with the composer's 70th birthday, the Royal Academy of Music has released a sequence of Birtwistle recordings made by staff and students in 2001. *Five Distances* for wind quintet (1992) has been recorded before, and this version risks substituting a generalised resonance for a strong sense of actual separation between the players. Yet it's very well played and persuasively shaped. Distance and resonance are even more basic to *The Silk House Tattoo* (1993) with its circling, echoing trumpets kept in line by a peremptory drummer, and to *17 Tate Riffs* (2000), Birtwistle's characteristically ritualised response to a commission for the opening ceremony of Tate Modern, with 15 players spread around the cavernous Turbine Hall. No recording can match the far-flung aural vistas of the original location, but this one is well worth having as a reminder of how – even on the smallest timescale – Birtwistle can hint at the wider formal perspectives and grander mythic themes which form his usual terrain.

Piano Works

The Axe Manual[a]. Harrison's Clocks. Hector's Dawn. Berceuse de Jeanne. Précis. Sad Song. Oockooing Bird. Ostinato with Melody. Betty Freeman: Her Tango. Saraband: The King's Farewell
Nicolas Hodges pf [a]**Claire Edwardes** perc
Metronome METCD1074 (71' · DDD)   Ⓕ

Though most of the items in this indispensable collection of Birtwistle's keyboard music last five minutes or less, two are on a scale commen-

surate with the orchestral *Triumph of Time* or *Secret Theatre*.

In *Harrison's Clocks* (1997-8) simultaneously unfolding strata demonstrate that 'interdependent independence' of which Birtwistle often speaks. On one level, the music is potently mechanical, welded together from clearly defined rhythmic patterns which recur and collide like meshing cogs. Yet lying behind these mechanics is that background of complex associations with myth and ritual that's never far away in any Birtwistle composition, even the shortest and simplest.

The first recording of *The Axe Manual* (2000), reveals it as an exuberant, and, in its central stages, delicate essay in 'extending' piano sound by means of metal and wood percussion. It turns fascination with tone-colour and texture into an absorbing musical drama, a battle with and against time that has an intensely human urgency and passion. It's a tribute to the quality of the WDR Cologne recording, excellent throughout, that the balance between the two performers seems so effortlessly right.

Nicolas Hodges is an accomplished guide to these varied perspectives, never over-nuancing the understated poetry of the miniatures, but meeting with total authority all the technical and interpretative challenges of the larger works.

Harrison's Clocks
Joanna MacGregor pf
SoundCircus SC004 (26' · DDD)   Ⓜ

Even if Harrison Birtwistle was not knowingly named after John Harrison, the 18th-century clockmaker discussed in Dava Sobel's recent best-seller *Longitude*, his recurrent concern with musical mechanisms whose 'ticking' regularity is the perfect foil for other, much less predictable elements, makes him the ideal composer to celebrate the pioneer of navigational chronometers. The recurring patterns which dominate the first of these five pieces (composed in 1998) are deceptive in that they create a relatively mild-mannered, even static effect, with contrast confined to brief episodes marking the movement's main formal divisions. But if this leads you to expect a sequence of neoclassical toccatas, the explosive fragmentation of the second piece will soon disabuse you, and in the hair-raisingly intense third movement the implacable power of the composer's invention takes the breath away. Joanna MacGregor meets the demands with interest, bringing the music vividly to life, and the recording is excellent. Indispensable.

The Woman and the Hare

The Woman and The Hare[a]. Nine Settings of Lorine Niedecker[b]. Duets for Storab[c]. An Interrupted Endless Melody[d]. Entr'actes and Sappho Fragments[e]

abeClaron McFadden *sop* aJulia Watson *spkr* Nash Ensemble (acePhilippa Davies, acHelen Keen *fls* aRichard Hosford *cl* deGareth Hulse *ob* eSkaila Kanga *hp* Ian Brown dpf/acels aeSimon Limbrick *perc* aeMarianne Thorsen, aElizabeth Wexler *vns* aeLawrence Power *va* abPaul Watkins *vc*) / aeMartyn Brabbins
Black Box BBM1046 (77' · DDD) Notes and texts included   Ⓕ

The Woman and the Hare (1999) shares its sound world with such close contemporaries as *Pulse Shadows*, *The Last Supper* and (near the end, in particular) with Birtwistle's music for the 2002 Royal National Theatre production of *The Bacchae*. The composer's genius for moving swiftly and imperceptibly between austerity and warmth is evident in both works, his characteristically fragmentary forms generating more than enough expressive continuity to ensure a powerful dramatic charge. This is equally true of the recent settings for soprano and cello of Lorine Niedecker, whose aphoristic poems about the threats and rituals of interactions between nature and humanity might have been written expressly for Birtwistle.

The vocal compositions gain greatly from the assured direction of Martyn Brabbins and the effortless yet characterful singing of Claron McFadden. Birtwistle's decision to divide David Harsent's text for *The Woman and the Hare* between a narrator and a singer, coupled with some particularly graphic instrumental writing, make this one of his most unambiguously theatrical concert pieces, and this account emphasises the claustrophobic aura of Harsent's text. The cumulative impact of the whole is remarkable, with a visceral thrust that complements the more withdrawn lyricism of the *Sappho Fragments* and the Niedecker settings.

The instrumental works, *Duets for Storab* and *An Interrupted Endless Melody* are performed with the Nash Ensemble's special flair, and the sound, throughout, has admirable presence. Both compositions are already available on a valuable Deux-Elles release from the Galliard Ensemble, but the two discs complement each other well enough to make both essential purchases.

The Mask of Orpheus

The Mask of Orpheus
Jon Garrison *ten* Orpheus: Man **Peter Bronder** *ten* Orpheus: Myth, Hades **Jean Rigby** *mez* Euridice: Woman **Anne-Marie Owens** *mez* Euridice: Myth, Persephone **Alan Opie** *bar* Aristaeus: Man **Omar Ebrahim** *bar* Aristaeus: Myth, Charon; **Marie Angel** *sop* Aristeus: Oracle of the Dead, Hecate; **Arwel Huw Morgan** *bar* Caller; **Stephen Allen** *ten* Priest, First Judge; **Nicholas Folwell** *bar* Priest, Second Judge; **Stephen Richardson** *bass* Priest, Third Judge; **Juliet Booth** *sop* Woman, First Fury; **Philippa Dames-Longworth** *sop* Woman, Second Fury; **Elizabeth McCormack** *mez* Woman, Third Fury; **Ian Dearden** *sound diffusion* BBC Singers;

BBC Symphony Orchestra / Sir Andrew Davis, Martyn Brabbins
NMC NMCD050 ③ (162' · DDD) Notes and text included   Ⓜ〇〇〇

 Birtwistle's opera is about the Orpheus myth, but the familiar story has been fragmented. Each of the principal characters is represented by two singers and a (silent) dancer, and much of what happens isn't directly described in the libretto. Without following the libretto you won't be able to follow everything being sung; at times very little (the text is sometimes broken up; some passages, including much of Act 3, are sung in an invented language). Rituals are often at their most powerful when they appeal to the imagination rather than to reason, and here the sense of ritual is awesomely powerful. It's an extraordinarily patterned opera, with many varied repetitions, all meticulously labelled ('First Structure of Decision', 'Second Time Shift' and so on) in the score. The ritual repetitions, the elaborate patternings and allegorical structures make their own effect. In the boldest of these, the 17 'arches' over which Orpheus passes in his quest for Euridice in Act 2, Birtwistle aids comprehension by quite extensive use of speech. But the music says far more than the sometimes enigmatic words, and the ceremonial retelling of the whole story in Act 3, would perhaps have less impact if the words of the song verses were comprehensible. Birtwistle communicates his refracted but gripping myth with, above all, orchestral colour: an orchestra of wind, percussion and plucked instruments (plus tape, sampler and a small chorus) used with vivid mastery. The sheer sound of this opera is quite haunting and moving. *The Mask of Orpheus* is a masterpiece, and this performance is fully worthy of it. There are no weak links at all in the extremely fine cast. Although it's unfair to single out any singer for special mention, Jon Garrison's portrayal of Orpheus the Man is outstanding. The recording, direct and pungent but by no means lacking in atmosphere, leaves nothing to be desired.

Punch and Judy

Punch and Judy
Stephen Roberts *bar* Punch; **Jan DeGaetani** *mez* Judy, Fortune-teller; **Phyllis Bryn-Julson** *sop* Pretty Polly, Witch; **Philip Langridge** *ten* Lawyer; **David Wilson-Johnson** *bar* Choregos, Jack Ketch; **John Tomlinson** *bass* Doctor **London Sinfonietta / David Atherton**
Etcetera ② KTC2014 (103' · ADD) Recorded 1980. Notes and text included   Ⓕ〇〇〇

 Punch and Judy was composed in the mid-1960s, and since this recording first appeared on Decca we have had the remarkable 1984 Opera Factory production of the work, directed by David Freeman, seen on stage and television. As Punch, Stephen

Roberts is less consistently menacing and 'over the top' in vocal demeanour than Opera Factory's Omar Ebrahim. But Roberts remains a very satisfying interpreter of a part which is far from uniformly aggressive in character and in which a kind of crazy vulnerability offsets the ritual violence. In fact the general excellence of the singers on this set is impressive, with a spectacular contribution from Phyllis Bryn-Julson.

In the light of Birtwistle's finest later works (especially the opera The Mask of Orpheus), Punch and Judy can seem relatively anonymous in style, at least in those places which offer the kind of brittle, fragmented textures found in many composers at that time. Yet these are only moments, and as a whole the opera loses none of its powerful and sustained impact when compared with Birtwistle's more mature compositions. If anything, its startling primitivisms stand out more vividly, while its not inconsiderable moments of reflection and lyricism acquire an enhanced poignancy. The performance gains immeasurably from the alert control of David Atherton and the superlative musicianship of the London Sinfonietta. The analogue recording may lack depth, but it's as clear and immediate as this throat-grabbing music demands.

Georges Bizet   French 1838-1875

Bizet was trained by his parents, who were musical, and admitted to the Paris Conservatoire just before his tenth birthday. There he studied counter-point with Zimmerman and Gounod and composition with Halévy, and under Marmontel's tuition he became a brilliant pianist. Bizet's exceptional powers as a composer are already apparent in the products of his Conservatoire years, notably the Symphony in C, a work of precocious genius dating from 1855 (but not performed until 1935). In 1857 Bizet shared with Lecocq a prize offered by Offenbach for a setting of the one-act operetta Le Docteur Miracle; later that year he set out for Italy as holder of the coveted Prix de Rome.

During his three years in Rome Bizet began or projected many compositions; only four survive, including the opera buffa, Don Procopio (not performed until 1906). Shortly after his return to Paris, in September 1861, his mother died; the composer consoled himself with his parents maid, by whom he had a son in June 1862. He rejected teaching at the Conservatoire and the temptation to become a concert pianist, and completed his obligations under the terms of the Prix de Rome. The last of these, a one-act opéra comique, La guzla de l'emir, was rehearsed at the Opéra-Comique in 1863 but withdrawn when the Théâtre-Lyrique director, who had been offered 100 000 francs to produce annually an opera by a Prix de Rome winner who had not had a work staged, invited Bizet to compose Les pêcheurs de perles .

Bizet completed it in four months. It was produced in September 1863, but met with a generally cool reception: an uneven work, with stiff characterisa-

tion, it is notable for the skilful scoring of its exotic numbers. In the ensuing years Bizet earned a living arranging other composers' music and giving piano lessons. Not until December 1867 was another opera staged – La jolie fille de Perth, which shows a surer dramatic mastery than Les pêcheurs. It received a good press but had only 18 performances.

1868 was a year of crisis for Bizet, with more abortive works, attacks of quinsy and a re-examination of his religious stance; and his attitude to music grew deeper. In June 1869 he married Geneviève, daughter of his former teacher, Halévy, and the next year they suffered the privations caused by the Franco-Prussian war (Bizet enlisted in the National Guard). Bizet found little time for sustained composition, but in 1871 he produced the delightful suite for piano duet, Jeux d'enfants (some of it scored for orchestra as the Petite Suite), and he worked on a one-act opera, Djamileh. Both the opera and Daudet's play L'arlésienne, for which Bizet wrote incidental music, failed when produced in 1872, but in neither case did this have anything to do with the music.

Bizet was convinced that in Djamileh he had found his true path, one which he followed in composing his operatic masterpiece, Carmen. Here Bizet reaches new levels in the depiction of atmosphere and character. The characterisation of José, his gradual decline from a simple soldier's peasant honesty through insubordination, desertion and smuggling to murder is masterly; the colour and vitality of Carmen herself are remarkable, involving the use of the harmonic, rhythmic instrumental procedures of Spanish dance music, to which also the fate-laden augmented 2nds of the Carmen motif may owe their origin. The music of Micaela and Escamillo may be less original, but the charm of the former and the coarseness of the latter are intentional attributes of the characters. The opera is the supreme achievement of Bizet and of opéra comique, a genre it has transformed in that Bizet extended it to embrace passionate emotion and a tragic end, purging it of artificial elements and embuing it with a vivid expression of the torments inflicted by sexual passion and jealousy. The work, however, was condemned for its 'obscene' libretto, and the music was criticised as erudite, obscure, colourless, undistinguished and unromantic. Only after Bizet's death was its true stature appreciated, and then at first only in the revised version by Guiraud in which recitatives replace the original spoken dialogue (it is only recently that the original version has been revived). The reception of Carmen left Bizet acutely depressed; he fell victim to another attack of quinsy and, in June 1875, to the two heart attacks from which he died. **GROVE**music

Symphony in C

Symphony in C[a]. L'Arlésienne[b] – Suites Nos 1 & 2 **H**
[a]**French National Radio Symphony Orchestra;**
[b]**Royal Philharmonic Orchestra / Sir Thomas Beecham**
EMI 5672312 (65' · ADD) Recorded 1956-9   Ⓕ**OO**

In Beecham's hands the Symphony in C is made to sound wonderfully songful and although the French orchestral playing is less than ideally

BIZET'S CARMEN – IN BRIEF

Leontyne Price Carmen **Franco Corelli** Don José
Mirella Freni Micaëla **Robert Merrill** Escamillo;
VPO / **Herbert von Karajan**
RCA ② 74321 39495-2 (160' · ADD) Ⓜ●●
One of Price's greatest studio achievements,
one of Corelli's richest, and Freni at her most
charming. Conducted a little effortlessly.

Angela Gheorghiu Carmen **Roberto Alagna**
Don José **Inva Mula-Tchako** Micaëla **Thomas
Hampson** Escamillo; Toulouse Capitole
Orchestra / **Michel Plasson**
EMI ② 557434-2 (157' · DDD) Ⓕ●
The husband-and-wife team of Gheorghiu
and Alagna really strike sparks off each other,
and the tenor has rarely done anything better
on disc.

Jessye Norman Carmen **Neil Shicoff** Don José
Mirella Freni Micaëla **Simon Estes** Escamillo;
French National Orchestra / **Seiji Ozawa**
Philips ② 470 417-2 (161' · DDD) Ⓑ
A surprise success – Jessye Norman might
not appear to be a natural Carmen, but she
sings with real insight and intelligence.
Shicoff's José, too, is magnificent.

Tatiana Troyanos Carmen **Plácido Domingo** Don
José **Kiri Te Kanawa** Micaëla **José van Dam**
Escamillo; LPO / **Sir Georg Solti**
Decca ③ 414 489-2DH3 (160' · ADD) Ⓕ
Troyanos is a softer Carmen than many, and
Domingo in 1975 was in glowing voice. Te
Kanawa and van Dam are de luxe casting, and
Solti keeps everything buoyant and exciting.

Teresa Berganza Carmen **Plácido Domingo**
Don José **Ileana Cotrubas** Micaëla **Sherill Milnes**
Escamillo; LSO / **Claudio Abbado**
DG ③ 477 5342GOR2 (157' · DDD) Ⓜ●
Even the sluggishly delivered dialogue
can't detract from the theatricality of this
much-loved recording. Berganza is an aristocratic Carmen, and Cotrubas one of the
loveliest Micaëlas.

Grace Bumbry Carmen **Jon Vickers** Don José
Mirella Freni Micaëla **Paskalis** Escamillo;
Orchestre de Paris / **Rafael Frühbeck de Burgos**
HMV Classics ② HMVD572871-2 (152' · ADD) Ⓑ●
Two magnificent singing actors take the
central roles, and subtly leave no emotion
unexplored. Frühbeck de Burgos is a lively
and committed conductor.

Maria Callas Carmen **Nicolai Gedda** Don José
Andrea Guiot Micaëla **Robert Massard**
Escamillo; Orchestre de Paris / **Georges Prêtre**
EMI ② 556281-2 (146' · ADD) Ⓜ
Callas is Callas and demands to be heard: this
isn't conventional but, wow, it works.

polished, the *joie de vivre* of Beecham's performance is irresistible. What makes this disc doubly
desirable are the marvellous RPO wind solos
(and, of course, the haunting strings in the
Adagietto) in *L'Arlésienne*. The performances of
these two suites stand head and shoulders above
present CD competition, their loving finesse
mixes evocative magic (the 'Intermezzo' of No
2) with wonderful rhythmic vivacity (the closing
'Farandole'). The refurbishing of the recordings is remarkably successful, especially *L'Arlésienne*.

Carmen

Carmen
Angela Gheorghiu sop Carmen; **Roberto Alagna**
ten Don José; **Inva Mula** sop Micaëla; **Thomas
Hampson** bar Escamillo; **Elizabeth Vidal** sop
Frasquita; **Isabelle Cals** sop Mercédès; **Nicolas
Rivenq** ten Dancaïre; **Yann Beuron** ten Remendado;
Ludovic Tézier bar Moralès; **Nicolas Cavallier** bass
Zuniga; Toulouse Children's Choir; Les Eléments;
Toulouse Capitole Orchestra / **Michel Plasson**
EMI ③ 557434-2 (157' · DDD) Notes, libretto and
translation included Ⓕ●

Michel Plasson draws some very fine playing
indeed from the Toulouse orchestra, and his
choice of speeds seems just right, never resorting to extreme effects. The one moment when
things get a bit sluggish is in the Card scene, but
he is, perhaps rightly, more concerned with letting Gheorghiu have as much breathing space as
she needs; the chest tone she uses for the cries of
'La mort!' is amazingly forceful. Her portrayal
has little of the easy sensuality of such celebrated interpreters as Grace Bumbry or Teresa
Berganza. But Gheorghiu and Roberto Alagna
have obviously worked very hard to achieve
some fine moments, a beautifully soft ending to
'Là-bas, dans la montagne', and an almost visible change of mood towards the end of the
Séguedille, as Carmen begins to work her
charms. Gheorghiu can't help sounding rather
imperious at times, and there's no exchange of
remarks at the moment when she throws the
flower.
Alagna has done nothing better recently: he's
really inside the character, and portrays the
man's descent into degradation. There's little
sense of him pushing the tone – as in his Manrico – although his voice is much lighter than
many other famous Don Josés. This is all in his
favour, though, for moments such as the beautifully realised ending to 'Parle-moi de ma mère'.
Other roles are well taken: Thomas Hampson
presents Escamillo as a very jovial sort of fellow,
Inva Mula as Micaëla is better in the Act 1 duet
than she is in her aria. The sound is uncomplicated, though Carmen's castanets (some very
classy playing) seem to be coming from quite a
distance away from her.
With dozens of *Carmen*s available on disc, it's
impossible to recommend only one. This will be
a pleasure for the many admirers of Plasson,

Gheorghiu and Alagna. Once you get to the final duet in this 21st-century *Carmen*, you should find yourself completely gripped – by Alagna, who, while sounding distraught, still manages to produce some lovely tone, and by Gheorghiu, who, though she may never sing the role on stage, is a remarkably dramatic lady-in-distress for the microphone.

Carmen   Ⓗ
Victoria de los Angeles sop Carmen; **Nicolai
Gedda** ten Don José; **Janine Micheau** sop Micaëla;
Ernst Blanc bar Escamillo; **Denise Monteil** sop
Frasquita; **Marcelle Croisier** mez Mercédès;
Monique Linval sop Mercédès; **Jean-Christoph
Benoit** bar Dancaïre; **Michel Hamel** ten
Remendado; **Bernard Plantey** bass Moralès; **Xavier
Depraz** bass Zuniga; **Les Petits Chanteurs de
Versailles; French National Radio Choir and
Symphony Orchestra / Sir Thomas Beecham**
EMI Great Recordings of the Century ③ 567357-2
(162' · ADD) Recorded 1958/9   Ⓜ**○○○**

This classic Beecham set stands the test of time, sparkling, swaggering and seducing in a way that's uniquely Beecham's. It now comes in the EMI Great Recordings of the Century series, with brightened, freshened and clarified sound. As Richard Osborne points out in his brilliant, informative note, there were serious problems at the sessions – a second series was organised 15 months after the first (hence the two Mercédès) – but you would never realise there had been difficulties, either from the performance or the firmly focused, spacious recording in which the atmospheric off-stage effects are vividly caught.

What's so individual is the way that Beecham points rhythms to captivate the ear, as well as his persuasive moulding of phrases. Witness the sensuous way he coaxes the string phrase leading into the second half of the Don José/Micaëla duet in Act 2, 'Parle-moi de ma mère!' (disc 1, track 9, 3'47"). In those qualities Beecham is matched by Victoria de los Angeles in the title-role.

Osborne reveals that Beecham's original choice of heroine was the Swedish mezzo Kerstin Meyer. After all, de los Angeles – Mimì in Beecham's *Bohème* recording – is hardly an obvious candidate for such a fire-eating role. But there's far more to Carmen than is conveyed in that conventional approach, and de los Angeles instantly establishes her as a seductive, provocative character with wickedly sparkling eyes. In her opening solo, the Habanera, her delicious downward *portamento* on 'Je t'aime' is irresistible. The Carmen quality which de los Angeles doesn't have in her regular armoury, though, is a snarl. Instead she consistently uses her golden tone to tantalise and provoke, as in the magically sultry moment leading into 'Là-bas dans la montagne' in her Act 2 duet with José just after the Flower song (disc 2, track 13). At that point Beecham, too, subtly pressing the music forward, is a fellow magician. Then at the

very end, in Act 4, de los Angeles does finally muster a snarl in the culminating phrase 'laisse-moi passer' ('Well stab me then, or let me pass').

In a way, Nicolai Gedda's portrait of Don José is just as remarkable. He was at his peak, and sings not just with refinement and imagination but with deep passion, leading you on in the widest expressive range in the Flower song. Janine Micheau makes a bright, clear Micaëla, very French in tone, and Ernst Blanc, if not the most characterful Escamillo, makes the bullfighter a forthright, heroic character, singing with firm, clear tone. The rest of the cast, all French, make an excellent team, as is clear in ensembles: the sparkling account of the Act 2 Quintet or the opening of the Card scene, or the swaggering march ensemble as the smugglers depart in Act 3 (disc 3, track 6). A magic set now made all the more enticing in this mid-price reissue.

Carmen
Teresa Berganza sop Carmen; **Plácido Domingo**
ten Don José; **Ileana Cotrubas** sop Micaëla; **Sherrill
Milnes** bar Escamillo; **Yvonne Kenny** sop Frasquita;
Alicia Nafé mez Mercédès; **Robert Lloyd** bass
Zuniga; **Stuart Harling** bar Moralès; **Gordon
Sandison** bar Dancaïre; **Geoffrey Pogson** ten
Remendado; **Ambrosian Singers; London
Symphony Orchestra / Claudio Abbado**
DG ③ 477 5342GOR2 (157' · ADD) Recorded 1977.
Notes, text and translation included   Ⓜ**○○**

This notable recording followed immediately on from the famous Faggioni production at the 1977 Edinburgh Festival, a staging finely observed enough still to remain with those who were there. In it Berganza declared her aim of rescuing the role from bad traditions and from its insults to Spanish womanhood. Her reading was restrained, haughty, but no less attractive and haunting for that. She developed the character, as she does on the recording, from carefree gypsy to tragic woman and, in doing so, is scrupulous in her obedience to Bizet's notes, rhythms and dynamics. Nothing is exaggerated yet nothing is left out in this sensuous but never overtly sensual portrayal, bewitchingly sung. Maybe you don't feel the full engagement of her emotions in her entanglement with José, but better a slight reticence than overacting. Migenes, on the Maazel set, is more immediately seductive, and occasionally more varied in tonal colouring, but Berganza is the more subtle artist. She works in keen rapport with Abbado, who brings clarity of texture, Mediterranean fire and intense concentration to the score.

You may find more elegance, more Gallic wit in, say, Beecham's famous EMI set, but only Maazel of other conductors comes near Abbado's emphasis on close-knit ensemble and histrionic strength – and both their sets come as the result of experience of 'real' performances. Domingo benefits here, as on the Maazel set, in the same way, being more involved in affairs. Like his Carmen, he sometimes lacks variety of colour in his singing, but its sheer musicality and, in the last two acts, power, count for much. Sherrill Milnes is at once virile and fatuous as Escamillo should be. Cotrubas makes a vulnerable, touching Micaëla. The dialogue is heavily foreshortened compared to rival sets. Abbado chooses some of the questionable Oeser alternatives, but – apart from the one in the finale – they aren't disturbing. The recording is first-rate.

Carmen
Julia Migenes mez Carmen; **Plácido Domingo** ten Don José; **Faith Esham** sop Micaëla; **Ruggero Raimondi** bass Escamillo; **Lilian Watson** sop Frasquita; **Susan Daniel** mez Mercédès; **Jean-Philippe Lafont** bar Dancäire; **Gérard Garino** ten Remendado; **François Le Roux** bar Moralès; **John Paul Bogart** bass Zuniga; **French Radio Chorus; French Radio Children's Chorus; French National Orchestra / Lorin Maazel**
Erato ③ 2292-45207-2 (151' · DDD) Recorded 1992.
Notes, text and translation included   ⓕ**OO**

Too many recordings of *Carmen* have blown up the work to proportions beyond its author's intentions but here Maazel adopts a brisk, lightweight approach that seems to come close to what Bizet wanted. Similarly Julia Migenes approaches the title part in an immediate, vivid way, exuding the gipsy's allure and suggesting Carmen's fierce temper and smouldering eroticism; she develops the character intelligently into the fatalistic person of the card scene and finale. Her singing isn't conventionally smooth but it's compelling throughout. Plácido Domingo has made Don José very much his own, and here he sings with unstinting involvement and finesse. Ruggero Raimondi is a macho Toreador though Faith Esham is a somewhat pallid Micaëla.

Les pêcheurs de perles

Les pêcheurs de perles
Barbara Hendricks sop Leïla; **John Aler** ten Nadir; **Gino Quilico** bar Zurga; **Jean-Philippe Courtis** bass Nourabad **Toulouse Capitole Chorus and Orchestra / Michel Plasson**
EMI ② 749837-2 (127' · DDD) Recorded 1989
Text and translation included   ⓕ**O**

Let a tenor and a baritone signify that they're willing to oblige with a duet, and the cry will go up for *The Pearl Fishers*. It's highly unlikely that many of the company present will know what the duet is about – it recalls the past, proclaims eternal friendship and nearly ends up in a quarrel – but the melody and the sound of two fine voices blending in its harmonies will be quite sufficient. In fact there's much more to the opera than the duet; and the EMI recording goes further than previous versions in giving a complete account of a score remarkable for its unity as well as for the attractiveness of individual numbers. It's a lyrical opera, and the voices need to be young and graceful. Barbara Hendricks and John Aler fulfil those requirements, she with a light, silvery timbre, he with a high tenor admirably suited to the tessitura of his solos. The third main character, the baritone whose role is central to the drama, assumes his rightful place here: Gino Quilico brings true distinction to the part, and his aria in Act 3 is one of the highlights. Though Plasson's direction at first is rather square, the performance grows in responsiveness. It's a pity the accompanying notes aren't stronger in textual detail, for the full score given here stimulates interest in its history. One of the changes made in the original score of 1863 concerns the celebrated duet itself, the first version of which is given in an appendix. It ends in a style you'd swear owed much to the 'friendship' duet in Verdi's *Don Carlos* – except that Bizet came first.

Additional recommendation

Les pêcheurs de perles
Cotrubas Leïla **Vanzo** Nadir **Paris Opera Orchestra / Prêtre**
Classics for Pleasure CD-CFP4721   Ⓑ
(104' · ADD)
    Worth hearing for Cotrubas's Leïla. Alain Vanzo's voice had lost some of its bloom by the late 1970s, when this was made, and Prêtre's conducting is somewhat lacking in magic.

Sir Arthur Bliss   British 1891-1975

Bliss Studied with Wood at Cambridge and served in the army in France. Immediately after World War I he made a mark with works using nonsense texts and brittle Les Six-style irony (Rout, 1920), but successive orchestral works (A Colour Symphony, 1922; Introduction and Allegro, 1926; Music for Strings, 1935) established him as Elgar's successor. His three ballets (Checkmate, 1937 ; Miracle in the Gorbals, 1944 ; Adam Zero, 1946), a notable score for the film Things to Come (1935) and his opera The Olympians (1949) express his feelings for high drama and atmosphere. Among his other works are concertos for piano (1938), violin (1955) and cello (1970), songs, chamber and piano music, and choral works (notably the choral symphony Morning Heroes, 1930). In 1953 he was appointed Master of the Queen's Music.   GROVEmusic

Cello Concerto, T120

Cello Concerto, T120. Music for Strings, T54.
Two Studies, T16
Tim Hugh vc **English Northern Philharmonia / David Lloyd-Jones**
Naxos 8 553383 (64' · DDD)   ⓢ**O**

This is a first-rate performance of Bliss's Cello

Concerto from Tim Hugh, stylishly and sympathetically partnered by David Lloyd-Jones and the English Northern Philharmonia. The work is a delightful creation, ideally proportioned, impeccably crafted and full of the most beguiling invention. Hugh plays with commanding assurance, great beauty of tone and rapt commitment, and the accompaniment is sprightly and sensitive to match. What makes this release indispensable to all Bliss admirers is the inclusion of the *Two Studies*. These date from 1921 and were believed lost until they turned up in the composer's papers after his death in 1975. The first is a memorably chaste, coolly serene affair, scored with delicious poise, whereas the second is an energetic, good-humoured and occasionally face-pulling romp. That just leaves the tremendous *Music for Strings*, which is where, alas, reservations must be raised. This superb score displays and demands a formidable technical facility, and Bliss's exhilaratingly well-judged writing would surely test any string section. It would be idle to pretend that the hard-working strings of the English Northern Philharmonia are ideally secure exponents. The work is well served by Lloyd-Jones's clear-headed, expressive interpretation, but in the finale's crucial introductory bars his approach is oddly perfunctory. The Cello Concerto and the *Two Studies* alone though, will probably be enticement enough for many listeners. The recorded sound is excitingly realistic.

Piano Concerto T58

Piano Concerto in B flat. Concerto for Two Pianos and Orchestra[a]. Sonata for Piano
Peter Donohoe, [a]Martin Roscoe pfs **Royal Scottish National Orchestra / David Lloyd-Jones**
Naxos 8 557146 (73' · DDD)   Ⓢ

In recent times Bliss's swaggering Piano Concerto (written in 1938-9 for Solomon) has found a champion in Peter Donohoe, and it's good that he's been able to set down his powerful interpretation as part of Naxos's British Piano Concertos series. As those thunderous octaves at the outset demonstrate, Bliss's bravura writing holds no terrors for Donohoe and he generates a satisfying rapport with David Lloyd-Jones and the RSNO. Theirs is a beautifully prepared and attentive reading which grips from start to finish. The bittersweet central *Adagietto* casts an especially potent spell, while both outer movements harness blistering virtuosity to supple affection. All told, a worthy modern counterpart to the thrilling historic displays from Solomon and Mewton-Wood.

No less compelling is the buoyant account of the Concerto for Two Pianos: an infectiously enjoyable, single-movement work that began life in 1921 as a Concerto for Piano, Tenor and Strings (that same year, Bliss embarked on his *Colour* Symphony, of which there are fleeting echoes here). The present revision dates from

1950; 18 years later, Bliss overhauled the piece one last time for the three-hand partnership of Phyllis Sellick and Cyril Smith. As in the Piano Concerto, the recording's a touch bright and clangorous, but the ear soon adjusts.

No such technical qualms surround Donohoe's intelligent and accomplished performance of the Sonata composed in 1952 for Noel Mewton-Wood. With his commanding presence and rich tonal palette, Donohoe again exhibits a remarkable empathy with Bliss's red-blooded inspiration. This rewarding Naxos disc deserves every success.

Additional recommendation

Piano Concerto in B flat, T58[a]. Adam Zero, T67[b]
Solomon pf [a]**New York Philharmonic-Symphony Orchestra / Boult;** [b]**Royal Opera House Orchestra, Covent Garden / Lambert**
APR mono APR5627 (61' · DDD) Recorded [a]1939 (live), [b]1946   Ⓜ

Solomon, for whose sovereign technique the Concerto was designed, plays like a man possessed. His partnership with Boult operates at the highest level of excitement, eloquence and dedication.

A Colour Symphony

A Colour Symphony. Adam Zero
English Northern Philharmonia / David Lloyd-Jones
Naxos 8 553460 (74' · DDD)   ⓈOO

David Lloyd-Jones's exciting and idiomatic account of *A Colour Symphony* proves more than a match for all current competition, including the composer's own 1955 recording so spectacularly transferred by Dutton Laboratories. Speeds are judged to perfection – nicely flowing for the first and third movements, not too hectic for the flashing *Scherzo* – and countless details in Bliss's stunning orchestral canvas are deftly attended to. Phrasing is sensitive and affectionate, solo work is consistently excellent (the slow movement's delicate woodwind arabesques are exquisitely voiced), and *tuttis* open out superbly in a technically fine recording from Naxos (magnificently keen-voiced horns throughout). Whereas *A Colour Symphony* was inspired by the heraldic associations of four different colours (one for each movement), the theme of *Adam Zero* is the inexorable life-cycle of humankind. In its entirety, this 1946 ballet score does admittedly have its occasional *longueurs*, but for the most part Bliss's invention is of high quality. Certainly, the vivid exuberance and theatrical swagger of numbers like 'Dance of Spring' and 'Dance of Summer' have strong appeal. Equally, the limpid beauty of both the 'Love Dance' and the hieratic 'Bridal Ceremony' which immediately ensues isn't easily banished, while the darkly insistent 'Dance with Death' distils a gentle poignancy which is most haunting.

Checkmate – Suite

Bliss Checkmate – Suite. **Lambert** Horoscope –
Suite. **Walton** Façade – Suites Nos 1 & 2
English Northern Sinfonia / David Lloyd-Jones
Hyperion Helios CDH55099 (74' · DDD) Recorded
1990   ⒷⒷ

What a joy to welcome on CD, a major British
ballet score (comparable in appeal to Walton's
Façade with which, happily, it's coupled). Constant Lambert's *Horoscope* is a highly individual
score that's somehow very English. It's played
here with striking freshness and expansiveness.
Lloyd-Jones responds to Bliss's lyricism very
warmly. What makes this disc particularly
enticing is the inclusion of the two *Façade* suites,
welcome away from the spoken poems. This is
music that in a witty performance can make you
smile and even chuckle. So it is here, especially
the 'Tango Pasodoble' with a delicious lilt for 'I
do like to be beside the seaside' contrasting with
its Offenbachian gusto, the 'Swiss Yodelling
Song' with its droll Rossini quotation and
refined mock-melancholy, and the irresistibly
humorous 'Polka' that just manages not to be
vulgar. All are ideally paced and the solo wind
playing a delight. The recording is near perfect.

Chamber Works

Piano Quartet in A minor, T6a. Viola Sonata.
Oboe Quintet, T44
Maggini Quartet (Laurence Jackson, David Angel
vns Martin Outram *va* Michal Kaznowski *vc*) with
Peter Donohoe *pf* **Nicholas Daniel** *ob*
Naxos 8 555931 (62' · DDD)   Ⓢ

The Maggini Quartet and Peter Donohoe give
a commanding performance of the Piano Quartet, locating an underlying toughness of argument and urgency of expression in both outer
movements to make one regret all the more
forcefully the budding composer's decision to
withdraw the piece following his demobilisation
in 1919.

Otherwise unrepresented in the domestic catalogue, the Viola Sonata was written in 1933 for
Lionel Tertis. If Bliss's inspiration lacks the distinctive melodic profile and organic mastery of,
say, Walton's Viola Concerto of four years previously, the work as a whole is still worth getting
to know. The Maggini's violist, Martin Outram,
makes commendably light of the solo part's at
times hair-raising demands and Donohoe offers
exemplary support.

But the jewel in this anthology is the Oboe
Quintet that Bliss composed in 1927 for Leon
Goossens. Elegance and resourcefulness are the
watchwords in the first two movements, whose
bitter-sweet lyricism forms an effective contrast
with the exuberant festivities of the finale.
Nicholas Daniel and the Maggini give a spry,
ideally proportioned reading, more intrepid in
its expressive range than than that of Gordon
Hunt and the Tale Quartet. Production-values

throughout are of a high order. Very warmly
recommended.

String Quartets – No 1 in B flat; in A (1915).
Conversations[a]
[a]**Nicholas Daniel** *ob/cora* [a]**Michael Cox** *fl/afl*
Maggini Quartet (Laurence Jackson, David Angel
vns Martin Outram *va* Michal Kaznowski *vc*)
Naxos 8 557108 (64' · DDD)   Ⓢ

The earliest work here, the String Quartet in A
major, was completed around 1914. It's a fresh-
faced, skilfully wrought essay, tinged with English modal pastoralism and an occasional dash of
Ravel, and much admired by Lady Elgar (in a
letter to Bliss, who was on active service in
France, she wrote of the music's 'eager life and
exhilarating energy and hope'). In 1919 Bliss
withdrew the Quartet, travelling to Paris where
he fell under the spell of the chic radicalism of
Les Six. While in the French capital, he composed *Conversations*, a wittily mischievous, at
times strikingly memorable suite in five pithy
movements.

However, it's the First Quartet proper that
yields the most enduring rewards. Cast in four
movements and full of high-class invention, this
is a shrewdly argued piece which strikes an
enormously pleasing balance between captivating poise, formidable economy of thought and
fervent expression. As with the masterly *Music
for Strings* of 1935, Bliss's command and understanding of the forces at his disposal are complete, and the work as whole shows the composer at his consummate, intelligent best. The
Maggini Quartet deserve the heartiest plaudits
for their cogent and assured championship of
this music; if anything, their account of the B
flat Quartet surpasses that of the Delmé in its
clean-limbed authority and scrupulous commitment to the cause.

For *Conversations*, Nicholas Daniel and
Michael Cox join in the fun with exemplary
spirit and character. The sound is vivid and true.
This is, quite simply, another irresistible bargain from the Maggini Quartet and Naxos.

Clarinet Quintet. String Quartet No 2
David Campbell *cl* **Maggini Quartet** (Laurence
Jackson, David Angel *vns* Martin Outram *va* Michal
Kaznowski *vc*)
Naxos 8 557394 (59' · DDD)   Ⓢ⊙

Like its predecessor of 1940, Bliss's Second
Quartet (composed a decade later as a 20th-
birthday gift to the Griller Quartet) is an enormously rewarding work, its progress purposeful
and vital, and consummately laid out for the
medium. It receives an absorbed and absorbing
reading from the Magginis, who find a hush and
concentration in the *Sostenuto* slow movement
missing from the Delmé Quartet (Hyperion,
nla). Otherwise, there's little to choose between
the two, save for a crucial bit more composure
and cogency from these poised newcomers.

In the Clarinet Quintet (written in 1932 for the clarinettist Frederick Thurston) the Magginis are joined by David Campbell for a mellifluous and intelligent account that must be deemed a worthy modern counterpart to Thurston's world première recording with the Griller Quartet. Listeners new to the work should sample the songful dialogue of the nostalgic opening movement and the bite these artists bring to the dashing finale: make no mistake, this is exceptional chamber playing.

With its authoritative booklet-essay by Andrew Burn and intimate, judiciously blended recorded sound, this laudable release deserves the widest currency.

A Knot of Riddles

Two American Poems[ag]. Seven American Poems[cg]. Angels of the Mind[ag]. The Ballads of the Four Seasons[ag]. A Knot of Riddles[chi]. Two Love Songs[cg]. Two Nursery Rhymes[aef]. Three Romantic Songs[bg]. Three Songs[bg]. Four Songs[adf]. At the Window[bg]. Auvergnat[bg]. A Child's Prayer[ag]. Elegiac Sonnet[bhi]. The Fallow Deer at the Lonely House[bg]. The Hammers[bg]. Rich or Poor[cg]. Simples[bg]. Three Jolly Gentlemen[ag]. 'Tis time, I think, by Wenlock Town[bg]. The Tramps[cg]. When I was one-and-twenty[cg]. The Tempest[bcg] – The Storm; Overture and Act 1, Scene 1
[a]**Geraldine McGreevy** sop [b]**Toby Spence** ten [c]**Henry Herford** bar [d]**Leo Phillips** vn [e]**Michael Collins** cl [f]**John Lenehan** pf [g]**Kathron Sturrock** pf [h]**Nash Ensemble** / [i]**Martyn Brabbins**
Hyperion ② CDA67188/9 (123' · DDD) Texts included
Ⓕ**O**

Nearly all Bliss's songs are here (only a few orchestral ones are omitted) but they're of uneven quality and are presented in almost random order, with no sense given of Bliss's development as a songwriter. It was a mistake to include the *Two Love Songs*, which are in fact the vocal movements of Bliss's beautiful *Serenade* for baritone and orchestra. Kathron Sturrock, throughout a wonderfully musical and responsive accompanist, does her best to make Bliss's piano reductions seem pianistic; but despite her they just sound clumpy. The finest songs here are mostly on the second disc. Kathleen Raine's poems drew the best from the composer – simple eloquence, bold, shining gestures and memorable images including a fine nocturne: they're masterly, and would alone make investigating this pair of discs worthwhile. Geraldine McGreevy sings them simply, purely and very movingly, as she does the progression from lyric charm to bare strength of *The Ballads of the Four Seasons*. Also on CD2 is *The Tempest*; this vivid storm scene is all that survives of some 1921 incidental music to Shakespeare's play, set with striking originality for two voices, trumpet, trombone and five percussion players. Things of such quality are rarer on CD1, though the *Three Songs* to poems by W H Davies are all strong, Bliss's setting of *When I was one-and-twenty* has a blithe insouciance, and several of

the other sets contain pleasing discoveries, like the elegantly witty 'A Bookworm' from *A Knot of Riddles* or the charming 'Christmas Carol' that opens *Four Songs*. McGreevy is the best of the singers, but both Herford and Spence are committed advocates. The best of these songs (about half) are of a quality to make their present neglect seem inexplicable.

Ernest Bloch   Swiss/American 1880-1959

Bloch studied with Dalcroze in Geneva, in Brussels (1897-9) and with Knorr in Frankfurt (1900). In 1916 he went to the USA, thereafter spending most of his time there (he took citizenship in 1924). He also taught at Cleveland (1920-25), San Francisco (1925-30) and Berkeley (1940-52). His early works are eclectic: the opera Macbeth (1910) draws on Strauss, Musorgsky and Debussy. Then came a period of concern mostly with Jewish subjects (Schelomo for cello and orchestra, 1916), followed by a vigorous neo-classicism (Piano Quintet No 1, 1923; Concerto grosso No 1 for strings and piano, 1925). He returned to epic compositions in the 1930s with the Sacred Service (Avodath hakodesh, 1933) and the Violin Concerto (1937). His last works represent a summation of his career and lean towards a less subjective style.   **GROVE**music

Symphony in C sharp minor

Symphony in C sharp minor. Schelomo
Torleif Thedéen vc **Malmö Symphony Orchestra / Lev Markiz**
BIS CD576 (78' · DDD) Recorded 1990-92   Ⓕ

Bloch's early symphony is an endearing and at times impressive showcase for a young composer (he was 23) endowed by nature and nurture with all the gifts save individuality (though there are hints in the later movements that that too is on the way). He can write impressively strong, expansive melodies, develop them with real ingenuity and build them into monumental climaxes. Climax-building, indeed, is what young Bloch seems most interested in at this stage, that and a love for all the rich contrasts of colour and texture that a big orchestra can provide. He's so adept at pulling out still more stops when you thought there could hardly be any left that you're scarcely ever made impatient by the occasional feeling that this or that movement could have ended two or three minutes earlier.

It's a pleasure, too, to listen for fulfilled echoes of that youthful exuberance in the mature 'biblical rhapsody' *Schelomo*. Just as Lev Markiz adroitly avoids any impression of overpadded grossness in the symphony, so he and his fine soloist find more than richly embroidered oriental voluptuousness in this portrait of King Solomon; there's gravity and even poignancy to the music as well, and Thedéen's subtle variety of tone colour provides shadow and delicacy as well as richness. The recording is excellent.

America

America. Concerto grosso No 1
Patricia Michaelian pf **Seattle Symphony Chorale and Orchestra / Gerard Schwarz**
Delos DE3135 (61' · DDD) Recorded 1993. Text
included   Ⓕ

Ernest Bloch's 'Epic Rhapsody for Orchestra', *America*, is a warming musical flight across the history of the United States, and uses the anthem of the same name as a leitmotif that helps bind English, American Indian and Jewish-style themes into a homogeneous, accessible whole. There are three variegated movements, each a dramatic tone-poem reflecting such universal ideas as 'Struggle and Hardships' or 'Hours of Joy – Hours of Sorrow' (the second movement's subtitle), with the third visiting the world of jazz and culminating in a full-throated choral celebration of the anthem. However, Bloch's 'programme' is fairly specific. *America* might be best described as a great film score that never was, a highly emotive thanksgiving from a man who had only recently arrived in his new home, with tender references to such favourites as *John Brown's Body* and *Dixie*. There are also veiled references to other of Bloch's works, including *Schelomo* and *Concerto grosso* that Schwarz programmes as *America*'s coupling. Demonstration standard sound.

Violin Sonatas / Cello Suites

Violin Sonatas – No 1; No 2, 'Poème mystique'.
Suite hébraïque. Abodah. Melody
Miriam Kramer vn **Simon Over** pf
Naxos 8 554460 (75' · DDD)   ⓈⓄ

Baal Shem[a]. From Jewish Life[a]. Méditation
hébraïque[a]. Solo Cello Suites Nos 1-3
Peter Bruns vc [a]**Roglit Ishay** pf
Opus 111 OPS30-232 (67' · DDD)   Ⓕ

Bloch's unaccompanied Cello Suites are late works that, while taking an obvious cue from Bach, still have plenty to say. The First Suite (1956) opens with a 'Prelude' before progressing to a lively *Allegro* which, in terms of style, isn't too far removed from the racy 'folkisms' of Kodály's solo Sonata. The typically Blochian slow movement calls for simultaneous bowed and *pizzicato* playing, and the work closes with an appealing 'Gigue'. Both the First Suite and contemporaneous Second were dedicated to the distinguished Canadian cellist Zara Nelsova. No 2 is more chromatic than the First, Bloch widening his expressive vocabulary (the second movement is especially dramatic) and making greater technical demands on his soloist. The German cellist Peter Bruns takes everything in his stride and his grainy, nicely modulated tone helps focus the music's manifold rhythms and colours. Bach hovers nearest the Third Suite (1957), whereas memories of *Schelomo* are most pronounced in the *Méditation hébraïque*. While

Bruns isn't quite in Piatigorsky's league for quietly stated eloquence in the opening 'Prayer' from Bloch's suite *From Jewish Life*, he plays beautifully and makes a cogent case for the cello version of *Baal Shem*'s 'Nigun'.

Miriam Kramer's programme might usefully serve as a sort of 'Bloch starter-pack', with the delightful *Suite hébraïque* as its tuneful opener. 'Rapsodie', the Suite's first movement, harbours a noble melody reminiscent of top-drawer Max Bruch and Kramer's performance of it could hardly be more heartfelt. Both violin sonatas are given extremely good performances, that of the Second particularly fine especially in the ecstatic, double-stopped statements of the central theme. The combination of Kramer's musicianship and Naxos's price will be irresistible to most repertory explorers.

John Blow   British 1649-1708

Blow was trained as a Chapel Royal chorister and then worked as organist of Westminster Abbey, 1668-79. In 1674 he both became a Gentleman of the Chapel Royal and succeeded Pelham Humfrey as Master of the Children; from 1676 he was also an organist there. Henry Purcell served an apprenticeship under him and many others were influenced by his teaching. The 1680s and 1690s were his most productive years as a composer. While still active at the Chapel Royal (where he was named official composer in 1700), he was Almoner and Master of the Choristers at St Paul's Cathedral in 1687-1703, and in 1695 he returned to Westminster Abbey as organist, succeeding Purcell.

Blow was the most important figure in the school of musicians surrounding Purcell and a composer of marked individuality. His music uses a wide range of idioms and reflects his interest in structure. Foremost in his sacred output are c100 anthems, mostly verse anthems (some with instrumental movements); the powerful coronation work God spake sometime in visions (1685) combines features of both types. Blow also wrote several services and Latin sacred works. Most of his odes were written for court occasions; among the others are works for St Cecilia's Day such as Begin the song (1684). The highly original and poignant miniature opera Venus and Adonis (1685), also for the court, was his only dramatic work. A well-known part of his output was his secular vocal music, comprising c90 solo songs and several duets, catches etc; the Ode on the Death of Mr Henry Purcell (1696), a duet with instruments, is notable for its expressiveness. Blow's instrumental works include organ voluntaries and some 70 harpsichord pieces.   GROVEmusic

Ode on the Death of Purcell

Blow Sonata in A. Ground in G minor.   Ⓟ
Fugue in G minor. Suite in G. Ground in C minor.
An Ode on the Death of Mr Henry Purcell[ab]
Purcell Birthday Ode, Z331 – Sweetness of
Nature[ab]. Here let my life[a]. Oedipus – Music for a

while[a]. St Cecilia's Day Ode, Z328 – In vain the am'rous flute
[aba]**Gérard Lesne**, [b]**Steve Dugardin** *countertens*
La Canzona (Pierre Hamon, Sébastien Marq *recs*
Elisabeth Joyé *clav* Philippe Pierlot *va da gamba*
Vincent Dumestre *theorbo*)
Virgin Veritas 545342-2 (64' · DDD) Texts and
translations included   Ⓕ Ⓞ

The teacher who has even one pupil who becomes even more distinguished than himself is fortunate; in Purcell, Blow had one such. And when that pupil's death precedes his own he has cause for genuine grief, as Blow did. One of Purcell's songs, here alternated with instrumental pieces by Blow, contains the line 'Nor let my homely death embroider'd be with scutcheon or with elegy', but it's one with which Blow and others could not concur. In a programmatic tour de force Blow's profoundly beautiful vocal tribute to Purcell comes at the end. Few countertenors are as finely matched in artistry and vocal quality as Lesne and Dugardin who, in both the solo songs and duets, wring every drop of emotion from the texts with sincerity, technically effortless *messa di voce* and admirably clear diction. In Blow's *Ode on the death of Mr Henry Purcell*, the risk that the recorders may cover the singers is avoided. The instrumental support faithfully shadows every vocal nuance throughout. Much of Blow's instrumental music was unpublished in his time and has remained unrecorded – some first-time pieces here. Where violins were originally specified, as in the A major Trio Sonata, in this recording they're replaced by recorders, and the harpsichord Suite in G minor is a modern compilation from various sources. Altogether this album is pure, unalloyed delight.

Venus and Adonis

Venus and Adonis   Ⓟ
Rosemary Joshua *sop* Venus **Gerald Finley** *bar*
Adonis **Robin Blaze** *counterten* Cupid, Second
Grace **Maria Cristina Kiehr** *sop* Shepherdess, First
Grace **Christopher Josey** *counterten* Huntsman,
First Shepherd **John Bowen** *ten* Second Shepherd
Jonathan Brown *bass* Third Shepherd, Third Grace
**Clare College Choir, Cambridge; Orchestra of the
Age of Enlightenment / René Jacobs**
Harmonia Mundi HMX290 1684 (51' · DDD) Texts
included   Ⓜ Ⓞ

Historically in the shadow of Purcell's *Dido*, *Venus and Adonis* is fast becoming a recognised masterpiece of small-scale Baroque drama. Blow draws considerable inspiration from French chamber opera both in matters of constitution and balance, though *Venus and Adonis* is still a distinctly English work with its poised, understated dialogue and an emotional denouement where Adonis's death from the tusks of a boar is touchingly tender in its measured, if demonstrative grief; the effect isn't far removed from Dido's lament, though Purcell's tragic

vein is ultimately untouchable. There are, however, some superb examples of indigenous word-setting and declamatory *arioso* which put Blow in the Purcell bracket in several instances, not least in Cupid's forthright scene-setting, sung with increasing assurance by Robin Blaze.

Indeed, René Jacobs surrounds himself with many fine singers here, all of whom he marshals in lively and responsive performances. Rosemary Joshua is an irresistable Venus, who wastes not a word either in colourful representation or vocal suppleness, and Gerald Finlay's reflective longing accords with Jacobs's elegant and full-flavoured direction. There's a nobility in the initial exchanges between the characters which is elevated by a doleful shimmer of recorders, which augurs much in its funereal symbolism. These responsive instrumental interjections from the OAE are even more effective in 'Hark, hark the rural music sounds'. This admirable recording puts the work on another footing entirely.

Luigi Boccherini   Italian 1743-1805

The son of a cello or double bass player, Boccherini made his public début as a cellist at 13. After studying in Rome, he worked intermittently at the Viennese court, 1757-64. In 1760 he began to catalogue his compositions (though excluding cello sonatas, vocal music and certain other works). In 1764-6 he worked in Lucca, where he composed vocal music and in 1765 reputedly arranged the first string quartet performances in public. On tour with the violinist Filippo Manfredi in Paris, 1767-8, he had his six string quartets op.1 and six string trios Op 2 published. In 1769 the duo arrived in Madrid, where Boccherini became composer and performer to the Infante Don Luis. Up to the time of Luis death in 1785 he composed chamber music for his court, notably string quintets for two violins, viola and two cellos. From 1786, as chamber composer to Prince (later King) Friedrich Wilhelm of Prussia, he sent string quartets to the Prussian court, though probably never went there.

The chief representative of Latin instrumental music during the Viennese Classical period, Boccherini was especially prolific in chamber music: he wrote well over 120 string quintets, nearly 100 string quartets and over 100 other chamber works. At first he used a standard Italian idiom, but with unusually ornate melodies and frequent high cello writing. Later, reflecting his isolated position, his style became more personal, with delicate detail, syncopated rhythms and rich textures; he sometimes used cyclic forms. The orchestral music includes several virtuoso cello concertos and over 20 symphonies; the vocal works include an opera, two oratorios and a Stabat mater (1781). **GROVE**music

Cello Concertos

Cello Concertos – No 4 in C, G477; No 6 in D, G479;
No 7 in G, G480; No 8 in C, G481

Tim Hugh vc **Scottish Chamber Orchestra /**
Anthony Halstead
Naxos 8 553571 (74' · DDD)   ○⑤

This disc is a winner, the first of a series of all 12
Boccherini cello concertos, beautifully performed on modern instruments but with concern for period practice and superbly recorded.
Each concerto has its individual delights, but
the formula in all four works is similar, with
strong, foursquare first movements, slow movements that sound rather Handelian, and galloping finales in triple time. One minor snag is a
confusion over numbering. Naxos calls its first
selection of works Nos 1-4, whereas the *Gramophone* Database uses the new numbering shown
above.

Many collectors will be concerned about the
Boccherini Cello Concerto beloved of generations in Grützmacher's corrupt edition. Many
years ago Jacqueline du Pré was questioned
about choosing it for her recording: she
promptly justified herself, saying, 'But the slow
movement is so lovely.' She was quite right, as
her classic recording makes clear, but that
movement was transferred from another work,
in fact No 7 in G, one of the four works here.
Tim Hugh's dedicated account of this lovely G
minor movement is a high spot of this issue,
with rapt, hushed playing not just from the
soloist but also from the excellent Scottish
Chamber Orchestra under Anthony Halstead.
Hugh offers substantial cadenzas not just in the
first movements of each work, but in slow
movements and finales too, though none is as
extended as the almost two minute meditation
in the G minor slow movement. Halstead, as a
period specialist and a horn virtuoso as well as a
conductor, matches his soloist in the dedication
of these performances, clarifying textures and
encouraging Hugh to choose speeds on the fast
side, with easily flowing slow movements and
outer movements which test the soloist's virtuosity to the very limit, without sounding breathless. Not just for those who know only the old
Grützmacher concerto, all this will be a delightful discovery.

Simply Baroque   ℙ
Boccherini Cello Concertos – No 5 in D, G478;
No 7 in G, G480 **Bach** Cantatas: No 22, Jesus nahm
zu sich die Zwölfe: Choral – Ertöt' uns durch dein'
Güte; No 136, Erforsche mich, Gott, und erfahre
mein Herz: Choral – Dein Blut, der edle Saft; No 147,
Herz und Mund und Tat und Leben: Choral – Jesu
bleibet meine Freude; No 163, Nur jedem das Seine:
Aria – Lass mein Herz die Münze sein; No 167, Ihr
Menschen, rühmet Gottes Liebe: Choral – Sei Lob
und Preis mit Ehren. St Matthew Passion, BWV244 –
Erbarme dich. Orgel-Büchlein – Ich ruf' zu dir,
BWV639. Schübler Chorales – Kommst du nun, Jesu,
von Himmel herunter, BWV650. Orchestral Suite No
3 in D, BWV1068 – Air (all arr Koopman)
Yo-Yo Ma vc **Amsterdam Baroque Orchestra /**
Ton Koopman hpd/org
Sony Classical SK60680 (69' · DDD)   ℗○

This appealing compilation is extremely imaginative: nine movements from Bach sensitively
arranged for cello and chamber orchestra, plus
an attractive pair of Boccherini cello concertos.
Yo-Yo Ma's Stradivarius was altered for the
occasion by luthier Charles Beare, and Ma uses
a Baroque bow. As superior 'light' listening
goes, it's difficult to think of a happier 70 minutes' worth. It also provides an ideal 'soft-
option' introduction to the sound of period
instruments. The *St Matthew Passion*'s 'Erbarme
dich' becomes a cleverly worked duet for violin
and cello, always flowing and discreet, aided by
responsive strings and a tactile lute continuo.
Ton Koopman's harpsichord brushes *Jesu Joy of
Man's Desiring* into action with a flourish,
answered by a mellifluous mix of solo cello,
strings and winds. Bassoon and cello join forces
for a swaggering 'Lass mein Herz die Münze
sein', before the brief chorale 'Dein Blut, der
edle Saft'. Last comes the inevitable 'Air' from
the Third Orchestral Suite, tellingly arranged
(as a duet for cellos) and superbly played. In fact,
Koopman's 'second' cello – his lead cellist Jaap
ter Linden – is every bit as eloquent as the star
act.

Listening to the two Boccherini works on this
marvellous CD reminds you again of Ma's
uncanny technical facility, at once elegant and
unselfconsciously virtuosic. Ton Koopman provides the cadenzas and the performances are
pure delight.

String Quintets

String Quintets, Op 25 – No 1 in D minor, G295;   ℙ
No 4 in C, G298; No 6 in A minor, G300. String
Quintet, Op 11 No 5 – Minuet
Europa Galante (Fabio Biondi, Enrico Casazza vns
Ernesto Braucher va Maurizio Naddeo, Antonio
Fantinuoli vcs)
Virgin Veritas 545421-2 (60' · DDD)   ℗○○○

 The frustration of those who seek to
identify Boccherini's works by their
opus numbers may end in their being
taken into care by sympathetic men in white
coats. The first three of the six string sextets
listed in his own catalogue as Op 25 were first
published as Op 36, No 4, as Op 47 No 9, and
No 6 as Op 47 No 5. The six of his Op 11, from
the Fifth of which the 'amputated' and very
famous Minuet is taken, appeared as Op 13 and
his own Op 13 became Op 20.

Thank goodness for Gérard, here also the
annotator, by whom to be guided when in any
doubt! Given that Boccherini wrote 100 string
quintets it isn't surprising that none of the three
from Op 25 on this disc has any other listed
recording. These three quintets serve as a
persuasive introduction to his music, full of
melodic invention, harmony that knows when
and for how long to remain static or flowing, or
ready to spring surprises, great variety of form,
and a kaleidoscope of sounds that could have
been imagined only by an accomplished and

venturesome virtuoso – which Boccherini was of the cello.

If the music itself is persuasive it becomes irresistible in these performances on period instruments (or copies thereof) at slightly lower pitch than today's standard, wielded by players of the highest calibre and sensitivity. The Font family quartet with whom Boccherini played at the Madrid court of Don Luis must have revelled in these quintets; in these recordings we come as close to sharing that experience as it's possible to get. An absolute must.

String Quintets – in E, G275; in F minor, G348; in G minor, G351
Richard Lester vc **Vanbrugh Quartet** (Gregory Ellis, Keith Pascoe vns Simon Aspell va Christopher Marwood vc)
Hyperion CDA67287 (62' · DDD)   Ⓕ

With more than 100 Boccherini cello quintets to choose from, the problem for anyone wanting to make recordings is which to choose. The E major G275 (formerly Op 13 No 5) makes an obvious first choice, when the third movement is the music universally associated with the very name of Boccherini, his Minuet. It's particularly refreshing in the Vanbrugh performance to hear it set in context against the work's other three movements, with their approach, light and crisp, paying obvious tribute to period practice in the choice of tempo – far faster than one usually associates with 'Boccherini's Minuet'.

The format of a string quintet with two cellos instead of two violas was very much Boccherini's special genre. Himself a cellist, it allowed him to free at least one of the cellos from following the bass line, so as to soar lyrically. To have this fascinating music vividly recorded in such fine performances, both polished and refreshing, with Richard Lester a perfect partner for the prize-winning Vanbrugh Quartet, makes an ideal sampler disc.

String Quartets

String Quartets, Op 32 – No 3 in D, G203; No 4 in C, G204; No 5 in G minor, G205; No 6 in A, G206
Quartetto Borciani (Fulvio Luciani, Elena Ponzoni vns Roberto Tarenzi va Claudia Ravetto vc)
Naxos 8 555043 (79' · DDD)   Ⓢ

Boccherini was a little less indulgent in his string quartets than in his string quintets, which are more numerous: here he couldn't allow so many fanciful flights for the cello into the upper reaches of the treble clef, nor could he create textures of quite such luxuriance. But the range of invention in these four works, composed in his compositional prime in 1780, is extraordinarily wide. The gem of this group is the A major work, with its graceful 6/8 opening, its pathetic, chromatic *Andantino lentarello*, its haunting little minuet with its echoing open E strings, and its brilliant and ebullient finale.

This was recorded many, many years ago by the Carmirelli Quartet (for Decca), whose Boccherini style was a model. The present group, the Quartetto Borciani, probably play it more perfectly in a sense, but the magic isn't quite so well captured. Named after the leader of the much admired Quartetto Italiano, this group play in a manner close to their model, with passion, intensity and accuracy, and their soft playing is wonderfully smooth and controlled, with a fine, veiled sound. In the quick movements they're a little sharper, more incisive in articulation than sometimes seems ideal for this music (they use modern instruments), but certainly the result is enormously spirited. This is very fine quartet playing and immensely endearing music; you can hardly ask for more.

Harpsichord Sonatas, G25-30

Six Sonatas for Harpsichord with Violin, G25-30   Ⓟ
Jacques Ogg hpd **Emilio Moreno** vn
Glossa GCD920306 (77' · DDD)   ⒻⓄ

Boccherini originally wrote these six sonatas for violin and fortepiano but eventually published them, with modifications, for violin and harpsichord. This may have been for commercial reasons, since he was at that time (1768) in Paris where the harpsichord was still in greater favour – though their dedicatee, Mme Brillan de Jouy, was a talented player of both keyboard instruments. The freedom of the writing in the violin parts confirms that her partner, André Noël Pagin, was no less gifted. They remain his only works for this instrumental combination. These aren't sonatas in the fully 'classical' sense – thematic material often reappears in different keys but isn't significantly developed, and two of the six have only two movements.

These sonatas are beautifully played and recorded with an intimacy suggestive of that of the salons in which they were performed in their own time. For the most part the music is lightly pleasing but in the Adagio of G25 and the Largo of G26 it digs more deeply. The warm sound of Jacques Ogg's harpsichord (by Adlam Burnett, after Blanchet) and the lower pitch to which the instruments are tuned, make it a sympathetic partner to Emilio Moreno's violin (Antonio Gagliano, Naples, c1760). This is a most desirable disc and, moreover, the only available recording of these sonatas.

Stabat mater, G532

Boccherini Stabat mater, G532 (1800 vers)[a]
Astorga Stabat mater[b]
Susan Gritton, [a]**Sarah Fox** sops **Susan Bickley** mez **Paul Agnew** ten [b]**Peter Harvey** bass [b]**The King's Consort Choir; The King's Consort / Robert King**
Hyperion CDA67108 (73' · DDD) Texts and translations included   ⒻⓄ

These settings of the same text by two Italian

composers (more exactly, Sicilian in the case of Astorga), who spent much of their lives in Spain, vary from each other both by the different groupings of the lines into movements and by the stylistic changes that had taken place in music in the course of the at least half century that separates them. Astorga's earlier setting has a good deal more contrapuntal writing, especially in three of its four choruses, as well as some diversity of style: more ornate in the double duet 'Quis est homo' and, in particular, the extremely florid, almost operatic, final 'Amen', but gently pathetic in the instrumental introduction and the soprano solo 'Sancta mater'. Intensity of feeling is heard in the duet stanza voicing the desire to weep with the distraught Mary, and the chorus sings expressively throughout, though 'Virgo virginum praeclara' sounds altogether too cheerful, and in the initial chorus the tenor line obtrudes rather edgily. Boccherini's is by far the more remarkable and beautiful setting. Originally written in 1781 for solo soprano, it was expanded in 1800 for three solo voices: fears that this could lead to a more 'symphonic' sound are dispelled by King's use of only seven instrumentalists. Robert King has a fine team of vocalists who on the whole blend well, an important consideration since only four of the 11 sections of the work are single-voice settings. The anguished melancholy of the opening and the grave serenity of the ending enclose a finely planned diversity of treatments, from the intense 'Quae moerebat' or the lyrical 'Fac ut portem' (both admirably sung by Sarah Fox) to the vigorous 'Tui nati' or the vehemently passionate 'Fac me plagis vulnerari' (for all three singers). The performance is accomplished and polished, but the recording venue tends to amplify singers' higher notes out of proportion.

Antoine Boësset   French 1586–1643

Boësset held various appointments at the French court from 1613 and was widely recognized as the leading composer of airs de cour (nine books, 1617-42). He also wrote vocal music for ballets de cour and some sacred music. **GROVE**music

Airs de cour

Je meurs sans mourir
Anonymous Nos esprits libres et contents. Ballet des fous et des estropiés de la cervelle – Entrée de l'Embabouinée; Entrée des demy-fous; Entrée des fantasques. Ballet des vaillans combattans. Entrée des Laquais **Boësset** Frescos ayres del prado. Dove ne vai, crudele. A la fin cette bergère. Je meurs sans mourir. Départ que le devoir me fait précipiter. O Dieu, ce ne sont point vos armes. Una músiqua. Quel soleil hors de saison. Quels doux supplices. Quel beautés, Ô mortels. Quelle merveilleuse advanture. Ballet des voleurs – Récit: Bien que je vole toutes choses; Chorus: Aux voleurs, au secours,

accourez tous **Briçeño** La gran chacona **Constantin** La Pacifique
Le Poème Harmonique / Vincent Dumestre *bqtr*
Alpha ALPHA057 (57′ · DDD · T/t)   Ⓕ**OO**

This CD completes a trilogy devoted to the *airs de cour* which help redefine one's perception of French court song. The first two were devoted to Guédron and Moulinié, and this last one to Antoine Boësset, who succeeded Guédron at the French royal court on his death in 1620. In many ways it's the most diverse and complex of the three.

Some songs appear in a four-voice version with continuo accompaniment, departing from the voice-plus-lute format that once pervaded recordings of this repertory. Interspersed with the songs are instrumental *entrées* from *ballets de cour* to which Boësset contributed in the 1620s. (Louis XIII was an avid dancer.) The composer didn't confine himself to French texts; the fraught relations between the Bourbons and the Spanish Habsburgs wrought a certain fascination with Iberian idioms, and an Italian text is thrown in for good measure. These complex links and political undercurrents are explained in an informative booklet-note.

This diverse mixture of languages and ensemble may appear unsettling at first, but later it becomes clear how well managed is that diversity, and one begins to trace the threads in common. *Dove ne vai, crudele* is thoroughly Italianate, and wonderfully sung. Claire Lefilliâtre, in particular, continues to impress: the title track, *Je meurs sans mourir*, combines artifice and a restrained but genuine emotional depth.

Georg Böhm   German 1661-1733

Böhm was organist of the Johanniskirche, Lüneburg, from 1698. He is important for his influence on JS Bach and for his development of the organ chorale partita (and variations) in which he used different compositional techniques in a synthesis of national styles. Böhm's keyboard works display his strongest gifts: among them are 11 suites and a Prelude, Fugue and Postlude in G minor which is one of the finest organ works of the period, combining French grace and charm with north German intensity. He also composed motets, cantatas, sacred songs, and a St John Passion (1704) formerly attributed to Handel. **GROVE**music

Keyboard Music

11 Keyboard Suites. Prelude, Fugue and Postlude in G minor
Mitzi Meyerson hpd
Glossa ② GCD921801/2 (96′ · DDD)   Ⓕ

Bach knew a good thing when he heard it and Georg Böhm was one. Based in Luneburg (where Bach was, to all intents and purposes, a sixth-former at St Michael's School), Böhm had mastered the flamboyant keyboard styles prevalent in northern Germany while taking a particular interest in adapting French keyboard sensibility and technique to the high emotional stakes beloved of Germans. These discs are, above all, a celebration of sonority; you notice this in Böhm's splendid organ music too, where his command of the textural impact of strong harmonic movement has as much to offer as the actual progressions themselves.

Mitzi Meyerson brings considerable colour and suavity to these 11 Suites and the miscellaneous 'triptych' piece, the very original 'scena', Prelude, Fugue and Postlude (which Schumann described as an 'eerie caprice'). Playing on a responsive and lyrical 1998 double-manual harpsichord by Keith Hill, Meyerson homes in on the essential *Affekt* of each prelude and treads a fine line between those occasions when the specific dance is to be articulated and when it's plainly a servant to another expressive end. She's especially successful in the movements requiring incisive execution and portentous nobility. She does Böhm a great service here, and reminds us why Bach justly rated him in the top division of senior contemporaries.

juxtaposes with carefully calculated transitions in between. Some of the most memorable moments involve popular idioms, evoking his ragtime performances or the songs he recorded so vividly with his wife Joan Morris. The word-setting is straightforward, reflecting the strophic poems, and refreshingly free from elaboration. The *Songs of Innocence* are charming and pastoral but in the *Songs of Experience* there's real anger at the human predicament.

This recording is based on a live performance with massive forces comprising 10 soloists, three choirs totalling almost 350 singers and a full symphony orchestra plus a harmonica and various extra electronic players and percussion. Nathan Lee Graham is an actor-singer who can project his catchy tunes and spoken poems; Joan Morris exercises all her magic in a range of styles, but Thomas Young seems too consistently declamatory. Christine Brewer is magisterial in numbers that reflect the modernistic side of Bolcom, and Carmen Pelton has a rare purity of sound.

This unique Blake spectacular makes a cumulative impact that represents Bolcom's wide stylistic embrace at its most ambitious.

William Bolcom
American b1938

Bolcom studied with Milhaud at Mills College (1958-61) and Leland Smith at Stanford (1961-4) and began teaching at the University of Michigan in 1973. As a pianist he has taken a leading part in the revival of ragtime and other American vernacular music. His works are polystylistic and concerned with momentous philosophical and religious themes: they include a monumental setting of Blake's Songs of Innocence and Experience for soloists, choirs and orchestra (1956-81). GROVEmusic

Songs of Innocence and Experience

Songs of Innocence. Songs of Experience
Christine Brewer, Measha Brueggergosman, Ilana Davidson, Linda Hohenfeld, Carmen Pelton sops **Joan Morris** mez **Marietta Simpson** cont **Thomas Young** ten **Nmon Ford** bar **Nathan Lee Graham** sngr **Peter 'Madcat' Ruth** harc/sngr **Michigan State University Children's Choir; Orpheus Singers; Choir, Chamber Choir, Musical Society Choral Union, Contemporary Directions Ensemble and Symphony Orchestra of Michigan University / Leonard Slatkin**
Naxos American Classics ③ 8 559216/8   Ⓢ
🅓🅥🅓 ② 5 110083-84 (138' · DDD · T)   Ⓜ

This is a *magnum opus* that occupied Bolcom for 25 years, starting as early as 1956. He's drawn on a wide range of musical styles to parallel Blake's method of moving from sophisticated to almost folk idioms. In some features – diatonic writing, English text and children's voices – Britten's *Spring* Symphony is in the background, but Bolcom is defined by the styles he

Songs

I will breathe a mountain. Casino Paradise – Night make my day; My father the gangster. Greatshot – You cannot have me now (or The Military Orgy). The Digital Wonder Watch. The Last Days of Mankind. Mary. Songs to Dance. Tillinghast Duo. Three Songs from The Wind in the Willows. Dynamite Tonite – When we built the church
Carole Farley sop **William Bolcom** pf
Naxos American Classics 8 559249 (64' · DDD · T)
Ⓢⵔ

Bolcom has always exemplified his eclectic American heritage in a distinctly personal way. As a pianist he's known for superb LPs of ragtime, Gershwin, Milhaud and songs with his wife Joan Morris. This collection of his songs with piano with Carole Farley, another performer of remarkable versatility, covers a range of styles from various periods; there are cycles and single songs.

Most of the accompaniments are hyperactively virtuoso, drawing on the full compass of the piano – a refreshing change from so much of the literature, but you're left wondering who else could play them like this. There are moments of repose, some in the witty mini-cycle *Songs to Dance* from 1989. *I will breathe a mountain* (1990) sets 10 American women poets, each song reflecting their personalities in a different style. 'The Fish' is an amusing poem by Elizabeth Bishop, a helter-skelter ride as dizzy as some of Sondheim's patter-songs. 'Messing about in boats', one of three poems based on *The Wind in the Willows*, makes an easy-going habanera.

This is a fascinating collection from one of the most individual American composers, who shouldn't be forgotten in the minimalist onslaught. Full texts of songs are an asset, it's vividly recorded and is delivered with effervescent enthusiasm by both performers.

Alexander Borodin   Russian 1833-1887

As a youth Borodin developed parallel interests in music and chemistry, teaching himself the cello and qualifying in medicine (1856); throughout his life music was subordinated to his research and his activities as a lecturer (from 1862) at the Medico-Surgical Academy in St Petersburg. His predilection for the music of Mendelssohn and Schumann, together with his acquaintance with Musorgsky, Cui, Rimsky-Korsakov, Liszt and above all Balakirev gave shape to his compositional efforts. It was mainly through Balakirev's influence that he turned towards Russian nationalism, using Russian folksong in his music; he was one of 'The Five', the group eager to create a distinctive nationalist school.

Borodin's earliest completed works include the First Symphony in E flat (1867), showing a freshness and assurance that brought immediate acclaim, and No 2 in B minor (1876) which, though longer in the making, is one of the boldest and most colourful symphonies of the century, in the Russian context a mature, symphonic counterpart to Glinka's Ruslan and Lyudmila. The piece contributing most to his early fame, however, especially in western Europe, was the short orchestral 'musical picture' On the Steppes of Central Asia (1880; dedicated to Liszt). Among the important chamber pieces, including those works which give the lie most clearly to charges of inspired dilettantism still sometimes brought against him, are the early Piano Quintet in C minor (1862) – already showing the supple lyricism, smooth texture, neat design and heartfelt elegiac quality of his most characteristic music – and the two string quartets, the second famous for its beautiful Nocturne, with their craftsmanship and latent muscularity. His most substantial achievement was undoubtedly the opera Prince Igor (written over the period 1869-87; completed and partly orchestrated by Rimsky-Korsakov and Glazunov). Despite its protracted creation and weak, disjointed libretto (Borodin's own), it contains abundant musical richness in its individual arias, in its powerfully Russian atmosphere and its fine choral scenes crowned by the barbaric splendour of the Polovtsian Dances.

GROVEmusic

Symphonies

Symphony No 2 (two performances)   **H**
[a]**NBC Symphony Orchestra / Erich Kleiber;**
[b]**Stuttgart Radio Symphony Orchestra / Carlos Kleiber**
Hänssler Classic 93 116 (52' · ADD) Recorded live
[a]1947, [b]1972   Ⓕ

Keen collectors may have acquired these off-air recordings in previous, more or less illicit incarnations but, in placing them back to back, Hänssler's authorised release allows us to make instructive comparison between Kleiber father and son. It's obvious here that Carlos has lifted key interpretative features from his father's marked-up score, and, in all probability, the recording too. Even so, his is the more remarkable of the two performances. He takes the music seriously, imparting a unique level of intensity to the argument, without moulding melodic lines with what we think of as idiomatic 'Russian' warmth.

In the first movement, both Kleibers eschew the grandiose rhetoric; Carlos has the edge in the development, hurtling forward with astonishing power. Surprisingly, perhaps, he makes more of the second movement, too, even relaxing a little for the trio's local colour where Erich stiffens up. Neither *Andante* can boast a truly Russian-sounding horn but Carlos comes closer. He's also a notch faster than Erich; even if the Stuttgart players aren't always quite on top of his demands, they struggle manfully with his no doubt fanatical insistence on crisp and resilient rhythms at high speed. When everything comes together, as in the finale's dash for the finishing line, the results are sensational.

The SWR studio relay has come up reasonably well, whereas the 1947 NBC broadcast (with audience) is inevitably rather dry and limited, in the Toscanini manner. Enthusiasts shouldn't hesitate.

Additional recommendation

Symphony No 2[a]
Coupled with: Symphony No 3 (unfinished)[b]. Prince Igor – Overture; Polovtsian Dances[c]
[a]**London Symphony Orchestra / Martinon** [b]**Suisse Romande Orchestra / Ansermet** [c]**LSO / Solti**
Decca Eloquence 467 482-2 (66' · ADD) Recorded
1961-6)   ⒷO
Martinon draws a thrilling performance from the LSO, an orchestra on top form. Solti's contributions are equalling thrilling – what playing!

String Quartets

String Quartets – No 1 in A; No 2 in D. String Sextet in D minor[a]
The Lindsays (Peter Cropper, Ronald Birks vns Robin Ireland va Bernard Gregor-Smith vc) [a]**Louise Williams** va [a]**Raphael Wallfisch** vc
ASV CDDCA1143 (73' · DDD)   ⒻO

Borodin's two string quartets have been coupled several times, and for a long time the most idiomatic versions were those made by the Borodin Quartet, who set the standard and persuaded many that they should be heard more often. The Lindsays don't ape these interpretations: for instance, they take the *Scherzo* of No 1 much more steadily than the fleeting performance of the Borodins, more as a dance than a *scherzo*, and they tackle the rather problematic finale of No 2 after their own fashion, by means of well-judged structural emphases, making a strong and just conclusion to the work. It isn't an easy movement, and like some other parts of the quartet, such as the spectral central section of the *Scherzo*, they manage the textures beautifully.

There's a less easy flow to the opening of No 2, and sensitively as The Lindsays play the much-traduced *Andante*, it's difficult not to feel the well-loved melody coming more instinctively, less lavishly, from the Borodins. Nevertheless, these are characteristically sensitive, thoughtful interpretations from a quartet whose fine work has brought us so much.

Unusually, they find room for the two surviving movements of Borodin's String Sextet, a lively *Allegro* in which, as is often remarked, Borodin seems to be taking Mendelssohn on at his own game, and a pleasant *Andante*. It's an agreeable addition to an attractive coupling.

Prince Igor

Prince Igor
Mikhail Kit *bar* Igor **Galina Gorchakova** *sop*
Yaroslavna **Gegam Grigorian** *ten* Vladimir **Vladimir
Ognovenko** *bass* Prince Galitzky **Bulat Minjelkiev**
bass Khan Kontchak **Olga Borodina** *mez*
Kontchakovna **Nikolai Gassiev** *ten* Ovlour **Georgy
Selezniev** *bass* Skula **Konstantin Pluzhnikov** *ten*
Eroshka **Evgenia Perlasova** *mez* Nurse **Tatyana
Novikova** *sop* Polovtsian Maiden **Kirov Opera
Chorus and Orchestra / Valery Gergiev**
Philips ③ 442 537-2PH3 (209' · DDD) Recorded 1993.
Notes, text and translation included

Ⓕ●

Prince Igor, even after 18 years of work, remained unfinished at Borodin's death in 1887, and it was finally completed by Rimsky-Korsakov and Glazunov. Borodin's main problem with *Prince Igor* was the daunting task of turning what was principally an undramatic subject into a convincing stage work. In many ways he never really succeeded in this and the end result comes over more as a series of epic scenes rather than a musical drama.

Despite this, however, the impression is given of a rounded whole, and it contains some of Borodin's most poignant and moving music, rich in oriental imagery and full of vitality. Curious things happen long before the official surprises of this vitally fresh *Prince Igor*, not least in the Overture, where Gergiev takes the horn's beautiful melody at a very slow pace. Gergiev is anxious to prepare us for the weighty events which follow and his particular point with the theme is to relate it to its place in the opera as the heart of Igor's great aria. There, in league with the bass-baritonal timbre of Gergiev's prince, Mikhail Kit, it solemnly underlines the fact that this is an aria of potency frustrated, sung by a hero who spends most of the opera in captivity; and that's further emphasised by a second aria which no listener will ever have heard before. It's the most significant of the passages discovered among Borodin's papers, rejected by Rimsky-Korsakov in his otherwise sensitive tribute to Borodin's memory but specially orchestrated for this recording by Yuri Faliek.

The other problem with the *Prince Igor* we already know is the way that Act 3 rather weakly follows its much more imposing Polovtsian predecessor. Gergiev obviates both that, and the problem of too much time initially spent in Igor's home town of Putivl, by referring to a structural outline of Borodin's dating from 1883 which proposes alternating the Russian and Polovtsian acts. In the theatre, we might still want the famous Polovtsian *divertissement* as a centrepiece; but on the recording the new order works splendidly, not least because Gergiev is at his fluent best in the scenes of Galitzky's dissipation and Yaroslavna's despair, now making up the opera's Second Act. While Borodina executes Kontchakovna's seductive chromaticisms with astonishing breath control and focus of tone, Bulat Minjelkiev's Kontchak is a little too free and easy, at least next to Ognovenko's perfectly gauged Galitzky, a rogue who needs the extra rebellion music of the more recent version to show more threatening colours. There's just the right degree of relaxation, too, about his drunken supporters Skula and Eroshka. It takes two Russian character-singers to make sense of this pair – 'with our wine and our cunning we will never die in Russia', they tell us truthfully – and their comical capitulation on Igor's return wins respect for Borodin's daring happy-end transition here.

It's beautifully paced by Pluzhnikov, Selezniev and their conductor, and crowned by a choral cry of joy which brings a marvellous rush of tearful adrenalin. That leaves us with Gorchakova, so touching in Yaroslavna's first aria but not always projecting the text very vividly and clearly not at her best in the big scena of the last act. Still, in terms of long-term vision, orchestral detail and strength of ensemble, Gergiev is ahead of the competition.

Dmitry Bortnyansky
Ukrainian 1751-1825

Bortnyansky studied in Italy from 1769; his first operas were given there, 1776-8. Returning to Russia in 1779, he became Kapellmeister at the St Petersburg court and in 1796 director. His many Russian sacred pieces (later edited by Tchaikovsky) are notable for their Italianate lyricism and skilful counterpoint. He also wrote operas, cantatas and instrumental pieces, notably a Sinfonia concertante (1790). GROVEmusic

Sacred Concertos

Sacred Concertos – No 17, How amiable are thy tabernacles, O Lord of hosts!; No 18, It is a good thing to give thanks unto the Lord; No 19, The Lord said unto my Lord: sit thou at my right hand; No 20, In thee, O Lord, do I put my trust; No 21, He that dwelleth in the secret place of the most high; No 22, The Lord is my light and my salvation; No 23,

Blessed is the people that know the joyful sound
**Russian State Symphonic Cappella / Valéry
Polyansky**
Chandos CHAN9840 (66' · DDD) Recorded 1989-90.
Texts and translations included   Ⓕ●

Bortnyansky has been mostly ignored in the West until quite recently. Tchaikovsky's disparaging comments on editing his sacred concertos also show he was not universally appreciated in his native Russia, but he has never lost his place in the repertoire of the Russian Orthodox Church and, as this series shows, these works are finely crafted pieces with an endless variety of invention.

This is Volume 3, and it contains some real gems. Concerto No 19 is a *locus classicus* of Bortnyansky's considerable lyrical power, though he also employs his neo-Baroque fugal writing to impressive effect, but No 20 is even more convincing, each movement containing a substructure characterised by different musical moods. Tchaikovsky complained that the concertos used 'stagey or even operatic' techniques, and that's quite true, but it's done with consummate elegance, as you may hear in No 22. The Russian State Symphonic Cappella understand this music, in all its manifestations, completely, responding to its subtlest nuances.

Sacred Concertos for Double Choir – No 1, I will praise thee; No 2, Praise ye the Lord; No 3, Come and behold the works of God; No 4, Who shall ascend into the hill of the Lord?; No 5, The heavens declare the glory of God; No 6, What God is greater?; No 7, Glory to God in the highest; No 8, Ye people, sing a song; No 9, Praise ye the Lord; No 10, My heart is fortified
**Russian State Symphonic Cappella / Valeri
Polyansky**
Chandos CHAN9922 (75' · DDD) Notes, texts and
translations included   Ⓕ

The Russian State Symphonic Cappella under the energetic direction of Polyansky continue their traversal of Bortnyansky's monumental production of sacred concertos with an entire disc devoted to those for double choir. As always, Bortnyansky delights in the contrasting of textures and dynamics in a spontaneous way that very frequently recalls a composer such as Handel. The joyous antiphonal writing to be found in many of the works on this recording reinforce this impression, and the style is meat and drink to Polyansky's singers.

The feeling of cohesion in the Seventh, for example (*Glory to God in the highest*), is achieved, in spite of the colourful contrasts that characterise the work, completely naturally and convincingly. While grand quasi-operatic moments such as the first movement of the Fifth and the often Bachian writing characteristic of, for example, the Eighth, are given suitably splendid and powerful renditions, the more reflective passages – which are far more abundant in the works in double-choir format than you might

suppose – are also sung with tremendous sensitivity, and a vital feeling of sheer vocal strength underlying those *pianissimos*, as can be heard beautifully demonstrated in the Ninth.

Without a doubt this is another triumph in a series that has definitively rehabilitated the much-maligned Bortnyansky in Western eyes.

Rutland Boughton   British 1878-1960

Boughton studied briefly at the RCM but was mostly self-taught. While teaching in Birmingham (1905-11) he developed his ideas on the basis of Wagner and William Morris socialism, and put them into practice at his Glastonbury festivals (1914-27), where several of his operas were first produced, including The Immortal Hour (1914); this had immense success when staged in London in 1922. After the collapse of the Glastonbury venture he retired to farm, write and compose, and in 1945 completed his Arthurian cycle of five operas, in which Wagnerianism gives way to a simpler folk-song manner.
GROVEmusic

The Immortal Hour

The Immortal Hour
Roderick Kennedy *bass* Dalua **Anne Dawson** *sop*
Etain **David Wilson-Johnson** *bar* Eochaidh
Maldwyn Davies *ten* Midir **Geoffrey Mitchell Choir;
English Chamber Orchestra / Alan G Melville**
Hyperion ② CDD22040 (125' · DDD) Recorded 1983.
Notes and text included   Ⓜ

The Immortal Hour is part of theatrical folklore: in London in the early 1920s it ran, unprecedentedly, for 216 consecutive performances and, shortly afterwards, for a further 160 at the first of several revivals. Within a decade it had been played a thousand times. Many in those audiences returned repeatedly, fascinated by the other-worldly mystery of the plot (it concerns the love of a mortal king, Eochaidh, for the faery princess Etain and the destruction of their happiness by her nostalgic longing for the Land of the Ever Young) and by the gentle, lyrical simplicity of its music. In the bleak aftermath of 1918, with civil war in Ireland, political instability at home and the names of Hitler, Mussolini and Stalin emerging from obscurity into the headlines, what blessed escapism this blend of Celtic myth and folk-tinged pentatonic sweetness must have been. Boughton's score still has the power to evoke that world, immediately and effortlessly.

It's quiet, sweet music, muted in colour and softly plaintive, and whenever the plot demands more than this the opera sags. Midir, the visitant from the Land of the Ever Young who lures Etain away from the mortal world, really needs music of dangerously heady, Dionysiac incandescence, but Boughton's vocabulary can run to nothing more transported than the prettily lilting Faery Song and some pages of folksy lyricism with a few showy high notes. No less seriously the music has little dramatic grip. Despite all this, *The Immortal Hour* does have a quality, difficult to define, that's genuinely alluring. It's there in the touching purity of Etain's music (and how movingly Anne Dawson sings the role). It's there in the moments of true darkness that the music achieves: Dalua, the tormented Lord of Shadow conjures up something of the sombre shudder of the supernatural world. The performance could hardly speak more eloquently for the opera. Alan G Melville allows the music to emerge from and retreat into shadowy silences; all the principal singers are accomplished and the superb chorus has been placed so as to evoke a sense of space.

Lili Boulanger
French 1893-1918

Boulanger studied at the Paris Conservatoire and won the Prix de Rome. Her composing life was short but productive: most important are her psalm settings and other large-scale choral works in a strong, subtle style. **GROVE**music

Psalms

Psalms – 24[b]; 129[d]; 130, 'Du fond de l'abîme'[abd]. Pour les funérailles d'un soldat[cd]. D'un soir triste. D'un matin du printemps. Vieille prière bouddhique[bd]
[a]Sonia de Beaufort *mez* [b]Martial Defontaine *ten* [c]Vincent le Texier *bar* [d]Namur Symphonic Chorus; Luxembourg Philharmonic Orchestra / Mark Stringer
Timpani 1C1046 (67' · DDD) Texts and translations included Ⓕ**O**

The name of the remarkable teacher and conductor Nadia Boulanger is famous throughout the musical world, but her sister Lili (six years younger), phenomenally gifted – she was the first woman to win the Premier Prix de Rome (while Nadia had attained only a Second Prix) – showed promise of at least equal distinction. Always of delicate health, her death at the age of 24 was a tragedy for music. Apart from works written in her early teens, which she later destroyed, her composing career lasted a mere seven years; but the quality of these compositions is arresting.

Except for parts of *D'un matin du printemps* (originally for violin and piano, and orchestrated only two months before her death), a grave, even sombre air permeates her works, which are heavily tinged with modal thinking. Her idiom is strong, with a bold harmonic sense and an individual feeling for scoring (her stirring Psalm 24, for example, has the unusual combination of brass, timpani, harp and organ with the male voices): the beatific ending of Psalm 129 is heart-easing after the earlier harshness of 'Hard as they have harried me, they have not overcome me' (words significantly applicable to her own determined spirit). Her choral works are comparable to the best of Roussel or Honegger, but her Psalm 130 (dedicated to her father's memory), with its exotic scale and chromaticisms, has more affinity with Bloch and is, without much doubt, a masterpiece. A disc not to be missed.

Faust et Hélène

D'un matin du printemps. D'un soir triste. Faust et Hélène[a]. Psalm 24[b]. Psalm 130, 'Du fond de l'abîme'[c]
[a]Lynne Dawson *sop* [c]Ann Murray *mez* [a]Bonaventura Bottone, [bc]Neil MacKenzie *tens* [a]Jason Howard *bar* [bc]City of Birmingham Symphony Orchestra Chorus; BBC Philharmonic Orchestra / Yan Pascal Tortelier
Chandos CHAN9745 (74' · DDD) Texts and translations included Ⓕ**OOO**

 This disc largely duplicates Mark Stringer's programme on the Timpani label mentioned above (inevitably, since in her mere 24 years of life Lili's output was limited). The performances here are first class, and splendidly recorded too. The eloquent sombreness of *D'un soir triste* tugs at the heart, *D'un matin du printemps* is deliciously airy and optimistic, Psalm 24 is given tremendous attack by orchestra and chorus and the powerful Psalm 130 is presented as the masterly, heartfelt work it is. The major work here, though, is the 30-minute cantata *Faust et Hélène* in its first recording. No wonder that it won the 1913 Premier Prix de Rome: the jury must have been thunderstruck by the maturity of this entry from a 19-year-old. It blends lyricism of striking beauty, rapturous fervour, emotional anguish and tense drama with, for a young composer, an astonishing sureness of touch in overall structure, freshness of invention, technical brilliance and imaginative scoring. It seems to have inspired the present performers, among whom it's almost invidious to praise Bonaventura Bottone.

Pierre Boulez
French 1925

Boulez studied with Messiaen at the Paris Conservatoire (1942-5) and privately with Andrée Vaurabourg and René Leibowitz, inheriting Messiaen's concern with rhythm, non-developing forms and extra-European music along with the Schoenberg tradition of Leibowitz. The clash of the two influences lies behind such intense, disruptive works as his first two piano sonatas (1946, 1948) and Livre pour quatuor for string quartet (1949). The violence of his early music also suited that of René Char's poetry in the cantatas Le visage nuptial (1946) and Le soleil des eaux (1948), though through this highly charged style he was working towards an objective serial control of rhythm, loudness and tone colour that was achieved in the Structures for two pianos (1952). At this time he came to know Stockhausen, with whom he became a leader of the European avant garde, teaching at Darmstadt (1955-67) and elsewhere, and creating one of the key postwar works in his Le marteau sans maître (1954). Once more to poems by Char, the work is for contralto with alto flute, viola, guitar and percussion: a typical ensemble of middle-range instruments with an emphasis on struck and plucked sounds. The filtering of Boulez's earlier manner through his 'tonal serialism' produces a work of feverish speed, unrest and elegance.

In the mid-1950s Boulez extended his activities to conducting. He had been Barrault's musical director since 1946 and in 1954 under Barrault's aegis he set up a concert series, the Domaine Musical, to provide a platform for new music. By the mid-1960s he was appearing widely as a conductor, becoming chief conductor of the BBC SO (1971-4) and the New York PO (1971-8). Meanwhile his creative output declined. Under the influence of Mallarmé he had embarked on three big aleatory works after Le marteau, but of these the Third Piano Sonata (1957) remains a fragment and Pli selon pli for soprano and orchestra (1962) has been repeatedly revised; only a second book of Structures for two pianos (1961) has been definitively finished. Other works, notably Eclat/Multiples for tuned percussion ensemble and orchestra, also remain in progress, as if the open-endedness of Boulez's proliferating musical world had committed him to incompleteness. Only the severe memorial Rituel for orchestra (1975) has escaped that fate.

Since the mid-1970s Boulez has concentrated on his work as director of the Institut de Recherche et Coordination Acoustique/Musique, a computer studio in Paris where his main work has been Répons for orchestra and digital equipment. GROVEmusic

Rituel in memoriam Bruno Maderna

Rituel in memoriam Bruno Maderna[a].
Eclat/Multiples[b]
[a]**BBC Symphony Orchestra,** [b]**Ensemble Intercontemporain / Pierre Boulez**
Sony Classical SMK45839 (52' · ADD/DDD) Recorded 1976-82 Ⓜ

Whatever's involved in the 20-bit technology used by Sony Classical to enhance the original CBS recordings of these works, the result is a very immediate and clear sound-picture. The sound does justice to a disc that can be recommended without reservation: magisterial performances by fine musicians of two masterworks by a leading contemporary composer. Boulez's casting off of post-Debussian refinements in *Eclat/Multiples* is enormously invigorating, and there's little of the stately, Messiaen-like processional writing that dominates *Rituel*. Here, two very different facets of Boulez's musical personality come into mutually illuminating confrontation, and this recording is frustrating only to the extent that the work itself remains unfinished. Maybe what's most radical about Boulez is that Western music's traditional concern with preparing and achieving a definitive ending has ceased to be necessary. In which case, of course, the way in which *Rituel* draws to a close could

represent a concession to convention he now regrets. In its CD transfer *Rituel* seems more than ever in thrall to the chiming, clattering percussion spread through the orchestra, which shepherds the various instrumental groups like so many anxious guardians. The source of *Rituel* lies in Boulez's tribute to Stravinsky, and the music – a massive public act of mourning, not a private expression of grief – is in some respects more appropriate as a memorial for the great Russian than for the genial Maderna. Solemn, hieratic, carved from blocks of harmonic marble by a master musical sculptor, *Rituel* is a fitting homage for a composer who learned to keep his emotions under strict control.

Répons

Répons. Dialogue de l'ombre double[a]
[a]**Alain Damiens** cl **Frédérique Cambreling** hp
Vincent Bauer vib **Daniel Ciampolini, Michel Cerutti** perc **Dimitri Vassilakis, Florent Boffard** pfs
Ensemble InterContemporain / Pierre Boulez
DG 20/21 457 605-2GH (61' · DDD) ⒻⓄ

In 1981 *Répons* was hailed as a breakthrough in the integration of instruments and electronics in a dynamic sound continuum. It's a model of what it was possible to do creatively with sound in the late 20th century. The version here is the third, from 1984, although further expansions are always possible. A 24-piece ensemble is enclosed by the audience, who are in turn surrounded by six instrumental soloists, a physical immersion in sound startlingly conveyed here by the *spatialisateur* computer programme. Only the soloists are electronically transformed, and these 'real time' processes make the musical textures as sensuous as they are complex. Within this convincing overall trajectory, two sections – track 5, with the piano accumulating layers of sound at a relentless rate, and track 10, where the soloists' spiralling resonances carry their own expressive current – are as satisfying musically as anything Boulez has achieved. *Dialogue de l'ombre double* introduces a theatrical dimension, the clarinet's electronic double gradually becoming more mobile and more 'real' than the actual soloist.

Sur Incises

D'un Anthèmes 2[a]. Messagesquisse[b]
Sur Incises[c]
[a]**Hae-Sun Kang** vn [ab]**Jean-Guihen Queyras** vc
[a]**Andrew Gerzso** elec [bc]**Ensemble InterContemporain / Pierre Boulez**
DG 20/21 463 475-2GH (66' · DDD) ⒻⓄⓄⓄ

 Combine three pianos and three harps with a range of metal percussion, and the result is like a magically enhanced keyboard, intensely resonant, but with the kind of incisive, cutting edge to the sound suggested by the title *Sur Incises*. *Incises* was a piano piece on which Boulez based this work, composed between 1996 and 1998. It's divided into two substantial movements or – as Boulez ironically titles them – 'Moments', implying that the immediate event and context matter more than the way events and contexts combine to create large-scale forms. Yet there's unambiguous evidence of larger-scale shaping in the way the second 'Moment' offers a wider range of more broadly characterised material than the first, and it builds to a stunning climax in which boiling cascades of sound erupt volcanically, before the cooling and calming process through which *Sur Incises* ends.

For all its richness, the range of tone colours in *Sur Incises* is narrower than in those later works which involve electroacoustics, and this dimension is represented here by the relatively small-scale *Anthèmes 2*. This supremely well-performed disc is completed by the short 'sketched message' for seven cellos which Boulez wrote to celebrate Paul Sacher's 70th birthday in 1976. The music brilliantly characterises those oppositions between refinement and ferocity which form the essence of Boulez's distinctive style. An outstanding disc.

Piano Sonatas

Piano Sonatas Nos 1-3
Idil Biret *pf*
Naxos 8 553353 (64' · DDD)   Ⓢ●

It sometimes seems as if Boulez has spent a lifetime paying the penalty for having found composition so easy as a young man. The first two piano sonatas, works of his early twenties, are formidably assured in technique and tremendously rich in ideas. Those sections of the Third Sonata released for performance sound cold and tentative by comparison. Or is it that the Third Sonata's much more extreme rejection of tradition is itself a triumph, an authentic modernity that stands out the more prominently for its individualism? Such thoughts are inspired by Idil Biret's absorbing disc. In the first movement of the First Sonata the broader picture proves to be well fleshed out, the argument kept on the move, the young composer's impatience and arrogance palpable in Biret's steely touch and the rather dry but never harsh recorded sound.

The Second Sonata is no less confidently played. Its power suggests why such experiments as No 3 represents could never be a last word for Boulez. This disc isn't the first to bring us the three sonatas together, but Biret's musical persuasiveness, and the up-to-date sound, earn it a strong recommendation.

Pli selon pli

Pli selon pli
Christine Schäfer *sop* **Ensemble InterContemporain / Pierre Boulez**
DG 20/21 471 344-2GH (70' · DDD) Notes, texts and translations included   Ⓟ●

This is the third recording of *Pli selon pli*, with the Ensemble InterContemporain expanded to 57 players, fitting the composer's definitive conception of the work as enhanced chamber music. Moreover, this is in effect a first recording, since it incorporates the revisions which Boulez made to the first and fourth movements during the 1980s. The recording was, as he wryly notes, the result of assiduous preparation, with no insecurity or 'panic'. It's a remarkably polished, gravely expressive account, as if he now sees his 'portrait of Mallarmé' more as a ritual homage to the radical 19th-century poet than as a multivalent, urgent, even angry sketch of the kind of intransigent creativity that few of Boulez's contemporaries were committed to at the time of the work's genesis (1957-60). But, even without panic, there can be no such thing as a sanitised, lushly comforting *Pli selon Pli*. The music remains Boulez's most extended engagement with the modernist aesthetic.

The recording is technically immaculate, with the intricate tapestry woven around guitar, mandolin and harps and the labyrinthine interactions between families of flutes, horns and lower strings especially well managed. Christine Schäfer sings serenely and securely, with an admirable poetic presence. Although you can imagine other performances recapturing more of the score's original fire and fury, this is an imposing representation of a work which sums up the composer's vision of art and life in the years before he found his way to a viable electroacoustic technique and a more stable view of musical structure.

Pli selon pli[a]. Les soleil des eaux[b]. Le visage nuptial[c]. Figures, Doubles, Prismes
[abc]**Phyllis Bryn-Julson** *sop* [c]**Elisabeth Laurence** *mez* [bc]**BBC Singers; BBC Symphony Orchestra / Pierre Boulez**
Warner Classics Apex ② 2564 62083-2 (129' · DDD · T/t)   Ⓑ●●●

 This is a super-budget-price reissue of four of Boulez's most imposing earlier works. True, the 1981 *Pli selon pli* doesn't give you his most recent thoughts on his endlessly evolving Mallarmé portrait – for that you need the DG account from 2002. But this BBC version, a *Gramophone* award-winner in 1983, remains a very satisfying document of its time. A special strength of the set as a whole is the vividness with which it demonstrates what has been lost in Boulez's complete abandonment of writing for the voice since the 1980s.

The large-scale cantata *Le visage nuptial*, originally composed in 1946, but performed here in the revised version from 1988-9, has an expressive incandescence and a sustained dramatic power that not only reconcile you to René Char's convoluted verse but provoke the thought that Boulez might, after all, be contemporary music's greatest opera composer manqué. The BBC Singers have have probably never done anything finer on disc.

More subversive dynamism can be heard in the expansive, eruptive monumentality of the orchestral *Figures, Doubles, Prismes*, strikingly enigmatic in its commitment to strongly sustained oppositions, and bringing back the composer's own 1985 reading to set beside the recent version from David Robertson and the Lyon National Orchestra (Naïve Montaigne, 10/03). Add to all this the fascinating feline glitter of *Le soleil des eaux* and you have a 'portrait de Boulez' of exceptional quality.

Le Marteau sans maître

Le Marteau sans maître[a]. Dérive 1 & 2
[a]**Hilary Summers** *contr* **Ensemble Intercontemporain / Pierre Boulez**
DG 20/21 477 5327 (69' · DDD · T/t)   Ⓕ**OO**

After *sur Incises*, *Dérive 2* (1988/2002) is Boulez's most extended recent work. Like *sur Incises*, it's a sonic firework display in which three groups of relatively homogenous tone colours – wind quartet (cor anglais, clarinet, bassoon and horn), string trio, and a second quartet comprising vibraphone, marimbaphone, harp and piano – converge and diverge in an absorbing Dionysian ritual.

Apart from the brief *Dérive 1* for six instruments – from which, the notes assure us, *Dérive 2* isn't derived – this CD is notable for a new recording of *Le Marteau sans maître*: a score now half a century old and sounding more urgently volatile than ever in this superbly crafted performance. This seems to be Boulez's fifth recording of the work, and the first since the 1985 CBS version with Elizabeth Lawrence and the Ensemble Intercontemporain. This time Hilary Summers brings a highly effective quality of the *farouche*, as well as considerable finesse, to the vocal part: but, as often before, the thunder is stolen by the superbly characterised instrumental playing. Flute, guitar and viola are never overshadowed by the more resonant sounds of the percussion duo, and there's the kind of edge-of-the-seat interplay that can only be achieved by players who have the music in their bones as well as under their fingers. As for the final duet for flute and metal percussion, this stands out for its incantatory gravitas, and for the hint of un-Gallic pathos that underpins its eloquence.

With the finest present-day sound quality, this DG release is outstanding in every way.

York Bowen   British 1884-1961

Bowen studied at the Royal College of Music, London, played the violin and horn and became known as a fine pianist and a productive composer who wrote in a Romantic style and in many forms: as well as numerous chamber works and works for solo piano he also wrote three piano concertos. **GROVE**music

Viola Concerto

Bowen Viola Concerto **C Forsyth** Viola Concerto
Lawrence Power *va* **BBC Scottish Symphony Orchestra / Martyn Brabbins**
Hyperion CDA67546 (63' · DDD)   Ⓕ**OOO**

 During the decade leading up to the First World War, York Bowen, one of the brightest and most prolific young talents in British music, produced no fewer than three piano concertos, two symphonies, a concert overture, Symphonic Fantasia, *Concertstücke* for piano and orchestra and a tone-poem, *The Lament of Tasso*. His exquisitely polished and sure-footed Viola Concerto in C minor was written for Lionel Tertis (viola professor at the Royal Academy of Music), who first performed it in March 1908. Lasting nearly 36 minutes, each of its three movements serves up a heady flow of intoxicating melody, all clothed in the deftest orchestral garb (there's a definite Russian tang to proceedings – Bowen clearly knew and loved his Tchaikovsky, Borodin and Rimsky-Korsakov). This new performance is beyond criticism. Not only does Lawrence Power effortlessly surmount every technical challenge, he forms a scintillating parternship with Martyn Brabbins and an uncommonly well-prepared BBC Scottish SO.

A pupil of Stanford, Greenwich-born Cecil Forsyth (1870-1941) played the viola in Henry Wood's Queen's Hall Orchestra (as, indeed, did Bowen) and published two books (*Music and Nationalism* and *Orchestration*) before emigrating to the USA in 1914. His G minor Concerto (in all likelihood the first for viola by a British composer) was premiered in 1903 by the French virtuoso (and its dedicatee) Emile Férir. Beside its its present companion it strikes a rather more conventional note, but remains an appealingly lyrical and sturdily crafted achievement. The performance is everything one could desire, and the recording is wonderfully ripe and glowing.

String Quartets

String Quartets – No 2 in D minor, Op 41;
No 3 in G, Op 46*b*. Phantasy Quintet, Op 93[a]
[a]**Timothy Lines** *bcl* **Archaeus Quartet** (Ann Hooley, Bridget Davey *vns* Elizabeth Turnbull *va* Martin Thomas *vc*)
British Music Society BMS426CD (70' · DDD)   Ⓕ

Published in 1922 after scooping a Carnegie Trust Award, York Bowen's Second String Quartet proves a most endearing discovery. Brimful of sweet-toothed yet never cloying melodic charm and written with consummate virtuosity for the medium, it's a fluent, poised and readily assimilable creation which merits immediate investigation by anyone with a penchant for, say, Bax or Korngold. Its unpublished successor was probably conceived about the same time and again boasts a wealth of big-hearted, felicitous invention. Both works follow the same Classical ground-plan, comprising two soundly constructed, sonata-form outer movements which frame a tenderly reflective slow movement in straightforward ternary form, and both certainly merit their resuscitation here. A similar technical mastery, harmonic pungency and generously lyrical cast inform Bowen's later *Phantasy Quintet* for the unusual combination of bass clarinet and string quartet, a single-movement essay of considerable imagination and frequently haunting beauty.

The Archaeus Quartet are sterling advocates of all this rewarding material. Timothy Lines, too, contributes most sensitively in the Quintet, and the sound is vivid to match. A stimulating and enjoyable release.

Viola Sonatas

Viola Sonatas – No 1 in C minor; No 2 in F.
Phantasy, Op 54
James Boyd va **Bengt Forsberg** pf
Dutton Laboratories Epoch CDLX7126 (72' · DDD) Ⓜ

A valuable survey of three early Bowen offerings fashioned for that great British violist, Lionel Tertis (1876-1975). Not surprisingly, given Tertis's phenomenal technique and tone-production, each piece here makes exceptional demands. Happily, James Boyd is fully equal to the task. What's more, he forges a marvellously eloquent alliance with Bengt Forsberg, their playing brimful of affectionate understanding while retaining a sense of freshness in discovery.

Both sonatas date from 1905 and were premièred at London's Aeolian Hall by Tertis, with the 21-year-old composer at the piano, in May 1905 and February 1906 respectively. Described by its dedicatee as 'a vivacious and light-hearted work', the First Sonata comprises an expansive and confident *Allegro moderato*, a songful slow movement in ternary form (whose principal melody hints at Lowell Mason's 1856 hymn-tune for *Nearer, my God, to Thee*) and an unusually meaty finale, where sheer high spirits win out in the end. Its F major successor follows pretty much the same pattern, though the slow movement now quarries a darker vein of expression, while the concluding *Allegro giocoso* yields plenty of opportunity for cheeky display. Boasting admirable sound and balance, this is a gem of a disc.

Further listening

Bowen Flute Sonata
Coupled with: **Arnold** Flute Sonata **L Berkeley**
Sonatina **Hamilton** Spring Days **D Matthews** Duet
Variations **Maw** Sonatina
Khaner fl **Abramovic** pf
Avie AV0016 (65' · DDD)   Ⓕ
  The Bowen Sonata is a real discovery; a strong and
  characterful piece full of Gallic lyricism, under-
  pinned with ample, and always interesting, key-
  board writing. A fascinating programme.

William Boyce   British 1711-1779

Boyce was a St Paul's Cathedral chorister and an organ pupil of Maurice Greene, also studying with Pepusch. From 1734 he held organist's posts in London and from 1736 was a composer to the Chapel Royal, writing anthems and services. His oratorio David's Lamentation over Saul and Jonathan (1736) was followed by his first dramatic works, including a short opera, Peleus and Thetis (by1740), The Secular Masque (1746) and the highly successful pastoral The Chaplet (1749), the first of a series of works for Drury Lane theatre. Increasing deafness hindered him – his last stage work was Heart of Oak (1759) – but his output in other vocal genres continued, and as Master of the King's Musick from 1757 he composed over 40 court odes. Among his few instrumental works are 12 trio sonatas (1747), Eight Symphonys (from ode and opera overtures, 1735-41, published 1760) and Twelve Overtures (1770). Boyce was among the finest and most respected English composers of his time, though his Baroque idiom had become old-fashioned by the end of his life. His music has a fresh vigour, especially evident in fugues, dance movements and expressive vocal writing. The owner of a valuable music library, he gained lasting fame for his Cathedral Music (1760-73), an edition of earlier English services by Orlando Gibbons, Purcell and others.
GROVEmusic

Eight Symphonys, Op 2

Eight Symphonys, Op 2   Ⓟ
The English Concert / Trevor Pinnock hpd
Archiv Produktion 419 631-2AH (60' · DDD)
Recorded 1986   ⒻⓄ

William Boyce's eight Symphonys (his own spelling) aren't symphonies in the modern sense, but a collection, issued for concert use, of overtures he had composed over nearly 20 years for theatre pieces and court odes. They represent English 18th-century music at its unpretentious best, notably in their formal unorthodoxy. The performances are a delight – cleanly articulated, decisive in rhythm, just in tempo. The French overture-like movements that open Nos 6 and 7 are crisp and brilliant; the more Italianate first movements, like those of Nos 2 and 4, have a splendid swing. And the tone of gentle melancholy behind the fine, expansive D minor first movement of No 8 is particularly well caught. Three of the symphonies have middle movements marked *Vivace*, which often leads conductors into unsuitably quick tempos; but Pinnock obviously knows that, in 18th-century England, *Vivace* meant a speed not much above *Andante*, and for once these movements make proper sense: they're lively, to be sure, but not fast. This disc comfortably surpasses any rivals in both style and accomplishment. The sound of the modest-sized band is brightly and truly reproduced.

David's Lamentation

David's Lamentation over Saul and Jonathan   **P**
(Dublin vers[a] and London vers excs[b]). Ode for St
Cecilia's Day[c]
[c]**Patrick Burrowes** treb **William Purefoy**, [a]**Andrew
Watts** countertens [ab]**Richard Edgar-Wilson** ten
[c]**Michael George** bar **New College Choir Oxford;
Hanover Band / Graham Lea-Cox**
ASV Gaudeamus CDGAU208 (80' · DDD)   Ⓕ

This third disc in ASV's excellent Boyce series
offers an unfamiliar work that shows an unfamiliar side of the composer. In *David's Lamentation over Saul and Jonathan*, written in 1736,
when he was 24, Boyce is in elegiac vein. It starts
with a sombre G minor overture, using the typical 'lamentation' bass, falling chromatically;
this is followed by a succession of choruses and
airs, in sorrowful tone and minor keys, telling
the tale of Israel's defeat and the deaths of Saul
and Jonathan – and the slaying of the Amalekite.
Of course, it's hardly on the emotional or dramatic scale of Handel's oratorio of three years
later (of which the action of this work forms an
episode), but Boyce's musical language is, on its
more modest canvas, telling, and the work is full
of moving and affecting ideas.

The version given here, as the main text,
incorporates Boyce's revisions for a Dublin performance in 1744. Boyce in more familiar vein
is represented by the Cecilian ode. Graham
Lea-Cox directs with authority and obvious
affection; the rhythms are sturdy, and the particular flavour of the music of perhaps the greatest English 18th-century composer is happily
captured. He's helped by a capable band, the
admirable choir of New College, and an accomplished team of soloists. Michael George is in
good voice and gets his best chance in the ode,
with his energetic account of 'In war's fierce
alarms'; and Richard Edgar-Wilson shows a
full, elegant tenor in his airs in the cantata. Of
the two high men's voices William Purefoy produces some soft and sweet-toned, uncommonly
even singing, and Andrew Watts, higher in tessitura, fine in line, excels in the poignant numbers. Overall, then, a most enjoyable disc.

Peleus and Thetis

Peleus and Thetis. Corydon and Miranda   **P**
Incidental music – Florizel and Perdita; Romeo and
Juliet
Julia Gooding, Philippa Hyde sops **Robin Blaze**
counterten **Joseph Cornwell** ten **Andrew Dale**
Forbes **bass Jilly Bond, Jack Edwards** spkrs **Opera
Restor'd / Peter Holman** hpd
Hyperion CDA66935 (68' · DDD) Texts included   Ⓕ

Boyce was in his time one of the leading theatre
composers. *Peleus and Thetis* is a short masque,
based on a simple story reminiscent of *Acis and
Galatea*, except that here the jealous Jupiter
resigns his amorous claims on Thetis on learning that her son would outshine his father

(he was of course Achilles). Among the best
moments are Peleus's spirited song of defiance,
Jupiter's fine, richly contrapuntal one of renunciation and the lovers' duet at the end. Boyce's
music has a flavour all its own, and at its best a
very appealing one; Peter Holman conducts the
piece in lively fashion, and uses singers with a
good command of the style. Two of the other
items are incidental music to Shakespeare productions. The little amorous competition of
Mopsa and Dorcas for *The Winter's Tale* (in
Florizel and Perdita) recall Purcell. It's sung here
in something of a brogue, which would probably be more persuasive on stage than on a
recording. Then there's a dirge for Romeo and
Juliet, a touching, richly harmonised setting of
words as Juliet's body is carried across the stage.
The 'Pastoral interlude', *Corydon and Miranda*,
in which a shepherd chooses between rival
claimants for his love, consists of four airs,
mostly in a simple, melodious style, but a final
fiery one for the girl who loses, linked by recitative, and a final chorus. It isn't great music, but
it's tuneful, in a very English way.

Johannes Brahms   German 1833-1897

*Brahms studied the piano from the age of seven and
theory and composition (with Eduard Marxsen)
from 13, gaining experience as an arranger for his
father's light orchestra while absorbing the popular
alla zingarese style associated with Hungarian folk
music. In 1853, on a tour with the Hungarian violinist Reményi, he met Joseph Joachim and Liszt;
Joachim, who became a lifelong friend, encouraged
him to meet Schumann. Brahms's artistic kinship
with Robert Schumann and his profound romantic
passion (later mellowing to veneration) for Clara
Schumann, 14 years his elder, never left him. After
a time in Düsseldorf he worked in Detmold, settling
in Hamburg in 1859 to direct a women's chorus.
Though well known as a pianist he had trouble finding recognition as a composer, largely owing to his
outspoken opposition – borne out in his D minor
Piano Concerto Op 15 – to the aesthetic principles of
Liszt and the New German School. But his hopes for
an official conducting post in Hamburg (never fulfilled) were strengthened by growing appreciation of
his creative efforts, especially the two orchestral serenades, the Handel Variations for piano and the early
piano quartets. He finally won a position of influence
in 1863-64, as director of the Vienna Singakademie, concentrating on historical and modern a
cappella works. Around this time he met Wagner,
but their opposed stances precluded anything like
friendship. Besides giving concerts of his own music,
he made tours throughout northern and central
Europe and began teaching the piano. He settled permanently in Vienna in 1868.*

*Brahms's urge to hold an official position (con-
nected in his mind with notions of social respectability) was again met by a brief conductorship – in
1872-3 of the Vienna Gesellschaftskonzerte – but
the practical demands of the job conflicted with his*

even more intense longing to compose. Both the German Requiem (first complete performance, 1869) and the Variations on the St Antony Chorale (1873) were rapturously acclaimed, bringing international renown and financial security. Honours from home and abroad stimulated a spate of masterpieces, including the First (1876) and Second (1877) Symphonies, the Violin Concerto (1878), the songs of Opp 69-72 and the C major Trio. In 1881 Hans von Bülow became a valued colleague and supporter, 'lending' Brahms the fine Meiningen court orchestra to rehearse his new works, notably the Fourth Symphony (1885). At Bad Ischl, his favourite summer resort, he composed a series of important chamber works. By 1890 he had resolved to stop composing but nevertheless produced in 1891-4 some of his best instrumental pieces, inspired by the clarinettist Richard Mühlfeld. Soon after Clara's death in 1896 he died from cancer, aged 63, and was buried in Vienna.

Fundamentally reserved, logical and studious, Brahms was fond of taut forms in his music, though he used genre distinctions loosely. In the piano music, for example, which chronologically encircles his vocal output, the dividing lines between ballade and rhapsody, and capriccio and intermezzo, are vague; such terms refer more to expressive character than to musical form. As in other media, his most important development technique in the piano music is variation, whether used independently (simple melodic alteration and thematic cross-reference) or to create a large integrated cycle in which successive variations contain their own thematic transformation (as in the Handel Variations).

If producing chamber works without piano caused him difficulty, these pieces contain some of his most ingenious music, including the Clarinet Quintet and the three string quartets. Of the other chamber music, the eloquent pair of string sextets, the serious C minor Piano Quartet Op 60 (known to be autobiographical), the richly imaginative Piano Quintet and the fluent Clarinet Trio Op 114 are noteworthy. The confidence to finish and present his First Symphony took Brahms 15 years for worries over not only his orchestral technique but the work's strongly Classical lines at a time when programmatic symphonies were becoming fashionable; his closely worked score led him to be hailed as Beethoven's true heir. In all four symphonies he is entirely personal in his choice of material, structural manipulation of themes and warm but lucid scoring. All four move from a weighty opening movement through loosely connected inner movements to a monumental finale. Here again his use of strict form, for example the ground bass scheme in the finale of the Fourth Symphony, is not only discreet but astonishingly effective. Among the concertos, the four-movement Second Piano Concerto in B flat – on a grandly symphonic scale, demanding both physically and intellectually – and the Violin Concerto (dedicated to Joachim and lyrical as well as brilliant) are important, as is the nobly rhetorical Double Concerto.

Brahms's greatest vocal work, and a work central to his career, is the German Requiem (1868), combining mixed chorus, solo voices and full orchestra in a deeply felt, non-denominational statement of faith. More Romantic are the Schicksalslied and the Alto Rhapsody. Between these large choral works and the many a cappella ones showing his informed appreciation of Renaissance and Baroque polyphony (he was a diligent collector, scholar and editor of old music) stand the justly popular Zigeunerlieder (in modified gypsy style) and the ländler-like Liebeslieder waltzes with piano accompaniment. His best-loved songs include, besides the narrative Magelone cycle and the sublime Vier ernste Gesänge, Mainacht, Feldeinsamkeit and Immer leiser wird mein Schlummer.

GROVEmusic

Piano Concertos

No 1 in D minor, Op 15; **No 2** in B flat, Op 83

Piano Concertos Nos 1 & 2. Lieder, Op 91. Fünf Lieder, Op 105
Stephen Kovacevich pf **Ann Murray** mez **Nobuko Imai** va **London Philharmonic Orchestra /**
Wolfgang Sawallisch
EMI Double Forte ② 575655-2 (DDD) Texts and
translations included   Ⓜ**OOO**

This is an altogether exceptional account of this leonine, beautiful, but often elusive work. It's one of those profoundly musical performances, thought out in a myriad small details, that at the same time flows freely and spontaneously from the minds and imaginations of musicians for whom the work is no longer a thing to be mastered but an experience to be wonderingly relived. The disc also offers the most imaginative and raptly performed fill-ups imaginable on a Brahms concerto record.

Kovacevich has recorded the Second Concerto before, with Davis and the LSO in 1979 (for Philips), but his account here is cooler and more detached than his earlier reading. This may in part be an impression fostered by the EMI recording which seems thinner-toned and marginally more distant than the Philips. (Always a risk with a pianist whose skills include the ability to play with an extraordinary inner fineness of timbre and dynamic.) But it's also the conducting. There's a touch of coolness about the orchestral playing that you don't get from rival versions. Having said that, Kovacevich plays with great buoyancy, brilliance and charm. It's playing after the manner of Solomon; and it just about works.

Piano Concertos Nos 1 & 2. Seven Piano Pieces, Op 116
Emil Gilels pf **Berlin Philharmonic Orchestra /**
Eugen Jochum
DG The Originals ② 447 446-2GOR2 (125' · ADD)
Recorded 1972-5   Ⓜ**OO**
No 2 also available (coupled with Symphony No 1, Haydn Variations and Hungarian Dances) on
DG Panorama ②469 298-2GP2   Ⓜ

The booklet-notes make reference to the original Gramophone review, in which Gilels and

BRAHMS PIANO CONCERTOS – IN BRIEF

Emil Gilels; Berlin PO / Eugen Jochum
DG ② 447 446-2GOR2 (125' · ADD)   Ⓜ**OO**
This is a modern classic: awe-inspiring piano playing and accompaniments of weight, power and great sympathy. Unmissable.

Rudolf Serkin; Cleveland Orchestra / George Szell
Sony Classical ② SB2K89905 (111' · ADD)   Ⓑ
A fine memento of a great partnership and one of the glories of the US orchestra scene, the Cleveland Orchestra. These are wonderfully intense performances (especially in the slow movements) but the sound takes a bit of getting used to.

Stephen Hough; BBC SO / Sir Andrew Davis
Virgin Classics ② 561412-2 (100' · DDD)   Ⓑ
Hough's set of these two mightly concertos is remarkably successful with delicacy matched by considerable power, but there's a luminosity here that's very attractive.

Leon Fleisher; Cleveland Orchestra / George Szell
Sony Classical ② MH2K63225 (128' · ADD)   Ⓜ**O**
Pre-dating the Serkin set (above), Fleisher's is a stupendous achievement. His virtuosity and keyboard power allow him to take on Szell's Clevelanders as equals. He balances horse-power and musicality most effectively. Good sound for the mid-1950s.

Stephen Kovacevich; London PO / Wolfgang Sawallisch
EMI ② 575655-2 (122' · DDD)   Ⓜ**OOO**
🜚 The First Concerto won a *Gramophone* Award, and the Second is deeply impressive too. Sawallisch is a solicitous partner and the LPO play supremely. A very fine modern contender with excellent sound to match.

Daniel Barenboim; Philharmonia, Vienna PO / Sir John Barbirolli
EMI ② 572649-2 (146' · ADD)   Ⓜ
An often overlooked pair of performances but a superb one none the less. The First Concerto is magnficent, with the partnership of piano and conductor at its most inspired. There's a wonderful freshness about both finales, and the 1960s sound is excellent.

Stephen Bishop-Kovacevich; London Symphony Orchestra / Sir Colin Davis
Philips 442 109-2PM2 (141' · ADD)   Ⓜ**OO**
Recorded when he was still Stephen Bishop, Stephen Kovacevich's first recordings of these works remain deeply impressive: nothing is done for show, instead it all flows from sheer conviction and musical integrity. A fine low-price alternative.

Jochum were praised for 'a rapt songfulness that in no way detracts from Brahms's heroism, and so comes closer to that unique and complex combination of attitudes that for me is Brahms more than any other performances of these concertos I have ever heard, on records or otherwise'. It might be added that Jochum and the Berlin Philharmonic make plain sailing where others struggle with choppy cross-currents (admittedly sometimes to Brahms's advantage) and that the recordings don't sound their age. Other interpreters have perhaps probed a little deeper here and there; neither concerto rests content with a single interpretation, the Second especially. As for the Seven Piano Pieces, Gilels viewed the opus as a single piece, a musical novella in several chapters.

Brahms Piano Concerto No 1[a]   Ⓗ
Franck Symphonic Variations[b] **Litolff** Concerto symphonique No 4 in D minor, Op 102 – Scherzo[b]
Sir Clifford Curzon pf
[a]**London Symphony Orchestra / George Szell;**
[b]**London Philharmonic Orchestra / Sir Adrian Boult**
Decca Legends 466 376-2DM (74' · ADD)   Recorded
[a]1962, [b]1955   Ⓜ**OO**

It's debatable as to whether there's any other recording of the D minor Concerto that so instantly takes fire and which burns thereafter with so pure and steady a flame. To all outward appearances, Curzon and Szell were an oddly contrasted couple; yet they worked wonderfully well together, in Mozart and here in Brahms. The 1962 recording still comes up phenomenally well, despite some occasional muzzling of the orchestra's bass texturing. A merciful muzzling, you might think, given the frequency with which Szell detects and detonates the small arsenal of explosive devices Brahms has hidden in the undergrowth. We obviously don't lack great recordings of this concerto but this 1962 Decca version remains as collectable as any. As for the fill-ups, the Franck is beginning to sound its age technically but the performance is charming. As for the Litolff, it's a gem of a performance, well recorded.

Piano Concerto No 2
Maurizio Pollini pf **Berlin Philharmonic Orchestra / Claudio Abbado**
DG 453 505-2GH (49' · DDD)   Ⓕ**O**

Pollini's and Abbado's Second is among the most formidably single-minded on record. This doesn't mean a chilling exclusivity, one that, humanly speaking, omits too much in its quest for a crystalline perfection. On the contrary, the sense is of a granitic reading stripped of all surplus gesture, preening mannerism or overt display, intent only on the unveiling of a musical or moral truth. Again, this is hardly the sort of performance which allows you to savour this or that pianistic luxury, and there will be listeners who, more in love with pianism than with great music-making, will turn away.

Their opening at once suggests a promise of the epic journey to come and in that moment when, as Tovey once put it, 'the air seems full of whispering and the beating of mighty wings' their performance achieves a rare sense of transcendence, of an inspiration above and beyond the printed page. It's doubtful whether many artists have achieved such sublimity in the *Andante* where they combine, most notably in the *Più adagio*, to create an astonishing sense of 'the still centre of the turning world' (Tovey again). This recording is a memento of a grand occasion that stunned its audience – there's never a sneeze or sniffle – into submission. Here, surely, is a performance above the vagaries of changing taste and fashion.

Violin Concerto in D, Op 77

Brahms Violin Concerto
Schumann Violin Concerto in D minor, Op posth
Joshua Bell *vn* **Cleveland Orchestra / Christoph von Dohnányi**
Decca 444 811-2DH (68' · DDD) Recorded 1994 Ⓕ❍

Bell's first entry in the Brahms instantly reveals the soloist's love of bravura display, his gift for turning a phrase individually in a way that catches the ear, always sounding spontaneous, never self-conscious. Regularly one registers moments of new magic, not least when, in the most delicate half-tones, *pianissimos* seem to convey an inner communion, after which the impact of bravura *fortissimos* is all the more dramatic. He rounds off the movement with his own big cadenza and a magically hushed link into the coda, rapt and intense. The slow movement, sweet and songful, gains too from Bell's love of playing really softly, not least in stratospheric registers. In the finale the vein of fantasy is less apparent. Next to others this can seem a little plain. Dohnányi and the Cleveland Orchestra provide weighty and sympathetic support and the generous Schumann coupling in another commanding performance adds to the attractions of the disc. There too Dohnányi and the Cleveland Orchestra add to the weight and dramatic impact of a performance that defies the old idea of this as an impossibly flawed piece, with Bell bringing out charm as well as power. The central slow movement has a rapt intensity rarely matched, and the dance-rhythms of the finale have fantasy as well as jauntiness and jollity, with Bell again revelling in the bravura writing. The recording is full-bodied and well balanced.

Brahms Violin Concerto **Tchaikovsky** Violin Concerto in D, Op 35
Jascha Heifetz *vn* **Chicago Symphony Orchestra / Fritz Reiner**
RCA Victor Living Stereo 09026 61495-2 (64' · ADD) Recorded 1955, 1957 Ⓜ❍

This combination appears unbeatable. You may think that Reiner starts the opening *tutti* at an extraordinarily quick speed – until you remember that he's going to accompany no less a virtuoso than Heifetz, so he's merely taking it to match his soloist's performance. You'll like this if you think that this concerto is too often played in the kind of 'autumnal' manner often attributed to Brahms's compositions but which really shouldn't apply to many of them. With Heifetz it's played with respect but without any kind of reverent hushed awe. The slow movement is lovely and the finale is a winner, the playing of an exuberant young man, yet Heifetz was over 50 when he made this record. Reiner conducts the fast movement with a fiery rhythmic impetus that incandescently matches the exhilarating, yet unforced bravura of his great soloist. It's confident throughout – and just listen to his real *staccato*, a rare thing from violinists.

The RCA recording comes up extraordinarily well – although the soloist is balanced forwardly, he's naturally focused and the Chicago acoustic ensures a convincing concert-hall balance. If anything, the remastering of the Tchaikovsky is even more remarkable, considering that originally Heifetz was apparently placed right up against the microphone. You soon adapt to the closeness when the fiddle-playing is so peerless; and Heifetz colours Tchaikovsky's melodies ravishingly.

Violin Concerto[a] Double Concerto in A minor, Op 102
Gil Shaham *vn* **Jian Wang** *vc* **Berlin Philharmonic Orchestra / Claudio Abbado**
DG 469 529-2GH (71' · DDD)[a]Recorded live at the Philharmonie, Berlin May 2000 Ⓕ

Modern digital recordings of this generous coupling are rare, Kremer and Clemens Hagen on Teldec being the most notable one (reviewed below). Now comes Gil Shaham in a live recording of the Violin Concerto which in its urgency and sense of drama is one of the most impressive for a long time, coupled with a comparably strong and warm reading of the Double Concerto. Even in the opening *tutti* of the Violin Concerto Abbado establishes the incisiveness which is a mark of the whole performance. The tempo is a shade brisker than has become common, markedly so than that set by Haitink in the Szeryng version, and Shaham's first entry is comparably dramatic, bringing out the total contrast when he relaxes into the soloist's first lyrical statement of the main theme, a magical moment of transition. It's a reading marked by high contrasts not just of dynamic but of mood, all set within relatively consistent speeds.

Shaham crowns his performance with a brilliant account of the finale, a daringly fast *Allegro* which consistently brings out the second marking, *giocoso*, underlining the impulsive folk-dance element with a hint of wildness, in which he finds a perfect ally in Abbado.

There are similar qualities in this performance

BRAHMS VIOLIN CONCERTO – IN BRIEF

Joshua Bell; Cleveland Orchestra / Christoph von Dohnányi
Decca 444 811-2DH   Ⓕ●
Sweet-toned and subtle, Bell is an appealing soloist with a winning spontaneity that reveals great depths of feeling. Dohnányi displays his Brahmsian credentials to fine effect. (Coupled appropriately with the Schumann.)

Jascha Heifetz; Chicago SO / Fritz Reiner
RCA mono 09026 61495-2   Ⓕ●
This is a high-octane, high-velocity performance in which Heifetz's legendary virtuosity is matched by some staggering playing by the Chicago orchestra under Reiner. This is no autumnal vision of the work but an athletic, graceful display. (Coupled with the Tchaikovsky.)

Gil Shaham; Berlin Philharmonic Orchestra / Claudio Abbado
DG 469 529-2GH
Coupled with the Double Concerto, this is one of the most impressive of modern versions, intensity and full of imagination. Recorded live, it shows Shaham at his spontaneous best.

David Oistrakh; London Philharmonic Orchestra / Norman Del Mar
BBC Legends BBCL4102-2
This is great violin playing: Oistrakh is on superb form, playing with his customary warmth. Well accompanied by Norman Del Mar, this builds up to a finale of thrilling power. Inevitably, the 1960 recording shows its years.

Gidon Kremer; Royal Concertgebouw Orchestra / Nikolaus Harnoncourt
Teldec 0630 13137-2
A radical reassessment of this great work by two questing musicians. Kremer falls in with Harnoncourt's dramatic reappraisal, even offering Enescu's startling first-movement cadenza from 1903. The Amsterdam orchestra is on magnificent form.

Ginette Neveu; Philharmonia Orchestra / Issay Dobrowen
Dutton mono CDBP9710
Dutton improves on EMI's own transfer of this magnificent performance, giving it a winning warmth and body. Neveu was a commanding violinist and there's never a moment's doubt that she has the measure (and beyond) of this great work. Her technique is astounding and the accuracy of her playing an object lesson in great musicianship.

of the Double Concerto, which, though not recorded live, has similar tensions and sense of spontaneity simulating a live experience. Jian Wang's big opening solo is expansive, though not as much as Hagen's on the Teldec disc. Shaham and Abbado bring power as well as expressiveness, establishing this far more firmly as a first-movement *Allegro*. As for the slow movement, that brings the most extreme contrast between Shaham/Wang and Kremer/Hagen, with the latter taking almost two minutes less in a cool, almost perfunctory account. Altogether this is an outstanding issue and a clear recommendation.

Additional recommendation

Violin Concerto[a]
Coupled with: Tchaikovsky Violin Concerto in D, Op 35
Oistrakh vn [a]**London Philharmonic Orchestra / Sargent;** [b]**Royal Philharmonic Orchestra / Del Mar**
BBC Legends / IMG Artists mono BBCL4102-2
(74' · ADD) Recorded live [b]1960, [a]1961   Ⓕ
> Fiddle buffs will need no prompting. Oistrakh gives it buckets of empathy and plays with exceedingly warm tone. His muscle-ripping first entry, where he pulls on the tempo so as to maximise a feeling of power, has colossal impact. The Tchaikovsky is a feisty and dangerous performance, with Del Mar whipping up an accelerating storm.

Double Concerto, Op 102

Brahms Double Concerto **Schumann** Cello Concerto in A minor, Op 129
Ilya Kaler vn **Maria Kliegel** vc **National Symphony Orchestra of Ireland / Andrew Constantine**
Naxos 8 550938 (59' · DDD) Recorded 1994   Ⓢ

The Brahms and Schumann concertos make an excellent and apt coupling, here given warmly spontaneous-sounding performances, very well recorded. The violinist, Ilya Kaler, is as clean in attack and intonation as Maria Kliegel. Kliegel in her opening cadenza allows herself full freedom, but any feeling that this is to be an easygoing, small-scale reading is dispelled in the main *Allegro*, which is clean and fresh, sharp in attack, helped by full-bodied sound. Kaler and Kliegel make the second subject tenderly expressive without using exaggerated rubato. Similarly there's no self-indulgence in the soaring main melody of the central *Andante*, but no lack of warmth or tenderness either. The finale is then unhurried but has dance-rhythms so beautifully sprung and such delicate pointing of phrases that any lack of animal excitement is amply replaced by wit and a sense of fun.

In the Schumann Kliegel takes a spacious, lyrical view of the first movement, using a soft-grained tone at the start with wide vibrato. She then builds up the power of the performance, and with Constantine providing sympathetic accompaniment, the spontaneous expression is most compelling. So, too, is the simple, dedicated playing in the central Langsam, and, as in the Brahms, Kliegel brings witty pointing to the finale, not least in the second subject. The balance of the soloists is good.

Double Concerto in A minor, Op 102[a]. Symphony No 2 in D, Op 73
[a]**Gordan Nikolitch** vn [a]**Tim Hugh** vc **London Symphony Orchestra / Bernard Haitink**
LSO Live LSO0043 (75' · DDD)   ⑤**OO**

Labels such as LSO Live bring altered priorities and fresh perspectives. When did a studio-based company last contemplate recording Brahms's Double Concerto with soloists drawn from within the orchestra? Brahms wrote the work with Joachim and his colleague in the Joachim Quartet, Robert Hausmann, in mind. It has a chamber-music dimension to it, yet it's also a work of real symphonic power. Haitink's accompaniment is superb, allowing the soloists the space for the lyric outpourings at the heart of the work. The sweet-toned Gordan Nikolitch and the burlier-sounding, though endlessly responsive Tim Hugh are perfectly matched, and grow ever closer and more eloquent as the romantic, at times almost operatic, colloquy of the two opening movements unfolds. After which, slippered ease and remembered passion is the order of the day in a sweetly judged reading of the finale. The recording, rich and immediate, brings out the tactile quality of Brahms's writing.

Haitink's 1990 Boston recording of the symphony has a certain Mediterranean glow to it. In this imposing and beautifully shaded new LSO performance, we return north again with a reading that's weightier and even more cleanly articulated than his 1973 Amsterdam version.

Symphonies

No 1 in C minor **No 2** in D **No 3** in F **No 4** in E minor

---

Symphonies Nos 1-4. Variations on a Theme by Haydn. Tragic Overture
Staatskapelle Dresden / Kurt Sanderling
RCA Victor Classical Navigator ③ 74321 30367-2 (197' · ADD) Recorded 1971-2   ⑤ ⑧**OO**

Kurt Sanderling has recorded the Brahms symphonies twice (his first set, with the Berlin Symphony Orchestra, is available on Capriccio), but what started out as solid, patient and well built broadened significantly, and in doing so stressed the epic element that was always implicit in the first recordings: the first movement of the later First Symphony is slower than its predecessor by over two minutes. Sanderling's great strength is in the way he handles Brahms's choppy, obdurate string writing, whether in the First Symphony's strutting first movement *Allegro* or the opening *Allegro non troppo* of the Fourth. Tempos are con-

sistently held firm, the lyrical passages allowed their due only within a solid structural frame (the Third Symphony's middle movement, for example) and first-movement repeats omitted. As ever, it's the Third Symphony that underlines specific interpretative differences between conductors – the first movement especially, a vigorous *Allegro con brio* that, for some reason or other, defeats even the greatest maestros. Sanderling takes a majestic, even marmoreal option that seems misguided: the gestures are grand, certainly, but the music remains rooted to earth. And if ever a piece said 'come fly with me', it's the first movement of Brahms's Third Symphony.

In short, Sanderling is sturdy, intelligently phrased, warmly played, fairly well recorded (the strings are a little grainy) and supplemented by equally well-considered accounts of the *Haydn* Variations and *Tragic Overture*.

Symphonies Nos 1-4. Variations on a Theme by Haydn. Tragic Overture, Op 81. Academic Festival Overture, Op 80. Hungarian Dances – No 1 in G minor; No 3 in F; No 10 in F. Serenades – No 1 in D, Op 11; No 2 in A, Op 16
Concertgebouw Orchestra / Bernard Haitink
Philips Bernard Haitink Symphony Edition ④
442 068-2PB4 (291' · ADD) Recorded 1970-80   ⑧**O**

Concertgebouw standards at the time of Haitink's survey (1970-80) left little to be desired. Perhaps the clarinets don't always overcome reservations about their tone and intonation with the sensitivity of their phrasing; but the horns invariably do, and more often than not Brahms's favourite instrument is a source of joy in these recordings, blazing gloriously at appropriate moments (especially in the Fourth Symphony), or opening up and sustaining huge vistas in the 'dawn' of the First's finale. As to the strings, Haitink's insistence on firmly defined (though never over-emphatic) rhythms from the bass lines up is altogether exceptional; there are countless examples, but most memorable of all is the cellos' and basses' ostinato that sees the Second Symphony's finale in the home straight. What an articulate, integrated Brahms sound this is, too; a case of conductor and engineers easily achieving their aims working in a familiar acoustic. The only movement you may initially find overly sober is the first of the Third Symphony, taken very broadly, though it's determined and imposing, and the launching of the coda is stupendously powerful. There's no better way of getting to know Brahms's orchestral works on a budget.

Symphonies Nos 1-4. Variations on a Theme by Haydn. Academic Festival Overture. Tragic Overture
Berlin Philharmonic Orchestra / Nikolaus Harnoncourt
Teldec ③ 0630-13136-2 (214' · DDD)   ⑤**OO**

Any fears that Nikolaus Harnoncourt's Brahms will be quirky, provocative or abrasive can be

BRAHMS SYMPHONIES – IN BRIEF

Hallé Orchestra / James Loughran
CfP ④ 575753-2 (279′ · ADD)   ⒷО
A longtime favourite: honest, muscular, with
a fine sweep and sense of architecture. The
Second Symphony is magnificent

Berlin PO / Nikolaus Harnoncourt
Teldec ③ 0630 13136-2 (214′ · DDD)   ⒻОО
A fresh approach to four classics played with
total conviction by a band with a tradition.

Berlin PO / Herbert von Karajan
DG ② 453 097-2GTA2 (156′ · ADD)   ⓂО
From the late 1970s, the BPO's Brahms
sound glows under Karajan's total command.
(Don't confuse this with his later, more
expensive, very similar digital recordings.)

Staatskapelle Dresden / Kurt Sanderling
RCA ③ 74321 30367-2 (197′ · ADD)   ⒷОО
Perfectly proportioned, sturdy readings from a
master conductor and great ensemble.

Concertgebouw Orchestra / Bernard Haitink
Philips ④ 442 068-2PB4 (291′ · ADD)   ⒷО
Exquisitely phrased, elegant Brahms from
one of the world's great orchestras.

Berlin PO, Vienna PO / Wilhelm Furtwängler
EMI mono ③ 565513-2 (219′ · ADD)   ⓂО
Perhaps *the* historic choice (1948-52) and a fine
example of Furtwängler's incandescent art: the
Fourth positively drips with tragedy.

Philharmonia Orchestra / Arturo Toscanini
Testament ③ SBT3167 (200′ · ADD)   ⒻОО
From 1952, the Italian maestro's singing way
with Brahms is gloriously conveyed.

Berlin PO / Claudio Abbado
DG $ 435 683-2GH4 (246′ · DDD)   ⒻО
One of the finest of modern Brahms cycles
with stylish, sleek orchestral work.

North German RSO / Günter Wand
RCA ② 74321 89103-2 (158′ · DDD)   ⒻО
Wonderfully wise, beautifully prepared performances that speak of a lifetime's love of
this music and thorough familiarity with it.

Scottish CO / Sir Charles Mackerras
Telarc ③ CD80450 (199′ · DDD)   Ⓕ
An interesting historic approach that uses an
orchestra of the same size as the one Brahms
had at Meiningen – fresh and light on its feet.

London PO / Eugen Jochum (Nos 1, 2 & 3)
EMI ② 569515-2 (149′ · ADD)   Ⓕ
A fine and often overlooked cycle from
the mid-1970s from a fine Brahmsian. The
Third receives a magnificent reading.

dispelled. There are interpretative novelties
(freshly considered articulation and clarified
counterpoint) and the Berlin strings project
a smooth, curvaceous profile. Harnoncourt
makes a beeline for the brass, and the horns in
particular. The live recordings have remarkable
presence and are mostly cough-free.

The First Symphony's opening *Un poco
sostenuto* seems a trifle soft-grained but the
pounding basses from bar 25 are beautifully
caught and the first-movement *Allegro* is both
powerful and broadly paced. The *Andante
sostenuto* slow movement is both limpid and conversational, with trance-like dialogue between
oboe and clarinet and sparing use of vibrato
among the strings. Harnoncourt makes real
chamber music of the third movement, though
he drives the trio section to a fierce climax, and
the finale's first accelerating pizzicatos are truly
stringendo poco a poco – the excitement certainly
mounts, but only gradually.

The Second Symphony's first movement is
relatively restrained. Harnoncourt's strategy is
to deliver a sombre exposition and a toughened
development. Again, the slow movement is fluid
and intimate, with some tender string playing.
The third movement's rustling trio is disarmingly delicate and the finale, tightly held, keenly
inflected and heavily accented: the coda threatens to break free and the effect is thrilling.

First impressions of the Third suggest a marginal drop in intensity, yet the first movement's
peroration is so powerful that there's a retrospective suspicion that all the foregoing was
mere preparation. The middle movements work
well but the rough-hewn, flexibly phrased finale
really makes the performance.

Like the Third, the Fourth opens with less
import than some of its older rivals, yet the
development intensifies perceptibly, the recapitulation's hushed *piano dolce* opening bars are
held on the edge of a breath and the coda is
recklessly headstrong. The slow movement has
some heartfelt moments, the top-gear *Scherzo* is
quite exhilarating and the finale, forged with the
noble inevitability of a Baroque passacaglia.
Ultimately, Harnoncourt delivers a fine and
tragic Fourth.

Harnoncourt's Brahms is the perfect antidote
to predictability and interpretative complacency.

Symphonies Nos 1-4
**South West German Radio Symphony Orchestra /
Sergiu Celibidache**
DG ③ 459 635-2GH3 (166′ · ADD) Recorded live
1974-6. Includes bonus disc of rehearsal of
Symphony No 4   ⒻО

Most performances conducted by Sergiu Celibidache (or Celi as he was popularly known) harbour at least one incomparable 'Celi moment',
and this set includes plenty. He could galvanise,
mesmerise, enrapture and insinuate even the
most bizarre interpretative ideas into your
consciousness. As a musical magician, he was
peerless; but as an exponent of the Classics, he

constantly courted controversy. He abandoned the recording studio soon after the war, and it's only thanks to his son and family that the flood of pirate Celi CDs can at last be challenged by superior authorised alternatives. This particular set is better played and better produced than anything before it. The recorded balance is excellent. Textures are transparent (the woodwinds especially), instrumental perspectives are unusually true and the incredible force of fully scored passages is never compromised.

The First Symphony is awe-inspiring. The coda is broad, but it never drags and the slow movement is a minor miracle. It's another those moments, but there are more in store, notably in the finale, where slowly interweaving violin desks achieve a perfect *diminuendo*. Another occurs around the famous horn episode, where horns answer each other with incredible power. The celebrated string melody is leisurely and serene, but the tempo soon picks up and the rest of the movement is pure joy. This must be counted among the most imposing Brahms Firsts currently available.

Celi frequently alters Brahms's written dynamics. For example, near the beginning of the Second Symphony, where the strings take the lead, the horns remain much in evidence. The slow movement builds to an epic climax at 8'47" where full winds and brass declaim above a slow-moving tide of first-violin semiquavers, and the finale's accelerating coda is immensely exciting. Indeed, the whole score enjoys an unusually cogent interpretation.

By contrast, parts of the Third Symphony sound decidedly odd, yet there are some wonderful moments: the quieter episodes in the central development, the fire of the string playing in the recapitulation and the delicate balance of forces elsewhere. The Third's principal 'Celi moment' happens at 7'46" into the second movement, at the point where the strings draw a broad expressive arch, played here with the greatest intensity and mesmerising control. The finale receives a relatively straightforward reading, again with some first-rate string playing. But, viewed as a whole, this isn't a Brahms Third to live with.

For the Fourth Symphony, in addition to the complete performance, we're treated to a full rehearsal of the opening *Allegro non troppo* where a fully 'fired-up' Celi takes the greatest pains over matters of rhythm and articulation. The slow, sweet centre of the movement is addressed in almost mystical terms, far more effectively in concert than in the rehearsal. Cumulatively, the Fourth Symphony is taut, intimate, transparent and rich in incident, and only sometimes deprived of the 'long' view. Remarkable, inspiring, exasperating – Celibidache was all these, and more. And if the overall approach was sometimes excessively interventionist, you learn so much from listening that eccentricities soon cease to register. These discs enshrine the work of a man who obviously loved every note of Brahms's symphonies and was not afraid to express it.

Symphonies Nos 1-4. Tragic Overture, Op 81. Variations on a Theme by Haydn, 'St Antoni Chorale', Op 56a
Philharmonia Orchestra / Arturo Toscanini
Testament mono ③ SBT3167 (200' · ADD) Recorded live 1952 Ⓕ**OO**

The concerts recorded here preserve the two legendary occasions in the autumn of 1952 when in a Brahms cycle at the Royal Festival Hall Toscanini conducted the Philharmonia Orchestra, then only six years old but already the front runner among London orchestras. The recording itself, now legendary, has generated pirated versions, but never before has the original made by EMI, under the supervision of Walter Legge, been officially released. Testament's remastering is a revelation. This new set brings the clearest of demonstrations that the RCA recordings of Toscanini and the NBC Symphony Orchestra made during the last years of his life (including his Brahms cycle of the very same 12-month period) give only an imperfect picture of a conductor who at the time, and for a generation or so previously, was almost universally counted the greatest in the world. That reputation has been eroded over the years, but this issue may help to put the record straight.

Take for example the quite different NBC version of No 3 that he recorded in New York barely a month after this performance: as Alan Sanders says in his note, a 'rhythmically staid recording which entirely lacked the lyricism and eloquence of the Philharmonia performance'. His description points to the marked contrasts, not only in No 3 but in all four symphonies. Whereas the New York performances, resonant and superbly drilled, have a hardness and rigidity, with the dynamic contrasts ironed out, thus eliminating *pianissimos* (partly a question of recording balance), the Philharmonia's consistently bring a moulding of phrase and subtlety of rubato which bears out the regular Toscanini instructions to 'Sing!'. And in contrast with most Toscanini recordings, the hushed playing is magical. The New York players, by comparison, seem to have forgotten how to respond to the finer subtleties of this notorious taskmaster among conductors. The extra flexibility of the Philharmonia performances over the NBC has an interesting effect on tempo too. Whereas in No 1 the NBC speeds of 1951 are faster, not just than those of the Philharmonia but of the 1941 NBC performance, in the other three symphonies the Philharmonia timings tend to be a degree quicker, notably in No 3, where for example the *Andante* flows far better.

Walter Legge fought hard to get these live recordings officially released – now we can understand why.

Brahms Symphonies Nos 1[a] & 2-4[b]
Variations on a Theme by Haydn[a]. Hungarian
Dances[a] – No 1 in G minor; No 3 in F; No 10 in F
Beethoven Overtures – Coriolan, Op 62[a];
Leonore No 2, Op 72[b]

aVienna Philharmonic Orchestra; bBerlin
Philharmonic Orchestra / Wilhelm Furtwängler
EMI Références mono ③ 565513-2 (219' · ADD)
Recorded 1948-56   Ⓜ●●

These are extraordinary performances, the
Third and Fourth Symphonies especially. In the
Fourth it's almost as though Furtwängler, to a
Berlin audience in 1948, were saying 'You *still*
don't believe that this symphony is an appalling
tragedy? Listen!' It's desperately serious from
the very beginning: austere, big-phrased, with
sober grace amidst the intensity, but also suspense, troubled anxiety. The coda is wildly turbulent, and ends in blackness. The slow movement begins in an unearthly hush, soon giving
way to expressive warmth, but the rejoinder of
the strings is unutterably poignant: the movement is a mourning procession, relieved only by
vain defiance. And the *Scherzo*, which Brahms
marked *giocoso*? More like grim determination.
The finale is baleful, the strings returning to
their intense eloquence, the chorale subdued
and prayer-like, the fierce conflict terribly
urgent, ending in bleak despair.

You might find the Third Symphony even
more disturbing. Furtwängler notices all the
music's hushed shadows; he explores them,
lingers in them, and on emerging you realise
that the *Andante*'s serenity isn't untroubled, that
clouds are often apt to fall across the music's
warm colours. The finale has a funereal tread,
the noble string theme is determined, not
relaxed or exuberant; there's a feverish quality
that leaves the coda hushed.

In the First Symphony there's a palpable sense
of Brahms confronting the shade of Beethoven.
The theme of the finale isn't radiant at its first
appearance: after an almost distraught slow
movement and a strangely unstable *Scherzo* (the
whole symphony takes up where the *first* movement of Beethoven's Ninth left off, not its
fourth) that theme will have to struggle for its
victory. And thus, Furtwängler seems to say, the
forest horns at the outset of the Second, the
huge energy of its first movement, the intense,
impulsive romanticism of its *Adagio*; hence the
exuberant robustness of the finale: Brahms has
earned this romantic richness by what he
achieved in the First Symphony. Subjective? Of
course, and anyone who objects to interpretations so subjective that they can rule out alternative views may dislike them very much
indeed. But if one of a conductor's functions is
to reveal the composer's intentions, another is
to convince you that those intentions matter.
Furtwängler's Third has the power to make you
question whether it's as ripely autumnal as most
seem to think; his Fourth could keep you awake
at night; all four symphonies have a visionary
urgency that can sweep you along with it.

They are all live recordings, with some audience noise; the strings are a bit acid at times, the
climaxes occasionally dense, but you would
probably gladly put up with far worse for performances as toweringly eloquent as these.

Additional recommendation

Symphonies Nos 1-4
Coupled with: Violin Concertoa. Alto Rhapsodyb.
Hungarian Dances
aHasson *vn* bGreevy *mez* aLPO; Hallé Orchestra /
Loughran
Classics for Pleasure ④ 575753-2
(279' · ADD) Recorded mid-1970s   Ⓑ

Loughran's cycle had a very loyal following on LP.
It still sounds pretty good some 25 years on. He
knows how to build a Brahms symphony not only
towards its climax but from its bass line; his choice
of tempo rarely falters. And No 2 is a sheer delight.
Add a glorious *Alto Rhapsody* and a cultivated
Violin Concerto and you've a real bargain.

Brahms Symphony No 1 **Schumann** Symphony No 1
in B flat, Op 38, 'Spring'
**Berlin Philharmonic Orchestra / Herbert von
Karajan**
DG The Originals 447 408-2GOR (76' · ADD)
Recorded 1964, 1971   Ⓜ

The first of Karajan's three Berlin Brahms
cycles was, by general consent, his finest for
DG. Which was his finest 'phase' in general,
only time will tell. Few would deny that this C
minor Symphony has a 'halcyon days' feel. It's
certainly present in the first two movements,
the drive established in the main *Allegro* of the
first (no repeat) allowing Karajan to relax for the
second theme without loss of purpose. The second movement, ideally mobile, evolves freely
and seamlessly, with masterfully graded wide
dynamic contrasts felt rather than fashioned.
This orchestra's tone production is even, rich
and rounded. So far, so good. In the third
movement bar-by-bar dynamic contrasts are
smoothed out, with the route to the Trio's climax taken as one very gradual *crescendo*. The
finale's 'daybreak' is broad and awe-inspiring.
Karajan here has gauged tempo, dynamics and
accentuation so the strings can articulate without strain; all very impressive, but his *Allegro*'s
progress is thus relatively short on attack,
energy and the ability to fly.

The more you hear Karajan's Schumann First
Symphony, the more convinced you may be that
it's spring cultivated and monitored under laboratory conditions. The most unsettling of those
conditions is an effect common to a number of
his 1970s DG Berlin recordings, namely, for a
fairly closely balanced orchestra (particularly the
strings, which aren't entirely glare-free), as
dynamic levels drop, to walk off several paces
into a glowing Berlin sunset. This also exaggerates the conductor's own contrasts, neither
exactly redolent of the vitality and freshness of
spring: the resolutely robust and measured
delivery of the rustic *forte*, and the carefully
crafted confection of his *dolce piano*.

Symphony No 1. Gesang der Parzen, Op 89
Berlin Radio Chorus; Berlin Philharmonic

Orchestra / Claudio Abbado
DG 431 790-2GH (58′ · DDD) Recorded 1990 Ⓕ

Abbado's tempos are generally broad: his first movement boldly emphatic but he never stints on affection, and few would find fault with his warm, lyrical handling of the beautiful *Andante*, 'sostenuto', indeed! He ventures between the score's little nooks and crannies, highlighting small details without impeding the music's flow or weakening the performance's structure. When the finale breaks from *Più andante* to *Allegro non troppo, ma con brio*, Abbado really goes for the burn, very much as Furtwängler did before him. It's a truly inspired reading, grand but never grandiose; appreciative of Brahms's thick-set orchestration, but never stodgy. The fill-up is of enormous import, and opens with one of the composer's most inspired musical gestures: a bold, burgeoning *Maestoso*, anticipating the words 'The gods should be feared/by the human race…'. *Gesang der Parzen* is a setting of a particularly unsettling poem by Goethe, one that warns how the uplifted have particular reason to fear the gods, those who 'turn their beneficent eyes away from whole races.' Abbado surely sensed the terrible truth of that prophecy, and his reading of Op 89 breathes a deeply disquieting air.

Brahms Symphony No 1 **Wagner** Siegfried Idyll. Siegfried – Siegfried's horn-call Ⓗ
Dennis Brain *hn* **Philharmonia Orchestra / Guido Cantelli**
Testament mono SBT1012 (62′ · ADD) Recorded 1947-53 Ⓕ●

Cantelli conducts an interpretation which is free of any idiosyncrasy. Yet there's an extraordinary electricity in his conducting, a sense of concentration and conviction which lifts the performance into one of the greatest ever set down on record. The fiery young Italian makes the vintage Philharmonia play in an inspired fashion, and the 1953 mono recording is very acceptable. A slightly edgy string sound betrays the 1951 origin of the *Siegfried Idyll* recording, but the performance has a tenderness, warmth and eloquence which has never been surpassed. Dennis Brain's exuberant horn-call completes a very desirable Testament disc.

Symphony No 2. Academic Festival Overture
New York Philharmonic Orchestra / Kurt Masur
Teldec 9031-77291-2 (50′ · DDD) Recorded 1992 Ⓜ

Masur brings affection to the symphony. In the first movement he maintains a strong sense of line, and paces the music more objectively than Haitink. The structure is clearer, but there's also an unforced lyricism. The *Adagio* has a natural ebb and flow, and Masur makes the listener aware of the music's shape and argument very clearly. After a neatly pointed *Allegretto* the finale is given a beautifully balanced, strongly argued reading which eschews superficial excitement, but satisfies through the feeling of a symphonic argument brought to a logical conclusion. To sum up, Haitink caresses the music with more subjective warmth than Masur, whose reading by no means lacks affection, but is more architectural and objective. The New York Philharmonic responds to Masur with highly sensitive, very accomplished playing, and Teldec's attractively warm but clearly recorded disc is completed by a genial, uplifting *Academic Festival Overture*.

Symphony No 2. Alto Rhapsody, Op 53
Marjana Lipovšek *contr* **Ernst Senff Choir; Berlin Philharmonic Orchestra / Claudio Abbado**
DG 427 643-2GH (60′ · DDD) Recorded 1988 Ⓕ●

These sessions took place before the BPO elected Abbado as its Chief Conductor, but the orchestra responds to him with unmistakable enthusiasm. The BPO's sound under Abbado is different from the Karajan sound. It still has a wonderful depth and sonority, but whereas Karajan encouraged a homogeneous, ultra-refined quality Abbado persuades the orchestra to play with more separated, slightly lighter textures and greater translucency.

In the symphony's first movement Abbado opts for a good, spacious middle-of-the-road tempo, and lets the music unfold easily and lyrically, but with affectionate care. The music-making is quite unidiosyncratic and direct, but develops genuine fire and passion at climaxes. In the second movement the basic tempo is even a little on the slow side, but there's still an appealing lightness and a quiet, glowing quality in the orchestral sound. Abbado gently but firmly persuades the music on, maintaining an adroit balance between warmth of expression and clarity. The third movement has good balance and clarity, too, and if the middle section lacks its customary eager quality there's still plenty of vitality in the movement overall. The finale feels ever so slightly tame, and the climax doesn't quite have its usual impact. But in general it's a most satisfying performance of the symphony, very well recorded, adorned by Lipovšek's singing in the *Alto Rhapsody*. This has good tone and good sense – perhaps a slightly dry-eyed quality too – and Abbado's characterful conducting is impressive.

Symphony No 3. Tragic Overture, Op 81. Schicksalslied, Op 54
Ernst-Senff Choir; Berlin Philharmonic Orchestra / Claudio Abbado
DG 429 765-2GH (68′ · DDD) Recorded 1989 Ⓕ

This disc is gloriously programmed for straight-through listening. It gets off to a cracking start with an urgently impassioned *Tragic Overture* in which the credentials of the Berlin Philharmonic to make a richly idiomatic, Brahmsian sound are substantially reaffirmed. A wide-eyed, breathtaking account of the *Schicksalslied*

('Song of Destiny') follows to provide sound contrast before the wonders of the Third Symphony are freshly explored. This is a reading of the Symphony to be savoured; it's underpinned throughout by a rhythmic vitality which binds the four movements together with a forward thrust, making the end inevitable right from the opening bars. Even in the moments of repose and, especially, the warmly felt *Andante*, Abbado never lets the music forget its ultimate goal. Despite this, there are many moments of wonderful solo and orchestral playing along the way in which there's time to delight, and Abbado seems to bring out that affable, Bohemian-woods, Dvořák-like element in Brahms's music to a peculiar degree in this performance. The Symphony is recorded with a particular richness and some may find the heady waltz of the third movement done too lushly, emphasised by Abbado's lingering tempo. Nevertheless, this is splendid stuff, and not to be missed.

Symphonies Nos 1a & 3b   H
ªLondon Symphony Orchestra / Hermann
Abendroth; ᵇVienna Philharmonic Orchestra /
Clemens Krauss
Biddulph WHL052 (75' · ADD) Recorded ª1928,
ᵇ1930   Ⓜ

Symphonies Nos 2ª & 3ᵇ   H
ªNew York Symphony Orchestra / Walter
Damrosch; ᵇLondon Symphony Orchestra /
Hermann Abendroth
Biddulph WHL053 (79' · ADD) Recorded ª1928,
ᵇ1927   Ⓜ

Thank heavens for such independent labels as Biddulph and others like it, for if it weren't for their sterling efforts, valuable performances such as these would be lost. Much as we prize the Brahms of Furtwängler, Toscanini, Klemperer and Walter, anyone with active critical faculties – and the ability to listen 'through' old sound – is likely to enjoy Krauss, Abendroth or Damrosch virtually as much. All three conductors reflect a performing style that might well have been recognised by the composer himself. Flexibility is a constant attribute, though the three orchestras featured produce very different pooled sonorities. A good many of Abendroth's post-war East German recordings have latterly found their way on to CD, but most collectors will have first encountered the conductor through these Brahms 78s with the LSO. The original sound quality – although generally well balanced – is cramped and mono-dimensional, but the transfers make the best of a difficult job.

The First Symphony opens magisterially. The main body of the first movement is pliable but energetic, whereas the *Andante sostenuto* second movement flows nicely and the finale generates considerable visceral excitement. Abendroth leans on the initial upbeat of the big string tune then pushes forwards. Occasionally the tempo seems too fast, but the effect of Abendroth's approach is rugged and impulsive. The LSO's

strings are more expressive than its rather acid woodwinds, the cellos being especially fine. As in the First Symphony, wide tempo fluctuations are conspicuous but convincing, save perhaps in the Passacaglia where the flow is sometimes impeded. Most of Brahms's dynamics are faithfully observed and Abendroth's treatment of the interrelationship of the movements perceptive.

Clemens Krauss was even more celebrated as an opera conductor than Abendroth, and his symphonic records are few and far between. This Vienna Philharmonic account of the Third is distinguished by taut string playing, glorious contributions from the horn section and an unselfconscious approach to rubato. You could easily imagine that anyone who learned the *Andante* from this recording will have found all subsequent versions pallid and unconvincing. Krauss's handling of the opening bars – where violas, cellos and basses answer woodwinds and horns – suggests the intimacy of chamber music. Rarely has the writing breathed more naturally, or the underlying sentiment been more precisely gauged. Although some of the finale's faster passages are a little uncoordinated, the driving force of Krauss's approach marks a telling contrast with the symphony's reflective coda.

Among Walter Damrosch's many claims to musical fame are the first American performances of Brahms's Third and Fourth Symphonies, and his New York recording of the Second is in some respects the most interesting of the set. The second subject is very broadly paced, but the highlight of the performance is the *Adagio non troppo* slow movement, a minutely observed reading full of tender incident. On the debit side, violins tend to lack body at anything above *mezzo-forte* and some will question the finale's very fast speeds (especially later on in the movement). But viewed as a whole, Damrosch's Brahms Two is both lyrical and lively, a quietly individual reading that repays close scrutiny. With fine transfers and expert annotation, these CDs provide an invaluable historical supplement to existing recommendations. You may not always agree with what you hear, and yet all four performances should significantly extend your knowledge of these fine works.

Symphonies Nos 2 & 3
Columbia Symphony Orchestra / Bruno Walter
Sony Classical Bruno Walter Edition SMK64471
(75' · ADD) Recorded 1960   ⓂO

Bruno Walter (1876–1962) was, quite simply, a lovely man, gentle and kind beyond the ordinary. He was always a fine interpreter of Brahms's music, which seemed so suited to his temperament, for Brahms, too, was also a deeply human person. Whatever Walter's conception of the work as a whole, song-themes are always allowed to open out with glorious effect. There's something almost pianistic about Walter's subtle flexibility of tempo: this is how Brahms might have envisaged it as he played through these works on the piano.

Phrasing, too, has a marvellous feeling of controlled freedom about it: dynamics may rise and fall considerably during a short phrase, and yet Walter's shaping of longer lines is always masterly. The whole second group of the Second Symphony is like a huge, evolving tune with one point of climax and one final resolution. Perhaps there could be more tautness and inner tension in some of the *allegros*, but the generosity and sensitivity of Walter's readings more than compensate: emphasis is upon the lyrical continuity of the music – Brahms the Schubertian rather than Brahms the Beethovenian – and it's none the worse for that. The recordings have come up marvellously in their digital remastering, gaining clarity and depth.

Symphonies Nos 2ª & 4ᵇ   🅷
Concertgebouw Orchestra / Willem Mengelberg
Teldec mono 0927-42662-2 (77' · ADD) Recorded
ᵇ1938, ª1940   Ⓜ

No performance of Brahms's Second Symphony can be fairly accused of being too beautiful or too robust, certainly not this one, which in its sheer splendour of orchestral sound is both beautiful and robust. (It's pretty exciting, too. Mengelberg doesn't hang about.) For the tragic Fourth Symphony, additional virtues are needed and here it's possible to think that an expert presentation of the musical facts is all Mengelberg is willing to offer us.

Bryan Crimp's transfers are warm and vivid. A certain amount of residual surface noise persists but the ear soon adjusts – drawn to the stunning interplay of orchestral sonority and the matchless Concertgebouw acoustic which the Telefunken engineers really knew and understood. Cleaned up, this is a Rembrandt among Brahms Seconds. The Rijksmuseum should be sent a copy forthwith.

Brahms Symphony No 2 in D, Op 73ª   🅷
Beethoven Symphony No 2 in D, Op 36ᵇ
**Royal Philharmonic Orchestra / Sir Thomas
Beecham**
BBC Legends/IMG Artists mono BBCL4099-2
(70' · ADD) Recorded live at ᵇBBC Studios, Maida
Vale, London in 1956, ªUsher Hall, Edinburgh 1956
                                                   Ⓕⓞ

Beecham was no Brahmsian but he loved the Second Symphony and was one of its most persuasive interpreters. In 1936 he made a much-admired recording with the newly founded LPO. Reviewing Beecham's stereo remake in *The Gramophone* in June 1960, William Mann recalled: 'I grew up with his 78 set and remember it with keen pleasure. It was light and sunny and full of charm, though perfectly strong; some people probably thought it a reading that lacked nobility.' The remake, recorded in 1958-9, wasn't as well liked as the 78rpm original. This live 1956 Edinburgh Festival performance is superior in almost every respect to that laboriously assembled studio version, and left the festival audience flabbergasted, walking on air.

In the studio the rip-roaring conclusion seemed contrived, but here it electrifies sense. If there's a whiff of the circus about the Edinburgh performance – Beecham audibly urging his players on like a shiny-hatted ringmaster, the final chord sounding defiantly on even as it drowns in a sea of applause – it's largely to do with the fact that the performance is live. The actual reading is exemplary: a thrilling denouement thrillingly realised.

And in the earlier movements Beecham's reading is everything William Mann remembered it as – sunny and full of charm but also, by 1956, wise and wondering, too. The mono sound is first-rate.

The Beethoven is less interesting, though this Maida Vale broadcast is every bit as vital as the generally well-respected EMI studio recording which Beecham and the RPO made that same winter. Buy it for the Brahms.

Symphony No 4
Vienna Philharmonic Orchestra / Carlos Kleiber
DG The Originals 457 706-2GOR (40' · DDD)
Recorded 1981   Ⓜⓞⓞ

Kleiber's charismatic 1981 Vienna recording, a classic of sorts and still sounding exceptionally well, continues to stand its ground. From the beginning, he keeps the speed fairly steady. In the first movement's coda, he scores over many of his rivals with prominent horns and a particularly exciting conclusion. He opens the second movement in a rather perfunctory manner, but the Vienna cellos make a beautiful sound in the *piano dolce* second subject. In the *Scherzo*, Kleiber pulls back for the two accented notes that dominate the first theme, an interesting gesture that lends the music an appropriately swaggering gait. This, arguably, is his finest movement – also from 4'48", where he keeps the timpani's triplets crystal-clear, then pushes his horns very much to the fore. Overall, Kleiber in the Fourth is the knight with shining breast-plate, bold, handsome, outgoing, relatively straightforward and (this will court controversy) perhaps just a little superficial.

Serenade No 1, Op 11

Brahms Serenade No 1 in D, Op 11
Stenhammar Serenade in F, Op 31
**Royal Stockholm Philharmonic Orchestra /
Sir Andrew Davis**
Finlandia 3984-25327-2 (79' · DDD)   Ⓕ

It was a lovely idea to pair these two delightful works, though most collectors who fancy Brahms's First *Serenade* will probably also want the Second. Yet the pairing with Stenhammar suggests many interesting points of contrast, not least a questing inventiveness that recalls Sweden's other estimable early symphonist,

Franz Berwald. The very opening has a breezy, extrovert quality that recalls early Nielsen, but thereafter the twists and turns in Stenhammar's writing are more reminiscent of Sibelius, even Strauss or Reger. The waltz-like 'Canzonetta' is quietly melancholic, and the *Scherzo* is impishly playful (save for a sombre second episode that initially sounds like *Deep River*). The 'Notturno' fourth movement has the sort of absorbing fairy-tale atmosphere that recalls the glittering masterpieces of Rimsky's school. Stenhammar's original design incorporated six rather than five movements, but Davis makes as strong a case as anyone for the revision. He offers a lean, keen-edged reading that keeps squarely to the plot; the playing is expressive and energetic, and the recording captures it well.

The Brahms is an altogether more relaxed piece and is here given a fresh, unmannered reading, vigorous in the opening *Allegro molto*, bouncy in the closing Rondo and with plenty of light and shade between. Rather than make points merely for the sake of it, Davis keeps to a workable interpretative mean and has his players perform as if in a chamber ensemble. Again, the sound is unexceptional but pleasing.

21 Hungarian Dances

Stuttgart Radio Symphony Orchestra / Georges Prêtre
Forlane UCD16770 (57' · DDD)   Ⓕ

Georges Prêtre has been honorary guest conductor of the Stuttgart Radio Symphony Orchestra since 1995 and he brings a touch of Gallic flamboyance to these delightful, variously orchestrated dances. The playing is mostly spirited and responsive, and the recording pleasantly blended save that the brass are sometimes a mite recessed. The First *Hungarian Dance* is bouncy and keenly accented; the Fourth features a novel 'question-and-answer' effect between the two halves of the principal melody; the Fifth is more elegant than rustic; the 10th pleasingly vivacious; the 14th broad and bold (almost like a majestic fragment from one of Brahms's larger orchestral works); the 16th warmly impassioned (with some of the best string-playing on the disc) and the 20th employs some telling rubato. There's also a 'CD-ROM/extra multimedia' rehearsal and concert track – six minutes' worth – for use with your PC. An enjoyable disc.

String Sextets

No 1 in B flat, Op 18; **No 2** in G, Op 36

String Sextets Nos 1 & 2
Raphael Ensemble (James Clark, Elizabeth Wexler vns Sally Beamish, Roger Tapping vas Andrea Hess, Rhydian Shaxson vcs)
Hyperion CDA66276 (74' · DDD) Recorded 1988
                                          ⒻⓄⓄ

Completed after the First Piano Concerto, but still comparatively early works, the Sextets are typified by lush textures, ardent emotion, and wonderfully memorable melodic lines. The first is the warmer, more heart-on-the-sleeve piece, balancing with complete naturalness a splendidly lyrical first movement, an urgent, dark set of intricate variations, a lively rustic dance of a *Scherzo*, and a placidly flowing finale. The second inhabits at first a more mysterious world of half-shadows, occasionally rent by glorious moments of sunlight. The finale, however, casts off doubt and ends with affirmation. Both works are very susceptible to differing modes of interpretation, and the Raphael Ensemble has established distinctive views of each, allowing the richness of the texture its head without obscuring the lines, and selecting characteristically distinct tone qualities to typify the two works. The recording is clear and analytic without robbing the sound of its warmth and depth. An impressive recording début for this ensemble.

String Sextet No 1. Piano Trio No 1 in B, Op 8[a]   Ⓗ
[a]**Pablo Casals, Madeline Foley** vcs [a]**Isaac Stern, Alexander Schneider** vns **Milton Katims, Milton Thomas** vas [a]**Dame Myra Hess** pf
Sony Classical Casals Edition mono SMK58994 (77' · ADD) Recorded 1952   ⓂⓄ

Casals is, of course, the lynch-pin. A charismatic presence, he embraces each work with the passion of a devoted horticulturist tending his most precious flowers. Being a proud humanitarian, Casals had long refused to step foot in Franco's Spain, and it was Alexander Schneider who coaxed him from self-imposed retirement for a series of music festivals in the French town of Prades – hence these recordings. This is a majestic, big-boned account of the early B flat Trio and a sublime version of the sun-soaked B flat Sextet, one of the glories of the Casals Edition. If you need a prime sampling of the Casals manner at its most inspired, then try the Sextet's second movement and note his sullen, ghostly tone at 8'32" – like some ancient bard relaying a solemn but wise message.

Additional recommendation

Brahms String Sextets
Coupled with: Theme and Variations in D minor (arr from String Sextet, Op 18 – slow movement)[b]
Stern, Lin vns **Laredo, Tree** vas **Ma, Robinson** vcs [b]**Ax** pf
Sony Classical ② SM2K 87275 (90' · DDD) Recorded 1992   Ⓜ
  A delectable coupling by a stellar line-up. The sense of teamwork throughout is palpable, the artists audibly revelling in Brahms's vision.

Clarinet Quintet in B minor, Op 115

Clarinet Quintet. Clarinet Trio in A minor, Op 114
Thea King cl **Karina Georgian** vc **Clifford Benson** pf

Gabrieli Quartet (Kenneth Sillito, Brendan O'Reilly
vns Ian Jewel *va* Keith Harvey *vc*)
Hyperion CDA66107 (65' · DDD) Recorded 1983 ⓕ**O**

These players' tempo in the Clarinet Quintet is more leisurely than most of their rivals. In the faster flanking movements of the trio, a stronger forward drive mightn't have come amiss. On the other hand, they allow themselves time to savour every bar to the full. Strinking in both these performances is their underlying warmth of heart. You'll respond easily to their quality of good-natured, unforced civility. The ensemble is excellent, with the clarinet very much one of the team, never assuming the role of soloist in a quasi-chamber concerto. Thea King's phrasing is unfailingly perceptive and stylish, and her undemonstrative, wise artistry in both works is most appealing. In the Trio, the sumptuous-sounding cello is impressive, which at times makes you feel that Brahms could just as well have called the work a cello trio. This is a disc which will bear frequent repetition. Playing such as this, committed and serious, yet at the same time relaxed and spontaneous, isn't easy to contrive in the recording studio, and Hyperion has done well to capture these interpretations on the wing. The sound is very good indeed, mellow and natural.

Clarinet Quintet. String Quartet No 2 in A minor,
Op 51 No 2
Karl Leister *cl* **Leipzig Quartet** (Andreas Seidel,
Tilman Büning *vns* Ivo Bauer *va* Matthias
Moosdorf *vc*)
Dabringhaus und Grimm MDG307 0719-2
(71' · DDD) ⓕ

One of the most attractive qualities of this version of a well-loved quintet is the skill with which the artists, abetted by the record producer, have integrated the clarinet into the string textures. Having listened more creatively than any other composer to Mozart's example, Brahms allows the clarinet to become part of the tone colour in the string ensemble; and he has also followed the implications, as not all his interpreters seem to understand. Here, the little falling third theme, one of his lifelong obsessions, moves in and out of the musical texture with wonderful subtlety, so that the return of the opening figure at the very end needs no special emphasis but is a natural conclusion. Leister is an artist of long skill and experience, and also of great musical intelligence; the qualities tell. They also mean that there's no need to confer upon the performance anything approaching the sentimentality which can afflict it, in the name of 'nostalgia' as the old composer looks affectionately back on his life's work. This is quite a robust performance, clearly appreciated by the enthusiastic young string quartet, who give a suitably matching account of the Op 51 work. There are, of course, any number of performances of the quintet, but this is unique.

Clarinet Quintet. Trio for Horn, Violin and Piano Ⓗ
in E flat, Op 40
Reginald Kell *cl* **Aubrey Brain** *hn* **Rudolf Serkin** *pf*
Busch Quartet (Adolf Busch, Gosta Andreasson *vns*
Karl Doktor *va* Hermann Busch *vc*)
Pearl mono GEMMCD0007 (63' · ADD) Recorded
1938, 1933 Ⓜ**OO**

Also available on Testament mono SBT1001
(65' · AAD) ⓕ**OO**

There's no need, at this remove of time, for further praise to be lavished on these performances. This account of the Horn Trio remains at, or very near, the top of any list of recorded rivals. HMV's recording of this somewhat idiosyncratic combination of instruments survives well and has been cleanly, honestly transferred. However, the performance of the Clarinet Quintet will give you even deeper pleasure. Where nowadays do we hear playing of such emotional range, such probing intensity? Here the Busch Quartet and Reginald Kell out-sing and out-search most rivals in the work's autumnal aspect but also make everything seem alive and doubly intense with their fierce and intense response to the music's wild mood-swings. It helps to have a clarinettist who can coo like a dove and exult like a gipsy; but, in the end, the performance's genius rests in the players' profound and unflinching identification with Brahms's shifting moods.

Brahms Clarinet Quintet in B minor, Op 115
Mozart Clarinet Quintet in A, K581
David Shifrin *cl* **Emerson Quartet** (Philip Setzer,
Eugene Drucker, *vns* Lawrence Dutton *va* David
Finckel *vc*)
DG 459 641-2GH (70' · DDD) ⓕ

David Shifrin and the Emerson play both works easily, sweetly and leaning affectionately where the melody line calls for an extra spot of emphasis. Here, flexibility and precision form a helpful alliance. In Mozart's first movement (played with its repeat intact), the strings tense effectively for the development and the recapitulation is nicely inflected. The *Menuetto* opens with a real spring to the rhythm; the viola is notably supple at 2'50" into the *Andante con variazione* and the seemingly endless phrase that precedes the final return of the opening theme can rarely have been more beautifully played on disc. The Brahms is similarly sensitive, with the strings dipping considerably as the clarinet makes his first entry. Everything ebbs and flows; there are numerous varieties of dynamic shading, and the onset of the first movement's development could hardly be gentler. Note, too, the intimately shared string lines at the beginning of the *Adagio* and how, a little later on (ie at 2'48"), Shifrin sings his sullen reference back to the Quintet's opening theme. The gypsy interludes are more reflective than fiery, in keeping with the tempered melancholy of the performance as a whole. The last two movements are sonorous and colourful, the sound consistently fine.

Additional recommendation

Clarinet Quintet
Coupled with: **Mozart** Clarinet Quintet in A, K581
Leister *cl* **Berlin Soloists**
Warner Apex 0927-43502-2 (71' · DDD) Recorded
c1989   Ⓑ

Karl Leister gives most beautifully easy, charming, relaxed performances of both works, and the recordings are pleasantly fresh and immediate.

Piano Quintet in F minor, Op 34

Brahms Piano Quintet. **Schubert** Piano Quintet in A, D667, 'Trout'
Sir Clifford Curzon *pf* **Amadeus Quartet** (Norbert Brainin, Siegmund Nissel *vns* Peter Schidlof *va* Martin Lovett *vc*) **James Edward Merrett** *db*
BBC Legends ② BBCL4009-2 (82' · ADD) Recorded live 1974, 1971   Ⓜ**OO**

If you put this set on at the end of a long day you'll feel as if a new day has begun. Such is the power of great music-making…and these performances are indeed 'great'. Granted, the 1971 recording of the Schubert sounds marginally better than the 1974 Brahms, but the visceral excitement generated by the Brahms Quintet has to be heard to be believed. It would be fairly easy to imagine a tidier performance, but not one that's more spontaneous or inspired. Sir Clifford Curzon's grand vision registers within a few bars of the opening movement and heats to near boiling-point by the start of the recapitulation. The emotional temperature rises even higher for the second movement.

The distinction of the performance resides in the co-operation of all five players, which reaches unprecedented heights in the finale. No wonder the audience explodes: it's doubtful that anyone present has heard a finer performance since. The *Trout*'s repeated exposition is even more exciting than its first statement, and there's some gentle tempo acceleration during the development. True, the strings make a fractionally late entrance at the beginning of the *Andante*, but the vitality of the *Scherzo* would be hard to beat, while the Theme and Variations features notable playing from Lovett. There's an amusing spot of premature congratulation when applause momentarily breaks in at the end of the *Allegro giusto*'s exposition, but it soon withers to silence for a joyous finale. Here the recording rather favours the strings, but better that than have the piano drown everyone else out. Wonderful stuff, all of it.

Piano Quintet. Horn Trio in E flat, Op 40
Nash Ensemble (Marcia Crayford, Elizabeth Layton *vns* Roger Chase *va* Christopher van Kampen *vc* Frank Lloyd *hn* Ian Brown *pf*)
CRD CRD3489 (73' · DDD) Recorded 1991   Ⓜ

It would be hard to imagine more amiable performances of these two strongly characterised works. The Nash Ensemble's comfortable approach is intense as well as warm, plainly derived from long experience performing this music in concert. The speeds in both works are markedly slower than on other versions, and the ensemble is a degree less polished, but in their expressive warmth they're just as magnetic, with a sense of continuity that the higher-powered readings do not always convey. The Romanticism of the Nash approach comes out particularly strongly in the opening *Andante* of the Horn Trio, with the horn soloist, Frank Lloyd, producing an exceptionally rich, braying tone, reminiscent of Dennis Brain. After relaxed accounts of the first three movements the galloping finale is given with great panache. Thanks partly to the CRD recording, the Nash performances sound satisfyingly beefy, almost orchestral, though some may find the full-bodied sound a degree too reverberant, with the piano rather in front of the strings. The disc can be strongly recommended, particularly as this is the only available coupling of these two works.

Piano Quintet
Andreas Staier *pf* **Leipzig Quartet** (Andreas Seidel, Tilmann Büning *vns* Ivo Bauer *va* Matthias Moosdorf *vc*)
Dabringhaus und Grimm MDG307 1218-2 (39' · DDD)   Ⓜ**OO**

Here's something quite unusual! Andreas Staier is playing a Steinway model D dating from 1901; not exactly contemporary with the Quintet (1865), but producing a noticeably lighter sound than its modern counterpart, and taking us closer to what would have been familiar to Brahms. On this excellent recording we're aware that the dominating resonance of the present-day concert grand is missing; the balance shifts in favour of the strings, making the work seem more colourful, less sombre. The first movement and the *Scherzo* are especially successful, with full, resonant *tutti*s contrasting dramatically with the more tenuous, atmospheric music. The Leipzig Quartet maintain a notably pure sound, without excessive vibrato, adding to the feeling of transparency.

Other performers, such as Peter Serkin and the Guarneri Quartet, have delved more searchingly into the Quintet's emotional content, bringing out the moments of deep pathos or soaring lyricism. But Staier and the Leipzigers will expand your view of this great work.

String Quintets

No 1 in F, Op 88; No 2 in G, Op 111

String Quintets Nos 1 & 2
Gérard Caussé *va* **Hagen Quartet** (Lukas Hagen, Rainer Schmidt *vns* Veronika Hagen *va* Clemens Hagen *vc*)
DG 453 420-2GH (59' · DDD)   Ⓕ**O**

The affirmative *Allegro* that launches the Second String Quintet on its course is exhilarating and the recording by the augmented Hagen Quartet greets the air like an unexpected sunbeam. This particular recording combines clarity and substance; nothing is left to chance and the end result is notably colourful, both in tone and in feeling. The First Quintet is crisply pointed, with crystalline textures, a pleasantly laid-back account of the first movement's lovely second set and a finely tensed development section. Furthermore, the heavily contrapuntal finale is played with great precision and rhythmic *élan*. Both performances include first-movement exposition repeats and both represent the Hagens' 'stylistic grid' at its most convincing, with vividly attenuated dynamics, occasional volatility, a consistent sense of line, impressive internal clarity, equal distribution of voices and a remarkable degree of concentration. Very well recorded.

Piano Quartets

No 1 in G minor, Op 25; **No 2** in A, Op 26; **No 3** in C minor, Op 60

Piano Quartets Nos 1-3
Isaac Stern *vn* **Jaime Laredo** *va* **Yo-Yo Ma** *vc*
Emanuel Ax *pf*
Sony Classical ② S2K45846 (128' · DDD) Recorded 1986-9
Ⓕ❍❍❍

The piano quartets belong to the middle of Brahms's life. They have all the power and lyricism that we associate with his music; but alongside a wealth of melodic and harmonic invention there are some shadows: all we know of Brahms's life suggests that he was never a happy man. Even if this is reflected in the music, and especially the C minor Quartet, all is kept in proportion and there's no overt soul-bearing. These quartets are big pieces which often employ a grand manner, though less so in No 2 than the others. For this reason, the present performances with their exuberant sweep are particularly telling, and although no detail is missed the players offer an overall strength. Top soloists in their own right, they combine their individual gifts with the ability to play as a well-integrated team. The recording is close but not overwhelmingly so.

Piano Quartet No 1. Four Ballades, Op 10
Emil Gilels *pf* members of the **Amadeus Quartet**
(Norbert Brainin *vn* Peter Schidlof *va* Martin Lovett *vc*)
DG The Originals 447 407-2GOR (65' · ADD)
Recorded 1970, 1975
Ⓜ❍

This is an outstanding performance of Brahms's G minor Piano Quartet, unforgettable for its spontaneity and uninhibited Romantic warmth and verve. The booklet reminds us that this 1971

recording made history since 'a contract between an artist from the Soviet Union and a Western label was a sensational event in cultural diplomacy'. Reproduced with respect for the sound quality of its time, the playing has a glowing strength and intensity throughout. Only in the first movement's opulent textures does the keyboard occasionally dominate. From Emil Gilels we're also given a maturely unhurried, essentially 'inward' recording of Brahms's four youthful *Ballades*.

Brahms Piano Quartet No 1 **Schumann**
Fantasiestücke, Op 88
Martha Argerich *pf* **Gidon Kremer** *vn* **Yuri Bashmet** *va* **Mischa Maisky** *vc*
DG 463 700-2GH (58' · DDD)
Ⓕ

You'd expect this line-up of performers to give us something remarkable, and so they do; the powerfully projected emotions and great imaginative range of their Brahms could only come from players well used to being soloists. It's a very suitable approach for this exuberant, colourful quartet. What's less expected is how well the four of them play together – the excellent, easy ensemble throughout, and the fine blend of the strings, at the start of the second movement, for instance. In the *Andante*'s opening pages the strongly sustained melodic lines, with fairly intense vibrato, do rather clog up an already thick texture, but we're soon taken into another world as Argerich introduces the march tune in the middle section, with crystal clear sonority and an inspiring rhythmic élan. The high point of the performance is the gypsy-style finale, combining controlled virtuosity with unconstrained physical energy.

Argerich's pianistic prowess continually lights up the music. An obvious instance is the extraordinary way she plays the cimbalom flourish in the Brahms finale. Ideally, the first of the *Fantasiestücke* could sound more wistful, with the violin and cello inflections more restrained – the Florestan Trio achieve this – but in general Schumann's fantastical world, as well as Brahms's more overtly emotional one, is brought magnificently to life.

String Quartets

No 1 in C minor, Op 51 No 1; **No 2** in A minor, Op 51; **No 3** in B flat, Op 67

String Quartets Nos 1-3
Alban Berg Quartet (Günter Pichler, Gerhard Schulz *vns* Thomas Kakuska *va* Valentin Erben *vc*)
EMI ② 754829-2 (102' · DDD) Recorded 1991
Ⓕ❍

Whereas the C minor and B flat major Quartets were recorded at sessions in a Swiss church, the A minor Quartet is a live concert performance, as applause confirms. All three works emerge not only with technical fluency and finish but also with quite exceptional immediacy and vividness. The first and last movements of No 1 spring at you with all the drama Brahms invariably drew from C minor. Yet the music's cajoling lyricism is very lovingly cherished too. The players' wide dynamic range is faithfully reproduced right down to the most intimate confidence – and of course the ensuing *Romanze*, very tenderly and delicately interwoven, brings still stronger proof of their awareness of the eloquence of *pianissimo* in all its variations of colour and character.

In the B flat Quartet (No 3), which shares the first disc, they at once capture its carefree rustic verve with their bold dynamic contrasts and relish of the composer's rhythmic teasing. For the *Andante*'s confident F major song Pichler finds a glowing fervour. The A minor Quartet, recorded at St Petersburg's Palais Yusopov, monopolises the second disc – some might think a little extravagantly since the playing time is only just 35 minutes. Tonal production is no less clear and true, even if just a shade less vibrant and lustrous than in that resonant Swiss church. Or maybe this impression can be attributed to the players, in their desire to convey the work's retreat into a more elusive, wistful world that they evoke with effortless fluency, fluidity and grace.

A strongly recommended issue for anyone wanting a keen-edged reminder of this composer's warm and vulnerable romantic heart.

String Quartets Nos 1 & 2
Cleveland Quartet (William Preucil, Peter Salaff *vns* James Dunham *va* Paul Katz *vc*)
Telarc CD80346 (68' · DDD) Recorded 1993 Ⓕ

Though the Cleveland Quartet has changed both its leader and viola player in recent years, all the old tonal opulence is still very much there. So is all the old fire, and equally, the determination to wring the last drop of expression from even the most intimate confession. In short, you'd be unlikely to meet a more overtly romantic composer than the Brahms you meet here. In the C minor Quartet's *Romanze* some might in fact prefer the very mellow but more emotionally reticent Borodin Quartet, or the Alban Berg with their ethereally withdrawn *pianissimo*. In the bolder flanking movements it's as compulsive as the highly strung, impressionable Alban Berg while often finding a broader, suaver, melodic sweep. The venue was its favoured Mechanics Hall at Worcester, Massachusetts, a warmly reverberant building – as the sheer fullness of the sound makes plain.

String Quartet No 1. String Quintet No 2[a]
Belcea Quartet (Corina Belcea, Lara Samuel *vns* Krzysztof Chorzelski *va* Alasdair Tait *vc*) with [a]**Thomas Kakuska** *va*
EMI 557661-2 (62' · DDD) ⒻⓄ

The Belcea Quartet's repertoire continues to range widely. What's most impressive about them is the way they combine care for the overall sound – ensuring that it's beautifully balanced and remains euphonious even in the most overwhelming *fortissimo* – with a strongly communicative style with an air of spontaneity. The spontaneity may sometimes be a clever illusion: in the third movement of the Op 51 Quartet the triplet passages with violin and viola in octaves are performed with a very natural-sounding *rubato* that maintains impeccable ensemble. The finale, faster than usual, creates a sense of passionate abandon, but with all the rhythmic complexities expertly negotiated. The *Poco adagio*, played with great concentration and attractive, warm tone, perhaps misses out on some of the movement's expressive opportunities.

The grandeur of the first movement of the Op 111 Quintet is immediately apparent: the opening has a wonderfully sonorous sound, but it's a feature of this performance that *forte* is taken to mean a full sound, not necessarily a very loud one. So, at places where the texture lightens, when the first movement's second theme arrives, or at the start of the second movement, the music is able to relax. And when Brahms writes a *pianissimo*, the effect is often quite magical.

A disc every Brahms lover should hear.

Clarinet Trio in A minor, Op 114

Brahms Clarinet Trio **Frühling** Clarinet Trio in A minor, Op 40 **Schumann** Märchenerzählungen, Op 132. Kinderszenen, Op 15 – Träumerei (arr Hough)
Michael Collins *cl* **Steven Isserlis** *vc* **Stephen Hough** *pf*
RCA Red Seal 09026 63504-2 (69' · DDD) Ⓕ

Here is a conversation between kindred spirits for whom musical phrasing and mellifluous tone production are evident priorities. Even when playing quietly, Stephen Hough exhibits an acute sense of tonal colour: try from 2'23" into Brahms's finale, where he posits the main idea and his colleagues respond with like minds. Hough's transcription of Schumann's 'Träumerei' might appear an old-fashioned appendage to an otherwise enterprising programme. And yet the musical result – where Michael Collins holds the main melody line until near the end of the piece, when Steven Isserlis takes over just for a couple of bars – is utterly captivating.

Schumann's four *Märchenerzählungen* – performed here with a cello in place of the original viola – combine forcefulness with a certain fragility. For example, the *Lebhaft und sehr markiert* second movement opens emphatically, then skips off in heady abandon before settling to a mood where the two elements – dark resolution and aerial fantasy – combine.

The third major work in this well-planned Romantic programme is by Lvov-born Carl Frühling (1868-1937), a gifted composer who, according to Isserlis, partnered celebrated artists of the day and died in poverty. Many of Frühling's works still await discovery (literally, as no one knows their precise whereabouts) but the Trio is full of lovely things. It's eclectic, but anyone with an ear for Chausson, Korngold, Godowsky or Kreisler will love it. The finale is an ideal sampling point, especially 5'25", where Isserlis bows a wistful motive and Hough responds with music that momentarily edges towards Liszt's 'Vallée d'Obermann'.

A highly imaginative programme characterised above all by fine balancing – musically, interpretatively and technically.

Brahms Clarinet Trio **Holbrooke** Clarinet Quintet **H**
No 1 in G, Op 27 No 1 **Weber** Clarinet Concertino in E flat, J109
Reginald Kell cl **Anthony Pini** vc **Louis Kentner** pf
Willoughby Quartet (Louis Willoughby, Kenneth Skeaping vns Aubrey Appleton va Vivian Joseph vc)
orchestra / Walter Goehr
Testament mono SBT1002 (54' · ADD) Recorded 1941   Ⓕ

In the rapturous love-duet between clarinet and cello in the *Adagio* of the Clarinet Trio, Reginald Kell's tonal warmth and beauty seem more than ever appropriate. Elsewhere in this work, though, despite his liquid sound and finesse of dynamics he's all but outshone by the eloquent lyricism and passion of that superb player Anthony Pini. Together with Kentner's understanding collaboration, never over-assertive but always supportive, an admirably cohesive team is formed, alive to Brahms's interplay of interest and changes of mood. Kell is the star of the Quintet by Josef Holbrooke which has fallen into total neglect; frankly the present diffuse work (concocted out of previous compositions) will not prompt much revaluation of his status. Nevertheless, it offers great opportunities for *cantabile* clarinet playing in the central Canzonet and for fluent virtuosity in the finale: Kell excels in both. Not unexpectedly the Weber *Concertino*, every clarinettist's party-piece, finds him displaying, besides an easy technical brilliance, beauty of tone, a charming sense of phrase and sensitive dynamic nuances. Goehr's orchestral accompaniment is clean and alert.

Piano Trios

No 1 in B, Op 8; No 2 in C, Op 87;
No 3 in C minor, Op 101

Piano Trios Nos 1-3. Horn Trio in E flat, Op 40
Clarinet Trio in A minor, Op 114
Richard Hosford cl **Stephen Stirling** hn **Florestan Trio** (Anthony Marwood vn Richard Lester vc Susan Tomes pf)
Hyperion ② CDA67251/2 (137' · DDD)   Ⓕ O

Aided by an especially clear, vivid, yet spacious recording, the Florestan Trio and their two col-

leagues allow us to hear far more of this music than usual – the elaborate decoration of Op 114's *Adagio*, or the sinister detail of the more delicate passages in Op 8's *Scherzo*. Much of the credit for this goes to Susan Tomes; her playing is an object-lesson in sensitivity and in matching the other voices. Balance and blend are a special feature of these performances. Anthony Marwood and Richard Lester match their sounds perfectly for the lovely duet passages in the slow movements of Op 8 and Op 101. Less expected, and less usual, is the matching of violin and horn, cello and clarinet. But perhaps the single outstanding feature of all the performances is the way the music is shaped. It's not only that the phrases are projected clearly and expressively – the approach moves outwards to encompass the music's larger paragraphs and, indeed, whole movements. These are very desirable recordings, then. Pires, Dumay and Wang (DG) offer big-toned performances on the grand scale of Opp 8 and 87, splendidly recorded. It's not easy to choose between them and the wholehearted, but more intimate approach of the Florestan.

Piano Trios Nos 1 & 2
Augustin Dumay vn **Jian Wang** vc **Maria João Pires** pf
DG 447 055-2GH (67' · DDD)   Ⓕ O

The duo of Augustin Dumay and Maria João Pires have found themselves a true soul mate in the Chinese cellist Jian Wang, as this, their first disc of piano trios, engagingly shows. The B major Trio doesn't quite topple the Chungs' recording, still at the very top of the list; but it comes pretty near it. The *Scherzo*'s trio, likewise, pulls back to form a slow, soupy centrepiece. Here the rubato is a little mannered, lacking perhaps the instinctive lilt of other versions. Everything, though, can be traded in for the sheer wonder of this *Adagio*. As slow as any on disc, it reveals the real empathy between Dumay and Wang in moments of great beauty where the Milstein legacy in Dumay's playing is wonderfully apparent. For the C major Trio, Dumay, Pires and Wang offer a generally broad, spacious performance, and a suppleness of repartee in the slow movement's variations which matches their fluency of invention. The *Scherzo*'s niggling is as compact and securely balanced as any, before the players glide, then stride, into the bright sunlight of the Trio.

Cello Sonatas

No 1 in E minor, Op 38; No 2 in F, Op 99

Cello Sonatas Nos 1 & 2
Mstislav Rostropovich vc **Rudolf Serkin** pf
DG 410 510-2GH (58' · DDD) Recorded 1982   Ⓕ O

Our younger generation of cello soloists seems to favour a tone production which balances a refined upper range with a middle and lower register that's strong and well focused, rather than expansively rich and resonant. Readers will not need to be told that Rostropovich's solo image is definitely not of this ilk: his musical personality is in every sense larger than life and in this magnificent coupling of the cello sonatas, in partnership with Rudolf Serkin, the very forward balance of the recording exaggerates this impression in the most vivid way. By comparison the piano image – to the right of and behind the cello – is more reticent in timbre and seldom matches Rostropovich's rich flood of sound, which isn't, of course, to suggest that Serkin fails to project the music, merely that the microphone placing makes Rostropovich very much the dominating artist. This passionately warmhearted and ripely Brahmsian music-making almost overwhelms the listener in its sheer impact. But with playing of this calibre, with both artists wonderfully attuned to each other's responses, every nuance tells and Brahms's bold melodic lines soar out from the speakers to capture the imagination, and provide an enthralling musical experience in each and every work.

Violin Sonatas

No 1 in G, Op 78; **No 2** in A, Op 100; **No 3** in D minor, Op 108

Violin Sonatas Nos 1-3
Itzhak Perlman vn **Vladimir Ashkenazy** pf
EMI Great Recordings of the Century 566893-2 (70' · DDD) Recorded 1983   Ⓜ**OO**

If anyone doubts that these three sonatas represent Brahms at his most blissfully lyrical, then this is an essential set to hear. The trouble-free happiness of these mellow inspirations, all written after the main body of Brahms's orchestral music had been completed, comes over richly and seductively in these fine performances. In their sureness and flawless confidence, they carry you along cocooned in rich sound. Perlman consistently produces rich, full-bodied tone, an excellent illustration being the way that he evokes a happy, trouble-free mood in the melody which opens the second movement *Adagio* of No 3. The obverse of this is that with such consistent richness and warmth, the three sonatas come to sound more alike than they usually do, or maybe should, a point which comes out the more from playing them in sequence. It's true that Perlman does quite often play softly, but for some tastes he's placed too close to the microphone, and the actual dynamic level stays rather high, however gently he's playing. This isn't to say that with sharp imagination and superbly clean articulation from the pianist, these performances lack range of expression – in particular, there's the rhythmic pointing, which gives a Hungarian or a Slavonic tang to such passages as the first contrasting episode in the 'raindrop' finale of No 1

or the contrasting *Vivace* passages in the second movement of No 2, where the last pizzicato reprise is made totally delectable. These performances are both distinctive and authoritative. The recording is bright, with a good sense of atmosphere to give bite to the piano tone without diminishing the warmth of Perlman's violin.

Violin Sonatas Nos 1-3
Augustin Dumay vn **Maria João Pires** pf
DG 435 800-2GH (72' · DDD) Recorded 1991   Ⓕ**O**

Of the numerous recordings of the violin sonatas available, Dumay and Pires easily deserve to be considered amongst the best, for their playing is consistently mature, stylistically homogeneous and, above all, refined. They never waste a note of the music, and yet it's always allowed to unfurl naturally. A reflective eloquence at the opening of the G major Sonata sets the mood for the entire CD. Pires contributes many lovely delicate touches and there's great breadth to her phrasing when this is required. The first movement of the A major work may be slightly slack in its cohesiveness, but in the *Andante tranquillo* that follows it's clear that the duo sees Brahms above all else as a lyrical dreamer. Only in the D minor Sonata does the darkly intense aspect of the composer's character make itself felt; here the *Presto agitato* finale is everything it should be in terms of tempo and storminess. The recorded sound is pleasant on the ear, without being ideal. The piano tone is a bit muffled and wanting in colour; this is especially apparent when the two instruments are playing together. But overall this is a release of considerable distinction.

Piano Works

Piano Sonatas – No 1 in C, Op 1; No 2 in F sharp minor, Op 2; No 3 in F minor, Op 5[b] Variations on a Theme by Paganini, Op 35[b]. Variations and Fugue on a Theme by Handel, Op 24[b]. Four Ballades, Op 10[b]. Variations on a Theme by Schumann, Op 9. Variations on an Original Theme, Op 21 No 1. Variations on a Hungarian Song, Op 21 No 2. Waltzes, Op 39. Two Rhapsodies, Op 79[b]. Scherzo in E flat minor, Op 4. Piano Pieces – Op 76; Op 116; Op 117; Op 118[b]; Op 119. Hungarian Dances[a]
Julius Katchen, [a]**Jean-Pierre Marty** pfs
Decca London Ⓜ 455 247-2LC6 (388' · ADD) Recorded 1962-6   Ⓢ Ⓑ**OO**

Items marked [b] are also available on Double Decca ② 452 338-2DF2   Ⓑ

The American pianist Julius Katchen made his name in the early 1950s and died in 1969, but although he's generally though of as a distinguished figure from the last generation, it's salutary to realise that he would probably be performing today if his career had not ended when he was only 42. Even so, his legacy of recordings reminds us of his gifts and the breadth of his repertory, and the present Brahms cycle has distinction. It begins with an account of the *Paganini* Variations that gives ample proof of his assured technique: the playing tells us at once that the challenging variations in sixths (Nos 1 and 2 in Book 1) held no terrors for him, and the athleticism here is matched by a fluency in the *leggiero* writing of the variation that follows. In this work, though, you're generally made more aware of a keyboard virtuoso than a poet; there are other performances which balance these two qualities more finely. Tempos tend to rapidity, too, and the piano sound tends to have a hardish brilliance. However, he does bring a gentler quality to the three other sets of variations here, not least in his freer use of rubato and tonal nuance, as witness (say) the serene Variations Nos 11-12 in the big *Handel* set, where the recording from three years earlier is easier on the ear. Here, as elsewhere, there's a little tape hiss, but not enough to distract.

Poetry is to be found in good measure in Katchen's playing of the *Four Ballades*, Op 10. These pieces belie the composer's youth in their deep introspection, though the pianist takes a brisk view of the *Andante con moto* tempo in No 4. The 16 Waltzes of Op 39 are attractive too in their crispness and charm, and the early *Scherzo* in E flat minor has the right dour vigour. The three sonatas are also impressive in their strong, energetic interpretative grasp, though you could wish that the first-movement repeat of No 1 had been observed. Also, slow movements could have a still more inward quality to convey that brooding self-communion which is so characteristic of this composer (though that of Sonata No 3 in F minor is pretty near it). But the great F minor Sonata is spacious and thoughtful as well as leonine, and this is a noble performance, well recorded in 1966.

The shorter pieces are finely done also. Katchen is in his element in the Two Rhapsodies of Op 79, balancing the stormy and lyrical qualities to perfection. The *Fantasias*, Op 116, aren't so well recorded (the sound is a bit muffled). However, the playing is masterly, with tragedy, twilight mystery and storm and stress fully playing their part and giving a golden glow to such pieces as the lovely E major *Intermezzo* which is No 6 of the set and the A major *Intermezzo*, Op 118 No 2. Possibly more sensuous gipsy charm could be found in, say, the B minor *Capriccio* of Op 76, but it's very attractive playing and the playful C major *Intermezzo* in Op 119 is delightful, as is the tender lullaby that begins Op 117.

Only the first 10 of the 21 Hungarian Dances exist in the composer's own (very difficult) version for piano solo, and in the others, written for piano duet, Katchen is joined by Jean-Pierre Marty; there's plenty of fire here and much to enjoy. Altogether, this Brahms set is a fine memorial to Katchen and a worthy issue.

Piano Sonata No 3 in F minor, Op 5. Hungarian Dances – No 1 in G minor; No 2 in D minor; No 3 in F; No 6 in D flat; No 7 in A. Eight Pieces, Op 76 – No 2, Capriccio in B minor; No 7, Intermezzo in A minor
Evgeny Kissin pf
RCA Red Seal 82876 52737-2 (56' · DDD)　　　Ⓕ

Kissin opens the F minor Sonata with an imperious thrust, and in the octave outburst at 4'46" again proves himself a fearless virtuoso; few pianists of any generation would even consider such a whirlwind tempo. For some, his *rubato*, heated and intense, will seem overbearing, yet he finds the still centre at the heart of the *Andante*. He thunders to the heavens the final climax (*molto appassionata*) and launches the *Scherzo* as though with a rush of blood to the head. He may be a less subtle poet of the keyboard in this sonata than, say, Radu Lupu, but his searing projection carries its own rewards, and every bar of Brahms's early and rhetorical masterpiece is marked by his overwhelming technique and magisterial temperament.

In Op 76 No 2 you'd hardly mistake the pressure he exerts for Rubinstein's or Perahia's patrician grace, but it says much for his conviction that in No 7 he can so audaciously replace the composer's *semplice* direction with his own more elaborate notion of style. But it's in five of the *Hungarian Dances* that his extrovert nature finds its truest outlet: in No 6 his performance is of an astounding verve and resilience. Here's virtuosity in the grandest of grand manners, and RCA's sound, for once, is as red-blooded as the playing.

Brahms Piano Sonata No 3　　　　　　　　Ⓗ
Liszt La leggierezza, S144 No 2a. Années de pèlerinage, Première Année, S160, 'Suisse' – Au bord d'une source[a]. Hungarian Rhapsody No 15 in A minor, S244[b] **Schumann** Carnaval, Op 9
Solomon pf
Testament mono SBT1084 (79' · ADD) Recorded 1952; [a]1930, [b]1932　　　　　　　　　ⒻⓄⓄ

Solomon's 1952 recordings of Schumann's *Carnaval* and the Brahms Sonata in F minor are essential for the desert island, so this well-produced compilation, generously filled out with Liszt, recommends itself. If you've heard tell of Solomon's reputation but don't know his work, or perhaps know only his Beethoven, snap it up. The sound has come up astonishingly well, also in the Liszt pieces which were made in 1930 and 1932. Solomon's performance of 'Au bord d'une source' is a match for Liszt's poetic inspiration, as few recordings of it are. Technical address and refinement on this level constitute a small miracle.

Piano Sonata No 3 in F minor, Op 5. 16 Waltzes, Op 39
Antti Siirala pf
Ondine ODE1044-2 (62' · DDD)　　　　　　ⒻⓄⓄ

Antti Siirala has been a serial entrant of piano competitions. He wins most of them, including the Beethoven, London, Dublin and Leeds (2003) events. So he knows how to play for a jury. His first recording after the London competition (Naxos, 8/03), however, belied such cynicism: an imaginative disc of Schubert transcriptions. Which is a long way round of saying Siirala is a great deal more than a jury-pleaser. This is a strikingly good disc, notable both for the full-bodied, golden tone of the piano (superbly recorded) and his ability to hold together both long movements and large structures with playing of refined musicality. After the first two pages of the F minor Sonata other mighty performances spring to mind – Katchen, Solomon, of course, Grainger and Bauer from an even earlier era. After the leonine first movement comes the long nocturnal narrative of the second. To hear Siirala at his most expressive, try the final section (*andante molto*) from 9'02", sensitive to every nuance, deeply felt and aching with regret. He characterises the rumbustious *Scherzo* and its chorale-like Trio equally well, and builds to the impassioned climax of the finale with abandon.

Siirala brings colour and imagination to the Op 39 Waltzes. He makes subtle use of all the repeats, and the sighing falls of No 12 are beautifully done, though it's debatable whether almost all the left hand of the famous A flat waltz (No 15) should be played *staccato* (only the first four bars and six towards the end are so marked). It's a detail, to be sure, an aspect of the music to which Siirala, otherwise, pays admirable attention.

Two Rhapsodies, Op 79. Three Intermezzos, Op 117. Six Piano Pieces, Op 118. Four Piano Pieces, Op 119
Radu Lupu pf
Decca 417 599-2DH (71' · ADD) Recorded 1970s   Ⓕ

Here are 71 minutes of the finest Brahms piano music, played by one of the outstanding Brahms exponents of our day. What's most treasurable about it is the quiet rapture of some of the most quintessentially Brahmsian moments; for example, the way Lupu sleepwalks into the last section of Op 117 No 3 and the revelation in Op 118 No 2 that the inversion of the theme is even more beautiful than its original statement. The Op 79 *Rhapsodies* are perhaps a fraction less memorable. Decca's recording sounds a little bottom-heavy, in the manner of certain Ashkenazy records of this vintage, and in the heavier textures of the *Rhapsodies* Lupu compounds the problem by reinforcing the bass with octaves and even fifths. Still, this remains as fine a selection of Brahms's piano works as you're likely to find on one disc.

Variations and Fugue on a theme by Handel, Op 24. Variations on a theme by Paganini, Op 35[a]. Eight Piano Pieces, Op 76[b]. Two Rhapsodies, Op 79[b].

Fantasias, Op 116. Three Intermezzos, Op 117. Six Piano Pieces, Op 118. Four Piano Pieces, Op 119.
[a]**Adam Harasiewicz, Stephen Kovacevich**, [b]**Dinorah Varsi** pfs
Philips Duo 442 589-2PM2 (157' · ADD/DDD)
Recorded 1969-85   Ⓜ

Despite strong competition, in Opp 116, 117 and 119 Kovacevich is first choice. He finds the intimacy of the *Intermezzos* without self-conscious search and in the stormier *Capriccios* and *Rhapsodies* blends enormous verve with rock-like stability and strength. These are performances that go right to the composer's innermost, secretive heart. In Op 118 Kovacevich finds a melting tenderness for No 2, a lovely textural lightness for No 4 with its mystical Trio, and the gracious liquidity for No 5. The desolate opening and closing sections of No 6 in their turn are beautifully phrased and deeply moving. In the *Paganini* Variations Adam Harasiewicz doesn't quite send the temperature soaring but his accuracy of detail at certain more hair-raising moments such as Nos 6 and 7 of Book Two mustn't be under-estimated. Recommended.

---

16 Waltzes, Op 39. 10 Hungarian Dances
Idil Biret pf
Naxos 8 550355 (52' · DDD) Recorded 1992   Ⓢ

Both the *Waltzes* and the *Hungarian Dances* are extremely demanding in their two-hand form, and in the latter collection you could often believe that the 20 fingers of two duettists must be involved, so many notes are being played in all registers (for an example, try No 8 in A minor). However, the technical problems hold no terrors for this pianist and her performances are convincing and attractive. What more need be said about this playing of music in which Brahms portrayed, in turn, sophisticated Vienna and untamed Hungary? Well, not a great deal. The quicker *Waltzes* have plenty of vivacity, and the slower ones are lyrical in an aptly Viennese manner. Tempos, textures, phrasing, rubato and pedalling are well managed and the playing has a very convincing blend of subtlety and simplicity. She treats these 16 pieces as a sequence, as Brahms's key structure allows, and leaves relatively little gap between them. The *Hungarian Dances* have a darkly surging Magyar energy and sound that are very pleasing: indeed, Biret seems totally at home in this music. The recording is a bit larger than life, but perfectly acceptable.

Ein deutsches Requiem, Op 45

Ein deutsches Requiem
Elisabeth Schwarzkopf sop **Dietrich Fischer-Dieskau** bar **Philharmonia Chorus and Orchestra / Otto Klemperer**
EMI Great Recordings of the Century 566903-2 (69' · ADD) Recorded 1961. Notes, text and translation included   ⓂⓄⓄⓄ

Brahm's *German Requiem*, a work of great concentration and spiritual intensity, is rather surprisingly, the creation of a man barely 30 years old. Klemperer's reading of this mighty work has long been famous: rugged, at times surprisingly fleet and with a juggernaut power. The superb Philharmonia is joined by its excellent chorus and two magnificent soloists – Schwarzkopf offering comfort in an endless stream of pure tone and the superb solo contribution from Fischer-Dieskau, still unequalled, taking us closer to the work's emotional, theological and musical sources than any other. Digital remastering hasn't entirely eliminated tape noise, but the engineers appear to have encountered few problems with the original tapes. A uniquely revealing account of the work.

Ein deutsches Requiem   **P**
Charlotte Margiono sop **Rodney Gilfry** bar
**Monteverdi Choir; Orchestre Révolutionnaire et
Romantique / Sir John Eliot Gardiner**
Philips 432 140-2PH (66' · DDD) Recorded 1990. Text
and translation included   Ⓕ**OO**

Gardiner's performance is notable for its intensity and fervour, and for the superb singing of his choir: splendidly firm and secure attacks and phrasing, always with fine tonal quality, meticulous attention to dynamic nuances, and alertness to verbal meaning and nuance. The solo baritone is a real find: an admirably focused voice with cleanly projected words and sensitive tonal gradations: if the soprano, pure-voiced and consoling, seems slightly less distinguished, it may be that she's set a trifle too far from the microphone. Pains have been taken to bring out contrapuntal strands with clarity, in both the chorus and the orchestra; and here the employment of period instruments and of selective string vibrato makes a significant contribution. In the past Gardiner has been accused of minimising the spiritual quality of religious works; but not in this outstanding performance.

Ein deutsches Requiem
Harolyn Blackwell sop **David Wilson-Johnson** bar
**London Symphony Chorus and Orchestra /
André Previn**
LSO Live LSO0005CD (66' · DDD) Text and
translation included   Ⓑ

A version of the *German Requiem*, fresh and concentrated, to confound even more strikingly than usual the jaundiced strictures notoriously piled on it by Bernard Shaw. With incandescent singing from the London Symphony Chorus, finely shaded over the widest dynamic range, this performance emphasises the drama of the piece in high contrasts. Any idea of longueurs in these seven movements could not be more completely dispelled.

Brahms's markings may be predominantly measured, but Previn, by choosing flowing

BRAHMS'S EIN DEUTSCHES REQUIEM – IN BRIEF

**Schwarzkopf; Fischer-Diekau; Philharmonia
Chorus and Orchestra / Otto Klemperer**
EMI 566903-2 (69' · DDD)   Ⓜ**OOO**
A genuine Great Recording of the Century: two superb soloists, a great choir and orchestra, and a conductor whose rugged feeling for the music pays colossal dividends.

**Margiono; Gilfry; Monteverdi Choir; Orchestre
Révolutionnaire et Romantique / Sir John Eliot
Gardiner**
Philips 432 140-2PH (66' · DDD)   Ⓕ**OO**
Gardiner's magnificent choir cover themselves in glory here: this is a performance charactersied by great clarity and transparency that makes this a wonderfully light-filled spiritual experience. Beautiful playing from the period strings.

**Blackwell; Wilson-Johnson; London Symphony
Chorus and Orchestra / André Previn**
LSO Live LSO0005CD (66' · DDD)   Ⓑ ·
**M Price; Ramey Ambrosian Singers; Royal
Philharmonic Orchestra / André Previn**
Apex 8573 89081-2 (75' · DDD)   Ⓑ**O**
Two London-based German Requiems from André Previn and both at budget price. The LSO performances shaves ten minutes off the 1987 one from the RPO but loses nothing in intensity. Both choruses sing well, but the Apex soloists probably just have the edge. A tough choice, but not an expensive one!

**Janowitz; Waechter; Vienna Singverein; Berlin
Philharmonic Orchestra / Herbert von Karajan**
DG 463 661-2GOR (77' · ADD)   Ⓜ
Two glorious soloists – Waechter's mellow toned and wonderfully humane, Janowitz almost instrumental in her purity – add to Karajan's soft-grained performance. A long-time favourite that still sounds good.

**Bonney; Terfel; Swedish Radio Choir;
Eric Ericson Chamber Choir; Berlin PO /
Claudio Abbado**
TDJ **DVD** DV-MUSIK (140')   Ⓕ**O**
Though the CD version of this performance is currently available, the DVD makes a fine alternative. Made in Vienna's striking Musikverein, this has been sensitively filmed by Bob Coles and presents a deeply impressive reading in a beautifully understated way. Excellent performances.

**Grümmer; Fischer-Dieskau; St Hedwig's
Cathedral Choir; Berlin PO / Rudolf Kempe**
EMI mono 764705-2 (76')   Ⓜ
The earliest of Fischer-Dieskau's numerous recordings of the work finds him, in 1955, in glorious voice – as is Elisabeth Grümmer. Kempe's interpretation is deeply moving.

tempos, never for a moment lets them sag as they so easily can. Previn has long shown what a fine Brahmsian he is, not least in this taxing work (his superb 1986 Teldec recording was a revelation). But however dedicated the performance is, his speeds are markedly faster than most.. Yet there's no hint of haste, just dramatic intensity to devotional ends. So the entry of the chorus in the setting of the Beatitudes in the first movement, 'Selig sind' ('Blessed are they that mourn'), is as extreme as I have ever heard it, yet when the following setting of Psalm 126 erupts on the word 'Freude', Joy, the *fortissimo* is thrilling in its bite. Just as bitingly dramatic are the climaxes in the second movement on the words 'Denn alles Fleisch es ist wie Gras' ('For all flesh is as the grass'), with the *crescendos* on the repeated timpani beats superbly caught, adding a *frisson* of excitement to the fearful message. Then on the words 'Aber des Herrn Wort' ('But the Word of the Lord'), leading to a vigorous *fugato*, the suddenness of the *forte* attack has you sitting up. Equally, the vision of the Last Trump in the sixth movement couldn't be more dramatic. In every way this performance has you registering the words with new intensity.

The impact of the chorus is all the greater when the recording gives the impression of a relatively compact group – perhaps more a question of the Barbican acoustic rather than actual size. In *pianissimos* it almost feels like a chamber group, but the *fortissimos* bite home far more tellingly than in recordings where the chorus is set in a more reverberant acoustic.

The soloists are equally responsive. David Wilson-Johnson's tone isn't perhaps very beautiful, but the plaintive quality and his feeling for the words make it a most compelling performance, and Harolyn Blackwell in 'Ihr habt nun Traurigkeit' conveys in the sweetness of her tone a tender vulnerability. Altogether an outstanding, fresh and revealing version of a much-recorded work, at bargain price.

Ein deutsches Requiem (London Version)
Sandrine Piau sop **Stéphane Degout** bar **Boris Berezovsky, Brigitte Engerer** pfs **Accentus Chamber Choir / Laurence Equilbey**
Naïve V4956 (65' · DDD) Text and translation included   Ⓕ

It was in Wimpole Street in 1871, at the home of a leading surgeon and his musical wife, that the London first performance of Brahms's *Deutsches Requiem* was given, two years before it was introduced to the British public at large and with orchestral scoring. The arrangement for piano duet was the composer's own, made at the urgent request of his publisher. The occasion was essentially a domestic one, with a small invited audience, piano duettists and singers who, having sung of all flesh being grass, would doubtless have found cold meats laid out for them in the dining room and a glass of wine to refresh the spirits.

This recording successfully presents the

Requiem as chamber music. An earlier performance on Opus 111 suggested a final piano rehearsal, the orchestra being expected next week. Here the piano part is played on two instruments, achieving a far more satisfying musical finish. The playing is sensitive, with a singing tone most of the time, and a keen ear for the differentiation between parts or melodic strands. Sandrine Piau is clear-toned and well in control after a very slightly tremulous start; Stéphane Degout, a fine baritone, isn't particularly expressive here but admirable in quality and phrasing. The choir sing with fresh, well-matched tones and care for detail. Choice of tempo seems unerringly right: that is but one of many reasons we have to be grateful to Laurence Equilbey, the conductor.

Alto Rhapsody, Op 53

Brahms Alto Rhapsody[a] **Wagner/Henze** Wesendonck-Lieder **Mahler/Schoenberg** Das Lied von der Erde – Der Abschied
Stephanie Blythe contr [a]**A Sei Voci Vocal Ensemble; Ensemble Orchestral de Paris / John Nelson**
Virgin Classics 545702-2 (60' · DDD · T/t)   Ⓕ Ⓞ

This disc is notable both for its programme and execution. A fined-down account of Brahms's *Alto Rhapsody* precedes chamber-music arrangements, by distinguished composers, of two romantic classics. Together they comprise a most satisfying experience.

There's plenty of serious sentiment in the Brahms, but none of the sentimentality that sometimes mars its performance. Goethe's profound words are uttered with equal profundity by Stephanie Blythe, whose firm, rich voice, tinged with attractive vibrancy, is just right for the piece. Nelson and his small group of singers provide compact, finely limned support. This is a reading to set beside that of Dame Janet Baker.

Henze's orchestration of the *Wesendonck-Lieder* is initially disconcerting, but the slimline instrumental support is effective, especially in the context of Blythe's unaffected, well-crafted interpretation. It's far removed from the grand scale of performance we usually hear; some may also disapprove of the low keys adopted.

The CD is crowned by a deeply eloquent account of 'Der Abschied' from *Das Lied von der Erde*, where Blythe surpasses herself in terms of steady tone, expressive phrasing and keen word-painting. Nelson and his players make Schoenberg's rescoring seems as convincing as Mahler's original. Full marks, too, for the clearly balanced, warm recording.

Choral Works

Two Motets, Op 74. Fest- und Gedenksprüche, Op 109. Three Motets, Op 110. Missa Canonica. Two Motets, Op 29
RIAS Chamber Choir, Berlin / Marcus Creed

Harmonia Mundi HMC90 1591 (61' · DDD) Recorded
1994-5. Texts and translations included ⓕ

These are wonderful pieces, which, hearing,
you would suppose to be all heart, looking at,
you think must be all brain, and in fact are compounded of both, the one feeding upon and
stimulating the other. In no other area of his
work is Brahms quite so conscious of his heritage. Writing in the midday of Romanticism,
he finds the great formal, contrapuntal tradition
not a weight upon him but a refreshment. He
draws upon Schütz as upon Bach, and from the
Italian polyphonists and masters of the double
choir as well as from his own German background. The innocent ear would never suspect
the mathematical intricacies, the musical logic,
and yet it tells, even without conscious recognition: the workmanship is clear, and the emotion
which would in any case go out to greet such
strong, vivid word-setting is immeasurably
enhanced. A striking example is provided by the
three movements, all that survive, from the
Missa Canonica. The *Sanctus* is set in deeply reverential mood and, like the flowing triple-time
Benedictus, betrays nothing of its origin as an academic exercise. The *Agnus Dei* is overtly polyphonic, yet that too gives way to a gently lyrical
mode, in the 'Dona nobis pacem'. They were
published in 1984 and this is their first recording. The motets, of course, have been recorded
many times and very well too, yet, on balance,
no more satisfyingly than they are here. The
RIAS Chamber Choir produces a fine quality of
homogeneous tone and, under Marcus Creed,
shows itself fully responsive to both words and
music. This disc carries a strong recommendation, especially for its inclusion of the surviving
Missa Canonica fragments.

Gesänge – Op 17; Op 42; Op 104. Sieben Lieder,
Op 62. Deutsche Volkslieder, WoO33 – In stiller
Nacht
Stefan Jezierski, Manfred Klier hns a**Marie-Pierre
Langlamet** hp **RIAS Chamber Choir, Berlin /
Marcus Creed**
Harmonia Mundi HMC90 1592 (62' · DDD) Texts and
translations included ⓕ

The RIAS Chamber Choir's blend of voices is
impeccable and the tone-quality perfectly
lovely. They're sensitive to word and phrase,
responding as one to their conductor's shading
and shaping. The performances give pleasure
and complete satisfaction. The sheer beauty of
sound preserves the gentle, romantic qualities
of the music faithfully; and there's never any
question of dullness, for text and music are both
lovingly tendered. The pieces themselves
always have more to them than you think at
first, and the sureness of Brahms's feeling for
choral sound impresses immediately. All are
unaccompanied save Op 17, where the harp and
horns bring a delightful enrichment. This is
quiet, late-night listening, of the kind that helps
to ease the day into retrospective contentment.

Liebeslieder

Brahms Liebeslieder, Op 52 **Rossini** Soirées
musicales – La promessa; La partenza; La regata
veneziana; La pesca **Tchaikovsky** Duets, Op 46 –
No 1, Evening; No 3, Tears; No 4, In the garden;
No 6, Dawn
Heather Harper sop **Dame Janet Baker** mez **Sir
Peter Pears** ten **Thomas Hemsley** bar **Claudio
Arrau, Benjamin Britten** pfs
BBC Music Legends/IMG Artists Britten the Performer
BBCB8001-2 (62' · ADD) Recorded 1968-71 Ⓜ**OO**

Here's another archive treasure mined from the
catacombs of Broadcasting House: a reminder
of the old Aldeburgh, where the concert hall
became a drawing-room peopled with genius,
upon which we, the far-flung radio audience,
might eavesdrop for a precious hour or so. The
programme is odd, but a joy. First, Brahms's
Liebeslieder with Claudio Arrau partnering Britten at the keyboard. It hadn't been planned as
such; cancellations had caused the hosts to shuffle the musical house guests. The result is a performance of great strength and spontaneity, the
two pianists – the engine-room of this thoroughly 'instrumental' work – playing with a
breathtaking singleness and singularity of spirit.
Brahms occasionally allows solo voices to shine.
Here the tones of Baker and Pears shine characteristically through. In the end, though,and as it
should be, it's the power and charm of the whole
ensemble that provides the pleasure.

The Tchaikovsky songs, four of the six duets,
Op 46, he wrote for his niece, Tatyana Davï-
dova, are sung in English and are thus as accessible as 'Come into the garden, Maud'. Heather
Harper and Dame Janet Baker, accompanied by
Britten, sing them grandly, without inhibition,
but it's the piano writing that tends to catch the
imagination. Finally, there's Rossini, four of *Les
soirées musicales*. Should the singing be quite so
declamatory? Perhaps not, until you realise just
how grand and funny something like the performance of 'La partenza' really is; Baker imperiously parodying the heroic style, Britten's
playing of the 22-second postlude a model of
enigmatic humour. At one level, this, and the
performance of 'La regata veneziana' which
concludes the programme, are high parody. It's
in the mordant postlude to 'La partenza', however, that we have 'Essence de Rossini', distilled
to a recipe of the composer's own making by
Britten himself in another of those acts of musical empathy which made him one of the wonders of the musical world.

Liebeslieder, Op 52. Neue Liebeslieder, Op 65.
Three Quartets, Op 64
Edith Mathis sop **Brigitte Fassbaender** mez **Peter
Schreier** ten **Dietrich Fischer-Dieskau** bar **Karl
Engel, Wolfgang Sawallisch** pfs
DG 423 133-2GH (55' · DDD) Recorded 1982 Texts
and translations included ⓕO

These delightful works will be eagerly snapped

up by lovers of these seemingly simple but, in fact, quite complex settings for one, two or four voices. The performances are thoroughly idiomatic, both as regards the singers and pianists, with full value given to the words and their meaning. It isn't merely a question of fine singing, which with this quartet can be more or less taken for granted: the subtlety and charm of the interpretations makes what can all too often be a dreary sequence of three-four numbers into a poetic response to the nature of the waltz. There's an intelligent give-and-take between the soloists, so that voices move in and out of the limelight, as the skilful recording allows, and an extra dimension of the music is disclosed here that's too often obscured. The immediate sound is here a great advantage. This is a very worthwhile and welcome reissue of a most attractive individual record.

Songs

Vier ernste Gesänge, Op 121. Neun Lieder, Op 69.
Sechs Lieder, Op 86. Zwei Lieder, Op 91ª
Marie-Nicole Lemieux contr ªNicolò Eugelmi va
Michael McMahon pf
Analekta AN29906 (68' · DDD · T/t)   Ⓕ**OO**

The absorbing six songs that make up Op 86 are all easily encompassed by Marie-Nicole Lemieux, not least because her technique is so secure that she can pay attention to the meaning of each song. *Feldeinsamkeit*, so inwardly sung, and *Todessehnen* receive particularly thoughtful readings, all supported finely by Michael McMahon's perceptive playing.

The nine songs of Op 69 are expressly designed for a woman and have their moments, but they're among the less inspired in Brahms's large output of Lieder. Not so, of course, the two songs with viola – the admirable Nicolò Eugelmi here. To these gently lulling, timeless pieces, Lemieux brings the sovereign virtues of firm line and apt phrasing.

The CD reaches its zenith in Brahms last and greatest Lieder, his *Vier ernste Gesänge*. Lemieux rises to their challenge. The interpretations are properly earnest, but intimate, never overblown. Her partner is again exemplary in his discreet yet positive playing.

A natural acoustic adds to the pleasure to be gained from this sensibly planned recital, which is highly recommended.

Brahms Lieder – Op 32; Op 72; Op 94 **Liszt** Tre Sonetti di Petrarca, S270. Die Loreley, S273. O lieb, so lang du lieben kannst, S298. Es muss ein Wunderbares sein, S314
Thomas Quasthoff bar **Justus Zeyen** pf
DG 463 183-2GH (80' · DDD) Texts and translations included   Ⓕ**O**

Whereas most singers cherry-pick *Wie rafft ich mich auf in der Nacht*, *Du sprichst, dass ich mich täuschte* and the ecstatic *Wie bist du, meine Köni-*

gin, Quasthoff treats Op 32 as a quasi-cycle. The nine songs making up the set are linked thematically: lost love and quintessentially German Romantic *Todes-sehnsucht* ('longing for death') loom large in the emotional foreground. If this means a lack of variety, Quasthoff minimises the effect with the poetry of his singing and deeply considered inflexion of the German language. His voice, a pure lyric baritone with darker accents, resembles Fischer-Dieskau's – and the older singer is an obvious interpretative model, although its upper register sounds more robust, so in a turbulent song such as *Wehe, so willst du mich wieder* ('Alas, would you enclose me, restraining fetters?') he doesn't hector as Fischer-Dieskau tends to.

Apart from Quasthoff's virtues, the disc's main attraction is his partnership with Justus Zeyen, who has transposed the first (tenor) version of Liszt's Petrarch Sonnets into the keys of the second (baritone) version for Quasthoff. But it's his exquisite playing which enhances the desirability of this disc: his twinkling arpeggios depicting the 'Melodischer Wandel der Sterne' ('Melodious movement of the stars') in *Wie rafft ich* or his subtle mood-painting in Liszt's justly celebrated *Die Loreley*. Unlike Fischer-Dieskau and Barenboim in their Brahms edition, Quasthoff doesn't disdain to sing the fourth song of Op 94, *Sapphische Ode*, usually reserved for female singers. Many will prefer Fischer-Dieskau and Barenboim in this music, but Quasthoff's and Zeyen's rapt account of *Wie bist du, meine Königin* is treasurable: the singer exhales the repeated exclamations of 'Wonnevoll' ('Rapturous') with intoxicating exaltation, the pianist underlining the sentiment with playing of rare sensitivity.

Zigeunerlieder, Op 103 – Nos 1-7 & 11. Dort in den Weiden, Op 97 No 4. Vergebliches Ständchen, Op 84 No 4. Die Mainacht, Op 43 No 2. Ach, wende diesen Blick, Op 57 No 4. O kühler Wald, Op 72 No 3. Von ewiger Liebe, Op 43 No 1. Junge Lieder I, Op 63 No 5. Wie rafft' ich mich auf in der Nacht, Op 32 No 1. Unbewegte laue Luft, Op 57 No 8. Heimweh II, Op 63 No 8. Mädchenlied, Op 107 No 5. Ständchen, Op 106 No 1. Sonntag, Op 47 No 3. Wiegenlied, Op 49 No 4. Zwei Gesänge, Op 91ª
Anne Sofie von Otter mez **Bengt Forsberg** pf
ªNils-Erik Sparf va
DG 429 727-2GH (61' · DDD) Recorded 1989. Texts and translations included   Ⓕ**O**

Many of the Lieder here are but meagrely represented in current catalogues, so that this recital is all the more welcome, particularly in view of the perceptive musicality of both singer and pianist. They show a fine free (but unanimous!) flexibility in the *Zigeunerlieder*, with a dashing 'Brauner Bursche' and 'Röslein dreie' and a passionate 'Rote Abendwolken'; but there's also lightness, happy in 'Wisst ihr, wann mein Kindchen', troubled in 'Lieber Gott, du weisst'; and von Otter's coolly tender tone in 'Kommt dir manchmal in den Sinn' touches the heart. Also deeply moving are the profound yearning and the loving but anxious lullaby in the two songs with viola obbligato (most sensitively played). Elsewhere, connoisseurs of vocal technique will admire von Otter's command of colour and *legato* line in the gravity of *O kühler Wald*, the stillness of *Die Mainacht* and the intensity of *Von ewiger Liebe*, and her lovely *mezza voce* in the *Wiegenlied* and the partly repressed fervour of *Unbewegte laue Luft*; but to any listener her remarkable control, her responsiveness to words and, not least, the sheer beauty of her voice make this a most rewarding disc, aided as she is by Forsberg's characterful playing.

Neun Gesänge, Op 69. Vier Gesänge, Op 70. Fünf Gesänge, Op 71. Fünf Gesänge, Op 72
Juliane Banse *sop* **Andreas Schmidt** *bar* **Helmut Deutsch** *pf*
CPO CPO999 446-2 (56' · DDD) Texts and translations included ⓜ

Of all the leading composers of Lieder, Brahms suffers more than any other through neglect, with so little of his output in the field ever appearing on recital programmes. There's some reason for this, given that his contribution to the genre is uneven, as you can judge listening to the uninspired settings of minor poets comprising Op 69. But just when you think the composer might have been on auto-pilot in his songs of the mid-1870s, along come the four pieces of Op 70 to make you revise your opinion. The impressionistic 'Lerchengesang', the reflective 'Serenade' and the better-known 'Abendregen', all show the composer in his most imaginative mode, alive to words and their inner meaning. The inspiration is more intermittent in Opp 71 and 72, but the better of the songs here – the Hölty 'Minnelied' and Bretano 'O kühler Wald' – rank with the finest in Brahms's output.

Both Banse and Schmidt are at their appreciable best as regards voice and interpretation, Banse always inside her readings, Schmidt producing tone that's consistently warm and appealing. She alternates convincingly between passion and lighter emotions. He's particularly well suited by the whole of Op 72, giving a nicely ebullient account of 'Unüberwindlich', a Goethe setting that ends the programme. Deutsch is fully up to the exigent demands of the piano parts, often almost like solos in themselves. The recording is admirable.

---

49 Deutsche Volkslieder, WoO33 – Ach, englische Schäferin; Ach Gott, wie weh tut Scheiden; All' mein' Gedanken; Da unten im Tale; Dort in den Weiden steht ein Haus; Du mein einzig Licht; Erlaube mir, fein's Mädchen, Es Ging ein Maidlein zarte; Es reit' ein Herr und auch sein Knecht; Es ritt ein Ritter; Es steht ein' Lind'; Es war ein Markgraf über'm Rhein; Es wohnet ein Fiedler; Feinsliebchen, du sollst mir nicht barfuss geh'n; Gar lieblich hat sich gesellet; Gunhilde lebt' gar stille und fromm; Ich stand auf hohem

Berge; Ich weiss mir'n Maidlein hübsch und fein; In stiller Nacht, zur ersten Wacht; Jungfräulein, soll ich mit euch geh'n; Mein Mädel hat einen Rosenmund; Mir ist ein schön's braun's Maidelein; Sagt mir, O schönste Schäf'rin mein; Die Sonne scheint nicht mehr: Wach' auf mein' in Herzensschöne; Schönster Schatz, mein Engel; Soll sich der Mond nicht heller scheinen; Wie komm'ich denn zur Tür herein?
Stephan Genz *bar* **Roger Vignoles** *pf*
Teldec 3984-23700-2 (59' · DDD) Texts and translations included ⓜ **OO**

This is another outright winner from Genz and Vignoles. Even in the pieces calling for two voices, Genz isn't really outdone: his variation in timbre subtly differentiates in each case between two characters, and the unity of purpose predicated by one singer's voice has its own validity. In any case, Genz's absolute and innate gift for natural and spontaneous interpretation is reason enough to recommend this issue. The late William Mann, in examining the sources of these pieces, showed that many weren't folksongs at all but 19th-century inventions, some by Brahms himself, but the innocent ear would find it hard to discern which was authentic and which contemporaneous with the composer, such is Brahms's wonderful gift for writing in folk mode, as in 'Erlaube mir, fein's Mädchen'. This is one of the most winning pieces here, enhanced by the artless simplicity and charm of Genz's singing. His attractively straightforward approach is just as welcome in many other songs such as 'Es steht ein' Lind' and 'Ach, englische Schäferin'. With Vignoles nimble and characterful at the piano, and a perfect recording, this is a must-buy unless you insist on the (almost) complete set available from EMI.

Frank Bridge
British 1879-1941

Bridge studied with Stanford at the RCM (1899-1903) and made a reputation as a chamber musician (a violist) and conductor. His early works, including the orchestral suite The Sea (1911), the symphonic poem Summer (1914) and much chamber music, are close to Bax and Delius, but after World War I he developed rapidly. His Third (1926) and Fourth (1937) Quartets are highly chromatic, reflecting his admiration for Berg, though his music remained distinctively English. Also remarkable is the contrapuntal vigour and energy of his later orchestral works, which include the rhapsody Enter Spring (1927), Oration with solo cello (1930) and Phantasm with solo piano (1931). None of his more adventurous music was much regarded until the 1970s, his fame resting largely on his having been Britten's teacher. GROVEmusic

Orchestral Works

Lament, H117. Oration (Concerto elegiaco), H180[a]. Rebus, H191. Allegro moderato, H192. A Prayer[b]
[a]**Alban Gerhardt** *vc* **BBC National** [b]**Chorus and**

Orchestra of Wales / Richard Hickox
Chandos CHAN10188 (77' · DDD) Ⓕ

Here's probably the most appealing and varied instalment yet in Richard Hickox's Frank Bridge series for Chandos. The disc's highlight is a superb performance of the 1930 'Concerto elegiaco' *Oration*, in which Hickox teams up with the gifted German cellist Alban Gerhardt. High drama and emotional candour are the keynotes to a riveting display. But there's no want of intimacy or compassion in the more contemplative passages, and the result is a trenchant interpretation that does justice to one of the towering masterpieces of British music.

The 1940 *Rebus* overture is as invigorating and impeccably crafted a concert-opener as any British composer has yet produced. The touching *Lament* (1915) is sensitively done, but Hickox and company seem less comfortable in Anthony Pople's completion of the patiently argued opening *Allegro moderato* from a projected symphony for strings upon which Bridge was working at the time of his death in 1941. Fortunately, there's a glowing account of *A Prayer*, Bridge's only composition for chorus and orchestra, a moving and often hauntingly beautiful setting from 1916-18 of words from *The Imitation of Christ* by Thomas à Kempis.

Minor strictures notwithstanding, this is an essential purchase for *Oration* alone – and the music itself deserves the widest dissemination.

The Sea, H100. Summer, H116. Cherry Ripe, H119b.
Enter Spring, H174. Lament, H117
Royal Liverpool Philharmonic Orchestra / Sir Charles Groves
EMI British Composers 566855-2 (60' · ADD)
Recorded 1975 Ⓑ❍

An ideal introduction to the music of Frank Bridge, this much-loved programme was always one of the highlights of Sir Charles Groves's Liverpool tenure, and its reappearance is more than welcome. Although a handful of individual performances – most notably Vernon Handley and the Ulster Orchestra in a stunningly engineered account of *The Sea* (on Chandos) – may have surpassed them in terms of poetic rapture and beguiling finish, Groves's clear-headed, stirringly sympathetic *Enter Spring*, though at times a little too sturdy on its pins, easily outranks the competition. The transfer is the same as that used for an earlier mid-price EMI Studio offering from 1989, and the finished article sounds as resplendent and full-bodied as ever (with a touch less background hiss than before). Don't miss this reissue.

Bridge The Sea, H100[a]. Enter Spring, H174[b]
Britten The Building of the House, Op 79[c]
Holst Egdon Heath, H172[d]. A Fugal Concerto, H152[e]
[e]**Richard Adeney** *fl* [e]**Peter Graeme** *ob* [c]**East Anglian Choirs;** [ace]**English Chamber Orchestra,**

[b]**New Philharmonia Orchestra,** [d]**London Symphony Orchestra /** [abcd]**Benjamin Britten,** [e]**Imogen Holst**
BBC Legends/IMG Artists Britten the Performer
[d]mono/stereo BBCB8007-2 (70' · ADD) Recorded live [d]July 1961, [bc]June 1967, [a]June1971, [e]June 1969 Ⓕ

Britten conducts the music of Bridge, his mentor and teacher, with a heart-warming dedication. From the outset his radiant interpretation of *The Sea* grips with its pungent elemental force, mastery of the singing line and unforgettably rapt poetic instinct. The supple naturalness of the phrasing is a thing of wonder throughout, nowhere more so than during the strings' ineffably tender reprise of the main theme of 'Moonlight'. Similarly, Britten's faithful conception of *Enter Spring* possesses a fresh-faced capriciousness, cogent sweep and expressive ardour to make you fall in love all over again with Bridge's exuberant vision. As in *The Sea*, there's an acute concern for the grander scheme. And what reserves of poignant tenderness he conjures from his hard-working New Philharmonia strings in the ecstatic central portion. Britten's sparky *The Building of the House* Overture launches proceedings in dashing fashion. This was only its second performance (the world première having taken place two days earlier), and the chorus's initial entry is sharp, but this is readily forgiven in view of the quick-witted tension generated elsewhere. Britten's 1961 Orford Church performance of Holst's *Egdon Heath* brings with it some occasional insecurity from the LSO, yet his eloquent direction distils exactly the right chill and the interpretation as a whole evinces a compelling dignity, patience and lucidity. Finally Holst's daughter, Imogen, presides over a wonderfully poised and serene account of her father's engaging *Fugal Concerto* from a June 1969 concert at Blythburgh Church. Recordings of varying vintage have all come up very freshly.

Additional recommendation

The Sea, H100. Summer, H116. Two Poems, H118.
Enter Spring, H174
New Zealand Symphony Orchestra / James Judd
Naxos 8 557167 (63' · DDD) Ⓢ
A hearty, sensibly paced account of *Enter Spring*, a gorgeous *Summer*. Despite any minor reservations, an enjoyable concert and very decent value.

String Quintet, H7 / String Sextet, H107

String Quintet in E minor, H7[a]. String Sextet in E flat, H107[b]. Lament[c]
[b]**Raphael Ensemble** ([a]James Clark, [a]David Adams vns [ac]Louise Williams, [ac]Adsis Valdimarsdottir vas [a]Andrea.Hess, Tim Gill vcs)
Hyperion CDA67426 (66' · DDD) Ⓕ

Bridge was a star student at the RCM, and his E minor String Quintet from 1901, one of four chamber offerings he wrote at that time, reveals a burgeoning talent. Cast in four movements and lasting just over half an hour, it's an accomplished achievement. A scrupulous craft and pleasing sense of proportion attest to lessons well learnt under Stanford's tutelage, yet there's already a strongly emergent personality in pages such as the third-movement trio section. The finale, too, shows enviable skills, the poignant backward glance to the work's opening just before the close being particularly effective. It's preceded by a powerfully wrought Lament for two violas first performed by Lionel Tertis and the composer at London's Aeolian (now Wigmore) Hall in March 1912. Both works are worthy of resuscitation and both are superbly served here.

So too is the Sextet (1906-12) in an even more persuasive performance than that by the Academy of St Martin in the Fields Chamber Ensemble on Chandos. The Raphael Ensemble produce a leaner, more subtly shaded sonority, allied to an extra re-creative spark and expressive urgency (witness the edgy anxiety they locate in the *scherzo* at the heart of the work). And the opening *Allegro moderato* is surveyed with due appreciation of its lyrical grace and elegant architecture; likewise, the finale combines pliancy and thrust.

A delightful anthology, beautifully realised by the experienced Keener/Eadon production team and highly recommended.

String Quartets

String Quartets No 1 in E minor, 'Bologna', H70; No 3, H175
Maggini Quartet (Laurence Jackson, David Angel, vns Martin Outram va Michal Kaznowski vc)
Naxos 8 557133 (60' · DDD) Ⓢ

Even by the high standards of previous Maggini/Naxos offerings, this is an exceptionally fine disc. If you don't know Frank Bridge's First Quartet of 1906, its ardour and melodic fecundity compel investigation. The Maggini Quartet give a performance to match, of sweep, assurance and affection. At the same time, their rapt concentration and daring range of expression (especially in the slow movement) banish for good any vestige of salon-room cosiness; the return of the opening material at the quartet's close has never seemed more wistfully inevitable.

That the Magginis are no less attuned to the far more challenging sound world of the 1926 Third Quartet is at once evident from the articulate authority and thrust they impart to the introductory bars (which sow the seeds for so much that follows). Both this work and the searching Piano Sonata, completed the previous year, represent the first wholly convincing examples of Bridge's liberating brand of English expressionism.

The Magginis are scrupulously alive to anguished introspection which runs through the work: the ghostly visions that stalk the

central *Andante con moto* and finale's twilit coda linger long in the memory here. A superb coupling, impeccably captured by the Walton/Thomason production team and well annotated by Andrew Burn.

String Quartets – No 2; No 4. Phantasy[a]
Maggini Quartet ([a]Laurence Jackson, David Angel vns [a]Martin Outram va [a]Michal Kaznowski vc)
with [a]**Martin Roscoe** pf
Naxos 8 557283 (60' · DDD) Ⓢ**OOO**

 Bridge's glorious Second Quartet, written in 1915 and winner of that year's Cobbett Prize, is arguably his first true chamber masterwork, superbly realised on every level (the finale is a *tour de force* of motivic integration) and full of the most engagingly fresh invention and invigorating part-writing. The last of his four quartets (completed in 1937) represents more of a challenge, but strong emotions stir beneath its uncompromising surface. Once again, the finale proves a fitting summation, and Bridge's technical command of the medium is absolute. Leaner and more 'classically' compact than its towering predecessor from 1926, this searching score will afford the patient listener plentiful long-term rewards.

The Brindisi Quartet's coupling has served us handsomely over the past dozen years but must now yield to this Naxos release. These are exemplary, scrupulously prepared readings from the Magginis, who play with unquenchable fire, keen intelligence and immaculate polish throughout. Joined by the admirable Martin Roscoe, they also offer a considerable bonus in the shape of the lovely Phantasy Piano Quartet of 1909-10.

With vividly realistic, beautifully balanced sound from the experienced Walton/Thomason production-team and succinct annotation by Andrew Burn, this is an unmissable disc.

Piano Trio No 2

Phantasy Trio in C minor, H79. Piano Trio No 2, H178. Miniatures – H88: Romance; Intermezzo; H89: Valse russe; Hornpipe
Bernard Roberts Trio (Andrew Roberts vn Nicholas Roberts vc Bernard Roberts pf)
Box BBM1028 (57' · DDD) Ⓕ

These are utterly sympathetic, beautifully prepared performances from this fine family group, whose line-up comprises the distinguished pianist Bernard Roberts and his two sons, Andrew and Nicholas. The centrepiece is the Second Piano Trio, a truly magnificent creation that Anthony Payne has justly hailed as 'one of the masterpieces of 20th-century English, indeed European chamber music'. Cast in two interlinked movements, it's a work of searing intensity and astounding individuality, whose 1929 première provoked a shockingly ignorant and hurtful response from some quarters of the British musical establishment. Compared with the Dartington Trio on a rival Hyperion issue, these dedicated newcomers take a more restrained, less lingering view of this troubled music. Some will crave an altogether more palpable sense of numbing loss in the unnerving Andante molto moderato slow movement than the Bernard Roberts Trio chooses to convey; and the work's towering final climax perhaps lacks that last ounce of cumulative power and epic breadth. No matter, this is a shapely, thoroughly convincing conception all the same.

Winner of the 1907 Cobbett Composition Prize, the *Phantasy* Trio in C minor inhabits an entirely different world, its elegant arch-shaped form, superior craftsmanship and generous lyrical flow being typical of Bridge's early output. The present group gives a splendidly taut, agreeably unmannered account of this lovely piece, and lavishes similarly deft and affectionate treatment upon four of the nine *Miniatures* for piano trio published in three sets between 1909 and 1915 (the opening 'Romance' is a particularly touching morsel).

The sound is admirably vivid, though the piano timbre is perhaps just a touch clangorous. In all, a most desirable acquisition.

Cello Sonata in D minor, H125

Bridge Cello Sonata. Meditation. Spring Song. Serenade. Berceuse. Scherzo. Elégie. Mélodie. Cradle Song **Britten** Cello Sonata in C, Op 65
Øystein Birkeland vc **Vebjørn Anvik** pf
Simax PSC1160 (70' · DDD)   Ⓕ

The Norwegian duo of Øystein Birkeland and Vebjørn Anvik lend gloriously unaffected and formidably lucid advocacy to Bridge's masterwork, his Cello Sonata, the strength and nobility of their playing always ideally counterbalanced by tender restraint and songful intimacy. These superbly stylish performers prove no less responsive to the poetic charms of Bridge the miniaturist.

The winsome *Serenade* of 1903 is a fresh-faced delight here, while the 1902 *Scherzo* fairly twinkles with humour. How memorably, too, they sustain the long-breathed ardour of both the *Elégie* (1904) and *Mélodie* (written in 1911 and dedicated to the cellist Felix Salmond).

Sandwiched between the Bridge Sonata and a sequence of miniatures comes a really fine account of the Cello Sonata that Britten penned for Rostropovich in 1960-61. Here, too, Birkeland and Anvik form an intelligent, scrupulously observant partnership, their playing as thoughtful as it's intense, though not even they can match the extraordinary fluidity that Rostropovich and Britten bring to the work's opening bars on their inspirational première recording for Decca (a true classic of the gramophone – reviewed above).

Among digital contenders, however, this beautifully engineered and sensitively balanced recording is as good as any and more imposing

than most. Calum MacDonald contributes the exemplary booklet essay. All told, a very positive recommendation.

Benjamin Britten   British 1913-1976

Britten studied with Frank Bridge as a boy and in 1930 entered the RCM. In 1934 he heard Wozzeck and planned to study with Berg, but opposition at home stopped him. The next year he began working for the GPO Film Unit, where one of his collaborators was Auden: together they worked on concert works as well, Auden's social criticism being matched by a sharply satirical and virtuoso musical style (orchestral song cycle Our Hunting Fathers, 1936). Stravinsky and Mahler were important influences, but Britten's effortless technique gave his early music a high personal definition, notably shown in orchestral works (Bridge Variations for strings, 1937; Piano Concerto, 1938; Violin Concerto, 1939) and songs (Les illuminations, setting Rimbaud for high voice and strings, 1939).

In 1939 he left England for the USA, with his lifelong companion Peter Pears; there he wrote his first opera, to Auden's libretto (Paul Bunyan, 1941). In 1942 he returned and, partly stimulated by Purcell, began to concentrate on settings of English verse (anthem Rejoice in the Lamb and Serenade for tenor, horn and strings, both 1943). His String Quartet No 2 (1945), with its huge concluding chaconne, also came out of his Purcellian interests, but the major work of this period was Peter Grimes (1945), which signalled a new beginning in English opera. Its central character, the first of many roles written for Pears, struck a new operatic tone: a social outcast, he is fiercely proud and independent, but also deeply insecure, providing opportunities for a lyrical flow that would be free but is not. Britten's gift for characterisation was also displayed in the wide range of sharply defined subsidiary roles and in the orchestra's sea music.

However, his next operas were all written for comparatively small resources (The Rape of Lucretia, 1946; Albert Herring, 1947; a version of The Beggar's Opera, 1948; The Little Sweep, 1949), for the company that became established as the English Opera Group. At the same time he began writing music for the Aldeburgh Festival, which he and Pears founded in 1948 in the Suffolk town where they had settled (cantata St Nicolas, 1948; Lachrymae for viola and piano, 1949). And in this prolific period he also composed large concert works (The Young Person's Guide to the Orchestra, 1946; Spring Symphony with soloists and choir, 1949) and songs.

The pattern of his output was thus set, though not the style, for the operas show an outward urge to ever new subjects: village comedy in Albert Herring, psychological conflict in Billy Budd (1951), historical reconstruction in Gloriana (1953), a tale of ghostly possession in The Turn of the Screw (1954), nocturnal magic in A Midsummer Night's Dream (1960), a struggle between family history and individual responsibility in Owen Wingrave (1971) and, most centrally, obsession with a doomed ideal in Death in

Venice (1973), the last three works being intermediate in scale between the chamber format of Herring and The Screw, and the symphonic fullness of Budd and Gloriana, both written for Covent Garden. But nearly all touch in some way on the themes of the individual and society and the violation of innocence. Simultaneous with a widening range of subject matter was a widening musical style, which came to include 12-note elements (Turn of the Screw) and a heterophony that owed as much to oriental music directly as it did to Mahler (cycle of 'church parables', or ritualised small-scale operas: Curlew River, The Burning Fiery Furnace, The Prodigal Son, 1964-8).

Many of these dramatic works were written for the Aldeburgh Festival, as were many of the instrumental and vocal works Britten produced for favoured performers. For Rostropovich he wrote the Cello Symphony (1963) as well as a sonata and three solo suites; for Pears there was the Hardy cycle Winter Words (1953) among many other songs, and also a central part in the War Requiem (1961). His closing masterpiece, however, was a return to the abstract in the String Quartet No 3 (1975).

Britten was appointed a Companion of Honour in 1952, to the Order of Merit in 1965, and was awarded a life peerage in 1976. GROVEmusic

Piano Concerto in D, Op 13

Piano Concerto. Violin Concerto, Op 15
Mark Lubotsky vn **Sviatoslav Richter** pf **English Chamber Orchestra / Benjamin Britten**
Decca British Music Collection 473 715-2 (67' · ADD)
Recorded 1970 Ⓜ

Just after Britten's performances were released on LP in 1971, the composer admitted with some pride that Sviatoslav Richter had learned his Piano Concerto 'entirely off his own bat', and had revealed a Russianness that was in the score. Britten was attracted to Shostakovich during the late 1930s, when it was written, and the bravado, brittleness and flashy virtuosity of the writing, in the march-like finale most of all, at first caused many to be wary of it, even to think it somehow outside the composer's style. Now we know his music better, it's easier to accept, particularly in this sparkling yet sensitive performance. The Violin Concerto dates from the following year, 1939, and it, too, has its self-conscious virtuosity, but it's its rich nostalgic lyricism which strikes to the heart and the quiet elegiac ending is unforgettable. Compared to Richter in the other work, Mark Lubotsky isn't always the master of its hair-raising difficulties, notably in the *Scherzo*, which has passages of double artificial harmonics that even Heifetz wanted simplified before he would play it (Britten refused), but this is still a lovely account. Fine recordings, made at The Maltings at Snape.

Piano Concerto. Soirées musicales, Op 9. Matinées musicales, Op 24
Ralf Gothóni pf **Helsingborg Symphony Orchestra**

/ Okko Kamu
Ondine ODE825-2 (71' · DDD) Recorded 1994 Ⓕ

A perceptive, at times daring, always thought-provoking account of Britten's Piano Concerto. Indeed, pungent characterisation reigns, especially in the two middle movements. Here the 'Waltz' is teased out with sly seduction by Okko Kamu and his excellent Swedish group, yet at the same time the ominous undertones of this music have never been more unnervingly projected. Even more distinctive is Ralf Gothóni's provocatively expansive way with the opening of the 'Impromptu'. Britten's theme here emerges like some ravishingly intimate meditation, its quasi-improvisatory air compellingly conveyed. Yet such is the magnetic concentration of Gothóni's playing that the line never falters, and the rest of the movement is again memorably realised. We are also offered the concerto's original slow movement, a sharply inventive, capricious 'Recitative and Aria' (which Britten withdrew in 1945). No complaints about the fizz and bravura on show in the opening 'Toccata', nor about the finale, whose *largamente* climax struts forth in superbly grim fashion. Welcome contrast comes with the two Rossini-inspired suites, and Kamu does them both proud. The orchestral playing in Helsingborg has poise, affection and wealth of tender expression in the two most reflective numbers (the 'Canzonetta' from *Soirées* and 'Nocturne' from *Matinées*). Ondine's sound throughout is simply first rate.

Violin Concerto in D minor, Op 15

Britten Violin Concerto **Walton** Viola Concerto
Maxim Vengerov vn/va **London Symphony Orchestra / Mstislav Rostropovich**
EMI 557510-2 (64' · DDD) Ⓕ

When artists of the stature of Vengerov and Rostropovich tackle English music it's often a revelation, and here's some of the most ravishing string-playing ever heard in either of these masterpieces. But these readings don't always follow convention, let alone metronome markings, and there's at least one choice of tempo that may have traditionalists spluttering in protest. As you might expect with Rostropovich as conductor, the Britten is the less controversial of the two readings. The soloist's first entry over crisply sprung ostinato repetitions on bassoon and harp is marked *dolcissimo*, and the sweetness of Vengerov's playing in the high-lying cantilena is nothing short of heavenly. Here and throughout the work his free expressiveness, his use of *rubato*, far from sounding forced, reflects a seemingly spontaneous understanding, the creative insight of a major artist, rapt and intense. Rostropovich and the LSO match him in their warm expressiveness. The full-blooded recording not only covers the widest dynamic range throughout, but brings out many inner details in the orchestral writing normally obscured.

That's also true of the Russians' reading of the Walton Viola Concerto, with Vengerov evidently just as much at ease on the viola as the violin. Yet the timings alone will bear witness to the individuality of the reading. Vengerov is even more expansive than Kennedy or Bashmet, and the wonder is that, with Rostropovich in total sympathy, he sustains the slow tempo with rapt intensity, pure and tender with no hint of soupiness of the kind that mars the Kennedy version. Unconventional as it is, this is a reading that demands to be heard, even if Waltonians won't want it as their only choice.

Violin Concerto[a]. Symphony for Cello and Orchestra, Op 68[b]
[a]**Rebecca Hirsch** vn [b]**Tim Hugh** vc **BBC Scottish Symphony Orchestra / Takuo Yuasa**
Naxos 8 553882 (68' · DDD)   Ⓢ

Rebecca Hirsch follows up her invaluable coupling of the two Rawsthorne violin concertos for Naxos with this no less likeable account of the Britten concerto. Not only does she (for the most part) make light of the solo part's fiendish technical difficulties, her playing evinces a beguiling lyrical beauty that's breathtaking. By the side of both Ida Haendel and Lorraine McAslan, she perhaps lacks the last ounce of fiery temperament (and there are a handful of tiny misreadings), but generally she's a convincing, characterful advocate.

In the *Cello Symphony*, Tim Hugh displays a profound musicality, great subtlety of tone and affecting lyrical ardour that puts in mind Steven Isserlis's account with Richard Hickox, though not quite achieving the dark-hued individuality and unremitting logic of that distinguished 1987 production. Nor does it displace dedicatee Rostropovich's blisteringly intense, composer-directed versions of this gritty masterpiece, but Hugh's achievement is considerable and he more than holds his own alongside the formidable roster of current rivals.

Takuo Yuasa draws an eloquent response from his forces. However, at the Violin Concerto's opening *Moderato con moto*, some leisurely tempos tend to undermine the purposeful thrust of the whole. Sound and balance are generally very good indeed.

Double Concerto in B minor

Double Concerto[b]. Young Apollo[a]. Two Portraits[c]. Sinfonietta, Op 1[d]
[b]**Gidon Kremer** vn [bc]**Yuri Bashmet** va [a]**string quartet** (Lyn Fletcher, Dara De Cogan vns Tim Pooley va Peter Worrall vc) [a]**Nikolai Lugansky** pf **Hallé Orchestra / Kent Nagano**
Warner Elatus 0927-46718-2 (59' · DDD)   ⓂⓄ

This release contains three world-première recordings. Most striking is the Double Concerto, the short score of which the gifted 18-year-old completed by the early autumn of

1932. That same summer Britten also produced his 'official' Op 1, the dazzlingly inventive *Sinfonietta* for 10 instruments. The two works have plenty in common both formally and stylistically. The 'orchestral' version of the *Sinfonietta* heard here incorporates a full complement of strings as well as a second horn part.

Colin Matthews fashioned a performing edition of the Double Concerto from Britten's helpfully detailed sketches, the piece receiving its première at the 1987 Aldeburgh Festival. While not quite showing the effortless fluency and innovative thematic guile of the *Sinfonietta*, it remains an astonishing work for one so young, with numerous examples of sparky, head-turning inspiration. Likewise, the *Two Portraits* make intriguing listening. Composed in August 1930, the first is a 'sketch for strings describing David' (David Layton, a close friend of the 16-year-old Britten at Gresham's School), whose emotional vehemence and harmonic restlessness nod towards Janáček and even Berg.

Nagano directs a set of performances which are beyond praise in their luminous refinement and blistering commitment; all three distinguished soloists are on unimpeachable form. Warners' sound quality is sumptuously realistic to match.

Cello Symphony, Op 68

Cello Symphony[a]. Sinfonia da Requiem, Op 20[b]. Cantata misericordium, Op 69[c].
Mstislav Rostropovich vc **Sir Peter Pears** ten **Dietrich Fischer-Dieskau** bar [a]**English Chamber Orchestra,** [b]**New Philharmonia Orchestra,** [c]**London Symphony Chorus and Orchestra / Benjamin Britten**
Decca London 425 100-2LM (75' · ADD) Recorded 1964. Text and translation included   ⓂⓄⓄ

The Cello Symphony, written in 1963 as part of a series for the great Russian cellist Mstislav Rostropovich, was the first major sonata-form work written since the *Sinfonia*. The idea of a struggle between soloist and orchestra, implicit in the traditional concerto, has no part here; it's a conversation between the two. Rostropovich plays with a depth of feeling that has never quite been equalled in other recordings and the playing of the English Chamber Orchestra has great bite. The recording, too, is extraordinarily fine for its years.

From the opening drumbeat the *Sinfonia* employs a sonata form with dramatic power, although the tone is never fierce or savage; it has an implacable tread and momentum. The central movement, 'Dies irae', however, has a real sense of fury, satirical in its biting comment – the flutter-tongued wind writing rattling its defiance. The closing 'Requiem aeternam' is a movement of restrained beauty. The New Philharmonia play superbly. The *Cantata misericordium* was written in 1962 as a commission from the Red Cross. It takes the story of the Good Samaritan and is scored for tenor and baritone soloists, chorus, string quartet and orchestra. It's a universal plea for charity and receives a powerful reading.

A must for any Britten enthusiast.

Additional recommendations

Cello Symphony[a]
Coupled with: Sinfonia da Requiem[b]. Cantata misericordium, Op 69[c]
Rostropovich vc **Pears** ten **Fischer-Dieskau** bar [a]**English Chamber Orchestra,** [b]**New Philharmonia Orchestra,** [c]**London Symphony Chorus and Orchestra / Britten**
Decca London 425 100-2LM (75' · ADD) Recorded 1964. Texts and translation included Ⓜ❍❍

A formidable coupling and a must for any Britten enthusiast: Rostropovich plays with a depth of feeling that has yet to be equalled (reviewed in full under Sinfonia da Requiem).

Sinfonia da Requiem, Op 20[a]
Coupled with: **Holst** The Planets[b]
[b]**Ambrosian Singers;** [b]**Philharmonia Orchestra;** [a]**City of Birmingham Symphony Orchestra / Rattle**
EMI Encore 575868-2 (72' · DDD) Recorded [a]1984, [b]1980 Ⓑ

Rattle's *Sinfonia da Requiem* is a model of blistering fervour and scrupulous observation, and Rattle need fear little in comparison with any modern rival. EMI's recording is vivid and true. Buy it for the Britten – *The Planets* is disappointing (although admirably detailed, it lacks some depth).

'Frank Bridge' Variations, Op 10

Variations on a theme of Frank Bridge, Op 10.
The Young Person's Guide to the Orchestra, Op 34.
Four Sea Interludes, Op 33a. Passacaglia, Op 33b
BBC Symphony Orchestra / Sir Andrew Davis
Warner Apex 8573 89082-2 (68' · DDD) Recorded 1991 Ⓢ

The real reason for investing in this bargain reissue is Davis's exceptionally insightful account of the *Variations*. After a deceptively low-key 'Introduction and Theme', this quickly develops into a reading of striking application and abundant character, plumbing genuine depths in the 'Funeral March' and 'Chant', and conveying an overwhelming sense of pathos towards the close. Of course, no home should be without the composer's uniquely authoritative 1966 account with the ECO on Decca (still unsurpassed and perhaps unsurpassable), but, as 'big-band' contenders go, there's no more perceptive rendering than Davis's.

The couplings include a thoroughly professional, no-frills *Young Person's Guide*, finely played and with a delectable rhythmic snap in the variation for percussion in particular. What's missing is harder to define: that sense of playfulness, fun even, you hear in, say, Hickox's excellent account for Chandos, which remains the pick of the digital crop, though Britten's own classic LSO recording is also an absolute

must. Davis's *Four Sea Interludes* are agreeable enough in their comparatively breezy, uncomplicated manner, and it's always a pleasure to hear the imposing *Passacaglia* given with such intensity. Overall, well worth its modest outlay.

The Young Person's Guide ..., Op 34

The Young Person's Guide to the Orchestra. Simple Symphony, Op 4[a]. A Spring Symphony, Op 44 – Spring, the sweet spring. Noyes Fludde[b] – Noye, Noye, take thou thy company ... Sir! heare are lions. Serenade for Tenor, Horn and Strings, Op 31 – Nocturne. Folk Songs – The Plough Boy; Early One Morning. Billy Budd – Interlude and Sea Shanties. A Ceremony of Carols, Op 28 – Adam lay i-bounden. A Hymn to the Virgin. War Requiem – Lacrimosa. Peter Grimes – Interlude (Dawn)
Sir Peter Pears ten **Barry Tuckwell** hn **various soloists; choirs, choruses and orchestras, London Symphony Orchestra,** [ab]**English Chamber Orchestra / Benjamin Britten** pf [b]**Norman Del Mar**
Decca 436 990-2DWO (74' · ADD) Recorded 1963-8 Ⓜ❍

This reissue includes the composer's own 1963 recording of *The Young Person's Guide to the Orchestra* with the LSO and his complete 1968 ECO version of the *Simple Symphony*. The latter is delightfully fresh and is unforgettable for the joyful bounce of the 'Playful Pizzicato', helped by the resonant acoustic of The Maltings, Snape. In *The Young Person's Guide*, without the now somewhat rather dated text, he adopts quick, demanding tempos, with more spacious ones for the more introspective sections. This is beautiful playing, possessing wit and brilliance, with all kinds of memorable touches. Even if this transfer is a little dry in sonority, this disc is invaluable for these two performances alone. As a bonus we're offered ten short excerpts from other major Britten works.

String Quartets

No 1 in D, Op 25; **No 2** in C, Op 36; **No 3** Op 94

String Quartets Nos 1-3. Three Divertimentos
Belcea Quartet (Corina Belcea, Lara Samuel vns Krzysztof Chorzelski va Alasdair Tait vc)
EMI ② 557968-2 (115' · DDD) Ⓕ❍❍❍

The Belcea Quartet have become prominent players on the chamber-music scene. In the concert hall, their rather balletic style of performance can be alienating, but in these Britten recordings you can appreciate their high level of technical accomplishment without the risk of visual distraction.

Collectors familiar with any of the earlier sets of the quartets may not warm immediately to the Belcea's exceptionally dramatic way with the music's contrasting materials. But almost nothing is forced or eccentric here. The hell-for-leather tempo adopted for the First's finale is genuinely exciting, not a scramble, and although there are a few obtrusive, fussy details in the outer movements of No 2 the overall impression is powerfully convincing. No 3 is even better, at least in the earlier movements, bringing a sense of barely suppressed anger to some of Britten's most personal and allusive music. In the last movement the phrasing is occasionally over-pointed: yet, despite tempi that make this account significantly faster than the excellent Magginis and considerably faster than the stately Brodskys, the effect reinforces the true consistency of tone and character which underpins this notably diverse score.

Recorded at Potton Hall, this is one of the best-engineered quartet discs you might hope to hear.

String Quartets – Nos 2 & 3
Brodsky Quartet (Andrew Haveron, Ian Belton *vns*
Paul Cassidy *va* Jacqueline Thomas *vc*)
Challenge Classics CC72099 (61' · DDD)   Ⓕ

The Brodsky are the Britten team for the new century, and at full price they take advantage of the super-refined Snape Maltings acoustic to offer performances of great intelligence and expressive power. No other recording of No 2 manages to convey the dramatic passion and lyric sweep of Britten's marvellously idiomatic string writing more persuasively than this one does. At two points during the long finale, the inner voices don't sound, to these ears, sufficiently distinct, the presentation of the all-pervading chaconne theme under-articulated. But these are momentary quibbles rather than sustained reservations, and it can certainly be argued that the overall interpretation of the movement benefits from the kind of contrasts which these effects represent.

In general, No 3 unfolds at slightly broader tempi than those chosen by the Maggini (on Naxos), and the episodic recitative that opens the finale seems a shade too expansive for its own good. Otherwise, this is exemplary, with immaculate ensemble and a sense of spontaneous expressive engagement bringing out the full stature of this deeply felt, valedictory music. A memorable disc, then, and an outstanding Britten cycle.

String Quartet No 3. Alla marcia. Quartettino. Simple Symphony, Op 4
Maggini Quartet (Laurence Jackson, David Angel *vns* Martin Outram *va* Michal Kaznowski *vc*)
Naxos 8 554360 (65' · DDD)   Ⓢ

This second volume of the Maggini Quartet's Britten series amply fulfils the promise of the first. As before, the recording, made in St Martin's Church, East Woodhay (near Newbury) favours blend and immediacy: the leading full-price alternative, recorded at Snape by the Sorrel Quartet for Chandos, has a richer atmosphere and a stronger sense of space, but, as inter-

pretations, the Maggini's versions need fear nothing from the current competition. The major work here is the late Third Quartet, a score whose extreme contrasts of mood and texture, ranging from rapt serenity to explosive bitterness, are the more difficult to make convincing for the extraordinary economy of means which the ailing Britten summoned. The Maggini are hard to beat in the conviction they bring to all aspects of a notably well-focused, technically polished account. Their choice of basic tempos for the tricky outer movements is ideal, and they relish the elements of parody elsewhere without descending into caricature. This disc also provides the only currently available version of the early but radical *Quartettino*, and the quartet version of the *Simple Symphony*.

String Quartet No 2; String Quartets – in D (1931); in F (1928)
Sorrel Quartet (Gina McCormack, Catherine Yates *vns* Vicci Wardman *va* Helen Thatcher *vc*)
Chandos CHAN9664 (74' · DDD)   Ⓕⵔ

The Sorrel Quartet can claim a significant 'first' in its account of the recently resurrected F major Quartet from 1928. At 15 Britten was nothing if not precocious, and although the ideas in this substantial piece offer few hints of his mature style, he was already using the medium to excellent effect. Three years later, in the D major Quartet which has been a repertory item since Britten revised it in 1974, there are signs of a more individual voice; this is an attractive performance, well shaped and effectively characterised. Nevertheless, it's on the interpretation of the Quartet No 2 that the disc must be judged. The Sorrel's naturalness and feeling for line are much in evidence. Tempos for the first movement are broader than most rivals, but they serve an approach which makes a virtue of reticence, and still manages to be quite gripping. It has just about the best sound currently available (with The Maltings, Snape, providing an ideal acoustic), and the otherwise unrecorded F major Quartet adds strength to the recommendation of this noteworthy disc.

Solo Cello Suites

No 1, Op 72; **No 2**, Op 80; **No 3**, Op 87

Solo Cello Suites Nos 1 & 2. Cello Sonata, Op 65
Mstislav Rostropovich *vc* **Benjamin Britten** *pf*
Decca London 421 859-2LM (68' · ADD)   Recorded 1961-9   Ⓜⵔⵔⵔ

 This is a classic recording of the Cello Sonata, with Rostropovich and Britten playing with an authority impossible to surpass, and is here coupled with the unaccompanied First and Second Cello Suites. The suggestive, often biting humour, masks darker feelings. However, Britten manages, just, to keep his devil under control. Rostropovich's and Britten's characterisation in the opening *Dialogo* is stunning and their subdued humour in the *Scherzo-pizzicato* also works well. In the *Elegia* and the final *Moto perpetuo*, again, no one quite approaches the passion and energy of Rostropovich. This work, like the two Suites, was written for him and he still remains the real heavyweight in all three pieces. Their transfer to CD is remarkably successful; it's difficult to believe that these recordings were made in the 1960s.

Solo Cello Suites Nos 1-3
Jean-Guihen Queyras vc
Harmonia Mundi Les Nouveaux Interprètes
HMN91 1670 (65' · DDD)   ⑧○

Britten's three Cello Suites have all the strength of musical character to sustain a permanent place in the repertory. Inspired by the personality, and technique, of Mstislav Rostropovich, they're remarkable for the way in which they acknowledge yet at the same time distance themselves from the great precedent of Bach's Cello Suites. The best performers (like Rostropovich himself, though he has never recorded No 3) are equally at ease with the music's Bach-like contrapuntal ingenuity and its lyric intensity, where Britten's own most personal voice is heard. Queyras has such a fine sense of phrase that his slower speeds do not sound unconvincing, and his technically superbplaying has an impressive consistency of style. The quality of the recording is another plus, with the close focus needed to ensure that all the details tell. The only disappointment came in the final track, with the Russian Prayer for the Dead that ends Suite No 3. Here, of all places, Queyras is simply too fast. Nevertheless, this lapse isn't so great as to deprive the disc of a place in this guide.

War Requiem, Op 66

War Requiem[a]. Sinfonia da Requiem, Op 20. Ballad of Heroes, Op 14[b]
Heather Harper sop [a]**Philip Langridge,** [b]**Martyn Hill** tens **John Shirley-Quirk** bar [a]**St Paul's Cathedral Choir; London Symphony Chorus and Orchestra / Richard Hickox**
Chandos ② CHAN8983/4 (125' · DDD) Texts and translations included   ⑤○○○

Britten's *War Requiem* is the composer's most public statement of his pacifism. The work is cast in six movements and calls for massive forces: full chorus, soprano soloist and full orchestra evoke mourning, supplication and guilty apprehension; boys' voices with chamber organ, the passive calm of a liturgy which points beyond death; tenor and baritone soloists with chamber orchestra, the passionate outcry of the doomed victims of war. The most recent challenger to the composer's classic Decca version offers up-to-date record-

ing, excellently managed to suggest the various perspectives of the vast work, and possibly the most convincing execution of the choral writing to date under the direction of a conductor, Richard Hickox, who's a past master at obtaining the best from a choir in terms of dynamic contrast and vocal emphasis. Add to that his empathy with all that the work has to say and you've a cogent reason for acquiring this version even before you come to the excellent work of the soloists. In her recording swan-song, Harper at last commits to disc a part she created. It's right that her special accents and impeccable shaping of the soprano's contribution have been preserved for posterity.

Shirley-Quirk, always closely associated with the piece, sings the three baritone solos and duets with rugged strength and dedicated intensity. He's matched by Langridge's compelling and insightful reading, with his notes and words more dramatic than Pears's approach. The inclusion of two additional pieces, neither of them short, helps to give this version an added advantage even if the *Ballad of Heroes* is one of Britten's slighter works.

War Requiem
Stefania Woytowicz sop **Sir Peter Pears** ten **Hans Wilbrink** bar **Wandsworth School Boys' Choir; Melos Ensemble; New Philharmonia Orchestra and Chorus / Carlo Maria Giulini**
BBC Legends/IMG Artists BBCL4046-2 (79' · ADD)
Recorded live 1969. Texts included   Ⓜ○○

This performance is a revelation. As the authoritative note makes clear, Britten and Giulini had a mutual respect for and an admiration of each other's work. Here they combine to give a performance that's a true Legend, as this BBC series has it. Giulini's reading is as dramatic and viscerally exciting as any rival version. The music leaps from the page new-minted in his historically taut hands, the rhythmic tension at times quite astonishing. For instance, the sixth movement, 'Libera me', is simply earth-shattering in its effect, every bar, every word, every instrument sung and played to the hilt – and so it's throughout, with the live occasion added to the peculiar, and in this case peculiarly right, acoustics of the Albert Hall adding its own measure of *verité* to the inspired occasion.

The performance of the New Philharmonia forces, under the man who was at the time their favourite conductor after Klemperer, is at once technically assured and wholly dedicated. Only perhaps the classic Decca recording comes near equalling it in this respect, and that doesn't quite have the electrifying atmosphere, found on this astonishing occasion. Nor have the Wandsworth Boys' Choir, placed up in the Hall's gallery, been surpassed.

The soloists also seem to realise the special quality of the occasion. Pears surpasses even his own creator's reading on the Decca set, singing with the sustained concentration and vocal acuity that were so much his hallmarks in Britten's

BRITTEN'S WAR REQUIEM – IN BRIEF

Vishnevskaya, Pears, Fischer-Dieskau, Bach Choir, Highgate School Ch, London Symphony Chorus, Melos Ens, LSO / Benjamin Britten
Decca 414 383-2DH2 (131 mins: ADD) Ⓕ●○○
A true recording classic, sounding more resplendent than ever in its latest 24-bit remastering. It also now contains a fascinating 50-minute rehearsal sequence.

Söderström, Tear, Allen, Christ Church Cathedral Choir, City of Birmingham Symphony Chorus & Orchestra / Sir Simon Rattle
EMI 747034-8 (83 mins: DDD) Ⓕ
Simon Rattle presides over a refreshing, concentrated reading, his assembled forces responding with crisp discipline and keen vigour. A wide-ranging recording, if not always ideally balanced.

Vaness, Hadley, Hampson, American Boychoir, Westminster Symphonic Choir, NYPO / Kurt Masur
Teldec 0630 17115-2 (83 mins: DDD) Ⓕ
A compassionate, scrupulously prepared performance under Masur. Of the three soloists, Hampson in particular is keenly intelligent and consistently moving.

Haywood, Rolfe Johnson, Luxon, Atlanta Boy Choir, Atlanta Symphony Chorus & Orchestra / Robert Shaw
Telarc CD80157 (83 mins: DDD) Ⓜ
Superlative engineering shows off Shaw's stunning Atlanta Symphony Choir to fine advantage. Perhaps not as penetrating an interpretation as some others, but still enormously satisfying.

Harper, Langridge, Shirley-Quirk, St Paul's Cathedral Choir, London Symphony Chorus & Orchestra / Richard Hickox
Chandos CHAN8983/4 (125 mins: DDD) Ⓕ●●
Now available at mid-price, Richard Hickox's admirably incisive and dedicated realisation rightly triumphed in both the Choral and Engineering categories at the 1992 *Gramophone* Awards. Generously coupled with the *Sinfonia da Requiem* and *Ballad of Heroes*.

Woytowicz, Pears, Wilbrink, Wandsworth School Boys' Choir, Melos Ensemble / Britten, New Philharmonia Chorus & Orchestra / Carlo Maria Giulini
BBC Legends BBCL4046-2 (79 mins: ADD) Ⓜ●●
An unmissable live recording from April 1969. Giulini's thrustingly intense and superbly sung account fits snugly onto a single disc. Britten himself directs the chamber forces in the Wilfred Owen settings. A remarkable document.

music. The soprano Stefania Woytowicz, who at the time made something of a speciality of this work, has very much the vocal timbre of Vishnevskaya, for whom the part was written, and perhaps a shade more sensitivity. She's certainly the best soprano on any version, and Wilbrink comes near being the best baritone. He may not be quite as varied or subtle as Decca's Fischer-Dieskau, nor as confident as Chandos's Shirley-Quirk, but he has a more beautiful voice than either, with a plangency in his tone that's so right for this music.

Most of all it's the sum of the parts that so impresses here, as does the truthfulness of the sound, preferable to that on the Chandos set.

War Requiem
Galina Vishnevskaya sop **Sir Peter Pears** ten **Dietrich Fischer-Dieskau** bar **Simon Preston** org **Bach Choir; Highgate School Choir; Melos Ensemble; London Symphony Orchestra / Benjamin Britten**
Decca ② 414 383-2DH2 (132' · DDD) Recorded 1963.
Texts and translations included. Includes previously unreleased rehearsal sequence Ⓕ●●●

Decca has used the most recent digital and Cedar technology to improve the original sound, under the overall supervision of veteran technician James Lock. This is one of the great performances of recording history. As an imaginative bonus, Decca gives us the first issue of a long rehearsal tape made by the producer John Culshaw without Britten's approval. When Culshaw presented it to the composer on his 50th birthday, Britten was 'appalled', considering it 'an unauthorised invasion of a territory exclusively his own and his performers', as Donald Mitchell relates in the booklet. Now Mitchell believes that we should be allowed 'to assess the tape as a contribution to our knowledge of him [Britten] as a performer and interpreter of his own music and to our understanding of the *War Requiem* itself.'

Throughout this fascinating document you hear evidence of Britten's vision of his own music, his astonishing ear for timbre and intimate details, above all his wonderful encouragement of all his forces, culminating in his heart-warming words of thanks at the end of the sessions, not to mention his tension-breaking humour and a couple of sharp comments from Vishnevskaya, who's unsurpassed as soprano soloist. The merit of this ground-breaking performance is that it so arrestingly conveys Britten's intentions. We're lucky to have not only Britten's irreplaceable reading refurbished, but also his commentary suggested by the rehearsal sequences.

AMDG

AMDG. Choral Dances from 'Gloriana'. Chorale after an Old French Carol. Five Flower Songs, Op 47. A Hymn to the Virgin. Sacred and Profane, Op 91

Polyphony / Stephen Layton
Hyperion CDA67140 (62' · DDD)   ⓕ❍❍❍

 The programme is delightful and the choir excellent. *AMDG* presents as formidable a challenge to its singers as any of Britten's compositions for unaccompanied choir. In fact that's sometimes suggested as the reason why, having written it for an expert group in 1939 and realising that its chances of frequent performance were slim, Britten never prepared the work for publication. It's a pity he couldn't have heard Stephen Layton's Polyphony! Even more than the Finzi Singers, their predecessors on record, they've worked it into the system so that they have the sense of it clearly in their mind and can make the word-setting fresh and spontaneous. 'God's Grandeur' (*allegro con fuoco*) has the fire: the Finzis seem almost cautious by comparison. In 'The Soldier' Polyphony catch the swing of the triplets and dotted notes with more panache and make more of the words. They also bring out the tender lyricism in 'Prayer II' and grasp more decisively the *con moto, Vivace* and *Avanti!* markings in 'O Deus, ego amo te'.

In the *Five Flower Songs* Polyphony have a young tone and their numbers allow them to convey a sense of round-the-table intimacy. In the *Choral Dances* from 'Gloriana', Polyphony improve on the Finzi Singers' performance with crisper rhythms and a clearer acoustic. *Sacred and Profane*, like *AMDG* a work for virtuosos, is given with wonderful confidence and imagination. A wonderful disc.

Additional recommendation

AMDG
Coupled with: Hymns – to St Peter, Op 56a; of St Columba; to the Virgin; to St Cecilia, Op 27. Rejoice in the Lamb, Op 30. Choral Dances from 'Gloriana'
Finzi Singers / Spicer with **Lumsden** *org*
Chandos CHAN9511 (67' · DDD) Texts included   ⓕ
Very enjoyable performances from this expert choir, successfully directed by Paul Spicer.

The World of the Spirit

An American Overture. King Arthur – Suite (arr Hindmarsh). The World of the Spirit (arr Hindmarsh)
Susan Chilcott *sop* **Pamela Helen Stephen** *mez* **Martyn Hill** *ten* **Stephen Varcoe** *bar* **Hannah Gordon, Cormac Rigby** *spkrs* **Britten Singers; BBC Philharmonic Orchestra / Richard Hickox**
Chandos CHAN9487 (79' · DDD) Text included   ⓕ

Hickox's performance of the Coplandesque *An American Overture* has exemplary polish, commitment and dash. The remaining items owe their revival to the efforts of Paul Hindmarsh. Britten wrote his incidental music for a BBC radio dramatisation of the King Arthur legend in 1937. It was the first of his 28 radio commissions and contains much high-quality invention.

Hindmarsh has fashioned the 23-year-old composer's inventive inspiration into a terrific four-movement orchestral suite lasting some 25 minutes, which Hickox and the BBC PO devour with audible relish.

The 'radio cantata' *The World of the Spirit* dates from May 1938. Commissioned by the BBC as a successor to *The Company of Heaven* (1937), it intersperses sung and spoken texts chosen by R Ellis Roberts. Again, Britten's fertile compositional powers are much in evidence. The work contains a whole string of memorable numbers, from the lilting barcarolle-like treatment of Emily Brontë's 'With wide-embracing love', via the joyful strut and swagger of Part 2's concluding 'The Spirit of the Lord' with its unmistakable echoes of Walton's *Belshazzar's Feast*, to a strikingly imaginative setting of Gerard Manley Hopkins's *God's Grandeur*. Framing the 42-minute edifice are two radiant settings of the Whitsuntide plainsong, *Veni Creator Spiritus* – an idea possibly inspired by a recent encounter with Mahler's Eighth Symphony at the Queen's Hall under Sir Henry Wood. The recording is superbly wide in its range and offers a realistic quality.

A Ceremony of Carols, Op 28

A Ceremony of Carols. Missa brevis in D, Op 63. A Hymn to the Virgin. A Hymn of St Columba, 'Regis regum rectissimi'. Jubilate Deo in E flat. Deus in adjutorum meum
Sioned Williams *hp* **Westminster Cathedral Choir / David Hill** with **James O'Donnell** *org* Hyperion CDA66220 (49' · DDD) Recorded 1986. Texts included   ⓕ❍

A Ceremony of Carols sets nine medieval and 16th-century poems between the 'Hodie' of the plainsong Vespers. The sole accompanying instrument is a harp, but given the right acoustic, sensitive attention to the words and fine rhythmic control the piece has a remarkable richness and depth. The Westminster Cathedral Choir performs this work beautifully; diction is immaculate and the acoustic halo surrounding the voices gives a festive glow to the performance. A fascinating *Jubilate* and *A Hymn to the Virgin*, while lacking the invention and subtlety of *A Ceremony*, intrigue with some particularly felicitous use of harmony and rhythm. *Deus in adjutorum meum* employs the choir without accompaniment and has an initial purity that gradually builds up in texture as the psalm (No 70) gathers momentum. The *Missa brevis* was written for this very choir and George Malcolm's nurturing of a tonal brightness in the choir allowed Britten to use the voices in a more flexible and instrumental manner than usual. The effect is glorious. St Columba founded the monastery on the Scottish island of Iona and Britten's hymn sets his simple and forthright prayer with deceptive simplicity and directness. The choir sings beautifully and the recording is first rate.

Hymn to St Cecilia, Op 27

Rejoice in the Lamb, Op 30. Te Deum in C. Jubilate
Deo in C. Antiphon, Op 56b. A Hymn to the Virgin.
Festival Te Deum, Op 32. Missa brevis in D, Op 63.
Hymn to St Peter, Op 56a. A Hymn of St Columba.
Prelude and Fugue on a Theme of Vittoria.
Hymn to St Cecilia
**St John's College Choir, Cambridge / Christopher
Robinson** with **Ian Farrington** org
Naxos 8 554791 (74' · DDD)   Ⓢ

As with other recent records from St John's,
there's a freshness, almost a feeling of adventure
and a sense that all this choral discipline is an
easy yoke. These are excellent performances,
the opening item setting a standard which is to
be maintained throughout. Buoyant rhythms,
precise accentuations and well-pointed contrasts are features of the singing; and the playing
of Ian Farrington in accompaniments that are
often difficult and always demanding of maximum alertness, is outstanding. Outstanding,
too, is the contribution of the trebles. In tone
they preserve the traditional John's sound,
without exaggerating its so-called continental
element. But what impresses most is the sense
of imaginative involvement. It's there, for
instance, in the *Kyrie* of the *Missa brevis*, and
most of all in the 'I cannot grow' section of *A
Hymn to St Cecilia*. To this they bring a distinctive excitement, a wide-eyed, breathlessly playful feeling of childlike wonder. The programme
itself is highly attractive. The 'hymns' are fully
developed compositions, and the canticles are
notably independent of tradition (for instance, a
quietly meditative note of praise is struck at the
start of both Te Deums). The *Missa brevis*
makes inventive use of its forces; and *Rejoice in
the Lamb*, a masterly expression of the liberal
spirit, never ceases to amaze with its evocation of
the cat Jeoffry, valiant mouse and staff-struck
poet. Recorded sound isn't as vivid as the performances, but this remains a very likeable disc.

Serenade, Op 31

Serenade for Tenor, Horn and Strings, Op 31ª   Ⓗ
Folksongsᵇ – The Bonny Earl o' Moray; Avenging
and Bright; The Last Rose of Summer; Sally in our
Alley Walton Façadeᶜ
abcSir Peter Pears ten/spkr ᶜDame Edith Sitwell
spkr ªDennis Brain hn ᵇBenjamin Britten pf ªBoyd
Neel String Orchestra / Benjamin Britten; ᶜEnglish
Opera Group Ensemble / Anthony Collins
Decca 468 801-2DM (74' · ADD/DDD) Recorded
1953-4   ⓂⓄⓄ

This disc includes one of the great highlights of
the whole Britten discography, that first magical
recording of the *Serenade*, with Pears in fresh,
youthful voice and Dennis Brain's marvellous
horn obbligatos, creating *frisson*-making echoes
in Tennyson, dark melancholy in Blake, and
rippling away exuberantly in Johnson's 'Hymn
to Diana'. What playing! The transfer is faith-

ful; but why on earth couldn't Decca have
removed the surface rustle, and above all, the
clicks? The coupled Walton *Façade*, however,
was a consummate technical and artistic miracle
of Decca's mono era. Edith Sitwell and Pears
deliver the engagingly preposterous words with
bravura insouciance, Collins conducting the
English Opera Group Ensemble with matching
wit and flair, and even today the 1953 recording
sounds almost like stereo.

Serenadeª. Our Hunting Fathers, Op 8. Folk-song
arrangements – Oliver Cromwell; O waly waly
Ian Bostridge ten ªMarie Luise Neunecker hn
Britten Sinfonia / Daniel Harding; aBamberg
Symphony Orchestra / Ingo Metzmacher
EMI 556871-2 (58' · DDD) Texts and translations
included   ⒻⓄ

On each hearing, Britten's *Serenade* still has the
power to astonish anew for its amazingly apt setting of the diligently chosen poems and for the
dazzling horn part written for Dennis Brain.
There's something inevitable and predestined
about these pieces, as though they existed for all
time, an impression enhanced by this performance. Bostridge is spontaneous and immediate in
his responses to text and music. One small reservation concerns a weakness in the lower register
in the Keats Sonnet, 'Oh soft embalmer of the
still night'. In the horn contribution, Neunecker
is as lithe and full toned as any that has gone
before. Metzmacher follows tradition in tempo
matters and his players are alive to every nuance
of the scoring. This compilation also offers an
interesting conspectus of the composer when
young and culminates in the early, quirky masterpiece, *Our Hunting Fathers*, written in 1936
under the influence of Auden and echoes of terrible events in Germany. Ian Bostridge's well-
known affinity with the composer's music and
his virtue of verbal illumination are amply
demonstrated here. The folk-song settings
receive pertinent readings, the first plangent, the
second skittish, as is appropriate to their texts.

Songs

Harmonia Sacra – Lord! I have sinned; Hymn to God
the Father; A Hymn on Divine Musick. This way to
the Tomb – Evening; Morning; Night. Night covers
up the rigid land. Fish in the unruffled lakes. To lie
flat on the back with the knees flexed. A poison tree.
When you're feeling like expressing your affection.
Not even summer yet. The red cockatoo. Wild with
passion. If thou wilt ease thine heart. Cradle song for
Eleanor. Birthday song for Erwin. Um Mitternacht.
The Holy Sonnets of John Donne, Op 35
Ian Bostridge ten **Graham Johnson** pf
Hyperion CDA66823 (65' · DDD) Texts included   Ⓕ

Bostridge is in the royal line of Britten's tenor
interpreters. Indeed his imaginative response to
words and music may come closer than any to
Pears himself. He's heard here in a veritable

cornucopia of mostly unfamiliar and unknown songs (the Donne cycle apart), mainly from the earliest period of Britten's song-writing career when his inspiration was perhaps at its most free and spontaneous. The three settings from Ronald Duncan's *This way to the Tomb* nicely match that poet's florid, vocabulary-rich style as Britten was to do again two years later in *Lucretia*, with 'Night', based on a B minor ground bass, a particularly arresting piece. The Auden settings, roughly contemporaneous with *On this Island*, all reflect Britten's empathy with the poet at that time. The third, *To lie flat on the back*, evinces Britten's gift for writing in racy mode, as does *When you're feeling like expressing your affection*, very much in the style of *Cabaret Songs*. Much deeper emotions are stirred by the two superb Beddoes settings (*Wild with passion* and *If thou wilt ease thine heart*), written when the composer and Pears were on a ship returning home in 1942. *The red cockatoo* itself is an early setting of Waley to whom Britten returned in *Songs from the Chinese*.

All these revelatory songs are performed with full understanding and innate beauty by Bostridge and Johnson, who obviously have a close artistic rapport. The *Donne* Sonnets are as demanding on singer and pianist as anything Britten wrote, hence their previously small representation in the catalogue. Both artists pierce to the core of these electrifying songs, written after, and affected by, Britten's visit to Belsen with Menuhin in 1945. The recording catches the immediacy of these riveting performances. A richly satisfying issue.

Britten Four Cabaret Songs. When you're feeling like expressing your affection. On this Island – As it is, plenty. Blues (arr Runswick) – The Spider and the Fly; Blues; The clock on the wall; Boogie-Woogie **Porter** Paris – Let's do it. Gay Divorce – Night and Day. Leave it to Me – My heart belongs to daddy. Miss Otis Regrets. Nymph Errant – The Physician **Jill Gomez** sop **Martin Jones** pf instrumental ensemble (David Roach cl/sax Graham Ashton tpt Beverley Davison vn Chris Lawrence db John Constable pf Gregory Knowles perc)
Unicorn-Kanchana DKPCD9138 (52' · DDD) Recorded 1992. Texts included ⓕ

Britten's cabaret songs were written for the singing actress Hedli Anderson; there were more than four, but these are the only ones published so far. The texts by Auden are full of the spirit that William Coldstream described, writing of one of Anderson's performances, 'teaching of carefree lucidity and the non-avoidance of banality'. *When you're feeling like expressing your affection* which is published and performed here for the first time is one of the results of Auden and Britten's work for the GPO in the 1930s. Apart from references to 'any telephone kiosk' and 'Press button A' it would still serve well as an encouragement to make use of the telephone. 'As it is, plenty' from *On this Island*, being also in the ironic popular-music style,

rounds off the group nicely.

Jill Gomez's performances are perfect in every nuance, her beautiful tone, clear diction and just hinted-at irony, never overdoing it, give the songs the exact weight they need. The Cole Porter encores and Daryl Runswick's arrangements of four *Blues* by Britten complete what's, without doubt, a quite delicious record.

Albert Herring, Op 39

Albert Herring
Christopher Gillett ten Albert Herring **Dame Josephine Barstow** sop Lady Billows **Felicity Palmer** contr Florence Pike **Peter Savidge** bar Mr Gedge **Robert Lloyd** bass Superintendent Budd **Stuart Kale** ten Mr Upfold **Susan Gritton** sop Miss Wordsworth **Della Jones** mez Mrs Herring **Gerald Finley** bar Sid **Ann Taylor** mez Nancy **Yvette Bonner** sop Emmie **Témimé Bowling** sop Cis **Matthew Long** treb Harry **Northern Sinfonia / Steuart Bedford**
Naxos ② 8 660107/8 (142' · DDD) Libretto available with UK copies only ⓢⓢ○○

Vivid as Hickox's traversal of the score for Chandos may be, Bedford's is just that much more alert, crisper. With his long experience of Britten in the theatre, dating back to *Death in Venice* under the composer's aegis, his timing carries unique authority and, in better sound than the old Decca set can now offer, he even has the edge over the composer's obviously definitive reading. Bedford's players are at least as accomplished as Hickox's, and are caught in a more immediate, less reverberant acoustic.

As for the singers, in almost every case Bedford's are the equal of, or superior to, Hickox's and several surpass Britten's. For instance, Albert was never one of Peter Pears's happiest assumptions; Christopher Gillett makes a more credible mother's boy and does well when he decides to break loose. Where the crucial role of Lady Billows is concerned, Josephine Barstow's commanding performance may not quite be on a par with Sylvia Fisher for Britten, but the difference is small. Susan Gritton gives us a dotty and cleanly sung Miss Wordsworth (Margaret Ritchie, the role's creator must have sounded like this), Robert Lloyd is a simpleton of a Budd (as well sung as any) and Felicity Palmer makes a wonderfully fussy Florence Pike.

It only remains to laud once again the score's many delights as regards technical mastery and subtle characterisation, and to suggest you hurry off to enjoy a real bargain.

Albert Herring
Peter Pears ten Albert Herring **Sylvia Fisher** sop Lady Billows **Johanna Peters** contr Florence Pike **John Noble** bar Mr George **Owen Brannigan** bass Mr Budd **Edgar Evans** ten Mr Upford **April Cantelo** sop Mrs Wordsworth **Sheila Rex** mez Mrs Herring **Joseph Ward** ten Sid **Catherine Wilson** mez Nancy **English Chamber Orchestra / Benjamin Britten**

Decca London ② 421 849-2LH2 (138' · ADD) Recorded 1964. Notes and text included ⓕ

Having shown us the grim and nasty side of Aldeburgh life at the beginning of the 19th century in *Peter Grimes*, Britten had fun with its parochial aspects at the end of the century in his comic opera *Albert Herring*, a tale of a mother-dominated shop assistant elected May King because of his virtue, and who's is slipped a laced drink at his crowning and goes off for a night on the tiles, after which he asserts himself. For some tastes, it's proved too parochial; some who otherwise admire the composer are repelled by its self-regarding whimsicality. The possible cure for these people is to listen to Britten's own recording, here marvellously transferred to CD and showing again what a genius the producer John Culshaw was. Britten finds all the humour in the piece, but he gives it a cutting-edge and is totally successful in conveying the proximity of comedy to tragedy in the remarkable ensemble where Albert is thought to have been killed. With the English Chamber Orchestra on peak form, all kinds of Bergian echoes in the score are revealed and some, too, of Verdi's *Falstaff* (Act 3). There's also Sir Peter Pears's brilliant performance as Albert, a genuine piece of perceptive singing-acting. The cast is well-nigh ideal. If only Britten had written more comic operas.

Billy Budd, Op 50

Billy Budd. The Holy Sonnets of John Donne, Op 35[a]. Songs and Proverbs of William Blake, Op 74[a]
Peter Glossop bar Billy Budd [a]**Sir Peter Pears** ten Captain Vere **Michael Langdon** bass John Claggart **John Shirley-Quirk** bar Mr Redburn **Bryan Drake** bar Mr Flint **David Kelly** bass Mr Ratcliffe **Gregory Dempsey** ten Red Whiskers **David Bowman** bar Donald **Owen Brannigan** bass Dansker **Robert Tear** ten Novice **Robert Bowman** ten Squeak **Delme Bryn-Jones** bar Bosun **Eric Garrett** bar First Mate **Nigel Rogers** ten Maintop **Benjamin Luxon** bar Novice's Friend **Geoffrey Coleby** bar Arthur Jones [a]**Dietrich Fischer-Dieskau** bar; Ambrosian Opera Chorus; London Symphony Orchestra / Benjamin Britten [a]pf
Decca London ③ 417 428-2LH3 (205' · ADD) Recorded 1961. Notes and text included ⓕ**OO**

Billy Budd is remarkable in having been composed for male voices, yet not once is there any lack of colour or variety. Britten marvellously supports the tenor, baritone and bass voices with extraordinary flair in the use of brass and woodwind. This was the last operatic recording John Culshaw produced for Decca and he again showed himself unsurpassed at creating a theatrical atmosphere in the studio. Although there have been several striking and brilliant stage productions of this opera in recent years, not to mention Nagano's recording, it must also be said that both technically and interpretatively this Britten/Culshaw collaboration represents

the touchstone for any that follows it, particularly in the matter of Britten's conducting. Where Britten is superb is in the dramatic tautness with which he unfolds the score and his unobtrusive highlighting of such poignant detail as the use of the saxophone after the flogging. But most of all, he focuses with total clarity on the intimate human drama against the background of life aboard the ship.

And what a cast he had, headed by Peter Pears as Vere, conveying a natural authoritarianism which makes his unwilling but dutiful role as 'the messenger of death' more understandable, if no more agreeable. Peter Glossop's Billy Budd is a virile performance, with nothing of the 'goody-goody' about him. Nor is there any particular homo-eroticism about his relationship with Michael Langdon's black-voiced Claggart: it's a straight conflict between good and evil, and all the more horrifying for its stark simplicity. Add to these principals John Shirley-Quirk, Bryan Drake and David Kelly as the officers, Owen Brannigan as Dansker and Robert Tear and Benjamin Luxon in the small roles of the novice and his friend, and the adjective 'classic' can be applied to this recording with a clear conscience. Also on the discs are two of Britten's most sombre song cycles, the *Donne Sonnets* and the *Blake Songs and Proverbs*, the former with Pears, the latter with Fischer-Dieskau, and both incomparably accompanied by Britten. They make ideal complements to *Billy Budd*. This is without doubt a vintage set.

Billy Budd
Simon Keenlyside bar Billy Budd **Philip Langridge** ten Captain Vere **John Tomlinson** bass John Claggart **Alan Opie** bar Mr Redburn **Matthew Best** bass-bar Mr Flint **Alan Ewing** bass Lt Ratcliffe **Francis Egerton** ten Red Whiskers **Quentin Hayes** bar Donald **Clive Bayley** bass Dansker **Mark Padmore** ten Novice **Richard Coxon** ten Squeak **Timothy DuFore** bar Bosun **Christopher Keyte** bar Bosun **Richard Whitehouse** bar Second Mate, Gunner's Mate **Daniel Norman** ten Maintop **Roderick Williams** bar Novice's Friend, Arthur Jones **Alex Johnson** treb Cabin Boy **Tiffin Boys' Choir**; London Symphony Chorus and Orchestra / **Richard Hickox**
Chandos ③ CHAN9826 (165' · DDD) Notes, text and translation included ⓕ**O**

Britten's score is so often praised that we tend to neglect the distinction of Forster and Crozier's libretto, sung in this set with unerring conviction by its three principals. Keenlyside and Langridge deserve special mention for their arresting sensitivity throughout the final scenes, when they make the utterances of Billy and Vere so poetic and moving: refined tone allied to eloquent phrasing – the epitome of English singing at its very best. Keenlyside has a voice of just the right weight and an appreciation of how Billy must be at once sympathetic and manly. From first to last you realise the lad's personal magnetism in vocal terms alone, explaining the crew's admiration for his qualities. Langridge is the complete Vere, suggesting the man's easy command of men, his poetic soul, his agony of mind at the awful decision placed in his hands to sacrifice Billy. At the opposite end of the human spectrum, Claggart's dark, twisted being and his depravity of thought are ideally realised by Tomlinson, give or take one or two moments of unsteadiness when his voice comes under pressure. In supporting roles there's also much to admire. Mark Padmore conveys all the Novice's terror in a very immediate, tortured manner. Clive Bayley's Dansker is full of canny wisdom. Alan Opie is a resolute Mr Redburn. Matthew Best's is an appropriately powerful Mr Flint, though his large, gritty bass-baritone records uneasily.

Hickox conducts with all his old zest for marshalling large forces, searching out every cranny of the score, and the London Symphony forces respond with real virtuosity. Speeds now and again sound a shade too deliberate, and there's not always quite that sense of an ongoing continuum you feel in both of Britten's readings, which are by and large tauter. But the Chandos, using the revised two-act version, comes into most direct competition with Britten's later Decca set. The latter still sounds well, though inevitably it hasn't the aural range of the Chandos recording. Yet nobody will ever quite catch the creative tension the composer brings to his own work. For all that, the Chandos set benefits from this trio of imaginative singers, and most newcomers will be satisfied with its appreciable achievement.

Billy Budd
Thomas Hampson bar Billy Budd **Anthony Rolfe Johnson** ten Captain Vere **Eric Halfvarson** bass-bar John Claggart **Russell Smythe** bar Mr Redburn **Gidon Saks** bass Mr Flint **Simon Wilding** bass Mr Ratcliffe **Martyn Hill** ten Red Whiskers **Christopher Maltman** bar Donald **Richard Van Allan** bass Dansker **Andrew Burden** ten Novice **Christopher Gillett** ten Squeak **Matthew Hargreaves** bass Bosun **Ashley Holland** bass First Mate **Simon Thorpe** bar Second Mate, Arthur Jones **Robert Johnston** ten Maintop **William Dazeley** bar Novice's Friend **Manchester Boys' Choir; Northern Voices; Hallé Choir and Orchestra / Kent Nagano** Erato ② 3984-21631-2 (148' · DDD) Notes and text included   Ⓜ

This recording is an exciting achievement; it restores to circulation the original, four-act version of the score. The crucial difference between this and Britten's two-act revision is a scene at the close of what's here Act 1, in which 'Starry' Vere addresses his crew and is hailed by them as the sailors' champion, thus establishing the relationship between captain and foretopman. It's an important scene, though musically not particularly distinguished. You can quite see why Britten wanted a tauter two-act drama. Nagano gives us a wonderfully full-bodied and detailed account of the score. There are electrifying

moments, not least the battle scene, where the listener feels very much in the middle of things, and the end of Act 3 where those tremendous and ominous series of chords represent Vere telling Budd of the sentence of death. Britten, in his studio recording, prefers a leaner sound and a slightly tauter approach all-round – in his hands you feel the tension of the personal relationships even more sharply than with Nagano. Hampson is very good, singing with all his customary beauty of voice and intelligence of style, though he imparts a touch of self-consciousness that goes against the grain of the writing. Halfvarson, as Budd's antagonist, the evil Claggart, gives us a mighty presence, singing with power and bite, though not always a steady tone. Rolfe Johnson sings his heart out as he presents Vere's tormented soul. For the rest, Gidon Saks makes a dominant Mr Flint, the sailing-master, Richard Van Allan, is here, predictably, a characterful Dansker, and Andrew Burden stands out as a properly scared Novice, far preferable to Tear's placid reading on Decca. The sum here is greater than the parts, and this set can be heartily recommended. The recording possesses an amazingly wide spectrum of sound: indeed, sometimes the orchestra is simply too loud.

Curlew River, Op 71

Curlew River
Sir Peter Pears ten Madwoman **John Shirley-Quirk** bar Ferryman **Harold Blackburn** bass Abbot **Bryan Drake** bar Traveller **Bruce Webb** treb Voice of the Spirit **English Opera Group / Benjamin Britten** and Viola Tunnard
Decca London 421 858-2LM (69' · ADD) Recorded 1965. Text included   Ⓜ**OO**

Curlew River captured completely the composer's fascination with the Japanese Noh play on which it was based. The recording, produced by John Culshaw, was made in Orford Church, and the atmosphere of this unforgettable occasion is preserved. The procession of monks at the beginning and end comes towards us and recedes, just as if we were sitting in a pew. Pears's performance as the Madwoman is one of his finest and most touching, while Shirley-Quirk and Drake are equally authoritative. The voice of the Madwoman's dead son is devoid of the sentimentality that might have been a peril if any treble other than Bruce Webb had sung it, and the inventive and beguiling orchestral score is marvellously played. With the composer and Viola Tunnard directing the performance, this is in a class of its own.

Death in Venice, Op 88

Death in Venice
Sir Peter Pears ten Gustav von Aschenbach **John Shirley-Quirk** bar Traveller, Elderly Fop, Old Gondolier, Hotel Manager, Hotel Barber, Leader of the Players, Voice of Dionysus **James Bowman**

countertenor Voice of Apollo **Kenneth Bowen** ten
Hotel Porter **Peter Leeming** bass Travel Clerk
Neville Williams bass-bar **Penelope MacKay** sop
Strolling Players **Iris Saunders** sop Strawberry-seller
**English Opera Group Chorus; English Chamber
Orchestra / Steuart Bedford**
Decca London ② 425 669-2LH2 (145' · ADD)
Recorded 1973. Notes and text included   Ⓕ**OO**

In his insert-notes, Christopher Palmer has pertinent things to say about the sexual climate of
Britten's last opera, *Death in Venice*; but these
seem to become of less consequence as you listen to the music. Its potency and inventiveness
create this opera's disturbing and intense
atmosphere, each episode heightened dramatically by instrumental colouring. Under Bedford's direction each scene is fully integrated
into a fluent and convincing whole. This
recording was made while Britten was very ill; it
omits Aschenbach's first recitative ('I have
always kept a close watch over my development
as a writer …'), given as an optional cut in the
vocal score, which was published after the
recording was made, by which time Britten had
changed his mind about this cut and wished it
had been included in the recording. Pears's
Aschenbach, a very English conception, is a
masterly performance, matched by John
Shirley-Quirk's assumption of the six characters
who are Aschenbach's messengers of death and
the Voice of Dionysus.

Death in Venice
Philip Langridge ten Gustav von Aschenbach **Alan
Opie** bar Traveller, Elderly Fop, Old Gondolier, Hotel
Manager, Hotel Barber, Leader of the Players, Voice
of Dionysus **Michael Chance** counterten Voice of
Apollo **BBC Singers; City of London Sinfonia /
Richard Hickox**
Chandos ② CHAN10280 (152' · DDD · S/T/t/N)
                                                        Ⓕ**OO**

Although most of Britten's major operas are
established on the international circuit, *Death in
Venice* has yet to claim its rightful place. Hopefully, this new recording in Richard Hickox's
Britten series – the first audio set since Decca's
original, made nine months after the premiere –
will help advance its cause. The performance is
beautifully played and recorded, and in its all-
important central role reunites Hickox with
Philip Langridge, so compelling in their earlier
set of *Peter Grimes*.

Britten tailored the role of Aschenbach so perfectly for Peter Pears's inimitable tenor that it's
unlikely any other singer will find it an easy fit.
A few years ago Langridge might have been
more adept than he is now at handling some of
the high-lying lyrical lines, but the compromises in this department are worth making for a
singer who's so penetrating in dramatic insight.
Hardly a page of the score passes without his
vivid delivery opening up some new dimension
of the role. As the drama deepens he progressively strips the soul of Aschenbach bare.
His two main colleagues perform to an equally

high level. Alan Opie is still in his vocal prime
and all seven of his multifarious Dionysiac characters are sharply delineated. The excellent
Michael Chance is more ethereal as the Voice of
Apollo than James Bowman, and for that reason
is preferable by a whisker.

As always, Hickox takes his time over the
score, but there's less sense of self-indulgence
than in some of his earlier Britten recordings.
He raws playing of high quality and generosity
of feeling from the City of London Sinfonia.
Add an exemplary choral contribution from the
BBC Singers and a typically atmospheric Chandos recording, and there's no reason to resist.

Noye's Fludde / The Golden Vanity

Noye's Fludde, Op 58
Owen Brannigan bass Noye **Sheila Rex** mez Mrs
Noye **David Pinto** treb Sem **Darian Angadi** treb
Ham **Stephen Alexander** treb Jaffett **Trevor
Anthony** spkr The Voice of God **Caroline Clack** sop
Mrs Sem **Maria-Thérèse Pinto** sop Mrs Ham **Eileen
O'Donnovan** sop Mrs Jaffett **Chorus; English
Opera Group Orchestra; An East Suffolk
Children's Orchestra / Norman Del Mar**

The Golden Vanity, Op 78
Mark Emney treb Captain **John Wojciechowski** treb
Bosun **Barnaby Jago** treb Cabin-boy **Adrian
Thompson** treb Captain **Terry Lovell** treb Bosun
Benjamin Britten pf **Wandsworth School Boys'
Choir / Russell Burgess**
Decca London 436 397-2LM (66' · ADD) Recorded
1961, 1966. Texts included   Ⓕ

Britten wrote these two works for children, but
don't imagine that they're cosy and childish.
Many of his friends thought that there remained
much of the child in him, and this clearly comes
out in the boisterous high spirits of some of this
music. By and large, *Noye's Fludde* and *The
Golden Vanity* are happy works. *Noye's Fludde*
makes invigorating listening. This 1961 performance, recorded in Orford Church, where it
had its première three years before (at the 1958
Aldeburgh Festival), is immensely vivid, and the
enthusiasm of the young singers and instrumentalists is infectious. All the children of East Suffolk seem to be involved in the enterprise: consorts of recorders, bands of bugles, peals of
handbell-ringers, plenty of violins, a few lower
strings, seven percussion players, child soloists,
and a choir as big as you like, enough to give full
representation to the 49 different species of animal mentioned in the text. Then three grown-
ups, and the English Chamber Orchestra. The
skill and imaginative power with which Britten
has used these forces defy adequate description.
There are inevitably rough edges in the singing
and playing, but the spirit is there in abundance.
The same is true of *The Golden Vanity*, and
although there's more conscious vocal skill in
the singing of the Wandsworth School Boys'
Choir, it never gets in the way of the presentation, which bubbles with life.

Peter Grimes, Op 33

Peter Grimes   H
Sir Peter Pears *ten* Peter Grimes Claire Watson
sop Ellen Orford James Pease *bass* Captain
Balstrode Jean Watson *contr* Auntie Raymond
Nilsson *ten* Bob Boles Owen Brannigan *bass*
Swallow. Lauris Elms *mez* Mrs Sedley Sir Geraint
Evans *bar* Ned Keene John Lanigan *ten* Rector
David Kelly *bass* Hobson Marion Studholme *sop*
First Niece Iris Kells *sop* Second Niece Chorus and
Orchestra of the Royal Opera House, Covent
Garden / Benjamin Britten
Decca ② 467 682-2DL2 (142' · ADD) Recorded 1958.
Notes and text included   Ⓕ**OOO**

 The Decca set, which in 1958 introduced this opera to many listeners, has
never been superseded in its refinement or insight. Britten's conducting, lithe and
lucid, reveals his work as a complex, ambiguous
drama. Peter Pears, in the title-role written for
him, brings unsurpassed detail of nuance to
Grimes's words while never losing sight of the
essential plainness of the man's speech. The rest
of the cast form a vivid portrait gallery of characters. The recording is as live and clear as if it
had been made yesterday, and takes the listener
right onto the stage. The bustle of activity and
sound effects realise nicely Britten's own masterly painting of dramatic foreground and background.

Peter Grimes
Philip Langridge *ten* Grimes Janice Watson *sop*
Ellen Orford Alan Opie *bar* Captain Balstrode
Ameral Gunson *mez* Auntie John Graham-Hall
ten Bob Boles John Connell *bass* Swallow Anne
Collins *contr* Mrs Sedley Roderick Williams *bar* Ned
Keene John Fryatt *ten* Rector Matthew Best *bass*
Hobson Yvonne Barclay *sop* First Niece Pamela
Helen Stephen *mez* Second Niece London
Symphony Chorus; City of London Sinfonia /
Richard Hickox
Chandos ② CHAN9447/8 (147' · DDD) Notes and
text included   Ⓕ**OO**

Any reading that so potently confirms the
genius of this piece must have a distinguished
place in the discography. In the first place
there's Langridge's tense, sinewy, sensitive
Grimes. Predictably he rises to the challenge of
the Mad Scene; this is a man hugely to be pitied,
yet there's a touch of resignation, of finding
some sort of peace at last, after all the agony of
the soul. His portrayal is tense and immediate,
and a match for that of Pears in personal identification – listen to the eager touch at 'We
strained in the wind'. The next composite
heroes are the members of the chorus. Electrifying as their rivals are, the LSO singers, trained
by Stephen Westrop, seem just that much more
arresting, not least in the hue-and-cry of Act 3,
quite terrifying in its immediacy as recorded by
Chandos. Hickox's interpretation has little to
fear from the distinguished competition. Many

BRITTEN'S PETER GRIMES – IN BRIEF

Peter Pears *Peter Grimes* **Claire Watson** *Ellen
Orford* **James Pease** *Balstrode* **ROH Chorus &
Orchestra / Benjamin Britten**
Decca Legends ② 467 682-2DL2 (142 mins: ADD)
    Ⓕ**OOO**

A uniquely authoritative set. Britten's
Covent Garden forces respond magnificently, and Pears is simply unforgettable in
the title-role specially written for him. John
Culshaw's newly remastered 1958 production barely begins to show its years.

Jon Vickers *Peter Grimes* **Heather Harper** *Ellen
Orford* **Jonathan Summers** *Balstrode*
ROH Chorus & Orchestra / Sir Colin Davis
Philips ② 462 847-2PM2 (146 mins: ADD)   Ⓜ
Davis conducts an intensely refreshing per-
formance, dominated by Jon Vickers's sear-
ingly passionate Grimes. Heather Harper,
too, is quite superb in the role of Ellen
Orford.

Anthony Rolfe Johnson *Peter Grimes* **Felicity
Lott** *Ellen Orford* **Thomas Allen** *Balstrode*
ROH Chorus & Orchestra / Bernard Haitink
EMI ② 754832-2 (145 mins: DDD)   Ⓕ
Haitink's 1993 set boasts a strong cast,
most notably Felicity Lott's outstandingly
sympathetic and secure Ellen Orford.
Anthony Rolfe Johnson's Grimes is not
always as involving as one might wish, and
the whole venture lacks the whiff of grease-
paint that marks out the composer's own
classic version.

Philip Langridge *Peter Grimes* **Janice Watson**
Ellen Orford **Alan Opie** *Balstrode* **Opera
London, London Sym Chorus, City of London
Sinfonia / Richard Hickox**
Chandos ② CHAN9447/8 (147 mins: DDD)   Ⓕ**OO**
Philip Langridge's Grimes is one of the
glories of our age, and Alan Opie's Balstrode
is another triumphant assumption. Hickox is
in his element, and the Chandos engineers
capture it all with sumptuous immediacy.

Glenn Winslade *Peter Grimes* **Janice Watson**
Ellen Orford **Anthony Michaels-Moore** *Balstrode*
**London Symphony Chorus and Orchestra /
Sir Colin Davis**
LSO Live ③ LSO0054 (143 mins: DDD)   Ⓢ
A stunning achievement for conductor,
chorus and orchestra, and while the perform-
ances of the soloists may not match those of
Davis's earlier recording, the strikingly pow-
erful LSO forces on this live 2004 recording
demand to be heard.

details are placed with special care, particularly in the Interludes and the parodistic dances in Act 3, and whole episodes, such as the Grimes-Balstrode dispute in Act 1, have seldom sounded so dramatic. Once or twice one would have liked a firmer forward movement, as in the fifth Interlude, but the sense of total music-theatre is present throughout. Of the other soloists, the one comparative disappointment is Janice Watson's Ellen Orford. She sings the part with tone as lovely as any of her rivals on disc and with carefully wrought phrasing, but doesn't have the experience to stand out from the village regulars. Britten's set remains *hors concours*, but that recording stretches over three CDs. Hickox is the finest of the modern recordings: as sound it's quite spectacular, vast in range, with well-managed perspectives and just enough hints of stage action to be convincing.

Additional recommendation

Peter Grimes
Vickers Peter Grimes **Harper** Ellen Orford **Royal Opera House Chorus and Orchestra / C Davis**
Philips 462 847-2PM2 (146′ · ADD)   Ⓜ
A mid-price alternative which enshrines the wonderfully drawn Grimes of Jon Vickers and the touching, immensely human Ellen of Heather Harper. Colin Davis's conducting, too, displays his love of the score.

The Turn of the Screw, Op 54

The Turn of the Screw   Ⓗ
Sir Peter Pears ten Prologue, Peter Quint **Jennifer Vyvyan** sop Governess **David Hemmings** treb Miles **Olive Dyer** sop Flora **Joan Cross** sop Mrs Grose **Arda Mandikian** sop Miss Jessel **English Opera Group Orchestra / Benjamin Britten**
Decca London mono ② 425 672-2LH2
(105′ · ADD) Recorded 1955. Notes and text included
                                         ⒻOO

As Sir Colin Davis has shown on Philips, there's room for an alternative interpretation of this remarkable work, but this superb first recording will remain as documentary-historical evidence of the highest importance and value. Will there ever be a better performance, let alone recording, of *The Turn of the Screw* than this by the original cast, recorded less than four months after the 1954 Venice première?

This score is Britten at his greatest, expressing good and evil with equal ambivalence, evoking the tense and sinister atmosphere of Bly by inspired use of the chamber orchestra and imparting vivid and truthful life to every character in the story. As one listens, transfixed, all that matters is Britten's genius as a composer. Jennifer Vyvyan's portrayal of the Governess is a classic characterisation, her vocal subtleties illuminating every facet of the role and she has the perfect foil in Joan Cross's motherly and uncomplicated Mrs Grose. The glittering malevolence of Pears's Quint, luring David Hemmings's incomparable Miles to destruc-

tion; the tragic tones of Arda Mandikian's Miss Jessel; Olive Dyer's spiteful Flora – how fortunate we are that these performances are preserved. As with all the Decca/Britten reissues, the transfer is a triumph.

The Turn of the Screw
Ian Bostridge ten Prologue, Peter Quint **Joan Rodgers** sop Governess **Vivien Tierney** sop Miss Jessel **Julian Leang** treb Miles **Caroline Wise** sop Flora **Jane Henschel** sop Mrs Grose **Gustav Mahler Chamber Orchestra / Daniel Harding**
Virgin Classics ② 545521-2 (106′ · DDD) Notes, texts and translations included   ⒻOOO

Ⓖ This absorbing version of Britten's arresting masterpiece, derived from Henry James's ever-mysterious short story, is based on the stage performances given by London's Royal Opera in Deborah Warner's controversial staging. It offers a considerable challenge to both the première recording, conducted by the composer, and the more recent version conducted by Steuart Bedford. The new recording catches all the sinister fascination of Britten's most tautly composed opera score, so aptly matched to James's tale and to Myfanwy Piper's evocative libretto.

Daniel Harding extracts the greatest tension from both the finely wrought writing for the chamber ensemble and from the well-balanced and, by and large, exemplary cast. He's helped by the clearest and most detailed recording the work has yet received.

When discussing the merits of the casts one is comparing three teams of undoubted excellence. Nevertheless there are distinctions to be made. As on stage, Joan Rodgers nicely balances the need to suggest the ingenuous and the excitable side of the Governess's nature, which she conveys in a performance that combines clarity of diction with the vocal verities. Bostridge's ethereal, other-worldly, eerily magnetic Quint provides an interesting contrast with Philip Langridge's more forceful and present assumption for Bedford. Both are preferable to Pears's more mannered singing on the pioneering set, but that, needless to say, has its own authority. On the other hand neither Vivian Tierney nor Nadine Secunde (Bedford) quite match the searing sadness of Arda Mandikian's dark-hued Miss Jessel for Britten. In the case of Mrs Grose, Jane Henschel, imposingly as she sings, sounds a trifle too stock-operatic in her responses to words and notes beside the particular gentility of Joan Cross (Britten) or the marvellously detailed and intensely uttered interpretation of Phyllis Cannan (Bedford).

This is an utterly absorbing version. Given its masterly engineering and sense of atmosphere it's, by a hair's-breadth, preferable to the Bedford among stereo recordings. The composer's set remains both a historic document and the tautest reading, but most will prefer and be satisfied with the conviction and the sound of this newcomer.

Sébastien de Brossard
French 1655-1730

Lexicographer and composer Sébastien de Brossard was maître de chapelle at Strasbourg Cathedral, 1687-98, then held a similar post in Meaux, where he composed sacred music, chiefly motets. He was among the first in France to write violin sonatas, and his French cantatas are among the few based on biblical subjects. Of his writings on music the most important is his Dictionnaire (1701, rev. 1703), the first of its kind in France. His extensive library is now in the Bibliothèque Nationale, Paris.

GROVEmusic

Grands Motets

In Convertendo Dominus. Miserere mei, Deus. Canticum eucharisticum pro pace
Delphine Collot, Catherine Padaut sops **Jean-Paul Fouchécourt, Gilles Ragon** tens **Olivier Lallouette, Jérôme Corréas** basses **Accentus Chamber Choir; Limoges Baroque Ensemble / Christophe Coin**
Astrée Naïve E8607 (76' · DDD) Texts and translations included Ⓕ

The name of Sébastien de Brossard usually appears in music history books only when its owner is being quoted in his capacity as a revealing theorist and lexicographer. As a composer, mainly of church music, his achievements are less often considered next to those of notable contemporaries such as Charpentier and Lalande, but in 1995 the Centre de Musique Baroque de Versailles devoted one of its annual short festivals to him, and this recording arises from that occasion. The three *grands motets* – large-scale pieces for choir, soloists and orchestra – are surprisingly eventful music, seemingly conceived more for entertainment than for liturgical edification. *Canticum eucharisticum pro pace*, a 40-minute show-piece written to celebrate the joining of Strasbourg to France, depicts God/Louis XIV as both angry war hero and generous peacemaker, and even includes a dramatic solo for a singer representing the voice of God. The other two motets, too, contain interesting contrasts and a few good descriptive moments of their own. The performances are refined and attractive, even if the choir is occasionally a little unfocused.

Petits Motets

O Jesu! quam dulce nomen tuum, SdB24ª. O plenus irarum dies!, SdB31ᵇ. Beati immaculati, SdB49ᶜ. Silentium dormi, SdB52ᵈ. Miserere mei, SdB53ᵉ
ᵃᶜᵉ**Cyrille Dubois** treb ᵇᶜ**Alain Buett** bar ᵈ**Hervé Lamy** bass-bar **Juan-Sebastian Lima** theorbo **Jean-Marie Quint** vc ᵉ**Maîtrise de Caen / Robert Weddle** org
Assai 207582 (55' · DDD) Recorded 1999. Texts and translations included Ⓕ〇

Brossard's *Petits motets* exemplify the fluent melodic style and intimacy of the genre at its most engaging. Cyrille Dubois is a seasoned treble with an astonishingly natural flair for the conventions and declamatory 'délicatesse' of the French Baroque. Put simply, there isn't anyone quite like him. The idiom is in his blood. As the opening motet, *O Jesu! quam dulce nomen tuum* reveals, Dubois places notes with the accuracy and nonchalance of an old pro, naturally colouring vowels and embellishing cadences without a morsel of fear. Dubois is joined by the expressive and resonant bass of Alain Buett, a commanding presence in the harrowing and harmonically daring *O plenus irarum dies!*; Weddle, leading from the organ a sensitive accompaniment to a lilting *tripla* for the merciful Christ, judges the music's Italianate contrasts with sensual relief.

The fine duo motet, *Beati immaculati*, is sweetly set by Brossard (who reckoned it his best), and Dubois and Buett have a rollicking time in a splendid performance. *Silentium dormi* suffers in comparison: the tenor, Hervé Lamy, isn't in the same league vocally. Finally, we have an unpretentious and musicianly performance of a *Miserere* for treble, vocal consort and continuo. Again, few will doubt that treble singing of this quality, guided so intelligently, adds a delectable *frisson* to French Baroque music. A strong recommendation.

Leo Brouwer
Cuban 1939

Cuban composer and guitarist. He studied in New York (1960-61) but was most influenced by the new music he heard at the 1961 Warsaw Autumn Festival. He has been occupied with being an artist in a revolutionary society; his early works are nationalist, the later ones adopting avant-garde techniques.

GROVEmusic

Guitar Concerto

Guitar Concerto No 5, 'Helsinki' **Albéniz/Brouwer** Iberia Suite **Lennon-McCartney/Brouwer** From Yesterday to Penny Lane
Timo Korhonen gtr **Tampere Philharmonic Orchestra / Tuomas Ollila**
Ondine ODE979-2 (66' · DDD) Ⓕ〇

The Concerto No 5, *Helsinki*, was commissioned for the Helsinki Festival but contains no musical reference to that city. As Brouwer explains: 'I compose in Space or in Lightness and Heaviness,' referring to the titles of the first two movements, but whether he ever does so in 'Luminosity', the title of the third, we aren't told. It's a substantial work that's none the worse for its lack of memorable tunes – except to those who regard them as essential. Brouwer's fingerprints abound, especially in the first movement's gestures, made familiar in other (solo) pieces. He has an intimate knowledge of the guitar, and uses the orchestra skilfully and imaginatively. Renaissance composers didn't hesitate to use popular and folk tunes, so why shouldn't today's do likewise? Brouwer describes The Beatles' tunes as 'folk songs of today' and the seven in this recording are set in a variety of pastiche forms, *à la* Wagner, Hindemith, Stravinsky *et al*, a pleasing counterbalance to the serious business of the Concerto. Timo Korhonen is a superb guitarist who takes everything in his clean-fingered stride. The Tampere Philharmonic Orchestra shares his zest, and the recording is first-class. It adds up to a strong recommendation.

John Browne   English fl c1490

Browne may have been the John (or William) Browne, clerk of Windsor, who died in 1479 or the lawyer and rector of West Tilbury who died in 1498. The Eton Choirbook originally contained 11 antiphons and four Magnificats by him, of which only nine antiphons (two incomplete) and a fragment of a Magnificat remain. The eight-voice O Maria Salvatoris mater, which opens the MS, shows contrapuntal expertise, but more remarkable are the six-voice settings of the Stabat mater, Stabat virgo mater Christi and Stabat iuxta Christi crucem.
                                            GROVEmusic

Motets

Music from the Eton Choirbook
O Maria Salvatoris mater. Salve regina. Stabat iuxta Christi crucem. Stabat mater dolorosa. O regina mundi clara
The Tallis Scholars / Peter Phillips
Gimell CDGIM036 (71' · DDD · T/t)   Ⓕ**OOO**

By any other name, John Browne would surely be recognised as one of the very greatest English composers. The fact that fewer than 10 works survive intact in the Eton Choirbook (practically the only source transmitting his music anyway) only adds to his mysterious aura; the music sends normally dispassionate specialists reaching for superlatives. He stands head and shoulders above the other Eton composers, and it's high time he was accorded an anthology of his own. The discography of early polyphonic music has made such great strides that 'landmark' recordings are fewer and further between; yet this can hardly be described as anything else.

An index of Browne's stature is the variety of scorings he deploys. His eight-voice *O Maria Salvatoris mater* was considered extraordinary enough to be given pride of place in the Eton Choirbook, and each of the three six-voice pieces included here is scored differently. No other Eton composer wrote so much six-voice music excluding trebles. Two of his pieces in this mould (*Stabat iuxta Christi crucem* and *O regina mundi*) are here recorded convincingly for the first time. Phillips's line-up of men's

voices (especially on the top lines) is as superb as Browne's must have been, for an exceptional keenness of focus is needed to prevent the thick texture from becoming stodgy; as it is, the sound of six parts jostling in a compass of under two octaves is thrilling.

But the pieces with trebles have long been reckoned Browne's masterpieces; as such, they have been recorded several times before. Phillips sees Browne as a mystical figure, and his choice of tempi in the *Stabat mater* and *O Maria* reflects this. His singers articulate it so convincingly as to suspend disbelief absolutely. The Tallis Scholars are to be heard at their best in this repertory; this recording confirms that. If you don't know Browne's music, you simply must hear this.

Max Bruch   German 1838-1920

Bruch studied with Hiller and Reinecke and had some success with his cantata Frithjof Op 23 (1864) before taking posts in Koblenz, Sondershausen, Liverpool and Breslau. Official recognition came in 1891 when he became professor at the Berlin Academy. Although he composed three operas, his talent lay in epic expression; during his lifetime the secular choral works Odysseus and Das Feuerkreuz, with their solid choral writing and tuneful style, sometimes showing affinities with folk music, were considered particularly significant. Only his violin concertos (especially the appealing No 1 in G minor), the Scottish Fantasy for violin and orchestra and the Kol nidrei for cello and orchestra Op 47 have remained in the repertory.   **GROVE**music

Clarinet and Viola Concerto, Op 88

Clarinet and Viola Concerto in E minor, Op 88.
Romance, Op 85. Eight Pieces, Op 83
Paul Meyer *cl* **Gérard Caussé** *va* **François-René Duchâble** *pf* **Orchestra of the Opéra National de Lyon / Kent Nagano**
Apex 8573-89229-2 (65' · DDD) Recorded 1988   Ⓢ

The Double Concerto and the Eight Pieces both stem from Bruch's later years as a composer, by which time he was ill and tiring, also embittered and resentful of the successes being enjoyed by Strauss and Debussy (the latter 'an unqualified scribbler'). His Concerto isn't only a backward-looking and inward-looking work: it's the music of a weary composer with little more to say but the habit of a lifetime in saying it. The technique doesn't fail, though the last movement is thinly stretched; the manner is still lyrical, and makes graceful use both of the solo instruments and of the accompaniments. This is unusually disposed so that the chamber orchestra of the first movement gradually swells in numbers until it's virtually a full symphony orchestra for the finale. Some problems ensue for the viola, which is in any case cast in a secondary role to the clarinet. Parity is restored with the *Eight Pieces*, though Bruch wrote them for the talents of his son Max Felix, a gifted clarinettist whose performance of these pieces earned him favourable comparison with the great Richard Mühlfeld from the conductor Fritz Steinbach. They are pleasant pieces, sometimes drawing on the tonal companionship which Mozart discovered the instruments to have in his *Kegelstatt* Trio, sometimes contrasting them with opposing kinds of music.

Violin Concertos

No 1 in G minor, Op 26; **No 2** in D minor, Op 44; **No 3** in D minor, Op 58

Bruch Violin Concerto No 1ᵃ **Beethoven** Violin Concerto in D, Op 61ᵇ
Kyung Wha Chung *vn* ᵃRoyal Concertgebouw Orchestra; ᵇLondon Philharmonic Orchestra / Klaus Tennstedt
EMI 754072-2 (70' · DDD) ᵇRecorded live 1989
Ⓕ**OO**

Kyung Wha Chung has recorded both of these concertos before, but these performances not only have the benefit of more modern sound but are more spontaneous in their expressive warmth. The Bruch was recorded in the studio and reflects Chung's growing ease in a recording environment. Notoriously, she dislikes the constraints of recording, when she's so essentially spontaneous in her expressiveness. Here her rubato is freer, so that in the first movement the opening theme is more impulsive, and her freedom in the second subject conveys the sort of magic you find in her live performances. The slow movement brings extreme contrasts of dynamic and expression from orchestra as well as soloist, and the finale is again impulsive in its bravura. The Beethoven is a live recording. Chung sustains spacious speeds very persuasively indeed. She's freely flexible in her approach to Beethoven, as Tennstedt is too, but magnetically keeping an overall command. The element of vulnerability in Chung's reading adds to the emotional weight, above all in the slow movement, which in its wistful tenderness is among the most beautiful on disc. As for the outer movements, they're full of flair, with a live event bringing few if any flaws of ensemble. Altogether, an exceptionally attractive release.

Bruch Violin Concerto No 2 **Goldmark** Violin Concerto No 1 in A minor, Op 28
Nai-Yuan Hu *vn* **Seattle Symphony Orchestra / Gerard Schwarz**
Delos DE3156 (60' · DDD) Recorded 1993-4 Ⓕ

Hu is a virtuoso in the best sense of that word, with uncommon lyrical gifts, who can shape phrases with a sense of gentle rapture and coax his violin to produce the most lovely sounds. Even though the Bruch was specifically written for Sarasate, neither of these warm-hearted

BRUCH'S VIOLIN CONCERTO NO 1 – IN BRIEF

Nathan Milstein; NYPSO / Sir John Barbirolli
Biddulph LAB096 (77 mins: ADD) Ⓜ**O**
Milstein captured on peak form in this memorable 1942 alliance with Barbirolli. A generous sequence of assorted bon-bons make up the remainder.

Jascha Heifetz; New SO of London / Sir Malcolm Sargent
RCA 09026 61745-2 (65 mins: ADD) Ⓜ**O**
A delectable souvenir of Jascha Heifetz's incomparable gifts. Similarly superlative accounts of Bruch's *Scottish Fantasy* and Vieuxtemps's Fifth Concerto make for ideal bedfellows.

Josef Suk; Czech Philharmonic Orchestra / Karel Ančerl
Supraphon SU3663-2 (79 mins: ADD) Ⓜ**O**
An irresistibly songful, warm-hearted performance. Suk's sweet, silky tone gives much pleasure, and he generates a profoundly satisfying rapport with Ančerl.

Salvatore Accardo; Leipzig Gewandhaus Orchestra / Kurt Masur
432 282-2PSL3 (3 CDs, 214 mins: ADD) Ⓜ
Accardo and Masur form a selfless, dedicated partnership. Part of an appealing set devoted to all Bruch's music for violin and orchestra.

Kyung Wha Chung; London Philharmonic Orchestra / Klaus Tennstedt
EMI 754072-2 (70 mins: DDD) Ⓕ**OO**
A freer, more impulsive account than Chung's own earlier Decca recording with Kempe. Tennstedt and the LPO tender powerful support.

Cho-Liang Lin; Chicago Symphony Orchestra / Leonard Slatkin
Sony Classical Theta SMK89715 (73 mins: DDD) Ⓜ
Lin plays with a freshness and spark that make this warhorse sound newly minted. He's accompanied with total sympathy by Slatkin and the Chicagoans.

Maxim Vengerov; Leipzig Gewandhaus Orchestra / Kurt Masur
Teldec 4509-90875-2 (51 mins: DDD) Ⓜ**O**
The 19-year-old Vengerov's first concerto disc is a winner all the way. Wonderfully vital, raptly expressive playing that never fails to lift the spirits.

Nikolaj Znaider; London Philharmonic Orchestra / Lawrence Foster
EMI 556906-2 (66 mins: DDD) Ⓕ
No question that Znaider's is a powerful new talent. An unusually thoughtful, articulate performance, uniquely coupled with Nielsen's adorable Violin Concerto.

concertos impresses primarily by its brilliance. Here both gain from the understanding partnership attained by Hu with Schwarz and his excellent Seattle orchestra within a kindly acoustic. Having attended the première of Bruch's Second Concerto, Brahms wrote to Simrock: 'Hopefully a law will not be necessary to prevent any more first movements being written as an *Adagio*. That is intolerable for normal people.' Bruch's riposte was, 'If I meet with Brahms in heaven, I shall have myself transferred to Hell'. He could not understand why the popularity of the First Concerto precluded performance of the others, 'which are just as good if not better'. Certainly Hu's superb reading here bears out the composer's evaluation of the Second. The ardently simple presentation of the glorious main theme of that maligned *Adagio* goes right to the heart.

Scottish Fantasy, Op 46

Bruch Scottish Fantasy
Lalo Symphonie espagnole, Op 21
Tasmin Little vn **Royal Scottish National Orchestra / Vernon Handley**
HMV Classics HMV5 73041-2 (68' · DDD) Ⓑ❍

It's an excellent idea to couple Bruch's evocation of Scotland with Lalo's of Spain, both works in unconventional five-movement *concertante* form. Tasmin Little takes a ripe, robust and passionate view of both works, projecting them strongly, as she would in the concert hall, but neither is she lacking in poetry.

Her leisurely speeds give her freedom to point rhythms infectiously and play with an extra degree of individuality in her phrasing, daringly using *portamentos* or agogic hesitations in a way that adds to the character of the reading. Little has the gift of sounding totally spontaneous on disc, with no feeling of strict studio manners. In this she's greatly helped by the splendid, keenly polished playing of the Scottish orchestra under Vernon Handley, a most sympathetic partner. Handley is also excellent in pointing the rhythms of the fast movements of the Lalo, matching his soloist, and the recording is superb, with brass in particular vividly caught.

Additional recommendation

Scottish Fantasy[a]
Coupled with: **Hindemith** Violin Concerto[b] **Mozart** Sinfonia concertante[c]
[abc]**D Oistrakh** vn [c]**I Oistrakh** va [a]**LSO / Horenstein;** [b]**Hindemith;** [c]**Moscow Philharmonic Orchestra / Kondrashin**
Decca Legends 470 258-2DM (DDD) Recorded 1962-3

The Bruch is a joy from start to finish, an Ⓜ❍❍ inspirationally eloquent reading to rank alongside Heifetz's indelible 1961 stereo version. Equally indispensable is Oistrakh's superbly eloquent playing on the Hindemith. A superb coupling.

Serenade, Op 75

Serenade, Op 75. Scottish Fantasy, Op 46.
Maxim Fedotov vn **Russian Philharmonic Orchestra / Dmitry Yablonsky**
Naxos 8 557395 (73' · DDD) Ⓢ

Though the *Scottish Fantasy*, with its wealth of traditional melodies, ripely presented, is firmly based in the repertory, most of Bruch's other *concertante* works for violin are largely unknown. Here's one of the most ambitious, the Serenade, dating from 1900, 20 years after the Fantasy. Its breadth and weight belies the lightweight title. It's a warm and fluent work in Bruch's high-Romantic style, built on clearly defined themes that lack only the last degree of memorability of the Fantasy. The third of the four movements, a dreamy, lyrical *Notturno*, comes nearest to matching the Fantasy's natural glow, but the other movements have striking moments, too. Bruch had the idea of putting this substantial work among his numbered concertos but changed his mind.

Maxim Fedotov gives a warm, thrusting performance of both the Serenade and the Fantasy. Compared with Tasmin Little in her outstanding rival Fantasy on HMV, Fedotov may be a little short on the mystery and tenderness, but his bravura playing, helped by full-blooded accompaniment from Dmitry Yablonsky and the Russian Philharmonic, makes the results consistently compelling.

Anton Bruckner   Austrian 1824-1896

Bruckner was the son of a village schoolmaster and organist, with whom he first studied and for whom he could deputise when he was ten. His father died in 1837 and he was sent at 13 as a chorister to the St Florian monastery where he could study organ, violin and theory. He became a schoolmaster-organist, holding village posts, but in 1845 went to teach at St Florian, becoming organist there in 1851. During these years he had written masses and other sacred works. In 1855 he undertook a counterpoint course in Vienna with the leading theorist, Simon Sechter; the same year he was appointed organist at Linz Cathedral. He continued his studies almost to the age of 40, but more crucial was his contact, in 1863, with Wagner's music – first Tannhäuser, then Tristan und Isolde; these pointed to new directions for him, as the Masses in D minor, E minor and F minor, and Symphony No 1, all written in 1864-8, show.

In 1868, after Sechter's death, he was offered the post of theory teacher at the Vienna Conservatory, which he hesitantly accepted. In the ensuing years he travelled to Paris and London as an organ virtuoso and improviser. In Vienna, he concentrated on writing symphonies; but the Vienna PO rejected No 1 as 'wild', No 2 as 'nonsense' and 'unplayable' and No 3 as 'unperformable'. When No 3 was given, it was a fiasco. No 4 was successfully played, but No 5 had to wait 18 years for a performance and some of No 6 was never played in Bruckner's lifetime. He was crit-icised for his Wagnerian leanings during the bitter Brahms-Wagner rivalries. His friends urged him to make cuts in his scores (or made them for him); his lack of self-confidence led to acquiescence and to the formal distortion of the works as a result. Late in his life he revised several of his earlier works to meet such criticisms.

Bruckner taught at a teacher-training college, 1870-74, and at Vienna University – after initial opposition – from 1875. Only in the 1880s did he enjoy real success, in particular with Symphony No 7; his music began to be performed in Germany and elsewhere, and he received many honours as well as grants from patrons and the Austrian government. Even in his last years, he was asked to rewrite Sym-phony No 8, and when he died in 1896 No 9 remained unfinished.

Bruckner was a deeply devout man, and it is not by chance that his symphonies have been compared to cathedrals in their scale and their grandeur and in their aspiration to the sublime. The principal influ-ences behind them are Beethoven and Wagner. Beethoven's Ninth provides the basic model for their scale and shape, and also for their mysterious open-ings, fading in from silence. Wagner too influenced their scale and certain aspects of their orchestration, such as the use of heavy brass (from No 7 Bruckner wrote for four Wagner tubas) and the use of intense, sustained string cantabile for depth of expression. His musical forms are individual: his vast sonata-type structures often have three rather than two main tonal areas, and he tends to present substantial sec-tions in isolation punctuated by pregnant silences. Huge climaxes are attained by remorseless reitera-tions of motifs, or, in the Adagios, by the persistent use of swirling figural patterns in the violins against which a huge orchestral tutti is inexorably built up, often with ascending phrases and enriching har-monies. Secondary themes often have a chorale-like character, sometimes counterpointed with music in dance rhythms. Slow movements are often planned (as in Beethoven's Ninth) around the alternation of two broad themes. Scherzos are in 3/4, often with the kind of elemental drive of that in Beethoven's Ninth; they carry hints of Austrian peasant dances, and some of the trios show ländler-like characteristics. From No 3 onwards, Bruckner's symphonies each end with a restatement of the work's opening theme. Because of their textual complications, Bruckner's symphonies have mostly been published in two edi-tions: the Sämtliche Werke series (ed R Haas and others) usually give the work as first written, the Gesamtausgabe (ed L Nowak and others) the revised and cut versions.   GROVEmusic

Symphonies

No 00 in F minor, 'Study Symphony'; **No 0** in D minor, 'Die Nullte'; **No 1** in C minor; **No 2** in C minor; **No 3** in D minor; **No 4** in E flat, 'Romantic'; **No 5** in B flat; **No 6** in A; **No 7** in E; **No 8** in C minor; **No 9** in D minor

---

Symphonies – Nos 1 (Linz version), 2, 3 (1889 version, ed Nowak), 4-7, 8 (ed Haas) & 9

Berlin Philharmonic Orchestra / Herbert von Karajan
DG ⑨ Karajan Symphony Edition 429 648-2GSE9
(520' · ADD/DDD) Recorded 1975-81   Ⓜ○○○

 Karajan's understanding of the slow but powerful currents that flow beneath the surfaces of symphonies like the Fifth or Nos 7-9 has never been bet-tered, but at the same time he shows how much more there is to be reckoned with: strong emo-tions, a deep poetic sensitivity (a Bruckner sym-phony can evoke landscapes as vividly as Mahler or Vaughan Williams) and a gift for singing melody that at times rivals even Schubert. It hardly needs saying that there's no such thing as a perfect record cycle, and Karajan's collection of the numbered Bruckner symphonies (unfor-tunately he never recorded 'No 0') has its weak-nesses. The early First and Second Symphonies can be a little heavy-footed and, as with so many Bruckner sets, there's a suspicion that more time might have been spent getting to know the fine but elusive Sixth. However, none of these performances is without its major insights, and in the best of them – particularly Nos 3, 5, 7, 8 and 9 – those who haven't stopped their ears to Karajan will find that whatever else he may have been, there was a side to him that could only be described as 'visionary'. As for the recordings: climaxes can sound a touch overblown in some of the earlier symphonies, but overall the image is well focused and atmospheric. A valuable set, and a landmark in the history of Bruckner recording.

Additional recommendation

Symphonies Nos 1-9
Berlin Philharmonic Orchestra; Berlin Radio SO / Jochum
DG ⑨ 469 810-2GB9 (9 hours 12' · ADD) Recorded 1958-68   ⑤Ⓑ
If you're used to Karajan's Bruckner, Jochum's approach can appear rather stop-start. But he was a great Brucknerian, and his highly charged, romantically intense, seemingly spontaneous approach will appeal to many. This is a great set with few real weaknesses, except for the Eighth.

Symphony No 1 (Linz version). Te Deum
Jessye Norman *sop* **Yvonne Minton** *mez* **David Rendall** *ten* **Samuel Ramey** *bass***Chicago Symphony Chorus and Orchestra / Daniel Barenboim**
DG Galleria 435 068-2GGA (70' · DDD) Recorded 1980. Text and translation included   Ⓜ

There's still a relative lack of choice when it comes to single CDs of the boisterous First Symphony in its original Linz version, so the reissue of this Chicago recording under Baren-boim is a most attractive choice, particularly if you don't mind adding to your collection a superb – eloquently sung, expertly played, exceptionally well-recorded – account of Bruckner's mighty *Te Deum*. In the symphony, Barenboim is witty, affectionate and vital and the Chicago playing is sumptuous. Here and there you might long for the countrified tread of Eugen Jochum, a German Bruckner conductor of the old school, but you can understand DG's desire to give the best of this Barenboim Bruckner cycle another airing. Warmly recommended if the coupling suits.

Symphonies Nos 1 (ed Carragan) & 3 – Bewegt, quasi Andante (1876 version)
Royal Scottish National Orchestra / Georg Tintner
Naxos 8 554430 (76' · DDD)　　Ⓢ**O**

Some of the outstanding performances in the late Georg Tintner's Naxos Bruckner series have been of the early symphonies. 'Your young men shall see visions,' says the Prophet Joel. It has been Tintner's skill to conjure vision by marrying sharpness of detail and youthful diction with a daring breadth of utterance. He did this in his recording of the Symphony No 3 and he does it again here in a fine account of the First recorded in Glasgow's Henry Wood Hall with the RSNO at the top of its considerable form.

Timings of individual movements confirm a broad reading, as broad as Václav Neumann's on his old Leipzig set. But where Neumann's performance ended up sounding soulful and ponderous, Tintner's is as fresh as could be. Bruckner called this a 'cheeky little minx' of a symphony. Tintner shows it to be that, and more. (Bruckner's own generally unavailing pursuit of cheeky post-pubescent minxes clearly fed a rich and lively fantasy life which the symphony vividly charts. Or so Freudians might have us believe.)

The announcement that this is the 'world première recording' of the 'unrevised Linz version' shouldn't cause seasoned collectors to throw out cherished extant recordings of the 1866 'Linz' (as opposed to 1890-91 'Vienna') version. The emendations Bruckner made in 1877 to the 1866 text are fairly minor. That said, future interpreters may want to follow Tintner in using this plainer Haas/Carragan edition rather than the 1955 Nowak edition which, in typically meddling style, incorporates the 1877 changes into the original text. The plainness of the orchestration at the very end of the symphony is absolutely right for a peroration that's both prompt and ingenious.

The fill-up is rather more intriguing textually. It's the largely forgotten 1876 revision of the original 1873 version of the *Adagio* of the Third Symphony. The changes include a quicker tempo, a gentle elaboration of the violin figurations near the start, and a disastrous attempt to underpin the lead to the final climax with a new *Tannhäuser*-like violin accompaniment. Since this is funny in the wrong way, it could be said nicely to complement the main work on the disc which is funny (and fun) in all the right ways.

Symphony No 2 (ed Carragan)
National Symphony Orchestra of Ireland / Georg Tintner
Naxos 8 554006 (71' · DDD)　　Ⓢ**OO**

This exceptional recording by veteran Austrian conductor Georg Tintner is in a league of its own. It's a beautifully shaped performance, characterfully played and vividly recorded. What's more, it's, in effect, a gramophone 'first', for though the original, 1872 version of Bruckner's Second Symphony has been recorded elsewhere this is the first to reach a wider market. Not that the differences between editions are hugely significant. What the earlier 1872 version principally offers is the reversal of the order of the two inner movements (the *Scherzo* now comes before the *Andante*), a full clutch of repeats in the *Scherzo* and Trio, a rather longer development section in the finale, various small changes to the orchestration and the absence of some of the more meretricious tempo markings. What's appealing about the 'full monty' is the feeling it gives of the symphony's Schubertian pedigree: heavenly length joining hands with a deep sense of melancholy and melodic *Angst*. Which brings us to Tintner's reading of the symphony, which is shrewd and affectionate, tellingly phrased and beautifully paced, the moves away from and back to the basic pulse nicely handled. This is Bruckner conducting of the old school. There's also something reassuringly old-fashioned about the playing of the National Symphony Orchestra of Ireland. The entire orchestra has the character of a well-to-do country cousin who's blessedly innocent of the more tiresome aspects of metropolitan life. This is an exceptional recording.

Symphony No 2 (1877 Novak edition)
Vienna Symphony Orchestra / Carlo Maria Giulini
Testament SBT1210 (59' · ADD) Recorded 1974　　Ⓕ

Perhaps the greatest of all recordings of the work, spacious, involved, profoundly human. So persuasive is Giulini's interpretation, it makes it almost impossible to take seriously the attempt at a more detached, monumental approach found in Daniel Barenboim's relatively recent Teldec performance. Giulini's ability to convey fervour without sentimentality is little short of miraculous, and it's clear from the way the early stages of the first movement effortlessly project an ideal balance between the lyrical and the dramatic that this reading will be exceptional. The recording might not have the dynamic range of current digital issues, and resonance can sound rather artificial in louder passages. There's also an obtrusive extension of the trumpet triplets seven bars before the end of the first movement. But such things count for less than nothing in the face of a performance which culminates in a finale of such glowing spontaneity you could almost believe that the orchestra are playing it for the first time, and that neither they (nor any other orchestra) will ever play it better.

A fuller and more authentic text of the symphony is available at super-bargain price in Georg Tintner's fine account of the 1872 edition (on Naxos; reviewed above). Serious collectors will need both. Yet the last thing you're likely to feel after hearing Giulini is that there's something inauthentic about this Bruckner. Matters musicological fade to vanishing point, given such communicative genius.

Symphony No 3 (1877/78 version)
Wagner Lohengrin – Act 1, Prelude; Act 3, Prelude
South West German Radio Symphony Orchestra /
Michael Gielen
Hänssler Faszination Musik 93 031 (67' · DDD)
Ⓕ**OOO**

The Bruckner is the thing here. This is a truly inspired performance, keenly argued, swift and clean-limbed, yet one that's also sensitive to the characteristic Brucknerian musings in lyric subjects and at points of transitions. Haitink may create more space in the finale's polka-cum-chorale in his 1988 Vienna recording but his account of the finale runs into gearing problems of its own later on.

The Gielen was made over three days in May 1999 in the Festspielhaus in Baden-Baden. It was evidently made with care; yet it sounds live. It even 'settles' as a real performance might, the orchestra shifting focus a few minutes into the first movement as the players begin to illuminate the drama from within rather than merely sounding it from without. Like Haitink, Gielen includes the scampering coda to the third movement which Bruckner added to this 1877 revision in January 1878. It's a curious afterthought which can sound trite. Not so here. Gielen's performance of the *Scherzo* and Trio is so lithe and fiery you half expect the music to race on beyond its accredited end.

Brucknerians who lust after the weight and unfailing security of the Berlin or Vienna string ensembles may have a few reservations about this Gielen version. The Gielen is *hors concours* principally because of the intuitive brilliance of a reading which profiles so vividly the ardent, aspiring mood of a provincial musician, intoxicated by his craft, giving his all in the service of the god Wagner to whom the work was dedicated. The recording by South-West German Radio's Ute Hesse is everything it should be: bold, open and bright-toned.

Symphonies Nos 3 (1877 version) & 8ª
Vienna Philharmonic Orchestra / Bernard Haitink
Philips Duo ② 470 534-2PM2 (62' · DDD) Recorded
1988, ª1995
Ⓜ**OO**

This is the least perfect of the nine symphonies, though not the least magnificent. As a symphonic project it's both magnificent and characteristic. Unfortunately, the sweep of the musical vision outdistanced Bruckner's ability to control it structurally; in 1889 he returned to the text and radically revised it. For most Bruckner scholars, however, the 1877 text is the ideal. 'It is stylistically purer,' Robert Simpson has written 'and though its construction leaves much to be desired, its weaknesses are exacerbated, not propped, by the crude remedies of the later version.' The 1877 is the version to collect. The finale's polka subject, which has a certain sly wit and grace in Haitink's Concertgebouw recording, retains a certain slyness and grace but with the Vienna Phil it's more the slyness and grace some of us associate with that old darling of Chancery Lane, Mr Horace Rumpole. This newer recording, like the playing, is immensely forceful. Haitink, dedicated Brucknerian that he is, makes a wonderful job of the work without resort to all those unseemly cuts, revisions and reorchestrations that most of his rivals rely on. He's a Brucknerian bold and true, and the Vienna Phil, the brass in particular, plays gloriously, with particular thrust, spontaneity, and weight of tone in the much disputed finale.

This is a slightly disappointing Eighth. What it lacks, by comparison with Karajan's (not to mention the longer-drawn Giulini and Sinopoli versions), is the sense of sustained organic growth. At least, that's how it seems, hearing 'cold' on record what was by all accounts a compelling listen in the concert hall. And for whatever reason, the Vienna Phil playing is only moderately fine. Nevertheless, a disc worth buying for a fine account of the Third.

Symphony No 3 (1873 version)
Royal Scottish National Orchestra / Georg Tintner
Naxos 8 553454 (78' · DDD)
Ⓢ

This original (1873) version of Bruckner's Third is his longest symphony, a work of epic intent filled with youthful fire. It has rarely been recorded and is rarely played, yet this is the work as it was meant to be heard. The work's recorded history might have been very different if Robert Haas's fully prepared and engraved edition of the 1873 version hadn't been incinerated in a raid on Leipzig in 1944. (Happily, an uncorrected proof later turned up in Winterthur.) In the event it wasn't until 1977 that the Bruckner/Haas edition finally appeared in print, edited by Nowak, since when it has been recorded by Inbal and Norrington. The Inbal recording is admirable in almost every way, a consistently satisfying version orchestrally and technically. What it lacks is the danger and visionary daring of parts of Tintner's reading. The contrast is most marked in the first movement where Tintner, like Inbal but unlike Norrington, judges the written instruction *Gemässigt, misterioso* ('Moderate, mysterious') to be all-important, taking the *alla breve* instruction as a secondary consideration. Yet he goes further than Inbal. As early as fig A (1'23"), it's clear that persistence of pulse isn't a priority. Tintner conducts the Third as he (and, indeed, all other good Brucknerians) would conduct the Fifth. It makes for a revelatory reading of the first movement. 'Vivid yet profound' are the words that most come to mind immediately – Tintner at his greatest.

The sound he draws from the Royal Scottish National Orchestra – the strings in particular – has an almost Sibelian spareness to it, as does the recording, where space has been cleared for *tutti*s that are clear, fierce, and unclaustrophobic. Clearing space involves keeping the orchestra slightly at a distance, at some cost to the winds – and the woodwinds in particular – in the two outer movements and in the otherwise wonderfully vibrant and beautifully paced *Scherzo* and Trio. The finale makes less of a mark. The playing of the polka in the crucial polka-cum-chorale seems under-rehearsed, bland and uninvolved; a pity since this juxtaposition of dance hall and funeral rite is one of Bruckner's most graphic inventions.

Symphonies Nos 3-9. Choral Works
ab**Dame Margaret Price** sop/mez b**Doris Soffel**
mez a**Christel Borchers** contr a**Claes H Ahnsjö,**
b**Peter Straka** tens a**Karl Helm,** b**Matthias Hölle**
basses ab**Munich Philharmonic Chorus;** a**Munich Bach Choir; Munich Philharmonic Orchestra /**
Sergiu Celibidache
EMI ⑬ Celibidache Edition 556688-2 (712' · ADD/DDD) Recorded live 1982-95. Texts and translation included   Ⓕ**O**

As a thinker, Celibidache was part genius, part crank. (This Bruckner set reveals both aspects.) A bizarre aggregation of musical, spiritual and quasi-scientific ideas led him to believe that because of what he called 'epiphenomena' – the need for each note to sound, resonate and return – it was necessary to place round the music an inordinate amount of space: 'The richer the music, the slower the tempo.' It's Celibidache's overriding preoccupation with slowness, with temporal space, which helps conjure forth what has got to be one of the greatest Bruckner performances recorded – this 1987 account of the Fourth Symphony, a truly towering act of the re-creative imagination – and several that are well-nigh interminable. His initial tempos are often quite sprightly. It's when he gets to the second and third subjects – to the great *Gesangsperiode* in each movement – that he drops down many more gears than most Bruckner conductors would dare. What Celibidache gives us, in effect, is a sequence of slow movements within the symphonic continuum. In each case, the slow movement itself is the crown (what a revelation his reading of the slow movement of the Sixth Symphony is), the dark sun at the centre of the Bruckner universe around which the *adagio* sections of the opening and closing movements (and the third movement Trio) slowly circle. The problems come in the Seventh, Eighth and Ninth Symphonies. The Haas edition of the Eighth Symphony ('Celi' uses the slightly shorter Nowak edition) gives an estimated playing time of 78 minutes. Many conductors are quicker than this. Some are slower. But even these are as the flash of a swallow's wing alongside the dinosaur flap of Celi-

bidache's record-breaking 104 minutes. The performance of the Seventh is almost as odd. Here Haas gives an estimated playing time of 68 minutes. Par for the course is nearer 62 or 63 minutes. Celi takes nigh on 80. Since the symphonies and the F minor Mass are available separately, the performances to acquire are those of the Fourth and Sixth Symphonies. The Fifth, too, if you don't already have one of Jochum's performances or Karajan's 1975 Berlin recording to which the Celi is surprisingly close in tempo and style, even though the manner of the music-making is a good deal earthier.

The ensemble playing, even in the best performances, isn't faultless. Celibidache occasionally has trouble getting woodwind and brass in together; the solo flute can play like a seraph but the flutes *en masse* are tentative, and the clarinet-playing is chancy. The brass is generally first-rate, but it's the strings that one comes back to.

The recordings have weight, warmth and immediacy. The choral works, though, fare less well; in the *Te Deum*, the choir is a misty irrelevance and although you hear more of it in the F minor Mass, neither the recording nor the choral or solo singing is in the top flight. Despite Celibidache's occasional flashes of insight, there are better versions of both works to be had elsewhere. The transfers have been well done. Applause is separately banded, and the pauses between movements are 'live', and feel right in context. Thus we have the best of all worlds, live music-making sensitively preserved on record.

Symphony No 4
Berlin Philharmonic Orchestra / Günter Wand
RCA Victor Red Seal 09026 68839-2
(69' · DDD) Recorded live 1997   Ⓕ**OOO**

The pacing of each movement is majestic. Not too fast in the first movement; a slow, contemplative tread in the second; animated, but capable of opening out into something more leisurely in the Scherzo; varied, but with the sense of an underlying slow pulse in the finale. Wand allows himself some fairly generous rubato from time to time, halting slightly on the high unaccompanied cello phrase in the first movement second subject. From the start there's something about his performance that puts it in a different league from rivals. There's the depth and richness of the string sound in the opening tremolo. A few seconds later the Berlin Philharmonic's principal horn intones the opening phrases so magically and majestically that it's hard to believe you aren't listening to a real voice – a superhuman larynx, not just a contraption of brass and valves. The sound is, to some extent, the orchestra's own, but there's a feeling that the players are giving extra for Wand, something with more inner life; and the unaffected eloquence and shapeliness of the phrasing is all Wand. It carries you along even when the rubato ought to jar, as it does sometimes in other versions.

This is a concert performance, and feels like one. Things that work in concert aren't always ideal solutions on a repeatable commercial recording. Take Wand's big *ritardando* at the fleeting reference to Brünnhilde's Magic Sleep motif in the finale – the effect might pall after a couple of playings. But then he does ease very effectively into the weird *pianissimo* cello and bass figures that follow, triplet quavers gradually becoming triplet crotchets. The sound quality is excellent.

Symphony No 4
Vienna Philharmonic Orchestra / Karl Böhm
Decca Legends 466 374-2DM (68' · ADD)   Recorded 1973   Ⓜ❍❍❍

 Böhm's VPO account of the Fourth Symphony has the unmistakable stamp of greatness. It was made in the Sofiensaal in Vienna with its helpful acoustic; for though you can detect a whisper of tape-hiss if you put your ear against the loudspeaker, in almost every other way the sound is realistic and warm. There's a roundness in the brass tone with plenty of bite and fullness but no unwanted rasp – especially important in this symphony. Böhm's Fourth is at the head of the field irrespective of price. The warmth as well as the mystery of Bruckner are far more compellingly conveyed in Böhm's spacious view than with any other conductor.

Symphony No 4
Royal Concertgebouw Orchestra / Nikolaus Harnoncourt
Warner Elatus 2564-60129-2 (65' · DDD)   Ⓜ

If you're expecting something controversial here you'll probably be disappointed. Harnoncourt's Bruckner Fourth is nothing like as provocative as his Beethoven. It's relatively fast, but not startlingly so. If Harnoncourt's first movement is more gripping, more like a symphonic drama than usual, that has more to do with the crisp, clear rhythmic articulation than with the number of crotchets per minute. The solo woodwind and horn playing that follows is lovely, expansive enough; what else would you expect from the Concertgebouw in Bruckner? This is an unusually compelling Bruckner Fourth – exciting throughout the first movement and *Scherzo*, and in passages like the problematical Brucknerian Ride of the Valkyries that erupts after the finale's bucolic second theme. In many more traditional Bruckner performances the bass often seems to move in sustained, undifferentiated pedal points. In Harnoncourt's version you're often aware of a deep pulsation – like the throbbing repeated notes that open the finale – continuing, however discreetly, while the tunes unfold above. To hear the finale's second theme in this version is to be reminded that Bruckner was an excellent dancer, light on his feet until he was nearly 70. Of course, you shouldn't confuse

---

BRUCKNER SYMPHONY NO 4 – IN BRIEF

Vienna PO / Karl Böhm
Decca 446 374-2DM (68 mins: ADD)   Ⓜ❍❍❍
☼ A classic performance from 1973, in which both orchestra and conductor rise to the challenge with one of the freshest, most endearing interpretations ever recorded. (Also coupled with a fine No 3 on an excellent Double Decca, 448 098-2DM2.)

Berlin PO / Günter Wand
RCA 09026 68839-2 (69 mins: DDD)   Ⓕ❍❍❍
☼ Recorded live at the Philharmonie, Berlin in 1997, and taking a *Gramophone* Award on its release, this is a fine souvenir of the Wand way with Bruckner: thoughful, structurally as safe as houses and beautifully phrased, every note lavished with attention. Truly inspired.

Berlin PO / Herbert von Karajan
EMI 566094-2 (70 mins: ADD)   Ⓜ❍
Berlin PO / Herbert von Karajan
DG 439 522-2GGA (64 mins: ADD)   Ⓜ
The EMI was Karajan's first recording of the work (from 1970) and demonstrates his credentials as a Brucknerian. Beautifully recorded in the Jesus-Christus Kirche in Berlin, it still sounds splendid. The DG version, part of what became a complete cycle, dates from five years later and was made in the Philharmonie. Both show an innate grasp of the work's architecture and display a strong feeling for impetus in this most pastoral of Bruckner's symphonies.

Royal Concertgebouw Orchestra / Nikolaus Harnoncourt
Warner Elatus 2564-60129-2 (65 mins: DDD)   Ⓜ
A fresh and refreshing view of Bruckner's Fourth, more exciting than is usual with a delightful rustic gait and very light on its toes. Well worth considering for a slightly unconventional approach to Bruckner.

Royal Scottish National Orchestra / Georg Tintner
Naxos 8 554128 (73 mins: DDD)   Ⓢ
A CD that matches value with musical insight: Tintner was an experienced Brucknerian and gives a reading full of poetry and delightful incident. Good playing from the RSNO. A real bargain.

Philharmonia Orchestra / Lovro von Matačić
Testament mono SBT1050 (76 mins: ADD)   Ⓕ
Coupled with a stereo recording of the rarely encountered Overture in G minor, von Matačić's 1954 Bruckner Fourth is a fine one, though for many the Schalk edition used, with its substantial cuts, may count against it.

the man with the musical personality, but why should Bruckner always sound heavy, sedentary, as though slowly digesting a gigantic meal? Harnoncourt provides us with the light-footedness, while allowing the music to unfold at its own speed, to take time. There's no question that Harnoncourt must be considered a serious contender in Bruckner.

Symphony No 5
Staatskapelle Dresden / Giuseppe Sinopoli
DG 469 527-2GH (77' · DDD)　　　Ⓕ**OOO**

 Publishers publish 'study' scores, but no marketing guru has ever come up with the idea of the 'study' recording. They exist, of course: recordings which do us the singular honour of providing an interpretation while at the same time allowing us to hear all the notes. This doesn't suit every piece of music ('Gentleman,' Richard Strauss once said, 'Give me an *impression* of the music!'), nor does it suit all listeners. Here we have a study recording *par excellence*, as close as we have come on record to being provided with a sound facsimile of the symphony's printed page.

Such an undertaking requires immense discipline from the orchestra, the balance engineer and the conductor. On this form the Staatskapelle Dresden have no peer. The sound is characterful, the ensemble exact, the concentration absolute. There must be a quarter of a million notes in this symphony and we hear practically all of them more or less flawlessly delivered. Like Sinopoli's Bruckner Nine recording, the engineering is intensely concentrated: not cold as such but fiercely analytical. It entirely suits the Fifth, arguably the most intricately crafted of all Bruckner's symphonies.

Sinopoli is here more the alpha-quality Kapellmeister than the Bruckner 'interpreter'. The text is his passion; his trust in it is absolute, his patience immense. The first movement is one of Bruckner's most subtle and elusive. So much of it is marked to be delivered in an undertone, with *p*, *pp*, and *ppp* the principal markings. Cynics will argue that Bruckner wrote these in because he didn't trust the orchestras and conductors of his time, a theory Sinopoli gives us every reason to doubt.

After the enigma that's the first movement, Sinopoli senses a somewhat easier, more sunlit mood in the *Adagio*. He's wary, however, of what some conductors see as the Upper Austrian folksiness of the *Scherzo*. 'A formidable human power directly faced with heedless gaiety' is how Robert Simpson sums up this music, exactly how Sinopoli appears to see it, too.

The finale resolves fugue, chorale and a host of earlier considerations into a glorious homecoming, a process greatly helped here by Sinopoli's refreshingly swift, beautifully integrated treatment of the main exposition. There's an inevitability about the proceedings that has everything to do with the performance, yet without the performance in any way drawing

attention to itself. It's Bruckner and the impeccable logic of his musical thinking we are listening to (and very moving it proves to be).

Among rival versions, Karajan's 1976 Berlin recording, though rather grander in manner, comes closest to this (though the CD transfers have always seemed foggy and recessed). Welser-Möst's doesn't quite operate on this level and, in any case, is now eclipsed technically and orchestrally. Those who prefer the thrills and spills of a 'real' performance (the Sinopoli may be live but it doesn't seem so) will no doubt prefer Horenstein's 1971 Proms performance. But that's a very different kind of experience, more overtly dramatic, more mundane. Sinopoli's Bruckner Fifth has all the beauty of a great mathematical proof.

Symphony No 5 (ed Haas/Nowak)
Vienna Philharmonic Orchestra / Nikolaus Harnoncourt
RCA Red Seal 🔊 82876 60749-2 (73' · DDD/DSD)
Recorded live at the Musikverein, Vienna, 7-14 June
2004. Includes a disc of rehearsal excerpts　Ⓕ**OO**

Nikolaus Harnoncourt's Fifth is more a realisation than an interpretation, musically vivid but spiritually serene. Serene but now slow. By the clock, this is one of the quickest Fifths on record, though only the *Adagio* is taken more swiftly than usual. It was here that Bruckner began the symphony in the pit of despair in 1875 with a keening oboe melody he marked 'Sehr langsam' but scored *alla breve*. Harnoncourt treats it *allegretto* after the manner of a threnody by Bach or Mozart, whose Requiem is quoted during the course of the movement. Furtwängler, surprisingly, took a similar view of the movement, as does Welser-Möst.

The 'liveness' of the live performance owes much to Harnoncourt – his persona fuelling the music-making not the concept, which is as it should be – though the superlative playing of the Vienna Philharmonic is also a factor. The light-fingered realisation of the exquisite string traceries is a constant source of wonder; *tuttis* are glowing and unforced. The hall of the Musikverein helps, too; with an audience present it offers a uniquely natural-sounding Bruckner acoustic. This is a performance of rare vision and strength.

Symphonies Nos 7 & 6
Concertgebouw Orchestra / Bernard Haitink
Philips Duo ② 473 301-2PM2 (65' · ADD) Recorded
1970, 1979　　　Ⓜ**O**

Bernard Haitink's 1979 Concertgebouw account of Bruckner's Seventh Symphony was a change from and an advance on his 1966 Concertgebouw recording. Broader in pace and warmer-toned, it retained much of the earlier reading's classical integrity while also paying more attention to the music's Schubertian aspect. Haitink does not go as far down that particular road as Karajan does in his deeply reflective, pantheistically charged 1971 Berlin Philharmonic version. The velvet sonorities of the Berlin performance will not please everyone, though it has to be said that the Berliners' quiet, affective glow of colour is part and parcel of a reading which is deeply thought through and of a piece with itself. (The *Adagio* is especially fine, more *innig* than the Haitink and more of a piece.) But the return of this later Haitink recording to the catalogues is both timely and welcome for those in search of a fine, middle-of-the-road, mid-price recording of the symphony.

The recording of the Sixth is exceptionally fine – everything thrillingly immediate and finely 'terraced'. It's a quicker performance than Klemperer's classic version for EMI (reviewed above). The *Adagio* sounds particularly well, the keening Dutch oboe and bright trumpets the perfect foil for the Rembrandt colourings of the strings and lower brass.

Symphony No 7 (ed Haas)
Vienna Philharmonic Orchestra / Herbert von Karajan
DG Karajan Gold 439 037-2GHS (66' · DDD) Recorded 1989
Ⓕ**O**

The Vienna Philharmonic features on what was Karajan's last recording, an idiomatic account of Bruckner's Seventh Symphony, lighter and more classical in feel than either of his two Berlin recordings yet loftier, too. As for the Original-image bit-processing you need go no further than the first fluttered violin *tremolando* and the cellos' rapt entry in the third bar to realise how ravishingly 'present' the performance is in this reprocessing. Or go to the end of the symphony and hear how the great E major peroration is even more transparent than before, the octave drop of bass trombone and bass tuba 13 bars from home the kind of delightfully euphoric detail that in 1989 only the more assiduous score-reader would have been conscious of hearing. This remastered Seventh is definitely pure gold.

Symphony No 7 (ed Haas)
Royal Scottish National Orchestra / Georg Tintner
Naxos 8 554269 (66' · DDD)   Ⓢ

In the absence of recommendable budget or super-budget recordings of Bruckner's Seventh Symphony, this will do nicely. It's a finely schooled performance, chaste and discreet, with a notable reading of the *Adagio* which lies at the heart of the work. Tintner sees this very much as a piece, the first (G major) climax finely achieved, the later, greater climax splendidly 'placed'. The coda, Bruckner's lament for the dead Wagner, is played relatively swiftly, touchingly and without bombast. In general, his reading of the score is loyal without being in any sense dull or hidebound. In an ideal world, the playing of the first violins would be more con-

sistently secure *in alt*. In particular, you have the feeling that both the players and the engineers (the engineering is generally excellent) would have benefited from a chance to refine and tidy parts of the performance of the first movement. A notable bargain, none the less.

Symphony No 8 (ed Haas)
Vienna Philharmonic Orchestra / Herbert von Karajan
DG ② 427 611-2GH2 (83' · DDD) Recorded 1988
Ⓕ**OOO**

 As if by some strange act of providence, great conductors have often been remembered by the immediate posthumous release of some fine and representative recording. With Karajan it's the Eighth Symphony of Bruckner, perhaps the symphony he loved and revered above all others. It's the sense of the music being in the hearts and minds and collective unconscious of Karajan and every one of the 100 and more players of the Vienna Philharmonic that gives this performance its particular charisma and appeal. It's a wonderful reading, every bit as authoritative as its many predecessors and every bit as well played but somehow more profound, more humane, more lovable if that's a permissible attribute of an interpretation of this work. The end of the work, always astonishing and uplifting, is especially fine here and very moving. Fortunately, it has been recorded with plenty of weight and space and warmth and clarity, with the additional benefit of the added vibrancy of the Viennese playing. The sessions were obviously sufficiently happy for there to shine through moments of spontaneous eloquence that were commonplace in the concert hall in Karajan's later years, but which recordings can't always be relied upon to catch.

Symphony No 8 in C minor (ed Haas)
Hallé Orchestra / Sir John Barbirolli
BBC Legends BBCL4067-2 (74' · ADD) Recorded live 1970
Ⓕ**OO**

At the time of this concert in May 1970 there were just three recordings of Bruckner's Eighth Symphony in the catalogue; now there are more than 50, and counting. This performance is that rare thing, an intensely dramatic Bruckner Eighth. It isn't often that you hear an account of the turbulent first movement as thrilling as this. The jagged downward slashes of the trumpets are terrible to experience, yet the space that opens up after the vast and glorious E flat cadence 40 bars later is the very reverse, a way to heaven even from the gates of hell. The odd stumble in the brass, the occasional cough are immaterial. This isn't a performance for those who measure out their life in coffee spoons. The *Scherzo* is ferociously quick with a Trio of compensating loftiness. The loftiness returns in the *Adagio* which Barbirolli again projects urgently and with a full heart. Plaintive winds, trenchant

BRUCKNER'S SYMPHONY NO 8 – IN BRIEF

Vienna PO / Herbert von Karajan
DG ② 427 611-2GH2 (83 mins: DDD)   Ⓕ**OOO**
Bruckner's longest *Adagio* has perhaps never radiated such warmth as in Karajan's last and most integrated recording of the Eighth, with the Vienna Philharmonic more flexible than their Berlin rivals for the conductor.

Hallé Orchestra / Sir John Barbirolli
BBC Legends BBCL4067-2 (74 mins: ADD)   Ⓕ**OO**
An electric live performance – the last Barbirolli gave in London – in which the tragic first movement casts a baleful shadow over the rest. Not for the faint-hearted, or for those who like their Bruckner opulent.

Vienna PO / Carlo Maria Giulini
DG ② 445 529-2GMA2 (88 mins: DDD)   Ⓜ**OO**
Giulini takes such loving, paternal care over inner parts that his spacious tempi rarely register as such. Opulence never obscures the sure-footed journey from C minor to major.

Berlin PO / Günter Wand
RCA ② 74321 82866-2 (87 mins: DDD)   Ⓕ**OO**
The last of Günter Wand's recordings of the work, but one which shows an ever-deepening desire to present all of its many sides, from the unrelieved tension of the first movement, through the Olympian dance of the *Scherzo* to the finale's unifying triumph.

North German RSO / Günter Wand
RCA ② 09026 68047-2 (88 mins: DDD)   Ⓕ**OOO**
Wand's second recording of the work with 'his' orchestra, and many would say his finest of all. Lubeck Cathedral's acoustic bestows its own benediction – the audience is understandably awed into silence.

Vienna PO / Boulez
DG 459 678-2GH (76 mins: DDD)
TDK 📀 DV-VOPBR (95 mins)   Ⓕ**O**
Boulez's famed clarity of ear results not in the antiseptic traversal some might expect but lends a startling clarity and sense of purpose to Bruckner's symphonic argument. A superbly 'terraced' orchestral balance in the best Bruckner tradition.

Vienna PO / Furtwängler
Music & Arts CD-764 (77 mins: ADD)   Ⓜ**OO**
Furtwängler judged this work as the finest of all symphonies. Hear this terror-filled, mid-war performance and you understand why.

Munich PO / Celibidache
EMI ② 556696-2 (107 mins: DDD)   Ⓕ
Bruckner never sounds the same again once heard through Celi's patient, prismatic analysis. You'll love it or you'll hate it.

brass, and speaking strings, full-bodied and emotionally intent, build the heaven on earth that Bruckner envisions. To hear why this is great music-making, listen to the coda and the gloriously articulated long string recitative that underpins it. The finale, too, is fairly gripping, though there's a brief tired patch midway.

The Festival Hall's fierce acoustic suits the performance well and the engineering is spectacular for its day. Barbirolli was mortally ill when this concert took place. He died just 10 weeks later. 'This might be the old man's last, so let's make it a good one,' the players were saying at the time. By all accounts, Karajan's last live Bruckner Eighth was a lofty, out-of-life experience. Barbirolli's is the very opposite, a case of 'Do not go gentle into that good night/Rage, rage against the dying of the light.' It's a one-off, eloquent beyond measure: the boldest, bravest Bruckner Eighth on record.

Symphony No 8 (ed Nowak)
Vienna Philharmonic Orchestra / Carlo Maria Giulini
DG Masters ② 445 529-2GMA2 (88' · DDD) Recorded 1984   Ⓜ**OO**

Giulini's performance of the Eighth can confidently be claimed as also being among one of the great Bruckner recordings of the age. It's an immensely long-breathed performance, yet it's of a piece with itself and the music it serves. It's a reading that's suffused from start to finish with its own immutable logic, cast and voiced, you might say, like a great tenor bell. The playing of the Vienna Philharmonic is similarly whole: luminous as though lit from within, immensely strong, yet flawless in every aspect of tone and touch. You might argue that Giulini's case is helped by his use of the tidied Nowak text; that Karajan, in his last and greatest recording, goes one stage further by conjuring from the fuller Haas edition a performance of even greater grandeur and sweep. But the two aren't in contention. Both are miracles sufficient unto themselves; the Karajan a shade earthier, perhaps, a shade rougher hewn than the Giulini which glows, in this magnificent transfer, like Carrara marble lit by the evening sun.

Symphony No 8 in C minor (ed Haas)
Berlin Philharmonic Orchestra / Günter Wand
RCA Red Seal ② 74321 82866-2 (87' · DDD)
Recorded live 2001   Ⓕ**OOO**

Few readings have been more assiduously toured or generally acclaimed than Wand's Bruckner Eighth yet Wand himself struggled to better on record the exact and far-seeing account of the symphony he made with the Cologne RSO in 1979. In January 2001 he harnessed the Berlin Bruckner sound to his own particular ends, a potentially Sisyphean task for a man then nearing his 90th birthday.

And the rewards are here. This Eighth is exceptionally fine. When in the *Scherzo* you sense that the mountains themselves are beginning to dance, you know you're onto a good thing; on this occasion, Olympus itself seems to have caught the terpsichorean bug. Not that anything is exaggerated or overblown. Wand knows where each peak is and how best to approach it. His reading is broader than it was 20 years ago, yet nowhere is there any sense of unwanted stasis. Wand draws from the orchestra, the brass and strings in particular, sound of great power and transparency which the engineers have translated in a recording of uncommon reach and splendour. The three recordings by the Vienna Philharmonic (surely *the* Bruckner orchestra) are all incomparable in their way: the 1984 Giulini (closest to Wand IV but with greater spiritual rigour in the *Adagio*) and the 1989 Karajan (closest to Wand I in its plainspoken mastery of the whole). Suffice it to say, this is a grand and worthy memento for the tens of thousands who heard Wand conduct the symphony in the concert hall.

Symphony No 9
Berlin Philharmonic Orchestra / Daniel Barenboim
Elatus 0927-46746-2 (63' · DDD) Recorded live 1990
Ⓜ️Ⓞ

This is an outstanding version of Bruckner's Ninth Symphony. Like Karajan's reading on DG, it's essentially a 'central' account of the score that attempts neither extreme breadth of utterance nor sharp-edged drama. Rather it's a reading that combines long lines, flowing but astutely nuanced, and sonorities that are full-bodied yet always finely balanced. The outer movements have great rhetorical and emotional power; the *Scherzo* is thunderous and glinting by turns. The *Adagio* begins very slowly but, for once, Barenboim gets away with it, the movement growing organically rather than remaining still-born near the start. This is a live performance and, as you would expect, it's superbly executed, the playing every bit as fine as it is on the Karajan recording. But even that doesn't compete with the natural splendours of this issue. This is superb Bruckner sound, spacious and clear, with strings, woodwind and brass at once unerringly 'placed' and finely matched. Given good engineering and the kind of astute playing we have from Barenboim and the Berliners, the Philharmonie is far from being the acoustic lemon it's sometimes said to be. This is a front-runner for this symphony.

Symphony No 9
Vienna Philharmonic Orchestra / Carlo Maria Giulini
DG 427 345-2GH (68' · DDD) Recorded 1988   Ⓕ️Ⓞ

Giulini's Ninth is an idiosyncratic reading – nearly seven minutes longer than Karajan's – but it has a kind of immutable breadth and boldness of utterance. Despite the slowness, there's the sense of his being the master of his own brief. As a concept it's quite different from the musically dynamic readings of others. In the first movement's main *Gesangsperiode* it can seem dangerously broad, with the Vienna strings rather tensely following the contours of Giulini's protracted beat. The wary score-watcher may notice some unevenness in ensemble, but this is a reading which should be patiently heard rather than proof-read. The *Scherzo* is very effective, with drive and dynamism. After that, the orchestra is at its finest in the concluding *Adagio*, not only the Viennese horns, but the entire ensemble in the difficult broad transitions and terrifying C sharp minor climax. The recording is magnificent.

Symphony No 9
Vienna Philharmonic Orchestra / Nikolaus Harnoncourt
RCA Red Seal SACD/CD hybrid ② 82876 54332-2 (131' · DDD) Includes a workshop concert with commentary by Harnoncourt   Ⓕ️

Harnoncourt's flirtations with Bruckner haven't always impressed. He didn't seem to 'know' the symphonies as the old master Brucknerians did. But this live Salzburg Ninth is glorious. There's no sense here of fallible rhythms or a conductor not being able to see the wood for the trees. Like all great interpreters of the Ninth, Harnoncourt treats the opening movement as a vast tripartite structure – exposition, countervailing statement, and coda – which can be taken in a single glance. Nor is there any falling off in the *Scherzo* or the great concluding *Adagio*, both of which are beautifully paced and expertly realised in terms of each new harmonic salient. In beauty of sound and accuracy and articulacy of ensemble, the Vienna Philharmonic matches, even occasionally surpasses, its own high standards in this work. All of which must have helped the Teldex engineers, who make the acoustically problematic Grosses Festspielhaus sound like one of the great Bruckner halls.

Additional recommendations

Symphony No 9
Berlin Philharmonic Orchestra / Wand
RCA Red Seal 74321 63244-2 (62' · DDD)   Ⓕ️Ⓞ
The Berliners' playing is on the very highest level. Wand gives a performance that's marvellously directed, with moments of sublime frenzy and sublime quiet. The RCA recording is first rate.

Saarbrücken Radio Symphony Orchestra / Skrowaczewski
Arte Nova Classics 74321 80781-2 (61' · DDD)   Ⓢ️Ⓢ️
A very closely controlled performance. Skrowaczewski has taken enormous care over the preparation of the performance and the results tell in orchestral playing of a quality and articulacy that few ensembles could rival.

Masses

No 1 in D minor; **No 2** in E minor; **No 3** in F minor

Masses – Nos 1[a], 2 & 3[ba]
Edith Mathis, [b]**Maria Stader** sops [a]**Marga Schiml**,
[b]**Claudia Hellmann** mezzos [a]**Wiesław Ochman**,
[b]**Ernst Haefliger** tens [a]**Karl Ridderbusch**, [b]**Kim
Borg** basses **Bavarian Radio Chorus and
Symphony Orchestra / Eugen Jochum**
DG ② The Originals 447 409-2GOR2 (148' · ADD)
Recorded [a]1963, [b]1971, [c]1972. Text and translation
included   Ⓜ**OO**

Like Bruckner, Eugen Jochum came from a
devout Catholic family and began his musical
life as a church organist. He would have
known the Mass texts more or less inside out,
which explains why his readings focus not on
the sung parts – which, for the most part, present the text in a relatively four-square fashion
– but on the orchestral writing which, given
the gloriously full-bodied playing of the
Bavarian orchestra, so lusciously illuminates
familiar words. He approaches the Masses
with many of the same ideas he so eloquently
propounds in his recordings of the symphonies and the music unfolds with a measured, almost relaxed pace which creates a
sense of vast spaciousness. This can have its
drawbacks: you can be so entranced by the
beautifully moulded orchestral introduction
to the Benedictus from the D minor Mass that
the entry of a rather full-throated Marga
Schiml comes as a rude interruption. DG's
transfers are extraordinarily good – they really
seem to have produced a sound which combines the warmth of the original LP with the
clarity of detail we expect from CD.

Mass No 3. Psalm 150 in C
Juliet Booth sop **Jean Rigby** mez **John Mark
Ainsley** ten **Gwynne Howell** bass **Corydon Singers
and Orchestra / Matthew Best**
Hyperion CDA66599 (68' · DDD) Recorded 1992.
Texts and translations included   Ⓕ

The F minor Mass can certainly be regarded as
being among the finest music Bruckner ever
created. The intensity of religious feeling is
heightened rather than diminished by the
sumptuous orchestral support, and the soaring
melodies and opulent harmonies are somehow
purified and enriched by the devotional character of these familiar texts. Matthew Best's performance, by understating the music's abundant richness, gives tremendous point to the
inner conviction of Bruckner's faith. His
orchestra, sounding as if it has been playing
this music all its days, plays with commendable
discretion, balancing admirably with a relatively
small choral body. As with everything the
Corydon Singers and Best turn their hands
to, it's an impeccable performance, infused
with real artistry and sensitive musicianship.

Enhanced by the glorious solo voices from a
high-powered team this is a CD of rare depth
and conviction.

Te Deum

Bruckner Te Deum. **Verdi** Messa da Requiem   Ⓗ
Leontyne Price, Leonie Rysanek sops **Hilde
Rössl-Majdan, Christa Ludwig** mezzos **Fritz
Wunderlich, Giuseppe Zampieri** tens **Walter Berry**
bass-bar **Cesare Siepi** bass **Vienna Singverein;
Vienna Philharmonic Orchestra / Karajan**
EMI Salzburg Festival Edition mono ② 566880-2
(107' · ADD) Recorded live 1958, 1960   Ⓜ

Karajan recorded these works more than once
in the studio, in better sound, yet these live
recordings made at Salzburg have their own
validity in the vast Karajan discography because
they catch performances undoctored in any way
by the conductor or others, and recorded, obviously, at a single stretch. The 1960 Bruckner
was recorded in the new Festspielhaus, and is a
performance of breadth and conviction,
adorned by the singing of Leontyne Price and
the youthful Fritz Wunderlich. His Vienna
forces are on tremendous form, alive to the
nuances Karajan wants us to hear and to his
overview of the work's structure. The sound in
the Bruckner is very good, albeit mono.

The Verdi was recorded in the Felsenreitschule. In spite of Karajan's many better-
recorded versions, we recommend this one – it's
a more immediate, more spontaneous experience than those recorded in the studio (the 1967
film done at La Scala apart). It's true there are a
few noises off, including one incident that
sounds like a member of the audience falling off
their perch, and some questionable intonation
among the soloists, but these are worth tolerat-
ing for Karajan's visionary reading, one also
strong on orchestral detail. Heading the solo
team is Rysanek, her only recording of this
piece. After a tentative start she soon finds her
most responsive form, with the arching phrases
of 'Salva me' finely taken, a beautifully floated
entry at 'Huic ergo' and an even more ethereal
one at 'Sed' in the 'Domine Jesu Christe' movement. Ludwig is as ever strength personified in
the mezzo solos. Zampieri sings with vibrant
tone and great feeling, although his dynamic
range is limited. Siepi is his firm sympathetic
self on the bass line. .

Antoine Brumel   French c1460-c1515

*A singer at Notre Dame, Chartres, from 1483,
Brumel became Master of the Innocents at St Peter's,
Geneva, by 1486. He was installed as a canon at
Laon Cathedral by 1497 and the following year took
charge of the choirboys at Notre Dame, Paris. In*

1501-2 he was a singer at the Duke of Savoy's Court in ChambÈry, and from 1506 to 1510 acted as maestro di cappella to Alfonso I d'Este. He was prominent among the composers who ranked, after Josquin Desprez, as the most eminent masters of the late 15th and early 16th centuries. He was primarily a composer of sacred music, notably of masses (15 survive complete). They may be divided into three stylistic groups, the earliest depending primarily on a cantus firmus, the middle group (which includes the impressive Missa 'Et ecce terrae motus' for 12 voices) exhibiting greater rhythmic regularity, thinner textures and a closer relationship between text and music, and the later works tending towards concentration and brevity. He also wrote motets. The secular works also frequently use pre-existing melodies; the four-part pieces have texts but those in three parts are purely instrumental. **GROVE**music

Missa Et ecce terrae motus

Missa Et ecce terrae motus
Ensemble Clément Janequin; Toulouse Saqueboutiers / Dominique Visse
Harmonia Mundi HMC90 1738 (58' · DDD) Text and translation included ⒡

Until somebody finds Ockeghem's 36-voice motet (which almost certainly did exist) Brumel's so-called 'Earthquake Mass' must count as the earliest seriously large composition – not just in its 12 voices, used together almost throughout, but also in its sheer length.

Another reason it's so long is that Dominique Visse likes to linger over particular passages and bring out some of the inside details. This is most welcome, because the previous two recordings of the cycle (Paul Van Nevel in 1990 and Peter Phillips in 1992) tended to keep a steady tempo and charge past much of the lovely inner writing Visse makes more audible. Especially in the 'Benedictus' and the *Agnus Dei*, he reveals new glories in this enormously complicated score. His flexibility of tempo also makes it possible for the singers to give more value to the texts, which is again a welcome change.

His recording is fundamentally different in other ways, too. Whereas Phillips had 24 voices and no instruments, and Van Nevel had four instruments, Visse has 12 voices and 12 instruments. Whether Brumel is likely to have had such forces around 1500 seems unlikely, but it brings certain advantages: it makes it possible fto pitch the whole thing fairly low without losing clarity on the crucial bottom lines and to have men singing the top line.

The result has a slightly nasal quality that isn't at all in line with what we expect here; those who dislike this may be a lot happier with the direct brilliance of The Tallis Scholars under Peter Phillips. But it's a beautifully balanced ensemble with a coherent and unusual sound; and it brings out unexpectedly different qualities in the music. If you love this work, one of the most fascinating and original of the years around 1500, you'll want this recording alongside the others.

Gavin Bryars British 1943

Bryars studied philosophy at Sheffield University and music privately; in the 1960s he played in jazz groups and since 1970 he has lectured at Leicester Polytechnic. A leading experimental composer, influenced by Cage and Satie, he first wrote for indeterminate forces (The Sinking of the Titanic, 1969), but more recently his music has been influenced by theories of literature; it is often repetitive and witty. His opera Medea was staged in 1984. **GROVE**music

String Quartets

String Quartets – No 1, 'Between the National and the Bristol'; No 2; No 3
Lyric Quartet (Jonathan Carney, Edmund Coxon *vns* Nick Barr *va* David Daniels *vc*)
Black Box BBM1079 (63' · DDD) ⒡

A quiet strain of melancholy passes through all three of Gavin Bryars' string quartets, though the Third and latest – which was commissioned by, and is dedicated to, the Lyric Quartet – has a bardic feel to it that's quite unlike the others. Part of the reason lies in the use of pure intervals which in turn reflects a passing preoccupation with the world of early music.

Bryars' original plan for the First Quartet had been to create a sort of compositional séance where memories of such past masters as Ysaÿe, Hindemith and Schoenberg would be conjured musically. In the event it's the Second Quartet that's more suggestive of musical side references: to John Adams of *Shaker Loops* and the Schoenberg of *Verklärte Nacht*, though these are probably just coincidental similarities.

All that needs to be said about the music Bryars says himself in the booklet-note, much as he did for the Balanescu Quartet's Argo CD of the first two quartets. There the coupling is *Die letzten Tage* for two violins but this disc will hold the greater appeal for those building their quartet repertoire on CD. Comparing the two versions finds the colour-conscious Balanescu employing a subtler range of nuance while the Lyric press for greater emphases and rather more in the way of inner voice detail. Either disc will probably find you returning to this haunting, though by no means immobile, music again and again.

Adnan Songbook

Adnan Songbook. Cadman Requiem. Wonderlawn – Epilogue
Valdine Anderson *sop* **The Hilliard Ensemble; Fretwork; Gavin Bryars Ensemble / Dave Smith**
Point Music 462 511-2 (61' · DDD) Texts included ⒡

When Bryars' music is as well performed and recorded as on this disc, it achieves a power and inevitability that's rare in new music. The voice seems to suit his compositional approach. The very presence of a singer accords a subjective intensity that nicely complements the unwavering, dry-eyed clarity of Bryars's instrumental writing. Bryars says he attempts to write vocal material that will highlight the unique character of each singer's voice and that all the vocal works are being performed on this recording by the specific singers he had in mind. Though his writing for The Hilliard Ensemble reconstitutes the characteristic four-part sound, they're given every opportunity to be appreciated as soloists.

In composing the Adnan Songbook for the young British soprano Valdine Anderson, Bryars could almost have used Richard Strauss as a model, so expressive is his treatment of her highest tessitura. On the other hand, the blunt, even artless handling of the text and instrumental accompaniment is typical of Bryars. It's this oblique mixture of understatement and expressive warmth that makes the work so original. Cadman Requiem is also very impressive. Dedicated to the sound engineer Bill Cadman, who died in the Lockerbie aircrash in 1988, the piece was recorded with its two ensembles, Fretwork and The Hilliard Ensemble, facing each other. The resulting rich blend of timbres, well captured by the recording, makes for arresting listening. Overall, a hauntingly beautiful album that provides compelling evidence of the recent resurgence in Bryars's work.

Alan Bush $\qquad$ British 1900

Bush studied at the Royal Academy of Music and privately with John Ireland, going on to study musicology and philosophy at Berlin University. In 1925 he began teaching at the RAM and in 1936, already a committed communist, founded the Workers' Music Association. His earlier works (Dialectic for string quartet, 1929; First Symphony in C, 1940) are progressive, using his own 'thematic' method, in which each note must be thematically significant. After the war he simplified his style and began a series of operas expressing his political beliefs: Wat Tyler (1953), Men of Blackmoor (1960), The Sugar Reapers (1966) and Joe Hill (1970), all produced in East Germany. He has also composed much choral, chamber and solo vocal music. **GROVE**music

Violin Concerto

Violin Concerto, Op 32[a]. Dialectic, Op 15[b]. Six Short Pieces, Op 99[c]
[a]**Manoug Parikian** vn [c]**Alan Bush** pf
[b]**Medici Quartet** (Paul Robertson, David Matthews vns Ivo-Jan van der Werff va Anthony Lewis vc)
[a]**BBC Symphony Orchestra / Norman Del Mar**
Claudio CB51512 (52' · DDD) Recorded [a]1983, [b]1984, [c]1984 Ⓕ**Ⓞ**

Alan Bush – pupil of John Ireland, Professor of Composition at the Royal Academy of Music for half a century – was undoubtedly one of the major musical figures of British music in the 1920s, 30s and 40s. More importantly, in his earlier works he developed a promising 'thematic' variation of serialism, which retained a tonal base, convincingly and appealingly demonstrated here. Yet little of his output has been recorded, and performances in England have been, and are still, very rare indeed. However his music was regularly performed (including the four operas!) in the 1950s and 60s in Soviet Russia and East Germany, and was apparently much admired by Shostakovich.

The reason is simple. Bush joined the British Communist Party in 1935 and remained a devotee of the Soviet political mirage throughout his life, even moderating his sinewy early lyricism into a more easily communicative style in 1948, loyally following the Soviet directive. In England his firm political stance alienated many in positions of power, and his works in consequence went unheard.

Now, at last, time begins to make amends, and although the (splendid) recordings on this disc date from the 1980s, they're of the very highest quality. This CD includes two key works in Bush's output: the riveting *Dialectic* for string quartet of 1929, and the vividly attractive and much mellower Violin Concerto of 1948. This marked the composer's change to a more directly communicative, rhapsodical lyricism, which balances the work's pulsing, rhythmic opening and its closely related dance-like finale. The solo writing has an attractive neo-Classical element also reflected in the orchestral string-writing, while the brass interjections in the opening movement remind one of British film music during its golden era. This is a concentrated work which invites the listener's immediate participation, especially in a performance so persuasively assured and sympathetic as Manoug Parikian's, admirably accompanied by the BBC Orchestra.

As for the *Dialectic*, it's so marvellously played that one longs to hear it live. Tersely argued, but brimming over with passionate lyricism, it reaches a fugal climax of thrusting intensity, one which even recalls Beethoven's *Grosse Fuge*. In short, this CD can't be recommended too highly.

Chamber Works

Three Concert Studies, Op 31[abd]. Two Easy Pieces[ad]. Two Melodies, Op 47[ac]. Sonatina, Op 88[ac]. Concert Piece, Op 17[ad]. Summer Valley, Op 125[ad]
[a]**Catherine Summerhayes** pf **Adam Summerhayes** [b]vn/[c]va [d]**Joseph Spooner** vc
Meridian CDE84458 (67' · DDD) Ⓕ

The challengingly rhapsodic *Concert Piece* for cello and piano was written prophetically as war clouds were gathering in Europe. The music's angst expresses real despair, the harmony bleakly astringent. Yet there's a touching central cantilena of the utmost sadness before the malevolent closing section with its march rhythms builds to an urgent and uncompromising climax. One then turns to the balm of the Sonatina for viola with its pastoral atmosphere (the opening and close might almost be by Vaughan Williams) or the lovely, very English evocation of a *Summer Valley* (ravishingly played here). These three artists have obviously lived with this music and play very sympathetically indeed and with fine ensemble.

There's all the expressive power needed in Op 17, while the central 'Nocturne' of the Op 31 *Concert-Studies* for piano trio is haunting in its gentle atmospheric feeling, and the closing 'Alla Bulgaria' great fun. The two charming *Easy Pieces* for cello, and the pair for viola (both with piano) show Bush's disarming melodic gift.

In short, this CD combines excitement and real stimulation, lyrical strength and musical pleasure, in varying measure. Let John Amis, who wrote the booklet notes, have the final word. He tells us that 'Bush was a delightful man' who 'wrote music for head and heart, and many times managed to combine the two elements...these [works] are all masterly and endearing.'

Antoine Busnois   French c1430-1492

Busnois was possibly a pupil of Ockeghem in Paris, he was a much-favoured singer in the chapel of Charles the Bold and then of his daughter, Mary of Burgundy. After her death in 1482 he became attached to the church of St Sauveur, Bruges. Two masses, a Credo, a Magnificat, eight motets, two hymns and 61 songs for three or four voices are attributed to him with reasonable certainty. His music typifies the Burgundian style in the third quarter of the 15th century and he occupies a central position in the development of music between Dufay and Josquin His works are characterised by triadic sonority, strong harmonic progressions, clear structure and extensive use of imitation. The chansons, for many of which he probably wrote the texts, are his most original works. Most are three-part rondeaux or bergerettes and some are based on popular melodies. Both his masses are four-voice cantus firmus structures and the motets, like the chansons, exploit a wide variety of contrapuntal techniques. **GROVE**music

Missa L'homme armé

Busnois Anima mea liquefacta est. Missa L'homme armé. Gaude celestis domina[a] Domarto Missa Spiritus almus Pullois Flos de spina[a]
[a]Robin Tyson *counterten* **The Binchois Consort / Andrew Kirkman**
Hyperion CDA67319 (79' · DDD) Texts and translations included   Ⓕ**OO**

Few works embody the spirit of an age as eloquently as the *L'homme armé* Mass of Antoine Busnois. Teeming with incident, it engages the listener from the off, but retains throughout a classical balance and poise. No other Mass of the mid-15th century survives in as many sources, and no other setting of the famous tune was as influential.

The Binchois Consort improves on Pro Cantione Antiqua's magnificent 1976 recording in several ways. Kirkman takes an *a cappella* approach instead of using a chamber organ for *colla parte* voice-doubling as PCA do. Some courageously close miking captures the slightly rough-edged grain of these voices; by allowing an element of risk into the performance, the singers exhilaratingly replicate the balance of finely wrought detail and clarity of design that characterises the work itself. He also slows the basic tempo down just a notch: this dramatises one of the Mass's most sublime moments, when the inverted *cantus firmus* is momentarily exposed, the basses holding a low F for several seconds with a lone, static voice for company. One of the Mass's high-points, it ranks among the supreme inspirations of the 15th century. The Binchois Consort has never sounded more assured.

The remaining motets are nicely varied, too. *Anima mea liquefacta est* is surprisingly rhapsodic by Busnois' standards. *Gaude celestis domina* has only recently been identified as his work, but his stamp is unmistakeable. Finally, Pullois' *Flos de spina* is given a similarly involving rendition. This is musicianship of a very high order, transcending specialisms.

Missa O crux lignum

Missa O crux lignum. Anthoni usque limina.
In hydraulis. Magnificat sexti toni. Regina coeli
Kapel van de Lage Landen / Harry van der Kamp
Emergo Classics EC3954-2 (58' · DDD) Recorded c1994. Texts and translations included   Ⓕ

Busnois left only two securely ascribed Masses; the one on *L'homme armé* is easily the more famous, but this one, based on part of the sequence *Victimae Paschali*, is equally accomplished on a technical level, and stylistically very close to it. As to the motets that accompany it here, they're all top-drawer Busnois, and together with the Mass they paint a rounded, appealing portrait of that fastidiously elegant composer. Kapel van de Lage Landen uses an all-male, one-to-a-part approach, which sounds extremely well here, and the resulting performances – the Mass especially – give considerable enjoyment. A more interventionist producer would no doubt have sorted out most of the problems – occasional lack of rhythmic cohesion and melodic shape – but the sound-quality produced by these Flemish musicians (led by the incomparable Harry van der Kamp) lends the recording real character. Do these singers sound anything like their forebears at Charles the Bold's chapel? One could be seduced into thinking so, and ultimately the illusion wins out.

Ferruccio Busoni
Italian/German 1866-1924

Born to musician parents, an Italian father and a German mother, Busoni appeared from the age of eight as a pianist. In 1876 the family settled in Graz, where he had lessons with Wilhelm Mayer and produced his first published works. He then moved to Vienna, where he came to know Goldmark and Brahms, to Leipzig and eventually Berlin in 1894. Until he was 40 his output consisted mostly of piano and chamber music, including arrangements of Bach (these were eventually published in seven volumes). But in 1902 he began conducting concerts of modern music, including works by Debussy, Bartók, Sibelius and himself, and his music began to open itself to a wider range of influence. He adopted an aesthetic of 'junge Klassizität', by which he intended a return to the clarity and purely musical motivation of Bach and Mozart; yet such works as his Elegien (1907), the virtuoso Fantasia contrappuntistica (1910) and the Second Sonatina (1912), all for piano, show his awareness of the latest developments including Schoenberg's most recent music, along with his reverence of the past. His Sketch of a new Aesthetic of Music (1907) looks forward with enthusiasm to the use of microtones and electronic means.

The unresolved conflicts in his musical mind between futurism and classical recovery, Italian vocality and German substance, Lisztian flamboyance and Mozartian calm all inform his larger works, which include a Piano Concerto with choral finale (1904), several works on American Indian themes and operas – the ETA Hoffmann fantasy Die Brautwahl (1912), a commedia dell'arte double bill of Arlecchino and Turandot (1917) and the unfinished Doktor Faust (1924), where the protagonist's search after knowledge and experience is finally assuaged when he gives birth to a new future.

GROVEmusic

Piano Concerto, K247

Piano Concerto
Marc-André Hamelin pf **Men's Voices of the City of Birmingham Symphony Chorus and Orchestra / Mark Elder**
Hyperion CDA67143 (72' · DDD) Ⓕ**OO**

Busoni's Piano Concerto has never become a repertoire piece. It fits awkwardly into a concert programme, due to its length and its choral finale, and the extreme difficulty of its solo writing can't quite disguise the fact that it's really more of a symphony with an elaborate piano part than a real concerto. This new recording might just change all that, for like no other performance (not even Garrick Ohlsson's stunning account on Telarc) it proves what a richly enjoyable piece it is. Without in the least understating the grandeur of the central movement (or its Faustian pointers to Busoni's later style), it finds humour not only of the gallows kind in the first *Scherzo* (even a touch of irony to its nostalgic centre), while the brilliant tarantella second *Scherzo* is often very funny indeed: Busoni

celebrates his Italian ancestry, but at times bursts into helpless laughter at it as well. Hamelin obviously loves the work's opportunities for grand romantic pianism and barnstorming, and he has a fine ear for its stark boldness. Elder is splendidly eloquent, from the nobly Brahmsian introduction to the full-throatedly sung finale. Both are at their best in the central *Pezzo Serioso*, which is grand and grave, but alert to the presence of Chopin as well as Liszt. The recording is warm and spacious, the piano at times just a touch (but forgivably) close. This is a remarkable performance.

Additional recommendation

Piano Concerto, K247
Ogdon pf **John Alldis Choir, RPO / Revenaugh**
HMV Classics HMV5 73857-2 (69' · ADD) Ⓢ Ⓢ
Ogdon's pioneering 1968 recording of this marathon work was among the very finest of his records. It's a hugely impressive interpretation.

Orchestral Works

Turandot – concert suite, Op 41. Sarabande und Cortège: Zwei Studien zu Doktor Faust, Op 51. Berceuse élégiaque, Op 42
Hong Kong Philharmonic Orchestra / Samuel Wong
Naxos 8 555373 (71' · DDD) Ⓢ

Of the six works recorded here, two are essential for anyone interested in Busoni: the *Berceuse élégiaque* and the *Sarabande und Cortège*. Samuel Wong, the recently appointed music director of the Hong Kong Philharmonic, is on this reading a very interesting artist. He takes the *Berceuse élégiaque*, for example, at a very slow tempo and indeed its pace suggests mournful sighing rather than the rocking of a cradle. The extraordinary end of the piece, string chords with the dark glow of gong strokes, is quite magical, partly because it's so sombrely slow. In the *Cortège*, also a touch slow, he misses something of Busoni's mercurial quality but imparts a lovely nobility to its string counter-subject.

Every one of the *Turandot* suite's movements is entertaining, two are Busoni at his most imaginative (the strikingly malign fourth and the sinister seventh) and they're all brilliantly and charfterfully played. Wong's intriguing musicality and Naxos's bargain price make this a worthwhile issue.

Piano Works

Sieben Elegien. Perpetuum mobile. Prélude et Etude en Arpèges. Sieben Kurze Stücke zur Pflege des polyphonen Spiel
Roland Pöntinen pf
CPO CPO999 853-2 (73' · DDD) Ⓕ

Few composers have more resolutely avoided popularity than Busoni. Like Rachmaninov and

Liszt he took a jaundiced view of his career as a virtuoso pianist, seeing it as a vainglorious alternative to the serious business of composition. Is this why his work so often exudes an atmosphere of dark intellectuality and desolation? Such music, in Alfred Brendel's words, only 'begins to glow when the right eye falls on it', and in Roland Pöntinen it surely has an ideal interpreter. His playing is subtly and brilliantly judged and, whether in the far-reaching Elegies, the more didactic *kurze Stücke* or in the *Perpetuum mobile*, where Busoni temporarily rises from the slough of despond, his sympathy and virtuosity are unfailing. The recordings are excellent; those looking for an uneasy rather than comfortable experience need look no further.

Die Brautwahl

Die Brautwahl
Siegfried Vogel *bass* Voswinkel **Carola Höhn** *sop* Albertine **Graham Clark** *ten* Thusman **Vinson Cole** *ten* Lehsen **Pär Lindskog** *ten* Baron Bensch **Roman Trekel** *bar* Leonhard **Günter von Kannen** *bar* Manasse **Chorus of the Deutsche Staatsoper, Berlin; Staatskapelle Berlin / Daniel Barenboim**
Teldec ② 3984-25250-2 (116' · DDD) Notes, text and translation included ⒻO

Busoni's first mature opera occupied him for seven years (1905-11). He may not have been as natural a man of the theatre as Richard Strauss, but *Die Brautwahl* has plenty of fine music in it – at times foreshadowing the splendours of *Doktor Faust*. This 1992 Berlin production used a version made by Antony Beaumont, whose completion of *Doktor Faust* was a great success. As Beaumont explains in the booklet, we get only about two-thirds of the whole, and all aspects of the opera's subject-matter may not be ideally balanced. This 'fantastic comedy' is based on a story by E T A Hoffmann, with the climactic scene in which a bride is chosen (hence the title) leaning heavily on *The Merchant of Venice*. The action is set in Berlin, but there are echoes of Wagner's Nuremberg in the text and characterisation. Musically, Busoni keeps his distance from Wagner, and the music is attractive, ranging widely in character.

This performance is a strong one, with a certain, untroublesome amount of stage noise. No doubt reflecting the staging, the recording occasionally recesses the singers, but the energy and command of Barenboim's conducting are never in doubt. The energy does not mean that anything is rushed, and the romantic episodes are warmly moulded, the scenes of fantasy properly attentive to matters of colour and texture. Roman Trekel, a warm yet dramatically resonant baritone, makes a strong impression as Leonhard. He's the perfect foil to Graham Clark, who tackles the role of Thusman with relish, and with considerable technical skill in music which demands lyrical sensitivity as well as comic agility.

Doktor Faust

Doktor Faust
Dietrich Henschel *bar* Doktor Faust **Markus Hollop** *bass* Wagner, Master of Ceremonies **Kim Begley** *ten* Mephistopheles **Torsten Kerl** *ten* Duke of Parma **Eva Jenis** *sop* Duchess of Parma **Detlef Roth** *bar* Soldier **William Dazeley** *bar* Natural Philosopher **Eberhard Lorenz** *ten* Lieutenant **Frédéric Caton** *bass* Theologian **Jérôme Varnier** *bass* Jurist **Dietrich Fischer-Dieskau** *spkr* Poet **Geneva Grand Theatre Chorus; Chorus and Orchestra of the Opéra National de Lyon / Kent Nagano**
Erato ③ 3984-25501-2 (196' · DDD) Notes, text and translation included ⓂO

Finally we have a recording that not only provides the full, uncut text, as completed by Busoni's pupil Philipp Jarnach soon after the composer's death, but also offers as supplements Antony Beaumont's very different realisations of parts of the opera's later stages. So complete is this version, indeed, that it includes the spoken prologues and epilogues, with Dietrich Fischer-Dieskau providing a poignant link to DG's heavily cut 1969 recording.

Given that Beaumont worked from sketches and other information of which Jarnach was unaware (or chose to ignore), there can be no question as to which of the two is the more genuinely Busonian, and the extended closing scene in Beaumont's version has a persuasive gravity and sense of fulfilment quite different from Jarnach's more terse yet slightly melodramatic completion. Nevertheless, it will take a sensibility more refined than most not to be swept away by the sheer visceral power of Jarnach's rendering of the death of Faust.

Dietrich Henschel displays considerable style and stamina during his two extended monologues in the opera's final stages, and although his singing isn't entirely free of straining for effect, or of bluster, the character's tortured humanity is vividly conveyed. Kim Begley makes a considerable success of the other principal role, although, in an ideal world, Mephistopheles would manage more variety. But Begley tackles the many demanding aspects of the part with panache and, in the scintillating ballad, wit and menace are in perfect balance. Other parts are adequately taken, though articulation of the German text varies in clarity and accuracy.

This variability is one reason why the performance takes some time to take wing: another, more fundamental reason concerns the rather dry nature of the recording itself. At times, principal voices are backwardly placed, and, even when they aren't, one suspects that the brilliance of the orchestral sound is being damped down in order to ensure their audibility. Nevertheless, Nagano's shaping of this extremely demanding score is neither inflexible nor inexpressive. *Doktor Faust* can at last be heard in a recording that, in the end, reaches and reveals its essence, and whose documentary value is inestimable.

George Butterworth British 1885-1916

Butterworth was educated at Eton and Oxford and became associated with Vaughan Williams in collecting folksongs. His works include the orchestral rhapsody A Shropshire Lad (1912), based on his two sets of songs from the same collection (1911-12).

GROVEmusic

Songs

Two English Idylls[a]. The Banks of Green Willow[b]. Bredon Hill and other songs[c]. A Shropshire Lad – Rhapsody[d] Six Songs from A Shropshire Lad[e]
[ce]Benjamin Luxon *bar* [ce]David Willison *pf*
[abdf]ASMF / Sir Neville Marriner
Decca 468 802-2DM (56' · ADD/DDD) Recorded 1976.

Ⓜ

George Butterworth's music creates a perfect, idealised image of pastoral England before World War I (in which the composer met his death). His lovely songs are indelibly associated with the poetry of AE Housman, notably *A Shropshire Lad* (though Butterworth himself lived in Oxfordshire). Although they have a simple folk inspiration, they don't draw on actual folk tunes. Benjamin Luxon's performances are deeply felt and find the widest range of expression, always responsive to the words' meanings, never treating the songs just as charming miniatures. Marriner's superbly recorded accounts of the wonderful orchestral evocations, which are folk-song based, is full of passionate yearning as well as delicacy of feeling. Is there any more magically haunting opening in English orchestral pastoralism than the rhapsody *A Shropshire Lad*?

Dietrich Buxtehude German c1637-1707

Buxtehude's first studies were under his father, who held posts as organist in Hälsingburg and Helsingor (Elsinore), as did Buxtehude himself between c1657 and 1668, when he became organist at the Marienkirche at Lübeck, one of the most important posts in north Germany; he was also appointed Werkmeister (general manager) of the church. Later that year he married Anna Margarethe Tunder, his predecessor's daughter. Besides his normal duties on Sundays and feast days, he reinstated the practice of giving Abendmusik concerts in the church on five Sunday afternoons each year. These events attracted much interest and drew JS Bach from Arnstadt in Advent 1705.

Surviving texts from the Abendmusik performances show that he composed a number of oratorio-like works, but none has survived. The bulk of his known sacred music consists of cantatas or sacred concertos, the latter often settings of psalm texts, consisting of contrasting sections in which each line of the text is treated with a new motif. He used a concertato style, for voices and continuo (sometimes with other instruments), in which the motifs are treated in dia-

logue in a manner related to the Venetian polychoral style; there are also arioso sections. Buxtehude wrote a number of chorale settings, commonly with the melody in the soprano but with instrumental accompaniment and interludes; in ensemble settings he used the chorale motet style, in the manner of a sacred concerto but with motifs from the chorale melody, and he also set chorales with the melody in one voice and instrumental counterpoints. His sacred arias are mostly in strophic or varied strophic form, with a fluent, sometimes Italianate melodic style. Some extended vocal works, akin to Bach's cantatas, combine movements in the sacred concerto style with others of the aria type.

Most of Buxtehude's instrumental music is for the organ: about half consists of freely composed music, often using a toccata-like section with several fugues and incorporating virtuoso passage-work, while half consists of chorale settings, some of the variation and fantasia types, but mostly highly unified settings of a single stanza of the chorale with a richly ornamented melody. He composed suites and other music for the harpsichord; his courantes are variations of the allemandes and the gigues are loosely fugal. French influence is noticeable. He also wrote several variation sets. The only works published in his lifetime were two collections each of seven sonatas, for violins, viola da gamba and harpsichord continuo (seven more sonatas survive in MS); they are closer to the German tradition of improvisatory viol playing than to the Corelli tradition, with movements in contrasting tempo and texture. They include ground bass movements and fugues, usually only in two parts as the viol part is not always independent of the bass. Especially in his sacred vocal works and his organ music, Buxtehude represents the climax of the 17th-century north German school, and he significantly influenced Bach.

GROVEmusic

Membra Jesu nostri, BuxWV75

Membra Jesu nostri   Ⓟ
The Sixteen; Symphony of Harmony and Invention / Harry Christophers
Linn Records CKD141 (61' · DDD) Text and translation included

Ⓕ

Composed in 1680, this group of seven tiny cantatas – each meditating on a part of Christ's body (feet, knees, hands, side, breast, heart and face) – represents an extreme in formal compression. Each cantata has just six movements: an instrumental introduction, a choral setting of the relevant Biblical citation, three short solo arias, and a repeat of the chorus. Few of those movements last more than 90 seconds, and some are a lot shorter. But the real catch is that the solo arias are all on texts consisting of 80-syllable trochaic lines: Buxtehude sets the vast majority of them to four-bar phrases, which can lead to musical predictability. The first task of musicians is to counteract the numbing regularity of those phrases. They approach this by adopting a generally very smooth rhythmic style, benefiting much from the marvellous continuo group of Paul Nicholson (organ), Jane Coe (cello) and Elizabeth Kenny (theorbo): all three superbly resourceful in their range of colours and attacks, without ever interrupting the music's flow. Above this the violins of David Woodstock and Walter Reiter glow or sparkle as the music requires. In line with today's best practice, the choruses are taken just by the five excellent solo singers, led by Carolyn Sampson in luscious form. A wonderfully moving account of Buxtehude's remarkable cycle of cantatas.

Sacred Cantatas

Sacred Cantatas   Ⓟ
Fuga, BuxWV174. Ich habe Lust abzuscheiden, BuxWV47^{abc}. Ich halte es dafür, BuxWV48^{bc}. Jesu meine Freude, BuxWV60^{abc}. Mein herz ist bereit, BuxWV73^{cd}. Herr, wenn ich nur dich hab, BuxWV38^b. Salve, Jesu, Patris gnate unigenite, BuxWV94^{ab}. Jesu dulcis memoria, BuxWV56^{ab}. Cantate Domino, BuxWV12^{abc}
^aEmma Kirkby, ^bSuzie LeBlanc sops ^cPeter Harvey bass ^dClare Salaman vn Purcell Quartet (Catherine Mackintosh vn/va Catherine Weiss vn Richard Boothby bvio Robert Woolley org)
Chandos Chaconne CHAN0691 (76' · DDD) Texts and translations included   Ⓕ

Setting various German and Latin texts for solo voices, violins and continuo, these sacred cantatas are typical products of the late 17th century in their pragmatic approach to form.

Here are patchworks such as *Jesu dulcis memoria* and *Salve, Jesu, Patris gnate unigenite*; chorale or song variations such as *Jesu, meine Freude*; and others, like *Ich halte es dafür* and *Ich habe Lust abzuscheiden*, which combine the two. *Cantate Domino* is liltingly Italianate, *Mein Herz ist bereit* is an agile showpiece for solo bass, while *Herr, wenn ich nur dich hab* is a set of variations over a ground bass. The Purcell Quartet's essential string sound has always been sweet, airy and lucid, and it's interesting to hear how that has been transferred here from the instrumental sphere to the vocal. To this end the choice of singers is important, and on this occasion they could hardly have picked more shrewdly: Emma Kirkby and Suzie LeBlanc make an excellent pairing, distinguishable from each other in both voice and approach, yet at the same time superbly matched in duet; and Peter Harvey has the friendliest of bass voices, his alert account of *Mein Herz ist bereit*, set against the thrillingly radiant background of three violins, being one of the disc's highlights.

An expert recording in an amenable acoustic completes a release of many refined pleasures.

Nimm von uns, Herr, BuxWV78. Jesu, meines Lebens Leben, BuxWV62. Mit Fried und Freud, ich fahr dahin, BuxWV76. Führwahr, er trug unsere Krankheit, BuxWV31. Herzlich lieb, hab' ich dich o Herr, BuxWV41. Der Herr ist mit mir, BuxWV15
Claron McFadden sop **Franciska Dukel** mez **Jonathan Peter Kenny** counterten **Marius van Altena** ten **Stephan MacLeod** bass **Collegium**

Vocale; The Royal Consort; Anima Eterna Orchestra / Jos van Immerseel
Channel Classics CCS7895 (65' · DDD) Recorded 1994. Texts included (German only)   Ⓕ

The North German middleground between chorale *concertato* and the early cantatas of Bach is an interesting one, especially in the hands of composers of Buxtehude's stature. In these cantatas the disparate textual elements of Bible passage, hymn and devotional poetry are drawn together by the composer's skill in handling the comparably disparate musical ones of sonata, concertato principles, aria and chorale. That in itself might give these cantatas only an ephemeral charm, but Buxtehude was gifted in the art of word-painting and, above all, in the expression of deep, often grief-stricken emotions. He could be brilliant, too, in his lyrical approach to texts, but his sacred vocal music seems to be characterised most strongly by an all-pervading melancholy. These six works demonstrate Buxtehude's formal versatility with two large-scale chorale cantatas; a beautiful ostinato-based strophic aria, with an almost startling dissonance; the famous, austere and highly contrapuntal *Canticum Simeonis* ('*Mit Fried und Freud*') which Buxtehude performed at his father's funeral in 1674; and two *concertante* pieces. The performances respond to the highly charged emotional outpouring of these works but can lack polish. However, the music is first rate (the ostinato- and chaconne-based movements make particularly strong appeal) and Immerseel's direction is stylish and sensitive.

William Byrd   British 1543-1623

Brought up in London, Byrd was a pupil of Tallis. In 1563 he became Organist and Master of the Choristers at Lincoln Cathedral and married there in 1568. Though he remained at Lincoln until c1572 he was a Gentleman of the Chapel Royal from 1570 and its organist from 1575 (at first jointly with Tallis). In London he rapidly established himself as a composer, gaining influential friends and patrons and earning favour with Queen Elizabeth, who granted him a patent (with Tallis) in 1575 for the printing and marketing of part-music and MS paper. After his wife's death in the 1580s he remarried. He and his family were often cited as Catholic recusants, but he continued to compose openly for the Roman church. In 1593 Byrd moved to Essex, where he spent the rest of his life and was frequently involved in property litigation. His reputation was very high: he was described as 'Father of British Music'. Morley and Tomkins were among his pupils.

Much of Byrd's vast and varied output was printed during his lifetime. His sacred music ranges widely in style and mood, from the florid and penitential motets of the Cantiones sacrae to the concise and devotional ones in the Gradualia (motet sections intended to form an impressive scheme of complete

Mass Propers). His secular songs predate the true madrigal; they use intricate, flowing counterpoint derived from an earlier English style (eg Tallis, Taverner) and range from solemn lamentations to exuberant jests. His instrumental music is specially important: the many consort songs greatly influenced the later lute ayre, while the virginal pieces are unparalleled in richness of invention and contrapuntal brilliance. In all the genres in which he wrote Byrd was both traditionalist and innovator, channelling continental ideas into a native English tradition, and his expressive range was unusually wide for his day. He wrote for both Catholic and Anglican churches with equal genius. **GROVE**music

Chamber works

Byrd Fantasia a 6. Pavan and Galliard –   🅟
Kinbourough Good, MB32. The Queen's Alman,
MB20, 'Hugh Ashton's Ground'. Pavan and Galliard a
6. Pavan and Galliard, MB14. Browning. Pavan a 5.
The Carman's Whistle, MB36. The Irish March, MB94.
My Lord of Oxenford's Maske. Pavan, MB17.
A Fancie, MB25. Praeludium and Ground. Pavan and
Galliard, MB60 **Anonymous** Pavans – Mille regretz;
Belle qui tiens ma vie
Capriccio Stravagante / Skip Sempé hpd
Astrée Naïve E8611 (73' · DDD)   🅕🅞

This is technically superb and musically distinctive. Skip Sempé and his musicians grab hold of each piece and play it in a way that leaves no doubt why it was chosen; that is, they have something new and interesting to say musically about each work. The sound is also wonderful: Sempé plays on a Skowroneck harpsichord that he enthusiastically describes as 'one of the first truly admirable harpsichords of the 20th century'; the viols and the recorder group are beautifully recorded, with every detail of the dense polyphony clear. This is the kind of disc you could play to almost any music-lover as a way of explaining that Byrd isn't just a great composer but one of the greatest. On the other hand, those who know the music may well feel a touch uncomfortable. While Sempé plays with often truly dazzling skill and virtuosity, many may wish that his pavans were a touch steadier. He also has a slightly mannered way of overdotting cadential bass figurations. The ensemble pieces are sometimes heavily orchestrated: the great six-part *Fantasia* that opens the disc, for example, has recorders and continuo instruments added to the viols as though to underline contrasts that some would think were already there in the music. Caveats apart, this is an invigorating disc which gives you a new understanding of some of the finest masterpieces of English music.

---

yrd Fantasia a 5, BE17/8. Browning a 5, BE17/10.
Fantasias a 6, BE17/13-14. In Nomines a 5,
BE17/19-22 **Mico** Fancies a 4 Nos 4a, 5-7, 9, 10, 14,
18 & 19. Pavans a 4 Nos 2-4
Phantasm (Laurence Dreyfus, Wendy Gillespie,

Jonathan Manson, Markku Luolajan-Mikkola, *viols*)
with **Martha McGaughey, Alison McGillivray** viols
Simax PSC1143 (60' · DDD)   🅕

The odd juxtaposition of Byrd's very finest chamber music with pieces by Richard Mico may seem rather like pairing late Beethoven with Vanhal; but it works extremely well. Though Mico has been little regarded, much of his music shows absolute mastery (his Pavan No 4 is in some ways one of the most perfect and beautiful examples of the simple eight-bar pavane). The Mico selection includes two pieces that are by no means certainly his (*Fancies* Nos 18 and 19); but they're still fine work. Phantasm play this music with immaculate control and balance, finding many telling details that might elude less careful musicians. Some listeners may be a touch less happy with the Byrd, feeling that the honeyed sounds cover certain details, that the speed of *Browning* loses the work's harmonic and contrapuntal magic, that the myriad changes in the grand six-voice *fantasias* could benefit from greater lightness of touch. But that would be like saying that only the English can perform Elgar idiomatically. What Phantasm brings to this music is a clear and unusual view of the music. Moreover, they present what's absolutely the best of Byrd's consort work, omitting the troublesome first *In Nomine* and the less perfect first six-part *Fantasia*. The four *Fantasias* and the four *In Nomines* on this disc are the core of Byrd's claim to stand among the world's greatest composers of chamber music. The performances convincingly support that claim.

Complete Keyboard Works

23 Pavans and Galliards (with two additional   🅟
Pavans and five Galliards). 14 sets of Variations.
11 Fantasias. 11 Grounds. Nine Preludes.
Miscellanea and variant versions
Davitt Moroney chbr org/clav/hpd/muselar virg/org
Hyperion ⑦ CDA66551/7 (497' · DDD) Recorded
1991-7   🅜🅞🅞🅞
Selected highlights available on 🅕 CDA66558

The three volumes of keyboard music added in 1950 as an afterthought to Edmund Fellowes's edition of Byrd have only slowly made their full impact as containing one of the most remarkable and innovative repertories in the history of music. A much-needed new edition by Alan Brown (1969-71) was followed by Oliver Neighbour's important critical study (1978), which perhaps for the first time made it clear that Byrd wasn't just another of the 'Elizabethan Virginalists' but stood head and shoulders above all his contemporaries – in range, contrapuntal technique, melodic invention and above all formal control and imagination. Davitt Moroney has completed the picture by presenting the entire body of music on seven CDs. The results here are a triumph for all concerned. Moroney has the music in his hands, head and soul. There are so many fine details in his playing that it's hard to know where to begin in its praise: the wonderful clarity of the part-writing; the superb energy of the playing; the glittering virtuosity; the ability to vary the colours and move from the ineffably light and whimsical to the seriously confrontational; the constant delicate flexibility of his metre; or his compelling grasp of Byrd's often difficult formal designs.

Moroney approached this Everest of a project over many years, in constant consultation with Brown and particularly Neighbour (who, appropriately enough, plays the 'third hand' for the duet *Fantasia* on Disc 4). The engineers have coped well with the different recording venues and occasions. Six different instruments are used to vary the colour and to fit the different styles of the music. The most novel is the muselar virginal, a marvellously earthy instrument with a refreshingly noisy action. The others are plainly chosen with loving care. A harpsichord by Hubert Bédard (after Ruckers) tends to be used for the lighter pieces, while he chooses one by Reinhard von Nagel (after Couchet) for some of the more serious works. Neatly enough, the set ends with a prelude already heard on Ahrend's Toulouse organ, now played on four different instruments in turn (omitting only the chamber organ). Alongside all this, Moroney has provided the most detailed set of notes: 200 pages of wide-ranging erudition (in English and French) including a key to the 'BK' numbers of the Brown edition which are used throughout his running prose. So when you've got through the 497 minutes needed to listen to the discs, you still have several hours of reading to do.

Masses

Masses – for Three Voices; for Four Voices; for Five Voices (ed Skinner). Fantasias[a] – in G, 'A Voluntary for My Ladye Nevell'; in D minor; C, 'A Fancie for My Ladye Nevell'
[a]**Patrick Russill** *org* **The Cardinall's Musick /
Andrew Carwood**
ASV Gaudeamus CDGAU206 (79' · DDD) Texts and translations included · ⓅⓄⓄⓄ

This is incomparable music by one of the greatest English composers and it was high time for someone to take a fresh look at these works in the light of more recent research and changing attitudes to performance practice.

Byrd had composed his three settings of the Ordinary of the Mass in troubled times for the small recusant Catholic community that still remained in England in spite of persecution. The settings would have been sung, in all probability, during festive, albeit furtive, celebrations of the old time-honoured Roman liturgy, in private chapels in the depths of the country,

at places such as Ingatestone, the seat of Byrd's principal patron, Sir John Petre. Andrew Carwood has recorded them in the Fitzalan Chapel of Arundel Castle, a small but lofty building with a clear resonance that enables the inner voices of the part-writing to come through straight and clean. It hasn't the aura of King's College Chapel, but is probably easier to manage than, say, Winchester Cathedral or Merton College Chapel.

Carwood uses two voices to a part in all three Masses. In comparison with rival recordings he's alone in selecting high voices for the three-part Mass, transposed up a minor third, which introduces a note of surprising lightness and grace. He, too, is alone in taking the initiative of using an all-male choir for the four-part Mass – alto, tenor, baritone, bass. This close, low texture, together with the transposition down an augmented fourth, adds a fitting sense of gravity to the performance. In particular, it heightens the poignancy of such passages as the 'dona nobis pacem' in the *Agnus Dei*, with its series of suspensions in the drooping phrases leading to the final cadence.

That dimension of understanding is precisely what this recording by The Cardinall's Musick so keenly demonstrates. Theirs is a simplicity of style that belies simplistic criticism. Vibrato is used sparingly: 40 years on, some listeners might consider its constant use by a King's Choir of the late 1950s almost too overpowering. Carwood chooses his tempos with care, avoiding the modern tendency to speed everything up inordinately.

The interesting historical note on the whole background is a good pointer to what the listener may experience as the music unfolds.

Masses – Three Voices; Four Voices; Five Voices
Motet – Ave verum corpus a 4
The Tallis Scholars / Peter Phillips
Gimell CDGIM345 (67' · DDD) Recorded 1984 ⓅⓄⓄ

Byrd was a fervently committed Roman Catholic and he helped enormously to enrich the music of the English Church. His Mass settings were made for the many recusant Catholic worshippers who held services in private. They were published between 1593 and 1595 and are creations of great feeling. The contrapuntal writing has a much closer texture and fibre than the Masses of Palestrina and there's an austerity and rigour that's allowed to blossom and expand with the text. The beautifully restrained and mellow recording, made in Merton College Chapel, Oxford, fully captures the measure of the music and restores the awe and mystery of music that familiarity can dim.

Mass for Five Voices (with Propers for the Feast of Corpus Christi). Gradualia ac cantiones sacrae:
Part 2 – Corpus Christi. Gradualia seu cantionum sacrarum, liber secundum: Votive Mass for the Blessed Sacrament – Ab ortu solis; Alleluia:

Cognoverunt discipuli
Winchester Cathedral Choir / David Hill
Hyperion CDA66837 (73' · DDD) Texts and
translations included   (F)

On this CD the five movements of Byrd's Mass
for five voices are interspersed with the five
pieces of the Proper for the Feast of Corpus
Christi. We can therefore transport ourselves
back in time to the end of the 16th and beginning of the 17th century, and imagine their
being performed, in early summer, at a live celebration of Mass in one of the great houses of
the Catholic nobility. Winchester Cathedral
Choir has purposely sought out an enclosed
space in the great cathedral to make this recording, so that the sound captures something of the
immediacy of singers performing in a small hidden room. One is particularly struck by the
quality of the trebles – the slight edge to the
gentle tone of very young singers – and also by
the teamwork of the whole choir.

The secret of this recording lies in its unity of
theme and in its understanding of Byrd's triumphant statements of belief, expressed in
music of great tenderness as well as strength.

Cantiones Sacrae

Cantiones Sacrae (1575) – Tribue, Domine. Siderum
rector. Domine secundum. Fantasias – C; D. Attollite
portas. Miserere mihi. Aspice Domine. Peccantem
me quotidie. Salvator mundi II. O lux, beata Trinitas
**New College Choir, Oxford / Edward
Higginbottom** with **Timothy Morris** org
CRD CRD3492 (64' · DDD) Recorded 1994. Texts and
translations included   (M)

There's so much wonderful six-part writing in
this attractive selection from the 1575 *Cantiones
Sacrae* that such a medium appears in a new
light, particularly when performed by the choir
and in the acoustic of New College Chapel –
where, as Edward Higginbottom reminds us,
they 'have been rehearsing for 500 years'. The
beauty and balance of the musical architecture is
constantly conveyed to the listener, particularly
in the six-part writing. It doesn't matter
whether these compositions were intended for
liturgical or domestic use, or as a noble offering
to the Queen: from a purely musical point of
view they're superb. To give a single example,
the little Vespers hymn *O lux, beata Trinitas* displays consummate craftsmanship through the
ingenious use of the number three – three high,
then three low voices, three diverse voices, a
canon three-in-one, three strophes, triple time,
and so on, building up to a tremendous final
'Amen'. The point made by this recording is
that it all sounds natural, uncontrived, magnificent. The three organ pieces are a welcome
addition: with their brilliant fingerwork and
gentle registrations they present a charming and
lively contrast to the vocal settings.

Cantiones Sacrae (1589) – Vigilate; In resurrectione
tua; Aspice Domine de sede; Ne irascaris Domine.
Propers for the Feast of the Purification – Ave regina
caelorum; Adorna thalamum; O quam gloriosum;
Tribulationes civitatum; Domine secundum
multitudinem; Laetentur caeli
The Cardinall's Musick / Andrew Carwood
ASV Gaudeamus CDGAU309 (71' · DDD)   (F)

ASV's Byrd Edition presents Propers for
Candlemas (also known as the 'Feast of the
Purification'), and further motets from the 1589
Cantiones Sacrae, many of them composed to
strengthen the spirits of the Queen's loyal
Catholic subjects in those troubled and highly
dangerous times. Which goes to explain the
high proportion of sorrowful or penitential
texts, the frequent cries for deliverance (*Aspice
Domine, Ne irascaris, Tribulationes*), and the mastery with which Byrd sets them. This historical
background, vital to an understanding of the
music, doesn't exclude the possibility of a joyful
outcome: Byrd can also contemplate the ultimate joys of heaven, (*O quam gloriosum, Laetentur caeli*).

The choir enters deeply into an understanding
of what lies behind these pieces. And Byrd is
never averse to raising his singers' spirits by
introducing a jaunty rhythm – the crowing cock
in *Vigilate*, for example – or a bright, rising
theme to inspire hope. The choir responds with
sustained restraint, perfect balance and crisp
rhythms.

The settings of the Propers for Candlemas
offer a short recital of their own, this time in the
full context of the liturgy for this ancient feast,
and following the whole course of events as the
story unfolds. A thoroughly satisfying disc.

Gradualia

Gradualia – Volume 1: Saturday Lady Masses in
Advent. Domine quis habitabit. Omni tempore
benedic Deum. Christe redemptor omnium.
Sermone blando a 3. Miserere. Ne perdas cum
implis. Lamentations of Jeremiah. Christe, qui lux es
a 5. Christe qui lux es a 4. Sanctus. Audivi vocem de
caelo. Vide Dominum quoniam tribulor. Peccavi
super numerum (all ed Skinner)
The Cardinall's Musick; Frideswide Consort
(Caroline Kershaw, Jane Downer, Christine Garratt,
Jean McCreery recs) / **Andrew Carwood**
ASV Gaudeamus CDGAU170 (70' · DDD) Texts and
translations included   (F)

This is a great start to The Cardinall's Musick's
project to record Byrd's complete output. On
the disc, some of the shorter motets are
entrusted to The Cardinall's' habitual instrumental accomplices, the Frideswide Consort. A
full list of sources is given for each piece, along
with appropriate editorial commentary. Since
Byrd set certain texts a number of times, such
precision seems only sensible. Much of this

music is new to the CD catalogue, and even in this selection of largely unpublished motets, there are impressive finds (the nine-voice *Domine quis habitabit*, for instance). This repertory is the mother's-milk of English choristers, and of the younger generation of English vocal ensembles The Cardinall's Musick remains perhaps the closest to that tradition outside of actual choral establishments. So they respond to Byrd with a suavity and confidence born of longstanding acquaintance. The expansive penitential pieces, such as the early *Lamentations*, are far removed from the small-scale forms of the *Gradualia*. The Cardinall's Musick respond effectively to these different functions and moods, and the recording complements them admirably.

Gradualia – Volume 2: Nativity of our Lord Jesus Christ – Puer natus est; Viderunt ... omnes fines terrae; Dies sanctificatus; Tui sunt coeli; Viderunt omnes fines terrae; Hodie Christus natus est; O admirabile commercium; O magnum mysterium. Ave regina caelorum. O salutaris hostia. Confitemini DomiNo In exitu Israel (with Sheppard and Mundy). Laudate pueri Dominum. Decantabat populus. Deus in adjutorium. Ad Dominum cum tribularer (all ed Skinner)
The Cardinall's Musick / Andrew Carwood
ASV Gaudeamus CDGAU178 (73' · DDD) Texts and translations included   Ⓕ❶

This second volume of The Cardinall's Musick's Byrd edition is, if anything, more impressive than the first. It may be a matter of programming, for the works recorded here seem to be of a higher overall calibre: even an obviously experimental piece such as *O salutaris hostia* could have been included on merit alone – yet this appears to be its first recording. Complete surveys sometimes turn up items of lesser interest, yet they also allow one to hear pieces that might have difficulty in finding a home elsewhere: witness the responsory, *In exitu Israel*, an intriguing collaborative effort by Byrd and his contemporaries, Mundy and Sheppard. Finally, one can judge for oneself the authenticity of works that modern scholarship has deemed doubtful (such as the opening *Ave regina caelorum*). Most of the pieces here involve male altos on the top line. The centrepiece is a collection of Propers from the *Gradualia* of 1607, this time for the Nativity. As on their first set, Skinner's and Carwood's decision to structure each volume around a set of Propers proves an astute piece of programming, integrating shorter items as it does (such as the various *Alleluia* settings) within a framework that allows them their own space. The singers are on very fine form indeed. It takes confidence to carry off *O salutaris hostia*, whose fierce false relations could so easily have sounded merely wilful. Only in the final, extended settings does the pace flag: the disc's last moments are rather ponderous. That aside, this is a disc to delight Byrd-lovers everywhere.

Music for Holy Week and Easter

Plorans plorabit. Passio Domini nostri Jesu Christe secundum Johannem[a]. Adoramus te[bc]. Vespers for Holy Saturday[a]. Mass Propers for Easter Day. Haec dies. Angelus Domini. Mane vobiscum. Post dies octo. Christus resurgens
The Cardinall's Musick / Andrew Carwood [a]ten with [b]**Robin Tyson** counterten [c]**Patrick Russill** org
ASV Gaudeamus CDGAU214 (76' · DDD) Texts and translations included   Ⓕ❶❶❶

The sixth volume of The Byrd Edition is a landmark recording, covering most of Byrd's Holy Week and Easter music, from the St John's Passion choruses for Good Friday to the Octave day of Easter, and including miniature Vespers at the end of the Easter Vigil, and the whole of the Proper of the Mass for Easter Day.

The opening motet *Plorans plorabit*, recalling the Lamentations chanted earlier in the week, is a stern reminder of the recusant atmosphere in which Byrd lived out his religious beliefs. The straightforward Passion choruses are rightly set into their proper context, an edition of St John's Passion prepared by Byrd's Roman contemporary, Guidetti. Admirably sung, Carwood maintains throughout a remarkable balance between drama and restraint. A gentle consort song, *Adoramos te*, fills the space in the listener's imagination between the burial of Christ and his rising from the dead. The miniature Vespers follow, sung, almost with bated breath, to Byrd's simple three-part settings of the two antiphons, with a correction of Bretts' suggested psalmtone for the single – and shortest – psalm.

The Mass *Resurrexi* is exhilarating, with surging themes, rhythmic interplay and bursts of joy. Byrd, unable to resist word-painting suggestive of earthquake at the Offertory, introduces here a note of merriment into a particularly serious liturgy, and doesn't entirely avoid it elsewhere. Thankfully it was under- rather than overplayed.

The solemn final four-part processional *Christus resurgens* is a triumphant restatement of Easter: total joy.

Consort Songs

O Lord, within thy tabernacle. Quis me statim. With Lilies White. Wretched Albinus. Blame I Confess. Ye Sacred Muse. Rejoice unto the Lord. Fair Britain Isle. In Nomines a 5, BE17 Nos 18-22. Browning a 5, BE17 No 10. Fantasia a 5, BE17 No 8. Praeludium and Ground a 5
Gérard Lesne counterten **Ensemble Orlando Gibbons** (Wieland Kuijken, Kaori Uemura, Anne-Marie Lasla, Sylvie Moquet, Jérôme Hantaï viols)
Virgin Classics Veritas 545264-2 (65' · DDD)   Ⓕ

The five *In Nomines* reveal the growing maturity and control over form of the inventive fledgling Byrd, though you'll need to shuffle tracks to follow it in sequence. This is the only CD where the *In Nomines* are coupled with Byrd's consort songs. Of the other instrumental items, the *Praeludium and Ground* are treated with winsome lightness but the 20 remarkable variations on *Browning* hang more heavily than is suggested by the words of either version of the tune (the other is *The leaves be green*). Solemnity is the prevailing mood of the consort songs, four of them laments. *Wretched Albinus* refers to the disgracing of the Earl of Essex, attributed to a 'silly woman' – the same Queen Elizabeth whose protection of Byrd from anti-Catholic laws is obliquely celebrated in *Rejoice unto the Lord*, the only cheerful oasis in this desert of sorrow. Fortunately the sorrow is expressed in magnificent music of which *Ye Sacred Muse*, Byrd's tribute to the recently deceased Tallis, is the jewel in the crown. Magnificent vocal music calls for a matching singer and Gérard Lesne fills that requirement to the full. First-class recording and excellent booklet-notes provide additional reasons for acquiring this disc.

All in a garden green. La volta No 1 in G, 'Lady [P]
Morley'. O mistress mine I must. Wolsey's Wild.
O Lord, how vain are all our delights. Psalmes, Sonets
and Songs – Who likes to love; My mind to me a
kingdom is; Farewell, false love. Triumph with pleasant
melody. Truth at the First. Ad Dominum cum tribularer.
Cantiones sacrae – Attollite portas; da mihi auxilium;
Domine secundum actum meum; Miserere mihi,
Domine
Sophie Yates virg **I Fagiolini / Robert**
Hollingworth; Fretwork
Chandos Chaconne CHAN0578 (73' · DDD)
Recorded 1994. Texts and translations included (F)(O)

This disc adopts an imaginative approach to programming Byrd's music by presenting works in different genres grouped together to demonstrate a single stage in his development. It includes Latin motets, keyboard dances and variations on popular songs of the day, and sacred and secular songs (and a dialogue) with viols. There's so much here that wins our admiration: the dazzling contrapuntal elaboration of *Attollite portas*, the close-knit texture of *Da mihi auxilium* and the massive *Ad Dominum cum tribularer*; the exuberant variations on *O mistress mine* (neatly played by Sophie Yates) and Byrd's melodic gift in the strophic *O Lord, how vain*. The singers' adoption of period pronunciation – for example, 'rejoice' emerges as 'rejwace' – affects the tuning and the musical sound, it's claimed here, but without rather clearer enunciation the point remains not proven. Probably more upsetting to many will be the Anglicised pronunciation of Latin. The viol consort gives stylish support and is well balanced, the Fagiolini sopranos occasionally 'catch the mike' on high notes (eg in the passionate pleas of *Miserere mihi, Domine*), and the recorded level of the virginals might have been a little higher without falsifying its tone. But these are minor criticisms of a most rewarding disc.

Rejoice unto the Lord. Ah, silly soul. Come to me, grief, for ever. Constant Penelope. Lullaby my sweet little baby. O dear life. O God that guides the cheerful sun. O that most rare breast. Ye sacred muses. An aged dame. Psalmes, Songs and Sonnets – How vain the toils that mortal men do take; Who likes to love; All as a sea
Robin Blaze counterten **Concordia** (Emilia Benjamin, Reiko Ichise, Joanna Levine, Mark Levy, Alison McGillivray viols Elizabeth Kenny lte)
Hyperion CDA67397 (67' · DDD) Texts and translations included (F)

The subject-matter of these songs is wide ranging, from a triumphant celebration of an Elizabethan anniversary, *Rejoice unto the Lord*, to the two laments on the death of Sir Philip Sidney, the quietly poignant funeral song *Come to me, grief, for ever*, and the deeply felt sonnet *O that most rare breast*, the text attributed to Sir Edward Dyer, one of Sidney's circle of poets. A third lament, *Ye sacred muses*, was Byrd's personal, most moving tribute to his great master: 'Tallis is dead, and music dies'.

The performance brings out two seemingly contradictory points. One is the importance Byrd gives to the soloist's line. He admires the fine natural voice, so rare, he says, 'as there is not one among a thousand, that hath it …' He'd have appreciated the voice and art of Robin Blaze, whose sympathetic interpretation of Byrd's melodic style, the rests, the patterning of the phrases and the syncopation, is remarkable. The second point is the way in which viols and lute become an integral part of 'a carol for New Yeares Day' – *O God that guides the cheerful sun*. Their imitation of the movements of the voice in the little tableau of the old lady tumbling over on top of the hill, spilling her lapful of skulls, is equally delightful (*An aged dame*). And the sprightly rhythms in *All as a sea* brought home the analogy between human life and life on the ocean wave.

Fantasias – a 6 Nos 2 & 3. Pavan and Galliard a 6,
BE17/15. Gradualia, Vol 1/ii: Miscellaneous and
Office Text – In manus tuas, Domine. Constant
Penelope[a]. Content is rich[a]. My mistress had a little
dog[a]. The Noble famous Queen[a]. O Lord how vain
are all our delights[a]. O you that hear this voice[a].
Psalmes, Sonets and Songs[a] – My mind to me a
kingdom is; O that most rare breast. Truth at the
First[a]. Out of the Orient crystal skies[a]. O Lord, bow
down thine... He that all earthy pleasure scorns[a]
[a]**Emma Kirkby** sop **Fretwork** (Richard Boothby,
Richard Campbell, Wendy Gillespie, Julia Hodgson,
William Hunt, Susanna Pell viols)
Harmonia Mundi HMU90 7383 (75' · DDD · T/t) (F)

Byrd's consort songs reveal a homelier, more personal aspect than his sterner sacred music. Many have texts reflecting the earlier part of his life, the reign of Edward VI, a time of moralising peity: *He that all earthly pleasure scorns* would be an obvious example, or *Content is rich*. But that particular song becomes fast and witty in this performance, almost tongue-in-cheek: it's as if the singer has joining the viols and uses a vocal technique to match their bowing.

Emma Kirkby's versatile performance brings these delightful items to life, and Fretwork fill out the texture with sensitive imitative polyphony. Sometimes the soprano's almost-too-perfect clarity of articulation tends to obscure the subtlety of the musical phrasing: Byrd makes a point of measuring the English text with extreme care, and the gentle cross-rhythms he creates are essential, adding to the life and flow of the composition.

The well-chosen programme is interspersed with five instrumental pieces, three Fantasias for viols, and a delightful pairing and sharing Pavan and Galliard. Fretwork excel here with their vibrant rhythms and gorgeous interplay of parts.

John Cage
American 1912-1992

Cage left Pomona College early to travel in Europe (1930-31), then studied with Cowell in New York (1933-4) and Schoenberg in Los Angeles (1934): his first published compositions, in a rigorous atonal system of his own, date from this period. In 1937 he moved to Seattle to work as a dance accompanist, and there in 1938 he founded a percussion orchestra his music now concerned with filling units of time with ostinatos (First Construction (in Metal), 1939). He also began to use electronic devices (variable-speed turntables in Imaginary Landscape No 1, 1939) and invented the 'prepared piano', placing diverse objects between the strings of a grand piano in order to create an effective percussion orchestra under the control of two hands. He moved to San Francisco in 1939, to Chicago in 1941 and back to New York in 1942, all the time writing music for dance companies (notably for Merce Cunningham), nearly always for prepared piano or percussion ensemble. There were also major concert works for the new instrument: A Book of Music (1944) and Three Dances (1945) for two prepared pianos, and the Sonatas and Interludes (1948) for one.

During this period Cage became interested in Eastern philosophies, especially in Zen, from which he gained a treasuring of non-intention. Working to remove creative choice from composition, he used coin tosses to determine events (Music of Changes for piano, 1951), wrote for 12 radios (Imaginary Landscape No 4, also 1951) and introduced other indeterminate techniques. His 4'33" (1952) has no sound added to that of the environment in which it is performed; the Concert for Piano and Orchestra (1958) is an encyclopedia of indeterminate notations. Yet other works show his growing interest in the theatre of musical performance (Water Music, 1952, for pianist with a variety of non-standard equipment) and in electronics (Imaginary Landscape No 5 for randomly mixed recordings, 1952; Cartridge Music for small sounds amplified in live performance, 1960), culminating in various large-scale events staged as jamborees of haphazardness (HPSCHD

for harpsichords, tapes etc, 1969). The later output is various, including indeterminate works, others fully notated within a very limited range of material, and pieces for natural resources (plants, shells). Cage also appeared widely in Europe and the USA as a lecturer and performer, having an enormous influence on younger musicians and artists; he wrote several books. GROVEmusic

The Seasons

The Seasons. Suite for Toy Piano[a]. Concerto for Prepared Piano and Orchestra[b]. Seventy-Four (Versions A & B)[c]
Margaret Leng Tan [a]toy pf/[b]prepared pf **American Composers Orchestra / Dennis Russell Davies**
ECM New Series 465 140-2 (76' · DDD) Recorded [ab]1999, [c]2000 Ⓕ Ⓞ

This is an enchanting CD, every item a sheer delight. Margaret Leng Tan worked with Cage in the last decade of his life, and her earlier recordings show a special sympathy for Cage's keyboard music. The second of her New Albion CDs included the piano solo version of *The Seasons*, and Cage was honest enough to admit to her that he had help from Virgil Thomson and Lou Harrison in making the orchestral version recorded here. The result is Cage at his most poetic, evoking each of the four seasons in lovely changing colours. There are two realisations of one of the last of what are called Cage's 'Number Pieces', *Seventy-Four*, written for the American Composers Orchestra a few months before his death in 1992. This seamless garment of sustained sound in two overlapping parts is an immensely moving document from a unique human being at the end of his life. Anyone who responds to the spiritual minimalism of Pärt, Górecki or Tavener will understand, especially in these dedicated performances. The *Concerto for Prepared Piano* (1951) takes its rightful place as the major classic for the transformed instrument with orchestra – a status emphasised by this fastidious performance with its delicate sonic tapestry, including discreet radio, all reflecting Cage's absorption with oriental philosophy. Tan has recorded the *Suite for Toy Piano* (1948) before. This time the sound is closer, you can hear her in-breath just before some movements, and we could have done with more precise rhythms. Lou Harrison's orchestration is perfectly in the spirit and makes a fascinating complement – Cage writing memorable tunes! This disc shows that much of Cage has now entered the mainstream and that his music is unique.

Music for Piano

Music for Piano – 1; 2; 3; 4-19; 20; 21-36; 37-52; 53-68; 69-84; 85. Music for ... Two Pianos I/II; Three Pianos; Four Pianos; Five Pianos. Electronic Music for Two Pianos
Steffen Schleiermacher pf

Dabringhaus und Grimm ② MDG613 0784-2
(153' · DDD)   Ⓕ

This set is devoted to the *Music for Piano* series
almost entirely written in the 1950s, which is
neglected and mostly unavailable. You can see
why performers have found these pieces less
attractive. After Cage's crisis year of 1952,
which saw him produce the so-called silent
piece *4'33"*, he was obsessed with removing his
own tastes and desires from his compositions.
Before he became fully committed to the *I
Ching*'s random numbers he marked out imperfections in the manuscript paper he was using as
a way of getting the notes. He said he looked at
his paper and suddenly realised that all the
music was there. This procedure also settled the
density of notes on the page. In the whole series
the performer is left to decide dynamics and
pace in a continuity dominated by single notes.
If this sounds austere, we're reckoning without
Schleiermacher's ingenuity. Cage specifies various types of sound production, apart from the
use of the keys: primarily plucking the strings
from inside or muting them. As in Schleiermacher's prepared piano recordings, the quality of
sound has been carefully considered. A muted
low note or a single plucked string can be marvellously evocative in conjunction with conventionally produced pitches. The ambience of the
prepared piano isn't far away. Further, Schleiermacher avails himself of Cage's provision for
several of these pieces to be played together,
which he does at intervals in the series. Since
we've heard the same pieces solo, the superimposed versions bring back familiar material in a
fascinating way. Fastidiously researched and
performed, Schleiermacher says he's taken the
pieces seriously. In so doing he's begun a new
chapter of virtually unknown Cage.

Sonatas and Interludes

Sonatas and Interludes
Yuji Takahashi prpf
Fylkingen Records FYCD1010 (58' · ADD) Recorded
1965   Ⓕ

Written between February 1946 and March
1948, the *Sonatas and Interludes* were, at the time
of this recording, still quite new, although
already established as core contemporary
repertoire. Even when they were premièred
they were accepted as among the least controversial of Cage's works: the somewhat conservative journal *Musical America* welcomed them as
'quite enchanting'. Cage had devised the prepared piano in 1940. Wanting a percussion
ensemble for a dance piece but having room
only for a piano, he began to transform the
instrument into a substitute gamelan. In the
Sonatas and Interludes he explored the timbral
possibilities further, here and there extending
them by the use of contact mikes.

These pieces, often structured in accordance

with complicated mathematical schemes, leave
little to chance. The preparation of the piano
is a long and meticulous process, and Cage
provided precise directions. Nevertheless,
performers need to make choices, and the
results can be very different.

The benchmark recording by Aleck Karis (on
Bridge) is certainly an impressive, powerful, virtuoso performance. Yet, compared with Takahashi's fresh-sounding reading, with its endlessly subtle gradations and reflective approach,
evoking the image of a musical archaeologist's
brush carefully revealing ancient, magical
inscriptions, Karis sounds too burly, sometimes
seeming to fall prey to the contemporary tendency to confuse aggression with conviction.
Takahashi is a marvellous guide through the
mystery and strange beauty of these appealing
pieces.

Litany for the Whale

Litany for the Whale. Aria No 2. Five. The
Wonderful Widow of Eighteen Springs. Solo No
22. Experiences No 2. Thirty-six Mesostics re and
not re Marcel Duchamp. Aria (arr Hillier). The Year
Begins to Be Ripe
Theatre of Voices (Paul Elliott, Andrea Fullington,
Allison Zelles, Terry Riley vocs Alan Bennett
voc/closed pf Shabda Owens voc/electronics) / **Paul
Hillier** voc
Harmonia Mundi HMU90 7279 (72' · DDD) Texts
included   Ⓜ

This is a landmark for Cage, Paul Hillier's
group and everyone else. Hillier says he's been
interested in Cage for years and here his own
considerable advocacy has turned Cage into a
troubadour of our global village. The Theatre
of Voices' collection jumps right in at the deep
end with *Litany for the Whale* (1980), a 25-
minute monody with two uncannily similar
voices (Alan Bennett and Paul Elliott) using
only five notes in antiphonal phrases. Shut your
eyes and this ritual could almost be Gregorian
chant. The scope narrows to three notes in *The
Wonderful Widow*, where the closed piano part is
slightly subdued, and the same three recur in
Thirty-six Mesostics, spoken by American
minimalist Terry Riley and sung by Hillier.
Cage's *Aria* (1958), for Cathy Berberian, has
been associated with one voice but this realisation for seven voices and electronic sounds is
thoroughly idiomatic. *Experiences* No 2, another
monody to a poem by E E Cummings is beautifully sung, but the precisely notated pauses
aren't always accurate. *Aria* No 2 is a fastidious
mix of extended vocal techniques by Alan Bennett with weather sounds. Cage convinces us of
the musical beauty of rainfall, water and thunder. *Five* is a vocal version of one of Cage's late
number pieces. This type of sustained writing is
ideal for voices and there are meditative qualities in all these performances. The close-micro-
phone breathing in *Solo No 22* is, like everything else here, artistic and well engineered.

Antonio Caldara
Italian c1670-1736

Caldara was a chorister at St Mark's, Venice, and proficient on the viol, cello and keyboard. In the 1690s he began writing operas, oratorios and cantatas; his trio sonatas opp. 1 and 2 (1693, 1699) are his only known instrumental chamber works. He served as maestro di cappella da chiesa e dal teatro to the Duke of Mantua, 1699-1707, and maestro di cappella to Prince Ruspoli in Rome between 1709 and 1716, meanwhile composing for other cities. From 1716 until his death he was vice-Kapellmeister at the Viennese court. He was much favoured there for his dramatic works, cantatas liturgical music and oratorios; latterly he also composed stage works for the Vienna Carnival, for court celebrations and for Salzburg. His output (over 3000 works, almost all vocal) was one of the largest of his generation. His operas and oratorios make him a central figure in the creation of music drama in the tradition of Metastasio, many of whose texts he was the first to set. GROVEmusic

Maddalena ai piedi di Cristo

Maddalena ai piedi di Cristo
Maria-Cristina Kiehr, Rosa Dominguez *sops*
Bernarda Fink *contr* **Andreas Scholl** *counterten*
Gerd Türk *ten* **Ulrich Messthaler** *bass* Schola Cantorum Basiliensis / René Jacobs
Harmonia Mundi ② HMC90 5221/2 (126' · DDD)
Notes, text and translation included ⒻOOO

 Caldara was the most prolific and famous oratorio composer of his day and this one, written around 1700, is wonderfully rich in fresh and attractive invention. Practically devoid of external action, it's dramatically tense and concentrates on the struggle between the forces of good and evil, the sinner Magdalen being urged towards penitence by her sister Martha; the roles of Christ and a Pharisee are considerably smaller. The work opens arrestingly, with an agitated sinfonia followed by the hypnotic aria 'Dormi, o cara': then come another 27 brief *da capo* arias with their associated recitatives – ensembles scarcely exist. But there's no lack of variety: some arias, flanked by an orchestral ritornello, are accompanied only by a continuo instrument; others are furnished with different usages of the five-part strings. René Jacobs furthers the dramatic impact by his pacing; and his casting is flawless. He has the highly effective idea of differentiating the parts of Earthly and Celestial Love by allocating the former to a mezzo and the latter to a countertenor. Both are excellent, but so are all the participants. It seems invidious to single out highlights but outstanding are the aria 'Diletti' for Magdalen (Kiehr) and the succeeding ornate 'Vattene' for Martha (Dominguez) and, even more, two florid arias from Scholl rejoicing in the eventual triumph of good, and two passionately delivered by Fink, of fury by evil at its overthrow. You're urged to acquire this disc.

Cantatas

12 Suonate da camera, Op 2 – in B flat; in A; in F; in G minor. 12 Cantate da camera a voce sola, Op 3[a] – Il Silentio; L'anniversario amoroso; La Fama. Vicino a un rivoletto[a]
Four Nations Ensemble ([a]Jennifer Lane *mez* Ryan Brown, Claire Jolivet *vns* Loretta O'Sullivan *vc*) / **Andrew Appel** *hpd*
ASV Gaudeamus CDGAU347 (68' · DDD) Texts and translations included Ⓕ

This very agreeable disc samples the two chamber genres favoured by Caldara, prolific writer of operas and oratorios in Venice, Rome and Vienna. The sonatas are in the Corelli mould of *sonate da camera*, but half a generation on – more regular in their patterns, rather perkier in their manner, their counterpoint always beautifully dovetailed. The voice behind them isn't especially original, but the music is always pleasingly and elegantly formed. Four of the 12 sonatas of Op 2 are recorded here, including the last of the set, which in the Corelli tradition is an extended ground-bass movement, carried off with a lot of ingenuity. There's wit, too, in some of these pieces: try for example the sparkling little Corrente from No 8. The Four Nations Ensemble play them with real feeling for the idiom as well as impeccable technique, and the recorded sound is bright and true.

It's principally as a vocal composer that Caldara is known, and Jennifer Lane, possessor of a full and warmly musical voice, makes the most of his graceful and shapely lines while always giving due weight and sense to the words. There's plenty of appealing, if again not specially distinctive, music in the three cantatas here, but the gem is *Vicino a un rivoletto*, where the first aria has an *obbligato* for violin and the second one for cello, which, exquisitely played by Loretta O'Sullivan, unmistakably represents the heart swooning with pain, and coupled with Lane's singing does so to very moving effect.

Joseph Canteloube
French 1879-1957

Canteloube studied with d'Indy at the Schola Cantorum and collected and arranged folksongs from throughout France, especially from his native province (four volumes of Chants d'Auvergne for voice and orchestra, 1923-30). He also wrote two operas and other works. GROVEmusic

Chants d'Auvergne

Canteloube Chants d'Auvergne – La pastoura als camps; Baïlèro; L'io de rotso; Ound' onorèn gorda; Obal, din lou Limouzi; Pastourelle; L'Antouèno; La pastrouletta è lo chibaliè; La delïssádo; N'aï pas iéu de mio; Lo calhé; Lo fiolaïré; Passo pel prat; Lou boussu; Brezairola; Maluros qu'o uno fenno.

Jou l'pount d'o Mirabel; Oï, ayaï; Pour l'enfant;
Chut, chut; Pastorale; Lou coucut; Postouro sé
tu m'aymo; Quand z-éyro petituono; Té, l'co tèl;
Uno jionto postouro; Hél beyla-z-y-dau fél;
Obal, din lo combuèlo; Là-haut, sur le rocher;
Lou diziou bé **Villa-Lobos** Bachianas brasileiras
No 5
Dame Kiri Te Kanawa sop **English Chamber
Orchestra / Jeffrey Tate**
Double Decca ② 444 995-2DF2 (111' · DDD)
Recorded 1982-3. Notes, text and translation
included   Ⓜ

Te Kanawa's richly sensuous approach to these
delightful songs is very seductive, especially
when the accompaniments by Jeffrey Tate and
the ECO are so warmly supportive and the
sound so opulent. Her account of the most
famous number, 'Baïlèro', must be the most
relaxed on record, yet she sustains its repetitions
with a sensuous, gentle beauty of line, supported by lovely wind playing from the orchestra which seems to float in the air. There's a resonance given to the sound, which means that
certain of the brighter, more obviously folksy
numbers, lose a little of their rustic sharpness.
However, the overall effect is very appealing,
particularly when her voice (recorded in the
early 1980s) is so young and fresh. As an encore
we are offered the Villa-Lobos *Bachianas brasileiras* No 5, an 'Aria' for soprano and cellos. She
sings this in Portuguese and the result is ravishing, almost decadent at its softly intoned
reprise. An enticing disc.

Canteloube Chants d'Auvergne, Volume 2 – La
pastoura als camps; Baïlèro; L'ïo dè rotso; Ound'
onorèn gorda; Obal, din lou Limouzi; L'Antouèno; La
pastrouletta è lo chibaliè; N'aï pas iéu de mio; Lo
calhé; Maluros qu'o uno fenno; Pour l'enfant; Quand
z-éyro petituono; Hél beyla-z-y-dau fél; Là-haut, sur
le rocher; Lou diziou bé **Emmanuel** Chansons
bourguignonnes du Pays de Beaune, Op 15 – Quand
j'ai sôti de mon villaige; Il était une fille, une fille
d'honneur; Le pommier d'Août; Noël; Complainte
de Notre Dame; Aidieu, bargeire!
Dawn Upshaw sop **Orchestra of the Opéra de
Lyon / Kent Nagano**
Erato 0630-17577-2 (63' · DDD) Texts and translations
included   ⒻⓄ

Chants d'Auvergne – Baïlèro; L'ïo dè rotso; Ound'
onorèn gorda; Obal, din lou Limouzi; L'Antouèno; La
delïssádo; N'aï pas iéu de mio; Lo calhé; Lo fiolaïré;
Passo pel prat; Brezairola; Oï, ayaï; Pour l'enfant;
Chut, chut; Lou coucut; Tè, l'co, tè!; Uno jionto
postouro; La pastoura als camps; Pastourelle; La
pastrouletta è lo chibaliè; Lou boussu; Malurous qu'o
uno fenno; Jou l'pount d'o Mirabel; Pastorale
Frederica von Stade mez **Royal Philharmonic
Orchestra / Antonio de Almeida**
Sony Classical Essential Classics SBK63063
(73' · DDD) Recorded 1980s   Ⓑ

Maurice Emmanuel's arrangements of his local
Burgundian folk-songs are antecedents to what

Canteloube was to do a decade or two later.
This is the second disc that Dawn Upshaw has
devoted primarily to Canteloube's Songs of the
Auvergne. Upshaw and Nagano seem to have
taken a conscious decision to re-establish a link
with the music's folk texts and banish as much
sentimentality as they can. Their 'Baïlèro' is
keenly dramatised and refuses to wallow. The
simple 'Pour l'enfant' is bright-eyed with detail;
and 'L'ïo dè rotso' is given a more sarcastic edge
than usual. In general, there's a grittiness here
that sets it apart from most recordings, with
Upshaw's determination to put across the words
and Nagano's restraint in the orchestra, encouraging cool strings to let the bright Lyon wind
section pipe through clearly. The Sony selection with Frederica von Stade is an old friend.
Two sets of recordings have been combined and
all the best-known songs are here in more conventional performances than are found on the
Erato disc. Von Stade varies her tone according
to the sense of each song, but the overall mood
is less sharp, more comfortable if you like, than
with Upshaw. The RPO sounds a lot richer than
its Lyon counterpart and, at slower speeds,
Antonio de Almeida provides big-orchestra
accompaniments, where Nagano prefers chamber-music detail. You'll probably find that the
consoling romanticism of the Songs of the
Auvergne on this tried-and-trusted disc is more
what you had in mind.

Chants d'Auvergne – La pastoura als camps; Baïlèro;
L'ïo dè rotso; Ound' onorèn gorda; O bal, din lou
Limousi; Pastourelle; L'Antouèno; La delïssádo; N'aï
pas iéu de mïo; Lo calhé; Passo pel prat; Lou boussu;
Brezairola; Malurous qu'o uno Fenno; Jou l'pount
d'o Mirabel; Oï, ayaï; Lou coucut; Quand z-èyro
petituono; Uno jionto postouro; Là-haut, sur le
rocher; Lou diziou bé
Véronique Gens sop **Lille National Orchestra /
Jean-Claude Casadesus**
Naxos 8 557491 (62' · DDD · T/t)   ⒮Ⓞ

Each decade finds its favourite soloist for the
Chants d'Auvergne: in the 1960s it was Natania
Devrath, the 70s had Victoria de los Angeles,
the 80s Kiri Te Kanawa, the 90s Dawn Upshaw.
They weren't French, whereas Véronique Gens
is quite at home in the dialect, as she comes
from the Auvergne. Her singing is smooth and
delicate, with plenty of body in the tone for
some of the earthier moments.
    In all, five volumes of Auvergne songs were
published between 1923-54. Each singer naturally includes 'Baïlèro', the most famous, and
Gens doesn't disappoint in this. The 20 other
songs range from the sad 'Uno jionto postouro',
the lament of the girl whose lover has deserted
her, to 'Malurous qu'o ono Fenno', the jaunty
exposé of unhappy couples.
    Jean-Claude Casadesus and the Lille Orches-
tra bring out all the little details in the score,
such as the lovely woodwind solos that link the
three Bourrées. Perhaps this will become the
interpretation for the present decade.

Elliott Carter
American b1908

Carter studied at Harvard (1926-32), at the Ecole Normale de Musique in Paris (1932-5) and privately with Boulanger. Back in the USA he worked as musical director of Ballet Caravan (until 1940) and as a teacher. From boyhood he had been acquainted with the music of Schoenberg, Varèse, Ives and others, but for the moment his works leaned much more towards Stravinsky and Hindemith: they included the ballets Pocahontas (1939) and The Minotaur (1947), the Symphony No 1 (1942) and Holiday Overture (1944). However, in his Piano Sonata (1946) he began to work from the interval content of particular chords, and inevitably to loosen the hold of tonality. The development was taken further in the Cello Sonata (1948), already characteristic of his later style in that the instruments have distinct roles. A period of withdrawal led to the First Quartet (1951), a work of complex rhythmic interplay, long-ranging atonal melody and unusual form, the 'movements' being out of step with the given breaks in the musical continuity: effectively it is a single unfolding of 40 minutes' duration. It was followed by exclusively instrumental works of similar complexity, activity and energy, including the Variations for orchestra (1955), the Second Quartet (1959), the Double Concerto for harpsichord and piano, each with its own chamber orchestra (1961), the Piano Concerto (1965), the Concerto for Orchestra (1969), the Third Quartet (1971) and the Brass Quintet (1974). At that point Carter returned to vocal composition for a triptych of works for soloist and ensemble: A Mirror on which to Dwell (1975), Syringa (1978) and In Sleep, in Thunder (1981), with words by Elizabeth Bishop, John Ashbery and Robert Lowell respectively. But he has also continued the output of large instrumental movements with A Symphony of Three Orchestras (1976), the piano solo Night Fantasies (1980), the Triple Duo (1983) and Penthode for small orchestra (1985). His String Quartet No 4 (1986) is in a simpler style.
GROVEmusic

Piano Concerto

Piano Concerto. Concerto for Orchestra. Three Occasions
Ursula Oppens pf **South West German Radio Symphony Orchestra / Michael Gielen**
Arte Nova Classics 74321 27773-2 (62' · DDD)
Recorded 1992   Ⓢ

Oppens and Gielen have collaborated in a recording of the Piano Concerto before, and their long familiarity with the work brings an air of confidence to an account which is admirable in its feeling for the essential character as well as the formal logic of a score whose shoals of notes will defeat all but the most dedicated of interpreters. Gielen's ability to bring a convincing sense of shape and a persuasive expressive profile to complex music is no less apparent in an admirable reading of the *Concerto for Orchestra*. Again and again, the solo lines marked in the score are brought out, although the recording

isn't able to give ideal clarity to the highly detailed string writing (a compositional problem, perhaps). But Gielen's is as compelling a presentation of this turbulent yet strangely affirmative music as one could hope to hear.

In *Three Occasions* Gielen is weighty, perhaps to excess in the often delicate third piece. Nevertheless, the interpretation is full of character, and the orchestra confirms its excellence in this demanding repertory. Recommended, despite the inadequate insert-notes.

Symphonia

Symphonia: sum fluxae pretium speia. Clarinet Concerto[b]
[b]**Michael Collins** cl [a]**BBC Symphony Orchestra,** [b]**London Sinfonietta / Oliver Knussen**
DG 20/21 459 660-2GH (64' · DDD)   ⓟ❶❶❶

 Carter's three-movement *Symphonia* (1993-6) seems certain to provide the crowning glory to his orchestral output, just as his recent chamber opera *What Next?* should prove the summit of his vocal works. Nevertheless, *Symphonia*'s 45 minutes aren't a mere distillation of the techniques and moods developed over the previous half-century or so, and while it isn't radically innovative it has plenty of challenges to offer. The 'I' of *Symphonia*'s subtitle – 'I am the child of flowing hope' – is a 'charming, wanton, inconstant, beautiful, gleaming and noble' bubble, the subject of Richard Crashaw's extraordinary Latin poem *Bulla*. Carter transforms this image into a musical celebration of modernist instability and unpredictability: but in so doing he makes a permanent statement in a masterwork which deserves to endure, and to be heard and reheard. In Knussen's supremely authoritative interpretation, the sound quality has been meticulously managed in order to help the listener trace those gradually emerging and steadily unfolding arcs of eloquent melody. It takes time to appreciate how *Symphonia*'s extraordinary variety of pace contributes to the music's melodic and harmonic coherence. The Clarinet Concerto, written a short time later, is more immediately approachable, an exuberant tribute to Boulez's seminal *Domaines* in the way it moves the soloist around in dialogue with various well-contrasted instrumental groups. This performance will leave you breathless with admiration, not only for Carter's inventiveness but also for the brilliance with which the score is realised by these dedicated artists.

Francesco Cavalli
Italian 1602-1676

Cavalli received musical instruction from his father, GB Caletti, and probably sang in Crema Cathedral choir. In 1616 the governor, Federico Cavalli, persuaded Caletti to allow him to take Francesco to

Venice, where the boy (who adopted his patron's name) joined the cappella of St Mark's as a soprano and later tenor. In 1630 Cavalli made an advantageous marriage with a Venetian widow, Maria Sozomeno, and in 1639 he was appointed second organist at St Mark's. He began his opera career at the Teatro San Cassiano and in the 1650s was also active in other Venetian theatres and other Italian cities.

In 1660-62 Cavalli was in Paris, where his celebratory opera, Ercole amante, was played to a less than appreciative audience; when he returned to Venice he vowed never to work for the theatre again. In the event he composed six more operas, but his life centred more on St Mark's and in 1668 he succeeded Rovetta as its maestro di cappella. His wife had died in 1652; they had no children.

The modest quantity of Cavalli's extant sacred music is probably only a small part of a continuous production throughout his career. Most of it follows in the tradition of large concerted works for St Mark's, best represented by the Gabrielis and Monteverdi. The Musiche sacrae (1656) includes a mass and Magnificat for double choir with instruments as well as several motets, and the Vesperi (1675) consists of three Vespers services in eight parts with continuo. A requiem and another Magnificat are among other sacred pieces published during Cavalli's lifetime. He also left secular arias and cantatas, but his most important works were the nearly 30 operas composed for Venetian theatres. They run from the tentative beginnings of public opera to the establishment of Venice as the chief centre of Italian opera, and offer the only continuous view of Venetian operatic style over two decades. Modern revivals, notably of Didone, Ormindo, Calisto and Egisto, have shown Cavalli to be the most important opera composer in the quarter-century after Monteverdi.

GROVEmusic

Statira, Principessa di Persia

Statira, Principessa di Persia
Roberta Invernizzi sop Statira **Dionisia di Vico** mez Cloridaspe **Maria Ercolano** sop Ermosilla, Usimano **Giuseppe de Vittorio** ten Elissena **Giuseppe Naviglio** bass Plutone, Nicarico, Dario **Maria Grazia Schiavo** sop Floralba **Daniela del Monaco** contr Brimonte **Rosario Totaro** ten Vaffrino **Roberta Andalò** sop Maga, Eurillo **Stefano di Fraia** ten Marcurio, Brisante **Valentina Varriale** sop Messo **Cappella de' Turchini / Antonio Florio**
Opus 111 ② OP30382 (139' · DDD) Notes, libretto and translation included   Ⓕ

The plot of *Statira*, first produced in Venice in 1656, is a convoluted mixture of supernatural hatred and royal love triangles. It's given here in a revised form that includes comic scenes probably inserted for a performance at Naples ten years later as part of the festivities celebrating the coronation of King Philip IV of Spain. The Cappella de' Turchini present a refined performance. The prominent continuo section juggle the busy demands of the music with seeming ease. *Ritornelli* are consistently infectious and irresistibly dance-like. The playing is generally

first class, exemplified by the mournful yet tasteful string playing in Ermosilla's aria 'Menfi, mia Patria, Regno'.

There are few moments of intense drama in an opera that seems to have been devised primarily as entertainment rather than a profound experience. The final chorus declares that 'After all sufferings, all joy comes at last', but the preceding drama doesn't present a credible exploration of suffering. It's only when the plot grows more desperate in Act 3 that *Statira* becomes notably riveting, but there are delectable moments to enjoy. During the prologue the band plays beautifully, while a malcontent sorceress plots revenge on the Arabian King Cloridaspe with caustic glee. Meanwhile, the king has fallen in love with Statira, and their love is subsequently challenged and threatened before all ends happily. Roberta Invernizzi in the title-role is more muscular than most 'early music' sopranos, but lacks nothing in finesse and clarity in the rapturous night scene that opens the opera. The outstanding aria of the recording is Invernizzi's exuberantly heroic 'La tromba orgogliosa', although her lament 'Lassa che fo' is an equally potent moment.

The opera's plenteous comic scenes are hammed up, but the plain-speaking servant characters have dated worse than the conventional *opera seria* lovers that monopolise the best arias. Mountains of recitative are delivered with sparkle, and Antonio Florio judges each scene effectively. The quality of the recording is indisputable, and Opus 111 deserves immense credit for continuing to reveal fascinating lesser-known repertoire. This recording is an indispensable indication of operatic style in the under-represented period between Monteverdi and Handel, and those interested in buying it shouldn't hesitate.

Emmanuel Chabrier   French 1841-1894

Chabrier was trained as a lawyer and worked in the Ministry of the Interior until 1880, meanwhile developing his talents as a pianist and improviser, studying composition, publishing piano pieces and writing light stage works. His friends included Verlaine, Manet, Fauré and Chausson, who encouraged his admiration for Wagner. He produced several imaginative operas, among which the Wagnerian Gwendoline (1885) and the graceful opéra comique Le roi malgré lui (1887) were favourably received in Germany. He is best known for his sparkling orchestral rhapsody España (1883), but his natural talent for the lyric, the comic and the colourful is most apparent in his piano works, notably the Impromptu (1873), the ten Pièces pittoresques (1881), the Bourrée fantasque (1891) and the Valses romantiques (1883); they show free treatment of dissonance, modality, bold harmonic contrasts, rhythmic verve and dynamic inventiveness, and inspired subsequent generations of French composers, particularly Ravel.

GROVEmusic

Suite pastorale

Suite pastorale. Habanera. España. Larghetto.
Prélude pastoral. Joyeuse marche. Gwendoline –
Overture. Le roi malgré lui – Fête polonaise
Ronald Janezic vn **Vienna Philharmonic Orchestra
/ Sir John Eliot Gardiner**
DG 447 751-2GH (66' · DDD) Ⓕ**OO**

Gardiner enters territory previously occupied
by Paul Paray and the Detroit Symphony with
some superbly responsive playing by the Vienna
Philharmonic and a first-class recording that,
while warm, leaves all detail clear, and sweeps
the board with a set of outstanding, exuberant
performances. The early *Larghetto* for horn and
orchestra is the least characteristic of the composer, being a long-breathed, lyrical piece in the
Romantic tradition: it's played with quiet mastery by Ronald Janezic. But the *Suite pastorale* of
five years later is quintessential Chabrier.
Poulenc described the 'Idylle' as being as heady
as your first kiss; and light-footed as the 'Danse
villageoise' is here, with telling cross-accents
and a splendidly rowdy end. *España*, that ever-
fresh centrepiece, is enormously ebullient; but
for all its verve, its internal balance is excellent
throughout, the brass brilliant but never drowning out the ornamental subsidiary phrases. In
contrast the *Habanera* is suitably languorous.
The Overture to *Gwendoline* – the nearest
Chabrier came to Wagnerism – has you cling-
ing to the edge of your seat in the agitated
urgency of the opening and the blazing ferocity
of its final pages; Gardiner brings well-managed
rubato to the noisy orgy of the *Roi malgré lui*
scene. Judging by the speed at which he takes it,
he seems to have had French *chasseurs* in mind
for the brash *Joyeuse marche*, which the orchestra
obviously enjoyed. Altogether an exhilarating
disc.

Cécile Chaminade   French 1857-1944

*Chaminade studied privately with Godard and other
Conservatoire teachers and gave her first public concert at 18. She wrote several major works in the
1880s, including an orchestral suite, a symphonie
dramatique Les amazones, a Concertstück for piano
and orchestra and an opéra comique; thereafter she
wrote little besides piano pieces and songs, music of
considerable charm, perhaps influenced by what was
expected of a woman composer. She toured widely,
several times in England (from 1892) and in the
USA (1908).*   **GROVE**music

Songs

Mots d'amour

Alleluia[a]. L'amour captif[a]. L'anneau d'argent[a].
Attente (Au pays de Provence)[a]. Auprès de ma mie[a].
Bonne humeur[a]. Capriccio, Op 18[b]. Chanson triste[a].
Danse païenne, Op 158[c]. Ecrin[a]. Espoir[a]. L'Eté[a].
Je voudrais[a]. La lune paresseuse[a]. Malgré nous[a].
Ma première lettre[a]. Menuet[a]. Mignonne[a].

Nice-la-belle[a]. Mots d'amour[a]. Pas des cymbales,
Op 36 No 2[c]. Rondeau, Op 97[b]. Ronde d'amour[a].
Sérénade espagnole, Op 150[b]. Si j'étais jardinier[a].
Sombrero[a]. Valse carnavalesque, Op 73[c]. Viens!
mon bien-aimé![a]. Villanella. Voisinage[a]
[a]**Anne Sofie von Otter** mez [b]**Nils-Erik Sparf** vn
Bengt Forsberg, [c]**Peter Jablonski** pfs
DG Gramophone Awards Collection 476 7110
(76' · DDD) Ⓜ**OOO**

Here is something to delight all but the
most misanthropic listeners. Although
Cécile Chaminade's piano music has
never been entirely neglected, her songs have
remained firmly locked away. Chaminade composed over 125 *mélodies* at the height of her fame
between 1890 and 1910; she was equally popular as a pianist and composer, in 1907 giving a
25-concert tour in the USA.
Von Otter and Forsberg open with one of
Chaminade's most popular songs, *Ronde
d'amour*. It's also one of the very few to have
been recorded before – by the 80-year-old
Lucien Fugère in 1928. He sings it more as a
folksong, but von Otter tilts it towards the theatre, taking it very fast and with some lovely
playful half-spoken effects. *La lune paresseuse*
that follows, with a beautiful rippling melody in
the accompaniment, shows Chaminade in a
more ecstatic vein, the singer offering a prayer
to the moon. The recital moves back and forth
between the romantic, the exotic and the whimsical. In the hands and the voice of lesser artists,
Chaminade's songs might seem hoplessly dated,
but von Otter and Forsberg so obviously relish
the elegant vocal lines and the really imaginative
(and demanding) piano parts.
A totally entrancing CD from two of the
greatest explorers of repertory.

Marc-Antoine Charpentier   French 1643-1704

*Charpentier studied in Rome, probably with Caris-
simi, whose oratorios he introduced into France. On
his return to Paris he was employed as composer and
singer by the Duchess of Guise and also collaborated
with Molière in the theatre. In the early 1680s he
entered the service of the grand dauphin, for which
Louis XIV granted him a pension in 1683, and he
was for a time music teacher to Philippe, Duke of
Chartres (later Duke of Orleans and Regent of
France). Perhaps also in the 1680s Charpentier
became attached to the Jesuit church of St Louis in
Paris, and from 1698 until his death he held the
important post of maître de musique of the Saint-
Chapelle, for which he wrote some of his most
impressive works.*
*Charpentier's church music was based initially on
mid-century Italian models, but soon incorporated
French modes of expression – the 'official' grandeur
of the grand motet; the declamatory manner of the
court air and Lullian récit; the 'popular' simplicity of
noëls; and an often elaborately ornamented melodic*

line. Charpentier was the only Frenchman of his time to write oratorios of any quality. His theatre compositions are even more indebted to French models, and he was an important composer of airs sérieux and airs à boire.   GROVEmusic

Concert pour quatre violes, H545

Concert pour quatre parties de violes, H545.   **P**
Il faut rire et chanter: Dispute de bergers, H484.
La pierre philosophale, H501. Airs – Ah! Qu'ils sont courts les beaux jours, H442. Ah qu'on est malheureux, H443. Ah, laissez-moi rêver, H441. Auprès du feu l'on fait l'amour, H446. Ayant bu du vin claret, H447. Charmantes fleurs naissez, H449b. En vain rivaux assidus, H452. Fenchon, la gentile Fenchon, H454. Non, non je ne l'aime plus, H455. Quoi! Je ne verrai plus, H461. Quoi! rien ne peut vous arrêter, H462. Rentrez, trop indescrets soupirs, H464. Sans frayeur dans ce bois – Chaconne, H467. Tristes déserts, sombre retraîte, H469
Sophie Daneman, Adèle Eikenes, Patricia Petibon sops **Paul Agnew, Andrew Sinclair, François Piolino** tens **David le Monnier** bar **Alan Ewing** bass **Ensemble Orlando Gibbons; Les Arts Florissants / William Christie**
Erato 3984-25485-2 (74' · DDD) Texts and translations included   Ⓟ**O**

Here is a delightfully constructed programme, of which only the tenderly expressive *Concert pour quatre parties de violes* has made previous appearances on disc. But it's the way in which William Christie has dispersed its six movements irregularly within a longer sequence of mainly continuo airs for one and two solo voices that lends particular charm to the programme, ensuring at the same time a consistently high and diverting musical interest. The four-strand string *Concert* is a piece of outstanding merit, beautifully crafted and affectingly expressive. Ensemble Orlando Gibbons play with tonal warmth, rhythmic suppleness and insight into the subtle inflective nuances present in each and every section of the piece. The texture is light and transparent, which it needs to be in order to disclose the sheer beauty of the harmonies and phrase contours. After the *Concert* there are the *airs sérieux*, all but one of which are supported solely by continuo, that most readily engage your interest.

The odd one out is *Charmantes fleurs naissez* for two sopranos and, in this performance, sporting two recorders. It's a ravishing piece, sung with sensibility by Sophie Daneman and Adèle Eikenes. Paul Agnew has four solo airs which he sings with declamatory elegance and a feeling for their expressive intensity.

La pierre philosophale is a comedy by Thomas Corneille and Donneau de Visée, for which Charpentier provided music for one of its five acts. The story-line is Indian paper-thin, but Charpentier's score is characteristically animated and entertaining. Christie brings it to life with all his customary flair and the performance is captivating from start to finish. In short, this disc is a winner.

Mass, H1

Mass, H1. Te Deum, H147. Precatio pro filio regis, **P**
H166. Panis quem ego dabo, H275. Canticum Zachariae, H345, 'Benedictus Dominus Deus'
Le Concert Spirituel / Hervé Niquet ˙
Naxos 8 553175 (57' · DDD) Texts and translations included   Ⓢ

This early Mass is a beautiful piece, intimately scored for voices with two melody instruments and continuo. The Mass is harmonically richly inventive with passages of vivid word-painting. Taken as a whole the work is generously endowed with subtle inflexions, a pervasive element of contemplation, and effectively varied rhythmic juxtapositions which enliven the text and hold our attention.

The *Te Deum*, for four soloists, four-part choir and *colla parte* instruments, isn't that one for which Charpentier is renowned but a smaller, later piece belonging to the last years of his life. Modest in scale it may be but musically it's impressive and emotionally satisfying. The choir and instrumentalists of Le Concert Spirituel are on their usual lively form. Some of the solo vocal contributions are more focused than others but the choir maintains a high standard of vocal blend and secure intonation. The recorded sound is very good indeed and Niquet directs with stylistic assurance.

Messe pour les trépassés, H2

Messe en la mémoire d'un prince   **P**
Charpentier Messe pour les trépassés, H2[a]. Motet pour les trépassés, H311[b]. Miserere mei , H193[b]
L Couperin Les carillons de Paris[c] **Roberday** Fugue et Caprice VIII[c]
[a]**Caroline Pelon** sop [a]**Pascal Bertin** counterten [a]**Hans Jörg Mammel** ten [a]**Jean-Claude Sarragosse** bass [c]**Jean-Marc Aymes** org [ab]**Namur Chamber Choir,** [ab]**Ensemble La Fenice / Jean Tubéry** rec
Virgin Classics Veritas 545394-2 (63' · DDD) Texts and translations included   Ⓕ

This recording is the product of a close and fruitful collaboration between scholars (including the late Jean Lionnet, Jean Duron and Catherine Cessac) and performers. Together they have given us a deeply moving requiem service that reflects the latest thinking in period style. The performances are simple and dignified, like a rather exquisite string of pearls. The succession of musical forms, textures, instruments and voices is breathtaking and complex. Charpentier created individual musical architectural structures to enhance the individual lines of the Latin texts, exploiting seemingly endless combinations of voices (apparently eight) and instruments. To complete the sense of a religious occasion, church bells are rung at the beginning, and organ music by Charpentier's distinguished contemporaries, Louis Couperin and François Roberday, has been interleaved. The performances suit the notional occasion, and so while – appropriately – no one voice stands out among the solo singers, as a choir they produce strong clean lines, consistently in tune. The finely tuned continuo instrumentation and the added ornamentation are stunning refinements worthy of a jeweller.

Te Deum, H146

Te Deum, H146. Dixit Dominus, H202. Domine salvum fac regem, H291. In honorem S Ludovici Regis Galliae canticum, H365. Marches pour les trompettes, H547
Le Concert Spirituel / Hervé Niquet
Glossa GCD921603 (55' · DDD)   Ⓕ**O**

Hervé Niquet and his ensemble are old hands at the French *grand motet* for choir and instruments by now, and Charpentier in particular has been well served by them. Here they move into familiar ground in the form of the best-known of his *Te Deum* settings, prefaced by two scurrying, delightful little marches and coupled with three motets not currently available elsewhere. These last should be good enough reason to acquire the disc, but even for those who have a *Te Deum* or two in their collection already, Niquet's reading of it is another. With a choir of 12 and a one-to-a-part band, this is as limpid and lithe a performance of the piece as you're likely to hear. Niquet chooses some fleet tempos, but also injects the music with a catchy rhythmic lilt and an attention to declamatory detail that constantly keeps the music alive. And when a smoother arch is required, as in the choral soprano setting of 'te ergo quaesumus', he can touch the heart too. Good recorded sound and balance make this a disc to have.

Vesper psalms / Magnificat, H72

Charpentier Beatus vir, H221. Laudate pueri, H149. Laetatus sum, H216. Nisi Dominus, H150. Lauda Jerusalem, H210. Ave maris stella, H60. Magnificat, H72. Salve regina, H24 **Nivers** Antiphonarium Monasticum, Antiennes I-VI
Le Concert Spirituel / Hervé Niquet
Naxos 8 553174 (61' · DDD) Texts and translations included   Ⓢ

This release offers a liturgical reconstruction of the Vespers office. The five Vesper psalms and *Magnificat* belong to different periods in Charpentier's life and the six antiphons are by his organist-composer contemporary, Nivers. The reconstruction works well and Le Concert Spirituel, under Hervé Niquet, demonstrates its rapport with Charpentier's music. The vocal sound is fresh and the wide range of musical *Affekt* shows off a greater diversity of tonal colour. Tenors and basses incline towards a roughness of timbre here and there yet, overall, the bright and full-blooded choral sound is pleasing and vital. Some may find the recording balance of the psalms and canticle a fraction too

close, creating the atmosphere of a drawing-room Vespers rather than one in more spacious, ecclesiastical surroundings. The antiphons fare much better in this respect, having a deeper aural perspective. This is a richly rewarding programme of music which never disappoints.

Leçons de Ténèbres du Vendredi Saint

Leçons de Ténèbres de la Semaine Sainte de 1692 – H135; H136; H137. Méditations pour le Carême – H380; H381; H386; H387; H388
Thibaut Lenaerts, Cyril Auvity countertens **Pierre Evreux, Ian Honeyman** tens **Alain Buet, Ronan Nédélec** bars **Le Concert Spirituel / Hervé Niquet**
Glossa GCD921604 (59' · DDD) Notes, texts and translations included   Ⓕ

Messe de Monsieur de Mauroy, H6
Marie-Louise Duthoit, Claire Gouton sops **Serge Goubiod** counterten **Pierre Evreux** ten **Christophe Sam** bass **Le Concert Spirituel / Hervé Niquet**
Glossa GCD921602 (66' · DDD) Notes, texts and translations included   Ⓕ

It almost goes without saying that a Hervé Niquet recording of Charpentier is going to be a thing of beauty. Whether it's in the long build-up to the top of the grand arch that's the opening *Kyrie* of the *Messe de Monsieur de Mauroy*, or the ardent twists and dissonances with which the first of the *Leçons de Ténèbres* announces itself, it only takes a few moments for Niquet's expert team of singers and instrumentalists to draw us into the achingly expressive world of 17th-century France.

Composed around 1691, this is the longest of his 11 Masses, and its many sections seem to move effortlessly from one to another, creating a constantly shifting range of subtle responses to text – some sweet, some stirring, some lilting and some weighty – while successfully maintaining the work's continuity.

Charpentier composed 31 incomplete sets of *Leçons de Ténèbres*, those intense settings of the Lamentations of Jeremiah that were so popular in Holy Week in France during the mid-Baroque period, and which produced some of its most ravishing musical moments. Scored for six male voices, strings, flutes and continuo, this set moves between straightforward declamation and music of increasing harmonic and dramatic urgency to present a striking evocation of the desolation of the ruined Jerusalem.

These performances are exquisitely judged, showing an unerring feel for the music's expressive ebb and flow. Two releases of thorough desirability.

Dialogus inter angelum et pastores, H406

Dialogus inter angelum et pastores, H406[a]. Mors Ⓟ Saülis et Jonathae, 'Cum essent congregata ad praelium', H403[b]. Sacrificium Abrahae, H402[c]
[bc]**Jaël Azzaretti**, [bc]**Marie-Louise Duthoit** sops

Gérard Lesne, bcBenjamin Clee countertens Jean-
François Novelli, bcNicholas Bauchau tens Ronan
Nédélec, bcRaimonds Spogis basses Il Seminario
Musicale / Gérard Lesne
Naïve Astrée E8821 (68' · DDD)   Ⓕ O

French countertenor Gérard Lesne and Il Seminario Musicale manage to bring Charpentier's
three miniature oratorios vividly to life. The
works employ narrators – sometimes a solo
voice, sometimes the chorus – in a highly dramatic series of instrumental and vocal movements, carefully tinged with suspensions and
chromatic inflections. Both *Mors Saülis et
Jonathae* and *Sacrificium Abrahae* rely on tightly
constructed dialogues cast in recitative. Lesne
intensifies the characterisation by associating
particular combinations of continuo instruments and organ stops with each of the inter-
locutors. Melodic, melismatic movements are
reserved for moments of powerful emotion, as
when David weeps for his brother Saül.

Although Il Seminario Musicale take pride in
performing without a conductor, they wouldn't
produce the precision of ensemble so evident in
this recording but for the vigilance of the continuo players. The absence of a principal interpreter is audible and here, as in less complex
chamber music, the effect is highly desirable.
Lesne delivers a string of inspiring performances in a raft of roles – as do Jean-François
Novelli as David and Abraham and the bass Raimonds Spogis as Samuel. This recording should
definitely top your shopping list.

Christmas Music

Canticum in nativitatem Domini, 'Usquequo avertis',
H416. Dialogus inter angelos et pastores Judeae in
nativitatem Domini, H420. Noël: un flambeau,
Janette, Isabelle!, H460c
Aradia Ensemble / Kevin Mallon
Naxos 8 557036 (62' · DDD)   Ⓢ O

Perhaps few composers have produced as much
beautiful Christmas music as Charpentier. Both
oratorios recorded here are generously laid out
for soloists, chorus and a sweet-toned, atmospherically nocturnal ensemble of recorders and
strings, a grand motet-style line-up which
Charpentier uses to create a work with clear
dramatic pretensions. Thus, in addition to the
ravishing choral writing of the kind at which
Charpentier excelled, each oratorio has a gentle
instrumental number to represent night (an
archetype taken straight from the dreamy *som-
meils* of French Baroque opera), followed by a
tootly little dance-chorus to represent the
'awakening of the shepherds', and later on a
perky march to send them off to Bethlehem. In
this way Charpentier's faultless music brings
together his own contemporary world and that
of the New Testament in an utterly beguiling
mixture of richness and simplicity.

The Toronto-based Aradia Ensemble are
superbly attuned to the music's atmosphere.

Perhaps an extra ounce of vocal refinement
could have been drawn from the choir, but more
important is that these performances show an
unfailing appreciation of style, taste and sheer
beauty of sound. The result is a Christmas treat
for us all.

Actéon, H481

Actéon   Ⓟ
Dominique Visse counterten Actéon **Agnès Mellon**
sop Diane **Guillemette Laurens** mez Junon **Jill
Feldman** sop Arthébuze **Françoise Paut** sop Hyale
Les Arts Florissants Vocal Ensemble
La Comtesse d'Escarbagnas/Le Mariage Forcé, H494
– Ouverture
Michel Laplénie ten **Philippe Cantor** ten
Les Arts Florissants Ensemble / William Christie
Harmonia Mundi Musique d'abord HMA195 1095
(47' · ADD) Recorded 1981   Ⓑ OOO

Charpentier's little vignette opera is an
astonishingly rich score containing
most, if not all, the ingredients of a
tragédie-lyrique. There's a profusion of fine choruses and dances but an overture which departs
somewhat from the standard Lullian pattern.
Actéon is made up of six well-contrasted short
scenes. The first of them is musically the most
colourful with appealing evocations of *La chasse*
and a riotous dance as the hunters go in search
of their quarry. The second scene is much gentler with a tender air for Diana, pastoral reflections from her followers and a recurring chorus
of nymphs which recalls passages in Blow's
Venus and Adonis. Jill Feldman as Arthebuze,
one of Diana's attendants, is admirably languid
in her air disdaining love's ardour. Scene 3 discloses a pensive Actéon who, while reflecting on
matters of the heart, stumbles upon Diana and
her retinue in a state of *déshabillé*. Actéon's
defence is touching and is delicately portrayed
by Dominique Visse. The fourth tableau begins
with Acteon's discovery that he has been turned
into a stag: 'A horrible fur enwraps me', he cries
and, at this point Visse cleverly alters the character of his voice: 'Ma parole n'est plus qu'une
confuse voix.' A poignant symphonie follows. In
the fifth tableau Actéon is torn to pieces by his
own hounds and, in the sixth and final scene,
Junon imperious as ever explains to the hunters
what they have just done. A chorus of grief mingled with anger sung by Acteon's followers
brings this little *opera de chasse* to an end.

Christie directs the work from beginning to
end with conviction and assurance. The action
is well paced and there's an intensity of expression, a fervour, which gives a touching emphasis
to the drama.

Médée, H491

Médée   Ⓟ
Lorraine Hunt sop Médée **Bernard Deletré** bass
Créon **Monique Zanetti** sop Créuse **Mark Padmore**

ten Jason **Jean-Marc Salzmann** bar Oronte **Noémi Rime** sop Nérine **Les Arts Florissants / William Christie**
Erato ③ 4509-96558-2 (195' · DDD) Recorded 1994.
Texts and translations included　　　　　　Ⓕ○○

Lorraine Hunt's Medea is something of a *tour de force*. She invests every word with meaning and produces the widest range of colour to express all the emotional nuances in Medea's complex character – jealousy, indignation, tenderness, sorrow, fury, malignity and outright barbarism: she's outstanding in Act 3, one of the most superb acts in all Baroque opera, in which she has no fewer than four great monologues, the first with affecting chromatic harmonies, the second accompanied by feverish rushing strings, the third the sombre 'Noires filles du Styx' with its eerie modulations, the fourth with dark orchestral colours. Charpentier's orchestration and texture, indeed, are wonderfully effective: string writing varies between extreme delicacy (beautifully played here) and savage agitation; the cool sound of the recorders is refreshing and the many dances featuring recorders and oboes are enchanting. As Jason, Mark Padmore, a real *haute-contre*, sings with admirable ease and intelligence and the tragic Creusa, poisoned by the vengeful Medea is the light-voiced Monique Zanetti, the very embodiment of youthful innocence and charm: her death scene, still protesting her love for Jason, is most moving. A notable detail in all the principals, incidentally, is their absorption of *agréments*, with Hunt showing special mastery in this regard. There's a large cast for the numerous minor roles, all well taken; and the chorus sings cleanly and with evident commitment. All told, a considerable achievement, and a triumph for Christie.

Ernest Chausson　　　French 1855-1899

Chausson grew up in comfortable and cultured circumstances but turned to music only after being trained in law. Studying with Massenet at the Paris Conservatoire, he came under Franck's influence and visited Germany to hear Wagner. His friends in Paris included Mallarmé, Debussy, Albéniz and Cortot. He died prematurely in a cycling accident but his output reflects his growing maturity from dependence on Massenet, Franck and Wagner, seen in the prettiness of early songs and the orchestration of the symphonic poem Viviane (1882), to a more elaborate, intensely dramatic style in the Poème de l'amour et de la mer (1882-93) and the opera Le roi Arthus (1886-95), and finally to a period of serious melancholy which produced the Turgenev-inspired Poème op.25 for violin and orchestra (1896) and some concise chamber music. Once criticised for being vague and Wagnerian, his music took on a more classical expression from about 1890, when he turned towards older Gallic and Italian resources and to Couperin and Rameau.　　　　**GROVE**music

Symphony in B flat, Op 20

Symphony in B flat, Op 20. Viviane, Op 5. Soir de fête, Op 32. La têmpete – Air de danse; Danse rustique
BBC Philharmonic Orchestra / Yan Pascal Tortelier
Chandos CHAN9650 (67' · DDD)　　　　　　Ⓕ○

There are at least two misconceptions to put right about Franck's arguably most gifted pupil. The first, which this disc dispels admirably, is that the majority of Chausson's music, in the manner of his *Poème*, is endlessly melancholic or elegiac. The second, which the disc doesn't dispel quite so well, is that in his orchestral writing never managed to free itself from Wagner's embrace. Never *entirely* perhaps, but by the time the 43-year-old composer came to write his last orchestral piece, the nocturnal *Soir de fête* included here, his escape from Wagner was well under way, and who knows where it might have led, had it not been for his tragically early death the following year? The outer sections of *Soir de fête* have something about them of 'the vibrating, dancing rhythms of the atmosphere' of Debussy's later *Fêtes*. The programme as a whole, the overall richness of the orchestral process – whether Wagnerian, Franckian, Straussian or Chaussonian – is well served by the full-bodied sound of Tortelier's BBC Philharmonic. The Symphony, like Franck's, is cyclical, but not otherwise as indebted to the older composer as is often suggested. There are none of Franck's organ-loft sonorities anywhere in this wonderfully variegated, open-air orchestration. This is the finest modern recording of the Symphony now available. Each movement is superbly built, and Chandos's recording is truly impressive although in the excerpts from Chausson's incidental music for *The Tempest*, the sound is perhaps a little bulky.

Piano Trio in G minor, Op 3

Piano Trio in G minor, Op 3. Poème, Op 25 (arr cpsr). Andante et Allegro. Pièce, Op 39
Charles Neidich cl **Philippe Graffin** vn **Gary Hoffman** vc **Pascal Devoyon** pf **Chilingirian Quartet** (Levon Chilingirian, Charles Sewart vns Asdis Valdimarsdottir va Philip de Groote vc)
Hyperion CDA67028 (62' · DDD)　　　　　　Ⓕ

The opulent sound of this disc is ideal for Chausson; it especially suits the impassioned early Trio. Devoyon plays the demanding piano part in the grand style, yet the strings are never swamped. In particular, Philippe Graffin's sensuous, unforced tone sails above the texture without any of the strenuous feeling we experience in other performances. All three players sound completely at home, whether in the rhetorical gestures of the work's big moments, or the poised delicacy of the second movement. This Trio, though an early work, is already fully characteristic of Chausson – the way the carefree, day-in-the-country atmosphere at the start of the finale is gradually overtaken by tragic portents demonstrates his melancholic nature. The *Andante et Allegro* is less individual, but here, too, the performance rises to the occasion. Neidich's playing is remarkable for its breadth of expression in the *Andante* as well as for the extraordinarily brilliantly articulated *Allegro*. Hoffman and Devoyon are equally convincing in the beautiful, dreamy *Pièce* for cello and piano The most novel aspect of the disc, paradoxically, concerns the most familiar music: this is the first recording of a newly rediscovered version of the *Poème*, with string quartet and piano accompaniment. As a chamber work, the music's essentially intimate tone is felt more strongly, and Graffin gives a plangent account of the solo part, with something of that sense of freedom that Ysaÿe, the work's sponsor, would certainly have conveyed. The only trouble with the arrangement is the loss of perspective between the soloist and an 'orchestra' led by another solo violin. But the Chilingirian and Devoyon play the sustained *tutti* music beautifully.

Poème de l'amour, Op 19

Chausson Poème de l'amour et de la mer, Op 19
Debussy Cinq poèmes de Charles Baudelaire (arr Adams) – Le balcon; Harmonie du soir; Le jet d'eau; Recueillement **Ravel** Shéhérazade
Susan Graham sop **BBC Symphony Orchestra / Yan Pascal Tortelier**
Warner Classics 2564 61938-2 (63' · DDD · T/t)
Ⓕ **000**

Only a brave, or foolhardy, composer sets about reorchestrating Debussy. Yet that's what John Adams has done, in 'Le jet d'eau', the third of Debussy's *Cinq poèmes de Charles Baudelaire*, the first four of which Adams has chosen to score for a modern orchestra. He's done an effective job, and if it makes the songs sound more boisterous, less mysterious than in the usual version for voice and piano, he's probably doing his soloist a big favour. By common consent, these are the most difficult of all Debussy's early songs. Susan Graham seems totally in command, her *diminuendo* on the words 'Et le charme des soirs' is tender, and is echoed a few bars later by Adams providing a nostalgic woodwind for the reference to those firelit evenings, 'par l'audeur du charbon'.

There's a lovely photograph, taken in 1893, the year of *Poème de l'amour et de la mer*. It shows Debussy, at Chausson's house, playing the piano. Both composers are in white shirts, surrounded by a peaceful group of family and friends, all in summer clothes, the windows openThis is the sort of mood this disc evokes. Yan Pascal Tortelier and Susan Graham give Chausson's work a well-nigh perfect performance, capturing the sense of quiet regret at the memory of springtime love that has faded, and of a story that is never quite told.

As for Ravel's *Shéhérazade*, like nearly all mezzo-sopranos, Graham is stretched to the limits of her resources by the big climactic phrases in 'Asie'. She sings a hushed, beautiful 'La flûte enchantée' and a rather too sad 'L'indifférent', but it's all done with a fine line, with the BBC Symphony Orchestra playing Ravel's music with a good deal of passion.

Carlos Chávez   Mexican 1899-1978

Chávez studied with Ponce (1910-14) and Ogazón (1915-20) but was self-taught as a composer, being most influenced by his experience of Indian culture. A visit to Europe in 1922-3 was unproductive, but his first trip to the USA (1923-4) began a close association: in 1926-8 he lived in New York and formed friendships with Copland, Cowell and Varèse. On his return to Mexico he became founder-director of the Mexico SO (1928-48) and director of the National Conservatory (1928-33), having a decisive influence on Mexican cultural life. His works include seven symphonies (the Sinfonía india is no.2, 1936) and two Aztec ballets (El fuego nuevo, 1921; Los cuatro soles, 1925). He was a master of orchestration, particularly of wind writing, and explored concerto writing; characteristic are the four Soli (1933-66) for small groups and orchestra. **GROVE**music

Piano Sonatas

Sonatas – Nos 2 & 6. Cinco caprichos. Seven Pieces. 10 Preludes
Hsuan-Ya Chen pf
Elan ② CD82406 (123' · DDD)   Ⓕ

Chávez's piano music presents a very different picture of the composer from that we are familiar with through his orchestral music, even the more abstract later symphonies (Vóx). There are precious few indications of the folkloric exoticism of the Sinfonía india in the five works played here, indeed little enough to suggest their Mexican origin.

The three large movements of the Second Sonata (1919-20) possess a Lisztian bravura which persuaded Ignaz Friedman, no less, to arrange for its publication in 1923. By that time Chávez was moving to a more modernistic, angular style in a series of miniatures collated in 1930 as the *Seven Pieces*. The *10 Preludes* (1937) are radically different again. Starting out as a set based on the seven Gregorian modes, Chávez exchanged the percussive, overtly colouristic manner of earlier pieces for a more contrapuntal style. Deceptively simple-sounding, the *Preludes* form a wonderfully expressive sequence that deserves exposure in the recital room.

So, too, does the excellent *Cinco caprichos* (1975), his final solo piano work. The quicker, odd-numbered movements are capricious, twisting and turning through a variety of moods, offset by the second and fourth, with their evocative bass-up writing for the left hand. The biggest surprise, though, is the Sixth Sonata which is convincingly Mozartian in every fibre, but without a hint of pastiche. If ever a work was meant to be heard with the innocent ear then this is it. Across a full half-hour Chávez recreates the spirit of the classical sonata, however modern the inner structure.

Hsuan-Ya Chen plays with admirable authority, and the sound is nicely clear and resonant.

Luigi Cherubini
Italian 1760-1842

Cherubini was a dominant figure in French musical life for half a century. At 18, with 36 works (mainly church music) to his credit, he began a period of study with Sarti in Bologna and Milan (1778-80). The resulting Italian operas he produced in Italy and London (1784-5), and his work as an Italian opera director (1789-90) in Paris (where he had settled in 1786), pale in significance next to the triumphant première of his second French opera, Lodoïska (Paris, 1791). He was appointed inspector at the new Institut National de Musique (from 1795 the Conservatoire), his status soon being enhanced by the successes of Médée (1797) and Les deux journées (1800). As surintendant de la musique du roi under the restored monarchy, he turned increasingly to church music, writing seven masses, two requiems and many shorter pieces, all well received (unlike his later operas). National honours, a commission from the London Philharmonic Society (1815) and the directorship of the Conservatoire (1822) and completion of his textbook, Cours de contrepoint et de fugue (1835), crowned his career.

Cherubini's importance in operatic history rests on his transformation of merely picturesque or anecdotal opéra comique into a vehicle for powerful dramatic portrayal (eg Médée's depiction of psychological conflict) and for the serious treatment of contemporary topics.

His best church music, notably the C minor Requiem (specially admired by Beethoven, Schumann, Brahms and Berlioz), unites his command of counterpoint and orchestral sonority with appropriate dramatic expression, while his non-vocal works, chiefly the operatic overtures, Symphony in D and six string quartets, make their effect through the creative use of instrumental colour. GROVEmusic

Mass No 1 in C minor

Mass No 1 in C minor. Marche funèbre
Corydon Singers; Corydon Orchestra / Matthew Best
Hyperion CDA66805 (54' · DDD) Text and translation included Ⓕ

It would be an oversimplification to suggest that Matthew Best emphasises the Beethoven rather than the Berlioz aspect of the main work here; but he does seem less interested in the fascinating use of colour as an element in the actual invention than in the rugged moral strength and the force of the statements. The recording reflects this emphasis, and is firm and clear

without being especially subtle over orchestral detail. The choir delivers the *Dies irae* powerfully, and much dramatic vigour is recalled in the fugue traditionally reserved for 'Quam olim Abrahae'. Berlioz, however, was satirical about Cherubini's fugues, and saved his admiration for the wonderful long *decrescendo* that ends the *Agnus Dei*. This is beautifully controlled here. Best includes the tremendous *Marche funèbre*, inspiration here again for Berlioz. Best handles this superbly, opening with a merciless percussion crash and sustaining the pace and mood unrelentingly. It sounds more original than ever, a funeral march that, rather than mourn or honour, rages against the dying of the light.

Requiem in C minor

Requiem in C minor[a]. Marche funèbre
[a]**Gruppo Vocale Cantemus; Italian Swiss Radio**
[a]**Chorus and Orchestra / Diego Fasolis**
Naxos 8 554749 (56' · DDD) Text and translation included Ⓢ

Cherubini's C minor Requiem was admired by both Berlioz and Beethoven, with good reason, since both owed a great deal to a work that isn't far short of a masterpiece. For Beethoven, the music's rugged strength and the force of the statements held much; Berlioz, often mocking and unfair to Cherubini, responded warmly to the use of instrumental colour as part of the actual invention. To oversimplify, if Christoph Spering and his Cologne artists (Opus 111) give a more colourful, 'Berliozian' performance, Matthew Best and the Corydon Singers (Hyperion) respond to the 'Beethovenian' aspect of the music. Of course, there's much more to it than that. Both are excellent performances.

So is the present one. Certainly it has more of an emotional charge in the 'Dies irae' than Spering's which, once the trump has sounded, gathers the voices with nervous intensity rather than the urgent drama that both Best and Fasolis discover. Best and Fasolis also produce great vigour for the 'Quam olim Abrahae' fugue. No one can make very much of the *Sanctus*, a surprisingly weak movement; all respond sensitively to the strange 'Pie Jesu', Best and Fasolis with rather sharper definition of phrasing.

All three open with the tremendous *Marche funèbre*, another piece that inspired Berlioz when he came to write his *Hamlet* funeral march. Excellent as the new performance is, those who acquired Best, in particular, can rest content.

Médée

Medée Ⓗ
Maria Callas *sop* Medea **Gino Penno** *ten* Jason **Maria Luisa Nache** *sop* Glauce **Giuseppe Modesti** *bass* Creon **Fedora Barbieri** *mez* Neris **Angela Vercelli** *mez* Maidservant I **Maria Amadini** *mez* Maidservant II **Enrico Campi** *bass* Captain of the

Guard **La Scala, Milan Chorus and Orchestra /
Leonard Bernstein**
EMI mono ② 567909-2 (129' · ADD) Recorded live
at La Scala Theatre, Milan, 1953. Notes, text and
translation included   Ⓜ**O**

It was Callas's particular genius to find exactly
the appropriate mode of expression for every
role she tackled. Here we have Callas the avenging tigress as Medea. But there are also a hundred different individual inflections to reflect
the emotion of the moment: indeed, as John
Steane points out in one of his illuminating
notes, it's often a small aside that reveals as
much about the character she's portraying as a
big set-piece. That said, it's the shattering outburst of Act 3 that makes her Medea such a terrifying experience. This is a reading of the central solo that has seldom, if ever, been surpassed.
De Sabata was intended as the conductor of
Medea but fell ill. Serafin wasn't available, so
Callas asked for Bernstein, of whom she had
heard good things. The results are revelatory.
Bernstein, in his first operatic assignment anywhere, breathes new life into Cherubini's score,
in spite of some rude cuts, and finds much more
immediate drama in it than did an ageing Serafin in Callas's commercial recording. In consequence she's in absolutely terrific form, the very
incarnation of a woman who has been crossed in
love.

And it isn't only Callas and Bernstein who
make this set so unmissable. Here is a house at
the peak of its form. La Scala produces just the
apt singer for each role. Gino Penno has the
right heroic, *spinto* sound for Jason. Giuseppe
Modesti is a warm Creon.

This is a feast not only for Callas aficionados
but for anyone interested in Italian opera at its
most potent.

Additional recommendation

Medea
Sass Medea **Luchetti** Jason **Kováts** Creon
**Budapest Symphony Orchestra; Hungarian Radio
and Television Chorus / Gardelli**
Hungaroton ② HCD11904/5 (137' · rec 1977) Notes,
text and translation included   Ⓕ

Sass is impressive, managing to capture the
humanity as well as the horror. She has a vivid
vocal personality essential for the recording of
such a role. The other soloists are equally fine.

Fryderyk Chopin   Polish 1810-1849

*The son of French émigré father (a schoolteacher
working in Poland) and a cultured Polish mother,
Chopin grew up in Warsaw, taking childhood music
lessons (in Bach and the Viennese Classics) from
Wojciech Zywny and Jósef Elsner before entering the
Conservatory (1826-9). By this time he had performed in local salons and composed several rondos,*

*polonaises and mazurkas. Public and critical acclaim
increased during the years 1829-30 when he gave
concerts in Vienna and Warsaw, but his despair over
the political repression in Poland, coupled with his
musical ambitions, led him to move to Paris in 1831.
There, with practical help from Kalkbrenner and
Pleyel, praise from Liszt, Fétis and Schumann and
introductions into the highest society, he quickly
established himself as a private teacher and salon
performer, his legendary artist's image being
enhanced by frail health (he had tuberculosis),
attractive looks, sensitive playing, a courteous manner and the piquancy attaching to self-exile. Of his
several romantic affairs, the most talked about was
that with the novelist George Sand – though
whether he was truly drawn to women must remain
in doubt. Between 1838 and 1847 their relationship,
with a strong element of the maternal on her side,
coincided with one of his most productive creative
periods. He gave few public concerts, though his playing was much praised, and he published much of his
best music simultaneously in Paris, London and
Leipzig. The breach with Sand was followed by a
rapid deterioration in his health and a long visit to
Britain (1848). His funeral was attended by nearly
3000 people.*

*No great composer has devoted himself as exclu-
sively to the piano as Chopin. By all accounts an
inspired improviser, he composed while playing,
writing down his thoughts only with difficulty. But
he was no mere dreamer – his development can be
seen as an ever more sophisticated improvisation on
the classical principle of departure and return. For
the concert-giving years 1828-32 he wrote brilliant
virtuoso pieces (eg rondos) and music for piano and
orchestra the teaching side of his career is represented
by the studies, preludes, nocturnes, waltzes,
impromptus and mazurkas, polished pieces of moderate difficulty. The large-scale works – the later
polonaises, scherzos, ballades, sonatas, the Barcarolle
and the dramatic Polonaise-fantaisie – he wrote for
himself and a small circle of admirers. Apart from
the national feeling in the Polish dances, and possibly
some narrative background to the ballades, he
intended notably few references to literary, pictorial
or autobiographical ideas.*

*Chopin is admired above all for his great original-
ity in exploiting the piano. While his own playing
style was famous for its subtlety and restraint, its
exquisite delicacy in contrast with the spectacular
feats of pianism then reigning in Paris, most of his
works have a simple texture of accompanied melody.
From this he derived endless variety, using wide-
compass broken chords, the sustaining pedal and a
combination of highly expressive melodies, some in
inner voices. Similarly, though most of his works are
basically ternary in form, they show great resource in
the way the return is varied, delayed, foreshortened
or extended, often with a brilliant coda added.*

*Chopin's harmony however was conspicuously
innovatory. Through melodic clashes, ambiguous
chords, delayed or surprising cadences, remote or sliding modulations (sometimes many in quick succession), unresolved dominant 7ths and occasionally
excursions into pure chromaticism or modality, he
pushed the accepted procedures of dissonance and key
into previously unexplored territory. This profound*

influence can be traced alike in the music of Liszt, Wagner, Fauré, Debussy, Grieg, Albéniz, Tchaikovsky, Rachmaninov and many others.

GROVEmusic

Piano Concertos

No 1 in E minor, Op 11; **No 2** in F minor, Op 21

Piano Concertos Nos 1 & 2
Martha Argerich *pf* **Montreal Symphony Orchestra / Charles Dutoit**
EMI 556798-2 (69' · DDD)   Ⓕ**OOO**

 Martha Argerich's first commercially released recordings of the Chopin concertos were for DG; No 1 in 1968, No 2 in 1978. Here she revisits both concertos and offers an act of re-creative daring, of an alternating reverie and passion that flashes fire with a thousand different lights. Indeed, her earlier performances are infinitely less witty, personal and eruptive, less inclined to explore, albeit with the most spontaneous caprice and insouciance, so many new facets, angles and possibilities. Now, everything is accomplished without a care for studios and microphones and with a degree of involvement that suggests an increase rather than a diminution of her love for these works. The recordings are impressively natural and if Dutoit occasionally seems awed if not cowed into anonymity by his soloist (the opening *tuttis* to the slow movements of both concertos are less memorable than they should be) he sets off Argerich's charisma to an exceptional degree. Argerich's light burns brighter than ever. Rarely in their entire history have the Chopin concertos received performances of a more teasing allure, brilliance and idiosyncrasy.

Piano Concertos Nos 1 & 2
Murray Perahia *pf*
Israel Philharmonic Orchestra / Zubin Mehta
Sony Classical SMK87323 (76' · DDD) Recorded live 1989   Ⓜ**O**

Perahia has never made any secret of his liking for the 'inspirational heat-of-the-moment' of a live performance as opposed to a studio recording, where 'sometimes things get tame'. As enthusiastic audience applause (discreetly rationed on the disc) makes plain, these two concertos were recorded live at Tel Aviv's Mann Auditorium. Whether they were subsequently 'doctored' we don't know, but the finished product brings us a Perahia miraculously combining exceptional finesse with an equally exceptional urgency. In all but the finale of No 1 (where Pollini on EMI beats him by a minute) his timings throughout both works are considerably faster than most of his rivals on disc. Was this prompted by 'inspirational heat-of-the-moment'? Or was it a deliberate attempt to come closer than others do to the surprisingly briskish metronome markings printed in the

Eulenburg scores? The two slow movements are distinguished by exquisitely limpid *cantabile* and superfine delicacy of decorative detail while again conveying urgent undercurrents. But in a guessing-game perhaps it would be the two finales that would most betray the identity of the soloist. Not only are they faster, but also of a more scintillating, *scherzando*-like lightness. The recording is first rate.

Piano Concertos Nos 1 & 2
Polish Festival Orchestra / Krystian Zimerman *pf*
DG ② 459 684-2GH2 (82' · DDD)   Ⓜ**O**

Krystian Zimerman was in his early twenties when he recorded the Chopin concertos for DG two decades ago, with Carlo Maria Giulini conducting the Los Angeles Philharmonic. For his long-anticipated remakes he directs the Polish Festival Orchestra from the keyboard, an ensemble he founded and trained from scratch. Are the results worth all the extraordinary effort (and no doubt expense) that went into this project? In many ways, yes. Helped by DG's exquisite engineering, Chopin's oft-maligned orchestrations emerge with the clarity of a venerable painting scrubbed clean and fully restored. Not one string phrase escapes unaccounted for. Every dynamic indication and accent mark is freshly considered, and each orchestral strand is weighed and contoured in order for each instrument to be heard, or, at least, to make itself felt. Some listeners may find the strings' ardent vibrato and liberal *portamentos* more cloying than heartfelt, yet the vocal transparency Zimerman elicits from his musicians underscores the crucial influence of *bel canto* singing on this composer. If he downplays many of Chopin's dynamic surges and enlivening accents, he compensates with carefully pinpointed climaxes in both concertos' slow movements. The slow timings, incidentally, have less to do with fast versus slow than the pianist's insidiously spaced *ritardandos* and broadening of tempos between sections. More often than not he lets his right hand lead, rather than building textures from the bottom up, or bringing out inner voices as Argerich does in her more forceful, impulsive renditions. By contrast, some of Zimerman's salient expressive points have calcified rather than ripened with age. Having said that, he has clear ideas of what he wants, and commands the formidable means to obtain the desired results, both at the keyboard and in front of his hand-picked musicians. Of the many offerings made to celebrate Chopin's 150th anniversary, Zimerman's achievement stands out.

Piano Concertos Nos 1ᵃ & 2ᵇ   Ⓗ
Noel Mewton-Wood *pf* ᵃ**Netherlands Philharmonic Orchestra,** ᵇ**Zurich Symphony Orchestra / Walter Goehr**
Dante Historical Piano Collection HPC105 (69' · ADD) Recorded c1951, 1948   Ⓕ

Inconsolable after the death of his partner Bill Fredricks, Noel Mewton-Wood (1922-53) committed suicide and robbed the world of a musical genius. Born in Melbourne, he included, in his London-based career, work with Schnabel, a début (in Beethoven's Third Concerto) with Sir Thomas Beecham, the frequent replacement of Benjamin Britten as Peter Pears's musical collaborator and, mercifully for the present generation, the making of several recordings taken from his eclectic and enterprising repertoire.

Amazingly, in his incomparably sensitive and robust hands, the Chopin concertos seem as though heard for the first time, their passions and intimacies virtually re-created on the spot. Who of today's pianists would or could risk such candour or phrase and articulate Chopin's early intricacy with such alternating strength and delicacy? The notes (in French only) suggest parallels with Solomon, Anatole Kitain and Murray Perahia, yet as with all truly great artists, Mewton-Wood's playing defies comparison, however exalted. No more vital or individual performances exist on record. The orchestra is hardly a model of precision or refinement, but the recordings have come up remarkably well.

Piano Concerto No 1. Ballade in G minor, Op 23 .
Nocturnes, Op 15 – No 1 in F; No 2 in F sharp minor.
Nocturnes, Op 27 – No 1 in C sharp minor; No 2 in D flat. Polonaise No 6 in A flat, Op 53, 'Heroic'
Maurizio Pollini pf **Philharmonia Orchestra / Paul Kletzki**
EMI 5675482 (73' · ADD) Recorded 1960-68   Ⓜ**OO**

This disc is a classic. The concerto was recorded shortly after the 18-year-old pianist's victory at the Warsaw competition in 1959. Nowadays we might expect a wider dynamic range to allow greater power in the first movement's *tutti*s, but in all other respects the recording completely belies its age, with a near perfect balance between soloist and orchestra. This is very much Pollini's disc, just as the First Concerto is very much the soloist's show, but effacing as the accompaniment is, Pollini's keyboard miracles of poetry and refinement could not have been achieved without one of the most characterful and responsive accounts of that accompaniment ever committed to tape. The expressive range of the Philharmonia on top form under Kletzki is exceptional, as is the accord between soloist and conductor in phrasing and shading. The solo items are a further reminder of Pollini's effortless bravura and aristocratic poise.

Piano Concerto No 2. Preludes, Op 28
Maria João Pires pf **Royal Philharmonic Orchestra / André Previn**
DG 437 817-2GH (74' · DDD) Recorded 1992   Ⓕ**OO**

Here, beautifully partnered by Previn and the RPO, and recorded with the greatest warmth and clarity, Pires gets the treatment she

deserves. What gloriously imposing breadth as well as knife-edged clarity she brings to each phrase and note. The stylishness of her rubato reminds us that the inspiration behind the F minor Concerto was Constantia Gladkowska, a young singer and Chopin's first love. Listen to Pires's *fioritura* in the heavenly *Larghetto* or her way of edging into the finale's scintillating coda and you'll gasp at such pianism and originality. Indeed, the opening of her finale may surprise you with its dreaminess (*Allegro vivace*?) but as with all great pianists, even her most extreme ideas are carried through with unshakeable conviction and authority.

Pires's 24 Preludes, too, remind us that she's the possessor of one of the most crystalline of all techniques. Understatement plays little part in her conception; those who prefer the more classical playing of artists such as Pollini are in for some surprises. You rarely hear Chopin playing of greater mastery or calibre. In her own scrupulously modern way she surely embodies the spirit of the great pianists of the past; of Kempff, Edwin Fischer and, most of all, Cortot.

Piano Concerto No 2 in F minor, Op 21[a].   Ⓗ
Ballade No 1 in G minor, Op 23. Mazurka in C minor, Op 56 No 3. Etudes, Op 10 – No 6 in E flat minor; No 8 in F; No 9 in F minor. Scherzo No 4 in E, Op 54. Andante spianato and Grande Polonaise, Op 22
Artur Rubinstein pf [a]**Philharmonia Orchestra / Carlo Maria Giulini**
BBC Legends/IMG Artists mono BBCL4105-2 (78' · ADD) Recorded live 1959; [a]1961   Ⓕ**O**

Rubinstein remains the most elegant and life-affirming of all great Chopin pianists, his patrician ease and stylistic distinction the envy and despair of lesser mortals. Above all he understood a central paradox, that Chopin was in love with the human voice yet sensing the limitation of words and a single vocal line confided his deepest, most fiery and intimate thoughts to the piano, an instrument of a supposed percussive limitation. No pianist has played Chopin with a more translucent and uncluttered tone, with a greater sense of singing 'line', of vocal breathing and inspiration. His *rubato* was personal and inimitable, a subtle bending of the phrase, an ebb and flow. Above all there was his sovereign naturalness. Audiences felt transported, indeed transfigured by his playing.

These wondrous performances transport you to another world. True, there are tiny slips of finger and concentration, yet they do nothing to qualify a sense of supreme mastery. In the Concerto, where, despite a once traditional and disfiguring cut in the opening *tutti*, he's memorably partnered by Giulini, Rubinstein achieves a flawless balance between Chopin's ever-elusive mix of poise and intensity. In his recital his reading of the great C minor Mazurka surely numbers among the greatest of all Chopin performances in its play of light and shade, of brio and introspection.

But all these performances are memorable,

haunting one over the years and now, thankfully, available in beautifully remastered sound.

Piano Concertos Nos 1 & 2 (chamber versions)
Fumiko Shiraga pf **Jan-Inge Haukås** db **Yggdrasil Quartet** (Fredrik Paulsson, Per Oman vns Robert Westlund va Per Nyström vc)
BIS CD847(72' · DDD)   Ⓕ●

This is one of the most exciting Chopin recordings in recent years because it confronts and deepens the uneasiness that Chopin lovers have with his concertos. They are more comfortable as chamber works, the chamber works he never succeeded in writing when he confronted that form head on. If you find Chopin's ideas inflated when cast in orchestral form, this recording will remove the last traces of doubt. Pianist Fumiko Shiraga has reduced the scope of the music, and wisely so. The heroism and grandeur is of the sort one finds in Schumann's piano-chamber context, the dynamic and expressive extremes that Shiraga achieves are no less compelling than a pianist unleashed against a large orchestra. Shiraga doubles in some *tutti* passages – a surprise at first, but again a wise decision. She adds gravity and fullness to the Yggdrasil Quartet's excellent accompaniment while remaining hidden, diligently underscoring but never overbearing.

Piano Trio in G minor, Op 8

Piano Trio. Cello Sonata in G minor, Op 65. Introduction and Polonaise brillant in C, Op 3 (versions for pf, vc & pf, arr Feuerman)
Pamela Frank vn **Yo-Yo Ma** vc **Emanuel Ax, Eva Osinska** pfs
Sony Classical SK53112 (72' · DDD) Recorded 1989-92   Ⓕ

This most welcome reminder of the 'chamber music' Chopin starts with his G minor Piano Trio dedicated to his compatriot, the would-be composer-cum-cellist, Prince Radziwill. Rarely has it enjoyed what might be termed 'bigger-named' rescue on disc. For even if Chopin's beloved piano gets the best of it, a performance as imaginatively characterised as this makes you salute the teenage work anew. Despite the procrustean (for Chopin) demands of sonata-form, the minor-key challenges of the opening *Allegro con fuoco* are conveyed with appealing urgency before the amiable grace of the *Scherzo*, the smouldering romance of the *Adagio sostenuto* and the dance-like gaiety of the finale. Shortly after accepting the Trio's dedication, Prince Radziwill invited Chopin to stay at his country estate – hence the Op 3 *Polonaise brillant* in C for the Prince to play with his bewitching 17-year-old pianist daughter. Here, Yo-Yo Ma chooses Emanuel Feuermann's reworking of the cello part – as Chopin himself might well have enhanced it with decorative *fioriture* had the Prince's fingers been as agile as his daughter's.

The mature Cello Sonata receives a tactfully balanced, persuasively fluid performance from Ma and Ax that ranks with the best of its rivals. The recording is vivid and true.

Cello Works

Cello Sonata in G minor, Op 65. Polonaise brillante in C, Op 3 (ed Feuermann). Grande duo concertante in E on themes from Meyerbeer's 'Robert le Diable'. Nocturne in C sharp minor, Op posth (arr Piatigorsky). Etude in E minor, Op 25 No 7 (arr Glazunov). Waltz in A minor, Op 34 No 2 (arr Ginzburg). Etude in D minor, Op 10 No 6 (arr Glazunov)
Maria Kliegel vc **Bernd Glemser** pf
Naxos 8 553159 (64' · DDD) Recorded 1994   Ⓢ

Here are Chopin's complete works for cello and piano complemented by an intriguing garland of encores. Performed with youthful relish, impressively balanced and recorded, this is a notable offering. Clearly, Kliegel and Glemser have few reservations concerning the sonata's surprisingly Germanic overtones. Recognisably Chopin in virtually every bar there remains an oddly Schumannesque bias, particularly in the finale's tortuous argument – an irony when you consider that Chopin had so little time for his adoring colleague. Yet this awkward and courageous reaching out towards a terser form of expression is resolved by both artists with great vitality and, throughout, they create an infectious sense of a live rather than studio performance. Kliegel and Glemser are no less uninhibited in Chopin's earlier show-pieces, written at a time when the composer had a passing passion for grand opera and for what he dismissed as 'glittering trifles'. Their additions (transcriptions by Glazunov, Piatigorsky and Ginzburg) remind us how singers, violinists and cellists beg, borrow or steal Chopin from pianists at their peril. As Chopin put it, 'the piano is my solid ground; on that I stand the straightest', and his muse has proved oddly and magically resistant to change or transcription. Still, even though the selection often suggests an alien opacity, the performances are most warmly committed.

Cello Waltzes, Volume 1
Etude in C sharp minor, Op 25 No 7 (arr Glazunov). Grande valse brillante in D, Op 18 (arr Davïdov). Mazurkas – G minor, Op 67 No 2; C, Op 67 No 3; A minor, Op 67 No 4; A minor, Op 68 No 2; B flat, Op posth (arr Wispelwey/Lazić). Preludes, Op 28 – No 2 in A minor; No 3 in G; No 4 in E minor; No 6 in B minor; No 7 in A (arr Wispelwey/Lazić). Waltzes – No 2 in A flat, Op 34 No 1; No 3 in A minor, Op 34 No 2; No 5 in A flat, Op 42 (arr Davïdov). Nocturne No 20 in C sharp minor, Op posth (arr Piatigorsky). Introduction and Polonaise brillante in C, Op 3. Cello Sonata in G minor, Op 65 – Scherzo
Pieter Wispelwey vc **Dejan Lazić** pf
Channel Classics CCS16298 (59' · DDD)   Ⓕ●●

Chopin's music, so beautifully conceived for the piano's sonority and technique, is treacherous territory for an arranger. But a good case can be made for transcription to Chopin's next most favoured instrument, the cello. The performances, full of verve and expressive sensitivity, provide an even stronger argument. The *valse* arrangements by the 19th-century cellist Davïdov transform Chopin's pianistic evocations into virtuoso cello pieces, most spectacularly so in the case of Op 34 No 1, with its rocketing scales and sparkling passagework. That the original character often changes – the repeated-note figure at the start of Op 18 has a quite different effect when articulated by a bouncing bow – seems not to matter when the music sounds so idiomatic in its new dress.

Glazunov's beautiful arrangement of the famous slow Etude from Op 25 and Piatigorsky's version of the Nocturne are just as successful. The artists' own arrangements are simpler in scope. The Mazurkas are, no doubt, specially chosen for their appropriateness as cello pieces, and the lyrical Preludes sound most impressive, if more overt and operatic than usual. Only the third Prelude seems a mistake; the semiquavers are a cellistic tour de force, but the long notes added to the piano bass introduce an earthbound quality that's not there in the original. Very good recorded sound, and brilliant and imaginative cello playing.

Piano Sonatas

No 1 in C minor, Op 4; No 2 in B flat minor, Op 35; No 3 in B minor, Op 58

Piano Sonatas Nos 2 & 3. Etudes – Op 10 Nos 1-12 (two versions); Op 25 Nos 1-12 (two versions). Waltzes Nos 1-14. Ballades Nos 1-4. Preludes Nos 1-24. Impromptus Nos 1-3. Nocturnes Nos 2, 4, 5, 7, 15 & 16. Polonaise No 6. Berceuse (two versions). Fantasie in F minor, Op 49. Tarantelle in A flat, Op 43. Barcarolle. Chants polonais, Op 74 – No 2, Spring (trans Liszt); No 12, My darling; No 14, The ring. Piano Concerto No 2
Alfred Cortot pf orchestra / **Sir John Barbirolli**
EMI mono ⑥ 767359-2 (429' · ADD) Recorded 1920-43   Ⓜ

Has there ever been a more bewitching or endearing virtuoso than Alfred Cortot? His touch was of a crystalline clarity, his coloration alive with myriad tints and hues. Combined with a poetic passion that knew no limits, such qualities created an idiosyncrasy and style that usually survived a fallible and bewildering confused keyboard mechanism. His left hand in particular had a way of drifting in and out of focus and leading a wayward and disobedient life of its own. Yet Cortot's famous errors surely resulted not from incompetence, but from his nervous, high-pitched intensity; a sheer involvement that could easily cloud his composure or unsettle his equilibrium. Importantly,

Chopin's elusive essence emerged, for the greater part, unscathed from his inaccuracy and caprice.

Here on six glorious CDs is Cortot's Chopin in all its infinite richness and variety. The transfers are outstanding, with no attempt made to mask the glitter of his brilliance in the interests of silent surfaces or to remove other acoustical hiccups. Although not everything is included, the selection is wonderfully enterprising, offering several alternative performances of the same work. The only quibble is the preference shown for the 1942 set of the *Preludes* when the earlier 1933 recording seems infinitely superior. The 1931 B minor Sonata is far superior to a later version from 1933. Cortot's 1933 B flat minor Sonata is also a far cry from one made in 1953, where his powers failed him almost totally and is, indeed, of a dizzying aplomb and brio.

There's elaboration in the Second *Ballade*, the volcanic interjections ablaze with added notes, and in the opening of the last and glorious Fourth *Ballade* there's a convulsive leap across the rhythm. However, the gem is surely the Third *Ballade* with the opening pages played as if improvised on the spot, the figuration foaming and cascading with a freedom and liberality unknown to most players. The F minor *Fantasie* also suggests that Cortot never compromised where his intensity of vision was concerned. Cortot's *Barcarolle* is as insinuating as it's blisteringly intense, even though the hectic rush through the final pages shows him at his least eloquent. In the *Etudes* (the 1934 is preferable to the 1942 set; both are included) he reaches out far beyond mere pedagogical concerns. The final and awe inspiring Op 25 No 12, too, isn't the *cantus firmus* of a traditional view but an elemental declamation and upheaval.

In the Waltzes there's a near operatic freedom in the melody of Op 42 with its cunning mix of duple and triple rhythm, a charming decorative aside at bar 20 in the E flat, Op 18 (only in the 1943 version), and a puckish mercurial touch throughout that banishes all possible monotony from so many pieces in three time. There's a comically confused start to the A flat, Op 64 No 3, and an unholy muddle at the end of the final Waltz in E minor. The Second Concerto, heard in Cortot's own arrangement or refurbishment with some marginal retexturing here and there, shows him at his most excitingly rhetorical. Barbirolli's accompaniment may be rumbustious rather than subtle, yet the music sounds as if newly minted. Six *Nocturnes* are included in the set and, while hardly examples of the stylistic purity to which we have become accustomed in the post-Cortot era, they're brilliantly alive with his own heady alternative. You won't easily find a more absorbing boxed set of piano discs.

Piano Sonatas Nos 2[a] & 3[b]. Scherzo No 3 in C sharp minor, Op 39[c]
Martha Argerich pf
DG 419 055-2GGA (56' · ADD) Recorded [a]1975, [b]1967, [c]1961   Ⓜ●●

Here, simply and assuredly, is one of the most magisterial talents in the entire history of piano playing. She's hardly a comfortable companion, confirming your preconceptions. Indeed, she sets your heart and mind reeling so that you positively cry out for respite from her dazzling and super-sensitive enquiry. But she's surely a great musician first and a great pianist second. From her, Chopin is hardly the most balanced or classically biased of the romantics. She can tear all complacency aside. How she keeps you on the *qui vivre* in the Second and Third Sonatas. Is the Funeral March too brisk, an expression of sadness for the death of a distant relative rather than grief for a nation? Is the delicate rhythmic play at the heart of the Third Sonata's *Scherzo* virtually spun out of existence? Such qualms or queries tend to be whirled into extinction by more significant felicities. Who but Argerich, with her subtle half-pedalling, could conjure so baleful and macabre a picture of 'winds whistling over graveyards' in the Second Sonata's finale, or achieve such heart-stopping exultance in the final pages of the Third Sonata (this performance is early Argerich with a vengeance, alive with a nervous brio). And if her free spirit leaves us tantalised, thirsting for Chopin's First, Second and Fourth as well as his Third *Scherzos*, for example, she has also left us overwhelmingly enriched, for ever in her debt.

Chopin Piano Sonata No 3. Polonaise in A flat, 'Heroic', Op 53
Schumann Kinderszenen, Op 15. Papillons, Op 2
Alex Slobodyanik pf
EMI Debut 573500-2 (69' · DDD) Ⓑ

Alex Slobodyanik (the son of Alexander Slobodyanik, a celebrated pianist of the 60s and 70s) is Russian-born but American-based and the possessor of a truly prodigious talent. His Schumann *Papillons* are among the most engaging on record, delicate and piquant in No 4, immaculately virtuosic in No 6 and with the sort of haunting nuance and *cantabile* in No 7 that usually only comes later in a pianist's career. Rarely has carnival night (the coda) died away more magically, its gaiety lost in a mist of distant chimes, while Slobodyanik's *Kinderszenen* shows a no less breathtaking rapport with Schumann's poetry. His 'Dreaming' is memorable, while 'Child Falling Asleep' evolves into a lullaby of exquisite joy and pain, of childhood revisited through adult eyes and perceptions.

Chopin's Third Sonata begins more flamboyantly, if no less poetically, with a fierce thrust that's hardly *maestoso*, yet contains such zest and ardour that you listen as if mesmerised. There's no repeat – the authenticity of the first-movement repeats in either of the mature sonatas is in any case debatable – and, throughout, some of Chopin's most richly ornate pages are allowed to blossom and expand in glorious profusion (the reverse of the gaunt and death-haunted Second Sonata). Again, there's absolutely no sense of the studio, but rather of live and imme-

CHOPIN'S PIANO SONATA NO 2 – IN BRIEF

Martha Argerich
DG 419 055-2GGA (56' · ADD) ⓂOO
Coupled with the Third Sonata and the *Scherzo* No 3, this disc shows off Argerich's mastery of this music. You never quite know what will happen next, which only adds to the excitement! Red-blooded Chopin, for sure.

Vladimir Ashkenazy
Decca 448 123-2DM (76' · ADD) Ⓜ
Ashkenazy's Chopin is wonderfully poetic, and this disc contains all three sonatas. His way with the slow movements – try the Funeral March – is very appealing.

Murray Perahia
Sony Classical MK76242 (50' · DDD) ⓂO
Beautifully played, intellectually probing Chopin with an great emphasis on detail and incidental delights. Coupled with the Third Piano Sonata – another joy.

Artur Rubinstein
RCA 09026 63046-2 (61' · ADD) ⓂOO
Rubinstein is the Chopin pianist *par excellence* for many people, and listening to him in the Second and Third Sonatas it's easy to agree. Poetry flows from his fingers with ease, and his way with the most subtle nuance is quite breathtaking.

Maurizio Pollini
DG 415 346-2GH (52' · DDD) ⒻO
This is Chopin playing of great power and feeling: there's no hint of the chilliness of which Pollini is occasionally accused.

Ivo Pogorelich
463 678-2GOR (73' · ADD) ⒷO
Perhaps Pogorelich's most controversial recording, but in 1981, as his recorded début, it established him as a player of quite extraordinary technique and temperament. It's coupled, unusually, with Ravel's *Gaspard de la nuit* and Prokofiev's Piano Sonata No 6.

Leif Ove Andsnes
Virgin Classics ② 561618-2 (111' · ADD) Ⓜ
An appealing Chopin collection (it includes the three sonatas as well as some Etudes and Mazurkas) from the young Norwegian. It makes one long for more Chopin from this talented pianist.

Emil Gilels
Testament SBT1089 (64' · ADD) Ⓕ
The great Russian pianist, far too little represented on record in Chopin, proves to be a magnificent interpreter, full of majestic gesture and noble utterance. This is resonant playing (coupled, oddly, with Mozart and Shostakovich).

diate responses caught on the wing. Only a touch of diffidence mars the A flat *Polonaise*, yet even here the playing reveals the most exceptional refinement and musicianship. The English-based recordings are virtually ideal and, overall, this is a début of débuts.

Piano Sonatas Nos 1-3
Vladimir Ashkenazy *pf*
Decca Ovation 448 123-2DM (76' · ADD) Recorded
1976-81   Ⓜ

Ashkenazy's grouping of the three sonatas is particularly valuable as he makes such a good case for the early (1827) C minor Sonata, and his account of No 3 is undoubtedly very fine, with an excitingly spontaneous account of the last movement. But it's the 'Funeral March' Sonata that one especially remembers. He obviously identifies with the music profoundly and after the concentration of the first two movements the dazzling finale seems the more mercurial. The analogue piano recording is very real and vivid.

Piano Sonatas Nos 2 & 3
Maurizio Pollini *pf*
DG 415 346-2GH (52' · DDD) Recorded 1986   ⒻⒶ

These two magnificent sonatas are Chopin's longest works for solo piano The passion of the B flat minor Sonata is evident throughout, as is its compression (despite the overall length) – for example, the urgent first subject of its first movement is omitted in the recapitulation. As for its mysterious finale, once likened to 'a pursuit in utter darkness', it puzzled Chopin's contemporaries but now seems totally right. The B minor Sonata is more glowing and spacious, with a wonderful *Largo* third movement, but its finale is even more exhilarating than that of the B flat minor, and on a bigger scale. Pollini plays this music with overwhelming power and depth of feeling; the expressive intensity is rightly often disturbing. Magisterial technique is evident throughout and the recording is sharp-edged but thrilling.

Piano Sonatas Nos 2 & 3. Fantasie in F minor, Op 49
Artur Rubinstein *pf*
RCA Victor Red Seal 09026 63046-2 (61' · ADD)
Recorded 1960s   Ⓜ

In the Chopin sonatas it's difficult to think of which performance to choose as the greatest. Aside from the Funeral March itself, Rubinstein's account of the Second Sonata is a bit too imperious; the Third is much more thrilling, with considerable technical risks being taken both in the first movement and the finale. His own feeling for quiet nuances in the *Largo* of this work is quite superb, and here too Pollini on DG achieves an innocence that's disarming. Pollini's disc is the most perfect, both in terms

of the pianist's technical accomplishment and the lucid piano sound, with nothing that offends the ear. The middle treble range in Rubinstein's piano sound has a hollow resonance. Rubinstein tackles the F minor *Fantasie* in rather a heavy-handed manner, with more power than searching drama. To sum up this release, if you want your Chopin sonatas balanced and formally cohesive, then Rubinstein is for you.

Piano Sonata No 3. Mazurkas Nos 36-38. Nocturne
No 4. Polonaise No 6. Scherzo No 3
Martha Argerich *pf*
EMI 556805-2 (52' · ADD) Recorded 1965   Ⓕ

Argerich's pianism is remarkable for combining seemingly effortless technical resource with temperamental volatility. Yet the vehemence of her playing is seldom to the disadvantage of the extraordinary subtlety of her art. Moreover, despite the limits she places on her repertory, such is the spontaneity of her approach that each of her interpretations, no matter how familiar in broad outline, is characterised by a profusion of contrasting details beneath the surface. In the B minor Sonata she omits the first-movement repeats. Such a formal contraction can contribute to the momentum with which the movement unfolds. Ironically, however, she seems to rein in the propulsive power for which she's renowned, appearing instead to be seeking at every turn to exploit a deeply felt exprssive lyricism to offset the febrile intensity of the most energetic figurational devices. This has the virtue of allowing us a less hectic view of subsidiary elements within the music, which elsewhere can too often be overwhelmed by the sheer turbulance of the action. Some of the most satisfying playing on the disc comes in her account of the Op 59 *Mazurkas*. There's a vulnerability as well as an affecting wistfulness about the playing which captures the elusiveness of the idiom, with its harmonic ambiguities, with rare acuity. At the other end of the scale, the excitement she generates in the A flat *Polonaise* is of an order that goes far beyond mere effect. If these accounts do not necessarily outstrip her other recordings, they nevertheless offer an intriguing insight into ongoing 'work in progress' from a pianistic giant whose artistry continues to fascinate and perplex.

Piano Sonata No 3. Mazurkas – A minor, Op 17 No 4;
B flat minor, Op 24 No 4; D flat, Op 30 No 3; D, Op
33 No 2; C sharp minor, Op 50 No 3; C, Op 56 No 2;
F sharp minor, Op 59 No 3; B, Op 63 No 1; F minor,
Op 63 No 2; C sharp minor, Op 63 No 3; F minor,
Op 68 No 4
Evgeni Kissin *pf*
RCA Victor Red Seal 09026 62542-2 (65' · DDD)
Recorded live 1993   ⒻⒶ

Kissin is among the master-pianists of our time. What magnificence and assertion he finds in the B minor Sonata's opening, what menace in the following uprush of chromatic scales, his deliberate pedal haze capturing one of Chopin's most truly modernist moments. He may relish left-hand counter-melody in the return of the second subject and elsewhere, yet such detail is offered within the context of the whole. A momentary failure of concentration in the *Scherzo* comes as reassuring evidence of human fallibility but elsewhere one can only marvel at a manner so trenchant, musicianly and resolutely unsentimental. The equestrian finale is among the most lucid on record and concludes in a controlled triumph that has the audience cheering to the heavens. The 12 *Mazurkas* are no less remarkable for their strength and discretion. Everything unfolds with complete naturalness and authority. The beautifully idiomatic rubato is so stylishly applied that you're only aware of the finest fluctuations of pulse and emotion. Few pianists have gone to the heart of the matter with such assurance (always excepting Artur Rubinstein). The recording captures Kissin's clear, unnarcissistic sonority admirably and audience noise is minimal.

Piano Sonata No 3. Polonaise-Fantaisie in A flat, Op 61. Nocturne No 1. Scherzo No 4. Barcarolle. Ballade No 4
Nelson Goerner pf
EMI Debut 569701-2 (77' · DDD)   Ⓑ

Nelson Goerner is Argentinian, a student of Maria Tipo, and devotes his most personal and inflammatory recital to Chopin's later masterpieces. How fearlessly he launches the B minor Sonata's imperious opening, never using Chopin's *maestoso* instruction as an excuse for undue rhetoric or inflation. Even the startling sense of hiatus in the first movement repeat (can this really be authentic?) makes sense given such intensity. His second movement *Scherzo* is as colourful as it's volatile and in the *Largo* the playing is, again, gloriously free-spirited and keenly felt. His transition out of the *Polonaise-Fantaisie*'s central *Più lento*, back to Chopin's principal idea, shows a compelling sense of the composer's depth and introspection, and if his choice of the Fourth *Scherzo* is surprising, given such seriousness, he's brilliantly attuned to one of Chopin's most mercurial flights of fancy. The C minor *Nocturne* pulses with profound elegy, its central octaves fired off like so many ceremonial cannons, and Goerner makes something very special out of the Fourth *Ballade*'s coda, tempering Chopin's bravura with fine melodic intricacy. EMI has provided this most personal and distinctive artist with an impressively bold and spacious recording.

Four Ballades

No 1 in G minor, Op 23; **No 2** in F, Op 38;
No 3 in A flat, Op 47; **No 4** in F minor, Op 52

Ballades Nos 1-4. Mazurkas – No 7 in F minor, Op 7 No 3; No 13 in A minor, Op 17 No 4; No 23 in D, Op 33 No 2. Waltzes – No 1 in E flat, Op 18; No 5 in A flat, Op 42; No 7 in C sharp minor, Op 64 No 2. Etudes, Op 10 – No 3 in E; No 4 in C sharp minor. Nocturne No 1 in F, Op 15
Murray Perahia pf
Sony Classical SK64399 (61' · DDD) Recorded 1994
Ⓟ**OOO**

This is surely the greatest, certainly the richest, of Perahia's many exemplary recordings. Once again his performances are graced with rare and classic attributes and now, to supreme clarity, tonal elegance and musical perspective, he adds an even stronger poetic profile, a surer sense of the inflammatory rhetoric underpinning Chopin's surface equilibrium. In other words the vividness and immediacy are as remarkable as the finesse. And here, arguably, is the oblique but telling influence of Horowitz whom Perahia befriended during the last months of the old wizard's life. Listen to the First *Ballade*'s second subject and you'll hear rubato like the most subtle pulsing or musical breathing. Try the opening of the Third and you'll note an ideal poise and lucidity, something rarely achieved in these outwardly insouciant pages. From Perahia the waltzes are marvels of liquid brilliance and urbanity. Even Lipatti hardly achieved such an enchanting lilt or buoyancy, such a beguiling sense of light and shade. In the mazurkas, too, Perahia's tiptoe delicacy and tonal irridescence (particularly in Op 7 No 3 in F minor) make the music dance and spin as if caught in some magical hallucinatory haze. Finally, two contrasting *Etudes*, and whether in ardent lyricism (Op 10 No 3) or shot-from-guns virtuosity (Op 10 No 4) Perahia's playing is sheer perfection. The recording beautifully captures his instantly recognisable, glistening sound world.

Ballades Nos 1-4. Barcarolle in F sharp, Op 60. Berceuse in D flat, Op 57. Scherzo No 4 in E, Op 54
Evgeni Kissin pf
RCA Red Seal 09026 63259-2 (62' · DDD)   Ⓕ

Kissin plays Chopin with a rhetorical drama, intensity and power that few could equal. His technique is of an obliterating command, enough to make even his strongest competitors throw up their hands in despair, and yet everything is at the service of a deeply ardent and poetic nature. Listen to his slow and pensive *Andantino* in the Second *Ballade*, its rhythm or thought-pattern constantly halted and checked, the following *presto* storms of such pulverising force that they will make even the least susceptible hackles rise and fists clench as Jove's thunder roars across the universe. The first subject of the First *Ballade* is daringly slow and inward-looking, the start of the glorious Fourth evoking the feelings of a blind man when first granted the gift of sight, while the *Berceuse* is seen through an opalescent pedal haze that creates its own hallucinatory and rarified atmosphere. The final page of the *Barcarolle* – always among music's most magical homecomings – is given with an imaginative brio known to very few, and the Fourth *Scherzo* is among the most Puckish and highly coloured on record. The recordings are less than ideally beautiful but more than adequate. An astonishing achievement.

Four Ballades. Four Scherzos
Stephen Hough *pf*
Hyperion CDA67456 (72' · DDD)   Ⓕ**OO**

This is astonishing piano playing; Chopin interpretation that, at its best, fully measuring up to the greatness of these pieces. Stephen Hough's accounts offer plenty of refreshment to spirit and senses.

The distribution is interesting, chronological but alternating one of each, which may not make a recital to consume at one go, but helps to point up their diversity and individual character, as well as Chopin's mastery of large forms. Hough is unfailingly thoughtful; there isn't a note that hasn't been cared for. Just a few of them (Third Ballade, for example) are picked out of the texture and strung together for our delectation in a way that might strike you as otiose if you're in a sober-sides kind of mood. The surfaces of his presentations are very 'worked', more indicative of application, maybe, than of organic growth. But this isn't superficial playing – the performances catch fire.

He inclines to the accepted view that Chopin's large forms have a 'plot' that culminates in a tumult or a whirlwind of activity. The tempest in the coda of the Fourth Ballade might have been a mite less furious, to let the ear have more time to register what's going on. The closing pages of No 1, on the other hand, have an exemplary finish and allure. Most distinguished of the Ballades is No 2, where Hough perceives the invasion of one kind of music by another in all its subtlety and lays out a spellbinding seven-minute drama.

He has interesting points to make in the *Scherzos*, too. Where many a player is content to let recurring sections and paragraphs register simply as the music we heard before, with him they sound different in some degree, affected by what's come in between. Hough is always doing something, though sometimes you might wish he were doing less. This is an issue out of the ordinary; welcome, too, for being handsomely recorded and produced.

Four Ballades – No 3 in A flat, Op 47; No 4 in F minor, Op 52. Mazurkas – No 36 in A minor, Op 59 No 1; No 37 in A flat, Op 59 No 2; No 38 in F sharp minor, Op 59 No 3; No 39 in B, Op 63 No 1; No 40 in F minor, Op 63 No 2; No 41 in C sharp minor, Op 63 No 3; No 49 in F minor, Op 68 No 4. Polonaises – No 5 in F sharp minor, Op 44; No 6 in A flat, 'Heroic', Op 53
Piotr Anderszewski *pf*
Virgin Classics 545619-2 (60' · DDD)   Ⓕ**OO**

Following his celebrated earlier discs of Beethoven, Mozart and Bach, 34-year-old Piotr Anderszewski gives us an exceptionally powerful and seductive Chopin recital. He prefers a subtly chosen programme to complete sets of the Mazurkas, Ballades or Polonaises, and his often phenomenally acute and sensitive awareness of Chopin's constantly shifting perspective has you reliving every bar of such incomparable music.

In the three Op 59 Mazurkas (a notably rich part of Chopin's deeply confessional diary) he achieves a rare sense of brooding introspection, close to neurosis, with bittersweet mood swings that shift from resignation to flashes of anger. Then there's the F minor Mazurka, Op 63 No 2, taken for once at a true *lento*, a dark place indeed for Anderszewski, with only relative light in the central idea to lessen the mood of heart-stopping despondency. Again, in both the Ballades his sharply original ideas combine with a total responsibility to the score; seldom can the letter and spirit of the composer be united so flawlessly.

Eyebrows may be raised in the A flat Polonaise, but this is no obvious celebration of triumph over adversity, rather a re-creation of music which lives again in all its initial audacity. Here, in this great young pianist's incomparable hands, and in Virgin's excellent sound, is living proof that Chopin's music is forever new, forever revelatory.

Etudes

Etudes – Opp 10 & 25
Murray Perahia *pf*
Sony Classical SK61885 (56' · DDD)   Ⓕ**OOO**

Perahia brings order and lucidity to the heart of Chopin's most audacious fire-storms and in, for example, Etudes Nos 1 and 4 from Op 10, you're made aware of an incomparable mix of poetry and precision. Perahia's may be a wholly modern voice yet he truly speaks in the spirit of his revered masters of the past, of Cortot and Fischer in particular, and this, allied with his immaculate infinitely polished and shaded pianism, gives his performances the rarest distinction and quality.

How superb and unfaltering is his mastery in No 1, that magnificent curtain-raiser to Op 10, how magical his improvisatory touch in its closing page. His textural translucency and musical breathing, his *rubato* in No 3, like that of Rubinstein, is that of a great and natural singer of the keyboard. Chopin would surely have cried out once again, 'ah, mon patrie!' if he had heard this performance.

No 8 is delightfully rumbustious and just when you note a touch of evasion in his rapid spin through the morbid near-Wagnerian chromaticism of No 6 you find yourself relishing his cool tempo, a musical ease and flexibility that give new meaning to Chopin's prescribed *con molto espressione*. On the other hand No 7 from

Op 25 unfolds with the truest, most memorable sense of its *lento* elegy. And where else have you heard a more impassioned or articulate *Revolutionary* Etude?

Faced with artistry of this calibre, criticism falls silent; one can only listen and wonder at such unalloyed perfection. Perahia's is the finest of all modern discs of the Etudes, and Sony's sound captures all his artistry.

Etudes, Opp 10 & 25
Maurizio Pollini *pf* DG 413 794-2GH (56' · ADD)
Recorded 1972   ⓕⷞ

The 24 *Etudes* of Chopin's Opp 10 and 25, although dating from his twenties, remain among the most perfect specimens of the genre ever known, with all technical challenges – and they are formidable – dissolved into the purest poetry. With his own transcendental technique (and there are few living pianists who can rival it) Pollini makes you unaware that problems even exist – as for instance in Op 10 No 10 in A flat, where the listener is swept along in an effortless stream of melody. The first and last of the same set in C major and C minor have an imperious strength and drive, likewise the last three impassioned outpourings of Op 25. Lifelong dislike of a heart worn on the sleeve makes him less than intimately confiding in more personal contexts such as No 3 in E major and No 6 in E flat minor from Op 10, or the nostalgic middle section of No 5 in E minor and the searing No 7 in C sharp minor from Op 25. Like the playing, so the recording itself could profitably be a little warmer at times, but it's a princely disc all the same.

Etudes, Opp 10 & 25. Ballades. Waltzes – Nos 1–19
Augustin Anievas *pf*
EMI Double Forte ② 574290-2 (146' · ADD) Recorded 1966-75   Ⓜⷪⷪⷪⷪ

These recordings celebrate the sadly far-distant heyday of American pianism, a time when New York's Juilliard School turned out keyboard athletes of an enviable prowess and charisma. Here is a pianist whose dismissal of every daunting difficulty of the 24 Etudes is so nonchalant that it allows him total freedom to turn pragmatism into the purest poetry, and achieve a glamorous perfection. His scintillating play of light and shade in the opening curtain-raiser is as delectable as it's masterly, and he's even more magically deft in No 2, where his impeccable right-hand flight is counterpointed by the most witty relish of the left hand's tic-toc momentum. Listen to the lift he gives each phrase in the etude in sixths, or hear him in the so-called 'Winter Wind', and you'll be aware of the most imperious command combined with the most elegant musicianship.

In the Ballades Anievas may offer a less potent or focused experience than, say, Zimerman or Perahia, yet all these readings are alive with spe-

cial insights. In the Waltzes Anievas is once more in his element, a ballroom dancer of rare urbanity and ease. In short, few more beguiling recordings of the Waltzes exist.

The recordings have come up admirably. This is an invaluable issue by a superlative pianist.

Fantasie, Op 49

Fantasie in F minor, Op 49. Waltzes – No 2 in A flat, Op 34 No 1; No 3 in A minor, Op 34 No 2; No 5 in A flat, Op 42. Polonaise No 5 in F sharp minor, Op 44. Nocturnes – No 1 in C sharp minor, Op 27 No 1; No 2 in D flat, Op 27 No 2; No 10 in A flat, Op 32 No 2. Scherzo No 2 in B flat minor, Op 31
Evgeni Kissin *pf*
RCA Victor Red Seal 09026 60445-2 (67' · DDD)
Recorded live 1993   ⓕ

Evgeni Kissin's playing at 21 (when these performances were recorded) quite easily outmatches that of the young Ashkenazy and Pollini – and most particularly in terms of the maturity of his musicianship. The programme launches off with a reading of the great F minor *Fantasie*, which, though a bit measured, is integrated to perfection. The power and determination of the performance certainly make one sit up and listen, but at the same time it would be difficult not to be moved by the heartfelt lyricism of the melodic passages. Although Kissin may be a little unsmiling in the three waltzes, at least he has admirable sophistication in being able to add interest to the interpretations. His control in the tricky A flat, Op 42, is quite amazing. The *Nocturne* in C sharp minor is a jewel. This reading is among the most darkly imaginative and pianistically refined on disc. The disc ends with a powerfully glittering performance of the Second *Scherzo*.

Mazurkas

Nos 1-64: Op 6 Nos 1-4 **(1-4)**; Op 7 Nos 1-5 **(5-9)**; Op 17 Nos 1-4 **(10-13)**; Op 24 Nos 1–4 **(14-17)**; Op 30 Nos 1-4 **(18-21)**; Op 33 Nos 1-4 **(22-25)**; Op 41 Nos 1-4 **(26-29)**; Op 50 Nos 1-3 **(30-32)**; Op 56 Nos 1-3 **(33-35)**; Op 59 Nos 1-3 **(36-38)**; Op 63 Nos 1-3 **(39-41)**; Op 67 Nos 1-4 **(42-45)**; Op 68 Nos 1-4 **(46-49)**; Op posth **(50-64)**

Mazurkas Nos 1-51
Artur Rubinstein *pf*
RCA Victor Red Seal ② 09026 63050-2 (140' · ADD)
Recorded 1960s   Ⓑⷪⷪ

Recording in the studio, rather than at a live concert, quite naturally leads to a safe and uniform approach, which doesn't really serve the inspired inventiveness of the music. In some ways these recordings suffer from this. If you compare Rubinstein's readings here with those he recorded on 78rpm discs in 1938-9, you immediately notice that an element of fantasy and caprice has given way to a more sober view of the music. The *Mazurkas* are so intricate in their variety of moods that the successful pianist has to be able to treat each one as an entity, contrasting the emotional content within the context of that particular piece. Rubinstein, with his serious approach, lends the music more weight than is usual and he wholly avoids trivialising it with over-snappy rhythms. With him many of the lesser-known *Mazurkas* come to life, such as the E flat minor, Op 6 No 4, with its insistent little motif that pervades the whole piece. His phrasing is free and flexible and he has utter appreciation of the delicacy of Chopin's ideas. He doesn't, however, take an improvisatory approach. Rubinstein judges to perfection which details to bring out so as to give each piece a special character. He convinces one that he has made this music his own. When you hear Rubinstein tackle the C sharp minor Mazurka, Op 53 No 3, you at once know that he fully comprehends the depth of this, perhaps the greatest of them all. He ranges from the pathos of the opening to a persuasive tonal grandeur in the more assertive parts, and yet is able to relate the two. The recording has a number of blemishes: the piano is too closely recorded, the loud passages are hollow-toned, especially in the bass, and little sparkle to the sound.

Mazurkas Nos 1-52, 55, 56, 59-62
Vladimir Ashkenazy pf
Double Decca 448 086-2DF2 (143' · DDD/ADD)
Recorded 1976-85　　　　　ⓈⒷ**OO**

Vladimir Ashkenazy made his integral set of the *Mazurkas* over a decade. He has always played outstandingly. He does so again here, giving complete satisfaction. The set includes all those published posthumously and the revised version of Op 68 No 4; so his is the most comprehensive survey in the current catalogue. Ashkenazy memorably catches their volatile character, and their essential sadness. Consider, for example, the delicacy and untrammelled spontaneity with which he approaches these works. He shows the most exquisite sensibility, each item strongly, though never insistently characterised. His accounts of the Mazurkas, Op 6 and Op 7, for instance, offer a genuine alternative to Rubinstein. Nine pieces in all, they were Chopin's first published sets and their piquancy, the richness of their ideas, is here made very apparent. One is given a sense of something completely new having entered music. Although there are fine things in all the groups, Op 24 is the first Mazurka set of uniformly high quality and No 4 is Chopin's first great work in the genre. On hearing them together like this one appreciates the cumulative effect which the composer intended, and Ashkenazy makes a hypersensitive response to their quickly changing moods. The recorded sound has the warmth, fullness and immediacy typical of this series, with a nice bloom to the piano tone.

Mazurkas Nos 1-51[a]; No 23 in D, Op 33 No 2[b];　Ⓗ
No 35 in C minor, Op 56 No 3[e]; No 41 in C sharp minor, Op 63 No 3[f]. Waltzes – No 2 in A flat, Op 34 No 1[c]; No 7 in C sharp minor, Op 64 No 2[d]
Artur Rubinstein pf
Naxos Historical mono ② 8 110656/7
(137' · ADD) Recorded [cd]1928-30, [bef]1930-32, [a]1939
　　　　　Ⓢ**OOO**
Nocturnes[a] – Opp 9, 15, 27, 32, 37, 48, 55, 62　Ⓗ
71. Scherzos[b] – Opp 20, 31, 39 & 54
Artur Rubinstein pf
Naxos Historical mono ② 8 110659/60
(132' · ADD) Recorded [b]1932, [a]1936-7　　　　Ⓢ

It's controversial to say so, but such playing makes a mockery of present-day standards. All these performances prove that Rubinstein played the piano as naturally as a bird flies or a fish swims. He was simply in his element, and never more so than in Chopin. Who else has given us the Nocturnes with such ravishing inwardness, pianistic sheen and a bel canto to rival the finest singer? Decorative fioriture are spun off like so much silk, and whether or not you consider Op 15 No 2 'inseparable from champagne and truffles' and Op 27 No 1 a portrait of 'a corpse washed ashore on a Venetian lagoon', or hear the nightingales of Nohant in Op 62 No 1 and the chant of the monks of Valdemosa in Op 15 No 3 and Op 37 No 1, you can hardly remain unaffected by Rubinstein's unique artistry. His feline ease in the double-note flow of Op 37 No 2, or the way he lightens the darkness of the great C minor Nocturne without losing an ounce of its tragedy, all form part of the genius that made him the most celebrated of all Chopin pianists.

Rubinstein's Mazurkas are equally the stuff of legends. Chopin's most subtle and confessional diary, they transcend their humble origins and become in Rubinstein's hands an ever-audacious series of miniatures extending from the neurasthenic to the radiant, from Chopin's nagging child (Op 17 No 3) to the unfurling of proud ceremonial colours (Opp 63 No 1). What heartache he conveys in Op 63 No 3; and when has Op 67 No 3 been more intimately confided, its banal association with Les sylphides more blissfully resolved? Chopin's final composition, Op 68 No 4, becomes a valediction encouraging rather than forbidding weeping, Rubinstein's rubato the caressing magic that created a furore at his unforgettable recitals.

Finally the Scherzos, played with an outrageous but enthralling disregard for safety. Only a pedant will underline the odd mis-hit or pockmark in the context of such sky-rocketing bravura and poetic impulse. As an added bonus there are additional recordings of three Mazurkas and two Waltzes, the A flat Op 34 No 1 alive with dizzying virtuoso trickery. The sleeve-note writer may comically mistake the Mazurkas for the Polonaises in referring to Schumann's oft-misquoted description, 'guns [sic] buried in flowers', but that's a mere spot on Naxos's blazing sun. No more life-affirming Chopin exists.

Nocturnes

No 1 in B flat minor, Op 9; **No 2** in E flat, Op 9;
No 3 in B, Op 9; **No 4** in F, Op 15; **No 5** in F sharp,
Op 15; **No 6** in G minor, Op 15; **No 7** in C sharp
minor, Op 27; **No 8** in D flat, Op 27; **No 9** in B flat,
Op 32; **No 10** in A flat, Op 32; **No 11** in G minor, Op
37; **No 12** in G, Op 37; **No 13** in C minor, Op 48; **No
14** in F sharp minor, Op 48; **No 15** in F minor, Op 55;
No 16 in E flat, Op 55; **No 17** in B flat, Op 62; **No 18**
in E, Op 62; **No 19** in E minor, Op 72; **No 20** in C
sharp minor, Op posth; **No 21** in C minor, Op posth

Nocturnes Nos 1-19
Maria João Pires pf DG ② 447 096-2GH2 (109' ·
DDD)   ⓔ**OOO**

Passion rather than insouciance is
Pires's keynote. Here is an intensity
and drama that scorn all complacent
salon or drawing-room expectations. How she
relishes Chopin's central storms, creating a
vivid and spectacular yet unhistrionic contrast
with all surrounding serenity or 'embalmed
darkness'. The *con fuoco* of Op 15 No 1 erupts in
a fine fury and in the first *Nocturne*, Op 9 No 1,
Pires's sharp observance of Chopin's *appassionato* marking comes like a prophecy of the coda's
sudden blaze. Chopin, he informs us in no
uncertain terms, was no sentimentalist. More
intimately, in Op 15 No 3 (where the music's
wavering sense of irresolution led to the sobriquet 'the Hamlet Nocturne') Pires makes you
hang on to every note in the coda's curious,
echoing chimes, and in the *dolcissimo* conclusion
to No 8 (Op 27 No 2) there's an unforgettable
sense of 'all passion spent', of gradually ebbing
emotion. Pires with her burning clarity has
reinforced our sense of Chopin's stature and
created a new range of possibilities (showing us
that there's life after Rubinstein). Naturally,
Rubinstein's legendary cycles possess a gra-
ciousness, an ease and elegance reflecting, perhaps, a long-vanished *belle époque*. Yet moving
ahead, one has no hesitation in declaring Maria
João Pires among the most eloquent master-
musicians of our time.

Polonaises

No 1 in C sharp minor, Op 26; **No 2** in E flat minor,
Op 26; **No 3** in A, Op 40, 'Military'; **No 4** in C minor,
Op 40; **No 5** in F sharp minor, Op 44; **No 6** in A flat,
Op 53, 'Heroic'; **No 7** in A flat, Op 61, 'Polonaise-
fantaisie'; **No 8** in D minor, Op 71; **No 9** in B flat,
Op 71; **No 10** in F minor, Op 71; **No 11** in B flat
minor; **No 12** in G flat; **No 13** in G minor; **No 14** in B
flat; **No 15** in A flat; **No 16** in G sharp minor

Polonaises Nos 1-7. Andante spianato and   Ⓗ
Grande Polonaise in E flat, Op 22
Artur Rubinstein pf
Naxos Historical mono 8 110661 (64' · ADD) Recorded
1934-5   ⓈⒶ**OOO**

Here, in all their glory, are Rubinstein's 1934-5 recordings of Chopin's
six mature Polonaises framed by examples of his early and late genius (Opp 22 and 61
respectively). Together with his early discs of
the Mazurkas, Scherzos (EMI) and Nocturnes,
these performances remain classics of an unassailable calibre, their richness and character
increased rather than diminished by the passage
of time.

For Schumann, the Polonaises were 'canons
buried in flowers' and whether epic or confiding, stark or florid their national and personal
fervour is realised to perfection by Rubinstein.
Listen to the *Andante spianato* from Op 22 and
you'll hear a matchless *cantabile*, a tribute to a *bel
canto* so often at the heart of Chopin's elusive
and heroic genius. Try the central *meno mosso*
from the First Polonaise and witness an imaginative freedom that can make all possible rivals
sound stiff and ungainly by comparison. The
colours of the A major Polonaise are unfurled
with a rare sense of its ceremonial nature, and
the darker, indeed tragic, character of its sombre C minor companion is no less surely caught.
The two 'big' Polonaises, Opp 44 and 53, are
offered with a fearless bravura (you can almost
hear the audience's uproar after Rubinstein's
thunderous conclusion to the latter), rhythmic
impetus and idiomatic command beyond criticism.

The simple truth is that Rubinstein played the
piano as a fish swims in water, free to phrase and
inflect with a magic peculiarly his own, to make,
in Liszt's words, 'emotion speak, weep and sing
and sigh'. The sound may seem dated but
Naxos's transfers are excellent, and to think that
all this is offered at a bargain price…

Polonaises Nos 1-7
Maurizio Pollini pf
DG The Originals 457 711-2GOR (62' · ADD)
Recorded 1975   Ⓜ**OO**

This is Pollini in all his early glory, in expertly
transferred performances. Shorn of all virtuoso
compromise or indulgence, the majestic force of
his command is indissolubly integrated with the
seriousness of his heroic impulse. Rarely will
you be compelled into such awareness of the
underlying malaise beneath the outward and
nationalist defiance of the *Polonaises*. The tension and menace at the start of No 2 are almost
palpable, its storming and disconsolate continuation made a true mirror of Poland's clouded
history. The C minor *Polonaise's* denouement,
too, emerges with a chilling sense of finality,
and Pollini's way with the pounding audacity
commencing at 3'00" in the epic F sharp minor
Polonaise is like some ruthless prophecy of every
percussive, anti-lyrical gesture to come. At
7'59" Chopin's flame-throwing interjections
are volcanic, and if there's ample poetic delicacy
and compensation (notably in the *Polonaise-
fantaisie*, always among Chopin's most profoundly speculative masterpieces), it's the more

elemental side of his genius, his 'canons' rather than 'flowers' that are made to sear and haunt the memory. Other pianists may be more outwardly beguiling, but Pollini's magnificently unsettling Chopin can be as imperious and unarguable as any on record. That his performances are also deeply moving is a tribute to his unique status.

Polonaises Nos 1-16. Allegro de concert in A, Op 46. Etudes – F minor, Op posth; A flat, Op posth; D flat, Op posth. Tarantelle in A flat, Op 43. Fugue in A minor. Albumleaf in E. Polish Songs, Op 74 – Spring. Galop marquis. Berceuse. Barcarolle. Two Bourrées
Vladimir Ashkenazy pf
Double Decca ② 452 167-2DF2 (145' · DDD/ADD)
Recorded 1974-84   Ⓑ

Ashkenazy's Chopin hardly needs any further advocacy. His distinguished and virtually complete survey rests alongside the Rubinstein recordings in general esteem. The 16 *Polonaises* were not recorded in sets but individually, or in small groups, which is one reason why they sound so fresh, with Ashkenazy striking a sensitive artistic balance between poetic feeling and the commanding bravura that one takes for granted in the more extrovert pieces, with their Polish patriotic style. The recordings vary between analogue and digital, and the recording venues are as different as the Kingsway Hall, St John's, Smith Square, and All Saints, Petersham; but the realism of the piano sound is remarkably consistent. A series of shorter pieces is included on the second disc and the playing is always distinguished. Among the major items, the gentle *Berceuse* is quite melting, while the *Allegro de concert* and *Barcarolle* are hardly less memorable.

Preludes, Op 28

No 1 in C; No 2 in A minor; No 3 in G; No 4 in E minor; No 5 in D; No 6 in B minor; No 7 in A; No 8 in F sharp minor; No 9 in E; No 10 in C sharp minor; No 11 in B; No 12 in G sharp minor; No 13 in F sharp; No 14 in E flat minor; No 15 in D flat; No 16 in B flat minor; No 17 in A flat; No 18 in F minor; No 19 in E flat; No 20 in C minor; No 21 in B flat; No 22 in G minor; No 23 in F; No 24 in D minor; No 25 in C sharp minor; Op 45; No 26 in A flat, Op posth

---

Preludes Nos 1-26[a]. Barcarolle[b]. Polonaise No 6[c]. Scherzo No 2 in B flat minor, Op 31[d]
Martha Argerich pf
DG Galleria 415 836-2GGA (62' · ADD) Recorded
[a]1977, [b]1961, [c]1967, [d]1975   Ⓜ●

Professor Zurawlew, the founder of the Chopin Competition in Warsaw, was once asked which one of the prize-winners he would pick as having been his favourite. The answer came back immediately: 'Martha Argerich'. This disc could explain why. There are very few record-

ings of the 24 Preludes (Op 28) that have such a perfect combination of temperamental virtuosity and compelling artistic insight. Argerich has the technical equipment to do whatever she wishes with the music. Whether it's in the haunting, dark melancholy of No 2 in A minor or the lightning turmoil of No 16 in B flat minor, she's profoundly impressive. It's these sharp changes of mood that make her performance scintillatingly unpredictable. In the *Barcarolle* there's no relaxed base on which the melodies of the right hand are constructed, as is conventional, but more the piece emerges as a stormy odyssey through life, with moments of visionary awareness. Argerich is on firmer ground in the *Polonaise*, where her power and technical security reign triumphant. The CD ends with a rippling and yet slightly aggressive reading of the second *Scherzo*. This is very much the playing of a pianist who lives in the 'fast lane' of life. The sound quality is a bit reverberant, an effect heightened by the fact that Argerich has a tendency to overpedal.

Op 47; in F minor, Op 52 No 4. Nocturnes – in C minor, Op 48 No 1; in D flat, Op 27 No 2; in E, Op 62 No 2
Nikolai Lugansky pf
Erato 0927-42836-2 (78' · DDD)   Ⓕ●

Nikolai Lugansky is the young Russian protégé of the late Tatiana Nikolayeva who, confident of his dazzling talent, pronounced him 'the next one'. His first prize in the 1994 Tchaikovsky Competition entirely justified her claim and this disc offers formidable evidence of her unswerving belief. Here we see Chopin gaunt and intense, his inner rage and torment dramatically exposed, the salon figure of popular imagination erased for ever. For Lugansky it's all or nothing, and, indeed, there's 'something of the dark' (and not only in the Nocturnes) about the seething passions he evokes. Hear him in the B major Nocturne and note the tonal richness and imaginative freedom of the greatest Russian singers. How daringly he underlines the sense of elegy in the great C minor Nocturne, how menacingly he weights Prelude No 18, telling its violence with an uncompromising strength.

True, there are, thankfully, other approaches to Chopin. But if some turn for relief to Cortot's careless rapture or Rubinstein's urbanity they will surely admit that Lugansky's Chopin is of a formidable commitment and audacity; Chopin 'through a glass darkly'.

Preludes
Grigory Sokolov pf
Opus 111 OP30-336 (47' · DDD) Recorded live 1990Ⓕ

Grigory Sokolov is an uncompromising, exclusively serious rather than commercial artist and has consequently paid a price. Even today, he remains an awe-inspiring figure to connoisseurs rather than a wider public. His recordings, too, are sadly few, though this reissue reaffirms him as among the most formidable and characterful pianists of our time. So deeply is every bar, indeed, every note, weighed and considered that each Prelude emerges in a new and arresting light. True, he can bear down so intensely that Chopin isn't always allowed his truest or most natural voice. But glories far outweigh queries. Prelude No 2 is authentically *lento* and lugubrious, its morbidity realised quite without a cool and over-familiar evasion. Again, just as you wonder whether No 13, an idyllic Nocturne, needs such strenuous pleading, you find yourself at No 16, played with a thunderous and lavishly pedalled aplomb, and to a reading of No 17 inflected with rare affection. What daring in No 18, what imaginative delicacy in No 19 (that flight into a cloudless azure), what aerial magic in No 23 with its audacious close, and when have you heard a more dramatic dip from *fortissimo* to *pianissimo* in the elegiac and processional C minor Prelude (No 20)?

The sound captures Sokolov's immense dynamic range exceptionally well, and even if you're a lover of understatement or of Cortot's careless and unforgettable rapture you'll surely admit that this is among the most powerfully individual òf all Chopin recordings.

Chopin 24 Preludes[a] **Mendelssohn** Ⓗ (arr Rachmaninov) A Midsummer Night's Dream[b] – Scherzo **Prokofiev** Suggestion diabolique, Op 4 No 4[c] **Rachmaninov** Lilacs[d]. Moment musical in E minor, Op 16 No 4[e] . Preludes – G, Op 32 No 5[f]; B minor, Op 32 No 10[g] **Schumann** Kinderszenen, Op 15[h] **Stravinsky** Etude, Op 7 No 4[i] **Vallier** Toccatina[j] **Weber** Piano Sonata No 1 in C – Rondo, 'Perpetuum mobile'[k]
Benno Moiseiwitsch pf
Testament SBT1196 (78' · ADD) Recorded [h]1930, [i]1938, [b]1939, 91940, [ad]1948, [cj]1950, [ef]1956 Ⓕ🅾🅾

Benno Moiseiwitsch's love affair with the piano spawned numerous fine recordings, though few match this superlative 1948 set of Chopin's Preludes. The first Prelude is candid and forthright, whereas No 4's *Largo* projects an outspoken top line (and note how sensitively Moiseiwitsch negotiates the accompaniment's constantly shifting harmonies). Desynchronised chords mark the opening of Prelude No 6, while the same Prelude's quiet close *segues* almost imperceptibly into the gnomic A major (a parallel sense of transition marries Preludes 10 and 11). Bryce Morrison, in his bookletnotes for Testament, singles out No 16 for its dexterity, but the more oratorical Nos 18 and 22 are particularly notable too for their especially keen sense of narrative.

But the greatness of these performances lies beyond detail. Much of the magic resides in Moiseiwitsch's ability to balance close-up and landscape, cultivating the individual phrase while keeping an eye on whole paragraphs. His touch, pedalling and attention to contrapuntal side-play are remarkable. These are profoundly

individual readings that positively teem with incident. But which CD to choose? Testament's transfer achieves a marginally clearer sound frame, APR a touch more warmth but a tad more surface noise. One minor criticism of Testament's disc: there's a very slight drop in pitch between the end of the 14th Prelude and the beginning of the 15th – not a full semitone, but noticeable enough to trouble those with perfect or relative pitch. APR's transfer is spot-on.

Choosing between the two programmes is more problematic. APR's all-Chopin sequence includes fluent accounts of the four Ballades, the Fourth a first-ever release. Odd smudges hardly matter in the face of such compelling musicianship. In the B flat Polonaise it's fascinating to compare Moiseiwitsch with fellow Leschetizky pupil Ignaz Friedman, the one restrained and elegant, the other (Friedman) pointed and rhythmically fierce. Likewise in the A flat Ballade, where Friedman invests the 'Galloping Horse' second set (Sir Winston Churchill's description) with extra impetus, Moiseiwitsch's musical manners are far milder.

Testament's makeweights highlight Moiseiwitsch's virtuosity, most memorably in Rachmaninov's reworking of the *Scherzo* from the *Midsummer Night's Dream*, which is heard to even better advantage than on the arranger's own recording. So much happens, so quickly and at so many dynamic levels, you can hardly credit the results to a single pair of hands. A Rachmaninov sequence includes a stereo G major Prelude (Op 32 No 5) and a justly famous 1940 account of the sombre B minor Prelude, Op 32 No 10. His primary-coloured 1930 recording of *Kinderszenen* is a joy. In contrast, lightning reflexes benefit textually bolstered Weber and the dry wit of Prokofiev, Stravinsky and John Vallier.

Those fancying an 'Essential Moiseiwitsch' collection should plump for Testament, though Chopin's magnificent Ballades are a significant enough draw to push the scales in APR's direction. It really is a matter of repertory preferences. Both discs are extremely well annotated.

Scherzos

No 1 in B minor, Op 20; **No 2** in B flat minor, Op 31; **No 3** in C sharp minor, Op 39; **No 4** in E, Op 54

Chopin Scherzos Nos 1-4
Schumann Bunte Blätter, Op 99
Sviatoslav Richter pf
Olympia OCD338 (75' · ADD) Recorded 1970-77 Ⓕ

Remarkably well recorded considering the source, one performance after another here is so memorable as to rank among the best versions around of the piece in question. There's nothing amid all the glorious playing here that won't keep your attention galvanised to the music. Richter isn't usually thought of as a very credible Chopin player, and yet he strides through the four *Scherzos* with an abundance of technique and deftly coloured textures that make this version a definite front-runner. His Chopin is finely controlled, spaciousness being the watchword rather than overt passion. His Schumann, on the other hand, has always been dazzling, because he has a temperament that convincingly responds to the extreme swings in mood. Many of the *Bunte Blätter* are amazingly fast and unnerving. Don't miss these performances.

Scherzos Nos 1-4
Ivo Pogorelich pf
DG 439 947-2GH (42' · DDD)   Ⓕ Ⓞ

Love him or hate him, Pogorelich guarantees a response. Chopin for the faint-hearted this isn't; original, provocative, challenging, daring, it emphatically is. Nevertheless, if Pogorelich's most unconventional ideas approach wilful eccentricity, the rewards far outweigh any reservations. True, if they weren't reinforced by such transcendental pianism Pogorelich's interpretations wouldn't carry nearly the same authority or conviction; but it's precisely the marrying of his imaginative scope with his extraordinary technical resource that opens up such startling expressive possibilities.

The first and second *Scherzos* show the juxtaposition of extremes at its most intense, stretching the limits of the musically viable. Predictably, the outer sections of the B minor *Scherzo* are incredibly fast, possessed with an almost demonic drive, while the central Polish carol (*Sleep, little Jesus*) is unusually slow and luxuriously sustained. But such extremes, of character as much as tempo, place enormous tension on the musical structure, and this is most evident in the B flat minor *Scherzo*. Make no mistake, Pogorelich's playing is astounding, from the imperious opening to the lingering and ravishing middle section, where his sublime lyrical simplicity is of the deepest inward poetry.

To sum up, a recording like this isn't easy. Some may find Pogorelich's probing individualism too overwhelming. There are more ideas crammed into under 42 minutes than on many discs almost twice the length, although most collectors will still feel short-changed by the playing time. This may not be Chopin for every day, but the force of Pogorelich's musical personality subtly and irrevocably shapes one's view of the music. A truly extraordinary disc.

Waltzes

No 1 in E flat, Op 18; **No 2** in A flat, Op 34 No 1;
No 3 in A minor, Op 34 No 2; **No 4** in F, Op 34 No 3;
No 5 in A flat, Op 42; **No 6** in D flat, Op 64 No 1;
No 7 in C sharp minor, Op 64 No 2; **No 8** in A flat,
Op 64 No 3; **No 9** in A flat, Op 69 No 1; **No 10** in
E minor, Op 69 No 2; **No 11** in G flat, Op 70 No 1;
No 12 in F minor, Op 70 No 2; **No 13** in D flat, Op
70 No 3; **No 14** in E minor, Op posth; **No 15** in E,

Op posth; **No 16** in A flat, Op posth; **No 17** in E flat,
Op posth; **No 18** in E flat, Op posth.; **No 19** in
A minor, Op posth

Waltzes Nos 1-14
Artur Rubinstein pf
RCA Red Seal 09026 63047-2 (50' · ADD) Recorded
1960s   Ⓑ Ⓞ

There has in recent years been a tendency to take Rubinstein's imposing series of Chopin recordings from the mid-1960s for granted, but to hear them digitally refurbished soon puts a stop to that. His tone doesn't have much luxuriance, being quite chiselled; yet a finely tuned sensibility is evident throughout. This is at once demonstrated by his direct interpretation of Op 18, its elegance explicit. His reading of Op 34 No 1 is *brillante*, as per Chopin's title. In Op 34 No 2 Rubinstein judges everything faultlessly, distilling the sorrowful yet cannily varied grace of this piece. The two finest here are Opp 42 and 64 No 2, and with the former Rubinstein excels in the unification of its diverse elements, its rises and falls of intensity, its hurryings forward and holdings back. This is also true of his reading of Op 64 No 2, the yearning of whose brief *più lento* section is memorable indeed. The sole fault of this issue is that conventional programming leads to the mature Waltzes, which were published by Chopin himself, coming first, the lesser, posthumously printed, items last. Not all of these are early but they have less substance than Opp 18-64, and should come first.

Waltzes Nos 1-14. Mazurka in C sharp minor,   Ⓗ
Op 50. No 3. Barcarolle. Nocturne in D flat, Op 27
No 2
Dinu Lipatti pf
EMI Great Recordings of the Century mono 566904-2
(65' · ADD) Recorded 1947-50   Ⓜ Ⓞ Ⓞ Ⓞ

 As a former pupil of Cortot, it wasn't perhaps surprising that Lipatti always kept a special place in his heart for Chopin. And thanks primarily to the 14 Waltzes, played in a non-chronological sequence of his own choosing, it's doubtful if the disc will ever find itself long absent from the catalogue. Like the solitary *Mazurka*, they were recorded in Geneva during his remarkable renewal of strength in the summer of 1950. The *Nocturne* and *Barcarolle* date back to visits to EMI's Abbey Road studio in 1947 and 1948 respectively. Just once or twice in the Waltzes you might feel tempted to question his sharp tempo changes for mood contrast within one and the same piece – as for instance in No 9 in A flat, Op 69 No 1. However, for the most part his mercurial lightness, fleetness and charm are pure delight. His *Nocturne* in D flat has long been hailed as one of the finest versions currently available. And even though we know he himself (one of the greatest perfectionists) was not completely happy about the *Barcarolle*, for the rest of us this glowing performance has a strength of direction and shapeliness all its own. In fuller contexts there's just a trace of plumminess in the recorded sound.

Waltzes Nos 1-19
Vladimir Ashkenazy *pf*
Decca 414 600-2DH (56' · ADD/DDD) Recorded 1976-83   Ⓕ

No one has served Chopin's cause more faithfully than Ashkenazy. He always preferred miscellaneous programmes which, while wholly understandable from his own point of view, occasionally posed problems for the collector wanting conveniently packaged sets of this or that genre in its entirety. So hats off to Decca for this reissue. All 19 known waltzes are here, including the last six posthumous publications. Rubinstein and Lipatti have long been the heroes in the sphere of the waltz. Ashkenazy must now join their number. From all three of these outstanding artists the waltzes emerge as true 'dance poems'. Ashkenazy also finds the ideal, translucent sound world for this composer, without excessive weight in the bass or injudicious use of the right pedal. What lessons he can teach certain younger contenders about exaggerated point-making (especially in the spotlighting of inner parts), and whirlwind spontaneity in faster numbers achieved without loss of grace or finesse. There's no need to be worried by any suggestion of inconsistency arising from date, level or system of recording.

Waltzes Nos 1-17. Polonaises – G minor, Op posth; B flat, Op posth
Allan Schiller *pf*
ASV Quicksilva CDQS6149 (60' · DDD) Recorded 1994   Ⓢ

Allan Schiller's playing has a wholesomely musical, straightforward directness that could be described as quintessentially English. Far more sparing than his rivals in resorting to cajoling rubato, he avoids personal idiosyncrasies of all kinds so that the music, as printed, can tell its own tale. The recording itself has a similar unforced naturalness to it. That said, sometimes Schiller's well-trained, obedient fingers are a little too impersonal in more nostalgic moods – Op 64 No 2 in C sharp minor, Op 69 No 1 in A flat (inspired by a youthful love, Maria Wodzinska) and even Op 69 No 2 in B minor. In several more agile contexts a little more light-fingered fancy and charm would not have come amiss. However, in both contexts Schiller's imagination seems to be given freer rein as the set progresses. And he certainly comes close to the truth in the spirited Op 70 No 1 in G flat, as is indeed also the case in the warmly benign posthumous E flat major Waltz with which he concludes. Both *Polonaises* are played with an engaging youthful purity of sound and sentiment.

Piano Works, various

Solo Piano Music – Volume 1   Ⓗ
Andante spianato and Grande Polonaise, Op 22°. Four Ballades^d. Barcarolle in F sharp, Op 60°. Berceuse in D flat, Op 57 (2 recordings)$^{e/k}$. Ecossaise in D, Op 72 No 3 (2 recs)$^{b/k}$. Etude in G flat, Op 10 No 5^c. Fantaisie-impromptu in C sharp minor, Op 66 (2 recs)$^{b/h}$. Fantasie in F minor, Op 49^q. Three Impromptus – No 1 in A flat, Op 29^j; No 2 in F sharp, Op 36^e; No 3 in G flat, Op 51°. Piano Sonatas – No 2 in B flat minor, Op 35^n; No 3 in B minor, Op 58^l. Preludes, Op 28 – Nos 1-24^e; No 7 in A^c; No 15 in D flat^f. Scherzos – No 1 in B minor, Op 20°; No 2 in B flat minor, Op 31^a; No 3 in C sharp minor, Op 39°; No 4 in E, Op 54^j. Waltzes – No 1 in E flat, Op 18 (2 recs)$^{e/l}$; No 2 in A flat, Op 34 No 1 (4 recs)$^{e/i/l/o}$; No 3 in A minor, Op 34 No 2e; No 4 in F, Op 34 No 3 (2 recs)$^{e/p}$; No 5 in A flat, Op 42 (2 recs)e/r; No 6 in D flat, Op 64 No 1 (2 recs)$^{e/g}$; No 7 in C sharp minor, Op 64 No 2 (3 recs)$^{e/l/m}$; No 8 in A flat, Op 64 No 3^e; No 9 in A flat, Op 69 No 1^e; No 10 in B minor, Op 69 No 2^e; No 11 in G flat, Op 70 No 1^e; No 12 in F minor, Op 70 No 2^e; No 13 in D flat, Op 70 No 3^e; No 14 in E minor, Op posth (2 recs)$^{e/n}$
^{a}**Arturo Benedetti-Michelangeli**, ^{b}**Alexander Brailowsky**, ^{c}**Ferruccio Busoni**, ^{d}**Robert Casadesus**, ^{e}**Alfred Cortot**, ^{f}**Ignaz Friedman**, ^{g}**Walter Gieseking**, ^{h}**Leopold Godowsky**, ^{i}**Josef Hofmann**, ^{j}**Vladimir Horowitz**, ^{k}**Raoul Koczalski**, ^{l}**Dinu Lipatti**, ^{m}**Ignace Jan Paderewski**, ^{n}**Sergey Rachmaninov**, ^{O}**Artur Rubinstein**, ^{P}**Emil von Sauer**, ^{q}**Solomon**, ^{r}**Magda Tagliaferro** *pfs*
Andante mono ④ AND1150 (5 hours: ADD) Recorded 1917-51   Ⓜ

We should never judge a book by its cover, but in this instance the one matches the other in quality and desirability, the classiest and best-packaged four-disc set you're likely to see in a long while. The trilingual notes are attractively designed and boast some rare and well-produced illustrations.

The contents are an idea that has been begging to be done by someone for years: an historical survey of the greatest Chopin pianists. What to choose? It's the ideal after-dinner game for piano anoraks. Jed Distler has made a judicious, imaginative and occasionally, of course, contentious selection. He also contributes a thorough critique of the recordings and thumbnail biographies of each pianist.

Who'd be without Rachmaninov in the Second Sonata and Lipatti in the Third? Or Cortot in any Chopin? His luminous 1943 set of Preludes is preferred to his better-known 1933-4 recording while Andante bravely champions his much-criticised 14 Waltzes. With all Cortot's anachronisms and finger-slips, he's pure piano poetry and provides a welcome antidote to the blemish-free, chilly perfection of Lipatti. Cortot is a rare exception in successfully bringing off the collections that were never intended to be played as *intégrales*: the complete Waltzes, *Scherzi* or Ballades from a single pianist are seldom satisfactory.

Seasoned pianophiles will have long cherished

most of these recordings in one format or another (the transfers, incidentally, are uniformly superb and frequently a marked improvement on previous reincarnations), but this volume makes a fantastic introduction to Chopin's genius.

Muzio Clementi   Italian/British 1752-1832

Clementi trained first in Rome, but in 1766-7 went to Dorset, England, to study the harpsichord. Moving to London in 1774, he became conductor at the King's Theatre and from 1770 gave concerts, often including his well-known keyboard sonatas Op 2 (1779).

Clementi travelled widely as a pianist in 1780-85, and in 1781 took part in a piano contest with Mozart in Vienna. In 1785-1802 he was a frequent piano soloist in London and conductor of his own symphonies, but in the 1790s he was overshadowed by the visiting Haydn. He was in great demand as a teacher. In 1798 he established a music publishing and piano-making firm, touring Europe (initially with his pupil John Field) as its representative in 1802-10. Among the firm's publications were major works by Beethoven. Clementi continued to conduct his symphonies in London and abroad; his last major works were three piano sonatas Op 50 (1821).

Foremost in Clementi's large output are c70 keyboard sonatas, spanning some 50 years. Counterpoint, running figuration and virtuoso passage-work are constant elements. Dramatic writing (which strongly influenced Beethoven) appears increasingly, and works such as Op 13 (1785) feature motivic unity and powerful expression. The sonatas of after c 1800 tend to be more diffuse. Only six of the symphonies and one piano concerto (1796) survive. Clementi also wrote keyboard duets, chamber music and two influential didactic works, Introduction to the Art of Playing on the Piano Forte (1801) and the comprehensive keyboard collection Gradus ad Parnassum (1817-26). **GROVE**music

Keyboard Sonatas

Keyboard Sonatas – F minor, Op 13 No 6; F,   **P**
Op 33 No 2; G minor, Op 34 No 2. Musical
Characteristics, Op 19 – Preludio I alla Haydn;
Preludio I alla Mozart. Capriccio in B flat, Op 17.
Fantasie with Variations, 'Au clair de lune', Op 48
Andreas Staier *fp*
Teldec Das Alte Werk 3984 26731-2 (68' · DDD)
Ⓟ**❍❍❍**

One's inclined to think of Clementi as a rather dry composer, however brilliant, but there's nothing remotely dry about this CD, which is full of expressive and often powerful music. Partly it's the instrument: on the fortepiano Clementi's music has a sharpness of impact that it lacks on a modern grand, and also a gently poetic, often almost mysterious ring that carries overtones of early Romanticism, especially in some of the slower music. But the chief responsibility belongs with Andreas Staier, who's clearly fired by the music and discovers so many layers of expression in it.

Essentially he plays three sonatas with a framework of single pieces surrounding them. Two of those pieces come from Clementi's *Musical Characteristics*, a group of short preludes published in 1787 and imitating Haydn and Mozart as well as Sterkel, Kozeluch and Vaňhal. Interestingly, these lively pieces indicate the features of the two composers that Clementi regarded as distinctive. Then there's a *Capriccio*, a charming piece demanding (and receiving) crisp and athletic fingerwork. The final item is a brilliant and imaginative fantasy on *Au clair de lune*, which Clementi varies in some highly inventive ways. This is a late work, from about 1820, and its style is comparable with mature Beethoven.

Of the three sonatas, the last (Op 33 No 2, 1794) is an elegantly written piece, in effect in two movements. Staier is masterly in his command of Clementi's dialectic and of the slightly quirky character of some of his themes, as in the first movement's finale. Op 34 No 2 is a big G minor work: its *Adagio* draws beautifully shapely and pointed playing from Staier, and the finale, another elaborate and extended movement, is impassioned music, powerfully done. The first of the sonatas, the earlier F minor work (1785), seems in some ways the most 'Romantic' in tone, with its *Allegro agitato* carrying hints of menace and darkness (enhanced by Staier's sensitive pedalling and misty textures), its eloquent *Largo*, where the melodic line is enunciated with real pathos, and its stormy final *Presto*. In all, Staier's reconciliation of the poetic and imaginative content of this music, with his command of its structure and its arguments, makes this one of the most impressive fortepiano discs in memory.

Eric Coates   British 1886-1957

Coates studied at the Royal Academy of Music, worked as an orchestral viola player, and wrote light orchestral music and c100 songs. He is best known for the suite London *(1933) and* The Dam Busters *march from his film score.* **GROVE**music

Light orchestral works

Saxo-Rhapsody. Wood Nymphs   **H**
Music Everywhere (Rediffusion March). From
Meadow to Mayfair. The Dam Busters – march;
London. Cinderella – Phantasy. London Again
**Royal Liverpool Philharmonic Orchestra /
Sir Charles Groves**
The Merrymakers – Miniature Overture. Summer
Days – At the dance. By the Sleepy Lagoon.
The Three Men – Man from the sea. The Three

Bears – Phantasy
London Symphony Orchestra / Charles Mackerras
Calling all Workers – March. The Three Elizabeths
City of Birmingham Symphony Orchestra /
Reginald Kilbey
HMV Classics ② HMV5 72327-2 (129′ · ADD)
Recorded 1956-71   Ⓢ Ⓑ

Eric Coates reached a vast public through the use of his music as signature tunes for radio programmes, and the cinema furthered the cause with the huge success of *The Dam Busters* march. There's much more to his music, though, than mere hit themes. Suites such as *London, London Again, From Meadow to Mayfair* and *The Three Elizabeths* offer a wealth of delights and are all the better for the juxtaposition of their contrasted movements. The two tone-poems for children, *Cinderella* and *The Three Bears*, are splendidly apt pieces of programme music – simple to follow, ever charming, never trite. The miniature overture *The Merrymakers* and the elegant waltz 'At the dance' are other superb pieces of light music, while the *Saxo-Rhapsody* shows Coates in more serious mood. Throughout there's a rich vein of melody, and an elegance of orchestration that makes this music to listen to repeatedly with ever-increasing admiration. The three conductors and orchestras featured adopt a no-nonsense approach that modestly suggests that his music should not be lingered over, never taken too seriously. Considering that the Mackerras items were first issued in 1956 (the rest being from 1968-71), the sound is of astonishingly good quality. This is a veritable feast of delightful music.

Sweet Seventeen. Summer Afternoon. Impressions of a Princess[a]. Salute the Soldier. Two Light Syncopated Pieces. For Your Delight. The Unknown Singer[a]. I Sing to You. Coquette. Over to You. Idyll. Under the Stars. By the Tamarisk. Mirage. Last Love. The Green Land[a]
[a]**Peter Hughes** sax **BBC Concert Orchestra / John Wilson**
ASV White Line CDWHL2107 (79′ · DDD)   Ⓜ

The title of these pieces won't ring much of a bell with any but the most avid Coates fans. Indeed, four pieces are here recorded for the first time. But what delights there are! It goes without saying that Coates's craftsmanship is in evidence from start to finish. Yet so often, one wonders just *why* a particular piece never quite made it in the way his most popular works did. Isn't *Summer Afternoon* every bit as delightful as *By the Sleepy Lagoon*? And wouldn't *Salute the Soldier* have served just as well as other marches as a radio signature tune? Most simply, aren't *Under the Stars, For Your Delight* and others just simply such utter charmers? The BBC Concert Orchestra plays beautifully, and the conductor seems thoroughly imbued with the Coates style. The recorded sound is crisp and clean, too. You are urged to sample the pleasures of this splendid collection.

Samuel Coleridge-Taylor
British 1875-1912

Coleridge-Taylor's father was from Sierra Leone and his mother was English. He studied the violin, singing and composition (with Stanford) at the RCM, producing anthems, chamber music and songs. His fame rests mainly on the cantata Hiawatha's Wedding Feast *(1898), once popular for its exotic flavour, and on choral works commissioned for provincial festivals, including further* 'Hiawatha' *scenes and* A Tale of Old Japan *(1911). He wrote incidental music for His Majesty's Theatre and was a composition professor and an excellent conductor, making three visits to the USA and maintaining contacts with prominent African-Americans who shared his mission to establish the dignity of blacks. Stylistically close to the music of his idol Dvor̆k, some of his works are modelled on African-American subjects and melodies, though some lack harmonic inventiveness. He was at his best in smaller pieces, including the* Petite suite de concert *for orchestra (1910).* **GROVE**music

Violin Concerto

Coleridge-Taylor Violin Concerto in G minor, Op 80
Dvořák Violin Concerto in A minor, B108
Philippe Graffin vn **Johannesburg Philharmonic Orchestra / Michael Hankinson**
Avie AV0044 (63′ · DDD)   Ⓕ

The resurgence of interest in the music of Samuel Coleridge-Taylor reaches another milestone with this long-overdue first recording of his Violin Concerto. Coleridge-Taylor completed it in 1911 for the American virtuoso Maud Powell but never lived to hear a note. Abetted by polished and passionate playing from the recently formed Johannesburg PO under its British-born chief Michael Hankinson, Philippe Graffin triumphantly demonstrates what an effective, endearing work it is, acutely responsive as he is to its bittersweet lyricism while equally relishing the many opportunities for solo display in both outer movements.
The choice of Dvořák's concerto as a coupling would no doubt have pleased Coleridge-Taylor; the Czech master was his favourite composer. Again, there's no missing the wholehearted commitment of all involved. Admittedly, there are times when you're aware that the orchestra isn't in the luxury class, but Graffin plays with such vibrant character and imagination, and the whole venture radiates such a life-affirming spontaneity and joy in music-making that any drawbacks dwindle into insignificance.

Additional recommendation

Violin Concerto
Coupled with: **Somervell** Violin Concerto
Marwood vn **BBC Scottish SO / Brabbins**
Hyperion CDA67420 (65′ · DDD)   Ⓕ
The coupling with Arthur Somervell's English

pastoral concerto of 1930 is interesting. Marwood's unflashy sweet-toned playing lends the right note of enchantment and authenticity to these forgotten scores.

Aaron Copland   American 1900-1990

Copland studied with Goldmark in New York and with Boulanger in Paris (1921-4), then returned to New York and took a leading part in composers organisations, taught at the New School for Social Research (1927-37) and composed. At first his Stravinskian inheritance from Boulanger was combined with aspects of jazz (Music for the Theatre, 1925) or with a grand rhetoric (Symphonic Ode, 1929), but then he established an advanced personal style in the Piano Variations (1930) and orchestral Statements (1935). Growing social concerns spurred him towards a popular style in the cowboy ballets Billy the Kid (1940) and Rodeo (1942), but even here his harmony and orchestral spacing are distinctive. Another ballet, Appalachian Spring (1944) – a continuous movement towards a set of variations on a Shaker hymn – brought a synthesis of the folksy and the musically developed.

Other works from the 'Americana' period include the Lincoln Portrait for speaker and orchestra (1942), the Fanfare for the Common Man (1942), the 12 Poems of Emily Dickinson for voice and piano (1950), two sets of Old American Songs (1950-52) and the opera The Tender Land (1954). But there were also more complex developments, especially among the chamber and instrumental works: the Piano Sonata (1941), Violin Sonata (1943), Piano Quartet (1950) and Piano Fantasy (1957). In the orchestral Connotations (1962) and Inscape (1967) he completed a journey into serialism, though again the sound is individual. Other late works, including the ballet Dance Panels (1963), the String Nonet (1960) and the Duo for flute and piano (1971), continue the cool triadic style. He was conductor, speaker and pianist, a generous and admired teacher, and author of several books, among them Music and Imagination (1952).   GROVEmusic

Symphony No 3

Copland Symphony No 3[a] **Hanson** Symphony No 2, 'Romantic'[b]
[a]**Dallas Symphony Orchestra / Eduardo Mata**
[b]**Saint Louis Symphony Orchestra / Leonard Slatkin**
HMV Classics HMV5 73544-2 (72' · ADD) Recorded 1986   ⒷO

This release is a superb coupling of two of the very greatest American symphonies. Mata's account of the Copland may seem understated when compared with Bernstein's – the *scherzo* has a taut, spare energy but much less weight, while the slow movement has a fine intensity, capable of relaxing into grace and lyrical purity but never approaches Bernstein's transported, slightly Thespian poignancy. The colours of the finale are bright and crisp, the mood exhilarat-

ingly joyous, but the sudden grinding of brakes and the gaze into the abyss beneath all this exuberance is less of a shock than in Bernstein's version. In short, the work doesn't seem quite such a huge gesture of a symphony in Mata's hands, but in compensation for this the quieter emotions are more gravely stated (the first movement, after all, is marked 'with simple expression', and throughout the work Mata often comes closer to this injunction than Bernstein). The strings in the *scherzo*'s trio section, too, have a hushed lyricism more touching than Bernstein's heartfelt but over-the-top eloquence, while the reminder of this mood at the centre of the slow movement seems a natural progression. Mata's players aren't quite a match for the NYP but they're splendidly recorded; DG's live recording glares rather at times.

Turning to the coupling, anyone who has been moved by the Barber *Adagio for strings* must respond to the yearning lyricism of the string writing of Hanson's *Romantic* Symphony, composed for the Boston Symphony Orchestra's 50th anniversary in 1930. This splendid work has real tunes – the *Andante* is its melodic focal point. It's convincing structurally, too, with the finale quoting earlier themes succinctly and powerfully (it's neither too long or too rhetorical) and without false optimism. Some will find Hanson's harmonic language not daring enough, but his music communicates. This performance is very fine. Perhaps, it has rather less grip and fervour than the composer's own, but it has breadth and a natural response to the atmosphere of the piece, while the orchestral playing is committed and fresh and the spacious acoustics add to the evocative effect.

Symphony No 3. Billy the Kid – Suite
New Zealand Symphony Orchestra / James Judd
Naxos American Classics 8 559106 (64' · DDD)   ⓈO

The first of Copland's three popular ballets is coupled here with what's arguably the greatest American symphony. Judd's first movement has more dynamic range than Eiji Oue's performance (Reference Recordings) and the long lines feel better paced. The second movement is the rumbustious *Scherzo* in Copland's most extrovert manner. Judd's interpretation works, and makes Oue seem a trifle pedestrian, closer to Copland's own performances than the dazzle that Bernstein brought to this kind of texture. The New Zealand strings aren't as precise in the taxing high opening as Oue's Minnesota players but, when it eventually comes, the fanfare and the subtle textures surrounding it are completely convincing.

The verdict on this efficient and sympathetic performance will be affected by its being the best buy around now. The suite from *Billy the Kid* gets thoroughly idiomatic treatment too and the coupling will encourage lovers of the most folksy Copland to recognise and enjoy the same composer in the big symphony.

Symphony No 3. Appalachian Spring. Fanfare for the
Common Man
Minnesota Orchestra / Eiji Oue
Reference Recordings RR-93CD (72' · DDD)　　　ⒻO

As an opening salute, the *Fanfare for the Common
Man* makes a good centenary tribute and prepares listeners for its appearance in the finale of
the Third Symphony. It also shows off the
prowess of the Minnesota brass. The version of
Appalachian Spring here is the suite, not the full
ballet, and it's well paced under Oue although
occasionally lacking attack in the strings, for
example at 15'22", where Copland said he
wanted 'bitten out *marcato*'.

Significant earlier versions of the Third Symphony have included Copland's rather understated treatment with the New Philharmonia
and Bernstein's much better projected interpretation on DG, considered by some the best. Yet
Oue's approach is compelling, falling midway
between Copland's objectivity and Bernstein's
dramatisation. The soft, long lines of the first
movement move inexorably towards the first
climax, and Copland's translucent scoring tells
in its purely personal way. The *scherzo* is a controlled riot, again showing off the brass – the
orchestra's best feature – and the finale is convincing. The recorded sound is spectacular too.

Ballets

Appalachian Spring. Billy the Kid. Rodeo
**San Francisco Symphony Orchestra / Michael
Tilson Thomas**
RCA Red Seal 09026-63511-2 (77' · DDD)　　ⒻOOO

 For *Appalachian Spring* Tilson Thomas
boldly opts for the rarely heard full
orchestral version of the complete ballet score. This includes an extra 10 or so minutes of fretful, dark-hued music omitted from
the familiar suite, after which that glorious final
statement of *Simple Gifts* seems to emerge with
even greater éclat and emotional release than
usual. Elsewhere, these newcomers distil all the
tender poetry and dewy freshness you could
wish for, while bringing a marvellously supple
spring and athletic purpose to any faster music.

Under Tilson Thomas, the suite from *Billy the
Kid* opens with a real sense of 'once upon a time'
wonder, the illimitable expanses of the prairie
stretching out before our very eyes. The ensuing street scene soon generates an infectious
rhythmic snap, and there's a wonderfully affecting contribution from the SFSO's principal
trumpet during the card game at night. Best of
all is 'Billy's death', as poignantly intoned as
you've ever heard it. Absolutely no grumbles,
either, about the four *Rodeo* dance episodes.
Tilson Thomas sees to it that 'Buckaroo Holiday' packs all the requisite punch and high-kicking swagger, while the two middle numbers ravish the ear in their disarming beauty. Moreover,
the concluding 'Hoe-Down' goes with terrific,
toe-tapping gusto, though the orchestra's

COPLAND'S APPALACHIAN SPRING – IN BRIEF

San Francisco SO / Michael Tilson Thomas
RCA 09026 63511-2 (77' · DDD)　　　ⒻOOO
The complete 35-minute score in its
guise for full orchestra, surveyed with
acute perception by Tilson Thomas and his
peerlessly refined band. Sensational, spectacularly natural sound.

Atlantic Sinfonietta / Andrew Schenck
Koch International 37019-2 (62' · DDD)　　　Ⓕ
A sensitive and shapely realisation of Copland's ballet in its original scoring for
13 instruments. Close-set recording, but by
no means lacking atmosphere.

Los Angeles PO / Leonard Bernstein
DG 439 528-2GGA (54' · DDD)　　　ⓂO
The popular 1945 suite in the performance of
a lifetime. Lenny at his most charismatic and
raptly understanding. Marvellous orchestral
playing.

Boston SO / Serge Koussevitzky
Biddulph WHL050 (80' · ADD)　　　Ⓜ
Koussevitzky's 1945 account was the suite's
world première recording, a blazingly committed display with a coda as touchingly
serene as you could hope to hear.

London SO / Aaron Copland
Sony SMK89874 (77' · ADD)　　　Ⓜ
The suite receives an eminently sprightly,
forthright performance under Copland's
lead, though it's perhaps neither quite as distinctive nor as radiant as his own 1959 RCA
Boston predecessor.

Atlanta SO / Robert Spano
Telarc CD80596 (69' · DDD)　　　ⒻO
A beautifully sprung account of the suite
from this burgeoning partnership. Barber's
tremendous First Symphony and approachable new works by Jennifer Higdon and
Christopher Theofanidis complete a varied
programme.

Detroit SO / Antál Dorati
Decca 430 705-2DM (74' · DDD)　　　Ⓜ
Glowingly caught by the Decca microphones, Dorati's uncomplicated Detroit
account of the 1945 suite will give pleasure.
Part of a supremely enjoyable all-Copland
concert.

Seattle SO / Gerard Schwarz
Delos DE3154 (62' · DDD)　　　Ⓕ
Another lucid, gently perceptive reading of
the 1945 suite. Enterprisingly coupled with
the Piano Concerto and *Symphonic Ode*, and
handsomely engineered by Delos.

delirious whoops of delight may perhaps strike some listeners as too much of a good thing.

Boasting some opulent, exhilaratingly expansive sonics, this is a corker of a release.

El salón México[a]. Danzón cubano[b]. An Outdoor Overture[b]. Quiet City[b]. Our Town[b]. Las agachadas[a]. Fanfare for the Common Man[b]. Lincoln Portrait[b]. Appalachian Spring – suite[b]. Rodeo – Four Dance Episodes[b]. Billy the Kid – orchestral suite[b]. Music for Movies[c]. Letter from Home[b]. John Henry[b]. Symphony No 3[c]. Clarinet Concerto[d]
Benny Goodman cl **Henry Fonda** narr [a]**New England Conservatory Chorus;** [b]**London Symphony Orchestra;** [c]**New Philharmonia Orchestra;** [d]**Columbia Symphony Orchestra / Aaron Copland**
Sony Classical ③ SM3K46559 (226' · ADD) Recorded 1963-76 Ⓜ

Single 'Copland conducts Copland' disc available on Sony Classical Ⓜ SMK89874 (includes El salón México, Appalachian Spring, Fanfare for the Common Man, Rodeo – Four Dance Episodes, Three Latin American Sketches & An Outdoor Overture)

This offers a welcome gathering of a lot of Copland's own performances. Only *Las agachadas* ('The shake-down song') for unaccompanied chorus is new to the British catalogue; this is a rather lame performance and nobody would buy the three-CD set for that. The oldest recording is the Clarinet Concerto with Benny Goodman – the second of the two he made under Copland. *Lincoln Portrait* with Henry Fonda is disappointing, but apart from earlier recordings in Spanish and Portuguese, this, made in 1968, is the only one under Copland. He was surprisingly modest about interpretation and wrote (in *Copland on Music*; New York: 1960): 'Composers rarely can be depended upon to know the correct tempi at which their music should proceed'. All the same it's a pleasure to have Copland as both composer and interpreter in some of his most delightful shorter works such as *Letter from Home*, *John Henry*, *Quiet City* and *An Outdoor Overture*. All told, this is an economical way to build up a collection of his performances which provide such an insight into his personality.

El salón México. Dance Symphony. Fanfare for the Common Man. Rodeo – Four Dance Episodes. Appalachian Spring – suite
Detroit Symphony Orchestra / Antál Dorati
Decca Ovation 430 705-2DM (74' · DDD) Recorded 1980s Ⓜ

This glorious disc shows how well Antál Dorati assimilated the music of Aaron Copland. The big-boned swagger of 'Buckaroo Holiday' from *Rodeo* with its vision of open spaces and clear blue skies is established straightaway in Dorati's performance with keen rhythmic drive and fine orchestral articulation. The 'Hoe Down' is properly exciting while the other two dance episodes are wonderfully expressive. In the 1945 suite of *Appalachian Spring* Dorati secures marvellous phrasing and dynamics but tends to understate the score's poetic elements. Decca's exemplary sound quality is of demonstration standard in *Fanfare for the Common Man*, as it is in the enjoyable curtain-raiser, the sturdy, bighearted *El salón México*. Dorati's vast experience as an interpreter of Stravinsky and Bartók pays fine dividends in Copland's gruesome *Dance Symphony*. A most welcome mid price release.

Piano Quartet

Movement[a]. Two Pieces[a]. Vitebsk[b]. Piano Quartet[c]. Sextet[d]
[d]**Michael Collins** cl [bcd]**Martin Roscoe** pf
[ad]**Vanbrugh Quartet** ([bc]Gregory Ellis, Keith Pascoe vns [c]Simon Aspell va [bc]Christopher Marwood vc)
ASV CDDCA1081 (65' · DDD) Ⓟ

This fine collection of Copland's small output of chamber music offers the first British recording of *Movement*, a characteristically introspective piece from his student years in Paris which shares a theme with the *Symphony for Organ and Orchestra*. The *Two Pieces* (1928) are also rarities well worth having, the rapid second one embodying to perfection the ideals of Nadia Boulanger's teaching.

Then there are the three major chamber works, starting with *Vitebsk*, the 1929 trio based on a Jewish folk theme. This is a commanding performance, which makes the most of the off-key quarter-tones and is thoroughly adroit in the central *Allegro*. The Sextet is a genuine chamber piece, although it was an arrangement of the *Short Symphony* which was found too difficult for most orchestras in 1933 and had to wait until 1944 for its American première. With Collins and Roscoe the Vanbrugh give an accomplished performance of the Sextet's sparklingly affirmative rhythms.

The Piano Quartet (1950) is in the same slow-quick-slow layout as *Vitebsk*. Like the final slow movement of the Piano Sonata its outer movements have a sublime immobility. Written while Copland was working on his great cycle, *Twelve Poems of Emily Dickinson*, the first two movements of this impressive quartet enter new territory, Copland tentatively exploring serial techniques. A few exposed string phrases lack finesse, and some soft details in the piano are almost lost – at the end of the first movement and more seriously at the end of the last movement when the dissonant note in the last chord is inaudible. But this is a valuable collection, well worth acquiring to have all these works together, played – and recorded – like this.

12 Poems of Emily Dickinson

Four Piano Blues. 12 Poems of Emily Dickinson. Night. Pastorale. Poet's Song. Old American Songs –

Set 1; Set 2
Susan Chilcott *sop* **Iain Burnside** *pf*
Black Box BBM1074 (69' · DDD) Texts included Ⓕ●

In this excellent selection Susan Chilcott and
Iain Burnside grasp the subtlety of Copland's
idiom. The two sets of *Old American Songs* are
rightly sung in an American accent in a range of
styles from the soulful-nostalgic of 'Long time
ago' to the knockabout comedy of 'I bought me
a cat'. But 'Simple Gifts', so well known from
Appalachian Spring, is taken well below the
marked tempo.

Copland's settings of Emily Dickinson are
given with the commanding authority that this
great cycle deserves. The competition on CD
consists of Roberta Alexander with Roger Vignoles, where there are minor flaws, and Barbara
Bonney with André Previn, which isn't an all-
Copland disc. Neither of Copland's own
recordings is still available. Even in this company Chilcott is impressive, with an enviable
control of the wide leaps from top to bottom.
Her breath control is so good that she can easily
sustain the last note of 'I could not stop for
death' for its full length, symbolising eternity.
In each song every mood is right, although the
recorded balance varies.

The early songs are interesting. Copland set
his friend Aaron Schaffer's poem *Night* when he
was only 18 and Debussy's impressionism still
avant-garde. But *Pastorale* three years later, just
before he went to study with Nadia Boulanger
in Paris, shows real personality.

Arcangelo Corelli   Italian 1653-1713

*Corelli studied in Bologna from 1666, and was
admitted to the Accademia Filarmonica at 17. By
1675 he was in Rome, where he became the foremost
violinist and a chamber musician to Queen
Christina of Sweden, to whom he dedicated his 12
trio sonatas da chiesa Op 1 (1681). His 12 trio
sonatas da camera Op 2 (1685) were dedicated to
Cardinal Pamphili; Corelli was his music master,
1687-90. His next patron, Cardinal Pietro Ottoboni, received the dedication of the trio sonatas Op 4
(1694). Corcilli came to dominate Rome musical life,
and also directed opera performances there and in
Naples. After 1708 he retired from public view.*

*Corelli was the first composer to derive his fame
exclusively from instrumental music. His works were
immensely popular during his lifetime and long
afterwards, and went through numerous reprints
and arrangements (42 editions of the op.5 violin
sonatas had appeared by 1800). They were seen as
models of style for their purity and poise. His small
output – six published sets and a few single pieces –
contains innovations of fundamental importance to
Baroque style, reconciling strict counterpoint and
soloistic violin writing, and using sequential progressions and suspensions to give a notably modern sense
of tonality. Distinctions between 'church' (abstract)
and 'chamber' (dance) idioms are increasingly*

*blurred in his sonatas. The op.6 concerti grossi
(1714) resemble trio sonatas with orchestral reinforcement and echo effects. They were especially popular in England, preferred even to Handel's concertos well into the 19th century. There were many
imitations of Corelli's music, notably of the folia
variations in the violin sonata Op 5 No 12 (1700),
and some composers used his music as a springboard;
Bach borrowed a theme from the trio sonata Op 3 No
4 (1689) for an organ fugue. As a violinist Corelli
was the finest, most influential teacher of his day; as
an ensemble director he imposed high standards of
discipline.*   GROVEmusic

Concerti grossi

12 Concerti grossi, Op 6 – No 1 in D; No 2 in F; Ⓟ
No 3 in C minor; No 4 in D; No 5 in B flat; No 6 in F;
No 7 in D; No 8 in G minor; No 9 in F; No 10 in C;
No 11 in B flat; No 12 in F
The English Concert / Trevor Pinnock
Archiv Produktion Gramophone Awards Collection
② 474 907-2 (130' · DDD) Recorded 1988   Ⓜ●○○

 In his working life of about 40 years
Corelli must have produced a great
deal of orchestral music, yet the 12
Concerti grossi, Op 6, form the bulk of what's survived. Their original versions are mostly lost;
what we know today are those published in
Amsterdam by Estienne Roger. These had been
assembled from movements Corelli had written
over a period of years, and which he'd carefully
polished and revised. The first eight are of the
da chiesa type, the last four the *da camera* type,
which essentially means that the latter have
dance movements; the former don't. The number of movements in each varies from four to
seven. All feature the interplay of a group of
soloists, the *concertino* (two violins and a cello)
and the orchestra, the *ripieno*, whose size, as
Corelli wrote, could be flexible. These are
masterpieces of their genre, much admired in
their day, and very influential. The scores leave
scope for embellishment, and the players of The
English Concert take full advantage of them.

Trio Sonatas

Trio Sonatas, Op 1ᵃ,2ᵇ,3ᶜ, 4ᵈ
Purcell Quartet (Catherine Mackintosh,
ᵃᵇᶜElizabeth Wallfisch, ᵈCatherine Weiss vns Richard
Boothby vc) **Jakob Lindberg** *theorbo* **Robert
Woolley** ᵇᵈhpd/ᵃᶜorg
Chaconne Classics ④ CHAN0692/4 (276' · DDD)
Recorded 1990s   Ⓜ●

Corelli's chamber music was reprinted 84 times
during his lifetime and 31 more during the rest
of the 18th century, a record most composers
would envy even today. The Sonatas of Ops 1
and 3 are *da chiesa*, those of Ops 2 and 4 are *da
camera* (with dance-titled movements). They
are small gems: most have four movements, and
their durations range from five and a half to
seven and a half minutes, within which they

pack a wealth of invention, pure beauty and variety of pace and mood. Surviving evidence suggests that they were played at a much lower pitch than today's standard, the lower string tension adding warmth and opulence to the sound. Catherine Mackintosh takes full advantage of the works' opportunities for pliant phrasing and added embellishments; Elizabeth Wallfisch 'converses' with her in her own characteristic way, while Catherine Weiss follows her example more closely. The Purcell Quartet's oneness of thought and timing is a joy to hear and the recording is superb in all respects.

Violin Sonatas, Op 5

Violin Sonatas, Op 5
Andrew Manze vn **Richard Egarr** hpd
Harmonia Mundi ② HMU90 7298/9 (131' · DDD)
Ⓜ**OO**

Considering the acknowledged status of Corelli's Op 5 violin sonatas, it's surprising how few of today's star Baroque violinists have recorded them. Published as a clear statement of intent on January 1, 1700, they're a benchmark not only in the history of the violin but of chamber music in general; yet despite being an accepted model of compositional purity and refinement which lasted throughout the 18th century and beyond, for many music-lovers – even Baroque music-lovers – they're still relatively little-known territory. Perhaps it's their finely honed perfection which has counted against them. Maybe they just seem too polite. Accounts of Corelli's violin-playing tell us that his eyes would glow 'red as fire' and his face contort, but evidence of this volatile character has not not always been easy to detect in the written notes of the violin sonatas.

If anyone is going to find him, however, it's Andrew Manze, who has repeatedly demonstrated that the heart of Baroque music lies beyond what's on the printed page. At a time when improvisational flair and spontaneity have never been a more exciting part of Baroque music-making, Manze and his accompanist Richard Egarr are the masters of it, and here they have produced a Corelli recording which is nothing short of revelatory.

Not that it's unthinkingly wild or bizarre. Manze may have adorned the music with his customarily liberal decoration of extra double-stops, flowery arabesques and emphatic gestures – and Egarr may have performed his usual extraordinary feats at the keyboard, devising an array of inventive keyboard textures which ranges from luxurious feather-bed arpeggios and swirls to daring, stabbing left-hand double octaves (no other continuo player manages to sound so much as if his fingers were a direct extension of his imagination) – but this is still Corelli with a measure of north Italian dignity.

The resulting balance between restraint and urgency is compelling, because the performers, you feel, aren't out to shock but to search for something new and real. This really is Corelli as

you haven't heard him before. The performances reach a high technical standard, as does the recording, though strangely long gaps are left between some of the movements. This vital, ear-opening disc is in a category of its own, classic music in a-classic – maybe even an epoch-making – recording.

William Cornysh   British 1468-1523

After being at court (from 1494) Cornysh became Master of the Children at the Chapel Royal, a post he held until his death. From 1509 he was the leading figure in the plays and entertainments that enlivened court life. In 1513 he made the first of several visits to France with the Chapel Royal, in Henry VIII's retinue. Several of his sacred vocal works are in the Eton Choirbook; their style ranges from the flamboyance of the Stabat mater to the simplicity of the Ave Maria Mater Dei. His notable secular part-songs (in MSS are similarly versatile, Yow and I and Amyas being simple and chordal and A robyn a three-part canon apparently incorporating elements of pre-existent melody. Several other musicians with the surname Cornysh were active in the late 15th century and early 16th.   **GROVE**music

Magnificat

Salve regina. Ave Maria, mater Dei. Gaude virgo mater Christi. Magnificat. Ah, Robin. Adieu, adieu, my heartes lust. Adieu courage. Woefully arrayed. Stabat mater
The Tallis Scholars / Peter Phillips
Gimell CDGIM014 (65' · DDD) Recorded 1988. Texts and translations included   Ⓕ

Cornysh's music is a riot of abundant, often seemingly wild melody, constantly in search of wanton, abstract, dare-devil ideas. Take, for example, the extraordinary conclusion to the five-part *Magnificat*, where pairs of voices are challenged with music of gradually increasing complexity, peaking in an exchange of quite hair-raising virtuosity between the sopranos – and all this just for the words 'and ever shall be, world without end'! As far as the sacred works are concerned, The Tallis Scholars respond magnificently to Cornysh's audacious imagination. Theirs is a majestic and glorious sound, to be relished in full in the *Stabat mater*, a huge piece that survives incomplete and for which the late Frank Harrison composed treble parts that may even trump Cornysh himself in their sheer bravura. Marginally less striking in The Tallis Scholars' performances are the short partsongs and the carol *Woefully arrayed*, robbed as they are here of some of their latent expressiveness and strength by being sung (admittedly very beautifully) in an inappropriately resonant building, and in rounded modern English vowels. But judged as a whole this disc must be reckoned an outstanding success.

François Couperin   French 1668-1733

Couperin was the central figure of the French harp-sichord school. He came from a long line of musicians, mostly organists, of whom the most eminent was his uncle, Louis Couperin, though his father Charles (1638-79) was also a composer and organist of St Gervais. François succeeded to that post on his 18th birthday; his earliest known music is two organ masses. In 1693 he became one of the four royal organists which enabled him to develop his career as a teacher through his court connections. He was soon recognised as the leading French composer of his day through his sacred works and his chamber music and, from 1713, his harpsichord pieces. In 1716 he published an important treatise on harpsichord playing and the next year he was appointed royal harpsichordist.

Among the music Couperin composed for Louis XIV's delectation were his Concerts royaux, chamber works for various combinations. He had written works in his own elaboration of trio-sonata form in the 1690s following the Italianate style of Corelli but retaining French character in the decorative lines and rich harmony. Later, he published these alongside French-style groups of dances as Les nations; they include some of his emotionally most powerful music. He was much concerned with blending French and Italian styles; he composed programmatic tributes to Lully and Corelli and works under the title Les goûts-réünis. He also wrote intensely expressive pieces for bass viol.

But it is as a harpsichord composer that Couperin is best known. He published four books with some 220 pieces, grouped in 27 ordres or suites. Some movements are in the traditional French dance forms, but most are character pieces with titles that reflect their inspiration: some are portraits of individuals or types, some portray abstract qualities, some imitate the sounds of nature. The titles may also be ambiguous or metaphorical, or even intentionally obscure. Most of the pieces are in rondeau form. All are elegantly composed, concealing a complex, allusive and varied emotional world behind their highly wrought surface. Couperin took immense pains over the notation of the ornaments with which his harpsichord writing is sprinkled and animated. These, and his style generally, are expounded in his L'art de toucher le clavecin.

Couperin's children were also musicians: Nicholas (1680-1748) succeeded his father at St Gervais, and probably composed, while Marie-Madeleine (1690-1742) was probably an abbey organist and Marguerite-Antoinette (1705-c1778) was active as a court harpsichordist, c1729-1741. GROVEmusic

Pièces de clavecin

L'art de toucher le clavecin – Prelude No 6 in B minor. Troisième livre de pièces de clavecin – Treizième ordre; Quatorzième ordre; Quinzième ordre
Robert Kohnen hpd **Barthold Kuijken** fl
Accent ACC9399D (64' · DDD) Recorded 1993   Ⓔ

Kohnen's playing is rhythmically incisive, fas-tidious in detail – Couperin was hot on that – and full of character. If, on first acquaintance, his realisation of Couperin's vignette 'Les lis naissans' (*Ordre* No 13) seems a shade spiky then his lyrical approach to the flowing 6/8 melody of the rondeau 'Les rozeaux', which follows, reassures us that Kohnen does have the poetry of the music at heart, and intends that it should be so. Less appealing are Kohnen's somewhat intrusive vocal introductions to 'Les folies françoises'. This information is provided in the booklet so it hardly needs to be reiterated. In a concert recital such snatches of actuality can be effective; on a disc, after repeated listening, they become an unwelcome interruption. Occasional departures from the norm in the following two *ordres* are of an altogether more agreeable nature. In 'Le rossignol-en-amour' (*Ordre* No 14) Kohnen takes Couperin up on his suggestion to use a transverse flute, played here with a beautifully rounded tone by Barthold Kuijken. Likewise, in the jaunty rondeau, 'La Julliet', the trio texture is realised by flute and harpsichord rather than the more usual two-harpsichord texture. This piece is beautifully done, as is the subtly bell-like 'Carillon de Cithère' which follows it. In short, a stylish and entertaining release which is as likely as any to draw the cautious listener into Couperin's refined, allusory and metaphor-laden idiom.

Louis Couperin   French c1626-1661

Louis Couperin was the first important member of a major dynasty of French composers, influential for more than two and a half centuries. He settled in Paris and by 1653 was organist of St Gervais; he also held a post as treble viol player at the royal chapel. He wrote pieces for wind and strings, but most of his music is for keyboard: some 70 fugues, plainchant settings and other pieces for organ, notable for their vigorous counterpoint and expressive force, and some 135 for harpsichord, consisting of preludes and dances, longer than most from this period and remarkable for their lively ideas, their grandeur and their intensity. GROVEmusic

Suites

L Couperin Suites – in F; in A; in D; in A; in F; in C. Pavane in F sharp minor **Froberger** Le Tombeau de Monsieur Blancheroche
Skip Sempé hpd
Alpha ALPHA066 (79' · DDD)   Ⓕ**OO**

Louis Couperin, less famous than his nephew, François 'Le Grand', was nevertheless one of the greatest harpsichord composers of the 17th century, a creator of suites of beautifully honed miniatures cast predominantly in the standard French dance-forms of the day (Allemande, Courante, Sarabande and so on) exuding all the noble expressiveness and lyrical melancholy of their age.

He finds an ideal interpreter in Skip Sempé, a player who relishes the sheer sound of the harpsichord and knows how to exploit its glorious resonance. Sempé achieves this by means of probably the most exquisite touch you'll ever hear on the instrument, leaving him in control of the tone at every turn. Chords are spread lovingly, ornaments tumble easily into one another, all without a hint of unwelcome percussiveness or jangliness – every note seems to have been deftly caressed into being.

He also shows us just how much he enjoys the bass sonority of his harpsichord (a compliant French copy by Bruce Kennedy) by throwing in a low-lying transcription of a Marais gamba piece; another guest composer is Froberger, who answers Couperin's *Prélude* in explicit imitation of his style, with his sombrely magnificent *Tombeau de Monsieur Blancheroche*. A minute lack of improvisatory flow in the unmeasured *Préludes* is scarcely worth mentioning when so much else in Sempé's playing gives unalloyed pleasure. This is demonstration-class musicianship at the harpsichord.

Henry Cowell   American 1897–1965

(Before he had had any formal training in composition Cowell wrote piano pieces using clusters and other new effects. He then studied in California and New York (1916-18), though continued an independent path as composer, publisher (through his New Music Edition, founded in 1927 and providing scores of Ives, Ruggles and others) and spokesman (through his book New Muscial Resources, 1930). He taught at the Peabody Conservatory (1951-6) and Columbia University (1949-65). Apart from piano clusters (Advertisement, 1914), he pioneered strumming on the instrument's strings (Aeolian Harp, 1923; The Banshee, 1925), complex rhythms, mobile form (Mosaic Quartet, 1935) and unusual combinations. But from 1936 he composed in a more regular, tonal style influenced by American and Irish folk music (18 Hymns and Fuguing Tunes for various forces, 1943-64). In his last 15 years he returned to clusters and other unconventional means while drawing on non-European musical cultures. His immense output includes over 140 orchestral works (including 21 symphonies and many concertos), c 60 choral and c 170 chamber works, over 200 piano pieces, and operas, incidental and film music, showing him to have been an indefatigable musical explorer. **GROVE**music

Miscellaneous Works

Deep Color[a]. Fabrica. Fairy Answer[a]. Tiger[a]. Violin Suite[b]. Quartet for Flute, Oboe, Cello and Harpsichord[c]. Polyphonica[d]. Three Anti-Modernist Songs[e]. Irish Suite[f]
[e]**Ellen Lang** *mez* [c]**Jayn Rosenfeld** *fl* [c]**Marsha Heller** *ob* [b]**Mia Wu** *vn* [c]**Maria Kitsopoulos** *vc* **Cheryl Seltzer** [bef]*pf/*[c]*hpd* [df]**Continuum /**[de]**Joel Sachs** [a]*pf*
Naxos American Classics 8 559192 (66' · DDD)   Ⓢ

Set of Five[a]. The Banshee[b]. Vestiges[b]. Euphoria[b]. What's This?[b] Elegie[b]. Six Casual Developments[c]. Homage to Iran[d]. Piece for Piano with Strings[e]. Two Songs[f] – Sunset; Rest
[f]**Raymond Murcell** *bar* [c]**David Krakauer** *cl* [a]**Gordon Gottlieb** *perc* [d]**Mark Steinberg**, [a]**Marilyn Dubow** *vns* [bdef]**Cheryl Seltzer** *pf* [be]**Continuum /** **Joel Sachs** [a]*pf/*[d]*perc*
Naxos American Classics 8 559193 (60' · DDD)   Ⓢ

Henry Cowell was an avant-garde pioneer with his tone-clusters; became a multi-culturalist, some of whose music falls midway between East and West; and was an inspiration to younger American composers such as John Cage and Lou Harrison. His use of the insides of the piano has borne fruit in the work of George Crumb. Cowell said he wanted to 'live in the whole world of music' and wrote almost 1,000 works to prove it. Many of these are unknown but his position in the record catalogue has been improving steadily since his centenary in 1997.

Cowell recorded three of the group of four piano pieces on the first CD in 1962; his aggressive *Tiger* is better phrased and slower than Joel Sachs's and thus more comprehensible but *Deep Color* is barely known. Both the Suite for Violin and Piano (1925) and the much later Quartet for flute, oboe, cello and harpsichord are neo-Baroque. The Bach-with-clusters approach at first seems surreal but the *Andante calmato* is magical. *Polyphonica* is a bracing study in the kind of dissonant textures fashionable in the late 1920s but the *Irish Suite* is quite different. It's an expanded version for piano and small orchestra of three earlier pieces played directly on the piano strings. The first is *Banshee* (the original version is on the second CD) named after the ghost which wails at the time of a death. The ravishing new sounds in all three pieces – amazing for 1929 – are uniquely Cowell's.

In 1956 he spent some time in the Middle East; one result was the *Homage to Iran* for violin, piano and drums. As elsewhere, he ingeniously adapts ethnic materials in a manner that falls midway between the two cultures. The *Six Casual Developments* (1933) for clarinet and piano are vivid epigrammatic miniatures. The *Set of Five* (1952) is for violin, piano and varied percussion, used to provide an ethnic flavour. The final *vigoroso* is spacious and declamatory with a surprise in the middle – a duet for celesta and prepared piano.

These two CDs provide a judiciously chosen sample of Cowell's work on a small scale; the performances are fine, although some of the recordings date back to LP; enthusiasts for Cowell will certainly want both CDs and, thanks to Naxos, will be able to afford them.

Jean Cras   French 1879-1932

Cras showed early promise as a composer, but followed family tradition and entered the French navy, where he pursued a successful career, rising to the rank of rear admiral. He pursued his musical interests as an amateur. In 1900 he studied composition with Henri Duparc, who became a close friend. His small output includes the five-act opera Polyphème.

Polyphème

Polyphème
Armand Arapian bar Polyphème **Sophie Marin-Degor** sop Galatée **Yann Beuron** ten Acis **Valérie Debize** mez Lycas **Rémi Corbier** sngr Un Sylvain **Laure Baert** sngr Une Nymphe **Vittoria Regional Choir, Ile de France; Luxembourg Philharmonic Orchestra / Bramwell Tovey**
Timpani ③ 3C3078 (161' · DDD) Notes, libretto and translation included   Ⓕ

Cras was a pupil of Duparc, although by the time the two met Cras was an experienced naval officer, having seen service in various French colonial skirmishes. *Polyphème*, his only opera, was composed in 1914, but not performed until 1922.

The libretto, by Albert Samain, takes the legendary figure of the Cyclops Polyphemus, and his jealousy fired by the love of the nymph Galatea for the handsome herdsman Acis. Polyphemus is torn between love and self-loathing: he puts out his own eye, after witnessing the love scene between Acis and Galatea.

Cras's music is atmospheric, beautifully scored, and with its overtones of impressionistic symphonic works, larded with Wagnerian touches, it sounds at times reassuringly familiar. It's hard to imagine any staging rescuing it from its static, uneventful story, but it makes a perfect opera on disc.

Cras's love of the sea pervades the whole work. Armand Arapian in the title-role sounds anguished and sinister; the moment when he describes seeing his own ugliness for the first time, reflected from other depictions of the character. Sophie Marin-Degor as Galatea and Yann Beuron as Acis are never overwhelmed by the orchestra – Cras certainly knew how to write for the voice.

His opera takes a while to insinuate itself. The sound is first rate, the large forces of the Luxembourg Philharmonic, and especially the Vittoria Regional Choir, play and sing for Bramwell Tovey to create a fine and important addition to the recorded repertory of French opera.

Bernhard Crusell   Finnish 1775-1839

Crusell studied the clarinet from the age of eight and at 12 joined a military band in Sveaborg; in 1791 he went to Stockholm where he became a court musician two years later. He studied the clarinet in Berlin in 1798 with Tausch and in 1803 went to Paris to study composition with Gossec and Berton and the

clarinet with Lefèvre. He later held posts as music director in the Swedish court chapel and royal regiment. His compositions include three clarinet concertos (1811, 1816, 1829), an air and variations for clarinet and a Concertante for clarinet, bassoon and horn (1816); he also wrote chamber music, including three clarinet quartets (1812, 1816, 1823), an opera Den lilla Slafvinnan (1824, Stockholm) and 12 songs. He was a fluent composer with a fresh vein of melody. He also made Swedish translations of operas by Mozart, Rossini and others.

GROVEmusic

Clarinet Concertos

Crusell Clarinet Concerto No 2 in F minor, 'Grand'
Baermann Adagio in D flat **Rossini** Introduction and Variations in C minor **Weber** Concerto Concertino in C minor, J109
Emma Johnson cl **English Chamber Orchestra / Sir Charles Groves**
ASV CDDCA559 (55' · DDD) Recorded 1985   Ⓕ

It was this Crusell Grand Concerto which Emma Johnson played when she won the BBC Young Musician of the Year competition in 1984. That occasion was the first time she had played a concerto with a full symphony orchestra, and her special affection for the piece, her total joy in each of the three movements, comes over vividly in this performance. The uninhibited spontaneity of her playing, exactly matching a live performance, brings an extra compulsion and immediacy of expression. Emma Johnson in each movement translates the notes with very personal phrasing and expression, always taking risks and bringing them off. This is a daring performance, naughtily lilting in the outer movements, happily songful in the *Andante pastorale* of the slow movement. In the three shorter pieces Johnson may not have the same technical perfection, but the free expressiveness could not be more winning. Her moulding of *legato* melodies in the Weber and Rossini works, as well as the Baermann, brings warm expressiveness, with free rubato and sharp contrasts of tone and dynamic. The orchestral sound is full and bright, with Groves a lively, sympathetic accompanist.

Clarinet Concertos – No 1 in E flat, Op 1; No 2 in F minor, Op 5; No 3 in B flat, Op 11
Kari Kriikku cl **Finnish Radio Symphony Orchestra / Sakari Oramo**
Ondine ODE965-2 (64' · DDD)   Ⓕ

With full, bright, immediate sound, the Finnish clarinettist Kari Kriiku gives dazzling performances of these three delightful clarinet concertos. In many ways he's even more daring than the two excellent rivals Karl Leister (BIS) and Emma Johnson (ASV and Regis Records), regularly choosing speeds that stretch virtuosity to the limit, particularly in the finales. Those of Nos 1 and 2 may be marked *allegretto* merely, but Kriiku, by choosing exceptionally fast speeds, brings out an extra *scherzando* quality, often sharp and spiky, in which Crusell's characteristically dotted rhythms are delightfully crisp. The almost impossibly rapid tonguing never seems to get in the way of detailed characterisation.

Johnson in her recordings is altogether more relaxed, regularly adopting speeds rather broader, extremely so in the *Alla Polacca* which ends No 3. Consistently, her pointing of rhythm brings out the fun in the writing, and in her comparably broad approach to slow movements she finds extra poetry. Partly as a result of the immediacy of the recording, Kriiku's *pianissimos* aren't as extreme, yet in flair and panache Kriiku is second to none, superbly supported by the crisp, purposeful playing of the Finnish National Radio orchestra under Sakari Oramo.

An excellent disc, guaranteed to win friends for these sparkling works.

Peter Maxwell Davies   British 1934

Davies studied at the Royal Manchester College of Music (1952-6); his fellow students included Goehr and Birtwistle They studied the music of Boulez, Nono and Stockhausen which, together with early English music, provided him with the roots of a style (Trumpet Sonata, 1955). He then studied with Petrassi in Rome (1957-9) and extended his range to orchestral works (St Michael for 17 wind, 1957; Prolation, 1958). But a period of teaching at Cirencester Grammar School (1959-62) encouraged him to reconsider not only school music (drawing out children's creative potential) but also his own: he began to write in a more expressively focussed, dramatic way and to recover aspects of symphonic largeness, particularly as he found them in Mahler (second In Nomine Fantasia for orchestra, 1964). Much work was done at the universities of Princeton (1962-4) and Adelaide (1966).

Back in England, Davies and Birtwistle formed the Pierrot Players in 1967 (re-formed as the Fires of London, 1970) and Davies began a sequence of music-theatre pieces for them (Eight Songs for a Mad King and Vesalii icones, both 1969). These exploited a fiercely expressionist style that came out of Pierrot lunaire and from work on his opera Taverner (1967), concerning the war between creed and creativity in the mind of the Tudor composer. Another symptom of disintegration was his use of foxtrots in works of desperate seriousness (St Thomas Wake for orchestra, 1969), though at the same time he was working, in the big orchestral movement Worldes Blis (1969), towards a more integrated style.

Since 1970 he has pursued that style, with occasional expressionist throwbacks, while living remotely in Orkney, where in 1977 he founded the St Magnus Festival; there many of his works have been introduced, often reflecting on the landscapes, legend and literature of the islands (e.g. the opera The Martyrdom of St Magnus, 1977, children's operas, choral pieces). At the same time he has been

writing large-scale symphonic works (three symphonies, 1976, 1980, 1983; Violin Concerto, 1985).
GROVEmusic

Second Taverner Fantasia

A Portrait

Seven in Nomine[a]. O magnum mysterium[b]. Second Fantasia on John Taverner's 'In Nomine'[c]. Antechrist[d]. Missa super 'L'homme armé'[e]. From Stone to Thorn[f]. Lullaby for Ilian Rainbow[g]. Hymn to St Magnus[h]
[fh]**Mary Thomas** sop [e]**Vanessa Redgrave** spkr [defh]**The Fires of London** (Judith Pearce fls/picc Alan Hacker cls Duncan Druce vn/va Jennifer Ward Clarke vc Stephen Pruslin kybds/perc Gary Kettel perc Timothy Walker gtr) [b]**Cirencester Grammar School Choir and Orchestra** / [bdefh]**Peter Maxwell Davies**; [a]**London Sinfonietta** / **David Atherton**; [c]**New Philharmonia Orchestra** / **Sir Charles Groves** Decca ② 475 6166 (155' · ADD)   Ⓜ

This is a portrait of a musician who, in the 12 years covered (1960-72), evolved from being a schoolmaster to prominence on the professional musical scene as composer and conductor. These well-filled discs illustrate most aspects of Maxwell Davies's work from this period.

The earliest compositions are the carols and instrumental sonatas from *O magnum mysterium* (1960) performed by the schoolboys for whom they were written. The brief *Seven in Nomine* (1965) and the large-scale *Second Fantasia on John Taverner's 'In Nomine'* (1964) both relate to the opera *Taverner*, first performed in 1972. The Fantasia is a particular rarity. Although this performance can't mask the immense challenges it poses to its interpreters, Groves and the New Philharmonia leave one in no doubt as to its substance and quasi-symphonic stature.

Antechrist (1967) and the *Missa super 'L'homme armé'* (1968, rev. 1971) portray Max the swinging-60s parodist, with their sardonic reflections on cruelty and betrayal. But for a more balanced expressive character, in which foxtrots and other 'foreign' styles give way to a more refined though still intensely expressionistic idiom, there are *From Stone to Thorn* (1971) and the *Hymn to St Magnus* (1972), representing the composer's early encounter with the poetry of George Mackay Brown and with the Orkney culture bound up with the story of Saint Magnus.

This is a substantial and vivid sampling of a composer revelling in his new-found maturity and individuality. The recordings are of variable quality, though most still sound well.

String Quartets

Naxos Quartets Nos 1 & 2
Maggini Quartet (Laurence Jackson, David Angel vns Martin Outram va Michal Kaznowski vc)
Naxos 8 557396 (75 ' · DDD)   Ⓢ**OO**

This first instalment of Sir Peter Maxwell

Davies's ambitious series of 10 Naxos Quartets indicates that it's shaping up to be quite a journey. The septuagenarian composer rises superbly to the technical challenges of the medium. The first two movements of the First Quartet evince a formal strength, expressive scope and thematic ingenuity that launch the cycle in sure-footed fashion; both attain a dramatic and emotional resolution in some arresting unison writing. The compact concluding *scherzo* could hardly provide a bolder contrast; its ghostly, Will-'o-the-wisp dialogue will re-emerge in the Third Quartet.

There are four movements in the Second Quartet, the second and third of which comprise a self-contained diptych (and the former's recitative first half harks back to No 1's *Largo* centrepiece). The outer movements are more expansive. An expectant *Lento* introduction leads to a bracing *Allegro*, its progress stimulating and satisfyingly proportioned. The *Lento flessibile* finale is finer still: a memorably serene and utterly inevitable essay.

The Magginis are most accurate and cogent guides, realistically recorded within the sympathetic acoustic of Potton Hall in Suffolk. A most rewarding coupling.

Naxos Quartets Nos 3 & 4
Maggini Quartet (Laurence Jackson, David Angel vns Martin Outram va Michal Kaznowski vc)
Naxos 8 557397 (56' · DDD)   Ⓢ

The impression of great things given by the first two quartets in the Naxos cycle is amply confirmed by this no less rewarding second volume. Work on the Third Quartet during the spring of 2003 was profoundly affected, the composer informs us in his booklet-note, by news of the invasion of Iraq. Presumably, then, it's not too fanciful to ascribe certain aspects of the score to his dismay at that conflict. Sample the development section of the first-movement March (described by its creator as a 'military march of a fatuous and splintered nature'), the queasily wide vibrato that discolours the short hymn marked *stucchevole* (meaning 'cloying' or 'nauseating') towards the end of the third movement ('Four Inventions and a Hymn'), or the questioning demeanour of the finale ('Fuga'). At the same time, the quartet (whose four movements span some 31 minutes) stands up convincingly on its own terms. Impressive is its unerring sense of growth, proportion and contrapuntal ingenuity (Davies states that, before composition, he embarked upon a fruitful re-examination of Bach's Two- and Three-part Inventions), while the slow movement ('In nomine') incorporates the magical return of the ghostly, ethereal dialogue 'left hanging in the air' at the end of the First Quartet.

Cast in a single movement lasting just under 25 minutes, No 4 takes its cue from Bruegel's *Children's Games* (a canvas which also inspired Davies's Sixth Strathclyde Concerto, for flute and orchestra). The composer had originally intended it to be 'lighter and much less fierce than its predecessor', but a fretful mood underpins the relentless logic of this music with its protean motivic transformations and intriguing harmonic byways. The immaculately judged part-writing displays a bracing mastery of the idiom and, needless to say, the Magginis once again play with superlative poise and intelligence.

Both sound and balance are first-rate.

Choral music

Missa parvula[ab]. Mass[abc]. Dum complerentur[a]. Veni Sancte Spiritus[a]. Veni Creator Spiritus[b]. Reliqui Domum Meum[b]
[a]**Westminster Cathedral Choir / Martin Baker**, with [b]**Robert Quinney**, [c]**Robert Houssart** orgs
Hyperion CDA67454 (67' · DDD) Texts and translations included   Ⓕ

Under David Hill and subsequently James O'Donnell the choir of Westminster Cathedral established a tradition of excellent recordings for Hyperion. That tradition is as strong as ever under Martin Baker, who became Master of the Music in 2000. Like his immediate predecessors, Baker is exploring repertoire which isn't just challenging and unusual, but of real value.

The *Missa parvula* for unison boys' voices vividly recalls Britten's *Missa Brevis* both in its terse musical language and understated emotion. The opening of the Mass occupies the same sound-world as the *Missa parvula* and it's only with the thrilling and lavishly scored *Gloria* that it's apparent we are now into a work of much greater depth and impact. This is a hugely impressive performance, as much for the astonishing effect of the two organs as for the often magical choral effects. Baker entices some of the most wonderful singing from his choir here while Roberts Quinney and Houssart revel in their virtuoso interplay. Hyperion's recording captures the full effect of Maxwell Davies' astonishing writing.

A revelatory disc for those keen to know what sort of 'establishment' music we might expect from the new Master of the Queen's Music.

Walford Davies   English 1869-1941

Davies studied with Parry and Stanford at the RCM, where he joined the staff in 1895, also working as a conductor, organist (of St George's Chapel, Windsor, 1927-32) and broadcaster. His works include church music. In 1934 he became Master of the King's Music.   GROVEmusic

Everyman

Everyman
Elena Ferrari sop **Jennifer Johnston** contr **Andrew Staples** ten **Pauls Putnins** bass **London Oriana**

Choir; Kensington Symphony Orchestra / David
Drummond
Dutton Laboratories Epoch CDLX7141 (69' · DDD · T)
Ⓜ

Henry Walford Davies's splendid oratorio was
written and first heard in 1904, in the shadow of
Elgar's *Gerontius*. Yet it was an immediate success and widely performed. But by the end of
the First World War it had fallen into oblivion,
apart from an isolated revival in 1929. Like
Gerontius, it's based on a vision of a human soul
crossing into the next world, where Everyman
has to justify his life to God. It, too, offers dialogues between Everyman and the subsidiary
characters, here representing Good Deeds (a
particularly lovely duo) and Knowledge (jointly,
the equivalent of Elgar's Angel). There's no 'Go
forth' at the end of Part 1: here the choral
sequences are more lyrical. Instead, Everyman
learns that the attributes he's taken for granted
in life (friends, possessions, physical attributes)
will be left behind when he dies; riches, too, are
sneeringly dismissed. The choral Epilogue
brings a thrillingly optimistic conclusion. The
solo parts must be very grateful to sing, and the
soloists here rise to the occasion. The frequently inspired choral writing is at times
Elgarian, though there's no hint of plagiarism,
and the music is communicative and appealing.
David Drummond's direction has a powerful
yet lyrical thrust, with the feeling of a live performance. The recording is first class, too. If
you enjoy the English choral tradition don't
miss this: *Everyman* is a real find.

Claude Debussy   French 1862-1918

*Debussy studied with Guiraud and others at the
Paris Conservatoire (1872-84) and as prize-winner
went to Rome (1885-7), though more important
impressions came from his visits to Bayreuth (1888,
1889) and from hearing Javanese music in Paris
(1889). Wagner's influence is evident in the cantata
La damoiselle élue (1888) and the Cinq, poèmes de
Baudelaire (1889) but other songs of the period,
notably the settings of Verlaine (Ariettes oubliées,
Trois mélodies, Fêtes galantes, set 1) are in a more
capricious style, as are parts of the still somewhat
Franckian G minor String Quartet (1893); in that
work he used not only the Phrygian mode but also less
standard modes, notably the whole-tone mode, to create the floating harmony he discovered through the
work of contemporary writers: Mallarmé in the
orchestral Prélude à 'L'après-midi d'un faune'
(1894) and Maeterlinck in the opera Pelléas et
Mélisande, dating in large part from 1893-5 but not
completed until 1902. These works also brought forward a fluidity of rhythm and colour quite new to
Western music.*

*Pelléas, with its rule of understatement and decep-
tively simple declamation, also brought an entirely
new tone to opera – but an unrepeatable one. Debussy
worked on other opera projects and left substantial
sketches for two pieces after tales by Poe (Le diable*

*dans le beffroi and La chûte de la maison Usher), but
nothing was completed. Instead the main works were
orchestral pieces, piano sets and songs.*

*The orchestral works include the three Nocturnes
(1899), characteristic studies of veiled harmony and
texture ('Nuages'), exuberant cross-cutting ('Fêtes')
and seductive whole-tone drift ('Sirènes'). La mer
(1905) essays a more symphonic form, with a finale
that works themes from the first movement, though
the centrepiece ('Jeux de vagues') proceeds much less
directly and with more variety of colour. The three
Images (1912) are more loosely linked, and the
biggest, 'Ibéria', is itself a triptych, a medley of Spanish allusions. Finally the ballet Jeux (1913) contains
some of Debussy's strangest harmony and texture in
a form that moves freely over its own field of motivic
connection. Other late stage works, including the
ballets Khamma (1912) and La boîte à joujoux
(1913) and the mystery play Le martyre de St
Sébastien (1911), were not completely orchestrated
by Debussy, though St Sébastien is remarkable in
sustaining an antique modal atmosphere that otherwise was touched only in relatively short piano pieces
(e.g. 'La cathédrale engloutie').*

*The important piano music begins with works
which, Verlaine fashion, look back at rococo decorous-
ness with a modern cynicism and puzzlement (Suite
bergamasque, 1890; Pour le piano, 1901). But then,
as in the orchestral pieces, Debussy began to associate
his music with visual impressions of the East, Spain,
landscapes etc, in a sequence of sets of short pieces. His
last volume of Etudes (1915) interprets similar
varieties of style and texture purely as pianistic exercises and includes pieces that develop irregular form
to an extreme as well as others influenced by the
young Stravinsky (a presence too in the suite En
blanc et noir for two pianos, 1915). The rarefaction
of these works is a feature of the last set of songs, the
Trois poèmes de Mallarmé (1913), and of the
Sonata for flute, viola and harp (1915), though the
sonata and its companions also recapture the inquisitive Verlainian classicism The planned set of six
sonatas was cut short by the composer's death from
rectal cancer.* **GROVE**music

Orchestral Works

Images. Berceuse héroïque[a]. Danse sacrée et danse
profane[b]. Jeux. Nocturnes. Marche écossaise sur un
thème populaire. Prélude à l'après-midi d'un faune.
La mer. Première rapsodie[c][b]
Vera Badings hp [c]**George Pieterson** cl
Concertgebouw Orchestra / [a]**Eduard van Beinum,
Bernard Haitink**
Philips Duo ② 438 742-2PM (141' · ADD) Recorded
[b]1957, 1976-9   Ⓜ**OOO**

 Philips has repackaged Haitink's late-
1970s recordings on two CDs for the
price of one. Space has also been found
for Debussy's last orchestral work, the short
Berceuse héroïque conducted by Eduard van
Beinum (in excellent 1957 stereo). In every
respect this package is a bargain. In *La mer*, like
the 1964 Karajan on DG Galleria, there's a concern for refinement and fluidity of gesture, for a
subtle illumination of texture; and both display

a colourist's knowledge and use of an individually apt variety of orchestral tone and timbre. It's the wind playing that you remember in Haitink's *Images*: the melancholy and disconsolate oboe d'amore in 'Gigues'; and from 'Ibéria', the gorgeous oboe solo in 'Les parfums de la nuit', and the carousing clarinets and raucous trumpets in the succeeding holiday festivities. And here, as elsewhere in the set, the Concertgebouw acoustic plays a vital role. Haitink's *Jeux* is slower and freer than average, and possessed of a near miraculous precision, definition and delicacy. The jewel in this set, for many, will be the *Nocturnes*, principally for the purity of the strings in 'Nuages'; the dazzling richness and majesty of the central procession in 'Fêtes'; and the cool beauty and composure of 'Sirènes'. Haitink opts for an ethereal distance; there may be passages where you're unsure if they're singing or not, but the effect is magical.

Debussy La mer. Prélude à l'après-midi d'un faune
Ravel Daphnis et Chloé – Suite No 2. Boléro
Berlin Philharmonic Orchestra / Herbert von Karajan
DG Galleria 427 250-2GGA (64' · ADD) Recorded 1964-5 ⓜ**OOO**
Also available on DG ②474 278-2GX2 (coupled with Saint-Saëns 'Organ' Symphony, Ravel Pavane & Rapsodie espagnole) ⓜ

 Beautifully recorded, controlled and aristocratic, these performances show a scrupulous regard for the composers' wishes. The sound of the Berlin strings is sumptuous, with detail well placed and in a generally natural perspective. It's a joy to relish the beauty of the playing in such clear, well-defined sound. It has that indefinable quality that one can more readily recognise than describe, a magic that makes one forget the performer and transports one into the composer's world. You can either be seduced by some of the most sheerly beautiful orchestral sound recorded, or appreciate it for its wide-ranging imagery and its properly mobile pacing; whichever, it's one of the great recorded *La mer*s and one of the classics of the gramophone. Karajan's interpretation of *Prélude à l'après-midi d'un faune* remains one of the most beautiful readings committed to record – the first flute, Karlheinz Zöller, plays like a wizard. *Boléro* is slow and steady (but Karajan risks floating the early solos). This is also a ravishing account of the Second Suite from *Daphnis et Chloé*.

Debussy La mer **Stravinsky** The Rite of Spring
Boulez Notations VII
Chicago Symphony Orchestra / Daniel Barenboim
Teldec 8573-81702-2 (69' · DDD) ⒡

Barenboim's *La mer* is formidable, and you'll need to turn to other accounts, like Haitink's or Karajan's, if you expect a gentler touch and fewer turbulent undercurrents in Debussy.

You'll find yourself completely won over by the emotional force and intellectual grasp of this reading, as well as by the spectacular Chicago sound. Barenboim takes risks, as in the broad presentation of the first movement's climactic chorale, but because his rhythms are never stodgy, his response to contrast vividly immediate yet always coherent with respect to the larger whole, he brings a strength of character and depth of expression to this music which few other conductors have matched.

Barenboim's *Rite of Spring* comes hard on the heels of Valery Gergiev's ultra-theatrical version with the Kirov Orchestra, and differences aren't hard to hear. Gergiev is recorded with a warmer resonance, but this does his brass players, especially the horns, no favours, and – at least compared to Barenboim – there's some loss of pungency and force of attack in the later stages, as well as a melodramatically drawn-out final cadence. So, although other versions of *The Rite*, like Markevitch's, might convey greater spontaneity, Barenboim's formidable yet never mechanical interpretation is even more compelling in music which seems to present a grimmer, more unsettling message the further we get from its time of composition.

Not to mince words, this recording captures some great music-making in all three works. However many versions of the Debussy and Stravinsky you have, you're urged to try it.

Debussy La mer **Mahler** Symphony No 2, 'Resurrection'[a]

[a]**Eteri Gvazava** sop [a]**Anna Larsson** contr [a]**Orféon Donostiarra; Lucerne Festival Orchestra / Claudio Abbado**
DG ② 477 5082GH2 (106' · DDD). Recorded live
Ⓕ**OO**

This most exalted of all *ad hoc* orchestras consists largely of alumni of Abbado's youth projects. The Mahler Chamber Orchestra provides core personnel with a guest list that includes distinguished present and former Berlin Philharmonic principals. They play as if performing chamber music for friends. You feel that they genuinely want to make music with and for their vulnerable-looking maestro, whose reliance on the willing co-operation of co-workers can give his music-making a faceless quality when the playing is anything less than radiant.

Fortunately it's sensationally good here, every phrase beautifully shaped. The formula works best in *La mer*. The jewel-like colour and élan are indicative of more southerly climes, with superb solos and freshly imagined balances. The glorious, brassy blaze of sunlight at the end of the first movement isn't allowed to obscure the filigree of the woodwind. Though his final pages don't lack fervour, one marvels at the seemingly effortless transparency. The central panel, 'Jeux de vagues', is more scintillating than ever, in a different league from its modern rivals on disc.

And has there ever been a suaver, more transparent Mahler performance or one in which everything stays so beautifully in tune? In spite of the fragility of Abbado's health, his music-making is a celebration of the purest joy.

Nocturnes – Nuages; Fêtes   Ⓗ
Prélude à l'après-midi d'un faune. Le martyre de Saint-Sébastien – symphonic fragments. La mer
Philharmonia Orchestra / Guido Cantelli ·
Testament mono SBT1011 (67' · ADD) Recorded 1954-5   Ⓕ**O**

The death of Guido Cantelli in an air crash at the age of 36 in 1956 was a terrible loss. In a career lasting just 13 years he made his way right to the top, although at the end of his life he was still developing and maturing, and would surely have been one of the most important artists of our time. Fortunately he made a number of superlative recordings and this disc, which contains all his Debussy, shows why concert audiences in the 1950s were bowled over by him.

It's a pity that he never conducted all three *Nocturnes*, for 'Nuages' flows beautifully and expressively and he chooses just the right tempo for 'Fêtes'. He doesn't press this piece too hard as most conductors do, and its colour and piquant personality thus flower freshly and easily. *L'après-midi* is also given plenty of room to breathe: the playing cool, elegant, beautifully poised, yet very eloquent. In *La mer* Cantelli avoids the ham-fisted, overdramatic approach of so many conductors, and instead we have a performance with clear, gleaming textures. The first movement ebbs and flows in a movingly poetic fashion: every detail makes its effect and everything is perfectly in scale. The middle movement is taken quite briskly, but phrasing is hypersensitive and appropriately fluid. In the last movement there's plenty of drama and excitement, although climaxes are kept within bounds in a way which paradoxically makes for a greater effect than if they were given Brucknerian proportions, as they often are.

During Cantelli's lifetime *Le martyre de Saint-Sébastien* was strangely regarded as a tired, feeble work, yet he conducted the 'Symphonic fragments' quite frequently. His approach is very much of the concert hall in that he gives the four pieces a life of their own rather than relating them to the unfolding drama. However, he still captures the music's peculiarly fervent, religious-cum-exotic flavour very effectively. The Philharmonia plays with extraordinary subtlety, and the recordings sound very well indeed.

Prélude à l'après-midi d'un faune[a]. Images[b]. Jeux[c].
Danse sacrée et danse profane[d]
[b]**František Kimel** ob [d]**Karel Patras** hp **Czech Philharmonic Orchestra / Serge Baudo**
Supraphon Archiv SU3478-2 (70' · ADD) Recorded 1966, 1977   Ⓜ**O**

Serge Baudo's Debussy collection brings together three of the most outstanding recordings Supraphon gave us in the analogue era.

Indeed the rich, balmy sound is perfect for the ravishing Czech playing in the *Prélude à l'après-midi d'un faune*, with a wonderfully limpid flute solo, and Baudo letting the music flow onwards in the most natural way. Debussy's translucent colours gleam vividly at the very opening of *Images*, and the piquant oboe solo is ear-catching. 'Les parfums de la nuit' waft softly and languorously in the evening breeze, and the opening of 'Le matin d'un jour de fête' is hauntingly mysterious before the orchestra blazes into life. Finest of all is *Jeux*, always an elusive work on record, but here presented with richly glowing colouristic magic, ravishingly seductive string textures, and a subtle feeling for the music's ebb and flow. The transfer is ADD, and if you're one of those collectors who think that a digital CD can't transfer analogue hall ambience and decay properly, sample this.

String Quartet

Debussy String Quartet in G minor, Op 10 **Ravel** String Quartet in F **Dutilleux** Ainsi la nuit
Belcea Quartet (Corina Belcea, Laura Samuel vns Krzysztof Chorzelski va Alasdair Tait vc)
EMI Debut 574020-2 (71' · DDD) ⓑ**ooo**

This CD is the work of a highly talented, exceptionally well-integrated ensemble. Their excellent balance is highlighted by crystal-clear recording. This is quartet-playing of great musicality, with a wonderful sense of interaction. They find a near ideal transparency in the Ravel, its subtleties beautifully articulated.

The denser, less light-filled style of the Debussy, too, is perfectly weighted – this is a work they've clearly played on numerous occasions, and their performance has a feeling of a work truly inhabited by its players. And the Dutilleux is exquisitely observed, its fragmentary structure creatively embraced by these young musicians. And if all that weren't enough, this disc comes at budget price.

Debussy String Quartet in G minor, Op 10 **Ravel** String Quartet in F
Quartetto Italiano (Paolo Borciani, Elisa Pegreffi vns Piero Farulli va Franco Rossi vc)
Philips Silver Line 420 894-2PSL (57' · ADD)
Recorded 1968 ⓜ**o**

Coupling the Debussy and Ravel String Quartets has become a cliché of the record industry, but as someone has said, a cliché is only a great truth made stale by repetition, and these two wonderful pieces do make a satisfying pair. The account of them by the Quartetto Italiano is over 30 years old but none the worse for that. They are marvellously vital performances in which intensity of feeling doesn't preclude refinement. The only quibble is about the high-level transfer to CD which may send you reluctantly to the volume control of your amplifier.

But when the necessary adjustment is made, the result as sound is satisfactory and the playing good enough to make this Philips issue a first choice at medium price despite its age.

Piano Trio

Debussy Piano Trio in G **Fauré** Piano Trio in D minor, Op 120 **Ravel** Piano Trio in A minor
Florestan Trio (Anthony Marwood vn Richard Lester vc Susan Tomes pf)
Hyperion CDA67114 (66' · DDD)   Ⓕⵔ

The Florestan Trio has the ability to adapt its style to different kinds of music without any loss of conviction. After Brahms and Schumann comes this French disc showing it equally adept at entering the 1880 salon world of Debussy's youthful Trio, Ravel's brilliant exotic idiom, and the intimate, intense thoughts of Fauré's old age. In the quicker movements Susan Tomes's playing is remarkably light and precise. The finale of the Fauré, for example, has a *scherzando* quality that throws into relief the seriousness of the strings' initial gesture. The string players are always ready to modify their sound to produce special expressive effects – the eerily quiet unison passage in Fauré's *Andante* (track 2, 2'54") or the vibrato-less duet in the Ravel *Passacaille* (track 10, 5'15") – sounding wonderfully remote and antique. The clarity of the Hyperion recording allows the fantastical detail in the Ravel *Pantoum* to emerge. In the Debussy, the Florestan favour elegance rather than trying to search out expressive depths. Their freshness, imagination and purposeful directness makes this a top choice.

Sonata for Flute, Viola and Harp

Sonata for Flute, Viola and Harp[a]. Prélude à l'après-midi d'un faune (arr Samazeuilh)[b]. Syrinx[b]. La flûte de Panc. Chansons de Bilitis[d]
[cd]Irène Jacob spkr Philippe Bernold, [d]Mathieu Dufour fls [a]Gérard Caussé va [ad]Isabelle Moretti, [d]Germaine Lorenzini hps Ariane Jacob [b]pf/[d]celesta
Harmonia Mundi HMC90 1647 (50' · DDD) Texts included   Ⓕ

The high point of this disc is a beautifully sensitive performance of Debussy's elusive late sonata, a 'terribly sad' work according to the composer himself, but also containing in its latter two movements an uneasy kind of high spirits born of desperation. The opening and close of the first movement provide two of those haunting moments at which French composers seem to excel. Philippe Bernold is a player of delicate, refined tone whose descents to the edge of sound are hypnotic in their effect; and with his two partners the performance rivals those recordings hitherto cherished as yardsticks – the classic Melos of 1962 and the Nash of 1991. Bernold captures the spirit of rapture in

Syrinx, which is heard both in its usual form as an unaccompanied solo and as it was originally intended, as incidental music to a play, *Psyché*. Unfortunately Irène Jacob, who reads the text admirably, is too distantly placed in relation to the flute. The same criticism applies to the erotic *Chansons de Bilitis* poems. It was Debussy's own idea to make a transcription for flute and piano of the *Prélude à l'après-midi d'un faune*; but imaginatively as Samazeuilh wrote this and Ariane Jacob plays the piano part, the sensuous magic of this score suffers from this reduction of colour.

Violin Sonata

Debussy Violin Sonata **Franck** Violin Sonata in A **Ravel** Berceuse sur le nom de Gabriel Fauré. Pièce en forme de habanera. Tzigane
Augustin Dumay vn **Maria João Pires** pf
DG 445 880-2GH (56' · DDD) Recorded 1993   Ⓕ

There's a spacious, eloquent view here of Franck's Sonata. Dumay's sweet tone has the requisite strength; Pires accompanies where necessary, yet can offer a partner's contribution too, as well as being equal to the composer's considerable pianistic demands. Although the recorded balance favours the violinist, the brilliant second movement is very effective, as is the flowing canonic finale, in which the players rightly think in long phrases. Debussy's emotionally fragile world fares even better: this playing has the right flexibility of time and tone, and the rapidly shifting moods of this essentially sad music, so different from Franck's with its emotional assurance, are unerringly captured; and the sound is excellent here. Dumay and Pires are also at home in Ravel's music with its delicate tenderness and – in *Tzigane* at least – glittering virtuosity.

Complete Piano Works

Préludes, Books 1[a] & 2[a]. Pour le piano[a].   Ⓗ
Estampes[a] . Images, Sets 1a & 2a. Children's Cornera. 12 Etudes. D'un cahier d'esquisses. Rêverie. Valse romantique. Masques. L'îsle joyeuse. La plus que lente. Le petit nègre. Berceuse héroïque. Hommage à Haydn. Danse bohémienne. Mazurka. Deux Arabesques. Nocturne. Tarantelle styrienne. Ballade. Suite bergamasque. Fantaisie
Walter Gieseking pf **Hessian Radio Orchestra, Frankfurt / Kurt Schröder**
EMI mono ④ 565855-2 (276' · ADD) Recorded 1951-5   Ⓜⵔⵔⵔ

The complete Préludes with items marked [a] are also available on HMV Classics ② HMVD5 73192-2   Ⓑ
and (Préludes only) on EMI Great Recordings of the Century 567233-2   Ⓜ

 Gieseking's insight and iridescence in Debussy are so compelling and hypnotic that they prompt either a book or

a blank page – an unsatisfactory state where criticism is concerned! First and foremost, there's Gieseking's sonority, one of such delicacy and variety that it can complement Debussy's witty and ironic desire to write music 'for an instrument without hammers', for a pantheistic art sufficiently suggestive to evoke and transcend the play of the elements themselves ('the wind, the sky, the sea…'). Lack of meticulousness seems a small price to pay for such an elemental uproar in 'Ce qu'a vu le vent d'ouest', and Puck's elfin pulse and chatter (*pp aérian*) are caught with an uncanny deftness and precision. The final Debussian magic may not lie in a literal observance of the score, in the unfailing dotting and crossing of every objective and picturesque instruction, yet it's the start or foundation of a great performance. More domestically, no one (not even Cortot) has ever captured the sense in *Children's Corner* of a lost and enchanted land, of childhood re-experienced through adult tears and laughter, as Gieseking does here. 'Pour les tierces', from the *Etudes*, may get off to a shaky start but, again, in Debussy's final masterpiece, Gieseking's artistry tugs at and haunts the imagination. Try 'Pour les sonorités opposées', the expressive centre of the *Etudes*, and you may well wonder when you've heard playing more subtly gauged or articulated, or the sort of interaction with a composer's spirit that can make modern alternatives seem so parsimonious by comparison. So here's that peerless palette of colour and texture, of a light and shade used with a nonchalant but precise expertise to illuminate every facet of Debussy's imagination. An added bonus, a 1951 performance of the *Fantaisie* for piano and orchestra, completes an incomparable set of discs. The transfers are a real triumph – these discs should be in every musician's library.

Etudes

Etudes – Books 1 & 2
Mitsuko Uchida pf
Philips 50th Edition 464 698-2PH (47' · DDD)
Recorded 1989 Ⓜ Ⓞ

The harmonic language and continuity of the *Etudes* is elusive even by Debussy's standards, and it takes an artist of rare gifts to play them 'from within', at the same time as negotiating their finger-knotting intricacies. Mitsuko Uchida is such an artist. On first hearing perhaps rather hyperactive, her playing wins you over by its bravura and sheer relish, eventually disarming criticism altogether. This isn't just the finest ever recorded version of the *Etudes*; it's also one of the finest examples of recorded piano playing in modern times, matched by sound quality of outstanding clarity.

Etudes. Images
Pierre-Laurent Aimard pf
Teldec 8573 83940-2 (72' · DDD) Ⓕ ⓄⓄ

Debussy once remarked that he'd like to get rid of the percussive attack of the piano's hammers on the strings. He's said to have regarded the piano as Balinese musicians do their gamelan orchestras, interested not so much in the single tone heard when a note was struck as in the patterns of resonance that it set up. Many of his pieces are built entirely on this acoustical sense of the piano.

With Pierre-Laurent Aimard the sheer freshness and novelty of it come across strongly. So does the ardour; whereas some players are content with mood and atmosphere, his communication of feeling is acute. There are passages of extraordinary violence in this music, especially in the Etudes; he makes them still sound modern. Others would favour letting sonorities hang longer in the air. You couldn't ask for more colour, or greater sensibility, but he isn't a charmer. He has edge and likes sonority to work directly on the business in hand. He always goes for the movement and the thrust of what's written; those used to a more spacious and laid-back view of the Images, in particular, may occasionally be disconcerted.

This is a Debussy record of high class, hugely stimulating. Aimard's version of the *Etudes* is up there with the very best. Technically, he's a wizard, without a chink in his armour; but he's the best kind of technician, playing like a composer, and letting the music drive him.

Images

Images. Le petit nègre. Children's Corner. La plus que lente. Valse romantique. Tarantelle styrienne. Mazurka. Suite bergamasque. Hommage à Haydn. Elégie. Berceuse héroïque. Page d'album. Etudes. Etude retrouvée
Jean-Yves Thibaudet pf
Decca ② 460 247-2DH2 (151' · DDD) Recorded 1994-8 Ⓕ

Jean-Yves Thibaudet's Debussy cycle is a cornucopia of delights. The 12 *Etudes* could hardly be presented more personally or vivaciously. Nos 6 and 7 are marvels of bright-eyed irony and humour, while Nos 8 and 9 contrast a haunting alternation of lassitude and hyperactivity with razor-sharp cascades of repeated notes. His timing in the central *lento, molto rubato* of No 12 is memorably acute; throughout, you're aware of a pianist with a penchant for spare pedalling and a refined brilliance, far remote from, say, Gieseking's celebrated, opalescent magic. He takes a brisk hand to the *Children's Corner* suite (*allegro* rather than *allegretto* in 'Serenade for the Doll', hardly *modérément animé* in 'The Snow is Dancing') but even here his spruce technique and vitality are never less than enlivening. In the *Suite bergamasque* he dances the 'Menuet' with an unusual sense of its underlying grace and gravity, and his 'Clair de lune' is exceptionally silvery and transparent. Both books of *Images* are given with a rare sense of epiphany or illumination, of flashing fins and

DEBUSSY'S PRÉLUDES – IN BRIEF

Walter Gieseking
EMI 567233-2 (71' · AAD)   Ⓜ❍❍❍
Gieseking's classic recording of the *Préludes* dates from 1953-4 and remains unsurpassed in extracting the elusive poetry of the more delicate pieces.

Krystian Zimerman
DG ② 435 773-2GH2 (84' · DDD)   Ⓜ❍❍❍
Larger in scale if perhaps less obviously idiomatic, Zimerman's compelling revivification tips over onto a second disc. This is high-octane playing for our own times, with the widest dynamic range and very tangible digital sound. It took a *Gramophone* Award on its release.

Noriko Ogawa
BIS BIS-CD1205 (76' · DDD)   Ⓕ❍❍
The second instalment of Ogawa's Debussy survey includes a fine account of the First Book of *Préludes* in unbeatably natural sound.

Arturo Benedetti Michelangeli
DG ② 449 438-2GH2 (128' · ADD/DDD)   Ⓕ❍
The crystalline perfection of Michelangeli's Debussy has at times an imperious quality that continues to divide audiences. The *Préludes* have been recoupled with his earlier accounts of *Children's Corner* and the two sets of *Images*, performances which enjoy more nearly universal acclaim.

Martino Tirimo
Regis RRCD1111 (78' · DDD)   Ⓢ❍
Complete on one super-bargain CD, Tirimo's set offers excellent value, his sensitive playing enhanced by fine digital sound.

Jean-Yves Thibaudet
Decca ② 452 022-2 (157' · DDD)   Ⓕ
Always a crisp and articulate pianist, Thibaudet's *Préludes* display greater freedom and imagination than is sometimes the case with him. The eruptive, lightly pedalled *Feux d'artifice* is a particular highlight. This is volume 1 of his first-rate survey of the complete Debussy piano music.

Jos van Immerseel
Channel Classics CCS4892 (54' · DDD)   Ⓕ
This is something of a curiosity and certainly isn't a prime recommendation: van Immerseel uses an 1897 Erard piano for the First Book of *Préludes*, as well as the *Images Oubliées*. It's certainly worth hearing for its special note of authenticity. When not played loudly the piano makes a delightful sound, but Immerseel isn't the most imaginative of players.

sunlight in 'Poissons d'or' and of a timeless sense of archaism in 'Hommage à Rameau'. Decca's presentation and sound are, respectively, lavish and natural. If you want to hear Debussy new-minted, with air-spun and scintillating textures, Thibaudet is your man.

Images – Sets 1 & 2. D'un cahier d'esquisses. L'isle joyeuse. Deux arabesques. Hammage à aydn. Rêverie. Page d'album. Berceuse héroïque
Zoltán Kocsis
Philips Gramophone Awards Collection 475 2102
(62' · DDD) Recorded 1988   Ⓕ❍❍❍

Zoltán Kocsis stands out as an especially idiomatic exponent of Debussy's piano style. Here he offsets the familiar with the less known, bringing playing of exceptional finesse, and, at times, of exceptional brilliance and fire. The main work is *Images*, its two sets completed in 1905 and 1907, by which time the composer was already master of that impressionistic style of keyboard writing so different from anything before. For sensitivity to details of textural shading Kocsis is at his most spellbinding in the first two numbers of the second set, 'Cloches à travers les feuilles' and 'Et la lune descend sur le temple qui fût'. He's also successful in reminding us of Debussy's wish to 'forget that the piano has hammers' in the atmospheric washes of sound he conjures (through his pedalling no less than his fingers) in *D'un cahier d'esquisses*. The sharp clear daylight world of *L'isle joyeuse* reveals a pianist exulting in his own virtuosity and strength, as he also does in the last piece of each set of *Images*, and even in the second of the two familiar, early *Arabesques* – neither of them mere vapid drawing-room charmers here. The recording is first rate. Highly recommended.

Préludes

Préludes – Books 1 & 2   Ⓗ
Walter Gieseking pf
EMI Great Recordings of the Century 567233-2
(71' · ADD) (in USA: 5 67262-2) Recorded 1953-4
Ⓜ❍❍❍

Gieseking's set of both Books of the *Préludes* is one of the great classics of the gramophone. The individual insights are endless, so is the extraordinary feeling for the music's evocation and atmosphere. The 1953-4 recordings just missed the stereo era, but the Abbey Road mono sound is first-class. Don't miss it.

Préludes – Books 1 & 2
Krystian Zimerman pf
DG ② 435 773-2GH2 (84' · DDD) Recorded 1991
Ⓜ❍❍❍

Two discs, retailing at a high mid-price and playing for a total of 84 minutes? The playing and the recording had better be in the luxury class. Fortunately they are. Zimerman is the very model of a modern virtuoso. His overriding aim is vivid projection of character. His quasi-orchestral range of dynamic and attack, based on close attention to textual detail (there are countless felicities in his observation of phrase-markings) and maximum clarity of articulation, is the means to that end. As a result, he draws out the many connections in this music with the romantic tradition, especially in pianistic *tours de force* such as 'Les collines d'Anacapri', 'Ce qu'a vu le vent d'ouest' and 'Feux d'artifice', which are treated to a dazzling Lisztian *élan*.

At the other extreme Zimerman displays an exquisite refinement of touch that makes the quieter pieces both evocative and touching. Such sensitively conceived and wonderfully executed Debussy playing stands, at the very least, on a level with a classic recording such as Gieseking's. The instrument selected is itself something of a star and DG's recording combines opulence with razor-sharp clarity.

Préludes – Book 1. D'un cahier d'esquisses. Morceau de concours. La plus que lente. Hommage à Joseph Haydn. The little nigar. Children's Corner
Noriko Ogawa pf
BIS BIS-CD1205 (76' · DDD)　　　　　Ⓕ**OO**

Every bar of these performances confirms Ogawa as a most elegant, scrupulously sensitive interpreter of 'music like a dream from which one draws away the veil' (Debussy). She achieves a magical transparency throughout Book 1 of the *Préludes* with her refined pedalling and cool command of texture and colour. In 'Voiles' she makes you readily recall Cortot's heady description of 'the flight of the white wing on the crooning sea toward the horizon bright with the setting sun' while maintaining her own individuality. Her hushed start before the start of the whirling tarantella in 'Les collines d'Anacapri' is one of many haunting touches; and her playing of 'Des pas sur la neige', the Arctic centre of Book 1 of the *Préludes*, suggests some ultimate desolation. In *Children's Corner* she never turns 'Doctor Gradus', marked *modérément animé*, into a glittering *presto* and finds time to convey its mix of guile and sophistication. You could hardly find a more skilful or sympathetic artist from a younger generation. BIS's demonstration sound quality crowns this superb issue.

Préludes – Books 1 & 2ᵃ. Images. Children's Corner
Arturo Benedetti Michelangeli pf
DG ② 449 438-2GH2 (128' · ADD/ᵃDDD) Recorded 1971-88　　　　　　Ⓕ**O**

Of Debussy playing his own music Alfredo Casella said 'he made the impression of playing directly on the strings of the instrument with no intermediate mechanism – the effect was a miracle of poetry'. This isn't Michelangeli's way.

He can certainly be poetic and produce miracles, but his manner isn't ingratiating. Generalised 'atmosphere' doesn't interest him. His superfine control is put at the service of line and movement, above all, and the projection of perspectives. He gives you a sense not just of foreground and background but of many planes in between. He was capable of a transcendental virtuosity that had nothing to do with playing fast and loud, and everything to do with refinement, and it's very much in evidence here – in many *Préludes* and especially in the first two *Images* of the Second Book. The clarity of texture and the laser-like delineation can sometimes be disconcerting if you're accustomed to a softer, more ethereal style, but they have a way of making Debussy's modernism apparent and thrilling. He sounds here as if he has had nothing to do with the 19th century. The *Images* and *Children's Corner* are among the finest versions ever recorded. But in some of the *Préludes*, particularly in Book 1, the sound is rather close and dry – maybe how Michelangeli wanted it. He uses as little pedal as he can get away with.

There are people who regard Gieseking as unparalleled in this music, but after a quarter of a century the best of Michelangeli, similarly, will run and run. Today's generation of Debussy pianists will be expected to work from a less corrupt text, but they'll have far to go before they can rival the penetrating qualities of Michelangeli's Debussy at its best. He could take your breath away, and he was illuminating in this repertoire in a rare way.

Additional recommendation

24 Preludes – Books 1 and 2
Tirimo pf
Regis RRCD1111 (78' · DDD)　　　　Ⓢ**ⒼO**
It would be hard to find a more quietly stylish or subtle account than that offered by Tirimo. His undemonstrative mastery makes him among the finest Debussy interpreters on disc.

Pelléas et Mélisande

Pelléas et Mélisande　　　　　　　　　Ⓗ
Jacques Jansen bar Pelléas **Irène Joachim** sopMélisande **Henri Etcheverry** bar Golaud **Paul Cabanel** bass Arkel **Germaine Cernay** mez Geneviève **Leila ben Sedira** sop Yniold **Emile Rousseau** bass Shepherd **Armand Narçon** bass Doctor **Yvonne Gouverné Choir; symphony orchestra / Roger Desormière**
EMI Références mono ③ 761038-2 (196' · ADD) Recorded 1941. Booklet with translation included
　　　　　　　　　　　　　　　　Ⓜ**OO**

The strength of the performance owed much to the fact that Irène Joachim, Jacques Jansen and Henri Etcheverry had already sung the work many times under Desormière at the Opéra-Comique. Irène Joachim had studied the role of Mélisande with its creator, Mary Garden; and both she and Jansen had been coached by Georges Viseur, who with Messager had been

DEBUSSY'S PELLÉAS ET MÉLISANDE – IN BRIEF

Jacques Jansen Pelléas **Iréne Joachim**
Mélisande **Henri Etcheverry** Golaud **Yvonne**
Gouverné Choir / Roger Desormière
EMI ③ 761038-2 (196' · AAD)   Ⓜ○○
A truly historic 1941 recording that transcends limited sound with superbly idiomatic
performances by a native French cast, a great
advantage in this opera, with Jacques Jansen's
still youthful Pelléas and Irene Joachim's
glass-clear Mélisande.

Wolfgang Holzmair Pelléas **Anne Sofie von**
Otter Mélisande **Laurent Naouri** Golaud
Radio France Chorus, French National
Orchestra / Bernard Haitink
Naïve ③ V4923 (160' · DDD)   Ⓜ○
Though the international cast is quite
impressive, Haitink's conducting, luminous
but highly dramatic, is the star of this concert
recording.

Didier Henry Pelléas **Colette Alliot-Lugaz**
Mélisande **Montreal Symphony Chorus and**
Orchestra / Charles Dutoit
Decca ② 430 502-2DH2 (151' · DDD)   Ⓕ
A French-speaking cast and fine orchestral
playing are outstanding features of Dutoit's
straightforward set, recorded under perform-
ance conditions.

Richard Sitwell Pelléas **Frederica von Stade**
Mélisande **José van Dam** Golaud **Deutsche Oper**
Berlin Chorus, Berlin PO / Herbert von Karajan
EMI ③ 567057-2 (162' · ADD)   Ⓜ
Pelléas meets Tristan in this extraordinary set
– for many – misguided set, with a decent cast
and superb orchestral playing subjected to an
over-romantic, glutinous interpretation.

George Shirley Pelléas **Elisabeth Söderström**
Mélisande **Chorus and Orchestra of the Royal**
Opera House / Pierre Boulez
Sony ③ SM3K47265 (154' · ADD)   Ⓜ
Based on a legendary Covent Garden production, Boulez's intense, gush-free interpretation
brings out Wagnerian undertones more
authentically than Karajan, and a top-flight
international cast headed by Elizabeth Söderström and George Shirley, lacking only
absolutely natural French.

François Le Roux Pelléas **Maria Ewing** Mélisande
José van Dam Golaud **Vienna State Opera**
Chorus, Vienna PO / Claudio Abbado
DG ② 435 344-2GH2 (148' · DDD)   Ⓕ
A large-scale but beautifully translucent and
poetic performance, very well recorded, with
probably the best modern cast on disc,
appropriately Francophone except for Maria
Ewing's unconventional and strikingly
seductive Mélisande.

the répétiteur for the opera's first performance.
Jansen with his free, youthful-toned production
and Joachim with her silvery voice and intelligent response to every verbal nuance, set
standards for the doomed lovers that, though
nearly equalled, have never been surpassed; but
even more impressive is Etcheverry's interpretation of Golaud, a role in which, arguably, he
has yet to be rivalled. Leila ben Sedira gives one
of the most convincing portrayals ever heard of
the child Yniold; and Germaine Cernay and
Paul Cabanel (who alone is just a trifle free with
the text in places) fill the parts of the older characters with distinction. In this recording, the
placing of the voices is such that every single
word is crystal clear. More important every
word is invested with meaning by a native
French cast – in other versions allowances
sometimes need to be made for non-French
singers – which had immersed itself totally in
the emotional nuances and overtones of the
text. Every shade of expression is caught, but
nevertheless the overall feeling is of subtle
Gallic understatement – with Golaud's self-
tormenting jealousy and Pelléas's final inability
to resist declaring his love for his brother's
mysterious, fey wife creating the great emotional climaxes.

Keith Hardwick's alchemy in transforming
these old recordings into sound of improved
quality (and with only minimal vestiges of the
78rpm surfaces) is nothing short of amazing. He
hasn't, of course, been able to correct the thin
1941 recording of the woodwind, but one soon
comes to terms with the dated instrumental
sound because of Desormière's inspired pacing
and moulding of the score, the committed
orchestral playing, and the well-nigh perfect
casting.

Pelléas et Mélisande
Wolfgang Holzmair bar Pelléas **Anne Sofie von**
Otter sop Mélisande **Laurent Naouri** bar Golaud
Alain Vernhes bass Arkel **Hanna Schaer** mez
Geneviève **Florence Couderc** sop Yniold **Jérôme**
Varnier bar A Doctor, A Shepherd **Radio France**
Chorus; French National Orchestra / Bernard
Haitink
Naïve ③ V4923 (160' · DDD) Notes, texts and
translations included   Ⓜ○

Bernard Haitink has always had a soft spot for
French music, where his control of texture and
pace often brings out beauties and strengths
that other conductors do not find. Pelléas et
Mélisande, for which long-term flow is a crucial
requirement, is ideally suited to his talents. He
has the ability, like a good games player, to create his own time and space.

Throughout, the beauty, energy and brilliance
of the orchestral playing ride over an undertow
of melancholy and impending disaster, echoing
that 'strange air' Mélisande has of someone
who, in Arkel's words, 'is always waiting for
some great sorrow in the sunshine in a lovely
garden'. Haitink is well served by his singers.

Holzmair is a fresh-voiced, ardent but elegant Pelléas, and innocent enough to make his entrapment plausible. Even the slight signs of tiring on his high notes in Act 4 can be heard as portraying vulnerability. Anne Sofie von Otter plays Mélisande in the traditional way as timid and fatally seductive. But von Otter brings more vibrato to her top notes than some other interpreters and this gives her timidity a slightly used, passive-aggressive colouring, as though she has employed her don't-touch-me gambit several times in the past, and has found it works.

Laurent Naouri is a supremely intelligent Golaud, slow to jealousy and anger, but terrifying when the dam finally bursts. By contrast, in the final act he's the image of a spiritually lost soul and his choked cries of 'Mélisande!' are truly heartrending. Alain Vernhes's Arkel has that 'goodness' in his tone that the composer wanted, though his pitching, hitherto perfect, wanders somewhat in Act 5.

Members of the French National Orchestra are, apparently, still talking two years later of this *Pelléas* as a high point in their professional lives. It isn't to be wondered at: Haitink gives us a deeply serious and powerful interpretation of the opera.

Additional recommendation

Stilwell *Pelléas* **von Stade** *Mélisande*
Berlin Philharmonic Orchestra / Karajan
EMI 567057-2 (162' · ADD)   Ⓜ

A controversial recording: too 'hot-house' for some but full of breathtaking playing and a heartbreakingly touching pair of lovers. This was clearly a labour of love for the great Austrian conductor.

Rodrigue et Chimène

Rodrigue et Chimène
Laurence Dale *ten* Rodrigue **Donna Brown** *sop* Chimène **Hélène Jossoud** *mez* Iñez **Gilles Ragon** *ten* Hernan **Jean-Paul Fouchécourt** *ten* Bermudo **José van Dam** *bass-bar* Don Diègue **Jules Bastin** *bass* Don Gomez **Vincent le Texier** *bass-bar* King **Jean-Louis Meunier** *ten* Don Juan d'Arcos **Jean Delescluse** *ten* Don Pèdre de Terruel **Chorus and Orchestra of the Opéra de Lyon / Kent Nagano**
Erato ② 4509-98508-2 (109' · DDD) Recorded 1993-4.
Notes, text and translation included   Ⓜ

It may come as a surprise to many who treasure the unique magic of *Pelléas et Mélisande* that Debussy toyed with some 30 other plans for operas, and two years before *Pelléas* had all but completed his first operatic venture. Debussy very soon realised that the libretto's blustering tone was alien to his ideals of half-hinted action in short scenes, and became increasingly restive, finally abandoning it and claiming that it had been accidentally destroyed. In reality it survived complete in a sketch in short score, though some pages have since been lost. Richard Langham Smith reconstructed the work

from the manuscripts in the Piermont Morgan Library in New York, it was completed and orchestrated, with a remarkable insight into Debussian style, by Edison Denisov, and in 1993 it was presented by the Opéra de Lyon to mark the opening of its new house. Inconsistencies of style reveal something of Debussy's uncertainties and doubts over a subject inappropriate for him. There's little in Act 3 that would lead anyone to identify him as the composer, and virtually the only sections of the work with a harmonic idiom that was later to become characteristic of him are Rodrigue's and Chimène's mutual declaration of love at the start of Act 1, the orchestral prelude to Act 2 and the unexpected quiet interlude that precedes Rodrigue's mortal challenge to his beloved's father Don Gomez, who had shamed his own father. Debussy is less at home with the choral scene leading up to the angry conflict between the two initially friendly houses, the heroic and warlike atmosphere of much of Act 2, and the bombastic assembling of the royal court; but all these are tackled, if not with individuality, at least with vigour. Don Gomez's death scene is affecting, and the unaccompanied choral requiem for him makes an effective close to Act 2.

Unlike *Pelléas*, there are a number of extended set pieces for the singers, including Rodrigue's dutiful dilemma, Don Diègue's hymn to the concept of honour, Chimène's lament for her father and her final anguish as she's torn between love and hate for Rodrigue. As a performance and recording, this is in the highest class. Nagano's orchestra plays for him with finesse, and the work is cast from strength. Laurence Dale is a near-perfect Rodrigue – youthful, ardent and sensitive to changes of mood; Donna Brown makes a passionate Chimène, though occasionally just too close to the microphone for sudden outbursts; and José van Dam is his reliable self, with nobility in his voice. Clarity of enunciation throughout (except, at times, from the chorus) is to be applauded.

Léo Delibes   French 1836-1891

A church, organist until 1871, Delibes was drawn to the theatre, first writing light operettas in the style of his teacher Adolphe Adam (roughly one a year from 1856 to 1869), then becoming chorus master at the Théâtre-Lyrique and the Opéra. He is best known for his appealing classical ballets Coppélia (1870), with its charming character numbers, and the tuneful but more sophisticated Sylvia (1876), both admired by Tchaikovsky. Meyerbeer's influence is evident in his serious opera Jean de Nivelle (1880), and a gift for witty pastiche in his dances for Hugo's play Le roi's'amuse (1882). His masterpiece is Lakmé (1883), a highly successful opera indebted to Bizet and memorable for its oriental colour, strong characterisation and fine melodies. **GROVE**music

Sylvia

Delibes Sylvia **Saint-Saëns** Henry VIII – Ballet-divertissement
Razumovsky Sinfonia / Andrew Mogrelia
Naxos ② 8 553338/9 (114' · DDD)   ⑤

Of Delibes's two full-length ballets, *Coppélia* is the more obviously popular, the one with the bigger tunes and the greater number of recordings. However, *Sylvia* is also a superbly crafted score, full of haunting melodies. Andrew Mogrelia's Naxos series is one to be collected and treasured: there's loving care applied to selection of tempos, shaping of phrases, orchestral balance and refinement of instrumental detail. Here you thrill to *Sylvia*'s Act 1 Fanfare, marvel at the control of tempo and refinement of instrumental detail in the 'Valse lente' and 'Entrée du sorcier', and revel in the sheer ebullience of Sylvia's return in Act 2. The inclusion of the ballet music from Saint-Saëns's *Henry VIII* was an admirably enterprising move, even though it doesn't amount to anything major apart from the 'Danse de la gitane', being essentially a collection of mock 'Olde Britishe' dances. All the same, a quite remarkable bargain.

Lakmé

Lakmé
Natalie Dessay *sop* Lakmé **Gregory Kunde** *ten*
Gérald **José van Dam** *bass-bar* Nilakantha **Delphine Haidan** *mez* Mallika **Franck Leguérinel** *bar* Frédéric **Patricia Petibon** *sop* Ellen **Xenia Konsek** *sop* Rose **Bernadette Antoine** *sop* Mistress Bentson **Charles Burles** *ten* Hadji **Toulouse Capitole Chorus and Orchestra / Michel Plasson**
EMI ② 556569-2 (144' · DDD) Text and translation included   ⒻⒹ

Opera audiences in 19th-century Paris may never have visited India, but they loved to dream about it. After the successes enjoyed by *Les pêcheurs de perles* and *Le roi de Lahore* Delibes knew what he was doing when he chose to set an adaptation of Pierre Loti's exotic Indian novel *Rarahu* and duly scored a hit with his opera *Lakmé* at the Opéra-Comique in 1883. The opera is nothing without a star in the title-role. Natalie Dessay is certainly that and yet she never fails to remember that Delibes's heroine must be fragile and sensitive. Her Bell Song, brilliantly sung, is also intent on telling a story. Her singing of the death scene, with its delicate *fil de voce* perfectly poised each time the high A comes round, is heartfelt and leaves no doubt that this is a Lakmé who deserves to go to heaven. EMI found a worthy tenor to partner her. Gregory Kunde, as Gérald, is at ease at the top of his voice. At the first entrance of the colonial Brits, Frédéric describes Gérald as a poet and Kunde lives up to the promise by phrasing his opening solo, 'Fantaisie aux divins mensonges', with poetic sensibility. In the duets he

and Dessay are tender young love personified. The supporting cast is also a decent one.

Michel Plasson gives the music room to breathe and is able to conjure a dreamy atmosphere in the scenes of romance. His Toulouse orchestra is adequate, if not exceptional, and the recording is of a good standard. What reason is there to resist?

Additional recommendations

Lakmé

Sutherland Lakmé **Vanzo** Gérald **Monte-Carlo Opera Orchestra / Bonynge**
Decca Double 460 741-2DF2 (138' · ADD)   Ⓜ
One for Sutherland fans (don't even try to understand her French) or those wanting a mid-price set. The largely French cast helps convey the spirit of this elusive score.

Robin Lakmé **L de Luca** Gérald   Ⓗ
Orchestra / Sebastien
Pearl mono ② GEMS0181 (139' · ADD) Recorded 1951   ⓂⓄⓄ
This is a classic, outshining even the superb 1998 Natalie Dessay on EMI. Mado Robin was a famous Lakmé, and you can hear why in her tender, plaintive and technically astonishing performance. The transfer is exemplary.

Frederick Delius   British 1862-1934

Delius's father lent him money to set up as a citrus grower in Florida (1884-6), where he had lessons with Thomas Ward; he then studied at the Leipzig Conservatory (1886-8) and met Grieg. He settled in Paris as a man of bohemian habits, a friend of Gauguin, Strindberg, Munch and others, until in 1897 he moved to Grez with Jelka Rosen, later his wife. There he remained.

He had written operas, orchestral pieces and much else before the move to Grez, but nearly all his regularly performed output dates from afterwards while looking back at the musical and other experiences of earlier years: the seamless flow of Wagner, the airier chromaticism of Grieg, the rich colouring of Strauss and Debussy, the existential independence of Nietzsche. His operas A Village Romeo and Juliet (1901) and Fennimore and Gerda (1910) are love stories cast in connected scenes and examining spiritual states within a natural world. Nature is important too in such orchestral pieces as In a Summer Garden (1908), A Song of the High Hills (with wordless chorus, 1911) or A Song of Summer (1930), though there are other works in which the characteristic rhapsodising is made to serve symphonic forms, notably the Violin Concerto (1916) and three sonatas for violin and piano (1914, 1923, 1930). The choral works include two unaccompanied, wordless songs 'to be sung of a summer night on the water' (1917), the large-scale A Mass of Life with words from Nietzsche (1905) and a secular Requiem (1916). In the

early 1920s he grew blind and paralysed as a result
of syphilitic infection, and his last works were taken
down by Eric Fenby.   GROVEmusic

Concertos

Violin Concerto[a]. Piano Concerto in C minor[b]. On
Hearing the First Cuckoo in Spring[c]. Brigg Fair[d].
Caprice and Elegy[e]
[a]Tasmin Little vn [b]Jean-Rodolphe Kars pf [e]Julian
Lloyd Webber vc [e]Bengt Forsberg pf [ac]Welsh
National Opera Orchestra, [bd]London Symphony
Orchestra / [d]Anthony Collins, [b]Alexander Gibson,
[ac]Sir Charles Mackerras
Decca British Music Collection ② 470 190-2
[a]Recorded 1991   Ⓜ

The basic pace of Mackerras and Little's
account of the Violin Concerto is faster than
that of Ralph Holmes (reviewed below), though
progress is in no way metronomic. Decca's
sound offers a closer view of both soloist and
orchestra, and this immediacy goes hand in
hand with the more purposeful manner. But
after the relative vigour of the first movement,
how gloriously the central section develops.
Little and Mackerras breathe as one, even in the
accompanied cadenza, which like Holmes has a
properly *ad lib* feel to it. This account will
undoubtedly win the Concerto and its composer new friends, and has the added bonus of
some great couplings.

Paris: The Song of a Great City. Cello Concerto.
Double Concerto
Tasmin Little vn **Raphael Wallfisch** vc **Royal
Liverpool Philharmonic Orchestra / Sir Charles
Mackerras**
Classics for Pleasure 575803-2 (64' · DDD)
Recorded early 1990s   Ⓢ Ⓑ ◐◐

Mackerras's *Paris* is vividly characterised, with
the dancing propelled to wild, whirling climaxes. Not even Beecham in 1934 was this
uninhibited. Mackerras isn't afraid to push the
orchestra into genuine *prestissimos* in an instant,
or relax to the most lingering *molto adagio*, and
the control at both extremes is total. The engineering paints a deceptively distant picture at
the start, but as the city's nocturnal wheel
begins to turn the whole orchestral fabric suddenly lights up before your amazed ears; the
sheer immediacy of it all may be too much for
some, but it aligns perfectly with Mackerras's
uncompromisingly vital, impetuous reading of
the score. This *Paris* has to be heard. And so it's
with the Cello Concerto. Wallfisch and Mackerras manage to inject a fair measure of vigour
into the work's faster moving sections and in the
Allegramente of the finale, thus avoiding any
uniformity of mood. This *Allegramente* now
dances as well as sings; the pace sounds instinctively right. They also find plenty of space to
relax, and the solo cello's musings at the start of
the slow movement, for example, have a lovely
improvisatory feel.

Tasmin Little joins them for the much underrated Double Concerto that, in the drive and
energy of its outer sections here, often recalls
the work that inspired it (the Brahms Double).
Again this concerto receives a performance of
great confidence, security and unanimity of
purpose; and the expressive range of the
soloists' playing lifts this heavenly meditation
on to another level altogether. All this at budget
price!

Orchestral Works

Appalachia, RTVII/2[d]. Brigg Fair, RTVI/16[a].   Ⓗ
Koanga[b] – La Calinda (arr Fenby). Hassan[c] – Closing
scene. Irmelin Prelude, RTVI/27[b].
[c]Jan van der Gucht ten [c]Royal Opera House
Chorus, Covent Garden; [d]BBC Chorus;
[a]Symphony Orchestra; [bcd]London Philharmonic
Orchestra / Sir Thomas Beecham
Naxos Historical mono 8 110906 (66' · AAD) Recorded
[a]1928-9, 1938   Ⓢ Ⓢ ◐

There always was a unique alchemy between the
art of Sir Thomas Beecham and the music of
Frederick Delius, to be heard in every bar of this
remarkable January 1938 recording of *Appalachia*. It's a performance of beaming dedication,
wistful heartache and rapt wonder leaves the listener in no doubt about Sir Thomas's boundless
love for a work that served as his introduction to
the composer. (He later recalled how the 1907
London première under Fritz Cassirer left him
'startled and electrified'.) By July 1938 Beecham
and the LPO had committed to disc the three
remaining items that eventually made up The
Delius Society's lavishly presented third and
final volume of the composer's music issued by
Columbia Records; suffice it to say, *La Calinda*
skips along entrancingly here, while no true
Delian could fail to respond to Beecham's ineffably poignant way with both the closing scene
from *Hassan* and the lovely *Irmelin Prelude*.

Naxos's curtain-raiser, *Brigg Fair*, was
recorded towards the end of the previous
decade. Some seven months separated the two
days required to produce a reading of unforgettable tenderness and bewitching poetry (the
results of an even earlier session in July 1928
having been rejected altogether), although
some will still hold a slight preference for the
second of Sir Thomas's three versions (a gloriously intuitive display with the newly formed
RPO from November 1946).

David Lennick's transfers have been
admirably managed, *Appalachia* now sounding
rather more open and full bodied than on a rival
Dutton compilation. Throw in a lively and
informative booklet-essay from Lyndon Jenkins, not to mention the absurdly low price-tag,
and it should be abundantly clear that this is a
self-recommending issue.

Fantastic Dance. A Dance Rhapsody No 1[a]. A Dance
Rhapsody No 2. A Song of the High Hills. Three

Preludes. Zum Carnival
Maryetta Midgley sop **Vernon Midgley** ten **Eric Parkin** pf **Ambrosian Singers**
Royal Philharmonic Orchestra / Eric Fenby,
[a]**Norman Del Mar**
Unicorn-Kanchana Souvenir UKCD2071 (65' · DDD)
Recorded 1981-90 Ⓜ

Irmelin Prelude. A Song of Summer. A Late Lark.
Piano Concerto in C minor[a]. Violin Concerto[b]
Anthony Rolfe Johnson ten **Ralph Holmes** vn **Philip Fowke** pf **Royal Philharmonic Orchestra / Eric Fenby,** [a]**Norman Del Mar,** [b]**Vernon Handley**
Unicorn-Kanchana Souvenir UKCD2072 (71' · DDD)
Recorded 1981-90 Ⓜ

Koanga – La Calinda (arr Fenby). Idyll: Once I passed through a populous city. Songs of Sunset. A Village Romeo and Juliet – The Walk to the Paradise Garden[a]
Felicity Lott sop **Sarah Walker** mez **Thomas Allen** bar **Ambrosian Singers; Royal Philharmonic Orchestra / Eric Fenby,** [a]**Norman Del Mar**
Unicorn-Kanchana Souvenir UKCD2073 (73' · DDD)
Recorded 1981-90 ⓂⓄ

The unique insight that the late Eric Fenby would bring as an interpreter of Delius was the reason for many of these Unicorn recordings, but we owe the idea and its realisation to their producer, the late Christopher Palmer. As well as providing Delians with some of the most illuminating text on the music, Palmer, in the studio, and especially in a work like *A Song of the High Hills*, was able to put his understanding (and Fenby's, of course) into practice. You don't need the score of *A Song of the High Hills* to tell you that the passage from 9'54" represents 'The wide far distance, the great solitude'. What you're listening to – totally spellbound – couldn't be anything else (or by anyone else).

Ralph Holmes's recording of the Violin Concerto is a warm, leisurely reading. The Piano Concerto, as recorded here, is a grand showstopper in the best Romantic piano concerto tradition, yet Fowke and Del Mar alert you to all the Delian reverie in the making (the dynamic range of Fowke's piano is colossal). But the outlay for Vol 2 is justified by Anthony Rolfe Johnson alone, in the all too brief six-minute *A Late Lark* ('one of Delius's works that is surely entirely without flaw', as Trevor Harvey put it in his original review).

In Vol 3, Fenby's control in *Songs of Sunset* doesn't always match his insight (choral work is often sloppy and too distantly recorded); the recent Hickox, or the 1957 Beecham is to be preferred. But without Fenby in the recording studio (or at Grez!), we would never have had *Idyll*: Whitman texts combined with a late reworking of music from an earlyish opera, *Margot la Rouge*, to provide a reflective then rapturous love duet that looks back to Delius's Paris as well as to his *Paris* – this makes Vol 3 indispensable, especially as sung and played here.

And a very considerable bonus to be found in

Vol 3 is Del Mar's previously unissued *Walk to the Paradise Garden*. This isn't the Beecham version for reduced orchestra, though it incorporates many of Beecham's dynamics and tempo indications. Most assuredly, it's a *Walk* on the grandest (11'00" to Beecham's 8'38"), most passionate scale (there's not a barline in earshot, either), and turns out to be yet another of these three discs' memorials to inspired Delians who died in our, but before their, time.

On Hearing the First Cuckoo in Spring. Brigg Fair. In a Summer Garden. Paris: The Song of a Great City. Summer Night on the River. A Village Romeo and Juliet – The Walk to the Paradise Garden
BBC Symphony Orchestra / Sir Andrew Davis
Warner Apex 8573-89084-2 (77' · DDD) Recorded 1992 Ⓢ

This *Brigg Fair* is unique. What a lovely surprise to hear real London sparrows sharing the air space of St Augustine's Church with Delius's translated Lincolnshire larks (flute and clarinet) in the opening minutes of the work, albeit much more distantly. Very effective too are those almost still pools of string sound (early morning mists?), given the extended boundaries of this acoustic, and the familiar warmth and depth of tone Davis draws from the orchestra's strings. In the final magnificently broad climax (pealing bells, for once, very clear), you can't fail to be impressed by the depth, coherence and articulacy of the sound – hallmarks, indeed, of the entire disc. Davis's strings come into their own in the *Walk to the Paradise Garden*. For *In a Summer Garden*, Davis mutes his strings more often than Delius asks; but the reading's delicacy of texture and hazy, suffusing warmth are difficult to resist.

American Rhapsody. Fantastic Dance. Marche caprice. Three Small Tone Poems. Two Pieces for Small Orchestra. A song before sunrise. A Village Romeo and Juliet – The walk to the Paradise Garden
Royal Scottish National Orchestra / David Lloyd-Jones
Naxos 8 557143 (64' · DDD) Ⓢ

A chronologically wide-ranging programme startis with Bizet-meets-Elgar in *Marche caprice* (composed in Paris in 1889) and finishes with the flourishes of the 1931 *Fantastic Dance* that Delius inscribed to his amanuensis Eric Fenby. There are two further rarities: the fragrant *Spring Morning* of 1890, which breathes a distinctly Norwegian air, and the colourful *American Rhapsody* of 1896, an embryonic (and purely orchestral) dry run for the towering *Appalachia* of six years later.

Lloyd-Jones's flowing yet deeply felt way with *The Walk to the Paradise Garden* leaves a less artfully self-conscious impression than Mark Elder's silky Hallé version. The only reservation applies to the Two Pieces for Small Orchestra, *On hearing the first cuckoo in Spring* and

Summer night on the river, both of which are too robust to work their full magic. (Thomas Beecham and Norman Del Mar remain unsurpassed in this 1911-12 diptych; the same goes for *A song before sunrise*.) Otherwise, the RSNO respond attentively throughout.

Additional recommendations

Brigg Fair – An English Rhapsody. Dance ⊞
Rhapsody No 2. On Hearing the First Cuckoo in Spring. Summer Night on the River. A Song Before Summer. Intermezzo (arr Fenby). Irmelin Prelude. Sleighride. Summer Evening (ed & arr Beecham). Florida Suite (rev & ed Beecham) – Daybreak, Dance
Royal Philharmonic Orchestra / Beecham
EMI Great Recordings of the Century 567552-2
(77' · ADD)   Ⓜ

Brigg Fair A Song Before Sunrise. Songs from ⊞
the Norwegian. Hassan – excerpts. Dance Rhapsodies Nos 1 & 2. On Hearing the First Cuckoo in Spring. Summer Night on the River. Danish Songs. Irmelin Prelude.
Suddaby *sop* **Thomas** *contr* **Royal Philharmonic Orchestra / Beecham**
Dutton CDLX7028 (77' · ADD)   Ⓜ

Two superb reissues containing superlative performances from Beecham and the RPO, both beautifully remastered and at mid-price. At least one of these discs of these should be on every classical enthusiast's shelf.

Appalachia. In a Summer Garden.   ⊞
North Country Sketches
Royal Philharmonic Orchestra / Beecham
Sony Classical SMK89429 (76' · ADD) Recorded 1950s
Delians will almost certainly want this CD.   Ⓜ
Keenly and clearly recorded. Beecham fully demonstrates his sensitivity for Delius's music.

Brigg Fair. In a Summer Garden. The Walk to the Paradise Garden. A Song of Summer. Summer Night on the River. A Song before Sunrise. Eventyr
Hallé Orchestra; London Philharmonic Orchestra / Handley
Classics for Pleasure 575 315-2 (DDD) Recorded 1981
                                                              Ⓑ
Handley keeps things moving with a springing rhythm and doesn't overstress the romantic side of Delius (unlike Barbirolli). This treasurable recording – one that can be lived with very easily – comes warmly recommended.

In a Summer Garden. Brigg Fair. Paris. A Village Romeo and Juliet – The Walk to the Paradise Garden. Two Pieces for Small Orchestra – On Hearing the First Cuckoo in Spring; Summer Night on the River
BBC Symphony Orchestra / A Davis
Warner Apex 85730-89084-2 (77' · DDD)   Ⓢ
Davis is a sensitive and elegant Delian, full of good ideas, scoring high marks in Brigg Fair and In a Summer Garden, the latter's achingly beautiful central melody floating on the breeze to perfection. The sound is ripe and true.

Violin Sonatas

Violin Sonatas – B; Nos 1-3
Tasmin Little *vn* **Piers Lane** *pf*
Conifer Classics 75605 51315-2 (77' · DDD)   Ⓕ

Tasmin Little's Delian instincts are formidable, here amply confirmed by Conifer's rewarding coupling. The wonderful First Sonata receives big-hearted, confident advocacy here. These marvellously sensitive performers strike a near-ideal balance between flexibility and purposeful concentration, even by the standards of Holmes and Fenby. Little and Lane aren't out of place in such august company. Likewise, the Second Sonata is given a commandingly articulate, thoughtful interpretation that never once threatens to hang fire. In the Third Sonata Little's playing glows with fervour and understanding. Moreover, she and Lane see to it that the fine Sonata in B major (1892) emerges in infinitely convincing fashion. To both outer movements they bring fiery propulsion as well as a firm sense of direction, while the haunting central processional of the lovely *Andante molto tranquillo* (which so impressed Grieg) captures the imagination. The recording is full bodied, though the piano focus could be sharper within a church acoustic that's too expansive for such intimate repertoire. The sessions (as Little relates in her touching notes) were lent an extra poignancy by the news of Eric Fenby's death on the first day of recording.

Violin Sonatas Nos 1-3. Cello Sonata
Ralph Holmes *vn* **Julian Lloyd Webber** *vc* **Eric Fenby** *pf*
Unicorn-Kanchana Souvenir UKCD2074
(65' · ADD/DDD) Recorded 1972-81   Ⓜ

This is selfless, utterly dedicated music-making, always spontaneous-sounding yet never losing the organic thread of Delius's remarkable, free-flowing inspiration. There's a slight fragility to Holmes's distinctive, silvery tone that's extremely moving, and Fenby, though no virtuoso practitioner, accompanies with intuitive sympathy. The recording of the piano (the instrument used is the three-quarter Ibach grand left to Fenby by Delius himself) remains a touch boxy and wanting in bloom, though the balance is otherwise natural and the overall effect nicely intimate. In the Cello Sonata Lloyd Webber and Fenby adopt a mellow, notably ruminative approach.

A Mass of Life

A Mass of Life[a]. Requiem[ba]
[a]**Joan Rodgers**, [b]**Rebecca Evans** *sops* [a]**Jean Rigby** *mez* [a]**Nigel Robson** *ten* **Peter Coleman-Wright** *bar* **Waynflete Singers; Bournemouth Symphony Chorus and Orchestra / Richard Hickox**
Chandos ② CHAN9515 (129' · DDD) Texts and translations included   Ⓕ

This is only the third commercial recording of *A Mass of Life*. The previous two recordings were the 1952 Beecham (no longer available) and the 1971 Groves on EMI. You might imagine modern recording would best place this vast canvas between your loudspeakers. And yes, Hickox's dynamic peaks are marginally higher, his perspectives marginally wider and deeper. Actually, some of this has as much to do with Hickox's own pacing and shading as the engineering. In general, this 'idealised' light- and air-filled sound brings a sharper, bright presence for the chorus, and such things as the piccolo trilling atop the final 'Hymn to Joy'. What it doesn't bring is the sense of performers in a specific acoustic space. But the chorus shines in the prominent role which the Chandos balance gives them, with ringing attack for all entries where it's needed, and singing as confident as it's sensitive; even if one has to make the odd allowance for not quite perfect pitching on high (Delius's demands are extreme) and moments where they're too loud. The soloists are fine; Hickox's baritone has a good line in stirring, virile address, though little of Benjamin Luxon's nobility, inwardness and true *legato*. What makes the Hickox *Mass* preferable to the Groves (but only just) is the conductor's inspired handling of each part's central dance panels. Hickox makes you believe in them, with a judicious drive, lift to the rhythms, and really incisive, eager singing and playing. As a coupling, Hickox has only the second-ever commercial recording of the Requiem: more Nietzsche, but this time dogma not poetry, all the more unpalatable/ embarrassing (regardless of your faith) for being in English, but containing much unique Delius.

Additional recommendation

Mass of Life   **Ⓗ**
Raisbeck *sop* Sinclair *contr* **Craig** *ten* Boyce *bar* **London Philharmonic Choir and Orchestra / Beecham**
Sony Classical mono ② SM2K89432 (111′ · ADD) Recorded 1952-3   Ⓜ

A classic recording in a generally clear, full-bodied transfer. An incandescent performance from choir and soloists; the persuasiveness of Beecham in Delius remains irresistible.

Sea Drift

Sea Drift. Songs of Sunset. Songs of Farewell
Sally Burgess *mez* **Bryn Terfel** *bass-bar* **Waynflete Singers; Southern Voices; Bournemouth Symphony Chorus and Orchestra / Richard Hickox**
Chandos CHAN9214 (77′ · DDD) Recorded 1993. Texts included   Ⓕ**❍❍❍**

 Sea Drift is a sublime conjunction of Whitman's poetry and Delius's music describing love, loss and unhappy resignation, with the sea (as Christopher Palmer put it) as 'symbol and agent of parting'. Written

in 1903-4 (the same years as Debussy's *La mer*), it's surely Delius's masterpiece; right from the swaying opening bars its spell is enduring and hypnotic. Hickox in his second recording of the work now gives us the finest recorded post-Beecham *Sea Drift*. The shaping of the opening falling woodwind figures at a slow tempo more than usually (and very beautifully) portends the sad turn of events; and the climax is broad and superbly co-ordinated. Terfel's bar-by-bar characterisation (and glorious voice), conveys the full expressive range of the role from impassioned appeal to gentle call without artifice; and the choral singing is superb. The whole is recorded with warmth, spaciousness, depth and clarity.

Songs

The Song of the High Hills, RTII/6[b] Eventyr, 'Once upon a time', RTVI/23. Sleigh ride (Winter night), RTVI/7. Five Songs from the Norwegian, RTV/5[a] (arr Holten)
[a]**Henriette Bonde-Hansen**, [b]**Helle Høyer Hansen** *sops* [b]**John Kjøller** *ten* [b]**Aarhus Chamber Choir;** [b]**Aarhus University Choir; Aarhus Symphony Orchestra / Bo Holten**
Danacord DACOCD592 (66′ · DDD) Texts and translations included   Ⓟ**❍❍❍**

 Bo Holten and the excellent Aarhus Symphony Orchestra include here a collection of Delius works inspired by Norway, a country to which he was specially attracted. His first major visit was in 1887 during a summer vacation while studying at the Leipzig Conservatory, when he spent more than six weeks joyfully exploring fjords, moors and mountains.

Later that year his Leipzig contemporary, Christian Sinding, introduced him to Grieg, for whom as a Christmas present Delius wrote *Sleigh Ride*, a piano piece buried for many years that finally surfaced in the composer's orchestration in 1946 long after his death. It's a jolly little piece, not at all Delian in style, that by rights should have been a popular hit from the start; here it's given a delightful, lightly sprung performance.

The *Five Songs from the Norwegian* were written the following year in 1888 in gratitude for Grieg's intervention with Delius's father over giving him an allowance so as to devote himself to composition. Dedicated to Grieg's wife, they're charming pieces, setting poems by Bjornsen and others that Grieg himself had set, and are here made the more seductive in Bo Holten's sensitive orchestrations, with Henriette Bonde-Hansen the fresh, pure-toned soprano. The most ambitious Delius work inspired by Norway is *The Song of the High Hills*, the most substantial item on the disc. Though Beecham recorded it in the days of 78, it has been curiously neglected on disc when over its 25-minute span it offers some of the most hauntingly atmospheric music that Delius ever wrote, notably in the passages for wordless choir. Holten conducts a beautiful, refined performance which keeps the music moving, never letting it meander, building to powerful climaxes thrillingly recorded. With a wide dynamic range the sound is evocatively atmospheric, not least in the offstage choral passages.

Fennimore and Gerda – Intermezzo. Lebenstanz, RTVI/15. An Arabesque, RTII/7[bc]. Sakuntala[b]. The Page Sat in the Lofty Tower[a]. In Bliss we Walked with Laughter[a]. Two Brown Eyes[a]. I Hear in the Night[a]. Two Danish Songs, RTV/21 – The Violet[b]; Autumn[a]. Seven Danish Songs, RTIII/4[a]. Summer Landscape, RTV/24[b]
[a]**Henriette Bonde-Hansen** sop [b]**Johan Reuter** bar
[c]**Danish National Opera Chorus;** [c]**Aarhus Chamber Choir; Aarhus Symphony Orchestra / Bo Holten**
Danacord DACOCD536 (70' · DDD) Texts and translations included   Ⓕ

This collection of Delius's Danish inspirations, beautifully performed and recorded, makes a delightful disc, including as it does rarities that are otherwise unavailable. Even if 'masterworks' is a bit of an exaggeration, the pieces here all show Delius at his most characteristic, drawing on his deep sympathy for Scandinavia and its culture.

Significantly, the performances under Bo Holten tend to be faster and often more passionate than those on rival recordings, such as in Unicorn's admirable Delius Collection.

An Arabesque dates from 1911, but all the other vocal items were written much earlier. In many ways the conventional picture we have of Delius, as the blind and paralysed composer of his later years, is misleading, failing to reflect what we know of the younger man, active and virile, a point that Bo Holten has clearly registered. It's good to have the *Seven Danish Songs* of 1897 as a group in Delius's own sensuous orchestrations. The self-quotations in the ballad-like 'Irmelin Rose' are the more telling in orchestral form, and the most beautiful song of all, 'Summer Nights', is magically transformed in its atmospheric evocation of a sunset.

Delius also orchestrated two separate Danish songs, 'The Violet' and *Summer Landscape* as well as *Sakuntala*, prompting Holten to orchestrate the five other Danish songs, which here form another orchestral cycle. These, too, are more beautiful than with piano, even though Holten is less distinctive than Delius himself in his use of orchestral colour, notably in woodwind writing. All these songs are sung in the original language, where the Unicorn series opted for the English translations which Delius either made himself or approved. The two singers here may not be as characterful as such British soloists as Felicity Lott, Sarah Walker or Thomas Allen (in *An Arabesque*), but they both have fresh young voices, clear and precise, with Henriette Bonde-Hansen shading her bright soprano down to the gentlest *pianissimos*. The choral singing, too, is excellent in *An Arabesque*.

The *Fennimore and Gerda* 'Intermezzo' (drawn from two of that opera's interludes) is relatively well known, but *Lebenstanz* ('Life's Dance'), inspired by a play of Helge Rode, is a rarity, otherwise available only on Unicorn conducted by Norman Del Mar. Here, too, Holten opts for marginally faster speeds in a piece depicting (in the composer's words) 'the turbulence, the joy, energy, great striving of youth'. The dance sections – one of them surprisingly Straussian – are punctuated by typically reflective passages, and the depiction of death at the end is peaceful and not at all tragic.

The Aarhus Symphony Orchestra respond warmly to Holten's idiomatic direction, and the refined playing is quite closely balanced in a helpful acoustic.

Five Partsongs (1887). Her ute skal gildet staa. Irmelin Rose (arr Lubin). On Craig Dhu. Wanderer's Song. Midsummer Song. The splendour falls on castle walls. Two Songs for Children. To be sung of a summer night on the water. A Village Romeo and Juliet – The dream of Sali and Vrenchen (arr Fenby). Appalachia – Oh, Honey, I am going down the river (arr Suchoff). Irmelin – Away; far away to the woods. Hassan – Chorus behind the scenes; Chorus of Beggars and Dancing Girls
Joanna Nolan sop **Stephen Douse** ten **Andrew Ball** pf **Mark Brafield** org **Elysian Singers of London / Matthew Greenall**
Somm Recordings SOMMCD210 (50' · DDD) Texts and translations included. Recorded 1992   Ⓕ

Delius had a special relationship with the collective human voice, and the songs here are presented chronologically, which allows us to follow pleasurably the development of his style. The extracts from *A Village Romeo and Juliet* and *Appalachia* prolong what would otherwise be a rather brief encounter and their accompaniments also provide contrast of timbre, but they do no need to be heard in context to 'take off'. The 'essential' Delius comes with *On Craig Dhu* – experience of nature not so much tinged by melancholy as perceived through it; a haunting evocation in grey; and the setting of Tennyson's *The splendour falls on castle walls*, as characteristically Delius as Britten's setting of it, in his *Serenade*, is Britten.

Though the singing itself deserves a generally warm welcome, not all Delius's chromatic wanderings are as confidently charted as they might be. The sopranos seem the strongest contingent, and the ones most often in the expressive spotlight. Nor are the soloists ideal, the tenor sounding unhappy in the higher regions of the second of the two songs, *To be sung of a summer night on the water*. And on occasions, as in the first of those two songs, one might have wished for more varied pacing and dynamic shading from the conductor. But the world of Delius performance is one where devotees are used to taking the roundabouts with the swings, and this is the only all-Delius collection of its kind on the market.

A Village Romeo and Juliet

A Village Romeo and Juliet
Benjamin Luxon bar Manz **Noel Mangin** bar Marti
Corin Manley treb Sali as a child **Wendy Eathorne**
sop Vreli as a child **Robert Tear** ten Sali **Elizabeth
Harwood** sop Vreli **John Shirley-Quirk** bar Dark
Fiddler **Stephen Varcoe** bar First Peasant, Shooting
Gallery Man **Bryn Evans** bar Second Peasant **Felicity
Palmer** sop First Woman, Slim Girl **Mavis Beattie**
sop Second Woman **Doreen Price** sop Gingerbread
Woman **Elaine Barry** sop Wheel of Fortune Woman
Pauline Stevens contr Cheap Jewellery Woman
Martyn Hill ten Showman **John Huw Davies** bar
Merry-Go-Round-Man **Sarah Walker** contr Wild Girl
Paul Taylor ten Poor Horn Player **Franklyn Whiteley**
bass Hunchbacked Bass Player **Robert Bateman** bar
First Bargeman **John Noble** bar Second Bargeman
Ian Partridge ten Third Bargeman **John Alldis
Choir; Royal Philharmonic Orchestra / Meredith
Davies**
EMI ② 575785-2 (138' · ADD) Recorded 1971
Includes an illustrated talk by Eric Fenby   Ⓜ**OO**

Central to this Swiss slant on the *Romeo and
Juliet* story (based on a novella by Gottfried
Keller) is a sustained sequence of duets between
the lovers, Sali and Vreli, as their calf-love blossoms into something deeper: Davies' inspired
pacing of the score avoids any risk of stagnation
– the music never meanders, and its dramatic
contrasts are sharply brought out. As much as it
evokes *Romeo and Juliet*, the plot is a variant of
Tristan and Isolde, leading to the final love-death
as the lovers, in an ecstatic suicide pact, drift
down the river in their sinking barge.
Beecham's phrasing may be a degree more flexible than Davies', but Davies is, if anything,
even more passionate, as at the climax of the
great orchestral set-piece, 'The Walk to the
Paradise Garden'. Davies is most successful at
contrasting the love-duets with the vigorous
writing, whether in the urgent opening prelude,
the quarrel between the lovers' fathers, the
choral writing in the dream sequence when the
lovers imagine their wedding ceremony, and,
above all, the lively fair scene. The plot unfolds
with a feeling of inevitability, and the overall
freshness is enhanced by the use of Tom Ham-
mond's radically revised text for the libretto in
place of the grotesquely stilted original by
Delius himself in collaboration with his wife,
Jelka.
Elizabeth Harwood and Robert Tear are both
outstanding as Vreli and Sali, characterful and
clearly focused. Benjamin Luxon and Noel
Mangin can hardly be bettered as the warring
fathers, dark and incisive, while John Shirley-
Quirk as the Dark Fiddler – representing the
spirit not of evil but of raw nature – is firm and
forthright with an apt hint of the sinister. The
rest of the cast includes many of the starriest
names among British singers of the period,
though none of them gets more than a few lines.
The 1971 recording, with the classic team of
Christopher Bishop as producer and Christopher Parker as balance-engineer, still sounds

well, with plenty of body. The evocative off-
stage effects are beautifully handled, even if the
strings aren't quite as sweet as they might be.
The only serious snag is that there's no libretto.
Instead, Eric Fenby provides a detailed synopsis, and as a supplement on the second disc
comes a talk by him, with a fascinating reconstruction of how the blind and paralysed composer dictated his final inspirations – a terrifying
exercise.

Henry Desmarest   French 1661-1741

*As a boy chorister in the royal chapel Desmarest
became a disciple of Lully. He maintained court links
and his first opera was given at Versailles in 1682.
Later he was maître de chapelle at a Jesuit college.
An amorous imbroglio led to his exile in 1699, and
in 1701 he took a court post in Madrid. From 1707
he was surintendant de la musique to the Duke of
Lorraine at Lunéville, where he expanded musical
activities. He wrote c20 stage works; the tragédies
lyriques, such as Iphigénie en Tauride (1704), use
more adventurous harmony and more flexible recitative than Lully's. His other works include impressive
grands motets, cantatas, airs and sonatas.*
                              GROVEmusic

Grands Motets Lorrains

Grands Motets Lorrains – Usquequo, Domine;   Ⓟ
Lauda Jerusalem; Domine, ne in furore
Sophie Daneman, Rebecca Ockenden sops **Paul
Agnew** ten **Laurent Slaars** bar **Arnaud Marzorati**
bass **Les Arts Florissants / William Christie**
Erato 8573-80223-2 (68' · DDD) Texts and translations
included   Ⓕ**OO**

If Henry Desmarest hasn't yet joined other
French Baroque composers among the ranks of
the Great Rediscovered, here's a disc which
ought to help him on his way. These three
grands motets were composed between 1708 and
1715, the early years of his time as musical
director to the court of the Duke of Lorraine.
Scored for soloists, choir and orchestra, each is
a multi-sectional psalm-setting lasting about 20
minutes. What's immediately striking isn't only
how strong-boned and well-written the music
is, but also how contrasted; here are moments of
supreme tenderness, powerful intensity, robust
grandeur and uplifting rhythmic vigour. And if
a tendency towards melancholy is unsurprising
given that two of these psalm-texts are penitential, who's to say that we aren't also witnessing a
reflection of the unhappy circumstances of this
composer's life?
Such music couldn't have fallen into better
hands than Christie's. His talent is to see the
work as a totality, with the result that the music
never fails to punch its full expressive weight.
With Sophie Daneman and Paul Agnew excellent among the soloists, and choral singing

which remains unfailingly vivid and alert throughout, these are vibrant performances that don't put a foot wrong. The recording is clear and nicely balanced, though an unusual profusion of extraneous noises is an irritant. Even so, this is a must-buy for French Baroque fans.

James Dillon   Scottish b1950

He studied music and linguistics at London University, but was self-taught as a composer. His music, influenced by Ferneyhough and Finnissy, is characterised by wild complexity and extreme instrumental demands. His early works are for solo instruments or small ensembles – Once Upon a Time for eight instruments (1980), East 11th St NY 10003 for six percussionists (1982) – but in Überschreiten for 16 instruments (1986) and his first orchestral score Helle Nacht (1987) he began to extend his techniques to larger forces. **GROVE**music

Chamber Works

String Quartet No 2[a]. Parjanya-vata[b]. Traumwerk[c]. Vernal Showers[d]
[a]**Arditti Quartet** ([cd]Irvine Arditti vn David Alberman vn Garth Knox va [b]Rohan de Saram vc) [c]**Graeme Jennings** vn [d]**Nieuw Ensemble / Ed Spanjaard**
Auvidis Montaigne MO782046 (67' · DDD) Recorded 1993   Ⓕ

For a composer with James Dillon's avant-garde credentials, the title *Vernal Showers* might lead you to expect a send-up of English pastoralism. In fact, there's nothing the least frivolous or forbidding about this response to Coleridge's *The Nightingale*. The music invokes the glittering cascades of sudden downpours while the sun still shines, and even the nocturnal song of the nightingale, without compromising Dillon's very personal blend of inventiveness and carefully weighted structuring.

Parjanya-vata is an appropriate partner for *Vernal Showers*, its title involving two Sanskrit words for rain and wind. This exhilarating essay for solo cello is executed with charismatic brilliance by Rohan de Saram. That there's far more to his music than mere sound-effects is confirmed by the Second String Quartet, a fizzing firework display as exuberant as it's poetic and a supremely imaginative rethinking of the traditional quartet. In *Traumwerk*, 12 miniatures for two violins, Dillon seizes the opportunity to devise a sequence of sharply drawn character pieces whose variety of mood ranges from sly comedy to unbridled ferocity. As always with this composer, nothing about the medium – like the contrast between playing vibrato and non vibrato – is taken for granted. The persuasive technical and interpretative virtuosity of all the performers on this CD should not be taken for granted either, and the various recordings are all superb.

The Book of Elements

The Book of Elements
Noriko Kawai pf
NMC ② NMCD091 (83' · DDD)   ⒻOO

There's a marvellously flamboyant spontaneity and exuberance *The Book of Elements*, demonstrating his view of the elements – air, water and so on – as standing for 'different forms of energy'. Energy is life, life is both time and transience, and the composer's over-riding concern is with images of impermanence and flux. These determine musical processes that speak of the inherent fragility of life and the essential sadness of attempts to construct something relatively stable and permanent in sound.

The work, composed between 1996 and 2003, is in five volumes with a clear formal trajectory, comprising 11, 7, 5, 3 and 1 pieces respectively. The listener is kept enthralled, not only by allusions to familiar generic prototypes (*toccata* or *moto perpetuo* at one extreme, nocturne or threnody at the other), but also by a musical language that plays with perceptions about centricity: repeated notes or chords reconfigure traditional, even tonal identities as much as they contradict them. All this is accomplished with a mastery of piano style in which the entire history of keyboard virtuosity from Frescobaldi to Ligeti is thrown into the melting pot.

The Book of Elements began with a commission from Roger Woodward, and Rolf Hind, Nicolas Hodges and Ian Pace have all been associated with individual volumes. But Noriko Kawai has become most closely involved with this music, and she offers an unfailingly persuasive realisation, helped by a recording of exemplary immediacy and atmosphere. While she has ample reserves of strength for the many episodes of turbulence, the delicacy with which she plays the soft yet immensely intricate polyphony of the third piece of Volume 3 is even more remarkable.

Dillon manages to use all the instrument's traditional technical devices for prolonging sound with barely a hint of cliché. The final dispersal of energy at the end of the fifth volume, coming as it does after a positive *Hammerklavier* of trills and tremolos, is one of the great moments of early 21st-century music, simply because it speaks as much of affirmation as of dissolution. It sets the seal on a memorable release.

Ernö Dohnányi   Hungarian 1877-1960

Dohnányi studied with Thomán and Koessler at the Budapest Academy (1894-7) and came quickly to international eminence as both pianist and composer. After teaching at the Berlin Hochschule (1905-15) he returned to Budapest and worked there as pianist, teacher, conductor and composer. His influence reached generations in all spheres of musical life and he is considered one of the chief architects of 20th-

century Hungarian musical culture; he championed the music of Bartók and Kodály. He also toured internationally as a pianist, ranking among the greatest of his time, and as a conductor (his pupils included Solti). He left Hungary in 1944 and in 1949 settled in the USA. His works are in a Brahmsian style, crossed with Lisztian virtuosity and thematic transformation; they include two symphonies (1901, 1944), two piano concertos (1898, 1947), two piano quintets (1895, 1914) and two violin concertos (1915, 1950), the popular Variations on a Nursery Song for piano and orchestra (1914) and three string quartets (1899, 1906, 1926).

GROVEmusic

Symphony No 1

Symphony No 1 in D minor, Op 9. American Rhapsody, Op 47
BBC Philharmonic Orchestra / Matthias Bamert
Chandos CHAN9647 (67' · DDD)   Ⓕ**O**

The First Symphony is a fascinating if uneven work. Sundry influences spontaneously spring to mind: Tchaikovsky, Brahms and Richard Strauss. The five-movement structure has its obvious models in Beethoven and Berlioz, but the scoring, although tending towards Wagnerian sonorities, is frequently individual, and so is the 23-year-old Dohnányi's command of symphonic argument. Bamert offers a broad reading, with much drama, most notably at the beginning of the *Scherzo* and the furious *fugato* passage 12'00" into the finale, where the BBC lower strings dig in with a vengeance. Bamert and Chandos also offer us an excellent performance of the much later *American Rhapsody* (1950, as opposed to 1900 for the Symphony). Here, Dohnányi's sound world recalls the Delius of *Appalachia* and the *Florida* suite and his use of American traditional tunes are reminiscent of Charles Ives's Second Symphony. If all this sounds as if Dohnányi didn't have an original idea in his head, it's certainly not meant to. The references are intended to focus superficial similarities but should not mask the fact that Dohnányi had plenty to say, and said it well. As for the recording, it's in the demonstration class.

Variations on a Nursery Theme

Dohnányi Variations on a Nursery Theme, Op 25
Brahms Piano Concerto No 1 in D minor, Op 15
Mark Anderson pf **Hungarian State Symphony Orchestra / Adám Fischer**
Nimbus NI5349 (75' · DDD) Recorded 1994   Ⓕ

Mark Anderson gives a glittering performance of the Dohnányi, and a spontaneous one at that; he's superbly accompanied by Adám Fischer and the Hungarian State SO. Nimbus's recording is admirable in everything but the backward placing of the woodwind in general and the bassoons in particular. One thing that the Dohnányi *Variations* share with the D minor

Brahms Concerto is a passionate minor key opening. Again Fischer and his Hungarian orchestra are quite superb, the playing incisive and gloweringly vivid. It's a measure, too, of the accord that exists between conductor and soloist that the pianist enters the fray with the perfectly groomed musical manners of a soloist in a Baroque concerto. And it's the logic of Anderson's playing, his sweet reasonableness, that holds the attention, even though Brahmsians may find Anderson a shade light-toned in bravura passages. The Brahms obviously faces tough competition, but the Dohnányi is without doubt a fine performance in its own right.

Variations on a Nursery Theme, Op 25[a]. Der Schleier der Pierrette – Pierrot's Love-lament; Waltz-rondo; Merry Funeral March; Wedding waltz. Suite in F sharp minor, Op 19
[a]**Howard Shelley** pf **BBC Philharmonic Orchestra / Matthias Bamert**
Chandos CHAN9733 (70' · DDD)   Ⓕ

Dohnányi's penchant for quality musical entertainment bore popular fruit with his perennially fresh *Variations on a Nursery Theme*. Howard Shelley's performance is a model of wit and style, blending in with the orchestra whenever the moment seems right and employing an ideal brand of *rubato*. Bamert's conducting is properly portentous in the Introduction and charming elsewhere, whether in the music-box delights of the fifth variation, the animated bustle of the sixth or the seventh's novel scoring (plenty for the bassoons and bass drum). Kocsis and Fischer's is still marginally the best version overall, but Shelley and Bamert are no less musical.

Lovely, too, is the F sharp minor Suite, especially the opening *Andante con variazioni* which seems to straddle the worlds of Dvořák and Elgar (try the serene string choirs from 9'35"). The stamping *Scherzo* brings to mind the *Scherzo* from Bruckner's Ninth, and the tuneful Rondo finale has a striking resemblance to a key passage in the *Rondo-burleske* in Mahler's Ninth.

Also included is the very first recording of *The Veil of Pierrette*, four scenes from a mimed entertainment dating from 1908-9. The best movement is the exuberant 'Wedding Waltz' (track 21), rumbustious music, carefree and beautifully scored. Chandos has come up with a dazzlingly realistic recording. A peach of a disc.

Piano Quintets

Piano Quintets[a] – No 1 in C minor, Op 1; No 2 in E flat minor, Op 26. Suite in the Old Style, Op 24
[a]**Vanbrugh Quartet** (Gregory Ellis, Elizabeth Charleson vns Simon Aspell va Christopher Marwood vc) **Martin Roscoe** pf
ASV CDDCA915 (70' · DDD) Recorded 1994   Ⓕ

Dohnányi's First Piano Quintet, Op 1, written when the composer was only 18, is a work of abounding confidence and energy that's played here with suitable verve and exuberance. Roscoe and the Vanbrugh Quartet luxuriate in lush, romantic textures in the first movement, and delight in the melodic exchanges of the warmly expressive *Adagio*. Moreover, their expression of Hungarian flavour, evident in the *Scherzo's* jaunty cross-rhythms and the engagingly dance-like finale, has considerable charm.

The Second Quintet, written some 19 years later, shows a striking advance in technique. Sensitive evocation of atmosphere in the first movement by Roscoe and the Vanbrugh Quartet highlights both Dohnányi's more searching harmonic language and his remarkably fresh and imaginative approach to form.

The performers deftly blend the *Intermezzo's* faintly Viennese character with the flamboyant toccata material, and the final movement's fusion of slow movement and finale is ingeniously turned from sombre minor to radiant major. Both the quintets display Dohnányi's considerable pianistic skills; the *Suite in the Old Style* being a highly effective display of the composer's parody of Baroque keyboard techniques. Roscoe's evident sympathy for his music contributes to this arrestingly persuasive account, which fully exploits the work's rich variety of style and technique.

String Quartets

Dohnányi String Quartets – No 2 in D flat, Op 15; No 3 in A minor, Op 33 **Kodály** Intermezzo
Lyric Quartet (Patricia Calnan, Harriet Davies vns Nick Barr va David Daniels vc)
ASV CDDCA985 (60' · DDD)   Ⓕ

Dohnányi's output is nothing if not rich in contrasts: both slow movements of these appealing quartets are visited by animated, mood-changing faster sections, stormy and passionate in the Second Quartet and skittish in the Third. The earlier quartet is the more wholesomely romantic of the two, with a *Presto acciacato* second movement that recalls the orchestral storm sequence at the beginning of Wagner's *Die Walküre*. The Second Quartet's heart is in its poignant slow movement finale which incorporates references to previous movements. Dohnányi's musical language suggests something of Strauss, Brahms and Mendelssohn, with the Third Quartet's cynically argumentative first movement providing the grittiest musical activity on the disc. The earliest work programmed is by Kodály, a pleasant but uncharacteristic *Intermezzo* from 1905 that the Lyric Quartet performs – like everything else – with gusto and warmth.

Gaetano Donizetti   Italian 1797-1848

Donizetti was of humble origins but received help and a solid musical education (1806-14) from Mayr, producing apprentice operas and many sacred

and instrumental works before establishing himself at Naples with La zingara (1822). Here regular conducting and a succession of new works (two to five operas a year) marked the real start of his career. With the international triumph of Anna Bolena (1830, Milan) he freed himself from Naples; the further successes of L'elisir d'amore and Lucrezia Borgia (1832, 1833, Milan), Marino Faliero (1835, Paris) and the archetype of Italian Romantic opera, Lucia di Lammermoor (1835, Naples), secured his pre-eminence. Some theatrical failures, however, as well as trouble with the censors and disappointment over losing the directorship of the Naples Conservatory to Mercadante, caused him to leave for Paris, where besides successful French versions of his earlier works he brought out in 1840 La fille du régiment and La favorite. His conducting of Rossini's Stabat mater (1842, Bologna) and enthusiasm in Vienna for Linda di Chamounix (1842) led to his appointment as Kapellmeister to the Austrian court. Declining health began to affect his work from this time, but in Don Pasquale (1843, Paris) he produced a comic masterpiece, and in the powerful Maria di Rohan (1843, Vienna), Dom Sébastien, roi di Portugal (1843, Paris) and Caterina Cornaro (1844, Naples) some of his finest serious music.

Donizetti's reputation rests on his operas: in comedy his position has never been challenged but in the tragic genre, though his work sums up a whole epoch, no single opera can be considered an unqualified masterpiece. His works survive through the grace and spontaneity of their melodies, their formal poise, their effortless dramatic pace, their fiery climaxes and above all the romantic vitality underlying their artifice. Like Bellini, Donizetti epitomised the Italian Romantic spirit of the 1830s. Having imitated Rossini's formal, florid style for ten years (1818-28) he gradually shed heavily embellished male-voice parts, conceiving melodies lyrically and allowing the drama to determine ensemble structures.

From 1839 his style was further enriched by fuller orchestration and subtler, more varied harmony. If he contributed nothing so distinctive to the post-Rossinian tradition as Bellini's 'heavenly' melody, he still showed a more fluent technique and a wider-ranging invention, from the brilliant to the expressive and sentimental. He was particularly responsive to the individual qualities of his singers, including Persiani (Lucia), Pasta and Ronzi de Begnis (Anna Bolena, Maria Stuarda, Roberto Devereux), the baritone Giorgio Ronconi and the tenors Fraschini and Moriani (L'elisir d'amore, Lucia).

Although his practical facility and readiness to adapt scores themselves constructed of 'spare-part' set forms once brought criticism, since 1950 revivals and reassessment as well as a fuller understanding of the theatrical practices of his day have restored Donizetti to critical and popular favour. **GROVE**music

Concertos

Sinfonia in G minor (recons Päuler). Sonata in C minor (orch Hoffmann). Oboe Sonata in F (orch Hoffmann). Concerto for Violin, Cello and Orchestra in D minor (recons Wojciechowski). Cor Anglais Concerto in G. Clarinet Concertino in B flat (recons Meylan). Sinfonia in D minor (recons Andreae)

Donizetti Opera

Budapest Camerata / László Kovács
Marco Polo 8 223701 (64' · DDD) Recorded 1994   Ⓕ

This is an intriguing issue of instrumental concertos, recorded for the first time. As in his string quartets, Donizetti's dramatic flair and imaginative instrumentation provide the main points of interest, while the G major Concerto for cor anglais – a theme and variations – allows us to sample Donizetti's formal ingenuity and thematic invention. After a crisp performance of the buoyant G minor *Sinfonia*, the Budapest Camerata offers a group of solo concertos featuring a variety of instruments. The C minor flute *Concertino* and F major oboe *Concertino* – originally intended as instrumental sonatas – are presented in Wolfgang Hoffmann's sensitive orchestrations. Contrasts (textural, dramatic and dynamic) are well defined, with admirably clear recording. The exuberant *allegros* aren't especially profound, but Donizetti's slow movements are often most effective. The D minor Concerto for violin, cello and orchestra is the longest and most impressive work here. The Budapest Camerata balances solo and ensemble forces with subtle refinement throughout this charming piece, whose brief *Andante* has genuine pathos, and smiling finale has engaging wit.

Anna Bolena

Anna Bolena
Maria Callas *sop* Anna Bolena **Nicola Rossi-Lemeni** *bass* Enrico VIII **Giulietta Simionato** *mez* Ⓗ
Giovanna Seymour **Gianni Raimondi** *ten* Riccardo Percy **Plinio Clabassi** *bass* Rochefort **Gabriella Carturan** *mez* Smeton **Luigi Rumbo** *ten* Hervey **Chorus and Orchestra of La Scala, Milan / Gianandrea Gavazzeni**
EMI mono ② 566471-2 (140' · ADD) Recorded live 1957. Notes, text and translation included Ⓜ

One of Callas's unique qualities was to inspire an audience with the sense of a great occasion, and to key-up a sympathetic conductor into the production of something to match her own intensity and the public's expectations. Here she gives one of her finest performances. The first impression is a vocal one, in the sense of the sheer beauty of sound. Then, in the first solo, 'Come innocente giovane', addressing Jane Seymour, she's so clean in the cut of the voice and the style of its usage, delicate in her *fioriture*, often exquisite in her shading, that anyone, ignorant of the Callas legend, would know immediately that this is an artist of patrician status. There are marvellous incidental moments, and magnificent *crescendos*, into, for instance, 'per pietà delmio spavento' and 'segnata è la mia sorte', culminating in the Tower scene.

Unfortunately, the singers at her side hardly measure up. Simionato has a splendid voice that nevertheless bumps as it goes into the low register and isn't reliably steady in many passages, while the manner is too imperious and unresponsive. The tenor role has been reduced by Gavazzeni's cuts, but Gianni Raimondi makes limited impression in what remains; and, as the King, Rossi-Lemeni produces that big but somewhat woolly tone that became increasingly characteristic. Even so, the great ensembles still prove worthy of the event, and the recording, which is clear without harshness or other distortion, conveys the special quality of this memorable evening with remarkable vividness and fidelity. For those who insist on a modern recording, there's an imaginatively conducted 1994 performance on Nightingale Classics by Elio Boncompagni, with Edita Gruberová in the title-role. But this Callas/Gavazzeni set is in a different class altogether.

Don Pasquale

Don Pasquale
Renato Bruson *bar* Don Pasquale **Eva Mei** *sop* Norina **Frank Lopardo** *ten* Ernesto **Thomas Allen** *bar* Malatesta **Alfredo Giacomotti** *bass* Notary **Bavarian Radio Chorus; Munich Radio Orchestra / Roberto Abbado**
RCA Victor Red Seal ② 09026 61924-2 (120' · DDD) Recorded 1993. Notes, text and translation included
  Ⓕ

Roberto Abbado balances equally the witty and more serious sides of this score, finding a gratifying lightness in the 'A quel vecchio' section of the Act 1 finale and creating a delightful sense of expectancy as Pasquale preens himself while awaiting his intended bride. Abbado plays the score complete and respects Donizetti's intentions. This set has many strengths and few weaknesses. Pasquale is usually assigned to a veteran singer and with Bruson you hear a voice hardly touched by time and a technique still in perfect repair. Apart from weak low notes, he sings and acts the part with real face, and his vital diction is a pleasure to hear. He works well with Thomas Allen's nimble, wily Malatesta, an inspired piece of casting. Like Bruson, Allen sings every note truly and relishes his words.

Eva Mei's Norina is an ebullient creature with a smile in her tone. The edge to her voice seems just right for Norina though others may find it tends towards the acerbic under pressure. Her skills in coloratura are as exemplary as you would expect from a reigning Queen of Night. Lopardo is that rare thing, a tenor who can sing in an exquisite half-voice, yet has the metal in his tone to suggest something heroic in 'E se fia', the cabaletta to 'Cercherò lontana terra', which in turn is sung in a plangent, loving way, just right. The recording here is exemplary.

L'elisir d'amore

L'elisir d'amore
Mariella Devia *sop* Adina **Roberto Alagna** *ten* Nemorino **Pietro Spagnoli** *bar* Belcore **Bruno Praticò** *bar* Dulcamara **Francesca Provvisionato** *mez* Giannetta **Tallis Chamber Choir; English Chamber**

Orchestra / Marcello Viotti
Erato ② 4509-98483-2 (129' · DDD) Recorded 1992.
Notes, text and translation included   Ⓜ

This set is a delight, making one fall in love all over again with this delightful comedy of pastoral life. Roberto Alagna, disciple of Pavarotti, sings Nemorino with all his mentor's charm and a rather lighter tone appropriate to the role. He also evinces just the right sense of vulnerability and false bravado that lies at the heart of Nemorino's predicament. He's partnered by Mariella Devia who has every characteristic needed for the role of Adina. With a fine sense of buoyant rhythm, she sings fleetly and uses the coloratura to enhance her reading. She can spin a long, elegiac line where it's needed, and her pure yet full tone blends well with that of her colleagues. She also suggests all Adina's high spirits and flirtatious nature. The other principals, though not as amusing in their interpretations as some predecessors, enter into the ensemble feeling of the performance. All are helped by the lively but controlled conducting of Viotti and by the ideal recording.

L'elisir d'amore
Mary Plazas *sop* Adina **Barry Banks** *ten* Nemorino
Ashley Holland *bass* Belcore **Andrew Shore** *bar*
Dulcamara **Helen Williams** *sop* Giannetta
**Geoffrey Mitchell Choir; Philharmonia Orchestra /
David Parry**
Chandos Opera in English Series ② CHAN3027
(133' · DDD) Sung in English. Notes and text included
    Ⓕ

'Prima la musica' no doubt, but in this instance the words should perhaps take their share of the credit first. The late Arthur Jacobs, who was an expert on Arthur Sullivan, provides a translation that might almost be the work of W S Gilbert. A resourceful vocabulary and a keen ear for verbal rhythms are its main technical assets, and a natural sense of humour rather than the untiring facetiousness of a self-conscious clever-dick is the source of its wit. Dulcamara is a Gilbertian figure to start with, so the translator isn't forcing an entrance for his hobby-horse, and any inventions are all in the spirit of the thing. The Gilbertian element emerges again when Andrew Shore, in the Barcarolle, sings his part of 'elderly Senator' in the tones of Sir Henry Lytton. Generally his portrayal is well sung and gracefully turned, as is Ashley Holland's Sergeant Belcore. The lovers have light, well-matched voices, Mary Plazas avoiding the pert, hard character-note and vocal tone that can make Adina so unsympathetic, and Barry Banks giving particular pleasure with the freedom and clarity of his upper notes.

The playing of the Philharmonia under David Parry calls for special remark: from the Overture onwards (with its delightfully chirruping woodwind) there are passages in the score that find a flavour, their own by rights but usually lost because not sought-out. The recording is one of the series' best.

La favorita

La favorita
Fiorenza Cossotto *mez* Leonora **Luciano Pavarotti**
ten Fernando **Gabriel Bacquier** *bar* Alfonso **Nicolai
Ghiaurov** *bass* Baldassare **Ileana Cotrubas** *sop* Ines
Piero de Palma *ten* Don Gasparo **Chorus and
Orchestra of the Teatro Comunale, Bologna /
Richard Bonynge**
Decca Grand Opera ③ 430 038-2DM3 (168' · ADD)
Recorded 1974. Text and translation included   Ⓜ

La favorita's lack of popularity has been attributed to the lack of an important soprano role, which is a pity, for it really is a very fine opera. Though there are passages where it fails to rise to the situation, and unfortunately the final duet is one of them, it has much in it that goes to the heart within the drama, and it's richly supplied with melody and opportunities for fine singing. The opportunities are well taken here. The recording has Pavarotti in freshest voice. That understates it: his singing is phenomenal. Wherever you care to test it, it responds. Of the two best-known solos, 'Una vergine' in Act 1 is sung with graceful feeling for line and the shape of the verses; the voice is evenly produced, of beautifully pure quality and with an excitingly resonant top C sharp. Throughout the opera he gives himself sincerely to the role dramatically as well as vocally. Cossotto, who in her absolute prime was one of the most exciting singers ever heard, is just fractionally on the other side of it here; she still gives a magnificent performance, gentle as well as powerful, in a part she made very much her own at La Scala. The role of Alfonso attracted all the great baritones in the time when the opera was heard regularly. Here, Gabriel Bacquier sings with a somewhat colourless tone. Yet Alfonso emerges as a credible character, a man of feeling, whose 'A tanto amor' has, in context, a moving generosity of spirit and refinement of style. Ghiaurov brings sonority, Cotrubas sweetness, Piero de Palma character.

The chorus is poorly recorded but that may be to its advantage. The orchestra does well under Bonynge, especially in the 20-minute stretch of ballet music, which would be 10 too many if less well played. Recorded sound is fine.

La fille du régiment

La fille du régiment
Joan Sutherland *sop* Marie **Luciano Pavarotti** *ten*
Tonio **Spiro Malas** *bass* Sulpice **Monica Sinclair**
contr Marquise **Edith Coates** *contr* Duchess **Jules
Bruyère** *bass* Hortensius **Eric Garrett** *bar* Corporal
Alan Jones *ten* Peasant **Chorus and Orchestra of
the Royal Opera House, Covent Garden / Richard
Bonynge**
Decca ② 414 520-2DH2 (107' · ADD) Recorded 1968.
Notes, text and translation included   ⒻⓄⓄ

Even Joan Sutherland has rarely, if ever, made an opera recording so totally enjoyable and involving as this. With the same cast (including chorus and orchestra) as at Covent Garden, it was recorded immediately after a series of live performances in the Royal Opera House, and both the comedy and the pathos come over with an intensity born of communication with live audiences. That impression is the more vivid on this superb CD transfer. As with some of Decca's early CD transfers, you could do with more bands to separate items and it strikes one as odd not to indicate separately the most spectacular of Luciano Pavarotti's contributions, his brief but important solo in the finale to Act 1, which was the specific piece which prompted the much-advertised boast 'King of the High Cs'. For those who want to find it, it comes at 2'58" in band 13 of the first disc. Dazzling as the young Pavarotti's singing is, it's Sutherland's performance which, above all, gives glamour to the set, for here in the tomboy Marie she found a character through whom she could at once display her vocal brilliance, her ability to convey pathos and equally her sense of fun. The reunion of Marie with the men of her regiment and later with Tonio makes one of the most heartwarming operatic scenes on record.

The recording is one of Decca's most brilliant, not perhaps quite so clear on inner detail as some, but more atmospheric. Though there are one or two deliberately comic touches that approach the limit of vulgarity, the production is generally admirable. The sound at once takes one to the theatre, without any feeling of a cold, empty studio.

Lucia di Lammermoor

Lucia di Lammermoor
Maria Callas sop Lucia **Ferruccio Tagliavini** ten **H**
Edgardo **Piero Cappuccilli** bar Enrico **Bernard Ladysz** bass Raimondo **Leonard del Ferro** ten Arturo **Margreta Elkins** mez Alisa **Renzo Casellato** ten Normanno **Philharmonia Chorus and Orchestra / Tullio Serafin**
EMI Callas Edition ② 556284-2 (142 minutes)
Recorded 1959. Notes, text and translation included
ⒻⓄⓄⓄ

 Callas was certainly more fallible here than in her first Lucia for Serafin in 1953, but the subtleties of interpretation are much greater; she's the very epitome of Scott's gentle, yet ardently intense heroine, and the special way she inflects words and notes lifts every passage in which she's concerned out of the ordinary gamut of soprano singing. In that sense she's unique, and this is certainly one of the first offerings to give to an innocent ear or a doubter to help convince them of Callas's greatness. The earlier part of the Mad scene provides the most convincing evidence of all. Then the pathos of 'Alfin son tua', even more that of 'Del ciel clemente' are here incredibly eloquent, and the coloratura is finer than it was in 1953, if not always so secure at the top. Tagliavini, after a rocky start, offers a secure, pleasing, involving Edgardo. Cappuccilli, then in his early prime, is

a forceful but not insensitive Enrico, Bernard Ladysz a sound Raimondo. Serafin is a far more thoughtful, expressive Donizettian than his rivals on other sets, confirming this as the most persuasive account of the opera ever recorded.

Lucia di Lammermoor
Cheryl Studer sop Lucia **Plácido Domingo** ten Edgardo **Juan Pons** bar Enrico **Samuel Ramey** bass Raimondo **Jennifer Larmore** mez Alisa **Fernando de la Mora** ten Arturo **Anthony Laciura** ten Normanno **Ambrosian Opera Chorus; London Symphony Orchestra / Ion Marin**
DG ② 459 491-2GTA2 (138' · DDD) Recorded 1990. Notes, text and translation included Ⓜ

With Studer and Domingo in the leading roles, this version is certainly fit as a whole to stand alongside its eminent predecessors. The fine deep colours of the orchestra, the sturdy dramatic cohesion and well-wrought climaxes, are well brought out; passages traditionally omitted are in place (and deserve to be). The role of Lucia's confidante is sung with distinction by Jennifer Larmore, and though Juan Pons could do with more bite to his tone and Samuel Ramey with more expressiveness in his vocal acting these have their strengths too. Studer combines beautiful tone, technical accomplishment and touching pathos. Details include an extended cadenza in the Mad scene, which ends on a not too exposed high E flat (D being the ceiling elsewhere). Domingo triumphantly overcomes the difficulties such a role must pose at this stage of his career: Edgardo di Ravenswood in this recording is as firmly at the centre of the opera as is its eponymous heroine.

Additional recommendations

Lucia di Lamermoor
Callas Lucia **di Stefano** Edgardo **Berlin RIAS Symphony Orchestra / Karajan**
EMI mono 566438-2 (119' · ADD) Recorded live Ⓜ
A great event: two great musicians striking sparks off each other. Karajan directs a white-hot performance and Callas sings with huge passion.

Sills Lucia **Bergonzi** Edgardo **Orchestra / Schippers**
Westminster ② 471 250-2GWM2 (ADD) Recorded 1970 ⓂⓄⓄ
Sills's typical style is here: the tense commitment, wonderful use of hushed, intimate tone, but also that slightly fluttery quality and the fondness for elaborate decorations. Devotees of Callas won't be won over, but for those seeking a thoroughly dramatic and full version of the score with a strong cast, this this should go high on your list.

Maria Stuarda

Maria Stuarda
Janet Baker mez Maria Stuarda **Rosalind Plowright** sop Elisabetta **David Rendall** ten Leicester **John Tomlinson** bass Talbot **Alan Opie** bar Cecil **Angela**

Bostock *sop* Anna **English National Opera Chorus and Orchestra / Sir Charles Mackerras**
Chandos Opera in English Series ② CHAN3017 (136' · ADD) Recorded live 1982. Sung in English. Notes and English text included   Ⓜ❶

Pelizzoni *ten* Felice **Virgilio Carbonari, Giuseppe Morresi** *basses* Christians **Chorus and Orchestra of La Scala, Milan / Antonino Votto**
EMI mono ② 565448-2 (111' · ADD) Recorded live 1960. Notes, text and translation included   Ⓜ

This revival celebrates the association of Janet Baker and Charles Mackerras within the context of the ENO company and one of its most memorable productions. For those who saw this, the set will call the stage back to mind with wonderful vividness; but the appeal goes well beyond that, preserving a performance stamped with the strong individuality that confers the status of a gramophone classic. This brought a personal triumph for Janet Baker and it impresses afresh by the distinctiveness of her vocal characterisation. It isn't every singer who reflects, or re-creates, the distinctive identities through vocal colour and 'registration'. Everyone who was there will remember the 'Royal bastard!' in confrontation with Elizabeth, but equally powerful, and more regal, is her command – 'Be silent! Leave me!' – to the Lord Chancellor of England who brings to Fotheringay news of her condemnation to death. By contrast, the quieter moments can be immensely moving, as, for instance, in the line in which she acknowledges an unexpected generosity in her great opponent. In that role, Rosalind Plowright gives what surely must have been one of the supreme performances of her career. The writing for Elizabeth makes immense demands of the singer, and in these fearsome opening solos the technical challenges are triumphantly met.

John Tomlinson's massive bass commands attention (which it doesn't then always reward with evenness of production). The male soloists have not the most grateful of roles, but Alan Opie's Cecil shows its quality in the duet with Elizabeth, and David Rendall endows the ineffectual Leicester with plenty of Italianate ardour. The chorus has limited opportunities, and has certainly been heard to better advantage on other occasions.

A word of warning must be added concerning texts which involve cuts and adaptations. The transpositions are defended as standard practice when an exceptional mezzo-soprano (such as Malibran) took a soprano role, in the present instance merely conforming to the lower orchestral pitch of Donizetti's time. However, it's unlikely that at this date the set would be bought or rejected with this kind of consideration foremost. What remains are the strong positives, most notably the vitality of Mackerras's conducting and the glory of Baker's singing. Also, for those to whom this is a priority, the opera is given in clear English.

Poliuto

Poliuto   Ⓗ
Franco Corelli *ten* Poliuto **Maria Callas** *sop* Paolina **Ettore Bastianini** *bar* Severo **Nicola Zaccaria** *bass* Callistene **Piero de Palma** *ten* Nearco **Rinaldo**

This is the first appearance of this recording in the official canon, by incorporation into EMI's Callas Edition; and the quality is certainly an improvement on the previous 'unofficial' incarnation. The sound is clear and faithful to the timbre of the voices, which are slightly favoured in the balance at the expense of the orchestra. With it comes unforgettable testimony to what was clearly a great night at La Scala. Its place in the Callas history owes less to the importance of this new role in her repertory than to the triumph of her return to the house she had left in high dudgeon in 1958. The part of Paolina in this Roman tragedy is restricted in opportunities and leaves the centre of the stage to the tenor. In other ways it suits her remarkably well, the Second Act in particular involving the heroine in grievous emotional stress with music that here runs deep enough to give it validity.

There's a big part for the chorus, which sings with fine Italian sonority. Nicola Zaccaria, La Scala's leading *basso cantabile*, has not quite the sumptuous quality of his predecessors, Pasero and Pinza, but is still in their tradition. Ettore Bastianini is rapturously received and, though wanting in polish and variety of expression, uses his firm and resonant voice to exciting effect. The tenor *comprimario*, Piero de Palma cuts a by no means inadequate vocal figure by the side of Corelli, who's mostly stupendous: it isn't just the ring and range of voice that impress, but a genuinely responsive art, his aria 'Lasciando la terra' in Act 3 providing a fine example. It's for his part in the opera, quite as much as for Callas's, that the recording will be valued.

Rosmonda d'Inghilterra

Rosmonda d'Inghilterra
Renée Fleming *sop* Rosmonda **Bruce Ford** *ten* Enrico II **Nelly Miricioiu** *sop* Leonora di Guienna **Alastair Miles** *bass* Gualtiero Clifford **Diana Montague** *mez* Arturo **Geoffrey Mitchell Choir; Philharmonia Orchestra / David Parry**
Opera Rara ② ORC13 (150' · DDD) Recorded 1994. Notes, text and translation included   Ⓕ

The performance of this, Donizetti's 41st opera, could hardly be improved. And there's scarcely more than a single item in which Donizetti seems not to be writing with genuine creativity. Parry conducts with what feels like a natural rightness and the playing of the Philharmonia is of unvaryingly high quality – the Overture is one of Donizetti's best, and the orchestral score shares interest on equable terms with the voice-parts. These include two virtuoso roles for sopranos, who in the final scene confront each other in duet. As Rosmonda, Renée Fleming shows once again that not only has she

325

one of the most lovely voices of our time but that she's also a highly accomplished technician and a sympathetic stylist. Nelly Miricioiu is the older woman, the Queen whose music encompasses a wide range of emotions with an adaptable vocal character to match. She fits the Second Act more happily than the First, where for much of the time the tone appears to have lost its familiar incisive thrust. Bruce Ford is an excellent, incisive Enrico, and Alastair Miles makes an authoritative father and councillor as Clifford. The *travesto* role of Arturo is taken by the ever welcome Diana Montague, and it's good to find that a solo has been dutifully included for 'him' in Act 2, even if it's a less than inspired piece of music. The only complaint concerns balance, which sometimes accords prominence and recession in a somewhat arbitrary way. The opera and performance, however, are strong enough to take that on board.

John Dowland
British c1563-1626

Dowland became a Catholic while serving the English ambassador in Paris (1580-84) and in 1588 graduated at Oxford. In 1592 he played the lute to the queen, then travelled in Europe, visiting the courts of Brunswick, Kassel, Nuremberg and cities in Italy, where he met Marenzio. He was back in London in 1597, then became a lutenist at the Danish court (1598-1603, 1605-6). On his return he served Lord Walden (1609-12) and eventually achieved his ambition, the post of court lutenist, in 1612. He had been awarded a doctorate by 1621 and played at James I's funeral in 1625. He was succeeded by his son Robert (c 1591-1641), also known for the lute collections he edited.

Though known in his day as a virtuoso lutenist and singer, Dowland was also a prolific, gifted composer of great originality. His greatest works are inspired by a deeply felt, tragic concept of life and a preoccupation with tears, sin, darkness and death. In the best of his 84 ayres for voice and lute (published mainly in 4 vols., 1597, 1600, 1603, 1612), he markedly raised the level of English song, matching perfectly in music the mood and emotion of the verse; in his best songs, such as In darknesse let mee dwell, he freed himself of almost all conventions, accompanying the singer's strange, beautiful melody with biting discords to express emotional intensity to an extent unsurpassed at the time. His 70-odd pieces for solo lute include intricate polyphonic fantasias, expressive dances and elaborate variation sets; foremost among his other instrumental music is the variation set Lachrimae, which contains the famous 'Semper Dowland semper dolens', characterising his air of melancholy. But he could also write in a lighter vein, as in the ballett-like Fine Knacks for Ladies. He also wrote psalm settings and spiritual songs.

GROVEmusic

Lute Works

A fancy, P73. Pavana Dowlandi Angli. Doulands   **P**

rounde battell galyarde, P39. The Erle of Darbies galiard, P44. Mistris Norrishis delight, P77. A jig, P78. Galliard, P76. Une jeune fillette, P93. Gagliarda, P103. Squires galliard. A fancy, P72. Sir Henry Umptons funerall. Captayne Pipers galliard, P88. A fantasie, P1 **Bacheler** (arr ?) The Earl of Essex galliard, P89 **Moritz, Landgrave of Hessen** (arr Dowland?) Pavin **Joachim Van Den Hove** Pavana Lachrimae **Holborne** Hasellwoods galliard **R Dowland** Sir Thomas Monson, his Pavin and Galliard. Almande
Paul O'Dette lte
Harmonia Mundi HMU90 7164 (73' · DDD)   Ⓕ

Given the odd transmission of John Dowland's lute music, any 'complete' recording of it's inevitably going to include a fair number of works that can have had little to do with him. Paul O'Dette has boldly put most of these together in his fifth and last volume, adding for good measure the three surviving works of the master's son, Robert Dowland. O'Dette is engagingly candid in expressing his views about the various works and their various degrees of authenticity. The only works he seems to think authentic are the *Sir Thomas Monson* pavan and galliard that survive only under the name of Robert Dowland. The collection is none the less fascinating for all that. They are nearly all thoroughly worthwhile pieces, some of them very good indeed; and he ends with what he considers a late adaptation of one of Dowland's most famous fantasies. O'Dette continues to show that in terms of sheer freedom of technique he's hard to challenge among today's lutenists: the often complicated counterpoint is always crystal clear; and he invariably conveys the strongest possible feeling for the formal design of the works. Anyone who's fascinated by the work of the prince of lutenists will want to have this disc.

Preludium, P98. Fantasias – P6; P71. Pavans –   **P**
Lachrimae, P15; The Lady Russell's Pavan, P17; Pavana Johan Douland, P94; La mia Barbara, P95. Galliards – Frog Galliard, P23; Galliard (upon a galliard by Dan Bachelar), P28; The Lord Viscount Lisle, his Galliard, P38; The Earl of Essex, his Galliard, P42a; Galliard to Lachrimae, P46; A Galliard, P82; Galliard on 'Awake sweet love', P92. An Almand, P96. My Lord Willoughby's Welcome Home, P66a. Loth to departe, P69. The Shoemakers Wife, a Toy, P58. Coranto, P100. Come away, P60
Paul O'Dette lte
Harmonia Mundi HMU90 7163 (64' · DDD)   Ⓕ

Cadential trills played on one string are a recurrent problem for performers; the less well equipped use a *rallentando* or slur them, while guitarists tend to play them across two strings. No one is more adept at delivering them cleanly and in tempo than O'Dette. It's in the suppleness of his phrasing, clarity of his contrapuntal lines and attention to the functional purpose of every note, that he's pre-eminent – and has the edge over Lindberg. This disc has all the virtues of its predecessors, and though it's doubtful that the Earl of Essex would have been happy to dance his galliard at O'Dette's pace, you can share the sentiment of its last track – you'll be loath to leave it.

Lute Songs

The First Booke of Songes or Ayres – If my   **P** complaints could passions moue; Can she excuse my wrongs with vertues cloake; Deare if you change ile neuer chuse againe; Go Cristall teares; Sleepe wayward thoughts; All ye whom loue or fortune hath betraide; Come againe: sweet loue doth now enuite; Awake sweet loue thou art returnd. The Second Booke of Songs or Ayres – I saw my Lady weepe; Flow my teares fall from your springs; Sorrow sorrow stay, lend true repentant teares; Tymes eldest sonne, old age the heire of ease; Then sit thee down, and say thy 'Nunc Dimitis'; When others sings 'Venite exultemus'; If fluds of tears could clense my follies past; Fine knacks for Ladies, cheap, choise, braue and new; Come ye heauie states of night; Shall I sue, shall I seeke for grace

Paul Agnew ten **Christopher Wilson** lte   **F**
Metronome METCD1010 (59' · DDD) Texts included

Love-songs and Sonnets of John Donne   **P**
and Sir Philip Sidney

G Tessier In a grove most rich of shade. **Dowland** O sweet woods, the delight of solitarie-nesse. Sweete stay a while, why will you? Preludium. **Morley** Who is it that this darke night. **Coprario** Send home my long strayde eies to mee. **A Ferrabosco II** So breake off this last lamenting kisse. **Corkine** The Fire to see my woes for anger burneth. 'Tis true, 'tis day, what though it be? **Hilton II** A Hymne to God the Father. **Anonymous** Come live with me. So breake off this last lamenting kisse. Goe my flocke, goe get you hence. Goe and catch a fallinge star. O deere life when shall it be. Sir Philip Sidney's Lamentacion. Dearest love I doe not goe

Agnew ten **Christopher Wilson** lte
Metronome METCD1006 (62' · DDD) Recorded 1994. Texts included   **F**

In the Dowland, Paul Agnew is light of step in the quicker songs, and he languishes longer than most over the variously sorrowful ones. Many of his choices now enjoy 'pop' status, but his inclusion of the beautiful trilogy of which 'Tymes eldest sonne' is the first part is particularly welcome. He receives the most sensitive of support from Wilson, clearly articulated, warm in tone, and perfectly complementary in completing the contrapuntal textures – neither intrusively nor coyly balanced with the voice. Dowland's lute songs have generated many fine recordings, as they richly deserve, and here's one more, beautifully presented, with a booklet containing all the texts.

Love is a familiar peg on which to hang a song recital, and if there's a further focus it's usually on the composer of the music; Agnew and Wilson turn the tables, for once, by spotlighting the writers of the texts, namely Sir Philip Sidney

and John Donne. Sidney's sonnets *Astrophel and Stella*, written between 1581 and 1583, may have been addressed to the daughter of the Earl of Essex but she was unwillingly married to Lord Rich in 1581, so Sidney may have had in mind the daughter of Sir Francis Walsingham, whom he married in 1583. The emotional range of Donne's *Songs and Sonets* may also mirror the fluctuating fortunes of his own, basically happy marriage. The recording also includes two well-chosen lute solos by way of interludes from Wilson.

Lachrimae, or Seven Teares

Lachrimae, or Seaven Teares.   **P**
First Booke of Songs[a] – Come heavy sleepe; Go teares. Second Booke of Songs[a] – Sorrow stay; I saw my Lady weepe; Flow my teares
Paul O'Dette lte **The King's Noyse** ([a]Ellen Hargis sop Robert Mealy, Scott Metcalfe, Margriet Tindemans vas Emily Walhout bvn) **David Douglass** vn
Harmonia Mundi HMU90 7275 (75' · DDD) Texts and translations included   **F** **OO**

The Seaven Teares are the heart of *Lachrimae*; the purpose of the other 14 items is unknown – were they intended to be played together with the Pavans, and if so, in what order?

This present recording is superb in every way. Ellen Hargis sings in sensitive response to her texts and her diction is almost clear enough to make the printed ones in the inlay booklet redundant. The violins of The King's Noyse have a rounder and less edgy sound than those of The Parley of Instruments, and their dynamic ebb and flow is as eloquent as that of Ellen Hargis's voice. The recording itself and the annotation are superb.

With so many options available you pays your money and you takes your choice. Our choice rests firmly with this recording.

Guillaume Dufay   French c1400-1474

Dufay was acknowledged by his contemporaries as the leading composer of his day. Having been trained as a choirboy at Cambrai Cathedral, where he probably studied under Loqueville, he seems to have entered the service of the Malatesta family in Pesaro some time before 1420. Several of his works from this period were written for important local events. After returning briefly to Cambrai and establishing links with Laon, where he held two benefices, he was a singer in the papal choir in Rome from 1428 until 1433, when he became associated with the Este family in Ferrara and the Dukes of Savoy. He rejoined the papal choir (1435-7), and composed the famous motet Nuper rosarum flores for the dedication of Brunelleschi's dome of Florence Cathedral in 1436, but spent his later years (apart from 1451-8, when he was again in Savoy) at Cambrai, where he was visited as a celebrity by such musicians as Binchois, Tinctoris and Ockeghem. Although he composed up to his death, most of his late works are lost.

Working in a period of relative stability in musical style, Dufay achieved distinction rather by consummate artistry than bold innovation. More than half his compositions, including most of his antiphons, hymns, Magnificats, sequences and single items of the Mass, are harmonisations of chant, with the melody usually in the upper part. Most of his motets are imposing compositions written to celebrate a political, social or religious event; four- and five-part textures, often alternating with duos, are common, two or more texts may be set simultaneously, and isorhythm is sometimes used. Others, in a three-voice, treble-dominated style, are more direct and intimate expressions of religious sentiment. Moving from early paired mass movements to the developing form of the cyclic tenor mass, he was apparently the first to base a cycle on a secular melody. Outstanding among his masses is the Missa 'Ave regina celorum', perhaps his last composition. He also composed secular songs, three-quarters of them rondeaux. As an artist of international fame, he is represented in some 70 MSS in many countries. GROVEmusic

Sacred Music

Sacred Music from Bologna Q15

O sancte Sebastiane. Supremum est mortalibus bonum. Vasilissa, ergo gaude. O gemma, lux et speculum. Kyrie, 'Fons bonitatis'. O beate Sebastiane. Gloria, Q15 No 107. Credo, Q15 No 108. Sanctus and Benedictus, Q15 No 104. Inclita stella maris. Agnus Dei, Q15 No 105. Gloria, 'Spiritus et alme'
The Clerks' Group (William Missin *counterten* Lucy Ballard *alt* Chris Watson, Matthew Vine *tens* Jonathan Arnold *bass*) / **Edward Wickham** *bass*
Signum SIGCD023 (60' · DDD) Notes, texts and translations included ℗○

This recording focuses on sacred works by Dufay from a 15th-century manuscript preserved at Bologna and known as Q15. This is a complex source, compiled over a number of years in northern Italy, and containing a wide range of polyphonic repertory, including diverse works by the great Dufay.

This CD isn't in any sense a reconstruction, but a carefully selected anthology of not necessarily very familiar pieces by Dufay. Indeed, this is a really superb recording: vocal lines are well shaped and the sonorities achieved through accuracy of ensemble and pacing result in performances that are decidedly sensual, even dance-like, at times.

Just try the four-voice *Gloria* or the isorhythmic motet *Supremum est mortalibus bonum*, in praise of peace. This extraordinary work composed to commemorate the signing of a peace treaty between the Pope and Holy Roman Emperor-elect in 1433 combines just about every musical technique and idiom available to a composer in the first half of the 15th century, complete with, in this interpretation by The

Clerks' Group, improvised vocal flourishes on the block chords declaiming the names of the signatories.

Vocal agility – notably in the faster-moving upper parts of *Inclita stella maris* – and a text-centred intensity of projection are hallmarks of this excellent group: only in the three-voice setting of *O beate Sebastiane*, a plea for delivery from the plague, does the approach seem too cool. Elsewhere, even in familiar texts such as the *Sanctus*, there's a real sense of engagement. If you've yet to discover the delights of Dufay, this is an excellent place to start; Dufay fans can't fail to be delighted.

Missa S Jacobi

Missa S Jacobi. Rite majorem Jacobum canamus. Balsamus et munda cera. Gloria 'Resurrexit dominus' and Credo 'Die Maria'. Apostolo glorioso
The Binchois Consort (Mark Chambers, David Gould, Fergus McLusky, Robin Tyson *countertens* James Gilchrist, Chris Watson, Andrew Carwood, Edwin Simpson *tens*) / **Andrew Kirkman**
Hyperion CDA66997 (67' · DDD) Texts and translations included ℗○○○

Here the Binchois Consort shows absolute mastery of Dufay's difficult early style, with immaculate balance, wonderfully free phrasing, and crystalline clarity. Moreover in the *Missa S Jacobi* Andrew Kirkman shows an uncanny ability to set the perfect tempo every time, so that the music emerges with its full force. The *Missa S Jacobi* is an odd but supremely important work. It's one of two early Dufay Mass cycles that have rarely been recorded, partly because they're less obviously part of the grand tradition than his later four-voice *cantus firmus* Masses. And this one is particularly difficult because its many different textures and styles present a severe challenge if it isn't to seem fragmented and incoherent. Here it stands as a glorious masterpiece, its nine movements spanning over 40 minutes, with the various styles acting as necessary contrast and culminating in the famous Communion that Heinrich Besseler many years ago argued was the earliest example of *Fauxbourdon* writing. Strangely, two of the motets work less well: both the earlier *Rite majorem* and the later *Balsamus* seem to go too fast for the details to have their full effect, perhaps because they're so strikingly different in style from the other works performed here. And it seems a touch perverse to use the now fashionable 'old French' pronunciation of Latin, particularly in a motet composed for a papal ceremony (even if the original singers would have been Franco-Flemish): in all his early motets the text seems centrally important, and this kind of pronunciation loses too many of the consonants. But the Italian-texted *Apostolo glorioso* is again quite superb, as is the astonishing *Gloria* and *Credo* pair.

Briefly, then, this is as close to a perfect Dufay CD as any available.

Paul Dukas
French 1865-1935

Dukas studied with Guiraud at the Paris Conservatoire (1881-9) and became a friend of Debussy, d'Indy and Bordes. His Franckian leanings are evident in his first published work, the overture Polyeucte (1891), though Beethoven is also suggested, as again in his Symphony in C (1896). But the symphonic scherzo L'apprenti sorcier (1897) is more individual, not least in its augmented-triad and diminished-7th harmonies, which influenced Stravinsky and Debussy. The next years were devoted to the opera Ariane et Barbe-Bleue (1907), though at the same time he produced two piano works of Beethovenian range and power: the Sonata in E flat minor and the Variations, interlude et final sur un thème de Rameau. Dukas self-criticism constricted his later output. Apart from the exotic ballet La péri (1912) he published only a few occasional works. He cultivated craftsmanship to an extreme degree and his orchestration has been widely admired and imitated. His voluminous criticism reveals an unusual breadth of sympathy and he was a conscientious editor of Beethoven, Couperin, Rameau and Scarlatti and an admired teacher at the Conservatoire. **GROVE**music

Symphony in C major

Symphony in C. Polyeucte – overture
BBC Philharmonic Orchestra / Yan Pascal Tortelier
Chandos CHAN9225 (56' · DDD) Recorded 1993 Ⓕ●

Before *L'apprenti sorcier*, the tradition Paul Dukas was following was that of César Franck, and he was also heavily influenced by the Wagnerianism which held French composers in thrall during that period. Both models can be discerned in the overture *Polyeucte*: nevertheless, and despite extensive Wagnerian use of the brass, there's a clarity (even delicacy in the third of its five sections) and an imaginative sense of colour which are individual to him. The finely crafted Symphony composed four years later, in 1896 – daringly in C major at a time when tonality was undergoing such general buffeting – shows Dukas as essentially a classicist, although the middle section of the central movement reveals that Nature romanticism hadn't passed him by. The eloquent performance here gives the vigorous first movement a splendid *élan* while also luxuriating in the Franckian secondary subjects, there's lovely warm, lyrical playing and sensitive nuance in the second movement, and the finale (even more Franckian in its harmonic thinking) bubbles over with nervous energy. Exemplary recording quality.

The Sorcerer's Apprentice

Dukas The Sorcerer's Apprentice (L'apprenti sorcier)
Saint-Saëns Symphony No 3 in C minor, Op 78, 'Organ'
Simon Preston *org* **Berlin Philharmonic Orchestra /**

James Levine
DG 419 617-2GH (47' · DDD) Ⓕ

Levine's account of Dukas' masterpiece is still the best in the catalogue. Levine chooses a fast basic tempo, but justifies his speed by the lightness of his touch and the clean articulation and rhythmic bounce of the Berlin Phil playing help considerably. The climax is thrilling, but Levine reserves something for the moment when the sorcerer returns to quell the flood. In all, it provides a marvellous finish to an exhilarating listening experience. Levine's performance of Saint-Saëns' Third Symphony is also among the best available. The balance between the orchestra and organ, here played powerfully by Simon Preston, is well judged and the overall acoustic very convincing. Levine directs a grippingly individual reading, full of drama and with a consistently imaginative response to the score's detail. The organ entry in the finale is quite magnificent, the excitement of Preston thundering out the main theme physical in its impact. The music expands and blossoms magnificently, helped by the spectacular dynamic range of the recording.

Henry Du Mont
French 1610-1684

Du Mont was organist at Maastricht Cathedral before studying in Liège with Hodemont. In 1638 he moved to Paris as organist at StPaul and later compositeur de musique de la Chapelle Royale (1672) and maître de la musique de la Reine (1673-81). The petits motets in his Cantica sacra (1652), influenced by Italian motets, are the first in France with figures and a separate continuo part. Some of the 30 in the Motets à deux voix avec la basse continue (1668) show Du Mount's exploitation of dramatic monody. The Motets à II, III et IV parties (1671) move closer to French models; italianate dialogues co-exist with French dance rhythms, which also affect his Airs à quatre parties (1663). His 20 grand motets, published 1684-6, show him as a miniaturist, excelling in the more intimate moments. **GROVE**music

Grands motets

Grands motets pour la chapelle de Louis XIV au Louvre
Allemandes. Allemande grave. Dialogus de anima. Super flumina Babylonis. Benedic anima mea. Ecce iste venit. Pavane
Pierre Robert Ensemble / Frédéric Desenclos *org*
Alpha ALPHA069 (73' · DDD · T/t) Ⓕ●●

Henry Du Mont has long been credited as one of the creators, alongside Lully, of the *grand motet*, the opulent style of church composition for soloists, choir and orchestra associated with Louis XIV's chapel at Versailles. The Pierre Robert Ensemble (named after another of the genre's founding fathers) take a different view.

Noting that Du Mont's 20 *Motets pour la Chapelle du Roy*, printed two years after his death in 1684, contain the kind of clumsy viola parts reconcilable with the work of a publisher's hack, they propose that such 'posthumous tawdry' can be dispensed with to reveal the originals as more intimate works for five solo singers, two violins and continuo, probably written for pre-Versailles times at the Louvre palace. It's in this form that they present three of the motets here, emphasising their argument by adding the semi-dramatic *Dialogus de anima*, scored for the same line-up.

When performed and recorded as beautifully and sensitively as they are here, Du Mont's plangent harmonies and dissonances reach into the listener's heart with sensuous clarity. These are near-perfect performances by an ensemble ideal for such ravishing music, and who, in Marcel Beekman, have an *haute-contre* of striking quality. Frédéric Desenclos's tidy organ solos break up the programme nicely, but the motets are the stars.

John Dunstaple
British c1390-1453

Dunstaple is acknowledged as the most eminent of the Englishmen who strongly influenced the generation of Dufay and later continental composers. Little is certainly known about his career; he was probably not the John Dunstavylle who was at Hereford Cathedral, 1419-40, but may have been in the service of the Duke of Bedford before 1427. He was in the service of Queen Joan of Navarre, second wife of Henry IV, 1427-36, and was serviteur et familier domestique in the household of Henry, Duke of Gloucester, in 1438. In the late 1430s he held lands in northern France. There is evidence that he was also an astronomer. He was buried at St Stephen's, Walbrook, where his epitaph described him as 'prince of music'.

Most of his surviving music is in continental sources. 51 compositions are consistently stated in MS sources to be his, but many others, anonymous or with conflicting ascriptions, are probably by him. Stylistically, his music can be divided into four categories: isorhythmic works in which a plainchant tenor forms the lowest of three or four parts; non-isorhythmic works based on a plainchant that may be in any of the three parts; works in 'free treble' or 'ballade' style, consisting of a freely composed melodic line (which may however incorporate traces of elaborated plainchant) and two slower supporting parts; and declamatory works in a syllabic style with careful accentuation of the text.

Two of the earliest mass cycles, Rex seculorum and Da gaudiorum premia, are ascribed to him in some sources and some of his other mass movements may originally have belonged to complete cycles. Most of his works are in three parts, except for the isorhythmic motets which are mostly in four, and, while nearly all begin in triple time, there is often a change to duple near the middle and sometimes a shorter return to triple towards the end. His melodies are

characterised by stepwise and triadic movement, and the harmony, reflecting the English predilection for 3rds and 6ths, is predominantly consonant.

GROVEmusic

Sacred Works

Descendi in ortum meum. Ave maris stella. Gloria in canon. Speciosa facta es. Sub tuam protectionem. Veni, Sancte spiritus / Veni creator spiritus. Albanus roseo rutilat / Quoque ferundus eras / Albanus domini laudus. Specialis virgo. Preco preheminencie / Precursor premittitur / textless / Inter natos mulierum. O crux gloriosa. Salve regina mater mire. Missa Rex seculorum
Orlando Consort
Metronome METCD1009 (74' · DDD) Texts and translations included
Ⓟ**○○○**

This disc contains three of Dunstaple's well-known motets – *Preco preheminencie*, *Veni veni* and *Albanus* – but the rest are rarely performed. For some of the delicious antiphons, it's hard to see why: *Salve regina mater mire* is particularly striking – one of those pieces that sounds far more impressive than it looks on the page. There are also some total novelties. The canonic *Gloria* was discovered in Russia: it's a massively inventive work that adds a substantial new dimension to our knowledge of Dunstaple. And *Descendi in ortum meum*, though discovered and published a quarter of a century ago, surely stands as the latest known work of its composer: a magnificent piece that builds an entirely new kind of edifice with the materials of his characteristic style. Most impressive of all, though, is the Mass, *Rex seculorum*, which ends the disc. This may or may not be by Dunstaple – which is probably why it has never been recorded. Whoever the composer, though, it's a key work in the history of the polyphonic mass cycle, brimming with invention. The Orlando Consort has a wonderfully forward style that beautifully matches the music and helps the listener to understand why Dunstaple achieved such an enormous reputation on the continental mainland. If they're occasionally a touch rough, these are classic performances that will be hard to challenge.

Henri Duparc
French 1848-1933

Duparc studied the piano and composition with Franck, writing works that he later destroyed; this loss, together with a crippling psychological condition that caused him to abandon composition at the age of 36, has resulted in a legacy of just 13 songs (composed 1868-84). An important influence is Wagner, seen in the ambitious harmonic structure of Chanson triste and the shifting chromaticism of Soupir. Yet Duparc's feeling for poetic atmosphere and the craftsmanship he used to communicate it, as in the sinister drama of La manoir de Rosemonde, were unique, giving the French mélodie a rare musical substance and emotional intensity. From 1885 he led a quiet life, remaining close to Ernest Chausson and cultivating his aesthetic sensibility through reading and drawing. ❋ **GROVE**music

Mélodies

L'invitation au voyage. Sérénade florentine. Extase. Chanson triste. Le manoir de Rosemonde. Lamento. Au pays où se fait la guerre. La fuite. La vague et la cloche. Sérénade. Testament. Phidylé. Romance de Mignon. Elégie. Le galop. Soupir. La vie antérieure
Danielle Borst *sop* **François Le Roux** *bar* **Jeff Cohen** *pf*
REM REM311049 (63' · DDD) Recorded 1987. Texts and translations included ⒡

If you consider Duparc's songs the most rewarding in the French language you'll rejoice at this issue. Without hesitation, we would say Le Roux's are the most successful performances of these masterpieces in miniature since the war. In his foreword to this issue the veteran composer Henri Sauguet comments: 'The interpretations of François Le Roux and Danielle Borst are remarkable, not just for their vocal qualities and their emotional commitment but also for their exemplary use of words, which illustrates perfectly the profound unity of poetry and music.' That almost says all that needs to be said, at any rate about Le Roux who has the lion's share of the burden. His voice can sometimes take on a rough edge but his understanding of the Duparc idiom is second to none, rivalling that of Panzéra and Bernac in the distant past, precisely because he realises what French can convey when sung with scrupulous care over diction.

Added to that he and his admirable pianist, Jeff Cohen, seem almost always to find exactly the right tempo for each *mélodie*. Le Roux is partnered in *La fuite* by Borst, another dedicated Duparcian who catches some of its trance-like beauty. The recorded sound is ideal. A 'must' for anyone interested in great performances of *mélodies*.

Marcel Dupré   French 1886-1971

Dupré studied with Guilmant, Vierne and Widor at the Paris Conservatoire (1902-14), returning as professor of organ (1926-54) while also serving as organist of St Sulpice (1934-71) and appearing internationally as a recitalist. His works introduced a Lisztian virtuosity and a contemplative modality into organ music; he also wrote religious symphonic poems. Alain and Messiaen were among his pupils. **GROVE**music

Organ Works

Complete Organ Works, Volume 9
Entrée, méditation, sortie, Op 62. Les nymphéas, Op 54. Suite bretonne, Op 21. Poème héroïque, Op 33 (arr cpsr)
Jeremy Filsell *org*

Guild GMCD7188 (63' · DDD) Recorded on the organ of St Boniface Episcopal Church, Florida, USA, 1998
⒡●

It's sometimes the case that the reputation of great composers rests on a handful of works. With Dupré it's the two symphonies, the Op 7 Preludes and Fugues and the *Noël* Variations for which he's best known, but these compositions form a tiny proportion of his entire output. One of the many benefits of Guild's series is the discovery of hidden treasures, and much of the music on Volume 9 deserves to be heard more frequently.

The revelation here is *Les nymphéas*. This is a beautiful work, even as original as Debussy's *Images, Nocturnes* or the quieter moments of *Jeux*. It would make a marvellous orchestral suite; indeed, much of Dupré's organ writing has a quasi-orchestral character, and reflects his love and knowledge of the vast tonal palette of 20th-century instruments. You can also tell that, like Messiaen, he was an experienced writer of piano and chamber music.

We're indebted to Filsell for his special arrangement of *Les nymphéas* for this CD, and for his excellent performances throughout this volume. The choice of the organ at St Boniface, Florida, was a good one as it provides sensuous colours for the softer movements, plus glockenspiel effects for the *Suite bretonne*. The playing is backed up by fine recorded sound and comprehensive programme notes. There's no doubt that this series is setting the standard for Dupré interpreters of the future and will be a landmark in the history of organ recordings.

Complete Organ Works, Volume 10
Le chemin de la croix, Op 29
Jeremy Filsell *org*
Guild GMCD7193 (56' · DDD) ⒡●●

Complete Organ Works, Volume 11
Vêpres du commun des fêtes de la Sainte-Vierge, Op 18. Choral et Fugue, Op 57. Regina coeli, Op 64
Vocal Quartet; Jeremy Filsell *org*
Guild GMCD7198 (55' · DDD) ⒡●●

Complete Organ Works, Volume 12
79 Chorales, Op 28
Jeremy Filsell *org*
Guild GMCD7203 (72' · DDD) ⒡●●
All recorded on the organ of St Boniface Episcopal Church, Sarasota, Florida, USA

Thinking about 20th-century French music after Debussy and Ravel, the names of Messiaen and the members of Les Six would probably spring to mind. However, at the same time organists like Vierne, Tournemire, Alain, Langlais and Dupré himself were writing music every bit as original and as intense as the aforementioned composers. One of the many benefits of Guild's series (which concludes with these three volumes) is the opportunity to discover just how fine a composer Dupré was. Perhaps more than any of his contemporaries he managed to embrace both the sacred and the secular with utter conviction. *Le chemin de la croix* is one of his major works, and is a landmark piece of musical drama. One can hear links with the *Symphonie-Passion* of six years earlier, and David Gammie in his comprehensive accompanying notes points out the influence of these works on Duruflé's Requiem and Messiaen's *Les corps glorieux*. Filsell gives a suitably dramatic performance with some telling *rallentandos* at climactic moments.

All three compositions on Volume 11 were inspired by Gregorian chant, and each movement is preceded on this CD by the singing of the verse on which it's based. The vocal quartet includes the CD's producer Adrian Peacock and Filsell himself – an inspired and appropriate piece of programming. Listening to Filsell's flowing, atmospheric playing it's easy to imagine oneself sitting in a vast, incense-laden Parisian church, with glorious improvised music coming from the west-end grand orgue.

Dupré is remembered for writing music of extreme technical complexity, but Volume 12 shows that he was well capable of composing pieces for organs and organists of modest resources. The 79 Chorales take hymn tunes which were all used by Bach as the basis for chorale-preludes. Many of Dupré's chorales are effective Bachian pastiches, but a handful have the unmistakable 20th-century French idiom. Again, Filsell's performances are beyond reproach, and he shows that Dupré was able to match JSB for solemnity and piety.

As is so often the case Naxos provides healthy competition, and Volume 11 of its Dupré series has a very fine performance of *Le chemin de la croix* from Mary Preston. She brings a greater clarity to the music, helped by the drier acoustic of the Meyerson Symphony Center at Dallas. However, Filsell in the more resonant acoustic of St Boniface Church, Sarasota, Florida brings more warmth, passion and drama to his interpretations, and this, coupled with Gammie's excellent insert-notes sways the balance in favour of the Guild series.

In all 12 volumes Filsell's playing has been consistently superb, and what has been most impressive is that his virtuosity has always been the servant of the music. The St Boniface organ may not have the éclat of a Cavaillé-Coll, but its clarity and attack enhance Dupré's complex textures, and the recordings are suitably warm and atmospheric. We must salute Filsell for what must surely rank as one of the greatest achievements in organ recordings.

Prelude and Fugue in F minor, Op 7 No 2. Cortège et Litanie, Op 19 No 2. Symphonie-Passion, Op 23. Symphony No 2 in C sharp minor, Op 26. Evocation, Op 37 – Allegro deciso
John Scott *org*
Hyperion CDA67047 (71' · DDD) Recorded on the organ of St Paul's Cathedral, London 1998   Ⓕ

This is an impressive release on every account.

As we have come to expect from John Scott, the playing is superb – that perfect combination of technical virtuosity and intense musicianship which is so rare among organists – and numerous Hyperion recordings from the cavernous St Paul's over the past 15 years have fine-tuned its engineering to such an extent that we no longer admire the sound, *per se*, but find that the acoustic positively enhances it. That awesome echo, as the final chord of Scott's vehement account of the *Symphonie-Passion* is cast adrift to fend for itself in the cathedral's vastness, adds a tangible sense of presence. Yet the clarity is there; the precision of Scott's fingerwork is captured in microscopic detail in his stunning performance of the Second Symphony's 'Preludio' and 'Toccata' movements. The Prelude and Fugue receives a richly atmospheric performance which makes you wonder why this deeply moving piece, with its strong melodic ties with the popular Requiem, has been so overshadowed by its companions. Musically, technically and emotionally these are truly distinguished recordings.

Le chemin de la croix, Op 29
Ben van Oosten *org*
Dabringhaus und Grimm MDG316 0953-2
(62' · DDD) Played on the Cavaillé-Coll Organ, Saint-Ouen, Rouen   Ⓕ

Many collectors will instinctively be drawn to Ben van Oosten's choice of a genuine French organ. And not just any old French organ, but one of the finest extant Cavaillé-Colls captured in a recording of exemplary clarity, depth and presence. Against Jeremy Filsell's incisive precision and intensity (on Guild) van Oosten seems somewhat flabby and cumbersome. But his is a performance which exposes the very heart of Dupré's creation. The work was originally conceived as an improvisation to accompany spoken verses from Paul Claudel's *Le chemin de la croix*. Van Oosten re-creates a tangible feeling of a 'living improvisation' and portrays a compelling sense of emotional reflection and musical response to the drama of these 14 scenes. Despite rare opportunities for open exhibitions of virtuosity or bravura display, *Le chemin de la croix* places as daunting and formidable technical demands on the player as any of Dupré's works. But here those technical demands are overshadowed by van Oosten's powerful visionary zeal, hauntingly revealed in the portrait of the disconsolate Mary (Station IV), the nervous energy of Simon the Cyrenean as he attempts to bear the burden of the cross (Station V), and the compassion of Jesus as he comforts the tormented women of Jerusalem (Station VIII). A release to be wholeheartedly recommended whatever the competition.

Choral Works

Dupré La France au Calvaire, Op 49ª **Alain**
O Salutaris Langlais Festival Alleluia **Messiaen**

O sacrum convivium!
[a]Helen Neeves *sop* [a]Catherine Denley *mez*
[a]Matthew Beale *ten* [a]Colin Campbell *bar* Jeremy
Filsell *org* Vasari Singers / Jeremy Backhouse
Guild GMCD7239 (78' · DDD) Texts and translations
included   Ⓕ **OO**

La France au Calvaire is an astonishing work,
setting, to quote the booklet note, 'a curious
libretto' by René Herval who, like Dupré, was a
native of Rouen. Appalled by the devastation
wrought on his native city during the Second
World War, Dupré vents all his anger and passion into this 65-minute oratorio, its movements dedicated to six French saints and framed
by a Prologue and Final. Principally known for
his organ music, it might seem strange to question Dupré's use of the organ here as the sole
means of instrumental accompaniment. But
despite Jeremy Filsell's stunning virtuosity and
brilliant handling of the not always perfectly in
tune Douai Abbey organ, the score seems to cry
out for an orchestra.

No such reservations about the performance:
in a word, stunning. The bleak ugliness of
Christ nailed to the cross is compellingly portrayed by Matthew Beale, Catherine Denley
makes an arresting France appealing for forgiveness for her misguided people, Colin
Campbell fulfils the dual roles of St Denis and
the voice of Christ with suitable gravitas and
authority, and Helen Neeves is a beautifully
innocent St Clotilde (magically set against a
decidedly Messiaenic organ backdrop).

As for Jeremy Backhouse and his superb
Vasari Singers, they excel even by their own
high standards. The three motets which share
the disc seem in comparison a trifle disappointing. But that disappointment is only because the
motets precede a work of extraordinary emotional impact and a performance of exceptional
power.

Quatre motets, Op 9ª. De profundis, Op 18. Ave
verum, Op 34 No 1. La france au Calvaire, Op 49 –
Final. Deux motets, Op 53
Vasari Singers / Jeremy Backhouse with Jeremy
Filsell, [a]Ian Curror *orgs*
Guild GMCD7220 (80' · DDD)Texts and translations
included   Ⓕ

For all but a handful of devotees Marcel Dupré
is inseparably associated with the organ. Dupré
himself conceded this: 'I do not think of myself
as a composer. I have specialised in the organ,
and I do not have the reputation that composers
have.' However, any thoughts that Dupré's
choral music might merely be organ music with
words are immediately quashed by even the
briefest snatch of the extended *De profundis*
(particularly the thrilling 'Et ipse redimet Israel'
with the organ's great pillars of sound underpinning the richly textured and rhythmically
exhilarating chorus). Here is truly impressive
choral music. True, the organ does figure
prominently, occasionally assuming a decidedly

virtuoso role, but it's clearly always the servant
of the choir, and for the most part it's the choral
lines rather than the organ accompaniments
which require the greatest virtuosity. To that
end it's hard to imagine a choral group more
ideally suited to the task. The Vasari Singers are
one of the most accomplished small choral
groups of our time and for this compelling, passionate, often deeply moving and always technically demanding music, every ounce of their
artistry is called into play. Guild's recording is
wonderfully spacious yet crystal-clear, and
Jeremy Filsell's organ support immaculate.

Maurice Duruflé   French 1902-1986

*Duruflé studied with Tournemire, whose deputy at
SteClotilde he became, and then at the Paris Conservatoire (1920-28) with Gigout and Dukas. In 1930
he was appointed organist of StEtienne-du-Mont
and he toured internationally as a recitalist. His
works are few, in a vivid modal style, and include a
Requiem (1947).*   **GROVE**music

Organ Works

'Veni Creator: The Complete Organ Music' Scherzo,
Op 2. Prélude, Adagio et Choral varié sur le thème
de 'Veni Creator', Op 4. Suite, Op 5. Prélude et
Fugue sur le nom d'Alain, Op 7. Fugue sur le thème
du Carillon des Heures de la Cathédrale de Soissons,
Op 12. Prélude sur l'Introït de l'Epiphanie, Op 13.
Meditation, Op posth
Hans Fagius *org*
BIS BIS-CD1304 (71' · DDD) Played on the 1928
Frobenius organ at Århus Cathedral, Denmark   Ⓕ

Listeners to his *Requiem* will recognise Duruflé's conservative and intensely personal musical
language as heard in his organ music. The influence of Debussy, Dukas, Ravel, Tournemire
and Vierne is evident, and like these composers
Duruflé provides detailed performance indications. Hans Fagius, a former student of Duruflé's, scrupulously observes all the scores' markings, and this is one reason why he's now the top
recommendation for this repertoire.

His performances have a flexible, seamless
flow, and the playing has a slight understated
quality which gives more clarity and impact
than Eric Lebrun's flamboyant accounts. Fagius's interpretations are close in spirit to the
recordings by the composer and his wife Marie-
Madeleine Duruflé-Chevalier, and it's a shame
that their authoritative performances are
marred by poor sound quality. By contrast,
BIS's recording of the 89-stop four-manual
organ in Århus Cathedral is superbly realistic.
The choice of this instrument was inspired; it
has all the appropriate colours and it's set in a
warm, generous acoustic.

Another bonus is the inclusion of the sensuous
and recently discovered *Meditation*. Although

the recordings by Lebrun and the Duruflés are very good, they must now stand aside and let this BIS disc take the place of honour, for this is a truly distinguished release of one of the finest corpus of organ music you'll ever hear.

Duruflé Requiem. Prélude et Fugue sur le nom d'Alain, Op 7. Quatre Motets sur des thèmes grégoriens, Op 10 **Fauré** Requiem, Op 48. Cantique de Jean Racine, Op 11. Messe basse **Poulenc** Mass in G. Salve Regina. Exultate Deo. Litanies à la vierge noire
Jonathon Bond, Andrew Brunt, Robert King trebs
Benjamin Luxon bar **Christopher Keyte** bass
St John's College Choir, Cambridge; Academy of St Martin in the Fields / George Guest with
Stephen Cleobury org
Double Decca ② 436 486-2DF2(149' · ADD)
Recorded 1969-76   Ⓜ

Here's almost two and a half hours of bliss. These are recordings to set aside for the time when, as the prayer says, 'the busy world is hushed'. Asked to characterise Fauré's and Duruflé's Requiems as compared with others, we might suggest words such as 'delicate', 'meditative', 'undramatic'; but that last would be a mistake. These performances certainly do not go out of their way to 'be' dramatic or anything else other than faithful to the music, but one is struck by the power exercised by those rare moments that rise to a *forte* and above. The choir is surely at its best, the trebles with their fine clear-cut, distinctive tone, the tenors (so important in the Fauré) graceful and refined without being precious, the altos exceptionally good, and only the basses just occasionally and briefly plummy or obtrusive in some way.

The Poulenc works further test a choir's virtuosity yet in the extremely difficult Mass, the choir seems secure, and in the *Salve Regina* they catch the necessary tenderness. The treble soloists sing beautifully, Christopher Keyte dramatises almost too convincingly in Duruflé's 'tremens factus', and Benjamin Luxon, his production less even, builds finely in Fauré's *Libera me*. These recordings have a vividness, certainly in the choral sound, that modern recordings generally lack.

Duruflé Requiem[a] **Fauré** Requiem, Op 48[b]
[a]**Kiri Te Kanawa,** [b]**Lucia Popp** sops **Siegmund Nimsgern** bass-bar **Ambrosian Singers;**
[a]**Desborough School Choir;** [a]**New Philharmonia Orchestra,** [b]**Philharmonia Orchestra / Sir Andrew Davis**
Sony Classical Essential Classics SBK67182
(79' · ADD) Recorded 1977   Ⓑ

These recordings, made within six months of each other with substantially the same forces and in the same church, were issued separately but obviously go together. Both had outstandingly good reviews in *Gramophone* and although textural matters have arisen to enrich the choice and complicate the issue, if what were then

regarded as the standard versions (in full orchestral score) are required, then the recommendations can remain. Davis's superiority over more recent versions is especially apparent in the Duruflé. His way with the opening is typical: the flow, the gentle wave-like motion, is beautifully caught and in the 'Libera me' he discovers the full richness of Duruflé's colours. Te Kanawa sings with feeling and incomparably lovely sound. There may be misgivings about the remastered sound, but it settles down (or one's ears do).

Henri Dutilleux   French 1916

Dutilleux studied with the Gallons, Büsser and Emmanuel at the Paris Conservatoire (1933-8), where he was appointed professor in 1970 after periods with French radio (1943-63) and at the Ecole Normale de Musique (from 1961). His first works suggest influences from Debussy, Ravel, Roussel and Honegger, but he developed as an isolated and independent figure, producing a relatively small output of great breadth and originality, predominantly of instrumental works; they include two symphonies (1950, 1959) and other orchestral pieces, piano music and the string quartet Ainsi la nuit (1976).
GROVEmusic

Concertos

Cello Concerto, 'Tout un monde lointain'. Métaboles. Mystère de l'instant
Boris Pergamenschikov vc **BBC Philharmonic Orchestra / Yan Pascal Tortelier**
Chandos CHAN9565 (60' · DDD)   Ⓕ

This is the third issue in Chandos's Dutilleux series with the BBC Phil and Yan Pascal Tortelier. The virtues of those earlier issues remain evident here, with meticulously prepared, well-played performances, and recordings carefully adapted to the coloristic subtlety and textural delicacy of the music. *Métaboles* is particularly tricky to bring off, but this version is admirable in the way it builds through some dangerously episodic writing to underline the power of the principal climaxes, though a more sharply delineated sound picture could have reinforced these contrasts even more appropriately. Boris Pergamenschikov is an eloquent soloist in the Cello Concerto. Tortelier's account of *Mystère de l'instant* – using a full orchestral complement of strings – is excellently done. As with *Métaboles*, the structure is shaped with great flexibility and feeling for its ebb and flow, and this emerges as a highly dramatic score, despite the inherent reticence of Dutilleux's style.

Dutilleux Violin Concerto, 'L'arbre des songes'. Timbres, espace, mouvement. Deux Sonnets de Jean Cassou (orch cpsr) **Alain** (orch Dutilleux) Prière pour

nous autres charnels
Olivier Charlier vn **Martyn Hill** ten **Neal Davies** bar
BBC Philharmonic Orchestra / Yan Pascal Tortelier
Chandos CHAN9504 (58' · DDD) Texts and
translations included   Ⓕ Ⓞ

Timbres, espace, mouvement (1978, revised 1991)
can be counted as Dutilleux's best orchestral
composition, at once rooted in tradition yet
persistently sceptical about conventional 'symphonic' values. It's a tricky score to bring off,
and Tortelier is successful in negotiating its
twists and turns of form. In the Violin Concerto
(1985) Tortelier again favours a symphonic
approach, and very effective it is too, with a
soloist who's authoritative without being overly
self-assertive. In the rival Decca recording
(reviewed below) Pierre Amoyal is more intense
in tone, with a volatility from which all sense of
effort hasn't been completely purged. Is the
Charlier/Tortelier version too staid, or does
this richly perfumed music demand a response
that keeps its more flamboyant qualities under
firmer control than that provided by the Decca
team? Amoyal and Dutoit make the more
immediate impact, but it could be that Charlier
and Tortelier prove more satisfying in the
longer run. The Chandos disc also includes
Dutilleux's orchestral arrangement of his Cassou settings, and also his orchestration, made in
1944, of Jehan Alain's touching prayer. Well-
characterised contributions from Martyn Hill
and Neal Davies complete this valuable release.

Symphonies

Symphonies – No 1; No 2, 'Le double'
BBC Philharmonic Orchestra / Yan Pascal Tortelier
Chandos CHAN9194 (60' · DDD) Recorded 1993
                                                Ⓕ Ⓞ Ⓞ Ⓞ

 This pair of relatively early works,
completed in 1951 and 1959 respectively, show him poised to inherit the
Honegger/Martinů strand of the symphonic
tradition. Yet, while an almost Simpsonian *élan*
in the first movement of No 2 promises a rich
vein for further exploration, the Stravinskian
strategies of the finale, ending with a virtual
recomposition of the chorale that concludes the
Symphonies of Wind Instruments, reveals a more
modernist tendency, and leads away from the
well-made, tonally resolving symphony altogether. With their broad thematic vistas and
persuasive adaptations of traditional forms,
Dutilleux's symphonies offer considerable
rewards to interpreters and listeners alike. Yan
Pascal Tortelier and the BBC Philharmonic
allow the music all the space it needs in strongly
characterised, rhythmically well-sprung performances with uniformly excellent solo playing
in No 2, and the sound is rich and natural.

Symphony No 1. Cello Concerto, 'Tout un monde
lointain'a. Timbres, espace, mouvement
a**Jean-Guihen Queyras** vc **Bordeaux-Aquitaine**

National Orchestra / Hans Graf
Arte Nova 74321 92813-2 (80' · DDD)   Ⓢ

The traditional French virtues of lightness, elegance, wit and so on are all very well, but they
don't take us far with Dutilleux's music on their
own. It's wonderfully inspiriting to hear, albeit
under an Austrian conductor, an orchestra from
the long underfunded French provinces finding
this music's power, passion and eloquence.
  Hans Graf enjoys Dutilleux's confidence, and
from this recording it's easy to see why. The
detail is all here, but so is the control of long
paragraphs – few recordings of the slow movement of the First Symphony are as moving as
this. The sound may not have quite the brilliance of the Chandos set, but do we always have
to have brilliance?
  Similarly, Jean-Guihen Queyras may not produce Rostropovich's matchless tone high up on
the A string; but he has his own things to say and
says them with authority. In *Timbres, espace,
mouvement*, Graf impresses on us the sheer curi-
ousness of many of the textures, just as van
Gogh's 1889 picture *La nuit étoilée*, which
inspired the work, stands far apart from so much
contemporary painting.
  The First Symphony is especially welcome.
Amid all the congratulations after its first public
performance in 1952, Pierre Boulez pointedly
turned his back on the composer. The usual
explanation is that Dutilleux, eschewing the 12-
note system, was clearly one of those who were,
in Boulez's words, 'inadequate to the times'. Or
was the younger man all too aware of this
music's quality? Happily, these fences have
been mended since. But the work is undoubtedly a masterpiece and the final resolution on to
D flat major one of the great moments of 20th-
century music.

The Shadows of Time

The Shadows of Timea. Cello Concerto, 'Tout un
monde lointain'b. Métaboles.
a**Joel Esher**, a**Rachael Plotkin**, a**Jordan Swaim**
trebs; b**Arto Noras** vc **Boston Symphony Orchestra
/ Seiji Ozawa**
Warner Elatus 09274-9830-2 (64' · DDD)   Ⓜ

Warner boldly gambled that the interest and
appeal of the first substantial work by Henri
Dutilleux for almost a decade would justify this
issue of a CD single. We can only commend the
enterprise and the finely engineered recording.
The Shadows of Time is an unambiguously
emotional, even angry work, and may well stand
as the musical testament of a composer who,
while seeking to celebrate 'the unity of time and
place' (as his brief note accompanying the disc
puts it), can only do so from the basis of considerable pessimism about the ability of the real
world to achieve the kind of harmonious, classical ideals to which he, as an artist, aspires. Pessimism and anger are most explicit in the way
the first and last sections depict the inexorable

passage of time, and in the increasing density and urgency of the orchestral lament which explodes out of a central episode in which childrens' voices repeat the questions, 'Why us? Why the star?'. This is a reference to Anne Frank and 'all the innocent children of the world', Dutilleux declares, yet there's nothing mawkish here, rather an almost *Wozzeck*-like pathos in the way the music searches for consolation without, in the end, quite achieving it. By the time of these performances Ozawa, his orchestra and the three assured young singers, had achieved absolute authority in this often testing music. The result is a moving and memorable document of a very special occasion, and a very special work.

In short, this set makes a great introduction to one of Europe's most distinguished living composers. The Cello Concerto is almost a modern classic, with Arto Noras a fine soloist, and *Métaboles* is a vivid concerto for orchestra. Thoroughly recommended.

Chamber Works

Piano Sonata[a]. Ainsi la Nuit[b]. Les citations[c]. Figures de résonances[d]. Trois préludes[e]. Deux sonnets de Jean Cassou[f]. Trois strophes sur le nom de Sacher[g]
[f]**Gilles Cachemaille** bar [c]**Maurice Bourgue** ob
[g]**David Geringas** vc [c]**Bernard Cazauran** db
[c]**Bernard Balet** perc [c]**Huguette Dreyfus** hpd [ade]
Geneviève Joy, [df]**Henri Dutilleux** pfs
[b]**Sine Nomine Quartet** (Patrick Genet, François Gottraux vns Nicolas Pache va Mars Jaermann vc)
Ultima ② 8573 88047-2 (88' · DDD) Recorded 1988 Ⓢ

The pieces on these discs cover a wide range of compositional concerns, from the atmospheric piano writing of the *Trois préludes* and *Figures de résonances*, through the use of quotations in *Les citations*, to the memories of the Second World War embodied in the *Deux sonnets de Jean Cassou* (subsequently developed so memorably in his orchestral work *The Shadows of Time*). Dutilleux is dismissive about his own piano technique, and it's true that, for all Gilles Cachemaille's persuasive advocacy, the *Sonnets* do come over better in their original orchestral garb. Otherwise the performances are excellent in every respect. Dutilleux has recently spoken highly of the Arditti's 1993 version of *Ainsi la nuit*, but this one by the Quatuor Sine Nomine, where the crucial dynamic contrasts are well observed, also retains his favour. Geringas is tidier in the *Trois strophes* than Haimovitz, though not always as vigorous.

Geneviève Joy remains without equal in the Piano Sonata written for her, both in execution and in understanding – it's worth noting that the movement durations of this 1988 performance are still only a few seconds away from those of her first recording, made in 1955! The strong architecture and profound poetry of this wonderful work have never been so memorably caught.

Antonin Dvořák   Bohemian 1841-1904

Dvořák studied with Antonín Liehmann and at the Prague Organ School (1857-9). A capable viola player, he joined the band that became the nucleus of the new Provisional Theatre orchestra, conducted from 1866 by Smetana. Private teaching and mainly composing occupied him from 1873. He won the Austrian State Stipendium three times (1874, 1876-7), gaining the attention of Brahms, who secured the publisher Simrock for some of his works in 1878. Foreign performances multiplied, notably of the Slavonic Dances, the Sixth Symphony and the Stabat mater, and with them further commissions. Particularly well received in England, Dvořák wrote The Spectre's Bride (1884) and the Requiem Mass (1890) for Birmingham, the Seventh Symphony for the Philharmonic Society (1885) and St Ludmilla for Leeds (1886), besides receiving an honorary doctorate from Cambridge. He visited Russia in 1890, continued to launch new works in Prague and London and began teaching at the Prague Conservatory in 1891 (where Joseph Suk was among his most gifted pupils). Before leaving for the USA he toured Bohemia playing the new Dumky Trio. As director of the National Conservatory in New York (1892-5) he taught composition, meanwhile producing the well-known Ninth Symphony ('From the New World'), the String Quartet in F, the String Quintet in E flat and the Cello Concerto. Financial strain and family ties took him back to Prague, where he began to write symphonic poems and finally had his efforts at dramatic music rewarded with the success of the fairytale opera Rusalka (1901). The recipient of honours and awards from all sides, he remained a modest man of simple tastes, loyal to his nationality.

In matters of style Dvořák was neither conservative nor radical. His works display the influences of folk music, mainly Czech (furiant and dumky dance traits, polka rhythms, immediate repetition of an initial bar) but also ones that might equally be seen as American (pentatonic themes, flattened 7ths); Classical composers whom he admired, including Mozart, Haydn, Beethoven and Schubert; Wagner, whose harmony and use of leitmotifs attracted him; and his close friend Brahms (notably his piano writing and mastery of symphonic form). Despite his fascination with opera, he lacked a natural instinct for drama for all their admirable wit and lyricism, his last five stage works rank lower than his finest instrumental music. Here his predilection for classical procedures reached its highest level of achievement, notably in the epic Seventh Symphony, the most closely argued of his orchestral works, and the Cello Concerto, the crowning item in that instrument's repertory, with its characteristic richness and eloquence, as well as in the popular and appealing Ninth Symphony and the colourful Slavonic Dances and Slavonic Rhapsodies. Among his chamber works, landmarks are the String Sextet in A Op 48, a work in his national style which attracted particular attention abroad; the F minor Piano Trio Op 65, one of the climaxes of the more serious, classically 'Brahmsian' side of his output – unlike the E minor Op 90, a highly original series of dumka movements alternately brooding and spirited; the exuberant

Op 81 Piano Quintet; and several of the string quar-tets, notably the popular 'American' Op 96, with its pentatonic leanings, and the two late works, the deeply felt op.106 in G and the warm and satisfying Op 105 in A flat. GROVEmusic

Cello Concerto

Dvořák Cello Concerto in B minor, B191 **Tchaikovsky** Variations on a Rococo Theme, Op 33
Mstislav Rostropovich vc **Berlin Philharmonic Orchestra / Herbert von Karajan**
DG The Originals 447 413-2GOR (60' · ADD)
Recorded 1968 Ⓜ❍❍❍

 This splendid disc offers a coupling that has justifiably held its place in the catalogue at full price (both on LP and CD) for over 30 years. The upper surface of the CD itself is made to look like a miniature repro-duction of the original yellow label LP – com-plete with light reflecting off the simulated black vinyl surface. There have been a number of outstanding recordings of the Dvořák Con-certo since this DG record was made, but none to match it for the warmth of lyrical feeling, the sheer strength of personality of the cello playing and the distinction of the partnership between Karajan and Rostropovich. Any moments of romantic licence from the latter, who's obvi-ously deeply in love with the music, are set against Karajan's overall grip on the proceed-ings. The orchestral playing is superb. You've only to listen to the beautiful introduction of the secondary theme of the first movement by the Principal Horn to realise that the BPO is going to match its illustrious soloist in elo-quence, while Rostropovich's many moments of poetic introspection never for a moment inter-fere with the sense of a spontaneous forward flow. The recording is as near perfect as any made by DG in that vintage analogue era. The CD transfer has freshened the original and gives the cello a highly realistic presence, and if the passionate *fortissimo* violins lose just a fraction in fullness, and there seems to be, comparably, just a slight loss of resonance in the bass, the sound picture has an impressively clear and vivid focus.

In the coupled Tchaikovsky *Rococo* Variations, Rostropovich uses the published score rather than the original version. However, he plays with such masterly Russian fervour and ele-gance that any criticism is disarmed. The music itself continually demonstrates Tchaikovsky's astonishing lyrical fecundity, as one tune leads to another, all growing organically from the charming 'rococo' theme. The recording is marvellously refined. The description 'legend-ary' isn't a whit too strong for a disc of this calibre.

Dvořák Cello Concerto in B minor, B191[a] **Schumann** Cello Concerto in A minor, Op 129[b] **Tchaikovsky** Pezzo capriccioso in B minor, Op 62[c]
Mstislav Rostropovich vc [a]**USSR State Symphony Orchestra / Evgeni Svetlanov;** [b]**London Symphony**

Orchestra; [c]**English Chamber Orchestra / [b][c]Benjamin Britten**
BBC Legends/IMG Artists [ab]mono BBCL4110-2 (71' · ADD) Recorded live [a]1968, [b]1961, [c]1968 Ⓟ❍

Truly legendary performances are rare, but this heroic account of the Dvořák Concerto deserves its place on collectors' shelves along-side such classics as Mravinsky's Shostakovich Eighth or Horenstein's Mahler *Symphony of a Thousand*. This concert offers us a piece of his-tory in sound that raises questions about music and politics, music and personality, music and identity.

In the Cold War era, no Western tour by Russian artists was entirely without political resonance, and this London Prom took place on the very day that Soviet tanks rolled into Prague. With demonstrators outside the Royal Albert Hall, there was also dissent within. The performers might not have been directly to blame, yet had they not been dispatched know-ingly, as cultural ambassadors? Svetlanov, at least, was something of an apparatchik. More-over, the programme featured the Dvořák Con-certo – an intensely nostalgic and nationalistic score, a natural focus for strong emotions.

On this privately sourced, somewhat com-pressed-sounding mono tape, you can hear the unease as Svetlanov and his raw-toned band tear into the work as if determined to get it over with as quickly as possible. It's the cellist, already in tears, whose transparently honest playing wins the audience over, as his sense of guilt and fury is transmuted into a potent requiem for the Czech Spring. The restated second subject is forcefully projected, suitably gutsy and passion-ate at the start, but it's the development which strikes deepest. Never has the first theme's metamorphosis from resolute, relatively short-breathed march to elegy struck home so mov-ingly. The finale is almost too rushed until the tender, unmistakably tragic, coda arrives, pre-senting an extreme and all the more moving contrast.

The Schumann, though scarcely epoch-mak-ing in the same way, was recorded on the occa-sion of the cellist's first visit to the Aldeburgh Festival. It receives a glorious interpretation. The sound, considerably more refined and open, is still mono only with the orchestra rather backwardly placed. Strongly recom-mended.

Dvořák Cello Concerto **Herbert** Cello Concerto No 2 in E minor, Op 30
Yo-Yo Ma vc **New York Philharmonic Orchestra / Kurt Masur**
Sony Classical SK67173 (61' · DDD) Ⓕ

Ma's and Masur's version of the Dvořák is among the very finest, matched by few and out-shining most, including Ma's own previous ver-sion with Maazel and the Berlin Philharmonic (also available on Sony Classical). It's fascinat-ing to compare Ma's two versions, the newer

DVOŘÁK CELLO CONCERTO – IN BRIEF

Mstislav Rostropovich; Berlin PO / Herbert von Karajan
DG 447 413-2GOR   Ⓜ❍❍❍

☀ A longtime favourite, with sympathetic accompaniment from Karajan and his Berlin orchestra and pliant, flexible playing from Rostropovich at his most charismatic.

Mstislav Rostropovich; USSR SO / Yevgeni Svetlanov
BBC Legends BBCL4110-2   Ⓕ❍

Recorded at London's Royal Albert Hall the very day in 1968 when Soviet tanks rolled in Prague, this is a performance of extremes: orchestra and conductor sound like they want to dispatch it as quickly as possible, while the soloist uses the piece to project his pain and guilt. It is hugely powerful, though the mono sound is somewhat constricted.

Yo-Yo Ma; New York PO / Kurt Masur
Sony Classical SK67173   Ⓕ

A very fine modern version of this popular work: Yo-Yo Ma betters his already fine first version, offering playing of both powerful discipline and apparent free-flying spontaneity. This is not Ma in sophisticated mode but rather offering a direct, simplicity that plays huge dividends in this ebulliently melodious music.

Pablo Casals; Czech PO / George Szell
Dutton mono CDEA5002   Ⓜ

Casals's 1937 recording with the Czech Philharmonic is a classic with wonderfully idiomatic playing by the orchestra, gloriously directed by George Szell. This is a performance of incandescent beauty, the cellist's bow seemingly striking sparks off the string as he launches into the work's richly Romantic melodies.

Pierre Fournier; Berlin PO / George Szell
DG 423 881-2GGA   Ⓜ❍

What an elegant player Fournier was! And with Szell again on top form, this remains a highly recommendable mid-price version.

János Starker; London SO / Antal Dorati
Mercury 423 001-2MM   Ⓜ

With slightly fierce recorded sound, this is still well worth seeking out for Starker's blazing commitment and for Dorati's masterly accompaniment.

Pierre Fournier; Philharmonia / Rafael Kubelík
Testament SBT1016   Ⓕ

The first of Fournier's three recordings dates from 1948 and displays his customary ease and grace as a soloist. Kubelík conducts idiomatically drawing excellent playing from the young Philharmonia.

one more readily conveying weight of expression despite the less spotlit placing of the soloist, more disciplined yet more spontaneous-sounding. This time Ma's expressiveness is simpler and more noble, and the recording (made in Avery Fisher Hall, New York), once a trouble-spot for engineers, is fuller and more open than the Berlin one, cleaner in *tutti*s, with only a touch of unwanted dryness on high violins. Ma and Masur together encompass the work's astonishingly full expressive range, making it the more bitingly dramatic with high dynamic contrasts.

Herbert's concerto, first given in 1894, was almost certainly what prompted Dvořák to write his own concerto later that same year. Here it receives a high-powered performance, but one which doesn't overload the romantic element with sentiment, whether in the brilliant and vigorous outer movements or in the warmly lyrical slow movement. Ma's use of rubato is perfectly judged, with the slow movement made the more tender at a flowing speed. The finale is then given a quicksilver performance, both brilliant and urgent.

Additional recommendations

Cello Concerto
Coupled with: Symphony No 9   Ⓗ
Casals vc **Czech Philharmonic Orchestra / Szell**
Dutton CDEA5002 (74' · ADD)   Ⓑ

    Casals's legendary 1937 account of the Dvořák, described at the time as 'seemingly played with a sword rather than a bow', still exercises a powerful effect. Szell's powerful performance of the *New World* makes this transfer particularly desirable.

Coupled with: Elgar Cello Concerto.
Fournier vc **Berlin Philharmonic Orchestra / Szell; Wallenstein**
DG Galleria 423 881-2GGA (65' · ADD)   Ⓜ

    The third of Fournier's three accounts, and for some the most satisfying. Of the dozens of recordings of this work, this still stands as a first-class recommendation.

Coupled with: **Bruch** *Kol Nidrei*. **Tchaikovsky** Variations on a Rococo Theme.
Starker vc **London Symphony Orchestra / Dorati**
Mercury Living Presence 432 001-2MM   Ⓜ
(64' · DDD)

    Janos Starker's admirers will not want to be without this issue, for there's much that's eloquent and moving in the Dvořák. The recorded sound is a little harsh, though.

Coupled with: **Saint-Saëns** Cello Concerto No 1.   Ⓗ
Le Carnival des animaux – excerpt. **Fauré** Elégie. Berceuse. **Ravel** Pièce en forme de habanera. **Debussy** Rêverie.
Fournier vc **Lush, Moore** pfs **Philharmonia / Kubelík; Susskind**
Testament SBT1016 (77 minutes)   Ⓕ

    This is the first (1948) of three recordings made Fournier of the Dvořák. Here his customarily aristocratic, beautifully fashioned playing has an extra quality of spirituality which lifts his performance to great heights.

Piano Concerto

Dvořák Piano Concerto in G minor, B63
Schumann Piano Concerto in A minor, Op 54
Paolo Giacometti *pf* **Arnhem Philharmonic Orchestra / Michel Tilkin**
Channel Classics CCS17898 (71' · DDD) Ⓕ

To say that Paolo Giacometti measures up well to the classic versions is to say a great deal. His playing has all the energy, sparkle, poetry and technical finish you could wish. He approaches the Dvořák with an admirable mixture of respect and enjoyment. And his Schumann is as urgent as the composer's markings suggest it should be, yet without sacrificing natural characterisation for the sake of making that point. Nor do the Dutch orchestra and conductor sound in any way out of their depth; on the contrary, they're clearly as engaged as their soloist in warm, lively music-making. The Channel Classics recording is also rich and well balanced. If the Schumann/Dvořák coupling is just what you're looking for, there's no need to hesitate.

Piano Concerto in G minor, B63[a]. The Golden Spinning-Wheel, B197
[a]**Pierre-Laurent Aimard** *pf* **Royal Concertgebouw Orchestra, Amsterdam / Nikolaus Harnoncourt**
Teldec 8573 87630-2 (68' · DDD) Ⓕ●

Straight to the top of the list for this one! Even on its best showings – Richter and Carlos Kleiber, Firkušný under Somogyi – Dvořák's Piano Concerto has never quite managed to cast off its Cinderella rags. With this recording, the ball beckons, and there's no time limit. Granted, Brahms is still securely in the background and the concerto is hardly as pianistic as the best of its concerto-peers but the beauty of this performance is its utter naturalness, Pierre-Laurent Aimard easing around the solo part as if he's been playing it all his life, and Nikolaus Harnoncourt's sympathy for the work is obvious from the start. Together they make the most of the score's drama, giving the lie to Dvořák's supposedly ineffective piano writing. Albrecht Gaud's excellent booklet note credits the long-prevalent revision by Vilém Kurz as giving the part 'not only a more effective form' but also the virtue of extra clarity. Yet it appears that the original is used here and redeemed. Richter's clarity and Firkušný's knowing accent remain attractive, but Aimard's combination of intelligence and informality win the day. A magnificent CD.

Violin Concerto

Violin Concerto in A minor, B108[a]. Piano Quintet in A B155[b]
Sarah Chang, [b]**Alexander Kerr** *vns* [b]**Wolfram Christ** *va* [b]**Georg Faust** *vc* [b]**Leif Ove Andsnes** *pf* [a]**London Symphony Orchestra / Sir Colin Davis**
EMI 557521-2 (72' · DDD) Ⓕ

What an excellent idea for the brilliant young violinist Sarah Chang to couple her warm and powerful reading of the Dvořák Violin Concerto not with another concerto but with one of Dvořák's most popular chamber works. She shows again what a warmly sympathetic chamber-player she is. This time she shares the leadership with pianist Leif Ove Andsnes, an equally imaginative artist who similarly conveys a sense of spontaneity in almost every phrase.

As a group they give the impression of making music for fun, great artists enjoying themselves in the interplay of free expression, each challenging the others. So the first movement brings rapt playing from Chang, with Andsnes wonderfully clean in his articulation of fast triplets, and the viola player Wolfram Christ satisfyingly rich-toned in the second subject theme. The *Dumka* slow movement again sounds almost improvisatory, a fantasy movement, totally idiomatic, while the *Scherzo* is exceptionally light, taken at a challengingly fast tempo; the jauntiness of the finale is also lightly presented. Though the recording, made in the Mozartsaal of the Konzerthaus in Vienna, has less presence than some, it's clean and well balanced.

The performance of the Concerto with Sir Colin Davis, a powerful and understanding Dvořákian, similarly draws expressive playing from Chang in a performance which treats the unconventional structure of the first movement as rhapsodic without letting tensions slip. The sense of fantasy is again irresistible, with Chang exploiting dynamic extremes, as she does in the wistfully tender slow movement, while the slavonic dance of the finale is given a winning spring. The recording made at the Watford Colosseum enhances the feeling of a big-scale performance with full-bodied sound set in a lively acoustic.

Dvořák Violin Concerto[a] **Elgar** Violin Sonata in E minor, Op 82[b]
Maxim Vengerov *vn* [b]**Revital Chachamov** *pf* [a]**New York Philharmonic Orchestra / Kurt Masur**
Teldec 4509 96300-2 (58' · DDD) Ⓕ●●●

This makes a winning coupling, unexpected though it may be. Maxim Vengerov, always an inspirational artist, gives positive, passionate performances of both works, finding a purposeful logic in music that can in lesser hands seem wayward. He's helped in the Dvořák Violin Concerto by being recorded live (in Avery Fisher Hall): though the orchestra sound a little congested, the violin is beautifully caught, the daringly wide dynamic and tonal range of Vengerov's playing on his 1723 Stradivarius being fully exploited. He's masterly in conveying the sharp changes of mood in this unconventionally shaped work, at one moment purposeful, at another deeply reflective. This, more than most rivals – even Tasmin Little and Itzhak Perlman – conveys an improvisational quality, intensifying the Slavonic flavours, making the music sparkle, bringing out the fun and fantasy.

The slow movement is yearningly beautiful, heartstoppingly tender thanks to Vengerov's use of the subtlest half-tones, while the finale is as light and resilient as a Slavonic dance. In this, Masur is the most sympathetic accompanist, persuading his American players to evoke the music's Czech flavours.

In some ways, particularly for the British listener, the Elgar Sonata is an even more exciting choice, and certainly it gives wonderful promise of what this inspired young virtuoso will do when he tackles the Elgar Violin Concerto, as surely he must. Outstanding.

Additional recommendations

Violin Concerto
Coupled with: **Suk** Fantasy
Suk vn **Czech Philharmonic Orchestra / Ançerl**
Supraphon SU1928-2 (69' · ADD)　　　Ⓜ
　A distinguished performance from this all-Czech line-up.

Symphonies

No 1 in C minor, B9, 'The Bells of Zlonice'; **No 2** in B flat, B12; **No 3** in E flat, B34; **No 4** in D minor, B41; **No 5** in F, B54; **No 6** in D, B112; **No 7** in D minor, B141; **No 8** in G, B163; **No 9** in E minor, B178, 'From the New World'

Complete Symphonies

Symphonies Nos 1-9. Scherzo capriccioso, B131. Overtures – In Nature's Realm, B168; Carnival, B169; My Home, B125a
London Symphony Orchestra / István Kertész
Decca Ⓑ 430 046-2DC6 (431' · ADD) Recorded 1963-66　　　　　ⒷⓄⓄ

István Kertész recorded the Dvořák symphonies in the mid-1960s, and his integral cycle quickly achieved classic status; his exhilarating and vital account of the Eighth Symphony rapidly became a special landmark in the catalogue. The original LPs are now collectors' items. These magnificent interpretations became available again in 1992, in glitteringly refined digitally remastered sound, and it's a tribute to the memory of this tragically short-lived conductor that this cycle continues to set the standard by which others are judged. He was the first conductor to attract serious collectors to the early Dvořák symphonies, and his jubilant advocacy of the unfamiliar First Symphony has never been superseded. This work offers sur-

prising insights into the development of Dvořák's mature style, as does the Second Symphony. Kertész shows that Symphonies Nos 3 and 4 have much more earthy resilience than many commentators might have us believe, insisting that Dvořák's preoccupation with the music of Wagner and Liszt had reached its zenith during this period. The challenging rhetoric of the Fourth has never found a more glorious resolution than here, with Kertész drawing playing of quite gripping intensity from the LSO. The Fifth Symphony and, to a still greater extent, the Sixth reveal Dvořák's clear affinity with the music of Brahms. Kertész's superb reading of the Sixth, however, shows just how individual and naturally expressive this underrated work actually is, while the playing in the great climax of the opening movement and the vigorous final peroration remains tremendously exciting. In the great final trilogy, he triumphs nobly with the craggy resilience of the Seventh Symphony, and he brings a dynamic thrust and momentum to the Eighth. His *New World* is by turns indomitable and searchingly lyrical.

The six-disc set also offers assertive and brilliant readings of the Overtures *Carnival*, *In nature's realm* and the rarely heard *My home*, together with a lucid and heroic account of the *Scherzo capriccioso*. These definitive performances have been skilfully reprocessed, the sound is astonishingly good, even by modern standards, and the playing of the London Symphony Orchestra is often daringly brilliant.

Symphonies – selected

Symphony No 6. The Wild Dove
Czech Philharmonic Orchestra / Jiří Bělohlávek
Chandos CHAN9170 (63' · DDD) Recorded 1992　Ⓕ

Bělohlávek has referred to his Czech orchestra's 'singing art of playing' and its 'mellow sound' and indeed it's Bohemia's woods, fields and wildlife, rather than energetic village green festivities, that linger in the memory here. Perhaps you shouldn't expect a Czech Philharmonic performance to 'go' or leap about excitedly in the manner of Kertész's with the LSO; in these days of high adrenalin, high contrast and high definition, there's a lot to be said for a less assertive and vigorous approach, always artlessly sung, and for this orchestra's Old World timbres a Brahmsian fireside glow, for example, to the Symphony's first movement second subject on cellos and horns (beautifully eased in by Bělohlávek). These horns, always more rounded in tone than their rasping counterparts in London (Kertész), bear an obvious family resemblance to the woodwind, not only in timbre, but also in the use of vibrato (again, that 'singing art of playing'). And the 'silver moon' flute is one of this disc's principal joys. Bělohlávek also projects the drama of *The wild dove* with relish. Chandos, as ever, guarantees a sepia-toned warmth throughout.

Symphony No 6 in D, B112. The Golden Spinning-Wheel, B197
Czech Philharmonic Orchestra / Sir Charles Mackerras
Supraphon SU3771-2 (71' · DDD)   Ⓕ

Sir Charles Mackerras's vibrant interpretation easily holds its own in the most venerable company. Not only are the Czech Philharmonic, recorded live in October 2002, at their articulate and spirited best, but Mackerras directs the outer movements with a pliancy and keen sense of long-term proportion reminiscent of his mentor Talich, as well as Rowicki's magnificent 1965 LSO account (Philips Duo, nla). He also extracts every ounce of songful poetry from the sublime slow movement, while the *Furiant* cross-rhythms of the *scherzo* skip to the manner born. If the trio hasn't quite the seraphic wonder of Sejna's (Supraphon, nla) or Kubelík's live version, the performance as a whole has a spine-tingling thrust, meriting a place alongside any of its distinguished rivals.

The Golden Spinning-Wheel is a studio recording from June 2001. A splendidly opulent and atmospheric reading, observant and affectionate, if without quite the narrative flair and expressive scope of Harnoncourt's riveting Concertgebouw account.

Symphonies Nos 6 & 8
Vienna Philharmonic Orchestra / Myung-Whun Chung
DG 469 046-2GH (77' · DDD)   Fmm

Drawing playing of infectious eagerness and disarming poise from his distinguished band, Myung-Whun Chung directs an exhilaratingly purposeful and memorably fresh account of the Sixth. The wonderful opening *Allegro non tanto* at once sets the template for Chung's mobile, yet affectionately pliant approach. Unfortunately there's no repeat, but, by way of compensation, Chung does impart a riveting expectancy to the start of the development section. Likewise, the succeeding *Adagio* enshrines an unusually flowing conception, though there's no gainsaying the flexibility and poetry of Chung's conducting, not to mention the chamber-like intimacy and concentration of the VPO's sublimely poised response (such heart-warming *dolce* tone from the first violins).

Chung's Scherzo must be just about the swiftest on disc. With the VPO on its toes, the effect is undeniably exciting, though more of those delicious *ben marcato* violas · cutting through the texture would have been welcome. On the other hand, the dare-devil tempo does throw into sharper relief both the blissful innocence of the Trio (with its sublime piccolo writing) as well as the deceptively relaxed launch pad of the finale, which is paced to perfection, its giddy coda as thrillingly judged. In fact Chung's Sixth is the best we've had in years, meriting a place way up there alongside the likes of Kubelík, Rowicki and Ančerl.

Chung's earlier Gothenburg SO Eighth for BIS was full of good things, but this April 1999 remake operates at an altogether higher level of intensity. The first movement is a generously moulded, spontaneous-sounding affair, its sunshine and storm gauged with arresting flair. The slow movement, though not as distinctive as Harnoncourt's 'back to nature' restoration, is very fine indeed, its dark-hued eloquence counterbalanced by a touching lyrical simplicity. Elsewhere, the *Allegretto grazioso* is a great success, its Trio etched with open-mouthed wonder, while the scampering coda fairly chortles with mischief. The finale, too, brings plenty of incident, not least that grandly theatrical ritenuto for the trombones' four-bar flourish at fig M or 4'45" (by no means the only instance where memories of Talich and Kubelík came flooding back).

DG's sound is immensely ripe and full-bodied, this great orchestra's burnished glow and mahogany-like timbre exceptionally well captured. However, some *tuttis* (especially in the Eighth) may fall a little too aggressively on the ears for some tastes, and at times the ample Musikverein acoustic precludes the last ounce of clarity. No matter, Chung's remains a cherishable pairing overall.

Symphony No 7. Nocturne in B, B47. The Water Goblin
Czech Philharmonic Orchestra / Jiří Bělohlávek
Chandos CHAN9391 (69' · DDD) Recorded 1992   Ⓕ

Bělohlávek is a lucid, sure-footed guide through Dvořák's mightiest symphonic utterance, and his sympathetic direction combines both warmhearted naturalness as well as total fidelity to the score (dynamics are scrupulously attended to throughout). If it sounds just a little under-energised next to other vividly dramatic accounts, the sheer unforced eloquence and lyrical fervour of the playing always give enormous pleasure. Certainly, the first movement's secondary material glows with affectionate warmth, while the sublime *Poco adagio* emerges seamlessly, its songful rapture and nostalgic vein captured as to the manner born by this great orchestra (listen out for some gorgeous work from the principal flute, clarinet and horn). The *Scherzo* trips along with an infectious, rhythmic spring, as well as an engaging poise and clarity; moreover, the dark-hued unsettling Trio (a casualty in so many rival performances) is handled with equal perception. The finale, too, is immensely pleasing, marrying symphonic thrust with weighty rhetoric rather in the manner of Colin Davis's distinguished Amsterdam account. The closing bars are very broad and imposing indeed. A performance of considerable dignity and no mean stature, benefiting from vibrant Chandos engineering. The symphony is followed by a long-breathed, slumbering account of the *Nocturne* (gloriously played by the Czech PO strings) and the disc concludes with a fine *Water goblin*.

Again, the orchestral response is as disciplined and poised as you could hope to hear.

Symphonies Nos 7-9[a]. Symphonic Variations, B70[b]
[a]**Concertgebouw Orchestra;** [b]**London Symphony Orchestra / Sir Colin Davis**
Philips Duo ② 438 347-2PM2 (139' · ADD) Recorded
[a]1975-8, [b]1968　　　　　　　　　　Ⓜ**OO**

Colin Davis's magnificent Amsterdam Dvořák Seventh remains one of the most compellingly taut available: gloriously played and paced to perfection, it has a dark, searing intensity wholly apt for this, the Czech master's most tragic utterance; certainly, only a select handful of rivals on disc have matched this performance's irresistible symphonic drive. The Eighth is excellent, too: it's notable for its keen vigour, textural transparency and unfailing sense of purpose – only a little more nudging affection might not have gone amiss. Davis's finely sculpted *New World* (first-movement repeat included) is another powerful, involving affair – the sublimely articulate orchestral response alone ensures enormous pleasure. Although not as endearingly flexible or evocative a reading as some would prefer, Davis's directness is always refreshing and never brusque. The result: an impressively cogent, concentrated conception. Apart from some distractingly close balancing in the finale of No 8, all three symphonies are blessed with Philips engineering of the highest analogue quality. Davis's 1968 version of the masterly *Symphonic Variations* is very fine: sounding admirably fresh still, it's an effective and unfussy rendering.

Symphony No 8. The wood dove
Scottish National Orchestra / Neeme Järvi
Chandos CHAN8666 (57' · DDD) Recorded 1987　Ⓕ

Järvi's account of the Eighth Symphony underlines the expressive warmth of the piece, the rhapsodic freedom of invention rather than any symphonic tautness. That the result seems so warm and natural is due above all to the responsiveness of the SNO players, who seem to feel Järvi's wonderfully free rubato and affectionate moulding of phrase with collective spontaneity. It's a joy to have this from an orchestra, without any feeling of mannerism. The score, to take an obvious example, is marked *allegro con brio* from the first bar, and anyone wanting a more firmly structured reading will be happier with a version such as the Davis/Philips. But Järvi is here doing no more than follow a long-established tradition, and one which in a performance such as his – always purposeful, marked by strong dramatic contrasts – hardly sounds wayward. Though he allows himself fair breadth, his speeds are never eccentric. The finale is marginally slower than usual, but his relaxation goes with a control of tension that almost suggests the telling of a story, easy and natural in its sharp changes of mood. In all four movements there are many incidental delights. In *The Wood Dove*, as in the symphony, Järvi's feeling for the rhapsodic side of Dvořák's invention makes for a persuasive performance, warm and colourful. The Chandos sound has a characteristic bloom.

Symphonies Nos 8 & 9
Berlin Philharmonic Orchestra / Rafael Kubelík
DG The Originals 447 412-2GOR (73' · ADD)
Recorded 1972　　　　　　　　　　　　Ⓜ

These accounts are quite magnificent, and their claims on the allegiance of collectors remain strong. Their freshness and vigour remind one of what it was like to hear these symphonies for the first time. The atmosphere is authentic in feeling and the sense of nature seems uncommonly acute. Kubelík has captured the enthusiasm of his players and generates a sense of excitement and poetry. The playing of the Berlin Philharmonic is marvellously eloquent and, as is often the case, a joy in itself. The woodwinds phrase with great poetic feeling and imagination, and all the departments of this great orchestra respond with sensitivity and virtuosity. The recording has great dynamic range and encompasses the most featherweight string *pianissimos* to the fullest orchestral *tutti* without discomfort. The listener is placed well back in the hall so that the woodwind, though they blend beautifully, may seem a little too recessed for some tastes, though it should be said that there's no lack of vividness, power or impact. The balance and the timbre of each instrument is natural and truthful; nothing is made larger than life and Kubelík has a natural warmth and flexibility. This will remain high on any list of recommendations for it has a vernal freshness that's wholly reviving.

Symphonies Nos 8 & 9
Budapest Festival Orchestra / Iván Fischer
Philips 464 640-2PH (78' · DDD)　　　Ⓕ**OO**

Ten years ago Fischer recorded the Eighth Symphony with the same orchestra at the same venue. In terms of timings, the two readings are remarkably similar, and yet the newer performance is warmer, more malleable and significantly more spontaneous. Both employ expressive string slides (a Fischer characteristic in Slavic music), most noticeably at the end of the *Scherzo*, where a snappy portamento on fiddles is echoed by the brass. Philips' recording has an extended dynamic range and a fuller, closer string sound.

While the Eighth, then, is given a bouncy, lyrical performance, 'localised' with the odd gypsy inflection, the *New World*, on the other hand, is intense and energetic. Indeed, it's some tribute to Fischer's musical perception that he views the two works in entirely different terms. Small dynamic details tell with a new-found freshness. Just try sampling the difference between *forte* and *sforzando* among the basses in the first movement and the softness of the second subject, for once a genuine *ppp*. These and similar markings register even if you're not following the music with a score. Accents, too, are keenly observed, articulation is carefully judged and the string choirs have real bite. Indeed, there isn't a more enjoyable digital *New World* on the current market, although Kurt Masur's beautifully considered 1991 New York Philharmonic performance makes a fine alternative. It's not as energetically driven as Fischer's, but as an interpretation it's extremely well balanced. As is Harnoncourt who, though more obviously idiosyncratic than Fischer, brings a host of personalised insights to both symphonies. But Fischer's CD is a consistent joy, and is thoroughly recommended.

Dvořák Symphony No 9. American Suite in A, B190
Smetana Má vlast – Vltava
Prague Symphony Orchestra / Libor Pešek
Classic fM The Full Works 75605 57043-2 (71' · DDD)
Ⓜ

Symphony No 9. The Water Goblin, Op 107
Royal Concertgebouw Orchestra / Nikolaus Harnoncourt
Teldec 3984-25254-2 (64' · DDD) ⒻО

Harnoncourt has some distinguished Concertgebouw forebears, not least structure-conscious Sir Colin Davis and combustible Antál Dorati (both Philips). This, though, beats them all. Auspicious happenings register within the first few pages: carefully drawn woodwind lines; basses that calm meticulously from fierce *fortissimo* to tense *pianissimo*; provocative bassoons and an effortless passage into the lovely flute melody at 2'58". At the start of the development section *piano* violins really are played *leggiero* (lightly), a significant detail that most rivals gloss over. Middle and lower voices are granted their full flavour and the violin desks are divided. Harnoncourt's *Largo* is something of a minor miracle. Undulating clarinets register against shimmering string *tremolandos* and, beyond the beautifully judged approach to the *Meno* passage (bar 78), you suddenly hear quiet second-violin *pizzicato* chords (7'00") that you almost never notice in concert. The finale itself never sags, and for the home strait Harnoncourt treads a course somewhere between the printed *Allegro con fuoco* and the expressive broadening that Dvořák later sanctioned. Most admirable about Harnoncourt's Dvořák is its close proximity to nature: barely a minute passes that isn't somewhere touched by verdure or sunshine.

Compared to Pešek's earlier recording with the Royal Liverpool Philharmonic, his Prague Symphony remake is faster, fresher and more spontaneous. Again, the first-movement repeat is observed and, while some speeds catch the Prague players sounding hard pressed, a compensating sense of excitement suits the impulsive nature of the music. Pesek's 10'12" *Largo* is at times more like a *Larghetto* (Harnoncourt clocks up 12'17") but the mood is right (more

---

DVOŘÁK'S SYMPHONY NO 9, 'FROM THE NEW WORLD' – IN BRIEF

Czech PO / Karel Ančerl
Supraphon SU 3662-2 (71' · ADD) Ⓜ
As cogent and delectably unforced a *New World* as any in the catalogue. The Czech PO respond to the manner born for their distinguished chief.

Berlin PO / Rafael Kubelík
DG 447 412-2GOR (73' · ADD) ⓂО
One of the most lovable, vibrantly communicative versions ever committed to disc. Coupled with a scarcely less distinguished account of the Eighth Symphony.

London SO / Witold Rowicki
Philips ② 456 327-2PM2 (156' · ADD) Ⓜ
An unusually intelligent, trenchant interpretation from this underrated Polish maestro, who draws consistently spry playing from the LSO. Rowicki's rugged Seventh and lithe Eighth also command respect, while Leppard's 1973 LPO account of the *Legends* makes a attractive bonus.

Concertgebouw Orchestra / Sir Colin Davis
Philips ② 438 347-2PM2 (139' · ADD) ⓂОО
Given its purposeful drive, untrammelled eloquence and architectural splendour, Davis's 1978 performance is hard to fault. The Amsterdam orchestra, too, are at their considerable best; ditto the Philips sound-team.

Vienna PO / Kirill Kondrashin
Decca Ovation 430 702-2DM (63' · DDD) Ⓜ
If demonstration-worthy sonics are your top priority, look no further than Kondrashin's warmly sympathetic 1979 traversal. Aptly and imaginatively paired with Dorati's RPO *American* Suite.

Berlin PO / Ferenc Fricsay
DG 463 650-2GOR (72' · ADD) Ⓜ
A lovely performance, chock full of personality and beaming affection, yet strongly argued too. Fricsay's stupendous readings of Smetana's *Vltava* and Liszt's *Les Préludes* round off an irresistible anthology.

Royal Concertgebouw Orchestra / Nikolaus Harnoncourt
Teldec 3984 25254-2 (64' · DDD) ⒻО
One of the great recordings of Dvořák's perennial favourite. Harnoncourt really does make you listen anew, and the orchestral playing is breathtakingly accomplished. Harnessed to a scarcely less riveting account of *The Water Goblin*.

elegiac than solemn) and the finale is full of vigour. For recording quality, Teldec yields the greater warmth, Classic FM the sharper edge.

For the couplings, Harnoncourt gives us *The Water Goblin*, the most folk-like of Dvořák's Erben tone-poems where, as in the Symphony, middle voices rise to the fore and the stamping outer sections are played with great rhythmic bite. Pešek makes winsome music of the lovely *American Suite*, adding a forthright 'Vltava' (faster by a minute than his Liverpool recording) into the bargain. If you think that you know the *New World* back-to-front then Harnoncourt will have you thinking again.

Additional recommendations

Symphony No 5
Coupled with: Three Slavonic Rhapsodies
Czech Philharmonic Orchestra / Sejna
Supraphon SU1917-2 (75' · ADD)   Ⓜ
Irreproachably idiomatic music-making, evincing both tingling vitality and fresh-faced wonder – a classic, life-enhancing document.

Symphony No 6
Coupled with: **Janáček** Sinfonietta
Bavarian Radio Symphony Orchestra / Kubelík
Orfeo C552011B (70' · ADD) Recorded live 1981   Ⓕ
A cherishable document captured in wholly acceptable sound and a must-buy for all devotees of this conductor. Live performance lends the Sixth an easy, free-wheeling spontaneity and a songful poetry that his studio version lacks. The slow movement is an especial delight.

Symphony No 6
Coupled with: Hussite. My Home. Carnival
Czech Philharmonic Orchestra / Ančerl
Supraphon 11 1926-2 (75' · ADD)   Ⓜ
One of the most distinguished versions of a simply glorious symphony – intelligent observation and purposeful thrust in perfect accord.

Symphonies Nos 6 and 7
Czech Philharmonic Orchestra / Sejna
Supraphon SU1918-2 (74' · ADD)   Ⓜ
Sejna's Sixth remains a miracle of joyous musicality and endearing spontaneity; the Seventh is less compelling, though still worth while.

Symphony No 7
London Symphony Orchestra / C Davis
LSO Live LSO0014 (40' · DDD)   Ⓢ Ⓢ
Davis masterminds a performance of authority. His approach is more flexible and generously expressive than his outstanding 1975 account, but there's no want of symphonic thrust. That set still reigns supreme but at the price this is one to snap up.

Symphonies Nos 7, 8 and 9
Coupled with: Romance in F minor[a]. Symphonic Variations
[a]**Gonley** vn [a]**English Chamber Orchestra, London Philharmonic Orchestra / Mackerras**
Classics for Pleasure ② 575761-2 (150' · DDD)   Ⓢ Ⓑ

These are winning performances – rhythms delightfully sprung, detail closely observed and completely without point scoring. The Seventh and Eighth are the gems here, but the rest in no way disappoints.

Symphony No 8
Coupled with: Cello Concerto[a]
[a]**Tortelier** vc [a]**London Symphony Orchestra / **[a]**Previn Hallé Orchestra / Barbirolli**
HMV Classics HMV5 73454-2 (75' · ADD)   Ⓢ
The Eighth shows the inimitable Hallé/Barbirolli partnership at its most inspirationally fresh. Here is truly life-enhancing, hugely spontaneous music-making.

Symphony No 8
Coupled with: The Noon Witch
Concertgebouw / Harnoncourt
Teldec 3984 24487-2 (51' · DDD)   Ⓕ
A typical Harnoncourt interpretation with a freshness of approach and attention to colour and detail that spell winner.

Symphony No 9
Coupled with: Slavonic Dances, B83: Nos 6, 8; B147: No 2
New York Philharmonic Orchestra / Masur
Apex 8573-89085-2 (60' · DDD) No 9 recorded live 1991   Ⓢ Ⓞ
The slow movement is particularly outstanding, with straight, simple phrasing conveying a deeply emotional intensity. Though recorded live, Masur achieves a precision of ensemble to rival that of a studio performance.

Symphony No 9
Coupled with: Othello. In Nature's Realm.
Czech Philharmonic Orchestra / Ančerl
Supraphon SU3662-2 (70' · ADD)   Ⓜ
A truly great, remarkably unforced interpretation, consistently illuminating and displaying an iron grip unmatched on disc.

Symphony No 9
Coupled with: **Beethoven** Leonore Overture No 3.
Prokofiev The Love for Three Oranges – Suite
BBC Symphony Orchestra / Kempe
BBC Legends/IMG Artists BBCL4056-2 (71' · ADD) Recorded live 1975   Ⓜ
A visionary reading, deeply meditative in the slow movement.. The BBC SO, on exceptional form, have *pianissimos* of breathtaking delicacy. The extreme dynamic contrasts are beautifully caught and the sound is vivid and fresh.

Czech Suite

Czech Suite, B93. Festival March, B88. The Hero's Song, B199. Hussite, B132
Polish National Radio Symphony Orchestra / Antoni Wit
Naxos 8 553005 (65' · DDD) Recorded 1993-4   Ⓢ

The Hero's Song, a colourful, rather sprawling tone-poem, was Dvořák's last orchestral work and isn't an easy piece to bring off. Wit finds genuine nobility in it, while his gentle, mellow way with the lovely *Czech Suite* also gives much pleasure. The opening 'Praeludium' is just a touch sleepy, but there's no want of lyrical affection or rhythmic bounce elsewhere and the whole performance radiates an idiomatic, old-world charm that really is most appealing. As for the *Hussite* overture, Wit's clear-headed reading impressively combines dignity and excitement. Given such finely disciplined orchestral playing, the results are again both eloquent and characterful. This just leaves the rousing *Festival March* of 1879, splendidly done here, with the excellent Katowice brass sounding resplendent in their introductory call to arms. Recordings throughout possess a most agreeable bloom and transparency.

Legends

Legends, B122. Nocturne in B, B47. Miniatures, B149. Prague Waltzes, B99
Budapest Festival Orchestra / Iván Fischer
Philips The Rosette Collection 476 2179PR
(69' · DDD)   Ⓜ**OO**

Dvořák's 1881 *Legends* are like Brahmsian *Slavonic Dances* – intimate music, mostly reflective and invariably light hearted. You might also think of the scherzos from Dvořák's symphonic and chamber pieces, where elements of the dance are weighted with a certain gravitas. The eighth *Legend* occasionally anticipates the Seventh Symphony's *Scherzo*, and the sixth, parts of the Eighth Symphony. This is the Dvořák of woodland and foliage, eventful, piquantly scored and with generously nostalgic codas. Iván Fischer has often professed a deep fondness for 'Dvořák miniatures', and his affection registers afresh in performances that combine certain old-style expressive devices (lots of violin *portamentos*) with taut execution and acute feeling for the shape of a phrase. The remainder of Fischer's programme is somewhat lighter, excepting the beautiful *Nocturne* which Dvořák reworked from earlier chamber-music sources. The performance is seamless and fluid.

This is an enchanting programme, especially as the playing and conducting are so consistently imaginative. To call it 'light' music is to court the misguided notion that the *Legends* in particular fail to tap our deeper responses. 'Gentle' would be a better word, and – once you've taken the music to heart– 'indispensable' would be another.

Additional recommendation

Legends
Coupled with: Stabat mater.
English Chamber Orchestra / Kubelík
DG 453 025-2GTA2 ② (129' · ADD)   Ⓜ
  New-minted conducting from a great Dvořákian, with the ECO responding to the manner born.

Slavonic Dances

Slavonic Dances, B83 and B147
Chamber Orchestra of Europe / Nikolaus Harnoncourt
Teldec 8573-81038-2 (73' · DDD)   Ⓕ**OO**

Each dance on this exciting disc is granted its rightful, rustic character. The *furiants* really move (Harnoncourt's readings of Op 46 Nos 1 and 8 are among the fastest on disc) and the Dumka of No 2 oscillates between tender reflection and feverish high spirits.

Harnoncourt's high energy levels never preclude delicacy, or transparency or even the occasional suggestion of sentiment. Tempo relations have been thought through to the last semiquaver though in general they're more dramatic than rival Iván Fischer's (Philips). That Harnoncourt loves this music is beyond doubt, and that he understands it beyond question. He delves among Dvořák's inner voices, pulling them to the fore like a magician freeing a rabbit, while others seem happier to let the music speak for itself. The Chamber Orchestra of Europe play superbly, all swelling curves and attenuated lines, with their pooled individuality shedding fresh light on virtually every piece. If you don't know the music, Harnoncourt will make you love it. And if you do know it, he'll make you love it even more.

Slavonic Dances
Cleveland Orchestra / George Szell
Sony Classical Essential Classics SBK48161
(74' · ADD) Recorded 1963-5   Ⓑ

This reissue is something of a revelation. Both discs have been lovingly remastered and the quality is an amazing improvement over the old LPs. The remastering engineers seem to have discovered a whole bottom octave in the sound, which before had appeared to lack richness and weight to support the brilliant upper range. The *Slavonic Dances* are offered as Szell recorded them, with no repeats cut, so the phenomenal orchestral virtuosity is revealed in all its glory. There's much evidence of the conductor's many captivatingly affectionate touches of rubato and, throughout, this large orchestra follows Szell's every whim, with playing full of lyrical fervour and subtlety of nuance, wonderful precision and a lilting rhythmic pulse. The recordings were made within the acoustics of Cleveland's Severance Hall, usually a pair of dances at a time. The result is infectiously spontaneous and this disc can't be recommended too highly; even if the close balance prevents any real *pianissimos* to register, the dynamic range of the music-making is still conveyed.

Additional recommendations

Slavonic Dances
Czech Philharmonic Orchestra / Sejna

Supraphon SU1916-2 (72' · ADD)　　　　Ⓜ
Sejna secures some wonderfully lithe and vivacious playing from his superb Czech band – an
exhilarating treat.

Bavarian Radio Symphony Orchestra / Kubelík
DG Eloquence 469 760-2 (71' · ADD)　　　Ⓑ●
Inspirationally re-creative, scrupulously prepared
performances under Kubelík's intensely charismatic direction.

Piano Quintet in A, B155

Piano Quintet in A[a]. Piano Quartet No 2 in
E flat, B162
András Schiff pf **Panocha Quartet** (Jiří Panocha,
[a]Pavel Zejfart vns Miroslav Sehnoutka va Jaroslav
Kulhan vc)
Teldec 0630-17142-2 (72' · DDD)　　　　Ⓕ

The ease of musical passage in Dvořák's Second
Piano Quartet was confirmed by the composer
himself, who once confessed that the melodies
positively 'surged' upon him. Indeed, the endless cello line that opens the second movement
would have done even Wagner proud (in principle if not in style) and the dramatic opening
Allegro con fuoco is similarly well endowed in
terms of melody. Any sensitive listener sampling the first movement's haunting coda will
encounter some of the most ravishing modulations in the whole of Dvořák's voluminous output. András Schiff and the Panocha Quartet
seem acutely alive to most of this varied musical
incident. Articulation is crisp (especially from
the pianist) and the general approach is rhythmically alert, with lively characterisation all
round in the 'folky' finale. The better-known
Second Piano Quintet is rather more relaxed,
though Schiff's detail-studded playing again
engages one's interest and the important first-
movement repeat allows us a few seconds' worth
of extra music that most rival versions omit.
Generally, the pianist has the strongest musical
voice; very occasionally with the Panocha inner
voices could be more clearly defined.

Piano Quintet in A. String Quintet in G, B49
Gaudier Ensemble (Marieke Blankestijn, Lesley
Hatfield vns Iris Juda va Christoph Marks vc Stephen
William db Susan Tomes pf)
Hyperion CDA66796 (66' · DDD)　　　　Ⓕ

The pianist here is Susan Tomes, who matches
even Pressler in imagination, encouraging a
performance lighter than that for DG, full of
mercurial contrasts that seem entirely apt. For
example, in the second movement *Dumka*
there's more light and shade, and the *Scherzo*
sparkles even more, leading to a jaunty, exuberant finale. The G major String Quintet, the earliest of the two which Dvořák wrote, the one
with extra double bass, is similarly lighter than
the Chilingirian Quartet on Chandos. The
Chilingirian is just as strongly characterised as

the Gaudier, with a firmer, fuller tone. Marieke
Blankestijn's violin is thinner than Levon
Chilingirian's, but it can be just as beautiful, as
in the lovely high-floating second subject of the
slow movement. A fine disc.

Piano Quintet[a]. Piano Quartet No 2 in E flat, B162
Menahem Pressler pf **Emerson Quartet** (Eugene
Drucker, [a]Philip Setzer vns Lawrence Dutton va David
Finckel vc)
DG 439 868-2GH (75' · DDD) Recorded 1993　Ⓕ

If the Piano Quintet with its wealth of memorable melody is by far the better known, Pressler
and the Emersons demonstrate how the Piano
Quartet, sketched immediately after the other
work and completed two years later in 1889, is
just as rich in invention and in some ways even
more distinctive in its thematic material. If
there's one movement that above all proves a
revelation, it's the *Lento* of the Quartet. Opening with a duet for cello and piano, it's played
here with a rapt, hushed concentration to put it
among the very finest of Dvořák inspirations.
The performance of the Quintet, too, is comparably positive in its characterisation. Many will
prefer the easier, even warmer reading from
Domus in the Piano Quartet, which is neatly if
not so generously coupled with the much earlier
Piano Quartet in D, B53. In this music it isn't
always the high-powered reading that makes its
mark most persuasively, and the Hyperion
sound for Domus is far warmer than the DG
New York recording for this disc, which gives
an unpleasant edge to high violins, making the
full ensemble rather abrasive. None the less, if
the volume is curbed, one can readily enjoy
these passionate and intense accounts of two of
Dvořák's most striking chamber works.

String Quintets

String Quintets – G, B49; E flat, B180. Intermezzo in
B, B49
Chilingirian Quartet (Levon Chilingirian, Mark Butler
vns Louise Williams va Philip De Groote vc) **Simon
Rowland-Jones** va **Duncan McTier** db
Chandos CHAN9046 (69' · DDD) Recorded 1990-91Ⓕ

The G major String Quintet is thoroughly
engaging. Though it was originally in five
movements, Dvořák removed the 'Intermezzo'
second movement, revising and publishing it
separately eight years later as the haunting *Nocturne* for string orchestra. Enterprisingly, this
Chandos disc includes that 'Intermezzo' in its
original string quintet garb. The E flat Quintet
from 1893, on the other hand, is a wholly
mature masterpiece. Completed in just over two
months during Dvořák's American sojourn, it
replaces the double bass of the earlier Quintet
with the infinitely more subtle option of a second viola. Brimful of the most delightfully
fresh, tuneful invention, the score also shares
many melodic and harmonic traits with the

popular *American* Quartet – its immediate predecessor.

The Chilingirian Quartet, ideally abetted by double bassist Duncan McTier and violist Simon Rowland-Jones, are enthusiastic, big-hearted proponents of all this lovely material, and the excellent Chandos recording offers both a realistic perspective and beguiling warmth.

Additional recommendation

String Quintet in G
Coupled with: Serenade, Op 44.
Lincoln Center Chamber Music Society / Shifrin
Delos DE3152 (66' · DDD)   Ⓕ

A strongly communicative, memorably perceptive reading of a marvellous work, expertly engineered into the bargain.

Piano Quartets

Piano Quartets – No 1 in D, B53; No 2 in E flat, B162
Domus (Krysia Osostowicz vn Timothy Boulton va
Richard Lester vc Susan Tomes pf)
Hyperion CDA66287 (70' · DDD) Recorded 1987   Ⓕ

These are two very enjoyable works. Hans Keller's description of the opening pages of the E flat Quartet as 'childish' is staggering – this from the leading campaigner against 'posthumous critical torture'! Childlike would be much more suitable, and this appealing characteristic is well brought out by the members of Domus: Susan Tomes's descent from incisive *fortissimo* clarity to *pianissimo* mystery in the opening bars is a delight, and fully prophetic of the kind of musicianship we're to hear. Two other unforgettable moments from this performance: the lovely return of the first movement second subject, with its heart-easing B major/E flat major modulation – very sensitive use of rubato here – and cellist Richard Lester's richly expressive solos at the beginning of the *Lento*. The D major Quartet is a delightful, if not fully mature piece – it does tend to rely rather heavily on sequence and repetition. Domus makes sure we don't miss any of its virtues, but it doesn't force anything: the timing in the magical opening shift from D major to B major is finely judged, and Dvořák's wonderfully effortless melodies are affectionately shaped and shaded; admirable too the way Susan Tomes finds so much beauty in what often looks like conventionally decorative piano writing. In general the sound is very pleasing, intimate enough to draw one right into the performances without being intimidating, even in the somewhat histrionic second theme of the E flat Quartet's *Lento*. A richly rewarding disc.

String Quartets

No 1 in A, B8; No 2 in B flat, B17; No 3 in D, B18;
No 4 in E minor, B19; No 5 in F minor, B37; No 6 in A

minor, B40; **No 7** in A minor, B45; **No 8** in E, B57;
No 9 in D minor, B75; **No 10** in E flat, B92; **No 11** in
C, B121; **No 12** in F, B179, 'American'; **No 13** in G,
B192; **No 14** in A flat, B193

String Quartets Nos 1-14; F, B120 (Fragment).
Cypresses, B152. Quartettsatz. Two Waltzes, B105
Prague Quartet (Břetislav Novotny, Karel Přibyl vns
Lubomír Malý va Jan Sírc vc)
DG ⑨ 463 165-2GB9 (589' · ADD) Recorded 1975-7
                                                        Ⓑ**OO**

Like Schubert, Dvořák turned to the string quartet early in his career. The three complete quartets included in Vol 1 (Nos 1-3) show considerable facility in writing for strings (after all, Dvořák was a violinist), but it took him some time to arrive at a fully idiomatic quartet style. He also had to learn to rein in his natural expansiveness: the Third Quartet spins out its modest material to an astonishing 70 minutes – the first movement alone is longer than the whole *American* Quartet! The outer movements of the No 4 in E minor (Vol 2) show him concentrating admirably, though the later shortened version of the central *Andante religioso* is a considerable improvement. So the interest of Vol 1 (three discs) is largely musicological. Despite this, with playing so fresh and authoritative even the impossibly long-winded Third Quartet has rewards to offer. Each performance has a strong sense of purpose, but that doesn't mean an inability to enjoy all those charming Dvořákian byways. Technically the playing is admirable. The enjoyment increases through Vol 2. The violin cavatina in the *Andante* of the Fifth Quartet has just the right gentle lilt. Listening to the Prague in the first movement of No 7 you realise how what looks on the page like very simple music can come glowingly to life in the right hands – and the way they handle the slightly tricky *poco più mosso* at the second subject is very impressive. The finest work in Vol 2 (discs 4-6) is undoubtedly the D minor Quartet, No 9. Volume 3 contains three gems: the E flat Quartet (No 10), the *American* and No 13 in G major – the outstanding work of the collection. The Prague are very sensitive to dynamic contrast (Dvořák's markings are often surprisingly detailed). There's plenty of fine music on these nine well-filled discs, all of it well performed, and the recordings are generally creditable.

String Quartets Nos 12 & 13
Vlach Quartet, Prague (Jana Vlachová, Ondřej Kukal
vns Petr Verner va Mikael Ericsson vc)
Naxos 8 553371 (69' · DDD)   Ⓢ

On the face of it, the Vlach Quartet's credentials would seem to be impeccable – the group's leader, Jana Vlachová, is the daughter of the great Josef Vlach – and, indeed, the players make a most pleasing impression on this vividly recorded Naxos coupling. They certainly produce a beguilingly rich, beautifully blended sound and bring to this music a big-hearted, songful fervour as well as textural mastery. What's more, Dvořák's characteristic, chugging cross-rhythms are handled with particular felicity. Interpretatively, their approach contrasts strongly with other readings in that the Vlach team adopt a coaxing, lyrically expressive stance (with the gorgeous slow movement of the *American* a highlight). In the case of the masterly G major Quartet, these gifted newcomers show fresh insights (they're especially perceptive in those wistful reminiscences at the heart of the finale).

Additional recommendation

String Quartet Nos 12, 'American', and 13
Lindsay Quartet
ASV CDDCA797 (66' · DDD) Ⓕ

Sedicated, typically probing accounts from the Lindsays; the great G major Quartet comes off especially well here.

Piano Trios

Piano Trios – No 3 in F minor, B130; No 4 in E minor, B166, 'Dumky'
Florestan Trio (Anthony Marwood vn Richard Lester vc Susan Tomes pf)
Hyperion CDA66895 (68' · DDD) Ⓕ

A favourite and appropriate pairing – Dvořák's most passionate chamber work in harness with one of his most genial. The F minor Piano Trio (1883) was contemporaneous with the death of Dvořák's mother; it anticipates something of the storm and stress that characterises the great D minor Seventh Symphony (1884-5) and the Florestan Trio serves it well. All three players allow themselves plenty of expressive leeway and yet the musical line is neither distorted nor stretched too far. The second movement *Allegretto* is truly *grazioso* and the qualifying *meno mosso* perfectly judged. The finale is buoyant rather than especially rustic, whereas the more overtly colourful *Dumky* Trio inspires a sense of play and a vivid suggestion of local colour. Throughout the performance, the manifest 'song and dance' elements of the score (heartfelt melodies alternating with folk-style faster music) are keenly projected. The recordings are first rate, as are the insert-notes. If you're after a subtle, musically perceptive coupling of these two works, then you could hardly do better.

Violin Sonata in F

Violin Sonata in F, B106. Ballad in D minor, B139. Four Romantic Pieces, B150. Violin Sonatina in G, B183. Nocturne in B, B48a (arr cpsr)
Anthony Marwood vn **Susan Tomes** pf
Hyperion CDA66934 (67' · DDD) ⒻⓄ

This delectable release enshrines music-making of sensitivity and eloquence. Marwood may not produce as luscious a sound as that of some of his rivals, but his subtly variegated tone colouring more than compensates; Tomes, too, displays the deftest touch throughout. The F major Sonata receives a wonderfully pliable reading, full of imaginative touches. You'll especially warm to their unhurried, yet purposeful way with the opening movement (Dvořák's *ma non troppo* marking ideally judged). The beautiful ensuing *Poco sostenuto* has both Brahmsian warmth and hushed intimacy; the finale is joyous and articulate. Marwood's and Tomes's account of the captivating *Sonatina* is less 'glamorous' and high powered than the Gil and Orli Shahams' 1995 account on DG – and altogether more personable as a result. Similarly, the second of the *Four Romantic Pieces* has an earthy tang reminiscent of Janáček, while the *Allegro appassionato* third movement unfolds with just the right flowing ardour. Hyperion also offers the haunting *Nocturne* in B major and a sombre, vividly characterised *Ballad* in D minor. This anthology must now take the palm, not least in view of the marvellously balanced recording.

Requiem Mass, B165

Requiem Mass, B165. Mass in D, B153
Pilar Lorengar sop **Neil Ritchie** treb **Erzesébet Komlóssy** contr **Andrew Giles** counterten **Robert Ilosfalvy, Alan Byers** tens **Tom Krause** bar **Robert Morton** bass **Nicholas Cleobury** org **Ambrosian Singers; Christ Church Cathedral Choir, Oxford / Simon Preston; London Symphony Orchestra / István Kertész**
Double Decca ② 448 089-2DF2 (138' · ADD)
Recorded 1968. Texts and translations included Ⓜ

Requiem Mass also available (coupled with Kodály Psalmus Hungaricus) on Decca ② 468 487-2DL2 Ⓜ

Kertész's Requiem dates from 1968 and on all counts but one, it surpasses Karel Ančerl's classic 1959 set, reissued on DG in 1995 and coupled with Fischer-Dieskau's 1960 set of Dvořák's *Biblical Songs* with Jörg Demus. The exception is the rather too soft-grained singing of Pilar Lorengar as compared with the clear, more vibrant soprano of Maria Stader. But Lorengar's singing is particularly sensitive and appealing in the quieter passages. The lovely quality of Robert Ilosfalvy's voice tells beautifully in 'Liber scriptus proferetur' and in the opening section of the quartet, 'Recordare, Jesu pie'. Dvořák distributes short passages among the soloists impartially. They combine beautifully in the quartet, and the chorus with them in 'Pie Jesu Domine'. The hero of the occasion is Kertész. He gets choral singing and orchestral playing of the finest quality. It's abundantly evident that he cherishes a great love for this work. The Mass in D (sung in the original version with organ) sits well with the Requiem; Simon Preston produces a fine, well-balanced performance, with the Christ Church choristers on excellent form.

Mass in D

Dvořák Mass in D, Op 86 Eben Prague Te Deum
1989 Janáček Our Father
Dagmar Masková sop **Marta Benacková** mez
Walter Coppola ten **Peter Mikulás** bass **Lydie
Härtelová** hp **Josef Ksica** org **Prague Chamber
Choir / Josef Pancík**
ECM New Series 449 508-2 (59' · DDD) Recorded
1993. Texts and translations included   (F)

This imaginative coupling brings together three
fine pieces of Czech church music in skilled and
sympathetic interpretations. Dvořák's Mass has
received a number of good recorded performances; this one, in the original 1887 version with
organ, has a very well-matched quartet of
soloists who blend smoothly with each other
and with the chamber choir. It's a work of particular intimacy and charm, and these qualities
mark this performance.

Janáček's setting of the Lord's Prayer dates
from 1906, and is in turn a meditative piece, not
without vivid illustrative touches appropriate to
a work originally designed to accompany a
sequence of devotional pictures; and Petr
Eben's *Prague Te Deum* coincided, in 1969, with
a moment of apparent release from political
oppression. It has something of Janáček's
suddenness in the invention, and a graceful
melodic manner. Each of these works is in its
way inward, personal and reflective, but they all
share a Czech character.

Stabat mater

Stabat mater. Psalm 149
Lívia Aghová sop **Marga Schiml** contr **Aldo Baldin**
ten **Luděk Vele** bass **Prague Children's Choir;
Prague Philharmonic Choir; Czech Philharmonic
Orchestra / Jiří Bělohlávek**
Chandos ② CHAN8985/6 (96' · DDD) Recorded
1991. Notes, texts and translations included   (F)O

The 10 sections of the *Stabat mater* are well laid
out for the different vocal and instrumental
forces and so avoid the monotony which might
seem inherent in this contemplative and deeply
sombre text. This performance was recorded in
Prague Castle, and in it we feel the full dignity
and drama of the work, an oratorio in all but
name. The four solo singers convey genuine
fervour and one feels that their sound, which is
quite unlike that of British singers, must be akin
to what the composer originally imagined. If
they're a touch operatic, that doesn't sound misplaced and they perform well together, as in the
second verse quartet 'Quis est homo'. The
choral singing is no less impressive, and indeed
the whole performance under Bělohlávek gets
the balance right between reverent simplicity
and intensity of feeling. Psalm 149 is a setting of
'Sing unto the Lord a new song' for chorus and
orchestra and its celebratory mood provides a
fine complement to the other work.

Additional recommendations

Coupled with: Legends
Mathis sop **Reynolds** mez **Ochman** ten **Shirley-Quirk**
bar **Bavarian Radio Chorus and Symphony
Orchestra; English Chamber Orchestra / Kubelík**
DG 453 025-2GTA2 ② (129' · ADD)   (M)
This warm-hearted work well deserves all the care
and attention lavished upon it by the performers,
who respond with evident enthusiasm to Kubelík's
inspiring direction.

Zvetkova sop **Donose** mez **Botha** ten **Scandiuzzi**
bass **Saxon State Opera Theatre Chor;
Staatskapelle Dresden / Sinopoli**
DG ② 471 033-2GH2 (88' · DDD)   (F)
A very appealing performance; Sinopoli draws a
more operatic response – both colourful and
dramatic – than is usual from his forces, and his
soloists are superb.

Cypresses

Cypresses, B11ª. Cypresses, B152ᵇ
ª**Timothy Robinson** ten ª**Graham Johnson** pf
ᵇ**Delmé Quartet** (Galina Solodchin, John Trusler vns
John Underwood va Jonathan Williams vc)
Somm SOMMCD236 (80' · DDD · T/t)   (F)

The charming sequence of 12 pieces for string
quartet that Dvořák called *Cypresses* has been
recorded fairly often, but the set of 18 folk-like
songs on which they're based has been neglected. So this disc setting the two cycles side by
side makes an illuminating coupling. His first
essays in song-writing were inspired by his
unrequited love for the elder of two sisters (he
later married the younger one), and were not
published in his lifetime. The cycle had to wait
until 1983 for a first complete public performance. In their reflection of youthful love they
provide a touching portrait of the young composer. Predictably, the quartet versions are
subtler. The vocal line is generally transferred to
violin or viola, with masterly transcription of the
piano accompaniments, disguising their origin.
A number were radically expanded.

The recording sets Timothy Robinson at a
slight distance, and there's an occasional roughness to the top of his range. Still, he responds
with warmth, and in idiomatic Czech, aided by
responsive accompaniment from Graham Johnson. In the instrumental versions the Delmés
phrase expressively within relatively broad
speeds.

Songs

Dvořák Four Songs, B124 . In Folk Tone, B146. Eight
Love Songs, B160 Janáček Moravian Folk Poetry in
Songs Martinů New Miniatures. Mélodies pour une
amie de mon pays. Lullaby. Seven Songs on One
Page. New Slovak Songs
Magdalena Kožená mez **Graham Johnson** pf
DG 463 472-2GH (68' · DDD) Texts and translations
included   (F)OOO

For most of us the songs of what was Czechoslovakia have amounted, in direct knowledge, to a few by Dvořák, principally *Songs my mother taught me*, and though not included here, the programme is never short of interest. The basis of folk melody is common to all, much of the distinctive character of each lying in the writing for piano. Probably no accompanist in the world today would bring a surer insight and rightness of touch to this relatively unfamiliar music, and in the young Czech mezzo Graham Johnson has a singer to whom it's home ground. Kožená's expressive powers would probably have to be judged by a Czech speaker: they aren't of the kind which supersede language or which send one eagerly to consult text and translation. That isn't to say she's bland, and certainly her diction is remarkably clear. But the great gift of her singing at present is the exceptional beauty of her voice, rich, firmly placed, ample in power and range, and now in its freshest bloom. For many, these songs and this singer will be a most welcome discovery.

Gypsy Melodies, B104. In Folk Tone, B146. Love Songs, B160. Biblical Songs, B185
Dagmar Pecková *mez* **Irwin Gage** *pf*
Supraphon SU3437-2 (69' · DDD) Texts and translations included ⒡

These four cycles make an excellent and generous coupling, with Dagmar Pecková, brilliantly supported by Irwin Gage, a most persuasive advocate. Hers is an ideal voice, unmistakably Slavonic in timbre, yet firm and pure as well as rich. She retains a freshness specially apt for the songs inviting a girlish manner, including Dvořák's most famous song, the fourth of the seven *Gypsy Melodies*, 'Songs my mother taught me', sounding fresh and new.

The four cycles represent the full span of Dvořák's career. The eight *Love Songs*, B160 may officially date from 1888, but Dvořák in fact reworked a selection from 18 songs he'd written passionately at high speed over 20 years earlier – charming pieces which already reveal his unquenchable lyrical gift. Next chronologically are the *Gypsy Songs* of 1800, bold and colourful, here nicely contrasted by Pecková and Gage with four simpler, less exotic songs, *In Folk Tone*, of six years later. Last and longest is the cycle of ten *Biblical Songs*, written in the United States in 1894, when he was feeling homesick. They are more often sung by male singers, gaining from weight and gravity, but here with the mezzo, Pecková, they prove just as moving and intense. The sound is clear and well balanced.

Seven Gypsy Melodies, B104. In Folk Tone, B146. Eight Love Songs, B160. Four Songs, B124 – Oh what a perfect golden dream; Downcast am I, so often. Four Songs, B157 – Over her embroidery; Springtide; At the brook. Four Songs, B23 – Obstacles; Medita-

tion; Lime trees. Songs from the Dvur Králové Manuscript, B30
Bernarda Fink *mez* **Roger Vignoles** *pf*
Harmonia Mundi HMC90 1824 (69' · DDD) ⒡

An all-Dvořák song recital may still seem a luxury. The *Gypsy Songs*, and not just their famous fourth ('Songs my mother taught me'), have found a secure place in the repertoire, but not much else is heard at all regularly either in recital or on disc. They may lack the variety of mood to constitute a fully satisfying programme on their own, but they never fail to give pleasure. One cause of the continued unfamiliarity of the B160 set is that Czech is an alien language to most recitalists. Not, however, to the Argentinian mezzo Bernarda Fink, who comes from a Slovenian family, lived in Prague for a while and has made a special study of Czech music. Her diction is very clear. Her tone is rich and deep, and the manner has warmth and dignity, though these seem to be its limits. If you come to the *Gypsy Songs* with Anne Sofie von Otter's recording in mind, you'll miss, in Fink's singing, a lot of colour, imagination and temperament. But there may be some relief, too. Her recording with Bengt Forsberg is exciting but assertive. Fink and Vignoles may prove more companionable. But this new issue is most welcome: tasteful and often lovely performances and a generously comprehensive selection.

The Jacobin

The Jacobin
Václav Zítek *bar* Bohuš **Vilém Přibyl** *ten* Jiří **Daniela Sounová** *sop* Terinka **Karel Průša** *bass* Count Vilém **René Tuček** *bar* Adolf **Marcela Machotková** *sop* Julie **Karel Berman** *bass* Filip **Beno Blachut** *ten* Benda **Ivana Mixová** *mez* Lotinka **Kantilena Children's Chorus; Kühn Chorus; Brno State Philharmonic Orchestra / Jiří Pinkas**
Supraphon ② 11 2190-2 (155' · ADD) Recorded 1977. Notes, text and translation included ⒡

This was the first (and, so far, only) recording of Dvořák's charming village comedy – for the Jacobin of the title isn't a political activist but a young man, Bohuš, returning from exile in Paris to his stuffy old father, Count Vilém. The subplots include all manner of misunderstandings, and set in the middle of them is the touching figure of Benda, the fussy, rather pedantic but wholly moving music-master. Dvořák is known to have had in mind his own boyhood teacher, Antonín Liehmann, whose daughter gives her name, Terinka, to Benda's daughter. Beno Blachut celebrated his 64th birthday during the making of this set. His was a long career, as well as one of great distinction; he's still well able to get round the lines of this part, and gives an affecting picture of the old musician, never more so than in the rehearsing of the welcome ode. This is an idea that's cropped up in opera before, but it's charmingly handled here.

Václav Zítek sings Bohuš pleasantly and

Marcela Machotková trips away lightly as Julie. Vilém Přibyl sounds less than his most energetic, though his voice is in good fettle; and there's some lack of drive from Jiří Pinkas, who might have done more to bring out the often witty touches in Dvořák's scoring. Never mind: this revived version of a delightful piece can be safely recommended.

Kate and the Devil

Kate and the Devil
Anna Barová contr Kate **Richard Novák** bass Devil Marbuel **Miloš Ježil** ten Shepherd Jirka **Daniela Suryová** contr Kate's mother **Jaroslav Horáček** bass Lucifer **Jan Hladík** bass Devil the Gate-keeper **Aleš Stáva** bass Devil the Guard **Brigita Sulcová** sop Princess **Natália Romanová** sop Chambermaid **Pavel Kamas** bass Marshall **Oldřich Polášek** ten Musician **Brno Janáček Opera Chorus and Orchestra / Jiří Pinkas**
Supraphon ② 11 1800-2 (119' · AAD) Recorded 1979. Notes, text and translation included   Ⓕ

Though this was never one of the best Supraphon recordings, it's perfectly serviceable. The plot is complicated, and broadly speaking concerns the bossy Kate who, finding herself a wallflower at the village hop, angrily declares that she would dance with the Devil himself. Up there duly pops a junior devil, Marbuel, who carries her off to hell, where her ceaseless chatter wearies Lucifer himself. The diabolical company is only too happy to allow the shepherd Jirka to remove her again. Jirka, attractively sung by Miloš Ježil, also manages to help the wicked but later repentant Princess to escape the Devil's clutches, and all ends well. The work has a proper coherence, and much good humour besides. Anna Barová's Kate is strong and full of character, but manages not to exclude the charm that should underlie her rantings at Marbuel, who's handsomely sung by Richard Novák. Brigita Sulcová similarly makes much of the unsympathetic Princess. Jaroslav Horáček enjoys himself hugely as Lucifer and Jiří Pinkas accompanies them well.

Rusalka

Rusalka
Renée Fleming sop Rusalka **Ben Heppner** ten Prince **Franz Hawlata** bass Watergnome **Dolora Zajick** mez Witch **Eva Urbanová** sop Foreign Princess **Iván Kusnjer** bar Hunter, Gamekeeper **Zdena Kloubová** sop Turnspit **Lívia Aghová** sop First Woodsprite **Dana Burešová** mez Second Woodsprite **Hana Minutillo** contr Third Woodsprite **Kühn Mixed Choir; Czech Philharmonic Orchestra / Sir Charles Mackerras**
Decca ③ 460 568-2DHO3 (163' · DDD) Notes, text and translation included   ⒻⓄⓄⓄ

 Renée Fleming's tender and heartwarming account of Rusalka's Invocation to the Moon reflects the fact that the role of the lovelorn water nymph, taken by her in a highly successful production at the Met in New York, has become one of her favourites. Ben Heppner also has a special relationship with the opera, for the role of the Prince was the first he studied in depth as a student. He has sung it repeatedly since then, often opposite Renée Fleming, and both he and Mackerras have long harboured the ambition to make a complete recording.

The joy of this magnificent set, which won Gramophone's Record of the Year 1999, is that in almost every way it fulfils every expectation and more, offering a recording with glowing sound that more than ever before reveals the richness and subtlety of Dvořák's score. As interpreted by Fleming and Mackerras, Rusalka's big aria at the start of Act 3, when having been rejected by the Prince, she seeks consolation in returning to the water, is as poignantly beautiful as the more celebrated Invocation to the Moon in Act 1, when she laments over loving a human. In addition, the climactic moments bring glorious top notes, firm and true up to B flat and B. Heppner, like Fleming, conveys his special affection for this music, unstrained up to top C, combining heroic power with lyric beauty.

Dolora Zajick as the Witch, Jezibaba, is characterful and fruity. Franz Hawlata as the Watergnome, Rusalka's father, is firm and dark, bringing a Wagnerian weight to the role. The engineers also thrillingly capture the off-stage effects so important in this opera, with the Watergnome balefully calling from the lake. Even the smaller roles have been cast from strength, all of them fresh, true and idiomatic. Strikingly, there isn't a hint of a Slavonic wobble from any of the singers. In the orchestra, too, the Czech horns are consistently rich and firm. And if anyone is worried about having four non-Czech principals, they're as idiomatic as any rivals.

The final glory of the set lies in the warmly understanding conducting of Charles Mackerras. In every way this matches and even outshines his supreme achievement in the Decca series of Janáček operas. In those you had the Vienna Philharmonic, but here the Czech Philharmonic is both a degree more idiomatic and just as opulent in tone, with superb solo work. The balance between voices and orchestra is well managed, with voices never drowned.

Rusalka
Milada Subrtová sop Rusalka **Eduard Haken** bass Watergnome **Marie Ovčačíková** contr Witch **Ivo Zídek** ten Prince **Alena Míková** mez Foreign Princess **Jadwiga Wysoczanská** sop First Woodsprite **Eva Hlobilová** sop Second Woodsprite **Věra Krilová** contr Third Woodsprite **Ivana Mixová** sop Turnspit **Václav Bednář** bar Hunter, Gamekeeper **Prague National Theatre Chorus and Orchestra / Zdeněk Chalabala**
Supraphon ② SU0013-2 (149' · ADD) Recorded 1961. Notes, text and translation included   ⒻⓄ

This excellent set boasts Eduard Haken, one of the great interpreters of the Watergnome, in robust voice, infusing the character with a rueful gentleness as well as a firmness of utterance. Ivo Žídek as the Prince was in his mid-thirties and in his prime at the time of this recording, singing ardently and tenderly and with a grace of phrasing that matches him well to Milada Subrtová's Rusalka. Hers is a beautiful performance, sensitive to the character's charm as well as to her fragility and pathos. The Slavonic tradition of the old watersprite legend places her in the line of the suffering heroine and it's a measure of Dvořák's success that her delicate appeal holds throughout quite a long opera, and her sinuous but never oversensual lines and the piercing harmony associated with her give her a unique appeal. Subrtová sings the part with unfaltering sensitivity. Zdeněk Chalabala, who died only a couple of months after completing this recording, handles the score with great tenderness and an affection that shines through every bar. This is a beautiful performance. The recording comes up remarkably well, too.

Sir George Dyson
British 1883-1964

Dyson studied at the Royal College of Music (1900-1904) and later taught there (director from 1938), and at several schools. His works include choral and orchestral pieces (notably The Canterbury Pilgrims, 1931) and books. GROVEmusic

Quo Vadis

Quo Vadis
Cheryl Barker sop **Jean Rigby** mez **Philip Langridge** ten **Roderick Williams** bar **Royal Welsh College of Music and Drama Chamber Choir; BBC National Chorus and Orchestra of Wales / Richard Hickox**
Chandos ② CHAN10061 (102' · DDD) Text and translation included (F)**OO**

Like so many British composers Dyson, even before he died in 1962, suffered neglect through writing in a conservative idiom that critics were all too ready to label 'out of date'. Originally written for the Three Choirs Festival in Hereford in 1939, its first performance was cancelled because of the outbreak of war, and it was only given its première in Hereford a decade later. Dyson draws on the widest array of sources, boldly picking out passages from such poets as Campion, Vaughan, Herrick, Shelley, Newman and Bridges in an elaborate kaleidoscope, mixing them together in all but one of the nine substantial movements, even rearranging individual lines from Wordsworth's *Intimations of Immortality*. He also includes such well-known hymns as *God be in my head* and *New every morning* without hinting at the respective hymn tunes. Such a scheme might be expected to sound disjointed or bitty, but Dyson's response

to each section of his text gives a seamless quality to each movement, with ecstatic choral climaxes designed to exploit the all-embracing acoustics of a great cathedral. The warm but well-defined recording helps to heighten the impact of the singing of the Welsh choristers. All four soloists are in superb voice, each of them strong, firm and characterful; and both choruses sing with fresh, incandescent tone. Dyson's idiom may not be as distinctive as that of those other 'agnostics at prayer', but with its lyrical warmth and fine control of texture, the result will delight all devotees of the English choral tradition.

The Canterbury Pilgrims

The Canterbury Pilgrims. In Honour of the City.
At the Tabard Inn
Yvonne Kenny sop **Robert Tear** ten **Stephen Roberts** bar **London Symphony Chorus and Orchestra / Richard Hickox**
Chandos ② CHAN9531 (118' · DDD) Texts included (F)**OOO**

This superb offering of a full-length cantata based on the Prologue to Chaucer's *Canterbury Tales* bears out its reputation as Dyson's masterpiece. It's a fresh, tuneful work, aptly exuberant in its celebration of Chaucer. Following the scheme of Chaucer's Prologue, the 12 movements, plus Envoi, present a sequence of portraits, deftly varying the forces used, with the three soloists well contrasted in their characterisations and with the chorus acting as both narrator and commentator, providing an emotional focus for the whole work in two heightened sequences, the sixth and twelfth movements, moving and noble portraits of the two characters who aroused Dyson's deepest sympathy, the Clerk of Oxenford and the Poor Parson of a Town. If the idiom is undemanding, with occasional echoes of Vaughan Williams's *A Sea Symphony* and with passages reminiscent of Rachmaninov's *The Bells*, the cantata sustains its length well.

Outstanding among the soloists is Robert Tear who not only characterises brilliantly but sings with admirable fullness and warmth. The beautiful, fading close, when Tear as the Knight begins the first tale, moving slowly off-stage, is most atmospherically done. Yvonne Kenny and Stephen Roberts sing well too, but are less distinctive both in timbre and expression. The London Symphony Chorus sings with incandescent tone, superbly recorded, and the orchestra brings out the clarity and colourfulness of Dyson's instrumentation.

Sir Edward Elgar
British 1857-1934

Elgar had violin lessons in Worcester and London but was essentially self-taught, learning much in his father's music shop. From the age of 16 he worked locally as a violinist, organist, bassoonist, conductor and teacher, also composing abundantly though not yet very individually: the accepted corpus of his works belongs almost entirely to the period after his 40th birthday.

His first attempt to establish himself in London was premature. He moved there with his wife Alice in 1889, but in 1891 they returned to Malvern, and he began to make a reputation more steadily with choral works: The Black Knight, The Light of Life, King Olaf and Caractacus. These were written within a specifically English tradition, but they were influenced also by German music from Weber, Schumann and Mendelssohn to Brahms and Wagner. The orchestral Enigma Variations (1899), in which each variation portrays a different friend of Elgar's, then proclaimed the belated arrival of a fully formed original style, taken further in the oratorio The Dream of Gerontius (1900), where the anxious chromaticism of a post-Parsifal manner is answered by the assurances of the Newman text: Elgar was himself a Roman Catholic, which may have been one cause of his personal insecurity. GROVEmusic

Cello Concerto

Elgar Cello Concerto[a] **Bloch** Schelomo[a] **Kabalevsky** Cello Concerto No 2 in G, Op 77[b] **Tchaikovsky** Variations on a Rococo Theme, Op 33[c]. Nocturne, Op 19 No 4[c]. Pezzo capriccioso, Op 62[c]. Andante cantabile, Op 11[c] **R Strauss** Don Quixote[d]
Steven Isserlis vc [a]**London Symphony Orchestra / Richard Hickox;** [b]**London Philharmonic Orchestra / Andrew Litton;** [c]**Chamber Orchestra of Europe / Sir John Eliot Gardiner;** [d]**Minnesota Orchestra / Edo de Waart**
Virgin Classics 561490-2 (51' · DDD) Recorded 1988
Ⓜ●

Cellists are apt to 'come of age' in recordings of the Elgar. Isserlis was no exception. This is a wonderful account of the Concerto – brave, imaginative, individual – indeed, quite the most personal in its perception of the piece since the treasurable Du Pré on EMI. And that, you'll appreciate, is saying something though not, we hasten to add, that the two readings are in any outward sense similar. Far from it. With Isserlis, the emotional tug is considerably less overt, the emphasis more on shadow and subtext than open heartache. Yet the inner light is no less intense, the phrasing no less rhapsodic in manner than Du Pré. On the contrary. This is free-range Elgar all right, and like Du Pré it comes totally without affectation. Both Isserlis and Du Pré take an appropriately generous line on the first movement's sorrowful song, with Isserlis the more reposeful, the more inclined to open out and savour key cadences. The Scherzo itself is quite simply better played than on any previous recording; the articulation and definition of the semiquaver 'fours' would, we're sure, have astonished even the composer himself. From a technical point of view Isserlis is easily the equal, and more, of any player currently before us. And if you still feel that Du Pré really did have the last word where the epilogue is concerned, then listen to Isserlis sinking with heavy heart into those pages preceding the return of

the opening declamation. He achieves a mesmerising fragility in the bars marked lento – one last backward glance, as it were – and the inwardness of the final diminuendo is something to be heard and remembered. Hickox and the LSO prove model collaborators. Don't on any account miss these performances.

Elgar Cello Concerto **Dvořák** Cello Concerto in B minor, B191
Maria Kliegel vc **Royal Philharmonic Orchestra / Michael Halász**
Naxos 8 550503 (73' · DDD)   Ⓢ

The technical accomplishment of Kliegel's playing is balanced by a richness of musical insight that won't disappoint. The boldness of the opening soliloquy recalls Du Pré at her finest, and yet Kliegel shares a yet deeper cup of grief in the world-weariness of the main first subject, carried with noble conviction. She takes a more improvisatory view in the lilting second group than Du Pré, though Schiff (Philips) is the most convincing of all in the transition back to the 9/8 at the close of the movement. The *Scherzo* is brilliantly done, and at a very fast tempo, but the conductor Michael Halász overlooks Elgar's precisely noted *A tempo* indication in response to the soloist's cantabile *largamente* statements at the end of each main section. The effect isn't only tedious, but is quite the reverse of the composer's intention, clearly stated in the score. The *Adagio* is thoughtfully played, avoiding unwelcome posturing or empty affectation, though Kliegel is, if anything, a little too cool and dispassionate here. The finale is superbly paced, with the rumbustious militarism of the orchestration never allowed to dominate. The recording was made at Henry Wood Hall, and is full bodied and emphatic in major *tutti*s, yet one might have wished the overall balance to favour the soloist more than it does.

Elgar Cello Concerto in E minor, Op 85a   Ⓗ
Bruch Kol nidrei, Op 47[b] **Dvořák** Cello Concerto[c]
Pablo Casals vc [a]**BBC Symphony Orchestra / Sir Adrian Boult;** [b]**London Symphony Orchestra / Sir Landon Ronald;** [c]**Czech Philharmonic Orchestra / George Szell**
EMI Références mono 763498-2 (75' · ADD)
Recorded 1936-45   Ⓜ●●

It scarcely seems necessary to write anything further about Casals's famous recordings of the Dvořák and Elgar concertos, which have long been recognised as classics of the recorded repertoire. The former, destined to mark a standard for generations, and seemingly played with a sword rather than a bow, still exercises a powerful effect: the incandescent solo playing is so mesmeric that one can accept the rather harsh and dry orchestral sound which betrays its age (from 1937). Some of Casals's passionate quality may have been due to his decision to break out of his self-imposed restricted activities caused

ELGAR'S CELLO CONCERTO – IN BRIEF

Beatrice Harrison; New SO / Sir Edward Elgar
EMI British Composers 567298-2 (75' · ADD) Ⓜ
For all her occasional falliblity, Harrison displays enormous conviction, compassion and tender vulnerability. Elgar's accompaniment is a miracle of flexiblity and grace.

Pablo Casals; BBC SO / Sir Adrian Boult
Biddulph LAB144 (79' · ADD) Ⓜ
Backed by Boult at his authoritative best, Casals brings an irresistible physicality and capricious temperament to Elgar's nostalgic inspiration. Despite one or two wayward touches from the soloist, an account to hear.

André Navarra; Hallé Orchestra / Sir John Barbirolli
Testament SBT1204 (65' · ADD) Ⓕ
A real, breathing performance, captivating in its bright-eyed, lean manners and intensely warm-hearted, with a slow movement that approaches perfection in its songful restraint.

Jacqueline du Pré; London SO / Sir John Barbirolli
EMI 556806-2 (54' · ADD) ⒻⓄⓄⓄ
For countless collectors the world over, du Pré's immortal 1965 recording with Barbirolli and the LSO tugs at the heartstrings like no other version before or since.

Steven Isserlis; London SO / Richard Hickox
Virgin Classics ② 561490 2 (156' · DDD) ⓂⓄ
Unusually self-effacing, Isserlis eschews any vestige of overheated, heart-on-sleeve exaggeration. Intimacy and wistfulness are the keynotes.

Maria Kliegel; Royal PO / Michael Halász
Naxos 8 550503 (73' · DDD) Ⓢ
Kliegel is a most accomplished, passionate soloist, though sentiment occasionally topples over into sentimentality. Eminently acceptable, wide-ranging sound.

Truls Mørk; CBSO / Sir Simon Rattle
Virgin Classics 545356 2 (65' · DDD) Ⓢ
Mørk and Rattle form an intelligent, dignified and irreproachably stylish partnership. Top-notch production-values. Comes with an equally compelling Britten Cello Symphony.

Pieter Wispelwey; Netherlands RPO / Jac van Steen
Channel Classics CCS12998 (54' · DDD) Ⓕ
Wispelwey is acutely alive to the strong strain of classicism that runs through Elgar's autumnal masterpiece. An unforced, deeply satisfying reading, with splendidly bright-eyed orchestral playing.

by the Spanish civil war: the astute Fred Gaisberg, hearing that he had consented to appear with Szell in Prague, talked them into making a recording the day after the concert. About Casals's Elgar there has always been controversy: his reading was heavily criticised as over-emotional ('un-English') when he first played it in London before the war, but when he returned in 1945 and performed it, according to Boult, in exactly the same way, it was said that 'in the deeply meditative sections...it reached an Elgarian mood of wistfulness that few artists understand.'

Additional recommendation

Coupled with: **Lutosławski** Cello Concerto
Wispelwey vc **Netherlands Radio Philharmonic Orchestra / Van Steen**
Channel Classics CCS12998 (54' · DDD) Ⓕ
The utterly sympathetic performance of the Elgar displays both elasticity and plentiful re-creative fantasy. A notable achievement in every way.

Violin Concerto in B minor

Elgar Violin Concerto **Vaughan Williams** The Lark Ascending
Nigel Kennedy vn **City of Birmingham Symphony Orchestra / Sir Simon Rattle**
EMI 556413-2 (72' · ADD) ⒻⓄ

Astonishingly, in the case of the first two movements at least, this release, recorded during the week following a live concert at Birmingham's Symphony Hall in July 1997, fully re-creates the heady excitement of that memorable event. From every conceivable point of view – authority, panache, intelligence, intuitive poetry, tonal beauty and emotional maturity – Kennedy surpasses his 1985 *Gramophone* Award-winning EMI Eminence recording (now on HMV Classics). The first movement is a magnificent achievement all round, with tension levels extraordinarily high for a studio project. Rattle launches the proceedings in exemplary fashion, his direction passionate, ideally flexible and texturally lucid (the antiphonally divided violins help). The CBSO, too, is on top form. But it's Kennedy who rivets the attention from his commanding initial entry onwards. There's no hiding in this of all scores and Kennedy penetrates to the very essence of 'the soul enshrined within' in his melting presentation of the 'Windflower' theme – Elgar's *dolce semplice* realised to tear-spilling perfection. The slow movement is almost as fine. Only the finale oddly dissatisfies. Not in terms of technical address or co-ordination (both of which are stunning); rather, for all the supreme accomplishment on show, the results aren't terribly moving. Despite any lingering doubts about this last movement we're still left with an enormously stimulating and well-engineered display. The fill-up is a provocative account of *The Lark Ascending*, which Kennedy (whose tone is ravishing) and Rattle spin out to 17 and a half minutes.

Violin Concerto[a]. Cello Concerto[b]   H
[a]**Yehudi Menuhin** vn [b]**Beatrice Harrison** vc
[a]**London Symphony Orchestra,** [b]**New Symphony Orchestra / Sir Edward Elgar**
EMI Great Recordings of the Century mono
566979-2 (75' · AAD) Recorded 1932, 1928   Ⓜ**OOO**

 Elgar's conducting for Menuhin in the Violin Concerto's opening orchestral *tutti* is magnificent, as is his solicitous, attentive accompaniment throughout the work. Menuhin's youthful, wonderfully intuitive musicianship in fact needed little 'instruction', and the success of the recording may be judged from the fact that there have been few periods in the years since it was first issued when it hasn't been available in some shape or form. Beatrice Harrison first studied the Cello Concerto for an abridged, pre-electric recording with Elgar conducting. So impressed was the composer then that he insisted that she should be the soloist whenever he conducted the work again. Their authoritative performance is deeply felt and highly expressive, but it has a quality of nobility and stoicism which comes as a refreshing change from some overindulgent modern performances.

Since the original matrices were destroyed, EMI's engineers had to return to the 1957 tape for this transfer; although the 1957 engineers did not quite capture all the body of the originals there's an impressive clarity in the transfer, now brightened a little more for CD. The 1970s transfer of the Harrison/Elgar Cello Concerto was impressively managed, and this reissue has given still more presence to the sound without any sense of falsification.

Elgar Violin Concerto in B minor, Op 61[b]   H
Delius Violin Concerto[a]
Albert Sammons vn [a]**Liverpool Philharmonic Orchestra / Malcolm Sargent;** [b]**New Queen's Hall Orchestra / Henry Wood**
Naxos Historical mono 8 110951 (67' · ADD)
Recorded [b]1929, [a]1944   Ⓢ**OOO**

 Albert Sammons' 1929 account of Elgar's Violin Concerto with Sir Henry Wood and the New Queen's Hall Orchestra remains the finest version ever made, outstripping even the legendary Menuhin/Elgar collaboration from three years later in terms of authoritative grip, intuitive poetry and emotional candour. Previous transfers to CD have varied from satisfactory to merely tolerable and unacceptably botched. So it's a pleasure to encounter Mark Obert-Thorn's judicious restoration for Naxos.

Delius heard Sammons perform the Elgar in May 1915, and was so bowled over that he set about writing a concerto for the formidable virtuoso. Sammons premièred the work with Boult

in January 1919 but had to wait a full quarter of a century before committing it to disc. Here is another irreplaceable document: Sammons was an assiduous champion of this glorious music, and although the solo playing hasn't quite the effortless technical mastery of its companion here, his wise and unforced interpretation penetrates to the very core of Delius's lovely vision. An admirable introduction to a truly great fiddler, irresistible at the price.

Additional recommendation

Violin Concerto
Kennedy vn **London Philharmonic Orchestra / Handley**
Classics for Pleasure 575 139-2 (54' · DDD)   Ⓑ
Kennedy's superb first recording of the Elgar Violin Concerto won the *Gramophone* Record of the Year in 1985 and is now at bargain price.

Symphonies

No 1 in A flat, Op 55; **No 2** in E flat, Op 63; **No 3** in C minor, Op 88

Symphony No 1[a]. Falstaff, Op 68[b]   H
London Symphony Orchestra / Sir Edward Elgar
EMI 567296-2 (80' · ADD) Recorded [a]1930, [b]1931
      Ⓜ**OO**

Symphony No 2   H
London Symphony Orchestra / Sir Edward Elgar
EMI 567297-2 (57' · ADD) Recorded 1927   Ⓜ**OO**

Cello Concerto in E minor, Op 85[a]. Cockaigne,   H
Op 40[b]. Falstaff, Op 68[c] – Interludes. Froissart,
Op 19[d]. In the South, Op 50[e]
[a]**Beatrice Harrison** vc [d]**London Philharmonic Orchestra;** [b]**Royal Albert Hall Orchestra;** [e]**London Symphony Orchestra;** [ac]**New Symphony Orchestra / Sir Edward Elgar**
EMI 567298-2 (75' · ADD) Recorded [b]1926, [a]1928, [c]1929, [e]1930, [d]1933   Ⓜ**OO**

The blockbuster coupling here (clocking in at nearly 80 minutes) has to be that of the First Symphony and *Falstaff*, both of which receive readings that leave you gasping in wonder at the astonishing vitality, entrancing poetry and daring flexibility of Elgar's conducting. Certainly, this is a *Falstaff* brimful of humanity, irresistible narrative flair and (at the close) heart-rending poignancy. As for the symphony, never was there a more wistful treatment of the *Scherzo*'s enchanting trio section, while the work's thrilling closing pages have surely never resounded with greater cumulative swagger.

Similarly, the composer's 1927 version of the Second Symphony enshrines another inspirational display, its huge expressive fervour and blistering intensity shining like a beacon across the decades. First-timers should listen out for the generous use of *portamento*, to say nothing of the staggering reserves of *sostenuto* tone Elgar

ELGAR'S SYMPHONIES – IN BRIEF

London PO / Sir Georg Solti
Decca ② 443 856-2DF2 (135' · ADD)   Ⓜ
Solti drives hard in any faster music but both slow movements have a tingling concentration and rapt hush that are deeply affecting. The LPO respond brilliantly throughout; lustrous Decca sound, too.

Philharmonia Orchestra / Bernard Haitink
EMI ② 569761-2 (118' · DDD)   Ⓜ
Noble, reflective and meticulously etched readings under the Dutch maestro, beautifully played by the Philharmonia. Discerning Elgarians will find much to reward them here.

SYMPHONY NO 1

London SO / Sir Edward Elgar
EMI 567296-2 (80' · ADD)   Ⓜ**OO**
As ever on the podium, Elgar is very much his own man. This 1930 recording of the First enshrines an extraordinarily malleable, uniquely involving document. Generously paired with Elgar's inspirational 1931 version of his 'symphonic study' *Falstaff*.

London SO / Sir Colin Davis
LSO Live LSO0017 (55' · DDD)   Ⓢ
Sir Colin's unhurried conception is crowned by a superbly exciting reading of the finale that sweeps all before it. The Barbican acoustic is not ideally opulent, but don't let that minor caveat put you off.

SYMPHONY NO 2

Hallé Orchestra / Sir John Barbirolli
EMI 764724-2 (66' · ADD)   Ⓜ**O**
A richly expansive performance, delivered by the Hallé *con amore*, with the slow movement in particular rising to an indescribable peak of emotion. One to snap up.

BBC SO / Sir Andrew Davis
Apex 0927-49586-2 (78' · DDD)   Ⓢ**OO**
Few rivals come close to equalling the all-round perception displayed by Sir Andrew Davis in his 1991 account of Elgar's multi-faceted masterpiece. With its meaty coupling of *In the South*, this is an exceptional bargain.

SYMPHONY NO 3

London SO / Sir Colin Davis
LSO Live LSO0019 (58' · DDD)   Ⓢ
Recorded live at the Barbican in 2001, Sir Colin Davis's dedicated interpretation more than matches both its predecessors on NMC and Naxos. The slow movement is the kernel here, almost unbearably moving in its intimacy and heartache.

draws from the LSO strings (hardly a top-ranking group at the time). Recorded over just one day, this rapt performance was rush-released in time for Elgar's 70th birthday on June 2. Six weeks later Elgar remade the first side of the *Rondo* third movement (producer Fred Gaisberg having meanwhile noticed 'foreign noises' in the original take), and it was from those July 1927 sessions that the tantalising five-minute rehearsal sequence derives (the unique shellac pressing of which Elgar was extremely fond of playing to visitors at his home).

The third disc kicks off with a rivetingly characterful *Froissart* from February 1933, followed by an astoundingly charismatic *Cockaigne* with the Royal Albert Hall Orchestra (Elgar's very first recording for the electric microphone, set down in April 1926). Exhilarating is the only word to describe the 1930 account of *In the South* with the LSO, the music's thrusting grandeur and intimacy of feeling seamlessly integrated into a searingly cogent whole. We also get an agreeably bluff, aptly rustic rendering of the two 'Dream Interludes' from *Falstaff*, and the anthology concludes with Beatrice Harrison's big-hearted, wonderfully touching 1928 performance of the Cello Concerto.

The First Symphony's scherzo still sounds pretty uncongenial. Otherwise, the sound is often remarkably vivid, with a commendable truthfulness of timbre on the third disc not quite matched by the first two (containing the symphonies and *Falstaff*).

Symphony No 1. Serenade for Strings. Chanson de nuit, Op 15 No 1. Chanson de matin, Op 15 No 2
London Philharmonic Orchestra / Sir Adrian Boult
EMI 764013-2 (70' · DDD) Recorded 1968-76 Ⓜ**OOO**

Ⓖ   Boult in Elgar on CD: the combination is irresistible, particularly when in addition to the symphony it comes with substantial and valuable makeweights. The 1976 recording of the symphony is among the last that Boult made of Elgar, a noble, unforced reading with no hint of extreme speeds in either direction. In Boult's view the flow of the music is kept free and direct, with *rallentandos* and *tenutos* reduced to the minimum in the links between sections. The sound in this digital transfer is first rate, every bit as fine as the original LP. The brass is gloriously full, which with Elgar is one of the main necessities.

On the fill-ups, more than in the symphony, the analogue original is revealed in the degree of tape-hiss, noticeable but not distracting, and if anything the 1973 recording of the *Serenade* brings sound even more vivid in its sense of presence than that of the bigger ensemble. Boult so naturally conveys the tenderness and delicacy of the inspiration, and so it is too in the two shorter pieces from 1968 with violin tone noticeably less full and rounded but still sweet enough. The couplings will for many be irresistible.

Symphony No 1 in A flat, Op 55. Introduction and Allegro, Op 47
Hallé Orchestra / Sir John Barbirolli
BBC Legends/IMG Artists BBCL4106-2 (67' · ADD)
Recorded live 1970   Ⓕⓞ

On July 24, 1970 Sir John Barbirolli conducted (and recorded) this inspired Hallé performance of Elgar's First Symphony in St Nicholas's Chapel, as his major contribution to the King's Lynn Festival. Four days later he suffered a fatal heart attack. There could be no finer memorial, for the acoustic of the chapel provides a wonderfully warm glow and the richest amplitude for the Hallé brass and strings, without blunting the *fortissimo*s. The depth of feeling and power in the performance has the genuine thrill of live music-making. For instance, there's an extraordinary central climax in the first movement, with the brass outbursts given a terrifying intensity; the apotheosis of the finale has similar emotional strength. Barbirolli invests the symphony's slow sad motto theme with a poignant nostalgia each time it appears; but most memorable of all is the richness of the opening of the *Adagio*, sustained throughout with Barbirolli's characteristic warmth of feeling, while the impassioned Hallé string playing is as rich in tone as it's heartfelt.

Fascinatingly, the interpretation looks back to his first 1956 Pye recording with his own orchestra (available on Dutton Laboratories). Both performances play for a little over 52 minutes, and the timings of each movement and the flexible inner relationships of tempo are very close. But this final version matches and even surpasses that first venture in its surging forward momentum, and the sound is far richer, obviously more modern. Everyone has their favourite version among the six, but no Elgarian will be disappointed with this account.

Symphony No 1 in A flat, Op 55
London Symphony Orchestra / Sir Colin Davis
LSO Live LSO0017 (55' · DDD)   Ⓢ Ⓢⓞⓞ

This thrillingly combustible account easily holds its own in the most exalted company. Davis's is a patient, noble conception, yet lacking absolutely nothing in thrusting drama, fresh-faced character and tender poetry. Certainly, Sir Colin steers a marvellously confident course through the epic first movement, the music-making always comprehensive in its emotional scope and hitting genuine heights in the development. The *Scherzo* is another great success, the glinting, defiant swagger of the outer portions counterbalanced by the delectable grace and point these eloquent players lavish on the Trio. Just one small interpretative quibble: Davis's inorganic slackening of tempo during the sublime transition into the slow movement (listen to Barbirolli's unforgettable 1956 Hallé account to hear how it should be done). As for the great *Adagio* itself, Davis's intensely devotional approach works beauti-

fully. The finale positively surges with purposeful bite, fire and sinew, while the glorious closing pages really do raise the roof. The expertly balanced sound doesn't have quite the bloom that EMI and Decca achieved for Boult and Solti on their classic analogue versions, but it amply conveys the tingling electricity and physical impact of a special event. At this price, this is one to snap up.

Symphony No 1[a]. In the South, 'Alassio', Op 50[b] Ⓗ
London Philharmonic Orchestra / Sir Adrian Boult
Testament mono SBT1229 (69' · DDD) Recorded
[a]1949, [b]1955   Ⓕⓞⓞⓞ

The first wonder of this very welcome transfer fis the astonishing quality of the sound, mono only but full-bodied and finely detailed to give a keener sense of presence than the rather disappointing CD transfer of the 1976 stereo version, with a surprisingly wide dynamic range for a 1949 recording. When Boult recorded that final stereo version, he was already 87, and though as ever the reading is a noble one, beautifully paced, it has nothing like the same thrust and tension as this recording of nearly three decades earlier. In particular the heavenly *Adagio* has an extra meditative intensity in the way that Boult presents each of the great lyrical themes. The finale in particular has a bite and thrust far beyond that of the later account.

Boult's recording of *In the South*, made in 1955, brings out his thrustful side even more strikingly, with urgent speeds giving way in the lovely *Canto popolare* section to a honeyed beauty before an urgent yet finely controlled account of the coda. Sadly, the 1955 sound is shallower than that of six years earlier for the symphony, though there's ample weight for the brass theme of the second section.

Symphony No 2. In the South
BBC Symphony Orchestra / Sir Andrew Davis
Warner Apex 0927-49586-2 (78' · DDD) Recorded
1992   Ⓢ Ⓢⓞⓞ

In his finest achievement on record, Andrew Davis penetrates to the dark inner core of this great symphony. In the opening *Allegro vivace e nobilmente*, for example, how well he and his acutely responsive players gauge the varying moods of Elgar's glorious inspiration: be it in the exhilarating surge of that leaping introductory paragraph or the spectral, twilight world at the heart of this wonderful movement, no one is found wanting. In fact, Davis's unerring structural sense never once deserts him, and the BBC Symphony Orchestra plays its heart out. Above all, it's in the many more reflective moments that Davis proves himself an outstandingly perceptive Elgarian, uncovering a vein of intimate anguish that touches to the very marrow; in this respect, his account of the slow movement is quite heart-rendingly poignant – undoubtedly the finest since Boult's incomparable 1944 performance with this very same orchestra – while the radiant sunset of the symphony's coda glows with luminous beauty. Prefaced by an equally idiomatic, stirring *In the South*, this is an Elgar Second to set beside the very greatest. In every way a treasurable release.

Symphony No 2
BBC Philharmonic Orchestra / Sir Edward Downes
Naxos 8 550635 (56' · DDD) Recorded 1993　　Ⓢ●

Here's further proof that Edward Downes is an Elgarian to be reckoned with. This account of the Second Symphony is up there with the very best. In the first movement, Downes steers a clear-sighted course: here's the same unexaggerated, splendidly authoritative conception heard from this conductor in the concert hall. Unlike some rivals on record, Downes resists the temptation to give too much too soon, and this feeling of power in reserve lends an extra cumulative intensity to the proceedings; indeed, the coda here is absolutely thrilling. The ensuing *Larghetto* sees Downes striking a near-perfect balance between introspection and heart-warming passion. Both the *Rondo* and finale are ideally paced – the former not too hectic, the latter flowing to perfection, culminating in an epilogue of rare delicacy. Throughout, the BBC Philharmonic plays outstandingly for its former chief: the orchestra's golden-toned cello section must be singled out for special praise. Just a touch more clarity in *tuttis*, and the recording would have been ideal. A deeply sympathetic reading, possessing qualities to match any rival.

Additional recommendations

Symphony No 2

Coupled with: Symphony No 1. Pomp and Circumstance March No 5
Philharmonia / Haitink
EMI Double Forte ② 569761-2 (118' · DDD)　　Ⓜ
The cumulative intensity of Haitink's interpretation is overwhelming in its clear-sightedness and emotional impact.

Coupled with: Sea Pictures
Greevy *mez* **London Philharmonic Orchestra / Handley**
Classics for Pleasure 575 306-2(DDD) Recorded 1980
Another superb account. An unerringly　　Ⓑ
paced reading, this is plainly a version which all Elgarians will want.

Coupled with: Serenade
Hallé Orchestra / Loughran; Academy of St Martin in the Fields / Marriner
ASV Quicksilva CDQS6087 (70' · DDD)　　Ⓢ
This super-budget Second is well worth anyone's money. The Hallé respond with sure-footed discipline and their playing lacks nothing in whole-hearted application or fervour.

Symphony No 3
Bournemouth Symphony Orchestra / Paul Daniel
Naxos 8 554719 (55' · DDD)　　ⓈOO

How thrillingly urgent Elgar's unforgettably gaunt introductory bars sound here – a magnificent launch-pad for an interpretation of unswerving dedication, plentiful character and intelligence. Audibly galvanised by Paul Daniel's direction, the Bournemouth orchestra responds with infectious eagerness, polish and, most important, all the freshness of new discovery. In these newcomers' hands there's a rhythmic snap and athletic drive about the mighty opening movement that exhilarate. Where Davis perhaps scores over Daniel is in the spiritual, 'inner' dimension he brings to those ineffably beautiful bars at the start of the development section. Come the succeeding *Allegretto*, and Daniel's approach is more urgent, less evocative. The anguished slow movement welds a penetrating textural and harmonic clarity to a noble strength that's very moving. Best of all is the finale, which now emerges in a rather less piecemeal fashion than it does under Davis. Particularly good is the dark swagger that Daniel locates in both the *nobilmente* paragraphs, while the closing bars are magical, the final soft tam-tam stroke disappearing into the ether like some vast unanswered question. The sound is excellent in every respect. Another jewel in the Naxos crown, not to be missed.

Additional recommendation

Symphony No 3
BBC Symphony Orchestra / A Davis
NMC NMCD053 (56' · DDD)　　Ⓕ
An eloquent, profoundly involving performance with demonstration-worthy sound.

Enigma Variations

Variations on an Original Theme, 'Enigma', Op 36.
Cockaigne Overture, Op 40. Introduction and Allegro, Op 47. Serenade for Strings
BBC Symphony Orchestra / Sir Andrew Davis
Warner Apex 0927-41371-2 (74' · DDD) Recorded 1991　　Ⓢ

These are four of the best Elgar performances on disc available. First, the recording is superb, with near-perfect balance and a really natural sound. Second, the playing of the BBC Symphony Orchestra is first rate. Andrew Davis's conducting of all four works is inspired, as if he had forgotten all preconceived notions and other interpretations, gone back to the scores and given us what he found there. In *Cockaigne*, for example, the subtle use of *ritardando*, sanctioned in the score, gives the music that elasticity which Elgar considered to be an ideal requisite for interpreting his works. The poetry and wit of this masterpiece emerge with renewed freshness. As for the *Enigma* Variations, instead of wondering why another recording was thought necessary, you'll find yourself rejoicing that such a fine performance has been preserved to be set alongside other treasured versions. Each of the 'friends pictured within' is strongly characterised by Davis, but without exaggeration or interpretative quirks. Tempos are just right and the orchestral playing captures the authentic Elgarian sound in a manner Boult would have recognised. Similarly, in the *Introduction and Allegro*, how beautifully the string quartet is recorded, how magical are the gentle and so eloquent pizzicatos which punctuate the flow of the great melody. The fugue is played with real zest and enjoyment. This is music on a large scale and is played and conducted in that way, whereas the early *Serenade* is intimate and dewy-eyed and that's how it sounds here.

Elgar 'Enigma' Variations[e] Three Bavarian Dances, Op 27 – Lullaby[d]. **Barbirolli** An Elizabethan Suite[a] **Bax** The Garden of Fand[b] **Butterworth** A Shropshire Lad[c] **Ireland** The Forgotten Rite[f]. Mai-Dun[g]. These Things Shall Be[h] **Purcell** Suite for Strings[i] **Vaughan Williams** Fantasia on 'Greensleeves'[j]. Fantasia on a Theme by Thomas Tallis[k].
[h]**Parry Jones** *ten* **Hallé** [h]**Choir and Orchestra / Sir John Barbirolli**
Dutton Laboratories mono ② CDSJB1022 (140' · ADD) Recorded at Houldsworth Hall, Manchester [k]1946, [e]1947, [ih]1948; [d]Kingsway Hall, London 1947; [fg]Abbey Road Studio, London 1949; Free Trade Hall, Manchester [a]1954, [bci]1956   Ⓑ**O**

The long-buried treasure here is Barbirolli's very first recording of Elgar's Enigma Variations, never previously issued. It was recorded in Manchester in May 1947, only months before Barbirolli made his first published recording at EMI's St John's Wood studio. This newly unearthed version narrowly becomes the favourite rather than the later one. Both versions are perfectly satisfying in terms of sound, but interpretatively this unpublished version brings added advantages. The opening statement of the theme is lighter, more flowing and less emphatic, while even more important, 'Nimrod' is more warmly emotional, more spontaneous in expression, and the 'EDU' finale, taken at a marginally slower tempo, has no hint of the breathlessness which slightly mars the October performance at the end, again more warmly spontaneous sounding. Significantly Barbirolli's later stereo version of Enigma also adopts the slightly broader, less hectic speed.

The two Vaughan Williams items have never appeared before on CD, and both are very welcome. They may be less weighty than Barbirolli's stereo remakes, but the *Tallis Fantasia*, featuring a vintage quartet of Hallé principals, separates the quartet more clearly from the main body than the version with the Sinfonia of London, and again is more warmly expressive. The extra lightness of *Greensleeves*, too, sounds more spontaneous. Disc one contains the shorter works of Bax, Butterworth and Ireland.

ELGAR ENIGMA VARIATIONS – IN BRIEF

Royal Albert Hall Orchestra / Sir Edward Elgar
EMI 566979-2 (67' · ADD)   Ⓜ
Elgar's own 1926 recording positively oozes spontaneity and fantasy. Harnessed to the 14-year-old Menuhin's legendary 1932 version (with the composer) of the Violin Concerto.

Hallé Orchestra / Sir John Barbirolli
Dutton ② CDSJB1022 (140' · ADD)   Ⓑ**O**
The first of Sir John's four recordings. Never previously issued, it features irrepressible playing and conducting of rare perception. Other Hallé/Barbirolli highlights on this Dutton double-pack include Bax's *Garden of Fand* and Ireland's *Mai-Dun* and *The Forgotten Rite*.

Hallé Orchestra / Sir John Barbirolli
EMI/IMG Artists ② 575100-2 (150' · ADD)   Ⓜ
Barbirolli's first stereo *Enigma*, originally engineered by a Mercury production-team for Pye, is a gloriously uninhibited conception. A heartwarming, indeed life-enhancing experience.

London SO / Pierre Monteux
Decca 452 303-2DCS (78' · ADD)   Ⓜ
Another vernally fresh interpretation from a great conductor. Monteux brings plenty of revealing insights to bear, the LSO are on top form and Decca's 1958 Kingsway Hall sound is astonishingly undated.

London SO / Sir Adrian Boult
EMI 567748-2 (79' · ADD)   Ⓜ**O**
Sir Adrian's noble 1970 *Enigma* (the last of his four versions) dates from towards the start of his Indian summer in the recording studio, and remains a central recommendation.

Royal PO / Norman Del Mar
DG 429 713-2GGA (58' · ADD)   Ⓜ
The voluble expressive freedom of this interpretation owes much to the composer's own. Similarly, Del Mar invests the *Pomp and Circumstance Marches* with terrific élan.

Czech PO / Leopold Stokowski
Cala CACD0524 (76' · ADD)   Ⓜ
Stokowski's only Elgar recording enshrines an interpetation of abundant charisma and glowing affection. The sheer energy of it all is astounding, especially when you remember that the Old Magician had just turned 90!

Baltimore SO / David Zinman
Telarc CD80192 (62' · DDD)   Ⓜ
Now reissued at mid-price, Zinman's eagle-eyed, exceptionally poised account is a real tonic, and receives top-drawer Telarc sound to boot.

The performances all have a passionate thrust typical of Barbirolli, with the tenor, Parry Jones, and the Hallé Chorus matching the orchestra in their commitment.

'Enigma' Variations[a]. Pomp and Circumstance Marches, Op 39[b]
[a]**London Symphony Orchestra,** [b]**London Philharmonic Orchestra / Sir Adrian Boult**
EMI 764015-2 (55' · ADD) Recorded 1970, 1976 Ⓜ**OO**

Boult's 1970 recording of the *Enigma* Variations offers similar riches to those of Barbirolli with the additional bonus of a slightly superior recorded sound. Boult's account has authority, freshness and a beautiful sense of spontaneity: each variation emerges from the preceding one with a natural feeling of flow and progression. There's warmth and affection, coupled with an air of nobility and poise, and the listener is always acutely aware that this is a performance by a great conductor who's lived a lifetime with the music. You need only sample the passionate stirrings of Variation 1 (the composer's wife), the athletic and boisterous 'Troyte' variation, or the autumnal, elegiac glow of the famous 'Nimrod' variation to realise that this is a very special document indeed. The LSO, on top form, plays with superlative skill and poetry and the excellent recording has been exceptionally well transferred to CD. The *Pomp and Circumstance* Marches, recorded six years later with the London Philharmonic Orchestra, are invigoratingly fresh and direct – indeed the performances are so full of energy and good humour that it's hard to believe that Boult was in his late eighties at the time of recording! A classic.

Additional recommendations

'Enigma' Variations
Coupled with: Cockaigne. Serenade. Salut d'amor
Baltimore Symphony Orchestra / Zinman
Telarc CD80192 (62' · DDD)   Ⓕ
 An impressive performance. Zinman has the feel for the ebb and flow, the elasticity of the music, and he obtains idiomatic playing from the excellent Baltimore SO.

Coupled with: Serenade in E minor, Op 20[a].
Vaughan Williams The Lark Ascending[a]. Tallis Fantasia[b]. Fantasia on Greensleeves[b]
[a]**London Philharmonic Orchestra;** [b]**Royal Liverpool Philharmonic Orchestra / Handley**
Classics for Pleasure 574 880-2 (76' · DDD)   Ⓑ
 The LPO have an ease with the *Variations* and the freshness of the *Serenade* that reveal deep acquaintance. The depth of understanding in the VW recordings is just as acute, with Handley bringing control and intensity to the *Tallis* Fantasia.

Falstaff

Falstaff. 'Enigma' Variations. Grania and Diarmid – Incidental Music; Funeral March

City of Birmingham Symphony Orchestra / Sir Simon Rattle
EMI British Composers 555001-2 (79' ·DDD)
Recorded 1992-3   Ⓕ

Rattle gives us perhaps the most meticulously prepared and subtly blended *Falstaff* ever committed to disc. His keen intellect and almost fanatical fidelity to the letter of the score team up to produce the most invigorating, wittily observant results. However, it's a bit like viewing a pristinely restored portrait of Shakespeare's fat knight, whereas Barbirolli presents us with the lovable, vulnerable creature of flesh and blood himself – his epilogue really does touch to the marrow every time. In *Enigma* the results are always enjoyable and refreshing, with myriad details in Elgar's lovingly woven, orchestral canvas adroitly pinpointed. A fine, deeply felt performance. The most completely successful item here is the glorious *Grania and Diarmid* incidental music: the magnificent 'Funeral March' is one of Elgar's most inspired creations, and Rattle gauges its brooding melancholy most eloquently. Balance is impeccable (and the transfer level comparatively low) in all three works, although the quality in *Falstaff* isn't quite as rich and glowing as it's elsewhere. Overall, this is an exceedingly stimulating release.

Pomp and Circumstance Marches

Pomp and Circumstance, Op 39 – No 1 in D[a];   Ⓗ
No 2 in A minor[a]; No 3 in C minor[b]; No 4 in G[a]; No 5 in C[b]. The Dream of Gerontius, Op 38 – Prelude[c]. Serenade in E minor, Op 20[d]. Improvisation No 4[f]. Salut d'amour, Op 12[e]. Chanson de nuit, Op 15 No 1[e]. Chanson de matin, Op 15 No 2[b]. Land of Hope and Glory[b]. Cockaigne, Op 40[a]
[a]**BBC Symphony Orchestra,** [b]**London Symphony Orchestra,** [c]**Royal Albert Hall Orchestra,** [d]**London Philharmonic Orchestra,** [e]**New Symphony Orchestra / Sir Edward Elgar**[f] pf
HMV Classics mono HMV5 74001-2 (77' · ADD)
Recorded 1926-33   Ⓑ**O**

The five *Pomp and Circumstance* marches are taken from recordings of different vintages. The earliest, No 3, made in 1927, is thinner in sound than No 5, recorded in 1930 when it was new, and Nos 1, 2 and 4. Those are among Elgar's last recordings, made with the BBC Symphony Orchestra in 1932 and 1933. As with the *Cockaigne Overture*, also performed by the then recently founded BBC Symphony Orchestra, the sound as transferred is splendidly full bodied, the Elgarian trombones rasping out wonderfully well. As for the performances, one can almost see Elgar's great moustache bristling at the panache of the playing, and the delightful lilt he gives to such a motif as the Dvořákian theme in No 3. Broadly, as ever, Elgar favours speeds on the fast side, here and elsewhere, but then allows ripely romantic expansion in big expressive moments, as in the dedicated account of the *Gerontius* Prelude. Recorded live in 1927 at the Royal Albert Hall, that comes in limited but wonderfully atmospheric sound, leading on to the tenor's first entry. Setting the seal on this issue are two of the shortest and most moving items – one of the strangely intense piano improvisations he recorded for HMV with uninhibitedly splashy playing, and the brief account of *Land of Hope and Glory* he recorded with the LSO for a Pathé newsreel at the opening of the EMI Studios in Abbey Road in 1931. That brings a gruff but moving speech from Elgar: 'Gentlemen, please play this tune as though you've never heard it before.' That alone is worth the money.

Piano Quintet

Piano Quintet in A minor, Op 84. String Quartet in E minor, Op 82. In Moonlight (for viola and piano)
Piers Lane *pf* **James Boyd** *va* **Vellinger Quartet**
Classics for Pleasure 575980-2 (65' · DDD) Recorded 1994   ⓑ〇

This set represents an outstanding bargain. When it first appeared on EMI Eminence, the Vellinger Quartet's coupling fairly bowled this critic over. These are performances to which you'll return again and again, for their ardour, spontaneity and impeccable address – though just a fraction more wistful intimacy would not have gone amiss. Sandwiched between the two main items here, the miniature for viola and piano, *In Moonlight*, leaves a haunting impression. Vividly engineered and at bargain price, this is an issue to treasure.

Violin Works

Romance in C minor, Op 1. Pieces, Op 4 – No 1, Idylle; No 3, Virelai. Mazurka in C minor, Op 10 No 1. Salut d'amour. Bizarrerie in G minor, Op 13 No 2. Chanson de nuit. Chanson de matin. La capricieuse, Op 17. Gavotte in A. Etude-Caprice (cpted Reed). Serenade. May Song. In Hammersbach. Carissima. Adieu. Etudes characteristiques
Marat Bisengaliev *vn* **Benjamin Frith** *pf*
Black Box BBM1016 (67' · DDD)   Ⓕ

Born in 1962, Marat Bisengaliev is a prize-winning graduate from the Moscow Conservatory. On the evidence of this most enjoyable disc he's a violinist of great technical accomplishment and communicative warmth, and he generates a really fine rapport with Benjamin Frith. As the opening *Romance* immediately reveals, these artists bring an affectingly uncloying, totally unforced naturalness of expression to this charming repertoire. Even such well-worn nuggets as the two *Chansons* and *Salut d'amour* emerge with a new-minted freshness. Only in *La capricieuse* do you feel that the *rubato* lacks the last ounce of spontaneity. Elsewhere, the programme usefully plugs a number of gaps in the Elgar discography, not least the delec-

table *Bizarrerie*, Op 13 No 2, *Virelai* (1884) and a cheeky *Gavotte* from the following year. The winsome *In Hammersbach* will be more familiar as the second of the *Three Bavarian Dances*. Eagle-eyed enthusiasts will also have spotted two world-première recordings in the contents listed above: it was left to violinist W H Reed to complete the *Etude-Caprice* that Elgar first sketched as long ago as 1877, while the ferocious difficulty of the five solo *Etudes characteristiques* of 1878 has long put off any potential champions on disc (and Bisengaliev rises to the challenge with fearless aplomb). Piano tone seems a touch metallic at the outset, but the ear soon adjusts, and balance within is generally excellent.

Elgar Violin Sonata in E minor, Op 82 **Finzi** Elegy in F, Op 22 **Walton** Violin Sonata
Daniel Hope *vn* **Simon Mulligan** *pf*
Nimbus NI5666 (62' · DDD)   Ⓟ〇〇〇

The coupling of the violin sonatas by Elgar and Walton is a most satisfying one, not unique on disc, and one which provides fascinating parallels. The Finzi *Elegy* is a very apt makeweight, the only surviving movement from a projected Violin Sonata written in a hectic period for the composer at the beginning of the World War II. The Elgar elicits a performance of high contrasts both in dynamic range – Hope uses daringly extreme *pianissimos* – and in flexibility of tempo. So in the first movement the opening at an urgent speed gives way to a very broad reading of the second subject, hushed and musingly introspective. Yet such freedom of expression goes with deep concentration, so that the structure is still firmly held together. In the finale, Hope conveys an improvisational quality, again using the widest dynamic range, finely matched by Simon Mulligan. With Hope's sweet, finely focused violin tone beautifully caught in the Nimbus recording – full and warm but less reverberant than some – and well balanced against the piano, this set makes an outstanding recommendation.

Organ Works

Organ Sonatas – No 1 in G, Op 28; No 2 in B flat, Op 87a (arr Atkins). Vesper Voluntaries, Op 14. Cantique in C, Op 3 No 1. Loughborough Memorial Chime
John Butt *org*
Harmonia Mundi HMU90 7281 (67' · DDD) Played on the organ of King's College Chapel, Cambridge   Ⓕ

These five works represent Elgar's complete output for solo organ. Indeed, in the case of the Sonata in B flat, the music is as much the work of Elgar's close friend, Ivor Atkins, as of Elgar himself, but in spite – maybe because – of that, it's probably the most successful of all the works here. Having been largely overlooked on disc, it's good to report that John Butt's suitably self-confident if at times slightly idiosyncratic performance makes truly riveting listening.

Strongly redolent in style of the period (1890), the nine tiny *Vesper Voluntaries* have all but disappeared from the repertory in recent years. They are, nevertheless, full of Elgar hallmarks, and Butt's sensitive handling of both the music and, more especially, the organ, breathes new life into these miniature gems. The Sonata in G is Elgar's largest and best-known organ work, and Butt's authoritative performance, at times magisterial, occasionally deliciously sentimental and frequently breathtakingly virtuoso, has no equal in the current catalogue. The unusually clear and focused recording of the famous King's instrument is the ideal partner to Butt's playing. Elgar's music for organ has never been served so well on record as it is here.

The Black Knight, Op 25

The Black Knight. Scenes from the Bavarian
Highlands, Op 27
**London Symphony Chorus and Orchestra /Richard
Hickox**
Chandos CHAN9436 (61' · DDD) Texts included   Ⓕ

Elgar completed *The Black Knight* in 1893 and it provided him with his first big success. The text tells of a sinister, unnamed 'Prince of mighty sway', whose appearance at the King's court during the feast of Pentecost has disastrous consequences. Elgar's score boasts much attractive invention, some of it strikingly eloquent and prescient of greater offerings to come. The choral writing is always effective, the orchestration already vivid and assured. Richard Hickox and his forces are dab hands at this kind of fare and their performance has great bloom and spaciousness. Similarly, in the tuneful, vernally fresh *Scenes from the Bavarian Highlands*, Hickox and his colleagues respond with commendable spirit and pleasing polish. Typical of Chandos, the recording is bright and clear, tonally beyond reproach and with just the right balance between choir and orchestra.

The Light of Life, Op 29

The Light of Life
Judith Howarth sop **Linda Finnie** mez **Arthur
Davies** ten **John Shirley-Quirk** bar **London
Symphony Chorus and Orchestra / Richard Hickox**
Chandos CHAN9208 (63' · DDD) Recorded 1993.
Text included   Ⓕ

In the glorious orchestral 'Meditation' Hickox's conducting demonstrates a noble flexibility, sensitivity to dynamic nuance and feeling for climax. Equally the engineering, sumptuous yet detailed, comes close to the ideal. The LSO and Chorus contribute to proceedings in exemplary, disciplined fashion. As The Blind Man, Arthur Davies could hardly be more ardent, but his

slightly tremulous timbre won't be to all tastes. John Shirley-Quirk, so eloquent and firm-toned a Jesus for Groves (on EMI) back in 1980, now shows signs of unsteadiness in the same part. On the other hand, Linda Finnie and Judith Howarth make a creditable showing. Hickox's reading excels in precisely the areas where the Groves was deficient, and *vice versa*. If you already have the Groves reissue, hang on to it, for it's by no means outclassed by the Hickox. However, for anyone coming to this underrated score for the first time, Hickox's must now be the preferred version.

The Dream of Gerontius, Op 38

The Dream of Gerontius[a]. Cello Concerto[b]   Ⓗ
Gladys Ripley contr **Heddle Nash** ten **Dennis Noble**
bar **Norman Walker** bass **Paul Tortelier** vc
Huddersfield Choral Society; [b]**BBC Symphony
Orchestra;** [a]**Liverpool Philharmonic Orchestra /
Sir Malcolm Sargent**
Testament mono ② SBT2025 (120' · ADD) Recorded
1945-53.Text included   Ⓕ Ⓞ

This pioneering set of *Gerontius* has come up newly minted in these superbly engineered transfers taken from 78rpm masters. That only enhances the incandescence and fervour of the reading itself, in virtually all respects the most convincing the work has received. Sargent's conducting, influenced by Elgar's, is direct, vital and urgently crafted with an inborn feeling for the work's ebb and flow and an overall picture that comprehends the piece's spiritual meaning while realising its dramatic leanness and force. Heddle Nash's Gerontius is unrivalled in its conviction and inwardness. He'd been singing the part since 1930, and by 1945 the work was in his being; he sang it from memory and had mastered every facet. 'Take me away' is like a searing cry of pain from the depth of the singer's soul. Gladys Ripley is a natural and communicative Angel, her flexible and appealing tone always a pleasure. The Liverpool Philharmonic lives up to its reputation at the time as the country's leading orchestra (in particular the sonorous string section), and the members of the Huddersfield Choral Society sing as if their lives depended on it.

Tortelier's Cello Concerto presents the Classical approach as compared with the Romantic one of du Pré, and is the best of Tortelier's readings of the work on disc, with his tone and phrasing at their firmest and most telling. A considered and unaffected reading among the best ever committed to disc.

Elgar The Dream of Gerontius **Parry** Ode at a Solemn
Music, 'Blest Pair of Sirens'. I was glad
Felicity Palmer sop **Arthur Davies** ten **Gwynne
Howell** bass **London Symphony Orchestra and
Chorus / Richard Hickox**
Chandos CHAN8641/2 (114 minutes : DDD) Recorded
1988   Ⓜ

Hickox gives us a peculiarly immediate and urgent interpretation – not dissimilar from Rattle's on EMI – that has us thinking more than ever that *Gerontius* is an opera in everything but name, or at least a dramatic cantata, not an oratorio. His speeds tend to be quick, but only once, in 'Sanctus fortis', does the tempo feel hurried. Being a choral trainer of many years' standing, he naturally enough persuades them to sing with an impressive unanimity of purpose and with perhaps a wider range of dynamics than any other conductor. Perhaps an element of dignity and grandeur such as you find in Boult's and Barbirolli's EMI readings, both appreciably more measured, is missing, but little else. The sound of the chorus and excellent orchestra surpasses that on the Rattle version, Watford Town Hall proving as ever a good venue for the recording of large forces.

Arthur Davies has a stronger, more secure voice than any other tenor who has recorded Gerontius and, unlike several of them, he's in his prime as a singer. 'Mary, pray for me' and 'Novissima hora est' are sung with the appropriate sweet sadness, the duet with the Angel tenderly, and he enters with terrified power at 'Take me away'. He doesn't have the individuality of utterance or special affinity with the text, as for instance at 'How still it is!' that you get with Heddle Nash (for Sargent) and Sir Peter Pears (for Britten), or even quite the agony of the soul projected by Mitchinson (for Rattle), but it's an appreciable performance, firmly projected. Felicity Palmer's Angel is less successful. The intentions are right, the understanding is there, but the means to carry them forward are faulty: her singing, once she puts pressure on the tone, is uncomfortable to hear. Gwynne Howell is just about the best Priest and Angel of the Agony in any version. His warm, firm bass-baritone easily encompasses the different tessituras of the two 'parts'.

This is a fine modern version, better than the Rattle for all its élan, and with the bonus of the Parry works. But probably the greatest conducting in this work comes from Sargent, Barbirolli and Britten.

The Kingdom, Op 51

The Kingdom[a]. Coronation Ode, Op 44[b]
[a]Margaret Price, [b]Felicity Lott *sops* [a]Yvonne Minton *mez* [b]Alfreda Hodgson *contr* [a]Alexander Young, [b]Richard Morton *tens* [a]John Shirley-Quirk, [b]Stephen Roberts *bars* [a]London Philharmonic Choir and Orchestra / Sir Adrian Boult; [b]Cambridge University Musical Society Chorus; [b]Choir of King's College Cambridge; [b]New Philharmonia Orchestra / Philip Ledger
EMI British Composers ② 764209-2 (130' · ADD) Ⓜ❍

Boult was a passionate admirer of *The Kingdom* and, as ever, the unaffected devotion and authority of his advocacy is hard to resist. The two formidable contenders in the work are Leonard Slatkin and Richard Hickox. All three

ELGAR DREAM OF GERONTIUS – IN BRIEF

Nash, Ripley, Noble, Walker; Huddersfield Choral Society, Liverpool PO / Sir Malcolm Sargent
Testament ② SBT2025 (120' · ADD)   Ⓜ❍
Recorded as long ago as 1945, and still the interpretative and artistic touchstone. Sargent secures a searingly eloquent response from his massed forces, Heddle Nash is unforgettable and Gladys Ripley's 'Softly and gently' never fails to activate the tearducts.

Lewis, Thomas, Cameron; Huddersfield Choral Society, RLPO / Sir Malcolm Sargent
CfP ② 585904-2 (129' · ADD)   Ⓑ
Sargent re-recorded *Gerontius* for the then new LP format with the same orchestral and choral team. Not as compelling as his legendary 1945 account, but worth hearing for Richard Lewis and Marjorie Thomas alone.

Lewis, Baker, Borg, Hallé Choir, Sheffield Philharmonic Chorus, Ambrosian Singers, Hallé Orchestra / Sir John Barbirolli
EMI ② 573579-2 (98' · ADD)   Ⓜ❍❍
Newly remastered at budget price, Barbirolli's 1964 set should not be passed over. Richard Lewis is not quite as fresh-voiced as he was for Sargent a decade earlier, and Kim Borg's a bit woolly, but otherwise it's a performance to cherish.

Pears, Minton, Shirley-Quirk, King's CCC London Symphony Chorus & Orchestra / Benjamin Britten
Decca ② 448 170-2DF2 (140' · ADD)   Ⓜ
In Britten's classic 1972 version scrupulous preparation goes hand in hand with a profound musicality and dramatic strength that illuminate every bar. As Gerontius, Peter Pears is occasionally taxed, but sings with unflagging commitment.

Gedda, Watts, Lloyd, John Alldis Choir, London Philharmonic Choir, New Philharmonia Orchestra / Sir Adrian Boult
EMI ② 566540-2 (135' · ADD)   Ⓜ
Opulently engineered, Boult's 1975 set features the distinctive, Italianate timbre of Nicolai Gedda in the title-role. Boult directs with commendable energy and typical humanity. A document to be treasured.

Davies, Palmer, Howell, London Symphony Chorus & Orchestra / Richard Hickox
Chandos ② CHAN8641/2 (114' · DDD)   Ⓜ
Now retailing at mid-price, Hickox's début disc for Chandos brought this finely sung and played *Gerontius*, with Arthur Davies engagingly ardent in the title-role. Parry's *Blest Pair of Sirens* and *I was glad* make welcome bonuses.

performers have much going for them. In short, Boult enjoys the strongest team of soloists, Hickox obtains the most disciplined and full-bodied choral work, and Slatkin secures the finest orchestral playing – indeed, the LPO are on inspired form, responding with an exemplary sensitivity, commitment and concentration which also marked out Slatkin's magnificent account of the Symphony No 2 set down with this same group some 17 months later. Slatkin also benefits from perhaps the best engineering, with Boult's Kingsway Hall production now sounding just a little pale and hard-edged in comparison. Where the EMI release really comes up trumps, though, is in the shape of its generous fill-up, Philip Ledger's superb, swaggering reading of the *Coronation Ode*. Ultimately, then, the Boult, must take the palm, especially at mid-price, though no devoted Elgarian should miss hearing Slatkin's gloriously lucid conception either.

Additional recommendation

The Kingdom
Coupled with: Sospiri. Sursum corda
Marshall, Palmer sops **Davies** ten **Wilson-Johnson** bar **London Symphony Chorus and Orch / Hickox**
Chandos ② CHAN8788/9 (108' · DDD)   Ⓕ
  Particularly impressive and moving 'Breaking of the Bread'; the orchestra play with fire and sensitivity.

Sea Pictures, Op 37

Sea Pictures. Cello Concerto.
Janet Baker mez **Jacqueline du Pré** vc **London Symphony Orchestra / Sir John Barbirolli**
EMI 556219-2 (54' · ADD) Recorded 1965   ⒻⓄⓄⓄ

 Until this recording, *Sea Pictures* had tended to be underprized even among Elgarians; but the passion, intensity and sheer beauty of this performance with each of the five songs sharply distinct rebutted any idea that – in reflection of verse of varying quality – it had anything of sub-standard Elgar in it. It's a work you'll probably never be able to listen to again without hearing in your mind Janet Baker's deeply individual phrasing on this disc. What strikes you most is the central relevance to Baker's whole career of the last stanza in 'Sabbath morning at sea', a radiant climax. 'He shall assist me to look higher' says the Barrett Browning poem, and the thrust of meaning as she sings it invariably conveys a *frisson* such as you rarely get on record. It's coupled with du Pré's outstanding Cello Concerto. What more could you want?

Sea Pictures, Op 37. The Music Makers
Felicity Palmer mez **London Symphony Chorus and Orchestra / Richard Hickox**
EMI British Composers 565126-2 (62' · DDD)
Recorded 1986. Texts included   Ⓜ

These idiomatic Elgar performances from Richard Hickox well merit their mid-price resuscitation within EMI's British Composers series. Hickox's admirable London Symphony Chorus impresses in matters of intonation and diction. Felicity Palmer sings commandingly, though her contribution in *The Music Makers* doesn't always generate the tear-laden intensity the part requires. However, Hickox doesn't quite match Sir Andrew Davis's Teldec account – he evinces a personal identification with Elgar's inspiration that's rather special. In the *Sea Pictures*, however, Hickox and Palmer form an intelligent, distinctive partnership, less endearing, perhaps, than many would like in 'In Haven' and 'Where corals lie', yet tough and dramatic in 'Sabbath morning at sea' and 'The swimmer'. It's a thrusting, unsentimental view which is most refreshing. The orchestral playing is excellent.

George Enescu   Romanian 1881-1955

Enescu studied at the Vienna Conservatory (1888-94) and at the Paris Conservatoire (1895-9). Paris remained the centre of his professional life, though he spent much time in Romania as a teacher and conductor. He is regarded as the greatest and most versatile Romanian musician and was widely admired as a violinist. Apart from the two Lisztian Rhapsodies roumains for orchestra (1901) his music has been neglected, perhaps partly because of the complexity and diversity of his stylistic allegiances: Romanian folk music is a recurrent influence, but so too are Wagner and Reger and early Schoenberg. His output includes the opera Oedipe (1936), five symphonies (1905, 1914, 1921, 1934, 1941) and much chamber music. **GROVE**music

---

Vox maris

Poème roumain, Op 1. Vox maris, Op 31[a]. Vox de la nature, Op posth
[a]**Florin Diaconescu** ten **George Enescu Bucharest Philharmonic** [a]**Choir and Orchestra / Cristian Mandeal**
Arte Nova Classics 74321 65425-2 (62' · DDD)   ⓈⓈ

If all you know of Enescu are his First *Romanian Rhapsody* and Third Violin Sonata, then the 26-minute symphonic poem *Vox maris* – which preoccupied its composer for some 20 years – will likely come as a profound shock. Even Scriabin would have drowned in these waters, with their pungent harmonic cross-currents, exotic colours and densely crowded textures. The orchestra is huge, involving quadruple woodwinds, six horns, percussion (five players), two harps, piano and off-stage chorus. The opening recalls the Romanticised antiquity of Pfitzner's *Palestrina*, but the overwhelming impression is of vast, tonal tidal waves that ultimately defeat the sailor of the story (a death at sea) and draw cries of 'Miserere, Domine' from the soprano.

Enescu's expansive *Romanian Poem* is an outrageously precocious essay for a teenager, redolent of Saint-Saëns in its slow first section and with elements of Romanian dance in the second. Of the available versions this release packs the weightiest wallop, and is certainly the best recorded. *Voix de la nature* emerges as a close-knit tapestry of sound that has an air of ancient legend about it.

The interpretation is convincing (though the playing isn't front-rank), the sound excellent and the musical journey well worth making. At a fiver, you won't find a cheaper ticket to a more interesting destination.

String Quartets, Op 22

String Quartets, Op 22 – No 1 in E flat; No 2 in G
Ad Libitum Quartet (Adrian Berescu, Serban
Mereuta vns Bogdan Bisoc va Filip Papa vc)
Naxos 8 554721 (74' · DDD)   Ⓢ Ⓢ Ⓞ

Enescu's 1920 First Quartet crams so much into 45-odd minutes that even two or three hearings barely scratch its surface. It's a veritable forest of invention, fairly Brahmsian in texture, organic in its thinking and frequently dramatic. The second movement incorporates sundry embellishments and effects (including the use of *sul ponticello*), and the finale features variations on a march-like theme. It will make wonderful if challenging listening for anyone who values quality ideas above economical structuring.

Although the two quartets share the single opus number, they're years apart chronologically, aeons if you consider their contrasting styles. The Second Quartet was Enescu's penultimate work, and breathes the heady aroma of Romanian folk music, especially in the slow movement and finale, which recall the world of the far better-known Third Violin Sonata. Shorter than the First Quartet by almost half, the Second feels tighter and more agile.

The Ad Libitum Quartet do a fabulous job. They attend to Enescu's endless technical demands with a devotion that translates to apparent effortlessness. Their generally soft-spoken, conversational mode of playing is in marked contrast to the tougher-grained Voces Quartet on Olympia, another good group, but hardly flattered by a hard analogue recording.

Naxos's superior production is a secure top recommendation and unbeatable value too.

Violin Sonatas

Violin Sonatas[a] – No 2 in F minor, Op 6; No 3 in A
minor, 'dans le caractère populaire roumain', Op 25.
Caprice roumain[b]. Impressions d'enfance, Op 28[a]
Sherban Lupu vn [a]**Valentin Gheorghiu** pf [b]**George
Enescu Philharmonic Orchestra / Cristian Mandeal**
Electrecord ② EDC324/5 (93' · DDD)   Ⓕ

Listening to Sherban Lupu is like confronting a

composite violinistic genius made up of Enescu himself (elegance, tonal allure, recreative flare), Dinicu (fire, seduction) and Isaac Stern (intellectual fibre, toughness of attack). Lupu's timing is immaculate. Try the opening of *Impressions d'enfance*, or the many instances in the Third Sonata where Enescu leaps to his feet, kicks sadness aside and starts to dance. Lupu's quietly sighing bow is like the breathy frame favoured by certain jazz saxophonists, and his mastery of gypsy-style devices is quite unique.

Pianist-composer Valentin Gheorghiu proves himself an ideal collaborator. His subtle negotiation of colour, dynamics and rhythm mirror Lupu's controlled rhapsodising to perfection.

The relatively early Second Sonata recalls César Franck, picking up folk-like speed only towards the end, where it makes an unexpected move in the direction of its successor. Again, the performance is superb: ardent, well judged and imaginative.

Cristian Mandeal and his Bucharest players cope well with the lavish demands that Enescu and Taranu make on them, and Lupu's handling of the solo part has all the temperament and colour that inform his performances of the chamber works. Good sound.

Enescu Violin Sonata No 3, 'dans le caractère populaire roumain', Op 25. Impressions d'enfance, Op 28
Ravel Sonata for Violin and Piano in G. Tzigane
Leonidas Kavakos vn **Péter Nagy** pf
ECM New Series 476 053-2 (78' · DDD)   Ⓕ Ⓞ Ⓞ

A compelling programme based principally around the figure of Georges Enescu, both as composer and as a performing phenomenon, the latter probably inspiring Ravel's Violin Sonata of 1897, a lavish essay redolent of early Debussy. Both Ravel pieces respond handsomely to Leonidas Kavakos's agile and refined approach, *Tzigane* in particular being meticulously prepared, the partnership with Péter Nagy ensuring clarity in matters of articulation and the 'pick-up' of motives between violin and piano; you're unlikely to hear a more supportive or better gauged account of the piano part.

These aren't 'showy' performances. Though Kavakos is audibly appreciative of the folk flavouring in Enescu's Third Sonata, he treats the abstract element as paramount, suggesting keen parallels with the violin sonatas of Bartók. Again Nagy takes the greatest care over such issues as rhythm, texture and the shape of individual phrases: his precise musical thinking could serve as an object lesson in such matters. The high-spot of the performance is the cantorial closing section of the *Andante* second movement, so exquisitely turned and sustained. The graphic *Impressions d'enfance*, with its lullaby, caged bird and cuckoo-clock, chirping cricket and ecstatic dawn, is endlessly fascinating, again rich in folk references, the sort that Enescu worked in to his *Romanian Rhapsodies*.

These performances justify consideration for their warmth, intelligence and superb sound.

Einar Englund Finnish 1916-1999

Englund studied with Palmgren and Carlsson at the Helsinki Academy (1933-41), with Copland at Tanglewood, and in Russia, where he was impressed by Prokofiev and Shostakovich. His works include five symphonies (1946-77), concertos and piano pieces. GROVEmusic

Symphonies

Symphonies – No 2, 'Blackbird'; No 4, 'Nostalgic'.
Piano Concerto No 1[a]
[a]**Niklas Sivelöv** pf **Turku Philharmonic Orchestra / Jorma Panula**
Naxos 8 553758 (76' · DDD) Ⓢ**O**

Einar Englund was the finest Finnish symphonist between Sibelius and Kokkonen, and the *Blackbird* Symphony is one of his best. You can hear why he so named it from the woodwind writing, particularly the solos for flute, although he grew wary of emphasising the title in later life. One of the most attractive features of all his music is its orchestration. Panula's account is superbly played, with excellent sound. The Fourth (1976), written in memory of Shostakovich, is less epic, though no less inventive. A chamber symphony for strings and percussion, its most effective movement is the sparkling but macabre *Scherzo*, 'Tempus fugit', haunted by the chiming of bells and the manic ticking of some outlandish clock. Here, as well as in the darkly poetic third span, 'Nostalgia', and concluding 'Epilogue', Panula finds great poetry. Naxos's centrepiece, though, is the first of Englund's two piano concertos. Englund's own recording disappeared from the catalogue long ago, but Niklas Sivelöv proves a fine advocate.

Symphonies – No 4, 'Dedicated to the Memory of a Great Artist'; No 5, 'To the Memory of JK Paasikivi'.
The Great Wall of China
Tampere Philharmonic Orchestra / Eri Klas
Ondine ODE961-2 (65' · DDD) Ⓕ

The first cycle of Englund's seven symphonies is completed here with the Fourth and Fifth and an exuberantly parodistic theatre suite. Paavo Pohjola set the pace in the Fourth Symphony (1976) in the 1980s; not until 1993 did a second appear, from Geza Szilvay's fine youth orchestra. The Fifth Symphony (1977) was recorded on LP by Jukka-Pekka Saraste; Englund once said this was too fast, so he would probably have approved of Klas's better-judged version. Although titled *Sinfonia Fennica* ('Finnish' Symphony), the composer claimed it contained more of his wartime experiences than his famous *War* Symphony (No 1, 1946). In a bold, riveting single span, its full orchestration pairs very effectively with the strings and percussion of No 4. The suite from the incidental music to Max Frisch's *The Great Wall of China* (1949) is great fun. 'The Green Table Tango' and 'Rumba' reveal what an adept light/jazz composer he also was (under the pseudonym, Marcus Eje). The Tampere band are really put through their paces here and come through very well. If Panula's Naxos disc is still perhaps the best introduction to Englund's music, this disc should certainly be the next stop.

Manuel de Falla Spanish 1876-1946

Falla studied in Cádiz. and from the late 1890s in Madrid, where he was a pupil of Tragó for the piano and Pedrell for composition. In 1901-3 he composed five zarzuelas in the hope of making money; then in 1905 came his first important work, the one-act opera La vida breve, which he revised before its first performance, in Paris in 1913. He had moved to Paris in 1907 and become acquainted with Dukas, Debussy, Ravel, Stravinsky and Albéniz, all of whom influenced his development of a style using the primitive song of Andalusia, the cante jondo, and a modern richness of harmony and colour. This was not an immediate achievement: he wrote little before returning to Madrid in 1914, but then came the piano concerto Noches en los jardines de España (1915) and the ballets El amor brujo (1915) and El sombrero de tres picos (1919), the latter presented by Dyagilev and designed by Picasso.

Like Stravinsky a few years before, he turned to a much sparer style and to the format of touring theatre in El retablo de maese Pedro (1923). He also began to concern himself with the medieval, Renaissance and Baroque musical traditions of Spain, reflected in his Concerto for harpsichord and quintet (1926). Most of the rest of his life he devoted to a vast oratorio, Atlántida, on which he worked in Granada (where he had settled in 1919) and after 1939 in Argentina. With Albéniz and Granados he was one of the first Spanish composers to win international renown and the most gifted of the three. GROVEmusic

Harpsichord Concerto

Harpsichord Concerto. El sombrero de tres picos
Maria Lluisa Muntada sop **Tony Millan** hpd **Jaime Martin** fl **Manuel Angulo** ob **Joan-Enric Lluna** cl **Santiago Juan** vn **Jorge Pozas** vc **Spanish National Youth Orchestra / Edmon Colomer**
Astrée Naïve V4642 (56' · DDD) Recorded 1989 Ⓕ

Falla's *El sombrero de tres picos* (The three-cornered hat) started life as a 'mimed farce', but Diaghilev then persuaded him to revise and enlarge it as a one-act ballet which had its première in London in 1919. Besides the orchestra, it features a soprano solo warning wives to resist temptation, and cries of 'Olé' from men's voices representing a bullring crowd. Much of the score consists of dances such as the *fandango* and *seguidilla*, while the finale is a *jota*. This performance by Maria Lluisa Muntada and the Spanish National Youth Orchestra, playing under the direction of its founder Edmon

Colomer, brings us all the vivid colours, intense melodies and vigorous rhythms that evoke that southernmost province of Spain which is Andalusia. These artists clearly love and understand this music, and bring tremendous gusto to the famous 'Miller's Dance' (the longest single number) with its chunky chords getting louder and faster.

The Harpsichord Concerto shows us another side of Falla, and was among the first 20th-century compositions for the instrument. It's less obviously Spanish in style, more neo-classical – indeed, Stravinsky was probably the chief model – although we may detect an Iberian element in its directness and even toughness. With just five instruments playing alongside the soloist, it's really a chamber work, but the writing is so powerful that the composer's title is doubtless justified. Here, too, the playing is fine and the recording of both these works is full blooded and atmospheric.

Noches en los jardines de España

Falla El amor brujo – ballet (complete)[a]. Noches en los jardines de España[b] **Rodrigo** Concierto de Aranjuez[c]
[a]**Huguette Tourangeau** *mez* [c]**Carlos Bonnell** *gtr*
[b]**Alicia de Larrocha** *pf* [a][c]**Montreal Symphony Orchestra / Charles Dutoit;** [b]**London Philharmonic Orchestra / Rafael Frühbeck de Burgos**
Decca Ovation 430 703-2DM (71' · DDD) Recorded 1980-83   Ⓜ︎⊙

Decca's hugely enjoyable disc of Spanish music includes Rodrigo's most famous work, the *Concierto de Aranjuez*, which has never lost its popularity since its Barcelona première in 1940. Here Carlos Bonnell imparts a wistful, intimate feeling to the work, aided by a thoughtful accompaniment from Charles Dutoit's stylish Montreal Orchestra. The famous string tune in the *Adagio* enjoys a fulsome rendition. Dutoit's beautifully played interpretation of *El amor brujo* captures the wide range of emotions that this fiery, mysterious piece requires and his performance of the famous 'Ritual Fire Dance' must be among the best in the catalogue. A cooler mood is captured in *Nights in the gardens of Spain* with Alicia de Larrocha as the distinguished soloist. Her smooth, effortless playing matches the mood of the piece exactly and de Burgos's accompaniment with the London Philharmonic is equally sympathetic, with ripe tone colour and careful dynamics. Those unfamiliar with these great Spanish works will be hard pressed to find a better introduction than this superbly recorded disc.

Falla Noches en los jardines de España
Albéniz (orch Halffter). Rapsodia española, Op 70
Turina Rapsodia sinfónica, Op 66
Alicia de Larrocha *pf* **London Philharmonic Orchestra / Rafael Frühbeck de Burgos**
Decca 410 289-2DH (52' · DDD) Recorded 1983   Ⓕ

The three magically beautiful nocturnes which make up Falla's *Nights in the gardens of Spain* express the feelings and emotions evoked by contrasted surroundings, while Albéniz's enjoyably colourful *Rapsodia española* is a loosely assembled sequence of Spanish dances such as the *jota* and the *malagueña*. Like Falla's *Nights* the work was conceived as a piano solo, but this disc contains a version with orchestra arranged by Cristóbal Halffter. The disc is completed by Turina's short, two-part work for piano and strings. All three pieces are excellently performed, but it's the Falla work which brings out the quality of Larrocha's artistry; her ability to evoke the colour of the Spanish atmosphere is remarkable. Frühbeck de Burgos supports her magnificently and persuades the LPO to produce some very Latin-sounding playing. The recording is suitably atmospheric.

Noches en los jardines de España[a] El sombrero de tres picos[b]
[b]**Jennifer Larmore** *mez* **Chicago Symphony**
[b]**Chorus and Orchestra /** [a]**Plácido Domingo,**
[b]**Daniel Barenboim** [a]*pf*
Teldec 0630-17145-2 (63' · DDD) Text and translation included   Ⓜ︎

In *Noches en los jardines de España* Barenboim and Domingo make a wonderfully understanding partnership, wafting the great Chicago orchestra into the Spanish night with its balmy warmth, and glittering background of flamenco dance rhythms. The rustling opening of the evocation of the 'Generalife' is beautifully managed by Domingo, and Barenboim's crystal-clear entry somehow suggests the water flowing in those astonishing centuries-old Moorish fountains. The orchestral detail is full of subtle colouring, and the ebb and flow of tempo and tension seem totally spontaneous. The central 'Danza lejana' glimmers and glitters, and leads into the final sequence with sparkling pianistic dash and a most volatile response from the Chicago players. The languorous closing pages create a richly sensuous sunset-like apotheosis, Domingo's expansive *rallentando* boldly underlined by the piano. *The Three Cornered Hat*, conducted by Daniel Barenboim, opens with a fierce, brash briskness from trumpet and timpani, and Jennifer Larmore is a vibrant if not especially individual soloist. Again this superb orchestra revels in the vivid colouring and flashing rhythms, and no less so in the gentler moments. The live recording is full blooded, yet has plenty of transparency. Strongly recommended.

El sombrero de tres picos

El sombrero de tres picos[b]. El amor brujo[a]   Ⓗ
La vida breve – Interlude and Dance
[b]**Teresa Berganza** *sop* [a]**Marina de Gabarain** *mezzo*
Suisse Romande Orchestra / Ernest Ansermet
Decca Legends 466 991-2DM (69' · ADD) Recorded
[a]1955, 1961   Ⓜ︎⊙⊙⊙

Ansermet's vintage 1961 recording of *El sombrero de tres picos* with the Suisse Romande Orchestra is an electrifyingly great performance, and the sound remains in the top demonstration class – four decades after it was made!

Ansermet's opening with hard-sticked timpani, extrovert trumpeting and fervently spirited 'Olés' creates an altogether different sound-world of dramatic primary colours and rhythmic pungency. He has the characterful Teresa Berganza as his soloist, and the ballet swings along spontaneously, with infectious zest, the Swiss orchestra on its toes and clearly enjoying every minute. Every detail of Falla's superb score is sharply and richly focused, the colours lighting up radiantly. The finale grabs the listener, and carries the music along with thrilling impetus to make an expansive climax. This is a truly marvellous performance, and the spectacular Victoria Hall recording could hardly be better had it been made yesterday.

Ansermet's *El amor brujo* is very early stereo (1955) and not as opulent as *El sombrero*, but it still sounds remarkably lustrous. The performance isn't quite as distinctive as its companion, but is still brightly etched, 'El círculo mágico' being quite bewitching; and the strings and horns bring splendid bite to the 'Fire Dance'. The finale does expose the weakness of the Suisse Romande Orchestra in the middle strings, but it's none the less passionately played. A reissue worthy of its legendary status.

La vida breve

La vida breve[a]. Canciones populares españolas[b]. El sombrero de tres picos[c] El amor brujo[d] Soneto a Córdoba[e]. Psyché[f]
Victoria de los Angeles sop Salud [a]**Ana Maria Higueras** sop Carmela/Street Vendor I & III [a]**Inès Rivadeneyra** mez Grandmother, Street Vendor II [a]**Carlo Cossutta** ten Paco [a]**Victor de Narké** bass Uncle Salvador [a]**Gabriel Moreno** bar Singer [a]**Luis Villarejo** bar Manuel [a]**José Maria Higuero** ten Voice in smithy/Voice in distance [a]Juan de Andia ten Voice of a hawker [b]**Gonzaleo Soriano** pf [ef]**Annie Challan** hp [f]**Jean-Claude Gérard** fl [f]**French String Trio** (Gérard Jarry vn Serge Collot va Michel Tournus vc) [a]**Orfeón Donostiarra;** [a]**Spanish National Orchestra / Rafael Frühbeck de Burgos; Philharmonia Orchestra /** [c]**Raphael Frühbeck de Burgos;** [d]**Carlo Maria Giulini**
EMI Great Recordings of the Century ② 567587-2 (150' · ADD) Recorded 1962-71 Ⓜ**OO**

It was a broadcast of *La vida breve* that began Victoria de los Angeles' international career, and although her 1952 recording is worth treasuring for its pitifully vulnerable portrayal of youthful heartbreak, this successor is in every other way preferable. Her portrayal has deepened, the supporting cast has no weak links, the recording is spacious and brilliant; above all, in Frühbeck de Burgos it has a conductor in perfect sympathy with Falla's maturing, mordantly

original genius. He shows this even more in *El sombrero*, with its vivid detail and pungent timbres. Even Giulini is slightly cast into the shade: his *El amor brujo* is powerful but not quite as idiomatic. But here also we have several treasurable passages of los Angeles's dark, gypsyish mezzo register. In the *Canciones populares* and the other songs close recording brightens her tone, but how fearlessly she launches the proud phrases of the *Soneto a Córdoba*! And the *Canciones populares*, perhaps too often projected with peasant vehemence, are here sung as by one of Goya's majas. For its indication of her vocal and expressive range and Frühbeck's stature this is an indispensable reissue.

Gabriel Fauré   French 1845-1924

Fauré was trained at the Ecole Niedermeyer (1854-65) as organist and choirmaster, coming under the influence of Saint-Saëns and his circle while working as a church musician (at Rennes, 1866-70; St Sulpice, 1871-3; the Madeleine, from 1874) and giving lessons. Though he met Liszt and was fascinated by Wagner, he sought a distinctive style in his piano pieces and numerous songs, which had to be composed during summer holidays. Recognition came slowly owing to the modernity of his music. In 1892 he became national inspector of the provincial conservatories, and in 1896 chief organist at the Madeleine and composition teacher at the Conservatoire, where his pupils included Ravel, Koechlin, Roger-Ducasse, Enescu and Nadia Boulanger; from 1905 to 1920 he was the Conservatoire's resolute and influential director, becoming celebrated for the vocal and chamber masterpieces he produced until his death.

Fauré's stylistic development can be traced from the sprightly or melancholy song settings of his youth to the bold, forceful late instrumental works, traits including a delicate combination of expanded tonality and modality, rapid modulations to remote keys and continuously unfolding melody. Widely regarded as the greatest master of French song, he produced six important cycles (notably the novel La bonne chanson op.61) and three collections each of 20 pieces (1879, 1897, 1908). In chamber music he enriched all the genres he attempted, while his works for piano (chiefly nocturnes, barcarolles and impromptus) embody the full scope of his stylistic evolution. Among his few large-scale works, the popular and delicately written Requiem op.48 and the 'song opera' Pénélope (1913) are noteworthy. GROVEmusic

Ballade, Op 19

Fauré Ballade, Op 19 **Franck** Symphonic Variations, Op 46 **d'Indy** Symphonie sur un chant montagnard français in G, Op 25
François-Joël Thiollier pf **National Symphony Orchestra of Ireland / Antonio de Almeida**
Naxos 8 550754 (55' · DDD) Recorded 1993 Ⓢ

The renamed RTE Symphony Orchestra taped

this programme in their Dublin concert hall (acoustically clean, bright and airy, but warm, if this disc's sound is representative). François-Joël Thiollier's playing is individual, often impulsive but always idiomatic, helped by the sensitive, guiding hand of a conductor well acquainted with the music. A more high-profile production would probably have retaken those passages where piano and orchestra co-ordination is occasionally fractionally awry, such as in the last variation of the Franck, but it might also have seemed less spontaneous. Thiollier's rubato is always distinctive and attractive; the style, particularly and crucially in the Fauré, properly fluid. Both the piano and the orchestra's woodwind are discreetly prominent, but internal balances are generally excellent.

Fauré Ballade, Op 19ª **Leigh** Concertino for Piano and Strings^b **Mozart** Piano Concertos – No 15 in B flat, K450^c; No 24 in C minor, K491^d
Kathleen Long pf ^{ac}**National Symphony Orchestra;** ^b**Boyd Neel String Orchestra / Boyd Neel;** ^d**Concertgebouw Orch / Eduard van Beinum**
Dutton Laboratories CDBP9714 (75' · ADD) Recorded 1940s   Ⓢ Ⓢ ⓞⓞ

A richly experienced chamber musician, Kathleen Long (1896-1968) was partnered and praised by Casals, played Ravel's 'Ondine' to the composer and gave over 60 National Gallery concerts during the Second World War. Though her playing may initially seem too restrained, you find yourself wondering why you've never enjoyed music so much or been made so aware, however unobtrusively, of its innermost spirit. It's in Fauré's *Ballade* that she makes her finest impression. Indeed, it's difficult to imagine this magical work played more serenely or inwardly. Even French critics wary of foreign interpreters marvelled over this recording. Her affection is evident in every caressing bar and makes for a perfect conclusion to a delectable disc. Long was a born aristocrat of the keyboard and you'll look in vain for any overt or disfiguring drama in her lucid and stylish performance of Mozart's C minor Concerto. The recordings have come up well and the inclusion in the booklet of a 1950 *Gramophone* interview is an illuminating bonus.

Orchestral Works

Pelléas et Mélisande, Op 80 (with Chanson de Mélisande – orch Koechlin). Three Songs, Op 7 – Après un rêve (arr vc/orch Dubenskij). Pavane, Op 50. Elégie, Op 24. Dolly Suite, Op 56 (orch Rabaud)
Lorraine Hunt sop **Jules Eskin** vc **Tanglewood Festival Chorus; Boston Symphony Orchestra / Seiji Ozawa**
DG 423 089-2GH (56' · DDD) Recorded 1986. Texts and translations included   Ⓕ

Fauré's music for Maeterlinck's play *Pelléas et Mélisande* was commissioned by Mrs Patrick

Campbell. To the usual four-movement suite Ozawa has added the 'Chanson de Mélisande', superbly sung here by Lorraine Hunt. Ozawa conducts a sensitive, sympathetic account of the score, and Jules Eskin plays beautifully in both the arrangement of the early song, *Après un rêve*, and the *Elégie*, which survived from an abandoned cello sonata. The grave *Pavane* is performed here in the choral version of 1901. *Dolly* began life as a piano duet, but was later orchestrated by the composer and conductor Henri Rabaud. Ozawa provides us with a pleasing account of this delightful score and the recording is excellent.

Masques et bergamasques, Op 112. Ballade, Op 19. Pavane, Op 50. Fantaisie, Op 79. Pénélope – Overture. Elégie, Op 24. Dolly Suite (orch Rabaud)
Richard Davis fl **Peter Dixon** vc **Kathryn Stott** pf **BBC Philharmonic Orchestra / Yan Pascal Tortelier**
Chandos CHAN9416 (72' · DDD)   Ⓕ

Masques et bergamasques, which takes its title from Verlaine's sad, mysterious poem *Clair de lune*, is a late stage work that the composer himself described as melancholy and nostalgic, but it's hardly romantic, being instead pointedly neo-classical in character and shape, recalling Bizet's youthful C major Symphony and Grieg's *Holberg Suite*. The playing here under Yan Pascal Tortelier is very satisfying, as are the elegant flute solos of the exquisitely delicate *Pavane*, performed here without the optional chorus, and in *Dolly*. The rarely heard Overture to the opera *Pénélope* is also effectively presented here.

The biggest *concertante* work here, the *Ballade* of 1881, is Fauré's orchestration of his piano piece of the same name; it's gentle music that persuades and cajoles in a very Gallic way. Though not an overtly virtuoso utterance, it makes its own exacting technical demands on the soloist, among them being complete control of touch and pedalling. The highly regarded Fauréan Kathryn Stott meets these with consistent success.

There's little rhetoric and no bombast in Fauré's art, but how civilised he was, and what sympathetic interpreters serve him here! The recording is warm yet also delicate.

Piano Quintets

Piano Quintets – No 1 in D minor, Op 89; No 2 in C minor, Op 115
Domus (Krysia Osostowicz vn Timothy Boulton va Richard Lester vc Susan Tomes pf) **Anthony Marwood** vn
Hyperion CDA66766 (60' · DDD) Recorded 1994   Ⓕ ⓞⓞⓞ

This isn't music that yields its secrets easily. Despite pages pulsing with all Fauré's sustained radiance and energy, the abiding impression is of music of such profound introspection that you often feel like an interloper who's stumbled into a private conversation. But perseverance reaps the richest rewards, and moments like the opening of the D minor Quintet, where Fauré achieves what's referred to in the insert-notes as a 'rapt weightlessness', or the closing pages of the C minor Quintet's *Andante moderato* send out resonances that finally embrace the entire work. The otherworldly dance beginning the finale of the First Quintet, the wild catch-as-catch-can opening and elfin close of the C minor Quintet's *Allegro vivo*, or the grave serenity of the following *Andante moderato* – all these are at the heart of Fauré's simultaneously conservative and radical genius. Simply as a person he remained conscious of an elusiveness that baffled and tantalised even his closest friends, companions who felt themselves gently but firmly excluded from his complex interior world. Domus fully suggests this enigma, yet plays with an ardour and élan that would surely have delighted the composer ('people play me as if the blinds were down'). The recordings are superb.

Piano Quartets

Piano Quartets – No 1 in C minor, Op 15; No 2 in G minor, Op 45
Domus (Krysia Osostowicz vn Robin Ireland va Timothy Hugh vc Susan Tomes pf)
Hyperion CDA66166 (62' · DDD)   Ⓕ**ooo**

 The First Piano Quartet reveals Fauré's debt to an earlier generation of composers, particularly Mendelssohn. Yet already it has the refined sensuality, the elegance and the craftsmanship which were always to be hallmarks of his style and it's a thoroughly assured, highly enjoyable work which could come from no other composer's pen. The Second Quartet is a more complex, darker work, but much less ready to yield its secrets. The comparatively agitated, quicksilver *Scherzo* impresses at once, however, and the complete work possesses considerable poetry and stature. Occasionally one might wish that Domus had a slightly more aristocratic, commanding approach to these scores, but the overall achievement is impressive, for their playing is both idiomatic and technically impeccable. The recording is faithful and well balanced.

Cello Works

Romance in A, Op 69[b]. Elégie, Op 24[b]. Cello Sonatas[b] – No 1 in D minor, Op 109; No 2 in G minor, Op 117. Allegretto moderato[a]. Sérénade, Op 98[b]. Sicilienne, Op 78[b]. Papillon, Op 77[b]. Andante[c]
Steven Isserlis, [a]**David Waterman** vcs [b]**Pascal Devoyon** pf [c]**Francis Grier** org
RCA Victor Red Seal 09026 68049-2 (62' · DDD)
Recorded 1993-4   Ⓕ

This, surely, is the most 'complete' of Fauré's complete works for cello yet to appear. Isserlis has unearthed the original version of the

Romance, Op 69 (entitled *Andante*), with a sustained, chordal accompaniment for organ in place of the piano's broken chordal semiquavers, and a gracious flourish from the cello by way of adieu. Mystically accompanied by Francis Grier at the organ of Eton College Chapel, the cello's song, restored to the church, seems to acquire more depth.

In the more familiar version of this work, as throughout the disc, Pascal Devoyon is a partner in a thousand, keenly aware of Isserlis's respect for the 'discretion, reticence and restraint' once hailed as the hallmarks of Fauré's style. In fact only in the noble *Elégie* do we discover the full breadth and richness of this cello's (a 1745 Guadagnini) tonal range.

A world war, plus the private trauma of incipient deafness, helps to explain the yawning gulf between the miniatures and the two sonatas of 1918 and 1922. Skipping through the score of the First you notice that only once does Fauré use a dynamic marking above *forte*, relying on the word *espressivo* to elicit just that little extra intensity at moments of climax. This is appreciated by both artists, most movingly in the central *Andante*. In the first movement, however, it's Devoyon's piquant accentuation that brings home the music's menace. The urgency and *Elégie*-evoking heart-throb of the G minor work again benefit from the immediacy of keyboard characterisation, and the variety of keyboard colour, underpinning this poetically introspective cellist's fine-spun line.

Additional recommendation

Cello Sonatas
Coupled with: Elégie. **Debussy** Cello Sonata
Tortelier vc **Hubeau** pf
Warner Elatus 0927-49012-2 (55' · ADD)   Ⓜ
Tortelier's tone can express true grandeur (in the *Elégie* and in the Second Sonata's sombre *Andante*); in the outer movements of this Sonata his lighter but still intense sound soars aloft to create an atmosphere of elation.

Violin Sonatas

No 1 in A, Op 13; **No 2** in E minor, Op 108

Fauré Violin Sonatas Nos 1 & 2[a] **Franck** Violin Sonata in A[b]
Arthur Grumiaux vn [a]**Paul Crossley**, [b]**György Sebok** pfs
Philips Musica da Camera 426 384-2PC (73' · ADD)
Recorded 1979   Ⓜ**oo**

Those Fauré-lovers who long prayed for a CD reissue of the two sonatas from Grumiaux and Paul Crossley won't be disappointed. The sound itself is pleasing – better, even, than it was on LP. And there's a radiance in the playing suggesting an unerring understanding of structure and style that goes hand in hand with the joyous spontaneity of new discovery. The hyper-sensitive suppleness of Grumiaux's shading and phrasing is a particular delight, as is his awareness that just as much of the musical message comes from the piano, particularly in the Second Sonata. Not for nothing has Crossley come to be recognised as one of this country's most dedicated Fauré specialists. It would be difficult to over-praise the subtlety of the two artists' interplay in both works. Their immediacy of response often finds outlet in a slightly faster tempo than most of their rivals, not least in both slow movements, where they rise more urgently to moments of heightened excitement. Despite the slightly plummier-sounding reproduction of György Sebok's piano, much pleasure is also to be found in the open-hearted warmth brought by both artists to the Franck Sonata, where you have the impression that Grumiaux himself might have put aside a silken Strad in favour of a throatier Guarnerius.

The Fauré Album
Andante in B flat, Op 75. Berceuse, Op 16. Piano Trio in D minor, Op 120[a]. Romance in B flat, Op 28. Violin Sonata No 1 in A, Op 13. Sérénade toscane, Op 3 No 2 (arr Ronchini). Clair de lune, Op 46 No 2 (arr Périlhou). Pelléas et Mélisande, Op 80 – Fileuse (arr Auer); Sicilienne. Morceau de lecture. Après un Rêve (arr Eguchi)[a]
Gil Shaham vn [a]**Brinton Smith** vc **Akira Eguchi** pf
Canary Classics/Vanguard Classics ATMCD1239
(77' · DDD)   ⒡**O**

Two major works have been well chosen as the cornerstones of this attractive compilation: the ardently lyrical First Violin Sonata and the Piano Trio, one of the finest examples of Fauré's late flowering in chamber music. In the sonata Shaham and Akira Eguchi bring out the contrasts between the passion of the first movement, the hushed opening of of the slow movement, the sparkling fantasy of the quirky *Scherzo* and the easy warmth of the finale. In the Piano Trio there's a similar urgency; this is a more freely expressive reading than, say, that of the Beaux Arts Trio. The programme is rounded off with a piano trio arrangement by Eguchi of *Après un Rêve*, with the cello and violin intertwining as they share the melody. Other favourites among the eight shorter pieces are two more songs, arranged for violin and piano: *Clair de lune* and *Sérénade toscane*. Shaham plays with a phenomenal range of tone and dynamic, always caressing the ear. The haunting Berceuse brings ravishing *pianissimos* with the violin again muted, fading into a magical silence.

Piano Works

Five Impromptus. Impromptu, Op 86. Thème et Variations in C sharp minor, Op 73. Romances sans paroles, Op 17. Quatre valses-caprices. 13 Barcarolles. Ballade in F sharp, Op 19. 13 Nocturnes. Souvenirs de Bayreuth[a]. Pièces brèves, Op 84. Dolly, Op 56[a]. Nine Préludes, Op 103.

Mazurka in B flat, Op 32
Kathryn Stott, [a]**Martin Roscoe** pfs
Hyperion ④ CDA66911/4 (297' · DDD) Recorded 1994   Ⓜ**OO**

Fauré's piano works are among the most subtly daunting in all keyboard literature. Encompassing Fauré's entire creative life, they range through an early, finely wrought eroticism via sporting with an aerial virtuosity as teasing and light as the elements themselves (the *Valses-caprices*) to the final desolation of his last years. There, in his most powerful works (*Barcarolles* Nos 7-11, *Nocturnes* Nos 11-13), he faithfully mirrors a pain that 'scintillates in full consciousness', a romantic agony prompted by increasing deafness and a lack of recognition that often seemed close to oblivion. Few compositions have reflected a darker night of the soul, and Fauré's anguish, expressed in both numbing resignation and unbridled anger, could surely only be exorcised by the articulation of such profound and disturbing emotional complexity. The task for the pianist, then, is immense, but in Kathryn Stott Fauré has a subtle and fearless champion. How thrilled Fauré would have been by the sheer immediacy of Stott's responses. Time and again she throws convention to the winds, and although it would be surprising if all her performances were consistent successes, disappointments are rare. Sometimes her *rubato* and luxuriant pedalling soften the outlines of Fauré's starkest, most austere utterances. But such quibbles remain quibbles. The Fourth *Nocturne* is gloriously supple, and the 13 *Barcarolles* show Stott acutely responsive to passion and finesse alike. The *Pièces brèves*, too, are played with rare affection. Stott proves herself a stylish and intriguing pianist.

---

13 Barcarolles   **H**
Germaine Thyssens-Valentin pf
Testament mono SBT1215 (72' · ADD)

13 Nocturnes
Germaine Thyssens-Valentin pf
Testament mono SBT1262 (80' · ADD)

4 Valses caprices. 6 Impromptus Pièces brèves, Op 84
Germaine Thyssens-Valentin pf
Testament mono SBT1263 (73' · ADD)
All recorded 1956-9   ⒡**OOO**

 Germaine Thyssens-Valentin (1902-87) was a great and inspired pianist; occasionally one hears Fauré playing that approaches, or even occasionally equals hers, but none that surpasses it. This review could be filled with a catalogue of her qualities, but her intimacy of expression demands first place. Fauré's music has a confiding quality to it, as though it were a message intended for an audience of one, and Thyssens-Valentin is in perfect accord with this. Those messages, however, especially in the later *Nocturnes* and *Barcarolles*, are often of great profundity, and she has both the heart and the technique to convey them.

Why isn't Thyssens-Valentin better known? Perhaps being a superlative interpreter of Fauré wasn't a reliable passport to international fame in the middle years of the 20th century; she also retired from the concert platform for a lengthy period, in order to bring up a family of five children. And she seems to have recorded mainly for the Ducretet-Thomson company, whose decline coincided with the arrival of stereo. The recordings here, by the way, are admirably clean and the remastering is beyond praise. Her sound, first of all, is wonderfully beautiful, a combination of the subtlest colour and great delicacy of touch ensuring that contrapuntal voices are in perfect balance. She's a mistress of the most refined *rubato*, extreme finesse of articulation and smooth, singing line. Although she excels in quiet delicacy, her strength when required is formidable but even in the strongest *fortissimo* she never makes an ugly sound. She is, blessedly, aware that Fauré had a sense of humour, and not only in the frank exuberance of the *Valses caprices*. Nor is she one of those artists that it takes a while to get used to. On each of these discs the first track is immediately characteristic of her. The first Nocturne has immaculate voice-leading and the lightest-fingered *leggierissimo* playing imaginable; the first Barcarolle is wonderfully tender, its second idea poised and liquid; the first *Valse caprice* has rich fantasy, dazzling brilliance and adorable wit.

The exploration of Fauré's emotional and technical range through the *Barcarolles* and especially the *Nocturnes* has never seemed so absorbing, the companion on that voyage never so prodigal with insight. Truly, a great pianist.

Requiem

Requiem (original version – ed Rutter). Motets –
Ave verum corpus; Tantum ergo; Ave Maria; Maria,
Mater gratiae. Cantique de Jean Racine, Op 11
(orch. Rutter). Messe basse
Caroline Ashton, Ruth Holton *sops* **Stephen
Varcoe** *bar* **Simon Standage** *vn* **John Scott** *org*
**Cambridge Singers; City of London Sinfonia /
John Rutter**
Collegium COLCD109 (63' · ADD/DDD) Recorded
1984. Texts and translations included   Ⓕ**OOO**

Fauré began his Requiem in 1885, under the impact of the death of his father, but the work didn't take on the form in which we now know it until 15 years later. The familiar 1900 score, therefore, can't really be regarded as 'definitive'; it's a compromise, rather, between Fauré's original conception and what his publisher no doubt saw as the practicalities of concert performance. It's Fauré uncompromised that John Rutter has sought to restore in his edition of the seven-movement 1892 version, and his performance of it, using a chamber orchestra, a small choir and, in the 'Pie Jesu', a soprano who could easily be mistaken

for a treble (Fauré's own early performances used a boy soloist) is a most convincing argument for accepting this score as more 'authentic' than the customary 1900 version.

The differences are audibly obvious, and most are no less obviously improvements. The almost omnipresent organ now sounds more like a continuo instrument than (as can easily happen with the 1900 score) an unwelcome thickening of an already dark orchestra. Above all, one is more aware than in any other recording that the sound in Fauré's head when he conceived the work wasn't that of a conventional orchestra but the rich, dark graininess of divided violas and cellos, the radiant luminosity of the work provided not by violins or woodwind but by the voices. It's thus more unified than the later revision as well as being more intimate. Rutter's chorus is a fine one, immaculate of diction and pure of line; Stephen Varcoe's light and unforced baritone could well be just what Fauré had in mind and Caroline Ashton's absolute purity in her brief solo is most moving. The recording is excellent.

Requiem[a]. Pavane, Op 50
[a]**Robert Chilcott** *treb* [a]**John Carol Case** *bar* [a]**King's
College Choir Cambridge; New Philharmonia
Orchestra / Sir David Willcocks**
EMI 764715-2 (42' · ADD) Recorded 1967. Text and
translation included   Ⓜ**OO**

This is the Fauré Requiem to come home to. It's tempting to describe it as a recording as near as can be to absolute perfection from start to finish. If an earlier version of the score is wanted, the smaller orchestra being in some ways preferable, then the recording by the Cambridge Singers under the text's editor, John Rutter, might be tried instead. But for what we used to mean by the Fauré Requiem in days when ignorance of textual complications was bliss, then this is still the best. Willcocks neither sentimentalises nor hurries; the choir is on top form; Robert Chilcott sings the *Pie Jesu* with the most touchingly beautiful purity and control, and John Carol Case brings to his solos a style that exactly matches that of the famous choir. If anything, time has enhanced appreciation, for the recorded sound compares so favourably, giving due prominence to the choir and obtaining an immediacy of sound that these days is exceptional. The only matter for regret is that the *Pavane* wasn't performed in its choral version, but as it's such an exquisite composition in either form the regret is short lived.

Fauré Requiem, Op 48 (1901 version)[a]   Ⓟ
Franck Symphony in D minor
[a]**Collegium Vocale;** [a]**La Chapelle Royale; Champs
Elysées Orchestra, Paris / Philippe Herreweghe**
Harmonia Mundi HMC90 1771 (76' · DDD) Notes,
texts and translations included   Ⓕ**O**

Philippe Herreweghe's earlier recording of the

Fauré *Requiem* (also Harmonia Mundi) used Jean-Michel Nectoux's edition of the original 1891 'chamber' score. This is the familiar 1901 version, with its full if curious orchestration, but in other respects this is a more 'authentic' reading than the earlier one. Period instruments are used, gut strings giving the sound a gentle luminescence, and instead of an organ Fauré's permitted alternative, a large harmonium, adds a reedy quality to the wind scoring. A shade more controversially, the work is sung in 'Gallican' Latin – 'Pié Zhesü' instead of 'Pie Yesou', 'Lüx perpétüa', and so on. Together with the other period details it makes the work sound distinctly Gallic: an admirable antidote to the Anglicised or even Anglicanised Fauré presented by the archetypally English cathedral and college choirs that have so often recorded it. Both soloists are excellent, Herreweghe's tempos are a little more alert than before and the recording is splendidly ample. Alongside gut strings the big advantage of a period orchestra in Franck is the beautifully smooth sound of the horns. The overall sound is more transparent than usual, and Franck's reputation for dense over-scoring seems more than ever unjustified. It's a fine and idiomatic performance and hugely enjoyable. A fascinating coupling, strongly recommended.

Requiem, Op 48[a]. Pavane, Op 50. Cantique de Jean Racine, Op 11. La Naissance de Vénus, Op 29[b]
[a]**Libby Crabtree**, [b]**Mary Plazas** *sops* [b]**Pamela Helen Stephen** *mez* [b]**Timothy Robinson** *ten* [ab]**James Rutherford** *bass-bar* **City of Birmingham Symphony Chorus; BBC Philharmonic Orchestra / Yan Pascal Tortelier**
Chandos CHAN10113 (70' · DDD) Texts and translations included ⒻO

It was the French music publisher Hamelle who suggested that Fauré expand his 'petit Requiem' (1893 version – as restored by John Rutter) into a 'version symphonique' (1900). However, if you like Fauré's evergreen sung by a large chorus supported by symphonic-strength strings and brass then this new recording will suit nicely.

The disc's sound is consistently warm, reverberant and engaging. The chorus are in committed form: unanimous, well blended and balanced. Aside from one ugly glitch from the sopranos in the Requiem's *Sanctus* ('hosanna-RIN-excelsis'), they should be congratulated on their clear diction. Unlike Philippe Herreweghe's 'authentic' recording, no attempt has been made to sing the Latin text with a French accent. Yan Pascal Tortelier's tempos are perfectly sensible, though the opening *Kyrie* is well below the metronome marking. Both soloists control their fervour admirably, and the organist Jonathan Scott conjures up a wide variety of (presumably) electronic organ tone, including a delicious hamonium-type combination in the 'Pie Jesu'.

The enjoyable makeweights *Pavane* and *Cantique de Jean Racine* both breathe the calm air of

FAURÉ REQUIEM – IN BRIEF

BBC PO / Yan Pascal Tortelier
Chandos CHAN10113 (70' · DDD)   ⒻO
A warm and spacious mainstream performance that comes as part of an all-Fauré collection taking in the rarely heard *La naissance de Vénus*.

City of London Sinfonia / John Rutter
Collegium COLCD109 (63' · ADD)   ⒻOOO
Rutter's recording of his own edition of the original 1893 score retains its fascination. The sound is more closely balanced than is usually the case with the larger-scale traditional readings.

New Philharmonia / David Willcocks
EMI 764715-2 (42' · ADD)   ⓂOO
A much-loved LP version, documenting the excellence of the King's College Choir at its mid-1960s peak, and still sounding well.

Champs Elysées Orchestra / Herreweghe
Harmonia Mundi HMC90 1771 (76' · DDD)   ⒻO
Herreweghe, the first to tape Jean-Michel Nectoux's reconstruction of the composer's lightly scored original (Harmonia Mundi HMC90 1292), here gives new life to the 1901 version, again favouring surprisingly broad tempos. The coupling is unique: a period instrument performance of the Franck Symphony.

ASMF / George Guest
Decca ② 436 486-2DF2 (149' · ADD)   Ⓜ
Fresh, vivid and relatively small-scale, the Choir of St John's College, Cambridge, as taped in 1975, shines in a twofer of French choral classics.

Philharmonia / Andrew Davis
Sony Classical SBK67182 (79' · ADD)   Ⓑ
The natural pairing of Requiems, Fauré's plus Duruflé's, with big orchestral textures and star sopranos taking solos in both works.

ASMF / Sir Neville Marriner
Philips 446 084-2PH (54' · DDD)   Ⓕ
With Sylvia McNair and Thomas Allen the outstanding soloists, Sir Neville Marriner's 1993 version uses the fuller orchestration but never lets the music drag. His unusual makeweight is a select group of French orchestral miniatures, exquisitely played.

BBC SO / Nadia Boulanger
BBC Legends BBCL4026-2 (75' · ADD)   Ⓕ
A blast from the past, Nadia Boulanger's performance has dignity and gravitas, while the rest of the programme, featuring music by Nadia's short-lived sister Lili, has even greater authority.

the Requiem. But the disc's revelation is a wonderful performance of the rarely heard *La Naissance de Vénus*, a 23-minute 'mythological scene' completed in 1895. Often criticised for its supposedly banal text, it's a little gem. The solo quartet, chorus and orchestra are first rate throughout.

Songs

The Complete Songs – 1, Au bord de l'eau

Les Matelots. Seule! La chanson du pêcheur. Barcarolle, Op 7 No 3. Au bord de l'eau. Tarentelle, Op 10 No 2. Les berceaux. Larmes. Au cimetière. Cinq Mélodies de Venise. Pleurs d'or. La fleur qui va l'eau. Accompagnement. Mirages. C'est la paix!. L'horizon chimérique
Felicity Lott, Geraldine McGreevy, Jennifer Smith *sops* Stella Doufexis *mez* John Mark Ainsley *ten* Stephen Varcoe, Christopher Maltman *bars* Graham Johnson *pf*
Hyperion CDA67333 (69' · DDD · T/t)   ⒡**OO**

This is the first of four projected CDs to cover all Fauré's *mélodies*. It's been attempted three times before, by Dalton Baldwin, with Gérard Souzay and Elly Ameling (EMI), then by Malcolm Martineau, with Sarah Walker and Tom Krause (CRD), most recently by Jeff Cohen, with François Le Roux and Béatrice Uria-Monzon (REM). Few singers would give over a whole evening to Fauré's songs on the concert platform, and choosing a way of presenting them on disc obviously poses problems. The EMI set had all the songs in chronological order; the others chose poets or moods: Graham Johnson and company have begun with songs about water. This means a lot of dreaming and melancholy, whether in Gautier's *Chanson du pêcheur* ('Ma belle amie est morte', also set by Berlioz), or Richepin's *Au cimitière*. The latter is given a most beautiful rendition by John Mark Ainsley, who otherwise only sings on two tracks, with Jennifer Smith in the sentimental *Pleurs d'or*, and the homage to Venice and its lovers in Marc Monnier's *Barcarolle*.

Three cycles are the main items here. Felicity Lott sings the *Cinq Mélodies de Venise*, which includes some of Fauré's best-known songs, 'Mandoline', 'En sourdine' and 'Green'. She brings to bear on them a lifetime's devotion to French song. Her other contribution is *Au bord de l'eau*, to a poem by Sully-Prudhomme. This is made to sound very sad; taken faster it can be quite merry; it's a celebration of love, as well as a meditation on the passing of time.

Stephen Varcoe sings *Mirages*, Fauré's penultimate cycle (1919). As Graham Johnson writes in his fascinating notes, these poems by Brimont permitted Fauré 'uneventful passion'. Christopher Maltman is the other featured singer, in five separate songs and *L'horizon chimérique*. All the performances are elegant and well-balanced, but one misses the extra slight note of acid that native French singers bring to Fauré's songs.

Hyperion's sound is impeccable and in both his playing and accompanying essay, Graham Johnson penetrates to the heart of one of music's most subtle and enigmatic geniuses.

The Complete Songs – 2, Un paysage choisi

Mai, Op 1 No 2[f]. Dans les ruines d'une abbaye, Op 2 No 19. Sérénade toscane, Op 3 No 2[e]. Lydia, Op 4 No 2[f]. Three Songs, Op 59 – No 1, Chant d'automne; No 3, L'Absent. Tristesse, Op 6 No 2[b]. Après un rêve, Op 7 No 1[e]. Puisqu'ici-bas, Op 10 No 1[bd]. Three Songs, Op 18 – No 2, Le voyageur[h]; No 3, Automne[b]. La fée aux chansons, Op 27 No 2[b]. Noël, Op 43 No 1[e]. Clair de lune, Op 46 No 2[a]. Spleen, Op 51 No 39. Prison, Op 83 No 1[h]. Dans la forêt de septembre, Op 85 No 19. Chanson, Op 949. Les jardins clos, Op 106[c]. Il est né, le divin Enfant[b]. En prière[b]
[a]Felicity Lott, [b]Geraldine McGreevy, [c]Jennifer Smith *sops* [d]Stella Doufexis *mez* [e]John Mark Ainsley, [f]Jean-Paul Fouchécourt *tens* 9Stephen Varcoe, [h]Christopher Maltman *bars* Graham Johnson *pf*
Hyperion CDA67334 (68' · DDD · T/t)   ⒡

Volume 2 of Hyperion's superb Fauré song series takes its theme from *Clair de lune* and an idealised landscape peopled with dreaming birds and sobbing fountains. It follows the composer from youth to old age, from the young charmer to the mature master to the inscrutable sage, imaginatively side-stepping all possible monotony. Fauré's dream world is a mirror of an occasionally innocent nature that received too many cruel knocks, reflected in music of light and darkness, courage and despair. All the singers involved in this ideally presented and recorded offering perform with a special ardour and commitment; Graham Johnson is, as always, a matchless partner and commentator.

Robert Fayrfax   British 1464-1521

Fayrfax was a Gentleman of the Chapel Royal by 1497, graduated MusB (1501) and MusD (1504) at Cambridge and was incorporated DMus at Oxford (1511). From 1509 until his death he was senior lay clerk there, and received many payments from Henry VIII for music MSS. 29 compositions by him survive (more than by any other English composer of his generation), including two Magnificats, ten votive antiphons and secular pieces. He is important for his cultivation of the cyclic mass, of which six of his are known, all except one are based on a plainsong cantus firmus in the tenor of the full sections. His music is less elaborate than that of Cornysh and Taverner and uses restrained, carefully wrought melodic lines.   GROVEmusic

Missa Regali ex Progenie

(ed Skinner). Antiphona Regali ex Progenie. Missa Regali ex Progenie. Lauda Vivi Alpha et O. Magnificat

Regali. Alas, for lak of her presens.
That was my woe
The Cardinall's Musick / Andrew Carwood
ASV Gaudeamus CDGAU185 (78' · DDD) Texts and
translations included   Ⓕ

Fayrfax's *Missa Regali ex Progenie* and *Magnificat Regali* are both early works, written before 1504, perhaps to impress his royal patron, and both, particularly the mass, show signs that the composer had yet to settle into his stride. The longer, wordy movements of the Mass (the *Gloria* and *Credo*) seem elusive, as though he were note-spinning rather than weaving the contrapuntal texture, even if the hallmarks of greatness are all there. The Cardinall's Musick, with its by now almost instinctive understanding of his music, gives as convincing a performance as anyone could, or likely will, for some considerable time to come.

The votive antiphon *Lauda Vivi Alpha et O*, with its coda in praise of Henry VIII, probably dates from the time of or shortly after his coronation in 1509. This extended homage to the Virgin is rich in textural resonances, and a double meaning of 'O rosa gratie redolentissima' ('Most sweetly scented rose') was surely intended. Here the long-drawn-out vocal lines, shifts in scoring, intellectual transitions of harmony of Fayrfax's mature style are much in evidence and the work's richness is given its full due here. There's a striking contrast between this full-blown rose of a piece and the closed, but equally perfectly formed rosebud that is the duo 'That was my woe': it was a long way from ceremonial homage to semi-private entertainment in Tudor London. It's sung perfectly by Robin Blaze and Steven Harrold.

Magnificat, 'O Bone Ihesu'

Magnificat, 'O Bone Ihesu'. Missa, O Bone Ihesu.
Salve regina. Most clere of colour. I love, loved and
loved wolde I be. Benedicite! What dreamed I?
(all ed Skinner)
The Cardinall's Musick / Andrew Carwood
ASV Gaudeamus CDGAU184 (76' · DDD) Texts and
translations included   ⒻO

The Cardinall's Musick put the focus here on Fayrfax's Mass *O bone Ihesu*. Tragically, only a single voice survives of the antiphon that was probably its model, so in that respect their recording can't be complete, unless David Skinner is prepared to indulge in the massive and quixotic task of reconstruction for this and other fragmentary survivals. But we do have a glorious *Magnificat* built on the same materials, one of the most widely distributed of all early Tudor works. By far the most commanding performance here is of that *Magnificat*: wonderfully controlled and perfectly tuned. The group is slightly rougher in the mass and the *Salve regina*, a work that stands rather apart from the style we otherwise know from Fayrfax, and which may be one of his earliest surviving

works. Intriguingly, this is the piece that seems to show the strongest debts to composers from the Continent (especially Brumel), giving important insights into the evolution of his music. Similarly, the three songs presented here, in performances that are skilled but slightly wooden, show a remarkable affinity with other mainland music, particularly that of Alexander Agricola. These little three-voice works, with their beautifully evocative texts, can without any doubt be counted among the glories of early Tudor music.

John Field   Irish 1782-1837

Field's early musical training came from his father and from Tommaso Giordani in Dublin, after which he was apprenticed to Muzio Clementi in London. He probably studied with Salomon. By 1801 he had established a reputation as a concert pianist and published his first important works, the piano sonatas Op 1. As a result of a successful continental tour with Clementi (1802-3) he remained in St Petersburg, becoming an idol of fashionable society there and in Moscow, teaching, giving concerts and composing until 1823, when illness overwhelmed him; he died in Moscow, having made one return visit to London and to other European cities.

During his lifetime Field was known chiefly for the sensitivity of his playing, especially his expressive touch, singing phrases and extreme delicacy, a striking contrast to the fashion for virtuoso display. This legendary playing style was supported by the publication of his 17 nocturnes, each a self-sufficient piece evoking a dreamy mood of sadness consoled; song-like in manner and texture, they anticipated Chopin's pieces of the same type by nearly 20 years and influenced Liszt and Mendelssohn. Among Field's other, more numerous works, the most important are the rondos and fantaisies for piano, the Kamarinskaya variations (1809) and the Air russe varié for piano duet (1808), and the seven piano concertos. At his best, he was the equal of any of the Romantic pianist-composers.   **GROVE**music

Piano Concertos

No 1 in E flat, H27; No 3 in E flat, H32
Benjamin Frith *pf* **Northern Sinfonia / David
Haslam**
Naxos 8 553770 (52' · DDD)   Ⓢ ⓈO

Benjamin Frith presents a very formidable challenge to rival versions, at super-budget price. Both works are played with effortless fluency, plus all the immediacy and freshness of new discovery. In No 1 Frith is acutely responsive to the delicate charm of the Scottish-inspired ('*Twas within a mile of Edinboro' Town*) slow movement. He makes one aware of Field's teasing delight in the unexpected in the smiling outer movements, to which he brings a wide range of tone, and piquant accentuation in the last. There's warm, sympathetic support from the Northern Sinfonia under David Haslam. The performers revel in the composer's surprises of modulation, rhythm and orchestral colouring, while from the soloist there isn't a trace of the perfunctory in passagework. The recording (in a resonant venue) might be thought overforward and full, but it remains a true bargain.

Piano Concertos – No 2 in A flat, H31;   **P**
No 3 in E flat, H32
Andreas Staier *fp* **Concerto Köln / David Stern**
Warner Elatus 0927-49610-2 (62' · DDD)   **Ⓜ❍**

For those who love the sound and capabilities of the modern piano, the fortepiano's thinner tone, distinctive timbre and more intimate dynamic scope (or, put another way, the lack of power) take some adjusting to. But once one is attuned to its tonal and colouristic possibilities, the daring nature of the piano writing emerges with striking force. Take the soloist's first entry in the Second Concerto, where the virtuosic power and originality delivers its full intended *frisson* and physicality when heard on an instrument being pushed to its limit. Andreas Staier is a brilliant pianist who allies dazzling technical élan to his acute musical insight and imagination. In the outer movements, his fingerwork is as precise and crystalline as his musical intelligence, with passagework assuming a quasi-melodic purpose, elevated to the level of what Gerald Abraham called 'significant line'.

The slow movement of the A flat Concerto, a brief contrasting *molto espressivo* song without words, is played with unaffected simplicity and clarity of line, while in the E flat major Concerto, Staier follows Field's own practice of interpolating one of his nocturnes as a slow movement by playing the well-known work in C minor. Staier is a most poetic and inspiring advocate, yet the success of these performances is as much due to the extraordinary clarity and impact of the Concerto Köln's orchestral playing. There's such an infectious generosity of spirit, such vivid character and crispness, with beautifully poised wind playing and a real bite from the brass and timpani. Try the opening of the finale of the Second Concerto, where, after the lilting melody is presented by the soloist, the full orchestra respond with invigorating gusto and rusticity, never losing their tonal blend or refinement. The recorded sound, too, is wonderfully clear and detailed.

Piano Concertos – No 5 in C, 'L'incendie par l'orage';
No 6 in C
Benjamin Frith *pf* **Northern Sinfonia / David Haslam**
Naxos 8 554221 (57' · DDD)   **Ⓢ Ⓢ❍**

Benjamin Frith proves an ideal soloist in these attractive, decorative pieces. Like his close contemporary, Hummel, Field is much more adept

at embroidering the themes which bubble from him than at developing them in a conventional way. The passagework which can seem just trivial needs both the virtuosity and the artistry of a pianist of charm such as Frith if it's to come fully alive and compel attention, as it does here.

Frith's articulation is sparklingly clear throughout with rapid scales and decorations pearly and wonderfully even, helped by the relatively intimate acoustic of the theatre in Gosforth where the recordings were made.

The title of the Fifth Concerto, *L'incendie par l'orage* ('Fire from the Storm'), is inspired by the passage of storm music towards the end of the central development section in the first movement. Surprisingly Field, the inventor of the nocturne and inspirer of Chopin, here avoids a full slow movement, contenting himself instead with a slow introduction to the jaunty finale. At least he makes amends in the Sixth Concerto, where the central *Larghetto* slow movement is a nocturne in everything but name, with soaring cantilena for the piano which might well have inspired Bellini. The finale is a sparkling polka-like movement, with passagework breathtakingly elaborate, which Frith rightly treats as fun music, a fine pay-off. Haslam and the Northern Sinfonia are well recorded, too, in the relatively small-scale acoustic.

Gerald Finzi   British 1901-1956

Finzi studied privately with Farrar (1914-16) and Bairstow (1917-22) and lived most of his life in the country. Influenced by Elgar and Vaughan Williams as well as his teachers, he developed an intimate style and concentrated on songs, particularly settings of Hardy. Other works include a clarinet concerto (1949) and Dies natalis for high voice and strings (1939).   **GROVE**music

Cello Concerto

Finzi Cello Concerto, Op 40[a] **Leighton** Cello Concerto, Op 31[b]
Raphael Wallfisch *vc* [a]**Royal Liverpool Philharmonic Orchestra / Vernon Handley;** [b]**Royal Scottish National Orchestra / Bryden Thomson**
Chandos CHAN9949 (72' · DDD) Recorded 1986, 1989   Ⓕ

The Cello Concerto is arguably Finzi's finest work, written at the very end of his life under the stress of knowing he was terminally ill. At just under 40 minutes it's planned on a massive scale. The first movement brings the darkest music, an extended *tutti* establishing a brooding tone of voice. The slow movement is in more characteristically tender pastoral vein, with a poignant tinge of melancholy, music originally conceived many years before its actual completion in 1951. Leighton's Cello Concerto is almost equally ambitious. Helped by full, warm

pioneering Lyrita recording, yet with no loss of composure. A wordless female chorus intensifes the atmosphere of mystic awe that permeates the succeeding 'Mantra of Bliss'. The concluding 'Mantra of Will' strictly employs the seven-note modal scale of a South Indian raga. A daring, extended pause ushers in a flamboyantly savage pay-off (here rather more transparent and tidier in execution than under Wordsworth).

Next comes *Lyra Celtica*, a concerto for wordless voice and orchestra written between 1917 and the mid-1920s for his wife, the soprano Maud McCarthy. In the event Foulds completed only two of the three movements (the finale remains a 150-bar fragment). It's an alluring discovery, which deploys both microtones and quarter-tones (a Foulds trademark). Mezzo Susan Bickley rises valiantly to the challenge.

By comparison, *Apotheosis* (1909) and *Mirage* (1910) strike a rather more conventional note, though Daniel Hope's contribution in the former locates the lyrical beauty in this heartfelt elegy in memory of Joachim. Richard Strauss looms large in *Mirage*, an opulent 23-minute tone-poem with much arresting incident, which Oramo and the CBSO do proud.

The sound is hugely vivid and Calum Mac-Donald's annotation a model of its kind. Don't miss this gem of a release.

César Franck Belgian/French 1822-1890

Franck, French composer, teacher and organist of Belgian birth, was intended by his ambitious father for a career as a piano virtuoso. He studied at the Liège (1830-35) and Paris (1837-42) conservatories but found his true vocation only later through organist's appointments in Paris, chiefly that of Ste Clotilde (from 1858) and part-time teaching. His improvisatory skill attracted notice and led to his first major work, the remarkable Six pièces (1862), though another decade passed before he was appointed organ professor at the Conservatoire. From the mid-1870s until his death his creative powers lasted unabated. He wrote large-scale sacred works, notably the oratorio Les béatitudes (1879), and several symphonic poems such as Le chausseur maudit (1882) and Psyché (1888). But his achievements are evident especially in the symphonic, chamber and keyboard works in which he made one of the most distinguished contributions to the field by any French musician. Here, in the Piano Quintet (1879), the Prélude, choral et fugue for piano (1884), the Violin Sonata (1886), the Symphony in D minor (1888) and the String Quartet (1889), his inherent emotionalism and a preoccupation with counterpoint and traditional forms found a balance, in turn decisively impressing his band of disciples, from Duparc, d'Indy and Chausson to Lekeu, Vierne, Dukas and Guilmant. Features of his mature style, indebted alike to Beethoven, Liszt and Wagner, are his complex, mosaic-like phrase structures, variants of one or two motifs; his rich chro-

maticism, often put to structural use in the 'chord pair'; and his fondness for cyclic, tripartite forms.

GROVEmusic

Symphony in D minor

Symphony in D minor. Symphonic Variations[a].
Les Eolides
[a]**Louis Lortie** pf **BBC Philharmonic Orchestra /
Yan Pascal Tortelier**
Chandos CHAN9875 (62' · DDD)   Ⓕ❍

With so many versions of the Symphony and the *Symphonic Variations* available, it's surprising that these two favourite orchestral works aren't coupled more often. Here Tortelier adds an attractive bonus in the evocative tone-poem *Les Eolides*.

His reading of the Symphony is no less than five minutes shorter than both the Karajan and Chailly versions. The reading isn't in any way perfunctory, rushed or trivial, but one made fresher, eliminating any suspicion of the glutinous or sentimental, helped by a cleanly defined yet atmospheric recording. The slow introduction, promptly repeated, is all the more effective for being taken at a flowing speed, with no feeling of haste, and the main *Allegro* is fresh and alert, less smooth than with either Karajan or Chailly. However, Monteux's account, which has a very different coupling (*Petrushka*), is still the most idiomatic performance of all, bitingly dramatic, too, with the 1959 sound astonishingly full and vivid. Tortelier is far closer to Monteux in his feeling for the idiom than either Karajan or Chailly, both taking a weighty view. In tempo Tortelier is very similar to Karajan and Monteux in the central *Allegretto*, with fine gradations of dynamic and a slightly raw-sounding cor anglais adding to the freshness. It's in the finale that Tortelier is most distinctive, his fast, urgent speed for the *Allegro non troppo* challenging the players of the BBC Philharmonic to produce exciting rather than genial results.

Louis Lortie is the excellent soloist in the *Symphonic Variations*, spontaneously poetic in the slow sections, sparkling and light in the *scherzando* finale. Tortelier is again at his most warmly understanding in *Les Eolides*, a work that can seem wayward, but which here is made light and fanciful in its luminously scored evocation of the breezes of heaven.

Franck Symphony in D minor[a] **Mendelssohn**
Symphony No 5 in D, 'Reformation', Op 107[b]
[a]**Berlin Radio Symphony Orchestra,** [b]**Berlin
Philharmonic Orchestra / Lorin Maazel**
DG The Originals 449 720-2GOR (64' · ADD)
Recorded 1961   Ⓜ

This CD preserves a phenomenon: a living legend in the making. Appreciative insert-notes describe features of Maazel's work of the period – freshness of vision and youthful vitality tempered by a feeling for line and a classical poise – to which might be added a more timeless characteristic: a sensational command of the orchestra. In 1961 both orchestras were at their finest, and there are countless examples of expressive shaping, pointing and shading. Just occasionally, you're aware of command over-exercised: the finale of the Franck has one or two radical swells and drastic *diminuendos* and *pianissimos*. And some of Maazel's more racy tempos are questionable. But the very mobile *Allegretto* central movement of the Franck works like a dream. The finale of the Mendels-sohn is admittedly a 'problem' movement, and inclined to sound foursquare if not dispatched with a certain dash. Maazel's quick march solves the problem, but leaves little room for airy cele-bration and final elation. The recordings con-tribute to the lean-and-hungry impression of the performances: always superbly clear, but wanting warmth and space in *fortissimo tutti*s (those of the Franck are often strident and hec-toring).

Piano Quintet

Franck Piano Quintet in F minor[a] **Mozart** Clarinet Quintet in A, K581[b] **R Strauss** Capriccio – Prelude[c]
Amadeus Quartet (Norbert Brainin, Siegmund Nissel *vns* Peter Schidlof *va* Martin Lovett *vc*)
[b]**Gervase de Peyer** *cl* [a]**Clifford Curzon** *pf* [c]**Cecil Aronowitz** *va* [c]**William Pleeth** *vc*
BBC Legends/IMG Artists *amono* BBCL4061-2
(77' · ADD) Recorded live [a]1960, [b]1966, [c]1971

Ⓜ❍❍❍

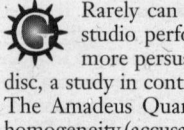
Rarely can a case for live rather than studio performances have been made more persuasively than by the present disc, a study in contrasts if ever there was one. The Amadeus Quartet was celebrated for its homogeneity (accusations from critics of a plush or *de luxe* style were rare), yet this superb ensemble could easily accommodate other radi-cally different players, and here Curzon's leg-endary nervous intensity is accentuated by the Amadeus, who join him in a performance of the Franck Quintet so supercharged it virtually tears itself apart. Taken from a 1960 Aldeburgh Festival concert, it eclipses all others (even Cur-zon's revelatory Decca disc). Curzon and his colleagues hurl themselves at music which clearly they see as hardly needing a cooling agent. How free and rhapsodic is Curzon's reply to the Amadeus's opening *dramatico*, and what a savage explosion of pent-up energy from all the players at 7'02"! Intonation may suffer in the finale's equestrian nightmare, but the conclud-ing pages are overwhelming, and Curzon's dart-ing *crescendo*s at 3'56" and 58" are like snarls of defiance.

At the opposite end of the spectrum is Mozart's Clarinet Quintet, that assuaging and elusive glory of the repertoire, played with all Gervase de Peyer's serenity and elegance. Yet again, the performance is essentially live, and has the sort of vitality and imaginative subtlety less easy to achieve or even countenance in the studio. And the same could be said of Cecil

Aronowitz and William Pleeth, who join the Amadeus for Strauss's Prelude to *Capriccio*, aptly described in the notes as 'a sumptuous effusion of very late romanticism'. The recordings (1960-71) are vivid and immediate, and odd noises off only add to the sense of occasion. Finally, a word of warning; this performance of the Franck isn't for late-night listening: you'll sleep more peacefully after the Mozart.

Cello Sonata

Franck Cello Sonata in A **Lekeu** Cello Sonata in G **Ysaÿe** Solo Cello Sonata, Op 28. Rêve d'enfant, Op 14
Raphael Wallfisch *vc* **John York** *pf*
Cello Classics CC1009 (78' · DDD) Ⓕ❍❍

Raphael Wallfisch's and John York's playing in the Franck has an air of spontaneity and enjoy-ment which exudes a very natural ebb and flow, while the ample ambience allows them to make the most of the 'big' moments, such as the cen-tral climax in the finale.

The disc also scores through its imaginative programming, placing the two Franco-Belgian sonatas alongside music by the great violinist who inspired them. Ysaÿe's unaccompanie Cello Sonata is an impressive, sombre work; as in the more familiar violin sonatas, echoes of the Baroque are placed within an impressionistic context. Wallfisch's account is magnificent – full-blooded, yet very clear and precise.

The Lekeu, with its opulent, passionate piano part and predominately lyrical string writing, transcribes just as effectively for the cello as does the Franck. And its grand emotions inspire a very wholehearted response. Thoroughly rec-ommended.

Violin Sonata

Debussy Violin Sonata. Sonata for Flute, Viola and Harp **Franck** Violin Sonata in A **Ravel** Introduction and Allegro
Kyung-Wha Chung *vn* **Osian Ellis** *hp* **Radu Lupu** *pf*
Melos Ensemble
Decca 421 154-2DM (67' · ADD) Recorded 1962-77
Ⓜ❍❍❍

Here we have masterpieces from the French tradition in excellent perform-ances that have won the status of recording classics. Kyung-Wha Chung and Radu Lupu are a fine duo who capture and con-vey the delicacy and poetry of the Franck Sonata as well as its rapturous grandeur, and never can the strict canonic treatment of the great tune in the finale have sounded more spontaneous and joyful. They are no less successful in the differ-ent world of the elusive Sonata which was Debussy's last work, with its smiles through tears and, in the finale, its echoes of a Neapoli-tan tarantella. The 1977 recording is beautifully balanced, with a natural sound given to both the violin and piano. The Melos Ensemble recorded the Ravel *Introduction and Allegro* 15 years before, but here too the recording is a fine one for which no allowances have to be made even by ears accustomed to good digital sound; as for the work itself, this has an ethereal beauty that's nothing short of magical and Osian Ellis and his colleagues give it the most skilful and loving performance. A wonderful disc and a must-buy.

Piano Works

Prélude, choral et fugue. Prélude, aria et final. Grand caprice. Les plaintes d'une poupée. Danse lente. Choral No 3 in A minor (arr Hough)
Stephen Hough pf
Hyperion CDA66918 (68' · DDD)   Ⓕ◐

Hough has a dream-ticket combination of virtues – astonishing agility, a faultless ear for texture, fine-tuned stylistic sensibility and an exceptional understanding of harmonic and structural tensions. He acknowledges all Franck's nuances, notated and implied, without ever disturbing the broader flow; he gives full rein to the heroic Lisztian cascades, without ever tipping over into melodrama. The only hint of a nit to be picked would be that the *fortissimo* arpeggiations in the 'Choral' don't ring as resonantly as they might. One can't imagine the calm at the end of the 'Aria' being better judged. In their very different ways the almost comical bravura of the *Grand caprice* and the salon charm of the *Danse lente* and *Les plaintes d'une poupée* are extremely difficult to bring off with success. Yet anyone who has followed Hough's recording career will know that this sort of thing is meat and drink to him. As for his own transcription of the A minor *Chorale*, the unavoidable adjective is 'awesome'.

Organ Works

Pièce héroïque in B minor. Cantabile in B. Fantaisie in A. Grande pièce symphonique in F sharp minor, Op 17. Pastorale in E, Op 19. Fantaisie in C, Op 16. Prélude, fugue et variation in B minor, Op 18. Trois chorales – No 1 in E; No 2 in B minor; No 3 in A minor. Prière in C sharp minor, Op 20. Final in B flat, Op 21
Marie-Claire Alain org
Erato ② 0630-12706-2 (152' · DDD) Recorded on the Cavaillé-Coll organ, Saint-Etienne, Caen, France 1995   Ⓜ

Alain is a completely involved communicator. More than anyone else she delves into the very soul of these works. Thus we have an intensely prayerful *Prière*, a majestically statuesque *Grande pièce symphonique* while the *Chorales* are delivered with an unexpected degree of fervour; perhaps the Third is a shade overfervent since some of the semiquaver figurations lack absolute clarity – something which after one or two hearings serves to heighten the excitement

but which might, after repeated listening, become irritating. This is a highly authoritative release not just in terms of playing but also in Alain's accompanying notes. The Caen organ is a particularly fine specimen of a Cavaillé-Coll, dating from 1884 – 25 years after the St Clotilde organ for which Franck wrote much of this music. The recording captures it, and the church's atmosphere, effectively.

Girolamo Frescobaldi
Italian 1583-1643

Frescobaldi studied with Luzzaschi at Ferrara, where he also came under Gesualdo's influence. Soon after 1600 he went to Rome where in 1607 he became organist of S Maria in Trastevere. The same year he travelled with his patron, Guido Bentivoglio, to Brussels, but his experience of this centre of keyboard music left little imprint on him, except perhaps in the fantasias of 1608. In July 1608 Frescobaldi was elected organist of St Peter's, Rome; during the following years he was employed also by Cardinal Pietro Aldobrandini and other patrons.

In 1615 Frescobaldi secured a position with Duke Ferdinando Gonzaga at Mantua, but after three months he returned to Rome, remaining there until 1628 when he became organist at the Medici court in Florence. By the time he returned once more to Rome, in 1634, his fame was international and he was moving in the highest circles of patronage. In 1637 Froberger came from Vienna to study with him. Little is known of his other pupils, but his influence on keyboard playing and composition remained important for a century or more.

Frescobaldi is remembered chiefly for his keyboard music, much of which was published in 12 volumes (1608-14) with toccatas, canzonas, ricercares, dances and variations. The most famous is Fiori musicali (1635), with pieces for use in the Mass: the Kyrie-Christe unit from the Ordinary, toccatas to be played during the Elevation and other pieces corresponding to items of the Proper (introit, gradual, offertory, communion). Bach owned a copy and learnt from it.

Frescobaldi's vocal music is of relatively small importance. His sacred works, including c40 motets, mostly for one to three voices and continuo, show none of the complexity and expressive intensity of the keyboard works. Perhaps his most characteristic vocal music is in an early volume of madrigals (1608), but two volumes of Arie musicali published during his years in Florence (1630) are also of interest.

GROVEmusic

Canzonas

Il Primo libro delle canzoni – La Bernadina; La Donatina; L'Altera; La Tucchina o La Superba; L'Ambitiosa; La Plettenberger; La Lievoratta; La Samminiata; La Diodata; La Nobile; Canzona Prima a due bassi; Canzona Quinta a due canti; Canzona Seconda a due canti e basso; Canzona Quinta a 4; Canzona Quarta a due canti e basso; Tre Canzona a

canto e basso; Canzona Prima a 4; Canzona Seconda
a 4; Canzona trigesima quinta
Les Basses Réunies / Bruno Cocset *vion*
Alpha ALPHA053 (65' · DDD)　　　　　　　　Ⓕ

As this ensemble's name implies, viols are the
start here, and part of the disc's attraction lies in
the novelty of hearing these pieces, which are
played often enough, in an instrumentation that
largely dispenses with the more usual winds.
The only touch of non-string colour is provided
by the cornetto.

The role of the continuo is immeasurably
enhanced, becoming not so much a backdrop to
the solo lines as their foundation. And the continuo section is rich indeed: harp, claviorganum,
theorbo and harpsichord. When everything
comes together the result is as colourful and
ear-tickling as anything to be heard on other
recordings of this repertoire.

The performances rise to the music's challenges with elegance and barely any technical
strain. This is a disc that grows on you with
repeated listening, and demonstrates that Frescobaldi's canzonas are no less inventive than his
keyboard music.

Keyboard Works

Il Primo libro di Ricercari et Canzoni francese　　Ⓟ
Il Primo libro delle fantasie
Sergio Vartolo *hpd/org*
Naxos ② 8 553547/8 (132' · DDD)　　　　　Ⓢ●

The *Fantasie* (1608) and *Ricercari* (1615) are the
earliest of Frescobaldi's keyboard publications,
and as neither has been issued complete before;
to get both together, and at super-budget price,
is treasure-trove indeed. Frescobaldi fanatics
need read no further.

Vartolo's tendency to spin out the music at
twice the length of most other interpreters can
be rather off-putting, and doesn't always help
the listener to grasp the overall design of formally complex pieces like the Toccatas. But
these Fantasias and Ricercars are imitative,
fugal pieces, more abstract in conception than
the exuberant toccatas; recognising this, Vartolo avoids extreme tempi, and instead gives
measured performances that gain in clarity what
they have lost in eccentricity. These are (and
this isn't intended to damn with faint praise)
sensible performances, that give both composer
and audience their due. Vartolo loosens up a bit
in the playful *Canzoni Francesi* that conclude the
book of Ricercars, but in this he follows the
composer's lead, and demonstrates his own sensitivity to style.

Vartolo mostly performs on a modern copy of
an Italian harpsichord, and on the organ of the
Chiesa del Spirito Santo, Pistoia (built a few
years after Frescobaldi's death). Suffice it to say
that this recording would be a must-have at full
price; as it is, you won't find better value anywhere.

Andrea Gabrieli　　　　Italian 1533-1585

*Possibly a pupil of Willaert, in 1557-8 Andrea
Gabrieli was organist of S Geremia, Cannaregio,
and in 1562 was working in Munich, where he met
Lassus. In 1566 he became organist of St Mark's,
Venice, where he remained all his life. A prolific and
exceptionally versatile composer, he was a leading
figure in Venice, respected as a performer and
teacher, 1576) and psalms (1583), as well as secular
and instrumental works (1566-80); many pieces
were published posthumously by his nephew Giovanni. He is chiefly famous for his sacred ceremonial
music (notably Concerti, 1587), in which he brilliantly exploited the architecture of St Mark's, sepa-
rating voices and instruments into cori spezzati to
create imposing stereophonic effects, a style that
greatly influenced other Venetian and German composers. His madrigals are more lightweight and
homophonic than others of the time, some showing
Lassus's influence.*　　　　　　　**GROVE**music

Madrigals

A Gabrieli 21 Madrigals – Caro dolce ben mio,
perchè fuggire; Sento, sent'un rumor ch'al ciel si
estolle; Mentr'io vi miro, vorrei pur sapere. Del gran
Tuonante. Sassi, palae. Felici d'Adria. I'vo
piangendo. Asia felice. O beltà rara. Laura soave.
O passi sparsi. Amami, vita mia. Lasso, Amor mi
transporta. Hor ch'a noi torna. Voi non volete,
donna. Io mi sento morire. Mirami, vita mia. Chi'nde
darà la bose. Ancor che col partire. Fuor fuori a sì bel
canto. Dunque il commun poter **G Gabrieli** Canzoni
– Canzon la spiritata
**I Fagiolini; The English Cornett and Sackbut
Ensemble / Robert Hollingworth**
Chandos Chaconne CHAN0697 (77' · DDD) Texts and
translations included　　　　　　　　　Ⓕ

Andrea Gabrieli has always been something of a
textbook composer, whose reputation falls
under the shadow of his more famous nephew,
Giovanni, the composer *par excellence* of the
grand Venetian polychoral manner. Though
Andrea's music may not plumb the depths of
Giovanni's best pieces, his compositional range
displays a versatility that the writing of his more
considered relation surely lacks. Whereas Giovanni concentrated on liturgical composition,
Andrea explored the gamut of contemporary
styles and forms, from madrigals and lighter
secular writing to dialect texts, church music,
instrumental works, experimental theatre-
pieces and music for Venetian festivities.

This imaginatively constructed disc, punctuated by instrumental items, presents as a main
course a selection of Andrea's settings of Italian
texts. These reveal an unexpected emotional
complexity, robust and lively works being contrasted with more reflective ones. The former
are characterised by an energetic rhythmic drive
and bright sonorities in the upper registers, the
latter by a mellifluous and sensitive approach.

There are also a few oddities, notably 'Asia
felice', composed for an outdoor celebration

of the Battle of Lepanto in 1571 – suitably enlivened here with unscripted interventions of organ, sackbuts and cornets – and the boisterous rendition of the dialect text 'Chi'nde darà la bose al solfizar', which evocatively breathes the air of the streets and squares of Renaissance Venice. Anyone smitten with the musical traditions of this most fascinating of all cities, shouldn't hesitate to buy this record.

Giovanni Gabrieli   Italian c1553/6-1612

Giovanni Gabrieli, like his uncle Andrea Gabrieli, with whom he studied, worked briefly at the Munich court (c1575-8) and in 1585 he became organist of S Mark's, Venice, and of the confraternity of S Rocco, posts he held for the rest of his life. After Andrea's death, he edited many of his works for publication. His own fame and influence were widespread and crucial, notably in northern Europe – Schütz was among his many pupils – and he represents the highest point of the High Renaissance Venetian school. He composed motets and mass movements (Symphoniae sacrae, 1597, 1615, MSS), instrumental ensemble music (1597, 1615, MSS) and organ works (1593, MSS), as well as a few madrigals (1587 and anthologies). Much of his sacred ceremonial music exploits the architecture of St Mark's, using contrasting groups of singers and players to create cori spezzati effects, but often in a more intense and dissonant style than his uncle's. His music for wind ensemble is lively and colourful and includes up-to-date concertato writing; the organ ricercares are in a well-developed and specific keyboard style.   **GROVE**music

Canzonas

Sacrae symphoniae (1597) – Canzon a 8: primi   **P**
toni, septemi toni (2), noni toni, duodecimi toni;
Canzon a 10: primi toni, duodecimi toni, echo
duodecimi toni; Sonata octavi toni, a 12.Canzoni
(1608) – Canzon seconda a 4. Canzoni et Sonate
(1615) – Canzon a 7: V, VI. Canzon a 8: VIII, X-XII;
Canzon XIV, a 10; Canzon XVI, a 12. Ricercar del
primo tono
Concerto Palatino / Bruce Dickey, Charles Toet
Harmonia Mundi HMC90 1688 (76' · DDD)   Ⓕ**OO**

Gabrieli's instrumental music is as evocative of the sonorous interior spaces of St Mark's Basilica and the grandeur of the Venetian Renaissance as his better-known large-scale motets, yet they aren't so often performed except as 'fillers'. This single-minded recording, which above all provides an opportunity to re-evaluate the canzonas, will bring a number of surprises to many. One is the sheer variety of styles and techniques which Gabrieli deploys, even among the early pieces which might be thought to be written in a comparatively limited idiom. Not so, for this early group ranges from the sparkling *Canzon septimi toni*, which achieves its effect by adopting all the characteristics of the

double-choir motet, to the far more serious *Canzon noni toni*, which plays with chromatic inflection, another vocal device, as a way of making its effect. Although the double-choir technique and quasi-counterpoint are still the mainstay of the pieces from the 1615 collection, there are also intrusions of idiomatic writing, as with the exuberant passagework for cornetts in the Canzon VIII.

As might be expected, Concerto Palatino are well up to the challenges. These readings are characterised by just the kind of sensitive articulation and modulated phrasing that's often absent from performances of this repertory. Above all there's a sense of kaleidoscopic colour, a subtlety of interpretation based on exploration of the variety of texture in Gabrieli's writing, which stands in contrast to the more usual 'blockbuster' performances relying on sudden dynamic shifts and full brilliance. Highly recommended for specialists and newcomers alike.

Sacrae Symphoniae

The 16 Sonatas and Canzonas from Sacrae   **P**
symphoniae. Toccata quinti toni. Three Toccatas.
Intonatione del noni toni
**His Majesties Sagbutts and Cornetts / Timothy
Roberts** org
Hyperion CDA66908 (75' · DDD)   Ⓕ

Giovanni Gabrieli is arguably the earliest composer to write a significant body of instrumental music to a formula which can be said to be truly idiomatic and timelessly palatable. The *Sacrae symphoniae* publication of 1597 is a mixed set of vocal and instrumental pieces and, in its grand design, preserves a glorious heyday of textural opulence, intimate and playful dialogue between galleries and unashamedly ostentatious virtuosity. His Majesties Sagbutts and Cornetts have augmented their chamber consort to form, as cornettist David Staff proudly proclaims, 'the largest group of cornett and sagbutt players to have been assembled from one city since the 17th century'. These wonderful 16 canzonas and sonatas make up the complete instrumental music of the 1597 collection. In essence it's the extensive juxtaposition between sombre blocks and glittering small-scale exchanges which gives the music its seminal quality of moving both inevitably and eventfully towards a self-assured resolution, befitting its aristocratic gait. Having a 'moderator' (in this case the fine keyboardist, Timothy Roberts), as opposed to an artistic director, is pragmatic and democratic but there's the odd moment where a strong artistic presence at the helm would have, ironically perhaps, empowered the musicians towards a more flexible and varied approach to articulation and colour. That said, there are some glorious and majestic sounds: you can fly to the buzzing *Canzon duodecimi toni a 10*, bathe in the fragrant harmonic mosaic of the three-choir *Canzon quarti toni a 15* and relish elsewhere the peculiarly delicate and sweet sounds of this ensemble. Overall, a notable and distinctive achievement. Recommended to a broad listenership.

Niels Gade   Danish 1817-1890

Danish composer, the most important figure in 19th-century Danish music. He trained as a violinist and played in the Royal Orchestra, Copenhagen, producing his official op.1, the prize-winning concert overture Efterklange af Ossian in 1840. Encouraged by Mendelssohn, who was enthusiastic about his First Symphony (1841-2), he went to Leipzig as an assistant conductor of the Gewandhaus Orchestra, also meeting Schumann and composing the Mendelssohnian Third Symphony (1847) and String Octet (1848). In Copenhagen he reorganised the Musical Society, establishing a permanent orchestra and choir which gave the premières of his Symphonies nos. 4-8 and his large choral works ('Koncertstykke'), notably Comala (1846), and serving as co-director of the Copenhagen Academy of Music. Although the personal, Scandinavian colouring of his early works gave way to the German Romantic influence in his music after c 1850, he had an immense influence on the next generation of Danish composers. **GROVE**music

Symphonies

Symphony No 1 in C minor, Op 5. Hamlet Overture, Op 37. Echoes from Ossian, Op 1
Danish National Radio Symphony Orchestra / Dmitri Kitaienko
Chandos CHAN9422 (61' · DDD)   Ⓕ●

Gade's First Symphony, championed in Leipzig by Mendelssohn, launched him on his long and successful career. Its subtitle, *On Sjøland's fair plains*, alludes to one of the folk-songs collected and published by his teacher Andreas Peter Berggreen, though it isn't the only folk-song to figure in the score. Kitaienko's reading is to be preferred to either of his rivals – the performance is both vital and sensitive and the recording is splendidly natural, with a good perspective and no want of detail. The *Echoes from Ossian* Overture is Gade's first opus, which he composed two years earlier in 1840. Its second group has a charm that's difficult to resist. Readers beginning a Gade collection would do well to start here. Recommended.

Symphonies – No 1 in C minor, 'On Zealand's fair plains', Op 5; No 5 in D minor, Op 25[a]
[a]**Ronald Brautigam** pf **Danish National Symphony Orchestra / Christopher Hogwood**
Chandos CHAN10026 (58' · DDD)   Ⓕ

Symphonies – No 3 in A minor, Op 15; No 6 in G minor, Op 32. Andante (Discarded First Movement from Symphony No 3). Echoes from Ossian, Op 1
Danish National Radio Symphony Orchestra /

Christopher Hogwood
Chandos CHAN9795 (77' · DDD)   Ⓕ

If not the most adventurous of composers, and in his later years over-conservative, Gade in his youth certainly had his moments. his inventiveness is evident in all four symphonies presented here, albeit in very different ways. The Sixth (1856-7) is perhaps the most perfect, Classical in design although with a minatory feel suggestive at times of middle-period Haydn. If it stays within its own clearly defined harmonic and stylistic limits, the First, Third and Fifth do not. No 1 (1842), based on an old ballad and incorporating his own earlier setting of it, is bright and full of life: no wonder Mendelssohn and the Leipzig audience were enchanted. The Third (1846-7) is a different proposition, more Romantic in tone, its first movement too much so causing the composer to replace it with a less radical opening span (the *Presto* tempo marking of which must still have raised a few eyebrows). The original *Andante – Allegro energico* is included here in its first recording, proving a fine if turbulent sonata *Allegro*. The Fifth (1852) has a Mendelssohnian poise and grace plus one startling – if ultimately still-born – innovation: the piano as an orchestral instrument. The Fifth is definitely not a concerto, but a true symphony with an extended keyboard part, sometimes as soloist, sometimes as colouristic device. The performances are all very nicely drawn, the First and Fifth particularly so.

Symphonies – No 4, Op 20; No 7, Op 45 Concert Overture No 3, Op 14
Danish National Radio Symphony Orchestra / Christopher Hogwood
Chandos CHAN9957 (65' · DDD)   Ⓕ

Both symphonies on this second volume in Hogwood's Gade cycle are fine examples of the Dane's mastery of Classical balance, with perhaps less overt Romanticism than their dates of composition (1850 and 1864) might suggest – consider what Wagner was writing in those years. Hogwood's general approach is bright and lively, the rhythmic precision caught beautifully by Chandos's recording. The third concert overture is a real rarity, reputedly inspired by the figure of Achilles, its character is broadly heroic.

Gautier de Coincy   French 1177/8-1236

Gautier may have studied at Paris University; in 1214 he became prior at Vic-sur-Aisne and in 1233 abbot at Soissons. He wrote a massive verse narrative, Miracles de Nostre-Dame, in 1214-33, including songs, and composed religious chansons. His work represents the earliest substantial collection of sacred, Marian songs in the vernacular, and drew on secular melodies, which are set to sacred or devotional words. **GROVE**music

Miracles of Notre-Dame

Anonymous Benedicamus Domino. Hyer matin a l'enjournee. S'amours dont sui espris **Gautier de Coincy** Miracles de Nostre-Dame – Amours dont sui espris; Entendez tuit ensemble; Ma viele; D'un amour coie et serie; Quant ces floretes florir; Hui matin a l'ajournee; Roine celestre; Esforcier m'estuet ma vois; Amours qui set bein enchanter; Puisque voi la flour novele; Cui donrai je mes amours; Douce dame; De la sainte Leocade; Talens m'est pris orendroit; Pour Dieu traiez vous en la; Je pour yver
Harp Consort / Andrew Lawrence-King hp
Harmonia Mundi HMU90 7317 (70' · DDD)
Texts and translations included   Ⓕ

There are so many difficulties for performers of Gautier de Coincy. Quite aside from the problems of all monophonic song from the 13th century (whether to use instruments or not, how literally to take the written notes, how much can be improvised and so on), most of the music is demonstrably not by him, but adaptations of well-loved pieces of his time. His main contribution is therefore the poetry. So an important feature of this issue is that the texts are treated with the utmost seriousness: the seven songs that form the core of this CD are all sung complete, all treated as coherent poems without gratuitous repetition of sections, all with the words taking absolute primacy in the performance, and all done in ways that makes it quite clear that the performers know exactly what they are singing about. There's something marvellously refreshing in the way they relish the sound of their texts, enunciated with a deliciously hard-edged approach to medieval French.

Around these seven songs, Andrew Lawrence-King has created a frame designed from shorter fragments. Many are instrumental renditions of the melodies, with some particularly remarkable and fascinating performances by Ian Harrison on cornett and shawm, alongside some astonishingly attractive examples of group improvisation.

Francesco Geminiani Italian 1687-1762

Geminiani studied in Rome with Corelli and A Scarlatti, and in 1711 became leader of the opera orchestra in Naples. Settling in London in 1714, he earned instant success as a violin virtuoso and became one of the most influential teachers (of the violin and composition). He published a series of instrumental works, starting with the highly acclaimed violin sonatas Op 1 (1716). In the 1730s he made two lengthy visits to Ireland, and later spent time in the Netherlands and Paris. He settled in Dublin in 1759, giving his last known concert in 1760.

Geminiani's principal works are solo sonatas and concerti grossi. His model was Corelli, but he composed with originality, writing for a wider range of solo instruments and using a more sonorous and chromatic idiom; his music is more expressive and dramatic than Corelli's (though still contrapuntal). Most works have the traditional four-movement plan still popular in England. The violin sonatas Op 1 and Op 4 (1739) are especially difficult to play, and include cadenzas. Geminiani revised the former set as trio sonatas (c1757), and also made arrangements of others of his works. His 45 concerti grossi have a concertino of two violins, viola and cello; they include arrangements of sonatas by Corelli.

GROVEmusic

Concerti grossi

Geminiani Concerti grossi (after Corelli, Op 5)[a]. 🅿
Cello Sonata in D minor, Op 5 No 2[b]
Corelli/Geminiani Sonata for Violin and Cello in A, Op 5 No 9[c]
[bc]**David Watkin** vc [b]**Alison McGillivray** vc
[b]**Richard Egarr** hpd [a]**Academy of Ancient Music / Andrew Manze** [c]vn
Harmonia Mundi ② HMU907261/2 (144' · DDD)
                                               Ⓕ**OO**

Eighteenth-century English music lovers, it seems, were obsessed with the music of Corelli, in particular his *concerti grossi*; Manze's notes quote a lovely account of how, when the Op 6 concertos were first published in 1714, one London orchestra of gentlemen amateurs, led by a Mr Needler, couldn't stop themselves from playing through all 12 at one sitting. They were Corelli's only published concertos, however, so it isn't hard to see what a welcome sight the works presented on this disc must have been when they first appeared in the mid-1720s; immensely skilful arrangements by Corelli's London-based pupil Francesco Geminiani of the master's 12 violin sonatas, Op 5, they were to all intents a new set of Corelli concertos.

What held for Londoners back then should hold equally well for Baroque enthusiasts today; these ingeniously crafted *concerti grossi* are a delight, their musical effectiveness in no way compromised by their origins. Listeners familiar with Corelli's Op 5 will doubtless have fun spotting what Geminiani has done with them (which goes well beyond straightforward orchestration); those who do not know the originals can just enjoy the music for what it is, which is to say bright, tuneful and invigorating. Where Manze's particular success lies is in conjuring the atmosphere of the past and in the sheer joyousness and freshness which these performances convey. It's as if Mr Needler and his friends were before us, revelling in an unexpected Corellian bonus. Listen to the Academy of Ancient Music lustily laying into the thick chords in the final movement of Concerto No 4, dragging back the tempo and then charging off again, and you can almost see the complicit grins on their faces; or the way in which the ending of the well-known *La folia* (Concerto No 12) sweeps them up into a fit of orchestral scrubbing, to be capped by an excited ornamental whinny from Manze's violin.

Manze is free with his embellishments, throwing in double-stops, blue notes and all manner of flourishes with an abandon that won't be to everyone's taste, but which contributes hugely to the enthusiastic tenor of the music-making as a whole. The orchestra is in fine form, offering a full sound whose occasional slight rawness is no bad thing in performances of such strength, directness and honesty.

The Inchanted Forrest

The Inchanted Forrest. Two Concertos – First in D; Second in G
Italian Baroque Orchestra / Ryo Terakado vn
Stradivarius STR33630 (49' · DDD)   Ⓕ

Geminiani's incidental music to *The Inchanted Forrest* dates from his last period (*c*1756). Its first performances don't seem to have been particularly successful, but it was one of his first works to be recorded. A great variety of effects are contained in little space (the work lasts about half an hour), ranging from the wistful to the heroic (perhaps even the mock-heroic), and a reasonably varied orchestration (there are horns in the first part, trumpets in the second, and a flute doubles the violins throughout, imparting the sense of mystery inherent in the work's programme). At times it calls to mind the melodic idiom that Stravinsky was to put to such good use in *Pulcinella* (try the finale of the Second Act music, or the start of the fifth). It's a beguiling piece, and even though the programme duration verges on the miserly, the disc is worth recommending on the strength of it.

The Italian Baroque Orchestra nicely match the music's light touch, which belies some tricky passagework. In general they cope well with the latter: only the build-up to the Fourth Act's *Allegro moderato* seems to misfire slightly. At any rate, it's an 'inchanting' piece, well worth discovering.

Roberto Gerhard
Spanish/British 1896-1970

Gerhard studied in Barcelona with Granados and Pedrell and in Vienna and Berlin with Schoenberg (1923-8), returning to Barcelona to take an active part in musical life. His compositions from this period are few: they include the Schoenbergian Wind Quintet (1928), the cantata L'alta naixença del rei en jaume (1932) and the ballet Ariel (1934). In 1939 he left Spain and eventually settled in England, where he became much more productive, in a distinctly Spanish style. There were three more ballets (Don Quixote, 1941; Alegrias, 1942; Pandora, 1944), an opera (The Duenna, 1947), the symphony Homenaje a Pedrell (1941) and songs, besides the Violin Concerto (1943), which looks back to the early atonal works and forward to the dynamic, boldly colourful, serial compositions of his last two decades. This late development was rapid, from the Schoenbergian style of the First Quartet (1955) to the athematic, block-form, effect-filled Second (1962). It can be seen too in the cycle of four symphonies (1953, 1959, 1960, 1967) and the Concerto for Orchestra (1965), which move towards a Varèsian sound-drama (the Third Symphony has the sub-title 'Collages' and includes tape). Other late works include electronic pieces, much incidental music and pieces for ensemble (Concert for Eight, 1962; Hymnody, 1963; Libra, 1968; Leo, 1969).   **GROVE**music

Symphonies

Symphony No 2. Concerto for Orchestra
BBC Symphony Orchestra / Matthias Bamert
Chandos CHAN9694 (55' · DDD)   Ⓕ

Although the avowed purpose of Gerhard's *Concerto for Orchestra* (1965) was to highlight the orchestra as an entity rather than its constituent sections or instruments, and while it may not have the immediate universal appeal of, say, Kodály's or Bartók's works with the same title (written in a very different idiom some 20 or so years earlier), it has never been surpassed for its imaginative handling of instrumental sonorities or for its virtuoso demands on the players. It has to be said right away that this is a stunning performance: not merely does the BBC SO rise spectacularly to the work's demands, but Bamert shows himself exceptionally skilful at securing internal balances. It's worth quoting Gerhard's own words: 'My favourite listener is one who does not read explanatory programme notes … I stand by the *sound* of my music, and it is the sound that must make the sense…a work of music takes shape only in the mind of the listener.' Gerhard's Second Symphony has been represented on disc only by the revised version (*Metamorphosis*) which had had to be completed by Alan Boustead (available on Auvidis Montaigne); although Gerhard may have felt the original too cerebral, it was at least all his, and tough going as it undoubtedly is, it's very welcome to all interested in the mental processes of this quite exceptional musician. The opening of the work's second section, with its clicking percussion, is hauntingly mysterious, and the final nightmare palindrome *Scherzo* (of which only a fraction exists in the Boustead version) is one of his most astonishing creations. With first-class recording throughout, this must be regarded as an essential disc for all admirers of Gerhard.

Symphony No 4, 'New York'. Pandora Suite
BBC Symphony Orchestra / Matthias Bamert
Chandos CHAN9651 (54' · DDD)   ⒻО

Roberto Gerhard attached *New York* to the title of his Fourth Symphony (1967) because it was commissioned for performance there. Thirty years on, the music's frequent recourse to imposing brass clusters suggests common ground with Varèse's *Déserts* (1954), and its subtext of urban menace and decay. Varèse would probably have scorned the way Gerhard introduces allusions to Catalan folk music as a way of humanising his bleak landscape, and the two kinds of material do indeed seem distinctly uneasy associates. But that might have been Gerhard's point; not to integrate atonal symphonism and nostalgic folklorism, but to let them stand side by side as symbols of a fractured culture and an uprooted life. Bamert and the BBCSO provoke such thoughts through the clarity with which they project the symphony's constant shifts of mood: and the sound has rather greater range and presence than that of Víctor Pablo Pérez's reading for Auvidis Montaigne. The Chandos coupling, the suite from the ballet *Pandora*, was written a quarter of a century before the symphony, and here folklorism is at the heart of music which has nothing to do with mere exoticism. This wartime score is as evocative of deep, dark feelings as anything Gerhard ever wrote. Good though the Auvidis Montaigne version of *Pandora* is, this one is better recorded, and lingers even more potently in the mind's ear.

Chamber Music

Piano Trio. Cello Sonata. Chaconne. Gemini
Cantamen (Caroline Balding vn Jo Cole vc Timothy Lissimore pf)
Metier MSVCD92012 (77' · DDD)   Ⓕ

Between Gerhard's Piano Trio, written in 1918 at the age of 22, and *Gemini*, composed nearly half a century later, yawns a stylistic gulf that almost defies credence; but of the genuineness of his convictions in each case there's no question. The sensuous warmth of the Trio demonstrates the influence of Ravel, with clear reminiscences of the Frenchman's String Quartet in the finale. The second movement is exquisitely seductive, and Cantamen plays the whole work with tenderness and sympathy. Five years later, everything was to change when Gerhard went to study in Vienna with Schoenberg; but his perpetually enquiring mind and ultra-sensitive ear, along with his strong sense of Catalan identity, led him to temper the dodecaphonic system, so that later works broke free of serial dogma and frequently incorporated references to Spanish turns of phrase. This is so in the 1956 Cello Sonata which, for all the trenchant energy of its outer movements, is never less than euphonious: its deeply lyrical slow movement is beautifully shaped by Jo Cole. The Chaconne for solo violin is more uncompromising in idiom but Caroline Balding fulfils its virtuosic demands with distinction. Gemini, with its plucked piano strings and keyboard clusters, its violin scurries and its frenetic outbursts, shows Gerhard's love of experimentation in sonorities and the two instruments are presented as antagonists rather than partners. The performance has real fire and conviction.

Leo. Nonet. Hymnody
Barcelona 216 / Ernest Martínez Izquierdo
Stradivarius STR33615 (54' · DDD)   Ⓕ

This disc focuses on the remarkably fruitful final 15 years of Gerhard's career. It's a satisfying programme, excellently performed, and recorded with due attention to the music's pungent colours and innovative instrumental balances.

In the Nonet for wind and brass octet and accordion (1956-7) the compatibility between serialism and neo-classicism which Gerhard took over from his teacher Schoenberg is much in evidence. Although the slow start to the first movement may be rather austere, the main part of the movement expertly avoids predictability through rhythmic contrast and textural variety, in music of considerable elegance and wit. But the two later scores are more flexibly designed and stronger in thematic character, and in *Hymnody* (1963) there are passages of such dramatic intensity you suspect that the later Gerhard – whose last stage work was his version of Sheridan's *The Duenna* (1947-9, with revisions in the 1950s) – was, above all, a frustrated opera composer.

Hymnody alludes to the Psalms, and proceeds by alternations between relatively calm and turbulent material which suggest the emotional extremes of the biblical texts. The unusual scoring, with a wind septet set alongside two pianos and percussion (two players) inspires some rather melodramatic piano writing in the early stages, but this proves to be an absorbing work of powerful expressive command.

Leo (1969) – Gerhard's last completed score – has an even stronger appeal, not only in its thematic character, but in its *scherzo*-like volatility, admirably realised in this performance. It has been available for some time on a Largo disc of Gerhard's instrumental music, but this new version is now the one to have. *Leo* may be Gerhard's swansong, but its quiet citation of a (probably Peruvian) folk tune at the end – echoing the slightly earlier *Libra* – is delightfully understated. Neither overt nostalgia nor lamenting self-pity were Gerhard's way, and all three works provide salutary reminders of the kind of strong musical thinking that was such a positive feature of the 1950s and 60s.

George Gershwin   American 1898-1937

Gershwin was essentially self-taught. He was first a song plugger in Tin Pan Alley and an accompanist. In his teens he began to compose popular songs and produced a succession of musicals from 1919 to 1933 (Lady, be Good!, 1924; Oh, Kay!, 1926; Strike up the Band, 1927; Funny Face, 1927; Girl Crazy, 1930; the lyrics were generally by his brother Ira (1896-1983). In 1924 he became famous: he wrote Rhapsody in Blue as a concerto for piano and Paul Whiteman's jazz band. Its success led him to devote increasing energy to 'serious' composition. His more ambitious works include the Piano Concerto in F (1925) and the tone poem An American in Paris

387

GERSHWIN RHAPSODY IN BLUE – IN BRIEF

Columbia SO / Leonard Bernstein pf
Sony Classical SMK63086 (64' · ADD)　Ⓜ●
The free-wheeling zip and chutzpah of this famous 1958 recording are irresistible. Coupled with Lenny's abundantly charismatic renderings of Gershwin's *An American in Paris* and Grofé's *Grand Canyon* Suite.

Earl Wild; Boston Pops Orch / Arthur Fieldler
RCA 74321 68019-2 (70' · ADD)　Ⓢ
A brilliant performance from Earl Wild, the opening item in a vintage all-Gershwin anthology featuring Fiedler and the Boston Pops. RCA's late-1950s sound hardly begins to show its age.

New World SO / Michael Tilson Thomas pf
RCA 09026 68798-2 (68' · DDD)　Ⓕ
A performance of unshackled freedom and improvisatory daring, marvellously well recorded. Part of a terrific jazz-inspired anthology including music by Adams, Antheil, Bernstein, Milhaud and Stravinsky.

Aalborg SO / Wayne Marshall pf
Virgin Classics 561478-2 (70' · DDD)　Ⓜ
Wayne Marshall performs with teasing wit and edge-of-seat bravado on this strongly recommendable anthology devoted to all of Gershwin's piano *concertante* works.

London SO / André Previn pf
EMI 566981-2 (65' · ADD)　Ⓜ●
Previn's endearingly laid-back 1971 account sounds more glowing than ever in EMI's latest remastering. These artists' *An American in Paris* and Piano Concerto complete a fondly regarded Gershwin triptych.

Pittsburgh SO / André Previn pf
Philips 412 611-2PH (64' · DDD)　Ⓕ
Although the piano tone is shallower, many will prefer the extra transatlantic tang of Previn's identically coupled Pittsburgh digital collection for Philips.

George Gershwin pf roll **Columbia Jazz Band / Michael Tilson Thomas**
Sony Classical MK42240 (71' · ADD)　Ⓕ
Tilson Thomas's earliest recording cleverly fuses the composer's 1925 piano roll with Grofé's original jazz-band instrumentation. Coupled with *An American in Paris* and six of Gershwin's Broadway overtures.

Los Angeles PO / Michael Tilson Thomas pf
Sony Classical SMK60028 (77' · DDD)　Ⓜ
Tilson Thomas's second version (and his first directing from the piano) has heaps of temperament, and again employs the original 1924 scoring. Brightly recorded, this could well be a first choice for many.

(1928). But he continued composing for the musical theatre, and some of his most successful musicals (*Strike up the Band*, *Girl Crazy*, *Of Thee I Sing*) date from this period. In 1934-5 he wrote his 'American folk opera' *Porgy and Bess*, which draws on African-American idioms; given on Broadway, it was only a limited success. Gershwin went to Hollywood in 1936 and wrote songs for films. He was a sensitive songwriter of great melodic gifts and did much to create syntheses between jazz and classical traditions in his concert music and black folk music and opera in *Porgy and Bess*.　GROVEmusic

Rhapsody in Blue

Gershwin Rhapsody in Blue. An American in Paris　Ⓗ
Grofé Grande Canyon Suite
New York Philharmonic Orchestra / Leonard Bernstein pf
Sony Classical SMK63086 (64' · ADD) Recorded 1958-59　Ⓜ●

Bernstein conducted and played the music of Gershwin with the same naturalness he brought to his own music. Here, *An American in Paris* swings by with an instinctive sense of its origins in popular and film music; no stilted rhythms or four-squareness delay the work's progress, and where ripe schmaltz is wanted, ripe schmaltz is what we get, devoid of all embarrassment. *Rhapsody in Blue* is playful and teasing, constantly daring us to try to categorise its style, and then confounding our conclusions. Although the solo passages from individual players are beautifully taken, the orchestra captures the authentic flavour of Gershwin's and Bernstein's idiom, and Bernstein pushes them to transcend the printed scores. His own playing in the *Rhapsody* is tantalisingly unpredictable. The recording is clear and bright, perhaps a touch hard-edged, and a little of the richness of the original LP issue might have been preferred by some, especially as the editing is now made more obvious.

Additional recommendation

Rhapsody in Blue　Ⓗ
Coupled with: An American in Paris. Piano Concerto in F. Variations on 'I got rhythm'
Wild pf **Boston Pops Orchestra / Fiedler**
RCA Red Seal 74321 68019-2 (70' · ADD) Recorded 1959-61　Ⓢ
Wild's pianism is often scintillating, and he generates an infectiously sparky rapport with Fiedler and the Bostonians, whose exuberant, gently affectionate *American in Paris* is a treat. RCA's sound is astonishingly undated.

Gershwin Piano Rolls

Akst Jaz-o-mine[a] **Berlin** For Your Country and My Country[ac] **Conrad** Singin' the Blues ('till My Daddy Comes Home)[a] **Frey** Havanola[a] **O Gardner** Chinese Blues[d] **Gershwin** La La Lucille – From Now On[a]. Rialto Ripples[a] **B Grant** Arrah Go On I'm Gonna Go Back to Oregon[a] **Kern** Zip Goes a Million – Whip-

Poor-Will[a] **Matthews** Pastime Rag No 3[e] **M Morris** Kangaroo Hop[a] **Pinkard** Waitin' for Me[a] **Schonberg** Darling[ab] **Schonberger** Whispering[a] **Various** Greenwich Village Follies of 1920 – Just Snap Your Fingers at Care[a] **P Wendling** Buzzin' the Bee[a] [a]**George Gershwin,** [b]**Cliff Hess,** [c]**Rudy Erlebach,** [d]**Bert Wynn,** [e]**Fred Murtha** *pfs*
Nonesuch 7559-79370-2 (42' · DDD) Derived from piano rolls cut 1916-21   Ⓕ

There are some curiosities here but only two numbers are by Gershwin himself. The first of these is *Rialto Ripples*, a catchy rag Gershwin wrote in collaboration with Will Donaldson and put on to a roll in September 1916. It's fascinating to compare Gershwin's own 1916 performance with the sheet music published a year later. The roll has much more of the ragtime idiom in oom-pah left-hand chords and even reveals a few misprints in the score. Another ragtime connection is the 1916 roll, under one of Gershwin's pseudonyms (Fred Murtha), of *Pastime Rag No 3*, one of only five polished rags in different styles by black composer Artie Matthews. Again there are interesting differences between the sheet music published in the same year and Gershwin's roll – he doesn't play repeats but he returns to the A strain at the end.

The rest of the song arrangements, which sometimes employ two players, show the ragtime background of this piano style, especially in the earlier rolls. These are also good examples of the techniques of the roll arrangers, who hyped it all up by adding notes to create the effect of a whole team of pianists.

Piano Works

Of Thee I Sing – Prelude[a]; Jilted. Second Rhapsody[a]. The Shocking Miss Pilgrim – For you, for me, for evermore. Cuban Overture[a]. Pardon My English – Isn't it a pity? Variations on 'I got rhythm'[a]. Catfish Row[a]. Shall we dance? – Let's call the whole thing off[a]; They can't take that away from me[a]. Goldwyn Follies – Our love is here to stay
Jack Gibbons *pf*
ASV White Line CDWHL2082 (77' · DDD) Recorded 1992-3. Items marked [a] arr Gibbons.   Ⓜ

This disc is mostly comprised of Gibbons's own arrangements, based on Gershwin's film music, two-piano pieces, and in the case of the 'Catfish Row' *Porgy and Bess* suite, his orchestrations. The longest work is the *Second Rhapsody*, composed for a scene in the Gershwins' first Hollywood movie, *Delicious*. The film starred Janet Gaynor and Charles Farrell, and in this sequence the heroine wanders frightened through Manhattan – it might be rechristened *A Scotswoman in New York*. George Gershwin referred to the main tune as his 'Brahmsian theme' but today no one would mistake it for anything but Gershwin.

The solo version of the *Cuban Overture* is Gibbons's own adaptation of Gershwin's four-hand arrangement; like the 'Catfish Row' suite it

makes formidable demands on the pianist and Gibbons gives them both virtuoso performances. The recital ends with three of the standards Gershwin wrote in Hollywood during the last months of his life. 'They can't take that away from me' must be a strong contender for the greatest songs of the 20th century, and no one hearing 'Our love is here to stay' can doubt that a premonition of death lingered somewhere in the composer's heart in the autumn of 1936.

Porgy and Bess

Porgy and Bess
Willard White bass Porgy **Cynthia Haymon** sop Bess **Harolyn Blackwell** sop Clara **Cynthia Clarey** sop Serena **Damon Evans** bar Sportin' Life **Marietta Simpson** mez Maria **Gregg Baker** bar Crown **Glyndebourne Chorus; London Philharmonic Orchestra / Sir Simon Rattle**
EMI ③ 556220-2 (189' · DDD) Recorded 1988. Notes and text included   ⒻⓄⓄⓄ

 The company, orchestra and conductor from the outstanding 1986 Glyndebourne production re-create a very real sense of Gershwin's 'Catfish Row' community on this complete recording. Such is its atmosphere and theatricality, we might easily be back on the Glyndebourne stage. From the very first bar it's clear just how instinctively attuned Rattle and this orchestra are to every aspect of a multi-faceted score. The cast, too, are so *right*, so much a part of their roles, and so well integrated into the whole, that one almost takes the excellence of their contributions for granted. Here is one beautiful voice after another, beginning in style with Harolyn Blackwell's radiant 'Summertime', which at Rattle's gorgeously lazy tempo, is just about as beguiling as one could wish. Willard White conveys both the simple honesty and inner strength of Porgy without milking the sentiment and Haymon's passionately sung Bess will go wherever a little flattery and encouragement take her. As Sportin' Life, Damon Evans not only relishes the burlesque elements of the role but he really *sings* what's written a lot more than is customary. But the entire cast deliver throughout with all the unstinting fervour of a Sunday revivalist meeting. Sample the final moments of the piece – 'Oh Lawd, I'm on my way' – if that doesn't stir you, nothing will.

Carlo Gesualdo   Italian c1561-1613

A nobleman and amateur musician, Gesualdo is notorious for having his first wife and her lover murdered in 1590; he married Leonora d'Este of Ferrara three years later. While at the Ferrarese court (1594-6) he played the lute and showed a passion for music and came to be accepted as a serious composer. He eventually retired to his castle at Gesualdo, sunk into a deep melancholy from which music alone could provide relief. His music was strongly influenced by Luzzaschi and Nenna, particularly the former in his use of serious, expressive, richly worked music even for quite light texts. He took great pains over word setting, allowing texts to be clearly heard and strongly expressed. Much of the music in his six madrigal books (1594-1611) and three sacred books (1603-11) uses unexpected harmonies and changes of key, dissonances and striking chromaticism in a highly original way, usually prompted by the emotions of the texts. Stravinsky made arrangements of some of his madrigals. **GROVE**music

Madrigals

Il quarto libro di madrigali
La Venexiana (Rossana Bertini, Emanuela Galli sops Lucia Sciannimanico mez Giuseppe Maletto, Sandro Naglia tens Daniele Carnovich bass Franco Pavan, Gabriele Palomba ltes Fabio Bonizzoni hpd) /
Claudio Cavina counterten
Glossa GCD920907 (68' · DDD) Text and translation included   ⓕ**OOO**

These performances brilliantly advocate Gesualdo as a voice of lasting substance, not just originality. This exquisitely modulated Italian ensemble is wonderfully discriminating, extracting the eloquence of the mercurial lines and unobtrusively seeking architectural sense behind the text. The internalised 'Sparge la morte' could so easily degenerate into a series of arcane indulgences and yet one is gracefully invited by La Venexiana to inhabit the intense fabric of the finely wrought melodic contours.

Book 4 is heady stuff, indeed, if less peculiarly other-worldly and intense than some from the more established Fifth Book, but stuffed full of delectable passages. Subtle inflections of timbre and balance abound here, be it the warm immediacy of 'Mentre gira' or the softly radiant and reflective beauty of 'Ecco, morirò'. Thoroughly recommended.

Ahi, disperata vita. Sospirava il mio cor. O malnati messaggi. Non t'amo, o voce ingrata. Luci serene e chiare. Sparge la morte al mio Signor nel viso. Arde il mio cor. Occhi del mio cor vita. Mercè grido piangendo. Asciugate i begli ochi. Se la mia morte brami. Io parto. Ardita Zanzaretta. Ardo per te, mio bene. Instrumental items – Canzon francese. Io tacerò. Corrente, amanti
Les Arts Florissants / William Christie
Harmonia Mundi HMC90 1268 (55' · DDD) Texts and translations included   ⓕ

To many, Gesualdo is known above all for the *crime passionnel* that left his wife and her lover impaled on the same sword, but the notion that his highly charged music is the product of a tortured and unstable mind is, no doubt, over-romanticised. For this foray into the schizophrenic world of Gesualdo's five-voice

madrigals, Les Arts Florissants have selected their programme from the last three books, pieces in which the highly mannered and exaggerated aspects of the composer's style reach their most extreme expression. Nevertheless, we should not think of all these works being undifferentiated in style, and one of the fascinations of this disc, which has been very carefully planned, is the insight it offers into the gradual emergence and sharpening of the features which characterise Gesualdo's late madrigalian manner.

Some of those elements can already be heard in *Sospirava il mio cor* from the Third Book, and by the last tracks they're present, with all their compositional distortions in full dress. William Christie and Les Arts Florissants are no strangers to the aesthetic of the Italian madrigal in its last decades. This recording, like so many of their productions, is full of surprises on both the large and small scales. The first, of a general kind, is the decision to add continuo accompaniments *avant la lettre*. This is justifiable on historical grounds, though less certain is the precise way it has been done with some passages within a piece still left *a cappella*. Less justifiable, if only on artistic grounds, is the performance of two madrigals on instruments alone (*Io tacerò* and *Corrente, amanti*); it makes little sense to attempt such highly charged word-driven music in this way. What may also surprise is the rather understated, almost classically pure character of the interpretations, though it is a relief that the calculatedly neurotic and deliberately out-of-tune manner so often turned out for Gesualdo has here been eschewed. These are technically very fine and dramatically convincing and coherent readings which are certainly preferable to any other recordings of Gesualdo's madrigals currently available.

Tenebrae Responses

Responsoria et alia ad Officium Hebdonadae Sanctae spectantia
Taverner Choir / Andrew Parrott
Sony Classical SK62977 (67' · DDD) Text and translation included   ⓕ

Gesualdo's *Tenebrae* have a distinguished discography – the Hilliard Ensemble's recording of all three days of the *Triduum sacrum* for ECM achieved considerable popularity. This recording from the Taverner Choir is no less compelling, and it includes the plainsong which ought to frame Gesualdo's polyphony, an essential detail the Hilliards left out. The composer's tough vision comes across all the more forcefully, betraying not a hint of complacency. Liturgical reconstruction is a rock on which many fine performances have foundered, but can be very effective when the plainchant is interpreted as consciously as the polyphony. Here there are no lush, rounded cadences to the chant, but carefully chosen voices whose pleasing edge keeps the music firmly anchored to earth. Listening to the polyphony, one is struck by the care with which Parrott has chosen his singers. The countertenors in particular seem to rise out of the chest tone of the lower voices: a 'bottom-up' approach to timbre more typical of continental ensembles than of English ones. It has always been a great strength of Parrott's that he ensures that the stable core of singers comprising the Taverner Choir can adapt its sound to the music under consideration. And right from the first polyphonic entry, the acerbic quality of Gesualdo's chordal progressions have a deeply involving dynamism. Those who treasure the Hilliards' recording need not fear duplication, and for the first-time buyer one can recommend either version.

Tenebrae Responsories for Maundy Thursday
King's Singers (David Hurley, Robin Tyson *countertens* Paul Phoenix *ten* Philip Lawson, Gabriel Crouch *bar* Stephen Connolly *bass*)
Signum Records SIGCD048 (66' · DDD)   Ⓕ

It's perhaps in his music for Holy Week that Gesualdo's claim as a composer of real substance lies. By transferring his madrigal idiom to the sacred sphere so consummately, he shows he can work effectively within formal constraints that the secular works rarely impose. The formal severity of these Responses places in sharp relief his striking melodic turns and startling contrapuntal progressions. It's no wonder that vocal ensembles have been so attracted to them.

This recording joins a select and distinguished group, starting with the Hilliard Ensemble's complete set for ECM, and continuing with the Taverner Consort's set for Good Friday. The King's Singers have a brighter tone than the Hilliards, which makes for a more extrovert reading. In qualitative terms there's little to choose: perhaps in matters of intonation the Hilliards and the Taverners retain a slight edge. But this newcomer naturally takes its place alongside them in the front row, which speaks volumes for its quality.

Orlando Gibbons   British 1583-1625

Gibbons came from a musical family and was a chorister (1596-8) and student (1599-1603) at King's College, Cambridge. He joined the Chapel Royal in c 1603 and was one of its organists by 1615 (senior organist, 1625). In 1619 he became a virginal player at court and in 1623 organist at Westminster Abbey. He took the MusB at Cambridge (1606) and the DMus at Oxford (1622). One of the most important English composers of sacred music in the early 17th century, he wrote several Anglican services, popular in their day, and over 30 anthems, some imposing and dramatic (e.g. O clap your hands), others colourful and most expressive (See, the word is incarnate; This is the record of John). His instru-

mental music, also important, includes over 30 elaborate contrapuntal viol fantasias and over 40 masterly keyboard pieces. His madrigals (1612) are generally serious in tone (eg The Silver Swanne).
GROVEmusic

Viol Works

Fantasias – a 3: Nos 1-4; a 6: Nos 1-6. Pavan and Galliard a 6. Three In Nomines a 5 – No 1; No 2. Pavan and Galliard in A minor, 'Lord Salisbury', MBXX/18-19. Hosanna to the Son of David. O Lord, in thy wrath rebuke me not. Go from my window. Peascod time. The Silver swan
Phantasm (Wendy Gillespie, Jonathan Manson, Markku Luolajan-Mikkola *viols*) / **Laurence Dreyfus** *viol* with **Asako Morikawa, Susanna Pell** *viols*
Avie AV0032 (72' · DDD)   Ⓕ**OOO**

 Phantasm is a superb ensemble. They now turn their attention to the viol music of Orlando Gibbons, with a focus on the central works that are definitely for viols and definitely by Gibbons: the six great fantasies for six viols; the four marvellous fantasies for three viols and a selection of what is otherwise best of his viol music in five and six parts. They play with vast assurance and verve, always attractive, always with fresh and varied textures, always beautifully balanced. This is often playing of a breathtaking virtuosity that communicates the music with irresistible vitality. Some listeners may feel that they hit poor Gibbons a little hard, occasionally losing track of the poetry that's his own special contribution; others could feel that some tempos are chosen simply for bravado, especially in the dazzling performance of *Go from my window* that ends the disc. But this is classy playing and a major contribution to the catalogue.

As a slightly eccentric *bonne bouche* they steer away from the music with a violone, preferring to offer arrangements of keyboard pieces and vocal anthems. This is presumably to stress the unquestionable truth that music in those days wasn't often genre-specific; but in the event it emphasises that the greatest of Gibbons' viol pieces are perfectly suited to that particular ensemble.

Keyboard Works

The Woods So Wild   Ⓟ
Fantasias – in D minor, MBXX/5; in G, MBXX/6; in D minor, MBXX/7 (for double organ); in D minor, MBXX/8; in G minor, MBXX/9; in A minor, MBXX/10; in A minor, MBXX/11; in A minor, MBXX/12; in C, MBXX/13; in C, MBXX/14; Ground, MBXX/26. Italian Ground, MBXX/27. Pavan and Galliard in A minor, 'Lord Salisbury', MBXX/18-19. The Fairest Nymph, MBXX/43. Preludes – in A minor, MBXX/1; G, MBXX/2; in D minor, MBXX/3; in A minor, MBXX/4; The Woods So Wild, MBXX/29. Galliard, MBXX/23. Pavans – MBXX/16; MBXX/17. Coranto, MBXX/39
John Toll *org/hpd*
Linn Records CKD125 (73' · DDD)   Ⓕ

John Toll succumbed to cancer in his early fifties, thus depriving the world of a supreme continuo player, in many ways unchallenged in his generation. This disc's quality deepens the sense of loss. The choice of Gibbons is itself intriguing for a man whose main career was in Baroque music. But it's clear from every note that this was a composer very close to Toll's heart, that he acknowledged the quiet poet who has perhaps the most distinctive voice of all composers from the age of Shakespeare.

Toll has focused on the most substantial works. All the Fantasias are here, as well as most of the Pavans; but most of the smaller dances are omitted. So we have a Gibbons of considerable seriousness, which Toll underlines by controlled playing that has not the slightest trace of self-indulgence. What we hear in Toll is the composer who was not just the 'best finger of that age' but also one of the finest contrapuntists and a man of marvellous musical imagination. The music is divided between two instruments. The late 17th-century organ at Adlington Hall sounds absolutely glorious, beautifully caught by the engineers, and played with sympathetic mastery; it's used not just for Fantasias but also for some of the music that one would more instinctively have thought intended for a harpsichord – with fascinating results. A modern Flemish-style harpsichord by Michael Johnson serves for the rest, but again not just for the dances. This is top-quality playing.

Sacred Vocal Works

O clap your hands. Great Lord of Lords. Hosanna to the Son of David. Prelude in G^a. Out of the deep. See, see, the Word is incarnate. Preludes – No 3 in D minor, MBXX/3^a. Lift up your heads. Almighty and everlasting God. First (Short) Service – No 6, Magnificat; No 7, Nunc dimittis. Second Service – No 3, Magnificat; No 4, Nunc dimittis. Fantazia of four parts^a. O God, the king of glory. O Lord, in Thy wrath rebuke me not
Oxford Camerata / Jeremy Summerly with ^{a}**Laurence Cummings** org
Naxos 8 553130 (65' · DDD) Recorded 1994. Texts included ⑤

The Oxford Camerata provides a representative selection of choral works by Gibbons, together with three of his organ pieces. The programme is introduced by a bright and busy performance of the eight-part *O clap your hands*, followed by the noble verse anthem *Great Lord of Lords* – and it's pleasing to hear in this piece, and in the other verse-anthems, the rich timbre of the countertenor Robin Blaze, a welcome acquisition for the Camerata, which has a great deal of vocal talent in its make-up. They tackle the gently moving *See, see, the Word is incarnate* with great confidence, together with the First and Second Services and the quiet collects with all the knowledge and aplomb of cathedral lay clerks or choral scholars from Oxford and Cambridge. Laurence Cummings plays two

short preludes, the one in G major – a real test of agility – from *Parthenia* and that in D minor from Benjamin Cosyn's *Virginal Book*. The *Fantazia of four parts* is a most extraordinary work, quite hard to steady and control. Nevertheless, it's a welcome addition to the programme.

Secular Vocal Works

Pavan and Galliard a 6. Fantasia a 2 No 1. Go from my window. Fantasias a 6 – Nos 3 & 5. Fantasia a 4 No 1 'for the great double bass'. Galliard a 3. In Nomine a 4. Pavan and Galliard in A minor, 'Lord Salisbury'. Prelude in G. Masks – Lincoln's Inn mask; The Fairest Nymph. Alman in G. Behold, thou hast made my days. Glorious and powerful God. The First Set of Madrigals and Mottets – Daintie fine bird; Faire is the rose; I weigh not fortune's frown; I see ambition never pleased; I feign not friendship where I hate; The silver swanne
Tessa Bonner sop **Timothy Roberts** keybds **Red Byrd; Rose Consort of Viols**
Naxos 8 550603 (68' · DDD) Recorded 1992   ⑤

Beautifully performed and finely recorded, this selection of Gibbons's music is especially attractive for its variety. At its richest it presents writing for voice and viols combined, five parts to each, or for viols alone, sometimes in six parts. In lightest, most transparent texture there's a charming piece for two viols. Three keyboard instruments are used for solos: virginals, harpsichord and organ. A soprano also sings solos to viol accompaniment. Moods and styles vary correspondingly. The *Masks* and *Alman* for virginals have a high-spirited, almost popular manner; the Fifth *Fantasia* includes some unusual chromaticism and harmonic developments that for a while almost anticipate Purcell. Tessa Bonner sings with unvibrant purity; but most striking here is the pronunciation. It's one of the distinguishing marks of this curiously named group, Red Byrd, that they sing such music with vowel sounds modified to fit theories about the English in which it would originally have been sung. Thus the 'daintie fine bird' tells 'oi sing and doy', and the 'u' acquires a sort of umlaut in *I weigh not fortune's frown*, 'weigh' and 'frown' also having a measure of rusticity. Perhaps it's a good idea, but it does increase the desirability of printed texts in the booklet. The instrumental music is finely played, the viols avoiding any imputation of belonging to the squeeze-and-scrape school, and Timothy Roberts's keyboard solos are particularly skilful, in *legato* and fluency.

Eugène Gigout   French 1844-1925

Gigout studied with Saint-Saëns at the Ecole Niedermeyer and associated with Fauré and Franck. In 1863 he became organist of St Augustin, Paris, and in 1911 began teaching at the Conservatoire. Most of his music is for organ. **GROVE**music

Organ Works

The Complete Organ Works, Volume 1
Rhapsodie sur des airs catalans. Suite de six pièces.
Trois pièces
Gerard Brooks *org*
Priory PRCD761 (77' · DDD) Played on the organ of
Perpignan Cathedral, France   Ⓕ

For lovers of organ sound this disc is an absolute treasure. Perpignan's sumptuous Cavaillé-Coll isn't an organ of memorable solo stops but of deliciously blended, exquisitely balanced choruses. Full organ is warm and robust while its plentiful soft-stops have a subtlety and charm which, even in the face of the omnipresent action clatter, this recording captures with almost magical delicacy. The fourth of the *Suite de six pièces*, an *Andantino* in E minor, is lent distinction by the utter charm of the contrasting soft flute and string choruses, while the first of the *Trois pièces* dances across the manuals revealing tantalising glimpses of colour richly enhanced by the atmospheric acoustic of Perpignan's cathedral. All this is superbly captured in Priory's rich, mellow recording.

In his deft handling of the instrument and his keen sense of colour, Brooks proves that there's much more to organ playing than big virtuoso gestures. Which may be as well since there's little scope for such things here. Not only do all 10 pieces on this disc completely avoid the virtuoso and emotional excesses of Liszt, Widor and Vierne, but none stretches much over 10 minutes in duration. With the exception of the captivating *Rhapsodie sur des airs catalans*, all are relatively youthful works revealing a composer with a keen sense of structure and a penchant for contrapuntal argument. A most attractive release.

The Complete Organ Works, Volume 2
Suite de six pièces (pub 1881). Deux pièces.
Interludium. Méditation
Gerard Brooks *org*
Priory PRCD762 (72' · DDD) Played on the Cavaillé-
Coll organ of St Ouen, Rouen   Ⓕ

The Complete Organ Works, Volume 3
Dix Pièces. Pièce Jubilaire. Poèmes Mystiques
Gerard Brooks *org*
Priory PRCD763 (75' · DDD) Played on the Cavaillé-
Coll organ of St Etienne, Caen   Ⓕ

Before Gerard Brooks embarked on his complete cycle, only two of Gigout's solo organ pieces figured consistently on the *Gramophone* database. One of those, the 'Grand choeur dialogué' (the sixth of the 1881 *Suite de six pièces*), appears on the second disc of the series in a performance that makes it a highly treasurable release. Brooks imbues it with great majesty and splendour, letting it unfold with all the opulence

of a regal procession. Such spacious playing allows us ample opportunity to savour the glorious sonic spectacle of the wonderful St Ouen organ in Rouen, an instrument frequently recorded, though never before with such stunning sound.

The third disc includes the most familiar of Gigout's organ works; the *Dix Pièces* published in Paris in 1892. There can be few organists who don't possess this tome, if only for the scintillating B minor Toccata, and it's been recorded frequently. Brooks's may not be the most impressive of these but he's impeccably faithful to the score and, playing on what's described as 'one of the finest surviving examples of Cavaillé-Coll's work', we have here an unquestionably authoritative version, not just of the Toccata but all ten pieces. Even those that pass most organists by are revealed as musical gems ideally suited to a resourceful organ. Organ recordings of this calibre are few and far between.

Alberto Ginastera
Argentinian 1916-1983

Ginastera studied at the National Conservatory (1936-8) and made an early reputation with his ballet Panambí; (1940). Another nationalist ballet, Estancia, followed in 1941, when he was also appointed to the staff of the National Conservatory. During an extended visit to the USA (1945-7) he attended Copland's courses at Tanglewood; thereafter his life was divided between Argentina and abroad, his travels sometimes necessitated by changes of government. In 1971 he settled in Geneva.

Until the mid-1950s his music was essentially nationalist in a manner comparable with Bartók, Falla and Stravinsky, but he moved towards an atonal expressionism that has links with Berg and Penderecki: this made possible his late emergence as a composer of highly charged opera in which magic and fantastic elements are prominent (Don Rodrigo, 1964; Bomarzo, 1967; Beatrix Cenci, 1971). Other works include two piano concertos (1961, 1972), the Cantata para América mágica for soprano and percussion (1960) and three string quartets (1948, 1958, 1973). **GROVE**music

Orchestral Works

Overture to the Creole 'Faust', Op 9. Pampeana
No 3, Op 24. Estancia, Op 8a. Glosses on Themes of
Pablo Casals, Op 48
Berlin Symphony Orchestra / Gabriel Castagna
Chandos CHAN10152 (66' · DDD)   Ⓕ

Overture to the Creole 'Faust', Op 9. Pampeana
No 3, Op 24. Estancia, Op 8a. Ollantay, Op 17
Odense Symphony Orchestra / Jan Wagner
Bridge 9130 (57' · DDD)   Ⓕ

Either of these two well-produced discs would make a near-ideal introduction to this versatile composer's output, featuring three of his finest orchestral inspirations. If the suite from his ballet *Estancia* (1942) remains his best-known work, and its malambo finale one of the most famous pieces in Latin American music, the *Overture to the Creole Faust* (1943) can't be far behind. Both are outgoing, 'popular' items, whereas the 'symphonic pastoral' *Pampeana* No 3 (1954) is more obviously serious.

All three works receive committed performances on both discs. Castagna and the Berliners find a touch more magic in the *Pampeana*'s slower outer movements aided by Chandos's sumptuous sound, but the Danish players, led by their Venezuelan-born conductor, often have the edge in the swifter sections. In *Estancia*, the resonance of Chandos's recording works against the music: Bridge's drier, cleaner sound in the Carl Nielsen Hall in Odense is more successful. And while some of Jan Wagner's tempos seem a shade deliberate compared to Castagna's, he mostly justifies them by the pacing of each work *in toto*.

If there's little overall to choose between the newcomers, the fourth item on each may decide the matter. On Chandos comes a scintillating account of the second, full-orchestral version of the more harmonically advanced *Glosses on Themes of Pablo Casals*, originally written for strings to celebrate the Catalan cellist's centenary in 1976 and rescored a year later. In contrast, Bridge restores to the CD catalogue Ginastera's *Ollantay* (1947), a darkly colourful and dramatic folk-triptych that could be thought of as an Argentinian *Taras Bulba*.

If you want only one version of these pieces the Bridge is recommended.

Umberto Giordano   Italian 1867-1948

Giordano studied with Serrao at the Naples Conservatory between 1880 and 1890 and was commissioned, after showing promise in a competition, to write an opera: this was Mala vita, a verismo opera of some violence and crudity, given at Rome in 1892. After another failure (an old-fashioned romantic melodrama), he moved to Milan, where his Andrea Chenier was given, at La Scala, in 1896; with its French Revolutionary subject and its fervent, assertive style, it was an immediate success and has remained popular in Italy and beyond. Comparable success, at least in Italy, was met by Fedora (1898, Milan), but of his seven later operas only the comic Il re (1929, Milan), which was taken up by coloratura sopranos, enjoyed any real success although he remained a master of the intense, vehement, Massenet-influenced, theatrically effective style that gives Andrea Chenier its appeal. **GROVE**music

Andrea Chénier

Andrea Chénier
Luciano Pavarotti *ten* Andrea Chénier **Leo Nucci**
bar Gerard **Montserrat Caballé** *sop* Maddalena
Kathleen Kuhlmann *mez* Bersi **Astrid Varnay** *sop*
Countess di Coigny **Christa Ludwig** *mez* Madelon
Tom Krause *bar* Roucher **Hugues Cuénod** *ten*
Fleville **Neil Howlett** *bar* Fouquier-Tinville, Majordomo **Giorgio Tadeo** *bass* Mathieu **Piero De Palma** *ten* Incredible **Florindo Andreoli** *ten* Abate
Giuseppe Morresi *bass* Schmidt **Ralph Hamer** *bass*
Dumas **Welsh National Opera Chorus; National Philharmonic Orchestra / Riccardo Chailly**
Decca ② 410 117-2DH2 (107' · DDD) Recorded 1982-84. Notes, text and translation included   Ⓕ**O**

This is certainly the best-recorded and probably the best-conducted *Andrea Chénier* yet. Chailly overconducts the score, drawing attention to himself rather than to Giordano, but by and large he's sympathetic to both the score and his singers. *Chénier* isn't easy to interpret; it bustles along busily all the time, but not always with much distinction or to any very strong purpose. For the many and important small roles, Decca has assembled half a dozen old faithfuls in various states of vocal health. Varnay goes rather over the top as the old Countess in Act 1. The three *comprimario* tenors, whose combined ages must be more than 200, all make the mark with Piero De Palma the most potent as the spy Incredible, an object-lesson in acting with the voice. Giorgio Tadeo, a *buffo* bass of distinction, here turns himself into the nasty Mathieu. Krause is an honourable Roucher. But Christa Ludwig is better than any, making old Madelon's brief appearance into a moving vignette. Of the younger singers, Kathleen Kuhlmann is a rather anonymous Bersi, while Neil Howlett is a snarling Fouquier-Tinville.

But *Chénier* stands or falls by its three principals. All three here perform eloquently. Pavarotti tends to rasp his way through the Improvviso, but improves no end in his first love duet with Maddalena, and defies the court in Act 3 with real heroism. But it's in the final act that his tone recaptures its old refulgence in his poetic musings and death-going duet. Again and again a phrase will set Caballé apart as a uniquely subtle artist. There are occasionally those self-regarding mannerisms that she indulges in, also a want of sheer tonal weight, but you'll warm to her portrayal. Nucci's Gérard is excellent, a nice balance between line and punch. Pavarotti and Caballé enthusiasts will need to have this set; others should perhaps endeavour to hear the pros and cons of Levine.

Andrea Chénier
Plácido Domingo *ten* Andrea Chénier **Renata Scotto** *sop* Maddalena **Sherrill Milnes** *bar* Carlo Gérard **Michael Sénéchal** *ten* Incredible **Maria Ewing** *mez* Bersi **Gwendolyn Killebrew** *mez* Madelon **Jean Kraft** *mez* Countess **Allan Monk** *bar* Roucher **Terence Sharpe** *bar* Fléville **Stuart Harling** *bass* Fouquier-Tinville **Isser Bushkin** *bass* Schmidt **Malcolm King** *bass* Dumas **Piero De Palma** *ten* Abate **Nigel Beavan** *bass-bar* Maestro di casa **Enzo Dara** *bar* Mathieu **John Alldis Choir; National**

Philharmonic Orchestra / James Levine
RCA ② 74321 39499-2 (114' · ADD) Recorded 1976.
Notes, text and translation included Ⓜ

Choosing between these two recordings, it might seem sensible to start with the tenor in the title-role, and here a strong inclination would be to plump for RCA and Domingo: he's in splendid voice, with a touch of nobility to his manner that makes for a convincing portrayal of a poet. Pavarotti (Chailly) begins with a rather leather-lunged Improvviso, but he later finds poetry in the role as well, especially when responding to his soprano, Caballé, who's rather stretched by the more exhausting reaches of her role and sounds audibly grateful for the occasional opportunities he gives her to float rather than belt a high-lying phrase. However, Pavarotti is an *Italian* tenor, and his Italianate sense of line adds one per cent or so of elegance to some phrases that even Domingo can't match. Caballé does many things beautifully, and her fine-spun *pianissimos* and subtle shadings only occasionally sound mannered, but the role is undeniably half a size too big for her. So it's for Scotto, you might say, and a hint of strain is audible once or twice, in her timbre rather than her phrasing. It's her phrasing that tips the balance back to RCA: Scotto is as subtle a vocalist as Caballé, but she gives meaning and eloquence to every phrase without ever breaking the long line, which one can't always say of the Spanish soprano. Matters are about even as far as the baritones are concerned: Milnes acts admirably, but refrains from over-acting, and the voice is rich and characterful. In the supporting cast, but RCA's striking Bersi, vividly characterised Incredible, and their Roucher, too, aren't outmatched (only their Madelon, both fruity and acid – a grapefruit of a voice – is disappointing).

A lot of people will enjoy the huge energy and bustle of Levine's direction. It's vividly characterful, but a shade exhausting and overassertive. The flow of the music seems more natural in Chailly's hands, and orchestral detail is clearer. The Decca recording, too, is warmer.

Madame Sans-Gêne

Mirella Freni *sop* Caterina Giorgio Merighi *ten* Lefebvre Mauro Buda *bar* Napoleone Andrea Zese *bar* Fouche Valter Borin *ten* Neipperg Antonio Feltracco *ten* Vinaigre, Despreaux Marzia Giaccaia *sop* Toniotta, Carolina Muriel Tomeo *sop* Giulia Federica Bragaglia *sop* Principessa Elisa, La Rossa Valerio Marletta *bar* De Brigole Riccardo Ristori *bar* Gelsomino, Roustan Alfio Grasso *bar* Leroy Muriel Tomeo *sop* Madame Bulow Modena Teatro Comunale Chorus; Emilia Romagna 'Toscanini' Symphony Orchestra / Stefano Ranzani
Dynamic CDS247 (123' · DDD) Notes, text and translation included Ⓕ

In the not-so-distant past most 'serious' musicians thought Giordano beneath notice while opera-goers of a certain kind felt he was everything they stood for. These opinions were usually based on *Andrea Chenier* and (with slightly less conviction) *Fedora*. Otherwise a few excerpts from one or two lesser-known operas were gratefully heard but didn't allay suspicions that a wider acquaintance might prove disheartening. This set from the Italian-based company Dynamic invites us all to think again. The plot of *Madame Sans-Gene* is a rather charming variant on the theme of the Emperor's clothes; it's also about a star-struck girl who learns sense and returns to home and boyfriend. The première at La Scala in 1929 failed to impress, though Toscanini conducted and Toti Dal Monte sang the leading role. The score is elegantly lyrical and lively, modern in relation to Chenier as (say) *Gianni Schicchi* is in relation to *Manon Lescaut*.

Madame Sans-Gene is a comedy whose story takes a serious turn in Act 3, which for a while seems about to topple over into tragedy. Napoleon, previously a figure in the background, appears in person and in a bad mood, but is charmed and shamed into a talk about old times with the genial heroine and all ends well. At first Madame Sans-Gene, so-called, seems to be one of those tireless life-and-soul-of-the-party people who can be so wearing, but she develops into less of a turn and more of a character, while her chirpy vocal line eventually settles for a more rewarding warmth and lyricism. It's understandable that the role should be attractive to a star soprano who late in her career looks for something out of the way in which much is accomplished by personality. Mirella Freni's voice is still full bodied and to a large extent pure in quality, but for many years now has forfeited the firm evenness of its prime. She gives a genuine performance – and (not far off her 64th birthday) a remarkable one. The best singing, however, is that of the tenor, Giorgio Merighi. Mauro Buda as Napoleon shows an almost tenorial baritone which it would be good to hear in a part with more opportunities. Ranzani conducts with spirit. As a recording this is a great deal more satisfactory than the currently available alternative, taken from an Italian radio transmission in 1957.

Mauro Giuliani   Italian 1781-1829

In Vienna from 1806, Giuliani became famous as the greatest living guitarist, teaching, performing and composing a rich repertory for the guitar. He was also a cellist, playing in the première of Beethoven's Symphony no.7 (1813). In 1814 he became honorary chamber musician to Napoleon's second wife. He returned to Italy in 1819 and was patronised by the nobility. His works include three guitar concertos, sonatas, studies and variations for solo guitar, quartets and many duos (with flute or violin) for guitar and songs. GROVEmusic

Guitar Concerto No 1

Giuliani Guitar Concerto No 1 in A, Op 30 **Schubert**
Sonata for Arpeggione and Piano in A minor, D821
(arr Williams)
John Williams gtr **Australian Chamber Orchestra**
Sony Classical SK63385 (52' · DDD)   Ⓕ

The guitar has played a part in several adaptations of the Schubert A minor Sonata, substituting for either the arpeggione or the piano, but never before with a string orchestra in the supporting role, reversing the bowed/percussive relationship. Good arranging doesn't consist of literal adherence to the original score but, as here, in making small changes to take advantage of the new instrumentation. Rarely has such a transmutation been accomplished with greater conviction. Put any doubts or prejudices you may have on the back burner and enjoy familiar beauty in new clothing. The Giuliani is familiar in every respect – except that of interpretation. What we have in this recording is the recognition of the relationship between instrumental and vocal music in Giuliani's work; it's apparent in his (and others') frequent adaptation of operatic music for the guitar, but has more or less escaped the attention of guitarists on record. The vocal quality of the writing is fully realised here, producing what might even be regarded as the first stylistically faithful recording of the First Concerto. The performances from both John Williams and the Australian Chamber Orchestra are exemplary and praise should also extend to the engineers who recorded them with such clarity and ideal balance. If you already have these works, don't let it deter you from adding this revelatory one to your collection.

Philip Glass   American 1937

Glass studied at the Juilliard School and with Boulanger in Paris (1964-6) and worked with the Indian musicians Ravi Shankar and Alla Rakha. His minimalist works of 1965-8 (eg Two Pages) are 'experimental and exploratory' but later ones, for his own amplified ensemble, are more complicated (eg Music in Fifths). Since 1975 his works have nearly all been for the theatre. When Einstein on the Beach was given at the Met (1976) he became famous; further full-scale operas, Satyagraha (1980), Akhnaten (1984), The Making of the Representative for Planet 8 (1988) and The Voyage (1992), chamber operas and music theatre works followed. One of the most popular serious composers in the USA, he has also performed in rock and jazz.   **GROVE**music

Cello Concerto

The Concerto Project, Volume 1
Cello Concerto[a]. Concerto Fantasy for Two
Timpanists and Orchestra[b]
[a]**Julian Lloyd Webber** vc [b]**Evelyn Glennie**,
[b]**Jonathan Haas** perc **Royal Liverpool Philharmonic Orchestra / Gerard Schwarz**
Orange Mountain Music OMM0013 (45' · DDD)   Ⓕ

The Cello Concerto was conceived when Julian Lloyd Webber asked Glass to compose a work for the cellist's 50th birthday. Lloyd Webber says the piece, premièred in October 2001, contains technical hurdles he had not seen before, particularly in the opening cadenza, but for the listener it's not a difficult work. That cadenza, underpinned by muffled, percussive figures from the orchestra, is dramatic, with an undercurrent of ambiguous emotion, but it's also lithe and attractive, evocative of the classics of cello literature, not least Bach and Elgar. There are passages where the debate between orchestra and soloist seems to contrast those often-copied, easily parodied Glass mannerisms with his more melodically and harmonically expansive work of recent years. The result is one of the most engaging, impressive and beautiful things Glass has done. The slow movement, lyrical and graceful, sets us up perfectly for the shock of the opening of the finale, which bursts in with one of those 'accelerating train' episodes he does so effectively.

The gestation of the timpani concerto was more problematic. Despite their tuneful capabilities, timpani are associated primarily with melodrama and bombast and aren't an ideal choice for a concerto solo instrument. There are 14 of them here, presumably due to the need to negotiate fairly rapid movement through different keys. It all works remarkably well in the event. The fast first movement has exciting, ritualistic solo parts, perhaps influenced by South-East Asian and Japanese traditions. The slow movement manages to make the drums sound lyrical, embedded in settings of regal brass and pastoral woodwind. The cadenza preceding the third movement, highly athletic as it is, proves to be a warm-up for Evelyn Glennie and Jonathan Haas before the technical *tour de force* of the finale.

Symphonies

Symphony No 2. Orphée – Interlude. Concerto for
Saxophone Quartet and Orchestra
Raschèr Saxophone Quartet (Carina Raschèr sop
sax Harry Kinross White alto sax Bruce Weinberger
ten sax Kenneth Coon bass sax) **Vienna Radio
Symphony Orchestra, Stuttgart Chamber
Orchestra / Dennis Russell Davies**
Nonesuch 7559-79496-2 (69' · DDD)   Ⓕ

Glass isn't a symphonist in the conventional sense, but neither was Messiaen. Glass himself has indicated that his large-scale orchestral works are conceived with their probable role in the conventions of concert programming in mind. This sounds outrageously manipulative when stated explicitly, but in fact it's nothing more than a description of the context of the symphonic form since its inception. He's also said that he devoted his earlier career to subtracting elements from his music and is now deciding what to put back in. In the case of this symphony, the specified element is polytonality, the presence of which in much 20th-century music is perhaps taken for granted. However, when it's added into this stripped-down and austere idiom, the results are certainly striking. The opening movement recalls the prelude to *Akhnaten*, the third and final movement reprises the chattering arpeggios of the composer's earlier works, closing with an exciting – and, indeed, viscera-loosening – *crescendo*. After recovering during the snippet from *Orphée*, we come to the marvellous Concerto. Conceived for performance either as a quartet or in this quartet-plus-orchestra version, this is a gloriously animated work, almost Coplandesque in many respects, yet remaining true to Glass's own vision. Despite being presented as the secondary work on this disc, its presence makes the whole recommendable.

Symphony No 3[a]. The CIVIL WarS – Interludes Nos 1 & 2[a]. The Voyage – Mechanical Ballet[b]. The Light[b]
[a]**Stuttgart Radio Symphony Orchestra,** [b]**Vienna Radio Symphony Orchestra / Dennis Russell Davies**
Nonesuch 7559-79581-2 (61' · DDD)   Ⓕ

Comparing Glass's Third Symphony with his Second finds the forces reduced from full orchestra to strings, the overall timing reduced by virtually half and the number of movements increased from three to four. Glass No 2 is long breathed, atmospheric and occasionally suggestive of Brucknerian vistas, whereas Glass No 3 is texturally lean and harmonically more adventurous than much of his previous work. It also seems to have taken in influences from some fairly unexpected sources.

The first movement is sombre and march-like while the second, which is built on compound meters, kicks out in all directions, switching to a gutsy *staccato* at 2'59". The pulse is constant, but the tone has altered, sometimes sidling nearer to Sibelius, sometimes a stone's throw from Shostakovich. At the start of the brief finale, there's even a hint of Kurt Weill, but one thing is for sure: if you play the Symphony blind, you might never guess that it's by Glass. The stylistic shift from mellow, arpeggiated dreamscape (a familiar Glassian aura that holds sway for most of *The Light*) to a sort of ecstatic acerbity, follows through to the rest of the work. But there's another presence – less of a surprise, perhaps – later in the long third movement when the Arvo Pärt of *Cantus* seems to join the fray.

The idea of external influence extends to the interludes from *The CIVIL WarS*, where, as annotator David Wright tells us, Tchaikovsky's *Nutcracker* gets a look in, particularly in the Second Interlude with its *pas-de-deux*-like downward scales. 'Mechanical Ballet' (from *The Voyage*) and the expansive *The Light* are rather more

what you'd expect from Glass: haunting narratives, always on the move yet tinged with melancholy. Even if you don't care for Glass's more familiar 'arpeggiated' style, do try the Third Symphony. It's different, and the performance is excellent.

The Hours

The Hours – original soundtrack
Michael Riesman *pf* **Lyric Quartet** (Rolf Wilson, Edmund Coxon *vns* Nicholas Barr *va* David Daniels *vc*) **Chris Laurence** *db* **orchestra / Nick Ingham**
Nonesuch 7559-79693-2 (58' · DDD)   ⒻⒺ

'I love Glass's music,' writes Michael Cunningham in the note included with this recording, 'almost as much as I love [Virginia] Woolf's *Mrs Dalloway*, and for some of the same reasons. Glass, like Woolf, is more interested in that which continues than he is in that which begins, climaxes and ends; he insists, as did Woolf, that beauty often resides more squarely in the present than it does in the present's relationship to past or future.' Seldom has there been such a concisely eloquent description of Glass's work. And the analogy with Woolf is in this case quintessentially correct, for *The Hours* is a film with deals with Mrs Woolf, her creation Mrs Dalloway and, as we eventually learn, a Los Angeles housewife, Mrs Brown. The *present-ness* of their situations is what connects these three women, eternally containing the potential to leap into the future or regress into the past... Was there ever a more perfect film for Glass's current lyrical manner? He himself refers to his own past, quoting from his 'Glassworks' and 'Solo Piano' collections, and from as far back as his opera *Satyagraha*, but the way in which the material is treated here, clothed in nostalgic colours by piano, string quartet and orchestra, transforms it inevitably into that eternal present. This album of music has a fragile beauty that never lapses into mere sentimentality.

Naqoyqatsi

Naqoyqatsi – Original Film Soundtrack
Yo-Yo Ma *vc* Members of the **Philip Glass Ensemble** (Lisa Bielawa *sop* Jon Gibson, Richard Peck *saxs* Andrew Sterman *fl, picc, cl* Michael Riesman *kbd*) **orchestra / Michael Riesman**
Sony Classical SK87709 (77' · DDD)   ⒻⒺ

This is another colourful, barnstorming film score from Glass, and one that contains enough material of substance that it can stand quite successfully on its own. There are the expected Glass fingerprints – the powerful, pulsing, dark-hued 'heartbeat' opening, the rippling arpeggios of 'Religion', the clangorous vocal and orchestral writing in 'Intensive Time' and 'Point Blank', both of which recall parts of his opera *Akhnaten* – but there are also moments when he creates something quite new. In 'Mass-man' he explores the higher regions of the solo cello in some hauntingly lyrical music; and lyricism, of a non-Western kind, also characterises two remarkable sections for solo cello and percussion, 'New World' and 'Old World'. A more purely romantic sensibility is at work in 'Media Weather', as in other sections in passing, but it seems all of a piece with this interesting mixture of the familiar pulsing, glowing Glass and the less familiar, introspective lyrical composer. The performance is superb, and beautifully recorded.

Itaipú

The Canyon. Itaipú[a]
Atlanta Symphony [a]**Chorus and Orchestra / Robert Shaw**
Sony Classical SK46352 (56' · DDD) Recorded 1990
Ⓕ Ⓞ

The idea of spacious natural vistas has always been central to Glass's work. *Itaipú* and *The Canyon* are the second and third of his 'portraits of nature'. Itaipú is located on the Paraná River, which in turn forms the border between Brazil and Paraguay. It's the location of a massive hydro-electric dam with individual generators large enough to house a full symphony orchestra. So it's little wonder that Itaipú provided Glass with instant inspiration. The score itself is divided into four separate sections and calls on substantial orchestral and choral forces. Although consistent with his other work, *Itaipú* has an especially dark, rugged tonal profile. The hub of the work – 'The Dam' itself – is in the third movement, where brass and winds abet a pounding ostinato and a series of modulations redolent of such scenically aware late-Romantics as Sibelius, Bruckner and Roy Harris. It's one of the most arresting passages in Glass's output, and gives a vivid impression of the dam's overwhelming physical presence.

The Canyon is purely orchestral; it's built around two basic ideas, with a jagged middle section that heats up for a powerful climax. Less heavily scored than *Itaipú*, *The Canyon* utilises a large array of percussion, which Glass exploits with his usual ear for nuance. But *Itaipú* is the disc's main 'event' – a patient, cumulatively powerful essay, easily assimilated and well enough crafted to repay repeated listening. The recordings are cleanly balanced, the performances neat.

Music in similar motion

Music in similar motion[a]. Strung Out[d]. Piece in the shape of a square[b]. Gradus[c]. Music in contrary motion[a]
[a]**Alter Ego** ([b]Manuel Zurria *fl* [c]Paolo Ravaglia *cl* [d]Francesco Peverini *vn* Francesco Dillon *vc* Oscar Pizzo *kybd* Gianluca Ruggeri *mari*) Stradivarius STR33602 (78' · DDD)
Ⓕ Ⓞ Ⓞ

Alter Ego's disc of music by Glass, written between 1967 and 1969, is quite stunning. They kick off with a tremendous performance, powerful and sensitive in equal measure, of *Music in similar motion*, undoubtedly one of Glass's most powerful and enduring works. Violinist Francesco Peverini's gives a dazzling rendition of the solo *Strung Out*, which is such a *tour de force* that one is left quite out of breath just by listening. *Piece in the shape of a square*, for two flutes, was recorded using overdubbing. It's a literal tongue-twister, with its exhilarating quick-fire exchanges between the two lines receiving a transcendent performance from Manuel Zurria. The disc closes with another blazing ensemble piece, *Music in contrary motion*. Their beautiful performance, while evincing a tremendous rhythmic precision, also flows in the most extraordinary way. An essential disc for anyone interested in Glass's work.

La Belle et la Bête

La Belle et la Bête
Janice Felty *mez* La Belle **Gregory Purnhagen** *bar* La Bête, Avenant, Ardent, Port Official **John Kuether** *bass* Father, Usurer **Ana Maria Martinez** *sop* Felicie **Hallie Neill** *sop* Adelaide **Zheng Zhou** *bar* Ludovic **Philip Glass Ensemble / Michael Riesman**
Nonesuch ② 7559-79347-2 (89' · DDD) Recorded 1994. Notes, text and translation included Ⓕ Ⓞ

This is one of Glass's most innovative and impressive works. It isn't exactly an opera, but nor is it film music; cantata is the nearest term, yet even that won't really convey the idea. What Glass has done is to make a setting of the script for Jean Cocteau's 1946 film *La Belle et la Bête*, using every word as it's spoken in the film, but having it sung, the whole thing designed to be performed in concert, with a print of the film being projected silently. Of all Cocteau's movies, *La Belle et la Bête* is visually the most stylised, with its images of the Beast's castle, and the Vermeeresque settings for the family home of the merchant whose search for a rose to give to his youngest daughter sets off the nightmarish story. Cocteau described his film as 'the illustration of the border that separates one world from the other'. For all its surreal photography and extravagant décor by Christian Bérard (the arms-bearing candelabra, poking out from the wall, have influenced hundreds of interior decorators), the dialogue in the film is delivered in a naturalistic way. The words are sung in an ethereal way, and the music itself trembles with characteristic Glass motifs.

La Belle et la Bête hovers somewhere between genteel beat music and Messiaen-influenced *mélodie* and defies categorisation. As Beauty, Janice Felty's voice matches the image of Josette Day in the film, but Gregory Purnhagen's light baritone would never suggest Jean Marais, whose smoky tones were such an inspiration to Cocteau. Most people prefer the Beast with his hairy face and claws to the rather effete-looking

Prince Charming who emerges at the end, and Glass's music seems to make an ironic commentary on this transformation. Well worth investigating.

Alexander Glazunov

Russian/USSR 1865-1936

Glazunov studied privately with Rimsky-Korsakov (1879-81) and had his First Symphony performed when he was 16. He became a member of the circle around the patron Belyayev, who took him to meet Liszt in Weimar, and in 1899 was appointed to the St Petersburg Conservatory, which he directed from 1905 until leaving the Soviet Union in 1928. During these later years he composed relatively little: the bulk of his output, which includes nine symphonies, much else for orchestra, the ballet Raymonda (1897) and seven quartets, dates from before World War I. He has a significant place in Russian music in that he reconciled Russianism and Europeanism. He absorbed Balakirev's nationalism, Rimsky-Korsakov's orchestral virtuosity, Tchaikovsky's lyricism, Borodin's epic grandeur and Taneyev's contrapuntal skill. GROVEmusic

Violin Concerto in A minor, Op 82

Violin Concerto. Meditation, Op 32[a] The Seasons, Op 67
[a]**Aaron Rosand** *vn* **Malaysian Philharmonic Orchestra / Kees Bakels**
Vox Classics VXP7907 (61' · DDD)   Ⓕ●

Aaron Rosand began recording for Vox in the late 1950s. Now in his seventies, his timbre and technique are as sure as ever. Moreover Rosand's very stylish playing of the delightful Glazunov Concerto brings a sense of having lived with this music over the decades, yet returning to it as to an old friend, with no possible hint of staleness. The beguiling opening theme floats off the bow with the most engaging warmth and an easy, natural *rubato*, which the conductor follows admirably. The richly shaped melody of the *Andante*, too, goes straight to the heart of the music: again Rosand's timbre is warm, his phrasing ravishingly lyrical. The finale dances away jauntily, its spirited rhythmic charisma echoed by the orchestra.

In short, this performance is very good indeed, worthy of comparison with the finest on disc (including Vengerov, Shaham, Mutter) and, in its security of the solo line, even approaches Heifetz. The gentle, rhapsodic *Meditation* makes a splendid encore while the recording is admirable, with a completely natural balance.

Glazunov Violin Concerto[a] **Prokofiev** Violin Concertos Nos 1 & 2[b]
Maxim Vengerov *vn* [a]**Berlin Philharmonic Orchestra / Claudio Abbado;** [b]**London Symphony Orchestra / Mstislav Rostropovich**

Warner Elatus 0927-49567-2 (DDD) Recorded 1994-5
Ⓜ●

Vengerov turns Glazunov's war-horse concerto from a display piece into a work of far wider-ranging emotions. It's a remarkable account, with Vengerov making you appreciate afresh what a wonderful and varied sequence of melodies Glazunov offers. It's characteristic of Vengerov how he shades and contrasts his tone colours. He reserves his big, Romantic tone for the third theme, where most rivals let loose sooner with less subtle results. His *rubato* is free but always spontaneous sounding, and the lolloping fourth section brings some delicious *portamento*. Predictably the dashing final section is spectacular in its brilliance, with orchestral textures fresh and clean.

Vengerov and Rostropovich take an unashamedly epic, wide-open-steppes view of Prokofiev's First Concerto rather than the pseudo-Ravelian one posited by Chung/Previn and Mintz/Abbado, but it works at least as well. His tone is gloriously rich, every note hit dead centre. No 2 is slightly less successful. The balance is partly to blame – the soloist rather too closely scrutinised – but there's also a lack of intimacy in the interpretation itself. Nevertheless, this is an extremely fine disc and comes thoroughly recommended.

Symphony No 8

Symphony No 8 in E flat, Op 83. Cantata in Memory of Pushkin's 100th Birthday, Op 65[a]. Lyric Poem in D flat, Op 12
[a]**Ludmila Kuznetsova** *mez* [a]**Vsevolod Grivnov** *ten* **Russian State Symphony** [a]**Cappella and Orchestra / Valéry Polyansky**
Chandos CHAN9961 (67' · DDD) Text and translation included   Ⓕ

Glazunov's Symphony No 8 opens confidently and lyrically, conductor Valéry Polyansky maintaining an easy-going momentum, later pressing forward, yet always holding the argument together. There's some lovely woodwind playing in the *Mesto* slow movement and the strings create a genuinely passionate climax. The *Scherzo* is given a purposeful thrust, and the finale doesn't outstay its welcome, with the chorale theme splendidly sonorous at the opening, the drive and tension of the playing well maintained to the end.

Also well captured here is the lovely *Poème lyrique* was admired by Tchaikovsky for its rich flow of Russian melancholy. But what makes this Chandos disc so very attractive is the *Cantata in Memory of Pushkin's 100th Birthday*, which is full of warmly lyrical ideas. Glazunov's flow of invention more than compensates for the doggerel poetry he was forced to set by the Grand Duke Constantine Romanov. The work is framed and interlaced by splendid, powerfully sung and very Russian choruses of gratitude. There's a lovely 'Berceuse' for the mezzo, here radiantly sung by Ludmila Kuznetsova, who redeems its sentimentality; a later aria of praise for the tenor is relished by Vsevolod Grivnov; finally comes a hymn in which the two soloists join, exultantly taken up by the chorus, with a burst of joy at the close. This one of those happy works, full of melody, that makes you feel glad to be alive. A truly memorable performance then, and the Chandos recording is well up to house standards.

Suite caractéristique

Suite caractéristique in D, Op 9. Le chant du destin, Op 84. Deux Préludes, Op 85
Moscow Symphony Orchestra / Igor Golovschin
Naxos 8 553857 (75' · DDD) ⑤○

The eight-movement Suite caractéristique is vintage Glazunov, an orchestral transcription of piano pieces. Slavic melancholy characterises the 'Introduction', which serves to usher in an engaging 'Danse rustique'. The central, delicately scored 'Pastorale' is particularly charming and the following 'Danse orientale' is at first piquant, in the best Russian pseudo-oriental manner, but reaches an expansive climax, and the gentle beginning of the 'Elégie' is followed by a passionate interjection (in a surprisingly Tchaikovskian manner). The grand closing 'Cortège' makes a resplendent, very Russian ending. The two Préludes date from 1906 and 1908 respectively. One remembers, in a grave, valedictory mood, Vladimir Stassoff; the second (much more extended) opens surprisingly like Tchaikovsky's Francesca da Rimini and this curious leitmotif dominates the early part of the piece, which later produces a gentle, disconsolate chorale and a sonorously Wagnerian coda. It's played most impressively, as indeed is the Suite. The recording is good too.

Reyngol'd Glière
Ukraine/USSR 1875-1956

Glière studied at the Moscow Conservatory, where he became professor of composition (1920-41). His works, in the Russian epic tradition of Borodin and Glazunov, include three symphonies (the third subtitled 'Il'ya Muromets', 1911), concertos (one for coloratura soprano, 1943) and ballets (notably The Red Flower), as well as operas on central Asian themes using indigenous musical traditions, and chamber and piano music. **GROVE**music

Concerto for Coloratura Soprano

Ginastera Harp Concerto, Op 25 Glière Harp Concerto, Op 74. Concerto for Coloratura Soprano and Orchestra, Op 82
Eileen Hulse *sop* **Rachel Masters** *hp* **City of London Sinfonia / Richard Hickox**

Chandos CHAN9094 (65' · DDD) Recorded 1992 Ⓕ

Glière was among the comparatively few front-rank Russian composers who stayed on in their homeland after the 1917 Revolution. The music he composed there adopted a middle-of-the-road conservative style which helped him to steer clear of the more viscous controversies of the 1920s and 1930s. The Concertos for harp and coloratura soprano are unashamedly ingratiating, high-grade mood-music, here played and recorded in a manner that those with a sweet tooth should find irresistible. Ginastera's Harp Concerto is made of sterner stuff, but only slightly – it's Bartókian acerbities are tempered by an engaging Latin American swing. Again the performance is crisp and bouncy, though the reverberant recording takes some of the edge off the rhythmic bite.

Symphonies

Symphony No 2 in C minor, Op 25. The Red Poppy – Ballet Suite, Op 70
New Jersey Symphony Orchestra / Zdenek Macal
Delos DE3178 (73' · DDD) Ⓕ

This performance of Glière's colourful late-Romantic Second Symphony is extremely satisfying, with a fine blend of transparency and warmth. Glière never puts a foot wrong, but that's because he's going along trails blazed for him by others long before 1908. Although the Romantic parts of *Firebird* are audibly just round the corner, here the magic is tamed and the amount of repetition can even become slightly irksome. The New Jersey cor anglais plays with peerless refinement in the slow movement, and Macal coaxes suave phrasing from his musicians. For newcomers to Glière, the *Red Poppy* Suite is a useful choice as filler.

Symphony No 3, 'Il'ya Mouromets', Op 42
London Symphony Orchestra / Leon Botstein
Telarc CD80609 (72' · DDD) Ⓕ○

Recognisably breathing the same air as Stravinsky's *Firebird*, Scriabin's *Poem of Ecstasy* and Suk's *Asrael* Symphony, Glière's *Il'ya Mouromets* makes up in lusciousness and sweep what it slightly lacks in individuality, offering a superb vehicle for the modern orchestra and, indeed, for state-of-the-art hi-fi systems. The LSO and Leon Botstein have the edge in almost every respect over rival performances. Comparable to Downes in his tempos, albeit with a rather fleeter-footed finale, Botstein is less insistent in his accentuation and more emotionally generous with his phrasing, so the overall effect is less strenuous, more sensuously appealing, with the climaxes standing in higher relief. The LSO, on terrific form, command a slighter wider range of nuance, and Telarc's recording is a degree or two more spacious, without ever feeling overblown. Altogether, a very collectable disc.

Mikhail Glinka · Russian 1804-1857

Having come to know rural folk music in its purer forms, and receiving an unsystematic musical education in St Petersburg and on his sojourn in Italy (1830-33), Glinka neither inherited a tradition of sophisticated composition nor developed a distinctive and consistent personal style. But he exerted a profound and freely acknowledged influence on Balakirev, Rimsky-Korsakov, Mussorgsky, Borodin and Tchaikovsky, as well as on Prokofiev and Stravinsky. His first important compositions, written in Berlin (1834), where he studied briefly with Siegfried Dehn, were a Capriccio for piano duet and an unfinished symphony, both applying variation technique to Russian themes.

It was his opera A Life for the Tsar (1836; originally Ivan Susanin) that established him overnight as Russia's leading composer. Though its national character derives from melodic content alone (mostly merely quasi-Russian), it is nevertheless significant for its novel, expressive Russian recitative and for its use of the leitmotif. His next opera, Ruslan and Lyudmila (1842), based on Pushkin's fantastic, ironic fairy-tale, was less well received, being structurally unsuited to the stage and musically haphazard, yet it contains elements of striking originality, including Chernomor's grotesque little march, pungent touches of chromatic colour, exuberant rhythms, the use of the whole-tone scale and the 'changing background' technique for folktune presentation. Inspiring the oriental and 'magic' idioms of later Russian composers, this opera proved to be seminal in the history of Russian music. At Paris (1844-5) Glinka enjoyed Berlioz's music and in Spain (1845-7) folk music and fresh visual impressions; two Spanish Overtures resulted, exceeded in inventiveness however by the kaleidoscopic orchestral variations Kamarinskaya (1848). Among the rich legacy of his songs, the Pushkin settings Where is our rose?, I recall a wonderful moment, Adèle and The toasting cup are particularly fine. GROVEmusic

Orchestral Works

Capriccio brillante on the 'Jota aragonesa'. Souvenir d'une nuit d'été à Madrid. Symphony on Two Russian Themes. Overture in D. Kamarinskaya. Valse-fantaisie. Ruslan and Lyudmila – Overture; Dance; Chernomor's March
BBC Philharmonic Orchestra / Vassily Sinaisky
Chandos CHAN9861 (71' · DDD) Ⓕ

This is a more comprehensive survey than that available on ASV with the Armenian Philharmonic under Loris Tjeknavorian. Both conductors include the two 'Spanish Overtures', the *Valse-fantaisie* and *Kamarinskaya* in closely matched performances. Sinaisky is rather faster and brighter in the first 'Spanish Overture', *Capriccio on the jota aragonesa*, and in the second, *Souvenir d'une nuit d'été*, he reflects more subtly the French grace that also lies within the music. Both conductors give good, vivid performances of the *Valse-fantaisie* and *Kamarinskaya*, with recordings that do justice to Glinka's brilliant orchestration. Thereafter the repertoire parts company. While Tjeknavorian gives the rest of his record up to a suite of six pieces from *A Life for the Tsar*, Sinaisky prefers *Ruslan and Lyudmila*, with a lively performance of the overture and then the Act 3 dances and the dwarf Chernomor's grotesque little march. This gives him room for the early Overture in D minor, which doesn't often feature on records, and for the *Symphony on Two Russian Themes*. The work survives in only a single movement, but fascinatingly anticipates *Kamarinskaya*. For a highly enjoyable introduction to Glinka's orchestral music, indeed to his whole original way of thinking, this Chandos disc is the one to go for.

Christoph Gluck · Bohemian 1714-1787

Gluck's father was a forester in the Upper Palatinate (now the western extreme of Czechoslovakia); Czech was his native tongue. At about 14 he left home to study in Prague, where he worked as an organist. He soon moved to Vienna and then to Milan, where his first opera was given in 1741. Others followed, elsewhere in Italy and during 1745-6 in London, where he met Handel's music. After further travel (Dresden, Copenhagen, Naples, Prague) he settled in Vienna in 1752 as Konzertmeister of the Prince of Saxe-Hildburghausen's orchestra, then as Kapellmeister. He also became involved in performances at the court theatre of French opéras comiques, as arranger and composer, and he wrote Italian dramatic works for court entertainments. His friends tried, at first unsuccessfully, to procure a court post for him; but by 1759 he had a salaried position at the court theatre and soon after was granted a royal pension.

He met the poet Calzabigi and the choreographer Angiolini, and with them wrote a ballet-pantomime Don Juan (1761) embodying a new degree of artistic unity. The next year they wrote the opera Orfeo ed Euridice, the first of Gluck's so-called 'reform operas'. In 1764 he composed an opéra comique, La rencontre imprévue, and the next year two ballets; he followed up the artistic success of Orfeo with a further collaboration with Calzabigi, Alceste (1767), this time choreographed by Noverre; a third, Paride ed Elena (1770), was less well received.

Gluck now decided to apply his new ideals to French opera, and in 1774 gave Iphigénie en Aulide (as well as Orphée, a French revision of Orfeo) in Paris; it was a triumph, but also set the ground for a controversy between Gluck and Italian music (as represented by Piccinni) which flared up in 1777 when his Armide was given, following a French version of Alceste (1776). Iphigénie en Tauride followed in 1779 – his greatest success, along with his greatest failure, Echo et Narcisse. He now acknowledged that his career was over; he revised Iphigénie en Tauride for German performance, and composed some songs, but abandoned plans for a journey to London to give his operas and died in autumn 1787, widely recognised as the doyen of Viennese composers and the man who had carried through important reforms to the art of opera.

Gluck's opera reforms – they are not exclusively his own, for several other composers (notably Jommelli and Traetta) had been working along similar lines – are outlined in the preface he wrote, probably with Calzabigi's help, to the published score of Alceste. He aimed to make the music serve the poetry through its expression of the situations of the story, without interrupting it for conventional orchestral ritornellos or, particularly, florid and ornamental singing; to make the overture relevant to the drama and the orchestration apt to the words; to break down the sharp contrast between recitative and aria: 'in short to abolish all the abuses against which good sense and reason have long cried out in vain'. Orfeo exemplifies most of these principles, with its abandonment of simple recitative in favour of a more continuous texture (with orchestral recitative, arioso and aria running into one another) and its broad musical-dramatic spans in which different types of solo singing, dance and choral music are fully integrated. It also has a simple, direct plot, based on straightforward human emotions, which could appeal to an audience as the complicated stories used in opera seria, with their intrigues, disguises and subplots, could not.

He had a limited compositional technique, but one that was sufficient for the aims he set himself. His music can have driving energy, but also a serenity reaching to the sublime. His historical importance rests on his establishment of a new equilibrium between music and drama, and his greatness on the power and clarity with which he projected that vision; he dissolved the drama in music instead of merely illustrating it. **GROVE**music

Opera Arias

Italian Arias   P
Antigono – Berenice, che fai?. **La clemenza di Tito** – Tremo fra' dubbi miei; Ah, taci, barbaro…Come potesti, oh Dio!; Se mai senti spirarti sul volto. **La corona** – Quel chiaro rio. **Ezio** – Misera, dove son!…Ah! non son io che parlo. **Il Parnaso confuso** – Di questa cetra in seno. **La Semiramide riconosciuta** – Ciascun siegua il suo stile…Maggior follia
Cecilia Bartoli mez **Akademie für Alte Musik Berlin / Bernhard Forck**
Decca 467 248-2DH (68' · DDD) Notes, texts and translations included   Ⓕ❍❍❍

This is something very much out of the ordinary. These eight arias, taken variously from Gluck's early operas (those preceding his 'reforms' that began with *Orfeo* in 1762) or his non-reform later ones, are almost wholly unfamiliar, but they have great power and character; and they're sung with an extraordinary emotional force and technical skill, not to say a sheer beauty of tone, that can't be matched by any other singer today. Cecilia Bartoli's range is formidable. In the first aria, from *La clemenza di Tito*, she sings with trumpet-like tone and brilliance of attack, throwing off widespanning arpeggios with evident abandon and dispatching coloratura with fluency and precision, each note articulated and perfectly tuned.

The second, an elegantly pathetic little piece from the later *Il Parnaso confuso*, is a tour de force of delicate, tender *pianissimo* singing. The third, from *Ezio*, begins with an orchestral recitative of thrilling dramatic urgency and goes on to an aria of great passion. Bartoli is described as a mezzo-soprano here, and her voice does indeed chiefly lie in that range; but most of these are soprano arias, and she happily goes well above the stave – there's one slightly squally high C sharp in the first aria but she's usually pretty comfortable in her top register. The accompaniments are splendidly sensitive and alert. A quite outstanding disc that no one who loves fine singing can miss.

Gluck Paride ed Elena – O del mio dolce ardor.   P
Orfeo ed Euridice – Che puro ciel!; Che farò senza Euridice. Alceste – Non vi turbate **Haydn** Il mondo della luna – Una donna come me. Orlando Paladino – Ad un sguardo, a un cenno solo. La fedeltà premiata – Deh soccorri un'infelice **Mozart** Le nozze di Figaro – Voi che sapete. Don Giovanni – Batti, batti; Vedrai, carino; In quali eccessi…Mi tradì quell'alma ingrata. Lucio Silla – Dunque sperar…Il tenero momento. La finta giardiniera – Dolce d'amor compagna. La clemenza di Tito – Ecco il punto, oh Vitellia…Non più di fiori
Anne Sofie von Otter mez **The English Concert / Trevor Pinnock** hpd
Archiv Produktion 449 206-2AH (71' · DDD) Texts and translations included   Ⓕ❍

For the sake of both vocal and family wellbeing, Anne Sofie von Otter has always followed the wise course of self-rationing in opera. This disc, an entirely personal selection of arias from the Viennese Classical period, means all the more to her including, as it does, arias sung by dramatic and passionate women 'most of whom', she admits in the accompanying notes, 'I have never performed on stage and, alas, probably never will'. They include *La clemenza di Tito*'s Vitellia, whom she has irresistibly observed in her own role as Sesto: here she at last voices her guilt at implicating Sesto in her crime of passion, and expresses that unique fusion of sadness and desperation of 'Non più di fiori' in the eloquent company of Colin Lawson's basset horn, followed by Gluck's *Alceste*, again keenly observed by von Otter in a *comprimario* role. Gluck's *Orfeo* is familiar to her at first hand, and here The English Concert's introduction to the recitative preceding 'Che farò' creates exquisitely the 'nuova serena luce' of the Elysian fields against which her grief is the darker, the more plangent. The Mozart arias evoke memorable stage and concert performances by von Otter: a Cherubino whose phrasing combines with that of the wind soloists to create the warm breath of burgeoning sensuality in 'Voi che sapete'; a Cecilio (*Lucio Silla*) whose coloratura captures the thrilled anticipation of that 'tenero momento'; and a moustachioed Ramiro (*La finta giardiniera*) who pays ecstatic *cantabile* tribute to the power of love.

Alceste

Alceste   P
Teresa Ringholz sop Alcestis **Justin Lavender**
ten Admetus **Jonas Degerfelt** ten Evander **Miriam
Treichl** sop Ismene **Lars Martinsson** bar Herald
Voice of Apollo **Adam Giertz** treb Eumelo **Emilie
Clausen** treb Aspasia **Johan Lilja** bass High Priest
Hercules, God of the Underworld **Mattias Nilsson**
bar Bandit **Drottningholm Court Theatre Chorus
and Orchestra / Arnold Östman**
Naxos ③ 8 660066/8 (147' · DDD) Notes, text and
translation included   S

Almost all critics of Gluck's two versions of
Alceste – the Italian original, first given in
Vienna in 1767, and the French revision or
recomposition given in Paris in 1776 – regard
the latter as superior: musically richer, more
flexible, dramatically more persuasive, deeper in
its treatment of the emotions and the humanity
of the two central characters. But this performance of the Italian version treats the 1767 text
on its own terms. Like the original *Orfeo*, the
original *Alceste* is an opera pared down, in accordance with Gluck's and his librettist Calzabigi's
reform principles, to deal with just a single
issue: it's concerned exclusively with Alceste's
sacrifice of her life to save that of her husband,
Admeto, King of Thessaly, and the emotions
that each of them and those around them feel.
The performance is deftly paced and transparent in its textures. There's no portentousness
about Östman's direction, and the Drottningholm orchestra ensures that the detail of accompanying textures is clearly heard, playing gently
and lightly in the dances.

Teresa Ringholz has a voice of modest dimensions, which she uses in a natural way, with little
vibrato, firm, surely tuned, clear and well
focused. She catches Alceste's increasingly passionate determination, at the close of Act 1, as
her resolution to die to save her husband hardens, with its magnificent climax in 'Ombre,
larve'. Her controlled manner – there's no outburst of grief when she bids her children
farewell at the end of the act, for example –
catches well the stylised nature of Gluck's
expression. Justin Lavender, as Admeto, is
slightly less successful. He has a generous tenor
– fuller and weightier than that of the other
tenor, Jonas Degerfelt, who sings gracefully and
also with vitality – and he brings to the music a
good deal of passion that occasionally threatens
to go beyond the scale of the performance as a
whole. The smaller roles are very adequately
done. This recording conveys effectively the
intensity and the integrity of Gluck's vision.

Armide

Armide   P
Mireille Delunsch sop Armide **Charles Workman**
ten Renaud **Laurent Naouri** bar Hidraot **Ewa Podles**
mez Hate **Françoise Masset** sop Phénice, Mélisse
Nicole Heaston sop Sidonie, Shepherdess, Lucinde

Yann Beuron ten Artémidore, Danish Knight **Brett
Polegato** bar Ubalde **Vincent le Texier** bar Aronte
Magdalena Kožená mez Pleasure **Valérie Gabail**
sop Naiad **Choeur des Musiciens du Louvre; Les
Musiciens du Louvre / Marc Minkowski**
Archiv Produktion ② 459 616-2AH2 (139' · DDD)
Notes, text and translation included   F O

'Perhaps the best of all my works', said Gluck of
his *Armide*. But this, the fifth of his seven
'reform operas', has never captured the public
interest as have *Orfeo*, *Alceste*, the two *Iphigénies*
and even *Paride ed Elena*. Its plot is thinnish,
concerned only with the love of the pagan sorceress Armide, princess of Damascus, for the
Christian knight and hero Renaud, and his
enchantment, disenchantment and finally his
abandonment of her. But *Armide* has two features that set it apart. One is the extraordinary
soft, sensuous tone of the music; Gluck said that
it was meant 'to produce a voluptuous sensation', and that if he were to suffer damnation it
would be for the passionate love duet in Act 5.
Certainly his orchestral writing here has a
warmth, a colour and a richness going far
beyond anything in his other reform operas
(apart from parts of *Paride ed Elena*). Second,
there are several great solo dramatic scenes, two
of them for Armide.

The success of *Armide*, then, depends critically on the Armide herself. Here it goes to
Mireille Delunsch, who brings to it a good deal
of intensity but doesn't have command of a wide
range of tone, and doesn't seem to make much
use of her words. There's some graceful singing
in the softer music and the scene where she can't
bring herself to kill Renaud is finely done,
though ultimately perhaps her singing lacks real
emotional tension. Renaud is sung by Charles
Workman, in a strong tenor, sounding almost
baritonal at times, but then singing the sleep
song, 'Plus j'observe ces lieux', with soft, sweet
tone and much delicacy. The lovers' duet in Act
5 is sung gently and with much charm. Among
the other singers, Ewa Podles makes a strong
impression as Hate with her large and steady
voice. And Laurent Naouri shows a pleasant,
firm baritone as Hidraot.

Minkowski makes much of the score's colour
and flow. He uses a substantial orchestra, which
plays lightly and flexibly and with rhythmic
spring. He has a tendency towards quickish
tempos here and there but is always attentive to
the characterisation of individual numbers.

Iphigénie en Aulide

Iphigénie en Aulide
Lynne Dawson sop Iphigénie **José van Dam** bass
Agamemnon **Anne Sofie von Otter** mez
Clytemnestre **John Aler** ten Achille **Bernard
Deletré** bass Patrocle **Gilles Cachemaille** bass
Calchas **René Schirrer** bass Arcas **Guillemette
Laurens** mez Diane **Ann Monoyios** sop First Greek
woman, Slave **Isabelle Eschenbrenner** sop Second

Greek woman **Monteverdi Choir; Lyon Opéra Orchestra / Sir John Eliot Gardiner**
Erato ② 2292-45003-2 (132' · DDD) Recorded 1987.
Notes, text and translation included   ⑤**OO**

Gluck's first reform opera for Paris has tended to be overshadowed by his other *Iphigénie*, the *Tauride* one. But it does contain some superb things, of which perhaps the finest are the great monologues for Agamemnon. On this recording, José van Dam starts a little coolly; but this only adds force to his big moment at the end of the Second Act where he tussles with himself over the sacrifice of his daughter and – contemplating her death and the screams of the vengeful Eumenides – decides to flout the gods and face the consequences. The cast in general is strong. Lynne Dawson brings depth of expressive feeling to all she does and her Iphigénie, marked by a slightly grainy sound and much intensity, is very moving. John Aler's Achille too is very fine and sings both with ardour and vitality. There's great force too in the singing of Anne Sofie von Otter as Clytemnestre. Gardiner's Monteverdi Choir sings with polish, perhaps seeming a little genteel for a crowd of angry Greek soldiers baying for Iphigénie's blood. But he gives a duly urgent account of the score, pressing it forward eagerly and keeping the tension at a high level even in the dance music. A period-instrument orchestra might have added a certain edge and vitality but this performance wants nothing in authority. Securely recommended.

Iphigénie en Tauride

Iphigénie en Tauride   **P**
Christine Goerke sop Iphigénie; **Vinson Cole** ten Pylade; **Rodney Gilfry** bar Oreste; **Sharon Baker** sop 1st Priestess, Greek woman; **Jayne West** sop 2nd Priestess, Diana; **Stephen Salters** bar Thoas; **Mark Andrew Cleveland** sngr Scythian; **Mark Risinger** sngr Minister of the Sanctuary; **Boston Baroque / Martin Pearlman**
Telarc Classics ② CD80546 (134' · DDD) Text and translation included   ⑤**OO**

'With Gluck, there's a long sweep to the drama,' says Martin Pearlman towards the end of his introductory talk about *Iphigénie*, included here at the end of the second CD. It's obvious from his performance that this is how he sees the work; and it's his capacity to sustain that 'long sweep' that makes this version so compelling.

Pearlman, using period instruments, draws vivid and dramatic playing from his admirable group. He's particularly successful in the various dances in the course of the opera, which, beautifully alive and springy in rhythm, never permit the drama to flag, but emerge as an integral part of it, not as decorative interludes. With these clear textures, Gluck's orchestral colouring comes across sharply as, too, does the lofty,

hieratic quality of the work. There's tenderness as well, and it's thanks partly to Pearlman's sensitive timing that the opera's climactic moment – the sacrifice scene, where brother and sister at last recognise each other – is so intense and poignant.

Although it lies quite high, the role of Iphigenia is often assigned to a mezzo, as if to heighten the intensity. Christine Goerke is a true soprano, which allows softer tones and more femininity than one generally hears, but there's metal in her voice, too (she doesn't altogether forgo vibrato), and the weight of the tragedy is by no means underplayed: listen to 'O malheureuse Iphigénie' – enhanced by the fine line of the oboe obbligato – or to her impassioned singing of the noble aria at the beginning of Act 4. Rodney Gilfry provides a strong, manly Orestes and is successful in conveying the tortures he's suffering. Vinson Cole gives a sympathetic reading of Pylades – lyrical, shapely and expressively phrased. There's excellent choral singing.

The principal rival recordings both have rather starrier casts. Muti's is a big, modern opera-house performance, powerful and exciting, Gardiner's more stylish, more concentrated dramatically. But this set is just about first choice.

Orfeo ed Euridice

Orfeo ed Euridice   **P**
Derek Lee Ragin counterten Orfeo **Sylvia McNair** sop Euridice **Cyndia Sieden** sop Amore
Monteverdi Choir; English Baroque Soloists / Sir John Eliot Gardiner
Decca Compact Opera Collection
② 470 424-2DOC2 (89' · DDD) Recorded 1991   Ⓜ**O**

This version of *Orfeo*, played on period instruments and following the original text, has a degree of spiritual force to which other recordings scarcely aspire, and that's to the credit primarily of the conductor, John Eliot Gardiner. It begins with a taut, almost explosive account of the overture, moves to a deeply sombre opening chorus and then a *ballo* of intense expressiveness, finely and carefully moulded phrases (but plenty of air between them) and a lovely translucent orchestral sound. Every one of the numerous dances in this set is the subject of thoughtful musical characterisation, shapely execution and refined timing of detail. Derek Lee Ragin excels as Orpheus; the sound is often very beautiful, the phrasing extraordinarily supple and responsive for a countertenor voice. Eurydice is sung clearly and truly, and with due passion, by Sylvia McNair, and the casting of Cyndia Sieden, with her rather pert, forward voice, as Amore proves to be very successful.

Orfeo ed Euridice   **P**
Bernarda Fink contr Orfeo **Veronica Cangemi** sop

Euridice **Maria Cristina Kiehr** sop Amore **Berlin RIAS Chamber Choir; Freiburg Baroque Orchestra / René Jacobs**
Harmonia Mundi ② HMU90 1742/3 (91' · DDD)
Notes, text and translation included   Ⓕ

Orfeo comes in many guises. There's Gluck's original Italian version, composed for Vienna in 1762, his adjusted version for Parma in 1769, his French revision of 1774 for Paris, and then the numerous, posthumous compromise texts that seek the best of both worlds by incorporating sections of the French version within the framework of the Italian. This version is 'pure' Italian, and although this means forgoing such famous and affecting music as the Dance of the Blessed Spirits, 'Cet asile' and the enhanced ending to 'Che farò', as well as the big D minor Dance of the Furies, it does offer a much more concentrated experience.

The tone of the performance is set by the highly energetic overture, with its forceful accents and its sharply defined textures and dynamics. Jacobs takes pains throughout to give a clear yet also rich quality to Gluck's highly original orchestral textures and to shape his phrases with style and awareness of the omnipresence of dance. However, it's the singer of Orpheus, even more than the conductor, who gives character to a performance of this work. Often nowadays it's sung by a countertenor in preference to the contralto long favoured in the role, which was composed for a castrato anyway. So which voice better suits the semi-divine Orpheus? Ultimately it depends on the artistry of the singer. Bernarda Fink sings the role here very beautifully and quite unaffectedly. Her great strength lies in her smooth, natural and very even tone and her command of line.

This is probably the best version of the Italian original with a woman as Orpheus, and can be recommended without hesitation to anyone who prefers to avoid the male alto voice. If you prefer to stick with the male voice the choice lies between Michael Chance's beautifully sung version under Frieder Bernius (Sony) and Derek Lee Ragin's ardent impersonation in Gardiner's account; both are revealing, in quite different ways, of this very special work.

Orphée et Eurydice   Ⓟ
Richard Croft ten Orphée **Mireille Delunsch** sop
Eurydice **Marion Harousseau** sop Amour
Claire Delgado-Boge sop Blessed Spirit
Les Musiciens du Louvre / Marc Minkowski
Archiv Produktion ② 471 582-2AH2 (111' · DDD · T/S/t/N). Recorded live   ⒻⓄ

As always, Minkowski proves to be a livewire conductor, never afraid of an outpouring of emotions that might sweep the music off its feet. This isn't a simple matter of speed, though some instrumental movements like the Overture and the 'Air de Furies' are propelled along by a force of energy that's almost explosive. Turn to other conductors such as Gardiner or

GLUCK ORFEO ED EURIDICE – IN BRIEF

Derek Lee Ragin Orfeo **Sylvia McNair** Euridice **Cyndia Sieden** Amor **Monteverdi Choir; English Baroque Soloists / Sir John Eliot Gardiner**
Decca 470 424-2DOC2   ⓂⓄ
A very fine, period-instrument performance of the original version of Gluck's opera: Derek Lee Ragin and Sylvia McNair are superb in the title-roles, and Gardiner directs with heart-breaking sympathy.

Bernarda Fink Orfeo **Veronica Cangemi** Euridice **Maria Cristina Kiehr** Amor **Berlin RIAS Chamber Choir; Freiburg Baroque Orchestra / René Jacobs**
Harmonia Mundi HMU901742/3   Ⓕ
Bernarda Fink's Orfeo is superb, natural and extremely beautiful; opposite her is Veronica Cangemi, on excellent form. If you want a period-instrument version of the Italian original with a female Orpheus, this is the one to have.

Richard Croft Orphée **Mireille Delunsch** Eurydice **Marion Harousseau** Amour **Les Musiciens du Louvre / Marc Minkowski**
Archiv Produktion 471 582-2AH2   ⒻⓄ
This is a very vigorous performances of the 1774 revision Gluck made for Paris, so it is sung – excellently – in French. Richard Croft is a strong Orphée with an interesting half-tenor, half-countertenor voice. Mireille Delunsch is a fine Euridice. But be prepared to be shaken up by Minkowksi's approach!

Anne Sofie von Otter Orphée **Barbara Hendricks** Eurydice **Brigitte Fournier** Amour **Lyon Opera Orchestra / Sir John Eliot Gardiner**
EMI 556885-2   Ⓜ
This is Berlioz's version in French and Gardiner does it proud, drawing excellent playing from the Lyon Opera Orchestra from Anne Sofie von Otter and Barbara Hendricks.

Kathleen Ferrier Orfeo **Ann Ayars** Euridice **Zoë Vlachopoulos** Amor **Southern PO / Fritz Stiedry**
Dutton mono CDBP9730   ⓂⓄ
This is the classic 1947 recording with the incomparable Orfeo of Kathleen Ferrier: an interpretation that goes from the heart to the heart. The sound takes a bit of getting used to, even though Dutton has done its best to clean it up.

Dame Janet Baker Orfeo **Elizabeth Speiser** Euridice **Elizabeth Gale** Amor **London PO / Raymond Leppard**
Erato 2292-45864-2   ⓂⓄ
A wonderful memento of Baker's Orfeo, a glorious characterisation with its ardent, heatfelt emotional response. Strong, sinuous accompaniment from Leppard.

Ostman, and suddenly we're on firm land again, rooted by rhythms that are clear and regular and dependable. What's different about Minkowski is his fluid impulsiveness – unsettling to anybody used to old-style Gluck perhaps, but how involving this performance is, and how staid and formal most others sound in retrospect.

The other main point of interest here is the edition. Critical opinion has tended to prefer the classically simple version composed for Vienna in 1762. Minkowski has chosen the 1774 Paris revision, for which the opera was recast in French, Orpheus became a tenor, and a substantial amount of new music was added. Only one other recording of the 1774 *Orphée* with a tenor hero graces the catalogue, and that dates from almost half a century ago. Why the reluctance? Possibly because Gluck made this version for an *haute-contre*, a legendary beast – half countertenor, half tenor. Richard Croft could plausibly pass for one, displaying both a good head for heights and also the agility necessary for 'L'espoir renaît dans mon âme'. His Orpheus is a sensitive soul, singing for the most part in soft and tender tones that can be very touching, though when he does press harder, he can sound stressed. What Croft lacks is the stature of a mythological hero.

The other two principals – Mireille Delunsch and Marion Harousseau – could hardly be bettered, Delunsch conveying a lovely human warmth in the short time available to her, Harousseau fresh and spirited. Minkowski's choir and players are caught in full flight by Archiv's lively recording, which puts the listener in the best seat of the house. Collectors of Gluck have no reason to hesitate: they'll want the only period-instrument recording of *Orphée* with its tenor hero. But they'll also be glad to know that it captures a performance well worth having anyway.

Additional recommendations

Orphée et Eurydice
von Otter Orfeo **Hendricks** Euridice **Fournier** Amor
Lyon Opera Orchestra / Gardiner
EMI 556885-2 (89' · DDD)   Ⓕ
  Berlioz's edition of Gluck's masterpiece (sung in French) receives powerful advocacy from Sir John Eliot Gardiner, Anne Sofie von Otter and Barbara Hendricks. An extremely fine interpretation of this version of the work.

Orfeo ed Euridice (abridged recording)   Ⓗ
Ferrier Orfeo **Ayars** Euridice **Vlachopoulos** Amor
Glyndebourne Festival Chorus; Southern Philharmonic Orchestra / Stiedry   ⓈⓄ
Dutton mono CDBP9730 (63' · ADD) Recorded 1947
  Though the sound may initially prove a little distracting, Dutton have done their best to clean it up, and Ferrier's singing more than makes up for it. Its beauty goes straight to the heart: a noble and intensely human Orfeo which deserves its place on every collector's shelves.

Leopold Godowsky
Polish/American 1870-1938

An American pianist and composer of Polish birth, Godowsky toured widely from the age of nine, making his American début in Boston in 1884. Tours of the USA and Canada followed and until 1900 he taught in Philadelphia and Chicago. Until World War II he continued to appear in Europe; his reputation as a Chopin interpreter was not enhanced by a series of elaborate Studies on the Etudes. His concert career ended in 1930.   GROVEmusic

Studies

53 Studies on Chopin's Etudes
Marc-André Hamelin pf
Hyperion ⓐ CDA67411/2 (158' · DDD)   ⒻⓄⓄⓄ

Godowsky's 53 studies on Chopin's 27 studies are the *ne plus ultra* of Romantic intricacy. Godowsky's wily disclaimer that, far from wanting to 'improve' on Chopin's matchless originals, he merely wished to extend the parameters of technique, hardly convinces purists, who dismiss his *magnum opus* as an outrageous gilding of the lily, an unforgivable powdering and rouging of Chopin's genius. For others, Godowsky's ingenuity, his ear-tickling wit and elegance, create edifices, indeed 'miracles of rare device'. But if heated debate still rages around the music, the quality of Hamelin's recording is entirely uncontroversial. Rarely can such a gargantuan task have been accomplished with such strength, grace and agility, with an ease bordering on nonchalance. His virtuosity is pre-eminent because it's so musical, and it's impossible to think of another living pianist who could have carried off this enterprise with comparable success. In lesser hands these *Etudes* can seem overweight; with Hamelin, even the densest, seemingly impenetrable textures are kept as light as air and everything is mobile, fluent and adroit. And so, to evoke Schumann, it's 'hats off, gentlemen' to this handsomely presented and finely recorded set. A truly phenomenal achievement.

Alexander Goehr
British 1932

Goehr's father, the conductor Walter Goehr, brought the family to England in 1933, and Alexander studied with Hall at the Royal Manchester College (1952-5), where fellow students included Birtwistle and Davies. He then followed Messiaen's classes at the Paris Conservatoire (1955-6). Family and education thus fitted him to marry Schoenbergian with post-Webernian influences, which he did in two cantatas, The Deluge (1958) and Sutter's Gold (1960), and in instrumental pieces of this period. With the Violin Concerto (1962) and Little Symphony (1963) he moved into a broader style made possible by greater understanding of serialism.

His first opera, *Arden Must Die* (1967), is a morality on the borders of Weill, and a triptych of music-theatre pieces (1968-70) also shows a concern with social behaviour. Orchestral and chamber works of this period move still closer to the ethos of the two Viennese schools, but in doing so display a more confident individuality (String Quartet No 3, 1976). His second opera, *Behold the Sun* (1985), is about the clash between revolutionary and established thought in 16th-century Germany. In 1976 he became professor of music at Cambridge.

GROVEmusic

Arianna

Arianna
Ruby Philogene sop Arianna **Angela Hickey** mez Venus, Dorilla **Juliet Schiemann** sop Cupid **Lawrence Zazzo** counterten Bacchus **Timothy Dawkins** bass Jupiter, First Messenger **Philip Sheffield** ten Theseus **Jeremy Huw Williams** bar Counsellor **Andrew Hewitt** ten Herald **Stephen Rooke** ten Second Messenger **Arianna Ensemble / William Lacey**
NMC ② NMCD054 (132' · DDD)   Ⓕ

The title-page of *Arianna* describes it as a 'lost opera by Monteverdi, composed again by Alexander Goehr'. Precisely. At its heart is Ariadne's lament, all that survives of Monteverdi's score, richly and movingly sung by Ruby Philogene. The vocal line is embedded in an elaborate instrumental texture in Goehr's own manner, in which the modernism he grew up with is enriched with a modality that owes a lot to Goehr's own teacher, Olivier Messiaen, but a good deal also to Monteverdi himself. Whether Monteverdi ever set these lines we may never know. Goehr has set them effectively and very beautifully, in Monteverdi's manner. Indeed, at times, it's as though Goehr and Monteverdi had collaborated on this opera, the vocal lines, brilliant toccatas and madrigalesque choruses often sounding very much like the earlier composer, even the instrumentation suggesting that Monteverdi has been so excited by the sound of the modern keyed flute, the soprano sax and bass clarinet that he can't resist using them. Goehr's score is at once a loving homage and a vivid evocation for the 1990s of how dazzling and emotionally hard-hitting Monteverdi's lost original must have been to its first audiences in 1608. The soloists are almost without exception excellent, and Lacey is clearly a conductor of real gifts. The live recording is admirable.

Nicolas Gombert   Flemish c1495-c1560

Probably a native of Flanders and possibly a pupil of Josquin (he composed a déploration on Josquin's death, 1545), Gombert was a singer (from 1526) and maître des enfants (from 1529) in Emperor Charles V's court chapel, with which he travelled in Europe and for which he also served unofficially as

composer. He was canon of Notre Dame, Tournai, by 1534. By 1540 he had been dismissed from the imperial chapel but was probably pardoned (and granted a benefice) c1552. Highly regarded by his contemporaries as a great innovator, he favoured dense textures and often used dark, rich timbres. He used pervading imitation more consistently than anyone of his own or an earlier generation, creating textures in which the voices tend to be equally important. All but two of his ten extant masses elaborate existing motets or chansons. His motets (over 160 survive) (from books, 1539, 1541, many in collections), are his most representative works, each phrase of text having its own expressive motif worked through the texture. Other sacred works include eight fine Magnificats and multi-voice works. His chansons (over 70) are like the Netherlands motet only more animated and often conceived on a broad scale. His music continued to be printed until long after his death.

GROVEmusic

Missa Tempore paschali

Missa Tempore paschali. Magnificat octavi toni. Adonai, Domine Iesu Christe. In illo tempore loquente Jesu. O Rex gloriae
Henry's Eight / Jonathan Brown
Hyperion CDA66943 (65' · DDD) Texts and translations included   Ⓕ Ⓞ

This disc reinforces the impression of Gombert as the most involving composer of his generation; the booklet-note aptly describes his music as a cross between the imitative processes of Josquin's generation and the seamless style of Ockeghem. The *Missa Tempore paschali* is thought to be a fairly early work, whereas the *Magnificat* is one of a set that probably dates from Gombert's last years. The mass is most ambitious, culminating in a 12-voice *Agnus Dei* modelled on Brumel's Mass, *Et ecce terrae motus*. The singing is confident and assured, with a good grasp of large-scale form in the *Credo*. The final *Agnus Dei* seems to crown the mass in a more credible manner. An added feature is the more inventive, and highly convincing, use of false relations in the readings prepared for Henry's Eight by John O'Donnell. The result has invigorating harmonic incident throughout. The mass is complemented by some of the composer's most well-known works; the motet, *In illo tempore* is particularly lovely and Henry's Eight respond with some particularly sensitive singing. Those familiar with their very English, yet full-bodied sound won't be disappointed; those who aren't can start here. In Henry's Eight Gombert has found worthy champions.

Henryk Górecki   Polish 1933

Górecki studied with Szabelski at the Katowice Conservatory (1955-60) and with Messiaen in Paris. His music has connections with Penderecki, but its deepest affinities are with ancient Polish religious music, and it often shows a saintly simplicity. Most of his works are for orchestra or chamber ensemble; they include the chamber trilogy Genesis (1963) and three symphonies, the third of which achieved striking public success in the early 1990s. GROVEmusic

Symphonies

Symphony No 2, 'Copernican', Op 31^a. Beatus vir, Op 38
^aZofia Kilanowicz *sop* Andrezej Dobber *bar*
Silesian Philharmonic Choir; Polish Radio Choir;
Polish National Radio Symphony Orchestra /
Antoni Wit
Naxos 8 555375 (67' · DDD)   Ⓢ

Górecki composed his Second Symphony in 1972 in response to a commission to mark the 500th anniversary of the birth of the Polish astronomer Nicolas Copernicus. It possesses a certain Janus-like quality in that it forms a bridge between his earlier 'modernist' works and his later 'reductionist' style, into which the ubiquitous Third Symphony falls. The Second Symphony comprises two movements, the first glancing back to the dissonance of earlier works, the second looking forward to more tonal pastures in which the seeds of the Third Symphony are in abundant evidence. Górecki's Copernican Symphony is an unsung masterpiece, and a greater and more impressively constructed work than the Third.

Beatus vir was composed in 1977 in response to a commission to mark the 900th anniversary of the martyrdom of the Bishop of Cracow, Stanisław of Szczepanów. The opening pages are particularly striking and there are some marvellously scored moments in the remaining 24 minutes or so, though it doesn't attain the stature of the Second Symphony. That said, this disc is thoroughly recommended to anyone wanting to expand their appreciation of Górecki beyond the Third. The Copernican Symphony more than justifies the price of the disc alone and the performances and recorded sound throughout are exceptionally fine.

Symphony No 3, 'Symphony of Sorrowful Songs',
Op 36
Dawn Upshaw *sop* London Sinfonietta / David
Zinman
Nonesuch 7559-79282-2 (54' · DDD) Recorded 1991
                                    Ⓕ OOO

Górecki's Third Symphony has become legend. Composed in 1976, it's always had its champions and admirers within the contemporary music world, but in 1993 it found a new audience of undreamt-of proportions. A few weeks after its release, this Elektra Nonesuch release not only entered the top 10 in the classical charts, but was also riding high in the UK Pop Album charts. It became the biggest selling disc of music by a contemporary classical composer.

The Symphony, subtitled *Symphony of Sorrowful, Songs* was composed during a period when

Górecki's musical style was undergoing a radical change from avant-garde serialism to a more accessible style firmly anchored to tonal traditions. The Symphony's three elegiac movements (or 'songs') form a triptych of laments for all the innocent victims of World War II and are a reflection upon man's inhumanity to man in general. The songs are beautifully and ethereally sung by Dawn Upshaw, and David Zinman and the London Sinfonietta provide an intense and committed performance of the shimmering orchestral writing. The recording quality is excellent.

Symphony No 3, 'Symphony of Sorrowful Songs',
Op 36^a. Three Pieces in Old Style
^aZofia Kilanowicz *sop* Katowice Radio Symphony
Orchestra / Antoni Wit
Naxos 8 550822 (66' · DDD) Recorded 1993 Text and
translation included   Ⓢ●

This recording is virtually as good as the better-known Zinman version. The performance is exceptionally fine, although the acoustic is more resonant, the orchestral choirs less closely balanced and Antoni Wit isn't as meticulous as Zinman in his observance of minor details. Interpretatively, Wit leaves the more austere impression. His relative inwardness squares convincingly with the symphony's harrowing texts and 'Sorrowful Songs' sub-title. If spectacular singing is your main priority, then Upshaw's is the vocal tour de force. Zofia Kilanowicz displays stronger lower registers and a brilliant, bleached-white soprano that reflects the score's innate pathos, its sense of shock. Her enunciation is more idiomatic, while her partial suspension of vibrato is a powerful interpretative ploy. What's most impressive about this performance is its spirituality; and given the overall excellence of the recording, the conducting and the singing, it's strongly recommended, particularly to those who have yet to discover the Symphony's hypnotic sound-world. It's also commended to those who do know the work but who find Upshaw and Zinman too 'plush'.

Kleines Requiem für eine Polka

Kleines Requiem für eine Polka, Op 66^a. Harpsichord
Concerto, Op 40^b. Good Night, 'In memoriam
Michael Vyner', Op 63
Dawn Upshaw *sop* Sebastian Bell *fl* John
Constable *pf* Elisabeth Chojnacka *hpd* David
Hockings *perc* London Sinfonietta / ^aDavid
Zinman, ^bMarkus Stenz
Nonesuch 7559-79362-2 (59' · DDD) Recorded
1993-4   Ⓕ●

Like a small café huddled within the shadow of some ancient church, Górecki's *Kleines Requiem für eine Polka* (1993) evokes feelings of paradox. The opening movement suggests distracted tranquillity. This is followed by a grating *Allegro* which approximates the sort of vicious 'knees-up' that Shostakovich penned whenever he bared his teeth at empty celebration. Later, we're back within the tranquil interior of Górecki's imagination – and it's there that we stay until the work ends. The *Kleines Requiem für eine Polka* displays a profundity expressed via the simplest means. It's a pity, then, that the Harpsichord Concerto breaks the mood so quickly: one's initial impression is of a further violent 'episode' from the first work, although the stylistic contrast breaks the illusion soon enough. This is probably the most famous 20th-century harpsichord concerto after Falla's. Bach served as its creative prime mover, while Elisabeth Chojnacka is its dedicatee and most celebrated interpreter. Here she revels in the piece's playful aggression. It's an unrelenting display and in total contrast to *Good Night*, Górecki's deeply felt memorial to one of his staunchest supporters, Michael Vyner. The language is sombre, but never merely mournful. Mostly quiet and contemplative, *Good Night* is scored for alto flute, piano and tam-tam with Dawn Upshaw intoning Hamlet's 'flights of angels' in the closing movement. The work ends in a spirit of veiled ritual with a sequence of quiet gong strokes. The performance and recording are consistently fine.

Choral Works

Miserere, Op 44ª. Amen, Op 35ª. Euntes ibant et flebant, Op 32ª. My Vistula, grey Vistula, Op 46ᵇ. Broad waters, Op 39ᵇ
ªChicago Symphony Chorus; ªChicago Lyric Opera Chorus / John Nelson; ᵇLira Chamber Chorus / Lucy Ding
Nonesuch 7559-79348-2 (67' · DDD) Recorded 1994. Texts and translations included Ⓕ

Miserere is an intensely spiritual, prayerful work in which Górecki responds with heartfelt passion to the political events of 1981 (a sit-in by members of Rural Solidarity which ultimately led to the democratisation of Poland). It's as intellectually demanding and emotionally compelling as anything by Górecki released on disc. Lovers of the Third Symphony will fall under its spell straight away, but it should gain respect from those less easily swayed by the opulent orchestral textures of that work, for here Górecki is using what's probably his favourite medium, the unaccompanied choir. The voices enter in a series of layered thirds until all ten parts begin an electrifying ascent through the word 'Domine' to the work's climax which, with the first statement of 'Miserere', suddenly bathes us in a quiet chord of A minor – a moment as devastatingly effective as an orchestra full of banging drums and crashing cymbals. John Nelson directs a hypnotic performance full of impact, his choral forces emotionally committed and technically excellent. The recording itself isn't technically excellent – there are a number of persistent background rattles and bangs; the church acoustic is a little cloudy and there's a haze of surface noise. But in the end, it only serves to reinforce this grainy aural picture of those dark times in Poland's recent history.

François-Joseph Gossec
French 1734-1829

At Paris Gossec was a violinist in La Pouplinière's orchestra, c 1751-1762, as well as a composer. In 1762-70 he directed the Prince of Condé's theatre at Chantilly, from c 1766 also serving the Prince of Conti; meanwhile he composed opéras comiques, notably Les pêcheurs (1766, Paris). He founded the Concert des Amateurs in 1769 and directed it until 1773; the orchestra was one of Europe's finest. In 1773-7 he was a director of the Concert Spirituel. From 1775 he held posts at the Opéra and presented various stage works there; the ballets were the most successful. From 1784 he directed the new Ecole Royale de Chant. At the Revolution he directed the band of the Garde Nationale and wrote numerous Revolutionary works for large forces. After 1799 his output declined, and he concentrated on teaching at the Conservatoire.

Gossec's c50 symphonies, showing many Mannheim traits, are his most important works and contributed significantly to the development of the genre in France. One of them (1761) was among the first French orchestral works to use clarinets. Novel effects of scoring also appear in his Messe des morts (1760) and oratorio La nativité; (1774). He also wrote other sacred works, songs, symphonies concertantes, chamber music and treatises. **GROVE**music

Missa pro defunctis

Salomé Haller, Ingrid Perruche sops Cyril Auvity ten Alain Buet, Benoît Haller bars Namur Chamber Choir; La Grande Ecurie et La Chambre du Roy / Jean-Claude Malgoire
K617 ② K617152 (91' · DDD) Text and translation included Ⓕ

Gossec is a name more often found in history books than on record collectors' shelves. During his long life he contributed to opera reform in Paris before the arrival of Gluck, was one of the directors of the Concert Spirituel, and wrote 50 symphonies. In old age he became the foremost composer of French revolutionary themes, and the first anniversary of the fall of the Bastille was commemorated with a performance of his *Te Deum* that featured over a thousand performers. The *Missa pro defunctis* had more modest origins. It was first performed in 1760, and aroused notable reaction due to the use of trombones, a novelty. The *Dies Irae* – featuring horns, clarinets and drums – became a popular concert item. The composer revised and revived it several times over the next two decades, and parts of the Mass were used for large-scale patriotic commemorations during the revolutionary period.

This recording, made in the chapel at Versailles in 2002, efficiently captures a special event. Occasionally the most intricate details in the accompaniment of soloists seem slapdash, but the rich and imposing grandeur of Le Grande Écurie et La Chambre du Roy's woodwind and brass remind us that Gossec's fiery dramatic work was a clear influence on Berlioz's colossal choral works. The music sounds astonishingly Mozartian, despite its earlier origin. Jean-Claude Malgoire's strongest asset has always been to give performances with immediacy and character, albeit sometimes sacrificing technical perfection. But when his forces are on form, as they are here, the results are emotionally natural, musically dramatic and neatly direct.

Louis Moreau Gottschalk
American 1829-1869

At 13 Gottschalk went to Paris for piano and composition lessons, and by 19, through the success of his 'Creole' piano pieces Bamboula, La savane and La bananier (the so-called Louisiana trilogy), his name was a household word throughout Europe. He was hailed as the New World's first authentic musical spokesman and his keyboard virtuosity was compared with Chopin's. After another charming genre piece, Le mancenillier (1851), and tours of Switzerland, France and Spain, 1850-52, he made his New York début. In touring the USA to increase his income, 1853-6, he catered ever more to the public taste for sensational effects (eg in Tournament Galop and The Last Hope). His most fruitful period, 1857-61, was spent in the Caribbean, where he wrote some of his finest works, including Souvenir de Porto Rico, Ojos criollos (four hands), the Symphony no.1 ('La nuit des tropiques') and the one-act opera Escenas campestres. A second extended tour of the USA, 1862-5, produced little but the well-known Dying Poet and the duet La gallina. From his last years in South America, feverishly devoted to concert-giving, the most notable works are Pasquinade, the Grand scherzo and the Grande tarantelle for piano and orchestra. Although not an 'advanced' composer, Gottschalk was sensitive to local colour and often used quotation as both a musical and psychological device, as well as syncopated rhythms and jagged melodic lines – all traits associated with later music.
GROVEmusic

Piano Works

Sospiro, RO214 Op 24. Marguerite, RO158 Op 92. Bataille, RO25 Op 64. Réponds-moi RO225 Op 50 (arr Wachtmann). Solitude, RO239 Op 65. Ballade No 8, RO16 Op 90. Tremolo, RO265 Op 58. Orfa, RO186 Op 71. El cocoyé, RO57 Op 80. Polka de salon, RO207 Op 1. Rayons d'azur, RO220 Op 77. La chasse du jeune Henri, RO54 Op 10
Philip Martin *pf*
Hyperion CDA67248 (68' · DDD)   Ⓕ

There's very little of Gottschalk's piano music on CD that hasn't been recorded by Philip Martin, the ideal exponent, but here's another whole collection of surprises – again a real enchantment from start to finish. It's interesting to hear Gottschalk's Op 1, the *Polka de salon*, published in Paris, which he wrote in his midteens. No particular character yet but genuine charm. More typical of the pianist-composer as pop star is *El cocoyé*, which gives a local carnival tune a flashy setting and brought the house down for Gottschalk's first recital in Havana in 1854. *Solitude* is a pretty nocturne inspired by Lamartine, Chopinesque but simpler. The middle section is a fine example of Martin's totally natural, relaxed melodic playing which perfectly fits the serenity of Gottschalk's lyricism. Martin knows how to pace Gottschalk's Caribbean syncopations, too, and is up to all the pyrotechnics. Another immaculate Hyperion production.

O ma charmante, épargnez-moi, RO182. Grande fantaisie triomphale sur l'hymne national brésilien, RO108. Melody in D flat. Bamboula, RO20. The Dying Poet, RO75. Grande étude de concert, RO116, 'Hercule'. The last hope, RO133. Murmures éoliens, RO176. Symphony No 1, RO5, 'La nuit des tropiques' – Andante (arr Napoleão). La chute des feuilles, RO55. Tournament Galop, RO264
Philip Martin *pf*
Hyperion CDA66915 (73' · DDD)   ⒻⓄ

It isn't only the playing here which gives such satisfaction, but the whole package is stylishly produced – Rousseau on the booklet cover and fine notes from Jeremy Nicholas. The piano sound from the fastidious Hyperion team is flawless. Martin, operating in a context where some pianists can hardly play softly at all, has a ravishing *pianissimo*. This makes *O ma charmante* and the perennial – but highly original – *The last hope* simply enchanting. Gottschalk is a real melodist. Martin understands the intimacies of the salon but he also lacks nothing in his transcendental virtuosity. The more flamboyant numbers, such as *Tournament Galop* prove this. About 10 years after Gottschalk's death, his pianist colleague, Artur Napoleão, made a piano arrangement of the first movement of Symphony No 1 (*Night in the tropics*) which Martin includes here. It's slightly drab compared with the orchestral version and soon feels repetitive. But don't let that put you off this outstanding continuation of Martin's Gottschalk series.

La colombe, RO60. La moissonneuse, RO173. Le songe d'une nuit d'été, R0240. Pensée poétique. L'étincelle, RO80. Souvenir de Cuba, RO245. La gitanella, RO103. Morte!!, RO174. Polonia, R0210. Fantôme de bonheur, R094. Forest Glade Polka, R098. Ossian ballades, RO187. Ricordati, RO227. Reflets du passé, R0223. Apothéose, RO8
Philip Martin *pf*
Hyperion CDA67118 (72' · DDD)   Ⓕ

Piano Works for Two and Four Hands

Réponds-moi, RO225[a]. Printemps d'amour, RO214[a]. Marche de nuit, RO151[a]. Ses yeux, RO234[a]. La jota aragonesa, RO130[a]. Le bananier, RO21[a]. Ojos criollos, RO184[a]. Orfa, RO186[a]. L'étincelle, RO80[a]. Marche funèbre, RO148[a]. La gallina, RO100[a]. Radieuse, RO217[a]. Grande tarantelle, RO259[a]. Souvenir d'Andalousie, RO242[b]. Le banjo, RO22[b]. Grand scherzo, RO114[b]. Pasquinade, RO189[b]. Berceuse, RO27[b]. Tournament Galop, RO26[b]. Mazurkah. Union, RO269[b]. The Last Hope, RO133[b]. Scherzo-romantique, RO233[b]. Le mancenillier, RO142[b]. The Dying Poet, RO75[ab]
[a]**Nerine Barrett,** [b]**Alan Marks** pfs
Nimbus ② NI7045/6 (107' · DDD) Recorded 1984-91
Ⓜ

It was once necessary to explain who Gottschalk was. Now the virtuoso from New Orleans has taken his place as a composer of some of the most colourful and charming Romantic piano music, thanks largely to Martin's advocacy in this immaculately produced Hyperion series. Compared with Gottschalk's syncopated masterpieces such as *Souvenir de Porto Rico*, which ends Volume 1, this collection may be slighter, but every track is a delight. Martin's feeling for this music is so convincing and the recorded sound so good that even the more trivial pieces are a joy – Gottschalk appears as a real melodist. A superficial crowd-pleaser such as *Apothéose* is good for a laugh. But *Morte!!* is moving in its simplicity. The piano duets on the two-disc set from Nimbus feature the magnificent team of Marks and Barrett, well recorded, who sparkle in infectious enjoyment of this vivid music.

Charles François Gounod
French 1818-1893

Gounod studied privately with Reicha and at the Paris Conservatoire with Halévy (counterpoint) and Le Sueur (composition), winning the Prix de Rome in 1839. At Rome (1840-42) he was deeply impressed by the 16th-century polyphonic music (particularly Palestrina's) he heard in the Sistine Chapel and wrote some rather austere masses; for a time a church organist in Paris, he considered joining the priesthood. The climax of his liturgical work came in 1855 with the florid Messe solennelle de Ste Cécile, a favourite setting scarcely superseded by his 12 later ones (1870-92). Meanwhile he wrote a Gluckian, then a Meyerbeerian opera, both failures; the succeeding five, all first performed at the Théâtre-Lyrique, are the works by which he is remembered, namely the small-scale Le médecin malgré lui (1858) and Philémon et Baucis (1860), the triumphant Faust (1859), in which sensitive musical characterisation and a refreshing naturalness set new standards on the French operatic stage, and the major successes Mireille (1864) and Roméo et Juliette (1867).

In 1870 Gounod took refuge in England from the Franco-Prussian War, staying some four years to exploit the English demand for choral music. The first conductor of the Royal Albert Hall Choral Society (1871), he produced dozens of choruses and songs. But he experienced considerable intrigue in his private life, effectively marking the end of his fruitfulness as a composer. His oratorios for Birmingham, La rédemption and Mors et vita, if banal and facilely emotional, were nonetheless successful. Gounod's influence on the next generation of French composers, including Bizet, Fauré and especially Massenet, was enormous. Tchaikovsky and later Poulenc, Auric and Ravel admired his clean workmanship, delicate sentiment, gift for orchestral colour and, in his best songs, unpretentious lyrical charm. GROVEmusic

Symphonies

Symphony No 1 in D. Symphony No 2 in E flat
Orchestra of St John's, Smith Square / John Lubbock
ASV CDDCA981 (65' · DDD) Ⓕ

Gounod's symphonies aren't brow-furrowing and don't represent any advance in symphonic thought beyond Schumann and Mendelssohn, but they reveal Gounod in the Gallic tradition of elegantly crafted works with a light touch. The melodious, classically built and witty First Symphony, with its delicate second-movement fugue and vivacious finale, isn't to be peremptorily brushed aside. The longer Second Symphony makes an attempt to sound more serious, especially in the first movement and the dramatic *Scherzo* – the cantilena of the *Larghetto* is beautifully shaped here – but high spirits return in the finale. John Lubbock and his St John's orchestra are adept at the crisply neat treatment that this music demands. His wind section is outstanding, but in the finale of No 1 the violins too show real virtuosity. A warm but clean recorded sound adds to our pleasure.

Mélodies

Où voulez-vous aller?[a]. Le soira. Venise[a]. Ave Mariab. Sérénade[b]. Chanson de printemps[a]. Au rossignol[b]. Ce que je suis sans toi[a]. Envoi de fleurs[a]. La pâquerette[b]. Boléro[b]. Mignon[a]. Rêverie[a]. Ma belle amie est morte[b]. Loin du pays[b]. Clos ta paupière[a]. Prière[b]. L'absent[a]. Le temps des roses[a]. Biondina[c]. The Worker[c]. A lay of the early spring[c]. My true love hath my heart[b]. Oh happy home! Oh blessed flower![c]. The fountain mingles with the river[a]. Maid of Athens[c]. Beware! The Arrow and the Song[a]. Ilala: stances à la mémoire de Livingston[c]. If thou art sleeping, maiden[c]
[a]**Dame Felicity Lott** sop [b]**Ann Murray** mez
[c]**Anthony Rolfe Johnson** ten **Graham Johnson** pf
Hyperion ② CDA66801/2 (136' · DDD) Recorded 1993. Texts and translations included Ⓕ

This well-filled two-CD set is surely the most wide-ranging single issue of Gounod's *mélodies*. The first of the discs confirms the commonly held view of Gounod. Almost without exception the songs are pleasing and sentimental, a sweetly scented posy of hymns to flowers, of

411

rêveries and serenades. The selection includes two settings of poems that Berlioz had used in *Les nuits d'été*, plumbing the depths of the poetry, where Gounod is content to skim across the surface. In chronological order, the songs show how little Gounod's music deepened, but also how evergreen was his inspiration in melody and harmony.

To turn to the second disc is to have all your prejudices overturned. This comprises non-French settings, for which Gounod dons first Italian garb for the song cycle *Biondina*, and then English for a group of ten songs written during his stay in London in the 1870s. The Italian cycle is a delight. It would be impossible to guess the composer, as Gounod exchanges his customary flowing themes and rippling arpeggios for an ardent, Tosti-like vocal line over dry *staccato* chords. Anthony Rolfe Johnson catches its mix of sunny lyricism and Gallic sensitivity to perfection.

All three singers are on their best form, Rolfe Johnson bringing an air of intimate seductiveness to Byron's *Maid of Athens*.

Gounod L'Arithmétique. Au printemps. D'un coeur qui t'aime. O ma belle rebelle. Mignon. Par une belle nuit. Sérénade. La siesta. Fleur des bois. Les vacances. Le banc de pierre. Donne-moi cette fleur Lalo Puisqu'ici bas. Aubade. Dansons! **Saint-Saëns** Clair de lune. Dans les coins bleus. El desdichado. Pastorale. Rêverie. Le rossignol. Le soir descend sur la colline. Viens!
Les Demoiselles de ... (Sophie Marin-Degor *sop* Claire Brua *mez* Serge Cyferstein *pf*)
Alpha Productions ALPHA033 (70' · DDD) Texts and translations included   Ⓕ**OO**

Every now and then a disc comes along that paralyses the critical faculties: you know you should be trying to be objective, but somehow cold analysis seems almost obscene. So it is here. Though just one word of warning: for some tastes, Sophie Marin-Degor's soprano may seem a little shrill at *forte* in the higher reaches. But then French sopranos have been taxed with this since forever, and we probably have to accept that it goes with the territory.

In all other respects that territory, as explored here, is the land where the oranges bloom; or, if you prefer, 'l'île heureuse'. Both Marin-Degor and Claire Brua come to this repertory from the world of Baroque music, and they bring with them a cleanness of articulation and phrasing that's wholly delightful, sensitively and tactfully supported by Serge Cyferstein. Apart from the sheer sonorous pleasure of the disc, the balance all three artists maintain between expressive moment and formal shaping is almost perfection itself: key words come over with just a little emphasis, but not so much that we're aware of some vocal coach in the background saying 'Bring out the verb here!' Similarly, rhythms are accurately observed, and delicate *rubato* generally reserved for cadences.

This disc is stylish, responsive, impeccable in

ensemble and tuning, sensuous, witty, moving... (that's enough epithets): utterly unmissable.

Faust

Faust
Richard Leech *ten* Faust **Cheryl Studer** *sop* Marguerite **José van Dam** *bar* Méphistophélès **Thomas Hampson** *bass* Valentin **Martine Mahé** *mez* Siébel **Nadine Denize** *sop* Marthe **Marc Barrard** *bar* Wagner **French Army Chorus; Toulouse Capitole Choir and Orchestra / Michel Plasson**
EMI ③ 556224-2 (204' · DDD) Recorded 1991 Notes, text and translation included   Ⓕ**O**

Richard Leech as the hero sings his part with the fresh, eager tone, the easy *legato*, the sense of French style that it has so badly been wanting all these years, certainly since Nicolai Gedda essayed the role on the now rather aged Cluytens/EMI sets from 1953 and 1958. Gedda's voice may be more lyrical in the role, but Leech encompasses it with less effort, and creates a real character. It's extremely distinguished singing. Beside him he has an equally impressive loved one in Studer and antagonist van Dam. Studer finds herself another amenable *métier* in Gounod; her Marguerite isn't only sung with innate musicality, firm tone and expressive phrasing but also with a deep understanding of this style of French music in terms of nuance and the lighter touch. The Jewel song is a treasure, and to add to one's satisfaction Studer's French seems faultless.

Van Dam is a resolute, implacable Devil with a firm, even tone to second the insinuating characterisation. His voice may have dried out a little, but he remains a paragon of a stylist in all he attempts. The three French-speaking singers excel in subsidiary roles. Thomas Hampson is in places overextended as Valentin, a role that needs experience and perfect French.

Plasson almost but not quite kills the score with kindness. He so loves the piece that his tempos, especially in the more reflective moments, such as the start of the Garden scene, become much slower than the score predicates and demands. Against that must be set his respect for the minutiae of Gounod's often inspired writing for orchestra and a general warmth that lights the score from within. It was an inspired stroke to invite the French Army Chorus to sing the Soldiers' Chorus, delivered with such verve as to make it seem unhackneyed.

Faust
Jerry Hadley *ten* Faust **Cecilia Gasdia** *sop* Marguerite **Samuel Ramey** *bass* Méphistophélès **Alexander Agache** *bar* Valentin **Susanne Mentzer** *mez* Siébel **Brigitte Fassbaender** *mez* Marthe **Philippe Fourcade** *bass* Wagner **Welsh National Opera Chorus and Orchestra / Carlo Rizzi**
Teldec ③ 4509-90872-2 (211' · DDD) Recorded 1993.

Notes, text and translation included   Ⓕ

The tender, sweet-toned and idiomatically French singing and style of Gasdia and Hadley quite exceed expectations in these days of homogenised and uniform interpretation. These two principals step outside predictable parameters to give us readings of high individuality, favouring their music with delicately etched line, varied dynamics and real involvement in their characters' predicaments.

Both their happiness and later remorse are eloquently expressed. Gasdia gives a well-nigh faultless performance – light-hearted, elated in the Jewel song, ardent in the Garden duet, ecstatic in the bedtime solo that follows, ineffably sad in her 'Il ne revient pas'. She's no less touching when she has lost her reason. Subtle timbres, poised high notes inform all her singing. Hadley, with the ideal weight of voice for Faust, has done nothing better. 'Je t'aime' at the first meeting with Marguerite is whispered in wonder. In the love duet he sings to her as a gentle lover, caressing his music, and Gasdia replies in kind.

The good news continues with Mentzer. She sings both Siébel's regular solos with vibrant, properly virile tone, the quick vibrato attractive. It's a real coup to have Fassbaender as Marthe, making so much of little. Ramey is the one singer to give a standardised performance. His Mephisto is as soundly and resolutely sung as one would expect from this sturdy bass, but it doesn't have the Francophone smoothness and subtlety of other interpretations. The only drawback is the often lax conducting. Rizzi conducts an often alarmingly slow account of the score and in compensation the more exciting passages are given rather too much verve. However, he's aware of the sensuous nature of Gounod's scoring and the WNO Chorus and Orchestra are excellent. The recording is open, full of presence and well balanced.

Faust (sung in English)
Paul Charles Clarke ten Faust **Mary Plazas** sop Marguerite **Alastair Miles** bass Méphistophélès **Gary Magee** bar Valentin **Diana Montague** mez Siébel **Sarah Walker** mez Marthe **Matthew Hargreaves** bass Wagner **Geoffrey Mitchell Choir; Philharmonia Orchestra / David Parry**
Chandos Opera in English Series ③ CHAN3014 (208' · DDD) Notes and text included   Ⓕ

After listening to this *Faust*, one can feel something very like awe. The structure is massive, the workmanship infinitely thorough, the boldness of stroke (dramatic and musical) almost breathtaking. No doubt the performance contributes to the awe. That's because in many ways it's a very good one, and partly because it underlines seriousness and grandeur. But it appears that David Parry has joined the swelling ranks of the slowcoaches. The Church scene and Faust's solo in the garden, for instance, are probably the slowest on record. Happily, there's

nothing boring about it. This recording and its production keep the stage in view, and it's particularly good to have the chorus in such clear focus.

The principals, too, form a strongly gifted team. Paul Charles Clarke, the Faust, is an interesting tenor, thrustful both in tone and manner yet capable of gentleness and delicacy. He never lets us forget that this is *his* story; when he sings everything counts. By comparison, Alastair Miles's Méphistophélès seems a mild-mannered type with reserves of authority and a magnificent voice. The absence of overt devilry may pass as a virtue, but the absence of character is surely taking the disguise too far. Gounod's Mephisto is a joker, a man of the world and an exhibitionist; this one, rarely in the spotlight, loses it entirely when Marthe enters the garden in the person of Sarah Walker.

The Valentin, Gary Magee, has a fine, vibrant baritone and rises well to his high notes and big moments. Diana Montague is an excellent Siébel (and how she rises to hers). The Marguerite, Mary Plazas, is totally likeable, ingenuous but not winsomely so, touchingly sincere in her love and her loss, clean in the scale-work of her Jewel song, a little underpowered in the grand melody of the Church scene, but having a powerful high C in reserve. The English version by Christopher Cowell reads well, sounds natural and doesn't affect the artless colloquialism that can be an embarrassing feature of modern translations.

Additional recommendation

Faust
Nash Faust **Licette** Marguerite **Easton** Mephistopheles **BBC Choir; orchestra / Beecham; Raybould**
Dutton Laboratories mono ② 2CDAX2001 (138' · ADD)   Ⓜ

Recorded in 1929-30, Beecham's English version enshrines two wonderful performances by Heddle Nash and Miriam Licette. They are object lessons in style and diction. Beecham conducts with the lightest of touches.

Roméo et Juliette

Roméo et Juliette
Roberto Alagna ten Roméo **Angela Gheorghiu** sop Juliette **José Van Dam** bass-bar Frère Laurent **Simon Keenlyside** bar Mercutio **Marie-Ange Todorovitch** sop Stéphano **Alain Fondary** bar Capulet **Claire Larcher** mez Gertrude **Daniel Galvez Vallejo** ten Tybalt **Didier Henry** bar Paris **Till Fechner** bar Grégorio **Guy Flechter** ten Benvolio **Alain Vernhes** bar Duc **Christophe Fel** bass Frère Jean **Toulouse Capitole Chorus and Orchestra / Michel Plasson**
EMI ③ 556123-2 (180' · DDD) Notes, text and translation included   Ⓕ**●**

Michel Plasson is no stranger to this opera. He's recorded it once before for EMI in 1983, but compared with his earlier self Plasson is more assuredly his own man here, taking a broader view of the turbulent, dramatic opening. Then comes the chorus's introductory narration; the earlier Plasson recording puts great emphasis on story-telling, and isn't nearly as imaginative as the quieter, more intimate style he favours here, the chorus having more light and shade, better rhythmic pointing, more 'face'.

As Juliette Gheorghiu immediately makes her listeners echo the chorus's 'Ah! qu'elle est belle!', for the sound matches the imagined sight. Its beauty is more mature than Catherine Malfitano's (Plasson's earlier Juliette), but as the part develops towards tragedy so her warmer, richer tone is better able to embody the depth of feeling, and she brings a fine conviction to the despairing scene with Friar Laurence and to the scene of the potion.

Alagna's Romeo has youth on his side, and though he doesn't always sound too happy with the B flats of 'Ah, lève-toi, soleil', there are many, many things to enjoy. The opera also abounds in rewarding secondary roles – José Van Dam as the Friar is gravely firm and as fine as ever, while Simon Keenlyside is also excellent. The only slight question-mark hangs over the third disc – there to contain the ballet music, but which the opera is better off without. Nevertheless, this is now the version to go for.

Percy Grainger

American/Australian 1882-1961

Grainger studied with Knorr and Kwast at the Hoch Conservatory in Frankfurt (1895-9), where he became linked with Balfour Gardiner, Quilter and C Scott, and settled in London in 1901. Another close friend was Grieg. During the next decade he appeared widely as a concert pianist; he also took part in the folksong movement, collecting and arranging numerous songs. He was an unconventional man, in his attitudes, his lifestyle and his music where he experimented with a variety of techniques, including rhythm freed from regular metre, polytonality, improvisation and highly unusual instrumentation. In 1914 he moved to the USA, where he taught in Chicago and New York; he visited Australia several times, helping the establishment of the Grainger Museum at Melbourne. His large output, complicated by the fact that he often made several versions of a piece, includes both original works and folksong arrangements. He has suffered the fate of being remembered more for what he called his 'fripperies' (Country Gardens, Handel in the Strand, Molly on the Shore) than his larger works, but even in them his originality of spirit comes through.

GROVEmusic

The Warriors

Grainger The Warriors **Holst** The Planets, H125[a]

[a]women's voices of the **Monteverdi Choir;**
Philharmonia Orchestra / Sir John Eliot Gardiner
DG 445 860-2GH (68' · DDD) Recorded 1994 Ⓕ●

Grainger's *magnum opus*, *The Warriors*, was the 'music for an imaginary ballet', a commission set up by Sir Thomas Beecham for Diaghilev's Ballets Russes, but one that failed to materialise. Grainger wrote it anyway, his imagination running riot with visions of a great tribal pageant, a 'wild sexual concert', the ghostly clans of all humankind spirited together in celebration of life's prime. *The Warriors* was its corrective, a symphony of dissolution. It's excessive, vulgar, as strange as it's beautiful. The rhythmic excitement of the piece is totally irresistible.

Gardiner's Classical and pre-Classical explorations have set great store by rhythmic matters, and what a boon they are in *The Planets*. His insistence on precise articulations keeps fleet-footed 'Mercury' airborne, brings the opening of 'Jupiter' into sharp relief, making it shine all the brighter. There are other moments where a little more theatrical rhetoric wouldn't have gone amiss. But the marmoreal beauty of 'Venus' and 'Neptune', the sensitivity of the Philharmonia's playing, leave their impression. The recorded sound is superb.

Orchestral Works

Green Bushes, BFMS12. Lord Maxwell's Goodnight, BFMS14 (both ed Barry Peter Ould). Hill Song No 2. The Merry King, BFMS39[a]. Eastern Intermezzo. Colonial Song, S1. Spoon river, AFMS2. The Power of Rome and the Christian Heart. The Immovable Do. County Derry Air, BFMS29. Ye Banks and Braes O' Bonnie Doon, BFMS31. English Dance No 1
[a]**Paul Janes** pf **BBC Philharmonic Orchestra / Richard Hickox**
Chandos CHAN9839 (70' · DDD) Ⓕ●●

Here's a recipe guaranteed to delight Grainger acolytes and inquisitive newcomers alike: a liberal sprinkling of old friends, three of the composer's most ambitious creations and no less than four world première recordings. Falling into the last two categories comes the giddily inventive *English Dance* No 1. Bearing the inscription 'For Cyril Scott with long love', this is the work of which Gabriel Fauré exclaimed: 'It's as if the total population were a-dancing.' Hickox and company have already set down this remarkable piece in its final scoring from 1924-9; the present orchestration dates from 1906-9 and wears an even more exuberantly colourful demeanour than its successor.

Originally conceived in 1907 for 24 winds (in which guise it can be heard on Chandos), the bracing, somewhat Delian *Hill Song* No 2 is played in its final incarnation from 1948 for symphony orchestra. That same year, Grainger accepted a commission for an even more ambitious wind-band creation, *The Power of Rome and the Christian Heart*, based on ideas from as far back as 1918 and given here with the optional string parts. It's an imposing, oddly moreish affair, whose second half borrows material from the 1943 orchestral essay *Dreamery* (Chandos) as well as the first movement ('The Power of Love') of the marvellous *Danish Folksong Suite*. From a clutch of indelible favourites, to be singled out are the well-upholstered 1919 orchestration of the supremely touching *Colonial Song*, *Green Bushes* and that memorably tangy 1920 harmonisation of the *Irish Tune from County Derry*.

Hickox secures a set of performances that are simply past praise in their combination of stylish swagger and heartwarming commitment to the cause. Wonderful Chandos sound, too, irrepressibly vivid. Terrific stuff!

Youthful Suite. Molly on the Shore, BFMS1. Irish Tune from County Derry, BFMS15. Shepherd's Hey, BFMS16. Country Gardens. Early one Morning, BFMS unnum. Handel in the Strand, RMTB2. Mock Morris, RMTB1. Dreamery (ed Ould). The Warriors (ed Servadei)
BBC Philharmonic Orchestra / Richard Hickox
Chandos Grainger Edition CHAN9584 (75' · DDD)
Ⓕ●

Featuring some ripe, beautifully clean-cut sonics, this collection is a great success for all involved. As the opening, chest-swelling 'Northern March' of the *Youthful Suite* immediately shows, Hickox draws playing of infectious swagger from the ever-excellent BBC Philharmonic (marvellous brass sounds especially). The suite boasts some striking invention, not least in the central 'Nordic Dirge' (a hauntingly eloquent processional, incorporating plenty of 'tuneful percussion') and a winsome, at times almost Ivesian 'English Waltz'. There follow seven of Grainger's most popular miniatures in the orchestrations Gershwin made for Leopold Stokowski. Hickox gives us Grainger's original thoughts and a delectable sequence they comprise, full of truly kaleidoscopic textural and harmonic variety. By the side of Rattle's CBSO version, Hickox's *Country Gardens* is perhaps marginally lacking in twinkling good humour and entrancing lightness of touch, but his infectious energy and evident affection more than compensate. *Dreamery*, described by Grainger as 'Slow Tween-Play' (an epithet which, annotator Barry Peter Ould suggests, 'could be construed as his particular term for an intermezzo'), appears here in the extended orchestral version.

For *The Warriors*, Hickox uses a new critical edition prepared by the Australian Grainger authority, Alessandro Servadei. Grainger's orchestral palette has never sounded more gloriously extravagant. Then again, this impression is just as much a tribute to Hickox's performance, which is breathtaking in its virtuosic brilliance and stunning co-ordination.

Music for Wind Band

The Power of Rome and the Christian Heart.

Children's March: Over the Hills and Far Away, RMTB4. Bell Piece[a]. Blithe Bells. The Immovable Do. Hill Songs – No 1; No 2. County Derry Air, BFMS29. Marching Song of Democracy
[a]**James Gilchrist** ten **Royal Northern College of Music Wind Orchestra / Timothy Reynish, Clark Rundell**
Chandos Grainger Edition CHAN9630 (65' · DDD)
Recorded 1992-7
Ⓕ●

Rundell's compelling realisation of the extraordinary *Hill Song* No 1 – regarded by Grainger as one of his finest achievements and performed here in its original guise for two piccolos, six oboes, six cors anglais, six bassoons and double bassoon – was actually made by BBC Manchester back in 1992; the remaining items date from 1997 and benefit from the splendid sound and balance achieved by Chandos.

Another of Grainger's most striking wind-band compositions opens the disc, namely the 12-minute *The Power of Rome and the Christian Heart*. Both the *Children's March* and *Bell Piece* feature some unexpected vocal contributions. In the latter – a charming 'ramble' on John Dowland's *Now, O now I needs must part* – Grainger incorporates a bell part specially written for his wife, Ella. The delightfully piquant arrangements of *Blithe Bells* and *The Immovable Do* date from March 1931 and November/December 1939 respectively. These fine players equally revel in the 'scrunchy' harmonies of the eventful version of *Irish Tune from County Derry* (made in 1920 for military band and pipe-organ). That just leaves the boisterous *Marching Song of Democracy*, which Rundell again directs as to the manner born.

Piano Works

Piano Music for four hands, Volume 3
Rondo. Crew of the Long Dragon. Fantasy on George Gershwin's 'Porgy and Bess'. Ye Banks and Braes, BFMS32. Tiger-Tiger, KS4/JBC9. Walking Tune, RMTB3. **C Scott** Three Symphonic Dances. **Delius** A Dance Rhapsody No 1, RTVI/18. **Grieg** Knut Lurasens Halling II. **Addinsell** Festival. **Le Jeune** La Bel'aronde. **Gershwin** Girl Crazy – Embraceable you (all trans Grainger)
Penelope Thwaites, John Lavender pfs
Pearl SHECD9631 (78' · DDD) Recorded 1989-91 Ⓕ

Volume 3 of Grainger's music for four hands (Volume 2 is no longer available) contains short original compositions and a number of his transcriptions. These latter are fascinating in their admirable combination of scrupulous fidelity and creative rethinking for an entirely different medium. You wouldn't necessarily think that a transcription, even for two pianos, of Delius's First *Dance Rhapsody* could possibly work with any real degree of success. However, the reality is that it works so well that some may even prefer Grainger's version to the original. In the *Porgy and Bess Fantasy* he treats the tunes with loving respect, but as a pianist he can't help seeing different ways of presenting them: the very big gestures in 'My man's gone now'; a searching little prelude to 'It ain't necessarily so' implying all sorts of interesting things that Grainger could have done with that slithery little tune if he weren't obliged to play it straight – which he then does, and with sparkling enjoyment.

Grainger Jutish Medley, DFMS8. Colonial Song, S1. Molly on the Shore, BFMS1. Harvest Hymn. Spoon River, AFMS1. Country Gardens, BFMS22. Walking Tune, RMTB3. Mock Morris, RMTB1. Ramble on Themes from Richard Strauss's 'Der Rosenkavalier'. Shepherd's Hey, BFMS4. Irish Tune from County Derry, BFMS6. Handel in the Strand, RMTB2. The Hunter in his career, OEPM4. Scotch Strathspey and Reel, BFMS37. In a Nutshell Suite – No 4, The Gumsuckers March. The Merry King, BFMS38. In Dahomey **Stanford** (arr Grainger) Four Irish Dances, Op 89 – No 1, A March-Jig; No 4, A Reel
Marc-André Hamelin pf
Hyperion CDA66884 (73' · DDD)   Ⓕ

This is perhaps one of the most riveting and satisfying anthologies of Grainger's music. Hamelin's superb control and artistry just about sweep the board if you're looking for a disc that not only brings you all the old favourites but also explores some of the less familiar music, such as Grainger's arrangements of two of Stanford's *Irish Dances*, the Cakewalk Smasher, *In Dahomey* or some of the rather less familiar folk-music settings such as *The Merry King* – the latter a delightful discovery. The deceptive ease with which Hamelin presents these pieces is quite breathtaking. The *Irish Tune from County Derry*, for instance, contains some exacting problems which call on the pianist to play *ppp* in the outer fingers and *mf* with the middle in order to bring out the melody which Grainger places almost entirely within the middle register of the piano, and yet Hamelin makes it sound incredibly natural.

Piano Transcriptions

Grainger Beautiful fresh flower. Lullaby. Paraphrase on the Waltz of the Flowers from Tchaikovsky's Flower Waltz. Free Settings of Favourite Melodies – Brahms: Wiegenlied, Op 49 No 4; Handel: Hornpipe from the Water Music; Fauré: Nell, Op 18 No 1; Fauré: Après un Rêve, Op 7 No 1; R Strauss: Rosenkavalier Ramble; Dowland: Now, O Now, I Needs Must Part. Gershwin Transcriptions – The Man I Love; Love Walked In Scott Handelian Rhapsody Stanford Irish Dances, Op 89 **Byrd** The Carman's Whistle **Delius** Air and Dance, RTVI/21
Piers Lane pf
Hyperion CDA67279 (75' · DDD)   Ⓕ ❶❶

These short pieces range from simplicity to elaboration, from innocence to experience; most of them are homages to many of Grainger's friends and honour his trenchant

belief in the sort of folk-melody that crosses all barriers. Wherever you turn you'll hear music 'like a breath of spring air' (to quote Barry Peter Ould's excellent note) and, more paradoxically, transcriptions that show Grainger's originality.

Cyril Scott's *Handelian Rhapsody*, receiving its first recording, may suggest Scott and Grainger more than Handel but it's an intriguing oddity and one which rises to an impressive grandeur. Stanford's Leprechaun is gentle and confiding rather than mischievous and the 'Ramble on Love' from *Der Rosenkavalier* is a sophisticated 'dish-up' of introspection and open-hearted virtuosity. All this music makes a wide variety of subtle and fierce demands, but Piers Lane, weaving his expertise with the lightest of touches, meets them with warmth and brio. Heartache, heart-ease or a tantalising mix of both all come within his style and everything is played with unfaltering command. Grainger's 'woggles' (his idiosyncratic term for *tremolandi*) can rarely have sounded more convincing and the Tchaikovsky Waltz is taken by storm in a magnificent display of red-blooded virtuosity.

The recording and presentation are immaculate. This is a dazzling, affectionate tribute to the composer and pianist who once said: 'To know a world of beauty and not to be able to spread the knowledge of it is agonising.'

Songs

David of the White Rock[a]. Died for Love, BFMS10[a]. The Sprig of Thyme, BFMS24[a]. Willow, Willow, OEPM1[a]. Near Woodstock Town[a]. Early one morning[a]. In Bristol Town (arr Gibbs)[d]. Songs of the North[a] – No 2, This is no my plaid; No 3, Turn ye to me; No 4, Skye Boat Song; No 5, Weaving Song. The Bridegroom Grat[a]. The Land O' the Leal[a] (both arr Ould). Proud Vesselil[a] (ed Thwaites). Under a bridge[ac]. Hubby and Wifey, DFMS5[ac]. The Lonely Desert-Man sees the Tents of the Happy Tribes, RMTB9[abc]. Colonial Song[ab]. The Only Son, KS21[ab]. The Love Song of Har Dyal, KS11[ac]. A Song of Autumn[a]. Five Settings of Ella Grainger[a]. O Glorious, Golden Era[a]. Little Ole with his Umbrella[a]. Variations on Handel's 'The Harmonious Blacksmith'[a] (ed Ould). Harvest Hymn[ae]. After-word[a]
Della Jones mez [a]**Penelope Thwaites** pf with [b]**Mark Padmore** ten [c]**Stephen Varcoe** bar [d]**George Black** gtr [e]**John Lavender** pf
Chandos Grainger Edition CHAN9730 (74' · DDD)
Texts included   Ⓕ❶

Again Grainger amazes, amuses, arouses, intrigues. These 'Songs for mezzo' originate in Britain (with an excellent sequence of Scottish songs), Jutland and Australia. Some are folk-songs collected in the early years of the century; two have words by Kipling, five by Ella, Grainger's wife, and some have no words at all. The latter are fortifying antidotes to those text-merchants who think that song is essentially 'about' the communication of words, whereas everybody knows that you sing (la-la, dee-dee, as in these of Grainger) because a tune has taken your fancy and singing it makes you feel better.

It's really Della Jones's record, or hers and that of the admirable Penelope Thwaites. But the menfolk appear occasionally and always to effect. Mark Padmore is a resourceful tenor with hints here that he has in reserve a vibrant, rather Italianate body of tone. Jones hereself is a natural for Grainger: she has the spirit to match, and, like him, a certain ambiguity in her forth-rightness, so that at times we're not quite sure what's serious and what's a bit of fun. The *Colonial Song* ('Sentimental No 1') is unashamedly nostalgic, but with an element of send-up too: in the piano solos especially a joyful passage of inspired improvisation that's both a joke and 'for real'. Also for real is the prime quality of this disc, with 15 tracks 'première recordings' and 14 'première recordings in this version'.

Rudyard Kipling Settings – Dedication, KS1; Dedication II; Anchor Song; The Widow's Party, KS7; Soldier, Soldier; The Sea-wife; Ganges Pilot; The First Chantey; The Young British Soldier. Three Settings of Robert Burns. Songs of the North – Fair Young Mary, SON7; The Woman are a Gane Wud, SON9; My Faithful Fond One, SON10; O'er the Moor, SON12. The Power of Love, DFMS4. The Twa Corbies. A Reiver's Neck-Verse. Lord Maxwell's Goodnight, BFMS14
Martyn Hill ten **Penelope Thwaites** pf
Chandos Grainger Edition CHAN9610 (69' · DDD)
Texts included   Ⓕ**O**

Grainger cared for neither rules nor forms; he wrote what he wanted and for whom he wanted, and you see him flinging down collar and tie to do it. A singer probably needs to shed a few inhibitions in coping with these songs, and if Martyn Hill had any to start with he's got rid of them. His magnificent performances are matched by Penelope Thwaites, who seems un-erringly to make sense of the idiosyncratic piano parts. Some are folk-songs or settings of Burns. In at least one of these, *Afton Water*, a compari-son with Britten's way with folk-song inevitably comes to mind, Grainger being similarly deter-mined and single-minded in working out his concept, but exquisite in the delicacy of his mur-murous water-colouring. In others he stands almost in reproach of Britten, for the traditional melody so 'takes' him that he wants little more than to present it, lovingly, almost reverently, in its own unadorned beauty. As for the eight poems of Kipling – one of them being set twice – they inspire him with a sense of strange, fierce compassion and unquenchable energy. To the 'character' songs – *The Widow's Party* and the relentless *Young British Soldier* for instance – Martyn Hill brings an unfailingly right touch, directed by a sense of passionate, imaginative conviction. His voice isn't now beautiful, at any rate not above a *mezzo-forte*; but it's pliant and resourceful, and at times capable of most lovely 'pure' singing. He has made many good record-ings, but this, surely, is his masterpiece.

The Power of Love, DFMS4. Early one morning. Scherzo. Random Round, RMTB8. O Gin I Were Where Gadie Rins, SON13. Skye Boat Song, SON3: Danny Deever, KS12. Irish Tune from County Derry (all.ed Ould). Mock Morris, RMTB1. Died For Love, BFMS10 (ed Perna). Love Verses from 'The Song of Solomon'. Shepherd's Hey, RMTB3.The Three Ravens, BFMS41. Youthful Rapture. The Merry King, BFMS39 (ed Rogers). Dollar and a Half a Day, SCS2. Molly on the shore, BFMS1
Susan Gritton sop **Pamela Helen Stephen** mez
Mark Tucker ten **Stephen Varcoe** bar **Tim Hugh** vc
Joyful Company of Singers; City of London Sinfonia / Richard Hickox
Chandos Grainger Edition CHAN9653 (62' · DDD)
Texts included   Ⓕ**O**

Once considered the musical equivalents of Bet-jeman's 'chintzy chintzy cheeriness', *Molly on the shore*, *Mock Morris* and *Shepherd's Hey* now raise a delighted smile in appreciation of their energy, wit, skill, grace and joy. Like most of the items here, they're short pieces, and it would be unthinkable to call any of them 'major works'. But in each instance, for the space of three or four minutes, Grainger is the Jupiter of com-posers: the unfeigned, unforced, Bringer of Jol-lity. He is other things as well. In all his folksong arrangements there's scarcely one that doesn't at some moment make the heart jump, as (for instance) he feels his way towards the secretive beauty of the *Brigg Fair* tune in *Died For Love*, or as he commits himself with unstinting sympathy and inflamed musical imagination to the protest of *Dollar and a Half*. His *Random Round*, meant for improvisation but eventually (in 1943) writ-ten out, begins as casual fun and ends in some-thing very like ecstasy.

Among the soloists, Susan Gritton brings a pure tone and a ready understanding, and Stephen Varcoe leads a haunting performance of *The Three Ravens*. The Joyful Company of Singers deserves to remain so, and with Richard Hickox, the City of London Sinfonia sound as though they're playing for pleasure too. With fine sound and a good booklet, the disc is a stayer.

I'm seventeen come Sunday BFMS8. Brigg Fair, BFMS7. Love Verses from 'The Song of Solomon'. The Merry Wedding. Shallow Brown, SCS3. Father and Daughter. My Dark-Haired Maid, 'Mo Nighean Dhu'. The Bride's Tragedy. Irish Tune from County Derry, BFMS5. Scotch Strathspey and Reel, BFMS8. The Lost Lady Found, BFMS33. The Three Ravens, BFMS41. Danny Deever. Tribute to Foster.
Monteverdi Choir, English Country Gardiner Orchestra, Sir John Eliot Gardiner
Philips Gramophone Awards Collection 475 2132 (75' · DDD)   Ⓜ**OOO**

 The startling thing about all these set-tings is the way in which Grainger unlocks the inner life of each text, each melody. He'll digest it, understand it, respect it, and then in his response he'll elaborate, creating as little or as much subtext as appropriate. Like Britten in his folksong settings, Grainger knew how and when to get out of the way. The plaintive *Brigg Fair* is no more no less than the tenor solo and chiefly wordless chorus will allow us – a tune so precious to Grainger that even the harmony is almost an intrusion. Then there's the *Londonderry Air* – no words, just voices – a harmony that's so rich, so expressive, so integrated, that it always shrouds the melody in the imagination. Then what, you may ask, could be more extraordinary than the *Love Verses from 'The Song of Solomon'*? Well, *Shallow Brown* for a start, which is astounding. A sea shanty with the reach of a spiritual, it's set as the sailors will have yelled it, the vocal line straining to be heard over furious oceanic tremolandos in guitars and strings. This is a fabulous disc. Gardiner is hot in his response to this music's rhythmic zest, as are his wonderfully articulate and impeccably tuned Monteverdi singers and players. The singing is, by turns, fleet, spry, fireside-cosy and cathedral-rich – or plain raucous. the recorded sound is brilliant and revealing.

Enrique Granados Spanish 1867-1916

Granados studied in Barcelona with Pedrell and in Paris (1887-9), then returned to Barcelona to work as a teacher, pianist and composer. His greatest success came with the piano suite Goyescas (1911), a sequence of highly virtuoso studies after paintings by Goya he expanded them to form an opera of the same title, produced in New York in 1916. His other works include songs, orchestral pieces and more piano music. **GROVE**music

Danzas españolas

Granados 12 Danzas españolas, Op 37. 7 Valses poéticos. Allegro di concierto. El pelele. Danza lenta. Goyescas **Montsalvatge** Divagación. Sonatine for Yvette
Alicia de Larrocha *pf*
RCA Victor Red Seal ② 74321 84610-2 (147' · DDD)
Recorded 1994 ⓑⓞ

Alicia de Larrocha, that incomparable interpreter of the Spanish repertoire, is here revisiting many of her favourite musical haunts. And if some of her former edge and fire, her tonal and stylistic luxuriance are now replaced by more 'contained' and reflective qualities, her warmth and affection remain undimmed. Her *rubato*, while less lavishly deployed than before, is potent and alluring, and each and every dance is played with rare naturalness and authority. But if a touch of sobriety occasionally blunts the fullest impact of these fascinating, most aristocratic idealisations of local Spanish life and colour, the actual playing is never less than masterly. The *Valses poéticos* are offered as an engaging encore. The recordings have much less range and reverberance than her previous ones on Decca; however, all lovers of this repertoire will want to add this to their collection.

Goyescas

Granados Goyescas **Albéniz** Iberia. Navarra
Alicia de Larrocha *pf*
Double Decca ② 448 191-2DF2 (141' · ADD)
Recorded 1972-6 ⓜⓞⓞ

Alicia de Larrocha has been playing these works, the greatest in the repertoire of Spanish piano music, all her life. Complete technical assurance in these extremely demanding works has now become taken for granted, and Larrocha isn't unique in mastering their terrors; but though there have been other distinguished interpreters, her readings have consistently remained a touchstone. She employs plenty of subtle *rubato* but possesses the ability to make it sound as natural as breathing. In the true sense of that much misused word, this is classical playing, free from any superimposed striving for effect but responding fully to the music's sense of colour; and even in the densest of textures she's able to control conflicting tonal levels. *Goyescas*, which can tempt the unwary into exaggerated 'expressiveness', brings forth a wealth of poetic nuance, without losing shape. The recorded quality throughout always was good and here emerges as fresh as ever. Anyone who doesn't already possess these recordings should not hesitate to acquire them now – all the more since the two discs together cost the same as one full-price one.

Goyescas. El pelele
Eric Parkin *pf*
Chandos CHAN9412 (61' · DDD) Recorded 1993 Ⓕ

The *Goyescas* are profoundly Spanish in feeling, but the folk influence is more of court music than of the flamenco or *cante hondo* styles which reflect gypsy and Moorish influence. A direction in the score at the beginning of the *Goyescas* is *con garbo y donaire* ('with charm and elegance'). The description aptly fits Parkin's performances. His readings have an element of free *rubato*, but this is never excessive, and it serves to underline the improvisatory nature of these pieces. Aided by a clean technique in this sometimes complex texture he gives persuasive performances that also contain much poetry. He captures the dignified flamboyance of the traditional dance in the 'Fandango by candlelight', carefully observing the direction *avec beaucoup de rythme*. Two of the hardest tests for a pianist in this collection are the preservation of coherence in the long 'Serenata del espectro' and the avoidance of mawkishness in 'La maja y el ruiseñor': Parkin emerges successfully from both. A piano with bright top octaves was perhaps not the ideal instrument for this recording, but there's no lack of colour or nuance from the performer.

Alexandr Grechaninov

Russian/American 1864-1956

Grechaninov studied at the Moscow Conservatory (1881-90) and with Rimsky-Korsakov at the St Petersburg Conservatory (1890-93) and worked as a piano teacher and folksong arranger; in 1910 he received a pension for his liturgical music. But that ceased with the Revolution, and in 1925 he settled in Paris, moving to the USA in 1929. His large output (nearly 200 opus numbers) includes operas, five symphonies, masses, songs and piano music.

GROVEmusic

Piano Trios

No 1 in C minor, Op 38; No 2 in G, Op 128
Bekova Sisters (Elvira Bekova vn Alfia Bekova vc Eleonora Bekova pf)
Chandos CHAN9461 (53' · DDD)   Ⓕ

Composed in 1906, Grechaninov's First Piano Trio is a typical product of Russia's 'Silver Age': typical in its expert, school-of-Rimsky craftsmanship, typical in its languishing lyricism, typical in its fundamental complacency. The first movement draws heavily on the figurations from Tchaikovsky's Fourth Symphony but divests them of all emotional immediacy or dangerous intensity. This makes for pleasant, undemanding listening, and throws into relief the achievements of Rachmaninov, Scriabin and Stravinsky. But don't expect more than that. Grechaninov is one of several candidates for the label of 'the Russian Brahms'. That fits him as unsatisfactorily as it does Taneyev or Glazunov, but the finale of his Second Trio at least shows why it sticks. This playful, yet sturdy and well-crafted music has a feel of 1881 rather than 1931. Composed in California, its childlike escapism is touching, and its sounds agreeable and rewarding to play. Strong, enjoyable, upfront performances from the talented Bekova sisters; the recording is well lubricated with resonance, but not absurdly so.

All-Night Vigil

All-Night Vigil, Op 59. Nunc dimittis, Op 34 No 1. Ⓟ
The Seven Days of the Passion, Op 58 – No 3, In Thy Kingdom[a]; No 6, Now the Powers of Heaven
[a]**James Bowman** *counterten* **Holst Singers / Stephen Layton**
Hyperion CDA67080 (63' · DDD) Texts and
translations included   ⒻOO

The *All-Night Vigil* is an outstanding achievement. Like Rachmaninov's famous setting, it's a selection of texts from the services of Vespers and Matins celebrated as a Vigil, though in current parish practice this lasts rather less than an entire night. Grechaninov sets fewer texts: the duration of the work is just over 47 minutes. Here we find the sustained chordal writing and slow-moving melodies oscillating around a few notes familiar from Rachmaninov, but Grechaninov has his own distinctive harmonic vocabulary, and his writing is less text-driven. Chant is an inspiration, but is also used in a different way from Rachmaninov: none is quoted in its entirety, the composer preferring instead to use fragments of various chants which are combined and juxtaposed with considerable freedom. He's a master of texture: listen to the astonishing darkness of sound produced by the scoring for lower voices in *Ot yunosti moyeya*, for example. Overall there's a feeling of luminosity in the writing, however, as well as an undeniable grandeur. To round off the disc we're given three other liturgical works, including a dramatic setting of the Beatitudes (sung at the Divine Liturgy) with James Bowman as soloist. The Holst Singers under Stephen Layton are superb: they have a complete mastery of the style and the fine, rich choral timbre which the music demands. Very highly recommended.

José Luis Greco

American b1953

Born in New York, Greco studied at the City College of New York and Columbia University. The son of two dancers, he was a dancer himself for some years. He was based in the Netherlands for 10 years, where he was closely involved with Cloud Chamber, a dance and theatre company. Since 1994 he has lived in Madrid. His early work includes many ballets and dance theatre pieces, but more recently he has written predominantly for the concert hall.

Orchestral Works

Triptych – Perfume; Violin Concerto, 'Ardour'[a]; Forbidden Tonic. I'm Superman! Pastel
[a]**Mariana Todorova** vn **Gran Canaria Philharmonic Orchestra / Adrian Leaper**
ASV CDDCA1153 (69' · DDD)   Ⓕ

José Luis Greco, the son of two celebrated Spanish dancers, and danced, himself, with Balanchine's New York City Ballet. As a composer he first came under the influence of John Lewis, pianist of the Modern Jazz Quartet, and studied composition at Columbia University. It isn't surprising that his music has absorbed many influences, but it's essentially 'classical', and the rhythmic influences stretch from Iberian dance and jazz to classical ballet. Moreover, he shows a Mediterranean ear for orchestral colours, which are predominant in the Iberian nocturnal fragrances of *Perfume*, the opening movement of *Triptych*, and provide a glittering backcloth for the second, *Ardour*, where the solo violinist (the excellent Mariana Todorova) takes a fantasy-like *concertante* role. *Forbidden Tonic*, written especially for this recording, completes the triptych, and brings more vehement, often thunderous rhythmic pulsing, with its percussive effects (including bizarre *glissandi*, a police whistle and wind machine), but an atmospheric central section recalls the exotic bouquet of *Perfume*.

Pastel, although still innovatively scored, has a more direct appeal: a serene idea builds up emotionally on the strings, is taken up more fragmentally by the woodwind, then reaches an exultant orchestral apotheosis. Last comes the unashamedly populist, lilting, *I'm Superman*, full of witty surprises (rather like the sardonic light music of Shostakovich), and including a famous parodied funeral march. Essentially a miniature set of variations, the work would make a splendid closing item in concert.

The performances demonstrate the excellence of the Gran Canaria Philharmonic Orchestra, who play with fine ensemble and relish under Adrian Leaper. Good recording, too.

Edward Gregson British b1945

Gregson studied composition with Alan Bush at the Royal Academy of Music, 1963-7. He has held various teaching positions, including Professor of Music at Goldsmiths College, University of London. Since 1996 he has been Principal of the Royal Northern College of Music. He has written music for a broad range of orchestral, instrumental and vocal forces, with a particular predilection for brass ensembles.

Clarinet Concerto

Clarinet Concerto[a]. Violin Concerto[b]. Blazon. Stepping Out
[a]Michael Collins cl [b]Olivier Charlier vn
BBC Philharmonic Orchestra / Martyn Brabbins
Chandos CHAN10105 (75' · DDD) (F)

Edward Gregson is a remarkably individual composer who writes in the mainstream of 20th-century English music, influenced by Walton, Malcolm Arnold and Vaughan Williams. He proves a superb craftsman, with great orchestral flair and genuine melodic gifts. The concertos are among the most rewarding written in the late 20th century.

Blazon (1992) is a miniature concerto for orchestra, resourcefully compressed into ten minutes, yet overflowing with energy and ideas. Opening and closing with regal brass fanfares, it introduces each orchestral group in turn, their myriad contributions underpinned by a lyrical theme which sets the whole piece in perspective.

The splendid Clarinet Concerto (1994), sensitively and exuberantly played by Michael Collins, opens with the musing soloist exploring the basic material inquisitively, and from this grow the spirited, impetuous, rhymically spiky main themes. The second half begins *pianissimo* on high strings, creating magical textures and an atmosphere of serene tranquillity which sends shivers down the spine. But the dynamism of the first part returns and from this Gregson fash-

ions a richly heart-warming tune which resolves all that has gone before.

Each movement of the Violin Concerto (1999) is prefaced by lines of poetry as inspirational starting points. The brash sardonic waltz climax of the first movement catches something of Oscar Wilde's 'Love passed into the house of lust' (from *The Harlot's House*). The elysian, mystical slow movement, rapturously played by Olivier Charlier, takes the listener far deeper than the quoted lines of Paul Verlaine's *Chanson d'automne*, and the Irish reel of the athletic finale is at one with Yeats's 'And the merry love the fiddle, And the merry love to dance': the soloist leads that dance wildly, even drawing on the energy of the ideas in *Blazon*.

Stepping out (1996), for string orchestra, briefly dallies in the world of John Adams; but Gregson is no minimalist and the brief polyphonic second section shows how his compositional skills were honed under Bush, while he adds a spontaneous lyrical momentum all his own.

The recordings are vivid and warmly atmospheric; this CD is highly recommend to anyone who cares about contemporary British orchestral music.

Edvard Grieg Norwegian 1843-1907

Grieg studied with EF Wenzel at the Leipzig Conservatory (1858-62), where he became intimately familiar with early Romantic music (especially Schumann's), gaining further experience in Copenhagen and encouragement from Niels Gade. Not until 1864-5 and his meeting with the Norwegian nationalist Rikard Nordraak did his stylistic breakthrough occur, notably in the folk-inspired Humoresker for piano Op 6. Apart from promoting Norwegian music through concerts of his own works, he obtained pupils, became conductor of the Harmoniske Selskab and helped found the Christiania Musikforening (1871), meanwhile composing his Piano Concerto (1868) and the important piano arrangements of 25 of Lindeman's folksongs (Op 17, 1869). An operatic collaboration with Bjornson came to nothing, but his incidental music to Ibsen's Peer Gynt (1875), the best known of his large compositions, produced some of his finest work. Despite chronic ill-health he continued to tour as a conductor and pianist and to execute commissions from his base at Troldhaugen (from 1885); he received numerous international honours. Among his later works, The Mountain Thrall Op 32 for baritone, two horns and strings, the String Quartet in G minor Op 27, the popular neo-Baroque Holberg Suite (1884) and the Haugtussa song cycle Op 67 (1895) are the most distinguished.

Grieg was first and foremost a lyrical composer; his Op 33 Vinje settings, for example, encompass a wide range of emotional expression and atmospheric colour, and the ten opus numbers of Lyric Pieces for piano hold a wealth of characteristic mood-sketches.

But he also was a pioneer, in the impressionistic uses of harmony and piano sonority in his late songs and in the dissonance treatment in the Slåtter Op 72, peasant fiddle-tunes arranged for piano.

GROVEmusic

Piano Concerto

Grieg Piano Concerto[a] **Schumann** Piano Concerto 🅗 in A minor, Op 54[a]. Romance in F sharp, Op 28 No 2. Vogel als Prophet, Op 82 No 7 **Palmgren** West-Finnish Dance, Op 31 No 5. Refrain de berceau
Benno Moiseiwitsch pf [a]**Philharmonia Orchestra / Otto Ackermann**
Testament mono SBT1187 (70' · ADD) Recorded 1941, [a]1953   Ⓟ Ⓞ

Few pianists have played the silken aristocrat more engagingly than Benno Moiseiwitsch. His outward impassivity hid an imaginative delicacy and stylish nonchalance often mistaken for diffidence. Playful, individual, debonair, occasionally mischievous (why not expand on the last pages of the Grieg Concerto's cadenza if you feel like it?), he invariably had one more surprise up his sleeve than you expected.

The Grieg Concerto sounds newly minted, with markings such as *tranquillo e cantabile* observed with special affection. The catalogue may be filled with more openly confrontational performances but Moiseiwitsch, who took music more by stealth than storm, elegantly eclipses the readings of so many more assertive keyboard tigers. For encores there are classic performances of Palmgren and Schumann.

Both the Grieg and Schumann Concertos were central to Moiseiwitsch's immense repertoire but, as with so many other Russian pianists, Schumann remained his greatest love. His opening to the Schumann Concerto is under-stated (like a great actor throwing away his lines), but his projection of the principal theme has a matchless tonal bloom and subtlety. How many other pianists have eased their way through the central A flat dreams with such unaffected charm? In the opening of the Intermezzo he's delightfully *grazioso*, emphasising the *staccatos* as much as the manifold feelings and colours, and in the finale his play of light and shade are, again, inimitable Moiseiwitsch. Ackermann's partnership is arguably more able than inspiring, but Testament's transfers of recordings dating from 1941 to 1953 are superb.

Grieg Piano Concerto in A minor, Op 16[b] **Debussy** Préludes – Book 1[a]
Arturo Benedetti Michelangeli pf [b]**New Philharmonia Orchestra / Rafael Frühbeck de Burgos**
BBC Legends/IMG Artists [b]mono/[a]stereo
BBCL4043-2 (69' · DDD/ADD) Recorded live [b]1965, [a]1982   Ⓜ Ⓞ Ⓞ Ⓞ

 Somehow you feel it must be possible to deliver the hackneyed opening flourishes of the Grieg Concerto with real abandon and impetuosity, to get the orchestra to respond to them with genuine ardour, then for the soloist to combine flow, virtuoso dash, fantasy and noble eloquence and to crown the structural highpoints in a way that lifts you out of your seat. Yet until you hear a performance like this one you may never quite believe it can be done. A sense of joyous rhapsody buoys up Michelangeli's playing from first note to last, yet everything is founded on a bedrock of high intelligence, taste and natural authority. Witness too the fabulous tone-colours he draws from the instrument. His slow movement is by turns balmy and ecstatic, and the finale has terrific drive. And the virtuosity...! If your hair isn't standing on end in the finale's coda you need an urgent medical check-up. Forget the boxy recording and the hissy background. This is a performance that entirely merits the hysterical cheers that greet it.

Seventeen years on, Michelangeli's Debussy also provokes rapturous applause, but in this instance it was probably partly a tribute to his by this time legendary status – he was 63 and rapidly becoming as famous for his cancellations as for his performances. There are marvels of pianism here, but an air of calculation hangs over much of the playing. Those who have Michelangeli's 1978 DG studio version will find little to prefer here, apart from the slightly warmer acoustic.

Grieg Piano Concerto in A minor, Op 16 **Schumann** Piano Concerto in A minor, Op 54
Stephen Kovacevich pf **BBC Symphony Orchestra / Sir Colin Davis**
Philips 50 Great Recordings 464 702-2PM (60' · ADD) Recorded 1970-71   Ⓜ Ⓞ Ⓞ

Stephen Kovacevich's Philips recording has been tirelessly celebrated for its freshness and poetic vitality, and it remains a benchmark offering. His virtuosity is both inclusive and discreet, and his Grieg Concerto remains among the finest on record. The cadenza flashes fire with the best of them and in the central *Adagio* his playing has all the luminous magic lacking in Michelangeli's otherwise masterly performance on his BBC archive CD. Indeed, there's little of the Prussian officer about Kovacevich, and as he makes the final *quasi presto* dance on air you may well wonder when you've heard a performance of greater skill and affection.

True, some may find Kovacevich's Schumann too polite, bathed as it were in an often pale and silvery light rather than in more brilliant hues. Certainly he would be more characterful, even confrontational today.

Davis and the BBC Symphony Orchestra are beautifully sensitive to their soloist's subtle and acute musicianship, and the transfers have come up more than successfully. A treasurable reissue.

Grieg Piano Concerto in A minor, Op 16 **Schumann** Piano Concerto in A minor, Op 54

GRIEG PIANO CONCERTO – IN BRIEF

Dinu Lipatti; Philharmonia Orchestra / Alceo Galliera
EMI Références 574802-2 (71' · ADD) Ⓜ
Very special playing from Dinu Lipatti; the poetry and rapt beauty of this famous 1947 performance linger long in the memory.

Sir Clifford Curzon; London PO / Øivin Fjeldstad
Decca 448 599-2DCS (69' · ADD) Ⓜ
Curzon's patrician, enchantingly lyrical contribution is the very epitome of tasteful discretion. Fjeldstad and the LPO also deserve great credit. Expertly refurbished 1959 sound.

Murray Perahia; Bavarian RSO / Sir Colin Davis
Sony Classical SK44889 (60' · DDD) ⒻOO
A performance to delight all admirers of this aristocrat of the keyboard. Sir Colin Davis and the Bavarian RSO also distinguish themselves, as do the Sony engineers.

Benno Moiseiwitsch; Philharmonia Orchestra / Otto Ackermann
Testament SBT1187 (70' · ADD) ⒻO
Moiseiwitsch's vintage 1953 recording was one of the mainstays of HMV's early LP catalogue. (Check out, too, this magical soloist's arguably superior wartime account with Heward on Naxos 8 110683.)

Leif Ove Andsnes; Berlin PO / Mariss Jansons
EMI 557562 2 (59' · DDD) ⒻOOO
☼ A commanding, intrepidly imaginative account from one of the supreme pianists of our times, its pleasures enhanced by Jansons's immaculate, powerfully responsive backing with the Berliners.

Leif Ove Andsnes; Bergen PO / Dmitri Kitaenko
Virgin The Classics 561996-2 (78' · DDD) Ⓜ
Andsnes's earlier recording continues to holds its own at mid-price. A softer-spoken affair than his EMI remake, with poetry and delicacy in perfect equilibrium.

Stephen Kovacevich; BBC SO / Sir Colin Davis
Philips 464 702-2PM (61' · ADD) ⓂOO
Kovacevich's indelibly fresh performance has enchanted for over three decades now. Felicities abound, not least the agile bravura of the first-movement cadenza and captivating skip of the finale.

Arturo Benedetti Michelangeli; New Philharmonia Orch / Rafael Frühbeck de Burgos
BBC Legends BBCL4043-2 (69' · ADD) ⓂOOO
☼ Simply breathtaking artistry from the great Italian pianist. This June 1965 performance generates a joyous, edge-of-seat ardour that grips from the first bar to the last.

Murray Perahia pf **Bavarian Radio Symphony Orchestra / Sir Colin Davis**
Sony Classical SK44899 (60' · DDD) Recorded live 1987, 1988 ⒻOO

Despite the hazards, Murray Perahia delights in the inspirational heat-of-the-moment of a live recording. Though there are no claps, coughs or shuffles betraying the presence of an audience, we're told both concertos were recorded live at Munich's Philharmonie Gasteig. Of the two works, the Grieg is better served by the immediacy and warmth of Perahia's response, whether through rhythmic bite in livelier dance tempo or total surrender to lyrical nostalgia elsewhere. Never is there the slightest sacrifice of artistic sensitivity or keyboard finesse. His Schumann is no less ardent. In the spirited finale, as throughout the Grieg, any collector would be as happy with this performance as that of Kovacevich for Philips. But in the first two movements, it's Kovacevich who finds a simpler, more confiding note – as well as more artfully weaving the piano into the comparatively light texture as if it were part of the orchestra instead of a spot-lit outsider. Davis goes all the way in both works to uphold Perahia in his open-hearted point-making, and the Bavarian Radio Symphony Orchestra gives him all he asks. The sound is more clear-cut than the old Philips.

Grieg Piano Concerto in A minor, Op 16 **Schumann** Piano Concerto in A minor, Op 54
Leif Ove Andsnes pf **Berlin Philharmonic Orchestra / Mariss Jansons**
EMI 557562-2 (59' · DDD) ⒻOOO

 It was the Grieg Concerto that first made the name of Leif Ove Andsnes on disc in 1990. The interpretation remains broadly the same, except that speeds are now rather brisker. However many times he's performed the Grieg, Andsnes retains a freshness and expressiveness that always sounds spontaneous. That inspirational quality is more markedly perceptible with the new version's faster tempos, but the expressive flights remain just as broad. In that contrast, he's firmly supported by Jansons and the Berlin Philharmonic, with playing not just refined but dramatic too in fiercely exciting *tuttis*. Schumann's cello melodies are gloriously warm, with textures in both works admirably clear, and Andsnes fully responds to Schumann's *espressivo* and *ritardando* requests.

Though both Stephen Kovacevich and Murray Perahia are equally spontaneous, they tend not to be quite so free in their expressive flights; EMI's finely balanced digital sound and the playing of the Berlin Philharmonic are also in this version's favour. Andsnes also offers slightly faster basic speeds than his rivals; particularly enjoyable is the free-flowing tempo for the central *Andantino grazioso* of the Schumann, which you'd never mistake for a simple *Andante*.

Peer Gynt Suites

Grieg Peer Gynt – Suites Nos 1 & 2, Opp 46 & 55.
Holberg Suite, Op 40 **Sibelius** Legends, Op 22 –
No 2, The Swan of Tuonela. Kuolema – Valse triste,
Op 44. Finlandia, Op 26
**Berlin Philharmonic Orchestra / Herbert von
Karajan**
DG Karajan Gold 439 010-2GHS (78' · DDD)
Recorded 1981-4   Ⓜ**OO**

Very impressive indeed. Somehow one feels
that one could stretch out and touch the players,
so vivid is the sound here. In the *Peer Gynt*
movements, there's much greater range and
separation. *Peer Gynt* is most beautifully done.
At times you might think the wind could have
been a shade more distant, particularly in the
'By the seashore' movement but there's no want
of atmosphere here – quite the contrary! Not to
put too fine a point on it, this is a marvellous
recording. In the *Holberg Suite*, the sound has
marvellous clarity and definition as well as
exemplary range. For some tastes it may be a little too sophisticated but one's admiration for it
remains undimmed. The playing throughout is
beautifully cultured and there's wonderful
lightness and delicacy. The present issue is
Karajan's third account of 'The Swan of
Tuonela' and it's regrettable that he never committed to disc the four *Legends* in their entirety.
It's as powerful and atmospheric an account as
ever recorded, and the remaining two pieces,
'Valse triste' and *Finlandia*, reinforce the feeling
that this partnership has never been equalled.
The stirring account of *Finlandia* is incredibly
wide-ranging – the orchestral playing is really in
a class of its own.

Grieg Peer Gynt – Suites Nos 1 & 2, Opp 46 & 55
Saeverud Peer Gynt, Op 28 – Suites Nos 1 & 2
Anne-Margrethe Eikaas *sop*
Norwegian Radio Orchestra / Ari Rasilainen
Finlandia 0630-17675-2 (74' · DDD)   Ⓕ**O**

To juxtapose the *Peer Gynt* music of Grieg and
Saeverud on record is such an obvious idea that
it's astonishing that no one has thought of it
before. It was inevitable that there should be a
reaction against the pictorialism and Romanticism of Grieg's *Peer Gynt*, particularly after the
upheaval of the Second World War and the
Nazi occupation of Norway, and when
Saeverud was approached by Hans Jacob Nilsen
to compose his incidental music, it was for a
realistic production shorn of sentiment and
glamour. Saeverud's score for the play has no
vestige of Romanticism, not a trace of gentility,
and its musical language is robust and uncouth.
It's full of character, whether it's in 'Peer-
ludium', the portrayal of the cocky Peer himself,
the wild and lascivious 'Anitra' (nothing demure
about her) or the splendidly earthy 'Devil's
Five-hop' and the equally brilliant 'Dovretroll
jog'. The Norwegian Radio Orchestra is a
highly accomplished body with great refine-

ment of colour and tone, and Ari Rasilainen
draws splendid, well-characterised playing from
them. The familiar Grieg suites are hardly less
fine. The recording is refined.

Peer Gynt – Suites: Nos 1 & 2, Opp 46 & 55.
In Autumn, Op 11. Symphonic Dances, Op 64
**City of Birmingham Symphony Orchestra / Sakari
Oramo**
Erato 8573-82917-2 (74' · DDD)   Ⓕ**O**

As soon as the strings respond to the flute near
the beginning of *Peer Gynt*'s 'Morning' – longingly leaning on an expressive *ritardando* – you
sense this is a quality production. Done to death
it may be, but Grieg's vernal score still holds the
potential to seduce, enthral and entertain. Here,
charm and drama form a seductive alliance.
Sakari Oramo has an architect's sense of proportion and an athlete's sense of pacing. He also
knows how to shape and colour musical textures. Ase's death ends with a full-bodied *pianissimo* while the bassoon counter-subject that follows Peer through 'The Hall of the Mountain
King' can rarely have sounded more mischievous. Rather than push an unworkable *accel-
lerando*, Oramo moves with stealth, tightening
the rhythm as he goes, letting in an element of
swagger before speeding for the final chase.
'Ingrid's Lament' enjoys powerfully drawn
basses and an unusually dramatic climax and
'Peer Gynt's Journey Home' allows ample space
for the elements to rage. Note how, at around
1'14", woodwinds goad lower strings into action
and the ensuing tumult gradually gains momentum. As for 'Anitra' and the 'Arabian Dance',
both benefit from the CBSO's vivid but
unforced characterisations.

The Concert Overture *In Autumn* takes its
point of departure from a song called *Autumn
Storms*. And if there's one aspect of Oramo's
performance that pips Beecham's stereo version
to the post, it's a feeling of what one might call
'weatheredness'. True, the superb recording
helps, but so do Oramo's rock-steady control of
rhythm and sense of atmosphere.

The *Symphonic Dances* are by turns lyrical or
exuberant, the last of them – the partially pensive A minor – being faster than Järvi's thinner-
sounding Gothenburg version by a good two
minutes. The Birmingham orchestra are consistently responsive to Oramo's very specific
demands. Credible rivals are headed by piquant
Sir Thomas in *Peer Gynt* and *In Autumn*, and by
Järvi in the *Symphonic Dances*. Oramo's Grieg
matches both, being less fussy than keen-eared
and with a sense of play that does credit both to
Ibsen's dramatic prompt and the folk-music
roots of the concert works.

String Quartets

Grieg String Quartets – No 1 in G minor, Op 27; No
2 in F, CW146 **Schumann** String Quartet No 1 in A
minor, Op 41 No 1

Petersen Quartet (Conrad Muck, Gernot Süssmuth vns Friedemann Weigle va Hans-Jakob Eschenburg vc)
Capriccio 10 476 (75' · DDD) Recorded 1993   Ⓕ

Grieg String Quartet No 1 in G minor, Op 27
Mendelssohn String Quartet No 2 in A minor, Op 13
Shanghai Quartet (WeiGang Li, HongGang Li vns Zheng Wang va James Wilson vc)
Delos DE3153 (64' · DDD) Recorded 1993   Ⓕ**O**

Since Grieg owed much to Schumann, coupling their quartets seems a good idea. These G minor and A minor Quartets were written when the composers were in their thirties, although Grieg was a few years older. Yet it's his work that sounds more youthfully passionate, while the Schumann is a rather self-conscious homage to his friend Mendelssohn and classical models. The Petersens invest the Grieg G minor Quartet with *gravitas* and are skilful in linking the disparate sections of its structure. Their recording has a natural balance and an impressively wide dynamic rang; it also copes well with Grieg's forceful, semi-orchestral string writing. The whole performance has vigour and tenderness in good proportion, and a truly Scandinavian feeling. The unfinished F major Quartet is another sensitive performance and the work sounds no more incomplete than Schubert's *Unfinished* Symphony.

The Schumann is no less enjoyable; the artists are fully inside his idiom and make a consistently beautiful and meaningful sound. The Shanghai Quartet's brightly lit account of the Mendelssohn suggests a rich store of interpretative potential. Theirs is a sizzling, multicoloured performance. The Grieg coupling is, if anything, even finer, with an *Allegro molto* first movement that truly is *ed agitato*, a warming *Romanze* and a superbly characterised *Intermezzo*. It's arguably the most compelling performance of this score since the original Budapest Quartet's trail-blazing HMV 78s from 1937. It's richly recorded.

Violin Sonatas

No 1 in F, Op 8; **No 2** in G, Op 13;
No 3 in C minor, Op 45

Augustin Dumay vn **Maria João Pires** pf
DG 437 525-2GH (70' · DDD) Recorded 1993   Ⓕ**O**

Grieg's violin sonatas span his creative life, the first two dating from his early twenties, before his Piano Concerto, and the Third Sonata of 1887 belonging to the last decade of his life. Augustin Dumay brings to this music a youthful *seigneur*, manifest in the impetuosity, charm and command of his playing. He and Pires are at their considerable best in the G major Sonata, with its vivid first movement, lilting *Allegretto* and triumphant finale – whose conclusion they lift to the skies. The recording does full justice

to Dumay's silky and resourceful tone. Pires is rightly an equal partner, and both artists bring an infectiously fresh response to the music. The finale of the C minor Sonata, which anticipates Sibelius in its urgency and elemental force, is compellingly played.

Violin Sonatas Nos 1-3
Henning Kraggerud vn **Helge Kjekshus** pf
Naxos 8 553904 (67' · DDD)   Ⓢ

This disc gives us consistently enjoyable performances. The two young Norwegians play with idiomatic style, and give the impression of expressing every aspect of the music. Their eagerness at the start of Op 8's first *Allegro* sets the tone; the *doloroso* opening of Op 13, the delicacy and serenity of the E major section of that sonata's middle movement, and the exciting 'Hall of the Mountain King' atmosphere they generate in the finale of Op 45 – these are just a few of the places where the pair convince us they've found exactly the right sound and manner of expression. Dumay and Pires on DG are magnificently recorded, causing one to regret the slight lack of brilliance in the Naxos recording and wish that the violin in particular had been given a more glamorous presence. They are as deeply involved as the Norwegians but play with far greater freedom. However, Kraggerud's account of the 'big tune' in the last movement of Op 45, respecting all Grieg's marks of expression and phrasing, has a nobility that Dumay, more heart-on-sleeve and cavalier about dynamics and slurs, misses. The Naxos disc is, in short, highly recommendable – as a contrast to Dumay/Pires or simply as an excellent bargain.

Piano Works

Volume 1: Piano Sonata in E minor, Op 7. Funeral March for Rikard Nordraak, CW117. Melodies of Norway – The sirens' enticement. Stimmungen, Op 73. Transcriptions of Original Songs I, Op 41 – No 3, I love thee. Four Humoresques, Op 6. Four Piano Pieces, Op 1
Einar Steen-Nøkleberg pf
Naxos 8 550881 (72' · DDD) Recorded 1993   Ⓢ

Volume 2: Two Improvisations on Norwegian Folksongs, Op 29. Melodies of Norway – A Ballad to Saint Olaf. 25 Norwegian Folksongs and Dances, Op 17. Transcriptions of Original Songs II, Op 52 – No 2, The first meeting. 19 Norwegian Folksongs, Op 66
Einar Steen-Nøkleberg pf
Naxos 8 550882 (70' · DDD) Recorded 1993   Ⓢ

Volume 3: Four Album Leaves, Op 28. Six Poetic Tone-pictures, Op 3. Melodies of Norway – Iceland. Three Pictures from life in the country, Op 19. Three Pieces from 'Sigurd Jorsalfar', Op 56 – Prelude. Ballade in G minor, Op 24, 'in the form of variations on a Norwegian melody'
Einar Steen-Nøkleberg pf

Naxos 8 550883 (64' · DDD) Recorded 1993 ⑤●

Volume 4: Holberg Suite, Op 40. Melodies of
Norway – I went to bed so late. Six Norwegian
Mountain Melodies, CW134. Peer Gynt Suite No 1,
Op 46 – Morning. 17 Norwegian Peasant Dances,
Op 72
Einar Steen-Nøkleberg pf
Naxos 8 550884 (71' · DDD) Recorded 1993 ⑤

These are the first four volumes of a complete
Grieg cycle which stretches to no fewer than 14
discs. Since they are all at super-budget price
they make a very competitive alternative to
other complete or near-complete surveys. Einar
Steen-Nøkleberg came into prominence during
the 1970s and won numerous Norwegian and
other prizes. He was professor of the piano at
the Hanover Musikhochschule for a number of
years and is the author of a monograph on
Grieg's piano music and its interpretation.

8 550881: The first disc juxtaposes early
pieces, the Sonata, Op 7, the Op 6 *Humoresques*
and the *Funeral March for Rikard Nordraak*, all
written in the mid-1890s with his very last piano
work, *Stimmungen* (or 'Moods'), Op 73. He
plays these bold and original pieces with great
flair and understanding. Whatever its limitations there's much greater range in Grieg's
piano music than is commonly realised and
Steen-Nøkleberg is attuned to the whole spectrum it covers, whether in the Bartókian
'Mountaineer's Song' from the Op 73 to the
charm and innocence of the *Allegretto con grazia*,
the third of the *Humoresques*, Op 6. 8 550882:
The *19 Norwegian Folksongs* (1896) are remarkable pieces as Grieg himself knew. He wrote to
the Dutch composer, Julius Röntgen, of having
'put some hair-raising chromatic chords on
paper. The excuse is that they originated not on
the piano but in my mind.' Readers will recognise No 14 as the source of the theme for
Delius's *On hearing the first cuckoo in spring*.
Steen-Nøkleberg plays them with great tonal
finesse and consummate artistry.

8 550883: The most substantial work on this
disc is the *Ballade* which Grieg wrote on his parents' death. This recording can hold its own
with the best in this healthy area of the catalogue – even if there are moments when Steen-
Nøkleberg seems too discursive. Yet what an
imaginative colour he produces in the *Adagio*
variation when the music suddenly melts *pianissimo*.

8 550884: The *Norwegian Peasant Dances* are
amazing pieces for their period, and though
their audacity and dissonance were later overtaken by Bartók, they still retain their capacity
to surprise. The playing conveys the extraordinary character and originality of these pieces as
do few others. The smaller pieces contained on
this disc – as well as on its companions – are full
of rewards.

Lyric Pieces, Book 1, Op 12 – No 1, Arietta; No 2,
Waltz; No 5, Folksong; No 6, Norwegian; Book 2,

Op 38 – No 6, Elegy; No 7, Waltz; No 8, Canon; Book
4 Op 47 – No 2, Album Leaf; No 3, Melody; No 4,
Norwegian Dance; Book 5, Op 54 – No 3, March of
the Trolls; No 4, Nocturne; Book 6, Op 57 – No 2,
Gade; No 3, Illusion; No 6, Homesickness; Book 7,
Op 62 – No 1, Sylph; No 4, Brooklet; No 5, Phantom;
No 6, Homeward; Book 8, Op 65 – No 6, Wedding
Day at Troldhaugen; Book 9, Op 68 – No 3, At your
Feet; No 4, Evening in the Mountains; No 5, Cradle
Song; Book 10, Op 71 – No 6, Gone; No 7,
Remembrances
Leif Ove Andsnes pf
EMI 557296-2 (68' · DDD) Played on Grieg's piano at
the Grieg Troldhaugen Museum, Bergen ℗●●●

 Once again on home ground, Andsnes
reminds you of his capacity to go
directly to the heart of the matter.
Taking you on a journey of increasing subtlety
and introspection, he makes you aware that so
much of this music is for those long winter
nights. At the same time the music is so richly
varied: 'Melody's insistent dactylic rhythm creates a strange unsettling poetic ambience, while
the central oasis of calm in 'Wedding Day at
Troldhaugen' would surely melt a heart of
stone.

All Andsnes's performances have that deceptive simplicity which is his touchstone. His playing is always sensitive, never sentimental and
with a bracing and essential 'touch of the cod-
fish' (Grieg) when required. And while one
would never want to be without Gilels' rapt DG
performances (see below), praise could hardly
be too high for a pianist who so enviably captures the poignant nature of a composer who
Tchaikovsky once claimed had 'a glance like a
charming and candid child'. Grieg's piano, with
its distinctive timbre, provides an added touch
of nostalgia.

Lyric Pieces – Arietta, Op 12 No 1. Berceuse, Op 38
No 1. Butterfly, Op 43 No 1. Solitary Traveller, Op 43
No 2. Album Leaf, Op 47 No 2. Melody, Op 47 No 3.
Norwegian Dance, 'Halling', Op 47 No 4. Nocturne,
Op 54 No 4. Scherzo, Op 54 No 5. Homesickness,
Op 57 No 6. Brooklet, Op 62 No 4. Homeward,
Op 62 No 6. In ballad vein, Op 65 No 5.
Grandmother's Minuet, Op 68 No 2. At your feet,
Op 68 No 3. Cradle Song, Op 68 No 5. Once upon
a time, Op 71 No 1. Puck, Op 71 No 3. Gone, Op 71
No 6. Remembrances, Op 71 No 7
Emil Gilels pf
DG The Originals 449 721-2GOR (56' · ADD)
Recorded 1974 Ⓜ●●●

 Here, surely, is a classic recording, one
of calibre and status for all time. Rarely
can a great artist have declared his love
with such touching candour. By his own admission Gilels discovered in Grieg's Lyric Pieces a
'whole world of intimate feeling' and at the sessions where these were recorded fought tirelessly to capture their intricate mix of innocence
and experience. The results are of an unblemished purity, grace and contained eloquence.

He brings the same insight and concentration to these apparent trifles as he did to towering masterpieces of the classic repertoire. The programme proceeds chronologically and one can appreciate the gradual but marked development in Grieg's harmonic and expressive language – from the folk song inspired early works to the more progressive and adventurous later ones. Gilels's fingerwork is exquisite and the sense of total involvement with the music almost religious in feeling. Never can Debussy's sniping estimate of Grieg', 'a pink bonbon filled with snow' (or DG's dreary accompanying notes), have seemed wider of the mark. The recordings remain as impeccable as the playing. This is a disc for everyone's desert island.

Peer Gynt

Peer Gynt – The Bridal March passes by; Prelude; **H**
In the Hall of the Mountain King; Solveig's Song;
Prelude; Arab Dance; Anitra's Dance; Prelude;
Solveig's Cradle Song. Symphonic Dance, Op 64 –
Allegretto grazioso. In Autumn, Op 11. Old
Norwegian Romance with Variations, Op 51
Ilse Hollweg sop **Beecham Choral Society; Royal
Philharmonic Orchestra / Sir Thomas Beecham**
EMI Great Recordings of the Century 566914-2
(77' · ADD) Recorded 1957　　　　　　Ⓜ**OO**

Grieg's incidental music was an integral part of Ibsen's *Peer Gynt* and from this score Grieg later extracted the two familiar suites. This recording of excerpts from *Peer Gynt* goes back to 1957 but still sounds well and is most stylishly played. Included is the best known ('Anitra's Dance' is a delicate gem here) together with 'Solveig's Song' and 'Solveig's Cradle Song'. Beecham uses Ilse Hollweg to advantage, her voice suggesting the innocence of the virtuous peasant heroine. There's also an effective use of the choral voices which are almost inevitably omitted in ordinary performances of the two well-known suites: the male chorus of trolls in the 'Hall of the Mountain King' are thrilling, and the women in the 'Arab Dance' are charming. The other two pieces are well worth having too; *Symphonic Dances* is a later, freshly pastoral work, while the overture *In Autumn* is an orchestral second version of an early piece for piano duet. This reissue is further enhanced by the first release in stereo of the *Old Norwegian Romance*.

Songs

Haugtussa, Op 67. Two brown eyes, Op 5 No 1.
I love but thee, Op 5 No 3. A swan, Op 25 No 2.
With a waterlily, Op 25 No 4. Hope, Op 26 No 1.
Spring, Op 33 No 2. Beside the stream, Op 33 No 5.
From Monte Pincio, Op 39 No 1. Six Songs, Op 48.
Spring showers, Op 49 No 6. While I wait, Op 60
No 3. Farmyard Song, Op 61 No 3
Anne Sofie von Otter mez **Bengt Forsberg** pf
DG Gramophone Awards Collection 476 1815GGR

(68' · DDD) Recorded 1992. Texts and translations
included　　　　　　　　　　　　　Ⓜ**OOO**

Von Otter is at the peak of her powers here, glorying in this repertoire. In the *Haugtussa* cycle she projects her imagination of the visionary herd-girl with absolute conviction. She's no less successful in the German settings that follow. The sad depths of *One day, my thought* from Six Songs, Op 48, the hopelessness of Goethe's *The time of roses* (Op 48 No 5), a setting of great beauty, are encompassed with unfettered ease, but so are the lighter pleasures of *Lauf der Welt*. Even the familiar *A dream* (Op 48 No 6) emerges as new in her daringly big-boned reading. Her readings are immeasurably enhanced throughout by the imaginative playing of Bengt Forsberg. They breathe fresh life into *A swan* and in the almost as familiar *With a waterlily*, another superb Ibsen setting, the questing spirit expressed in the music is marvellously captured by the performers. This should be regarded as a 'must' for any collector.

Twelve Songs, Op 33. Five Songs, Op 26. For LM Lindemans's Silver Wedding. My little bird. She walked to the church. The Odalisque. To Christian Tønsberg. The Blueberry. The girl Gjenta. On Hamar's Ruins. The White and Red Roses.
Monica Groop mez **Roger Vignoles** pf
BIS BIS-CD1257 (68' · DDD) Texts and translations
included　　　　　　　　　　　　　　　Ⓕ

The important item here is the complete set of the Op 33 songs. Only the second song of the Op 33 set, *Våren* ('Last Spring'), has had many takers – Schwarzkopf and Tauber among them. The rest are lucky to have a single recording in the catalogue, if that.

Grieg had been recovering from the deaths of his parents and was going through a bad patch in his marriage when he set 12 poems by AO Vinje for his Op 33 set, hence their preoccupation with darker themes of mortality and mankind. Groop does well by them, making full use of her deep mezzo colouring. Her singing is beautiful, sympathetic, typically bringing a sense of calm and understanding to 'The Spring' ('Våren') and stretching to the weightier seriousness needed for a song such as 'First Things' ('Det fyrste').

Groop and accompanist Roger Vignoles are well paired, as both like to let the music flow naturally. This puts them in the opposite corner to Anne Sofie von Otter and Bengt Forsberg, whose award-winning Grieg recital (DG) comes with their personalities stamped on every bar.

Where they're in competition (only three songs here), Von Otter and Forsberg are instantly memorable, achieving lift-off with a tremendous sense of elation in 'Hope' ('Et Håb') from the Op 26 set, albeit at the expense of some pulling-around of the tempo from the pianist. There are people who are resistant to the Swedish couple's bold way with Grieg and for them the more traditional approach of Groop and Vignoles will be preferable. The recording quality is first rate.

pathetic throughout, and there are neatly delivered solos from many of the Buffalo players. This is a revelatory Griffes release, decently recorded with a wide dynamic range: strongly recommended.

Charles Griffes   American 1884-1920

Griffes studied with Mary Selena Broughton in Elmira and with Humperdinck in Berlin, where he lived, 1903-7. He returned to teach in Tarrytown, NY. Up to c1911 his music was within the German Romantic tradition but he then developed a more Debussian style in piano pieces (The Pleasure-Dome of Kubla Khan, 1912; Roman Sketches, 1915-16) and songs (Tone-images, 1912-14; Four Impressions, 1912-16). He became closely concerned with oriental culture (Five Poems of Ancient China and Japan, 1916-17; ballet Sho-jo, 1917), while his last works, including the Piano Sonata (1918), show a free handling of dissonance paralleling Scriabin.
GROVEmusic

Orchestral Works

Bacchanale. Clouds. Poem for Flute and Orchestra. The Pleasure-Dome of Kubla Khan. The White Peacock. Three Poems of Fiona McLeod. Three Tone-Pictures
Barbara Quintiliani *sop* **Carol Wincenc** *fl* **Buffalo Philharmonic Orchestra / JoAnn Falletta**
Naxos 8 559164 (56' · DDD)   ⑤❶

Griffes represents the high point of American post-Romanticism. From his European training he inherited both the German and French traditions of Strauss and Debussy, fused them into something rich and strange, and in his later years became involved with Scriabin and oriental music. Much of his music has been regularly available on record, but this all-Griffes CD now makes the best showing for his hyper-sensitive responses to both literature and landscape.

Many of the works here are piano pieces fastidiously scored, with significant additions. *The White Peacock*, just possibly a cousin of Stravinsky's firebird, is the first of the *Roman Sketches* for piano, all prefaced with stanzas by Fiona McLeod (a *nom-de-plume* for William Sharp): the impressionistic *Clouds* is the last of these. The orchestral opulence of the *Three Poems of Fiona McLeod*, steeped in baleful Celtic twilights, makes the piano version seem anaemic; they're compellingly sung here by Barbara Quintiliani.

In the *Three Tone-Pictures* every picturesque detail of harmonically qualified melody is subtly imagined. The same applies to the *Poem* for flute and orchestra, where the continuity has the instinctive flow of Delius, beautifully realised by Carol Wincenc. *The Pleasure-Dome of Kubla Khan*, the most extended work in this anthology, is an ecstatic response to Coleridge's opium-saturated masterpiece.

Conductor JoAnn Falletta is completely sym-

Sofia Gubaidulina   Russian b1931

Gubaidulina studied with Peyko and Shebalin at the Moscow Conservatory (1954-62). During the 1960s and 70s she wrote primarily chamber music, which is characterised by a radical expansion of the range of musical sound and by use of serial techniques, as in Noch'v Memfise ('Night in Memphis', 1968). She then explored the potential of orchestral and vocal genres, paying particular attention to the role of rhythm and time; her experiments in the role of rests culminated in the solo for conductor in the symphony Stimmen Verstummen (1986). In Alleluja (1990) she gives coloured light a rhythmic function and this determines the structure of the work. Her music has a strong religious basis.
GROVEmusic

Orchestral Works

Music for Flute, Strings and Percussion[a] The Canticle of the Sun[b]
[b]**Emmanuel Pahud** *fls* **Simon Carrington, Neil Percy** *perc* [b]**John Alley** *celeste* [a]**London Symphony Orchestra / Mstislav Rostropovich** [b]*vc/perc* [b]**London Voices / Ryusuke Numajiri**
EMI 557153 2 (76' · DDD)   Ⓕ

Since the death of Alfred Schnittke, Sofia Gubaidulina has come to represent the best of contemporary Russian music, even though she lives and works in Germany. In both *Music for Flute, Strings and Percussion* (1994) and *Canticle of the Sun* (1997) Gubaidulina's special kind of meditative minimalism is offset by more intense, even neo-Romantic material. *Music for Flute* is a mightily impressive work, with the various members of the flute family set against abundant percussion and two string orchestras. Similar inventiveness is to be heard in *Canticle of the Sun*. The composer has spoken of this work as a tribute to Rostropovich's 'sunny energy', and she uses St Francis of Assisi's *Canticle of the Sun* as a basic text. Yet there's as much unquiet, brooding music here as the celebration of faith and light.

The material of both pieces seems a little thinly stretched in places, but Gubaidulina's blazing conviction (matched by Rostropovich as both cellist and conductor) is such that your attention is unlikely to waver for a moment.

De profundis[a]. Seven Words[b]. Ten Preludes[c]
[ab]**Elsbeth Moser** *bayan* [c]**Boris Pergamenschikov** *vc* [b]**Munich Chamber Orchestra / Christoph Poppen**
ECM New Series 461 897-2 (72' · DDD)   Ⓕ

Recordings of Sofia Gubaidulina's music differ markedly as to presentation. Elsbeth Moser and Boris Pergamenschikov interpret *Seven Last Words*, meditations rather than commentaries on the biblical texts, with chamber-like inwardness. Their fervent confrontation in movement IV has a transparency of texture, incisive strings kept to the rear, which offsets the gestural immediacy of the experience. The final movement isn't so much valedictory as implosive, draining away in a haze of sound and emotion. The première recording by Friedrich Lips and Vladimir Tonkha, briefly available on Melodiya, has an impact like no other, while the Naxos account offers a very acceptable overview, but this new recording has a distinct and searching identity of its own. It's enhanced by the companion pieces. The *Ten Preludes* have become staples of the modern repertoire, harnessing technique to a range of moods which work perfectly as a sequence. *De profundis* is a classic of its medium, and while Gerd Draugsvoll on BIS draws visceral emotion from this quirky mix of dissonance and incantation, Moser's lucid unfolding probes deeper. Sound, here and in the *Preludes*, is a model of solo balance.

Chamber Works

In croce[a]. 10 Preludes. Quaternion[b]
Alexander Ivashkin, [b]Natalia Pavlutskaya, [b]Rachel Johnston, [b]Miranda Wilson vcs [a]**Malcolm Hicks** org
Chandos CHAN9958 (56' · DDD) Ⓕ

A quaternion may be a mathematical operation, but there's nothing calculated or contrived about *Quaternion* for four cellos (1996), which here receives its first recording. At its best – as it certainly is here – Gubaidulina's music manages to combine a fiercely improvisatory freedom with a satisfying sense of balance and coherence. On one level *Quaternion* concerns the contrast between the mundane and the transcendent. Yet although the music contains strikingly immediate evocations of both the earthy and the uncanny, it never suggests the withdrawn serenity of a spirituality that regards the real world as 'lost'. Ivashkin and his colleagues achieve marvels of co-ordination, as well as an astonishingly wide range of colour, qualities enhanced by a truthful and well-balanced recording.

Two earlier works complete the programme. The *Ten Preludes* for solo cello (1974) encapsulate energy and expressiveness to highly charged poetic effect. *In Croce* for cello and organ (1979) transforms what could have been a simplistic exercise in the crossing over of two very different sound sources into a grippingly unpredictable drama of convergence and divergence. Both pieces have been recorded before, and you might welcome the chance to acquire the bargain-price version of *In Croce* in its alternative arrangement for cello and accordion (Naxos). But Alexander Ivashkin is a fine player, unsurpassed in Gubaidulina's music.

Francisco Guerrero   Spanish 1528-99

Guerrero was a pupil of Morales. He also taught himself the vihuela, harp, cornett and organ. He was maestro de capilla of Jaén Cathedral (1546-9) and then vice-maestro (1551) and maestro (1574-99) of Seville Cathedral. He visited Rome (1581-2), Venice and the Holy Land (1588-9). The most important 16th-century Spanish composer of sacred music after Victoria, he published 18 masses and c150 motets; because of their singable, diatonic lines, they remained in use in Spanish and Spanish-American cathedrals for more than two centuries after his death. He also published secular songs; many other works survive in anthologies and MSS.

GROVEmusic

Missa de la Batalla Escoutez

Missa de la Batalla Escoutez[ab]. Pange lingua[a]. Ⓟ
In exitu Israel[ab]. Duo Seraphim[a]. Regina coeli[b]
Magnificat[a]. Conditor alme siderum[a]
[a]**Westminster Cathedral Choir; [b]His Majestys Sagbutts and Cornetts / James O'Donnell**
Hyperion CDA67075 (72' · DDD) Texts and
translations included   Ⓕ**OO**

Despite his suggestive name, Guerrero's parody of Janequin's *La Bataille de Marignan* isn't the work of a fighting man: fanfares and alarums are definitely off the agenda while he develops, in an often rather sober manner, the smooth counterpoint of his model. Only in the 'Osanna' does Guerrero let rip, a moment seized on with gusto by the choir and His Majestys Sagbutts and Cornetts. Guerrero spent his career at Seville Cathedral, where the chapter was one of the first in Spain to agree to the establishment of a permanent, salaried wind band to participate in processions and at other points in divine worship. It appears to have been one of Guerrero's duties to sort out what and when, and even how (scoring and ornamentation were part of his brief) the minstrels played.

The instruments (shawms, cornetts, sackbuts, dulcian and organ) subtly double the voices, adding depth to the sound, and strengthening major cadence points. Particularly striking is the earthy tone of the *bajón* (dulcian) reinforcing the bass line in proto-continuo fashion. In fact, it's in the other items on this CD that the combination of voices and instruments really comes into its own. The setting of the psalm *In exitu Israel* experiments with Guerrero's forces (including cornetts and recorders), resulting in an opulence of sound more readily associated with Venetian music of the period. But this isn't just an exercise in applied musicology. These are well-paced, intelligent performances that get inside the skin of Guerrero's marvellous music. Don't be surprised to find yourself humming the Spanish chant for the hymn *Conditor alme siderum* after this compelling rendition. The musicianship is superb, the technical element entirely satisfactory and satisfying.

Reynaldo Hahn

Venezuelan/French 1875-1947

Hahn studied with Massenet at the Paris Conserva-toire. While in his teens he gained a reputation as a composer of songs, which he sang to his own accompa-niment in fashionable salons, gaining admittance to Proust's circle. But after 1900 he concentrated on the theatre, as conductor (at the Opéra from 1945) and as a composer of ballets, operas and operettas (Ciboulette, 1923; Mozart, 1925). GROVEmusic

Violin Concerto

Violin Concerto[ch]. Piano Concerto[dh]. Suite Hongroise[cdh]. Violin Sonata in C[ce]. Romance in A[ce]. Nocturne[ce]. Piano Quintet[eg]. Les feuilles blessées[bf]. Amour sans ailes[af]. Cinq petites chan-sons[af]. Neuf mélodies retrouvées[bf]. Méduse[af] – Chanson au bord de la fontaine; Danse, petite sirène. La dame aux camélias[af] – Mon rêve était d'avoir; C'est à Paris!; Au fil de l'eau
[a]**Catherine Dune** sop [b]**Didier Henry** bar [c]**Denis Clavier** vn [d]**Angeline Pondepeyre**, [e]**Dimitris Saroglou**, [f]**Stéphane Petitjean** pfs [g]**Quatuor Clavier** (Denis Clavier, Marie-France Razafimbadà vns Florian Wallez va Claire Breteau vc); [h]**Lorraine Philharmonic Orchestra / Fernand Quattrocchi**
Maguelone ③ MAG111 111 (203' · DDD) Texts and translations included ⓂⓂ

Both the Violin Concerto and the Piano Con-certo belong to a period in Hahn's life when he knew that strange mixture of happiness and regret that comes to us all in our fifties. The great figures he had known in his youth were nearly all dead, the First World War had claimed many of his contemporaries, and the glamour that had once surrounded his name had faded. Yet in the Paris of the 1920s he had his biggest stage successes (*Ciboulette* and *Mozart*) and entered on the longest and happiest rela-tionship of his life with the tenor Guy Ferrant; all this seems to be expressed in the slow move-ment of the Violin Concerto. Here we have Hahn spinning a slow, languorous tune that hovers between dance and delirium. It's marked throughout *Tranquillo*, *Très calme*, *Amoroso* and *Sans rigueur*. Denis Clavier plays it with just the right air of restraint: as Jean Gallois writes in the notes, it's 'a song from the soul without pathos'.

The better-known Piano Concerto from 1930 is a slighter work. Perhaps its curious structure – the second movement lasts less than three min-utes – makes it seem a little jokey. Those who already have a recording should not be deterred from hearing this excellent performance: Ange-line Pondepeyre takes the opening somewhat slower than Magda Tagliaferro in the historic recording conducted by the composer, but she brings out the jazzy element more.

The second CD starts with the Violin Sonata, composed in 1926. Denis Clavier and Dimitris Saroglou give a first-rate performance, the opening movement a beautiful questioning theme which gives way to a second, more romantic melody. The *Romance* and *Nocturne* are both real salon pieces, and the *Romance* in particular has a haunting tune. As for the Piano Quintet, this has some of Hahn's most passion-ate music in the slow movement. It's impossible not to believe that this piece – composed in 1920-21 – isn't a commentary on the tragic events of 1914-18.

The Quintet may be Hahn's personal reaction to the war, but while actually in the trenches, he composed music which was as far removed from the horrors as possible. His *Five Little Songs* were dedicated to Jan Bathori; it's very difficult for modern singers to hit off the mood of delib-erate naivety in these songs, but it's good to have at least this performance.

Most of the other songs on the third CD in this set have not been recorded before: it's not difficult to see why; the heavy sentiment is so hard to take. *Feuilles blessées*, a cycle of 11 songs, is one of Hahn's most ambitious works. Didier Henry sings them with the right mixture of robust tone and detailed articulation.

The *Neuf mélodies retrouvées* were published a few years after Hahn's death. The final song, 'Sous l'oranger', is the most fun, a 'tango-habanera' that seems to hark back to the Second Empire, that frivolous, dangerous period for which Hahn felt such nostalgia.

This set can't be recommended too highly. Three CDs might seem too much to the unini-tiated, but if you only know his songs or operettas, these is a lot to surprise here.

Chamber Works

Premières valses[a]. Venezia (arr Pidoux)[b]. Piano Quartet[c]. Soliloque et forlane[d]. Cello Concerto (unfinished, ed Pollain)[e]
[be]**Roland Pidoux**, [b]**Pierre Cordier**, [b]**Renaud Guieu**, [b]**Antoine Lederlin**, [b]**Matthieu Lejeune**, [b]**Christophe Morin** vcs [c]**Quatuor Gabriel** ([ade]Yoko Kaneko pf Guillaume Plays vn [d]Vincent Aucante va Jérôme Pinget vc)
Maguelone MAG111 117 (72' · DDD) Ⓕ

According to Jean Gallois's notes for this invaluable disc, the Quartet in G for violin, viola, cello and piano, was completed just a month before Hahn died in January 1947. If that's so, it can be listened to as a farewell, something that inevitably invokes Hahn's friendship with Marcel Proust. And even if one were told that he'd composed the quartet when he was young and happy, it would still evoke a mood of regret and yearning. It's the beautiful *Andante*, the third movement, that's the heart of the piece. A song without words that seems to speak of the pain of long parting, of thoughts unspoken, it ends on a reflective note of accept-ance. Even the dance-like final movement, which contains a perhaps unconscious quote from some of the music for Hahn's musical comedy *Mozart*, also has a bittersweet quality. The Quatuor Gabriel play it eloquently, with-out undue sentimentality.

The suite *Premières valses* for piano was composed in 1898, when Hahn was at the height of his youthful celebrity in Parisian society. The fifth waltz is subtitled 'A l'ombre rêveuse de Chopin', and the whole sequence seems to be a tribute to the style of the 1840s. Yoko Kaneko plays it with more emphasis on the Polish mood than Catherine Joly in her 1988 recording on Accord. This performance reveals more of the rhythmic inventiveness in these miniatures.

The romantic *Soliloque et forlane* was composed in 1937 as a test piece for the Conservatoire. Vincent Aucante and Kaneko bring out the playful Spanish quality in the *allegro scherzando* finale. Finally, Roland Pidoux's arrangement of Hahn's song cycle *Venezia* for cello sextet must be such an expensive proposition that you're unlikely to encounter it in the concert hall. The tunes are adorable.

Songs

A Chloris. Le rossignol des lilas. L'enamourée. Trois jours de vendange. Etudes latines – Lydé; Tyndaris; Phyllis. Les fontaines. Automne. Infidélité. Dans la nuit. D'une prison. Quand la nuit n'est pas étoilée. Fumée. Le printemps. Je me souviens. Quand je fus pris au pavillon. Paysage. Fêtes galantes. Nocturne. Mai. L'heure exquise. Offrande. Si mes vers avaient des ailes
Susan Graham sop **Roger Vignoles** pf
Sony Classical SK60168 (62' · DDD) Texts and translations included ⒻⓄⓄ

Susan Graham brings to these songs a voice of lovely quality, excellent French and – in keeping with Hahn's own insistence – gives overriding importance to clarity of enunciation, the verbal meaning governing the vocal colour. It's certainly better to savour these songs a few at a time, but the programme has been well put together to show Hahn's range, from the Bachian pastiche of A Chloris or the antique simplicity of Lydé to the adventurous harmonic progressions of Fumée, Le printemps or Je me souviens, from the despairing pathos of D'une prison to the light-heartedness of Quand je fus pris au pavillon, from the quiet rapture of Nocturne to the passion of Dans la nuit (a splendid miniature). His outstanding gift for lyricism is evident throughout; Le rossignol des lilas, for example, is enchanting. Susan Graham perfectly captures these songs' elegant intimacy with a wealth of nuance, from the gentle tone of L'enamourée to the fullness of L'automne; and the way she floats the words 'l'heure exquise' is haunting. Roger Vignoles provides most sensitive partnership throughout: he has more scope in songs like Les fontaines or Dans la nuit, but equally noteworthy is his subtle treatment of the repeated pattern of Infidélité.

Douze rondels. Etudes latines. Si mes vers avaient des ailes. Paysage. Rêverie. Offrande. Mai. Infidélité. Seule. Les cygnes. Nocturne. Trois jours de vendange. D'une prison. Séraphine. L'heure exquise. Fêtes galantes. Quand la nuit n'est pas étoilée. Le plus beau présent. Sur l'eau. Le rossignol des lilas. A Chloris. Ma jeunesse. Puisque j'ai mis ma lèvre. La nymphe de la source. Au rossignol. Je me souviens. Mozart – Air de la lettre. O mon bel inconnu – C'est très vilain d'être infidèle. Ciboulette – C'est sa banlieue; Nous avons fait un beau voyage. Une revue – La dernière valse
Dame Felicity Lott sop **Susan Bickley** mez **Ian Bostridge** ten **Stephen Varcoe** bar **Graham Johnson, Chris Gould** pfs **London Schubert Chorale / Stephen Layton**
Hyperion ② CDA67141/2 (134' · DDD) Texts and translations included ⒻⓄ

The two cycles, *Douze rondels* and *Etudes latines*, are linked by a common fascination with the past. The *Douze rondels* were composed to poems in a medieval metre, which allowed Hahn to try his hand at pastiche madrigals and courtly ballads. The *Etudes latines* cast their gaze back still further in time to Classical antiquity. For Hahn, that era seemed to represent the ultimate in purity and sensuality rolled into one. This collection of 10 songs is a real discovery and rivals late Fauré, both in its refinement and mesmerising simplicity of utterance. Apart from a few moments when one would like a more substantial tone, Stephen Varcoe's light baritone suits Hahn very well and he's a refreshingly unaffected interpreter, who sings with grace and feeling. Susan Bickley is better at the larger canvas of a piece like Quand la nuit n'est pas étoilée than the more intimate songs but the most celebrated pair of all Hahn's *mélodies* goes to Dame Felicity Lott, whose sympathy for the French style could have no happier outlet. Both Si mes vers avaient des ailes and L'heure exquise are included here, the latter if not an hour, then at least two and a half minutes that are truly exquisite. They are both beautifully sung and are undisturbed by the discomfort around the top of the stave that sometimes mars Lott's singing elsewhere. At the end, she offers four operetta solos as an encore. Graham Johnson's accompaniments are as sensitive as ever. The piano could have been placed a little closer, but the voices have been well captured.

Haflidi Hallgrímsson   Icelandic b1941

Hallgrímsson studied music in Reykjavik, at the Accademia Santa Cecilia in Rome and the Royal Academy of Music, London. He was subsequently a composition student of Alan Bush and Peter Maxwell Davies. He was Principal Cello with the Scottish Chamber Orchestra until 1983, when he devoted himself to composition. His catalogue of works includes orchestral, instrumental and chamber music.

Passia, Op 28

Mary Nessinger mez **Gardar Thór Cortes** ten

Hallgrímskirkja Motet Choir and Chamber
Orchestra / Hördur Askelsson
Ondine ODE1027-2 (61' · DDD) Text and translation
included   ⓕ◐

Hallgrímsson's music is impressive in its depth
and originality. *Passia*, first performed in 2001,
may be his finest achievement to date. Written
to celebrate the millennium of Christianity in
Iceland, it combines a monumental, timeless
quality with an acute sense of human fragility in
music of deft orchestration and highly effective
vocal writing. Text drawn from a variety of Icelandic sources forms a continuous narrative
which relates to the choruses and arias of the
traditional Passion structure. Moments of blazing light to punctuate the tenebrous journey
travelled by soprano and tenor soloists (Mary
Nessinger and Gardar Thór Cortes are outstanding in these demanding roles), The theme
of the work is one of hope and optimism arrived
at after a tortuous journey, turning around the
combination of physical brutality and divine
mercy of the crucifixion scene. The use of the
orchestra is extremely effective; textures are
essentially spare, thus making the more thickly
scored passages stand out. A notable feature is
the colour provided by the organ, the magnificent instrument of the Hallgrimskirkja in Reykjavik.

An outstanding release, and one that should
help to give Hallgrímsson the prominence he
deserves.

George Frideric Handel

German/British 1685-1759

Handel was the son of a barber-surgeon who
intended him for the law. At first he practised music
clandestinely, but his father was encouraged to allow
him to study and he became a pupil of Zachow, the
principal organist in Halle. When he was 17 he was
appointed organist of the Calvinist Cathedral, but a
year later he left for Hamburg. There he played the
violin and harpsichord in the opera house, where his
Almira was given at the beginning of 1705, soon followed by his Nero. The next year he accepted an invitation to Italy, where he spent more than three years,
in Florence, Rome, Naples and Venice. He had
operas or other dramatic works given in all these
cities (oratorios in Rome, including La resurrezione)
and, writing many Italian cantatas, perfected his
technique in setting Italian words for the human
voice. In Rome he also composed some Latin church
music.

He left Italy early in 1710 and went to Hanover,
where he was appointed Kapellmeister to the elector.
But he at once took leave to take up an invitation to
London, where his opera Rinaldo was produced early
in 1711. Back in Hanover, he applied for a second
leave and returned to London in autumn 1712.
Four more operas followed in 1712-15, with mixed
success; he also wrote music for the church and for
court and was awarded a royal pension. In 1716 he
may have visited Germany (where possibly he set

Brockes's Passion text); it was probably the next year
that he wrote the Water Music to serenade George I
at a river-party on the Thames. In 1717 he entered
the service of the Earl of Carnarvon (soon to be Duke
of Chandos) at Edgware, near London, where he
wrote 11 anthems and two dramatic works, the evergreen Acis and Galatea and Esther, for the modest
band of singers and players retained there.

In 1718-19 a group of noblemen tried to put Italian opera in London on a firmer footing, and
launched a company with royal patronage, the Royal
Academy of Music; Handel, appointed musical director, went to Germany, visiting Dresden and poach-
ing several singers for the Academy, which opened in
April 1720. Handel's Radamisto was the second
opera and it inaugurated a noble series over the ensuing years including Ottone, Giulio Cesare,
Rodelinda, Tamerlano and Admeto. Works by
Bononcini (seen by some as a rival to Handel) and
others were given too, with success at least equal to
Handel's, by a company with some of the finest
singers in Europe, notably the castrato Senesino and
the soprano Cuzzoni. But public support was variable and the financial basis insecure, and in 1728 the
venture collapsed. The previous year Handel, who
had been appointed a composer to the Chapel Royal in
1723, had composed four anthems for the coronation
of George II and had taken British naturalisation.

Opera remained his central interest, and with the
Academy impresario, Heidegger, he hired the King's
Theatre and (after a journey to Italy and Germany
to engage fresh singers) embarked on a five-year
series of seasons starting in late 1729. Success was
mixed. In 1732 Esther was given at a London musical society by friends of Handel's, then by a rival
group in public; Handel prepared to put it on at the
King's Theatre, but the Bishop of London banned a
stage version of a biblical work. He then put on Acis,
also in response to a rival venture. The next summer
he was invited to Oxford and wrote an oratorio,
Athalia, for performance at the Sheldonian Theatre.
Meanwhile, a second opera company ('Opera of the
Nobility', including Senesino) had been set up in
competition with Handel's and the two competed for
audiences over the next four seasons before both
failed. This period drew from Handel, however, such
operas as Orlando and two with ballet, Ariodante
and Alcina, among his finest scores.

During the rest of the 1730s Handel moved
between Italian opera and the English forms, oratorio, ode and the like, unsure of his future commercially and artistically. After a journey to Dublin in
1741-2, where Messiah had its première (in aid of
charities), he put opera behind him and for most of
the remainder of his life gave oratorio performances,
mostly at the new Covent Garden theatre, usually at
or close to the Lent season. The Old Testament provided the basis for most of them (Samson, Belshazzar, Joseph, Joshua, Solomon, for example), but
he sometimes experimented, turning to classical
mythology (Semele, Hercules) or Christian history
(Theodora), with little public success. All these works,
along with such earlier ones as Acis and his two
Cecilian odes (to Dryden words), were performed in
concert form in English. At these performances he
usually played in the interval a concerto on the organ
(a newly invented musical genre) or directed a con-

certo grosso (his Op 6, a set of 12, published in 1740, represents his finest achievement in the form).

During his last decade he gave regular perform-ances of Messiah, usually with about 16 singers and an orchestra of about 40, in aid of the Foundling Hospital. In 1749 he wrote a suite for wind instru-ments (with optional strings) for performance in Green Park to accompany the Royal Fireworks cele-brating the Peace of Aix-la-Chapelle. His last orato-rio, composed as he grew blind, was Jephtha (1752); The Triumph of Time and Truth (1757) is largely composed of earlier material. Handel was very eco-nomical in the re-use of his ideas; at many times in his life he also drew heavily on the music of others (though generally avoiding detection) – such 'bor-rowings' may be of anything from a brief motif to entire movements, sometimes as they stood but more often accommodated to his own style.

Handel died in 1759 and was buried in Westmin-ster Abbey, recognised in England and by many in Germany as the greatest composer of his day. The wide range of expression at his command is shown not only in the operas, with their rich and varied arias, but also in the form he created, the English oratorio, where it is applied to the fates of nations as well as individuals. He had a vivid sense of drama. But above all he had a resource and originality of inven-tion, to be seen in the extraordinary variety of music in the Op 6 concertos, for example, in which melodic beauty, boldness and humour all play a part, that place him and JS Bach as the supreme masters of the Baroque era in music. **GROVE**music

Organ Concertos, Op 4

No 1 in G minor; No 2 in B flat; No 3 in G minor; No 4 in F; No 5 in F; Op 7 – No 1 in B flat; No 2 in A; No 3 in B flat; No 4 in D minor; No 5 in G minor; No 6 in B flat. Harp Concerto in B flat, Op 4 No 6
Paul Nicholson *org* **Frances Kelly** *hp* **The Brandenburg Consort / Roy Goodman** *hpd*
Hyperion ② CDD220952 (154' · DDD)   Ⓜ

This recording was made at St Lawrence Whitchurch on an organ Handel must certainly have played. It sounds well under Paul Nichol-son's hands. There's plenty of brightly glitter-ing passagework and rich diapason sound in such movements as the passacaglia-like first of Op 7 No 1; while the softer side of the instru-ment is particularly appealing in Op 4 No 5, where Nicholson, doubtless conscious that this is a transcription of a recorder sonata, draws from it some very sweet sounds. It has a mechanical action, and here and there the inci-dental noise may be disconcerting. Still, it's authentic, so possibly we should be grateful to have it reproduced. There's some very lively and at times virtuoso playing from Nicholson in the quick movements, with sturdy rhythms, and some of the dance movements go with a good swing too.

Nicholson gives good, precise accounts of the various solo fugues and the transcriptions and improvisatory movements used here when Handel offered merely an *ad lib*. He's a thought-

ful player; his added ornamentation is always musical, intelligent and stylish. However, in several movements overdeliberate orchestral phrasing or accentuation can be damaging; this happens quite often and sometimes affects Nicholson's playing. Op 4 No 6 is played on the harp, with some very delicate timing from Frances Kelly. The bright, clear recording cap-tures happily the acoustic of this moderate-sized church.

Concerti grossi

Op 3, HWV312-17; **Op 6**, HWV319-30

Concerti grossi, Opp 3 & 6   Ⓟ
Vienna Concentus Musicus / Nikolaus Harnoncourt
Teldec ④ 4509-95500-2 (237' · ADD/DDD) Recorded 1982-85   ⒷⓄ

The somewhat perfunctory look of these recou-pled reissues (there are no insert-notes) masks just what extraordinary music-making lies within. These recordings come from a time when even Harnoncourt's supporters were find-ing him a little too eccentric to handle. But lis-tening now to these searching, unceasingly imaginative performances of Handel's finest instrumental music, you can't help feeling that Harnoncourt was simply ahead of his time.

The fact is that there's ferocious creativity in every bar. Every opening slow movement is the prelude to a drama, every fugue a precisely related episode. You can find imposing exam-ples of the former in Op 6 No 5 (its opening solo violin notes are like being tickled under the nose with a feather) or Op 6 No 6 (like the start of some great operatic scena), and stunning demonstrations of the latter in Op 3 No 3 or Op 6 No 1 (both broadly painted but leading to very different types of climax). There's hardly a place where Handel's music is allowed to just play itself; Harnoncourt is everywhere busy with thunderous dynamic contrasts or the sort of vivid articulation that at one moment has us enthralled by a grippingly minimal *staccato*, at another swept up by the warm embrace of a sud-den but grandly *legato* phrase (quite a Harnon-court trademark, this).

The Vienna Concentus Musicus plays for the most part with a virtuosity and precision that's well highlighted by the slightly dry but trans-parent acoustic in which they're recorded. To Harnoncourt this is big music, and these are big performances. There's no denying that they sound eccentric, even now. Not everything works and we'd hesitate to recommend them as one's only encounter with this music. But their consistent and often audacious probing at the music's meaning is a spirit-reviving antidote to what by comparison seems like bland cautious-ness on the part of some of Harnoncourt's rivals.

Concerti grossi, Op 6 Nos 1-5   **P**
Collegium Musicum 90 / Simon Standage vn
Chandos Chaconne CHAN0600 (62' · DDD)   Ⓕ**O**

Concerti grossi, Op 6 Nos 6-9   **P**
Collegium Musicum 90 / Simon Standage vn
Chandos Chaconne CHAN0616 (58' · DDD)   Ⓕ**O**

Concerti grossi – Op 6 Nos 10-12; C, HWV318, **P**
'Alexander's Feast'
Collegium Musicum 90 / Simon Standage vn
Chandos Chaconne CHAN0622 (56' · DDD)   Ⓕ**O**

The first disc of the ever-fresh Op 6 *Concerti grossi* includes the oboe parts that Handel later added to Nos 1, 2, 5 and 6. The performances are brimful of vitality, and the clean articulation and light, predominantly detached style give the music buoyancy and help to bring out Handel's often mischievous twinkle in the eye. Speeds are generally brisk, with boldly vigorous playing, but Standage's team can also spin a tranquil broad line. Dynamics throughout are subtly graded, and except in one final cadence ornamentation is confined to small cadential trills.

On the second disc, except, in the sombre colours in the splendid G minor Concerto (No 6) – here with oboe and the agreeable addition of a theorbo to the continuo – there's a general air of cheerfulness that's most engaging. The fugue in No 7 is wittily buoyant, the *Allegro* in No 9, borrowed from the *Cuckoo and the nightingale* Organ Concerto, could scarcely be more high-spirited, the final Passepied of No 6 and the Hornpipe of No 7 are spring-toed; and Standage's feeling for convincing tempos is nowhere better shown than in the long Musette of No 6, which in other hands can drag. Phrasing everywhere is shapely, and the surprise chords that interrupt the flow of No 8's Allemande are admirably 'placed'.

On the final disc the playing is always on its toes – positively twinkling in dance movements such as the concluding fugal gigue of No 12. The last two concertos, No 11 in particular, give Simon Standage an opportunity to shine as a soloist; his *ad lib* sections are tastefully done, without excesses; his semiquavers in the variants of the A major *Andante* are feather-light. All dynamics are well contrasted in a natural way, and the tempos nicely judged; a slightly faster repeat of the first half of No 10's fifth movement suggests the splicing of a different take. As a fill-up, we're presented with the *Alexander's Feast* concerto grosso, for which the string group is joined by oboes and bassoon. The excellent concertino of two violins and cello is thrown into high relief and the *Allegro* movements are performed with a delightful spring.

12 Concerti grossi, Op 6   **P**
Academy of Ancient Music / Andrew Manze vn
Harmonia Mundi ② HMU90 7228/9 (157' · DDD) Ⓕ**O**

With one stride, Harmonia Mundi has stolen a march on Chandos Chaconne's rival set of Han-

del's Op 6 with Simon Standage's Collegium Musicum 90; by juggling with the order, the 12 concertos have been accommodated on only two CDs. The AAM is on sparkling form, clearly enjoying itself under Andrew Manze's leadership. Performances are invigoratingly alert, splendidly neat (all those semiquaver figurations absolutely precise) and strongly rhythmical but not inflexible, with much dynamic gradation which ensures that phrases are always tonally alive and sound completely natural (even if more subtly nuanced than Handel's players ever dreamt of). Manze's basically light-footed approach is particularly appealing, and he sees to it that inner-part imitations are given their due weight. Speeds are nearly all fast, occasionally questionably so (though exhilarating), as in the first *Allegro* of No 1, the big *Allegro* of No 6 and the *Allegro* in No 9. But Manze successfully brings out the character of all the movements, and the listener can't fail to love the vigorous kick of his No 7 hornpipe. He's mostly sparing in embellishing solo lines except in Nos 6 and 11. Altogether this is an issue of joyous vitality.

Water Music, HWV348-50

Water Music   **P**
Simon Standage, Elizabeth Wilcock vns
The English Concert / Trevor Pinnock hpd
Archiv Produktion Blue 471 723-2ABL (54' · DDD)
Recorded 1983   Ⓜ**OO**

It's unlikely that George I ever witnessed performances that live up to this one. They are sparkling; tempos are well judged and there's a truly majestic sweep to the opening F major French overture; that gets things off to a fine start but what follows is no less compelling with some notably fine woodwind playing, so often the disappointing element in performances on period instruments. In the D major music it's the brass department that steals the show and here, horns and trumpets acquit themselves with distinction. Archiv Produktion has achieved a particularly satisfying sound in which all strands of the orchestral texture can be heard with clarity. In this suite the ceremonial atmosphere comes over particularly well, with resonant brass playing complemented by crisply articulated oboes. The G major pieces are quite different from those in the previous groups, being lighter in texture and more closely dance-orientated. They are among the most engaging in the *Water Music* and especially, perhaps, the two little 'country dances', the boisterous character of which Pinnock captures nicely. Pinnock's is still the best performance of the *Water Music* on the market.

Water Music   **P**
Le Concert des Nations / Jordi Savall
Auvidis Astrée ES9920 (74' · DDD) Recorded 1993   Ⓜ**O**

Of the period-instrument couplings of these

two 'elemental' suites, particularly the *Fireworks Music*, Savall's must be placed at the top of the list. It's strange, however, that though the book-let-notes acknowledge that the *Water Music* falls into 'three suites' and that the Suite in G major was probably played during supper, the recorded performance ends with the one in F major (described as 'Suite II') preceded by the rest ('Suite I') – neither the published nor the 'logical' order. The movements from the earlier Concerto in F aren't included and there's also the familiar retitling and juggling with the order of movements. What splendid performances these are though, spirited, clean-edged and ele-gantly embellished – by a solo trumpet in the *Adagio* of the Overture of the *Fireworks Music*, where the preceding section is repeated as marked. The orchestral force is substantial, and the comparatively high-level recording and generous acoustic give a deliberate sense of being close to the performers – just as, on the Thames, King George I may have been in a barge adjacent to the musicians – rather than of hearing them from the riverside.

Water Music. Music for the Royal Fireworks
Scottish Chamber Orchestra / Nicholas McGegan
Classic fM The Full Works 75605 57044-2 (68' · DDD)
Ⓜ Ⓞ

The only punch that's pulled here to use mod-ern instruments and pitch, but Nicholas Mc-Gegan is too wise and experienced to allow that to count for much. He places Handel's *Water Music* Suites in the order usually accepted as appropriate to a single excursion along the Thames – F major on the outward journey, D major on the way back, and the gentler G major during supper – one that's equally effective in a recording. Identifying the move-ments by their titles provides the usual occupa-tion for a relaxed winter's evening, but no mat-ter – the music is magnificent in whatever order it's played, and by whatever titles it bears. The flanking Suites are recorded in a more spacious acoustic, as befits the postulated outdoor loca-tion of their original performances. The begin-ning and end of the *Music for the Royal Fireworks* are ablaze with the brilliant sounds of the trum-pets and drums that the King loved. Authentic or not, these beautifully balanced performances are most enjoyable.

Water Music. Il pastor fido – Suite, HWV8c   Ⓟ
Tafelmusik / Jeanne Lamon vn
Sony Classical Vivarte SK68257 (76' · DDD)   Ⓕ Ⓞ

The jubilant spirit of the *Water Music* is splen-didly captured here. This Canadian group has a good grasp of Handelian style, and lots of energy; there's plenty of vigour to its playing but no roughness. There are many nicely and unobtrusively managed details of timing and accent, yet always perfectly natural and justified from within. The tempos in the main are on the quick side but not hurried. The flowing *Andante*

for the famous Air, which so readily becomes sticky if done slowly, is particularly likeable; here it sounds just right and no less expressive than usual. Only the D major *Lentement* seems heavy and ponderous, and perhaps the *Bourrée* is also a little clumsily done. The horn playing, recorded well forward, is particularly impressive – clean and clear, with a fine ring; it would have sounded well across the Thames. The move-ments are done here with the F major music first, then the D major and G major mixed, an unusual arrangement these days but one that probably has Handel's authority: and it works well. Tafelmusik gets through the *Water Music* in some 52 minutes, and there's room for a sub-stantial suite of dances from the second version of *Il pastor fido*. These are charming and lively pieces and the final Chaconne, with its inventive textures, is particularly appealing. The sound here is a shade middle- and bottom-heavy, rather more so than in *The Water Music*, but again the playing is splendidly fresh and spir-ited.

Water Music, HWV348-50. Music for the Royal
Fireworks, HWV351
Le Concert Spirituel / Hervé Niquet
Glossa GCD921606 (62' · DDD)   Ⓕ

Hervé Niquet celebrated the 15th anniversary of his group Le Concert Spirituel by assembling a hundred musicians at the Arsenal de Metz to produce what is claimed as 'the first historical recording' of the *Fireworks Music* and *Water Music*. We've had many versions on period instruments but till now only one recording of the *Fireworks Music* has attempted to assemble period instruments in the numbers that Handel is known to have had originally. That's the 1989 version for Hyperion by Robert King with the King's Consort, but he was content with 62 wind, brass and percussion players; Niquet, as in the *Water Music*, adds massed strings too. Sir Charles Mackerras's flamboyant recording of the Fireworks Music using vast wind forces has reappeared on Testament with great success, but that dates from the days of Handel on mod-ern instruments.

Niquet goes further than most of his rivals, not only in assembling these numbers, but in applying early performance techniques. When he reports that the nine horn players 'performed their parts without "correcting" the natural intonation of their instruments', with mean-tone temperament imposed on the whole orchestra, it makes one apprehensive that the results would be painful to the modern ear. Happily this isn't so. The rawness of brass tone is so well controlled that it tickles the ear delightfully.

The massed woodwind players (24 oboes, 15 flutes and recorders, and 14 bassoons) add to the weight and tang of the sound, and though only two percussionists are listed, they're balanced to give maximum impact, with a spectacular tim-pani cadenza in the Overture to the Fireworks

Music. The bass drum and timpani in the 'Gigue' which ends the G major Water Music Suite have similar panache.

The string sections are comparably large, but inevitably on gut strings their playing is less prominent, counterbalanced by such elaborations as the sparkling little cadenza for solo violin that links the 'Prelude' and 'Hornpipe' of the D major Water Music Suite.

As you'd expect, fast speeds predominate, sometimes so fast that they sound breathless: one marvels at the articulation of the wind and brass players in coping. Helped by atmospheric recording, one has a vivid impression of a grand ceremonial celebration. Niquet's is a fine achievement.

Music for the Royal Fireworks, HWV351

Music for the Royal Fireworks, HWV351[d] **P**
Berenice, HWV38 – Overture (arr Whittaker)[a].
Concerti a due cori in F, HWV333 (arr Mackerras)[b].
Concertos[c] – in D, HWV335a; F, HWV331. Water Music, HWV38-50 (arr Harty)[e] – Allegro; Bourrée; Hornpipe; Allegro decisio
[d]Wind Ensemble; [ce]London Symphony Orchestra; Pro Arte Orchestra[b] / Charles Mackerras
Testament SBT1253 (76' · ADD) Recorded [ae]1956, [bd]1959, [c]1977   Ⓕ➍

Over the night of 13-14 April 1959 in St Gabriel's Church, Cricklewood, a recording session took place, historic in every way, when the young Charles Mackerras conducted a band of 62 wind players plus nine percussionists in Handel's *Music for the Royal Fireworks*. With no fewer than 26 oboists topping the ensemble, it was only possible to assemble such a band after all concerts and operas had finished for the day.

They began at 11pm and finished at 2.30 in the morning, yet so far from sounding tired or jaded, the players responded to the unique occasion with a fizzing account of Handel's six movements. The success of this extraordinary project fully justified Mackerras's determination to restore the astonishing array of instruments that Handel himself had assembled for the original performance in Green Park in April 1749.

It's thrilling to hear that 1959 recording, at last transferred to CD, with sound that's still of demonstration quality, full and spacious, with a wide stereo spread. It's true that Mackerras takes the introduction to the overture and the 'Siciliana' at speeds far slower than he would choose today, but this was a recording which marked a breakthrough in what later developed as the period performance movement.

As a coupling for the *Fireworks Music*, Mackerras devised a composite *Concerto a due cori* which draws on two works written with that title around 1747. It makes a splendid piece, in which the massed horns bray gloriously.

Whatever the degree of authenticity, this is an electrifying collection, superbly transferred.

HANDEL FIREWORKS AND WATER MUSIC – IN BRIEF

Le Concert Spirituel / Hervé Niquet
Glossa BDC921606 (62' · DDD)   Ⓕ
This comes closest of all 'authentic' recordings to gathering the forces Handel originally wrote for in both *Water* and *Fireworks*, with massed winds – horns using the natural intonation of their instruments to piquant effect – and some splendid drumming sessions! The sound is rather recessed to cope with the wide dynamic range, but the overall effect is stunning.

Le Concert des Nations / Jordi Savall
Astrée Naive ES99220 (74' · DDD)   Ⓕ➍
Using smaller though still substantial forces, Savall's performances are more refined than Niquet's but still very characterful, with a delightful sense of rhythmic swing, caught in less recessed sound.

London Classical Players / Roger Norrington
Virgin 545265-2 (69' · DDD)   Ⓕ
Neatly articulated, 'cleaner' playing than either Niquet or Savall, though perhaps lacking something of the character they find. Nonetheless the grandeur of the brass in the *Fireworks* is stirring.

Boston Baroque / Martin Pearlman
Telarc CD80594 (73' · DDD)   Ⓕ
Again, not quite at the same level of characterisation as Niquet and Savall, but rhythmically well-sprung performances, taken at generally swift speeds.

Scottish CO / Nicholas McGegan
BMG 75605 57044-2 (69' · DDD)   Ⓜ➍
One to delight those who want the fuller, more rounded sound of modern instruments. Though the orchestra inevitably lacks the grain and 'juiciness' of authentic wind instruments, translucence is maintained by vibratoless string playing, neatly articulated phrasing and lively speeds.

ASMF / Neville Marriner
Decca 414 596-2 (63' · ADD)   Ⓜ
Another good version for those who prefer modern instruments. This 1971 recording is one of Neville Marriner's finest with the ASMF, full of energy and rhythmic vitality which still compares well with the light-footed versions of more recent vintage.

LSO / Charles Mackerras (Fireworks only)
Testament SBT1253 (76' · ADD)   Ⓕ➍
An historic first attempt to gather the forces Handel originally scored the *Fireworks* for, but using modern instruments. Some of the speeds are a touch ponderous by today's standards, but the sound is excellent and the overall effect breathtaking.

Music for the Royal Fireworks. Concertos – F,   ⓟ
HWV331; D, HWV335a. Passacaille, Gigue and
Minuet in G. Occasional Suite in D (both arr Pinnock)
The English Concert / Trevor Pinnock hpd
Archiv Produktion 453 451-2AH (60' · DDD)   ⓕ

Trevor Pinnock uses George II's preferred scoring rather than Handel's – that is, just wind and percussion. What we know about the first performances of the work seems to indicate that Handel had his way and strings were used, along with a massed wind; probably the wind version was never heard in Handel's day. Well, here it is, with 24 oboes, 12 bassoons, double bassoon, nine each of trumpets and horns and six percussion. It's certainly rousing stuff, and a noble noise. With his direct and unaffected rhythm, Pinnock sets up a sturdy momentum for the Overture and the effect is grand and imposing. The dances too receive straightforward performances, with plenty of spirit and energy. This disc offers some welcome rarities. The F major Concerto is made up of versions of two movements from the D major part of the *Water Music*, here in F major; one is the movement generally labelled in the 18th century 'Mr Handel's Water Peice', again, with some interesting and very characteristic differences from the familiar version and the other is the *Alla Hornpipe*. In between Pinnock plays, as a slow movement, an *Adagio* from Op 3 No 5. The D major Concerto consists of what are probably early versions of two movements from the *Fireworks Music* with a version of a movement from a violin sonata, on the organ, in between. The Passacaille, Gigue and Minuet come from a trio sonata and the *Occasional Suite* draws on the *Occasional Oratorio* overture, the *Ariodante* ballet and music composed for *Joshua* and *Alessandro Severo*. It all works pretty well, although some of the music in this last isn't Handel's most distinguished. But the concertos especially are well worth having, and certainly George II's vision of the *Fireworks Music* is to be relished in its way.

Music for the Royal Fireworks   ⓟ
Concerti a due cori – No 1 in B flat, HWV332;
No 2 in F, HWV333; No 3 in F, HWV334
Tafelmusik / Jeanne Lamon vn
Sony Classical Vivarte SK63073 (66' · DDD)   ⓕⓞ

It makes excellent sense to devote a CD to the three *Concerti a due cori* and the *Music for the Royal Fireworks*. Here the *Fireworks Music* is done in the form, with strings as well as wind, that Handel preferred. The less familiar *Concerti a due cori* were composed in the late 1740s for use in the intervals of oratorio performances. They borrow freely from other works – in particular *Messiah* and *Belshazzar* – and some movements seem a little odd in shape because the structure is dictated, in the originals, by the texts; but they're cheerful pieces and make very attractive listening.

These performances are splendidly spirited and enjoyable on every plane. Tafelmusik tends to favour speedy tempos. In the *Fireworks Music* 'La paix' is taken steadily but it's all very nicely judged, and the jauntiness they bring to the main *Allegro* of the overture is particularly likeable, making it a shade more detached than usual. Once or twice there's a stylish lilt, almost a hint of *inégalité*, in the dances.

The band sounds a big one, but the strings are only 5.6.3.3.2, with a fair number of wind – six oboes, three bassoons, four horns and three trumpets, with percussion (their collective intonation is as good as one has any right to expect). In the concertos there's some first-rate wind playing and a fine, earthy ring from the horns. One or two tempos may strike you as quickish; no one would think of singing 'And the glory of the Lord' as fast as Tafelmusik plays Handel's transcription of it, but there's no reason why it shouldn't be done this way.

Orchestral and Ballet Music

Orchestral and Ballet Music from Alcina,   ⓟ
Ariodante, Arminio. Berenice, Rinaldo, Rodelinda
and Serse
Collegium Musicum 90 / Simon Standage vn
Chandos Chaconne CHAN0650 (67' · DDD)   ⓕⓞ

Handel's music is never more winsome than when it's written for special occasions, not least operas. Several of the items in this programme are arias, but they aren't sung. Like today's musicals, though not for calculated commercial reasons, some became what we would now term pops, and Handel reworked them as instrumental pieces, so no liberty has been taken here in presenting them in that form. The charm of this music hasn't escaped the notice of others in recording studios, but it has never been more persuasively captured than it is by Collegium Musicum 90. Other recordings exist of the complete operas and some of the individual instrumental items, but *Arminio* is represented by only one aria; there's nothing run-of-the-mill about the fugal subject of the Overture, or its treatment, and the Minuet is winsome and light of step. Collegium Musicum 90 fields a team of 32 players but their sound is marvellously light and transparent even when in full flood, and their use of period instruments (or copies thereof) leads also to a natural, revelatory balance. Flawless recording and excellent notes by Standage complete an outstanding issue.

Trio Sonatas

Trio Sonatas, Op 2, HWV386-391
Sonnerie (Wilbert Hazelzet fl Monica Huggett, Emilia
Benjamin vns Joseph Crouch vc Matthew Halls hpd)
Avie AV0033 (66' · DDD)   ⓕ

With their boldness of invention, their expressive range and their extraordinary variety of three-part textures, Handel's six Op 2 sonatas represent a peak of the trio sonata as a genre.

Yet for some time there's been no complete recording of the set in the catalogue.

These are polished and sophisticated performances fill the gap admirably. There's much exquisitely turned detail, subtle timing, graceful shaping, and a happy sense of the musical logic. The two violinists play as if they were identical twins. Some listeners may feel these finely modulated performances lack the energy and freshness that ideally belong to the music, but there's a great deal to compensate for that, and you won't often hear this music more attentively, more lovingly played.

Trio Sonatas – Op 2 No 5 in G minor, HWV390; 🅟
Op 5 Nos 4 & 7. Tra le fiamme, HWV170. Notte
placida e cheta, HWV142
Catherine Bott sop **Caroline Kershaw, Jane
Downer** recs/obs **Nigel Amherst** violone **Jonathan
Manson** vc **Purcell Quartet** (Catherine Mackintosh,
Catherine Weiss vns Richard Boothby va da
gamba/vc Robert Woolley hpd)
Chandos Chaconne CHAN0620 (70' · DDD) Texts
and translations included   🅕🅞

The idea of alternating trio sonatas with cantatas is a happy one, based perhaps on the idea that people play CDs for pleasure and not simply for reference. The two cantatas are rarities on record. *Tra le fiamme* is a spectacularly scored piece, its textures enriched by a viola da gamba obbligato and wind instruments (recorders in some numbers, oboes in another) as well as strings. *Notte placida e cheta* is a delightful evocation of night, sleep and amorous reflection, with its opening aria full of sinuous, voluptuous interweaving violin lines and its soft, gently accompanied recitatives; it ends – a slightly rude awakening, perhaps, to chime with the words – with a fugal aria in which the singer takes one of the four contrapuntal parts along with the violins and the bass. Catherine Bott sings them very responsively, both to the words and to the sense of Handel's lines, with neatly placed detail and some attractively floated phrases. The viol obbligato is done in accomplished style by Richard Boothby, who supplies much of the continuo harmony with multiple stops. In the Trio Sonatas there's some splendidly athletic playing from the violins of the Purcell Quartet, which plays with its usual spruce rhythms and conversational give and take. These are probably the most appealing performances currently available of these works.

Violin Sonatas

Violin Sonatas. Andante in A minor, HWV412. 🅟
Allegro in C minor, HWV408
Andrew Manze vn **Richard Egarr** hpd
Harmonia Mundi HMU90 7259
(77' · DDD)   🅕

Uncertainty over the authenticity of the violin sonatas, coupled with the fact that Handel and his publisher were notoriously imprecise about which instruments his various solo sonatas were even intended for, has no doubt prevented many violinists from embracing them as they might in these scholarly times. But there's certainly a good CD's worth of material to be had, even if only five sonatas are thought to be definitely by Handel. Andrew Manze and Richard Egarr offer these, plus three questionable works originally published in one or other of two versions of Handel's Op 1 set of mixed solo sonatas and two authentic one-movement fragments. There isn't an unenjoyable note.

The recording was made immediately after this pair's *Gramophone* Award-winning set of sonatas by Pandolfi (Harmonia Mundi), and it shows them in the same world-beating form. These are performances brimming with vitality and imagination, transforming these sonatas from the polite, even rather staid music you might expect, into grand dramas full of incident, excitement and many little moments that make you sit up and listen. Manze's violin sings with wonderful, glowing tone (he's not afraid to use vibrato to achieve it), to which he adds a joyous assortment of flowery ornaments and emphatic double-stoppings. Egarr's contribution is no less crucial; surely the most inspired continuo improviser around at present, he draws an astounding and mercurial array of colours and textures from his harpsichord. Whatever he does, though, it's never routine. This is a great chamber-music recording, made by a duo who complement each other to perfection.

Flute Sonatas

Flute Sonatas – in E minor, HWV359b; in G, 🅟
HWV363b; in B minor, HWV367b; in A minor,
HWV374; in E minor, HWV375; in B minor, HWV376;
in D, HWV378; in E minor, HWV379
Barthold Kuijken fl **Wieland Kuijken** va da gamba
Robert Kohnen hpd
Accent ACC9180 (73' · DDD) Recorded 1991   🅕🅞

In this recording of solo flute sonatas Barthold Kuijken plays pieces unquestionably by Handel as well as others over which doubt concerning his authorship has been cast in varying degrees. Certainly not all the pieces here were conceived for transverse flute – there are earlier versions of HWV363b and 367b, for example, for oboe and treble recorder, respectively; but we can well imagine that in Handel's day most, if not all, of these delightful sonatas were regarded among instrumentalists as more-or-less common property. Barthold Kuijken, with his eldest brother Wieland and Robert Kohnen, gives graceful and stylish performances. Kuijken is skilful in matters of ornamentation and is often adventurous, though invariably within the bounds of good taste. Dance movements are brisk and sprightly though he's careful to preserve their poise, and phrases are crisply articulated. This is of especial benefit to movements such as the lively *Vivace* of the B minor Sonata

(HWV367*b*) which can proceed rather aimlessly when too *legato* an approach is favoured; and the virtuosity of these players pays off in the *Presto (Furioso)* movement that follows. In short, this is a delightful disc which should please both Handelians and most lovers of Baroque chamber music.

Recorder Sonatas

Sonatas for Recorder and Continuo – G minor,   Ⓟ
HWV360; A minor, HWV362; in C, HWV365; in F,
HWV369; in B flat, HWV377. Sonata for Flute and
Continuo in B minor, HWV367b
Marion Verbruggen *rec/fl* **Jaap ter Linden** *vc*
Ton Koopman *hpd/org*
Harmonia Mundi HMU90 7151 (58' · DDD) Recorded
1994   Ⓕ●

These are lively, intelligent performances. The recorder playing is outstandingly fine, sweet in tone, pointed in articulation, perfectly tuned, technically very fluent, and informed by a good understanding of the art of ornamentation. Marion Verbruggen's real command of Handel's language makes this CD is out of the ordinary. Some of Ton Koopman's accompaniments are a little busy (half are on the organ, half on the harpsichord), but it's all part of the sense of lively music-making that runs through this attractive disc.

Recorder Sonatas – in G minor, HWV360;   Ⓟ
in A minor, HWV362; in C, HWV365; in D minor,
HMW367a; in F, HWV369; in B flat, HWV377.
Keyboard Suite in E, HWV430
Pamela Thorby *rec* **Richard Egarr** *hpd/org*
Linn Records CD/SACD 🔊 CKD223 (74' · DDD)
                                   Ⓕ●

The recorder sonatas included on this disc were composed in the mid-1720s. We can't be sure for whom they were written or when they were performed. Pamela Thorby, regular member of the Palladian Ensemble, claims it's easy to imagine Handel wrote them for members of his opera orchestra to perform during intervals at the King's Theatre. Though this is open to debate, her performances are lively and committed, beautifully recorded at the National Centre for Early Music in York.

She demonstrates versatility and virtuosity beyond question and is imaginatively accompanied by Richard Egarr, who also contributes a sparkling account of the Harpsichord Suite in E major. The recording was made from facsimiles of the autograph manuscripts, and the performances are commensurately vivid and immediate. One feels constantly gripped by the music, as if every single note matters, although you may prefer the gentler and more relaxed performances by Dan Laurin and the Suzukis on BIS.

There's no compulsive need for a cello on the basso continuo part, and on this occasion Thorby and Egarr manage perfectly well without one. Egarr uses a chamber organ on some of

the sonatas, and although it's not historically likely in Handel's chamber sonatas, its musical effect is pleasing, and increases textural variety while removing the threat of monotony across 74 minutes of intense brilliance.

Keyboard Works

Handel Keyboard Suites – in F, HWV427; in D minor,
HWV428; in E, HWV430. Chaconne in G, HWV435
D Scarlatti Keyboard Sonatas – in B minor, Kk27; in
D, Kk29; in E, Kk206; in A, Kk212; in C sharp minor,
Kk247; in D, Kk491; in A, Kk537
Murray Perahia *pf*
Sony Classical SK62785 (69' · DDD)   Ⓕ●●●

 In his projection of line, mass and colour Perahia makes intelligent acknowledgement of the fact that none of this is piano music, but when it comes to communicating the forceful effects and the brilliance and readiness of finger for which these two great player-composers were renowned, inhibitions are thrown to the wind. Good! Nothing a pianist does in the *Harmonious Blacksmith* Variations in Handel's E major Suite, or the Air and Variations of the D minor Suite could surpass in vivacity and cumulative excitement what the expert harpsichordist commands, and you could say the same of Scarlatti's D major Sonata, Kk29; but Perahia is extraordinarily successful in translating these with the daredevil 'edge' they must have. Faster and yet faster! In the Handel (more than in the Scarlatti) his velocity may strike you as overdone; but one can see the sense of it. It's quite big playing throughout, yet not inflated. Admirable is the way the piano is addressed, with the keys touched rather than struck, and a sense conveyed that the music is coming to us through the tips of the fingers rather than the hammers of the instrument. While producing streams of beautifully moulded and inflected sound Perahia is a wizard at making you forget the percussive nature of the apparatus. There are movements in the Handel where the musical qualities are dependent on instrumental sound, or contrasts of sound, which the piano just can't convincingly imitate. And in some of the Scarlatti one might have reservations about Perahia's tendency to idealise, to soften outlines and to make the bite less incisive.

If you can't bear to hear it on anything other than the harpsichord, this record won't be for you. But Perahia is an artist, not just a pianist, and has an experience to offer that's vivid and musically considered at the highest level – not at all second best. The virtuosity is special indeed, and there isn't a note that hasn't been savoured.

Keyboard Suites – in F sharp minor, HWV431;   Ⓟ
in G minor, HWV432; in F minor, HWV433; in B flat,
HWV440; in G, HWV441; in G, HWV442 – Preludio
Sophie Yates *hpd*
Chandos CHAN0688 (71' · DDD)   Ⓕ●

Sophie Yates brings formidable technique and strong dramatic feeling to these suites. The works of the first collection (1720, HWV426-33) are the more demanding, each of them opening with a prelude (or overture) – complex, pensive, often sombre – with a large-scale, fully worked fugue. Yates plays these in an appropriately rhetorical manner, rhythmically taut yet with enough flexibility and attentiveness to the music's caesuras to shape and characterise it, at the same time giving it some sense of the improvisatory. Then she takes the fugues at a lively pace, just a touch too fast for the music to sound comfortable: this is brilliant and exciting playing that keeps you on the edge of your seat.

Her playing, with its thoughtful details of timing, clearly conveys the structure of the music. She finds the same grandeur of manner in the *Passacaille* that ends the G minor Suite. For the rest, it's mainly dance music: some lively *courantes* and exuberant gigues, sober and deliberate allemandes, spacious and noble sarabandes – the crisp and precise fingerwork in that of the B flat Suite in the Second Set (1733), with its intensely detailed line, is a delight.

These are the most appealing versions of Handel's suites: fresh, alive, with a real command of style and technique but also just a hint of risk about the playing. Handel's harpsichord music has sometimes been called dull, but there isn't a moment here when you'd believe that.

Keyboard Suites – in A, HWV426; in G minor, **Ⓟ**
HWV432; in D minor, HWV437. Chaconne in G,
HWV435. Prelude in D minor. The Lady's Banquet –
Sonata in C; Capriccio in F, HWV481; Preludio ed
Allegro in G minor, HWV574; Fantaisie in C, HWV490
Olivier Baumont *hpd*
Erato 0630-14886-2 (63' · DDD)   Ⓕ

A splendid disc, imbued with freshness and vitality. Employing two different instruments – a Flemish harpsichord (1652) by Couchet, a shallower, 'dustier'-toned anonymous Italian instrument of 1677, and a wonderfully rich 1707 French instrument by Dumont – all tuned to a pitch a whole tone lower than that of today, Olivier Baumont presents two of Handel's 1720 'grand suites', the D minor Suite from the 1733 collection, which is seldom heard, the great C major Chaconne (one of Handel's favourites), which is played with every variant repeated, and a handful of very early shorter pieces. Two things in particular are striking about these performances – Baumont's stylishness and spontaneous-sounding skilful free decorations of Handel's text (not only in repeats but, for example, in the minor-key variants of the Chaconne). Definitely a disc to raise the spirits.

Dixit Dominus, HWV232

Dixit Dominus. Laudate pueri Dominum, HWV237
Saeviat tellus, HWV240. Salve regina, HWV241
Annick Massis *sop* **Magdalena Kožená** *mez*
Chœur des Musiciens du Louvre; Les Musiciens du
Louvre / Marc Minkowski
Archiv Produktion 459 627-2AH (78' · DDD) Texts and
translations included   Ⓕ**OO**

These pieces, written in Handel's early twenties, embody a kind of excitement and freedom, and a richness of ideas, that come from his contact with a different tradition and a sudden realisation that the musical world was larger and less constricted than he had imagined, tucked away in provincial middle and north Germany. You can hear him stretching his musical wings in this music. And it certainly doesn't fail to take off in these very lively performances. The quickish tempos habitually favoured by Marc Minkowski are by no means out of place here. The *Saeviat tellus*, although little recorded, is pretty familiar music, as Handel recycled most of it, notably the brilliant opening number in *Apollo e Dafne* and the lovely 'O nox dulcis' in *Agrippina*. This is a solo motet, as too is the *Salve regina*, notable for the expressive vocal leaps and chromatic writing in the 'Ad te clamamus' and the solo organ and string writing in the 'Eia ergo' that follows. *Laudate pueri*, which uses a choir, is another fresh and energetic piece: the choir of the Musiciens du Louvre do their pieces in rousing fashion, and there's some happy oboe playing, as well as fine singing from Kožená, earlier on, in particular in the hugely spirited 'Excelsus super omnes'. The biggest item is the *Dixit Dominus*, where the choir sings very crisply. The illustrative settings of 'ruinas' tumbling down through the registers, and the 'conquassabit' that follows, are truly exciting; and the long closing chorus is done with due weight at quite a measured pace. These splendid performances truly capture the spirit of these marvellous pieces.

Handel Dixit Dominus, HWV232. **Caldara** Crucifixus.
Missa Dolorosa
**Balthasar-Neumann Choir and Ensemble / Thomas
Hengelbrock**
Deutsche Harmonia Mundi CD/SACD ⊛
82876 58792-2 (63' · DDD) Texts and translations
included   Ⓕ**OO**

Handel's *Dixit Dominus*, the magnificent psalm setting composed in Rome in 1707, seems to have an eternal power to startle and delight in equal measure. This performance captures the flamboyant tension and precocious genius that must have struck the 22-year-old's Roman patrons like a thunderbolt. The superb Balthasar-Neumann Choir possess laudable clarity and precision, although the in-house male soloists are less impressive than their rivals for John Eliot Gardiner and Andrew Parrott.

The soprano duet 'De torrente' is ideally hushed and plaintive, but apocalyptic moments such as 'Juravit Dominus' make Thomas Hengelbrock's version comparable with the most striking in the catalogue. The *staccato* chords on 'conquassabit' are delivered with impeccably controlled aggression. The orchestra is magnif-icent, with the contrast between first and second violins presented in thrilling SACD sound. Two theorbo players drive the music along with firm determination and make the opening of the 'Gloria' snap with an energetic bite.

Some of Hengelbrock's most important work has been the championing of Italian Baroque sacred music (especially Lotti). This time it's the turn of Antonio Caldara, a Venetian active in Rome at about the same time as Handel and was subsequently the most popular and prolific composer at the Viennese court of Emperor Charles VI. The *Kyrie* of the *Missa dolorosa*, composed in 1735, instantly establishes that Caldara was infinitely more than a mediocre tal-ent blessed by good fortune, although the feel-ing persists that the Mass was made to fit cir-cumstances rather than to endure for posterity. Its splendid moments range from the graceful bassoon solo in 'Domine Fili' to an abrasively dramatic 'Et resurrexit'. Caldara's reputation is further restored by the gorgeous 16-part *Cruci-fixus* which rounds off this exceptional disc. Highly recommended.

Utrecht Te Deum

Handel Utrecht Te Deum and Jubilate, HWV278-79
Blow I was glad when they said unto me **Boyce** Lord, thou hast been our refuge
Julia Gooding, Sophie Daneman *sops* **Edward Burrowes, Timothy Burtt, Alastair Cook** *trebs* **Robin Blaze, Ashley Stafford** *altos* **Rogers Covey-Crump, Mark Le Brocq** *tens* **Andrew Dale Forbes** *bass* **St Paul's Cathedral Choir; The Parley of Instruments / John Scott**
Hyperion CDA67009 (74' · DDD) Texts included   Ⓕ

Anyone who's tried to listen to music in St Paul's Cathedral might be forgiven for hesitat-ing before buying a recording made there: however, by some magic the Hyperion engi-neers have succeeded in producing a recording that's a model of clear sound, even in the fullest *tutti*s, while capturing something of the cathe-dral ambience. This CD happily celebrates the tercentenary, which fell in 1997, of the official opening of the cathedral, offering three of the finest pieces written for performance there. The Blow anthem was written for the opening event and also to give thanks for the Peace of Ryswick. It's an attractive work, including a countertenor duet, exquisitely done here by Robin Blaze and Ashley Stafford, and a tenor solo sung fluently and with much refined detail by Rogers Covey-Crump, supported by a pair of obbligato trum-pets. The Boyce anthem was written in 1755 for the Festival for the Sons of the Clergy, still held annually at St Paul's; again, there's distin-guished solo singing from Covey-Crump in the expressive 'Yea, like as a father pitieth his own children', and from Blaze in 'The eyes of all wait upon thee'; but perhaps the most appealing number is the trio sung here, in very accom-plished style, by three of the boys. And there are rousing choral Hallelujahs to end with.

However, the main item is Handel's *Te Deum and Jubilate* for the Peace of Utrecht, given at St Paul's in 1713 and Handel's first serious ven-ture into Anglican church music. It's a colourful piece, full of original ideas, and it's done here under John Scott, the incumbent St Paul's organist, with great vitality, breadth, excellent discipline and clear verbal articulation. Sopra-nos are used for the solos here, with Julia Good-ing and Sophie Daneman singing with delicacy, and the other soloists, plus the bass Andrew Dale Forbes, shine again. A disc worthy of its subject.

Chandos Anthems

No 4a, HWV249a, 'O sing unto the Lord'; No 6, HWV251, 'As pants the hart'; No 11, HWV256, 'Let God arise'
Ensemble William Byrd; Académie Sainte-Cécile / Graham O'Reilly
L'Empreinte Digitale ED13072 (57' · DDD) Texts included   Ⓕ Ⓞ

Graham O'Reilly is clearly a fine musician with a keen and true feeling for this music. He uses very small forces, modelled on those Handel is likely to have had available. This produces not only lucid and well-balanced textures but also an intimacy of atmosphere that the more tradi-tional type of choral performances rules out. It also allows O'Reilly to phrase the music sensi-tively. Listen for example to the opening Sonata of *O sing unto the Lord*, with its slightly detached articulation and its gently sprung rhythms, or to the vigorous but poised Sonata beginning *As pants the hart*. The sound in the first chorus here has an almost sensuous quality, with its rich sus-pensions and chromaticisms; and later, in 'Why so full of grief', taken at a nicely measured tempo, the effect is of highly expressive, devo-tional chamber music. In *Let God arise* there's some happy interplay between soprano and oboe in 'Let the righteous be glad', and spirited ensemble singing in the closing items. The recording is beautifully clear.

Odes & Anthems

Coronation Anthems, HWV258-61. Ode for the Birthday of Queen Anne, 'Eternal Source of Light Divine', HWV74
Susan Gritton *sop* **Robin Blaze** *counterten* **Michael George** *bass* **King's College Choir, Cambridge; Academy of Ancient Music / Stephen Cleobury**
EMI 5557140-2 (61' · DDD)   Ⓕ

Recordings of the Coronation Anthems are usually winners – the old Willcocks one from King's, and the Preston from Westminster Abbey certainly were in their day – and this one certainly hits the mark. It's a traditional enough reading, without eccentricities, with plenty of energy and duly grand in scale: listen to the noble opening of *Zadok the Priest*, the introduction beautifully sustained and shaped, and then overwhelmingly grand at the choral entry, whose weight and power may surprise you, bearing in mind the quite modest size of the King's choir. They know just how to manage this kind of music in the chapel acoustic, which is naturally appropriate to the music.

The other three are no less enjoyable. The clear young voices, free of the fuzziness and soft edges of most choirs, help in such movements as the first of 'Let thy hand be strengthened', or the lightly sprung first of 'My heart is inditing' and its vigorous finale too. The *Ode for the Birthday of Queen Anne*, one of Handel's earliest settings of English words is more of a rarity. This is a lively performance, with clear and light solo singing, notably from Robin Blaze. There are also admirable contributions from Susan Gritton and Michael George. Excellent choral singing, and the Academy of Ancient Music are on their toes throughout.

Ode for St Cecilia's Day, HWV76. Cecilia, volgi un sguardo, HWV89
Carolyn Sampson sop **James Gilchrist** ten **Choir of The King's Consort; The King's Consort / Robert King**
Hyperion CDA67463 (78' · DDD) Texts and translations included Ⓕ**OOO**

This completes the series of recordings exploring the smaller works Handel inserted into his glorious setting of Dryden's *Alexander's Feast*. Robert King has previously recorded *The Choice of Hercules*, which was created for the 1751 revival. The tenor cantata *Look down, harmonious Saint* was intended as the interlude for the original run in 1736, but was rejected in favour of *Cecilia, volgi un sguardo*. It's a splendid idea to pair this seldom-heard Italian cantata with Dryden's sublime *Ode for St Cecilia's Day* that Handel created to fulfil the same function three years later.

This is a mouth-watering performance of Handel's colourfully gorgeous ode. 'The trumpets' loud clangour' features Crispian Steele-Perkins on fine form, flautist Rachel Brown enchants in 'The soft complaining flute', and Jonathan Cohen's cello solo in 'What passion cannot Music raise and quell!' is sweetly inspired. The King's Consort and Choir perform with perfect juxtaposition of flamboyance and taste. James Gilchrist sings with authority: he's a Handel tenor of the highest order. This recording is in a class of its own when it comes to the seemingly effortless, beautiful singing of Carolyn Sampson, now the best British early music soprano by quite some distance. She's sensitively partnered by organist Matthew Halls in the sublime 'But oh! what art can teach', which has a breathtaking poignancy. Notwithstanding many agreeable past achievements, King has seldom produced a disc of such outstanding conviction.

L'Allegro, il Penseroso HWV55

L'Allegro, il Penseroso, ed il Moderato ⓟ
Patrizia Kwella, Marie McLaughlin, Jennifer Smith sops **Michael Ginn** treb **Maldwyn Davies, Martyn Hill** tens **Stephen Varcoe** bar **Monteverdi Choir; English Baroque Soloists / Sir John Eliot Gardiner**
Erato ② 2292-45377-2 (116' · ADD) Recorded 1980. Notes, text and translation included Ⓜ**OOO**

The score of *L'Allegro, il Penseroso ed il Moderato* is presented here virtually complete. The soprano aria 'But O, sad virgin' is omitted, which if you look at the marvellous opening for two cellos, seems savage indeed, but the music does rather lose its way in the long decorative passages for both voice and instruments, and its absence need not be regretted. The band is small and so is the superbly alert chorus. Playing and singing constantly delight by their delicacy. The three soprano soloists sound poised and clean cut. Jennifer Smith's high notes are an especial joy. Handel wanted a boy treble for two arias and presumably knew that their words were never very clear; this one produces some pretty sounds. The succession of charming miniatures is interrupted in the middle of Part 2 by more substantial items and a blaze of brilliant coloratura from several soloists. Martyn Hill's 'These delights' is triumphantly good, and the choral singing is excitingly precise. The final chorus in Part 2, a fugue with four subjects, is sublime, but he did not bother himself unduly with the final chorus in Part 3. But in general this is very likeable music, its charm, conciseness and emphasis on word-painting unlike anything else in Handel. The sound quality is very good.

L'Allegro, il penseroso ed il moderato ⓟ
Lorna Anderson, Susan Gritton, Claron McFadden sops **Paul Agnew** ten **Neal Davies** bass **The King's Consort Choir; The King's Consort / Robert King**
Hyperion ② CDA67283/4 (138' · DDD) Text and translation included Ⓕ

This is the first truly complete recording of Handel's delectable pastoral ode. The early numbers of *L'Allegro* – literally 'the cheerful man' – have a spontaneous exuberance barely matched in Handel's output, while much of the music of *Il penseroso* ('The melancholy man') attains a contemplative ecstasy found elsewhere only in parts of *Theodora*. The whole work is suffused with an almost pantheistic sense of wonder and delight in the natural world. While alive to the *al fresco* gaiety of numbers such as 'Mirth, admit me of thy crew' and 'O let the merry bells', Robert King gives full value to the tranquil reflectiveness that lies at the core of the work, favouring broad tempos and gravely expressive phrasing. Occasionally, as in the soprano aria 'Straight mine eye hath caught new pleasures', his approach seems a shade too reverential. But for the most part he directs this glorious music with affection and relish, abetted by vivid orchestral playing and a typically responsive contribution from the chorus.

Susan Gritton is a soprano of rare accomplishment, with a warm, pure, yet highly individual timbre and a wonderful feeling for the broad Handelian line. Both the *scena* 'Come pensive nun' and the romantic nocturne 'Oft on a plat of rising ground', with its haunting evocation of 'the far-off curfew', are intensely moving; and, with the cellist Jane Coe, she makes an eloquent case for the long florid aria 'But O! sad virgin', omitted in the Gardiner recording. Lorna Anderson, if a mite less secure above the stave, brings an appealing plangent tone to the nightingale aria 'Sweet bird' (done complete here, whereas Gardiner makes drastic cuts) and a trancelike absorption to the sublime 'Hide me from Day's garish eye'. Some slightly odd vowel sounds apart, Claron McFadden's bright, eager tones and nimble coloratura serve the more extrovert arias well; Neal Davies is sturdy in his bucolic hunting number and mellifluous in his minuet aria in *Il moderato*; and Paul Agnew is personable and stylish, though his *legato* is rather shown up by Susan Gritton's in 'As steals the morn'.

Acis and Galatea, HWV49b

Acis and Galatea, HWV49b   P
Sophie Daneman sop Galatea **Paul Agnew** ten Acis
Patricia Petibon *sop* Damon **Alan Ewing** bass
Polyphemus **Joseph Cornwell** ten Coridon **François
Piolino, David Le Monnier, Andrew Sinclair** tens
Les Arts Florissants / William Christie
Erato ② 3984-25505-2 93' · DDD) Texts included
                                                        Ⓕ**OOO**

Christie has elected to give a 'chamber version' of the work, that is, with forces akin to those Handel used for his original Cannons performances: probably five singers and between seven and a dozen instrumentalists. He doesn't, however, follow the original Cannons text, but adds a choral 'Happy we' after the duet, and assigns the role of Damon to a soprano: these changes aren't without Handelian authority, but it comes from his 1739 revival, which embodied other departures and used much larger forces. Never mind: there's nothing that any modern conductor would do that's half as shocking as the violences that Handel himself did to *Acis* on some of its revivals.

Christie strongly emphasises the work's central division. He adopts rather speedy tempos throughout Act 1 (that is, up to 'Happy we'), which is concerned with pastoral love: Acis's 'Where shall I seek' and Damon's 'Shepherd, what art thou pursuing?' don't seem, respectively, like Larghetto and Andante, but the urgency and the joy of the lovers' mutual desire is strongly caught. In Act 2, where Polyphemus's shadow falls over their love, the sparkle and vitality give way to the pathetic and the elegiac. Christie's tempos here are steady, and his shaping of the act seems something of a departure: its climaxes here come not in 'The flocks

shall leave the mountains' (when Acis is killed) and 'Heart, the seat of soft delight' (when he's immortalised as a river) – arguably the most powerful musical numbers – but in the ensembles, 'Mourn, all ye Muses!' and 'Must I my Acis still bemoan', where the sustained, gentle singing of Christie's ensemble lends the music an emotional weight that it does not usually achieve. There are other, mostly smaller, points where Christie does new and different things, and some will not like them all. Christie's orchestra is one-to-a-part, as Handel's may have been: this seems to produce a slightly oboe-heavy balance in some items, and in the lightly scored pieces the continuo line seems overweighted.

The opening scenes, then, are done more lustily, in two senses, than usual. The choral opening is remarkably hearty and robust. Sophie Daneman sings Galatea with something more than stylised pastoral sensuality: there's real intensity in her airs, with a pretty warbling recorder, very chirrupy, and sharply moulded phrasing, and particular sensuality in 'As when the dove'. If her 'Heart, the seat', at the end, seems to carry rather less emotional weight, that's part of the overall reading of the work. Paul Agnew makes an elegant Acis in Act 1, with an eager 'Where shall I seek' and 'Love in her eyes sits playing' done with quiet passion. 'Love sounds th'alarm', later, is lively but not quite stirring. Patricia Petibon's Damon is prettily sung, with a nice ring to the voice, and Alan Ewing's Polyphemus, done with spirit and humour in a well-focused, firm-edged voice and articulated with precision, is excellent.

Gardiner's 1976 version long held the field in this work, and to some extent still does, although Robert King's smaller-scale reading has many virtues, too. Christie's new version may not be everyone's answer, but it's a polished and strongly characterised performance, and is certainly the first we would urge anyone to try.

Alexander Balus, HWV65

Alexander Balus   P
Lynne Dawson, Claron McFadden sops **Catherine
Denley** mez **Charles Daniels** ten **Michael George**
bass **New College Choir, Oxford; The King's
Consort and Choir / Robert King**
Hyperion @ CDA67241/2 (156' · DDD) Notes and
text included   Ⓕ

Alexander Balus has never been one of Handel's more popular oratorios. That's mainly because its plot is by modern standards lacking in drama and motivation, and accordingly doesn't call forth the vein of his music that nowadays has the strongest appeal. It's essentially a sentimental drama, in which the interest centres on the characters' emotional reactions to their situations, amatory, political and religious, and these are rather static in the first two acts but much more powerful in the more eventful third with the deaths of both Alexander and Ptolomee.

Here we have a very capable, idiomatic, sensibly cast performance under Robert King. The choruses are especially accomplished. The New College Choir, supported by men from The King's Consort Choir, is confident, bright-toned and vigorous, clean in line and well balanced. Lynne Dawson sings beautifully in her firm and resonant soprano and her usual poised and unaffected style. Her singing of the lamenting music in the final act is particularly moving. Cleopatra has a couple of duets, one with some attractive interplay with the secondary character Aspasia, sung with much assurance by Claron McFadden. As Alexander, Catherine Denley sings with much confidence and directness in music that isn't all of special individuality. Jonathan is sung fluently and warmly, but very plainly, by Charles Daniels. Lastly there's Michael George, who's ideally suited to the villainous Ptolomee, with his forceful (but always musical) manner and the touch of blackness in his tone. The orchestral playing is accomplished, and often rather carefully shaped. The recitative moves at a steady but natural pace; ornamentation is generally modest. All Handelians will want to acquire this set, and others should not be put off by the indifferent press *Alexander Balus* has received from time to time.

Athalia, HWV52

Athalia   Ⓟ
Joan Sutherland sop Athalia **Emma Kirkby** sop
Josabeth **Aled Jones** treb Joas **James Bowman**
counterten Joad **Anthony Rolfe Johnson** ten
Mathan **David Thomas** bass Abner **New College
Choir, Oxford; Academy of Ancient Music /
Christopher Hogwood**
Decca Gramophone Awards Collection ② 475 207-2
(122' · DDD) Recorded 1985. Notes and text
included   Ⓜ**ⓄⓄⓄ**

Athalia, composed for Oxford in 1733 to a libretto that draws on Racine's play, tells of the usurping, apostate Jewish queen Athalia, and her overthrow when the prophet Joad and his wife Josabeth bring the true heir, the boy Joas, to the throne. The action is feebly handled by the librettist, Samuel Humphreys; but several of the characters are quite strong and Handel grasps the opportunities offered him for striking music.

Athalia fares best of all, musically, as one would expect; and it was a brilliant stroke of imagination to ask Joan Sutherland to take the role here. She's a great Handelian, but not a figure you expect to see in early-music circles. In the event, the slight disparity of approach between her and the other members of the cast serves ideally to symbolise the separation of Athalia from her fellow-Israelites. She uses more vibrato than the rest of the cast, but the singing is magnificent in its grandeur and its clear, bell-like, perfectly focused tone. Among the rest, Emma Kirkby is on her very best form, singing coolly, with poised musicianship, and with quite astonishing technical command at

times. James Bowman, as Joad, has his moments, and always sounds well. David Thomas is dependable in the often very vigorous music for Abner; and as Athalia's priest, Mathan, Anthony Rolfe Johnson sings in shapely fashion. The boy Joas is sung, as it should be, by a boy, in this case Aled Jones, who gives a very controlled, exact performance, perhaps rather careful but of intense tonal beauty. At its best, the choral singing is first-rate, spirited, forthright and accurate, but it can have an air of the routine. There's much good, crisp orchestral playing, though some of the AAM's less positive characteristics are evident: an occasional moment of unsure ensemble, and a lack of broad shaping. These are however perfectionist quibbles: these discs, excellently recorded, give an admirable and often striking realisation of a choice work.

Israel in Egypt, HWV54

Israel in Egypt   Ⓟ
Nancy Argenta, Emily Van Evera sops Timothy
Wilson counterten **Anthony Rolfe Johnson** ten
David Thomas, Jeremy White basses **Taverner
Choir and Players / Andrew Parrott**
Virgin Classics Veritas ② 562155-2 (135' · DDD)
Recorded 1989. Text included   Ⓑ

Israel in Egypt, of all Handel's works, is the choral one *par excellence* – so much so, in fact, that it was something of a failure in Handel's own time because solo singing was much preferred to choral by the audiences. Andrew Parrott gives a complete performance of the work, in its original form: that's to say, prefaced by the noble funeral anthem for Queen Caroline, as adapted by Handel to serve as a song of mourning by the captive Israelites. This first part is predominantly slow, grave music, powerfully elegiac; the Taverner Choir shows itself to be firm and clean of line, well focused and strongly sustained. The chorus has its chance to be more energetic in the second part, with the famous and vivid Plague choruses – in which the orchestra too plays its part in the pictorial effects, with the fiddles illustrating in turn frogs, flies and hailstones. And last, in the third part, there's a generous supply of the stirring C major music in which Handel has the Israelites give their thanks to God, in some degree symbolising the English giving thanks for the Hanoverian monarchy and the Protestant succession. Be that as it may, the effect is splendid. The solo work is first-rate, too, with Nancy Argenta radiant in Miriam's music in the final scene and distinguished contributions from David Thomas and Anthony Rolfe Johnson.

Jephtha, HWV70

Jephtha   Ⓟ
Lynne Dawson, Ruth Holton sops **Anne Sofie von
Otter** mez **Michael Chance** counterten **Nigel**

Robson ten Stephen Varcoe bar Alastair Ross hpd
Paul Nicholson org Monteverdi Choir; English
Baroque Soloists / Sir John Eliot Gardiner
Philips ③ 422 351-2PH3 (158' · DDD) Recorded live
1988. Text included   Ⓕ●○○

Jephtha has the same basic story as several eastern Mediterranean myths familiar to the opera-goer (in *Idomeneo* and *Iphigénie en Aulide*, for example), of the father compelled to sacrifice his child. In the event Jephtha's daughter Iphis isn't sacrificed: when, Abraham-like, her father has shown himself willing to perform God's will, and she has shown herself ready to accept it, an angel happily intervenes and commutes her sentence to perpetual virginity. But not before the tragic situation has provoked some of the noblest music Handel wrote. From the moment that Jephtha sees that it's his daughter who has to fall victim to his improvident oath, the music, hitherto on a good but not outstanding level, acquires a new depth, above all in the sequence at the end of Act 2. This recording does the work full justice. It could scarcely have been better cast. Nigel Robson seems ideal as Jephtha. He has due weight as well as vigour, style as well as expressive force. Lynne Dawson's Iphis is also a real success. Sometimes this role is done in a girlishly 'innocent' vein; she does more than that, establishing the character in the appealing love duet in Part 1. Her firm, well-focused, unaffected singing is just right for this role.

The other outstanding contribution comes from Michael Chance as Hamor, her unfortunate betrothed. Stephen Varcoe sings Zebul's music with due resonance and spirit, and Anne Sofie von Otter makes a distinguished contribution in Storgè's music: 'Scenes of horror' has a splendid attack and depth of tone, and 'Let other creatures die!' is spat out with rare power. Ruth Holton makes a pleasantly warm and mellifluous angel. The Monteverdi Choir is in fine voice, responsive to all that Gardiner asks of them. Here and there one might cavil at some of the dynamic shaping in the choruses, for example in 'Doubtful fear' in Act 3; and the Overture can be a trifle fussy in detail. But the broad vision of the work, the rhythmic energy that runs through it and the sheer excellence of the choral and orchestral contributions speak for themselves. Cuts are very few, and amply justified by authentic precedent. This recording is firmly recommended as the standard version of this great work.

Joseph and his Brethren, HWV59

Joseph and his Brethren   Ⓟ
Yvonne Kenny sop Catherine Denley mez Connor
Burrowes treb James Bowman counterten John
Mark Ainsley ten Michael George bass
New College Choir, Oxford; The King's Consort
Choir; The King's Consort / Robert King
Hyperion ③ CDA67171/3 (164' · DDD) Text
included   Ⓕ

There's never been a complete, professional recording of *Joseph and his Brethren*, a neglect out of proportion to the merits of its music. It's full of good and characteristic things, and there are several scenes, including the extended denouement in the last act, that are very moving. The work begins splendidly, with an unusual overture heralding a deeply felt opening scene for Joseph, languishing in an Egyptian prison. The setting of his prophecy is effective, with seven bars of darting arpeggios for the years of plenty and seven of sparse harmonic writing, *adagio*, for the famine years. The rest of Act 1 celebrates Joseph's foresight, preferment and marriage to Asenath, Pharaoh's daughter. The highlights of Act 2 include a prison scene for Simeon, an agonised G minor accompanied recitative and aria, a beautiful, nostalgic idyll for Joseph, and scenes for Joseph with his brothers which incorporate a splendid outburst from Simeon, an aria from Benjamin and a moving chorus from the brothers, a sustained prayer and a richly worked fugue.

The soloists dispatch all this music with spirit and accuracy. James Bowman is in excellent voice in the title-role, full, rich and duly agile in the rapid music. *Joseph* is well suited to Robert King's way of conducting Handel. This isn't a specially dramatic performance, but carefully moulded and intelligently paced. The choir produces a sound that's bright and firm and the singing is resolute. King is particularly good at shaping the dynamics in a natural and unanimous way.

Messiah, HWV56

Messiah   Ⓟ
Arleen Auger sop Anne Sofie von Otter mez
Michael Chance counterten Howard Crook ten
John Tomlinson bass The Choir of the English
Concert; The English Concert / Trevor Pinnock
Archiv Produktion ② 423 630-2AH2 (150' · DDD)
Recorded 1988. Text included   Ⓕ●○

How authentic is authentic? Trevor Pinnock and The English Concert, while using period instruments, are guaranteed to appeal very widely to traditional lovers of Handel's masterpiece, who might as a rule opt for a performance with modern instruments. Pinnock gets the best of both worlds. A distinctive point is that, even more than his rivals, he brings out the impact of timpani and trumpets, above all in the 'Hallelujah' and 'Amen' choruses. There he stirs the blood in a way that even Sargent would have envied. Another point is that a genuine, dark, firm, bass soloist has been chosen, John Tomlinson, who's ripely resonant here. Traditionalists who lament the lack of dark bass tone and the predominance of baritonal shades in Handel today will doubtless raise a cheer, and if it comes to authenticity, Handel must surely have been thinking of just such a voice, rather than anything thinner or more discreet. Not only Tomlinson but Arleen Auger too will delight listeners of all Handelian persuasions. She has one of the sweetest, most ravishing soprano sounds on any of the current versions, and the warmth of expressiveness, whether strictly authentic or not, brings many of the most memorable moments in the whole performance. Try the close of 'I know that my Redeemer liveth', where the dramatic contrasts of dynamic are extreme and masterfully controlled, without a hint of sentimentality. The male alto, Michael Chance, also outshines his direct rivals in artistry and beauty of tone, but he's given only a proportion of the alto numbers. The majority are given to Anne Sofie von Otter. Hers is another beautiful voice, finely controlled. The recording is one of the finest available, with plenty of bloom and with inner clarity never making textures sound thin or overanalytical.

Messiah   **H**
Dame Isobel Baillie sop **Gladys Ripley** contr **James Johnston** ten **Norman Walker** bass **Huddersfield Choral Society; Royal Liverpool Philharmonic Orchestra / Sir Malcolm Sargent**
Dutton Laboratories Essential Archive mono
② 2CDEA5010 (146' · ADD) Recorded 1946   ⓑ●

From the 1940s until the early 1960s one of the greatest of regular British musical events (every bit as important as the Proms) was Malcolm Sargent's *Messiah*. He conducted it up and down the country, always to packed houses; indeed, to be able to attend the performance at Huddersfield Town Hall, you needed very special connections, for tickets were scarcer than an invitation to Buckingham Palace! Sargent usually omitted – as he does here – three numbers from Part 2 and four from Part 4. Even then, the performance time was two and a half hours without the interval. Apart from spacious tempos, He had his own ideas about Handelian style. Today we usually listen to a quite different kind of *Messiah*: brisker, often exchanging grandeur for exhilaration; so it's heart-warming to have the opportunity to return to a great tradition that Sargent kept alive for so many years.

This is made possible by one of Dutton Laboratories' most miraculous 78rpm transfers – the finest ever heard taken from 78s of any music – of Sargent's extraordinarily vivid and expansive recording (the most spontaneous of the three he made). The four splendid soloists – that queen of oratorio sopranos, Dame Isobel Baillie; the rich-voiced Gladys Ripley; the warmly lyrical James Johnson; and the vibrant Norman Walker – are right inside their parts. But the star of the performance is undoubtedly Isobel Baillie. Her first entry in 'There were shepherds' is a truly ravishing moment, while her gloriously beautiful 'I know that my Redeemer liveth' has never been surpassed on record. Sargent opens the work with a sumptuous presentation of the Overture, while his tempos for the choruses now sound very slow to ears used to 'authenticity'. He believed deeply in this music and he carried the listener with him. The hushed close of

HANDEL'S MESSIAH – IN BRIEF

English Concert and Choir / Trevor Pinnock
Archiv ② 423 630-2AH2 (150' · DDD)   Ⓕ●●
Grace and liveliness are the characteristics of Pinnock's fine performance that uses instruments Handel would have recognised, though, arguably, a smaller choir than he would have ideally wanted. Arleen Auger is outstanding in the aria 'I know that my redeemer liveth'.

Gabrieli Consort & Players / Paul McCreesh
Archiv ② 453 464-2AH2 (130' · DDD)   Ⓕ●●
McCreesh favours drama above gracefulness, often to striking effect, though his chorus often sound slick rather than engaged with their text. However, he has a number of fine soloists, with Susan Gritton memorably touching in her two big arias.

London Sym Chorus & Orch / Sir Colin Davis
Philips ② 438 365-2PM2 (144' · ADD)   Ⓜ
This 1966 *Messiah*, once thought to be a fresh reinterpretation of a very British institution, ironically became the 'traditional' *Messiah* many of us knew before the rise of such conductors as Pinnock and Norrington. Colin Davis's intelligent direction, using modern orchestral forces, has moments of high drama, and he has a sterling line up of soloists.

Collegium Musicum 90 / Richard Hickox
Chandos ② CHAN0522/3 (141' · DDD)   Ⓕ
Although using authentic instruments, this is another fine performance in the post-Colin Davis tradition, with an excellent line-up of soloists (including the young Bryn Terfel) and excellent choral singing.

Boston Baroque / Martin Pearlman
Telarc ② CD80322 (132' · DDD)   Ⓕ
A fleet performance of *Messiah*, with a well-disciplined choir able to make light work of 'His Yoke is Easy'! The soloists give committed interpretations, though their degree of ornamentation may be excessive for some tastes.

Bach Collegium Japan / Masaaki Suzuki
BIS ② BIS-CD891/2 (140' · DDD)   Ⓕ
An attempt to re-create forces used in a specific performance directed by Handel. The results are clean, transparent textures and well-sprung rhythms with alert, committed choral singing.

Huddersfield Choral Society; Liverpool PO / Malcolm Sargent
Dutton mono ② 2CDEA5010 (146' · ADD)   ⓑ●
For a generation of British listeners Sir Malcolm Sargent owned *Messiah*; here his 1946 recording has been lovingly cleaned up for the digital age.

'All we like sheep' almost brings tears to the eyes. The sound itself is truly astounding. At bargain price it's an ideal investment for anyone who relishes an old-fashioned, large-scale approach to Handel's *Messiah*.

The Occasional Oratorio, HWV62

The Occasional Oratorio
Susan Gritton, Lisa Milne *sops* **James Bowman** ▣
counterten **John Mark Ainsley** *ten* **Michael George**
bass **New College Choir, Oxford; The King's**
Consort / Robert King
Hyperion ② CDA66961/2 (144' · DDD) Recorded
1994. Text included   Ⓕ

The occasion that called forth this work was the Jacobite rising of 1745 and its impending defeat. The Duke of Cumberland's victory at Culloden was yet to come. Handel, anticipating it, hit off the mood of the moment with a rousing piece full of appeals to patriotic feeling, partly through the traditional identification between the English Protestant culture of Hanoverian times with that of the biblical Hebrews. Much of the music comes from existing works, notably *Israel in Egypt*. The 'plot' pursues the familiar route of Anxiety-Prayer-Victory-Jubilation, but the work lacks the unity of theme and purpose of the great dramatic oratorios; if, however, you value Handel primarily because the music is so splendid you'll find a lot to relish here. King rises to the challenge of this sturdier side of Handel's muse and produces playing and singing full of punch and energy, and with that command of the broad Handelian paragraph without which the music lacks its proper stature.

The grand eight-part choruses, with the choir properly spaced, antiphonally, over the stereo span, make their due effect. King has a distinguished solo team. John Mark Ainsley's singing is particularly touching in the highly original 'Jehovah is my shield', where the rocking figures in the orchestra eventually turn out to symbolise sleep. Also very enjoyable is Susan Gritton's soprano, a sharply focused voice with a fine ring and due agility in the lively music and handled with taste and a keen feeling for the shape of phrases in the contemplative airs. A fine set.

Saul, HWV53

Saul
Nancy Argenta, Susan Gritton, Susan Hemington
Jones *sops* **Andreas Scholl** *counterten* **Paul Agnew,**
Mark Padmore, Tom Phillips, Angus Smith *tens*
Julian Clarkson, Neal Davies, Jonathan Lemalu
basses
Gabrieli Consort and Players / Paul McCreesh
Archiv Produktion ③ 474 510-2AH3 (166' · DDD) Text
and translation included   ⒻO

The special strengths of Paul McCreesh's performance lie in the drama and the urgency he brings to the work, the keen sense of character he imparts to the music, the vigorous pacing that carries the action forward with the inevitability of a Greek tragedy. But *Saul* is a tragic work, and there's sometimes a want of the necessary gravitas. Nevertheless, this is a gripping and very inspiriting performance. The precision and flexibility of the Gabrieli Consort is a constant delight; the voices are fresh and bright, the words well articulated. The Gabrieli Players, too, produce a fine and distinctive period orchestral timbre. Andreas Scholl makes an ideal David, with sweetness and unusual depth of tone, exceptional precision of rhythm and perfectly clear words: if you try 'O Lord, whose mercies' you will buy this set. Enjoyable, too, is Nancy Argenta's natural, delicately phrased singing of Micah's music, and Susan Gritton's telling portrayal of Saul's elder daughter, Merab. Saul himself, sometimes fiery, nearly always agonised, is effectively drawn by Neal Davies; and Mark Padmore's warm and gently graceful tenor is ideal for Jonathan's music.

There's no shortage of good recordings of this work. Gardiner's weighty version holds the field, but this version presents a serious challenge; the lightness and clarity, the livelier drama and the solo singing of Scholl in particular tell in favour of McCreesh.

Solomon, HWV67

Solomon   ▣
Andreas Scholl *counterten* **Inger Dam-Jensen,**
Susan Gritton, Alison Hagley *sops* **Susan Bickley**
mez **Paul Agnew** *ten* **Peter Harvey** *bass* **Gabrieli**
Consort and Players / Paul McCreesh
Archiv Produktion ③ 459 688-2AH3
(161' · DDD) Notes and text included   ⒻOO

Solomon is universally recognised as one of Handel's finest masterpieces, not only with magnificent choruses, but more importantly containing rapturous love music, nature imagery, affecting emotion and the vividly portrayed dramatic scene of Solomon's famous judgement over the disputed infant. This is in fact the only dramatic part of the oratorio; and each of the female characters appears in only one of the work's three parts. Paul McCreesh, responsive to the work's stature, employs an orchestra of about 60 (including a serpent as the bass of the wind group) and presents the oratorio in the original 1749 version, full and uncut.

It's been argued that even in so splendid a work Handel was fallible enough to include some dead wood. McCreesh, however, stoutly defends the original structural balance. In one respect, though, he does depart from Handel's intentions. By the time *Solomon* was written, he was using no castratos in his oratorios, and the title-role was deliberately designed for a mezzo-soprano; but here the chance to secure the pre-eminent countertenor Andreas Scholl was irresistible. The colour of Handel's predominantly female vocal casting (only Zadok and the smaller-part Levite being exceptions) is thus slightly modified. This historical infidelity is one of the few possible reservations about the set, which is a notable achievement. McCreesh is fortunate in his cast, too. Predictably, Scholl becomes the central focus by his beauty of voice, calm authority, charm and intelligent musicianship. Inger Dam-Jensen, as Solomon's queen, sounds suitably ecstatic in the florid 'Blessed the day' and amorous in 'With thee th'unsheltered moor', and her duet with Solomon flows with easy grace. To Susan Gritton falls the sublime 'Will the sun forget to streak', with its wonderful unison oboe-and-flute obbligato. As the high priest Zadok, Paul Agnew shines in the ornate 'See the tall palm'. A more positive and audible keyboard continuo would have been welcome, but this is a minor shortcoming, and the effect of the performance as a whole is deeply impressive, with such things as 'Will the sun', the grave interlude to 'With pious heart' and the elegiac chorus 'Draw the tear from hopeless love' haunting the listener's mind.

Theodora, HWV68

Theodora   P
Susan Gritton sop **Susan Bickley** mez **Robin Blaze** counterten **Paul Agnew, Angus Smith** tens **Neal Davies** bass **Gabrieli Consort and Players / Paul McCreesh**
Archiv Produktion ③ 469 061-2AH3 (184' · DDD) Text and translation included   ⓕ○○○

Theodora, Handel's penultimate oratorio, was a failure in his own time. Until relatively recently it remained a rarity, but lately has come to be recognised as a masterpiece, although quite different in mood and treatment from most of his more familiar oratorios. This recording encourages attentive listening to its subtleties, because it's done with such affection, care and refinement. There's nothing sensational about it, no singer who overwhelms you with brilliance or virtuosity. But all the solo music is finely sung. Theodora herself is taken by Susan Gritton, who's won golden opinions recently, and will win more here for a great deal of lovely, clear and musicianly singing, with a quiet seriousness and unaffected intensity that are ideally suited to the role. Her presence at the centre of the tragic drama elevates it as a whole.

Irene, her fellow Christian, is sung with scarcely less distinction by Susan Bickley, coolly expressive in most of her music, more passionate in 'Defend her Heaven' in Act 2, a shapely performance with subtleties of timing. Didymus, originally a castrato role (very rare in oratorios), is sung by Robin Blaze, whose focused, even-toned countertenor – not a hint of the traditional hoot – serves well: this is fluent singing, with no great depth of tone, but very steady and controlled, with the detail precisely placed. As Septimius, Paul Agnew is in good voice, firm and full in tone, phrasing the music elegantly (although the Act 3 air is unconvincing, too

bouncy and cheerful for the situation). Lastly, there's Neal Davies as the Roman ruler, Valens, whose excellent singing makes as persuasive a case as can be imagined for torturing Christians – his is a pleasantly grainy voice, with considerable warmth and fullness of tone, well suited to a figure representing authority, and he despatches the divisions with assurance.

Ornamentation is appropriate and tasteful, and McCreesh takes the recitative at a natural and relaxed pace. His main contribution, however, is in the well-sprung rhythms he draws from his Gabrieli singers and players, in the way he allows the lines to breathe, and in the sense of purpose and direction he imparts to the bass line. Add to this a keen sense of the right pace for each number, and you've the recipe for an outstanding reading of this noble work.

Theodora
Sophie Daneman sop Theodora **Juliette Galstian** mez Irene **Daniel Taylor** counterten Dydimus **Richard Croft** ten Septimus **Nathan Berg** bar Valens **Laurent Slaars** bar Messenger **Les Arts Florissants / William Christie**
Erato ③ 0927 43181-2 (178' · DDD) Notes, libretto and translation included   ⓕ○

Theodora is reputed to have been Handel's favourite of his own works, and we seem to have come around to sharing his high opinion. In 1996 William Christie conducted an Peter Sellars' intense production at Glyndebourne; since then Handelians have awaited his seminal interpretation on disc, despite admirable versions by Paul McCreesh and Peter Neumann.

The eventual release of this recording is vindicated by a magnificent and deeply satisfying performance. Sophie Daneman strikes a perfect blend of virtue and vulnerability as Theodora. Daniel Taylor is ideal as the devoted Didymus, and there's a tangible sense of poetry in his sensitive performance. The sole survivor from the Glyndebourne cast is Richard Croft, whose portrayal of the Roman soldier Septimius undergoing a crisis of faith is his finest achievement on disc yet. Christie's management of speeds, theatrical pacing, and melodic phrasing is almost perfect: a brisk dance-like treatment of animated music is thoughtfully balanced elsewhere by patient sustained expression. His conducting brings out orchestral subtleties and varied emotions in Handel's score that previous recordings have failed to sufficiently explore, and evidently understands that Handel's greatness as an artist is rooted in his humanity. This is an exceptional recording.

Il trionfo del Tempo ..., HWV46a

Il trionfo del Tempo e del Disinganno   P
Deborah York, Gemma Bertagnolli sops
Sara Mingardo contr **Nicholas Sears** ten Concerto Italiano / **Rinaldo Alessandrini** org
Opus 111 ② OPS30-321/2 (133' · DDD)   ⓕ

Il trionfo del Tempo e del Disinganno, of 1707, was Handel's first oratorio; in its third and final incarnation 50 years later it was to be his last. It has all the hallmarks of the finest music of his Italian years – tremendous verve, originality of invention, freshness. It calls for four soloists, representing Beauty, Pleasure, Time and Truth. This is the work in which Handel in effect invented the organ concerto, with the 'Sonata' in Part 1, seemingly the first piece for solo organ and orchestra. The Handelian will find it, *Hamlet*-like, full of quotations; in it Handel drew on some of the music of his German years, and it served in turn as a quarry for many later works, including *Agrippina* and *Rinaldo*.

This new version is done with prodigious energy and rather rapid tempos. The young Italianate Handel can readily take these fast tempos, generally speaking, but here and there the music would have profited from being allowed more time to unfold. But the rhythms do have plenty of spring and vitality, and the players, and the singers too, usually cope. The star is undoubtedly Deborah York, as Beauty, whose bright, diamantine tone and incisive articulation, not to mention her agility serve well. The other soloists are just as fine. This is certainly the most dramatic of the three versions of *Il trionfo* in the catalogue. Dazzlingly played and sung, it comes highly recommended.

Cantatas

Aci, Galatea e Polifemo, HWV72   P
Sandrine Piau *sop* **Sara Mingardo** *contr* **Laurent Naouri** *bar* **Le Concert d'Astrée / Emmanuelle Haïm** *hpd*
Virgin Classics ② 545580-2 (99' · DDD) Text and translation included   FOO

The cantata or serenata *a 3* (for three), *Aci, Galatea e Polifemo*, dates from Handel's visit to Naples in 1708, and it has almost nothing in common, except for its subject matter, with his exquisite English pastoral, *Acis and Galatea* for the Duke of Chandos's house at Cannons of 1718. As with so many of his Italian compositions, Handel used this enchanting creation of his youth as a sort of melody bank, lifting whole arias for insertion into his subsequent operas, so even if there are Handelians new to this work some of the music won't be entirely unfamiliar.

Aci, cast originally, one presumes, with a high soprano castrato, has two sublime arias, 'Qui l'augel da pianta in pianta' and his dying lament, 'Verso già l'alma col sangue' ('My soul pours out with my blood'). Both belong to Handel's most ravishing early inspirations, the first a simile aria in which the soprano voice 'competes' with birdsong supplied by oboe and violin solos, the second a wonderfully evocative representation of the dying hero's throbbing heart and intense anguish. This is top-flight stuff, and Aci's music is superbly sung by Sandrine Piau with her brilliant, steely yet still sweet soprano, used with quasi-instrumental technical accomplishment.

Even though Galatea's music, written for a contralto, is less interesting, the Arcadian nymph is cast with the best singer here, the wonderful Sara Mingardo, one of the truly sublime Handelians of our time, who brings a dark sensuality to her love music and a heartbreaking outpouring of grief in the recative following Aci's death. Haïm's spirited and imaginative direction, her singers and a pristine modern recording weigh the balance in favour of this set.

No se emenderá jamás, HWV140. Tra le fiamme, P
HWV170. Alcina – Sì; son quella!; Tornami a vagheggiar; Mi restano le lagrime. Giulio Cesare – V'adoro, pupille; Che sento? Oh Dio!; Se pietà di me non senti; Da tempeste il legno infranto. Rinaldo – Lascia ch'io pianga
María Bayo *sop* **Capriccio Stravagante / Skip Sempé**
Astrée Naïve E8674 (64' · DDD) Texts and translations included   FOO

Bayo starts with an aria that's always a sure winner, Cleopatra's celebration in *Giulio Cesare* of her brother's defeat and her amorous conquest of Caesar: 'Da tempeste' is sung with tremendous vivacity, precise articulation and beautifully clean pitching. In 'V'adoro, pupille', from much earlier in the same opera, she's gently seductive, conveying just a hint of sensual languor, singing on a chamber-music scale with a delicately colourful accompaniment from Capriccio Stravagante. In 'Se pietà', one of the more tragic utterances, at a dark moment in the opera, she's not over-intense, but the tone is richer, the lines expressively shaped. The performance of the cantata *Tra le fiamme* is notable for the brilliance and accuracy of Bayo's duetting in the opening aria with the obbligato viola da gamba. She sings 'Lascia ch'io pianga' with a refined line, but perhaps more vibrato than one might wish, and there's some gently alluring ornamentation in the *da capo*. As a Spaniard, she naturally includes Handel's little Spanish cantata, *No se emenderá jamás*, a light piece with guitar accompaniment, which is delicately done. Of the arias from *Alcina*, Morgana's 'Tornami a vagheggiar' is a delight for its high spirits and Bayo's easy, natural mode of delivery. 'Mi restano le lagrime', where Alcina faces her downfall, is done with pathos and poignancy – and again in the *da capo* her ornamentation allows for heightening of the expression.

Armida abbandonata, HWV105. Agrippina condotta P
a morire, HWV110. La Lucrezia, HWV32
Véronique Gens *sop* **François Fernandez, Mira Glodeanu** *vns* **Les Basses Réunies** (Bruno Cocset *vc* Pascal Monteilhet *theorbo* Blandine Rannou *hpd* Richard Myron *db*)
Virgin Classics Veritas 545283-2 (53' · DDD) Texts and translations included   FO

Composed during Handel's youthful years in Italy, these cantatas contain some of the boldest music he ever wrote, and certainly among the most passionate. They aren't set to the pastoral, amorous texts that were widely favoured: two of them deal with tragic episodes in Roman history (the rape of Lucretia and the condemnation to death of Agrippina by her son Nero), the other, after Tasso, with the betrayal of Armida.

These performances by Véronique Gens amply capture this passionate character. She brings to them a full, warm, large voice, not entirely without hints of vibrato, but handled with real feeling for style; she uses the words and their sound effectively, phrases expressively and sometimes subtly, varies her colour a good deal, and brings particular emotional energy to the recitatives. *Lucrezia* draws some remarkably intense singing from her, in the highly chromatic F minor aria and in the lament-like 'Alla salma infedel'. In this lament, the main continuo accompaniment is assigned to the theorbo, which emphasises the intimate tone of the music. The violin playing in *Armida* is particularly enjoyable – brilliant in the *furioso* recitative, stylish and sweet-toned in 'Venti, fermate'. They play with admirable spirit and rhythmic spring in the lively second aria of *Agrippina*, too, where again Gens sings commandingly, impassioned in the first aria ('Orrida, oscura'), with lightness in the second and then with much intensity in the beautiful 'Come, o Dio!' and also in the concluding recitatives. Les Basses Réunies supplies excellent continuo support. In all, highly impressive performances of some superlative music.

Apollo e Dafne, 'La terra e liberata', HWV122. **P**
Crudel tiranno amor, HWV97
Nancy Argenta sop **Michael George** bass
Collegium Musicum 90 / Simon Standage
Chandos Chaconne CHAN0583 (58' · DDD)
Recorded 1994. Texts and translations included ⓕ

Handel's *Apollo e Dafne* is a difficult work to put in context. Completed in Hanover in 1710 but possibly begun in Italy, its purpose isn't clear, while, as secular cantatas go, it's long (40 minutes) and ambitiously scored for two soloists and an orchestra of strings, oboes, flute, bassoon and continuo. But this isn't just a chunk of operatic experimentation: it sets its own, faster pace than the leisurely unfolding of a full-length Baroque stage-work, yet its simple Ovidian episode, in which Apollo's pursuit of the nymph Dafne results in her transformation into a tree, is drawn with all the subtlety and skill of the instinctive dramatic genius that Handel was.

This recording features the expert Handelian voices of Nancy Argenta and Michael George, and both convey their roles convincingly. Argenta's hard, clear tone seems just the thing for the nymph, who isn't required to be especially alluring but who does have to sound quick to anger and (literally) untouchable; and George strikes the right note as Apollo, bragging loudly at the opening of his superior skill in archery to Cupid before succumbing more gen-

tly, and in the end extremely touchingly, to Cupid's arts. The orchestra is bright and efficient, and the pacing of the work seems just right. This is superb Handel then, and, as if that were not enough, there's a bonus in the form of a shorter cantata for soprano and strings, *Crudel tiranno amor*. It's a beautiful piece indeed, and Argenta performs it perfectly.

German Arias

Handel German Arias, HWV202-10[a] **Telemann** **P**
Musique de table – 'Paris' Quartets: G, E minor
[a]**Dorothea Röschmann** sop **Academy for Ancient Music, Berlin**
Harmonia Mundi HMC90 1689 (79' · DDD) Texts and translations included ⓕⓞⓞ

Handel's nine *German Arias* aren't as well known nor as often recorded as they deserve, perhaps because, being devotional music, they're generally rather solemnly, even earnestly performed. Dorothea Röschmann sings them delightfully. There's no lack of seriousness, or intensity, where it's called for. The instrumental support is highly polished, but arguably too varied in colour: what's the justification for switching bass instruments for an aria's middle section? The obbligato part is shared between violin, flute and oboe: the oboe seems to be a mistake in the high part of 'Meine Seele', with a rather squealy effect – although Röschmann's exuberance at 'Alles jauchzet, alles lacht' ('all rejoice, all laugh') is happy. The Telemann 'Paris' quartets set off the arias well. Some of the playing in the E minor work is a little sober, but the lively G major is done in lively and elegant fashion, with spruce rhythms. But Röschmann's Handel is the real joy: listen to 'Die ihr aus dunklen Grüften' and you won't be able to resist it.

Oratorio & Opera Arias

Belshazzar – Destructive War; Oh sacred oracles of truth. **Jephtha** – Dull delay, in piercing anguish; Up the dreadful steep ascending. **Messiah** – He was despised. **Saul** – O Lord, whose mercies; Brave Jonathan. **Semele** – Despair no more shall wound me; Your tuneful voice. **Theodora** – The raptur'd soul; Deeds of kindness; Kind Heav'n; Sweet Rose and Lilly
David Daniels counterten **Paris Orchestral Ensemble / John Nelson**
Virgin Classics 545497-2 (67' · DDD) Notes and texts included ⓕⓞ

The world's leading 'operatic' countertenor has sung on precious few of the abundant complete Handel recordings of the last decade so this selection of oratorio arias fills some of the gaps in the Daniels discography.

The American was to have sung Didymus in Paul McCreesh's Archiv recording of *Theodora* – the role of his Glyndebourne début in Peter

Sellars's controversial 1995 staging – but he was unable to fit the preceding concerts into his burgeoning international schedule and was replaced by Robin Blaze. Not surprisingly, he includes four of Didymus's arias in his oratorio album, and rejoices in the wonderful music Handel composed for the young Italian castrato, Gaetano Guadagni. The sensuous colours of Daniels' falsetto are ideal in this music, which he sings with beguiling erotic ambiguity.

The same goes for David's ravishing 'O Lord, whose mercies numberless' – a prayer whose yearning melismata suggest passions more earthly than godly – from *Saul*. There's little cause for complaint, except perhaps about the use of the modern instrument Ensemble Orchestral de Paris rather than a period band, but at least John Nelson's conducting – particularly in the fast-moving numbers – is livelier than on his complete *L'allegro*. In excellent sound, this glorious disc comes highly recommended.

Acis and Galatea – I rage, I melt, I burn!...O ruddier than the cherry. **Alcina** – Verdi prati, selve amene. **Alexander's Feast** – Revenge, revenge, Timotheus cries...Behold a ghastly band. **Berenice** – Si, tra i ceppi e le ritorte. **Giulio Cesare** – Va tacito e nascosto. **Judas Maccabaeus** – I feel the Deity within ... Arm, arm, ye brave!. **Messiah** – Thus saith the Lord...But who may abide?; Why do the nations?; Behold I tell you a mystery...The trumpet shall sound. **Orlando** – O voi del mio poter...Sorge infausta una procella. **Samson** – Honour and arms scorn such a foe. **Semele** – Where'er you walk. **Serse** – Fronde tenere...Ombra mai fù. **Te Deum in D, 'Dettingen'** – Vouchsafe, O Lord
Bryn Terfel bass-bar **Scottish Chamber Orchestra / Sir Charles Mackerras**
DG 453 480-2GH (73' · DDD) Texts and translations included   Ⓕ

'I feel', sings Terfel with assurance in his voice matching the solemnly, expectantly, ceremonious opening bars; and then, the second time, 'I feel', but now with the awed conviction of one who has experienced 'the Deity within'. The adjustment, the change of expression, is small, and no doubt when described sounds obvious enough; but it's typical of the imaginative intelligence Terfel brings. And what of his singing, his voice production, his care for *legato*? As to the latter, conflict always lurks as expressive emphasis, shading and verbal naturalism assert their rights in the face of pure beauty and the evenness of the singing line. Terfel is one in whom the rival claims work their way to a compromise, though if one side has to win it will generally be the expressive element. A good example of the compromise is the second track, the 'Vouchsafe, O Lord', quietly and simply sung, preserving the movement's unity and yet with a power of feeling that, at 'let thy mercy lighten upon us', is as overtly emotional as an operatic aria.

The adapted arias, 'Where'er you walk',

'Verdi prati' and 'Ombra mai fù', justify their inclusion readily enough, and it's good to hear Terfel in the solos from *Messiah*. The singing here incorporates a good deal of embellishment, some of it of Mackerras's devising. He's excellent, sharing with Terfel an appreciation of the zest in Handel. The recording is vivid and clean.

Ariodante – E vivo ancora … Scherza infida in   Ⓟ
grembo al drudo. **Giulio Cesare** – Cara speme, questo core; Va tacito e nascosto; L'angue offeso mai riposa; Al lampo dell'armi; Dall' ondoso periglio...Aure, deh, per pietà. **Rinaldo** – Cara sposa; Venti, turbini, prestate. **Rodelinda** – Pompe vane di morte!...Dove sei?; Vivi tiranno!. **Serse** – Fronde tenere...Ombra mai fù. **Tamerlano** – A dispetto
David Daniels *counterten* **Orchestra of the Age of Enlightenment / Sir Roger Norrington**
Virgin Classics Veritas 545326-2 (69' · DDD) Texts and translations included   Ⓕ**OO**

The ever-increasing popularity of Handel and his contemporaries, and their employment of alto castratos, has encouraged the development of countertenors capable of similar vocal feats to the original interpreters of the heroic roles in these works. Among these David Daniels can certainly be counted as a leading contender. He displays and deploys his talent here in a wide range of arias reflective and dramatic. His amazing technique runs through Tamerlano's virtuoso 'A dispetto' and Bertarido's 'Vivi tiranno!' without a blemish in the sound and with every division in its place yet part of a confidently delivered whole: by and large Daniels's runs and embellishments are smoothly accomplished. In more reflective pieces such as Giulio Cesare's 'Aure, deh, per pietà' (he also tackles Sesto's 'Cara speme' from *Giulio Cesare*, a particularly liquid, subtle piece of singing), Bertarido's 'Dove sei?' and Ariodante's sad lament, 'Scherza infida', written for the great Senesino, he uses his impeccable Italian to express wide-ranging emotions. Throughout, Roger Norrington and the Orchestra of the Age of Enlightenment give excellent support. The recording is blameless so there's every reason for readers to sample this fine exposition of the countertenor's art.

Alcina – Mi lusinga il dolce affetto; Verdi prati,   Ⓟ
selve amene; Stà nell'Ircana. **Ariodante** – E vivo ancora?... Scherza infida; Dopa notte. **Giulio Cesare** – Va tacito e nascosto; Se in fiorito ameno prato; Piangerò, la sorte mia; Dall' ondoso periglio...Aure, deh, per pietà. **Serse** – Fronde tenere e belle...Ombra mai fù; Se bramate d'amar, chi vi sdegna; Crude furie degl'orrido abissi
Ann Murray *mez* **Orchestra of the Age of Enlightenment / Sir Charles Mackerras**
Forlane UCD16738 (75' · DDD) Recorded 1994. Texts and translations included   Ⓕ

The cautious tread of the watchful huntsman, with the lovely dialogue of voice and basset horn in Caesar's first aria, makes a delightful start to this recital. The arias here range from the simple ease and beneficence of 'Verdi prati' to the florid outburst of the frustrated Xerxes in 'Crude furie'. In between are Cleopatra's lament, Caesar's love song, Ariodante's sadness and his new-found joy. Handel and Mackerras have long been associated, and with the Orchestra of the Age of Enlightenment he provides the singer with a stylish accompaniment that's never assertive or doctrinaire but scrupulous in its care for phrasing and texture. Ann Murray responds with singing which has not only her customary expressiveness and energy but also a generally well-preserved beauty of tone. Occasionally a harsher, less firmly placed tone threatens to emerge, as at the start and *da capo* of 'Stà nell' Ircana', but such moments are short-lived and instead she encourages a mellower, warmer sound which also has the advantage of being precise in its focus. The voice is quite closely recorded.

Alessandro – Brilla nell' alma un non inteso ancor **Amadigi di Gaula** – Ah spietato **Arianna in Creta** – Son qual stanco **Deidamia** – M'hai resa infelice **Faramondo** – Combattuta da due venti **Giulio Cesare** – Che sento? oh Dio!; Se pietà di me non senti **Orlando** – Verdi piante, erbette liete **Partenope** – L'amor ed il destin **Rodelinda** – Ombre, piante **Scipione** – Scoglio d'immota fronte **Tamerlano** – Cor di padre
Sandrine Piau sop **Les Talens Lyriques / Christophe Rousset**
Naïve E8894 (67' · DDD · T/t)   Ⓕ**ⓞⓞⓞ**

Sandrine Piau and Christophe Rousset have been consistently stylish and perceptive Handelians together. Their musical flair and dramatic intelligence is marvellously captured here, and they have chosen arias that explore the full range of Handel's genius.

The experience starts with the spectacular 'Scoglio d'immota fronte', and the subsequent sequence weaves through wonderful contrasts. It's hard to capture the full dramatic sense and vivid personality of Handel's opera characters in a studio recital, yet they hit the bullseye every time, bringing out Cleopatra's despair, Rodelinda's eloquent grief for her apparently deceased husband, the heartbroken sorceress Melissa in *Amadigi di Gaula*, Deidamia's distress at losing Achilles to the Trojan war, and Partenope's gorgeous charisma.

Although some *da capo* sections stray a little too far from Handel's notation for the comfort of scholars, they all enhance the drama of the text, and each cadenza, showing panache and taste, is a breath of fresh air. The playing of Les Talens Lyriques is a model of clarity, vitality and theatrical wit. It was an inspired decision to close the recital with the sublime understatement of 'Son qual stanco', featuring a heartbreaking cello solo by Atsushi Sakaï.

Rousset and Piau achieve the perfect synthesis

of elegance, extravagance and emotion. This is may be the finest recital of Handel arias ever recorded.

Heroes and Heroines
Alcina – Act 3, Sinfonia; Sta nell'Ircana; Mi lusingha il dolce affetto; Entrée des songes agréables; Verdi prati **Ariodante** – Act 2, Sinfonia; Scherza infida; Dopo notte **Hercules** – Act 2, Sinfonia; Cease, ruler of the day; Where shall I fly **Solomon** – Arrival of the Queen of Sheba; Will the sun forget to streak
Sarah Connolly mez **The Symphony of Harmony and Invention / Harry Christophers**
Coro COR16025 (65' · DDD)   Ⓕ

Sarah Connolly is an exemplary Handel singer. Her recital is dominated by two roles she's performed at ENO, with arias from *Alcina* and *Ariodante*. 'Scherza infida' is an addictive mixture of vocal elegance and poignant desolation, and 'Mi lusingha' is sung with a beautiful simplicity that lacks for nothing in drama or passion. In contrast, the extravagant coloratura in 'Dopo notte' and the robust 'Sta nell'Ircana' capture the virtuoso thrills of heroic joy. In Dejanira's 'Where shall I fly?', she reminds us that taste and subtlety have an important place even in Handel's tormented and emotionally unstable creation. She avoids contrived intensity and allows the quality of the vocal writing to speak for itself.

Harry Christophers' direction is judicious, supportive yet never intrusive. It's pleasant to hear performances that are musically sensible, dramatically sensitive, and brave enough to apply understatement.

Overture in D, HWV337/338. **Giulio Cesare** – Caro! Bella!; Overture; Da tempeste il legno infranto[ab]. **Rinaldo** – Sinfonia, Act 1; Scherzano sul tuo volto[ab]; Cara Sposa[b]; Lascia ch'io pianga[a]. **Rodelinda** – Ombre, piante[a]; Io t'abbraccio[ab]. **Serse** – Ombra mai fù[b]. Tolomeo – Se il cor ti perde[ab]
[a]**Suzie LeBlanc** sop [b]**Daniel Taylor** counterten **Arion / Stephen Stubbs**
ATMA Classique ACD2 2260 (57' · DDD) Texts and translations included   Ⓕ

This disc is outstandingly well performed, partly through the contribution of Stephen Stubbs, better known as lutenist than conductor, whose beautifully sprung rhythms and sensitive orchestral phrasing animate the whole. The singing is no less distinguished. Suzie LeBlanc's reading of such an old favourite as 'Lascia ch'io pianga' brings it freshly to life, with her unaffected expression, her shapely phrasing and beauty of tone. In the *Rodelinda* aria her moulding of the music again adds to the poignancy of the climactic top notes, while the semiquavers are bright, precise and duly jubilant in Cleopatra's triumphal final aria from *Giulio Cesare*.

Daniel Taylor gives a moving account of 'Cara sposa', sweet and clear of tone and with some telling *messa di voce*, and he excels, too, in the purity of his expression of 'Ombra mai fù'.

And when they sing together the pleasure is more than doubled – both have admirable clarity of articulation, and they know how to make the most of the expressive content, as, for example, in their handling of the dissonances on 'amara' ('bitter') in the *Tolomeo* duet, or their quite modest but tasteful ornamentation in the *da capo* sections where often they echo each other. Listen, too, to their moving account of the elegiac duet in *Rodelinda*.

Alessandro – Overture; Sinfonia; Che vidi?; No, più soffrir; Placa l'alma; Solitudine amate … Aure, fonti; Pur troppo veggio…Che tirannia d'Amor; Svanisci, oh reo timore…Dica il falso. **Admeto** – Il ritratto d'Admeto; La sorte mia vacilla; Quest'è dunque la fede…Vedrò fra poco. **Riccardo Primo** – Morte vieni…A me nel mio rossere … Quando non vede. **Siroe** – A costei, che dirò?; L'aura non sempre; Si diversi sembianti…Non vi piacque, ingiusti dei. **Tolomeo** – E dove, e dove mai … Fonti amiche; Ti pentirai, crudel
Catherine Bott, Emma Kirkby sops **Brandenburg Consort / Roy Goodman**
Hyperion CDA66950 (76' · DDD) Texts and translations included   Ⓕ**OO**

It was a happy idea to assemble a selection of Handel's arias written for the two sopranos whose famous rivalry coloured the last years of the first Royal Academy. Francesca Cuzzoni – impersonated here by Catherine Bott – was Handel's principal soprano from 1723, creating among other roles Cleopatra and Rodelinda. Faustina Bordoni – her roles here go to Emma Kirkby – arrived in 1726 and the two sang together in several operas including five new ones by Handel, all represented on this recording. Both were superlative singers and each had a characteristic style.

In his music composed for them, Handel clearly differentiated between their capacities, as this disc illustrates. The 'rival queens' first sang together in *Alessandro*, which is the opera most fully represented here. There are two of Cuzzoni's arias, one brilliant piece with rapid divisions, which Bott throws off in splendidly free fashion, and a pathetic one, a typical F minor *siciliano*, taken very slowly here, allowing plenty of time for some expressive elaboration in the *da capo*. Of Faustina's music we have the exquisite *scena* that opens Act 2, including the aria, 'Aure, fonti', and the lively one with which the act closes. The aria typifies, in the way it demands and rewards precisely detailed singing, Handel's writing for her, and Kirkby's refinement of detail is remarkable. There's beautifully managed interplay between the singers in the *Alessandro* duet; they seem to feed one another with opportunities.

The programme is imaginatively put together and Goodman is a prompt and stylish accompanist. A thoroughly enjoyable disc.

Admeto – Alma mia, dolce ristoro **Atalanta** – Amarilli?; Amarilli? Oh Dei! che vuoi? **Faramondo** – Del destin non mi lagno; Caro, tu m'accendi **Flavio** – Ricordati, mio ben **Muzio Scevola** – Vivo senz'alma, o bella **Orlando** – Finché prendi **Poro** – Caro amico amplesso!; Perfidi! Ite di Poro a ricercar nel campo; Se mai più sarò geloso; Se mai turbo il tuo riposo; Act 3, Sinfonia; Lode agli Dei!; Se mai turbo il tuo riposo **Rinaldo** – Scherzano sul tuo volto **Rodelinda** – Non ti bastò, consorte; Io t'abbraccio **Serse** – Gran pena e gelosia! **Sosarme** – Per le porte del tormento **Teseo** – Addio, mio caro bene **Silla** – Mio diletto, che pensi?; Sol per te, bell'idol mio
Patrizia Ciofi sop **Joyce Di Donato** mez **Il Complesso Barocco / Alan Curtis** hpd
Virgin Classics 545628-2 (74' · DDD) Texts and translations included   Ⓕ**OOO**

GThe duets in his operas are the special treats, coming at climactic points – most often, two lovers' supposedly final parting, or their ultimate reunion. Try 'Io t'abbraccio', from *Rodelinda*, or the wonderful 'Per la porte del tormento' from *Sosarme*. We have several pieces from *Poro*, first the intense little love duet in Act 2, and later the two arias in which Poro and Cleofide swear eternal fidelity – which they fling back at each other when, in a duet we also hear, both believe themselves betrayed. Then there's the delightful little minor-key duet from *Faramondo*, the quarrel duet from *Atalanta*, the charmingly playful piece from *Muzio Scevola*, and the extraordinary one for the pleading Angelica and the furious, maddened Orlando. Handel's understanding of the shades and accents of love are something to marvel at.

All are most beautifully sung by Patrizia Ciofi and Joyce DiDonato, who has just the right firmness and focus for a castrato role (as the mezzo voices almost always are here); both phrase beautifully, articulate and express the words clearly and tellingly, and ornament the *da capo* sections in a natural and tasteful fashion. The accompaniments, done by a chamber group under Alan Curtis with much refined timing of detail, add to the pleasures of this truly delectable CD.

Admeto, HWV22

Admeto, Re di Tessaglia   Ⓟ
René Jacobs counterten Admeto **Rachel Yakar** sop Alceste **Ulrik Cold** bass Ercole, Apollo **Rita Dams** mez Orindo **James Bowman** counterten Trasimede **Jill Gomez** sop Antigona **Max van Egmond** bar Meraspe, A Voice **Il Complesso Barocco / Alan Curtis**
Virgin Classics Veritas ③ 561369-2 (217' · ADD) Recorded 1979. Notes, text and translation included   Ⓕ

Admeto is full of fine things, particularly in its music for the two women – Alceste, the nobly self-sacrificing wife of King Admetus, and Antigona, the princess he'd once wooed but then rejected, who now returns after the supposed death of Alceste. The plot, then, is akin to Gluck's *Alceste*, but with an extra subplot that allows for touches of wit and irony and insights into human character. When it was first released, the recording was something of a pioneer in the use of period instruments and performing conventions. Things have moved on, of course: it seems a bit dated now, heavier in manner than most Handel opera recordings of recent years. And some of the cast aren't wholly at home in a Baroque style where little vibrato is wanted. One thinks in particular of Rachel Yakar, but although her articulation and attack aren't always ideally clean she does bring a good deal of spirit to some of the arias. Jill Gomez's lighter, bell-like voice is more convincingly Handelian: she sings Antigona's music charmingly and with due agility, and expressively too in the beautiful Act 2 *siciliana*. James Bowman is in his best voice as Trasimede, Admetus's brother who loves Antigona. René Jacobs, however, lacks the heroic tones and the incisiveness that the role demands. Ulrik Cold makes a strong Ercole, with appropriately sturdy, masculine tone, and Meraspe is neatly and very stylishly sung by Max van Egmond. Alan Curtis's direction is attentive to matters of style, but he sometimes lets the bass-line plod. Even so, Handelians needn't hesitate.

Alcina, HWV34

Alcina   P
Renée Fleming sop Alcina **Natalie Dessay** sop
Morgana **Kathleen Kuhlmann** mez Bradamante
Susan Graham mez Ruggiero **Juanita Lascarro** sop
Oberto **Timothy Robinson** ten Oronte **Laurent
Naouri** bass Melisso **Les Arts Florissants / William
Christie**
Erato ③ 8573-80233-2 (191' · DDD) Notes, text and
translation included   Ⓕ●

Alcina, musically and dramatically, is among the finest of Handel's operas. This performance shows the typical Christie touch: polished and sweet-toned playing, well-judged balance, care for detail. No doubt it's a consequence of performing in a large house (the Palais Garnier, Paris) that tempos are on the slower side of average, generally speaking, although there's no lack of fire in the big virtuoso pieces. The orchestral playing, with a good-sized band, is always warm and shapely, from the sparkling overture onwards – where Christie takes the Un *peu lentement* of the musette quite literally. The opera is given virtually complete, following the Chrysander score; the only ballet music included (besides the dances in the overture) are the *entrée* and *tamburino* in the final scene.

There have been some magnificent Alcinas in the past, headed by the two on record, Dame Joan Sutherland and Arleen Auger. Renée Fleming is in the same class. Less conscious a stylist, perhaps, than Auger, less obviously brilliant than Sutherland, she sings with great intensity. Her performance of this marvellous

role is of a very high order. There are others to match. Susan Graham, in the *primo uomo* role of Ruggiero, has some of the opera's finest music, and brings to it a firm, full mezzo, clear and agile. The famous 'Verdi prati', her poignant farewell to the enchantments of Alcina's realm, is very simply and beautifully sung, with no ornamentation at all, and the result amply justifies it. Kathleen Kuhlmann sings Bradamante with great vigour and resource, the semiquaver runs done with absolute precision, the tone rich and warm with an attractive gleam. Natalie Dessay brings her full and warm soprano to Morgana's music, and a touch of the coquettish where called for.

The orchestra is less aggressively 'period' in tone than some. But the opera is done with the spirit and passion that its superb music calls for, and can be recommended without hesitation as the finest to be had.

Ariodante, HWV33

Ariodante   P
Anne Sofie von Otter mez Ariodante **Lynne
Dawson** sop Ginevra **Veronica Cangemi** sop
Dalinda **Ewa Podles** mez Polinesso **Richard Croft**
ten Lurcanio **Denis Sedov** bass King of Scotland **Luc
Coadou** ten Odoardo **Choeur des Musiciens du
Louvre; Les Musiciens du Louvre / Marc
Minkowski**
Archiv Produktion ③ 457 271-2AH3 (178' · DDD) Text
and translation included   Ⓕ●

Lynne Dawson is the star of this show. In Act 2, where Ginevra finds herself inexplicably rejected and condemned by everyone, Dawson brings real depth of tone and feeling to her E minor lament, 'Il mio crudel martoro'; in the final act she shines in the desolate miniature 'Io ti bacio' and brings much fire to the outburst 'Sì, morro'. But she never transgresses the canons of Baroque style. Von Otter, too, has much marvellous music – the aria 'Scherza infida' is one of Handel's greatest expressions of grief – and she sings it beautifully, but she isn't really at one with his idiom and seems to lack a natural feeling for the amplitude of Handel's lines.

Yet there's much to enjoy here too, the beauty of the actual sound, the immaculate control, the many telling and musicianly touches of phrasing. But the noble, climactic triumphant aria, 'Dopo notte' doesn't have quite the effect it should. For that, however, Minkowski is partly to blame. Carried away, it almost seems, by the passion of the music, he's often inclined to go at it baldheaded, too fast and with a ferocity of accent that seems foreign to the style and dangerously close to ugly.

Veronica Cangemi makes a charming Dalinda, light, spirited and duly agile, with some gently pathetic expression in the delightful *siciliana* song early in Act 2. Ewa Podles brings her large, resonant voice to Polinesso's music; and the King of Scotland's fatherly music is done with due fullness and warmth by Denis

Sedov, who covers the two-octave range with comfort and resonance.

Despite the driven quality of Minkowski's performance, especially in the high dramatic music of the latter part of the opera, the sheer passion of this set does give it claims to be considered first choice. The admirable McGegan performance is possibly a safer buy, and in some respects it's a more stylish performance, but the singing here, Lynne Dawson's above all, is on balance superior.

Arminio, HWV36

Arminio   P
Vivica Genaux sop Arminio **Geraldine McGreevy** sop Tusnelda **Dominique Labelle** sop Sigismondo **Manuela Custer** mez Ramise **Luigi Petroni** ten Varo **Syste Buwalda** counterten Tullio **Riccardo Ristori** bass Segeste **Il Complesso Barocco / Alan Curtis** Virgin Veritas ② 545461-2 (147' · DDD) Notes, text and translation included   F

On the evidence of this very fine recording, *Arminio* can stand among the best of Handel's operas, full of beautiful and imagination. The first number, a minor-key duet largely in dialogue for Arminio and his wife Tusnelda, is done with an intensity and vitality that immediately involves you in the action. In Act 2 a series of more expansive arias unfolds: a pair for Arminio, one noble and the other furious, a striking one, austerely scored for Tusnelda, a more playful piece for Arminio's sister Ramise, and a spacious one – also almost an oboe concerto movement – for Sigismondo. This sequence is crowned by a sombre aria for Arminio, with hints of a music that foreshadows 'He was despised', and a soft-textured, sensuous *siciliana* aria for Tusnelda. This is musically one of Handel's finest acts.

The performance is excellently directed by Alan Curtis, who paces the opera well, keeping the recitative moving and characterising the arias clearly. Dominique Labelle is of star quality, delicate, precise, rhythmic, powerful where she needs to be. The lower castrato part, the title-role, is sung by Vivica Genaux, whose focused, slightly grainy voice serves ideally – there's singing of real brilliance here. Geraldine McGreevy gives a lot of pleasure too with her commanding singing in the *prima donna* role. *Arminio* isn't of the stamp of, say, *Giulio Cesare* or *Alcina*, but it has a lot of splendid music in it and is hugely enjoyable. Recommended.

Flavio, HWV16

Flavio, re de' Langobardi   P
Jeffrey Gall counterten Flavio **Derek Lee Ragin** counterten Guido **Lena Lootens** sop Emilia **Bernarda Fink** contr Teodata **Christina Högman** sop Vitige **Gianpaolo Fagotto** ten Ugone **Ulrich Messthaler** bass Lotario **Ensemble 415 / René Jacobs** Harmonia Mundi ② HMX290 1312/3 (156' · DDD)

Recorded 1989. Notes, text and translation included   M

Flavio is one of the most delectable of Handel's operas. Although it comes from his 'heroic' period, it's rather an ironic tragedy with a good many comic elements. Does that sound confusing? – well, so it is, for you never know quite where you are when King Flavio of Lombardy starts falling in love with the wrong woman; it begins as an amusing idle fancy but develops into near-tragedy, since he imperils everyone else's happiness, ultimately causing the death of one counsellor and the dishonour of another. The delicately drawn amorous feeling is like nothing else in Handel, and in its subtle growth towards real passion and grief is handled with consummate skill. The opera, in short, is full of fine and exceptionally varied music, and it's enhanced here by a performance under René Jacobs that, although it takes a number of modest liberties, catches the moods of the music surely and attractively, with shapely, alert and refined playing from the admirable Ensemble 415. And the cast is strong. The central roles, composed for two of Handel's greatest singers, Cuzzoni and Senesino, 18th-century superstars, are sung by Lena Lootens, a delightfully natural and expressive soprano with a firm, clear technique, and the countertenor Derek Lee Ragin, who dispatches his brilliant music with aplomb and excels in the final aria, a superb minor-key expression of passion. The singers also include Bernarda Fink as the lightly amorous Teodata and Christina Högman, both fiery and subtle in the music for her lover, and the capable Jeffrey Gall as the wayward monarch. Altogether a highly enjoyable set, not flawless but certainly among the best Handel opera recordings.

Giulio Cesare, HWV17

Giulio Cesare   P
Jennifer Larmore mez Giulio Cesare **Barbara Schlick** sop Cleopatra **Bernarda Fink** mez Cornelia **Marianne Rørholm** mez Sextus **Derek Lee Ragin** counterten Ptolemy **Furio Zanasi** bass Achillas **Olivier Lallouette** bar Curio **Dominique Visse** counterten Nirenus **Concerto Cologne / René Jacobs** Harmonia Mundi ③ HMX290 1385/7 (243' · DDD) Recorded 1991. Notes, text and translation included   M○○○

Handel's greatest heroic opera sports no fewer than eight principal characters and one of the largest orchestras he ever used. Undoubtedly this, and the singing of Francesca Cuzzoni (Cleopatra) and Senesino (Caesar), helped to launch *Giulio Cesare* into the enduring popularity that it enjoys to this day. But it's primarily the quality of the music, with barely a weak number in four hours of entertainment, that's made it such a favourite with audiences. Here the period instruments are an immediate advantage in giving extra 'bite' to the many moments of high drama without threatening to drown the singers in forte passages.

This performance is a particularly fine one with an excellent cast; Caesar, originally sung by a castrato, is here taken by the young mezzo, Jennifer Larmore. She brings weight and integrity to the role, seemingly untroubled by the demands of the final triumphant aria, 'Qual torrente'. Occasionally her vibrato becomes intrusive, but that's a minor quibble in a performance of this stature. Handel could just as well have called his opera 'Cleopatra' as she's the pivotal element in the drama, a role taken here by Barbara Schlick and sung with acuity and imagination. If Cleopatra represents strength in a woman, then Cornelia is surely the tragic figure, at the mercy of events. Her first aria, 'Priva son', here taken very slowly, shows Bernarda Fink to be more than equal to the role, admirable in her steady tone and dignity of character. Derek Lee Ragin's treacherous Ptolemy is also memorable, venom and fire injected into his agile voice.

A first-rate cast is supported by René Jacobs and Concerto Cologne on fine form, though the continuo line is sometimes less than ideally clear. The recording is excellent.

Giulio Cesare
Dame Janet Baker mez Giulio Cesare **Valerie Masterson** sop Cleopatra **Sarah Walker** mez Cornelia **Della Jones** mez Sextus **James Bowman** counterten Ptolemy **John Tomlinson** bass Achilles **Christopher Booth-Jones** bar Curio **David James** counterten Nirenus **English National Opera Chorus and Orchestra / Sir Charles Mackerras**
Chandos Opera in English Series ③ CHAN3019
(183' · DDD) Recorded 1984. Sung in English. Notes and English text included   Ⓕ⭕

This opera was a personal triumph for Dame Janet. As Caesar, she arms the voice with an impregnable firmness, outgoing and adventurous. Valerie Masterson shares the honours with Dame Janet, a Cleopatra whose bright voice gains humanity through ordeal. The tinkle of surface-wear clears delightfully in her later arias, sung with a pure tone and high accomplishment. As a total production, *Julius Caesar* was an outstanding achievement in ENO's history. Strongly cast, it had a noble Cornelia in Sarah Walker, a high-spirited Sesto in Della Jones, and in James Bowman a Ptolemy whose only fault was that his voice lacked meanness of timbre appropriate to the odious character. John Tomlinson's massive bass also commands attention. At the time of this recording the cuts and adaptations in the texts were severely condemned in some quarters. Mackerras's conducting is impeccable and the opera is given in clear, creditable English.

Hercules, HWV60

Hercules
Gidon Saks bass-bar Hercules **Anne Sofie von** Ⓟ **Otter** mez Dejanira **Richard Croft** ten Hyllus **Lynne Dawson** sop Iole **David Daniels** counterten Lichas

HANDEL GIULIO CESARE – IN BRIEF

Jennifer Larmore Giulio Cesare **Barbara Schlick** Cleopatra **Concerto Köln / René Jacobs**
Harmonia Mundi HMX290 1385/7   Ⓜ⭕⭕⭕
☀ A superb performance that took a *Gramophone* Award back in 1991. Jennifer Larmore is a powerful and technically magnificent Caesar, Barbara Schlick an imaginative and sweet-voiced Cleopatra, and Derek Lee Ragin a suitably poisonous Ptolemy. Jacobs demonstrates his mastery of 18th-century theatre with the superb Concerto Köln.

Dame Janet Baker Giulio Cesare **Valerie Masterson** Cleopatra **ENO / Sir Charles Mackerras**
Chandos CHAN3019   Ⓜ⭕
An outstanding performance from 1984 that enshrines Janet Baker's extraordinarily complete portrayal of Caesar. Valerie Masterson is a superb Cleopatra, bright toned and coquettish. James Bowman sings well as Ptolemy, though he could perhaps be nastier! Mackerras's command of the score is magnificent.

Dame Janet Baker Giulio Cesare **Valerie Masterson** Cleopatra **ENO / Sir Charles Mackerras**
ArtHaus Musik ◊ 100 308   Ⓜ⭕
John Copley's English National Opera production is here taken into the studio and reveals the magnificent cast on top form, all revolving around Baker's emotionally powerful Caesar. Mackerras drives the score forward with his customary élan ensuring a performance of real dramatic intensity.

Marijana Mijanovic Giulio Cesare **Magdalena Ko@ená** Cleopatra **Les Musiciens du Louvre / Marc Minkowski**
Archiv 474 210-2AH3   Ⓕ⭕
A strong challenger to the Jacobs set, with Majanovic a strong Caesar and Ko0ená a fine Cleopatra (though perhaps lacking the nth degree of voluptuousness). Anne Sofie von Otter is a superb Sesto and Charlotte Hellekrant a noble Cornelia. Minkowski's direction is generally pretty swift, though he can linger at particularly lovely moments.

Graham Pushee Giulio Cesare **Yvonne Kenny** Cleopatra **Australian Opera / Richard Hickox**
Euroarts ◊ 205 3599   Ⓕ
A countertenor Cesare heads a straightforward and most satisfying performance. Hickox directs his modern-instrument orchestra with style and exemplary timing. Some of the women are a little wayward vocally but nothing too alarmingly so. Francisco Negrin's production does Handel proud and shows enormous affection for this great work.

Marcos Pujol bar Priest of Jupiter **Chœur des Musi-
ciens du Louvre; Les Musiciens du Louvre / Marc
Minkowski**
Archiv Produktion ③ 469 532-2AH3 (176' · DDD)
Notes, texts and translations included   Ⓕ**O**

Hercules has never quite occupied the place it
merits in the Handel canon, even though it
includes some of his most powerfully dramatic
music. This is understood by Marc Minkowski,
whose intentions towards the work are made
clear frm the start of the Overture. But he's also
intent on maintaining its dramatic pace and
emphasising its range of feeling. His cast is well
able to share his dramatic vision. Von Otter
excels as Dejanira. This, rather than Hercules
himself, is the central role, carrying the work's
chief expressive weight. There's some beautifully shaped singing as in her opening air
she mourns Hercules' absence, and she copes
well with Minkowski's demanding tempo in
'Begone, my fears'. Lynne Dawson makes a
delightful Iole, crystalline, airy, rhythmic, but
able to call on more intensity where needed.
'My breast with tender pity swells' is truly
lovely. Lichas' music is done with refinement
but also vigour by David Daniels. Richard
Croft, though often hurried by Minkowski,
sings much of Hyllus' music with elegance, and
his delicate sustained *pianissimo* in the *da capo*
of 'From celestial seats descending', one of the
most inspired pieces in the score, is remarkable.
The choral singing is strong, secure, responsive,
though the French choir is rather less euphonious than the best English ones. The orchestral playing is duly alert. This account benefits
from fewer cuts than his rival Gardiner and
superior solo singing.

Orlando, HWV31

Orlando   Ⓟ
Patricia Bardon *mez* Orlando **Rosemary Joshua** *sop*
Angelica **Hilary Summers** *contr* Medoro **Rosa
Mannion** *sop* Dorinda **Harry van der Kamp** *bass*
Zoroastro **Les Arts Florissants / William Christie**
Erato ③ 0630-14636-2 (168' · DDD) Notes, text and
translation included   Ⓕ

Christie is very much concerned with a smooth
and generally rich texture and with delicacy of
rhythmic shaping. His management of the
recitative could hardly be bettered and moments of urgency or of other kinds of emotional
stress are tellingly handled. Sometimes he
favours a rather sustained style in the arias,
making the textures seem airless and heavy, and
the lines within them too smooth. However, to
set against it there's his exceptional delicacy of
timing, his careful but always natural-sounding
moulding of cadences and other critical
moments in the score. Not many Handel interpreters show this kind of regard for such matters
and it's a delight to hear Handel's music so
lovingly nurtured; it also helps the singers to
convey meaning. The cast is very strong. The

title-role is taken by a mezzo, Patricia Bardon,
who draws a firm and often slender line, with
that gleam in her tone that can so enliven the
impact of a lowish mezzo – the famous Mad
Scene is magnificent. The Sleep Scene, with
very sweet, soft-toned playing of the *violette
marine*, is lovely.

Hilary Summers offers a very sensitively sung
Medoro, pure and shapely in line. Harry van der
Kamp makes a finely weighty Zoroastro, with
plenty of resonance in his lower register; the last
aria in particular is done in rousing fashion. As
Angelica, Rosemary Joshua's musicianship
comes through in her attractive phrasing and
timing. Rosa Mannion's Dorinda is no less full
of delights, catching the character to perfection.
Hogwood's lighter orchestral textures are
appealing but the refinement of detail in the
newer set is equally admirable.

Rinaldo, HWV7

Rinaldo   Ⓟ
David Daniels *counterten* Rinaldo **Cecilia Bartoli**
mez Almirena **Gerald Finley** *bar* Argante **Luba
Orgonasova** *sop* Armida **Bejun Mehta** *counterten*
Christian Sorcerer **Mark Padmore** *ten* Herald **Daniel
Taylor** *counterten* Eustazio **Bernarda Fink** *contr*
Goffredo **Catherine Bott** *sop* Siren I **Ana-Maria
Rincón** *sop* Donna, Siren II **Academy of Ancient
Music / Christopher Hogwood**
Decca L'Oiseau-Lyre ③ 467 087-2OHO3 (179' · DDD)
    Ⓕ**OOO**

In a sense, *Rinaldo* is at once Handel's
most familiar and unfamiliar opera:
familiar because, as his lavish first stage
work for London, it has been much written
about both by modern historians and by the
composer's contemporaries; unfamiliar because
the Handel opera revival of recent years has
largely passed it by. Although there are numerous recordings of its two hit slow arias – 'Lascia
ch'io pianga' and 'Cara sposa' – this is its first
complete studio recording for over 20 years. It
may not be Handel's most dramatically effective
work (Act 3 marks time rather), and its magic
effects and transformation scenes no doubt
make it a tricky prospect for opera companies,
but in many ways its rich orchestration and
impressive set-piece arias make it ideal for
recording. That much makes this release a welcome sight already; add the de luxe cast Decca
has assembled for the purpose and it begins to
look irresistible.

Top of the bill come David Daniels as the
eponymous crusader knight and Cecilia Bartoli
as his love Almirena. Daniels' heart-stopping
countertenor voice is one of the marvels of our
age. It isn't big, and though he's technically
untroubled by the virtuoso runs of the quicker
arias, some may feel it lacks some of the heroic
power expected of a warrior; but there's an
inner strength to it, and in the love music he's
utterly convincing. Bartoli is equally impressive,
though her singing is less well suited to Handel.
She can deliver the most demanding music with

almost frightening ease and force, and, as ever, she throws herself into her role, but one can't help thinking that a more natural and unaffected style would have been more appropriate for arias such as 'Lascia ch'io pianga' and 'Augeletti che cantate'. The rest of the cast is almost unwaveringly strong. Daniel Taylor is slightly less technically secure or forceful than the others (which is hardly a criticism), but he does well enough with the opera's least effective role as Goffredo's brother Eustazio.

Christopher Hogwood's direction is typically neat and well-mannered. He isn't a natural opera conductor – others may have found more magic in the enchanted gardens and more sensuality in the sirens who lure Rinaldo, and you sometimes get the feeling that he's rushing the singers at important moments – but he has an unerring sense of tempo, and the opera as a whole is well paced. The Academy of Ancient Music plays to a high standard, backed up by a startlingly virtuoso performance on the Drottningholm thunder machine and by some genuine birdsong at the beginning of Act 2.

Competition for this recording consists of Jean-Claude Malgoire's pioneering 1977 account, and from a performance recorded live under John Fisher in 1989. The latter is notable for having an impressive Marilyn Horne in the title-role, but little else. The former is altogether a better piece of work – it features notable singing from, among others, Carolyn Watkinson as Rinaldo and Ileana Cotrubas as Almirena – but it suffers some less distinguished contributions lower down the cast, and in general it treads a bit too carefully throughout. Decca's newcomer may not be the last word on the opera, but for all-round standard of performance and production it currently wins hands down and it will take some beating.

Rodelinda, HWV19

Rodelinda, regina de' Langobardi Ⓟ
Sophie Daneman sop Rodelinda **Daniel Taylor** counterten Bertarido **Adrian Thompson** ten Grimoaldo **Catherine Robbin** mez Eduige **Robin Blaze** counterten Unulfo **Christopher Purves** bass Garibaldo **Raglan Baroque Players / Nicholas Kraemer** hpd
Virgin Classics Veritas ③ 545277-2 (173' · DDD)
Notes, text and translation included Ⓕⓞ

Composed just after *Giulio Cesare* and *Tamerlano*, *Rodelinda* must rank in many people's top half-dozen of the Handel operas, with its complex plot of dynastic intrigue revolving around the powerful, steadfast love of Bertarido (the ousted king of Milan) and his queen Rodelinda: just the kind that unfailingly drew strong music from Handel. Nicholas Kraemer gives a very direct and unaffected reading of this score. The pacing is sensible, if anything slightly on the slow side, especially perhaps in the recitative; the playing of the Raglan Baroque Players is alive and rhythmically well sprung, with a firmly

defined bass line. There's some modest ornamentation in the *da capo* sections of the arias.

What you don't get very strongly is much sense of urgency or boldness, of an unfolding drama, or indeed of the musical characterisation of individual numbers. There's just a hint here of the 'concert in costume'. Its star is Sophie Daneman. The voice is bright and intense, very firm in focus, dead sure in pitch, with only the faintest and most discriminatingly used hint of vibrato. It's ideally suited to Rodelinda's character, as the poignant singing of her lovely, elegiac opening aria makes clear – and that's immediately followed by a defiant one, vigorously thrown off. Adrian Thompson is also particularly enjoyable as the would-be usurper Grimoaldo. Thompson's easy and natural delivery, his natural feeling for the shape of Handel's phrases and his elegant manner make all his music a pleasure to listen to, and perhaps especially his final aria, which is a delight.

Catherine Robbin sings Eduige's music with spirit and rhythmic life. The two castrato roles, Bertarido and Unulfo, are taken by countertenors. Daniel Taylor is a very accomplished singer, even toned and accurate, well able to realise the pathos of Bertarido's prison scene, and the famous 'Dove sei' is touchingly done. But this role was written for Senesino, one of the great expressive singers of his day, and Taylor (or indeed the countertenor voice) isn't quite capable of conveying emotion on the scale the music demands. Unulfo's rather smaller part is neatly and clearly done – and some exceedingly awkward passagework is surely negotiated in his Act 1 aria – by Robin Blaze, although the general effect is rather bland.

This may not be the most dramatic of Handel opera recordings, but it gives an excellent account of the music and there's some first-rate singing – and in one of the very finest and most compelling of the Handel operas.

Rodrigo, HWV5

Rodrigo Ⓟ
Gloria Banditelli mez Rodrigo **Sandrine Piau** sop Esilena **Elena Cecchi Fedi** sop Florinda **Rufus Müller** ten Giuliano **Roberta Invernizzi** sop Evanco **Caterina Calvi** mez Fernando **Il Complesso Barocco / Alan Curtis** hpd
Virgin Classics Veritas ② 545897-2 (155' · DDD)
Notes, text and translation included Ⓕ

The music of Handel's Italian years has a unique freshness, a boldness of invention, a novelty in textures and lines – characteristics which distinguish his first Italian opera, *Rodrigo*, written in 1707 for the Medici court at Florence. This recording restores all that survives of the lyrical music, with one item composed in a more-or-less Handelian manner by Curtis and other Handel music imported to fit the original text. Curiously, the dances aren't included here, and – presumably in the interest of keeping the set to two CDs – there are many large cuts in the recitative. As a result some quite important sections are omitted and the often very close succession of lyrical numbers gives a slightly misleading impression of the opera. Even so the recording of this fine, often very moving and mostly inspiriting piece is warmly welcome.

Like most Italian operas of its time, it's essentially a succession of arias, mostly shorter ones than those of Handel's mature operas. As so often with Handel, much of the finest music comes in Act 2, with a pair of arias for Esilena (the second a furious outburst), and at the beginning of the next act, with Rodrigo and Esilena apparently facing death, Handel finds that marvellous vein of pathos familiar in his later operas. Alan Curtis, a man of the theatre, keeps the score moving along at a good pace. He conducts, as it were, from a 17th-century standpoint, with a flexibility over accent and metre that allows the music to move unusually freely. Yet he's rather predictable in his use of cadential *rallentandos*, and there are points where the orchestral discipline is a shade loose.

Sandrine Piau sings Esilena's part beautifully, with much attention to detail, to timing and to phrasing, as well as with fluency and with a richness of tone unusual for her. Gloria Banditelli makes a sturdy Rodrigo, direct and accurate, and very controlled in the fast semiquaver passages. Elena Cecchi Fedi perhaps overdoes the characterisation of Florinda as a shrew, singing shrilly at times and with rather more shouting and pouting than is consistent with musical enjoyment. But the singing is powerful and brilliant in its way. There's competent and spirited playing from Il Complesso Barocco, and excellent notes from Anthony Hicks and Curtis.

Serse, HWV40

Serse   P
Judith Malafronte *mez* Serse **Jennifer Smith** *sop* Romilda **Brian Asawa** *counterten* Arsamene **Susan Bickley** *mez* Amastre **Lisa Milne** *sop* Atalanta **Dean Ely** *bar* Ariodate **David Thomas** *bass* Elviro **Hanover Band and Chorus / Nicholas McGegan**
Conifer Classics ③ 75605 51312-2 (177' · DDD)
Notes, text and translation included   Ⓕ

Handel's *Serse* has proved to be one of the most popular of his operas over recent years – certainly in England. Wit may not be a part of most people's image of Handel's operas, and rightly: but from time to time, and especially when he was using a libretto of Venetian origins, Handel and his London librettists permitted themselves touches of ironic humour and sometimes rather more than that – *Serse* has one truly comic character, a servant, and King Xerxes himself is in some degree made a figure of fun by his unruly amorous whims. But as in all the best comedy, the situations give rise to serious emotion too, and in Act 2 of *Serse*, when events provoke first Xerxes, then Romilda (whom he thinks he loves) and then Amastre (who loves him) into forceful expressions of passion, touchingly followed by a

gentle aria from Xerxes's brother Arsamene (Romilda's true lover), the music springs into real life and enters more than a purely entertaining plane. Otherwise, however, it's inclined to be elegant, thin-textured and short-breathed. Although the cast here isn't obviously starry it's evenly accomplished and the performance holds together very well under Nicholas McGegan's assured direction. His own personal touch is unmistakable – the light textures, quickish tempos, spruce rhythms, dapper cadences, faintly ironic tone – and it works well for this opera, perhaps better than it does for a big heroic piece. The soloists are exemplary, too. This set must surely be the choice for anyone wanting a stylish version of this lively and appealing work.

Teseo, HWV9

Teseo   P
Eirian James *mez* Teseo **Julia Gooding** *sop* Agilea **Della Jones** *mez* Medea **Derek Lee Ragin** *counterten* Egeo **Catherine Napoli** *sop* Clizia **Jeffrey Gall** *counterten* Arcane **François Bazola** *bar* Sacerdote di Minerva **Les Musiciens du Louvre / Marc Minkowski**
Erato ② 2292-45806-2 (148' · DDD) Recorded 1992.
Texts and translations included   Ⓜ

Teseo was Handel's third opera for London, given at the beginning of 1713. Exceptionally, its libretto was based on a French original, written by Quinault for Lully; it's a spectacular piece, in five acts, with Medea (after the events of *Médée*) and Theseus (before the events of *Hippolyte* or the Ariadne operas) as its central characters. It's Medea who, as slighted lover and jealous sorceress, provides the principal musical thrills; but the score is, in any case, an unusually rich and inventive one, with much colourful orchestral writing even before she turns up at the beginning of Act 2. When she does, she introduces herself with a *Largo* aria, 'Dolce riposo', of a kind unique to Handel in its depth of poetic feeling, with a vocal line full of bold leaps above throbbing strings and an oboe obbligato; but, lest we should think her docile, Medea hints at her true colours in the ensuing C minor aria, and by the end of the act she's singing furious recitative and fiery, incisive lines – real sorceress music. Her biggest scene comes at the start of the final act, a *Presto* vengeance aria, packed with raging rapid semiquavers. Handel scored the opera for a more varied orchestra than usual; there are recorders, flutes, oboes, bassoons and trumpets called for. The arias themselves tend to be rather shorter than usual for Handel. The work needs first-rate singing, and by and large receives it here. The role of Medea falls to Della Jones, a singer with a superb technique and a remarkable ability to identify with the role; she truly lives Medea's part and brings to it great resources of spirit and technique. Except when allowed to play too fast, too loudly or too coarsely, the Musiciens du Louvre are impressive. Several numbers are accompanied with only a continuo instrument, to good effect. The recitative always moves well, and appoggiaturas are duly observed.

Howard Hanson   American 1896-1981

Hanson studied with Goetschius in New York and became director of the Eastman School (1924-64), where he was an influential teacher and founded the Institute of American music; he also promoted modern American music through his work as a conductor. His own music shows the influence of Sibelius, Grieg and Respighi (his teacher in Rome in the early 1920s). Among his works are seven symphonies, symphonic poems, choral pieces, chamber and piano music and songs.   GROVEmusic

Symphonies

Symphony No 1 in E minor, 'Nordic', Op 21. Merry Mount Suite. Pan and the Priest, Op 26. Rhythmic Variations on Two Ancient Hymns
Nashville Symphony Orchestra / Kenneth Schermerhorn
Naxos 8 559072 (61' · DDD)   Ⓢ

The *Nordic* Symphony was completed when Hanson was in Rome studying with Respighi – stylistically it brings Sibelius south to Italy. The Nashville performance can be compared with the Seattle orchestra under that fine Hanson interpreter, Gerard Schwarz. Schermerhorn is more spacious, taking a good two minutes longer overall – no bad thing in such hyperactive music, as it constantly strives towards the next climax. Schwarz is faster in the final *Allegro* but both performances are exciting and well recorded: the issue is settled by coupling and price.
There are many attractive features in the *Merry Mount Suite* – Charleston syncopation in the 'Children's Dance' and characteristic Hanson harmony oscillating between two chords at the start of the ecstatic 'Love Duet'. All supremely operatic, but the stage work still remains in limbo. The least-known piece here is the *Rhythmic Variations*, considered lost until recently, and cited as such in the *New American Grove*. This seems distinctly careless of someone, since Hanson recorded this late work himself in 1977. It's serenely spacious, utterly diatonic but no great rediscovery. *Pan and the Priest*, a vivid symphonic poem reaching pagan intensity, completes a bargain Hanson package that's well recorded, too.

Symphonies – Nos 2, 4 & 6; No 7, 'A Sea Symphony'. Fantasy Variations on a Theme of Youth. Elegy in memory of Serge Koussevitzky. Serenade, Op 36. Mosaics
Carol Rosenberger pf **New York Chamber Symphony Orchestra; Seattle Symphony Chorale and Orchestra / Gerard Schwarz**

Delos ② DE3705 (136' · DDD) Recorded 1988-92 Ⓜ𝐎

Gerard Schwarz's red-blooded 1988 account of the Second Symphony (*Romantic*) remains a match for any rival. Schwarz and his excellent Seattle band do full justice to its dark opulence, concision and organic power. Similarly, there's no missing the communicative ardour and clean-limbed security of Schwarz's lucid reading of the Sixth. Commissioned in 1967 by the New York Philharmonic for their 185th anniversary season, it boasts a formidable thematic economy and intriguing formal scheme of which Hanson himself was justifiably proud. Its successor, *A Sea Symphony* from 1977, sets texts from Walt Whitman's *Leaves of Grass*. In the unashamedly jubilant finale Hanson fleetingly quotes from his *Romantic* Symphony of more than four decades earlier: it's a spine-tingling moment in a score of consummate assurance and stirring aspiration. Schwarz's traversal finds the Seattle Symphony Chorale on rousing form. We also get exemplary renderings of the pretty 1945 Serenade for flute, harp and strings (a gift for Hanson's wife-to-be, Margaret Elizabeth Nelson) and characteristically inventive *Fantasy Variations on a Theme of Youth* from 1951 (with Carol Rosenberger a deft soloist), both these featuring Schwarz directing the New York Chamber Symphony. The present warm-hearted accounts of both the *Elegy in memory of Serge Koussevitzky* and *Mosaics* (which is a highly appealing set of variations written in 1957 for Szell and the Cleveland Orchestra) need not fear comparison with the composer's own Mercury recordings. The engineering is wonderfully ripe.

Symphonies – No 2, Op 30, 'Romantic'; No 4, Op 34, 'The Requiem'. Elegy in memory of Serge Koussevitzky
Jena Philharmonic Orchestra / David Montgomery
Arte Nova Classics 74321 43306-2 (60' · DDD)   Ⓢ𝐎

Here's enticingly off-the-beaten-track repertory from this super-budget label. The Fourth (*Requiem*) was apparently Hanson's own favourite of his seven symphonies. Inscribed 'in memory of my beloved father', it's a darkly intense, neo-Sibelian outpouring which won the composer the first Pulitzer Prize given to music in 1944. The tuneful, opulently scored *Romantic* (No 2) has remained a firm favourite with American orchestras and audiences since its première in November 1930 under Serge Koussevitzky. More recently, its use on the soundtrack of the 1979 feature film *Alien* won Hanson an entirely new band of admirers. The *Elegy* (1956) is a supremely touching memorial to a close friend and great conductor to whom American music this century owes an incontestably profound debt of gratitude. Performances are capable and shapely, and the sound is very good too.
The orchestra responds with enthusiasm to David Montgomery, who knows his way round

these scores. That said, nothing here poses a serious challenge to Gerard Schwarz and the splendid Seattle Symphony in terms of orchestral finesse or interpretative insight: Montgomery's provincial band don't possess the ingratiating tonal lustre and sheer muscle of their American counterparts, while Schwarz's direction displays just that little bit of extra commitment to the cause. None the less, at its absurdly low price, this issue will find many new friends for Hanson's ripely romantic vision.

Solo Piano Works

Sonata in A minor, Op 11. Two Yuletide Pieces, Op 19. Poèmes érotiques, Op 9. Three Miniatures, Op 12. Three Etudes, Op 18. Enchantment. For the First Time. Slumber Song
Thomas Labé pf
Naxos 8 559047 (76' · DDD)   Ⓢ

Much of this CD is an orgy of romantic piano music. Admirers of Hanson's *Romantic* Symphony (Arte Nova) or his one-time smash-hit opera *Merry Mount* (Naxos) will surely devour this collection, which includes unknown and unpublished music. A first impression is that the earliest works here, written around 1920, have the sort of ecstatic luxuriance that might be expected of a pupil of Respighi. But this influence came later since Hanson didn't start his three-year residence in Rome until 1921. His background was Swedish and there's a Nordic, Sibelian intensity about his whole approach, although the fulsome piano style clearly stems from Liszt.

The earliest piece is probably the *Slumber Song*, a pure salon morsel, and the latest is the suite *For the First Time*. The three *Poèmes érotiques* (the fourth has disappeared) are what Hanson called his 'first studied attempt at psychological writing'. They are powerful in a surging melodic style where in several pieces the climaxes stem from an almost Tchaikovskian cathartic need to unburden tensions.

The striking three-movement Sonata (1918) has had to be completed from the composer's shorthand by Thomas Labé since it was never published, although Hanson performed it in 1919. The vivid improvisatory keyboard writing, at times extravagantly rhetorical, causes Labé to hit the piano rather hard in the last two movements. One can understand his enthusiasm, but there are times when a little more *cantabile* might have helped. However, nothing must detract from the real service that this CD does in bringing Hanson's piano music to public attention for the first time.

Merry Mount

Lawrence Tibbett *bar* Wrestling Bradford **Göta**   Ⓗ
Ljungberg *sop* Lady Marigold Sandys **Gladys Swarthout** *mez* Plentiful Tewke **Edward Johnson** *ten* Sir Gower Lackland **Alfredo Gandolfi** *bar* Myles

Brodrib **Giordano Paltrinieri** *ten* Jonathan Banks **Arnold Gabor** *bar* Faint-not-Tinker **James Wolfe** *sngr* Samoset **Irra Petina** *mez* Desire Annable **Louis d'Angelo** *bar* Praise-God-Tewke **Chorus and Orchestra of the Metropolitan Opera, New York / Tullio Serafin**
Naxos Historical mono ② 8 110024/5 (126' · ADD)
Recorded live 1934   ⒷⓄ

Hanson's only opera was a considerable success when first given. This is the first opportunity to register the impact of the entire work. The recording itself is a lucky scoop taken from 78rpm acetate and metal discs of the broadcast. No doubt technical wonders have been worked on the original sound but the result is still patchy, although, with announcements, commentary and applause included, the recording has a powerful sense of occasion. The story started with a grisly episode in New England history (about 1625) concerning feuding Puritan and Cavalier colonists. This was the basis of a slender short story by Nathaniel Hawthorne and considerably embroidered in a libretto by Richard L Stokes. The crowd scenes gave Hanson the opportunity to write some magnificent choruses, and the dances before the maypole in Act 2 were so exciting at this première that they stopped the show. When Bradford gives his soul to the devil (scene 3) the choral and orchestral panoply is as vivid as anything in the Shakespeare film scores of Walton, and similar in style.

Lawrence Tibbett is magisterial in conveying all the horrors of repressive Puritanism souring into devil-worship but Göta Ljungberg (Marigold/ Astoreth) is resplendent in her lyrical role, specially the climactic Act 3 lament. Their joint immolation must have made a convincing peroration on stage, judging by the reports of 50 curtain calls. What's remarkable is that a composer with so little experience in the theatre could deliver such an operatic grand opera. It has everything opera houses like – star roles, crowd scenes, violence and spectacle.

Karl Amadeus Hartmann
German 1905-1963

Hartmann studied with Haas at the Munich Academy (1924-7), with Scherchen and with Webern (1941-2). After the war he started the Musica Viva festival in Munich to present music that had been banned during the Nazi years, and most of his published works date from after this period. They include most importantly a cycle of eight symphonies (1936, 1946, 1947, 1949, 1950, 1953, 1958, 1962), which have a Brucknerian breadth while suggesting the influences of Reger, Berg, Stravinsky, Bartók and Blacher. He also wrote several concertos and vocal music including a chamber opera Simplicius Simplicissimus (1949), a strongly expressive work combining popular song, chorale and psalm-like recitation with symphonic method. **GROVE**music

Symphonies

Symphonies – Nos 1[a], 2 – Adagio[b], 3[c], 4-6[b], 7
(1957-8)[d] and 8[b]. Gesangsszene (1963)
Doris Soffel contr **Dietrich Fischer-Dieskau** bar
Bavarian Radio Symphony Orchestra / [a]**Fritz**
Rieger, [b]**Rafael Kubelík,** [c]**Ferdinand Leitner,**
[d]**Zdenek Macal**
Wergo ④ WER60187-50 (225' · ADD)   ⒻO

In the 1930s Hartmann was beginning to establish a reputation, but as a known opponent of the Nazi regime, he was forced to withdraw himself and his works from public musical life. During the war he destroyed or radically revised most of his previous output, and these eight symphonies (five of which are based on, or are revisions of, earlier works) appeared between 1946 and his death in 1963. Together they show his broad sympathies with the 20th-century masters.

You can hear the presence of Bruckner in the monumental sense of structure, of Reger in the densely chromatic counterpoint and an intense, tortured lyricism derived from Berg. There's a tribute to the neo-classical Stravinsky in the Fifth Symphony, and more than a hint of Bartók in the irresistible momentum of the fugues that conclude the Sixth. Mahler is present in the Whitman settings of the First Symphony, significantly entitled 'Attempt at a Requiem' and in the upheavals of the first movement of the Eighth. The spectral Funeral March in Webern's Pieces, Op 6, haunts sections of the First, Third and Eighth Symphonies.

Whether Hartmann managed to forge a demonstrably personal idiom is questionable. What's indisputable is the power of his music to communicate, and its capacity to fascinate. On the debit side, not all the vigorously contrapuntal sections of the later works avoid sounding academic. The dates of these live recordings aren't given, but they're all naturally balanced, with excellent clarity – Hartmann's torrents of tuned percussion are thrillingly captured, and the orchestra plays with polish and conviction.

Symphony No 4. Concerto funèbre[a]. Chamber Concerto[b]
[a]**Isabelle Faust** vn [b]**Paul Meyer** cl [b]**Petersen Quartet** (Conrad Muck, Gernot Sussmuth vns Friedemann Weigle va Hans-Jakob Eschenburg vc) **Munich Chamber Orchestra / Christoph Poppen**
ECM New Series 465 779-2 (78' · DDD)   Ⓕ

When Hartmann opted for internal exile during the Nazi era, he took with him some key influences from the free musical world. Beam up around 0'33" into the third movement of the 1939 Concerto funèbre and you have a virtual quote from the first movement of Bartók's 1934 Fifth String Quartet. Hartmann completed his Chamber Concerto for Clarinet, String Quartet and String Orchestra in 1935, seven years after Bartók wrote his Fourth Quartet – which in turn barges headlong into Hartmann's second

movement (0'07" into track 9, an unmistakable reference to the Quartet's finale).

In the Chamber Concerto the melodic and structural profile of the first movement follows the profile of Kodály's 1933 Dances of Galánta (try following through from 1'09" until around 3'22" into track 8, taking particular note of the clarinet line). The language of the work is Magyar-inspired (even aside from the Galánta references) and the scoring lively and luminous.

The Concerto funèbre opens with a quotation (fully acknowledged this time) of the Hussite chorale 'Ye Who are God's Warriors', best known to Brits for its use in Smetana's Má vlast. The reference commemorates the Nazi betrayal of Czechoslovakia, though Hartmann's anger finds controlled expression in the Allegro di molto third movement.

The Fourth Symphony is scored for strings, and frames a lively Allegro di molto with two profound Adagios that, again, draw you in by virtue of their intense arguments. All three performances do Hartmann proud. Isabelle Faust's eloquent playing of the Concerto funèbre draws maximum effect from extremes in mood and temperature and outplays her rivals, while Rafael Kubelík offers an admirably pliant live account of the Fourth Symphony, and while Ingo Metzmacher's Fourth is occasionally more intense than this version under Christoph Poppen (especially in the unison opening pages), Poppen's central Allegro has the stronger sense of propulsion.

With fine sound and programming, this is the ideal Hartmann primer.

Hartmann Symphony No 6 **Bruckner** Symphony No 6 in A
South West German Radio Symphony Orchestra / Ferdinand Leitner
Hänssler Faszination Musik 93 051 (80' · ADD)
Recorded 1982   ⒻO

'Truth prepared by joy and bound up with sorrow' was Hartmann's motto. Nazism and war blighted his career yet fired his imagination, as we can hear in the brief, thrilling and often moving Sixth Symphony which Ferdinand Leitner conducts here with rare acumen and power. The Symphony, premièred by Jochum in 1953 and recorded by Fricsay in 1955, is in two movements: an at times apocalyptic but ultimately serene slow opening movement and a searing Toccata variata in which two of the three fugue subjects are variants of the first. If there are influences to be found, they're Berg in the first movement, Bartók in the second. This is white-knuckle-ride music, though the ride itself has you looking at the stars. Leitner eclipses all rivals, not least because the recording is itself a tour de force. Leitner and his engineers place timpani, piano and xylophone with pin-point accuracy, ensuring that the music's explosive force is generated from within, not imposed from without. Leitner's Bruckner has grand moments but some less-than-convincing times in between. He's good on headlines, less good on argument and fine detail. Nevertheless, this disc is worth the price for the Hartmann alone.

Jonathan Harvey
British 1939

Harvey studied at Cambridge, privately with Erwin Stein and Hans Keller, and with Babbitt at Princeton (1969-70). He has taught at the universities of Southampton (1964-77) and Sussex. His early music shows enthusiasms ranging from Britten and Messiaen to Stockhausen and Davies, but since the early 1970s he has developed a more integrated style and has emerged as an outstanding composer of electronic music (Mortuos plango, vivos voco, 1980). Later pieces include Madonna of Winter and Spring (1986).
GROVEmusic

Death of Light / Light of Death

Death of Light/Light of Death. Advaya. Ricercare una melodia (performed on oboe). Ricercare una melodia (performed on trumpet). Tombeau de Messiaen. Wheel of Emptiness
Ictus / Georges-Elie Octors
Cyprès CYP5604 (77' · DDD)   Ⓕ

Three of the compositions on this disc offer ideal introductions to Jonathan Harvey's work, showing how music centering on a single line, or instrument, can evolve into a potently imaginative discourse when that line or instrument is manipulated electronically. In *Ricerare una melodia* the moment of revelation comes when the electronic material opens out a much wider registral spectrum than that 'naturally' available on the trumpet or oboe. Something similar happens both in the brief *Tombeau de Messiaen*, where the interaction of piano and electronics unleashes a torrential, joyously uninhibited commemoration of the French master, and also in *Advaya*. All three of these works have been recorded before, but Harvey enthusiasts should still find it difficult to resist this new release, not only for its outstanding recording quality, but for the interest and substance of the programme as a whole. The disc ends with the most striking evidence of Harvey's versatility. *Death of Light/Light of Death* is scored for five performers, without electronics, but with the harpist doubling on tam-tam. It offers music of an intensity and, in the end, ceremonial solemnity which few composers today can match. With performances of supreme technical assurance and magnificently lucid sound, this is an outstanding disc in every respect.

Madonna of Winter and Spring

Madonna of Winter and Spring[a]. Percussion Concerto[b]. Song Offerings[c]
[c]**Penelope Walmsley-Clark** *sop* [b]**Peter Prommel** *perc* [ab]**Netherlands Radio Philharmonic Orchestra**

/ **Peter Eötvös;** [c]**London Sinfonietta /**
George Benjamin
Nimbus NI5649 (78' · DDD) Text and translation included   ⒻOO

This is an impressive disc indeed: a strong cast, a varied programme, and music of great integrity and beauty. In relation to many British scores that have garnered recent critical praise, Harvey more than holds his own. The three pieces – two of them recorded here for the first time – date from the 1980s and 90s. Each introduces a 'foreign' element to the orchestra in a slightly different way. There are elements of the competitive streak between soloist and orchestra in the Percussion Concerto; in *Song Offerings* relations between the two elements are more symbiotic, as one might expect; but in *Madonna of Winter and Spring*, the most extended piece here, the 'foreign' element is assumed by synthesisers and electronics. This piece, in particular, sums up Harvey's preoccupations: the interaction of the different media, and the programmatic elements derived from the composer's faith.

At intervals the orchestra recedes, creating electro-acoustic 'windows' reminiscent of similarly mixed-media scores (Birtwistle and Boulez come to mind); at others, individual instruments appear in a quasi-soloistic context, adding an extra dimension to the texture. Moreover, the quality of these interpretations gives this recording a special appeal. The electro-acoustic element is well captured, and conveys something of the spatial imaging mentioned in the composer's insert-notes.

All three pieces receive committed, dynamic interpretations: if only contemporary music could always enjoy such advocacy.

Passion and Resurrection

Passion and Resurrection
Carolyn Foulkes, Alison Smart *sops* **Kim Porter** *contr* **Andrew Mackenzie-Wicks** *ten* **Stuart Macintyre** *bar* **BBC Singers; Sinfonia 21 / Martin Neary**
Sargasso ② SCD28052 (85' · DDD · T) Recorded live   Ⓕ

Were the audience were warned that they'd be called on to lend their voices to this performance, recorded by the BBC in 1999? This score is as much a 'liturgical action' as an oratorio (or 'church opera', as it's described in the booklet). It was written for a community celebration at Winchester Cathedral, and most of the text is a translation of extant Passion Plays.

Harvey's ability to combine chant-like idioms (and actual plainchant hymnody) within a predominantly atonal context is quite uncanny. The work opens with a familiar passage from the Book of Common Prayer which gradually morphs into more angular cadences, but there's nothing wilful in the transformation.

The libretto faithfully follows Christ's Passion

and Resurrection. In the Passion men's voices and low brass predominate, and the writing is harsher, more angular, the treatment of pacing more earth-bound. The Resurrection sequence points out the greater involvement of women (through their voices); the register is consistently higher, the sense of time more suspended. There's little abstraction in the score – in fact, Harvey allows himself a surprising degree of literal-mindedness: you can even hear the nails being driven in at the Crucifixion.

The action is set in a most direct way, yet never 'talks down' to the congregation or the listener, and the performance is dramatic and well shaped. The BBC Singers and Sinfonia 21 have plenty of body; the strings have much to do; and the brass interventions are most striking. The postlude is quite literally 'recessional', as very low instruments gradually disperse throughout the church of St John's, Smith Square: this spatial element stands in for many of Harvey's preoccupations, and the effect is nicely rendered by the engineers.

Choral Works

I love the Lord. Carols. Lauds (with **Paul Watkins** vc). Sobre un éxtasis alte contemplación. Come, Holy Ghost. O Jesu, nomen dulce. Two Fragments. The Angels. Forms of Emptiness **The Joyful Company of Singers / Peter Broadbent**
ASV CDDCA917 (63' · DDD) Recorded 1994. Texts and translations included   Ⓕ

Compare Jonathan Harvey's *Come, Holy Ghost* with one of his large-scale instrumental works and you might suspect that they're the work of different Jonathan Harveys, one providing short pieces for cathedral choirs, the other active on the avant-garde concert scene. So it's a particular virtue of this disc that by providing such a generous cross-section of Harvey's choral music it makes it easier to hear how the two Harveys are in fact one far from inconsistent composer. Since Harvey himself has progressed from choir school to electronic studio it isn't so surprising that his music can relate to both worlds so effectively, and most of the compositions here take a fresh look at aspects of the English cathedral tradition without attempting to force those aspects into an unholy alliance with modernist techniques. From the early *Fragments* (1966) to *The Angels* (1994) we can hear versions of the kind of contemplative intensity that informs some of Harvey's finest concert works (for example, *Bhakti*), and these choral pieces are never poor relations. The short *Sobre un éxtasis alte contemplación* works within its own essential sounds, and in exploring speech as well as song it develops the more dramatic dialogue to be found in the larger-scale *Forms of Emptiness* (1986) and *Lauds* (1987).

The Joyful Company of Singers prove to be the ideal interpreters to project all facets of this often quite challenging music.

Joseph Haydn   Austrian 1732-1809

Haydn, the son of a wheelwright, was trained as a choirboy and taken into the choir at St Stephen's Cathedral, Vienna, where he sang from c1740 to c1750. He then worked as a freelance musician, playing the violin and keyboard instruments, accompanying for singing lessons given by the composer Porpora, who helped and encouraged him. At this time he wrote some sacred works, music for theatre comedies and chamber music. In c1759 he was appointed music director to Count Morzin; but he soon moved, into service as Vice-Kapellmeister with one of the leading Hungarian families, the Esterházys, becoming full Kapellmeister on Werner's death in 1766. He was director of an ensemble of generally some 15-20 musicians, with responsibility for the music and the instruments, and was required to compose as his employer – from 1762, Prince Nikolaus Esterházy – might command. At first he lived at Eisenstadt, c30 miles south-east of Vienna by 1767 the family's chief residence, and Haydn's chief place of work, was at the new palace at Eszterháza. In his early years Haydn chiefly wrote instrumental music, including symphonies and other pieces for the twice-weekly concerts and the prince's Tafelmusik, and works for the instrument played by the prince, the baryton (a kind of viol), for which he composed c125 trios in 10 years. There were also cantatas and a little church music. After Werner's death church music became more central, and so, after the opening of a new opera house at Eszterháza in 1768, did opera. Some of the symphonies from c1770 show Haydn expanding his musical horizons from occasional, entertainment music towards larger and more original pieces, for example Nos 26, 39, 49, 44 and 52 (many of them in minor keys, and serious in mood, in line with trends in the contemporary symphony in Germany and Austria). Also from 1768-72 come three sets of string quartets, probably not written for the Esterházy establishment but for another patron or perhaps for publication (Haydn was allowed to write other than for the Esterházys only with permission); Op 20 clearly shows the beginnings of a more adventurous and integrated quartet style.

Among the operas from this period are Lo speziale (for the opening of the new house), L'infedeltà delusa (1773) and Il mondo della luna (1777). Operatic activity became increasingly central from the mid-1770s as regular performances came to be given at the new house. It was part of Haydn's job to prepare the music, adapting or arranging it for the voices of the resident singers. In 1779 the opera house burnt down; Haydn composed La fedeltà premiata for its reopening in 1781. Until then his operas had largely been in a comic genre; his last two for Eszterháza, Orlando paladino (1782) and Armida (1783), are in mixed or serious genres. Although his operas never attained wider exposure, Haydn's reputation had now grown and was international. Much of his music had been published in all the main European centres; under a revised contract with the Esterháza his employers no longer had exclusive rights to his music.

His works of the 1780s that carried his name

further afield include piano sonatas, piano trios, symphonies (Nos 76-81 were published in 1784-5, and Nos 82-7 were written on commission for a concert organisation in Paris in 1785-6) and string quartets. His influential Op 33 quartets, issued in 1782, were said to be 'in a quite new, special manner': this is sometimes thought to refer to the use of instruments or the style of thematic development, but could refer to the introduction of scherzos or might simply be an advertising device. More quartets appeared at the end of the decade, Op 50 (dedicated to the King of Prussia and often said to be influenced by the quartets Mozart had dedicated to Haydn) and two sets (Opp 54-5 and 64) written for a former Esterházy violinist who became a Viennese businessman. All these show an increasing enterprise, originality and freedom of style as well as melodic fluency, command of form, and humour. Other works that carried Haydn's reputation beyond central Europe include concertos and notturnos for a type of hurdygurdy, written on commission for the King of Naples, and The Seven Last Words, commissioned for Holy Week from Cadíz Cathedral and existing not only in its original orchestral form but also for string quartet, for piano and (later) for chorus and orchestra.

In 1790, Nikolaus Esterházy died; Haydn (unlike most of his musicians) was retained by his son but was free to live in Vienna (which he had many times visited) and to travel. He was invited by the impresario and violinist JP Salomon to go to London to write an opera, symphonies and other works. In the event he went to London twice, in 1791-2 and 1794-5. He composed his last 12 symphonies for performance there, where they enjoyed great success; he also wrote a symphonie concertante, choral pieces, piano trios, piano sonatas and songs (some to English words) as well as arranging British folksongs for publishers in London and Edinburgh. But because of intrigues his opera, L'anima del filosofo, on the Orpheus story, remained unperformed. He was honoured (with an Oxford DMus) and fêted generously, and played, sang and conducted before the royal family. He also heard performances of Handel's music by large choirs in Westminster Abbey.

Back in Vienna, he resumed work for Nikolaus Esterházy's grandson (whose father had now died); his main duty was to produce masses for the princess's nameday. He wrote six works, firmly in the Austrian mass tradition but strengthened and invigorated by his command of symphonic technique. Other works of these late years include further string quartets (Opp 71 and 74 between the London visits, op.76 and the Op 77 pair after them), showing great diversity of style and seriousness of content yet retaining his vitality and fluency of utterance; some have a more public manner, acknowledging the new use of string quartets at concerts as well as in the home. The most important work, however, is his oratorio The Creation in which his essentially simple-hearted joy in Man, Beast and Nature, and his gratitude to God for his creation of these things to our benefit, are made a part of universal experience by his treatment of them in an oratorio modelled on Handel's, with massive choral writing of a kind he had not essayed before. He followed this with The Seasons, in a similar vein but more a series of attractive episodes than a whole.

Haydn died in 1809, after twice dictating his recollections and preparing a catalogue of his works. He was widely revered, even though by then his music was old-fashioned compared with Beethoven's. He was immensely prolific: some of his music remains unpublished and little known. His operas have never succeeded in holding the stage. But he is regarded, with some justice, as father of the symphony and the string quartet; he saw both genres from their beginnings to a high level of sophistication and artistic expression, even if he did not originate them. He brought to them new intellectual weight, and his closely argued style of development laid the foundations for the larger structures of Beethoven and later composers. **GROVE**music

Cello Concertos

No 1 in C, HobVIIb/1; **No 2** in D, HobVIIb/2

Cello Concertos Nos 1 & 2
Academy of St Martin in the Fields / Mstislav Rostropovich vc
EMI 5672342 (49' · ADD) Recorded 1975   Ⓟ **OO**

This deserves a place on any collector's shelf. With Rostropovich directing from the bow the ASMF sounds a little less sturdy than usual, a little more lithe in the First Concerto. The scale of its first movement is little short of perfection: everything a Moderato should be, with Rostropovich humming along non-chalantly in its second theme. He's leisurely in the Adagio, playing it as an extended meditation which exists almost outside time. Without ever losing the life of the melodic line, Rostropovich progresses as slowly as it's humanly possible to do without total stasis; and, to wonderfully joyful effect, breaks all records for speed in the finale. Every note, every sequential phrase is there in its place, secured by glintingly true intonation and needle-sharp dramatic timing. The almost complete absence of physical stick and finger sound which Rostropovich and his engineers manage between them makes the latter two movements of the Second Concerto a most pleasing experience. Rostropovich takes deep, long breaths: the surface of his slow movement is glassy, every fragment of bowing and phrasing given the microscopic hair-pin treatment. For his deep, instinctive understanding of scale, and for Britten's cadenzas, many collectors' preferences in these concertos will remain with Rostropovich.

Cello Concertos – Nos 1 & 2; No 4 in D, HobVIIb/4 (formerly attributed to Haydn)
Gautier Capuçon vc **Mahler Chamber Orchestra / Daniel Harding**
Virgin Classics 545583-2 (66' · DDD)   Ⓟ **OO**

Barely 22, Gautier Capuçon plays the cello with the control and wisdom of a much older musician. The lightness of his touch and the consistent clarity of his bow strokes are quite admirable in themselves, but when combined with an uncanny sweetness of tone in the higher registers they're breathtaking. These qualities suit the two Haydn concertos very well indeed and bestow upon the modest little anonymous D major Concerto unexpected dignity and charm.

Daniel Harding, conducting the Mahler Chamber Orchestra, opts for *galant* rather than driven tempi. The scale of his orchestral forces enables him to establish a relationship with the soloist more akin to chamber music than is usually heard in these works. There's lightness of articulation throughout, conveying both intimacy and vitality.

Their reading of the C major Concerto, while not strongly imprinted, is truly Classical in its delicacy and refinement. It's shapely and spirited but never forced. It's the second item, the D major Haydn, which proves the highlight. In the opening movement Capuçon conjures the darting image of a water sprite, who can nevertheless steal time in all the right moments. The doublestops are dizzying and the chords in the poetic cadenza are exquisitely rolled. The *Adagio* takes on the aura of a meditation; Capuçon seems detached while gently supported by the orchestra, in a reverie of his own. When it comes, the elaboration that serves in the place of a cadenza is perfectly attuned to the moment. The final *Allegro* is never allowed to go 'peasant', remaining instead in the aristocrat's drawing room where it sparkles and glows.

Cello Concertos Nos 1 & 2. Sinfonia concertante in B flat, HobI/105. Symphony No 13 in D – Adagio cantabile
Steven Isserlis vc **Douglas Boyd** ob **Matthew Wilkie** bn **Marieke Blankestijn** vn **Chamber Orchestra of Europe / Sir Roger Norrington**
RCA Victor Red Seal 09026 68578-2 (75' · DDD) Ⓕ●

What a versatile artist Steven Isserlis is. Having made his name as a sympathetic interpreter of a wide variety of romantic and modern music, here he shows he can be just as persuasive in 18th-century repertoire. His stylistic awareness is evident in beautiful, elegant phrasing, selective use of vibrato and varied articulation, giving an expressive range that never conflicts with the music's natural language. In the cello concertos he's helped by an extremely sensitive accompaniment, stressing the chamber musical aspects of Haydn's pre-London orchestral writing. The *Adagios* are taken at a flowing speed, but Isserlis's relaxed approach means they never sound hurried. The *Allegro molto* finale of the C major Concerto, on the other hand, sounds poised rather than the helter-skelter we often hear.

Mørk's vivacious, imaginative performances characterise the music very strongly, but some may prefer Isserlis's and Norrington's lighter touch and greater refinement. And this isn't taking into account the extras – the lovely symphony movement (a cello solo throughout) and

what many may find the highlight of the disc – the *Sinfonia concertante*. The first movement's *tutti*s have excessively prominent added dynamics that detract from the music's vigour and grandeur, but the serenade-like *Andante*, the robust and witty finale and, throughout, the conversational exchanges of the four soloists, are an unalloyed delight.

Keyboard Concertos

Piano Concertos – in G, HobXVIII/4; in F, HobXVIII/3; in D, HobXVIII/11
Norwegian Chamber Orchestra / Leif Ove Andsnes pf
EMI 556960-2 (54' · DDD) Ⓕ

 Like Emanuel Ax on Sony, Leif Ove Andsnes confines himself to the three concertos that have been fully authenticated. Had the works generally known as 'the Haydn piano concertos' been these three and not a rag-bag of juvenilia and pieces attributed to Haydn, the canon might have been more highly thought. But even the slightest work can dazzle and delight if it's performed as well as these are here. Where Ax's performances have a slightly monochrome feel, everything tapped out (there's much audible fingerwork) with the same well-adjusted mix of energy and sensibility, Andsnes's playing is altogether more various, while perfectly at one with itself stylistically. Ax's Franz Liszt Chamber Orchestra is the more idiomatic of the two ensembles in the D major Concerto's *Rondo all'Ungarese*, but that's about the only occasion on which it has the edge over Andsnes's stylish and highly articulate Norwegian Chamber Orchestra; and even here Andsnes himself scores points for a less noisy plunge into the interlude in D minor and a more sunlit and finely flighted way with the episode which follows. The Norwegian players are never afraid to play full out, a strategy which the explicit but carefully balanced recording is happy to underwrite. Thus the players make much of the 'look here, young man' chromaticisms in the first movement of the D major Concerto as the piano chatters irrepressibly on; and they contribute decisively to the superbly articulated – nay, revelatory – performance of the G major Concerto with which the disc begins. After a splendidly jaunty account of the first movement, Andsnes pushes this G major Concerto to its limits with a decidedly skilfully shaped account of the glooming C major slow movement and a dashing account of the concluding *Presto*. His playing of the *Largo cantabile* of the F major Concerto – the concerto's centrepiece and its *raison d'être* – is the very embodiment of sweetness and light. This is a simply marvellous disc.

Keyboard Concertos – in G, HobXVIII/4; in F, HobXVIII/6ᵃ; in D, HobXVIII/11
Andreas Staier fp **Freiburg Baroque Orchestra /**

Gottfried von der Goltz [a]vn
Harmonia Mundi HMC90 1854 (64' · DDD)   ⓕ**OO**

Many concertos are attributed to Haydn but these three are undisputedly authentic. The keyboard part in No 4 falls in a narrow compass; Andreas Staier introduces variety by ornamenting the slow movement and decorating fermatas in all movements. His embellishments are very good indeed, even if he is ornate in places. (If you dislike ornament, you should choose the Andsnes, who sticks to the letter and does so most artistically.)

A rarity is No 6 for violin and keyboard, its outer movements the least interesting with sequential passages. The emotive slow movement (mostly a conversation between the two soloists) redeems matters and gives Gottfried von der Goltz a chance to show his mettle as a sensitive violinist.

In the finest work, No 11, the orchestral exposition is an ideal *Vivace*, the first theme lilting over repeated quavers generating the right degree of forward tension, and the bass line given its full due, oboes and horns colouring the texture tellingly. A similar degree of perception, with Staier's contribution equally telling, is heard throughout. The recording is expertly balanced and tonally truthful. An outstanding disc.

Trumpet Concerto

Haydn Trumpet Concertos in E flat, HobVIIe/1; in C[a]
Albinoni Trumpet Concerto in B flat, Op 7 No 3[b];
Adagio (transcr. Orsomando) **Corelli** Trumpet Concerto in D[b] **Hertel** Trumpet Concertos in D & E flat[a] **Hummel** Trumpet Concerto in E flat **JM Molter** Trumpet Concerto No 1 in D[a] **Mozart** Trumpet Concerto in D **FX Richter** Concerto for Trumpet and Strings in D[a] **J Stamitz** Trumpet Concerto in D. Plus works by JS Bach, Clarke and Gounod
Håkan Hardenberger tpt **Simon Preston** org **Academy of St Martin in the Fields / Sir Neville Marriner;** [a]**London Philharmonic Orchestra / Elgar Howarth;** [b]**I Musici**
Philips Duo ② 464 028 (148' · DDD) Recorded 1986, 1989, 1991, 1993   Ⓜ**O**

This is probably the finest single collection of trumpet concertos in the catalogue. Hardenberger offers an interesting programme, including a performance of a recently discovered trumpet concerto either by Stamitz or a musician called JG Holzbogen. The trumpeting on this disc is truly splendid and Hardenberger (or the record's producers) have ensured that the accompaniments are distinguished and full of characterful detail by asking Marriner and the ASMF to provide the backing.

Hardenberger opens with the famous Hummel Concerto, played in E major rather than the usual E flat, which makes the work sound bolder and brighter than usual. The finale with its crisp articulation, fantastic tonguing and tight trills,

displays a genial easy bravura, yet overflows with energy and high spirits. In the Haydn, soloist and orchestra alike find an elegant style for the more lyrical side of the first movement and the *Andante* too is nicely relaxed, the noble melody obviously relished, then the finale swings off joyously to make a sparkling conclusion.

The Stamitz (or Holzbogen) piece seems to have a very doubtful lineage. Whoever it was written for was a formidable virtuoso: the writing lies consistently in the trumpet's stratospheric tessitura and includes some awkward leaps. It's an inventive piece, though, and even the second movement *Adagio* moves along quite briskly; the finale, however, is the most catchy section and Hakan Hardenberger dispatches it with panache, having taken all the earlier histrionics in his stride.

They are warmly and truthfully balanced in Philips's best manner and while the trumpet is well up front most trumpet fanciers will enjoy the realistic projection. A superb issue.

Symphonies

No 1 in D; No 2 in C; No 3 in G; No 4 in D; No 5 in A; No 6 in D, 'Le matin'; No 7 in C, 'Le midi'; No 8 in G, 'Le soir'; No 9 in C; No 10 in D; No 11 in E flat; No 12 in E; No 13 in D; No 14 in A; No 15 in D; No 16 in B flat; No 17 in F; No 18 in G; No 19 in D; No 20 in C; No 21 in A; No 22 in E flat, 'Philosopher'; No 23 in G; No 24 in D; No 25 in C; No 26 in D minor, 'Lamentatione'; No 27 in G; No 28 in A; No 29 in E; No 30 in C, 'Alleluja';

No 31 in D, 'Hornsignal'; No 32 in C; No 33 in C; No 34 in D minor; No 35 in B flat; No 36 in E flat; No 37 in C; No 38 in C; No 39 in G minor; No 40 in F; No 41 in C; No 42 in D; No 43 in E flat, 'Mercury'; No 44 in E minor, 'Trauersinfonie'; No 45 in F sharp minor, 'Farewell'; No 46 in B; No 47 in G, 'Palindrome'; No 48 in C, 'Maria Theresia'; No 49 in F minor, 'La passione'; No 50 in C; No 51 in B flat; No 52 in C minor; No 53 in D, 'Imperial';

No 54 in G; No 55 in E flat, 'Schoolmaster'; No 56 in C; No 57 in D; No 58 in F; No 59 in A, 'Fire'; No 60 in C, 'Il distratto'; No 61 in D; No 62 in D; No 63 in C, 'La Roxelane'; No 64 in A, 'Tempora mutantur'; No 65 in A; No 66 in B flat; No 67 in F; No 68 in B flat; No 69 in C, 'Loudon'; No 70 in D; No 71 in B flat; No 72 in D; No 73 in D, 'La chasse'; No 74 in E flat; No 75 in D; No 76 in E flat; No 77 in B flat; No 78 in C minor; No 79 in F; No 80 in D minor;

No 81 in G; No 82 in C, 'L'ours'; No 83 in G minor, 'La poule'; No 84 in E flat; No 85 in B flat, 'La reine'; No 86 in D; No 87 in A; No 88 in G, 'Letter V'; No 89 in F; No 90 in C; No 91 in E flat; No 92 in G, 'Oxford'; No 93 in D; No 94 in G, 'Surprise'; No 95 in C minor; No 96 in D, 'Miracle'; No 97 in C; No 98 in B flat; No 99 in E flat; No 100 in G, 'Military'; No 101 in D, 'Clock'; No 102 in B flat; No 103 in E flat, 'Drumroll'; No 104 in D, 'London'.

Orchestral **Haydn**

Symphonies – boxed sets

Symphonies – Nos 1-104; 'A' in B flat; 'B' in B flat.
Sinfonia concertante in B flat, Hobl/105, 'No 105'
Philharmonia Hungarica / Antál Dorati
Decca 448 531-2LC33 (33 discs: ADD) Recorded
1969-73   Ⓑ**O**

Dorati's famous integral recording of all 104 of the published Symphonies now returns in a Decca bargain box containing 33 CDs. It still holds its place in the catalogue as the only complete set to contain everything Haydn wrote in this medium, including the Symphonies 'A' and 'B', omitted from the original numbering scheme because at one time they were not thought to be symphonies at all. The survey also encompasses additional alternative movements for certain works (notably Nos 53 and 103) and alternative complete versions of the *Philosopher* Symphony and No 63, which are fascinating. The remastering confirms the excellence of the vintage Decca sound. No more needs to be said, except that the one minus point in these very convincing modern-instrument performances is Dorati's insistence on measured, often rustic tempos for the minuets. For those who can run to the complete series this is self-recommending – a source of inexhaustible pleasure.

Symphonies, Nos 1-104
Austro-Hungarian Haydn Orchestra / Adám Fischer
Brilliant Classics 99925 (33 discs: DDD)
From Nimbus originals recorded 1987-2001 Ⓢ Ⓢ**OO**

It was little short of tragic that the very last box of symphonies in Adám Fischer's Haydn series for Nimbus, Nos 21 to 39 plus the Symphonies A and B, appeared just as the demise of that label was announced in January 2002. The final box was the finest of the series, but all too few copies reached the shops, making this 33-disc box covering all the symphonies very welcome indeed, even if over the 14 years that it took to complete the project, the quality and style varied.

That final box of 20 symphonies was a superb culmination to the project. Not only are they a fascinating sequence of works written in the 1760s when the young Haydn was busy experimenting, the performances are outstanding. They were recorded as recently as 2000 and 2001, and far more than the earliest recordings in the series, they take full note of period practice while staying faithful to modern instruments. More than ever one registers the individual virtuosity of the various soloists in the orchestra, often challenged to the limit by fast speeds. So a movement like the variation finale of No 31, the *Hornsignal*, features a sequence of brilliant soloists such as Haydn might have been writing for in his Esterházy orchestra – violin, cello, horn and so on, even double bass. It's a performance full of panache, with the four horns braying out superbly.

Other striking symphonies in the group

include No 22 in E flat, *The Philosopher*, with its extraordinary parts for two cors anglais. Also the *Alleluia* Symphony, No 30 in C, with trumpets and drums dramatically added to the usual published scoring – brought in later, according to HC Robbins Landon, by Haydn as an option. The minor-key works in this last batch, such as the *Lamentatione*, No 26 in D minor, and best of all, No 39 in G minor, are fine examples of Haydn's *Sturm und Drang* manner, with Fischer heightening dynamic contrasts to good effect. No 39 brings an example of Fischer's mastery when he enhances the tension of the nervy opening and exaggerates the pauses; he's far more effective in that movement than Dorati .

While with those symphonies recorded at the beginning of the project, from 1987 to 1990, comparisons with the Dorati series have the merits of each balanced fairly evenly, the advantage certainly tips in favour of Fischer as the project developed. For the *London* Symphonies, Nos 93 to 104, the first to be recorded, the Nimbus engineers – working in the very hall at the Esterházy Palace which Haydn used – produce rather washy sound, whereas the works recorded later benefit from a sharper focus. In those early recordings, too, the slow movements tend to be taken at the sort of broad speeds of tradition, with warmly expressive phrasing.

At that point, no doubt, Fischer was just beginning to woo his select band of Austrian and Hungarian musicians away from their usual Romantic manners. In his notes Fischer makes a point of describing the unfolding development of the project over 14 years. He becomes increasingly aware of historically informed style, notably in faster speeds for both slow movements and *minuet*s (which increasingly acquire a *scherzo*-like flavour), giving him a clear advantage over Dorati. Also the string playing comes closer to that found in period orchestras, with lighter phrasing and less marked use of vibrato.

That development is noticeable as early as the recordings made in 1994-5, when most of the *Sturm und Drang* symphonies were covered – broadly those in the late 40s and early 50s in the regular Breitkopf numbering. Finales in particular, taken fast, have all the bite and wildness one could want, with pinpoint attack. The very earliest symphonies in numerical order, Nos 1 to 20, were recorded early in the project between 1989 and 1991, with results that are more variable. The finale of No 12, for example, marked *Presto*, is taken surprisingly slowly, almost like a *minuet*. No 13, very adventurously for that early period, uses four horns, yet because of the reverberant acoustic they don't ring out as prominently as those used in works like the *Hornsignal*, recorded later.

Even in these early symphonies, recorded near the beginning of the project, the trios in *Minuet*s have solo strings, and regularly the vigour and thrust of *Allegro*s is exhilarating, with rhythms lifted and admirably crisp ensemble.

This is a set guaranteed to encourage collectors to delve into works which from first to last

HAYDN'S 'LONDON' SYMPHONIES (NOS 93-104) – IN BRIEF

Orchestra of the 18th Century / Frans Brüggen
Philips ② 468 546-2PM2 (Nos 93, 94, 97, 99, 102, 103) (153' · ADD) & ② 468 927-2PM2 (Nos 95, 96, 98, 100, 101, 104) (152' · DDD) Ⓜ
Not Brüggen at his best, but he always has good ideas, and if at times he makes this beautifully proportioned works feel somewhat Beethovenian, his rhythmic snap invariably charms.

Concertgebouw Orchestra / Sir Colin Davis
Philips 442 614-2PM2 (Nos 93, 94, 97, 99, 100, 101) (147' · ADD/DDD) & 442 611-2PM2 (Nos 95, 96, 98, 102, 103, 104) (151' · ADD/DDD) ⓂⓄⓄ
A magnificent achivement from Sir Colin Davis: urbane, witty and stylish with superb playing by the Concertgebouw Orchestra. Tempi and are beautifully judged and inter-related, and the whole cycle has an effortless ease. A real treasure trove. The recordings, made in Amsterdam's Concertgebouw, are excellently done.

Philharmonia Hungarica / Antál Dorati
Decca ② 452 256-2DM2 (Nos 93, 94, 97, 100, 103, 104) (154' · ADD) & ② 452 259-2DM2 (Nos 95, 96, 98, 99, 101, 102) (154' · ADD) Ⓜ
Antál Dorati's complete Haydn symphony cycle was a pioneering project that has stood the test of time. There is no sign of fatigue in the course of this enormous undertaking, and all the works have a *joie de vivre* that's truly infectious. The scale and temperament looks forward to recent trends.

London PO / Eugen Jochum
DG ⑤ 474 364-2GC5 (329' · ADD) Ⓜ
With extra performances of Nos 88, 91 and 98 (from the Berlin PO and Bavarian RSO), this is a real bargain. The LPO play superbly and Jochum gives a series of gloriously cultivated, fresh and often quite enchating performances. He lavishes great affection on this music, and since it's Haydn, that affection is returned in plenty. The LPO recordings from 1970-71 are excellent, the 'extras' are from the 1950s and early 60s. Packaged in a little slimline box, this set is as economical of your shelving as your wallet.

London Festival Orchestra / Ross Pople
Arte Nova ④ 74321 72109-2 (286' · DDD) Ⓢ
A sympathetic rather than earth-shattering set of the 'London' Symphonies from Pople and his London-based band. The string section is relatively small, and the recording acoustic is quite tight and dry. Pople's direction is straightforward, sprightly and sensitive to Haydn's many opportunities for solo display (invariably stylishly done).

convey the joy in creation that's the unfailing mark of this ever-welcoming master.

Symphonies – 'Sturm und Drang', 'Paris', 'London': Nos 26, 35, 38, 39, 41-52, 58, 59, 65, 82-89, 90-104 Ⓟ
Orchestra of the Age of Enlightenment, Orchestra of the Eighteenth Century / Frans Brüggen
Philips Collectors Edition ⑬ 473015-2PB13 (DDD)
Recorded 1990-96 ⓈⒷⓄ

Although increasingly rejected by scholars, the label *Sturm und Drang* is still widely used to describe the symphonies Haydn wrote during the late 1760s and early 1770s. Storm and stress is most evident in the half-dozen minor-key symphonies of this period. Several of the major-key works here also have their share of turbulence, above all No 46. Others, though, employ the cheerful, Italianate musical language of the day with a new force, originality and, as in movements like the 'limping' Minuet of No 58, comic eccentricity. No 48, the erroneously named *Maria Theresia*, is one of the noblest and most imposing in a line of 18th-century C major ceremonial symphonies. Stormy, majestic or playful, virtually every work here reflects Haydn's restless exploration of the symphony's expressive and intellectual potential during these years.

These symphonies have been well served by previous period-instrument recordings, but this set more than holds its own. Brüggen is the most 'Romantic' of the conductors in this repertoire: and he has little truck with the smart tempos and clean-cut phrasing favoured by Hogwood and Weil, in particular. Outer movements are often broad, and Brüggen phrases the lyrical music as expressively as any traditional conductor, and reveals a strong control of cumulative symphonic tensions. Slow movements are shaped with all the refinement and chamber-musical delicacy heard on Pinnock's recordings, and often with more affection. In one or two of the faster movements Brüggen's tempo is arguably a notch too expansive, above all in the first movement of the C major, No 41. He also shows an intermittent fondness for shading away at cadences, notably in the opening movement of the *Lamentatione*, No 26. Equally controversial is his speeding up for the trios of several of the minuets, most blatantly in that of *La Passione*, though his tempos for the minuets themselves are thoughtfully chosen, ranging from the measured, elegiac No 26 to the stinging one-in-a-bar quasi-*Scherzo* of No 52.

Brüggen eschews a harpsichord continuo, though he rightly reinforces the bass line with a clearly audible bassoon. And he omits second-time repeats in all but a few sonata movements, a small price to pay for an average of nearly four symphonies per disc. His performances, though occasionally questionable, are the most individual in their shaping and characterisation.

Haydn's so-called *Paris* Symphonies, written in 1785-6 for the famed orchestra of the Concert de la Loge Olympique, have fared pretty well on CD: there are three rival period-instrument accounts from Sigiswald Kuijken, Roy Goodman and Bruno Weil. Brüggen is crisp and vital in the *allegros*, yet always allows the music plenty of breathing space. And his phrasing of the lyrical themes is more expressively moulded than on any of these rival versions. The main theme of No 85's opening *Vivace*, for instance, glides with a feline grace, and the first movement of No 84 has an airy, dancing elegance. Yet Haydn's dramatic coups, such as the barbaric dissonances in the first movement of No 82, are played for all they're worth; and throughout Brüggen shows a shrewd grasp of long-range structure, knowing just when to tighten the screws (as in the fiercely modulating developments in the finales of Nos 83 and 85, both unusually tense and truculent here, and the thrilling, brassy codas to the finales of Nos 82 and 86). He judges nicely the pace and character of each of the minuets, too, ranging from the red and gold pomp of No 82 to the brisk and breezy No 85, with its whiplash accents and whooping high horns. And, predictably, his phrasing in the slow movements is more affectionate, more highly nuanced, than on any of the competing versions. Also, his tempos here are all aptly chosen.

It would be rash to recommend an outright 'winner' among period versions of the *Paris* Symphonies when all competitors have so much going for them, but in Brüggen's favour is his stronger sense of drama in sonata movements, his more expressive phrasing, and his superlative wind players, who in refinement and imagination eclipse all their rivals. The live Philips recordings are remarkably consistent, combining transparency with a pleasing ambient warmth.

Symphonies – smaller sets

Symphonies Nos 93-4, 97, 99 & 100-101
Concertgebouw Orchestra / Sir Colin Davis
Philips Duo ② 442 614-2PM2 (ADD/DDD) Recorded 1975-81   Ⓜ◐◐

Symphonies Nos 95-6, 98 & 102-104
Concertgebouw Orchestra / Sir Colin Davis
Philips Duo ② 442 611-2PM2 (ADD/DDD) Recorded 1975-81   Ⓜ◐◐

A superb achievement. It's nigh-on impossible to imagine better 'big-band' Haydn than you encounter here on Colin Davis's four well-filled CDs. His direction has exemplary sparkle and sensitivity. Minuets are never allowed to plod, outer movements have an ideal combination of infectious zip and real poise, and the humour is always conveyed with a genial twinkle in the eye. Quite marvellous, wonderfully unanimous playing from the Amsterdam orchestra, too (the woodwind contributions are particularly distinguished), with never a trace of routine to betray the six-year recording span of this acclaimed

project. The Philips engineering, whether analogue or digital, is of the very highest quality, offering a natural perspective, gloriously full-bodied tone and sparkling textures within the sumptuous Concertgebouw acoustic. Invest in this set: it will yield enormous rewards for years to come.

Additional recommendations

Symphonies Nos 6-8
Northern Chamber Orchestra / Ward
Naxos 8 550722 (59' · DDD) Recorded 1993   Ⓢ
A lot to enjoy in the popular Times of Day trilogy, with their colourful and entertaining *concertante* writing. The Northern Chamber Orchestra is a lively, responsive group, and fields a personable bunch of soloists No one staking a fiver on this disc could possibly be disappointed.

Symphonies Nos 22, 29 & 60
Northern Chamber Orchestra / Ward
Naxos 8 550724 (60' · DDD) Recorded 1992-3   Ⓢ
A winning performance that fully captures the composer's infectious wit.

Symphonies Nos 43, 46 & 47
Cologne Chamber Orchestra / Müller-Brühl
Naxos 8 554767 (64' · DDD)   Ⓢ
A beefier sound than from many chamber orchestras but with ample detail. Müller-Brühl's speeds can't be faulted, with *Allegros* crisp and alert and slow movements kept flowing. A worthy rival for existing versions, whether on period or modern instruments.

Symphonies Nos 55-69
Austro-Hungarian Haydn Orchestra / Fischer
Nimbus ⑤ NI5590/4 (317' · DDD)   Ⓢ
A most attractive collection, on modern instruments in the helpful acoustic of the Haydnsaal of the Esterházy Palace at Eisenstadt. Fischer's fine control of dynamics is illustrated in the subtlety of echo phrases, clear but unexaggerated.

Symphonies arr Chamber Ensemble

London Symphonies arr Salomon, Volume 1
Symphonies (arr Salomon) Nos 93[a], No 94[b], 101[a]
Florilegium Ensemble (Ashley Solomon *fl* James Johnstone *fp* [a]Kati Debretzeni, [b]Rodolfo Richter *vns* Jane Rogers *va* Jennifer Morsches *vc*)
Channel Classics SACD hybrid CCSSA19603 (72' · DDD)   Ⓕ

Johann Peter Salomon, violinist, composer and impresario, was a shrewd businessman. Not only did he organise Haydn's two triumphant visits to London in the 1790s, visits which directly prompted the composition of the 12 *London* Symphonies, but he bought the rights to those masterpieces on Haydn's final return to Vienna in August 1795. Instead of issuing them in full score, in 1798 he published versions for domestic music-making. The basic ensemble is a string quartet and flute, plus a full keyboard part. This music is readily available in its original garb, but these arrangements are worth hearing. Some effects that must have sounded so original to early listeners stand out even more with this chamber ensemble than they do with a full orchestra. The extra transparency generally benefits fast movements. First-movement development sections strike the listener more sharply in their chamber guise, particularly the minor-key darkness of the *Surprise*, which recalls Haydn's *Sturm und Drang* style. The famous 'surprise' itself is intensified by Florilegium's dynamic response. These arrangements, well recorded with stylish if occasionally abrasive period performances and the advantage of an SACD alternative, can be warmly recommended to anyone who's intrigued.

Flute Quartets

Cassation in F, HobII/20. Divertissement in B flat, HobII/B4. Flute Quartet in A, HobII/A4. Notturno No 1 in C, HobII/25
Linos Ensemble
Capriccio 10 719 (68' · DDD). Recorded 1994   Ⓕ

These highly polished, enthusiastic performances have a compelling immediacy. The diverse choice of pieces amply shows the excellent soloistic skills of Linos's members and its deftly balanced ensemble. Close recording presents the group's eloquence and vitality in fine, clear detail. The delightful, open-air qualities of this repertoire are exemplified by the F major *Cassation*, whose good humour is captured with buoyant vigour in the opening *Allegro*; with stately elegance in the two minuets, affecting melodiousness in the *Adagio*, and an engaging swing in the final rondo. The extrovert B flat *Divertissement* offers a charming display of fluent, conversational playing, a style the Linos exploits to particular effect in the lively alternation of different instrumental groupings in the elegant A major Quartet for flute and strings. The infectiously high-spirited, effervescent exchanges between flute and oboe in the witty C major *Notturno* sum up the allure of this entertaining issue.

String Quartets

Op 0 in E flat
Op 1: No 1 in B flat, 'La chasse' No 2
in E flat No 3 in D No 4 in G No 5 in E flat No 6 in C
Op 2: No 1 in A No 2 in E No 3 (spurious) No 4 in F
No 5 (spurious) No 6 in B flat
Op 3 Nos 1-6 (spurious)
Op 9: No 1 in C No 2 in E flat No 3 in G No 4 in
D minor No 5 in B flat No 6 in A
Op 17: No 1 in E No 2 in F No 3 in E flat No 4 in
C minor No 5 in G No 6 in D
Op 20, 'Sun': No 1 in E flat No 2 in C No 3 in
G minor No 4 in D No 5 in F minor No 6 in A
Op 33 'Gli Scherzi': No 1 in B minor No 2 in E flat,

'Joke' No 3 in C, 'Bird' No 4 in B flat No 5 in G
No 6 in D
Op 42 in D
Op 50 'Prussian': No 1 in B flat No 2 in C No 3 in
E flat No 4 in F sharp minor No 5 in F, 'Dream'
No 6 in D, 'Frog'
Op 54 'Tost': No 1 in G No 2 in C No 3 in E
Op 55 'Tost': No 1 in A No 2 in F minor, 'Razor' No 3
in B flat
Op 64 'Tost': No 1 in C No 2 in B minor No 3 in B
flat No 4 in G No 5 in D, 'The Lark' No 6 in E flat
Op 71 'Apponyi': No 1 in B flat No 2 in D No 3 in
E flat
Op 74 'Apponyi': No 1 in C No 2 in F No 3 in
G minor, 'Rider'
Op 76 'Erdödy': No 1 in G No 2 in D minor, 'Fifths'
No 3 in C, 'Emperor' No 4 in B flat, 'Sunrise' No 5 in
D No 6 in E flat
Op 77 'Lobkowitz': No 1 in G No 2 in F
Op 103 in D minor (unfinished)

Complete String Quartets

Op 0; Op 1 – Nos 1[a], 2, 3, 4[a] & 6 in C[a]; Op 2 –
Nos 1, 2[a], 4[a] & 6; Opp 9, 17, 20, 33, 42[a], 50[a], 54, 55,
64, 71, 74, 76, 77 & 103
Angeles Quartet (Kathleen Lenski, Steven Miller,
[a]Sara Parkins *vns* Brian Dembow *va* Stephen
Erdody *vc*)
Philips (21 discs) 464 650-2PX21(140' · DDD)   Ⓜ**OO**

The most relevant comparisons for this collection are the Aeolian Quartet on Decca and the Kodály Quartet on Naxos. The all-digital Naxos series features performances that are, in the main, musically reliable and technically proficient. But turn back to the 1973-6 Aeolian series, and every work becomes an event, every quirk of harmony, rhythm or timing is etched with maximum relish.

Comparative disc layouts begin to differ from CD 3, and the Angeles omit *The Seven Last Words*, a work which, beautiful as it is, wasn't originally written for string quartet. Recording-wise, Philips favours a warm, open sound, balanced much as you would hear it from the centre stalls in a smallish-size concert hall. Decca's analogue recordings are closer, dryer, more sensitive to extraneous noise and commonly balanced in favour of Emanuel Hurwitz's first violin. It's a clear and intimate sound frame and the leader bias actually suits the divertimento-style early quartets, but Philips's more refined engineering makes for less strenuous listening in concert-length sessions. A handful of edits are the only blots on Philips's otherwise immaculate aural landscape.

The svelte texture of the Angeles' pooled sound, their consistent evenness in full chords and the musical like-mindedness of individual players, whether in excited *prestos* or in shared *rubato* is admirable. As to contrasts in playing styles, think of the relatively smooth-toned Juilliard or Emerson Quartets (Angeles) as compared with the internally differentiated Amadeus Quartet (Aeolian). The Angeles are generally lighter, faster and subtler in their use of tone colouring whereas the Aeolians' roster of virtues includes strong (even emphatic) characterisation, consistently flexible phrasing and a more pungent approach to rhythm.

Surfing the set for good sampling points brings us, initially, to the early quartets, where both groups sport some superb first-violin solo work, tastefully inflected with Lenski, more candidly expressive with Hurwitz. A particularly telling comparison is provided by the quietly contrapuntal Minuet of Op 17 No 1, where the Angeles'- seamless *legato* contrasts against the Aeolians' near *staccato*. The exquisite *Adagio* of Op 20 No 6 is another good place to compare, the Angeles with their perfectly timed pauses, warm cello line and overall restraint set against the more romantic, even rhapsodic, Aeolian. Listening to the first bars of Op 33 No 1 is like eavesdropping on a small gathering mid-conversation, where the cello line gradually gains in urgency. The Angeles' *sotto voce* handling of the *scherzo* to Op 33 No 3 is wonderful: it's rather more pensive than the Aeolians and marks much more of a contrast with the chirping trio.

Op 50 No 4's *Andante* anticipates the dramatic interjections that trouble various late Schubert slow movements. Both groups are effective here, though when the cello marks an expected change of key two minutes or so into the movement, it's the Aeolian's Derek Simpson who makes the biggest impact: you can almost see the rosin erupt from his strings. In Op 50 No 5 late Beethoven springs more readily to mind, but there the Angeles' extra speed and restraint is more effective. Note how beautifully they negotiate the quiet alternation between upper and lower voices towards the end of Op 50 No 6's *Poco adagio* and the sudden blossoming that follows. Then again, Op 54 No 1's mobile *Allegretto* second movement harbours the potential to switch from tenseness to lyrical effusiveness, which the Angeles exploit to the full, as they do for the rhapsodising *Adagio* of Op 54 No 2. Late Beethoven is evoked once more, this time the Cavatina from Op 130.

Beam up around three minutes into the *Adagio* of the *Lark* Quartet (Op 64 No 5) and you'll note how skilfully the Angeles cue a *ritardando*, while the bracing finale to Op 74 No 3 has just the right bounce to offset all the breathless excitement. The *Sunrise* Quartet (Op 76 No 4) opens like a spring flower (never more so than in the Angeles' ecstatically controlled performance) and Op 77 No 1's cheeky *Allegro moderato* bounds in with perfectly modulated high spirits.

Turning to other competition, the Lindsays, Amadeus, Vienna Konzerthaus, Quatuor Mosaïques, Pro Arte and Takács, all have added substantiallyto the Haydn quartet discography, and all have their value. However, in this particular context it really is a head-to-head contest between two 'complete' sets similarly presented.

Richard Wigmore contributes detailed annotation, quite different from Lindsay Kemp's overview for Decca, but just as useful and equally well written. The Angeles appeal per-

haps primarily for their restrained expressiveness and consistent attention to detail. Philips's superior recording is another bonus. The Aeolians generate more immediate heat but, ultimately, the Angeles' intelligence and cooler blending pay the higher musical dividends.

String Quartets: Op 1 No 1. Op 20 Nos 2 & 5. **H**
Op 50 No 3. Op 54 Nos 1-3. Op 64 Nos 3 & 4.
Op 74 No 3. Op 76 Nos 3 & 4. Op 77 No 2
Pro Arte Quartet (Alphonse Onnou, Laurent
Halleux *vns* Germain Prévost *va* Robert Maas *vc*)
Testament mono ③ SBT3055 (229' · ADD) Recorded
1931-8 ⓕⓞ

Haydn String Quartets: Op 1 No 6. Op 20 **H**
Nos 1 & 4. Op 33 Nos 2, 3 & 6. Op 50 No 6. Op 55
Nos 1 & 3. Op 64 No 6. Op 71 No 1. Op 74 Nos 1 &
2. Op 77 No 1 **Hoffstetter** String Quartets, Op 3 –
No 4 in B flat; No 5 in F
Pro Arte Quartet (Alphonse Onnou, Laurent
Halleux *vns* Germain Prévost *va* Robert Maas *vc*)
Testament mono ④ SBT4056 (243' · ADD) Recorded
1931-8 ⓕⓞ

The Pro Arte Quartet's first London appearance in 1925 prompted *The Times* to declare, 'One has never heard it surpassed, and rarely equalled, in volume and beauty of tone, in accuracy of intonation and in perfection of balance between the parts' – and that could well be the verdict on these sets. The musicians' tempos invariably seem just right and their phrasing has an inner life that's extraordinarily potent. Alphonse Onnou and Laurent Halleux were superbly matched, and Halleux often led in their early days. Such virtuosity as the quartet exhibits is effortless and totally lacking in ostentation. Though the actual sound is dated – the string tone is wanting in bloom and freshness – the ear soon adjusts; but these transfers might have made a little more space between movements.

String Quartets, Op 1

String Quartets, Op 1 Nos 1-6
Petersen Quartet (Conrad Muck, Gernot Sussmuth
vns Friedemann Weigle *va* Hans-Jakob Eschenburg *vc*)
Capriccio ② 10 786/7 (99' · DDD) ⓕⓞ

The history of the string quartet in effect began with these cheerful, compact *Divertimenti a quattro*, as the composer titled them; and though they contain only spasmodic hints of future glories, their freshness and exuberance make for highly pleasurable listening.

The Petersen Quartet responds vividly to the music's youthful verve, with polished ensemble, keen attack and a wide spectrum of colour and dynamics. Purists may raise an eyebrow at the special effects the players deploy in repeats, especially in minuets – added touches of imitation, pizzicato and even *col legno*. But the young Haydn, famed for his mischievous humour, may have enjoyed these liberties. The recording combines clarity with an attractive church resonance.

String Quartets, Op 9

String Quartets, Op 9 Nos 1, 3 & 4
Kodály Quartet (Attila Falvay, Tamás Szabó vns Gábor Fias va János Devich vc)
Naxos 8 550786 (52' · DDD) Recorded 1993   Ⓢ

String Quartets, Op 9 Nos 2, 5 & 6
Kodály Quartet (Attila Falvay, Tamás Szabó vns Gábor Fias va János Devich vc)
Naxos 8 550787 (58' · DDD). Recorded 1993   Ⓢ

Overshadowed by four dozen later masterpieces, Haydn's Op 9 has usually received short shrift from players and commentators. The most familiar is the D minor, No 4, described by Hans Keller as 'the first great string quartet in the history of music'. The minor mode at this period (1769-70) invariably drew something special from Haydn, and this work stands apart from the others for its intensity of expression, its mastery of texture and development and the sheer character of its ideas. The opening *Allegro moderato* could well have been at the back of Mozart's mind when he came to write his own great D minor Quartet, K421. The Kodály Quartet is, as ever, a sympathetic Haydn exponent, impressing with its slightly old-fashioned warmth of sonority, the natural musicality of its phrasing and care for blend, balance and intonation, though the boomy church acoustic hardly helps.

String Quartets, Op 20

String Quartets, Op 20 Nos 1-6   ℗
Quatuor Mosaïques (Erich Höbarth, Andrea Bischof vns Anita Mitterer va Christophe Coin vc)
Astrée Naïve ② E8802 (147' · DDD) Recorded 1990
Ⓕ**OOO**
Also available separately: E8785 – Nos 1, 5 & 6.
E8786 – Nos 2-4

The Op 20 String Quartets date from the composer's so-called *Sturm und Drang* period, though Haydn's increasingly frequent use of the more dramatic and 'serious' minor mode in these pieces can perhaps be attributed just as much to the fruitful influence of the three operatic projects he had been working on just a few years previously. Moreover, these quartets reveal a greater preoccupation with counterpoint than any of his music to that date, and the great fugal finales of Nos 2, 5 and 6 clearly herald the consummate craftsman so overwhelmingly displayed in the mature quartets to come. These wonderfully flexible performances display an altogether breath-taking refinement, sensitivity and illumination. Indeed, in terms of expressive subtlety, imaginative intensity and sheer depth of

feeling, the Mosaïques' achievement in these marvellous works is unmatched.

String Quartets, Op 20 Nos 1, 3 & 4
The Lindsays (Peter Cropper, Ronald Birks vns Robin Ireland va Bernard Gregor-Smith vc)
ASV CDDCA1027 (79' · DDD)   Ⓕ**O**

String Quartets, Op 20 Nos 2, 5 & 6
The Lindsays (Peter Cropper, Ronald Birks vns Robin Ireland va Bernard Gregor-Smith vc)
ASV CDDCA1057 (66' · DDD)   Ⓕ**O**

The Lindsays are Haydn interpreters of rare understanding and communicative flair. Their characterisation is bold and decisive, enhanced by a scrupulous observation of the composer's expression and dynamic markings. Faster movements tend to be more urgent, less ruminative, than those from the Quatuor Mosaïques. The *zingarese* cross-rhythms of No 4's Minuet have an abrasive edge, and the *Presto e scherzando* finale is no mere frolic in The Lindsays' hands – its wit can scathe and sting, and the closing theme, with its gypsy *acciaccaturas*, has an almost manic insistence. Elsewhere they bring an ideal warmth and lyricism to the opening movement of No 1, characteristically phrasing in long, eloquent spans, and a quixotic energy to the outer movements of the G minor, No 3, where the Quatuor Mosaïques is broader and tougher. In the Minuet The Lindsays' singing line and flexibility of pulse realise to the full Haydn's searching harmonic progressions; and the lulling E flat Trio is exquisitely floated. Each of the slow movements reveals dedication and profound identification. The players vindicate their dangerously slow tempo in the sublime *Affettuoso e sostenuto* of No 1 with the breadth and intensity of their phrasing, subtlety of colour and feeling for harmonic flux. As ever, the occasional moment of impure intonation is a small price to pay for performances of such colour, character and spontaneity. The Lindsays observe all the important marked repeats and the recording is vivid and truthful. Characterisation of the sharply contrasted Nos 2, 5 and 6 is invariably vivid, phrasing is alive and inventive, and the players combine a scrupulous care for Haydn's dynamic and expression markings with a strong feeling for the music's larger contours.

String Quartets, Op 33

String Quartets, Op 33 Nos 1-6   ℗
Quatuor Mosaïques (Erich Höbarth, Andrea Bischof vns Anita Mitterer va Christophe Coin vc)
Auvidis Naïve ② E8801 (121' · DDD)   Ⓕ**OOO**

Nos 1, 4 & 6 are also available separately on Auvidis Naïve E8570   Ⓕ**O**

 The Mosaïques, at a rather slower tempo than usual, find in the theme-and-variation finale of the G major

Quartet, No 5, an unsuspected reflective tenderness. The theme itself is played with a characteristic touch of flexibility and a gentle lift to the dotted rhythms; in the first variation Erich Höbarth shapes his decorative semiquavers *fioriture* with apparently spontaneous fantasy; the luminous, high-lying textures of the second are exquisitely realised; and even the *Presto* send-off has a delicacy and whimsy in keeping with what has gone before. The Mosaïques' readings of the slow movements in the so-called *Joke* (No 2) and *Bird* (No 3) Quartets are again outstanding in their grave tenderness, their sensitivity to harmonic flux and the improvisatory freedom Erich Höbarth brings to his ornamental figuration. The *Bird*, in particular, receives as searching a performance as ever heard: in the first movement the players steal in almost imperceptibly, respond vividly to the music's richness and wit, and bring a spectral *pianissimo* to the mysterious lull in the development. The Slavonic finale, one of several movements to benefit from the lighter, more flexible period bows, goes with terrific fire and panache.

From the teasingly timed initial upbeat of the D major Quartet, No 6, the Mosaïques' performances have all the familiar hallmarks: inventive phrasing, subtly varied colour, a sure sense of organic growth and a spontaneous-sounding delight in Haydn's inspired unpredictability. Tempo and manner in the opening *Vivace assai* of No 6 are, typically, gentler than that of the equally imaginative Lindsays, the articulation lighter and more delicate, as you would expect from period strings. They catch ideally the music's glancing *scherzando* spirit, with a delightfully eager, quick-witted give-and-take between the instruments. Like The Lindsays, the Mosaïques vividly play up the contrast between the perky, high-stepping D major theme and alternating D minor melody. But the Mosaïques flex the tempo more freely and play with the length of Haydn's upbeats, to witty or pathetic effect.

In the *Andante* of the B minor Quartet (No 1) the Mosaïques arguably overdo the whimsical hesitations. However, their unusally reflective way with this movement, and the sense of remoteness they bring to the strange, spare second theme is very appealing. The undervalued B flat Quartet (No 4) is a delight throughout, from the puckish opening movement, with its quasi-improvisatory freedom to the comic exuberance of the finale; the vitality and point of the inner voices' semiquavers in the finale's G minor episode are typical of the character brought to seemingly routine accompanying figuration.

This set has playing that marries uncommon style, technical finesse and re-creative flair. The recording has an attractive ambient warmth.

String Quartets, Op 33 Nos 1, 2 & 4
The Lindsays (Peter Cropper, Ronald Birks *vns* Robin Ireland *va* Bernard Gregor-Smith *vc*)
ASV CDDCA937 (62' · DDD) Recorded 1994 ℗○

The Lindsays' is chamber-music-making of unusual flair, untouched by the faintest hint of routine. In their uncommonly grave, inward readings of the slow movements of the E flat and B flat Quartets they sustain a daringly slow tempo magnificently, phrasing in long, arching spans, always acutely sensitive to harmonic movement, as in their subtle colouring of Haydn's breathtaking tonal excursions in No 4. Beethoven is evoked in The Lindsays' swift, mordant reading of No 1's epigrammatic *Scherzo*: rarely have the waspish part-writing and the abrupt, disconcerting contrasts in dynamics and articulation been so vividly realised. Typically, it makes the most of the complete change of mood and texture in the major-key Trio, finding an almost Viennese sweetness of tone and phrase, complete with touches of *portamento*. The finale, fast, fierce, utterly uncomical, has a distinct whiff of the Hungarian *puszta* here, both in the wild gypsy figuration and the mounting passion of the sequence in the development. The Lindsays bring an ideal spaciousness and flexibility to the urbane, quietly spoken first movement of the E flat Quartet, No 2, taking due note of Haydn's *cantabile* marking. In the finales of this Quartet and No 4 they bring vital, inventively varied phrasing, palpably relishing Haydn's exuberance and comic sleight of hand.

String Quartets, Op 33 Nos 3, 5 & 6
The Lindsays (Peter Cropper, Ronald Birks *vns* Robin Ireland *va* Bernard Gregor-Smith *vc*)
ASV CDDCA938 (61' · DDD) ℗○○

The Lindsays eclipse all comers in range of colour, vital, creative phrasing and emotional penetration. They respond gleefully to the subversive comedy that pervades each of the three works – most overtly in the Slavonic-influenced finale of *The Bird* (No 3), and in the outrageous *Scherzo* of No 5, where with explosive *sforzandos* and sly touches of timing they relish to the full Haydn's rhythmic and dynamic mayhem. But time and again in this music wit is suddenly suffused with poetry; and they bring a glancing delicacy and grace of interplay to, say, the startling tonal deflexions in the opening *Vivace assai* of No 6. With their slower-than-usual tempo and wonderfully tender, contained *sotto voce*, the second movement of No 3, where Haydn transmutes the Minuet-scherzo into a hymn, becomes the expressive core of the quartet. The Lindsays constantly provoke you to respond afresh to Haydn; to his wit, comic exuberance and his often unsuspected profundity.

String Quartet, Op 42

Haydn String Quartet, Op 42 **Schumann** String Quartet No 3 in A, Op 41 No 3
Shostakovich String Quartet No 3 in F, Op 73
Allegri Quartet (Peter Carter, David Roth *vns* Jonathan Barritt *va* Bruno Schrecker *vc*)

Naim Audio NAIMCD016 (73' · DDD) Ⓕ

Haydn's exquisite Op 42 is given an especially winning rendition, the *Andante ed innocentemente* first movement donning a degree of understatement that reflects its equivocal personality. Following it with Shostakovich's Op 73 was an inspired idea: the former ends quietly and the latter opens with a sort of distracted innocence, marking time before the real drama starts. The argument suddenly intensifies, playfully, provocatively, though characterisation is cleverly differentiated. In the second movement, Prokofiev is an obvious point of reference and there has rarely been a more delicately pointed account of the weird, tiptoe *staccato* passage that emerges out of the first idea. The third movement is a striking precursor of the 10th Symphony's violent 'Stalin' *Scherzo*, the slow movement redolent of the 12th Symphony's noble opening and the long finale ending in a mood of veiled mystery. Above all, this is profoundly natural playing and the recordings maintain a realistic 'small concert-hall' ambience throughout. The disc ends with an affectionate, flexible performance of Schumann's loveliest string quartet. The opening *Andante espressivo* sets the mood while the ensuing second set (1'19") is limpid and rapturous, and the finale – which in some hands can seem repetitive – is given precisely the right degree of rhythmic emphasis. Again one senses wholehearted identification between the repertoire and its interpreters – and while one may question the wisdom of mixed-repertory CD programmes, this one is so well planned and well played, that it can be recommended even to those who already own recordings within cycles.

String Quartets, Op 54

String Quartets, Op 54 Nos 1-3
The Lindsays (Peter Cropper, Ronald Birks vns Robin Ireland va Bernard Gregor-Smith vc)
ASV CDDCA582 (66' · DDD) Fmm

All three quartets are in the usual four-movement form but they contain many surprises: in No 1, the false recapitulation in the first movement, the dark modulations in the following sonata-form *Allegretto* and the Hungarian gipsy flavour (anticipated in the Minuet) and mischievousness of the final rondo. No 2 has a rhapsodic fiddler in its second movement, a nostalgic minuet with an extraordinarily anguished trio, and an *Adagio* finale in which a *Presto* section turns out to be no more than an episode. A notable feature of No 3 is ternary-form *Largo cantabile*, the centre of which is more like a mini-concerto for the first violin; 'Scotch snaps' pervade the Minuet, and pedal points the finale. The performances and the recording are superb, marked by unanimity, fine tone, suppleness of phrasing, and acute dynamic shaping; in the second movement of No 1 there are hushed passages whose homogeneity and quality of

sound are both quite remarkable. Overall, this recording is irresistible.

String Quartets, Op 55

String Quartets, Op 55 Nos 1-3
The Lindsays (Peter Cropper, Ronald Birks vns Robin Ireland va Bernard Gregor-Smith vc)
ASV CDDCA906 (64' · DDD) Recorded 1994 ⒻO

Most immediately striking of the trilogy is the F minor work, No 2, with its searching double variations on related minor and major themes (a favourite form in Haydn's later music), spiky, rebarbative second movement *Allegro* and strangely spare contrapuntal Minuet. The A major, No 1, has much of this key's traditional brilliance, with ample scope for the leader's creative virtuosity in the outer movements and the stratospheric trio of the minuet; in contrast the noble, wonderfully scored *Adagio cantabile* prefigures the profound slow movements of Haydn's final years. The more inward-looking No 3 in B flat is specially remarkable for the varied recapitulations in the flanking movements, astonishingly free and inventive even for Haydn, and the subtle chromatic colouring in all four movements which may just owe something to the quartets Mozart had dedicated to Haydn three years earlier. Here and there The Lindsays' intonation is less than true, but as so often with this group, this is a small price to pay for performances of such colour and penetration. The balance, as with many recent quartet recordings, is a shade closer than ideal but the overall sound picture is very acceptable.

String Quartets, Op 64

String Quartets, Op 64 Nos 1-3
Kodály Quartet (Attila Falvay, Tamás Szabo vns Gábor Fias va János Devich vc)
Naxos 8 550673 (64' · DDD) Recorded 1992 Ⓢ

String Quartets, Op 64 Nos 4-6
Kodály Quartet (Attila Falvay, Tamás Szabo vns Gábor Fias va János Devich vc)
Naxos 8 550674 (65' · DDD) Recorded 1992 Ⓢ

The so-called *Lark* (No 5), with its soaring opening melody and *moto perpetuo* finale, is perhaps the most immediately fetching of all Haydn's quartets. But No 6 is at least as fine, with its intimate and intensely argued opening movement, its poignant, exquisitely textured *Andante* and a finale full of instrumental fooling and insouciant contrapuntal virtuosity. Of the other works, No 2 is one of Haydn's most astringent pieces, from its tonally deceptive opening to the mordant, unsettling humour of the finale. Quartets Nos 3 and 4 return to a more familiar vein of sociable wit. Both are endlessly subtle and surprising in their arguments, with *cantabile* slow movements of peculiar candour and eloquence. Quartet No 1, the least favoured of the six is certainly the plainest in its thematic ideas. But it's an absorbing, immensely sophisticated piece, exploring an astonishing range of textures; the recapitulation of the leisurely first movement opens up marvellous new harmonic vistas, while the central development of the finale is a canonic *tour de force*. The Kodály Quartet has rightly won plaudits for its wonderfully civilised playing; mellow and lyrical, far removed from the highly strung brilliance cultivated by many modern quartets. Ensemble and intonation are first class, tempos generally spacious, with broad, natural and beautifully matched phrasing. It's at its very finest where Haydn is at his most searching; and the Quartets Nos 2, 5 and 6 each receive outstanding, deeply considered performances. In one or two movements the Kodály's penchant for slowish tempos leads to a slight dourness. Against that, it brings a deliciously lazy *Ländler* lilt, enhanced by the first violin's *portamentos*, to the Trio of No 6, and a grave, inward intensity to each of Haydn's slow movements. The recording, made in a Budapest church, is resonant and less intimate than is ideal in this music.

String Quartets, Opp 71 and 74

String Quartets, Op 71 Nos 1-3
Kodály Quartet (Attila Falvay, Tamás Szabo *vns* Gábor Fias *va* János Devich *vc*)
Naxos 8 550394 (62' · DDD) Recorded 1989 Ⓢ

String Quartets, Op 74 Nos 1-3
Kodály Quartet (Attila Falvay, Tamás Szabo *vns* Gábor Fias *va* János Devich *vc*)
Naxos 8 550396 (63' · DDD) Recorded 1989 Ⓢ

The Kodály Quartet plays with evident joy and an easy neatness of ensemble. There's never a hint of routine and the inter-communication is matched by enormous care for detail. Just sample the elegant *Andante* with variations which form the slow movement of Op 71 No 3, or the witty Minuet which follows, or any of the consistently inspired Op 74 set. The hushed intensity of playing in the *Largo assai* of Op 74 No 3 is unforgettable. The recordings are wholly natural and balanced within a well-judged acoustic; the sound is of the highest quality and documentation is excellent. At their modest price this pair of CDs is irresistible.

String Quartets, Op 76

String Quartets, Op 76 Nos 1-6 🄷
Tátrai Quartet (Vilmos Tátrai, Mihály Szücs *vns* György Konrád *va* Ede Banda *vc*)
Hungaroton ② HCD12812/3-2 (128' · ADD)
Recorded 1964-5 Ⓕ

Your reaction to this recommendation may be, for heaven's sake, why not a modern recording in stereo? Play them and you'll know the answer. The performances are breathtaking – for each player's sensitivity and brilliance, their intimately interwoven ensemble and, most of all, their revelatory characterisation. Even the recording is remarkable for its age. When writing these six works in his mid-sixties Haydn was at the peak of his powers. You'll be bowled over as much by their unpredictable ingenuity as by their startling range and variety of experience. The Tátrai's musical response is very immediate. This finds outlet in readiness to risk fast tempos for livelier movements (always with a touch of virtuoso brilliance when needed) as well as great intensity in slow movements. Pungency of accentuation and clarity of articulation also contribute to its youthful vividness, as does its wide range of dynamics and colour – arrestingly demonstrated in the dramatic opening movement of No 2. Though the sound quality may not compare with the best on offer today, its clarity is admirable: microphones seem less close than on many modern recordings, permitting everything to emerge in better perspective. But it's Haydn's genius that overwhelms you, and just as Haydn's own imagination seems progressively to take wing in the course of the six works, so does the players' own commitment.

String Quartets, Op 76 Nos 1-3
The Lindsays (Peter Cropper, Ronald Birks *vns* Robin Ireland *va* Bernard Gregor-Smith *vc*)
ASV CDDCA1076 (75' · DDD) Ⓕ●

These are among the finest Haydn quartet recordings heard in years, performances which will quickly establish themselves as classics. They are consistently a degree more refined in texture and control of dynamic than the Lindsays' earlier live recordings, and the ensemble is more polished. Yet the feeling of spontaneity is just as intense, with Haydn's witty moments pointed even more infectiously, as in the finale of Op 76 No 2, where in the main theme the little upward *portamentos* at the end of the eighth bar are delectably timed on each occurrence. The studio sound is fuller, too, and far better balanced, so that one can register far more clearly than before the first violin's rapid triplets in the finale of the *Emperor*; it's ideally crisp articulation. Matching the new performances of the *Fifths* and the *Emperor*, The Lindsays' account of Op 76 No 1 is just as strongly characterised. The sense of fun in the opening *Allegro con spirito* is deliciously brought out, leading on to an account of the sublime *Adagio*, both dedicated and refined, which conveys a Beethovenian depth of expression, making most rivals sound superficial.

String Quartets, Op 76 – Nos 4-6
Lindsay Quartet (Peter Cropper, Ronald Birks *vns* Robin Ireland *va* Bernard Gregor-Smith *vc*)
ASV CDDCA1077 (78' · DDD) Ⓕ●●

Here, in the last three Op 76 quartets, you've Haydn interpretations that bring forth the full range of expression in these inspired works of his official retirement. They aren't just polished and refined but communicate with an intensity that simulates live performance. No 5 in D was one of the works which The Lindsays recorded earlier live at the Wigmore Hall, but the extra subtlety this time means that rhythms are a degree more liltingly seductive, in which humour is more delightfully pointed, as in the repeated cadence-figure at the start of the finale, with comic pauses beautifully timed.

The quiet opening of No 4, which gave rise to the nickname 'Sunrise', gently insinuates itself before the full thrust of the *Allegro* takes over; with its heightened contrasts, it could not be more captivating. Most strikingly, too, the slow movements in each of these three quartets are given a visionary intensity, matching The Lindsays' treatment of the slow movement of No 1 in the companion disc.

Here is music from the last years of Haydn's career which in these performances has you thinking forward to middle or late Beethoven and the new world of the 19th century. So the *Adagio* of No 4 brings a hymn-like dedication, not least in the dark E flat minor episode, and the astonishing modulations in the *Fantasia* slow movement of No 6 convey the tingle of new discovery, with magical *pianissimos* for contrast. This was a work which for Donald Tovey marked a tailing-off of inspiration, but one registers the opposite with The Lindsays, when the *adagio* Fantasia gives way to such witty treatment both in the *presto* Minuet (in fact a *scherzo*), with its weird leaps, and the *Allegro spirituoso* finale.

With refined sound that draws out the subtleties of balance between these players, here's another disc of Haydn from The Lindsays that sets the highest standards.

String Quartets, Op 76 Nos 2-4
Alban Berg Quartet (Günter Pichler, Gerhard Schulz *vns* Thomas Kakuska *va* Valentin Erben *vc*)
EMI 556166-2 (66' · DDD) Recorded 1993-4   Ⓕ

This disc is uncommonly fine, above all the performance of the D minor, No 2. The Berg take both outer movements more spaciously than most of their rivals. The opening *Allegro* is tough and austere, the players thinking and phrasing in long spans, bringing an urgent sweep to the development and a true sense of climax to the coda. And with its broader tempo the Berg realise details like the repeated hairpin *crescendos* on the sequence of tied notes in the second group. The Hungarian-tinged finale has great trenchancy and symphonic weight, with an imaginative variety of colour and accent.

The *Emperor* and the *Sunrise* are hardly less fine, marrying impressive formal control with a vivid sense of character and felicity of detail: listen, for instance, to the subtle timing and hushed, veiled tone at the sudden dip to E flat in the first movement of No 3; the rapt tenderness and breadth of phrase in the sublime *Adagio* of

the *Sunrise*, the melody unfolding in a single unbroken span; or the deft management of the progressive speed increases in the finale of the same work. The leader's very fluid, ruminative phrasing in the Quartet's opening makes it seem even more than usual like a slow introduction, with the first phrase stealing in magically from nowhere.

At their best, the Berg bring rare imaginative insight to this inexhaustible music. The recording is both clear and sympathetic.

String Quartets, Op 77

String Quartets – Op 77 Nos 1 & 2; Op 103 in   Ⓟ
D minor (unfinished)
Quatuor Mosaïques (Erich Höbarth, Andrea Bischof *vns* Anita Mitterer *va* Christophe Coin *vc*)
Astrée Naïve E8800 (62' · DDD)   Ⓕ

Anyone who thinks that period-instrument performance means austerity and coolness should listen to this disc. Here's playing full of expressive warmth and vigour. The opening of Op 77 No 1 is done duly gracefully, but with a sturdy underlying rhythm and the *Scherzo* is crisp and alive. Then the first movement of the F major work is beautifully done, with many sensitive details; and the lovely second movement is ideally leisurely, so that the players have ample room for manoeuvre and the leader makes much of his opportunities for delicate playing in the filigree-like high music. The players show a real grasp of structure and illuminate the key moments with a touch more deliberation or a little additional weight of tone. These performances, clearly recorded, are competitive not merely within the protected world of 'early music' but in the bigger, 'real' world too!

Additional recommendation

String Quartets – Op 20, No 5; 'The Joke', Op 33
No 2; Op 54 No 1; 'The Lark', Op 64 No 5; 'The
Rider', Op 74 No 3; 'Fifths', Op 76 No 2; Op 77 No 1
Emerson Quartet
DG ③ 471 327-2GH2 (141' · DDD)   Ⓕ
A magnificent set – the Emersons' playing is lively, poised and expressive. An excellent introduction to Haydn's mature quartets.

Seven Last Words, Op 51

The Seven Last Words, Op 51, HobIII Nos 50-56
Rosamunde Quartet
ECM New Series 461 780-2 (66' · DDD)   ⒻⓄⓄ

This reading is alert not only to musical texture, but to the modulating phrase and the dramaturgy of key changes between movements. The playing is limpid and subtly coloured, sparing of vibrato (in that respect the Rosamunde are heedful of various period-instrument models) and, at the beginning of the third movement, suspended in a sense of rapture. Another imaginative aspect of this performance is the way it reflects the sense of the text, just as Haydn does in those movements that seem to follow the pattern of the words he set. This feeling of narrative is especially keen in the fourth movement, 'Woman, behold thy son!' and the closing 'Earthquake'.

The list of virtues is fairly simple to enumerate: variety and refinement of tone, internal clarity, historical awareness, imagination and a certain poise that not all its rivals can claim in equal measure. It serves well as a compromise between period-instrument clarity and modern-instrument warmth. Against strong competition its fuller instrumental sonority is marginally to be preferred. First-rate reportage of a wonderful score.

Seven Last Words, Op 51ª (interspersed with Seven Gregorian Responsories for Holy Weekᵇ)
ªCarmina Quartet (Matthias Enderle, Susanne Frank vns Wendy Champney va Stephan Goerner vc)
ᵇSchola Romana Lucernensis / Father Roman Bannwart
Claves 50-2002 (74' · DDD) Text and translation included   Ⓕ Ⓞ

Haydn's *Seven Last Words* was designed for performance in Holy Week, in the Santa Cueva grotto in Cádiz, with discourses from the bishop on each of the seven utterances followed by Haydn's musical meditation. Originally these were orchestral pieces, not the string quartet versions (arranged by Haydn to widen access to the music) which are more often given today. Haydn was concerned that 'seven *Adagios*' would be exhausting to the listener, and probably wouldn't have favoured performing them without a break. The idea of interspersing them with Holy Week Gregorian responsories is certainly an appropriate solution.

The group singing them here is a mixed choir, although we hear either the men or the women, never the two together. They sing in a carefully moulded style, cadences softly rounded off; ensemble is precise, from the women especially. The Carmina Quartet plays with a remarkably wide range of expression. The Introduction is quite fiercely done, and the 'Terremoto' at the end has a violence and is taken at a pace that almost obscures the pulse of the music.

In between, they play the 'seven *Adagios*' (as Haydn called them – actually three *Largos*, two *Graves*, a *Lento* and an *Adagio*) as they would any other Haydn slow movement. The first is quite relaxed and lyrical, although its accents are well marked, and it has touches of added ornamentation. Refinement and delicacy of line characterise the second, and the third, the E major meditation on 'Mother, behold thy son', is done with much tenderness.

In the fourth their realisation of Haydn's notated ornaments – the appoggiaturas in bars 2 and 4, and at several points later – are oddly perverse and disturbing: one played short, the

other long, although the second phrase is a clear echo of the first. No 5 ('I thirst') again draws some very telling soft playing from the quartet, but also pained *forzato* accents, and there's forceful expression of 'Consummatum est', along with moments of tenderness. They play the E flat No 7 with the sense of calm and fulfilment that Haydn surely sought. Their tempos, generally, are well chosen, perhaps faster at times than many quartets take these pieces, but this helps bridge the gulf between Haydn's normal mode of expression and the special significance of this remarkable music.

Additional recommendation

Fitzwilliam Quartet   Ⓟ
Linn Records CKD153 (62' · DDD)   Ⓕ
A chaste, inward reading on period instruments, deeply musical, swifter than some but always thoughtfully articulated. A compelling recording, beautifully balanced.

Piano Trios

HobXV – No 1 in G minor; No 2 in F; No 5 in G; No 6 in F; No 7 in D; No 8 in B flat; No 9 in A; No 10 in E flat; No 11 in F minor; No 12 in E minor; No 13 in C minor; No 14 in A flat; No 15 in G; No 16 in D; No 17 in F; No 18 in A; No 19 in G minor; No 20 in B flat; No 21 in C; No 22 in E flat; No 23 in D minor; No 24 in D; No 25 in G, 'Gypsy Trio'; No 26 in F sharp minor; No 27 in C; No 28 in E; No 29 in E flat; No 30 in E flat; No 31 in E flat minor; No 32 in G; No 34 in E; No 35 in A; No 36 in E flat; No 37 in F; No 38 in B flat; No 39 in F; No 40 in F; No 41 in G; No C1 in C; No f1 in E flat

---

Piano Trios: HobXV – Nos 18, 24, 25 & 29
Vienna Piano Trio (Wolfgang Redik vn Marcus Trefny vc Stefan Mendl pf)
Nimbus NI5535 (60' · DDD)   Ⓕ Ⓞ

The *Gypsy* Trio, No 25, may have been written in and for London, but this ensemble's short, snappy bowing, stomping piano accents and instinctive fluctuations of tempo and pulse in the finale, locate the work in the grape-treading, Romany heart of the Burgenland. The steps of the dance shape and pervade the E flat Trio, too, in the jaunty rhythms of the opening *Allegretto*, and the boisterous and cross-accented Allemande of its finale. Among countless delights in these bold performances is the sensitivity to the power of silence, and the short, hushed half-tones within the long-breathed lines of the *Andante* of the A major Trio. And, not least, the perceptive understanding and judgement of the shifting qualities of an *Allegro* which so well supports the structure of the outer movements of the D major, as well as enabling many a clearly articulated yet fanciful variation in the *Gipsy* Trio. These recordings are close, sometimes breathy, always thrillingly true.

Keyboard Sonatas

HobXVI: No 1 in C **No 2** in B flat **No 3** in C **No 4** in D **No 5** in A (doubtful) **No 6** in G **No 7** in C **No 8** in G **No 9** in F **No 10** in C **No 11** in G **No 12** in A (doubtful) **No 13** in E (doubtful) **No 14** in D **No 15** in E flat (doubtful) **No 17** (spurious) **No 18** in B flat **No 19** in D **No 20** in C minor **No 21** in D **No 22** in E **No 23** in F **No 24** in D **No 25** in E flat **No 26** in A **No 27** in G **No 28** in E flat **No 29** in F **No 30** in A **No 31** in E **No 32** in B minor **No 33** in D **No 34** in E minor **No 35** in C **No 36** in C sharp minor **No 37** in D **No 38** in E flat **No 39** in G **No 40** in G **No 41** in B flat **No 42** in D **No 43** in A flat **No 44** in G minor **No 45** E flat **No 46** in A flat **No 47** in F **No 48** in C **No 49** in E flat **No 50** in C **No 51** in D **No 52** in E flat **Deest** E flat (doubtful)

Piano Sonatas: HobXVI – Nos 20, 32, 34, 37, 40, 42, 48-52. HobXVII – No 4, Fantasia in C; No 6, Variations in F minor; No 9, Adagio in F
Alfred Brendel pf
Philips ④ 416 643-2PH4 (205' · ADD/DDD) Booklet included Ⓕ**OOO**

![G]These sonatas are magnificent creations, wonderfully well played by Alfred Brendel. Within the order and scale of these works Haydn explores a rich diversity of musical languages, a wit and broadness of expression that quickly repays attentive listening. It's the capriciousness as much as the poetry that Brendel so perfectly attends to; his playing, ever alive to the vitality and subtleties, makes these discs a delight. The sophistication innate in the simple dance rhythms, the rusticity that emerges, but above all, the sheer *joie de vivre* are gladly embraced. Brendel's continual illumination of the musical ideas through intense study pays huge dividends. The recording quality varies enormously between the different works and though the close acoustic on some of the later discs could be faulted for allowing one to hear too much of the keyboard action, it certainly brings one into vivid contact with the music.

Piano Sonatas: HobXVI – Nos 20, 34, 40, 44, 48-52. HobXVII No 4, Fantasia in C
András Schiff pf
Teldec ⓐ 0630-17141-2 (147' · DDD) Ⓕ**O**

András Schiff has consistently championed Haydn, not only the sonatas but also the glorious late piano trios. If his way with Haydn tends to be more intimate, less robust and less gleefully subversive than Brendel's, Schiff is equally acute in his responses to the music's drama, wit and poetry, and in his control of narrative line. His 'centred' tone and limpid, subtly coloured soft playing are a constant delight, as is his variety of articulation and nuance. He plays all the marked repeats, embellishing and dramatising them as appropriate; and he's alive to Haydn's manipulations of silence, timing pauses and fermatas with an ear for their exact comic or dramatic significance. Schiff's great C minor Sonata is one of the most searching readings on record: the outer movements combine refinement of detail with bold dramatic contrasts and a terrific overall sweep. The finale, a notch slower than Brendel's, is also more impassioned and disturbing, rising (especially in the repeat) to a final climax of desperate intensity. Schiff's virtuoso technique – and his understanding of Haydn's silences – pays special dividends in a dazzling performance of the C major *Fantasia*. And he wonderfully realises the richness and sophistication of the final three sonatas. In the first movement of the C major, where Haydn conjures miracles from his initial vision of dry bones, Schiff's playing is as crisp and as vividly orchestrated as Brendel's. He's also more spacious in the E flat sonata, a magnificent, probing reading which realises the music's reach, poetry and harmonic daring as completely as any. The recording captures the beautiful, luminous sonorities of his Bösendorfer, and provides just the right amount of space around the sound.

Piano Sonatas: HobXVI – Nos 26, 32, 36-7, 49
Leif Ove Andsnes pf
EMI 556756-2 (58' · DDD) Ⓕ**O**

This disc offers delectable performances of five shrewdly contrasted works: two troubled, trenchant minor-key sonatas from the 1770s juxtaposed with a pair of lightweight pieces from the same period and culminating in the great E flat Sonata. Andsnes is responsive to the individual character of these sonatas, to their richness and variety of incident, and their sheer unpredictablility. With his wide spectrum of colour and dynamics he makes no apologies for using a modern Steinway. But his playing, founded on a pellucid *cantabile* touch and diamantine passagework, marries classical refinement and clarity with a spontaneous exuberance, a sense that the next phrase is yet to be created. Andsnes is always ready to add stylish and witty touches of embellishment to the repeats. The opening movements of both minor-key sonatas have a lithe, sinewy urgency, above all in the vehement sequences of their developments, together with a rare delicacy of nuance: and here, as elsewhere, you notice how alive and concentrated is his *piano* and *pianissimo* playing. Andsnes brings a bright, buoyant yet lyrical approach to the E flat Sonata's outer movements, to the wonderful *Adagio* a limpid line, a subtly flexed pulse and, in the B flat minor central episode, a true sense of passion. This is just the sort of playing – joyous, imaginative, involving – to win Haydn's sonatas a wider following. The recording of the E flat, made in a church in Oslo, has slightly more ambient warmth than that of the remaining sonatas, recorded at EMI's Abbey Road studios. But throughout, the piano sound is natural and present without being too closely miked.

Haydn Piano Sonatas: HobXVI – Nos 30 & 52
Schubert Piano Sonata No 14 in A minor, D784.
Marche militaire No 1 in D, D733 (arr Tausig)
Evgeni Kissin pf
Sony Classical SK64538 (62' · DDD) Recorded 1994
                                                        Ⓕ Ⓞ

This is Haydn playing of high style and verve – also affectionate, articulate, colourful and expressive. Its vitality seems authentic even when Kissin asks you to admire the means with which he achieves it. This isn't wilful or eccentric playing. By the end of the A major work, an engaging and unconventional sonata, even by Haydn's standards, you feel its stature has been enhanced. Kissin meets the greater challenge of Haydn's last sonata equally well. The breadth as well as the brilliance of the first movement is there, and its warmth; his tempo may be a little brisker than usual but it still allows for weight. The last movement *Presto* really is breakneck, at a speed which would be unwise for most others; once again the impression is of allure allied to perfectly judged dramatic tension and articulate speech. Maybe he sustains the phrases of the *Adagio* with less success: they tend to emerge a bar at a time instead of as an arching span. How difficult this is to do when tone on the piano dies so quickly. But it's precisely this kind of growth and building through sentences and long paragraphs – and through silences – that he manages so well in the first movement of the Schubert sonata. Above all, there's a commanding vision of the whole. The recording balance isn't too close; the sound pleasingly open and natural.

Piano Sonatas: HobXVI Nos 35-9
Jenö Jandó pf
Naxos 8 553128 (62' · DDD) Recorded 1993   Ⓢ Ⓞ

The exquisite, classical balance evident in these six sonatas makes them rewarding examples of Haydn's exploitation of the piano's broad expressive range and rich textural variety. This volume in Jenö Jandó's complete edition presents these pieces in a compelling, modern-instrument version. For example, there's brilliance and sparkle in the opening movements of the D major and E flat Sonatas; warmth and dramatic intensity in the slow movements (most notably in the Baroque echoes of the Sonatas in C major and D major), and an appealing blend of wit and elegance in finales such as the third movement of the D major Sonata. Most remarkable, though, is the G major, where Jandó's precision and sensitive balance of linear and harmonic dimensions convey its concerto character and Haydn's imaginative approach to form. Try Jandó's engaging account of the opening *Allegro*, his deft balance of the slow movement's effective blend of major and minor, and his exuberant virtuosity in the finale.

The keyboard sonatas which Haydn originally intended for piano, such as the four considered here, show hi's exploration of the instrument's capacity for greater dynamic variation. Jandó is sensitive to the relationship between motif and dynamics which is particularly evident in the E flat and D major Sonatas respectively. Aided by clear recorded sound, Jandó's warmth in the lyrical passages provides a dramatic contrast to his crisp, positive approach in the livelier music. Jandó's glittering technique has a high profile in the other two sonatas in the programme. His well-turned readings are uncontroversial, but they lack nothing in excitement. Sample the finale of the E flat Sonata, where the wealth of expressive detail at an extremely fast tempo is breathtaking.

The Complete Piano Sonatas, Volume 2
Piano Sonatas HobXVI Nos 2, 5, 6, 14; E flat, Deest
Roland Batik pf
Camerata CM472 (64' · DDD)   Ⓕ

Piano Sonatas HobXVI Nos 20, 46, 49
Hélène Couvert pf
Zig Zag Territoires ZZT030502 (71' · DDD)   Ⓕ

HobXVI No 5 and No 16 on Roland Batik's disc probably aren't by Haydn. There's scholarly disagreement about No 2 and the E flat sonata, Hob/Deest. That leaves No 6 and No 14 as the undisputedly real articles – No 6 is the finer, bearing the imprint of incipient greatness. Batik reserves his most committed playing for this work; he invests the melancholic slow movement with feeling but doesn't inflate its proportions, improvises small cadenzas at fermatas, and tactfully judges the dynamics that are needed. Here's playing of high refinement, and the Bösendorfer piano is a delight.

No questioning the authorship of the sonatas chosen by Hélène Couvert. They're definitely by Haydn, and are mostly interpreted in a manner that recognises their value. Purists might quail at the suggestions of 'romanticism' in the treatment of phrases, and the hint of *notes iné-gales* in the opening movement of No 46. They might also take umbrage that the through-composed coda in the first movement of No 49 is only played when the second half is repeated. Maybe it's a liberty: this 'tail' should have been heard both times, but a single appearance undoubtedly enhances its impact. Couvert never slights Haydn; nor is she slighted by Ax, Brendel and Schiff, who by their longer experience often find more in the music than she does. If the last movement of No 49, isn't dance-like and is too jaunty to convey the shadows of the E flat minor episode, No 20 is fine enough to stand alongside the best. She's a cultivated pianist and a potentially distinguished musician.

Piano Sonatas: HobXVI Nos 49-52
Jenö Jandó pf
Naxos 8 550657 (62' · DDD) Recorded 1992   Ⓢ

Piano Sonatas HobXVI No 33, 36, 43, 45 & 46
Emanuel Ax pf
Sony Classical SK89363 (78' · DDD)   Ⓕ

Harpsichord sonorities are never far away here; indeed, they're clearly suggested in the outer movements of No 45. Since it's an early work, Haydn is likely to have written it for this instrument. Not that Emanuel Ax is concerned; he takes the modern piano on its own terms and shuns imitation without alienating these sonatas from their period. Perhaps the sharp transients of a harpsichord or fortepiano might have sharpened the rhetoric of Haydn's musical language. But if some of the force has been blunted by the nature of the piano, then grace, melancholy or lyricism are enhanced. The *Adagio* of No 46 shows how much feeling he can bring to the music through tonal inflexions, and broadening or telescoping the line without breaking stylistic boundaries. In the last movement he's adroit and incisive. Witty, too, in his timing of the demisemiquaver flourishes in the first movement of No 33; but inexplicably straitlaced in the finale because he doesn't decorate any of the repeats in the variations. The contrasts in the last movement of No 36 don't escape his notice. He's sombrely circumspect in the C sharp minor Menuet, brightly expressive in the Trio, perceptive in the Menuet's *da capo* return, as if as a shadow of its former self. The recording is a bit close and bass-shy, but offers no impediment to concentrated listening.

Masses

Mass in B flat , Missa Sancti Bernardi de Offida ℗ (Heiligmesse), HobXXII/10. Mare Clausum, HobXXIVa/9. Insanae et vanae curae. Motetti de Venerabili Sacramento, HobXXIIIc/5a-d. Te Deum in C, HobXXIIIc/2
Jörg Hering ten **Harry van der Kamp** bass
Tölz Boys' Choir; Tafelmusik / Bruno Weil
Sony Classical SK66260 (63' · DDD) Recorded 1994
Texts and translations included   Ⓕ

A special attraction for Haydn lovers is the first-ever recording of the unfinished ode *Mare Clausum*, commissioned in 1794 by Haydn's English friend Lord Abingdon, and abandoned when the nobleman was imprisoned for libel. The gauche, crudely chauvinistic verses, trumpet England's sovereignty of the sea. But the two numbers Haydn completed are worthy of his ripest style: a noble F major bass aria with rich, inventive writing for woodwind, authoritatively sung by Harry van der Kamp, and a D major chorus whose verve and contrapuntal power presage the late Masses and oratorios. Under Bruno Weil's spirited direction the Tölz Boys' Choir, with their bright-edged, slightly breathy tone, and the period orchestra, Tafelmusik, are on first-rate form throughout this enterprisingly planned disc, which includes the thrilling, majestic, late *Te Deum* and the motet *Insanae et vanae curae.*

Weil's reading is eagerly responsive to the music's drama, with taut rhythms, sharp dynamic contrasts and keen instrumental detailing; and he maintains the initial pulse through the tranquil D major section. Between these masterpieces the four little *Motetti de Venerabili* from the 1750s (another recorded first) inevitably sound tame, for all their easy tunefulness and skilful marshalling of rococo cliché. The largest work here is the so-called *Heiligmesse*, first of the six magnificent Mass settings of Haydn's old age. This receives an energetic, uplifting reading, with brisk tempos, fresh, incisive choral work and strongly etched orchestral colours. In one or two sections Weil can drive too hard and Harry van der Kamp sometimes overwhelms the excellent boy soloists. But there's no doubting the vigour and joyfulness of Weil's reading, nor the skill and commitment of his forces. Quite apart from its pioneering value, this is an inspiring Haydn collection whose appeal is enhanced by vivid sound.

Masses – in C, Missa in tempore belli (Paukenmesse), HobXXII/9; in B flat, Missa Sancti Bernardi von Offida (Heiligmesse), HobXXII/10. Insanae et vanae curae
Joanne Lunn sop **Sara Mingardo** contr **Topi Lehtipuu** ten **Brindley Sherratt** bass **Monteverdi Choir; English Baroque Soloists / Sir John Eliot Gardiner**
Philips 470 819-2PH (79' · DDD) Texts and translations included   ⒻⓄ

This rounds off Gardiner's excellent series of the six late masses, all supreme masterpieces, which Haydn wrote for the nameday each year of the Princess Esterhazy. There's also room for a valuable extra in the motet *Insanae et vanae curae*. Haydn salvaged it from his Italian oratorio *Il ritorno di Tobia*, after he had pruned it, saying that it was 'too good to waste'. With a Latin text replacing the original Italian, it inspires Gardiner and his brilliant team to a searing performance, very different from those you'd get from a cathedral choir.

The masses also find Gardiner on incisive form. The contrast with Hickox's Chandos cycle is most striking in the *Gloria* of the *Heiligmesse*. Where Hickox makes the music swagger happily, Gardiner directs a biting, crisp reading, with spotlit drums and trumpets and marginally less spring in the rhythm. Contrasts elsewhere are similar, if less marked; Hickox is warmer and more joyful where Gardiner, with some extreme speeds is consistently crisp and fresh.

Both masses were written in 1796 and the *Heiligmesse* first performed on the Princess's nameday that year. The *Paukenmesse* was held over until 1797, though it had been heard in Vienna the previous December. Not only are both masses smaller in scale than the succeeding four, the *Paukenmesse* at least is more lyrical, less grandly symphonic that those masterpieces. Haydn is still intent on springing surprises; he characteristically ends each with vigorous, even military settings of the 'Dona nobis pacem' which foreshadow Beethoven' illustration of war in the *Missa Solemnis*.

The Philips recording is clear and well balanced, bringing out more inner detail than the

Hickox recordings and highlighting the pin-point ensemble of Gardiner's Monteverdi Choir, with his excellent team of solists, led by the boyish-sounding Joanne Lunn.

Masses – in G,Missa 'Rorate coeli desuper', **P**
HobXXII/3;in B flat (Schöpfungsmesse), HobXXII/13
(with alternative setting of the Gloria)
Susan Gritton sop **Pamela Helen Stephen** mez
Mark Padmore ten **Stephen Varcoe** bar **Collegium**
Musicum 90 Chorus; Collegium Musicum 90 /
Richard Hickox
Chandos Chaconne CHAN0599 (62' · DDD) Texts
and translations included   Ⓕ**O**

The *Creation* Mass is no less resplendent or searching than, say, the *Nelson* Mass or the *Harmoniemesse*, a glorious affirmation of Haydn's reverent, optimistic yet by no means naive faith. Even by Haydn's standards, the work is startling in its exploitation of colourful and dramatic key contrasts, as in the sudden swerve from F major to an apocalyptic *fortissimo* D flat at 'Judicare vivos'; the *Benedictus*, characteristically, moves from serene pastoral innocence (shades of 'With verdure clad' from *The Creation*) to urgent intensity in its central development; and the sublime G major *Agnus Dei* has a profound supplicatory fervour extraordinary even among the composer's many memorable settings of this text.

This reading eclipses previous recordings in the quality of its choir and soloists, the subtlety of Hickox's direction and the vividness and transparency of the recorded sound. In faster movements like the *Kyrie* and the openings of the *Gloria* and *Credo* Hickox strikes just the right balance between dignity and happy, pulsing energy, relishing each of Haydn's dramatic *coups*; and he brings a marvellous clarity and verve, and a sure sense of climax, to the chromatically inflected fugues in the *Gloria* and at 'Dona nobis pacem'. Abetted by his first-rate orchestra, Hickox is always alive to the felicities of Haydn's scoring, while the 24-strong professional choir is superbly responsive throughout.

We also get the alternative version of the *Gloria*, and the ultra-compressed (6'49") and instantly forgettable *Missa rorate coeli desuper*, which David Wyn Jones, in his excellent note, wryly describes as 'a reminder of how perfunctory church music in 18th-century Austria could be'. It's neatly dispatched by Hickox and his forces, but inevitably comes as an anticlimax.

Masses – in E flat (Great Organ Mass), HobXXII/4ª;
in C, Missa Celensis (Mariazeller), HobXXII/8
Susan Gritton sop **Louise Winter** mez **Mark Pad-**
more ten **Stephen Varcoe** bar **Alan Watson** org
Collegium Musicum 90 / Richard Hickox
Chandos Chaconne CHAN0674 (71' · DDD)   Ⓕ**OO**

This concluding issue in Richard Hickox's prize-winning Haydn Mass series follows a similar pattern to earlier discs, offering exhilarating

performances which wear their period style lightly. Gardiner for Philips is by a fraction the more crisply incisive, with pinpoint attack and clean textures: Hickox generally prefers slightly broader speeds, with full, immediate sound, more clearly bringing out the joy of Haydn's inspiration as well as the drama.

Both of these Masses are relatively neglected, even on disc. The *Great Organ* Mass, dating from 1768-9, seems not to have been composed for a special occasion, but, exceptionally, because Haydn wanted to write it. It's a distinctive work, both in its choice of key, E flat, rare for a Mass of the time, and for replacing oboes in the orchestra with two cor anglais.

The role of the organ is far more important, though; its Baroque figuration attractively decorative, while the *Benedictus* includes a concertante organ part, accompanying the quartet of soloists. Choosing light registration, Ian Watson produces delightful sounds throughout, with delicate organ decorations set in contrast with the relatively plain choral writing. As in the rest of the Hickox series, the singing and playing of Collegium Musicum 90 is most stylish.

Hickox has a special relish for Haydn's rhythmic exuberance, as in the syncopated Amens in the *Sanctus* and the robust 6/8 rhythms of the 'Dona nobis pacem' at the very end.

The *Mariazeller* Mass, written much later in 1782, was the last Mass setting that Haydn composed before the final six masterpieces, and already points forward. As in those late Masses, the *Kyrie* is in a compressed sonata form: a slow introduction leads to a vigorous *Allegro*, with the 'Christe eleison' as the development section. Clearly, Haydn was already thinking of his Mass settings in symphonic terms, with striking key-changes also relating to Haydn's symphonic writing. Even more than in the *Great Organ* Mass, Hickox brings out the vitality of the writing, as in the extraordinary 'Dona nobis pacem' at the end, so wildly syncopated it's almost jazzy. A splendid culmination to an outstanding series.

Masses – in D minor, Missa 'Sunt bona mixta',
HobXXII/2; in C, Missa Cellensis (Cäcilienmesse),
HobXXII/5.
Susan Gritton sop **Pamela Helen Stephen** mez
Mark Padmore ten **Stephen Varcoe** bass
Collegium Musicum 90 / Richard Hickox
Chandos CHAN0667 (70' · DDD) Texts and
translations included   Ⓕ**O**

This is the only current recording of the fragmentary *Missa sunt bona mixta malis*, consisting only of a brief setting of the *Kyrie* followed by a more expansive setting of the *Gloria*, which is cut off after the 'Gratias agimus tibi'. Improbably, the score was discovered as recently as 1983 in a farmhouse in the north of Ireland. Dating from 1768, it's tantalising having only a fragment when the contrapuntal writing presents Haydn at his most striking in this period. It makes a fascinating supplement to Hickox's superb account of the longest setting of the liturgy that Haydn ever composed. The title of the *Missa cellensis* – referring to the small Austrian town of Mariazell – is misleading in two ways. It's obviously so when there's another, later Mass also entitled *Cellensis*, but equally because it seems highly unlikely that so ambitious a work as this was ever designed for such a place as Mariazell: it was more probably written for a grand occasion in Vienna. So it would surely be less confusing to return to the usual title for this work, 'St Cecilia Mass'.

This is a 'cantata-mass' very different from Haydn's usual settings which involve a single movement for each of the six sections of the liturgy. Here instead, the liturgy is divided into 18 separate movements. Hickox's new version gains over the fine Preston issue from the late 1970s in weight and warmth of expression, helped by the Chandos recording which, while warm, allows ample detail in the many splendid contrapuntal passages. The choir's sopranos are amply bright and boyish and achieve a crisp ensemble. The soloists make an outstanding, responsive team.

Masses – in G, Missa Sancti Nicolai (Nikolaimesse), HobXXII/6; in B flat, Missa Sancti Bernardi von Offida (Heiligmesse), HobXXII/10
Lorna Anderson sop **Pamela Helen Stephen** mez **Mark Padmore** ten **Stephen Varcoe** bar **Collegium Musicum 90 / Richard Hickox**
Chandos Chaconne CHAN0645 (62' · DDD) Text and translation included Ⓕ

With fresh, inspiriting work from soloists, chorus and orchestra, the performance of the so-called *Heiligmesse* captures the symphonic impetus and the spiritual and physical exhilaration of this gloriously life-affirming music. Hickox opts for Haydn's original scoring, minus the horn parts and the enhanced parts for clarinets that he later added for a performance in Vienna's Court Chapel. Hickox is ever responsive to the drama and colour of Haydn's orchestral writing, while the 24-strong chorus sings with firm, well-nourished tone over a wide dynamic range and a real care for the meaning of the text. The many high-lying entries are always true, never strained or overblown, and the sopranos rise unflinchingly to their frequent high B flats. The soloists have less to do here than in Haydn's other late Masses: but, led by the plangent, beseeching soprano of Lorna Anderson, they sing with a chamber-music grace and intimacy.

The appealing *Missa brevis* is cast in the 'pastoral' key of G major. Again, the soloists make their mark both individually and in ensemble, with Anderson floating a beautiful line in the 'Gratias' and Mark Padmore launching the expressive G minor 'Et incarnatus est' with gently rounded tone and graceful phrasing. The recorded sound is clear, spacious and carefully balanced, combining vivid orchestral detail with plenty of impact from the chorus.

Masses – in B flat, HobXXII/7, Missa brevis Ⓟ Sancti Johannis de Deo ('Little Organ Mass'); in B flat (Theresienmesse), HobXXII/12
Janice Watson sop **Pamela Helen Stephen** mez **Mark Padmore** ten **Stephen Varcoe** bar **Collegium Musicum 90 Chorus; Collegium Musicum 90 / Richard Hickox**
Chandos CHAN0592 (60' · DDD) Texts and translations included Ⓕ◐

Hickox generates the physical and spiritual elation essential to this music, calling to mind Haydn's own much-quoted remark that whenever he praised God his heart leapt with joy. In the glorious *Theresienmesse* of 1799 Hickox's manner is particularly fine in the exultant, springing *Gloria* and the rough-hewn vigour of the *Credo*. He understands, too, the Mass's dramatic and symphonic impetus, bringing a powerful cumulative momentum to the sonata-form 'Dona nobis pacem' and thrillingly tightening the screws in the closing pages. The choir is placed forward, though never at the expense of orchestral detail, keenly observed by Hickox. His uncommonly well-integrated solo quartet framed by the sweet-toned Janice Watson and the gentle, mellifluous Stephen Varcoe, sings with a chamber-musical grace and refinement in the 'Et incarnatus est' and the *Benedictus*. And their supplicatory tenderness in the 'Dona nobis pacem' contrasts arrestingly with the choir's urgent demands for peace. Hickox also captures the peculiar serenity and innocence of the much earlier *Missa brevis Sancti Johannis de Deo*, or *Little Organ Mass*, its intimacy enhanced here by the use of solo strings. A disc guaranteed to refresh the spirit.

Mass in C, Missa in tempore belli (Paukenmesse), HobXXII/9. Te Deum in C, HobXXIIIc/1. Te Deum in C, HobXXIIIc/2. Alfred, König der Angelsachsen, HobXXX/5 – Aria des Schutzgeistes; Chor der Dänen
Nancy Argenta sop **Catherine Denley** mez **Mark Padmore** ten **Stephen Varcoe** bar **Jacqueline Fox** spkr **Collegium Musicum 90 Chorus and Orchestra / Richard Hickox**
Chandos Chaconne CHAN0633 (64' · DDD) Texts and translations included Ⓕ◐

Few other conductors on disc convey so happily the drama, symphonic power and spiritual exhilaration of these glorious works than Richard Hickox. He's fully alive to the ominous unease that permeates the great *Mass in Time of War*, but while others strive for maximum dramatic and rhetorical effect, he directs the Mass with a natural, unforced sense of phrase and pace. The playing of Collegium Musicum 90, led by Simon Standage, is polished and athletic, with detail sharply etched, while the chorus sings with fresh tone and incisive attack. The four soloists are well matched in the anxious C minor *Benedictus*; elsewhere Nancy Argenta brings a pure, slender tone, and a graceful sense of phrase to the *Kyrie*, while in the 'Qui tollis'

Stephen Varcoe deploys his mellow baritone with real sensitivity.

The fill-ups are imaginatively chosen. The two *Te Deum* settings epitomise the immense distance Haydn travelled during his career, the rococo exuberance and strict species counterpoint of the little-known early work contrasting with the grandeur and massive, rough-hewn energy of the 1799 setting.

The two numbers of incidental music Haydn completed for the play *King Alfred* in 1796, shortly before embarking on the Mass, are a real collectors' item. Argenta sings the first hymn-like E flat aria with chaste elegance, while choir and orchestra palpably enjoy themselves in the following number, a rollicking, brassy celebration of the Danes' victory over the Anglo-Saxons. Invigorating performances and first-class recorded sound, with an ideally judged balance between chorus and orchestra.

Mass in D minor (Nelsonmesse), HobXXII/11.   **P**
Te Deum in C, HobXXIIIc/2
Dame Felicity Lott sop **Carolyn Watkinson** contr
Maldwyn Davies ten **David Wilson-Johnson** bar
The English Concert and Choir / Trevor Pinnock
Archiv Produktion 423 097-2AH (50' · ADD) Texts and
translations included   ℗**OOO**

The British Admiral had ousted the Napoleonic fleet at the Battle of the Nile just as Haydn was in the middle of writing his *Nelson* Mass. Although the news could not have reached him until after its completion, Haydn's awareness of the international situation was expressed in the work's subtitle, 'Missa in Augustiis', or 'Mass in times of fear'. With its rattle of timpani, pungent trumpet calls, and highly strung harmonic structure, there's no work of Haydn's which cries out so loudly for recording on period instruments; and it's the distinctive sonority and highly charged tempos of this performance which set it apart. The dry, hard timpani and long trumpets bite into the dissonance of the opening *Kyrie*, and the near vibrato-less string playing is mordant and urgent. The fast-slow-fast triptych of the *Gloria* is set out in nervously contrasted speeds, and the *Credo* bounces with affirmation. Just as the choral singing is meticulously balanced with instrumental inflexion, so the soloists have been chosen to highlight the colours in Pinnock's palette.

Masses – in D minor (Nelsonmesse), HobXXII/11;   **P**
in B flat (Theresienmesse), HobXXII/12. Te Deum in C,
HobXXIIIc/2
Donna Brown sop **Sally Bruce-Payne** mez **Peter
Butterfield** ten **Gerald Finley** bass Monteverdi
Choir; English Baroque Soloists / **Sir John Eliot
Gardiner**
Philips ② 470 286-2PH (89' · DDD) Texts and
translations included   Ⓜ**OO**

Dating respectively from 1798 and 1799, the

Nelsonmesse and the *Theresienmesse* are the third and fourth of the six Masses written for the nameday of the Princess Esterházy. That was a period during the Napoleonic wars when Prince Esterházy, Nikolaus II had economised by dismissing his Harmonie or windband. Even so, in 1798 for the *Nelsonmesse*, Haydn, seeking to reflect the mood of the times (hence the official title, *Missa in angustiis* – 'Mass in straitened times'), brought in three trumpets and timpani, and their impact is all the greater when set against strings and organ alone.

That heightened contrast is a point which comes out with thrilling attack in Gardiner's performance at the very opening of the *Kyrie*. This vigorous *Allegro*, typical of Haydn but totally untypical of Mass-settings, introduces martial fanfares, which recur through the whole work. Though Haydn composed the Mass in a mere 53 days in the summer of 1798, just when Nelson was winning the Battle of Aboukir, Haydn knew nothing of that victory till later, and the Nelson association dates from two years later when the admiral visited Eisenstadt, and the Mass was given in his honour.

Gardiner's treatment of the fanfares offers only the first of dozens of examples where his crisp, incisive manner highlights the extraordinary originality of this work. The *Theresienmesse* brings similar revelations. Here, in addition to trumpets and timpani, Haydn scored for two clarinets, and though this is a less sharply dramatic, more lyrical work, a martial flavour is again introduced. There are surprises aplenty, as in the sudden silence of the orchestra in the setting of the word 'miserere' at the end of the 'Gratias agimus tibi', or the setting of 'Et incarnatus' in the *Credo* in the rare key (in this context) of B flat minor, and 'Et vitam venturi' set in a galloping 6/8 time or the bold, square opening of *Agnus Dei* in bare octaves at an unapologetic *forte*. Such points must have startled early listeners, and Gardiner's treatment makes one appreciate that with new ears.

In this respect he even outshines Richard Hickox, whose prize-winning Mass series for Chandos brings equally enjoyable performances of both these works, just as energetic and a degree warmer, thanks in part to the recording acoustic. Gardiner's team, on the other hand, has markedly cleaner separation of textures, with soloists and chorus more sharply defined. Gardiner's Monteverdi Choir as ever sings with passion, brilliance and fine precision, and his soloists are all outstanding, fresh and youthful-sounding with firm clear voices.

As a splendid, very apt bonus there's a superb account of the magnificent ceremonial C major *Te Deum*.

Mass in B flat (Harmoniemesse), HobXXII/14. Salve
regina in E, HobXXIIIb/1
Nancy Argenta sop **Pamela Helen Stephen** mez
Mark Padmore ten **Stephen Varcoe** bar **Collegium
Musicum 90 Chorus; Collegium Musicum 90 /
Richard Hickox**

HAYDN NELSON MASS – IN BRIEF

Soloists; The English Concert and Choir / Trevor Pinnock
Archiv Produktion 423 097-2AH　　Ⓕ **OOO**
A thrilling performance from 1989 of Haydn's 'Mass in times of fear'. Pinnock directs with a winning buoyancy that doesn't neglect the work's charged mood. His soloists are superb and The English Concert Choir sing with tremendous precision and power.

Soloists; Monteverdi Choir; English Baroque Soloists / John Eliot Gardiner
Philips 470 286-2PH　　Ⓕ **OO**
Another superb performance characterised by magnificent choral work and thrilling orchestral playing. Gardiner brings his characteristic feel for a work's drama thrillingly to bear on this great work.

Soloists; Collegium Musicum 90 and Choir / Richard Hickox
Chandos CHAN0640　　Ⓕ **O**
Part of Hickox's fine Haydn Mass series, this is well worth hearing, but it's outclassed by the Pinnock and Gardiner for the sheer precision and intensity of their approach. Splendidly recorded, though.

Soloists; London Symphony Chorus; City of London Sinfonia / Richard Hickox
Decca 448 983-2　　Ⓑ
If you like Hickox's way with this music but prefer modern instruments, this is well worth acquiring. Excellent solo singing with Barbara Bonney the radiant soprano, and firm, focused choral work from the London Symphony Chorus.

Soloists; Choir of King's College, Cambridge; London SO / Sir David Willcocks
Decca 448 518-2 or 458 623-2　　Ⓑ
Sir David Willcocks's 1962 King's College performance of the Nelson Mass takes its place alongside the excellent series of Haydn Masses recorded by George Guest at St John's College, Cambridge. It's a fine interpretation and is available as part of a seven-CD set as well as singly.

Chandos Chaconne CHAN0612 (59' · DDD) Texts and translations included　　Ⓕ **O**

Haydn's first major work, the *Salve regina* of 1756, is here juxtaposed with his last, the *Harmoniemesse* of 1802, so-called because of its exceptionally full scoring for woodwind. The gulf between the two works, in sophistication, mastery and emotional range, is predictably vast. Yet, in their very different ways, both reconcile the formal liturgical conventions of their era with the expression of Haydn's own life-affirming religious faith. Hickox and his forces ideally capture this sense of celebratory spiritual energy. Tempos are lively, rhythms alert and vital. In the Mass Hickox generates an exhilarating symphonic momentum in, say, the opening sections of the *Gloria* and *Credo*, and, aided by an outstandingly clear, well-balanced recording, realises to the full such dramatic *coups* as the sudden swerve into A flat in the recapitulation of the 'Benedictus' and the martial fanfares that slew the music from D major to B flat at the start of the 'Dona nobis pacem'. The steely edged valveless trumpets are thrilling here; and elsewhere the wind players do rich justice to Haydn's glorious writing, nicely balancing rusticity and refinement.

Nancy Argenta's innocent, bell-like tones and graceful sense of line are heard to touching effect in the 'Et incarnatus est' of the Mass. In the *Salve regina*, she also reveals her deft, fluent coloratura technique. No great depths in this youthful work, but Haydn's setting of the Marian antiphon is elegant and affecting, with a command of shapely, Italianate melody and a feeling for dramatic contrast. This is certainly the most memorable work of Haydn's from the 1750s and aptly complements Hickox's fervent, inspiring reading of the *Harmoniemesse*.

Masses – in B flat (Harmoniemesse), HobXXII/14[a]; 🄿
in B flat (Schöpfungsmesse), HobXXII/13[b]
[b]**Ruth Ziesak,** [a]**Joanne Lunn,** [a]**Angharad Gruffydd Jones** sops [b]**Bernarda Fink** mez [b]**Susanna Spicer,** [a]**Sara Mingardo** contrs [b]**Christoph Prégardien,** [b]**Peter Butterfield,** [a]**Andrew Busher,** [a]**Topi Lehtipuu** tens [b]**Oliver Widmer** bar [a]**Brindley Sherratt** bass **Monteverdi Choir; English Baroque Soloists / Sir John Eliot Gardiner**
Philips ② 470 297-2PH (84' · DDD) Notes, texts and translations included　　Ⓜ **O**

Gardiner adds to the attractions of Philips' mid-price package by choosing outstanding teams of soloists. Particularly notable is the soprano for the *Harmoniemesse*, Joanne Lunn, with her fresh, at times almost boyish tone nicely set against the creamy contralto of Sara Mingardo.

Gardiner takes a dramatic, incisive view of these last two of the Masses, which in many ways can be said to continue Haydn's symphonic sequence. The contrasts between Gardiner and Hickox (on Chandos) bring out the positive qualities of each. Both inspire superb performances. Where Hickox is warmer in his approach with bouncing rhythms which bring out the joy of the old composer's inspiration, Gardiner is more incisive, with the Monteverdi Choir singing with pinpoint attack and exceptionally clean textures, helped by warm but relatively transparent recording quality. The Chandos sound for Hickox is a degree fuller and more immediate.

Gardiner also tends to favour speeds a shade faster than Hickox, often challengingly so in furious speeds for the settings of 'Et resurrexit', though in such a slow movement as the *Sanctus* of the *Schöpfungsmesse* Gardiner takes a broader view, moulding the phrases. Any lover of these works will be happy with either view, and the differences of coupling might well dictate choice.

Stabat mater

Stabat mater, HobXX*bis*
Jeni Bern sop **Jeannette Ager** mez **Andrew Carwood** ten **Giles Underwood** bass **David Goode** org **Christ Church Cathedral Choir, Oxford; London Musici / Stephen Darlington**
Griffin GCCD4029 (60' · DDD)   Ⓕ

Haydn's *Stabat mater*, the first of his vocal works to establish his reputation internationally, is an ambitious cantata, and like the *Cecilia* Mass, from that same early period. It was written in 1767 soon after Haydn took over responsibility for Prince Esterházy's church music, having succeeded as full Kapellmeister on the death of Gregor Werner.

There's strong competition among current versions, but Griffin's disc finds a distinctive place among them. Like the Heltay version, and unlike Pinnock and Harnoncourt, it uses an orchestra of modern instruments, but far more than Heltay Stephen Darlington takes note of period practice, lightening string textures, finding extra detail. He also tends to adopt fast speeds, at times challengingly so, as in the big tenor aria, 'Vidit sum', stylishly sung by Andrew Carwood. The other distinctive point is that not only does it use a church choir with boy trebles, it offers a warmly atmospheric cathedral acoustic. The others were recorded in churches, though all markedly smaller than Christ Church Cathedral. The line-up of soloists may not be as starry as those on the rival discs, but these are young singers with fresh, clear voices and with keen experience of the choral repertory.

The Creation (Die Schöpfung)

Die Schöpfung   Ⓟ
Sylvia McNair, Donna Brown sops **Michael Schade** ten **Rodney Gilfry, Gerald Finley** bars **Monteverdi Choir; English Baroque Soloists / Sir John Eliot Gardiner**
Archiv Produktion ② 449 217-2AH2 (101' · DDD) Text included   Ⓕ**❍❍❍**

 With Gardiner's first down-beat it's obvious that Chaos's days are numbered. Not that 'days' (strictly speaking) are in question till the mighty words have been spoken, and then, in this performance, what an instantaneous blaze! No premonitory intimation (of pre-echo in the old days whereas now even the faintest stirring in the ranks of the choir will do it), but a single-handed switching-on of the cosmic power-grid and a magnificently sustained C major chord to flood the universe with light. This is one of the great characteristics here: the superbly confident, precise attack of choir and orchestra. Enthusiasm, then, in plenty; but how about the mystery of Creation? It's certainly part of the aim to capture this, for the bass soloist's 'Im Anfange' ('In the beginning') with pianissimo chorus has rarely been so softly and so spaciously taken: the Spirit that moved upon the face of the waters is a veiled, flesh-creeping presence, felt again in the first sunrise and the 'softer beams with milder light' of the first moon. Even so, others have incorporated this element more naturally. Gardiner has an excellent Raphael in Gerald Finley, and gains from having extra singers for Adam and Eve, especially as the Eve, Donna Brown, brings a forthright style doubly welcome after the somewhat shrinking-violet manner and breathy tone of Sylvia McNair's Gabriel. On the whole, Gardiner is sound: yet his is a fun Creation and a real enrichment of the library. Against others of comparable kind, Gardiner stands firm as an easy first choice: a re-creator of vision, a great invigorator and life-enhancer.

Die Schöpfung   Ⓟ
Ann Monoyios sop **Jörg Hering** ten **Harry van der Kamp** bass **Tölz Boys' Choir; Tafelmusik / Bruno Weil**
Sony Classical Vivarte ② SX2K57965 (91' · DDD) Recorded 1993. Text and translation included   Ⓑ

Bruno Weil's reading, using a period orchestra of up to 45 players and an all-male choir of similar strength, is above all a luminous, joyous affair, with generally fleet tempos, nimble, dancing rhythms and a richly communicated sense of delight in the work's sublime, pre-lapsarian innocence. Tafelmusik equals and sometimes surpasses rival period orchestras in the point and relish of its playing, and the Tölz Boys' Choir sings with brio, accuracy and characteristically fresh, bright-edged tone. Weil's direction mingles a sense of spontaneous discovery with a strong feeling for shape and structure and a sharp ear for Haydn's wonderful orchestral detail. Weil's eager pacing and judgement of tempo relationships almost invariably feel right, though occasionally you long for a deeper sense of mystery and reverence.

The three soloists are all stylish singers, clean of line and tone (vibrato used quite sparingly) and notably flexible in coloratura. They make

HAYDN'S CREATION – IN BRIEF

Janowitz; Ludwig; Wunderlich; Krenn; Fischer-Dieskau; Berry; Vienna Singerverein; Berlin PO / Herbert von Karajan
DG ② 449 761-2GOR2 (109' · ADD)　　Ⓜ❍❍❍

☀ A *de luxe* line-up for Karajan's *Creation* (Wunderlich's death halfway through the recording meant that Werner Krenn recorded the recitatives). Karajan's feeling for the music is considerable, and he brings drama as well as intimacy to it. Everyone gives his or her all. A classic.

McNair; Brown; Schade; Finley; Gilfry; Monteverdi Choir; English Baroque Soloists / Sir John Eliot Gardiner
Archiv Produktion ② 449 217-2AH2 (101' · ADD)　　Ⓕ❍❍❍

☀ A very fine period-instrument version full of drama and imaginative response to the text. Gardiner's wonderful choir sings superbly and his EBS play with fiersome commitment.

Popp; Döse; Hollweg; Moll; Luxon; Brighton Festival Chorus; Royal PO / Antál Dorati
Decca ② 443 027-2DF2 (129' · ADD)　　Ⓑ
A fine budget version with wonderfully characterised solo performances and vigorous imaginative direction from that veteran Haydn interpreter Dorati. Generously it has a coupling: a 1771 *Salve regina*.

Kermes; Mields; Davislim; Mannoc; Chung; Balthazar-Neumann Choir and Ensemble / Thomas Hengelbrock
Deutsche Harmonia Mundi ② 05472 77537-2 (99' · DDD)　　Ⓕ
A swift, exciting period-instrument recording that has a freshy, appealing youthful feel to it. The soloists are delightful and Hengelbrock's excellent chorus cover themselves with glory.

Röschmann; Schade; Gerhaher; Arnold Schoenberg Choir; Concentus Musicus Wien / Nikolaus Harnoncourt
Deutsche Harmonia Mundi ② 82876 58340-2 (107' · DDD)　　Ⓕ❍
Harnoncourt returns to *The Creation* after 18 years, this time on period insturments, and gives a wise, spiritually satisfying performance. The soloists are superb and the chorus sing magnificently. A period version to rival the Gardiner.

Kirkby; Rolfe Johnson; Michael George; New College Choir, Oxford; AAM / Christopher Hogwood
Decca ② 430 397-2OH2 (99' · DDD)　　Ⓕ
A period-instrument *Creation* in English. Great soloists. Hogwood has an invigorating, bracing way with the orchestral writing.

their mark in recitative and aria, and blend and balance unusually well in ensemble. If Ann Monoyios's soprano lacks the hint of tonal depth ideally required, her purity, freshness and shapely sense of phrase are delectable. And like her male colleagues, she ornaments tastefully at fermatas and cadences. Jörg Hering is a compact, elegant tenor with no hint of bleat or strain. To sum up, Weil conveys most infectiously the work's unique joy and exhilaration. The recording has a fine depth of perspective and an almost ideal balance between voices and orchestra.

Die Schöpfung　　Ⓟ
Sunhae Im *sop* Jan Kobow *ten* Hanno Müller-Brachmann *bass* Cologne Vocal Ensemble; Capella Augustina / Andreas Spering
Naxos ② 8 557380/1 (105' · DDD)　　Ⓢ❍❍

Recorded in Cologne in July 2003 by German Radio, this issue offers a first-rate period performance of Haydn's masterpiece, lively and well sung. Since other issues of *Die Schöpfung* in the super-budget category use modern instruments it fills an important gap, particularly as the digital sound is so clear and transparent. Andreas Spering successfully brings out the composer's eternal freshness.

The prelude representing Chaos is taken slowly, markedly more so than by Gardiner or Brüggen, but that brings out all the more the abrasiveness of Haydn's daring dissonances. After the extreme hush of that opening the choral cry of 'Licht' is shattering in its impact; in the following tenor aria Spering shows his true colours in a crisp, faster-than-usual *Andante* that's exhilaratingly carefree, not least at the felicitous passage, marked *sotto voce*, when the chorus sings of 'eine neue Welt'. His speeds are generally on the fast side, but when, as in the prelude, the marking is *Largo* as opposed to *Andante* or *Adagio*, he takes a measured view.

The Cologne Vocal Ensemble is a relatively compact body, incisive in its attack, and set in a helpful but not over-large acoustic. The three soloists are all excellent and youthful-sounding.

An outstanding bargain.

The Seasons (Die Jahreszeiten)

The Seasons　　Ⓟ
Barbara Bonney *sop* Anthony Rolfe Johnson *ten* Andreas Schmidt *bar* Monteverdi Choir; English Baroque Soloists / Sir John Eliot Gardiner
Archiv Produktion ② 431 818-2AH2 (127' · DDD)
Recorded 1990. Text and translation included　　Ⓕ❍❍

The comparative unpopularity of Haydn's *The Seasons* when considered against *The Creation* is understandable perhaps, but it isn't all that well deserved. Less exalted its subject and libretto may be, but its depiction of the progress of the year amid the scenes and occupations of the Austrian countryside drew from its composer music of unfailing invention, benign warmth and constant musical-pictoral delights. As usual, John Eliot Gardiner and his forces turn in disciplined, meticulously professional performances, though the orchestra is slightly larger – and consequently a tiny bit less lucid – than the sort you might nowadays find playing a classical symphony. The choir, however, performs with great clarity and accuracy, and brings, too, an enjoyable sense of characterisation to their various corporate roles.

The soloists all perform with notable poise and intelligence: Barbara Bonney's voice is pure and even, Anthony Rolfe Johnson sounds entirely at ease with the music, and Andreas Schmidt is gentle-voiced but certainly not lacking in substance. Perhaps in the end this is a performance which just lacks that last inch of necessary warmth to make it unbeatable, but it's a first-rate recommendation none the less.

Die Jahreszeiten
Marlis Petersen sop **Werner Güra** ten **Dietrich Henschel** bar **RIAS Chamber Choir, Berlin; Freiburg Baroque Orchestra / René Jacobs**
Harmonia Mundi CD/SACD ⊛ ② HMC80 1829/30 (125' · DDD) Text and translations included Ⓕ**OO**

It would be hard to imagine a more joyful account of Haydn's culminating masterpiece. René Jacobs and his outstanding team perfectly capture the exuberance with which the composer seemed to be defying the years. Infectious rhythms bring out the fun of *The Seasons* from the start, and when in Simon's first aria Haydn quotes from the slow movement of the *Surprise* Symphony, Jacobs nudges the music persuasively. And in the final chorus of 'Summer', the lowing cattle and quail's cry, and chirping crickets and croaking frogs, sound witty, not naive.

In all this Jacobs is helped by a clear and immediate recording that has more presence than Gardiner's 1992. The RIAS Chamber Choir is a fair match for Gardiner's Monteverdi Choir, and the soloists are first-rate, fresh and youthful-sounding. A final choice is a matter of taste – in its way Gardiner's is just as recommendable – but this newer account's greater sense of relaxation and feeling for the fun in the writing make its claims second to none.

Additional recommendation

The Seasons (highlights)
Janowitz sop **Hollweg** ten **Berry** bar **Chor der Deutschen Oper, Berlin; Berlin Philharmonic Orchestra / Karajan**
EMI Encore 574977-2 (DDD) Ⓑ
A fine, polished reading, well recorded.

L'anima del filosofo

L'anima del filosofo, ossia Orfeo et Euridice Ⓟ
Uwe Heilmann ten Orfeo **Cecilia Bartoli** mez Euridice, Genio **Ildebrando d'Arcangelo** bass

Creonte **Andrea Silvestrelli** bass Pluto **Angela Kazimierczuk** sop Baccante **Roberto Scaltriti** bar First Chorus **Jose Fardilha** bass Second Chorus **Colin Campbell** bar Third Chorus **James Oxley** ten Fourth Chorus **Chorus and Orchestra of the Academy of Ancient Music / Christopher Hogwood**
L'Oiseau-Lyre ② 452 668-2OHO2 (124' · DDD) Notes, text and translation included Ⓕ**O**

Christopher Hogwood builds his band on the model of those prevalent in late 18th-century London theatres. Not only does his phrasing and articulation discover no end of witty and poignant nuances, but the grave austerity of the string playing, and the plangency of the early woodwind instruments are eloquent advocates of an opera whose uncompromisingly tragic ending owes more to Ovid and Milton than to operatic tradition. Hogwood also remembers that Haydn was writing for a Handelian London choral tradition: his chorus, be they cast as Cupids, Shades or Furies, have robust presence, and sculpt their lines with firm muscle.

Cecilia Bartoli takes the role of Euridice. In her very first aria, 'Filomena abbandonata', she understands and eagerly re-creates the type of coloratura writing which simultaneously fleshes out the central nightingale simile and incarnates the single word 'crudeltà'. Her unmistakable, melting half-voice comes into its own as emotion first clouds reason, only to create the fatal emotional extremes to which she gives voice so thrillingly. Uwe Heilmann is just the tenor of rare agility and wide vocal range vital for this particular Orfeo. The minor parts are strongly profiled: Ildebrando d'Arcangelo is a stern, noble Creonte, Andrea Silvestrelli a fearsome, stentorian Pluto – and there's even a convincing *strepito ostile* off-stage as Euridice's abduction is attempted in Act 2. Beyond the detail, it's the poignancy of the musical drama at the heart of this strange, grave *Orfeo* which Hogwood reveals with such sympathetic and imaginative insight.

Michael Haydn · Austrian 1737–1806

Michael Haydn, younger brother of Joseph Haydn, sang with his brother at St Stephen's Cathedral, Vienna, and in 1757-63 was Kapellmeister to the Bishop of Grosswardein. From 1763 he was court musician and Konzertmeister to the Prince-Archbishop of Salzburg, also writing music for the court. He had much contact with the Mozart family, and he, Mozart and Adlgasser wrote an act each of the oratorio Die Schuldigkeit des ersten Gebots (1767). He became organist at the Holy Trinity Church in 1777, and cathedral organist (succeeding Mozart) in 1781. Under the church reforms of the 1780s he wrote simpler sacred music; meanwhile his reputation grew, and he later composed several works for the Empress Maria Theresia. Among his pupils was the young Carl Maria von Weber.

Haydn contributed most in the field of sacred music, writing 38 masses and over 300 other church works; most are for four solo voices, four-part choir and orchestra (sometimes with wind instruments). Fugues often appear, and some masses are in a strict contrapuntal style; there is less florid solo writing than in many sacred works of the day. His Requiem in C minor (1771) probably influenced Mozart's later setting. His instrumental works include c40 symphonies, many of them vigorous and inventive and some having fugal finales, concertos, minuets etc, and chamber music including many divertimentos, 12 string quartets and four duets for violin and viola (which Mozart made into a set of six). He also composed Singspiels, incidental music to Voltaire's Zaire (1777), an opera seria (1787), oratorios, cantatas and other secular vocal works. His partsongs for unaccompanied male voices were among the earliest written.   **GROVE**music

Requiem

Requiem (Missa pro defuncto Archiepiscopo Sigismundo), MH155 KI I/8. Missa in honorem Sanctae Ursulae, MH546 KI I/18
Carolyn Sampson sop **Hilary Summers** contr **James Gilchrist** ten **Peter Harvey** bass **The King's Consort Choir; The King's Consort / Robert King**
Hyperion ② CDA67510 (84' · DDD · T/t)   Ⓜ❍❍❍

Robert King suggests that Michael Haydn's Requiem of 1771 for the Archbishop-Prince of Salzburg reflects a personal outpouring of grief for the loss of Haydn's beloved patron and the recent death of his infant daughter. The fervent expressions of grief, consolation and hope must have made some impression on the 15-year-old Mozart. A comparison with Mozart's Requiem setting of 20 years later is inevitable: Haydn didn't give his solo quartet anything that compares with the immediacy of Mozart's 'Tuba mirum', but the older man's masterful choral writing, brilliant orchestral scoring and sensitive use of solo voices created plenty of musical riches and dramatic moods, such as the brooding Kyrie and the bursting energy of the 'Dies irae'.

The quartet of soloists is impeccable; the choir and orchestra of The King's Consort prove to be increasingly assured and dynamic with each recording released. Robert King's measured and emphatic direction makes it easy to appreciate why the Requiem was performed at his brother Joseph's funeral in 1809.

His interpretation of the sunnier, extrovert Missa in honorem Sanctae Ursulae (1793) helps the music to sound natural and spontaneous. In some respects the Mass is an even finer composition, full of charismatic and inventive musical charms (it's worth buying for Carolyn Sampson's ravishing 'Benedictus' alone).

Anybody who enjoys the choral works of Mozart and Joseph Haydn will be delighted by this double-disc set, and will probably concur that Michael Haydn's neglect in the shadow of his younger friend and older brother is substantially corrected by these exquisite performances.

Johann Heinichen   German 1683-1729

Initially an advocate, German composer and theorist Heinichen composed music for the Weissenfels court, then moved to Leipzig (1709), where he presented operas and directed a collegium musicum. He also worked at Zeitz and Naumburg. In 1710-16 he lived in Italy and had two operas staged in Venice in 1713. From 1717 he was Kapellmeister (with JC Schmidt) at the Dresden court. He wrote serenatas, cantatas, sacred works, and instrumental music for the court, combining German, French and Italian features; his concertos and sonatas are italianate, with unusual instrumental combinations and sonorities. He wrote two versions of a thoroughbass treatise, the second (1728) among the major musical writings of the period.   **GROVE**music

Concertos

Concertos – C, S211; G, S213; G, S214,'Darmstadt'; Ⓟ S214, Venezia'; G, S215; G, S217; F, S226; F, S231; F, S232; F, S233; F, S234; F, S235. Serenata di Moritzburg in F, S204. Sonata in A, S208. Movement in C minor, S240
Musica Antiqua Köln / Reinhard Goebel
Archiv Produktion ② 437 549-2AH2 (137' · DDD)
Recorded 1992   Ⓕ❍❍❍

Johann David Heinichen was a contemporary of Bach and one of an important group of musicians employed by the Dresden court during the 1720s and 1730s. As well as being an inventive composer, Heinichen was also a noted theorist and his treatise on the continuo bass was widely admired. All the music collected here was probably written for the excellent Dresden court orchestra and most of it falls into that rewarding category in which north and central German composers were pre-eminent. Vivaldi had provided effective models but the predilection for drawing upon other influences, too, gives the concertos of the Germans greater diversity. Heinichen admittedly doesn't so readily venture into the Polish regions whose folk-music gives such a piquancy to Telemann's concertos and suites, but the wonderful variety of instrumental colour and deployment of alternating 'choirs' is every bit as skilful. Your attention will be held from start to finish. Much of the credit for this must go to Reinhard Goebel and his impeccably drilled Musica Antiqua Köln. Some of these pieces might well seem less entertaining in the hands of less imaginative musicians and it would be untruthful to claim that everything is of uniform interest. Each concerto fields its own distinctive wind group drawing variously upon recorders, flutes, oboes, bassoons and horns, the latter always in pairs, in addition to concertante parts in many of them for one or more violins and cellos. There's little need to say more. The recorded sound is first-rate, and Goebel's painstaking essay is fascinating to read.

Te Deum

Christmas at the Court of Dresden
Heinichen Pastorale in A, 'Per la notte della
Nativitate Christi'. Te Deum **Ristori** Messa per il
Santissimo Natale di Nostro Signore. Motetto
pastorale **Schürer** Christus natus est nobis. Jesu
redemptor omnium **Seger** Praeludium
Christine Wolff sop **Britta Schwarz** contr **Martin
Petzold** ten **Sebastian Knebel** org **Dresden
Körnerscher Singverein; Dresden Instrumental-
Concert / Peter Kopp**
Carus 83 169 (78' · DDD · T/t)   Ⓕ

This charming disc has been lovingly
researched and produced: the liturgical model is
the Christmas Eve service used at the Dresden
Court during the mid-18th century. All the
composers were closely associated with Dresden, and the choir, orchestra and conductor are
all from that city too.

Peter Kopp is a stylish director, and his youthful choir and orchestra are magnificent. The
soloists are capable, although the soprano and
alto don't always blend convincingly in
Schürer's *Christus natus est*. Heinichen's *Te
Deum* is replete with brilliant horns, exhilarating choruses and moments of pastoral tenderness. Giovanni Alberto Ristori, a Bolognese
musician who settled in Dresden, composed his
Messa per il Santissimo Natale in 1744. It's full of
glorious and lyrical moments evoking shepherds and the Nativity. The elegant performance of Ristori's *O admirabile mysterium* goes to
show what we lost when most of his church
music was destroyed during World War II.
Almost all the works here are receiving their
first recordings; Carus deserves credit for its
illuminating exploration of the rich Dresden
school of Baroque sacred music.

Hans Werner Henze   German 1926

*Henze studied at a music school in Brunswick and,
after war service, with Fortner at the Institute for
Church Music in Heidelberg (1946-8). At first he
composed in a Stravinskian neo-classical style (First
Symphony, 1947), but lessons with Leibowitz in
1947-8 encouraged his adoption of 12-note serialism. Unlike such contemporaries as Stockhausen,
however, he held his music open to a wide range of
materials. Occasionally he made his obeisance to
Darmstadt (Second Quartet, 1952), but his large,
varied output of this period also shows the continuing
importance to him of neo-classicism, Schoenbergian
or Bergian expressionism and jazz. Nor was he dismissive of old forms or, in particular, the theatre: he
conducted the Wiesbaden ballet (1950-53) and composed ballets (Jack Pudding, 1951; Labyrinth,
1951) and operas (Boulevard Solitude, 1952).*

*In 1953 he moved to Italy, where his music became
more expansive, sensuous and lyrical and he concentrated on a sequence of operas (König Hirsch, 1956;
Elegy for Young Lovers, 1961) and cantatas (Kam-*

*mermusik, 1958; Cantata della fiaba estrema,
1963). The climax to this period came with a rich
and elaborate but also dynamic treatment of The
Bacchae in the opera The Bassarids (1966), followed
by a period of self-searching; that was externalised in
the Second Piano Concerto (1967) and eventually
gave rise to an outspoken commitment to revolutionary socialism. Henze visited Cuba (1969-70), where
he conducted the first performance of his Sixth Symphony, incorporating the tunes of revolutionary
songs. He also developed a bold, poster style in music-
theatre works (El Cimarrón, 1970), leading to his
dramatisation of class conflict in the opera We Come
to the River (1976).*

*But he was also continuing his exploration of an
expressionist orchestral sumptuousness in such works
as Heliogabalus imperator (1972) and Tristan
(1974), and an enjoyment in reinterpreting old
musical models (Aria de la folía española for chamber
orchestra, 1977). Later works, including the opera
The English Cat (1983) and the Seventh Symphony
(1984), continue his highly personal synthesis of past
and present, lyricism and rigour.*   GROVEmusic

Piano Concerto No 2

Piano Concerto No 2[a]. Telemanniana
[a]**Rolf Plagge** pf **North-West German Philharmonic
Orchestra / Gerhard Markson**
CPO999 322-2 (62' · DDD) Recorded [a]1997, 1995 ⒻO

In an interview with Oliver Knussen for DG's
1996 reissue of the Second Piano Concerto
(1967), Henze stated he felt it had 'made a
breakthrough towards a vaster area of musical
expression'. Manifest in every bar of this rich
and intense score is a sense of release and discovery, of standing on the brink of a new musical landscape utterly different from what had
gone before. Henze only had a couple of years
to explore this before the storm over *The Raft of
the Medusa* burst around his head, changing
irrevocably the course of his career. Henze
wrote the Concerto for Christoph Eschenbach,
who premièred it in 1968, recording it under
the composer's direction in London two years
later. That performance still sounds splendid
and has unassailable authority, but shouldn't
deter anyone from investigating this newcomer,
which is brilliantly played and prepared. If
Eschenbach and Henze occasionally wring
more excitement out of the notes, Plagge and
Markson are only just behind, and CPO's terrific recording captures even more of the subtle
orchestral detail. The orchestra also turns in a
very fine performance of Henze's Suite of Telemann arrangements, written in the same year as
the Concerto. Recommended with enthusiasm.

Nachtstücke und Arien

Drei sinfonische Etüden. Quattro poemi.
Nachtstücke und Arien[a]. La selva incantata[a]
[a]**Michaela Kaune** sop **North German Radio
Symphony Orchestra / Peter Ruzicka**
Wergo WER6637-2 (61' · DDD)   Ⓕ

This attractive compilation fills significant gaps in the current discography of Henze's earlier compositions. The main work, *Nachtstücke und Arien*, dates from 1957, and mortally offended avant-garde puritans at its première by its revival of full-blooded lyricism, less than 10 years after Strauss's *Four Last Songs* was supposed to have said a final farewell to such self-indulgence. This sumptuous, at times explosively dramatic music, comes across well in this performance. Michaela Kaune sings with poise and, where necessary, an apt operatic flair. The recorded sound throughout is adequate, though not especially well defined.

Like the other works on the disc, *Nachtstücke und Arien* owes far more to the post-Romantic *espressivo* of Berg and Schoenberg than it does to Strauss. It's most directly indebted to Henze's own opera *König Hirsch*, the major work of the 1950s in which he gave his new-found love of melody the fullest rein. With *La selva incantata* (The enchanted forest, 1991) we find Henze revisiting *König Hirsch* and recasting some of its most characterful music in purely orchestral form. *Three Symphonic Studies* and *Four Poems* for orchestra were both written in the 1950s, and although less fully rounded than *Nachtstücke und Arien*, they all have Henze's typical blend of turbulent emotionalism and spacious, questing lyricism. In the relatively extended first *Study* the risk of aimless drifting isn't altogether avoided. But this lapse is corrected with interest in the shorter, more tightly controlled *Poems*. The romantic resonances confirm how fruitful the experience of composing for the theatre, and engaging with earlier German traditions, had become for Henze. Those resonances continue in most of his finest later works, but the idiomatic performances on this disc let you hear some of their earliest manifestations.

Louis Hérold — French 1791-1833

Hérold studied at the Paris Conservatoire with Louis Adam, Kreutzer, Catel and Méhul (who became the dominant influence on his style), composing his first opera in Italy in 1814. For several years he had difficulty finding adequate texts and his works frequently failed. Not until the delightful Marie (1826) did he score a triumphant success, meanwhile working as an accompanist at the Théâtre-Italien in Paris and later as singing coach at the Opéra, where he composed music for five ballets, including La somnambule and La fille mal gardée. The two operas for which he is remembered – Zampa, ou La fiancée de marbre (1831; originally Le corsaire) and the finer Le pré aux clercs (1832) – were both popular successes, the first full of effective theatrical situations and showing the brilliant tenor Chollet to advantage, the second treating thoughtfully a controversial subject. Such accomplished scores suggest that had Hérold lived longer, he might have fulfilled his ambitions to compose grand opera. **GROVE**music

La fille mal gardée

La fille mal gardée – excerpts (arr Lanchbery)
Orchestra of the Royal Opera House, Covent Garden / John Lanchbery
Decca Ovation 430 196-2DM (51' · ADD) Recorded 1962 Ⓜ︎Ⓞ

The Royal Ballet's *La fille mal gardée* remains a source of perpetual delight, not least for the music that John Lanchbery arranged largely from Hérold's patchwork score for the 1828 version. The Clog dance is the obvious highlight; but there are felicitous moments throughout, with snatches of Rossini, Donizetti *et al* cropping up all over the place. This recording is the original one that Lanchbery conducted when the ballet proved such a success in the Royal Ballet's repertoire in 1960. More recently he has recorded the score complete; and ballet lovers will consider this fuller version essential. However, others will find that the complete score rather outstays its welcome by comparison with this constantly uplifting selection. A most compelling recommendation.

Hildegard of Bingen — German 1098-1179

German composer, abbess and mystic Hildegard of Bingen's writings include much lyrical and dramatic poetry which has survived with monophonic music. The Symphonia armonie celestium revelationum contains musical settings of 77 poems arranged according to the liturgical calendar. The poetry is laden with imagery and the music, based on a few formulaic melodic patterns, is in some respects highly individual. Her morality play Ordo virtutum contains 82 melodies in a more syllabic style. She also wrote medical and scientific treatises, hagiography and letters and recorded her many visions. **GROVE**music

Vocal Works

A Feather on the Breath of God
Columba aspexit. Ave, generosa. O ignis spiritus Paracliti. O Jerusalem. O Euchari, in leta vita. O viridissima virga. O presul vere civitatis. O Ecclesia
Gothic Voices / Christopher Page with **Doreen Muskett** symphony **Robert White** reed drones
Hyperion CDA66039 (44' · DDD) Recorded 1981 Ⓟ︎ⓄⓄⓄ

Here's a collection of choice gems from one of the greatest creative personalities of the Middle Ages. We've limited means of assessing how these inspired pieces were performed in Hildegard's time; but the refreshingly unsophisticated timbre of the four sopranos and the reedy, almost boyish, vocal quality of the contralto are convincing enough to transport the listener right back to the unpolluted atmosphere of her cloister. Most to be savoured are the unaccompanied items, amounting to 50 per cent of the total. Indeed, since the notes make a point of telling us us that 'distractions such as the intrusion of instrumental decorations' were to be avoided, why did the producer go out of his way to introduce symphony and reed drones in the performance of the other 50 per cent? However, this is a delightful recording. When it was first released it sparked new interest in the music of the Middle Ages, and it remains a jewel in Hyperion's crown.

Favus distillans. Et ideo puelle. O tu illustrata. O vos angeli. Studium divinitatis. O ignee Spiritus. O rubor sanguinis. O orzchis Ecclesia. O gloriosissimi lux vivens angeli. Rex noster promptus est. Deus enim in prima muliere. De patria. Sed diabolus in invidia. Nunc gaudeant materna viscera Ecclesia
Sinfonye (Jocelyn West, Vivien Ellis, Stevie Wishart, Emily Levy, Vickie Couper, Julie Murphy) **members of the Oxford Girls' Choir**
Celestial Harmonies 13127-2 (62' · DDD) Texts and translations included ⒻO

Stevie Wishart succeeds in putting Hildegard's music across chiefly by her imaginative choice of singers, which includes quite young girls. The tuneful, unsophisticated timbre of the youngest voices acts as a foil to the sturdy chest voices of the older women – which have a quality of their own, somewhat akin to that of Hungarian folk singers. Such contrasts seem typical of the whole Hildegardian picture. Hildegard herself was made up of contrasts: she's both ecstatic and quietly tender; she can be passionate while maintaining a sense of decorum; she's erotic but also chaste. We could do without the hurdy-gurdy and dispense with the drones and improvised organum. What's left is a penetration of Hildegard's music that rarely comes through in other interpretations. One thinks particularly of the composer's portrayal of the mystery of the Incarnation in *O tu illustrata* and also, particularly, of the remarkably sustained lines of ecstasy in *O vos angeli* – this extraordinary outpouring ranging over two octaves, but which yet has shape and structure for all Hildegard's protestations that she'd never studied her art formally.

The Origin of Fire
Anonymous Beata nobis gaudia. Veni creator spiritus. Veni spiritus eternorum alme **Hildegard von Bingen** Caritas habundat in omniam. O felix anima. O ignis Spiritus Paracliti. O quam mirabilis. O igne Spiritus. O eternae Deus
Anonymous 4 (Marsha Genensky, Susan Hellauer, Jacqueline Horner, Johanna Rose sngrs)
Harmonia Mundi HMU90 7327 (66' · DDD · T/t) Ⓕ

This well-planned recording presents four of Hildegard's visionary experiences and several of her antiphons, including her best-known, *Caritas habundat in omniam*, with its spontaneously soaring phrases. Anonymous 4, with their smooth and restrained unison singing, are in many ways ideal interpreters; their careful avoidance of over-emphasising the rapture of the composer's outpourings marks this performance.

Anonymous 4 also introduce a degree of variety by setting some of her prose texts to ancient invitatory and reading tones, including one or two early two-part settings. They're perhaps on less certain ground here, though I find the tones intriguing, especially the one used for the opening vision of Vision 4 – *In vere visione spiritus*. The group hasn't been able to resist the temptation of adding discreet drones.

The programme is bounded by two hymns for Pentecost from a 12th-century Swiss Troper-Proser. The first is the well-known ninth-century Vespers hymn *Veni creator spiritus*, which acts as a prologue and is followed by an 11th-century paraphrase. The last item is the Lauds hymn *Beata nobis gaudia*, with a rather beautiful and unusual *tetradus* setting. One wonders how much opportunity Hildegard would have had to hear any music other than the traditional monastic chant of her abbey, which she would have sung every day of her life. But within the limits of her musical vocabulary she's astonishingly and outstandingly creative.

Paul Hindemith   German 1895-1963

Hindemith studied as a violinist and composer (with Mendelssohn and Sekles) at the Hoch Conservatory in Frankfurt (1908-17) and made an early reputation through his chamber music and expressionist operas. But then he turned to neo-classicism in his Kammermusik No 1, the first of seven such works imitating the Baroque concerto while using an expanded tonal harmony and distinctively modern elements, notably jazz. Each uses a different mixed chamber orchestra, suited to music of linear counterpoint and, in the fast movements, strongly pulsed rhythm.

During this early period Hindemith lived as a performer: he was leader of the Frankfurt Opera orchestra, and he played the viola in the Amar-Hindemith Quartet (1921-9) as well as in the first performance of Walton's Viola Concerto (1929). Much of his chamber music was written in 1917-24, including four of his six quartets and numerous sonatas, and he was also involved in promoting chamber music through his administrative work for the Donaueschingen Festival (1923-30). However, he also found time to compose abundantly in other genres; including lieder (Das Marienleben, to Rilke poems), music for newly invented mechanical instruments, music for schoolchildren and amateurs, and opera (Cardillac). In addition, from 1927 he taught at the Berlin Musikhochschule.

His concern with so many branches of music sprang from a sense of ethical responsibility that inevitably became more acute with the rise of the Nazis. With the beginning of the 1930s he moved from chamber ensembles to the more public domain of the symphony orchestra, and at the same time his music became harmonically smoother and less intensively contrapuntal. Then in the opera Mathis der Maler (preceded by a symphony of orchestral excerpts) he dramatised the dilemma of the artist in society, eventually opposing Brechtian engagement and insisting on a greater responsibility to art. Nevertheless, his music fell under official disapproval, and in 1938 he left for Switzerland, where Mathis had its first performance. He moved on to the USA and taught at Yale (1940-53), but spent his last decade back in Switzerland.

His later music is in the style that he had established in the early 1930s and that he had theoretically expounded in his Craft of Musical Composition (1937-9), where he ranks scale degrees and harmonic intervals in order from most consonant (tonic, octave) to most dissonant (augmented 4th, tritone), providing a justification for the primacy of the triad. His large output of the later 1930s and 1940s includes concertos and other orchestral works, as well as sonatas for most of the standard instruments. His search for an all-encompassing, all-explaining harmony also found expression in his Kepler opera Die Harmonie der Welt. **GROVE**music

Cello Concerto

Cello Concerto. The Four Temperaments
Raphael Wallfisch vc **Howard Shelley** pf
BBC Philharmonic Orchestra / Yan Pascal Tortelier
Chandos CHAN9124 (52' · DDD) Recorded 1992   Ⓕ

These two concertos, both from Hindemith's maturity (1940), make a good pairing. The outwardly conventional Cello Concerto contrasts a relatively small voice (the cello) which carries the work's lyrical message, with a large orchestra used initially for active statements delivered with great power. Hindemith's plan would seem to be to gradually to reconcile these apparently contradictory modes of address. The Four Temperaments is a concerto for piano and string orchestra, a much more evenly balanced combination, using theme and variations form to integrate and relate the contrasted 'humours'. Hindemith's treatment of his material appears to argue that all temperaments, whatever the dominant disposition, are closely related. His portraiture, in fact, reveals characterisation of great depth and dimension. Performances are superbly accomplished, indeed this is the finest of many currently available recordings of the work. And Chandos has resisted the temptation to move in on the soloist in the Cello Concerto. The sound is open and spacious.

Violin Concerto

Hindemith Violin Concerto[a] **Bruch** Scottish Fantasy[b] **Mozart** Sinfonia concertante[c]
[abc]**David Oistrakh** vn [c]**Igor Oistrakh** va [b]**LSO /**
Horenstein; [a]**Hindemith;** [c]**Moscow Philharmonic**
Orchestra / Kondrashin
Decca Legends 470 258-2DM (DDD) Recorded 1962-3   ⓂⒶ○○○

 What makes this disc indispensable is the 30-minute Violin Concerto with Oistrakh playing at his legendary best and the composer conducting. The late Deryck Cooke, in his original Gramophone review, wrote of Oistrakh as 'superbly poised and eloquent...and as performed here the Concerto shows that behind Hindemith's stony neo-classical facade beats a romantic German heart'. Listening to this recording it's hard to understand the concerto's relative neglect, but easy to imagine current star violinists finding Oistrakh an impossible act to follow. The 1962 sound gives him a discreet dominance, and the engineers flatten out the slow movement's central climax, but thankfully no other allowances need be made for preserving a classic recording. Bruch's Scottish Fantasy makes a fine coupling; a joy from start to finish, this is an inspirationally eloquent reading to rank alongside Heifetz's indelible 1961 stereo version.

Additional recommendation

Coupled with: Konzertmusik for Brass and Strings. Symphonic Metamorphosis
Kavakos vn **BBC Philharmonic Orchestra / Tortelier**
Chandos CHAN9903 (66' · DDD)   Ⓕ
A splendid modern alternative in superb sound to Oistrakh's classic account; Kavakos is, if anything, even more fleet-fingered than the Russian.

Wind Concertos

Clarinet Concerto. Horn Concerto. Concerto for Trumpet, Bassoon and Strings. Concerto for Flute, Oboe, Clarinet, Bassoon, Harp and Orchestra
Walter Buchsel fl **Liviu Varcol** ob **Ulrich Mehlhart** cl
Carsten Wilkening bn **Reinhold Friedrich** tpt **Marie Luise Neunecker** hn **Charlotte Cassedanne** hp
Brigitte Goebel spkr **Frankfurt Radio Symphony Orchestra / Werner Andreas Albert**
CPO CPO999 142-2 (70' · DDD) Recorded 1990-93   Ⓑ

Hindemith's four wind concertos (1947-9) have never enjoyed the success of the Kammermusik concertos with which they have much in common; that for clarinet came first, to a commission from Benny Goodman, and its lack of overt display may have militated against its popularity. Ulrich Mehlhart's performance more than bears comparison with that of any rival, and is served by the best sound. The 1949 Horn Concerto was written for Dennis Brain. If not quite in Brain's class, Marie Luise Neunecker's is nevertheless a fine, highly musical account. The declamation of Hindemith's poem in praise of the horn, inscribed over its wordless setting, may be thought intrusive. The other two concertos are rarities. In them Hindemith most nearly approaches his 1920s manner, for instance in the woodwinds and harp Concerto with the finale's quotations from Mendelssohn's Wedding March, occasioned by his silver anniversary. Albert's tempos in the Clarinet and

Horn Concertos are brisker than the composer's own; in all four works the soloists and Frankfurt orchestra are committed advocates.

Symphonic Metamorphosis

Mathis der Maler. Symphonic Metamorphosis on Themes of Carl Maria von Weber. Nobilissima Visione
Philadelphia Orchestra / Wolfgang Sawallisch
EMI 555230-2 (71' · DDD) Recorded 1994   Ⓕ

The Philadelphia players for Sawallisch give taut performances that simply outclass the competition. Another plus point is the unusual running order that achieves a better musical balance, starting with the most brilliant piece, the *Symphonic Metamorphosis*, and increasing in weight to the resounding brass Alleluias at the climax of the *Mathis* Symphony. Sawallisch's interpretations rank with Blomstedt in the *Mathis* Symphony and *Symphonic Metamorphosis*. Though many will prefer the leaner sound of the San Francisco Orchestra, EMI's sound for Sawallisch is relatively recessed. Given the spacious acoustic of Memorial Hall and the conductor's largeness of vision this is entirely apposite, with no loss of detail.

Kammermusiken

Kammermusiken – No 1, Op 24 No 1; No 2; No 3, Op 36 No 2; No 4, Op 36 No 3; No 5, Op 36 No 4; No 6, Op 46 No 1; No 7, Op 46 No 2. Kleine Kammermusik No 1 for Wind Quintet, Op 24 No 2
Konstanty Kulka vn **Kim Kashkashian** va **Norbert Blume** va d'amore **Lynn Harrell** vc **Ronald Brautigam** pf **Leo van Doeselaar** org **Royal Concertgebouw Orchestra / Riccardo Chailly**
Double Decca ② 473 722-2DF2 (138' · DDD) Recorded 1990   Ⓜ**OOO**

 Even were the performances and recordings not outstanding (and they are) this would be a very valuable set. Hindemith's series of *Kammermusik* ('Chamber Music') began in 1921 as an iconoclastic response to the hyper-intense emotionalism of German Expressionist music over the previous 15 years. It continued until 1927, at which point he began to rationalise the harmonic and expressive foundations of his style. This, then, is neo-classicism with a German accent; as such it was to be a vital force in sweeping away the cobwebs of late romanticism; Walton, Prokofiev, Shostakovich and Britten were among those who, however indirectly, would feel the benefit. The music is also immensely enjoyable in its own right. Hindemith cheekily throws together disparate idioms and sheer force of personality is all that guards against anarchy. All this is done with more than half an eye on the performers' enjoyment of recreation, and the fine array of artists assembled by Chailly savour every detail. Recording quality is exemplary.

String Quartets

Hindemith String Quartet No 3, Op 22   Ⓗ
Prokofiev String Quartet No 2 in F, Op 92
Walton String Quartet in A minor
Hollywood Quartet (Felix Slatkin, Paul Shure vns Paul Robyn va Eleanor Aller vc)
Testament mono SBT1052 (74' · ADD) Recorded 1951   Ⓕ

Although many accounts of the Prokofiev have appeared over the years, none has approached, let alone surpassed, the Hollywood version of the Second Quartet. The same would no doubt apply to the Hindemith but for the fact that there have been fewer challengers. What a wonderful feeling for line these players had, what an incredible, perfectly matched and blended ensemble – and how well these transfers sound! That goes for the Walton, too: there's no other account of it that makes so positive a case for it.

Viola Sonatas

Viola Sonatas – F, Op 11 No 4; Op 25 No 4; C (1939). Nobilissima visione – Meditation. Trauermusik
Paul Cortese va **Jordi Vilaprinyó** pf **Philharmonia Orchestra / Martyn Brabbins**
ASV CDDCA978 (70' · DDD) Recorded 1993   Ⓕ

The late-Romantic lyricism of the early F major Sonata, Op 11 No 4, comes over as slightly saccharine, with a tendency for the extremes to be evened out – a common problem with works from Hindemith's most radical decade. But in the more acerbic Second, Op 25 No 4 (1922), Cortese's warmth is persuasive. He's at his best in No 3 (1939), where he gives a performance of real depth that edges out even the composer's own from the top spot – though some might prefer a quicker pace. This can be recommended as first choice in the sonatas and *Meditation* (from *Nobilissima visione*). The *Trauermusik* is a bonus, though it doesn't supplant the Walther-Blomstedt version.

Violin Sonatas

Violin Sonatas – E flat, Op 11 No 1; D, Op 11 No 2; E (1935); C (1939)
Ulf Wallin vn **Roland Pöntinen** pf
BIS CD761 (56' · DDD)   Ⓕ**O**

The E major Sonata of 1935 is brief (under 10 minutes long) and uncomplicated, yet it's familiar Hindemith from first note to last. The C major work (1939) is more complex and grave, and probably the finest of them. The longest sonata, and most conservative in idiom, is the D major. Both Op 11 works were written in 1918 while Hindemith was on active service, and are remarkable for bearing few traces of either the grimness of the Great War or the composer's personal voice. Both deserve wider currency. This issue is also welcome in including the fragmentary abandoned finale of Op 11 No 1, a rustic dance not in keeping with the symmetry of the whole. The sweet-toned Ulf Wallin is fully attuned to Hindemith's wavelength, and Pöntinen provides exemplary support. The recording is typical BIS (ie excellent). A splendid disc.

Requiem for those we love

When Lilacs Last in the Door-yard Bloom'd (Requiem for those we love)
Jan DeGaetani mez **William Stone** bar **Atlanta Symphony Chorus and Orchestra / Robert Shaw**
Telarc CD80132 (62' · DDD) Text included. Recorded 1986 Ⓜ**O**

Hindemith's *Requiem* is a setting of Whitman's poem – the lilacs piled on President Lincoln's coffin as it was taken across the country after his assassination just as the Civil War was over, the thrush symbolising his own mourning, and the then fallen Western star (hailed at Lincoln's inauguration as a good omen) – further layers of association were added when, 80 years later almost to the day, President Roosevelt died as the Second World War was coming to an end. It includes a tragedy-laden sinfonia, arias, recitatives, marches, a massive double fugue and a passacaglia. It isn't, however, the great technical virtuosity – in places as close-packed as Whitman's verse – which leaves the most lasting impression, but the haunting beauty of much of the setting.

Robert Shaw gives a superlative and moving performance and receives an outstandingly vivid recording. He knows the work perhaps more intimately than anyone (having commissioned it from Hindemith in 1945 for his Collegiate Chorale in New York), and he makes the most of every expressive nuance, every shade of dynamics, though without losing the overall shape. There's greater subtlety in the playing of the prelude than ever before; the big brass chords have weight and fullness without stridency, and the orchestral playing generally is first-rate; it would scarcely be possible to find a more sympathetic baritone than William Stone, an unforced lyrical singer with clean technique and exemplary enunciation, or a sweeter or purer-voiced mezzo than Jan DeGaetani.

Das Unaufhörliche

Das Unaufhörliche
Ulrike Sonntag sop **Robert Wörle** ten **Siegfried Lorenz** bar **Berlin Radio Children's Choir; Berlin Radio Chorus and Symphony Orchestra / Lothar Zagrosek**
Wergo ② WER6603-2 (95' · DDD) Text and translation included Ⓕ

The oratorio *Das Unaufhörliche* ('The One Perpetual') was Hindemith's longest concert work. It never established itself in the repertoire

(although Boult conducted the UK première as early as 1933). It's cast in three parts, the first describing the 'one perpetual' itself, the second its effect on diverse areas of activity (including art, science and love), the third Humankind's reaction away from it and final acquiescence. How closely Hindemith accorded with the poet Gottfried Benn's viewpoint is a matter for conjecture, but his evanescent score matched the poem's expansiveness of theme and nobility of utterance. In this alone it pointed the way to *Mathis der Maler*, for there's nothing here akin to the *Kammermusiken* or *Neues vom Tage* (a smash-hit in Berlin at the time).

This is the work's first recording and the performance is a fine one with good sound. Flies in the ointment? Soprano Ulrike Sonntag, who seems too often to be straining for her notes and whose intonation isn't always secure, and Wergo's failure to provide a translation of Benn's spoken introduction, recorded in 1932 and included as the final track. These are quibbles, however, and should not deter anyone from investing in this important release.

Die Harmonie der Welt

Die Harmonie der Welt
Arutiun Kotchinian bass Kaiser Rudolf II, Kaiser Ferdinand II, Sun **François Le Roux** bar Kepler, Imperial Mathematician, Earth **Robert Wörle** ten General Wallenstein, Jupiter **Christian Elsner** ten Ulrich, Kepler's assistant, Late soldier, Mars **Michael Burt** bass Pastor in Linz, Mercury **Reinhard Hagen** bass Tansur, Saturn **Michael Kraus** bar Baron Starhemberg **Daniel Kirch** ten Kepler's brother **Tatiana Korovina** sop Susanna, Venus **Michelle Breedt** contr Kepler's mother, Luna **Sophia Larson** sop Little Susanna **Berlin Radio Symphony Chorus and Orchestra / Marek Janowski**
Wergo ③ WER6652-2 (161' · DDD) Notes, libretto and translation included Ⓕ

Die Harmonie der Welt is one of Hindemith's major works, perhaps his major post-war work. He first seems to have contemplated an opera on the polymath Johannes Kepler in the late 1930s, in the wake of *Mathis der Maler*. But it wasn't until 1955 that serious work was started on the libretto, although, as with *Mathis* two decades before, he had already written a symphony using themes reserved for the opera.

There are also superficial similarities in subject treatment between the two stage works. *Die Harmonie* is an opera about an astronomer-cum-philosopher rather than science, just as *Mathis* had been about an artist, not painting. Kepler's career is set in the context of his time, culminating in the tumultuous Thirty Years' War, just as Grünewald's had been set against the 16th-century Peasants' Revolt. Yet Kepler isn't as involved in the whirl of events as Mathis; he stands apart from them, concerned increasingly just to resolve his theories about the harmony of the world. In the end his search is vain and he dies with the word 'Futile' on his lips.

By the time of the première, Hindemith's star had waned and some critics regarded the opera also as futile, especially when compared to *Cardillac* and *Mathis*. But in several respects it's just as successful musically, its symphonic coherence and integration more consistently achieved than in earlier stage works and the composer had grown as an artist. If some of the characterisation is two-dimensional, this is made to serve the symbolic aspects of the whole, most clearly in the final scene as the main characters assume celestial roles in a cosmic passacaglia, the incandescent culmination of which truly raises the roof.

Marek Janowski directs a splendidly paced and committed performance, with some fine singing and playing from the forces of Berlin Radio. François Le Roux turns in a thoughtful and multi-faceted account of Kepler, with Robert Wörle's conniving but ultimately doomed Wallenstein and Christian Elsner's Ulrich the pick of the rest. Recorded in the Jesus-Christus-Kirche, Berlin, the sound is clear and spacious, the acoustic and balance serving the music better than in most theatres. A marvellous achievement, strongly recommended.

Mathis der Maler

Mathis der Maler
Roland Hermann bar Mathis **Josef Protschka** ten Albrecht **Gabriele Rossmanith** sop Regina **Sabine Hass** sop Ursula **Harald Stamm** bass Riedinger **Heinz Kruse** ten Hans Schwalb **Victor von Halem** bass Lorenz von Pommersfelden **Hermann Winkler** ten Wolfgang Capito **Ulrich Hielscher** bass Truchsess von Waldberg **Ulrich Ress** ten Sylvester von Schaumberg **John Cogram** ten Der Pfeiffer des Grafen von Helfenstein **Marilyn Schmiege** mez Helfenstein **North German Radio Chorus; Cologne Radio Chorus and Symphony Orchestra / Gerd Albrecht**
Wergo ③ WER6255-2 (166' · DDD) Recorded 1990. Notes and text included ⓕ

Mathis der Maler is one of the pinnacles of 20th-century German opera. It's become axiomatic to see in it a parable of the times, with Hindemith using the turbulent world of 16th-century Germany to mirror the Nazi Reich and his place in it. But in reality *Mathis* is a spiritual and historical opera, not a political one. Rudolf Stephan in his essay for Wergo plays down the political angle; if Hitler hadn't risen to power until, say, 1936, one doubts that *Mathis* would have turned out much different. Gerd Albrecht's acquaintance with Hindemith's music goes back to the early 1960s, before the composer's death. Hindemith even sanctioned some retouching of the orchestration in *Mathis* made by Albrecht for a festival performance, though it isn't made clear whether Albrecht has applied this here, nor to what extent. Rarely have Hindemith's often heavy textures sounded so clear.

As to the music, isn't the brief concluding 'Alleluia' duet that crowns the sixth tableau one of *the* great moments in 20th-century opera? You'll be convinced from your first hearing of it. There are fine moments aplenty in Albrecht's reading, not least where familiar passages from the *Mathis* Symphony surface and precipitate some of the most intense music of the opera.

Roland Hermann is, perhaps, a shade stolid in places as the painter (though his world-weariness in the final scene is just right); Josef Protschka makes a most authoritative Cardinal, acting as a perfect foil to Hermann's Mathis. They head a fine cast, supported by some lusty singing and playing from the combined forces of Cologne and North German Radios.

Sancta Susanna

Sancta Susanna
Susan Bullock sop Susanna **Della Jones** mez Clementia **Ameral Gunson** mez Old Nun **Mark Rowlinson** spkr Farmhand **Maria Treedaway** spkr Maid **Leeds Festival Chorus**

Drei Gesänge, Op 9. Das Nusch-Nuschi, Op 20 – Dances. Tuttifäntchen – Suite
Susan Bullock sop **BBC Philharmonic Orchestra / Yan Pascal Tortelier**
Chandos CHAN9620 (70' · DDD) Notes, text and translations included ⓕ

Sancta Susanna is one of three early stage works Hindemith composed in the wake of the First World War, its companions being *Mörder, Hoffnung der Frauen* and *Das Nusch-Nuschi*, based on a play for Burmese marionettes and represented here by its dances. He earned a living at the Frankfurt Opera during this period, so it's natural that he nurtured operatic ambitions. *Sancta Susanna* enjoyed a certain notoriety in its day. Fritz Busch refused to conduct the première on account of its blasphemous plot. It tells briefly of a young nun, Susanna, inflamed by the legend she hears from Sister Clementia, of a girl coming naked to the altar to embrace the life-size figure of Christ on the Cross. For this blasphemy she's buried alive. Aroused and undeterred, Susanna strips off and rips the covering from Christ's torso. She's terrified when a huge spider falls on to her head from the crucifix and, horrified by her deed, begs the nuns to wall her up. A drastic cure for arachnophobia or blasphemy! The opera is short, concentrated, highly imaginative and resourceful in its use of sonority; and its expressionist musical language is so powerful that at the end of its barely 23 minutes you feel you've heard a much longer piece. It's superbly done here. No praise can be too high for the singers and for the delicacy, eloquence and power of the playing Tortelier draws from his orchestra. The recorded sound is of demonstration quality in its unforced naturalness.

The gorgeous Straussian *Drei Gesänge*, Op 9, are very vehement and passionate, and at times wildly over the top, but their assured craft and confident ambition is breathtaking. Susan Bullock performs them with thrilling panache. The dances from *Nusch-Nuschi* are just as expertly done.

Leopold Hofmann   Austrian 1738-1793

After a period as Kapellmeister at St Peter's, Vienna, Hofmann became court keyboard teacher (1769); from 1772 he was second court organist and also Kapellmeister at St Stephen's Cathedral. He enjoyed wide fame as both player and composer. His many sacred works (including over 30 masses) combine Austrian Baroque and Neapolitan traits, while his c55 symphonies are in a galant style. Among his other works are Lieder, concertos and chamber music. GROVEmusic

Cello Concertos

Cello Concertos – D, B:D3; C, B:C3; D, B:D1; C, B:C1
Northern Sinfonia / Tim Hugh vc
Naxos 8 553853 (68' · DDD)   Ⓢ

The supremacy of Haydn and Mozart has always cast a shadow over the other Viennese composers of their time. In his day Leopold Hofmann, Kapellmeister at St Stephen's Cathedral from 1772, was one of the most eminent, as a composer of church music, symphonies, concertos and chamber works. His cello concertos – there are eight in all – belong to the 1760s or early 1770s, much the time of the Haydn C major Concerto, which they resemble in style. They are attractive, agreeable pieces, technically and formally assured if without very much individuality. The longest of the four concertos here, the one catalogued as D3, is more mature in style than the others and makes greater demands on the soloist. Tim Hugh's advocacy certainly makes the revival of these concertos worthwhile. He brings a very sound modern technique to the music, throwing off the rapid passages with evident ease, and there's a breadth to his phrasing that gives some amplitude to Hofmann's writing. His intonation is faultless, his tone full and warm, and he brings a keen feeling for *galant* expression to the slow movements. There's vivacity in the quick movements too. The Northern Sinfonia plays responsively. Those who relish good cello playing, should try this disc.

Violin Concertos

Violin Concertos – B flat, B:Bb1; A, B:A2. Concerto for Violin, Cello and Strings in G, B:G1
Lorraine McAslan vn **Tim Hugh** vc
Northern Chamber Orchestra / Nicholas Ward
Naxos 8 554233 (60' · DDD)   Ⓢ

For a composer long represented in the catalogue only by a concerto that masqueraded as Haydn's (HobVIIf:D1), this is a welcome issue of orchestral works, admirably edited and presented by the scholar Allan Badley. These Viennese concertos, probably from the 1760s, are *galant* works, with florid solo parts and elaborate lines, a leisurely harmonic pace and a good deal of sequence, but they're shapely and effective music, with tenderness in the slow movements – and also wit: the finale of the B flat Concerto is especially ingenious. Then there's the double concerto, for violin and cello, which has much attractive dialogue and duetting, rather in the manner of the Mozart violin-viola *Sinfonia concertante*. The *Adagio* is also eloquent. The performances are excellent, with clean, perfectly tuned and expressive violin playing from Lorraine McAslan. Tim Hugh plays equally securely and with a keen sense of style. Tempos are well chosen by Nicholas Ward who obtains spruce accompaniments from his orchestra.

Joseph Holbrooke   British 1878-1958

A pupil of Corder at the Royal Academy of Music, Holbrooke was influenced by Wagner and early Strauss. His large output, dating mostly from the beginning of the century, includes operas (among them the huge trilogy The Cauldron of Anwyn), symphonies, symphonic poems, chamber music and much for piano. GROVEmusic

Piano Concerto No 1

Holbrooke Piano Concerto No 1, Op 52, 'The Song of Gwyn ap Nudd' **Wood** Piano Concerto in D minor
Hamish Milne pf **BBC Scottish Symphony Orchestra / Martyn Brabbins**
Hyperion CDA67127 (69' · DDD) Text included Ⓕ**ⓄⓄ**

Holbrooke's ambitious First Piano Concerto is by some margin the most impressive orchestral piece of his to appear on disc. Dubbed a symphonic poem by its creator, it follows the narrative of a poem based on a Welsh legend by his patron Lord Howard de Walden entitled *The Song of Gwyn ap Nudd*. Yet the work can also be appreciated perfectly well as a red-blooded Romantic concerto in the grand tradition. Holbrooke handles proceedings with deft resourcefulness and a vaulting sweep. It receives outstandingly eloquent and tirelessly committed treatment in this performance.

An altogether more straightforward confection is the D minor Piano Concerto by Haydn Wood (1882-1959), who, before he made his name in the field of light music, was a gifted violinist and composition pupil of Stanford. Indeed, Stanford conducted the Queen's Hall première of Wood's big-boned D minor Concerto in July 1909. Grieg's Concerto is the obvious template, and there are stylistic echoes of Tchaikovsky, Rachmaninov and MacDowell.

The opening movement is full of effective display, and boasts a ravishing secondary idea. By far the best music comes in the central *Andante* – a haunting, deeply felt essay, boasting some wistfully fragrant orchestral sonorities. Not a great work, by any means, but incurable romantics will devour it.

Heinz Holliger   Swiss b1939

Holliger studied with Veress, in Paris, and with Boulez in Basle. Since the mid-1960s he has appeared internationally in a repertory ranging from Baroque oboe concertos to works written for him by Berio, Henze and LutosLawski. He has a bright tone and extraordinary phrasing technique and has introduced new effects (e.g. harmonics, double trills, chords). His compositions were initially Boulezian but have drawn nearer to Berio and Kagel in making the actual performance the main point (String Quartet, 1973). GROVEmusic

Violin Concerto

Holliger Violin Concerto, 'Hommage à Louis Soutter'[a] **Ysaÿe** Solo Violin Sonata in D minor, 'Ballade', Op 27 No 3
Thomas Zehetmair vn [a]**South West German Radio Symphony Orchestra, Baden-Baden and Freiburg / Heinz Holliger**
ECM New Series 476 1941 (54' · DDD)   ⓕ**OO**

During 1993-5 Heinz Holliger composed a three-movement Violin Concerto of about half an hour. Shortly before this recording of 2002 he added a 17-minute Epilogue: 'I want to show that music can age, be sapped of vital energy and end in agony.' The concerto is inscribed as homage to Louis Soutter, a Swiss-born violinist and painter (1871-1942) whose troubled images of violence and despair haunted Holliger for many years. The Epilogue is called 'Before the massacre', after one of Soutter's macabre paintings from 1939.

The concerto clearly isn't a lighthearted piece, but neither is it emptily depressing or disheartening. Soutter studied with Ysaÿe, so Holliger starts from Ysaÿe's short Third Sonata, played here as a prelude. The first three movements offer a dazzling portrait of virtuosity under strain. The Epilogue is much tougher, but Holliger does not totally renounce all suggestions of compassion for human victims of violence and fanaticism. This may be ageing, agonised music, but its effect is less of futility than of hushed awe in the face of a creative impulse that refuses to lie down and die.

These positive impressions owe much to the artistry of Thomas Zehetmair, who has been associated with the concerto from the beginning. The recording gives a needle-sharp aural image of the progress from bright colours and brittle textures to dark evanescence.

Robin Holloway   British 1943

Holloway studied with Goehr (from 1960) and at Cambridge, where in 1974 he was appointed lecturer. His large output covers many genres (including numerous songs) and shows a remarkable command of diverse styles: some pieces lovingly reinterpret Romanticism (Scènes from Schumann for orchestra,1970); others are strikingly positive in their modernism (The Rivers of Hell for chamber ensemble,1977). His first opera, Clarissa, a study of rape, was given by the English National Opera in London in 1990. GROVEmusic

Concertos for Orchestra

Second Concerto for Orchestra, Op 40
BBC Symphony Orchestra / Oliver Knussen
NMC NMCD015M (34' · DDD) Recorded 1993
Ⓜ**OOO**

A North African holiday was the stimulus for Robin Holloway's Second Concerto for Orchestra. The extremes of contrast, he tells us ('opulence and austerity, richness and drabness, brilliant light and dense shadow … And above all, the noises … the polyphony of hammering, tapping, thudding, tinkling, bashing …'), haunted him and were soon demanding to be turned into music. The experience seems also to have set him off on a more enigmatic, private voyage through his musical past. We hear a few particularly aching bars from Act 2 of *Tristan*, and rather more of Chopin's F sharp major Barcarolle; while a strange, broken tune on muted trombone metamorphoses neatly into Parry's *Jerusalem*. It's bewildering, but gripping. Holloway can swerve from lush, late Romanticism to strident modernism and back again with the alarming speed of an opium dream; but as with any really revelatory dream, the more you probe it, the more lucid it seems. When you reach the end, you feel you want to go back and soak in the experience all over again, and then go away somewhere and ponder its riddles.

The members of the BBC Symphony Orchestra play as though each one of them were engaged on his or her own voyage of discovery. Oliver Knussen's triumph in pulling it all together, and then shaping and shading it so lovingly, is just one of the technically miraculous aspects of this disc; another is that the production team have somehow turned BBC Maida Vale Studio No 1 into a fine, spacious acoustic, with details beautifully focused. It all adds up to a quite fascinating disc.

Third Concerto for Orchestra, Op 76
London Symphony Orchestra / Michael Tilson Thomas
NMC NMCD039 (45' · DDD) Recorded live 1996 ⓕ**O**

The first ideas for No 3 came during a trip through South America: there are sound pictures of Lake Titicaca, riotous New Year's Day celebrations in the Bay of Bahia, the slow train-crossing of the Great Brazilian Swamp and the huge, satanic slag heap at the Potosì Silver Mine. Holloway jotted them all down on the spot: then his notebook was stolen, and it took another 13 years to recall them and finish the piece. By then, the alchemical processes of memory had transformed the original musical impressions into something quite different. What might have been simply a descriptive tone-poem finally emerged as a powerful and unusual musical argument – a huge slow movement, with a moderately fast dance-like finale, which evolves from tiny scraps of motifs (there's hardly a 'theme' in sight). And yet much of the original 'illustrative' character of the piece remains.

String and woodwind textures recall dense, overripe rain forest foliage; the dark, 'sluggish' first movement suggests the movement of a vast, slow, muddy river; extravagant sensuousness contrasts with clangorous bells or craggy brass. This recording, based on its 1996 première, is quite an achievement. It's rare for a conductor and an orchestra to show such a compelling grasp of the shape and atmosphere of a work at its first performance. Technically the sound has none of the usual problems associated with a live recording – virtually no intrusive noise, good balance, warm tone.

Fantasy-Pieces on...'Liederkreis'

Holloway Fantasy-Pieces on the Heine 'Liederkreis' of Schumann, Op 16. Serenade in C, Op 41*b*
Schumann Liederkreis, Op 24
Toby Spence *ten* **Ian Brown** *pf* **Nash Ensemble /**
Martyn Brabbins
Hyperion CDA66930 (75' · DDD) Texts and
translation included   Ⓕ**O**

A contemporary composer takes a 19th-century classic, Schumann's song cycle *Liederkreis*, and sets it in a musical frame of his own devising: a short, astringent 'Praeludium' and four extended movements, the style hovering between pure homage and what the composer calls 'phantasmagorical collage'. Certainly sufficient to cause hackles to rise! But the result, entitled *Fantasy-Pieces on the Heine 'Liederkreis' of Schumann* is uniquely fascinating, haunting and increasingly rewarding the more one goes back to it. Brief though it is, the 'Praeludium' is just enough to tell the ear that the performance of *Liederkreis* that follows isn't going to be the whole story. Holloway picks up magically on Schumann's ending, in a short movement, 'Half asleep' (what follows is, at times, intensely dream-like). Then come an *Adagio*, a *Scherzo* and a finale – on one level, symphonic, on another, an intricate series of references and cross-references based on Schumann's songs (not all from *Liederkreis*). The manner drifts between masterful irony and fleeting moments of intense self-revelation. *Liederkreis* remains *Liederkreis*, and yet something profound and (in

the wider sense) modern is added. The Serenade in C is a kind of post-modern *divertimento*. Scored for the same forces as Schubert's Octet, it alternates, charmingly and teasingly, between sensuous Viennese cosiness, something closer to the salon Elgar, and delightful, end-of-the-pier vulgarity – though with a more acerbic harmonic colouring from time to time. Play a short extract to a musical friend and he/she might well date it before the First World War. But nothing is ever what it seems for very long; the disruptive subtlety of *Fantasy-Pieces* is here too, despite the seeming holiday feeling. Splendid performances from the Nash Ensemble – colourful, precise and sensitive to Holloway's kaleidoscopic shifts in mood. The recordings are quite excellent: the change in perspective for the Schumann songs makes perfect aural sense.

Gilded Goldbergs

Gilded Goldbergs (for two pianos after JS Bach),
Op 86
Micallef-Inanga Piano Duo (Jennifer Micallef, Glen
Inanga *pfs*)
Hyperion ② CDA67360 (98' · DDD)   Ⓜ**OO**

Holloway's initial prompt for these stunning two-piano transcriptions of Bach's *Goldbergs*, was his frustration as a single pianist at his 'inability to clarify the close-weave canons or manage the more fiendish hand-crossing numbers so idiomatic on a two-manual harpsichord'. So far, so pleasurable – but then inevitably the full artistic implication of what he was doing struck home. It was only later, after much agonised self-questioning, that he decided to 'go for the gilding and lose the guilt!' Bach's original is thrown in at the deep centre of a swelling harmonic sea, sometimes as a moment of ineffable calm (Variation 18, a 'canon in sixths'), at other times more like an oncoming tidal wave (Variation 29, 'Toccata with clusters'). The use of modulation is often alarming but always musically effective and never more so than in an ingenious re-working of the closing 'Quodlibet' (Variation 30), which traverses 'all 12 keys', ending in D. Holloway's ear for nuance, and the ingenuity of his invention, will leave you open-mouthed with admiration. Whatever your CD priorities to date, this one surely has to fly straight to the top of your wants list.

Vagn Holmboe   Danish 1909-1996

Holmboe studied with Hoffding and Jeppesen in Copenhagen, and with Toch in Berlin, then returned to Copenhagen to work as a teacher (at the conservatory), critic and composer. He is the leading Danish symphonist after Nielsen (he has composed 11, 1935-82) and composer of a series of 14 string quartets (1949-75), regarded as the most important Scandi-

navian contributions to the genre since World War Two. He has also written operas, vocal and chamber music. His style is unproblematic if not immediately accessible, influenced by Nielsen, Hindemith and Stravinsky. **GROVE**music

Chamber Concertos

Chamber Concertos – No 8, 'Sinfonia Concertante', Op 38; No 10, 'Wood, Brass and Gut', Op 40. Concerto giocondo e severo, Op 132. The Ill-Tempered Turk, Op 32b
Aalborg Symphony Orchestra / Owain Arwel Hughes
BIS BIS-CD917 (68' · DDD) Ⓕ

Holmboe the concerto writer had a very different agenda from Holmboe the symphonist, and nowhere does that become more apparent than in *Chamber Concerto* No 8 (1945), subtitled *Sinfonia concertante*, a splendid work that's a direct precursor of the magnificent *First Chamber Symphony* (1953). Owain Arwel Hughes underscores the music's internal cohesion and plays down the Hindemithian overtones. No 10 (1945-6) is a bracing early example of Holmboe's metamorphosis technique, its nine sections acting like variations within a traditional concerto format: the sections in pairs respectively form an introduction and three 'movements', with the last acting as coda.

Holmboe devotees will be particularly keen on the other two works, both novelties. The *Cheerful and Severe* Concerto is a single (12-minute) movement, though like the Tenth, divided into sections; here, though, they are compressed to form a compellingly fluent design in the composer's late, luminous style. More fascinating still is the suite, made (with some recomposition) in 1969 from the music of the still-unperformed ballet *Den Galsindede Tyrk* (1942-4). The opening 'Dance of the Executioner' has echoes of the contemporaneous Fifth Symphony, while later movements – for instance, the central 'Dance of the Trees' – point towards the Sixth and Seventh (1947-50). But the music also seems eminently danceable, making its neglect all the more astonishing. Heartily recommended.

Chamber Concertos – No 11 for Trumpet and Orchestra, Op 44; No 12 for Trombone and Orchestra, Op 52; Tuba and Orchestra, Op 127. Intermezzo concertante, Op 171
Håkan Hardenberger *tpt* **Christian Lindberg** *tbn* **Jens Bjørn-Larsen** *tuba* **Aalborg Symphony Orchestra / Owain Arwel Hughes**
BIS CD802 (55' · DDD) Ⓕ

The Trumpet Concerto has a leanness of texture and neo-classical air that will surprise those familiar with Holmboe's symphonies. Hardenberger's first entry creates an electricity that's maintained throughout the work – indeed, the disc as a whole. No 11's tripartite design recurs, condensed into a single movement, in No 12: a

brief, expressively crucial slow section framed by a large-boned *Allegro* (rather grave in character in the trombone work), and a good-humoured, rollicking finale. The Tuba Concerto (1976), by contrast, requires a full orchestral complement, its one integrated span bearing little semblance of traditional three-movement form. It's the most dramatic and exploratory work here, both in mood and sonority, the demands of which on tuba virtuosos over the years have occasioned it to be played in slightly differing versions, especially with regard to the taxing cadenza. The short *Intermezzo concertante* reaffirms that the tuba really can sing. Wonderful music, wonderfully performed and recorded.

Chamber Concertos – No 1, Op 17[a]; No 3, Op 21[b]; No 7, Op 37[c]. Beatus parvo, Op 117[d]
[c]**Gordon Hunt** *ob* [b]**Martin Fröst** *cl* [a]**Noriko Ogawa** *pf* [d]**Danish National Opera Chorus; Aalborg Symphony Orchestra / Owain Arwel Hughes**
BIS BIS-CD1176 (78' · DDD · T/t) ⒻⓄ

A word about nomenclature. Holmboe composed 13 chamber concertos between 1939 and 1956 as a series with small-orchestral accompaniment, similar but not so homogeneous a set as Hindemith's *Kammermusiken*. Much later BIS renamed them just concerti, which is how BIS in its continuing series (coupled with other concertante works; this is the third issue) refers to them. Dacapo's integral set of the 13 curiously retained the chamber tag.

Irrespective of titles, they make a fine set. The concertos are extremely diverse and may surprise those who know only the symphonies and quartets. Hannu Koivula's nicely paced and well-thought-through interpretations for Dacapo, although a touch studio-bound, set a formidable standard to follow. As with the Brass and Orchestral Concertos, Owain Arwel Hughes more than rises to that challenge with tempi usually a touch swifter and more urgent, and the recorded sound more resonant, giving a warmer sound picture of each work.

This is particularly true in the First Concerto for piano, strings and timpani, where Ogawa is more sympathetically placed and not recessed as was Anne Øland. Ogawa's technique is also the stronger and she shapes Holmboe's neo-romantic lines even more splendidly than her rival.

In the Clarinet and Oboe Concertos honours are a little more even, though Martin Fröst and Gordon Hunt just shade the decision. There's a 'bigness' to Fröst's tone that Niels Thomsen cannot quite match and Hunt's incisive playing that's just about perfect. There's nothing inadequate about the Dacapo issues, but if you're in two minds about buying this newcomer consider the bonus of Holmboe's charming cantata *Beatus parvo*, a kind of concerto for amateur forces full of that marvellous luminosity that characterised so much of his music in his last decades. Strongly recommended.

Symphonies

Symphonies – No 11, Op 144; No 12, Op 175; No 13, Op 192
Aarhus Symphony Orchestra / Owain Arwel Hughes
BIS CD728 (63' · DDD) Recorded 1994 ⓕ●

Few who have invested in this series so far can doubt that these are among the most commanding symphonies to have emerged in post-war Europe. Some might even argue that they're *the* finest since Sibelius and Nielsen. All credit to Owain Arwel Hughes and the Aarhus orchestra for their committed advocacy and to BIS for recording them in such vivid, naturally balanced sound. The 11th, composed in 1980, is quintessential Holmboe, and its atmosphere resonates in the mind long after you've heard it. To quote Knud Ketting's notes, 'the symphony's climax in dynamic and emotional terms comes in the second movement and it then slowly retreats within itself…[it] is cast as a strong arch, which impresses at first hearing, and commands increasing admiration on closer acquaintance'. The arabesque that opens the symphony seems to come from another world and the transparent, luminous textures communicate the sense of a spiritual quest that one rarely encounters in modern music. The 12th is a taut, well-argued piece, and is, like its two companions on this disc, in three movements. No one listening to the 13th, written at the instigation of Owain Arwel Hughes, would think that it was the work of an 85-year-old. There have been other octogenarian symphonies, but none that sounds quite so youthful or highly charged as this.

Sinfonias

Symphonias I-IV, Op 73. Chairos
Danish Radio Sinfonietta / Hannu Koivula
Dacapo ② (Two-for-the-price-of-one) 8 226017/8 (114' · DDD) ⓕ●

Holmboe's reputation resides principally on his cycles of 17 symphonies and 20 string quartets. He clearly relished the opportunities and challenge of cycles; and these four sinfonias for strings (1957-62) form another. They can be played either as independent pieces or – in a very particular sequence – as a large meta-symphony, *Chairos*, in which the four movements of Sinfonia IV frame and interlock with the single spans of I-III. Dacapo present, intelligently, both versions, each on its own disc.

Holmboe explained that 'Chairos means "time" in the psychological sense, that is the passage of time as we sense it', in contrast to measured time (Chronos). Sinfonias I-III all embrace the main elements of traditional symphonism in their unbroken designs, the first two adopting broadly a slow-fast ground plan, III the reverse. If IV's sequence of prelude, interludes and postludes suggests something lightweight, this is misleading, for it's a highly impressive structure; the movement titles are relevant mostly for the larger composition. It's unclear when Holmboe conceived this unusual double-form. The expressive characters and relative brevity of I and III suggest that he may have had a larger design in mind at first, though II, at 19 minutes, the longest by far of the four, hints at a totally separate genesis.

However the music started out, the achievement of *Chairos* is splendid testament to Holmboe's near-unique skill as a composer in the 20th century. In its larger form, it evinces a freedom of line and spontaneity of incident that suggests the tyranny of beat and bar-line had been cast off, yet in reality all is closely argued and achieved by total precision of means. Koivula and the Danish Radio Sinfonietta embrace this dichotomy in the music's soaring lines (which in the highest registers can sound just a touch thin) and multi-faceted fantasy. Dacapo's sound is of demonstration quality. Very strongly recommended.

Symphonic Metamorphoses

Symphonic Metamorphoses – No 1, Op 68, 'Epitaph'; No 2, Op 76, 'Monolith'; No 3, Op 80, 'Epilog'; No 4, Op 108, 'Tempo variabile'
Aalborg Symphony Orchestra / Owain Arwel Hughes
BIS CD852 (75' · DDD) ⓕ●

In form the symphonic metamorphosis is an offshoot of the symphonic fantasia (but of a kind radically different from Sibelius's *Pohjola's Daughter*), each of these four very different from its companions. The vigour and luminous orchestration of the symphonies are present, as are many of the internal developmental processes, but not the level of integration. Holmboe's priorities here are unlike those of many others of his pieces, yet the music coheres perfectly on its own terms. Hughes is fully inside Holmboe's idiom, whether in the single-minded determination of *Monolith* or in the visionary *Epilog*, one of the composer's most searching utterances, prefiguring both the Ninth Symphony (1969) and *Requiem for Nietzsche*. This is extraordinary music.

Gustav Holst   British 1874-1934

Holst studied at the Royal College of Music with Stanford, and in 1895 met Vaughan Williams, to whom he was close for the rest of his life. From 1905 he taught at St Paul's Girls' School in Hammersmith. Like Vaughan Williams, he was impressed by English folksong, but also important was his reading in Sanskrit literature (chamber opera Savitri, composed 1908; Choral Hymns from the Rig Veda, 1912) and his experience of the orchestral music of Stravinsky and Strauss (he had played the trombone professionally). In The Planets (1916) he produced a suite of seven highly characterful movements to represent human dispositions associated with the planets in astrology, and his interest in esoteric wisdom is expressed too in his cantata The Hymn of Jesus (1917). But his very varied output also includes essays in a fluent neo-classicism (A Fugal Concerto for flute, oboe and strings, 1923; Double Violin Concerto, 1929), a bare Hardy impression (Egdon Heath, 1927) and operas.　　　**GROVE**music

Egdon Heath

A Somerset Rhapsody, H87. Beni Mora, H107.
Invocation, H75. A Fugal Overture, H151. Egdon
Heath, H172. Hammersmith, H178
Tim Hugh vc **Royal Scottish National Orchestra /
David Lloyd-Jones**
Naxos 8 553696 (69' · DDD)　　　　　　Ⓢ

This superb recording was made in the Henry Wood Hall, Glasgow. Lloyd-Jones has as his two weightiest items the Hardy-inspired *Egdon Heath*, arguably Holst's finest work, as well as the prelude and fugue *Hammersmith*, comparably dark and intense. In the latter he chooses the wind-band version, achieving a subtlety of shading in phrasing and dynamic amply to justify that striking choice. The Naxos sound is vividly atmospheric while letting one hear inner detail. Lloyd-Jones generally adopts flowing speeds and is objective in his interpretation while bringing out to the full the tenderness and refinement of the writing. Particularly beautiful is the performance of *A Somerset Rhapsody* which opens the disc, with the cor anglais solo ravishingly played. The six works are neatly balanced, three dating from before the climactic period of *The Planets* and *The Hymn of Jesus*, and three after. Particularly valuable is the atmospheric *Invocation* for cello and orchestra of 1911, rather dismissed by Imogen Holst, but here given a yearningly intense, deeply thoughtful performance with Tim Hugh as soloist. This is a highly recommendable offering, whether for the dedicated Holstian or the newcomer wanting to investigate work outside *The Planets*.

The Planets

The Planets
**Women's voices of the Montreal Symphony
Chorus and Orchestra / Charles Dutoit**
Decca Gramophone Awards Collection 476 1724
(53' · DDD) Recorded 1986　　　　Ⓜ❶❶❶

 The Planets is Holst's most famous work, and its success is surely deserved. The musical characterisation is as striking as its originality of conception: the association of 'Saturn' with old age, for instance, is as unexpected as it's perceptive. Bax introduced Holst to astrology, and while he wrote the music he became fascinated with horoscopes, so it's the astrological associations that are paramount, although the linking of 'Mars' (with its enormously powerful 5/4 rhythms) and

war also reflects the time of composition. Throughout, the work's invention is as memorable as its vivid orchestration is full of infinite detail. No recording can reveal it all but this one comes the closest to doing so. Dutoit's individual performance is in a long line of outstanding recordings.

Holst The Planets[a] **Elgar** Variations on an Original Theme, Op 36, 'Enigma'[b]
[a]**Geoffrey Mitchell Choir;** [a]**London Philharmonic Orchestra,** [b]**London Symphony Orchestra /
Sir Adrian Boult**
EMI Great Recordings of the Century 567748-2
(78' · ADD) Recorded [a]1978, [b]1970　　　Ⓜ❶

From the famous first run-through – for it can scarcely have been more – at the Queen's Hall in 1919, Boult had a long association with *The Planets*. This splendid set from 1978 has been admirably remastered. Boult, in the composer's words, 'first made the *Planets* shine' and he always had something special to say about the music on all his recordings. Apart from public performances, he made five recordings of the work, and this is considered by many to have been the finest. His interpretation varied very little throughout his long association with the suite, only being temporarily shaken when he heard the reissue of Holst's own very different 1926 performance. However, he stuck to his own view, which Holst thoroughly approved of.

The actual performance has an indefinable 'rightness' about it, a supreme authority that makes it difficult to imagine the score being interpreted in any other way. Has 'Mars' ever resounded with more terrifying ferocity? In 'Venus' the playing has a translucent beauty, while the impish 'Mercury' really sparkles. 'Jupiter' has marvellous exuberance and sparkle, its big tune lent enormous dignity and humanity. 'Saturn', too, is paced to perfection (the central climax has a massive inevitability about it), and 'Uranus' goes about his mischievous antics with terrific swagger.

If you've never heard Boult's *Planets*, you should investigate this set immediately. Plenty of *Enigma* recordings have been added to the catalogue since 1970, but none has surpassed it in authority and fidelity. There's also a slightly elegiac feel to the phrasing, as if Boult, no sentimentalist, was nevertheless aware that his *Enigma* days must be numbered. Yet the faster variations have the vitality and brio you might expect from a younger conductor. The LSO's performance is excellent, and the recording too.

Holst The Planets[a] (includes extra version of Neptune with original ending). Lyric Movement
C Matthews Pluto
Tim Pooley va **Hallé Orchestra and** [a]**Choir**
(Women's Voices) / **Mark Elder**
Hyperion CDA67270 (75' · DDD)　　　　Ⓕ

Unusually popular repertoire for Hyperion; but

HOLST'S THE PLANETS – IN BRIEF

BBC SO / Sir Adrian Boult
Beulah 2PD12 (70' · ADD)   Ⓜ
Set down in January 1945, this is the earliest
and most exciting of the five recordings
under the maestro, who, in the words of the
composer, 'first caused *The Planets* to shine'.

London PO / Sir Adrian Boult
EMI 567748-2 (79' · ADD)   ⓂⓄ
Dedicatee Boult's final, unerringly paced
account of a work with which, perhaps more
than any other in his vast repertoire, he was
most closely associated.

Montreal SO / Charles Dutoit
Decca 476 1724 (53' · DDD)   ⓂⓄⓄⓄ
☀ Holst's colourful canvas has rarely been
captured with such lustre or transparency by a recording team. Dutoit conducts with infectious bounce and plenty of
twinkling affection.

Philharmonia Orchestra / Sir John Eliot Gardiner
DG 445 860-2GH (68' · DDD)   Ⓕ
Gardiner's is a consistently effervescent performance, preceded by a roistering account of
Grainger's amazing 'imaginary ballet' from
1913-16 *The Warriors* (composed at almost
exactly the same time as *The Planets*).

London SO / André Previn
EMI 492399-2 (75' · ADD)   Ⓕ
Originally made in quadrophony, Previn's
memorable version leaps out of the speakers
with startling impact, and is stunningly well
played by the LSO at its early-70s peak. At
present only available in DVD-Audio format.

Boston SO / William Steinberg
DG 463 627-2GOR (76' · ADD)   Ⓜ
Anyone seeking a different angle on this
much-traversed showpiece would do well to
seek out this hugely spirited and strongly
characterised American offering. Resonant,
full-bodied 1971 sound.

BBC SO / Sir Andrew Davis
Warner Apex 8573 89087-2 (64' · DDD)   Ⓢ
Davis's admirably prepared account won't
break the bank and enjoys sumptuous, stunningly well-defined recording – try 'Saturn'
with its devastating climax and floorboard-
throbbing organ pedals.

Royal Liverpool Philharmonic Orchestra /
Sir Charles Mackerras
Virgin @ 561510-2 (121' · DDD)   Ⓢ
Mackerras invariably achieves spontaneous,
communicative results on disc and this highly
enjoyable 1990 *Planets* is no exception.

the special interest here is *Pluto*, commissioned
by the Hallé's outgoing director Kent Nagano
to illustrate the eighth planet, discovered only
in 1930. For proper effect, though, it obviously
demands a decent *Planets*, which happily it
receives. If the Hallé lack the glitz and sheen of
Dutoit's and Karajan's orchestras, then they
offer a warmly idiomatic sound which suits the
generally expansive yet detailed approach of
their new director Mark Elder, as well as the
full-blooded, rather forward recording.

Mars, with balefully clear percussion, steers a
middle way between the machine-gun tempo
favoured by the composer and Haitink's leaden
grimness. *Venus* and *Mercury* are sensuous, even
lingering, but *Jupiter* is refreshingly vibrant and
dancing. Tension slackens somewhat in *Saturn*,
but spaciousness and detail make more sense of
Uranus than usual, although the transcendent
organ *glissando* is somewhat underwhelming.
Neptune is suprisingly lush, with a chorus as
alluring as ethereal. Which, in the main version
here, fades out to *Pluto* – a flashing *scherzo*,
inspired by the rushing particles of the so-called
'solar wind'. Matthews wisely avoids Holstian
pastiche, linking it to the original by tempo –
Holst's favoured 5/4 – and sound; celesta,
glockenspiel and jittery percussion create fleeting reminiscences of the other planets. The
result is appealing, postmodern but lyrical, yet
ultimately unsatisfying. Like a spectacularly
modern wing grafted onto a classic building, it
stimulates by contrast, yet the uneasy lack of
unity diminishes both. A separate piece, linked
companionably rather than umbilically, might
have been more effective. As the composer disarmingly admits, Pluto's planetary status is
pretty dubious, anyway. The *Lyric Movement*,
with a fine soloist, raises hopes for some more
rare Holst from this particular team.

The Planets. Egdon Heath, H172
BBC Symphony Chorus and Orchestra /
Sir Andrew Davis
Warner Apex 8573-89087-2 (64' · DDD) Recorded
1993   Ⓢ

This is a mightily impressive account of *The
Planets*. The high is undoubtedly 'Saturn',
whose remorseless tread has rarely seemed
more implacable. Aided by orchestral playing
that's both memorably concentrated and rapt,
Holst's textures in the closing section acquire a
breathtaking translucency, and how memorably
the BBC SO brass thrusts home the terrifying
central climax at 5'34". 'Neptune', too, is exceptionally successful: ethereally delicate *tremolando* harps set the scene for a tone picture of
exquisite beauty, graced by choral work of
notable purity from the women of the BBC
Symphony Chorus. Elsewhere, 'Mercury' darts
hither and thither in suitably impish fashion.
'Venus' is cool and chaste: if the BBC violins
can't quite command the bloom and sheen of
the very finest groups, the liquidity and poise of
the woodwind are most striking. And the burst

of energy at the close of 'Jupiter' is genuinely exhilarating. The spectacularly ample sound certainly makes the mischievous antics of 'Uranus' a feast for the ears, and Davis handles the coda superbly, plunging the listener into a world which is unnerving in its bleakness. He shows comparable perception in the similarly remote terrain of *Egdon Heath*, and succeeds in conveying much of the sombre intensity of Holst's cloud-hung evocation.

Additional recommendations

A Somerset Rhapsody

Coupled with: Beni Mora. A Fugal Overture. Hammersmith. Japanese Suite. Scherzo
London Philharmonic Orchestra; LSO / Boult
Lyrita SRCD222 (62' · ADD)   (F)
 Conducted by one of the composer's greatest friends and staunchest advocate, this release is still in the front rank.

Coupled with: **Holst** Egdon Heath. Brook Green Suite. **Vaughan Williams** In the Fen Country. Five Variants of Dives and Lazarus. Norfolk Rhapsody No 1
Bournemouth Sinfonietta / Del Mar; various artists
HMV Classics HMV5 73461-2 (66' · DDD/ADD)   (M)
 The *Somerset Rhapsody* builds from the quietest of beginnings to a fine climax – a vivid recording.

The Hymn of Jesus

The Hymn of Jesus, H140[a].
First Choral Symphony, H155[b]
[b]**Felicity Palmer** sop [a]**St Paul's Cathedral Choir;**
[a]**London Symphony Chorus; London Philharmonic**
[b]**Choir and Orchestra** / [a]**Sir Charles Groves,**
[b]**Sir Adrian Boult**
EMI British Composers 565128-2 (72' · ADD)
Recorded 1974,1977, Texts included   (M)

When it first appeared in 1978 Groves's account of *The Hymn of Jesus* was generally rated a finer effort than Boult's 1961 Decca recording. The authority and honesty of the former's direction is impressive. True, orchestral discipline could at times be tighter, but the choral singing is never less than very commendable. It should, however, be pointed out that Groves's achievement has since been outshone by Richard Hickox, who in turn can't quite match the extraordinary fervour and intensity of Sir Malcolm Sargent in his pioneering 1944 account. The really good news here, though, is Boult's powerful 1974 première recording of the awesome *Choral Symphony*. This was one of Holst's most ambitious, imaginative and questing creations, still under-appreciated to this day. It contains pages that are among the most original he conceived, not least the opening 'Invocation to Pan' and extraordinarily intense setting of the *Ode on a Grecian Urn*. The sound is satisfyingly full and immediate.

The Cloud Messenger, H111[aef]. The Hymn of Jesus, H140[ef]. A Choral Fantasia, H177[bdg]. A Dirge for Two Veterans, H121[dg]. Ode to Death, H144[eg]. Ave Maria, H49[c]. Motets, H159-60[c] – The Evening-Watch. This have I done for my true love, H128[c]. Seven Partsongs, H162[bdg]. O lady, leave that silken thread, H4[c]. Short Partsongs, H13[c] – Soft and gently through my soul. The autumn is old, H1[c]. Winter and the birds, H App I/40[c]
[a]**Della Jones** mez [b]**Patricia Rozario** sop [c]**Finzi Singers / Paul Spicer;** [d]**Joyful Company of Singers; London Symphony** [e]**Chorus and** [f]**Orchestra,** [g]**City of London Sinfonia / Richard Hickox**
Chandos Two for One ② CHAN241-6 (147' · DDD)
Recorded 1990   (M)(O)

The Cloud Messenger is a 43-minute work of considerable imaginative power. Before its previous single-issue release it had been virtually forgotten since its disastrous première under Holst's baton in 1913. It shows the composer already working on an epic scale – something that casts light on the subsequent eruption of *The Planets*. It's marvellous to have the work on disc, though, as you might expect, it's uneven. Those who admire the ascetic rigour of his later music may share Imogen Holst's reservations, and find the score disappointingly 'backward'. There are certainly echoes of Vaughan Williams's *A Sea Symphony* and several older models. On the other hand, the glittering approach to the sacred city on Mount Kailasa and the stylised orientalism of the climactic dance are new to British music; another world, that of 'Venus', is foreshadowed in the closing pages. The text is Holst's own translation from the Sanskrit.
 One of the few incontrovertible masterpieces in Holst's output, the familiar *Hymn of Jesus* has seldom received a better performance on disc. The choral singing itself is splendidly crisp, but the grand acoustics of London's St Jude's impart a certain warm imprecision that can blunt the impact of Holst's acerbic harmonies.

Seven Partsongs

Seven Partsongs, H162. A Choral Fantasia, H177. A Dirge for Two Veterans, H121. Ode to Death, H144
Patricia Rozario sop **London Symphony Chorus; Joyful Company of Singers; City of London Sinfonia / Richard Hickox**
Chandos CHAN9437 (59' · DDD) Recorded 1994.
Texts included   (F)

The First World War is the unnamed, ever-felt presence here. 'I float this carol with joy, with joy to thee O Death', chants Walt Whitman with that willed mystical intoxication that proved surprisingly attractive to both Holst and Vaughan Williams, composers who could face reality soberly enough, and in Holst's case often with a bleak, spare beauty of sound that takes and bestows only a hard-won comfort. Listening even to the relatively 'light' and partially happy Bridges settings (the *Seven Partsongs*), one becomes aware of a hollow, half-anxious feeling, located in that mysterious area of midriff wherein these undefined apprehensions take their dwelling. With it comes a musician's cherishing of silence, as though the music which intrudes upon it must be most finely attuned if it's to justify the presumption. Death emerges from its temporary hiding place in the seventh ('Assemble, all ye maidens') and then, for the rest of the recital, comes into its kingdom. Most explicitly, the *Dirge for Two Veterans* takes up the 'full-keyed bugles' of war, and that was written in the last months of 1914. In the *Ode to Death* (1931) and even the partsongs for women's voices, it's surely the dreadful sadness of that war which fills the hollow places and so, for comfort, enhances the apprehension of beauty in music. The programme has a very special value, and the performances are worthy of it.

Songs

Hymns from the Rig Veda, H90^c. Six Songs, H69^a. Four Songs, H132^{ad}. 12 Songs, H174^b. Margrete's cradle song, H14 No 2^a. The Heart Worships, H95^a
^{a}**Susan Gritton** sop ^{b}**Philip Langridge** ten
^{c}**Christopher Maltman** bar ^{d}**Louisa Fuller** vn
Steuart Bedford pf
Naxos 8 557117 (76' · DDD) Texts included ⑤

The Four Songs for voice and violin, settings of medieval texts, were inspired by the composer hearing one of his pupils singing to herself and playing her violin in Thaxted Church. They're singularly moving, especially in this plangently toned performance by Susan Gritton. She is no less remarkable in the Six Songs, early pieces in which Holst perfectly responds to an eclectic choice of poetry, nowhere more so than in the opening piece from Tennyson's 'In Memoriam'.

Philip Langridge is equally well suited to the 12 Humbert Wolfe settings, to which he brings his customary gift of an immediate response to the texts in hand. His empathy with poet and composer here couldn't be closer. The *Vedic Hymns* are more rarified, mystical territory and not so easy for singer or listener to encompass. Christopher Maltman does well by them, except where an incipient beat sometimes spoils pleasure in his singing.

Pianist Steuart Bedford is responsive to all the varying moods of these groups, and in the opening group Louisa Fuller is the sensitive violinist.

Arthur Honegger
French/Swiss 1892-1955

Honegger studied from 1911 at the Paris Conservatoire, then returned to Switzerland for military service (1914-15), though Paris remained his home.

He was a member of Les Six, and set Cocteau's libretto in his stylised opera Antigone (1927), but he had no time for Satie or for the group's flippancy: he was acutely aware of artistic responsibility and took his guidelines from Bach and Beethoven.

His harmony, though fundamentally tonal, is often dense and wide-ranging, set in motion by a vigorous rhythmic propulsion that suggests Baroque formality wielding modern means: that is the manner of his oratorio-style stage works, including Le roi David (1921) and Jeanne d'Arc au bûcher (1938). His other works include five symphonies (1930, 1941, 1946, 1946, 1951), three 'symphonic movements' (Pacific 231, 1923; Rugby, 1928; No 3, 1933), chamber pieces, songs and much incidental music.
GROVEmusic

Symphonies

No 1 in C; **No 2** for Strings and Trumpet obbligato in D, H153; **No 3**, H186, 'Liturgique'; **No 4** in A, H191, 'Deliciae basiliensis' **No 5** in D, H202, 'Di tre re'

Symphonies Nos 1-5. Three Symphonic Movements – Pacific 231, H53; Rugby, H67; No 3, H83. Pastorale d'été, H31
Suisse Romande Orchestra / Fabio Luisi
Cascavelle ③ RSR6132 (174' · DDD) Ⓕ◯

In most respects this recording is excellent. The textures are clearer and sharper than Dutoit's for Erato, and passages like the contrapuntal *tour de force* in the last movement of the Fourth Symphony are all the more impressive for it. The Suisse Romande's solo woodwind are fresh and seductive, with a particularly fine first oboe while, on the other hand, the clarity of the recording can bring with it a certain bleakness, entirely appropriate at the beginning of the Fifth Symphony, which here comes over rather like Sibelius.

Where Dutoit sometimes scores is in the more tender moments (his *Pastorale d'été* is a touch more loving than Luisi's) and in generally faster tempos for the symphony finales. In those of the first two symphonies, Luisi's tempos sound just a little heavy. But his penchant for slower speeds brings notable rewards both in the central movement of the Third Symphony and in the final *Adagio* of the third *Symphonic Movement*. This latter passage, only marginally affected by a few flat alto saxophone notes at the top of the range, makes Dutoit's *Adagio* seem like a lightweight *Andante*.

Luisi is alive to the strong element of melancholy and disillusion in this music – strong also in Honegger himself. Where, in the opening of the Second Symphony, Jansons allows himself to get increasingly excited by the repeated viola figure, Luisi recognises it as the call of fate, that changeth not. A large measure of Honegger's disillusion came from what he saw as the triumph of the forces of collectivism over the individual human spirit, and in the Third Symphony Luisi brings out the solo cello line in the third movement as the voice of the composer crying out against the waste of war. Luisi also obeys one of the composer's rare dictats over tempo: Honegger knew that conductors weren't going to like the slow speed of crotchet = 52 for the central *Adagio mesto* of the Second Symphony, but he stuck by it none the less. If you compares this tempo even with Jansons' very nearly obedient crotchet = 56, you can't help concluding that Honegger and Luisi are both right. And that goes for most of the music on these three discs.

Honegger Symphonies Nos 2 & 3 **Stravinsky** Concerto in D
Berlin Philharmonic Orchestra / Herbert von Karajan
DG The Originals 447 435-2GOR (72' · ADD)
Recorded 1969   Ⓜ**OOO**

 Karajan's performances of these Honegger symphonies enjoy legendary status – and rightly so. This recording remains in a class of its own for sheer beauty of sound and flawless ensemble. The French critic, Bernard Gavoty, once spoke rather flightily of Karajan 'transcending emotions and imparting to them that furnace heat that makes a work of genius give off light if brought to the desired temperature' – but it's true! There's a luminous quality and an incandescence about these performances. The Stravinsky Concerto in D major was written within a year of the *Symphonie liturgique* and may perhaps be a little too 'cultured' and not spiky enough for some tastes. The lightness of touch, sprightliness of rhythm and flawless ensemble of the Berlin Philharmonic Orchestra are an absolute joy in themselves.

Symphonies Nos 3 & 5. Three Symphonic Movements – No 1
Danish National Radio Symphony Orchestra / Neeme Järvi
Chandos CHAN9176 (57' · DDD) Recorded 1992   Ⓕ

There's a resemblance in the Fifth to the opening bars (with their triads in contrary motion) to Milhaud's *Moses* and one wonders whether it was a deliberate tribute or merely fortuitous. Be that as it may, the Fifth remains one of Honegger's most individual scores, and this recording serves it well. There's nothing restrained here and even if the finale doesn't quite match the sheer exhilaration and gusto of Serge Baudo's wonderful Supraphon account from the early 1960s (which now sounds far more full bodied in its new transfer), the Järvi isn't far behind: moreover it's very well recorded. So, too, is the rest of the programme and although the playing of the Danish orchestra for Järvi in the Third doesn't outshine that of the BPO for Karajan this is a very convincing and compelling account. The *Pacific 231* also thunders mightily along the track.

Additional recommendation

Symphonies Nos 1-5
Coupled with: Three Symphonic Movements – No 1, H53; 'Pacific 231'; No 2, H67, 'Rugby'
Bavarian Radio Symphony Orchestra / Dutoit
Erato Ultima ② 3984-21340-2 (141' · DDD) Recorded 1982-4)   Ⓑ
Dutoit's cycle is a considerable achievement; at the price this is an attractive starting-point for the symphonies.

Alan Hovhaness   American 1911-2000

Hovhaness studied with Converse at the New England Conservatory. His earliest music, though Romantic in harmony, reflects his interest in Renaissance style; from 1943 he began to incorporate elements of his Armenian heritage, and in the 1950s, when he travelled widely, he embraced non-Western and experimental procedures. From c1960 he took a keen interest in Japanese and Korean music, which affected his style; only in the 1970s did he return to a more Western style, richer and more spacious. An individual feature is his way of treating elements (harmony, tone colour etc) as either predominant or else neutral; any note may be exclusively linear, vertical, textural or rhythmic. Most of his work is broadly religious in inspiration; he is enormously prolific, having reached his first 60 symphonies in the mid-1980s, with corresponding production in other orchestral music, choral and solo vocal works, piano and chamber music.   **GROVE**music

Cello Concerto

Symphony No 22, 'City of Light', Op 236[a]. Cello Concerto, Op 17[b]
[b]**János Starker** vc **Seattle Symphony Orchestra /** [a]**Alan Hovhaness**, [b]**Dennis Russell Davies**
Naxos 8 559158 (61' · DDD)   Ⓢ

City of Light (1970) has some lovely ideas, like the surprisingly sweet and simple string melody in the middle of the 'Angel of Light' movement, and the third movement, *Allegretto grazioso*, which sounds like a minuet in oriental garb. The outer movements, however, outstay their welcome. On the other hand, the Cello Concerto (1936) is required listening for Hovhaness admirers. The composer destroyed several hundred of his compositions during a period of self-reflection in the early 1940s, but the concerto survived the cull, finally receiving its première in 1999. The music's modal tinge is pure Hovhaness, but there is a spareness to the writing that sets it apart from its successors. Indeed, the tone is unrelievedly elegiac, making the Elgar Concerto seem positively jovial by comparison. János Starker brings sad nobility to the ruminative solo part, and Dennis Russell Davies makes the most of the *Das Lied von der Erde*-like orchestral texture in a warmly recommended disc.

Symphonies

Symphonies – No 2, 'Mysterious Mountain', Op 132;
No 50, 'Mount St Helens', Op 360; Symphony No 66,
'Hymn to Glacier Peak', Op 428. Storm on Mount
Wildcat, Op 2 No 2
**Royal Liverpool Philharmonic Orchestra / Gerard
Schwarz**
Telarc CD80604 (72' · DDD)   (F)

It's easy to dismiss the music of Hovhaness, who
was was suspiciously prolific, with opus numbers nearing 500. But despite such sustained
productivity over more than seven decades, his
work is stylistically consistent – so much so, in
fact, that some only half-jokingly claim he wrote
the same symphony 67 times. Certainly, the
profusion of sing-song fugues and modal,
hymn-like tunes throughout his output can give
a feeling of predictability.

And yet listening to the opening movement of
the *Mount St Helens* Symphony (1982), it's difficult not to be entranced, even awed, by the
music's sensuous beauty – those luminous
clouds of strings, that majestic rising theme in
the horns, then, a little later, the delicate spinning of the harp and a procession of ecstatic,
exotic woodwind solos. Perhaps the depiction of
the volcano's eruption is a bit primitive, though
it's fascinating that Hovhaness seems to view
the explosion not only as an elemental event but
also as a ritualistic one.

Hymn to Glacier Peak (1992), the composer's
penultimate symphony, is also appealing. As the
title suggests, it has a preponderance of hymn-
like melody, yet there's a touching valedictory
quality to the music. The finale is particularly
effective, moving from hymn to one of Hovhaness's most tuneful fugues via a darkly atmospheric interlude.

Warmly recommended: this would make an
excellent introduction to Hovhaness's music.

Khaldis, Op 91

Khaldis, Op 91[a]. Mount Katahdin, Op 405[b].
Fantasy, Op 16[c]
[ab]**Martin Berkofsky**, [c]**Alan Hovhaness** pfs [a]**William
Rohdin**, [a]**Dan Cahn**, [a]**Francis Bonny**, [a]**Patrick
Dougherty** tpts [a]**Neal Boyar** perc
Crystal CD814 (52' · ADD) Recorded [c]1970, [a]1972,
[b]1999   (F)

Khaldis (1951) has a connection with the late
Hovhaness's well-known *St Vartan* symphony
(1950) in their common use of a quartet of
trumpets: the composer wanted a piece he could
play with them and a percussionist alone. It's a
striking work – named from the god of the universe of the pre-Armenian Urarduan people –
full of apocalyptic visions. The even-movement
structure has the feel of a set of studies rather
than an integrated concerto, the brass tending
to play en bloc and one movement scored as if
for some primordial trio of giants.

The sonata *Mount Katahdin* (1986-7) doesn't

sound almost a career later than *Khaldis*. The
four movements resemble the sequence of a
Bach orchestral suite, with the imposing opening 'Solenne', succeeded by three tiny movements, lighter in character and acting as foils for
the first. The central 'Jhala of Larch Trees' is
particularly lovely. Berkofsky plays with evident
love and conviction, and these are persuasive
performances, whether from 1972 or 1999
(*Mount Katahdin*).

Most fascinating of all is Hovhaness's own
account of the *Fantasy*, written *c*1936 and also
once available on a Poseidon LP. A mesmeric
performance of a mesmeric piece, the 10 sections or 'steps' built from Indian ragas utilise
Cowellesque devices such as playing the strings
inside the instrument with fingers, plectrum,
marimba mallet or timpani stick. The sound
overall is acceptable but the remastered *Khaldis*
and *Fantasy* are a touch lacking in depth.

String Quartets

Hovhaness Four Bagatelles, Op 30. String Quartets
– No 1, Op 8, 'Jupiter'; No 3, Op 208 No 1,
'Reflections on my Childhood'; No 4, Op 208 No 2,
'The Ancient Tree'. Suite from String Quartet No 2 –
Gamelan in Sosi Style; Spirit Murmur; Hymn **Z Long**
Song of the Ch'in
Shanghai Quartet (WeiGang Li, HongGang Li vns
Zheng Wang va James Wilson vc)
Delos DE3162 (69' · DDD) Recorded 1994   (F)(O)

The likeable First Quartet of 1936 boasts, like
Mozart's *Jupiter* Symphony, a four-part fugue
of impressive rigour (hence the work's subtitle).
Next come three out of the seven pithy movements that comprise the Second Quartet from
1952: the concluding 'Hymn' is a particularly
affecting creation. The Third and Fourth Quartets were inspired by childhood memories. The
former basks in a soothing, supplicatory glow,
with some occasional touches of Eastern promise (reminders of the composer's Armenian
roots), whereas its more nostalgic companion is
a sweetly lyrical essay of beguiling euphony and
striking resonance.

Delos's collection begins with the haunting,
perfectly crafted *Four Bagatelles* (delightful
miniatures) and ends with *Song of the Ch'in* by
the Chinese composer, Zhou Long: the *ch'in* is a
traditional Chinese zither; this imaginative
piece attempts to convey the piquant sounds of
that ancient instrument through the 'modern'
medium of the string quartet. These are consistently pure-toned, beautifully rapt performances from the talented young Shanghai Quartet, and Delos's sound is warm and true.

Herbert Howells   British 1892-1983

*Howells studied with Stanford and Wood at the
Royal College of Music, where he taught from 1920
almost to his death. He also succeeded Holst at St*

Paul's Girls' School (1932-62) and was professor of music at London University. His music is within an English diatonic tradition embracing Elgar, Walton and Vaughan Williams. The earlier works include two piano concertos and chamber pieces, but most of his music is choral, including c15 anthems, a concert Requiem (Hymnus Paradisi, 1938, first performed 1950), masses, anthems and motets and some fine songs. Deeply tinged by the English choral tradition, Howells's music reflects a subtle and fastidious craftsman who was capable of a restrained, individual eloquence.   GROVEmusic

Piano Concertos

Piano Concertos[a] – No 1 in C minor, Op 4; No 2 in C, Op 39. Penguinski
[a]Howard Shelley pf BBC Symphony Orchestra / Richard Hickox
Chandos CHAN9874 (71' · DDD)   Ⓕ●

An astonishing revelation, especially to anyone who still thinks of Herbert Howells as a nostalgic English rhapsodist, more at home in an organ loft than a concert hall. The First Piano Concerto is very early (1914 – Howells was 22) and hasn't been performed for many years because its last few bars are missing (John Rutter has provided them). It reveals the young Howells as more Russian than English – the dazzlingly flamboyant keyboard writing is strongly reminiscent of Rachmaninov – and with hardly a trace of English reserve as he brandishes theme after theme, intensifying many of them to heights of impassioned eloquence.

One or two lyrical paragraphs suggest the 'real' Herbert Howells. But who, the Second Piano Concerto demands, was he? This work was abused at its première (one critic shouted 'Thank God that's over!') and Howells, deeply wounded, withdrew it immediately. Indeed, although it's a lot closer to 'real' Howells in its rhapsodic lyricism, there's another quality which is angular, sometimes dissonant, tough and determined.

Surely we shall get closer to the real Howells, lifelong admirer of the arch-conservative Stanford, in Penguinski, from its title an obvious satire on Stravinsky? But in fact the sidelong glances at him are admiring and affectionate, and the robust humour is Howells' own. There's more to him than we had imagined, and his stature is increased, not diminished, by the realisation that he was once an exuberant Romantic, that his ears were sharp and that he had a sense of humour.

Enthusiastic, virtuoso, very slightly rough-cornered performances and a sumptuously rich recording.

Threnody

King's Herald. Paradise Rondel. Fantasia[a].
Threnody[a]. Pastoral Rhapsody. Procession
[a]Moray Welsh vc London Symphony Orchestra /
Richard Hickox
Chandos CHAN9410 (58' · DDD)   Ⓕ●

This delightful, moving disc offers a whole sequence of orchestral works which for whatever reason Howells hid from the world. Only since his death have such pieces as these emerged, and one can only marvel that so accomplished and imaginative a writer for the orchestra should have let any of them be buried. Howells completed the short score of Threnody with piano accompaniment in 1935, his first task after his son's death. Probably planned as the slow movement of a three-movement cello concerto, it's given here in the orchestration made by Christopher Palmer for the Howells centenary concert in 1992. More direct in style and structure, it's an effective pendant to the Fantasia, with the two movements together forming a rhapsodic concerto.

The other major piece is the Pastoral Rhapsody, written earlier in 1923 and more conventionally English except for a radiant climax with anglicised echoes of Daphnis and Petrushka. The Rhapsody is totally distinct, and so is the Paradise Rondel, named after a Cotswold village: a generally vigorous movement dating from 1925, which over a shorter span is full of sharp contrasts, including one passage which in its addition of a piano offers clear echoes of the 'Russian Dance' from Petrushka.

The collection opens with the boldly extrovert King's Herald, bright with Waltonian fanfares. Drawn from a brass band piece of 1934, it was arranged for orchestra as a Coronation offering in 1937. Procession, which closes the sequence, is the earliest work here, adapted from a piano piece written in 1920, and in this orchestration of 1922 brings more echoes of Petrushka, again reflecting Howells's response to appearances in London by Diaghilev's Ballets Russes. Helped by rich, atmospheric sound, Hickox draws performances both brilliant and warmly persuasive from the LSO, with Moray Welsh a movingly expressive soloist in the concertante works.

Suite for Orchestra, 'The B's'

Suite for Orchestra, 'The B's'. Three Dances[a]. In Green Ways[b]
[b]Yvonne Kenny sop a[Lydia] Mordkovitch vn
London Symphony Orchestra / Richard Hickox
Chandos CHAN9557 (65' · DDD) Text and translation included   Ⓕ●

Both The B's (1914) and Three Dances (1915) are from Howells's student days. The former is a delightful orchestral suite celebrating Howells's circle of closest friends at the Royal College of Music, each of the five movements bearing as its subtitle the nickname of a colleague. As with many of Howells's student offerings, the infectious confidence and sheer craft are remarkable. Completed just a couple of months after The B's, the Three Dances for violin and orchestra reveal a similarly assured touch and charm. Perhaps the most captivating of the set is the wonderfully serene *Quasi lento*, with its seraphically lovely melody. By contrast the first dance is all sunny, carefree vigour and the brief third like a boisterous Irish jig. Lydia Mordkovitch plays with enormous fervour, but in the middle dance she doesn't have quite the radiance or security of RLPO leader Malcolm Stewart on Hyperion; Hickox's accompaniment, too, is marginally 'bluffer' than that of Handley's, though still full of appealing bonhomie. *In Green Ways* had its origins in a song cycle for high voice and small orchestra written the same year as the *Three Dances*. It takes its name from a collection of poetry by James Stephens, whose poem 'The Goat Paths' forms the emotional kernel of the whole sequence in Howells's sublime treatment. Yvonne Kenny sings radiantly, with Hickox and the LSO as model partners. The airy recording complements this hugely enjoyable release.

Chamber Works

Howells String Quartet No 3, 'In Gloucestershire'
Dyson Three Rhapsodies
Divertimenti (Paul Barritt, Rachel Isserlis *vns* Gustav Clarkson *va* Sebastian Comberti *vc*)
Hyperion Helios CDH55045 (64' · DDD) Recorded 1984   Ⓑ

The reappearance of Divertimenti's shapely account of Howells' masterly *In Gloucestershire* (the last of his three works for string quartet) is all the more valuable now that the Britten Quartet's magisterial 1995 version on EMI British Composers has disappeared from the catalogue. If you don't yet know this exquisitely wrought, hauntingly atmospheric creation (Howells' most extended chamber offering), then immediate investigation is recommended.

The coupling, too, is a delight. Completed between 1905 and 1912, Dyson's youthful *Three Rhapsodies* form a most appealing triptych, uncommonly fluent, tightly knit and always evincing an engaging, at times positively Straussian lyrical grace. Divertimenti give another first-rate display brimful of commitment and communicative warmth. The airy, natural sound complements a budget-priced reissue that isn't to be missed.

Further listening

Howells Rhapsodic Quintet
Coupled with: **Frankel, Holbrooke, Arnold Cooke** and **Maconchy** Clarinet Quintets
King *cl* **Britten Quartet**
Hyperion Helios CDH55105 (66' · DDD)   Ⓑ
  Howells' *Rhapsodic Quintet* is a jewel, while no one could fail to be touched by the elegiac last movement of Frankel's eloquent Quintet. Thea King forms a stylish and sensitive partnership with the much-missed Britten Quartet. At budget price, don't miss it.

Organ Sonata No 2

Organ Sonata No 2. Six Pieces (1940-45)
Graham Barber *org*
Priory PRCD524 (67' · DDD) Recorded on Hereford Cathedral organ in 1995   Ⓕ

These are powerful, authoritative performances which ooze the spirit of Howells – that odd mixture of emotional detachment with a hint of deep personal passion, an undercurrent of tragedy and an almost improvisatory fluidity of structure. The Sonata has a formal structure which makes it easy to follow while the *Six Pieces* give such a kaleidoscopic array of organ colours that the ear is continually enchanted. The Hereford organ is a lovely instrument. Priory has, in focusing the microphones on the organ, expunged much of the building's aural ambience, but the sound is an utter delight to the ear.

Evening Services

Evening Services – G; Collegium Sancti Johannis Cantabrigiense; New College, Oxford; Collegium Regale; Sarum; York. Magnificat and Nunc Dimittis
The Collegiate Singers / Andrew Millinger with **Richard Moorhouse** *org*
Priory PRCD745 (65' · DDD)   ⒻⓄ

Howells wrote 20 settings of the evening canticles. His first setting (1918), the freshly vigorous work of the Stanford pupil, sets out on the long life's musical journey with bone and muscle. The gentler passages have a light-footed grace, and in exultation the spirit flares; this is the music of purposeful movement, where the more 'Howells' he becomes the more the firm lines of the Stanford pupil dissolve, and the nearer he draws to a music of mystical stasis. The opening of the Collegium Regale *Magnificat* has something of this, the great thing being that he can still pull out of it (with the strong-boned 'He hath shown strength with his arm', for instance). It's a pity that the series hasn't been arranged chronologically; it would have been good to follow the order of composition, seeing which parts of his musical system he developed and which he left unexercised.

The other slightly faltering element in this welcome release concerns the choice of a choir of mixed voices. The women scrupulously adhere to the tonal ideal, but boy trebles and male altos have a distinctive quality, and Howells's own sound is less distinctive without them. It's an extremely good choir, and they're under careful, intelligent direction, yet making a chance comparison with the choir of Bristol Cathedral in the G major setting one can't help rejoicing in a character (individual as a face) which those trebles possessed and for which the Collegiate sopranos substitute a collective identity somewhat depersonalised.

The recorded sound is fine, balance between choir and the excellent organist is well judged, and the acoustic resonance is sufficient to form an appropriate setting while preserving the clear articulation. The selection here also includes two première recordings (the York Service and the 1941 setting for men's voices, performed, as the score suggests, by women).

Requiem

Requiem[a]. Choral and Organ Works. Collegium Regale – Communion Service[ab]. St Paul's Service[ab]. Like as the hart[a]. Long, long ago[a]. Take Him, Earth, for Cherishing[a]. Organ Rhapsody No 3[b]. Paean[b]
[b]Ian Farrington *org* [a]St John's College Choir, Cambridge / Christopher Robinson
Naxos 8 554659 (76' · DDD) Texts included ⓢ

Howells, probably more than any other composer, extended the cathedral repertoire in the 20th century. Here his music is performed by one of the best choirs. Under Christopher Robinson, St John's has preserved its distinctive character (the bright tone of its trebles a famous part of it) and, as this record demonstrates, has gained in vigour and clarity of purpose. Immediately notable is the choice of relatively quick speeds. Howells sometimes appears to invite a relaxed style of performance which isn't to his advantage.

St John's tempo suits the acoustic. This applies to a similar comparison with the Choir of King's College in its more reverberant chapel, singing the Communion Service dedicated to it: the more opulent sound matches the broader tempo, St John's achieving (as in the *Sanctus*) clearer effects within a narrower spectrum. Their discs also have in common the *Rhapsody No 3* for organ, and whereas the expansive performance at King's includes a murmurous *pianissimo* next-thing-to-silence, the quicker, more sharply defined one at St John's has a dramatic urgency.

The choice of programme is particularly happy, with one of the lesser-known Evening Services (the 'St Paul's') and one of the best known of Howells's anthems (*Like as the hart*).

Additional recommendation

Requiem
Coupled with: Take him, earth, for cherishing.
Vaughan Williams Mass in G minor. Te Deum
Coxwell, Seers *sops* **Chance** *counterten* **Salmon** *ten* **J Best** *bass* **Corydon Singers / M Best**
Hyperion CDA66076 (DDD) Ⓕ
A fine performance of the *Requiem* and attractive couplings.

Missa Sabrinensis

Janice Watson *sop* Della Jones *mez* Martyn Hill *ten* Donald Maxwell *bar*
London Symphony Chorus and Orchestra / Gennadi Rozhdestvensky
Chandos CHAN9348 (76' · DDD) Recorded 1994.
Text and translation included ⒻⓄ

Along with the *Stabat Mater* this 'Mass of the Severn', the river which together with the Wye defined the composer's homeland, shows even more than *Hymnus Paradisi*, the daunting accomplishment of Howells's complex choral-orchestral polyphonic technique and harmonic language. In *Hymnus Paradisi* and the *Stabat Mater* Howells movingly delineates spiritual and sensual responses to the grief of loss. The *Missa Sabrinensis* naturally encompasses a wider, different emotional spectrum, but without sacrificing self-consistency or intensity. It's unique, in English music, analogous perhaps to Janáček's *Glagolitic Mass*, though it could hardly be more different in temper and texture. A richly imploring *Kyrie* (subtly reworked for the *Agnus Dei*), a 20-minute *Gloria* of magnificent range and brilliantly balanced lyricism and exaltation, an exquisitely delicate *Benedictus* – all this is Howells at his most characteristic and inspired. The performance isn't always ideal. In the proliferating polyphonic complexes Rozhdestvensky is rather too broad-brush in matters of detail. And the generous-spirited chorus sometimes sound a degree under-prepared or under-directed – or both.

Of the soloists, an authoritative Martyn Hill and outstanding Janice Watson more than compensate for less certain colleagues. But the dominant impression of the performance – helped by a spacious, warm recording – is Rozhdestvensky's full-blooded communication of the rich emotional content, impulsively pointing-up the extremes, the climactic conflagrations, the fragrant lyrical pastures.

Tobias Hume   English c1570-1645

An officer in the Swedish and Russian armies, Hume played the viol and entered Charterhouse almshouse in London in 1629. His two published lyra viol tablatures (1605, 1607) contain all his known works – dances, descriptive and programmatic pieces and songs.   **GROVE**music

Musicall Humors

Captaine Humes Pavan. A Souldiers Resolution. Deth. Life. Captaine Humes Galliard. Touch me lightly. A Pavane. My hope is decayed. A Souldiers Galliard. Beccus an Hungarian Lord. The Second part. A Question. An Answere. The new Cut Good againe. The Duke of Holstones Almaine. Hark! Hark!. The Spirit of Gambo: The Lord Dewys favoret Humorous Pavin. Love's Farewell
Jordi Savall *va da gamba*
Alia Vox AV9837 (70' · DDD) ⒻⓄ

Tobias Hume was a professional soldier and a 'gentleman' (read amateur) composer, and virtuoso of the bass viol. His *Musicall Humors* (1605), a large collection of solo pieces, is the first publication devoted to the lyra viol, a style of playing that treated the instrument poly-phonically, like a lute. Hume reveals himself as a distinct, even eccentric, personality, and an inventive composer, expanding the viol's nor-mal range with such unusual devices as *col legno* ('Drum this with the backe of your Bow').

Jordi Savall's cultivated, elegant style is very appropriate for much of the music; occasionally he adopts a more earthy manner to great effect – for example in *A Souldiers Resolution*, with its trumpet and drum imitations. When Captain Hume's *Humors* become more reflective, in a piece like *Beccus an Hungarian Lord*, Savall uses varied bow strokes and dynamic shadings with great artistry, to bring out the music's dignified, sombre character.

In characterising the music so strongly, Savall's rhythms are often very free; the rushing scalic divisions and lingering approaches to cadences balance one another, and prevent the music ever seeming stiff or mechanical. It's a finely produced disc, too, with a fascinating essay about the composer by David Pinto.

Johann Hummel   Austrian 1778-1837

A child prodigy and a pupil of Mozart (Vienna, 1786-8), Hummel undertook an extended tour (1789-92) throughout northern Europe with his father, arousing particular interest in England, where he met Haydn. Back in Vienna he studied with Albrechtsberger, Salieri and Haydn, giving les-sons to support himself. He held a position as Konz-ertmeister to Prince Nikolaus Esterházy (1804-11) and, after a period of writing piano and chamber music for Vienna, returned to the concert platform. He was Kapellmeister in Stuttgart (1816-18) and Weimar (from 1819), where he conducted the court theatre and many concerts, knew Goethe and other luminaries and still had time to teach and compose; he toured regularly as a pianist and worked tirelessly on his important piano method (1828). The climax of his career came in 1830 with a trip to Paris and London. Despite his public and financial success – he had an excellent business sense and systematised multinational music publishing – he remained a warm and simple person. His playing was praised for its clarity, neatness, evenness, superb tone and deli-cacy, products of his preference for the light-toned Viennese piano; he excelled at improvisation. Ferdi-nand Hiller was among his pupils. Hummel wrote some of the finest music of the last years of Classicism, with ornate Italianate melodies and virtuoso embroi-dery; his later music shows more expression and vari-ety, including imaginative harmony and long flights of lyricism. GROVEmusic

Piano Concertos

Piano Concerto No 4 in E, Op 110. Double Concerto in G, Op 17
Hagai Shaham vn **London Mozart Players /**
Howard Shelley pf
Chandos CHAN9687 (63' · DDD) ⓕⓞ

Shelley is outstanding in this music, blending classical and Romantic elements perfectly. These two concertos are wonderfully infec-tious. The E major occupies a kind of bridge between Mozart and Chopin, although Moz-art's depth and subtlety are in a different vein. Hummel is more of a show-off, and his music almost smiles at you, its charm and sparkle eschewing any pretentiousness. Throughout, Shelley conveys the music's *joie de vivre*, revel-ling in the figurative passagework. The Double Concerto may have been inspired by Mozart's *Sinfonia concertante*, K365; it doesn't have the same harmonic or lyrical variety as the E major Concerto, but it's a charming work, especially when so persuasively played. Shelley's well-pro-portioned piano part is perfectly complemented by Hagai Shaham's sweet-toned violin. Shelley fulfils his dual role admirably, and the London Mozart Players respond well to his playing and conducting. The recorded sound is first-rate. A lovely disc.

Piano Concertos – No 2 in A minor, Op 85; No 3 in B minor, Op 89
Stephen Hough pf **English Chamber Orchestra /**
Bryden Thomson
Chandos CHAN8507 (66' · DDD) ⓕⓞⓞⓞ

 This is a staggering disc of Hummel's piano concertos played by Stephen Hough. The most obvious comparison is with the piano concertos of Chopin, but whereas those works rely on the grace and panache of the piano line to redeem an often lacklustre orchestral role, the Hummel works have finely conceived orchestral writing and no shortage of original ideas. The piano part is for-midable, combining virtuosity of a very high order with a vigour and athleticism that does much to redress Hummel's somewhat tarnished reputation. The A minor Concerto is probably the better known of the works here, with a thrilling rondo finale, but the B minor is no less inventive with some breath-taking writing in the piano's upper registers. This disc makes strong demands to be heard: inventive and exciting music, a masterly contribution from Stephen Hough, fine orchestral support from the ECO under Thomson and a magnificent recording.

Piano Concerto No 5 in A flat, Op 113. Concertino in G, Op 73. Gesellschafts Rondo in D, Op 117
London Mozart Players / Howard Shelley pf
Chandos CHAN9558 (59' · DDD) ⓕ

These are decorous rarities played with an assured brilliance and affection. Hummel's Mozartian rather than Chopinesque bias declares itself most obviously in his Op 73 *Con-certino*, though even here the figuration has a recognisably Hummelian froth and sparkle. Too charming to be vacuous, such surface brio has little in common with Mozart's depth and subtlety, and for music of greater romantic range and ambition we turn to the A flat major Concerto, with its fuller scoring and lavishly decorated solo part. Lovers of a fine-spun, operatic cantilena will warm to the central 'Romanze'. The *Gesellschafts Rondo* commences in solemn *Adagio* vein before turning to a bustling and ceremonious *Vivace*. It may be that Hummel 'puffed, blew and perspired' when he played but he won the admiration of Chopin (a hard master to please) and his style is infectious when projected with such unfailing expertise by Howard Shelley in his dual role as pianist and conductor. The Chandos recordings are exceptionally well balanced.

Trumpet Concerto

Hummel Trumpet Concerto in E flat **Haydn** Trumpet Concertos in E flat, HobVIIe/1; in Cª·Concertos by **Albinoni, Corelli, Hertel, JM Molter, Mozart, FX Richter, J Stamitz**. Works by JS Bach, Clarke and Gounod
Håkan Hardenberger tpt **Simon Preston** org **Academy of St Martin in the Fields / Sir Neville Marriner;** ªLondon Philharmonic Orchestra / Elgar Howarth; ᵇI Musici
Philips Duo ② 464 028 (148' · DDD) Recorded 1986, 1989, 1991, 1993   ⓂO

This is probably the finest single collection of trumpet concertos in the catalogue. When it first appeared in 1987 (the Hummel and Haydn have since been recoupled with a later set as listed here) it created overnight a new star in the firmament of trumpeters.

The two finest concertos for the trumpet are undoubtedly those of Haydn and Hummel, and Hardenberger plays them here with a combination of sparkling bravura and stylish elegance that are altogether irresistible. Hardenberger opens with the famous Hummel Concerto, played in E major rather than the usual E flat, which makes the work sound bolder and brighter than usual. The finale with its crisp articulation, fantastic tonguing and tight trills, displays a genial easy bravura, yet overflows with energy and high spirits. Marriner and his Academy accompany with characteristic finesse and warmth, with the lilting dotted rhythms of the first movement of the Hummel, seductively jaunty. The lovely *Andante* of the Haydn is no less beguiling, and both finales display a high-spirited exuberance and an easy bravura which make the listener smile with pleasure.

The recording gives him the most vivid realism and presence, but it's a pity that the orchestral backcloth is so reverberant; otherwise the sound is very natural. A superb disc.

Solo Piano Works

Piano Sonatas – No 3 in F minor, Op 20; No 5 in F sharp minor, Op 81; No 6 in D, Op 106
Stephen Hough pf

Hyperion CDA67390 (69' · DDD)   ⒻO

Stephen Hough's splendid issue is in its way as revelatory as his *Gramophone* Award-winning recordings of the piano concertos. He revels in the element of display which Hummel, one of the leading pianists of his day, must have brought out in his own performances.

These three works are arguably the most interesting of Hummel's nine solo sonatas. The most radical is No 5, with the composer in 1819 enthusiastically throwing himself behind the new romantic movement. A strikingly angular opening motif leads to an argument which, in a very free rendering of sonata form, brings surges of energy set against moments of reflection; there are many unexpected melodic and harmonic twists and few passages of conventional figuration, such as those that weaken the piano concertos. The slow movement, too, opens surprisingly, with a heavyweight *fortissimo* gesture, before settling down to a yearning melody, anticipating Chopin's Nocturnes but more bare in texture, with cantilena echoing *bel canto* opera. The finale is a wild Slavonic dance, fierce and energetic in headlong flight, again dotted with unexpectedly angular ideas.

In the Sixth Sonata in 1824 Hummel was rowing back from the romantic stance of Op 81. The first movement establishes a much lighter tone and is more conventional in structure, exceptionally clear in its presentation of sonata form. The opening theme, for all its lightness of texture, has characteristically quirky twists, and leads to a warmly lyrical second subject, rather like Weber. The second movement *Scherzo*, the most striking of the four, is a fast mazurka, leading to a slow movement rather like a Mendelssohn *Song without Words* and a virtuoso finale, light in texture at the start and ending, after all the display, in an unexpected throwaway cadence.

Sonata No 3 in F minor, dating from 1807, again starts gently before developing quirks typical of Hummel. The slow movement then surprisingly has the marking *Maestoso*, majestic, strong and forthright rather than conventionally lyrical, leading to another virtuoso finale, relatively brief, with cross-hand, Scarlatti-like leaps for the left hand.

Rondo in E flat, Op 11. Piano Sonata No 2 in E flat, Op 13. Capriccio in F, Op 49. Variations on a theme from Gluck's 'Armide' in F, Op 57. Bagatelles, Op 107 – La contemplazione; Rondo all'ungherese. La bella capricciosa, Polonaise in B flat, Op 55
Howard Shelley pf
Chandos CHAN9807 (73' · DDD)   ⒻO

This attractive recital shows several sides of Hummel's creative personality, from the classical sonata to the fanciful early Romantic character piece, with a good deal of virtuosity thrown in. Most relishable are some of the more contemplative items, including the 'Contemplazione' from his Op 107 bagatelles, a beautiful piece that takes a short theme and weaves a poetic fabric around and beyond it. The other bagatelle here, the 'Rondo all'ungherese', is quite a different piece, exploiting ideas of gypsy themes and rhythms with a good deal of wit. Both respond splendidly to Howard Shelley's playing, his attentive shaping, his sense of the music's poetry, his springy rhythms. The rather earlier *Capriccio*, Op 49, is another particular success, notable for Shelley's exquisite timing and aristocratic poise in the slow music and his brilliant fingerwork in the fast.

The recital begins with the earliest piece, an 1804 *Rondo* to which Shelley brings crisp phrasing, precise ornaments and happily judged touches of *rubato*. He ends with a sonata of 1805, more classical than much of what has gone before: easy to say that the style is Beethovenian with less exalted content, but the central *Adagio* is a fine piece with a vein of nobility of its own. The other items are the ingenious Gluck variations, in which Shelley shows a fine command of piano sonorities and rhythms, as well as ample brilliance in the closing pages, and the polonaise *La bella capricciosa*, which moves from an unassuming start to a coruscating finish. The recording is a model of clear and rich piano tone.

Masses

Mass in B flat, Op 77. Mass in D, Op 111.
Offertorium, 'Alma Virgo', Op 89a^a
^a**Susan Gritton** sop **Collegium Musicum 90 /
Richard Hickox**
Chandos Chaconne CHAN0681 (76' · DDD) Texts
and translations included   Ⓟ**OOO**

 When the glories of Haydn's late Masses have been widely appreciated, it's sad that Hummel's have been so neglected. They are for chorus and orchestra alone, without soloists, which may have deterred potential performers. However, while they can't quite match late Haydn or Beethoven in originality, they're lively, beautifully written, and full of striking ideas, inspiring Hickox and his team to performances here just as electrifying as those they have given of Haydn, and just as vividly recorded.

Hummel follows Haydn in both Masses in his fondness for fugues. Similarly, he follows Haydn in offering joyfully energetic settings of 'Dona nobis pacem', only unlike Haydn he doesn't end either Mass on a *fortissimo* cadence, instead fading down the final phrases, maybe for liturgical reasons in the context of a church performance. Hummel, like Haydn and Beethoven before him, fully brings out the drama of the liturgy, though in both settings of 'Et resurrexit' he begins not with a sudden *fortissimo* but with a rising *crescendo*, as though a crowd of bystanders are gradually appreciating the wonder of it.

Another symbolic point is that the Mass in B flat, dating from 1810, the year before Hummel left the Esterházy court, includes a setting of the

Credo with distinctive unison and octave passages for the chorus, as though to emphasise unity of belief. In both masses the settings of the *Sanctus* are surprisingly brief, even perfunctory, yet the musical ideas could not be more striking, with a gently flowing 6/8 setting in the D major work and a bold setting in the B flat Mass which crams into the shortest span surprisingly varied ideas.

Thanks to the imagination of Richard Hickox, we're finally able to discover the joys of Hummel's Masses. An extremely fine disc.

Mass in E flat, Op 80. Quod quod in orbe, Op 88.
Te Deum in D
Susan Gritton sop **Ann Murray** mez **James
Gilchrist** ten **Stephen Varcoe** bar **Collegium
Musicum 90 / Richard Hickox**
Chandos Chaconne CHAN0712 (62' · DDD · T/t)
                               Ⓟ**OO**

The second in Richard Hickox's Hummel Mass edition concentrates on works written soon after Hummel was appointed *Konzertmeister* to Prince Esterházy in 1804. Hummel was keen – the Mass was completed four months before the September deadline. In his booklet-note David Wyn Jones suggests the composer may have been trying to pre-empt his potential rival, Johann Fuchs, who was nominally in charge of church music for the prince. The result has a winning freshness. As in the first disc, Hickox captures the joy of Hummel's inspiration, with clean attack and fine diction from chorus and soloists.

That clarity extends to the superb setting of the *Te Deum*, written at high speed to celebrate peace with Napoleon in 1805. Each section of the elaborate text is strikingly characterised without holding up the urgency established in the opening fanfares. The graduale *Quod quod in urbe* is another fine, neglected work. The Blackheath Concert Hall recording is full and clear: this is shaping up to be an outstanding series.

Missa solemnis in C, W12. Te Deum, W16
Patricia Wright sop **Zam McKendree-Wright** contr
Patrick Power ten **David Griffiths** bar **Tower Voices
New Zealand; New Zealand Symphony Orchestra
/ Uwe Grodd**
Naxos 8 557193 (57' · DDD)   Ⓢ

Richard Hickox's splendid *Gramophone* Award-winning Chandos issue of two of Hummel's Masses alerted us to the vigour and imagination of his choral writing, with none of the note-spinning that occasionally mars his keyboard writing. This, the longest of Hummel's five Masses, is another invigorating example, coupled with an electrifying setting of the *Te Deum*. Both were written in 1806 and feature martial reminders that this was the period of the Napoleonic Wars.

The *Te Deum* opens with a rousing march, and with one or two relaxed passages for contrast – illustrating this long and varied prayer-text –

continues in a single span. It ends with a brisk and triumphant *fugato*, quite different from the sombre close most often heard in Anglican settings. It's a delight. Uwe Grodd draws an exhilarating performance from his forces.

The performance of the Mass is equally successful. The grandeur of the writing is established in the slow introduction to the *Kyrie*, leading to a brisk main *Allegro* (following Haydn's lively practice in *Kyries*) in a rhythmic triple time. The martial flavour of the writing is evident from the *Gloria*'s opening fanfares and continues into the *Credo*, until a sharp change of key to a warm A major brings a relaxed and lyrical setting of 'Et incarnatus', followed by the clashing discords of the 'Crucifixus'. 'Et resurrexit' restores the military mood. One moment to relish comes after the last of the calls of 'Credo' on 'Et vitam venturi' (track 4, 9'09") with two rising scale passages clearly intended to send you up to Heaven in their exhilaration.

Brodd opts to use his admirable soloists throughout the *Benedictus*, even though the autograph suggests otherwise. It works very well, with imitative writing for the soloists set against the four-square tread of the orchestra. With the *Agnus Dei* Hummel at last writes a meditative movement, slow and hushed, which develops into chromatic writing in a minor key, before the 'Dona nobis pacem', as in Haydn's masses, brings a joyful close. Grodd inspires vigorous playing and singing from his forces, who are freshly and cleanly recorded.

Engelbert Humperdinck
German 1854-1921

Humperdinck studied at the Cologne Conservatory (1872-6) and at the Royal Music School in Munich (1877-9), meeting Wagner in Naples and assisting him with Parsifal at Bayreuth (1881-2). After interludes in Paris, Spain, Cologne and Mainz (working for B Schotts Sohne), he moved to Frankfurt as a teacher and opera critic, also writing his most famous work, Hänsel and Gretel (1890-93; given its début at Weimar under Richard Strauss); by 1900 he was in Berlin, teaching, composing operas and writing Shakespearean incidental music (among his most successful work). The operatic version of Königskinder, another characteristic piece in his naive, folklike style, was first performed in New York in 1910; like Hänsel und Gretel it started from simple song settings and went through an intermediate stage to a full opera, showing Wagnerian harmonic and textural influences. GROVEmusic

Hänsel und Gretel

Hänsel und Gretel   Ⓗ
Elisabeth Grümmer *sop* Hänsel **Elisabeth Schwarzkopf** *sop* Gretel **Maria von Ilosvay** *mez* Gertrud **Josef Metternich** *bar* Peter **Anny Felbermayer** *sop* Sandman, Dew Fairy **Else Schürhoff** *mez* Witch **Choir of Loughton High**

School for Girls; Bancroft's School Choir; Philharmonia Orchestra / Herbert von Karajan
EMI Great Recordings of the Century mono ②
567061-2 (108' · ADD) Recorded 1953. Notes, text and translation included   Ⓜ**OO**

This new CD transfer has opened up the mono sound, putting air round the voices and instruments, giving presence. Where EMI's earlier transfer of this set sounds disappointingly flat, a little gauzy, damped down, this one is brighter, clearer, fuller, with textures clarified. The voices better defined and separated. A full stereo recording would have been better still, but it was this recording which Walter Legge would often cite in conversation, when he mounted his curious hobby-horse, questioning the value of stereo over mono. The scene he picked on was where children hear the cuckoo in the forest: there the distancing of the cuckoo-call does indeed simulate stereo atmosphere, but that's far clearer this time than last. The performance remains a classic, with Karajan plainly in love with the music, and the two principals singing immaculately. This isn't for those who resist the child-voice inflexion of Schwarzkopf and Grümmer, but everyone else will register the mastery in singing and acting. The thinness of Anny Felbermayer's voice as the Sandman is an unwelcome contrast, but this is otherwise a satisfyingly Germanic team.

Additional recommendation

Hänsel und Gretel
Fassbaender Hänsel **Popp** Gretel **Vienna Philharmonic Orchestra / Solti**
Decca ② 470 567-2 (108' · ADD)   Ⓜ
A fine mid-price alternative, though there's nothing cut-price about the casting. Fassbaender and Popp are delightful in the title-roles, and other treats include Walter Berry as the Father and the lovely Norma Burrowes as the Sandman. Solti draws gorgeous playing from the VPO.

Sigismondo d'India   Italian c1582-1629

As a young man d'India travelled in Italy, notably to Florence, and in 1611 he became chamber music director at the Turin court; he left in 1623, working in Modena and Rome. His five books Le musiche (1609-23) contain chamber monodies, varied in style but often of great emotional intensity, and duets; he also published eight volumes of madrigals (1606-24), some highly chromatic and expressive, villanellas and motets. GROVEmusic

Madrigals

Il primo libro de madrigali
La Venexiana (Valentina Coladonato, Nadia Ragni *sops* Lucia Sciannimanico *mez* Giuseppe Maletto, Sandro Naglia *tens* Daniele Carnovich *bass*) / **Claudio Cavina** *counterten*

Glossa GCD920908 (49' · DDD) Texts and translations
included   Ⓔ

The northern and southern Italian madrigal
traditions meet in the person of Sigismondo
d'India. The date of publication of this, his *First
Book of Madrigals* (1606) reveals him to be one of
the last of the genre's most significant figures.
By this time the majority of Monteverdi's publications were already in existence, and Gesualdo's too. The influence of both is clearly audible, and not just in the music. One of the most
memorable tracks is *Felice chi ti miro*, although
much of the tripartite *Interdette speranze* is
equally impressive. Sometimes you feel that a
phrase or sentiment might have been more dramatically and elastically projected, or lingered
over and savoured. As to tuning, it's generally
very accurate, and the slightest slip stands out.
But that's the problem with tuning: standards
are so high nowadays that critics risk expecting
something inhuman, or at least superhuman.
This will do just fine. A movingly dramatic
account.

John Ireland   British 1879-1962

*Ireland studied at the Royal College of Music, first as
a pianist, then as a composer under Stanford (1897-
1901), under whom he gained command of a solid
Brahmsian style radically altered during the next
two decades by the impressions of Debussy, Ravel and
Stravinsky. The result was a sequence of lyrical piano
pieces, but also substantial chamber works, including
two piano trios (1906, 1917) and two violin sonatas
(1909, 1917). Meanwhile he served as organist and
choirmaster at St Luke's, Chelsea (1904-26), later
returning to the RCM to teach (1923-39). Postwar
works include the symphonic rhapsody Mai-Dun
(1921, one of many works suggestive of English
landscape), the Piano Concerto (1930), a classic of
20th-century English music, and Legend for piano
and orchestra (1933).*   GROVEmusic

A Downland Suite

A Downland Suite (arr Ireland and Bush). Orchestral
Poem in A minor. Concertino pastorale. Two
Symphonic Studies (arr Bush)
City of London Sinfonia / Richard Hickox
Chandos CHAN9376 (64' · DDD) Recorded 1994   ⒻО

Hickox gives a sensitive account of the *Downland Suite* and extracts great expressive intensity
from the glorious second movement 'Elegy'.
The *Concertino pastorale* is another fine work,
boasting a most eloquent opening 'Eclogue' and
tenderly poignant 'Threnody', towards the end
of which Ireland seems to allow himself a
momentary recollection of the haunting opening phrase of his earlier orchestral prelude, *The
Forgotten Rite*. In 1969 Ireland's pupil, Geoffrey
Bush, arranged two sections of the score for
the 1946 film *The Overlanders* which were not

incorporated into the 1971 concert suite compiled by Sir Charles Mackerras. The resulting,
finely wrought *Two Symphonic Studies* were
recorded many years ago by Sir Adrian Boult for
Lyrita – no longer available – and Hickox proves
just as sympathetic an interpreter, whereas the
Orchestral Poem in A minor is here receiving its
recorded début. This is a youthful essay, completed in 1904, some three years after Ireland's
studies with Stanford.

It's a worthy rather than especially inspiring
effort, with hardly a glimpse of the mature manner to come, save for some particularly beautiful
string writing. Hickox makes out a decent
enough case for it. However, with rich, refined
Chandos sound, this is most enjoyable.

Violin Sonatas

Violin Sonatas – No 1 in D minor[a]; No 2 in   Ⓗ
A minor[b]. Phantasie Trio in A minor[c]. The Holy Boyd
[ac]**Frederick Grinke,** [b]**Albert Sammons** *vns*
[cd]**Florence Hooton** *vc* [ab]**John Ireland,** [c]**Kendall
Taylor,** [d]**Lawrence Pratt** *pfs*
Dutton Laboratories Historic Epoch mono CDLX7103
(73' · ADD) Recorded 1930-45?   ⓂОО

Such was the critical acclaim that greeted the
March 1917 première of Ireland's Second Violin Sonata that the 37-year-old composer's reputation was cemented virtually overnight. The
performers on that momentous occasion were
the legendary Albert Sammons and pianist
William Murdoch. Some 13 years later Sammons finally set down his thoughts on this glorious music with Ireland himself at the piano.
Quite why this valuable document never saw the
light of day until now is a mystery, so all gratitude to Dutton for granting a long overdue lease
of life to a nobly spacious rendering of such
palpable feeling and insight.

As for the First Violin Sonata, Frederick
Grinke's 1945 Decca recording (again with the
composer) continues to strike as, quite simply,
the most perceptive interpretation of this early
offering ever encountered, possessing a compelling sweep and tingling concentration that
grip from first measure to last. The November
1938 recording of the *Phantasie Trio* is yet
another cherishable display, the playing wonderfully alive and always radiating a most winning understanding and spontaneity.

Good, if not exceptional transfers, the spook-
ily quiet background is obtained at the expense
of some naturalness of timbre. Urgently recommended all the same.

Additional recommendation

Violin Sonatas Nos 1 and 2
Coupled with: Fantasy-Sonata. Cello Sonata. The
Holy Boy. Phantasie Trio. Trios Nos 2 and 3
Mordkovitch *vn* **Georgian** *vc* **Brown** *pf*
Chandos ② CHAN9377/8 (147' · DDD)   Ⓕ
  Whole-hearted, affectionate performances.

Piano Works

Piano Works, Volume 1
Sarnia. London Pieces. In Those Days. Prelude in E flat. Ballade. Columbine. Month's Mind
John Lenehan pf
Naxos 8 553700 (60' · DDD)　　　　　Ⓢ**O**

The pleasures here are many. John Lenehan is a very accomplished performer: not only is his technical address impeccable, but he also has a strikingly wide dynamic range and sophisticated variety of tone colour, both of which he uses to poetic effect throughout. That Lenehan has a real affinity for Ireland's muse is immediately evident from his raptly intimate delivery of the gentle opening diptych, *In Those Days*. Similarly, in the extraordinarily imaginative, harmonically questing *Ballade* of 1929 he rises superbly to the elemental fury of the remarkable central portion, with its brooding echoes of the 'Northern' Bax from the same period. Elsewhere, *Columbine* is a treat, as is the ravishing *Month's Mind* and the haunting Prelude in E flat. Lenehan's supremely affectionate and articulate advocacy will surely win Ireland many friends.

Piano Works, Volume 2
Merry Andrew. The towing-path. Rhapsody. Two Pieces (1924-5). Decorations. Leaves from a Child's Sketchbook. The darkened valley. Sonatina. Three Pastels. Two Pieces (1921). Summer evening
John Lenehan pf
Naxos 8 553889 (71' · DDD)　　　　　Ⓢ**O**

Ireland's piano music, intriguingly titled, exudes a deeply personal, bittersweet fragrance. The sense of autobiography is strong. Nostalgia is his keynote, his pantheistic and wistful Gallic delicacy subsumed into a wholly English reticence. On this release there's a strong feeling of how purely local influences (Pangbourne and the Thames Valley in *The towing-path*, Le Fauvic beach, Jersey in 'The Island Spell', to take two examples) are transcended to become statements of wider poetic import.

The large-scale *Rhapsody*, with its powerful Fauréan overtones, is relished by John Lenehan, a strong, sympathetic interpreter, and time and again he makes you wonder at works aptly described as 'some of the most appealing English piano music written this century, too long neglected.'

Additional recommendation

London Pieces
Coupled with: In Those Days. Leaves from a Child's Sketchbook. The darkened valley. Two Pieces. Equinox. Sonatina. Prelude. Ballade. Greenways
Parkin pf
Chandos CHAN9140 (74' · DDD)　　　　　Ⓕ
　The best of Ireland's piano music, revealing a subtle, nostalgic sensibility.

Charles Ives　　　American 1874-1954

Ives was influenced first by his father, a bandmaster who had libertarian ideas about what music might be. When he was perhaps 19 (the dating of his music is nearly always problematic) he produced psalm settings that exploit polytonality and other unusual procedures. He then studied with Parker at Yale (1894-8) and showed some sign of becoming a relatively conventional composer in his First Symphony (1898) and songs of this period. He worked, however, not in music but in the insurance business, and composition became a weekend activity – but one practised assiduously: during the two decades after his graduation he produced three more symphonies and numerous other works.

The only consistent characteristic of this music is liberation from rule. There are entirely atonal pieces, while others are in the simple harmonic style of a hymn or folksong. Some are systematic and abstract in construction; others are filled with quotations from the music of Ives's youth: hymns, popular songs, marches etc. Some, like the Three Places in New England, are nostalgic; others, like the Fourth Symphony, are fuelled by the vision of an idealist democracy. He published his 'Concord' Sonata in 1920 and a volume of 114 songs in 1922, but composed little thereafter. Most of his music had been written without prospect of performance, and it was only towards the end of his life that it began to be played frequently and appreciated.　　　　**GROVE**music

Symphonies

Symphony No 2. Robert Browning Overture
Nashville Symphony Orch / Kenneth Schermerhorn
Naxos 8 559076 (67' · DDD)　　　　　Ⓢ

Ives' Second Symphony isn't as well served on CD as might be expected. Bernstein gave the première in 1951 some 40 years after the work's composition. His 1958 recording, showing its age, is still available and so is his live recording from 1987.

What's new about this Nashville release is that it uses Jonathan Elkus's edition made for the Charles Ives Society for both works. The main difference for the listener is that the exposition of the second movement of the Symphony is repeated. That this helps the overall balance in this extended, somewhat repetitive movement is debatable. When it comes to Bernstein, he quite unnecessarily cut 16 measures from the last movement. His tempos may be considered slow in the third and fourth movements, but in both his recordings the work luxuriates in a way that nobody else achieves.

The *Robert Browning Overture* is one of Ives' most visionary pieces, with declamatory trumpet parts that make Scriabin's *Poème de l'extase* seem reticent. The mystical calm of the opening is memorably caught in the Nashville performance; the energetic passages are vivid, although some textures inevitably get submerged. It's a great relief to have the obvious errors in the

IVES THREE PLACES IN NEW ENGLAND – IN BRIEF

San Francisco SO / Michael Tilson
RCA 09026 63703-2   Ⓕ●
Placed at the centre of a wonderfully conceived programme of mainly vocal works, Ives's masterpiece receives an outstanding performance from MTT's excellent West Coast ensemble.

Boston SO / Michael Tilson Thomas
DG 463 633-2   Ⓜ
Dating from 1970, and with still superb sound, the youthful MTT nails his Ivesian credentials to the mast with a finely sculpted performance. Appealingly coupled with more Ives, Piston and Ruggles.

Cleveland Orchestra / Christoph von Dohnányi
Decca 466 745-2   Ⓑ
Forming part of an inexpensive Double Decca, this digital version of the *Three Places* is very fine with outstanding sound. Dohnányi's modernist sympathies play dividends in pointing up the work's novelty.

Eastman-Rochester Orchestra / Howard Hanson
Mercury 432 755-2   Ⓜ
Howard Hanson proves a splendid advocate for the music by his fellow American, and well coupled with works by Mennin and Schuman, presents a fine portrait of 20th-century orchestral Americana. Great sound from 1957 (only available in the US).

Philadelphia Orchestra / Eugene Ormandy
Sony Classical SBK89290   Ⓑ
As the coupling to a fine Stokowski's led performance of Ives's First Symphony, Ormandy directs a straightforward, sensitive account of the *Three Places* on a generously filled CD.

score corrected. This puts earlier recordings such as Stokowski's beyond the pale and it's well worth buying this CD for the *Browning Overture* alone, although both works in these carefully considered editions make a bargain pair.

Symphony No 2. The Gong on the Hook and Ladder. Tone Roads – No 1. A Set of Three Short Pieces – Largo cantabile, Hymn. Hallowe'en. Central Park in the Dark. The Unanswered Question
New York Philharmonic Orchestra / Leonard Bernstein
DG 429 220-2GH (68' · DDD) Recorded 1987-8 Ⓕ●●

Although Bernstein thought of Ives as a primitive composer, these recordings reveal that he had a deep understanding of, his music. The Second Symphony (written in 1902 and first performed in 1951) is a glorious work, still strongly rooted in the 19th century yet showing those clear signs of Ives's individual voice that are largely missing from the charming but lightweight First Symphony. Bernstein brings out all its richness and warmth without wallowing in its romantic elements, and he handles with utter conviction the multi-textures and the allusions to popular tunes and snatches from Bach, Brahms and Dvořák, to name but a few. The standard of playing he exacts from the NYPO, both here and in the disc's series of technically demanding shorter pieces, is remarkably high with the depth of string tone at a premium – and the engineers retain this to a degree unusual in a live recording. An essential disc for any collection.

Symphony No 3, 'The Camp Meeting'. The Unanswered Question. Central Park in the Dark. Overture and March, '1776'. Holidays – Washington's Birthday. Country Band March
Northern Sinfonia / James Sinclair
Naxos 8 559087 (52' · DDD)   Ⓢ

James Sinclair has been a dedicated Ives scholar and performer for more than 30 years, which means this CD has to be something special. First on this issue comes the hymn-saturated Third Symphony, where Sinclair uses some of the thinly sketched options in the manuscripts. This means there's a bit extra in the distance at the end of the first two movements and slighty more of the barely audible bells, ingeniously made to sound like an outdoor carillon, at the end of the last movement, compared with Slatkin and the St Louis Orchestra. There are more distant effects if you listen carefully.

In *The Unanswered Question* Sinclair uses the version with two flutes and two clarinets rather than four flutes for the attempted answers to the questioning trumpet. Then, in *Central Park in the Dark*, he uses a battered upright piano for the bits taken from the 1899 hit-song 'Hello! ma Baby' which suggests the tavern scene in Berg's *Wozzeck*. It works, but unfortunately the piano, marked *fff*, almost fades out at the climax.

There are two little-known early pieces which Ives drew on for 'Putnam's Camp', the second of *Three Places in New England*. The *Country Band March* has hilarious junketings as an affectionate reflection of the mistakes of amateur players – Sinclair takes an option without the final chord which leaves the dilatory saxophonist exposed after the end. Then the *Overture and March, '1776'* goes to town with a brass player using the wrong instrument so that quite a lengthy passage comes out in parallel semitones! Vintage Ives, all played with completely idiomatic feeling and adequately recorded.

Symphony No 4 – Fugue[c]. Orchestral Set No 1, 'Three Places in New England'. Charlie Rutlagea[d]. The Circus Band[bc]. From the Steeples and the Mountains[c]. General William Booth Enters into Heaven[bc]. In Flanders Fields[ad]. Memories[ad]. The Pond[abc]. Psalm 100[bc]. Serenity[ac]. They are There![abc]. The Things our Fathers Loved[ad]. Tom Sails Away[ad]. The Unanswered Question[c]
[a]**Thomas Hampson** bar [b]**San Francisco Girl's Chorus; San Francisco Symphony Chorus and** [c]**Orchestra / Michael Tilson Thomas** [d]pf
RCA Red Seal 09026 63703-2 (65' · DDD) Recorded live 1999 Ⓕ**O**

If anyone has a hot-line to the cortex of Ives's imagination, it's Michael Tilson Thomas. The programme he's devised here isn't so much a journey, more a stream of consciousness through the hinterlands of Ives Americana. It's about the things that mattered to Ives: the times, places, events that fashioned the nation and enabled it to find its own way. It's a landscape of ballad songs and snatches, of hymns, marches, tall tales and short orders, assembled exactly as the man remembered them and entirely in keeping with the chaotic comedy of life. But above all, it's about the spirit within us all – great and small.

From the Steeples and the Mountains is classic Ives: a visionary statement fashioned from bare essentials, bells and brass dissonances always just a whisper away from a recognisable hymn tune. Then from the mountains to the back yard – recollections of a very American childhood. Picket fences and parlour songs. Like *The Things Our Fathers Loved* written 16 years after the craggy bell and brass piece. You can be sure the Ives chronology will constantly wrong-foot you. Thomas Hampson is the man entrusted with these rich pickings from the Ives songbook. He lustily makes a drama out of a crisis in *Charlie Rutlage*, a cowboy song turned operatic *gran scena*. Later he's the Salvation Army's General William Booth banging the drum for all his pimps, floosies, and drunks – his 'saved souls' – as he leads them towards that great courthouse in the sky. Then one of the most heartfelt of all Ives songs, *Tom Sails Away* – a life in a song from cradle to grave.

Such juxtapositions make this all-live compilation especially affecting. Hard to believe that this is a live recording, so astonishingly lucid and transparent is the multi-layered orchestral sound. Tremendous impact, too.

Finally, a beautiful performance of that little masterpiece *The Unanswered Question*, as close as we get to an understanding of what spirituality actually meant to Ives. A superb disc.

String Quartets

String Quartets No 1, 'From the Salvation Army'; No 2. A set of three short pieces – Scherzo, 'Holding Your Own' **Barber** String Quartet, Op 11
Emerson Quartet (Eugene Drucker, Philip Setzer vns Lawrence Dutton va David Finckel vc)
DG 435 864-2GH (65' · DDD) Ⓕ**O**

The First Quartet (1896) is a student work, saturated in hymn-tunes: each movement was probably used as an organ voluntary. But, like the Third Symphony, it assembles an affectionate archive of religious forms of musical expression ranging from mystical intensity to almost ecstatic fervour. The Fugue, which forms the first movement of the First Quartet, crops up again as the third movement of the Fourth Symphony. In the performance the Emerson has everything under control even if the third movement is slightly cold. Ives's Second Quartet (1913) is wildly different. With the first movement called 'Discussions' and the second 'Arguments' there's free scope for all Ives's photographic realism with textures as violent as middle-period Bartók later on. The Emerson brings hard-edged attack to the 'Arguments' but the ironic 'Andante Emasculata', a burlesque cadenza at 0'43", and similar moments are a little short-changed. The last movement, 'The Call of the Mountains', has a real chill when it opens largely without vibrato: and it climaxes resoundingly on 'Nearer my God', linking this peroration to the last movement of the Fourth Symphony. The Scherzo is a rarity – a brief comic study in rhythmic juxtapositions with the occasional diatonic tune sticking out of the melée. A fine, well-recorded performance.

Violin Sonatas

Violin Sonatas – No 1; No 2; No 3; No 4, 'Children's Day at the Camp Meeting'
Curt Thompson vn **Rodney Waters** pf
Naxos 8 559119 (77' · DDD) Ⓢ

The four violin and piano sonatas are at the core of Ives's chamber music output. The style oscillates because Ives was uncertain about his more radical visions and admitted he'd tried to compromise. But this gives all four of them an enlarged frame of reference, saturated with quotations as usual, but relating to European sonata traditions as well. There's everything to savour from these performances on Naxos: lovely soft textures in the transcendental meditations, well recorded, and everything hectic is under control. Warning: the distant violin in the second movement of No 1 isn't a balance fault – Ives specified that the pianist should overwhelm the defenceless muted violin! This is now the version to choose.

Piano Sonata No 2, 'Concord'

Piano Sonata No 2, 'Concord, Mass.: 1840-60'[a]. Ann Street[b]. The Cage[b]. The Circus Band[b]. A farewell to land[b]. The Housatonic at Stockbridge[b]. The Indians[b]. Like a sick eagle[b]. Memories[b]. September[b]. Serenity[b]. Soliloquy[b]. Songs my mother taught me[b]. Swimmers[b]. The things our fathers loved[b]. Thoreau[b]. 1, 2, 3[b]. A sound of distant horn[b]
[b]**Susan Graham** sop [a]**Emmanuel Pahud** fl [a]**Tabea Zimmermann** va **Pierre-Laurent Aimard** pf
Warner Classics 2564 60297-2 (79' · DDD)　Ⓕ**OO**

Charles Ives to complaining pianist: 'Is it the composer's fault that man has only ten fingers?' Listening to Pierre-Laurent Aimard play the *Concord* Sonata it isn't Ives's dry wit but the assertion that man has only ten fingers that you begin to question. Nothing he wrote was 'reasonable' as in playable, singable. Everything was a stretch, a note or chord or counterpoint too far. Technically optimistic, spiritually aspirational. In a sense Aimard is almost too good, the realisation of everything Ives was striving for in this piece. You can almost hear Ives thinking: 'OK, if that's possible, let's go somewhere else…'

Actually, the *Concord* Sonata goes wherever you want it to go. Its starting point is American literature but its substance is in ideas. Ives the transcendentalist: beyond the American dream. An amazing stream of consciousness. Concord is a town in Massachusetts, it's where American Independence was bloodily born; but it's also a word for harmony, and for Ives there's harmony in extreme diversity. The big moments in the sonata are all born out of flux. Ideas and notes boil over in the second movement, 'Hawthorne', but at its heart is the basic conflict between the earthly body and its free spirit. The body resists, the spirit meditates. There are moments here where you'd swear two pianists were involved. You'd also swear that the sorrowful song so fleetingly alluded to by solo viola (Tabea Zimmerman) in the first movement or the remnant of solo flute (Emmanuel Pahud) in the last are figments of your imagination.

Ives's imagination – his rampant theatricality – should have made for great operas. Instead he wrote songs: capsule dramas laid out not in scenes or acts but moments in time. Susan Graham inhabits 17 such moments – nostalgic ('Songs my mother taught me'), visionary ('A sound of distant horn'), cryptic ('Soliloquy'), brutal ('1, 2, 3'), expectant ('Thoreau') – and the feminine and masculine qualities of her voice, to say nothing of her musical sensibility, easily encompass the 'expectancy and ecstasy' prom-

ised by the song 'Memories' – which appropriately enough recalls her (and others like her) as a little girl 'sitting in the opera house'. Aimard is again a one-man band. Almost literally so in 'The Circus Band'. When Graham shouts 'hear the trombones', you really do.

Additional recommendation

Ives Piano Sonata No 2, 'Concord, Mass.: 1840-60'
Barber Piano Sonata
Marc-André Hamelin pf
Hyperion CDA67469 (62' · DDD)　　　　Ⓕ
A superb recital of two sharply opposed American sonatas. Hamelin subdues his awe-inspiring command to a purely musical end. Hyperion's sound is immaculate.

Elisabeth Jacquet de la Guerre
French 1666/67-1729

Elisabeth-Claude Jacquet de la Guerre was the daughter of Claude Jacquet (d 1702), member of a well-known family of harpsichord makers and organists. An accomplished harpsichordist with a talent for improvisation, she became a protégée of Louis XIV and Mme de Montespan. She wrote music for the Théâtres de la Foire. Her surviving music includes a ballet, an opera Cephale et Procris (1694), three collections of cantatas (1708-c1715), solo and trio sonatas with violin and bass viol, and two sets of Pièces de clavecin (1687, 1707). She was among the first in France to use the sonata and cantata genres, was the only woman to write a tragédie lyrique and among the earliest to publish harpsichord collections.
GROVEmusic

Pièces de clavecin

Premier livre de pièces de clavecin.　　　　　Ⓟ
Pièces de clavecin
Carole Cerasi hpd
Metronome METCD1026 (79' · DDD)　　　Ⓕ**OOO**

 A member of a family of musicians, at the age of only five Elisabeth Jacquet attracted the benevolent attention of Louis XIV by her harpsichord playing, and subsequently was taken under the wing of his favourite, Mme de Montespan. At 18 she married the organist Marin de la Guerre and became famous for the concerts she gave at her home, in which her powers of improvisation were greatly admired. Her first book of harpsichord pieces was published as early as 1687 and contains in its four suites, apart from partly unmeasured preludes, sequences of dances that have real individuality and feeling for expressive harmony, a very unusual *Tocade* (to open the F major Suite) and a couple of chaconnes. Twenty years later, after a series of family deaths, she produced two more harpsichord suites 'that can be played on the violin'. All this music is performed with flair, vitality, panache and character by the Swedish-born harpsichordist Carole Cerasi. Her playing on a rich-toned Ruckers instrument is deeply impressive and rewarding, and a model of clarity.

Jacquet of Mantua   French 1483-1559

Jacquet was a singer to the Modenese house of Rangoni and in 1525, with Willaert, served at the Este court at Ferrara. The following year he settled in Mantua, where for 30 years he dominated musical life. He was also titular maestro di cappella of the Cathedral of SS Peter and Paul there (1534-59). Jacquet was the leading master of sacred polyphony between Josquin and Palestrina and a prolific composer. In his sacred music (which includes over 20 masses and numerous motets) he appears a skilled craftsman alert to new ideas: smoothly arched lines, symmetry of phrase and fluency. His later motets show clearly his stylistic change to pervading imitation as the generating principle.   GROVEmusic

Lamentations of Jeremiah

Lamentations of Jeremiah
Michel Lonsdale spkr **Ensemble Jachet de Mantoue** (Raoul de Chenadec counterten Thierry Bréhu, Eric Raffard tens James Gowings bar Philippe Roche bass)
Calliope CAL9340 (64' · DDD) Text and translation included   Ⓕ

Both Jews and Christians use these texts liturgically, the Jews to commemorate the destruction of Jerusalem in 586BC, the Western Christian Church during the Office of Tenebrae on the last three days of Holy Week. Jacquet of Mantua's set of *Lamentations* for Holy Week was published posthumously in 1567, but probably dates from several decades earlier, when he was employed by Ercole Gonzaga, Cardinal Bishop of Mantua.

The singers, a recently formed ensemble based in Brittany, are joined for the recording by the Parisian actor Michel Lonsdale. The recital is planned so that the different sections fall into place in a natural sequence of three days, each divided into three lessons and each lesson into a series of verses, introduced by Hebrew letters. Before each of the lessons Lonsdale reads, quietly and most beautifully, an early 16th-century French translation of what's to follow. The singers continue with the same spirit of deep and utter sorrow, expressed with totally controlled emotion throughout the performance. It's never overdone. The vocal blend is excellent, and the spoken voice adds just enough relief.

The booklet notes are of interest and importance, the illustrations discreet and sober. The whole CD is a model of beauty and perfection.

Leos Janáček   Moravian 1854-1928

Janáček was a chorister at the Augustinian 'Queen's' Monastery in Old Brno, where the choirmaster Pavel Križkovský took a keen interest in his musical education. After completing his basic schooling he trained as a teacher and, except for a period at the Prague Organ School, he spent 1872-9 largely as a schoolteacher and choral conductor in Brno. In 1879 he enrolled at the Leipzig Conservatory, where he developed his interest in composition under the strict and systematic supervision of Leo Grill. After a month in Vienna he returned to Brno in May 1880; there he became engaged to one of his pupils, Zdenka Schulzová, whom he married in July 1881.

In Brno, Janáček took up his former activities, and also founded and directed an organ school and edited a new musical journal, Hudební listy. After composing his first opera, Sárka, he immersed himself in collecting Moravian folk music, which bore fruit in a series of orchestral suites and dances and in a one-act opera, The Beginning of a Romance. This was favourably received in 1894, but Janáček withdrew it after six performances and set to work on Jenůfa.

During the long period of composition of Jenůfa (1894-1903), Janáček rethought his approach to opera and to composition in general. He largely abandoned the number opera, integrated folksong firmly into his music and formulated a theory of 'speech-melody', based on the natural rhythms and the rise and fall of the Czech language, which was to influence all his ensuing works and give them a particular colour through their jagged rhythms and lines. Jenůfa was soon followed by other operatic ventures, but his reputation in Brno was as a composer of instrumental and choral music and as director of the Organ School. Outside Moravia he was almost unknown until the Prague première of Jenůfa in 1916. The creative upsurge of a man well into his 60s is explained partly by the success of Jenůfa in Prague and abroad, partly by his patriotic pride in the newly acquired independence of his country, and perhaps most of all by his passionate, though generally distant, attachment to Kamila Stösslová, the young wife of an antique dealer in Pisek, Bohemia.

Between 1919 and 1925 Janáček composed three of his finest operas, all on subjects with special resonances for him: Kát'a Kabanová with its neglected wife who takes a lover, The Cunning Little Vixen with its sympathetic portrayal of animals (and particularly the female fox), and The Makropoulos Affair with the 'ageless' woman who fascinates all men. Each was given first in Brno and soon after in Prague. His 70th birthday was marked by a doctorate from the Masaryk University in Brno. Early in 1926 he wrote the Sinfonietta for orchestra, characteristic in its blocks of sound and its forceful repetitions, and later that year his most important choral work, the Glagolitic Mass. While performance of his music carried his fame abroad, he started work on his last opera, From the House of the Dead, which he did not live to see performed. It received its première in April 1930 in a version prepared by his pupils Bretislav Bakala and Osvald Chlubna.

Janáček's reputation outside Czechoslovakia and

German-speaking countries was first made as an instrumental composer. He has since come to be regarded not only as a Czech composer worthy to be ranked with Smetana and Dvořák, but also as one of the most substantial and original opera composers of the 20th century.   GROVEmusic

Orchestral Works

Sinfonietta. The Cunning Little Vixen – Suite. Taras Bulba. Jealousy. Šárka – Overture. Kát'a Kabanová – Prelude. Schluk und Jau
Czech Philharmonic Orchestra / Sir Charles Mackerras
Supraphon ② SU3739-2 (92' · DDD)   ⓕ**OO**

Issued to celebrate the 150th anniversary of the composer's birth, this two-disc set of orchestral works may be the last Janáček recording from our greatest advocate of his work, Sir Charles Mackerras. Where his pioneering Pro Arte recording of the *Sinfonietta* has an earthy quality and Decca's Vienna version is ripe and resonant, the new one is generally lighter and more flexible. The live performance brings dividends in its flow and the build-up of excitement, thrillingly caught when the fanfare theme returns to cap the finale.

Where most versions of the *Cunning Little Vixen* Suite use Václav Talich's reorchestration, Mackerras has gone back to the original. As he says, the orchestral writing may seem unusual, but it certainly isn't amateurish, where Talich's version, for all its beauty, 'rather emasculates the acid sounds produced for the insects'.

Mackerras includes two tiny interludes for *Kát'a Kabanová* which he discovered in Prague, written when the German Theatre needed more time for scene changes. Rightly, he regards them as little jewels, well worth preserving.

The rarity is the incidental music for Gerhardt Hauptmann's play, *Schluck und Jau*, which Janáček was writing at the time of his death. The first of the two completed movements brings intriguing echoes of the fanfares in the *Sinfonietta* and the second in 5/8 time is equally original in its instrumentation, with deep trombones and stratospheric violins.

The helpful acoustic of the Rudolfinum gives a mellow quality to the refined playing of the Czech Philharmonic, with ample space round the sound, without underplaying the contrasts of wind and strings which are so typical of the composer.

Janáček Taras Bulba. The Cunning Little Vixen – ⒣
Suite **V Novák** Slovak Suite, Op 32
Czech Philharmonic Orchestra / Václav Talich
Supraphon Historical mono 11 1905-2 (71' · AAD).
Recorded 1953-54   Ⓜ**OO**

Talich's *Taras Bulba* is hugely imposing. Aided by playing of brazen fervour from the Czech PO, his reading has a rare dignity, culminating in an apotheosis of overwhelming grandeur and

majesty (magnificent brass sounds). Not that there's any want of energy and momentum: in Talich's hands, the battle scenes of the first two tableaux possess thrilling snap and vigour. Some might crave a leaner, harder-edged orchestral sonority, but the impact and stature of this music-making isn't in question. It's followed by the affectionate orchestral suite from *The Cunning Little Vixen* which Talich himself compiled in 1937. Not all Janáčekians will approve of the great conductor's 'sensualising' of the original instrumentation, but many collectors will be grateful to have this classic 1954 recording restored to circulation at long last, and its sense of enchantment and magical atmosphere remain utterly intoxicating. The Novák coupling is an unmitigated delight. Talich's wonderful conception has all the tangy affection and lithe, rhythmic punch one could wish for, but he also locates and taps into a vein of tangible, old-world nostalgia that's extremely moving. You won't hear better performances than these.

Additional recommendation

Sinfonietta. Taras Bulba. Concertino
Rudolf Firkušný pf **Bavarian Radio Symphony Orchestra / Rafael Kubelík**
DG/The Rosette Collection 476 2196PR
(61' · ADD)   Ⓜ
A reissue of Kubelík's all-conquering 1970 account of Janáček's *Sinfonietta* together with classic versions of *Taras Bulba* and the Concertino (with Rudolf Firkušný) complete an unmissable survey

String Quartets

String Quartets – No 1, 'Kreutzer Sonata'; No 2, 'Intimate Letters'. Along an Overgrown Path (1906-8) – Suite No 1
Radoslav Kvapil pf **Talich Quartet** (Petr Messiereur, Jan Kvapil vns Jan Talich va Evzen Rattai vc)
Calliope CAL5699 (73' · DDD) Recorded 1986   Ⓜ**O**

This recording doesn't give a true balance, and in places the sound itself is rather grey. At first blush, too, the Talich Quartet's manner can seem tentative. Yet this is exactly what's right. The music is sudden, questing, unpredictable, by turns mysterious, vehement in its emotions, passionately lyrical. The whole programme of the Second Quartet, with its reference in the title to secret affections, indicates the extraordinariness of the emotion for the younger woman that overcame Janáček; and its exceptional and impossible nature finds ideal expression in the idiom of Janáček's astonishing final years. The Talich Quartet suggests secrecy, fear even, in the quick shifts between musical gestures; yet it can allow Janáček's beautiful phrases declaring his full heart to find passionate expression. It's a more restrained manner of playing than that adopted by other groups, and it can make its effect by skilful understatement; but repeated hearings increasingly find it to yield subtle and true performances of both works. Room is also found for the First Suite of *Along an Overgrown Path*. Kvapil is direct and eloquent in his approach to Janáček's oblique statements and half-hidden memories, both passionate and tragic; but he never overstates, and his allusive manner is very effective indeed.

String Quartets – No 1, 'Kreutzer Sonata'; No 2, 'Intimate Letters'
Skampa Quartet (Pavel Fischer, Jana Lukášová *vns* Radim Sedmidubský *va* Peter Jarůšek *vc*)
Supraphon SU3486-2 (41' · DDD)   Ⓕ**O**

Janáček changed his mind a great deal, especially about the Second Quartet, on the way from composition to performance and even after that. Most records use the scores published in Prague respectively in 1945 and 1949 as 'revised editions'. However, Milan Skampa published further revisions in 1975 and 1979, and these are what are used here by the quartet which studied under him at the time of its formation in 1989.

The differences depend mostly upon dynamic markings and emphases. To these the present players give great attention, stressing the sudden changes of tempo or dynamics and the consequent abrupt changes of mood which mark the music. They also pay particular attention to coloration of tone. In the First Quartet, for instance, where the seducer of the Tolstoy-inspired 'plot' makes his mincing entrance, the sound is deceptively warm within the delicacy; other quartets play the theme with almost disdainful thinness, but theŠkampa allow him his dangerous charm. In the final movement of the Second Quartet, there's a searing discord marked to be played *fortississimo* but right up near the bridge where string tone is weakest: the outcome is a horrible sound, and theŠkampa believe that that's what's meant. In short, these are sharp, well-considered performances, vivid in detail and excellently judged in structure. They take their place in the catalogue beside the marvellous Talich Quartet (reviewed above).

SBT1074 – **Janáček** String Quartet No 1, 'The Kreutzer Sonata' **Dvořák** String Quartet No 12 in F, 'American', B179. Piano Quintet in A, B155[a]

SBT1075 – **Janáček** String Quartet No 2, 'Intimate Letters' **Dvořák** Terzetto in C, B148. String Quartet No 14 in A flat, B193

Smetana Quartet (Jiří Novák, Lubomir Kostecký *vns* Milan Skampa *va* Antonín Kohout *vc*) [a]**Pavel Stěpán** *pf*
Testament ② SBT1074/5 (oas: 79' & 77' · ADD)
Recorded 1965-6   Ⓕ**O**

Listening to these discs tempts one to think that in the 1960s the Smetana was the Berlin Philharmonic of quartets – just as in the 1950s the Hollywoods might have been fancifully called

JANÁČEK STRING QUARTETS – IN BRIEF

Talich Quartet
Calliope CAL5699   Ⓕ**O**
Full of imagination and idiomatic touches, the Talich must top the list of superb interpretations. These are superb performances that really drill to the core of the works.

The Lindsays
ASV CDDCA749   Ⓕ
Another pair of superb performances, The Lindsays play with febrile intensity and minute attention to the numerous shifts of mood and emotional temperature.

New Helsinki Quartet
Warner Apex 0927 40603-2   Ⓢ
A super-budget coupling worth considering: stylish playing and a real sense of the music's variety. Generously coupled with Dvořák's delightful *Cypresses*.

Vlach Quartet
Naxos 8 553895   Ⓢ
Played with passion and imagination, here's another well-filled and competitively priced coupling well worth considering.

Skampa Quartet
Supraphon SU3486-2   Ⓕ**O**
Tremendous performances that are not afraid to explore some of Janáček's more extreme sonic demands: they almost revel in making sounds that are simply ugly, but they justify it by the intelligence of their overall approach.

Smetana Quartet
Testament SBT1074/5   Ⓕ**O**
Slightly awkwardly spread over two individual full-price discs, each coupled with Dvořák, the Smetana Quartet really convey the passion and intensity of these two great works. The 1960s sound is outstanding.

the Philadelphia Orchestra of quartets. Much of the playing here is in a class of its own, only later equalled by the Borodin and Alban Berg Quartets in terms of finesse and ensemble. The Dvořák performances must be numbered among the very best now in the catalogue: their phrasing has none of the artificiality that marks some professional quartets. (A phrasing once rehearsed can become mechanically reproduced, so that while the line rises and falls it doesn't genuinely breathe.) It's an enormous relief to hear genuine *pianissimo* tone and so natural and unforced an ensemble. There are numerous recordings of each of the Janáček Quartets, but, in terms of tonal finesse, perfection of ensemble and depth of feeling, the present issues would be difficult to beat.

Piano Sonata 1.X.1905

Piano Sonata 1. X. 1905, 'From the street'.
On an Overgrown Path. In the mists. Reminiscence
Charles Owen pf
Somm SOMMCD028 (73' · DDD)   Ⓕ**O**

It says much for Charles Owen and his understanding of this composer that a young British pianist should present this music with such a distinctive voice. As is evident from the first of the two movements of the Sonata, he's even more strikingly successful than Rudolf Firkušný (reviewed below), doyen of Czech pianists, at bringing out the quirky side of Janáček's writing. So the jagged little flurries of notes that bite away in contrast to the poetic lyricism of the opening are presented in sharper focus than with either Firkušný or Mikhail Rudy, an effect which directly echoes Janáček's orchestral writing. Here and throughout the disc Owen is helped by the clarity of the recording.

The qualities which distinguish Owen's performance of the sonata recur in the other works. Where Firkušný is regularly faster in a freely expressive style, and Rudy (on EMI) markedly slower, with *rubato* not always so idiomatic, Owen's middle way offers sharper focus and more refined dynamics. So his performances of the two series of miniatures which make up *On an Overgrown Path* reflect the composer's folk influences in their lyrical freshness, both in the songful pieces and the dances. In the four movements of *In the Mists*, Owen matches Firkušný in spontaneity; indeed, he gives an almost improvisatory feel to the suite. The tiny *Reminiscence*, a product from the year Janáček died, makes a moving supplement.

Glagolitic Mass

Glagolitic Mass[a]. Sinfonietta, Op 60[b]
Felicity Palmer sop **Ameral Gunson** mez **John Mitchinson** ten **Malcolm King** bass **Jane Parker-Smith** org [a]**City of Birmingham Chorus and Orchestra;** [b]**Philharmonia Orchestra / Sir Simon Rattle**

EMI Great Recordings of the Century 566980-2 (62' · DDD) Recorded 1980s. Text and translation included   Ⓜ**O**

'I am not an old man, and I am not a believer – until I see for myself.' Thus Janáček replied angrily to a critic after the première of his *Glagolitic Mass*. This is a gritty, masterful performance of a jagged, uncomfortable masterpiece. Its unusual title stems from the script of the ancient Slavonic text (*Glagol*) which Janáček set to music. Rattle's is a full-blooded, urgent view of the work, with particularly fine solo contributions from Felicity Palmer and John Mitchinson. That the language is an unfamiliar one is occasionally evident in the chorus, though they, like the orchestra, give totally committed performances under Rattle's inspired leadership. Also included on this disc is the *Sinfonietta*, which is as much a study in orchestration as form, with the melody of the fourth movement appearing unaltered no fewer than 14 times, changed only in orchestral colour. It's brilliantly played here, with the 12 trumpets coming up gleaming in the final climax.

Janáček (ed Wingfield) Glagolitic Mass (original version) Kodály Psalmus Hungaricus, Op 13[a]
Tina Kiberg sop **Randi Stene** contr **Peter Svensson** ten **Ulrik Cold** bass **Per Salo** org [a]**Copenhagen Boys' Choir; Danish National Radio Choir and Symphony Orchestra / Sir Charles Mackerras**
Chandos CHAN9310 (63' · DDD) Recorded 1994. Texts and translations included   Ⓕ**OO**

Mackerras's version of the *Glagolitic Mass* is of particular interest as it embodies one of the painstaking reconstructions of Janáček's original intentions in different works as his stature has drawn greater scholarly interest. This one was made by Paul Wingfield. Briefly, his restorations involve the playing of the Intrada at the beginning and the end, in the Introduction a very complex rhythmic pattern and in the 'Gospodi pomiluj' ('Kyrie') use of quintuple metre instead of the familiar four-in-a-bar (both far more effectively), and fierce timpani interjections in the wild organ solo. There are other points; but in any case, most interested listeners will care less for them in detail than for the heightened force and impact of the music. This it certainly now (or once again) has. These matters make it the more regrettable that, despite marvellous handling of the work by Mackerras, there are problems with a quartet of soloists that's less than exciting, and a recording that even with the most modern techniques can obscure the detail and clarity. This shouldn't detract from the interest of the disc, which every lover of the work will surely want to hear. Those who acquire it will have the additional benefit of a fine performance of Kodály's *Psalmus Hungaricus*, though the restored Mass is naturally the occasion here for recommendation and choice.

The Cunning Little Vixen

The Cunning Little Vixen. The Cunning Little Vixen – orchestral suite (arr V Talich)
Lucia Popp sop Vixen, Young vixen **Dalibor Jedlička** bass Forester **Eva Randová** mez Fox **Eva Zikmundová** mez Forester's wife, Owl **Vladimir Krejčik** ten Schoolmaster, Gnat **Richard Novák** ten Priest, Badger **Václav Zítek** bar Harašta **Beno Blachut** ten Pásek **Ivana Mixová** mez Pásek's wife, Woodpecker, Hen **Libuše Marová** contr Dog Gertrude Jahn mez Cock, Jay **Eva Hríbiková** sop Frantik **Zuzana Hudecová** sop Pepik **Peter Saray** treb Frog, Grasshopper **Miriam Ondrášková** sop Cricket **Vienna State Opera Chorus; Bratislava Children's Choir; Vienna Philharmonic Orchestra / Sir Charles Mackerras**
Decca ② 417 129-2DH2 (109' · DDD) Recorded 1981.
Notes, text and translation included   Ⓕ**OOO**

Janáček used the most unlikely mate-rial for his operas. For *The Cunning Little Vixen* his source was a series of newspaper drawings, with accompanying text, about the adventures of a vixen cub and her escape from the gamekeeper who raised her. The music is a fascinating blend of vocal and orchestral sound – at times ludicrously roman-tic, at others raw and violent. Mackerras's Czech training has given him a rare insight into Janáček's music, and he presents a version faith-ful to the composer's individual requirements. In the title-role, Lucia Popp gives full weight to the text while displaying all the richness and beauty of her voice. There's a well-chosen sup-porting cast of largely Czech singers, with the Vienna Philharmonic to add the ultimate touch of orchestral refinement. Decca's sound is of demonstration quality.

House of the Dead / Makropulos Affair

From the House of the Dead[a]. Mládí[b]. Nursery rhymes[c]
Dalibor Jedlička bar Goryanchikov **Jaroslava Janská** sop Alyeya **Jiří Zahradníček** ten Luka (Morosov) **Vladimir Krejčík** ten Tall Prisoner **Richard Novák** bass Short Prisoner **Antonín Svorc** bass-bar Commandant **Beno Blachut** ten Old Prisoner **Ivo Zídek** ten Skuratov **Jaroslav Souček** bar Chekunov, Prisoner acting Don Juan **Eva Zigmundová** mez Whore **Zdeněk Soušek** ten Shapkin, Kedril **Václav Zítek** bar Shishkov **Zdeněk Svehla** ten Cherevin, A Voice **Vienna State Opera Chorus; Vienna Philharmonic Orchestra / Sir Charles Mackerras;** [c]**London Sinfonietta Chorus;** [bc]**London Sinfonietta / David Atherton**
Decca ② 430 375-2DH2 (123' · DDD/ADD) Recorded 1980. Notes, texts and translations included Ⓕ**OOO**

The Makropulos Affair. Lachian Dances[a]
Elisabeth Söderström sop Emilia Marty **Peter Dvorský** ten Albert Gregor **Vladimir Krejšík** ten Vítek **Anna Czakova** mez Kristina **Václav Zítek** bar Jaroslav Prus **Zdeněk Svehla** ten Janek **Dalibor Jedlička** bass Kolenatý **Jiří Joran** bass Stage technician **Ivana Mixová** contr Cleaning woman **Beno Blachut** ten Hauk-Sendorf **Blanka Vitková** contr Chambermaid **Vienna State Opera Chorus; Vienna Philharmonic Orchestra / Sir Charles Mackerras;** a**London Philharmonic Orchestra / François Huybrechts**
Decca ② 430 372-2DH2 (118' · ADD) Recorded 1978.
Notes, text and translation included   Ⓕ**OOO**

From the House of the Dead (the 1980 *Gramophone* Record of the Year) was here recorded for the first time in its proper, original version; and this revealed it as even more of a masterpiece – a work, indeed, to count among the handful of masterpieces of 20th-century opera. The loss of the final cho-rus, a sentimental addition, is but the most strik-ing of the clarifications: throughout, the sound is sharper, the textures are sparer, and this serves to sharpen the effect and to give the singers more clearly differentiated support. The cast is led, nominally, by Goryanchikov, but the character isn't really the hero of an opera that has no heroes, and in which all are heroes, though Dalibor Jedlička sings him warmly and well. The prisoners are skilfully contrasted in Janáček's writing so as to make an apparently random yet actually well-structured group; there isn't a weak performance among them.

The Makropulos Affair does have a heroine, in the tragic figure of Emilia Marty; and here Elis-abeth Söderström gives one of her greatest recorded performances. She succeeds amaz-ingly in conveying the complexity of the charac-ter, the elegance yet flinty cynicism, the aloof-ness yet vulnerability, the latent warmth that can flower into such rich expressive phrases and then be reined in with a sense of nervy panic. She's only really alarmed by Prus, the most for-midable of the men around her, powerfully sung by Václav Zítek. Mackerras is again masterly. This is a recording to set among great perform-ances of it. As with *From the House of the Dead*, there's an essay by John Tyrrell that not only gives the listener the best possible introduction to the opera but is also a contribution to scholarship. The fill-ups, *Mládí* and the *Nursery rhyme*, come from David Atherton's splendid 1981 set of five LPs devoted to Janáček; the *Lachian Dances* set is a rather less successful companion to *Makropulos*.

Jenůfa

Jenůfa
Elisabeth Söderström sop Jenůfa **Wieslaw Ochman** ten Laca **Eva Randová** mez Kostelnička **Petr Dvorskü** ten Steva **Lucia Popp** sop Karolka **Marie Mrazová** contr Staŕenka **Václav Zitek** bar Stárek **Dalibor Jedlička** bass Rychtar **Ivana Mixová** mez Rychtarka **Vera Soukopová** mez Pastuchyňa, Tetka **Jindra Pokorná** mez Barena **Jana Janasová** sop Jano **Vienna State Opera Chorus; Vienna Philharmonic Orchestra / Sir Charles Mackerras**
Decca ② 414 483-2DH2 (130' · DDD) Recorded 1982 Ⓕ**OOO**

Janáček's first operatic masterpiece is a towering work, blending searing intensity with heart-stopping lyricism. It tells of Jenůfa and the appalling treatment she receives as she's caught between the man she loves and another who finally comes to love her. But dominating the story is the Kostelnička, a figure of enormous strength, pride and inner resource who rules Jenůfa's life and ultimately kills her baby. Randová's characterisation of the role of the Kostelnička is frightening in its intensity yet has a very human core. The two men are well cast and act as fine foils to Söderström's deeply impressive Jenůfa. The Vienna Philharmonic plays beautifully and Mackerras directs magnificently. The recording is all one could wish for and the booklet is a mine of informed scholarship.

Additional recommendations

Jenůfa (Brno version, 1908)

Mattila Jenůfa **Silvasti** Laca **Silja** Kostelnička **Hadley** Steva **Royal Opera House Orchestra / Haitink**

Erato ② 0927-45330-2 (139' · DDD) Recorded live 2001. Notes, libretto and translation included Ⓕ

Haitink may not topple the Mackerras version from its pedestal but it makes a deeply rewarding and valid alternative, especially collectable for Mattila's heroine and Silvasti's superlatively sung Laca.

Jenůfa (Brno version, 1908; sung in English)

Watson Jenůfa **Robson** Laca **Barstow** Kostelnička **Wedd** Števa **Welsh National Opera Chorus and Orchestra / Sir Charles Mackerras**

Chandos/Peter Moores Foundation Opera in English ② CHAN3106 (120' · DDD) Notes, libretto and translation included Ⓜ

A superb issue rivalling Mackerras's Award-winning Decca recording. If anything, the intense emotion comes over even more powerfully. For those who prefer opera in translation, this is the one to choose.

Kát'a Kabanová

Kát'a Kabanová. Capriccio[a]. Concertino[a]

Elisabeth Söderström sop Kát'a Kabanová **Petr Dvorsky** ten Boris **Naděžda Kniplová** contr Kabanicha **Vladimír Krejčík** ten Tichon **Libuše Márová** mez Varvara **Dalibor Jedlička** bass Dikoj **Zdeněk Svehla** ten Kudrjáš **Jaroslav Souček** bar Kuligin **Jitka Pavlová** sop Glaša **Gertrude Jahn** mez Fekluša **Vienna State Opera Chorus; Vienna Philharmonic Orchestra / Sir Charles Mackerras;** [a]**Paul Crossley** pf [a]**London Sinfonietta / David Atherton**

Decca ② 421 852-2DH2 (140' · ADD) Recorded 1976-8. Notes, text and translation included Ⓕ**OOO**

 Kátá, a free spirit, is imprisoned by marriage into, and domicile with, a family in a provincial Russian town on the Volga. The family is manipulated by her widowed mother-in-law. The only son (Kátá's

husband) is spineless, and Kátá looks for escape in love. She finds the love, but true escape only in suicide. Janáček focuses on his heroine, giving her at least two of the most moving scenes in opera: the first where, to music of shimmering, seraphic beauty she describes her childhood imagination given free rein by sunlight streaming through the dome in church; and the second in the last scene where, after confessing her adultery, she concludes that 'not even God's own sunlight' gives her pleasure any more. Söderström has the intelligence and a voice which guarantees total credibility; and of the superb all-Czech supporting cast one might only have wished for a slightly younger-sounding sister-in-law. Mackerras obtains the finest playing from the VPO; and Decca reproduces the whole with clarity, atmosphere, ideal perspectives and discernible stage movement – only a detectable levelling of the score's few extreme *fortissimos* points to the recording's vintage.

As a bonus, Decca adds the late chamber concertos, both excellently performed and engineered, and equally essential Janáček.

John Jenkins   English 1592-1678

A lutenist and lyra viol player, Jenkins was in London in 1634 and was appointed a court theorbo player in 1660. He lived with several East Anglian families, including Roger North's at Kirtling, Cambs. (1660-66), but was never officially attached to any. He was important for his consort music, notably for viols, which were widely popular among amateur players; his c 800 surviving pieces are pre-eminent in lyrical invention, structural organization and sonority. He had a command of the English virtuoso 'division' style. He composed both in the traditional many-voice consort style and in the new Italian three-part manner, often writing for treble, two basses and organ or two trebles and bass, moving towards a new violin-influenced phrase structure.
GROVEmusic

Consort music

19 Divisions on a Ground – Division in A. 12 Fantasias in six parts – No 3; No 8; No 5. Two Fantasia-Suites in two parts fantasia-air-corant – A minor. Eight Fantasia-Suites in four parts – No 3. Two In Nomines in six parts. Pavan and Galliard, 'Newarke Seidge'. Two Pavans in six parts – No 2. Galliard

Ensemble Jérôme Hantaï

(François Fernandez, Simon Heyerick vns Jérôme Hantaï, Kaori Uemura, Catherine Arnoux, Alix Verzier viols Brian Feehan lte Maude Gratton, Pierre Hantaï orgs)

Naïve Astrée E8895 (60' · DDD) Ⓕ

It's common enough to find recordings of Purcell or Byrd from Continental ensembles, but to have a distinguished group such as this playing a more insular figure like John Jenkins comes as something of a pleasant surprise. English composers of his generation have something very distinctive to offer, even though they may not score as highly as some of their Continental contemporaries in terms of historical eminence.

Jenkins's idiom isn't as angular as that of his contemporary William Lawes, though he can trade in 'those sourest sharps and uncouth flats' along with the best of them, and match Lawes' energy (as in the *Newark Siege*, one of the gems of this collection). The generous tone of Hantaï's ensemble (in which the continuo is an audibly well-nourished presence) lends the gentler pieces a warm glow. And when required, they certainly can play their socks off: the *Newark Siege* sees them switch from swashbuckling truculence to more melancholy repose at the end with barely a hint of changing gear.

This is chamber-music, and chamber music-making, of real distinction.

Josquin Desprez   French c1440-1521

Josquin was a singer at Milan Cathedral in 1459, remaining there until December 1472. By July 1474 he was one of the 'cantori di capella' in the chapel of Galeazzo Maria Sforza. Between 1476 and 1504 he passed into the service of Cardinal Ascanio Sforza, whom he probably accompanied in Rome in 1484. His name first appears among the papal chapel choir in 1486 and recurs sporadically; he had left the choir by 1501. In this Italian period Josquin reached artistic maturity.

He then went to France (he may also have done so while at the papal chapel) and probably served Louis XII's court. Although he may have had connections with the Ferrara court (through the Sforzas) in the 1480s and 1490s, no formal relationship with the court is known before 1503 when, for a year, he was maestro di cappella there and the highest-paid singer in the chapel's history. There he probably wrote primarily masses and motets. An outbreak of plague in 1503 forced the court to leave Ferrara (Josquin's place was taken by Obrecht, who fell victim in 1505). He was in the north again, at Notre Dame at Condé, in 1504; he may have been connected with Margaret of Austria's court, 1508-11. He died in 1521. Several portraits survive, one attributed to Leonardo da Vinci.

Josquin's works gradually became known throughout western Europe and were regarded as models by many composers and theorists. Petrucci's three books of his masses (1502-14) reflect contemporary esteem, as does Attaingnant's collection of his chansons (1550). Several laments were written on his death (including Gombert's elegy Musae Jovis), and as late as 1554 Jacquet of Mantua paid him tribute in a motet. He was praised by 16th-century literary figures (including Castiglione and Rabelais) and was Luther's favourite composer.

Josquin was the greatest composer of the high Renaissance, the most varied in invention and the most profound in expression. Much of his music can-

not be dated. Generally, however, his first period (up to c1485) is characterised by abstract, melismatic counterpoint in the manner of Ockeghem and by tenuous relationships between words and music. The middle period (to c1505) saw the development and perfection of the technique of pervasive imitation based on word-generated motifs. This style has been seen as a synthesis of two traditions: the northern polyphony of Dufay, Busnois and Ockeghem, in which he presumably had his earliest training, and the more chordal, harmonically orientated practice of Italy. In the final period the relationship between word and note becomes even closer and there is increasing emphasis on declamation and rhetorical expression within a style of the utmost economy.

His many motets span all three periods. One of the earliest, the four-part Victimae paschali laudes (1502), exemplifies his early style, with its dense texture, lack of imitation, patches of stagnant rhythm and rudimentary treatment of dissonance. Greater maturity is shown in Planxit autem David, in which homophonic and freely imitative passages alternate, and in Absalon, fili mi, with its flexible combination of textures. His later motets, such as In principio erat verbum, combine motivic intensity and melodic succinctness with formal clarity; they are either freely composed, four-part settings of biblical texts, or large-scale cantus firmus pieces. Transparent textures and duet writing are common.

Josquin's 18 complete masses combine elements of cantus firmus, parody and paraphrase techniques. One of the earliest, L'ami Baudichon, is a cantus firmus mass on a simple dance formula the simplicity of melody and rhythm and the clarity of harmony and texture recall the Burgundian style of the 1450s and 1460s. Fortuna desperata, on the other hand, is an early example of parody. Canonic writing and ostinato figures are features. His last great masses, notably the Missa de beata virgine and the Missa 'Pange lingua', were preceded by works in which every resource is deployed with bravura.

Josquin's secular music comprises three settings of Italian texts and numerous chansons. One of the earliest, Cela sans plus, typifies his observance of the formes fixes and the influences of the Burgundian styles of Busnois and Ockeghem. Later works, such as Mille regretz, are less canonic, the clear articulation of lines and points of imitation achieved by a carefully balanced hierarchy of cadences. Some, like Si j'ay perdu mon ami, look forward to the popular 'Parisian' chanson, of Janequin.   **GROVE**music

Masses

Missa L'homme armé sexti toni. Missa L'homme armé super voces musicales
A Sei Voci / Bernard Fabre-Garrus; Maîtrise des Pays de Loire / Bertrand Lemaire
Astrée Naïve E8809 (74' · DDD) Texts and translations included   Ⓕ**OO**

Josquin's Masses on *L'homme armé* have one of the most impressive recording pedigrees of the early Renaissance, but A Sei Voci's is probably the finest so far. There's superlative singing, a compelling, enveloping acoustic presence, and above all an interpretative logic, a sure-footed-ness of tempo and of phrasing that makes sense of some of Josquin's most prolix and demanding music. First comes *Sexti toni*, which is sung for the first time in the range that the sources' low clefs seem to imply. Where all the previous recordings have women on the top line (in a correspondingly higher tessitura), here it's taken by countertenors, supplemented on occasion by the children of the Maîtrise des Pays de Loire. The sunny, almost genial tone of previous recordings gives way to a quite unsuspected, darker and more interiorised but still luminous sound world.

The contrapuntal intensity of the final *Agnus Dei* is wonderful to hear, especially after the restrained scoring of much of what precedes it. Still more impressive, perhaps, is the performance of *Super voces musicales*, Josquin's most extended work, and certainly one of his most abstract and intellectually challenging. In the past, its very abstraction bred a suspicion that here was a work easier to admire than to love. Fabre-Garrus and his singers change all that: the intellectual toughness is still there, but in addition they make clear the Mass's rhetorical logic in a way that previous recordings never quite managed. Rarely has Josquin's achievement appeared so compelling. In short, this recording is a revelation.

Missa 'Malheur me bat'. Virgo prudentissima. Liber generationis Jesu Christi. Ave Maria…virgo serena. Baiséz moy. Que vous ma dame/In pace in idipsum. Victimae paschali laudes. Comment peult avoir joye
The Clerks' Group / Edward Wickham
ASV Gaudeamus CDGAU306 (71' · DDD) Texts and translation included   Ⓕ

The Clerks' Group once again earn our gratitude by heading straight for the top-class works that lack modern, top-class recordings. The Mass *Malheur me bat* is one of Josquin's most resourceful treatments of received material, taking all three voices of a secular piece and treating each separately, each in different ways; and in the magnificent final movement he follows an almost comical two-voice canon at the second with a broad treatment in six voices with two canons running simultaneously. As a display of contrapuntal techniques, this may well be his most stunning composition.

The Clerks' Group can seem less polished than previously. Intonation isn't always out of the top drawer. And the speeds chosen often seem perplexing, but on further listening, it seems that they're trying to tackle different musical problems; they're going for the music, and that has to be good.

This is particularly the case in the most welcome novelty here, the *Liber generationis*, Josquin's setting of the genealogy from St Matthew's gospel. How wonderful to have this and the other works here in seriously skilled performances.

Missa Pange lingua. Missa La sol fa re mi
The Tallis Scholars / Peter Phillips
Gimell CDGIM009 (62' · DDD) Recorded 1986
    ℗⦿⦿⦿

This is absolutely superb. We must accept that Josquin is unlikely to have heard this music with two women on the top line, but they do it so well that only a fundamentalist would mark the disc down for that. It should also be said that the least successful performance on the entire disc is in the opening *Kyrie* of this Mass where there's a certain brutality in the approach; and although The Tallis Scholars make much of the 'Benedictus' and the last *Agnus Dei*, there may still be better ways of doing it. On the other hand, as just one example among many, these were the first musicians to make the 'Osanna' truly successful and understand why Josquin should have chosen to compose it that way. But they sing even better in the Mass, *La sol fa re mi*. Again and again in the singing one has the feeling that Josquin's lines are projected with an understanding and clarity that have rarely been heard before. The *La sol fa re mi* of the title denotes (among other things) the melodic passage which appears over 200 times in the course of the work with its intervals unchanged – which may not seem a recipe for the kind of music one would want to hear. But Josquin treats his material with such astonishing sophistication that you're rarely aware of the melodic fragment as such; and Phillips is scrupulously careful never to emphasise the melody except in places – such as the end of the second 'Osanna' – where it's clearly intended to work as an ostinato. This performance shows that the *La sol fa re mi* belongs with the greatest works of its era.

Missa, 'Hercules Dux Ferrarie'. Salve regina. Miserere mei, Deus. Virgo salutiferi
De Labyrintho / Walter Testolin
Stradivarius STR33674 (60' · DDD · T)   Ⓕ

Josquin's Mass for Ercole, Duke of Ferrara, is one of his finest, and has received several good recordings. De Labyrintho's performance has a rhythmic fluidity that relieves the Mass's inflexibly four-square construction. This ensemble is one to watch out for: its blend is full and focused, yet softly rounded; and the individual voices (heard in the sections with reduced scoring) are of similar quality. Walter Testolin uses countertenors on the top line in the Mass, and women in the motets. Such decisions seem sensible in principle, and prove just as effective in practice. There is a pleasing variety of atmosphere: compare to the twilit first *Agnus dei* with the *Credo*'s robust conclusion.

The motets are anything but fillers; sufficiently contrasted to confirm the first impression of De Labyrintho's versatility. It's heartening to hear an Italian ensemble tackling Josquin so felicitously: after all, most of the music on this disc was composed in Ferrara.

Additional recommendation

Josquin Hercules Missa Dux Ferrariae. **Josquin, Gombert, Compère** Motets & chansons
Hilliard Ensemble
Virgin Veritas 562346-2 (118' · DDD)　　Ⓑ
The Hilliards take a different approach to the Mass from Labyrintho, and maintain a rugged emphasis on the tactus. A fine bargain.

Josquin Desprez Missa de beata virgine
Mouton Nesciens mater. Ave Maria virgo serena. Ave sanctissima Maria. O Maria piissima. Ave Maria gemma virginum
Theatre of Voices / Paul Hillier
Harmonia Mundi HMU90 7136 (53' · DDD) Recorded 1993. Texts and translations included　　Ⓕⵔ

Jean Mouton was a composer who, in the eyes of 16th-century musicians, most successfully challenged the peerless Josquin Desprez. So it was a good idea to assemble a programme that juxtaposes the two composers: for Josquin it's his most successful Mass; and for Mouton a group of motets on the same theme – varied, but all luscious and exhilarating. Effectively Paul Hillier divides up the Mass, as it would have been divided in a celebration, and puts Mouton's motets into the gaps. This works particularly well, the constant juxtaposition of the two similar yet contrasting styles clarifying one's perception of both composers. The music is also superbly performed. The 15 singers of the Theatre of Voices are effortlessly clear, wonderfully in tune and beautifully balanced. You hear the lines and spaces of Josquin just as you hear the immaculately modulated colours of Mouton; and that's partly because the singers have such good control of a range of vocal timbre. But beyond that there's an energy in the performances that keeps everything marvellously alive: even if you occasionally feel that Hillier takes the music a touch briskly, there's constant delight in the shapes that result. An issue of true distinction.

Missa Gaudeamus. Recordare virgo Mater. Regina caeli. Missa Ave maris stella: Virgo salutiferi/Ave Maria
A Sei Voci; Maîtrise des Pays de Loire / Bernard Fabre-Garrus bass
Auvidis Astrée E8612 (68' · DDD) Texts and translations included　　Ⓕ

Bernard Fabre-Garrus has long been experimenting with different ways of performing renaissance polyphony. It seems that each of his recordings offers a new sound; and in this particular case his novelty is to use the children of the Maîtrise des Pays de Loire – both boys and girls – to sing the top line of Josquin's Mass *Gaudeamus*. This is one of Josquin's most rhythmically intricate works, so there's a major challenge here; just occasionally the rhythms slip a little. But to compensate for that there's a stir-

ring energy to their singing; and part of the elegance of Fabre-Garrus performances has always been in his fluid, linear approach to polyphony, which works splendidly here. Moreover, with just six singers on the three lower lines, he always manages to produce a beautifully clear and balanced texture. This is a very successful and exciting performance of one of Josquin's most stunning masterpieces. His astonishingly varied treatment of the *Gaudeamus* melody ranges from straight imitation through unusually long-held tenor notes (that have a stunning effect on the work's harmonic rhythm), via bravura exercises in ostinato, to the heart-stopping modulations of the final *Agnus Dei*. The plainchants are sung with an unusual lucidity and energy. The motets include the rarely heard *Recordare virgo Mater*, which gives a special opportunity for the children to sing in three parts; and they end with a superlatively eloquent and clear performance of one of Josquin's most famous five-voice motets, *Virgo salutiferi*.

Songs and Instrumental Music

Master of Musicians – Songs and instrumental music by Josquin des Prez, and his pupils and contemporaries
Includes **Josquin** Adieu mes amours[b]. Bergerotte savoysienne[c]. Comment peult avoir joye. De tous biens pleine – à 3; à 4. Dido – Fama malum à 4[abcd]. Dulces exuviae à 4. El grillo[abcd]. Faulte d'argent[ab]. Je me complains[bc]. Mille regretz[abcd]. Pauper sum ego[d]. Petite camusette[ab]. Pleine de dueil[bc]. Se congié prens[ab] – Recordans de mia segnora; à 6. Si j'avoys Marion. Si j'ay perdu mon amy – à 3; à 4. Le villain. Also includes works by **Agricola, Alonso, Anon, Févin, Gerle, Isaac, Japart, Orto, Le Roy** and **Spinacino**
[a]**Belinda Sykes** contr [b]**John Potter** ten [c]**Jennie Cassidy** mez [d]**Robert Evans** bar **London Musica Antiqua** (John Bryan rec/crumhn/viol Alison Crum rec/crumhn/viol/hp Jacob Heringman viol/lte/gtr Roy Marks crumhn/viol Rebecca Miles rec) / **Philip Thorby**
Signum SIGCD025 (68' · DDD) Texts and translations included　　Ⓕⵔ

The secular music of Josquin has not always been very successful in recordings. Many of the pieces are very short – some can seem like exercises for something else, and others make little sense unless they're understood in the wider context of other settings based on the same material. The last problem is solved here by the inclusion of a lot of the related settings alongside those of Josquin. And the recording solves the first problem by unapologetically offering no fewer than 37 tracks, with the pieces grouped together so they flow cleanly from one to the next; it also resists some of the more outgoing pieces, so that the whole disc occupies a consistent sound world.

That sound world is mostly a gentle one, with the lines flowing quite fast in an easy playing style that can occasionally lose a few details but compensates with clarity of design. The musicians also cultivate a sound that favours vivacity and flair over constant attention to all the details of intonation; but that, too, is good, because everything is lively and full of variety. The instruments used range from viols and lutes to an ensemble of recorders and even one of crumhorns (played with an admirable restraint). And the singers offer all the variety of tone-colour one might expect from a group spear-headed by John Potter.

Many pieces here have never been recorded before; and the disc has the twin benefits of being remarkably accessible for easy listening as well as providing a marvellous basis for closer understanding. Most enjoyable.

tion. This is followed by a sinuous Armenian theme from the wind which the cello takes up ruminatively, with well-judged *espressivo*. Yet it's the energetic main theme that dominates and the soloist is carried along on its impetus, while ardently recalling the secondary material, finally leading to an exciting sequential coda. The finale offers the busy, rumbustious Khachaturian we know so well from the Violin Concerto. This composer's major works (with the exception of the Violin Concerto) can seem rather inflated, but here the combined concentration of Lidström and Ashkenazy minimises this impression. As an encore we're given a beautiful, restrained account of Rachmaninov's *Vocalise*. The recording is of high quality and well balanced, but a shade over-resonant, though the ear adjusts.

Dmitry Kabalevsky
Russian/USSR 1904-1987

Kabalevsky had a liberal education, wrote poetry and painted and showed promise as a pianist. The family moved to Moscow in 1918, where he studied the piano with Selyanov and from 1925 at the Moscow Conservatory with Catoire and Myaskovsky, the latter a formative influence; in 1932 he returned to teach at the conservatory (full professor from 1939). He was also involved in organisational and union activities, and worked in the music publishing house. The period 1932-41 was prolific, with much dramatic music (including the first version of his opera Colas Breugnon) and the first three symphonies. In the war years he turned to topical works on heroic patriotism. After the party decree of 1948 he worked towards a more lyrical idiom, as seen in his concertos of the ensuing years; later he worked in operetta and topical cantatas. Kabalevsky occupied an important role in Soviet music, as writer, spokesman on cultural policy, teacher and administrator as well as composer. GROVEmusic

Cello Concerto No 2

Kabalevsky Cello Concerto No 2 in G, Op 77
Khachaturian Cello Concerto **Rachmaninov** (trans Rose) Vocalise, Op 34 No 14
Mats Lidström vc Gothenburg Symphony Orchestra / **Vladimir Ashkenazy** pf
BIS CD719 (65' · DDD) Recorded live 1995   ⓕ

This coupling offers performances of two works which, if not masterpieces, are still sufficiently rewarding to be in the regular concert repertory. Ashkenazy creates an evocative opening atmosphere for the first movement of the Kabalevsky, when after mysterious string pizzicatos the soloist steals in with a gentle, singing tone. The soliloquy continues, for the work's unusual structure, with its three unbroken sections linked by cadenzas, invites an improvisational approach well understood by Mats Lidström. The Khachaturian Concerto opens with a flamboyantly coloured orchestral declamation before the cello sails off with vigorous anima-

Imre Kálmán
Hungarian 1882-1953

Kálmán studied with Koessler at the Budapest Academy. The success of his first operetta, The Gay Hussars (1908), led him to settle in Vienna, where he produced more such works in Viennese-Hungarian style (Die Csárdásfürstin, 1915; Gräfin Mariza, 1924). In 1939 he moved to Paris, and from there in 1940 to the USA. GROVEmusic

Die Csárdásfürstin

The Gypsy Princess **Yvonne Kenny** sop Sylva Varescu **Michael Roider** ten Edwin Ronald **Mojca Erdmann** sop Countess Stasi **Marko Kathol** ten Count Boni **Karl-Michael Ebner** ten Feri von Kerekes, Notary **Hellmuth Klumpp** spkr Rohnsdorff **Heinz Holecek** bar Prince **Yvonne Kálmán** spkr Princess
Plus orchestral excerpts from Der Zigeunerprimás, Die Faschingsfee, Das Hollandweibchen and Der Teufelsreiter
Slovak Philharmonic Chorus; Slovak Radio Symphony Orchestra / Richard Bonynge
Naxos ② 8 660105/6 ⟐ 6 110075-76
(114' · DDD · S/N)   Ⓢ**OO**

The English title of Kálmán's most celebrated operetta is a misnomer. The heroine is a princess not of gypsies but (as the German title, *Die Csárdásfürstin*, indicates) of the *csárdás*; she's a Budapest cabaret-singer in love with a young aristocrat. Its score shows Kálmán at his most fluent, with a succession of gloriously tuneful hit numbers that mix spicy Hungarian rhythms with the more graceful strains of the Viennese waltz. Individual numbers have often been committed to disc, but complete recordings have been much less frequent. Yet to appreciate the overall structure of Kálmán's operetta scores you really need to hear his elaborately constructed act finales, in which musical reprises are interspersed with passages of dialogue and melodrama.

Apart from sensibly reducing the opening orchestral flourishes from three to one, Bonynge typically gives us total fidelity to what Kálmán actually wrote. He brings out to the full Kálmán's highly charged rhythms, every detail of the exotic orchestration, and the contrasts of mood between the fiery big numbers and the moments of melancholy and sadness in the Acts 1 and 2 finales. Among a wholly admirable cast, Yvonne Kenny provides the vocal strength, fire and beauty required by the title role.

At the low Naxos price, this is a wonderful bargain.

Giya Kancheli

Georgian 1935

Kancheli studied at the Tbilisi Conservatory (1958-63), where he has taught since 1972. He is recognised as one of the most radical thinkers in Georgian music. His works, using folk music, include six symphonies (1967-81), jazz pieces and musicals.

GROVEmusic

Liturgy for Viola and Orchestra

Liturgy for Viola and Orchestra, 'Mourned by the Wind'. Bright Sorrow
Ian Ford, Oliver Hayes trebs **France Springuel** vc
Cantate Domino Chorus; I Fiamminghi / Rudolf Werthen
Telarc CD80455 (72' · DDD) Ⓕ●

Givi Ordzhonikidze, the editor of a well-known book on Shostakovich, was one of Kancheli's closest friends and staunchest supporters, and it was the sense of loss after his death in 1984 that prompted the composition of the heart-rendingly beautiful *Liturgy* (subtitled *Mourned by the Wind*). The other inspiration was Yuri Bashmet, for this four-movement lament was originally a Viola Concerto. It goes superbly on the cello too, thanks to France Springuel's passionate advocacy, and in this form it inevitably invites comparisons with Tavener's *The Protecting Veil*.

A common feature of these two pieces is that they can seem almost unbearably moving if they catch you in the right mood and yet almost unbearably protracted if they don't. Yet for all the obvious gestures of lamentation and assuaging, *Liturgy* isn't a tear-jerking piece. In fact the texture is for the most part quite transparent, and Kancheli constantly steers away from potentially manipulative clichés on to stonier paths.

The Flemish orchestra gives a wonderfully controlled performance and Telarc's recording quality is superb. *Bright Sorrow* again draws from the bottomless well of lamentation which is the ex-USSR composer's special curse and privilege. It bears the dedication, 'To children, the victims of war', hence the choice of two boy soloists, symbolising the innocent victims of the

last world war addressing themselves to the present-day generation. The soloists sing only slow, fragmented lines, conveying the fragility of innocence. The second half of the work seems to be gaining strength and optimism, but these are soon obliterated, leaving behind only a heart-broken crippled waltz.

Highly recommended, whether or not you already have the Kancheli 'bug'.

...à la Duduki

...à la Duduki. Trauerfarbenes Land
Vienna Radio Symphony Orchestra / Dennis Russell Davies
ECM New Series 457 850-2 (57' · DDD) Ⓕ●

...à la Duduki (a 'duduki' is a Georgian folk-reed instrument) should prove the ideal introduction to Kancheli's current style. And while a momentary encounter might suggest familiar territories revisited (vast terrains sparsely but dramatically populated), the musical material is more immediately striking, the scoring more texturally variegated, and the time sequences – even the rhetorical uses of silence – quite different from those in Kancheli's other recent work. Furthermore, echoes of modern jazz frequently fall within earshot. *Trauerfarbenes Land* ('Country the Colour of Mourning') employs a large orchestra and is different again, being nearly twice as long as *...à la Duduki* and darker in tone.

The opening has solo piano and *fortissimo* trombones hammer what sounds like a recollection of Carl Ruggles before six significant quavers (which turn up again later, in different hues and keys) mark a dramatic dynamic contrast. Time and again Kancheli's penchant for 'cliffhanger' climaxes bring us to the edge of a towering aural precipice. This is the music of personal displacement: desolate, spacious, occasionally cryptic, and with sudden pangs of sweetened nostalgia that flutter across the canvas like torn diary jottings tossed by the wind. Dennis Russell Davies and producer Manfred Eicher conjure between them a precision-tooled sound picture where every grade of nuance is meticulously reported. Performance standards are unusually high throughout, so much so that it's hard to imagine either work being better played. An exceptional release of some extraordinarily powerful music.

Lament

Lament (Music of mourning in memory of Luigi Nono)
Maacha Deubner sop **Gidon Kremer** vn
Tbilisi Symphony Orchestra / Jansug Kakhidze
ECM New Series 465 138-2 (42' · DDD) Text and translation included Ⓕ

Music of lamentation has long been Kancheli's preoccupation, and this *Lament*, inscribed to the memory of Luigi Nono, has all the familiar Kanchelian moods: damaged soulfulness, peremptory outbursts and transfigured sadness, invoked aphoristically yet stretched to a hypnotic unbroken 42-minute span. Initial dots of sound on the solo violin grow into painfully sweet bursts of melody, suggesting a context only the composer himself knows and which the listener has to grope towards. Meanwhile a non-vibrato singer intones prayerful fragments. Kremer's violin becomes an eloquent voice; Maacha Deubner's soprano becomes a celestial instrument. Just as you sense the need for new ideas, the orchestra's sculpted orchestral chords gain a pulverising force, and before long all hell breaks loose. The slight residual rawness of the Tbilisi brass is a treasurable authentic feature here, and the entire score is conducted faithfully by the man who knows Kancheli's music better than any musician alive. Eventually the text of Hans Sahl's poem, *Strophen*, reveals the under-lying substance. The recording is first-rate.

Nikolai Kapustin
Russian b1937

Kapustin, born in the Ukraine, graduated from the Moscow Conservatoire in 1961 and for some years made a living as a jazz pianist and arranger. His music is nearly all instrumental or orchestral, and is characterised by its use of jazz and rock idioms.

Piano Sonata No 6

Suite in the Old Style, Op 28. Eight Concert Etudes, Op 40. Variations, Op 41. Bagatelle, Op 59 No 9. Piano Sonata No 6, Op 62. Five Etudes in Different Intervals, Op 68. Sonatina, Op 100
Marc-André Hamelin pf
Hyperion CDA67433 (78' · DDD)   ⓅO

'Crossover' is an old rather than recent tradition, whether the jazz elements are peripheral as in Ravel or central as in Kapustin. Jed Distler, writing for Hamelin's disc in a style as witty and engaging as the music itself, speaks of a Chick Corea-based language that lifts a romantic virtuoso tradition into a beguiling quasi-improvisational style and holds it up to a fun-house mirror. Such high-pitched claims arguably fail to account for too many family likenesses (be they variations, studies or sonatas) or a style that too often suggests composition as a facile rather than arduous process (like Saint-Saëns, Kapustin 'produces music as an apple-tree produces apples'). Nonetheless, there are many scintillating surprises. The Variations' gawky theme blossoms into the sort of elaboration that would have made Bill Evans envious, while the second of the Op 40 Etudes ends with a passing memory of Liszt's *Au bord d'une source*, reminding you of Kapustin's work as a virtuoso pianist with Alexander Goldenweiser. No 6, *Pastoral*, a

dream encore, sends a tiny cell-like motif spinning through a variety of guises. The Bagatelle's perky tune would not be out of place 'in a Brazilian Chorino' (Distler) and everything on this remarkable disc is played with a nonchalant aplomb and magical dexterity hard to imagine from any other pianist. Hamelin is in his element, and he's been immaculately recorded.

Mieczysław Karłowicz
Polish 1876-1909

Trained as a violinist, he was active in the Warsaw Music Society and a strong supporter of the 'Young Poland' artistic movement, advocating the newest techniques in Polish orchestral music. Among his works are symphonic poems using thematic transformation and reflecting pantheism, sorrow and Wagnerian ideas of love and death, including Eternal Songs (1908) and StanisLaw i Anna Oswiecimowie (1912).   GROVEmusic

Eternal Songs

Eternal Songs, Op 10. Lithuanian Rhapsody, Op 11. Stanisław and Anna of Oświecim, Op 12
BBC Philharmonic Orchestra / Yan Pascal Tortelier
Chandos CHAN9986 (67' · DDD)   ⒻOOO

 What a fine composer Mieczysław Karłowicz might have become, had he not died at the age of 32 in an avalanche in the Tatra mountains. He had already produced a clutch of symphonic poems in a post-Wagnerian style, strongly pantheistic in outlook and, in the case of *Stanisław and Anna of Oświecim*, with a dash of illicit love thrown in. These luxuriant works set him broadly beside such near-contemporaries as Rachmaninov, Zemlinsky or Suk, and there are even signs in the 'Song of Eternal Being' (third and last of the *Eternal Songs*) of an individuality that might one day have become as powerful as Janáček's. This is, for the most part, sultrily ecstatic music, that hangs fragrantly or ominously in the air and seems to be constantly about to break through to some visionary realm. Even the relatively jaunty *Lithuanian Rhapsody* eventually turns wistful in a rather moving way.

If you've a taste for lush late-Romanticism but haven't yet encountered Karłowicz, you've a treat in store, not least because these are fine performances. His music has never been more than fleetingly represented in the catalogue. Back in 1990 there was a two-disc Chant du Monde compilation of the symphonic poems from the Silesian Philharmonic; but their courageous efforts are easily outclassed by the BBC Philharmonic and Yan Pascal Tortelier, as is the recording by Chandos's customary rich sound-stage.

Symphony in E minor, 'Rebirth', Op 7. Serenade in C,
Op 2. Bianca da Molena, Op 6
BBC Philharmonic Orchestra / Gianandrea Noseda
Chandos CHAN10171 (73' · DDD)   Ⓕ**O**

This second BBC Philharmonic Karłowicz disc complements the first with three earlier works. Composed in the first two years of the 20th century, Karłowicz's 40-minute *Rebirth* Symphony is very much of its time – not just in its ambitious programmatic span from existential despair to world-saving apotheosis, but in its opulent post-Tchaikovskian idiom. Though he clearly overreached himself, this is a need-to-know piece for anyone interested in the aspirational *Zeitgeist* prevalent before the First World War. Most immediately appealing, perhaps, is the slow movement, which features a tender song-like theme that British listeners may connect with the hymn 'My song is love unknown'.

The symphonic prologue *Bianca da Molena* is extracted from music for a now forgotten Polish play; not surprisingly it contains many echoes of Wagner. The Serenade for String Orchestra is an apprentice piece with a certain charm, notably in the vaguely *Parsifal*ian slow movement, which helps to compensate for the disappointment of the cursory finale.

The BBC Philharmonic's playing and Chandos's recording uphold their customary high standards.

Reinhard Keiser   German 1674-1739

Keiser wrote operas for Brunswick from c1693 and in 1694 became court chamber composer. From 1696-7 he was Kapellmeister at Hamburg, and from 1700-1701 also Kapellmeister to the Schwerin court. As joint director of the Hamburg Theater-am-Gänsemarkt, 1702-7, he presented 17 of his own operas. Der Carneval von Venedig (1707), which included local dialect, was especially successful. He remained active in Hamburg until 1718. After a period as a guest Kapellmeister at Stuttgart he served intermittently at Copenhagen. He was back in Hamburg by 1723 and in 1728 became Kantor of the cathedral. The Singspiel Der hochmüthige, gestürtzte und wieder erhabene Croesus (1730), a version of a 1710 opera, was among his last stage works.

Keiser was the central and most original figure in German Baroque opera, and wrote over 80 stage works. Most have serious German texts, which cover a wide range of subjects and often include allegorical or comic elements. They are notable for their dramatic flavour and skilful characterisation. Italian and French musical elements appear (including Italian arias from 1703), with dramatic recitatives and ariosos, varied aria forms and inventive instrumentation. His several Passions, oratorios and cantatas show similar features. Among his other works are sacred music and trio sonatas. Handel drew heavily on his works in his own. **GROVE**music

Croesus

Croesus
Roman Trekel *bar* Croesus; **Werner Güra** *ten* Atis; **Salomé Haller** *sop* Clerida; **Brigitte Eisenfeld** *sop* Trigesta; **Johannes Mannov** *bass* Cyrus; **Markus Schäfer** *ten* Eliates; **Dorothea Röschmann** *sop* Elmira; **Graham Pushee** *counterten* Halimacus; **Johanna Stojković** *sop* Nerillus; **Klaus Häger** *bass* Orsanes; **Kwangchul Youn** *bass* Solon; **Kurt Azesberger** *ten* Elcius; **Hanover Boys' Choir; Berlin RIAS Chamber Choir; Akademie für Alte Musik Berlin / René Jacobs**
Harmonia Mundi ③ HMC90 1714/6 (188' · DDD)
   Ⓕ**OOO**

Reinhard Keiser was principal opera composer at Hamburg's celebrated Theatre on the Goosemarket from 1697 to 1704 and from 1707 to 1718, returning intermittently, under Telemann's direction, between 1722 and 1735 when he retired after the death of his wife. During the first of these periods, a young man called Georg Friedrich Händel joined his theatre's orchestra and during his temporary absence composed three operas for the Goosemarket opera house, including *Almira* (1705) to a libretto set by Keiser.

Keiser's opera, given the catchy title *Die Unbeständigkeit weltlicher Ehre und Reichthums der hochmüthige/gestürzte/und wieder erhabene Croesus* ('The inconstancy of earthly glory and riches of the proud, deposed and rehabilitated Croesus') at its first performance in 1711, is called by the *New Grove* one of 'a handful of masterpieces' and René Jacobs concurs in his evangelising essay, 'Why Produce *Croesus* today?' printed in Harmonia Mundi's lavish booklet. The answer to Jacobs's question lies in the quality of the music, which will come as a delightful surprise to Baroque lovers.

The music itself is sheer bliss from first to last, and has a succession of variously characterised arias – the most exquisite are alloted to the heroine Elmira, ravishingly sung by Dorothea Röschmann, the most moving to the deposed Croesus (Roman Trekel) in his prison or facing his death in the flames of a sacrificial fire. The beauties of the work are manifold – the beginning of Act 2 is a pastoral scene in which peasants sing folksongs, and there's a delicious chorus for the peasant children extolling the joys of kissing lips as sweet as nuts. Suffice it so say that anyone who has enjoyed Handel's operas will be delighted by Keiser's.

The solo singing is uniformly first class, with eloquent performances from Trekel as Croesus, and from Werner Güra as his dumb son Atis, whose speech is restored by the shock of an assassination attempt on his father. Klaus Häger as Elmira's villainous, unwanted admirer is first-class, too. There are also vivid contributions from Graham Pushee, Salomé Haller and the performers of the two comic servants, Brigitte Eisenfeld and Kurt Azesberger. This is another outstanding Jacobs resurrection and a great Baroque operatic discovery too.

Albert Ketèlbey

British 1875-1959

Ketèlbey appeared as a solo pianist and conducted internationally. He was a popular composer of light orchestral pieces (In a Monastery Garden, 1915; In a Persian Market, 1920). GROVEmusic

In a Persian Market

In a Persian Market[a]. In a Monastery Garden[a] The Adventurers. Chal Romano Suite romantique. Caprice pianistique. The Clock and the Dresden Figures. Cockney Suite – No 3, At the Palais de Danse; No 5, Bank Holiday. In the Moonlight. Wedgwood Blue. Bells across the Meadows. Phantom melody.
[a]**Slovak Philharmonic Male Chorus; Bratislava Radio Symphony Orchestra / Adrian Leaper**
Marco Polo 8 223442 (74' · DDD) Recorded 1992 Ⓕ⦿

The obvious Ketèlbey favourites (*In a Monastery Garden, In a Persian Market, Bells across the Meadows*) are played with a grace and sensitivity that never invites unfavourable comparison with earlier recordings of the same pieces. If others in the same somewhat maudlin vein (*In the Mystic Land of Egypt, In a Chinese Temple Garden, Sanctuary of the Heart*) are missing, it's to give us the opportunity to hear some of his unjustly overshadowed compositions. And what delights there are! Over-exposure to Ketèlbey's more stereotyped, highly perfumed compositions has disguised what varied and inventive music he composed. Once you acquaint yourself with the charms of *The Clock and the Dresden Figures, In the Moonlight* and the invigorating open-air spirit of *Chal Romano*, you'll want to hear them again and again. With the playing, conducting and recording of a high standard, this is a collection that demands to be heard.

Aram Khachaturian

Russian/USSR 1903-1978

Khachaturian, a bookbinder's son, at first studied medicine; he received his musical education comparatively late, studying the cello and composition under Myaskovsky at the Moscow Conservatory (1929-37). He came to wider notice in 1936 with his Piano Concerto and his Violin Concerto (1940), and was active from 1937 in the Union of Soviet Composers. Most of his best-known works, including the ballet Gayane, date from the 1940s. In common with other Soviet composers, he was subject to official criticism in 1948; but his colourful, nationally tinged idiom was far removed from modernistic excess. He concentrated on film music in the ensuing years, and took up conducting and teaching (at the Gnesin Institute and the Conservatory).

His later works include 'concert rhapsodies' which re-interpret concerto form. His career represents the Soviet model of the linking of regional folklorism with the central Russian tradition; his Armenian heritage is clear in his melodies and his vitality, but in disciplined form. His greatest strengths lie in colourful orchestration and effective pictorialism. GROVEmusic

Flute Concerto

Ibert Flute Concerto[a]. Pièce **Khachaturian** Flute Concerto (transcribed from the Violin Concerto by J-P Rampal)[a]
Emmanuel Pahud *fl* [a]**Tonhalle Orchestra, Zurich / David Zinman**
EMI 557563-2 (64' · DDD) Ⓕ

Most flute concertos are lightweight, so it isn't surprising that flautists are keen to expand the repertory, adapting more ambitious works. That's how, on the suggestion of the composer himself, Jean-Pierre Rampal in 1968 came to prepare a brilliant transcription of Khachaturian's Violin Concerto. In the concert-hall a soft-grained flute can't cut through orchestral textures in the way a violin can, but on disc careful balancing has produced a successful result.

The flute naturally lacks the required incisiveness for the first subject, but there are obvious gains in the lyrical second subject: Emmanuel Pahud's gentle tone and fine shading bring out echoes of Dvořák in *New World* vein, where the violin had more of a gypsy flavour. Rampal and Pahud effectively replace the cadenza's double-stops with little arpeggiated flourishes, and surprisingly little seems changed. Better still is the slow movement, where Pahud's exquisitely hushed playing finds a mystery and tenderness in the hypnotic, Satie-like melody. In place of the finale's brilliant extroversion on the violin, Pahud's flute offers a cheeky lightness.

Ibert's unaccompanied *Pièce* makes an interlude between the concertos: a work which owes its easily improvisatory flow to Debussy's *Syrinx*. The Flute Concerto was written for Marcel Moyse in 1934; the finale's mix of 6/8 and 3/4 metres brings a sharp, jazzy flavour. What sets Pahud's performance apart is the depth of feeling he conveys in the slow movement: poignantly mysterious, with breathtaking *pianissimo*s matched by the strings of the Tonhalle Orchestra under David Zinman. The long, slow middle section in the finale, too, has a slinky quality, as in a *valse grise*. The recording is full and clear.

Piano Concerto

Piano Concerto. Dance Suite. Five Pieces for Wind Band – Waltz; Polka
Dora Serviarian-Kuhn *pf* **Armenian Philharmonic Orchestra / Loris Tjeknavorian**
ASV Platinum PLT8510 (59' · DDD) Ⓜ⦿

In the Piano Concerto Dora Serviarian-Kuhn and her Armenian compatriot, Loris Tjeknavorian, are in every way first-class: both identify naturally with the sinuous oriental flavour of the melodic lines and understand that the outer movements need above all to convey thrusting vitality; here there's plenty of drive and rhythmic lift. But what primarily makes this performance memorable is Serviarian-Kuhn's sense of fantasy, so that her various cadential passages, for all their brilliance, are charismatically quixotic rather than merely bravura displays.

The other works on the disc are small beer. The 'Waltz' for wind band has an engaging carousel flavour; the somewhat vulgar 'Polka' which follows roisterously suggests the circus. The *Dance Suite* goes through the usual Khachaturian routines with which he likes to clothe his agreeable but at times rather insubstantial Armenian folk ideas. Easily the most memorable movement is the first and much the longer of the two Uzbek dances, which opens gently and touchingly.

The performances here are excellent and vividly recorded.

Violin Concerto

Khachaturian Violin Concerto in D minor. **Sibelius** Violin Concerto in D minor, Op 47
Sergey Khachatryan vn **Sinfonia Varsovia /**
Emmanuel Krivine
Naïve V4959 (70' · DDD)   Ⓕ●

Sergey Khachatryan is among the most compelling players of his generation. Being the youngest-ever winner of the Sibelius Competition (2000) he was bound to record the Sibelius Concerto. Interestingly, his conductor, Emmanuel Krivine, had already recorded the work with a star player of a slightly older generation, Vadim Repin. Common to both is a mellow, fairly soft-core approach to the orchestral score, the new Sinfonia Varsovia recording, probably using a smaller band, warmer overall and with superior sound quality. Khachatryan's approach is smoother and more flexible, especially in the first movement's first cadenza, which he accelerates by stages, and the great leap that launches the second cadenza, which he edges into on a finely calculated *crescendo*. He moves around the score with comparative ease, always intense though with a mode of attack that stops short of roughness. His sound in the lower registers is rich and fulsome, yet even at *piano* or thereabouts, he still manages to sustain a full-bodied tone.

Similar qualities inform the Khachaturian Concerto with a crisp, lightly articulated opening and seductive handling of the first movement's second set. In the finale Khachatryan knows how to coax a workable ebb and flow, ease his tone, lighten tension to facilitate a change in musical current. Again, Krivine and his team are sympathetic collaborators for a highly commendable performance.

Khachaturian Violin Concerto **Glazunov** Violin Concerto **Prokofiev** Violin Concerto No 1
Julia Fischer vn **Russian National Orchestra /**

Yakov Kreizberg
Pentatone ⬚ PTC5186 059 (80' · DDD/DSD) Ⓕ●●

As Julia Fischer explains in the booklet-notes to this, her first CD, she has an abiding love of the Khachaturian Concerto, a work she found impossible to sell to concert-promoters. The freshness of her way with the Khachaturian is immediately striking in the chattering figuration of the opening, and she brings a rare tenderness to the lyrical second subject. The orchestral sound is impressive, too. Though Itzhak Perlman and Lydia Mordkovitch produce a beefier sound, the refinement of Fischer's performance makes it equally compelling. This concerto has claims to be the composer's finest work, claims which the yearning tenderness of the slow movement support. The clarity of Fischer's performance in the finale brings lightness and sparkle.

In the Glazunov, too, it's the clarity and subtlety of Fischer's playing that marks out her reading. She finds the tenderness of the slow middle section of this one-movement work, and gives an easy swing to the bouncy rhythms of the final section. In the Prokofiev she takes a meditative view of the wistful melodies, the element, she says, that most attracts her, even if she does not quite reach the depths of Kyung-Wha Chung's version.

A unique coupling, superbly recorded, that could hardly be more recommendable.

Gayaneh – Suite No 2

Khachaturian The Widow of Valencia – Suite. Gayaneh – Suite No 2 **Tjeknavorian** Danses fantastiques
Armenian Philharmonic Orchestra / Loris Tjeknavorian
ASV CDDCA884 (65' · DDD)   Ⓕ●

The Widow of Valencia is an early work (1940), yet already reveals the composer's fund of good tunes. He admitted its lack of authentic Spanishness, and though the 'Introduction' opens with flashing southern Mediterranean gusto, it soon makes way for a sultry Armenian melody of best local vintage. But why worry? Altogether this is a most winning suite, without a dull bar, piquantly scored and brilliantly presented by an orchestra that's completely at home and clearly enjoying themselves. They also give us another suite, comprising six indelible numbers – for the most part little known – from Khachaturian's masterpiece, *Gayaneh*. Tjeknavorian's own *Danses fantastiques* frequently burst with energy and the gentler dances have that Armenian flavour so familiar in *Gayaneh*. Brilliant playing in glittering yet spacious sound.

Spartacus

Spartacus – Ballet suites Nos 1-3
Royal Scottish National Orchestra / Neeme Järvi

Chandos CHAN8927 (63' · DDD) Recorded 1990 Ⓕ

Khachaturian's ballet, *Spartacus*, first produced in 1956, was a judicious and highly successful artistic response to the demands of Soviet populist realism. For its dramatic narrative of a Roman slave rebelling against his captors, eventually to be betrayed and killed, the composer created a score of striking vitality, at once full-blooded and crude, passionate and tuneful, and yet individual. The ballet's most famous number, the 'Adagio of Phrygia and Spartacus', is justly popular. Elsewhere there are many expressions of joyous extroversion and scenes of wild revelry, in which the music erupts with great energy, for example the 'Entrance of the Merchants' and the wild 'Dance of the Pirates', both in Suite No 2.

Järvi and his Scottish players respond exuberantly to the near vulgarity of the unbuttoned animation and revel in the lusher evocations. The resonant acoustics of the Henry Wood Hall, Glasgow, cast a rich ambient glow over Khachaturian's vivid primary colours. Recommended.

Oliver Knussen

British 1952

Knussen studied in London and with Schuller at Tanglewood. His works display a fine ear for complex textural blendings; they include three symphonies (1967, 1971, 1979) and the operas Where the Wild Things Are *(1983) and* Higglety Pigglety Pop! *(1985).* **GROVE**music

Orchestral Works

Whitman Settings, Op 25a[a][b]. Flourish with Fireworks, Op 22[a]. The Way to Castle Yonder, Op 21a[a]. Two Organa, Op 27[a]. Horn Concerto, Op 28[a][c]. Music for a Puppet Court, Op 11[a]. '...upon one note'[d]
[b]**Lucy Shelton** sop [d]**Michael Collins** cl [c]**Barry Tuckwell** hn [d]**Clio Gould** vn [d]**Paul Silverthorne** va [d]**Christopher van Kampen** vc [d]**John Constable** pf [a]**London Sinfonietta / Oliver Knussen**
DG 20/21 474 322-2GH (51' · DDD) Ⓕ

'Nothing is likely about masterpieces, least of all whether there will be any.' So Stravinsky is supposed to have remarked in a conversation with Robert Craft. None of the pieces on this disc lasts as much as a quarter of an hour, but several might just qualify. Is there a more scintillating concert-opener than Knussen's four-minute *Flourish with Fireworks*? Woven from ciphers based on the initials of Michael Tilson Thomas and the London Symphony Orchestra plus allusions to Stravinsky's own *Fireworks*, Op 4, it's brilliantly rendered here.

Oliver Knussen is – or ought to be – a national treasure. His idiom has loosened up just a little in recent years, but he still offers plenty to satisfy the obsessive analyst, while presenting a field day to sonic sensualists. Not that he's ever

exactly easy listening. There are almost always lots of notes, great flashing skirls of them, and when they aren't there, as in the Purcell fantasia '...*upon one note*' that concludes this disc, you may even feel short-changed.

In his original review Michael Oliver had doubts only about the post-Expressionist vocal writing in the Whitman settings. It's this aspect of the modernist inheritance that's most likely to irk non-specialists. Lucy Shelton copes manfully with Knussen's demands even so, and the orchestral sounds are magical. If you missed this superb collection first time round, you have no excuse now: it has been attractively repackaged and comes with full annotations.

Where the Wild Things Are

Higglety Pigglety Pop!
Cynthia Buchan mez Jennie **Lisa Saffer** sop Potted Plant, Baby, Mother Goose **Rosemary Hardy** sop Rhoda, Voice of Baby's Mother **Christopher Gillett** ten Cat-Milkman, High voice of Ash-tree **David Wilson-Johnson** bass-bar Pig-in-Sandwich Boards, Low voice of Ash-tree **Stephen Richardson** bass-bar Lion

Where the Wild Things Are
Lisa Saffer sop Max **Christopher Gillett** ten Wild Thing with Beard, Goat Wild Thing **David Wilson-Johnson** bass-bar Rooster Wild Thing **Stephen Richardson** bass-bar Bull Wild Thing **Mary King** mez Mama, Tzippy **Quentin Hayes** bass Wild Thing with Horns **London Sinfonietta / Oliver Knussen**
DG 20/21 ② 469 556-2GH2 (102' · DDD) Notes and texts included ⒻO

The stories and drawings of Maurice Sendak upon which both these operas are based explore a vein of surreal dreaming and of the delight that children take in both fantasy and disorder, and all these things appeal to something close to the centre of Oliver Knussen's creativity. An obvious model for both operas is Ravel's *L'enfant et les sortilèges*, and Knussen shares Ravel's pleasure in mechanisms that work immaculately well. He also has much of Ravel's mastery of orchestration, and one of the most enjoyable aspects of both scores is their kaleidoscopic sequence of brilliantly imagined and faultlessly executed instrumental textures.

Knussen's music reveals profundities and a childlike awe in Sendak that you might not have expected. The Ash-tree in *Higglety Pigglety Pop!*, for example, is at one level a straightforward comic character ('You are taller than I am', says the Sealyham terrier Jennie; 'Sixty feet taller, to be precise', replies the tree, primly), but Knussen's setting of its words for two singers, tenor and bass, and his evocative orchestra make of it a magic voice of nature as well. The Lion in the same opera is a relative of the amiable beast in *The Wizard of Oz*, but at the same time formidable. Knussen's Wild Things, roaring gibberish, are anarchically comic and their 'Wild Rumpus' hugely inventive fun, but they have also the musical equivalent of the pointed teeth and glaring yellow eyes that Sendak gave them; and something of pathos when the child Max leaves them on their island. In the best sense both of these operas are for children of all ages, or indeed for any listener who's inclined to respond to wonder, humour and meticulous intricacy.

Both recordings were made following staged performances, and have benefited from it: the singers, all first class, are audibly enjoying themselves, and the orchestra takes no less obvious pleasure in Knussen's magical sounds.

Additional recommendation

Songs without Voices, Op 26. Whitman Settings, Op 25. Hums and Songs of Winnie-the-Pooh, Op 6. Variations, Op 24. Four Late Poems and an Epigraph of Rainer Maria Rilke, Op 23. Sonya's Lullaby, Op 16. Océan de terre, Op 10

Shelton, Shaffer sops **Serkin** pf **Chamber Music Society of Lincoln Center / Knussen**
EMI British Composers 575296-2 (DDD) Recorded 1970-92   Ⓑ

An authoritative survey and perfect introduction to the work of Oliver Knussen at budget price.

Zoltán Kodály   Hungarian 1882-1967

Kodály was brought up in the country; he knew folk music from childhood and also learnt to play the piano and string instruments, and to compose, all with little tuition. In 1900 he went to Budapest to study with Koessler at the Academy of Music, and in 1905 he began his collaboration with Bartók, collecting and transcribing folksongs. They also worked side by side as composers, and Kodály's visit in 1907 to Paris, bringing back Debussy's music, was important to them both: their first quartets were played in companion concerts in 1910, marking the emergence of 20th-century Hungarian music.

Kodály, however, preferred to accept rather than analyse folk material in his music, and his style is much less contrapuntal and smoother harmonically. His major works, notably the comic opera Háry János, *the* Psalmus hungaricus *and the 'Peacock' Variations for orchestra and the Dances of Marosszék and Galánta draw on Magyar folk music (unlike Bartók, he confined himself to Hungarian material). His collecting activity also stimulated his work on musical education, convincing him of the value of choral singing as a way to musical literacy. He taught at the Budapest Academy from 1907, and after World War Two his ideas became the basis of state policy, backed in part by his own large output of choral music, much of it for children, as well as other exercise pieces, and was widely used as a model abroad.*
GROVEmusic

Symphony in C

Symphony in C. Summer Evening. Magyar Rondo
Christopher Warren-Green vn **Philharmonia**

Orchestra / Yondani Butt
ASV CDDCA924 (54' · DDD) Recorded 1994   Ⓕ

Kodály's only Symphony has an engagingly pastoral quality, with mild but memorable thematic material, lively – even somewhat overwrought – musical arguments and notably scenic orchestration. Yondani Butt presents a volatile view of the piece, with weighty textures and a fairly intense delivery, especially in the first movement's emphatic development section. The slow movement, an elegiac *Andante* based on folk-style motives, is appealingly atmospheric, while the fresh-faced finale generates plenty of rustic excitement. *Summer Evening* underlines the music's alternation of dance and reverie, whereas Butt's invigorating performance of the rarely heard but strangely more-ish *Magyar Rondo* (shades of Bartók's *Romanian Folk Dances*) has the Philharmonia playing like a generously augmented gipsy band, with stylish solo work from Christopher Warren-Green. Enthusiasm and sincerity are much in evidence throughout this well-recorded concert, while the odd spot of executive ruggedness is fairly appropriate to the music's outdoor character.

Dances from Galánta

Dances from Galánta[a]. Dances of Marosszék[a]. Háry János[a] – concert suite; The Flute-Playing Hussar; The Old Woman; The Jewish family; Háry riding Lucifer; The two gipsies. Dancing Song[b]. St Gregory's Day[c]. See the gipsies[b]
[b]**Budapest Children's Choir Magnificat;**
[c]**Kecskemét Children's Choir Miraculum;**
[a]**Budapest Festival Orchestra / Iván Fischer**
Philips 462 824-2PH (66' · DDD) Texts and translations included   ⒻOO

Iván Fischer and his Hungarian band join the most august company in this wonderful repertoire. As both sets of dances amply demonstrate, Fischer's Budapest Festival Orchestra is no less virtuosic than Ormandy's dazzling Philadelphians or Ferenc Fricsay's exemplary Berlin RSO, and its impassioned playing melds an earthy physicality, tangy exuberance and improvisatory flair to consistently telling effect. Add to the mix Fischer's wittily observant direction (an abundance of affectionate *rubato* in the opening section of the *Marosszék Dances* especially, allied to a generous quotient of 'gypsy' slides from the strings elsewhere), and the results are irresistible. Similarly, their *Háry János* Suite is immensely engaging. After a spectacularly good introductory 'sneeze', Fischer sees to it that Kodály's great arcs of melody are truly *espressivo cantabile* as marked. Napoleon's battlefield antics are hilariously depicted (splendidly bolshy trombones), while Fischer's thrusting 'Intermezzo' has joyous swagger. Moreover, for all the giddy festivities of the brassy 'Entrance of the Emperor and his Court', Fischer still manages to extract plenty of ear-burning detail. Five miniatures from the original *Singspiel* are also included, programmed separately from the suite; in 'The two gypsies' Fischer shares fiddling duties with Gábor Takács-Nagy. Last but not least we get three choral offerings from 1925-9, which are delivered with captivating freshness and charm by the two admirable children's choirs here.

A peach of an issue, complemented by an irrepressibly vivid recording.

Cello Sonatas

Solo Cello Sonata, Op 8. Cello Sonata, Op 4. Three Chorale Preludes (after Bach)
Maria Kliegel vc **Jenö Jandó** pf
Naxos 8 553160 (64' · DDD) Recorded 1994-5 ⑤❶

Maria Kliegel rises to the challenge of Kodály's Solo Sonata with considerable gusto: harmonics, *glissandos*, *sul ponticello*, fiery arpeggios – all are expertly employed and delivered via a nicely rounded tone. Kliegel's lustrous account of the *Adagio* underlines harmonic similarities with late Liszt and the folky, one-man-band finale has ample panache. The appreciative booklet-note relates Bartók's enthusiasm for the Solo Sonata's 'unusual and original style…[and] surprising vocal effects'. In fact, no other work by Kodály is so profoundly Bartókian in spirit. The Sonata, Op 4, is a far milder piece, though forthright expressive declamation sits at the centre of the first movement and the second is infused with the spirit of folk music. Kliegel and Jenö Jandó are in musical accord, and the recording is very good – although if you listen to the 'Bach-Kodály' tracks and wait for the Solo Sonata to start, you'll note a huge expansion in the cello's recorded profile. The three *Chorale Preludes* that open the programme are 'attributed Bach' and enjoy the rich trimmings of a thunderous piano part (Busoni-cum-Liszt, with a snatch of Bartók for good measure) and a warm flood of tone from Kliegel.

Solo Cello Sonata, Op 8. Cello Sonata, Op 4[a].
Adagio[a]. Sonatina[a]
Sung-Won Yang vc [a]**Ick-Choo Moon** pf
EMI Debut 575685-2 (67' · DDD) ⑧❍❍

These two Korean artists are clearly seasoned performers, approaching their interpretive task with the sort of confidence and certainty that only comes from considerable experience.

Sung-Won Yang, who studied in Paris and in the US, produces a notably rich, expressive tone, ideal for the Solo Sonata's extensive explorations of the lower register – the opening of the *Adagio* sounds magnificently dark and resonant. It's obvious that he and Ick-Choo Moon feel a strong affinity with Kodály, and perform his long, arching melodies with a fine sense of line and of rising and falling tension. And they have no trouble in finding just the right Hungarian idiom, whether for the florid rhetorical outbursts that open the Solo Sonata and (on the

piano) the Sonatina, or for the dance styles that predominate in the finales of both sonatas.

The whole programme is indeed very finely and sympathetically played, but the major achievement has to be the Solo Sonata. It takes a player of Sung-Won Yang's technical brilliance and expressive boldness to make one feel the work's full grandeur. 'One of the greatest masterpieces', asserts Yang. As you listen, you're inclined to agree.

Kodály Solo Cello Sonata, Op 8. Cello Sonata, Op 4[a]
Novák Cello Sonata, Op 68[a]
Jiří Bárta vc [a]**Jan Cech** pf
Supraphon SU3515-2 (73' · DDD) Ⓕ

Kodály's Solo Cello Sonata is among the strongest, most searching of all his works, arguably the finest of all works for unaccompanied cello since Bach's suites, and here it receives a performance of exceptional power, precision and clarity from Jiří Bárta. His command in tackling the most formidable of technical problems means that he's able to keep a steady tempo and clarify textures with clean attack on double stopping, all seemingly without strain. Yet the intensity of his performance never flags, with a rare depth of concentration in the dark central *Adagio*. In the folk-dance rhythms of the *Allegro* finale he's volatile and thrusting, again using a formidable dynamic range that's well caught by the recording.

The same goes for the accompanied Cello Sonata. Bárta is well-matched by his pianist, Jan Cech: they make light of the problems presented by the many tempo changes in both movements, an opening Fantasia and a weighty finale, by giving an improvisatory feel. The folk element is heightened by an element of rawness, with the players striking sparks off each other.

The Supraphon disc has a substantial supplement in one of Vitezslav Novák's late works, a Cello Sonata. Written in 1941 during the Nazi occupation of Czechoslovakia, it represented an eruption of hatred against the invaders. Though it may not quite match the two Kodály works in emotional power, the passionate character of this closely argued single movement – bringing together elements of a multi-movement sonata structure – is most impressive, particularly in a performance as commanding as this.

Kodály Cello Sonata, Op 4 Janáček Pohádka Liszt Elégies – No 1, S130; No 2, S131. La lugubre gondola, S134
Anne Gastinel vc **Pierre-Laurent Aimard** pf
Astrée Naïve V4748 (50' · DDD) Ⓕ

This is an imaginative piece of programme planning, with arrangements of Liszt's *Elégies* and *La lugubre gondola* separated by Kodály's Sonata and Janáček's *Pohádka*. Liszt, writing in the 1870s and early 1880s, sounds as modern as either of the composers writing in 1910; indeed, there's much in his augmented-chord harmony and his fondness for unusual scales that influenced Kodály, while Janáček also admired him and used his religious music for teaching. This is Romantic music outside the mainstream of European musical romanticism. Gastinel and Aimard give performances as intelligent as these juxtapositions suggest, oblique and dark in the linking figure of Liszt, especially with *La lugubre gondola*, one of the most extraordinary late piano pieces. Kodály's sonata is played with a quiet intensity, rhapsodic in manner but strongly held together by the clarity of emphasis on the motto theme and its musical implications. Janáček's pieces can sound sharper and quirkier than here, and in such performances make their point more strongly; but this playing is of a piece with the whole approach. Gastinel has a clean, resinous tone, and a strong sense of line; she's well partnered by Aimard, and the recording is balanced.

Missa brevis

Kodály Laudes organi. Missa brevis **Janáček** (ed Wingfield) Mass in E flat
Andrew Reid org **Westminster Cathedral Choir / James O'Donnell**
Hyperion CDA67147 (73' · DDD) Texts and translations included   Ⓕ**OO**

Janáček began his Mass around 1908, left it to gather dust for 20 years, then turned it into the first draft of the *Glagolitic Mass*. Paul Wingfield's reconstruction draws substantially on the original draft of the *Glagolitic Mass* to the extent of including a complete movement (the *Sanctus*) from it. Clearly Janáček knew best, and the only distinguishing moments are those bits recognisably from the *Glagolitic Mass*. Unquestionably, though, both the *Missa brevis* and *Laudes organi* are among Kodály's most inspired creations. Yet new recordings of favourite works are prone to disappoint. Not this one. If anything, this stunning performance, crowned by Andrew Reid's masterly organ playing, raises this setting of dog-Latin verses in praise of the organ and commissioned by the American Guild of Organists even higher. About 20 years before *Laudes organi*, the *Missa brevis* was first performed in this version for organ and chorus (it was originally an organ solo) in a bomb shelter during the 1944-5 Siege of Budapest. From such an inauspicious start, the work has fared remarkably well on record and this release represents an undoubted climax. It's a simply glorious performance and, in short, should not be missed.

Charles Koechlin
French 1867-1950

Koechlin studied with Massenet, Gédalge and Fauré at the Paris Conservatoire from 1890 and was associated with such contemporaries as Ravel, Schmitt

and Debussy (whose Khamma he largely orchestrated in 1913). As a public figure he soon became noted more for his writings on music and for his teaching (Milhaud and Poulenc were pupils) than for his composing, which at all periods was prolific. His output is enormous: there are over 200 works with opus numbers, many of them big symphonic, choral or chamber pieces. His symphonic poem Les bandar-log (1939), one of seven works based on the Jungle Book stories, shows his knowledgeable and sometimes satirical view of a wide range of contemporary musical languages, as does his Seven Stars' Symphony (1933), a portrait gallery of the contemporary cinema. Other works include symphonic poems, choral works, songs and instrumental sonatas, as well as numerous small pieces for diverse combinations. Some reflect his communist sympathies, some are polytonal, some influenced by his love of Bach. His uncompromising and unworldly nature contributed to his unjust neglect. GROVEmusic

Orchestral Works

La course de printemps, Op 95ᵃ. Le buisson ardent, Opp 171 & 203ᵇ
Stuttgart Radio Symphony Orch / Heinz Holliger
Hänssler Classic Faszination Musik 93 045
(73' · DDD) Recorded live ᵃ2000, ᵇ2001   Ⓕ**OO**

The influence of Rudyard Kipling's *Jungle Book* on Koechlin was profound and *La course de printemps*, which gestated over a very long period, was the finest of the tone poems he gathered together under the composite title *Le livre de la jungle*. Although the events depicted are certainly connected with the character and life of Mowgli, the music itself is above all evocative of the jungle itself, its exotically humid atmosphere and unpredictable bursts of violence and animal energy. The underlying sinister ambience is balanced by a Ravelian sensuality (there's even is a hint of *Daphnis* in the dawn evocation of the opening), while the mysteriously gentle but lustrous string monody which closes the work is other-worldly in its vision of a voluptuous moonlit spring night. Koechlin's scoring is headily brilliant and one is engulfed in its rich panoply, so that for all the music's ecclecticism, it has a life and individuality of its own.

Le buisson ardent makes an ideal coupling. An evocation of rebirth – at times passionately intense in the strings, but with the ondes martenot later used to represent the ethereal voice of the reborn spirit. The work climaxes with a lusciously positive affirmation, but closes gently and rapturously. Heinz Holliger, justly famous as oboist, shows himself equally sensitive with the baton, inspiring a splendid orchestral response from the Stuttgart players (especially the strings). They in turn are served by a first-class recording. A superb introduction to Koechlin's exotic sound-world.

Vers la voûte étoilée. Le Docteur Fabricius
Christine Simonin onde **Stuttgart Radio Symphony Orchestra / Heinz Holliger**

Hänssler Classic 93 106 (64' · DDD) Ⓕ

Much of Koechlin's highly individual orchestral music remains unexplored: indeed, both works here are premiere recordings. Before he became a composer, Koechlin wanted to be an astronomer and his fascination with the 'starry firmament', and the dream-world it evoked, is sensuously created in the arch-like structure of *Vers la voûte étoilée* ('Towards the vault of stars'). Written in the early 1920s and revised in 1939, this demonstrates the composer's exotic sound-world in a nocturnal piece that doesn't outstay its welcome.

The stars in the heavens return in *Le Docteur Fabricius*, written 1941-4, a more ambitious, large-scale symphonic poem with a philosophical underlay, based on a short story by the composer's uncle. The narrative describes a visit to the mysterious house in which the nihilistic Doctor Fabricius has cut himself off from the world. After an austere opening, dolorous chorales symbolise the philosophical disillusion, interrupted by a strident, fugal revolt and interwoven with moments of sadness. A powerfully scored chorale suggests that human hope always re-emerges. The visitor looks out to the starry firmament (the ondes martenot-rich scoring suggests Messiaen) and then, in a passage of radiant exultation, the spirit of Ravel hovers over the music to evoke the consolation of Nature. After an explosion of joy the music returns to the serene, withdrawn evocation of the opening.

Koechlin's powers as an orchestrator ensure his vision is powerfully communicated. Heinz Holliger is very much at home here, and the Stuttgart Radio orchestra play most responsively. The recording is full and atmospheric, though one ideally needs a more voluptuous ambience. But this is well worth trying.

Erich Wolfgang Korngold
Austro/Hungarian 1897-1957

Korngold, an American composer of Austro-Hungarian origin, was the son of the music critic Julius Korngold (1860-1945). He studied with Zemlinsky and had spectacular early successes with his ballet Der Schneemann (1910, Vienna) and operas Violanta (1916) and Die tote Stadt (1920). In 1934 he went to Hollywood and wrote some fine film scores. After World War II he wrote orchestral and chamber pieces, including a Violin Concerto and Symphony in F sharp, in a lush, Romantic style.
GROVEmusic

Violin Concerto

Korngold Violin Concerto[a]. **Rózsa** Violin Ⓗ
Concerto, Op 24[b]. Tema con variazioni,
Op 29a[b].**Waxman** Fantasy on Bizet's 'Carmen'[c].
Jascha Heifetz *vn* **Gregor Piatigorsky** *vc*
[b]**Chamber Orchestra;** [a]**Los Angeles Philharmonic**

Orchestra / **Alfred Wallenstein;** [b]**Dallas Symphony Orchestra / Walter Hendl;** [c]**RCA Victor Symphony Orchestra / Donald Voorhees**
RCA Victor Gold Seal [ac]mono/[b]stereo
09026 61752-2 (70' · ADD) Recorded 1946-63 Ⓜⓞ

Heifetz's legendary recording of the Korngold Concerto serves a double purpose: as an effective introduction to Korngold's seductive musical style, and as the best possible example of Heifetz's violin artistry. The work itself was written at the suggestion of Bronislaw Huberman, but it was Heifetz who gave the première in 1947. It calls on material that Korngold had also used in three of his film scores, although the way he welds the themes into a three-movement structure is masterly enough to suggest that the concerto came to him 'of a piece'. The very opening would be enough to seduce most listeners. Miklós Rózsa's Concerto has its roots in the composer's Hungarian soil, and echoes of Bartók are rarely absent. But whereas Korngold's score is taken from movie music, Rózsa's (or parts of it) became a film score – namely, *The Private Life of Sherlock Holmes*. Rózsa's self-possessed, skilfully written *Tema con variazoni* was taken, in 1962, from a much larger work then in progress, but Heifetz and Piatigorsky play it in a reduced orchestration. As to the *Carmen Fantasy* by Franz Waxman (another notable film composer), its luscious tunes and frightening technical challenges were written with the great violinist in mind. It's a stunning piece of playing, and wears its years lightly. The other recordings sound far better, and the Rózsa items are in stereo.

Additional recommendation

Coupled with: **Korngold** Much Ado about Nothing – Maiden in the Bridal Chamber; Dogberry and Verges; Intermezzo; Hornpipe **Barber** Violin Concerto, Op 14
Shaham *vn* **LSO / Previn** *pf*
DG 439 886-2GH (71' · DDD) Ⓕ
Shaham is yearningly warm without being sentimental, and clean and precise in attack. The suite from *Much Ado About Nothing* provides a delightful makeweight.

Film Music

The Sea Hawk (excerpts). The Prince and the Pauper (excs). The Private Lives of Elizabeth and Essex (excs). Captain Blood (excs). (Scores reconstructed and assembled by Patrick Russ)
London Symphony Orchestra / André Previn
DG 471 347-2GH (68' · DDD) Ⓕⓞ

Erich Korngold was the pioneer composer of the Hollywood film score during the 1930s and 40s. Errol Flynn starred in the films whose scores are featured on this CD, playing assorted dashing heroes swashbuckling their way through four slices of English history.

The line-up assembled here could not be bettered. Previn knows just how this music should go while the LSO bring the prerequisite pizzazz and élan that the music needs to take wing. The dexterity with which they negotiate the heavily scored cue 'Duel Continued' from *The Sea Hawk* (track 8) would prompt anyone to give a spontaneous round of applause.

The brilliant panoply of brass and strings that opens *The Sea Hawk* at once denotes these as 'action' films, but Previn's way with the music isn't to let the mood be dictated by the 'separate card' by which each moment in the credits was given a specific number of seconds on the screen. So the broad string theme of *The Sea Hawk* unfolds with a symphonic breadth akin to that majestic opening of Vaughan Williams's *A Sea Symphony*. In *The Prince and the Pauper* the LSO respond in true Romantic style to Korngold's luxuriant expansion of his material, and it comes across in this most affectionate performance as Korngold's finest cinematic achievement. A marvellous recording sets the seal on a definitive account of this splendid music.

Suite, Op 23

Suite, Op 23. Piano Quintet in E, Op 15
Claire McFarlane, Jan Peter Schmolck vns **Schubert Ensemble of London** (Simon Blendis vn Douglas Paterson va Jane Salmon vc William Howard pf)
ASV CDDCA1047 (69' · DDD)   Ⓕ

This supremely stylish interpretation of the Op 23 Suite (1930) has much to commend it, occupying a satisfying middle ground between the Czech Trio's endearingly homely view and the far more grandly virtuoso approach espoused by Sony's starry team. Not for the first time on disc, William Howard's superior brand of pianism is a real boon, and the whole performance radiates an affection and gentle purposefulness that are genuinely appealing. Anyway, Korngoldians will surely want to acquire this ASV coupling for the marvellous Piano Quintet, which here receives a reading that marries refreshing spontaneity to notable architectural elegance. Dating from 1921 and composed just after *Die tote Stadt*, it's an exuberantly confident offering cast in three movements. These artists audibly revel in Korngold's taxing, yet sumptuously rewarding writing, and the recording is handsome and true.

Suite, Op 23. Piano Trio in D, Op 1
Jana Vlachová vn **Czech Piano Trio** (Dana Vlachová vn Jan Páleníček vc Milan Langer pf)
Supraphon SU3347-2 (62' · DDD)   Ⓕ

Supraphon's well-recorded version of the Suite is remarkably fast. Where this Czech team scores over recorded rivals is in the 'Lied', which Korngold asks to be played *Nicht zu langsam*. Their timing is a nifty 3'09". The coupling is Korngold's outrageously precocious – and utterly unmissable – Op 1 Piano Trio. No other musical 12-year-old could have penned

such a memorable – and meaningful – opening theme (a premonition of Korngold's film scores), not to mention the *Scherzo*'s Trio and the brief *Larghetto* third movement. Astonishing! It's no surprise that, following the Trio's New York première, W J Henderson wrote (in the New York *Sun*), 'if we had a little boy of 12 who preferred writing this sort of music to hearing a good folk tune or going out and playing in the park, we should consult a specialist.' Fortunate for us, folk tunes and football took second place to chronicling some quite marvellous musical ideas.

Violin Sonata, Op 6

Violin Sonata in D, Op 6. Sonett für Wien, Op 41. Much Ado About Nothing – Dogberry and Verges; Intermezzo; Hornpipe; Bridal Morning. Das Wunder der Heliane – Gesang der Heliane. Der Schneemann – Serenade. Die tote Stadt – Glück, das mir verblieb; Mein Sehnen, mein Wähnen (all arr cpsr). Märchenbilder, Op 3 – The Gnomes (arr Révay)
Detlef Hahn vn **Andrew Ball** pf
ASV CDDCA1080 (70' · DDD)   ⒻOO

This is an indispensable disc gathering together the complete works for violin and piano – all superbly performed – including no fewer than three world-première recordings.

The disc opens with the remarkably early, but emotionally mature, Violin Sonata in D – a ravishing work that ranks among Korngold's major compositions. The Sonata is lyrical and expansive and has all the characteristics of Korngold's melodic and harmonic idiom – there's certainly nothing apprentice about this piece. Hahn and Ball give a beautifully crafted performance indeed and have truly absorbed the essence of this masterly score.

Korngold's suite of incidental music for *Much Ado About Nothing* has enjoyed a certain amount of currency in its original orchestral version, but less so in Korngold's own arrangement for violin and piano heard here. The transition works marvellously, being ideally suited to the intimacy of chamber music. The second movement, 'Dogberry and Verges', a grotesque march depicting the two drunken night-watchmen, pays passing homage to Korngold's childhood idol Gustav Mahler, and elsewhere in the suite there are constant intimations of the film scores of later years.

The remainder of the disc is devoted to smaller arrangements of works, including two extracts from the opera *Die tote Stadt* and one from *Das Wunder der Heliane* as well as the gorgeous song setting *Sonett für Wien* (In Memoriam), Op 41, the theme of which Korngold also used in the 1946 film *Escape Me Never*. The sound recording is excellent.

Complete Piano Music

Sonatas – Nos 1-3. Don Quixote. Der Schneemann.

Märchenbilder. Four Waltzes for Piano. Four little caricatures for children. What the woods tell me. Zwischenspiel – Act 3 Intermezzo. Piano Trio. Potpourri from 'Der Ring des Polykrates' (arr Ruffin)[a]. Much Ado About Nothing. Geshichten von Strauss. Der Schneemann – Four easy pieces. Schauspiel Overture. Grand Fantasy on 'Die tote Stadt' (arr Rebay)[a]
Martin Jones, [a]**Richard McMahon** *pfs*
Nimbus ④ NI5705/8 (5h · DDD)   Ⓢ

A hearty three cheers to this complete Korngold cycle from the indefatigable and inexplicably underrated Martin Jones. The first two discs have those extraordinary works composed between 1908 and 1910 that put the infant Korngold into the Mozart-Mendelssohn prodigy class – the first two piano sonatas, *Don Quixote*, the ballet-pantomime *Der Schneemann*, *Was der Wald erzählt*, and seven *Märchenbilder*. The final 'Epilog' contains one of his most beautiful melodies, and here Jones captures the *Weltschmerz* of the composer's own treasurable 1951 recording (nla).

The Piano Trio in D major, completed just before Korngold's 13th birthday, is played in the previously unrecorded four-hand version. In this and the 1911 *Schauspiel* Overture (arranged by Korngold's friend Ferdinand Rebay), Jones is joined by Richard McMahon. Written in language of pre-nascent maturity that was to develop little over the composer's lifetime, these pieces constitute one of Western music's more noteworthy miracles.

These four well-filled discs are completed by Rebay's substantial (18'31") Grand Fantasy on themes from *Die tote Stadt*, and Korngold's fantasy on Johann Strauss themes. Stylish, lovingly prepared, classily played and with an excellent 10-page booklet from Korngold's biographer Brendan G Carroll, this valuable addition to the catalogue cannot be praised too highly.

Vocal Works

Abschiedslieder, Op 14[a]. Tomorrow, Op 33[ac]. Einfache Lieder, Op 9[a]. Much Ado About Nothing, Op 11 – Overture; Maiden in the Bridal Chamber; Dogberry and Verges; Intermezzo; Hornpipe; Garden Music. Prayer, Op 32[bc]
[a]**Gigi Mitchell-Velasco** *mez* [b]**Stephen Gould** *ten*
[a]**Jochem Hochstenbach** *pf* [c]**Ladies of the Mozart Choir, Linz; Bruckner Orchestra, Linz / Caspar Richter**
ASV CDDCA1131 (66' · DDD)   Ⓕ●

Caspar Richter and his fresh-faced band give a polished and affectionate performance of the delightful suite Korngold drew from his 1918 incidental score to a Vienna Burgtheater production of *Much Ado about Nothing*. They include the fragrant (and previously unrecorded) 'Garden Music' that opens Act 3, the haunting main theme of which Korngold subsequently incorporated into the third movement of his violin and piano arrangement (beloved of such legendary fiddlers as Heifetz, Kreisler,

Elman and Seidel). Other rarities include the first recording of the Op 32 *Prayer* for tenor, female choir and organ, as well as a long-overdue digital successor to Charles Gerhardt's pioneering RCA performance of *Tomorrow*, a six-minute work for mezzo-soprano, female choir and orchestra, originally written for the 1943 film *The Constant Nymph*.

Another first recording is the orchestral version of 'Nachtwanderer' from the six *Einfache Lieder*. Korngold orchestrated these songs in 1917, and in this guise most of the rest of the set has been recorded by Barbara Hendricks on EMI. Six years later, in 1923, Korngold orchestrated his masterly *Abschiedslieder* of 1920, whose demandingly wide-ranging melodic lines occasionally strain the otherwise appealing mezzo here, Gigi Mitchell-Velasco. That apart, these consistently communicative performances – captured in decent, truthfully balanced sound – arouse nothing but praise. A must for all Korngold fans.

Sursum corda

Sursum corda, Op 13. Die kleine Serenade ('Baby Serenade'), Op 24. Der Schneemann – Prelude; Serenade. Die tote Stadt – Prelude to Act II[a]. Das Wunder der Heliane – Interlude
[a]**Karen Robertson** *sop* [a]**Tibor Pazmany** *org*
Linz Bruckner Orchestra / Caspar Richter
ASV CDDCA1074 (62' · DDD)   Ⓕ

This disc is a must for newcomers to Korngold. Richter presents a beautifully rounded and balanced programme, headed by a virtuoso, highly charged account of the Prelude to Act 2 from the opera *Die tote Stadt*, with a finely sung, if brief contribution from soprano Karen Robertson. Although there's no film music by Korngold on this disc, the symphonic overture *Sursum corda*, with its uplifting, heroic themes, did eventually provide material for the film score to *The Adventures of Robin Hood* some 18 years later. Richter and his players deliver a wonderfully impassioned and incident-packed performance. The *Baby Serenade* was composed shortly after the birth of Korngold's second son Georg, and is a delightful five-movement suite describing a day in the life of his baby son. Korngold's perceptive and often humorous sketches are brilliantly matched in a performance that simply exudes affection and fun – check out the wonderfully characterised performances in the jazzy 'Baby tells a story', track 6. The disc is nicely rounded off with the orchestral Interlude from *Das Wunder der Heliane* – more voluptuous playing in what must be some of Korngold's most voluptuous music. Excellent sound: a disc not to be missed.

Die Kathrin

Die Kathrin
Melanie Diener *sop* Kathrin **David Rendall** *ten*

François **Robert Hayward** bass-bar Malignac **Lilian Watson** sop Chou-Chou **Della Jones** mez Monique **Brabbins**
BBC Singers; BBC Concert Orchestra / Martyn **Brabbins**
CPO ③ CPO999 602-2 (162' · DDD) Notes, text and translation included ⒻO

This is the first modern performance and recording of Korngold's last stage work. *Die Kathrin* is separated by 10 years from its predecessor, *Das Wunder der Heliane*. Between *Heliane* and *Die Kathrin*, Korngold's career had changed. From being the wunderkind of the 1910s, he had developed into the film composer and arranger of large-scale operettas. If *Heliane* is the most grandiose of his operas, *Die Kathrin* is the most unpretentious; Korngold had thought of labelling it a folk-opera. The story is simple. The hero, François, is a singer who has been conscripted into the army. He falls in love with Kathrin, leaving her pregnant. She loses her job, follows him to Marseilles, where in a vaguely *Tosca*-like plot-twist François is implicated in the murder of the villain, who has actually been shot by one of the cabaret girls. Five years pass, François returns to find Kathrin and his child. The opera ends with a rapturous love duet. The music is full of typically lush Korngold scoring. In the night-club scene, obligatory in any 1930s opera, there are two catchy numbers, and Korngold brings in such fashionably jazzy instruments as a trio of saxophones and a banjo. The cast is exceptionally strong. Diener has just the right weight of voice for Kathrin, and Rendall makes François into a very positive hero. Brabbins brings out the essentially Puccinian side of the score; in its structure the opera resembles *La rondine* more than a little: *verismo* didn't die with *Turandot*. Devotees of Korngold's music won't need any encouragement. Those with a taste for tuneful, Romantic opera, sometimes bordering on operetta, should give it a chance.

Fritz Kreisler   Austrian 1875-1962

After study at the Vienna Conservatory and the Paris Conservatoire Kreisler toured the USA (1888-9). Real recognition came in 1899, after a concert with the Berlin PO under Nikisch. His London début was in 1902 and in 1910 he gave the première of Elgar's Concerto. He lived in Berlin, 1924-34, and in 1939 settled in the USA, becoming an American citizen in 1943. His last concert was in 1947. Kreisler played with grace, elegance and a sweet, golden tone with a pronounced vibrato. His repertory included brief pieces of his own, some of them semi-pastiche pieces which he initially ascribed to composers such as Tartini and Pugnani, some of them sugary Viennese morsels, all beautifully written to display brilliant, subtle and expressive violin playing. **GROVE**music

Compositions and Arrangements

Original Compositions and Arrangements – Ⓗ works by Kreisler and arrangements of works by Bach, Brandl, Dvořák, Falla, Glazunov, Heuberger, Poldini, Rimsky-Korsakov, Schubert, Scott, Tchaikovsky and Weber
Fritz Kreisler vn with various artists
EMI Références mono 764701-2 (78' · ADD)
Recorded 1930-38 ⓂOO

Kreisler Praeludium and Allegro in the style of Pugnani. Schön Rosmarin. Tambourin chinois, Op 3. Caprice viennois, Op 2. Précieuse in the style of Couperin. Liebesfreud. Liebesleid. La Gitana. Berceuse romantique, Op 9. Polichinelle. Rondino on a theme by Beethoven. Tempo di Menuetto in the style of Pugnani. Toy Soldier's March. Allegretto in the style of Boccherini. Marche miniature viennoise. Aucassin and Nicolette, 'Canzonetta medievale'. Menuet in the style of Porpora. Siciliano and Rigaudon in the style of Francoeur. Syncopation
Joshua Bell vn **Paul Coker** pf
Decca 444 409-2DH (63' · DDD) Ⓕ

Years of encores have guaranteed the cult longevity of Kreisler's music – certainly among violinists. Kreisler's disc consists of his own pieces and a large number of arrangements. Some of the latter are pretty feeble musically, yet the great violinist's unique artistry and magical tone-quality shine through. Sometimes he doesn't land right in the middle of a note, but always plays with the timing and phrasing of a great singer. Nothing is routine or set in his playing, which has a continual feeling of discovery and freshness. The transfers are excellent.

Joshua Bell learned Kreisler from his teacher, the late Josef Gingold, yet his approach is anything but 'old school'. He habitually avoids the pitfalls of imitation, flashiness and patronising overkill, preferring instead to revisit the music with modern ears. His *Caprice viennois* is light-years removed from the composer's own, a fresh-faced, strongly characterised reading that trades sentimentality for just a hint of jazz. And there's that inseparable twosome, *Liebesfreud* and *Liebesleid*, the latter displaying Bell's tone at its most alluring. The longest piece here is the *Praeludium and Allegro in the style of Pugnani* which he gives the full treatment, deftly pointing the *Allegro*, relishing passagework and double-stopping with impressive accuracy. Some pieces seem indivisible from Kreisler's own very individual tone and phrasing, *Polichinelle*, for example, and *Marche miniature viennoise*, both of which paraded the sort of personalised *rubato*, timing and tone-production that have for so long seemed part of the music's very essence.

Bell's smooth, witty and keenly inflected readings make for elevated entertainment: they may not replace the composer's own, but they do provide a youthful and in many ways illuminating alternative. The recordings are excellent, but Coker's fine accompaniments occasionally seem overprominent.

Viennese Rhapsody
Albéniz/Kreisler Tango, Op 165 No 2
Dvořák/Kreisler Slavonic Dances – B78: No 2 in E
minor; B145: No 2 in E minor **Falla/Kreisler** La vida
breve – Danse espagnole **Granados/Kreisler**
Andaluza, Op 37 No 5 **Kreisler** Caprice viennois,
Op 2. Tambourin chinois, Op 3. Berceuse roman-
tique, Op 9. Viennese Rhapsodic Fantasietta. Zige-
uner-capriccio. La gitana. Polichinelle. Aucassin and
Nicolette. Liebesleid. Liebesfreud. Slavonic Fantasie
Scott/Kreisler Lotus Land, Op 47 No 1 **Wieniawski/
Kreisler** Etude-Caprice in A minor, Op 18 No 4
Leonidas Kavakos vn **Péter Nagy** pf
BIS CD1196 (71' · DDD)   F**OO**

Leonidas Kavakos's Kreisler is authentic in the
best meaning of that term, namely a keen
approximation both of the music's spirit and of
the composer's inimitable playing style. Few
Kreisler recitals have recalled, in so much
minute detail, the warmth, elegance and gentle-
manly musical manners of the master himself. It
was an inspired idea to open the programme
with that nostalgic evocation of Old Vienna, the
eight-minute *Viennese Rhapsodic Fantasietta*, a
Korngold sound-alike that can't waltz without
smiling wistfully or even shedding the odd tear.
Kavakos has mastered that lilting 3/4 to a T. His
tone is uncannily familiar – cooler and less
vibrant perhaps than Kreisler's own during the
earlier part of his recording career but with a
similarly consistent (though never overbearing)
vibrato. But don't imagine that these performances are mere imitations: an individual personality does come through, it's just that a Kreisler-
ian accent has become part of the mix – at least
for the purposes of this recital. The programme
has been very well chosen, ending with what are
surely Kreisler's three most famous miniatures
– *Liebesleid*, *Liebesfreud* and *Caprice viennois*. The
Slavonic Fantasie after Dvořák is among the most
interesting, incorporating as it does the first of
the four *Romantic Pieces*. Cyril Scott's *Lotus Land*
is haunting and exotic, while Kreisler's own
Zigeuner-capriccio provides a fine example of
Kavakos's slightly melancholy puckishness.
Péter Nagy's stylish accompaniments add yet
more flavour to the menu.

*his best-known work, the Biblical Sonatas, which
describe in music, sometimes naively but with enterprising use of the harpsichord's resources, the emotional states aroused by particular stories from the
Bible.*   GROVEmusic

Tristis est anima

Ihr Himmel jubilirt von oben. Weicht ihr Sorgen aus
dem Hertzen. Gott, sei mir gnädig nach deiner Güte.
Wie schön leuchtet der Morgenstern. Tristis est
anima mea. O heilige Zeit
Deborah York sop **Gary Cooper** org **The King's
Consort Choir; The King's Consort / Robert King**
Hyperion CDA67059 (75' · DDD) Texts and
translations included   F

Johann Kuhnau was Cantor at St Thomas's,
Leipzig until his death, crossing paths with
Bach and inspiring the younger man to borrow
the title *Clavier-Übung* for the prime repository
for Bach's published keyboard works. This
splendid and varied cross-section of his choral
music leaves us in no doubt that Kuhnau is far
more than merely a confident practitioner who
followed the plot of changing fashion. Through
a keen sense of assimilation comes a singular,
mainly sober, yet highly accomplished church
composer. *Gott, sei mir gnädig* is a fine, evocative
work full of rhetorical detail and inference,
while in *Wie schön leuchtet der Morgenstern* the
declamation straddles the concentrated world
of the Bach motet, *Komm, Jesu, komm*, yet punctuated by the secular ostentation and chuckling
horns of another world.

Robert King and his consort of singers and
players highlight the multi-layered references
in Kuhnau's cantatas, from the graceful Bach-
aria lilt of *Weicht ihr Sorgen*, with the sympathetic colouring, if questionable diction, of
Deborah York offset by an affectionate and
responsive band of strings and unison oboes, to
the decidedly pietist world of the *accompagnato*
recitative in *Wie schön leuchtet*.

The beguiling and antiquated *Tristis est anima
mea* is worth its weight in gold. Vocally colourful (all the soloists are on fine form, especially
Robin Blaze and Peter Harvey) and instrumentally outstanding, this is an important recording
of a woefully neglected figure whose music has
real stature.

Johann Kuhnau   German 1660-1722

*German composer and theorist Kuhnau studied in
Dresden and Zittau, where he briefly served as Kantor and organist, and then at Leipzig, where in 1684
he became organist at the Thomaskirche and, in
1701, Kantor. His secular vocal music is all lost, but
many sacred works survive, mostly cantatas, anticipating the style of Bach, his successor: they show lyrical vocal writing, powerful fugues and dramatic contrasts of texture which stress the rhetorical sense. He
published four sets of keyboard pieces, including two
sets called Clavier-Übung (each with seven suites,
one set in the major keys and one in the minor) and,*

György Kurtág   Romanian 1926

*Kurtág studied with Veress and Farkas at the
Budapest Academy (1946-55) and with Milhaud
and Messiaen in Paris (1957); in 1967 he began
teaching at the Budapest Academy. His works are
few and mostly short, suggesting a combination of the
most abstract Bartók and late Webern, though with
a strong lyrical, expressive force (and sometimes
ingenious wit). Most of his compositions are for
chamber forces, sometimes with solo voice. Among*

the best known are The Sayings of Péter Bornemisza (1968), a 'concerto' for soprano and piano in 24 short movements, and Messages of the Late RV Troussova (1980) for soprano and orchestra. Some of his pieces (eg 15 songs, 1982) use the cimbalom.

GROVEmusic

String Quartets

Aus der Ferne III. Officium breve, Op 28. Ligatura, Op 31b. String Quartet, Op 1. Hommage à Mihály. András (12 Microludes), Op 13
Keller Quartet (András Keller, János Pilz vns Zoltán Gál va Ottó Kertész vc) **Miklós Perényi** vc **György Kurtág** celesta
ECM New Series 453 258-2 (49' · DDD)   Ⓕ

This disc, devoted exclusively to Kurtág's music for string quartet, is of great significance, and both performance and recording are equal to the enterprise. The Keller Quartet have secure technique as well as emotional commitment, while ECM has provided a warm yet spacious acoustic for this expressive music. The journey begins with Kurtág's Op 1 of 1959, in a world, dominated by expressionistic fragmentation, of which he's clearly the master. Eighteen years later, in the Op 13 *Microludes*, Kurtág has perfected his own personal style, in which small, separate forms are linked together, and the music's allusions – to Bartók and Webern, in particular – are subsumed into a lyrical, dramatic discourse. The fruits of Kurtág's long apprenticeship are most evident here in the superb *Officium breve* of 1988-9, a miracle of textural imagination and musical thought whose richly varied language is distilled further into the two miniatures – *Ligatura* (also 1989) and *Aus der Ferne* (1991). By now Kurtág's music is characterised by a concentrated homogeneity, and by a harmony whose tensions, and stability, are the result of bringing convergence and divergence into confrontation. The result is memorable, and these fine recordings provide immensely rewarding listening.

Játékok

Játékok – excerpts from Books 1-5 & 8.
Transcriptions from Machaut to Bach – No 46, Gottes Zeit ist die allerbeste Zeit (Bach: BWV106); No 48, Aus tiefer Not (Bach: BWV687); No 50, Trio Sonata in E flat (Bach: BWV525/1); No 52, O Lamm Gottes unschuldig (Bach: BWVdeest)
György Kurtág, Márta Kurtág pf duet
ECM New Series 453 511-2 (50' · DDD)   Ⓕ

If any contemporary composer can persuade the musical world that compositions of between 30 seconds and four minutes in length are the natural vehicle for progressive post-tonal music, that composer is Kurtág. This sequence of pieces, the longest of which lasts just over five minutes, offers a very special experience. The disc contains a selection from his ongoing

sequence of 'games' (*Játékok*) for solo piano and piano duet. They're a mixture of studies and tributes, not explicitly pedagogic in *Mikrokosmos* mode, but ranging widely in technical demands and style, from fugitive fragments, in which even the smallest element tells, to the extraordinary flamboyance of a *Perpetuum mobile* containing nothing but *glissandos*. Most are sombre in tone, and even the more humorous items have a bitter side. For access to another musical world, Kurtág has included four Bach transcriptions, music whose serenity and confidence speaks immediately of utter remoteness from the real present. The performances risk overprojection but they're supremely characterful, and the close-up recording reinforces the impression of music that's mesmerically persuasive in its imagination and expressiveness.

Helmut Lachenmann   German b1935

Lachenmann studied with David at the Stuttgart Musikhochschule (1955-8) and with Nono in Venice (1958-60). In 1966 he began teaching. In later works he simplified his forms and lessened the extent of aesthetic intervention in his material.

GROVEmusic

Das Mädchen mit den Schwefelhölzern

Das Mädchen mit den Schwefelhölzern (Tokyo version, 2000)
Nicole Tibbels, Eiko Morikawa sops **Helmut Lachenmann** spkr **Mayumi Miyata** shô **Yukiko Sugawara, Tomoko Hemmi** pfs **Stuttgart Vocal Ensemble; South West German Radio Symphony Orchestra, Baden-Baden and Freiburg / Sylvain Cambreling**
ECM New Series ② 476 1283 (113' · DDD)   Ⓕ

Das Mädchen mit den Schwefelhölzern, the composer's first piece of music theatre, is based on Hans Christian Andersen's The *Little Match Girl*, which he interprets as an attack on a cold and indifferent society. The piece has appeared previously on the Kairos label. There isn't much to choose between the two recordings in terms of performance, but the new ECM version has a pleasing precision that suits Lachenmann's vision well. The chief difference between the two versions lies in a substantial revision undertaken by the composer. The oft-recorded '...zwei Gefühle...' scene is here abridged, subtly altering the work's balance while not quite diminishing the sequence's importance to the whole. Though the work has been shortened only barely, it's possible that a greater concision results, aided perhaps by the slightly tauter sound. Lachenmann's music demands the listener's active engagement, a determined effort at understanding, but here are rewards to be reaped from perseverance.

Edouard Lalo
French 1823-1892

Lalo studied at the Lille Conservatory and in Habe-neck's class at the Paris Conservatoire. As a violinist and teacher in Paris in the 1850s he showed an unfashionable inclination towards chamber music, playing Classical string quartets and composing string trios and a noteworthy quartet. During the 1870s he attracted attention for his instrumental works, especially for the Symphonie espagnole (1874), a five-movement violin concerto, and the powerful Cello Concerto (1877). After disappoint-ment at the poor reception of his opera Fiesque (1866-7), he took up stage music again in 1875, winning success with Le roi d'Ys (1888), on which his operatic fame has rested; his ballet score Namouna (1881-2) became popular as a series of orchestral suites. Among the hallmarks of Lalo's music, the vigour of which stands in contrast to the style of Franck's pupils and the impressionists, are his strongly diatonic melody, piquant harmony and ingenious orchestration. GROVEmusic

Cello Concerto

Lalo Cello Concerto **Massenet** Fantaisie **Saint-Saëns** Cello Concerto No 1 in A minor, Op 33
Sophie Rolland vc **BBC Philharmonic Orchestra /**
Gilbert Varga
ASV CDDCA867 (65' · DDD) Recorded 1993 (F)(O)

Sophie Rolland's performance of the Lalo Con-certo is surely as fine as any recorded. It opens with great character, thanks to Gilbert Varga's strong accompaniment, and the solo playing is joyously songful. But Rolland is at her finest as she plays her introduction to the finale with commanding improvisatory spontaneity. The orchestra bursts in splendidly and she shows her technical mettle with some bouncing bowing in the attractive closing Rondo. The Saint-Saëns Concerto brings similar felicities. Massenet's *Fantaisie* opens dramatically and is rhythmically vital, flowing onwards boldly to produce a win-ningly sentimental yearning melody which the soloist clearly relishes. A cadenza then leads to a charming, very French Gavotte, and the piece ends jubilantly. It really is a find, and it could hardly be presented more persuasively. The recording is near perfect.

Cello Concerto in D minor[a]. Cello Sonata[b]. Chants russes, Op 29[b]
Maria Kliegel vc [b]**Bernd Glemser** pf [a]**Nicolaus Esterházy Sinfonia / Michael Halász**
Naxos 8 554469. (60' · DDD) (S)

Maria Kliegel views the Concerto as a strong, dramatic work, and she has just the qualities – impressive, powerful tone and brilliant tech-nique – to bring it off. The early exchanges with the orchestra establish her heroic presence, which she then relaxes to give a soft, delicate account of the second theme. The orchestral

interruptions sound suitably stern and implac-able – although the many loud, *staccato* chords for full orchestra become somewhat wearisome. The finale is excellent; a robust, serious approach allied to energetic, bouncy rhythms. Throughout, the orchestra sounds warmly Romantic, the important solo wind parts full of character.

The Sonata, too, is well worth hearing. Writ-ten 20 years before the Concerto, it's still a fully mature work, mixing grand Lisztian gestures with classical formal outlines and ingenious, colourful harmony. Kliegel and Glemser play with fine style and intense commitment, encompassing the high Romanticism and, in the outer movement, Lalo's characteristically forceful rhythmic manner. *Chants russes* is an arrangement of the middle movement of the *Concerto russe* for violin – it's very effective as a cello piece. Kliegel's soft, refined sound near the end is especially memorable.

Violin Concerto

Violin Concerto in F, Op 20[a]. Concerto russe, Op 29[a]. Scherzo. Le roi d'Ys – Overture
[a]**Olivier Charlier** vn **BBC Philharmonic Orchestra /**
Yan Pascal Tortelier
Chandos CHAN9758 (72' · DDD) (F)

This collection opens splendidly with a spank-ingly good performance of the Overture to *Le roi d'Ys*, with its melodrama, brassy splashes and a rather memorable swooning cello solo. It has all the gusto and panache of a Beecham per-formance and is certainly the finest account on disc since Paray's old Mercury version. Then come the two *concertante* violin works, both written with Sarasate in mind (separated by the comparatively familiar *Scherzo*, given here with rumbustious zest). Why are they not better known? The Violin Concerto has plenty going for it, a nicely coloured palette, a disarmingly nostalgic lyrical melody to haunt the first move-ment, followed by a delightful, songful *Andante*, which Olivier Charlier plays with engaging del-icacy. But the real surprise is the *Concerto russe*, virtually another *Symphonie espagnole*, but with Slavic rather than Spanish ideas, and very good ones too. Its lovely slow movement, the 'Chant russe', opens with a chorale and the violin steals in with a genuine Russian folk tune, which (with its rhythmic snaps) is astonishingly reminiscent of the Bruch *Scottish Fantasy*. Charlier plays it most tenderly and the result is gently ravishing. The 'Intermezzo', with its off-beat timpani interjections and catchy main theme, is deli-cious, rhythmically sparkling in Charlier's hands, and there's another luscious secondary theme to come in the middle. The finale opens with a burst of sombre Slavonic passion from the strings, and another folk melody arrives. Soon the music quickens, culminating in a viva-cious conclusion, with Charlier's contribution always lightly sparkling. Highly recommended.

Symphonie espagnole

Lalo Symphonie espagnole, Op 21[a] **Vieuxtemps** Violin Concerto No 5 in A minor, Op 37[b]
Sarah Chang vn [a]**Royal Concertgebouw Orchestra**, [b]**Philharmonia Orchestra / Charles Dutoit**
EMI 555292-2 (52' · DDD) Recorded [a]live 1995, [b]1994
Ⓕ

The *Symphonie espagnole* is a more ambitious piece than the Vieuxtemps, and Lalo's inventive Spanishry holds up well throughout the five movements. Dutoit's approach has impetus, so when the *malagueña* secondary theme arrives, it makes a shimmering contrast. The delicious piping woodwind *crescendo* and *decrescendo* which begins the finale sets the scene for scintillating *salterello* fireworks from the soloist. The dash to the home straight brings vociferous applause, which makes one realise that the concentration and spontaneity of the performance has been helped by the presence of an audience, who aren't apparent until this point. Certainly the splendidly resonant Concertgebouw sound and perfect balance would never give the game away.

Vieuxtemps's Fifth Concerto opens disarmingly, but the *tutti* gathers strength in Dutoit's hands before Chang steals in silkily and proceeds to dominate the performance with her warm lyricism and natural, flowing *rubato*. In a performance like this it remains a small-scale work to cherish, for it hasn't a dull bar in it. The recording is warm and full, the balance treating the relationship between the violin and the Philharmonia Orchestra as an equal partnership.

Constant Lambert   British 1905-1951

Lambert entered the Royal College of Music when he was 17, and was becoming well known by the time he was 20. He was the first English composer commissioned by Dhiagilev (Romeo and Juliet, 1926), initiating a lifelong association with ballet as a conductor and composer: he wrote Pomona (1927) for Nizhinska and Horoscope (1938) for the Vic-Wells Ballet, of which he was founder musical director (from 1931). But he also wrote concert pieces, preferring unconventional genres and anti-traditional tastes for jazz and Stravinsky: such works include The Rio Grande for piano, chorus and orchestra (1927), the Concerto for piano and nonet (1930-31) and the choral orchestral 'masque' Summer's Last Will and Testament (1932-5). He stood in sharp relief against the background of English musical life and had wide-ranging interests. A lively critic, he wrote the stimulating Music Ho! a Study of Music in Decline (1934). **GROVE**music

Piano Concerto

Concerto for Piano and Chamber Orchestra[a].
Merchant Seamen Suite. Pomona. Prize-Fight

[a]**David Owen Norris** pf **BBC Concert Orchestra / Barry Wordsworth**
ASV White Line CDWHL2122 (66' · DDD)   Ⓜ ⓞⓞ

More gaps in the Lambert discography are enterprisingly plugged by these sensitive and shapely performances, which display most agreeable dash and commitment. The Piano Concerto recorded here isn't that unnervingly bleak 1930-31 creation for soloist and nine players but one from 1924 that remained in short score, never to be heard in the composer's lifetime. Now, thanks to the editorial skills of Giles Easterbrook and the late Edward Shipley, we can at last savour another astonishingly mature and skilful product of Lambert's youth. Not only is the concerto tightly organised and brimful of striking invention, it also plumbs expressive depths, not least in the *Andante* slow movement which contains music as achingly poignant as any he penned. David Owen Norris does full justice to the glittering solo part, and he receives splendid support from Barry Wordsworth and the BBC Concert Orchestra.

Prize-Fight (Lambert's first ballet score) is earlier still, begun in 1923, completed the following year and overhauled one last time in 1927. It's a veritable romp, pungently scored in the manner of Satie and Milhaud, and with something of the anarchic spirit of Georges Auric's deliciously daft contributions to those glorious Ealing Comedies. In point of fact, Lambert had long been a connoisseur of the silver screen before he finally embarked on his first film score in 1940, for a flag-waving documentary entitled *Merchant Seamen*. Two years later, he compiled the present five-movement suite, and a superior specimen it is. *Pomona* we've had before. Wordsworth's spacious realisation occasionally lacks something in sheer effervescence and dry wit. But this is a most enjoyable and valuable compilation and the recording is vivid and truthfully balanced.

Tiresias

Tiresias. Pomona
English Northern Philharmonia / David Lloyd-Jones with [a]**Michael Cleaver** pf
Hyperion CDA67049 (72' · DDD)   Ⓕ ⓞ

Constant Lambert's *Tiresias* was commissioned for the Festival of Britain in 1951 and the subject had been preoccupying the composer for over 20 years. In the event, the ailing Lambert struggled to meet his July deadline and called upon colleagues like Robert Irving, Alan Rawsthorne, Elisabeth Lutyens, Gordon Jacob, Denis Apivor, Humphrey Searle and Christian Darnton to help him finish the orchestration. Lambert directed eight performances in all, but the work was coolly received and he died the following month, just two days before his 46th birthday.

The instrumentation of *Tiresias* calls for neither violins nor violas and features a notably

varied battery of percussion as well as an important role for piano obbligato (brilliantly played
here by Michael Cleaver). The music has a
dark-hued intimacy and at times starkly ritualistic demeanour which probably baffled that
glitzy first-night audience. However, Lambert's
achievement is ripe for reassessment, and David
Lloyd-Jones's meticulously prepared realisation
allows us to revel anew in the score's many
effective set-pieces. Stravinsky and Ravel are
prime influences, but the work is suffused with
that distinctive mix of keen brilliance and bleak
melancholy so characteristic of its creator. The
present account is all one could wish for.

Pomona (1927) is much earlier and altogether
lighter in tone. Deftly scored for a chamber
orchestra of 34 instrumentalists, *Pomona* comprises eight delightfully inventive numbers
whose neo-classical spirit breathes very much
the same air as that of Stravinsky and Les Six
from the same period. Again, the performance is
first-rate and the sound quite admirable.

Romeo and Juliet

The Bird Actors. Pomona. Romeo and Juliet
Victoria State Orchestra / John Lanchbery
Chandos CHAN9865 (56' · DDD)   Ⓕ⚫

The really good news here is the CD début of
Romeo and Juliet, one of only two ballet scores
that Diaghilev commissioned from British composers for his Ballets Russes (the other being
Lord Berners' *The Triumph of Neptune*, also
staged in 1926). It's a frothy romp firmly in the
Stravinsky/Poulenc/ Milhaud mould – and a
brilliantly confident achievement for a 20-year-
old student – but, strange to relate, there's
barely a glimpse of the sheer expressive scope of
either *Pomona* or *The Rio Grande* (not to mention the remarkable Piano Concerto). We've
long needed a worthy successor to Norman Del
Mar's affectionate Lyrita version with the ECO;
happily, Lanchbery and company have plugged
the gap with notable success. Not only does the
orchestral playing evince infectious zest and
unswerving dedication to the cause, Lanchbery
directs with palpable relish throughout.

He also gives us an enjoyably lithe account of
Pomona and a sparkling curtain-raiser in the
guise of *The Bird Actors*, a three-minute overture
which originally began life as the finale of an
even earlier ballet entitled *Adam and Eve*. The
sound throughout is lively and full-bodied,
without perhaps being in the very top flight.

Rued Langgaard   Danish 1893-1952

*Aged 11, Langgaard made his début in Copenhagen
as organist and improviser. A series of trips to Berlin
led to the performance of his hour-long Symphony
No 1 (1908-11) by the Berlin PO in 1913. The
musical community in Denmark, however, regarded*
*the highly productive but reserved and solitary com-
poser with scepticism. After his opera Antikrist was
turned down by Copenhagen's Royal Theatre in
1925, he turned his back on modernism and openly
criticised Danish musical life and Nielsen's influence
on it. His Straussian music, coloured by religion and
symbolism, did not concur with the anti-Romantic
and sober attitude dominant in Denmark around
1930. Interest in his work was reawakened in the
1960s, Music of the Spheres in particular being seen
as anticipating the avant-garde music of the 60s.*

GROVEmusic

Symphonies

Symphonies – No 9, 'From Queen Dagmar's City',
BVN282; No 10, 'Yon Hall of Thunder', BVN298;
No 11, 'Ixion', BVN303
**Danish National Radio Symphony Orchestra /
Thomas Dausgaard**
Dacapo 8 224182 (54' · DDD)   Ⓕ

Incalculability is essential for prolific symphonists – think of the diversity of Haydn or Shostakovich – but rarely so extreme as with Langgaard, neatly encapsulated in this new disc of
three works written in just four years (1942-5).
The style of the anachronistic Ninth is more in
keeping with early Wagner (the opening movement sounds like Siegfried's Rhine Journey!).
The *scherzo* looks to Tchaikovsky (filtered
through early Sibelius), while the lowering
Lento, 'Ribe Cathedral', starts with chords out of
Don Giovanni. This eclecticism switches to
Strauss and Mahler in No 10, another of his
large-scale, nature-based orchestral fantasias
and one of his best. Its title, *Yon Hall of Thunder*,
hints at its grandiose character, but there's subtlety here too. The Danish Radio orchestra play
with greater refinement for Dausgaard than for
Ole Schmidt in the 1970s, the more tellingly as
Dausgaard takes it at a ferocious pace in a compelling reading. No 11, *Ixion*, is one of the oddest works in Langgaard's symphonic canon.
Running for some six minutes, it seems like a
foreshadowing of Minimalism, albeit maximally
orchestrated with four tubas adding their baleful tone to its monothematic round. As overture
or finale it convinces, but a whole symphony?
Dausgaard's accounts are superior to all rivals
and excellently recorded. Eccentric but fascinating.

The End of Time

The End of Time, BVN243[a]. From the Song of
Solomon, BVN381[b]. Interdikt, BVN335. Carl Nielsen,
Our Great Composer, BVN355[c]
[ab]**Nina Pavlovski** sop [ab]**Stig Andersen** ten [a]**Per
Høyer** bar [b]**Per Salo** org **Danish National Radio
[abc]Choir and Symphony Orchestra / Gennadi
Rozhdestvensky**
Chandos CHAN9786 (60' · DDD) Texts and
translations included   Ⓕ

The End of Time, a concert suite dating from

1939-40, is based on the original 1921-3 version of the opera *Antikrist*. It's a cantata in four movements (a prelude and three self-contained 'arias') to which Langgaard made further revisions as he assembled it, the whole making a highly effective work that doesn't betray its origins. The text as retained also illustrates, in brief, the radical differences between the two versions of the opera. The shorter *From the Song of Solomon* (1949) is one of his last works, and typically strays very little from the Straussian opulence of the opening. There's more than a touch of Wagner in the latter stages. Langgaard's selective use of the Biblical text had a moralistic point that was aimed at what he felt to be the degenerate Danish society of the time. The orchestral *Interdikt* (1947-8) is targeted rather more personally; specifically, at the interdict he believed the Danish musical establishment had placed on him. It's quintessential Langgaard – eruptive, memorable and not a note too long. The role of the organist is an acute autobiographical touch. *Carl Nielsen, Our Great Composer* (1948; the title is also the complete text) presents the less attractive, paranoid side of his creative persona. This sarcastic little hymn is pure doggerel, attacking Nielsen's posthumous pre-eminence. Rozhdestvensky has the measure of Langgaard's idiom, and secures top-notch performances, while Chandos's sound quality is both rich and clear.

Music of the Spheres

Music of the Spheres. Four Tone Pictures
Gitta-Maria Sjöberg sop **Danish National Radio Choir and Symphony Orchestra / Gennadi Rozhdestvensky**
Chandos CHAN9517 (53' · DDD)　　Ⓕ●

Music of the Spheres (1916-18) is probably Langgaard's most important – certainly most original – work. So radical did its sonic experiments seem even in the late 1960s that Ligeti no less, when inspecting the score, quipped that he had merely been a 'Langgaard imitator' all along. The manipulation of blocks of sound rather than conventional thematic development does have much in common with trends in post-Second World War avant-garde composition (though stemming from impressionism), but other contemporaries of Langgaard's, such as Schoenberg and Scriabin, had traversed similar terrain at least in part. The main difference between Langgaard and Ligeti lies in the former's reliance on a fundamentally tonal language, however eccentrically deployed, but *Music of the Spheres* seems in hindsight to be a bridge between two other highly virtuosic scores with celestial connotations: Holst's *The Planets* and Ligeti's *Atmosphères*. The *Tone Pictures* (1917) were written alongside this extraordinary work, yet possess none of its stature: four charming songs, they seem effusive and outmoded by comparison. Chandos's sound is superb.

Orlande de Lassus
Franco/Flemish 1532-1594

Lassus served Ferrante Gonzaga of Mantua from c1544, accompanying him to Sicily and Milan (1546-9). He worked for Constantino Castrioto in Naples, where he probably began to compose, then moved to Rome to join the Archbishop of Florence's household, becoming maestro di cappella at St John Lateran in 1553. After returning north, to Mons and Antwerp, where early works were published (1555-6), he joined the court chapel of Duke Albrecht V of Bavaria in Munich as a singer (1556). He married in 1558. Although a Catholic, he took over the court chapel in 1563 and served the duke and his heir, Wilhelm V, for over 30 years, until his death. In this post he consolidated his position by having many works published and travelling frequently (notably to Vienna and Italy, 1574-9), establishing an international reputation. The pope made him a Knight of the Golden Spur in 1574.

One of the most prolific and versatile of 16th-century composers, Lassus wrote over 2000 works in almost every current genre, including masses, motets, psalms, hymns, responsorial Passions and secular pieces in Italian, French and German. Most of his masses are parody masses based on motets, chansons or madrigals by himself or others; the large number of Magnificats is unusual. His motets include didactic pieces, ceremonial works for special occasions, settings of classical texts (some secular, e.g. Prophetiae Sibyllarum, 1600), liturgical items (offertories, antiphons, psalms, eg Psalmipoenitentiales, 1584) and private devotional pieces. He issued five large volumes of sacred music as Patrocinium musices (1573-6), and after his death in 1594 his sons assembled another (Magnum opus musicum, 1604).

Admired in their day for their beauty, technical perfection and rhetorical power, the motets combine the features of several national styles – expressive Italian melody, elegant French text-setting and solid northern polyphony – enhanced by Lassus's imaginative responses to the texts. His secular works reveal a cosmopolitan with varied tastes. The madrigals range from lightweight villanellas (Matona mia cara) to intensely expressive sonnets (Occhi, piangete); the chansons include 'patter' songs and reflective, motet-like works; and among the German lieder are sacred hymns and psalms, delicate love-songs and raucous drinking-songs. This versatility and this wide expressive range place Lassus among the most significant figures of the Renaissance period.

Lassus's sons Ferdinand (c1560-1609) and Rudolph (c1563-1625) also served the Bavarian court chapel and were responsible for assembling many of their father's works for publication. Ferdinand succeeded to his father's post at court; Rudolph composed much sacred music. **GROVE**music

Masses

Missa Entre vous filles. Missa Susanne un jour. Infelix ego
Oxford Camerata / Jeremy Summerly
Naxos 8 550842 (68' · DDD) Recorded 1993. Text and

translation of *Infelix ego* included ⑤

The Masses *Entre vous filles* and *Susanne un jour* show Lassus at his best, full of variety and invention, music of an immediate impact; in fact, they display exactly the same qualities as the better-known motets. The Oxford Camerata has understood this well, taking considerable care with the nuances of the text and really enjoying the music's rich sonorities. Sometimes a slight imprecision in the playing of chords is detectable, but this is more than outweighed by the sense of melodic contour and the powerful, somewhat dark and austere sound which conveys so well the spirit of the music. With over 68 minutes of some of the finest 16th-century polyphony available at such a low price, no one should hesitate.

king on campaigns; he was killed during the battle to relieve the garrison at Chester.

Lawes was a gifted, versatile and prolific composer. The stylised dance suite is the basic vehicle for his chamber music, often with a preceding fantasia or pavan. In his viol consorts he exhibited late Renaissance traits, but the larger part of his chamber music uses violins in the concertante style of early Baroque violin music with continuo. It includes the 'Harpe' consorts, a unique collection of variation suites for violin, bass viol, theorbo and harp. Of Lawes's vocal music, over 200 songs are extant, many of them composed for court masques and other theatrical entertainments. He is considered the leading English dramatic composer before Purcell. Much of his church music – c50 anthems and ten sacred canons or rounds – is also of high quality, The Lord is my Light *being one of the finest verse anthems of its period.*

GROVEmusic

Lagrime di San Pietro

Lagrime di San Pietro
Ensemble Vocal Européen / Philippe Herreweghe
Harmonia Mundi HMX298 1483 (60' · DDD)
Recorded 1993. Texts and translations included Ⓜ**O**

Lassus completed his swan-song days before his death in 1594. The decision to set 20 stanzas from Luigi Tansillo's unfinished meditation on 'the tears of St Peter' must have been a highly personal one. The poet's portrayal of a man driven nearly insane with remorse allowed Lassus to exorcise the mental illness that engulfed him in his last years. The result is perhaps his most moving work, for in these *madrigali spirituali* there's a distilled mannerism that evokes the understated passion of late-period Brahms. Philippe Herreweghe captures the detached expression of pain that makes this music so haunting. This is partly a matter of vocal timbre: individually the singers' tone is a shade cool, but collectively they sound full-bodied. Their interpretative acuteness is best illustrated by their approach to rubato: Herreweghe ever so slightly *stretches* the pulse when the voices achieve a poignant inflexion or come to a standstill. Such moments acquire an intensity that clearly identifies them as the key moments in a psychological drama, making the cycle as a whole compulsive listening. Quite simply, Herreweghe's singers achieve something that's very, very special indeed.

William Lawes   British 1602-1645

William Lawes, the younger brother of Henry Lawes, was probably a chorister at Salisbury Cathedral until the Earl of Hertford placed him under the tutelage of his own music master, John Coprario. In 1635 Lawes was appointed 'musician in ordinary for the lute and voices' to Charles I, though he was probably in Charles's service before then. In 1642 he enlisted in the royalist army and accompanied the

Consort Setts

Consort Setts a 6 – in G; in C; in F; in B; in C.
Fantazy a 6 in F
Phantasm (Wendy Gillespie *viol* Jonathan Manson,
Varpu Haavisto *tvios* Susanne Braumann, Markku
Luolajan-Mikkola *bvios*) / **Laurence Dreyfus** *viol*
Channel Classics CCS17498 (60' · DDD)   Ⓕ**OO**

Dreyfus writes passionately about the music, referring to 'a Dionysian frenzy hell-bent on breaking civilised taboos' and 'jubilant incantations'. So what do we hear? A subtly resonant, particularised landscape: in effect an Elysian soundscape. Gone is the corporate consort sound we learned to relish in former decades, replaced with rather more democratic textures. With seeming ease, the voice of each viol emerges and withdraws on cue as the music unfolds with sublime logic and unquestionable momentum.

The best setts are perhaps the two in minor keys, which offered Lawes a richer harmonic palette and the players greater expressive possibilities. The harmonically bizarre first Fantazy of the C minor Sett must have excited 17th-century ears, which, if they were lucky, were treated as we are here to an excitingly paced second Fantazy, then an 'Inomine' ('sinewy' and sustained at first, then quicker in the second section, the plainchant exquisitely interwoven and at the same time plain for all to hear), and finally a vibrant Aire, resplendent in its swaggering repeated notes and syncopated dash. Whether it would make so vivid an impression from another ensemble is doubtful. Dreyfus's unselfconscious hyperbolic enthusiasm aside, these are beautifully thought-out, sympathetic performances, worthy of a cultivated monarch and the composer's quatercentenary.

A superb disc – Phantasm is truly in a class of its own.

Royall Consorts

Royall Consorts – No 2 in D minor; No 4 in D;   Ⓟ

No 5 in D; No 8 in C; No 10 in B flat
The Greate Consort (Anne Schumann vn Emilia
Benjamin, Reiko Ichise va da gambas Elizabeth
Kenny, William Carter theorbos) / **Monica Huggett** vn
ASV Gaudeamus CDGAU147 (68' · DDD)   Ⓕ○

These formalised dances give us a less familiar
view of this composer: the broody cavalier
reflecting, in exquisitely fashioned thematic
strains, the unequivocal decorum of musical
conceits in Charles I's cultivated time-bomb of
a court. The soft-grained and unforced string
timbre of The Greate Consort is underpinned
by delightfully subtle and undemonstrative theorbo playing. For some, the characterisation in,
say, the Aires of Consort No 4 will seem a touch
under-explored but given the Pavan's wonderful concentration of seamless allusions, gently
passed back and forth, the sense of an integral
suite is strongly and vitally projected. Monica
Huggett leads by example with tonal sweetness
and exemplary musicianship. Rare qualities
indeed, and treasure from which she has
effected chamber music playing of the very
highest quality.

Jean-Marie Leclair   French 1697-1764

*French composer and violinist Leclair was initially a
dancer. He lived from 1723 in Paris, where he
became a prominent soloist and began producing violin sonatas (from 1723). He also appeared abroad,
and in 1733 became ordinaire de la musique du roi
at the French court. In 1738-43 he served the court
of Orange in the Netherlands and (in 1740-43)
Franç;ois du Liz at The Hague. He then lived
mainly in Paris, where he was murdered (probably
by his nephew). Foremost in Leclair's output are over
60 solo, duet and trio sonatas for violin. In these he
imbued the Italian style with French elements more
successfully than most of his contemporaries, using
short ornamented phrases and colourful harmonies;
the idiom reflects his own virtuoso technique. He also
composed concertos, minuets, suites etc, ballet music,
an opera (Scylla et Glaucus, 1746) with many striking features and other vocal music. He was an influential teacher and is considered the founder of the
French violin school.*   GROVEmusic

Violin Concertos

Violin Concertos – Op 7: No 4 in F; No 6 in A.   Ⓟ
No 2 in A, Op 10. Flute Concerto No 3 in C, Op 7.
Rachel Brown fl **Collegium Musicum 90 / Simon
Standage** vn
Chandos Chaconne CHAN0564 (65' · DDD)
Recorded 1994   Ⓕ○

Of the violin concertos here, Op 10 No 2 is the
richest harmonically. The solo instrument in
Op 7 No 3 is Leclair's stated alternative of flute,
the only one of his 12 violin concertos to be
so designed. Accordingly, it lacks the double-
stopping so much favoured by this greatly

admired violinist-composer. Otherwise it exploits the graceful sequential passagework
found in the other concertos, though here with
a fuller accompanying texture, with more movement in inner parts. Rachel Brown's playing
throughout is deliciously cool and poised. Virtuoso violin fireworks abound in the vigorous
first movements of the other two Op 7 concertos here and the ebullient finale of the A major:
as expected, Simon Standage throws off their
difficulties with panache and an apparent ease
that allows him also to add stylish embellishments of his own. The extensive multiple-stop-
ping on which the elegant minuet-like Aria of
Op 7 No 6 relies is performed with well-nigh
impeccable intonation.

Violin Concertos – Op 7: No 1 in D minor.   Ⓟ
Op 10: No 3 in D; No 4 in F; No 6 in G minor
Collegium Musicum 90 / Simon Standage vn
Chandos Chaconne CHAN0589 (59' · DDD)   Ⓕ○

This disc contains Leclair's most vivacious and
attractive works, played with great élan, sensitivity and neatness, and recorded with exemplary clarity and balance. The concertos represent a high-water mark in 18th-century violin
technique, with extensive double-stopping, an
extended range that soars up to heights scarcely
ventured previously, rapid scales and flying
arpeggios, and elaborate figurations of all kinds.
To all of this Standage brings a seasoned virtuosity which he places totally at the service of the
music's grace: his bowing in particular commands admiration. From the stylistic viewpoint
these concertos are interesting for their mingling of French and Italian elements. There are
Vivaldian unisons, but French dance forms for
the middle movements – a pair of minuets in the
D minor, minuets en rondeau in the G minor, a
pair of gavottes with unusual interplay between
solo and tutti in the F major, and an ornate solo
line over supporting reiterated chords in the D
major. Standage adds spontaneous embellishments of his own on repeats.

Violin Sonatas

Violin Sonatas, Op 1 – No 1 in A minor;   Ⓟ
No 3 in B flat; No 8 in G; No 9 in A
François Fernandez vn **Pierre Hantaï** hpd **Philippe
Pierlot** va da gamba
Astrée Naïve E8662 (64' · DDD)   Ⓕ

Leclair's Op 1 set was so successful when it was
first published in 1723 that it had to be
reprinted four times. Though it makes considerable technical demands on the violinist, the
composer himself was at pains not to employ
virtuosity as an end in itself and to condemn the
'trivialisation' of players who exaggerated the
speed of quick movements. Leclair also, like
Couperin, was insistent that performers should
not add ornamentation of their own – though in
the four sonatas here only the initial *Adagio* of

549

No 3 is much decorated. Rather did he place emphasis on 'le beau chant' – expressive *cantabile*, which is well exemplified in the first movements of Nos 1, 8 and 9. The crisp *Allegro*, with its rapid dipping across strings, and the *Largo* of No 3 make play with multiple stopping, including double trills, and there's vigorous cross-string work too in the ebullient Giga of No 1. Leclair shows himself fond of the rondeau form with long episodes, and the Sarabande of No 9 is a set of variations. This last has an athletic gamba line, as does the whole of the G major Sonata; and the alert and positive continuo playing here (from both gamba and harpsichord) is a special pleasure. But naturally the main spotlight falls on François Fernandez, whose lively, pointed bowing, delicate fast movements and graceful slow ones (like the gentle G major Musette) do full justice to Leclair's attractive invention.

Ernesto Lecuona   Cuban 1895-1963

Born into a musical family, he played the piano from an early age and wrote his first song when he was 11. He graduated from the National Conservatory in Havana in 1913 and soon made his first appearance as a composer-pianist. Then, after further studies with Joaquín Nin, he made several tours of Latin America, Europe and the USA as the leader of a dance band, Lecuona's Cuban Boys, which became quite well known. For some years he lived in New York, where he wrote for musicals, films and the radio. In his concerts he usually performed his songs and dances for piano, as well as light pieces by other late 19th-century and early 20th-century Cuban composers. His salon piano pieces, using 'white' peasant and Afro-Cuban rhythms, found wide favour, and many of his songs, too, achieved great popularity. **GROVE**music

Songs

On a Night Like This
Siempre en mi corazón. Como presiento. Allá en la sierra. Tu no tienes corazón. Mi corazón se fué. Dame de tus rosas. ¡No es por ti! La habanera – ¡Mira! Dame el amor. Que risa me da. La comparsa. Al fin. Se abrieron las flores. Conga Cuba. Amor tardio. En una noche así. Devuélveme el corazón. Primavera de ilusión. Un amor vendrá. Me has dejado. No me engañarás. Rumba mejoral. No me mires ni me hables. Mi amor fue una flor. Canción del amor triste.
Carole Farley *sop* **John Constable** *pf*
BIS BIS-CD1374 (70' · DDD) Texts and translations included   Ⓕ Ⓞ

It's curious to think that Paul Hindemith and Ernesto Lecuona were almost exact contemporaries, born a couple of months apart in 1895 and dying within five weeks of each other at the end of 1963. Yet, despite this closeness in time, their music had no real common ground.

Hindemith was no mean song-writer, though not especially prolific, unlike the Cuban Lecuona for whom song was a paramount form of expression: he wrote around 400 of them.

For this recording Carole Farley undertook a protracted detective hunt through libraries, publishers, basements and packing cases to arrive at her selection of 25 love songs. Hers is a fine and varied choice, highlighting Lecuona's undeniable gifts as a melodist and word-setter, ranging between the overtly romantic – as in the opening *Siempre en mi corazón* ('Always in my heart') and *Primavera de ilusión* ('Spring of Illusion') – to fast and lively songs such as *Que risa me da* ('Oh, what a laugh') and *Conga Cuba*. In between these are more lilting songs such as *Como presiento* ('The feeling I have') and *Amor tardio* ('Belated love'), directly Latin numbers such as *Allá en la sierra* ('High in the Sierra') and the dramatic, scena-like *Canción del amor triste*.

Farley sings all the songs with great finesse and warmth of feeling. Very occasionally, as in *Se abrieron las flores* ('The flowers opened'), her vibrato doesn't suit Lecuona's clean lines. She's accompanied sympathetically by the excellent John Constable, whose playing is a model of precision yet catches that feeling of improvisation that is an essential part of these songs. The recording is wonderfully pure and clear.

Franz Lehár   Austro/Hungarian 1870-1948

The son of a military bandmaster and composer, Lehár studied in Prague with Foerster and Fibich and followed his father in an army career. In 1902 he resigned to work in Vienna as a conductor and composer, notably of operettas, achieving spectacular international success with Die lustige Witwe (1905), Der Graf von Luxemburg (1909) and Zigeunerliebe (1910). These and others restored the fortunes of the Viennese operetta and opened the genre to a greater musical and dramatic sophistication. After World War One his time seemed to have passed, but then came new successes, many written for Richard Tauber: Paganini (1925), Der Zarewitsch (1927), Friederike (1928), Das Land des Lächelns (1929) and Giuditta (1934). His other works include waltzes, marches and songs. **GROVE**music

Concertino for Violin and Orchestra

Tatjana – Prelude, Act 1; Prelude, Act 2; Prelude, Act 3; Russian Dances. Fieber. Il guado. Concertino for Violin and Orchestra in B flat minor. Eine Vision: meine Jugendzeit. Donaulegenden, 'An der grauen Donau'
Robert Gambill *ten* **Latica Honda-Rosenberg** *vn* **Volker Banfield** *pf* **North German Radio Philharmonic Orchestra / Klauspeter Seibel**
CPO CPO999 423-2 (70' · DDD) Texts and translations included   Ⓑ

Lehár's mastery of the orchestra has never been in doubt; and here's further evidence of his technical accomplishment. Such touches of the operetta composer as are here are of the more ambitious operetta scores such as *Zigeunerliebe*. More often it's Wagner, Richard Strauss and Korngold who come to mind. Throughout, the music is tastefully and evocatively written, and with a supreme confidence in the handling of a large orchestra. *Tatjana* was an early operatic attempt of which Lehár was especially fond, and its preludes and dances capture the starkness of its Siberian setting. *Il guado* ('The Ford') and the concert overture *Eine Vision* are works from the *Lustige Witwe* years, when Lehár was still seeking to determine in which direction his future lay. The former is a symphonic poem with some attractively rippling writing for the piano, the latter a recollection of the Bohemian countryside of his youth. The elegant *Concertino* for violin and orchestra, which has been recorded previously, is a student work that demonstrates his affection for his own instrument. *Fieber* is the starkest piece in the collection – a bitter First World War portrayal of a soldier in the throes of a deadly fever. *Donaulegenden* gives glimpses of the familiar waltz-time Lehár, but a Lehár looking back sadly at a bygone age. What other operetta or waltz composer could have written music as powerful, gripping and spine-tingling as this? Do try it!

Waltzes / Overtures

Gold und Silber, Op 79. Wiener Frauen – overture. **H**
Der Graf von Luxemburg – Waltz; Waltz Intermezzo.
Zigeunerliebe – overture. Eva – Wär' es auch nichts als ein Traum von Glück; Waltz Scene. Das Land des Lächelns – overture. Die lustige Witwe – concert overture
Zurich Tonhalle Orchestra / Franz Lehár
Dutton mono CDBP9721 (66' · ADD) Recorded 1947
⑤●

These were the 77-year-old composer's last recordings. Most were reissued on LP (latterly on the Eclipse label), but here they're complete for the first time. Mostly the selections represent obvious items from Lehár's melodic output. However, the inclusion of the *Wiener Frauen* overture is an especial joy, representing Lehár at his less familiar but most melodic and inventive. The operetta's principal character was a piano tuner, and the overture includes an ingenious passage where one hears the piano being tuned up before launching into one of Lehár's most luxuriant and beautiful waltzes.

In his excellent notes Malcolm Walker aptly describes these recordings as, in a sense, Lehár's last will and testament. Slower and more indulgent than his earlier recordings they may be; but never for a moment the slightest bit ponderous. Rather they're full of nostalgia, wonder and joyful pride – lovingly caressed performances by a master melodist, master orchestrator and master conductor. The transfers have been excellently done from original shellac discs. Filtering may be required to minimise hiss; but it's more than worth while for uniquely beautiful recordings of some of the most heavenly melodies ever created.

Frühling

Frühling. Elfentanz. Hungarian Fantasy, Op 45[a]
Stefanie Krahnenfeld *sop* Hedwig **Alison Browner** *sop* Toni **Robert Wörle** *ten* Lorenz **Markus Köhler** *bar* Ewald [a]**Mark Gothoni** *vn* **Deutsche Kammerakademie Neuss / Johannes Goritzki**
CPO CPO 999 727-2 (78' · DDD) Notes, text and translation included ⑤

A completely unfamiliar Lehár operetta is a surprise indeed, and an utterly delightful treat it turns out to be. Set against the background of a Viennese housing shortage, it's a 'show-within-a-show' piece, featuring amorous goings-on between a composer, his librettist and two office typists. And it's the composer who gets the girl!

It's cast on an altogether smaller scale than usual for Lehár: just four soloists, without chorus, and for smaller orchestra. Though the style is unmistakable, the music is geared to a more intimate environment – no big, cloying waltzes, everything altogether more airy and light.

Actually the recording appears to be not so much of *Frühling* but its later manifestation *Frühlingsmädel*, produced in Berlin in 1928. For this the composer added brass instruments, composed one new number, inserted orchestral arrangements of three earlier piano compositions, and most importantly added a couple of popular dance numbers. The last two numbers – the syncopated 'Wenn eine schöne Frau befiehlt' and 'Komm, die Nacht gehört der Sünde' – show Lehár at his most seductive. The score also has a wonderful duet for the two male characters discussing the delights of a lady's wardrobe, as well as a typical Lehár march duet for the two lovers.

CPO have given the piece a winning performance, admirably capturing its lightheartedness and in splendidly clear sound. This CD is altogether a sheer delight.

Giuditta

Giuditta
Deborah Riedel *sop* Giuditta **Jerry Hadley** *ten* Octavio **Jeffrey Carl** *bar* Manuele Biffi, Antonio **Andrew Busher** *spkr* Duke **Naomi Itami** *sop* Anita **Lynton Atkinson** *ten* Pierrino **William Dieghan** *ten* Sebastiano **English Chamber Orchestra / Richard Bonynge**
Telarc CD80436 (78' · DDD) Sung in English. Text included ⑤

Giuditta was Lehár's last stage work and the peak of his compositional development. Written for the Vienna State Opera, it's a highly ambitious score, containing some fiendishly difficult vocal writing and using a large orchestra featuring mandolin and other exotic instruments. For this recording some two hours of music have been compressed into 78 minutes by means of snips here and there and the omission of a couple of subsidiary numbers. The piece has a *Carmen*-like story, about the disenchanted wife of an innkeeper who persuades a soldier to desert, before eventually abandoning and ruining him as she goes from lover to lover. The best-known number is Giuditta's 'On my lips every kiss is like wine', here gloriously sung by Deborah Riedel; the leading male role was written for Tauber, and there are some marvellous and demanding tenor solos, equally superbly sung by the impressive Jerry Hadley. Despite writing for the opera house, Lehár remained faithful to his formula of interspersing the music for the principal couple with sprightly dance numbers for a comedy pair, here in the hands of Naomi Itami and Lynton Atkinson. Assisted by Richard Bonynge's lilting conducting, these contribute richly to the appeal of the recording.

Das Land des Lächelns

Das Land des Lächelns
Anneliese Rothenberger sop Lisa **Harry Friedauer** ten Gustl **Nicolai Gedda** ten Sou-Chong **Renate Holm** sop Mi **Jobst Moeller** bar Tschang **Bavarian Radio Chorus; Graunke Symphony Orchestra / Willy Mattes**
EMI ② 565372-2 (87' · ADD) Recorded 1967   Ⓜ️**O**

The great glory of this *Das Land des Lächelns*, Lehár's portrayal of the clash of western and eastern cultures, is the singing of Nicolai Gedda, who brings off 'Dein ist mein ganzes Herz' and the other Richard Tauber favourites to quite splendid effect. Anneliese Rothenberger is on excellent form vocally and full of charm, and she and Gedda make an excellent partnership. Renate Holm is a smiling Mi and the other principals, chorus and orchestra all play their full parts. Willy Mattes is an experienced and sympathetic conductor of operetta. The score here isn't the one given in London when the operetta was first produced there in 1931. Apparently, Tauber was in and out of the cast every other day, providing his understudy, Robert Naylor, with plenty of opportunities. The show had only a short run. It seems that people wanted to hear Tauber rather than Lehár. This reissue should be in every Viennese operetta collection.

Die lustige Witwe (The Merry Widow)

Die lustige Witwe
Cheryl Studer sop Hanna **Boje Skovhus** bar Danilo **Bryn Terfel** bass-bar Zeta **Rainer Trost** ten Camille **Barbara Bonney** sop Valencienne **Uwe Peper** ten Raoul **Karl-Magnus Fredriksson** bar Cascada **Heinz Zednik** ten Njegus **Richard Savage** bar Bogdanowitsch **Lynette Alcantara** sop Sylviane **Philip Salmon** ten Kromow **Constanze Backes** mez Olga **Julian Clarkson** bass Pritschitsch **Angela Kazimierczuk** sop Praskowia **Wiener Tschuschen-**

kapelle; **Vienna Philharmonic Orchestra / Sir John Eliot Gardiner**
DG 439 911-2GH (80' · DDD) Recorded 1994. Notes, text and translation included   Ⓕ**OO**

This is a truly great operetta interpretation. Gardiner's approach is on an altogether more inspired plane than his rivals. In the Viennese rhythms, he shows himself utterly at home – as in the Act 2 Dance scene, where he eases the orchestra irresistibly into the famous waltz. But there are also countless instances where Gardiner provides a deliciously fresh inflexion to the score. The cast of singers is uniformly impressive. If Cheryl Studer's 'Vilja' isn't quite as assured as some others, her captivatingly playful 'Dummer, dummer Reitersmann' is typical of a well-characterised performance. As Danilo, Boje Skovhus acquits himself well with a polished performance and he offers a natural, more human characterisation than his rivals, while Barbara Bonney is superb. Not the least inspired piece of casting comes with Bryn Terfel, who transforms himself outstandingly well into the bluff Pontevedran ambassador. As for Gardiner's personally selected chorus, they make Monteverdi to Montenegro and Pontevedra seem the most natural transition in the world. DG's recorded sound has an astonishing clarity and immediacy, as in the way the piccolos shriek out at the Widow's Act 1 entrance or in the beautiful *pianissimo* accompaniment to the 'Vilja-Lied'.

Die lustige Witwe   **H**
Dame Elisabeth Schwarzkopf sop Hanna **Erich Kunz** bar Danilo **Anton Niessner** bar Zeta **Nicolai Gedda** ten Camille **Emmy Loose** sop Valencienne **Josef Schmidinger** bass Raoul **Ottakar Kraus** bar Cascada **Philharmonia Orchestra and Chorus / Otto Ackermann**
EMI mono 5858222 (72' · ADD) Recorded 1953
Ⓕ**OOO**

This is a star-studded performance. Emmy Loose has exactly the right appealing kind of voice for the 'dutiful wife' who plays with fire, and Nicolai Gedda is a superb Camille, sounding extraordinarily like Tito Schipa at his best. His high notes ring out finely and his caressing lyrical tones would upset a far better-balanced woman than the susceptible Valencienne. These two sing their duets beautifully, both excelling in the second act duet, in which Gedda has the lion's share. Nothing in this recording, except Schwarzkopf's 'Vilia', is so ravishing as his soft tone in the second half of the duet ('Love in my heart is waking'), which begins 'Sieh' dort den kleinen Pavillon' ('See over there the little pavilion') which is perhaps the loveliest in the score. Erich Kunz has not the charm but more voice and a perfect command of the style the music requires; and he's very taking in the celebrated Maxim's song. He speaks the middle section of the little song about the Königskinder possibly because the vocal part lies uncomfortably high for him; and perhaps his rich laughter would not be considered quite the thing in the diplomatic service. But his is, in most ways, a very attractive and lively performance. The Baron's part was probably much written up for George Graves but here what little he has to do is done well by Anton Niessner.

Elisabeth Schwarzkopf sings Hanna radiantly and exquisitely. She commands the ensembles in no uncertain manner and makes it clear that the 20-million-francs widow would be a personage even if she had only 20 centimes. It's a grand performance, crowned with the sensuous, tender singing of the celebrated waltz in Act 3. The chorus singing is first-rate and its Viennese abandon sounds absolutely authentic, whatever its address. Otto Ackermann conducts with total understanding, and notable sympathy for the singers, and the members of the Philharmonia Orchestra play like angels for him. The recording is as good as one can reasonably expect and, very important in such a score, the string tone is lovely throughout.

Tatjana

Tatjana
Roland Schubert bass **Sergej; Dagmar Schellenberger** sop Tatjana **Herbert Lippert** ten Alexis **Karsten Mewes** bar Sasha **Carsten Sabrowski** bass-bar Djerid, Nikolajev **Sebastian Bluth** bar Pimen **Olaf Lemme** bar Punin **Hanne Fischer** mez Raisa **Dieter Scholz** bass Starost von Uslon **Berlin Radio Chorus and Symphony Orchestra / Michail Jurowski**
CPO ② CPO999 762-2 (122' · DDD) Notes, text and translation included   Ⓕ

Franz Lehár was a reluctant operetta composer. His ambitions lay in serious music. When his three-act *Kukuška* was produced in Leipzig in 1896 he promptly resigned his job as military bandmaster, only to resume the drudgery of military service when it failed. Not until 1902, when he was 32, did conducting and composition enable him to give up the uniform for good. He didn't abandon *Kukuška* but later revised the work as *Tatjana*, achieving productions in 1905 at Brno, and in 1906 at the Vienna Volksoper. By then *Die lustige Witwe* had begun its triumphant progress around the globe. Lehár conducted a Leipzig radio performance of *Tatjana* in 1937; but that was it until the Berlin Radio concert performance in April 2001 that's preserved on these two CDs.

The opera opens on the banks of the Volga in the 1840s, moves on to the mines of Siberia, and ends on the Russian steppes. There, in the snow, the lovers Alexis, a soldier, and Tatjana, the daughter of a Volga fisherman, die together.

Lehár's musical language is very much of its time. There are hints of Wagner, perhaps rather more of Tchaikovsky's own Tatyana in *Eugene Onegin*, and something of the ill-fated love-match of Puccini's *Manon Lescaut*. The setting reminds us specifically of Giordano's *Siberia*. Yet the composer the music most obviously evokes is Lehár himself – the orchestral master who so expertly captured local colour and who could weave instrumental strands into a ravishing orchestral whole. The performance is very capably done, if with the atmosphere of a concert performance rather than a full staging. Herbert Lippert's Alexis is sung with clarity and brilliance, if a touch short on true passion. Dagmar Schellenberger's Tatjana is a shade too mature, lacking purity in her upper ranges, and yet overall agreeably done. It remains a piece of beautiful lyrical writing, brilliant orchestral colouring and impassioned melody.

Jón Leifs   Icelandic 1899-1968

Leifs studied in Leipzig (1916-22) and conducted various German orchestras. He wrote orchestral, vocal and piano music based on Icelandic folk music, which he championed.   GROVEmusic

Organ Concerto

Concerto for Organ and Orchestra, Op 7ª. Dettifoss, Op 57ᵇ. Fine II, 'Farewell to Earthly Life', Op 56ᶜ. Variazioni pastorale, Op 8
ªBjörn Steinar Sólbergsson org ᵇLoftur Erlingsson bar ᶜReynir Sigurdsson vib ᵇHallgrím's Church Motet Choir; Iceland Symphony Orchestra / En Shao
BIS CD930 (56' · DDD)   ⒻO

Well received at its 1935 première in a Nazi-arranged Nordic music festival, Leifs' Organ Concerto was execrated later once the Jewish connections of Leifs's wife had become known. A piece long heard-of but unheard, this performance reveals the concerto to be a truly original utterance. Björn Steinar Sólbergsson gives a consummate rendition of what sounds like a monstrously difficult solo part.

The orchestra is given music of unusual delicacy (for this composer) in the *Variazioni pastorale* (on a theme from Beethoven's *Serenade*, also Op 8), though the pastoralism is more redolent of Roy Harris than Beethoven. In this work, also completed in 1930, Leifs's real voice again emerges gradually, and the return of Beethoven's theme at the close is wonderfully surreal – though the tonal framework remains more conventional than in the later works. *Fine II* (1963) is one of two orchestral endings Leifs penned for his unfinished Edda oratorio, *Twilight of the Gods*. *Dettifoss* (1964) is the third of Leifs's tone paintings (the others are *Geysir* and *Hekla*) of Icelandic natural wonders, though here he conceived of a dialogue between poet Einar Benediktsson and the huge waterfall rather than straight depiction. Thumpingly good performances from all concerned, captured in spectacular sound to match the landscape.

Hekla

Elegy, Op 53[c]. Hekla, Op 52[bc]. Icelandic Overture, Op 9[ac]. Loftr-Suite, Op 6a[c]. Réminiscence du Nord, Op 40[c]. Requiem, Op 33b[a]
[a]**Hallgrím's Church Motet Choir;** [b]**Schola Cantorum;** [c]**Iceland Symphony Orchestra / En Shao**
BIS CD1030 (65' · DDD) Texts and translations included   Ⓕ

Hekla (1961) is, like *The Rite of Spring*, enormously complex in texture, such that it's practically impossible to achieve a truly definitive account in which everything can be heard. Highlight one passage and another is likely to be submerged. So it proves when comparing recordings of it. The bells that feature prominently early on do not ring out in this newcomer, although rather more other detail does than in the competitors. En Shao's is a more measured approach and the benefits of the slower speeds outweigh any minor losses. The rival accounts from Leif Segerstam and Paul Zukofsky are still very fine, but this new release is the one to have. It's a signal tribute to Leifs's growing popularity that all but one of the works here have alternatives to compare them with.

En Shao and Petri Sakari (Chandos) are fairly close in terms of expressive intent and tempo here, as indeed they are in the exuberant if loosely constructed *Icelandic Overture* (1926). The latter work and the extended and searching *Réminiscence du Nord* for strings (1952) have a flavour suggestive of Roy Harris about them, which is remarkable given that the Overture pre-dates the American's famous Third Symphony by some 12 years. The *Elegy* for strings (1961, in memory of his mother) and *Requiem* show the private side to Leifs not heard much in works composed in his more 'public' manner. The *Elegy* is less interesting, however deeply felt, than *Réminiscence du Nord* or Requiem (1947, to a non-liturgical text assembled by Leifs). The motet is without doubt a gem, a lullaby to a dead child whom the parent seems frightened to wake. Beneath the surface gentleness is an undertow of dissonance like a barely suppressed howl of anguish.

Kenneth Leighton   British 1929-1988

Leighton studied at Oxford and with Petrassi in Rome, and in 1970 was appointed professor at Edinburgh University. His music is in a 12-note but fundamentally diatonic style; its romanticism is expressed in lyrical melody, instrumental colour and virtuoso solo writing. It includes Catholic church music, concertos, chamber and instrumental pieces.
GROVEmusic

Chamber Works

Piano Trio, Op 46[abc]. Partita, Op 35[ac]. Metamorphoses, Op 48[ab]. Elegy, Op 5[ac]

[a]**Michael Dussek** *pf* [b]**Lorraine McAslan** *vn* [c]**Andrew Fuller** *vc*
Dutton Epoch CDLX7118 (77' · DDD)   Ⓜ

Although a fair amount of his music for voices has been recorded, Kenneth Leighton's orchestral and instrumental music is seriously underrepresented in the catalogue. This most impressive disc gives a good idea of what we're missing: superbly crafted music of at times overwhelming intensity. The craft and the intensity are inseparable: there's as little here of mere technical cleverness as there is of self-indulgent emotional display; the emotion both needs and is concentrated by tight control.

The Piano Trio is a characteristic example, its first movement building from close working of a broad, sweeping theme and a more subdued and shadowy one to a bitter eloquence slightly reminiscent of Shostakovich before a shadowy, drained conclusion. Calm is eventually achieved, but not serenity. The Partita has similar energy but a less fraught quality; there's even a sort of bony wit, again recalling Shostakovich, to some of the variations of the finale.

Metamorphoses, although ostensibly a single 21-minute movement, could be read as a monothematic sonata, with a quite violent *scherzo* and a slow finale, by turns poignant and ghostly. The very early *Elegy* reveals some of Leighton's English roots: descendants of its sustained lyrical theme can be heard in the later pieces, but there are some harmonic shifts that John Ireland would have approved.

The programme, in short, is an ideal introduction to this important but still underrated composer. He's not underrated by these artists, however, who play with passionate conviction and splendid risk-taking attack; they're admirably recorded.

Additional recommentation

Sacred Choral Music
Crucifixus pro nobis, Op 38. An Easter Sequence, Op 55. Evening Service, 'Collegium Magdalenae Oxoniense'. Evening Service, Op 62. Give me the wings of faith. Rockingham. Veni creator spiritus. What love of this is thine?
Oxley *ten* **Whitton** *org* **Steele-Perkins** *tpt* **St John's College Choir, Cambridge / Robinson**
Naxos 8 555795 (67' · DDD)   Ⓢ

Our reviewer summed up: 'In this business of record-reviewing I find, on the positive side, music and performances I like, more that I admire, some that I love, but not much that evokes affirmation from the soul. This does.'

God's Grandeur

God's Grandeur. What love is this of thine?. Give me wings of faith[a]. Crucifixus pro nobis, Op 38[a]. Lully, lulla, thou little tiny child, Op 25b. Mass, Op 44[a]. Laudate pueri, Op 68

Finzi Singers / Paul Spicer with [a]Andrew
Lumsden org
Chandos CHAN9485 (71' · DDD) Recorded 1993.
Texts and translations included   (F)

There's a fine unease in Kenneth Leighton, a
sense that fulfilment, musical and spiritual,
must be striven for, that nothing worthwhile is
gained without what Hardy called 'a full look at
the worst'. Every new phrase in these choral settings sounds like the outcome of innumerable
rejections: nothing is facile. In several of them,
comfort is found – in *God's Grandeur* 'There
lives the dearest freshness', in *What love is this of
thine?* 'Oh, that thy love might overflow my
heart' – and with it a sweetness that means so
much more when hard won out of bleakness.
He's a composer for the pilgrimage – not joyless
by any means, but serious. In this excellent
programme never does anything compromise
this integrity. The works range from a student
composition, his fine, independent setting of
the Coventry Carol, to the anthem, *What love is
this of thine?*, written not very long before his
death.

The performances have all that could be
desired in textual responsiveness and technical
control. Somewhere among the sopranos is a
voice (or it may be two voices) which at a *forte*
has a worn or otherwise obtrusive edge; but
clearly all members are valuable singers, as is
shown by the ample supply of soloists from the
ranks. Most of the works here are sung *a cappella*, those that aren't being accompanied with
clarity and discretion by Lumsden. The acoustic
of All Saints', Tooting, is resonant but not
excessively so. This disc is a most welcome addition to the catalogue.

Ruggiero Leoncavallo
Italian 1858-1919

*Italian composer and librettist Leoncavallo studied
literature at Bologna University. The failure of an
early opera, I Medici (1893), conceived as the first of
a Renaissance trilogy (unrealised) and written for
Giulio Ricordi who rejected it, prompted him, in a
defiant quest for fame, to write the poem and music
of Pagliacci (Milan, 1892), the single work for
which he is widely known. In its economy and consistent impetus, notably with the commedia dell'arte
playlet and the Zola-inspired prologue invoking naturalism, the opera represents a skilful exploitation of
the 1890s verismo trend; it made Leoncavallo a
celebrity overnight. That success was never repeated.
However, he set La bohème (1897) in opposition to
Puccini and the sentimental Zazà (1900) was
favourably received. One of the first composers to
become involved with gramophone records, he
wrote the popular song Mattinata (recorded by
Caruso, 1904) and conducted Pagliacci (1907), both
for the G and T Company.* **GROVE**music

Pagliacci

Pagliacci
José Cura ten Canio; **Barbara Frittoli** sop Nedda;
Carlos Alvarez bar Tonio; **Simon Keenlyside** bar
Silvio; **Charles Castronovo** ten Beppe; **Adrian
Folea** ten First Villager; **Gert Jan Alders** bass
Second Villager; **National Children's Choir**;
Netherlands Radio Choir; **Royal Concertgebouw
Orchestra / Riccardo Chailly**
Decca 467 086-2DH (73' · DDD)   (F)**OOO**

The big point in favour of this version
of *Pagliacci* is the glorious playing of
the Royal Concertgebouw Orchestra
under their long-time music director. If Riccardo Chailly in previous *verismo* opera recordings – with Italian opera orchestras – has tended
to sound aggressive and paradoxically not fully
Italianate, this is quite different. The opening
orchestral prelude instantly alerts you to the
refinement of the playing, not just in the polished ensemble but in the subtle shading of tone
and dynamic. When speeds in ensembles are on
the fast side, the results are never breathless.
Rather, they tingle with excitement, and the
scherzando wit of much of the writing comes
over with new point.

Happily Decca has lined up a first-rate cast to
match. José Cura's voice hasn't quite the glowing freshness it once had, having acquired
something of a baritonal quality, but his feeling
for detail as well as the heroic power of his voice
make his reading of Canio strong and intense,
far more than the loud rant it can become even
with leading tenors. 'Vesti la giubba' is nicely
shaped, moving without being too lachrymose,
and Cura reserves his finest singing of all for the
climactic 'No! Pagliaccio non son'.

Barbara Frittoli proves an excellent choice as
Nedda, giving a finely detailed performance,
with singing on almost every phrase showing
that she has rethought the role and its implications, rather as Callas did in her classic performance, but with more sensuous, more beautiful
tone. Another rising star, Carlos Alvarez, with
his big heroic baritone, makes an impressive
Tonio from the Prologue onwards, even if he
doesn't sound as sinister as some in his menaces.
He's well contrasted in scale and timbre with
Simon Keenlyside as Nedda's lover Silvio,
lighter and more lyrical. The *pianissimo* close to
Silvio's big duet with Nedda couldn't be subtler
from either singer, while Charles Castronovo as
Beppe in the final Play scene sings with comparable refinement.

There are few digital versions of this perennially popular opera not marred by poor recording if not flawed singing, and so this new one is
particularly welcome. Vintage versions may
offer individual performances of each role
which in various ways outshine these, but in the
power, beauty and refinement of the Royal
Concertgebouw's playing we have something
incomparable, enhanced by Decca's rich, spacious and brilliant recording.

Pagliacci

Carlo Bergonzi *ten* Canio **Joan Carlyle** *sop* Nedda
Giuseppe Taddei *bar* Tonio **Rolando Panerai** *bar*
Silvio **Ugo Benelli** *ten* Beppe **Chorus and Orchestra
of La Scala, Milan / Herbert von Karajan**
DG The Originals 449 727-2GOR (78' · ADD)
Recorded 1965. Notes, texts and translations
included   Ⓜ **OO**

Cav and Pag have been bedfellows for many
years. Lasting for about 75 minutes each, the
two operas have similarities. Each concerns the
passions, jealousies and hatred of two tightly
knit communities – the inhabitants of a Sicilian
town and the players in a travelling troupe of
actors. *Cavalleria rusticana* ('Rustic chivalry')
concerns the triangular relationship of mother,
son and his rejected lover. Played against a rich
musical tapestry, sumptuously orchestrated, the
action is played out during the course of an
Easter day. Bergonzi is a stylish, ardent Turiddu
whose virile charms glitter in his every phrase
and Fiorenza Cossotto makes a thrilling Santuzza motivated and driven by a palpable conviction; her contribution to the well-known
Easter hymn scene is gripping. But the real hero
of the opera is Karajan, whose direction of this
powerful work is magnificent. Conviction and
insight also instil *Pagliacci* with excitement and
real drama. A troupe of actors arrives to give a
performance of a *commedia dell'arte* play. The
illustration of real love, life and hatred is portrayed in the interplay of Tonio, Silvio, Nedda
and her husband Canio. As the two rivals, Caro
Bergonzi and Giuseppe Taddei are superb.
Taddei's sinister, hunch-backed clown, gently
forcing the play-within-the-play closer to reality until it finally bursts out violently is a masterly assumption, and Karajan controls the slow
build-up of tension with a grasp that few conductors could equal. The Milan La Scala forces
respond wholeheartedly and the 1965 recording
sounds well. The third disc is filled by a selection of very rich, very soft-centred opera intermezzos.

Leoncavallo Pagliacci   Ⓗ
Giuseppe di Stefano *ten* Canio **Maria Callas** *sop*
Nedda **Tito Gobbi** *bar* Tonio **Rolando Panerai** *bar*
Silvio **Nicola Monti** *ten* Beppe

Mascagni Cavalleria rusticana
Maria Callas *sop* Santuzza **Giuseppe di Stefano** *ten*
Turiddu **Rolando Panerai** *bar* Alfio **Anna Maria
Canali** *mez* Lola **Ebe Ticozzi** *contr* Lucia **Chorus and
Orchestra of La Scala, Milan / Tullio Serafin**
EMI mono ② 556287-2 (141' · ADD) Recorded 1954.
Notes, texts and translations included   Ⓕ **OO**

The sound here is much more confined than on
the Karajan set, though more immediate. Serafin conducts swifter-moving performances, yet
ones quite as notable as Karajan's for pointing
up relevant detail. All four interpretations carry
with them a real sense of the theatre and are
quite free from studio routine. It's difficult to

choose between the casts on these two sets.
Callas lives the characters more vividly than
anyone. The sadness and anguish she brings to
Santuzza's unhappy plight are at their most
compelling at 'io piango' in 'Voi lo sapete' and
at 'Turiddu mi tolse' in her encounter with
Alfio, where the pain in Santuzza's heart is
expressed in almost unbearable terms. As
Nedda, she differentiates marvellously between
the pensiveness of her aria, the passion of her
duet with Silvio, and the playfulness of her *commedia dell'arte* acting.
   Her partner in both operas is di Stefano They
work up a huge lather of passion in the big
Cavalleria duet, and the tenor is wholly believable as the caddish Turiddu. In the immediacy
of emotion of his Canio, it's the tenor's turn to
evoke pity. Di Stefano does it as well as any
Canio on record without quite having the
heroic tone for the latter part of the opera. Panerai is a strong Alfio on the Serafin set, but
Guelfi, with his huge voice, is possibly better
suited to this macho part. It's impossible to
choose between the two Tonios, both perti-
nently cast. Taddei plays the part a little more
comically, Gobbi more menacingly. Callas or
Karajan enthusiasts will have no difficulty making their choice. Others may be guided by quality of sound. With either you'll be ensured
hours of memorable listening.

Pagliacci (In English)
Dennis O'Neill *ten* Canio **Rosa Mannion** *sop* Nedda
Alan Opie *bar* Tonio **William Dazeley** *bar* Silvio
Peter Bronder *ten* Beppe **Geoffrey Mitchell Choir;
Peter Kay Children's Choir; London Philharmonic
Orchestra / David Parry**
Chandos Opera in English Series CHAN3003
(80' · DDD) Sung in English. Notes and text included
                                                Ⓕ

'Hello … Hello' is the neat rendition of 'Si può
… si può'. 'A slice of life as we live it' replaces
'life with its laughter and sorrow', 'Will ye hear
then the story?' becomes 'Now you know what
we're here for', and 'Ring up the curtain' is now
'Bring up the curtain'.
   The text is one thing, the performance
another. Opera singers are trained to pronounce their words in a very pure English which
nowadays sounds more upper-class than it did
not so long ago when all 'official' pronunciation
was 'pure' in this sense. The 'slice of life'
involves travelling players and villagers, but
they all sound like ladies and gentlemen: it takes
some of the verity out of *verismo*. Dennis
O'Neill's Canio is fine as to vocal resource and
avoidance of cheapness; but 'Un tal gioco' wants
ironical bite, 'Vesti la giubba' more sense of
occasion, 'No, Pagliaccio non son' more tension, bitterness and (at one point) sweetness.
Rosa Mannion is an admirable Nedda, and both
baritones do well, Alan Opie excellent in the
Prologue, William Dazeley a lyric baritone of
pleasing quality and tasteful style. The off-stage
serenade is nicely sung by Peter Bronder, and
the chorus is fine. David Parry's conducting has

grown in authority, and in the climax (menace in the accompaniment to 'No, Pagliaccio' for instance) more than fulfils expectations. With effective work by producer and sound engineers, this *Pagliacci* will much enhance appreciation of the opera.

Gyorgy Ligeti
Hungarian 1923

Ligeti studied with Farkas, Veress and Járdányi at the Budapest Academy, where he began teaching in 1950. During this period he followed the prevailing Kodály-Bartók style in his works while also writing more adventurous pieces (First Quartet, 1954) that had to remain unpublished. In 1956 he left Hungary for Vienna. He worked at the electronic music studio in Cologne (1957-8) and came to international prominence with his Atmosphères (1961), which works with slowly changing orchestral clusters. This led to teaching appointments in Stockholm (from 1961), Stanford (1972) and Hamburg (from 1973).

Meanwhile he developed the 'cloud' style in his Requiem (1965) and Lontano for orchestra (1967), while writing an absurdist diptych for vocal soloists and ensemble: Aventures (1966) and Nouvelles aventures (1966). His interests in immobile drifts and mechanical processes are seen together in his Second Quartet (1968) and Chamber Concerto (1970), while the orchestral Melodien (1971) introduced a tangle of melody. The combination of these elements, in music of highly controlled fantasy and excess, came in his surreal opera Le grand macabre (1978). His subsequent output has been diminished by ill-health, although it includes a Horn Trio (1982) in which perverse calculation is carried into Romanticism. Other later works include Monument, Selbstporträt, Bewegung, for two pianos (1976), two pieces for harpsichord (1978), two Hungarian studies for chorus (1983) and a book of piano studies (1985).
GROVEmusic

Concertos

Violin Concerto[a]. Cello Concerto[b]. Piano Concerto[c]
[a]**Saschko Gawriloff** vn [b]**Jean-Guihen Queyras** vc
[c]**Pierre-Laurent Aimard** pf **Ensemble**
InterContemporain / Pierre Boulez
DG 439 808-2GH (67' · DDD) Recorded 1992-3
Ⓕ**OOO**

The Violin Concerto (1992) is music by a composer fascinated with Shakespeare's *The Tempest*: indeed, it might even prove to be a substitute for Ligeti's long-mooted operatic version of the play. There are plenty of 'strange noises', the result not just of Ligeti's latter-day predilection for ocarinas, but of his remarkable ability to play off natural and artificial tunings against each other. This work is superior to the Piano Concerto because the solo violin is so much more volatile and poetic as a protagonist, an animator who 'fires up' the orchestra, functioning as a leader at odds with the led. Saschko Gawriloff is a brilliantly effec-

tive soloist, and well served by a sharply defined yet expressive accompaniment – Boulez at his most incisive – and a totally convincing recording. The other works are played and recorded with similar success. The Cello Concerto (1966) is a particularly powerful reminder of the strengths of the earlier Ligeti, where simple, basic elements generate anything but minimal consequences.

Cello Concerto[b]. Violin Concerto[c]. Clocks and Clouds[a]. Sippal, dobbal, nádihegedüvel, 'With pipes, drums, fiddles'[d]
[d]**Katalin Károlyi** mez [c]**Frank Peter Zimmermann** vn [b]**Siegfried Palm** vc [d]**Amadinda Percussion Group;** [a]**Cappella Amsterdam;** [abc]**Asko Ensemble;** [abc]**Schönberg Ensemble /** [abc]**Reinbert de Leeuw**
Teldec 8573 87631-2 (67' · DDD)
Ⓕ**O**

This CD forms an ideal overview of Ligeti's work and a great introduction to his music. The Cello Concerto (1966) juxtaposes the primary Ligetian musical 'types' of this period – frozen, imperceptibly changing planes of sound, and surreal gestures which collide in manic and unpredictable ways. Good that Siegfried Palm was able to record a work he himself premièred, in an account less perfectly realised but more characterful than that by Jean-Guihen Queyras (reviewed above). As the title implies, *Clocks and Clouds* (1973) superimposes rigour and freedom – with a nod towards Minimalist thinking of the period – to create the archetypal Ligeti composition. In what is surprisingly its first commercial recording, balance between voices and ensemble could have had greater spatial depth, but the ethereal nature of the soundscape comes through unimpeded.

In just a decade, the Violin Concerto has established itself as a modern classic, combining Ligeti's love of polyrhythmic interplay and varied tunings with a heady recall of his Bartókian heritage. Frank Peter Zimmermann yields to Saschko Gawriloff in the finely judged poise of the opening *Vivacissimo* and Intermezzo. Elsewhere, however, his greater immediacy pays off, with a visceral edge to the closing cadenza that's truly hair-raising. If marginally less accurate than Boulez in his handling of the orchestra, Reinbert de Leeuw is more alive to its extremes of emotional anguish and deadpan humour, bringing the music vividly to life.

With personable notes from the composer, this is certainly the Ligeti disc that should be in everyone's collection.

Piano Concerto[a]. Chamber Concerto. Melodien. Mysteries of the Macabre[b] (arr Howarth)
[b]**Peter Masseurs** tpt [a]**Pierre-Laurent Aimard** pf
ASKO Ensemble; Schönberg Ensemble / Reinbert de Leeuw
Teldec New Line 8573 83953-2 (64' · DDD)
Ⓕ**O**

It's good that Teldec has picked up where Sony left off in issuing a complete edition of Ligeti's authorised works. *Melodien*, in particular, has been ill-served on disc: surprisingly so, as its 13 minutes are a microcosm of Ligetian practice at its most refined and accessible, the transitions between apparent activity and real stasis magically effected. The ASKO Ensemble has greater dynamic nuance than the London Sinfonietta's pioneering account on Decca, reaffirming just why this music has had such an impact on a generation of European (not least British) composers. The Chamber Concerto has been better represented. This paring down to essentials of the harmonic and textural mesh familiar from earlier works, out of which melodic lines can then reassert themselves, is deftly achieved with no little humour. Compared with Boulez, de Leeuw feels a shade deadpan, but 'Calmo' has real plangency and 'Movimento' is pungently mechanistic.

Whether through familiarity or a more integrated balance with the orchestra, Aimard doesn't quite recapture the sense of daring in his 1992 account of the Piano Concerto, notably the opening *Vivace*'s freewheeling polyrhythms and the fractured energy of the fourth movement, where Boulez's precision still allows for a more spontaneous interplay. Yet the *Lento*'s folk inflections are fervently expressive, and the overall impression is of a work that seems far more unsettling than it did a decade ago: a sure sign of interpretative flexibility and musical durability.

It was a neat touch to sign off with Elgar Howarth's *Macabre* paraphrase. Masseurs is fully equipped to deliver the necessary pyrotechnics, while this first recording with ensemble accompaniment gives the music a more strident feel, in keeping with its operatic context. Ligeti can feel well served.

Lontano

Lontano[a]. Atmosphères[a]. Apparitions.
San Francisco Polyphony[a]. Concert Românesc
Berlin Philharmonic Orchestra / Jonathan Nott
Teldec 8573-88261-2 (55' · DDD) [a]Recorded live 2001
Ⓕ●

Here at last are the scores with which the composer first made his name in the early 1960s (*Apparitions* and *Atmosphères*); here also is *Lontano* (1967), one of the finest orchestral scores of the 20th century, and *San Francisco Polyphony* of 1974, which inaugurates the more self-consciously virtuosic and referential approach that characterises Ligeti's subsequent works for large forces (*Le Grand Macabre*, and the concertos for piano, violin and horn); and, as a postscript of sorts, an early score from the composer's pre-Western period. The latter has its first recording here; rather more incredibly (given its position in Ligeti's output), so does *Apparitions*. On the last count alone, this recording is simply a must for anyone interested in 'new music'.

The two premières here are studio recordings,

whereas *Atmosphères*, *Lontano* and *San Francisco Polyphony* were recorded live. A previous recording of *Atmosphères* and *Lontano* with the Vienna Philharmonic under Claudio Abbado was also live, and unsatisfactory on a number of counts (not least unwanted audience 'participation'). Thankfully there are very few such problems here: the general accuracy is commendable, considering the difficulty of co-ordinating dozens of individual lines (for example, getting 80-odd instruments to attack *pianissimo* together at the beginning of *Atmosphères*: the Berliners just about manage it; at any rate, they're nearer the mark than any of the other recordings). The sound-quality has all the requisite impact and delicacy, and the orchestra's shaping of line and continuity (and, when required, their opposites) is equally persuasive.

String Quartets

String Quartets – No 1, 'Métamorphoses nocturnes'; No 2
Artemis Quartet (Heime Müller, Natalia Prischepenko vns Volker Jacobsen va Eckart Runge vc)
Ars Musici AM1276-2 (43' · DDD)   Ⓕ●

Few string quartets of the late 20th century are as often performed as these, and it was only a matter of time before one of the up-and-coming younger ensembles took up the challenge thrown down by the Arditti Quartet in their recent re-recording of both pieces for Sony (their earlier reading on Wergo dates from the late 1970s). The First Quartet, *Métamorphoses nocturnes*, dates from Ligeti's Hungarian period, and the evident debt to Bartók notwithstanding, his approach to mass and textural transformation is recognisable to anyone familiar with his later music. To their credit, the Artemis let the music breathe, and make much of Ligeti's impish humour: both works are theatrical and benefit from being 'played up', which the Artemis do perhaps more freely than the Ardittis.

But the real test comes with the Second Quartet, where the Arditti's pre-eminence is more obvious and the composer's demands rather fiercer. Here the acoustic makes a perceptible difference. The Arditti's ambience is very resonant and has been recorded at a certain distance – presumably a lesson learnt from the Wergo session, which was miked so closely that one heard the players' tense breathing. This brings a psychological distance to the performance, and slightly blurs the sudden cuts and changes of texture on which the musical drama depends.

The Artemis are miked more closely than the Sony recording, but the sound still allows for some beautifully differentiated, 'atmospheric' timbres (like the 'organ-stops' of bar 71, first movement). There's also a more palpable sense of immediacy, and a more riotous climax in the most abrupt passages (the *ferocissimo* fourth movement, most obviously). The Artemis offer a sufficiently different view from the Ardittis to make for an unmissable alternative. First-time buyers may defer to the Arditti's pedigree but need not hesitate to start here.

Horn Trio

Horn Trio[a]. Six Bagatelles[b]. 10 Pieces[b]. Sonata for Solo Viola[c]
[a]**Marie Luise Neunecker** hn [a]**Saschko Gawriloff** vn [c]**Tabea Zimmermann** va [a]**Pierre-Laurent Aimard** pf
[b]**London Winds** (Philippa Davies fl Gareth Hulse ob Michael Collins cl Robin O'Neill bn Richard Watkins hn)
Sony Classical SK62309 (71' · DDD) Recorded 1994-6
(F)**O**

Those looking for a specific reason to buy this disc need look no further than the account of the Horn Trio, Ligeti's homage to Brahms, a work which has become a classic of its kind. What distinguishes this version is the astonishing horn-playing of Marie Luise Neunecker – the impression of near-effortlessness and breadth of dynamic range she conveys are unlikely to be bettered. As to her companions, they have both recorded the Trio before, and their experience is audible.

This interpretation is especially effective at projecting the music's multiple levels and layers. As to its expressive power, even those who find Ligeti's later music problematic can hardly deny the poignant, tragic beauty of the concluding *Lamento*. The two sets of wind pieces are given polished, bravura performances by London Winds. The *Bagatelles* are among the composer's most convincing music from his pre-Western period; as to the *10 Pieces*, they plough the same furrow as those two masterpieces from the same year (1968), the Second String Quartet and *Continuum* for harpsichord; but they're altogether more lightweight, their brevity almost provocative when heard against the broader canvas of those other works. Provocative in a very different way is the Viola Sonata, completed in 1994. Listen to Tabea Zimmermann's commanding and expressive playing, and hear a composer for whom confounding the critics' expectations has always been second nature.

Etudes

Etudes Books 1-3. Musica ricercata
Pierre-Laurent Aimard pf
Sony Classical SK62308 (65' · DDD)   (F)**OOO**

Pierre-Laurent Aimard is not just a modern-music specialist but an artist of phenomenal gifts, and excellently recorded here. First impressions of the music are likely to be of its immediacy. The complexities are a problem only for the pianist – whatever the sources of Ligeti's inspiration, his ideas serve only a musical/poetic purpose. Central to these dazzling pieces is his longstanding interest in composing with layers of material in different metres or different tempos and in producing what he calls 'an illusion of rhythm'; evident,

too, are his more recent preoccupations with modern mathematics, in particular the young science of dynamical systems which seeks to explain the precarious balance between pattern and chaos, order and disorder. Ligeti's powerful imagination is fuelled by many things, but there's no question of needing a special key to enter his world. The music is enough. There can be no doubt that Ligeti's *Etudes* belong with the greatest piano music of this or any other century. They are amazing.

African Rhythms

Ligeti Etudes[a] – Fanfares; Fém; Entrelacs; Pour Irina; A bout de souffle **Reich** Clapping Music[b]. Music for Pieces of Wood[a] **Traditional** Bossobe[c]. Bobangi[c]. Yangissa[c]. Anduwa[c]. Zoboko[c]. Mohunga[c]. Mai[c]. Banga Banga[c]
Pierre-Laurent Aimard [a]pf/[b]perc cAka Pygmies
Teldec 8573-86584-2 (51' · DDD)   (F)

Highlighting the première recordings of Ligeti's Etudes 16-18, this is the perfect remedy for overexposure to the composer's polyrhythms, and abounds in thrilling contrasts. Above all, it sensitises the ear in a remarkable way to his innovations in phrasing and musical structure. The Ligeti pieces are offset by two entirely different but significant elements. The first is the complex, predominantly vocal music of the Aka Pygmies from sub-Saharan Africa, a crucial structural element of which is an instrumenal ostinato in fast time, against which the voices set short-breathed phrases of irregular length. The second element is the music of Steve Reich: *Clapping Rhythm* for two sets of hands, where the same rhythm is heard in different canonic relationships to itself, and *Music For Pieces of Wood*, which applies the processes of gradual rhythmic addition and subtraction to the same rhythmic pattern.

There are marvellous insights to be found in the juxtapositions, moving in both directions: the effect of hearing *Clapping Music* followed by the Aka Pygmies' *Bobangi*, where two pieces of iron hammer out a similar rhythm for its ostinato background, followed immediately by the ostinato of Ligeti's Fourth Etude, which is in the same 'key' as *Bobangi*.

Aimard's playing of the Ligeti is without parallel, but this is no surprise. Just as rewarding, though, are *Clapping Music* and *Music For Pieces of Wood*, where he is found clapping and playing overdubbed on himself – outstandingly exciting and revealing accounts.

At just 51 minutes, this disc is perfect for anybody hungry for a new kind of listening experience. It's also a perfect introduction to the very particular world of Ligeti's piano études.

Le grand macabre

Le grand macabre
Sibylle Ehlert sop Venus, Gepopo **Laura Claycomb** sop Amanda **Charlotte Hellekant** mez Amando

Derek Lee Ragin *counterten* Prince Go-Go **Jard van Nes** *contr* Mescalina **Graham Clark** *ten* Piet the Pot **Willard White** *bass* Nekrotzar **Frode Olsen** *bass* Astradamors **Martin Winkler** *bar* Ruffiak **Marc Campbell-Griffiths** *bar* Schobiak **Michael Lessiter** *bar* Schabernack **Steven Cole** *ten* White Minister **Richard Suart** *bass* Black Minister **London Sinfonietta Voices; Philharmonia Orchestra / Esa-Pekka Salonen**
Sony Classical Ligeti Edition ② S2K62312 (102' · DDD) Recorded live 1998. Text and translation included ⑫⊙

Le grand macabre, a comedy about the end of the world, an elaborate game of musical time-travel, an ambiguous dance on the brink of an abyss, looks more and more like the key opera of the end of the 20th century. Direct comparison between this version and Elgar Howarth's splendid 1987 Wergo performance is difficult, because Ligeti extensively revised the score in 1996, and it's that 'final version', as he calls it, that's recorded here. He's made a number of cuts, a great deal of what was originally spoken dialogue is now sung and there have been many changes to the scoring, making it more practical but also thinning it out. The reduction of spoken dialogue and the lightening of the orchestral texture make life a little easier for the singers (though not for the soprano singing Gepopo, which Ligeti has described as an attempt to out-Zerbinetta Zerbinetta) and for the players. The whole performance is rather more assured than Howarth's and the score's beauties are more lovingly polished. It now sounds rather closer to a 'normal' opera and, perhaps inevitably, lacks a degree of Howarth's alarming impact.

Interestingly enough, it's Salonen's performance, sung in English to a French audience, that draws more laughs at the jokes. Sibylle Ehlert is spectacularly virtuoso and Willard White's gravity is effective in the role of Nekrotzar. Graham Clark is hugely exuberant as Piet the Pot, and Steven Cole and Richard Suart make a splendid double-act of the two Ministers. Jard van Nes and Frode Olsen are perhaps inhibited by the English language from making Mescalina and Astradamors as grotesque as they can be, though both sing well, as does every other member of the cast. The recording, like the performance, is a little more comfortable, rather less in-your-face, than Howarth's. This version is the one to have – Ligeti's revisions are all improvements, and the performance is a fine one – but the older one has a shade more of the quality that Ligeti says he has hoped for in stage productions of the opera, that of 'demoniacal farce'.

Further listening

Ligeti Aventures. Nonsense Madrigals. Mysteries of the Macabre. Nouvelles Aventures. Der Sommer. Three Weores Songs. Five Arany Songs. Four Wedding Dances

Soloists; **Philharmonia Orchestra / Salonen**
Sony Classical SK62311 (72' · DDD) ⑫
A richly entertaining collection, a sort of auto-biography, ranging from Ligeti's early folk-song arrangements to the hugely inventive and funny *Nonsense Madrigals*.

Magnus Lindberg   Finnish 1958

Following piano studies, Lindberg entered the Sibelius Academy where his composition teachers included Rautavaara and Heininen. Heininen encouraged his pupils to explore the works of the European avant-garde, and this led c1980 to the founding of the informal grouping known as the Ears Open Society, through which Lindberg and his contemporaries aimed to encourage a greater awareness of mainstream modernism. Lindberg's compositional breakthrough came with two large-scale works, Action-Situation-Signification (1982) and Kraft (1983-5). Action, the work in which Lindberg first turned to musique concrète, led to his founding with Esa-Pekka Salonen the experimental Toimii Ensemble. This group, in which he plays piano and percussion, has provided him with a laboratory for his sonic development. During the late 1980s Lindberg's music approached a new modernist classicism, in which many of the communicative ingredients of a vibrant musical language (harmony, rhythm, counterpoint, melody) were reinterpreted. Key scores in this period were the orchestral/ensemble triptych Kinetics (1988), Marea (1989-90) and Joy (1989-90), reaching fulfilment in Aura (1993-4) and Arena (1994-5). Recent works, including Feria (1997), Fresco (1997) Cantigas (1999) the Cello Concerto (1999) and most recently Gran Duo (2000) have established Lindberg's international reputation as one of Finland's leading orchestral composers. **GROVE**music

Cello Concerto

Cello Concerto[b]. Cantigas[a]. Parada. Fresco
[a]**Christopher O'Neal** *ob* [b]**Anssi Karttunen** *vc* **Philharmonia Orchestra / Esa-Pekka Salonen**
Sony Classical SK89810 (80' · DDD) ⑫

A rebel whose early work was a poke in the eye for the Finnish musical establishment, Lindberg has repositioned himself in the mainstream with a series of pieces that depend less on the theatrics of live performance and more on traditional, 'classical' notions of virtuoso orchestral writing and long-range harmonic thinking. The idiom is very much his own but, if it helps, think Berio, Lutosławski, Sibelius and a lot of extra notes and apocalyptic drum thwacks.

Cantigas begins calmly, the interval of a perfect fifth permeating its opening oboe melody. The argument quickly turns dark, extravagant and very loud, with the exceptionally busy surfaces that are a hallmark of this composer's work. Some find the effect exhilarating. Others suspect that the near-constant presence of rapid figuration coruscating over slower-moving harmonies is driven by the availability of appropriate software. Wonderfully limpid passages, as exquisitely scored as anything in Oliver Knussen, coexist with near-cacophony. There may be a lack of heart, but, as in much of Lindberg's recent music, the musical current is immensely compelling.

While *Parada*'s ravishing invention is easy to enjoy, this may or may not be the place to start for the uninitiated. If the Cello Concerto makes more sense, that isn't because its idiom is less advanced but because there's a soloist whose progress we can follow. And Lindberg provides Anssi Karttunen with some fantastical technical challenges along the way. One could not describe the results as emotionally compelling. Rather, they constitute an unmissable show. The performances are brilliant and the recorded sound top-notch.

Franz Liszt
Hungarian 1811-1886

Liszt was taught the piano by his father and then Czerny, establishing himself as a remarkable concert artist by the age of 12. In Paris he studied theory and composition with Reicha and Paer; he wrote an opera and bravura piano pieces and toured France, Switzerland and England before ill-health and religious doubt made him reassess his career. Intellectual growth came through literature, and the urge to create through hearing opera and especially Paganini, whose spectacular effects Liszt transferred to the piano in original works and operatic fantasias. Meanwhile he gave lessons and began his stormy relationship (1833-44) with the (married) Countess Marie d'Agoult. They lived in Switzerland and Italy and had three children.

The greatest pianist of his time, Liszt composed some of the most difficult piano music ever written and had an extraordinarily broad repertory, from Scarlatti onwards; he invented the modern piano recital. To help raise funds for the Bonn Beethoven monument, he resumed the life of a travelling virtuoso from 1839-47; he was adulated everywhere he went. In 1848 he took up a full-time conducting post at the Weimar court, where, living with the Princess Carolyne Sayn-Wittgenstein, he wrote or revised most of the major works for which he is known, conducted new operas by Wagner, Berlioz and Verdi and, as the teacher of Hans von Bülow and others in the German avant-garde, became the figurehead of the 'New German school'. In 1861-9 he lived mainly in Rome, writing religious works (he took minor orders in 1865); from 1870 he journeyed regularly between Rome, Weimar and Budapest. He remained active as a teacher and performer to the end of his life.

Two formal traits give Liszt's compositions a personal stamp: experiment with large-scale structures (extending traditional sonata form, unifying multimovement works), and thematic transformation, or subjecting a single short idea to changes of mode, rhythm, metre, tempo or accompaniment to form the thematic basis of an entire work (as in Les préludes, the Faust-Symphonie). His 'transcendental' piano technique was similarly imaginative, springing from a desire to make the piano sound like an orchestra or as rich in scope as one. In harmony he ventured well beyond the use of augmented and diminished chords and the whole-tone scale; the late piano and choral works especially include a strikingly advanced chromaticism.

Piano works make up the greater part of Liszt's output; they range from the brilliant early studies and lyric nature pieces of the first set of Années de pèlerinage to the finely dramatic and logical B minor Sonata, a masterpiece of 19th-century piano literature. The piano works from the 1870s onwards are more austere and withdrawn, some of them impressionistic, even gloomy (Années, third set). Not all the piano music is free of bombast but among the arrangements, the symphonic transcriptions (notably of Berlioz, Beethoven and Schubert) are often faithful and ingenious, the operatic fantasias more than mere salon pieces.

Liszt invented the term 'sinfonische Dichtung' (symphonic poem) for orchestral works that did not obey traditional forms strictly and were based generally on a literary or pictorial idea. Whether first conceived as overtures (Les préludes) or as works for other media (Mazeppa), these pieces emphasise musical construction much more than story-telling. The three-movement Faust Symphony too, with its vivid character studies of Faust, Gretchen and Mephistopheles, relies on technical artifice (especially thematic transformation) more than musical narrative to convey its message; it is often considered Liszt's supreme masterpiece. Although he failed in his aim to revolutionise liturgical music, he did create in his psalm settings, Missa solemnis and the oratorio Christus some intensely dramatic choral music.

GROVEmusic

Piano Concertos

No 1 in E flat, S124; **No 2** in A, S125; **No 3** in E flat, S125a, Op Posth (ed Rosenblatt)

Liszt Piano Concertos Nos 1ᵃ & 2ᵃ. **Beethoven** Piano Sonatas Nos 10, 19 & 20
Sviatoslav Richter pf **London Symphony Orchestra / Kyrill Kondrashin**
Philips 50 Great Recordings 464 710-2PM (70' · ADD) Recorded ᵃ1961, 1963 ⓜ❍❍❍

 These were recognised as classic performances virtually from their first appearance. They're characterised not only by the intense expressiveness of Richter's playing, but also by very careful balances of orchestral texture which hitherto hadn't been much apparent in recordings of these works. Throughout, the emphasis is on poetic insight, dramatic impact; these interpretations have in these and other regards exerted a considerable influence. Yet even if sensitive readings of Liszt's concertos are now less rare, this in no way weakens the impression made by Richter's and Kondrashin's. In short, these are among the great Liszt recordings.

Piano Concertos Nos 1 & 2. Totentanz, S126
Krystian Zimerman pf **Boston Symphony
Orchestra / Seiji Ozawa**
DG 423 571-2GH (56' · DDD)   Ⓕ Ⓞ

This is playing in the grand manner. From the start of First Concerto you're aware of a consciously leonine approach. Zimerman even deliberately takes risks in a few technically perilous places where some of his colleagues, at least in the studio, play safe; and indeed his octaves in the opening cadenza are an example. The result sounds spontaneous and, yes, even brave. Ozawa and the orchestra are behind the soloist in all this. Not only do lyrical sections sing with subtlety, the big passages also are shapely. There's plenty of drive in this Concerto. In the Second Concerto Zimerman adopts a different approach; he evidently considers it a more poetic piece and the playing style, strong though it is, is to match. Finely though he handles the gentler music, there are odd sniffs and hums in the *molto espressivo* passage following the D flat major cello solo, and also in the last of the work's quiet sections. In the gorgeously grisly *Totentanz*, both the music and the playing should make your hair stand on end. The sound has a depth that suits the music and the piano is especially impressive. Zimerman's freshness (he reminds us that this is a young man's music), and the coupling, makes this disc a most desirable one.

Piano Concertos Nos 1-3. Concerto Pathétique, S365a (orch Reuss).
Louis Lortie pf **The Hague Residentie Orchestra /
George Pehlivanian**
Chandos CHAN9918 (69' · DDD)   Ⓕ

This recording triumphantly concludes Louis Lortie's Chandos cycle of Liszt's works for piano and orchestra. Once again his mastery is as fluent as it's scintillating. He's less heart-stopping or intense than his finest rivals in the two concertos (Richter and Zimerman, and Argerich in No 1 only), but his occasional distance lends enchantment, and his aristocratic brilliance brings a special distinction to pages inviting heaviness and theatricality. He does all that's humanly possible with Concerto No 3, which received its première in 1990, yet even he, alive to moments of authentic Lisztian rhetoric, can do little to erase the sense of music in urgent need of revision. Likewise the *Concerto Pathétique*, judiciously arranged from a variety of sources, storms and rants with the sort of self-conscious drama that came too easily to Liszt; never more so than in the all-guns-blazing *Allegro trionfante* conclusion. But again, the performance is exemplary; George Pehlivanian and The Hague Residentie Orchestra prove themselves admirable partners, even when they're hardly *maestoso* at the start of the First Concerto. The recordings of demonstration quality with a sensible rather than spectacular balance.

Liszt Piano Concerto No 1 **Chopin** Piano Concerto
No 1 in E minor, Op 11
Martha Argerich pf **London Symphony Orchestra /
Claudio Abbado**
DG The Originals 449 719-2GOR (56' · ADD)
Recorded 1968   Ⓜ Ⓞ

These performances, in DG's beautifully refurbished sound, remain as fanciful and coruscating as the day they were made. Argerich's fluency and re-creative spark dazzle and dumbfound to a unique degree but, given her reputation for fire-eating virtuosity, it's perhaps necessary to say that both performances quiver with rare sensitivity as well as drama. Time and again she gives a telling and haunting poetic counterpoint to her, arguably, more familiar way of trailing clouds of virtuoso glory. Abbado partners his mercurial soloist as to the manner born, finding (in the Chopin in particular) a burgeoning sense of wonder where others sound dry and foursquare.

Additional recommendations

Piano Concertos
Coupled with: Fantasia on Hungarian Folk Themes,
S123 **Chopin** Andante spianato and Grande
polonaise in E flat, Op 22
Richter pf **LSO / Kondrashin**
BBC Legends/IMG Artists mono BBCL4031-2
(69' · ADD) Live recording   Ⓜ
    Richter's London début concerts in July 1961 were the sensation of the season, and the Liszt piano concertos at the Royal Albert Hall were the climax. Solos are miked very close by today's standards but only in this respect do the concertos yield to the famous Philips studio versions, made a little later during the same London visit.

Piano Concertos[ab]
Coupled with: Mephisto Waltz. Transcendental
Study, S139 No 1[c]. Grand Fantaisie de bravoure sur
La Clochette de Paganini
Ogdon pf [a]**Bournemouth Symphony Orchestra /
Silvestri;** [b]**BBC Symphony Orchestra / C Davis**
BBC Legends/IMG Artists [c]mono BBCL4089-2
(73' · ADD) Recorded live, 1967-71   Ⓕ
    Ogdon plays here with all those characteristics inseparable from his genius: his improvisatory daring, his thrills, spills and poetry. An invaluable issue with excellent sound, he plays as if his life depended upon it.

A Dante Symphony, S109

A Dante Symphony, S109[a]. Années de pèlerinage –
deuxième année, S161, 'Italie' – No 7, Après une
lecture du Dante (fantasia quasi sonata)[b]
[a]**Berlin Radio Women's Chorus;** [a]**Berlin
Philharmonic Orchestra / Daniel Barenboim** [b]pf
Teldec 9031-77340-2 (67' · DDD) Item marked [a]
recorded live 1992   Ⓜ

This disc proves conclusively that the *Dante Symphony*, a contemporary of the *Faust Symphony*, no longer needs its apologists. Tone, full and rounded, firm and true, and rock-steady pacing elevate the opening beyond its all-too familiar resemblance to a third-rate horror-film soundtrack. As the work progresses, together with the countless examples of Berlin tone and artistry filling out, refining or shaping gestures in often revelatory ways, one becomes aware of Barenboim's skill in maintaining the large-scale tension he's created. As for the final choral Magnificat, if Liszt owed Wagner a debt of gratitude for persuading him to conclude the symphony with the 'noble and softly soaring' bars that precede a more noisily affirmative appended coda, in Barenboim's Magnificat (and much else in the symphony), it's Wagner's debt to Liszt that's more readily apparent; the *Parsifal*ian radiance of these final pages is unmistakable. More importantly, for once they sound convincingly conclusive. The live recording is spacious, focused and expertly balanced.

The *Dante* Sonata was recorded with the kind of risk-taking abandon and occasionally less than perfect execution that you might expect from a live event. Improvisatory, impulsive and full of extreme contrasts, Barenboim's *Dante* Sonata is vividly pictorial. The instrument itself (closely miked and widely spaced) sounds larger than life. This recording is riveting.

A Faust Symphony
András Molnár ten **Hungarian State Choir; Orchestra of the Franz Liszt Academy / András Ligeti**
Naxos 8 553304 (73' · DDD) Recorded 1994   Ⓢ

There's a lot right with this performance, not least being its outspoken acknowledgement of Faust's stormy character. Liszt's first-movement portrait receives zestful advocacy, less polished than some, perhaps, but fired by immense gusto. The recording, too, is endowed with plenty of body, while András Ligeti's vocal promptings vie with Toscanini's in *La bohème*! Gretchen is quite comely and Ligeti effectively traces both her darker moods and those passages associated with Faust's yearning. Mephistopheles is more angry than 'ironico' and if you want confirmation of Ligeti's Lisztian mettle, then try from 5'49" through the following minute or so: it's quite thrilling. True, woodwind pointing isn't as vivid as under, say, Leonard Bernstein, but there's certainly no lack of enthusiasm. The Orchestra of the Franz Liszt Academy gives its all and the Hungarian State Choir makes noble music of the final chorus, even though András Molnár's wobbly tenor proves to be something of a distraction. It's a compelling if flawed production, less carefully prepared than its best rivals but more spontaneous than most.

A Faust Symphony, S108

A Faust Symphony
Kenneth Riegel ten
Tanglewood Festival Chorus; Boston Symphony Orchestra / Leonard Bernstein
DG The Originals 447 449-2GOR (77' · ADD) Recorded 1976   Ⓜ Ⓞ

David Gutman's absorbing booklet-note for the Leonard Bernstein release tells how at a Tanglewood concert in 1941 Bernstein scored a triumph in modern American repertoire and Serge Koussevitzky conducted the first two movements of *A Faust Symphony*. Some 20 years later Bernstein himself made a distinguished recording of the work, faster than this superb 1976 Boston remake by almost five minutes yet ultimately less involving. The passage of time witnessed not only an easing of tempo but a heightened response to individual characters, be it Faust's swings in mood and attitude, Gretchen's tender entreaties or the unpredictable shadow-play of 'Mephistopheles'. Orchestral execution is first-rate, the strings in particular really showing their mettle (such biting incisiveness), while Bernstein's pacing, although often slower than average, invariably fits the mood. The sound too is far warmer and more lifelike than its rather opaque New York predecessor, although when it comes to the tenor soloist in the closing chorus, Kenneth Riegel is rather strident.

Hungarian Rhapsodies, S359

(Orch cpsr/Doppler) – **No 1** in F minor (piano No 14); **No 2** in D minor (piano No 2 in C sharp minor); **No 3** in D (piano No 6 in D flat); **No 4** in D minor (piano No 12 in C sharp minor). **No 5** in E minor (piano No 5); **No 6** in D, 'Carnival in Pest' (piano No 9 in E flat)

Hungarian Rhapsodies Nos 1-6
Budapest Festival Orchestra / Iván Fischer
Philips 456 570-2PH (60' · DDD)   Ⓕ Ⓞ Ⓞ

Fischer's idiomatic foray into this well-worn repertoire is distinguished by tonal lustre and high spirits, with the authentic gipsy violin of József 'Csócsi' Lendvay lending a touch of added spice to No 3 (i.e. the piano No 6) and a tangy cimbalom much in evidence throughout. Rubato is legion, though more improvisatory than schmaltzy. Liszt's orchestrations are used for Nos 4-6, with Liszt and Doppler in No 3, and Doppler alone in No 2. Even if you've never particularly liked Doppler's version of the Second, Fischer's performance is so vivid, so imaginative of phrasing, that you may well be won over. Charm abounds. There's plenty of power, too, with meaty brass and growling *crescendos* at the start of No 4, and a riot of colour to close No 6. Fischer's *Hungarian Rhapsodies* are as frisky as foals and as flavoursome as goulash, as dashing and as dancing as anyone might want. They are further aided by excellent, full-bodied sound (especially impressive at high playback levels).

Symphonic Poems

Les Préludes, S97. Mazeppa, S100. Tasso, S96.
Orpheus, S98. Mephisto Waltz No 2
Leipzig Gewandhaus Orchestra / Kurt Masur
EMI Encore 575623-2 (72' · DDD) Recorded late
1980s   ⓈOO

These are strong, exciting and idiomatic performances. Masur draws impassioned playing
from the Gewandhaus orchestra in the best
known of the tone poems, *Les Préludes*, but he
drives the music along forcefully in Mazeppa's
ride without the sense of self-indulgence that's a
danger in such virtuoso romantic pieces: the
energy is made to come from within, rather than
being applied from without. *Tasso* is always
described as rather a gloomy and unsatisfactory
work; it can be made to hold together effectively, as here. So can *Orpheus*, which includes
some of Liszt's most beautiful effects. These, as
well as the vehemence of the playing in *Mazeppa*
and *Les Préludes*, are well contained by the
recording, even if once or twice there's some
slightly artificial balance (some improbably
prominent pizzicato, for instance). But the disc
is a safe recommendation for anyone who loves
Liszt, and a fine introduction to some superb
music for anyone who doesn't.

Tasso, S96. Trois Odes funèbres, S112
Berlin Radio Men's Chorus; Berlin Radio Symphony
Orchestra / Karl Anton Rickenbacher
Koch Schwann 317682 (57' · DDD) Recorded 1994 Ⓕ

Rickenbacher's is a strong and sombre reading
of *Tasso* that responds to the powerful opening –
much the best music in a very uneven work –
and does well with the minuet passage and with
the later pages in which Liszt is at his most
assertive and least creative. Nevertheless, the
record has a claim on Lisztians for the inclusion,
as what appears to be a first recording, of three
very fine works that have lain neglected. Two
are personal elegies. Though his neglect of his
children is one of the least appealing aspects of
his normally benign and generous character, he
felt very deeply the deaths of his son Daniel and
his eldest daughter Blandine. 'Les morts', a so-
called Oration for Orchestra for Daniel, makes
use of a chorus to intone words by the Abbé
Lammenais, who at one stage affected Liszt
profoundly . 'La notte', for Blandine, is based on
Il penseroso, from the Italian book of the *Années
de pèlerinage*, but also includes some haunting
Hungarian reminiscences. He asked for these
two works to be played at his funeral. Dying
half-ignored in Bayreuth, he went to his grave
without any proper music, and the *Odes* weren't
performed until 1912. The third is a kind of
pendant to *Tasso*, and uses some of its themes.
The *Odes* are strong and moving works, perhaps
difficult to programme in concerts even individually. To have them available at last, in an ideal
recording, in very sympathetic performances, is
a cause for some gratitude.

Piano Sonata in B minor, S178

Liszt Piano Sonata. Hungarian Rhapsody No 6
Brahms Two Rhapsodies, Op 79 **Schumann** Piano
Sonata No 2 in G minor, Op 22
Martha Argerich pf
DG Galleria 437 252-2GGA (64' · ADD) Recorded
1963-72   ⓂOOO

 No one could accuse Martha Argerich
of unstructured rêverie or dalliance
and her legendary DG performance of
the Liszt Sonata from 1972 suggests a unique
level of both technical and musical achievement. Her prodigious fluency unites with a
trail-blazing temperament, and Valhalla itself
never ignited to such effect as at the central
Andante's central climax. Both here and in the
final *Prestissimo* there are reminders that Argerich has always played octaves like single notes,
displaying a technique that few if any could
equal. There are times when she becomes virtually engulfed in her own virtuosity yet this is a
performance to make other pianists turn pale
and ask, how is it possible to play like this?
Argerich's Schumann, too, is among her most
meteoric, headlong flights. In terms of sheer
brilliance she leaves all others standing yet,
amazingly, still allows us fleeting glimpses of
Eusebius (the poetic dreamer in Schumann, and
one of his most dearly cherished fictions). The
Brahms and Liszt *Rhapsodies*, taken from Argerich's very first 1963 DG disc, are among the
most incandescent yet refined on record. The
sound, when you bother to notice it, is excellent.
(The Liszt and Brahms works, are also included
in a compilation disc reviewed in the Collections section; refer to the Index.)

Piano Sonata. Nuages gris, S199. Unstern: sinistre,
disastro, S208. La lugubre gondola, S200, No 1.
R W – Venezia, S201
Maurizio Pollini pf
DG 427 322-2GH (46' · DDD)   Ⓕ

No prizes for predicting that this Liszt B minor
Sonata is technically flawless and beautifully
structured. What may come as more of a shock
is its sheer passion. To say that he plays as if his
life depended on it is an understatement, and
those who regularly accuse him of coolness
should sit down in a quiet room with this
recording, a decent hi-fi system and a large
plateful of their own words. The opening creates a sense of coiled expectancy, without
recourse to a mannered delivery, and Pollini's
superior fingerwork is soon evident. His virtuosity gains an extra dimension from his ability at
the same time to convey resistance to it – the
double octaves are demonstrably a fraction
slower than usual and yet somehow feel faster,
or at least more urgent.
There's tensed steel in the very fabric of the
playing. By the two-minute mark so much passion has been unleashed one is bound to wonder
if it has not all happened too soon. But that's to

underestimate Pollini's unerring grasp of the dramatic structure and its psychological progression from paragraph to paragraph; it's also to underestimate his capacity to find extra technical resources when it would seem beyond the power of flesh and blood to do so. Another contributing factor, is his determination to maintain the flow in lyrical paragraphs, at tempos slightly more forward-looking and with breathing-spaces slightly less conspicuous than usual. The final page is pure mastery, a fitting conclusion to a spell-binding performance. It seems not so much that Pollini has got inside the soul of the music but that the music has got inside him and used him, without mercy, for its own ends. In Pollini's hands *Unstern* certainly has a fine inexorable tread and *La lugubre gondola* and *R W – Venezia* are both beautifully weighted. The audience adds nothing to the sense of involvement in any of the three live recordings. The background ambience changes suddenly in *La lugubre gondola*. Still, after such a classic account of the Sonata, anything would have been an anti-climax.

Piano Sonata. Two Légendes, S175. Scherzo and March, S177
Nikolai Demidenko pf
Helios CDH55184 (67' · DDD) Recorded 1992   Ⓕ

Even in an impossibly competitive field Demidenko's Liszt Sonata stands out among the most imperious and articulate. His opening is precisely judged and once the Sonata is under its inflammatory way his virtuosity is of a kind to which few other pianists could pretend. The combination of punishing weight and a skittering, light-fingered agility makes for a compulsive vividness yet his economy in the first *cantando espressivo*, sung without a trace of luxuriance or indulgence, is no less typical. There are admittedly times when he holds affection at arm's length, but just as you're wondering why he commences the central *Andante* so loudly he at once withdraws into a wholly apposite remoteness or reticence. The final climax, too, is snapped off not only with a stunning sense of Lisztian drama but also with an even truer sense and understanding of Liszt's score and instructions. Demidenko's couplings are no less autocratic, with a capacity to make seemingly arbitrary ideas sound unarguable. His *Légendes* are far from benign, yet his tautness and graphic sense of their poetic power carry their own authority. He's in his element in the *Scherzo* and March's diablerie, music which, coming after the two *Légendes*, affects one like an upside-down crucifix, or some dark necromancy. The recording is outstanding.

Piano Sonata in B minor. Années de pèlerinage – Première année: Suisse – 'Vallée d'Obermann'. Two Concert Studies. Harmonies poétiques et réligieuses – No 3, 'Bénédiction de Dieu dans la solitude'
Claudio Arrau pf

LISZT PIANO SONATA – IN BRIEF

Martha Argerich
DG 437 252-2GGA   Ⓜ**OOO**
A performance of torrential passion and technical mastery, Argerich's Sonata is a work of huge emotional range. Dating from 1972, this is a roller-coaster ride that still thrills and moves.

Maurizio Pollini
DG 427 322-2GH   Ⓕ
Technically immaculate? Of course. But what you mightn't expect is the passion and soul: Pollini wears his heart on his sleeve, and offers a performance of great temperament.

Mikhail Pletnev
DG 476 7237   Ⓜ
A real demonstration of Pletnev's pianist mastery: he demonstrates a staggering range of colour and texture, all couched with spectacular technical ease.

Nikolai Demidenko
Hyperion Helios CDH55184   Ⓜ
An imperious and beautifully conceived performance that veers between playing of terrific weight and fingerwork of a filigree lightness. There's phenomenal authority in Demidenko's approach that some might find dauting, but it's most impressive pianism.

Claudio Arrau
Philips 464 713-2PM   Ⓜ
Few pianists coveyed the opulence of Liszt's work as did Claudio Arrau, a master of the Olympian stance. This is a towering achievement and a great memento of a major artist.

Paul Lewis
Harmonia Mundi HMC90 1845   Ⓕ
A deeply impressive recording by a pianist of the younger generation demonstrating aristocratic playing and a real sense of poetry.

Arnaldo Cohen
BIS BIS-CD1253   Ⓕ
A powerful and technically hugely impressive performance from Cohen which sets this mighty work in an interesting context. Fine recorded sound.

Yundi Li
DG 471 585-2   Ⓕ
A splendid second disc from this impressive young Chinese pianist (a Chopin Piano Concerto winner). He is clearly a Lisztian of serious credentials and draws a host of fabulous colours from his instrument which have been sensitively captured by DG.

Philips 50 Great Recordings 464 713-2PM (74' · ADD)
Ⓜ️Ⓞ

Listening once more to Arrau's Liszt is to recollect those many occasions in the concert hall when he seemed like Atlas holding aloft the universe, absorbed in a gargantuan feat that left his audience limp with exhaustion. Opulent, magisterial and of a range that few other pianists would contemplate, Arrau's Liszt B minor Sonata remains a towering achievement. The build to the climax of the central *Andante sostenuto* seems so choked on its own emotion it can scarcely move and, love it or hate it, that stammering climb through the final *Allegro moderato* is pure Arrau; the playing of a man possessed and not given to half measures. The 'Bénédiction' is taken very slowly, yet the result – apart from a curiously choppy and didactic view of the central *Andante* or blessing – is ineffable rather than literal. No more subtly lit recording of 'Waldesrauschen' exists, and the final triumphant home-coming in 'Vallée d'Obermann' is overwhelming. In other words Arrau joins 'those who, by the dint of glass and vapour,/ Discover stars, and sail in the wind's eye.' (Byron).

Piano Sonata in B minor, S178. Fünf Kleine Klavierstücke, S192 – in E; in A flat; in F sharp; in F sharp. Nuages gris, S199. La lugubre gondole, S200 (2nd version). RW Venezia, S201. Schlaflos, Frage und Antwort, S203. En rêve, S207. Unstern: sinistre, disastro, S208
Paul Lewis pf
Harmonia Mundi HMC90 1845 (60' · DDD)
Ⓕ️Ⓞ

Once considered musically incomprehensible and technically unplayable, the Liszt Sonata is now part of the repertoire of virtually every pianist of note. Yet even in a crowded marketplace (where Horowitz, Gilels, Richter, Argerich, Brendel, Pollini and others jostle for attention) Paul Lewis's recording stands out for its breadth, mastery and shining musicianship.

Eschewing all obvious display, he concentrates on the Sonata's monumental weight, grandeur and ever-elusive inner poetry. His sense of drama is dark and intense, and his reading of the central *Andante sostenuto* alone puts his performance in the highest league. Lewis's octaves in the final *Prestissimo* blaze before the retrospective coda are of a pulverising strength; with him the Sonata regains its stature among music's most formidable milestones.

Moving to the music of Liszt's final years, Lewis ranges from *Nuages gris*, much admired by Stravinsky, its language anticipating Debussy, Bartók and even Schoenberg, to *Unstern* (literally, and in Shakespearean terms, 'unstarred'), music of a sinister violence. If there's solace in the relatively benign world of the four *Little Pieces* and *En rêve* it's quickly shattered by *La lugubre gondole II*, a desolate elegy anticipating Wagner's funeral.

This isn't music for late-night listening, more an invitation to 'sleepless question and answer'.

But these pieces are played with a rapt and haunting sense of their attenuated beauty, making this one of the finest, most intelligently planned Liszt recitals for many years. Harmonia Mundi's sound is of demonstration quality.

Piano Sonata in B minor. Vallée d'Obermann. Funérailles. Rapsodie espagnole
Arnaldo Cohen pf
BIS BIS-CD1253 (73' · DDD)
Ⓕ️ⓄⓄ

Arnaldo Cohen's playing blazes with the risk-taking, spontaneity and urgency of a live concert. His *Funérailles* is a truly great performance, perfectly structured, a real sense of angry desolation, and the central 'cavalry charge' emerging more logically from its context than in any other account. In the Rhapsody, he provides the requisite bravura thrills but also does Liszt the honour of eschewing the vapidity which so many bring to it. *Vallée d'Obermann* emerges as an inspired dramatic tone poem, to which Cohen adds the element of white-hot improvisation; in colour and temperament he yields little to Horowitz's famous RCA recording (nla). The Liszt Sonata, Cohen's second recording, mingles narrative and textual clarity with a musical maturity and heady virtuosity in the Richter class.

Années de pèlerinage

Années de pèlerinage – Première année. Venezia e Napoli, S162
Sergio Fiorentino pf
APR APR5583 (72' · ADD) Recorded 1962-3
Ⓜ️Ⓞ

The third volume of Sergio Fiorentino's early Liszt recordings made during the 60s unites the contemplative (volume 1) and the virtuoso (volume 2). These performances are of a rare virtuosity and imaginative delicacy, and it's doubtful whether the sense of bells ringing gently and exultantly through the crystalline Swiss air in 'Les cloches de Genève' has often been caught more evocatively. He rightly makes the gloomy and Byronic 'Vallée d'Obermann' the nodal and expressive centre of the cycle, fully justifying and sustaining his audaciously slow tempo (after all, it's marked *lento*) and, throughout, his performances are alive with the sort of fantasy and freedom that eluded Jorge Bolet in his more cautious *Gramophone* Award-winning Decca recording. Sadly Fiorentino recorded only one work from the official Italian *Annèe* ('Sposalizio') so this disc ends with its supplement, *Venezia e Napoli*, a garland of encores that show off his poetic resource and, in the 'Tarantella', quicksilver brilliance. His early Saga recordings often suggested an enviable, if occasionally flippant facility, but here he's at his finest; even when he playfully tampers with the score (in 'Les cloches de Genève) it's usually to Liszt's advantage. The transfers have come up trumps.

Années de pèlerinage – Première année; Deuxième
année; Troisième année. Venezia e Napoli, S162
Lazar Berman pf
DG Collectors' Edition ③ 471 447-2GB3
(176' · ADD) Recorded 1977   Ⓜ**O**

Liszt's three volumes of *Années de pèlerinage* are
rarely recorded complete, largely because many
pianists remain baffled by the dark-hued
prophecy and Romanticism of the third and
final book. Berman's resource here is remarkable, and his performance of the entire book is
hauntingly inward and sympathetic to both the
radiance of 'Les jeux d'eau à la Villa d'Este' and
to Liszt's truly dark night of the soul, and to his
desolate lack of spiritual solace elsewhere. He's
hardly less persuasive in the first two books.
'Chapelle de Guillaume Tell' is a true celebration of Switzerland's republican hero with
alpine horns ringing through the mountains,
while in 'Au lac de Wallenstadt' Berman's gently undulating traversal is truly *pianissimo* and
dolcissimo egualamente. His 'Orage' is predictably
breathtaking, and in the gloomy Byronic 'Vallée
d'Obermann' the severest critic will find himself
mesmerised by Berman's free-wheeling eloquence. These superb recordings have been
finely remastered.

Additional recommendation

Années de pèlerinage – Deuxième année: Après une
lecture du Dante
Coupled with: Valse oubliée No 4,. Mephisto Waltzes
Nos 1, 2 and 4. Die Zelle in Nonnenwerth. Ballade
No 2. Harmonies poétiques et réligieuses No 9
Andsnes pf
EMI 570022-2 (74' · DDD)   Ⓕ
    Leif Ove Andsnes's *Dante* Sonata is outstandingly
    well paced and his Ballade excitingly coloured and
    powerfully projected.

12 Grandes Etudes, S137

Complete Solo Piano Music, Volume 34
Douze Grandes Etudes, S137. Morceau de salon,
S142
Leslie Howard pf
Hyperion CDA66973 (76' · DDD) Recorded 1994   Ⓕ

In this first recording of the concert version of
the *Douze Grandes Etudes* (1837), Leslie Howard
brings his customary technical wizardry to bear
on this outrageously difficult music in an arresting virtuoso display that demonstrates Liszt's
consummate skill at transforming musical material. Moreover, despite Liszt's exhortation that
only the later revisions of the studies should be
played, there's a great deal to recommend the
1837 set, as these performances attest. The
extreme technical demands of these pieces have
led to critical scorn, but the challenges they
contain aren't designed merely for display, but
are the result of the composer's comprehensive
exploitation of the piano's expressive capabilities. Saint-Saëns said that 'in Art a difficulty

overcome is a thing of beauty' and, in the present instance, Howard's own triumph over the
monumental difficulties posed by these pieces
reveals the astonishing beauty of Liszt's 'orchestral' use of tone colour and sparkling virtuosity.

19 Hungarian Rhapsodies, S244

No 1 in C sharp minor; **No 2** in C sharp minor; **No 3**
in B flat; **No 4** in E flat; **No 5** in E minor, 'Héroïde-
Elégiaque'; **No 6** in D flat; **No 7** in D minor; **No 8** in
F sharp minor, 'Capriccio'; **No 9** in E flat, 'Carnival in
Pest'; **No 10** in E; **No 11** in A minor; **No 12** in C
sharp minor; **No 13** in A minor; **No 14** in F minor;
No 15 in A minor 'Rákóczy'; **No 16** in A minor, 'For
the Munkascy festivities in Budapest'; **No 17** in D
minor; **No 18** in F sharp minor, 'On the occasion of
the Hungarian Exposition in Budapest'; **No 19** in D
minor

Hungarian Rhapsodies Nos 1-19. Rhapsodie
espagnole, S254
Roberto Szidon pf
DG ② 453 034-2GTA2 (156' · ADD) Recorded 1972
                                           Ⓜ**O**
This well-known set has been in and out of the
catalogue a number of times, always to considerable acclaim. And the performances are every
bit as good as everybody has always said.
Although individual readings of isolated *Rhapsodies* may surpass Szidon's, taken as a whole this
is certainly the most pleasurable set available.
Szidon's technique is especially geared towards
clarity of passagework and rhythmic precision
and he also possesses a convincingly dreamy
temperament that enables the slow passages to
emerge with a rare distinction. His technical
mastery is in no doubt and this is playing of
great flair, with a natural feeling for rubato. The
Rapsodie espagnole is a welcome bonus. The
sound is sympathetic and vivid.

Harmonies poétiques ..., S173

Harmonies poétiques et religieuses, S173
Steven Osborne pf
Hyperion ② Two-for-the-price-of-one CDA67445
(84' · DDD)   Ⓕ**OO**

Steven Osborne follows his superlative Hyperion recording of Messiaen's *Vingt Regards sur
l'Enfant-Jésus* with Liszt's *Harmonies poétiques et
religieuses*, surely a precursor of Messiaen's masterpiece. Attuned to the mystic heart at the centre of Liszt's Catholicism, Osborne once more
shows the sort of stylistic ease and tonal magic
that come to very few young pianists. Sacred
and profane love blend with a wholly Lisztian
alchemy.
    In 'Invocation', the magnificent gateway to
the cycle, Osborne offers up its quasi-orchestral
rhetoric with immense power but without bombast. The 'Bénédiction' is daringly understated
in pages that can all too easily topple into lavish,

tear-laden emotionalism. 'Pensées des morts' is a triumph of alternating anguish and exultation. If all conventional pomp and circumstance are erased by the brisk tempo in the opening of 'Funérailles', Osborne's performance is still a marvel of concentrated musicianship and individuality. In the *Andante lagrimoso* he conjures an uncanny stillness in music whose painful climbing looks ahead to the dark, attenuated utterances of Fauré's final years, while the final 'Cantique d'Amour' resolves all past torment in a paean of praise for the union of two traditionally opposed ideas of love.

Few more radiant or deeply considered Liszt recordings have ever been made. Hyperion's sound is immaculate.

Hungarian Themes ..., S242

Complete Solo Piano Music, Volume 29. Hungarian Themes and Rhapsodies, S242
Leslie Howard *pf*
Hyperion ② CDA66851/2 (159' · DDD) Recorded 1993   Ⓕ

When listening to these 22 pieces, officially entitled *Magyar Dalok* and *Magyar Rapszódiák*, you at once realise you've heard many a snatch of them before. And not surprisingly, for in fact they're the source of most of what eventually emerged as Liszt's world-wide best-sellers, the *Hungarian Rhapsodies*. The composer revels in the lavishly decorative, cimbalom-coloured, improvisational style of the gypsies, in the process making demands on the pianist variously described by Leslie Howard in his insert-notes as 'devil-may-care, frighteningly difficult, frenetic, hand-splitting' and so on. Whether because of Liszt's own waning interest in platform pyrotechnics, or the fact that only he could really bring them off, simplification seems to have been the primary aim when recasting these first flings as *Hungarian Rhapsodies*. But as Howard reveals, there are losses as well as gains in the maturer Liszt. Despite moments of protracted rodomontade there's a vast amount of enjoyment to be had.

Petrarch Sonnets

Complete Solo Piano Music, Volume 21
Soirées musicales, S424. Soirées italiennes, S411. Nuits d'été à Pausilippe, S399. Tre sonetti del Petrarca, S158. Venezia e Napoli, S159. La serenata e L'orgia (Grande fantaisie sur des motifs des Soirées musicales), S422. La pastorella dell'Alpi e Li marinari (Deuxième fantaisie sur des motifs des Soirées musicales), S423
Leslie Howard *pf*
Hyperion ② CDA66661/2 (157' · DDD) Recorded 1991-2   Ⓕ

The two discs comprising Vol 21 of Howard's enormous cycle remind us of the young Liszt's love affair with Italy, the spotlight now falling primarily on frolics with Rossini, Mercadante and Donizetti in lighter, lyrical vein. The special interest of the two original sets of pieces included, i.e. the three *Sonetti del Petrarca* and the four *Venezia e Napoli*, is that Howard introduces them as first written (*c*1839 and 1840 respectively) before Liszt's characteristically painstaking later revisions. There's much to enjoy in the playing itself, especially in simpler contexts when gondolas glide through calm waters, or lovers dream, or shepherds dance. Melody, so important throughout, is nicely sung.

Totentanz

Impromptu in F sharp, S191. Nuages gris, S199. La lugubre gondola, S200 Nos 1 & 2. Unstern: sinistre, disastro, S208. Totentanz, S525. Danse macabre (Saint-Saëns), S555. Réminiscences des Huguenots (Meyerbeer), S412
Arnaldo Cohen *pf*
Naxos 8 553852 (71' · DDD)   Ⓢ

Arnaldo Cohen is as poetically and imaginatively intrepid as he's technically coruscating, and all these performances offer refinement and ferocity in equal proportion. Few pianists could identify or engage so closely with music that hovers on the edge of silence or extinction (*Nuages gris*, *La lugubre gondola* Nos 1 and 2), or that sparks and sports with a truly devilish intent (*Danse macabre*, *Totentanz* and so on). In the *Danse macabre* the music emerges from Cohen's fingers supercharged with malevolence. On the other hand he can send the F sharp *Impromptu* spiralling into a true sense of its ecstasy, or momentarily inflect *Nuages gris* in a manner that accentuates rather than detracts from its abstraction and economy. He makes something frighteningly bleak out of *Unstern* (or 'Evil Star'), with its savagely dissonant climax and its unresolved hymnal solace, yet is no less at home in *Réminiscences des Huguenots*, dismissing ambuscades of treacherous skips, octaves and every other technical terror with a telling mix of verve and nonchalance. These, then, are performances of rare lucidity, virtuoso voltage and trenchancy, and all quite excellently recorded.

Transcendental Etudes

12 Etudes d'exécution transcendante, S139
Jenö Jandó *pf*
Naxos 8 553119 (64' · DDD) Recorded 1994   Ⓢ

The 12 *Transcendental Etudes* are the ultimate test of quasi-orchestral virtuosity and of the capacity to achieve nobility and true eloquence. Jandó perhaps lacks diabolic *frisson* in the more ferocious numbers but his performances, overall, aren't disfigured by wilful, sensational attributes or hysteria. No 1 is an impressive, dramatically pointed, curtain-raiser, and he can hell-raise with assurance in 'Mazeppa'. His

'Feux follets' hardly sparks with the brilliance of, say, some of the full-blooded accounts of certain Russian artists, but even when it hardly modulates from study to tone-poem it's still more than capable (higher praise than you might think where such intricacy is concerned). He flashes an impressive rapier at the start of 'Eroica' and there's plenty of swagger and facility in the so-called 'Appassionata' *étude*. 'Chasse-neige', too, proceeds with a fine sense of its menacing start to a howling, elemental uproar before returning to distant thunder. Jandó is less assured in introspection, yet it has to be said that all-encompassing versions of the *Transcendental Etudes* are hard to come by. Jandó is impressively recorded.

Transcriptions

Oberon – Overture, S574 (Weber). Fantasia on themes from Le nozze di Figaro and Don Giovanni, S697 (Mozart). Ernani Paraphrase, S432. Miserere du Trovatore, S433. Rigoletto Paraphrase, S434. Réminiscences de Boccanegra, S438 (Verdi). Valse de concert sur deux motifs du Lucia et Parisina, S214/3 (Donizetti). Réminiscences de Robert le diable (Meyerbeer) – Cavatine; Valse infernale, S413. Les Adieux – Rêverie sur un motif de Roméo et Juliette, S409 (Gounod). Schwanengesang and Marsch from Hunyadi László, S405 (Erkel). Lohengrin – Elsa's Bridal Procession, S445/2; Two Pieces, S446. Fantasy on themes from Rienzi, S439 (Wagner)
Leslie Howard pf
Hyperion ② CDA66861/2 (153' · DDD) Recorded 1993   Ⓕ

Liszt's operatic outings range from literal transcriptions, such as the opening *Oberon* Overture, to the most free fantasias, like that on motives from *Rienzi* at the end of the disc. The sequence is artfully planned to provide the maximum contrast between Liszt as lion and dove, with four of the 16 items earmarked as 'first recordings'. Of these, the Gounod *Roméo et Juliette* Rêverie is a tender, nocturne-like idyll that not for a second outstays its welcome. Liszt scholars may nevertheless be still more grateful for Howard's rescue of the other three, and first and foremost the nearly 22-minute long Fantasia on themes from *Le nozze di Figaro and Don Giovanni*. Though self-indulgently protracted (as Busoni surely realised when preparing his own shortened version), its thematic interweavings *en route* still take your breath away. With Verdi and Wagner we're on more familiar ground, where it goes without saying that Howard has formidable CD rivals. But throughout the disc there's a spaciousness in his characterisation that far more often than not compensates for momentary technical strain or loss of finesse. His tonal range is certainly wide, ranging from the deep, dark, brooding intensity he finds for the *Ernani* and *Il trovatore* excerpts to his translucent delicacy in the upper reaches of Gounod's Rêverie. Apart from a slightly metallic touch above a certain dynamic level in

the treble, the recorded sound quality can best be described in a nutshell as ripe.

Adelaïde, S466. Sechs geistliche Lieder, S467. An die ferne Geliebte, S469. Lieder von Goethe, S468 (Beethoven). Lieder, S547 (Mendelssohn). Lieder, S485 (Dessauer). Er ist gekommen in Sturm und Regen, S488. Lieder, S489 (Franz). Two songs, S554 (Rubinstein). Lieder von Robert und Clara Schumann, S569. Provenzalisches Lied, S570. Two songs, S567. Frühlingsnacht, S568. Widmung, S566 (Schumann)
Leslie Howard pf
Hyperion ② CDA66481/2 (147' · DDD) Recorded 1990   Ⓕ

Few composers have ever shown a more insatiable interest in the music of others than Liszt, or devoted more time to transcribing it for the piano. Here Howard plays 60 of Liszt's 100 or so song transcriptions, including several by the lesser-known Dessauer, Franz and (as composers) Anton Rubinstein and Clara Schumann, alongside Beethoven, Mendelssohn and Robert Schumann. The selection at once reveals Liszt's variety of approach as a transcriber no less than his unpredictability of choice. Sometimes, as most notably in Beethoven's concert aria, *Adelaïde*, the keyboard virtuoso takes over: he links its two sections with a concerto-like cadenza as well as carrying bravura into an amplified coda. But after the dazzling pyrotechnics of many of his operatic arrangements, the surprise is the self-effacing simplicity of so much included here.

The five songs from Schumann's *Liederalbum für die Jugend* are literal enough to be played by young children. Even his later (1880) fantasy-type transcriptions of Rubinstein's exotic *The Asra* has the same potent economy of means. Howard responds keenly to mood and atmosphere, and never fails, pianistically, to emphasise the 'singer' in each song – in response to the actual verbal text that Liszt was nearly always conscientious enough to write into his scores. The recording is clean and true.

Christus, S3

Christus
Henriette Bonde-Hansen sop **Iris Vermillion** mez
Michael Schade ten **Andreas Schmidt** bar **Cracow Chamber Choir; Stuttgart Gächinger Kantorei Stuttgart Radio Symphony Orchestra / Helmuth Rilling**
Hänssler Classic Exclusive Series ③ CD98 121 (162' · DDD) Recorded live 1997. Text and translation included   Ⓕ

Christus is essentially a contemplative work and so could really be said to exist in a different time-scale to most music. Much of the opening part, the 'Christmas Oratorio', uses very simple melody and harmony, and is studiously undramatic. Helmuth Rilling does well not to charge it with too much colour, and, if listened to as meditation rather than drama, what can seem static takes on a positive atmosphere as a group of long reflections on the Christmas events. This is a far cry from the sensational Liszt of the early virtuoso years, not yet reaching the terse, inward pieces of the last years. There's greater drama in the middle part, 'After Epiphany', especially in the superb scene of Christ walking on the water. Although there's still the suggestion that a wonder is being contemplated, Liszt stirs up a terrific storm. This part also includes the beautiful setting of the Beatitudes, sung by Andreas Schmidt with a degree of uncertainty which he entirely sheds when he comes to pronounce the sentences in Part 3 ('Passion and Resurrection') for the scene of the Agony in the Garden. The long *Stabat mater* is beautifully controlled by Rilling. His soloists support him well, though Iris Vermillion can seem rather operatic; Henriette Bonde-Hansen sings with a beautiful, clear tone. The recording does excellent justice to Liszt's wide-ranging orchestration.

Henry Litolff French 1818-1891

French composer and pianist. He was a concert artist, conductor, music publisher, festival organiser, piano teacher and salon composer but is remembered chiefly for his four piano concertos entitled concertos symphoniques (c1844-67); their conception as symphonies with piano obbligato greatly impressed Liszt (who dedicated his Concerto no.1 to Litolff), and their scherzos contain some of his most brilliant writing. **GROVE**music

Concertos symphoniques

Concertos symphoniques – No 3 in E flat, Op 45;
No 5 in C minor, Op 123
Peter Donohoe *pf* **BBC Scottish Symphony Orchestra / Andrew Litton**
Hyperion CDA67210 (66' · DDD)   ⒻO

Litolff's dauntingly ambitious structures accommodate every possible style, looking forwards and backwards Janus-style, yet reaching out in the strange almost Alkanesque oddity of the Fifth Concerto's last two movements towards a more personal and distinctive style. Admired by Tchaikovsky, Liszt and Berlioz (though with some telling reservations), Litolff enjoyed a hectic career which is mirrored in writing of a formidable intricacy. So even if claims that he was 'the English Liszt' and that his development sections are similar to late Beethoven seem far-fetched, the sheer energy and resource of Litolff's writing are absorbing. Few pianists could approach, let alone top, Peter Donohoe's blistering virtuosity in these works. His performances throughout are as rock-steady as they're dazzling, sweeping aside torrents of notes with both affection and authority. Hear him in the exultant whirl which

opens the Third Concerto's finale, and you can only marvel at such unfaltering command, ideally complemented by Andrew Litton and the BBC Scottish Symphony Orchestra. An invaluable issue for lovers of intriguing repertoire.

Alonso Lobo Spanish c1555-1617

A choirboy at Seville Cathedral, Lobo studied at Osuna University and was a canon there by 1591. He assisted Guerrero at Seville Cathedral from 1591, becoming maestro de capilla of Toledo Cathedral in 1593 and of Seville in 1604. He published masses and motets, some for double choir (1602); many other sacred works are in MSS. Victoria esteemed him as an equal and he was long regarded as one of the finest Spanish composers. **GROVE**music

Masses

Lobo Missa Maria Magdalene. O quam suavis est, Domine. Quam pulchri sunt. Ave regina caelorum. Versa est in luctum. Credo quod Redemptor. Vivo ego, dicit Dominus. Ave Maria **Guerrero** Maria Magdalene
The Tallis Scholars / Peter Phillips
Gimell CDGIM031 (63' · DDD) Texts and translations included   Ⓕ

Alonso Lobo is best known for one work, his setting of the funerary *Versa est in luctum*. This is undoubtedly a masterpiece of its kind but to have it placed alongside other pieces from his 1602 collection affords a welcome chance to assess his composition skills more fully. Lobo's music is sonorous in a manner that's direct and unfussy in effect, though often highly expressive, and always structured with the utmost technical control. Take, for example, the *Ave Maria*, an 8-in-4 canon (in other words, four more voices are generated from the original quartet) which emanates a sense of absolute serenity. In fact, each of the motets explores a different aspect of the compositional techniques brought to the genre, and the Mass is equally fine, Lobo making the spacious textures of the motet, *Maria Magdalene* by his teacher Guerrero a distinguishing feature of his own setting of the Ordinary. The Tallis Scholars are on superb form, the overall sound vibrant and immediate with solo sections providing contrast through a more introspective approach. Even if you've never bought a CD of late-Renaissance polyphony, try this one. You'll be bowled over.

Ego flos campi. Lamentations. Missa O rex gloriae. Missa Simile est regnum caelorum
Choir of King's College London / David Trendell
ASV Gaudeamus CDGAU311 (75' · DDD) Texts and translations included   Ⓕ

This CD confirms the high calibre of Lobo's

sacred polyphony: the excellent mixed choir present two masses (*O rex gloriae* and *Simile est regnum caelorum*, based on motets by Palestrina and Guerrero respectively, and printed in Madrid in 1602), together with a magnificent setting of the *Lamentations* and the motet *Ego flos campi*.

The masses have carefully honed vocal lines and that sense of vertical spaciousness that characterises the sacred polyphony of 16th-century Iberian composers. The choir sing with absolute conviction and total security, as if they really know the music rather than as if it were a very competent read-through. Trendell paces it all well, the tempo never seeming forced or plodding. The motet is deservedly popular, but the recently discovered six-voice setting of the *Lamentations* is an absolute winner, with meltingly beautiful suspensions, often in the upper voices, in the Hebrew letter sections; the choir again captures just the right degree of intensity without slipping into over-indulgence.

The fresh sound of this student choir (rather larger at 27 voices than the professional groups that have previously recorded this repertory) combines energy and clarity in a most appealing way. This fine recording will enrich anyone's collection of Renaissance polyphony.

Pietro Locatelli   Italian 1695-1764

Locatelli studied the violin in Rome and in 1717-23 played in the basilica of S Lorenzo in Damaso. He was appointed to the Mantuan court in 1725 but gave concerts elsewhere (especially Germany), gaining a high reputation; his playing was noted for its virtuosity and sweetness. From 1729 he worked mostly as a teacher and orchestral director in Amsterdam. Locatelli wrote almost exclusively sonatas and concertos. The first of his four concerto grosso sets (1721) is the most Corellian (particularly its Christmas Concerto); his later music is more progressive. His influential L'arte del violino (1733) contains 12 solo violin concertos in a Venetian idiom like Vivaldi's and 24 caprices for solo violin. Among Locatelli's other works are solo and trio sonatas.

GROVEmusic

Sonatas, Op 8

10 Sonatas, Op 8   Ⓟ
Locatelli Trio (Elizabeth Wallfisch *vn* Richard Tunnicliffe *vc* Paul Nicholson *hpd*) **Rachel Isserlis** *vn*
Hyperion ② CDA67021/2 (116' · DDD) Recorded 1994   Ⓔ

There's a sense of the decadent about Locatelli's music. But decadence can be fun, and it would be an austere spirit that took little pleasure in these sonatas, and especially the playing of them here. This two-disc set of his Op 8 (published in 1744) contains six violin sonatas and four trio sonatas, three for two violins and continuo and one using the much less common

combination of violin, cello and continuo. A number of them have a slowish movement and most end with a quick triple-metre piece, again in brilliant violinistic style. The most attractive is No 5, with its interesting gestures and hints of wit in the second movement. The most demanding is No 6, with its final minuet with variations, quite breathtaking (and improbably set in E flat, a perverse gesture): here Elizabeth Wallfisch clambers unruffled through the technical thickets, which include an extraordinary variation with trills on one string and moving parts on another and dashes from one end of the compass to the other and back again, and much more besides. This is amazing violin playing of a kind of virtuosity rarely heard from a period instrument player. The three trio sonatas for two violins aren't virtuoso music in quite the same way, and musically not generally very inventive. The performances are admirable; no one who admires good violin playing will want to miss Wallfisch's crisp, rhythmic playing.

Matthew Locke   British 1621-1677

Locke was a chorister and secondary at Exeter Cathedral, where he became friendly with Christopher Gibbons. In 1653 he and Gibbons wrote the music for James Shirley's masque Cupid and Death and in 1656 he joined with others in writing the music (all lost) for Davenant's opera The Siege of Rhodes, in which he also sang. After the Restoration in 1660 he was awarded three posts at court, to which in 1662 he added that of organist to the queen (facilitated by his conversion to Roman Catholicism). He continued to write for the theatre and also engaged in a polemical exchange with Thomas Salmon over the latter's proposals for a new form of musical notation.

Locke's importance lies in his chamber music and dramatic music, which influenced Purcell's. His consort music and other ensemble works, mainly suites and separate dances, display robust and daring melody, harmony and form, as well as a conscious preoccupation with contrasting rhythms, tempos and dynamics. Although sometimes experimental, it is the work of a gifted and inspired craftsman. His extant sacred music, while not as maturely conceived, is often of high quality. His dramatic music, best represented by Cupid and Death, the masque in The Empress of Morocco (1673) and the vocal music for Psyche (1675), shows a sure dramatic instinct, especially in the recitatives and in several of the curtain tunes. Locke's other music includes the well-known pieces 'ffor His Majesty's Sagbutts and Cornetts', probably performed on the eve of Charles II's coronation, and Melothesia (1673), a collection of keyboard works with an important preface giving the first extant English rules for realising a figured bass.

GROVEmusic

Consort of Fower Parts

Consort of Fower Parts, Suites Nos 1-6.   Ⓟ

The Flatt Consort – Suite No 1 in C minor
Phantasm (Laurence Dreyfus, Wendy Gillespie,
Jonathan Manson, Markku Luolajan-Mikkola viols)
Global Music Network GMNC0109 (55' · DDD) ℗**O**

Matthew Locke, the irascible and xenophobic
Anglo-Catholic, is usually remembered in the
'predecessor of Purcell' category, a classifica-
tion that's easy to understand when listening to
works such as the four-movement consort suites
on this disc, composed around the 1650s. Each
has an opening *fantasie* full of the brooding,
angular and often dissonant expressiveness one
associates with Purcell's own later viol fantasies,
and Purcell is known to have admired Locke,
composing an elegy on his death in 1677. But
Locke had a personality of his own: the dances –
courantes, ayres and sarabandes – that follow
the *fantasies* in each suite have an idiosyncratic
rhythmic snap to them. Writing in the booklet,
Laurence Dreyfus also draws attention to
Locke's 'striking muscularity' and also to his
'purest lyricism and…most generous warmth',
dubbing his work 'true music of consolation'.
Changeable and abrupt though it may at first
seem, it's certainly music that grows on you with
repeated listenings.

Phantasm play with their customary expertise.
Their combination of vibrant tone quality and
strong rhythmic attack allows them to make the
most of Locke's mercurial musings, bringing
lyrical gravity to the *Fantasies* and an exhilarating spring to the faster dances. A fairly close
recording helps, giving them at times the clarity
and substance almost of a string quartet. By
comparison the equally accomplished Fretwork
have a thinner and less defined sound, and their
performances are less consistent in offering
moment-to-moment excitement. Their generally more subdued approach has power to
charm, as does their enlivening use of archlute,
organ or spinet continuo in some of the suites,
but Phantasm tend to make more of this
intriguing music.

Carl Loewe
German 1796-1869

*Loewe, a pupil of Türk at Halle, began composing
songs and instrumental pieces at an early age, also
singing his own ballads to great acclaim. Among his
finest early solo vocal works are settings of Goethe's
Erlkönig (1818) and Byron's Hebrew Melodies
(Opp 4, 5, 13 and 14). He was a prolific composer in
many media, but his other works, including the
operas (notably Emmy, 1842) and oratorios, string
quartets and piano works (in particular some programmatic sonatas and the tone poem Mazeppa, Op
27), were not as acclaimed as his narrative songs.
Their accompaniments and modified strophic style,
incorporating dramatic and lyrical passages, make a
vivid impression (eg Archibald Douglas, Op 128);
the fairy element in many of his folklore settings (eg
Herr Oluf and Tom der Reimer) creates colour and
melodic interest. From 1820 to 1865 Loewe worked*

*in Stettin as a conductor, organist and teacher, yet it
was through his recital tours that he won international fame; the Viennese called him 'the north German Schubert'.*　　　　　　　　　　**GROVE**music

Lieder

Drei Balladen, Op 1 – Edward; Erlkönig. Drei
Balladen, Op 2 – Herr Oluf. Drei Balladen, Op 3 –
Elvershöh; Die drei Lieder. Lieder, Gesänge,
Romanzen und Balladen, Op 9 – Book 1: Wandrers
Nachtlied; Book 3: Ich denke dein; Book 8:
Türmwachter Lynkeus zu den Füssen der Helena;
Lynkeus, der Türmer, auf Fausts Sternwarte singend;
Gutmann und Gutweib. Drei Balladen, Op 20. Die
Gruft der Liebenden, Op 21. Zehn Geistliche
Gesänge, Op 22 – Book 1: Gottes ist der Orient!.
Drei Balladen, Op 44 – Der getreue Eckart; Der
Totentanz. Drei Balladen, Op 56 – Heinrich der
Vogler. Drei Balladen, Op 59 – Der Schatzgräber.
Zwölf Gedichte, Op 62 – Book 1: Süsses Begräbnis;
Hinkende Jamben. Kleiner Haushalt, Op 71. Vier
Legenden, Op 75 – Der heilige Franziskus. Sechs
Gesänge, Op 79 – Frühzeitiger Frühling. Fünf Lieder,
Op 81 – In Vorübergehen. Prince Eugen, Op 92 Drei
Balladen, Op 97 – Der Mohrenfürst auf der Messe.
Odins Meeresritt, Op 118. Drei Gesänge, Op 123 –
Trommelständchen; Die Uhr. Archibald Douglas,
Op 128. Drei Balladen, Op 129 – Der Nöck. Tom der
Reimer, Op 135a. Fünf Lieder, Op 145 –
Meeresleuchten. Canzonette. Freibeuter. Wenn der
Blüten Frühlingsregen
Dietrich Fischer-Dieskau bar **Jörg Demus** pf
DG ② 449 516-2GX2 (156' · ADD) Recorded 1968-79.
Texts and translations included　　　　　Ⓜ**OO**

All the best-known ballads are included here,
magnificently sung by a great artist at the height
of his powers. *Edward, Herr Oluf, Heinrich der
Vogler, Prince Eugen, Der Zauberlehrling*: these
and others are sung with a wonderful sense of
the graphic, conveyed through an appreciation
of the colour of the words that never descends
into overemphasis and that's beautifully attuned
to Loewe's illustrative manner. Fischer-
Dieskau and Demus are ideal partners, Demus
responding quickly and with an ear for the sinister that often marks the piano writing and its
subtle use of motive. Not just a composer of ballads, Loewe was also a Lieder writer in the great
German tradition, and this is too often overlooked, but not by Fischer-Dieskau.

Two songs alone, from this magisterial collection, are witness to Loewe's stature. They are
settings of the wonderful poems from the second part of *Faust* in which Lynceus, the lynx-
eyed watcher on the tower, sees the magical
appearance, of Helen of Troy herself. He,
incarnating the gift of the perception of visual
beauty, after a life of watching from his tower
can conceive of nothing that could surpass this
wonder; and, in the second song, hymns his
gratitude to the gift of sight. Loewe's two settings are beautiful responses to the poetry of a
great artist with the gift of an ideal simplicity.
These two songs alone should persuade the
responsive listener to make the exploration.

Paolo Lorenzani
Italian 1640-1713

Lorenzani was a chorister in the Cappella Giulia in the Vatican and a pupil of Benevoli. After an early career as maestro di cappella in Rome and Messina, he fled during the wars of 1678 to Paris and became an important figure in the struggle to gain recognition for Italian music and thus to break Lully's monopoly. He gained the support of Louis XIV (who helped him become director of the queen's music) and leading aristocrats (who arranged performances of his dramatic music), but after Queen Marie-Thérèse's death in 1683 his influence waned, despite successful Roman-style oratory performances he arranged as maître de chapelle to the Theatine order (from 1685) and an opera, Orontée, given at Chantilly. In 1694 he returned to Italy as director of the Cappella Giulia. Although rooted in the Roman tradition, his style was readily adaptable to French taste, and the instrumental writing particularly shows Lully's influence. Among his surviving works are airs, cantatas, motets and a mass and Magnificat, both for two choirs. **GROVE**music

Grands motets

Antienne à la Vierge. Motet pour l'élévation. Motet pour tous les temps. Dialogue entre Jésus et l'Ame. Motet pour les confesseurs. Litanies à la Vierge
Le Concert Spirituel / Hervé Niquet
Naxos 8 553648 (63' · DDD) Texts and translations included   Ⓢ

Paolo Lorenzani was a Roman-born composer who towards the end of the 17th century spent 16 years in France, where he tried to raise the profile of Italian music. In this he had little success, especially ashe inevitably came up against the machinations of the tyrannical Lully. Their rivalry seems to have become quite acrimonious, and eventually Lorenzani returned to Italy to finish his days as director of the Cappella Giulia at the Vatican. This rarity to the catalogue offers five of the *grands motets* for soloists, choir, violins and continuo which he published in Paris in 1693, plus a *Litany of Our Lady* for voices and continuo which he probably wrote when back in Rome. The lack of success the *motets* enjoyed at the time – for all that the King liked them and that they were very much in the French style – no doubt hastened Lorenzani's departure, but listening to them now, musico-political distractions put aside, it's hard to understand why they should have failed; this is highly attractive music, easily on a par with that of some of the better-known *grand motet* composers of the time, and there's some clever responsiveness to text as well.

The performances, too, are very enjoyable. Hervé Niquet's experience in this type of music pays off in a well-balanced and lithe ensemble, good stand-out solos, and an intelligent, quick-witted approach to the music's interpretation. Lorenzani may not be a forgotten genius exactly, but his music is well worth unearthing. Lully has plenty to answer for.

Antonio Lotti
Italian c1667-1740

Lotti, a pupil of Legrenzi in Venice, became an organist at St Mark's in 1690, eventually becoming maestro di cappella (1736). He also taught at the Ospedale degli Incurabili (Galuppi was one of his pupils); he wrote sacred music for both institutions. From 1692 he composed operas, mostly serious: he presented c30, the last four (1717-19) in Dresden. His large output includes oratorios, secular cantatas, duets, madrigals, instrumental pieces and numerous masses, motets and psalms. Most of his sacred choral works have no orchestral accompaniment; many, such as a Miserere of 1733, remained in use long after his death. His output bridges the late Baroque and early Classical styles and his late works are notable for their elegance and skilful counterpoint. **GROVE**music

Missa Sapientiae

Lotti Missa Sapientiae in G **Bach** Magnificat in E flat, BWV243a
Balthasar-Neumann Choir and Ensemble / Thomas Hengelbrock
Deutsche Harmonia Mundi 05472 77534-2
(62' · DDD) Texts and translations included   Ⓕ

Thanks to his only well-known piece, the eight-part *Crucifixus*, Antonio Lotti has a reputation as a Baroque conservative, fuddy-duddily turning out nothing but church music in old-fashioned, Palestrina-inspired counterpoint. Yet, if there were such men in 18th-century Italy, Lotti – singer, organist and later *maestro* at St Mark's in Venice, but also composer of around 20 operas – wasn't one of them. For proof one need only sample this impeccably 18th-century short Mass for soloists, choir and orchestra, a work that Bach and Handel made copies of, and which evidently left its mark on both of them.

Handel actually 'borrowed' two bits of it for oratorios, but further stylistic resemblances are plain to hear. As for Bach, it's hard to believe that the meandering choral chromaticisms and coaxing accompaniment of the 'Qui tollis' weren't in his mind when he fashioned the 'Crucifixus' of the B minor Mass. Furthermore, Lotti must have known Vivaldi personally; we don't who wrote first, but anyone familiar with the Vivaldi *Gloria* will spot similarities of approach in several movements. This is a fascinating find, and well performed by the pleasingly cohesive Balthasar-Neumann Ensemble, who convey its mood of bright confidence.

The coupling is Bach's *Magnificat* in its original E flat version, which differs from its better-known D major revision in several respects: the most significant are four irresistible extra movements for Christmas. Recordings are rare, though there is recent competition from Philippe Herreweghe. Of the two, Herreweghe's is the more 'traditional' performance, with a polished chorus, fine soloists and brassy trumpets. Hengelbrock achieves greater intimacy, and he's also more urgent.

Requiem

Requiem in F. Credo. Miserere
Balthasar-Neumann Choir and Ensemble / Thomas Hengelbrock
Deutsche Harmonia Mundi 05472 77507-2
(68' · DDD) Ⓕ

Lotti's Requiem Mass in F major is considered by Thomas Hengelbrock the most important Requiem before Mozart's. It's full of expressive contrast: Lotti has an affection for a quasi-Palestrina style on the one hand and the skill to deploy more up-to-date techniques on the other. This Requiem is essentially in the late Baroque idiom, occasionally recalling certain of Vivaldi's larger sacred vocal pieces. The sections differ from the sequence usually encountered in later 18th-century Requiem Masses. There's neither *Sanctus*, 'Benedictus' nor *Agnus Dei*, but instead a very extended 'Dies irae' as well as a much shorter 'Requiem aeternam', *Kyrie* and Offertory. Full of theatrical gestures, supple polyphony, warmly seductive harmony and some beautiful melodies, the Requiem holds attention from start to finish. The contrasts are often striking, as between the hushed opening section and the awesome introduction to the 'Dies irae'. The *a cappella Miserere* is sung with clarity and finesse. The five-movement *Credo* is a supple piece for choir and strings with some affecting, shimmering harmonies in the 'Crucifixus'. As well as full mass settings, Lotti seems also to have favoured separate autonomous sections such as this, themselves subdivided into short units. The splendid performances bring this highly charged music to life.

Jean-Baptiste Lully
Italian/French 1632-1687

A French composer of Italian birth, Lully was taken from Florence to Paris in 1646 by Roger de Lorraine, Chevalier de Guise, who placed him in the service of his niece, Mlle de Montpensier. At her court in the Tuileries Lully got to know the best in French music and, despite his patroness's dislike of Mazarin and her involvement in the Fronde, he was no stranger to Italian music either. After the defeat of the Frondists, Mlle de Montpensier was exiled to St Fargeau. Lully obtained release from her service and on the death of his friend Lazzarini, in 1653, was appointed Louis XIV's compositeur de la musique instrumentale. From 1655 his fame as dancer, comedian and composer grew rapidly, and his disciplined training of the king's 'petite bande' earned him further recognition. In 1661 he was made surintendant de la musique et compositeur de la musique de la chambre and in 1662 maître de la musique de la famille royale. By then he was a naturalised Frenchman, and in July 1662 he married Madeleine Lambert.

Lully then collaborated with Molière on a series of comédies-ballets which culminated in Le bourgeois gentilhomme (1670). After that he turned to opera, securing the privilege previously granted to Perrin and forestalling potential rivals with oppressive patents granted by the king. He chose as librettist Philippe Quinault, with whom he established a new and essentially French type of opera known as tragédie lyrique. Between 1673 and 1686 Lully composed 13 such works, 11 of them with Quinault.

During this time Lully continued to enjoy the king's support. His greatest personal triumph came in 1681 when he was received as secrétaire du Roi. After the king's marriage to Mme de Maintenon in 1683 life at court took on a new sobriety; it was perhaps in response to this that Lully composed much of his religious music. During a performance of his Te Deum in January 1687 he injured his foot with the point of a cane he was using to beat time. Gangrene set in, and within three months he died, leaving a tragédie lyrique, Achille et Polyxène, unfinished.

At his death Lully was widely regarded as the most representative of French composers. Practically all his music was designed to satisfy the tastes and interests of Louis XIV. The ballets de cour (1653-63) and the comédies-ballets (1663-72) were performed as royal entertainments, the king himself often taking part in the dancing.

The tragédies lyriques (1673-86) were kingly operas par excellence, expressing a classical conflict between la gloire and l'amour; Louis himself supplied the subject matter for at least four of them and certainly approved the political sentiments of the prologues. Lully's music was correspondingly elevated, in the stately overtures, the carefully moulded 'récitatif simple' and the statuesque choruses; many of the airs, too, draw as much attention to the galant mores of the court as to the stage action. Finally, the Versailles grand motet, of which the Miserere is an outstanding example, was designed to glorify the King of France as much as the King of Heaven.

GROVEmusic

Suites

L'Orchestre du Roi Soleil Ⓟ
Première Suite: Le bourgeois gentilhomme.
Deuxième Suite: Le divertissement royal. Troisième Suite: Alceste
Le Concert des Nations / Jordi Savall
Alia Vox AV9807 (64' · DDD) ⒻⓄ

Le Concert des Nations offers here a compendium of Lully's music from the heyday of the court of Louis XIV (widely assumed to have been at Versailles, but in fact from before the move from Paris). The pieces, drawn from a variety of Lullian sources to make up three entertainments (or *divertissements*), provide Savall with opportunities to present his musicians in Lully's spectrum of ensemble textures. The players respond to the rhythmic vitality of the music, adding ornamentation with tremendous precision and flair, but the secret of the obvious success of this recording is the rightness of the tempos, whether for a dance, a battle, a gust of wind or a funeral. Those who saw the film *Tous les matins du monde* will be familiar with Lully's 'March pour la Cérémonie turque' and will immediately hear the difference even a few years has made to Savall: the playing on this new recording more effectively captures the military character without caricaturing the janissary element. The real stars of the recording, however, are the percussion players, Michèle Claude and Pedro Estevan, whose command of the possibilities for accompanying this repertory would have impressed even Lully. Whole evenings of Lully are still an acquired taste, but a recording of highlights as good as this is something anyone who enjoys Baroque music would wish to own.

Grands Motets

Miserere. Quare fremuerunt. Domine salvum fac regem. Jubilate Deo
Amel Brahim-Djelloul sop **Howard Crook, Damien Guillon** countertens **Hervé Lamy** ten **Arnaud Marzorati** bass **Les pages et les chantres de la Chapelle; Musica Florea / Olivier Schneebeli**
K617 K617157 (53' · DDD)   Ⓕ

Grands motets, requiring lavish vocal and instrumental resources, always signalled important occasions at the French court. Until the advent of public concerts in Paris in the 1720s they were performed exclusively by the king's musicians for the court. Olivier Schneebeli has assembled an admirable survey of these large-scale settings of psalm texts, which were excerpted and arranged to convey *doubles entendres* flattering to Louis XIV and his policies. The music employs an orchestra with a full continuo complement, a choir and a *petit chœur* of soloists that relies on high male voices. The only concession to modern times is the use of sopranos instead of castrati in the top part and the inclusion of girls among the pages.

The survey begins with Lully's first *grand motet*, the *Jubilate Deo* (1660), celebrating both the marriage of the king and a peace treaty. The *Miserere* (1663), frequently performed during Lully's lifetime, has remained his best-known work. *Quare fremuerunt* (1685) was composed at a difficult time, when he most needed to please the king. From first to last, one can easily hear the ways in which Lully experimented with his forces, refining the role of the orchestra, the ways in which the soloists relate to the choir, and how he was influenced by his experience of opera.

The singers are attentive to Schneebeli's direction; the five soloists contribute singly, in dialogue with one another and in concert with the choir. Musica Florea's sweet sound suggests a refreshing departure from current ideas of Lullian style.

Acis et Galatée

Acis et Galatée   Ⓟ
Jean-Paul Fouchécourt ten Acis **Véronique**

Gens sop Galatée **Monique Simon** sop Diane, Second Naiad **Jean-Louis Meunier** ten Comus **Howard Crook** ten Apollon, Télème, Priest of Juno **Françoise Masset** sop Scylla, Dryad **Rodrigo del Pozo** counterten Tircis **Mireille Delunsch** sop Aminte, Abundance, First Naiad **Laurent Naouri** bar Polyphème **Thierry Félix** bar Neptune, Sylvan **Choeur des Musiciens du Louvre; Les Musiciens du Louvre / Marc Minkowski**
Archiv Produktion ② 453 497-2AH2 (107' · DDD)
Notes, text and translation included   ⒻOO

Acis et Galatée was Lully's last completed opera, and one of his greatest. A *pastoral héroïque* performed in 1686 to entertain the Dauphin during a hunting party at the Duc de Vendôme's château, it employs many features of his *tragédies en musique* – vocal ensembles, instrumental movements and an enhanced use of the orchestra in general; and each act contains a *divertissement* with choruses and dances. One of the glories of the score is the concluding *passacaille*, which with instrumental sections builds up from single voices to chorus. There's also a small but affecting chaconne for Galatea in Act 2; but another glorious moment is the lengthy scene in which she discovers the body of her lover and calls on her father, Neptune, who guarantees Acis immortality by transforming him into a river. Marc Minkowski brings out all the drama of the work by thoughtful treatment of the verbal text, intelligent pacing and varied instrumental articulation and weight: especially striking are the rough sonorities of the march in which Polyphemus first appears, and the intensity of the lovers' angry confrontation in Act 2. Jean-Paul Fouchécourt projecting the image of an ardent youthful lover, and Véronique Gens that of a passionate goddess, are both excellently cast, but Laurent Naouri almost steals the scene from them with his fearsomely powerful Polyphemus: Howard Crook contributes valuably in various roles, though he's ill at ease in the very highest register. There's considerable finesse in the chorus singing, and the theorbo continuo is admirable. An altogether splendid performance of a masterpiece.

Roland

Roland
Nicolas Testé bass Roland **Anna Maria Panzarella** sop Angélique **Olivier Dumait** counterten Médor **Monique Zanetti** sop Témire, Bélise **Robert Getchell** counterten Astolfe **Salomé Haller** sop Logistille **Evgueniy Alexiev** bass Ziliante, Demogorgon **Emiliano Gonzalez-Toro** ten Tersandre **Anders J Dahlin** counterten Coridon **Marie-Hélène** Essade sop Une pastourelle **Delphine Gillot** sop La Gloire **Lausanne Opera Chorus; Les Talens Lyriques / Christophe Rousset**
Ambroisie ③ AMB9949 (161' · DDD) Notes, libretto and translation included   ⒻO

Coming from a composer who relied so much on spectacle, it's astonishing how vividly this opera's drama comes to life on disc. *Roland* is about the power of love to persuade the knight Roland to put aside his pursuit of glory and, when thwarted in love, to drive him to a short-lived madness, from which he recovers sufficiently to return to the battlefield. There are no mythological gods within earshot, although Glory, Fame and Terror put in cameo appearances at the end. The agile chorus members of the Opéra de Lausanne adapt their tone to evoke fairies, oriental islanders, shepherds and shepherdesses and the ghosts of dead heroes.

Lully's music displays emotion and wit, and is often ravishing, and in Christophe Rousset's experienced hands, beautifully paced. Five acts slip by quickly, abetted by a succession of musical triumphs. There's exquisite chamber music and moments of extreme drama. (Not even Lully's orchestra could have performed the mad scene with the speed and clarity of Les Talens Lyriques.) But Lully's trademark masterstroke is the series of monologues and dialogues over ground basses delivered by Angélique and Médor which culminates in the great chaconne with orchestra and chorus that ends Act 3.

The role of Roland is sung with dignity and touching vulnerability by Nicolas Testé. Angélique is sympathetically characterised by Anna Maria Panzarella, as is gentle, steadfast Médor, by Olivier Dumait. Emiliano Gonzalez-Toro delights us with fluent ornamentation, and Salomé Haller with the beauty of her tone.

This recording is destined to win accolades. Recommended highly.

Witold Lutosławski   Polish 1913-1994

Lutosławski studied with Maliszewski at the Warsaw Conservatory (1932-7) and soon made his mark as a pianist and composer, though few works from before 1945 have been published. He then developed a clear, fresh tonality related to late Bartók displayed in the Little Suite for orchestra (1951), the Concerto for Orchestra (1954) and the Dance Preludes for clarinet and piano (1954). But that style was short-lived: in the late 1950s he was able to essay a kind of serialism (Funeral Music for strings,1958) and to learn from Cage the possibility of aleatory textures, where synchronisation between instrumental lines is not exact (Venetian Games for chamber orchestra, 1961). Most of his subsequent works were orchestral, fully chromatic, finely orchestrated in a manner suggesting Debussy and Ravel, and developed from an opposition between aleatory and metrical textures. These include his Second (1967), Third (1983) and Fourth (1993) symphonies, concertos for cello (1970) and for oboe and harp (1980), and settings of French verse with chorus (Three Poems of Henri Michaux, 1963), tenor (Paroles tissées, 1965) and baritone (Les espaces du sommeil, 1975). During this period he was also internationally active as a teacher and conductor of his own music. **GROVE**music

Cello Concerto

Cello Concerto. Livre pour orchestre. Novelette. Chain 3
Andrzej Bauer vc **Polish National Radio Symphony Orchestra / Antoni Wit**
Naxos 8 553625 (73' · DDD)   Ⓢ

This is an excellent disc; fine music, well played and recorded, and all at the special Naxos price. The earliest composition, *Livre* (1968), was the first work completed by Lutosławski after the Second Symphony, and it shows him at his freshest and boldest, as if relieved to be free (if only temporarily) from the burden of one of music's weightiest traditions. With its well-nigh surreal juxtapositions of strongly contrasted materials, and the unusual ferocity of its tone – the 'book' in question must have been of the blood and thunder variety – *Livre* reveals a Lutosławski quite different from the relatively benign, ironic master of the later works. Coming immediately after *Livre*, the Cello Concerto has an even wider expressive range: indeed, in the balance it achieves between lamenting melodic lines and mercurial scherzo-like writing, coupled with a tendency to home in on crucial pitch-centres, it sets out the basic elements of the composer's later style.

This performance owes a great deal to Antoni Wit's skilful shaping of the music's alternations between relatively free and precise notation, and this skill is even more evident in the remaining orchestral scores. *Novelette*, completed in 1979, is Lutosławski's response to his first American commission; it's far more cogent and concentrated than its title might lead you to expect. *Chain 3* (1986) is one of the best later works, let down only by some rather perfunctory quasi-tonal harmony near the end. But this doesn't undermine the impression the disc as a whole conveys of some of the most characterful and individual music of the last 30 years.

Concerto for Orchestra

Concerto for Orchestra. Funeral Music. Mi-parti
BBC Philharmonic Orchestra / Yan Pascal Tortelier
Chandos CHAN9421 (55' · DDD) Recorded 1993   Ⓟ**OO**

Tortelier's virtues as a conductor – expressive warmth allied to a special rhythmic buoyancy – are apparent in a sizzling account of the *Concerto for Orchestra*. The musical flow is firmly controlled, yet the effect is never inflexible, and the technical precision and the alertness of the playing is something for the listener to revel in. The sound is bright, well differentiated dynamically, and even if the BBC's Manchester studio lacks some of the depth and atmosphere of Chicago's Orchestra Hall, as caught in Barenboim's version, this recording is generally more vivid, in keeping with a performance which has precisely the kind of bite and energy that the score demands. It's good that Chandos and Tortelier chose *Mi-parti* to complete the disc, since of all

Lutosławski's later instrumental works this one makes out the best possible case for his radical change of technique around 1960.

Symphonies

Symphony No 1. Chantefleurs et Chantefables[a].
Jeux vénetiens. Postlude No 1. Silesian Triptych[a]
[a]**Olga Pasiecznik** sop **Polish National Radio
Symphony Orchestra / Antoni Wit**
Naxos 8 554283 (73' · DDD)   Ⓢ

Juxtaposing Lutosławski's early Symphony No 1 with the late *Chantefleurs et Chantefables* reinforces the fundamentally French associations of this composer's very personal musical voice; to contemplate how the symphony's exuberant embrace of a Roussel-like idiom was complemented, more than 40 years later, by the subtle Ravellian overtones of *Chantefleurs et Chantefables* is to recognise that the radical gestures of *Jeux vénetiens* (1961) have worn less well than Lutosławski's more 'conservative' qualities. Indeed, the wild piano cadenza in *Jeux vénetiens* now evokes the high jinks of Ibert's *Divertissement* rather than the liberated avant-garde ethos of more determinedly progressive musical minds. The downbeat ending is far more memorable.

Olga Pasiecznik's singing is outstanding, especially in *Chantefleurs*, where she easily surpasses Dawn Upshaw in subtlety and Antoni Wit turns in strongly characterised, well-shaped accounts of all the scores. The playing is eloquent as well as energetic, and although, as with earlier Naxos volumes, the recordings are rather glassy and generalised, the music's range of colour and variety of texture is never in doubt. With such a well-filled disc, why did Naxos decide to include the first of the Three Postludes? The composer himself was clearly happy for the piece to appear on its own, but in a series with pretensions to completeness the full set is surely a must.

Symphonies – Nos 1 & 2. Symphonic Variations.
Funeral music. Concerto for Orchestra. Jeux
vénitiens. Livre pour Orchestre. Mi-parti
**Polish National Radio Symphony Orchestra /
Witold Lutosławski**
EMI Double Forte ② 573833-2 (149' · ADD) Recorded
1976-7   Ⓑ Ⓞ

The works here illustrate Lutosławski's progress from relatively traditional to relatively radical styles. The *Concerto for Orchestra* fully deserves to stand alongside Bartók's slightly earlier, similarly exuberant essay in the genre, and this performance, by turns punchy and passionate, proves that Lutosławski was not always an overly reticent conductor of his own scores. The playing and recording lack some of the refinement of Barenboim's Chicago version, but it has an attractively raw energy, the composer contemplating 'youthful' excesses with enjoyment rather than embarrassment.

Hearing *Jeux vénitiens* immediately after the concerto supports the argument that Lutosławski's change of direction, around 1960, risked losing much that was most substantial in his earlier music. The aleatory jam sessions of *Jeux vénitiens* seem especially dated in this rather cluttered, airless recording, but at least the performance doesn't attempt to add spurious solemnity to a liberating *jeu d'esprit*. *Livre* and *Mi-parti* are both much finer works, and the blend of formal mastery with vivid, well-contrasted materials – especially in *Mi-parti* – offers one of the most satisfying and distinctive musical experiences of recent times.

The first two symphonies, *Symphonic Variations* and *Funeral music* share an acute sense of texture, with the *Symphonic Variations* (1938) serving as a sort of changing room where the composer busily experiments with all manner of musical dress.

The *Funeral music* for Bartók (1956-8) is a powerful synthesis of original thought and active homage, with plentiful reminders of the master himself. The real ground-breaker, however, is the Second Symphony, a seething, structured mass in two parts: the first, nervous and diffuse (with strikingly original passagework for piano and percussion), the second initially dense, but ultimately ethereal.

With performances that are authoritative and engaging, this bargain-priced reissue is an indispensable Lutosławski release.

Symphony No 3. Concerto for Orchestra
Chicago Symphony Orchestra / Daniel Barenboim
Warner Elatus 0927-49015-2 (58' · DDD) Recorded
live 1992   Ⓜ

Lutosławski's Third Symphony was commissioned by the Chicago SO and first performed by them under Sir Georg Solti in 1983, but only nine years later did the orchestra record the work. None of the versions made in the interim can equal Barenboim's blend of refined detail and cumulative power, and the Warner recording is also more faithful to the dynamics marked in the score. The *Concerto for Orchestra*, completed almost 30 years before the symphony, is comparatively conservative in style, but it possesses ample substance to match its panache. It also remains a formidable challenge to an orchestra. As with the symphony, Barenboim's strength is the large-scale creation and sustaining of tension, and the recording contains the heavy climaxes without draining them of clarity or impact.

Sergey Lyapunov   Russian 1859-1924

Lyapunov studied at the Moscow Conservatory but, attracted by the nationalism of the new Russian school, became a pupil of Balakirev, a dominating influence. He taught and conducted in St Peters-

burg, also appearing as a pianist and composing pro-lifically, often in the style of other composers (Schumann, Chopin, Mendelssohn, Balakirev and above all Liszt); his brilliant technical studies op.12 recall Liszt's Transcendental Studies. Besides piano show-pieces (still in the repertory), he wrote distinctive, lyrical piano miniatures, orchestral works, notably the Solemn Overture on Russian Themes (1896), and many songs. **GROVE**music

Piano Concertos

Piano Concertos – No 1 in E flat minor, Op 4; No 2 in E, Op 38. Rhapsody on Ukrainian Themes, Op 28
Hamish Milne *pf* **BBC Scottish Symphony Orchestra / Martyn Brabbins**
Hyperion CDA67326 (59' · DDD)   Ⓕ**OO**

Hyperion celebrates the 30th release in its invaluable The Romantic Piano Concerto series with a disc of Lyapunov's works for piano and orchestra as beautiful as it's comprehensive. Whether in Opp 4, 28 or 38, you could never fail to guess the composer's nationality, and even when you sense Balakirev's eagle-eyed scrutiny of the First Concerto or Liszt's influence in the Second, Lyapunov's style invariably transcends the sources of his inspiration. Indeed, it's no exaggeration to say, as Edward Garden does in his excellent accompanying essay, that the hushed nocturnal opening to the Second Concerto is among the loveliest in the repertoire, setting the stage for every starry-eyed wonder.

The writing is as lavish and ornate as even the most ardent lover of Russian Romantic music could wish – at 3'35" it's like some richly embroidered cloth winking and glinting with a thousand different lights and colours. More generally, everything is seen through such a personal and committed perspective that all sense of derivation or of a tale twice told is erased.

Such an overall impression wouldn't, occur if the performances were less skilful or meticulously prepared. Hamish Milne holds his head high, lucidly and affectionately throughout, commanding cascades of notes; he's stylishly partnered by Martyn Brabbins. There's competition in the Second Concerto from the urbane and scintillating Howard Shelley who is rather more immediately recorded on Chandos. But to have all three works on a single disc is an irresistible bonus.

Symphony No 1

Symphony No 1, Op 12. Polonaise, Op 16 Piano Concerto No 2, Op 38[a]
[a]**Howard Shelley** *pf* **BBC Philharmonic Orchestra / Vassily Sinaisky**
Chandos CHAN9808 (65' · DDD)   Ⓕ

Sergei Lyapunov has always been a shadowy figure, his derivative yet distinctive voice drowned by his more celebrated compatriots and even by his contemporaries Taneyev, Liadov and Arensky. Yet hearing the First Symphony in a performance of this calibre you're reminded of the way Lyapunov's melodic appeal is complemented by brilliant craftsmanship.

The opening motif is sufficiently brief to invite elaboration and to play a key role in music as coherent as it's heartfelt. The chromatic undertow as the music eases into the *poco più tranquillo*, its mix of sweetness and unrest looks ahead to Rachmaninov's Second Symphony, and if the themes are less memorable than in that towering Romantic masterpiece they're marshalled and directed with great compositional skill. Vassily Sinaisky and the BBC Philharmonic Orchestra allow the long sinuous lines of the *Andante sostenuto* to unfold with an unfaltering tact and commitment, and in the balletic *Scherzo*, with its memories of Tchaikovsky, he realises all of the music's captivating grace and charm.

If Borodin is a key influence in the symphony then Liszt is central to the thinking behind the Second Piano Concerto. Lyapunov, after all, paid an eloquent tribute to Liszt in his 12 *Transcendental Etudes* for solo piano, a magnificent if uneven creation, and not surprisingly the lavish and intricate pianism in the Second Concerto is a Romantically inclined pianist's dream. Certainly its succulent themes and star-dust decoration could hardly be spun off more beguilingly than by Howard Shelley. His relaxed mastery and enviably elegant style inform every bar of this most seductive work.

The recordings are magnificent; no lover of Russian Romantic by-ways can afford to be without this.

Edward MacDowell
American 1860-1908

MacDowell studied the piano in Paris (with Marmontel), Wiesbaden and Frankfurt (Carl Heymann), as well as composition (with Raff, at the Hoch Conservatory in Frankfurt), taking his first post at the Darmstadt Conservatory. Liszt heard his First Modern Suite and First Piano Concerto and strongly encouraged him; by 1884 German firms had published 10 of his works. After several years in Wiesbaden he moved to Boston in 1888 to pursue a performing career. His Second Piano Concerto and First and Second Orchestral Suites won success there and in New York, and he was increasingly accepted as a leading figure in American musical life. Compositions of the Boston years included his popular Woodland Sketches, Sonata tragica and Sonata eroica and the Six love Songs. In 1896 he became the first professor of music at Columbia University; besides organising the new department, he conducted a New York men's glee club and composed some of his best piano music – Sea Pieces, the Third and Fourth Sonatas, New England Idyls – and many male choruses. He left Columbia in 1904 but continued to teach privately; after his death his summer home at

Peterborough, New Hampshire, was converted into an artists' colony (still active).

MacDowell was a Romantic by temperament, with a musical imagination shaped by nature and literature (notably poetry and Celtic and Nordic legends). His style derives largely from Schumann, Liszt, Wagner, Raff and especially Grieg and, though not innovatory, influential or distinctively American, retains a certain melodic freshness and attractive orchestral colouring.   GROVEmusic

Piano Concertos

Piano Concertos – No 1 in A minor, Op 15[a];
No 2 in D minor, Op 23[a]. Hexentanz, Op 17 No 2[a].
Romance for Cello and Orchestra, Op 35[b]
[a]**Stephen Prutsman** pf [b]**Aisling Drury Byrne** vc
National Symphony Orchestra of Ireland / Arthur Fagen
Naxos 8 559049 (56' · DDD)   Ⓢ

Music of another time, another age, the Mac-Dowell piano concertos can, in the right hands, seem more endearing than quaint or overblown. Both may satisfy conventional notions of dark and light, of tragedy and skittishness, but their heart-easing, lavishly decorated themes understandably attracted Liszt. Stephen Prutsman, a brilliant and versatile pianist, plays with ease and fluency, tossing aside the *Presto* movements from both concertos with an enviable sheen, though arguably without a necessarily committed or potent romanticism. Suave and engaging in the Grieg-haunted *Andante tranquillo* from the A minor Concerto, he loses his poise in the deeply welling *più mosso, con passione* from the D minor Concerto's first movement, and it's here, in particular, that one misses Van Cliburn's unforgettable warmth and virtuosity. No pianist has played this concerto with such magisterial command or emotional generosity; indeed, it sounds as if it was written for him. Eugene List, too, shows a higher degree of involvement than Prutsman, though it must be admitted that the latter's occasional reticence results from Naxos's recessed sound, which irons out much sense of dynamic perspective or variety. Too often Prutsman is confined to the shadows when he should be centre-stage. The National Symphony Orchestra of Ireland has its uneasy moments, but world-première recordings of the *Hexentanz*, in an arrangement for piano and orchestra, and the *Romance* for cello and orchestra make this a tempting issue.

Guillaume de Machaut
French c1300-1377

Machaut entered the service of John of Luxembourg, King of Bohemia, as a royal secretary, c1323. The king helped him to procure a canonry in Reims, which was confirmed in 1335; Machaut settled there c1340, although he continued in royal service until the king's death (1346). He then served various members of the French high nobility, including John, Duke of Berry, his later years being dedicated to the manuscript compilation of his works.

With his prolific output of motets and songs, Machaut was the single most important figure of the French Ars Nova. He followed and developed the guidelines of Philippe de Vitry's treatise Ars nova and, in particular, observed Vitry's unprecedented advocation of duple time in many of his works, even in his setting of the Ordinary of the Mass. Only in some of his lais and virelais and the Hoquetus David did he consistently adhere to 13th-century rhythmic patterns and genres. His own rhythmic style is novel in its use of variety and motivic interest, particularly through syncopation, and in his development of isorhythmic techniques: all but three of his 23 motets, and four of the movements of the Messe de Nostre Dame –one of the earliest polyphonic settings of the Mass Ordinary – are isorhythmic. In secular music, Machaut set a wide range of poetic forms, all of which are illustrated in his long narrative poem, the Remede de Fortune (probably an early work). While the relationship between text and music is most closely observed in the monophonic lais and virelais, a highly flexible approach is adopted in the three-voice motets so that the subtle treatment of the text avoids the symmetricality of complete isorhythm. More progressive features of Machaut's style – an increased awareness of tonality, the use of unifying rhythmic motifs – are found in his polyphonic settings of rondeaux and ballades, while melodic considerations are to the fore in his virelais.   GROVEmusic

Messe de Nostre Dame

Messe de Nostre Dame. Je ne cesse de prier (Lai 'de la fonteinne'). Ma fin est mon commencement
Hilliard Ensemble / Paul Hillier
Hyperion CDA66358 (54' · DDD) Texts and translations included   Ⓕ**Ⓞ**

Machaut's *Messe de Nostre Dame* is the earliest known setting of the Ordinary Mass by a single composer. Paul Hillier avoids a full reconstruction on this release: his deference to 'authenticity' restricts itself to the usage of 14th century French pronunciation of the Latin. His ensemble sings two to a part, with prominent countertenors. It's arguable whether the musicians sing the chant at too fast a tempo but they're smooth and flexible, and the performance as a whole is both fluid and light in texture. Also included on this release are two French compositions. The wonderful *Lai 'de la fonteinne'* is admirably sung by three tenors and is pure delight – providing food for the heart as well as for the intellect. The rather more familiar *Ma fin est mon commencement*, with its retrograde canon, completes this admirable disc.

Motets

De souspirant cuer, M2. Fine Amour, qui me vint navrer, M3. Puis que la douce rousée, M4. Qui plus aimme, M5. Lasse! Je suis en aventure, M7. Ha! Fortune, M8. O livoris feritas, M9. Helas! Où sera pris

confors, M10. Fins cuers dous. Eins que ma dame
d'onnur, M13. Faus Samblant m'a deceü, M14. Se
j'aim mon loyal ami, M16. Bone pastor, M18. Diligen-
ter inquiramus, M19. Biauté parée de valour, M20.
Veni creator spiritus, M21. Plange, regni respublica,
M22. Inviolata genitrix, M23

The Hilliard Ensemble (David Gould, David James
countertens Rogers Covey-Crump, Steven Harrold
tens Gordon Jones *bar*)
ECM New Series 472 402-2 (63' · DDD) Texts and
translations included ⓕ**OO**

This is a landmark recording and a courageous
venture. It's probably the first devoted to
Machaut's motets, containing no fewer than 18
of the 23 that survive. It's certainly the first to
present them in the order in which Machaut
himself presented them in his own manuscripts.
And the performances are of a truly mandarin
refinement. Here are The Hilliard Ensemble
with goodness knows how many combined
years of experience performing this kind of
music in public; they aren't just on the top of
their form but also constantly showing the fruits
of that experience.

The results of that refinement may surprise
some listeners. Tempos tend to be rather slower
than on earlier recordings: it's as though they
feel no need for lily-gilding, no need to apologise for the music, where earlier performances
injected possibly gratuitous energy into
Machaut's lines. Dissonances are often made to
disappear almost without trace, which will disappoint those who thought the clashes to be the
very lifeblood of Machaut's music. (It must be
absolutely clear that this was an informed decision by The Hilliards, many of whom have performed this music with other groups over the
years.) Diction tends to be clearer than in some
recent recordings, and – perhaps most surprising of all – they refrain from adopting current
views on the early French pronunciation of
Latin. These are all features that could make
some listeners find it a touch dull; they might
even find that they scarcely recognise old
favourites. But they're superbly done, and the
performances give the best avenue yet to gaining access to Machaut's still perplexing but
always irresistible art.

Sir Alexander Mackenzie

British 1847-1935

*Mackenzie studied in Germany and at the Royal
Academy of Music, by 1865 becoming known in
Edinburgh as a violinist and conductor. In the 1880s
he won a reputation as one of England's leading composers, chiefly with the oratorio The Rose of Sharon
(1884). From 1885 he lived in London, conducting
the Novello Oratorio Concerts and, from 1888, serving as an influential principal of the RAM he also
conducted for the Philharmonic Society (1892-9)
and occasionally for the Royal Choral Society, making a tour of Canada in 1903. He received a knight-*

*hood (1895) and created KCVO (1922). A work-
manlike composer, Mackenzie produced successful
choral works, vocal settings (many of Scottish poets)
and descriptive orchestral pieces, often imaginative
and satisfying if also somewhat derivative.*
GROVEmusic

Scottish Concerto

Mackenzie Scottish Concerto, Op 55 **Tovey** Piano
Concerto in A, Op 15
Steven Osborne *pf* **BBC Scottish Symphony
Orchestra / Martyn Brabbins**
Hyperion CDA67023 (62' · DDD)   ⓕ

From the horns' call to arms at the outset of the
piece to the irrepressible merrymaking of the
closing pages, Edinburgh-born Sir Alexander
Mackenzie's *Scottish Concerto* (1897) spells firm
enjoyment, and it's astonishing that this is its
first recording. Cast in three movements, each
of which employs a traditional Scottish melody,
it's a thoroughly endearing and beautifully
crafted work which wears its native colours
without any hint of stale cliché or cloying sentimentality; indeed, the canny wit, genuine freshness and fertile imagination with which
Mackenzie treats his material are in evidence
throughout the work.

By contrast, Edinburgh-based Sir Donald
Tovey's Piano Concerto (1903) exhibits a rather
more formal demeanour, its three movements
brimful of youthful ambition and possessing a
very Brahmsian solidity and dignity. Tovey's
idiomatically assured writing isn't always
entirely untouched by a certain academic
earnestness, but on the whole any unwanted
stuffiness is deftly kept at bay. In fact, repeated
hearings only strengthen one's admiration for
this work.

No praise can be too high for Steven
Osborne's contribution, while the excellent
Martyn Brabbins draws a splendidly stylish and
alert response from his fine BBC group. Sound
and balance are excellent too.

James MacMillan

British 1959

*MacMillan studied at Edinburgh University and
then with Casken at Durham University. In 1990
he became affiliate composer of the Scottish Chamber
Orchestra he has since become visiting composer for
the Philharmonia (London) and artistic director of
its Contemporary Music Series. His music is noted
for its energy and emotional power, its religious and
political content and its references to Scottish folk
music. Recent works include The Beserking (1990),
a piano concerto for Peter Donohoe; Sinfonietta
(1991); and Veni, Veni, Emmanuel (1992), a percussion concerto for Evelyn Glennie.* **GROVE**music

The Confession of Isobel Gowdie

The Confession of Isobel Gowdie. Tryst.

BBC Scottish Symphony Orchestra/Jerzy Maksymiuk
Koch Gramophone Awards Collection 476 2646
(54' · DDD)   Ⓜ**OOO**

 The Confession of Isobel Gowdie tells a stirring story. If MacMillian's programme – the martyrdom of a Scottish Catholic 'witch' – seems over-pictorial, no problem: the progression from rapt modal string threnody through mounting violence to the re-emergence and transformation of the modal lament is as easy to follow as the 'narrative' of a Mahler symphony – and the aftereffect isn't all that dissimilar. Some may be bothered by undisguised echoes of other composers: Copland, Messiaen, Stravinsky, Ives, the famous single-note crescendo from Berg's *Wozzeck...* But lack of disguise is part of their strength. Maksymiuk and the BBC SSO give the kind of penetrating performance that usually only comes from long involvement.

Tryst too emerges well: the forces may be smaller, but the head-on confrontation of violence with calmer, more humane sounds again generates a compelling musical drama, and the ending, though less spectacular than Isobel Gowdie's final one-tone immolation, works both as an imaginative conclusion and a challenge to go back and dig deeper. Away with caution! Give this a try.

Tryst

Tryst[a]. Adam's Rib[b]. They Saw the Stone had been Rolled Away[a]. Ì (A Meditation on Iona)[a]
[b]**Scottish Chamber Orchestra Brass;** [a]**Scottish Chamber Orchestra / Joseph Swensen**
BIS CD1019 (59' · DDD)   Ⓕ

This is the third recording of *Tryst* – extraordinary for a contemporary orchestral work. But its individuality is still as striking now as when it first appeared: especially so in this taut, gripping version. MacMillan touches, as warmly and directly as Mahler. The sounds can be violent, acerbic or prickly (as indeed they can in Mahler!); the keening string lament at the heart of the work isn't always easy on the ear, and yet it all speaks – it's plainly the work of someone who urgently wants to tell us something. So too are the performances. Joseph Swensen brings the passionate enthusiasm to *Tryst*, and to *Ì*, that has made his concerts with the Scottish Chamber Orchestra such events in Scotland. *Ì* (pronounced 'ee') is a quite astonishing work. The subtitle, 'A Meditation on Iona', might suggest something romantically atmospheric, with soft, lilting Celtic accents. In fact this is hard, intense, sometimes eerie music: a tribute to St Columba, the muscular, fiercely contentious monk who brought Christianity to Scotland and founded the monastic college of Iona – perhaps also a reminder of St Paul's words about working out one's salvation with 'fear and trembling'. Along with this come two short, brooding

pieces, which are dominated by the sound of brass: *Adam's Rib* and *They saw the Stone had been Rolled Away*, the latter giving more than a foretaste of MacMillan's Symphony, *Vigil* – the concluding part of the trilogy *Triduum*. As with *Triduum*, the success is total: powerful, concise works, powerfully and understandingly performed, in crisp, clear recordings.

String Quartets

String Quartets – No 1, 'Visions of a November Spring'; No 2, 'Why is this night different?'.
Memento. Tuireadh[a]
[a]**Robert Plane** cl **Emperor Quartet** (Martin Burgess, Clare Hayes vns Fiona Bonds va William Schofield vc)
BIS BIS-CD1269 (74' · DDD)   ⒻO

Visions of a November Spring, James MacMillan's First String Quartet, was completed in 1988 and already bears many a stylistic trait of the composer who was to create such a stir two years later with *The Confession of Isobel Gowdie*, not least a mastery of the singing line and the distinctive, 'keening' quality of the string writing itself. The work is cast in two movements, the much lengthier second of which perhaps doesn't quite add up to the sum of its impressive parts.

No such reservations, however, apply to the Second Quartet from 1998, whose title, *Why is this night different?*, comes from the question posed by the youngest member of the family during the Jewish rite of Seder on the first night of Passover. The father answers by telling of the flight of the children of Israel from Egypt. The result is an arrestingly powerful and sure-footed masterwork, ideally proportioned, economically argued and always evincing a riveting narrative and emotional scope. Similarly, *Tuireadh* (Gaelic for 'lament') for clarinet and string quartet packs a wealth of pungent and varied expression into its single-movement frame. MacMillan wrote it in 1991 as a 'musical complement' to Sue Jane Taylor's sculpture in memory of the victims of the Piper Alpha oil rig disaster, having also been greatly moved by a letter from a grieving mother who recalled how, during the memorial service, 'a spontaneous keening sound rose gently from the mourners assembled on the boat'. *Tuireadh* is a deeply compassionate threnody, as is the much briefer *Memento* for string quartet (1994), which (as so often with this composer) shows the influence of the ancient oral tradition of Gaelic psalmody still practised in the Western Isles today. Performances throughout are as superlatively disciplined as they're tirelessly eloquent; sound, balance and presentation are all beyond reproach. Another MacMillan/BIS triumph.

The Birds of Rhiannon

The Birds of Rhiannon. Magnificat. Exsultet. Nunc

dimittis. Mairi. The Gallant Weaver
BBC Singers; BBC Philharmonic Orchestra / James MacMillan
Chandos CHAN9997 (71' · DDD)   ⓕⓞ

MacMillan's colours can be garish, his gestures histrionic, but his is an art of passion and commitment: these are the effects of a composer seeking to make you feel and react strongly as well as think deeply. His admixture of Celtic cultural nationalism, leftist politics and Catholicism may be too rich for the blood of some 21st century connoisseurs, but it provides affecting and memorable listening experiences. This CD resolutely demonstrates the point.

The setting of Burns's *Gallant Weaver* (1997) is MacMillan at his gentlest and most intimate, but this only softens you up for *Rhiannon* (2001), inspired by a tale from the Mabinogion, an ancient Welsh collection. *The Times* described its Proms première as unwieldy and florid with overworked and impoverished motifs. Maybe the performance has since been refined: here it sounds polymorphous and full of incident. More importantly, there's a cogent musical argument, even if not of the most sophisticated or subtle kind.

The *Magnificat*, a BBC Millennium commission heard here in the version for choir and orchestra, still includes an organ part which powers the violent ensemble interjections in the closing minutes.

He's already handsomely represented on disc, but this is as good an introduction as you'll get.

Mass

Mass[ab]. A New Song[ab]. Christus vincit[a].
Gaudeamus in loci pace[b]. Seinte Mari moder
milde[ab]. A Child's Prayer[a]. Changed[ab]
[a]**Westminster Cathedral Choir / Martin Baker** with
[b]**Andrew Reid** *org*
Hyperion CDA67219 (66' · DDD) Texts and
translations included   ⓕⓞⓞ

MacMillan's choral music is more often than not a direct response to his own Christian faith. The Mass recorded here was commissioned by Westminster Cathedral for the 'Glory of God in the Millennium Year of the Jubilee' and unlike MacMillan's two previous Masses, which were composed for congregational use, was specifically written for performance by a professional choir. It's through-composed and this provides a sense of structure, continuity and flow that greatly enhances its accessibility when heard out of context – on disc rather than celebrated. That MacMillan intended the Mass for practical use is apparent by his choice of vernacular rather than the Latin text. His often eclectic style is very much in evidence; the score glimmers with echoes of Howells and Duruflé, especially in the Kyrie and in his often quasi-orchestral organ writing, but in general it's MacMillan's individual voice that shapes this impressive and deeply felt setting. The Gloria

contains some particularly effective music, not least some marvellously atmospheric organ writing, and the crepuscular Agnus Dei lingers in the mind long after the final notes die away. Of the remaining works on the disc, A New Song and A Child's Prayer (dedicated to the victims of the Dunblane tragedy) stand out as particularly fine examples of MacMillan's choral writing. As a bonus we're treated to the wonderfully translucent organ solo Gaudeamus in loci pace, beautifully performed by Andrew Reid. Performances throughout are exceptionally fine, the recorded sound radiantly atmospheric. A must.

Raising Sparks

Raising Sparks[a]. Piano Sonata. Barncleupédie.
Birthday Present. For Ian.
[a]**Jean Rigby** *mez* **John York** *pf* [a]**Nash Ensemble**
(Ian Brown *pf* Philippa Davies *fl* Richard Hosford *cl*
Marianne Thorsen, Elizabeth Wexler *vns* James Boyd
va Paul Watkins *va* Skaila Kanga *hp*) / **Martyn
Brabbins**
Black Box BBM1067 (57' · DDD)   ⓕ

Martyn Brabbins and the Nash Ensemble here offer a superb recording première of a major work by James MacMillan. Like much of his music, it has a religious base. The big difference this time is that whereas his source of inspiration generally lies at the heart of his Roman Catholicism, this time is it the Jewish tradition. *Raising Sparks*, a 35-minute cantata on the theme of creation and redemption, is inspired by a poem by Michael Symmons Roberts and by the writing of the Jewish author, Menahem Nahum; the work takes one inexorably through a kaleidoscopic sequence of symbolic images, with one vivid simile piled on another in Roberts's striking language. MacMillan, for whom the poems were written, responds to the poet's verbal colour with musical ideas, often onomatopoeic but always striking and dramatic, within a taut musical structure. The vocal line, though taxing, is more lyrical than in many new works, superbly sung by Jane Rigby, while the instrumental accompaniment is endlessly inventive, with the piano (the masterly Ian Brown) generally the central instrument in the ensemble, with the fifth of the songs accompanied simply by the occasional note sounded on the piano and no more. Otherwise Brown leads the Nash players in a totally committed performance, very well recorded.

The four piano works which come as coupling find the pianist John York just as dedicated. The Piano Sonata of 1985 in three movements is much the most demanding, far grittier than the rest, inspired by the extreme winter of that year. It remains so potent in MacMillan's mind that he used it as the basis for his Second Symphony of 1999. The first of the piano pieces, *For Ian*, then brings release into pure tonality and lyricism, a strathspey full of Scottish-snap rhythms. After that *Birthday Present* seems a sombre gift, musically striking nonetheless, and the final

Barncleupédie (1990) rounds things off light-heartedly. Backing up a masterly major work, these are occasional pieces which readily earn their place.

Veni, veni, Emmanuel

Veni, veni, Emmanuel[a]. After the tryst[b]. '... as others see us ...'[c]. Three Dawn Rituals[c]. Untold[c]
[a]**Evelyn Glennie** *perc* [b]**Ruth Crouch** *vn* [b]**Peter Evans** *pf* [ac]**Scottish Chamber Orchestra** / [a]**Jukka-Pekka Saraste**, [c]**James MacMillan**
Catalyst 09026 61916-2 (68' · DDD)   Ⓕ**OO**

Taking the Advent plainsong of the title as his basis, MacMillan reflects in his continuous 26-minute sequence the theological implications behind the period between Advent and Easter. The five contrasted sections are in a sort of arch form, with the longest and slowest in the middle. That section, 'Gaude, Gaude', expresses not direct joy as the Latin words might suggest but a meditative calm, using the four relevant chords from the plainsong's refrain as a hushed ostinato. Over that the soloist on the marimba plays an elaborate but gentle and intensely poetic cadenza. The main sections on either side are related dances based on hocketing repeated notes and full of jazzy syncopations, with powerful sections for Advent and Easter respectively framing the work as a whole. The plainsong emerges dramatically as a chorale at the climax of the second dance section, a telling moment.

The composer's notes are most helpful, but they deliberately keep quiet about the coda, where MacMillan brings off another dramatic coup. After the soloist has worked through the widest range of percussion in the different sections, there's a gap when players in the orchestra pick up and start playing little jingling bells, and the soloist progresses up to the big chimes set on a platform above the rest of the orchestra. The very close of the work brings a *crescendo* of chimes intended to reflect the joy of Easter in the Catholic service and the celebration of the Resurrection. Disappointingly though, the preparatory jingles are gentle and discreet, and even the final chimes are devotional rather than exuberant. Even so, this is a magnificent representation of one of the most striking and powerful works written by any British composer of the younger generation.

Leevi Madetoja   Finnish 1887-1947

Madetoja studied with Sibelius in Helsinki (1906-10), with d'Indy in Paris (1910-11), and in Vienna and Berlin (1911-12), then worked in Helsinki as a teacher, critic and composer. His works, often using Ostrobothnian folk music and French techniques, are skilfully orchestrated; they include the operas The Ostrobothnians (1923) and Juha (1934), three symphonies (1916, 1918, 1926) and much choral music. GROVEmusic

Lieder

The Land in our song. Lieder, Op 2 – Since thou didst leave; Alone; Winter morning; Starry night: Dark-hued leaves, Op 19 No 1. Serenade, Op 16 No 1. Folk Songs from Northern Ostrobothnia, Op 18. Songs of Youth, Op 20b. Take up that fair kantele again. A flower is purest when opening. Lieder, Op 25 – From afar I hear them singing; Wintry road; Birthplace; Sometimes weeping in the evening. I would build a hut, Op 26 No 3. Song at the plough, Op 44 No 1. Lieder, Op 49 – Hail, O daylight in the North; Finland's Tree. Lieder, Op 60 – My longing; Evening. Lieder, Op 71 – I want to go home; The word of the Master. Song of the winter wind
Gabriel Suovanen *bar* **Gustav Djupsjöbacka** *pf*
Ondine ODE996–2 (79' · DDD) Notes, texts and translations included   Ⓕ**O**

The 32 songs are chronologically laid out. After the late-Romantic elegiac *lingua franca* of the Op 2 set, the first of Op 9, 'Dark-hued leaves', startles with its affinities with Rachmaninov; this gem of a piece is on the short list for all Finnish song recitals. Composed in 1913, the first of the *Songs of Youth*, Op 20b, couldn't be published until Finland's independence from Russia after the First World War, which is no surprise, given that its text is demonstratively nationalistic ('Arise, O young sons of Finland…Saved and cherished shall our homeland soon be!') and its melody strong and catchy. This is an altogether impressive opus, whose concluding 'Christmas song' has become one of Finland's best-loved carols. With Op 25 we're back to the ecstatic tone of the earlier songs. Perhaps most impressive of this set is No 2, 'Wintry Road', with its tolling Brittenish ostinato and air of painful asceticism. Swedish-born baritone Gabriel Suovanen is well attuned both to the late-Romantic manner of Madetoja's early songs and to the ardent national-patriotic tone of his later ones. And his pianist, Gustav Djupsjöbacka, supplies stylish accompaniments. Recording quality is fine, and collectors of Nordic and/or song repertoire should not hesitate.

Albéric Magnard   French 1865-1914

Magnard, of a serious disposition, produced severe, formalistic works – mainly orchestral and chamber music and operas – taking Wagner, Beethoven, Gluck and his teacher d'Indy as models. Canon and fugue pervade much of his output, though the Third Symphony (1896) and the opera Bérénice (1909), his masterpiece, show a refreshing clarity of scoring and a lyric simplicity. GROVEmusic

Symphonies

Symphonies – No 1 in C minor, Op 4. No 2 in E, Op 6
BBC Scottish Symphony Orchestra / **Jean-Yves Ossonce**
Hyperion CDA67030 (67' · DDD)   Ⓕ**O**

Symphonies – No 3 in B flat minor, Op 11. No 4 in
C sharp minor, Op 21
**BBC Scottish Symphony Orchestra / Jean-Yves
Ossonce**
Hyperion CDA67040 (73' · DDD)   Ⓕ●

The name of Albéric Magnard began to
impinge on us only 30 years ago, and there have
been recordings of three of his symphonies, the
opera *Guercoeur*, and a five-disc set of his chamber music and songs; but he seems doomed to be
a composer whose music survives only via
recordings: his impact on the concert life of this
country has been virtually nil; nor has he been
much better served in his native France. Not
that he would have cared overmuch: during his
life (brought to an abrupt end at the start of the
First World War by German invaders who set
fire to his country house) he made little attempt
to get his music performed, being paranoically
sensitive to any suspicion of nepotistic influence, as his father was a powerful newspaper
proprietor. By all accounts he was withdrawn
and austere; perhaps in keeping with that image
his music isn't for the casual listener who looks
for facile attractiveness, but in a somewhat Teutonic way is rewarding for the serious-minded
in its skilfully crafted and thoughtfully lyrical
character.

The First Symphony (1890) shows the unmistakable influence of Wagner in the *religioso* slow
movement. Despite the adoption of the cyclic
principle championed by his teacher Vincent
d'Indy, under whose watchful eye the work was
written and who must have smiled approvingly
at his pupil's fluent contrapuntal technique,
Magnard's proliferation of ideas threatens
structural continuity, especially in the first
movement. In contrast to that movement's initial brooding atmosphere, the Second Symphony begins more sunnily and spiritedly, and
the following *Scherzo* (which replaced an earlier
fugue) is a bucolic 'Danses' tinged with introspection. The emotional core of the symphony
is the luxuriant *Chant varié*, and the work ends
in an almost light-hearted mood. The Third
Symphony's striking organum-like opening
leads to an *Allegro* by turns vigorous and contemplative. Next comes a *Scherzo* headed
'Danses' (as in the previous symphony), a mocking soufflé with a wistful central section – an
altogether captivating movement that's anything but austere. The movingly tense slow
movement's long lines are subverted by menacing outbursts that build to a stormy climax
before subsiding; and there's a finale which
combines exuberance and lyricism with a return
to the symphony's very first theme. This is certainly the work to recommend to newcomers to
Magnard.

Several years elapsed before the appearance of
his last symphony in 1913, and by then his overall mood had darkened. The turbulent passion
that characterises the first movement, presented
in dramatically colourful orchestration, is also
mirrored in the finale: between them come a
highly individual *Scherzo* with strange oriental-

type passages and a lengthy, anguished slow
movement. The BBC Scottish Symphony
Orchestra is on splendid form throughout; their
efforts have been recorded in exemplary fashion.

Gustav Mahler   Austrian 1860-1911

*From 1875 to 1878 Mahler was at the Vienna Con-
servatory, where he studied the piano, harmony and
composition. After that he attended university lec-
tures, worked as a music teacher and composed Das
klagende Lied, a cantata indebted to the operas of
Weber and Wagner but also showing many conspicuously Mahlerian features.*

*In 1880 he accepted a conducting post at a summer
theatre at Bad Hall, and was engaged in a similar
capacity in 1881 and 1883 at the theatres in Ljubl-
jana and Olomouc. In autumn 1883, he became
music director at Kassel. He found conditions uncongenial, but an unhappy love affair with one of the
singers led to his first masterpiece, the song cycle
Lieder eines fahrenden Gesellen, and the inception of
the closely related First Symphony.*

*Early in 1885 Mahler secured the post of second
conductor at the Neues Stadttheater in Leipzig, to
begin in July 1886. The intervening year he spent at
the Landestheater in Prague, where he had the
opportunity of conducting operas by Gluck, Mozart,
Beethoven and Wagner. At Leipzig, in January
1887, he took over the Ring cycle from Arthur
Nikisch, who fell ill, and convincingly established
among critics and public his genius as an interpretative artist. The following year he completed Weber's
unfinished comic opera Die drei Pintos (its successful
performances in 1888 made Mahler famous and
provided a useful source of income) and fell in love
with the wife of Weber's grandson. It was through
the Webers that he discovered in 1887 the musical
potential of Des Knaben Wunderhorn, a collection of
folklike texts by Arnim and Brentano which provided Mahler with words for all but one of his songs
for the next 14 years.*

*Disagreements with colleagues led to Mahler's res-
ignation at Leipzig in May 1888 and to his dismissal
a few months later from Prague, but within a few
weeks he secured a far more important appointment
at the Royal Opera in Budapest. His first year there
was overshadowed by the illness and deaths of his
parents and his sister. Though he was successful in
bringing the opera house into profit and improving
standards and repertory, the imminent appointment
of an Intendant with artistic control made his situation untenable; he resigned and became first conductor at the Stadttheater, Hamburg. Despite a stifling
artistic atmosphere and a heavy workload, Mahler
returned to composition and at his summer retreat in
the Salzkammergut completed the Second and Third
Symphonies. 1895 brought both tragedy, when his
youngest brother committed suicide, and success, with
the première of the Second Symphony in Berlin in
December. Now a conductor of international stature
and a composer of growing reputation, he turned his
attention to the Vienna Hofoper. The main obstacle*

was his Jewish origins; so he accepted Catholic baptism in February 1897 and was appointed Kapellmeister at two months later.

At Vienna Mahler brought a stagnating opera house to a position of unrivalled brilliance. In 1901 he had a villa built at Maiernigg on the Wörthersee in Carinthia, where he spent the summers composing. In 1902 he married Alma, daughter of the artist Emil Jakob Schindler, and though their life together was not untroubled the security benefited his creative life. At Maiernigg he completed Symphonies Nos 5-8 and in 1904 the Kindertotenlieder, settings of five poems by Rückert on the death of children. The death of Mahler's own elder daughter, Maria, from scarlet fever three years later left him distraught. In Vienna Mahler was surrounded by radical young composers, including Schoenberg, Berg, Webern and Zemlinsky, whose work he supported and encouraged. His propagation of his own music, however, aroused opposition from a section of the Viennese musical establishment, and when the campaign against him, led by an anti-semitic press, gained momentum he turned to New York, where he spent his last winters as conductor, first of the Metropolitan Opera and, from 1910, of the New York PO. He continued to spend the summers in Europe, where he undertook further conducting and completed the valedictory Ninth Symphony and Das Lied von der Erde. This last, a setting of six Chinese poems in German translation, took the shape of a large-scale symphony for two voices and orchestra but Mahler, whose fear of death and sense of fate had been intensified by the diagnosis of a heart condition in 1907, refused to number the work 10, citing Beethoven, Schubert and Bruckner. He did, however, start work on a 10th symphony, but died before he could complete it.

Although as a conductor Mahler achieved fame primarily in opera, his creative energies were directed almost wholly towards symphony and song. Even in the early Das klagende Lied, there are stylistic features to be found in his mature music, for example the combining of onstage and offstage orchestras, the association of high tragedy and the mundane, the drawing on folksong ideas and the dramatic-symbolic use of tonality. This last reappeared in his early masterpiece, the Lieder eines fahrenden Gesellen, which has an evolutionary tonal scheme paralleling the changing fortunes of the travelling hero. In the 1890s Mahler was much influenced by the Wunderhorn poems, in his symphonies as well as his songs, for he often used song to clarify an important moment in the structure of a symphony, for example 'Urlicht' in No 2, which he found himself unable to continue after writing the imposing first movement. No 3 is more idiosyncratic; again, its dramatic scheme evolved with recourse to song and chorus. No 4 returns to tradition, in a first movement of rare wit and subtlety; here the poetic idea is the progress from experience to innocence (with a Wunderhorn song finale). While No 2, 'The Resurrection', moves from C minor to E flat, No 4 goes from G major to the 'heavenly' E major. Parody, irony and satire are important in Mahler's thinking during these years, with popular invention (like the children's round in no.1 and the march tunes of No 3) and elements of distortion.

Nos 5, 6 and 7 are sometimes regarded as a trilogy, although No 5 is a heroic work, with a narrative running from its opening funeral march through the agitated Allegro to a Scherzo and a triumphant conclusion. The symphony moves from C sharp minor to D major. No 6, a tragic work – and in many musicians' view, his greatest symphony for its equilibrium between form and drama – begins and ends in A minor; the finale makes it clear that there is no escape for the implied hero and indeed his death is symbolically enacted in the movement's shattering climax. The shape of No 7, which moves from E minor to C major, is less satisfying; possibly, with its dark, nocturnal middle movement, it is consciously built round the poetic concept of darkness moving towards the light of the finale. The largest-scale of Mahler's symphonies is No 8, the so-called 'Symphony of a Thousand', in which the second part is a vast synthesis of forms and media embodying the setting of the final scene of Goethe's Faust as an amalgam of dramatic cantata, oratorio, song cycle, Lisztian choral symphony and instrumental symphony. This public pronouncement was followed by one of his most personal, Das Lied von der Erde, influenced in its vocal writing and woodwind obbligatos by Mahler's new interest in Bach. His last two symphonies return to the four-movement scheme of the middle-period ones, incorporating extensions of the character movements of his earlier works with the new type of slow first movement (followed up in the unfinished 10th) and ending with an Adagio in a mood of profound resignation. Mahler's extension of symphonic form, of the symphony's expressive scope and the use of the orchestra (especially the agonised timbres he obtained by using instruments, particularly wind, at the top of their compass) represent a pained farewell to Romanticism; different aspects were followed up by the Second Viennese School, Shostakovich and Britten.   GROVEmusic

Symphonies

No 1 in D; **No 2** in C minor, 'Resurrection'; **No 3** in D minor; **No 4** in G; **No 5** in C sharp minor; **No 6** in A minor; **No 7** in E minor; **No 8** in E flat, 'Symphony of a Thousand'; **No 9** in D; **No 10** in F sharp minor

Complete Symphonies

Symphonies – No 1[a]; No 2[b] (with **Cheryl Studer** sop **Waltraud Meier** mez **Arnold Schoenberg Choir**); No 3[b] (**Jessye Norman** sop **Vienna Boys' Choir; Vienna State Opera Chorus**); No 4[b] (**Frederica von Stade** mez); No 5[a]; Nos 6[c] & 7[c]; No 8[a] (**Studer, Sylvia McNair, Andrea Rost** sops **Anne Sofie von Otter** mez **Rosemarie Lang** contr **Peter Seiffert** ten **Bryn Terfel** bass-bar **Jan-Hendrik Rootering** bass **Tölz Boys' Choir; Berlin Radio Chorus; Prague Philharmonic Chorus**) Nos 9[b] & 10[b] – Adagio [a]**Berlin Philharmonic Orchestra**; [b]**Vienna Philharmonic Orchestra**; [c]**Chicago Symphony Orchestra / Claudio Abbado**

DG ⑫ 447 023-2GX12 (718' · ADD/DDD) Texts and translations included Recorded 1977-94   Ⓜ**OO**

The current pre-eminence of Gustav Mahler in the concert hall and on disc isn't something that could have been anticipated – other than by the composer himself. Hard now to believe that his revival had to wait until the centenary celebrations of his birth in 1960. And yet by 1980 he was more widely esteemed than his longer-lived contemporaries Sibelius and Strauss and could suddenly be seen to tower over 20th-century music much as Beethoven must have done in a previous age. By this time too, a new generation of conductors had come to the fore, further transforming our perceptions of the composer. Claudio Abbado is arguably the most distinguished of this group and, while his interpretations will not satisfy every listener on every occasion, they make an excellent choice for the library shelves, when the price is reasonably competitive (and the performances so emblematic (and arguably central to our understanding) of Mahler's place in contemporary musical life.

Of the alternatives, Haitink's package has the fewest expressive distortions while Bernstein's is the most ceaselessly emotive of them all; neither has Abbado's particular combination of qualities. It's probably no accident that Donald Mitchell's notes for this set are focused on the nature of Mahler's 'modernity'. For it's that ironic, inquisitive, preternaturally aware young composer who haunts this conductor's performances. Not for Abbado the heavy, saturated textures of 19th-century Romanticism, nor the chilly rigidity of some of his own 'modernist' peers. Instead an unaffected warmth and elegance of sound allows everything to come through naturally – in so far as the different venues and DG's somewhat variable technology will permit – even in the most searingly intense of climaxes.

Abbado presents Mahler as a fluent classicist, and is less concerned to characterise the surface battle of conflicting emotions than to elucidate the underlying symphonic structure. The lack of Solti's brand of forthright theatricality can bring a feeling of disappointment. But even where he underplays the drama of the moment, sufficient sense of urgency is sustained by a combination of well-judged tempos, marvellously graduated dynamics and precisely balanced, ceaselessly changing textures. The propulsion comes from within.

It was in November 1907 that Mahler famously told Sibelius that 'the symphony must be like the world. It must embrace everything.' And perhaps it's only today that we see this as a strength rather than a weakness in his music. He wrote music that's 'about' its own past while at the same time probing into all our futures, music that's so all-embracing and communicates with such directness that we can make it 'mean' whatever we want it to, confident that we alone have really understood the code. Abbado lacks Bernstein's desire to explore these limitless possibilities, but some will count that as a blessing. These are committed and authoritative performances.

The Mahler Broadcasts 1948-82 〔H〕

Symphonies – No 1 (recorded live 1959)[ac]; No 2 (**Kathleen Battle** *sop* **Maureen Forrester** *contr* **Westminster Choir;** rec 1982)[afm]; No 3 (**Yvonne Minton** *mez* **Camerata Singers; Little Church around the Corner Boys' Choir; Trinity Church Boys' Choir** rec 1976)[adm]; No 4 (**Irmgard Seefried** *sop* rec 1962)[ah]; No 5 (rec 1980)[akm]; No 6 (rec 1955)[ag]; No 7 (rec 1981)[ae]; No 8 (**Frances Yeend, Uta Graf, Camilla Williams** *sops* **Martha Lipton, Louise Bernhardt** *contrs* **Eugene Conley** *ten* **Carlos Alexander** *bar* **George London** *bass-bar* **Schola Cantorum; Public School No 12 Boys' Choir, Manhattan;** rec 1950)[bj]; No 9 (rec 1962)[ac]; No 10 – Adagio; Purgatorio (rec 1960 & 1958)[ag]. Lieder eines fahrenden Gesellen (**Dietrich Fischer-Dieskau** *bar* rec 1964)[ai]. Das Lied von der Erde (**Kathleen Ferrier** *contr* **Set Svanholm** *ten* rec 1948)[bl]

[a]**New York Philharmonic Orchestra,** [b]**Philharmonic Symphony Orchestra of New York /** [c]**Sir John Barbirolli,** [d]**Pierre Boulez,** [e]**Rafael Kubelík,** [f]**Zubin Mehta,** [g]**Dimitri Mitropoulos,** [h]**Sir Georg Solti,** [i]**William Steinberg,** [j]**Leopold Stokowski,** [k]**Klaus Tennstedt,** [l]**Bruno Walter** New York Philharmonic mono/[m]stereo ⑫ NYP9801/12 (903' · ADD) Also contains interviews and reminiscences about Mahler Ⓕ**OO**

Available from selected Tower Records stores or by mail order; in North America call (toll free) 1-800-557-8268; worldwide 1-317-781-1861; web: www.newyorkphilharmonic.org

Not your average collection of Mahler symphonies, but one which, with pride, charts in words and music, the impact of the composer's final two years (1909-11) in and on New York and the important part the city's orchestra subsequently played in spreading the Mahler message. Consideration was given, when choosing what to include, to the New York players' own views and memories of the concerts or conductors; and to featuring symphonies from conductors who never took them into the studio. Bernstein is conspicuous by his absence, but it would seem that rights aren't currently available for the release of his Mahler broadcast tapes. We hear, though, from the man whose Mahler was Bernstein's model; and Mitropoulos's 1960 Sixth Symphony must have been a hard act for Bernstein to follow. Mitropoulos delivers the symphony's integrity and unpalatable truths with a grim and arguably more compelling single-mindedness. Apart from the slow movement (placed second, and gloriously played), there's little relief from the symphony's battering march to tragedy.

Latterly interpreters have also been more protean in the Eighth's expansive Faust fantasy, and it would be idle to pretend that other conductors don't make more than Stokowski of the contrasts explicitly indicated in Mahler's score. Stokowski in 1950 opted for an unusually moderate range of tempos (starting with a swift *Andante*), and it's impossible to say whether he was playing safe, attempting to dignify the folksy inspiration, or bringing us something of the manner in which Mahler himself conducted the work (Stokowski was present at the Eighth's Munich world première in 1910). Whatever the case, along the way there are as many attractions as there are inevitable insecurities, and it's worth hearing, not least for the First Part of the symphony, which bears the unmistakable stamp of greatness, and the sound is a marvel for its years.

The earliest recording here is a vital, controlled and incisive 1948 *Das Lied von der Erde* from Walter, with Kathleen Ferrier making her American début. Set Svanholm tends to press ahead of the beat, but it's a rare pleasure to hear the tenor songs as resolutely conquered and characterised. As for Ferrier's contribution, there's little to choose between this and her famous 1952 Decca Vienna account made with a more relaxed Walter. The later recording perhaps presents the richer portrait of a unique vocal phenomenon, and a cathartic release of emotion in the final pages not matched in New York. Aptly enough for this enterprise, applause has been retained at the end of the works, even if, in the case of *Das Lied*, one wishes that the audience had waited a few seconds longer. But audience noise during the music can be frustrating. Time may well be standing still at the start of Barbirolli's 1959 First Symphony, but the audience is still finding its way to the seats.

Matters improve, possibly because, as one of the concert's critical notices informs us, only part of the audience stayed to the end. And the part that did was witness to some engaging features, such as the pronounced, and for the time, deeply unfashionable string *portamentos*, and a *Scherzo* with big boots and rustic charm laid on by the barrow-load. The *Scherzo* of Barbirolli's 1962 New York Ninth Symphony is of a consistently coarser cut than his 1964 Berlin studio recording for EMI, and arguably benefits from it, though there's little evidence for the booklet's general assessment of the Berlin Ninth as 'rather disengaged from the work's churning emotions'. And the brightly analytical (and stereo) Berlin recording does allow clearer perception of the details of – future archival revelations apart – Barbirolli's finest taped Mahler symphony interpretation. Solti's Fourth Symphony (also 1962), as we know from his two Decca studio recordings, was unexpectedly graceful, with a long-breathed slow movement, and admirable discipline and refinement, even if that refinement streamlines the work's bolder colours and sardonic edge.

All the New York recordings enjoy good balances; those already mentioned are all in very decent, if occasionally pale, mono sound. The stereo tapings aren't ideally flattering to New York's violins, but benefit from a wider dynamic range. The deployment of the various on- and off-stage forces in Mehta's 1982 Second is a major achievement for a live recording. This was a special occasion for all involved (the orchestra's 10,000th concert), and although Mehta's view of the work is neither particularly lofty nor radical, the excitement in the hall has

MAHLER'S SYMPHONIES – IN BRIEF

Various orchs / Claudio Abbado
DG ⑫ 447 023-2GX12 (11 hr 58′ · DDD)　Ⓜ**OO**
The Italian conductor's dramatic, carefully moulded way with Mahler is best experienced live, but there's no lack of polish or refinement from his *de luxe* performers.

New York Philharmonic / various
NYP9801/12 ⑫ (15 hr 3′ · ADD)　Ⓕ**OO**
A valuable box for connoisseurs, documenting the orchestra's long Mahler tradition (dating back to when the composer was its music director). Boulez in No 3, Mitropoulos in No 6 and Kubelík in No 7 are highlights.

Concertgebouw Orchestra / Bernard Haitink
Philips ⑩ 442 050-2PB10 (11 hr 32′ · DDD)　Ⓜ**O**
Haitink's grasp of the music's many contrasts has sharpened since he made these recordings, but their unaffected clarity stands the test of time, and the Concertgebouw are in a Mahlerian class of their own.

London PO / Klaus Tennstedt
EMI ⑪ 572941-2 (12 hr 19′ · ADD)　Ⓢ**OO**
Mahler's music seemed to live within Tennstedt even more intensely than Bernstein. Not as unforgettably demanding of attention as later, live accounts, but the Eighth is worth the price of the set alone.

Frankfurt RSO / Inbal
Brilliant ⑮ 92005 (14 hr 40′ DDD)　Ⓢ
Denon's fine engineering, the Alte Oper's welcoming acoustic and Inbal's headstrong interpretations are an even more tempting proposition at super-budget price.

NYPO / Bernstein
Sony ⑫ SX12K89499 (11 hr 53′ · ADD)　Ⓢ**OO**
The heartfelt passion of possibly the composer's most famous interpreter is well known; his unerring composer's ear for the traffic of Mahler's vast forces and structures is often overlooked. Still definitive in its way.

SWR Orchestra Baden-Baden / Gielen
Hänssler ⑬ 931330 (12 hr 31′ ADD)　Ⓑ**O**
Age has mellowed and deepened the Mahler interpretations of this one-time colleague of the avant-gardistes. Fine sound shows off Gielen's forensic ear for detail; Mahler's stature as pivotal figure between centuries is clearer than ever.

Bavarian Radio SO / Kubelík
DG ⑩ 463 738-2 (10 hr 51′ · ADD)　Ⓑ**O**
The Czech conductor brings an unfussy clarity to Mahler's dance rhythms that can be even more moving than the breast-beating approach. Ideal for those new to Mahler.

transferred to disc admirably. The pleasures of Boulez's 1976 performance of the Third Symphony include a typical (and often very sensuous) cultivation of inner workings, concern for outer structure, very precisely graded dynamics, and a strikingly individual *rubato*. Rarely has the sudden tumult and its immediate aftermath at the end of the third movement – proclamatory brass receding over shimmering strings – cast such a spell.

Tennstedt had the ability, at the moment of performance, to persuade listeners that the music could and should sound no other way, and his 1980 New York Fifth Symphony runs the full gamut of 'no tomorrow' intensity, intervention, riotous colour and perfectly formed details.

In contrast, the years between Kubelík's Bavarian Radio Seventh (recorded for DG in 1970) and this 1981 New York account appear to have prompted a radical rethink. Or maybe Kubelík is responding to the extra heft of the New York orchestra and ephemeral concert conditions to push out the boundaries. Still recognisable, if moderated, are the sharp features and deliberately soured tone lending menace to both the second and third movements, and an *Andante amoroso* cajoled into a diversion of wonderfully graceful, fresh-voiced charm. But the much broader manner maximises the far-flung sonorities, in the first movement, at the expense of line and general decorum.

Naturally there are fluffs, early entries and an occasional *rubato* prompting untidiness, but the vast majority demonstrates a level of professionalism and innate ability to produce the right sort of sound at the right time that have made and maintained the orchestra as one of the world's ideal Mahler instruments.

Symphonies – Nos 1 & 2 (**Elly Ameling** *sop*
Aafje Heynis *contr* **Netherlands Radio Chorus**);
No 3 (**Maureen Forrester** *contr* **St Willibrord Church Boys' Choir; Netherlands Radio Chorus**);
No 4 (**Ameling**); Nos 5-8 (**Ileana Cotrubas, Heather Harper, Hanneke van Bork** *sops* **Birgit Finnila** *mez* **Marianne Dieleman** *contr* **William Cochran** *ten* **Hermann Prey** *bar* **Hans Sotin** *bass* **St Willibrord and Pius X Children's Choir; Collegium Musicum Amstelodamense; Amsterdam Toonkunst Choir; Amsterdam Stem des Volks Choir**); No 10 – Adagio
Concertgebouw Orchestra / Bernard Haitink
Philips Bernard Haitink Symphony Edition ⑩
442 050-2PB10 (692' · ADD) Recorded 1962-71   Ⓜ●

If space is at a premium, this set is undeniably attractive, though the multilingual illustrated booklet dispenses with texts and translations, and several symphonies are awkwardly spread between discs. For a generation of record buyers it was these sane, lucid, sometimes insufficiently demonstrative Concertgebouw readings that represented a way into music previously considered unacceptable in polite society. Haitink's phrasing has an appealing natural simplicity, his rhythmic almost-squareness providing welcome reassurance. The preoccupation with conventional symphonic verities of form and structure doesn't preclude striking beauty of sound and the recordings have come up well in the remastering. There's some residual hiss.

Haitink's early No 1 (1962), his first taping of a Mahler symphony, is usually reckoned the least satisfactory of his career. True, the third movement doesn't quite work: Haitink's attempts at 'Jewishness' are so self-conscious that the results sound rhythmically suspect, not quite together rather than convincingly ethnic. The real problem is the boxed-in sound, uncharacteristically rough and ready, with none of the cool tonal lustre which characterised subsequent LPs from this source.

The Fourth receives a similarly straightforward account with a wonderfully hushed *Poco adagio* and few if any of the aggressive mannerisms which have marred more recent versions. The restraint can border on inflexibility at times. The first movement lacks a certain element of fantasy with everything so very accurate and together, and, while Elly Ameling makes a lovely sound in the finale, the orchestra's animal caricatures aren't really vulgar enough, the sense of wonder and awe in the face of heaven rather muted at the close. Though inevitably lacking the gut-wrenching theatricality and hallucinatory colour of Bernstein, the Seventh has none of the staidness and rigidity that occasionally prompts doubts about Haitink's Mahlerian credentials. It emerges here as a high point of the series, second only to the celebrated Ninth. The opening is deceptively cool and brooding; thereafter the interpretation is unexpectedly driven and intense, even if Mahler's fantastical sonorities are left to fend for themselves. Only those who feel the nth degree of nightmarish 'exaggeration' to be vital to the expression of the whole need have any doubts. The finale is effectively held together but should perhaps sound more hollow than this.

If you must have the Mahler symphonies under a single conductor, Haitink could arguably be the man to go for. His objectivity won't spoil you for alternative readings. Nevertheless you wouldn't want to miss out on Bernstein, unrelenting in his desire to communicate the essentials of these scores, taking his cue from Mahler's remark that 'the symphony must be like the world. It must be all-embracing'. Haitink is more circumspect, the music's vaunting ambition knowingly undersold.

Symphony No 1

Symphony No 1. Lieder eines fahrenden Gesellen
Dietrich Fischer-Dieskau *bar* **Bavarian Radio Symphony Orchestra / Rafael Kubelík**
DG The Originals 449 735-2GOR (67' · ADD)
Recorded 1967. Text and translation included   Ⓜ●

Rafael Kubelík is essentially a poetic conductor and he gets more poetry out of this symphony than almost any other conductor who has recorded it. Although he takes the repeat of the first movement's short exposition, it's strange that he should ignore the single repeat sign in the *Ländler* when he seems so at ease with the music. Notwithstanding a fondness for generally brisk tempos in Mahler, Kubelík is never afraid of rubato here, above all in his very personally inflected account of the slow movement. This remains a delight. The finale now seems sonically a little thin, with the trumpets made to sound rather hard-pressed and the final climax failing to open out as it can in more modern recordings. The orchestral contribution is very good even if absolute precision isn't guaranteed.

Dietrich Fischer-Dieskau's second recording of the *Lieder eines fahrenden Gesellen* has worn rather less well, the spontaneous ardour of his earlier performance (with Furtwängler and the Philharmonia) here tending to stiffen into melodrama and mannerism. There's much beautiful singing, and he's most attentively accompanied, but the third song, 'Ich hab' ein glühend Messer', is implausibly overwrought, bordering on self-parody. By contrast, Kubelík's unpretentious, Bohemian approach to the symphony remains perfectly valid. A corrective to the grander visions of those who conduct the music with the benefit of hindsight and the advantages of digital technology? Perhaps.

Symphony No 2

Symphony No 2
Arleen Auger sop **Dame Janet Baker** mez
City of Birmingham Symphony Chorus and Orchestra / Sir Simon Rattle
EMI ② 747962-8 (86' · DDD) Recorded 1986. Text and translation included ℗ **OOO**

Where Simon Rattle's interpretation is concerned, we must go into the realm of a giant Mahlerian like Klemperer. For we're dealing here with conducting akin to genius, with insights and instincts that can't be measured with any old yardstick. Rattle's sense of drama, of apocalyptic events, is so strong that at the final chords one is awed. None of this could have been achieved without the CBSO, which here emerges as an orchestra of world class. Such supple and rich string playing, such expressive woodwind and infallibly accurate and mellow-toned brass, could be mistaken as belonging to Vienna, Berlin or Chicago. Attention to dynamics is meticulous, and contributes immeasurably to the splendour of the performance. A double *pianissimo* is really that, so when triple *forte* comes along its impact is tremendous. Some outstanding features can be pinpointed: the haunting beauty of the *portamento* horn playing and the strings' sensitive and perfectly graded glissandos at fig 23; the magical entry of flute and harps just after fig 3 in the second movement; and the frightening eruption of the two *fortissimo* drum notes just after fig 51 in the same movement. Dame Janet Baker is at her most tender in 'Urlicht', with Arleen Auger as

the soul of purity in the finale. The CBSO Chorus is magnificent. Indeed the whole finale is an acoustic triumph. This in a spiritual class of its own and the recording is superb.

Symphony No 2
Elisabeth Schwarzkopf sop **Hilde Rössl-Majdan** mez **Philharmonia Chorus and Orchestra / Otto Klemperer**
EMI Great Recordings of the Century 567235-2 (72' · ADD) Text and translation included **ⓂO**

You emerge from Klemperer's first movement unharrassed, unsettled in the knowledge that this extraordinary music has something much more to yield. You miss those elements of high risk, the brave rhetorical gestures, the uncompromising extremes, in Klemperer's comparatively comfortable down-the-line response. He knocks minutes off most of the competition (yes, it's a fallacy that Klemperer was always slower), paying little or no heed to Mahler's innumerable expressive markings in passages which have so much to gain from them. Take, for example, the magical shift to remote E major with the *ppp* emergence of the second subject where Klemperer allows himself no lassitude whatsoever in the *rubato* despite Mahler's explicit requests to the contrary. Likewise the grisly procession of cellos and basses which begins the approach to the awesome climax of the development. How little Klemperer makes of their cadaverous first entry or Mahler's long backward glance just prior to the coda. But then, come the deceptive second movement minuet, something happens, the performance really begins to find its space. Klemperer's scherzo is ideally big-boned with fine rollicking horns and a lazy trio with lovely old-world close-harmony trumpets. And the finale, growing more and more momentous with every bar, possesses a unique aura. Not everyone is convinced by Klemperer's very measured treatment of the Judgement Day march. The grim reaper takes his time but the inevitability of what's to come is somehow the more shocking as a result. Klemperer's trumpets peak thrillingly in the bars immediately prior to the climax itself – and what a seismic upheaval he and his orchestra pull off at this point. The rest is sublime: marvellous spacial effects, off-stage brass and so on, an inspirational sense of the music burgeoning from the moment the chorus breathe life into the Resurrection Ode. It's a pity that in those days so many technical blemishes were allowed to make it to the final master, though EMI's digital remastering of this almost legendary reading is superb.

Symphony No 3

Symphony No 3
Norma Procter contr **Wandsworth School Boys' Choir; Ambrosian Singers; London Symphony Orchestra / Jascha Horenstein**

Unicorn-Kanchana Souvenir ② UKCD2006/7
(97' · ADD) Recorded 1970. Text and translation
included Ⓜ○

Horenstein's interpretation of the Third Symphony is an outstanding example and its reissue
on CD at mid-price is a major addition to the
Mahler discography. No other conductor has
surpassed Horenstein in his total grasp of every
facet of the enormous score. Even though the
London Symphony Orchestra strings of the day
were not as powerful as they later became, they
play with suppleness and a really tense sound,
especially appropriate in the kaleidoscopic first
movement, where changes of tempo and mood
reflect the ever-changing face of nature. Horenstein gives the posthorn solo to a flügelhorn, a
successful experiment. His light touch in the
middle movements is admirable, and Norma
Procter is a steady soloist in 'O Mensch! Gib
acht!', with the Wandsworth School Boys'
Choir bimm-bamming as if they were all Aus-
trian-born! Then comes the *Adagio* finale, its
intensity sustained by Horenstein without dragging. The recording isn't as rich as more recent
ones, but is still a classic.

Symphony No 3. Four Rückert Lieder.
Kindertotenlieder
Martha Lipton *mez* **Dietrich Fischer-Dieskau** *bar*
**Women's chorus of the Schola Cantorum; Boys'
Choir of the Transfiguration; New York
Philharmonic Orchestra / Leonard Bernstein**
Sony Classical ② SM2K61831 (142' · ADD) Recorded
1962 Ⓜ

Few who experienced Bernstein's passionate
advocacy of Mahler's musical cause in the 1960s
were left untouched by it. These recordings
date from those years and the flame of inspiration still burns brightly about them almost 40
years later. The CBS recordings were clearly
manipulated, but the sound – at best, big and
open but trenchant and analytically clear –
suited Mahler's sound world especially well.
Bernstein's account of the Third Symphony is
as compelling an experience and as desirable a
general recommendation now as when it first
appeared. The New Yorkers are on scintillating
form under the conductor they have most obviously revered in the post-war period. This is a
classic account, by any standards. Bernstein
himself is a subtle and self-effacing pianist. Fischer-Dieskau scales the musical heights in several of the *Rückert* Lieder.

Symphony No 3
Anne Sofie von Otter *mez* **Vienna Boys Choir;
Women's Chorus of the Vienna Singverein; Vienna
Philharmonic Orchestra / Pierre Boulez**
DG ② 474 038-2GH2; SACD 474 298-2GSA2
(96' · DDD) Text and translation included Ⓕ○

In the context of Pierre Boulez's Mahler series,
this Third stands high and is in many ways an

outstanding achievement, even if its merits may
be more properly attributable to the strengths
of the players and of DG's sound team. Boulez's
refusal to engage with Mahler's 'theatricality'
won't be to all tastes, though in music so excessive, this might be counted a virtue.

The opening movement is unexpectedly slow,
but never drags, such is the conductor's tight
control. While there are fewer discontinuities
than you might be used to, the impression is
dark and even glowering, anything but superficial or merely neutral. And always there's the
magnificent sonority of the Vienna Philharmonic – in a spacious acoustic that will open up
still further for surround sound. The weakest
passages are those requiring a modicum of local
charm, the strongest those in which the music
perhaps needs saving from itself.

Anne Sofie von Otter is more pungent than
sentimental in the potentially cloying fifth
movement, and the slow finale is kept moving
naturally forward, never wearing its heart on its
sleeve. On the other hand, some may find the
second and third movements inappropriately
flat. In the Nietzsche setting, while much is
made of the *hinaufziehen* marking as revived by
Sir Simon Rattle and Michael Gielen, Boulez
seems less concerned to evoke the concrete
image of bird song at night.

Technically speaking, Boulez and his collaborators accomplish precisely what they set out to
achieve and at the very least his set will be in
demand for its considerable sonic virtues.

Symphony No 4

Symphony No 4[a]. Lieder eines fahrenden Gesellen[b]
[a]**Judith Raskin** *sop* [b]**Frederica von Stade** *mez*
[a]**Cleveland Orchestra / George Szell;** [b]**London
Philharmonic Orchestra / Sir Andrew Davis**
Sony Classical Essential Classics SBK46535
(75' · ADD/DDD) Recorded 1966 Ⓑ○○

Collectors who waited for years in anticipation
of the reappearance on CD of Szell's famous
Cleveland Fourth Symphony will not be disappointed. Sony Classical has come through with
a pristine digital remastering of the open and
exceptionally well-balanced Columbia original.
Some hardening of tone under pressure was
always a problem, even on LP, but on the whole
you would never credit that this was a 1960s
recording. As to the performance, the assurance
and precision of its execution is something quite
remarkable – an orchestra in the very peak of
condition: ensemble absolutely unanimous,
rubato finely turned to a man, not a blemish in
earshot. There's no better tribute to Szell's
achievements in Cleveland. Some people have
found it dispassionate and calculated in effect
and would willingly sacrifice some of the precision for a greater sense of spontaneity at the
moment of performance (Szell was always at his
best in the concert hall). That's a very subjective
reaction, and the cool, pellucid beauty of Szell's
Cleveland strings in the slow movement is

beyond dispute. The strong and characterful readings of the *Lieder eines fahrenden Gesellen* will provide much pleasure. They sound fresh and alert, and the tone colouring is quite beautifully controlled.

Symphony No 4 in G[a]. Das Lied von der Erde[c]   [H]
Symphony No 2 in C minor, 'Resurrection'[a]; Lieder aus 'Des Knaben Wunderhorn'[b] – Wer hat dies Liedlein erdacht?; Wo die schönen Trompeten blasen. Rückert-Lieder – No 1, Ich atmet' einem linden Duft[b]
[b]**Maria Cebotari,** [a]**Hilde Güden** sops [c]**Kathleen Ferrier,** [b]**Rosette Anday** contrs [c]**Julius Patzak** ten [b]**Vienna State Opera Chorus; Vienna Philharmonic Orchestra / Bruno Walter**
Andante mono ④ 4973 (201' · ADD) Recorded live at the Musikverein, Vienna [b]1948, [c]1952, [a]6, 1955.
Texts and translations included   Ⓜ Ⓞ

Of the several Mahler disciples whose recordings provide us with a line back to Mahler himself, none is more important than Bruno Walter. He was 18 when Mahler engaged him as an assistant at the Hamburg Opera in 1894. The following year, he attended the première of the Second Symphony in Berlin and was himself destined to conduct the posthumous premières of the Ninth Symphony and *Das Lied von der Erde*, both of which he recorded for 78s and LP. He also made influential post-war studio recordings of the First, Second, Fourth and Fifth symphonies.

So what's special about this latest anthology, given the fact that the readings are already 'known' quantities? Rather a lot, is the short answer. Had copyright considerations allowed the publication of these live Vienna radio recordings of *Das Lied von der Erde* and the Fourth Symphony at the time they were made, they would have become overnight library recommendations. Walter's 1946 New York account of the Fourth Symphony is very fine. Yet the string playing alone puts this 1955 Vienna Philharmonic performance into a different league. In the slow movement in particular, it's more tender, more inward, more purely beautiful and – since this is still recognisably the 'old' Vienna Philharmonic Walter remembered from his Mahler-inspired youth – more authentic. Significantly, the occasion itself was special, an unrepeatable, memory-laden concert which took place in the Musikverein the morning after the post-war reopening of the Vienna Opera.

As usual, the 'heavenly' finale brings us down to earth with a bump when the human voice enters and Mahler humours us with his child's view of the afterlife; but Hilde Güden is an agreeable soloist and the end is properly magical. The mono recording – cleared by Walter himself for release by Philips, a deal vetoed by CBS – is first rate.

The live 1952 account of *Das Lied von der Erde* – in effect, the concert version of the celebrated Decca recording with Patzak and Ferrier which was being made at the same time – is as a reading identical with that on the studio recording. What's different can best be described as a certain airiness and ease due to the natural rhythms of the live performance and to the altogether more natural balance of the radio sound, something that benefits Patzak, Ferrier and the orchestra whose playing is superbly concentrated and sure-footed.

Ferrier is phenomenal, and benefits more than anyone from the more natural balance of the radio recording. Already in thrall to the condition which would end her life, she sings with line and beauty, great intensity and huge courage. The voice never did convey a sudden shiver on 'ein kalter Wind' in 'Der Einsame im Herbst' but what she does with 'gold'nen Blätter' and the fire-and-ice intensity of the line about the drying of bitter tears more than compensates. In the 'Abschied' her singing is fragile and vulnerable in human terms yet thrillingly secure musically. Her rendering of the recitative-like passage in which the friend arrives to take his last farewell removes Mahler's writing into the realm of Passion music. In the closing pages, her singing is a miracle of quiet transfigured beauty, perfectly paced by Walter and supremely well accompanied.

The 1948 Mahler Second has been on CD before, more a yellowing newspaper clipping for one's scrapbook than a volume for the library, though Andante's technical and editorial presentation is vastly superior to that of any of its predecessors. The second and third movements are all wistfulness and charm though something like the cry of disgust at fig 49 (8'12") of the St Antony *Scherzo* is plain enough. Rosette Anday gives a graphic account of the 'Urlicht', after which the end is vivid and uplifting, despite the restricted nature of the recording. This is a set no Mahlerian will want to live without.

Symphony No 4
Amanda Roocroft sop **City of Birmingham Symphony Orchestra / Sir Simon Rattle**
EMI 556563-2 (59' · DDD)   Ⓕ

Rattle springs two big surprises in the first four bars. The first tempo might strike you as over-cautious, but check Mahler's score, and note the words: *Bedächtig – Nicht eilen* ('Cautious; prudent – don't hurry'). In keeping with the accepted view among seasoned Mahlerians that the *poco ritard* in the third bar doesn't apply to the sleigh bells, Rattle then effects a fleeting moment of disarray as the bells jangle roughshod over this elegant turn into the first theme. A gauche, childlike moment. But then comes the real surprise. The tempo for this charming theme-with-airs (*gemächlich* – 'leisurely') is faster, not slower, than the opening tempo. Leisurely, yes, but eager too. The adventure playground of Mahler's youth is up and running. The benefits of this become plainer as the movement unfolds. The second subject sounds completely new (the CBSO cellos manage to persuade us that they've only just discovered it). The first horn is youth's magic horn, the woodwinds beckon raucously. And all the while those startling swings of mood and manner just happen – no rhyme, no reason; just a child's fancy. But beware the bogeyman fiddler. His dance of death – all the sharper, all the more sour for being so flatly dispatched – comes as a timely reminder that childhood fears are no less real for being the stuff of fairy-tales. Rattle contrasts this beautifully with the rubicund Trio. The transfiguration at its heart, swathed in woozy *portamento*, is quite simply gorgeous. So, too, the opening of the slow movement, the cellos' legato so fine as to suggest little or no contact with the strings. Rattle's reading is perhaps the most inquisitive (and therefore the most intriguing) of recommendable versions.

Symphony No 4
Dame Margaret Price *sop*; **LPO / Jascha Horenstein**
Classics for Pleasure 5 74882-2 (59' · ADD) Recorded 1970 ⓑ

The Mahler Four with Horenstein is a must-have, a version at last reissued on CD. Its short-comings as a recording are of little account; the sound does lack depth but in a reading of such distinction the ear compensates. The LPO play beautifully, and with Margaret Price as the singer in the finale this is more than a good introduction to the Symphony; it's a performance of uncompromising integrity, brilliant colour, pinpoint vividness, and a blend of tenderness and strength that seems to go to the heart of the matter. When first issued in 1971, it cost 89p. Snap it up now.

Symphony No 5

Symphony No 5
Berlin Philharmonic Orchestra / Sir Simon Rattle
EMI 557385-2 (69' · DDD) Recorded live 2002 Ⓟ **OOO**

 Mahler's Fifth is a terror to bring off but, brought off, is a joy beyond measure. It made a fine nuptial offering for Rattle and the Berliners on 7 September 2002 – festive yet challenging, a tragi-comic revel and a high-wire act to boot. 'The individual parts are so difficult,' wrote Mahler, 'they call for the most accomplished soloists.' Rattle brought the prodigious first horn to the apron of the stage for his obbligato contribution in the *Scherzo*. Mengelberg's conducting score, which Mahler used for the work's Amsterdam première in 1906, has an annotation to this effect, and the practice was followed at the work's English première in 1945, but we're left wondering what would have happened if Rattle hadn't brought the player forward. EMI's recording is splendidly explicit, but the horn section, which plays a crucial role at key moments, seems oddly distant on CD.

The *tutti* sound Rattle draws from the orchestra is clean and sharply profiled, not unlike the Mahler sound Rafael Kubelík tended to favour. Rattle's tempo for the *Adagietto* is a good one by modern standards (not too slow) and the string playing has a lovely diaphanous quality, but you may find the playing over-nuanced.

Nowadays it isn't unusual to hear rhythm and line sacrificed to detail and nuance as old-established symphony orchestras are made to rethink their readings by conductors schooled in the arcana of ancient performance practice. Rattle has done his fair share of this. What's interesting about this live Mahler Fifth is the degree to which the detail is absorbed and the line maintained.

Like most latter-day conductors, Rattle tends to underplay the march element in the first movement. Mahler in his 1905 piano roll, Walter, and Haitink in his superb 1969 Concertgebouw recording all preserve this. Some may find the approach too dry-eyed in the long-drawn string threnody at figure 2. But an excess of feeling can damage both opening movements (the second is a mirror of the first) if the larger rhythm is obscured. Rattle, like Barbirolli and Bernstein in his superb Vienna Philharmonic recording, treats the threnody more as a meditation than a march, but the pulse isn't lost and the attendant tempos are good. The frenzied B flat minor Trio is particularly well judged. The second movement is superb (the diminished horn contribution notwithstanding) and none but the most determined sceptic could fail to thrill to the sense of adventure and well-being Rattle and his players bring to the *Scherzo* and finale, even if Barbirolli (studio) and Bernstein (live) both reach the finishing line in rather more eloquent and orderly fashion that this talented but still occasionally fragile-sounding Berlin ensemble.

As a memento, the CD is a triumph of organisation and despatch. As a performance and as a recording, it has rather more character and bite than Abbado's much admired 1993 Berlin version. Indeed, it can safely be ranked among the half dozen or so finest performances on record. It isn't perfect, but do you know of one that is?

Symphony No 5
New Philharmonia Orchestra / Sir John Barbirolli
EMI Great Recordings of the Century 566910-2 (74' · ADD) Recorded 1969 Ⓜ**OO**

Sir John Barbirolli's Fifth occupies a special place in everybody's affections: a performance so big in spirit and warm of heart as to silence any rational discussion of its shortcomings. Some readers may have problems with one or two of his sturdier tempos. He doesn't make life easy for his orchestra in the treacherous second movement, while the exultant finale, though suitably bracing, arguably needs more of a spring in its heels. But against all this, one must weigh a unity and strength of purpose, an entirely idiomatic response to instrumental colour and texture (the dark, craggy hues of the first two movements are especially striking); and most important of all that very special Barbirollian radiance, humanity – call it what you will. One point of interest for collectors – on the original LP, among minor orchestral mishaps in the *Scherzo*, were four bars of missing horn obbligato (at nine bars before fig 20). Not any more! The original solo horn player, Nicholas Busch, has returned to the scene of this momentary aberration (Watford Town Hall) and the absent bars have been ingeniously reinstated. There's even a timely grunt from Sir John, as if in approval. Something of a classic, then; EMI's remastering is splendid.

Symphony No 5
Vienna Philharmonic Orchestra / Leonard Bernstein
DG 423 608-2GH (75' · DDD) Recorded live 1987
Ⓕ**OO**

Bernstein's tempo for the Funeral march in the first movement of the Fifth Symphony became slower in the 23 years that separated his New York CBS recording from this one, made during a performance in Frankfurt. The strings only passage at fig 15 in the first movement is exquisitely played, so is the long horn solo in the *Scherzo*. And there's one marvellously exciting moment – the right gleam of trumpet tone at one bar before fig 29 in the second movement. Best of all is Bernstein himself, here at his exciting best, giving demonic edge to the music where it's appropriate and building the symphony inexorably to its final triumph.

Thanks to a very clear and well-balanced recording, every subtlety of scoring, especially some of the lower strings' counterpoint, comes through as the conductor intended. One is made aware of the daring novelty of much of the orchestration, of how advanced it must have sounded in the early years of this century. Here we get the structure, the sound and the emotion. The *Adagietto* isn't dragged out, and the scrupulous attention to Mahler's dynamics allows the delightfully silken sound of the Vienna strings to be heard to captivating advantage, with the harp well recorded too. Bernstein is strongest in Mahler when the work itself is one of the more optimistic symphonies with less temptation for him to add a few degrees more of *Angst*.

Symphony No 6

Symphony No 6 in A minor
San Francisco Symphony Orchestra / Michael Tilson Thomas
SFS Media/Avie ② 821936-0001-2 (87' · DDD)
SACD/CD player compatible   Ⓜ**O**

This recording of Mahler's Sixth Symphony was made from performances planned long before the events of September 11 gave the San Francisco Symphony's choice of repertory

extraordinary resonance. And it's a credit to both Michael Tilson Thomas and the orchestra that this ferocious performance is carried out without hysteria or self-indulgence. Tempos are judiciously chosen. In the first movement, for example, Tilson Thomas's *Allegro energico, ma non troppo* is only a hair's breadth slower than Bernstein's in his Vienna Philharmonic recording, yet the difference is enough to give proper weight to the march. Indeed, the SFS strings dig very deep to produce a dark, throaty tone of startling vehemence. Ardently played and generously phrased, the 'Alma' theme provides welcome consolation – and how longingly Tilson Thomas clings to the final peaks of its melody.

Gunshot-like *sforzandos* from the timpani introduce the *scherzo*, sharply etched here with stinging dotted rhythms. The trios are similarly pointed – though affectionately *grazioso*, as Mahler requests – and rather deliberately paced, like a long-forgotten dance now remembered in slow motion. The *Andante moderato* is also treated expansively, but the tension never sags. Tilson Thomas mis-steps only once in the sprawling finale, pressing too hard at the end of the introduction so that the orchestra arrives prematurely at the main tempo – a minor flaw and quickly forgiven.

A more impressive start to Tilson Thomas and the SFS's Mahler cycle is difficult to imagine. Less mannered than Bernstein, and more emotionally engaged than Karajan, this is an exceptionally intense and, under the circumstances, remarkably coherent performance that isn't to be missed. Very good sound quality, too, from the orchestra's new in-house label.

Symphony No 6. Kindertotenlieder
Thomas Hampson *bar* **Vienna Philharmonic Orchestra / Leonard Bernstein**
DG ② 427 697-2GH2 (115' · DDD) Recorded live 1988   Ⓕ**O**

Mahler's tragic Sixth Symphony digs more profoundly into the nature of man and Fate than any of his earlier works, closing in desolation, a beat on the bass drum, a coffin lid closing. Bernstein's reading was at a concert, with all the electricity of such an occasion, and the VPO responds to the conductor's dark vision of Mahler's score with tremendous bravura. Fortunately, the achingly tender slow movement brings some relief, but with the enormous finale lasting over 30 minutes we must witness a resumption of a battle to the death. The coupling is a logical one, for the *Kindertotenlieder* takes up the theme of death yet again. But it's in a totally different, quieter way: these beautiful songs express a parent's grief over the loss of a child, and although some prefer a woman's voice, the sensitive Thomas Hampson makes a good case here for a male singer. The recording of both works is so good one would not know it was made 'live', particularly as the applause is omitted.

Symphony No 6. Kindertotenlieder· Rückert-Lieder
Christa Ludwig *mez* **Berlin Philharmonic Orchestra
/ Herbert von Karajan**
DG The Originals ② 457 716-2GOR2 (129' · ADD)
Recorded 1974-5   Ⓜ**OO**

Karajan's classic Sixth confirmed his belated
arrival as a major Mahler interpreter. Only
Bernstein, in his more emotive, less consciously
beautifying way, left recorded performances of
comparable strength and conviction. Karajan's
understanding of Mahler's sound world – its
links forward to Berg, Schoenberg and Webern
as opposed to retrospective links with Wagner –
is very acute. Combining this with a notable
long-term control of rhythm, Karajan is sustains not only the composer's lucidly stated
tragic case but also Mahler's exploration of
materials drawn from different sound worlds
and even, in the Scherzo, from different areas of
the inherited musical tradition. This Scherzo is
a masterly achievement by composer, conductor, and. orchestra alike. Also, the engineers
have tidied up the very end of the symphony,
where the bass tuba's entry over drum and *ff
pizzicato* basses no longer betrays quite so obviously its origin as part of a separate take. The
Rückert Lieder are memorably sung by Christa
Ludwig who is eloquently supported by the
Berlin wind players who are recorded with gratifying immediacy.

Additional recommendation

Symphony No 6 in A minor
London Symphony Orchestra / Jansons
LSO Live ② LSO0038 (82' · DDD)   Ⓢ
A considerable achievement, and a plausible best
buy for those looking for digital sound at bargain
price. Jansons sets out his Mahlerian credentials
with real verve, sharply defining timbre and instrumental detail. He succeeds in unearthing new facets
of this extraordinary score without necessarily
plumbing its depths of terror and despair.

Symphony No 7

Symphony No 7
Chicago Symphony Orchestra / Claudio Abbado
DG Masters 445 513-2GMA (79' · DDD) Recorded
1984   Ⓕ**OO**

Abbado's account of Mahler's Seventh was
always a highlight of his cycle and remains the
ideal choice for collectors requiring a central
interpretation in modern sound. Steering a
middle course between clear-sightedness and
hysteria, and avoiding both the heavy, saturated
textures of 19th-century romanticism and the
chilly rigidity of some of his own 'modernist'
peers, he is, as the original review reported,
'almost too respectable'. That said, it's all to the
good if the forthright theatricality and competitive instincts of the Chicago orchestra are held
in check just a little. Even where Abbado underplays the drama of the moment, a sufficient

sense of urgency is sustained by a combination
of well-judged tempos, marvellously graduated
dynamics and precisely balanced, ceaselessly
changing textures. For those put off by Mahler's
supposed vulgarity, the unhurried classicism of
Abbado's reading may well be the most convincing demonstration of the music's integrity.
This is a piece Abbado continues to champion
in concert with performances at the very highest
level.

Symphony No 7
**New York Philharmonic Orchestra / Leonard
Bernstein**
Sony Classical Bernstein Century Edition SMK60564
(80' · ADD) Recorded 1965   Ⓜ

We are often assured that great conductors of
an earlier generation interpreted Mahler from
within the Austrian tradition, encoding a sense
of nostalgia, decay and incipient tragedy as distinct from the in-your-face calamities and neuroses proposed by Leonard Bernstein. Well,
this is one Bernstein recording that should convince all but the most determined sceptics. It
deserves a place in anyone's collection now that
it has been transferred to a single disc at mid-
price. The white-hot communicative power is
most obvious in the finale which has never
sounded more convincing than it does here; the
only mildly questionable aspect of the reading is
the second *Nachtmusik*, too languid for some.
The transfer is satisfactory, albeit dimmer than
one might have hoped. It sounds historic, but
historic in more ways than one.

Symphony No 7
**City of Birmingham Symphony Orchestra /
Sir Simon Rattle**
EMI 754344-2 (77' · DDD) Recorded live 1991
           Ⓕ**O**

You may wonder about the choice of venue –
The Maltings, Snape: a great sounding hall –
one of the most natural and focused in the world
– but for Mahler? Well, there are times here
where the hefty *tuttis* of the outer movements
sound fit to burst at the seams. The tonal quality is first class, the immediacy is to some extent
exciting; one can see right into the phantasmagorical scoring of the inner movements – a
clear, gently ambient sound serving both intimacy and atmosphere. Last things first. The
finale is for once a sensation. From the quasi-
Baroque splendour of the opening procession
right through to a coda which truly flings wide
its glorious excess, the adrenalin really pumps.
Rattle pulls off a mad kind of coherence, a
wholeheartedly vulgar apotheosis of Viennese
dance with no apologies for Mahler's seemingly
irrational changes of gear and direction. Even
the most unruly transitions are met head-on
with ferocious energy, episodes falling over
each other in the jostling for centre-stage. The
characterisation is acute, the colours wonderfully garish. Mahler was not one to mince his

notes, and neither is Rattle.

Not even Bernstein is as uncompromising in the *Scherzo*. The nightmare comes quickly into focus: the shrieking *glissando* on two clarinets at 00'28" is at once surreal, a flash of grinning skull behind the face. Rapier violin *sforzandos* claw the texture, an emaciated string bass slithers from behind a bellowing tuba and the strings really relish their grotesque waltz. The dynamic extremes are vicious. Rattle is unique in making it sound thus. On either side of these grisly goings on, the two *Nachtmusiks* could hardly be more beguiling. Only the first movement slightly disappoints – there isn't the almost euphoric release that one experiences with Bernstein. But trombones proudly take command in the coda and the first trumpet's fearless ascent to his high-stopped *forte* into Tempo 1 brings a genuine tingle of excitement. Few orchestras play the score this well; few conductors have explored it so exhaustively. Against these considerations, any reservations count for little.

Symphony No 8, 'Symphony of a Thousand'

Symphony No 8
Heather Harper, Lucia Popp, Arleen Auger sops
Yvonne Minton mez **Helen Watts** contr **René Kollo** ten **John Shirley-Quirk** bar **Martti Talvela** bass
Vienna Boys' Choir; Vienna State Opera Chorus; Vienna Singverein; Chicago Symphony Orchestra / Sir Georg Solti
Decca 460 972-2DM (80' · ADD) Recorded 1971. Text and translation included Ⓜ️OO

Of the so-called classic accounts of the Eighth Symphony, it's Solti's which most conscientiously sets out to convey an impression of large forces in a big performance space, this despite the obvious resort to compression and other forms of gerrymandering. Whatever the inconsistencies of Decca's multi-miking and over-dubbing, the overall effect remains powerful even today. The remastering has not eradicated all trace of distortion at the very end and, given the impressive flood of choral tone at the start of the 'Veni creator spiritus', it still seems a shame that the soloists and the Chicago brass are quite so prominent in its closing stages. As for the performance itself, Solti's extrovert way with Part 1 works tremendously without quite erasing memories of Bernstein's ecstatic fervour. In Part 2, it may be the patient Wagnerian mysticism of Tennstedt that sticks in the mind. Less inclined to delay, Solti makes the material sound more operatic. Yet for its gut-wrenching theatricality and great solo singing, Solti's version makes a plausible first choice – now more than ever. Also, it has been squeezed onto a single CD, albeit at full price.

Symphony No 8. Des Knaben Wunderhorn[a]
Elizabeth Connell, Edith Wiens, Dame Felicity Lott sops **Trudeliese Schmidt, Nadine Denize**

contrs **Richard Versalle** ten **Jorma Hynninen** bar **Hans Sotin** bass [a]**Lucia Popp** sop [a]**Berndt Weikl** bar **Tiffin Boys' School Choir; London Philharmonic Choir and Orchestra /** [a]**David Hill, Klaus Tennstedt**
EMI Double Forte ② 575661-2 (DDD) Recorded 1986. Notes included 💲 Ⓜ️OOO

 Mahler's extravagantly monumental Eighth Symphony, which is often known as the *Symphony of a Thousand*, is the work that raises doubts in even his most devoted of admirers. Its epic dimensions, staggering vision and sheer profligacy of forces required make it a 'difficult work'. Given a great live performance it will sway even the hardest of hearts; given a performance like Tennstedt's, reproduced with all the advantages of CD, home listeners, too, can be mightily impressed (and so, given the forces involved, will most of the neighbourhood!) – the sheer volume of sound at the climax is quite overwhelming. The work seeks to parallel the Christian's faith in the power of the Holy Spirit with the redeeming power of love for mankind and Tennstedt's performance leaves no doubt that he believes totally in Mahler's creation. It has a rapt, almost intimate, quality that makes his reading all the more moving. The soloists are on excellent form and the choruses sing with conviction.

Additional recommendations

Symphony No 8
Juliane Banse, Christine Brewer, Soile Isokoski sops **Jane Henschel, Birgit Remmert** contrs **Jon Villars** ten **David Wilson-Johnson** bar **John Relyea** bass **Toronto Children's Choir; London Symphony Chorus; City of Birmingham Symphony Youth Chorus, Chorus and Orchestra / Sir Simon Rattle**
EMI 557945-2 (74' · DDD · T/t) Ⓕ
Recorded live at Symphony Hall, Birmingham, June 2004

Thrilling, euphoric, hair-raising – Rattle holds the score in a perpetual state of wonder. This is is arguably the best Mahler Eighth we've had since Solti's sensationally recorded Decca account.

Symphony No 9

Symphony No 9. Kindertotenlieder. Five Rückert-Lieder
Christa Ludwig mez **Berlin Philharmonic Orchestra / Herbert von Karajan**
DG Double ② 453 040-2GTA2 (132' · ADD) Recorded 1979-80 Ⓜ️OOO

 Mahler's Ninth is a death-haunted work, but is filled, as Bruno Walter remarked, 'with a sanctified feeling of departure'. Rarely has this symphony been shaped with such understanding and played with such selfless virtuosity as it was by Herbert von Karajan and the BPO.

For this reissue the tapes have been picked over to open up the sound and do something about the early digital edginess of the strings. There's still some occlusion at climaxes; and if those strings now seem more plasticky than fierce, it's impossible to say whether the conductor would have approved. Karajan came late to Mahler and yet, until the release of his rather more fiercely recorded 1982 concert relay, he seemed content to regard this earlier studio performance as perhaps his finest achievement on disc.

The attraction is greatly enhanced by Christa Ludwig's carefully considered Mahler performances of the mid-1970s. The voice may not be as fresh as it was when she recorded the songs in the late 1950s, but there are few readings of comparable nobility. She articulates the text with unrivalled clarity, and 'In diesem Wetter' at least is positively operatic. How much of the grand scale should be attributed to Karajan? It's difficult to say; the voice is sometimes strained by the tempos. This collection isn't to be missed.

Symphony No 9
**Berlin Philharmonic Orchestra /
Herbert von Karajan**
DG Gramophone Awards Collection ② 474 5372
(85' · DDD) Recorded live 1982   Ⓜ❍❍❍

 Choice between the 1982 Karajan classic and the analogue studio recording is by no means easy. Both versions won Gramophone Awards in their day. The live performance remains a remarkable one, with a commitment to lucidity of sound and certainty of line. There's nothing dispassionate about the way the Berlin Philharmonic tears into the Rondo-Burleske, the agogic touches of the analogue version ironed out without loss of intensity. True, Karajan doesn't seek to emulate the passionate immediacy of a Barbirolli or a Bernstein, but in his broadly conceived, gloriously played Adagio the sepulchral hush is as memorable as the eruptive climax. The finesse of the playing is unmatched.

Symphony No 9
Berlin Philharmonic Orchestra / Claudio Abbado
DG 471 624-2GH (81' · DDD) Recorded live at the
Philharmonie, Berlin 1999   Ⓕ❍❍

Claudio Abbado began his career with Mahler and has been conducting the composer for his entire professional life. The Ninth and, above all, the Seventh, have consistently brought out the best in him.

Abbado's previous recording of No 9, taped live in Vienna, is now only available in his boxed set of the complete symphonies (DG, reviewed above). Much acclaimed as an interpretation, its airless sound wasn't to all tastes. This account is another multi-miked extravaganza with sonic shortcomings that are immediately apparent. The opening bars establish a wide open sound stage (complete with hiss) that implodes with

the appearance of the harp. That harp is always on the loud side, trumpets are almost always too reticent, the bass feels synthetic and there are troublesome changes of perspective. None of which is enough to nullify the obvious sincerity and conviction of a performance that simply gets better and better as it proceeds. This really is live music-making (the last big first movement climax at 16'54" isn't together), but the inner movements are beyond reproach, ideally paced and characterised and superbly realised. The finale is content to plumb the depths in its own way – as sensitive as any of its celebrated rivals if without the point-scoring you may be used to.

Where some interpreters feel bound to choose between structural imperatives and subjective emotions, proffering either proto-Schoenbergian edginess or late Romantic excess, Abbado has the confidence to eschew both the heavily saturated textures of his predecessors and the chilly rigidity of some of his own 'modernist' peers. Instead, his unaffected warmth allows everything to come through naturally. There remains something self-effacing about his musical personality. And yet there's sunlight – and a certain tenderness – in this account of the Ninth that you won't find anywhere else, a fluency and ease that's something to marvel at. For those put off even now by the composer's supposed vulgarity, Abbado's readings constitute a convincing demonstration of the music's integrity.

The awed silence that greets the expiration of the Ninth may or may not be stage-managed, but it seems genuine.

Mahler Symphony No 9 **R Strauss** Metamorphosen,
AV142
Vienna Philharmonic Orchestra / Sir Simon Rattle
EMI ② 556580-2 (108' · DDD) Recorded live 1993,
1997   Ⓕ

This may not be a Mahler Ninth for all seasons and all moods, but how thrilling it is to hear the score projected at white heat! Even if Sir Simon Rattle is less frankly emotive than a Barbirolli or a Bernstein, his is still a performance that goes for broke – fidgety, raw and intense. Listeners exclusively committed to the eloquent lucidity of Karajan should perhaps give it a wide berth. This is at various times the loudest, softest, fastest and slowest Mahler Ninth on disc. There are passages where the nuancing is *echt*-Viennese (with some pronounced string *portamentos*), others where the music is driven forward harshly and with surprising rigidity. There are big rhetorical effects which threaten to reduce a glorious symphonic canvas to a series of neurotic episodes, others where the power and commitment of the playing take the breath away.

Test the waters – if you can – with the first movement. This is overwhelming, edge-of-the-seat stuff, yet ultimately a little monochrome. Despite the impulsive, agitated approach, the mood of brutal obstinacy is oppressively sustained. In music that responds equally to the tragic subjectivity of a Bernstein and the elevated sense of eternal calm evoked by Karajan, Rattle continues to press home the attack, conveying rather an unquenched commitment to life. Nor does he seek the kind of linear clarity delivered by Bruno Walter, whose remastered stereo recording is much more revealing than its previous LP incarnations.

If in the final analysis, the vehemence of execution isn't always allied to the generosity of spirit you find in the great performances of the past, is that any more than a recognition that we live in different times? There's little space to discuss the Strauss, except that there's a sense in which it tells the same story, abandoning the familiar berth of Karajan-inspired smoothness for altogether choppier seas. Rattle's music-making lives in the here and now and the immediacy of the performance – passionate but dry-eyed – is gripping.

Symphony No 9
Berlin Philharmonic Orchestra / Sir John Barbirolli
EMI Great Recordings of the Century 567925-2
(78' · ADD) Recorded 1964 Ⓢ Ⓜ**OO**
Also available on HMV Classics HMV5 74364-2 Ⓑ

This remastered transfer to CD supports the views of those who regard it as one of the classic interpretations, worthy to be ranked with Walter's and Karajan's. There's an almost imperceptible tape hiss to remind us of the recording's age; otherwise the late Kinloch Anderson's sensitive production wears well. The rapport between Sir John and the Berliners is obvious in the warmth, flexibility and richness of the playing, with the principal horn in particular movingly expressive. Barbirolli's shaping of the great first movement, like a broad arch, has all the intensity that one so admired in his conducting and also an architectural structure for which he did not always receive full credit. The savagery of the *Rondo Burleske* is a feature of this performance with Mahler's scoring sounding years ahead of its time. Barbirolli takes fewer than 23 minutes over the *Adagio*-finale, with the result that the melodic pulse never falters. The string playing is wonderfully heartfelt.

Additional recommendation

Symphony No 9 Ⓗ
Vienna Philharmonic Orchestra / Walter
Dutton Laboratories mono CDBP9708 (71' · ADD)
Recorded 1938 Ⓢ**OO**
This is a historic document – the Ninth's first commercial recording conducted by its dedicatee. Few modern performances offer more intensity in the first movement (Rattle and Bernstein perhaps excepted). Don't be taken aback by the technical lapses of the VPO; this is music-making in which scrappiness and fervour are indissolubly linked. The original surface noise is filtered to near inaudibility – Dutton's restoration is a must-have.

Symphony No 10

Symphony No 10
Berlin Philharmonic Orchestra / Sir Simon Rattle
EMI 556972-2 (77' · DDD) Ⓕ**OOO**

 Rattle previously recorded Deryck Cooke's performing version of Mahler's incomplete 10th in June 1980 and the passionate sensitivity of his reading helped win over a sceptical public at a time when we were much less keen to tamper with the unfinished works of dead or dying artists. These days, it's almost as if we see in their unresolved tensions some prophetic vision of the life to come. Over the years, Rattle has performed the work nearly 100 times, far more often than anyone else. Wooed by Berlin, he repeatedly offered them 'Mahler ed Cooke' and was repulsed. He made his Berlin conducting début with the Sixth. But, after the announcement in June 1999 that he had won the orchestra's vote in a head-to-head with Daniel Barenboim, he celebrated with two concert performances of the 10th. A composite version is presented here. As always, Rattle obtains some devastatingly quiet string playing, and technical standards are unprecedentedly high in so far as the revised performing version is concerned. Indeed, the danger that clinical precision will result in expressive coolness isn't immediately dispelled by the self-confident meatiness of the violas at the start. We aren't used to hearing the line immaculately tuned with every accent clearly defined. The tempo is broader than before and, despite Rattle's characteristic determination to articulate every detail, the mood is, at first, comparatively serene, even Olympian. Could Rattle be succumbing to the Karajan effect? But no – somehow he squares the circle. The neurotic trills, jabbing dissonances and tortuous counterpoint are relished as never before, within the context of a schizoid *Adagio* in which the Brucknerian string writing is never undersold.

The conductor has not radically changed his approach to the rest of the work. As you might expect, the scherzos have greater security and verve. Their strange hallucinatory choppiness is better served, although parts of the fourth movement remain perplexing despite the superb crispness and clarity of inner parts. More than ever, everything leads inexorably to the cathartic finale, brought off with a searing intensity that has you forgetting the relative baldness of the invention.

Berlin's Philharmonie isn't the easiest venue: with everything miked close, climaxes can turn oppressive but the results here are very credible and offer no grounds for hesitation. In short, this new version sweeps the board even more convincingly than the old. According to reports of the first night, Rattle was called back and accorded two Karajan-style standing ovations after the orchestra had left the stage. There's no applause here, but it isn't difficult to imagine such a scene. Rattle makes the strongest case for an astonishing piece of revivification that only the most die-hard purists will resist. Strongly recommended.

Symphony No 10
Berlin Symphony Orchestra / Kurt Sanderling
Berlin Classics 0094422BC (74' · ADD) Recorded 1979
Ⓕ**OO**

Sanderling's own pioneering account of the 10th is – or ought to be – a classic, representing as it does a crucial stage in its performance history. Chronologically speaking, it comes after the analogue LP versions of Eugene Ormandy and Wyn Morris, but predates Sir Simon Rattle's much praised first (Bournemouth) set, let alone the piece's wider acceptance as a repertoire staple. Sanderling made his recording 18 months after conducting the East German première in May 1978. Astonishingly, it wasn't released in the UK until 2001.

Though other conductors of his generation rejected the whole notion more or less out of hand, Sanderling has suggested that while we can't know *how* Mahler would have said it, we can feel what it is he wished to say. He pored over the 'completion' for more than a year, perhaps looking for a way to hold everything together in 'classical' balance without neglecting the more disruptive elements of Mahler's invention; he also exchanged ideas with project veteran Berthold Goldschmidt. The result is tremendous – a balder sort of reading than we're used to, still hugely emotive but with slightly faster speeds, fewer subtle inflections and a radically altered text. There can be nothing wrong in principle with such tinkering – Cooke's confederates have continued their search for an ideal version ever since his death – and, although it's sometimes claimed that Cooke added nothing of his own save patches of instrumentation, there are portions of the score that call for something more if they're going to be played at all. Several of the changes unveiled by Sanderling were taken up by colleagues.

That said, Sanderling stands apart from the minimally interventionist tradition of Rattle and Chailly. He not only preserves some of the speculative scoring suggested and then abandoned by Cooke, such as the xylophone in the second *Scherzo*, but also appends additional percussion throughout, lending the music an uncomfortable edge reminiscent of Hindemith or Weill. While such micro-surgery is fascinating, it's the visceral conviction and rigorous continuity that impress just as much. The recording, almost too immediate, with hard-working strings miked close, remains vivid and true. The less-than-prestigious Berlin orchestra is even better prepared than the Bournemouth Symphony, engagingly 'provincial' horns and all. Inevitably, Sir Simon's Berlin Phil sounds more refulgent than either. This recording of the Tenth may well be Sanderling's finest hour.

Symphony No 10
Berlin Radio Symphony Orchestra / Riccardo

Chailly
Decca 466 955-2DH (79' · DDD) Recorded 1986 Ⓕ**O**

This, the third incarnation of Riccardo Chailly's 1986 studio recording, is the first to fit its 79 minutes onto a single sound carrier. In terms of recorded sound, Chailly is ahead on points: his orchestra (and inevitably you'll notice his violas) may lack the deep pile of the Berlin Philharmonic, but his strings are sympathetically laid out in the warm acoustic of the Jesus-Christus Kirche.

Unsurprisingly, Chailly's interpretation is on the cool side, though one never has the feeling that he's merely going through the motions. The reticence is of a piece with what we know of Chailly's subsequent Mahler conducting. And part of the collectability of Chailly's reading, for admirers of Mahler ed Cooke, are the many points at which he departs from Rattle's solutions and/or follows the score published in 1976 as opposed to the 1989 revision of it.

Thus, where Rattle enlivens the denouement of the first *Scherzo* with a cymbal clash, Chailly in the mid-80s is being literal: the effect was not restored until the 1989 edition. On the other hand, Chailly gives us the chance to hear xylophone and side drum parts subsequently excised from the fourth movement. Rattle, like Sanderling, cuts out a (not-so-muffled) drum stroke to pass seamlessly from the fourth to the fifth movement; this isn't explicitly authorised scorewise, although it has made such good sense in performance that unsuspecting listeners might attribute an editing fault to the Chailly. In the finale, the Italian isn't among those who underwrite the return of the *Adagio*'s dissonant 'break-down' chords with added percussion, and he surely has a point.

Swings and roundabouts? Even for those not interested in the minutiae, this represents a worthwhile addition to the collection – a 10th to live with perhaps.

Kindertotenlieder / Rückert-Lieder

Kindertotenlieder[a]. Rückert-Lieder[b] Lieder eines fahrenden Gesellen[a]
Dame Janet Baker *mez* [a]**Hallé Orchestra,** [b]**New Philharmonia Orchestra / Sir John Barbirolli**
EMI 566981-2 (65' · ADD) Texts and translations included
Ⓕ**O**

The songs of the *Lieder eines fahrenden Gesellen* ('Songs of a Wayfarer') are quoted from Mahler's First Symphony and the fresh, springtime atmosphere is shared by both works. The orchestration has great textural clarity and lightness of touch. The *Kindertotenlieder*, more chromatically expressive than the earlier work, tap into a darker, more complex vein in Mahler's spiritual and emotional make-up. The *Rückert-Lieder* aren't a song cycle as such but gather in their romantic awareness and response to the beauties of the poetry a unity and shape that binds them. Baker and Barbirolli reach a transcendental awareness of Mahler's inner musings. Barbirolli draws from the Hallé playing of delicacy and precision, establishing a clear case for having this CD in your collection.

Kindertotenlieder[a]. Lieder eines fahrenden Gesellen[b]. Fünf Rückert-Lieder[c]
[a]**Anne Sofie von Otter**, [c]**Violeta Urmana** mezs
[b]**Thomas Quasthoff** bar **Vienna Philharmonic Orchestra / Pierre Boulez**
DG 477 5329GH (62' · DDD · T/t)   (F)

As you'd expect, Boulez clarifies orchestral textures, often with magical results. 'Ging heut morgen übers Feld', the second of the *Wayfarer Songs*, gleams and glistens like the dewiest of spring mornings. And the exquisite gossamer fabric of 'Blicke mir nicht in die Lieder' in the *Rückert-Lieder* is also breathtaking. In the *Kindertotenlieder*, he underlines the spareness of the scoring; with playing of great gravity from the winds of the Vienna Philharmonic, the effect is especially disconsolate.

Equally absorbing, though not always as satisfying, is the chemistry between Boulez and each of the singers. Thomas Quasthoff elicits the most highly charged reading. With plangent, aching tone and carefully weighted emphases, he indicates how deeply bitterness has seeped into this wayfarer's veins. With its attention to detail and faultless pacing, this is a performance to set alongside Dietrich Fischer-Dieskau's.

Violeta Urmana's reading of the *Rückert-Lieder* is cooler. Her graceful agility and pure tone are a delight in 'Blicke mir nicht in die Lieder.' Elsewhere, though, her singing is unaccountably plain – rigid and squarely phrased. The Apollonian poise she conveys in 'Ich bin der Welt abhanden gekommen' is convincing but not sufficiently moving.

Anne Sofie von Otter's long-awaited recording of the *Kindertotenlieder* is deeply felt and noble; if this is a bereaved parent, it's surely an aristocratic one. Perhaps the effect results partly from her relatively bright, svelte tone – both Janet Baker and Kathleen Ferrier are more earthy and maternal – though von Otter's smoothing out of the written accents at the climax of the first song definitely mutes the music's inherent volatility.

Clearly, there's plenty here to gratify and provoke the devoted Mahlerian, and although it's not entirely persuasive this is a disc that deserves to be heard.

Kindertotenlieder. Lieder eines fahrenden Gesellen. Fünf Rückert-Lieder. Lieder und Gesänge – No 1, Frühlingsmorgen; No 3, Hans und Grethe; No 5, Phantasie aus Don Juan; No 10, Zu Strassburg auf der Schanz; No 11, Ablösung im Sommer; No 12, Scheiden und Meiden; No 13, Nicht wiedersehen!
Stephan Genz bar **Roger Vignoles** pf
Hyperion CDA67392 (73' · DDD · T/t)   (F)

Stephan Genz's voice and style place him above

his many noted contemporaries. His mellifluous baritone recalls that of a young Thomas Hampson, but his understanding of the Lieder genre is even more penetrating, as this Mahler recital reveals. Each song is shaped as a whole yet with subtleties of phrase and word-painting that seem inevitable in every respect, especially as the chosen tempi always seem the right ones.

Performing and listening to these songs with piano is inevitably a more intimate experience than when they are heard in their orchestral garb. The pair's rapport is evident throughout. Memorable are the poise and stillness of 'Ich atmet' einen Linden duft' from the *Rückert-Lieder*, the eloquent sadness of 'Nicht Wiedersehen' and the restrained sorrow of the whole of *Kindertotenlieder*. No a hint of sentimentality, such a danger in Mahler, spoils the experience of the composer's deeply felt emotions.

Hyperion's recording, beautifully balanced, catches the true quality of Genz's voice and the refinement of Vignoles's playing. This disc is an experience not to be missed by any lover of Mahler and/or of Lieder.

Das klagende Lied

Das klagende Lied[a] (complete version including 'Waldmärchen'). Kindertotenlieder. Rückert-Lieder. Lieder eines fahrenden Gesellen. Lieder aus Des Knaben Wunderhorn – Das irdische Leben; Des Antonius von Padua Fischpredigt; Urlicht
Brigitte Fassbaender mez [a]**Markus Baur** treb [a]**Susan Dunn** sop [a]**Werner Hollweg** ten [a]**Andreas Schmidt** bar; [a]**Städtischer Musikverein, Düsseldorf, Radio Symphony Orchestra, Berlin; Deutsches Symphony Orchestra, Berlin / Riccardo Chailly**
Double Decca ② 473 725-2 (DDD) Recorded 1988-9.
Texts and translations included   (M)(O)

Few would realise that *Das klagende Lied* is the work of a teenager. It's as self-assured as anything he was to write in later life. Enthusiastic Mahlerians will recognise here passages which crop up in other works, most notably the Second Symphony. Those same Mahlerians might not recognise much of this recording, however, since only two movements of *Klagende Lied* are usually performed: the 30-minute first movement is considered too rambling. But no one could arrive at that conclusion from this tautly directed, electrifying performance, and it contains wonderfully imaginative music, including some delightful forest murmurs.

For this movement alone this CD is a must for any Mahler fan, but more than that this is a spectacular recording of a one-in-a-million performance. The soloists, choir and orchestra achieve near perfection under Chailly's inspired direction, and the decision to substitute for the marvellous Brigitte Fassbaender a boy alto (Markus Baur) to represent the disembodied voice of the dead brother is pure genius. His weird, unnatural voice provides a moment of sheer spine-tingling drama.

MAHLER'S DAS LIED VON DER ERDE – IN BRIEF

Urmana; Schade; Vienna PO / Pierre Boulez
DG ⏺ 471 635-2 (61' · DDD)   Ⓕ🟢🟢🟢

A real ensemble effort whose guiding light is Boulez. With the help of DG's sound, textures glint with unprecendented clarity; the very end is possibly the most evocative on record.

Ferrier; Patzak; Vienna PO / Bruno Walter
Decca 466 576-2DM (89' · ADD)   Ⓜ🟢🟢

This classic meeting of minds in mono now has a better depth of sound than ever before in Decca's latest remastering. The human appeal of Ferrier's 'Farewell' is still magnetic.

Ludwig; Wunderlich; Philharmonia / Otto Klemperer
EMI 566892-2 (64' · ADD)   Ⓜ 🟢🟢

Another conductor who knew Mahler and worked with him: both singers are in gloriously full voice.

Hodgson; Mitchinson; BBC Northern SO / Jascha Horenstein
BBC Legends BBCL4042-2 (61' · ADD)   Ⓜ🟢🟢

Horenstein's live legacy of long-breathed Mahler is at last gaining deserved recognition. This is a meditative, deeply felt *Das Lied*. Hodgson eclipses many greater names.

Ferrier; Lewis; Hallé / Sir John Barbirolli
Appian mono APR5579 (77' · ADD)   Ⓕ🟢🟢

Ferrier is in even fuller, finer voice here than for Walter, with a richer, more expansive canvas painted by the Hallé and that most passionate of Mahlerians, Barbirolli. Restricted sound.

Baker; Kmentt; Bavarian RSO / Rafael Kubelík
Audite 95491 (62' · ADD)   Ⓑ🟢

No survey could be without Janet Baker's sensitive, heartfelt response to the long final 'Farewell': in Kmentt she finally has a partner who is almost her equal, and, in concert, Kubelík finds new expressive heights and depths.

Fischer-Dieskau; King; Vienna PO / Leonard Bernstein
Decca 466 381-2DM (67' · ADD)   Ⓜ

If you want Mahler's sanctioned alternative, with a baritone singing the mezzo songs, this is a first choice: Fischer-Dieskau's vast experience in Lieder is telling here, and so are King's credentials as a Wagnerian.

Rigby; Tear; Première Ensemble / Mark Wigglesworth
RCA 09026 68043-2 (69' · ADD)   Ⓕ

Schoenberg's arrangement reduces the orchestra to a chamber ensemble, and allows the singers to project with more subtlety while exerting an authentic Mahlerian pull.

Similar characteristics inform a deeply eloquent interpretation of *Kindertotenlieder*. The world-weary tone and verbal illumination in the first song catch at the heart and suggest personal responsibility for the children's deaths. Baker/Barbirolli, with the singer in lovely voice, must be a 'safer' recommendation than the more daring Fassbaender, but the latter is an inviting proposition – and a searing experience.

Fassbaender's emotionally charged way of singing is ideally matched to Mahler yet she's just as able to smile and sing gently, wittily. It's in the dramatic declamation, however, that the true flavour of her singing is caught. Throughout the *Fahrenden Gesellen* it's the immediacy, the fearlessness of attack and her particular intensity, that make these readings so arresting. The swiftish speeds throughout keep sentimentality at bay; so does Chailly's and the orchestra's biting precision and light touch.

Des Knaben Wunderhorn

Des Knaben Wunderhorn – Revelge[b]. Das irdische Leben[a]. Verlor'ne Müh[ab]. Rheinlegendchen[a]. Der Tamboursg'sell[b]. Der Schildwache Nachtlied[ab]. Wer hat dies Liedlein erdacht?[a]. Lob des hohen Verstandes[b]. Des Antonius von Padua Fischpredigt[b]. Lied des Verfolgten im Turm[ab]. Trost im Unglück[ab]. Wo die schönen Trompeten blasen[a]
[a]**Elisabeth Schwarzkopf** *sop* [b]**Dietrich Fischer-Dieskau bar London Symphony Orchestra / George Szell**
EMI Great Recordings of the Century 567236-2 (50' · ADD) Recorded 1968. Texts and translations included   Ⓜ🟢🟢🟢

EMI's classic recording made in 1968 by Schwarzkopf, Fischer-Dieskau and Szell more or less puts all rivals out of court. Even those who find Schwarzkopf's singing mannered will be hard pressed to find more persuasive versions of the female songs than she gives, while Fischer-Dieskau and Szell are in a class of their own most of the time. Bernstein's CBS version, also from the late 1960s but with less spectacularly improved sound than EMI now provide, is also very fine, but for repeated listening Szell, conducting here with the kind of insight he showed on his famous Cleveland version of the Fourth Symphony, is the more controlled and keen-eared interpreter. Also, few command the musical stage as Fischer-Dieskau does in a song like 'Revelge' where every drop of irony and revulsion from the spectre of war is fiercely, grimly caught. Strongly recommended.

Lieder aus Des Knaben Wunderhorn
Jard van Nes *contr* **John Bröcheler** *bass* **Arnhem Philharmonic Orchestra / Roberto Benzi**
Ottavo OTRC79238 (55' · DDD) Recorded 1992. Texts included   Ⓕ

Jard van Nes is a natural for Mahler, vocally and

interpretatively. Particularly admirable is her fresh, spontaneous approach, free from both the shadow of past performance or awe before such familiar songs. She catches ideally the folk-like charm of 'Rheinlegendchen' and 'Wer hat dies Liedlein erdacht?'. She's also appropriately earthy in 'Das irdische Leben', then marvellously tender as the distant lover in 'Des Schildwache Nachtlied'. Her unadorned mastery of word and tone can't be praised too highly – listen to the *keck* delivery of 'Verlor'ne Muh': just right – and she crowns her performance with her grave utterance in 'Urlicht'. Bröcheler is among the best, characterising 'Lob des hohen Verstandes' with vivacity and revelling in St Antony's sermon. Benzi and his orchestra never make the mistake of over-egging the pudding. Although the detail is all clearly projected and keenly played, in a perfectly balanced recording, the music is kept on the move.

Das Lied von der Erde

Das Lied von der Erde
Christa Ludwig *mez* **Fritz Wunderlich** *ten*
Philharmonia Orchestra, New Philharmonia Orchestra / Otto Klemperer
EMI 566892-2 (64' · ADD) Recorded 1964-6 ⓜⓞⓞ

In a famous BBC TV interview Klemperer declared that he was the objective one, Walter the romantic, and he knew what he was talking about. Klemperer lays this music before you, even lays bare its soul by his simple method of steady tempos (too slow in the third song) and absolute textural clarity, but he doesn't quite demand your emotional capitulation as does Walter. Ludwig does that. In the tenor songs, Wunderlich can't match Patzak, simply because of the older singer's way with the text; 'fest steh'n' in the opening song, 'Mir ist als wie im Traum', the line plaintive and the tone poignant, are simply unsurpassable. By any other yardstick, Wunderlich is a prized paragon, musical and vocally free. So natural is the sound on the revived EMI that it easily beats the mono Decca. With voice and orchestra in perfect relationship and everything sharply defined, the old methods of the 1960s have nothing to fear here from today's competition. These two old recordings will never be thrust aside; the Walter for its authority and intensity, the feeling of being present on an historic occasion, the Klemperer for its insistent strength and beautiful singing.

Additional recommendations

Coupled with: Symphony No 5
Baltsa *mez* **König** *ten* **London Philharmonic Orchestra / Tennstedt**
EMI Double Forte ② 574849-2 (DDD) ⓜ
The LPO play with alternating intensity and delicacy throughout, and Klaus König proves one of the best tenor soloists on disc. A bargain.

Hodgson *contr* **Mitchinson** *ten* **BBC Northern Symphony Orchestra / Horenstein**
BBC Legends/IMG Artists BBCL4042-2 (73' · ADD) Recorded live ⓜ
Horenstein gives us a deeply eloquent, valedictory reading. Its sustained intensity, revelatory attention to orchestral detail and wonderful overview of the work make it a classic worthy to be set alongside readings by Walter, Klemperer and Reiner.

Gian Francesco Malipiero
Italian 1882-1973

Malipiero studied with Bossi at the Licei Musicali in Venice (1899-1902) and Bologna (1904-5), and began transcribing the music of Monteverdi and other early Italians in 1902; he also learnt much from serving as amanuensis to Smareglia. In 1913 he visited Paris, where he formed a lasting friendship with Casella and heard The Rite of Spring: he then suppressed everything he had previously written. The influences of Stravinsky and particularly Debussy were to remain fundamental, and they gave rise to his first masterpieces: the orchestral Pause del silenzio I (1917), the ballet Pantea (1919, perf.1932) and the seven miniature operas Sette canzoni (1919).

In 1924 he retired to Asolo in the Veneto and in 1926 embarked on his complete Monteverdi edition, while continuing to compose copiously. Archaic and contemporary elements were combined in the operas, his main works of the 1920s, including San Francesco d'Assisi (1922) and Torneo notturno (1931). His enormous later output includes more operas, orchestral music, eight string quartets and vocal pieces. He was the most original and inventive Italian composer of his generation. **GROVE**music

Il Capricci di Callot

Il Capricci di Callot
Martina Winter *sop* Giacinta **Markus Müller** *ten* Giglio **Gro Bente Kjellevold** *mez* La Vecchia Beatrice **Bernd Valentin** *bar* Il Principe Travestito da Ciarlatanto **Burkhard Ulrich** *ten* Il Poeta **Jörg Sabrowski** *bar* Una Maschera **Kiel Philharmonic Orchestra / Peter Marschik**
CPO ② CPO999 830-2 (93' · DDD) Notes, text and translation included ⓕ

Malipiero was one of the most original and provocative operatic composers of the 20th century, but with the exception of the weird, impressive trilogy *L'Orfeide*, this was the first of his 23 major full-length operas to be recorded. *I Capricci di Callot* is relatively brief, musically easy of access (its characteristic tone is gracefully lyrical, at times oddly close to Vaughan Williams) and absolutely typical of Malipiero's anti-realistic dramaturgy. We receive warning of this when an elegantly neo-classical seven-minute overture is followed by a nine-minute danced prologue: nobody sings a note until more than a sixth of this opera's duration has passed, and there are long mimed scenes later.

The plot concerns a poor seamstress, Giacinta, who loses her own personality when she tries on a sumptuous dress she has been making, and becomes, in her imagination, a princess. The most lyrical and moving music comes in a mad scene where she imagines herself in a fabulous palace waiting for the magical arrival of her imaginary prince. The world of masks, illusions and ambiguities was central to what Malipiero called 'my opera', and the serene beauty of this scene is due to it. In many of his operas the most exquisite moments are the most perplexingly irrational ones. Or rather those where he casts his strange spells: the passage in which Giacinta puts on the fabulous dress and her friend Beatrice exclaims in wonder and fills the room with lighted candles. Or the gentle flute solo that accompanies the smashing of a doll representing the mythic princess; it's followed by a curiously formal and haunting funereal dance.

All the singers are good, Peter Marschik clearly understands Malipiero's alluring oddness and projects the score strongly. The live recording is very close, which adds a touch of gawkiness to the strings at times, but in what sounds like a small auditorium the voices gain from not needing to force. An accomplished issue, and an important one.

Marin Marais   French 1656-1728

Marais, the central figure in the French bass viol school, spent his life in Paris, much of it in royal service. A pupil of Sainte-Colombe and protégé of Lully, he composed four operas (1693-1709 – notably Alcione, 1706, famous for its storm scene) that form an important link between Lully and Campra. But his greatest significance lies in his five collections of music for one to three bass viols (1686-1725), comprising over 550 pieces. As well as the usual dances, they include character pieces that are among his finest works, and they possess an eloquence and refinement of line and richness of ornamental detail that perfectly display the qualities of his instrument. The Pieces en trio (1692) are recognised as the first appearance of the trio sonata in France.

GROVEmusic

Alcyone

Alcyone – Suites   P
Le Concert des Nations / Jordi Savall
Astrée Naïve ES9945 (53' · DDD) Recorded 1993   MO

As one of the greatest exponents of the solo viol tradition perfected by Marais, Savall focuses his insights upon this music and interprets the scoring as Marais might have done. He experiments with all the chamber music combinations of the day and, typically, hazards some of his own, particularly in the Chaconne. Occasionally, Savall uses winds and sometimes miscalculates his effects, as in the 'Bourrée pour les Bergers et Bergères'. His command of Maraisian ornamentation is, however, everywhere evident and indeed very welcome because of the constant melodic echoes of the solo repertoire in the opera score. With chamber music come more transparent textures, revealing the harmonic and textural richness of the post-Lullian style; cross-rhythms, syncopations and sequences have more impact. By contrast, the opera performances can often sound sluggish and four-square. Savall also includes music that was left out of the opera recording, including the delicately syncopated 'Air pour les Faunes et les Driades' from the Prologue, the exquisitely scored Sarabande, with its beautifully shaded cadences, and the Gigue from Act 1 as well as the 'Sarabande pour les Prêtresses de Junon' from Act 2. In the Prologue and the March and Air 'pour les Matelots' in Act 3, Savall orchestrates passages that were once vocal solos to maintain the proportions of the movements.

Pièces de viol

Le labyrinthe & autres histoires   P
Pièces de viole – Deuxième livre: Cloches ou carillon; La polonaise; Sarabande à l'espagnol; Chaconne en rondeau; Troisième livre: Plainte; La musette; La guitarre; Quatrième livre: Rondeau Le bijou; Le tourbillon; Le labyrinthe; Cinquième livre: Le tombeau pour Marais le cadet; La georgienne dite La maupertis; Le jeu du volant; Prélude en harpegement; Marche persane dite La sauvigny
Paolo Pandolfo bass viol **Mitzi Meyerson** hpd
Thomas Boysen theorbo/gtr
Glossa GCD920404 (67' · DDD)   FOO

Paolo Pandolfo stands alone in his generation as the master of his instrument and of a repertory that depends upon a deep affinity with its socio-historical context. Labyrinths form the theme of this recording: Louis XIV's passion for them, the monumental *Labyrinthe* Marais composed to amuse him, and the labyrinthine character of Marais' output when taken as a whole. Pierre Jacquier has contributed a thought-provoking essay and Pandolfo (rather courageously) offers notional monologues related to the *pièces* he selected to represent a hypothetical route through Marais' musical maze. The CD begins, appropriately enough, with a freely expressed prélude that sets the tone for the recording and ends with a playfully unstuffy performance of a chaconne. Along the way there are spine-tingling allusions to a harp, bells, a musette and a guitar; a yearning polonaise, a lascivious sarabande and a pompous Persian march. But in Pandolfo's hands none eclipse the dramatically conceived and passionately realised *Labyrinthe* itself. It isn't simply that Pandolfo is completely at ease with the instrument and the idiom; he creates new sounds and new combinations of effects with his continuo forces (in *Cloches ou carillon* and *La musette*) – sounds and effects not precisely notated in the music and probably unimagined by Marais, but within the scope and idiom of the instruments. Pandolfo himself can play so softly, almost without attack, so clearly, so quickly and yet so apparently effortlessly. He can play a chord a dozen different ways, and appears to relish the 'growl-ish' effects the lower strings of the bass viol can produce, making them sound truly beautiful and even exotic. So expertly has the ensemble been recorded that for once the CD listener can imagine being among the privileged few invited to the king's private rooms at Versailles. This is a thrilling disc.

Pièces de viole, Livre 2 – Part 1: Ballet en rondeau; **P**
Couplets de folies; Prélude; Cloches ou carillon. Part 2: Prélude lentement; Chaconne en rondeau; Tombeau pour M de Ste Colombe; Prélude; Allemande; Courante; Pavan selon de goût des anciens compositeurs de luth; Gavotte; Rondeau en vaudeville; Gigue; Chaconne; Fantaisie
Markku Luolajan-Mikkola, Varpu Haavisto *vas da gamba* **Eero Palviainen** *lte* **Elina Mustonen** *hpd*
BIS CD909 (73' · DDD)　　　　　　　　Ⓕ

The most substantial pieces here are the set of variations of *La folia*, and the *Tombeau pour M de Ste Colombe* in memory of Marais's mentor. His idiom embodies a paradox that's peculiarly French, in that it demands a very high technical standard, yet its proper expression requires the utmost restraint. The young Finnish viol-player, Markku Luolajan-Mikkola, is a founder-member of Phantasm. Here he holds his own with elegance and reserve, although in the slower pieces one might have wished for more rhythmic flexibility. The continuo section consists of another viol-player, and a theorbo or harpsichord (though in the variations on *La folia*, the two are combined). This works well for the most part, though the high partials of the harpsichord tend to drown the viols: the lute is far less obtrusive. The problem of balance also intrudes when the soloist is in the lower range. But as an introduction to Marais's art this is hard to fault – try his Pavan 'in the style of the bygone lute composers': a real treat.

Further listening

Tous les matins du monde (soundtrack)　　**P**
Music by **Couperin, Lully, Marais** and **Sainte-Colombe**
Le Concert des Nations / Savall *va da gamba*
Alia Vox AV9821 (76' · DDD) Recorded 1991　Ⓕ
This magical disc occupies the more inward world of the solo gamba repertoire, taking in moving and thoughtful compositions such as Marais' *La rêveuse* and Sainte-Colombe's deeply moving *Les pleurs*. Savall shows himself throughout to be a master worthy of these great viol-playing composers.

Luca Marenzio　　　Italian 1553/4-1599

Possibly a pupil of Contino in Brescia, Marenzio moved to Rome in c1574 and served cardinals and other wealthy patrons (including Luigi d'Este) until 1586. During these years he published copiously and gained an international reputation. He travelled in 1587, visiting Verona, and briefly served Ferdinando de' Medici in Florence, where in 1589 he composed intermedi for the ducal wedding festivities. He returned to Rome later that year, residing with the Duke of Bracciano untilc 1593, when he entered Cardinal Cinzio Aldobrandini's service; he held a Vatican apartment in 1594. In 1595-6 he visited the Polish court, returning to Rome in 1598.

One of the most prolific madrigalists of the period, Marenzio published over 400 madrigals and villanellas in at least 23 books (1580-99). They range widely, from light pastorals to serious sonnets (these mostly from later years), and are notable for their striking mood- and word-painting. They long remained popular in Italy and elsewhere, especially England. His motets, though less well known, also feature much verbal imagery and religious symbolism.　　　　　　　　　GROVE*music*

Madrigals

Madrigals – Book 1: Così moriro i fortunati amanti; Deh rinforzate il vostro pianto; Dolorosi martir, fieri tormenti; Frenò Tirsi il desio; Liquide perle Amor da gl'occhi sparse; Per duo coralli ardenti; Tirsi morir volea; Book 2: Là dove sono i pargoletti Amori; E s'io doglio, Amor; Fuggi speme mia, fuggi; Vaghi e lieti fanciulli; Book 4: Caro Aminta pur voi; Donne il celeste lume; Nè fero sdegno mai donna mi mosse; Non può Filli più; Book 5: Basciami mille volte; Consumando mi vo di piaggia in piaggia; Book 6: O verdi selv'o dolci fonti o rivi; Udite, lagrimosi; Book 7: Cruda Amarilli; Ma grideran per me le piagge; Book 9: Cosí nel mio parlar; Et ella ancide, e non val c'huom si chiuda **Philips** Tirsi morir volea **Terzi** Intavolatura di liuto, libro primo – Liquide perle Amor, da gl'occhi sparse
Il Concerto Italiano / Rinaldo Alessandrini *hpd*
Opus111 OP30245 (74' · DDD)　　　　　Ⓕ**ооо**

 Marenzio's music was known throughout Europe during his lifetime; its success was based on what one contemporary identified as its 'new, fresh style, pleasing to the ear, with some simple counterpoint and without excessive artifice', a characterisation that applies more to the earlier books than to the late ones. It's this style which lies at the heart of Rinaldo Alessandrini's selection (though there are plenty of pieces from the later books as well), and the performances nicely capture its essential spirit, its communicability and transparent craftmanship occasionally disturbed (as in 'Dolorosi martir') by more serious intent. These beautifully paced and architecturally controlled performances, many of which make intelligent and appropriate use of added continuo instruments, present the most persuasive argument for understanding the reasons for

Marenzio's enormous reputation, throughout Italy and beyond, at the start of the 1580s. Highly recommended.

Il sesto libro de Madrigali
La Venexiana (Valentina Coladonato, Nadia Ragni sops Paola Reggiani mezz Sandro Naglia, Giuseppe Maletto tens Andrea Favari, Daniele Carnovich basses Gabriele Palomba, Franco Pavan ltes) /
Claudio Cavina counterten
Glossa GCD920909 (54' · DDD) Text and translations included ⓕ〇

La Venexiana have already successfully explored the world of Marenzio's late madrigals with their quite stunning recording of the Ninth Book, a collection that's far from eas to interpret persuasively. The overall style of the Sixth Book is quite different; the most important trend here is towards a declamatory style which critically depends upon a new kind of rhetoric. The group is superbly equipped to elucidate the details of intimate music-text relations without resorting to over-mannered gestures. The overall tone of the Sixth Book is pastoral-elegiac, and the group responds with a sense of pacing that's gentle and spacious, allowing the music plenty of opportunity to speak clearly. Accurate tuning and carefully balanced chording, backed up by exquisite phrasing, are the keys to La Venexiana's delicate interpretations of some of the most poetic music written by one of the most important Italian madrigalists before Monteverdi. This is a must.

Frank Martin   Swiss 1890-1974

Martin, the son of a Calvinist minister, was deeply impressed by a performance of the St Matthew Passion he heard at the age of 10. He studied with Joseph Lauber and worked from 1926 with Jaques-Dalcroze, then in his Piano Concerto no.1 (1934) and Symphony (1937) adopted Schoenbergian serialism while retaining an extended tonal harmony that looked to Debussy: the mature fusion of these elements into a style marked by dissonant chords, smooth part-writing and 'gliding tonality' did not come until the dramatic chamber oratorio Le vin herbé (1941), soon followed by two larger oratorios, In terra pax (1944) and Golgotha (1948), as well as by the Petite symphonie concertante for harp, harpsichord, piano and strings (1945) and the Sechs Monologe aus 'Jedermann' (1943, orchestrated 1949). In 1946 he moved to the Netherlands; he also taught at the Cologne Musikhochschule (1950-57). His later works include the operas Der Sturm (1956, Vienna Staatsoper) and Monsieur de Pourceaugnac (1963, Geneva), a large-scale Requiem (1972) and many concertante pieces, among them concertos for violin and harpsichord (both 1952) and a second for piano (1969).
GROVEmusic

Piano Concertos

Piano Concertos – No 1[a]; No 2[b]. Ballade[a]
Danse de la peur[ab]
[a]**Sebastian Benda**, [a]**Paul Badura-Skoda** pfs
Svizzera Italiana Orchestra / Christian Benda
ASV CDDCA1082 (74' · DDD)   ⓕ

What Martin's music needs is performances of understanding but also affection, and ASV deserves congratulation for the shrewd casting of this disc. Sebastian Benda was a composition pupil of Martin's, and once recorded the *Ballade* with him conducting. The Second Piano Concerto was written for Paul Badura-Skoda, and he too recorded it with the composer. The conductor here is too young to share the two pianists' warm memories of Martin, but he's Sebastian Benda's son, and the sense of all three collaborating in a tribute is strong.

Martin is often described as a serialist, but this isn't true. He used 12-note rows, but only to discipline his melodic language, which is tonal, strong and lyrical. The First Concerto might just as well have been subtitled 'The Dramatic' and Benda plays it with flair and great enjoyment, as he does the gentler but no less varied *Ballade*. The Second Concerto, a late work, is one of Martin's finest, with a profusion of bold, striking ideas and opportunities for grand rhetoric. Badura-Skoda plays it as though he were delighted to make its acquaintance again.

Perhaps the orchestra could have done with two or three extra desks of strings, but the recording is excellent and the performances all that could be desired.

Maria-Triptychon

Der Sturm – Overture; Mein Ariel, hast du, der Luft nur ist; Ein feierliches Lied; Hin sind meine Zauberei'n. Maria-Triptychon. Sechs Monologe aus Jedermann
Linda Russell sop **David Wilson-Johnson** bar
Duncan Riddell vn **London Philharmonic Orchestra / Matthias Bamert**
Chandos CHAN9411 (68' · DDD) Recorded 1994   ⓕ

The *Maria-Triptychon* was written in the late 1960s in response to a request from Wolfgang Schneiderhan for a work for violin, soprano and orchestra that he could perform with his wife, Irmgard Seefried. Although their recording under the composer himself emanating from a Swiss Radio tape is authoritative, it doesn't match this Chandos recording in sheer beauty of sound. Linda Russell sings the solo part with great sympathy and intelligence, and Duncan Riddell assumes the mantle of Schneiderhan with no mean success. The transparency of texture that Chandos achieves shows this visionary score in the most favourable light. It makes a stronger impression than in any earlier performance, thanks to the dedication of the LPO and its conductor. Bamert distils a strong atmosphere and sense of mystery in all these scores. Wilson-Johnson is on impressive form in the *Jedermann* Monologues (one of the great song cycles of the century). His is as perceptive and moving an account as any – and he's no less impressive in the magical *Der Sturm*.

Requiem

Requiem
Elisabeth Speiser sop **Ria Bollen** contr **Eric Tappy** ten **Peter Lagger** bass **Lausanne Women's Chorus; Union Chorale; Ars Laeta Vocal Ensemble; Suisse Romande Orchestra / Frank Martin**
Jecklin Disco JD631-2 (47' · ADD) Recorded live 1973. Text and translation included   Ⓕ

Astonishingly, this beautiful score still remains grievously neglected – it deserves to be heard as often as the Fauré Requiem. It's a work of vision and devotion of spirit, and casts a strong spell. It's one of those pieces that leaves you with a feeling of enormous tranquillity. The musical language is familiar enough, for there are the same subtle shifts of colour and harmony that you'll find in Martin's *Petite Symphonie concertante*. However, there's a dramatic power (*Dies irae*) and a serenity (*In Paradisum*) that are quite new. The short *In Paradisum* is inspired, and has a luminous quality and radiance that are quite otherworldly. Martin certainly put all his consummate musical skills into this score with organ and orchestra of equal importance. He conducts a completely dedicated and authoritative performance: it might well be improved upon in one or two places in terms of ensemble or security, but the spirit is there. The Swiss Radio recording is eminently truthful and well balanced, and offers a natural enough acoustic.

Mass for Double Choir

Martin Mass for Double Choir. Passaille[a] **Pizzetti** Messa di requiem. De profundis
Westminster Cathedral Choir/James O'Donnell [a]org
Hyperion CD CDA67017 (71' · DDD) Texts and translations included   ⒻⓄⓄⓄ

🅖   These are magnificent performances. Written in 1922, the *Agnus Dei* being added four years later, the Mass is one of Martin's most sublime compositions. Surprisingly it gains enormously from using boys' rather than female voices. It's a measure of James O'Donnell's achievement with Westminster Cathedral Choir that the gain in purity and beauty is never at the expense of depth and fervour. This is an altogether moving and eloquent performance, often quite thrilling and always satisfying.

This disc brings us a fine performance by O'Donnell of the *Passacaille* and the Pizzetti *Messa di Requiem*, also composed in 1922. The received wisdom is that it is in his *a cappella* music that Pizzetti is at his finest; in his 1951 monograph Guido Gatti spoke of his setting as 'the most serene and lyrical of all ... from

Mozart's to Gabriel Faure's'. Serene and lyrical it most certainly is, and it will come as a revelation to those encountering it for the first time. There is a fervour and a conviction about the Westminster performances of both the Requiem and the 1937 *De profundis*. The luminous tone this choir produce in both these inspired and masterly works will ring in your ears long after you have finished playing this splendidly recorded disc.

Vicente Martín y Soler
Spanish 1754-1806

Martín y Soler was in the service of the Spanish Infante by 1780 and composed operas and ballets for Italian cities in 1779-85; he also wrote zarzuelas. He then began a famous collaboration with the librettist Da Ponte in Vienna, presenting three Italian opera buffe (notably Una cosa rara, 1786). In 1788-94 he was at the Russian court as a composer and teacher, returning there in 1796 after a period in London, and becoming inspector of the Italian court theatre. He composed some 20 stage works in all; his ten opere buffe, among the finest of the period, contain expressive and dance-like melodies.
GROVEmusic

La capricciosa corretta

La capricciosa corretta
Josep Miquel Ramon bar Fiuta **Marguerite**   Ⓟ
Krull sop Donna Ciprigna **Yves Saelens** ten Lelio **Enrique Baquerizo** bar Bonario **Katia Velletaz** sop Isabella **Carlos Marin** bar Don Giglio **Raffaella Milanesi** sop Cilia **Emiliano Gonzalez-Toro** ten Valerio **Les Talens Lyriques / Christophe Rousset**
Naïve ② E8887 (135' · DDD) Notes, libretto and translation included   Ⓕ

Mozart's affectionate quotation from Martín y Soler's *Una cosa rara* in the *Don Giovanni* dinner music suggests he admired his Spanish contemporary, whose music was praised by others as 'sweet' and 'graceful'. Such descriptions remain apt for a charming and brilliantly executed performance that's essential for anybody curious about late 18th-century opera beyond Mozart.

The best operas of his later years were produced in London. *La capricciosa corretta* was first performed at the King's Theatre in 1795 under the title *La scuola dei maritati*; Its plot concerns the marriage of an older man to a young second wife whose excessive vanity and capriciousness makes life miserable for everybody else.

The libretto was by Lorenzo da Ponte. There are illuminating musical and dramatic parallels with, most notably, *Così fan tutte* and *Le nozze di Figaro*. 'Se figli vi siamo' is a gorgeous lyrical quintet, graced with sensitive woodwind colour, that wouldn't be out of place in *Così*. 'Qui vive, e respira' is a tender tenor aria in which Lelio softly enthuses about the woman he loves: it's a striking counterpart of Ferrando's 'Un' aura amorosa'. Valerio's mock-martial aria 'Un fucil, un spadon' is an intriguing close descendant of Figaro's 'Non più andrai', with a lightly scored military accompaniment illustrating a text about taking up a post in the army.

Individual personalities aren't portrayed to quite such memorable effect as in Mozart, of course, but there's plenty of distinctive music to overcome the inevitable comparisons.

Christophe Rousset's cast of relative unknowns deliver a competent and committed team performance. Les Talens Lyriques savour the music with their customary zest and astute musical intelligence.

pated fast movements is very infectious, indeed unforgettable, and his slow movements are often deeply expressive, most potently, perhaps, in that of the Third Symphony which is imbued with the tragedy of war. The Bamberg orchestra plays marvellously and with great verve for Järvi, whose excellently judged tempos help propel the music forward most effectively. His understanding of the thrust of Martinů's structures is impressive and he projects the music with clarity. The recordings are beautifully clear, with plenty of ambience surrounding the orchestra, a fine sense of scale and effortless handling of the wide dynamic range Martinů calls for. It's enthusiastically recommended.

Bohuslav Martinů   Bohemian 1890-1959

Martinů studied at the Prague Conservatory (1906-10), then worked as a teacher and orchestral violinist before going to Paris in 1923. There he studied with Roussel and developed a neo-classical style, sometimes using jazz (La bagarre, 1926; Le jazz, 1928, both for orchestra). He began to apply himself to Czech subjects (ballet S˘palícek, 1933; operas The Miracles of Mary, 1935, Comedy on the Bridge, 1937; Field Mass for male voices, wind and percussion,1939), but not exclusively: this was also the period of his fantasy opera Julietta (1938) and of numerous concertos. In 1940 he left Paris, and the next year arrived in New York, where he began to concentrated on orchestral and chamber works, including his first five symphonies. From 1948 his life was divided between Europe and the USA: this was the period of his Sixth Symphony (1953), Frescoes of Piero della Francesca for orchestra (1955) and opera The Greek Passion (1961). He was one of the most prolific composers of the 20th century, imaginative in style, with energetic rhythms and powerful, often dissonant harmony, but uneven in quality.

GROVEmusic

Symphonies

Symphonies Nos 1 & 2
Bamberg Symphony Orchestra / Neeme Järvi
BIS CD362 (61' · DDD)   Ⓕ

Symphonies Nos 3 & 4
Bamberg Symphony Orchestra / Neeme Järvi
BIS CD363 (63' · DDD)   Ⓕ

Symphonies Nos 5 & 6
Bamberg Symphony Orchestra / Neeme Järvi
BIS CD402 (59' · DDD) Recorded 1988   ⒻO

Despite his travels throughout his formative years as a composer, Martinů remained a quintessentially Czech composer and his music is imbued with the melodic shapes and rhythms of the folk-music of his homeland. The six symphonies were written during Martinů's America years and in all of them he uses a large orchestra with distinctive groupings of instruments which give them a very personal and unmistakable timbre. The rhythmic verve of his highly synco-

Symphonies Nos 3 & 4
Czech Philharmonic Orchestra / Jiří Bělohlávek
Supraphon SU3631-2 (63' · DDD)   ⒻOO

This is Jiří Bělohlávek's third recording of Martinů's life-enhancing Fourth Symphony (1945) and his second with the Czech Philharmonic. Both these predecessors possess considerable merits but must now yield to this newcomer. Not only is the orchestral playing in the luxury class, but Bělohlávek's reading is as shapely as it's involving. He masterminds a selfless and unforced ccount of the Third (1944), an altogether more troubled work than its successor, and whose homesick undertow is potently realised here (the heartrending closing pages are precisely that). Bělohlávek's, too, is a meticulously prepared performance of compassion and insight that does justice to a riveting work. Throughout, the inimitable, silvery sonority of this great orchestra has been admirably captured by the Supraphon engineers.

Symphony No 4. Memorial to Lidice. Field Mass[a]
[a]Ivan Kusnjer *bar* Czech Philharmonic [a]Chorus and Orchestra / Jiří Bělohlávek
Chandos CHAN9138 (65' · DDD) Text and translation included   ⒻO

The luscious, intricately scored pages of the big-hearted Fourth Symphony sound opulent in this recording. For the most part, the playing is glorious, intoxicating in its richness and sure-footed poise. But there's some lack of intensity and temperament, so, for a more considered Bělohlávek account, look to his more recent Supraphon disc, reviewed above.

His performance of the *Field* Mass, on the other hand, is an undoubted success. It's wonderfully fervent, boasting a noble-toned, impassioned contribution from the baritone, Ivan Kusnjer, and disciplined, sonorous work from the men of the Czech Philharmonic Chorus. Chandos's recording captures it all to perfection: blend and focus impeccably combined. The moving *Memorial to Lidice* completes this ideally chosen triptych. Bearing a dedication 'To the Memory of the Innocent Victims of Lidice', Martinů's score was written in response to the destruction of that village by the Nazis in June 1942. One of the composer's most deeply felt creations, this is an eight-minute orchestral essay of slumbering power, incorporating at its climax a spine-chilling quotation from Beethoven's Fifth. It, too, receives sensitive advocacy here.

Chamber Works

Piano Quartet. Quartet for Oboe, Violin, Cello and Piano. Viola Sonata. String Quintet
Joel Marangella ob **Isabelle van Keulen, Charmian Gadd, Solomia Soroka** vns **Rainer Moog, Theodore Kuchar** va **Young-Chang Cho, Alexander Ivashkin** vcs
Daniel Adni, Kathryn Selby pfs
Naxos 8 553916 (73' · DDD) Recorded 1994 Ⓢ

The Quartet for oboe, violin, cello and piano is a highly attractive piece in the busy yet unfussy neo-classical style that Martinů made so much his own. Its opening theme is quite captivating, but all three movements have charm. The other music is hardly less delightful. The Viola Sonata is an eloquent work from the mid-1950s, composed three years after the *Rhapsody-Concerto* for the same instrument and orchestra. These were vintage years in Martinů's creativity. The String Quintet is the earliest work, dating from his Paris years, and shows the influence of Roussel. Although the first movement is perhaps not top-drawer Martinů, the slow movement is most imaginative. The performances are often touched with distinction and are never less than eminently serviceable. Adni could perhaps be a little more supple in the Piano Quartet of 1942 though in general he plays with spirit. There's plenty of air round the players and the recording is lifelike and well balanced.

Duo for Violin and Viola, H331. Duos for Violin and Cello – No 1, H157; No 2, H371. Three Madrigals. Piece for Two Cellos, H377. String Trio No 2, H238
Pavel Hula vn **Josef Kluson** va **Michal Kanka** vc
Praga Digitals PRD250 155 (68' · DDD) Ⓕ

It doesn't look promising: a whole disc of string duos and trios by a composer that even his warmest admirers admit was both over-prolific and uneven. Maybe it has something to do with the fact that Martinů was a string player himself, but the level of invention here is very high, and it often emerges in the forms of nervous, energetic *toccata* and folk-rooted lyricism that those admirers will recognise as 'real Martinů'. The *Three Madrigals*, for the apparently austere combination of violin and viola, in fact combine both those veins with such a sheer enjoyment of virtuoso string technique that you'll be convinced that at least four players are involved. In the central movement an archetypal Martinů melody blissfully emerges from clouds of trills and double stopping, while in the third he delightfully manages to suggest that Domenico

Scarlatti was very probably born in Moravia.

There are pleasures like those in most of the movements here. Martinů quite often, notably in his only surviving String Trio, rewards his players for negotiating his energetic toccatas with brilliant but never merely showy cadenzas, and these fine players respond with ample tone and real sympathy for his idiom and for the touching nostalgia that often underlies it. The recording is satisfyingly full. Warmly recommended.

Works for Violin and Piano, Volumes 1 & 2
Volume 1: Sonatas – C, H120; D minor, H152; No 1, H182. Concerto, H13. Elegy, H3. Impromptu, H166. Five Short Pieces, H184.
Volume 2: Sonatas – No 2, H208; No 3, H303. Sonatina, H262. Seven Arabesques, H201. Ariette-Vocalise, H188a. Czech Rhapsody, H307. Sept études rythmiques, H202. Intermezzo, H261. Five Madrigal Stanzas, H297
Bohuslav Matoušek vn **Petr Adamec** pf
Supraphon ② SU3412-2 (121' & 111' · DDD) ⒻⓄ

A handsome gathering of all 16 of Martinů's compositions for violin and piano. Supraphon's decision to present the music in more or less chronological order makes it all the easier to chart a fascinating stylistic journey spanning some 36 years. The 19-year-old Martinů wrote his impassioned *Elegy* in 1909, and the comparatively straightforward violin writing contrasts dramatically with the piano's big-boned, unashamedly dramatic contribution. Strangely, the following year's Concerto proves to be anything but. Indeed, one wonders whether its title was a leg-pull on the young composer's part, for its 27-minute progress totally eschews any ostentatious display in favour of a sunny simplicity and open-hearted playfulness. With the ambitious Sonata in C from 1919, we encounter an increasing confidence and fluency, though there's still little sign of the composer's mature voice.

Volume 2 kicks off with the winsome *bonne-bouche* of 1930, the *Ariette-Vocalise*, while the following year saw the creation of the concise and poised Second Violin Sonata. The 1937 *Sonatina* radiates a treasurable serenity and joy. Composed in New York during 1943, the *Five Madrigal Stanzas* bear an inscription to a certain amateur violinist by the name of Professor Albert Einstein.

The more meaty Third Sonata, written towards the end of 1944, possesses a pungent emotional scope that relates it to his Symphonies Nos 3-5 from the same period. Matoušek and Adamec form a consistently stylish partnership, and the recordings are rich and airy to match. A truly notable achievement.

Piano Sonata

Bagatelle, H323. Dumka No 3, H285bis. Fantasie a toccata, H281. The Fifth Day of the Fifth Moon,

H318. Piano Sonata, H350. Eight Préludes, H181
Eleonora Bekova *pf*
Chandos CHAN9655 (60' · DDD)   Ⓕ

Martinů hardly wrote the sort of music where every note is worth its weight in gold. Criticised for his failure to sense that 'all kinds of heterogeneous elements mixed together do not constitute an independent style', he unsettlingly reminds you of an actor happiest when adopting a wide variety of masks but uncomfortable when compelled to be himself. Yet the powerful Sonata and *Fantasie a toccata* show that Martinů was capable of a genuine eloquence and stature beyond a merely elegant and impersonal expertise. As Graham Melville-Mason tells us in his notes, the Sonata was much admired by Rudolf Serkin, who programmed it alongside Beethoven's *Hammerklavier* Sonata.

Eleonora Bekova's performances show a uniform and unswerving command. Her full-blooded sonority and technique proclaim her Moscow training and, musically enriched by her success in chamber music, she makes light of every difficulty. Whether in chic Parisian asides directed at jazz and ragtime (the First and Second *Préludes*), in the greater weight and substance of the Sonata (which has, perhaps surprisingly, failed to enter the mainstream repertoire beside the sonatas of, say, Copland, Janáček, Barber and Dutilleux, for example) or in a garland of encores including the perky *Bagatelle*, her performances are exemplary. Chandos's excellent sound, too, makes this a prime issue.

Steve Martland   British b1959

Martland studied at Liverpool University, then with Louis Andriessen at the Hague Conservatory. Though he later followed his teacher's example in rejecting the orchestra on social grounds (he is a very political animal), an early work includes the large-scale orchestral Babi Yar (1983); works typical of his later style – Principia (1989) and Dance Works (1993) – are written for amplified, wind-dominated ensembles. More recently, The Steve Martland Band has become the principal exponent of his work (from 1992).   GROVEmusic

Horses of Instruction

Horses of Instruction. Kick. Beat the Retreat. Mr Anderson's Pavane. Principia. Thistle of Scotland. Eternal Delight. Re-Mix. Terminal
The Steve Martland Band
Black Box BBM1033 (70' · DDD)   Ⓕ**o**

This is a superb disc, an indispensable guide to Steve Martland's music and a showpiece for his marvellous band. There's playing of such virtuosity that it beggars belief, particularly in *Beat the Retreat* and *Terminal*. The title-work, *Horses of Instruction*, is one of those pieces that never

fails to arouse a sense of eager anticipation that you're about to hear something truly pleasurable, a feeling that you might expect for *Four Last Songs* but one that's all too rare for contemporary music. The band play the piece unconducted, and you sense it's become almost an emblem of their identity.

The composer writes movingly in the CD booklet text about his ensemble. He states that these recordings 'could not be achieved without the faith, commitment or, indeed, criticisms of a group of people whose individual and collective musicianship makes me humble'. In a sense, Martland is right to show humility. He writes music with a directness and single-mindedness that's both its greatest strength and a potential cause of exasperation for the unconvinced listener. You hear the joins in his music and when they don't work, there's no hiding place.

What's special about the Steve Martland Band is the extent to which individual members assert ownership over the music, something symbolised by the aforementioned unconducted performance of *Horses of Instruction*. Take for instance *Re-Mix*, a transcription of viol music by Marin Marais. It's always seemed a rather shoddy piece of work on Martland's part, but the performance here, replete with klezmer-like yowling from the saxes and braying brass, is quite simply a *tour de force*. The same could be said for the exceptional rhythm guitar and soprano sax playing which so beguiles the ear in *Terminal*, a work originally composed for the rock band Spiritualized.

This recording recaptures the energy of the Steve Martland Band's performance at the Queen Elizabeth Hall in 1997, which was quite simply one of the best concerts ever.

Giuseppe Martucci   Italian 1856-1909

Martucci studied at the Naples Conservatory. As a touring piano virtuoso, he won praise from Liszt and Anton Rubinstein in 1874, but from 1880-81 was professor of the piano (in 1902, director) at the Naples Conservatory. He was an enthusiastic conductor of the German (sometimes English and French) repertory in Naples and Bologna, where he was director of the Liceo Musicale (1886-1902). Besides piano music, he composed distinctive chamber works, often Schumannesque or Elgarian in their gentle lyricism and caprice (eg the popular Notturno, Op70 No 1, and Novelletta, Op 82 No 2); his attractive Second Symphony has been called 'the starting point of the renaissance of non-operatic Italian music'.   GROVEmusic

Nocturne

Martucci Nocturne, Op 70 No 1. La canzone dei ricordi **Respighi** Il tramonto
Brigitte Balleys *mez* **Lausanne Chamber Orchestra / Jésus López-Cobos**
Claves CD50-9807 (51' · DDD)   Ⓜ

Martucci, once director of conservatoires in both Bologna and Naples, and conductor of the first performance in Italy of *Tristan*, is a curious case of a composer totally unfamiliar to the UK's concert life but surprisingly well represented on disc. His warmly nostalgic and tender *Nocturne* would make a worthy alternative to the Mahler *Adagietto* or Barber's overplayed *Adagio*; and the seven poems of his elegiac cycle, *La canzone dei ricordi* are haunting examples of a refined Italian lyricism a world away from his contemporary, Puccini. The setting of Shelley's *Il tramonto* by Martucci's pupil Respighi is suitably poignant but more lush in texture.

The admirable Brigitte Balleys sings with her accustomed artistry, but from time to time her voice 'catches' the mike: the playing of the Lausanne Chamber Orchestra is seductively affectionate.

Pietro Mascagni   Italian 1863-1945

Mascagni studied with Ponchielli and Saladino at the Milan Conservatory (1882-4), then worked as a touring conductor and wrote Guglielmo Ratcliff (c1855). His next opera was the one-act Cavalleria rusticana, which was staged in Rome in 1890 and won him immediate international acclaim: it effectively established the vogue for verismo. None of his later operas was anything like so successful, though some numbers from L'amico Fritz (1891) and the oriental Iris (1898) have survived in the repertory. Later works include the comedy Le maschere (1901), the unexpectedly powerful Il piccolo Marat (1921) and Nerone (1935), this last testifying to his identification with fascism. GROVEmusic

Cavalleria rusticana

Cavalleria rusticana
Renata Scotto *sop* Santuzza **Plácido Domingo** *ten* Turiddu **Pablo Elvira** *bar* Alfio **Isola Jones** *mez* Lola **Jean Kraft** *mez* Lucia **Ambrosian Opera Chorus; National Philharmonic Orchestra / James Levine**
RCA Red Seal 74321 39500-2 (71' · ADD) Recorded 1978. Notes, text and translation included   Ⓕ Ⓞ

This was a strong contender in an overcrowded field when it was first released. You'd be hard pressed to find either a more positive or a more intelligent Turiddu or Santuzza than Domingo or Scotto. Scotto manages to steer a precise course between being too ladylike or too melodramatic. She suggests all the remorse and sorrow of Santuzza's situation without resorting to self-pity. Her appeals to Turiddu to reform could hardly be more sincere and heartfelt, her throbbing delivery to Alfio, 'Turiddi mi tolse l'honore', expresses all her desperation when forced to betray her erstwhile lover, and her curse on Turiddu, 'A te la mala pasqua', while not resorting to the lowdown vigour of some of her rivals, is filled with venom. Domingo proved how committed he was to his role when

the part was first given to him at Covent Garden in the mid-1970s. He gives an almost Caruso-like bite and attack to Turiddu's defiance and (later) remorse, and finds a more appropriate timbre than Bergonzi (for Karajan, reviewed under Leoncavallo). He also delivers the Brindisi with an appropriately carefree manner, oblivious of the challenge awaiting him. Pablo Elvira's Alfio is no more than adequate, and the other American support is indifferent.

Levine's direction, as positive as Karajan's, is yet quite different. He goes much faster, and time and again catches the passion if not always the delicacy of Mascagni's score. He's well supported by the superb National Philharmonic Orchestra. With a bright and forward recording, this reading of the work is wholly arresting.

Cavalleria rusticana
Nelly Miricioiu *sop* Santuzza **Dennis O'Neill** *ten* Turiddu **Phillip Joll** *bar* Alfio **Diana Montague** *mez* Lola **Elizabeth Bainbridge** *mez* Lucia **Geoffrey Mitchell Choir; London Philharmonic Orchestra / David Parry**
Chandos Opera in English CHAN3004 (79' · DDD) Sung in English. Notes and text included   Ⓕ

One of the most magical beginnings in opera is beautifully played here, and at this early stage you aren't getting restive over the slow speeds. Dennis O'Neill sings his *siciliana* like a lover, with touches of an imaginative tenderness that are rare unique in this music. His voice distances effectively, and very effective too is the mingling of the church bells with the singing of the off-stage chorus. Santuzza, Nelly Miricioiu, must have been born in another village, but that doesn't matter; her voice has some raw patches but that also troubles less than it might, as she brings such concentrated feeling to the part. On the other hand, when Alfio arrives you can't go on saying it doesn't matter: it does. We want a vibrant Italianate voice if possible, and a firm one at least. Elizabeth Bainbridge is a vivid Mamma Lucia, but Diana Montague, immensely welcome as a singer, has quite the wrong voice-character for Lola, who should be either the local Carmen or a shallow, pert flirt. Still, for those collecting Chandos's Opera in English series this isn't to be missed. The drama keeps its hold, the grand old melodies surge, the score reveals more of its inspired detail, and the English language does itself worthwhile credit.

Jules Massenet   French 1842-1912

Massenet entered the Conservatoire at the age of 11 as a piano pupil of Adolphe Laurent. He later studied harmony with Reber and composition with Ambroise Thomas, winning the Prix de Rome in 1863. In Rome he got to know Liszt and, through him, Constance de Sainte Marie, who became his pupil and, in 1866, his wife. The following year his opera La 'grand'tante was given at the Opéra-Comique, and in1873 Marie-Magdeleine at the Théâtre de l'Odéon initiated a series of drames sacrés based on female biblical characters. Many of his secular operas, too, are in effect portraits of women.

In 1878 Massenet was made a teacher of composition at the Conservatoire, where he remained all his life, influencing many younger French composers, including Charpentier, Koechlin, Pierné and Hahn. In his own music he began to move away from the suave, sentimental melodic style derived from Gounod and to adopt a more Wagnerian type of lyrical declamation. The change is apparent in Manon (1884), which placed Massenet in the forefront of French opera composers, and still more in Werther (1892). But as early as 1877, in Hérodiade, Massenet had begun to modify the symmetry and loosen the syntax of his melodies to give them a more speaking, intimate, conversational character. Repetitions are usually masked or transferred to the orchestra while the voice takes a lyrical recitative line in the Wagnerian manner; literal repetitions are carefully calculated to provide an insistent, emotional quality. Often his melodies have a swaying, hesitant character. By Werther, the relationship of voice and orchestra is more sophisticated, and that opera contains clear examples of Massenet's dissolution of formal melody into rhapsodic recitative-like writing as evolved by Wagner. Massenet's music is harmonically conservative, rarely venturing beyond modest chromaticisms; rhythmically, it is original in the variations he uses to give the melody a more caressing, intimate character. He had a characteristically French ear for orchestral nuance. Though primarily a lyrical composer, he was also a master of scenes of action, as for example at the opening of Manon.

After Sapho (1897) Massenet scored few major successes. His conception of opera became outdated long before his death and his position as France's leading opera composer was finally challenged when Debussy's Pelléas et Mélisande was given at the Opéra-Comique in 1902. **GROVE**music

Ballet music

Massenet Le Cid. Scènes pittoresques. La vierge – le dernier sommeil de la vierge. **Saint-Saëns** Wedding Cake
City of Birmingham Symphony Orchestra / Louis Frémaux
EMI Encore 575871-2 (72' · ADD) Recorded c1971
Ⓑ⚫

Frémaux's Massenet collection provides most enjoyable listening. This is highly tuneful music, and it's directed with appropriate vigour and refinement as the individual numbers require. The ballet music from *Le Cid* is full of the authentic rhythms of Spain, and there's real excitement in such numbers as the 'Aragonaise', where the members of the CBSO respond most admirably to Frémaux's demands for dynamic variation and instrumental shading. At the quieter end of the spectrum, the delightful 'Madrilène', with its solos for cor anglais and flute, is most charmingly done. Similar sensitivity is shown throughout the contrasted *Scènes pittoresques*. The further inclusion of the 'Last

Sleep of the Virgin' – once a Beecham lollipop – was an inspired idea. The recorded sound throughout is spacious and well balanced.

Arias

Amoureuse: Sacred and Profane Arias
La Grand' Tante – Je vais bientôt quitter. **Marie Magdeleine** – O mes soeurs. **Eve** – O nuit.
La Vierge – O mon fils; Rêve infini. **Hérodiade** – Il est doux, il est bon. **Le Cid** – Plus de tourments; Pleurez mes yeux. **Sapho** – Ce que j'appelle beau; Solitude-demain, je partirai; Vais-je rester ici? **Grisélidis** – Loÿs! Loÿs! **Chérubin** – Vous parlez de péril. **Ariane** – Avec tes compagnes guerrières; Je comprends un héros! Un roi; Ils mentaient! A quoi bon. **Songs** – Sainte Thérèse prie; Amoureuse
Rosamund Illing sop **Australian Opera and Ballet Orchestra / Richard Bonynge**
Melba Recordings 301080 (75' · DDD) Notes, texts and translations included Ⓕ

Most of the items here are rarities, some unpublished, all attractive. The performances are excellent: Rosamund Illing is a soprano well-known over here, but never heard on records to better advantage, and Richard Bonynge's convinced advocacy and feeling for style constitute another guarantee of value. To this should be added a proviso. Everything is tuneful in the grand, late 19th-century understanding of the word; but everything is also rather sweet on the palate. Still, for anyone in the least interested it's not a record to miss.

Among the operas, *Sapho* will still be unfamiliar to most, and *Ariane* to practically all. The three excerpts here are arias for Ariadne herself, and include the final pages with the call of the Sirens and a hauntingly plaintive B minor melody for the dying heroine, who descends into the sea holding a high A natural of heavenly softness, firm to the end.

These roles were written for a diverse range of singers, but the Australian soprano adapts easily and, except on a few slightly worn *fortissimo* high notes, sings most beautifully. The orchestra is recorded with vivid immediacy and makes the most of Massenet's imaginative scoring. One for the shopping list.

Massenet: Le Cid – Ah! tout est bien fini... O souverain. **Grisélidis** – Je suis l'oiseau. **Le Mage** – Ah! Parais ! Parais, astre de mon ciel[b]. **Manon** – Enfin, Manon... En fermant les yeux[a]; Je suis seul!... Ah! fuyez, douce image. **Le Roi de Lahore** – Voix qui me remplissez d'une innefable ivresse. **Roma** – Je vais la voir! Tout mon être frémit[b]. **Werther** – Lorsque l'enfant revient d'un voyage; Ah! bien souvent mon rêve s'envole... Pourquoi me réveiller **Gounod: Faust** – Quel trouble inconnu me pénètre!; Salut, demeure chaste et pure. **Mireille** – Mon cœur est plein d'un noir souci!; Anges du paradis. **Polyeucte** – Stances: Source délicieuse. **La Reine de Saba** – Inspirez-moi, race divine. **Roméo et Juliette** – L'amour! l'amour; Salut! tombeau sombre

Rolando Villazón ten with [a]**Natalie Dessay** sop
French Radio [b]**Chorus and Philharmonic**
Orchestra / Evelino Pidò
Virgin Classics 545719-2 (67' · DDD · T/t) Ⓕ**OO**

This is mostly well-planned and executed recital
mixes favourites with extracts from operas that
have remained rarities, even with the increased
interest in late 19th-century repertory. It begins
with Rodrigue's great prayer, 'O souverain'
from Act 3 of *Le Cid*. Rolando Villazón sings
this with an attractive quiet introspection to
start with, but then there is metal and passion in
his voice for the climax. Of the other well-
known Massenet items, it's good to hear
Werther's 'Lorsque l'enfant' as well as the
show-stopping 'Pourquoi me réveiller?'. In 'En
fermant les yeux' from *Manon*, Natalie Dessay
provides Manon's brief phrases, and Villazón
makes a really sensitive dreamer. 'Ah, fuyez'
goes well too, but it will be the arias from *Roma*,
Grisélidis and *Le Mage* that will attract most listeners. In all Massenet's output is there a more
seductive tune than the one that forms the centre of the *Roma* scene, 'Soir admirable'? This is
done very well by Warren Mok in the complete
recording, but Villazón outshines him.

Of the Gounod arias, Faust's 'Salut demeure'
fares the best, but again it will be the extracts
from *Polyeucte* and *La Reine de Saba* that will
please immediately.

Villazón has established himself as one of the
most promising among the new generation of
tenors. His French has improved recently, but
there is the odd difficulty still with certain vowels. Accompaniment, recording and presentation are first-rate.

Hérodiade

Hérodiade
Nadine Denize mez Hérodiade **Cheryl Studer** sop
Salomé **Ben Heppner** ten Jean **Thomas Hampson**
bar Hérode **José van Dam** bass-bar Phanuel **Marcel**
Vanaud bar Vitellius **Jean-Philippe Courtis** bass High
Priest **Martine Olmeda** mez Young Babylonian
Jean-Paul Fouchécourt ten Voice in the Temple
Toulouse Capitole Chorus and Orchestra / Michel
Plasson
EMI ③ 555378-2 (166' · DDD) Recorded 1994 Notes,
text and translation included Ⓕ**O**

Written in 1880, *Hérodiade* is typical of the early
grand operas with which Massenet courted popularity. It offers five magnificent roles to singers
who have the wherewithal to make the most of
them, with some glorious show-pieces which
are – as always with Massenet – gratefully written for the voice.

Michel Plasson conducts the opera uncut and
has the advantage of a good studio recording.
He's not one for taking an objective view of the
music and there are times when he rushes fre-
netically ahead, as if he's as possessed by the
lurid goings-on in the drama as the characters
on stage. The sense of atmosphere is palpable.

In Plasson's hands the heavy chords at the opening of Act 3 resound with a potent mysticism
that presages Klingsor's castle (Massenet knew
his Wagner too). In fact, we're at the dwelling of
Phanuel the sorcerer, a less threatening proposition. José van Dam is marvellous in this big
solo, leaning on the opening words of 'Dors, ô
cité perverse' with a sinister gleam in his voice
that sends shivers down your back. Silvery pure
in tone, Studer's Salomé throws herself into the
drama with lustful abandon and Heppner
phrases the music with remarkable breadth and
seems to have heroic top notes to spare.

Manon

Massenet Manon[a] **Berlioz** Les nuits d'été, Op 7[b] Ⓗ
Debussy La damoiselle élue[c]
Victoria de los Angeles sop Manon [c]**Carol Smith**
mez [a]**Henri Legay** ten Des Grieux [a]**Michel Dens**
bar Lescaut [a]**Jean Borthayre** bass Comte des
Grieux [a]**Jean Vieuille** bar De Brétigny [a]**René**
Hérent ten Guillot [a]**Liliane Berton** sop Poussette
[a]**Raymonde Notti** sop Javotte [a]**Marthe Serres** sop
Rosette [c]**Radcliffe Choral Society; Boston**
Symphony Orchestra / Charles Munch; [a]**Opéra-**
Comique Choir and Orchestra / Pierre Monteux
Testament mono ③ SBT3203 (213' · ADD)
Recorded in 1955. Texts and translations included
Ⓕ**OO**

As EMI now has its highly praised new set of
Manon with Gheorghiu and Alagna, it has fallen
to Testament to bring back this earlier HMV
set. Compared to its previous CD release, the
sound here has been carefully restored with
greatly reduced hiss, a less wiry treble and
firmer bass – a successful facelift for a *Manon*
who no longer sounds her age.

Recorded in mono in 1955, the set fell at a
unique point in the opera's history on disc. Previous recordings from the 78rpm era had captured the special Opéra-Comique spirit for posterity, but they hold limited sonic appeal to
present-day collectors; later recordings have
up-to-date sound, but their international casts
generally can't claim the same sense of style.
Only with this 1955 set do we get the best of
both worlds.

Already at the time a practised exponent of
Manon on stage, de los Angeles makes a vivid
heroine, allowing us to *see* every expression
passing across her face, almost as if we were
watching a video. Maybe the role lies a little
high for her, but de los Angeles surprised herself
on the day of recording by hitting the high D in
the Cours-la-Reine scene. Monteux's skill in his
native French repertoire is second to none, and
he brings exemplary sparkle to the music. ↑It
would be possible to find fault with various
members of the supporting cast, but that's to
miss the point. They sing with a grace and wit
that nobody from outside the Opéra-Comique
tradition can replicate easily. Henri Legay did
not have a great tenor voice, but the poetry and
the passion of Des Grieux come as second
nature to him. Michel Dens' lively Lescaut and

Jean Borthayre's serious Comte des Grieux are no less idiomatic; and the delectably perfumed Guillot of René Hérent is a collector's item in the best sense of the term, as he had been singing this role with the company since his début in 1918.

There's now a clear choice between this reissue and EMI's fine new Pappano set. Opera collectors will probably want both.

Manon
Angela Gheorghiu sop Manon; **Roberto Alagna**
ten Des Grieux; **Earle Patriarco** bar Lescaut; **José van Dam** bass-bar Comte des Grieux; **Nicolas Rivenq** bar De Brétigny; **Gilles Ragon** ten Guillot; **Anna Maria Panzarella** sop Poussette; **Sophie Koch** mez Javotte; **Susanne Schimmack** mez Rosette; **Nicolas Cavallier** bar Innkeeper; **Chorus and Symphony Orchestra of La Monnaie / Antonio Pappano**
EMI ③ 557005-2 (163' · DDD) Notes, text and translation included Ⓕ**OOO**

 EMI has had the good sense to build this set around Pappano's own company at La Monnaie, a Francophone group of singers who give an authentic flavour that non-French-speakers can't hope to match. The piece is given absolutely complete, including the splendidly played ballet.

Nothing of the myriad character of Massenet's popular work escapes Pappano's eye and ear. He has a near-perfect idea of how to pace the score and he persuades his orchestra and chorus to play and sing with the utmost respect for pertinent detail, so important in Massenet, and to follow, as do the soloists, the many expressive markings demanded by the composer.

Gheorghiu's is a Manon to savour in practically every respect. Suitably coquettish in her first solo, she turns ruminative, plangent for her second, 'Voyons, Manon'. The farewell to her little table is inward and pensive, tone subtly shaded with the 'larmes dans la voix' so admired in native French singers. To the Gavotte and the recitative preceding it, Gheorghiu brings the outward aplomb and, in the second verse, the hint of sadness required. The prayer at St Sulpice has all the urgency and the sense of apprehension as to how Des Grieux, now a servant of the church, will respond to her. Throughout these solos, Gheorghiu prudently follows Massenet's scrupulous instructions as to dynamics and phrasing with unforgettable results, not to mention the sheer glory of her singing, outclassing her compatriot, the sensitive Ileana Cotrubas, who recorded the role for Plasson too late in her career.

If Alagna doesn't quite equal his wife's example, he's an ardent, French-sounding Des Grieux, always suggesting the Chevalier's obsessive love for his 'Sphinx étonnant'. The Dream, finely phrased as it is, hasn't quite the individuality that Ansseau, Heddle Nash (in the famous pre-war broadcast now on Dutton) or

Gedda and others, brought to it, mainly because his tone has become a shade occluded. At St Sulpice, it rings out more truly. 'Ah fuyez, douce image' begins in nicely reflective fashion and the B flat climaxes are suitably impassioned. In most respects he surpasses the ageing Kraus for Plasson, even when he isn't quite as elegant.

Earle Patriarco, a young American baritone, proves an excellent Lescaut, keen with the text and properly cynical in manner. Still better is José van Dam as Le Comte (he sang the part for Plasson), words shaped so meaningfully onto tone, his spoken contribution faultlessly timed.

All the smaller parts are enthusiastically taken, small decorations on a masterly interpretation. Given an exemplary recording for balance and presence, this set is about as good as you'll get today (or maybe any day) of this adorable piece.

Many will have an affection for the 1956 EMI set with Victoria de los Angeles's *nonpareil* of a Manon and Monteux as her elegant conductor, but the work is cut, the recording is dated. This new version is the one to introduce a new generation to a work of which Beecham declared: 'I would give up all the *Brandenburgs* for *Manon* and would think that I had profited by the exchange.'

Thaïs

Thaïs
Renée Fleming sop Thaïs; **Thomas Hampson** bar Athanaël; **Giuseppe Sabbatini** ten Nicias; **Estefano Palatchi** bass Palémon; **Marie Devellereau** sop Crobyle; **Isabelle Cals** mez Myrtale; **Enkelejda Shkosa** mez Albine; **Elisabeth Vidal** sop La Charmeuse; **David Grousset** bass Servant; **Bordeaux Opera Chorus; Bordeaux-Aquitaine National Orchestra / Yves Abel**
Decca ② 466 766-2DHO2 (147' · DDD) Text and translation included Ⓕ**OO**

At last – a modern recording of *Thaïs* with a soprano who can sing the title-role. All we need is a soprano with a fabulously beautiful voice, idiomatic French, a sensuous *legato*, pure high notes up to a stratospheric top D, and the ability to leave every listener weak at the knees. Where was the problem? Renée Fleming makes it all sound so easy. Her success a couple of years ago at the Opéra Bastille in Paris with Massenet's Manon showed that she has an affinity for this composer. As Thaïs, a role with a similar vocal profile, she proves equally well cast. Within minutes of her entrance it's clear that neither of the other sets from the last 25 years will be able to touch her. Fleming simply has a vocal class that puts her in a different league from the unsteady Beverly Sills on Maazel's EMI set or the outrageously voiceless Anna Moffo on the now long-forgotten set from RCA. There's just enough individuality in her singing to give Fleming's Thaïs a personality of her own, and vocal loveliness brings a bloom to her every scene.

The Athanaël she leaves behind is Thomas

Hampson, who is her match in sensitivity and roundness of tone. Their duet at the oasis in the desert is beautifully sung, every word clear, every phrase shaped with feeling. If only Hampson were equally good at getting beneath the skin of the operatic characters he plays. In the case of Athanaël there's plenty of psychological complexity down there to uncover, but Hampson seems unwilling to engage the character's dark side.

Occasionally, one regrets that Abel doesn't have the New Philharmonia at his disposal, as Maazel does, but the subtlety of colour and accent that he draws from the Orchestre National Bordeaux-Aquitaine are a world apart from Maazel's constant up-front aggression. The famous 'Méditation', elegantly played by the young French violinist Renaud Capuçon, and featuring swoony background chorus is a dream. Add in a first-class Decca recording and it will be clear that this new *Thaïs* has pretty well everything going for it.

Werther

Werther
José Carreras *ten* Werther **Frederica von Stade** *mez* Charlotte **Thomas Allen** *bar* Albert **Isobel Buchanan** *sop* Sophie **Robert Lloyd** *bass* Bailli **Malcolm King** *bass* Bailli's friend **Paul Crook** *ten* Bailli's friend **Linda Humphries** *sop* Kätchen **Donaldson Ball** *bar* Brühlmann **Royal Opera House Orchestra, Covent Garden; Children's Choir / Sir Colin Davis**
Philips Gramophone Awards Collection ② 475 4962 (131' · AAD/ADD) Recorded 1980. Notes, text and translation included ⓂOOO

The ebb and flow of word and music, the warm, tremulous life of the string playing, and the pacing of each *tableau vivant* is handled so superbly by Sir Colin Davis that there isn't a single moment of *longueur*. The Royal Opera House orchestra plays at its very best: the solo detail and the velocity of its every response to Massenet's flickering orchestral palette operates as though with heightened awareness under the scrutiny of the laser beam. The casting polarizes this Werther and Charlotte. José Carreras is very much a Werther of action rather than of dream, of impetuous self-destruction rather than of brooding lyricism. The *élan* he brings to lines like 'Rêve! Rêve! Extase! Bonheur!' is more impressive than the conjuring of 'l'air d'un paradis', where the voice can be over-driven at the top. So far as style, line and inflection are concerned, Frederica von Stade's performance can hardly be faulted. Her voice is the very incarnation of Charlotte's essential simplicity of character; but there are times when one could perhaps wish for a darker *tinta* to find the shadows in the role, and to bring a greater sense of the undercurrent of emotional conflict as it grows towards the last two acts. Thomas Allen finds unusual breadth in this Albert, noting the slightest giveaway flutter in the line: when he sings 'j'en ai tant au fond du

coeur' one does actually begin to believe that there may be depths there of which one is too often kept ignorant. Isobel Buchanan's is a small-scale and a straightforward Sophie, a real 'oiseau d'aurore'.

Werther
Patricia Petibon *sop* Sophie **Angela Gheorghiu** *mez* Charlotte **Roberto Alagna** *ten* Werther **Jean-Paul Fouchécourt** *ten* Schmidt **Thomas Hampson** *bar* Albert **Jean-Philippe Courtis** *bass* Magistrate **Jean-Marie Frémeau** *bass* Johann **London Symphony Orchestra / Antonio Pappano**
EMI ② 556820-2 (128' · DDD) Notes, text and translation included ⒻO

Alagna is the first French-speaking tenor to record the role for a long time and his diction throughout is clear and full of emotion. At the climax of his big aria, 'Pourquoi me reveiller?' in Act 3, he sings 'O souffle du printemps?' with a beautiful head tone. And he can't resist singing it full out the second time around – just as Alfredo Kraus and many others often did.

Whether or not Angela Gheorghiu would be suitably cast as Charlotte on stage, she makes a vivid impression on disc. The obvious comparisons with Gheorghiu are two other sopranos who have recorded the part, Ninon Vallin in the historic set under Cohen, and Victoria de los Angeles in the Prêtre version, itself now sounding close to historic. But both Vallin and de los Angeles were also Carmens – on disc at least – and both sound more mature as characters than Gheorghiu does.

The sound on this new recording is fine, the conducting of Pappano taut and passionate. But, oh dear, what a lot of recordings of Werther there are now to choose from. The historic Cohen is probably the most completely satisfying version. Not everyone, however, wants to listen to historic mono. Amongst the new Werthers the Pappano scores mostly because of Alagna's heroic assumption of the title-role.

Werther
Jerry Hadley *ten* Werther **Anne Sofie von Otter** *mez* Charlotte **Gérard Théruel** *bar* Albert **Dawn Upshaw** *sop* Sophie **Jean-Marie Frémeau** *bar* Magistrate **Gilles Ragon** *ten* Schmidt, Brühlmann **Frédéric Caton** *bass* Johann **Geneviève Marchand** *sop* Kätchen **Chorus and Orchestra of the Opéra National de Lyon / Kent Nagano**
Erato ② 0630-17790-2 (121' · DDD) Notes text and translation included Ⓜ

The opening scene of this recording promises very well; the orchestra certainly knows how to play Massenet, and Nagano avoids the extremes of quasi-*verismo* style that can mar this essay in masochistic, unrequited passion. Jerry Hadley suggests convincingly the impulsive, romantic young poet. As Charlotte, Anne Sofie von Otter has just the right balance between sounding young (she's meant to be 20) but emotionally mature. She and von Stade (Davis) are among the finest interpreters of the role. Dawn Upshaw makes a very positive, flirty Sophie and Gérard Théruel a good Albert. There's a grandeur about the Davis recording which this version doesn't quite attain. However, von Otter and Hadley sound every bit as dramatic, but in a more intimate, neurotic way.

Nicholas Maw   British 1935

Maw studied with Berkeley at the Royal Academy of Music (1955-8) and Boulanger and Deutsch in Paris (1958-9). He has taught in England and the USA. His music represents the extension of a solid tonal tradition, traceable back through Britten, Tippett, Bartók and Strauss, all influences on a style of fresh vigour. Among his works are two comic operas, One Man Show (1964) and The Rising of the Moon (1970), orchestral pieces and chamber music. His monumental orchestral work Odyssey was given in 1987. GROVEmusic

Violin Concerto

Violin Concerto
Joshua Bell vn
London Philharmonic Orchestra / Sir Roger Norrington
Sony Classical SK62856 (42' · DDD)   Ⓕ**O**

For over a quarter of a century Maw has been investigating lines of musical development that were left dangling when modernism cut them. He's not so much writing 'neo-Brahms' or 'neo-Strauss' as exploring the enticing paths that they opened up, but which post-Schoenbergians have not pursued. The enormous orchestral *Odyssey* that he began in the early 1970s (impressively recorded by Sir Simon Rattle and the City of Birmingham Symphony Orchestra on EMI) has had many satellites and successors, but the roots of his mature style have never been clearer than in this concerto, written for a virtuoso of the most archetypally romantic instrument of them all. It's a concerto that Joseph Joachim would have loved as much as Joshua Bell so evidently does. Full of warmly eloquent melody, the concerto is fundamentally lyrical in all four of its movements, but there's vital energy too, plentiful opportunity for sparkling virtuosity, many beautifully expressive orchestral solos and, in the *Scherzo* and finale especially, magnificently rich multi-layered climaxes. The performance is remarkably fine, the recording clean but not clinical. A violin concerto for all who love the violin and its music.

Hymnus

Hymnus[a]. Little Concert[b]. Shahnama[b]
[a]**Oxford Bach Choir**; [a]**BBC Concert Orchestra**,
[b]**Britten Sinfonia / Nicholas Cleobury**

ASV CDDCA1070 (74' · DDD)   Ⓕ

Hymnus is firmly rooted in the tradition of large-scale English choral works, full of luminous harmonies, rich choral textures and fine, eminently singable lines. The music is compelling, accessible and distinctive and the choral writing clearly designed to be demanding yet well within the scope of a large amateur choral society. Maw wrote it in 1996 to mark the centenary of the 200-voice Oxford Bach Choir and, as it was intended primarily to display a large chorus, there are no solo parts and the orchestral accompaniment is relatively discreet. The net result of this is that the choir has virtually no respite throughout the work's 33-minute duration, which probably accounts for the sense of tiredness and strain that permeates this recording. Climaxes (and there are a great many of those in the work) appear to overstretch the choir while the gentler passages fail to exhibit the kind of precision and polish which characterises the choir's live performances. The BBC Concert Orchestra also seems to lack that final polish, but much of this may well be attributed to a strangely boxy and claustrophobic recording. It's a splendid work and there are some worthy performers, all of which deserve rather better than this.

The other two works on the disc more than compensate for any shortcomings to be found in *Hymnus*. Nicholas Daniel produces an amazing range of moods and colours – from the exquisitely lyrical to the robustly athletic – in the *Little Concert* for oboe, two horns and strings, while the atmospheric and evocative *Shahnama*, nine brief movements inspired by an 11th-century Persian epic, is beautifully captured in Nicholas Cleobury's nicely spaced and tautly directed performance.

La vita nuova

Ghost Dances. La vita nuova. Roman Canticle
Carmen Pelton sop **William Sharp** bar
Twentieth Century Consort / Christopher Kendall
ASV CDDCA999 (65' · DDD) Texts and translations included   Ⓕ

Maw's originality may not be the kind that leaps up and yells in your face; but original he certainly is. He can draw on influences as diverse as Britten and Richard Strauss in *La Vita Nuova*, blend elements of Schoenberg's *Pierrot* and Stravinsky's *Petrushka* with the sounds of Latin American and African folk instruments in *Ghost Dances*, and still come up with something that feels like nobody else. The sound of the soprano's sultry tonal phrases in *La Vita Nuova* is a long way from the eerie tone of the African Kalimba at the end of *Ghost Dances* – beautifully described by Malcolm MacDonald in his notes as 'like a phantom piano played with a bony finger'. And yet in context they're obviously the same composer: a romantic with a fertile imagination and a superb technical palate, who clearly delights in enticing and surprising the ear. The performances are of outstanding warmth and finesse. The sound world of *La Vita Nuova* emerges with such richness and depth that it's hard to believe that only 10 instruments are playing and Carmen Pelton has a strong sense of the way the vocal lines soar and dip over long periods. William Sharp is eloquent and quite distinct throughout the short *Roman Canticle*. And everything in *Ghost Dances* seems as clear as it should be, with no loss of atmosphere – an excellent recording. It adds up to a perfect introduction to a composer who offers genuine, long-term rewards, not instant, transient gratification.

Billy Mayerl
British 1902-1959

Mayerl studied in the junior department of Trinity College of Music (1914-19) and worked as a pianist for silent filme and in hotel bands playing American popular music. His first composition Egyptian Suite was published in 1919. In 1921 he joined Bert Ralton's band (later called the Savoy Havana Band) which regularly broadcast in the early years of the BBC. In 1926 he left that band for the music hall and founded his own school of music which pioneered teaching by post, using records. With Nippy (1930) his career moved to music theatre and he composed and directed several musical comedies which were successful at the time. He was a regular broadcaster before World War Two but the War marked the end of his celebrity. He continued as a performer despite ill health and was editor of The Light Music Magazine (1957-8). GROVEmusic

Piano Works

Mayerl Crystal Clear. Orange Blossom. Piano Exaggerations. Pastorale Exotique. Wistaria. Canaries' Serenade. Shy Ballerina. Puppets Suite, Op 77. Piano Transcriptions – Body and Soul; Deep Henderson; Tormented; Sing, you sinners; Cheer up; Have you forgotten?; The object of my affection; Is it true what they say about Dixie?; I need you; Love was born; I'm at your service **Parkin** Mayerl Shots, Sets 1 & 2. A Tribute to Billy Mayerl
Eric Parkin pf
Priory PRCD544 (80' · DDD)　　　　　Ⓕ

Nobody since the master himself has come anywhere near Parkin's easy technical mastery and fastidious musicianship in this delightful music. Some pianists hit the more demanding pieces quite hard: Parkin, like Mayerl, knows better and his playing is consistently light and subtle. This has always been his approach, allied to a faultless sense of pace and rhythm. However, Mayerl, apart from perfecting the piano novelty, also contributed to the English pastoral tradition, which Parkin knows equally well. *Shy Ballerina* is charmingly done with *rubato* which would be quite out of place in Mayerl's numbers. The three-movement *Puppets Suite* is a *tour de force*.

As a bonus Parkin adds two sets of his own

pieces called *Mayerl Shots*. He explains that, as a result of practising lots of Mayerl, further ideas surfaced spontaneously in a similar idiom. These are all fluent tributes and there are even quotations for the specialists. The piano sound is sharp and clear. Essential listening.

Mayerl Scallywag. Jasmine. Oriental. Minuet for Pamela. Fascinating Ditty. Funny Peculiar. Chopsticks. Carminetta. Mignonette. Penny Whistle. Piano Transcriptions – Me and my girl; Blue velvet; Sittin' on the edge of my chair; The pompous gremlin; My heaven in the pines; Alabamy bound; Stardust; Please handle with care; Two lovely people; Two hearts on a tree; You're the reason why. Studies in Syncopation, Op 55 – Nos 7, 10, 14, 15 & 18
Parkin Mayerl Shots, Set 3
Eric Parkin pf
Priory PRCD565 (76' · DDD)　　　　　Ⓕ

This release, 'Scallywag', has its own discoveries, notably the *Studies in Syncopation*, which parallel Bartók's *Mikrokosmos* in this field. There are three books of six pieces each, dating from 1930-31, and Parkin plays five of them, proving that they aren't just exercises but real music. There are gems in the transcriptions – Carmichael's *Stardust*, Mayerl's own 'You're the reason why' from his 1934 show *Sporting Love*, and a forgotten but lovely tune by Peter York called *Two hearts on a tree*. The Spanish *Carminetta* is Mayerl's equivalent of Joplin's *Solace*. And there's real comedy – totally appreciated and effectively realised by Parkin – in *Chopsticks* and *Penny Whistle*.

In addition, Eric Parkin gives us his own response to Mayerl in a similar idiom – a third set of his *Mayerl Shots*. The recording is adequate although there's occasionally some background noise.

Piano Transcriptions

Piano Transcriptions, Volume 3

There's a small hotel; The mood that I'm in; So rare; I'm always in the mood for you; Turkey in the straw; For only you; Thanks for the memory; The Highland Swing; I got love; Amoresque; There's rain in my eyes; Patty cake, patty cake, baker man; Blame it on my last affair; I have eyes; Like a cat with a mouse; Phil the Fluter's Ball; Fools rush in; Peg o' my heart; All the things you are; The Musical Earwig; Transatlantic Lullaby; Tell me I'm forgiven; Japanese Juggler; Poor little rich girl
Eric Parkin pf
Priory PRCD468 (63' · DDD) Recorded 1993　　Ⓕ

This is pure 1930s music. This isn't Mayerl as the lightning-fingered whizz-kid of the 1920s, although many of the transcriptions are tricky enough: it's the style he taught through the Billy Mayerl School of Music, a success story here and abroad until the war. These transcriptions – popular songs of the period arranged in Mayerl's inimitable English accent – are a wonderful encapsulation of an era and they transcend it – as long as they're played like this. The demands on the performer are similar to studying the style of the period at any time. Classically trained pianists have to work hard to play Joplin, Gershwin and Mayerl. But Mayerl belongs to them, as long as their left hand is strong enough, because this is basically a notated tradition rather than an improvised one. Parkin understands it all – the effortless lilt, the light touch, not too much pedal, nothing overdone, everything speaking for itself.

John McCabe   British 1939

McCabe studied at the Royal Manchester College and with Genzmer in Munich, then returned to England to work as a pianist, critic and composer; in 1983 he became director of the London College of Music. His works, in an extended tonal style relating to Hartmann and Nielsen, include three symphonies (1965, 1971, 1978), much other orchestral music, chamber and keyboard pieces. **GROVE**music

Piano Concerto No 2

Piano Concerto No 2 (Sinfonia Concertante)[a].
Concertante Variations on a Theme of Nicholas Maw.
Six-minute Symphony. Sonata on a Motet
[a]**Tamami Honma** pf **St Christopher Chamber Orchestra / Donatas Katkus**
Dutton Laboratories Epoch CDLX7133
(64! · DDD)   Ⓕ

This is an intriguing orchestral programme of pieces dating mostly from the 1970s. Despite the disparity in dates there's remarkable stylistic consistency, even to the extent of the occasional twang of Tippett in the string writing, as in the delightful *Six-minute Symphony* (1997) – invigoratingly rattled off in 5'18" – as in the *Concertante Variations* of 1970.

Why this latter work should be better known: it may lack the exuberance and virtuosity of Britten's *Frank Bridge* Variations but is subtler and more integrated. So, too, is the wonderful *Sonata on a Motet* (1976), McCabe's atmospheric, closely argued fantasia on Tallis's *Spem in alium*. Curiously, it's in the *Sonata*, rather than the *Concertante Variations*, that he allows his source to be distinctly heard, as for example in the climactic, rip-roaring fugue on the Elizabethan's ground bass. By contrast, the *Six-minute Symphony* eschews variation form for a real symphonic plan in miniature.

The largest piece, by virtue of its internal cohesion and gravitas rather than mere duration, is the Second Piano Concerto (1970). Subtitled *Sinfonia Concertante*, the music plays out on three levels: solo piano, a concertino group of nine instruments and the orchestra. Listen past the dissonance of the opening minute: what emerges, like order from chaos, is one of the finest post-war piano concertos.

Tamami Honma, something of a McCabe expert, plays brilliantly, as do the splendid St Christopher Chamber Orchestra of Vilnius under Donatas Kalkus's smart direction. Excellent sound, too. Very strongly recommended.

Symphony No 4

Symphony No 4, 'Of Time and the River'. Flute
Concerto[a]
[a]**Emily Beynon** fl **BBC Symphony Orchestra / Vernon Handley**
Hyperion CDA67089 (56' · DDD)   Ⓕ●

John McCabe's Fourth Symphony, some half an hour in duration, has something Sibelian about its utterly inevitable, ever-evolving progress. Behind the frequently prodigal surface activity, one is acutely aware of the inexorable tread of a grander scheme – a preoccupation with time mirrored in Thomas Wolfe's novel *Of Time and the River*, from which the work derives its subtitle. The very opening idea is momentarily reminiscent of Britten, and there's a magnificent passage in the second movement that recalls Vaughan Williams at his visionary best. Yet McCabe's score possesses a strong individuality, formal elegance and abundant integrity too. With dedication and scrupulous perception, Handley secures a disciplined and alert response from the BBC SO. The engaging Flute Concerto composed for James Galway in 1989-90 proves both resourceful and communicative. There's much that genuinely haunts here, not least the gently lapping opening idea (inspired by watching the play of waves on a Cornish beach), the ravishing dialogue between the soloist and orchestral flutes and the delightful emergence soon afterwards of an entrancingly naive, folk-like theme (heard again on alto flute at the pensive close, magically fading into the ether). Emily Beynon gives a flawless account of the demanding solo part, and is immaculately partnered by Handley and his BBC forces.

Edward II

Royal Ballet Sinfonia / Barry Wordsworth
Hyperion ② CDA67135 (114' · DDD)   Ⓕ●

Commissioned by the Stuttgart Ballet, choreographed by David Bintley and first given in April 1995, *Edward II* is McCabe's third ballet score, and draws its story-line from Christopher Marlowe's eponymous drama and the medieval courtly satire, *Le roman de Fauvel*. Quite apart from the meaty intrigue, complex character relationships and psychological pathos of the plot, McCabe's music communicates with a captivating expressive fervour. It isn't just the superbly judged orchestration (colourful extras include triple woodwind and electric guitar) and wealth of memorable invention that impress. Above all, it's his ability to forge his tightly knit material into a dramatically convincing and organically coherent whole that marks him out as a composer of exceptional gifts. No praise can be too high for Barry Wordsworth's fluent, pungently theatrical direction, not to mention the unstinting application of the excellent Royal Ballet Sinfonia. Tony Faulkner's excitingly truthful Walthamstow sound allies razor-sharp focus to a most pleasing bloom, too.

String Quartets

String Quartets Nos 3-5
Vanbrugh Quartet (Gregory Ellis, Elizabeth Charleson vns Simon Aspell va Christopher Marwood vc)
Hyperion CDA67078 (68' · DDD)   Ⓕ

John McCabe's Third Quartet has both fastidious craft and satisfying logic to commend it, its five movements laid out to form an elegant arch in three parts. The resourcefulness with which McCabe handles his material calls to mind the towering example of such figures as Bartók, Bridge, Britten and Simpson (yes, the music really is that rewarding!), while anyone who loves the Tippett quartets will surely recognise a kindred humanity and tumbling lyricism in, say, the memorable *Lento* episode which launches the 'Passacaglia' finale.

The Fourth Quartet dates from three years later (1982) and was composed in joint celebration of two birthdays, namely the Delmé Quartet's 20th and Joseph Haydn's 250th. Cast in one movement and lasting just under 20 minutes, the spectral unison theme heard at the outset fuels nine formidably inventive and contrasting variations, whose ever-evolving progress and ambitious emotional scope again repay the closest scrutiny (an enormous pleasure in a performance as cogent as the present one).

A viewing of Graham Sutherland's *The Bees* (a series of copper etchings) provided the impulse for McCabe's Fifth Quartet (1989). Uncompromising in its relentless organic growth, the Fifth none the less yields an ingratiating lyrical flow and vaulting grace. In fact, it's the most immediately approachable of Hyperion's valuable clutch and, like its colleagues, must be deemed a major addition to the catalogue. The Cork-based Vanbrugh Quartet proves to be an inspirational proponent, its performances flawlessly prepared and magnificently authoritative.

Nikolay Medtner   Russian 1880-1951

Medtner studied the piano under Safonov at the Moscow Conservatory (1897-1900) and had composition lessons with Arensky and Taneyev, though was mostly self-taught. In 1921 he left Russia. He settled in Paris (1925-35), but was out of sympathy with musical developments there and found a more receptive audience in London, where he spent his last 16 years. He belonged in the line of Russian composer-pianists, though his music is close too to the Schumann-Brahms tradition. His works include three piano concertos (1918, 1927, 1943), much solo piano music, three violin sonatas and songs. GROVEmusic

Piano Concertos

No 1 in C minor, Op 33; **No 2** in C minor, Op 50; **No 3** in E minor, Op 60

Piano Concerto No 1. Piano Quintet in C, Op posth
Dmitri Alexeev pf **New Budapest Quartet** (András Kiss, Ferenc Balogh vns Laszlo Barsony va Karoly Botvay vc) **BBC Symphony Orchestra / Alexander Lazarev**
Hyperion CDA66744 (59' · DDD) Recorded 1994   Ⓕ

For Dmitri Alexeev the First Concerto is Medtner's masterpiece, an argument he sustains in a performance of superb eloquence and discretion. Even the sort of gestures later vulgarised and traduced by Tinseltown are given with an aristocratic quality, a feel for a love of musical intricacy that takes on an almost symbolic force, but also for Medtner's dislike of display. Time and again Alexeev makes you pause to reconsider Medtner's quality, and his reserve brings distinctive reward. The early *Abbandonamente ma non troppo* has a haunting improvisatory inwardness and later, as the storm clouds gather ominously at 11'55", his playing generates all the necessary electricity. How thankful one is, too, for Alexeev's advocacy of the Piano Quintet where, together with his fully committed colleagues, the New Budapest Quartet, he recreates music of the strangest, most unworldly exultance and introspection. Instructions such as *poco tranquillo (sereno)* and *Quasi Hymn* take us far away from the turbulence of the First Concerto (composed in the shadow of the First World War) and the finale's conclusion is wonderfully uplifting. The recordings are judiciously balanced in both works, and the BBC Symphony Orchestra under Lazarev are fully sympathetic.

Piano Concertos Nos 2 and 3
Nikolai Demidenko pf **BBC Scottish Symphony Orchestra / Jerzy Maksymiuk**
Hyperion CDA66580 (74' · DDD) Recorded 1991
ⒻOOO

 This splendid disc is given a fine recording, good orchestral playing from a Scottish orchestra under a Polish conductor and, above all, truly coruscating and poetic playing from the brilliant young Russian pianist Nikolai Demidenko. Medtner was a contemporary and friend of Rachmaninov; he settled in Britain in the 1930s, and like Rachmaninov he was an excellent pianist. But while the other composer became immensely popular, Medtner languished in obscurity, regarded as an inferior imitation of Rachmaninov who wrote gushing music that was strong on gestures but weak on substance. The fact is that he can be diffuse (not to say long-winded) and grandiose, and memorable tunes are in short supply, so that his music needs to be played well to come off. When it is, there's much to enjoy, as here in Demidenko's hypnotically fiery and articulate accounts.

Piano Concertos Nos 2 and 3. Arabesque in   **H**
A minor, Op 7 No 2. Fairy Tale in F minor, Op 26 No 3
Nikolay Medtner pf **Philharmonia Orchestra /
Issay Dobrowen**
Testament mono SBT1027 (77' · ADD) Recorded
1947   Ⓕ

The strong Russian flavour of the ornate writing is evident, as is the composer's masterly understanding of the piano. Listening to the composer himself in the Second's first *molto cantabile a tempo, ma expressivo* or the Third's *dolce cantabile* is to be made doubly aware of his haunting and bittersweet lyricism. The streaming figuration in the Second Concerto's *Romanza* is spun off with deceptive ease, a reminder that while Medtner despised obvious pyrotechnics he was a superb pianist. Two exquisitely played encores are included (the ambiguous poetry of the A minor *Arabesque* could be by no other composer), and the 1947 recordings have been superbly remastered.

Piano Concertos – No 1 in C minor, Op 33;
No 3 in E minor, Op 60
Konstantin Scherbakov pf **Moscow Symphony
Orchestra / Vladimir Ziva**
Naxos 8 553359 (70' · DDD)   Ⓕ⬤

Naxos completes its Medtner concerto cycle with Scherbakov. To have such Romantic richness – once the province of specialists – offered on a bargain label is cause for celebration in itself; to have it performed and recorded with such tireless commitment is a double blessing. That said, the performances on the first disc suffered from the soloist's poetic parsimony and an oppressive ill balance from Naxos. But this second disc is successful on all counts. Scherbakov, praised by Richter and recently hailed as a 'modern Rachmaninov', is now more attuned to Medtner's widely fluctuating idiom, complementing his virtuosity with inwardness and conviction. Sample the passage beginning at 6'30" in the Third Concerto's finale and you'll hear the sort of eloquence that warms the hearts of all true Russians.

Commissioned by Moiseiwitsch, an early and courageous champion of Medtner, the Third Concerto, subtitled 'Ballade', flows like some primeval river of the imagination, its burgeoning course inspired by Lermontov's *Water Spirit*, while the First Concerto's often epic gestures blend a bittersweet Russian Romanticism with themes of an almost Elgarian cut. Scherbakov's agility at, say, the *con moto* (8'38") is never at the expense of a composer whose

bravura is always poetically motivated. Lovers of Romàntic piano concertos need look no further.

There's stiff competition from Alexeev in the First Concerto, to an even greater extent from the *Gramophone* Award-winning Demidenko in the Third (both Hyperion) and from the composer himself in the Second and Third Concertos. Yet even at this exalted level Scherbakov holds his own.

Violin Sonatas

No 1 in B minor, Op 21; **No 2** in G, Op 44;
No 3 in E minor, Op 57, 'Epica'

Violin Sonatas Nos 1 and 2
Lydia Mordkovitch vn **Geoffrey Tozer** pf
Chandos CHAN9293 (60' · DDD) Recorded 1993 Ⓕ⬤

Mordkovitch's readings emphasise a lyrical and relaxed approach, and this is particularly so in the lyrical first movement of the short, attractive First Sonata – a little too relaxed perhaps in the outer sections of the lilting second movement 'Danza'. Elsewhere (for instance the *Allegro appassionato* and Finale-Rondo of the Second Sonata), Mordkovitch has an intuitive grasp of structure, allowing the music to unfold with a high degree of ease and direction. These artists are persuasive interpreters of these works and can be strongly recommended to the first-time explorer. Recorded sound is warm and balanced.

Medtner Violin Sonata No 3 **Ravel** Violin Sonata
Vadim Repin vn **Boris Berezovsky** pf
Erato 0630-15110-2 (61' · DDD)   Ⓕ

Of Medtner's three sonatas this is perhaps the most intricately worked and, at over 40 minutes, certainly the most substantial. At times it seems almost too long for its own good and for that reason it needs a very persuasive and masterly performance in order to project its strengths. Fortunately this one is about as persuasive as you can get – Repin is lyrical and passionate and has plenty of fiery temperament for this music, and he's ideally complemented by Berezovsky's equally splendid playing. Much is made of the sonata's lyrical and melodic abundance (the *Scherzo* is delivered with great panache) and Repin's choice of tempo for all movements is expertly judged. In the Ravel, Repin and Berezovsky are perhaps even more impressive. As a vehicle for Repin's talent it shows what a marvellous colourist he is, what exceptional subtlety and nuance he brings to the music and, in the 'Blues' movement especially, the *frisson* he's capable of generating. One can't understate the superb ensemble playing either, with Berezovsky perfectly attuned to every twist and turn of Repin's playing. The sound is very realistic and naturally balanced.

Piano Works

Sonata in F minor, Op 5. Two Fairy Tales, Op 8.
Sonata Triad, Op 11. Sonata in G minor, Op 22.
Sonatas, Op 25 – No 1 in C minor, 'Sonata-Skazka';
No 2 in E minor, 'The Night Wind'. Sonata-Ballade in
F sharp, Op 27. Sonata in A minor, Op 30. Forgotten
Melodies – Set I, Op 38; Set II, Op 39. Sonata
romantica in B flat minor, Op 53 No 1. Sonata
minacciosa in F minor, Op 53 No 2. Sonate-Idylle in
G, Op 56
Marc-André Hamelin pf
Hyperion ④ CDA67221/4 (279' · DDD)　　Ⓜ️Ⓞ

With this classic recording of the 14 piano
sonatas, Medtner's star soared into the ascendant. Superlatively played and presented, it
effects a radical and triumphant transition from
years of indifference to heady acclaim. True,
Medtner was celebrated by Rachmaninov as
'the greatest composer of our time' and championed by pianists such as Moiseiwitsch,
Horowitz and Gilels, yet his music fell largely
on deaf ears. Such irony and enigma lie in the
music itself, in its distinctive character, colour
and fragrance. Listeners were understandably
suspicious of music that yields up its secrets so
unreadily, almost as if Medtner wished it to
remain in a private rather than public domain.
Moments of a ravishing, heart-stopping allure,
and heroics on the grandest of scales are apt to
occur within an indigestible, prolix and recondite context. On paper everything is comprehensible, yet the results are never quite what
you expect. Much of the writing, too, is formidably complex, with rhythmic intricacies deriving from Brahms and whimsicalities from Schumann supporting a recognisably Slavic yet
wholly personal idiom.

Such writing demands a transcendental technique and a burning poetic commitment, a
magical amalgam achieved with delicacy, drama
and finesse by Marc-André Hamelin. Interspersing the sonatas with miniatures containing
some of Medtner's most felicitous ideas, he
plays with an authority suggesting that such
music is truly his language. Hamelin achieves an
unfaltering sense of continuity, a balance of
sense and sensibility in music that threatens to
become submerged in its own passion. Readers
uncertain of Medtner's elusive art should try the
Forgotten Melodies (and most of all 'Alla reminis-
cenza'). Such heaven-sent performances will set
you journeying far and wide, their eloquence
accentuated by Hyperion's sound.

Two Pieces for Two Pianos, Op 58[a].
Sonatina in G minor. Morceaux, Op 4 – Moment
musical; Prelude. Sonata in C minor, 'Sonata-Skazka',
Op 25 No 1. Piano Quintet in C, Op posth[b]
Hamish Milne, [a]**Boris Berezovsky** pfs [b]**Kenneth Sil-
lito,** [b]**Malcolm Latchem** vns [b]**Robert Smissen** va
[b]**Stephen Orton** vc
CRD CRD3515 (70' · DDD)　　　　　　Ⓕ

Milne presents a rich and fascinating miscellany, with music ranging from Medtner's
teenage years (the Sonatina) to old age and,
finally, to a work (the Piano Quintet) which
occupied him throughout a life dogged by ill
fortune and lack of recognition. For Medtner
the Quintet was his *summa*, his 'hymns of old
Russia' dedicated to God. The echoes of others,
most notably Brahms, criss-cross its deeply
affecting pages, whether giving us a 'serene variant' on the *Dies irae*, the modal harmonies of the
Russian Orthodox Church or a finale concluding in a whirl of defiance and exultance. At the
other end of the scale, Milne's performance of
the Sonatina is as crystalline and sensitive as
even the most ardent Medtnerian could wish.
His robust partners in the Quintet are the Pro
Arte Piano Quartet, and his performance has all
his instinctive quality and commitment, most
notably a capacity to allow the composer his
own voice and to present his music with affection and clarity. Finally, Milne is joined by Boris
Berezovsky in the Op 58 'Round Dance' and
'Knight Errant' for two pianos, both performed
with total authority and conviction. Medtner
and Moiseiwitsch, who recorded the 'Round
Dance', would surely have been among the first
to applaud.

Dithyramb in E, Op 10 No 3. Two Fairy Tales, Op 20.
Four Lyric Fragments, Op 23. Four Fairy Tales, Op 26.
Theme and Variations in C sharp minor, Op 55. Fairy
Tale in G minor, Op 48 No 2. Two Elegies, Op 59
Geoffrey Tozer pf
Chandos CHAN9899 (63' · DDD)　　　　　Ⓕ

Medtner's moods, particularly in this seventh
volume of Tozer's cycle, are primarily introspective, whether simply or floridly expressed.
Most of the ideas, too, bear a family likeness,
suggesting a continuous return to a fabric or
dreamscape of happier times and places; nostalgia was always central to Medtner's haunting
genius. Tozer's long and complex journey
through these pages is always a labour of love
rather than duty. For him the Third *Dithyramb*
is 'a hymn of angels' and the third of the Op 26
Fairy Tales 'perfection'. His verbal tribute is ideally matched in performances of unfailing mastery and warmth. His tempo for the second of
the two Op 20 *Fairy Tales* allows every note of
its menacing tread or chime to be heard. The
delightfully ornate Op 55 *Variations* are spun off
with a true sense of their greater accessibility
and the Op 59 *Elegies* – rich, powerful, disconsolate and with a Brahmsian textural density –
provide a magnificent close to his programme.

Eight Mood Pictures, Op 1. Three Improvisations, Op
2. Three Novelles, Op 17. Improvisation, Op 31 No 1.
Etude 'of medium difficulty'. Three Hymns in Praise
of Toil, Op 49
Geoffrey Tozer pf
Chandos CHAN9498 (70' · DDD)　　　　　Ⓕ

Dithyramb in E flat, Op 10 No 2. Fairy Tale in F minor,

'Ophelia's song', Op 14 No 1. Sonatas, Op 25 – No 1
in C minor, 'Sonata-Skazka'; No 2 in E minor, 'The
Night Wind'. Sonate-Idylle in G, Op 56
Geoffrey Tozer pf
Chandos CHAN9618 (72' · DDD)   Ⓕ

Medtner's piano music contains glories and
riches indeed – an unending sense of intricacy
from Russia's most subtle and recondite composer. Even when Medtner reminds you of his
debt to others (to, say, Brahms and Schumann)
he remains inimitably himself, ranging effortlessly from lyric to epic and essaying everything
in between. Take the 'Prologue', from Op 1,
composed when Medtner was 18 and prefaced
by some lines from Lermontov telling of a soul
carried to earth by an angel. Such serenity and
other-worldly preoccupation are expressed in
music of rippling complexity, soaring to
declamatory heights before resuming its pensiveness and quiet ecstasy. In total contrast *The
Night Wind* Sonata is among the most daunting
of all sonatas; of heroic length and ambition.
The *Improvisation*, Op 31 No 1, is another of
Medtner's finest, most imaginative offerings,
and if the *Dithyramb* exults in Brahmsian fullness, its final pages, which seem to engulf the
entire keyboard, are of a vehemence peculiar to
Medtner.

Playing with an enviable strength, grace and
subtlety and with an unfailingly beautiful sonority, Geoffrey Tozer is more than equal to every
occasion. Hearing him, for example, in the
Sonata, Op 25 No 2 or in the slow movement
from the *Sonata-Skazka*, you'll be aware of his
warmth and affection, as well as his imper-
turbable fluency and skill. The recordings are of
the highest quality.

Songs

The Angel, Op 1a. Winter Evening, Op 13 No 1.
Songs, Op 28 – No 2, I cannot hear that bird; No 3,
Butterfly; No 4, In the Churchyard; No 5, Spring Calm.
The Rose, Op 29 No 6. I loved thee well, Op 32 No 4.
Night, Op 36 No 5. Sleepless, Op 37 No 1. Songs,
Op 52 – No 2, The Raven; No 3, Elegy; No 5, Spanish
Romance; No 6, Serenade. Noon, Op 59 No 1. Eight
Songs, Op 24
Ludmilla Andrew sop **Geoffrey Tozer** pf
Chandos CHAN9327 (60' · DDD) Recorded 1993.
Texts and translations included   Ⓕ

Musical Opinion, reviewing the newly published
Op 52 in 1931, concluded that, Medtner could
hardly be considered 'a born song writer'. It says
something for the achievement of Ludmilla
Andrew that the 'unvocal' character of Medtner's writing is hardly evident at all, though, to
be fair, the first three songs from Op 52 are perhaps the very ones in which the voice is most
hard-pressed and in which it's even possible to
feel that they might do very well as piano solos.
In the 'Serenade' (No 6), the piano part *is* an
accompaniment, and the singer brings to it a
charm and delicacy worthy of its dedicatee,

Nina Koshetz. Geoffrey Tozer is an excellent
accompanist. His playing of 'Winter Evening',
with its evocative rustling start, is superb; but
always, along with the sheer virtuosity, there's a
responsive feeling for mood and coloration.
There are songs in which the piano takes over.
Yet in many the interest is evenly distributed,
and these are among the most delightful in the
repertoire.

Fanny Mendelssohn-Hensel
German 1805-1847

*Sister of Felix Mendelssohn, Fanny was a gifted
pianist and composer of songs (some published under
her brother's name), piano music and a few large-
scale dramatic works. In the 1830s she became the
central figure in a flourishing salon, for which she
created most of her compositions and where she performed on the piano and conducted. Her diary and
correspondence provide vivid and essential material
on the musical life of her time.* GROVEmusic

Lieder

Fanny Mendelssohn Lieder – Opp 1, 7, 9 and 10. Ich
wandelte unter den Bäumen. Die Schiffende. Traum.
Suleika. Dämmrung senkte sich von oben. Nach
Süden. **Felix Mendelssohn** Italien, Op 8 No 3
Susan Gritton sop **Eugene Asti** pf
Hyperion CDA67110 (72' · DDD) Texts and
translations included   Ⓕⵔ

A few single songs by Fanny Mendelssohn have
appeared in concert programmes and have registered as pleasant, delightful even, but rather
too comfortable and conventional to reward any
more sustained attention. This is now proved to
be untrue. Heard in sequence, as here, the songs
reveal their strength. The melodies are more
athletic, the piano parts more varied, the modulations more expressive than one may have
thought. The choice of text – more of Goethe
than of any other poet – challenges thoughtfulness. There's also a curious feature of the music:
though the excellent commentary on the songs
often suggests a reminiscence on Fanny's part
(of Bach or Schubert or Schumann), the associations in a present-day listener's mind are likely
to be forward as often as back. Die frühen Gräber
(Op 9 No 4), for instance, is compared to 'a
Bach organ chorale'; and yet as one searches in
the mind to identify a kinship for that unusually
deep-toned piano writing, the name which surfaces isn't Bach but Brahms. In less sensitive
hands than Eugene Asti's this could sound
muddy; but his clarity and feeling for rhythm
and harmony obviate that. Similarly, a spring-
like voice such as Susan Gritton's could have
confirmed the impression that pleasantness was
all, whereas she's remarkably good at deepening
the colours (as in *Der Ersehnte*, Op 9 No 1) and
concentrating the mind (as in *Im Herbste*, Op 10
No 4). An excellent record: enterprising programme, fresh young artists, fine presentation.

Felix Mendelssohn German 1809-1847

Mendelssohn came from a distinguished intellectual, artistic and banking family in Berlin (the family converted from Judaism to Christianity in 1816, taking the additional name 'Bartholdy'). He studied the piano with Ludwig Berger and theory and composition with Zelter, producing his first piece in 1820; thereafter, a profusion of sonatas, concertos, string symphonies, piano quartets and Singspiels revealed his increasing mastery of counterpoint and form. Besides family travels and eminent visitors to his parents' salon, early influences included the poetry of Goethe (whom he knew from 1821) and the Schlegel translations of Shakespeare; these are traceable in his best music of the period. His gifts as a conductor also showed themselves early: in 1829 he directed a pioneering performance of Bach's St Matthew Passion at the Berlin Singakademie, promoting the modern cultivation of Bach's music.

A period of travel and concert-giving introduced Mendelssohn to England, Scotland (1829) and Italy (1830-31). In 1833 he took up a conducting post at Düsseldorf, concentrating on Handel's oratorios. Among the chief products of this time were The Hebrides, the G minor Piano Concerto, Die erste Walpurgisnacht, the Italian Symphony and St Paul. But as a conductor and music organiser his most significant achievement was in Leipzig (1835-47), where to great acclaim he conducted the Gewandhaus Orchestra, championing both historical and modern works, and founded and directed the Leipzig Conservatory (1843).

Composing mostly in the summer holidays, he produced Ruy Blas Overture, a revised version of the Hymn of Praise, the Scottish Symphony, the Violin Concerto Op 64 and the fine Piano Trio in C minor (1845). Meanwhile, he was intermittently (and less happily) employed by the king as a composer and choirmaster in Berlin, where he wrote highly successful incidental music, notably for A Midsummer Night's Dream (1843). Much sought after as a festival organiser, he was associated especially with the Lower Rhine and Birmingham music festivals. His death at the age of 38, after a series of strokes, was mourned internationally.

With its emphasis on clarity and adherence to classical ideals, Mendelssohn's music shows alike the influences of Bach (fugal technique), Handel (rhythms, harmonic progressions), Mozart (dramatic characterisation, forms, textures) and Beethoven (instrumental technique), though from 1825 he developed a characteristic style of his own, often underpinned by a literary, artistic, historical, geographical or emotional connection; indeed it was chiefly in his skilful use of extra-musical stimuli that he was a Romantic. His early and prodigious operatic gifts, clearly reliant on Mozart, failed to develop, but his penchant for the dramatic found expression in the oratorios as well as in Ruy Blas Overture, his Antigone incidental music and above all the enduring Midsummer Night's Dream music, in which themes from the overture are cleverly adapted as motifs in the incidental music. The oratorios, among the most popular works of their kind, draw inspiration from Bach and Handel and content from the composer's personal experience, St Paul being an allegory of Mendelssohn's own family history and Elijah of his years of dissension in Berlin. Among his other vocal works, the highly dramatic Die erste Walpurgisnacht, Op 60 (on Goethe's poem greeting springtime) and the Leipzig psalm settings deserve special mention; the choral songs and lieder are uneven, reflecting their wide variety of social functions.

After an apprenticeship of string symphony writing in a classical mould, Mendelssohn found inspiration in art, nature and history for his orchestral music. The energy, clarity and tunefulness of the Italian have made it his most popular symphony, although the elegiac Scottish represents a newer, more purposeful achievement. In his best overtures, essentially one-movement symphonic poems, the sea appears as a recurring image, from Calm Sea and Prosperous Voyage and The Hebrides to The Lovely Melusine. Less dependent on programmatic elements and at the same time formally innovatory, the concertos, notably that for violin, and the chamber music, especially some of the string quartets, the Octet and the two late piano trios, beautifully reconcile classical principles with personal feeling; these are among his most striking compositions. Of the solo instrumental works, the partly lyric, partly virtuoso Lieder ohne Worte for piano (from 1829) are elegantly written and often touching.

GROVE**music**

Piano Concertos

No 1 in G minor, Op 25; **No 2** in D minor, Op 40; **A minor** (piano and strings); **E; A flat** (both two pianos)

Piano Concertos – Nos 1 and 2. Capriccio brillant in B minor, Op 22. Rondo brillant in E flat, Op 29. Serenade and Allegro giocoso, Op 43
Stephen Hough pf **City of Birmingham Symphony Orchestra / Lawrence Foster**
Hyperion CDA66969 (75' · DDD)   Ⓟ**OO**

With Stephen Hough's Mendelssohn we enter a new dimension. The soft, stylish arpeggios that open the first work here, the *Capriccio brillant*, announce something special. But this is just a preparation for the First Concerto. Here again, 'stylish' is the word. One can sense the background – especially the operatic background against which these works were composed. The first solo doesn't simply storm away, *fortissimo*; one hears distinct emotional traits: the imperious, thundering octaves, the agitated semiquavers, the pleading appoggiaturas. The revelation is the First Concerto's slow movement: not a trace of stale sentimentality here, rather elegance balanced by depth of feeling. Some of the praise must go to the CBSO and Foster; after all it's the CBSO violas and cellos that lead the singing in that slow movement. Foster and the orchestra are also effective in the opening of the Second Concerto – too often dismissed as the less inspired sequel to No 1. The first bars are hushed, sombre, a little below the main tempo, so that it's left to Hough to energise the argument and set the pace – all very effective.

Piano Concerto in A minor. 🅿

Concerto for Violin, Piano and Strings in D minor

Rainer Kussmaul vn **Andreas Staier** fp

Concerto Köln

Teldec Das Alte Werk 0630-13152-2 (72' · DDD) 🄵🅾

These two works, dating from Mendelssohn's early teens, make an excellent coupling. Given that these works were first heard in the Sunday salons at the Mendelssohns' home, it's logical that they should be recorded here not just on period instruments but with a small band of strings, in places one instrument per part. What's less welcome is that the strings of Concerto Köln adopt what might be regarded as an unreconstructed view of period string-playing, so that the orchestral *tuttis* are rather trying, not least in slow movements, even on an ear well adjusted to period performance.

The soloists, both outstanding, provide a total contrast, and there the violinist, Rainer Kussmaul, is if anything even more impressive than Andreas Staier, for many years the harpsichordist of Concerto Köln and here the director as well as soloist. Throughout the Double Concerto Kussmaul plays with rare freshness and purity, allowing himself just a measure of vibrato, and if Staier takes second place, that isn't just a question of balance between the violin and an 1825 fortepiano by Johann Fritz of Vienna, but of the young composer's piano writing, regularly built on passagework, often in arpeggios, rather than straight melodic statements. No doubt that had something to do with the pianos of the day, with their limited sustaining power. That applies to the piano writing in the Piano Concerto too, and it's striking that though each work is astonishing from a composer so young, the Double Concerto, written just a year later, reveals a clear development. The material isn't as memorable in either work as it is in such a masterpiece as the Octet of two years later, yet in every movement, and not least the finales of both works, the composer is clearly identifiable as Mendelssohn.

Double Piano Concertos – E; A flat

Benjamin Frith, Hugh Tinney pfs

RTE Sinfonietta / Prionnsías O'Duinn

Naxos 8 553416 (74' · DDD) 🅂

Mendelssohn was 14 when he completed his first two-piano Concerto in E major, and still only 15 when he followed it with a considerably longer (rather too long) and more ambitious second in A flat. Both concertos were first heard at the family's Sunday morning music parties, with the composer's sister Fanny at the second piano. As her talents were akin to his own, the two solo parts are indistinguishable in their challenges. And it's to the great credit of Benjamin Frith and Hugh Tinney that without a

score at hand, you would be hard-pressed to guess who was playing what.

You'll be as impressed by their attunement of phrasing in lyrical contexts as by their synchronisation in all the brilliant semiquaver passagework in which both works abound. Their uninhibited enjoyment of the imitative audacities of the later work's finale is a real tour de force.

Under Prionnsías O'Duinn the RTE Sinfonietta plays with sufficient relish to allow you to forget that the recording is perhaps just a little too close. In short, a not-to-be-missed opportunity to explore the young Mendelssohn at bargain price.

Violin Concerto in E minor

Mendelssohn Violin Concerto **Bruch** Violin Concerto No 1 in G minor, Op 26 **Schubert** Rondo in A, D438

Kennedy vn **English Chamber Orchestra / Jeffrey Tate**

EMI 749663-2 (71' · DDD) Recorded 1987 🄵

These are exceptionally strong and positive performances, vividly recorded. When it comes to the two main works, Kennedy readily holds his own against all comers. His view of the Mendelssohn has a positive, masculine quality established at the very start. He may at first seem a little fierce, but fantasy goes with firm control, and the transition into the second subject on a descending arpeggio (marked *tranquillo*) is radiantly beautiful, the more affecting by contrast with the power of what has gone before.

Kennedy is unerringly helped by Jeffrey Tate's refreshing and sympathetic support. Though it's the English Chamber Orchestra accompanying, there's no diminution of scale. With full and well-balanced sound, the piece even seems bigger, more symphonic than usual. In the slow movement Kennedy avoids sentimentality in his simple, songful view. The coda is always a big test in this work, and Kennedy's and Tate's reading is among the most powerful and exciting on record.

The Bruch brings another warm and positive performance, consistently sympathetic, with the orchestra once more adding to the power. Kennedy's more than a match for rival versions, again bringing a masculine strength which goes with a richly expressive yet unsentimental view of Bruch's exuberant lyricism as in the central slow movement. Thoroughly recommended.

Additional recommendation

Coupled with: **Berg** Violin Concerto **Bruch** Violin Concerto No 1 in G minor, Op 26

Suk vn **Czech Philharmonic Orchestra / Ančerl**

Supraphon SU3663-2 (79' · ADD) Recorded 1966-8 🄵

Josef Suk gives an outstanding performance of the Mendelssohn – his playing combines his usual technical polish and fine tone with unaffected expression. The orchestra has exemplary internal balance and rhythmic poise. The Bruch has similar virtues, and there's more great music-making in the Berg. The sound has been remastered and is uncommonly clear: highly recommended.

Symphonies / Overtures

Symphonies – **No 1** in C minor, Op 11; **No 2** in B flat, Op 52, 'Hymn of Praise'; **No 3** in A minor, Op 56, 'Scottish'; **No 4** in A, Op 90, 'Italian'; **No 5** in D, Op 107, 'Reformation'.

Overtures – Die Hochzeit des Camacho, Op 10; A Midsummer Night's Dream, Op 21; The Hebrides, Op 26, 'Fingal's Cave'; Meeresstille und glückliche Fahrt, Op 27; The Fair Melusina, Op 32; Athalie, Op 74; Ruy Blas, Op 95

Symphonies Nos 3 and 4
London Symphony Orchestra / Claudio Abbado
DG 3-D Classics 427 810-2GDC (71' · DDD) Recorded 1984   Ⓜ**OO**

Abbado's coupling of the *Scottish* and *Italian* Symphonies makes a pretty clear first choice for those wanting these works paired together (the full set is reviewed above). The sound is fresh within a pleasing ambience and the performances show this conductor at his very finest. *Allegros* are exhilarating, yet never sound rushed, and the flowing *Adagio* of the *Scottish* is matched by the admirably paced *Andante* in the *Italian*, with the mood of the 'Pilgrim's March' nicely captured. The *Scherzo* of the *Scottish* is a joy, and the recording clarifies textures that can often sound muddled, especially at the exuberant horn arpeggios. Both first-movement exposition repeats are included.

Symphonies Nos 3 and 4   Ⓟ
London Classical Players / Sir Roger Norrington
Virgin Classics 561735-2 (65' · DDD) Recorded 1989
Ⓜ**O**

Schumann Symphonies – No 3 in E flat,   Ⓟ
'Rhenish', Op 97; No 4 in D minor, Op 120
London Classical Players / Sir Roger Norrington
Virgin Classics 561734-2 (57' · DDD) Recorded 1989
Ⓜ**O**

Issued originally in 1990 and 1991, both these discs represented an extension of repertory for Norrington and the London Classical Players, moving a stage further in period performances of the central romantic repertory. If in Beethoven Norrington has always been wedded to the doctrine of obeying the composer's challengingly fast metronome markings, it's different here. Both in Mendelssohn and in Schumann the outer movements at least are relatively unrushed. It's a special delight to hear textures so lightened and clarified in both the Mendelssohn symphonies – the first movement of the *Italian* skipping infectiously, and the flute

MENDELSSOHN'S VIOLIN CONCERTO – IN BRIEF

Yehudi Menuhin; Colonne Concerts Orchestra / George Enescu
Naxos 8 110967 (75' · ADD)   Ⓢ
The youthful Menuhin at his most mercurial and dauntingly accurate. A captivating display, as are its bedfellows, the 17-year-old prodigy's legendary 1933 Lalo *Symphonie espagnole* and Chausson *Poème*.

Josef Suk; Czech PO / Karel Ančerl
Supraphon SU3663-2 (79' · ADD)   Ⓢ
Suk at his incomparably eloquent, unaffected best. Ančerl and the Czech PO provide luminous support, and Supraphon's mid-60s sound has come up very freshly.

Alfredo Campoli; London PO / Sir Adrian Boult
Beulah 1PD10 (74' · ADD)   Ⓜ
This lovely performance dates from May 1958; the slow movement in particular has a homely, fireside glow that's irresistible. Pleasing early stereo. Paired with these artists' underrated account of the Elgar Concerto.

Cho-Liang Lin; Philharmonia Orchestra / Michael Tilson Thomas
Sony Classical SMK89715 (73' · DDD)   Ⓜ
There's a delightful purity and freshness about this reading. The Philharmonia is on top form throughout for Tilson Thomas, and the Abbey Road balance is a model of its kind.

Nigel Kennedy; English Chamber Orchestra / Jeffrey Tate
EMI 749663-2 (71' · DDD)   Ⓕ
One of Kennedy's first forays into mainstream repertory, this 1987 account of the Mendelssohn has not a hint of routine about it. As well as the ubiquitous Bruch G minor, the disc also contains Schubert's little-known Rondo.

Kyung Wha Chung; Montreal SO / Charles Dutoit
Decca 460 976-2DM (79' · DDD/ADD)   Ⓕ
A personable and polished alliance from Chung and Dutoit, glowingly engineered. Now generously coupled with Chung's classic 1971 pairing of Bruch's First Concerto and *Scottish Fantasia* with Kempe.

Joshua Bell; Camerata Academica Salzburg / Sir Roger Norrington
Sony Classical SK89505 (70' · DDD)   Ⓕ
Not everyone will go a bundle on Bell's own first-movement cadenza, but this remains a likeable, stimulating account. Perky, clean-limbed playing from the Salzburg chamber orchestra under Norrington, and very realistic sound.

MENDELSSOHN'S SYMPHONIES NOS 3, 4 & 5 – IN BRIEF

London SO / Claudio Abbado (Nos 3 & 4)
DG 427 810-2GDC (71' · ADD) Ⓜ ⓞⓞ
Abbado imparts a winning sense of structural direction and emotional abandon to these works. The myth of Mendelssohn the simple prodigy is satisfyingly exploded.

LCP / Roger Norrington (Nos 3 & 4)
EMI 561735-2 (65' · ADD) Ⓜ ⓞ
Right from the start of No 4, this offers something different: period instruments and good engineering give a radically altered view of balances and textures without stopping one from revelling in the joy Norrington himself clearly takes in these works.

Berlin PO / James Levine (Nos 3 & 4)
DG 427670-2GH (71' · DDD) Ⓕ ⓞ
Levine whips up the Berliners in performances of fizzing energy and airborne grace: the edgy dance of the *Italian*'s finale is as exhilarating as any on disc.

Madrid SO / Peter Maag (Nos 3 & 4)
Arts 47506-2 (70' · ADD) Ⓑ ⓞⓞ
The orchestra may not be top-rank but Peter Maag has trained it to give wonderfully wise, humane performances of Mendelssohn and Mozart. A clear budget choice.

Orchestra of the 18th Century / Frans Brüggen (Nos 3, 4 & 5)
Philips 456 267-2PH2 (120' · DDD) Ⓜ
Another period set, with a more reflective approach: Nos 3 & 5 are especially intriguing.

Vienna PO / John Eliot Gardiner (Nos 4 & 5)
459 156-2GH (77' · DDD) Ⓑ ⓞ
DG's engineering, the VPO at their most twinkle-toed and Gardiner's zeal for contrapuntal clarity combine to offer amazing levels of clarity and rhythmic buoyancy. The revised version of the Fourth is an illuminating bonus.

Leipzig Gewandhaus / Kurt Masur (Nos 3 & 4)
Warner Apex 0927 49817-2 (67' · DDD) Ⓢ
Masur has always been renowned for his joyful, straightforward performances of a composer for whom he has a special affection. Mendelssohn was director of the Leipzig orchestra and they play with an authenticity all their own.

COE / Nicolaus Harnoncourt (Nos 3 & 4)
Warner Classics 9031 72308-2 (69' · DDD) Ⓕ
No speed-merchant, ultra-authentic versions these: the young virtuosos of the Chamber Orchestra of Europe respond zestfully to Harnoncourt's cultured direction, which does much to reveal Mendelssohn's sophisticated sense of symphonic direction.

articulation wonderfully clean in the *Saltarello* finale.

Here and elsewhere it helps to have a rather less resonant body of strings, so giving extra prominence to brass and woodwind. The different entries in the *Scherzo* of the *Scottish* Symphony are given extra clarity, while the great horn entry in the coda of the finale is gloriously resonant (track 4, 8'05"), a moment to send you heavenwards.

If Mendelssohn as an orchestrator has always been counted a master of transparency, it's so different with Schumann. Yet Norrington in these exhilarating performances – like Gardiner in his set of the Schumann symphonies – demonstrates that period performance alongside skilful balancing can undermine the old myth, with textures at least as clear as you would expect in Brahms. Again speeds are unexaggerated, even if the three middle movements of the *Rhenish* Symphony flow rather faster than in most performances with modern instruments. The second and third movements become interludes, but the fourth loses none of its gravity, thanks largely to heightened dynamic contrasts. The Fourth Symphony in its revised version brings similar qualities, with the successive *accelerandos* in the coda to the finale clear and unexaggerated, full of excitement but without hysteria. Two welcome reissues at mid-price.

String Symphonies

String Symphonies Nos 1, 6, 7 and 12
Nieuw Sinfonietta Amsterdam / Lev Markiz
BIS CD683 (70' · DDD) Recorded 1994 Ⓕ

Amazing stuff, brilliantly performed. The first of the symphonies fair bursts from the staves, with a chuckling finale that would surely have delighted Rossini. And although the Sixth Symphony's finale harbours hints of miracles to come, Mendelssohn's mature personality is more comprehensively anticipated in the Seventh. Again, the finale suggests the ebullient, life-affirming manner of the orchestral symphonies, albeit sobered by a spot of fugally formal writing later on. The 12th Symphony opens with a Handelian sense of ceremony, goes on to incorporate a characteristically tender *Andante* and ends with a finale that, to quote Stig Jacobsson's enthusiastic notes, 'dies away to *pizzicato* and a subsequent *accelerando* which recalls Rossini'. This is truly delightful music, the playing both sensitive and exciting, while BIS's sound is impressively full-bodied.

Octet

Octet, Op 20[a]. Song Without Words, Op 109[b].
Variations concertantes, Op 17[b]. Assai tranquillo[b]
[a]**Ensemble Explorations** (Christine Busch, Lydia Forbes, Zhang Zhang, Francis Reusens *vns* Guus Jeukendrup, Marten Boeken *vas* Geert Debiève *vc*)

with **Roel Dieltiens** vc b**Frank Braley** pf
Harmonia Mundi HMC90 1868 (50' · DDD)   Ⓕ**OO**

It's easy to love the Mendelssohn Octet, and the account from Ensemble Explorations is irresistible. True, the recorded sound is rather too resonant, but the playing has real fire and vitality, and the more soulful solo passages, violinist Christine Busch's especially, are truly eloquent; at the first movement's climactic moments her tone rings out effortlessly above the texture. The recent Emerson version is more sharply recorded, with much finely polished detail, yet their earnestly projected tone doesn't give the sense of joyful flight that characterises this new recording. The *Scherzo* may seem a little tame after the brilliant, high-speed Emersons, but it catches the nocturnal atmosphere and leaves room for an exciting increase in speed for the *Presto* finale. The cello and piano items are played with beautiful expression; Frank Braley clearly enjoys his 1874 Steinway.

String Quintets

String Quintets – No 1 in A, Op 18[a]; No 2 in B flat, Op 87[b]
Raphael Ensemble (Anthony Marwood, Catherine Manson vns Timothy Boulton, Louise Williams vas [a]Andrea Hess, [b]Michael Stirling vcs)
Hyperion CDA66993 (58' · DDD)   Ⓕ**O**

These quintets – both masterpieces – emanate from opposite ends of Mendelssohn's career, Op 18 being much of a piece with the Overture to *A Midsummer Night's Dream*, Op 87, presenting more ardent lyricism. The Raphael Ensemble's smoothly mellifluous performances and ecstatic involvement is tellingly exemplified in the first movement of Op 18, where converging string lines set up gloriously full textures, whereas the *Scherzo*'s contrapuntal scurryings inspire quiet-voiced virtuosity. Both performances convey the shimmer and bustle of Mendelssohn's string writing without forcing the issue and score full marks for imagination, tonal integration and musicality. The recordings are well-nigh ideal.

String Quartets

No 1 in E flat, Op 12 **No 2** in A, Op 13 **No 3** in D, Op 44 No 1 **No 4** in E minor, Op 44 No 2 **No 5** in E flat, Op 44 No 3 **No 6** in F minor, Op 80

String Quartets Nos 3-5, Op 44
Talich Quartet (Jan Talich Jr, Petr Macecek vns Vladimir Bukac va Petr Prause vc)
Calliope CAL9302 (80' · DDD)   Ⓕ**OO**

Here is a set of brilliant but not dazzling performances of Mendelssohn's Op 44 Quartets: that's to say, they illuminate the music but never

blind the listener with empty demonstration of the players' virtuosity. Certainly the speeds are fast, but the fingerwork is so deft and the textures (helped by excellent recording) so lucid that everything Mendelssohn asks for is clear. Of the three works in this marvellous set, it's the third, in E flat (No 5), which stands highest, with one of the finest of all his first movements and an Adagio of a pensiveness that the players reflect in their just tempo and in a slight greying of tone. The scherzo and the finale (*Allegro con fuoco*) are classic examples of how the rigorous contrapuntal teaching Mendelssohn received in his youth from old Carl Zelter gave him the technique for music of not merely pace but of wit and ingenuity. It's music to enliven the spirit, and so is this performance of it.

The quartet's sense of tempo serves them well in the D major Quartet (No 3), Mendelssohn's own favourite, with a Menuetto whose harmonic originality encourages a wistfulness in the playing, and in the E minor Quartet (No 4) with an *Andante* that keeps gently moving. One might regret that none of the first movement repeats are observed, but as there's already 80 minutes' music here, such a complaint would be unreasonable. Altogether an outstanding issue.

String Quartets Nos 1-6. String Quartet in E flat (1823). Andante, Scherzo, Capriccio and Fugue, Op 81 Nos 1-2
Melos Quartet (Wilhelm Melcher, Gerhard Voss vns Hermann Voss va Peter Buck vc)
DG ③ 415 883-2GCM3 (199' · ADD) Recorded 1976-81   Ⓜ**OO**

The familiar and misleading cliché of Mendelssohn as the cheerful chappie of early Romanticism vanishes at the sound of the F minor Quartet, Op 80 (No 6). Here is the intensity, anguish and anger that everyone thought Mendelssohn incapable of. His beloved sister Fanny died in May 1847 (his own death was merely months away), and the ensuing summer saw him leave Berlin for Switzerland, where he began to 'write music very industriously'. And what remarkable music it is. Right from the opening *Allegro assai* one senses trouble afoot, an unfamiliar restlessness mixed in with the more familiar busyness. Furthermore the second movement is surely the most fervent and punishing that Mendelssohn wrote – wild, insistent and unmistakably tragic in tone. This gradual intensification and darkening that occurs throughout Mendelssohn's quartet cycle makes it a most revealing guide to his creative development. But much of the earlier music is profoundly 'Mendelssohnian' in the accepted sense of that term: fresh, dynamic, light-textured, beautifully crafted and full of amiable melodic invention.

The very early E flat Quartet, Op posth (composed when Mendelssohn was only 14), although fashioned in the style of Haydn and Mozart, points towards imminent developments – a song-like A minor Quartet, already taking its lead from late Beethoven in the same key, the E flat, Op 12, with its delightful Can-zonetta and the eventful Op 44 set, three of Mendelssohn's most concentrated full-scale works. And DG also adds the four separate pieces, Op 81, thus treating us to the entire Mendelssohn string quartet canon.

The Melos Quartet comes up trumps with a really superb set of performances – technically immaculate, transparent in tone and full of enthusiasm. The recordings have presence and clarity.

String Quartets Nos 1 & 2
Alban Berg Quartet (Günther Pichler, Gerhard Schulz vns Thomas Kakuska va Valentin Erben vc)
EMI 557167-2 (51' · DDD)   Ⓕ

These are live performances; no audience noise, apart from applause at the end of No 2, and any tiny imperfections are outweighed by a strong sense of immediacy. Partly this comes from the way the music is shaped and articulated. The ABQ are less interested than others in smooth, sustained phrasing: in the *Adagio* of No 2, for instance, they make little gaps – breathing places – and more prominent local dynamic variations. The speaking quality this gives to their performance is clear from the opening bars of No 1. They bring winning charm and sweetness to the *Allegretto*s that take the place of *Scherzo*s in the two works; the faster, fairyland middle sections of both movements are done with delightful lightness. Although ABQ's tempo changes aren't always entirely persua-sive, they're at their best in the passionate, Beethoven-inspired outer movements of No 2, where their vocal, rhetorical manner rivals the intense commitment of the Leipzig Quartet.

If you love this music, you're bound to enjoy this splendid disc.

String Quartets Nos 1 & 6
Henschel Quartet (Christoph Henschel, Markus Henschel vns Monika Henschel va Mathias D Beyer-Karlshøj vc)
Arte Nova 74321 96521-2 (49' · DDD)   ⓈⒷ

The Henschel Quartet is a strong, well-unified group (three of the four are siblings); its ardent, robust approach suits Mendelssohn, and they sustain the lyrical expansiveness of Op 12's first movement and *Andante* in fine style. Christoph Henschel uses fingerings that involve many audible changes of position, as early 19th-cen-tury violinists are known to have done. By the mid-20th century, violin slides had become a no-go area, but, performed as stylishly as they are here, they contribute powerfully to the music's emotional effect.

Refinement clearly isn't a priority for the Op 80 Quartet, Mendelssohn's last major work, which he composed in Switzerland in the wake of the sudden death of his sister Fanny. It's uninhibited confessional music, like the two Smetana quartets. Only the *Adagio* offers some

tentative relief from the prevailing bleak, almost desperate mood: this is the least satisfactory part of the Henschels' interpretation – the many slurred moving parts need a stronger sense of direction. In the other three movements they demonstrate in memorable fashion just how stark and uncompromising the music is. If you think Mendelssohn is rather bland and well mannered, try this!

String Quartets Nos 3 & 4. Four Pieces for String Quartet, Op 81
Henschel Quartet (Christoph Henschel, Markus Henschel vns Monika Henschel va Mathias D Beyer vc)
Arte Nova 82876 60848-2 (76' · DDD)   Ⓢ

String Quartets Nos 1 & 4. 12 Fugues – in D minor; in F; in G minor; in C minor
Vogler Quartet (Tim Vogler, Frank Reinecke vns Stefan Fehlandt va Stephan Forck vc)
Profil Medien PH04091 (58' · DDD)   Ⓕ

The Henschel Quartet's Mendelssohn set, now complete, is a fine achievement and an extraor-dinary bargain. Impressive is the intense involvement that makes the outer movements of No 3, for example, sound not merely brilliant but truly joyful. The two sparkling, quicksilver *scherzi* (in No 4 and Op 81) are admirably light and well controlled, but the Henschels are less convincing in serene or wistful music (in the *Andante*s of Nos 4 and 3, respectively), tending to sound too active and forceful.

The *Andante* of No 4 is certainly more poetic on the Vogler disc, which offers performances full of colour and expressive detail. The Voglers play very freely, with added dynamics, un-marked tempo changes and even, at one place in No 4's finale, some unusual notes. Most of these liberties are a natural part of a creative interpre-tation, but at 5'09" on track 4 (Op 12's finale) where Mendelssohn, who up to this point has been in the 'wrong' key, finally returns to E flat, the Voglers suddenly hare off at a faster speed, destroying what should be a majestic effect (as the Leipzig Quartet, for example, show). The fugues date from 1821 – academic exercises, no doubt, but amazing for a 12-year-old – and are played with suitable objectivity, and very styl-ishly.

With so many new Mendelssohn quartet recordings, these marvellous works seem to grow in stature as different facets are empha-sised – the Emersons demonstrating the bril-liance and variety of the string writing, the Hen-schels showing the composer's restless, forceful personality, while for the Voglers he's a roman-tic poet, evoking a multiplicity of scenes and moods.

Piano Trios

Piano Trios – No 1 in D minor, Op 49; No 2 in C minor, Op 66

Prague Guarneri Trio (Ivan Klánský *pf* Ceněk Pavlík
vn Marek Jerie *vc*)
Praga Digitals PRD250 154 (56' · DDD)   Ⓕ

Fifty-five and a half minutes for a full-price CD
is less than generous in terms of quantity. But
quality is a different matter. For this maturely
musical, 1986-formed Czech trio, not widely
known on these shores, has the power to make
you enjoy these two trios more than any other
recording to date. The pianist's role in both
trios demands scarcely less virtuosity than in
Mendelssohn's two earlier piano concertos. So
let's start by saluting Ivan Klánský, who
throughout dispatches a multiplicity of notes at
dare-devilishly fast tempos with a delectably
light-fingered fluency, clarity and immediacy
that never for a moment flags. All this without
'prettification' of the music, not even among the
supernatural sprites of both *Scherzo*s. The *con
fuoco* Mendelssohnian drive is never forgotten,
especially in the higher, Beethoven-inspired
voltage of the later work with its triumphant
chorale-infused C major homecoming.

Both violinist and cellist play glowingly mellow-toned Guarneri instruments with intuitively affectionate phrasing – not least in the
two unassumingly songful slow movements.
Ensemble and balance throughout are excellent.

Cello Sonatas

Cello Sonatas – No 1 in B flat, Op 45; No 2 in D,   Ⓟ
Op 58. Variations concertantes, Op 17. Assai
tranquillo. Song without words, Op 109
Steven Isserlis *vc* **Melvyn Tan** *fp*
RCA Red Seal 09026 62553-2 (62' · DDD) Recorded
1994   ⒻⓄ

Isserlis and Tan offer idiomatic, well-turned
performances full of freshness and vigour. Try
the First Sonata in B flat major (which Mendelssohn wrote for his brother, Paul, in 1838),
where the second movement's dual function as
scherzo and slow movement is convincingly
characterised, and the music's passionate outbursts sound arrestingly potent. Isserlis's and
Tan's fine blend of subtlety and panache affectingly conveys the nostalgic mood of the *Variations concertantes*, and culminates powerfully in
the work's conclusion. In the D major Second
Sonata, Isserlis's and Tan's spontaneity and
energy in the outer movements, skilfully controlled variety of timbre and touch in the
Scherzo, and dramatic opposition of chorale
(piano) and recitative (cello) in the third movement sound immensely compelling. In the *Assai
tranquillo*, as in the charming *Song without words*,
Op 109, sympathetic tonal balance between
cello and fortepiano in the softly lit recording
brings out the music's sentiment. Isserlis and
Tan effectively draw out the work's inconclusive ending to create a telling analogy of the
eternal nature of friendship. Excellent balance
and crisp, restrained recording helps vividly to
evoke this music's Romantic atmosphere.

Variations sérieuses, Op 54

Variations sérieuses in D minor, Op 54. Piano Sonata
in E, Op 6. Three Preludes, Op 104a. Three Studies,
Op 104b. Kinderstücke, Op 72, 'Christmas Pieces'.
Gondellied in A. Scherzo in B minor
Benjamin Frith *pf*
Naxos 8 550940 (65' · DDD) Recorded 1994-5   Ⓢ

The multiplicity of notes in Mendelssohn's
piano music sometimes lays him open to the
charge of 'note-spinning'. So what higher praise
for Benjamin Frith than to say that thanks to his
fluency, not a single work outstays its welcome
here. The unchallengeable masterpiece is the
Variations sérieuses, so enthusiastically taken up
by Clara Schumann, and still a repertory work
today. Frith characterises each variation with
telling contrasts of tempo and touch without
sacrificing the continuity and unity of the
whole. Equally importantly, he never lets us
forget the *sérieuses* of the title.

No less impressive is his sensitively varied
palette in the early E major Sonata (unmistakable homage to Beethoven's Op 101) so often
helped by subtle pedalling. But surely the
recitative of the *Adagio* at times needs just a little more intensity and underlying urgency. Of
the miniatures the six *Kinderstücke* ('Christmas
Pieces' – written for the children of a friend)
emerge with an unforced charm. As music they
lack the romance of Schumann's ventures into a
child's world, just as the *Three Studies* do of
Chopin's magical revelations in this sphere.
However, Frith's fingers never let him down. In
the first B flat Study he even seems to acquire a
third hand to sustain its middle melody. For
sheer seductive grace, the independent *Gondellied* haunts the memory most of all.

With pleasantly natural sound, too, this disc is
quite a bargain.

Elijah

Elijah
Helen Donath, Kerstin Klein *sops* **Jard van Nes**
contr **Donald George** *ten* **Alistair Miles** *bass*
**Leipzig Radio Chorus; Israel Philharmonic
Orchestra / Kurt Masur**
Teldec ② 9031-73131-2 (110' · DDD) Recorded live
1992. Sung in German. Text and translation included
                                          ⒻⓄⓄⓄ

 This is a tremendous performance on
almost every count. Never before on
disc had the work been treated with
such an accent on vivid drama: the Old Testament text and its setting sounds as if it had been
created on the spot, all Victorian plush and sentiment disposed of. Nor had any previous
recording anything like the immediacy, both
choral and orchestral, as this. The chorus is
fiery yet disciplined. They sound wholly confident in tone, articulation and accent, responsive
to all the roles they have to play, obedient to
Mendelssohn's dynamic markings, and totally
committed to the discipline imposed on them
by Masur's incisive beat. The pace of his reading

can be judged by the 110 minutes duration, as compared with the customary, say, 125. No doubt the live recording has something to do with the sense of electricity in the performance. Chorus and conductor seem to have struck up an ideal rapport with the Israel Philharmonic, which plays with verve allied to a technical skill capable of keeping up with Masur's demands. In consequence, sections (especially in Part 2) that can seem weak or uninspired in other hands here have a dynamic, driving force that carries all before it. Masur also gains credit for choosing soloists rather than the choir as demanded by Mendelssohn for the trios, quartets and double quartets.

Most of the solo singing is worthy of what surrounds it. With a voice of the right weight and timbre for the part, Alistair Miles sings an honest, strongly limned Elijah. He, more than the other soloists, would sometimes like a little more time than Masur permits him to phrase with more meaning, especially in 'Es ist genug': by and large he stands up well to current competition, both in voice and in delivery. Helen Donath is rightly urgent as the grieving widow, though one or two high notes discolour, and mostly belies her years. Jard van Nes makes a fiery Queen and sings her solos gravely but without any hint of sentimentality. The only blot on the escutcheon is the wiry tenor and tight vibrato of Donald George, whose voice doesn't record well. Otherwise, a superb issue.

Elijah
Renée Fleming, Libby Crabtree sops **Patricia** 🅿
Bardon, Sara Fulgoni mezzos **Matthew Munro** treb
John Mark Ainsley, John Bowen tens **Neal Davies**
bar **Bryn Terfel** bass-bar **Geoffrey Moses** bass
Edinburgh Festival Chorus; Orchestra of the Age
of Enlightenment / Paul Daniel
Decca ② 455 688-2DH2 (131' · DDD) Sung in English.
Text included   Ⓕ

Paul Daniel and Bryn Terfel ensure that this is one of the most dramatic performances of the oratorio on disc. The young conductor, with the advantage of an excellent period instrument orchestra, has looked anew at the score and as a reveals much of the rhythmic and dynamic detail not always present in other performances, at least those available in English. His accomplishment in terms of pacing and balance is also praiseworthy, and he earns further marks for using the trio, quartet and double quartet of soloists Mendelssohn asks for in specific pieces, so as to vary the texture of the music. Terfel simply gives the most exciting and vivid account of the prophet's part yet heard. His range, in terms of vocal register and dynamics, is huge; his expression, mighty and immediate, befits a man of Elijah's temperament. As the score demands, anguish, anger and sympathy are there in full measure, displayed in exceptional definition of words, and when this Elijah calls on the Lord for the saving rain, the Almighty could hardly resist such a commanding utter-

ance. Yet there's always the inwardness part of the role demands. As far as the other soloists are concerned, for the concerted numbers Daniel has chosen voices that nicely match each other in timbre. The chorus is alert and unanimous in both attack and well thought-through phrasing, but its actual sound can be a little soft-centred, partly because all-important consonants are ignored. The orchestral playing is exemplary.

Elijah
Christine Schäfer sop **Cornelia Kallisch** contr
Michael Schade ten **Wolfgang Schöne** bass-bar
Stuttgart Gächinger Kantorei; Stuttgart Bach
Collegium / Helmuth Rilling
Hänssler Classic ② 98 928 (128' · DDD) Recorded
1994. Sung in German. Text and translation included
                                                                      Ⓕ

Rilling brings out arrestingly the drama of the piece, turning it into a well-varied, exciting quasi-opera, a far from traditional view of the oratorio. The vicissitudes of the prophet's eventful life, his reaction to events, the challenge to Baal, the encounter with Jezebel, have never sounded so electrifying. For that we have to thank Rilling's disciplined chorus biting in diction, precise and convincing in attack. Yet they can also provide the most sensitive, ethereal tone, as in Nos 28 and 29, trio and chorus, 'Siehe, der Hüter Israels'. The orchestral playing is no less arresting. Furthermore, as Elijah, Schöne unerringly or authoritatively captures his many moods. Here is the courageous man of action as he confronts Baal's followers and ironically taunts them, the sense of fiery conviction in 'Ist's nichts des Herrn Wort', of doubt in 'Es ist genug', and finally the wonderful Bachian serenity in 'Ja, es sollen wohl Berge weichen', all evoked in the most positive and imaginative delivery of the text. The voice itself, a firm, expressive bass-baritone, is ideal for the role, one on which the singer has obviously lavished much time and consideration – to excellent effect. The same can be said for Schäfer, who brings a Silja-like conviction to all her work. Anyone hearing her declaim 'Weiche nicht' would never be afraid again. The voice itself is interesting, gleaming and yet not without a fair degree of warmth in the tone. Kallisch is almost as convincing in the mezzo solos and gives us a wonderfully malign portrayal of Jezebel. Schade is a fresh-voiced, communicative Obadiah, and he's another who's vivid with his words. The recording, however, is slightly too reverberant, but the added space around the voices doesn't preclude immediacy of impact.

Lieder

Lieder – Op 8: No 8, And'res Maienlied. No 10,
Romanze. Op 9: No 1, Frage; No 5, Im Herbst; No 7,
Sehnsucht; No 8, Frühlingsglaube; No 9, Ferne; No
10, Verlust; No 12, Die Nonne. Op 19a: No 3,
Winterlied; No 4, Neue Liebe. Op 34: No 2, Auf
Flügeln des Gesanges; No 3, Frühlingslied; No 4,

Suleika; No 5, Sonntagslied. Op 47: No 3, Frühlingslied; No 5, Der Blumenstrauss; No 6, Bei der Wiege. Op 57 No 3, Suleika. Op 71: No 2, Frühlingslied; No 6, Nachtlied. Op 86: No 3, Die Liebende schreibt; No 5, Der Mond. Op 99: No 1, Erster Verlust; No 5, Wenn sich zwei Herzen Scheiden; No 6, Es weiss und rät es doch keiner. Pagenlied, Op posth
Barbara Bonney *sop* **Geoffrey Parsons** *pf*
Teldec 2292-44946-2 (60' · DDD) Recorded 1991.
Texts and translations included   Ⓕ

The charm of these songs lies in their simple style and almost endless stream of delightful melody. Unlike other Lieder composers Mendelssohn avoided blatant word-painting or vivid characterisations and the most satisfying songs here tend to be settings of texts which don't on the surface offer much scope for musical expression. But while this disc may not give us the very best of Mendelssohn, or indeed the finest examples of 19th-century Lied, the singing of Barbara Bonney makes this a CD not to be missed. Here is a rare example of a singer caught on record at the very height of her technical and artistic powers, able to exercise seemingly effortless vocal control in portraying the subtle colours and understated moods of each songs. The partnership with that ever-sensitive accompanist Geoffrey Parsons is inspired. Listen to how Bonney seems to float ethereally above the rippling piano figures in that most famous of all Mendelssohn songs, *Auf Flügeln des Gesanges* ('On wings of song') – a performance which can surely never have been bettered on record.

Gian-Carlo Menotti   American b1911

An American composer of Italian origin, Menotti studied at the Milan Conservatory and the Curtis Institute (with Scalero, 1928-33), where a co-student was Samuel Barber, his close friend for whom he later wrote librettos. He won success with his comic one-act opera Amelia al ballo (1937), which was taken up by the Metin 1938 and led to an NBC commission for a radio opera, The Old Maid and the Thief (1939). A grand opera, The Island God (1942, Met), was a failure; but it was followed after the war by the chamber opera The Medium (1946), a supernatural tragedy notable for its sinister atmosphere; it was paired with his short comedy The Telephone (1947) for a Broadway run of 211 performances, 1947-8. The full-scale political melodrama The Consul (1950), in a post-Puccini verismo style, and The Saint of Bleecker Street (1954), an effective drama in the same serious style, enjoyed much success, as had the television Christmas opera Amahl and the Night Visitors (1951). His later works include more operas and orchestral pieces, including several works for children written in a direct and appealing style. More ambitious works (such as Goya, 1986) have been criticised as musically thin and too derivative. In 1958 he founded the Spoleto

Festival of Two Worlds, which he directed until 1967.   **GROVE**music

Violin Concerto

Violin Concerto[a]. The Death of Orpheus[b]. Muero porque no muero[c]. Oh llama de amor viva[d]
[c]**Julia Melinek** *sop* [b]**Jamie MacDougall** *ten*
[d]**Stephen Roberts** *bar* [a]**Jennifer Koh** *vn*
[bcd]**Spoleto Festival Choir and Orchestra / Richard Hickox**
Chandos CHAN9979 (61' · DDD)   Ⓕ

Gian-Carlo Menotti's lyrical Violin Concerto, one of his most popular instrumental works, is here neatly coupled with première recordings of three cantatas written in the last 20 years, products of his active old age in his seventies and eighties. Hickox, as music director of the Spoleto Festival, has already established himself as a fine interpreter of Menotti's music. He draws from the Festival Orchestra warmly persuasive readings of works which may be unashamedly eclectic, but are powerfully convincing in such committed performances. The young American violinist, Jennifer Koh, is the excellent soloist. The first movement with its sequence of flowing melodies could easily seem to meander, but Koh and Hickox give it a clear shape, with each new idea emerging seductively. The slow movement, played with hushed dedication, has a tender poignancy here; an intrusive brass motif leads to the central cadenza, technically demanding but not showy. The vigorous finale features a jaunty main theme and ends with virtuoso fireworks, rounding off a piece that deserves resurrecting not just on disc but in the concert-hall too.

The two Spanish language cantatas were written respectively in 1982 and 1991 for the Catholic University in Washington. Menotti confesses to having lost his religious faith, and perhaps understandably here writes sensuous music closer to Puccini's opera, *Suor Angelica*, than to any religious model. Julia Melinek is the vibrant soloist in the St Teresa setting, with her marked vibrato well-controlled. Stephen Roberts, the responsive soloist in the St John of the Cross setting, is caught less happily, his voice ill focused.

The Death of Orpheus, to an English text by Menotti himself, is even more dramatic, based on the legend of Orpheus being killed by Thracian women in a bacchanalian frenzy. Orpheus's song emerges as a broad diatonic melody, with choral writing of Delian sensuousness and the tenor's part with Britten-like echoes. Jamie MacDougall is the expressive soloist, with the chorus fresh and incisive in all three cantatas.

Aarre Merikanto   Finnish 1893-1958

Aarre Merikanto, son of the composer Oskar Merikanto (1868-1924), studied with Reger in Leipzig

(1912-14) and Vasilenko in Moscow (1915-16), and taught at the Helsinki Academy (1936-58). His opera Juha (1922) invites comparison with Janáček; other works, in a highly coloured, chromatic style, include three symphonies (1916, 1918, 1953), three piano concertos (1913, 1937, 1955) and chamber music.   GROVEmusic

Piano Concertos

Piano Concertos Nos 2 & 3. Two Studies. Two Pieces
Matti Raekallio pf **Tampere Philharmonic Orchestra / Tuomas Ollila**
Ondine ODE915-2 (55' · DDD)   Ⓕ

Merikanto's Second and Third Piano Concertos (from 1937-8 and 1955 respectively) are typical of his later output – contrapuntally inventive and impressionistic in scoring. Both have an engaging Prokofievan brio in the brisk outer movements and a Rachmaninovesque Romanticism in the lyrical central adagios. Yet Merikanto never entirely forsook his adventurous harmonic writing, and especially in the Second the result – allied to considerable formal lassitude – is suggestive of (of all people) Villa-Lobos. Granted it's with a Nordic not a Brazilian accent, but think here of works such as Momoprecoce and Bachiana No 3 as much as the piano concertos; those who know both will appreciate the similarity. Matti Raekallio is a pianist of real technical ability and musical sensibility. He has the measure of both concertos, and the Second in particular could well become popular as an alternative to Prokofiev's Third or the Paganini Rhapsody. The purely orchestral Two Studies and Two Pieces (1941), though much slighter affairs, are by no means insignificant trifles. Tuomas Ollila secures more than competent performances from the Tampere orchestra, matched by excellent sound. A real delight.

Pan, Op 28

Lemminkäinen, Op 10. Pan, Op 28. Four Compositions. Andante religioso. Scherzo
Tampere Philharmonic Orchestra / Tuomas Ollila
Ondine ODE905-2 (54' · DDD)   Ⓕ

Aarre Merikanto's career divided broadly into three phases, those of apprentice, radical and conservative, and there are works from each present on this valuable issue. Critical hindsight accords (quite rightly) that the brief radical phase, roughly corresponding to the 1920s, was the most valuable, though at the time Merikanto's modernistic approach – and that of his like-minded contemporaries, Ernest Pingoud and Väinö Raito – was derided. Only one piece here represents this period, the highly accomplished tone-poem, Pan (1924), a wonderful, evocative, yet robust score, possessed of a very Nordic brand of impressionism. Lemminkäinen (1916), by contrast, seems immature, and rather parochial. A Sibelian shadow lies heavily

across its quarter-hour duration, yet without a trace of the older composer's own Lemminkäinen tone-poems. There's little of the latter's emotional and psychological depth – or musical range – but instead a prevailing rollicking good humour broken occasionally by more serious moments. The remaining works all date from the early stages of Merikanto's post-modern period, when he reverted to a simpler, more accessible idiom. The Four Compositions (1932) make a very effective and satisfying set, and whereas the Andante religioso (1933) seems like a piece out of context, the Scherzo (1937) is entirely convincing on its own. The performances are sympathetic and well recorded.

Olivier Messiaen   French 1908-1992

Messiaen studied at the Paris Conservatoire (1919-30) with Dukas, Emmanuel and Dupré, and taught there (1941-78) while also serving as organist of La Trinité in Paris. Right from his first published work, the eight Preludes for piano (1929), he was using his own modal system, with its strong flavouring of tritones, diminished 7ths and augmented triads. During the 1930s he added a taste for rhythmic irregularity and for the rapid changing of intense colours, in both orchestral and organ works. Most of his compositions were explicitly religious and divided between characteristic styles of extremely slow meditation, bounding dance and the objective unfolding of arithmetical systems. They include the orchestral L'ascension (1933), the organ cycles La nativité du Seigneur (1935) and Les corps glorieux (1939), the song cycles Poèmes pour Mi (1936) and Chants de terre et de ciel (1938), and the culminating work of this period, the Quatuor pour la fin du temps for clarinet, violin, cello and piano (1941).

During the war he found himself surrounded by an eager group of students, including Boulez and Yvonne Loriod, who eventually became his second wife. For her pianistic brilliance he conceived the Visions de l'amen (1943, with a second piano part for himself) and the Vingt regards sur l'enfant Jésus (1944), followed by an exuberant triptych on the theme of erotic love: the song cycle Harawi (1945), the Turangalîla-symphonie with solo piano and ondes martenot (1948) and the Cinq rechants for small chorus (1949). Meanwhile the serial adventures of Boulez and others were also making a mark, and Messiaen produced his most abstract, atonal and irregular music in the Quatre études de rythme for piano (1949) and the Livre d'orgue (1951).

His next works were based largely on his own adaptations of birdsongs: they include Réveil des oiseaux for piano and orchestra (1953), Oiseaux exotiques for piano, wind and percussion (1956), the immense Catalogue d'oiseaux for solo piano (1958) and the orchestral Chronochromie (1960). In these, and in his Japanese postcards, Sept haïkaï for piano and small orchestra (1962), he continued to follow his junior contemporaries, but then returned to religious subjects in works that bring together all aspects of his

music. These include another small-scale piano concerto, *Couleurs de la cité céleste* (1963), and monumental *Et exspecto resurrectionem mortuorum for
wind and percussion* (1964). Thereafter he devoted
himself to a sequence of works on the largest scale: the
choral-orchestral *La Transfiguration* (1969), the
organ volumes *Méditations sur le mystère de la Sainte
Trinité* (1969), the 12-movement piano concerto
Des canyons aux étoiles (1974) and the opera *Saint
François d'Assise* (1983).   GROVEmusic

Turangalîla-symphonie

Turangalîla Symphony (1990 revised version)
Pierre-Laurent Aimard pf **Dominique Kim** ondes
Berlin Philharmonic Orchestra / Kent Nagano
Teldec 8573 82043-2 (73' · DDD)   Ⓕ⭙

Turangalîla is a difficult score, and to record it
live is risky. Even when the orchestra is the
Berlin Philharmonic? Yes, since the work is very
far from the centre of their repertoire. Whether
despite or because of that risk this is a splendidly
exciting performance; more surprisingly it's
also for the most part a very accurate and
detailed one. The textures and colours of the
third movement are finely balanced, as they are
even in the headlong exuberance of its successor. Although the precision of the seventh
seems to understate its balefulness the complex
textures and superimposed rhythms of the ninth
are outstandingly clear and fascinating. The
soloists are admirable; the extremes of the piano
part, in particular, are just what Aimard is good
at. There are one or two imprecisions of balance, but this is among the two or three best
accounts of *Turangalîla* available.

Additional recommendations

Coupled with: **Poulenc** Concert Champêtre. Organ
Concerto
Beroff pf **Loriod** onde **LSO / Previn**
EMI Double Forte ② 569752-2 (129' · ADD)   Ⓑ
Also available (without couplings) on EMI DVD-Audio
DVC4 92398-9
   If you're happy with the couplings, Previn's is the
   top recommendation at less than full price.

Coupled with: L'ascension
[a]**François Weigl** pf **Thomas Bloch** ondes **Polish
National Radio Symphony Orchestra / Antoni Wit**
Naxos ② 8 554478/9 (107' · DDD)   Ⓢ
   Strong contrasts and surging intensity ; the sound
   is bold and forwardly balanced, and the spirit of
   the music survives and prospers.

Thibaudet pf **Harada** onde **Concertgebouw /
Chailly**
Decca ⬫ CD/SACD hybrid 470 627-2DSA
(77' · DDD)   Ⓕ
   A 1992 recording, remixed for SACD, that gives
   new insights into this fascinating score and, in the
   quieter movements, reveals a sympathetic balance
   between the sound stage and the lovely Concertgebouw acoustic.

Et exspecto resurrectionem...

Et exspecto resurrectionem mortuorum.
Chronochromie. La ville d'en-haut
Cleveland Orchestra / Pierre Boulez
DG 445 827-2GH (58' · DDD) Recorded 1993   Ⓕ⭙

Boulez has spoken of his pleasure at performing
Messiaen with an orchestra relatively unfamiliar
with his music. It sounds as though the Cleveland Orchestra must have enjoyed it too. You
would expect them to, perhaps, in such a passage as that in the fourth movement of *Et
exspecto*, where the two superimposed plainchant melodies return together with the noble
'theme of the depths' – it has great splendour, as
does the chorale melody of the finale, rising at
the end to a satisfyingly palpable *fffff*. And in
this performance of *Chronochromie* you can hear
why Messiaen said that certain pages of it were a
double homage to Berlioz and Pierre Schaeffer,
the French pioneer of electronic music. In the
work's penultimate section, the famous 'Epode'
in which 18 string players impersonate different
birds, the obvious problems of clarity and
precistion are expertly negotiated: the players
really seem to enjoy their dawn chorus.
   Absolute rhythmic precision and the clarity of
colour that comes from meticulous balance are
among the other pleasures of these performances. They make a most satisfying coupling,
too. The recordings are excellent: clean but not
clinical and ample in range.

Visions de l'Amen

Visions de l'Amen[a]. Fantaisie burlesque. Pièce pour
le tombeau de Paul Dukas. Rondeau
Steven Osborne, [a]**Martin Roscoe** pfs
Hyperion CDA67366 (61' · DDD)   Ⓕ⭙

It's axiomatic (to use a favourite word of the
French) that the Messiaens' own 1962 disc of
Visions is irreplaceable. At the same time it raises
the common interpretative problem when composers play their own music: should we follow
what they say in musical and verbal notes, or
what they do?
   Such problems don't arise with the three early
pieces, which hardly show Messiaen at his best,
but the metronome mark for the very slow first
movement of *Visions*, which literally sets the
groundwork for the cycle, dictates a duration of
6'15". He and his wife, Yvonne Loriod, dispatch
it in 4'30". Steven Osborne and Martin Roscoe
(like the old Regis recording by Peter Hill and
Benjamin Frith) prefer to believe the score, and
the result is an impressively relentless sweep
from the faintest *pppp* to a searing *fff*.
   Messiaen's library was full of astonomical pic-
ture-books, and his interpretation of the whole
work brings out the violence and local disorder
involved in the act of creation, even if the ultimate goal (here, a resplendent A major chord) is
always in view. This superbly engineered Hyperion disc is true to his Technicolor vision.

Indeed, it's in the rich and immediate piano sound that this version scores most notably over Hill and Frith's, where the playing is no less accurate or intense. Particularly beautiful is a sudden *pianissimo* early in the fourth movement, and there are some decidedly upfront birds from Osborne in the next. (Messiaen always insisted that townspeople, who knew only the sparrow, had no idea how deafening birds in a forest could be.) In the final movement Osborne and Roscoe throw authenticity aside; their *Modéré, joyeux* goes uninhibitedly for the second epithet. And wonderfully exciting it is.

Catalogue d'oiseaux

Catalogue d'oiseaux
Roger Muraro pf
Accord ③ 465 768-2 (DDD) Ⓕ**O**

Until recently the French Accord label wasn't available in the UK: hard luck for Roger Muraro, who seems to record primarily for that company; harder luck for us, since we have been kept in ignorance of a pianist of great gifts.

Muraro demonstrates both formidable pianism and an outstandingly imaginative response to Messiaen's imaginative world. The dynamic range is wide, the colouring often subtly beautiful, the virtuosity quite breathtaking at times. The virtuoso and the poet are in ideal balance here – magnificent rocky landscapes, vivid greens and blues! This is an outstanding reading throughout, and one can only echo the audience's applause after 'The Wood Lark' and their cheers at 'Cetti's Warbler'. Recommended.

Huit préludes

Huit préludes. Etudes de rythme – No 1, Île de feu I; No 4, Île de feu II. Vingt regards sur l'Enfant-Jésus – No 4, Regard de la Vierge; No 10, Regard de l'esprit de joie; No 15, Le baiser de l'Enfant-Jésus
Angela Hewitt pf
Hyperion CDA67054 (76' · DDD) Ⓕ

Hewitt has few equals in Messiaen. The very early *Préludes* (Messiaen was studying with Dukas when he wrote them) mightn't seem the ideal repertory in which to demonstrate this, but she plays them with exquisitely controlled colour, clarity and eager love for the music. In this performance they're full of luminous shot and shaded colours that are typical of the mature Messiaen, and in the final virtuoso number she seems even to have discovered an early draft for a theme in the *Turangalîla* Symphony. Her melodic lines are strong, her sonorities rich, but her loud playing is never noisy or forced. She has that crucial quality needed of a Messiaen pianist: patience. Patience to let a chord register and fade, patience never to pre-empt a climax. In the two *Île de feu* pieces she shows that she can produce hard-edged sonori-

ties as well as subtle ones. And all her gifts as a Messiaen pianist are evident in 'Le baiser de l'Enfant-Jésus': the tempo is patient, the contemplation rapt, the embellishments delicately precise, with a magical change of colour as the sunlit *hortus conclusus* at the centre of the movement is reached. The recording is finely sensitive to the exceptional beauty of Hewitt's sound.

Vingt regards sur l'enfant Jésus

Vingt regards sur l'enfant Jésus
Pierre-Laurent Aimard pf
Teldec ② 3984-26868-2 (116' · DDD) Ⓕ**OO**

Any review of the *Vingt regards* should begin by discussing how well the pianist conveys the cycle's visionary awe and builds its disparate sections into a true cycle. But here the virtuosity is so remarkable that even listeners with a profound distaste for Messiaen – for whom the 15th *Regard* ('The kiss of the infant Jesus') is a byword for sentimental religiosity – may listen open-mouthed. Sheer virtuosity is an important part of the cycle's language: one of the functions of *Regard* No 6 ('By Him all was made') is to astonish, and the power and excitement of Aimard's playing are indeed astonishing. Virtuosity is also desirable if Messiaen's demands for a huge palette of colour and orchestral or super-orchestral sonorities are to be met. In No 14 ('The gaze of the angels') his notes evoke 'powerful blasts of immense trombones'; Aimard's prodigious range of timbre and dynamic provide just the sound that Messiaen must have imagined. The penultimate *Regard* makes a more extreme demand: that in the hushed coda the player should recall a passage from the *Fioretti* of St Francis where 'the angel drew his bow across the string and produced a note so sweet that if he had continued I should have died of joy'. Here the effect is suggested not by virtuosity but intense concentration, stillness and purity of colour. Could it have been a little slower? Possibly; Aimard's timing is faster than most and a few of his silences could have been held longer but his dazzling technique and fabulous range of colour make this the most spectacular reading of the *Vingt regards* yet.

Vingt regards sur l'enfant Jésus
Steven Osborne pf
Hyperion ② CDA67351/2 (127' · DDD) Ⓕ**OOO**

There are a number of recordings of *Vingt Regards* available, most of them very good indeed. Even the finest, though, provoke very slight reservations: an occasional suspicion of hurry in Pierre-Laurent Aimard's outstanding account, a few misjudgments in Roger Muraro's, and so on. There are no such reservations about the reading by Steven Osborne, who's revealed as a pianist of exceptional gifts.

Messiaen's widow, Yvonne Loriod, invited

Osborne to study the work with her after she heard him playing other music by her late husband. One can hear throughout not only her influence but, even more, the qualities in his playing that led her to make the offer. His command of sonority is prodigious: if you've never been able to take Messiaen's talk about the 'colour' of particular chords seriously, then Osborne's playing may change your mind. He also has a remarkable dynamic range. These two qualities combine to provide both clarity and a tremendous climax in the virtuoso quasi-fugal textures of No 6 ('By Him was everything made') and, at the other end of the spectrum, to make perfect sense of Messiaen's description of the opening bars of No 17 ('The Gaze of Silence'): 'The music seems to emerge from silence as colours emerge from the night.' Nor is he insensible to the fact that some of the *Regards* are frankly showy. No 10 ('Gaze of the Spirit of Joy') is dazzling; No 16 ('Gaze of the Prophets, the Shepherds and the Magi') is barbarously colourful. Perhaps most significant of all, he finds in No 15 ('The kiss of the child Jesus') not only the sweet quietness of its opening but the spectacular Lisztian display of its later pages. The recording is ideally responsive to the wide range of sound he draws from the instrument.

Additional recommendation

Complete Keyboard Works
Hill *pf*
Regis ⑦ RRC7001 (8 hours 5' · DDD) Recorded mid-1980s (also available separately)   Ⓑ
  Peter Hill delivers immaculate readings of some of the most technically and philosophically challenging works in the repertoire. The series enjoyed the close support of Messiaen, and you can hear why. The sound in the early volumes occasionally suffers from too close a recording.

Complete Organ Works

Complete Organ Works
Jennifer Bate *org*
Regis ⑥ RRC6001 (454' · DDD) Recorded on the organs of L'Eglise de la Sainte-Trinité, Paris, and St Pierre de Beauvais Cathedral, 1981, 1983, 1987   Ⓑⵔ

Messiaen was of towering importance to the world of 20th-century music, yet the seven-and a-half hours of his compositions for organ are a salutary reminder of how little time he had for that century's secular and humanistic aspirations. It's therefore only proper that recordings of the organ works should be made in church, not concert hall or studio. Jennifer Bate made the first recording of Messiaen's last and longest cycle, *Livre du Saint Sacrement*, switching from Beauvais to the composer's own Parisian church, Sainte-Trinité. Though hailed as 'a monumental achievement' when new, later judgements have been more critical. But Bate's set stands up well, especially in the *Livre du*

Saint Sacrement, where she relishes the extraordinary diversity of material and mood even more intensely than the cooler though never-less-than commanding Olivier Latry (DG). The other large-scale later cycle, *Méditations sur le mystère de la Sainte Trinité*, reinforces this basic distinction between the two interpreters, and although Latry has the more refined instrument and the more sophisticated recording, his slow tempos (Messiaen never gives metronome marks) can seem too slow, as in the eighth *Méditation*, 'Dieu est simple – les Trois sont Un'. Bate's set makes an excellent bargain-price recommendation.

La nativité du Seigneur

La Nativité du Seigneur. Apparition de l'église éternelle. Le banquet céleste.
Gillian Weir *org*
Priory PRCD921 (75' · DDD) Recorded on the 1928 Frobenius organ of Århus Cathedral 1994   ⵔⵔ

Remastered, these outstanding recordings made in Århus Cathedral are a model of how to combine atmosphere and clarity in this music, and no other player seems quite to equal Weir's remarkable identification with the reflective and dramatically explosive extremes of Messiaen's idiom. At the risk of being accused of heresy, it's possible to doubt whether *La Nativité du Seigneur* really works as a compositional whole, given the surely undeniable imbalance between mediative and more dynamic music. But Weir evidently has no such doubts, sustaining the long, quiet episodes with particular sensitivity and irresistible conviction: if you're to perform the work complete, this is how it has to be. So, despite the achievements of both Olivier Latry and Jennifer Bate across the full range of Messiaen's organ works, Gillian Weir's performances again claim the definitive status which they were accorded when they were first released.

La nativité du Seigneur. Le banquet céleste
Jennifer Bate *org*
Unicorn-Kanchana DKPCD9005 (62' · DDD) Recorded on the organ of Beauvais Cathedral 1980
                                         Ⓕⵔ
La nativité du Seigneur comprises nine meditations on themes associated with the birth of the Lord. Messiaen's unique use of registration gives these pieces an extraordinarily wide range of colour and emotional potency and in Bate's hands (and feet) it finds one of its most persuasive advocates. She was much admired by the composer and is so far the only organist to have recorded his complete works for the instrument. *Le banquet céleste* was Messiaen's first published work for the organ and is a magical, very slow-moving meditation on a verse from St John's Gospel (VI, 56). The faithful recording captures both the organ and the large acoustic of Beauvais Cathedral to marvellous effect.

La Transfiguration

La Transfiguration de Notre Seigneur Jésus-Christ
Thomas Prévost *fl* **Robert Fontaine** *cl* **Roger
Muraro** *pf* **Francis Petit** *mari* **Renaud Muzzolini** *xylr*
Emmanuel Curt *vib* **Eric Levionnois** *vc* **Radio
France Chorus; Radio France Philharmonic Orchestra / Myung-Whun Chung**
DG ② 471 569-2GH2 (100' · DDD) Text and
translation included   ⒡**OO**

La Transfiguration is an important turning point
in Messiaen's work, at once a sort of summation
of what he'd achieved so far and a preparation
for the richness of his late music, culminating in
his opera *Saint Francois d'Assise*. There are, as
ever, bird songs and glinting piano flourishes,
his characteristic, rich, 'coloured' harmonies
and complex rhythms. But not for some while in
his music had there been such resplendent tonal
chorales and sonorous unisons. Compared to
most of his major works, however, it's been seldom recorded. The reason no doubt is the enormous forces it demands: you could perhaps get
by with fewer than the 68 strings he stipulates,
but you still need quadruple woodwind, six
horns, six percussion players and seven instrumental soloists. And, most crucially, a large chorus (Messiaen suggested 100 singers) of whom
vaultingly angular lines are sometimes required
and who at one point are divided into 20 parts.
Until now there have been only three recordings. Those by Antál Dorati and Reinbert de
Leeuw are unavailable, but Karl Anton Rickenbacher's on Koch Schwann is admirable in most
respects. Where Chung is superior is in his
greater readiness to allow events time in which
to register, and the solemn chorales which end
each half of the work really do need to be as slow
as he takes them; each chord needs to be
savoured, and Rickenbacher doesn't quite do
this. Chung also has an edge in sheer splendour
of orchestral sound, aided by a recording which
balances the large orchestra, the *concertante*
group and the chorus very well indeed.

Poèmes pour Mi

Poèmes pour Mi. Réveil des oiseaux. Sept Haïkaï
Françoise Pollet *sop* **Pierre-Laurent Aimard, Joela
Jones** *pfs* **Cleveland Orchestra / Pierre Boulez**
DG 453 478-2GH (72' · DDD) Recorded 1990s Texts
and translations included   ⒡**O**

All the performances here are excellent,
virtuoso indeed, and the recordings are first
class. *Poèmes pour Mi* represent Messiaen at his
most lyrically passionate and sensuous, the
Réveil des oiseaux his 'bird style' at its most
intransigent, while the *Sept Haïkaï* stand both
for Messiaen's love-affair with Asia and his
attempts to convey vivid colour in music. In
Françoise Pollet the *Poèmes* get as close as any
reading has to Messiaen's specification of a
grand soprano dramatique as the ideal solo voice.
She can sustain a long arch of melody splendidly

and, assisted by Boulez's firm control, generates
great rhythmic excitement in the fourth and
ninth songs of the set. This latter quality gives
exhilaration to *Réveil des oiseaux*, as the tangle of
exuberant melodies grows ever more complex;
Aimard is glitteringly precise here. But it's the
Sept Haïkaï that are most crucial to Messiaen's
later development, with pairs of movements
reflecting each other, their searing saturated
colours, their use of juxtaposed 'refrains' and
their central homage to the sound of a Japanese
orchestra. Boulez has expressed reservations
about some of his great teacher's theories, but
evidently has few if any about the fantastic
sound world imagined by his astonishingly precise ear.

Saint François d'Assise

Saint François d'Assise
Dawn Upshaw *sop* L'Ange **José Van Dam** *bass-bar*
Saint François **Chris Merritt** *ten* Le Lépreux **Urban
Malmberg** *bar* Frère Léon **John Aler** *ten* Frère
Massée **Guy Renard** *ten* Frère Elie **Tom Krause** *bar*
Frère Bernard **Akos Banlaky** *ten* Frère Sylvestre **Dirk
d'Ase** *bass* Frère Rufin **Jeanne Loriod, Valerie
Hartmann-Claverie, Dominique Kim** *ondes
martenots* **Arnold Schoenberg Choir; Hallé
Orchestra / Kent Nagano**
DG 20/21 ④ 445 176-2GH4 (236' · DDD) Notes, text
and translation included   ⒡**OO**

The breakthrough for Messiaen's only opera
came with the Salzburg Festival production
unveiled in August 1992, Esa-Pekka Salonen
conducting. Van Dam and his monks still wore
habits, but Peter Sellars's production concept
broke with the composer's 'realistic' Umbrian
spectacle to put Dawn Upshaw's Angel in a grey
business suit, while his trademark video moni-
tors relayed associated imagery. He even
invented a second Angel, one that doesn't exist
in the score, who dances and mimes.
    Nagano took up the reins for the 1998
Salzburg revival as captured here in DG's live
recording, and there's no mistaking the remarkable authority and technical self-confidence of
the results. Van Dam's definitive Saint François
is a remarkable achievement for an artist on the
cusp of his sixth decade and his identification
with the role is profound. Upshaw too is well
cast, with just enough tonal weight to underpin
her fresh, ardent, mobile singing. It's mostly
plain sailing in the subsidiary roles, although
Malmberg's French is still as dodgy as the
choir's. The musicians of the Hallé have been
drilled to the peak of perfection, closely scrutinised by vivid, upfront sound that doesn't
always give their glittering sonorities a natural
perspective in which to expand.
    All Messiaen's trademarks are here: the bird-
song, the modal rigour (especially for the word
setting which is crystal clear), the basic triads
given new harmonic context and heft, the post-
Stravinskian dances. There are also distant
echoes of *Boris Godunov* and *Pelléas et Mélisande*.

Uninitiated listeners should perhaps try Act 1 scene 3 (the curing of the leper) where the mosaic construction permits a breathtaking conjunction of ideas from timeless chant through 1960s modernism, to childlike eruptions of joy and premonitions of holy minimalism. *Saint François d'Assise* can make *Parsifal* seem like an intermezzo, but it exerts a uniquely hypnotic spell. Strongly recommended.

Giacomo Meyerbeer
German 1791-1864

Meyerbeer was born into a wealthy Jewish merchant family in Berlin and studied composition with Zelter (1805), B. A. Weber (1808) and Abbé Vogler in Darmstadt (1810-11), winning success more as a pianist than a composer. After a study tour in Italy (1816-25), where he met artists, librettists and impresarios and wrote six notable operas (especially the impressive Il crociato in Egitto, 1824), he gained a reputation equal to Rossini's. From 1825 he worked chiefly in Paris but was always on the move, taking cures, producing his operas in major European cities and auditioning new singers; in 1842, indisputably the world's leading active opera composer, he became Prussian Generalmusikdirektor – he was dismissed in 1848 but directed the Berlin royal court music until his death. Having first conquered the Paris Opéra with the five-act Robert le diable (1831), he and his most important collaborator Eugène Scribe created the famous Les Huguenots (1836), then began work on Le prophète and L'africaine, both of which suffered long delays from casting difficulties; Le prophète was eventually received enthusiastically with Pauline Viardot as Fidès (1849), while the première of L'africaine (1865) became a brilliant posthumous tribute to its composer.

Cultivating a consistently realistic style, 'expressive monumentalism', Meyerbeer conceived of grand opera as a whole, blending social content, historical material and local colour; exploitation of the horrific was an essential ingredient, along with massive crowd scenes building up a grandiose volume of sound and long passages of demanding solo singing. But these were allied to innovations, notably in the orchestra and in the deliberate creation of 'unbeautiful' sound. He was widely admired for his care over historical details, his melodic invention in ballet scenes and his grasp of the capabilities of individual singers. GROVEmusic

Opera arias

Il crociato in Egitto – Queste destre l'acciaro di morte[a]; Ah! Non ti son piú cara[b]; Cara mano dell'amore[c]; Sogni, e ridenti[d]. **Emma di Resburgo** – Di gioia, di pace[e]. **L'esule di Granata** – Sí, mel credi[f]. **Margherita d'Anjou**[g] – Pensa e guarda; Amico, all erta! **Romilda e Costanza** – Che barbaro tormento[h]. **Semiramide riconosciuta** – Il piacer, la gioja scenda[i] [eh]Bronwen Mills, [d]Linda Kitchen, [e]Maria Bovino, [bdi]Yvonne Kenny *sops* [h]Anne Mason, [bde]Diana

Montague, [f]Patricia Spence, [cd]Della Jones *mezs* [ad]Bruce Ford, [h]Chris Merritt, [e]Harry Nicoll, [e]Paul Nilon, [d]Ugo Benelli *tens* [eg]Geoffrey Dolton, [d]Ian Platt, [g]Russell Smythe *bars* [fg]Alastair Miles *bass* Geoffrey Mitchell Choir; [abcd]Royal Philharmonic Orchestra; [efghi]Philharmonia Orchestra / David Parry
Opera Rara ORR222 (69' · DDD) Recorded 1990-95. Notes included   Ⓕ

Meyerbeer, born 1791, was in Italy from 1816 to 1824. On this showing, you're tempted to think he should have stayed there. He's remembered for the big Paris operas, such as *Les Huguenots*, *Le prophète* and *L'Africaine*, hugely successful in their time but latterly somewhat buried in their own grandeur. The Italian period was nearer to the 18th century and Mozart. There was also the presence of Rossini (almost exactly Meyerbeer's age); and the music is that of a young man, gifted, energetic, confident and wealthy. The operas were admired and, remarkably, he was accepted by the public, despite being a German and having an unfashionable interest in orchestration.

These excellent selections include something of all six operas from the eight years in Italy, with *Il crociato in Egitto* returning regularly like the theme in a rondo. All the recordings are drawn from previous issues in the Opera Rara catalogue. One of the most attractive numbers is the semi-comic trio from *Margherita d'Anjou* in which Margaret's protectors pit their wits against those of Richard, Duke of Gloucester. In fact, it seems fairly typical of Meyerbeer at this stage: his genius seems to lie in the light touch, the graceful phrase, the felicitous orchestral scoring; if there's a weakness, it's revealed in the grandly dramatic moments, for which his music remains incorrigibly jolly.

The other great delight of the disc is the singing. Meyerbeer's vocal line, like Rossini's, is written for virtuosos, and that, almost without exception, is a description to which the soloists can lay claim. Each has to negotiate passage-work of a kind that half a century ago would have made everybody shake their head and say it couldn't be done by 'today's' singers. Bruce Ford, particularly, performs wonders in the revised (Trieste) version of *Crociato*; Alistair Miles is on top form in *L'esule di Granata*; but all do well, carrying off their respective prizes with easy competence and no fuss.

Margherita d'Anjou

Margherita d'Anjou
Annick Massis *sop* Margherita d'Anjou **Bruce Ford** *ten* Duke of Lavarenne **Daniela Barcellona** *mez* Isaura **Alastair Miles** *bass* Carlo Belmonte **Fabio Previati** *bar* Michele Gamautte **Pauls Putninš** *ten* Riccardo **Colin Lee** *ten* Bellapunta **Roland Wood** *bar* Orner **Geoffrey Mitchell Choir; London Philharmonic Orchestra / David Parry**
Opera Rara ③ ORC25 (172' · DDD) Notes, libretto and translation included   Ⓕ

Margaret of Anjou, the widow of Henry VI, is more familiar to us as the embittered old crone in Shakespeare's *Richard III*. In the opera she's relatively young and beautiful, and loved by the tenor, a married man. The action takes place in Scotland where Margaret's forces are being pursued by Richard's. The tenor's dilemma is whether to follow his strong inclination to remain the Queen's lover or to return to his loving wife, Isaura, who, unknown to him, has followed him to Scotland in disguise.

The opera is called a *melodramma semiseria*, which is appropriate partly because from the very first bars of the Overture it's clear that we can't be expected to take it seriously, and partly because another principal role is that of the comical army surgeon, Michele, who in the nick of time summons a doughty troop of Highlanders to thwart Richard, who at that point has the rest of the cast at his mercy.

The first notes – 'diddly-diddly um-pompom' – may well deter the listener from going further, especially as the fatuous motif is heard six times more, plus twice in the minor and several times referentially in *crescendo*. But that would be a pity. The singing and orchestration are good, and the *semiseria* element stimulates invention and interest: Isaura's plaintive aria and hopeful cabaletta are combined with a *buffo* subtext for Michele, and in the cottage scene of Act 2 the tension of Richard's unsocial visit is partly diffused, partly increased, by Michele's prevarications, a surreal situation along the lines of Richard III-meets-Benny Hill. Margherita has a gentle and rather beautiful solo. Particularly charming are the choruses that come just before, slightly suggestive of the villagers in *Cavalleria rusticana*.

Daniela Barcellona as Isaura has a rich contralto that takes flight in the final solo, surprisingly snatched from the eponymous soprano. She, Annick Massis, is a great find, pure and warm in tone, and accomplished in technique. Bruce Ford gives special pleasure in his *cantabile* aria 'Tu, che le vie segrete'. Fabio Previati plays Michele effectively, singing well and keeping the patter on its toes without too much clowning. Alastair Miles's Carlo, potentially the most interesting character, is admirably fluent in passagework but rather lacking in colour and bite. Chorus and orchestra are in good form, David Parry helping to bring out the best in them, as in Meyerbeer, too. As ever in this series, the booklet is an example to all.

Nikolay Miaskovsky Russian 1881-1950

Miaskovsky studied for a military career but entered the St Petersburg Conservatory (1906-11), where his teachers included Lyadov and Rimsky-Korsakov. He served in the war, and from 1921 taught at the Moscow Conservatory. He was not an innovator but was an influential, individual figure working within the Russian tradition. His large output is dominated by the cycle of 27 symphonies (1908-50), highly regarded in and outside Russia in his lifetime. He also wrote 13 string quartets (1913-49), choral and chamber music. GROVEmusic

Sinfonietta No 1

Sinfonietta No 1 in B minor, Op 32 No 2. Theme and Variations. Two Pieces, Op 46 No 1. Napeve
St Petersburg Chamber Ensemble / Roland Melia
ASV CDDCA928 (56' · DDD) Recorded 1994   Ⓕ

Miaskovsky's Variations are consistently attractive, as are the shorter works, despite disconcerting reminiscences of the *Skye Boat Song* in the first of the Op 46 Pieces. That's not to say that the music 'holds' you in the way that Stravinsky, Martinů, Honegger or Tippett do. And, as so often with Miaskovsky, there are slack moments where ideas seem to be coming back for no better reason than to fill out a preallocated space. The fact remains that if you've got the Miaskovsky bug, or if you want the fullest possible picture of middle-of-the-road Soviet music, you'll find confident, full-bodied performances here which are the equal of any.

Darius Milhaud   French 1892-1974

Milhaud studied with Widor, Gédalge and Dukas at the Paris Conservatoire and became associated with Claudel, who took him to Rio de Janeiro as his secretary (1916-18): he wrote incidental music for Claudel's translation of the Oresteia (1922), making innovatory use of chanting chorus and percussion; he also drew on Brazilian music in his ballet L'homme et son désir (1918). But Claudel's influence was briefly succeeded by Cocteau's, and he became a member of Les Six; works of this period include the ballet Le boeuf sur le toit (1919). In 1922 he sought out jazz in Harlem and used the experience in another ballet, Le création du monde (1923). Thereafter he travelled widely, taught on both sides of the Atlantic and produced a colossal output in all genres, normally in a style of fluent bitonality. His operas include Les malheurs d'Orphée (composed 1925), Le pauvre matelot (1926), Christophe Colomb (1928), Maximilien (1930), Bolivar (1943), David (1952) and Saint Louis (1970). There are also 12 symphonies and much other orchestral music, sacred and secular choral music, 18 quartets and songs. GROVEmusic

Le boeuf sur le toit / La création du monde

La création du monde. Harp Concerto, Op 323.
Le boeuf sur le toit, Op 58.
Frédérique Cambreling *hp* **Lyon Opéra Orchestra / Kent Nagano**
Erato MusiFrance 2292-45820-2 (59' · DDD) Recorded 1992   Ⓜ

Here is music to delight, with performances to match. Milhaud's ballet *Le boeuf sur le toit* was written for Jean Cocteau in 1919 and is set in an American bar during the Prohibition period (forbidding the manufacture and sale of alcohol) that was then just beginning. Kent Nagano shows more Gallic taste and sophistication, and the playing is above all musicianly, while the more uproarious moments come over all the more effectively for this very reason. The playing by the accomplished Lyon orchestra is excellent, not least the wind players who have plenty to do. Written four years later, *La création du monde* was one of the first works by a European composer to take its inspiration from African folklore and the raw black jazz that Milhaud heard in New Orleans. This ballet on the creation myth ends with a mating dance and the whole work is powerfully and darkly sensual. Nagano and his French orchestra bring out all the character of this music and take the jazz fugue in Scene 1 more urgently than usual, to excellent effect. The Harp Concerto dates from 1953, three decades further on into Milhaud's career, and inevitably it has a brighter character, though here, too, there's some jazz influence, if of a gentler kind. Cambreling is a fine player – an ideal interpreter of this uneven but nearly always fascinating composer.

Milhaud Le boeuf sur le toit, Op 58. La création du monde **Ibert** Divertissement **Poulenc** Les biches – Suite
Ulster Orchestra / Yan Pascal Tortelier
Chandos CHAN9023 (68' · DDD) Recorded 1991　Ⓕ

Here is 1920s French music directed by a conductor who's completely in the spirit of it, and plenty of spirit there is, too. Except for Ibert's *Divertissement*, this is ballet music. Poulenc's suite from *Les biches*, written for Diaghilev's ballet company and first heard in Monte Carlo, is fresh and bouncy and stylishly played here, although Chandos's warm recording, good though it's, takes some edge off the trumpet tone; the genial nature of it all makes us forget that it's a unique mix of 18th-century *galanterie*, Tchaikovskian lilt and Poulenc's own inimitable street-Parisian sophistication and charm. As for Ibert's piece, this is uproariously funny in an unbuttoned way, and the gorgeously vulgar trombone in the Waltz and frantic police whistle in the finale are calculated to make you laugh out loud. Milhaud's *Le boeuf sur le toit* also has Parisian chic and was originally a kind of music-hall piece, composed to a scenario by Cocteau. It was while attending a performance of it in London in 1920 that the composer first heard the American jazz orchestra that, together with a later experience of New Orleans jazzmen playing 'from the darkest corners of the Negro soul' (as he later expressed it), prompted him to compose his masterly ballet *La création du monde*. Tortelier and his orchestra understand this strangely powerful music no less than the other pieces. This is a most desirable disc.

Violin Sonatas

Saudades do Brasil, Op 67 – Leme; Ipanema (arr Lévy). Suite for Violin, Viola and Piano, Op 157b. Quatre Visages, Op 238. Sonatine for Violin and Viola, Op 226. Sonatas for Viola and Piano – No 1, Op 240; No 2, Op 244. Sonatine for Viola and Cello, Op 378
Paul Cortese va **Michel Wagemans** pf with **Joaquín Palomares** vn **Frank Schaffer** vc
ASV CDDCA1039 (78' · DDD)　Ⓕ

Paul Cortese here brings his rich, warm tone and flawless technique to Milhaud's viola music. Of the seven works presented here, four were written in the 1940s while Milhaud was teaching at Mills College in the USA. Exceptions are the two arrangements from the early *Saudades do Brasil*; the Suite (which includes a jaunty Provençal-flavoured overture, and an engagingly cheery finale); and the much later *Sonatine* for violin and cello, which contains an unexpectedly emotional slow movement. Of the four other works, the *Sonatine* is easy-flowing small-talk, unmemorable save for the energetic final fugue; *Quatre Visages*, however, reveals Milhaud's sly wit in its characterisations of four women – a sunnily contented Californian, a chatterbox from Wisconsin, an earnest creature from Brussels and a vivacious Parisienne. The First Viola Sonata is one of his most endearing works, indulging to the full his penchant for canonic writing. The Second Sonata is less overtly bracing; its central *Modéré* is charged with expressive drama, while the finale is a rough-and-tumble which tempts Michel Wagemans, alert as he is, into being too loud for his partner – as he sometimes is elsewhere, notably in the early Suite.

Scaramouche (arr two pianos)

Le boeuf sur le toit, Op 58a (arr cpsr). Scaramouche, Op 165b. La libertadora, Op 236a. Les songes, Op 237. Le bal martiniquais, Op 249. Carnaval à la nouvelle-orléans, Op 275. Kentuckiana, Op 287
Stephen Coombs, Artur Pizarro pfs
Hyperion CDA67014 (62' · DDD)　Ⓕ

Milhaud was an inveterate traveller who absorbed influences from many national styles. The music here exudes infectious dance impulses, languid geniality, knockabout humour and *joie de vivre*. It may inhabit a limited expressive sphere, but providing you don't expect introspection or searching profundity you won't be disappointed. There's enjoyment at every turn, whether in the foot-tapping 'Brazileira', the Satie-esque simplicity of the 'Valse' from *Les songes*, or the breezy music-hall atmosphere of *Le boeuf sur le toit*, with its wonderfully imaginative piano writing. The performances are exemplary. Stephen Coombs and Artur Pizarro both enjoy the byways of the piano repertory, and, even if Pizarro is the more starry soloist, they're well matched as a duo. Coombs's top part is suitably bright and sharply lit, and is offset by Pizarro's more subtle colouring. They revel in the protracted playfulness of *Le boeuf sur le toit* (the only work here for piano duet, incidentally, although if anything there's a greater wealth of inner detail than in the two-piano works), where their feeling for Hispanic exoticism is matched by their virtuosity. The recorded sound is excellent.

Ernest Moeran   British 1894-1950

Moeran studied at the Royal College of Music (1913-14) then, after war service, with Ireland (until 1923) who, with Delius, was a dominant influence on his early music. In the early 1930s he retired to the Cotswolds, where he wrote his Symphony in G minor (1937), a work of Nature lyricism drawing on Sibelian thematic methods. His other works, all marked by meticulous craftsmanship, include the Sinfonietta (1944) and orchestral Serenade (1948), concertos for violin (1942) and cello (1945), chamber music and songs. **GROVE**music

String Quartets

String Quartets – No 1 in A minor; No 2 in E flat. String Trio in G
Maggini Quartet (Laurence Jackson, David Angel vns Martin Outram va Michal Kaznowski vc)
Naxos 8 554079 (59' · DDD)   ⑤〇

The A minor Quartet dates from 1921, when Moeran was a pupil of John Ireland at the Royal College of Music. It's an enormously fluent, folk-song-inspired creation, full of Ravelian poise; indeed the last movement of the three (an exhilarating rondo) owes much to the finale of the French master's F major Quartet. The Maggini Quartet accords the piece wonderfully assured, flexible advocacy. The E flat Quartet, discovered among Moeran's papers after his death, appears to be another early effort. It's cast in just two movements, the second of which is an ambitious linked slow movement and finale, full of ambition and tender fantasy, and containing some truly magical inspiration along the way. Perhaps this movement's intrepid thematic and emotional diversity engendered sufficient niggling doubts in Moeran's mind for him to suppress the whole work. Certainly, in a performance as convinced and convincing as this, its melodic fecundity and unpretentious, out-of-doors charm will endear it to many. That leaves the masterly String Trio of 1931, which, in its impeccable craft, rhythmic pungency (the opening *Allegretto giovale* is in 7/8), gentle sense of purpose and unerring concentration (above all in the deeply felt slow movement), represents one of Moeran's finest achievements. The Magginis reveal a relish for Moeran's exquisitely judged part-writing and give an admirably polished, affectionate rendering. Sound and balance are excellent throughout this enterprising, hugely enjoyable collection.

Federico Mompou   Spanish 1893-1987

Mompou studied in Barcelona and with Motte-Lacroix and Samuel-Rousseau in Paris, where he remained until 1941 except for a return to Barcelona in 1914-21; he then settled in his native city. His output consists almost entirely of small-scale piano pieces and songs in a fresh, naive style indebted to Satie and Debussy; he aimed for maximum expressiveness through minimum means, often achieving a melancholy elegance. **GROVE**music

Música callada

Música callada
Herbert Henck pf
ECM New Series 445 699-2 (63' · DDD) Recorded 1993   Ⓕ

Listening to this disc is rather like entering a retreat. There's a rapt, contemplative atmosphere around these 28 miniatures written between 1959 and 1967 as an attempt to express St John of the Cross's mystic ideal of 'the music of silence'. Practically all slow-moving, using repetition as a structural device but avoiding keyboard virtuosity, and rarely rising even to a *forte*, they seem to acknowledge descent from Erik Satie via the impressionists, though harmonically much freer and sometimes harsher – even, occasionally, stepping inside the area of atonality. No 3 has a childlike innocence in its folkloric theme: Mompou's fascination with bell-sounds finds echoes in Nos 5, 17 and 22. Overall there's a sense of tranquil self-communion which, paradoxically, exerts a strange spell on the listener. Herbert Henck, a specialist in 20th-century music, plays this collection with tender sensitivity and an ideally suited luminosity of tone, and he's finely recorded. An exceptional and haunting issue.

Preludes

Cançons i danses – Nos 1, 3, 5, 7, 8 & 9. Preludes – Nos 1, 5, 6, 7, 9 & 10. Cants màgics. Charmes. Variations. Dialogues. Paisajes
Stephen Hough pf
Hyperion CDA66963 (77' · DDD)   Ⓕ〇〇〇

 The music of Federico Mompou may appear at first to consist of little more than charming, delicately scented but dilettantish salon near-improvisations with marked overtones of Erik Satie; but it's significant that his earliest works (in the 1920s) are imbued with a sense of mystery and wonder. Later he was to progress from an ingenuous lyricism (in the *Songs and dances*) to a profounder contemplation and mysticism, to greater harmonic and keyboard complexity (*Dialogues*) and finally, in the 1946-60 *Paisajes* ('Landscapes'), to a more experimental, less tonal idiom. In the hands of an imaginative pianist like Stephen

Hough this other-worldly quality becomes revelatory. Hough's command of tonal nuance throughout is ultra-sensitive, he catches Mompou's wistful moods to perfection, and on the rare occasions when the music lashes out, as in *Prelude* No 7, he's scintillating. In the more familiar *Songs and dances* he's tender in the songs and crisp rhythmically in the dances. He treats the 'Testament d'Amelia' in No 8 with a good deal of flexibility, and because Mompou declared (and demonstrated in his own recordings) that 'it's all so free', he takes the fullest advantage of the marking *senza rigore* in No 5, which reflects Mompou's lifelong fascination with bell sounds.

---

12 Préludes. Suburbis. Dialogues. Cants magics.
Chanson de berceau. Fêtes lointaines
Jordi Masó pf
Naxos 8 554448 (79' · DDD)   Ⓢ

Vol 1 of Jordi Masó's Mompou cycle was given the warmest of welcomes and Vol 2 is no disappointment, either. Everything is presented with crystalline clarity, and if the manner is unusually robust it's never less than musicianly. Directions such as *énergiquement* and *très clair* (Prélude No 2), the *forte* climax of Prélude No 6 or the sudden blaze of anger that erupts in Prélude No 7 are arguably more sympathetically conveyed than Mompou's gentler, more characteristic instructions (*con lirica espressione* in Prélude No 8 or *un peu plus calme* in the second 'Gitanes' from *Suburbis*). It's almost as if Masó, a vibrant and articulate pianist, wished to draw attention away from sentimental or salon associations, and direct us towards Mompou's underlying fervour and what Wilfrid Mellors calls (in his invaluable book *Le jardin retrouvé*) the 'pre-melodic' nature of Mompou's vocal lines (in *Cants magics*) or the evocation of a remote, prehistoric world (see Stephen Hough's notes to his *Gramophone* Award-winning Hyperion disc). Masó's boldness is potent and arresting and his comprehensive undertaking makes comparison with Hough and Martin Jones a marginal issue. So although he's less tonally subtle than Jones, his playing is vital and idiomatic, qualities highlighted by the bright, immediate sound.

Jean-Joseph de Mondonville
French 1711-1772

In the 1730s violinist and composer Mondonville was in Lille; then he settled in Paris, where he won fame as soloist and composer. He became sous-maître to the royal chapel in 1740 and intendant in 1744. His music is notable for its imaginative textures. Best known were his sonatas for harpsichord and violin (1734), among the earliest accompanied keyboard music, and those for harpsichord, violin and voice

(1748); his 17 grands motets (among the finest since Lalande's and like his, much performed at the Concert Spirituel) and 10 stage works (1742-71) were also popular.   GROVEmusic

Grands motets

Grands motets – Dominus regnavit; In exitu Israel; ▣
De profundis
Sophie Daneman, Maryseult Wieczorek sops **Paul Agnew, François Piolino** tens **Maarten Koningsberger** bar **François Bazola** bass **Les Arts Florissants / William Christie**
Erato 0630-17791-2 (72' · DDD) Texts and translations included   ⊙Ⓕ

Mondonville's *grands motets* were enormously popular for many years at the Concert Spirituel in Paris. They follow the pattern laid down by Lalande and continued by Rameau, but with more independent instrumental parts and incorporating Italian influences (e.g. *da capo* arias) and operatic elements. These three on psalm texts are deeply impressive. *Dominus regnavit* (1734) was perhaps the earliest of Mondonville's *grands motets* and, besides its polyphonic opening chorus, is notable for two verses entirely for high-register voices and instruments, an operatic *tempête*, and a stunning complex 'Gloria patri'. *De profundis* (1748), written for the funeral of a Chapel Royal colleague, is by its nature sombre, and ends not with the usual 'Gloria patri' but with 'Requiem aeternam' and a fugue. The initial chorus was praised to the sky by contemporaries: other highlights are a baritone aria over a free chaconne bass, and a chorus illustrating 'morning' and 'night' by high and low voices respectively. There's even more illustrative music in the 1755 *In exitu Israel*: what amounts to a dramatic scena, with agitated strings and rushing voices for the 'fleeing sea', dotted figures for the mountains 'skipping like rams', and tremolos and vocal melismas for the 'trembling earth'. The performances are vivid, with very good soloists, an alertly responsive chorus and a neat orchestra.

Philippe de Monte
Flemish 1521-1603

Flemish composer. He was a choirboy at Mechlin and then served the Pinelli family in Naples (1542-51). In 1554 he was in Antwerp and then England (where he met Byrd), serving in the private chapel of Philip II of Spain (Mary Tudor's husband). He was next in Rome, probably with Cardinal Orsini, and from 1568 until his death he was Kapellmeister at the Habsburg court in Vienna (later Prague). Prolific, successful and progressive in outlook, he composed over 1100 madrigals in 34 books (1554-1600, often reprinted), spiritual madrigals (5 bks, 1581-93) and chansons (1585), as well as some 40 masses (mostly MS) and over 250 motets (10 bks, 1572-1600).   GROVEmusic

Missa Aspice Domine

Monte Missa Aspice Domine. Factum est silentium. Miserere mei, Domine. Pie Jesu, virtus mea. Clamavi de tribulatione mea. O suavitas et dulcedo **Jacquet of Mantua** Aspice Domine
Christ Church Cathedral Choir, Oxford / Stephen Darlington
Metronome METCD1037 (58' · DDD)   Ⓕ

What a feast for lovers of Renaissance polyphony, and the only available recording of Philippe de Monte's parody mass *Missa Aspice Domine*, based on a motet by an earlier composer, Jacquet of Mantua, also included here. In general Stephen Darlington adopts a faster tempo for the mass than for the slow-moving motet, but the mood is still quietly pleading. One of the loveliest forward-looking movements is the Angus Dei: the trebles lead with the finely structured melody, the lower voices being more of an accompaniment than a clearly defined part of the polyphonic texture. Two of de Monte's original motets that follow are again settings of texts of earnest supplication. The most moving is the *Miserere*, with its opening phrases marked by an imaginative chord progression. Of the other three, we hear the composer's surprisingly loud-sounding 'silence in heaven' as Michael does the dragon in (*Factum est silentium*).

Claudio Monteverdi   Italian 1567-1643

Monteverdi studied with Ingegneri, maestro di cappella at Cremona Cathedral, and published several books of motets and madrigals before going to Mantua in about 1591 to serve as a string player at the court of Duke Vincenzo Gonzaga. There he came under the influence of Giaches de Wert, whom he failed to succeed as maestro di cappella in 1596. In 1599 he married Claudia de Cattaneis, a court singer, who bore him three children, and two years later he was appointed maestro di cappella on Pallavicino's death. Largely as the result of a prolonged controversy with the theorist GM Artusi, Monteverdi became known as a leading exponent of the modern approach to harmony and text expression. In1607 his first opera, Orfeo, was produced in Mantua, followed in1608 by Arianna. The dedication to Pope Paul V of a grand collection of church music known as the Vespers (1610) indicated an outward looking ambition, and in 1613 Monteverdi was appointed maestro di cappella at St Mark's, Venice.

There Monteverdi was active in reorganising and improving the cappella as well as writing music for it, but he was also able to accept commissions from elsewhere, including some from Mantua, for example the ballet Tirsi e Clori (1616) and an opera, La finta pazza Licori (1627, not performed, now lost). He seems to have been less active after c1629, but he was again in demand as an opera composer on the opening of public opera houses in Venice from 1637. In 1640 Arianna was revived, and in the following two years *Il ritorno d'Ulisse in patria, Le nozze d'Enea con Lavinia (lost)* and *L'incoronazione di Poppea were given first performances. In 1643 he visited Cremona and died shortly after his return to Venice.*

Monteverdi can be justly considered one of the most powerful figures in the history of music. Much of his development as a composer may be observed in the eight books of secular madrigals published between 1587 and 1638. The early books show his indebtedness to Marenzio in particular; the final one, Madrigali guerrieri et amorosi, includes some pieces 'in genere rappresentativo' – Il ballo delle ingrate, the Combattimento di Tancredi e Clorinda and the Lamento della ninfa – which draw on Monteverdi's experience as an opera composer. A ninth book was issued posthumously in 1651.

Orfeo was the first opera to reveal the potential of this then novel genre; Arianna (of which only the famous lament survives) may well have been responsible for its survival. Monteverdi's last opera L'incoronazione di Poppea, though transmitted in not wholly reliable sources and including music by other men, is his greatest masterpiece and arguably the finest opera of the century. In the 1610 collection of sacred music Monteverdi displayed the multiplicity of styles that characterise this part of his output. The mass is a monument of the prima prattica or old style. At the other extreme the motets, written for virtuoso singers, are the most thorough-going exhibition of the modern style and the seconda prattica. **GROVE**music

Selva morale

Selva morale e spirituale   Ⓟ
Cantus Cölln; Concerto Palatino / Konrad Junghänel
Harmonia Mundi ③ HMC901718/20
(230' · DDD) Texts and translations included   Ⓕ**OOO**

Monteverdi's last publication has always been something of a stepchild in his output, perhaps partly because of its sheer size and variety: there's lots of music in it that's hard to pigeon-hole. It's a massive assembly of some 40 pieces, some apparently very early, many from those mysterious years after the 1610 *Vespers*, and a few perhaps very late. In style they range from the purest academic polyphony of the *stile antico* to the most elaborate concerted music with intricate and showy instrumental parts, from the simplest melodic writing to virtuoso floridity with extreme vocal ranges. In this complete recording Konrad Junghänel has effectively made the first and third CDs into approximate vespers collections, with the second CD containing most of the music that can't be fitted into the others. This works extremely well, not least because those who aren't ready to sit through it all at one sitting can get a satisfying musical unit from any one of the discs.

The 12 singers of Cantus Cölln have among them enough variety of colour to keep the sound lively and interesting. They are always clear, disciplined and balanced; and Junghänel directs the often episodic works with a firm control of their shape. The peerless Johanna Koslowsky leads much of the time in the larger pieces and contributes marvellous solo numbers. For the large-range bass solos Stephan MacLeod makes the impossible lines sound almost effortless. This set is a remarkable achievement.

1610 Vespers

Vespro della Beata Virgine (ed Parrott/Keyte)   Ⓟ
Taverner Consort; Taverner Choir; Taverner Players / Andrew Parrott
Virgin Classics Veritas Double ② 561662-2
(106' · DDD) Recorded 1984   ⒷO

The technical and interpretative problems of the Monteverdi *Vespers* of 1610 are legion. Should the entire volume be performed as an entity, or just the psalms, or perhaps a mixture of psalms and motets? Since the vocal lines in the original are heavily ornamented, does this preclude the addition of further embellishment after the manner of contemporary instruction books? Which portions should be sung chorally (and how large should such a 'choir' be?), and which by the soloists? How should the continuo be realised?

The central controversy concerns five non-liturgical compositions inserted among the Marian psalms, hymn and 'Magnificat'. These, the sacred *concerti* described on the title-page as 'suitable for the chapels or private chambers of princes', don't conform textually to any known Marian office but occur in Monteverdi's collection in positions normally occupied by psalm antiphons. Here the *concerti* are performed as substitutes for the antiphons missing from Monteverdi's collections. One effect is to make this version feel more unified and monumental.

Both physically and emotionally the *concerti* are presented here as the focal points of the *Vespers*. Certainly they're the occasion for some of the most spectacular singing. The essential ingredient is the performance of Nigel Rogers, surely the most accomplished and convincing singer of the early 17th-century Italian virtuoso repertory. He gives persuasive and seemingly effortless performances in three of the *concerti* in his mellifluous, dramatic yet perfectly controlled manner. In two cases, 'Audi coelum' and 'Duo Seraphim', he's well matched with Andrew King and Joseph Cornwell. 'Pulchra es', sung by Tessa Bonner and Emma Kirkby, seems comparatively rather understated.

One important feature of Andrew Parrott's interpretation is its fundamental conception, historically accurate, of the *Vespers* as chamber work rather than a 'choral' one. Thus only one instrument is used per part, the harpsichord is employed very sparingly, and the basic continuo group is restricted to organ and chitarrone. Following the same principle, one voice per part is taken as the norm. The result is a clarity of texture, evident from the opening bars, which allows correct tempos to be used without sti-

fling often intricate rhythmic features. Another fundamental choice represents something of a novelty. Both 'Lauda Jerusalem' and the 'Magnificat' are transposed down a fourth here, as they should be according to the convention relating to the clef combinations in which they were originally notated. This brings all the vocal parts into the tessitura of the rest of the work, and restores the instruments to their normal ranges. Whether or not the result is less 'exciting' than the version we're used to hearing has only partly to do with questions of musicality. For the rest, one of the lasting virtues of this well-balanced, unobtrusive recording is that it allows us to hear the *Vespers* sounding something along the lines that Monteverdi intended.

Cima Concerti ecclesiastici – Sonata per il violino,   Ⓟ
cornetto e violone; Sonata per il violino e violone
Monteverdi Vespro della Beata Vergine
Sophie Marin-Degor, Maryseult Wieczorek sops
Artur Stefanowicz, Fabián Schofrin countertens
Paul Agnew, Joseph Cornwell, François Piolino tens **Thierry Félix, Clive Bayley** basses
Les Sacqueboutiers de Toulouse; Les Arts Florissants / William Christie hpd/org
Erato ② 3984-23139-2 (100' · DDD) Text and translation included   ⒻO

This is in some ways an oddly old-fashioned approach to the 1610 *Vespers*. With a substantial choir and sometimes highly varying orchestration, William Christie creates a warm and glowing sound. Part of his emphasis is on texture and flow, so Monteverdi's often sharp dissonances tend to have a soft edge; and there are some occasionally irrelevant pitches buried in the polyphonic web. He faces the challenge of putting the 'Lauda Jerusalem' and the 'Magnificat' at a pitch standard a fourth lower than the rest (which he has at a modern concert pitch). And that's where the rich orchestration pays its dividends; the resulting almost impossibly low bass lines, particularly in the 'Et misericordia' section of the 'Magnificat', sound clear and lucid with their instrumental doubling. He also benefits from the splendid low range of the tenors he uses: they manage to make the 'Gloria Patri' section a true climax to the work, and they give the 'Duo Seraphim' perhaps the most convincing performance available anywhere because they're so beautifully matched. Christie prefaces each of the psalms with a chant introit; and he follows the order of the print except in putting 'Duo Seraphim' before the 'Sonata sopra Sancta Maria'. To fill the gap where Monteverdi put 'Duo Seraphim' he introduces a sonata by Cima, superbly played by a team led by the violinist, François Fernandez; another sonata by Cima separates the 'Lauda Jerusalem' from 'Duo Seraphim'. There's a warmth and generosity here that are undeniably attractive; the movements mentioned go better than anything else available; and everything is done at the level of skill and musicality that we've come to expect from Christie and his group.

MONTEVERDI'S VESPERS – IN BRIEF

Taverner Consort / Andrew Parrott
Virgin Veritas ② 561662-2 (148' · DDD) ·   Ⓑ**O**
The first recording to engage fully with the scholarly debates regarding the form, purpose and pitch of the work, this 1984 version is a comprehensive and radical attempt to reconstruct a festal Vespers service, the music reordered so that it no longer seems to work towards a proto-Wagnerian climax.

Les Arts Florissants / William Christie
Erato ② 3984 23139-2 (100' · DDD)   Ⓕ**O**
Christie's version, made with relatively large choral and instrumental forces in a resonant venue, conveys the flair, spontaneity and warmth of his live music-making.

Concentus Musicus / Nikolaus Harnoncourt
Teldec ② 0630-18955-2 (105' · DDD)   Ⓑ
Harnoncourt in 1986 prefers more rugged sonorities and bigger scoring than those modern rivals who look above all for clarity and simplicity.

English Baroque Soloists / John Eliot Gardiner
Archiv ② 429 565-2AH2 (106' · DDD)   Ⓕ
This large-scale live recording (Gardiner's second) was made in Venice's St Mark's Basilica. It captures the drama as well as the ceremonial aspect of the work, despite sometimes cloudy recorded sound (See Archiv 073 035-9 for the spectacular DVD).

Concerto Itaiano / Rinaldo Alessandrini
Naïve ② OP30403 (105' · DDD)   Ⓕ**OO**
A striking and thought-provoking performance from Alessandrini that uses a 'soloistic' approach to impressive effect. Try and hear a little before you buy: it will either repel or entrance. We think the latter…

Concentus Musicus / Réné Jacobs   Ⓕ
Harmonia Mundi ② HMC90 1566/7 (104' · DDD)
More intimate than most, with a dramatic flair that eludes most English versions. Jacobs relates the work to its madrigal inspirations.

New London Consort / Philip Pickett
Decca ② 425 823-2OH2 (91' · DDD)   Ⓕ
Pickett and his band go hell for leather in seizing the work's theatricality by the scruff of the neck – and revelling in its moments of secular, sensuous sensibility.

Monteverdi Choir etc / John Eliot Gardiner
Decca ② 429 565-2AH2 (106' · ADD)   Ⓜ
Gardiner's first version was made with some of the finest English singers of the day and the legendary Philip Jones Brass Ensemble. It may not be as polished, but its vitality stands up well to the later version.

Vespro della Beata Vergine   Ⓟ
Roberta Invernizzi sop Monica Piccinini, Anna Simboli mezs Sara Mingardo contr Francesco Ghelardini counterten Luca Dordolo, Vincenzo Di Donato, Gianluca Ferrarini tens Pietro Spagnoli, Furio Zanasi bars Daniele Carnovich, Antonio Abete basses Concerto Italiano / Rinaldo Alessandrini
Naïve ② OP30403 (105' · DDD · T/t)   Ⓕ**OO**

Rinaldo Alessandrini has waited long before committing to disc his thoughts on Monteverdi's most famous sacred publication. On the issues that have divided modern performers he's unflappably pragmatic. In keeping with Concerto Italiano's general approach, the vocal lines in 'choral' pieces are taken by soloists who step out of the ensemble, on the grounds, he says in the notes, that 'We possess no sources attesting choral performance of this music.' He sticks to the published order, observing that no single liturgical event can account for the presence of every piece in the collection. Finally, he transposes the *Lauda Jerusalem* and the *Magnificat* on the grounds that failure to do so would entail enlarging the overall ensemble. These are decisions that continue to divide scholars. Suffice it to say that a clear vision results which has the virtue of coherence, though it comes at the cost of dramatic effects that many continue to hold dear. But the notion that this work wasn't conceived on the grand scale in which some performers dress it up in no way diminishes the greatness of the music.

Other details of execution aren't quite so persuasive. In some of the later psalms, rhythmic detail tends to get lost in the overall sound, lessening one's appreciation of Monteverdi's contrapuntal virtuosity, and giving a certain 'floaty' quality that can be distracting. Not for Alessandrini the pinpoint precision and analytical clarity of, say, the Monteverdi Choir. However, the instruments give wonderfully punchy accounts of the Sonata, and at times the sackbuts and continuo come wonderfully close to impersonating a percussion section.

Those with a fixed conception of the work may fail to be convinced. Put mischievously, there's something here to displease nearly everyone. But there are many moments that will return you to the music more violently; and you have to take seriously what so distinguished a Monteverdian has to say.

Madrigals

Madrigals – Book 2, Il secondo libro de' madrigali
La Venexiana / Claudio Cavina counterten
Glossa GCD920922 (70' · DDD · T/t)   Ⓕ

La Venexiana's cast for Book 2 is virtually identical to Concerto Italiano's a decade earlier. Here La Venexiana has the edge. Concerto Italiano zipped through the whole book in just under an hour; given that the same singers take more than 10 minutes longer in the new version it's perhaps surprising that the two approaches don't sound more different. Claudio Cavina doesn't fragment the text in the manner of his rival, but his more leisurely readings generate a more effective charge by lingering over Monteverdi's climactic build-ups (as in the last line of *Mentr'io mirava fiso*, to mention just one instance), and he has the edge on intonation.

Madrigals – Book 3, Il terzo libro de madrigali
La Venexiana (Rossana Bertini, Valentina Coladonato, Nadia Ragni *sops* Paola Reggiani *mez* Giuseppe Maletto, Sandro Naglia *tens* Daniele Carnovich *bass*) / **Claudio Cavina** *counterten*
Glossa GCD920910 (63' · DDD) Text and translation included   Ⓕ**OOO**

The masterly anthology of styles in Book 3 presents very specific challenges in performance precisely because of its variety. La Venexiana have an excellent understanding of the essentially polyphonic nature of such works as *La giovinetta pianta* and are therefore quite superb in the more difficult mixed style of *O dolce anima mia*, *Stracciami pur il core* or *Se per estremo ardore*, whose complicated rhetorical devices are brought off with perfection. Such brief transcendent moments as 'non può morir d'amor alma fedele' in *Stracciami pur il core*, or 'ingiustamente brami' in *O dolce anima mia*, far from seeming isolated jewels, arise here naturally from their context, which is no mean achievement for the uncharted waters that Monteverdi was navigating in these experimental but masterly works. The singers also have the full measure of the Tasso cycles of Book 3 entering fully into the polychrome, storm-lit intensity of the emotional and musical landscape. La Venexiana's dark hues and dramatic but not histrionic approach sound unbeatable. A very fine disc indeed.

Madrigals – Book 4, Il quarto libro de madrigali Ⓟ
Concerto Italiano / Rinaldo Alessandrini
Opus 111 OPS30-81 (62' · DDD) Recorded 1993.
Texts and translations included   Ⓕ**OOO**

Book 4, first published in 1603, is a wide-ranging collection written during the previous 10 years. Originally written for performance before a select audience by professional virtuoso singers, these madrigals, many of which are set to the sensuous, emotional and epigrammatic verses of Guarini and Tasso, show Monteverdi's seemingly inexhaustible ability to unite words and music in expressively effective ways. A complete and profound understanding of textual nuance is, then, central to any successful performance and here Concerto Italiano begins with a considerable advantage over any group of non-Italians. Some of the finest madrigals in the Fourth Book are those involving direct speech, which allowed Monteverdi to make full use of the court virtuosi, famed for their abilities to combine clear

declamation with dramatic gestures and subtle shadings of dynamics and speed. These are performances infused with a flexible approach to tempo and strong projection of text geared to a determination to allow each detail of the words to speak with due force. The singing style is muscular without losing its ability to move into a gentler mood, the vocal balance good, the sound bright and clear. At its best this record is simply without equal.

Madrigals – Book 7, Il settimo libro de' madrigali
La Venexiana / Claudio Cavina *counterten*
Glossa ② GCD920927 (137' · DDD · T/t)   Ⓕ

Book 7 (1619) gathers together works that must have been written many years apart. The common denominator is its consistent use of instruments in conjunction with the voices. Recording the complete book is a considerable undertaking, only previously achieved by the Consort of Musicke (Virgin Veritas, nla).

La Venexiana's free approach to rhythm is alive to the spirit of the music. *Ohimé, dov'è il mio ben* manages to be a set of variations on the Romanesca theme, and something else entirely: they convince you that this double-reading is precisely what Monteverdi intended. Though not everything reflects the multi-faceted Monteverdi aesthetic, the pieces that are recorded less often still shed a useful light on his working process. As the first *intégrale* by a modern Italian ensemble, this is a significant addition to the catalogue.

Madrigals – Book 8, Il ottavo libro de madrigali Ⓟ
('Madrigali guerrieri et amorosi') – Sinfonia; Altri canti d'amor; Non havea Febo ancora, 'Lamento della ninfa'; Vago augelletto; Perchè t'en fuggi, O Fillide?; Altri canti di Marte; Ogni amante è guerrier; Hor ch'el ciel e la terra; Gira il nemico insidioso Amore; Dolcissimo uscignolo; Ardo, ardo, avvampo, mi struggo
Concerto Italiano / Rinaldo Alessandrini
Opus 111 OPS30-187 (75' · DDD) Texts and translations included   Ⓕ**OOO**

Book 8, issued with the eye-catching title of *Madrigali guerrieri et amorosi* ('Madrigals of Love and War'), was published in 1638. Taking their cue from the prominent position allocated to his cherished *genere concitato* in both the preface and contents of the collection, Rinaldo Alessandrini has made an unusual selection of pieces in which this kind of writing, which in practice involves much rapid chordal repetition, triadic formulas and scale passages to imitate the sounds of war, is prominent. It's a brave choice. The rhetorical gestures of the *genere concitato* are few, simple, obvious and rapidly pall when over-used. Nor are they confined to the *madrigali guerrieri* alone, since the agitation caused by the pains of love can also call them up. The real interpretative difficulty is to invest these moments with sufficient drama and character that they emerge from their somewhat textbook status and come to life.

Concerto Italiano's dramatic readings of the texts involve the familiar devices of contrast, changes of pace, subtle underscorings at cadences and the highlighting of dissonant moments. The star performance is 'Hor ch'el ciel e la terra' which begins with a magically poetic evocation of the stillness of the night before settling into a depiction of the lover's pain, achieved through sharp stabbing motions of almost mannerist exaggeration. Their account of the second part is remarkable, not least for its inspired isolation of vocal lines of great lyrical power passed between the voices; it's a revelation.

Madrigals – Book 8, Il ottavo libro di madrigali; 'Madrigali guerrieri et amorosi'
Maria Cristina Kiehr, Salomé Haller sops **Marisa Martins** mez **Bernarda Fink** contr **Christophe Laporte** counterten **John Bowen, Jeremy Ovenden, Mario Zeffiri, Kobie van Rensburg** tens **Victor Torres** bar **Antonio Abete, Renaud Delaigue** basses Concerto Vocale / **René Jacobs**
Harmonia Mundi ② HMC90 1736/7 (156' · DDD)
Texts and translations included   ⒻOO

This appears to be the first ever complete recording (and at any rate, the only one currently available) of Book 8. The blurb on the jacket says, 'Indispensable', and this is hardly an exaggeration. A complete Book 8 would be enough to whet any Monteverdian's appetite; but fortunately, completeness isn't the only reason to hail the new arrival. Jacobs's well-rounded team of singers is perhaps most effective in the large ensembles, which have a festive opulence about them, while allowing the necessary shadings to come into play: such things as the opening of 'Hor che'l ciel' and 'Ardo, avvampo' are admirably done, the one suitably mysterious and opaque, the other happily (but convincingly) chaotic. And with one or two exceptions the soloists acquit themselves handsomely, too: Bernarda Fink's title-role in the *Lamento della ninfa* is very affecting – one of the high-points of the set.

Jacobs's deployment of instruments, even on the continuo, is measured – even sparing, by his standards – but rich enough to evoke the splendid courtly entertainments for which these pieces were conceived. The instrumentalists are perhaps too easily overlooked in this repertoire: they don't draw attention to themselves here, but sound very solid and grounded.

Jacobs's feeling for the music's dramatic qualities is keen, and unsurprisingly encompasses the largest pieces, the 'one-act' operas *Il ballo delle ingrate* and *Combattimento di Tancredi e Clorinda*. For these, some may prefer Concerto Italiano's recording, which includes both pieces on a single disc, but Jacobs's less wilful readings are still most involving. By any objective criteria, Jacobs has pulled it off. So if you're looking for a single recording, this is a natural first choice.

L'incoronazione di Poppea

L'incoronazione di Poppea   Ⓟ
Helen Donath sop Poppea **Elisabeth Söderström** sop Nerone **Cathy Berberian** mez Ottavia **Paul Esswood** counterten Ottone **Giancarlo Luccardi** bass Seneca **Rotraud Hansmann** sop Virtue, Drusilla **Jane Gartner** sop Fortune, Pallas, Darmigella **Maria Minetto** contr Nurse **Carlo Gaifa** ten Arnalta **Philip Langridge** ten Lucano **Enrico Fissore** bass-bar Lictor, Mercury **anonymous** treb Love **Margaret Baker** sop Valletto **Vienna Concentus Musicus / Nikolaus Harnoncourt**
Teldec ④ 2292-42547-2 (215' · ADD) Recorded 1973-4. Notes, text and translation included   ⓂO

L'incoronazione di Poppea has always had its staunch admirers, many claiming it to be Monteverdi's greatest masterpiece, even the finest opera of the 17th century. However, what's left of the opera amounts to little more than a vocal score, and even then with some scenes missing, others evidently added by other hands. To turn the sketchy sources into something that Monteverdi might have recognised as his work requires self-confidence. Harnoncourt's production is still the best recording of it ever made. With its strong, sensitive cast and excellent pacing, this is a performance that shows the work's true potential, even if the realisation is calculated to raise a few eyebrows. There are reservations about the use of loud wind instruments, above all in vocal contexts, and about the heavy ornamentation that their players use. Even the scoring of the string orchestra is heavy handed on occasion. These effects are entirely of Harnoncourt's own making, since there's nothing in the sources to indicate the size and nature of the orchestra. His decision to associate certain timbres with specific situations could also be seen as regrettable. Trumpets for the gods is acceptable, but there's nothing subtle about the pair of oboes that accompanies the comic characters. What saves this performance, however, is the fine cast of singers. There isn't a single weak link. It was an imaginative move to cast Elisabeth Söderström as Nerone, and one can forgive her palpable femininity on the grounds that she finds so much to convey in her playing of the part. Equally sure of her role as Ottavia is Cathy Berberian. The lesser characters are played superbly well – Jane Gartner as Fortune/Darmigella/Pallas, for example, or Philip Langridge as Lucano. It's as if every member of the cast recognises the latent power of this marvellous music, and that's what makes this recording such an enduring one.

L'incoronazione di Poppea   Ⓟ
Sylvia McNair sop Poppea **Dana Hanchard** sop Nerone **Anne Sofie von Otter** mez Ottavia, Fortune, Venus **Michael Chance** counterten Ottone

Francesco Ellero d'Artegna *bass* Seneca
Catherine Bott *sop* Drusilla, Virtue, Pallas, Athene
Roberto Balcone *counterten* Nurse **Bernarda Fink**
contr Arnalta **Mark Tucker** *ten* Lucano, First Soldier
Julian Clarkson *bass* Lictor, Mercury **Marinella
Pennicchi** *sop* Love **Constanze Backes** *sop* Valleto
Nigel Robson *ten* Liberto, Second Soldier **English
Baroque Soloists / Sir John Eliot Gardiner**
Archiv Produktion ③ 447 088-2AH3 (191' · DDD)
Recorded live 1993. Notes, text and translation
included   Ⓕ

The central question was always about how
much needs to be added to the surviving notes
in order to make. *Poppea* viable on stage. Gardiner and his advisers believe that nothing needs
adding and that the 'orchestra' played only
when explicitly notated in the score and was a
very small group. To some ears this will have a
fairly ascetic effect, but it's firmly in line with
current scholarly thinking. To compensate,
there's a rich group of continuo players who
play with wonderful flexibility. And Gardiner's
spacious reading of the score bursts with the
variety of pace you might expect from a seasoned conductor of early opera. Sylvia McNair
is a gloriously sensuous Poppea: from her sleepy
first words to the final duet she's always a thoroughly devious character, with her breathy,
come-hither tones. Complementing this is
Dana Hanchard's angry-brat Nerone, less even
in voice than one might hope, but dramatically
powerful nevertheless. Whether they quite
challenge Helen Donath and Elisabeth Söderström for Harnoncourt is a matter of opinion,
but they certainly offer a viable alternative.

The strongest performances here, though,
come from Michael Chance and Anne Sofie von
Otter as Ottone and Ottavia, both of them
offering superbly rounded portrayals. Again
they face severe challenges from Harnoncourt's
unforgettable Paul Esswood and Cathy Berberian, but here the challenge is more equal.
Francesco Ellero d'Artegna is perhaps the most
vocally skilled Seneca to date.

The fact that this was recorded at a public concert is noticeable only occasionally.

L'Orfeo

L'Orfeo   Ⓟ
Laurence Dale *ten* Orfeo **Efrat Ben-Nun** *sop*
Euridice, Music **Jennifer Larmore** *mez* Messenger
Andreas Scholl *counterten* Hope **Paul Gérimon**
bass Charon **Bernarda Fink** *contr* Proserpina **Harry
Peeters** *bass* Pluto **Nicolas Rivenq** *bar* Apollo
Concerto Vocale / René Jacobs
Harmonia Mundi ② HMC90 1553/4 (120' · DDD)
Notes, text and translation included   ⒻOO

It's clear right from the start, with the almost
aggressive snarling brass and thudding drums of
the opening Toccata, that René Jacobs's reading of *L'Orfeo* is a full-blooded one. The tone is
set by Efrat Ben-Nun, whose approach to the
two roles she sings is refreshingly direct and

dramatic. Laurence Dale is powerful in the
title-role, capable of negotiating the sudden
changes of emotional state that characterise the
part. Among the other soloists Bernarda Fink
delivers a convincingly urgent account of Proserpina's appeal at the opening of the Fourth
Act, while Harry Peeters's Pluto presents his
measured responses with an attractively lyrical
authority. Charon's strangely angular lines,
with their air of menace appropriate to one who
spends time in contact with the Underworld,
are expertly managed by Paul Gérimon, who
shows himself to be a true Monteverdi bass.

Jacobs's approach to the thorny question of
orchestration is robust. The score is notoriously
difficult to interpret in this respect, and in the
end any solution can only be judged against
some notion of what Monteverdi's sound world
might have been. Jacobs's version was originally
given at the Salzburg Festival in 1993, and his
instrumental resources, based around three
continuo instruments spatially separated, are
more a reflection of the acoustical properties of
a modern pit rather than those of the sort of
room in the ducal palace of Mantua where
L'Orfeo was first performed. The result is successful and rarely over-elaborate.

L'Orfeo   Ⓟ
Ian Bostridge *ten* Orfeo **Patrizia Ciofi** *ten* Euridice
Natalie Dessay *sop* La Musica **Alice Coote** *ten*
Messenger **Sonia Prina** *ten* Speranza **Mario Luperi**
ten Caronte **Véronique Gens** *ten* Prosperina
Carolyn Sampson *ten* Nymph **Lorenzo Regazzo** *ten*
Plutone **Christopher Maltman** *ten* Apollo Shepherd
III **Paul Agnew** *ten* Eco Shepherd II **Pascal Bertin**
ten Shepherd I **Richard Burkhard** *ten* Shepherd IV
**European Voices; Le Concert d'Astrée /
Emmanuelle Haïm**
Virgin Classics Veritas ② 545642-2 (96' · DDD)   ⒻOO

Instead of attempting an intellectual reconstruction of *L'Orfeo*, Emmanuelle Haïm presents a full-blooded reinvention of the opera
that's firmly modernistic. The cast is primarily
composed of world-class opera and recital
singers: the overall result is even, cohesive and
without vocal blemishes. Some sopranos represent the legacy of 'authenticity' better than others. Natalie Dessay's forthright declamation as
La Musica in the exquisite prologue is emotive,
but can't eclipse Gardiner's astute Lynne Dawson. In contrast, Carolyn Sampson's fleeting
contribution as a Nymph is gorgeously refined
and elegantly poised, suggesting that she might
make a fine La Musica if given the chance.
Véronique Gens is a creamy Prosperina whose
tangible pity for Orfeo makes her a very human
goddess. Alice Coote's Messenger provides the
most compelling moment with a haunted voice
full of eloquent pain. The title-role suits Ian
Bostridge, and his thoughtfully considered
singing effortlessly ranges between smouldering gestures in 'Vi ricorda ò bosch' ombrosi'
and shivering disbelief when the messenger tells
him Euridice is dead.

MONTEVERDI'S ORFEO – IN BRIEF

John Mark Ainsley *Orfeo* **Jane Gooding** *Euridice*
Catherine Bott *Musica, Messenger, Prosperina*
New London Consort / Philip Pickett
L'Oiseau-Lyre ② 433 545-2OH2 (108' · DDD) Ⓕ**O**
A wonderfully vital account with a superbly
florid and intense performance of the title-role
from John Mark Ainsley. The rest of the cast is
very fine, and Pickett directs with great flair.

Anthony Rolfe Johnson *Orfeo* **Julianne Baird**
Euridice **Lynne Dawson** *Musica* **Anne Sofie von
Otter** *Messenger* **Monteverdi Choir; English
Baroque Soloists / Sir John Eliot Gardiner** Ⓕ
Archiv Production ② 419 250-2AH2 (106' · DDD)
Rolfe Johnson's performance is superb, and
Gardiner builds around him a musical struc-
ture that captures both the initimacy and,
where appropriate, the grandeur of the piece.
The Montverdi Choir, not surprisingly, rise to
the challenge with terrific vitality.

Nigel Rogers *Orfeo* **Patrizia Kwella** *Euridice*
Emma Kirkby *Musica* **Jennifer Smith** *Proserpina*
**Chiaroscuro; London Baroque; London Cornett
and Sackbutt Ensemble / Nigel Rogers**
EMI ② 764947-2 (104' · DDD) Ⓜ
A recording that really captures the extraordinary colours Monteverdi draws from his
instrumental ensemble: Medlam uses a
smaller group than other versions but they
play with great flexibility and style. The cast
is well chosen and Rogers makes a powerful
hero, surmounting the vocal challenges with
ease.

Laurence Dale *Orfeo* **Efrat Ben-Nun** *Euridice,*
Music **Jennifer Larmore** *Messenger* **Andreas
Scholl** *Hope* **Paul Gérimon** *Charon* **Bernarda
Fink** *Prosperina* **Concerto Vocale / René Jacobs**
Harmonia Mundi ② HMC90 1553/4 (120' · DDD)
Ⓕ**OO**
A thrilling and very exciting account with
great care lavished on the accompanying
ensemble. The cast is a strong one, and Lau-
rence Dale is well able to capture the numer-
ous shifts of character throughout the work.
A strong rival to the Gardiner set.

Ian Bostridge *Orfeo* **Patrizia Ciofi** *Euridice*
Natalie Dessay *Musica* **Alice Coote** *Messenger*
Véronique Gens *Proserpina* **Le Concert
d'Astrée / Emmanuelle Haïm**
Virgin Classics ② 545642-2 (96' · DDD) Ⓕ**OO**
A world-class cast and one of the most inspirational of today's Baroque specialists make for
an outstanding performance. Bostridge's
histrionic Orfeo is wonderfully drawn but to
single him out is invidious. Vividly recorded.

European Voices incline towards a full-
blooded operatic sound rather than a cool
choral blend. Le Concert d'Astrée serve as a
linchpin that propels the drama forward with
obsessive momentum. The pumping sackbuts
during the introductory toccata indicate that
the ensuing drama isn't going to be dull, and
Les Sacqueboutiers also provide a splendid
regal entrance to a vision of Dante's Inferno in
Act 3. The strings produce *ritornellos* of magnificent sensitivity and resonating eroticism. Haïm
does, though, excessively pepper Monteverdi's
score with prominent and improvisational percussion.

Haïm's performance has a much stronger Italianate sense than the comparatively English
school that's hitherto dominated the discography, and her compelling perspective possesses a
lively spirit that makes the listening hours fly by.
Purists will be divided over the liberties she
takes, but her performance is a stimulating
alternative to the fine pedigree of recordings
that has preceded it.

Il Ritorno d'Ulisse in Patria

Il Ritorno d'Ulisse in Patria Ⓟ
Christoph Prégardien *ten* Ulisse **Bernarda Fink**
contr Penelope **Christina Högmann** *sop* Telemaco,
Siren **Martyn Hill** *ten* Eumete **Jocelyne Taillon** *mez*
Ericlea **Dominique Visse** *counterten* Pisandro,
Human Fragility **Mark Tucker** *ten* Anfinomo **David
Thomas** *bass* Antinoo **Guy de Mey** *ten* Iro **Faridah
Subrata** *mez* Melanto **Jörg Dürmüller** *ten* Eurimaco
Lorraine Hunt *sop* Minerva, Fortune **Michael
Schopper** *bass* Nettuno, Time **Olivier Lallouette**
bass Giove **Claron McFadden** *sop* Giunone **Martina
Bovet** *sop* Siren, Love **Concerto Vocale / René
Jacobs**
Harmonia Mundi ③ HMX290 1427/9 (179' · DDD)
Recorded 1992. Notes, text and translation included
Ⓜ**O**

The only surviving manuscript score of this
major musical drama, preserved in Vienna,
presents an incomplete version of three acts.
For this recording, René Jacobs has, within the
spirit of 17th-century music-making, added
more music by Monteverdi and others to
expand the work to a satisfying five-act structure suggested by some surviving librettos. He
has also considerably expanded the scoring, very
much enlivening the instrumental palette that
Monteverdi would have had available to him for
his original production in Vienna in 1641, and
the result is powerful and effective.

The extensive cast, led by Christoph Prégardien in the title-role, is excellently chosen, not
only for vocal quality but also for a convincing
awareness of Monteverdi's idiom. Without
that, the performance could have seemed tame,
and that's nowhere better exemplified than in
Act 1, Scene 7 where Ulysses awakes, wondering where he is and what's to happen to him.
Prégardien here manages to convey as much
depth of feeling as a Pagliaccio yet stays clearly
within the bounds of Monteverdi's expressive

style. The result is a *tour de force*, one of the many within this production. The adept instrumental contribution certainly helps to maintain variety throughout the work, and an accompaniment suited to the sentiments expressed by the vocalists is always possible with these resources. Ultimately, this production is very much one for our time. It's a practical solution to the problems of performing music of another age, and one that turns out to be inspired, moving and totally compelling.

Cristóbal de Morales

Spanish c1500-1553

Morale is recognised as the most important figure in early 16th-century Spanish sacred music. He received his early musical education in Seville and in 1526 was appointed maestro de capilla of Avila Cathedral. In 1531 he resigned and by September 1535 was a singer in the papal chapel in Rome. He left in 1545 and was appointed maestro de capilla at Toledo Cathedral. He then fell ill and in 1547 renounced the position. On returning to Andalusia he became maestro de capilla to the Duke of Arcos at Marchena (1548-51). In 1551 he became maestro de capilla at Málaga Cathedral.

His works, almost all liturgical, include over 20 masses, 16 Magnificats, two Lamentations and over 100 motets. The Magnificats, perhaps the best known of his works, are permeated by Gregorian cantus firmi ; his Lamentations are characterised by a sober homophonic style. In his motets he often used chant associated with the text, as a melodic point of departure (eg Puer natus est) or as an ostinato figure (eg the five-voice Tu es Petrus), but he seldom borrowed entire melodies. Their texture is characterised by free imitation with exceptional use of homophonic sections to stress important words or portions of text. The two masses for the dead and the Officium defunctorum are the most extreme examples of Morales's sober style. He had thorough command of early 16th-century continental techniques and his style is better compared to Josquin, Gombert and Clemens than to his Spanish contemporaries. He favoured cross-rhythms, conflicting rhythms, melodic (but not harmonic) sequence and repetition, harmonic cross-relations, systematic use of consecutives and occasional daring use of harmony.

GROVEmusic

Masses

Missa 'Si bona suscepimus' **Crecquillon** Andreas **P**
Christi famulus **Verdelot** Si bona suscepimus
The Tallis Scholars / Peter Phillips
Gimell CDGIM033 (56' · DDD) Texts and translations included   Ⓕ**OO**

The Tallis Scholars move into new territory for them: Cristóbal de Morales is perhaps the most admired Spanish composer of all time, to judge from the distribution and longevity of his works. But not nearly enough of his music has appeared on disc. In particular, the six-voice Mass *Si bona suscepimus* appears not to have been recorded before. It was printed in his first book of Masses (1544) and undoubtedly comes from his years in the papal chapel. At first listening, there may be something almost too serene about its flawless counterpoint that flows with effortless invention. But there's an abundance of arresting detail in here, and he uses the six voices with an astonishing variety of textures.

The Tallis Scholars are up to their usual standards of magnificent sound colour, nicely judged balance and extremely pure intonation. There's nothing overtly Spanish in the performance: they simply sing what's in the music, without imposing too much externally. They hardly ever rush or slow down severely, preferring to allow the music to unfold at its own flexible pace. That could seem bland until you compare the sound with the introductory five-voice motet of Verdelot on which the Mass is based, or indeed the marvellous Crecquillon motet that ends the disc; these immediately sound quite different (and indeed make you wonder why the Crecquillon motet passed for so long as a work of Morales).

Morales Mass for the feast of St Isidore of Seville. **P**
Missa 'Mille regretz'. Emendemus in melius
Guerrero O Doctor optime Instrumental and organ works by **Cabézon, Rogier, Guerrero, Gombert, Santa María**
Gabrieli Consort and Players / Paul McCreesh
Archiv Produktion Blue 474 228-2ABL (76' · DDD)
Texts and translations included   Ⓜ

The instrumental *canciones* by Guerrero and Rogier which open the disc are played with delightful sensitivity: one can understand why instrumentalists were so prized in Spanish cathedrals at this time if they played like this. Morales's Mass itself, performed by an all-male consort, is sung splendidly. There's a real feeling for the work's direction (not easily discerned in music so seamlessly polyphonic as Morales) which, in combination with the seductively rich sonority of the choir, make it a performance of genuine stature. The only reservations concern the stodgy singing of the 'Hosanna' which would surely benefit from a lighter, more rhythmic approach. The plainchant is for the feast of St Isidore of Seville, taken from unspecified 16th- and 17th-century sources by Robert Snow. It's sung accompanied by a dulcian, as indeed is the polyphony, common Spanish practice of the time. Instruments and choir come together only in Guerrero's motet, *O Doctor optime*, sung at the Offertory, which is an object lesson in how to achieve blend and balance. Another *canción* by Rogier acts as a recessional, and the disc closes with a short piece by Tomás de Santa María followed by a magnificent performance of Morales's motet *Emendemus in melius*.

Assumption Mass – Toledo Cathedral, c1580 ⊡
Morales Ave regina caelorum. Exaltata est sancta
Dei genitrix. Missa Benedicta est regina caelorum
Cabezón Beata viscera Mariae Virginis. Tiento sobre
el hymno, 'Ave Maris stella' **Ceballos** O pretiosum et
admirabile sacrementum **F Guerrero** Ave Maria.
Dulcissima Maria **Ribera** Beata mater **Torrentes**
Asperges Mej **Plainchants** – Introitus; Oratio;
Graduale and Alleluia; Offertorium; Prefacio; Pater
noster; Communio; Postcommunio
Orchestra of the Renaissance / Richard Cheetham
and Michael Noone
Glossa GCD921404 (76' · DDD) Texts and translations
included   Ⓕ

This is a reconstruction of a Mass for the
Assumption as it might have been heard in
Toledo Cathedral in about 1580. It follows very
much the pattern established by the group's
previous discs, with a mixture of musical items
that can be pegged, however loosely, to a particular occasion or type of occasion. Here the
research into the rich musical repertory and the
musico-liturgical practice of Toledo Cathedral
by guest conductor Michael Noone makes for a
particularly compelling example of the reconstruction genre. The ways in which instruments
and voices are used is well thought out, and the
music, including those pieces by the less well-
known Toledan *maestros* Ribera and Torrentes,
is of the highest quality. Similar care has been
taken over the sources for the plainchant which,
as on earlier recordings by the Orchestra of the
Renaissance, is performed with just the right
inflections and sense of pace by the bass Josep
Cabré.

It's clear that Morales' music continued to be
performed in Spanish cathedrals throughout
the 16th century and beyond, and the superb
Mass *Benedicta est regina caelorum* makes it easy
to see why. It's performed well by singers and
instrumentalists alike, the harp and dulcian
adding a distinctive shimmer and depth to the
overall soundpool of voices, shawms and sackbuts. Overall, the performances are restrained
with a good sense of natural flow, if perhaps
occasionally lacking in intensity. An impressive
and very attractive CD that grows with repeated
listening into one of the most convincing 'occasional' recordings in the catalogue.

Motets

In illo tempore cum turba magna. In illo tempore
stabant autem. Fantasia. In illo tempore dixit Jesus
modicum. In illo tempore assumpsit Jesus. Missus
est Gabriel. Virgo Maria. Descendit Angelus. Manus
tuae Domine. Job, tonso capite, corruens in terram.
Vae Babylon, civitas magna. Similie est regnum. Iam
nom dicam vos servos. Accepit Jesus panes.
Clamabat autem mulier. Quanti mercenari. Quanti
mercenari (instrumental)
Consortium Carissimi / Vittorio Zanon org
ASV GaudeamusCDGAU343 (72' · DDD · T/t)   Ⓕ

Morales is presented in some textbooks as a pre-

cursor of Palestrina on account of the clarity of
his polyphony and the balance of his lines. He's
certainly one of the more distinctive voices of
his generation, even though he eschews the
startling false relations of (say) Gombert. All
this comes across in these performances. Consortium Carissimi give pleasant and generally
convincing accounts of some fine music, though
what is an instructive discovery on a budget
label mightn't be quite so enthusiastically recommended at full price. Morales's motets certainly deserve a hearing; on that basis, so does
this recording.

Ignaz Moscheles   German 1794-1870

*A pupil of B. D. Weber in Prague and of Albrechts-
berger and Salieri in Vienna, Moscheles became a
piano recitalist, travelling throughout Europe
(1815-25). Settling in London (1825-46), he
taught at the RAM established a series of 'historical
soirées' (in which he performed Bach and Scarlatti
on the harpsichord), wrote fashionable salon music
and conducted the Philharmonic Society; he was a
friend of Mendelssohn, conducted the London première of Beethoven's Missa solemnis (1832) and
translated Schindler's biography as The Life of
Beethoven (1841). From 1846 he was professor at
the Leipzig Conservatory. His best compositions are
his piano sonatas (some for duet), in which a classical
balance is tempered with an early Romantic
dynamism, and his studies (still used).*
                                              GROVEmusic

Piano Concertos

Piano Concertos – No 2 in E flat, Op 56; No 3 in G
minor, Op 58. Anticipations of Scotland: A Grand
Fantasia, Op 75
Tasmanian Symphony Orchestra / Howard
Shelley pf
Hyperion CDA67276 (76' · DDD)   Ⓕ**OO**

Both the Second and Third Concertos bristle
with enough savage jumps and hurdles to throw
a less than first class performer; woe betide the
pianist without flawless scales and arpeggios
(often twisting into awkward and unpredictable
patterns). Moscheles' contemporaries, hungry
for heart-stopping acrobatics, surely left the
concert hall thrilled and gratified. But there are
also many fascinating purely musical surprises.

Most engagingly, Moscheles was highly
responsive to local colour, paying tribute to his
adopted city of London in his Fourth Concerto
by quoting the 'March of the Grenadiers' and,
in his *Anticipations of Scotland: A Grand Fantasia*,
to folk songs and dances north of the border.
Who can resist the assurance of 'Auld Robin
Grey' (though even he breaks out into a flash of
virtuosity) or a strathspey sufficiently perky to
set all true Scotsmen's blood tingling.

The recordings, made in Tasmania, are excellent, and the Tasmanian Symphony Orchestra

enter into the spirit of things with verve and affection. In short, a disc of aristocratic brilliance and distinction.

Wolfgang Amadeus Mozart

Austrian 1756-1791

Mozart, son of Leopold Mozart, showed musical gifts at a very early age, composing when he was five and when he was six playing before the Bavarian elector and the Austrian empress. Leopold felt that it was proper, and might also be profitable, to exhibit his children's God-given genius (Mozart's sister was a gifted keyboard player), so from mid-1763-6 the family set out on a European tour. Mozart astonished his audiences with his precocious skills; he played to the French and English royal families, had his first music published and wrote his earliest symphonies. In 1767 they were off again, to Vienna, where hopes of having an opera by Mozart performed were frustrated by intrigues. 1770-73 saw three visits to Italy, where Mozart wrote two operas (Mitridate, Lucio Silla) and a serenata for performance in Milan, and acquainted himself with Italian styles. Summer 1773 saw a further visit to Vienna where he wrote a set of string quartets and, on his return, a group of symphonies including Nos 25 in G minor and 29 in A. Apart from a journey to Munich for the première of his opera La finta giardiniera early in 1775, the period from 1774 to mid-1777 was spent in Salzburg, where Mozart worked as Konzertmeister at the Prince Archbishop's court; his works of these years include masses, symphonies, all his violin concertos, six piano sonatas, several serenades and divertimentos and his first great piano concerto, K271.

In 1777 he was sent, with his mother, to Munich and to Mannheim, but was offered no position (though he stayed over four months at Mannheim, falling in love with Aloysia Weber). His father then dispatched him to Paris: there he had minor successes, notably with his Paris Symphony, no.31, deftly designed for the local taste. But prospects there were poor and Leopold ordered him home, where a superior post had been arranged at the court. He returned slowly and alone; his mother had died in Paris. The years 1779-80 were spent in Salzburg, playing in the cathedral and at court, composing sacred works, symphonies, concertos, serenades and dramatic music. But opera remained at the centre of his ambitions, and an opportunity came with a commission for a serious opera for Munich. He went there to compose it late in 1780; his correspondence with Leopold is richly informative about his approach to musical drama. The work, Idomeneo, was a success. In it Mozart depicted serious, heroic emotion with a richness unparalleled elsewhere in his works, with vivid orchestral writing and an abundance of profoundly expressive orchestral recitative.

Mozart was then summoned to Vienna, where the Salzburg court was in residence on the accession of a new emperor. Fresh from his success, he found himself placed between the valets and the cooks; his resentment towards his employer, exacerbated by the

Prince-Archbishop's refusal to let him perform at events the emperor was attending, soon led to conflict, and in May 1781 he resigned, or was kicked out of, his job. He made his living over the ensuing years by teaching, by publishing his music, by playing at patrons' houses or in public, by composing to commission; in 1787 he obtained a minor court post as Kammermusicus, which gave him a reasonable salary and required nothing beyond the writing of dance music for court balls. He earned, by musicians standards, a good income, but lavish spending and poor management caused him financial difficulties. In 1782 he married Constanze Weber, Aloysia's sister.

In his early years in Vienna, Mozart built up his reputation by publishing, playing the piano and, in 1782, having an opera performed: Die Entführung aus dem Serail, a German Singspiel which went far beyond the usual limits of the tradition with its long, elaborately written songs. The work was successful and was taken into the repertories of many provincial companies (for which Mozart was not however paid). In these years, too, he wrote six string quartets which he dedicated to the master of the form, Haydn: they are marked not only by their variety of expression but by their complex textures, conceived as four-part discourse, with the musical ideas linked to this freshly integrated treatment of the medium.

In 1782 Mozart embarked on the composition of piano concertos, so that he could appear both as composer and soloist. He wrote 15 before the end of 1786, with early 1784 as the peak of activity. They represent one of his greatest achievements, with their formal mastery, their subtle relationships between piano and orchestra (the wind instruments especially) and their combination of brilliance, lyricism and symphonic growth. In 1786 he wrote the first of his three comic operas with Lorenzo da Ponte as librettist, Le nozze di Figaro: here and in Don Giovanni (given in Prague, 1787) Mozart treats the interplay of social and sexual tensions with keen insight into human character that – as again in the more artificial sexual comedy of Così fan tutte (1790) – transcends the comic framework, just as Die Zauberflöte (1790) transcends, with its elements of ritual and allegory about human harmony and enlightenment, the world of the Viennese popular theatre from which it springs.

Mozart lived in Vienna for the rest of his life, though he undertook a number of journeys to Salzburg, Prague, Berlin and Frankfurt. The last Prague journey was for the première of La clemenza di Tito (1791), a traditional serious opera written for coronation celebrations, but composed with a finesse and economy characteristic of Mozart's late music. Instrumental works of these years include some piano sonatas, three string quartets written for the King of Prussia, some string quintets, which include one of his most deeply felt works (K516 in G minor) and one of his most nobly spacious (Kn C), and his last four symphonies – one (No 38 in D) composed for Prague in 1786, the others written in 1788 and forming, with the lyricism of No 39 in E flat, the tragic suggestiveness of No 40 in G minor and the grandeur of No 41 in C, a climax to his orchestral music. His final works include the Clarinet Concerto and some pieces for masonic lodges (he had been a freemason since 1784). At his death from a feverish illness whose precise nature has given rise to much speculation (he was not poisoned), he left unfinished the Requiem, his first large-scale work for the church since the C minor Mass of 1783, also unfinished. Mozart was buried in a Vienna suburb, with little ceremony and in an unmarked grave, in accordance with prevailing custom. GROVEmusic

Clarinet Concerto in A, K622

Clarinet Concerto. Clarinet Quintet in A, K581
Thea King basset cl [b]**Gabrieli String Quartet**
(Kenneth Sillito, Brendan O'Reilly vns Ian Jewel va
Keith Harvey vc) [a]**English Chamber Orchestra /
Jeffrey Tate**
Hyperion CDA66199 (64' · DDD) Recorded 1985 (F)O

The two works on this disc represent Mozart's clarinet writing at its most inspired; however, the instrument for which they were written differed in several respects from the modern clarinet, the most important being its extended bass range. Modern editions of both the Clarinet Concerto and the Quintet have adjusted the solo part to suit today's clarinets, but Thea King reverts as far as possible to the original texts, and her playing is both sensitive and intelligent. Jeffrey Tate and the ECO accompany with subtlety and discretion in the concerto, and the Gabrieli Quartet achieves a fine rapport with King in the Quintet. Both recordings are clear and naturally balanced, with just enough distance between soloist and listener.

Clarinet Concerto. Oboe Concerto in C, K314
Jack Brymer cl **Neil Black** ob **Academy of St Martin in the Fields / Sir Neville Marriner**
Philips 416 483-2PH (50' · ADD) Recorded 1973(F)OO

For all the classic status of Jack Brymer's recordings with Beecham (available on EMI with various couplings), we wouldn't now choose them in preference to this version with Marriner. His recording here is of the highest distinction, coupled with Neil Black's delightful performance of the Oboe Concerto. They are fine performances, even great ones; with Marriner, Brymer seems to have rethought his approach to a work he must have known almost too well. He's shed none of his elegance, but there's a greater touch of wistfulness, a hint of tragedy, which lends the music fuller substance. Even in the finale, there's the suggestion that the liveliness is the more precious for an awareness of a darker element. It's the finest of all the recordings, displaying Brymer's art at its greatest in one of the greatest works ever written for the instrument.

Additional recommendation

Coupled with: Beethoven Violin Concerto (arr Pletnev for cl)
Collins cl **Russian National Orchestra / Pletnev**
DG 457 652-2GH (70' · DDD) (F)

Wonderfully agile playing from Michael Collins on the basset clarinet. His is an elegant but powerful reading, with a deeply poetic slow movement. Pletnev's Russian National Orchestra give refined support.

Flute Concertos

No 1 in G, K313/K285c; **No 2** in C, K314/K285d.
Andante in C major, K315/K285e. **Flute and Harp Concerto** in D, K299/K297c

---

Flute Concerto No 1. Andante. Flute and Harp Concerto
Susan Palma fl **Nancy Allen** hp **Orpheus Chamber Orchestra**
DG 427 677-2GH (58' · DDD) Recorded 1988 (F)
Also available (coupled with Horn Concertos Nos 1-4; Clarinet Concerto in A, K622; Sinfonia concertante in E flat; Bassoon Concerto in B flat, K191; Oboe Concerto in C, K314) on
DG ③ 469 362-2GX3 (B)

Mozart's G major Flute Concerto is a charming work, not without depth. This is an admirable performance by Susan Palma, a remarkably gifted player and member of the Orpheus Chamber Orchestra, a conductorless ensemble of 24 musicians, who play with skill and unanimity so that all is alert, lithe and yet sensitive. Palma's tone is liquid and bright, with fine tonal nuances. The Concerto for flute and harp was written for the flute-playing Count de Guines to play with his harpist daughter, and combines these two beautiful instruments to fine effect. Again the soloists are highly skilled and their playing nicely matched, tonally and stylistically. Palma is as delightful as in the other work and the spacious *Andante* in C major that separates the two concertos, while Nancy Allen makes an exquisite sound and also articulates more clearly than many other harpists. The attractive cadenzas are by Palma and Bernard Rose. The balance between the soloists and the orchestra is natural and the recording from New York's State University has a very pleasing sound.

Flute and Harp Concerto[a]; Concerto for Bassoon and Orchestra in B flat, K191[b]; Sinfonia concertante in E flat, K297[bc]
[a]**Kate Hill** fl [c]**Nicholas Daniel** ob [c]**Joy Farrall** cl [bc]**Julie Andrews** bn [b]**Lucy Wakeford** hp [c]**Stephen Bell** hn **Britten Sinfonia / Nicholas Cleobury**
Classic fM The Full Works 75605 57038-2 (74' · DDD) (M)

A delightful recording in every way. These three works are brimful of Mozartian melody of the most beguiling kind. Julie Andrews, the bassoonist, has a spring in her step from the very opening of her solo concerto – after Nicholas Cleobury has set the pace in his spirited and stylishly turned opening ritornello. Her articulation is most winning: there's geniality here without clowning. The melody of the *Andante* brings a touchingly doleful mood, while the Minuet finale is so deftly decorated that you can't help being captivated. The Flute and Harp Concerto also swings off elegantly; and what fragility of texture the soloists, Kate Hill and Lucy Wakeford, create between them! The flute playing is exquisite in the slow movement, and the harp's delicate filigree brings a sense of caressing to the background embroidery. The finale dances off with great charm. The support provided by the Britten Sinfonia throughout has the right degree of robustness to set off the airy tracery of the two soloists. The *Sinfonia concertante* is a team work, and the solo response is first class. In the slow movement the bassoonist winningly takes the lead: the finale brings a delectably light-hearted gait; and how these players enjoy their divisions, with each taking the spotlight in turn, and then chortling in concert infectiously. The recording is vividly real, the kind that leaps out of the speakers. Highly recommended.

Additional recommendation

Flute Concerto No 1
Coupled with: Flute and Harp Concerto. Oboe Concerto
Snowden *fl* **Thomas** *harp* **Hunt** *ob*
London Philharmonic Orchestra / Mackerras
Classics for Pleasure 575 1442 (76' · DDD)   Ⓑ
Jonathan Snowden performs the Flute Concerto quite gloriously. The equally stylish Gordon Hunt plays the Oboe Concerto, and Mackerras directs with his customary flair.

Horn Concertos

No 1 in D, K412; **No 2** in E flat, K417; **No 3** in E flat, K447; **No 4** in E flat, K495

Horn Concertos Nos 1-4. Piano Quintet in E flat,   Ⓗ
K452
Dennis Brain *hn* **Philharmonia Orchestra / Herbert von Karajan**
EMI mono 566898-2 (55' · ADD) Recorded 1953
Ⓕ❰❰❰

Ⓖ Dennis Brain was the finest Mozartian soloist of his generation. Again and again Karajan matches the graceful line of his solo phrasing (the *Romance* of No 3 is just one ravishing example), while in the *Allegros* the crisply articulated, often witty comments from the Philharmonia violins are a joy. The glorious tone and the richly lyrical phrasing of every note from Brain himself is life-enhancing in its radiant warmth. The *Rondos* aren't just spirited, buoyant, infectious and smiling, although they're all these things, but they have the kind of natural flow that Beecham gave to Mozart. There's also much dynamic subtlety – Brain doesn't just repeat the main theme the same as the first time, but alters its level and colour. His

legacy to future generations of horn players has been to show them that the horn – a notoriously difficult instrument – can be tamed absolutely and that it can yield a lyrical line and a range of colour to match any other solo instrument. He was tragically killed, in his prime, in a car accident while travelling home overnight from the Edinburgh Festival. He left us this supreme Mozartian testament which may be approached by others but rarely, if ever, equalled, for his was uniquely inspirational music-making, with an innocent-like quality to make it the more endearing. It's a pity to be unable to be equally enthusiastic about the recorded sound. The remastering leaves the horn timbre, with full Kingsway Hall resonance, unimpaired, but has dried out the strings. This, though, remains a classic recording.

Horn Concertos Nos 1-4. Horn Quintet in E flat, K407/K386c
David Pyatt *hn* **Kenneth Sillito** *vn* **Robert Smissen, Stephen Tees** *vas* **Stephen Orton** *vc* **Academy of St Martin in the Fields / Sir Neville Marriner**
Warner Elatus 0927-46723-2 (70' · DDD)   Ⓜ

David Pyatt, Gramophone's Young Artist of the Year in 1996, provides performances in which calm authority and high imagination fuse; and this disc comlements the nobility and urbanity of Dennis Brain. Although there can be no direct comparison with Anthony Halstead, Pyatt's is very much in that mode of supple, understated and often witty playing, accompanied by truly discriminating orchestral forces. Soloist and orchestra create a constantly shifting and lively pattern of dynamic relationships. Pyatt makes the music's song and meditation his own. Compared with the dark, dream-like *cantabile* of Brain, he offers in the Second Concerto an *Andante* of cultivated conversation and, in the Third, a *Romanza* of barely moving breath and light. His finales trip the light fantastic. The Second Concerto's springing rhythms reveal wonderfully clear high notes; the Third is nimble and debonair without being quite as patrician as Brain's; and the Fourth creates real mischief in its effervescent articulation. The cadenzas by Terry Wooding (to the first movements of the Third and Fourth Concertos) epitomise Pyatt's performances as a whole: longer and more daringly imaginative than those of Brain, while remaining sensitively scaled and fancifully idiomatic. The concertos are imaginatively and unusually coupled with a fine performance of the Horn Quintet in E flat.

Horn Concertos Nos 1-4; E, KAnh98a/K494a. Rondos for Horn and Orchestra – D, K514 (cptd Süssmayr); E flat, K371. Fragment for Horn and Orchestra in E flat, K370b (both reconstr Humphries)
Bournemouth Sinfonietta / Michael Thompson *hn*
Naxos 8 553592 (76' · DDD)   Ⓢ

This isn't just an excellent bargain version of the

MOZART'S HORN CONCERTOS – IN BRIEF

Dennis Brain; Philharmonia Orchestra / Herbert von Karajan
EMI mono 566898-2 (77' · ADD) Ⓜ❍❍❍
Timelessly neat and elegant orchestral playing under Herbert von Karajan accompanies Dennis Brain's flawless and characterful playing – truly an all-time classic which transcends the mono sound.

Anthony Halstead; Academy of Ancient Music / Christopher Hogwood
Decca 443 216-2OH (60' · DDD) Ⓕ❍
Flawless, graceful performances on period instruments. Halstead's playing on valveless horns, involving some hand-stopping, results in characterful and witty playing with an extra nuance on chromatic notes!

Michael Thompson; Bournemouth Sinfonietta
Naxos 8 553592 (76' · DDD) Ⓢ
Sparkling performances on modern instruments by the Bournemouth Sinfonietta under the direction of the soloist, Michael Thompson, who performs scholarly editions prepared by John Humphries. A top bargain choice.

English Chamber Orchestra / Barry Tuckwell *hn*
Decca 458 607-2DM (69' · DDD) Ⓜ
Fluent and charming performances by Barry Tuckwell, who also directs the English Chamber Orchestra's idiomatic accompaniment, in his third studio recording of these concertos

David Pyatt; ASMF / Neville Marriner
Elatus 0927-46723-2 (69' · DDD) Ⓜ
Though recorded in 1996, the slightly plush string tone and close-focus miking of David Pyatt's mellow-toned horn makes these accounts sound a tad old-fashioned even next to Karajan and Brain. Nonetheless, these are affectionate performances which will please those wanting modern instrumentation in stereo sound.

Eric Ruske; Scottish CO / Charles Mackerras
Telarc CD-80367 (64' · DDD) Ⓕ
Attractive performances with golden horn tone complemented by idiomatic orchestral playing in spacious sound. Richard Suart singing Flanders and Swann's *Ill wind* makes an unusual encore.

Alan Civil; Philharmonia / Otto Klemperer
Testament SBT1102 (72' · ADD) Ⓕ
Another historic performance. Alan Civil's tone is more full bodied and his humour more earthy than Brain's. The orchestral accompaniment, however, is not always ideally co-ordinated with the soloist.

horn concertos, superbly played and recorded, but a valuable example of Mozartian scholarship on disc. Michael Thompson, directing the Bournemouth Sinfonietta with point and flair, plays the four regular concertos in revised texts prepared by John Humphries, as well as offering reconstructions by Humphries of two movements, designed as the outer movements, an *Allegro*, K370b and a *Rondo*, K371, for an earlier horn concerto written soon after Mozart arrived in Vienna. The Rondo played here as the second-movement finale of K412 is Humphries' reconstruction from recently discovered sources, and is much more imaginative than the Süssmayr version. It's a revelation too in the most popular of the concertos, No 4, to have extra passages, again adding Mozartian inventiveness. For example, the *tutti* in the first movement before the development section is extended in a charming few extra bars. Thompson, for 10 years the Philharmonia's first horn, isn't only technically brilliant, but plays with delectable lightness and point, bringing out the wit in finales, and the tenderness in slow movements. As conductor and director, he also draws sparkling and refined playing from the Sinfonietta, very well recorded in clear, atmospheric sound. An outstanding issue for both specialist and newcomer alike.

Oboe Concerto in C, K314/K271k

Oboe Concerto. Flute Concerto No 1. Clarinet Concerto
Nicholas Daniel *ob* **Kate Hill** *fl* **Joy Farrall** *basset cl*
Britten Sinfonia / Nicholas Cleobury
Classic fM 75605 57001-2 (73' · DDD) Ⓜ

This collection of Mozart's finest solo woodwind concertos is a winner. All the soloists are distinguished British orchestral players, each having a distinct personality in his or her own right. Joy Farrall's clarinet style combines an easy freedom with warm classical directness. Her performance of the Clarinet Concerto is totally seductive, with Nicholas Cleobury's gracefully phrased opening ritornello setting the scene for the lightly pointed solo entry. Her fluid line is heard at its most ravishing in the *Adagio*, which is richly echoed by the strings of the Britten Sinfonia; and the delicacy of the reprise is particularly magical. It's followed by a delicious, bubbling finale with lilting secondary material. Nicholas Daniel is hardly less appealing in the more petite Oboe Concerto and his reedy sweetness of timbre never cloys. He, too, is at his finest in the slow movement, while in the infectious closing *Rondo* finale he provides a neatly succinct cadenza. The Flute Concerto is equally delectable, especially the tender *Adagio*, which Cleobury moves forward at exactly the right measured pace and which Kate Hill carols so touchingly. The neatly pointed Minuet finale is captivating. The recorded sound is excellent.

Mozart Oboe Concerto **R Strauss** Oboe Concerto in D
Douglas Boyd ob **Chamber Orchestra of Europe / Paavo Berglund**
ASV CDCOE808 (44' · DDD)   Ⓕ

This coupling links two of the most delightful oboe concertos ever written. Mozart's sprightly and buoyant work invests the instrument with a chirpy, bird-like fleetness encouraging the interplay of lively rhythm and elegant poise. Boyd's reading captures this work's freshness and spontaneity beautifully. If the Mozart portrays the sprightly side of the instrument's make-up the Strauss illustrates its languorous ease and tonal voluptuousness. Again Boyd allows himself the freedom and breadth he needs for his glowing interpretation; he handles the arching melodies of the opening movement and the witty *staccato* of the last with equal skill. Nicely recorded.

Piano Concertos

No 1 in F, K37; No 2 in B flat, K39; No 3 in D, K40; No 4 in G, K41; No 5 in D, K175; No 6 in B flat, K238; No 8 in C, K246; No 9 in E flat, K271, 'Jeunehomme'; No 11 in F, K413/K387a; No 12 in A, K414/K385p; No 13 in C, K415/K387b; No 14 in E flat, K449; No 15 in B flat, K450; No 16 in D, K451; No 17 in G, K453; No 18 in B flat, K456; No 19 in F, K459; No 20 in D minor, K466; No 21 in C, K467; No 22 in E flat, K482; No 23 in A, K488; No 24 in C minor, K491; No 25 in C, K503; No 26 in D, K537, 'Coronation'; No 27 in B flat, K595

Piano Concertos Nos 1-27
English Chamber Orchestra / Murray Perahia pf
Sony Classical ⑫ SX12K46441 (608' · ADD/DDD)
Recorded 1975-84   Ⓜ❍❍

Mozart concertos from the keyboard are unbeatable. There's a rightness, an effortlessness, about doing them this way that makes for heightened enjoyment. So many of them seem to gain in vividness when the interplay of pianist and orchestra is realised by musicians listening to each other in the manner of chamber music. Provided the musicians are of the finest quality, of course. We now just take for granted that the members of the English Chamber Orchestra will match the sensibility of the soloist. They are on top form here, as is Perahia, and the finesse of detail is breathtaking. Just occasionally Perahia communicates an 'applied' quality – a refinement which makes some of his statements sound a little too good to be true. But the line of his playing, appropriately vocal in style, is exquisitely moulded; and the only reservations one can have are that a hushed, 'withdrawn' tone of voice, which he's little too ready to use, can bring an air of self-consciousness to phrases where ordinary, radiant daylight would have been more illuminating; and that here and

there a more robust treatment of brilliant passages would have been in place. However, the set is entirely successful on its own terms – whether or not you want to make comparisons with other favourite recordings. Indeed, we now know that records of Mozart piano concertos don't come any better played than here.

Piano Concertos Nos 9 & 21
English Chamber Orchestra / Murray Perahia pf
Sony Classical SK34562 (59' · DDD)   Ⓕ❍

No 21 (coupled with No 23) also available on Sony Classical Theta SK89876   Ⓜ

Perahia's fine Mozart playing is a feature of the musical scene that has been with us for decades. There's a delightful freshness and crispness as well as the kind of authority that convinces us that this is the only way to perform the music – that is, until another masterly account comes along. Perahia's choice of tempos is a case in point, yet he seems natural rather than merely predictable and one recalls how even fine musicians can often go astray on this matter which Wagner and Stravinsky alike regarded as crucial. Are there any reservations? Well, perhaps the CD sound is just that little bit close and bright, but with music-making of this quality that doesn't seem to matter.

The grave *Andantino* of No 9 is given weight without exaggeration. In No 21 Perahia doesn't give the first movement the *maestoso* element suggested in some editions: instead there's a delightful flexibility and Leporello-like charm. However, it might be that the G minor passage before the second subject and the E minor one in the development are too soft and yielding, charming though they're in themselves. Perahia's own cadenza is effective and in keeping with his chosen approach. In the famous *Andante* also, Perahia plays with great feeling and poise.

Piano Concertos Nos 11, 12 & 14
English Chamber Orchestra / Murray Perahia pf
Sony Classical SK42243 (70' · ADD/DDD)   Ⓕ❍

Piano Concertos Nos 20 & 27
English Chamber Orchestra / Murray Perahia pf
Sony Classical SK42241 (63' · ADD/DDD)   Ⓕ❍

These discs happily epitomise some of the best qualities of the complete Perahia/ECO set. Always intelligent, always sensitive to both the overt and less obvious nuances of this music, Perahia is firstly a true pianist, never forcing the instrument beyond its limits in order to express the ideas, always maintaining a well-projected singing touch. The superb ECO reflects his integrity and empathy without having to follow slavishly every detail of his articulation or phrasing. K414 and K413 are charming and typically novel for their time, but do not break new ground in quite the way that K449 does. Here,

Mozart's success in the theatre may have suggested a more dramatic presentation and working of ideas for this instrumental genre. K595 is a work pervaded by a serenity of acceptance that underlies its wistfulness. Mozart had less than a year to live, and the mounting depression of his life had already worn him down, yet there's still a sort of quiet joy in this music. The vast range of styles, emotions, and forms that these few works encompass are evocatively celebrated in these performances, and admirably captured in civilised recordings.

Piano Concertos Nos 11-13 (arr cpsr)
Patrick Dechorgnat *pf* **Henschel Quartet**
(Christoph Henschel, Markus Henschel *vns* Monika Henschel *va* Mathias D Beyer *vc*)
EMI Debut 572525-2 (79' · DDD)   Ⓑ

Writing of these three concertos in 1782, Mozart made an impressive claim: 'They strike a happy medium, neither unnecessarily complex nor overly simple; colourful, pleasant to the ear – but not without substance. At certain moments only the *cognoscenti* will derive any enjoyment from them, but there's something to please the less discriminating too, even if they don't know why.' Heard here in Mozart's own arrangement for piano and string quartet they make a crystalline, tirelessly inventive trio played with much spirit, articulacy and affection. A faint suspicion that in the opening *Allegro* of K414 (among Mozart's most economical but endearing works) provided you're clear and tasteful the rest will follow is erased in a most affecting sense of interplay in the *Larghetto* from K413, a grave sense of serenity in the *Andante* from K414 and embellishments that are elegant and discreet throughout. Dechorgnat also achieves a special sense of Romantic delicacy in the second subject from the opening movement of K415 and time and again relishes the opportunity for improvisatory freedom in the cadenzas. He's superbly partnered by the Henschel Quartet, and balance and sound are exemplary.

Piano Concertos Nos 12 & 19
London Mozart Players / Howard Shelley *pf*
Chandos CHAN9256 (52' · DDD) Recorded 1993   Ⓕ

These are clear and stylish readings. The playing of Shelley and the London Mozart Players is assured, relaxed and enjoyable, allowing the music to unfold naturally. Shelley demonstrates his fine judgement of tempo, and textures are well served; the recording gives quite a bold sound to his modern piano, but its overall immediacy and warmth aren't excessive and the balance is just right. Phrasing also deserves praise: Shelley and his expert team shape the music gracefully without falling into the slightly mannered delivery which can affect other artists in this repertory. Finally, cadenzas have the right balance of freedom and formality. Perhaps the two 'slow' movements here – the quotes are

because that of K414 is an *Andante* and K459's is an *Allegretto* – are richer in style than will suit some tastes: they do not sound authentic in period-performance terms, but then this is another kind of performance and perfectly convincing. The recordings are of high quality.

Piano Concertos Nos 15[a], 23[b] & 24[b]   Ⓗ
Solomon *pf* **Philharmonia Orchestra /** [a]**Otto Ackermann,** [b]**Herbert Menges**
Testament mono SBT1222 (80' · ADD) Recorded 1953-55   Ⓕ

It was Abram Chasins, the American pianist and critic, who noted in Solomon a 'proportionate grandeur that instead of seeming to lack power appeared not to desire it.' Others have spoken of his 'matchless austerity', and listening once more to his Mozart is to be reminded of the essential truth of such comments. Mozart may have felt that K450 (No 15) is a concerto 'to make the pianist sweat', but it's difficult to imagine even a single bead of perspiration on Solomon's brow as he tosses off cascades of notes with superlative ease and elegance. In his hands the *Andante*'s set of variations comes as close to Elysium as you could wish, while the finale has a delectable lightness that makes it a true dance of the gods.

In K488 (No 23), Solomon's lucidity, in the canonic interplay, for example, is of a sort granted to very few pianists, and his refinement in the closing pages of the ineffable F sharp minor *Adagio* suggests all his inimitable but lightly worn authority. In K491 (No 24) he shares with Clara Haskil, another supremely prized Mozartian, a characteristic way of taking one of Mozart's two minor-key concertos by stealth rather than by storm, though he compensates for what some may see as undue restraint by giving us Saint-Saëns' storming cadenza. The 1953-5 recordings have been superbly remastered, and his musical partners, Otto Ackermann and Herbert Menges, are as inspired as their soloist.

Piano Concertos Nos 15 & 16
English Chamber Orchestra / Murray Perahia *pf*
Sony Classical SK37824 (50' · DDD)   Ⓕ**OOO**

This is an interpretation of the highest calibre: Perahia's delicious shaping of even the longest and most elaborate phrases, his unfailingly clear and arresting articulation, and his delicacy and refinement of tone are without parallel. Perahia's attention is, moreover, by no means restricted to the solo parts: even the tiniest details of the orchestral writing are subtly characterised, and the piano and orchestra take on the character of a dialogue – sometimes poignant, often witty or sparklingly humorous. The two works are admirably contrasted: the 15th is largely light and high spirited, while the first movement of the 16th is almost Beethovenian in its grandeur and purposefulness, and both concertos have typically beautiful slow movements. The recordings are superb.

Piano Concertos Nos 9 & 17   **P**
Concerto Köln / Andreas Staier fp
Teldec Das Alte Werk 4509-98412-2 (61' · DDD)   Ⓕ

Andreas Staier, speaking of the use of period instruments in this outstanding recording of Mozart's G major Concerto, K453, declares the piece has 'more of the farmyard about it' that way. He's right. From the braying and bellowing of the mid-phrase *crescendos*, the snuffling and snorting of the bassoons and the hee-hawing of the alternating loud and soft chords, Staier appears throughout it all the delighted child with a favourite picturebook. Conductorless, the string playing in the outer movements of both this and the E flat Concerto is buoyant with daring. The impetus and excitement of both dialogue and modulations in the slow movement of K453 is thrilling – and so is the dialogue within the orchestral writing in the finale. In K271 the music-making has a bracing immediacy as the almost percussive string playing cuts into the fortepiano's rhetoric, so imaginatively developed in Staier's fingers.

Piano Concertos Nos 9 & 25
Alfred Brendel pf **Scottish Chamber Orchestra / Sir Charles Mackerras**
Philips 470 287-2PH (68' · DDD)   ⒻO

This Brendel recording, of No 9, K271, and No 25, K503, is alive with provocation, subtlety and distinction. In both widely contrasted concertos he somehow manages to combine a sense of first love and discovery with the sort of unalloyed musicianship that only comes with years of experience. He's also ideally complemented by Sir Charles Mackerras and the SCO who are as alert to musical impetus and every passing felicity as their superb soloist.

Throughout, the sense of a chamber music-like interplay between Brendel and Mackerras is maintained with an ease and naturalness the reverse of a more obvious or immature approach. How withdrawn yet characterful is Brendel's entry at 4'52" in the ever-astonishing C minor *Andante*, and how subtly he differentiates between *Andantino* and *Andante* in the cadenza, finding all its prophecy of later autumnal sadness.

Mackerras opens K503 with a magnificent sense of its *maestoso* and the same musical qualities noted in K271 are present in every bar. Brendel's own cadenza for the first movement is impishly engaging yet unfailingly true to Mozart's spirit. The *Andante*'s lines are discreetly and stylishly embellished and in K271 Brendel chooses the second set of Mozart's cadenzas. Philips's sound and balance are exemplary.

Piano Concertos Nos 17[a] & 21
Maria João Pires pf **Chamber Orchestra of Europe / Claudio Abbado**
DG 439 941-2GH (58' · DDD) [a]Recorded live 1993
     ⒻO

It's clear from the opening of the G major Concerto that Claudio Abbado and the Chamber Orchestra of Europe were on good form at this concert in Italy. It springs along, yet unhastily, and the orchestral sound, while full-bodied, has none of the heaviness that detracts from good Mozartian style. Playing what sounds like a modern piano of unusual tonal crispness, Maria João Pires also satisfies, with shapely phrasing and lovely sonorities, and this whole first movement proceeds with both a keen sense of purpose and unmannered grace. The cadenza here is Mozart's own, and a model of what cadenzas in his concertos should be but often aren't; in other words suiting the music and not overlong. After these unalloyed pleasures, the touching *Andante* is no less satisfying, elegantly sculpted and with marvellous woodwind playing. The playful, variation-form finale is again perfectly judged, and indeed the performance of the whole concerto offers truly outstanding Mozart playing, among the best on disc and unquestionably in the Perahia class. The recording is worthy of it: beautifully balanced and clear while also refreshingly free of audience noise and applause. The C major Concerto is also excellent, the first movement strong yet not pompous. The famous 'Elvira Madigan' slow movement isn't at all romanticised but admirably poised, and the finale springs along.

Piano Concertos Nos 18 & 20
Richard Goode pf **Orpheus Chamber Orchestra**
Nonesuch 7559-79439-2 (58' · DDD)   ⒻOO

With a first-rate balance and quality of sound, here's a Mozart concerto record to transcend considerations of style and stance. The excellence of Richard Goode's playing isn't surprising, but the quality of his collaboration with the Orpheus Chamber Orchestra is special: and the beautiful thing about Mozart performance of this calibre is that the two seem inseparable. The freshness and placing of the detail are to be savoured, but it's the long view which holds and persuades. In the D minor Concerto's first movement the brilliant piano writing is so thrilling here because it's projected as being essential to the expression, not just a decoration of it. Goode is particularly impressive in the way he handles the three successive solo statements at the start of the development without slackening pace. They are subtly different in feeling, one from the other, and although he isn't the first player to have noticed this, it's characteristic of his distinction to have kept the detail and the overview in balance. He plays his own cadenza in the finale, in place of Beethoven's. He has some good ideas about dynamics in this last movement, and Mozart's lightening of mood at the turn to the major key towards the end has rarely sounded such an inspiration. The B flat Concerto, K456, is equally enjoyable. The outer movements are brisk and light on their feet, even balletic, but all the colours – and the shadows which pass over the face of the music – are there, just as one wants. At the end, you feel you've had glorious entertainment, and a discourse that has touched on the deepest things. You may well be puzzled as to how Goode achieves so much while appearing to do so little. In this the orchestra matches him, as it also matches his spontaneity.

Piano Concertos Nos 19 & 27
Orpheus Chamber Orchestra / Richard Goode pf
Nonesuch 7559-79608-2 (55' · DDD)   Ⓕ〇

The opening *tutti* of K595 (No 27, which comes first on the disc) makes a striking impact, not only thanks to the crisp, alert playing but to the full, bright, immediate recording. The piano enters with similarly full and immediate sound – very different from the more transparent piano sound on a rival Decca release with András Schiff – but then the orchestra seems to move further off. It's an inconsistency of balance that's disconcerting for no more than a moment or two, but might well make a hypercritical artist or producer have reservations.

What matters is the liveness of the experience that Goode and his partners provide. His approach is more purposeful, more direct than that of Schiff, who favours speeds consistently a shade broader than Goode's. The natural weight and gravity of Goode's playing, reflecting his equivalent mastery as a Beethovenian, emerges clearly in such moments as the hushed B minor opening or the development in the first movement of K595, an extraordinary modulation for a movement in B flat major, or in the opening solo of the *Larghetto* which follows. Not that Goode's Mozart has anything remotely heavy about it in the wrong way. His lightness and wit in the finales of both concertos is a delight.

In the finale of K459, Goode, like Schiff, opts for a very fast *Allegro assai*, drawing on his phenomenal agility. Some may prefer a slightly more relaxed tempo, such as Murray Perahia, for example, adopts, with more swagger and fun in it, but Goode's playing is thrilling from first to last.

Piano Concertos Nos 20 & 24
Alfred Brendel pf **Scottish Chamber Orchestra / Sir Charles Mackerras**
Philips 462 622-2PH (60' · DDD)   Ⓕ〇

Brendel's conception of Mozart's two minor-key concertos has altered in countless nuances and emphases but little in fundamentals since his 1973 Philips recordings with Marriner. His sensibility, pianistic refinement and sheer questing intelligence remain as compelling as ever. Neither performance will entirely please

those who favour a barnstorming approach.

More than in 1973, Brendel is at times concerned to draw out the music's elegiac resignation than to highlight its more obvious passion and turbulence. But more than most pianists he constantly illuminates the smaller and larger shapes of the music with his range of colour and dynamics. In both opening movements, for instance, he brings a speaking eloquence to the piano's initial solo theme and then in the development finds a subtly altered tone of voice, in response to the gradually darkening musical landscape, for each of its reappearances.

Another Brendel hallmark is his variety of tone and articulation in rapid passagework, which is purposefully directed in accordance with its place in the overall scheme. Again he provides apt and spontaneous-sounding embellishments and 'in-filling' at fermatas, this time allowing himself greater freedom in decorating the spare lines of the slow movements; again, he uses his own cadenzas in both concertos, more adventurous in their thematic development than any of Mozart's own surviving examples.

In the opening *tutti* of K491 one can hear the extra character Mackerras brings to the music compared to Marriner – the impact of raw, louring brass (tamed by Marriner) at strategic moments, for instance, or his attentive shaping of inner strands to enhance the tension. The recording has an attractive spaciousness and ambient warmth, though in K491 the keyboard occasionally obscures important thematic ideas on oboes, clarinets and bassoons.

Piano Concertos Nos 20[a], 23[b], 24[b], 26[c] & 27[a]
Sir Clifford Curzon pf [a]**ECO / Benjamin Britten;**
[bc]**LSO / István Kertész**
Decca Legends ② 468 491-2DL2 (154' · ADD)   Ⓜ〇

With the addition of Curzon's recently disinterred account of No 26, the present collection is a genuine best buy. There are odd pockets where the piano part feels sparse and unadorned without infilling, where the 'inauthentic' accompaniments feel a little thick and opaque, but to describe such music-making as merely dated would be grossly unfair. Britten's ECO contributes more sparkle and individuality than Kertész's LSO, only partly a matter of acoustics though the present transfer does tend to 'dry out' the Kingsway Hall. Curzon's playing is outwardly cool and controlled, at times almost self-effacing, and yet teeming with inner life. What makes it so special isn't easily put into words: Curzon seems able to respond to every nuance in a way that makes most performers seem superficial even as he eschews their effortful striving after profundity.

Piano Concertos Nos 23 & 24
Orpheus Chamber Orchestra / Richard Goode pf
Nonesuch 7559-79489-2 (56' · DDD)   Ⓕ〇

This is the third Mozart CD Richard Goode

and the Orpheus Chamber Orchestra have made, and collaborations of this kind must necessarily be rare. The demands this sort of music-making imposes on the players are considerable. But so are the potential rewards. They are evident here in the exceptional focus and concentration of the playing. Polished you might expect it to be, but the allure and spontaneity are a joy. First impressions are likely to be of details of scoring in the orchestral expositions of the first movements, details that may not go unnoticed in other performances but which rarely receive such voicing and definition. The pianist doesn't disappoint either. Judge him by his first entry in this concerto, in the solo theme: there's none more difficult to get right. Goode has the range, the control and the rhetoric. He passes another difficult test in this first movement by supplying an impressive cadenza. It's an outstanding account of this movement, to be returned to again and again. There's no falling off in the other two either.

The A major, K488, equally well illuminated, has light and air from a different world. Indeed, there's an airborne quality to the finale, done here with the utmost vivacity, and a hint of that too in the open textures and the easy, glorious buoyancy of the first movement. The recorded sound is exemplary.

Piano Concertos Nos 23 & 24 (plus Nos 20, 26, 27)
Sir Clifford Curzon pf **London Symphony Orchestra / István Kertész**
Decca Legends ② 468 491-2DM2 (ADD) Recorded 1967 ⓂⓄⓄ

In a list of all-time best recordings of Mozart piano concertos these should have a place. The balances of piano with orchestra are just right, and the sound has come up freshly on CD, with clarity and a nicely truthful character. In the No 24 the wind isn't as forward as recordings favour these days, but from the LSO as distinguished soloists and as a wind chorus their contributions tell. Kertész gives Curzon nicely judged support: it sets him off, in a frame, even if it does appear a mite neutral at times and strangely limp in the presentation of the variation theme at the start of the finale of the C minor Concerto. These days, some people might consider the interpretations dated, or unreconstructed. Curzon doesn't decorate the bare, leaping intervals at the close of the slow movement of K488, and he's restrained too in the C minor. But the performances seem to be beyond fashion. The slow movements are especially fine. In the Larghetto of No 24, unfolding at an ideal tempo, Curzon gives the impression of walking while he speaks to us. The gravity of the F sharp minor Adagio of No 23 is a different thing; but there, again, he's unaffected and completely unsentimental, direct in manner even while projecting the deepest feeling. He reminds us that the best interpreters do not impose but find a way of letting the music speak through them.

MOZART'S PIANO CONCERTOS NOS 20 AND 21 – IN BRIEF

English Chamber Orchestra / Murray Perahia
No 20: Sony SK42241 (62' · DDD) Ⓕ
No 21: Sony SK34562 (59' · DDD) Ⓕ
Perahia's remains the classic Mozart piano concerto cycle on modern instruments, his readings invariably informed by a natural Mozartian sensibility. Directing from the keyboard, he gets fine playing from the ECO, and the recordings convey the warmth and finesse of his own keyboard sound.

Alfred Brendel; ASMF / Marriner
Philips 442 269-2PM2 (159' · ADD) Ⓕ
A bargain twofer in the Philips Duo series offering both concertos, plus three more, in critically acclaimed performances from Brendel's middle years. Top notch analogue sound.

Maria-João Pires; COE / Claudio Abbado
No 21: DG 439 941-2GH (58' · DDD) Ⓕ
Producing unusually crisp sonorities from her modern grand, Maria-João Pires combines a keen sense of purpose with unmannered grace, one unusual feature being the use of a Rudolf Serkin cadenza in the first movement. Well-sprung accompaniments and excellent sound quality.

Robert Levin; AAM / Christopher Hogwood
No 20: Decca 455 607-2OH (61' · DDD) Ⓕ
An original-instrument performance in which the originality extends to the improvised nature of Levin's cadenzas and embellishments of line. That glittering fortepiano sound is well caught too.

Orpheus CO / Richard Goode
No 20: Nonesuch 7559 79439-2 (58' · DDD) Ⓕ
Richard Goode's sparkling Mozart series is distinguished by the closeness of his collaborations with the conductorless Orpheus Chamber Orchestra: his K466 shares a disc with an exceptional account of No 18 in B flat K456.

Vienna Philharmonic Orchestra / Bruno Walter
No 20: Pearl GEMMCD9940 (72' · ADD) Ⓕ
Affectionate Mozart from pre-War Vienna. Bruno Walter was an accomplished pianist in his prime, and his personable solo work in Mozart's D minor Concerto is a valuable supplement to his 1930s readings of *Eine kleine Nachtmusik* and the *Prague* Symphony.

Alfred Brendel; Scottish CO / Mackerras
No 20: Philips 462 622-2PH (60' · DDD) Ⓕ
Ever thoughtful and probing, Alfred Brendel has been revisiting Mozart concertos in the company of Sir Charles Mackerras and the Scottish Chamber Orchestra. In 1999 they set down K466 with No 24 in C minor K491.

Piano Concertos Nos 9 & 25
Orpheus Chamber Orchestra / Richard Goode pf
Nonesuch 7559-79454-2 (63' · DDD)   ⓕ**OO**

The opening of No 25 sounds tremendous, with a leathery thwack to the kettledrums and the orchestra suitably weighty. Although the acoustic is a bit dry, there's a satisfying depth to the sonority, and the balance and placing of the instruments is absolutely perfect. All the colours are vivid. In contrast to many players of the modern instrument, Goode doesn't pull his punches and makes this first movement a most glorious procession, imposing but never ponderous. His tempo has a propulsive energy and an underlying fitness that makes possible some relaxation of it in the broader paragraphs of the solo part. Wonderful slow movement too, flowing admirably, and it's a tricky one to get right.

This concerto has rarely been recorded so successfully, but the Ninth has been done better. Many of the virtues enjoyed by No 25 apply here also. It needs a different rhetoric, and Goode supplies it, but he waxes and wanes, and there's something a shade impersonal about him. The reservations concern the first movement principally, where it's as if he were saying: 'I do not need to attract your attention, this beautiful thing Mozart has made we are going to lay out before you'. However, this is still a Mozart concerto disc to give exceptional pleasure. And what teamwork! The musical focus sustained here isn't something often encountered outside chamber music.

Piano Concerto No 26. Rondos – D, K382; A, K386
English Chamber Orchestra / Murray Perahia pf
Sony Classical SK39224 (DDD)   ⓕ**O**

This is one of the most distinguished of Perahia's Mozart concerto recordings. The D major Concerto, No 26, isn't, perhaps, a work of such individuality as the 12 concertos which preceded it, or the only one which succeeded it (No 27), yet it used to be one of the most popular, probably because it has a convenient nickname (*Coronation*), stemming from the fact that Mozart performed it on 15October 1790, at the festivities accompanying the coronation of the Emperor Leopold II in Frankfurt am Main. Now, curiously enough, it isn't played all that often and of the available recordings, Perahia leads the field: dignified yet never aloof in the first movement, eloquent in the central *Larghetto*, and marvellously agile and dexterous in the florid concluding *Rondo*. He plays his own characteristically stylish cadenza in the first movement (Mozart's own has not survived). As a coupling Perahia gives us the two concert *Rondos*: K382 in D, a Viennese alternative finale for the Salzburg D major Concerto, K175; and K386 in A, presumably the original, rejected finale of K414. The A major *Rondo* has had an eventful history, having been cut into pieces in the 19th century for use as greeting cards (!), and patched together subsequently by numer-

ous editors, including Alfred Einstein, Paul Badura-Skoda, Sir Charles Mackerras, and Erik Smith. The version performed here has a different ending which was discovered by Peter Tyson. It was completed by Paul Badura-Skoda and this is its first recording. The performances are sheer delight and, as in the concerto, the ECO plays, quite literally, con amore – a spirit evidently shared by the Sony recording team.

Mozart Piano Concerto No 27. Concerto for Two Pianos and Orchestra in E flat, K365/K316a **Schubert** Fantasia, D940
Emil Gilels, Elena Gilels pfs **Vienna Philharmonic Orchestra / Karl Böhm**
DG The Originals 463 652-2GOR (59' · ADD)   Ⓜ**OO**

This is the most beautiful of Mozart playing, his last piano concerto given here by Emil Gilels with total clarity. This is a classic performance, memorably accompanied by the VPO and Böhm. Suffice it to say that Gilels sees everything and exaggerates nothing, that the performance has an Olympian authority and serenity, and that the *Larghetto* is one of the glories of the gramophone. He's joined by his daughter Elena in the Double Piano Concerto in E flat, and their physical relationship is mirrored in the quality, and the mutual understanding of the playing: both works receive marvellous interpretations. We *think* Emil plays first, Elena second, but could be quite wrong. The VPO under Karl Böhm is at its best; and so is the quality of recording, with a good stereo separation of the two solo parts, highly desirable in this work.

Additional recommendation

Piano Concertos Nos 9, 14, 15, 17, 18
Coupled with: Rondo in D, K382
Uchida pf; **English Chamber Orchestra / Tate**
Philips Duo ② 473 313-2PM2 (107' · DDD)   Ⓜ
Wonderfully imaginative interpretations that show soloist, orchestra and conductor in perfect rapport.

Violin Concertos

No 1 in B flat, K207; **No 2** in D, K211; **No 3** in G, K216; **No 4** in D, K218; **No 5** in A, K219; **D**, K271a

---

Violin Concertos Nos 1-5[a]. Adagio in E, K261[c]. Rondo in C, K373[a]. Sinfonia concertante in E flat, K364/K320d[b]
[a]**Arthur Grumiaux** vn [b]**Arrigo Pelliccia** va [ab]**London Symphony Orchestra / Sir Colin Davis;** [c]**New Philharmonia Orchestra / Raymond Leppard**
Philips Duo ② 438 323-2PM2 (153' · ADD) Recorded 1961-4   Ⓜ

The concertos are also available (coupled with violin sonatas nos 32 & 35) on Philips 50 Great Recordings 464 722-2PM2   Ⓜ

These performances of the five standard violin concertos, the *Sinfonia concertante* and a couple of other pieces were much admired when they came out on LP, and they continue to earn praise for their crispness, lightness and eloquence. Grumiaux was also fortunate in his partner in the *Sinfonia concertante*, for Pelliccià is also an expert Mozartian and they give a performance of this beautiful piece that's expressive but still avoids self-indulgent romanticism. In the solo concertos, too, Grumiaux plays cadenzas that suit the music in length and style. Both Sir Colin Davis and Raymond Leppard are sympathetic partners in this repertory, and since the playing of the two London orchestras is no less satisfying, this issue scores all round artistically. The 1960s recordings do not sound their age, and are pleasing save for a little tape hiss and an excess of bass that hardly suits the style of this translucent music. However, that's a small price to pay when so much else is admirable, and Grumiaux's fine tonal palette is well caught.

Violin Concertos Nos 1-5. Serenade No 7 in D, 'Haffner', K250/K248b – Andante; Menuetto; Rondo
Pamela Frank vn **Zurich Tonhalle Orchestra / David Zinman**
Arte Nova Classics ② 74321 72104-2 (139' · DDD) Ⓢ

What a good idea to include the violin concerto movements from the *Haffner* Serenade as a filler, rather than the more usual group of extra movements for violin and orchestra. The Serenade shows the 20-year-old Mozart with his imagination at full stretch; Frank, Zinman and the Zurich orchestra revel in the wit, the sensuous expressiveness and the melodic fecundity of this still neglected music. Throughout the two discs Pamela Frank gives us violin playing of great technical purity. The music speaks to us without any affectation, yet respecting Mozart's indications and such 18th-century conventions as tailing off the weak beats of the bar. She's given a splendidly positive, well-considered accompaniment. The bouncy rhythms and perfect orchestral balance of the opening *tutti* to K216 establish a sense of *joie de vivre* that carries over into the violin playing.

Zinman's care for detail ensures that nothing of importance is overlooked: on the many occasions where the bass is carried by the second violin or viola these lines are given a bit of extra emphasis to highlight the harmonic movement. The horns deserve special mention; their purity of tone and rhythmic poise give a real sparkle to the outer movements of K207 and to the middle section of the *Haffner* Minuet, spectacularly scored for violin and wind. Zinman also wrote the cadenzas (except in K219, where Frank plays the famous Joachim ones) – they're imaginative and stylish, but don't always sound improvisatory enough and occasionally seem too long. Frank is supported by an unusually characterful orchestra and very crisp, clear recording. A fantastic bargain.

Violin Concertos Nos 3-5
Camerata Academica Salzburg / Augustin Dumay
vn
DG 457 645-2GH (75' · DDD) Ⓕ Ⓞ

Taking a break from chamber music-making, Augustin Dumay makes his début as soloist and conductor in these vivid and immediate recordings from the Salzburg Mozarteum. The dual role is very much what sets these performances apart. High-fibre, robustly articulated orchestral playing acts as frame and foil for the imaginative *richesse* of Dumay's own free and airy spirit; and the excitement of the players' close mutual engagement gives a real sense of Mozart's youthful energy bursting out of its Salzburg prison walls.

Dumay's choice of tempos makes each slow movement appear to breathe the air of another planet: in the G major work, the *pizzicato* pulse becomes the plucking of a distant lyre, as the bow scarcely seems to shift on the string in a finely suspended song.

In the D major, the soloist is *primus inter pares* in a fine weave of wind and strings. And in the A major, whose piercingly true, birdlike first-movement song deliciously anticipates Joachim's larkrise of a cadenza, there's a fluency and sense of wonderment which makes other interpretations seem earthbound by contrast. Dumay can be earthy enough when the occasion demands: in the finales of the D major and A major Concertos, his little moments of rubato make a shapely leg point and stretch forward in a series of high-stepping open-air dances.

Overtures

Overtures – Le nozze di Figaro; Il re pastore; Die Entführung aus dem Serail; Die Zauberflöte; Idomeneo; Der Schauspieldirektor; Bastien und Bastienne; La clemenza di Tito; Lucio Silla; Così fan tutte; La finta giardiniera; Mitridate, Re di Ponto; Don Giovanni
Sinfonia Varsovia / Yehudi Menuhin
Classic fM The Full Works 75605 57032-2 (63' · DDD) Ⓜ

This is a highly recommendable issue, offering fresh and alert performances, vividly recorded. Not only that, the choice of overtures is markedly more generous than on any rival disc, including as it does the early pieces, *Il re pastore*, *Bastien und Bastienne* and *Mitridate*. The Overture to *Bastien und Bastienne* may be little more than a flourish, lasting just over a minute and a half, but its opening strikingly anticipates the first theme of the *Eroica*. Like the Overture to *Lucio Silla*, the most inspired of Mozart's teenage operas, the one for *Mitridate* is like a symphony in three movements, just as delightful only even more compact, lasting in all only five and a half minutes.

Menuhin's fresh, alert manner at relatively brisk speeds, is most refreshing. What above all makes this disc compelling is the overall sense of live communication, of players responding in fresh enjoyment. The excellent sound is full and clear, with ample bloom.

Serenades

No 3 in D, K185/167a; **No 4** in D, K203/K189b; **No 5** in D, K204/K231a; **No 6** in D, K239, 'Serenata notturna'; **No 7** in D, K250/K248b, 'Haffner'; **No 9** in D, K320, 'Posthorn'; **No 10** in B flat for 13 wind instruments, K361/K370a, 'Gran Partita'; **No 11** in E flat, K375; **No 12** in C minor, K388/K384a; **No 13** in G, K525, 'Eine kleine Nachtmusik'

Serenade No 3ª. March, K189/K167b. Five Contredanses, K609. Notturno in D, K286/K269a
ªArvid Engegard ᵛⁿ Salzburg Mozarteum
Camerata Academica / Sándor Végh
Capriccio 10 302 (66' · DDD) Recorded 1988-9   Ⓕ

The main work here is the big *Serenade*, K185, commissioned by the Antretter family of Salzburg and first performed in August 1773 to celebrate the end of the university year. Like other works of its kind it incorporates a miniature two-movement violin concerto within a loose symphonic framework: an *Andante* designed to display the instrument's powers of cantilena, and a brisk *contredanse* with plenty of opportunities for ear-catching virtuosity. There's also a violin solo in the glum D minor trio of the second minuet. But perhaps the finest movements are the sensuous A major *Andante grazioso*, with its *concertante* writing for flutes and horns, and the rollicking 6/8 finale, preceded by an unexpectedly searching *Adagio* introduction.

The performance by Végh and his handpicked Salzburg players is affectionate, rhythmically alive and beautifully detailed, with an imaginative, subtly coloured solo violin contribution from Arvid Engegard. The tempo and specific character of each movement is shrewdly judged: the two minuets, for example, are vividly differentiated, the first properly swaggering, with a nice lilt in the trio, the second spruce and quick-witted. Only in the finale is Végh arguably too leisurely, though here too the style and rhythmic lift of the playing are infectious. Végh follows the serenade with deft, colourful readings of five contredanses from Mozart's last year and a beguiling performance of the *Notturno* for four orchestras, exquisitely imagined open-air music, with its multiple echoes fading into the summer night. A delectable disc, offering a varied concert of Mozart's lighter music performed with exceptional flair and finesse. The recording is outstandingly vivid, with the spatial effects in the *Notturno* beautifully managed.

Serenades Nos 6, 12 & 13
Orpheus Chamber Orchestra
DG Galleria 439 524-2GGA (54' · DDD) Recorded 1985   Ⓜ

The *Serenata notturna* (No 6) can easily seem bland, but here it's attractively vivacious and alert. The use of light and shade is a constant source of pleasure, the playing itself is extremely fine, and it's altogether a splendid account. *Serenade* No 12 is a big piece in four movements. It's played so stylishly, and with such refinement and variety that you never become satiated with wind tone, as can happen with more ordinary performances.

The minor key Mozart chose for the C minor Serenade (No 12), a work described in Anthony Burton's booklet note as 'dramatic and sombre' is hardly conventional serenade material. But whatever the mystery of its nature, it's a splendid piece, with a tense first movement and a mirror canon for oboes and bassoons in its Minuet that's been described as suggesting 'the image of two swans reflected in still water'. The finale is a terse set of variations, and it's only the Andante (in E flat major) that offers real warmth. Since the recording is as successful as the playing, this is the most recommendable version available of this work.

There are many worthy recorded performances of Mozart's most famous Serenade, the one now universally called *Eine kleine Nachtmusik* (No 13), but this one by the string section of the Orpheus Chamber Orchestra has qualities of refinement and alertness that make it rather special. These players clearly enjoy the music, but bring to it a delightful precision as well as the necessary *joie de vivre* and spontaneity, and each of the four movements is beautifully shaped and characterised, so that this familiar music comes up as fresh as anyone could wish for.

Serenades Nos 6 & 13. Divertimento in D, K136. Adagio and Fugue in C minor, K546
Ferenc Liszt Chamber Orchestra / János Rolla
Hungaroton HCD12471 (50' · ADD/DDD)   Ⓕ

The *Eine kleine Nachtmusik Serenade* is a favourite which will never be in any danger of oblivion. The Hungarian Ferenc Liszt Chamber Orchestra plays splendidly with an exceptionally alert style, but with a slightly heavier sound, a slightly solider style, than the Orpheus Chamber Orchestra. Nevertheless, this is to point to minor differences in the two perfectly sensible approaches, not to suggest that either of the performances is in any way materially superior to the other. Another common factor of the two discs is their inclusion, along with the *Nachtmusik*, of *Serenade* No 6. The Divertimento here offers a degree of instrumental contrast, adding a few wind players to the basic orchestra of strings. Perhaps rather more of the built-in different sounds of these two groups could have been made in the present recording; but the *Serenade* remains an enchanting one. The Divertimento, also in D, lacks corresponding colour, but is nevertheless, quite a strong work; and the C minor *Adagio and Fugue* (an arrangement by Mozart himself from a piano duo) offers a very noticeably strong *Adagio*, and a fugue in which Mozart makes one of his few explorations – a successful one – of an earlier contrapuntal idiom.

Serenade No 11. Harmoniemusik on **P**
'Die Zauberflöte' (arr Stumpf)
Nachtmusique (Alf Hörberg *cl/basset hn* Danny Bond, Donna Agrell *bns* Claude Maury, Teunis Van der Zwart *hns*) / **Eric Hoeprich** *cl/basset hn*
Glossa GCD2K0601 (65' · DDD) **M**

This recording of K375 uses the relatively rare original version, without oboes. In some ways it makes better sense – the later one with oboes never quite justifies their presence. This performance is thoughtful, euphonious (the chording purer than is usual with period instruments) and very musicianly. The opening movement is taken rather deliberately, the central *Adagio* rather more quickly than usual and flowing very gracefully. Eric Hoeprich, who directs from the first clarinet, has a beautifully full and round tone and provides many happy details of expressive timing. There's some very neat and spirited playing in the finale; the clarinets in particular are tested and show themselves to be duly agile. If some of the emphatic chords in the opening movement are a little too loudly played, which leads to some coarsening of tone, this is nevertheless one of the best available recorded versions of the work, certainly in its sextet form.

The *Zauberflöte* wind arrangements are less familiar than those of the Da Ponte operas and they're particularly enjoyable; more than once the transcription virtually reproduces the original scoring. They follow the same formulae as the others, offering shortened versions of the overture and 13 favourite numbers. The arrangements are for the most part the work of JC Stumpf, although two pieces are indeed performed in other versions, for smaller ensemble, in order to create variety.

Mozart Serenade No 13. Adagio and Fugue in C minor, K546 **Anonymous** (arr L Mozart) Cassation in G, 'Toy Symphony' **Pachelbel** Canon and Gigue
Academy of St Martin in the Fields / Sir Neville Marriner
Philips 416 386-2PH (52' · DDD) Recorded 1984-5 **F**

Sir Neville Marriner here collects a miscellaneous group of popular classical and Baroque pieces in characteristically polished and elegant performances. The only roughness – and that deliberate – is in the extra toy percussion of Leopold Mozart's *Cassation*, with its long-misattributed *Toy* Symphony. The anonymous extra soloists enjoy themselves as amateurs might, not least on a wind machine, but what's very hard to take is the grotesquely mismatched cuckoo-whistle, an instrument which should readily be tunable.

Eine kleine Nachtmusik brings a performance plainly designed to caress the ear of traditional listeners wearied with period performance. The second-movement *Romanze* is even more honeyed than usual on muted strings. The oddity of the Pachelbel item is that the celebrated Canon – taken unsentimentally if sweetly at a flowing speed – is given a reprise after the fugue. The recording is warm and well balanced.

Divertimentos

Divertimentos – B flat, K287/K271h; D, K205/K167a
Salzburg Mozarteum Camerata Academica / Sándor Végh
Capriccio 10 271 (59' · DDD) Recorded 1988 **F O**

Mozart's Divertimento, K287 is a six-movement work cast on quite a large scale, and is scored for two violins, viola, two horns and bass, a combination that presents some difficulties of balance. Toscanini and Karajan solved the problem in a way by recording the work with a full orchestral string section, but this brings its own problems, for Mozart's score demands playing of virtuoso standard, and anything less is ruthlessly exposed. Sandor Végh's smallish string band is of high quality, and has a pleasantly rounded tone quality. The engineers have managed to contrive a satisfactory balance that doesn't sound at all unnatural, and the sound quality is very good. Végh directs an attractive, neatly pointed performance that steers a middle course between objective classicism and expressive warmth. The Divertimento, K205, has five movements, but none lasts longer than five minutes, so the work is much shorter and more modest than K287. Scoring is for violin, viola, two horns, bassoon and double bass, to provide another difficult but well resolved problem for the engineers. Végh directs another characterful, delightful performance, to round off a very desirable disc.

Divertimentos – F, K247; D, K334/K320b
Gaudier Ensemble (Jonathan Williams, Christiaan Boers *hns* Marieke Blankestijn, Lesley Hatfield *vns* Iris Juda *va* Stephen Williams *db*)
Hyperion CDA67386 (76' · DDD) **F**

How lucky the burghers of Salzburg, in Mozart's day, who had such music as this to accompany their family celebrations! Mozart wrote a small group of divertimentos for strings and horns for the local aristocracy during his later years there, to augment his salary and prestige, and he did it with a mastery of technique that enabled him to find exactly the right blend of high spirits, warmth of expression and wit.

When they've been recorded, it's nearly always been with an orchestra rather than a solo group. In Austria in Mozart's time, the word 'divertimento' signified solo performance, and there's a world of difference between what a sensitive solo fiddler and what a galumphing orchestra can do with that top line, in terms of technique, expressiveness and flexibility. And in these performances the bass part is played not by a cello, but, as was preferred in Salzburg, a double bass, which provides a different relationship to the upper voices, and the one that Mozart clearly intended.

The Gaudier Ensemble catch the mood of the music perfectly. The elegant sentiment of the slow movements (there are two in each work) is happily conveyed – listen to the sweetness of violinist Marieke Blankestijn's phrasing in the *Adagio* of K247 and her gentle, unassuming eloquence in that of K334. In the latter work the second violin is called on, too, for some degree of virtuosity, but it's to Blankestijn that most of the rapid and stratospheric music goes, and she copes in style. She also phrases the famous first minuet here gracefully. Mozart's second minuets (each divertimento has six movements) are usually more rumbustious, with the horns prominent, and these too are heartily done. Altogether this is a delectable record.

Mozart Divertimento in D, K334[a]   H
Schubert Quintet for Piano and Strings in A, 'The Trout', D667[b]
Members of the Vienna Octet (Willi Boskovsky, [a]Philipp Matheis *vns* Günther Breitenbach *va* Nikolaus Hubner *vc* Johann Krump *db* [a]Joseph Velba, [a]Otto Nitsch *hns* [b]Walter Panhoffer *pf*)
Pearl mono GEM0129 (72' · ADD) Recorded 1950   (F)

Mozart's Divertimento for two horns and strings, K334, is one of his ripest and most engaging *pièces d'occasion* and this is a marvellous performance of it. Indeed, some skimping of repeats and a couple of cuts in the finale notwithstanding, this classic, out of the catalogues now for more than 30 years, is still the version to have.

Like the still too little regarded Vienna Konzerthaus Quartet, the Vienna Octet was one of the glories of post-war Viennese musical life. Willi Boskovsky, one of its founders, was a particular inspiration. Boskovsky may not have been every recording producer's dream. A wonderfully inspirational player, he would not necessarily play a take the same way twice. The results, though, are a joy; his playing, and the playing of the ensemble as a whole, is always burnished, idiomatic, intensely alive. The same could be said of this famous 1950 recording of Schubert's *Trout* Quintet, though the Vienna Octet's remake, recorded with Sir Clifford Curzon in 1957 when Boskovsky was still leading, is one of those gramophone classics difficult to knock off its perch. The original Decca LPs of the present performances (Pearl hasn't had access to the original tapes) were often said to be wiry in sound and difficult to reproduce, though this isn't true of the Mozart. Here, it sounds a million dollars. Tracking the latter movements of the *Trout* LP, though, has clearly not been easy. A barely audible amount of surface noise and a tiny amount of incipient distortion persists. That said, the new disc is indispensable.

Ein musikalischer Spass, K522

Ein musikalischer Spass. Contredanses – C, K587, 'Der Sieg vom Helden Koburg'; D, K534, 'Das Donnerwetter'; C, K535, 'La Bataille'; G, K610, 'Les filles malicieuses'; E flat, K607/K605a, 'Il trionfo delle donne'. Gallimathias musicum, K32. German Dances – C, K567; K605; C, K611, 'Die Leyerer'. March in D, K335 No 1
Orpheus Chamber Orchestra
DG 429 783-2GH (69' · DDD) Recorded 1989   (F)

The celebrated *Musikalischer Spass* ('Musical Joke') is never so crudely funny that it wears thin, but make no mistake, the jokes are there in just about every passage, whether they're parodying third-rate music or wobbly playing, and oddly enough sound still more amusing when the performance is as stylishly flexible as this one by the conductorless Orpheus Chamber Orchestra. One of the tunes is that of the BBC's *Horse of the Year* programme – and what a good tune it is, even at the umpteenth repetition as the hapless composer finds himself unable to stop. The rest of the programme is no less delightful, and includes miniature pieces supposedly describing a thunderstorm, a battle, a hurdy-gurdy man and a sleigh-ride (with piccolo and sleigh-bells). There's also a *Gallimathias musicum*, a ballet suite of dainty little dances averaging less than a minute, which Mozart is supposed to have written aged 10. Whatever the case, this CD provides proof of his genius, though differently from his acknowledged masterpieces. The recording is as refined as anyone could wish, yet has plenty of impact.

Symphonies

No 1 in E flat, K16; **No 2** in B flat, K17 (attrib L Mozart); **No 4** in D, K19; **No 5** in B flat, K22; **No 6** in F, K43; **No 7** in D, K45; **No 7a** in G, K45a/KAnh221, 'Alte Lambach'; **No 8** in D, K48; **No 9** in C, K73; **No 10** in G, K74; **No 11** in D, K84/K73q; **No 12** in G, K110/K75b; **No 13** in F, K112; **No 14** in A, K114; **No 15** in G, K124; **No 16** in C, K128; **No 17** in G, K129; **No 18** in F, K130; **No 19** in E flat, K132; **No 20** in D, K133; **No 21** in A, K134; **No 22** in C, K162; **No 23** in D, K181/K162b; **No 24** in B flat, K182/K173dA; **No 25** in G minor, K183/K173dB; **No 26** in E flat, K184/K161a; **No 27** in G, K199/K161b; **No 28** in C, K200/K189k; **No 29** in A, K201/K186a; **No 30** in D, K202/K186b; **No 31** in D, K297/K300a, 'Paris'; **No 32** in G, K318; **No 33** in B flat, K319; **No 34** in C, K338; **No 35** in D, K385, 'Haffner'; **No 36** in C, K425, 'Linz'; **No 38** in D, K504, 'Prague'; **No 39** in E flat, K543; **No 40** in G minor, K550; **No 41** in C, K551, 'Jupiter'; **(No 42)** in F, K75; **(No 43)** in F, K76/K42a; **(No 44)** in D, K81/K73l; **(No 45)** in D, K95/K73n; **(No 46)** in C, K96/K111b; **(No 47)** in D, K97/K73m; **(No 55)** in B flat, KApp214/K45b; **F**, KAnh223/K19a; **B flat**, K74g/KAnh216/C11.03

Symphonies Nos 1-36; Nos 38-47; (No 7a) in G, 'Alte H Lambach', K45a/KAnh221; G, 'Neue Lambach'
Berlin Philharmonic Orchestra / Karl Böhm

DG ⑩ 453 231-2GX10 (749' · ADD) Recorded
1959-68 Ⓑ

Böhm's vintage Mozart recordings with the Berlin Philharmonic were in fact just as much a pioneering project as Antál Dorati's Haydn symphonic cycle, completed five years later. This was the first attempt on commercial disc to record the whole Mozart symphony cycle, at a time when virtually none of the works before the little known G minor, No 25, were at all familiar even to specialists. What the performances tell us, warm and genial, with bold contrasts of dynamic and well-sprung rhythms, is that for the players as well as the conductor this was a voyage of discovery, and their enthusiasm never wanes. On matters of scholarship these performances may have been supplanted by a whole series of recordings since, but as a welcoming way to investigate Mozart early and late they hold their place, with no hint of routine in the playing. As with Dorati in Haydn, minuets are slow and often heavy by today's standards, but some of the minuets in the early symphonies are taken more briskly, almost as fast *ländlers*. In finales Böhm rarely adopts an extreme speed, but always the springing of rhythm, and the clarity of articulation has the ear magnetised, even with a speed slower than we have grown used to.

When this set was first issued on CD, it involved 12 discs, and it's welcome to have these transfers squeezed on to 10 discs instead, particularly when the sound is fuller and more forward, with good body and presence. There's some inconsistency in the recording quality, but not enough to worry about, and even the earliest reading – of the *Haffner*, made in 1959 – is satisfyingly full-bodied, when one or two of the later ones are rather thinner. All the earlier symphonies were recorded in intensive sessions in 1968, and the present bargain box, unlike the previous, has such information included.

Böhm is inconsistent over such matters as exposition repeats. In the *Prague*, for example, though there's no repeat in the first movement, the exposition repeat is observed in the *Presto* finale, a question, one imagines, of Böhm wanting to balance two exceptionally long earlier movements. Then in No 40 he does observe the first movement repeat, but not in No 39 or the *Jupiter*, and it's probable that with the *Jupiter* the reason is that DG wanted the symphony to fit comfortably on an LP side. Whatever the reason, it means that the last three symphonies have been squeezed on to a single disc of 79 minutes, and only one of the other discs has a timing of less than 70 minutes, and most are over 75. An excellent bargain.

ances, but there's nothing hair-shirt about them. Pinnock caresses the slow movements with great affection, and throughout there's a sense of fun and enjoyment. What's exciting is the sweetness of the period-instrument sound and the suppleness and flexibility The English Concert brings to the music. They play, much of the time, as if it were chamber music, particularly in second subjects – the lyrical passages, that is, where they shape the phrases with a warmth and refinement you hardly expect in orchestral music. Timing is quietly witty, yet not at all contrived or artificial: it's the sort of expressive refinement that depends on listening to one another, not on the presence of a conductor. There's large-scale playing, too.

The middle symphonies are especially good. The opening of the brilliant K133 (No 20) has a splendid swing, with its prominent trumpets, and a real sense of a big, symphonic piece. K184 (No 26) is duly fiery and its accents are neatly judged. K201 and K202 (Nos 29 and 30) are both very impressively done: an eloquent rather than a fiery account (though something of that too) of the opening movement of K201, with a particularly euphonious and shapely *Andante*. The finales of both are done with exceptional vitality and the rhythmic resilience that's characteristic of these performances.

Pinnock's *Jupiter* (No 41) is truly outstanding. The first movement is duly weighty, but energetically paced, and its critical junctures timed with a keen sense of their role in the shape of the whole. In the *Andante* he draws an extraordinarily beautiful, almost sensuous sound from The English Concert, and the lines are moulded with tenderness. This, above all, is the quality that distinguishes Pinnock's recordings from all others, this natural and musical sound, deriving from the way the players are intently listening to one another; and it's fitting that it reaches its high point in the *Jupiter*. As for the finale: well, it's decidedly quick, giving the impression of a performance in which the orchestra is pressed to an extent that its ensemble playing is under stress, though it holds together. It's a very bold, outspoken reading, which leaves one gasping afresh at the music's originality.

In short, quite outstanding performances, unfailingly musical, wholly natural and unaffected, often warmly expressive in the slow music and always falling very happily on the ear, with no trace of the harshness that some think is inevitable with period instruments. They are excellently recorded, with the properly prominent wind balance helping to characterise the sound world of each work.

Complete Symphonies Ⓟ
The English Concert / Trevor Pinnock
Archiv Produktion 471 666-2AB11 (11 discs: 13 hours, 36' · DDD) Recorded 1993-4 Ⓑ❍

This set is pure joy. These are period perform-

Symphonies Nos 1, 2, 4 & 5
Abel (formerly attrib Mozart) Symphony, Op 7 No 3
Northern Chamber Orchestra / Nicholas Ward
Naxos 8 550871 (59' · DDD) Recorded 1994 Ⓢ

Symphonies Nos 6-10
Northern Chamber Orchestra / Nicholas Ward
Naxos 8 550872 (56' · DDD) Recorded 1993 Ⓢ

These two discs of Mozart's first 10 symphonies offer a unique view of the composer's earliest years of apprenticeship as a symphonist. Ward and his orchestra show a sensitive response to the wealth of stylistic influences apparent in these works. Purists may question the inclusion of two of the symphonies, Nos 2 and 3, since neither work is actually by Mozart. The former is attributed to the composer's father, Leopold, while the latter is Mozart's orchestration of C F Abel's E flat Symphony, Op 7 No 3. However, when they're played with such engaging style and elegance as here, these two works add a further important dimension to Mozart's early symphonic output. Where J C Bach's influence is most powerful (Symphonies Nos 1, 4, 5 and 6), the NCO presents the music's contrasting thematic characters with fine clarity, balancing the music's beautifully transparent textures with appropriate lightness of touch. The inclusion of trumpets and drums in the next three symphonies (Nos 7, 8 and 9) announces the young composer's growing brilliance and stature. In these pieces, the NCO moves into a higher gear, revealing Mozart's potent originality, with powerfully dramatic *tuttis* and expressively sung *andantes*. Mozart made his first trip to Italy in 1770, and the symphony he wrote in Milan that year (No 10) shows his enthusiastic incorporation of Italian stylistic models. Here the NCO's deliciously spacious orchestral playing shows Mozart's ravishing originality, with dramatic opposition of gesture and instrumentation in the exuberant *allegros* and a beguilingly graceful slow movement that winningly displays a keen awareness of the composer's innovative touches. These are indeed splendid performances, admirably complemented by vivid recordings (made in the spacious acoustic of the Concert Hall, New Broadcasting House, Manchester).

Symphonies Nos 15-18
Northern Chamber Orchestra / Nicholas Ward
Naxos 8 550874 (58' · DDD) Recorded 1994 ⓢ

After Mozart returned from his first extended tour of Italy in 1771 he embarked on a number of symphonic projects that show his astonishing assimilation and transformation of the Italian overture, with crisp, transparent orchestration and suppleness of expression. The influence of Sammartini and J C Bach – whose music could be heard at concerts in Salzburg during 1772 when these pieces were written – is especially apparent in the bold thematic gestures and civilised discourse between wind and strings. Nicholas Ward and the NCO bring their customary style and eloquence to this music in performances that evocatively portray its blend of formal unity, radiant vitality and occasionally – as in the rhythmically imaginative finale of the C major Symphony – rustic charm. Opening *allegros* are suitably vivacious, *andantes* are graceful and poignant and the vigorous finales bristle with energy. The first movement of the

C major Symphony offers a more potent dramatic formula, with subtly poetic triplets and tense tremolos; however, the highlight of the programme is the F major Symphony (No 18), which Saint-Foix described as 'the first of [Mozart's] great symphonies'. Here, Ward's and the NCO's dramatically compelling account, beautifully presented in a natural, spacious recording, brilliantly highlights the music's operatic qualities.

Symphonies Nos 21-24 & 26
Northern Chamber Orchestra / Nicholas Ward
Naxos 8 550876 (53' · DDD) Recorded 1993 ⓢ

This is a chance to enjoy Mozart's inexhaustibly imaginative assimilation and transformation of Italian operatic models. Ward's balanced orchestral textures reveal Mozart's fragrant orchestration with great clarity in the A major Symphony. Sample the second movement's deftly handled interplay of strings, woodwind and horns, and buoyantly stately Menuetto that culminates effectively in the finale's restless drive. The complete musical satisfaction provided by the four Italian-overture symphonies that comprise the remainder of the programme is due to the fullness and vigour of the orchestration itself, and to the Northern Chamber Orchestra's lively performances. The opening *allegros* and cheerfully effervescent finales bubble with infectious vitality, while the slow movements give the opportunity for more intimate instrumental ensembles. Most impressive, however, is the E flat major work, which originated as the overture to the play *Lanassa*. Here, Ward and the NCO compellingly portray the dramatic violence of the opening *Presto*, the despair of its minor-key *Andante* and the exuberant rhythms of its finale. The recording is atmospheric.

Symphonies Nos 25, 28 & 29
Prague Chamber Orchestra / Sir Charles Mackerras
Telarc CD80165 (78' · DDD) Recorded 1987 Ⓜ

Here are three symphonies from Mozart's late teens, written in Salzburg, in crisply articulated performances. The first of them is a *Sturm und Drang* piece in G minor, a key that the composer reserved for moods of agitation. Mackerras takes the orchestra through the big opening *Allegro con brio* of No 25 with drive and passion, although it's unlikely that Mozart would have expected a Salzburg orchestra in the 1770s to play as fast as this skilful body of Czech players. The gentle *Andante* comes therefore as a relief, though here too Mackerras keeps a firm rhythmic grasp on the music, and indeed a taut metrical aspect is a feature of all three symphonies as played here, so that minuets dance briskly and purposefully and finales bustle. However, the sunlit warmth of the beautiful A major Symphony, No 29, comes through and the bracing view of the other two symphonies is a legitimate one, though giving little or nothing in the direction of expressive lingering, much less towards sentimental indulgence. The Prague Chamber Orchestra is an expert ensemble, not overlarge for this style of music, and the recording is without doubt admirably clear although a little reverberant.

Symphony No 33. Serenade No 9
Academy of St Martin in the Fields / Iona Brown
Hänssler Classic CD98 129 (59' · DDD)   Ⓕ

Symphony No 35. Serenade No 7
Academy of St Martin in the Fields / Iona Brown vn
Hänssler Classic CD98 173 (72' · DDD)   Ⓕ

Each disc brings together a middle-period symphony and a contemporaneous Serenade. The sound recording has a sharpness of focus and sense of presence more often associated with the finest analogue recordings of the 1960s and 1970s. It's surprising to find that the venue was Henry Wood Hall, for this sounds rather more intimate than most recordings made there, with plenty of bloom but no excessive reverberation. This is Mozart sound, using modern instruments but with some concern for the crisper manners encouraged by period performance, that in its freshness and beauty makes one want to go on listening. The finale of the Symphony No 33, for example, brings a hectic speed which doesn't sound at all breathless, with featherlight triplets, and similarly in the finale of the *Posthorn* Serenade with which it's coupled. Exceptionally, in that Serenade, Iona Brown opts for a more relaxed speed and more moulded style in the lovely minor-key *Andantino* of the fifth movement. The posthorn in the Trio of the second Minuet is this time much more brazen and more forwardly balanced than before.

The coupling of the *Haffner* Symphony and *Haffner* Serenade is specially apt. Iona Brown herself is the virtuoso soloist in the Serenade, lighter than ever in the *moto perpetuo* scurryings of the fourth-movement Rondo. For those who continue to resist period performances in this repertory these are very refreshing discs.

Symphonies Nos 35-6 & 38-41   🄷
Berlin Philharmonic Orchestra / Karl Böhm
DG The Originals ② 447 416-2GOR2 (146' · ADD)
Recorded 1959-66   Ⓜ

These performances come from the first ever complete set of Mozart symphonies (reviewed above), and they still represent 'big orchestra' Mozart at its most congenial. The contrast between Böhm's sparkling Mozart, both elegant and vigorous, and the much smoother view taken by Karajan on his countless recordings with the same orchestra, works almost entirely in Böhm's favour here. Interpretatively, these are performances very much of their time, with exposition repeats the exception (as in the first

movement of No 40) and with minuets taken at what now seem like lumbering speeds. However, the slow movements certainly flow easily enough, and finales bounce along infectiously.

Consistently they convey the happy ease of Böhm in Mozart, even if the recording is beefy by today's standards, not as transparent as one now expects in this repertory, whether on modern or period instruments.

There's some inconsistency between the different recordings, all made in the Jesus-Christus Kirche in Berlin. The best sound comes from the sessions in 1966 for the *Linz* and No 39 – satisfyingly full without any perceptible edginess on violins – and the least good from 1959 for the *Prague*, where high violins sound rather fizzy. Yet the very precision of the CD transfers encourages one to highlight such points. In practice most collectors will find the sound more than acceptable enough in all six symphonies to convey the warmth of Böhm in Mozart without distraction.

Symphonies Nos 36 & 38
Prague Chamber Orchestra / Sir Charles Mackerras
Telarc CD80148 (66' · DDD) Recorded 1987   Ⓜ

Mozart wrote his *Linz* Symphony in great haste (five days to be precise), but needless to say there's little evidence of haste in the music itself, except perhaps that the first movement has all the exuberance of a composer writing on the wing of inspiration. The slow movement with its siciliano rhythm certainly has no lack of serenity, although it has drama too. The *Prague* Symphony was written only three years later, yet Mozart's symphonic style had matured and the work is more ambitious and substantial.

A glorious spaciousness surrounds Sir Charles's performances. The fullness of the sound helps to add weight to climaxes without going beyond the bounds of volume that Mozart might have expected. Sir Charles captures the joy and high spirits that these symphonies embody without in any way undermining their greatness. This vivacity is emphasised by the East European sound of the Prague Chamber Orchestra. Mackerras adopts some aspects of the modern approach to Mozart performance: he includes harpsichord continuo, his minuets are taken trippingly, one-to-a-bar, and he prefers bowing that's crisper, more detached, and pointed. The very rightness of the result is recommendation enough.

Symphony No 38. Piano Concerto No 25 in C, K503[a].
Ch'io mi scordi di te … Non temer, amato bene,
K505[b]
[b]**Bernarda Fink** *sop* **Lausanne Chamber Orchestra / Christian Zacharias** [ab]*pf*
Dabringhaus und Grimm MDG340 0967-2
(73' · DDD)   ⒻⓄ

Here Christian Zacharias successfully experiments with a nicely balanced Mozart group of

MOZART'S SYMPHONIES NOS 40 & 41 – IN BRIEF

Cleveland Orchestra / George Szell
Sony Classical SBK46333 (73' · ADD)   ⒷO
With No 35, the *Haffner*, thrown in, this is
great value. Szell's approach is stylish and,
obviously, 'big band', but he presents this
music with appropriate scale. The late-1950s
sound is pretty good.

English Baroque Soloists / Sir John Eliot Gardiner
Philips 426 315-2PH (75' · DDD)   ⓂOO
Vivid, dramatic period-instrument accounts
that in no way diminish the reach and ambition of these two masterpieces.

The English Concert / Trevor Pinnock
DG 474 229-2ABA (73' · DDD)   Ⓜ
Smaller in scale than Gardiner's readings,
Pinnock invests these works with great spring
and vitality – at times they almost dance
along.

Berlin PO / Karl Böhm
DG 439 472-2GCL (73' · ADD)   Ⓑ
Urbane, autumnal Mozart from one of his
greatest interpreters. The BPO are very
stylish, and a charming *Eine kleine Nachtmusik*
from the VPO adds to the CD's allure.

Vienna PO / Leonard Bernstein
DG 445 548-2GM (69' · DDD)   ⓂOO
Recorded in 1984, Bernstein's Mozart is
beautifully conceived: full of light and shade
with no sense of overweight or over-drama-
tising. A charmer of a disc.

Prague CO / Sir Charles Mackerras
Telarc CD80139 (75' · DDD)   Ⓜ
Period manners but modern instruments
make for a delightful ride from Mackerras.
Completists will respond to his inclusion of
all the repeats – making for a *Jupiter* of vast
proportions, but every minute is a delight!

Concertgebouw Orchestra / Nikolaus Harnoncourt
Warner Elatus 0927 49622-2 (74' · DDD)   Ⓜ
Harnoncourt always has someting fascinating to say in Mozart, but these are somewhat
eccentric readings: the *Jupiter* is epic and certainly more succesful than No 40, which
never quite settles down.

Academy of St Martin in the Fields / Sir Neville Marriner
EMI 569820 2 (71' · DDD)   Ⓜ
Stylish, well-proportioned with some glorious solo work – a typical ASMF/Marriner
production. Well priced, this is a fine middle-
of-the-road coupling of these two great symphonies.

symphony, aria and concerto. He himself takes
multiple roles, conducting a fresh and lively
account of the Prague Symphony, and acting as
piano soloist not only in the Concerto, directing
the weighty K503 from the keyboard, but also
providing a crisply pointed obbligato in the
most taxing of Mozart's concert arias, Ch'io mi
scordi di te. The sense of freedom and spontaneous enjoyment is enhanced by the clarity of
the recording, made in the Metropole, Lausanne. Though *tutti*s are big and weighty,
Zacharias finds rare transparency in lighter passages, and a vivid sense of presence throughout.
One of Zacharias's great merits as a Mozart
pianist is the crispness of his articulation; he
defines each note with jewelled clarity.

The Symphony, too, is given a refreshing performance, with due weight in the first movement and light, crisp articulation in the finale.
Some may feel that Zacharias underplays the
gravity of the central Andante, but nowadays
few will object to a flowing tempo such as one
expects in a period performance.

Most striking of all, though, is the concert
aria. Bernarda Fink, officially a mezzo, isn't just
untroubled by the soprano tessitura but gives a
characterful interpretation, pointing words and
phrases with delightful individuality. Using her
lovely creamy tone-colours, Fink offers one of
the most impressive of all readings since
Schwarzkopf's. Her contribution crowns a consistently enjoyable programme.

Symphonies Nos 39-41. Bassoon Concerto in B flat, K191a
[a]**Jane Gower** *bn* **Anima Eterna / Jos van Immerseel**
Zig Zag Territoires ② ZZT030501 (104' · DDD)   Ⓕ

Jos van Immerseel, better known as fortepianist
than conductor, sets quickish tempos in almost
all the movements of Symphonies Nos 39 and
40. The overall effect is of vitality, brightness
and clarity, with contrapuntal interplay much
more apparent than usual. There are few of the
usual tragic overtones in the gracefully played
Andante, of No 39, or the usual darkness and
foreboding in No 40. All this comes partly from
the period instruments, and the perceptive way
they're handled. Van Immerseel balances them
carefully, has little or no string vibrato and
clearly requires precise articulation. That's why
we hear more of the inner lines.

In the *Jupiter*, however, the approach is less
chamber-music-like. This is a trumpets-and-
drums symphony, so the manner is more forceful, sometimes rather abrupt; but the first movement is powerfully shaped. Again a quickish
Andante with Mozart's textures illuminated to
fine effect. The dense writing in the minuet
profits from a finely balanced texture, and so
above all does the finale, where you're constantly aware of all that's going on below the
surface. It's passionate, too: listen to those
timpani thwacks in the development and the
power of the extraordinary recapitulation. The

amazing five-part counterpoint of the coda is heard with unprecedented clarity.

These may not be everyone's performances. But they should be treasured: if you think you know these symphonies back to front, these versions will enable you to listen to the music afresh and hear new things in it.

The Bassoon Concerto filler is enjoyably played by Jane Bower on a period bassoon, delightfully uneven in tone but always beautifully tuned and with many neatly imaginative touches.

Clarinet Quintet in A, K581

Mozart Clarinet Quintet **Brahms** Clarinet Quintet in B minor, Op 115
Karl Leister cl **Berlin Soloists** (Bernd Gellermann, Bernhard Hartog vns Wolfram Christ va Jörg Baumann vc)
Warner Apex 0927-43502-2 (71' · DDD) Recorded c1989   Ⓑ

This is a familiar and successful coupling of two of the most beautiful works written for clarinet and strings. Karl Leister gives most beautifully easy, charming, relaxed performances of both works, and the recordings are pleasantly fresh and immediate. There's no lack of sparkle in Mozart's final variations, and the Hungarian tinges are beautifully touched upon in the Brahms; the slow music in both works is reflective and tender without any loss of poise. Here are two beautiful performances that can be warmly recommended.

Clarinet Quintet. String Quartet No 18 in A, K464
Janet Hilton cl **The Lindsays** (Peter Cropper, Ronald Birks vns Robin Ireland va Bernard Gregor-Smith vc)
ASV CDDCA1042 (74' · DDD)   ⒻО

The Clarinet Quintet is given with the finesse and care for phrasing and articulation that characterises all Lindsay Mozart issues. It's good for Mozart to sound suave, and Janet Hilton presents the melody of the *Larghetto* with lovely soft articulation, yet the music is more rhetorical and passionate than she allows, and the hint of vibrato only serves further to soften the expression. There are, however, fine features in this performance – the exciting, perfectly controlled first-movement development, a lively, beautifully shaped Minuet, a really melancholic viola in the finale and a splendidly robust concluding *Allegro*.

The Lindsays' interpretation of K464 is persuasive, barring a few minor quibbles – the first movement, though flexible and elegant, is perhaps slightly lacking in urgency and dynamic contrast, the finale, on the other hand, has all the drama and onward thrust you could wish for, but occasionally begins to lose its rhythmic poise. If you prefer to have modern instruments in this quartet, go for this recording, which is clear, intimate, but not dry.

String Quintets

No 1 in B flat, K174 No 2 in C minor, K406/K516b No 3 in C, K515 No 4 in G minor, K516 No 5 in D, K593 No 6 in E flat, K614

String Quintets Nos 1-6
Arthur Grumiaux, Arpad Gérecz vns **Georges Janzer, Max Lesueur** vas **Eva Czako** vc
Philips Trio ③ 470 950-2PTR3 (170' · ADD) Recorded 1973   Ⓜ ООО

 Of the six works Mozart wrote for string quintet, that in B flat major, K174, is an early composition, written at the age of 17. It's a well-made, enjoyable work, but not a great deal more than that. The C minor work, K406, is an arrangement by Mozart of his Serenade for six wind instruments, K398. It's difficult not to feel that the original is more effective, since the music seems to sit a little uncomfortably on string instruments. But the remaining four works, written in the last four years of Mozart's life, are a different matter. The last string quintets from Mozart's pen were extraordinary works, and the addition of the second viola seems to have pulled him to still greater heights. It has been suggested that Mozart wrote K515 and K516 to show King Friedrich Wilhelm II of Prussia that he was a better composer of string quintets than Boccherini, whom the King had retained as chamber music composer to his court. There was no response, so he offered these two quintets for sale with the K406 arrangement to make up the usual set of three. K593 and K614 were written in the last year of his life. Refinement is perhaps the word that first comes to mind in discussing these performances, which are affectionate yet controlled by a cool, intelligent sensitivity. The recordings have been well transferred, and Grumiaux's tone, in particular, is a delight to the ear.

String Quintet No 3. String Quartet No 16 in E flat, K428
Louise Williams va **The Lindsays** (Peter Cropper, Ronald Birks vn Robin Ireland va Bernard Gregor-Smith vc)
ASV CDDCA992 (67' · DDD)   Ⓕ

Here's a fine performance of the great C major Quintet. The Lindsays take the first movement at a true *Allegro*, so that it bowls along in top gear, the details vivid and sharply etched. Much of this grandest and most spacious movement in Mozart's chamber output is marked to be played softly: in the Lindsays' hands the wonderful counterpoint in the development section can be heard with exceptional clarity as the tension builds up, but not the dynamic. The *Andante* sounds the more touching for never being overplayed, and it's a special pleasure to hear how the most florid passages for first violin and first viola fit effortlessly into the rhythmic scheme. In the finale, Peter Cropper introduces some beautifully played portamentos in the main theme, and the whole movement sounds delightfully witty and happy. The E flat Quartet, K428, is cool and stylish, which suits this enigmatic work rather well. The Lindsays' way of using Mozart's marks of expression and articulation to make the music speak feels absolutely right, especially in their delicate, refined *Andante*, and it's good to hear the quartet played with all its repeats. The recording has a nice intimate quality.

Flute Quartets

Flute Quartet No 1 in D, K285. Oboe Quartet in F, K370/K368b. Clarinet Quintet
Jaime Martin *fl* **Jonathan Kelly** *ob* **Nicholas Carpenter** *cl* **Brindisi Quartet** (Jaqueline Shave, Patrick Kiernan *vns* Katie Wilkinson Krososhunin *va* Anthony Pleeth *vc*)
EMI Debut 569702-2 (64' · DDD)   Ⓕ

Do you like your Mozart refined and graceful? Or robust and spontaneously expressive? A combination of both would be perfect, you may think, but in practice it's not always easy to achieve. The Brindisi Quartet and their three colleagues play with exceptional finesse, and excellent balance and blend, well captured by the recording. These are predominantly light-toned performances, with the phrases shaped convincingly and with unfailing elegance. Their approach seems just about ideal in the Flute Quartet, where the joyful, vivacious atmosphere of the outer movements is enhanced by thoughtful attention to detail. Jaime Martin's sensitive, sensuous flute-playing in the *Adagio* provides a delightful contrast.

There are many good things in the other two pieces, too. Jonathan Kelly's virtuosity in the Oboe Quartet's finale is really exciting, as is the brilliant, superbly balanced development section in the Clarinet Quintet's first movement. But there are places where you might long for something less cool and detached. The recording of the Oboe Quartet by Nicholas Daniel and members of the The Lindsays (reviewed below with the String Quartet No 17 and the Horn Quintet) manages to combine stylishness with rather stronger expression, but nevertheless this is a nice little set, worth buying for the Flute Quartet alone.

Flute Quartets – D, K285; G, K285a; C, KAnh171/K285b; A, K298
Emmanuel Pahud *fl* **Christoph Poppen** *vn* **Hariolf Schlichtig** *va* **Jean-Guihen Queyras** *vc*
EMI 556829-2 (59' · DDD)   Ⓕ

There may be only one movement of any emotional weight, the B minor *Adagio* of the First Quartet, K285, but in that brief cantilena Pahud finds a mystery and subtlety of dynamic shading that outshine almost any rival. For the rest he consistently conveys the fun in the writing here. The A major work may run the dangerous course of parodying the banalities of the contemporaries whom Mozart despised, but Pahud still finds charm in the invention, helped by the warm, imaginative playing of his string partners. Pahud's lighter, more sparkling playing, with his fresh, clear tone is preferable to Galway's more Romantic approach at generally broader speeds, and with phrasing more heavily underlined in characteristically full flute tone. Pahud also observes second-half repeats as well as first in the sonata-form first movements of the first three quartets. Recommended.

Piano Quartets

No 1 in G minor, K478; **No 2** in E flat, K493

Piano Quartets – Nos 1 & 2; E flat, K452 (arr)   ℗
Sonnerie (Monica Huggett *vn* Emilia Benjamin *va* Alison McGillivray *vc* Gary Cooper *fp*)
ASV Gaudeamus CDGAU212 (76' · DDD)   Ⓕ

Sonnerie go one – rather a large one – better than their recorded rivals in the Mozart piano quartets by including an extra work: the piano quartet arrangement (not generally thought to be Mozart's own) of the Quintet for piano and wind. The work, so artfully composed around the sound and capacities of the oboe, clarinet, bassoon and horn, loses the motivation for its particular thematic structure in transcription but is nevertheless a worthwhile bonus.

Not that these performances need any bonus. They have exceptional musical vitality, as though the music is being freshly thought through as it unfolds and the players are newly fired by its ideas. The G minor Quartet in particular is given a large-scale, outspoken performance, vigorous, dark-toned in the first movement, with an almost alarmingly vivid and strongly shaped account of the development section. There's drama in the *Andante*, too, which is expansively done, and the finale of the E flat work, too, is done with great spirit – here the pianist is very much in the driving seat – and there are many happy details of timing and dynamic gradation.

Mozart's wit is beautifully captured in K493, yet this is a deeply serious performance, strongly argued, with the mystery and logic of his unusual modulations fully grasped. The first movement here, taken at a rather steady tempo, is particularly successful, with Cooper taking his time over the expression of its ideas and Monica Huggett and her colleagues playing the lyrical secondary material with much warmth.

Piano Quartets Nos 1 & 2
Isaac Stern *vn* **Jaime Laredo** *va* **Yo-Yo Ma** *vc*
Emanuel Ax *pf*
Sony Classical Theta SMK89794 (56' · DDD)
Recorded 1994   Ⓜ

This grouping of star names offers performances of imagination and insight. In the E flat Quartet, K493, it isn't just Isaac Stern and Yo-Yo Ma whose solo entries have one sitting up, but also Jaime Laredo in the rare moments when Mozart gives a solo to the viola. Speeds are beautifully chosen, and in both works the performances convey a happy spontaneity. Emanuel Ax shows what a natural, individual Mozartian he is. The G minor work is in many ways parallel to the great piano concertos of the period, with the piano regularly set against the strings in ensemble, and Ax readily establishes the sort of primacy plainly required. He's a shade robust at the start of the central *Andante* but in fast music as in slow his gift of pointing rhythms and moulding phrases is consistently persuasive and imaginative. The recording, made in the Manhattan Center, New York, is a degree drier than in many of the current rival versions, but there's ample bloom on the sound, fitting very well in a domestic listening room.

Piano Quartets Nos 1 & 2
Paul Lewis *pf* **Leopold String Trio** (Marianne Thorsen *vn* Scott Dickinson *va* Kate Gould **vc**)
Hyperion CDA67373 (63' · DDD)   Ⓕ**OO**

These are unusually expansive works, their first movements each close on 15 minutes' music, prolific in their thematic matter and richly developed. They demand playing that shows a grasp of their scale, playing that makes plain to the listener the shape, the functional character of the large spans of the music.

Paul Lewis and the Leopold String Trio, playing on modern instruments, excel in this, with their feeling for its structure and its tension, particularly in the first movement of the G minor, and especially at its great climax at the end of the development section, which is delivered with a compelling power and a sense of its logic. This performance is exemplified by its carefully measured tempo, its poise and its subtle handling of the balance between strings and piano. The *Andante* is unhurried, allowing plenty of time for expressive detail; and the darker colours within the finale, for all its G major good cheer, are there too.

The spacious and outgoing E flat work is no less sympathetically done, with plenty of feeling for its special kind of broad lyricism; particularly attractive are the gently springy rhythms and the tenderness of the string phrasing in the first movement, and Lewis's beautifully shaped phrasing in the *Larghetto*. A real winner, this disc: warmly recommended.

Additional recommendation

Piano Quartets
FP Zimmermann *vn* **T Zimmermann** *va* **Wick** *vc* **Zacharias** *pf*
EMI Encore 575874-2 (61' · DDD) Recorded 1988   Ⓑ
The players make their instruments sing, and

they're alert to all the drama in the music. Just one quibble: the viola sound is slightly too recessed.

String Quartets

No 1 in G, K80/K73f; **No 2** in D, K155/K134a; **No 3** in G, K156/K134b; **No 4** in C, K157; **No 5** in F, K158; **No 6** in B flat, K159; **No 7** in E flat, K160/K159a; **No 8** in F, K168; **No 9** in A, K169; **No 10** in C, K170; **No 11** in E flat, K171; **No 12** in B flat, K172; **No 13** in D minor, K173; **No 14** in G, K387; **No 15** in D minor, K421/ K417b; **No 16** in E flat, K428/K421b; **No 17** in B flat, K458, 'Hunt'; **No 18** in A, K464; **No 19** in C, K465, 'Dissonance'; **No 20** in D, K499, 'Hoffmeister'; **No 21** in D, K575; **No 22** in B flat, K589; **No 23** in F, K590

String Quartets Nos 14 -19 ('Haydn' Quartets)
Hagen Quartet (Rainer Schmidt, Lukas Hagen *vns* Veronika Hagen *va* Clemens Hagen *vc*)
DG ③ 471 024-2GH3 (173' · DDD)   Ⓕ**OO**

Mozart's dedication of six quartet masterpieces to Haydn extends, in the hands of the Hagen Quartet, to Bartók, Janáček and Shostakovich. This is Mozart viewed from the sensitised standpoint of the 20th century: the transforming power of 'Hagenisms' – tiny brush strokes from an amazingly varied tonal palette – makes every Mozartian nerve end glow. Hardly a bar passes without some heightened dynamic, rhythmic or colouristic effect. This might have been infuriating but there's good hard thinking here behind the notes, the sort of informed radicalism that Glenn Gould brought to Bach.

Everything here makes musical sense. Put on K387 and listen to the improvisational violin cadenzas at the start of the development. Think about it for a moment and, yes, that's precisely what the writing suggests. They also score in the imaginative way they handle the witty 'false ending', making the final climax sound conclusive – which, in the event, it isn't.

Broadly speaking, the Hagen's Mozart is a hive of interpretative activity with constantly shifting hues and just an occasional hint of self-consciousness. The keenest bargain competition comes from Philips and the aristocratic Quartetto Italiano and is probably still a first choice overall, but the Hagens offer so much food for musical thought that only the most closed-minded listener is likely to disapprove. Strongly recommended.

String Quartet No 17. Oboe Quartet in F, K370/K368b. Horn Quintet in E flat, K407/K386c
Nicholas Daniel *ob* **Stephen Bell** *hn* **The Lindsays** (Peter Cropper *vn* Ronald Birks *vn/va* Robin Ireland *va* Bernard Gregor-Smith *vc*)
ASV CDDCA968 (68' · DDD)   Ⓕ

The Lindsays really make the *Hunt* Quartet sparkle. One could describe their approach as middle-of-the-road; they're as meticulous as many period-instrument groups about details of phrasing, and avoid excessive accents and vibrato, yet their sound is modern, and the care over detail doesn't preclude a very spontaneous approach in which the music's feeling is compellingly communicated. In the Oboe Quartet Nicholas Daniel matches the string players' care over articulation and detailed expression, and plays with exceptional technical polish and brilliance. His gleaming tone is capable of great expressive range. The Horn Quintet is perhaps not quite such an individual or remarkable work as the two quartets. And you may find yourself longing for the extra character and beauty that a fine performance with the natural horn would have had. Yet this is a highly recommendable reading, too. The recording is very lifelike, with clear spacing of the instruments.

String Quartets Nos 20 & 22   P
Quatuor Mosaïques
Astrée Naïve E8834 (63' · DDD)   ⒻOO

This release completes the Mosaïques' recording of the 10 mature Mozart Quartets: an outstanding achievement. Apart from the clear, rich sound of the period instruments and the precise, beautiful tuning, what impresses about this Mozart playing is the care for detail, the way each phrase is shaped so as to fit perfectly into context while having its own expressive nuances brought out clearly. This often leads the quartet to use more *rubato*, to make more noticeable breathing spaces between sentences than many other groups do.

In the first movements of both these quartets, for instance, the Mosaïques adopt a very similar tempo and tone to the Quartetto Italiano, but the Italians aren't so rhythmically flexible. The Mosaïques make us listen to and appreciate the significance of each detail as it unfolds. With this approach there might be a danger of sounding contrived, but even when adopting a mannered style, as in the *Minuet* of K499, the Mosaïques retain a strong physical connection with the music's natural pulse – by comparison the Quartetto Italiano here seem a trifle heavy and humourless.

The slow movements of both quartets are taken at a flowing pace, making possible an unusual degree of expressive flexibility. All repeats are made, including those on the Minuet's *da capo* in K499. The longer the better when the playing is as exceptional as this.

Piano Trios

Piano Trios – No 1 in G, K496; No 3 in B flat, K502.
Divertimento in B flat, K254
Augustin Dumay *vn* **Jian Wang** *vc*
Maria João Pires *pf*
DG 449 208-2GH (73' · DDD) Includes bonus CD featuring short works by Brahms, Franck, Grieg, Mozart and Ravel.   Ⓕ

This disc of early Mozart trios is radiant with music-making which characterises this rare trio of friends – discriminating, fanciful and exuberant. A *crescendo* of joy shooting up through the opening scalic and arpeggio figures of K496 is answered by finely tapered violin playing and a cello which draws the ear to its contributions long before the true dialogue of the *Andante*. They find a truly lilting 6/8 (rather than the illusion of a sturdier 3/4) for the second movement, and the finale is full of a sense of wonder, in its platinum-tipped violin and the drawing back into finely nuanced tones of grey for the sombre fifth variation. For K502, Pires picks up on the forward impetus inherent in the rhythm of the opening theme and in the slow movment her phrasing makes its melody more shapely above the unsurpassed beauty of sustained tone in violin and cello. A delicious performance of the little *Divertimento*, K254 reveals the ancestry of these two trios; and there's another bonus in a 48-minute disc of extracts from the six recordings of Mozart, Brahms, Franck, Ravel and Grieg made over six years by the incomparable duo of Pires and Dumay.

Violin Sonatas

Violin Sonatas – No 1, K6; No 26, K378/K317d;
No 27, K379/K373a; No 36, K547
Rachel Podger *vn* **Gary Cooper** *fp*
Channel Classics ⊕ CCSSA21804 (77' · DDD/DSD)   ⒻOO

This is billed as Volume 1 of a complete set, and the series certainly gets off to a cracking start. The recording gives the fortepiano (an Adlam copy of a 1795 Anton Walther instrument) a full, rich, sound; the balance with the violin is excellent – it's as though we're listening in a small but resonant room.

The noble introductory *Adagio* of K379 sounds wonderfully colourful, and is followed by an unusually passionate, intense performance of the Sonata's G minor *Allegro*. It's taken at a faster tempo than usual, and we're persuaded to think of it as a worthy forerunner of the great G minor works to come. It's the CD's high point, perhaps, but the first two movements of K378 run it close; the opening *Allegro moderato* is spacious, flexible and expressive, and the second movement warm and sensuous.

Gary Cooper plays with considerable freedom, often spreading chords to soften their impact or for extra expressiveness, and ornamenting repeated passages most imaginatively. Rachel Podger doesn't generally ornament her part; her accompaniments are unforced and flow easily, and she enjoys taking the lead, playing boldly yet with sensitivity.

Mozart's first sonata, K6, begun when he was six, is a lively piece, but you'd never guess the composer. And K547, intended as an educational piece, has nothing of the expressive depth of the other late sonatas. But Cooper and Podger's playing remains suited to the music's character, unaffectedly bringing out its charm and vitality.

Piano Duets

Piano Sonatas Nos 15 & 16. Fantasia, K475
(all arr Grieg)
Sviatoslav Richter, Elisabeth Leonskaja pfs
Teldec 4509-90825-2 (62' · DDD) Recorded 1993 Ⓜ

When Grieg added an accompaniment for a second piano to Mozart's keyboard sonatas, he did it primarily with teaching in mind. But the resulting compositions soon found their way into the concert hall where, according to Grieg, 'the whole thing sounded surprisingly good'. And so it does today. In trying to 'impart to several of Mozart's sonatas a tonal effect appealing to our modern ears' Grieg left a telling little document or two on just what those late 19th-century Norwegian ears expected. If the C major 'Sonata facile' seems to sit even more sedately in the drawing-room, then it soon becomes clear that the light glinting through its windows isn't a million miles away from that bouncing off the fjord waters which lap around Troldhaugen.

The C minor *Fantasia* becomes a dark salon melodrama which moves from conversation with not a little chromatic prevarication to the hanging of whimsical icicles of figuration around the major-key section. These are Mozart-Kugeln with a *bonne bouche* or two of the finest Gravadlax on the side. And if these fond tributes are good enough for Elisabeth Leonskaja and Sviatoslav Richter, who could resist tasting them?

Piano Sonatas

No 1 in C, K279/K189d; **No 2** in F, K280/K189e; **No 3** in B flat, K281/K189f; **No 4** in E flat, K282/K189g; **No 5** in G, K283/K189h; **No 6** in D, K284/K205b; **No 7** in C, K309/K284b; **No 8** in A minor, K310/K300d; **No 9** in D, K311/K284c; **No 10** in C, K330/K300h; **No 11** in A, K331/K300i; **No 12** in F, K332/K300k; **No 13** in B flat, K333/K315c; **No 14** in C minor, K457; **No 15** in F, K533/K494; **No 16** in C, K545; **No 17** in B flat, K570; **No 18** in D, K576

Piano Sonatas Nos 1-18. Fantasia, K475
Mitsuko Uchida pf
Philips Complete Mozart Edition ⑤ 468 356-2PB5
(325' · DDD) ⑤Ⓑ❍❍❍

 By common consent, Mitsuko Uchida is among the leading Mozart pianists of today, and her recorded series of the piano sonatas won critical acclaim as it appeared and finally *Gramophone* Awards in 1989 and 1991. Here are all the sonatas, plus the *Fantasia* in C minor, K475, which is in some ways a companion piece to the sonata in the same key, K457. This is unfailingly clean, crisp and elegant playing, that avoids anything like a romanticised view of the early sonatas such as the delightfully fresh G major, K283. On the other hand, Uchida responds with the necessary pas-

sion to the forceful, not to say *Angst*-ridden, A minor Sonata, K310. Indeed, her complete series is a remarkably fine achievement, comparable with her account of the piano concertos. The recordings were produced in the Henry Wood Hall in London and offer excellent piano sound; thus an unqualified recommendation is in order for one of the most valuable volumes in Philips's Complete Mozart Edition. Don't be put off by critics who suggest that these sonatas are less interesting than some other Mozart compositions, for they're fine pieces written for an instrument that he himself played and loved.

Piano Sonatas Nos 5, 6 & 10
Maria João Pires pf
DG 437 791-2GH (73' · DDD) Recorded 1990 Ⓕ

Maria João Pires presents these sonatas with clear yet lightly pedalled textures and an overall directness that still allows room for tonal and rhythmic flexibility – which, generally speaking, isn't overdone. Largely, her playing seems to let the music speak for itself, although just offering the notes isn't enough, and what we appreciate here is the art that conceals art. However, the occasional detail might be questioned: for example, less than a minute into the G major Sonata, Pires's longish trill on the D preceding the second subject gives us a bar of four beats instead of three. The Andante of the same work begins with repeated Cs that seem too emphatically *staccato*, and its central section is a little overdramatised. The dance movement called *Rondeau en Polonaise* in K284 is on the slow side, though it still holds together, and the variation-form finale varies considerably in pace. Pires consistently observes repeats, including the second halves of movements (thus we get virtually every note of K283 twice), as is indicated. These are clear, commendable performances, and the kind of grace that Pires brings to this music, in which other pianists can sound a touch severe, is most appealing. The recording is pleasing and faithful.

Piano Sonatas Nos 12, 13 & 14. Adagio in B minor, K540
Alfred Brendel pf
Philips 468 048-2PH (75' · DDD) ⒻⓄ

Alfred Brendel isn't the first distinguished Mozartian to have embarked on a thoroughgoing exploration of the solo sonatas comparatively late in his career and to have found there a greater range than he had discovered hitherto. He's never played the F major Sonata, No 12 (K332), before; it was misdated by Köchel (five years too early) and so perhaps has been underestimated by many pianists. Bu it's mature Mozart, and when presented with Brendel's freshness of perception you wonder how its stature could ever have been overlooked. He uses a big range of dynamics and colour throughout No 14 (K457), and the rhythmic control which supports his quite free handling of line and *rubato* and dramatic pauses is wonderful. There's spontaneity of feeling too, without which a Mozart player can't attain the heights, and in the finales of the two earlier pieces a sparkle in the fingers that makes evident his delight in them.

The acoustic at The Maltings, Snape seems glorious for the sweep and Beethovenian force of gesture of No 14, contributing to the impression of music unconfined by the instrument and alive in the air around it. The other recordings were done at Glyndebourne and are very good too, but drier. The intimacy is just right for the *Adagio* in B minor, K540. Sample him in this, if you will, for an immediate revelation of his achievement here as a Mozart interpreter of the highest class. Then forget about him and go straight to the heart of the matter.

Piano Sonatas Nos 8 & 15. Courante, K399. Gigue, K574. Rondo, K511. March, K408/1.
Richard Goode *pf*
Nonesuch 7559 79831-2 (60' · DDD)   Ⓕ**ooo**

G A Mozart programme such as this, which includes two of the greatest sonatas and the A minor Rondo, leaves absolutely no margin for error or insufficiency, nor indeed for anything at all approximate or generalised. It's given to very few to play Mozart as well as Richard Goode, who seems to pitch the rhetoric just right and sustain an ideal balance of strength and refinement.

It's quite big playing, and the range of sonority is appropriate to the A minor Sonata, K310, in particular; no other recent recording realises so well the sharp contrasts, the cross-cut abutments of dynamics, which are such a striking feature in all three movements. Goode has a characteristic touch of urgency that has nothing to do with impetuosity or agitation of the surface, but rather with carrying the discourse forward and making us curious about what will happen next. In the *presto* finale, where Brendel is choppy and rather slow, Goode is exciting and articulate, wonderfully adept at getting from one thing to another.

There's little to choose between these players in the composite F major Sonata, K533/494. Brendel is at his finest in the dark, far-reaching middle movement; both of them relish the challenge of characterising the multifariousness of the first; Goode is especially convincing in the last movement.

He gives you the overview, too, often powerfully. While admiring the flux of intensities, dynamics, shapes and colours he sets before you in the Rondo, you might wonder three-quarters of the way through whether the totality was going to achieve enough weight. But the coda is to come – passionate and desolate, a close without parallel in Mozart's instrumental music – and at moments such as this you can be assured that Goode will surprise and certainly not disappoint. The shorter pieces, enterprisingly cho-

sen, set off the great works admirably. Exceptional sound throughout – like the playing, quite out of the ordinary run.

Fantasias

Adagio in B minor, K540. Fantasias – C minor, K396/385f; D minor, K397/K385g; C minor, K475. Gigue in G, K574. Kleiner Trauermarsch in C minor, K453a. Minuet in D, K355/576b. Rondos – D, K485; F, K494; A minor, K511
Christian Zacharias *pf*
Dabringhaus und Grimm MDG340 0961-2
(67' · DDD)   Ⓕ

Most of Mozart's single piano pieces are the product of some special stimulus: they aren't the daily bread of music-making, like the sonatas, but something rather more piquant. Christian Zacharias groups the pieces interestingly, starting with a D major-based section: the D minor *Fantasia*, the D major *Rondo*, the B minor *Adagio* and the D major *Minuet*, as if making a kind of free sonata of them. He omits the *Allegretto* portion of the *Fantasia* (on the grounds, it seems, that Mozart left it unfinished), and leads directly from the *Fantasia* into the *Rondo*. The B minor *Adagio* is one of Mozart's darkest, most inward pieces: written at a difficult moment in his life, it invites autobiographical interpretation with its sense of defeat and protest. Zacharias's sombre, subdued performance underlines such thoughts, and in the very chromatic K355 *Minuet*, too, his playing is dark and impassioned.

The C minor *Fantasia*, K396, is a rarity: a completion by Maximilian Stadler of a fragment that Mozart wrote for keyboard and violin. One can't imagine a performance much more persuasive than this; and in the authentic C minor *Fantasia* Zacharias plays beautifully, again with fire in the turbulent sections and with exquisite gentleness in the coolly reflective music such as the B flat episode. The K494 *Rondo* – more familiar in its revised version as finale of the K533 Sonata – is played in a more relaxed manner; in the A minor *Rondo*, K511, Zacharias beautifully captures the 'sentimental' tone and provides a performance of great delicacy and refinement, again drawing the full depth of expression from Mozart's harmonic subtleties.

Masses

Missae breves – G, K49/K47d[a]; D minor, K65/K61a[b]; **P** D, K194/K186ha; C (Spatzenmesse), K220/K196bb
[a]**Christine Schäfer,** [b]**Angela Maria Blasi** *sops*
[a]**Ingeborg Danz,** [b]**Elisabeth von Magnus** *mezzos*
[a]**Kurt Azesberger,** [b]**Uwe Heilmann** *tens* [a]**Oliver Widmer** *bar* [b]**Franz-Josef Selig** *bass* **Arnold Schoenberg Choir; Vienna Concentus Musicus / Nikolaus Harnoncourt**
Teldec Das Alte Werk 3984-21818-2 (69' · DDD)
Recorded 1994. Texts and translations included   Ⓕ

These youthful Masses, composed between 1768 and 1775, are among Mozart's most concise – K65, in particular, is a *Missa brevis* with a vengeance. Brevity was *de rigueur* in the Salzburg liturgy and we can hardly blame Mozart for rattling unceremoniously through the long texts of the *Gloria* and *Credo*. With minimal scope for musical development, much of the writing in the two earlier works, especially, is perfunctory – the 12-year-old composer dutifully going through the motions. As so often in late 18th-century Masses, the central mystery of the 'Et incarnatus est – Crucifixus' prompts a more individual musical response; and the *Benedictus* of K65 is a touching little duet for soprano and alto soloists based, surprisingly, on a descending chromatic motif, a traditional trope of lamentation. For all the conventional bustle of their faster movements, the two later Masses are more varied in their textures and more memorable in their ideas. Both the settings of the *Benedictus* have the grace and airiness of 18th-century Austrian churches. But the high point in each work is the *Agnus Dei*, especially that of K194, with its harmonic poignancy and dramatic alternations of solo and chorus. Occasionally Nikolaus Harnoncourt's direction can sound over-insistent – in, say, the *Kyrie* of K49, with its almost aggressive *marcato* articulation. But for the most part he chooses apt, mobile tempos, keeps the rhythms buoyant and characterises vividly without betraying the music's blitheness and innocence.

Both individually and in consort the soloists make the most of their limited opportunities, with delectable tone and phrasing from the two sopranos, Christine Schäfer and Angela Maria Blasi. The recorded balance is excellent, catching Harnoncourt's sharply etched orchestral detail while giving ample presence to the polished and responsive choir.

Mass in C (Coronation), K317. Vesperae solennes **P**
de confessore in C, K339. Epistle Sonata in C,
K278/K271e
Emma Kirkby *sop* **Catherine Robbin** *mez* **John
Mark Ainsley** *ten* **Michael George** *bass* **Winchester
Cathedral Choir; Winchester Quiristers
Academy of Ancient Music / Christopher
Hogwood** with **Alastair Ross** *org*
L'Oiseau-Lyre 436 585-2OH (54' · DDD) Recorded
1990. Texts and translations included   **Ⓕ**

It's difficult to think of many recordings of Mozart's church music that so happily captures its character – the particular mixture of confidence, jubilation and contemplation – as Hogwood's. His unfussy direction, broad phrasing, lively but generally unhurried tempos and happy details of timing serve splendidly in the Coronation Mass, the finest of Mozart's completed mass settings; the solemnity of the *Kyrie*, the fine swing of the *Gloria* and the energy of the *Credo*, with due pause for its rapt moment at the 'Et incarnatus', all these come over with due effect. Arguably the 'Osanna' is rather quick,

but its jubilation is splendid. And the sweetness of the *Benedictus* is ravishing.

Not more so, however, than the *Agnus*, for there, at a decidedly slow tempo, Hogwood allows Emma Kirkby to make the most of this very sensuous music, which she duly most beautifully does. The soloists are altogether an excellent team, with two refined voices in the middle and Michael George a firm and sturdy bass. The inclusion of the K278 Epistle Sonata is a happy notion. The Vesperae solennes de confessore is a setting of the five vesper psalms and the Magnificat, made in 1780, a year after the Mass, for some church feast in Salzburg. With admirable singing from the choir and a spacious recording with exceptionally good stereo separation that properly conveys the ecclesiastical ambience, this is a disc to treasure.

Mass in C minor, K427/K417a (ed Maunder) **P**
Arleen Auger, Lynne Dawson *sops* **John Mark
Ainsley** *ten* **David Thomas** *bass* **Winchester
Cathedral Choir; Winchester Quiristers; Academy
of Ancient Music / Christopher Hogwood**
L'Oiseau-Lyre Florilegium 425 528-2OH (51' · DDD)
Recorded 1988. Text and translation included

Ⓜ

Mozart left unfinished the work that ought to have been the choral masterpiece of his early Viennese years but there's enough of it to make up nearly an hour's music – music that's sometimes sombre, sometimes florid, sometimes jubilant. Hogwood avoids any charge of emotional detachment in his steady and powerful opening *Kyrie*, monumental in feeling, dark in tone; and he brings ample energy to the big, bustling choruses of the *Gloria* – and its long closing fugue is finely sustained. The clarity and ring of the boys' voices serve him well in these numbers. There's a strong solo team, headed by the late Arleen Auger in radiant, glowing voice and, as usual, singing with refined taste; Lynne Dawson joins her in the duets, John Mark Ainsley too in the trio. But this is essentially a 'soprano mass' – Mozart wrote it, after all, with the voice of his new wife (and perhaps thoughts of the much superior one of her sister Aloysia) in his mind – and Auger, her voice happily stealing in for the first time in the lovely 'Christe', excels in the florid and expressive music of the 'Et incarnatus' (where Richard Maunder has supplied fuller string parts than usual, perhaps fuller than Mozart would have done had he finished the work). Hogwood directs with his usual spirit and clarity.

Mass in C minor, K427/K417a (ed Eder)
Arleen Auger, Barbara Bonney *sops* **Hans Peter
Blochwitz** *ten* **Robert Holl** *bass* **Berlin Radio
Chorus; Berlin Philharmonic Orchestra / Claudio
Abbado**
Sony Classical Theta SBK89777 (53' · DDD) Recorded
1990. Text and translation included   **ⓂO**

'Comfortable' isn't a fashionable word to use

by way of praise; 'disturbing' is. However, Abbado's performance has to be described as comfortable. No doubt part of the warmth is due to another unfashionable feature, the use of a large orchestra that doesn't play on period instruments. That it plays magnificently and that the choir is a particularly fine one will have something to do with it too. Perhaps the balance of the recording overweights the orchestral bass, and a little less reverberance might not come amiss in the hall acoustic, but these are matters of degree, not disqualifying objections. Rather similarly, when it comes to the style of the performance, you might prefer a more jolly, a-hunting-we-will-go bounce for the rhythms of the *Credo*, but again this is a matter of degree for Abbado isn't lacking in vitality or colour. In tempo, too, he judges well. His singers are well forward and very distinct. He brings a vigorous touch to the *Kyrie* without impairing the profundity.

The other great strength is the excellence of the two sopranos. Auger has warmth, Bonney brightness, and she sings the 'Et incarnatus est' with blissfully assured control.

There have been many lovely accounts of this work on disc, but few better than here.

Mass in C minor, K427/K417a (ed Schmitt/Gardiner)
Sylvia McNair sop **Diana Montague** mez **Anthony Rolfe Johnson** ten **Cornelius Hauptmann** bass
Monteverdi Choir; English Baroque Soloists / John Eliot Gardiner
Philips 420 210-2PH (54' · DDD) Text and translation included
ⒻⓄ

Writers on Mozart sometimes take him to task for the alleged mixture of style in the C minor Mass, in particular the use of florid, 'operatic' solo writing amidst all the severe ecclesiastical counterpoint. To object is to misunderstand the nature of Mozart's religion, but it takes a performance as stylistically accomplished as this one to make the point in practice. The usual stumbling-block is the 'Et incarnatus', with its richly embellished solo line and its wind obbligatos. Sung as it is here, by Sylvia McNair, beautifully refined in detail, it's indeed passionate, but passionately devout. McNair is deeply affecting in the 'Christe', taken quite spaciously and set in a measured Kyrie of great cumulative power which also has some fine, clean singing from the Monteverdi Choir.

As with Gardiner's version of the Requiem you might wish for the sound of a boys' choir (why go to the trouble of having authentic instruments if you then use unauthentic voices?) but the bright, forward tone of his sopranos is very persuasive. The music is all strongly characterised: the 'Gloria' jubilant, the 'Qui tollis' grandly elegiac with its solemn, inexorable march rhythm and its dying phrases echoed between the choirs, the 'Credo' full of vitality. Some of the 'Cum sancto spiritu' fugue is too heavily accented, though. Nevertheless, a confident recommendation.

Requiem, K626

Requiem
Sylvia McNair sop **Carolyn Watkinson** contr
Francisco Araiza ten **Robert Lloyd** bass
Chorus and Academy of St Martin in the Fields / Sir Neville Marriner
Philips 432 087-2PH (50' · DDD) Recorded 1990. Text and translation included
ⒻⓄ

Mozart's Requiem may not be wholly Mozart's, as we all know: but performers show no reservations in the power or the conviction they bring to its music. Marriner's is among the noblest and most powerful of them all. The first thing that strikes you is the passionate nature of the choral singing, right from the start: the Academy chorus sings almost as if it were a personal protest against death, and the chromaticisms and dissonances of the 'Requiem aeternam' make their due effect. And the *Kyrie*, taken at a vigorous pace, has great energy. The dynamics in the 'Dies irae' are strongly made, almost exaggerated; there's a solemn 'Rex tremendae majestatis', with sharply dotted rhythms, a slow 'Lacrimosa' with detailed shaping, a lively 'Domine Jesu' and an *Agnus Dei* so grandly sombre that it emerges as the expressive climax of the whole work. There's superlative solo singing – Robert Lloyd in dark and noble voice in the 'Tuba mirum', Sylvia McNair as moving as always with her beautiful sound and refinement of nuance. This is a powerful and distinctive interpretation of the work: a consistent, considered view, faithfully and carefully carried through.

Requiem. Ave verum corpus in D, K618　　Ⓟ
Anna Maria Panzarella sop **Nathalie Stutzmann** contr **Christoph Prégardien** ten **Nathan Berg** bass
Les Arts Florissants / William Christie
Erato 0630-10697-2 (54' · DDD) Recorded 1994. Texts and translations included
ⓂⓄ

Les Arts Florissants provides a substantial, dramatic reading: the tempo for the 'Requiem aeternam' is slow but malleable, and Christie is ready to make the most of the changes in orchestral colour or choral texture and, indeed, to dramatise the music to the utmost. He has little truck with any notion that this is an austere piece: he sees it as operatic, almost romantic – and the result is very compelling. There are surprising things: 'Quantus tremor', in a very weighty account of the 'Dies irae', for example, is hushed rather than terrifying; the 'Recordare' is slow to the point of stickiness; there are rather mannered *crescendos* in the *Sanctus*; and often cadences are drawn out. The powerful choruses of the Sequence are imposingly done, and the grave 'Lacrimosa' wonderfully catches the special significance not only of the music itself but also of the fact that this is the moment where Mozart's last autograph trails off. The choral singing is sharply etched and generally distinguished. Although the solo singing isn't uniformly outstanding the soprano's melting tone can be very appealing, and Prégardien is an excellent stylist; the *Benedictus* is particularly impressive: shapely and refined. This is a reading full of character and imaginative ideas, very much a conscious modern interpretation of the work and very finely executed. The disc is completed by perhaps the only piece which can reasonably follow the Requiem, the *Ave verum corpus*, in a slow, hushed, rather romantic reading that's undeniably moving.

Requiem. Symphony No 25   H
Lisa della Casa *sop* **Ira Malaniuk** *contr* **Anton Dermota** *ten* **Cesare Siepi** *bass* **Vienna State Opera Concert Choir; Vienna Philharmonic Orchestra / Bruno Walter**
Orfeo D'Or mono C430961B (76' · ADD) Recorded live 1956   F

Listening to this is a moving experience. This was Walter's farewell to a festival with which he had been closely associated over 30 years: he conducted there from 1925 to 1937 after which he withdrew because of Austria's Anschluss with Nazi Germany. He returned in 1946 and off and on, until this final meeting with his beloved Mozart. Yet there's nothing sentimental here from a conductor nearing his 80th birthday. The performance is taut and closely worked. In the counterpoint of 'Quam olim Abrahae' you'll hear the sharp rhythms that characterise the whole. Even so, Walter's beloved VPO displays its warm, ethereal string tone as circumstances allow. Four of the leading soloists of the day contribute positively. Siepi inhabits the bass line as to the manner born, and della Casa provides tones fit for the contemplation of heavenly matters. The one drawback of the performance is the unsteady tone of the chorus sopranos. But as a whole, the choral singing is as dedicated as the rest. The recording is in well-focused mono. This was the best of Walter's Requiems and so worth an hour or so of anyone's time.

Requiem
Christine Schäfer, Bernarda Fink *sops* **Kurt Streit** *ten* **Gerald Finley** *bar* **Arnold Schoenberg Choir; Concentus Musicus Wien / Nikolaus Harnoncourt**
Deutsche Harmonia Mundi CD/SACD 🔊
82876 58705-2 (50' · DDD) Text and translation included   F**OO**

Nikolaus Harnoncourt's recent choral projects seem consciously to be reconciling some of the treasured values of his upbringing, alongside deeply held beliefs as to how a famous score can be illuminated through a 'period' lens. This recording integrates past and present in a way his previous reading from over 20 years ago simply couldn't. The main difference between the two is the interpretative assurance of his latest version; it's far clearer in its message, and articulated with greater rhetorical awareness.

While the *Dies Irae* is a set-piece of graphic,

MOZART'S REQUIEM – IN BRIEF

Schäfer; Fink; Streit; Finley; Arnold Schoenberg Choir; Concentus Musicus Wien / Nikolaus Harnoncourt
DHM 82876 58705-2 (50' · DDD)   F **OO**
Strong, sombre and punchy by turns, Harnoncourt's second recording is as idiosyncratic as one expects from him, while benefiting from a stellar line-up of soloists.

McNair; Watkinson; Ataiza; Lloyd; ASMF and Chorus / Sir Neville Marriner
Philips 432 087-2PH (50' · DDD)   F **O**
Consistent and considered, Marriner offers the conventional text with both dignity and polish. Exceptionally fine choral singing.

Panzarella; Stutzmann; Prégardien; Berg; Les Arts Florissants / William Christie
Erato 0630 10697-2 (54' · DDD)   M **O**
Using period instruments, Christie goes none the less for a big-scale, surprisingly emotive rendering. He employs a nicely balanced team of soloists.

Gritton; Rogers; Robinson; Rose; Scottish CO and Chorus / Sir Charles Mackerras
Linn CKD211 (55' · DDD)   F
Susan Gritton leads the soloists in Sir Charles Mackerras' recent rethink. He uses the Robert Levin edition in which the traditional text is retained only in so far as it agrees with 'idiomatic Mozartian practice'.

della Casa; Malaniuk; Dermota; Siepi; Vienna Philharmonic Orchestra / Bruno Walter
Orfeo C430961B (76' · ADD)   F
A taut and powerful account from Walter's final Salzburg Festival concert (1956) with soprano Lisa della Casa in glorious voice and the VPO playing with fierce commitment.

M Price; Schimdt; Schreier; Adam; Staatskapelle Dresden / Peter Schreier
Philips 475 205-2PGR (53' · DDD)   M
Peter Schreier won the *Gramophone* Choral Award in 1984 with this dedicated reading, a little heavy by contemporary standards, yet still compelling thanks to Margaret Price's ravishing singing and the magnificence of the Leipzig Radio Choir.

Harper; Hodgson; Pears; Shirley-Quirk; Aldeburgh Festival Chorus; English Chamber Orchestra / Benjamin Britten
BBC Legends BBCL4119-2 (77' · ADD)   F
Mono only, but Britten's live Aldeburgh Requiem has a force and compassion that transcends the mono sound. Heather Harper, Alfreda Hodgson, Peter Pears and John Shirley-Quirk make a uniquely impressive team. (Also includes a fascinating taped conversation with Britten.)

biting and eerie terror, the previous *Kyrie* is treated as a quasi-liturgical introit, unfolding gradually with an understated elegance. The *Tuba Mirum* is also unusual, less statuesque than normal, with a highly charged trombone solo both triumphant and imploring. The solo singers, individually and collectively, are tinged with a glow of deep regret; they sing with a palpable sense of interdependent ensemble and sustained poignancy.

As you'd expect from Harnoncourt, there's a studied punchiness, and the *Confutatis* leaves us with a series of striking contrasts, with 'salva me' as a gesture of impending loneliness for the *Recordare*: the strings shadow the soloists with questing and characterful figures, belying the restless and unsentimental approach to the *Lacrimosa*. The Arnold Schoenberg Choir is highly responsive in the modern way, yet unmodish in their soft-edged attack and heterogeneous timbre. Harnoncourt conceives of an almost jocular majesty in the *Domine Jesu* and *Benedictus*. Of course, there has to be a moment for the iconoclast in him: here it's the *Hostias*, taken at almost twice the usual speed.

This isn't a Requiem that comforts and stirs in the expected ways; instead, a curious and enigmatic undertow of human vulnerability emerges, presenting Mozart's valedictory essay in a striking new light.

Litaniae..., K243

Litaniae de venerabili altaris sacramento, K243   **P**
Mass in C, K257, 'Credo'
Angela Maria Blasi *sop* **Elisabeth von Magnus** *contr* **Deon van der Walt** *ten* **Alistair Miles** *bass*
Arnold Schoenberg Choir; Vienna Concentus Musicus / Nikolaus Harnoncourt
Teldec Das Alte Werk 9031-72304-2 (61 minutes: DDD)
Recorded 1991, Notes, texts and translations included   (F)

The *Litaniae de venerabili altaris sacramento* of 1775 has powerful claims to be reckoned the finest of Mozart's church works before the C minor Mass and Requiem; but it's never quite had the recognition it deserves. Or the performance until now. It's a deeply felt work, from the grave, warm opening of the *Kyrie*, through the imposing 'Verbum caro factum' and the graceful 'Hostia' that succeeds it, the 'Tremendum' with its almost Verdian menace and the appealing 'Dulcissum convivium' (a soprano aria with soft textures supplied by flutes and bassoons), the highly original 'Viaticum' and the resourcefully and lengthily developed 'Pignus' to the *Agnus*, a beautiful soprano aria with solo writing for flute, oboe and cello. The performance here under Nikolaus Harnoncourt rightly sees no need to apologise for the stylistic diversity of the work. The issue is made still more attractive by the inclusion of a Mass setting of the same year, one of Mozart's most inventive and original in its textures and its treatment of words. Altogether a very attractive record.

Exsultate, jubilate, K165/K158a

Mozart Exsultate, jubilate. Zaïde – Ruhe sanft, meine holdes Leben. Nehmt meinen Dank, ihr holden Gönner, K383. Mia speranza adorata ... Ah non sai qual pena sia, K416. Vorrei spiegarvi, oh Dio, K418. Ch'io mi scordi di te ... Non temer, amato bene, K505[a] **R Strauss** Morgen, Op 27 No 4. Liebeshymnus, Op 32 No 3. Der Rosenband, Op 36 No 1. Wiegenlied, Op 41 No 1. Das Bächlein, AV118
Christine Schäfer *sop* [a]**Maria João Pires** *pf* **Berlin Philharmonic Orchestra / Claudio Abbado**
DG 457 582-2GH (65' · DDD) Texts and translations included   (F)

Schäfer must now be rated in the royal line of Schwarzkopf, Seefried, Ameling, Popp and most recently Bonney as an interpreter of Mozart and Strauss. Yet, like those renowned singers, she's very much her own person, with her own distinctive voice and style. Her almost vibrato-less, at times slightly acerbic tone won't be to all tastes but her unadorned, clear and imaginative singing of all the Mozart arias holds attention. In *Nehmt meinen Dank*, the single word 'Geduld' carries a wealth of meaning; the whole of K416 has an intense feeling of farewell as Schäfer delivers it and again a single word, 'addio' at the end of the recitative, is drenched in sadness. In *Non temer, amato bene*, with Pires providing an ideal counterpoint to the singer, Schäfer etches into the mind the full import of the emotions being expressed, without a hint of sentimentality. *Ruhe sanft* disarms criticism, so touchingly, simply, is it sung, with the little cadenza before the reprise deftly touched in. The more extrovert pieces, *Exsultate, jubilate* and *Vorrei, spiegarvi* are sung more objectively. Abbado and the BPO support Schäfer in the most refined fashion possible, all the instrumental detail finely honed. They are just as ingratiating in Strauss. Most recent interpreters have had richer, warmer voices than Schäfer's. She's a throwback to, say, Elisabeth Schumann, who sang *Wiegenlied* with the same kind of artless, silvery beauty, combined with a pure, keen line – a real winner. But so is each of these beautifully composed and sung pieces, the texts fully understood so the words are ideally melded with their settings: note especially the extra intensity at the climax of *Liebeshymnus* and the ideal delineation of the elegiac *Morgen*'s reflective mood. Indeed it's in this last song, that one hears, as well as anywhere, the soprano's special gift of plaintive eloquence. The recording could not be better balanced.

Concert Arias

Ah! se in ciel, benigne stelle, K538; Vorrei spiegarvi, oh Dio!, K418; No, no che non sei capace, K419; Se tutti i mali miei, K83/K73p; Popoli di Tessaglia! ... Io non chiedo, eterni Dei, K316/K300b; Mia speranza adorata...Ah, non sai qual pena sia, K416; Alcandro, lo confesso...Non so d'onde viene, K294; Ma che vi fece, o stelle...Sperai vicino al lido, K368

Natalie Dessay *sop* **Orchestra of the Opéra de Lyon / Theodor Guschlbauer**
EMI 555386-2 (64' · DDD) Recorded 1994. Texts and translations included   Ⓕ**O**

Natalie Dessay's range extends upward far into the leger lines yet without incurring breathiness of a pallid coloration in the lower notes. She has a sylph's grace and lightness, and yet the timbre or character of her voice is thoroughly human. The profusion of scales and more intricate passagework common in some degree to all these pieces find in her an unostentatious virtuoso, mind and breath giving well-regulated support, and a sensitive feeling for phrase and line making good musical sense throughout.

Where vehemence and a dramatic quality of voice are in demand, as in the opening of *Popoli di Tessaglia*, we can find some reassurance in their absence, because at least the young singer doesn't try to force an effect. In less strenuous attack, as in *No, no che non sei capace*, she conveys the energy of a determined spirit yet still has some way to develop as an expressive artist. The more sorrowful and tender phrases of *Se tutti i mali miei*, for example, evoke only a mild response in her. Occasionally, too, Dessay's purity forfeits normal resonance and for what seems to be an involuntary note or two the voice flutes with a kind of disembodied hollowness. An instance occurs just before the second part of *Vorrei spiegarvi*, yet this is such a lovely performance, so graceful in its leisurely interplay of voice and instruments, that grumbling really is out of order.

Ah, lo previdi … Ah, t'invola, K272. A questo seno … Or che il cielo, K374. Alma grande e nobil core, K578. Grabmusik, K42a/K35a – Betracht dies Herz und frage mich. Vado, ma dove? oh Dei!, K583. Bella mia fiamma … Resta, o cara, K528. Misera! dove son … Ah! non son io, K369

Gundula Janowitz *sop* **Vienna Symphony Orchestra / Wilfried Boettcher**
DG The Originals 449 723-2GOR (61' · ADD) Recorded 1966. Texts and translations included Ⓜ**O**

An 'original' is exactly what this disc is, as it reproduces Janowitz's first solo recital record, issued in 1967. Listening back, we can marvel not just at the purity of tone and silken vocal line, but also a refinement of style that marks out a fully formed artist. Highlights include a delicate *Vado, ma dove?* and a performance of *Bella mia fiamma* which lights up the music with the subtlest of colours from within. Some recitatives might have been more dramatic, but Boettcher and the Vienna Symphony Orchestra provide alert accompaniment. There's also a bonus: the original LP didn't have room for the ravishing G minor lament 'Betracht dies Herz' from the *Grabmusik*, K42, a minor treasure which is issued here for the first time.

Un bacio di mano, K541[b]. Davidde penitente, K469 –

A te, fra tanti affanni[a]. Mentre ti lascio, K513[b]. Misero! o sogno … Aura, che intorno spiri, K431/K425b[a]. Per pietà, non ricercate, K420[a]. Si mostra la sorte, K209[a]. **Così fan tutte** – Al fato dan legge[ab]; Rivolgete a lui lo sguardo[b]; Secondate, aurette amiche[ab]; Un' aura amorosa[a]; Donne mie, la fate a tanti[b]. **Don Giovanni** – Deh! vieni alla finestra[b]. **La finta giardiniera** – Con un vezzo all'italiana[b]
[a]**Christoph Genz** *ten* [b]**Stephan Genz** *bar*
La Petite Bande / Sigiswald Kuijken
Deutsche Harmonia Mundi 82876 55782-2 (59' · DDD) Texts and translations included   Ⓕ

The Genz brothers are among the most promising of young singers. Regrettably, Mozart wrote only two duets for tenor and baritone (from *Così fan tutte*), both rather brief: both are sung here. Their programme gives us other music from from *Così*, including the testing tenor aria, 'Un' aura amorosa', which Christoph sings smoothly and sweetly in the traditional manner of German lyric tenors, with a faint hint of nasality and very little vibrato, although a touch more softness in the voice would have been welcome. He does find some of that in the superb concert aria *Misero! o sogno*, and gives a strong, large-scale reading of *Per pietà, non ricercate*.

Stephan sings 'Donne mie', a delightfully light and shapely performance, with the refinement of a Lied singer, and he also does the Guglielmo aria that Mozart (sensibly) rejected, 'Rivolgete a lui', where he catches delightfully the jocular swagger, the sexual braggadocio. He gives a duly impassioned account of *Mentre ti lascio*, even if the bottom of his voice in this rather low-lying aria isn't as powerful as the top. Don Giovanni's Serenade is admirable, but a touch more of soft sensuality, of covered tone, might have served. Here the voice is well forward, but for most of the disc the orchestra is unusually prominent, and the rich detail of Mozart's scoring comes through clearly, aided by the period instruments and Sigiswald Kuijken's sensitive and alert direction.

Additional recommendation

Lieder and Concert Arias
Schwarzkopf *sop* **Brendel, Gieseking** *pfs* **LSO / Szell**
EMI Références 574803-2 (ADD) Recorded 1955, 1968
A classic disc – the fruitful collaboration Ⓜ**OO** of great artists. Schwarzkopf was 39 when she recorded the Lieder, mature in resources but still amazingly capable of the clarity of youth.

Opera arias

La clemenza di Tito – Parto, parto; Deh, per questo; Ecco il punto, o Vitellia… Non piu di fiori. **Così fan tutte** – E'amore un ladroncello. **Don Giovanni** – Vedrai, carino **Le nozze di Figaro** – Non so più; Voi che sapete; Giunse alfin il momento … Deh vieni. **Concert Arias** – Chi sa, chi sa, qual sia,

K582; Alma grande e nobil core, K578; Ch'io mi scordi di te?, K505
Cecilia Bartoli mez **András Schiff** pf **Peter Schmidtl** basset cl/basset hn **Vienna Chamber Orchestra / György Fischer**
Decca 430 513-2DH (58' · DDD) Recorded 1989-90.
Texts and translations included   Ⓕ**O**

Mozart wrote some of his most appealing music for the mezzo-soprano voice with the roles of Cherubino and Susanna in *Le nozze di Figaro*, Dorabella in *Così fan tutte* and Zerlina in *Don Giovanni* each boasting at least one memorable aria. Alongside these this disc includes a handful of concert arias including *Ch'io mi scordi di te?* which was written for the farewell performance of the great mezzo Nancy Storace with Mozart playing the concertante piano role. Here with as innate an interpreter of Mozart's piano writing as András Schiff and a voice so remarkably self-assured as Cecilia Bartoli's the electricity of that first, historic performance seems almost to be recreated. And, here as elsewhere, György Fischer directs the splendid Vienna Chamber Orchestra with disarming sensitivity while the recording is wonderfully warm and vibrant.

Cecilia Bartoli boasts a voice of extraordinary charm and unassuming virtuosity: her vocal characterisations would be the envy of the finest actresses and her intuitive singing is in itself a sheer delight. But she also brings to these arias a conviction and understanding of the subtleties of the language which only a native Italian could. Listen to the subtle nuances of 'Voi che sapete', the depth of understanding behind Dorabella's seemingly frivolous 'E'amore un ladroncello'; these aren't mere performances, but interpretations which cut to the very soul of the music. No Mozart lover should be without this CD.

Così fan tutte – In uomini, in soldati; Temerari! ... Come scoglio; Ei parte ... Per pietà, ben mio. **Le nozze di Figaro** – E Susanna non vien! ... Dove sono; Giunse alfin il momento ... Al desio (K577a). **Don Giovanni** – Batti, batti, o bel Masetto; In quali eccessi ... Mi tradì quell' alma ingràta. **Sacred** – Davidde penitente, K469 – Lunghi le cure ingrate. Exsultate, jubilate, K165/K158a
Cecilia Bartoli mez **Vienna Chamber Orchestra / György Fischer**
Decca 443 452-2DH (61' · DDD) Recorded 1993.
Texts and translations included   Ⓕ**O**

There are few Italian mezzos, or sopranos for that matter, who sing a lot of Mozart and Bartoli's very Italian characteristics are immediately identifiable: brilliance of execution, vitality of words, sharpness of mind. She tears into the recitative before Donna Elvira's 'Mi tradì' with a blistering fury that leaves most interpreters of the role standing and has no problems with the *fioriture* of the aria itself. Her Fiordiligi has the bite for 'Come scoglio', but comparisons with a variety of lyric sopranos show up a want of depth to the tone, both here and in 'Per

pietà'. Her Countess delivers her lines with appropriate aristocratic weight, though one senses her natural temperament being suppressed with difficulty. However much she tries to disguise herself, the real Bartoli is likely to pop her head out.

There are unlikely to be any complaints about her effervescent Despina or Zerlina, both portrayals for which she has stage experience. In the concert hall she's also a spirited interpreter of *Exsultate, jubilate*. From the opening line Bartoli makes other singers seem bland by comparison, getting the Latin words to tingle with a sense of elation that only an Italian speaker would dare. The orchestral sound might be more firmly focused (the sound picture in 'Batti, batti' has the solo cello close, while the wind struggle to be heard from some deep recess) but Fischer accompanies his soloist with energy and tact.

Ascanio in Alba – Dal tuo gentil sembiante. Ⓟ
Die Entführung aus dem Serail – Welcher Wechsel; Traurigkeit ward mir zum Lose; Martern aller Arten. **Idomeneo** – Solitudini amiche; Zeffiretti lusinghieri. **Lucio Silla** – Vanne, t'affreta; Ah se il crudel periglio. **Zaide** – Ruhe sanft, mein holdes Leben; Tiger! Wetze nur die Klauen. **Die Zauberflöte** – O zittre nicht, mein lieber Sohn!; Zum Leiden; Der Hölle Rache; Ach, ich fühl's
Natalie Dessay sop **Orchestra of the Age of Enlightenment / Louis Langrée**
Virgin Classics 545447-2 (67' · DDD) Texts and translations included   Ⓕ**OOO**

G Nathalie Dessay has cornered the market at the world's poshest opera houses as the Queen of Night, whose two arias frame this recital programme. She can be heard in the role complete in William Christie's 1996 recording of *Die Zauberflöte* for Erato. Aided by Louis Langrée's marginally faster tempos, Dessay's 'star-blazing' accounts of these famous show-stoppers sound even more vehement than before – the angry staccatos of 'Der Hölle Rache' spat out with blinding accuracy and the *in altissimo* Fs effortlessly, cleanly attained.

Dessay's light, girlish timbre might not immediately suggest regal imperiousness, but she brings real depth of feeling to 'Zum Leiden bin ich auserkoren' and its magnificent recitative 'O zittre nicht' on the concluding track. Between these mainstay arias of what the Germans call her Parade-Rolle, she selects an enterprising mix of the familiar – a delicate, fragile, touching 'Ach, ich fühl's' suggesting she may soon hanker after the role of the Queen's daughter, Pamina – and the virtually unknown – the fawn's charming but virtuosic aria, 'Dal tuo gentil sembiante' from *Ascanio in Alba* (the *festa teatrale* written for the wedding of the Archduke Ferdinand to Maria Beatrice of Modena, in Milan, 1771). The instrumental quality of her florid technique is put to marvellous use here, as it is in Giunia's moment of truth in Act 2 of *Lucio Silla*, 'Ah se il crudel periglio'. Perhaps in the theatre one would crave a richer voice, but Dessay colours her tone so effectively that the aria touches all the right emotional spots. Langrée has recently garnered glowing credentials as a Mozartian at Glyndebourne, and his beautifully conceived and theatrical accompaniments here demonstrate why. In addition, the period instruments of the Orchestra of the Age of Enlightenment complement the astringency of the soprano's tone.

La clemenza di Tito – Deh per questo istante; Ecco il punto … Non più di fiori vaghe catene.
Così fan tutte – Temerari … Come scoglio; Ei parte … Per pietà, ben mio. **Don Giovanni** – Batti, batti; In quali eccessi … Mi tradì. **Le nozze di Figaro** – Non so più cosa son; Porgi, amor. **Concert arias** – Oh, temerario Arbace! … Per quel paterno amplesso, K79. Ch'io mi scordi di te … Non temer, amato bene, K505
Véronique Gens sop **Orchestra of the Age of Enlightenment / Ivor Bolton** with **Melvyn Tan** fp
Virgin Classics Veritas 545319-2 (59' · DDD) Texts and translations included ⓕ🔴

Véronique Gens is one of the most engaging and stylish Mozart sopranos around, as this sampler of her art confirms. Under the exacting baton of Ivor Bolton, the OAE show sharp and eager teeth to match her own highly strung recitative in 'In quali eccessi'. And this Donna Anna demonstrates more than one-dimensional *Angst* as the orchestra's wind soloists breathe in sympathy with every moment of *palpitando* in Gens's own supple phrasing. There's a similar focus on the emotional potential of breath in a 'Non so più' whose fierce frustration flies out of eloquent consonants. Steady control of breath and tone bring a moving poise to 'Non più di fiori', where Vitellia's horrified introspection finds empathy in the basset horn obbligato. And as Sesto, Gens moulds the moist clay of some of Mozart's most beautiful melodic contours in 'Deh, per questo istante'. There's her Countess and Zerlina to enjoy as well, with the two exquisitely sculpted and sparingly but powerfully ornamented arias from *Così fan tutte*.

La clemenza di Tito, K621

La clemenza di Tito   Ⓟ
Uwe Heilmann ten Tito **Della Jones** mez Vitellia **Cecilia Bartoli** mez Sesto **Diana Montague** mez Annio **Barbara Bonney** sop Servillia **Gilles Cachemaille** bar Publio **Academy of Ancient Music Chorus; Academy of Ancient Music / Christopher Hogwood**
L'Oiseau-Lyre ② 444 131-2OHO2 (137' · DDD) Recorded 1993. Notes, text and translation included ⓕ

Hogwood has assembled a remarkable cast, with certainly two, perhaps three, outstanding interpretations. First among them must be Cecilia Bartoli, who rightly establishes Sextus as the central character, the one whose actions and

whose feelings are the focal point of the drama. The opening number is the duet 'Come ti piace, imponi', where the firm and pure sound of Bartoli's voice, in contrast with the contained hysteria of Vitellia's, at once defines the opera's basis. It's clear from her singing that she reads Sextus, for all his weakness in giving way to Vitellia, as a man of integrity, one of the noblest Romans of them all.

Then there's Della Jones's remarkable Vitellia. There are lots of interesting and emotionally suggestive touches in her singing; her rich bottom register is magnificent and the top Bs have no fears for her. Uwe Heilmann's Titus is marked by much subtle and finely shaped singing and a keen awareness of how phrasing conveys sense. Occasionally the tone is inclined to be nasal, but that doesn't interfere with a very sympathetic and often moving reading. Hogwood's keen awareness of what, expressively speaking, is going on in the music, and his refusal to be tied to a rigid rhythmic pulse in order to make it manifest, is one of the strengths of this recording. The recitatives are sung with a great deal of life and awareness of meaning, not simply gabbled at maximum speed. These aren't Mozart's own work, and are usually heavily cut. While some may feel that the inclusion of every note is an advantage to the opera, others may not unreasonably take the opposite view. At any rate, the discs' tracking is arranged so that a new track begins for each aria, which enables listeners to make their own cuts without difficulty.

Così fan tutte, K588

Così fan tutte
Elisabeth Schwarzkopf sop Fiordiligi **Christa Ludwig** mez Dorabella **Hanny Steffek** sop Despina **Alfredo Kraus** ten Ferrando **Giuseppe Taddei** bar Guglielmo **Walter Berry** bass Don Alfonso **Philharmonia Chorus and Orchestra / Karl Böhm**
EMI Great Recordings of the Century ③ 567379-2 (165' · ADD) Recorded 1962. Notes, text and translation included Ⓜ🔴🔴🔴

 Così fan tutte is the most balanced and probing of all Mozart's operas, formally faultless, musically inspired from start to finish, emotionally a matter of endless fascination and, in the second act, profoundly moving. It has been very lucky on disc, and besides this delightful set there have been several other memorable recordings. However, Karl Böhm's cast could hardly be bettered, even in one's dreams. The two sisters are gloriously sung – Schwarzkopf and Ludwig bring their immeasurable talents as Lieder singers to this sparkling score and overlay them with a rare comic touch. Add to that the stylish singing of Alfredo Kraus and Giuseppe Taddei and the central quartet is unimpeachable. Walter Berry's Don Alfonso is characterful and Hanny Steffek is quite superb as Despina. The pacing of this endlessly intriguing work is measured with immaculate judgement. The emotional control of the characterisation is masterly and Böhm's totally idiomatic response to the music is arguably without peer. However, two modern recordings, using period instruments, do offer stimulating alternative views.

Così fan tutte **P**
Amanda Roocroft sop Fiordiligi **Rosa Mannion** sop Dorabella **Eirian James** mez Despina **Rainer Trost** ten Ferrando **Rodney Gilfry** bar Guglielmo **Carlos Feller** bass Don Alfonso **Monteverdi Choir; English Baroque Soloists / Sir John Eliot Gardiner**
Archiv Produktion ③ 437 829-2AH3 (134' · DDD) Recorded live 1992   **F**

Gardiner's is a *Così* with a heart, and a heart in the right place. It comes from a stage performance given in the Teatro Comunale at Ferrara – the city from which the sisters in the story hail – in 1992. The vitality and the communicativeness of the recitative is one result of recording a live performance; it's flexible, conversational and lively, as it ought to be, and the Italian pronunciation is remarkably good considering there isn't a single Italian in the cast. Amanda Roocroft makes a capable Fiordiligi, with a big, spacious 'Come scoglio', and shows real depth of feeling in a very beautiful account of 'Per pietà'; her tone is bright and forward. Rosa Mannion, as Dorabella, acts effectively with her voice in 'Smanie implacabili' and is full of life in her Act 2 aria. The Guglielmo, Rodney Gilfry, is outstanding for his light, warm and flexible baritone, gently seductive in Act 1, showing real brilliance and precision of articulation in 'Donne mie'. Eirian James's Despina is another delight, spirited, sexy and rich-toned, and full of charm without any of the silliness some Despinas show. Period instruments notwithstanding, this is a fairly traditional performance. Gardiner often uses quite generous rubato to highlight the shape of a phrase, and he's alert, as always, to how the orchestral writing can underline the sense.

Così fan tutte **P**
Soile Isokoski sop Fiordiligi **Monica Groop** mez Dorabella **Nancy Argenta** sop Despina **Markus Schäfer** ten Ferrando **Per Vollestad** bar Guglielmo **Huub Claessens** bass Don Alfonso **La Petite Bande and Chorus / Sigiswald Kuijken**
Accent ③ ACC9296/98 (181' · DDD) Recorded live 1992. Notes, text and translation included   **F**

Kuijken's live recording is lighter in mood than Gardiner's. Nearly all the tempos are quicker and there's more sense of spontaneity. Mozart very rarely wrote dynamic or accentuation marks into his singers' parts; the singers were expected to learn their music from a repetiteur (or Mozart himself) and take their cues from what they heard in performance. Gardiner has his singers follow, meticulously, the orchestral dynamics; Kuijken leaves them, more or less, to

sing with what they hear. This is a symptomatic difference: one performance is highly wrought, the other freer and more natural. The sisters in the Kuijken version are excellently done by Soile Isokoski, even in voice and with an attractive ring, and Monica Groop, again a pleasing and even voice intelligently and musically used. Their duets are very appealing, with a happy sense in 'Prenderò quel brunettino' that they might be getting up to a little mischief. The Alfonso here, Huub Claessens, more baritone than bass, is particularly successful in the recitative, which here again is done with much care for its meaning. A pleasing, lively *Così*, it would be a good recording with which to get to know the opera, whereas the Gardiner is a connoisseur's performance, subtle and sophisticated, and communicating important things about the opera.

Don Giovanni, K527

Don Giovanni **H**
Eberhard Waechter bar Don Giovanni **Joan Sutherland** sop Donna Anna **Elisabeth Schwarzkopf** sop Donna Elvira **Graziella Sciutti** sop Zerlina **Luigi Alva** ten Don Ottavio **Giuseppe Taddei** bar Leporello **Piero Cappuccilli** bar Masetto **Gottlob Frick** bass Commendatore **Philharmonia Chorus and Orchestra / Carlo Maria Giulini**
EMI Great Recordings of the Century ③ 567869-2 (162' · ADD) Recorded 1959. Notes, text and translation included   **Ⓜ OO**

Although this set is over 40 years old, none of its successors is as skilled in capturing the piece's drama so unerringly. It has always been most recommendable and Giulini captures all the work's most dramatic characteristics, faithfully supported by the superb Philharmonia forces of that time. At this stage of Giulini's career, he was a direct, lithe conductor, alert to every turn in the story and he projects the nervous tension of the piece ideally while never forcing the pace, as can so easily happen. Then he had one of the most apt casts ever assembled for the piece. Waechter's Giovanni combines the demonic with the seductive in just the right proportions, Taddei is a high-profile Leporello, who relishes the text and sings with lots of 'face'. Elvira was always one of Schwarzkopf's most successful roles: here she delivers the role with tremendous intensity. Sutherland's Anna isn't quite so full of character but is magnificently sung. Alva is a graceful Ottavio. Sciutti's charming Zerlina, Cappuccilli's strong and Italianate Masetto and Frick's granite Commendatore are all very much in the picture. The sound is so good, the set might have been recorded yesterday.

Don Giovanni **P**
Rodney Gilfry bar Don Giovanni **Luba Orgonasova** sop Donna Anna **Charlotte Margiono** sop Donna Elvira **Eirian James** mez Zerlina **Christoph**

Prégardien *ten* Don Ottavio **Ildebrando d'Arcangelo** *bass* Leporello **Julian Clarkson** *bass* Masetto **Andrea Silvestrelli** *bass* Commendatore **Monteverdi Choir; English Baroque Soloists / Sir John Eliot Gardiner**
Archiv Produktion ③ 445 870-2AH3 (176' · DDD)
Recorded 1994. Notes, text and translation included
Ⓕ

Gardiner's set has a great deal to commend it. The recitative is sung with exemplary care over pacing so that it sounds as it should, like heightened and vivid conversation, often to electrifying effect. Ensembles, the Act 1 quartet particularly, are also treated conversationally, as if one were overhearing four people giving their opinions on a situation in the street. The orchestra, perfectly balanced with the singers in a very immediate acoustic, supports them, as it were 'sings' with them. That contrasts with, and complements, Gardiner's expected ability to empathise with the demonic aspects of the score, as in Giovanni's drinking song and the final moments of Act 1, which fairly bristle with rhythmic energy without ever becoming rushed. The arrival of the statue at Giovanni's dinner-table is tremendous, the period trombones and timpani achieving an appropriately brusque, fearsome attack. Throughout this scene, Gardiner's penchant for sharp accents is wholly appropriate; elsewhere he's sometimes rather too insistent. As a whole, tempos not only seem right on their own account but also, all-importantly, carry conviction in relation to each other. Where so many conductors today are given to rushing 'Mi tradì', Gardiner prefers a more meditative approach, which allows his soft-grained Elvira to make the most of the aria's expressive possibilities.

Rodney Gilfry's Giovanni is lithe, ebullient, keen to exert his sexual prowess; an obvious charmer, at times surprisingly tender yet with the iron will only just below the surface. Suave and appealing, delivered in a real baritone timbre, his Giovanni is as accomplished as any on disc. Ildebrando d'Arcangelo was the discovery of these performances: this young bass is a lively foil to his master and on his own a real showman, as 'Madamina' indicates, a number all the better for a brisk speed. Orgonosova once more reveals herself a paragon as regards steady tone and deft technique – there's no need here to slow down for the coloratura at the end of 'Non mi dir' – and she brings to her recounting of the attempted seduction a real feeling of immediacy. As Anna, Margiono sometimes sounds a shade stretched technically, but consoles us with the luminous, inward quality of her voice and her reading of the role, something innate that can't be learnt.

Nobody in their right senses is ever going to suggest that there's one, ideal version of *Don Giovanni*; the work has far too many facets for that, but for sheer theatrical *élan* complemented by the live recording, Gardiner is among the best, particularly given a recording that's wonderfully truthful and lifelike.

MOZART DON GIOVANNI – IN BRIEF

Eberhard Waechter *Don Giovanni* **Joan Sutherland** *Donna Anna* **Elisabeth Schwarzkopf** *Donna Elvira* **Philharmonia Chorus & Orchestra / Carlo Maria Giulini**
EMI ③ 567869-2 (163' · ADD) Ⓜ**OO**
Among an increasingly vast choice this remains a prime recommendation, both for its rich-voiced, characterful singers and Giulini's mercurial conducting.

Rodney Gilfry *Don Giovanni* **Luba Orgonosova** *Donna Anna* **Charlotte Margiono** *Donna Elvira* **Monteverdi Choir; English Baroque Soloists / Sir John Eliot Gardiner**
Archiv ③ 445 870-2AH3 (176' · DDD) Ⓕ
An immensely dynamic, theatrical performance recorded live, with a magnetic young Don heading a splendidly fresh cast. Original instruments, but this is a field leader by any standards.

Bo Skovhus *Don Giovanni* **Christine Brewer** *Donna Anna* **Felicity Lott** *Donna Elvira* **Scottish Chamber Chorus & Orchestra / Sir Charles Mackerras**
Telarc ③ CD80420 (183' · DDD) Ⓕ
Mackerras conducts the excellent Scottish players with characteristically theatrical energy, uniting a fine cast in an unusual sense of ensemble.

Simon Keenlyside *Don Giovanni* **Carmela Remigio** *Donna Anna* **Soile Isokoski** *Donna Elvira* **Ferrara Music Chorus; Chamber Orchestra of Europe / Claudio Abbado**
DG ③ 457 601-2 (176' · DDD) Ⓕ
A dark, weighty reading, but Abbado boasts perhaps the finest contemporary cast, including Bryn Terfel's ripe Leporello and Carmela Remigio's striking Anna.

Thomas Allen *Don Giovanni* **Carol Vaness** *Donna Anna* **Maria Ewing** *Donna Elvira* **Glyndebourne Festival Chorus, London PO / Bernard Haitink**
EMI ③ 747037-8 (172' · DDD) Ⓕ**O**
Derived from Glyndebourne's legendary Peter Hall production, this has a fine dramatic atmosphere, with Thomas Allen's silken, sinister Giovanni confronting Carol Vaness under Haitink's urbane direction.

Thomas Allen *Don Giovanni* **Carol Vaness** *Donna Anna* **Andrea Rost** *Zerlina* **Cologne Opera Chorus; Cologne Gürzenich Orchestra / James Conlon**
ArtHaus Musik 🎦 100 020 (173') Ⓕ
A straightforward staging, visually acceptable, if not thrilling, but with a fine cast, even if Thomas Allen's Don has aged a little since Glyndebourne. Ferruccio Furlanetto is a live-wire Leporello, Conlon conducts with brio.

Don Giovanni

Bo Skovhus bar Don Giovanni **Christine Brewer** sop
Donna Anna **Dame Felicity Lott** sop Donna Elvira
Nuccia Focile sop Zerlina **Jerry Hadley** ten Don
Ottavio **Alessandro Corbelli** bar Leporello **Umberto
Chiummo** bass Masetto, Commendatore **Scottish
Chamber Chorus and Orchestra / Sir Charles
Mackerras**
Telarc ③ CD80420 (183' · DDD) Notes, text and
translation included   Ⓕ

This set has no astonishing or brilliant individual interpretations, but the whole is full of life
and energy and freshness. The Scottish Chamber Orchestra isn't a period-instrument group,
but Mackerras uses valveless horns and trumpets and something close to period timpani –
hence the alarming sound of the opening
chords. He also calls for sharper attack and
quicker decay from the string players and a very
forward wind balance. Tempos are often but by
no means always on the fast side. But he also
allows his singers plenty of time to phrase their
music expressively, for example in the Gio-
vanni-Zerlina scene in the first finale, in the trio
at the beginning of Act 2 (some wonderfully
sensual orchestral colours here), in Giovanni's
serenade, in the great sextet (very powerfully
done) and in the cemetery scene, which has a
proper sense of the hieratic and yet a knife-edge
tension too. This highly theatrical interpretation has you right on the edge of your seat.

Umberto Chiummo makes a good, incisive
Masetto and a truly formidable Commendatore
in the final scenes. Nuccia Focile provides a
beguiling Zerlina, with a sweet upper range and
more than a touch of sensuousness and charm.
Alessandro Corbelli, the Leporello, is a lively,
lowish baritone who uses the sound of the words
to advantage and can phrase with just the right
hint of elegance. His voice is very close,
arguably too close, in sound to that of the Giovanni, Bo Skovhus, yet the master-servant relationship is conveyed convincingly. Skovhus's
sharp vitality, his virile Champagne Aria and his
deeply sensual *portamentos* in the Serenade
stress those aspects of Giovanni's character that
underlie the plot. Jerry Hadley offers an Ottavio
of some intensity, not the smoothest or most
graceful, but stronger in expression than most,
and Dame Felicity is in full, creamy voice in a
role she has often sung with distinction. On the
question of versions, Mackerras gives the
Prague original first (with 'Dalla sua pace'
inserted in Act 1), so if you play the second disc
through to the end, you should then skip the
first 10 tracks of the third disc to continue; or, if
you want the Vienna version, you should skip
the last six of the second and pick up at the
beginning of the third, where you'll hear the
rare (and rather silly, though musically agreeable) Zerlina-Leporello duet and Elvira's scene
(but not 'Il mio tesoro'). This is an excellent
solution for listeners who can be bothered to
press a couple of buttons. All round, an
immensely enjoyable *Don Giovanni*.

Die Entführung aus dem Serail, K384

Die Entführung aus dem Serail[a]   Ⓗ
Exsultate, jubilate, K165/K158a[b]
Maria Stader sop Constanze (Beate Guttmann) **Rita
Streich** sop Blonde **Ernst Haefliger** ten Belmonte
(Sebastian Fischer) **Martin Vantin** ten Pedrillo
(Wolfgang Spier) **Josef Greindl** bass Osmin **Walter
Franck** spkr Bassa Selim [a]**Berlin RIAS Chamber
Choir and Orchestra,** [b]**Berlin Radio Symphony
Orchestra / Ferenc Fricsay**
DG The Originals [a]mono/[b]stereo ② 457 730-2GOR2
(125' · ADD) Recorded 1954. Notes, texts and
translations included   Ⓜ**O**

Fricsay was an advocate of crisp, zestful, pared-
down Mozart *avant la lettre*. This was the first in
his distinguished series of Mozart opera recordings, throughout which he used Berlin Radio
forces and singers familiar with his work. They
prove formidable advocates. The orchestra,
recorded in resonant, honest mono, plays
superbly. Stader was a particular favourite with
Fricsay. If not the most refulgent of sopranos,
she had both the consistency of voice and thor-
oughness of technique to cope with almost all
the demands of Constanze's music. Although
one ideally wants a more dramatic singer in the
part, her feeling for the shape of a Mozart
phrase is always admirable. She's suitably partnered by the fluent, lyrical Haefliger, who also
sang Belmonte at Glyndebourne in the 1950s.
Rita Streich is the ideal Blonde, singing with
pure tone and spirited attack: she has the individuality of voice, the hint of vibrato most
attractive. Vantin is a more than adequate
Pedrillo, who sings his Serenade in an appropriate *mezza voce*. Greindl brings a fully fledged
bass to bear on Osmin's music and fills it with a
nice combination of vicious sadism leavened by
comedy. Although his singing is occasionally
marred by intrusive aspirates, he's among the
most enjoyable Osmins on disc. Happily he and
Streich are allowed to speak their own dialogue
so that their Act 2 encounter goes particularly
well.

As was a dubious custom with DG at the time,
the other singers are doubled by speaking voices
that hardly match their own. Those who have
come to appreciate Fricsay's many attributes as
a conductor won't be disappointed by this reissue, and will gain as a generous bonus Stader's
delightful account of *Exsultate, jubilate*. In
absolute terms those without *Die Entführung* in
their collection should hear this one.

Die Entführung aus dem Serail
Ingrid Habermann sop Constanze **Donna Ellen** sop
Blonde **Piotr Bezcala** ten Belmonte **Oliver
Ringelhahn** ten Pedrillo **Franz Kalchmair** bass
Osmin **Harald Pfeiffer** spkr Bassa Selim **Linz
Landestheater Choir; Linz Bruckner Orchestra /
Martin Sieghart**
Arte Nova Classics ② 74321 49701-2 (115' · DDD)
Notes, text and translation included   Ⓢ

This is a real bargain, just about as enjoyable as any performance given by more prominent artists on better-known labels. Recorded live, it isn't surprising to find such a natural sense of ensemble among the principals or such a well-integrated account of the score from Sieghart, who's also aware of the latest research on this score in terms of orchestration and small embellishments. His reading is a shade strict and unsmiling, but it has the virtue of keeping the drama on the move in a work that can outstay its welcome in more self-indulgent performances, and the playing of the small band is exemplary. Dialogue is included but kept to the minimum essential to clarify the action.

Ingrid Habermann has the dramatic coloratura, the technique and all the notes to encompass the fearful demands of Constanze's role and shows the dramatic resolution it requires. The Polish tenor Piotr Bezcala has also been judiciously cast for his part: his voice is firm and sappy, and he discloses an ability to make his four taxing arias sound relatively simple. One or two unwanted lachrymose moments apart, he's a model of Mozartian style. The Canadian soprano, Donna Ellen, is a mettlesome Blonde, happy in the dizzy heights reached in her first aria. Her Pedrillo is a lively singer but one prone to questionable pitch, particularly in his Serenade. Best of all is the native Austrian, Franz Kalchmair as an Osmin with a rotund, pleasing bass, as happy at the bottom as at the top of his range, and he's obviously a formidable actor. The recording is reasonably good.

Idomeneo, re di Creta, K366

Idomeneo   **P**
Anthony Rolfe Johnson ten Idomeneo **Anne Sofie von Otter** mez Idamante **Sylvia McNair** sop Ilia
Hillevi Martinpelto sop Elettra **Nigel Robson** ten Arbace **Glenn Winslade** ten High Priest **Cornelius Hauptmann** bass Oracle **Monteverdi Choir; English Baroque Soloists / Sir John Eliot Gardiner**
Archiv Produktion ③ 431 674-2AH3 (211' · DDD)
Recorded 1990. Notes, text and translation included
Ⓕ**OOO**

This is unquestionably the most vital and authentic account of *Idomeneo* to date on disc (though see the more recent review of the Mackerras set below). We have here what was given at the work's first performance in Munich plus, in appendices, what Mozart wanted, or was forced, to cut before that première and the alternative versions of certain passages, so that various combinations of the piece can be programmed by the listener. Gardiner's direct, dramatic conducting catches ideally the agony of Idomeneo's terrible predicament – forced to sacrifice his son because of an unwise row. This torment of the soul is also entirely conveyed by Anthony Rolfe Johnson in the title role to which Anne Sofie von Otter's moving Idamante is an apt foil. Sylvia McNair is

a diaphanous, pure-voiced Ilia, Hillevi Martinpelto a properly fiery, sharp-edged Elettra. With dedicated support from his own choir and orchestra, who obviously benefited from a long period of preparation, Gardiner matches the stature of this noble *opera seria*. The recording catches the excitement which all who heard the live performances will recall.

Idomeneo
Ian Bostridge ten Idomeneo **Lorraine Hunt Lieberson** mez Idamante **Lisa Milne** sop Ilia
Barbara Frittoli sop Elettra **Anthony Rolfe Johnson** ten Arbace **Paul Charles Clarke** ten High Priest
John Relyea bass Oracle **Dunedin Consort; Edinburgh Festival Chorus; Scottish Chamber Orchestra / Sir Charles Mackerras**
EMI ③ 557260-2 (203' · DDD) Notes, text and translation included   Ⓕ**OO**

There were golden opinions for the *Idomeneo* given at 2001's Edinburgh Festival by these performers, and here it is. The work is given complete, at the marvellously extravagant length at which Mozart initially planned it, bar some small (and authentic) cuts in the *secco* recitative. And it works. It works triumphantly, in fact. That's partly due to Mackerras's truly inspired reading of the score, and his insights into the meaning of its musical gestures. This is a score full of gestures, heavy with emotional significance, not only in the arias and the ensembles but perhaps above all in the orchestral recitative that abounds in this score as in no other of Mozart's. It's partly the expressiveness of Mackerras's handling of what's, in effect, Mozart's emotional commentary on the unfolding of the plot that makes this performance so powerful. He has a clear vision of the expressive messages that Mozart transmits through texture or harmony or dynamic or rhythmic refinement.

The performance is also full of dramatic energy. During the Overture you experience that tingle in your spine that comes of the expectation of a curtain about to rise. Never mind that this isn't a 'period instrument' performance: the textures are as lucid as one could wish, the articulation as light and precise, the balance as just. Tempos are unhurried.

Ian Bostridge makes a strong Idomeneo. His opening aria, 'Vedrommi intorno', is exquisitely done, smoothly and lovingly phrased. Mozart wrote it in a traditional style to flatter the voice of his original singer, Anton Raaff. Just here and there, and especially in the closing aria, one might perhaps have liked more variety of tone and in particular more soft and lyrical colouring. Idamante, originally a castrato part, is sung by a mezzo, and one can't imagine one much better than Lorraine Hunt Lieberson: it's a lovely, focused sound, with the firm centre that a male part needs, and there are many happy details of phrasing. Lisa Milne provides a sympathetic yet not frail Ilia, with a clear and warm ring to the voice. The singing of Barbara Frittoli as Elettra has properly a bit more edge to it and there's plenty of tension and power to her first aria and especially her stormy final one, 'D'Oreste, d'Ajace'. With Anthony Rolfe Johnson to sing Arbace, both of that character's arias (as well as his important accompanied recitatives) are given, understandably, although the second in particular isn't on the level of most of the score – Mozart probably excluded both of them in his own performances. It's a joy to hear them so beautifully sung; the *legato* line and the smooth large leaps in the first are a delight.

The chorus is first-rate, and there's excellent orchestral playing. This set, enshrining Mackerras's profound and mature understanding of the music, is deeply moving; readers are urged to buy it.

Mitridate, K87/74a

Mitridate, re di Ponto   🄿
Giuseppe Sabbatini ten Mitridate **Natalie Dessay**
sop Aspasia **Cecilia Bartoli** mez Sifare **Brian Asawa**
counterten Farnace **Sandrine Piau** sop Ismene **Juan
Diego Flórez** ten Marzio **Hélène Le Corre** sop
Arbate **Les Talens Lyriques / Christophe Rousset**
Decca ③ 460 772-2DHO3 (179' · DDD) Notes, text
and translation included   Ⓕ

Mozart wasn't quite 15 when he composed *Mitridate*, as the first carnival opera for the Milan opera house, which was shortly to become La Scala. Operas of that period were composed specifically for the cast that created them: Mozart more than once referred to fitting an aria to the voice as a tailor fitted a suit to the figure. And some of the original cast of *Mitridate* thought their arias ill-fitting: Mozart was required to rewrite several of them. Many of the arias are expansive pieces, with a semi-*da capo*, and make heavy demands on the singers' agility and compass.

This set has a starry cast. The *primo uomo* role, Sifare, written for an unusually high-lying castrato voice, is sung, with great character, by Cecilia Bartoli. Perhaps the finest of her four arias is the slow one in Act 2 with horn obbligato, 'Lungi da te, mio bene', which is sung here with real depth of feeling, shapeliness of line and richness of tone. The only reservation is that the part does lie very high for her: the top B flats sound strained, and indeed the quality from G upwards is slightly impaired. Still, it's a marvellous performance and she brings to the music a real sense of drama and care for the words in the recitative and arias.

There's nothing but praise, too, for Natalie Dessay in the *prima donna* role of Aspasia, beloved of Sifare. Full, creamy tone, brilliantly thrown-off rapid music, a firmly sustained line, a keen sense of drama, high notes struck loud and clear and bang in the middle: one could ask for nothing more. Her duet with Bartoli, the single concerted number, at the end of Act 2, is a joy: they seem to have all the time in the world for sensitive phrasing and refined detail.

Brian Asawa, in the castrato role of Farnace,

offers some very fine countertenor singing, with a full, almost throaty tone, not at all in the usual countertenor manner, and extraordinarily even across a wide range. Giuseppe Sabbatini copes well in the role of Mitridate but doesn't always manage so happily either in the lyrical music or the expressions of anger. He's inclined to sing too loudly or too softly: there's no comfortable mean. His first aria, 'Se di lauri', the most beautiful piece in the score, is forceful and grandiose where softness and warmth are wanted, and the *pianissimo* recapitulation isn't persuasive. Still, this is accurate, technically accomplished and perfectly tuned singing. Rousset directs his period instrument band with vigour and conviction.

Le nozze di Figaro, K492

Le nozze di Figaro   🄷
Sesto Bruscantini bar Figaro **Graziella Sciutti** sop
Susanna **Franco Calabrese** bass Count Almaviva
Sena Jurinac sop Countess Almaviva **Risë Stevens**
mez Cherubino **Monica Sinclair** contr Marcellina **Ian
Wallace** bass Bartolo **Hugues Cuénod** ten Don
Basilio **Daniel McCoshan** ten Don Curzio **Gwyn
Griffiths** bar Antonio **Jeanette Sinclair** sop
Barbarina **Glyndebourne Festival Chorus and
Orchestra / Vittorio Gui**
EMI ② 573845-2 (158' · ADD) Recorded 1955 Ⓑ**〇〇〇**

This comes from what you might call the second generation of Glyndebourne performances, those dominated by Vittorio Gui, whose approach to Mozart was more volatile, more Italianate, possibly a little less warm than that of his equally individual predecessor Fritz Busch. This is immediately evident in the Overture, which tells us very definitely that we're to hear a tale of intrigue and emotional turmoil, da Ponte as prominent as Mozart. To achieve his purpose, Gui imported a cast that included three Italians. Bruscantini is a mercurial, light-voiced, mobile Figaro, Calabrese a dark-browed Almaviva, a dominant personality in his household. Graziella Sciutti, was brought in for the recording, and a lively, if a little thin-voiced Susanna she proves. Wonderful to hear all three pronouncing their own tongue so pointedly.

For all that, the most compelling reason for obtaining this set is the Countess of the irreplaceable Sena Jurinac, a noble, aristocratic assumption sung in the warmest, most palpitating tones – a lovable singer at the height of her powers. A drawback is Risë Stevens's tired-sounding and unidiomatic Cherubino, but even she fits well enough into the ensemble.

This was one of EMI's earliest stereo efforts, and the placings are well managed, with the sense of intimacy you get in the theatre at Glyndebourne, but the orchestral sound now seems a little confined and lacking in bloom. But the playing from the RPO is both disciplined and full of character.

Le nozze di Figaro   **H**
Cesare Siepi bass Figaro **Hilde Gueden** sop
Susanna **Alfred Poell** bar Count Almaviva
Lisa della Casa sop Countess Almaviva **Suzanne
Danco** sop Cherubino **Hilde Rössl-Majdan** contr
Marcellina **Fernando Corena** bass Bartolo **Murray
Dickie** ten Don Basilio **Hugo Meyer-Welfing** ten
Don Curzio **Harald Pröglhöf** bass Antonio **Anny
Felbermayer** sop Barbarina **Vienna State Opera
Chorus; Vienna Philharmonic Orchestra / Erich
Kleiber**
Decca Legends ③ 466 369-2DM03 (172' · ADD)
Recorded 1955   Ⓜ**OO**

Kleiber's *Figaro* is a classic of the classics of the
gramophone: beautifully played by the Vienna
Phil, conducted with poise and vitality and a real
sense of the drama unfolding through the
music. It's very much a Viennese performance,
not perhaps as graceful or as effervescent as
some but warm, sensuous and alive to the interplay of character. At the centre is Hilde Gueden, whose Susanna has echoes of operetta,
although she remains a true Mozartian stylist.
Lisa della Casa's Countess may not be one of
the most dramatic but the voice is full yet
focused. Suzanne Danco's Cherubino isn't
exactly impassioned, and is really as much girlish as boyish, but it's still neat and musical
singing. The balance among the men is affected
by the casting of Figaro with a weightier singer
than the Count. But Alfred Poell's Count makes
up in natural authority and aristocratic manner
what he lacks in sheer power, and he shows himself capable of truly sensual singing in the Act 3
duet with Susanna.

There are excellent performances, too, from
Corena's verbally athletic Bartolo and Dickie's
alert, ironic Basilio. However, the true star is
Erich Kleiber. The beginning of the opera sets
your spine tingling with theatrical expectation.
Act 1 goes at pretty smart tempos, but all
through he insists on full musical value. There's
no rushing in the confrontations at the end of
Act 2 – all is measured and properly argued
through. The sound is satisfactory, for a set of
this vintage, and no lover of this opera should be
without it.

Le nozze di Figaro   **P**
Bryn Terfel bass-bar Figaro **Alison Hagley** sop
Susanna **Rodney Gilfry** bar Count Almaviva **Hillevi
Martinpelto** sop Countess Almaviva **Pamela Helen
Stephen** mez Cherubino **Susan McCulloch** sop
Marcellina **Carlos Feller** bass Bartolo **Francis
Egerton** ten Don Basilio, Don Curzio **Julian Clarkson**
bass Antonio **Constanze Backes** sop Barbarina
**Monteverdi Choir; English Baroque Soloists /
Sir John Eliot Gardiner**
Archiv Produktion ③ 439 871-2AH3 (179' · DDD)
Recorded live 1993. Notes, text and translation
included   Ⓕ**O**

The catalogue of *Figaro* recordings is long, and
the cast lists are full of famous names. In this
version only one principal had more than half a

MOZART LE NOZZE DI FIGARO – IN BRIEF

Lorenzo Regazzo Figaro **Simon Keenlyside**
Count Almaviva **Véronique Gens** Countess
Almaviva **Collegium Vocale; Concerto Köln /
René Jacobs**   Ⓜ**OOO**
Harmonia Mundi ③ HMC90 1818/20 (172' · DDD)
☼ A new contender in a crowded field,
Jacobs's performance is idiosyncratic
but both finely detailed and entertaining,
with a particularly strong cast.

Sesto Bruscantini Figaro **Franco Calabrese**
Count Almaviva **Sena Jurinac** Countess Almaviva
**Glyndebourne Festival Chorus & Orchestra /
Vittorio Gui**
EMI mono ② 573845-2 (158' · ADD)   Ⓑ**OOO**
☼ The very image of Glyndebourne
Mozart at bargain price; sparkling, lively
and intimate in a way that suits this opera,
with a cast close to perfection.

Bryn Terfel Figaro **Rodney Gilfry** Count Almaviva
Hillevi Martinpelto Countess Almaviva
**Monteverdi Choir; English Baroque Soloists /
Sir John Eliot Gardiner**
Archiv ③ 439 871-2AH3 (179' · DDD)   Ⓕ**O**
A brilliant period-instrument set recorded
live. Brisker and lighter-hued than the old
school, with a superior cast but a rather
obtrusive audience.

Cesare Siepi Figaro **Alfred Poell** Count Almaviva
Lisa della Casa Countess Almaviva **Vienna State
Opera Chorus; Vienna PO / Erich Kleiber**
Decca ③ 466 369-2DMO3 (172' · ADD)   Ⓜ**OO**
In the great Viennese tradition, conducted
with fleetfooted dramatic energy, with a cast
of rather heavyweight but exceptionally
beautiful voices, albeit on a recording that
is showing its age.

Samuel Ramey Figaro **Thomas Allen** Count
Almaviva **Kiri Te Kanawa** Countess Almaviva
**London Opera Chorus, London PO /
Sir Georg Solti**
Decca ③ 410 150-2DH3 (169' · DDD)   Ⓕ**O**
Large-scale Mozart, but conducted with irre-
sistible verve and wit, and an outstanding
ensemble, all in a brilliant modern recording.

Walter Berry Figaro **Ingvar Wixell** Count
Almaviva **Claire Watson** Countess Almaviva
**Vienna State Opera Chorus, Vienna PO / Karl
Böhm**
TDK **DVD** DV-CLOPNDF (180')   Ⓕ
A 1966 Salzburg TV recording in mono
and monochrome, but featuring such superlative singers in a truly likeable, accessible
production, and Böhm's finely judged conducting, that it has to be a prime recommendation.

dozen recordings behind him, and some had none at all. Yet this version can stand comparison with any, not only for its grasp of the drama but also for the quality of its singing. It's more evidently a period-instrument recording than many under Gardiner. The string tone is pared down and makes modest use of vibrato, the woodwind is soft-toned. The voices are generally lighter and fresher-sounding than those on most recordings. and the balance permits more than usual to be heard of Mozart's instrumental commentary on the action and the characters. The recitative is done with exceptional life and feeling for its meaning and dramatic import, with a real sense of lively, urgent conversation.

Bryn Terfel and Alison Hagley make an outstanding Figaro and Susanna. Terfel has enough darkness in his voice to sound menacing in 'Se vuol ballare' as well as bitter in 'Aprite un po' quegli occhi'; it's an alert, mettlesome performance – and he also brings off a superlative 'Non più andrai'. Hagley offers a reading of spirit and allure. The interplay between her and the woodwind in 'Venite inginocchiatevi' is a delight, and her cool but heartfelt 'Deh vieni' is very beautiful. Once or twice her intonation seems marginally under stress but that's the small price you pay for singing with so little vibrato. Hillevi Martinpelto's unaffected, youthful-sounding Countess is enjoyable; both arias are quite lightly done, with a very lovely, warm, natural sound in 'Dove sono' especially. Some may prefer a more polished, sophisticated reading, of the traditional kind, but this is closer to what Mozart would have wanted and expected.

Rodney Gilfry provides a Count with plenty of fire and authority, firmly focused in tone; the outburst at the *Allegro assai* in 'Vedrò mentr'io sospiro' is formidable. Pamela Helen Stephen's Cherubino sounds charmingly youthful and impetuous. There's no want of dramatic life in Gardiner's direction. His tempos are marginally quicker than most, and the orchestra often speaks eloquently of the drama.

Le nozze di Figaro
Lorenzo Regazzo bass Figaro **Patrizia Ciofi** sop Susanna **Simon Keenlyside** bar Count Almaviva **Véronique Gens** sop Countess Almaviva **Angelika Kirschlager** mez Cherubino **Marie McLaughlin** sop Marcellina **Antonio Abete** bass Bartolo Antonio **Kobie van Rensburg** ten Don Basilio, Don Curzio **Nuria Rial** sop Barbarina **Ghent Collegium Vocale; Concerto Köln / René Jacobs**
Harmonia Mundi ③ HMC90 1818/20 (172' · DDD)
Notes, libretto and translation included   Ⓕ❍❍❍

René Jacobs always brings new ideas to the operas he conducts, and even to a work as familiar as *Figaro* he adds something of his own. First of all he offers an orchestral balance quite unlike what we are used to. Those who specially relish a Karajan or a Solti will hardly recognise the work, with its strongly wind-biased orchestral balance: you simply don't hear the violins as the 'main line' of the music. An excellent corrective to a tradition that was untrue to Mozart, to be sure, but possibly the pendulum has swung a little too far.

Jacobs is freer over tempo than most conductors. The Count's authoritarian pronouncements are given further weight by a faster tempo: it gives them extra decisiveness, though the music then has to slow down. There are other examples of such flexibility, sometimes a shade disconcerting, but always with good dramatic point. The Count's Act 3 duet with Susanna is one example: the little hesitancies enhanced and pointed up, if perhaps with some loss in energy and momentum. Tempos are generally on the quick side of normal, notably in the earlier parts of the Act 2 finale; but Jacobs is willing to hold back, too, for example in the Susanna-Marcellina duet, in the fandango, and in the G major music at the dénouement where the Count begs forgiveness.

The cast is excellent. Véronique Gens offers a beautifully natural, shapely 'Porgi amor' and a passionate and spirited 'Dove sono', The laughter in Patrizia Ciofi's voice is delightful when she's dressing up Cherubino, and she has space in 'Deh vieni' for a touchingly expressive performance. Then there's Angelika Kirschlager's Cherubino, alive and urgent in 'Non so più', every little phrase neatly moulded. Lorenzo Regazzo offers a strong Figaro, with a wide range of voice – angry and determined in 'Se vuol ballare', nicely rhythmic with some softer colours in 'Non più andrai', and pain and bitterness in 'Aprite'. The Count of Simon Keenlyside is powerful, menacing, lean and dark in tone. Marie McLaughlin sings Marcellina with unusual distinction.

Strongly cast, imaginatively directed: it's a *Figaro* well worth hearing

---

Additional recommendations

Le nozze di Figaro

Prey Figaro **Mathis** Susanna **Fischer-Dieskau** Count **Janowitz** Countess **Troyanos** Cherubino **Deutsche Oper Orchestra / Böhm**
DG The Originals 449 728-2GOR3 (173' · ADD)   Ⓜ
A strongly cast opera from 1968, with Böhm a near perfect Mozartian in charge. Fischer-Dieskau and Janowitz are ideally partnered as the aristocrats and Prey and Mathis are a lively pair of young lovers. Troyanos's Cherubino is finely drawn. Well worth considering.

Pinza Figaro **Réthy** Susanna **Stabile** Count   Ⓗ **Rautawaara** Countess **Novotna** Cherubino **Vienna State Opera Chorus; Vienna Philharmonic Orchestra / Walter**
Andante mono ③ 3981 (157' · ADD) Recorded live at the Salzburg Festival 1937. Notes, libretto and translation included   Ⓕ
An invaluable document: an edge-of-your-seat reading, devoid of Romanticism, aware of authentic practice even in the sense of brisk tempos and

use of harpsichord in the recitatives. The singers are superb, and the cast melds into a convincing whole. The transfers have been lovingly achieved. Thoroughly recommended.

Zaïde, K344/336b

Zaïde   P
Lynne Dawson sop Zaïde **Hans-Peter Blochwitz** ten
Gomatz **Olaf Bär** bar Allazim **Herbert Lippert** ten
Sultan Soliman **Christopher Purves** bass Osmin
Academy of Ancient Music / Paul Goodwin
Harmonia Mundi HMU90 7205 (75' · DDD) Notes,
text and translation included   F

Mozart began composing the work known as *Zaïde* in 1779-80, but left it unfinished, ostensibly because no performance was in prospect, but perhaps also because, very soon after he broke off, he came to see that this rather static kind of musical drama wasn't the sort of piece he wanted to write. Moreover, the character relationships are difficult to deal with: the libretto and the music (as far as it goes) imply a powerful attraction at the beginning between Zaïde and Gomatz, but in the final scene, which Mozart never reached, they turn out to be brother and sister: very touching, and well attuned to the sensibilities of the time, but cramping to the composer. Nevertheless, the music of *Zaïde* is full of fine things, often foreshadowing not only the similar *Entführung* but also *Idomeneo*. This recording captures its beauties and its depth of feeling beautifully. This is partly because of the sympathetic conducting of Paul Goodwin, who paces it with excellent judgement, bringing to it just the right degree of flexibility, and achieves orchestral textures that are clear and warm – much more so than usual from period-instrument groups. The melodramas, tellingly shaped, perfectly catch the tone of passion. The AAM plays at its best for him (notably, understandably, the principal oboist).

It's hard to imagine a better cast. Lynne Dawson sings the title-role with an appealing frail beauty. Hans-Peter Blochwitz's shapely lines and full, eloquent tone make Gomatz's arias a delight, too; and Herbert Lippert, the second tenor, as the Sultan (in love, or lust, with Zaïde), is almost his match in evenness and lyrical quality. It's also a luxury to have Olaf Bär as Allazim: the music is sung with great refinement of tone and ease of articulation. Christopher Purves sings Osmin cleanly without perhaps quite fully realising the comedy. This far excels any previous recording.

Die Zauberflöte, K620

Die Zauberflöte   P
Rosa Mannion sop Pamina **Natalie Dessay** sop
Queen of Night **Hans-Peter Blochwitz** ten Tamino
Anton Scharinger bass Papageno **Reinhard Hagen**
bass Sarastro **Willard White** bass Speaker **Steven
Cole** ten Monostatos **Linda Kitchen** sop Papagena

Anna Maria Panzarella sop **Doris Lamprecht** mez
Delphine Haidan contr First, Second and Third
Ladies **Damien Colin, Patrick Olivier Croset,
Stéphane Dutournier** trebs First, Second and Third
Boys **Christopher Josey** ten First Armed Man, First
Priest **Laurent Naouri** bass Second Armed Man,
Second Priest **Les Arts Florissants / William
Christie**
Erato ② 0630-12705-2 (150' · DDD) Notes, text and
translation included   M

With a background primarily in the French Baroque, William Christie comes to *Die Zauberflöte* from an angle quite unlike anyone else's; yet this is as idiomatic and as deeply Mozartian a reading as any. In the booklet-note Christie remarks on the unforced singing that's one of his objectives, much more manageable with the gentler sound of period instruments. All this is borne out by the performance itself, which falls sweetly and lovingly on the ear.

Overall the performance is quick and light-textured – and often quite dramatic. Some may find Christie less responsive than many more traditional interpreters to the quicksilver changes in mood, yet this is a part of his essentially broad and gentle view of *Die Zauberflöte*. His cast has few famous names, though there's Hans-Peter Blochwitz, probably the finest Tamino around these days. As Pamina, Rosa Mannion has much charm and a hint of girlish vivacity, but blossoms into maturity and passion in 'Ach, ich fühl's', whose final phrases, as the wind instruments fall away, leaving her alone and desolate, are very moving. Natalie Dessay's Queen of Night is forthright, clean and well tuned, with ample weight and tonal glitter.

The orchestral playing from Les Arts Florissants is polished, and the translucent sound is a joy. In short, Christie offers a very satisfying, acutely musical view of the work.

The Magic Flute (sung in English)
Rebecca Evans sop Pamina **Elizabeth Vidal** sop
Queen of Night **Barry Banks** ten Tamino **Simon
Keenlyside** bar Papageno **John Tomlinson** bass
Sarastro **Christopher Purves** bass Speaker **John
Graham-Hall** ten Monostatos **Lesley Garrett** sop
Papagena **Majella Cullagh** sop First Lady **Sarah Fox**
sop Second Lady **Diana Montague** mez Third Lady
**Geoffrey Mitchell Choir; London Philharmonic
Orchestra / Sir Charles Mackerras**
Chandos/Peter Moores Foundation Opera in English
② CHAN3121 (137' · DDD · S/T/N)   F**OO**

No work makes better sense in the vernacular than Mozart's concluding masterpiece. The composer and, assuredly, Schikaneder would have approved of giving the work in the language of the listeners, and when you have to hand such a witty, well-worded translation as that of Jeremy Sams, it makes even better sense. Sir Charles Mackerras, in his many performances at ENO and WNO, has always been an advocate of opera in English when the circumstances are right.

MOZART DIE ZAUBERFLÖTE – IN BRIEF

Ruth Ziesak *Pamina* **Uwe Heilmann** *Tamino*
Kurt Moll *Sarastro* **Vienna State Opera Choir;**
Vienna PO / Sir Georg Solti
Decca ② 433 210-2DH2 (152' · DDD) Ⓕ**OO**

Crisply brilliant yet warm and well-paced
conducting, with a superlative cast, clear-
voiced and refreshingly youthful – except for
Kurt Moll's appropriately grave Sarastro –
drawn from a stage production, and vividly
recorded. Solti's Mozart at its freshest.

Rosa Mannion *Pamina* **Hans-Peter Blochwitz**
Tamino **Reinhard Hagen** *Sarastro* **Les Arts**
Florissants / William Christie
Erato ② 0630 12705-2 (150' · DDD) Ⓜ

The best original-instrument version and
among the best ever, a graceful, well-paced
reading with plenty of magic and a memorable cast including Rosa Mannion's passionate Pamina, Natalie Dessay's cut-glass Queen
and Willard White the Speaker.

Tiana Lemnitz *Pamina* **Helge Rosvaenge** *Tamino*
Wilhelm Strienz *Sarastro* **Favres Solisten**
Vereinigung; Berlin PO / Sir Thomas Beecham
EMI mono ② 761034-2 (130' · AAD) Ⓜ**OO**

A pre-war classic in very reasonable sound,
albeit dialogue-free, vibrantly conducted by
Beecham with a memorable cast including
Tiana Lemnitz and the great Gerhard Hüsch
as Papageno.

Gundula Janowitz *Pamina* **Nicolai Gedda**
Tamino **Gottlob Frick** *Sarastro* **Philharmonia**
Chorus and Orchestra / Otto Klemperer
EMI ② 567388-2 (134' · ADD) Ⓜ

Old-fashioned, grave and monumental,
omitting dialogue, but enshrines some glorious singing from Nicolai Gedda, the young
Lucia Popp and Gundula Janowitz, and
Elisabeth Schwarzkopf and Christa Ludwig
among the Ladies.

Evelyn Lear *Pamina* **Fritz Wunderlich** *Tamino*
Dietrich Fischer-Dieskau *Papageno* **Berlin Radio**
Chamber Choir; Berlin PO / Karl Böhm
DG ② 449 749-2GOR2 (147' · ADD) Ⓜ

Böhm's luminous, beautifully paced reading
is something special, and among a generally
impressive cast Fritz Wunderlich and Dietrich Fischer-Dieskau are unmissable, even if
Evelyn Lear's Pamina is less ideal.

Elizabeth Norberg-Schulz *Pamina* **Herbert**
Lippert *Tamino* **Georg Tichy** *Papageno* **Failoni**
Orchestra, Budapest / Michael Halász
Naxos ② 8 660030/1 (149' · DDD) Ⓢ

A fine bargain-priced introduction, a satisfyingly theatrical performance with a cast
including rising stars such as Herbert Lippert
and Hellen Kwon, and Halász's lively conducting, very well recorded.

As ever, he proves himself a loving and perceptive Mozartian. Throughout he wonderfully
contrasts the warmth and sensuousness of the
music for the good characters with the fire and
fury of the baddies, and he persuades the LPO
to play with a lightness and promptness that's
wholly enchanting, quite the equal of most
bands on the other available versions.

In no way is his interpretation here inferior to
his German one on Telarc; indeed, in the central roles of Tamino and Pamina the casting for
Chandos is an improvement, and Keenlyside is
fully the equal of Thomas Allen on the Telarc
set. Keenlyside's loveable, slightly sad, very
human and perfectly sung Papageno is at the
centre of things. Rebecca Evans's voice has
taken on a new richness without losing any of its
focus or delicacy of utterance. Everything she
does has sincerity and poise, although her diction might, with advantage, be clearer.

The recording is fine apart from an over-use
of thunder and lightning as sound effects. Anyone wanting the work in English needn't hesitate to acquire this set, the first-ever on CD.

Additional recommendation

Die Zauberflöte
Janowitz *Pamina* **Popp** *Queen of Night* **Gedda**
Tamino **Berry** *Papageno*
Philharmonia Chorus and Orchestra / Klemperer
EMI Great Recordings of the Century ② 567388-2
(134' · ADD) Text and translation included Ⓜ

Gedda is a forthright Tamino, Popp a *nonpareil* of
a Queen of Night and Berry an enchanting
Papageno. However, Janowitz, beautifully as she
sings, is a detached Pamina. Note that Klemperer
decided that there should be no dialogue.

Modest Mussorgsky
Russian 1839-1881

*Mussorgsky's mother gave him piano lessons, and at
nine he played a Field concerto before an audience in
his parents' house. In 1852 he entered the Guards'
cadet school in St Petersburg. Although he had not
studied harmony or composition, in 1856 he tried to
write an opera the same year he entered the Guards.
In 1857 he met Dargomizbsky and Cui, and
through them Balakirev and Stasov. He persuaded
Balakirev to give him lessons and composed songs and
piano sonatas.*

*In 1858 Mussorgsky passed through a nervous or
spiritual crisis and resigned his army commission. A
visit to Moscow in 1859 fired his patriotic imagination and his compositional energies, but although his
music began to enjoy public performances his nervous
irritability was not entirely calmed. The emancipa-
tion of the serfs in March 1861 obliged him to spend
most of the next two years helping manage the family estate; a symphony came to nothing and Stasov
and Balakirev agreed that 'Mussorgsky is almost an
idiot'. But he continued to compose and in 1863-6
worked on the libretto and music of an opera,*

Salammbô, which he never completed. At this time he served at the Ministry of Communications and lived in a commune with five other young men who ardently cultivated and exchanged advanced ideas about art, religion, philosophy and politics. Mussorgsky's private and public lives eventually came into conflict. In 1865 he underwent his first serious bout of dipsomania (probably as a reaction to his mother's death that year) and in 1867 he was dismissed from his post.

He spent summer 1867 at his brother's country house at Minkino, where he wrote, among other things, his first important orchestral work, St John's Night on the Bare Mountain. On his return to St Petersburg in the autumn Musorgsky, like the other members of the Balakirev-Stasov circle (ironically dubbed the 'Mighty Handful'), became interested in Dargomïzhsky's experiments in operatic naturalism. Early in 1869 Musorgsky re-entered government service and, in more settled conditions, was able to complete the original version of the opera Boris Godunov. This was rejected by the Mariinsky Theatre and Mussorgsky set about revising it. In 1872 the opera was again rejected, but excerpts were performed elsewhere and a vocal score published. The opera committee finally accepted the work and a successful production was given in February 1874.

Meanwhile Mussorgsky had begun work on another historical opera, Khovanshchina, at the same time gaining promotion at the ministry. Progress on the new opera was interrupted partly because of unsettled domestic circumstances, but mainly because heavy drinking which left him incapable of sustained creative effort. But several other compositions belong to this period, including the song cycles Sunless and Songs and Dances of Death and the Pictures at an Exhibition, for piano, a brilliant and bold series inspired by a memorial exhibition of drawings by his friend Victor Hartmann. Ideas for a comic opera based on Gogol's Sorochintsy Fair also began to compete with work on Khovanshchina; both operas remained unfinished at Musorgsky's death. During the earlier part of 1878 he seems to have led a more respectable life and his director at the ministry even allowed him leave for a three-month concert tour with the contralto Darya Leonova. After he was obliged to leave the government service in January 1880, Leonova helped provide him with employment and a home. It was to her that he turned on February 23, 1881 in a state of nervous excitement, saying that there was nothing left for him but to beg in the streets; he was suffering from alcoholic epilepsy. He was removed to hospital, where he died a month later.

Many of Mussorgsky's works were unfinished, and their editing and posthumous publication were mainly carried out by Rimsky-Korsakov, who to a greater or lesser degree 'corrected' what Mussorgsky had composed. It was only many years later that, with a return to the composer's original drafts, the true nature of his rough art could be properly understood.

GROVEmusic

Pictures at an Exhibition (orch Ravel)

Pictures at an Exhibition (orch Ravel). St John's Night on the Bare Mountain (arr Rimsky-Korsakov). The

destruction of Sennacheriba. Salammbô – Chorus of priestesses[a]. Oedipus in Athens – Chorus of people in the temple[a]. Joshua[b]

[b]**Elena Zaremba** mez [a]**Prague Philharmonic Chorus; Berlin Philharmonic Orchestra / Claudio Abbado**
DG 445 238-2GH (65' · DDD) Recorded live
1993. Texts and translations included Ⓕ

St John's Night on the Bare Mountain is the original version of A Night on the Bare Mountain. Abbado relishes the odd grotesque spurts of colour from the woodwind and Mussorgskian ruggedness. The composer's structural clumsiness isn't shirked and the lack of the smooth continuity found in the Rimsky-Korsakov arrangement doesn't impede the sense of forward momentum; indeed at the close the Russian dance element is emphasised, rather than the sinister pictorialism. The choral pieces are gloriously sung and again Abbado brings out their Russian colour, especially in the glowing yet sinuous 'Chorus of priestesses'. Joshua is made to seem a minor masterpiece with its lusty opening and its touching central solo ('The Amorite women weep'). This is most eloquently sung by Elena Zaremba and the theme is then movingly taken up first by the women of chorus and then the men, before the exultant music returns. The performance of Pictures at an Exhibition, like the choral items, gains from the spacious ambience and sumptuous overall textures. It's very dramatic in its contrasts and very beautifully played.

The refinement and colour of the evocation, so characteristic of Abbado is most touching in 'The old castle', while 'Tuileries' is gently evoked with a flexibly fluid control of tempo. 'Bydlo' opens and closes mournfully, yet reaches a strong, positive immediacy as it finally comes close. The chicks dance with dainty lightness, then the hugely weighty lower orchestral *tutti* and bleating trumpet response of 'Samuel Goldenberg' demonstrate the extraordinary range of tone this great orchestra can command.

After the scintillating virtuosity of 'Market Place at Limoges' the sonorous Berlin brass makes a tremendous impact in 'Catacombe' and Abbado's tonal and dynamic graduations are astute; then after a ferociously rhythmic 'Baba-jaga' he steadily builds his three-dimensional 'Great Gate at Kiev', losing none of the grandeur of the gentle contrasts of the intoned chorale, with the tam-tam splashes at the end satisfyingly finalising the effect. A most enjoyable concert: there's nothing routine about anything here.

Mussorgsky Pictures at an Exhibition (orch Ravel)
Stravinsky The Rite of Spring
Philadelphia Orchestra / Riccardo Muti
EMI Encore 574742-2 (64' · ADD) Recorded 1978 ⓈО

Pictures at an Exhibition was the first commercial recording to do justice to the range and depth of sonority that the Philadelphia Orchestra could command. The recording venue was the Metropolitan Church of Philadelphia and the generous acoustic of the hall enabled this great orchestra to be heard to best advantage. The lower strings in 'Samuel Goldenberg and Schmuyle' have an extraordinary richness, body and presence, and 'Baba Yaga' has an unsurpassed virtuosity and attack. The glorious body of tone, the richly glowing colours, the sheer homogeneity of the strings and perfection of the ensemble is a consistent pleasure. Muti's reading is second to none and the orchestral playing is breathtaking. There are many other fine recordings of this work but they do not have quite that homogeneity of tone and the extraordinary sheen that's been the hallmark of the Philadelphians for many decades. The recording is amazingly lifelike and truthful.

Muti directs a performance of *The Rite of Spring* that's aggressively brutal but yet presents its violence not in coldly clinical terms but with red-blooded conviction. His tempo is a degree faster than usual, but no faster than Stravinsky recommends. The great compulsion of the performance lies in his ability to draw playing from his orchestra which isn't just precise and brilliant, but passionately committed. Wildness and barbarity are so clearly part of the mixture to a degree not matched by most other recordings, so it isn't surprising that Muti's interpretation remains among the front-runners. The recording is gloriously full and dramatic with wide dynamic range and fine separation. The brass and percussion are caught with special vividness helped by one of the most impressive bass responses to be heard in this work.

Mussorgsky Pictures at an Exhibition (orch Ravel). A Night on the Bare Mountain (arr Rimsky-Korsakov)
Ravel Valses nobles et sentimentales
New York Philharmonic Orchestra / Giuseppe Sinopoli
DG 429 785-2GH (67' · DDD) Recorded 1989   Ⓕ

Sinopoli's recording of *Pictures at an Exhibition* has great panache and is full of subtle detail and sharply characterised performances. None of this would be possible without the marvellous virtuosity of the New York Philharmonic Orchestra, whose brass section plays with a wonderful larger-than-life sonority and whose woodwind section produces playing of considerable delicacy and finesse, as for example in 'Tuileries' and the 'Ballet of the Unhatched Chicks'. Sinopoli revels in the drama of this work and this is nowhere more noticeable than in his sinister readings of 'Catacombs' and 'Baba-Yaga'. *A Night on the Bare Mountain* is no less impressive, where again the orchestra's flair and virtuosity have an almost overwhelming impact. Less successful are Ravel's *Valses nobles et sentimentales* which are perhaps too idiosyncratic for an individual recommendation despite some superb performances and moments of great beauty. The sound is very well balanced.

Pictures at an Exhibition[a] (orch Ravel). Night on the Bare Mountain (arr Rimsky-Korsakov). Khovanshchina – Prelude (orch Shostakovich). Sorochintsï Fair – Gopak (orch Liadov)
Vienna Philharmonic Orchestra / Valery Gergiev
Philips 468 526-2PH (52' · DDD) [a]Recorded live 2000
Ⓕ Ⓞ

This is a larger-than-life reading of *Pictures*, which underplays the subtleties of colouring introduced by Ravel in favour of more earthily Russian flavours. The coupling is an all-Mussorgsky one, surprisingly rare in the many versions of this work.

This live account brings some superb playing, with fast, brilliant movements dazzlingly well played, and with the speed bringing an edge-of-seat feeling from perils just avoided, something not usually conveyed in a studio performance. The opening 'Promenade', taken squarely, establishes the monumental Russian quality, enhanced by the immediacy of the sound. Even the 'Hut on Fowl's Legs' seems larger than life, and the performance culminates in an account of the 'Great Gate of Kiev' shattering in its weight and thrust.

That and the all-Mussorgsky coupling establish a clear place for this new issue in an overstocked market, even though the coupling isn't generous. The regular Rimsky version of *Night on the Bare Mountain*, though not recorded live, brings a performance to compare in power with *Pictures*, with very weighty brass, while Shostakovich's orchestration of the *Khovanshchina* Prelude, though less evocative than it can be, is warm and refined, with the Gopak added as a lively encore.

Pictures at an Exhibition (orch Ravel). A Night on the Bare Mountain – 2 versions: orch Mussorgsky; orch Rimsky-Korsakov. The Fair at Sorochintsï – Gopak. Khovanshchina – The departure of Prince Golitsïn
Ukraine National Symphony Orchestra / Theodore Kuchar
Naxos 8 555924 (63' · DDD)   Ⓢ Ⓢ

Ravel's orchestration of *Pictures at an Exhibition* was commissioned by Koussevitzky as a showpiece for his superb Boston orchestra, and it proves just as impressive here to demonstrate the excellence of the National Symphony Orchestra of the Ukraine. The colour palette of the woodwind is a joy, as we discover in both 'Tuileries' and the deliciously cheeping 'Unhatched Chickens'; and how beautifully the solo saxophone sings his sad serenade outside 'The Old Castle'. In representing the bold profile of 'Samuel Goldenberg', the massed lower strings show their splendid body of tone, and the punch of the brass entry in 'Catacombae' has the richest underlying resonance in a performance full of eerie menace. The percussion come fully into their own in 'The Hut on Fowl's Legs', where the bass drummer adds dramatic weight and point. The 'Great Gate of Kiev' is given with the full, rich orchestral sonority now thrillingly expansive, and Kuchar broadening the final statement of the great chorale to give the listener a tingling *frisson* of satisfaction.

It was an original and fascinating idea to record both the original Mussorgsky score of *Night on the Bare Mountain* alongside the Rimsky arrangement, for in many ways they're entirely different works, something Theodore Kuchar underlines by his contrasting interpretations. It may be unfashionable to say so, but however inspired and original Mussorgsky's draft score is in conception, the all-but-recomposed Rimsky-Korsakov piece is the finer work overall. With a superbly rasping opening from the heavy brass, and thrusting forward momentum, Kuchar readily captures its intitial and recurring malignant force, deftly amalgamating the jollity of Rimsky's interpolated brass fanfares, then producing a magically peaceful close, with radiant playing from the Russian woodwind.

To sum up, this is a quite remarkable CD on all counts – outstandingly fine orchestral playing, vividly exciting and very Russian music-making, and a very tangible sound picture, consistently in the demonstration bracket.

Pictures at an Exhibition (orch Ravel). A Night on the Bare Mountain (arr Rimsky-Korsakov). Khovanshchina – Prelude, Act 1, 'Dawn over the Moscow River'
Atlanta Symphony Orchestra / Yoel Levi
Telarc CD80296 (50' · DDD) Recorded 1991   Ⓕ

When this was released, Telarc established a position for it as sonically the most spectacular set of *Pictures* among the many in the current catalogue. And it's a very fine performance too. The programme opens with *A Night on the Bare Mountain* – the brass sound is special, with great richness and natural bite with no exaggeration. The performance overall is both well paced and exciting. Perhaps Levi's evil spirits aren't as satanic as some, but they make an impact and the contrasting melancholy of the closing section is very touching, with the tolling bell nicely balanced and the clarinet solo poignantly taking over from the gently elegiac strings.

The characterisation of *Pictures at an Exhibition* is no less successful, although it's an essentially mellower view than, for example, Sinopoli's highly praised DG version with the New York Philharmonic Orchestra. Levi's is a performance where the conductor makes the most of the colour, and brilliant orchestral effects of Ravel's inspired score, revealing much that often goes unheard – the grotesquerie of 'Gnomus' isn't accentuated, but one greatly enjoys the attack of the lower strings which are very tangible indeed; a doleful bassoon introduces 'The Old Castle' and the saxophone solo has a satin-like finish on the timbre to produce an elegant melancholy; the woodwind in 'Tuileries' is gentle in its virtuosity. Levi holds back a little for the delicate string entry and the whole piece has a captivating lightness of touch. The final climax is unerringly built and at the very close

MUSSORGSKY/RAVEL PICTURES AT AN EXHIBITION – IN BRIEF

Chicago SO / Fritz Reiner
RCA 09026 61958 2 (71' · ADD)   Ⓜ⒪
An all-time classic from Reiner's legendary days at the helm of the Chicago Symphony. Bold characterisation and orchestral playing of tremendous conviction. The astonishingly vivid stereo dates from 1957.

Boston SO / Serge Koussevitzky
RCA mono 09026 61392 2 (75' · ADD)   Ⓜ
It was Koussevitzky who commissioned and premièred Ravel's orchestration in 1922. This electrifying first recording from eight years later shows off the phenomenal articulation and tonal breadth of his fabulous Boston orchestra.

Cleveland Orchestra / George Szell
Sony SBK48162 (74' · ADD)   ⒷⓄⓄ
Dazzling stuff from Szell and his immaculate Clevelanders. This partnership's irresistibly swaggering suites from Kodály's *Hary János* and Prokofiev's *Lieutenant Kijé* make up an unbeatable bargain triptych.

Berlin PO / Claudio Abbado
DG 445 238-2GH (65' · DDD)   ⒻⓄ
Abbado has long been a doughty Mussorgsky conductor. These live *Pictures* from 1993 are studded with newly minted detail, outstandingly well played by the Berliners.

Atlanta SO / Yoel Levi
Telarc CD80296 (50' · DDD)   Ⓕ
Levi's is a thoughtful interpretation, but by no means lacking in sheer personality or heady excitement. The Telarc engineering astonishes in its sheer weight of sonority and X-ray-like transparency.

Philadelphia Orchestra / Riccardo Muti
EMI Encore 574581-2 (64' · ADD)   ⓈⓄ
An exhilaratingly sleek set of *Pictures*, the richness and depth of the famed Philadelphia strings recalling the heady days of Stokowski. EMI's 1978 sound approaches demonstration quality.

National SO of Ukraine / Theodore Kuchar
Naxos 8 555924 (63' · DDD)   Ⓢ
Kuchar conducts with palpable relish and secures an enthusiastic response from his hard-working band. A super bargain all round from Naxos.

Vienna PO / Valery Gergiev
Philips 468 526-2PH (52' ·DDD)   ⒻⓄ
Assembled from a series of live concerts in Vienna's Musikverein during April 2000. Gergiev takes the listener on an illuminating journey, culminating in a simply majestic evocation of 'The Great Gate of Kiev'.

the brass and strings produce an electrifying richness and weight of sound, to bring a *frisson* of excitement, with the tam-tam resounding clearly. Then there's silence, and out of it steals the exquisite opening of the *Khovanschchina* Prelude, with its poetic evocation of dawn over the Kremlin. Levi goes for atmosphere above all else and doesn't make too much of the climax, but the coda with its fragile woodwind halos is most delicately managed. This disc is a first choice if state-of-the-art recording is your prime consideration.

Pictures at an Exhibition (piano)

Mussorgsky Pictures at an Exhibition **Chopin** 27 Etudes, Opp 10, 25 & posth – E, Op 10/3 **Liszt** 12 Etudes d'exécution transcendante, S139 – No 5, Feux follets; No 11, Harmonies du soir. 4 Valses oubliées, S215 – No 1; No 2 **Prokofiev** Sonata for Piano No 6, Op. 82 – Sonata for Piano No 7, Op 83. Sonata for Piano No 8, Op 84 **Rachmaninov** 24 Preludes – G sharp minor, Op 32/12 **Schubert** Impromptus – No 2 in E flat; No 4 in A flat. 6 Moments musicaux, D780 – No 1 in C
Sviatoslav Richter pf
Philips ② 456 946-2PM2 (149' · ADD) Recorded live 1958 Ⓜ

Forced to select the greatest of Richter's performances for a two-disc set, Philips, understandably, have looked to his famous 1958 Sofia recital. Even at the height of his powers he could be an erratic player, but on this occasion the force was with him from first note until last. Not only did the recital help to spread the Richter 'legend' in the months leading up to his much-hyped London and New York débuts in 1960, his Mussorgsky *Pictures* made a decisive contribution to the rehabilitation of that piece as a staple of the piano repertoire. Here is virtuosity entirely at the service of the music, defying anyone to say a word against Mussorgsky's pianistic imagination or to want to hear Ravel's orchestral make-over ever again.

The rest of the recital displays Richter's view of the Romantic repertoire at its first mature flowering, after a period of occasionally experimental overstatement. His Schubert, Chopin and Liszt share a common core of determined resistance to buffeting emotions. Yet on the surface his Schubert is as beautiful and refined as anyone's (no controversial tempos either); and as all collectors of recorded piano music already know, his Liszt 'Feux follets' remains a benchmark performance to this day. As for his Prokofiev, has anyone taken the Scherzo of the Sixth Sonata more convincingly at this tempo (the fast end of *allegretto*), for instance, or found more wide-ranging yet integrated drama in all three movements of the Eighth? You could certainly wish for more refined recording quality on the first disc, though the Prokofiev sonatas are well enough recorded, especially the Eighth. Overall it's difficult to imagine a truer encapsulation of the Richter phenomenon.

Boris Godunov

Boris Godunov (first version)
Nikolai Putilin bar Boris Godunov **Viktor Lutsiuk** ten Grigory **Nikolai Okhotnikov** bass Pimen **Fyodor Kuznetsov** bass Varlaam **Konstantin Pluzhnikov** ten Shuisky **Nikolai Gassiev** ten Missail **Zlata Bulycheva** mez Fyodor **Olga Trifonova** sop Xenia **Yevgenia Gorokhovskaya** mez Nurse **Liubov Sokolova** mez Hostess **Evgeny Akimov** ten Simpleton **Vassily Gerello** bar Shchelkalov **Grigory Karassev** bass Nikitich **Evgeny Nikitin** bass Mityukha **Yuri Schikalov** ten Krushchov

Boris Godunov (second version)
Vladimir Vaneyev bass Boris Godunov **Vladimir Galusin** ten Grigory **Olga Borodina** mez Marina **Nikolai Okhotnikov** bass Pimen **Fyodor Kuznetsov** bass Varlaam **Konstantin Pluzhnikov** ten Shuisky **Nikolai Gassiev** ten Missail **Evgeny Nikitin** bass Rangoni, Mityukha **Zlata Bulycheva** mez Fyodor **Olga Trifonova** sop Xenia **Yevgenia Gorokhovskaya** mez Nurse **Liubov Sokolova** mez Hostess **Evgeny Akimov** ten Simpleton **Vassily Gerello** bar Shchelkalov **Grigory Karassev** bass Nikitich **Yuri Schikalov** ten Krushchov **Andrei Karabanov** bar Lavitsky **Yuri Laptev** ten Chernikovsky **Chorus and Orchestra of the Kirov Opera / Valery Gergiev**
Philips ⑤ 462 230-2PH5 (306' · DDD) Notes, texts and translations included Ⓜ〇〇

What we have here is, literally, two operas for the price of one. That's to say, the two discs containing Mussorgsky's first *Boris Godunov* and the three containing his second are available at five discs for the normal cost of three. And, in a real sense, what we're dealing with is two operas. First, a brief resumé of the facts. In 1868-9 Mussorgsky composed seven scenes: outside the Novedevichy Monastery, Coronation outside the Kremlin, Pimen's Cell, the Inn, the Tsar's rooms in the Kremlin, outside St Basil's Cathedral, Boris's Death in the Kremlin. When these were rejected by the Imperial Theatres in 1872, he made various revisions. To meet objections about the lack of female roles, Mussorgsky added the two scenes with the Polish princess Marina Mniszek; he also substituted the final Kromy Forest scene for the St Basil's scene. He made a large number of adjustments, some of a minor nature, some rather more significant (such as dropping Pimen's narration of the murder of the young Tsarevich), and one huge, the complete rewriting of the original fifth scene, in the Kremlin, sometimes known as the Terem scene. This was the work that he resubmitted, and which was first performed in St Petersburg in 1874. Rimsky-Korsakov's famous version (which does much more than reorchestrate) was first heard in 1896, and for many years superseded its predecessors.

However, it has increasingly been recognised that *Boris* II isn't a revision of *Boris* I but a different work, both as regards the view of the central character and his place in the historical narrative, and also as regards the rethought musical technique and sometimes change of idiom which this has brought about. Therefore the present set makes a real contribution to our understanding and enjoyment of Russia's greatest opera. It follows that there have to be two singers of the central role. Putilin (*Boris* I) is in general more capacious in tone, more brooding and lofty, in the Terem scene more embittered and harsh, willing to act with the voice. Vaneyev is a decidedly more immediate and human Boris, tender with his son Fyodor (a touching, engaging performance from Zlata Bulycheva) both in the Terem and at the end, not always as dominating as this Tsar should be but sympathetic, allowing his voice to blanch as death approaches, and especially responsive to the melodic essence of Mussorgsky's speech-delivered lines. This enables him to be rather freer with the actual note values. It doesn't necessarily matter that much: Mussorgsky changed his mind over various details, and the important thing is to use his notes to create character rather than be too literal with what the different versions propose. Pimen, strongly sung with a hint of the youthful passions that he claims to have abjured, is sung by Nikolai Okhotnikov more or less identically in both performances.

The only character, apart from Boris, to be accorded two singers is Grigory, the False Dmitri. Viktor Lutsiuk (*Boris* I) is strenuous, obsessed, vital; Vladimir Galusin (*Boris* II) can sound more frenzied, and has the opportunity with the addition of the Polish acts to give a convincing portrayal of a weak man assuming strength but being undermined by the wiles of a determined woman. Here, she's none other than Olga Borodina, moodily toying with her polonaise rhythms and then in full sensuous call. Yevgenia Gorokhovskaya is a jolly old Nurse in the *Boris* II Terem scene. The rest of the cast do not really change their interpretations from one *Boris* to another, and indeed scarcely need to do so: it isn't really upon that which the differences depend. Liubov Sokolova sings a fruity Hostess, welcoming in Fyodor Kuznetsov a Varlaam who can really sing his Kazan song rather than merely bawling it. Konstantin Pluzhnikov makes Shuisky move from the rather sinister force confronting Boris in the Terem to a more oily complacency in the Death scene: many Shuiskys make less of the part. Evgeny Nikitin is a creepy, fanatical Rangoni, Vassily Gerello a Shchelkalov of hypocritical elegance, Evgeny Akimov a sad-toned Simpleton. Gergiev directs strong, incisive performances, accompanying sympathetically and controlling the marvellous crowd scenes well.

However, it's a pity that he allows fierce whistles to drown the speeding violins opening the Kromy Forest scene (the music can be heard only when it returns), and he hasn't been given sufficient clarity of recording with the chorus. The words are often obscure, even with the boyars in the Death scene, and far too much is lost in the crowd exchanges. This is regrettable for a work that, in either incarnation, draws so much on realistic detail of articulation.

MUSSORGSKY BORIS GODUNOV – IN BRIEF

Vladimir Vaneyev *Boris* **Vladimir Galusin** *Grigory* **Olga Borodina** *Marina* **Nikolai Okhotnikov** *Pimen* **Kirov Opera / Valery Gergiev**
Philips 462 230-2PHS   Ⓜ○○
This is a mandatory purchase for *Boris* fans: a five-CD set which contains both the original 1869 version and the 1872 revision complete with its Polish scene. Gergiev's sympathy for this music is total, and he draws staggering performances from his excellent Kirov musicians.

Anatoly Kotcherga *Boris* **Sergei Larin** *Grigory* **Marjana Lipovšek** *Marina* **Samuel Ramey** *Pimen* **Berlin PO / Claudio Abbado**
Sony Classical S3K58977   Ⓜ○
A spectacular recording of the 1872-4 version (with some extra scenes). Anatoly Kotcherga is superb in the title-role, and the remainder of the cast is on splendid form. The ambience of the Berlin Philharmonie adds to the recording's magnificence.

Robert Lloyd *Boris* **Alexei Steblianko** *Grigory* **Olga Borodina** *Marina* **Igor Morosov** *Pimen* **Kirov Opera / Valery Gergiev**
Philips ◊ 075 089-9PH2   Ⓜ○
The superb 1990 Andrei Tarkovsky production seen here in an adaptation for the Kirov Opera comes up splendidly on DVD. Robert Lloyd is masterly in the title-role, and the remainder of the cast has been assembled from strength. Gergiev's direction is first-rate.

Evgeni Nesterenko *Boris* **Vladimir Atlantov** *Grigory* **Elena Obratsova** *Marina* **Alexander Ognivtsiev** *Pimen* **Kirov Opera / Mark Ermler**
Regis RRC3006   Ⓢ
With the excellent Evgeni Nesterenko in the title-role, this 1982 Bolshoi recording under the ever-dependable Mark Ermler makes a fantastic bargain. Obtratsova and Atlantov offer strong support.

Boris Christoff *Boris, Pimen, Varlaam* **Nicolai Gedda** *Grigory* **Eugenia Zareska** *Marina* **French Radio National Orchestra / Issay Dobrowen**
EMI mono 565192-2   Ⓜ○
This recording from 1952 enshrines Boris Christoff's *tour de force* in the three central roles (Boris, Pimen and Varlaam) – a feat he pulls off with tremendous flair. Nicolai Gedda as Grigory is on equally superb form. Something of a classic.

Nevertheless, these five discs form a fascinating set, one no admirer of this extraordinary creative achievement can afford to ignore.

Boris Godunov (1874 version)
Anatoly Kotcherga bass Boris **Sergei Larin** ten Grigory **Marjana Lipovšek** mez Marina **Samuel Ramey** bass Pimen **Gleb Nikolsky** bass Varlaam **Philip Langridge** ten Shuisky **Helmut Wildhaber** ten Missail **Sergei Leiferkus** bar Rangoni **Liliana Nichiteanu** mez Feodor **Valentina Valente** sop Xenia **Yevgenia Gorokhovskaya** mez Nurse **Eléna Zaremba** mez Hostess **Alexander Fedin** ten Simpleton **Albert Shagidullin** bar Shchelkolov **Wojciech Drabowicz** ten Mitukha, Krushchov **Slovak Philharmonic Chorus; Berlin Radio Chorus; Tölz Boys' Choir; Berlin Philharmonic Orchestra / Claudio Abbado**
Sony Classical ③ S3K58977 (200' · DDD) Recorded 1993. Notes, text and translation included
Ⓕ**Ⓞ**

Few conductors have been more diligent than Claudio Abbado in seeking the truth about this vast canvas. He chooses the definitive 1872-4 version, adding scenes, including the complete one in Pimen's cell and the St Basil's scene from 1869. His is a taut, tense reading – grand, virtuosic, at times hard-driven, favouring extremes of speed and dynamics. The orchestra is very much in the foreground, sounding more emphatic than would ever be the case in the opera house. Kotcherga has a superb voice, firmly produced throughout an extensive register. His is a Boris avoiding conventional melodrama and concerned to show the loving father. The ambitious lovers are well represented. Indeed, Larin is quite the best Grigory yet recorded on disc, sounding at once youthful, heroic and ardent, and quite free of any tenor mannerisms. Lipovšek characterises Marina forcefully: we're well aware of the scheming Princess's powers of wheeler-dealing and erotic persuasion. The recording is of demonstration standard: it's most potent in the way that it captures the incisive and pointed singing of the combined choruses in their various guises. Here all is vividly brought before us by conductor and producer in the wide panorama predicated by Mussorgsky's all-enveloping vision.

Boris Godunov (arr Rimsky-Korsakov) Ⓗ
Boris Christoff bass Boris, Pimen, Varlaam **Nicolai Gedda** ten Grigory **Eugenia Zareska** mez Marina, Feodor **André Bielecki** ten Shuisky, Missail, Krushchov **Kim Borg** bass Rangoni, Shchelkalov **Ludmila Lebedeva** sop Xenia **Lydia Romanova** mez Nurse, Hostess **Wassili Pasternak** ten Simpleton **Raymond Bonte** ten Lavitsky **Eugène Bousquet** bass Chernikovsky **Choeurs Russes de Paris; French Radio National Orchestra / Issay Dobrowen**
EMI Références mono ③ 565192-2 (178' · ADD) Recorded 1952
Ⓜ**Ⓞ**

Dobrowen's lean, vivid, acutely shaped direction, benefiting from taut rhythms and fastish tempos, is as vital as that on any version since. Its other main attribute is Christoff's first complete reading on disc of the tortured Tsar, whose role he sings with an enviable combination of firm tone, vital diction and concentrated histrionics, never over-stepping the mark. His assumption of two other parts has always been frowned on, but he so subtly varies his tone – softer, greyer for Pimen, rotundly rollicking for Varlaam – that the tripling only worries in the final scene when Pimen comes face to face with the dying ruler. The contrast of his finely shaded Pimen with Ramey's one-dimensional singing on the Abbado version is most marked. If that were not enough, there's the beauty and ardour of the young Gedda as Grigory to please the ear and Zareska's seductive, vocally appealing Marina. She also sings a likeable Feodor. Kim Borg doubles successfully as Shchelkalov and an oily Rangoni. The choral singing is good. We have heard much better on disc since, but few orchestras, in the West at least, have sounded so Russian as these French players but then few have had the benefit of being tutored by Dobrowen. The digital transfers bring out the excellence of the original engineering.

Additional recommendation

Nesterenko Boris **Atlantov** Grigory **Obraztsova** Marina **Ognivtsiev** Pimen **Eizen** Varlaam **Lissovski** Shuisky **Baskov** Missail **Mazurok** Rangoni **Bolshoi Theatre Chorus and Orchestra / Mark Ermler**
Regis ③ RRC3006 (190' · ADD · S/N) Recorded 1982
Ⓢ

A performance in the old Bolshoi style using the Rimsky-Korsakov edition. At its super-budget price, this magnificent 1982 set is an easy recommendation.

Khovanshchina

Khovanshchina
Aage Haugland bass Ivan Khovansky **Vladimir Atlantov** ten Andrey Khovansky **Vladimir Popov** ten Golitsin **Anatolij Kotscherga** bar Shaklovity **Paata Burchuladze** bass Dosifey **Marjana Lipovšek** contr Marfa **Brigitte Poschner-Klebel** sop Susanna **Heinz Zednik** ten Scribe **Joanna Borowska** sop Emma **Wilfried Gahmlich** ten Kouzka **Vienna Boys' Choir; Slovak Philharmonic Choir; Vienna State Opera Chorus and Orchestra / Claudio Abbado**
DG ③ 429 758-2GH3 (171' · DDD) Recorded live 1989. Notes, text and translation included
Ⓕ**⒪Ⓞ**

The booklet-essay suggests that Mussorgsky's music constantly poses a question to his Russian compatriots: 'What are the causes of our country's continuing calamities, and why does the state crush all that is good?'. Anyone who follows today's news from Russia and then experiences this opera will understand what's meant, and while we observe with sympathy we seem no nearer than the citizens of that great, tormented country to finding solutions for its endemic problems. However, Mussorgsky was not the least of those Russian musicians who found lasting beauty in her history and he expressed it in a powerfully dramatic idiom that drew on folk-music and had both epic qualities and deep humanity as well as an occasional gentleness. There's also an element here of Russian church music, since *Khovanshchina* has a political and religious theme and is set in the 1680s at the time of Peter the Great's accession. Since the work was unfinished when Mussorgsky died, performances always involve conjectural work, and the version here – which works convincingly – is mostly that of Shostakovich with the choral ending that Stravinsky devised using Mussorgsky's music. The cast in this live recording isn't one of star opera singers, but they're fully immersed in the drama and the music, as is the chorus and the orchestra under Abbado, and the result is deeply atmospheric.

Nikolay Myaskovsky
Russian 1881-1950

Myaskovsky studied for a military career but entered the St Petersburg Conservatory (1906-11), where his teachers included Lyadov and Rimsky-Korsakov. He served in the war, and from 1921 taught at the Moscow Conservatory. He was not an innovator but was an influential, individual figure working within the Russian tradition. His large output is dominated by the cycle of 27 symphonies (1908-50), highly regarded in and outside Russia in his lifetime. He also wrote 13 string quartets (1913-49), choral and chamber music. GROVEmusic

Violin Concerto

Myaskovsky Violin Concerto in D minor, Op 44
Tchaikovsky Violin Concerto in D, Op 35
Vadim Repin vn Kirov Orchestra / Valery Gergiev
Philips 473 343-2PH (72' · DDD) Ⓕ **❍❍❍**

It's the Myaskovsky that really makes this disc a 'must-have'. His Violin Concerto was premièred by David Oistrakh in Leningrad in 1939. As with Tchaikovsky's Concerto, the opening *tutti* plays for less than a minute and the slow movement is touchingly lyrical. The rather melancholy first movement is built on a grand scale and includes an expansive cadenza where Repin's mastery is virtually the equal of Oistrakh's. It's forceful music, epic in scale and earnestly argued, the sort of piece that Gergiev thrives on. Listening to Repin's Tchaikovsky Concerto (his second recording of the work) confirms just how far he's journeyed in a few years. Tone projection is stronger, attack more aggressive and his solo demeanour seems better focused than before, far more confident and spontaneous. Mixed in with these improvements are one or two affectations, but it's a cracking performance, one of the best from the younger generation. The recording sounds like a digital update of the sort of blowsy in-your-face sonics typical of the first stereo recordings of the late 1950s. Nevertheless, a fabulous disc.

Conlon Nancarrow Mexican 1912-1997

Nancarrow was born in the United States, and studied with Slonimsky, Piston and Sessions in Boston (1933-6), but lived in Mexico from 1940. From the late 1940s he composed exclusively for player piano. His studies exploit the instrument's potential for rhythmic complexity and textural variety, creating showpieces of virtuosity far beyond a human performer's capabilities, with arpeggios, trills, glissandos, leaps, widely spaced chords and complex counterpoint. He was concerned with tempo, especially the 'temporal dissonance' of several rates occurring simultaneously, and with formal structure. His music first received serious attention only in the 1970s. GROVEmusic

Instrumental works

Studies and Solos

Studies for Player Piano[a] – Nos 3b[h], 3c[e], 3d, 4f, 6f, 9d, 14d, 159, 18f, 19d, 26d. Prelude[a]. Sonatina[a]9.
Three Canons for Ursula[b]. Blues[b]. Three Two-Part Studies[c]. Tango?[c]
(trans [d]Helena Bugallo; [e]Bugallo-Williams; [f]Erik Ona; 9Yvar Mikhashoff; [h]Amy Williams)
[a]**Bugallo-Williams Piano Duo** ([b]Helena Bugallo, [c]Amy Williams pfs)
Wergo WER6670-2 (63' · DDD) Ⓕ

Conlon Nancarrow moved from the US to Mexico City in 1940 largely because of his communist affiliations. He spent the rest of his life there in almost total isolation, composing for player-pianos because he knew performers would never cope with his complex rhythms. Times have changed, and pianists and ensembles have been taking up the challenge by using transcriptions of some of his studies. Those used here are by composers Yvar Mikhashoff and Erik Ona and the Bugallo-Williams duo themselves. The results are simply stunning.

Nancarrow's experience as a jazz trumpeter and knowledge of *The Rite of Spring* were catalysts for a distinctive contrapuntal idiom, in which separate voices are superimposed at different speeds leading to acoustic overcrowding and apparent chaos. But it's all finely controlled: several pieces stop dead on a unison or a major chord.

By the late 1970s Nancarrow was beginning to be rediscovered and, in a more appreciative context, wrote for live performers again, including *Tango?* and *Three Canons for Ursula* (Oppens). The studies work just as well with live pianists as with the twangy sound of Nancarrow's own player-pianos. Obviously some of the very fast studies will never be playable, but, since he allowed some transcription, there's no harm when performers of this calibre can rise to the occasion so brilliantly. This wonderfully affirmative music not only questions conventional notions about rhythm but provides a uniquely exhilarating experience for the listener – well recorded and really attractive in every way.

José de Nebra   Spanish 1702-1768

José de Nebra was principal organist of the Spanish royal chapel and the Descalzas Reales convent at Madrid from 1724; in 1751 he became deputy director of the chapel and head of the choir school. A highly successful theatre composer, he had 57 stage works performed in Madrid and Lisbon in 1723-30 and 1737-51 (none in 1731-6). Whether secular or sacred, they combine comic, folklike and tragic elements, and all include spoken dialogue. He also wrote (especially from the 1740s) music for the royal chapel.   GROVEmusic

Miserere

Miserere. Iphigenia en Tracia – Allegro cantabile; 'Yo soy, tyrana'; 'Ha, ingrato'
Marta Almajano sop **Xenia Meijer** mez **Al Ayre Español / Eduardo López Banzo** hpd
Deutsche Harmonia Mundi 05472 77532-2
(58' · DDD) Texts and translations included   ℗○

This CD is an absolute stunner. It's the eighth recording in a sequence of increasingly polished and insightful performances exploring the almost uncharted territory of the vocal and instrumental repertory of the Spanish court and theatre in the 17th and 18th centuries.

José de Nebra, the 300th anniversary of whose birth is being celebrated in Spain with recordings and performances, is clearly one of the most interesting figures of the period. He wrote much theatre music, mostly for the public theatres in Madrid, before dedicating himself, from about 1750, to the composition of sacred music for the royal chapel. Al Ayre Español give us a taste of both theatre and chapel with his setting of the Miserere and two extracts from the *zarzuela* (a Spanish version of semi-opera) *Iphigenia en Tracia* of 1747.

As one might expect from such an experienced composer for the stage, the Miserere is a dramatic work, which in this excellent performance continually arrests the attention. Eduardo López Banzo, his small ensemble of strings and continuo and his two superb singers, Marta Almajano and Xenia Meijer, really seem to have got the measure of this piece. Clearly influenced by the Italian, and perhaps primarily the Neapolitan idiom, there are also more *galant* features and at times a penchant for the unexpected harmonic twist or melodic turn that's reminiscent of CPE Bach, though it isn't at all clear that Nebra would have known his music.

The psalm is set *in alternatim*, that is with alternate verses set for solo voice or duet and strings, leaving the remaining verses to be sung to plainchant, as here, or perhaps – something the group might experiment with – organ elab-

orations of the chant. It may take you a while to become accustomed to the aural shock of hearing plainchant and 18th-century operatic arias juxtaposed; just one slight criticism of this CD is the difference in acoustic aura between the two (both were recorded in the same venue but at different times). Both singers perform with utter conviction and panache, and the duets are beautifully matched.

The instrumental and vocal extracts from Nebra's *Iphigenia* are equally compelling. If you've yet to experience the Spanish Baroque, there could be no better introduction; if you're already a fan of Al Ayre Español you'll probably agree that this is their best recording yet.

Carl Nielsen   Danish 1865-1931

Nielsen had a poor, rural upbringing, though his father was a musician and he learnt to play the violin, brass instruments and the piano. He studied at the Copenhagen Conservatory (1884-6), then continued having lessons with Orla Rosenhoff. In 1890-91 he travelled to Germany, France and Italy, and began his Brahmsian First Symphony (1892); from 1889 to 1905 he played the violin in the Danish court orchestra.

During the decade from the First Symphony to the Second ('The Four Temperaments', 1902) he developed an extended tonal style, but compacted and classical in its logic: the relatively few works of this period include the string quartets in G minor and E flat, the cantata Hymnus amoris and the opera Saul and David. Here he showed a gift for sharp musical characterisation, pursued in his second opera, the comedy Maskarade (1906) and other works, while his parallel command of large-scale, dynamic forms was affirmed by the Third Symphony (Sinfonia espansiva, 1911) and the Violin Concerto (1911).

From this period he was an international figure and went abroad often to conduct his own music, while working in Copenhagen as a conductor and teacher. At the same time his music became still more individual in its progressive tonality (movements or works ending in a key different from the initial one), 'group polyphony' (the orchestra being treated as an assembly of ensembles in counterpoint), vigorous rhythmic drive and dependence on a harmony not so much of chords as of focal pitches. His chief works were still symphonies (no. 4 'The Inextinguishable', 1916; No.5, 1922) and chamber pieces (F major quartet, 1919; Serenata in vano for quintet, 1914), but he also produced numerous songs and hymn tunes, in addition to incidental scores.

The range of his output remained broad during his last decade, but his textures became still more polyphonic and his ideas still more vividly characterised, bringing a conversational style, intimate or dramatic, to such works as the Sixth Symphony (Sinfonia semplice, 1925), the Wind Quintet (1922) and the concertos for flute (1926) and clarinet (1928). His last works, going still deeper into the great contrapuntal tradition, include the Three Motets (1929) and Commotio for organ (1931).   GROVEmusic

Clarinet Concerto

Nielsen Clarinet Concerto, FS129 **Lutosławski** Dance
Preludes **Prokofiev** Flute Sonata in D, Op 94
(arr Kennan)
Richard Stoltzman cl **Warsaw Philharmonic
Orchestra / Lawrence Leighton Smith**
RCA Red Seal 09026 63836-2 (66' · DDD)　　Ⓕ

Richard Stoltzman's Nielsen, Prokofiev and
Lutosławski compilation is a fine achievement.
He brings to the Nielsen Concerto both virtuosity and depth of characterisation. There may
be other ways of presenting this complex musical character-study but hid fluency and broad
expressive range are as impressive as any modern recorded account. The Warsaw Philharmonic under Lawrence Leighton Smith sound
exceptionally well prepared. They lend a natural
idiomatic pliancy to the Lutosławski *Dance Preludes*, where Stoltzman is perkiness personified,
and make a fine foil for him in the Concerto.

Kent Kennan's orchestration of the Prokofiev
Flute Sonata is also well worth hearing – indeed,
well worth taking up by other clarinettists. This
is a tactful and adroit arrangement for chamber
orchestra. Stoltzman lavishes care on the solo
part, making a persuasive case for the *Scherzo* as
an *allegretto scherzando* rather than Prokofiev's
suggested *presto*. His romanticised approach to
the slow movement is less convincing, but his
earthy characterisation of the finale is admirable.

RCA's recording quality is outstanding.

Violin Concerto, FS61

Nielsen Violin Concerto[a]. **Sibelius** Violin Concerto in
D minor, Op 47[b]
Cho-Liang Lin vn [a]**Swedish Radio Symphony
Orchestra,** [b]**Philharmonia Orchestra / Esa-Pekka
Salonen**
Sony Classical Theta SMK89748 (69' · DDD)
Recorded 1987-8　　Ⓜ**OOO**

At the time it was first issued, this was
the best recording of the Sibelius Concerto to have appeared for over a
decade, and probably the best ever of the
Nielsen. It remains one of the classic concerto
recordings of the century. Cho-Liang Lin
brings an apparently effortless virtuosity to both
concertos. He produces a wonderfully clean and
silvery sonority, and there's no lack of aristocratic finesse.

Only half a dozen years separate the two concertos, yet they breathe a totally different air.
Lin's perfect intonation and tonal purity excite
admiration and throughout them both there's
a strong sense of line from beginning to end.
Esa-Pekka Salonen gets excellent playing from
the Philharmonia Orchestra in the Sibelius and
almost equally good results from the Swedish
Radio Symphony Orchestra.

Violin Concerto. Flute Concerto. Clarinet Concerto
Toke Lund Christiansen fl **Niels Thomsen** cl
Kim Sjøgren vn **Danish National Radio Symphony
Orchestra / Michael Schønwandt**
Chandos CHAN8894 (80' · DDD) Recorded 1990　Ⓕ

Kim Sjøgren may not command the purity of
tone of Cho-Liang Lin but he has the inestimable advantage of totally idiomatic orchestral support: Michael Schønwandt has an
instinctive feeling for this music – and it shows
throughout. The perspective between soloist
and orchestra is well judged (Sjøgren is never
larger than life) and so is the internal balance. In
the Flute Concerto, which veers from Gallic wit
to moments of great poetic feeling, Toke Lund
Christiansen is an excellent soloist. He has no
want of brilliance or of authority and his performance is also endowed with plenty of character. Niels Thomsen's account of the Clarinet
Concerto is one of the very finest now before
the public. If there's any music from another
planet, this is it! There's no attempt to beautify
the score nor to overstate it: every dynamic
nuance and expressive marking is observed by
both the soloist and the conductor. Thomsen
plays as though his very being is at stake and
Michael Schønwandt secures playing of great
imaginative intensity from the Danish Radio
Orchestra.

Symphonies

No 1 in G minor, FS16; **No 2** FS29, 'The Four
Temperaments'; **No 3**, FS60, 'Sinfonia espansiva';
No 4, FS76, 'The inextinguishable'; **No 5**, FS97;
No 6, FS116, 'Sinfonia semplice'

Symphonies Nos 1, 2 & 3[a]. Maskarade – Overture.
Aladdin – Suite, FS89
[a]**Nancy Wait Fromm** sop [a]**Kevin McMillan** bar **San
Francisco Symphony Orchestra / Herbert
Blomstedt**
Double Decca 460 985-2DF2 (134' · DDD) Recorded
1989　　Ⓜ**OOO**
The complete symphonies with San Francisco SO /
Blomstedt / are also available in a box set: Decca
443 117-2DH3　　Ⓕ

Nielsen always nurtured a special
affection for his First Symphony – and
rightly so, for its language is natural
and unaffected. It has great spontaneity of feeling and a Dvořákian warmth and freshness.
Blomstedt's recording is vital, beautifully
shaped and generally faithful to both the spirit
and the letter of the score. The recording is very
fine: the sound has plenty of room to expand,
there's a very good relationship between the
various sections of the orchestra and a realistic
perspective. The Second and Third are two of
Nielsen's most genial symphonies, both of
which come from the earliest part of the century, in performances of the very first order.

The Second (1902), inspired by the portrayal of *The Four Temperaments* (Choleric, Phlegmatic, Melancholic, Sanguine) that he had seen in a country inn, has splendid concentration and fire and, as always, from the right pace stems the right character. Moreover the orchestra sounds inspired, for there's a genuine excitement about its playing. Indeed Blomstedt's accounts are by far the most satisfying available. The Third, *Espansiva*, is even more personal in utterance than *The Four Temperaments*, for during the intervening years Nielsen had come much further along the road of self-discovery. His melodic lines are bolder, the musical paragraphs longer and his handling of form more assured. It's a glorious and richly inventive score whose pastoral slow movement includes a part for two wordless voices. Blomstedt gives us an affirmative, powerful reading and in the slow movement, the soprano produces the required ethereal effect. The sound is very detailed and full bodied, and in the best traditions of the company. Blomstedt's *Espansiva* has greater depth than most accounts; the actual sound has that glowing radiance that characterises Nielsen, and the tempo, the underlying current on which this music is borne, is expertly judged – and nowhere better than in the finale.

Symphonies Nos 1 & 2
Finnish Radio Symphony Orchestra / Jukka-Pekka Saraste
Finlandia 8573-85574-2 (64' · DDD)   Ⓕ

Saraste's characterisation of the Second Symphony is absolutely winning. The headlong momentum of the 'Choleric Temperament', the charm of the 'Phlegmatic' non-*scherzo*, the immensely sympathetic 'Melancholic' slow movement, and the tremendous sense of well-being in the 'Sanguine' finale: all these are spot-on. Alongside Blomstedt (reviewed above) I'm inclined to rate this the most successful modern recording of No 2, and for anyone interested in this particular coupling, Saraste's accounts are greatly preferable to Bryden Thomson's. Finlandia's recording quality is respectable, though Decca's larger sound-stage for Blomstedt makes for airier perspectives.

Saraste neither over-sells nor under-sells the First Symphony, and the balance he finds between feeling and flow in the slow movement is the sure sign of a conductor with a strong instinct for Nielsen. In the first movement he slightly overplays the music's Berliozian self-assertiveness; vital though that ingredient is, it needs to be set off by a more palpable sense of wonder in such places as the opening of the development section. Saraste launches the *scherzo* at an extraordinary lick. Not only are the rhythms uncomfortably bustled along as a result, but he has to rein in when the dotted figures appear. Most of the finale, though, is splendidly done.

This is a most likeable Nielsen cycle – not quite as classily played as Blomstedt's with his San Franciscans, and not always entirely persuasive in choice of tempo, but always well prepared and exuding both enthusiasm and intelligence.

Symphony No 1. Flute Concerto. Rhapsody Overture: An imaginary trip to the Faroe Islands, FS123
Patrick Gallois *fl* **Gothenburg Symphony Orchestra / Myung-Whun Chung**
BIS CD454 (63' · DDD) Recorded 1989   Ⓕ

This recording of the First Symphony is hardly less fine than that of Blomstedt. Tempos are generally well judged and there's a good feeling for the overall architecture of the piece. It gets off to a splendid start and Chung shapes the second group affectionately. He doesn't put a foot wrong in the slow movement, which has a splendid sense of line, and phrasing which is attentive but never overemphatic. The finale is exhilaratingly played. Throughout the work Chung knows how to build up to a climax and keep detail in the right perspective. As always, the Gothenburg Symphony plays with enthusiasm and spirit, as if it has always lived with this music and yet, paradoxically, is discovering it for the first time. The Rhapsody Overture, *An imaginary trip to the Faroe Islands*, begins most imaginatively but inspiration undoubtedly flags. The performance of the Flute Concerto is rather special. It's most strongly characterised by Patrick Gallois who plays with effortless virtuosity and an expressive eloquence that's never over- or understated. His purity of line in the first movement is quite striking and he has the measure of the poignant coda. His dynamic range is wide, the tone free from excessive vibrato and his approach fresh.

Symphonies Nos 2 & 3
National Symphony Orchestra of Ireland / Adrian Leaper
Naxos 8 550825 (68' · DDD) Recorded 1994   Ⓢ

The vital current on which every phrase must be borne in Nielsen needs to flow at higher voltage. This is music which needs to be played at white heat. Well, there's certainly no lack of electricity in Leaper's reading of the Second. He sets a cracking pace for the first movement, the choleric temperament, and hardly puts a foot wrong in its three companions. His tempos in the *Sinfonia espansiva* are well judged and sensible throughout all four of the movements. The finale, where many conductors get it wrong, seems to be just right. These are more than just serviceable performances: they're very good indeed and the Irish orchestra sounds well rehearsed and inside the idiom. You can pay more and do worse although some collectors will think the additional polish one gets from Blomstedt or Myung-Whun Chung is worth the extra outlay. These latter performances continue to grow in stature, and it's no mean compliment to the Naxos versions to say that they give them a very good run for their money. Naxos doesn't identify the singers in the slow movement of the *Espansiva*. No one investing in this issue and then going on to either of the Blomstedt accounts is going to feel that they have been let down. The recording team secures a very decent balance: well laid-back wind and brass, with good front-to-back perspective and transparency of texture.

Symphonies Nos 3 & 5
Catherine Bott *sop* **Stephen Roberts** *bar* **Royal Scottish Orchestra / Bryden Thomson**
Chandos CHAN9067 (71' · DDD) Recorded 1991 Ⓕ

Bryden Thomson and the Royal Scottish Orchestra give fresh and direct readings of the Espansiva and the Fifth which are eminently satisfying. At no point are we aware of the conductor interposing himself between composer and listener, and one can sense an evident enthusiasm on the part of the players. This is Nielsen plain and unadorned without any frills. Thomson has a very good feeling for Nielsen's tempos and his account of the finale feels exactly right. It's a splendidly sane performance with good singing from the fine soloists in the slow movement.

The Fifth Symphony is another unaffected and straightforward performance that has a great deal going for it – not least the beautiful clarinet playing in the coda, and the thoroughly committed second movement. One is, perhaps, more aware of the beat in the first movement than in Blomstedt's Decca account and it rarely seems to float or sound disembodied as it does with him. However, Thomson achieves very spirited playing from the orchestra and the recordings are very good and present, even if the sound lacks the transparency Decca achieves for Blomstedt. Eminently enjoyable, ardent performances that can hold their head high.

Symphonies Nos 4-6. Little Suite in A minor, FS6[a]. Hymnus Amoris[b]
[b]**Barbara Bonney** *sop* [b]**John Mark Ainsley,** [b]**Lars Pedersen** *tens* b**Michael W Hansen,** [b]**Bo Anker Hansen** *bars* **San Francisco Symphony Orchestra / Herbert Blomstedt;** [a]**Danish National Radio Symphony Orchestra /** [a]**Ulf Schirmer**
Double Decca 460 988-2DF2 (142' · DDD) ⓂⓄ
The complete symphonies with Blomstedt / San Francisco SO are also available in a box set: Decca 443 117-2DH3 Ⓕ

The Fourth and Fifth are two of Nielsen's most popular and deeply characteristic symphonies. Blomstedt's are splendid performances. The Fourth occupied Nielsen between 1914 and early 1916 and reveals a level of violence new to his art. The landscape is harsher; the melodic lines soar in a more anguished and intense fashion (in the case of the remarkable slow movement, 'like the eagle riding on the wind', to use Nielsen's own simile). Blomstedt's opening has splendid fire and he isn't frightened of letting things rip. The finale with its exhilarating dialogue between the two timpanists comes off splendidly.

The Fifth Symphony of 1922 is impressive, too: it starts perfectly and has just the right glacial atmosphere. The climax and the desolate clarinet peroration into which it dissolves are well handled. The recording balance couldn't be improved upon: the woodwind are well recessed (though clarinet keys are audible at times), there's an almost ideal relationship between the various sections of the orchestra and a thoroughly realistic overall perspective.

Blomstedt has a good rapport with his players who sound in excellent shape and respond instinctively to these scores.

Blomstedt's account of the Sixth Symphony is a powerful one, with plenty of intensity and an appreciation of its extraordinary vision. It's by far the most challenging of the cycle and inhabits a very different world from early Nielsen. The intervening years had seen the cataclysmic events of the First World War and Nielsen was suffering increasingly from ill health. Blomstedt and the fine San Fransisco orchestra convey the powerful nervous tension of the first movement and the depth of the third, the *Proposta seria*.

Symphonies Nos 4 & 5
Finnish Radio Symphony Orchestra / Jukka-Pekka Saraste
Finlandia 3984-21439-2 (72' · DDD) Ⓕ

Symphony No 5 also available (coupled with No 6) on Warner Elatus 0927-49424-2 Ⓜ

This is an impressive account of the Symphony No 4 which can hold its own among the very best. The Finnish RSO brings a feeling of urgent intensity to the slow movement and Saraste is attentive to matters of dynamics and phrasing. He builds up the musical argument powerfully to a convincing climax. Nor can No 5 be faulted: it's also powerfully conceived with a strong command of both detail and the overall architecture of the piece. The opening moves but is atmospheric, with careful attention to dynamic nuance and texture. The *tranquillo* section (two bars before fig 24: track 5) is most sensitively handled: it's both poetic and mysterious.

The engineers cope admirably with the dryish acoustic of the Helsinki Culture Hall: they produce exemplary clarity and it's only at the ends of movements or in the general pause that precedes the final *Allegro* of No 4 where one becomes aware of this. Among modern recordings, this issue deserves to be recommended alongside Blomstedt's San Francisco coupling. You may even prefer it.

Symphonies Nos 4 & 6
Royal Scottish National Orchestra / Bryden Thomson

Chandos CHAN9047 (70' · DDD) Recorded 1991 Ⓕ

Bryden Thomson's accounts of the Fourth and Sixth call to mind the ardent intensity of the pioneering Danish recordings (no longer available) by Launy Gróndahl and Thomas Jensen, such are their fire. The orchestra plays with total commitment and the underlying violence of No 4 makes a powerful impact, both at the opening and in the finale. But his Sixth is arguably the very finest version of the work on disc, notwithstanding the cultured and splendidly recorded account by Herbert Blomstedt.

Thomson strikes exactly the right tempo for the first movement and the problematic 'Humoreske' has never made better sense. He takes it at a steadier pace than most rival conductors, so that its questioning spirit registers. The third movement, the 'Proposta seria', is both eloquent and searching.

Even in a strongly competitive field this splendidly recorded Chandos account brings one closer to this extraordinary work than any other.

Wind Quintet, FS100

Nielsen Wind Quintet, FS100 **Fernström** Wind Quintet, Op 59 **Kvandal** Wind Quintet, Op 34. Three Sacred Folktunes, Op 23b
Oslo Wind Quintet (Tom Ottar Andreasson *fl* Lars Peter Berg *ob* Arild Stav *cl* Hans Peter Aasen *bn* Jan Olav Marthinsen *hn*)
Naxos 8 553050 (70' · DDD) Recorded 1993 Ⓢ

This thoroughly entertaining CD combines three very different and unfamiliar works with what's probably the finest wind quintet ever penned. The major item here is the Nielsen: a glorious work which achieves the rare combination of seriousness of expression as well as being utterly relaxed in tone. The Oslo ensemble is a little slower than usual, but its measured tempos are most convincing; indeed, in the finale they highlight musical connections with Nielsen's Fifth and Sixth Symphonies in ways rarely heard. The Swede John Axel Fernström was undeniably a minor composer. If his music doesn't possess many visionary qualities it's certainly well crafted and his 1943 Quintet is an engaging concert opener. Johan Kvandal from Norway is a weightier proposition and better-known outside of his native country than is Fernström. Kvandal's Quintet, Op 34 (1971), was written for the Oslo ensemble and is serious and high-minded in tone, contrasting effectively with both the Fernström and Kvandal's own *Sacred Folktunes* of 1963. In the Quintet's fast second movement Kvandal adopts a rather Shostakovichian manner, even alluding to the Soviet master's 12th Symphony, though to what purpose is unexplained. The idiomatic playing is reproduced in a slightly flat recording (made in the studios of Norwegian Radio), although the Naxos sound has great immediacy.

String Quartets

No 1 in G minor, FS4; **No 2** in F minor, FS11; **No 3** in E flat, FS23; **No 4** in F, FS36

String Quartets Nos 1 & 2
Oslo Quartet (Geir Inge Lotsberg, Per Kristian Skalstad *vns* Are Sandbakken *va* Oystein Sonstad *vc*)
Naxos 8 553908 (62' · DDD) Ⓢ Ⓞ

Nielsen wrote five quartets in all between 1882 and 1919, although two exist in different versions, and the opus numbering is contradictory. This may explain why Naxos gets itself into such a pickle over the numbering of the G minor and F minor Quartets here, the second and third he composed. (The early D minor of 1882-3 remains unnumbered.) The G minor, Op 13 (FS4; 1887-8 but thoroughly rewritten in 1898) is No 1 and the F minor, Op 5 (FS11; 1890) is No 2. The front cover cites the works correctly as 'Quartets No 1, Op 13. No 2, Op 5', but the back cover has 'Quartet No 1 in F minor, Op 5 (Rev 1898)' and 'No 2 in G minor, Op 13 (1890)', managing thus to confuse both dates and numbering. Although in his notes Keith Anderson lays out the composition history quite simply, he refers only to the opus numbers, which should be consigned to oblivion and replaced by the more accurate Fog-Schousboe numbers.

The performances are as clear-sighted as the labelling is a mess. As with the first volume, the Oslo are sympathetic exponents, and do not overlay any extraneous expression on the music as the disappointing Zapolski for Chandos did. Like the almost exactly contemporaneous early Sibelius quartets, there's barely a hint of the familiar, mature Nielsen in either work, but both are well crafted and beautifully written for the instruments. The Oslo seem completely at home in the style, more so than either the Kontra for BIS (who, like the Zapolski, have the benefit of top-quality sound) or Danish (Kontrapunkt) Quartets, making them come alive as none of their rivals manage. The recording is, like Volume 1, a touch confined but not constricted; that aside, this disc can be unreservedly recommended.

String Quartets Nos 3 & 4
Oslo Quartet (Geir Inge Lotsberg, Per Kristian Skalstad *vns* Are Sandbakken *va* Øystein Sonstad *vc*)
Naxos 8 553907 (57' · DDD) Ⓢ

Why is it that quartets of international standing have not taken up the Nielsen quartets (or the Berwald or Stenhammar for that matter). They are marvellous pieces and their neglect outside Scandinavia seems quite unaccountable. This release by the Oslo Quartet is refreshingly straightforward, full of vitality and spirit. Both scores are played with evident feeling but without any intrusive expressive exaggeration. The recordings are a little closely balanced, and as a result *fortissimo* passages can sound a touch fierce and wiry, for example in the closing page or so of the first movement of the F major (seven minutes into track 5). A pity the Oslo doesn't have as well-balanced a recording as Chandos and the Danish engineers provide for the Zapolski. The quartet is scrupulous in observing dynamic markings and gives totally dedicated, idiomatic performances. Artistically it's the finest at any price point.

String Quartets Nos 1-4. Movements for String Quartet, FS3c
Danish Quartet (Tim Frederiksen, Arne Balk-Møller *vns* Claus Myrup *va* H Brendstrup *vc*)
Kontrapunkt ② 32150/1 (138' · DDD) Recorded 1992
Ⓕ

Nielsen composed two quartets and a string quintet during his student years. There was a gap of eight years between the F minor Quartet and the Third, in E flat, Op 14 (FS23) during which Nielsen had written his First Symphony, and another eight before the F major, Op 44 (FS36) saw the light of day. By this time he had written his opera, *Saul and David* and the best part of *Maskarade* as well as the Second Symphony. The Danish Quartet is very sensitive to dynamic nuance and phrases imaginatively. The F major Quartet goes deeper than the Third. There's a grace, an effortless fluency and a marvellous control of pace. Ideas come and go just when you feel they should; yet its learning and mastery is worn lightly. Though the earlier quartets aren't such perfect works of art, they're always endearing. The Danish Quartet is completely inside this music and is totally persuasive. In spite of the closely balanced recording this set gives real pleasure and can be recommended with enthusiasm.

Aladdin

Aladdin
Mette Ejsing *contr* Guido Paevatalu *bar* Danish National Radio Chamber Choir; Danish National Radio Symphony Orchestra / Gennadi Rozhdestvensky
Chandos CHAN9135 (79' · DDD) Recorded 1992.
Text and translation included   Ⓕ

Nielsen's music to Adam Oehlenschläger's *Aladdin* comes from 1917-18, and was commissioned for a particularly lavish production of the play at the Royal Theatre in Copenhagen. More than half the music consists of orchestral interludes to accompany processions and dances, most of which come in the Third Act. Many are delightful and endearing, and once heard difficult to get out of your head. Robert Simpson summed the work up in his Nielsen monograph: 'The market-square in Isfahan where four orchestras play in four different tempos suggesting marvellously the clashing colours, movements and sounds of an eastern market-place is undoubtedly the most striking and orig-

inal part of the music. Some of it isn't very interesting (the rather commonplace Blackamoors' Dance, for instance) but most is intensely perceptive and colourful.' It's full of characteristic Nielsen-esque touches, and although it isn't the composer at his very best, it offers many irresistible delights. Performance and recording are both superb.

Maskarade

Maskarade
Aage Haugland *bass* Jeronimus **Susanne Resmark** *contr* Magdelone **Gert Henning Jensen** *ten* Leander **Bo Skovhus** *bar* Henrik **Michael Kristensen** *ten* Arv **Kurt Ravn** *bar* Leonard **Henriette Bonde-Hansen** *sop* Leonora **Marianne Rørholm** *contr* Pernille **Johan Reuter** *bar* Night Watchman, Master of the Masquerade **Christian Christiansen** *bass* Tutor
Danish National Radio Choir and Symphony Orchestra / Ulf Schirmer
Decca Gramophone Awards Collection ② 475 214-2 (145' · DDD) Notes, text and translation included
ⒻⓄⓄⓄ

If you can keep a straight face through the master/servant antics of the club addicts Leander and Henrik, if you can stay uncharmed by the ageing, repressed Magdelone when she shows she can still cut a caper, if you can stop your foot tapping in the Act 3 Maskarade itself, and if you can remain unmoved by the gentle pathos of the demasking scene, then you're made of very stern stuff. Not surprisingly, it's thoroughly idiomatic. Since the first production in 1906 *Maskarade* has been Denmark's national opera, and all the principals here have the music in their blood. Gert Henning Jensen may be a rather tremulous Leander, but he sounds appropriately youthful, and the duets with his well-matched Leonora, Henriette Bonde-Hansen, are wonderfully touching. Bo Skovhus is in superb voice as the Figaro-esque Henrik. Aage Haugland is in magnificent voice and almost steals the show in Act 1 as the crusty old Jeronimus. Ulf Schirmer conducts with excellently judged tempos and a deep affection for the idiom. Above all he has a grasp of the underlying momentum of each act.

This recording restores traditionally cut or displaced passages and corrects a host of textual and musical details. This is a life-enhancing comic opera, comparable in many ways to Britten's *A Midsummer Night's Dream*. It's wonderful to hear the piece done full justice.

Pehr Henrik Nordgren   Finnish 1944

Nordgren studied musicology at the University of Helsinki, taking an MA in 1967, and composition as a private student of Joonas Kokkonen from 1965 to 1969. From 1970 to 1973, he studied composition and traditional Japanese music at the Tokyo University of Art and Music. Nordgren is a composer who transcends divisions between schools and styles combining, in various ways, elements of twelve-tone technique, Ligetian field technique, the Western tonal tradition, a meditative minimalism related to the music of Arvo Pärt, and Finnish and Japanese folk music. He has acknowledged Shostakovich as a particularly strong influence, but the affinity is one of expressive aims rather than style. Significant works include Euphonie II (1967), The Turning Point (1972) and 10 piano ballades (1972-8) – both of which draw upon Nordgren's interest and study into Japanese traditional music – three symphonies (1974, 1989, 1993) and Beaivi, Ah...áñan (The Sun, My Father) for soloists, choir and orchestra (1987–89) – a setting of poems in the Sámi language. He has also composed a number of concertos, chamber works, a few vocal works and two operas.

GROVEmusic

Symphonies Nos 2 & 4

Symphonies – No 2, Op 74; No 4, Op 98
Finnish Radio Symphony Orchestra / Juha Kangas
Finlandia 3984-29720-2 (55' · DDD)   Ⓕ●

Cello Concerto No 1, Op 50[a]. Concerto for Strings, Op 54[b]. Violin Concerto No 3, Op 53[c]. Equivocations, Op 55[d]. Nine Kwaidan Ballades[e]
[c]**Kaija Saarikettu**, [d]**Reijo Tunkkari** vns [d]**Timo Kangas** va [a]**Erkki Rautio** vc [d]**Niiles Outakoski** vc [d]**Ritva Koistinen** kantele [e]**Izumi Tateno** pf [abc]**Ostrobothnian Chamber Orchestra / Juha Kangas**
Finlandia Meet the Composer ② 3984 23408-2 (154' · DDD) Recorded 1984,1990, 1992-3   Ⓜ●

The darkly eloquent, recent Fourth Symphony is an ideal introduction to the impressive sound world of Pehr Henrik Nordgren, though it's more richly scored and denser in texture than anything on the two-disc set (one of Finlandia's valuable Meet the Composer compilations). The Fourth begins turbulently, and often during its course rises to forbidding, dissonantly fraught climaxes. But, as often in his work, the complexity is built from simple constituents – a phrase from *Boris Godunov*, Finnish folk melodies – and at the centre and the end of the symphony the textures clear to reveal a solitary herdsman playing a pipe and a hushed, solemn string chorale. The effect is moving, but the presence of those simple motifs amidst the uproar that surrounds the islands of tense calm gives them a grandeur, even a nobility and the whole work a powerful sense of drama.

The Second Symphony (1989) is longer, its contrasts more violent, its unifying elements harder to perceive, but its coherence is striking. Even in a densely complex *tutti* or a texture thinned to nothing more than a string shimmer and a few isolated piano notes the sense of movement and destination is tangible.

On the two-disc set the ideal starting-point is the *Concerto for Strings*. Characteristic of Nordgren again is the way that the first movement is derived from two ideas, one unchanging (a simple, pulsing rhythm), the other a melodic figure which is both extended and simplified, becom-

ing intensely expressive in the process. The central movement is an exciting, virtuoso toccata; the finale a sombre meditation on two simple ideas. Both concertos also build great variety from simple material (the Cello Concerto begins with single notes so precisely judged that a four-note rising phrase from the soloist has real lyrical eloquence), while the gripping *Equivocations* uses the Finnish national instrument, the kantele, to evoke an archaic folk world without ever quoting folk melody.

There's an improvisatory element to Nordgren's music, too, a feeling of ideas suggesting other ideas and dictating their own form. The *Kwaidan Ballades*, each prompted by one of Lafcadio Hearn's Japanese ghost stories, often give the impression of a tale told not in words but in formidably pianistic gestures. Izumi Tateno plays them with great eloquence and resource; indeed all the performances here, by artists closely associated with the composer, are vividly communicative. Finely recorded.

Vítezslav Novák   Bohemian 1870-1949

Novák studied with Jiránek and Dvořák at the Prague Conservatory (1889-92) and was powerfully influenced by the folk music of Moravia and Slovakia, which he began to collect and study in 1896. The result was an outpouring of symphonic poems and songs, culminating in the dramatic cantata The Storm (1910) and the large-scale tone poem Pan for piano (1910). In 1909 he began teaching at the Prague Conservatory, and this occupied him more than composition in his later years, though he wrote several operas, much choral music and a few late instrumental scores, of which the Autumn Symphony (1934) and the South Bohemian Suite are representative. A skilled melodist and contrapuntist, he retained an essentially late Romantic style, which was supported by a meticulous technique.

GROVEmusic

De profundis

Toman and the Wood Nymph, Op 40. Lady Godiva, Op 41. De profundis, Op 67
BBC Philharmonic Orchestra / Libor Pešek
Chandos CHAN9821 (66' · DDD)   Ⓕ●

Vítězslav Novák was a keen walker and each piece on this absorbing CD testifies to his vivid sense of outdoors. He was also fascinated by the female psyche and two of the works programmed bring rival viragos to mind: Smetana's 'Šárka' (in the opening pages of *Lady Godiva*) and Strauss's *Salome* (the close of *Toman and the Wood Nymph*).

Yet for all their lustre, excitement and charm, even *Godiva* and *Toman* can't rival the oppressive power of Novák's wartime masterpiece *De profundis*, a work that surely levels with Martinů's *Lidice* as being among the most poignant musical memorials of the period. Composed during the Nazi occupation of Czechoslovakia, *De profundis* finds Novák employing a significantly darkened palette, though the exultant closing section (track 7) bears little resemblance to the various politically motivated 'happy endings' that were surfacing elsewhere. Novák's use of the organ runs parallel with Scriabin's in *The Poem of Ecstasy* (albeit to very different effect).

Libor Pešek shows obvious sympathy for this repertoire and the playing of the BBC Philharmonic reaches formidable heights of passion, notably at the close of *De profundis*. Alternative discs of Novák's music are few and far between, and hard to come by.

Piano Quintet, Op 12

Piano Quintet in A minor, Op 12. 13 Slovak Folksongs. Songs of a Winter Night, Op 30
Magdalena Koženã *mez* **Radoslav Kvapil** *pf* **Kocian Quartet** (Pavel Hůla, Jan Odstrčil *vns* Zbynek Padourek *va* Václav Bernášek *vc*)
ASV CDDCA998 (67' · DDD) Texts and translations included   Ⓕ

Novák's A minor Piano Quintet of 1896 was composed in the wake of his first fruitful study of the folk-song traditions of both Moravia and Slovakia. It's an accomplished creation, comprising a finely sustained *Allegro molto moderato*, an effective central theme and variations (based on a 15th-century Czech love-song) and a joyous finale. Seven years later, Novák produced his piano suite, *Songs of a Winter Night*. Its four movements make a charming set, ranging in mood from the wistful intimacy of 'Song of a moonlight night' to the gleeful merry-making of the last in the series ('Song of a carnival night'). Even during the ecstatic pealing that marks the climax of the memorable 'Song of a Christmas night', Novák's piano writing always remains wonderfully pellucid, a factor that also adds to the listener's enjoyment of his six volumes of Slovak songs, 13 of which are heard here.

Gems include the plaintive *Sedla mucha* ('A fly sat on a cornflower') with its bewitching piano traceries, the harmonically searching *Svic, mila, mas komu* ('Light the lamp, my love') and the tragic tale of *Chodzila Mariska* ('Mariska's walking along the bank').

Radoslav Kvapil and the Kocian Quartet form a thoroughly convincing alliance in the early Piano Quintet. The excellent Kvapil also shines in the solo suite (although the balance is slightly too close), and in the song sequence he provides some tenderly idiomatic support to the characterful mezzo, Magdalena Koženã.

Michael Nyman   British b1944

Nyman studied at the Royal Academy of Music with Alan Bush and with Thurston Dart at King's College, London. He wrote the seminal book Experi-mental Music: Cage and Beyond (1974). In his compositions he aims to break down the barrier between popular culture and 'serious' composition. He is best known for his film scores, including The Draughtsman's Contract (1982), The Cook, the Thief, his Wife and her Lover (1989), Prospero's Books (1991) and The Piano (1993). He has also written five operas, among which The Man who Mistook his Wife for a Hat (1986) amply demonstrates his musical style in its use of variation and modular form, lyrical vocal lines over restless, repetitive phrases and repeated harmonic blocks.
GROVEmusic

The Piano Concerto

The Piano Concerto. MGV (Musique à Grande Vitesse)
Kathryn Stott *pf* **Royal Liverpool Philharmonic Orchestra; Michael Nyman Band; orchestra / Michael Nyman**
Argo 443 382-2ZH (59' · DDD) Recorded 1994   Ⓕ

After the international success of Jane Campion's film *The Piano*, Nyman adapted his celebrated score into a concert piece. Though performed uninterrupted, the 32-minute concerto is divided into four clear-cut sections. The Scottish folk-songs on which much of it is based imbue the piece with a yearning, heartfelt quality not usually associated with this composer. Indeed, the whole concerto, as so convincingly advocated by Kathryn Stott and the RLPO, throbs with an unbridled Romantic fervency that may come as something of a shock to hardened Nymanites or those who appreciate the less grandiose scoring for the film. More recognisably Nymanesque is *MGV*, a sort of *Pacific 231* for the 1990s, composed for the inauguration of the TGV North-European line in France. Here the composer's abstract style is eminently suited to describing a non-stop, imaginary railway journey through five regions between Paris and Lille; his repeated phrases and chugging, insistently propulsive rhythms create a spellbinding effect, with the strings adding an especially effective sense of speed and visual sweep. A rewarding disc that will appeal to Nyman fans old and new.

String Quartets

String Quartets Nos 1-3
Balanescu Quartet (Alexander Balanescu, Johnathan Carney *vns* Kate Musker *va* Anthony Hinnigan *vc*)
Decca 473 091-2DM (63' · DDD) Recorded 1991   Ⓜ

So celebrated is Michael Nyman as a composer for the screen that it's easy to underestimate the extent of his commitment to the concert hall. This recording helps to redress that balance. The Balanescu – dedicatees of the Second and Third, and clearly ardent chamions of the First String Quartet – play with enthusiasm and great vigour. The First in particular is immensely enjoyable, drawing heavily (and audibly) on a keyboard piece by the Elizabethan virginalist John Bull, manipulated (far less audibly) by ideas extracted from Schoenberg's Second Quartet, and subjected to typical Nymanesque principles of variation, ground bass, dismemberment and, when the time seems right, rude parody. Thus poetry and banality rub shoulders; the elation of the opening, and the ecstasies of track 12 give way to some marvellous kitsch in the centre, only to metamorphose into an ending which, within the curious terms of the piece, achieves a remarkable apotheosis of sorts. This is the Nyman one knows and loves.

Dance informs the Second Quartet, which was commissioned for and partly organised to match the choreography of Shobana Jeyasingh. Nyman's notes acknowledge a debt to Karnatic music, and though the piece is full of energy, and must make a marvellous ballet, it's thinner on ideas than its predecessor. The Third is something quite different. It functions as a chain of variations on *Out of the Ruins*, Nyman's hypnotic and startlingly beautiful soundtrack for the BBC documentary on the 1988 Armenian earthquake. Those who view Nyman as a lightweight need look no further than this piece to have their views put into disarray.

Jacob Obrecht   Netherlands c1450-1505

Obrecht was zangmeester at Utrecht, c1476-8, then choirmaster for the Corporation of Notre Dame at St Gertrude, Bergen op Zoom, 1479-84. He then became singing master at Cambrai, and on 13 October 1486 was installed as succentor at St Donatien, Bruges. After a visit to Italy he was appointed maître de chapelle at Bruges in 1490. In 1494 his name appears in the records of Notre Dame, Antwerp, and from then until his retirement in 1500 he alternated between Antwerp and Bergen op Zoom. He died of the plague while on a visit to Ferrara. As early as 1475 Tinctoris had mentioned him with the best and most renowned musicians, and other evidence suggests that he commanded the greatest respect. He wrote mainly sacred music. In his masses, and to a lesser extent in his motets, he brought to a culmination certain aspects of style that appeared in Dufay's last works and were developed by his successors, notably Busnois. One of his earliest masses, Missa 'Forseulement', combines the earlier practice of quoting the cantus firmus literally with newer, more varied techniques, such as the combination of the cantus firmus with the traditional chant in the Credo. Such variety of treatment continued to be a feature of his later masses. He normally changed the type of statement from movement to movement and exploited part-quotation, a cantus firmus moving from part to part and the simultaneous statement of material in two or more voices. His ingenuity in the quoting of borrowed material was inexhaustible. His counterpoint ranges from the serene (e.g. the Kyrie of the Missa Graecorum) to the hyperactive (e.g. the Missa 'Caput') but, unlike Josquin, he rarely maintained a single motivic pattern throughout a section

and his counterpoint thus lacks long-range function. His style also features full and sonorous writing, parallel 10ths between outer voices, skilful use of canon and emphasis on root-position chords. GROVEmusic

Missa Sub tuum praesidium

Missa Sub tuum presidium. Salve regina. Ave Regina caelorum. Ave maris stella. Alma Redemptoris Mater. Magnificat. Beata es Maria
Ars Nova / Paul Hillier
Ars Nova VANCD02 (63' · DDD) Texts and translations included   Ⓕ

Missa Sub tuum praesidium. Factor orbis. Salve crux. Salve regina a 3. Beata es Maria. Benedicamus in Laude. Mille Quingentis
The Clerks' Group / Edward Wickham
ASV Gaudeamus CDGAU341 (70' · DDD) Texts and translations included   Ⓕ

Back in the days of LPs, *Sub tuum presidium* was one of the first of Obrecht's masses to appear, and a second recording followed soon after. But 30 years have elapsed since then, so these two CDs are long overdue.

The scholar Birgit Lodes recently suggested that *Sub tuum praesidium* may be one of Obrecht's last mass settings. It's concise, both in terms of length and economy of means; at the same time its rich scoring packs a real punch. Its premise is typical of Obrecht at his most rational, but also visionary. The *Kyrie* begins with three voices; each movement adds another, culminating in the seven-voice *Agnus dei*. The *cantus firmus* recurs virtually unchanged in each movement, a fixed point; but as new voices and new chants (all of them Marian) are progressively added, the identity of the original plainchant is increasingly obscured as the texture thickens.

The tension between these two complementary processes generates a peculiar magic, and Ars Nova's performance captures this crucial feature. There's a certain lack of security in matters of detail, that may be put down to the recording venue: the church acoustic seems to dull the rhythmic angularity that characterises much of the mass: bursts of rapid runs often seem to lose crispness and direction, and Hillier's brisk tempos at the start of sections have a tendency to slacken.

Though Hillier sets more consistent tempos (and in this work consistency is surely a virtue: the contrasts in tempo in The Clerks' *Kyrie* are a bit forced), Wickham makes his decisions tell more meaningfully. Where Ars Nova occasionally sound rushed, The Clerks hold every rhythmic detail, every imitative flourish in place.

The role of the title *cantus firmus* is nicely contrasted in the two versions: with Hillier (who has more than one soprano on each line, even when the music divides into several top lines) the additional voices superimpose themselves on the main chant, as though actively obscuring it; Wickham splits his two sopranos once occasion demands it, so that the plainsong gives the impression of receding gradually, as though of its own accord, into the distance.

In the *Sanctus* and *Agnus dei* Wickham takes his foot off the throttle: that's one solution to the score's increasing complexity, and though Hillier maintains the tension, it's Wickham and his singers who defend their conception more persuasively.

The accompanying Marian motets on the Ars Nova disc are generally well sung, even though in a few cases (such as the oft-recorded six-voice *Salve regina*) more characterful alternatives are available.

The Clerks' recording, a return to form for the group, is one of the strongest and well-rounded introductions to Obrecht in the catalogue. *Salve crux* and *Factor orbis* rank among his most impressive statements. The Clerks don't eclipse memories of the Orlando Consort in *Salve crux*, but their reading offers a most effective contrast. Even a slender-looking piece such as the three-voice *Salve regina* is handled with a sure-footedness that signals regained confidence; the astonishing conclusion has a delicacy one mightn't readily associate with its composer. Every piece contains similarly striking insights, where music and musicians are perfectly in sync. *Beata es, Maria* has been recorded many times but never more lucidly than here. This seems to be the first recording of *Mille quingentis*, Obrecht's memorial to his father, a work whose hieratic structure doesn't inhibit depth of feeling.

Johannes Ockeghem

Flanders c1410-1497

The earliest reference to Ockeghem as a singer shows that he was a vicaire-chanteur at Notre Dame, Antwerp, for a year from June 24, 1443. His déploration on Binchois' death (1460) suggests a connection with the Burgundian ducal chapel where Busnois and Dufay worked. He entered the service of Charles I, Duke of Bourbon, in Moulins in the mid-1440s and was a member of the chapel in 1446-8. In the year ending September 30, 1453 he is cited in the French court archives 'nouveau en 1451'. This service continued during Louis XI's reign, though he held other offices, including a canonry at Notre Dame, Paris (1463-70). In 1470 he visited Spain, in 1484 Bruges and Dammes. After Louis death he remained premier chapelain and was still on the payroll in 1488. He enjoyed an enviable personal and professional reputation.

His most imposing works are his mass settings. Several are based on pre-existing material, sacred or secular. One of the earliest is probably the Missa Caput which states the cantus firmus in the lowest voice, but in other (probably later) works, such as the Missa De plus en plus, he varied the treatment of the cantus firmus, assimilating it increasingly to the rhythmic and melodic character of the other voices; his two incomplete mass cycles are based on late chan-

sons of his own, and his polyphonic Requiem is the earliest known setting. Others of his masses, including the Missa prolationum and the Missa Mi-mi, are freely composed. The former is perhaps the most extraordinary contrapuntal achievement of the 15th century, while the other clearly shows his own characteristic style, with its variations in mensuration, texture and sonority. His motets display even greater inventiveness, combining homophonic textures, skilful cantus firmus treatments, sweeping melodic lines, energetic rhythmic figures and frequent imitation. Most of his chansons use traditional formes fixes and feature treble-dominated textures, though some are canonic and occasionally anticipate early 16th-century chanson style. The level of contrapuntal skill and artistic excellence of his music laid a foundation for the achievements of Josquin's generation.

GROVEmusic

Missa Ecce ancilla Domini

Ockeghem Missa Ecce ancilla Domini. Missa Dei mater. Ave Maria. **Josquin des Prez** Déploration sur la mort de Johannes Ockeghem **Obrecht** Salve regina
The Clerks' Group / Edward Wickham
ASV Gaudeamus CDGAU223 (64' · DDD) Recorded 1993   (F)

Ockeghem Missa travail suis. Mort tu as navré. S'elle m'amera/Petite Camusette. Permanent vierge/Pulchra es/Sancta Dei genetrix. Missa sine nomine a 5. Intemerata Dei mater **Barbigant** Au travail suis
The Clerks' Group / Edward Wickham
ASV Gaudeamus CDGAU215 (55' · DDD)   (F)

The Clerks Group's recording of the Mass *Ecce ancilla Domini* remains one of their most satisfying achievements; how exciting it was to hear one of Ockeghem's most perfect Masses sung with such authority. Indeed, there are very few recordings of 15th-century polyphony to match this one. Their more recent disc is scarcely less impressive, and it, too, includes works that express Ockeghem's art in contrasted but typical ways. The five-voice Mass *Sine nomine* may seem slight on paper, but the Clerks' men make clear its effectiveness. And *Au travail suis* is one of the most strikingly distinctive of all 15th-century cycles, a study in contrasted, kaleidoscopic textures. Here, as elsewhere, the Clerks are mellifluous and slick: at times this is to the detriment of the music's delicious asperities (try the end of the *Credo*), but those who find the rival Pomerium Musices' account too mannered will welcome this more measured approach.

Lovers of vocal polyphony owe Edward Wickham and his singers a vote of thanks.

Missa L'homme armé

Ockeghem Missa L'homme armé. Ave Maria. Alma redemptoris mater **Josquin Desprez** Memor esto verbi tui **Plainchant** Alma redemptoris mater. Immittet angelus Domini **Anonymous** L'homme armé

Oxford Camerata / Jeremy Summerly
Naxos 8 554297 (57' · DDD) Texts and translations
included ⑤**O**

The centrepiece here is Ockeghem's *L'homme
armé* Mass. It may be one of his earliest Masses,
dating perhaps from the early 1450s. It's also
one of his most curious. For the most part it lies
in a relatively high register, belying his usual
predilection for low bass ranges; but every now
and again the basses descend in spectacular
fashion. In the third *Agnus* they hold down the
tune in very long notes, while the other voices
seem to float above them. Seldom before in the
history of music can the articulation of time
have been so clear a feature of a piece's design: it
seems almost to have been suspended altogether. It's an extraordinary moment, difficult
to pull off in performance, but here the singers
seem to have got it right. Elsewhere, Summerly's approach is nicely varied, but on the
whole more meditative than emphatic. The performance grows in stature with each movement,
as though keeping pace with the cycle's ambition. The reading isn't without the odd glitch,
but taken as a whole it's a fine achievement. The
accompanying motets work very well, but it's a
shame that the choir's richness of sound isn't
quite matched by the acoustic. But the overall
impression is resoundingly positive: those new
to Ockeghem should find this disc too good an
opportunity to pass up.

Missa De plus en plus

Missa De plus en plus. Presque transi. Prenez sur moi
vostre exemple. O rosa bella o dolce anima mia.
Aultre Venus estés. Petite camusette. Tant fuz
gentement. Mort tu as navré
Orlando Consort (Robert Harre-Jones *counterten*
Charles Daniels, Angus Smith *tens* Donald Greig *bar*)
Archiv Produktion Blue 471 727-2ABL (73' · DDD)
Texts and translations included ⓜ

This is a superb recording of Ockeghem's Mass
De plus en plus. The Orlandos' mixed programme of sacred and secular music offers a
good, rounded picture of Ockeghem's art. In
the Mass they're obvious first choice for those
who prefer a soloistic approach, or those for
whom anything other than countertenors on
top lines smacks of heresy. They're experienced
singers with logical phrasing and breathing in
solo passages, great interpretative acuteness,
and a quality of ensemble that's of itself expressive. They seem to achieve more with less. The
accompanying songs make the case for Ockeghem's versatility as a song composer, a point
emphasised by the differences of scoring to
which they're especially sensitive. This recording demonstrates the very different worlds of
the sacred and the secular; if the Orlandos seem
to experience trouble shifting gears between
the two, they certainly aren't alone, either in
England or abroad.

Missa prolationum

Ockeghem Missa prolationum. **Obrecht** (attrib)
Humilium decus. **Busnois** Gaude coelestis Domina.
In hydraulis. **Pullois** Flos de spina. **Josquin Desprez**
Illibata Dei Virgo nutrix
The Clerks' Group / Edward Wickham
ASV Gaudeamus CDGAU143 (65' · DDD) Ⓕ

This recording focuses on one of the most
astonishing compositional feats of the second
half of the 15th century: Ockeghem's *Missa prolationum*. The successive movements of the
Ordinary of the Mass are based on double
canons that progress from the unison to the
octave, while at the same time the composer also
exploits the inherent ambiguity of the mensural
system (and hence the work's title) of the later
Middle Ages so that the rhythmic relationships
between the voices are constantly being transformed. The astonishing thing is how effortlessly Ockeghem weaves his complex polyphonic web, and this is reinforced here by the
unfettered, direct way in which The Clerks'
Group approaches the music. Although there
are only eight singers in the group, they bring a
very satisfactory mix of the vocal agility one
might expect from a small ensemble and the
ability to sing through the long-breathed lines
favoured by Ockeghem, without ever sounding
strained or thin. The overall sound is closely
recorded, but it never lacks richness or blend.

Although at first sight the five motets on the
disc seem only loosely related to each other and
to the Mass, there are potentially illuminating
links: several of the composers appear to pay
homage, whether directly or indirectly, to one
another's pieces and in general they all opt for
quite self-consciously complex structures yet
create a musical idiom that's lucid and full of
emotional responses to the texts they chose to
set. No one could seriously doubt that this is the
Franco-Netherlandish school at its best.

Requiem

Ockeghem Requiem. Fors seulement. Missa Fors
seulement **Brumel** Du tout plongiet/Fors seulement
La Rue Fors seulement
The Clerks' Group / Edward Wickham
ASV Gaudeamus CDGAU168 (71' · DDD) Texts and
translations included Ⓕ**OOO**

 Top billing goes to the Requiem,
Ockeghem's most widely recorded
work, and perhaps his most enigmatic
piece, stylistically very wide-ranging and
diverse. Aesthetic judgement is hard to pass,
since it may well be incomplete; but the surviving movements contain some of his most arresting inspirations. This is the first version of any
quality to feature sopranos on the top lines.
Incidentally, no recording of the Requiem is
uniformly excellent; on the other hand, the
words of the Mass for the dead conjure up many
associations, and The Clerks deserve praise for

the verve and imagination with which they respond to the work's interpretative challenges. The fillers are the works built on Ockeghem's song *Fors seulement* (which includes Antoine Brumel's *Du tout plongiet*). It's difficult to decide which to praise more highly: the pieces themselves, which are incomparable, or the singing, which represents The Clerks' finest achievement to date. *Fors seulement* inspired a flowering of astonishing pieces scored for very low voices (initiated, it appears, by the composer himself): in both the Mass and in *Du tout plongiet*, the basses descendo written low Cs. In addition, these pieces are exceptionally richly scored (the Mass and the La Rue song are five-voice works), creating polyphony as dense and as dark as a strong Trappist ale. The Clerks achieve almost miraculous linear definition here, without losing an iota of the music's sensuous appeal: that's quite a feat, given the low pitch and awesome contrapuntal complexity involved. This must be counted as a major achievement.

Jacques Offenbach

German/French 1819-1880

Offenbach's career began with a year's study at the Paris Conservatoire and several years experience as a solo and orchestral cellist; he became a theatre conductor in 1850, finally getting his own stage works performed in 1855. Writing mainly for the Bouffes Parisiens, he reached the peak of his international success in the 1860s; revivals and tours, as well as the score of his serious opera Les contes d'Hoffmann (unfinished, completed by Guiraud), dominated the 1870s.

With Johann Strauss II, Offenbach was one of the two outstanding composers in popular music of the 19th century and writer of some of the most exhilaratingly gay, tuneful music ever written. Les contes d'Hoffmann has retained a place in the international repertory for its fantasy and its strongly appealing music; but his most significant achievements lie in operetta: Orphée aux enfers (1858), La belle Hélène (1864), La vie parisienne (1866), La Grande-Duchesse de Gérolstein (1867) and La Périchole (1868) are striking examples. Moreover, it was through the success of Offenbach's works abroad that operetta became an established international genre, producing major national exponents in Strauss, Sullivan and Léhar and evolving into the 20th-century musical.

Offenbach's comic subjects, usually satirical treatments of familiar stories with a sharp glance at contemporary society and politics, are enhanced by none-too-subtle musical devices, including the quotation of well-known operatic music in incongruous settings: his tunes are often built upon a rising phrase in a major key and his finales are made exciting by gradual tempo acceleration and the use of brass at climaxes. He had a rare gift for catchy tunes, usually in dance rhythms, and telling harmonic touches. Through its famous overture (in fact composed by Carl Binder) and can-can, Orphée aux enfers has remained his best-known operetta. **GROVE**music

Arias

Arias from Barbe-Bleue, La belle Hélène, Les contes d'Hoffmann[b], Fantasio[a], La fille du tambour-major, La Grande-Duchesse de Gérolstein[c], Lischen et Fritzchen[f]. Madame l'archiduc[cdef], La Périchole, La vie parisienne[cef]. Le carnaval des Revues[f]
Anne Sofie von Otter *mez* [a]**Magali Léger,** [b]**Stéphanie d'Oustrac** *sops* [c]**Gilles Ragon,** [d]**Jean-Christophe Keck,** [e]**Jean-Christophe Henry** *tens* [f]**Laurent Naouri** *bar* [d]**Christophe Grapperon** *bass* **Choeur des Musiciens du Louvre; Les Musiciens du Louvre / Marc Minkowski**
DG 471 501-2GH (70' · DDD) Recorded live 2001.
Texts and translations included   Ⓕ**OOO**

GAnne Sofie von Otter immediately stamps her brilliance on this fascinating collection as Offenbach's voluptuous Grand-Duchess. Her commanding projection and phrasing in 'Ah, que j'aime les militaires' are followed by tender lyricism in 'Dites-lui'. Gilles Ragon trills irresistibly as a youthful and virile Lieutenant Fritz in the 'Chanson militaire', and there's a refreshing spring in the step of Minkowski's conducting. There follow two glorious numbers from *Fantasio*, a virtually forgotten pre-*Hoffmann* serious work. The beautiful ballad 'Voyez dans la nuit brune' especially shows the genuine feeling of which Offenbach was capable, as well as the sheer beauty of von Otter's singing. We scarcely needed another *Hoffmann* Barcarolle, and yet the image of the gondola floating along the Grand Canal has seldom been created as gracefully as here. The rest is conceived with intelligence and imagination, and performed with equal brilliance, with the range of supporting performers heightening the variety of the collection.

The collection encompasses all that's fascinating in Offenbach's output – tender and sparkling by turns, engaging throughout – and all quite wonderfully performed. Irresistible!

La belle Hélène

La belle Hélène   Ⓟ
Felicity Lott *sop* Hélène **Yann Beuron** *ten* Pâris **Michel Sénéchal** *ten* Ménélas **Laurent Naouri** *bar* Agamemnon **François Le Roux** *bar* Calchas **Marie-Ange Todorovitch** *mez* Oreste **Eric Huchet** *bar* Achille **Alain Gabriel** *ten* Ajax I **Laurent Alvaro** *bar* Ajax II **Hjördis Thébault** *sop* Bacchis **Les Musiciens et Choeur des Musiciens du Louvre / Marc Minkowski**
Virgin Classics ② 545477-2 (118' · DDD) Texts and translations included   Ⓕ**OO**

From its very first bars, this recording strikes a chord of authenticity. Too often Offenbach's works are recorded with large orchestra, huge chorus and swimming-bath acoustics. Offenbach himself was perfectly happy to accept larger forces when available, but they do rather swamp the gossamer lightness and piquancy of what he actually composed. This newcomer derives from a stage production received enthusiastically at the Châtelet in Paris in September 2000. The feeling of a stage production pervades the recording in its integration of dialogue and music, as also in the uninhibited singing and playing of Orestes' opening couplets. Marie-Ange Todorovitch performs with appropriately boyish high spirits throughout, and Michel Sénéchal as Ménélas, Laurent Naouri as Agamemnon and François Le Roux as Calchas ensure this recording is cast from strength. Although Felicity Lott's Hélène lacks that distinctive French way of wrapping the voice round the words in her great arias, she succeeded in capturing Paris (the city as well as the Trojan prince). What appeals especially is her lightness of voice compared with the mezzo tones of many other interpreters. Yet the voice and interpretation that captivate the ear most here are those of Yann Beuron as Pâris. His honeyed tones are heard to absolute perfection throughout, but his *pianissimo* singing of the final verse of the 'Judgement of Paris' makes it an especially model interpretation. Moreover, Beuron has music to sing that isn't in any previous recording – a lullaby, complete with dove cooing, preceding the Dream Duet. There's more, too. In the 1865 German version, the scene of the Game of Goose was longer than in the 1864 French original, and here it's longer still. But most importantly, this is a sparkling, beautifully paced recording and is now a clear first choice for what's surely Offenbach's most captivating operetta.

Les contes d'Hoffmann

Les contes d'Hoffmann
Plácido Domingo ten Hoffmann **Dame Joan Sutherland** sop Olympia, Giulietta, Antonia, Stella **Gabriel Bacquier** bar Lindorf, Coppélius, Dapertutto, Dr Miracle **Huguette Tourangeau** mez La Muse, Nicklausse **Jacques Charon** ten Spalanzani **Hugues Cuénod** ten Andrès, Cochenille, Pitichinaccio, Frantz **André Neury** bar Schlemil **Paul Plishka** bass Crespel **Margarita Lilowa** mez Voice of Antonia's Mother **Roland Jacques** bar Luther **Lausanne Pro Arte Chorus; Du Brassus Chorus; Suisse Romande Chorus and Orchestra / Richard Bonynge**
Decca ② 417 363-2DH2 (143' · ADD) Recorded 1968. Notes, text and translation included   Ⓕ**OO**

This is a wonderfully refreshing set, made the more sparkling in the CD transfer. The story emerges crystal-clear, even the black ending to the Giulietta scene in Venice, which in Bonynge's text restores the original idea of the heroine dying from a draught of poison, while the dwarf, Pitichinaccio shrieks in delight. One also has to applaud his rather more controversial decision to put the Giulietta scene in the middle and leave the dramatically weighty Antonia scene till last. That also makes the role of Stella the more significant, giving extra point

to the decision to have the same singer take all four heroine roles. With Dame Joan available it was a natural decision, and though in spoken dialogue she's less comfortable in the Giulietta scene than the rest, the contrasting portraits in each scene are all very convincing, with the voice brilliant in the doll scene, warmly sensuous in the Giulietta scene and powerfully dramatic as well as tender in the Antonia scene. Gabriel Bacquier gives sharply intense performances, firm and dark vocally, in the four villain roles, Hugues Cuénod contributes delightful vignettes in the four *comprimario* tenor roles, while Domingo establishes at the very start the distinctive bite in his portrait of Hoffmann; a powerful and a perceptive interpretation. The recording is vivid, and the listener is treated to some first-class playing from the Suisse Romande Orchestra.

Les contes d'Hoffmann
Raoul Jobin ten Hoffmann **Renée Doria** sop   Ⓗ Olympia **Vina Bovy** sop Giulietta **Géori Boué** sop Antonia **Fanély Revoil** mez Nicklausse **Louis Musy** bar Lindorf **André Pernet** bass Coppélius **Charles Soix** bass Dapertutto **Roger Bourdin** bar Dr Miracle **René Lapelletrie** ten Spalanzani **Camille Maurane** bar Hermann **Chorus and Orchestra of the Opéra-Comique, Paris / André Cluytens**
Naxos Historical ② 8110214/15 (130' · ADD) Recorded 1948. Notes and text included   ⒮**O**

In the 1930s in Paris, Raoul Jobin and José Luccioni were the two great opera matinée-idols. Jobin, a French Canadian, made his début in 1930 and was soon singing at both the Opéra, as Faust, Lohengrin and Raoul in *Les Huguenots*, and at the Opéra-Comique, where he was a favourite Hoffmann and Don José. This recording may perhaps find him just a little late in his career. His years at the Metropolitan (throughout the German occupation) obviously took their toll, when he sang roles that were too heavy for him in such a huge theatre. However, the splendour of this set is the authenticity of the vocal style and the diction of such stalwarts of the Opéra-Comique ensemble as Louis Musy, Roger Bourdin, Fanély Revoil (better known as an operetta singer) and, luxurious casting, Camille Maurane in the small part of Hermann.

The three heroines are well inside their roles, but they're afflicted with a little strain in the higher-lying passages. Renée Doria sang all these parts later in her career – when this recording was made she was just at the outset, having made her début in Paris in 1944. Her Olympia is strong on the *staccato* notes but a bit fragile in the long phrases – this doll broke quite easily, one imagines. In the same act, André Pernet, a great figure from pre-war Paris is a superb Coppélius. In the Venice act, Vina Bovy is dramatically convincing as Giulietta, but hasn't much vocal sheen left (she made her début in 1919). Géori Boué, the Antonia, is one of the great figures from French post-war opera, but one feels that Giulietta would have been her role ideally. As for Jobin, despite some strain, he makes a convincing poet. Although there's such strong competition on CD where *Hoffmann* is concerned, this historic version is without doubt essential listening for a sense of style if the work absorbs you.

vivid. But the real joy of this disc is *Offenbachiana*, music drawn from a handful of the stage works arranged by Rosenthal while forced to kick his heels in Berlin for a fortnight owing to a recording equipment breakdown in 1953. This is a subtler, wittier and, if anything, even more scintillating score. Absolutely not to be missed!

Gaîté parisienne

Offenbach Gaîté parisienne (arr M Rosenthal) **H**
Rossini (arr/orch Respighi) La boutique fantasque
Boston Pops Orchestra / Arthur Fiedler
RCA Victor Living Stereo 09026 61847-2 (64' · ADD)
Recorded 1954-6 **M**

Arthur Fiedler and the Boston Pops, for so long the guardians of traditional concert-hall light music in America, never made a better stereo recording than the amazing early (1954) complete Offenbach/Rosenthal *Gaîté parisienne* ballet score. It scintillates with effervescence and vitality, has just the right degree of brash vulgarity, yet the richly embracing acoustics of Symphony Hall ensure that the entry of the great 'Barcarolle' has warmth as well as allure. This transfer makes the very most of the outstanding mastertape. The coupling comprises some 27 minutes from the hardly less delectable Rossini/Respighi *La boutique fantasque* also brightly and atmospherically played and again given first-class sound from two years later. This release is a real collector's item, and not to be missed by anyone who cares about the history of stereo reproduction and also for the sheer *joie de vivre* of the music.

Gaîté Parisienne (arr Rosenthal). Offenbachiana (arr Rosenthal)
Monte Carlo Philharmonic Orchestra / Manuel Rosenthal
Naxos 8 554005 (68' · DDD) **S**

Manuel Rosenthal was 92 when he made this recording – his third – of *Gaîté Parisienne*, his ballet for Massine that had produced such a storm of applause in Monte Carlo back in 1938. He made very clear why he was anxious to do so: not only had there been poor recordings, cut versions and mauled arrangements of his score by others, but in his own previous recordings he had felt obliged to accommodate the dancers' wishes as regards tempos, and now he wanted to treat his work symphonically, with more spacious speeds that would enable details of the orchestration to emerge fully for the first time. So we can now accept this 45-minute version as authentic, and the more deliberate pace adopted in some places (beautifully and expressively so in the Barcarolle) in no way diminishes the brilliant impact of his treatment of Offenbach's heady tunes. The Monte Carlo orchestra, long familiar with the work, give their all to the aged maestro, with voluptuous string playing in lyrical sections; and the recording is exceptionally

Orphée aux enfers

Orphée aux enfers (ed Minkowski/Pelly)
Yann Beuron ten Orphée **Natalie Dessay** sop
Eurydice **Jean-Paul Fouchécourt** ten Aristée-Pluton
Laurent Naouri bar Jupiter **Lydie Pruvot** sop Juno
Ewa Podles mez Public Opinion **Steven Cole** ten
John Styx **Véronique Gens** sop Vénus **Patricia
Petibon** sop Cupid **Jennifer Smith** sop Diane **Etienne
Lescroart** ten Mercury **Virginie Pochon** sop Minerva
**Grenoble Chamber Orchestra; Chorus and
Orchestra of the Opéra National de Lyon / Marc
Minkowski**
EMI ② 556725-2 (110' · DDD) Notes, text and
translation included **F O**

Orphée aux enfers may be Offenbach's best-known operetta, but it's had limited attention on disc. The lightly scored original 1858 version was in two acts and four scenes. The spectacular 1874 version had lots of extra songs and ballet numbers. Since this latter demands huge forces, it's scarcely viable on stage today. The usual solution in the theatre is thus to add selected numbers from the 1874 version to the 1858 text, and this is what was done for the performances at Geneva, Lyons and Grenoble that formed the basis of this recording. Home listeners may prefer to make their own selections of numbers, and musicologically questionable decisions such as the rescoring of 1874 pieces for 1858 orchestral resources become more exposed. What matters most, though, is the quality of performance, and the pleasures of this one are formidable.

Above all, Natalie Dessay's exchanges in the First Act with her despised violinist husband (the admirable Yann Beuron) are superbly done. So is her sighing over Jean-Paul Fouchécourt's Aristeus, whose two big solos show equal elegance. Later come Laurent Naouri's formidable Jupiter and cameos such as Etienne Lescroart's agile performance of Mercury's song and Patricia Petibon's deliciously winning account of Cupid's 'Couplets des baisers'. Ensemble numbers are extremely well done and throughout, Marc Minkowski provides thoughtful, lively direction.

What causes doubt is the tendency towards overstatement, from the opening monologue of Eva Podles's Public Opinion where almost every word seems to be given exaggerated emphasis, through Aristeus's crude falsetto in his opening solo, to a curiously mechanical version of John Styx's 'Quand j'étais roi de Béotie' and some gratuitous vocal gymnastics in the 'Hymne à Bacchus'. Ultimately, however, those doubts are banished by the virtues. Whereas

ORFF CARMINA BURANA –
IN BRIEF

Janowitz; Stolze; Fischer-Dieskau; Deutsche Opera Chorus and Orchestra / Eugen Jochum
DG 447 437-2GOR (56' · DDD)   Ⓜ❍❍❍

🌞 Recorded in the presence of the composer back in 1968. The soloists are very vivid, with Janowitz quite ravishing in her restraint and purity of tone. The chorus is superb.

Armstrong; English; Allen; London Symphony Chorus and Orchestra / André Previn
EMI 566899-2 (63' · ADD)   Ⓜ❍❍

Still one of the great recordings of the work full of excitement, event and above all good humour. Allen is magnificent, and the sound, from 1975, still sounds amazingly vivid.

Walmsley-Clark; Graham-Hall; Maxwell; London Symphony Chorus and Orchestra / Richard Hickox
Regis RRC1136 (64' · DDD)   Ⓑ❍

Hickox the choral trainer is shown off here to great effect in an exciting and vivid performance reissued at budget price. The solo singing is good too, so definitely worth considering if you're on a budget.

Matthews; Brownlee; Gerhaher; Berlin Radio Chorus; Berlin PO / Sir Simon Rattle
EMI 557888-2 (60' · DDD)   Ⓕ❍

An invigorating revisiting of an ever-popular score: Rattle has stripped it down and rebuilt in a way that will either entrance or annoy. Thrillingly alive and superbly recorded.

Oelze; Kuebler; Keenlyside; Deutsche Oper Chorus and Orchestra / Christian Thielemann
DG 453 587-2GH (63' · DDD)   Ⓕ❍❍

DG returned to the Deutsche Oper for a new recording to succeed the classic Jochum (see above), and it paid off. Thielemann directs with great verve and clarity, and his Berlin Opera forces acquit themselves admirably. Marvellous soloists.

Hendricks; Aler; Hagegård; London Symphony Chorus and Orchestra / Eduardo Mata
RCA 09026 63981-2 (60' · DDD)   Ⓑ❍

Another stunning LSO *Carmina burana* that employs Mata's rhythmic virtuosity to spectacular effect. Full of character and beautifully sung. A superb budget version.

Popp; Van Kesteren; Prey; Bavraina Radio Chorus; Munich Radio Orchestra / Kurt Eichhorn
RCA 📀 74321 85259 (78')   Ⓕ

Jean-Pierre Ponnelle's racy video interpretation takes Eichhorn's fine 1975 performance as its soundtrack. It's all a lot of fun and gives the work a dramatic outlet that in concert it often so desperately seems to aspire too.

those who want virtually every note Offenbach composed for *Orphée aux enfers* must stick with the 1978 Plasson/EMI recording, Minkowski offers a more faithful impression of Offenbach's original compact creation, with selected 1874 additions as a bonus. It's a consistently imaginative performance, altogether livelier than its predecessor, and at its best a superbly musical version of Offenbach's sparkling creation.

Carl Orff   German 1895-1982

Orff studied at the Munich Academy and later, in 1920, with Kaminski. In 1924, with Dorothee Günther, he founded a school for gymnastics, music and dance, and out of this came his later activity in providing materials for young children to make music, using their voices and simple percussion instruments. His adult works also seek to make contact with primitive kinds of musical behaviour, as represented by ostinato, pulsation and direct vocal expression of emotion; in this he was influenced by Stravinsky (Oedipus rex, The Wedding), though the models are coarsened to produce music of a powerful pagan sensual appeal and physical excitement. All his major works, including the phenomenally successful Carmina burana (1937), were designed as pageants for the stage; they include several versions of Greek tragedies and Bavarian comedies. **GROVE**music

Carmina Burana

Carmina Burana
Gundula Janowitz *sop* **Gerhard Stolze** *ten* **Dietrich Fischer-Dieskau** *bar* **Schönberg Boys' Choir; Chorus and Orchestra of the Deutsche Oper, Berlin / Eugen Jochum**
DG The Originals 447 437-2GOR (56' · ADD)
Recorded 1967. Text and translation included
   Ⓜ❍❍❍

🌞 Since its original release, Jochum's performance has consistently been a prime recommendation for this much-recorded piece. Listening to it again in the superbly remastered sound, one can easily hear why. He pays great attention to detail – particularly with regard to tempo and articulation – yet the performance as a whole has a tremendous cogent sweep and the choruses have terrific power. The more reflective sections aren't neglected, however, and movements such as 'Stetit Puella', with Janowitz sounding alluring and fey, have surely never been more sensitively handled. Stolze is ideal as the roasted swan and Fischer-Dieskau encompasses the very varied requirements of the baritone's music with ease. This distinguished performance, authorised by the composer and here sounding better than ever, retains its place at the head of the queue.

Carmina Burana
Christiane Oelze *sop* **David Kuebler** *ten* **Simon Keenlyside** *bar* **Knabenchor Berlin; Chorus and**

Orchestra of the Deutsche Oper, Berlin / Christian Thielemann
DG 453 587-2GH (63' · DDD) Text and translation included ⓕ**OO**

Over the years there have been some impressive recordings of *Carmina Burana* from DG, starting with Jochum's electrifying version, recorded in 1967. Thielemann's harks directly back to that classic account, and not just because, like Jochum's, it has the chorus and orchestra of the Deutsche Oper, Berlin. The difference lies predominantly in the slow, lyrical sections. So, although with Thielemann the opening movement of the 'Primo vere' section is much longer, he loses nothing in tension, simply following the score's marking *molto flessibile*. His speeds in fast sections come very close to those of Jochum and there's a similarly bright incisiveness, with rhythms clipped and well sprung, and with a comparably high voltage generated.

Although Thielemann's version has impressively full and brilliant sound, with fine inner clarity and wonderfully sharp definition of the many antiphonal contrasts, not only the chorus but more particularly the semi-chorus sound distant. The *pianissimos* are magical, but closer recording would have made the results even more involving. The choral singing is superb, warm and dramatic, reflecting the work of singers from the opera house, and the Knabenchor Berlin in the penultimate movement of the 'Court of Love' section adds an aptly earthy tang.

The soloists too, like Jochum's, are as near ideal as could be. David Kuebler is totally unfazed by the high tessitura of so much of the tenor writing: not just clean and precise and characterising superbly in the 'roast swan' sequence, but singing most beautifully in his equally taxing solo in the 'Court of Love' section. Christiane Oelze even matches the lovely Gundula Janowitz (for Jochum) in the soprano sections, ravishingly pure and true both in 'In trutina' and 'Dulcissime'. But it's Simon Keenlyside's singing which crowns this brilliant performance, at once clear, fresh and characterful. It's good to have this much-recorded work sounding as fresh as it did in that historic model.

Additional recommendation

Carmina Burana
London Symphony Chorus and Orchestra / Previn
EMI Great Recordings of the Century 566899-2.
(63' · ADD) Ⓜ
A classic reading, with a wonderful swagger and seductive rhythmic pointing; splendid soloists, too.

Johann Pachelbel   German 1653-1706

Pachelbel was taught by two local musicians, Heinrich Schwemmer and GC Wecker. In 1669 he entered the university at Altdorf and was organist of the Lorenzkirche there, but left after less than a year for lack of money and in 1670 enrolled in the Gymnasium Poeticum at Regensburg, where he continued musical studies with Kaspar Prentz. After about five years as deputy organist at St Stephen's Cathedral, Vienna (1673-7), and a year as court organist at Eisenach, Pachelbel was appointed organist of the Predigerkirche at Erfurt in June 1678, where he remained for 12 years. During this time he was outstandingly successful as organist, composer and teacher (his pupils included JS Bach's elder brother, Johann Christoph) and was twice married. He left Erfurt in 1690 and, after short periods as organist in Stuttgart and Gotha, returned to Nuremberg, where he was organist at St Sebald until his death. Pachelbel was a prolific composer. His organ music includes c70 chorales (mostly written at Erfurt), 95 Magnificat fugues (for Vespers at St Sebald) and non-liturgical works such as toccatas, preludes, fugues and fantasias. His preference for a lucid, uncomplicated style found fullest expression in his vocal music, which includes two masses and some important Vespers music as well as arias and sacred concertos. His modest contributions to chamber music include a canon that is now his best-known work.
GROVEmusic

Canon

Pachelbel Canon and Gigue **Mozart** Serenade No 13. Adagio and Fugue in C minor, K546 **Anonymous** (arr L Mozart) Cassation in G, 'Toy Symphony'
Academy of St Martin in the Fields / Sir Neville Marriner
Philips 416 386-2PH (52' · DDD) Recorded 1984-5 Ⓕ

Sir Neville Marriner here collects a miscellaneous group of popular classical and Baroque pieces in characteristically polished and elegant performances. Pachelbel's celebrated Canon – taken unsentimentally if sweetly at a flowing speed – is given a reprise after the fugue; unusual but why not? Warm, well-balanced recording.

Keyboard Suites

Keyboard Suites – C, S25; D minor, S26; E minor, S28; E minor, S29; F, S32; G minor, S33; G minor, S33b; G, S34; A, S36
Joseph Payne hpd
BIS CD809 (74 minutes: DDD) Ⓕ

First-class recordings of fine organ music and motets by Pachelbel seem to have been unable to plant his name in the minds of the general musical public other than as the composer of that attractive but over-recorded canon. These suites (definitely for harpsichord, not organ) are all printed in the *Denkmaler der Tonkunst in Bayern* series, but except for Nos 29, 32 and 33b their authorship is very questionable. Whoever wrote them, however, they contain some very impressive movements, and Pachelbel displays some intriguing rhythmic quirks on occasion.

Each of the suites consists of an allemand, courant and saraband, plus a 'gyque' [sic] in all but two cases; No 33 includes a lively 'ballett', Nos. 25, 36 and 28 a gavotte (that in A major a very jolly one); there are doubles in Nos 29 and 36. Playing on a copy of a bright-toned early Flemish instrument, Joseph Payne offers clean and vital performances, with neat ornaments; now and then, in his desire for expressiveness or to draw attention to a point, he's a bit mannered, but in general his playing is most appealing and he's recorded with total fidelity.

Sacred Works

Magnificat in C. Jauchzet dem Herrn. Christ lag in Todesbanden. Deus in adjutorium. Christ ist erstanden. Halleluja! Lobet den Herrn
La Capella Ducale; Musica Fiata / Roland Wilson
CPO CPO999 916-2 (78' · DDD) Texts and translations included 　　　　　　　　　　　　　　　　　　Ⓟ**Ⓞ**

This is a stunning disc: under Roland Wilson, La Capella Ducale and Musica Fiata elevate period performance to new heights. While the actual sound they produce, the textural authority and the musical conviction of their performances are of a standard that's long been *de rigueur*, they add to these a fresh sense of character which makes for the most compelling listening, not least because of CPO's terrific recording. The choir's diction is most impressive. There's an unforced, totally unpretentious clarity about their words which has the intimacy of a captivating story-teller. Texts and translations are provided, but they seem unnecessary when every word is so clear, and the essence of the texts is so obvious in Pachelbel's ingenious writing.

This is the only serious survey of Pachelbel's sacred choral music on the *Gramophone* database. It shouldn't be: the gloriously ebullient *Halleluja! Lobet den Herrn*, complete with delightful instrumental effects, is a particular delight. In his notes Peter Wollny describes the composer as 'a trailblazer', and this music provides a dramatic bridge between the operatic style of the early 17th century and the full-blooded oratorios of the 18th century. But given performances of this quality, the historical perspective of the music seems irrelevant; what comes across most vividly here is its vitality.

Giovanni Pacini　　　　　Italian 1796-1867

Pacini studied singing with Marchesi in Bologna, then turned to composition. Between 1813 and 1867 he wrote nearly 90 operas, first modelling them on Rossini and later, after contact with Bellini's works, giving more attention to harmonic and instrumental colour. He was gifted with melodic invention, used to effect in a variety of cabaletta types; his accompaniments and ensemble writing are weak by comparison.

Among the earlier works, Alessandro nelle Indie (1824), L'ultimo giorno di Pompei (1825), Gli arabi nelle Gallie (1827) and Ivanhoe (1832) were notable successes. In 1833 increased competition from Bellini and Donizetti caused his five-year withdrawal from the stage and he established a music school at his home in Viareggio and composed sacred works for the ducal chapel in Lucca, of which he was director from 1837. But with the immensely successful Saffo (1840), considered his masterpiece, he entered a period of more mature opera composition, producing La fidanzata corsa (1842), Maria, regina d'Inghilterra and Medea (1843). Though his success and reputation outside Italy were limited, his musical weaknesses can be attributed chiefly to the circumstances in which he worked. In the face of formidable competition within Italy, he satisfied a sophisticated public for half a century.
　　　　　　　　　　　　　　　　　　GROVEmusic

Carlo di Borgogna

Carlo di Borgogna
Bruce Ford *ten* Carlo **Elizabeth Futral** *sop* Leonora di Jork **Roberto Frontali** *bar* Arnoldo **Jennifer Larmore** *mez* Estella **Helen Williams** *sop* Amelia **Dominic Natoli** *ten* Lord Athol **Gary Magee** *bar* Gugliemo d'Erlach **Geoffrey Mitchell Choir; Academy of St Martin in the Fields / David Parry**
Opera Rara ③ ORC21 (184' · DDD) Recorded in association with the Peter Moores Foundation. Notes, text and translation included 　　　　　　　Ⓟ**Ⓞ**

First, a word to enthusiasts, to those with a special interest in early 19th-century opera, who may, perhaps, have acquired and enjoyed other operas of Giovanni Pacini that have appeared on records in recent years for the first time and who may look with some eagerness at this review. Don't read it! To borrow a well-known slogan of our time: just do it!

The one point that's well known about Pacini's career is that it divides in two, with a four-year period of retirement for further thought and study. From this he emerged with his masterpiece *Saffo* (1840), and the general assumption has been that the operas from before the divide are inferior. In particular, it's understood that Pacini himself recognised this, his shortcomings being brought home to him by the relative failure of the last opera he wrote before 'resting'. That opera was *Carlo di Borgogna*. It's an opera well set-up with characters and situations; more importantly, one in which the forms themselves almost guarantee satisfaction if they're handled by such a master as Pacini was. We aren't necessarily looking here for originality but (in no debased sense) for entertainment. As a matter of fact, originality is to be found as well: it's a curious feature of Pacini's writing that, while he can at one moment follow his stated theme with a sequential phrase of disheartening banality, he may also at any moment provide a harmonic or rhythmic lift that delights as it surprises.

The dominant character is Estella, Charles's true-love who turns savage on being dropped in favour of an arranged marriage but changes tack again as she tries to warn him that he's going to his death. Jennifer Larmore takes full advantage of her opportunities, sings the difficult role with some depth of vocal colour, is the assured mistress of technique and gives her words a vivid intensity of expression. The lower men's voices are strongly cast, with Gary Magee wasted in a role with little to sing. Bruce Ford takes the name-part, his tone virile, runs and *gruppetti* delivered with fluency we used to be told had disappeared with singers of the golden age.

As ever, David Parry conducts with a conviction to which his players respond, and the Mitchell Choir sing with precision and fresh tone. As to recorded sound, slightly closer contact with the soloists might be preferable, but for many this will be just about the right balance.

Maria, Regina d'Inghilterra

Maria, Regina d'Inghilterra
Nelly Miricioiu sop Mary Tudor **Bruce Ford** ten
Riccardo Fenimoore **José Fardilha** bass Ernesto
Malcolm **Mary Plazas** sop Clotilde Talbot **Alastair
Miles** bass Gualtiero Churchill **Susan Bickley** mez
Page **Benjamin Bland** bass Raoul **Geoffrey Mitchell
Choir; Philharmonia Orch / David Parry**
Opera Rara ③ ORC15 (172' · DDD) Notes, text and
translation included   Ⓕ

Pacini wrote happily within the formal conventions of Italian opera in his time. Opening chorus, aria and cabaletta, duet likewise in two 'movements', big ensemble as finale of the middle act, 'brilliant' solo for *prima donna* just before the final curtain. A great point about the plot is the scope it provides for duets, which are both plentiful and good. There are choruses of merrymakers, soldiers and Londoners out for blood. The ensemble, an excellent example of its kind, comes at the point when Fenimoore is cornered and feelings run high. So do the voices. We're lucky to have Bruce Ford: at a *fortissimo* he may sound underpowered, and he doesn't play imaginatively with *mezza voce* effects, but in florid passages he moves swiftly and gracefully, he appears to be comfortable with the tessitura, and in the prison scene, which provided Ivanov with his greatest success, he sings with feeling and style.

The women have suitably contrasting voices, Mary Plazas's fresh and high, Nelly Miricioiu's older in tone, more dramatic in timbre. Both are expressive singers, and though Miricioiu too habitually resorts to the imperious glottal emphasis associated with Callas and Caballé, she brings conviction to all she does. The baritone, José Fardilha, has a touch of the flicker-vibrato that can give distinctive character, and Alastair Miles confers nobility of utterance upon the vindictive Chancellor. The cast, in fact, is worthy of the opera, which in this recording has probably its most important performance since the première of 1843. There's

fine work from the Philharmonia under Parry. Recorded sound is well balanced, and the production handles the drama well. You are likely to play it straight through from start to finish, chafing at any interruption; and that says something for both the music and the drama.

Ignacy Paderewski   Polish 1860-1941

Pianist, composer and statesman Paderewski studied at the Warsaw Music Institute, in Berlin and with Leschetizky in Vienna, his career as a pianist beginning in 1888 with an exhausting international concert schedule; as a performer he was noted for his individual treatment of rubato. Meanwhile he composed during the summers, producing the opera Manru *(1892-1901), the Symphony Op 24 and the* Fantaisie polonaise *Op 19 for piano and orchestra, typical products of the late Romantic Polish national school; perhaps better known are his programmatic piano miniatures and the Piano Concerto (1888). Between 1910 and 1921 he was active on behalf of Poland, making speeches, assisting victims of oppression and eventually becoming prime minister (1919). He also supported young Polish composers and worked on a new Chopin edition. He received numerous musical and national honours including a state burial in Arlington National Cemetery.*

GROVEmusic

Polonia Symphony

Symphony in B minor, Op 24, 'Polonia'
**BBC Scottish Symphony Orchestra / Jerzy
Maksymiuk**
Hyperion CDA67056 (74' · DDD)   Ⓕ

As well as being a legendary concert pianist and first Prime Minister of Poland in 1919, Paderewski also found time to compose. In 1903 he embarked on his vast *Polonia* Symphony, which cost him some five years of labour and was to be his final major creation. In its unashamedly epic countenance and theatrical sense of rhetoric, *Polonia* most closely resembles Liszt's two symphonies, as well as Tchaikovsky's *Manfred*, though it perhaps lacks the distinctive thematic profile of those masterworks. That said, the mighty opening movement (some half an hour in duration) is an impressive achievement, its stately introductory material sowing the seeds for much of what's to follow and acting as an effective foil to the rousingly patriotic, defiant *Allegro vivace* proper. At first, the central *Andante con moto* meanders along moodily in an introspective, Rachmaninovian manner, but, about half-way through, the skies darken, and the music acquires a troubled, sombre flavour that can't be dispelled (the bleak coda offers no consolation). The finale's truculent battle-cries (which incorporate a cleverly disguised motif based on the first two bars of the Polish national anthem) are temporarily assuaged by two tranquil episodes. The BBC Scottish SO and its longstanding Polish chief Jerzy Maksymiuk mastermind a performance of eloquence and dashing commitment (only in the closing minutes does any hint of raggedness creep into the violins' bustling passagework). The recording, too, is pretty resplendent, and collectors with a sweet tooth for this sort of heady, late-Romantic 'spectacular' shouldn't hesitate.

Philharmonic Orchestra have a mainly subordinate role, certainly when the soloist is playing, but they fulfil it well and follow Accardo through the rhythmic flexibilities which are accepted performing style in this music and which for all we know were used by the virtuoso performer-composer himself. The recording is faithful and does justice to the all-important soloist.

Nicolò Paganini   Italian 1782-1840

Through his technique and extreme personal magnetism Paganini was not only the most famous violin virtuoso but drew attention to the significance of virtuosity as an element in art. He studied with his father, Antonio Cervetto and Giacomo Costa and composition with Ghiretti and Paer in Parma. From 1810 to 1828 he developed a career as a 'free artist' throughout Italy, mesmerising audiences and critics with his showmanship; notable compositions were the bravura variations Le streghe (1813), the imaginative 24 Caprices Op 1 and the second and third violin concertos, surpassing in brilliance any that had been written before. After conquering Vienna in 1828 he was equally successful in Germany (Goethe, Heine and Schumann admired him), Paris and London (1831-4). His hectic international career finally shattered his health in 1834, when he returned to Parma. Apart from his unparalleled technical wizardry on the instrument, including the use of left-hand pizzicato, double-stop harmonics, 'ricochet' bowings and a generally daredevil approach to performance – all of which influenced successive violinists – he is most important for his artistic impact on Liszt, Chopin, Schumann and Berlioz, who took up his technical challenge in the search for greater expression in their own works.

GROVEmusic

Violin Concertos

No 1 in E flat, Op 6; **No 2** in B minor, Op 7, 'La campanella'

Violin Concertos Nos 1 & 2
Salvatore Accardo vn **London Philharmonic Orchestra / Charles Dutoit**
DG 415 378-2GH (69' · ADD) Recorded 1975   Ⓕ

Paganini's violin music was at one time thought quite inaccessible to lesser mortals among the violin-playing fraternity, but as standards of technique have improved master technicians are now able to do justice to such works as these concertos. Salvatore Accardo is certainly among them, and we can judge his skill as early as the opening violin solo of the First Concerto. This is typical of the style, with its authoritative and rhetorical gestures and use of the whole instrumental compass, but so is the second theme which in its refinement and songlike nature demands (and here receives) another kind of virtuosity expressed through a command of tone, texture and articulation. Dutoit and the London

Violin Concertos Nos 1 & 2
Ilya Kaler vn **Polish National Radio Symphony Orchestra / Stephen Gunzenhauser**
Naxos 8 550649 (67' · DDD) Recorded 1992   Ⓢ

Ilya Kaler is a Russian virtuoso, a pupil of Leonid Kogan. He's a first-rate fiddler and an excellent musician. Paganini's once fiendish pyrotechnics hold no terrors for him, not even the whistling harmonics, and how nicely he can turn an Italianate lyrical phrase, as in the secondary theme of the first movement of the First Concerto. Then he can set off with panache into a flying *staccato*, bouncing his bow neatly on the strings when articulating the delicious *spiccato* finales of both works. Stephen Gunzenhauser launches into the opening movements with plenty of energy and aplomb and is a sympathetic accompanist throughout. How nicely the violins shape the lyrical ritornello introducing the first movement of the Second, and there's some sensitive horn playing in the *Adagio*. Kaler's intonation is above suspicion and he's naturally balanced: there's none of the scratchiness that can ruin your pleasure in Paganinian pyrotechnics. With excellent notes, this is a superior product at super-bargain price. The recordings were made in the Concert Hall of Polish Radio in Katowice. It has an ideal ambience for this music: nicely warm, not clouded. Great value on all counts.

Paganini Violin Concerto No 1 **Saint-Saëns** Havanaise in E, Op 83. Introduction and Rondo capriccioso in A minor, Op 28
Sarah Chang vn **Philadelphia Orchestra / Wolfgang Sawallisch**
EMI 555026-2 (55' · DDD) Recorded 1993-4   Ⓕⵔ

Paganini would surely have been astonished at Sarah Chang's version of his No 1. She made her début with the piece in the Avery Fisher Hall at the age of eight, but had reached more advanced years (12) when she recorded it in Philadelphia for EMI. The performance is dazzling, particularly the finale where her light rhythmic touch and deliciously pert sliding 'harmonised harmonics' are a wonder of technical assurance. Note too, in the first movement, the relaxed ease of the decorated bouncing bow passages and the gently tender reprise of the second subject. The slow movement isn't overtly romantic, but the freshness is never in doubt. One doesn't expect her to sound maturely sophisticated like Perlman and she understates the sultry atmosphere of the Saint-Saëns *Havanaise* to pleasing effect, yet manages the coda with spruce flexibility of phrase and the most subtle graduations of timbre. The *Introduction and Rondo capriccioso* has plenty of dash and she catches the Spanish sunlight in the *Introduction* without an overtly sensuous response. The recording is a little too closely balanced. Sawallisch directs with verve and supports his soloist admirably.

Cantabile in D, Op 17[a]. Violin Concerto Nos 1[b]
& 2 (arr vn/pf)[a]. Introduction and Variations on 'Nel cor più non mi sento' from Paisiello's 'La Molinara', Op 38. Moses-Fantasie[a]
Ilya Gringolts vn [a]**Irina Ryumina** pf [b]**Lahti Symphony Orchestra / Osmo Vänskä**
BIS CD999 (72' · DDD)   Ⓕ

Ilya Gringolts (*b*1982 in St Petersburg) is an outstanding young Russian violinist; with this Paganini programme he began his recording career at the deep end. He's able to surmount the ferocious technical demands, and has, too, a notably rich, beautiful, unforced tone. In the unaccompanied *Nel cor più non mi sento* Variations, he seems rather careful – missing the passionate directness that Leila Josefowicz brings to this piece. But Gringolts's more expansive and delicate account is equally valid, the theme, with its freely expressive ornamentation, especially appealing. The other shorter items work well, too, in particular the elegant *Cantabile* – originally for violin and guitar. Only *La campanella* is a bit disappointing: one feels the need for a more vigorous approach, and despite the finesse of the playing it's difficult not to regret the absence of the orchestra. The First Concerto benefits from a truly outstanding accompaniment, performed (and recorded) with a wonderful sense of space and balance. Even the bass drum and cymbal parts are played with sensitivity – what can sound like a crudely overloaded score emerges here full of colour and grandeur. With such fine orchestral sonority, one might wonder what the concerto would sound like in its original key. Paganini played it in E flat, by tuning his strings a semitone higher, and wrote the orchestral parts in the higher key; his aim was to produce a more brilliant, penetrating sound. Present-day soloists, understandably, prefer the standard tuning for such a demanding work.

Gringolts plays with sweetness or brilliance as required, though perhaps the first movement didn't need so many extreme tempo changes and perhaps the *Adagio* should have had a more dramatic tone, to match the darkly romantic orchestration. But the finale is terrific, with all the verve and high spirits you could want.

Violin and Guitar Duos

Centone di sonate Nos 7-12
Moshe Hammer vn **Norbert Kraft** gtr
Naxos 8 553142 (72' · DDD) Recorded 1994   Ⓢ

The *Centone di sonate* (a 'hotchpotch of sonatas') consists of 18 'sonatas' which are really salon works with a variety of movements – none of them in sonata form. Whether Paganini, who wrote them sometime after 1828, intended these pieces for public performance or merely for the use of the then abundant amateur musicians isn't known. As usual in his works of this genre, it's the violin that hogs the limelight while the guitar remains a humble bag-carrier. The guitar parts are indeed so simple that they would have been within the reach of any amateur who was capable of keeping his end up with another musician; Segovia considered them beneath his dignity and refused many invitations to play them with famous partners! Nothing is harder than to be 'simple': Mozart managed it, while at the same time being deceptively complex; Paganini did it
at a far less sublime level, with sentimental, cheerful and pert tunes. Truth to tell, they aren't the kind of works which impel one to listen to them at one sitting except for the most devoted *aficionado* of Paganini's violinistic voice or of hearing the guitar in an unremittingly subservient but genuinely complementary role.

These splendid performances on modern instruments make no claim to 'authentic' status, but they're no less appealing for that. They squeeze every last drop from the music with (inauthentically) full sound, and a Siamese-twin tightness of ensemble that was probably rare amongst those who played these works in Paganini's own time. In the end, these works have a charm that's hard for any but the most straitlaced to resist. It's unlikely that the *Centone* will ever be better played and/or recorded.

Six Sonatas for Guitar and Violin, Op 3. Sonata concertata in A, Op 61. 60 Variations on 'Barucabà', Op 14. Cantabile in D, Op 17
Scott St John vn **Simon Wynberg** gtr
Naxos 8 550690 (54' · DDD) Recorded 1993   Ⓢ

Six Sonatas for Guitar and Violin, Op 2. Cantabile e Valtz, Op 19. Variazioni di bravura on Caprice No 24. Duetto amoroso. Sonata per le gran viola e chitarra
Scott St John vn **Simon Wynberg** gtr
Naxos 8 550759 (59' · DDD) Recorded 1993   Ⓢ

Several of the violin/guitar duos testify to Paganini's amorous inclinations: the sections of the *Duetto amoroso* spell out the course of an affair, from beginning to separation, and may have been aimed (unsuccessfully, one imagines) at the Princess Elisa Baciocchi in Lucca. His conservative harmonic vocabulary springs few surprises and his melodies sometimes verge on banality, but by dint of sheer charm and technical ingenuity he somehow gets away with it; only the po-faced could resist an admiring smile at his effrontery. Collectively, these works present the full range of Paganini's technical armoury – left-hand pizzicatos, high harmonics, double-stopping, 'sneaky' chromatic runs and the rest, and Scott St John betrays no difficulty in dealing with every googly that comes his way. More than that, in the daunting *Sonata per le gran viola e chitarra* (celebrating Paganini's acquisition of a Stradivarius instrument) cocks a snook at every viola joke that ever was. Wynberg proves as well matched a partner as St John could have wished for. Violinists, guitarists and lovers of winsomeness for its own sake should revel in these very well-recorded discs.

24 Caprices, Op 1

24 Caprices, Op 1
Itzhak Perlman *vn*
EMI Great Recordings of the Century 567237-2
(72' · ADD)   Ⓜ**O**

This electrifying music with its dare-devil virtuosity has long remained the pinnacle of violin technique, and the *Caprices* encapsulate the essence of the composer's style. For a long time it was considered virtually unthinkable that a violinist should be able to play the complete set; even in recent years only a handful have produced truly successful results. Itzhak Perlman has one strength in this music that's all-important, other than a sovereign technique – he's incapable of playing with an ugly tone. He has such variety in his bowing that the timbre of the instrument is never monotonous. The notes of the music are dispatched with a forthright confidence and fearless abandon. The frequent double-stopping passages hold no fear for him. Listen to the fire of No 5 in A minor and the way in which Perlman copes with the extremely difficult turns in No 14 in E flat; this is a master at work. The set rounds off with the famous A minor Caprice, which inspired Liszt, Brahms and Rachmaninov, amongst others, to adapt it in various guises for the piano.

24 Caprices, Op 1
Leonidas Kavakos *vn*
Dynamic CDS66 (77' · DDD) Recorded 1989-90   Ⓟ**O**

The Greek Leonidas Kavakos, who won first prize at the 1988 Paganini Competition in Genoa, as well as taking the 1991 *Gramophone* Concerto Award for the Sibelius Violin Concerto, is given a recorded sound that favours the lower strings of the violin, so much so that the sonority resembles a viola. He takes a truly intelligent view of the musical potential of Paganini's frequently tortuous-sounding Caprices. He also has a pretty formidable playing equipment and captures the mysterious and obsessive side of the music. The acoustic is spacious and affords an objective and balanced view of the music. He doesn't treat the *Caprices* as if they were merely *études*, but follows the composer's tempo markings with fidelity, notably in the Sixth Caprice. Kavakos saves his best playing for last: the final, and best-known, Caprice is quite superb.

Giovanni Palestrina
Italian c1525/6-1594

Palestrina was a pupil of Mallapert and Firmin Lebel at S Maria Maggiore, Rome, where he was a choirboy from at least 1537. He became organist of S Agapito, Palestrina, in 1544 and in 1547 married Lucrezia Gori there; they had three children. After the Bishop of Palestrina's election as pope (Julius III) he was appointed maestro di cappella of the Cappella Giulia in Rome (1551), where he issued his first works (masses, 1554); during 1555 he also sang in the Cappella Sistina. Two of Rome's greatest churches then procured him as maestro di cappella, St John Lateran (1555-60) and S Maria Maggiore (1561-6), and in 1564 Cardinal Ippolito d'Este engaged him to oversee the music at his Tivoli estate. From 1566 he also taught music at the Seminario Romano, before returning to the Cappella Giulia as maestro in 1571.

During the 1560s and 1570s Palestrina's fame and influence rapidly increased through the wide diffusion of his published works. So great was his reputation that in 1577 he was asked to rewrite the church's main plainchant books, following the Council of Trent's guidelines. His most famous mass, Missa Papae Marcelli, may have been composed to satisfy the council's requirements for musical cogency and textual intelligibility. He was always in tune with the Counter-Reformation spirit; after his wife's death in 1580 he considered taking holy orders, but instead he remarried (1581). His wife, Virginia Dormoli, was a wealthy fur merchant's widow; his investments in her business eased his financial strains, and his last years at St Peter's were among his most productive.

Palestrina ranks with Lassus and Byrd as one of the greatest Renaissance masters. A prolific composer of masses, motets and other sacred works, as well as madrigals, he was (unlike Lassus) basically conservative. In his sacred music he assimilated and refined his predecessors' polyphonic techniques to produce a 'seamless' texture, with all voices perfectly balanced. The nobility and restraint of his most expressive works established the almost legendary reverence that has surrounded his name and helped set him up as the classic model of Renaissance polyphony.

GROVEmusic

Masses

Missa Dum complerentur. Dum complerentur. Magnificat VI toni. Motets, Book 3 – Alleluia: Veni Sancte Spiritus. Veni sancte spiritus (plainchant). Spiritus sanctus replevit totam domum. Veni Creator Spiritus
Westminster Cathedral Choir / Martin Baker
Hyperion CDA67353 (71' · DDD) Texts and
translations included   Ⓟ**O**

The opening six-part motet, *Dum complerentur*, a vivid description of the coming of the Holy Spirit as a 'mighty rushing wind', has a text calculated to stimulate any composer. Palestrina's stirring motet reappears completely transformed in his Mass, quiet and pleading in the

Kyrie, exuberant in the *Gloria*. The choir catches the spirit of each movement with remarkable flexibility .

The choir's renowned, so-called Continental, vocal quality has persisted throughout its existence, even with a succession of very different choir directors. Due in part to the building's acoustic, this factor almost certainly affects their singing of the chant. The beautiful Carolingian *Alleluia: Veni Sancte Spiritus*, with its melisma on the word 'amoris', is an excellent illustration of the trebles in full flight, singing with enormous confidence in the vast cathedral. In alternation with the low voices in the sequence *Veni Sancte Spiritus*, they have the edge over the men who sound a trifle strained on their top notes.

Palestrina's double choir version of this text shows the whole choir in top form, revelling in the composer's exciting rhythmic acrobatics: while never departing from the noble majesty of his style, Palestrina describes with thrilling realism the many-voiced confusion when 'they all began to speak in a multitude of different tongues'. Highly recommended.

Missa Viri Galilaei. Missa O Rex gloriae.
Motets – Viri Galilaei; O Rex gloriae
Westminster Cathedral Choir / James O'Donnell
Hyperion CDA66316 (68' · DDD) Recorded 1988.
Texts and translations included ⒻⓄ

This is music in which Westminster Cathedral Choir excels: its response to the richly reverberant acoustic is warm and generous; it performs with the ease and freedom of kinship – a far cry from the studied perfection of many other choirs. Each motet is heard before its reworking as a Mass. The six-part scoring of *Viri Galilaei* (two trebles, alto, two tenors and bass) invites a variety of combinations and textures, culminating in the joyful cascading Alleluias at the end of Part I and the jubilant ascending series in Part II. In the Mass the mood changes from triumph to quiet pleading – a change partly due to revised scoring: the two alto parts beneath the single treble produce a more subdued sound.

The Choir clearly relishes this exploration of the deeper sonorities: in the *Creed* one entire section is entrusted to the four lowest voices. The four-part motet *O Rex gloriae* is lithe and fast-moving. The corresponding Mass, largely syllabic in style, gives the Choir the chance to show its superb command of phrasing and accentuation: the Latin comes over with intelligibility and subtlety. Listen, also, to the wonderful solo boys' trio in the 'Crucifixus', and for the carefully crafted canons in the *Benedictus* and *Agnus Dei*.

Missa ecce ego Johannes. Cantantibus organis. Laudate pueri. Magnificat IV toni. Peccantem me quotidie. Tribulationes civitatum. Tu es Petrus
Westminster Cathedral Choir / James O'Donnell
Hyperion CDA67099 (65' · DDD) Texts and translations included ⒻⓄ

For sheer beauty of sound, this recording is unsurpassed. The choice of a programme of music by Palestrina, the one composer ever to have been honoured by official ecclesiastical recognition, was inspired. This CD represents several high points of solemn liturgy; a six-part polyphonic Mass, *Ecce ego Johannes*, and two groups of motets, including a festal psalm, two penitential pieces, antiphons for the feasts of St Peter and St Cecilia and a solemn *alternatim Magnificat*. What's very admirable about the whole performance is the excellent integration of the choir. Ivan Moody underlines in his notes Palestrina's skill in the seamless interweaving of homophony and flowing counterpoint; the choir, in its turn, moves from one to the other with the utmost ease and art. In particular, the give-and-take of dovetailing produces a perfect balance. In this respect, top praise for the trebles, with a firm, mature tone and assured flexibility.

Missa Assumpta est Maria. Missa Sicut lilium inter spinas. Motets – Assumpta est Maria a 6; Sicut lilium inter spinas I. Plainchant: Assumpta est Maria
The Tallis Scholars / Peter Phillips
Gimell CDGIM020 (72' · DDD) Recorded 1989 Ⓕ

In this recording of *Missa Assumpta est Maria* Peter Phillips has included the motet on which this work is based, together with another parody mass, the *Sicut lilium* with its corresponding motet. It's illuminating to hear how the larger-scale compositions unfold with reference to the original motets: close study reveals much about the compositional processes of the High Renaissance, but any listener will be able to appreciate the organic relationship between motet and Mass.

In addition, Phillips has deliberately paired two sharply contrasted parody Masses: *Assumpta est Maria*, the better known, is thought to be one of Palestrina's last masses, while *Sicut lilium* dates from relatively early in his career. The former, with its major tonality and *divisi* high voices, is marvellously bright and open, and is given an outgoing performance; the latter, inflected with chromaticism and melodic intervals that constantly fall back on themselves, is darker-hued and more plaintive, a mood well captured here in the intensity of the singing. But what's perhaps most striking is the difference in compositional technique between the two works: *Sicut lilium* relies largely onimitative textures for the unfolding of its structure (though there are the customary block chords on phrases such as 'et homo factus est', performed here with magical effect), while *Assumpta est Maria* makes far greater use of vocal scoring as a formal device, and thus looks forward to the contrast principle of the Baroque. The Tallis Scholars make the most of the contrasted blocks of sound here, achieving an impressive vocal blend and balance. The phrasing, particularly in the *Kyrie*, is perhaps a little too mannered and the very beautiful *Agnus Dei* verges on the narcissistic and therefore becomes too static. The flow in the *Missa Sicut lilium*, though, is excellent throughout.

Music for Holy Week

Anonymous Hosanna filio David **Palestrina** Stabat mater. Domine Jesus in qua nocte. Improperia. Terra tremuit. Motets, Book 2 – Pueri Hebraeorum. Fratres ego enim accepi. Victimae Paschali. Crux fidelis/ Pange lingua. O Domine, Jesu Christe. Popule Meus. Ardens est cor meum. Congratulamini mihi omnes. Haec Dies. Crucem Sanctam Subiit. Magnificat III Toni a 6
The Cardinall's Musick / Andrew Carwood
ASV Gaudeamus CDGAU333 (79' · DDD) Texts and translations included   Ⓕ

This recording of Palestrina's music for Holy Week opens with the strong rising fifth of the Palm Sunday plainchant antiphon *Hosanna filio David*. We go on to experience the solemn moments of the liturgy through music of outstanding dignity and beauty. After the Procession, the stern Palm Sunday Offertory *Improperium*, a slow foreboding of what is to come, is viewed with quiet calm. The same mood is captured in two settings of the Institution of the Eucharist, the first subdued and hushed, despite the massive means – eight voices – the second even more so, with five low voices. The Good Friday *Reproaches* and *Crux fidelis* are expressed simply but effectively by choral homophony alternating with chant. Carwood's restraint, blending of timbres and careful phrasing can't be faulted.

In Palestrina's monumental *Stabat Mater* for double choir is central to the recording. Carwood highlights every articulation of the architecture, guiding the listener from suffering to hope. The subtle final entries of 'Paradisi gloria' reflect the calm of the earlier pieces, but with a glow foreshadowing the victory to come. Christ's resurrection is marked in *Terra tremuit* by great leaping octaves and fifths and rapid rising scales. Mary Magdalene's fruitless searching, followed by the gentlest possible singing of the Alleluias in the antiphon *Ardens est*, finally yields to total rejoicing in the double choir responsory *Congratulamini*: the singers capture her moment of ecstasy; she's seen the risen Lord, and her joy is complete. The Easter gradual *Haec dies* is all lightness and flight, with cries of 'exultemus' chasing each other. The final sequence, *Victimae paschali laudes*, is a brilliantly dramatic interpretation with vigorous and imaginative rhythmic variety.

Music for Holy Saturday   Ⓟ

Lamentations, Book III – I-III. Stabat mater. Benedictus for Holy Week. Sicut cervus. Responsories and Antiphons
Musica Contexta / Simon Ravens
Chaconne CHAN0679 (60' · DDD) Notes, texts and translations included   ⒻⓄ

This outstanding recording of music for Holy Saturday opens with two lessons from the third of Palestrina's four settings of texts from *Lamentations*, passages chanted during the Office of Tenebrae on the last three days of Holy Week. The third lesson is Palestrina's superb setting of the *Prayer of Jeremiah*.

The performance is objectively straightforward, allowing the music, in its utter poignancy expressed with marked restraint, to speak for itself. The clarity of the individual voices is remarkable and the acoustic clear, yet warm: even the six-part final cry, 'Jerusalem…convertere ad Dominum Deum tuum', comes across with perfect intelligibility. In the chanted liturgy each lesson is followed by a florid repository, and full marks should go to Musica Contexta for transcribing these chants from Giovanni Guidetti's edition of 1587, which naturally comes from the right place and is of the right date.

Though the responsories might have been better in a slower, more determinedly solemn style, these singers are well on the way to achieving perfection here. It's particularly interesting to hear them sing Palestrina's wonderful *Sicut cervus*, with its surging phrases, and also his famous *Stabat mater* for double choir, displaying that dramatic alternation between antiphonal choir and combined choral sections. For maximum effect, more antiphonal distinction might have helped in the choir – versus – choir sections; but overall this is a well-thought-out and moving performance.

Giovanni Antonio Pandolfi
Italian fl1660-1669

Italian composer and violinist Pandolfi is a shadowy figure known only for handful of violin sonatas. He was among the instrumentalists of Archduke Ferdinand of Austria at Innsbruck when his opp 3 and 4 violin sonatas were published in 1660 and there is little doubt a 1669 volume of sonatas attributed to 'D. Gio. Antonio Pandolfi' is by the same composer.
GROVEmusic

Violin Sonatas

Six Sonatas per chiesa e camera, Op 3.   Ⓟ
Six Sonatas for Violin and Continuo, Op 4
Andrew Manze vn Richard Egarr hpd
Harmonia Mundi HMU907241 (80' · DDD)   ⒻⓄⓄⓄ

 These are virtuoso performances of some quite extraordinary music. Each sonata has its own descriptive subtitle and a movement layout which seems reluctant to conform to any set pattern. Presumably the sections have their own tempo indications, though these aren't disclosed either in the booklet or in the listing on the reverse side of the box. A pity, since there are lots of interesting and unusual juxtapositions of a strikingly nonconformist nature. Much of the writing is characterised by virtuoso figurations which, especially in faster movements, might become a little wearisome in the hands of a lesser player. But Manze seems to sense this danger and averts it with panache and a highly developed sense of fantasy. Slow movements, on balance, are more interesting. There's an especially memorable one in *La Clemente*, the fifth sonata of Op 3, with a pathos-laden aria-like character. Manze plays it sensitively and the result is touching. Several movements have a strong ostinato element and, in *La Monella Romanesca*, the third piece from Op 4, we have a set of variations on a melody contained in the bass. Harpsichordist Richard Egarr is a lively and an imaginative accompanist throughout. In short, an exhilarating recital of music whose exoticism, melancholy and wild, passionate outbursts resist categorisation and convenient definition. Strongly recommended.

Roxanna Panufnik
British b1968

Roxanna Panufnik, the daughter of the composer Sir Andrzej Panufnik, studied composition at the Royal Academy of Music. She has writen opera, ballet, music theatre, choral works, chamber music and music for film and television.

Westminster Mass

Angels Sing!
Westminster Mass[a]. Douai Missa Brevis[b]. Spring[c]. Prayer[d]. The Christmas Life[e]. Angels Sing![f]
[bd]Bridget Corderoy, [c]Katherine Seaton, [ce]Helen Semple *sops* [be]David Rees-Jones *bass* [cef]Jeremy Filsell *org* [bcdef]Joyful Company of Singers / Peter Broadbent; [a]Westminster Cathedral Choir; [a]City of London Sinfonia / James O'Donnell
Warner Classics 2564 60292-2 (65' · DDD) Texts included   Ⓕ

This recording of the *Westminster Mass* first appeared in 1999 alongside music by Howells, Pärt and Tavener – strange bedfellows for such a vibrant and positive composer. Now Warner Classics has had the good sense to devote an entire disc to Roxanna Panufnik's choral music, and so reveals what a superb composer for choir she is.

More than her deft handling of choral forces, what stands out is her instinctive feel for words; whether they are the Latin text of the Mass (the *Douai* Mass; the Westminster one uses English), the complex poetry of Gerard Manley Hopkins, or simple Christmas verses for Polish children, she treats them with equal respect, and while there's some delicious word-painting, particularly in the Hopkins setting, *Spring*, her real skill lies in an ability to find, in musical language, the essence of the texts.

The passionate *Douai* Mass was composed in 2001 for a mixed *a cappella* group, and stretches choral technique to the highest professional level. It provides a glorious showcase for Peter

Broadbent and his outstanding Joyful Company of Singers; its highly effective quasi-Orthodox chanting and almost oriental decorative lines are magnificently sung by David Rees-Jones and a sumptuous-voiced Bridget Corderoy.

The disc takes its title from a setting of four Polish Christmas Carols composed for an Ealing Children's choir. *Angels Sing!* is full of youthful spirit and occasional naivety, but heard here performed by this exceptionally accomplished group, with Jeremy Filsell an astonishingly virtuoso accompanist, one wonders just how gifted those Ealing children must have been.

Sir Hubert Parry
British 1848-1918

Parry studied at Oxford and with Pierson and Dannreuther, publishing songs, church music and piano works from the 1860s. He taught at the Royal College of Music from 1883 (succeeding Grove as director in 1894), also becoming professor at Oxford (1900-1908) and president of the Musical Association (1901-8). Among his scholarly interests were Bach and the history of musical style, on which he wrote perceptively. His cantatas Scenes from Prometheus Unbound (1880), Blest Pair of Sirens (1887) and L'allegro ed il penseroso (1890) made a decisive impact for their poetic merit and advanced (Wagnerian) idiom. The anthem I was glad (1902), the choral Songs of Farewell (1916) and many of the unison songs including The Lover's Garland and Jerusalem show a similar regard for text and a fresh lyricism. His forceful personality and social position, together with his ethical views and intellectual vigour, enabled him to exercise a revitalising influence on English musical life in the late 19th century.
GROVEmusic

Complete Organ Works

Fantasia and Fugue in G (1882 & 1913 vers)[a]. Three Chorale Fantasias[a]. Chorale Preludes, Sets 1[a] & 2[b]. Elegy in A flat[a]. Toccata and Fugue in G[a]. Elégie[b]
Various A Little Organ Book in Memory of Sir Hubert Parry[b]
James Lancelot *org*
Priory ② PRCD682AB (135' · DDD) Recorded [a]1997, [b]2000   Ⓕ❶❶❶

It's all too easy to dismiss Parry's music as being workmanlike and living in the shadow of Bach and Brahms. Yet there's real beauty and passion here, and at his best Parry can match the intensity of his contemporary Max Reger.

The appeal of this recording is enhanced by the inclusion of both the published and unpublished versions of the C major Fantasia and Fugue, and also by *A Little Organ Book*. This latter collection is an intensely moving tribute to Parry by 13 of his friends, colleagues and pupils (including Stanford, Bridge and Thalben-Ball).

This recording presents the best possible advocacy for Parry, and the combination of

Lancelot and the Durham Willis/Harrison organ is, to coin a phrase, a 'dream ticket'. The greatness of Lancelot's playing lies in the perfect fusion of meticulously honed detail with an effortless flow to the whole performance. He fully exploits the beauty and grandeur of Durham's magical organ, and of all the available CDs, this one is the finest showcase for this most charismatic of cathedral instruments. The excellence of the playing is matched by the recording. Quite simply, this is a definitive, outstanding, glorious recording.

I was glad ... / Jerusalem

I was glad when they said unto me. Evening Service in D, 'Great'. Songs of Farewell. Hear my words, ye people. Jerusalem
Timothy Woodford, Richard Murray-Bruce trebs
Andrew Wickens, Colin Cartwright countertens
David Lowe, Martin Pickering tens **Bruce Russell,**
Paul Rickard bars **John Heighway** bass **Roger Judd**
org **Choir of St George's Chapel, Windsor /**
Christopher Robinson
Hyperion CDA66273 (58' · DDD) Recorded 1987.
Texts included   Ⓕ

The more of Parry's music one comes to know, the more apparent it becomes that the received opinion of him is askew. Take the 1882 settings of the *Magnificat* and *Nunc dimittis*, for instance. These, amazingly, were not published until 1982. This recording – another example of Hyperion's courageous policy – shows how un-Victorian in the accepted sense they're. In other words, they're bold, unconventional and unsanctimonious – like quite a lot of Victorian church music, one may add. Perhaps the big anthem, *Hear my words* (1894) shows more signs of conventionality, but it has an attractive part for solo soprano (treble here) and ends with the hymn 'O praise ye the Lord'. The St George's Chapel Choir, conducted by Christopher Robinson, sings these works with more ease than it can muster for the famous and magnificent Coronation anthem *I was glad*, ceremonial music that not even Elgar surpassed. A sense of strain among the trebles is always evident. Although a wholly adult choir in the *Songs of Farewell* might be preferable, these are assured and often beautiful performances – excellent diction – of these extraordinarily affecting motets. English music doesn't possess much that's more perfect in the matching of words and music than the settings of 'There is an old belief' and 'Lord, let me know mine end', invidious as it is to select only two for mention. A stirring *Jerusalem* completes this enterprising recording, which brings the sound of a great building into our homes with absolute fidelity.

Songs

Parry English Lyrics: Set 2 – O mistress mine; Take, O take those lips away; No longer mourn for me; Blow,

blow, thou winter wind; When icicles hang by the wall. Set 4 – Thine eyes still shine for me; When lovers meet again; When we two parted; Weep you no more; There be none of beauty's daughters; Bright star. Set 5 – A Welsh lullaby. Set 6 – When comes my Gwen; And yet I love her till I die; Love is a bable. Set 7 – On a time the amorous Silvy. Set 8 – Marian; Looking backward. Set 9 – There. Set 10 – From a city window **Vaughan Williams** Songs of Travel. Linden Lea
Robert Tear ten **Philip Ledger** pf
Belart 461 493-2 (77' · ADD) Recorded c1979   Ⓑ

This selection of Parry's songs is very welcome in these fine and intelligent performances by Robert Tear and Philip Ledger. Parry doesn't always measure up to his texts (in the sonnets of Keats and Shakespeare especially), and is best when renouncing his teatime-Brahms style in favour of a more personal and imaginative idiom, as in 'When icicles hang by the wall' and 'From a city window'.

Vaughan Williams's great song cycle, *Songs of Travel*, has a freshness partly deriving from the comparative rarity of hearing it in higher keys for the tenor voice. Both artists give the impression of having studied the songs as it were 'from scratch'. Tear's phrasing is a delight, showing exceptional sensitivity to the words, and Ledger's playing, with very sparing use of pedal, is scrupulously clean and careful over detail. The recorded sound is fine. No texts are included but it hardly matters: the diction is so clear you're unlikely to miss a word.

Arvo Pärt   Estonian b1935

Pärt was a pupil of Eller at the Tallinn Conservatory until 1963 while working as a sound producer for Estonian radio (1957-67); in 1962 he won a prize for a children's cantata (Our Garden) and an oratorio (Stride of the World). Early works followed standard Soviet models, but later he turned to strict serial writing, in rhythm as well as pitch (Perpetuum mobile,1963) and then collage techniques (Symphony no.2, 1966; Pro et contra for cello and orchestra,1966). In the 1970s he came into contact with plainchant and the music of the Orthodox Church, which affected his music both technically and spiritually. This is seen in, for example, Symphony no.3 (1971) and the cantata Song for the Beloved (1973) as well as Tabula rasa for three violins, strings and prepared piano (1977). The music of other composers is evoked, drawing on minimalist techniques of repetition, in such works as Arbos for chamber ensemble (1977, Janáček), Summa for tenor, baritone and ensemble (1980, Stravinsky), Cantus in Memory of Benjamin Britten for bell and strings (1980, Britten). Of more recent works, Pari intervalli echoes Bach chorale preludes, An den Wassern zu Babylon calls on 13th-century music and the St John Passion (1981) uses choral and instrumental heterophony recalling ancient incantation, always intense yet pure and ritualistic in effect. **GROVE**music

Symphony No 3

Symphony No 3. Tabula rasa[a]. Fratres[b]
[ab]**Gil Shaham**, [a]**Adele Anthony** vns [a]**Erik Risberg**
prepared pf [b]**Roger Carlsson** perc **Gothenburg
Symphony Orchestra / Neeme Järvi**
DG 20/21 457 647-2GH (59' · DDD)   Ⓕ

Pärt's panoramic, occasionally fragmented
Third Symphony of 1971 contrasts with his
gaunt but entrancing tintinnabulation works of
the late 1970s. There are beautiful things in the
symphony – ancient modes imaginatively rede-
ployed, sensitive orchestration (especially for
strings and tuned percussion), striking musical
development and a fair quota of aural drama.
There are occasional anticipations of the *Cantus
in memory of Benjamin Britten*, and the 'breathing' spaces between episodes are characteristic
of Pärt's later work. It's the voice of someone
stretching his musical wings, edging into areas
of harmonic invention that would help inform
his future style – a youthful late-Romantic
poised on the brink of greater things. One
might wonder how Gil Shaham might tackle a
style of music in which, in terms of overt expression, 'less' most definitely means 'more'. In the
event, his firm, silvery tone is ideal and his pin-
sharp arpeggios at the beginning of *Fratres* are
extraordinarily exciting. When Pärt drops the
pace and switches to a slow, gradual *crescendo*,
Shaham plays with a mesmerising combination
of control and reserved expressiveness.

The more expansive *Tabula rasa* is given a full-
bodied and unexpectedly dynamic performance,
especially in the opening movement, which
sounds like a cross between a jig and a quick
march. The long second movement conjures up
immeasurable spaces and the spasmodic interjections of a prepared piano – an incredible
effect, musically – is balanced virtually to perfection by the engineers. Kremer's ECM disc
(with Schnittke, no less, on prepared piano) is
sparer and marginally more ethereal, but the
sheer sense of presence on this disc adds a new
perspective to our experience of the piece.
Strongly recommended, even if you already
own alternative versions.

Symphony No 3. Summa. Fratres. Trisagion. Cantus
in memory of Benjamin Britten. Silouans Song.
Festina lente
Estonian National Symphony Orchestra / Paavo Järvi
Virgin Classics 545501-2 (73' · DDD)   Ⓕ**Ⓞ**

With Arvo Pärt the terms of comparison normally used for focusing differences between this
or that recording tend to fall redundant. Pärt's
mature music responds most readily to luminous textures, carefully timed silences and mastery of line, and only rarely to the more subjective impulses of dramatic conducting.

Paavo's performance of the first movement
suggests urgent parallels with the fraught confrontations in Nielsen's Fifth. And there's more
than a hint of 'the spring water purity of

Sibelius's Sixth Symphony' in the finale. Everywhere one senses the hovering spectre of early
music, but this Third Symphony is the ideal
stepping stone for first-timers who wish to journey from standard symphonic fare to Pärt's
cloistered tintinnabulation.

The more familiar tintinnabulation pieces
work very well, with Järvi opting in the *Cantus*
and *Festina lente* for warmer textures than some
rivals, which usefully underlines Pärt's quietly
cascading harmonies. There are those who will
still prefer a more chaste sonority, the sort
favoured on virtually all the ECM productions.
But Paavo Järvi's more central approach will
appeal to those who until now have heard in
Pärt's music ascetic denial rather than quiet
affirmation. Virgin's sound canvas is well
judged, especially at the lower end of the spectrum. Recommended.

Additional recommendation

Coupled with: Tabula rasa[a]. Collage on B-A-C-H.
[a]**Hatfield**, [a]**Hirsch** vns **Ulster Orchestra / Yuasa**
Naxos 8 554591 (52' · DDD)   Ⓢ
Yuasa's reading is somewhat akin to Järvi's first
(BIS) recording – certainly for tempo. The Ulster
brass are excellent and if the Orchestra's strings
aren't quite on a par with those in Bamberg and
Gothenburg, they're still pretty good. Quality
samplings of Pärt don't come any cheaper.

Fratres / Summa

Fratres (seven versions). Summa. Festina Lente.
Cantus in Memory of Benjamin Britten.
Peter Manning vn **France Springuel** vc **Mireille
Gleizes** pf **I Fiamminghi**
Telarc CD80387 (79' · DDD) Recorded 1994   Ⓕ

Telarc's Fratres-Fest proves beyond doubt that
good basic material can be reworked almost *ad
infinitum* if the manner of its arrangement is
sufficiently colourful. This sequence is particularly imaginative in that it alternates two varied
pairs of *Fratres* with atmospheric original string
pieces, then separates the last two versions with
the sombre pealing of *Festina Lente*. The first
Fratres opens to a low bass drone and chaste,
ethereal strings: the suggested image is of a slow
oncoming processional – mourners, perhaps, or
members of some ancient religious sect – with
drum and xylophone gradually intensifying
until the percussive element is so loud that it
resembles Copland's *Fanfare for the Common
Man*. One envisages aged figures who have been
treading the same ground since time immemo-
rial, whereas the frantically propelled, arpeggiated opening to the version for violin, strings
and percussion leaves a quite different impression. Still, even here the music does eventually
calm and Peter Manning provides an expressive
solo commentary.

Next comes the gentle cascading of Pärt's
Cantus in Memory of Benjamin Britten, with its
weeping sequences and lone, tolling bell. The

eight-cello *Fratres* uses eerie harmonics (as does the cello and piano version that ends the programme), whereas *Fratres* for wind octet and percussion is cold, baleful, notably Slavonic-sounding and occasionally reminiscent of Stravinsky. The alternation of *Summa* (for strings) and the quartet version of *Fratres* works nicely, the former more animated than anything else on the disc; the latter, more intimate. The performances are consistently sympathetic, and the recordings are excellent.

Berliner Messe

Berliner Messe. Magnificat. Seven Magnificat Antiphons. The Beatitudes. Annum per Annum. De profundis
Polyphony / Stephen Layton with **Andrew Lucas** org
CDA66960 (74' · DDD) Texts and translations included   Ⓕ

Pärt's music is about equilibrium and balance – balance between consonance and dissonance, between converging voices and, in the context of a CD such as this, between the individual works programmed. Stephen Layton has chosen well, starting with the variegated *Berliner Messe* and closing with the starkly ritualistic *De profundis*, a memorable and ultimately dramatic setting of Psalm 130 for male voices, organ, bass drum and tam-tam, dedicated to Gottfried von Einem. The Mass features two of Pärt's most powerful individual movements, a gently rocking 'Veni Sancte Spiritus' and a *Credo* which, as Meurig Bowen's unusually perceptive notes remind us, is in essence a major-key transformation of the better-known – and more frequently recorded – *Summa*. Everything here chimes to Pärt's tintinnabulation style, even the brief but fetching organ suite *Annum per Annum*, where the opening movement thunders an alarm then tapers to a gradual *diminuendo*, while the closing coda shoulders an equally well-calculated *crescendo*. The five movements in between are mostly quiet, whereas *The Beatitudes* flies back to its opening tonality on 'a flurry of quintuplet broken chords'. It's also the one place that witnesses a momentary – and minor – blemish on the vocal line, but otherwise Layton directs a fine sequence of warmly blended performances. Polyphony employs what one might roughly term an 'early music' singing style, being remarkably even in tone, largely free of vibrato and alive to phrasal inflexions.

If you're new to Pärt's music, then this disc would provide an excellent starting-point. We would suggest playing the individually shaded *Seven Magnificat Antiphons* first, then tackling the *Berliner Messe*, followed, perhaps, by the *Magnificat*.

Berliner Messe[a]. Bogoróditse Djévo. I am the True Vine. Kanon pokajanen – Ode IX. The Woman with the Alabaster Box. Tribute to Caesar.
Pro Arte Singers, [a]Theatre of Voices / Paul Hillier

bar with [a]**Christopher Bowers-Broadbent** org
Harmonia Mundi HMU90 7242 (58' · DDD) Texts and translations included   Ⓕ**O**

I am the True Vine was composed in 1996 for the 900th anniversary of Norwich Cathedral, whereas *Tribute to Caesar* and *The Woman with the Alabaster Box* were commissioned in 1997 for the 350th Anniversary of the Karlstad Diocese in Sweden. Both works bear witness to a widened expressive vocabulary and, like *I am the True Vine*, take their creative nourishment from the power of words.

The remaining items can also be heard, in one form or another, on alternative recordings. Hillier's reading of the beautiful Ninth Ode from *Kanon pokajanen* is slower by some two minutes than Tõnu Kaljuste's première recording of the parent work on ECM (an absolute must for Pärt devotees), which is surprising given the less reverberant acoustic on the new CD. Both here and in the *Berliner Messe*, ECM's sound-frame suggests greater space and tonal weight, though this latest production is equally effective in its own quite different way. Pärt's 'revision' of the *Messe* is an update of his original score (which is warmly represented in its full-choir guise on Hyperion). In a second version (the one featured on ECM), the organ part was replaced by a string orchestra, whereas a third version (the one offered here) features an organ revision of the string score. Comparing Hillier's vocal quartet recording with Kaljuste's string version with choir inclines one towards the silvery organ registrations in the *Credo* and depth of organ tone in the *Agnus Dei*. As for the rest, there's sufficient contrast between the two to warrant owning – or at least hearing – both. With fine sound quality, first-rate singing and concisely worded annotation (by Paul Hillier) this should prove a popular, indeed an essential, addition to Pärt's ever-growing discography.

Berliner Messe. Te Deum. Magnificat. Silouans Song, 'My soul yearns after the Lord …
Estonian Philharmonic Chamber Choir; Tallinn Chamber Orchestra / Tõnu Kaljuste
ECM New Series 439 162-2 (66' · DDD) Recorded 1993. Texts and translations included   Ⓕ**OO**

Pärt's *Te Deum* sets the standard liturgical text to a wide range of nuances, shades and dynamics; brief string interludes provide heart-rending wordless commentaries, and the work's closing pages provide a serenely moving affirmation of holiness. Although relatively static in its musical narrative, Pärt's *Te Deum* is both mesmerising and enriching. *Silouans Song* (1991), an eloquent study for strings, is as reliant on silence as on sonority. It's again austere and chant-like, although its dramatic interpolations approximate a sort of sacral protest. The brief *Magnificat* for *a cappella* choir (1989) positively showers multi-coloured resonances. However, the *Te Deum*'s closest rival – in terms of substance and appeal – is surely the 25-minute

Berliner Messe (1990-92). Here again Pärt employs the simplest means to achieve the most magical ends: 'Veni Sancte Spiritus' weaves a luminous thread of melodic activity either side of a constant, mid-voice drone, while the weighted phrases of the 'Sanctus' take breath among seraphic string chords. And how wonderful the gradual darkening of the closing 'Agnus Dei', where tenors initially answer sopranos and an almost imperceptible mellowing softens the work's final moments. Beautiful sounds – gripping yet remote, communicative yet deeply personal in their contemplative aura; the all-round standard of presentation – performance, engineering etc – serves Pärt as devotedly as Pärt serves the Divine Image.

Como cierva sedienta

Orient and Occident
Como cierva sedienta[a]. Orient and Occident.
Ein Wallfahrtslied[a]
Swedish Radio [a]**Choir and Symphony Orchestra /
Tonu Kaljuste**
ECM New Series 472 080-2 (47' · DDD)　　Ⓕ**ⓈⓈⓈ**

 This programme represents a retreat from the remote cloister where for so long Arvo Pärt invited us to join him, a definite shift from the aerated tintinabuli. The purity remains, so do the spare textures and, to a limited extent, earlier stylistic traits. Pärt's voice is always recognisable. And yet who, years ago, could have anticipated the tempered tumult that erupts in the third movement of *Como cierva sedienta*, a half-hour choral drama commissioned by the Festival de Música de Canarias?

This recording subscribes to ECM's well-tried aesthetic, in which clarity, fine-tipped detail and carefully gauged perspectives are familiar priorities. The texts come from Psalms 42 and 43, opening with 'As the hart panteth…' (Psalm 42). Even in the first few seconds, vivid instrumental colour signals a fresh departure. It's almost as if Pärt is relishing textures previously denied him, like a penitent released from fasting. Take the second movement, 'Why art thou cast down, my soul?', which opens among lower strings then switches to tactile *pizzicati* and woodwinds that are almost Tchaikovskian in their post-Classical delicacy. The long closing section is pensive but conclusive: a dramatic opening, drum taps that recall Shostakovich 11, expressively varied instrumental commentary, quiet string chords later on and a closing episode filled with equivocal tranquillity.

The two shorter works are also significant. *Wallfahrtslied* (1984, 'Song of Pilgrimage'), a memorial to a friend, is presented in the revised version for strings and men's choir. Again Pärt engages a lyrical muse, particularly for the emotionally weighted prelude and postlude whereas the accompaniment to the main text (Psalm 121, 'I lift up mine eyes unto the hills…'), a combination of *pizzicato* and shudderingbowed

phrases, suggests a lament tinged with anger.

The seven-minute string piece *Orient and Occident* has 'a monophonic line which runs resolutely through [it]', to quote Pärt's wife. Snake-like oriental gestures, coiled with prominent *portamenti* (the sort used by Indian orchestras) sound like an Eastern variant of Pärt's earlier string works. The choral pieces, though, are the prime reasons for investing in this exceptional and musically important release.

Passio

Passio Domini nostri Jesu Christi secundum Johannem
Mark Anderson *ten* **Robert Macdonald** *bass* **Tonus Peregrinus / Antony Pitts**
Naxos 8 555860 (62' · DDD)　　Ⓢ **Ⓢ ⓄⓄ**

Arvo Pärt's *Passio* is a shining beacon among countless late 20th-century religious works that confronted the formidable prospect of a new millennium. Put briefly, *Passio* sets St John's gospel to a simple but powerful triadic musical language, its prescribed forces limited to a small chorus, a handful of solo voices and a chamber-size instrumental line-up consisting of organ, violin, oboe, cello and bassoon. Pärt treats the text as paramount and yet there's scarcely a hint of word painting in the accepted sense of the term. Spiritual underlining, yes, with telling support from the solo instruments. There are no written dynamics save for the opening, marked *Langsam* and *forte*, and the close, a *Largo* that blossoms from *pianissimo* to triple *forte*. Which doesn't mean that the singers are expected to deliver monotonously uninflected lines. Thankfully, none of them does.

Tonus Peregrinus shape phrases with a certain degree of freedom, just as choirs on rival versions have done before them. And Antony Pitts comes up trumps in his ability to keep lines lively and fluid, blending or clarifying as the text dictates. His is an excellent reading, always alert to Pärt's shifting harmonic plane and with consistently fresh voices, the women especially. Robert Macdonald's 'inward' portrayal of Jesus is preferable to the vocally commanding but inappropriately operatic Jorma Hynninen on Finlandia, though the Hilliards' Michael George perhaps remains the most impressive of all. And if the rival instrumentalists have the edge, Pitts's group is more than adequate.

Viewed overall, Tonus Peregrinus and Naxos have done Pärt proud. If this is your first *Passio*, rest assured that all the essentials are there. And if you want a top-grade specimen of quality music from the past 40 years, you won't find better. *Passio* truly is a wonderful work.

Nunc dimittis

Triodion
Dopo la vittoria. Nunc dimittis. …which was the son of…. I am the true vine. Littlemore Tractus[a]. Triodion.

My heart's in the Highlands[ab]. Salve regina
[b]David Jones *counterten* a**Christopher Bowers Broadbent** *org* **Polyphony / Stephen Layton**
Hyperion CDA67375 (77' · DDD)   Ⓕ**OO**

Meurig Bowen's notes observe that choral pieces composed in the 1990s suggested Pärt was moving into 'more complex, exotic harmonic territory'. Some of his music began to give a glimpse of what was described as 'an attractively post-Minimalist aspect' of the composer's recent work. All rather premature, perhaps, since, as Bowen acknowledges, Pärt subsequently returned to a more strictly diatonic, triadic approach.

Even so, the staccato, carol-like episodes bracketing *Dopo La Vittoria*, commissioned in 1991 and delivered in 1997, come as a shock, but the bulk of the piece is more recognisably by Pärt, and the *Nunc Dimittis*, with its lovely, lambent solo part for soprano Elin Thomas, evoking Allegri's *Miserere*, assuages all doubts.

The idea of Pärt setting Burns might surprise, but *My heart's in the Highlands*, with its serene, Pachelbel-like organ line and pellucid vocal by countertenor David James, is a triumph. In the hymn-like *Littlemore Tractus* and *Salve Regina*, warm melodies and bursts of colourful chords mellow Pärt's sound without detracting from its sublime, ethereal beauty. Polyphony's performance is gorgeous.

Martin Peerson   English c1572-1651

A virginalist and organist active in London, Peerson was probably sacrist at Westminster Abbey, 1623-30. He was also almoner and master of the choristers at St Paul's Cathedral from 1624-5 until services ceased in 1642, and remained later as almoner. Experiments with form and unusual harmonic procedures are characteristic of his works. His two books of secular vocal music (1620, 1630) include settings for up to six voices with instruments and combine elements from the ayre, madrigal, consort song and verse anthem; the second – the earliest English published collection with figured bass – is strikingly sombre in mood. A more modern idiom appears in his 20 (mostly verse) anthems. He also composed motets, keyboard pieces and consort music. GROVEmusic

Latin Motets

Motets – Deus omnipotens (prima pars); Redemptor mundi (secunda pars); Pater Fili paraclete; Levavi oculos meos in montes (prima pars); Ecce non dormitabit (secunda pars); Mulieres sedentes (prima pars); Hora nona Dominus Jesus (prima pars); Christus factus est (secunda pars); Latus eius lancea miles perforavit (secunda pars); O Rex gloriae; Quid vobis videtur de Christo; O Domine Jesu Christe; Laboravi in gemitu meo; Nolite fieri sicut equus et mulus (prima pars); Multa flagella peccatoris (secunda pars)
Ex Cathedra Consort / Jeffrey Skidmore
Hyperion CDA67490 (66' · DDD)   Ⓕ

'Here being heard for the first time since the 17th century': the phrase is quietly slipped into Richard Rastall's introductory notes. These 15 motets were unknown to the extent that the writers in *New Grove* speak of them somewhat hypothetically. Rastall's edition, with the missing soprano line reconstructed, was published in 2003; this recording marks the fulfilment of that valuable work.

Peerson is remembered generally for a small set of keyboard pieces and the madrigal *The Primrose*. These motets are masterly not only in their deployment of polyphonic techniques and harmonic expressiveness, but also in a large-scale architectural vision. They group naturally, the first five comprising one 'movement', the next four another, and the remainder an impressive third. In the opening numbers particularly there's a remarkable directness of utterance – Peerson has a madrigalist's feeling for words, and the counterpoint is never allowed to obscure them. The listening mind is fully engaged throughout.

Singing in the clear, unflattering acoustic of St Paul's, Southgate, Ex Cathedra give an immaculate account, imaginatively directed.

Krzysztof Penderecki   Polish b1933

Penderecki was a pupil of Malawski at the Kraków Conservatory (1955-8), where he has also taught. He gained international fame with such works as Threnody for the Victims of Hiroshima for 52 strings (1960), exploiting the fierce expressive effects of new sonorities, but in the mid-1970s there came a change to large symphonic forms based on rudimentary chromatic motifs. Central to his work is the St Luke Passion (1965), with its combination of intense expressive force with a severe style with archaic elements alluding to Bach, and its sequel Utrenia, in which Orthodox chant provides musical material and at the same time a sense of mystery. His operas have been admired for their dynamic expression even if their discrete vignettes offer more opportunity for characterisation than development. GROVEmusic

St Luke Passion

St Luke Passion (Passio et mors Domini nostri Jesu Christi secundam Lucam)
Sigune von Osten *sop* **Stephen Roberts** *bar* **Kurt Rydl** *bass* **Edward Lubaszenko** *narr* **Cracow Boys' Choir; Warsaw National Philharmonic Chorus; Polish Radio National Symphony Orchestra / Krzysztof Penderecki**
Argo 430 328-2ZH (76' · DDD) Recorded 1989
Text and translation included   Ⓕ

The first performance in Münster Cathedral in 1966 of Penderecki's *Passio et mors Domini nostri Jesu Christi secundum Lucam* brought overnight fame and world recognition to the then 33-year-old composer, and succeeded, where many others had failed, in bringing the methods and language of the avant-garde to a much wider audience. Part of its immediate success must surely lie in his skilful fusion of past musical techniques (Renaissance-like polyphony, Gregorian melismata and Venetian *cori spezzati*) with the colouristic avant-garde devices that he had been developing in the years preceding its composition. Mind you, it was not without its detractors. Some critics, for the very reasons stated above, accused Penderecki of 'courting the masses' and of 'pure sensation-seeking', not to mention the fact that here was a young composer who had the audacity to court comparison with the sublime creations of Bach. Time, however, has proved some justification for the initial enthusiasm as the many hundreds (yes, hundreds!) of performances since its première testify.

It unfailingly creates an impressive impact on the listener with its dramatic energy and waves of tension, even if some of its language does sound a little dated.

The performance, under the guiding hand of the composer, is all one could wish for with splendid performances from orchestra, chorus and soloists alike, while the recording, made in the Cathedral of Christ the King, Katowice, has a beautifully spacious and resonant sound that gives the work a somewhat timeless quality

St Luke Passion – In pulverem mortis; Vulgata. Magnificat – Sicut locutus est. Agnus Dei. Song of Cherubim. Veni creator. Benedicamus Domino. Benedictus. Symphony No 2 – Finale; Allegro moderato
Tapiola Chamber Choir / Juha Kuivanen
Warner Apex 8573-88433-2 (52' · DDD) Recorded 1993. Texts and translations included ⑤

There's a neat correspondence in the way the earliest and most recent pieces included here – Stabat mater (1962) and Benedictus (1992) – both move to resolutions on simple major triads. The difference is in the extent to which the triads in the later work govern the musical fabric throughout. In the 1960s such common chords had to be fought for, and could even seem tacked on arbitrarily. In general, however, it's another kind of consistency that makes this disc musically worthwhile. Although all the works tend to be reflective and devotional, the contrapuntal medium of the unaccompanied chorus inspires the composer to an economical intensity all too often absent from his later instrumental works. Indeed, it's as part of that intensity that elements of his early, much more dissonant style, so powerfully represented in the three extracts from the St Luke Passion and the fragment from the Magnificat, re-emerge in the more traditional harmonic world of the later pieces – especially the Veni creator. Yet it should also be said that Penderecki's austere response to this celebratory text seems more than a little strange. Of the later works Song of Cherubim is the most powerful, ending with remarkably rapt 'Alleluias'. A note tells us that

the composer regards the Benedictus as a draft to be reworked at a later stage. These performances are on the whole models of pure-toned clarity. Recordings are full of atmosphere but well balanced.

Additional recordings

St Luke Passion
Hirzel *sop* **Le Roux** *bar* **Courtis** *bass* **Jung** *narr* **West German Radio Chorus; North German Radio Chorus; Mainz Cathedral Choir; Orchestra of the Beethovenhalle, Bonn / Soustrot**
Dabringhaus und Grimm MDG337 0981-2 (70' · DDD) Text and German translation only included Ⓕ
While Soustrot can't erase the disparity between the brief Passion narrative and the drifting choral meditations, he maintains plenty of ongoing tension: as a result, the performance is about six minutes shorter than Penderecki's. The sound has an appropriately raw edge with a touch of glare at climaxes. The performance is consistently excellent – a genuine team effort.

Izabella Klosinska *sop* **Adam Kruszewski** *bar* **Romuald Tesarowicz** *bass* **Krzysztof Kolberger** *spkr* **Jaroslaw Malanowicz** *org* **Warsaw Boys' Choir; Warsaw Philharmonic Choir; Warsaw National Philharmonic Orchestra / Antoni Wit**
Naxos 8 557149 (76' · DDD) Ⓢ
The relatively brief moments of almost expressionistic drama come off best, aided by a pungently immediate recording, complete with rasping organ and blazing brass. The soloists are all excellent. Given the importance of the spoken narration, the absence of text and translation is unfortunate, though Richard Whitehouse's track-cued synopsis is better than nothing.

A Polish Requiem

A Polish Requiem
Izabella Kłosinska *sop* **Jadwiga Rappé** *contr* **Ryszard Minkiewicz** *ten* **Piotr Nowacki** *bass* **Warsaw National Philharmonic Choir and Orchestra / Antoni Wit**
Naxos ② 8 557386/7 (99' · DDD · T/t) Ⓢ

The *Polish Requiem* had its origins in a setting of the *Lacrimosa* dedicated to Gdansk shipyard workers who died during clashes with the Communist authorities in 1970. Though the work's tendency to swing between bombast and sentimentality may make you long for the austerity of an Arvo Pärt, if you approach it as a valid attempt to continue the tradition of 19th-century concert Requiems – Verdi's, above all – then you may well feel it has much to offer.

This performance is well played and conducted, Antoni Wit ensuring that the big climaxes make their effect without labouring the less eventful episodes. The choral singing is robust, though the sustained high writing is demanding enough to give the Polish Philharmonic Choir some anxious moments. Of the vocal soloists, both Jadwiga Rappé and Piotr Nowacki are excellent, but the normally reliable Izabella Kłosinska was clearly under strain, and Ryszard Minkiewicz also sounds out of sorts in places. The sound is typical of Naxos's Polish recordings in being rather too bright and generalised for music that depends for its effect on such strong contrasts between the very quiet and the extremely loud.

Ubu Rex

Ubu Rex
Pawel Wunder ten Pa Ubu **Anna Lubanska** mez Ma Ubu **Józef Frakstein** bass King Wenceslas **Izabella Klosinska** sop Queen Rosmunde **Wielki Theatre Chorus and Orchestra / Jacek Kaspszyk**
CD Accord ② ACD133-2 (122' · DDD · T/S/t/N).
Recorded live at the Teatr Wielki, Warsaw, October 2003   Ⓕ

Here's the perfect antidote to the pious lamentations that pervade Penderecki's later choral and symphonic works. *Ubu Rex* was written for Munich in 1991, and had its Polish premiere in October 2003, the performance recorded here.

He planned an opera on Alfred Jarry's *Ubu Roi* for many years before the easing of political restrictions permitted a broad satire on the theme that, while all power corrupts, absolute power does so with maximum absurdity. The atmosphere of this self-declared *opera buffa* is for the most part raw and brash, as Jarry's original conception requires. But the overtly farcical episodes, depicting Ubu's improbable rise to kingship, are balanced by some of Penderecki's most probing, expressive music.

The pungent score involves a good deal of parody: most prominently, the kind of high-kicking, polka-cum-cancan style in which Rossini and Offenbach merge seamlessly into Shostakovich and Schnittke. This idiom can become rather relentless for the CD listener, but the booklet helps maintain interest by including plenty of production photographs.

Great demands are placed on the histrionic skills of the principals, notably Pawel Wunder as the grotesquely over-confident, sublimely indestructible Pa Ubu. He deploys his commanding high tenor alongside a wealth of guttural plosives and screechings which, miraculously, avoid tedium, and keep the story moving at breakneck speed.

This is an admirable ensemble effort. Special credit for the maintenance of both buoyancy and coherence goes to the conductor Jacek Kaspszyk. The recording provides a good balance. Given the high-energy production, stage noise isn't excessive, either.

Giovanni Pergolesi   Italian 1710-1736

While studying with Durante in Naples Pergolesi worked as a violinist, and in 1731 he presented his first stage work, a dramma sacro. He became maes-tro di cappella to the Prince of Stigliano in 1732 and to the Duke of Maddaloni in 1734. Several more stage works followed for Naples and an opera seria, L'Olimpiade (1735), for Rome.

Only moderately popular in his lifetime, Pergolesi posthumously attained international fame as a leading figure in the rise of Italian comic opera. He wrote two commedie musicali, with both buffo and seria elements, and three comic intermezzos, each staged with an opera seria by him. The intermezzo La serva padrona (1733, Naples) is a miniature masterpiece of buffo style, spirited, with touches of sentiment and with clear, lively characterisation; it was widely performed and in 1752 initiated the Parisian Querelle des Bouffons. Livietta e Tracollo, also known as La contadina astuta (1734, Naples), became popular too. His other works include sacred music (notably a Stabat mater of 1736), chamber cantatas and duets, and a few instrumental pieces.   **GROVE**music

Stabat mater

Stabat mater. Salve regina in C minor   Ⓟ
Emma Kirkby sop **James Bowman** counterten
Academy of Ancient Music / Christopher Hogwood
L'Oiseau-Lyre Florilegium 425 692-2OH (52' · DDD)
Recorded 1988. Texts and translations included   Ⓕ

Pergolesi's *Stabat mater*, written in the last few months of his brief life, enjoyed a huge popularity throughout the 18th century. But modern performances often misrepresent its nature, either through over-romanticising it or by transforming it into a choral work. None of these are qualities overlooked in this affecting performance, for Emma Kirkby and James Bowman are well versed in the stylistic conventions of Baroque and early classical music – and their voices afford a pleasing partnership. Both revel in Pergolesi's sensuous vocal writing, phrasing the music effectively and executing the ornaments with an easy grace. Singers and instrumentalists alike attach importance to sonority, discovering a wealth of beguiling effects in Pergolesi's part writing. In the *Salve regina* in C minor Emma Kirkby gives a compelling performance, pure in tone, expressive and poignant, and she's sympathetically supported by the string ensemble. The recording is pleasantly resonant.

La serva padrona

La serva padrona[b]. Livietta e Tracollo[a]   Ⓟ
[a]**Nancy Argenta** sop Livietta [a]**Werner van Mechelen** bass Tracollo [b]**Patricia Biccire** sop Serpina [b]**Donato di Stefano** bass Uberto
La Petite Bande / Sigiswald Kuijken vn
Accent ACC96123D (80' · DDD) Recorded live 1996.
Notes and texts included   Ⓕ

La serva padrona is given here with a rare but comparable companion-piece. *Livietta e Tracollo* is also for two characters, light soprano and *buffo* bass, with two sections, originally to be played in the intervals of the evening's *opera seria*. Rather more complicated and improbable than *La serva padrona*, it tells of a girl disguised as a French peasant (male) seeking vengeance on a robber who in turn appears disguised as a pregnant Pole. She succeeds in the first half, but in the second the man, now disguised as an astrologer, has more luck and they agree to get married. Musically it isn't so very inferior to *La serva*. Both have more wit in the music than in the libretto, with deft parodies of *opera seria* and a popular appeal in the repeated phrases of their arias.

The performance is a lively one, with Nancy Argenta a resourceful and not too pertly soubrettish Livietta. Kuijken's Petite Bande plays with a distinctively 'period' tone; the speeds are sprightly and the rhythms lightfooted. In both works, the women are better than the men, who lack the comic touch. Patricia Biccire sings attractively, especially in her 'sincere' aria, 'A Serpina penserate', and she paces her recitatives artfully. A lower Baroque pitch is used and the final number is the short duet, 'Per te io ho nel core', as in the original score.

Pérotin
French c1155/60-c1225

Pérotin was the most celebrated musician involved in the revision and re-notation of the Magnus liber (attributed to Léonin). Two decrees by the Bishop of Paris concerning the 'feast of the fools' and the performance of quadruple organum, from 1198 and 1199, have been associated with Pérotin since the theorist known as Anonymous IV stated that he composed four-voice settings of both the relevant texts. Attempts to identify him at Notre Dame have proved inconclusive. He may have been born c1155-60, revised the Magnus liber 1180-90 subsequently composed his three- and four-voice works and died in the first years of the 13th century; or he wrote the four-voice works early in his career, revised the Magnus liber in the first decade of the 13th century and died c1225. As regards his Magnus liber revisions, Anonymous IV refers to his abbreviations and improvement of the work by substituting succinct passages in discant style for the more florid organum; this would seem to be confirmed by one source of the Magnus liber, although the substitute sections are not attributed there to a specific composer. The creation of three- and four-voice organum c1200 is an important step in the development of polyphony which until then had been conceived in terms of two voices, and Pérotin's compositions show great awareness of the implications for structure and tonality. The confusion over dating derives from unresolved problems of notation. GROVEmusic

Viderunt omnes / Sederunt principes

Pérotin Viderunt omnes. Alleluia, Posui Adiutorium. Dum sigillum summi Patris. Alleluia, Nativitas. Beata viscera. Sederunt principes **Anonymous** Veni creator spiritus. O Maria virginei. Isias cecinit

Hilliard Ensemble (David James *counterten* John Potter, Rogers Covey-Crump, Mark Padmore, Charles Daniels *tens* Gordon Jones *bar*) / **Paul Hillier** *bar*
ECM New Series 837 751-2 (68' · DDD) Texts included ⓕⵔ

This is a superb and original recording. It gives musical individuality to a group of works that have hitherto tended to sound much the same. Moreover, as a special attraction for those wanting to see artistic individuality in early composers, it includes all but one of the identifiable works of Pérotin. Inevitably his two grand four-voice organa take up much of the record. At nearly 12 minutes each they may have been the most ambitious polyphonic works composed up to the end of the 12th century. The Hilliard Ensemble adopts a suave and supple approach to both *Viderunt* and *Sederunt*, softening the pervasive rhythms that can make them a shade oppressive and showing a clear view of the entire architecture of each piece. They surge irrepressibly from one section to another, creating a musical momentum that belies the admirably slow speeds they generally adopt. They also beautifully underline the musical differences between the two works, producing a sound which seems a credible reflection of what one might have heard at Notre Dame in the late 12th century. Particularly exciting is the way in which the musicians grasp at the individual dynamic of each work: the huge open spaces they create to project the text of the magical *O Maria virginei*; the breakneck virtuosity in their swirling performance of *Dum sigillum*, the gently modulated rhythms in the strophic *Veni creator*; the harder edge in their tone for *Alleluia Nativitas*; and so on. This is a recording of the highest distinction.

Allan Pettersson
Swedish 1911-1980

Pettersson, a pupil of Olsson and Blomdahl at the Stockholm Conservatory (1930-39), played the viola in the Stockholm PO (1939-51), then went to Paris for further study with Honegger and Leibowitz. Back in Sweden he concentrated on composition, in particular on large-scale, single-movement symphonies in an impassioned diatonic style (there were eventually 15, c1950-78); he also wrote concertos, songs and chamber pieces. GROVEmusic

Symphonies

Symphonies Nos 5 & 16
John-Edward Kelly *sax* **Saarbrücken Radio Symphony Orchestra / Alun Francis**
CPO CPO999 284-2 (65' · DDD) ⒷⒶ

The orchestral playing is full of commitment, the account of the 40-minute Fifth (1960-62) sounding tremendously vivid; Francis has the edge over rival versions where it counts, in his overall view of this magnificent work. Yet the coupling – the last symphony the Swede completed – is better still. No 16 was written in 1979 for the American saxophonist Frederik Hemke. Here Kelly, who has made some minor modifications to the solo part for reasons explained in the booklet (the ailing composer appears to have been uncertain of the instrument's range), glides through the hair-raising virtuosity with breathtaking ease. This is the kind of advocacy Pettersson, who never heard the work, can only have dreamed of. An excellent disc.

Symphonies Nos 7 & 11
Norrköping Symphony Orchestra / Leif Segerstam
BIS CD580 (70' · DDD) Recorded 1992   Ⓕ

Most of Pettersson's major works are constructed as large, unified movements (although he was an accomplished miniaturist) and Nos 7 and 11, respectively 46 and 24 minutes in length, are no exceptions. The former in some ways is unrepresentative of the composer; the obsessiveness of mood and hectoring tone are present, especially in the *Angst*-ridden first and third spans, but the range of expression is much wider than in most of his other works. Composed in 1967-8, it has a unique atmosphere, both haunting and haunted, which will stay with you for a long time. His melodic genius is confirmed in the long and heartfelt central threnody, as well as by the beautiful quiet coda, truly music to 'soften the crying of a child'; its delivery by the Norrköping players has just the right amount of detachment. Segerstam's tempos permit the work to breathe and resonate not unlike Mahler. The 11th Symphony (1974) is less combative in tone, although it has its moments, and isn't on the same elevated plane as the Seventh. The recording quality is first-rate, allowing both the devastating power and delicate fine detail of these scores to emerge equally well.

Hans Pfitzner   German 1869-1949

Pfitzner, a pupil of Knorr and Kwast at the Hoch Conservatory, Frankfurt, was a teacher in Berlin, Strasbourg and Munich until 1934, when he was relieved of his post. His earlier works, including the operas Der arme Heinrich (1895) and Die Rose vom Liebesgarten (1901), are Wagnerian, but in Palestrina (1917) he produced a remarkable piece of operatic spiritual autobiography, contrasting the pressures of the everyday world with the inner certainties of artistic genius. One of his certainties was of the supremacy of the German Romantic tradition – he was a powerful patriot – which he supported in polemical exchanges with Berg and implicitly in the cantatas (Von deutscher Seele, 1921; Das dunkle Reich, 1929) which were his main works after Palestrina. He also wrote three symphonies (1932, 1939, 1940), concertos for the piano (1922), the vio-

lin (1923) and two for the cello (1935, 1944), chamber music (including three string quartets) and c100 songs.   **GROVE**music

Piano Trio

Violin Sonata in E minor, Op 27. Piano Trio in F, Op 8[a]
Benjamin Schmid vn [a]**Clemens Hagen** vc **Claudius Tanski** pf
Dabringhaus und Grimm MDG312 0934-2
(70' · DDD)   ⒻⓄⓄ

The Sonata is a fine piece from Pfitzner's maturity, while the much earlier Piano Trio is one of the most extraordinary works for the medium you're likely to have ever heard. To be sure, enterprising chamber players hunting for neglected repertory may well have come across early critical reactions to both these pieces, and references to (for example, in the case of the Trio) Pfitzner's 'sick imagination' and the work's 'monstrous length' might put anyone off. When he wrote it Pfitzner was in despair at his financial and other problems; he told a friend that after finishing it all he wanted was to die. It does at times suggest a man at the end of his tether, but also a composer chronicling such a state when at the height of his powers.

It's long, extremely tense, at times weirdly obsessive, even hysterical, but all this takes place within a cunningly plotted ground plan. After the strange and powerful contrasts of the first movement, with its wild coda, the noble but perilously assaulted main theme of the slow movement, the dance-like but fraught and nervous *Scherzo*, Pfitzner begins his finale with a choleric gesture which soon fades to pathos and pallor. After 10 minutes of desperate attempts to climb out of this pit, a positive coda seems possible, but when the music turns instead to utterly euphonious calm the listener is likely to be moved by what seems in context heroic as well as wonderfully beautiful.

The Sonata, from 1918, sounds like a demonstration – with various modernisms obvious – that Pfitzner's late Romantic style and prodigious craft still had abundant life in them. Its inexhaustible inventiveness and the beauty of its themes are accompanied by a considerable enjoyment of virtuosity: Pfitzner, you realise, is having a high old time. Both works are vastly welcome, in short, but that they should be so superbly played goes beyond all reasonable expectations.

Palestrina

Palestrina
Nicolai Gedda ten Palestrina **Dietrich Fischer-Dieskau** bar Borromeo **Gerd Nienstedt** bass Master of Ceremonies **Karl Ridderbusch** bass Christoph Madruscht, Pope Pius IV **Bernd Weikl** bar Morone **Herbert Steinbach** ten Novagerio **Helen Donath** sop Ighino **Brigitte Fassbaender** mez Silla **Renate Freyer** contr Lukrezia **Victor von Halem** bass Cardinal of Lorraine **John van Kesteren** ten Abdisu

Peter Meven *bass* Anton Brus **Hermann Prey** *bar*
Count Luna **Friedrich Lenz** *ten* Bishop of Budoja
Adalbert Kraus *ten* Theophilus **Franz Mazura** *bass*
Avosmediano **Tölz Boys' Choir; Bavarian Radio
Chorus** and **Symphony Orchestra / Rafael Kubelík**
DG 20th Century Classics ③ 427 417-2GC3
(206' · ADD) Recorded 1970s. Notes, text and
translation included   Ⓜ❍

Kubelík's magnificent, sumptuously cast DG
recording of *Palestrina* is an almost impossible
act to follow, indeed it's hard to imagine such an
extravagance of vocal riches being encountered
in a German opera recording nowadays: Brigitte Fassbaender ardently impulsive in the brief
role of Palestrina's pupil Silla, Helen Donath
pure-voiced and touching as his son Ighino, and
an absolute constellation of superb basses and
baritones, often doubling quite small parts: Karl
Ridderbusch, Bernd Weikl, Hermann Prey,
Franz Mazura, with at their head Dietrich Fischer-Dieskau as a surely unsurpassable Borromeo: dangerously powerful, intensely concerned and in magnificent voice. And those are
just the 'secondary' roles! Pfitzner's text is one
of the finest librettos ever written, and Gedda's
singing gives the impression that the beauty of
the words and their portrayal of Palestrina's
dignity and suffering are more important to him
than concern for his own voice. Kubelík's
urgent conducting shows a visionary quality,
and he clearly has a marvellous ear for the radiance of this wonderful score.

Montague Phillips   English 1885-1969

*Philips studied organ and composition at the Royal
Academy of Music. He first made a name with popular ballads composed for his wife, the soprano Clara
Butterworth, who also starred in the work to which
his fame was due above all, the light opera The Rebel
Maid (1921) was a popular success. For the centenary of the RAM in 1922 he composed The Song of
Rosamund and he was for many years professor of
harmony and composition there. He composed many
works for orchestra, but only the lighter pieces, which
showed off his talents to greater advantage, made
any real mark.*   **GROVE**music

Orchestral Works

A Surrey Suite, Op 59. Moorland Idyll, Op 61. Revelry
Overture, Op 62. A Spring Rondo. A Summer
Nocturne. A Shakespearean Scherzo: Titania and her
Elvish Court. Sinfonietta in C, Op 70. Arabesque, Op
43 No 2. The Rebel Maid – Jig; Gavotte; Graceful
Dance; Villagers' Dance
BBC Concert Orchestra / Gavin Sutherland
Dutton Laboratories Epoch CDLX7140 (76' · DDD)
                                        Ⓜ❍
Along with Charles Ancliffe and Percy Fletcher,
Montague Phillips was one of the most obvious
gaps in Marco Polo's series devoted to British

light music composers. At last the means have
been found to record a selection of his orchestral works, and the result is highly rewarding.
  Phillips's music, like that of Sullivan, German
and Coleridge-Taylor, was on the more serious
side of 'light'. He had a thorough technical
musical grounding at the Royal Academy of
Music, where he was later professor of composition, and he was also a church organist and
accompanist. These are emphatically not radio
jingles but concert items of genuine symphonic
status. If the sparkling *Revelry* Overture, with
which the programme opens, evokes Eric
Coates's *Merrymakers* Overture, much of the
rest is Elgarian in its grandeur. The orchestration is bold and accomplished, with a use of
brass that, as Lewis Foreman's expert notes
indicate, sometimes suggests Phillips's Academy contemporary Bax.
  The once widely popular dances from *The
Rebel Maid* (a light opera whose entire score
merits rediscovery) may recall German's dance
sets in their concept, but they're made of sturdier stuff. The moving *Moorland Idyll*, the picturesque and varied Surrey Suite, the sparkling
Titania and her Elvish Court and the charming
Arabesque all constitute music to be treasured.
Phillips's voice, so eloquently served here by
fine performances and recording, deserves to be
heard not just as light music but in a wider
British music context.

Astor Piazzolla   Argentinian 1921-1992

*A child prodigy on the bandoneón, Piazzolla emi-
grated with his family to New York in 1924. In
1954 he won a scholarship to study with Boulanger,
who encouraged him in the composition of tangos.
Piazzolla's unique version of the tango, which initially met with opposition, included dissonance, jazz
elements and chromaticism. By the 1980s his work
had finally become accepted in Argentina and had
begun to be espoused by classical artists.*
                                        GROVEmusic

Tangos

Tangazo
Adiós Noninoc. Milonga del ángel[c]. Tres movimien-
tos tanguísticos porteños. Oblivion[ac]. Double Con-
certo for Bandoneon and Guitar[bc]. Danza criolla.
Tangazo
[a]**Louise Pellerin** *ob* [b]**Eduardo Isaac** *gtr* [c]**Daniel
Binelli** *bandoneon* **Montreal Symphony Orchestra /
Charles Dutoit**
Decca 468 528-2DH (76' · DDD)   Ⓕ

Piazzolla's objective was to establish the tango
as a viable art form in its own right and to fuse it
with jazz and more formal musical genres. In
essence the tango isn't the natural province of a
large orchestra, but Piazzolla came to accept
and embrace it in that form as a natural extension of his 'crusade'.

Many of Piazzolla's works bear specific reference to Buenos Aires, such as the *Movimientos tanguísticos poerteños*. But the most movingly memorable are arguably those which were emotionally personal to him: *Adiós Nonino* was his immediate reaction to the death of his father – 'Perhaps I was surrounded by angels,' he said of it. The eponymous Angel of the milonga signifies inspiration, the natural gift of artists. Only the bandoneon and guitar soloists have any direct connection with this music but one could not hope for more sympathetic and finely recorded performances than these. Piazzolla's musical 'voice' remains one of the most captivating in all South American art music and it's well served in this magnificent recording.

Aconcagua. Adiós Nonino (arr Morera)[a]. Oblivión (arr Morera). Tres tangos
Mika Väyrynen *accordion* [a]**Esko Hilander** *vn*
[a]**Petteri Karttunen** *pf* **Kuopio Symphony Orchestra / Atso Almila**
Finlandia 3984-29723-2 (54' · DDD)   ⒻＯ

The accordion, when handled as virtuosically as by Mika Väyrynen and in music which fits it like a glove – as in Piazzolla's *Tres tangos* and *Aconcagua* Concerto – is an irresistible instrument. The *Tres tangos* are an excellent set, more suite than concerto, and more intimate in scale than *Aconcagua* which, in keeping with its subject (Argentina's highest peak), possesses a greater massiveness of sound. Both were written for the bandoneon, a variant of the accordion, but Väyrynen uses a Russian Jupiter instrument, the sound of which 'is much akin to that of the bandoneon', so why not use the latter? Well, power and depth mainly; and questions of authenticity aren't as acute here as they are in, say, Bach or Scarlatti. The result is most satisfactory and, if nothing else, proves that for Piazzolla tango could be a means to an expressive end as much as a vehicle for enjoyment. And enjoyment is the watchword for the whole of this brilliantly played and recorded disc.

Piazzolla Libertango (arr Calandrelli). Tango Suite (arr S Assad) – Andante; Allegro. Le Grand Tango (arr Calandrelli). Sur – Regreso al amor. Fugata. Mumuki. Tres minutos con la realidad. Milonga del ángel. Histoire du Tango – Café 1930 (all arr Calandrelli)
Calandrelli Tango Remembrances
Yo-Yo Ma *vc* **Antonio Agri** *vn* **Nestor Marconi, Astor Piazzolla** *bandoneón* **Horacio Malvicino, Odair Assad, Sérgio Assad, Oscar Castro-Neves** *gtrs* **Edwin Barker, Héctor Console** *db* **Kathryn Stott, Gerardo Gandini, Leonardo Marconi, Frank Corliss** *pfs*
Sony Classical SK63122 (64' · DDD) Recorded 1987-97   Ⓕ

Yo-Yo Ma is the latest international artist to surrender to the spell of the Argentinian dance: he can also be heard on the soundtrack of the film, *The Tango Lesson*. Here, surrounded by a brilliant group of experts in the genre, he presents with wholehearted commitment a well-varied programme of Piazzolla pieces. They range from the melancholy or sultry to the energetic or fiery. Among the latter, *Fugata* is ingenious, *Mumuki* richly eloquent, and *Tres minutos con la realidad* nervily edgy: in this last, Kathryn Stott understandably earned the admiration of her Argentinian colleagues. She also shines with Yo-Yo Ma in an exciting performance of *Le Grand Tango*: his playing in the *Milonga del ángel* is outstandingly beautiful. Special mention must also be made of some spectacular virtuosity by the Assad brothers in the *Tango Suite*. The characteristic bandoneón is featured with the cellist in *Café 1930*; and by technological trickery Yo-Yo Ma partners Piazzolla himself (recorded in 1987) in a confection called *Tango Remembrances*. Those who are already fans of this genre will be in no need of encouragement to procure this disc.

María de Buenos Aires

María de Buenos Aires (arr Desyatnikov)
Julia Zenko, Jairo *vocs* **Horacio Ferrer** *narr* **Buenos Aires Coral Lírico; Kremerata Musica / Gidon Kremer** *vn*
Teldec ② 3984-20632-2 (94' · DDD) Notes, text and translation included   Ⓜ

María de Buenos Aires is victim, lover, heroine and *femme fatale*, a powerful illusion given substance and pathos by the approachable surrealism of the opera's librettist, Horacio Ferrer. Piazzolla's music harbours a Weill-like sense of foreboding; minor-key heartache invades almost everywhere, even when the dancing starts, the air thickens and the drink starts to flow.

If you want to sample prior to purchasing, then try disc 1, track 4, 'I am María', potentially the set's hit number; or the gorgeous, rambling bandoneón solo that opens the track 8 but which soon gives way to a rhythmically ferocious but heavily sentimental 'Accusation Toccata'. María is a textile-worker whose spirit is conjured from an asphalt-covered grave for various fresh encounters – not least with a gaggle of psychoanalysts who, in real life (Argentina around 1960) helped cope with a national neurosis caused by severe economic problems. Piazzolla's madcap 'Aria of the Analysts' (disc 2, track 4) recalls Bernstein's 'Gee, Officer Krupky' from *West Side Story*, but elsewhere the musical style has that air of ineffable sadness, melancholy and 'tragedy bravely borne' that's so typical of Piazzolla's music in general.

Leonid Desyatnikov's arrangement takes heed of various recorded predecessors, but centres mainly on the graphically stark style of the Astor Quartet. This latest set is fresher in tone, texturally more inventive and tellingly astringent than any rival. Julia Zenko is a sensually alluring singer and Jairo recalls the passionate, jazz-inflected delivery of that great tango master, Carlos Gardel. And then there's Kremer himself, agile, personable, a template in sound for the tragic but elusive main character, 'María tango, slum María, María night, María fatal, María of love'. Through him, you learn to love her.

Walter Piston   American 1894-1976

Piston trained as a draughtsman before studying composition at Harvard (1919-24) and with Dukas and Boulanger in Paris; he then returned to Harvard (1926-60), becoming a renowned theory teacher. His textbook Harmony (1941) has been widely used. His music is in a clear, tonal style suggesting the neo-classical Stravinsky, Fauré and Roussel: the main works include eight symphonies (1937-65), five string quartets (1933-62) and the ballet The Incredible Flutist (1938). GROVEmusic

Violin Concertos

Violin Concertos Nos 1 & 2. Fantasia for Violin and Orchestra
James Buswell vn **National Symphony Orchestra of Ukraine / Theodore Kuchar**
Naxos 8 559003 (61' · DDD)   ⓢⵔ

Piston's First Violin Concerto, written in 1939, has much in common with the Barber, including a similar abundance of individual melody. The heart of the work is in the moving, pensive central *Andantino molto tranquillo*. With just a hint of Gershwin in its bluesy opening, the movement is essentially searching and ruminative. This is a masterpiece, as will be confirmed when other violinists take it up.

The Second Concerto, written two decades later, is less obviously 'popular', its atmosphere more elusive. But its opening is similarly haunting and the more one hears it the more one is drawn by its depth of inner feeling. The extended, pensive *Adagio* introduces a serene and very beautiful theme, which later forms a canonic duet with the flute. The finale is another sparkling, jaunty rondo. The *Fantasia* is a late work, first performed in 1973. In five intricately related sections, its language more dissonant with almost feverish, bravura *allegros* framed by troubled, lonely *adagio* passages, dominated by the soloist, which have been described as 'painfully aware and transcendentally serene'. The closing section is profoundly gentle. It may seem remarkable that these works should make their CD début played by a Russian orchestra, but it plays the music with splendid commitment, much subtlety of expression and fine ensemble too. The sure idiomatic feeling is explained by the fact its conductor, Theodore Kuchar, moved to the Ukraine from Cleveland, Ohio. James Buswell is a superbly accomplished and spontaneous soloist, and the recording is first class.

Symphony No 4

Symphony No 4. Capriccio. Three New England Sketches
Seattle Symphony Orchestra / Gerard Schwarz
Naxos American Classics 8 559162 (52' · DDD)
Recorded 1990s   ⓢⵔ

Those unfamiliar with Piston's work should investigate this Naxos disc that repackages performances originally issued on Delos. This one is arguably the best of the lot as it features the Fourth Symphony (1951) and the *Three New England Sketches* (1959), two of the composer's greatest and most attractive scores.

The Fourth's rollicking syncopations show that Piston had been listening closely to Copland's ballets. This is a symphony in the true sense, though, and its musical ideas are as lucidly argued, profoundly uttered and strongly structured as any in the classical repertoire. Perhaps the surface dissonance of 'Seaside', the first of the *Sketches*, might be off-putting to some, but how could anyone resist the exquisite colours Piston conjures up. 'Summer Evening', with its flitting, twittering evocation of insect activity, is as vivid as the best of Mendelssohn's *scherzo*s, and the craggy majesty of 'Mountains' is truly awesome.

We also get the delightfully atmospheric *Capriccio for Harp and Strings*, and the quality of both the performances and recorded sound is as impressive as ever. At budget price, this disc should prove utterly irresistible.

Fantasy

The Incredible Flutist – Suite. Fantasy for English Horn, Harp and Strings. Suite for Orchestra. Concerto for String Quartet, Wind Instruments and Percussion. Psalm and Prayer of David
Scott Goff fl **Glen Danielson** hn **Theresa Elder Wunrow** hp **Juilliard Quartet** (Robert Mann, Joel Smirnoff vns Samuel Rhodes va Joel Krosnick vc)
Seattle Symphony Chorale and Orchestra / Gerard Schwarz
Delos DE3126 (68' · DDD) Recorded 1991-2   Ⓕ

Gerard Schwarz's flutist fixes you with his limpid tone. However, it will always be known as the score with the Tango. Schwarz goes with the flow, the sway of the melody, but it can never linger long enough. The *Fantasy* enters darkened Elysian fields – Piston's lyricism sits well with this distinctive voice of sorrow and regret. We can trace their kinship right back to the composer's first published work – the orchestral *Suite* of 1929. At its heart is a long and intense pastorale: the cor anglais is there at the inception. Framing it, motoric syncopations carry us first to a kind of drive-by the blues with bar-room piano and Grappelli violin. The finale is essentially a fugal work-out: high-tech Hindemith. Piston's very last work, the *Concerto*, is 10 eventful minutes where the imperative is once again pitted against the contemplative.

The mixing of timbres is masterly, a fleck of woodwind or a brush of tambourine or antique cymbal speaking volumes. But at the centre of gravity is the Juilliard Quartet, moving in mysterious ways. In fact, the last words uttered here are those of the *Psalm and Prayer of David* – a rare vocal setting for Piston, and as such, refreshingly open, unhackneyed, unhieratical. Performance and recording are superb.

Amilcare Ponchielli   Italian 1834-1886

After studying at the Milan Conservatory Ponchielli settled in the provinces as an organist and municipal band conductor, repeatedly attempting to establish himself as an opera composer. He finally won success in 1872 with the much-revised I promessi sposi, in 1874 with the Ricordi commission I lituani and above all in 1876 with La Gioconda. As professor of composition at the Milan Conservatory (from 1880) he taught Puccini and, briefly, Mascagni. He also composed much sacred music for S Maria Maggiore, Bergamo. Of his works, only La Gioconda, on a text drawn by Boito from Hugo, is in the modern repertory. An inspired stylisation of grand opera, it contains music that is alive, varied and sensitive, notably the tenor romanza 'Cielo e mar' and the famous 'Suicidio', and that foreshadows aspects of late Verdi and of verismo opera. Elsewhere Ponchielli's atmospheric colouring and symphonic treatment show remarkable imagination and workmanship, despite his lack of a strong personality.

GROVEmusic

La Gioconda

La Gioconda[a]   H
Bellini Norma – Casta diva[d]; Mira, o Norma[b]
Donizetti Lucrezia Borgia – Com'è bello!; M'odi, ah m'odi[d] **Rossini** Guglielmo Tell – Selva opaca[d] **Verdi** Ernani – Fa che a me venga[c]. La forza del destino[d] – Madre, pietosa Vergine; La Vergine degli angeli. I lombardi[d] – Te, Vergin santa; O madre dal cielo
Giannina Arangi-Lombardi *sop* La gioconda; [a]**Alessandro Granda** *ten* Enzo Grimaldi; [a]**Gaetano Viviani** *bar* Barnaba; [a]**Camilla Rota** *mez* La Cieca; [a]**Corrado Zambelli** *bass* Alvise Badoero; [ab]**Ebe Stignani** *mez* Laura Adorno; [a]**Aristide Baracchi** *bar* Zuàne; [a]**Giuseppe Nessi** *ten* Isèpo; [c]**Enrico Molinari** *bar*; [a]**Chorus and Orchestra of La Scala, Milan;** [bcd]**Orchestra / Lorenzo Molajoli**
Naxos Historical mono ③ 8 110112/4 (169' · ADD)
Recorded 1926-33   Ⓢ●

Outstanding among Italian operatic sets of the interwar years, this was also the first complete recording of Ponchielli's masterpiece. Inevitably the sound quality of 1931 is at some disadvantage; the carefully orchestrated score, large-scale ensembles and off-stage effects need more space and clarity to do them full justice. Yet, to compensate, the voices have the vivid immediacy of their period and the transfers are excellent.

The work of chorus and orchestra is certainly among the strengths of the performance. That in turn reflects on the conductor, Lorenzo Molajoli. The three male principals were also Scala singers, though not in this opera. Alessandro Granda, a Peruvian who made his Italian début in 1927, was also Columbia's Pinkerton and Cavaradossi; as Enzo in *La Gioconda* he's perhaps a little too slender and lacking in heroic potential, yet the tone is incisive and the characterisation convincing. The baritone Gaetano Viviani is most exciting, a Ruffo-imitator perhaps and a bit throaty, but rich, vibrant, grandly sinister and not unsubtle. These aren't qualities shared by the Alvise, Corrado Zambelli, who sings with dull authority and unimpressive low notes: a pity they did not have Tancredi Pasero for the part. Mind, if they had, that would have meant the addition to the cast of one more singer with a fast vibrato (Camilla Rota's La Cieca being another), which might have proved all too much for listeners of more modern times. Stignani, whose young voice was ideal for the part of Laura, is free of it, and Arangi-Lombardi relatively so. But she, the heroine of the recording, is one of the main reasons for acquiring this set, which also includes a selection of her solo recordings, giving a fuller portrait of a highly distinguished artist.

Regarded by her contemporaries as a singer of the old school, she presents a Gioconda more appealing to modern tastes than the overcharged *verismo*-style of predecessors such as Eugenia Burzio. She brought to the role the refinements heard in her arias from *Lucrezia Borgia*, *I lombardi* and *La forza del destino*. There's also a thrilling intensity about her singing, so that, although Lauri-Volpi in his book *Voci parallele* (Garzanti: 1955) recalls that as an actress she was never quite able to liberate the impulses of her personality, one would be most unlikely to guess as much from these records.

La Gioconda   H
Maria Callas *sop* La Gioconda **Fiorenza Cossotto** *mez* Laura Adorno **Pier Miranda Ferraro** *ten* Enzo Grimaldo **Piero Cappuccilli** *bar* Barnaba **Ivo Vinco** *bass* Alvise Badoero **Irene Companeez** *contr* La Cieca **Leonardo Monreale** *bass* Zuane **Carlo Forte** *bass* A Singer, Pilot **Renato Ercolani** *ten* Isepo, First Distant Voice **Aldo Biffi** *bass* Second Distant Voice **Bonaldo Giaiotti** *bass* Barnabotto **Chorus and Orchestra of La Scala, Milan / Antonio Votto**
EMI mono ③ 556291-2 (167' · DDD) Recorded 1959.
Notes, text and translation included   Ⓜ●

Ponchielli's old warhorse has had a bad press in recent times, which seems strange in view of its melodic profusion, his unerring adumbration of Gioconda's unhappy predicament and of the sensual relationship between Enzo and Laura. But it does need large-scale and involved singing – just what it receives here on this now historic set. Nobody could fail to be caught up in its conviction. Callas was in good and fearless voice when it was made, with the role's emotions perhaps enhanced by the traumas of her own life at the time. Here her strengths in declaiming recitative, her moulding of line, her response to the text are all at their most arresting. Indeed she turns what can be a maudlin act into true tragedy. Ferraro's stentorian ebullience is most welcome. Cossotto is a vital, seductive Laura. Cappuccilli gives the odious spy and lecher Barnaba a threatening, sinister profile, while Vinco is a suitably implacable Alvise. Votto did nothing better than this set, bringing out the subtlety of the Verdi-inspired scoring and the charm of the 'Dance of the Hours' ballet. The recording sounds excellent for its age.

La Gioconda[a] **H**
Maria Callas sop La Gioconda **Gianni Poggi** ten
Enzo Grimaldi **Paolo Silveri** bar Barnaba **Maria
Amadini** mez La Cieca **Giulio Neri** bass Alvise
Badoero **Fedora Barbieri** mez Laura Adorno **Piero
Poldi** ten Zuàne **Armando Benzi** ten Isèpo **RAI
Chorus and Orchestra, Turin / Antonino Votto**
Warner Fonit Cetra ③ 3984-29355-2 (165' · ADD) Live
broadcast 1952. Notes and text included **M**

Callas recorded La Gioconda twice, here in 1952 and then, for EMI, in 1959. The choice between these versions is finely balanced. What's beyond doubt is that you must hear her in this part if you want to understand why she was such a great interpreter. Ponchielli's tragic heroine must run Violetta pretty close for her best role, even though it wasn't as central to her career; in the final, inspired act of the melodrama all the tragedy of the wronged woman rising above her jealousy to allow her lover Enzo to escape with Laura, and then commit suicide, is expressed quite indelibly in words and music.

In her EMI recording she refined her interpretation; indeed, she declared that anyone who wanted to understand what she was about should listen to the final act. If you take the role as a whole, here she's in stronger, in fact in overwhelming voice throughout, mixing love, fury, pathos, desperation in equal measure as she imprints on our minds the woman at the end of her tether so marvellously described in the score. Above all, it's what she does in melding text and notes, and her complete emotional identification with the part that makes Callas's Gioconda the most emotion-laden in the work's history. Barbieri is a fit antagonist in the famous Act 2 duet and on her own a magnificent Laura. As evil incarnate, Silveri is a powerful if unsubtle Barnaba. Neri, as the forceful Alvise, shows what Italian basses used to sound like, rich and firm in tone, imposing in manner: sad that he died so young. The drawback of the set is the ungainly, raw singing of Poggi, a fine voice ill-used by its owner. Apart from his penchant for cutting the score, Votto – as in the 1959 version – makes the most of the work's many strong points and overlooks its weak ones. The refurbished sound is admirable. Don't miss it.

Francis Poulenc French 1899-1963

Poulenc's background gave him a musical and literary sophistication from boyhood, and he was already a publicly noted composer by the time he took lessons with Koechlin (1921-4): such works as his Apollinaire song cycle Le bestiaire (1919) and Sonata for two clarinets (1918) had shown the Stravinsky-Satie inclinations that assure him a place among Les Six. His ballet Les biches (1924), written for Dyagilev, established his mastery of the emotions and musical tastes of the smart set, opening a world of suavity and irony that he went on to explore in a sequence of concertante pieces: the Concert champêtre for harpsichord, the Aubade with solo piano and the Concerto for two pianos.

Around 1935 there came a change in his personal and spiritual life, reflected in a sizeable output of religious music, a much greater productivity and an important contribution to French song. Yet the basis of his style was unchanged: Stravinsky, Fauré and contemporary popular music continued to be his sources, even in the devotional music and the larger sacred works. The songs include four cycles. But his output of instrumental music, apart from the many piano pieces of a private character, continued to be modest: his most important later orchestral piece is the G minor organ concerto with strings and timpani (1938), which journeys between Bach and the fairground, while his main chamber works were the sonatas for flute, oboe and clarinet.

Music for the stage also continued to occupy him. There was another ballet, Les animaux modèles (1942), scores for plays and films, and a new departure into opera, begun with the absurd Apollinaire piece Les mamelles de Tirésias and pursued with more seriousness in his deeply felt tragedy of martyrdom, Dialogues des Carmélites (1957), as well as a setting of Cocteau's telephone monologue La voix humaine (1959). GROVEmusic

Organ Concerto

Concerto for Organ, Strings and Timpani in G minor.
Suite française, d'après Claude Gervaise. Concert
champêtre
Elisabeth Chojnacka hpd **Philippe Lefebvre** org
Lille Symphony Orchestra / Jean-Claude Casadesus
Naxos 8 554241 (59' · DDD) **S**

Elisabeth Chojnacka gets off to a head start against most others who have recorded the Concert champêtre by using the right kind of instrument: she understands that it's much sillier to play newish music on a period instrument than old music on a modern one. The effective proportions secured here between her deft playing and the orchestra also owe much to Jean-Claude Casadesus's nice sense of judgement and to the work of an excellent recording team. It was particularly perverse of Poulenc to ask a harpsichord to contend with large brass and percussion sections and then, a decade later, employ only strings and timpani in his concerto for the intrinsically far more powerful organ; and that perversity is underlined here by using the massive organ of Notre Dame, Paris – though once again the recording technicians have skilfully succeeded in producing a string sonority that doesn't suffer beside the organ's awesome thunders. You can't help wondering whether Poulenc really had such a giant sound in mind, but it's undeniably thrilling; and the quieter moments are captured with commendable clarity and calm. From the interpretative point of view, it's quite a performance. The wind and percussion of the Lille orchestra get a chance to demonstrate their quality in accomplished playing of the spry dances of the *Suite française*. This is an eminently recommendable disc.

Chamber works

Complete Chamber Works

Sextet for Piano and Wind Quintet[a]. Trio for Oboe, Bassoon and Piano[b]. Flute Sonata[c]. Oboe Sonata[d]. Clarinet Sonata[e]. Violin Sonata[f]. Cello Sonata[g]. Sonata for Two Clarinets[h]. Sonata for Clarinet and Bassoon[i]. Sonata for Horn, Trumpet and Trombone[j]. Villanelle[k]. Elégie[l]. Sarabande[m]
The Nash Ensemble (Philippa Davies [ac]fl/kpicc [abd]Gareth Hulse ob [aehi]Richard Hosford, [h]Michael Harris cls [abi]Ursula Leveaux bn [ajl]Richard Watkins hn [j]John Wallace tpt [j]David Purser tbn [f]Leo Phillips vn [g]Paul Watkins vc [m]Craig Ogden gtr) [a-g/kl]**Ian Brown** pf
Hyperion ② CDA672556 (146' · DDD)   (F)

Invidious as it may seem to pick out just one of these excellent artists, special mention must be made of Ian Brown, who plays in nine of the 13 works included and confirms his standing as one of the most admired and musicianly chamber pianists of our day. He knows, for example, how to control Poulenc's boisterous piano writing in the Sextet without sacrificing the sparkle, and as a result the work coheres better than ever before. Like the Trio (whose opening reveals Stravinskian influence), it's a mixture of the composer's madcap *gamin* mood and his predominantly melancholy bittersweet lyricism. The latter characteristic is most in evidence in his most enduring chamber works: the solo wind sonatas with piano, all three of which were in the nature of *tombeaux* , the Flute Sonata for the American patron Mrs Sprague Coolidge, that for clarinet for Honegger, and that for oboe for Prokofiev. All are given idiomatic, sensitive and satisfying performances by the Nash artists.

The *Elégie* for Dennis Brain was a not altogether convincing experiment in dodecaphony: Poulenc had earlier dabbled in atonality and polytonality in the little sonatas (really sonatinas) for, respectively, two clarinets and for clarinet and bassoon. There's a touching reading of the little *Sarabande* for guitar. A hint of the guitar's tuning at the start of the second movement is almost the only Spanish reference in the Violin Sonata, which was composed *in memoriam* the poet Lorca, whose loss is bitterly suggested in the angry finale. In this work Poulenc allotted

to the piano (his own instrument) rather more than equal status in the duo – a situation rather paralleled in the lighthearted Cello Sonata, over which the composer dallied longer than any other of his works – but balance in both is finely judged by the performers and the recording team. The whole issue wins enthusiastic recommendation: it bids fair to become the undisputed yardstick for the future.

Poulenc Oboe Sonata. Trio for Oboe, Bassoon and Piano **Britten** Temporal Variations. Six Metamorphoses after Ovid, Op 49. Two Insect Pieces. Phantasy, Op 2
François Leleux ob **Jean-François Duquesnoy** bn **Guillaume Sutre** vn **Miguel da Silva** va **Marc Coppey** vc **Emmanuel Strosser** pf
Harmonia Mundi Les Nouveaux Interprètes HMN91 1556 (76' · DDD)   (B)

The pairing of these composers is apt, for they were friends and their musical high spirits often have a darker side. The oboist here possesses an excellent technique and is a deeply sensitive artist. Both qualities quickly become evident in the flowing and quietly poignant opening melody of Poulenc's Sonata, where Leleux's tone isn't only beautiful but also admirably responsive to the subtle dynamic shading and rhythmic flexibility. However, this is far from the whole story, and the grotesquerie of the passage starting at 2'16" shows that there's more to his playing than gentleness – as does the mercurial *Scherzo*, delivered with delightful point and relish. The final *Déploration* of this sonata, as played here, is infinitely moving and nothing less than superb.

Fortunately Leleux and his pianist partner, who's equally attuned to Poulenc's world, have been extremely well recorded. This performance and that of the bouncy Trio both give keen pleasure. So do the Britten pieces, three of them early (the characterful *Six Metamorphoses* being the exception) and edgy. Performed as vividly as this, they're undoubtedly worth having. A fine and generously filled disc.

Gloria and Stabat mater

Gloria. Stabat mater
Janice Watson sop **BBC Singers; BBC Philharmonic Orchestra / Yan Pascal Tortelier**
Chandos CHAN9341 (56' · DDD) Recorded 1994.
Texts and translations included   (F)●

We are immediately struck, at the start of the *Gloria*, by the radiantly warm but clean orchestral sonority: only later does an uneasy suspicion arise that, apparently seduced by the sound, the recording engineers may be favouring it at the expense of the chorus, especially at orchestral *fortes*. But it's committed and thoroughly secure choral singing, perhaps most easily appreciated in some of the unaccompanied passages – tender in the almost mystic 'O quam tristis' and firm-toned at 'Fac ut ardeat' (both in the *Stabat mater*); it gives real attack at 'Quis est homo' (just holding its own against the orchestra); the sopranos can produce a bright, ringing tone; and only the very first line of the *Stabat mater*, lying low in the basses, needed to be a bit stronger (as in most performances). Janice Watson is a sweet-voiced soloist with very pure intonation; but she could with advantage have strengthened her consonants throughout. Tortelier gives intensely felt readings of both works – the murmurous ending of the *Stabat mater* and the thrilling *fortissimo* chords at 'Quoniam' in the *Gloria* spring to mind – and fortunately he keeps the vocal 'Domine Deus' entry moving at the same pace as at its introduction. He takes the Stravinskian 'Laudamus te' fast and lightly; the only questionable speed is of 'Quae moerebat', which sounds too cheerful for the words ('mourning and lamenting'). These are performances of undoubted quality.

Motets

Mass in G. Quatre motets pour un temps de pénitence. Quatre motets pour le temps de Noël. Exultate Deo. Salve regina
Berlin RIAS Chamber Choir / Marcus Creed
Harmonia Mundi HMC90 1588 (52' · DDD) Texts and translations included ⓕ

There has never been a more beautiful performance of the *Salve regina*. And elsewhere this virtuoso choir displays, beyond impeccably pure intonation and chording (chorus-masters everywhere will note with envy the sopranos' clean, dead-sure attacks on high notes), a sensitivity to verbal meaning, dynamics and vocal colour that argues not only skilful direction but a complete ease and absorption into the music's often chromatic nature by all the singers. They bring a bright-eyed tone to the *Exultate Deo*, awe to 'O magnum mysterium' (in the Christmas motets), and a striking diversity of timbre to 'Tristis est anima mea' (in the penitential motets); in the Mass they interpret to perfection the *doucement joyeux* indication of the *Sanctus*. They appear to have been recorded in some large church, but without any problems of resonance and the words are extremely clear throughout. In all, this is a first-class disc.

Figure humaine

Figure humaine. Sept chansons. Un soir de neige
Accentus Chamber Choir / Laurence Equilbey
Naïve Classique V4883 (39' · DDD) Texts and translations included ⓕⓞ

Poulenc's choral music is particularly treacherous territory. One moment you're singing what sounds like Janequin or Passereau, the next you're into jagged, almost atonal lines and harmonies that seem to tear at the ether. And the contrasts are often abrupt and have to be managed at speed with every syllable of the French in place. Incredibly, the Accentus Chamber Choir under Equilbey's direction meet all these challenges with flying colours. Not only that, but their phrasing is unfailingly sensitive to the verbal shifts of the poems and no less to the harmonic and textural shifts of Poulenc's music. It's unlikely that a non-French choir would be able to achieve these standards.

Tuning and ensemble are impeccable, tone quality excellent and the varied textures sharply characterised within a spacious acoustic and with slightly distant recording.

Mélodies

Banalités. Bleuet. Chansons gaillardes. Chansons villageoises. Dernier poème. Quatre poèmes. Métamorphoses – C'est ainsi que tu es. Montparnasse. Poèmes – C. Priez pour paix. Rosemonde. Tel jour, telle nuit – Bonne journée; Une ruine coquille vide; Une herbe pauvre; Je n'ai envie que de t'aimer;Nous avons fait la nuit
Michel Piquemal *bar* **Christine Lajarrige** *pf*
Naxos 8 553642 (67' · DDD) Ⓢⓞⓞ

The first time Michel Piquemal met Pierre Bernac, for whom most of these songs were written, Piquemal recalls that Bernac said: 'I am very moved, because what you're doing is exactly what Francis Poulenc was hoping for. He would have been happy.' Afterwards Piquemal studied both with Bernac and Denise Duval, the two singers who were closest to the composer, so this recital is part of a real, authentic tradition. The greatest challenge for a singer comes in the best-known songs, for instance *Montparnasse* and 'C'. Piquemal doesn't disappoint. He hasn't got the luxurious voice for the lyrical climax of the first, at the words 'Vous êtes en réalité un poète lyrique d'Allemagne / Qui voulez connaître Paris,' but he delivers all the complicated Apollinaire verse in this and the cycle *Banalités* with a complete understanding of the necessary balance between stressing the irony and maintaining the strict forward-moving musical line.

The one group that wasn't composed for a light baritone is *Chansons villageoises*, which, although sung and recorded by Bernac, was intended for a Verdi baritone; 'Un tour de chant symphonique' Poulenc called it. Like Bernac, Piquemal doesn't have the opulent vocal quality here that Poulenc was looking for, but instead he has an actor's way with the words that brings personality and humour to a text such as the opening 'Chanson du clair tamis' – *très gai et très vite* in Poulenc's marking. All the brilliance of Maurice Fombeure's poetry gains clarity from Piquemal's diction and sense of fun, while the ensuing sadness of 'C'est le joli printemps' and the macabre parable of 'Le mendiant' are sharply contrasted.

If you want to sample this disc, try *Bleuet*, and the 'sensitive lyricism' that Bernac wrote of. It's one of the saddest songs Poulenc composed, with its image of the young soldier, the blue referring to the uniform of the conscript who has seen such terrible things while he's still almost a child. It has to be sung 'intimately', wrote Poulenc; Bernac, however, thought that it should also be 'virile and serious'. The penultimate line in which the boy faces the reality – he knows death better than life – is sung by Piquemal with a natural feel for the simplicity of the poem, never overdoing the emphasis, and never becoming arch.

At Naxos's low price this is a first-rate introduction to Poulenc's songs, but more than that it's an example of the best kind of French singing. Christine Lajarrige is a sensitive accompanist, for Poulenc always acknowledged that his songs are duets, for voice and piano.

Le bestiaire ou Cortège d'Orphée. Cocardes. Trois poèmes de Louise Lalanne. A sa guitare. Tel jour, telle nuit. Miroirs brûlants – Tu vois le feu du soir. Banalités. Métamorphoses. Voyage. Le souris. La dame de Monte-Carlo
Dame Felicity Lott sop **Graham Johnson** pf
Forlane UCD16730 (64' · DDD) Recorded 1994
Texts and translations included ⒡

This programme of *mélodies* is perfectly chosen and balanced. Juxtaposing song cycles and single numbers from the whole of Poulenc's career, putting them in chronological order, it highlights the extreme modernity of Poulenc's choice of poetry with his universal appeal as a songwriter. *Le Bestiaire* from 1918, to Apollinaire's verses, is his earliest substantial group and it's remarkable how vivid and strong the Poulenc sound already was, when he was just 19. Of the three early Cocteau settings, *Cocardes*, Poulenc said he wanted 'the smell of French fries, the accordion, Piver perfume' – once one has that in mind, both pianist and singer do splendidly, with lines such as 'Lionoléum en trompe-l'oeil. Merci. Cinéma, nouvelle muse'. *Tel jour, telle nuit* was one of the great cycles composed for Pierre Bernac, but the brighter colours of Lott's voice make it more romantic than, for instance, Souzay's interpretation. Graham Johnson as accompanist is the worthy successor to Dalton Baldwin and the composer himself as the perfect interpreter of these *mélodies*.

Complete stage works

Dialogues des Carmélites[a]
Denise Duval sop Blanche de La Force **Régine Crespin** sop Madame Lidoine **Denise Scharley** mez Madame de Croissy **Liliane Berton** sop Soeur Constance **Rita Gorr** mez Mère Marie **Xavier Depraz** bass Marquis de La Force **Paul Finel** ten Chevalier de La Force **Janine Fourrier** sop Mère Jeanne **Gisèle Desmoutiers** sop Soeur Mathilde **Louis Rialland** ten L'Aumônier **René Bianco** bar Le Geôlier **Jacques Mars** bar L'Officier **Raphael Romagnoni** ten First Commissaire **Charles Paul** bar

Second Commissaire **Michel Forel** ten Thierry **Max Conti** bar Javelinot **Chorus and Orchestra of the Opera, Paris / Pierre Dervaux**

Le gendarme incompris[b]
Nicolas Rivenq bar Monsieur Médor **Jean-Paul Fouchécourt** ten Marquise de Montonson **Jean-Christoph Benoit** bar Pénultième **Soloists Ensemble of the Garde Républicaine / François Boulanger**

Les mamelles de Tirésias[c]
Duval sop Thérèse, Fortune-teller **Marguérite Legouhy** mez Marchande de journaux, Grosse Dame **Jean Giraudeau** ten Husband [c]**Emile Rousseau** bar Policeman **Robert Jeantet** bar Director **Julien Thirache** bar Presto **Frédéric Leprin** ten Lacouf **Serge Rallier** ten Journalist **Jacques Hivert** sngr Son **Gabriel Jullia** sngr Monsieur barbu **Chorus and Orchestra of the Opéra-Comique / André Cluytens**

Les chemins de l'amour[d]
Yvonne Printemps sop orchestra / **Marcel Cariven**

Fanfare[e]
Toulouse Capitole Orchestra / Stéphane Cardon

L'histoire de Babar[f]
Sir Peter Ustinov narr **Paris Conservatoire Orchestra / Georges Prêtre**

La dame de Monte Carlo[g]
Mady Mesplé sop **Monte Carlo Philharmonic Orchestra / Prêtre**

La voix humaine[h]
Duval sop La Femme **Orchestra of the Opéra-Comique, Paris / Prêtre**

Le bal masqué[i]
Benoit bar **Maryse Charpentier** pf **Soloists of the Paris Conservatoire Orchestra / Prêtre**

L'invitation au château[j]
David Grimal vn **Romain Guyot** cl **Emmanuel Strosser** pf

Sécheresses[k]
French Radio Choir; French New Philharmonic Orchestra / Prêtre

Figure humaine[l]. Un soir de neige[m]
The Sixteen / Harry Christophers

EMI Poulenc Edition acdmono/stereo ⑤ 566843-2 (380' · ADD/DDD) Recorded 1941-89. Texts included
Ⓜ **OO**

Poulenc's stage works might seem to be divided between those that hark back to his youth as a member of Les Six, and the more pessimistic mood that overtook him after the Second World War. It doesn't really work like that, however, since it was after composing *Dialogues des Carmélites* that he returned to the work of Jean Cocteau to produce two contrasting monologues – *La voix humaine* and *La dame de Monte Carlo* in which the frivolous and the tragic are mixed with exquisite irony. It must have been quite a long-term investment when *Les mamelles de Tirésias* was recorded in 1953. This classic version under André Cluytens can never be surpassed as a souvenir of the earliest performances of what's still Poulenc's most successful opera, but the orchestral detail is much more vivid on the modern Ozawa set. Denise Duval was Poulenc's favourite soprano and although her voice has that slightly astringent quality in the upper reaches typical of French female singers, her performances are so complete, musically and dramatically. Cocteau wanted Poulenc to compose *La voix humaine* for Callas but he would only consider Duval. Although many famous divas have tackled it, Duval's 'Elle' is sublime. Public and critics have always been somewhat divided by *Dialogues de Carmélites*. The *Gramophone* Award-winning Nagano version boasts an extremely strong cast, but again, Duval, Crespin, Berton and the others have an intensity that it's difficult to imagine ever being equalled.

EMI has provided texts but no translations. Monsieur Poulenc would not have been amused. He insisted that *Carmélites* should be performed in translation outside France. The other items that make up the set include Poulenc's humorous and really beautiful incidental music for Anouilh's play *L'invitation au château*. As in so many other instances this finds Poulenc using little quotations and self-quotations. The fourth number 'Mouvement de valse hésitation' is a delicate variation on the Berger-De Féraudy waltz *Amoureuse* and elsewhere there's a hint of his 15th *Improvisation*. Similarly in *Le bal masqué*, there's a little five-note phrase which is a pre-echo of the husband's demand 'Donnez-moi du lard' in *Mamelles*. At the end of the fourth CD we do get to hear Mme Fresnay, the delectable Yvonne Printemps, in her waltz-song from Anouilh's *Léocadia*, 'Les chemins de l'amour'. It was Poulenc himself who called her singing 'literally divine'.

La dame de Monte Carlo, composed as a concert number for Denise Duval, is beautifully sung by Mady Mesplé. It's a bit like an opera-composer's take on the 'Let's face the music and dance' scene from the Astaire-Rogers movie *Follow the Fleet*, the gambler facing ruin outside the casino. The secular cantatas that end the last CD, two of them newly recorded by The Sixteen, provide yet more scope for contrasting Poulenc's shifts of mood between the cabaret and the chapel. Poulenc wrote: 'The vocal style of the *Stabat* or that of *Dialogues des Carmélites* is in fact as far removed from the song as the string quartet is from the string orchestra.'

Dialogues des Carmélites

Dialogues des Carmélites
Catherine Dubosc *sop* Blanche de la Force **Rachel Yakar** *sop* Madame Lidoine **Rita Gorr** *mez* Madame de Croissy **Brigitte Fournier** *sop* Soeur Constance **Martine Dupuy** *mez* Mère Marie **José van Dam** *bass-bar* Marquis de la Force **Jean-Luc Viala** *ten* Chevalier de la Force **Michel Sénéchal** *ten* L'Aumônier **François Le Roux** *bar* Le Geôlier
Lyon Opéra Chorus and Orchestra / Kent Nagano
Virgin Classics ② 759227-2 (152' · DDD) Notes, text

and translation included Ⓟ**OOO**

Poulenc's *chef d'œuvre* is one of the few operas written since *Wozzeck* that has survived in the repertory – and deservedly so. It's written from, and goes to, the heart, not in any extrovert or openly histrionic way but by virtue of its ability to explore the world of a troubled band of Carmelite nuns at the height of the terrors caused by the French Revolution, and do so in an utterly individual manner. Poulenc unerringly enters into their psyches as they face their fatal destiny. Nagano responds with perceptible keenness to the sombre, elevated mood and intensity of the writing and unfailingly delineates the characters of the principals as they face their everyday martyrdom. The magisterial authority of Martine Dupuy's Mère Marie, the agony of Rita Gorr's Old Prioress, the inner torment of Catherine Dubosc's Sister Blanche, the restraint of Rachel Yakar's Madame Lidoine, the eager charm of Brigitte Fournier's Sister Constance are only the leading players in a distribution that's admirable in almost every respect. The score is for once given complete. The atmospheric recording suggests stage action without exaggeration.

La voix humaine

La voix humaine. La dame de Monte-Carlo
Felicity Lott *sop* **Suisse Romande Orchestra / Armin Jordan**
Harmonia Mundi HMC90 1759 (51' · DDD)　　　　Ⓕ

Poulenc was certainly in close touch with his anima. His heroines, often suffering, as in these two works, readily take upon themselves his own depressive and even hysterical character. But not only is the rejected woman in *La voix humaine* Poulenc himself (he admitted as much), she's also Denise Duval, the first interpreter of the work, for whom it was written. Duval said that both she and the composer were in what the tabloids call 'love tangles' at the time and that the work spoke for both of them. So it's a brave act for any other soprano to compete with her 1959 recording, let alone someone who isn't French. Felicity Lott is one of the few British sopranos who could hope to come close. And she does. The voice is in excellent shape, the French likewise. The recording doesn't place her so firmly in the limelight as Duval's, while Jordan draws fine playing from the orchestra – maybe not quite as explosive as Prêtre in the emotional outbursts, but if anything with more of the *sensualité orchestrale* that Poulenc asked for. And if she doesn't quite get the necessary hysteria and vulgarity, she very nearly does. She seems more at home in *La dame de Monte-Carlo*, also on a Cocteau text but this time in verse. The top of the voice is radiant where Mady Mesplé's is sometimes shrill and marred by heavy vibrato, and throughout she captures exactly the right tone of outraged dignity.

Michael Praetorius   German 1571-1621

*The son of a strict Lutheran, Praetorius was edu-
cated at Torgau, Frankfurt an der Oder (1582) and
Zerbst (1584). He was organist of St Marien,
Frankfurt (1587-90), before moving to Wolfenbüttel, where he was court organist from 1595 and
Kapellmeister from 1604. He temporarily served the
Saxon court (1613-16), chiefly at Dresden, where he
met Schütz and got to know the latest Italian music,
and he worked in many other German cities. The
most versatile German composer of his day, he was
also one of the most prolific. His 21 extant sacred
vocal publications include over 1000 Protestant
hymn-based works, many for multiple choirs, as well
as Latin music for the Lutheran service, motets,
psalms and instrumental dances (Terpsichore,
1612). His encyclopedic treatise Syntagma musicum
(published 1614-20), with detailed information on
instruments and performing practice, is of immense
documentary value.*   GROVEmusic

Christmas Music

Mass for Christmas Morning
Roskilde Cathedral Boys' Choir and   Ⓟ
Congregation; Gabrieli Consort; Gabrieli Players /
Paul McCreesh
Archiv Produktion 439 250-2AH (79' · DDD) Recorded
1993. Text and translation included   ⒻⓄ

The aesthetic of contrast, so central to early
Baroque spectacle (sacred or profane), is
inspired here by the traditional part played by
the congregation in Lutheran worship. Praetorius's music for the *figuraliter* (the vocal/ instrumental choirs) is greatly influenced by fashionable Venetian techniques. But what's striking is
the way the old *alternatim* practices of the
Protestant church blend so naturally with the
intricate textures and scorings of a colourful
Italian-style canvas, ranging from intimate dialogues to full grandiloquent sonority. What's
more, the centrality of the chorale is never compromised. Despite all these ingredients, it's
McCreesh's research and imagination that
make this service such a powerful testament to
the faith expressed by Lutherans of Praetorius's
generation, and indeed by subsequent generations to which Bach was so indebted.
  The service follows, to all intents and purposes, the Mass of the Roman rite (sung distinction by the Gabrieli Consort though the sopranos seem a little unsure in the *Kyrie*)
interspersed with a versatile array of motets,
hymns, prayers, intoned readings, a superbly
conceived and suitably mysterious Pavan by
Schein for the approach to Communion and
several rhetorically positioned organ preludes.
For a congregation, the Gabrieli Consort and
players are joined by the boys of Roskilde
Cathedral, Denmark and a some local amateur
choirs. The effect is remarkable for its fervour
in the hymns; now one can see why *Von Himmel
hoch da komm ich her* inspired so many settings in
the 17th century.

Other familiar tunes include *Quem pastores,
Wie schön leuchtet der Morgenstern* in a shimmering prelude by Scheidt followed by a delicately
nuanced motet on the same tune. *In dulci jubilo* is
treated to a flamboyant setting by Praetorius
featuring six trumpets. The spacious acoustic of
the cathedral exhibits McCreesh's acute timbral
sense; definition isn't ideally sharp but this is a
small price to pay for a natural perspective
which embraces the sense of community worship essential for this project.

Zbigniew Preisner   Polish b1955

*A self-taught musician, he studied history of art at
Kraków University. From 1978 he worked with the
legendary Kraków cabaret Piwnica pod Baranami
('The cellar beneath the sign of the ram'). He made
his début as a film composer in 1982 with Prognoza
pogody ('Weather Forecast'), and from 1985 collaborated regularly with the film director Krzysztof
Kieślowski until the latter's death in 1996. The success of Kieślowski's films, particularly La double vie
de Véronique and the trilogy 'Three Colours' led to
Preisner's flourishing career in Europe and the
USA.*   GROVEmusic

Requiem for my Friend

Requiem for my Friend
Elzbieta Towarnicka *sop* **Varsov Chamber Choir;**
Sinfonia Varsovia / Jacek Kaspszyk
Erato 3984-24146-2 (74' · DDD) Text and translation
included   Ⓕ

As the success of his film scores shows, Preisner
knows exactly how to compose effective and
immediately impressive music with an acute
sense of timing. *Requiem For My Friend*, his first
work written specifically for concert performance, also shows this ability, but placed in a
new context. Scored for five voices, organ,
string quintet and percussion, the first part,
'Requiem', employs words from the Latin *Missa
pro defunctis*, and one feels that the ghosts of
chant and the polyphonic tradition are often not
far away (particularly in the opening 'Officium'
and the *Kyrie*). A good deal of other music is
suggested during the course of the work: one
occasionally thinks of the Górecki of the Third
Symphony or *O Domina nostra*, or Pärt, and also
other composers of film music such as Vangelis
or Jerry Goldsmith. This said, however, the
work has its own sense of direction and cohesion
and the relatively limited resources are put to
very effective use: the only section that doesn't
work is the *Agnus Dei*, which relies too heavily
on sentiment. The most effective movement is
the unaccompanied 'Lux aeterna', simple and
folk-like, but there are memorable things particularly in the 'Lacrimosa', which attains a real
dramatic power with its repetitive melodic tag,
and the 'Offertory', whose character is defined
by the subtle use of recitative-like vocal writing.

The second part of the work, 'Life', for much larger forces and also in nine movements, is generally less successful in that it has less sense of unity and doesn't rely so much on distinctive musical material as on the kind of symphonic film music gestures which work excellently in context but which fail to sustain interest or to cohere as a concert work. There are nevertheless some fine things, such as the saxophone writing (and playing) in 'The beginning', or the hushed, valedictory 'Prayer'. This is music which wears its heart on its sleeve: as a personal memorial to a friend (the film director, Krzysztof Kieslowski) that's entirely appropriate.

André Previn   German/American 1929

American conductor, pianist and composer of German birth, Previn studied in Berlin and at the Paris Conservatoire and moved to Los Angeles in 1939. His early career was in the film industry and as a jazz pianist. He made his conducting début in 1963 and was conductor-in-chief of the Houston SO, 1967-70. From 1965 he has been heard with the LSO (principal conductor, 1969-79), notably in strongly coloured late Romantic or early 20th-century music. He conducted the Pittsburgh SO, 1976-86, and became music director of the Los Angeles PO in 1986. He has composed musicals and orchestral and chamber works. **GROVE**music

Violin Concerto

Bernstein Serenade after Plato's Symposium[a]
Previn Violin Concerto, 'Anne-Sophie'[b]
Anne-Sophie Mutter vn [a]**London Symphony Orchestra;** [b]**Boston Symphony Orchestra / André Previn**
DG 474 500-2GH (71' · DDD)   Ⓟ**O**

Previn's Violin Concerto begins with a deep sigh in the lower strings and a series of wistful horn calls that set up the solo violin's entrance – a singing, soaring tune of markedly Straussian character. Knowing that the work was composed expressly for his new bride, that's much to be expected. Indeed, the first movement is a modern equivalent of Korngold's sweetly nostalgic cinemascope romanticism. But the second movement comes as a shock, for the mood becomes overwhelmingly desolate and sometimes even grief-stricken. Previn's lyrical impulse is always apparent, but this hardly sounds like a love letter. The finale brightens a bit, with some humorous turns and plenty of ecstatic melodic flights that put a lump in one's throat, yet the concerto's tragic conclusion takes the breath away, not just because it's so unexpected but because it's so darkly beautiful. Mutter's performance is simply miraculous; she dances nimbly through the thorniest passages and gives a silky sheen to even the most stratospherically placed notes.

Bernstein's *Serenade* makes an excellent companion and not only because it dispels the melancholy of the Previn Concerto's 'surprise' ending. While Mutter's temperament mightn't be naturally suited to Bernstein's jazzy syncopations, she plays with great élan, and brings sinewy intensity to the lyrical sections. Previn is right at home in this repertoire, and he elicits a gutsy performance from the LSO.

A Streetcar Named Desire

A Streetcar Named Desire
Renée Fleming sop Blanche DuBois **Rodney Gilfry** bar Stanley Kowalski **Elizabeth Futral** sop Stella Kowalski **Anthony Dean Griffey** ten Harold Mitchell **Judith Forst** mez Eunice Hubbell **Matthew Lord** ten Steve Hubbell **Jeffrey Lentz** ten Young Collector **Josepha Gayer** mez Flower Woman
San Francisco Opera Orchestra / André Previn
DG ③ 20/21 459 366-2GX3 (163' · DDD) Recorded live 1998. Notes and text included   Ⓜ

Tennessee Williams always resisted the operatic stage. Requests to turn *Streetcar* into an opera were always denied. His plays were quite operatic enough without being sung. The music of his poetry was always implicit. And yet in 1964 he gave the composer Lee Hoiby, who underscored his ill-fated *Slapstick Tragedy*, the option to adapt any of his plays as an opera. Hoiby chose *Summer and Smoke*. But the door was open. André Previn came to it only in 1998. After almost half a century of writing dramatic music for the movies and stage, opera was impatient for his touch. But *Streetcar*? It's perfect and yet not. The greater part of Previn's success has to do with his respect for, and understanding of, the music of Williams's text. Librettist Philip Littell has done an excellent job of adaptation, preserving the play's narrative strength while losing more than an hour of its duration.

Previn's word-setting is well practised. His acute awareness of Williams's speech rhythms means you hear every word. The jokes all land; the poetry takes wing; the tone of the play rings true. The opera begins with the ominous lowing of a tuba and a sleazy, twice-sounded, trumpet-laden chord slurred through too much heat and booze. There's no jazz in the score, just an allusion to it. The sound world is late late Romantic – Berg crossed with Barber and suffused with Britten. The threat of violence agitates just below the surface. Previn takes Williams's lead in aspiring to a heady, ready lyricism where the play and players dare to dream of enchantment, tenderness, hope. As Blanche retreats further into her imagined world, so her music grows more fragrant, more voluptuous, transporting us to flightier regions. Renée Fleming must have been such an inspiration for Previn: you can't imagine another singer of this stature who sounds and looks so like Blanche should.

This is a considerable piece of work. Previn, Littell and their cast have gone further than you would have thought possible towards effecting the transition to the musical stage.

Sergey Prokofiev   Russian 1891-1953

Prokofiev showed precocious talent as a pianist and composer and had lessons from Glier from 1902. In 1904 he entered the St Petersburg Conservatory, where Rimsky-Korsakov, Lyadov and Tcherepnin were among his teachers; Tcherepnin and Myaskovsky, who gave him valuable support, encouraged his interest in Skryabin, Debussy and Strauss. He had made his début as a pianist in 1908, quickly creating something of a sensation as an enfant terrible, unintelligible and ultra-modern – an image he was happy to cultivate. His intemperateness in his early piano pieces, and later in such works as the extravagantly Romantic Piano Concerto No 1 and the ominous No 2, attracted attention. Then in 1914 he left the conservatory and travelled to London, where he heard Stravinsky's works and gained a commission from Diaghilev: the resulting score was, however, rejected (the music was used to make the Scythian Suite); a second attempt, Chout, was not staged until 1921.

Meanwhile his gifts had exploded in several different directions. In 1917 he finished an opera on Dostoyevsky's Gambler, a violently involved study of obsession far removed from the fantasy of his nearly contemporary Chicago opera The Love for Three Oranges, written in1919 and performed in 1921. Nor does either of these scores have much to do with his Classical Symphony, selfconsciously 18th-century in manner, and again quite distinct from his lyrical Violin Concerto No 1, written at the same period and in the same key. There were also piano sonatas based on old notebooks alongside the more adventurous Visions fugitives, all dating from 1915-19.

Towards the end of this rich period, in 1918, he left for the USA; then from 1920 France became his base. His productivity slowed while he worked at his opera The Fiery Angel, an intense, symbolist fable of good and evil (it had no complete performance until after his death, and he used much of its music in Symphony No 3). After this he brought the harsh, heavy and mechanistic elements in his music to a climax in Symphony No 2 and in the ballet Le pas d'acier, while his next ballet, L'enfant prodigue, is in a much gentler style: the barbaric and the lyrical were still alternatives in his music and not fused until the 1930s, when he began a process of reconciliation with the Soviet Union.

The renewed relationship was at first tentative on both sides. Romeo and Juliet, the full-length ballet commissioned for the Bolshoi, had its première at Brno in 1938, and only later became a staple of the Soviet repertory: its themes of aggression and romantic love provided, as also did the Eisenstein film Alexander Nevsky, a receptacle for Prokofiev's divergent impulses. Meanwhile his own impulse to remain a Westerner was gradually eroded and in 1936 he settled in Moscow, where initially his concern was with the relatively modest genres of song, incidental music, patriotic cantata and children's entertainment (Peter and the Wolf, 1936). He had, indeed, arrived at a peculiarly unfortunate time, when the drive towards socialist realism was at its most intense; and his first work of a more ambitious sort, the opera Semyon Kotko, was not liked.

With the outbreak of war, however, he perhaps found the motivation to respond to the required patriotism: implicitly in a cycle of three piano sonatas (Nos 6-8) and Symphony No 5, more openly in his operatic setting of scenes from Tolstoy's War and Peace, which again offered opportunities for the two extremes of his musical genius to be expressed. He also worked at a new full-length ballet, Cinderella. In 1946 he retired to the country and though he went on composing, the works of his last years have been regarded as a quiet coda to his output. Even his death was overshadowed by that of Stalin on the same day.   **GROVE**music

Piano Concertos

No 1 in D flat, Op 10; **No 2** in G minor, Op 16; **No 3** in C, Op 26; **No 4** in B flat, Op 53 (left-hand); **No 5** in G, Op 55

Piano Concertos Nos 1-5
Vladimir Ashkenazy pf **London Symphony Orchestra / André Previn**
Decca ② 452 588-2DF2 (126' · ADD) Recorded 1974-5   Ⓜ**OO**

While it's true that the Prokofiev piano concertos are an uneven body of work, there's enough imaginative fire and pianistic brilliance to hold the attention even in the weakest of them; the best, by common consent Nos 1, 3 and 4, have stood the test of time very well. As indeed have these Decca recordings. The set first appeared in 1975, but the sound is fresher than many contemporary digital issues, and Ashkenazy has rarely played better. Other pianists have matched his brilliance and energy in, say, the Third Concerto, but very few have kept up such a sure balance of fire and poetry. The astonishingly inflated bravura of the Second Concerto's opening movement is kept shapely and purposeful and even the out-of-tune piano doesn't spoil the effect too much. And the youthful First has the insouciance and zest its 22-year-old composer plainly intended.

Newcomers to the concertos should start with No 3: so many facets of Prokofiev's genius are here, and Ashkenazy shows how they all take their place as part of a kind of fantastic story. But there are rewards everywhere, and the effort involved in finding them is small.

Piano Concertos Nos 1-5
Vladimir Krainev pf **Frankfurt Radio Symphony Orchestra / Dmitri Kitaienko**
Teldec Ultima ② 3984 21038-2 (123' · DDD) Recorded 1991   Ⓜ

Far too little heard of in the West, Vladimir Krainev shows how sheerly exciting these concertos can be in the hands of a virtuoso on top form. Here are the dash and flamboyance, the spacious and rhythmic grasp, the balletic poise and acrobatic daredevilry which announce a born Prokofiev player. Only in the Third

Concerto, far and away the most popular of the five, does Krainev succumb to the temptations of smash-and-grab overstatement. In this case the first movement pushes forward in a crude, attention-grabbing manner, the second is laboured in places, and the finale is again rather roughly handled. Not that pussy-footing is what Prokofiev needs, but here the impression is of a foreground-only portrait of the music.

The finest performances are of the First, Fourth and Fifth Concertos, all of which have a splendid cut and thrust. Krainev revels in their extravagance and physicality, and he's backed up by beautifully prepared, sensitive orchestral playing. The massive Second Concerto is also fine, though here the recorded balance tends to swallow up important woodwind solo lines in a generalised warmth of ambience (elsewhere, for the most part, this warmth is a definite advantage). This set can hold its own against most of the competition.

Piano Concertos Nos 1 & 3[a]
Evgeni Kissin pf **Berlin Philharmonic Orchestra / Claudio Abbado**
DG 439 898-2GH (42' · DDD) [a]Recorded live 1993
Ⓕ**O**

Kissin always seems to have time to acknowledge the implications of Prokofiev's harmony, to allow the left hand to converse with the right (always naturally, never tricksily), and to gauge the relationship of his part to the orchestra. He's also scrupulous with dynamics. At the first entry in the C major Concerto he manages, as few pianists do, the *piano* contrast after the first three notes without losing soloistic presence. And he resists the temptation to shout out *forte* passages, so that Prokofiev's *fortissimos* stand in proper relief, as do his carefully placed accents (hear the opening theme of the same concerto's finale). Perhaps none of that strikes you as exceptional, but it's so in Prokofiev, where the sheer athletic demands are extreme and refinement seems like too much to ask. With a technique like his and an orchestra as responsive as the Berlin Philharmonic there are just a few places in the C major Concerto, such as the final pages, where Kissin might have allowed himself to be a bit more carried away. But there's no shortage of exhilaration in the youthful D flat Concerto, which is a model blend of attack, wit, poetry and drive. In fact there's little discernible difference between this studio recording and the live C major, either in accuracy or in excitement.

It would be wrong to say that Kissin surpasses Ashkenazy (reviewed above). Bronfman on Sony Classical is virtually a match for him and offers the Fifth Concerto in addition. But DG's recording is clearer than the 20-year-old Decca set, and Abbado and the Berliners are far superior to Mehta and the Israel Philharmonic. Full price for 42 minutes of music may seem a bit steep; but what Kissin and Abbado have to offer is certainly in the luxury class.

Prokofiev Piano Concertos Nos 1 & 3
Bartók Piano Concerto No 3, Sz119
Martha Argerich pf **Montreal Symphony Orchestra / Charles Dutoit**
EMI 556654-2 (70' · DDD) Ⓕ**OO**

Martha Argerich's return to the studios in two concertos she has not previously recorded is an uplifting moment. As always with this most mercurial of virtuosos, her playing is generated very much by the mood of the moment, and those who heard her in Prokofiev's First Concerto with Riccardo Muti at London's Royal Festival Hall some years ago – a firestorm of a performance – may well be surprised at her relative geniality with Dutoit. Her entire reading is less hard-driven, her opening arguably more authentically *brioso* than ferocious, her overall view a refreshingly fanciful view of Prokofiev's youthful iconoclasm. The central *Andante assai* is inflected with an improvisatory freedom she would probably not have risked earlier in her career and in the *Allegro scherzando* she trips the light fantastic, reserving a suitably tigerish attack for the final octave bravura display.

Again, while her performance of the Third Concerto is less fleet or nimble-fingered than in her early legendary disc for DG with Abbado (reviewed below); it's more delectably alive to passing caprice. Part-writing and expressive detail interest her more than in the past and there's no lack of virtuoso *frisson* in the first movement's concluding quasi-fugal *più mosso* chase. Once more Argerich is unusually sensitive in the central *Andantino*, to the fourth variation's plunge into Slavic melancholy and introspection. Personal and vivacious throughout, she always allows the composer his own voice.

This is true to an even greater extent in Bartók's Third Concerto where her rich experience in chamber music makes her often *primus inter pares*, a virtuoso who listens to her partners with the greatest care. Dutoit and his orchestra achieve a fine unity throughout. The recordings are clear and naturally balanced and only those in search of metallic thrills and rushes of blood to the head will feel disappointed.

Prokofiev Piano Concerto No 5[a] **Rachmaninov** Ⓗ
Piano Concerto No 2 in C minor, Op 18[b]
Sviatoslav Richter pf **Warsaw Philharmonic Orchestra** / [a]**Witold Rowicki**, [b]**Stanislaw Wislocki**
DG 415 119-2GH (58' · ADD) Recorded 1959 Ⓕ**OO**

Prokofiev was to find no more dedicated an advocate for his keyboard works than Sviatoslav Richter. So how good that this artist's now legendary account of the Fifth Piano Concerto has been granted a new lease of life on CD. Although it has never really enjoyed the popularity of Prokofiev's Nos 1 and 3, here, however, attention is riveted from the very first note to the last. Richter delights in the music's rhythmic vitality and bite, its melodic and harmonic unpredictability. Both piano and orchestra are so clearly and vividly reproduced that it's difficult to believe the recording is actually 35 years old. Though betraying its age slightly more, notably in the sound of the keyboard itself, Rachmaninov's No 2 is certainly no less gripping. Not all Richter's tempos conform to the score's suggested metronome markings, but his intensity is rivalled only by his breathtaking virtuosity. Never could the work's opening theme sound more laden, more deeply and darkly Russian.

Violin Concertos

No 1 in D, Op 19; No 2 in G minor, Op 63

Prokofiev Violin Concerto No 2 in G minor, Op 63
Glazunov Violin Concerto in A minor, Op 82
Tchaikovsky Souvenir d'un lieu cher, Op 42 – No 1, Méditation (orch Glazunov)
Nikolaj Znaider vn **Bavarian Radio Symphony Orchestra / Mariss Jansons**
RCA Red Seal 74321 87454-2 (57' · DDD)　　Ⓕ Ⓞ

Znaider's confident, abundantly characterful account of the Prokofiev is probably the finest since Vadim Repin's similarly stimulating 1995 version with Nagano and the Hallé. Znaider brings an extra lyrical ardour and tender intimacy to Prokofiev's soaring melodies, not to mention a greater rhythmic swagger in the finale. But what really lifts this account to special heights is the chamber-like rapport and concentration Znaider generates with Mariss Jansons and the Bavarian Radio SO, whose playing is a model of scrupulous observation and profound musicality. Time and again, these intelligent artists will have you gasping anew at the giddy beauty and wondrous fantasy of Prokofiev's stunningly inventive inspiration, and theirs is a strongly communicative performance which grips from first measure to last.

The Glazunov receives a reading notable for its refreshing thoughtfulness and unforced, 'old world' charm. By the side of the dazzlingly slick Vengerov, Znaider emerges as an altogether more personable and imaginative story-teller, yet there's heaps of panache and twinkling affection when needed, and his playing has none of the slight technical shortcomings that take the shine off Shaham's less distinctive account.

A slight niggle concerns the slightly up-front solo balance, which imparts a certain nasal wiriness to Znaider's tone in the upper reaches.

Prokofiev Violin Concertos Nos 1 & 2[a]
Glazunov Violin Concerto[b]
Maxim Vengerov vn [a]**London Symphony Orchestra / Mstislav Rostropovich;** [b]**Berlin Philharmonic Orchestra / Claudio Abbado**
Warner Elatus 0927-49567-2 (DDD) Recorded [a]1994, [b]1995　　Ⓜ Ⓞ

Vengerov and Rostropovich take an unashamedly epic, wide-open-steppes view of Prokofiev's First Concerto rather than the pseudo-Ravelian one posited by Chung/Previn and Mintz/Abbado, but it works at least as well. His tone is gloriously rich, every note hit dead centre. Closely observed digital recording uncovers a wealth of detail, most of it welcome. Towards the end of the first movement, the approach to the reprise of the opening melody on solo flute with harp, muted strings and lightly running tracery from the soloist is very deliberately taken, and the long-breathed finale builds to a passionate, proto-Soviet climax. The central scherzo is predictably breathtaking in its virtuosity. However committed you are to alternative interpretations, this demands to be heard.

No 2 is slightly less successful. The balance is partly to blame – the orchestra a remote presence, the soloist rather too closely scrutinised – but there's also a lack of intimacy in the interpretation itself. Even if the finale has its impressive passages, there isn't quite enough light-hearted Spanishry in a piece written not to Soviet order but for Robert Soëtans to play in Madrid. Vengerov's sometimes overwrought manner, though, fits this music like a glove.

Violin Concertos Nos 1 & 2. Solo Violin Sonata in D, Op 115
Gil Shaham vn **London Symphony Orchestra / André Previn**
DG 447 758-2GH (60' · DDD)　　Ⓕ

Rarely, if ever, have there been performances where soloist, orchestra and conductor all connect with such unerring intuition, where the music is treated so naturally. Previn ushers in the First Concerto's crystalline opening with gentle intensity, thereby raising the curtain for Gil Shaham's warmly tended first entry. Both make great play with the march theme that follows. The effect is almost like spicy gossip being shared between friends; the *Scherzo*, meanwhile, is equally rich in dialogue. Shaham's tone is at its most expressive at the beginning of the third movement, and at its most delicate just prior to the last big climax. This natural exegesis extends to the darker Second Concerto, even where Shaham or Previn linger about a particular phrase. The recording, too, is very impressive, with well defined string lines and a fine body of winds, brass and percussion. Note how, beyond the raucous happenings of the second movement's central episode, the violins waft back with the principal theme (at 6'56"). Similar felicities occur regularly throughout both concertos, while the Second's finale – a riotous and slightly tongue-in-cheek *danse macabre* – is here sensibly paced and very well articulated. As if all that weren't enough, Shaham treats us to a substantial encore in the lively Solo Sonata that Prokofiev intended to be performed in unison by a group of young players.

Additional recommendation

Violin Concertos Nos 1 and 2[a]
Coupled with: Overture on Jewish Themes. Classical
Symphony. March in B flat
Mintz vn; [a]**Chicago Symphony Orchestra,
Chamber Orchestra of Europe / Abbado**
DG Masters 445 607-2GMA (60' · DDD) Recorded
1983   Ⓜ

An impressive account. With lustrous tone and
immaculate technical address, Mintz cuts a commanding figure. Abbado secures immaculate
accompaniments, and the sound is bold yet
refined.

Symphony-Concerto (for cello)

Symphony-Concerto in E minor, Op 125[a]. Cello
Sonata in C, Op 119[b]
Han-Na Chang vc [a]**London Symphony Orchestra /
Antonio Pappano** [b]pf
EMI 557438-2 (62' · DDD)   Ⓔ**❍❍❍**

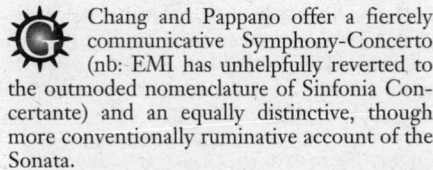

Chang and Pappano offer a fiercely
communicative Symphony-Concerto
(nb: EMI has unhelpfully reverted to
the outmoded nomenclature of Sinfonia Concertante) and an equally distinctive, though
more conventionally ruminative account of the
Sonata.

It's fair to assume that the Korean cellist is the
youngest exponent of these pieces on disc, and it
shows in the best possible way as her youthful
vivacity meets Prokofiev's mature style.
Although still in her teens, she's an experienced,
even mature recording artist with several fine
discs under her belt. Her taut, ardent conception of the main work here, music that can often
come across as rambling and discursive, is the
most radical thing she has done, knocking minutes off the timings of almost every previous
recording. The first movement is perfectly
pitched, never self-indulgent, and it's easy to
forgive any momentary lack of unanimity when
editing might have impaired the forward thrust
of the music-making. Chang's authoritative
style reaps huge rewards from 7'25", where the
theme sings out in the very highest register.

The central *scherzo* is sensationally swift and
articulate but deeply felt too, with more emotional as well as physical precision than in previous performances barring Rostropovich's own.
Prokofiev's sometimes wan lyricism is revivified
by Chang's refined sensibility; her phrasing
truly breathes with the music and the vulnerable, confessional quality she reveals may well
bring a tear to the eye. Autumnal half-lights are
usually more potent for being strictly rationed,
and Pappano is forthright as well as 'sensitive',
giving us some minatory, Soviet-sounding brass
interventions amid the hustle and bustle.

It's not only the refined direction that brings
new colour, clarity and lustre to Prokofiev's
orchestral fabric. EMI's sound is top-notch, and
you may be taken aback to discover just how ter-

rific this orchestra can sound in a sympathetic
recording studio. The cellist is placed closer
than would be the case in live concert, but such
technically invulnerable playing can take it.
Han-Na Chang's disc is quite superb.

Symphonies

No 1 in D, Op 25, 'Classical'; **No 2** in D minor, Op
40; **No 3** in C minor, Op 44; **No 4** in C, Op 47
(original 1930 version); No 4 in C, Op 112 **(revised
1947 version); No 5** in B flat, Op 100; **No 6** in E flat
minor, Op 111; **No 7** in C sharp minor, Op 131

Symphonies Nos 1-7
Royal Scottish National Orchestra / Neeme Järvi
Chandos ④ CHAN8931/4 (260' · DDD)   Ⓕ**❍❍❍**

Prokofiev wasn't a natural symphonist.
Albeit successful in emulating Haydn
in the *Classical* Symphony, the Sixth is
his only undisputed integrated symphonic
structure (and an epic-tragic utterance as
intense as any by Shostakovich). It has been suggested that his symphonies all have a sense of
some unstaged scenario, and the Third and
Fourth (and to a lesser extent, the Seventh)
Symphonies actually rework material from his
music for the stage. The Fourth (in both versions) in particular fails to convince as a symphony owing to the profusion and individuality
of its often strikingly beautiful thematic ideas –
it's a real patchwork quilt of a piece.

Enter Neeme Järvi, nothing if not a man of the
theatre, to give maximum dramatic intensity
and character to all Prokofiev's ideas, whether
they add up symphonically or not; capable of
overawing his Scottish forces into playing of
aerial lightness and easeful lyricism in the *Classical* Symphony, and pulling no punches where
Prokofiev's inspiration (as in the Second and
Third Symphonies) is at its most strident, violent and hysterical.

Make no mistake, though, these are also readings of real stature: where there's symphonic
'line', Järvi unerringly finds it. Drawbacks?
Some may feel the need for a deeper pile of
string sound, particularly in the Fifth Symphony; and these typically spacious Chandos
productions don't always ensure adequate projection for the woodwind, but more often than
not one can't fail to be impressed by the coherence and co-ordination, both musically and
technically, of some of this century's most fabulous and fraught orchestral essays. As a cycle,
this is unlikely to be challenged for some time.

Symphony No 1. Peter and the Wolf[a]. March in
B flat minor, Op 99. Overture on Hebrew Themes,
Op 34bis[b]
[a]**Sting** narr [b]**Stefan Vladar** pf **Chamber Orchestra
of Europe / Claudio Abbado**
DG 429 396-2GH (50' · DDD) Recorded 1986-9   Ⓕ**❍**

PROKOFIEV SYMPHONY NO 5 – IN BRIEF

Berlin PO / Herbert von Karajan
DG 463 613-2GOR (78' · ADD) Ⓜ️❍❍❍
DG 437 253-2GGA (71' · ADD) Ⓜ️❍❍❍

Recorded in 1968, Karajan's interpretation remains a classic. (The first listed CD couples it with his rather soft-grained Stravinsky *Rite of Spring*; the second, more appropriately, with the *Classical* Symphony, No 1.) Karajan's is a rich, long-breathed conception with full-blooded Berlin sonority.

Leningrad PO / Mariss Jansons
Chandos CHAN8576 (38' · DDD) Ⓕ❍
Short on playing time but heavy on temperament. Jansons gives a very fine performance and draws some superb playing from the St Petersburg orchestra, but he does force the work at times, over-pressuring lines that really don't need it.

City of Birmingham SO / Sir Simon Rattle
EMI 754577-2 (64' · DDD) Ⓜ️❍❍
Coupled with Prokofiev's ear-shattering *Scythian* Suite, Rattle's Fifth is a tremendous performance, lighter on its toes than either Jansons or Karajan, and sounding magnificent. This Rattle at his most re-creatively imaginative.

Royal Scottish National Orchestra / Neeme Järvi
Chandos CHAN8450 (57' · DDD) Ⓕ
A wonderful natural, unfussy reading with the RSNO on fine form and Chandos's recording is nicely handled – but for a modern version Rattle does have the edge. The coupling is a delightful *Waltz Suite*.

Paris Conservatoire Orchestra / Jean Martinon
Testament SBT1296 (72' · ADD) Ⓜ️
Coupled with the gorgeous No 7, Martinon's Fifth is a strong performance, muscular and imaginative. Obviously the 1959 sound leaves a little to be desired, but for those interested in fine conductors of yore this is well worth considering.

Slovak PO / Stephen Gunzenhauser
Naxos 8 550237 (61' · DDD) Ⓕ
Coupled with a rather lacklustre No 1, Gunzenhauser offers a very fine reading full of incident and nice detail. The Slovak band play superbly and the recording quality is very fine. An excellent budget price alternative.

Orchestre National de France / Mstislav Rostropvich
Warner Elatus 0927 46729-2 (58' · DDD) Ⓜ️
Very indulgent performances that could (or should) have been great, given Rostropovich's close relationship with Prokofiev.

Abbado's elegant and graceful reading of the *Classical* Symphony is one of the finest in the catalogue, and is particularly notable for its beautifully shaped phrasing, clarity of inner detail and crisp articulation. He seems to make all the right choices at all the right tempos. His first movement, the right side of measured, is dapper in the best sense and marked by keen detailing in the fugal development: note the clinching flourish in the timpani line – an exciting touch. Everywhere is elegance and rhythmic grace. Abbado's strings tread air through the *Larghetto*, the finale is indeed *molto vivace* with quicksilver articulation from the COE woodwinds, chortling and darting in and around the bar-lines. Abbado and the multi-talented Sting offer a lively and beautifully crafted account of Prokofiev's ever popular *Peter and the Wolf*. Any fears that the original freshness of Prokofiev's creation may be lost in favour of a less formal approach are soon dispelled – Sting is an effective and intelligent storyteller capable of capturing the imagination of adults and children alike, and there's never a feeling of contrivance or mere gimmickry.

The orchestral playing is a real delight too; sharply characterised and performed with great affection. The *Overture on Hebrew Themes* is more commonly heard in its drier, more acerbic version for clarinet, piano and string quartet, but makes a welcome and refreshing appearance on this disc in Prokofiev's own arrangement for small orchestra. The spry *March* in B flat is a wartime novelty which seems to scent victory: it's a little like *Kijé*'s Wedding march with a twist from a certain *Three Oranges* – this version of it will do very nicely.

Symphonies Nos 1 & 5
Berlin Philharmonic Orchestra / Herbert von Karajan
DG Galleria 437 253-2GGA (71' · ADD) Ⓜ️❍❍❍

 The playing throughout the First Symphony is beautifully cultured, and there's wonderful lightness and delicacy. The first movement could sparkle more and the same could be said of the finale, yet the slow movement is very beautiful indeed. The sound has marvellous clarity and definition as well as exemplary range.

Even more than 30 years after its first release, Karajan's Fifth Symphony still remains incomparable. The playing has wonderful tonal sophistication and Karajan judges tempos to perfection so that the proportions seem quite perfect. The recording, too, is extremely well balanced and has excellent ambience, and this reissue strikes you as smoother and more refined than both the original LP and any previous reissue. No other available version of this symphony begins to match this in distinction and stature. Even at full price this would still sweep the board and at its mid-price level it's a clear first choice.

Prokofiev Symphony No 5[a] **Stravinsky** The Rite of Spring[b]
Berlin Philharmonic Orchestra / Herbert von Karajan
DG The Originals 463 613-2GOR (78' · ADD)
Recorded [a]1968, [b]1977   Ⓜ**OOO**

Karajan's 1968 Prokofiev Fifth is a great performance. Whenever one compares it with later versions inevitably the DG account holds its place at the top of the list. The analogue recording was uncommonly good for its time. With the advantage of the Jesus-Christus Kirche acoustics, the sound is full and spacious, naturally defined and balanced; there's a slightly leonine quality to the strings and a natural bloom on woodwind and brass. Karajan lived with the work for a decade before he recorded it and this is immediately apparent in the way the first movement unfolds so inevitably. The ironic opening of the *Scherzo* with its flawless BPO articulation brings a splendid but unexaggerated bite, and in the more lyrical central section every subtle detail of colour comes over. The passionate string threnody of the *Adagio* (what playing, what intensity!) is superbly underpinned by darker wind murmurings; the tangibly hushed close leads naturally to the mellower opening of the essentially upbeat finale with its throbbing horns and instant echoes of *Romeo and Juliet*.

Karajan's *Rite of Spring* came a decade later and is more controversial. Stravinsky had been sarcastically scathing about the conductor's earlier 1964 account, even describing one section as 'tempo di hoochie-koochie'. So, Karajan let the work rest, and when he re-recorded it in January 1977 it was done in one single uninterrupted take. The result has less visceral excitement than the composer's own version and is without the brutally barbaric precision of Muti's Philadelphia account (HMV Classics), or the unrelenting thrust and tautness of Solti. But it's still very rewarding, combining both the symphonic and balletic aspects of this extraordinary score, with the BPO providing much sheer beauty of sound, as in the ravishing melancholy of the opening of Part II and the haunting 'Evocation des ancêtres', although other versions find more pungent drama when the horns enter later. The Philharmonie sound is excellent and both CD transfers are expertly managed to retain the full character of the originals.

Romeo and Juliet, Op 64

Romeo and Juliet
Kirov Theatre Orchestra / Valery Gergiev
Philips 50 Great Recordings ② 464 726-2PM2
(144' · DDD) Recorded 1990   Ⓜ

This great ballet score has been very lucky on records. Both Previn's EMI set and the Decca Maazel recording, are very distinguished and make a powerful impression on the listener.

This Russian recording could not be more different. It was made in the Kirov Theatre in Leningrad and has the fullness and amplitude characteristic of the finest western recordings, not surprising, as the recording team was from Philips. The orchestral playing, too, is superb by any international standard and has none of the sharp edges or raucousness we used to associate with Soviet *fortissimos*. If there were a criticism of the playing it would be to suggest that at times it's almost over-cultivated. The Introduction has a striking grace and flexibility, a sophistication of light and shade that some listeners mightn't expect. The action of the opening street scene and the sequence of events which follows is delineated with much delicacy of effect, crisp clear rhythms, great energy when called for, in the 'Morning dance', for instance and the most stylish instrumental response from all departments of the orchestra.

Perhaps it's all a shade mellow (Maazel demonstrated how pungent Prokofiev's scoring could sound) and the mood of the 'Balcony scene' is pure romanticism, relaxed and without sexual ardour: the strings float ethereally, there's a beautifully played violin solo, and at the climax the listener is quite carried away. The great climax of 'Juliet's funeral' generates richly intense string playing and resoundingly powerful brass. But there's no sense of utter despair. So this is a performance to enjoy for the lyric feeling of Prokofiev's score and for the marvellous orchestral playing, but the starkness of the tragedy is more heartrendingly conveyed elsewhere.

Cinderella, Op 87

Cinderella[a]. Symphony No 1[b]
London Symphony Orchestra / André Previn
EMI Double Forte ② 568604-2 127' · [a]DDD/[b]ADD)
Recorded [a]1983, [b]1977. Synopsis included   Ⓜ

Previn's admirable *Cinderella* appeared originally on LP in 1983 but was never transferred to CD in its entirety, EMI opting for a single-disc 'highlights' compilation. It has come up quite beautifully in this transfer, the Abbey Road production (Grubb/Parker) possessing a most appealing warmth and lustre. Previn's imaginative, highly sympathetic direction combines warm-hearted affection as well as a most seductive theatrical flair (the whole of Act 2 is particularly memorable in this regard). Throughout, the LSO responds with considerable dash and character: occasionally, the strings are wanting in the last ounce of finesse and absolute technical security, but the woodwind contribution is especially felicitous. Comparing it with the immaculately honed but comparatively chilly Pletnev set, many may prefer this keenly priced reissue. Unfortunately, the 'bonus' item – an enthusiastic, but distractingly scrappy *Classical Symphony* is far from ideal. No matter, a bargain all the same.

Peter and the Wolf, Op 67

Peter and the Wolf[a]. Symphony No 1. March in
B flat minor, Op 99. Overture on Hebrew Themes,
Op 34bis[b]
[a]**Sting** narr [b]**Stefan Vladar** pf **Chamber Orchestra
of Europe / Claudio Abbado**
DG 429 396-2GH (50' · DDD) Recorded 1986-90 Ⓕ⬤

Abbado and the multi-talented Sting offer a
lively and beautifully crafted account of
Prokofiev's ever popular *Peter and the Wolf*. Any
fears that the original freshness of Prokofiev's
creation may be lost in favour of a less formal
approach are soon dispelled – Sting is an effective and intelligent storyteller capable of capturing the imagination of adults and children alike,
and there's never a feeling of contrivance or
mere gimmickry. (The rest of the set is reviewed
under Symphony No 1 overleaf.)

Cello Works

Cello Concertino in G minor, Op 132 – Andante.
Cello Sonata in C, Op 119. Solo Cello Sonata in C
sharp minor, Op 134 (ed Giovale). Adagio in C, Op
97b No 10. Ballade in C minor, Op 15. Chout, Op 21a
(arr Sapozhnikov) – The Buffoon and his Wife; Dance
of the Buffoons' Wives; Dance of the Buffoons'
Daughters; In the Merchant's Bedroom; Quarrel of
the Buffoon and the Merchant
Alexander Ivashkin vc **Tatyana Lazareva** pf
Chandos CHAN10045 (68' · DDD)   Ⓕ

Captured in the Maly Hall of the Moscow Conservatory where much of Prokofiev's work was
first heard, it's surprising to find so many
aspects of the composer's style represented,
from the Romanticism of the early *Ballade*
through the spiky dissonances of *Chout* to the
elegiac, unfinished Solo Sonata. Aided by characterful piano-playing by Tatyana Lazareva,
Ivashkin's recital compares most favourably
with his similar programme on Ode for which
he was accompanied by a more reticent pianist;
although the earlier disc includes the Concertino movement in the guise of Rostropovich's cello quintet arrangement, the
absence of the *Chout* transmogrification makes
the Chandos collection appear better value.
We start with the familiar Cello (and piano)
Sonata, a highly polished and deeply felt
account with Lazareva providing a weighty,
authentically Russian accompaniment. The *Ballade* is surely the best version yet of this increasingly popular work. Good though Wallfisch's
expansive reading is, Ivashkin surpasses him in
his juxtaposition of the 19th-century style of the
opening and the ghostly second idea, hushed to
a real *pianissimo*. Instead of Wallfisch's 'March'
from *The Love for Three Oranges*, we get a *Chout*
selection arranged by the Russian cellist Roman
Sapozhnikov; again the rendition is technically
spotless. Finally comes the Sonata for cello
alone, its nostalgic opening brought off perfectly. Ivashkin's playful treatment of the cen-

tral gavotte-like section reminds us that he can
do humour as well.

Violin Sonatas

Violin Sonatas – No 1 in F minor, Op 80; No 2 in D,
Op 94a. Five Melodies, Op 35b
Vadim Repin vn **Boris Berezovsky** pf
Erato 0630-10698-2 (63' · DDD)   Ⓕ

A clear first choice in this repertoire and heartening confirmation of the young Vadim Repin's
considerable violinistic skills. Tension sets in
right from the First Sonata's opening bars: the
tone is bright, sweet, tremulous and warmly
expressive, while the music's sombre mood is
precisely gauged. Repin phrases with considerable sensitivity and his attack in the work's faster
episodes – the *Allegro brusco*'s outer sections and
most of the finale – has a Heifetzian 'edge'. Nervous energy is also much in evidence, while the
Andante – one of Prokofiev's most haunting creations – has a wistfully distracted air that Boris
Berezovsky matches with some notably perceptive piano playing. The *Allegrissimo* finale, too,
is arresting: deftly fingered, percussively insistent and with a truly heartfelt projection of the
work's tender closing phrase. One of Repin's
leading qualities is his obvious interpretative
sincerity; nowhere does one sense the suave
affectation that afflicts some of his contemporaries, a fact that registers with particular force
in the Second Sonata's opening *Moderato*. Here
lesser artists often sound either matter-of-fact
or uninterested, and even superior ones opt for
relative coolness. Repin and Berezovsky, on the
other hand, are both tender and relaxed; phrasal
'crossfire' and keen inflexion keep sparks flying
in the *Scherzo*, the *Allegretto leggiero e scherzando*
is appropriately limpid, and although the finale
could have swaggered more freely, there are
magical moments to spare. Both players achieve
an impressive range of colour throughout and
the five delightful *Melodies* make for a welcome
sequence of encores. Very well recorded.

Prokofiev Violin Sonata in D, Op 94a   🄷
K Khachaturian Violin Sonata, Op 1
Szymanowski Violin Sonata in D minor, Op 9
David Oistrakh vn **Vladimir Yampolsky** pf
Testament mono SBT1113 (65' · ADD) Recorded
1955   Ⓕ

David Oistrakh's playing is, at its best, a calming
force in an agitated world – intelligent, considered (just occasionally overcalculated), invariably poised, big-toned and confident. You know
what to expect and are rarely disappointed, and
these excellent refurbishments of key Oistrakh
performances from the 1950s lend a characteristic narrative quality to a wide variety of repertoire.
Best perhaps is the Prokofiev sonata, which
Oistrakh himself instigated in reaction to hearing the flute-and-piano original. The playing is

quietly confidential in the first and third movements, pert in the *Scherzo* and exuberant in the closing *Allegro con brio*. Oistrakh's phrasing is incisive without sounding aggressive (most notes retain their full measure of tone, even at speed), while his handling of rhythm is both supple and muscular. Szymanowski's post-Romantic Op 9 is lusciously full-toned and expertly negotiated by Yampolsky, while the reading of Karen Khachaturian's Op 1 – a pleasant piece reminiscent of Kabalevsky, the lighter Shostakovich and, occasionally, Gershwin – proves to be another masterly performance, especially in the delightful *Andante*.

This is a quite superb disc, expertly annotated and very well presented. The Prokofiev Second Sonata is as near definitive as anyone has a right to expect, while the remainder is typical of a violinist whose aristocratic playing and artistic diplomacy remain an inspiration to us all.

Piano Sonatas

No 1 in F minor, Op 1; **No 2** in D minor, Op 14; **No 3** in A minor, Op 28; **No 4** in C minor, Op 29; **No 5** in C, Opp 38/135; **No 6** in A, Op 82; **No 7** in B flat, Op 83; **No 8** in B flat, Op 84; **No 9** in C, Op 103; **No 10** in E minor, Op 137

Prokofiev Piano Sonata No 4 in C minor, Op 29 **Rachmaninov** Etudes-tableaux, Op 39 – No 3 in F sharp minor; No 4 in B minor **Scriabin** Piano Sonata No 9, 'Black Mass', Op 68 **Tchaikovsky** The Seasons, Op 37a – January; May; June; November
Sviatoslav Richter pf
BBC Legends/IMG Artists BBCL4082-2 (67' · ADD)
Recorded live 1966   Ⓕ **OO**

Recorded live at Richter's beloved Aldeburgh in 1966, this issue shows an incomparable pianist at the height of his powers. Indeed, it would be difficult to imagine a more authentic yet personal voice in Prokofiev's Fourth and Scriabin's Ninth Sonatas. Richter carved out a special niche in Prokofiev's Fourth Sonata, the most cryptic and ambiguous of the series written in a language that can seem oddly exclusive and inaccessible to those born outside Russia. No other pianist has approached Richter in this work, in his capacity to clarify so much awkward writing while at the same time (in the central *Andante assai*) acknowledging a wholly individual utterance full of dark confidences and, in the finale, a forced gaiety alive with stiff virtuoso challenges resolved in a mock-triumphant coda.

Few performances of the Scriabin have been more stealthily mobile or breathed a more satanic menace. For once, directions such as *avec une douceur de plus en plus caressante et empoisonnée* are made meaningful rather than merely idiosyncratic or eccentric. Yet, in more amiable territory Richter is enviably poised, less remote or enigmatic in Mozart's G major Sonata, K283, than one might have expected. His opening *Allegro* is gently flowing and is memorably

contrasted with his brilliantly vivacious finale.

The recordings have come up excellently, allowing us to appreciate Richter's range, unique empathy in Russian music and endlessly thought-provoking musicianship in all their glory.

Additional recommendation

Piano Sonatas Nos 7 and 8
Coupled with: Romeo and Juliet, Op 75 – Masks; Romeo and Juliet before departing Liszt Impromptu, S191. Mephisto Waltz No 1, S514
Ashkenazy pf
Decca Legends 468 497-2DM (72' · ADD)   Ⓜ
Ashkenazy's recording of Prokofiev's Seventh Sonata is among the most brilliant on disc, its slow movement less emollient than usual, the outer ones dispatched with fierce motoric energy. Tremendous playing.

Alexander Nevsky, Op 78

Alexander Nevsky Scythian Suite, Op 20
Linda Finnie sop **Scottish National Chorus and Orchestra / Neeme Järvi**
Chandos CHAN8584 (60' · DDD) Text and translation included   Ⓕ

At the chill opening of Järvi's fine version of *Alexander Nevsky* one can really feel the bitter wind of the Russian winter. The acoustics of the Caird Hall in Dundee where these Chandos recordings were made adds an extra atmospheric dimension to this splendidly recorded performance. The choral entry has an affecting poised melancholy, yet their geniality in the call to 'Arise ye Russian people' has a ring of peasantry. The 'Battle on the Ice' is the enormously spectacular climax, with the bizarre dissonance of the orchestral *scherzando* effects given tremendous pungency capped by the exhilarating shouts of fervour from the singers. Linda Finnie's contribution is most eloquent too and Järvi's apotheosis very moving. The *fortissimo* force of Chandos's recording is especially telling. As a coupling, Järvi chooses the ballet *Ala and Lolly*, originally written for Diaghilev which, when rejected by him, became the *Scythian Suite*. Its aggressive motoric rhythms are as powerful as anything Prokofiev wrote (indeed, their primitive force has an element of almost brutal ugliness to which you may not wholly respond) but the lyrical music is top-quality Prokofiev. 'It remains one of his most richly imaginative, harmonically sophisticated and wonderfully atmospheric scores', suggests Robert Layton in the notes. Certainly Järvi has its measure and so do the Chandos engineers, but it's not music for a small flat.

Prokofiev Alexander Nevsky[b]. Ivan the Terrible (arr Stasevich) – film music, Op 116[c]
Rachmaninov The bells[a]
[a]**Sheila Armstrong** sop [b]**Anna Reynolds**, [c]**Irina**

Arkhipova *mez* [a]Robert Tear *ten* [a]John Shirley-Quirk, [c]Anatoly Mokrenko *bar* [c]Boris Morgunov *narr* [ab]London Symphony Chorus and Orchestra / [ab]André Previn; [c]Ambrosian Chorus; [c]Philharmonia Orchestra / [c]Riccardo Muti
EMI Double Forte ② 573353-2 (78' · ADD) Recorded [b]1971, [a]1975, [c]1977 **ⓜ○○**

The previous EMI Studio reissue of these fine André Previn accounts of *The bells* and *Alexander Nevsky* has now been superseded by this EMI Double Forte release with *Ivan the Terrible* – one of Riccardo Muti's finest recordings. Made in the Indian summer of London's Kingsway Hall, it's a performance not to be missed. The fragmentary nature of the music – more evidently a collection of film score links than *Alexander Nevsky* – can be frustrating, but such is the fervour of the performance, the fulsome theatricality of Boris Morgunov's narration, that one is simply carried along by the 'visual' excitement of it all. The Ambrosian Chorus contribute an impressive imitation of the genuine Russian article, summoning up the requisite ballast for the big numbers, amply filling out one of the greatest of all Prokofiev 'tunes' in the 'Storming of Kazan' sequence: this is the noble *cantilena* that would later feature so prominently in *War and Peace*. If you would rather sample this re-release before buying, try the raucous 'Dance of the Oprichniki' and the finale. Was there ever a more resplendant final chord? All 28 seconds of it!

As for *The bells* and *Alexander Nevsky*, the soloists are first-rate. Sheila Armstrong is especially fine in *The bells* and Anna Reynolds provides genuine Slavonic intensity in her contribution to the Prokofiev. The chorals singing too, if without the special vocal timbre and enunciation of a Russian group, has undoubted fervour, while in the famous 'The Battle on the Ice' sequence in *Alexander Nevsky*, the orchestral playing has thrilling pungency and bite. The original analogue recordings were exceptionally well balanced and on LP the combination of ambient effect and sharpness of detail was ideally judged. The remastering increases the clarity and projection of the sound with, perhaps, a slight loss of warmth and atmosphere. However, the overall effect is vividly spectacular and compulsively dramatic. This disc is a real bargain for all three performances are very fine indeed.

Ivan the Terrible, Op 116

Ivan the Terrible
Liubov Sokolova *mez* Nikolai Putilin *bar* Chorus of the Kirov Opera; Rotterdam Philharmonic Orchestra / Valery Gergiev
Philips 456 645-2PH (65' · DDD) Text and translation included Ⓕ

This studio account of *Ivan* ranks with the best of Gergiev's opera recordings. Recommending just one version for the collection isn't easy

when the work, rather like the film itself, doesn't exist in a definitive form. Part 1 of Eisenstein's masterpiece was released in 1946 to worldwide acclaim, although Stravinsky for one didn't care for its mix of iconography and melodrama. Prokofiev's health was so poor that he recommended that Gavriil Popov take over composing Part 2. Later he was able to resume work on the project only to find it withheld from distribution. Soviet officials found its portrayal of Ivan's psychological decline too negative, and, no doubt, too close to home. The film was released in the USSR in 1958, by which time plans to complete the trilogy had been abandoned, its prime movers long dead. Prokofiev thought highly enough of the score to reuse sections, but he left no guidelines for presenting it in the concert hall. Reshaping the music to fit a chronological narrative, Abram Stasevich fabricated an overlong oratorio. Gergiev's version is based on Stasevich; only here the music is left to fend for itself without the interpolated Russian texts. The Russian choir and some notably forward timpani help Gergiev build the right atmosphere. The wide vibrato of his young mezzo is nothing if not authentic, and there will be no complaints about the robust singing of Nikolai Putilin. James Agee acclaimed the film as 'A visual opera, with all of opera's proper disregard of prose-level reality', but if you want to experience the music divorced from the images, then Gergiev's account is among the most dramatic.

Ivan the Terrible – complete film music
Irina Chistyakova *contr* Dmitry Stepanovich *bass* Vesna Children's Choir; Yurlov State Capella; Tchaikovsky Symphony Orchestra / Vladimir Fedoseyev
Nimbus ② NI5662/3 (99' · DDD) Ⓕ○

This is a must for completists, in that it's produced in association with a new edition of the score (1997), collating all that survives of the composer's contribution to the project. Indeed, Fedoseyev goes so far as to include music from the Russian Orthodox Liturgy that occurs in the completed films but isn't actually by Prokofiev.

Confused? Let's recap. Part 1 of Eisenstein's masterpiece was released in 1946 to worldwide acclaim, though Stravinsky for one did not care for its mix of iconography and melodrama. In poor health, Prokofiev recommended that Gavriil Popov take over as composer for Part 2. Later he did after all resume work – only to find the film withheld from distribution. Soviet officials found its portrayal of Ivan's psychological decline too negative and, no doubt, too close to home. Which isn't to say that Prokofiev intended to encode any criticism of Stalin in the notes. The film was released in the USSR in 1958, by which time plans to complete the trilogy had been abandoned, its prime movers long dead.

We know Prokofiev thought highly enough of the score to re-use sections of it, but he left no guidelines for presenting it in the concert hall. The oratorio we always used to hear was fashioned in 1962 by Abram Stasevich; it provided the missing element of continuity by reshaping the cues to fit a chronological narrative. Muti recorded this to superb effect. Christopher Palmer's solution for Järvi was to dispense with Stasevich's interpolated speaker, whereas Rostropovich revived the melodramatic element in an edition by Michael Lankester with English-language narration (Sony Classical). Gergiev's forceful version left the music to fend for itself, but was still based on Stasevich.

By cutting out the middleman, Fedoseyev now goes to the top of the heap as the most scholarly option. He produces a more convincing, well-prepared performance than many that have come out of Russia of late. Not all of what he presents is familiar even from the films, and there's a certain amount of crudely illustrative material. His orchestra, the present-day manifestation of the USSR broadcasting band with which Rozhdestvensky was associated in the 1960s and 1970s, acquits itself well: crude primary colours predominate, and the brass players avoid inauthentic finesse. Gergiev has only the mock-Soviets of the Rotterdam Philharmonic, though his Kirov chorus aren't outclassed by the Yurlov State Capella deployed here. Admittedly, Fedoseyev's contralto is extremely Russian, which you may find difficult in 'The song of the beaver'. Nor does he race in with quite Gergiev's irresistible flair. That said, Nimbus's Moscow-made recording is technically much better than you might expect.

The two-disc package includes a helpful account of the working methods of Prokofiev and Eisenstein, while key episodes are discussed in more depth and cross-referenced to the relevant tracks. Eisenstein's fraught relationship with the authorities and the suppression of *Ivan* Part 3 are also discussed, an attempt being made to disentangle the score from its inescapably propagandist aspect. True, the project's public role as a glorification of Soviet tyranny need not be as dominant as it can seem to be in Stasevich's oratorio. Whether it's better served here may depend on your attitude to listening to music in short, sharp (albeit authenticated) bursts.

The Fiery Angel, Op 37

The Fiery Angel
Galina Gorchakova *sop* Renata **Sergei Leiferkus** *bar* Ruprecht **Vladimir Galusin** *ten* Agrippa **Konstantin Pluzhnikov** *ten* Mephistopheles **Sergei Alexashkin** *bass* Faust **Vladimir Ognovanko** *bass* Inquisitor **Evgeni Boitsov** *ten* Jakob Glock **Valery Lebed** *bass* Doctor **Yuri Laptev** *ten* Mathias **Mikhail Kit** *bar* Servant **Evgenia Perlasova** *mez* Landlady **Larissa Diadkova** *mez* Fortune teller **Olga Markova-Mikhailenko** *contr* Mother Superior **Yevgeny Fedotov** *bass* Innkeeper **Mikhail Chernozhukov** *bass* First Neighbour **Andrei Karabanov** *bar* Second Neighbour **Gennadi Bezzubenkov** *bass* Third

Neighbour **Tatiana Kravtsova** *sop* First Nun **Tatiana Filimoniva** *sop* Second Nun **Chorus and Orchestra of the Kirov Opera / Valery Gergiev**
Philips Gramophone Awards Collection ② 476 1826 (119' · DDD) Recorded live 1993. Notes, text and translation included ⓜ❍❍❍

 The opera is no blameless masterpiece – Prokofiev's indulgence in lurid sensationalism sometimes gets the better of his artistic judgement. But that sounds a pretty po-faced judgement in the face of the overwhelming power which so much of this score exudes. This Maryinsky performance comes live from what's clearly a highly charged occasion in one of the world's great opera houses. That brings with it the disadvantage of a constrained opera-pit acoustic, which makes some of Prokofiev's over-the-top scoring seem pretty congested. But the immediacy and clarity of the sound, plus the orchestra's rhythmic grasp, ensures that the effect is still blood-curdling. If Leiferkus's distinctive rich baritone at first sounds a touch microphoney, the ear can soon adjust to that too, and Gorchakova brings intense beauty as well as intensity to Renata's hysterics, taking us right inside the psychological drama. The supporting roles are filled with distinction and this makes a huge difference to the sustaining of dramatic tension, the *crescendo* which Prokofiev aimed to build through his five acts. Considering the extent of the stage goings-on there's remarkably little audience distraction on the recording.

The Love for Three Oranges, Op 33

The Love for Three Oranges
Mikhail Kit *bass* King of Clubs **Evgeny Akimov** *ten* Prince **Larissa Diadkova** *mez* Princess Clarissa **Alexander Morozov** *bass* Leandro **Konstantin Pluzhnikov** *ten* Truffaldino **Vassily Gerello** *bar* Pantaloon **Vladimir Vaneev** *bass* Tchelio **Larissa Shevchenko** *sop* Fata Morgana **Zlata Bulycheva** *mez* Linetta **Lia Shevtsova** *mez* Nicoletta **Anna Netrebko** *sop* Ninetta **Grigory Karasev** *bar* Cook **Feodor Kuznetsov** *bass* Farfarello, Herald **Olga Korzhenskaya** *mez* Smeraldina **Yuri Zhikalov** *bar* Master of Ceremonies **Kirov Opera Chorus and Orchestra / Valery Gergiev**
Philips ② 462 913-2PH2 (102' · DDD) Texts and translations included ⓕ❍

Goldoni's play of 1761, adapted by Meyerhold in 1914 and set by Prokofiev four years later, was in many respects way ahead of its time. As Lionel Salter pointed out in his review of the Lyon Opera recording under Kent Nagano, it prefigured not only Brecht but also the Theatre of Cruelty and the Theatre of the Absurd. Prokofiev fell with relish on the scenario, seeing in it an opportunity to puncture the pretensions of the operahouse, rather as Stephen Sondheim's *Into the Woods*, working from the opposite direction and with more meagre compositional resources, has more recently used fairy-tale to try to add pretensions to the musical theatre.

Musically *The Love for Three Oranges* builds on Rimsky-Korsakov's *The Golden Cockerel*; and in turn Shostakovich's *The Nose* seeks to build on Prokofiev. It's a fabulously imaginative score, never reliant on cliché, always light on its feet and gloriously orchestrated. All credit to Gergiev and his Kirov players for provoking these observations. This is the fifth of their Prokofiev opera series, and it more than lives up to the high standards already set.

Among the evil conspirators at the court of the King of Clubs there are admittedly some dryish-sounding voices. But the main roles are superbly taken, most notably by tenor Evgeny Akimov as the whining, hypochondriac Prince. Other outstanding contributions come from Grigory Karasev as the giant cook who guards the Three Oranges, Feodor Kuznetsov as the demon Farfarello, and Anna Netrebko as the last of the three Princesses eventually released from the Oranges.

The Kirov recording was made live in Amsterdam in sessions spaced 10 months apart. There are no obvious joins, and the warmer ambience of the Concertgebouw amply compensates for the Maryinsky Theatre's more concentrated atmosphere. Though there's a certain amount of variance in the miking of the voices, this is never more than the action itself invites. Inevitably the audience misses out on the visual element, which is more than usually crucial with this opera. Even so, some of the verbal and situational humour clearly gets across, and the applause is tumultuous.

it's rather that the reactionary-collaborator father-in-law-to-be, Tkachenko, is so obviously a token of Soviet propaganda. Prokofiev would probably never have considered such subject-matter at all had it not been for the political climate of the late 1930s and he did his best to make a working compromise between the order of the day and the kind of melodious simplicity he wanted to cultivate. He took Katayev's prose-draft as it stood and sought to minimise its schematic and propagandist elements. In Act 3 he came up with two of his most effective 'dramatic *crescendos*', first for the arrival of the reactionary Ukrainian cavalry, then for the burning of Semyon's cottage.

There are more fine moments in Act 4, where the oppositional writing for Soviets and Germans has something of the power of *Alexander Nevsky*, composed just before the opera. There's also some attractively pungent folk-imitation writing in the second tableau of Act 1. Some less distinguished scenes suggest a rummaging through Prokofiev's cast-off ideas for all-purpose filler material, but such passages aren't so extensive or so deadly as to destroy all enjoyment. This splendid recording plugs another major gap in the discography of opera. Gergiev's interpretation is ardent and well paced, his orchestra is in fine fettle, and his soloists are of high quality. Prokofiev gives little or no opportunity for star turns, but Viktor Lutsiuk's Semyon is passionate and youthful-sounding, and Tatiana Pavlovskaya as his beloved Sofya is radiant. The recording is free from the dryness and sudden shifts of perspective that have dogged some previous issues in this Mariinsky series.

Semyon Kotko, Op 81

Semyon Kotko
Tatiana Pavlovskaya *sop* Sofya **Ekaterina Solovieva** *sop* Lyubka **Lyudmila Filatova** *mez* Semyon's mother **Olga Markova-Mikhailenko** *mez* Khivrya **Olga Savova** *mez* Frosya **Evgeny Akimov** *ten* Mikola **Nikolai Gassiev** *ten* Klembovsky, Workman **Viktor Lutsiuk** *ten* Semyon Kotko **Vladimir Zhivopistev** *ten* German interpreter **Viktor Chernomortsev** *bar* Tsaryov **Yuri Laptev** *bar* Von Wierhof **Gennady Bezzubenkov** *bass* Tkachenko **Grigory Karasev** *bass* Ivasenko **Andrei Khramtsov** *bass* German NCO, German sergeant **Yevgeny Nikitin** *bass* Remeniuk **Kirov Opera Chorus and Orchestra / Valery Gergiev**
Philips ② 464 605-2PH2 (137' · DDD) Text and translations included ⓕ

Valentin Katayev's tale of a local hero getting his girl despite strife with a prospective in-law is the kind of thing an opera-lover would normally take in their stride. What makes *Semyon Kotko* hard to live with isn't the fact that the soldier-boy returning to his village in the Ukraine at the end of the First World War is so unimpeachably virtuous, or even that the Germans who break up the wedding preparations and lay waste to the village are so one-dimensionally villainous –

War and Peace, Op 91

War and Peace
Lajos Miller *bar* Prince Andrei Bolkonsky **Galina Vishnevskaya** *sop* Natasha Rostova **Katherine Ciesinski** *mez* Sonya **Maria Paunova** *mez* Maria Akhrosimova **Dimiter Petkov** *bass* Count Ilya Rostov **Wieslaw Ochman** *ten* Count Pytor Bezukhov **Stefania Toczyska** *mez* Helena Bezukhova **Nicolai Gedda** *ten* Anatol Kuragin **Vladimir de Kanel** *bass-bar* Dolokhov **Mira Zakai** *contr* Princess Maria Bolkonsky **Malcolm Smith** *bass* Colonel Vasska Denisov **Nicola Ghiuselev** *bass* Marshal Mikhail Kutuzov **Eduard Tumagian** *bar* Napoleon Bonaparte **Radio France Chorus; French National Orchestra / Mstislav Rostropovich**
Erato Libretto ④ 2292-45331-2 (247' · DDD) Recorded 1986. Notes, text and translation included ⓜ

Over four hours long, 72 characters, 13 scene changes: is it any wonder that Prokofiev's *War and Peace*, adapted from Tolstoy's famously epic novel, has had few performances and even fewer forays into the recording studio? At the front of the booklet Rostropovich recalls how, as Prokofiev lay dying, he reiterated one wish, that Rostropovich should make this opera known to the world. It comes as no surprise, then, to find a deeply committed performance from both soloists (only 45 of them due to some adroit doubling), chorus and orchestra. Prokofiev adapted the novel into seven 'peace' and six 'war' tableaux, thus sustaining drama through contrast throughout its Wagnerian length. With few exceptions the multinational cast sings in good Russian and among them Lajos Miller is particularly affecting as Prince Andrei, pleasingly ardent in his opening moonlit aria. The central female role of Natasha is taken by Galina Vishnevskaya. She sang the role in the 1959 première and inevitably no longer sounds like an innocent 16 year old. Unfortunately, problems are compounded by a hardness in her tone and a lack of attention to detail in some of the quieter sections. Stefania Toczyska as the treacherous Helena makes a great impression, as does Katherine Ciesinski as Natasha's confidante, Sonya. Of the men, Nicolai Gedda as Prince Anatol sings with character and great style and Eduard Tumagian is an heroic and steadfast Napoleon. An added attraction of the recording are the sound effects, particularly in the war scenes, convincing but never too obtrusive. Good translations are provided in three languages, crowning a laudable achievement.

School, Francesco Provenzale. While scholars have argued that much of what's deemed 'Neapolitan' is really just 'Italian', this series from the Cappella de' Turchini has proved that such a view shows a limited knowledge of both the sources and the sheer range of musical idioms and 'dialects' which became established in the second half of the 17th century. Provenzale's three motets for two sopranos, published in 1689 (*Audite caeli* is for soprano and tenor) are hardly masterpieces but they're still good.

The bold challenges to the singer's techniques are often thrilling, but the flavour is less one of operatic transplantation than an indigenous sacred virtuosity which Provenzale jealously guarded; both the extensive *O Jesu mea spes* and *Angelicae mentes* see both Roberta Invernizzi and Emanuela Galli put through their paces, but they both sail through with well-matched timbres and nonchalant Mediterranean breeziness; only occasionally does their instinct for spontaneous moulding lead to questionable intonation. For the most part, the easy, imitative dialogue of Provenzale's motets are revitalised by textually alert and finely projected singing. Of the instrumental interludes, Marchitelli's Sonata II for three violins is a real winner.

Francesco Provenzale
Italian 1624-1704

Active in Naples, Provenzale had operas staged between 1654 and 1674 and became city maestro di cappella in 1665; he was later maestro di capella to the treasury of S Gennaro (1686-99) and served for two periods at the viceregal court. An important teacher, he worked as chief maestro at the conservatories S Maria di Loreto (1663-75) and the Turchini (1675-1701). He was the first prominent Neapolitan musician to compose opera and forerunner of the Neapolitan school of the 18th century. Il schiavo di sua moglie (1671) and La Stellidaura vendicata (1674), which survive complete, are largely modelled on the style of Venetians such as Cesti, but also include melodies of a dance-like, popular character. Provenzale wrote at least six other operas (two may have been adaptations of Cavalli's), secular cantatas and sacred music. GROVEmusic

Motets

Provenzale Cantemus, psallamus. O Jesu   **P**
mea spes. Audite caeli. Angelicae mentes **Avitrano**
Sonate a Quattro, Op 3 – No 2 in D, 'L'Aragona';
No 10 in C, 'La Maddaloni' **Marchitelli** Sonata II
Roberta Invernizzi, Emanuela Galli sops **Giuseppe
de Vittorio** ten **Cappella de' Turchini / Antonio
Florio** vc
Opus 111 OP20006 (62' · DDD) Texts and translations
included   **ⓂO**

This ambitious survey of the finest Baroque Neapolitan music turns to the well-nigh accepted father of the so-called Neapolitan

Giacomo Puccini (i)
Italian 1712-1781

Organist of S Martino in Lucca, 1739-72, and, from 1739 to his death, director of the republic's Cappella Palatina, Puccini was prominent in the organization of music in Lucca. He wrote much sacred music, marked by its good vocal writing, its skilful counterpoint and its varied treatment of the text; he also wrote dramatic music for the local election festivities, the tasche, consisting of orchestral pieces, recitatives and arias, and also an oratorio.
GROVEmusic

Requiem

Messa di Requiem[a]. Lucio Giunio Bruto – Overture.
Marzio Coroliano – Sinfonia
[a]**Ghislaine Morgan** sop [a]**Jonathan Peter Kenny**
counterten [a]**Joseph Cornwell** ten [a]**David Thomas**
bass [a]**Kantorei Saarlouis; Ensemble UnaVolta /
Joachim Fontaine**
Arte Nova 74321 98497-2 (64' · DDD)   Ⓢ

The composer here is the great-great-grandfather of the opera composer we all know, and a formidable figure in musical Italy in the mid-18th century. The Requiem harks back in its technique to traditional forms. If there's a parallel to be drawn between the two Giacomo Puccinis, it's their pragmatic eclecticism, drawing on the ideas or styles of others to create something fresh and individual. In the Requiem the elaborate eight-part contrapuntal writing regularly involves clashing discords and suspensions – the sort of effect that makes his choral writing so refreshing. He's also fond of chromatic bass lines, another notionally archaic device in his time, but invariably delighting the modern ear. The at-times Handelian choral passages are nicely set in contrast with relatively brief solo sections.

As fillers we also have a pair of overtures written for the secular oratorios that were performed annually in Lucca. These are very much of their time – one an Italian Overture in three movements, fast-slow-fast, the other a bright and breezy *Allegro* under four minutes long.

If Giacomo (i) lacks the gift of memorable melody that distinguishes Giacomo (ii)'s work, his liveliness and technical skill are never in doubt. Fontaine and his Saarland musicians bring out that vigour, even if the singing of the small professional choir isn't always polished. The four soloists are stylish and the recording focuses the performers cleanly and immediately in a helpfully warm acoustic. At super-budget price this is an issue that deserves the widest audience.

Giacomo Puccini (ii)   Italian 1858-1924

Puccini was fifth in a line of composers from Lucca. After studying music with his uncle, Fortunato Magi, and with the director of the Istituto Musicale Pacini, Carlo Angeloni, he started his career at the age of 14 as an organist at S Martino and S Michele, Lucca, and at other local churches. However, a performance of Verdi's Aida at Pisa in 1876 made such an impact on him that he decided to follow his instinct for operatic composition. With a scholarship and financial support from an uncle, he was able to enter the Milan Conservatory in 1880, where his chief teachers were Bazzini and Ponchielli.

While still a student, Puccini entered a competition for a one-act opera. He failed to win, but the opera Le villi came to the attention of the publisher Giulio Ricordi, who arranged a successful production at the Teatro del Verme in Milan and commissioned a second opera. The libretto, Edgar, was unsuited to Puccini's dramatic talent and the opera was coolly received at La Scala in April 1889. It did, however, set the seal on what was to be Puccini's lifelong association with the house of Ricordi.

Manon Lescaut, produced at Turin in 1893, achieved a success such as Puccini was never to repeat and made him known outside Italy. Among the writers who worked on its libretto were Luigi Illica and Giuseppe Giacosa, who provided the librettos for Puccini's next three operas. The first of these, La bohème, widely considered Puccini's masterpiece, but with its mixture of lighthearted and sentimental scenes and its largely conversational style was not a success when produced at Turin in 1896. Tosca, Puccini's first excursion into verismo, was more enthusiastically received by the Roman audience at the Teatro Costanzi in 1900.

Later that year Puccini visited London and saw David Belasco's one-act play Madam Butterfly. This he took as the basis for his next collaboration and he considered it the best and technically most advanced opera he had written. He was unprepared for the fiasco attending its first performance in February 1904, when the La Scala audience was urged into hostility, even pandemonium, by the composer's jealous rivals; in a revised version it was given to great acclaim at Brescia the following May. By then Puccini had married Elvira Gemignani, the widow of a Lucca merchant, who had borne him a son as long ago as 1896. The family lived until 1921 in the house at Torre del Lago which Puccini had acquired in 1891. Scandal was unleashed in 1909 when a servant girl of the Puccinis, whom Elvira had accused of an intimate relationship with her husband, committed suicide. A court case established the girl's innocence, but the publicity affected Puccini deeply and was the main reason for the long period before his next opera.

This was La fanciulla del West, based on another Belasco drama it was given its première at the Metropolitan Opera, New York, in December 1910. In all technical respects, notably its Debussian harmony and Straussian orchestration, it was a masterly reply to the criticism that Puccini repeated himself in every new opera. What it lacks is the incandescent phrase, and this is probably why it has not entered the normal repertory outside Italy.

Differences with Tito Ricordi, head of the firm since 1912, led Puccini to accept a commission for an operetta from the directors of the Vienna Karltheater. The result, La rondine, though warmly received at Monte Carlo in 1917, is among Puccini's weakest works, hovering between opera and operetta and devoid of striking lyrical melody. While working on it Puccini began the composition of Il tabarro, the first of three one-act operas (Il trittico) which follow the scheme of the Parisian Grand Guignol – a horrific episode, a sentimental tragedy (Suor Angelica) and a comedy or farce (Gianni Schicchi). This last has proved to be the most enduring part of the triptych and is often done without the others, usually in a double bill.

In his early 60s Puccini was determined to 'strike out on new paths' and started work on Turandot, based on a Gozzi play which satisfied his desire for a subject with a fantastic, fairy-tale atmosphere, but flesh-and-blood characters. During its composition he moved to Viareggio and in 1923 developed cancer of the throat. Treatment at a Brussels clinic seemed successful, but his heart could not stand the strain and he died, leaving Turandot unfinished. After his wife's death in 1930, his house at Torre del Lago was turned into a museum.

Puccini's choral, orchestral and instrumental works, dating mainly from his early years, are unimportant, though the Mass in A flat (1880) is still performed occasionally. His operas may not engage us on as many different levels as do those of Mozart, Wagner, Verdi or Strauss, but on his own most characteristic level, where erotic passion, sensuality, tenderness, pathos and despair meet and fuse, he was an unrivalled master. His melodic gift and harmonic sensibility, his consummate skill in orchestration and unerring sense of theatre combined to create a style that was wholly original, homogeneous and compelling. He was fully aware of his limitations and rarely ventured beyond them. He represents Verdi's only true successor, and his greatest masterpiece and swansong, Turandot, belongs among the last 20th-century stage works to remain in the regular repertory of the world's opera houses.

GROVEmusic

Messa di Gloria

Messa di Gloria[a]. Preludio sinfonico. Crisantemi
[a]**Antonello Palombi** ten [a]**Gunnar Lundberg** bar
Hungarian Radio Orchestra and [a]**Choir / Pier
Giorgio Morandi**
Naxos 8 555304 (60' · DDD) Notes, texts and
translations included ⑤❶

This recording is to be preferred to Antonio
Pappano's very fine account on EMI – and it's
not just a question of price. If the recorded
sound isn't as opulent as EMI's, it's very clear
and lets in the light. If the dynamic contrasts
aren't so big, they're also rather more refined.
Generally Giorgio Morandi prefers slightly
faster speeds, though not so fast as Pappano
when he really gets up some steam in the last
sections of the *Gloria*. But in context Morandi
brings out the inherent excitement very effectively and naturally whereas Pappano underlines it. With Pappano the majestic Verdian
unisons of the 'Qui tollis' broaden like a great
smile across a large face: it's grand fun but tends
towards vulgarity. Of the work as a whole,
Morandi and his forces give a more youthful
performance. There's an easy lightness of step
(the *Gloria* sets off with a dance). The chorus is
particularly fresh in tone and response, and the
tenor soloist, Antonello Palombi, is more gracefully lyrical and Italianate in timbre than either
Alagna (with Pappano) or his predecessor Carreras (with Scimone). The baritone is less apt
and certainly no match for Hampson (Pappano)
or Prey (Scimone); musical nevertheless, and
blending well with his colleague in the *Agnus
Dei*. In the string piece, *Crisantemi*, Morandi's
somewhat quicker tempo, still answering to the
marking *andante mesto*, is welcome, keeping
mawkishness at bay and limiting the over-exposure of rather thin material.

Opera Arias

La bohème – Sì, mi chiamano Mimì; Donde lieta uscì.
Gianni Schicchi – O mio babbino caro. **Madama
Butterfly** – Un bel dì vedremo; Che tua madre; Tu, tu,
piccolo iddio. **Manon Lescaut** – In quelle trine
morbide; Sola, perduta, abbandonata. **La rondine** –
Chi il bel sogno di Doretta. **Suor Angelica** – Senza
mamma, O bimbo. **Tosca** – Vissi d'arte. **Turandot** –
Signore, ascolta!; In questa reggia; Tu, che di gel sei
cinta
Julia Varady sop **Berlin Radio Symphony
Orchestra / Marcello Viotti**
Orfeo C323941A (52' · DDD) Recorded 1993 ⓕ❶❶

A lovely and somewhat surprising record by the
most fascinating and patrician lyric soprano of
the present age: 'surprising' because, though
Varady is associated closely enough with Verdi,
the Puccini connection is less readily made,

'lovely' because the voice is still so pure, the
style so musical and the response so intelligent,
immediate and full-hearted. She adjusts wonderfully well to the Italian idiom, lightening the
vowels, freeing the upper range, allowing more
portamento than she would probably do in other
music, yet employing in its use the finest technical skill and artistic judgement.

Her singing of Magda's song in *La rondine*
opens the record and introduces a singer who
sounds (give or take a little) half her actual age:
Varady's début dates back to 1962. In Mimì's
narrative she sings with so fine a perception of
the character – the hesitancies, the joy in 'mi
piaccion quelle cose' – that Schwarzkopf's exquisite recording comes to mind, just as, from
time to time, and especially in the *Madama Butterfly* excerpts, the finely concentrated, tragic
restraint of Meta Seinemeyer is recalled. It's
good to hear, too, how sensitively Varady differentiates between characters, Manon Lescaut
having that essential degree of additional
sophistication in tone and manner. What runs
as a thread through all these characterisations is
a feeling for their dignity. Mimì doesn't simper.
Sister Angelica doesn't sob. Lauretta has resolution in her pleading. Butterfly, Liù and Tosca
are what they should be: women whose pathos
lies not in their weakness but in a passionate,
single-minded fidelity. That leaves Turandot,
which is a mistake. That is, she's outside the
singer's scope and should remain so: it isn't
merely a matter of vocal thrust, weight and
stamina, but also of voice-character, although
the performance of her aria has clear merits.
None of which should deter purchase; overall
this is singing to treasure.

Madama Butterfly – Un bel dì vedremo; Tu, tu
piccolo iddio[a]. **La bohème** – Mi chiamano Mimì;
Quando m'en vo; Donde lieta usci. **Edgar** – Addio,
addio mio dolce amor?; Nel villaggio d'Edgar.
Gianni Schicchi – O mio babbino caro. **La fanciulla
del West** – Laggiù nel Soledad. **Manon Lescaut** –
In quelle trine morbide; Sola, perduta, abbandonata.
La Rondine – Chi il bel sogno di Doretta? **Suor
Angelica** – Senza mamma. **Turandot** – Signore,
ascolta!; Tu che di gel sei cinta; In questa reggia[a].
Le villi – Se come voi piccina
Angela Gheorghiu sop [a]**Roberto Alagna** ten
**Giuseppe Verdi Symphony Chorus and Orchestra,
Milan / Anton Coppola**
EMI 557955-2 (70' · DDD) ⓕ❶❶

This is a considerable addition to this ever-
enterprising artist's growing discography. Just
when many of us were declaring there would
never be anyone to take on Renata Tebaldi's
mantle in *spinto* roles, here's Angela Gheorghiu
doing just that. There is a similar strength of
tone, breadth of phrasing and attention to musical and verbal detail. Everything she achieves
here is technically assured, thought through and
emotionally rewarding.

Her Mimì in Decca's *La bohème* was an appealing, cleanly articulated reading, and it still is,

even if the youthful bloom isn't quite so much in evidence. Musetta, though, is now very much her role, her Waltz Song sung with zest adding to the fullness only a few others have brought to the piece. One can hear why EMI wanted 'Un bel dì vedremo' at its top: Gheorghiu's account is overwhelming, as is the death scene. She's almost as moving in *Suor Angelica*'s 'Senza mamma'. Magda's solo and 'O mio babbino caro' are as smiling and therefore as winning as they should be. From *Turandot*, Liù's pains and sorrows are encompassed with ease and an apt *morbidezza*, with finely poised *pianissimo* high notes.

This is a deeply satisfying traversal of the Puccini canon, well supported by the Milan orchestra and Anton Coppola, artistic director of Florida's Opera Tampa.

La bohème – Che gelida manina. **Edgar** – Orgia, chimera dall'occhio vitreo. **La fanciulla del West** – Una parola sola! ... Or son sei mesi; Risparmiate lo scherno ... Ch'ella mi creda libero. **Gianni Schicchi** – Avete torto! Firenze è come un albero fiorito. **Madama Butterfly** – Dipende dal grado di cottura ... Amore o grillo; Addio, fiorito asil. **Manon Lescaut** – Tra voi, belle; Donna non vidi mai; Ah! Manon, mi tradisce; Ah! non v'avvicinate!; Manon ... senti, amor mio ... Vedi, son io che piango. **La rondine** – Parigi! è la citta dei desideri ... Forse, come la rondine; Dimmi che vuoi seguirmi; **Il Tabarro** – Hai ben ragione; lo voglio la tua bocca ... Folle di gelosia!. **Tosca** – Recondita armonia; E lucevan le stelle. **Turandot** – Non piangere, Liù!; Nessun dorma!. **Le villi** – Ecco la casa ... Torna ai felici dì
José Cura ten Philharmonia Orchestra / **Plácido Domingo**
Erato 0630-18838-2 (71' · DDD) Texts and translations included ⓕ

For those who wish to feast on a good tenor voice, this is the goods. First, however, a peculiarity of this programme is that it goes backwards. It starts with *Turandot* and recedes along a strict chronological line to *Le villi*. That of itself is an attractive idea, but it means that the terminus is a long and somewhat inconclusive excerpt, while the starting-point is 'Nessun dorma!'. We all know what that means these days, and it looks suspiciously like making a bid for the market if not for the kingdom. A dark, rather throaty, big and uncharming voice reiterates the famous command. As it takes the high As we realise that this is special, rising easily and thrillingly out of the baritonal middle register; Cura holds his high B ('vincerò') for the maximum length compatible with holding on to the succeeding A for even longer. But he's a man with surprises in store. 'Non piangere, Liù!' begins quietly and is thoughtfully phrased. Similarly he shows his unpredictability in the *Tosca* arias: 'Recondita armonia' is stolid, almost routine, but then 'E lucevan le stelle' becomes the real expression of a man facing up to the prospect of imminent execution, and writing a poem. Throughout, Cura displays a thrilling

voice with an individual timbre. His 'face' wears too much of a scowl and he doesn't give the impression of thinking about the person he's nominally addressing, but this is a solo recital and perhaps it would be different in a complete opera. He's accompanied here with uncommon sympathy by a conductor who has a good deal more experience of singing than has the singer himself.

La bohème

La bohème ⓗ
Victoria de los Angeles sop Mimì **Jussi Björling** ten Rodolfo **Lucine Amara** sop Musetta **Robert Merrill** bar Marcello **John Reardon** bar Schaunard **Giorgio Tozzi** bass Colline **Fernando Corena** bass Benoit, Alcindoro **William Nahr** ten Parpignol **Thomas Powell** bar Customs Official **George del Monte** bar Sergeant **Columbus Boychoir; RCA Victor Chorus and Orchestra / Sir Thomas Beecham**
EMI Great Recordings of the Century mono ②
567750-2 (108' · ADD) Recorded 1956. Notes, text and translation included Ⓜ❍❍❍

The disadvantages of this famous Beecham *Bohème* are obvious. It's a mono recording and restricted in dynamic range. The sense of space for the complex crowd scene of Act 2 to emerge with the maximum impact is inevitably lacking; the climaxes here and elsewhere are somewhat constricted; no less important, it's sometimes harder to focus on the subtleties of Puccini's orchestration. It was also made in a great hurry, and this shows in a number of patches of slightly insecure ensemble, even a couple of wrong entries. But there's no other important respect in which it doesn't stand at least half a head (often head and shoulders) above its more recent rivals. Nobody has ever been so predestinately right for the role of Mimì than Victoria de los Angeles: right both in vocal quality and in sheer involvement with every word and every musical phrase that Mimì utters. Beyond a certain point (usually a certain dynamic level) most sopranos stop being Mimì and simply produce the same sound that they would if they were singing Aida or Tosca. De los Angeles rarely does this; even under pressure (and Beecham's unhurried tempos do put her under pressure at times), the very difficulties themselves are used as an expressive and interpretative resource. Hers is the most moving and involving Mimì ever recorded. And Björling's is the most musical Rodolfo. He has the reputation of having been a bit of a dry stick, dramatically (on stage he looked like the other Bohemians' elderly, portly uncle), but on record he's the one exponent of the role to be credible both as a lover and as a poet. His voice is fine silver rather than brass, it can caress as well as weep, and his love for Mimì is more often confided than it is bellowed for all Paris to hear. This, indeed, is one of the most conspicuous differences between

Beecham's account and most others: its simple belief that when Puccini wrote *pp* he meant it. Beecham (whose spell over his entire cast – in which there's no weak link – extends as far as teaching his Schaunard, John Reardon, an irresistibly funny, cut-glass English accent for the parrot-fancying milord) makes one realise what an intimate opera this is, how much of it is quiet, how many of its exchanges are *sotto voce*, and he thus enables his singers to use the full range of their voices and to employ subtleties of colour, phrasing and diction that are simply not available to a voice at full stretch (and in the process he largely cancels out the disadvantage of his recording's restricted dynamic range). It's the same with his handling of the orchestra: one would expect Beecham to seem understated, but again and again one turns back to his reading and discovers nothing missing – he has achieved as much or more with less. This is as complete a distillation of Puccini's drama as you're likely to hear.

La bohème
Mirella Freni *sop* Mimì **Luciano Pavarotti** *ten* Rodolfo **Elizabeth Harwood** *sop* Musetta **Rolando Panerai** *bar* Marcello **Gianni Maffeo** *bar* Schaunard **Nicolai Ghiaurov** *bass* Colline **Michel Sénéchal** *bass* Benoit, Alcindoro **Gernot Pietsch** *ten* Parpignol **Schoenberg Boys' Choir; Berlin German Opera Chorus; Berlin Philharmonic Orchestra / Herbert von Karajan**
Decca ② 421 049-2DH2 (110' · ADD) Recorded 1972.
Notes, text and translation included   Ⓕ**O**

Pavarotti's Rodolfo is perhaps the best thing he has ever done: not only the finest recorded account of the role since Björling's on the Beecham set, but adding the honeyed Italianate warmth that even Björling lacked. He can't quite match Björling's poetic refinement, and he's less willing to sing really quietly, but Pavarotti's sincerity counts for a great deal: his pride as he declares his vocation as a poet, the desperate feigning of his 'Mimì è una civetta' are points that most tenors miss or treat as mere opportunities for a big sing. His latter-day image may tend to hide it, but this recording is a reminder that Pavarotti is an artist of intelligence and delicacy as well as splendour of voice. His Mimì, Freni, sings beautifully and sensitively. Panerai is a strong, vividly acted Marcello. Harwood is an interesting Musetta: her tiny narration, in Act 4, of her meeting with the stricken Mimì is a gripping moment, and her waltz-song in Act 2 is a passionate (and irresistible) avowal to Marcello. Karajan is a great Puccini conductor who can linger over the beauties of orchestration without losing his grip on the drama or relaxing his support of the singers. There aren't many operas of which a better case can be made for having more than one account in your collection. For a modern *La bohème* to supplement the Beecham this Karajan set must go to the top of the list.

PUCCINI'S LA BOHÈME – IN BRIEF

Victoria de los Angeles *Mimì* **Jussi Björling** *Rodolfo* **Lucine Amara** *Musetta* **Columbus Boychoir; RCA Victor Chorus & Orchestra / Sir Thomas Beecham**
EMI mono ② 567750-2 (107' · AAD)   Ⓜ**OOO**
☀ A classic, with extra electricity derived from the hasty recording, with Beecham's living, vivid conducting and a superb cast, both stellar and supporting, even though the mono sound is less kind to the orchestra.

Mirella Freni *Mimì* **Luciano Pavarotti** *Rodolfo* **Elizabeth Harwood** *Musetta* **Schönberg Boys' Choir; Berlin Deutsche Oper Chorus; Berlin PO / Herbert von Karajan**
Decca ② 421 049-2DH2 (110' · ADD)   Ⓕ**O**
Karajan's lush but eloquent Puccini, with top-notch voices, Pavarotti in particular, that at least equal Beecham's. Magnificent orchestral playing in an equally fine recording.

(In English) **Cynthia Haymon** *Mimì* **Dennis O'Neill** *Rodolfo* **Marie McLaughlin** *Musetta* **Peter Kay Children's Choir; Geoffrey Mitchell Choir; Philharmonia Orchestra / David Parry**
Chandos ② CHAN3008 (111' · DDD)   Ⓕ
Despite the stilted old translation a highly enjoyable recording, warmly conducted and sung by a cast of international standing, and very directly communicative.

Angela Gheorghiu *Mimì* **Roberto Alagna** *Rodolfo* **Elisabeth Scano** *Musetta* **Chorus and Orchestra of La Scala, Milan / Riccardo Chailly**
Decca ② 466 070-2DHO2 (99' · DDD)   Ⓕ
A glittering ultra-modern recording starring opera's current 'dream team' Roberto Alagna and Angela Gheorghiu, both excellent, and with a fine supporting cast headed by Simon Keenlyside. Chailly's conducting can seem rather hard-driven.

Ileana Cotrubas *Mimì* **Neil Schicoff** *Rodolfo* **Marilyn Zschau** *Musetta* **Royal Opera House Chorus and Orchestra / Lamberto Gardelli**
NVC Arts 📀 4509 99222-2 (118')   Ⓕ
Of several DVD *Bohèmes*, this is the most convincing: an immensely vital production in richly atmospheric sets. Cotrubas, Allen and a vivid supporting cast are affectionately conducted by Gardelli.

Cheryl Barker *Mimì* **David Hobson** *Rodolfo* **Christine Douglas** *Musetta* **Australian Opera Chorus and Orchestra / Julian Smith**
Arthaus Musik 📀 100 954 (113')   Ⓕ**O**
The famous stage production by Baz Luhrman in its original and genuinely operatic approach. It's engaging, heartfelt and may well captivate opera newcomers with its 1950s Paris setting and youngish cast.

La bohème

Cynthia Haymon sop Mimì **Dennis O'Neill** ten
Rodolfo **Marie McLaughlin** sop Musetta **Alan Opie**
bar Marcello **William Dazeley** bar Schaunard
Alastair Miles bass Colline **Andrew Shore** bar
Benoit, Alcindoro **Mark Milhofer** ten Parpignol
Simon Preece bar Customs Official **Paul Parfitt**
bass-bar Sergeant **Peter Kay Children's Choir;**
Geoffrey Mitchell Choir; Philharmonia Orchestra /
David Parry
Chandos Opera in English ② CHAN3008
(111' · DDD) Sung in English. Notes and text
included   Ⓕ

The text (Grist and Pinkerton amended by
David Parry) is a very acceptable rendering of a
libretto which was, after all, first known in
England, in English. However well sung, that
first performance, at Manchester in 1897, is
unlikely to have offered orchestral playing as
fine as the Philharmonia's here, and Parry's
well-controlled tempo is another strong factor
in making this a special recording of the opera
irrespective of language.

The singers have that first requisite of a good
Bohème cast: they work as a team. Cynthia Haymon is a gentle Mimì, perfectly lovely in the
middle register of her voice, just a little worn on
top. Dennis O'Neill provides a rare pleasure in
this music, singing softly at the right moments;
he also produces such a very good top C in his
aria that he has no need to give us another at the
end of the Act instead of obliging with the composer's harmonies. Marie McLaughlin's isn't
quite the sparkler one had in mind as Musetta,
but the fellow Bohemians are capital, in voice as
in spirits. The ensemble in Act 2 is first-rate; the
contribution of the Peter Kay Children's Choir
even better than that. The recording is superb.

Additional recommendations

La bohème

Carreras Rodolfo **Ricciarelli** Mimì **Putnam** Musetta
Wixell Marcello **Royal Opera House Chorus and**
Orchestra / C Davis
Philips ② 442 260-2PM2 (106' · ADD)   Ⓜ
  Carreras and Ricciarelli make a wonderful pair of
  lovers – totally credible, their fresh, supple voices
  totally suited to the roles – while Davis conducts
  somewhat coolly.

Tebaldi Mimì **Bergonzi** Rodolfo **Orchestra**   Ⓗ
dell'Accademia di Santa Cecilia, Rome / Serafin
Decca Compact Opera Collection ② 470 431-2DOC2
(ADD) Recorded 1959   ⓂⓄ
  An all-Italian cast and an extremely fine account
  that matches and – some would say – surpasses
  Beecham's.

La fanciulla del West

La fanciulla del West
Carol Neblett sop Minnie **Plácido Domingo** ten
Dick Johnson **Sherrill Milnes** bar Jack Rance **Francis**

Egerton ten Nick **Robert Lloyd** bass Ashby **Gwynne**
Howell bass Jake Wallace **Paul Hudson** bass Billy
Jackrabbit **Anne Wilkens** sop Wowkle **Chorus and**
Orchestra of the Royal Opera House, Covent
Garden / Zubin Mehta
DG ② 419 640-2GH2 (130' · ADD) Recorded 1977.
Notes, text and translation included   ⒻⓄⓄⓄ

 This opera depicts the triangular relationship between Minnie, the saloon
owner and 'mother' to the entire town
of gold miners, Jack Rance, the sheriff and Dick
Johnson (alias Ramerrez), a bandit leader. The
music is highly developed in Puccini's seamless
lyrical style, the arias for the main characters
emerge from the texture and return to it effortlessly. The vocal colours are strongly polarised
with the cast being all male except for one travesti role and Minnie herself. The score bristles
with robust melody as well as delicate scoring,
betraying a masterly hand at work. Carol
Neblett is a strong Minnie, vocally distinctive
and well characterised, while Plácido Domingo
and Sherrill Milnes make a good pair of suitors
for the spunky little lady. Zubin Mehta conducts with real sympathy for the idiom and the
orchestra responds well.

Madama Butterfly

Madama Butterfly
Renata Scotto sop Madama Butterfly **Carlo**
Bergonzi ten Pinkerton **Rolando Panerai** bar
Sharpless **Anna di Stasio** mez Suzuki **Piero De**
Palma ten Goro **Giuseppe Morresi** ten Prince
Yamadori **Silvana Padoan** mez Kate Pinkerton **Paolo**
Montarsolo bass The Bonze **Mario Rinaudo** bass
Commissioner **Rome Opera House Chorus and**
Orchestra / Sir John Barbirolli
EMI Great Recordings of the Century ② 567885-2
(142' · ADD) Recorded 1966. Notes, text and
translation included   ⓂⓄ

This is Barbirolli's *Butterfly*; despite Scotto's
expressiveness and Bergonzi's elegance it's the
conductor's contribution that gives this set its
durability and its hold on the affections. The
Rome Opera Orchestra isn't the equal of the
Vienna Philharmonic for Karajan. However,
the rapport between conductor and orchestra
and their mutual affection for Puccini are evident throughout, and they make this the most
Italianate of all readings. It's hugely enjoyable,
not just in the big emotional outpourings (like
the Act 2 interlude, where Barbirolli's passionate gasps and groans spur the orchestra to great
eloquence) but in many tiny moments where
you can almost see the conductor and his players
lovingly and absorbedly concentrating on subtleties of phrasing and texture.

There's a lot of good singing, too. Scotto's
voice won't always take the pressure she puts on
it, but her portrayal is a touching and finely
detailed one. The ever stylish Bergonzi sings
with immaculate phrasing and perfect taste,
Panerai is an outstanding Sharpless (beautifully

sung, the embodiment of anxious, pitying concern) and di Stasio's Suzuki is attractively light-voiced and young-sounding.

The recording, however, is a bit narrow in perspective, rather close (really quiet singing and playing rarely register as such) and some of the voices are edged or slightly tarnished in loud passages. Barbirolli's set is perhaps for those who find the meticulously refined detail of Karajan studied (also ravishing and stunningly recorded); those, in short, for whom Latin warmth and impulsive open-heartedness are indispensable in this opera. They will find those qualities here, with singing to match, and won't mind the occasional strident patch.

Madama Butterfly
Mirella Freni sop Madama Butterfly **Luciano Pavarotti** ten Pinkerton **Robert Kerns** bar Sharpless **Christa Ludwig** mez Suzuki **Michel Sénéchal** ten Goro **Giorgio Stendoro** bar Prince Yamadori **Elke Schary** mez Kate Pinkerton **Marius Rintzler** bass The Bonze **Hans Helm** bass Commissioner **Vienna State Opera Chorus; Vienna Philharmonic Orchestra / Herbert von Karajan**
Decca ③ 417 577-2DH3 (145' · ADD) Recorded 1974. Notes, text and translation included ⑤

In every way except one the transfer of Karajan's radiant Vienna recording for Decca could hardly provide a firmer recommendation. The reservation is one of price – this Karajan is on three discs, not two, at full price. However it does allow each act to be self-contained on a single disc, and for such a performance as this no extravagance is too much. Movingly dramatic as Renata Scotto is on the Barbirolli set, Mirella Freni is even more compelling. The voice is fresher, firmer and more girlish, with more light and shade at such points as 'Un bel dì', and there's an element of vulnerability that intensifies the communication. In that, one imagines Karajan played a big part, just as he must have done in presenting Pavarotti – not quite the super-star he is today but already with a will of his own in the recording studio – as a Pinkerton of exceptional subtlety, not just a roistering cad but in his way an endearing figure in the First Act.

Significantly CD brings out the delicacy of the vocal balances in Act 1 with the voices deliberately distanced for much of the time, making such passages as 'Vienna la sera' and 'Bimba dagli occhi' the more magical in their delicacy. Karajan, in that duet and later in the Flower duet of Act 2, draws ravishing playing from the Vienna Philharmonic strings, getting them to imitate the *portamento* of the singers in an *echt-Viennes* manner, which is ravishing to the ear. Christa Ludwig is by far the richest and most compelling of Suzukis.

Madama Butterfly
Miriam Gauci sop Madama Butterfly **Yordi Ramiro** ten Pinkerton **Georg Tichy** bar Sharpless **Nelly**

Boschková mez Suzuki **Josef Abel** ten Goro **Robert Szücs** bar Prince Yamadori **Alzbeta Michalková** mez Kate Pinkerton **Jozef Spaček** bass The Bonze **Vladimir Kubovčik** bass Commissioner, Registrar **Slovak Philharmonic Chorus; Bratislava Radio Symphony Orchestra / Alexander Rahbari**
Naxos ② 8 660015/6 (141' · DDD) Recorded 1991. Notes and text included ⑤

Though this would never be a first-choice *Butterfly*, it might serve you could well find it a good introduction. It's consistently musical, avoids cheapness or exaggerated sentiment, and, while presenting worthily the enchanting and infinitely poignant score, it leaves plenty to be discovered with a widening knowledge of other and greater performances. An attractive feature is the youthfulness of the Butterfly and Pinkerton. The Pinkerton, a Mexican lyric tenor, Yordi Ramiro, gives as likeable, sincere a version of the character as any. And this isn't a falsification of the part, at the very heart of which is the painful truth that likeable people may do very unlikeable things. It's a good voice: limited, but well defined and with a youthful freshness in its tone. The Butterfly is also young-sounding: Miriam Gauci, born in Malta. She sings uncompromisingly as a light lyric soprano, with an especially lovely quality in the upper range. The lightness brings limitations in this colossal role, and they're compounded by the immaturity of her acting-portrayal: she does many of 'the right things' but it's rare to find in her the flash of expressiveness that illuminates a character from within. A newcomer to the opera isn't likely to be troubled by this, but will on the contrary be delighted by the quality of the voice and touched by the general appeal of the character. Rahbari conducts a performance that captures both the opera's charm and seriousness, not, however, its intensity.

Additional recommendation

Madama Butterfly

Coupled with: Arias by Bellini, Bianchini, ⒽDonizetti, Mascagni, Sadero and Verdi
Dal Monte Madama Butterfly **Palombini** Suzuki **Gigli** Pinkerton **Rome Opera Chorus and Orchestra / De Fabritiis**
Naxos Historical mono ② 8 110183/4 (153' · ADD) Recorded [a]1939, 1928-41 ⑤
This is the most complete performance of the role of Butterfly on record. Dal Monte's portrayal moves from 'child Butterfly' to create most movingly the maturing woman whose tragedy loses nothing in nobility as the last scene unfolds. Transfers are bright and clear. This *Butterfly* is definitely one for the collection.

Manon Lescaut

Manon Lescaut
Mirella Freni sop Manon Lescaut **Luciano Pavarotti** ten Des Grieux **Dwayne Croft** bar Lescaut **Giuseppe**

PUCCINI MADAMA BUTTERFLY –
IN BRIEF

Renata Scotto *Madama Butterfly* **Carlo Bergonzi**
Pinkerton **Rolando Panerai** *Sharpless* **Rome
Opera Chorus & Orch / Sir John Barbirolli**
EMI ② 567885-2 (142' · ADD)   Ⓜ️Ⓞ
In one of his rare operatic showings Barbirolli created a warmly idiomatic, Italianate
performance, fluent, detailed and superlatively sung by a distinguished cast, even if
the recorded sound is not up to the very best.

Mirella Freni *Madama Butterfly* **Luciano
Pavarotti** *Pinkerton* **Robert Kerns** *Sharpless*
**Rome Vienna State Opera Chorus, Vienna PO /
Herbert von Karajan**
Decca ③ 417 577-2DH3 (145' · ADD)   ⒻⓄ
A stunningly beautiful performance, in Karajan's conducting, measured and luxuriant
yet still dramatic, with two thrilling central
performances, sounding younger than Barbirolli's, a fine supporting cast and an outstanding recording.

Miriam Gauci *Madama Butterfly* **Yordi Ramiro**
Pinkerton **Slovak Philharmonic Chorus,
Bratislava RSO / Alexander Rahbari**
Naxos ② 8 660015/6 (141' · DDD)   Ⓢ
A fresh, engaging performance, not in the
class of the more star-filled productions,
but full of life and well recorded. A good
bargain-price set.

Maria Callas *Madama Butterfly* **Nicolai Gedda**
Pinkerton **Chorus & Orchestra of La Scala, Milan
/ Herbert von Karajan**
EMI ② 556298-2 (139' · AAD)   ⒻⓄ
Magnificently compelling despite the mono
sound, with Maria Callas a heartbreaking
Butterfly, Nicolai Gedda an intensely roman-
tic Pinkerton and Karajan more vividly thea-
trical than in his much later recording.

Svetlana Katchour *Madama Butterfly* **Bruce
Rankin** *Pinkerton* **Bremen Theatre Chorus,
Bremen PO / Günter Neuhold**
Naxos ② 8 660078/9 (140' · DDD)   Ⓢ
At super-budget price, a recording of the
1904 original score, restoring some valuable
extra music. Despite some heavy-handed
conducting, this is a likeable if not world-
class performance.

Ying Huang *Madama Butterfly* **Richard Troxell**
Pinkerton **Orchestre de Paris / James Conlon**
Columbia 📀 CDR24673 (128')   Ⓕ
A cinematic version, somewhat indulgently
directed by Frédéric Mitterand, with reasonable lip-sync. The very young Ying Huang is
a light-voiced but deeply touching Butterfly,
and though Richard Troxell is only serviceable as Pinkerton, this is still unusual and
enjoyable.

Taddei *bar* Geronte **Ramon Vargas** *ten* Edmondo
Cecilia Bartoli *mez* Singer **Federico Davia** *bass*
Innkeeper, Captain **Anthony Laciura** *ten* Dancing
Master **Paul Groves** *ten* Lamplighter **James
Courtney** *bass* Sergeant **Chorus and Orchestra of
the Metropolitan Opera / James Levine**
Decca ② 440 200-2DHO2 (120' · DDD) Recorded
1992. Notes, text and translation included   Ⓕ

With Luciano Pavarotti a powerful Des Grieux,
James Levine conducts a comparably big-boned
performance of *Manon Lescaut*, bringing out the
red-blooded drama of Puccini's first big success,
while not ignoring its warmth and tender poetry
in exceptionally full, vivid sound with the voices
well in front of the orchestra. In the title-role
Freni's performance culminates in an account of
the big Act 4 aria, more involving and passionate than any of the others on rival versions, with
the voice showing no signs of wear, and with her
sudden change of face at the words 'terra di
pace' ('a land of peace') bringing a magical lightening of tone. That aria makes a thrilling climax, when too often this act can seem a let-
down. In this as in so much else, Levine conveys
the tensions and atmosphere of a stage performance in a way that owes much to his experience
at the Metropolitan. More completely than
other versions, it avoids the feeling of a studio
performance. Reactions to Pavarotti as Des
Grieux will differ widely. The closeness of balance means that in volume his singing rarely
drops below *mezzo forte*, but there's little harm
in having so passionate a portrait of Des Grieux
as Pavarotti's. Needless to say, the hero's big
emotional climaxes in each of the first three acts
come over at full force. The rest of the cast is
strong too, with Dwayne Croft a magnificent
Lescaut. Many collectors will count this a clear
first choice among current versions.

Manon Lescaut   Ⓗ
Maria Callas *sop* Manon Lescaut **Giuseppe di
Stefano** *ten* Des Grieux **Giulio Fioravanti** *bar*
Lescaut **Franco Calabrese** *bass* Geronte **Dino
Formichini** *ten* Edmondo **Fiorenza Cossotto** *mez*
Singer **Carlo Forti** *bass* Innkeeper **Vito Tatone** *ten*
Dancing master **Giuseppe Morresi** *bass* Sergeant
Franco Ricciardi *ten* Lamplighter **Franco Ventrigilia**
bass Captain **Chorus and Orchestra of La Scala,
Milan / Tullio Serafin**
EMI ② 556301-2 (120' · ADD) Recorded 1957 Notes,
text and translation included   ⒻⓄⓄ

This performance is unique, with Act 4 for once
a culmination in Callas's supreme account of
the death scene. She may present a rather formidable portrait of a young girl in Act 1, but
here the final act with its long duet and the big
aria, 'Sola, perduta, abbandonata', is far more
than an epilogue to the rest, rather a culmination, with Callas at her very peak. Di Stefano,
too, is on superb form and Serafin's pacing of
the score is masterly. Di Stefano wipes the floor
with most of his rivals past and present: in Act 4
he has a concerned tenderness for Manon that

others can only sketch, his debonair charm in 'Tra voi belle' is incomparable and (rarest of virtues among tenors) he never sings past the limits of his voice. Fioravanti as Lescaut and Calabrese as Geronte sing well if not very characterfully.

However, digital CD remastering in this instance loses out. A break has to be made in Act 2 – in a fairly innocuous place before the duet 'Tu, tu, amore tu'. The first two acts make up a total timing only a few seconds over the 75-minute limit, but evidently it was enough to prevent them going on to a single CD. That said, the CD brings the same advantages in refining the original boxy sound without glamorising it in false stereo, plus the usual advantages of absence of background and ease of finding places. For an account of *Manon Lescaut* which comes fully to terms with the opera's huge contrasts of colour and mood you'll also have to have a modern recording, for with all its improvements the sound here remains very dry.

La rondine

La rondine. Le Villi – Prelude; L'Abbandono; La Tregenda; Ecco la casa … Torna ai felice dì. Morire!
Angela Gheorghiu *sop* Magda **Roberto Alagna** *ten* Ruggero **Inva Mula-Tchako** *sop* Lisetta **William Matteuzzi** *ten* Prunier **Alberto Rinaldi** *bar* Rambaldo **Patricia Biccire** *sop* Yvette **Patrizia Ciofi** *sop* Bianca **Monica Bacelli** *mez* Suzy **Riccardo Simonetti** *bar* Périchaud **Toby Spence** *ten* Gobin **Enrico Fissore** *bar* Crébillon **London Voices; LSO /
Antonio Pappano** *pf*
EMI ② 556338-2 (131' · DDD) Texts and translations included Ⓕ**OOO**

 It couldn't be more welcome when a recording transforms a work, as this one does, setting it on a new plane. *La rondine* ('The Swallow'), Puccini's ill-timed attempt to emulate Lehár in the world of operetta, was completed during the First World War. It's long been counted his most serious failure. Puccini's cunning has never been in doubt either, for he and his librettists interweave elements not just of *La traviata* but of *The Merry Widow* and *Die Fledermaus*, not to mention earlier Puccini operas. His melodic style may be simpler than before, but one striking theme follows another with a profusion that any other composer might envy. What Pappano reveals far more than before is the subtlety with which Puccini interweaves his themes and motifs, with conversational passages made spontaneous-sounding in their flexibility. Above all, Pappano brings out the poetry, drawing on emotions far deeper than are suggested by this operetta-like subject, thanks also to Gheorghiu's superb performance, translating her mastery as Violetta to this comparable character. Magda's first big solo, 'Che il bel sogno di Doretta', finds Gheorghiu at her most ravishing, tenderly expressive in her soaring phrases, opening out only at the final climax. From first

to last, often with a throb in the voice, her vocal acting convinces you that Magda's are genuine, deep emotions, painful at the end, intensified by the ravishing beauty of her voice.

As Ruggero, Alagna has a far less complex role, winningly characterising the ardent young student. What will specially delight Puccinians in this set is that he's given an entrance aria about Paris, 'Parigi e un citta', which transforms his otherwise minimal contribution to Act 1. The partnership of Gheorghiu and Alagna highlights the way that Puccini in the melodic lines for each of his central characters makes Ruggero's more forthright, Magda's more complex. Among much else, the role of the poet, Prunier, is transformed by the clear-toned William Matteuzzi in what's normally a *comprimario* role. Not only is his relationship with Magda beautifully drawn, his improbable affair with the skittish maid, Lisetta, is made totally convincing too, mirroring Magda's affair. For the fill-ups, the excerpts from *Le Villi*, warm and dramatic, make one wish that Pappano could go on to record that first of Puccini's operas, with Alagna giving a ringing account of Roberto's aria, as he does of the song, *Morire!* – with Pappano at the piano. Originally an album-piece written for a wartime charity, Puccini used it, transposed up a semitone, with different words, as the entrance aria for Ruggero. Altogether a set to treasure.

Il trittico

Il tabarro
Carlo Guelfi *bar* Michele **Maria Guleghina** *sop* Giorgetta **Neil Shicoff** *ten* Luigi **Riccardo Cassinelli** *ten* Tinca **Enrico Fissore** *bass* Talpa **Elena Zilio** *mez* Frugola **Barry Banks** *ten* Ballad-seller **Angela Gheorghiu** *sop* Lover **Roberto Alagna** *ten* Lover **London Voices; London Symphony Orchestra /
Antonio Pappano**

Suor Angelica
Cristina Gallardo-Domâs *sop* Suor Angelica **Bernadette Manca di Nissa** *contr* Princess **Felicity Palmer** *mez* Abbess **Elena Zilio** *mez* Monitoress **Sara Fulgoni** *mez* Mistress of the Novices **Dorothea Röschmann** *sop* Sister Genovieffa **Judith Rees** *sop* Sister Osmina **Rachele Stanisci** *sop* Sister Dolcina **Francesca Pedaci** *sop* Nursing Sister **Anna Maria Panzarella** *sop* First Almoner Sister, First Lay Sister **Susan Mackenzie-Park** *sop* Second Almoner Sister **Deborah Miles-Johnson** *contr* Second Lay Sister **Rosalind Waters** *sop* Novice **London Voices; Tiffin Boys' School Choir; Philharmonia Orchestra /
Antonio Pappano**

Gianni Schicchi
José van Dam *bass-bar* Gianni Schicchi **Angela Gheorghiu** *sop* Lauretta **Roberto Alagna** *ten* Rinuccio **Felicity Palmer** *mez* Zita **Paolo Barbacini** *ten* Gherardo **Patrizia Ciofi** *sop* Nella **James Savage-Hanford** *treb* Gherardino **Carlos Chausson** *bass* Betto di Signa **Luigi Roni** *bass* Simone **Roberto Scaltriti** *bar* Marco **Elena Zilio** *mez* La Ciesca **Enrico Fissore** *bass* Spinelloccio **Simon Preece** *bar*

Pinellino **Noel Mann** bass Guccio
London Symphony Orchestra / Antonio Pappano
EMI ③ 556587-2 (162' · DDD) Notes, texts and
translations included ⓕ

No previous recordings bring such warmth or
beauty or so powerful a drawing of the contrasts
between each of the three one-acters in Puccini's triptych as these. It's Pappano above all,
with his gift for pacing Puccini subtly, who
draws the set together. In each opera he heightens emotions fearlessly to produce unerringly at
key moments the authentic gulp-in-throat,
whether for the cuckolded bargemaster,
Michele, for Sister Angelica in her agonised suicide and heavenly absolution, or for the resolution of young love at the end of *Gianni Schicchi*.
It will disappoint some that the starry couple of
Angela Gheorghiu and Roberto Alagna don't
take centre-stage, but quite apart from their
radiant singing as Lauretta and Rinuccio in
Gianni Schicchi – not least in that happy ending,
most tenderly done – they make a tiny cameo
appearance in *Il tabarro* as the off-stage departing lovers, a heady 45 seconds. It's the sort of
luxury touch that Walter Legge would have
relished. No doubt Gheorghiu would have been
just as persuasive as Giorgetta in *Il tabarro* and
as Sister Angelica, but having different sopranos
in each opera sharpens the contrasts. Maria
Guleghina makes a warm, vibrant Giorgetta,
and the touch of acid at the top of the voice adds
character, pointing to the frustration of the
bargemaster's wife.

Even more remarkable is the singing of the
young Chilean soprano, Cristina Gallardo-
Domâs as Sister Angelica. Hers is a younger,
more vulnerable Angelica than usual. Her vocal
subtlety and commanding technique go with a
fully mature portrayal of the nun's agony, her
defiance of the implacable Princess as well as
her grief over her dead son. As with Gheorghiu,
the dynamic shading brings *pianissimos* of
breathtaking delicacy. The Princess is powerfully sung by Bernadette Manca di Nissa, her
tone firm and even throughout. Felicity Palmer,
with her tangy mezzo tone, is well contrasted as
the Abbess, and she's just as characterful as the
crabby Zita in *Gianni Schicchi*. The casting in
Suor Angelica is as near flawless as could be, with
Elena Zilio and Dorothea Röschmann outstanding in smaller roles. Zilio is the only singer
who appears in all three operas, just as effective
as Frugola in *Il tabarro*, though there her full,
clear voice isn't always distinguishable from
Guleghina as Giorgetta. Among the men Carlo
Guelfi makes a superb Michele, incisive, dark
and virile. He brings out not just the anger but
the poignancy of the bargemaster's emotions, as
in the duet with Giorgetta, when they lament
what might have been. Neil Shicoff makes a fine
Luigi, the nerviness in his tenor tone aptly
bringing out a hysterical quality in the character. The male *comprimarios* are vocally more
variable, if always characterful, as they are too in
Gianni Schicchi. As Schicchi himself José van
Dam's voice perfectly conveys the sardonic side

of the character, and the top Gs he has to negotiate are wonderfully strong and steady. Maybe
the full voice he uses for the name 'Gianni
Schicchi', when in impersonation of old Buoso
he's dictating the new will, makes too obvious a
contrast with the quavering old man imitation,
but it's what Puccini asked for.

Also worthy of praise is the sumptuous and
atmospheric sound. Off-stage effects are magical, and always thanks to Pappano and fine playing from both the LSO and Philharmonia, the
beauty and originality of the carefully textured
instrumentation can be appreciated with new
vividness. This is a set to renew your appreciation of operas that represent Puccini still at his
peak.

Il tabarro[a] Ⓗ
Tito Gobbi bar Michele **Margaret Mas** sop
Giorgetta **Giacinto Prandelli** ten Luigi
Piero De Palma ten Tinca **Plinio Clabassi** bass Talpa
Miriam Pirazzini mez Frugola

Suor Angelica[b]
Victoria de los Angeles sop Suor Angelica **Fedora
Barbieri** mez Princess **Mina Doro** mez Abbess,
Mistress of the Novices **Corinna Vozza** mez
Monitoress **Lidia Marimpietri** sop Sister Genovieffa,
First Almoner Sister **Santa Chissari** sop Sister
Osmina, Second Almoner Sister, Novice **Anna
Marcangeli** sop Sister Dolcina **Teresa Cantarini** mez
Nursing Sister **Silvia Bertona** sop First Lay Sister
Maria Huder mez Second Lay Sister

Gianni Schicchi[c]
Tito Gobbi bar Gianni Schicchi **Victoria de los
Angeles** sop Lauretta **Carlo del Monte** ten Rinuccio
Anna Maria Canali mez Zita **Adelio Zagonara** ten
Gherardo **Lidia Marimpietri** sop Nella **Claudio
Cornoldi** ten Gherardino **Saturno Meletti** bass Betto
di Signa **Paolo Montarsolo** bass Simone **Fernando
Valentini** bar Marco **Giuliana Raymondi** sop La Ciesca
Rome Opera Chorus; Rome Opera Orchestra /
[a]**Vincenzo Bellezza,** [b]**Tullio Serafin,** [c]**Gabriele
Santini**
EMI mono/[c]stereo ③ 764165-2 (161' · ADD)
Recorded [a]1955, [b]1957, [c]1958. Texts and
translations included Ⓜ**OO**

Unless you insist on the most up-to-date
recorded sound, or on buying the individual
operas of Puccini's trilogy separately, this is the
classic *Trittico*. Gobbi's blackly authoritative but
pitiful Michele in *Il tabarro* and his genially
authoritative Schicchi (the two outer panels of
the triptych *do* match, in an odd sort of way)
have seldom been equalled, let alone surpassed.
De los Angeles's Angelica is more purely and
movingly sung than any other on record, and
her Lauretta in *Gianni Schicchi* is enchanting.

Could it be said, even so, that *Il tabarro* is the
weak link in this trilogy? It's a three-hander,
surely, and neither the soprano nor the tenor
are quite in Gobbi's league. Mas is a bit plummy
and mezzoish, true, but the slight implication
this gives that Giorgetta's liaison with the

young stevedore Luigi is her last chance at escape from a hateful life and a marriage that has soured adds an extra twinge of pain to a plot in which all three principals are victims. And in this context Prandelli's slightly strenuous rawness of tone characterises Luigi rather well. In *Gianni Schicchi*, Carlo del Monte as Rinuccio also looks like under-casting but in fact he's one of the few tenors who've recorded the part who sounds convincingly young, and his ardent praise of Florence and the 'new men' who are reinvigorating the city is proudly sung. Here, too, Gobbi is surrounded by a constellation of pungent character actors, and de los Angeles in *Suor Angelica* is teamed with a charmingly girlish, impulsive Genovieffa and with Fedora Barbieri's rigidly implacable Princess. With generally very stylish conducting throughout (only Belezza in *Il tabarro* is a touch staid, and he omits nearly all Puccini's off-stage sound effects) only the rather elderly recordings might be seen as a drawback. EMI boldly labels the whole set 'stereo', but both *Il tabarro* and *Suor Angelica* sound like minimally 'processed' mono: a touch congested in fuller passages, a hint of fizzy brightness here and there, but all well worth putting up with for such performances as these.

Tosca

Tosca
Angela Gheorghiu sop Tosca **Roberto Alagna** ten
Cavaradossi **Ruggero Raimondi** bar Scarpia
Maurizio Muraro bass Angelotti **Enrico Fissore** bass
Sacristan **David Cangelosi** ten Spoletta **Sorin
Coliban** bass Sciarrone **Gwynne Howell** bass Un
carceriere **James Savage-Hanford** treb Un pastore
**Tiffin Children's Choir; Royal Opera House Chorus
and Orchestra / Antonio Pappano**
EMI ② 557173-2 (114' · DDD)   Ⓕ●

Antonio Pappano's conducting alone would make this a *Tosca* of distinction, whether in big matters (the voicing of those snarling opening chords) or tiny ones: the carefully measured pause after Tosca asks Cavaradossi whether he's happy at the prospect of stealing away to their villa: he's preoccupied and hasn't really been listening. The orchestral sound is splendidly full whenever it needs to be, but never at the expense of fine detail, and Pappano's pacing is admirable: the Act 2 dialogue between Tosca and Scarpia, for example, inexorably builds in tension instead of being feverish from the outset, as is too often the case.

Gheorghiu's Tosca responds to this. She's impetuous, nervously intense, but capable also of a lovely, quiet purity). She's a very complete Tosca, indeed, and intelligently capable of bringing her own perceptions to the role. After the killing of Scarpia, her 'And before him all Rome trembled!' is neither triumphant nor melodramatic but wondering and fearful: she's aghast at what she has done and already suspects that this isn't the end of the matter. Her 'Vissi

PUCCINI TOSCA – IN BRIEF

Angela Gheorghiu *Tosca* **Roberto Alagna**
Cavaradossi **Ruggero Raimondi** *Scarpia*
**Tiffin Children's Choir, Chorus and Orchestra of
the Royal Opera House / Antonio Pappano**
EMI ② 557173-2 (114' · ADD)   Ⓕ●
An excellent modern recording, distinguished by Gheorghiu's passionate, nervy Tosca and Pappano's dramatic conducting, with Alagna's lyrical Cavaradossi and Ruggero Raimondi's veteran Scarpia.

Monserrat Caballé *Tosca* **José Carreras**
Cavaradossi **Ingvar Wixell** *Scarpia*
**Chorus and Orchestra of the Royal Opera
House / Sir Colin Davis**
Philips ② 438 359-2PM2 (118' · DDD)   Ⓜ
Richly theatrical conducting by Davis, with Montserrat Caballé a compelling heroine and José Carreras at his ardent best, although Ingmar Wixell is an uncompelling Scarpia.

Leontyne Price *Tosca* **Giuseppe di Stefano**
Cavaradossi **Giuseppe Taddei** *Scarpia*
**Vienna State Opera Chorus, Vienna PO /
Herbert von Karajan**
Decca ② 466 384-2DM2 (114' · DDD)   Ⓜ●●
Much finer than Karajan's later recording. Leontyne Price and Giuseppe di Stefano are wonderfully rich-voiced and passionate, Taddei a hellishly charismatic Scarpia, with Karajan balancing detail and drama superbly.

Maria Callas *Tosca* **Giuseppe de Stefano**
Cavaradossi **Tito Gobbi** *Scarpia* **Chorus and
Orchestra of La Scala, Milan / Victor de Sabata**
EMI ② 562890-2 (110' · AAD)   Ⓜ●●●
EMI ② 585644 2 (110' · AAD)   Ⓑ●●●
✪ This could still be called a definitive *Tosca*, with Callas, Di Stefano and Gobbi striking sparks off the score and each other, supported by de Sabata's masterly conducting and a still impressive recording.

(In English) **Jane Eaglen** *Tosca* **Dennis O'Neill**
Cavaradossi **Gregory Yurisitch** *Scarpia* **Geoffrey
Mitchell Choir, Philharmonia Orchestra /
David Parry**
Chandos ② CHAN3000 (118' · DDD)   Ⓕ●
Exceptionally competitive English-language recording, with idiomatic performances from Jane Eaglen, Dennis O'Neill and Gregory Yurisitch, ripely conducted by David Parry.

Maria Callas *Tosca* **Renato Cioni** *Cavaradossi*
Tito Gobbi *Scarpia* **Chorus and Orchestra of
the Royal Opera House / Carlo Felice Cillario**
EMI ② 562675-2 (109' · AAD)   Ⓜ
A historic 1964 live broadcast from Covent Garden, with Callas and Gobbi splendidly fierce antagonists, Renato Cioni a fine Cavaradossi and well conducted by Cillario, although the mono sound is clear but rather lean.

d'arte' is most beautiful, her intimacy in the first scene with Cavaradossi tender and touching.

In that passage Alagna responds to her delicacy, and in Act 3 he receives her acting lesson with a touch of humour. Elsewhere he's in fine, mostly full voice, nowhere near as subtle as Gheorghiu. His tone hardens under pressure once or twice, and his *mezza voce* can sound thin, but he's never short of vocal glamour: a creditable but not especially interesting Cavaradossi.

Raimondi's Scarpia, on the other hand, is very interesting. The quieter shades of his voice now need careful management (and besides, it's darker and softer-grained than a true dramatic baritone), but although he may initially seem to lack authority his reading is full of finesse.

A very fine *Tosca*, in short, not quite in the same league as the celebrated Callas/di Stefano/Gobbi/de Sabata (see 'In Brief' box), but giving all the others an exciting run for their money. The recording is all that could be wished.

Tosca

Montserrat Caballé *sop* Tosca **José Carreras** *ten* Cavaradossi **Ingvar Wixell** *bar* Scarpia **Samuel Ramey** *bass* Angelotti **Piero De Palma** *ten* Spoletta **Domenico Trimarchi** *bar* Sacristan **William Elvin** *bar* Sciarrone, Gaoler **Ann Murray** *mez* Shepherd Boy **Chorus and Orchestra of the Royal Opera House, Covent Garden / Sir Colin Davis**
Philips Duo ② 438 359-2PM2 (118' · ADD) Recorded 1976   Ⓜ

Caballé's Tosca is one of the most ravishingly on record, with scarcely a less than beautiful note throughout, save where an occasional phrase lies a touch low for her. She doesn't quite have the 'prima donna' (in quotes, mind) temperament for the part (the coquettish malice of 'but make her eyes black!', as Tosca forgives Cavaradossi for using a blonde stranger as model for his altarpiece of the Magdalen, isn't in Caballé's armoury; either that or she knows that her voice would sound arch attempting it), but her portrayal is much more than a display of lovely sounds. She's precise with words, takes minute care over phrasing, and she knows to a split second where dead-centre precise pitching becomes crucial. Carreras's Cavaradossi is one of his best recorded performances: the voice untarnished, the line ample, and if he's tempted at times to over-sing one forgives the fault for the sake of his poetic ardour. Wixell is the fly in the ointment: a capable actor and an intelligent artist, but his gritty timbre lacks centre and thus the necessary dangerous suavity.

Davis's direction is flexible but dramatic and finely detailed, and the secondary singers are all very good. The recording, despite some rather unconvincing sound effects, still sounds very well, with space around the voices and a natural balance between them and the orchestra. It's pity Philips should have saved space by omitting the libretto.

Tosca

Leontyne Price *sop* Tosca **Giuseppe di Stefano** *ten* Cavaradossi **Giuseppe Taddei** *bar* Scarpia **Carlo Cava** *bass* Angelotti **Piero De Palma** *ten* Spoletta **Fernando Corena** *bass* Sacristan **Leonardo Monreale** *bass* Sciarrone **Alfredo Mariotti** *bass* Gaoler **Herbert Weiss** *treb* Shepherd Boy **Vienna State Opera Chorus; Vienna Philharmonic Orchestra / Herbert von Karajan**
Decca Legends ② 466 384-2DMO2 (114' · ADD) Recorded 1962. Text and translation included   Ⓜ〇

Karajan's classic version of *Tosca* was originally issued on the RCA label, but produced by John Culshaw of Decca at a vintage period. The first surprise is to find the sound satisfying in almost every way, with a firm sense of presence and with each voice and each section of the orchestra cleanly focused within the stereo spectrum. Less surprising is the superiority of this version as an interpretation. Karajan was always a master Puccinian, and this set was a prime example. A typical instance comes at the end of Act 1, where Scarpia's *Te Deum* is taken daringly slowly, and conveys a quiver of menace that no other version begins to match. An extra nicety is the way that in the instrumental introduction to Cavaradossi's first aria, 'Recondita armonia', he treats it as the musical equivalent of a painter mixing his colours, the very point Puccini no doubt had in mind. Karajan, though individual, and regularly challenging his singers is most solicitous in following the voices. It's fascinating to note what expressive freedom he allows his tenor, Giuseppe di Stefano, and he makes Leontyne Price relax, giving a superb assumption of the role, big and rich of tone; the voice is the more beautiful for not being recorded too closely.

Tosca (in English)

Jane Eaglen *sop* Tosca **Dennis O'Neill** *ten* Cavaradossi **Gregory Yurisich** *bar* Scarpia **Peter Rose** *bass* Angelotti **John Daszak** *ten* Spoletta **Andrew Shore** *bass* Sacristan **Christopher Booth-Jones** *bass* Sciarrone **Ashley Holland** *bass* Gaoler **Charbel Michael** *mez* Shepherd Boy **Peter Kay Children's Choir; Geoffrey Mitchell Choir; Philharmonia Orchestra / David Parry** Chandos Opera in English ② CHAN3000 (18' · DDD) Sung in English. Notes and text included   Ⓕ〇

This is an issue to delight far more than devotees of opera in English, a gripping account of Puccini's red-blooded drama. Above all, it offers the first major recording to demonstrate the powers of Jane Eaglen at full stretch in one of the most formidable, vocally satisfying portrayals of the role of Tosca in years. David Parry has already shown himself a sympathetic interpreter of rare repertory, but here he equally demonstrates his full understanding of Puccini. The bite and energy in the playing of the Philharmonia, not to mention the expressive warmth in the love music, will have you riveted as though hearing the music for the first time.

The opulent Chandos sound, cleanly focused with plenty of atmosphere and presence, adds to the impact, whether in the power of the big *tuttis* or in the subtlety of whispered string *pianissimos*. Off-stage effects are nicely evocative, though the sequence of bell sounds at the start of Act 3 is so clear it suggests an orchestra rather than a Roman landscape. Otherwise, the slightly forward balance of voices against orchestra is very well judged. Eaglen is well matched by Dennis O'Neill as Cavaradossi, aptly Italianate in every register, and betraying only a slight unevenness occasionally on high notes under pressure. Gregory Yurisich makes a powerful Scarpia, younger-sounding than most, and therefore a more plausible lover. The others are well cast too, notably Peter Rose, who's an outstanding, fresh-voiced Angelotti.

Turandot

Turandot
Dame Joan Sutherland *sop* Princess Turandot
Luciano Pavarotti *ten* Calaf **Montserrat Caballé**
sop Liù **Tom Krause** *bar* Ping **Pier Francesco Poli**
ten Pang, Prince of Persia **Piero De Palma** *ten* Pong
Nicolai Ghiaurov *bass* Timur **Sir Peter Pears** *ten*
Emperor Altoum **Sabin Markov** *bar* Mandarin
Wandsworth School Boys' Choir; John Alldis
Choir; London Philharmonic Orchestra / Zubin
Mehta
Decca ② 414 274-2DH2 (117' · ADD) Recorded 1972.
Notes, text and translation included   ⒻOO

Turandot is a psychologically complex work fusing appalling sadism with self-sacrificing devotion. The icy Princess of China has agreed to marry any man of royal blood who can solve three riddles she has posed. If he fails his head will roll. Calaf, the son of the exiled Tartar king Timur, answers all the questions easily and when Turandot hesitates to accept him, magnanimously offers her a riddle in return – 'What is his name?'. Liù, Calaf's faithful slave-girl, is tortured but rather than reveal his identity kills herself. Turandot finally capitulates, announcing that his name is Love. Dame Joan Sutherland's assumption of the title role is statuesque, combining regal poise with a more human warmth, while Montserrat Caballé is a touchingly sympathetic Liù, skilfully steering the character away from any hint of the mawkish. Pavarotti's Calaf is a heroic figure in splendid voice and the chorus is handled with great power, baying for blood at one minute, enraptured with Liù's nobility at the next. Mehta conducts with great passion and a natural feel for Puccini's wonderfully tempestuous drama. Well recorded.

Turandot   Ⓗ
Maria Callas *sop* Princess Turandot **Eugenio**
Fernandi *ten* Calaf **Dame Elisabeth Schwarzkopf**
sop Liù **Mario Borriello** *bar* Ping **Renato Ercolani**
ten Pang **Piero De Palma** *ten* Pong **Nicola Zaccaria**

Joan Sutherland *Turandot* **Luciano Pavarotti**
Calaf **Montserrat Caballé** *Liù* **John Alldis Choir;**
London PO / Zubin Mehta
Decca ② 414 274-2DH2 (117' · ADD)   ⒻOO
Slightly unexpected casting pays dividends in this exciting set, with Mehta luxuriating in the exotic textures, and all three principals bringing out the sheer beauty of the vocal writing.

Maria Callas *Turandot* **Eugenio Fernandi** *Calaf*
Elisabeth Schwarzkopf *Liù* **Chorus and**
Orchestra of La Scala, Milan / Tullio Serafin
EMI ② 556307-2 (118' · AAD)   ⓂOO
In this mono recording Callas is a less powerful ice-princess than many, but more compelling, despite an unexciting Calaf. With Serafin's vigorous support she and Schwarzkopf infuse the performance with memorable feeling.

Katia Ricciarelli *Turandot* **Plácido Domingo**
Calaf **Barbara Hendricks** *Liù* **Vienna State**
Opera Chorus, Vienna PO / Herbert von
Karajan
DG ② 423 855-2GH2 (DDD)   Ⓕ
Flawed by the casting of Katia Ricciarelli, game but overparted, this is still a very exciting set, with Plácido Domingo's thrilling Calaf, Barbara Hendricks' appealing Liù, and Karajan's monumentally lustrous reading.

Birgit Nilsson *Turandot* **Jussi Björling** *Calaf*
Renata Tebaldi *Liù* **Rome Opera Chorus and**
Orchestra / Erich Leinsdorf
RCA ② RD85932 (115' · ADD)   Ⓕ
With Molinari-Pradelli's more likeable version unavailable, this is the only way to enjoy Birgit Nilsson's spectacular Turandot, here alongside Jussi Björling's ardent Calaf, with Renata Tebaldi's creamy Liù and a good supporting cast.

Eva Marton *Turandot* **Michael Sylvester** *Calaf*
Lucia Mazzaria *Liù* **San Francisco Opera Chorus**
and Orchestra / Donald Runnicles
ArtHaus Musik ᴰⱽᴰ 100 088 (123')   Ⓕ
Marton is unsteady, Michael Sylvester a strong but unphotogenic Calaf, but with Runnicles' theatrical conducting and David Hockney's glowingly original sets, this is an enjoyable production, well worth considering.

Giovanna Casolla *Turandot* **Sergei Larin** *Calaf*
Barbara Frittoli *Liù* **Maggio Musicale Chorus**
and Orchestra, Florence / Zubin Mehta
RCA ᴰⱽᴰ 74321 60917-2   Ⓕ
The famous staging in Beijing's Forbidden City is robustly conducted by Mehta and well worth a look, even if Sergei Larin's Calaf and Barbara Frittoli's Liù outshine Gianna Casolla's serviceable Turandot.

bass Timur **Giuseppe Nessi** ten Emperor Altoum
Giulio Mauri bass Mandarin **Chorus and Orchestra
of La Scala, Milan / Tullio Serafin**
EMI mono ② 556307-2 (118' · ADD) Recorded 1957.
Notes, text and translation included ⓂOO

To have Callas, the most flashing-eyed of all
sopranos as Turandot, is – on record at least –
the most natural piece of casting. Other sopranos may be comparably icy in their command,
but Callas with her totally distinctive tonal
range was able to give the fullest possible characterisation. With her, Turandot was not just an
implacable man-hater but a highly provocative
female. One quickly reads something of Callas's
own underlying vulnerability into such a portrait, its tensions, the element of brittleness.
With her the character seems so much more
believably complex than with others. It was sad
that, except at the very beginning of her career,
she felt unable to sing the role in the opera
house, but this recording is far more valuable
than any memory of the past, one of the most
thrillingly magnetic of all her recorded performances, the more so when Schwarzkopf as
Liù provides a comparably characterful and distinctive portrait, far more than a Puccinian
'little woman', sweet and wilting.

Next to such supreme singers it was perhaps
cruel of Walter Legge to choose so relatively
uncharacterful a tenor as Eugenio Fernandi as
Calaf, but at least his timbre is pleasingly distinctive. What fully matches the positive character of the singing of Callas and Schwarzkopf
is Serafin's conducting, which is sometimes surprisingly free, but in its pacing invariably captures colour, atmosphere and mood, as well as
dramatic point. The Ping, Pang and Pong
episode has rarely sparkled so naturally, the
work of a conductor who has known and loved
the music in the theatre over a long career.

The conducting is so vivid that the limitations
of the mono sound hardly seem to matter. As
the very opening will reveal, the CD transfer
makes it satisfyingly full-bodied. Though with
its rich, atmospheric stereo the Mehta set
remains the best general recommendation, it's
thrilling to have this historic document so
vividly restored.

Additional recommendation

Turandot
Eaglen Turandot **O'Neill** Calaf **Plazas** Liù **Bayley**
Timur **New London Children's Choir; Geoffrey
Mitchell Choir; Philharmonia Orchestra / Parry**
Chandos/Peter Moores Foundation Opera in English
② CHAN3086 (135' · DDD) Sung in English. Libretto
and translation included Ⓜ

The great glory of this set is Jane Eaglen's Turandot. There's no strain even in the most taxing passages, a firmness and a clarity that hasn't always
marked her recordings. O'Neill gives a strong,
heroic reading, but with the occasional moment of
strain. And Parry carries the performance forward
magnetically. Thoroughly recommended.

Henry Purcell
British 1659-1695

*Purcell was a chorister in the Chapel Royal until his
voice broke in 1673. He was then made assistant to
John Hingeston, whom he succeeded as organ maker
and keeper of the king's instruments in 1683. In
1677 he was appointed composer-in-ordinary for the
king's violins and in 1679 succeeded his teacher,
Blow, as organist of Westminster Abbey. From 1680
he began writing music for the theatre. In 1682 he
was appointed an organist of the Chapel Royal. His
court appointments were renewed by James II in
1685 and by William III in 1689, and on each occasion he had the duty of providing a second organ for
the coronation. The last royal occasion for which he
provided music was Queen Mary's funeral in 1695.*

*Purcell was one of the greatest composers of the
Baroque period and one of the greatest of all English
composers. His works include the fantasias for viols
(masterpieces of contrapuntal writing in the old
style) and some of the more modern sonatas for violins which reveal an acquaintance with Italian models. In time Purcell became increasingly in demand as
a composer, and his theatre music in particular made
his name familiar to many who knew nothing of his
church music or the odes and welcome songs he wrote
for the court. During the last five years of his life
Purcell collaborated on five semi-operas in which the
music has a large share, with divertissements, songs,
choral numbers and dances. His only true opera (ie
with music throughout) was Dido and Aeneas, written for a girls school at Chelsea; despite the limitations of Nahum Tate's libretto it is among the finest
of 17th-century operas.* GROVEmusic

Complete Ayres for the Theatre

The History of Dioclesian, or The Prophetess, Z627[b].
King Arthur, Z628[b]. The Fairy Queen, Z629[b]. The
Indian Queen, Z630[b]. The Married Beau, Z603[a]. The
Old Bachelor, Z607[b]. Amphitryon, Z572[a]. The
Double Dealer, Z592[a]. Distressed Innocence, Z577[a].
The Gordian Knot Unty'd, Z597[a]. Abdelazer, Z570[a].
Bonduca, Z574[a]. The Virtuous Wife, Z611[a]. Sonata
While the Sun Rises in 'The Indian Queen'[b].
Overture in G minora, Z588 – Sir Anthony Love, Z588 –
Overture[a]. Timon of Athens, Z632[a]. The Indian
Queen, Z630 – Symphony[b]
[a]**The Parley of Instruments;** [b]**The Parley of
Instruments Baroque Orchestra / Roy Goodman**
Hyperion ③ CDA67001/3 (209' · DDD) Recorded
1994 Ⓕ

All these works were published within 18
months of Purcell's death. The 13 suites of
choice movements from plays and semi-operas,
entitled *A Collection of Ayres, compos'd for the Theatre, and upon other occasions*, may well have been
the editing work of Purcell's brother, Daniel.
Whoever it was had a rare combination of musical integrity and commercial flair: the pieces
lifted from Purcell's interpolations to plays are
often reordered and arranged with a deftness
and charm which conveys the spirit of the
theatre as well as heightening the loss and
poignancy of Purcell's passing. How moving

the Rondeau Minuet from *The Gordian Knot Unty'd* must have seemed to those who knew and loved Purcell.

As a major retrospective of Purcell's life in the theatre, the *Ayres for the Theatre* mainly comprise instrumental dances from their original sources, though there are several movements readapted from sung airs, such as 'Fairest isle' from *King Arthur* and 'If love's a sweet passion' from *The Fairy Queen*. The tunes are wonderful and varied, the inner part-writing skilful and the rhythmic imagination knows no bounds. Even so, this isn't music where more than a suite at a time can be recommended for ultimate satisfaction: stop while you still want more. And more you'll most certainly want with Roy Goodman's alert and distinctive direction. If a few of the movements sound a touch mundane and lack dynamism as one follows on from another, the positive side is that the performances are never forced and rarely mannered. For the semi-opera 'suites', Goodman employs a full orchestra. What The Parley of Instruments has in abundance is a cordiality of expression which seems so absolutely right, especially in the slower airs.

Fantasias

Fantasias – three part, Z732-4; four part,   P
Z735-43; five part, 'upon one note', Z745. In
Nomines – G minor, Z746; G minor, 'Dorian', Z747
Joanna Levine, Susanna Pell, Catherine Finnis *viols*
Phantasm (Laurence Dreyfus, Wendy Gillespie,
Jonathan Manson, Markku Luolajan-Mikkola *viols*)
Simax PSC1124 (51' · DDD) Recorded 1994   Ⓕ**OOO**

Purcell's contrapuntal mastery is dazzling, with the points of imitation in the various sections of each fantasia treated in double or triple counterpoint, inversion, augmentation and all other technical devices – for instance, the initial subjects of fantasias Z739, 742 and 743 at once appear in mirror images of themselves – but the music's deep expressiveness and the dramatic tension created by its chromaticisms and unpredictable harmonies make it clear that he certainly had performance in mind (a matter of some dispute), even if, because of the king's dislike of such intellectual pursuits, only privately by conservative-minded music-lovers. It's this expressiveness which Phantasm emphasises in this recording, both in their varied dynamics and in their use of vibrato. Speeds here are in general fast and there's great variety of bowing and hence of articulation.

Fantasia in F, Z745, 'Upon one note'.   P
Fantasias – three part, Z732-34; four part, Z735-43. In
Nomines – G minor Z746; G minor, Z747, 'Dorian'
Hespèrion XX (Sophie Watillon, Eunice,Brandao,
Sergi Casademunt, Wieland Kuijken, Marianne
Müller, Philippe Pierlot *viols*) / **Jordi Savall** *treb viol*
Auvidis Astrée ES9922 (54' · DDD) Recorded 1994
   Ⓜ**O**

Purcell's music for viols represents the final flowering of the English consort tradition. Viol consorts had been out of fashion for at least 20 years, ousted by the Italian violin sonatas and French ballet music. Purcell's polished essays in this antique form were neither published nor, apparently, widely circulated. Nevertheless, we cherish them today for their sublime expressiveness and craftsmanship. Jordi Savall and his group have achieved a state of abstraction seldom experienced in music. It almost goes without saying that Hespèrion's playing is always extremely beautiful: the music demands it. But any need to be rhetorical, to lean on a dissonance or pronounce a cadence, has been outgrown and discarded. The scale within which these features and more are articulated is so minimal, so subtle and yet ultimately so compelling, that from the first track the listener is transported into a rarefied aural dimension usually reserved for single movements or even phrases. Don't miss it.

Anthems and Services

Complete Anthems and Services, Volume 7   P
I was glad when they said unto me[b]. I was glad when they said unto me, Z19[a]. O consider my adversity, Z32[b]. Beati omnes qui timent Dominum, Z131. In the black dismal dungeon of despair, Z190. Save me, O God, Z51[b]. Morning and Evening Service in B flat, Z230 – Te Deum; Jubilate. Thy Way, O God, is Holy, Z60. Funeral Sentences for the death of Queen Mary II[b] – Drum Processional; March and Canzona in C minor, Z860; Man that is born of Woman, Z27; In the midst of Life, Z17[b]; Thou know'st Lord, Z58b; Thou know'st Lord, Z58c
Mark Kennedy, Eamonn O'Dwyer, James Goodman *trebs* **Susan Gritton** *sop* **James Bowman, Nigel Short** *countertens* **Rogers Covey-Crump, Charles Daniels, Mark Milhofer** *tens* **Michael George, Robert Evans** *basses* [a]**New College Choir,** **Oxford;** [b]**The King's Consort Choir; The King's Consort / Robert King**
Hyperion CDA66677 (70' · DDD) Recorded 1993   Ⓕ
Also available on Hyperion CDS44141/51 (11 discs) Ⓑ

This CD is made up predominantly of anthems, devotional songs and a morning service (a functional, though not perfunctory, setting of the *Te Deum* and *Jubilate*) most of which disclose the range and quality of the composer's sacred *oeuvre* near its best. Of the two settings of *I was glad*, the first was, until not long ago, thought to be the work of John Blow. This full anthem more than whets our appetite with its agreeable tonal and melodic twists; when the *Gloria* arrives, we're assured that this is vintage Purcell by the sensitive pacing as much as an exquisite contrapuntal denouement. The earlier setting is more poignant. Opening with a string symphony in the spirit of a Locke consort, the music blossoms into a deliciously Elysian melodic fabric. Good sense is made of the overall shape and the soloists are, as ever, excellent. *Beati omnes* is a positive gem; this may well have been written for the composer's wedding. Of the small-scale pieces, *In the black dismal dungeon* is the real masterpiece; it's delivered astutely by the secure and musicianly voice of Susan Gritton.

Finally to the funeral pieces. Here we have an ominous procession from the Guild of Ancient Fifes and Drums and the first appearance of four 'flatt' trumpets – as opposed to two plus two sackbuts; the effect of this subtle timbral change makes extraordinary sense of the music, engendering a new grandeur and uncompromising clarity as would have befitted such an occasion. The vocal performances are earthy and impassioned.

Odes & Welcome Songs

Odes for St Cecilia's Day – 'Hail, bright Cecilia', Z328; 'Welcome to all the pleasures', Z339
Susan Hamilton, Siri Thornhill sops **Robin Blaze, Martin van der Zeijst** countertens **Mark Padmore** ten **Jonathan Arnold, Peter Harvey, Jonathan Brown** basses **Collegium Vocale / Philippe Herreweghe**
Harmonia Mundi HMC90 1643 (73' · DDD) Texts included ⒡

The two famous St Cecilian Odes reflect a remarkable polarity in the composer's creative priorities: the shorter of the two, *Welcome to all the pleasures*, is a supreme amalgamation of Fishburn's words and Purcell's music, bursting with contained subtlety and enchantment. There's also a unique sense of conveying something novel, in this case an inaugural tribute on 22 November 1683, to the patron saint of music, henceforth annually celebrating 'this divine Science'. *Hail, bright Cecilia* from 1692 is three times longer and explores all the startling orchestral sounds which changed English music towards something approaching a Handelian palette. It's also truly *fin de siècle* (some might say Newtonian) in ambition and the imagery is as breathtakingly splendid now as it was when the Victorians first revered it for its boldness and scale. Such qualities clearly animate Herreweghe and he shapes this music with rapture and precision. The whole is infectiously fresh and never rushed. If not as brilliant or as full as McCreesh, Herreweghe is rather more sensitive to the nuances which irradiate from Purcell's colouring of words. He largely uses English voices. 'Hark! hark! each tree' boasts the versatile and effortless alto of Robin Blaze who, with the assured Peter Harvey, achieves a delightfully naturalistic lilt. This version certainly rivals McCreesh (for whom Peter Harvey also sings 'Wondrous machine' splendidly) for elevated characterisation. One blip here is the piping soprano in 'Thou tun'st this world' (Susan Hamilton) where the voice seems technically and expressively limited. For beauty of sound, then, Herreweghe is your man. For dramatic immediacy and excitement, it's McCreesh.

Odes for St Cecilia's Day – 'Hail, bright Cecilia', Z328; 'Welcome to all the pleasures', Z339. Birthday Ode, 'Come ye sons of art away', Z323. March and Canzona in C minor, Z860. Funeral Sentences for the death of Queen Mary.
Emily Van Evera sop **Timothy Wilson** counterten **John Mark Ainsley, Charles Daniels** tens **David Thomas** bass **Taverner Consort, Choir and Players / Andrew Parrott**
Virgin Classics Veritas Double ② 561582-2 (111' · DDD) Ⓑ

While McCreesh makes the score sparkle with his energetic view of tempos, Andrew Parrott parades his smooth and integrated forces with less instant theatricality. Instead we have a typically homogeneous and unfolding scenario which complements McCreesh's more effervescent and lush reading. The reappearance of Parrott's recordings of Purcell's earlier Cecilian ode, *Welcome to all the pleasures* and the time-honoured and particularly accessible *Come ye sons of art away* is also received with open arms. Some may distrust the low pitch (A=392) but the high tenor of Charles Daniels and the satisfying registral blend of Timothy Wilson and John Mark Ainsley in 'Sound the trumpet' are more than adequate recompense and the former's mellifluous rendering of 'Here the deities approve' is a real gem to be savoured.

Odes and Welcome Songs, Volumes 6-8 Ⓟ
Birthday Ode, 'Love's goddess sure was blind', Z331. Odes for St Cecilia's Day – 'Raise, raise the voice', Z334; 'Laudate Ceciliam', Z329. Welcome Song, 'From those serene and rapturous joys', Z326
Hyperion CDA66494 (68' · DDD) Ⓕ

Yorkshire Feast Song, 'Of old, when heroes thought it base', Z333. Welcome Songs – 'Swifter, Isis, swifter flow', Z336; 'What, what shall be done on behalf of the man?', Z341
Hyperion CDA66587 (66' · DDD) Ⓕ

Birthday Ode, 'Come ye sons of art, away', Z323. Welcome Songs – 'Welcome, viceregent of the mighty king', Z340; 'Why, why are all the Muses mute?', Z343
Hyperion CDA66598 (68' · DDD) Ⓕ

Gillian Fisher, Mary Seers, Susan Hamilton, Tessa Bonner sops **James Bowman, Nigel Short, Michael Chance** countertens **Mark Padmore, Andrew Tusa, Rogers Covey-Crump, Charles Daniels, John Mark Ainsley** tens **Michael George, Robert Evans** basses **New College Choir, Oxford; The King's Consort / Robert King**
Recorded 1991. Texts included

These three CDs represent the final instalments in Hyperion's complete recording of Purcell's Odes and Welcome Songs. Purcell composed a number of these celebratory works between 1680 and 1695, and 24 survive. They were written for a wide range of events: most for royal birthdays, of King James II and Queen Mary, but also for a royal wedding, educational celebrations, and the 'Yorkshire Feast' of 1689. Hyperion's edition is to be warmly welcomed, not only for bringing to the catalogue such magnificent music, but also for the extremely sympathetic performances by the The King's Consort under the direction of Robert King. Of all the works on these discs, probably the most well known is *Come ye sons of art, away* written for Queen Mary in 1694 (Volume 8). This joyous work contains some of Purcell's most ebullient music, typified by the duet for two countertenors, 'Sound the trumpet'. Like all the works in the set this is surrounded by a well contrasted group of solos and duets for individual voices, instrumental interludes, and the occasional chorus. Less famous, but equally full of Restoration pomp and ceremony is the Yorkshire Feast song (Volume 7).

Volume 6 contains four of the least well known if no less rich and varied odes, two of which are dedicated to the patron saint of music, St Cecilia. While composed for slightly smaller forces than the more ceremonial odes, these contain music which is equally jaunty and exhilarating. Throughout all three volumes the most striking fact is Purcell's extraordinary inventiveness, and his incredible facility at word setting: even the most lame texts come alive in his hands, and the variety of expression throughout is astonishing. Robert King's direction is always sensitive to both the broad span and individual nuances of Purcell's kaleidoscopic writing for voice and instruments. The King's Consort plays with great understanding throughout and has clearly absorbed the often elusive style of this music, in which many influences are combined. The vocal soloists are uniformly excellent, but special mention must be made of the soprano Gillian Fisher, and the countertenor James Bowman. The recordings are without fault, achieving both excellent internal balance and appropriate atmosphere and perspective.

Songs

She loves, and she confesses, Z413. Amintas, to my **P** grief I see, Z356. Corinna is divinely fair, Z365. Amintor, heedless of his flocks, Z357. He himself courts his own ruin, Z372. No, to what purpose, Z468. Sylvia, 'tis true you're fair, Z512. Lovely Albina's come ashore, Z394. Spite of the godhead, pow'rful love, Z417. If music be the food of love, Z379/3. Phyllis, I can ne'er forgive it, Z408. Bacchus is a pow'r divine, Z360. Bess of Bedlam, Z370, 'From silent shades'. Let formal lovers still pursue, Z391. I came, I saw, and was undone, Z375. Who can behold Florella's charms?, Z441. Cupid, the slyest rogue alive, Z367. If prayers and tears, Z380. In Chloris all soft charms agree, Z384. Let us, kind Lesbia, give away, Z466. Love is now become a trade, Z393. Ask me to love no more, Z358. O Solitude! my sweetest choice, Z406. Olinda in the shades unseen, Z404. Pious Celinda goes to prayers, Z410. When Strephon found his passion vain, Z435. The fatal hour comes on apace, Z421. Sawney is a bonny lad, Z412. Young

Thirsis' fate, ye hills and groves, deplore, Z473 **Barbara Bonney, Susan Gritton** sops **James Bowman** counterten **Rogers Covey-Crump, Charles Daniels** tens **Michael George** bass **Mark Caudle, Susanna Pell** vas da gamba **David Miller** lte/theorbo / **Robert King** org/hpd
Hyperion CDA66730 (76' · DDD) Recorded 1993-4. Texts included   Ⓕ

This third and last volume of Purcell's non-theatrical secular songs consummates a most rewarding survey of 87 songs with more of the same: a vocal palette of six singers who are by now so steeped in the nuances of Purcell's strains that even the slightest offering sparkles with something memorable. The treasure is shared between Barbara Bonney and Susan Gritton who complement each other superbly. Gritton, becoming more refined in characterisation and tonal colour by the day, is allotted the free-style and dramatic pieces while to Bonney's fluid and sensual melisma is designated the more strophic or *cantabile* settings. *Lovely Albina's come ashore* is one of the composer's most mature creations, tantalisingly hinting at a new, tautly designed and classically balanced type of song. This work, *If music be the food of love* (the best of the three versions) and *I came, I saw* are striking examples of how exceptionally Bonney negotiates Purcell's skipping and curling contours and makes these songs sound even finer creations than we previously thought. *From silent shades* ('Bess of Bedlam') is Purcell's quintessential mad-song and Gritton has the measure of it all the way; packed full of incident, imagery and musical detail, her narration is clear and finely judged, reporting the tale with irony and change of colour. The CD is beautifully documented.

Dido and Aeneas

Dido and Aeneas   **P**
Stephen Wallace counterten Second Witch **Gerald Finley** bar Aeneas **Rosemary Joshua** sop Belinda **Lynne Dawson** sop Dido **John Bowen** ten First Sailor **Dominique Visse** counterten First Witch **Maria Cristina Kiehr** sop Second Woman **Susan Bickley** mez Sorceress **Robin Blaze** counterten Spirit **Clare College Choir, Cambridge; Orchestra of the Age of Enlightenment / René Jacobs**
Harmonia Mundi HMX290 1683 (60' · DDD) Text and translation included   Ⓜ**O**

Dido is a conveniently short piece, one whose concentrated musical language and quicksilver dramatic juxtapositions are well suited to the recorded medium, giving full rein to Purcell's imagination and raising it out of its habitually stilted stage conventions. This is where Charles Mackerras's 1967 Archiv recording succeeded, especially in Tatiana Troyanos's exquisite pacing of Dido's noble and tragic demise; also successful in bringing out the work's full imaginative impact were the recent smaller-scale but atmospheric accounts from Andrew Parrott

(Emma Kirkby as Dido) and Ivor Bolton (Della Jones on Teldec) and – the pick of the crop until now – Christopher Hogwood, with the sensual immediacy of Catherine Bott as Dido.

René Jacobs was one of the very few luminaries of the current Baroque dramatic scene not to have tackled this singular masterpiece. He does so, like Hogwood, with a gaggle of top-class singers; when you can casually call on Maria Cristina Kiehr to sing her tuppenceworth of Second Woman, not to mention Robin Blaze as Spirit and Dominique Visse as First Witch, it augurs well for a new benchmark recording. Rosemary Joshua's Belinda is a straightforward, dramatically unobtrusive but essential presence, never manipulated to be more of an influence in Dido's life than Purcell clearly relates in the lady-in-waiting's offerings of advice, revealed in 'Pursue thy conquest love'. Act 2 is where things really get going, after the fairly perfunctory introduction to the solid hunk that is Aeneas. Whether you choose to cast your Sorceress as male or as a crooning hag, the part is crucial to the temperament of a performance, made neither to be too camp nor too earnest in delivery. Susan Bickley is a fine Sorceress of the old school, precise, yet retaining an authority through quality of tone rather than pantomine.

Jacobs' richly paletted, pacey and boldly theatrical reading will prove a breath of fresh air to those who feel that Purcell's music in general can withstand being 'un-Englished' for want of new approaches to colour, characterisation and the composer's inimitable lyrical undercurrent. The odd instrumental dance seems a touch lacking in native roughage, but the finely proportioned Orchestra of the Age of Enlightenment bound through the Grove's Dance are even more purposeful in the First Sailor's song that opens Act 3. Lynne Dawson will disappoint few in her devastated, long-breathed and honest 'Lament', elegantly turned (if not vocally peerless) and, crucially, consequential of so much that has passed before. The last chorus is more beautifully sung than you've ever heard: a true funeral rite. These are the elusive ingredients of a compelling and truly involved reading. Imaginative and invigorating, Jacobs has revitalised *Dido*.

Dido and Aeneas   **P**
Véronique Gens *sop* Dido **Nathan Berg** *bass-bar* Aeneas **Sophie Marin-Degor** *sop* Belinda **Claire Brua** *sop* Sorceress **Sophie Daneman** *sop* Second Woman, First Witch **Gaëlle Mechaly** *sop* Second Witch **Jean-Paul Fouchécourt** *ten* Spirit, Sailor **Les Arts Florissants / William Christie**
Erato 4509-98477-2 (52' · DDD) Recorded 1994.
Notes and text included   Ⓕ

William Christie's reading of *Dido* is very much in terms of the reputed French influence on Purcell. Overdotting, reverse dotting and *iné-galité* are used throughout; the lines are often heavily embellished in the manner of Lully. This is a perfectly justifiable approach to the music, since there's little direct evidence to say exactly how much the French style dominated in England. This version, with single strings, an excellent small choir and a slightly obtrusive harpsichord, stands well alongside what's available. Apart from a few moments' inattention in Belinda's 'Haste, haste to town', you'd hardly notice that most of the cast are Francophone, except in that Nathan Berg's imposing bass-baritone finds it slightly easier to exploit the colour and the meaning of Aeneas's words. Véronique Gens is a lucid and sensible Dido, partnered by a sprightly Belinda from Sophie Marin-Degor and a good Second Woman from Sophie Daneman. Claire Brua's Sorceress is a splendidly insinuating conception, with a slithering melodic style.

Perhaps the main musical distinction of this version is the way Christie presents the final paragraphs. Up to this point he's taken generally quick speeds, and he runs the final confrontation of Dido and Aeneas at a headlong tempo, which works well. Then he comes almost to a standstill at the moment when Aeneas leaves the stage, choosing an unusually slow speed for the chorus 'Great minds against themselves conspire'. This makes way for a dangerously slow Lament, which is heart-stopping, and the final chorus, which is not.

Dido and Aeneas
Susan Graham *mez* Dido **Ian Bostridge** *ten* Aeneas **Camilla Tilling** *sop* Belinda **Felicity Palmer** *contr* Sorceress **Cécile de Boever** *sop* Second Woman **David Daniels** *counterten* Spirit **Paul Agnew** *ten* Sailor **European Voices; Le Concert d'Astrée / Emmanuelle Haïm** *hpd*
Virgin Classics Veritas 545604-2 (53' · DDD) Notes and libretto included   Ⓕ**O**

It's hard to imagine another opera of less than an hour that swings so effortlessly from gently concordant characterisation to the depths of human loss. This is a work where common sense in recording markets doesn't appear to matter: every year a luminary of the Baroque will tackle it. And luminosity is indeed the key to Emmanuelle Haïm's evocative and atmospheric reading. You might have anticipated her questing mind and rigorous delving into the sinews of each line, but such cordial restraint at key moments is unexpected: 'Fear no danger' and 'In our deep vaulted cell' relieve tensions better kept in check for the set-pieces. 'Ah! Belinda' becomes a crucial set piece that displays a chilling prescience from the outset.

Susan Graham's Dido produces a supremely controlled range of emotional response. She may not glide through with the radiant and filtered sorrow of a Baker or Troyanos, but she's a flexible musician who brings a mesmerising degree of expressive nuance. Ian Bostridge's Aeneas is only serviceable, but then Aeneas is a wet and innocuous character anyway. Haïm has no truck with the somewhat statuesque exchange between the estranged lovers; in any case, the sense of danger in the air is what compels the listener at this stage. Most of this is brought about by Felicity Palmer's menacing and vengeful Sorceress.

Haïm uses her instrumentalists to excellent effect. There's an agreeable, studied rough edge to some of the numbers which brings liveliness and ensures the avoidance of anything remotely saccharine. Some will doubtless miss an indigenous quality to the reading but the work is surely bigger than its domestic provenance. Strongly recommended.

Additional recommendation

Dido and Aeneas
Baker Dido **Herincx** Aeneas **Clark** Belinda
English Chamber Orchestra / A Lewis
Decca 466 387-2DM (53' · ADD) Recorded 1961 Ⓜ

A very early recording by Janet Baker in a role she was to make her own. Lewis directs a traditional but sensitive account of the score.

Dioclesian

Dioclesian 🅿
Catherine Pierard *sop* **James Bowman** *counterten* **John Mark Ainsley, Mark Padmore** *tens* **Michael George** *bass* **Collegium Musicum 90 Chorus; Collegium Musicum 90 / Richard Hickox**
Chandos Chaconne CHAN0568 (54' · DDD)
Recorded 1994. Text included Ⓕ

It was *Dioclesian*, the least known of the four semi-opera masterpieces of Purcell, for which the composer initially earned a reputation for writing stage music. The 'opera' was by all accounts a roaring success, though music played a less important part in the stage works of the 1690s than it did in the masque-related works of the previous decades – ironically just at the time when England could at last boast a dramatic master who could stand tall amongst the 'greats' of France and Italy. If the paucity of tableaux means a less atmospheric scenic context, such as we experience in *The Fairy Queen* or *King Arthur*, there's still much fine music which deserves to be highly regarded. Hickox is evidently committed to this score: the instrumental movements are all disciplined and yet display the buoyancy and variety of expression of one who senses the freshness of Purcell's first foray into the theatre. His soloists are authoritative Purcellians and they never disappoint and he manages to sustain the tension and climate he sets from the start.

The Fairy Queen

The Fairy Queen 🅿
Gillian Fisher, Lorna Anderson *sops* **Ann Murray** *mez* **Michael Chance** *counterten* **John Mark Ainsley, Ian Partridge** *tens* **Richard Suart, Michael George** *basses* **The Sixteen Choir and Orchestra / Harry Christophers**
Coro ② COR16005 (133' · DDD) Recorded 1991.
Notes and texts included ⓂO

The Fairy Queen is hardly an 'opera' in the conventional sense: its musical virtues lie in the composer's uncanny ability to summon a discrete, potent atmosphere whose capacity to move the listener lies outside a sustained dramatic context. The masques draw heavily on vernacular situations and a form of tragicomedy which requires a crafty hand in performance.

Harry Christophers allows the music to breathe with a warm spontaneity, encouraged by a strong and diverse vocal cast. Gillian Fisher is a touch disappointing, but the likes of Ann Murray (who's both radiant and a misfit in one), Michael Chance, John Mark Ainsley, Ian Partridge, Richard Suart and Michael George present a greater array of characterisation than any other extant reading. Just sample the wonderful slapstick between Mopsa and Coridon.

It's clear from Sir Roger Norrington's rival account on Virgin Veritas that he's thought about *The Fairy Queen* a great deal but can never really let the human touch prevail: this is his greatest Achilles' heel. The whole feels rather studio-made, each scene a graceful vignette of layered perceptions. Overall, Christophers strikes most imploringly at the heart of Purcell's native sensibilities (Partridge's Phoebus sums it up) for a satisfying performance capturing the indigenous humour, grandeur and poignancy of Purcell's exquisite score.

The Indian Queen

The Indian Queen 🅿
Emma Kirkby, Catherine Bott *sops* **John Mark Ainsley** *ten* **Gerald Finley** *bar* **David Thomas** *bass* **Tommy Williams** *sngr* **Chorus and Orchestra of the Academy of Ancient Music / Christopher Hogwood**
Also includes additional Act by Daniel Purcell
Decca 475 052-2 (73' · DDD) Recorded 1994. Notes and text included Ⓜ

Christopher Hogwood makes us realise that for all the constraints, this score isn't inherently small-scale and warrants all the subtlety of colour that can be achieved using 12 soloists and a decent-sized choir and orchestra. Needless to say, he conveys a consistent, logical and meticulous understanding of the score. The orchestral playing is crisp and transparent, the AAM's articulation allowing the integrity of the inner parts to be heard to the full without compromising blend. Among a distinguished line-up of singers, John Mark Ainsley gets the lion's share and is perhaps marginally more effective as the Indian Boy than as Fame, but such gloriously mellifluous and controlled singing can only enhance the reputation of this work.

Emma Kirkby is in fine fettle and she executes the justly celebrated 'I attempt from love's sickness' with her usual communicative panache. Then comes the pleasurably contrasted voice of

Catherine Bott: 'They tell us that your mighty powers' could not be in better hands. David Thomas as Envy, with his two followers in the Act 2 masque, highlights this brilliant scene as the work of a true connoisseur of the theatre. Mature Purcell is most strongly felt in the deftly ironic invocation by the conjurer, Ismeron, whose 'Ye twice 10,000 deities' is delivered authoritatively by Gerald Finley, though the lulling to sleep, before the God of Dream's gloomy non-prediction, is unconvincing. The quality of music shines very brightly in this reading, though the performance is perhaps a touch calculated in places. Recommended.

The Indian Queen   **P**
Tessa Bonner, Catherine Bott sops **Rogers Covey-Crump** ten **Peter Harvey** bass **Purcell Simfony Voices; Purcell Simfony / Catherine Mackintosh** vn
Linn Records CKD035 (60' · DDD) Recorded 1994   Ⓕ

If *The Indian Queen* is less ambitious than the other three 'operas' there's the sure touch here of the composer at his most mature and adept. The Prologue, in which he had the rare opportunity to set an extended dialogue, is beautifully balanced, and the music in Act 3 – when Zempoalla's ill-fated love is prophesied by Ismeron the magician in 'Ye twice 10,000 deities' – ranks alongside the finest moments in Purcell's output. The small-scale character of the work, compared to its siblings, is taken a stage further by the Purcell Simfony, which employs a minute chamber-size group of four strings, doubling oboe and recorder, single trumpet and drums. The soloists sing with airy restraint but each responds to these Hilliard-esque proportions with a rhythmic buoyancy and direct intimacy which projects a finely gauged overall conception of the work.

If the expressive power of the music is at times rather glazed, there's a sure atmosphere which is captured by recorded sound that's both warm and yet never imposing. The ensemble isn't always first-rate but there's nothing too worrisome and the instrumental numbers are elegantly shaped. Tessa Bonner gets the lion's share of the solo soprano numbers, ahead of the more colourful Catherine Bott, though the former's comparatively brittle sound has a crystalline quality which suits Catherine Mackintosh's consistent, if austere, strategy. In short, this release is consistently touching, one which in a paradoxical way gets under the skin despite the recessed emotional climate it conveys.

King Arthur

King Arthur   **P**
Véronique Gens, Claron McFadden, Sandrine Piau, Susannah Waters sops **Mark Padmore, Iain Paton** tens **Jonathan Best, Petteri Salomaa, François Bazola-Minori** basses **Les Arts Florissants Chorus and Orchestra / William Christie**
Erato ② 4509-98535-2 (90' · DDD) Notes and text included   Ⓕ**OOO**

If the co-operation with John Dryden led to a unity of vision in terms of music's expressive role in the overall drama, Purcell was limited to a historical patriotic fantasy with little room for the magic and pathos of, say, the superior *Fairy Queen*. Yet in the context of a stage presentation, Purcell's music shines through strongly. On disc though, with just the music, not even the dramatic powers of William Christie can restore its place in the overall scheme. But never mind, this is a score with some magnificent creations and Christie is evidently enchanted by it. The choral singing is richly textured, sensual and long-breathed, yet always alert to a nuance which can irradiate a passage at a stroke, as Christie does in the bittersweet close of 'Honour prizing' – easily the best moment in Act 1. The instrumental movements are finely moulded so that sinewy counterpoint and rhythmic profile are always strongly relayed. The songs, too, have been acutely prepared and are keenly characterised without resorting to excess. All the basses deliver their fine music with aplomb. If there's one drawback to extracting the musical numbers from the 'opera' when they've so clearly been delivered in a theatrical context, it's that the contextual characterisations lend themselves less well to the musical continuity of a CD. *King Arthur* without the play is dramatically a nonsense, so why try to pretend? Christie doesn't, but makes the strongest case yet for this music.

Additional recommendation

King Arthur
Gens, Bayodi, Jarrige, Auvity, Cornwell, Harvey Le Concert Spirituel / Hervé Niquet
Glossa GCD921608 (76' · DDD) Notes, libretto and translation included   Ⓕ
The triumph of this reading is its joy and vigour. Unlike other non-British Purcellians, Niquet doesn't fall foul of projecting an excessive Frenchified view at the cost of the composer's indigenous and expressive language.

The Tempest

The Tempest[a]. Suite in G minor, Z770 –   **P**
Overture[b]. Chaconne for Strings in G minor, Z730[c]. Sonata for Trumpet and Strings No 2 in D, Z850[d]. If ever I more riches did desire, Z544[e]. The Indian Queen – Trumpet Overture[f]
[a]**Michael Colvin** ten Aeolus; [a][e]**Meredith Hall** sop Amphitrite; [a]**Rosemarie van der Hooft** mez Ariel; [a][e]**Gillian Keith** sop Dorinda; [a]**Brett Polegato** bar Neptune, First Devil; [a][e]**Paul Grindlay** bass-bar Second Devil; [a]**Robert Stewart** voc Third Devil; [e]**Nils Brown** ten [d][f]**Norman Engel** tpt **Aradia Baroque Ensemble / Kevin Mallon** vn
Naxos 8 554262 (76' · DDD) Texts included   Ⓢ

There's so much pleasure to be had from Purcell's semi-operas that it's easy to wish we had more of them. Much of *The Tempest* is thought to have been written by other hands, but that's no reason for refusing to give it shelf-room. The score is cast in the same mould as Purcell's fully accredited dramatic works and offers a similar range of music. Director Kevin Mallon doesn't fuss over shaping the slower music, and the fast numbers go with plenty of zest. The ensemble includes oboes, recorders and bassoons, quite sparingly used, and bells for the setting of Ariel's 'Full fathom five'. The line-up of solo singers has no weak links and a few real strengths. Brett Polegato may lack authority in the role of Neptune, but sings with a fine, warm, well-rounded tone. Meredith Hall brings a winning sensitivity to the long solo 'Halcyon days' and finds an ideal soprano partner in the young Gillian Keith. Purcell's setting of 'If ever I more riches did desire' and his Trumpet Sonata No 2 are substantial makeweights. The recording acoustic is more church than theatre, but lively enough. Recommended.

Sergey Rachmaninov
USSR/American 1873-1943

Rachmaninov studied at the Moscow Conservatory (1885-92) under Zverev (where Scriabin was a fellow pupil) and his cousin Ziloti for piano and Taneyev and Arensky for composition, graduating with distinction as both pianist and composer (the opera Aleko, given at the Bolshoi in 1893, was his diploma piece). During the ensuing years he composed piano pieces (including his famous C sharp minor Prelude), songs and orchestral works, but the disastrous première in 1897 of his Symphony No 1 brought about a creative despair that was not dispelled until he sought medical help in 1900: then he quickly composed his Second Piano Concerto. Meanwhile he had set out on a new career as a conductor, appearing in Moscow and London; he later was conductor at the Bolshoi, 1904-6.

By this stage, and most particularly in the Piano Concerto No 2, the essentials of his art had been assembled: the command of the emotional gesture conceived as lyrical melody extended from small motifs, the concealment behind this of subtleties in orchestration and structure, the broad sweep of his lines and forms and loyalty to the finer Russian Romanticism inherited from Tchaikovsky and his teachers. During the remaining years to the Revolution these provided him with the materials for a sizable output of operas, liturgical music, orchestral works, piano pieces and songs. In 1909 he made his first American tour as a pianist, for which he wrote the Piano Concerto No 3.

Soon after the October Revolution he left Russia with his family for Scandinavia; in 1918 they arrived in New York, where he mainly lived thereafter, though he spent time in Paris, Dresden and Switzerland. There was a period of creative silence until 1926 when he wrote the Piano Concerto No 4, followed by only a handful of works over the next 15 years, even though all are on a large scale. During this period, he was active as a pianist on both sides of

the Atlantic (though never again in Russia). As a pianist he was famous for his precision, rhythmic drive, legato and clarity of texture. GROVEmusic

Piano Concertos

No 1 in F sharp minor, Op 1; **No 2** in C minor, Op 18; **No 3** in D minor, Op 30; **No 4** in G minor, Op 40. **Rhapsody on a Theme of Paganini**, Op 43

Piano Concertos Nos 1-4. Paganini Rhapsody
Earl Wild pf **Royal Philharmonic Orchestra / Jascha Horenstein**
Chandos ② CHAN10078 (134' · ADD) Recorded 1965
Ⓜ️Ⓞ

Such is the luxuriance of sound revealed in these remasterings, it's difficult to believe the recording date; and such is the quality of the piano playing that it's easy to understand why Chandos should have wanted to go to such trouble. There aren't so many Rachmaninov pianists who dare to throw caution to the wind to the extent that Earl Wild does in the outer movements of the First Concerto, fewer still who can keep their technical poise in the process. The improvisatory feel to the lyricism of the slow movement is no less remarkable. Wild's panache is every bit as seductive in No 4, and the *Paganini* Rhapsody is a rare example of a performance faster than the composer's own – devilishly driven in the early variations and with tension maintained through the following slower ones so that the famous eighteenth can register as a release from a suffocating grip, rather than an overblown, out-of-context exercise in grandiosity. Because of his lightness and touch Wild's tempos never seem excessive. Undoubtedly he shifts the balance from languishing pathos and overwhelming grandeur towards straightforward exuberance; but that may be no bad thing for refreshing our view of the composer. It keeps us in touch with an earlier tradition. The RPO appears to be revelling in the whole affair, in a way one wouldn't have immediately associated with Horenstein. To pick on the very few weaknesses, the very relaxed clarinet tone in the slow movement of Concerto No 2 rather misses the character, and elsewhere in this work the balance engineers rather crudely stick a microphone under the cello section's nostrils. But then the solo playing in this concerto is generally a little disappointing too, as though Wild had actually played the piece rather too often. In No 3 there are the hateful cuts to contend with, and one senses that the performance has been rather thoughtlessly modelled on the composer's own, idiosyncrasies and all. None the less, for the sake of the outstanding performances of Nos 1 and 4 and the Rhapsody, and for the unique combination of old-style bravura and modern sound, this issue earns a strong recommendation.

Piano Concertos Nos 1-4
Vladimir Ashkenazy pf **London Symphony**

Orchestra / André Previn
Double Decca ② 444 839-2DF2 (135' · ADD) Recorded
1970-72   Ⓜ️OO

Despite the recording dates, the sound and balance are superb, and there's nothing to cloud
your sense of Ashkenazy's greatness in all these
works. From him every page declares Rachmaninov's nationality, his indelibly Russian
nature. What nobility of feeling and what dark
regions of the imagination he relishes and
explores in page after page of the Third Concerto. Significantly his opening is a very moderate *Allegro ma non tanto*, later allowing him an
expansiveness and imaginative scope hard to
find in other more 'driven' or hectic performances. His rubato is as natural as it's distinctive,
and his way of easing from one idea to another
shows him at his most intimately and romantically responsive. There are no cuts, and his
choice of the bigger of the two cadenzas is
entirely apt, given the breadth of his conception. Even the skittering figurations and volleys
of repeated notes just before the close of the
central *Intermezzo* can't tempt Ashkenazy into
display and he's quicker than any other pianist
to find a touch of wistfulness beneath Rachmaninov's occasional outer playfulness (the
scherzando episode in the finale).

Such imaginative fervour and delicacy are just
as central to Ashkenazy's other performances.
His steep unmarked *decrescendo* at the close of
the First Concerto's opening rhetorical gesture
is symptomatic of his Romantic bias, his love of
the music's interior glow. And despite his prodigious command in, say, the final pages of both
the First and Fourth Concertos, there's never a
hint of bombast or a more superficial brand of
fire-and-brimstone virtuosity. Previn works
hand in glove with his soloist. Clearly, this is no
one-night partnership but the product of the
greatest musical sympathy. The opening of the
Third Concerto's *Intermezzo* could hardly be
given with a more idiomatic, brooding melancholy, a perfect introduction for all that's to follow. If you want playing which captures Rachmaninov's always elusive, opalescent centre
then Ashkenazy is hard to beat. (The Second
Concerto, our first choice in this work, is available on a single disc and is reviewed below.)

Piano Concertos Nos 1-4. Paganini Rhapsody.
Vocalise
Zoltán Kocsis pf **San Francisco Symphony
Orchestra / Edo de Waart**
Philips Duo ② 468 921-2PM2 (DDD) Recorded 1982
                                                                 Ⓜ️O

Few if any readings of the piano concertos and
the *Paganini* Rhapsody spark or scintillate with
such daredevilry, are of such unapologetic virtuoso voltage, as these. True, Kocsis can sometimes be more voluble than poised, breezing
through the Third Concerto's haunting opening theme at the fastest flowing tempo and – for
lovers of the ever-romantic Var 18 from the
Paganini Rhapsody, in particular – sometimes

sacrificing heart's-ease for high-octane bravura.
Again, you may question his near *allegretto* spin
through the Second Concerto's central *Adagio*,
eagerly glimpsing so many dazzling athletic
opportunities ahead. Even so, try him in the
Third Concerto's cadenza (the slimmer and
better of the two) and you'll hear it topped and
tailed with a ferocious and almost palpable
aplomb. Listen to him snapping off phrase ends
in the intricate reel of the *Paganini* Rhapsody's
Var 15 or flashing fire in the *Allegro leggiero*
from the First Concerto's finale and you may
well wonder when you last encountered such
fearless brilliance, pace and relish. Even those
attuned to the darker, more introspective Rachmaninov of Ashkenazy will surely pause to wonder. Edo de Waart and the San Francisco Symphony Orchestra are no match for the LSO for
Previn; yet, overall, this is the most propulsive
and exciting set of the complete concertos. Kocsis's whirlwind tempos even allow him time for
an encore – his own ardent elaboration of the
Vocalise, a performance sufficiently ecstatic to
set even the least susceptible heart a-flutter.

Piano Concertos Nos 1-4. Rhapsody on a Theme of
Paganini, Op 43
Stephen Hough pf **Dallas Symphony Orchestra /
Andrew Litton**
Hyperion ② CDA67501/2; SACDA67501/2
CD/SACD ... (146' · DDD)   🅵OOO
Concertos recorded live at the Morton H Meyerson
Symphony Center, Dallas, April-May 2004

Ⓖ   Hough. Litton. Rachmaninov concer-
      tos. Hyperion. Already a mouth-water-
      ing prospect, isn't it? So, like the old
Fry's Five Boys chocolate advert, does Anticipation match Realisation in these five much-
recorded confections?

The answer is 'yes' on almost every level.
Culled from one or more live performances the
concertos may be, but they manifest a real sense
of occasion. Hough has clearly been burning to
record these pieces for years. Litton is one of the
world's most adept accompanists. He and his
Dallas players offer exemplary support, with
bright precision, purring strings and a judiciously blended brass section. A handsomely
voiced piano brings a near-perfect balance; only
in the final pages of the studio-made *Paganini*
Rhapsody does Hough struggle to make himself
heard.

Unlike most of his peers, he takes the composer at his word (scores and recordings) in
matters of tempo, dynamics and the performance practice of Rachmaninov's musical language, as he makes clear in a trenchant apologia
in the superb booklet-note (by David Fanning).

Where Wild and Argerich seem glib in the
cadenzas of the First and Third Concertos
respectively, Hough imparts the right sense of
heroic struggle; not even Rachmaninov caresses
the second subject of the First Concerto's finale
so beguilingly; the notoriously tricky opening
pages of the Second Concerto's finale are

dispatched with breathtaking élan, as is the last movement of the Third Concerto.

It's quite an achievement when each of Hough's five performances rivals the greatest versions recorded individually by other pianists (the younger Horowitz in the Third, for example, Michelangeli in the Fourth). As a competitive set, that from the much-lamented Rafael Orozco comes close to matching Hough's fleet-fingered ardour, but is less impressively recorded; Howard Shelley offers a convincing, slower alternative with powerful, weighty tone. Overall, though, only Earl Wild (1965) and, before that, Rachmaninov himself truly convey the composer's intentions with such miraculous fluency, passion and stylistic integrity.

Piano Concertos – Nos 1 & 2
Krystian Zimerman pf **Boston Symphony Orchestra / Seiji Ozawa**
DG 459 643-2GH (62' · DDD)   Ⓕ**OOO**

 The catalogue may bulge with recordings of these two concertos, yet the verve and poetry of these performances somehow forbid comparison, even at the most exalted level. Zimerman claims that Rachmaninov says everything there is to say about the First Concerto in his own performance. But had Rachmaninov heard Zimerman he might have been envious. Zimerman opens in a blaze of rhetorical glory before skittering through the first *Vivace* with the sort of winged brilliance that will reduce lesser pianists to despair. The cadenza is overwhelming, and at 4'36" in the central *Andante*'s starry ascent his *rubato* tugs painfully at the heartstrings. In the finale, despite a dizzying tempo, every one of the teeming notes is pinpointed with shining clarity.

The Second Concerto also burns and coruscates in all its first heat. A romantic to his fingertips, Zimerman inflects one familiar theme after another with a yearning, bittersweet intensity that he equates in his interview with first love. Every page is alive with a sense of wonder at Rachmaninov's genius. Seiji Ozawa and the Boston orchestra are ideal partners, and DG's sound and balance are fully worthy of this memorable release.

Piano Concerto No 1ᵃ. Paganini Rhapsodyᵇ
Vladimir Ashkenazy pf ᵃ**Concertgebouw Orchestra;** ᵇ**Philharmonia Orchestra / Bernard Haitink**
Decca 417 613-2DH (52' · DDD)   Ⓕ

Showpiece that it is, with its lush romantic harmonies and contrasting vigorous panache, the First Concerto has much to commend it in purely musical terms and although its debts are clear enough (most notably perhaps to Rimsky-Korsakov), it stands on its own two feet as far as invention, overall design and musical construction are concerned. The *Paganini* Rhapsody is one of the composer's finest works and arguably

---

RACHMANINOV PIANO CONCERTOS – IN BRIEF

Krystian Zimerman; Boston PO / Seiji Ozawa
DG 459 643-2GH (62' · DDD)   Ⓕ**OOO**
Zimerman's incendiary pianism trounces all-comers in the First Concerto, not excluding the composer himself. The Second, more ruminative in mood, comes over less well, thanks in part to a recording balance that attenuates the orchestral sound.

Stephen Hough; Dallas SO / Andrew Litton
Hyperion ② CDA67501/2; SACDA67501/2 (62' · ADD)   Ⓕ**OOO**
A stunning new set of the four concertos and *Paganini* Rhapsody played with towering virtuosity by Hough. A real winner.

Sviatoslav Richter; Warsaw PO / Stanislaw Wislocki
DG Originals 447 420-2GOR (71' · ADD)   Ⓜ
A classic account of the Second Piano Concerto taped as long ago as 1959. It's a performance of extremes, with the first two movements made grander than usual, and much of the finale a coruscating dash.

Arturo Benedetti Michelangeli; Philharmonia Orchestra / Ettore Gracis
EMI 567238-2 (47' · ADD)   Ⓜ**OO**
Less surgingly romantic than some, Michelangeli's transcendental pianism and refined sensibility come together in this classic coupling of Rach 4 and the Ravel G major, available continuously since the late 1950s.

Sergey Rachmaninov; Philadelphia Orchestra / Leopold Stokowski, Eugene Ormandy
Nos 2 & 3: Naxos 8 110601 (65' · ADD)   Ⓢ
Nos 1 & 4: Naxos 8 110602 (71' · ADD)   Ⓢ
Rachmaninov's own fastidious, never lugubrious 78 rpm performances remain indispensable, more than just historical documents despite their primitive recording technology.

Zoltán Kocsis; San Francisco SO / Edo de Waart
Philips 468 921-2PM2 (147' · DDD)   Ⓜ
Kocsis offers consistently bracing performances, fast enough to allow the Rhapsody to be accommodated, although the sound engineering is less than ideally natural.

Vladimir Ashkenazy; London SO / André Previn
Decca ② 444 839-2DF2 (135' · ADD)   Ⓜ**O**
Vladimir Ashkenazy's fresh and involving analogue stereo set with André Previn and the LSO dates from the early 1970s. The pianist demonstrates great poetic imagination and lightning reflexes as well as his formidable bravura and characteristic weight of sonority.

the most purely inventive set of variations to be based on Paganini's catchy tune ever written. The wealth of musical invention it suggested to Rachmaninov is truly bewildering and his control over what can in lesser hands become a rather laboured formal scheme is masterly indeed. Ashkenazy gives superb performances of both works and the Concertgebouw and the Philharmonia are in every way the perfect foils under Bernard Haitink's sympathetic direction.

There's weight, delicacy, colour, energy and repose in equal measure here, all conveyed by a full-bodied and detailed recording.

Piano Concerto No 2. Paganini Rhapsody
Vladimir Ashkenazy *pf* **London Symphony Orchestra / André Previn**
Decca Ovation 417 702-2DM (58' · ADD) Recorded 1970-72   Ⓜ**OO**

What emerges most obviously here is the keen poetic individuality of Ashkenazy as a Rachmaninov interpreter. The composer himself is far rougher with his music than Ashkenazy ever is. Those who like Rachmaninov concertos to sound forceful above all will no doubt have reservations, but rarely has this work sounded so magically poetic. That isn't just Ashkenazy's doing – his *rubato* is consistently natural – but the work of Previn and his players. Orchestral detail emerges more clearly than on other recordings, but thanks to finely balanced orchestral recording (no exaggeration of big violin tone) there are no gimmicks. The playing of both Ashkenazy and the LSO continually conveys the impression not of a warhorse but of a completely new work; even such a favourite passage as the return of the slow-movement main theme just before fig 26 is pure and completely unhackneyed. But the performance which clinches the success of this delightful venture is that of the *Paganini* Rhapsody, magical from beginning to end in its concentrated sense of continuity, with the varying moods over the 24 variations leading inevitably from one to another. There's no great splurge of emotion on the great eighteenth variation, but instead there's a ripe sense of fulfilment, which is utterly tasteful. Although the final surprising quiet cadence could be pointed with more wit, the rest has so much delicacy that it's a marginal reservation.

Piano Concerto No 3 in D minor, Op 30[a]. Cello Sonata in G minor, Op 19 – Andante (arr Volodos). Morceaux de fantaisie, Op 3 – No 5, Sérénade in B flat minor. Morceaux de salon, Op 10 – No 6, Romance in F minor. Preludes – F minor, Op 32 No 6. Prelude in D minor. Etudes-tableaux, Op 33 – No 9 in C sharp minor
Arcadi Volodos *pf* [a]**Berlin Philharmonic Orchestra / James Levine**
Sony Classical SK64384 (61' · DDD)   Ⓟ**OO**

Straight into the top flight of Rachmaninov

Thirds goes Arcadi Volodos's recording, made live at the Berlin Philharmonie. So many things about it are distinguished and thrilling. Volodos's phrasing is consummately tasteful, all the way through to the cadenza. There his textures are superbly graded, his tone never glaring, even under the pressure of torrents of notes. All's well, in fact, until mid-way in the first-movement cadenza, where he inserts a hiatus before the *Allegro molto*. It sounds terribly calculated, as does the way he steers the cadenza towards its main climax. A couple of mannerisms in a performance are neither here nor there, but what's bothersome – and this is increasingly noticeable in the slow movement and the finale – is that such initiatives don't feel part of an organically conceived interpretation. Just a whiff of self-consciousness can be enough to cancel out a host of poetic or virtuoso touches. So, while a listener may be amazed, and a pianist envious, at the clarity and velocity Volodos can bring to the toccata in the finale, in context it feels like a gratuitous display.

Though this isn't a world-beater, it's certainly one to assess at the highest level. Nothing but praise can be showered upon the BPO for their wonderfully cushioned accompaniment, and upon Levine for his avoidance of all the usual pitfalls. The piano is quite forwardly balanced, so that every tiniest note emerges bright as a new pin; and, given how wonderfully Volodos shapes everything, it's fine, although you do occasionally feel that you aren't hearing the orchestra in its full glory.

As for the solo pieces, the Cello Sonata arrangement is a marvel. It floats ecstatically, with air seemingly blowing through the textures as if through a Chekhovian country house on a cool summer evening. It's heavenly, and the other solos are little short of that.

Piano Concerto No 3 in D minor, Op 30[a]. Suite No 2 for Two Pianos, Op 17[b]
Martha Argerich, [b]**Nelson Freire** *pfs* [a]**Berlin Radio Symphony Orchestra / Riccardo Chailly**
Philips 50 Great Recordings 464 732-2PM (62' · DDD) Recorded live 1982   Ⓜ**OOO**

Rarely in her extraordinary career has Argerich sounded more exhaustingly restless and quixotic, her mind and fingers flashing with reflexes merely dreamt of by other less phenomenally endowed pianists. Yet her Rachmaninov is full of surprises, her opening *Allegro* almost convivial until she meets directions such as *più vivo* or *veloce*, where the tigress in her shows her claws and the music is made to seethe and boil. The cadenza (the finer and more transparent of the two) rises to the sort of climax that will make all pianists' hearts beat faster and her first entry in the 'Intermezzo' interrupts the orchestra's musing with the impatience of a hurricane. But throughout these pages it's almost as if she's searching for music that will allow her virtuosity its fullest scope. In the finale she finds it, accelerating out of the second movement with a sky-rocketing propulsion. Here the music races like wildfire, with a death-defying turn of speed at 7'21" and an explosive energy throughout that must have left audience, conductor and orchestra feeling as if hit by some seismic shock-wave.

Rachmaninov Piano Concerto No 3 **Tchaikovsky** 🄷
Piano Concerto No 1 in B flat minor, Op 23
Vladimir Horowitz pf **New York Philharmonic
Symphony Orchestra / Sir John Barbirolli**
APR mono APR5519 (66' · ADD) Recorded live 1940-41   Ⓕ●○○

This is the Rachmaninov Third to end all Rachmaninov Thirds, a performance of such super-human pianistic aplomb, pace and virtuosity that it makes all comparisons, save with Horowitz himself, a study in irrelevance. Horowitz's 1930 recording with Albert Coates made Artur Rubinstein pale with envy; goodness knows how he'd have reacted had he heard Horowitz and Barbirolli! Taken from a 1941 New York broadcast (with apologies from the producer for snaps, crackles, pops and the like) Horowitz's tumultuous, near-apocalyptic brilliance includes all his unique and tirelessly debated attributes; his swooning rubato, thundering bass and splintering treble, his explosive attack, his super-erotic inflexions and turns of phrase. Try the skittering *scherzando* variation just before the close of the central *Intermezzo* and note how the pianist's velocity eclipses even his legendary recording with Fritz Reiner. This ultimate wizard of the keyboard is in expansive mood in the Tchaikovsky. There are ample rewards, too, for those who rejoice in Horowitz at his most clamorous, for the thunder and lightning of this 'Tornado from the Steppes'. The performance ends in what can only be described as a scream of octaves and an outburst by an audience driven near to hysteria. Barbirolli and the New York Philharmonic Symphony Orchestra are equal to just about every twist and turn of their volatile soloist's argument and so these performances (and most notably the finale of the Rachmaninov) are simply beyond price.

Rachmaninov Piano Concerto No 4   🄷
Ravel Piano Concerto in G
Arturo Benedetti Michelangeli pf **Philharmonia
Orchestra / Ettore Gracis**
EMI Great Recordings of the Century 567238-2 (47' · ADD) Recorded 1957   Ⓜ●○○

In crude and subjective terms Michelangeli makes the spine tingle in a way no others can approach. How does he do it? This is the secret every pianist would love to know, and which no writer can ever pin down. But it's possible to give some general indications. It isn't a question of technique, at least not directly, because Ashkenazy, for example (on Decca) can match their most

virtuoso feats; indirectly, yes, it's relevant, in that there are dimensions in Michelangeli's pianism which allow musical conceptions to materialise which might not dawn on others. Nor is it a question of structure, in the narrow sense of the awareness of overall proportions, judicious shaping of paragraphs, continuity of thought; but the way structure is projected and the way it's transmuted into emotional drama; these things are critical.

In one way or another most of the recordings in this section respond vividly to the excitement of Rachmaninov's dramatic climaxes; but with Michelangeli these climaxes seem to burst through the music of their own volition, as though an irresistible force of nature has been released. It's this crowning of a structure by release, rather than by extra pressure, which gives the performance a sense of exaltation and which more than anything else sets it on a different level. It enables him to be freer in many details, yet seem more inevitable as a whole.

The impact of all this would be negligible without a sympathetically attuned conductor and orchestra. Fortunately that's exactly what Michelangeli has. Michelangeli's Ravel is open to criticism, partly because many listeners feel uncomfortable with his persistent left-before-right mannerism in the slow movement and with his unwarranted textual tinkerings (like changing the last note). But he's as finely attuned to this aloof idiom as to its temperamental opposite in the Rachmaninov.

And although the recording can't entirely belie its vintage, it does justice to one of the finest concerto records ever made.

Symphonies

No 1 in D minor, Op 13; **No 2** in E minor, Op 27; No 3 in A minor, Op 44. **Symphonic Dances**, Op 45

Symphonies Nos 1, 2ᵃ & 3ᵇ. Symphonic Dances, Op 45ᵇ. The isle of the dead, Op 29. Vocalise (arr cpsr). Aleko – Intermezzo; Gipsy Girls' Dance
London Symphony Orchestra / André Previn
EMI ③ 764530-2 (227' · ADD) Recorded 1974-6 Ⓜ●●

Items marked ᵃᵇ are also available on HMV Classics
ᵃHMV5 72833-2 & ᵇHMV5 73475-2   Ⓑ

Rachmaninov's three symphonies reflect three very different phases in his creative development: the first (1895) is a stormy synthesis of contemporary trends in Russian symphonic music, the Second (1906-7), an epic study in Tchaikovskian opulence, and the third (1935-6) a seemingly unstoppable stream of original ideas and impressions. The Second was the first to gain wide acceptance, and with good reason. It shares both the key and general mood of Tchaikovsky's Fifth. Cast in E minor, its initial gloom ultimately turns to triumph, and the symphony includes enough glorious melodies to keep Hollywood happy for decades.

RACHMANINOV SYMPHONY NO 2 – IN BRIEF

Leningrad PO / Kurt Sanderling
DG 449 767-2GOR (54' · ADD)　　　Ⓜ
Recorded in West Berlin while the Leningrad Philharmonic was on tour, Kurt Sanderling's 1965 recording distils a devastating emotional candour and symphonic thrust.

Philadelphia Orchestra / Eugene Ormandy
Sony ② SB2K63257 (137' · ADD)　　　Ⓜ
Ormandy and the Philadelphians gave us the first stereo Rachmaninov symphony cycle, and their account of the Second generates a heady sweep that makes it easy to forgive some niggling cuts.

Russian National Orchestra / Mikhail Pletnev
DG 439 888-2GH (64' · DDD)　　　ⒻOO
Pletnev's is a superbly controlled and enviably sure-footed performance, if a bit too cool and calculated for some tastes. Full bodied, though not ideally clear recording.

London SO / André Previn
EMI 566982-2 (74' · ADD)　　　ⓂOO
Many collectors maintain an unswerving allegiance to Previn's famous account from 1973, now sounding more refulgent than ever in its latest remastering.

Concertgebouw Orchestra / Vladimir Ashkenazy
Decca ② 448 126-2DF2 (139' · DDD)　　　ⓂO
An enjoyably red-blooded account with bags of temperament and athleticism. Ripe Decca engineering, albeit not quite as resplendent as on the two other instalments in Ashkenazy's Rachmaninov symphony cycle.

Berlin PO / Lorin Maazel
DG 457 913-2GGA (75' · DDD)　　　Ⓜ
Maazel's is an urgently intense conception, and accordingly he drives an unusually swift course through the first movments. High-powered orchestral playing, but the sound is just a tad fierce and unglowing.

National SO of Ireland / Alexander Anissimov
Naxos 8 554230 (58' · DDD)　　　Ⓢ
The Dublin orchestra may not be world-beaters but there's absolutely nothing slipshod about their contribution. Anissimov's deeply felt, keenly pondered conception enjoys realistic sound.

Budapest Festival Orchestra / Iván Fischer
Channel Classics CCSSA21698 (65' · DDD)　　　ⒻO
More musical alchemy from Iván Fischer and his Budapest orchestra. A real sense of dialogue permeates this malleable, joyous performance, whose textual revelations are legion.

The First Symphony had a difficult birth, largely through the incompetent musical midwifery of Alexander Glazunov whose conducting of the work's première apparently left much to be desired. However, it's an immensely promising piece and although undeniably the product of its times, prophetic not only of the mature Rachmaninov, but of other Northern voices, including – occasionally – the mature Sibelius. Both the Third Symphony and its near-contemporary, the *Symphonic Dances* find Rachmaninov indulging a fruitful stream of musical consciousness, recalling motives and ideas from earlier compositions, yet allowing gusts of fresh air to enliven and rejuvenate his style. Both works have yet to receive their full due in the concert hall, although the strongly evocative *Isle of the dead* is more securely embedded in the repertory.

What with these and a trio of warming shorter pieces, André Previn's mid-1970s LSO package is an excellent bargain. The performances are entirely sympathetic, avoiding familiar interpretative extremes such as slickness, bombast and emotional indulgence. Previn shows particular understanding of the Third Symphony, the *Symphonic Dances* and *The isle of the dead*, works that represent Rachmaninov at his most innovative and assured. The Second Symphony is played without cuts (not invariably the case, even today) and the recordings are generous in tone and revealing of detail.

Symphonies Nos 1-3
Concertgebouw Orchestra / Vladimir Ashkenazy
Double Decca ② 448 116-2DF2 (140' · DDD) Recorded 1980-82　　　ⓂOO

Ashkenazy has made few more distinguished discs as conductor than his Rachmaninov symphony recordings of the early 1980s. The downside of the repackaging in this 2CD format is that you have to put up with a change of disc half-way through the Second Symphony and lose the shorter orchestral works included in the Previn set. Previn is the most natural but not always the most electrifying of Rachmaninov interpreters and many will find Ashkenazy preferable, particularly in No 1. Although some of Ashkenazy's speeds seem unnaturally pressed – he fairly tips us into the first movement reprise having declined to cap the climax with unvalidated bells – the excitement is infectious. Previn's LSO isn't at its best in the *Larghetto*, but in the corresponding movement of the Second Symphony the boot is on the other foot. Not that Ashkenazy isn't convincing too – so long as you can forget the Previn. Ashkenazy's volatile approach is at its most extreme in the Third, the mood much less autumnal than it usually is, with the fruity Concertgebouw brass unconstrained. Such an unashamedly episodic rendering of the score has its drawbacks, but the virtuosic energy and Romantic gush are hard to resist. The recordings sound very well indeed.

Symphony No 2. The Rock, Op 7
Russian National Orchestra / Mikhail Pletnev
DG 439 888-2GH (64' · DDD) Recorded 1993 Ⓕ**OO**

Mikhail Pletnev's achievement is to make us hear the music afresh: a performance characterised by relatively discreet emotionalism, strong forward momentum and a fanatical preoccupation with clarity of articulation. When there's no Slavic wobble, it scarcely matters that his winds display an individuality which once or twice fails to transcend mere rawness – so much the better in this music! The strings, forceful and husky (with separated violin desks) are beyond reproach. The most remarkable playing comes in the finale. The lyrical effusions are superbly characterised without undermining the sense of inexorability, the climaxes not just powerful but affecting too. The closing pages bring a rush of adrenalin of the kind rarely experienced live, let alone in the studio. This is great music-making, the *rubato* always there when required, the long phrases immaculately tailored yet always sounding spontaneous.

DG's unexpected coupling is *The Rock*, a rather bitty piece which is however very deftly scored and intriguingly Scriabinesque in places. In Pletnev's hands, the central climax is surprisingly powerful, and the fabulous delicacy elsewhere is alone worth the price of admission.

Symphony No 3. Morceaux de fantaisie, Op 3 – No 3, Mélodie in E; No 4, Polichinelle in F sharp minor (both orch anon)
National Symphony Orchestra of Ireland / Alexander Anissimov
Naxos 8 550808 (52' · DDD) Ⓢ

Barely represented on disc a generation ago, Rachmaninov's orchestral works are firm favourites these days, and it's no surprise Naxos has entered the lists. Can Anissimov hope to compete in a field that includes Ashkenazy's high-octane digital accounts in sundry bargain formats? Perhaps surprisingly the answer is yes, for the conductor produces a highly distinctive performance of the Third, inspiring his orchestra to playing of considerable warmth and flair. Sound quality is excellent, too. String tone is crucially important with this composer, and here again any worries prove unfounded. Not for Anissimov the 'neurotic' Russianness of Ashkenazy's Rachmaninov. Like Jansons, he disregards the first-movement exposition repeat, but he makes the orchestral voices speak with a gentler tone. There are shattering climaxes when the music calls for them, and the symphony ends in rousing style; elsewhere the sophisticated languor and careful phrasing recall Previn's famous recording. Although some will be disappointed with the generally slow tempos, there's an unusual wholeness of musical vision and pacing which never sacrifices the needs of the larger structure to the lure of momentary thrills. Despite the short measure, this is thoroughly recommendable at the price.

Trios élégiaques

Trios elegiaques in G minor; D minor, Op 9
Copenhagen Trio (Søren Elbaek vn Troels Svane Hermansen vc Morten Mogensen pf)
Kontrapunkt 32187 (65' · DDD) Recorded 1994 Ⓕ**O**

The shade of Tchaikovsky haunts both these works. In the first, there are turns of phrase from his Trio, and much of the style and the textural approach to the problems derive from his example – not always a very good one, when it came to dealing with a virtuoso piano part against the weaker sound of the strings. Rachmaninov is ingenious, and handles his material expertly in a long, shapely movement. Tchaikovsky is more consciously the exemplar of the second Trio. Deeply impressed by the younger composer's *The Rock*, he had agreed to conduct the first performance in January 1894, a rare gesture of appreciation. On Tchaikovsky's death in October, the shocked Rachmaninov wrote his Trio 'in memory of a great artist', just as Tchaikovsky had once written a Trio in memory of another great artist, Nikolay Rubinstein. And here, too, there's a substantial variation movement, on a theme from *The Rock*. It's lyrically varied, not with conscious allusions after the manner of Tchaikovsky's elegy but with a sense of indebtedness that's unmistakable. Rachmaninov initially intended to have the opening statement of the theme played on the harmonium; he later revised the work, and it's the second version which is recorded here – and well, in a fine performance that does full justice to a lengthy but affecting piece.

Rachmaninov Trio élégiaque, op.9 **Shostakovich** Piano Trio No 2
Dmitri Makhtin vn **Alexander Kniazev** vc **Boris Berezovsky** pf
Warner Classics 2564 61937-2 (79' · DDD) Ⓕ

Rachmaninov's only substantial piano trio remains a relative rarity in the catalogue. It's not hard to see why, for this is more of an Ugly Sister than a Cinderella. True, there are many passages of beauty and poignancy, but overall it's an oddly structured piece, with two substantial movements followed by an almost throwaway finale.

This new reading comes closer than most to concealing the work's flaws. The opening movement is wonderfully realised, a single sweep of grief mingled with love and regret (it was written on the death of Tchaikovsky). And the second couldn't be more musically played. It's a highly piano-centric work, but you never feel that Berezovsky is hogging the limelight, superbly matched as he is by his compatriots. By contrast, the finale, despite its portentous, Brahmsian opening, is over all too soon, as if Rachmaninov simply ran out of steam.

It's tantalising that Rachmaninov left no recording of his own. But in the case of Shostakovich's Second Trio, we've had the composer at the keyboard on two occasions (various labels). Comparison is salutary: most modern interpretations seem sluggish by comparison (though admittedly Shostakovich plays fast and loose with his own tempo indications), particularly in the finale. Berezovsky, Makhtin and Kniazev are even more satisfying than the very good performance from the Wanderer Trio; their take on the following Passacaglia ideally balances profundity with unaffectedness. Their restraint is much more potent than the tacky exaggerations of Argerich, Kremer and Maisky, in a live performance from 1998.

Only a couple of niggles: like the Wanderer Trio, the string players apparently ignore the *con sordino* instruction in the finale, and at one point in the Passacaglia there's a very prominent exhalation from one of them – bothersome enough to make one wonder why it was left in. The recording is warm and convincingly balanced and complements the superb performances.

Complete Piano Music

Variations on a Theme of Chopin, Op 22. Variations on a Theme of Corelli, Op 42. Mélodie in E, Op 3 No 3. Piano Sonatas – No 1 in D minor, Op 28; No 2 in B flat minor, Op 36 (orig version); No 2 in B flat minor, Op 36 (rev version). 10 Preludes, Op 23. 13 Preludes, Op 32. Prelude in D minor. Prelude in F. Morceaux de fantaisie, Op 3. Morceau de fantaisie in G minor. Song without words in D minor. Pièce in D minor. Fughetta in F. Moments musicaux, Op 16. Fragments in A flat. Oriental Sketch in B flat. Three Nocturnes – No 1 in F sharp minor; No 2 in F; No 3 in C minor. Quatre Pièces – Romance in F sharp minor; Prélude in E flat minor; Mélodie in E; Gavotte in D. 17 Etudes-tableaux, Opp 33 & 39.
Transcriptions – **Bach** Solo Violin Partita No 3 in E, BWV1006 – Preludio, Gavotte, Gigue **Behr** Lachtäubchen, Op 303 (pubd as Polka de VR) **Bizet** L'Arlésienne Suite No 1 – Menuet **Kreisler** Liebesleid. Liebesfreud **Mendelssohn** A Midsummer Night's Dream, Op 61 – Scherzo **Mussorgsky** Sorochinsky Fair – Gopak **Rachmaninov** Daisies, Op 38 No 3. Lilacs, Op 21 No 5. Vocalise, Op 34 No 14 (arr Kocsis) **Rimsky-Korsakov** The Tale of Tsar Saltan – The Flight of the Bumble-bee **Schubert** Die schöne Müllerin, D957 – Wohin? **Tchaikovsky** Cradle Song, Op 16 No 1
Howard Shelley pf
Hyperion Ⓑ CDS44041/8 (449' · DDD) Recorded 1978-91   Ⓜ🅞

This Hyperion set is a significant testament to Howard Shelley's artistry. Pianistically impeccable, he understands what Rachmaninov was about. The original piano works span 45 years of the composer's life. The earliest pieces here, the *Nocturnes*, strangely owe allegiance neither to Field nor Chopin, but are very much in the mid- to late 19th-century Russian salon style. The Third, in C minor, has nothing whatever to do with its title. Nicely written too, but still uncharacteristic, are four pieces from 1888, which amply demonstrate that from his early

teens the composer had something individual to say. The *Mélodie* in E major is memorable for its hypnotic use of piano tone. Hyperion's recording quality can be heard at its very best here; there's real bloom and colour. Written shortly after his First Piano Concerto in the early 1890s, the *Morceaux de fantaisie*, Op 3 bring us to familiar Rachmaninov. The ubiquitous Prelude in C sharp minor is the second number but Shelley tries to do too much with it; he's more effective in the *Sérénade* with its Spanish overtones. In the E flat minor *Moment musical*, Op 16 one feels that he's able to master Rachmaninov's swirling accompaniments idiomatically. In Variation No 15 of the *Variations on a Theme of Chopin* he succeeds in bringing the notes to life, getting his fingers around the fleet *scherzando* writing.

The first set of Preludes is mainstream repertoire. In the warmly expressive D major Prelude he lends the piece a strong Brahmsian feel and it emerges as very well focused. He transforms the C minor into a restless mood picture. The First Sonata is often dismissed as being unwieldy but Shelley gives it a symphonic stature and allows it to be seen in conjunction more with the composer's orchestral writing. Shortly after the Third Concerto Rachmaninov wrote the Op 32 Preludes. Shelley conjures up an exquisite moonlit scene for the G major, but he's not as impressive in the B minor. However, with him it's always the music that dictates the course of the interpretation. In the two sets of *Etudes-tableaux* he excels, as he does too in the Second Sonata. He draws together the disparate elements of the finale with terrific mastery and is the equal of the 'Horowitz clones' for technique. In the *Corelli* Variations he's not quite in tune with the scope of the work but is outstanding in the transcriptions, if a little straight-faced. The recorded sound is never less than serviceable and is sometimes excellent.

Piano Sonata No 2

Piano Sonata No 2 in B flat minor, Op 36.
Etudes-tableaux, Op 39
Freddy Kempf pf
BIS CD1042 (67' · DDD)   Ⓕ🅞

Freddy Kempf's second disc in his series for BIS offers an enthralling example of that moment when early talent blossoms into fullness and individuality. Even if he lacks the concentrated intensity and force of more seasoned Rachmaninov pianists in the Second Sonata, his youthful play of light and shade, his innate musical grace and fluency are rich compensation for an occasional diffidence (the opening of the second and, more surprisingly, third movements show him at his least engaged). But in the Op 39 *Etudes* he comes entirely into his own. He paces No 2 more generously than on a previous occasion in New York, showing a nice sense of Rachmaninov's volatility (*poco più vivo*) beneath his despondent *Dies irae* surface. His rhythmic poise and vivacity in the reluctantly festive No 4 show an authentic feel for its bustle and urgency, and his deeply welling – rather than merely hectoring – start to No 5 leads to an inclusive sense of its *appassionata* rhetoric and declamation. And in No 7, an elegy that gives the lie to Rachmaninov's supposed conservatism), he achieves the sort of expressive freedom and elasticity that usually come to pianists far beyond his years. No 8 finds him clarifying Rachmaninov's ornate polyphony with rare artistry and, finally, his way with the *Liebesleid*, quite without preening idiosyncrasy or mannerism, re-creates a magical and touching sense of Rachmaninov's affection for Kreisler. BIS's sound is superb, fully capturing Kempf's dynamic range from whispering *pianissimos* to sonorous *fortissimos*. This is a very special record.

Etudes-tableaux

Etudes-tableaux, Opp 33 & 39
John Lill pf
Nimbus NI5439 (64' · DDD)   Ⓕ

The *Etudes-tableaux* are known to be musical evocations of various pictorial or perhaps narrative ideas, though quite rightly Rachmaninov did not let on where the stimuli came from; there's certainly no sign that John Lill is much preoccupied with such matters. He's a powerful keyboard technician, which is the first necessity in approaching these virtuoso studies, and this puts him in a strong position for dealing with the bold assertiveness of some of them, for instance the first piece of all. He also has a very vivid sense of tempo (balancing speed and texture sympathetically), and equally a sense for the slight lifting of pressure as well as slowing up, or the reverse, which is the essence of true romantic rubato. Where he can seem less responsive than some of his colleagues is with the more delicate pieces, whose fantasy he perhaps underrates. But if he also loses something in introspection, he can command admiration with his magisterial delivery. A very strong set of performances of some fascinating music.

24 Preludes

24 Preludes, Opp 23 & 32. Prelude in D minor. Morceaux de fantaisie, Op 3. Lilacs. Daisies. Mélodie in E. Oriental Sketch in B flat. Moments musicaux, Op 16
Dmitri Alexeev pf
Virgin Classics ② 561624-2(138' · DDD) Recorded 1987-9   ⒷO

Alexeev's all-Russian mastery has seldom been heard to such advantage and his technical force and authority throughout are unarguable. True, he hardly wears his heart on his sleeve in the quixotic Minuet of Op 23 No 3, is less than poetically yielding in the Chopinesque tracery

of Op 23 No 4. He does, however, capture the Slavonic malaise of No 1 with rare insight and his punishing weight and rhetoric in Op 23 Nos 2 or 7 will make even the most sanguine listener's pulse beat faster. He unleashes the central build-up of Op 32 No 7 with the impact of a Siberian whirlwind and time and again his icy, determinedly unsentimental approach gives added strength and focus to the composer's brilliant fury. Alexeev is more convincing in the more vertiginous numbers from the *Moments musicaux*, in Nos 2, 4 and 6 rather than in the opening rhythmic play of No 1 where he sounds altogether too literal and austere. Yet you only have to hear his way of making even *Polichinelle*'s well-worn phrases come up as fresh as paint or his trenchancy in *Oriental Sketch* to realise that you're in the presence of a master pianist.

The recordings are of demonstration quality and the accompanying essay mirrors the rare toughness and integrity of these performances; the essential nobility of Rachmaninov's genius.

Additional recommendation

Preludes, Op 23 – Nos 1, 2, 4, 5, 8; Op 32 – Nos 1, 2, 6, 7, 10, 12
Coupled with: **Beethoven** Piano Sonata No 11. Variations and Fugue on an Original Theme, 'Eroica' **Chopin** Nocturnes – Op 72 No 1; Op 15 No 1 **Haydn** Piano Sonata in E, HobXVI:22 **Schumann** Symphonic Etudes
Richter pf
BBC Legends/IMG Artists ② BBCL4090-2 (144' · ADD) Recorded live 1967-9   ⓂO
These performances took place when Richter was as his height, his early insecurity resolved in playing of imperious mastery. Richter's empathy for his great compatriot is overwhelming and the sound is excellent. This is phenomenal playing.

Liturgy, Op 31

Liturgy of St John Chrysostom, Op 31
King's College Choir, Cambridge / Stephen Cleobury
EMI 557677-2 (75' · DDD)   ⒻOO

Having recorded the much better known All-Night Vigil ('Vespers') in 1999, King's College here turn to Rachmaninov's earlier setting of the Divine Liturgy, written in 1910. This recording may well consolidate its place in the repertoire, for it's a triumph. Compared with the Vigil the writing is generally sober, though there are unforgettable moments such as the opening of the Second Antiphon, which allows the boys' crystalline tone to shine. In fact, the King's choir make a virtue of an apparent limitation, producing an astounding choral blend in the simple responses of the litanies that punctuate the Liturgy.

The most famous section of the work is the lovely Lord's Prayer, movingly sung with fine attention to detail. Other sections, such as the Beatitudes ought also to attract the attention of any discerning choir director. Only in the Creed do the choir slightly lose the spring in their step; perhaps inevitable with such a lengthy setting in an unfamiliar language.

The great majority of the priest's and deacon's intonations have been included. This makes sense of the whole, and proves, if it needed proving, that Rachmaninov knew all about liturgical pacing. This aspect of the recording benefits from the magnificent bass and fluent Slavonic of Protodeacon Peter Scorer, who has the lion's share. If Deacon Tobias Sims, singing the celebrant's parts, can't entirely disguise his English origins, the contrast between the two voices also helps convey the liturgical feeling. There are excellent booklet-notes by Archimandrite Kyril Jenner.

Vespers, Op 37

Vespers, Op 37
Olga Borodina *mez* **Vladimir Mostowoy** *ten* **St Petersburg Chamber Choir / Nikolai Korniev**
Philips 442 344-2PH (56' · DDD) Recorded 1993. Texts and translations included Ⓕ

The St Petersburg Chamber Choir sing the *Vespers*, or *All-Night Vigil*, dramatically. Korniev follows the composer's markings carefully, but he's evidently concerned to give a concert performance endowed with vivid immediacy, and there are places where this departs from the reflective or celebratory nature of music that's so strongly grounded in Orthodox tradition. This is most marked with Olga Borodina, who isn't the first fine singer to bring too operatic a note to her solo in 'Blagoslovi, dushe moya' ('Bless the Lord, O my soul'); Vladimir Mostowoy is more discreet in 'Blagosloven esi' ('Blessed art Thou').

The choir itself is excellent, with particularly fine sopranos who can chant high above the others in beautifully pitched thirds; while, as always in Russian church choirs, there's a splendid bass section that can underpin the textures with effortlessly rich low Cs, and find no difficulty with the famous descending scale down to a sonorous bottom B flat at the end of 'Nyne otpushchayeshi' (the *Nunc dimittis*). The recording isn't always as clear as it could be with the textures and especially the words. A strength of the issue, which distinguishes it from almost all others available, is the booklet, which includes not only the full text in transliteration (with English, German and French translations), but also excellent essays.

Additional recommendations

Vespers

National Academic Choir of Ukraine 'Dumka' / Savchuk
Regis Records RRC1043 (62' · DDD) Ⓢ

A first-rate bargain issue to compete with the very best. The Ukrainian choir is a superb body of singers, producing a beautifully warm, dark-hued sound and with an extraordinary sense of pacing. Their *piano* singing is unrivalled on disc.

Palmu *sop* **Wimeri** *contr* **Antoni** *ten* **Finnish National Opera Chorus / Eric-Olof Söderström**
Naxos 8 555908 (54' · DDD · T/t) Texts and translations included Ⓢ

This draws on the older Russian performance tradition. There's an operatic weight to the choral sound at the opposite extreme from the refinement of, say, King's College Choir. The soloists have an authentic air about them, and the choir is well-controlled and blended.

Songs

12 Songs, Op 21. 15 Songs, Op 26. Were you hiccoughing?. Night
Joan Rodgers *sop* **Maria Popescu** *mez* **Alexandre Naoumenko** *ten* **Sergei Leiferkus** *bar* **Howard Shelley** *pf*
Chandos CHAN9451 (72' · DDD) Recorded 1994-5. Texts and translations included Ⓕ●

Two figures in particular haunt this second volume of Chandos's survey of Rachmaninov's songs – Feodor Chaliapin and Rachmaninov himself. They had become friends in the years when they worked together in an opera company and when Rachmaninov was concentrating on developing his piano virtuosity. As a result the Op 21 songs are dominated by an almost operatic declamatory manner coupled with formidably difficult accompaniments. Leiferkus rises splendidly to the occasion, above all in 'Fate' (Op 21 No 1), and so throughout the songs does Howard Shelley. He's unbowed by the technical problems and he understands the novel proportions of songs in which the piano's participation has an unprecedented role. He also enjoys himself in the roisterous exchanges with Leiferkus in what's really Rachmaninov's only lighthearted song, *Were you hiccoughing?*

The songs for the other voices are less powerful, in general more lyrical and intimate. Alexandre Naoumenko only has five songs, and they aren't, on the whole, among the more striking examples, but he responds elegantly to 'The fountain' (Op 26 No 11). Maria Popescu gives a beautiful account of one of the most deservedly popular of them all, 'To the children' (Op 26 No 7), and of the remarkable Merezhkovsky setting, 'Christ is risen' (Op 26 No 6). Joan Rodgers is enchanting in 'The Lilacs' (Op 21 No 5) and moving in the song acknowledging that love is slipping away, 'Again I am alone' (Op 26 No 9). She has complete mastery of the style, and nothing here is finer than her arching phrase ending 'How peaceful' (Op 21 No 7) – 'da ty, mechta moya' (and you, my dream) – with Shelley gently articulating Rachmaninov's reflective piano postlude from the world of Schumann.

14 Songs, Op 34. Letter to K S Stanislavsky. From the Gospel of St John. Six Songs, Op 38. A prayer. All wish to sing
Joan Rodgers sop **Maria Popescu** mez **Alexandre Naoumenko** ten **Sergei Leiferkus** bar **Howard Shelley** pf
Chandos CHAN9477 (68' · DDD) Recorded 1994-5.
Texts and translations included ⒻО

This set opens with a powerful dramatic outpouring, *Letter to KS Stanislavsky*. In fact it's a formal letter of apology, for unavoidable absence from a gathering, which Rachmaninov sent for Chaliapin to sing to Stanislavsky; and one of the most touchingly elegant phrases is simply the date on the letter, October 14, 1908. Perhaps he was showing a rare touch of irony in using his full lyrical powers in such a context; but at any rate, the piece nicely prefaces the two collections of his last phase of song-writing, before he left Russia for exile.

Some of his greatest songs are here, coloured in their invention by the four great singers whose hovering presence makes the disposition of this recital between four similar voices a highly successful idea.

The Chaliapin songs go to Sergei Leiferkus, occasionally a little overshadowed by this mighty example (as in 'The raising of Lazarus', Op 34 No 6) but more often his own man, responding to the subtly dramatic, sometimes even laconic melodic lines with great sympathy for how they interact with the words, as with the Afanasy Fet poem 'The peasant' (Op 34 No 11). Alexandre Naoumenko inherits the mantle of Leonid Sobinov, and though he sometimes resorts to a near-falsetto for soft high notes, he appears to have listened to that fine tenor's elegance of line and no less subtle feeling for poetry. Pushkin's 'The muse' (Op 34 No 1) is most tenderly sung, and there's a sensitive response to line with 'I remember this day'.

Maria Popescu has only two songs, 'It cannot be' and 'Music' (Op 34 Nos 7 and 8), but she has a light tone and bright manner. Joan Rodgers is exquisite in the most rapturous and inward of the songs (the great Felia Litvinne was the original here). Of the Op 38 set, Rachmaninov was particularly fond of 'The rat-catcher' (No 4), and especially of 'Daisies' (No 3), which she sings charmingly, but it's hard to understand why he did not add 'Sleep'. He might have done had he heard Rodgers's rapt performance with Howard Shelley, the music delicately balanced in the exact way he must have intended between voice and piano as if between sleep and waking.

Jean-Philippe Rameau
French 1683-1764

Rameau's early training came from his father, a professional organist; he went to a Jesuit school, then had a short period of music study in Italy. In 1702 he was appointed maître de musique at Avignon Cathe-

dral, and spent the next 20 years in various organist posts in France.

By 1722 he was in Paris, where he was to remain; he had left his organist post at Clermont Cathedral to supervise the publication of his Traité de l'harmonie, a substantial and controversial work about the relationship of bass to harmony. The Traité brought him to wide attention. As a composer, he was known only for his keyboard music (a second collection appeared in 1729-30) and his cantatas, though he had written some church music.

His ambitions, however, lay in opera and at the age of 50 he had his first opera, Hippolyte et Aricie, given at the Opéra. It aroused great excitement, admiration, bewilderment and (among the conservative part of the audience) disgust. It was fairly successful, as were the operas that followed, including the opéra-ballet Les Indes galantes.

In 1745 Rameau was appointed a royal chamber music composer; thereafter several of his works had their premières at court theatres. Nine new theatre works followed in the mid-late 1740s, beginning with La princesse de Navarre and the comedy Platée; but from 1750 onwards only two major works were written, for Rameau was increasingly involved with theory and a number of disputes, with Rousseau, Grimm and even former friends, pupils and collaborators such as Diderot and D'Alembert. When Rameau died he was widely respected and admired, though he was seen too as unsociable and avaricious.

Rameau's harpsichord music is notable for its variety of texture, originality of line and boldness of harmony. But his chief contribution lies in his operas, especially those in the tragédie lyrique genre. He anticipated Gluckian reform by relating the overture to the ensuing drama. He brought to the numerous dances a wide range of moods using a richly varied orchestral palette and bold melodic lines. He wrote many fine pathetic monologues, usually at the beginnings of acts, with intense, slow-moving vocal lines and rich, sombre accompaniments. His recitative, while following the Lullian model, is more flexible in rhythms and more expressive in its declamation. Such tragédies as Hippolyte et Aricie and Castor et Pollux stand among the great creations of French musical drama. GROVEmusic

Ouvertures

Les fêtes de Polymnie; Les indes galantes; Ⓟ
Zäis; Castor et Pollux; Naïs; Platée; Les fêtes d'Hébé; Zoroastre; Dardanus; Les paladins; Hippolyte et Aricie; Le temple de la gloire; Pygmalion; Les surprises de l'Amour; Les fêtes de l'Hymen et de l'Amour; Acante et Céphise
Les Talens Lyriques / Christophe Rousset
L'Oiseau-Lyre 455 293-2OH (70' · DDD) ⒻOOO

Rameau was an orchestrator of rare and individual genius, and his operas, ballets and smaller entertainments are generously provided with some of the most original and alluring dance music to emerge from the 18th century. Roughly speaking, the music on this disc was written between 1733, the date of Rameau's first opera *Hippolyte et Aricie*, and 1761, when he produced his *comédie-*

lyrique, Les Paladins. Lovers of Rameau's music will be thoroughly familiar with most of the music played on the disc but will be delighted to find some rarities, too. The most remarkable of these is the overture to the *pastorale-héroïque, Acante et Céphise.* The overture to *Acante et Céphise* is different again, with its inclusion of specific 'occasional' references. Its three sections are marked 'Voeux de la Nation', 'Feu d'Artifice' (whose bass line is punctuated by cannon-fire) and 'Fanfare'. Les Talens Lyriques responds admirably to this music, relishing every bar of it in performances which are refined in ensemble and articulate in speech. Rousset proves himself a fine exponent of this rewarding repertoire.

Suites

Les fêtes d'Hébé; Acante et Céphise   **P**
Orchestra of the Eighteenth Century / Frans Brüggen
Glossa GCD921103 (67' · DDD) Recorded live 1996-7
   OF

Frans Brüggen's affection for Rameau's orchestral music is confirmed by the many previous issues of dances from his operas. Those are on the Philips label but, for this programme of suites from Rameau's *opéra-ballet, Les fêtes d'Hébé* and the *pastorale-héroïque, Acante et Céphise,* Brüggen has defected to the Spanish label, Glossa. In respect both of presentation and sound, this recently established label has, as they say, done him proud, for this is certainly the most satisfying issue so far in Brüggen's occasional series. While the music of *Les fêtes d'Hébé,* one of Rameau's most successful operas, is comparatively well known, that of *Acante et Céphise* isn't. It's an unjustly neglected piece, making Brüggen's suite of the overture and 15 dances all the more welcome.

The Orchestra of the 18th century responds atmospherically if not always unanimously to Brüggen's sensitive direction. He's a wonderfully rhythmic musician whose imagination is clearly and understandably fired by some of the most innovative and evocative orchestration to have emerged from the first half of the 18th century. *Acante et Céphise* was one of the earliest pieces in which Rameau introduced clarinets and these are at once heard to great effect in the brilliant overture, whose horn writing sometimes foreshadows Gluck. It's a splendid *pièce d'occasion* which many readers will find sufficient enticement to explore further. A captivating programme.

Naïs – Orchestral Suites. Zoroastre – Orchestral Suites
Orchestra of the Eighteenth Century / Frans Brüggen
Glossa GCD921106 (64' · DDD) Recorded 1998, 2000
   F

No corner of the operatic repertory offers a greater wealth of freestanding orchestral dances than the French Baroque, and no composer

wrote such a rich and enjoyable array of them as Rameau, that master blender of melodic inspiration, rhythmic irresistibility and orchestral colour. While Rameau's dances tend to be integrated into the action more than most, you do not really need to study the plots of these operas too much to enjoy the music they deliver. In the end the music is just there to be enjoyed, and in any case Rameau himself was not always that particular; those familiar with his harpsichord pieces will recognise a few old friends wearing hastily chosen new clothes.

As for the performances, little needs to be said about them save that they meet the Orchestra of the Eighteenth Century's normal high standards – impressively weighted sound, tight ensemble and excellent style – and are all the more admirable for being recorded live in concert, as usual.

Pièces de clavecin en concerts

Pièces de clavecin en concerts
Trevor Pinnock *hpd* **Rachel Podger** *vn* **Jonathan Manson** *va da gamba*
Channel Classics CCS19098 (67' · DDD)   F**OO**

Rameau's 1741 collection represents a major and entirely logical departure from the trio sonata and suite traditions that had held sway in Western European chamber music since the beginning of the 17th century. Rameau's textures are uniquely complex, demanding of the players a heightened awareness of their role in the musical texture at hand.

These are balanced and refreshingly musical performances that will draw you back again and again to savour the gracefulness and the kaleidoscopic blending of instrumental colours they bring to the music. Pinnock's playing is lively and engaging, inspiring and inspired. His accuracy is breathtaking, his ornamentation jewel-like. Podger and Manson respond with clarity and shapely phrasing, even in the hair-raising 'Tambourins' (Troisième Concert).

A movement such as 'La Boucon' (Deuxième Concert) is made wonderfully languid, 'La Timide' (Troisième Concert) sinuous but never oppressively so; and 'La Pantomime' (Quatrième Concert) is altogether civilised. And 'La Marais' (Cinquième Concert), which concludes the CD, reminds us how well the tone of a violin and viol can blend when produced by players of this calibre.

Pièces de clavecin

Premier Livre de pièces de clavecin (1706) – Suite   **P**
in A minor. Pièces de clavecin (1724, rev 1731) – Suite in E minor, Suite in D
Sophie Yates *hpd*
Chandos Chaconne CHAN0659 (71' · DDD)   F**OO**

The release of a CD devoted to Rameau's harpsichord music is relatively rare. But it's less

Rameau, and much more French keyboard music in general, that suffers neglect from an over-cultivated image. However, if Rameau's music is highly allusive, it's also possessed of an immediacy that makes it approachable today. Sophie Yates's firmly grounded yet sensitive and spirited playing will quickly dispel any lingering reservations, and she writes with authority and charm in the accompanying booklet (and plays here a copy of a 1749 Goujon harpsichord made by Andrew Garlick).

Yates's astute selection from Rameau's output is bound to please. The first suite, in A minor, is from the book of *Pièces de clavecin* published shortly after Rameau arrived in Paris in 1706, and displays a youthful brilliance that relies heavily on ornamentation (as, for example, in the Allemande 1 and the Courante) and, delightfully, occasionally reveals a certain provincialism – although Rameau never travelled to Italy, he clearly made certain assumptions about life there: his 'La Vénitienne' makes particular allusion to the beggars' bagpipe and hurdy-gurdy.

The second and third suites, from his later book of 1724 (rev 1731), are altogether more stylish and sophisticated. The E minor Suite begins sedately and with the gravitas befitting an Allemande, but is otherwise shot through with fashionable, pastoral *rondeaux*, and includes two of Rameau's best-known party pieces, 'Le rappel des oiseaux' and 'Tambourin'. The D minor Suite amuses with *pièces de caractère* (the flirtatious 'La follette', the devious 'Le lardon' and the pathetic 'La boiteuse') and amazes with the virtuosity of 'Les tourbillons' and 'Les Cyclopes'. But only a player of Yates's calibre can address the musical subtleties of 'Les soupirs', the deceptive 'Les niais de Sologne' and the sensuous 'L'entretien des muses'. A tour de force in every sense.

Premier livre de pièces de clavecin. Pieces de Ⓟ
clavecin en concerts. Nouvelles suites de pièces de
clavecin. Les petits marteaux de M Rameau.
La Dauphine
Christophe Rousset hpds
L'Oiseau-Lyre ② 425 886-2OH2 (129' · DDD)
Recorded 1989   ⒻⓄⓄⓄ

This recording of Rameau's solo harpsichord music outdistances most of the competition. Rousset doesn't include everything Rameau wrote for the instrument, but he does play all the music in the principal collections of 1706, 1724 and c1728, as well as *La Dauphine*. Rousset's phrasing is graceful and clearly articulated, the inflexions gently spoken and the rhythmic pulse all that one might wish for. Most tempos are well judged and the playing admirably attentive to detail and delightfully animated. Only occasionally does he just miss the mark with speeds that are uncomfortably brisk and lacking that choreographic poise that's such a vital ingredient in French Baroque music. However, when he's at his strongest he's

irresistible, and this is how we find him in 'Les niais de Sologne' and its variations, the reflective 'L'entretien des Muses', the animated 'Les cyclopes', 'La poule', 'L'enharmonique' and the dazzling A minor Gavotte and variations. In these and in many other of the pieces, too, his impeccable taste and seemingly effortless virtuosity provide the listener with constant and intense delight. The quality of the recording is ideal, as are the two instruments Rousset plays.

Motets

Deus noster refugium. In convertendo.   Ⓟ
Quam dilecta
Sophie Daneman, Noémi Rime sops **Paul Agnew**
ten **Nicolas Rivenq** bar **Nicolas Cavallier** bass
Les Arts Florissants / William Christie
Erato 4509-96967-2 (70' · DDD) Recorded 1994. Texts
and translations included   ⒻⓄⓄⓄ

All three motets date from relatively early in Rameau's career, before he had really made a name for himself, yet all show to a certain extent some of the characteristics that 20 years or so later would so thrillingly illuminate his operas. *Deus noster refugium*, for instance, features impressive depictions of nature in turmoil that would not sound out of place in *Hippolyte et Aricie*, and all three begin with long, expressive solos not unlike the opening of an act from a *tragédie-lyrique*. *Quam dilecta* does sound a little more 'churchy' than the others, with its impressive, rather Handelian double fugue, but *In convertendo* – a work which Rameau heavily revised well into his operatic Indian summer in 1751 – absolutely reeks of the theatre.

Drop anyone familiar with the composer's operas into the middle of this piece, and surely only its Latin text would give away that this is church music. It comes as no surprise to find Christie going to town on this dramatic element. The slightly dry acoustic of the Radio France studio is a help, as are the forceful, penetrating qualities of the solo and choral singers. But it's Christie's command of gesture, pacing and contrast which really gives these performances such an invigorating character.

Castor et Pollux

Castor et Pollux   Ⓟ
Howard Crook ten Castor **Jérôme Corréas** bass
Pollux **Agnès Mellon** sop Télaïre **Véronique Gens**
sop Phebe **René Schirrer** bar Mars, Jupiter **Sandrine
Piau** sop Venus, Happy Spirit, Planet **Mark Padmore**
ten Love, High Priest **Claire Brua** sop Minerve
Sophie Daneman sop Follower of Hebe, Celestial
Pleasure **Adrian Brand** ten First Athlete **Jean-
Claude Sarragosse** bass Second Athlete
Les Arts Florissants / William Christie
Harmonia Mundi ③ HMC90 1435/7 (173' · DDD)
Recorded 1992. Notes, text and translation included
                                              ⒻⓄ

Extracts available on HMA195 1501   Ⓑ

Castor et Pollux was Rameau's second *tragédie en musique*. Its first performance was in October 1737, but the opera was greeted with only moderate enthusiasm. It was only with the composer's thoroughly revised version of 1754 that it enjoyed the popularity that it deserved. The revision tautened a drama which had never been weak, but it dispensed with a very beautiful Prologue. Christie and Les Arts Florissants perform Rameau's first version, complete with Prologue. The librettist, Pierre-Joseph Bernard, was one of the ablest writers with whom Rameau collaborated and his text for *Castor et Pollux* has been regarded by some as the best of 18th-century French opera. Bernard focuses on the fraternal love of the 'heavenly twins' and specifically on the generosity with which Pollux renounces his immortality so that Castor may be restored to life. Christie's production was staged at Aix-en-Provence in the summer of 1991 and recorded by Harmonia Mundi a year later. This performance realises the element of tragedy, and Christie's singers sound very much at home with French declamation. A very beautiful score, affectionately and perceptively interpreted.

Dardanus

Dardanus   Ⓟ
John Mark Ainsley *ten* Dardanus **Véronique Gens** *sop* Iphise **Mireille Delunsch** *sop* Venus **Françoise Masset** *sop* Cupid, Pleasure, Phrygian Woman **Magdalena Kožená** *mez* Shepherdess, Phrygian Woman, A Dream **Jean-François Lombard** *counterten* A Dream **Russell Smythe** *bar* Teucer **Jean-Louis Bindi** *bass* Phrygian **Jean-Philippe Courtis** *bass* Isménor **Laurent Naouri** *bass* Anténor **Marcos Pujol** *bass* A Dream **Choeur des Musiciens du Louvre; Les Musiciens du Louvre / Marc Minkowski**
Archiv Produktion ② 463 476-2AH2 (156' · DDD)
Recorded live 1998. Text and translation included
    Ⓕ●

Between the Paris première of *Dardanus* in 1739 and its first revival in 1744, Rameau and his librettist revised the work so much that to combine its two versions is near impossible. Though the dramatic problems in the score perhaps remain insurmountable, for a recording a conductor can choose whichever version has the better music. For Minkowski, that's the 1739 original, but he can't resist importing a few numbers from 1744, even if most are relatively unimportant. The exception is the superbly intense monologue 'Lieux funestes' for Dardanus in chains, which here resurfaces at the opening of Act 4. Minkowski describes it as 'the finest *haute-contre* aria ever written'.

Dardanus, son of Jupiter, is in love with Iphise, the daughter of his enemy Teucer. Iphise is in fact promised to Teucer's ally Anténor, and much of the action concerns his and Dardanus's rivalry and Iphise's anguish. There's much use of the supernatural, something for which the opera was criticised in its day and which prompted its revision. There's a sea-monster, and the scene in which Anténor and Dardanus fight with it provides one of the more convincingly performed passages of dialogue on this recording, a significant point because ensemble acting is actually one of the least successful areas. This is a recording of a concert performance, and misses the vital spark of dramatic continuity and urgency of performers having lived their parts on stage. Laurent Naouri turns in a vivid performance as the hapless Anténor, Véronique Gens is noble and moving as the love-torn Iphise, and Mireille Delunsch is a powerful Venus, but the remaining singers, though vocally strong enough (especially Ainsley and Kožená), often struggle to bring their characters to life. What we get instead is more a series of splendid highlights. And then there are the dances, always such an enjoyable feature of Rameau's scores. Minkowski conducts with an appropriate mixture of drive and tenderness, and is rewarded by responsive and sound playing and singing from his orchestra and chorus.

Les fêtes d'Hébé

Les fêtes d'Hébé   Ⓟ
Sophie Daneman *sop* Hébé, Une Naïde, Eglé **Gaëlle Méchaly** *sop* L'amour **Paul Agnew** *ten* Momus, Le ruisseau, Lycurgue **Sarah Connolly** *mez* Sapho, Iphise **Jean-Paul Fouchécourt** *ten* Thélème, L'oracle, Mercure **Luc Coadou** *bass* Alcée **Laurent Slaars** *bar* Hymas **Matthieu Lécroart** *bar* Le fleuve **Maryseult Wieczorek** *mez* Une Lacédémonienne, Une bergère **Thierry Félix** *bar* Tirtée, Eurilas **Les Arts Florissants / William Christie**
Erato ② 3984-21064-2 (148' · DDD) Notes, text and translation included
    Ⓕ○○○

🌞 Rameau produced one of his most engaging scores for *Les fêtes d'Hébé*. The entertainment comprises a prologue and three *entrées*. All is prefaced with a captivating two-movement Overture whose playful second section has much more in common with a Neapolitan *sinfonia* than a traditional opera overture in the French mould. The dances belong to one of the composer's fruitiest vintages and Christie has capitalised upon this with a sizeable band which includes, where appropriate, a section of musettes, pipes and drums. The singers are carefully chosen for their contrasting vocal timbres and the line-up, by and large, is strong.

The leading roles in each of the opera's four sections are fairly evenly distributed between Sophie Daneman, Sarah Connolly, Jean-Paul Fouchécourt, Paul Agnew and Thierry Félix. The first three of this group are consistently engaging; their feeling for theatre, and their intuitive ability to seek out those aspects of Rameau's vocal writing which enliven it, seldom fail, and they bring considerable charm to their performances. Agnew, too, is on strong form though in the lower end of his vocal tessitura, required for the role of Momus in the Prologue, he sounds less secure than in his more accustomed *haute-contre* range. That can be heard to wonderful effect elsewhere and, above all, in a duet for a Stream and a Naiad (first *Entrée*) in which he's joined by Daneman. This beguiling little love-song is proclaimed with innocent fervour and tenderness. Félix has a rounded warmth and resonance and his occasional weakness of poorly focused tone has here been largely overcome. *Les fêtes d'Hébé* contains a wealth of inventive, instrumentally colourful and evocative dances. Small wonder that audiences loved it so much in the 1720s: with music of such vital originality, how could it be otherwise? Christie and Les Arts Florissants have possibly never been on crisper, more disciplined form than here, revelling in Rameau's beguiling pastoral images, tender and high-spirited in turn. A ravishing entertainment, from start to finish.

Hippolyte et Aricie

Hippolyte et Aricie   **P**
Mark Padmore *ten* Hippolyte **Anne-Maria Panzarella** *sop* Aricie **Lorraine Hunt** *sop* Phèdre **Laurent Naouri** *bass* Thésée **Eirian James** *mez* Diane **Gaëlle Mechaly** *sop* L'Amour, Female Sailor **Nathan Berg** *bass* Jupiter, Pluton, Neptune **Katalin Károlyi** *mez* Oenone **Yann Beuron** *ten* Arcas Mercure **François Piolino** *ten* Tisiphone **Christopher Josey** *ten* Fate I **Matthieu Lécroart** *bar* Fate II **Bertrand Bontoux** *bass* Fate III **Mireille Delunsch** *sop* High Priestess **Patricia Petibon** *sop* Priestess, Shepherdess **Les Arts Florissants / William Christie**
Erato ③ 0630-15517-2 (182' · DDD) Notes, text and translation included   **F OOO**

William Christie adheres throughout to the 1733 original (Rameau revised the start of Act 2 in 1757), in so doing opening up some passages previously omitted. He uses an orchestra with a good string weight and it plays with security both of ensemble and intonation, and with splendidly crisp rhythms. Despite the opera's title, the main characters are Theseus and his queen Phaedra, whose guilty passion for his son Hippolytus precipitates the tragedy. Phaedra is strongly cast with a passionate Lorraine Hunt who's particularly impressive in the superb aria, 'Cruelle mère des amours', which begins Act 3. Throughout the opera, one is also struck by the profusion of invention, the unobtrusive contrapuntal skill, the charm and colour of the instrumentation and the freedom allotted to the orchestra. The work's final scene, for example, set in a woodland, is filled with an enchanting atmosphere, ending, after the customary chaconne, with 'Rossignols amoureux' (delightfully sung by Patricia Petibon). Anna-Maria Panzarella makes an appealingly youthful Aricia, and Mark Padmore is easily the best Hippolytus on record. Pains have been taken with the whole cast over the expressive delivery

of words and neatness of ornamentation; and production values such as the proper perspective for the entry of the crowd rejoicing at Theseus's return have been well considered. All told, this is one of Christie's best achievements.

Zoroastre

Zoroastre   **P**
Mark Padmore *ten* Zoroastre **Nathan Berg** *bar* Abramane **Gaëlle Méchaly** *sop* Amélite **Anna Maria Panzarella** *mez* Erinice **Matthieu Lécroart** *bar* Zopire, God of Revenge **François Bazola** *bass* Narbanor **Eric Martin-Bonnet** *bass* Oramasès Ariman **Stéphanie Revidat** *sop* Céphie **Les Arts Florissants / William Christie**
Erato ③ 0927-43182-2 (157' · DDD) Notes, text and translation included   **F OO**

To describe *Zoroastre* as one of Rameau's most uncompromising music-dramas may seem strange when you consider that when it was revived in 1756, seven years after its première had met a rather lukewarm reception, it was in a heavily revised version in which the love interest had been stepped up. The story is of the endless struggle between good and evil which dominates the religion Zoroastre himself has founded.

Rameau's prime concern isn't with Zoroastrianism, but the elemental magic scenes and the intensely human emotions of love, jealousy, vengeance and rage thrown up by the story. Even so, there's a concentrated seriousness of intent about this work which sets it apart from standard *tragédie lyrique*. The French practice of blurring the distinction between recitatives and arias is intensified, so that choruses and snatches of melody fly past in a breathless, flexible flow of incident. And Rameau's music conjures massive dramatic contrasts, ranging from ineffably tender love scenes for Zoroastre and Amélite in Acts 3 and 5 to the almost oppressive demonic power of the subterranean incantations of Act 4, led by the strongly drawn characters of Abramane and Erinice.

The cast is in the best Les Arts Florissants tradition of dramatic commitment and intelligent treatment of text. Mark Padmore has the perfect high tenor for Zoroastre, able to charm in tender moments yet rage in the confrontational scenes without losing any of its essential sweetness, while Nathan Berg makes a strong and fearsome-sounding Abramane. Even more impressive, however, are the two principal sopranos: Anna Maria Panzarella gives her all as the tormented Erinice, while Gaëlle Méchaly is wonderfully bright and clear as Amélite. There are odd moments of vocal weakness among some of the other roles, but they cause no serious damage. The chorus and orchestra both perform for Christie with great vigour, the former contributing memorably to the underworld scenes, and the latter performing delightfully in the opera's many dances.

Opéra-ballets

Les Indes galantes   Ⓟ
Prologue: **Claron McFadden** sop Hébé **Jérôme
Corréas** bar Bellone **Isabelle Poulenard** sop
L'Amour, Le Turc généreux: **Nicolas Rivenq** bass
Osman **Miriam Ruggieri** sop Emilie; **Howard Crook**
ten Valère Les Incas du Pérou: **Bernard Deletré** bass
Huascar **Isabelle Poulenard** Phanie **Jean-Paul
Fouchécourt** ten Carlos

Les fleurs: **Fouchécourt** Tacmas **Corréas** Ali
Sandrine Piau sop Zaïre **Noémi Rime** sop Fatime
Les sauvages: **Rivenq** Adario **Crook** Damon **Deletré**
Don Alvar **McFadden** Zima
Les Arts Florissants / William Christie
Harmonia Mundi ③ HMC90 1367/9 (203' · DDD)
Notes, text and translation included   Ⓕⓞ

Les Indes galantes was Rameau's first *opéra-ballet*,
completed in 1735. *Opéra-ballet* usually consisted of a prologue and anything between three
and five *entrées* or acts. There was no continuously developing plot but instead various sections might be linked by a general theme, often
hinted at in the title. Such is the case with *Les
Indes galantes* whose linking theme derives from
a contemporary taste for the exotic and the
unknown. Following a prologue come four
entrées, 'Le Turc généreux', 'Les Incas du
Pérou', 'Les fleurs' and 'Les sauvages'. William
Christie and Les Arts Florissants give a characteristically warm-blooded performance of one
of Rameau's most approachable and endearing
stage works. Christie's control of diverse forces
– his orchestra consists of some 46 players – his
dramatic pacing of the music, his recognition of
Rameau's uniquely distinctive instrumental
palette and his feeling for gesture and rhythm
contribute towards making this a lively and satisfying performance. The choir is alert and the
orchestra a worthy partner in respect of clear
textures and technical finesse; this can be readily
appreciated in the spaciously laid out and tautly
constructed orchestral Chaconne which concludes the work. The music is recorded in a
sympathetic acoustic.

Einojuhani Rautavaara   Finnish b1928

*Rautavaara studied with Merikanto at the Helsinki
Academy (1948-52), where from 1966 he taught,
and with Persichetti at the Julliard School (1955-
6). His large output shows a variety of stylistic
resource (Russian nationalists, Hindemith and
advanced serialism) and he has written in many genres; notable is The True and False Unicorn (1971)
for chorus, orchestra and tape.*   **GROVE**music

Flute Concerto, Op 63

Flute Concerto, Op 63, 'Dances with the Winds'[a].
Anadyomene. On the Last Frontier[b]
[a]**Patrick Gallois** fl [b]**Finnish Philharmonic Choir;**
Helsinki Philharmonic Orchestra / Leif Segerstam
Ondine ODE921-2 (59' · DDD)   Ⓕⓞ

Anadyomene (1968) suggests a Turner canvas
recast in sound. It opens restlessly among undulating pastels, the tone darkens further, there
are brief comments from flute and bass clarinet,
the brass prompts a swelling climax, then the
mood gradually becomes more animated before
we're ferried back whence we came. It's 'a homage to Aphrodite, born of the sea foam, the goddess of love', and a very appealing one at that.
The colourful Flute Concerto *Dances with the
Winds* is a more extrovert piece with Nielsen as
a fairly certain forebear. It shares its material
between ordinary flute, bass flute, alto flute and
piccolo. The action-packed opening movement
withstands some fairly aggressive interjections
from the brass, the brief second movement
recalls the shrill sound world of fifes and drums;
the elegiac *Andante moderato* offers plenty of jam
for the alto flute, and the finale's striking mood-
swings have just a hint of Bernsteinian exuberance. Rautavaara's prompt for *On the Last Frontier* (1997) was an early encounter with *The
Narrative of Arthur Gordon Pym* by Edgar Allan
Poe. He calls it 'a seafaring yarn in the typical
boys' reading mould' and responds accordingly
with a 24-minute slice of descriptive musical
reportage, not of Poe's exact 'narrative', but of
an imagined *Last Frontier* based on ideas from
the story's closing section. It's an eventful,
majestic, slow-burning tone-poem, nourished
further by some distinctive instrumental solos
and with telling use of a full-blown chorus. No
texts are provided, and yet the aura of unexplored maritime depths and a sense of mystery
associated with them carry their own wordless
narrative. All three works are expertly performed and exceptionally well recorded.

Piano Concerto No 3

Piano Concerto No 3, 'Gift of Dreams'[a]. Autumn
Gardens
**Helsinki Philharmonic Orchestra / Vladimir
Ashkenazy** [a]pf
Ondine ODE950-2 (68' · DDD)   Ⓕⓞ

Autumn Gardens extends the Rautavaarian experience at least one step beyond the Seventh
Symphony. You sense it especially in the animated finale, which begins *giocoso e leggiero*
before a Baroque-style, four-note figure slowly
makes its presence felt. The figure is first heard
on the bassoon, then shifts timbre and focus
(timpani and bells play a crucial role later on),
inspiring the strings to lyrical heights. The
piquantly scored first movement conjures a gentle beating of wings, with glowing modulations
that sometimes darken, though they never
cloud the issue. The reflective central movement follows without a break.

The Third Piano Concerto (1998) is stronger
meat. More meditative than its predecessors
though visited by some cluster-like dissonances,

it seems to take its principal stylistic cue from the middle movement of Bartók's Second Piano Concerto. The opening string chord motive is simple, austere, the piano writing bold or decorative rather than overtly pianistic. As a whole, it's cast vaguely in the manner of Delius or Debussy, more an orchestral tone-poem with piano than a display piece. The most striking movement is the second, which incorporates some fairly harsh brass writing and memorably beautiful closing pages. The *Energico* finale calls in the big guns and is well served by Ondine's recording team, but one could imagine a more forceful performance. Otherwise, things go well. The disc closes with an interview, a disarmingly natural slice of dialogue where the composer relates to Ashkenazy how he views his works as received phenomena. That, for the most part, is precisely how his music sounds – like audible episodes drawn from nature, messages that, in a world seduced by banal artifice, are all too easily ignored.

Cantus arcticus, Op 61

Cantus arcticus, Op 61 (Concerto for Birds and Orchestra) with taped birdsong. Piano Concerto No 1, Op 45ª. Symphony No 3, Op 20
ªLaura Mikkola pf **Royal Scottish National Orchestra / Hannu Lintu**
Naxos 8 554147 (74' · DDD)   Ⓢ❍

No other new music stands to benefit more from extensive exposure, not so much because of its quality (which is beyond question), as because of an almost tangible connection with nature, than that by Rautavaara. One constantly senses the joy of a man alone with the elements: awe-struck, contented, inspired. Bird-song comes from all directions, literally in the 'Concerto for birds and orchestra' or *Cantus arcticus*, which sets taped bird-song against a rustic orchestral backdrop. The tape blends well with the music and is very atmospheric. The young Finnish conductor Hannu Lintu directs a fine performance. The First Piano Concerto and Third Symphony (out of seven) receive good performances, most notably the Brucknerian Symphony, an impressive and often dramatic work that begins and ends in the key of D minor. The orchestration incorporates four Wagner tubas, though some of the finest material is also the quietest. The slow movement is sullen but haunting, the *Scherzo* occasionally suggestive of Nielsen or Martinů and the finale brings the parallels with Bruckner fully within earshot. The First Piano Concerto has a brilliance and immediacy that should please orchestral adventurers and piano *aficionados*. The solo writing employs clusters and much filigree fingerwork, but it's the noble, chorale-like second movement that leaves the strongest impression. Laura Mikkola gives a good performance. Naxos gives a full sound picture and overall, this is an excellent CD, concisely annotated by the composer.

Symphony No 7, 'Angel of Light'

Symphony No 7, 'Angel of Light'. Annunciations
Kari Jussila org **Helsinki Philharmonic Orchestra / Leif Segerstam**
Ondine ODE869-2 (65' · DDD)   Ⓕ❍

The Seventh Symphony's opening *Tranquillo* evokes a calm though powerful atmosphere, with many Sibelian points of reference, especially in recognisable echoes of the *Largo* fourth movement from Sibelius's Fourth Symphony, whereas the closing *Pesante-cantabile* is more in line with the symphonic world of Hovhaness. The Angel idea originates in a series of works (*Angels and Visitations* and *Angel of Dusk*, for instance), the reference being to 'an archetype, one of mankind's oldest traditions and perennial companions'. This Jungian axis is reflected in monolithic chords, ethereal harmonic computations (invariably broad and high-reaching) and an unselfconscious mode of musical development. Readers schooled in the more contemplative works of Górecki, Pärt and Tavener will likely respond to this spatially generous essay, though Rautavaara's language is more a celebration of nature than any specific religious ritual. Comparisons with the *Annunciations*(for organ, brass quintet, wind orchestra and percussion) find the earlier work far harsher in tone, much more demanding technically (it calls for a formidable organ virtuoso) and more radical in its musical language. The style ranges from the primeval drone that opens the work through canon, 'bird forest' activity and the novel effect of having the 'notes of a dense chord weirdly circulating in the room' when the organ motor is switched off. Kari Jussila rises to the various challenges with what sounds like genuine enthusiasm (his fast fingerwork is amazing) while Leif Segerstam and his orchestra exploit the tonal drama of both works. The recordings are warm and spacious.

String Quartets

String Quartets Nos 1 & 2. String Quintet, 'Unknown Heavens'
Jan-Erik Gustafsson vc **Jean Sibelius Quartet**
(Yoshiko Arai-Kimanen, Jukka Pohjola vns Matti Hirvikangas va Seppo Kimanen vc)
Ondine ODE909-2 (62' · DDD)   Ⓕ

Here we encounter not one Rautavaara, but three: the fledgling student captivated by folklore; the dodecaphonic zealot stretching the expressive potential of 'the system'; and the triumphant melodist basking in his own unique brand of harmonic complexity. The stylistic leap from the Second Quartet to the Quintet, or *Unknown Heavens* is more a matter of tone than temperament. All three works are ceaselessly active, the First (1952) being perhaps the leanest, and the last (1997) the richest in texture. *Unknown Heavens* takes its name from an earlier work for male chorus, which Rautavaara quotes, initially in the second bar of the first movement ('when the second violin answers the question opposed by the first,' as Rautavaara writes), many times thereafter, and then significantly revised at the start of the fourth movement. The third begins as a cello duet, sure justification of why five players are employed where the Kuhmo Music Festival originally commissioned a piece for four. 'The work seemed to acquire a will of its own,' writes Rautavaara. The equally well-performed string quartets are stylistically rather more challenging. The First Quartet plays for just over 11 minutes and inhabits a mildly rustic world roughly akin to Kodály. Best here is the *Andante*'s haunting coda, whereas the 1958 Second Quartet is at its most inventive for the faster second and fourth movements. The current Rautavaara is more relaxed, more contemplative, wiser and softer-grained than his former self. He seems happier reflecting nature than organising abstract patterns: you sense that the Quintet is authentically self-expressive, whereas the quartets speak interestingly about nothing in particular. The recordings are full-bodied and well balanced.

Piano Works

Etudes, Op 42. Icons, Op 6. Partita, Op 34. Piano Sonatas – No 1, 'Christus und die Fischer', Op 50; No 2, 'The Fire Sermon', Op 64. Seven Preludes, Op 7
Laura Mikkola *pf*
Naxos 8 554292 (61' · DDD)   Ⓕ

The most interesting aspect of hearing piano music by a composer known primarily for his orchestral work is in spotting those inimitable harmonic fingerprints that help define his musical personality. Rautavaara's piano music is full of tell-tale signs, even in an early work like the Op 7 *Preludes*, where he indulged a sort of clandestine protest against the 'neo-classical' confines he experienced in Helsinki and America. Rautavaara was studying with Copland at the time but chose to keep his *Preludes* to himself. And yet it's Copland's Piano Sonata that spontaneously comes to mind during the austere opening of his 'The Black Madonna of Blakernaya' from *Icons*, perhaps the most striking of all his solo piano works. The translucent colours in 'The Baptism of Christ' make a profound effect, as does the serenity of 'The Holy Women at the Sepulchre'. Aspects of 'angels' seem prophetically prevalent – whether consciously or not – in the *Etudes* of 1969. Each piece tackles a different interval: thirds in the first, sevenths in the second, then tritones, fourths, seconds and fifths. The third is reminiscent of Messiaen, and the fifth of Bartók, but Rautavaara's guiding hand is everywhere in evidence. Spirituality is an invariable presence, especially in the two piano sonatas, though the Second ends with an unexpected bout of contrapuntal brutality. Perhaps the most instantly appealing track is the brief but touching central movement of the three-

and-a-half minute *Partita*, Op 34, with its gentle whiffs of Bartók. Laura Mikkola plays all 28 movements with obvious conviction. Naxos's recorded sound is excellent.

A Requiem in Our Time

A Requiem in Our Time, Op 3[a]. Playgrounds for Angels[b]. Tarantará[c]. Independence Fanfare[d]. A Soldier's Mass[e]. Octet for Winds[f]. Hymnus[g]
[f]**Petri Alanko** *fl* [f]**Jussi Jaatinen** *ob* [f]**Harri Mäki** *cl* [f]**Otto Virtanen** *bn* [f]**Esa Tapani**, [f]**Mika Paajanen** *hns* [d]**Jouko Harjanne**, [cg]**Pasi Pirinen**, [d]**Jorma Rautakoski**, [df]**Aki Välimäki** *tpts* [df]**Valtteri Malmivirta** *tbn* [g]**Seppo Murto** *org* [abe]**Finnish Brass Symphony / Hannu Lintu**
Ondine ODE957-2 (62' · DDD)   Ⓕ Ⓞ

There's little hint here of the escapist aura that frames most of Rautavaara's recent orchestral work. Latest to arrive is the atmospheric *Hymnus* for trumpet and organ, composed in 1998 for the Hampstead and Highgate Festival. *Hymnus* opens and closes in darkness, courting sunlight for a faster central section and couched in a language that's at once florid and austere. Six years earlier Rautavaara had produced a cantata in celebration of the 75th Anniversary of Finland's independence, and his unusually expressive, half-minute *Independence Fanfare* is fashioned from the same work's concluding hymn. Solo trumpet is represented by the ruminative but technically demanding *Tarantará*, superbly played – as is *Hymnus* – by Pasi Pirinen.

Rautavaara calls *A Requiem in Our Time* for brass and percussion his 'breakthrough work' in that it won him an international composition competition in Cincinnati. That was back in 1953, before his studies with Copland, and the musical language seems to give at least half a wink in Vaughan Williams's direction. It's a rather beautiful piece, more sorrowful than mournful and with some ingeniously crafted faster music.

A Soldier's Mass (1968) is the *Requiem*'s nearest musical relation. Rautavaara thinks of it as a 'companion work', though the forces called for are more generous and the overall spirit is far more extrovert. The 1962 *Octet* subscribes to an expressively varied dodecaphony, and the superb 12-minute *Playground for Angels* (1981) is a sort of musical hide-and-seek with lurking low brass and much quick-witted instrumental interplay. It reminds one at times of Janáček's *Capriccio*. It's a brilliant piece, fun to hear and probably just as much fun to play. The Finnish Brass Symphony does Rautavaara proud and Ondine's sound quality is spectacularly fine.

Vigilia

Vigilia
Pia Freund *sop* **Lilli Paasikivi** *mez* **Topi Lehtipuu** *ten* **Petteri Salomaa** *bar* **Jyrki Korhonen** *bass*
Finnish Radio Chamber Choir / Tino Nuoranne

Ondine ODE910-2 (64' · DDD) Text and translation included Ⓕ❍

Although grounded in the faith of the Finnish Orthodox Church, *Vigilia* somehow manages to excavate a spiritual path beyond the confines of denominational dogma. Rautavaara's delicious blend of ancient and modern modes is pointedly exemplified in the 'First Katisma', where soprano and contralto, then tenor and baritone, proclaim 'Blessed is the man that walketh not in the counsel of the ungodly'. There, the harmonic drift is decidedly 'post-Renaissance', whereas the 'Alleluias' that follow update to 'post-Romantic' and the subsequent assurance that 'the Lord knoweth the way of the righteous' brings us on line with the wistful, nature-loving Rautavaara of the Seventh Symphony and *Cantus arcticus*. Rautavaara's employment, or rather absorption, of ancient modes runs roughly parallel with Steve Reich's in works such as *Tehillim* and *Proverb*, though by contrast with Reich, harmonic colouring takes its lead from poetic imagery rather than from the sounds of specific words. *Vigilia* uses variation technique to impressive effect; it's a refreshingly open-hearted piece, one that – whether sombre or celebratory, traditional or innovative – grants ritual narrative a vibrant voice and should earn its composer wide-scale recognition. The performance is beautifully sung and the recording bold and realistic.

Aleksis Kivi

Aleksis Kivi
Jorma Hynninen bar Aleksis Kivi **Lasse Pöysti** spkr
August Ahlqvist; Eeva-Liisa Saarinen mez Charlotta
Helena Juntunen sop Hilda **Gabriel Suovanen** bar
Young Aleksis **Marcus Groth** buffo JL Runeberg **Lassi
Virtanen** ten Mikko Vilkastus **Jaako Kietikko** bass
Uncle Sakeri **Jyväskylä Sinfonia / Markus Lehtinen**
Ondine ② ODE1000-2D (98' · DDD) Libretto and
translation included Ⓕ

Idyll turned to nightmare, optimism to disillusionment, creative fruitfulness to barren schizophrenia and premature death. The tragic fate of the founder of Finnish-language literature has haunted Rautavaara ever since his youth. The opera *Aleksis Kivi* (1995-6) was the melodious crystallisation of a lifetime's pondering. Kivi (1834-72) was active while Swedish words still predominated in Finnish literature, the Finnish poet Johan Ludvig Runeberg having been the best-known Swedish-language exponent of the genre. Kivi's descent from lyrical flights of pastoral fancy to mental derangement was caused in part by damning assessments of his work from the poet and aesthetician August Ahlqvist, the only speaking role in the opera. Ahlqvist is portrayed here by the actor Lasse Pöysti, whose rhythmically inflected recitation is utterly bewitching. Musically *Aleksis Kivi* calls on a varied array of styles. The Prologue depicts Kivi as despondent, despairing and deranged, the

music dark and grainy, with a reptilian clarinet in the foreground and a skilfully deployed synthesiser. The scoring is economical throughout (strings, clarinets, percussion) but those who gravitate most readily to his 'angel' orchestral works will likely respond best to the First Act, music filled with mellow light which reflects, in its rich, constantly shifting hues, the protagonist's inspirational flights. The performance is consistently good, the mezzo Eeva-Liisa Saarinen excelling as Charlotta. Confidently conducted, keenly played and vividly recorded, *Aleksis Kivi* is a powerful narrative written with the kind of descriptive facility that Bartók employed for *Bluebeard's Castle*.

Maurice Ravel
French 1875-1937

Ravel's father's background was Swiss and his mother's Basque, but he was brought up in Paris, where he studied at the Conservatoire, 1889-95, returning in 1897 for further study with Fauré and Gédalge. In 1893 he met Chabrier and Satie, both of whom were influential. A decade later he was an established composer, at least of songs and piano pieces, working with luminous precision in a style that could imitate Lisztian bravura (Jeux d'eau) or Renaissance calm (Pavane pour une infante défunte); there was also the String Quartet, somewhat in the modal style of Debussy's but more ornately instrumented. However, he five times failed to win the Prix de Rome (1900-1905) and left the Conservatoire to continue as a freelance musician.

During the next decade he was at his most productive. There was a rivalry with Debussy but Ravel's taste for sharply defined ideas and closed formal units was entirely his own, as was the grand virtuosity of much of his piano music from this period, notably the cycles Miroirs and Gaspard de la nuit. Many works show his fascination with things temporally or geographically distant, with moods sufficiently alien to be objectively drawn: these might be historical musical styles, as in the post-Schubertian Valses nobles et sentimentales, or the imagination of childhood, as in Ma mère l'oye, the East (Shéhérazade) or on Spain (Rapsodie espagnole, the comic opera L'heure espagnole) or even ancient Greece in the languorous ballet Daphnis et Chloé, written for Diaghilev.

Diaghilev's Ballets Russes were also important in introducing him to Stravinsky, with whom he collaborated on a version of Mussorgsky's Khovanshchina, and whose musical development he somewhat paralleled during the decade or so after The Rite of Spring. The set of three Mallarmé songs with nonet accompaniment were written partly under the influence of Stravinsky's Japanese Lyrics and Schoenberg's Pierrot lunaire, and the two sonatas of the 1920s can be compared with Stravinsky's abstract works of the period in their harmonic astringency and selfconscious use of established forms.

However, Ravel's Le tombeau de Couperin predates Stravinsky's neo-classicism, and the pressure of musical history is perhaps felt most intensely in the ballet La valse where 3/4 rhythm develops into a

RAVEL PIANO CONCERTOS – IN BRIEF

Krystian Zimerman; London SO, Cleveland Orchestra / Pierre Boulez
DG 449 213-2GH (56' · DDD)　　　Ⓕ**OOO**

A *Gramophone* Award winner in 1999, this truly magnificent achievement enshrines musicianship of the highest calibre. Zimerman is on top form, his pianism quite astonishingly clear and precise and Boulez is a superb accompanist.

Louis Lortie; London SO / Frühbeck de Burgos
Chandos CHAN8773 (57' · DDD)　　　Ⓕ

Fine playing and rich, idiomatic accompaniment makes this a fine CD (the coupling is Fauré's *Ballade*). Lortie is best in the Concerto – his Left-Hand Concerto is slightly eccentric – but the sound he makes, and as captured by Chandos is most appealing.

Jean-Philippe Collard; French National Orchestra / Lorin Maazel
EMI 574749-2 (64' · DDD)　　　ⒷO

Another *Gramophone* Award winner – and the version to get if you're watching the pennies. Collard is on sparkling form, and Maazel is in his element in this music. There's real fizz here, and there are some generous solo piano works as coupling.

Anne Quéffelec; Strasbourg PO / Alain Lombard
Apex 8573 89232-2 (66' · ADD)　　　Ⓢ

Coupled with Debussy's *Fantaisie*, Anne Quéffelec gives thoughtful, very delicate performances of the two Ravel concertos and demonstrates why she is so highly regarded. Lombard accompanies sympathetically so if you're looking for these works and you're on a budget this makes a fine alternative to the Collard, more inward-looking, perhaps.

PIANO CONCERTO IN G

Martha Argerich; Berlin PO / Claudio Abbado
DG 447 438-2GGA (71' · ADD)　　　ⒻO

Coupled with a fiery Prokofiev Third Concerto, Argerch's G major Concerto is outstanding, with filligree-textured fingerwork, rhythmic vitality of crystal and a wonderful identification with the work's idiom. A magnificent performance.

Arturo Benedetti Michelangeli; Philharmonia / Ettore Gracis
EMI 567238-2 (47' · ADD)　　　ⓂOO

Simply the classic recording. Michelangeli demonstrates his total sympathy for the work. The Philharmonia on top form in this great disc from 1957. Coupled with Rachmaninov No 4, this is one of EMI's Great Recordings of the Century – and no one would surely question that accolade!

---

dance macabre: both these works, like many others, exist in both orchestral and piano versions, testifying to Ravel's superb technique in both media (in 1922 he applied his orchestral skills tellingly to Mussorgsky's Pictures at an Exhibition). Other postwar works return to some of the composer's obsessions: with the delights and dangers of the child's world (the sophisticated fantasy opera L'enfant et les sortilèges), Spanishness (Boléro and the songs for a projected Don Quixote film), and the exotic (Chansons madécasses). His last major effort was a pair of piano concertos, one exuberant and cosmopolitan (in G), the other (for left hand only) more darkly and sturdily single-minded. Ravel died after a long illness.
GROVEmusic

Piano Concertos

Piano Concerto in G[ab]. Piano Concerto for the Left Hand[ac]. Valses nobles et sentimentales (orch cpsr)[b]
[a]**Krystian Zimerman** pf [b]**Cleveland Orchestra,** [c]**London Symphony Orchestra / Pierre Boulez**
DG 449 213-2GH (56' · DDD) Recorded 1994　Ⓕ**OOO**

Zimerman's pianism is self-recommending. His trills in the first movement of the G major Concerto are to die for, his passagework in the finale crystal-clear, never hectic, always stylish. For their part Boulez and the Clevelanders are immaculate and responsive; they relish Ravel's neon-lit artificiality and moments of deliberate gaudiness. That goes equally for the *Valses nobles*, which have just about every nuance you'd want, and none you wouldn't. The recording is generous with ambience, to the point where some orchestral entries after big climaxes are blurred. Otherwise detail is razor-sharp and one of the biggest selling-points of the disc. Zimerman's humming may be a slight distraction for some listeners, especially in the Left-Hand Concerto, where you may not be always convinced that the LSO knew quite what it was supposed to do with the long notes of the main theme, and where there's a slight lack of tension in exchanges between piano and orchestra. There again, had the G major Concerto not been so wonderful those points might not have registered at all, for this is playing of no mean distinction. In the Left-Hand Concerto, Zimerman's phenomenal pianism sets its own agenda and brings its own rich rewards.

Orchestral Works

Boléro. Pavane pour une infante défunte. Daphnis et Chloé – Suite No 2. Ma mère l'oye – Pavane de la Belle au bois dormant; Les entretiens de la belle et la bête; Petit Poucet; Laideronnette, Impératrice des Pagodes; Apothéose: Le Jardin féerique
Cincinnati Symphony Orchestra / Paavo Järvi
Telarc CD80601 (63' · DDD)　　　Ⓕ**OOO**

Most of this disc is very enjoyable. Järvi is always in absolute control, and one or two moments of unscheduled *rubato*

in *La valse* can be forgiven, such was the tact and intelligence with which they were managed. Any conductor must balance the impulse to lilt *à la viennoise* against what appears to be Ravel's implicit instruction not to vary the tempo until around halfway. Järvi does it well and, notably, his speed for the return of the opening is spot on the original, not faster as so often happens.

His *Boléro* is on the quick side, but there's no feeling of scramble, and the only things to miss are the extra trombone slides from Ravel's disc, which unfortunately have never found their way into the score. The *Pavane* is lovely in all respects – steady but not stodgy – and the *Daphnis* suite has all the colour and warmth one could ask for. Just occasionally in *Ma mère l'oye* the balance isn't ideal: in the first movement the cor anglais momentarily obscures the clarinet, and in 'Laideronnette' the piccolo, too, is lost in its lower reaches. The only moment where Järvi's identification with the music seems to falter is with his handling of the 'Retenu/A tempo' marking leading into the final peroration of 'Le jardin féerique'. But these are small points to set against the quality of the whole.

Le tombeau de Couperin. Pavane pour une infante défunte. Ma mère l'oye. Une barque sur l'océan. Alborada del gracioso
Orchestra of the Opéra National de Lyon / Kent Nagano
Erato 0630-14331-2 (69' · DDD) Recorded 1994   Ⓕ**O**

The fairytale wonders and crystalline textures of *Ma mère l'oye* rarely fail to bring out the best in performers and sound engineers. And Nagano joins the score's other master magicians of the past decade, namely, Dutoit, Rattle and Boulez. But no consideration would be complete without putting into the frame Monteux's 1964 recording – it takes but a few seconds to hear 'through' a moderate degree of tape hiss to a group of crack musicians gathered around the revered *maître* and producing sublime chamber music, with the most finely gauged seeking out and savouring of expressive colour, character and period *charme*. Nagano enjoys perhaps the most present and tactile recorded sound of all available versions, with a fine bloom, if not quite the depth of the Dutoit or Boulez, or the focus for detail of the Rattle. Interpretatively, Nagano shares most with Rattle, preferring a wide variety of tempo; not as slow as him in Beauty's 'Pavane', though one might complain that 'Tom Thumb' suggests more movement than Nagano's tempo allows (he turns it into a dreamy woodland interlude). 'Pagodaland', by contrast, is more lively than usual, with the opening piccolo solo nicely inflected. Both the Boulez and Nagano discs offer *Une barque sur l'océan*, and Nagano's account is one of the most most gripping ever heard. It's a piece whose transcription tends to find more apology than advocacy among Ravel commentators, and is a less frequent inclusion among Ravel anthologies on disc. A pity, as its alternating gentle

sunlit sway (and what enchantment lies in the dappled detailing) and the huge waves of sound that arise from it are a gift to conductors who fancy themselves as Poseidon for eight minutes. The 'Prelude' of *Le tombeau de Couperin* is reminiscent of water music (an enchanted babbling brook?). Here Nagano eschews Dutoit's gentle rapids, facilitating more precise articulation and lovely colouring (wonderfully liquid woodwinds, so well caught by the recording). And in the 'Forlane', precise accentuation and articulation give the main theme a real lift. Questions of balance in *Le tombeau* between Baroque manners and romantic warmth tend to find different answers from different interpreters, and different expectations from listeners. And some may feel that Nagano's 'expressive' haltings in the central sections of the 'Forlane' and 'Rigaudon' are more affectation than affection. Still, it would be wrong to end with a complaint. This is a distinguished Ravel collection.

Daphnis et Chloé

Daphnis et Chloé. La valse
Berlin Radio Chorus; Berlin Philharmonic Orchestra / Pierre Boulez
DG 447 057-2GH (71minutes: DDD) Recorded 1993-4
Ⓕ**O**

Increasingly, for considering modern recordings of *Daphnis*, it seems you must banish memories of 1959 Monteux; put behind you the most playful, mobile, texturally diaphanous, rhythmically supple account of the score ever recorded; one that's uniquely informed by history and selfless conductorial wisdom. For some, Monteux's view may remain a rather moderate one – certainly in terms of basic tempo and basic dynamic range; and Ravel's score suggests tempos and dynamics which modern performances, and especially recordings, have more faithfully reproduced.

Boulez has acquired a wealth of experience of conductorial wisdom since his first New York recording of *Daphnis*. Here he has the Berlin Philharmonic Orchestra on top form to sustain and shape melody within some of his strikingly slow tempos (such as the opening, and Part 3's famous 'Daybreak'), and who remain 'composed' in his daringly fast ones (the 'Dance of the young girls around Daphnis' and the 'Danse guerrière' – one of the most exciting on disc). Just occasionally, you feel that there are parts of the work that interest him less than others. But anyone who doubts Boulez's ability to achieve, first, a sense of ecstasy should hear this 'Daybreak'; secondly, a refined radiance, should try the first embrace (track 5, 2'49"; at this point, this is also one of the very few recordings where you can hear the chorus); or, thirdly, to characterise properly the supernatural, listen to the 'flickering' accents he gives the string *tremolo* chords in the 'Nocturne'.

The chorus work, not least in the so-called 'Interlude', is outstanding; the harmonic boldness of this passage was just as startling in New

RAVEL DAPHNIS ET CHLOÉ
– IN BRIEF

Berlin Philharmonic Orchestra / Pierre Boulez
DG 447 057-2GH   Ⓕ**O**
A recording to banish any suggestions that
Boulez is a cool customer. This is a wonderfully sensuous, pliant reading which finds the
BPO on spectacular form. Boulez whips up
the moment of ecstatic frenzy with real abandon and seeks out the work's poise with equal
skill.

Boston SO / Charles Munch
RCA 09026 61846-2   Ⓕ**O**
A stunning stereo version from 1955 that
finds the Boston orchestra – the US's most
Gallic – on spectacular form. Munch is only
one of a handful of conductors who can rival
Pierre Monteux in this work. Astonishingly
good sound.

London Symphony Orchestra / Pierre Monteux
Decca 448 603-2   Ⓕ**OO**
Monteux conducted the work's premiere in
1912, and nearly half a century later made
this staggering recording with the LSO. For
range of colour and warmth of sound it has
rarely been equalled, never bettered.

London Symphony Orchestra / Claudio Abbado
DG 469 354-2GTR3   Ⓕ**O**
One of the gems in this marvellous three-CD
set of Ravel orchestral works, Abbado's
Daphnis is glorious, a worthy successor two
generations on from Monteux. Suave playing
from the LSO.

Montreal Symphony Orchestra / Charles Dutoit
Decca 458 605-2   Ⓕ**OO**
A wonderful modern recording in fabulous
Decca sound by one of the finest modern
interpreters of French music. It won a
Gramophone Award and still ranks as one of
the most attractive versions.

**City of Birmingham Symphony Orchestra /
Sir Simon Rattle**
EMI Encore 574750-2   Ⓑ
An almost Impressionist version of the ballet,
one in which the slightly hazy sound meshes
perfectly with the general approach. At
budget price, this is most enticing and well
worth acquiring.

York, but the Berlin chorus, unlike the New
York one, is here properly set back.
   In general, DG's recording strikes exactly the
right compromise between clarity and spaciousness, much as Decca's did for Dutoit. With the
added lure of an expansive and often massively
powerful *La valse* (spectacular timpani), this is
now the most recommendable modern *Daphnis*
available.

Daphnis et Chloé   Ⓗ
**New England Conservatory Choir; Boston
Symphony Orchestra / Charles Munch**
RCA Victor Living Stereo 09026 61846-2 (54' · ADD)
Recorded 1955   Ⓜ**O**

This landmark *Daphnis*, made in stereo, sounds
quite astonishing in this transfer. Robert Layton, writing in *Gramophone*, and comparing
Monteux with Munch 'succumbed more readily
to the heady intoxication, the dazzling richness
of colour and virtuosity' of the Munch. Both
Monteux and Munch understood the dangers of
extremes and excessive lingering in this score; of
sentiment turning into syrup and Ravel's 'Choreographic Symphony' falling apart. Though
their recordings balance Ravel's complex score
more skilfully and imaginatively than most
modern contenders, the score's huge range of
dynamics could not be fully realised by the technology of the time.

Additional recommendation

Daphnis et Chloé
Coupled with: Rapsodie espagnole. Pavane pour
une Infante défunte. La valse
**London Symphony Orchestra and Chorus /
Abbado**
DG Trio ③ 469 354-2GTR3 (200' · DDD)   Ⓜ**O**
   A very desirable set, with the LSO putting on its
   best, totally convincing, French accent. Abbado's
   Daphnis et Chloé is reminiscent of that from
   Monteux. The sophistication and power of these
   performances is something to marvel at.

String Quartet in F

String Quartet in Fᵃ. Violin Sonata in Gᵇ. Piano Trio
in A minorᶜ
ᵃ**Quartetto Italiano** (Paolo Borciani, Elisa Pegreffi
vns Piero Farulli *va* Franco Rossi *vc*) ᵇ**Arthur
Grumiaux** *vn* ᵇ**István Hajdu** *pf* ᶜ**Beaux Arts Trio**
(Daniel Guilet *vn* Bernard Greenhouse *vc* Menahem
Pressler *pf*)
Philips Solo 454 134-2PM (ADD) Recorded ᵃ1968,
ᵇᶜ1965   Ⓜ**O**

The playing by the Quartetto Italiano in the
String Quartet is superb. The first movement is
very languorous and though there isn't quite
enough contrast in the *Scherzo* between the loud
pizzicato at the start and the soft bowed music a
few seconds later – it sounds more like *mf* than

Ravel's *pp* and *ppp* – the movement goes well and the slow music in the middle is most sensitively managed. In the slow movement, the main tune on the viola (it comes 14 bars from the start) is covered by the second violin, and this happens later on as well whenever the tune recurs. Yet here again most of the movement is beautifully played. The balance of the recorded sound is splendid. (Incidentally, this same recording is also reviewed with the Debussy String Quartet – see the review under Debussy).

The Beaux Arts Trio is very much at home in Ravel. The account of the Trio is a fine one, sensitively paced and perceptive of the music's volatile ebb and flow, of its refined textures. The recording has the wide dynamic range this work needs and there's a good stereo balance between the three instruments. The sombre dignity of the *Passacaille* is particularly moving. It's still one of the best performances of this work in the catalogue. Grumiaux is very communicative in the Violin Sonata, main-taining a beautifully long line in the first movement, although here he could have sometimes employed a little more of a sense of fantasy. Both he and Hajdu make a convincing job of this work's central Blues section.

Complete Piano Works

Complete Solo Piano Works
Angela Hewitt pf
Hyperion ② CDA67341/2 (138' · DDD) ⒻO

Angela Hewitt's set of Ravel's piano music is a remarkable feat of the most concentrated imaginative delicacy, wit and style. Fresh from her success in Bach she shows how such prowess – namely a scrupulous regard for the score, an acute ear for part-writing, for polyphony, and for meticulous clarity and refinement – can bring extensive rewards. Everything in her performances betokens the greatest care and a special empathy for Ravel's neo-Classicism, for his way of paying affectionate tribute to the past while spicing its conventions with a wholly modern sensibility. Everything in the *Pavane* is subtly graded and textured, the pedalling light and discreet, with a special sense of luminous poetry when the theme makes its final and magical reappearance. No distorting idiosyncrasy is allowed within distance of *Le tombeau de Couperin*, yet nothing is taken for granted.

Her *Gaspard* is a marvel of evocation through precision. Gone are old-fashioned vagueness and approximation: her 'Le gibet' is surely among the most exquisitely controlled on record. Again, her opening to 'Scarbo' is alive with menace because all four of Ravel's directions are so precisely observed; and if she's too sensible to yearn for, say, Martha Argerich's chilling virtuoso *frisson* she makes no concessions to wildness, impetuosity or telescoped phrasing. Nothing is done in the heat of the moment; she keeps Ravel's nightmare under control rather than allowing it to engulf her.

RAVEL'S STRING QUARTET – IN BRIEF

Quartetto Italiano
Philips 464 699-2PM (52' · ADD) ⓂO
One of the cornerstones of the chamber catalogue. The Italians perform with a nimble grace and sense of wonder that never pall. The 1965 recording still sounds good to modern ears.

Vlach Quartet
Supraphon SU3461-2 (56' · ADD) Ⓜ
An interpretation of uncommon re-creative eagerness and genuine staying power. This distinguished Czech ensemble respond with all the freshness of new discovery. Admirably remastered 1959 sound.

Melos Quartet
DG Galleria 463 082-2GGA (53' · ADD) ⓂO
The Melos always put the music first and have both consumate artistic flair and impeccable technical address to commend them. DG's production-team strike a most natural balance.

Juilliard Quartet
Sony SK52554 (74' · DDD) ⒻOO
The Juilliards bring a wealth of experience and enviable sense of purpose to Ravel's masterly quartet. A heartfelt, concentrated reading, beautifully recorded.

Hagen Quartet
437 836-2GH (70' · DDD) Ⓕ
Chamber-music playing doesn't come much more stylish than this. The Hagens perform with rapt dedication, searching intelligence and judicious tonal blend.

Ad Libitum Quartet
Naxos 8 554722 (57' · DDD) Ⓢ
An arresting, sparkily individual rendering from this gifted young Romanian group, winners of the 1997 Evian String Quartet Competition. Coupled with a highly perceptive account of Fauré's elusive but alluring Quartet.

Petersen Quartet
Capriccio 10860 (68' · DDD) Ⓕ
Exceptionally refreshing and articulate music-making. Part of a hugely rewarding programme including Milhaud's First Quartet and attractive works by Chausson and Lekeu.

Belcea Quartet
EMI 574020-2 (71' · DDD) ⓈOOO
☼ An auspicious start to what promises to be a stellar career. Uncommonly well-integrated quartet playing and winner of the Best Debut Recording Prize at the 2001 *Gramophone* Awards.

RAVEL GASPARD DE LA NUIT – IN BRIEF

Martha Argerich
EMI 557101-2 (52' · ADD)   (F)**OO**
A wildly exciting concert performance from 1978, with Argerich live in Amsterdam shaving four minutes off the timing of her previous LP version (see below).

Martha Argerich
DG 447 438-2GOR (71' · ADD)   (M)**O**
For those who prefer studio recordings, Argerich's highly regarded 1974 taping has been added to her famous pairing of the Ravel G major and Prokofiev Third Piano Concertos. This one has both raw passion and wonderfully controlled gradations of touch and tone.

Ivo Pogorelich
DG 463 678-2GOR (73' · ADD)   (M)
The unpredictable Pogorelich at his very best, accomplishing miracles of tone colour, refinement and control, with a coruscating final 'Scarbo'. The couplings are both piano sonatas: a tremendous Prokofiev No 6 and a rather more eccentric Chopin B flat minor.

Arturo Benedetti Michelangeli
BBC Legends BBCL4064 (78' · ADD)   (F)
A scintillating BBC studio performance of 1959 in which Michelangeli seeks to convey the details of the score with what some hear as inhuman exactitude.

Pascal Rogé
Decca ② 440 836-2DF2 (142' · DDD)   (M)**OO**
Rogé eschews sensationalism in his elegantly achieved Ravel complete solo piano music. The set includes a *Gaspard* whose relative restraint and Gallic economy won't spoil you for other readings.

Angela Hewitt
Hyperion ② CDA67341/2 (138' · DDD)   (F)
The pellucid qualities of Hewitt's Bach playing are applied to the French master with compelling results in this set. An initially cool, slow-burn *Gaspard* with very clear textures in luminous sound.

Jean-Yves Thibaudet
Decca ② 433 515-2DH2 (130' · DDD)   (F)**O**
The complete Ravel piano music as pianistic *tour de force*. Thibaudet's high-flying *Gaspard* is given greater impact by the vigour and immediacy of Decca's recording.

Anne Quéffelec
Virgin Classics ② 561489-2 (128' · DDD)   (B)
A most appealing budget-price Ravel collection that includes a deeply musical *Gaspard* from this stylish French pianist.

Yet Hewitt can be as romantically yielding as she's exact. In the return of the principal idea from 'Oiseaux tristes' (*Miroirs*) she achieves an extraordinary sense of stillness, of 'birds lost in the sombre torpor of a tropical forest'.

Hyperion's sound is of demonstration quality. Hewitt joins Gieseking, Rogé, Thibaudet and Lortie among the most distinguished if entirely different Ravel cycles on record, and easily withstands comparison.

Gaspard de la nuit

Ravel Sonatine[b]. Gaspard de la nuit[a] **Schumann**
Fantasiestücke, Op 12[a]
Martha Argerich pf
EMI 557101-2 (52' · ADD) Recorded live [a]1978, [b]1979
                                            (F)**OO**
From the first note of 'Des abends' we're floating, thanks partly to Argerich's finely graded singing tone and partly to her taking the score's extraordinary pedal markings at something close to their face value. Once airborne, it seems all the worlds of Schumann's fantastical imagination are open to us. 'Aufschwung' is the epitome of ardour – a note of desperation never far beneath the surface. 'In der Nacht' skirts even closer to the borders of insanity, its post-*Appassionata* swirlings founded on staggeringly articulate fingerwork. Yet there's still room for an extra touch of dazzlement in the dartings of 'Traumes-Wirren'. Perhaps 'Ende vom Lied' might have relaxed a little more and offered a measure of consolation rather than more of the same kind of intensity; but the Coda is perfection.

The element of Latin American caprice in Argerich's Ravel *Sonatine* may not be everyone's idea of appropriate style; what it does, though, is take us close to the heart, if not of Ravel, then of the art of musical recreation itself. Everything here seems dictated by the feeling of the moment; yet the sheer beauty of sound, with textures once again bathed in fabulously imaginative pedalling, is no less overpowering. At the opening of the finale, Argerich's enthusiasm momentarily gets the better of her fingerwork, and around 0'50" to 0'55" her memory falters for an instant, an extra beat being added to put things back on course (in the parallel passage from 2'37" almost the opposite happens, and two beats are lost).

All this sits oddly with Bryce Morrison's perfectly reasonable description of the *Sonatine* in his essay as 'classically based, the epitome of distilled grace and Gallic understatement'. Yet he surely hits the nail on the head when he describes these performances as complementary to Argerich's studio accounts. For one thing her *Gaspard* is an astonishing four minutes faster than her by no means sedate DG recording from three years earlier. In expression it's polarised towards demonic flair and abandon, in a way scarcely imaginable under studio conditions. 'Ondine' flickers ravishingly and improvisatorily, but the later stages feel more like white-water rafting than the contemplation of a seductive water-nymph, and the big climax won't stand close scrutiny. On the other hand 'Le gibet' is as effective in its restraint as in its hallucinatory colourings – the passage from 2'23" is truly '*pp* sans expression'. Unsurprisingly, there's no shortage of horripilating malevolence in 'Scarbo'; the final stages have to be heard to be believed.

The sound picture may not be to all tastes, combining as it does a close-up image with a generous amount of ambience. This gives us simultaneously the clamorous impact of a super-pianist projecting to the back of a big hall and the atmosphere of a spellbound auditorium.

Gaspard de la nuit. Valses nobles et sentimentales. Jeux d'eau. Miroirs. Sonatine. Le tombeau de Couperin. Prélude. Menuet sur le nom de Haydn. A la manière de Borodine. Menuet antique. Pavane pour une infante défunte. A la manière de Chabrier. Ma mère l'oye[a]
Pascal Rogé, [a]**Denise-Françoise Rogé** *pfs*
Double Decca ② 440 836-2DF2 (142' · ADD) Recorded 1973-94　　　　　Ⓜ**OO**

Everything is expressed with a classic restraint, elegance and economy, an ideal absence of artifice or idiosyncrasy. Rogé knows precisely where to allow asperity to relax into lyricism and vice versa, and time and again he finds that elusive, cool centre at the heart of Ravel's teeming and luxuriant vision. True, those used to more Lisztian but less authentic Ravel may occasionally find Rogé diffident or *laissez-faire*. But lovers of subtlety will see him as illuminating and enchanting. How often do you hear *Ma mère l'oye* given without a trace of brittleness or archness, or find *Jeux d'eau* presented with such stylish ease and tonal radiance? Rogé may lack something of Thibaudet's menace and high-flying virtuosity in 'Scarbo' (also on Decca) but how memorably he re-creates Ravel's nocturnal mystery. Even if one misses a touch of cruelty behind Ondine's entreaty, few pianists can have evoked her watery realm with greater transparency. Arguably one of the finest Ravel recordings available.

Songs

Ravel Menuet antique. Pavane pour une infante défunte. Le Tombeau de Couperin. Shéhérazade **Debussy** Danse sacrée et danse profane. Trois Ballades de François Villon. Cinq Poèmes de Charles Baudelaire – Le jet d'eau
Alison Hagley *sop* **Anne Sofie von Otter** *mez* **Cleveland Orchestra / Pierre Boulez** DG 471 614-2GH (76' · DDD) Texts and translations included　　　　　Ⓕ**OO**

Anne Sofie von Otter is really exploiting the French repertory nowadays. After her Mélisande and Carmen, and Chaminade and Offenbach recitals, here she tackles Ravel's

Shéhérazade with total success. From the first cry of 'Asie' in the opening song, von Otter beguiles using a hushed, yet expectant quality. Throughout her soft singing is exquisite. The balance between voice and orchestra has all the subtlety this extended prologue requires. At the sinister line, 'Je voudrais voir des assassins', she employs a harsh edge to the voice that's immediately echoed in the orchestral climax. As the poet describes the story-telling, Boulez brings the song to its end with a perfect *diminuendo*, leading into the mysterious 'Flute enchantée'. Here again von Otter's control of dynamics pays off with a gorgeous 'mysterieux baiser'.

The final song is also the most difficult. In its ambiguity, 'L'indifférent' mustn't be overstressed, and yet that ironic remark at the end, 'Ta démarche feminine et lasse' needs to be not so much regretful as a sigh of half-amused resignation.

Le Tombeau de Couperin, in its orchestral version, is an equally difficult challenge which Boulez and the Cleveland orchestra bring off with precision. With the other two orchestral arrangements of piano pieces, the *Pavane* and the *Menuet Antique*, again Boulez achieves such clarity that even these over-familiar works sound surprising and fresh.

The Debussy *Danses*, for harp and strings, serve as a sort of interlude, leading into the other three-song event, the *Trois Ballades de François Villon*. These are so often sung by a baritone; indeed, they were premièred by Jean Périer, the first Pelléas, so it's a slight jolt to hear them done by a soprano. Alison Hagley deals well enough with what Jane Bathori used to call the 'rough and quite choppy' vocal lines of the first song, 'Ballade de Villon à s'amye', but the fuller, darker tones of a baritone might be more appropriate in the central prayer. The account of the chattering wives of Paris brings the programme to a merry conclusion. The disc is a most enjoyable combination of orchestral music and song. The sound throughout is exceptionally vivid, and Boulez, the orchestra and his soloists provide exemplary performances at almost every turn: heartily recommended.

Operas

L'enfant et les sortilèges[a]. Ma mère l'oye – Suite. **Andrée Aubery Luchini** *sop* Child **Geneviève Macaux** *mez* Mother, Chinese Cup, Dragonfly, She-cat **Michel Sénéchal** *ten* Wedgwood Teapot, Old Man, Frog, Tom-cat **Mady Mesplé** *sop* Fire, Princess, Nightingale **Coro di Voci Bianche; RAI Chorus and Orchestra, Rome / Peter Maag** Arts Archives 43039-2 (62' · ADD · T) [a]Recorded live at Radio Concert Hall, Rome, 16 March 1963　Ⓜ

L'heure espagnole[a] Valses nobles et sentimentales[b] **Andrée Aubery Luchini** *sop* Concepcion **Michel Sénéchal** *ten* Gonzalve **Eric Tappy** *ten* Torquemada **Pierre Mollet** *bar* Ramiro [a]**RAI Orchestra, Turin;** [b]**RAI Orchestra, Milan / Peter Maag** Arts Archives 43040-2 (63 · ADD · T) Recorded live at

Radio Concert Hall, Turin, [a]25 May 1962 , [b]4 March 1969 Ⓜ

In *L'enfant et les sortilèges* and *L'heure espagnol* Ravel for much of the time stays close to the spoken word, on the lines he'd explored in 1907 in his song cycle *Histoires naturelles*. For these recordings of the two operas Maag was wise enough to choose mainly French singers: non-French singers mostly lack the feeling for the rhythm of the syllables, even where their pronunciation is unexceptionable.

Throughout the two operas everything is in place and often a good deal more than that. Mady Mesplé is predictably superb in *L'enfant* as The Fire and The Princess, with astounding accuracy in her runs as the former, as is Michel Sénéchal, in the role of the Old Man which he'd sung on Lorin Maazel's DG set recorded two years earlier. In truth, vocally there's not a weak link anywhere. If Andrée Aubery Luchini's Concepcion in *L'heure espagnole* is a trifle approximate in her pitching at times, that's more than made up for by her spirited delivery.

There's a very slight tendency to hunkiness in Maag's interpretations of both operas. Quite frequently things can get too loud. And he misses some of Ravel's almost obsessive changes of tempo: for instance, the *rallentando* over Don Inigo's comment on how important it is that husbands should get out of the house and enjoy 'une occupation régulière et périodique'. There needs to be time for the audience to laugh here.

Maag's renderings of the *Valses nobles* and *Ma mère l'oye* aren't special: probably rehearsal time was insufficient. But both operas had obviously been well rehearsed, and the last page of *L'enfant* is deeply moving, with a wonderfully executed *crescendo* up to the chorus's final 'sage', confirming the child's arrival at a state of grace.

Alan Rawsthorne   British 1905-1971

Rawsthorne studied as a pianist at the Royal College of Music and abroad with Petri; only at the end of the 1930s did he begin to make a name as a composer. Influenced by Hindemith, he developed a highly crafted and abstract style, chiefly in concertos and other orchestral works. His inclination towards motivic thinking and variation structures brought some approximation to 12-note techniques, but tonal centres remained important. He wrote three symphonies (1950, 1959, 1964), two piano concertos (1939, 1951), two violin concertos (1948, 1956), three string quartets (1939, 1954, 1964) and sonatas for viola, cello and violin. **GROVE**music

Cello Concerto

Symphonic Studies. Oboe Concerto[a]. Cello Concerto[b]

[a]**Stéphane Rancourt** ob [b]**Alexander Baillie** vc
Royal Scottish National Orchestra / David Lloyd-Jones
Naxos 8 554763 (72' · DDD)   Ⓢ Ⓢ ○○

David Lloyd-Jones directs a swaggering, affectionate and ideally clear-headed account of Rawsthorne's masterly *Symphonic Studies* (1939), one of the most stylish and exuberantly inventive products of British music from the first half of the last century. The work's formal elegance, impeccable craftsmanship and healthy concision are exhilarating. It's an impressively assured orchestral début, its tightly knit 20-minute span evincing a remarkable emotional scope. The present performance is a great success, a worthy successor, to both Lambert's classic 1946 Philharmonia version (now happily restored on Pearl) and Pritchard's admirable 1975 Lyrita recording with the LPO.

First heard at the 1947 Cheltenham Festival, the Concerto for Oboe and String Orchestra was composed for Evelyn Rothwell. Brimful of gentle melancholy, it's another delectably clean-cut creation, whose touchingly eloquent first movement is succeeded by a wistfully swaying, at times cryptic *Allegretto con morbidezza* and a spirited, though never entirely untroubled *Vivace* finale. Impeccable solo work from RSNO principal oboe Stéphane Rancourt and a spick-and-span accompaniment to match.

There's another first recording in the guise of the Cello Concerto (1965). This is a major achievement, a work to rank beside Rawsthorne's superb Third Symphony and Third String Quartet of the previous year in its unremitting concentration and nobility of expression. A strongly lyrical vein runs through the notably eventful, ever-evolving opening movement, whereas the central *Mesto* mixes dark introspection with outbursts of real anguish. The clouds lift for the rumbustious finale. A substantial, deeply felt utterance, in short, which will surely repay closer study. Soloist Alexander Baillie gives a stunningly idiomatic rendering; Lloyd-Jones and the RSNO offer big-hearted, confident support. Apart from a hint of harshness in the very loudest *tutti*s of the *Symphonic Studies*, Tim Handley's engineering is immensely vivid and always musically balanced. Overall, a wonderfully enterprising triptych.

Piano Concertos

Piano Concertos – No 1; No 2. Improvisations on a theme by Constant Lambert
Peter Donohoe pf **Ulster Orchestra / Takuo Yuasa**
Naxos 8 555959 (57' · DDD)   Ⓢ Ⓢ ○

Rawsthorne's First Piano Concerto, originally written with just strings and percussion accompaniment, was introduced in its later full orchestral form at a 1942 Promenade Concert by Louis Kentner. The Second was commissioned by the Arts Council for the 1951 Festival of Britain and premièred by Clifford Curzon in the then-new Royal Festival Hall. He later recorded it with Sargent and the LSO on a 10-inch LP for Decca. *The Record Guide*'s review commented on the 'open air tune in the finale with an instant appeal' and suggested the work would achieve the 'wide popularity it certainly deserves'. Alas that never came about. Peter Donohoe plays the First with an effervescent lightness of touch that emphasises the *scherzando* element of the first movement. Yuasa provides witty orchestral detail – there's an engaging contribution from the bassoon – and yet still finds the underlying lyrical melancholy. He opens the Chaconne hauntingly, and the following dialogue with the piano has a compelling delicacy. The Tarantella finale brings an infectious élan and splendid momentum. Donohoe's brilliant solo contribution has all the sparkle you could want, and the gentle pay-off of the brief coda is neatly managed.

In the Second Concerto the fluidity of Donohoe's playing is particularly appealing, and the overall balance – though the opening flute solo is perhaps a little recessive – is mostly admirable. Donohoe and Yuasa deftly manage the quixotic changes of mood of the initally 'rather violent' *Scherzo* (the composer's description) and lead naturally into the wistful *Adagio semplice*, with its nostagic clarinet cantilena answered so exquisitely by the piano.

The *Improvisations* are based on a seven-note theme from Lambert's last ballet, *Tiresias*. They are widely varied in mood and style, and, even though Rawsthorne flirts with serialism, the variations are friendly and easy to follow, and the listener's attention is always fully engaged. Certainly this Naxos disc can be strongly recommended, especially to those who have not yet before encountered Rawsthorne's always rewarding music.

Violin Concertos

Violin Concertos Nos 1 & 2. Cortèges – fantasy overture
Rebecca Hirsch *vn* **BBC Scottish Symphony Orchestra / Lionel Friend**
Naxos 8 554240 (64' · DDD)   ⑤ ⑤●

Rawsthorne enthusiasts should waste no time in snapping up this disc, containing music-making of perceptive dedication and impressive polish. He completed his First Violin Concerto in 1947, dedicating the score to Walton (there's a quotation from *Belshazzar's Feast* just before the end). Cast in just two movements, it's a lyrically affecting creation that weaves a spell, especially in a performance as dignified and consistently purposeful as this. However, the revelation comes with the Second Concerto of 1956. Rebecca Hirsch and Lionel Friend locate a deceptive urgency and symphonic thrust in the opening *Allegretto* that genuinely compel. If anything, the succeeding *Poco lento* wears an even more anguished, nervy demeanour, the

music's questing mood very well conveyed. By contrast, the finale proceeds in serene, almost carefree fashion, its witty coda forming a delightfully unbuttoned conclusion to a striking, much-underrated work. As a curtain-raiser Naxos gives us the fantasy overture *Cortèges*. Commissioned by the BBC and premièred at the 1945 Proms by the LSO under Basil Cameron, it's a well-wrought essay, pitting an eloquent *Adagio* processional as against an irrepressible *Allegro molto vivace* tarantella. The composer develops his material with customary skill, and Friend draws a committed and alert response from the BBC Scottish SO. Boasting a spacious, bright and admirably balanced sound picture (no attempt to spotlight the soloist), here's an enormously rewarding issue and a bargain of the first order.

Concerto for String Orchestra

Concertante pastorale[a]. Concerto for String Orchestra. Divertimento. Elegiac Rhapsody. Light Music. Suite for Recorder and String Orchestra[b] (orch McCabe)
[a]**Conrad Marshall** *fl* [a]**Rebecca Goldberg** *hn* [b]**John Turner** *rec* **Northern Chamber Orchestra / David Lloyd-Jones**
Naxos 8 553567 (64' · DDD)   ⑤ ⑤●

The most substantial offering here, the resourceful and magnificently crafted *Concerto for String Orchestra*, dates from 1949. David Lloyd-Jones and his admirably prepared group give a performance which, in its emotional scope and keen vigour, outshines Boult's 1966 recording with the BBC Symphony Orchestra (nla). Not only does Lloyd-Jones achieve a more thrusting urgency in the outer movements, he also locates an extra sense of slumbering tragedy in the *Lento e mesto*. He gives a sparkling account of the immensely engaging *Divertimento*, written for Harry Blech and the London Mozart Players in 1962; the rumbustious concluding 'Jig' is as good a place as any to sample the spick-and-span response of the Northern Chamber Orchestra. The *Concertante pastorale*, written for the Hampton Court Orangery Concerts, is an atmospheric, beautifully wrought 10-minute essay for solo flute, horn and strings. It's succeeded by the perky *Light Music* for strings, composed in 1938 for the Workers' Music Association and based on Catalan folk-tunes. Then there's McCabe's expert orchestration of the miniature Suite for recorder and strings, the second of whose four linked movements is a reworking of a ballad from the *Fitzwilliam Virginal Book*. But the most exciting discovery has to be the 1963-4 *Elegiac Rhapsody*, a deeply felt threnody for string orchestra written in memory of Rawsthorne's friend, the poet Louis MacNeice. Not only does it pack a wealth of first-rate invention and incident into its 10-minute duration, it attains a pitch of anguished expression possibly unrivalled in this figure's entire output.

Symphonies

Symphonies – No 1; No 2, 'A Pastoral Symphony'[a]; No 3
[a]**Charlotte Ellett** sop **Bournemouth Symphony Orchestra / David Lloyd-Jones**
Naxos 8 557480 (75' · DDD · T)   Ⓢ

David Lloyd-Jones directs Rawsthorne's three symphonies with evident conviction, and secures a consistently enthusiastic and spruce response from the Bournemouth SO. He improves on Sir John Pritchard's 1975 Lyrita account of the terse, immaculately scored First Symphony (1950), bringing elegant proportion and thrusting purpose. As for its luminous and poignant successor, *A Pastoral Symphony* (1959), honours are more equally divided. Lloyd-Jones distils rather more in the way of gentle melancholy, whereas Nicholas Braithwaite and the LPO on Lyrita achieve the greater poise.

Norman Del Mar's BBC SO version of the imposing Third (1964) has done sterling service down the years, but Lloyd-Jones fully matches its blazing commitment, tying up the symphonic threads to even more clinching effect in the finale (whose peaceful coda recalls material from the opening movement), while distilling every ounce of brooding atmosphere and forceful emotion from the stately tread of the second movement 'Alla Sarabanda'.

A touch of rawness aside, the recording is hugely vivid, offering a pretty much ideal combination of bite and amplitude. The disc represents irresistible value for money.

Film Music

The Captive Heart – Suite. Lease of Life – Main Titles and Emergency. Burma Victory – Suite. Saraband for Dead Lovers – Saraband and Carnival (all arr Schurmann). West of Zanzibar – Main Titles. The Cruel Sea – Main Titles and Nocturne. Where No Vultures Fly – Suite. Uncle Silas – Suite. The Dancing Fleece – Three Dances (all arr and orch Lane)
BBC Philharmonic Orchestra / Rumon Gamba
Chandos CHAN9749 (73' · DDD)   Ⓕ●

Incapable of shoddy craftsmanship, and truly a 'composer's composer', Rawsthorne brought a professional integrity, great clarity of expression and unerring economy of thought to every field of music in which he worked, not least the 27 film scores he penned between 1937 and 1964. Here are selections from nine scores in all, the arranging and orchestrating duties being shared by the indefatigable Philip Lane and Gerard Schurmann. *The Cruel Sea* (1953) is the best-known offering, its evocative, slumbering power and noble defiance as eloquent as ever. Bernard Herrmann, who knew a thing or two about the genre, rated *Uncle Silas* (1947) one of the greatest film scores he'd ever encountered: try the delightfully flirtatious 'Valse caprice'. The charming 'Three Dances' from *The Dancing Fleece* (a Crown Film Unit production promoting British wool) can almost be viewed as a 'trial run' for *Madame Chrysanthème*, the one-act ballet Rawsthorne wrote in 1955for Sadlers Wells. The first track is an extended (18-minute) suite from the 1946 POW drama, *The Captive Heart*, and there are also generous excerpts from *Where No Vultures Fly* and the documentary *Burma Victory* (full of decidedly superior, stirring invention). Keller was especially complimentary about *Lease of Life* (1954), a Robert Donat vehicle for which Rawsthorne supplied a 'rich miniature score' lasting about 13 and a half minutes, and the collection concludes with a flourish in the shape of the superbly swaggering 'Prelude and Carnival' from *Saraband for Dead Lovers* (1948). Gamba draws playing of panache and infectious enthusiasm from the BBC Philharmonic, with spectacularly wide-ranging Chandos sound. Not to be missed!

Chamber Works

Piano Quintet[a]. Concertante for Violin and Piano[b]. Piano Trio[c]. Viola Sonata[d]. Cello Sonata[e]
[abc]**Nadia Myerscough**, [a]**Mark Messenger** vns [a]**Helen Roberts**, [d]**Martin Outram** vas [ace]**Peter Adams** vc [a]**John McCabe**, [bce]**Yoshiko Endo**, [d]**Julian Rolton** pfs
Naxos 8 554352 (70' · DDD)   Ⓢ Ⓢ○○

Here's a disc brimming with high-quality music and superlative performances. The Piano Quintet, from 1968, is cast in a single continuous movement divided into four contrasting sections. Although only 15 minutes long, the quintet abounds with musical ideas and interest. Much of the material is vigorous, powerful and concisely presented, but there's much poetry, too, particularly in the *Lento non troppo* section and the brief epilogue that closes the energetic opening section. The *Concertante* for violin and piano is a much earlier work dating from the mid-1930s and, although early influences such as Shostakovich and even Busoni in 'Faustian' mood can be detected, it's perhaps among the earliest of Rawsthorne's works in which his own voice begins to emerge. First performed by the distinguished Menuhin-Cassadó-Kentner Trio, the Piano Trio of 1963 contains much impressive and finely crafted material, as well as a good deal of colourful soloistic writing. The Viola Sonata dates from 1937, but the score was lost shortly after its première only to be rediscovered in a Hampstead bookshop and revised in 1954. The Sonata is something of a watershed in Rawsthorne's early output, and shows a considerable advance in style and technique from the *Concertante* of only a few years earlier, and both this and the equally fine Cello Sonata of 1948 are particularly valuable additions to the catalogue. Performances throughout are first class, although John McCabe's commanding reading of the Piano Quintet (he played for the work's première) stands out as exceptionally authoritative and compelling.

Theme and Variations

Rawsthorne Theme and Variations[d]. Violin Sonata[c]
McCabe Maze Dances[a]. Star Preludes[b]
Peter Sheppard Skaerve[d], [d]Christine Sohn vns
[bc]**Tamami Honma** pf
Metier MSV CD92029 (62' · DDD)   Ⓕ

Rawsthorne's *Theme and Variations* for two violins not only ranks as one of his masterpieces,
but is among the finest string writing for violin
duo this century. One of the work's major
strengths lies in the equality of writing and
invention in the two solo parts and the way in
which Rawsthorne treats the material as an
homogenous whole rather than two separate
contrapuntal strands. Quite why it's been so
neglected is something of a mystery, which
makes this new and exceptionally fine account
by Peter Sheppard Skaerved and Christine
Sohn all the more welcome. Another work that
deserves much wider recognition is the Violin
Sonata of 1958, originally written for Joseph
Szigeti, though never performed by him. It's
full of invention and memorable ideas, conveyed with the most economical of means.
Skaerved and pianist Tamami Honma give us a
particularly thoughtful, spirited reading of this
important Rawsthorne work. The music of John
McCabe, a long-time champion and biographer
of Rawsthorne, makes an ideal coupling. Good
recording. A must for all Rawsthorne admirers.

Jean-Féry Rebel   French 1661-1747

*After serving the Count of Ayen in Spain, 1700-
1705, Rebel became a leading member of the French
king's 24 Violons and the Académie Royale de
Musique orchestra. He later held court posts including that of chamber composer (from 1726) and was
active as a harpsichordist and conductor. An innovatory and esteemed composer, he wrote various vocal
works, string sonatas, 'symphonies' for the Académie
Royale dancers including Les caractères de la danse
(1715), Terpsichore (1720) and the much admired
Les élémens (1737), which begins with a famously
alarming dissonance to represent chaos.*
                                        GROVEmusic

Violin Sonatas

No 1 in A; No 3 in A minor; No 4 in E minor;   Ⓟ
No 5 in D; No 6 in B minor; No 7 in G minor; No 8 in
D minor; No 9 in F
Andrew Manze vn **Jaap ter Linden** va da gamba
Richard Egarr hpd
Harmonia Mundi HMU90 7221 (78' · DDD)   ⒻO

This is Andrew Manze's first foray into the
French Baroque repertory with eight of Rebel's
12 seldom-heard violin sonatas of 1713. Manze,
never short of genius or fire in the Italian and
Austrian repertory, here relaxes his sound,
making gentle and subtle use of tempo and

dynamics and only occasionally breaking out
into impassioned lyricism. But that doesn't
mean to say that he has simply plugged into the
fashionable French Baroque sound with its easy
grace and polite twiddles; one can easily imagine these sonatas being played in just such a
pretty manner, but Manze has instead looked
deep into the music and extracted from it a great
variety of expression, including in many places
an unexpected darkness, a brooding restraint
immediately apparent in the *Grave* movements
with which some of these sonatas open, but
seldom far away even in the apparently carefree
musettes, rondeaux or allemandes. It brings to
the music an unexpected emotional edge, even a
touch of menace. It would be a mean spirit who
couldn't admire the intelligence and imagination which is so lovingly brought to this neglected music. Combined with the sympathetic
contributions of Richard Egarr and Jaap ter
Linden, this is Baroque chamber music-making
of the highest order.

Max Reger   German 1873-1916

*Reger studied with Riemann (1890-95) in Munich
and Wiesbaden (where his drinking habits began);
in 1901 he settled in Munich and in 1907 moved to
Leipzig to take a post as professor of composition at
the university, though he was also active internationally as a conductor and pianist. He was appointed
conductor of the court orchestra at Meiningen in
1911 and in 1915 moved to Jena.*
*During a composing life of little more than 20
years, he produced a large output in all genres, nearly
always in abstract forms. He was a firm supporter of
'absolute' music and saw himself in a tradition going
back to Bach, through Beethoven, Schumann and
Brahms; his organ music, though also affected by
Liszt, was provoked by that tradition. Of his orchestral pieces, his symphonic and richly elaborate Hiller
Variations and Mozart Variations are justly
remembered; of his chamber music the lighter-tex-
tured trios have retained a place in the repertory,
along with some of the works for solo string instruments. His late piano and two-piano music places
him as a successor to Brahms in the central German
tradition. He pursued intensively, and to its limits,
Brahms's continuous development and free modulation, often also invoking the aid of Bachian counterpoint. Many of his works are in variation and fugue
forms; equally characteristic is a great energy and
complexity of thematic growth.*   GROVEmusic

Four Symphonic Poems, Op 128

Four Symphonic Poems after Arnold Böcklin,
Op 128. Variations and Fugue on a Theme of
JA Hiller, Op 100
Royal Concertgebouw Orchestra / Neeme Järvi
Chandos CHAN8794 (67' · DDD) Recorded 1989 ⒻO

Mention of Reger's name in 'informed' circles is
likely to produce a conditioned reflex: 'Fugue!'
In his day he was the central figure of the 'Back

to Bach' movement, but he was also a romantic who relished all the expressive potential of the enormous post-Wagnerian orchestra. Chandos exploits the open spaces of the Concertgebouw, forsaking some healthy transparency for an extra spatial dimension; a more sumptuous glow. With Järvi's instinct for pacing in late romantic music, and his great orchestra's evident delight in the copious riches of the discovery, for the *Hiller* Variations, this disc is very tempting. Anyone who warms to Vaughan Williams's *Tallis Fantasia* will immediately respond to the 'Hermit playing the violin', the first of the four *Böcklin* tone-poems; Debussy's 'Jeux de vagues' from *La mer* was obviously in Reger's mind for the second poem 'At play in the waves'; and the 'Isle of the dead' is Reger's no less doom- and gloom-laden response to the painting that so captured Rachmaninov's imagination. The final painting, 'Bacchanal', was described as a Munich beer festival in Roman costume – an entirely fitting description for Reger's setting of it!

Clarinet Quintet

String Quartet in E flat, Op 109. Clarinet Quintet in A, Op 146[a]
[a]**Karl Leister** *cl* **Vogler Quartet** (Tim Vogler, Frank Reinecke *vns* Stefan Fehlandt *va* Stephan Forck *vc*)
Nimbus NI5644 (72' · DDD)   (F)

Who could fail to smile at the winding lyricism that opens both these works, or at the self-possessed fugue that potters gleefully at the end of the Op 109 String Quartet? This is music that simply had to be written, complex music maybe, but with so much to say at so many levels that once you enter its world, you're hooked. Previous recordings of the gorgeous Clarinet Quintet have included two with Karl Leister, though for sheer naturalness, musicality and team spirit, this new production will be hard to beat. Reger's frequent allusions to early musical modes inspire playing of rare sensitivity. Humour surfaces in the *scherzo*'s rough and tumble, a downward scale idea backed by lively *pizzicatos*, teasingly discursive and with a sunny, song-like *Trio*. The slow movement recalls Brahms's Quintet but without the gypsy element, while the theme-and-variation finale reminds us that Reger's homage to Mozart extends beyond the chosen key of A major. The String Quartet is more openly argumentative, especially in the first movement. Hints of Taranto inform the tarantella-like *scherzo*, whereas the slow movement combines hymn-like nobility with more echoes of Brahms. The closing fugue is the work of a joyful creator drunk on counterpoint, though there's plenty to engage the heart as well as the mind. The Vogler commands a wider range of tonal colour than the Berne Quartet in their complete Reger quartet cycle but the present coupling is ideal for all Doubting Thomases who'd have you believe that Reger is a bore.

Piano Trios

Piano Trios – B minor, Op 2; E minor, Op 102
Gunter Teuffel *va* & **Parnassus Trio** (Wolfgang Schröder *vn* Michael Gross *vc* Chia Chou *pf*)
Dabringhaus und Grimm MDG303 0751-2
(67' · DDD)   (F)O

It was very wise to programme Reger's masterly Op 102 E minor Trio before its B minor predecessor. Unsuspecting listeners who jump straight in at Op 2 will discover a pleasing if discursive piece, forged in the shadow of Brahms, with an opening *Allegro appassionato* which, although half the length of its disc-companion's first movement, seems twice as long. The *Scherzo* is frumpish, the closing *Adagio con variazioni* sombre and somewhat long-winded. And yet the use of viola in place of a cello has its attractions, and there are numerous telling glimpses of the mature Reger.

The E minor Trio is something else again, a rugged masterpiece, with a finely structured opening *Allegro moderato, ma con passione* (the three stages of its argument are divided equally within a 15-minute framework), a mysterious *Allegretto* that opens in the manner of later Brahms then suddenly lets in the sunlight, and a noble, hymn-like *Largo* that recalls 'The Hermit with the Violin' from the *Böcklin* Portraits. Reger's Second Trio is full of audacious modulations and striking dramatic gestures; it *is* long (something in excess of 40 minutes), but never outstays its welcome. No one could reasonably ask for more than the Parnassus Trio offers, either in terms of drama or of interpretative subtlety. If you love Brahms, and fancy diving in among a plethora of stimulating musical complexities, invest without delay. If you love melody, there's plenty of that, too.

Violin Works

Solo Violin Sonata No 7 in A minor, Op 91[a]. Three Solo Viola Suites, Op 131d[b]
Luigi Alberto Bianchi [a]*vn*/[b]*va*
Dynamic CDS383 (56' · bADD/aDDD) Recorded [a]1992, [b]1977   (F)

Violin Sonata in C, Op 72. Little Sonata in A, Op 103b No 2. Tarantella in G minor. Albumblatt in E flat
Ulf Wallin *vn* **Roland Pöntinen** *pf*
CPO CPO999 857-2 (60' · DDD)   (M)OOO

 The variety of Reger's music could hardly be better suggested than by this pair of discs. Reger the wild modernist (by the standards of 1903) is vividly before us in the headlong, turbulent, disconcertingly chromatic outer movements of the Op 72 Sonata, with their huge variety of moods and frequent abrupt changes of direction. But the *Little Sonata* of only six years later is almost classical by comparison; it's much more direct, economically worked and tightly argued. And in all the unaccompanied music in Luigi Alberto

Bianchi's recital we meet Reger paying sincere and often touching homage to Bach.

Bianchi's disc is beautiful but poignant. The three Suites for viola were recorded in 1977 on a large and sumptuously rich-toned viola by the brothers Amati, the Medicea. It was stolen three years later; Bianchi began playing the violin instead and eventually acquired a fine Stradivari, the Colossus, upon which in 1992 he recorded the unaccompanied Violin Sonata. That too was stolen six years thereafter, and apart from the interest of the music and the eloquence of the playing this disc has the sad value of being perhaps the last that we shall hear of two exceptional instruments. Reger's love for the violin is as evident in the Op 91 Sonata as is his reverence for Bach. All the movements are like Bach in late-Romantic dress, and the finale is a magnificent chaconne.

Ulf Wallin plays with a slightly narrower tone than Bianchi, which works well in the tumultuous gestures of Op 72. But he and Roland Pöntinen are just as alive to Reger's moments of withdrawn pensiveness and long lines, which need care if their chromatic shifts aren't to make them seem diffuse; they never do here. The recordings are excellent.

Six Preludes and Fugues, Op 131a. Preludes and Fugues, Op 117 – No 1 in B minor; No 2 in G minor; No 3 in E minor; No 5 in G; No 6 in D minor; No 7 in A minor; No 8 in E minor
Mateja Marinkovič vn
ASV ② CDDCA876 (82' · DDD) Recorded 1993   Ⓜ︎Ⓞ

Reger's knowledge of, and feeling for, the violin were all-embracing, and although his winding melodic lines can sometimes prove maddeningly discursive, there's much beauty in the writing – the A minor Prelude, or the E minor Prelude, Op 131*a* providing particularly good sampling points. Bach is an overwhelming presence: quite apart from direct quotations there's the all-pervasive influence of the unaccompanied Sonatas and Partitas, especially with regard to Reger's fugues, which invariably start with a hint of Bachian *déjà-vu* before modulating way beyond the Baroque's customary orbit. All 13 works here are surprisingly varied in theme and tone, although even the most enthusiastic listener is advised not to take in more than a few at a time. The prize-winning violinist Mateja Marinkovič is professor at both the Royal Academy of Music and the Guildhall School of Music, and his warm-centred, tonally true performances serve Reger handsomely. A major addition to the solo violin repertory on CD, and a must for all Regerians.

Organ Works

Chorale Fantasias, Op 52 – Wachet auf, ruft uns die Stimme. Pieces, Op 145 – Weihnachten. Organ Sonata No 2 in D minor, Op 60. Symphonic Fantasia and Fugue, Op 57

Franz Hauk org
Guild GMCD7192 (73' · DDD) Played on the Klais organ of Ingolstadt Minster   Ⓕ︎Ⓞ

Opinions about Reger's music are polarised between admirers and detractors. The latter group would say of him, as Emperor Joseph II did of Mozart, that he wrote too many notes. Even in this new century the complexity of his scores still presents an awesome challenge to performers and listeners alike. Yet the rewards are immense; Reger is arguably even as great a composer as Liszt. His radical, eclectic approach took organ music to new dimensions, and he fully deserves a whole CD to himself. He's well served here by an inspired choice of player, instrument and venue. Hauk's performances are amazingly virtuoso; he brings clarity of rhythm and articulation to the faster passages and a serene poetry to the quieter moments. He plays the spectacular Klais organ of Ingolstadt Minster, which must be one of the best instruments in Europe. Its brilliant *tutti*, combined with a 12-second reverberation, does full justice to Reger's epic climaxes, and there are some ravishing colours in the softer sections. As resident organist, Hauk knows this instrument intimately, and exploits all the available colours and dynamics. Guild's fine recording stops the reverberation from becoming excessive, and captures the organ's full dynamic range. Whatever your views on Reger, this disc can be unreservedly recommended as an overwhelming and uplifting experience.

Choral Works

Drei geistliche Gesänge, Op 110. 3 Gesänge, Op 39
Danish National Radio Choir / Stefan Parkman
Chandos CHAN9298 (56' · DDD) Recorded 1993-4
Texts and translations included   Ⓕ︎

Mere mentions of Reger's *a cappella* music will send sensitive souls scurrying to the nearest Karaoke lounge. Visions of myriad notes covering the page would frighten most choirs away, but these singers are made of sterner stuff. They're undaunted by complex contrapuntal structures, devious chromatic harmonies and textures so thick you need a forage knife to get through them. They not only weave their way through Reger's characteristically tangled scores without a moment's doubt, but illuminate the paths so clearly one hardly notices the dense musical undergrowth all around. Parkman has a clear-sighted view of what's wanted, and, aided by singers whose pure, perfectly blended tone is a joy to hear, he follows his vision unfalteringly: everything falls neatly into place, making real musical sense. The hefty Op 110 Motets (ostensibly in five, but often diverging into as many as nine independent parts) can sound oppressively heavy, but here offer some of the most sublimely beautiful moments yet captured on CD. A triumph of skill over adversity if ever there was one.

Steve Reich
American b1936

Reich studied drumming when he was 14 with the New York Philharmonic Orchestra timpanist; later he took a degree in philosophy at Cornell (1953-7) and studied composition at the Juilliard School (1958-61) and at Mills College (1962-3) with Milhaud and Berio, also becoming interested in Balinese and African music. In 1966 he began performing with his own ensemble, chiefly of percussionists, developing a music of gradually changing ostinato patterns that move out of phase, creating an effect of shimmering surfaces; this culminated in Drumming (1971), a 90-minute elaboration of a single rhythmic cell. From c1972 he added harmonic change to his music, and later (Tehillim, 1981) melody. He has also worked with larger orchestral and choral forces (The Desert Music, 1983). Different Trains (1988), for string quartet and tape, won a Grammy for best new composition. GROVEmusic

Different Trains

Different Trains. Triple Quartet. The Four Sections.
Lyon National Orchestra / David Robertson
Naïve Montaigne MO782167 (65' · DDD)   Ⓕ●

This version of *Different Trains*, a reworking of the original string quartet version, impresses immediately by the richness of its vastly expanded sound palette. It reveals that inside that frenetic chamber work was a much larger piece trying to get out, and here it is, fully realised, as it were, in glorious technicolor. Some of the writing has an almost Beethovenian quality. It's a hugely impressive performance of a work that has, quite literally, grown in stature.

And, of course, if you're going to record Reich with 48 strings, you may as well include the largest version of *Triple Quartet* from 1999, scored for 36 of them.

If in going back to *The Four Sections* for orchestra from 1986 one has the feeling that much is inchoate, it's also true that all the elemental power of the more recent works is there, too, and the Lyon musicians react to it with fantastic energy and precision. A major addition to the Reich discography.

Drumming

Drumming
Synergy Vocals; Ictus / Georges-Elie Octors
Cyprès CYP5608 (55' · DDD)   Ⓕ

Drumming is from 1971, but it has lost none of its strength. The players of Ictus here put their hearts and souls into a work that demands ferocious concentration (though other approaches are possible – a composer friend once said that it was quite the best music for building bookcases), and which rewards accordingly. Now, we know that nobody likes the label 'minimalist' any more, but with music of this quality it's very hard to find that description insulting. This per-

formance is quite the equal of, and possibly more colourful than, Reich's second version, on Nonesuch, and clearly outstrips the original, less trim DG version.

Music for 18 Musicians

Music for 18 Musicians
Anonymous Ensemble / Steve Reich pf
ECM New Series 821 417-2 (57' · ADD) Recorded 1978   Ⓕ●

Reich's first recording of *Music for 18 Musicians* was a landmark release in the history of new music on record and showed what a towering masterpiece it is. The recording was produced by Rudolf Werner for DG, following the release of a three-LP set of *Drumming*, *Six Pianos* and *Music for Mallet Instruments, Voice and Organ*. Legend has it that Roland Kommerell, at that time head of German PolyGram, foresaw the commercial potential of Reich's piece but realised that DG was not the best vehicle to market the recording. Kommerell therefore offered the recording instead to Manfred Eicher of ECM, a company which had hitherto only released jazz and rock. The ECM release sold well over 100,000 copies, around 10 times higher than might be expected of a new music disc. This episode changed the nature of ECM and signalled a new approach to marketing new music that has since been taken up by other companies.

The 1978 recording still sounds beguilingly fresh. When Steve Reich and Musicians came to re-record *Music for 18 Musicians* for Nonesuch's 10-CD box set in 1996, their performance was amazingly 11 minutes longer than the ECM version. Normally, you would expect such a big difference to come from a slower tempo, but in fact the underlying pulse of both recordings is virtually identical. This is because of the unusual structure of *Music for 18 Musicians*, where the gradual fading-in and fading-out of different elements aren't given a fixed number of repetitions but are played simply as long as it takes for this process to happen. In the 1996 version these fade-ins and fade-outs are more finely graded and require more repetitions than in the 1978 version.

Electric Guitar Phase

Electric Guitar Phase (arr Frasca)[a]. Music for Large Ensemble[b]. Tokyo/Vermont Counterpoint (arr Yoshida)[c]. Triple Quartet[d]
[a]**Dominic Frasca** gtr [c]**Mika Yoshida** mari [d]**Kronos Quartet** (David Harrington, John Sherba vns Hank Dutt va Jennifer Culp vc) [b]**Alarm Will Sound;** [b]**Ossia / Alan Pierson**
Nonesuch 7559-79546-2 (54' · DDD)   Ⓕ●

Triple Quartet is Reich's first new work for the Kronos Quartet since writing his masterpiece *Different Trains* in 1988. It may disappoint –

there doesn't appear to be anything particularly new or different happening here. *Electric Guitar Phase*, on the other hand, shows precisely what's missing in *Triple Quartet*. The American guitarist Dominic Frasca has arranged *Violin Phase*, originally composed for four violins in the heady days of 1967, for four overdubbed guitars, and the result is sheer joy. Such is Frasca's sensitivity to every nuance of phrasing between the four lines that this recording is a classic for the minimalist genre, easily eclipsing the violin original in terms of intensity and tonal variety.

Up to now performances of Reich's music have been dominated by the composer's participative presence, even in larger concert works such as *The Desert Music*. His predilection for earthy, well-grounded tempos set the norm for performances of his music throughout the 1970s and 80s. Two recordings here are fascinating because they were made without Reich's active participation. In this recording of *Music For Large Ensemble*, the melodic invention at this jazzy, vibrant tempo sounds almost as if Reich had been listening to Ghanaian and Scottish folk music. Yet this is nothing compared to *Tokyo/Vermont Counterpoint*, where Mika Yoshida's articulation is so fast that at times you feel helium had escaped in the studio. This is compulsory listening for anyone who appreciates a little perversity now and again.

Violin Phase

Violin Phase[c]. Eight Lines[b]. New York Counterpoint[a]. City Life[d]
[a]Roland Diry cl [c]Jagdish Mistry vn [bd]Ensemble Modern / [b]Bradley Lubman, [d]Peter Rundel
RCA Red Seal 74321 66459-2 (66' · DDD) Ⓕ

The most focused work here, *Violin Phase* (1977), wears its purposefulness on its sleeve. Jagdish Mistry scintillates as the soloist, never letting go of the tension for a second, so when the end comes, you wait expectantly for that thread to be picked up again. *Eight Lines*, the reworked version of the *Octet* (1979/83) is also purposeful, moving gently from the early phase style to the melodic chanting-inspired style of the later *Tehillim*. While it's undeniably exciting, *New York Counterpoint* (1985) doesn't quite have that edge-of-the-seat adrenalin-powered quality that you can feel so clearly in *Violin Phase*. *City Life*, though beautifully written and, in many senses, a witty work (something that's caught wonderfully in the Ensemble Modern's sharp-edged performance), leaves one adrift, without any clear idea of its purpose. If you want unforgettable performances of *Violin Phase* and *Eight Lines*, Ensemble Modern's account is the one to go for.

City Life

Proverb. Nagoya marimbas. City Life
Bob Becker, **James Preiss** marimbas **Theatre of**

Voices (Andrea Fullington, Sonja Rasmussen, Allison Zelles *sops* Alan Bennett, Paul Elliott *tens*) **Steve Reich Ensemble / Paul Hillier; Bradley Lubman**
Nonesuch 7559-79430-2 (42' · DDD) ⒫Ⓞ

The Wittgenstein quotation 'How small a thought it takes to fill a whole life' serves as the basis of *Proverb* for three sopranos, two tenors, vibraphones and two electric organs, a composition that was premièred as a partial work 'in progress' at a 1995 Prom. The complete piece (it plays for some 14 minutes) holds together very well. Three sopranos 'sing the original melody of the text in canons that gradually augment, or get longer', whereas Perotin's influence can be heard in the tenor parts.

Reich's skill at inverting, augmenting and transforming his material has rarely sounded with such immediacy. After a virtuoso, pleasantly up-beat *Nagoya marimbas* lasting four and a half minutes, comes *City life*, probably Reich's best piece since *Different Trains*. The soundframe includes air brakes, pile drivers, car alarms, boat horns and police sirens, all of which are loaded into a pair of sampling keyboards and played alongside the instrumental parts. The first movement opens with what sounds like a distant relation of Stravinsky's *Symphonies of Wind Instruments* then kicks into action on the back of a Manhattan street vendor shouting 'Check it out'. The second and fourth movements witness gradual acceleration – the second to a pile driver, the fourth to a heartbeat – and the third has the two sampling keyboards engaging in top-speed crossfire based on speech samples. The last and most dissonant movement utilises material taped when the World Trade Centre was bombed in 1993.

City life is a tightly crafted montage, formed like an arch (A-B-C-B-A), lean, clever, catchy and consistently gripping. In fact the whole disc should thrill dyed-in-the-wool Reichians and preach convincingly to the as-yet unconverted. The sound is excellent.

Ottorino Respighi Italian 1879-1936

Respighi studied with Torchi and Martucci at the Liceo Musicale in Bologna (1891-1901), then had lessons with Rimsky-Korsakov during visits to Russia (1900-1903). In 1913 he settled in Rome, teaching and composing. He is best known as the composer of highly coloured orchestral pieces, capitalising on the most brilliant aspects of Rimsky-Korsakov, Ravel and Strauss: Fontane di Roma (1916), Pini di Roma (1924), Vetrate di chiesa (1925), Trittico botticelliano (1927), Gli uccelli (arrangements of pieces by earlier composers, 1927) and Feste romane (1928). His interest in the past is to be heard not only in his arrangements of Arie antiche for orchestra but in the use of plainchant and the church modes in such pieces as the Concerto gregoriano (for violin, 1921) and the Quartetto dorico (1924). He also wrote operas (La bella dormente nel bosco, 1921) and vocal works.

He was greatly helped by his wife, Elsa (b 1894),
herself a composer. GROVEmusic

Piano Concerto in A minor

Piano Concerto in A minor. Toccata. Fantasia slava
Konstantin Scherbakov pf **Slovak Radio Symphony**
Orchestra / Howard Griffiths
Naxos 8 553207 (51' · DDD) Recorded 1994   Ⓢ

All these pieces are otherwise available in decent
performances, but at this price how could anyone with the slightest weakness for Respighi
hesitate? Scherbakov and Griffiths do a good
deal more than dutifully go through the
motions, the soloist in particular playing with
delicacy and affection, grateful for the opportunities to demonstrate how well he would play
Liszt or Rachmaninov, but in the *Toccata* he's
interested as well in Respighi's more characteristic modal vein; as a Russian, he demonstrates
that this too, like so much in Respighi, was
influenced by the time he spent in Russia.

Russian soloist, English conductor and Slovak
orchestra all enjoy the moment in the *Fantasia
slava* where Respighi presents a morsel of
Smetana in the evident belief that it's a Russian
folk-dance, but the Concerto and the *Fantasia*,
both very early works, aren't patronised in the
slightest. The central slow section of the Concerto, indeed, achieves something like nobility,
and although there's a risk of the pianism in this
work seeming overblown, Scherbakov's fondness for Respighi's more fleet-footed manner
doesn't let this happen often.

The *Toccata* isn't so much an exercise in the
neo-Baroque, often though its dotted and florid
figures promise it, more of an essay on how far
one can be neo-Baroque without giving up a
post-Lisztian keyboard style and comfortable
orchestral upholstery. But in a slow and florid
central section, a rather melancholy aria that
passes from the soloist to the oboe, to the strings
and back again, there's a real quality of Bachian
utterance translated not unrecognisably into a
late Romantic language. Scherbakov sounds
touched by it, and obviously wants us to like it.
The recordings are more than serviceable, but
each work is given only a single track.

Roman Trilogy

Pines of Rome; Fountains of Rome; Roman Festivals

Roman Trilogy
Oregon Symphony Orchestra / James DePreist
Delos DE3287 (66' · DDD)   ⒻⓄ

The first essential of any new version of this
ideal coupling is to have brilliant recording to
bring out the splendour and atmospheric beauty
of Respighi's three musical picture-postcards.
That term may once have been used disparag-
ingly, but no longer when the glories as well as
the limitations of these highly attractive pieces

have long been recognised. On that first count
of recording quality, Delos provides a sensuously velvety, wrap-around quality that's both
warmly atmospheric and finely detailed, helped
by a sharp terracing of textures to make the
sound both immediate and vividly realistic.
Usually the *Pines of Rome*, with its thrusting first
movement of children-at-play, is presented
first, but DePreist prefers the *Fountains of Rome*,
with its gentle opening. The clean separation of
the recorded sound immediately conveys a fine
sense of presence.

DePreist, since he becoming music director of
the Oregon orchestra in 1980, has built it into a
virtuoso band more than able to hold its own in
international company, so these showpieces are
presented with the sort of panache they need.
DePreist and his players are no less brilliant
than their rivals. Often they gain from the extra
weight of the bass response, as when, in the second movement of the *Fountains*, 'The Triton
Fountain in the Morning', the pedal-notes from
the organ have the tummy-wobbling quality
usually experienced only in live performance.
The brash last movement of *Roman Festivals* has
sound slightly less vivid and immediate than the
rest, but on any count this is among the finest
versions of a much-duplicated coupling.

Roman Trilogy
Royal Philharmonic Orchestra / Enrique Bátiz
Naxos 8 550539 (61' · DDD) Recorded 1991   ⓈⓄ

This Naxos disc is an extraordinary bargain; it
would be recommendable at full price; in the
super-bargain area it's unbeatable. It has such
excitement and verve that you can accept an
extra degree of brazen extroversion, indeed
revel in it. In *Roman Festivals* the opening
'Circuses' is immensely spectacular, its character in the unfettered gladiatorial tradition of the
Coliseum: the trumpets and drums are quite
thrilling. The gossamer opening of 'The
Jubilee' leads to the most dramatic climax. In
the 'October Festival' the strings play their
Latin soliloquy very exotically for Bátiz. The
closing section brings a gentle mandolin serenade. The great clamour of the Epiphany celebrations which follow unleashes a riotous *mêlée*
from the RPO, which sounds as if it's enjoying
itself hugely, and the obvious affinity with the
final fairground scene of Petrushka is all the
more striking when the strings have that bit
more bite. The *Pines* and *Fountains* are also very
fine. When the unison horns signal the turning
on of the Triton Fountain, and the cascade
splashes through the orchestra, the RPO
unleashes a real flood. Yet the lovely, radiant
evocation of the central movements of *The
Pines*, and the sensuous Italian light of the sunset at the Villa Medici, are most sensitively
realised by the RPO, and at the very beginning
of the finale, 'The Pines of the Appian Way', the
ever present sound, with its growling bass clarinet, gives a sinister implication of the advancing Roman might.

Church Windows

Church Windows, Brazilian Impressions. Roman
Festivals
**Cincinnati Symphony Orchestra / Jesús López-
Cobos**
Telarc CD80356 (71' · DDD) Recorded 1993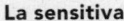

You might easily argue that neither *Church
Windows* nor *Brazilian Impressions* is quite as successful as the 'essential' Respighi of the Roman
Trilogy. The only answer to that, López-Cobos
seems to suggest, is to take the music perfectly
seriously and pay scrupulous attention not just
to its potential for sonorous spectacle but to its
wealth of beautifully crafted detail. The gong at
the end of the second movement of *Church
Windows* is magnificently resonant, as is the
organ in the finale, and the work is given an
extra inch or two of stature by sensitive handling
of those moments that need but don't always get
delicacy. He pays such care to character and
detail in 'Butantan', that creepy depiction of a
snake-farm in *Brazilian Impressions*, that you can
not only recapture the real, crawling horror that
Respighi experienced there, but discover in the
music also a queer sort of Debussian grace as
well. And as for *Roman Festivals*, well, what's
wrong with 20-odd minutes of wide-screen
spectacular once in a while? But if every colour
is precisely rendered, the quiet passages as affectionately turned as they are here, what skill is to
be found in it, what a gift for immaculately precise instrumental detail. With that sort of handling all three pieces sound quite worthy of
sharing shelf space with *Pines* and *Fountains*.
The recording is spectacular.

La Boutique fantasque

Respighi La Boutique fantasque. La Pentola magica
Bach Prelude and Fugue in D, BWV532 (orch
Respighi)
BBC Philharmonic Orchestra / Gianandrea Noseda
Chandos CHAN10081 (80' · DDD) Ⓕ

Noseda's vigorous account of *La Boutique fantasque* makes a fine coupling with two rarities
which similarly show off Respighi's brilliance as
an orchestrator of others' music. *La Pentola
magica* ('The magic pot') is a ballet score from
1920 whose scenario has been lost, though the
titles of the ten brief movements give an idea of
the Russian story behind it. Respighi drew on
relatively neglected Russian composers such as
Grechaninov, Arensky and Rubinstein, and Pol-
ish-born Pachulski, as well as including his
arrangements of Russian folk themes. Slow
music and a relaxed mood predominates in
evocative orchestration. His joy in orchestral
sound is even more striking in the exuberant
account of his arrangement of Bach's D major
Prelude and Fugue, with rich, weighty brass and
dramatic contrasts of timbre and dynamic. The
performance of *La Boutique fantasque* has similar
zest. The playing of the BBC Philharmonic is

expressive, with *rubato* that dancers wouldn't
welcome on stage. The speeds tend to be a trifle
extreme, bringing an apt and enjoyable sense of
danger in the pointing of the tricky woodwind
flurries dotted through the score. The Chandos
sound, satisfyingly full and bright, matches the
performance.

La sensitiva

La sensitiva[b]. Deità silvane[a]. Nebbie[b]. Aretusa[b]
[a]**Ingrid Attrot** sop [b]**Linda Finnie** mez **BBC
Philharmonic Orchestra / Richard Hickox**
Chandos CHAN9453 (60' · DDD) Texts and
translations included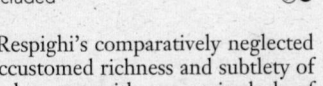

In some of Respighi's comparatively neglected
pieces, his accustomed richness and subtlety of
orchestral colour go with a certain lack of
melodic individuality. Once or twice in *Deità silvane* ('Woodland gods'), one wishes that the
poems' classical imagery would lead him
towards an evocation or even a direct quotation
from Italian music's 'classical' past of the kind
that so often renders his better-known music so
memorable. In *La sensitiva* ('The sensitive
plant'), however, his care for the imagery and
prosody of Shelley's poem (in Italian translation) was so responsive that striking melodic
invention was the result. The orchestral colour
of the piece is exquisite, the succession of ideas
(the sensitive plant is image both of unhappy
lover and spurned artist) a good deal more than
merely picturesque. In a performance as expressive as this it seems one of Respighi's best works,
and a good deal more sophisticated than he's
generally given credit for. *Aretusa* is fine, too,
with bigger dramatic gestures, even richer
colour and some magnificent sea music. The
much better-known *Nebbie* is another example
of Respighi finding a genuinely sustained
melodic line in response to a text which obviously meant a great deal to him. Everything
here is played with a real care for Respighi's line
as well as his sumptuous but never muddy
colours. First-class recording.

Songs

Cinque canti all'antica. Sei liriche. Deità silvane.
Ballata alla luna. Stornello. Stornellatrice. Contrasto.
Tanto bella. Invito alla danza. L'ultima ebbrezza.
Notturno. Luce
Leonardo de Lisi ten **Reinild Mees** pf
Channel Classics CCS9396 (60' · DDD) Texts and
translations included Ⓕ

Leonardo de Lisi is a lyric tenor of real quality
with a Lieder singer's subtlety, taste and
responsiveness to words. In fact by the colour of
the voice you might not take him to be an Italian
and his French diction is almost impeccable in
the two settings by Respighi (among the *Sei
liriche*) of French texts, the quite magical 'Le
repos en Egypte' and the striking 'Noël ancien'.

If you haven't so far thought of Respighi as a song composer you're in for a surprise. Sopranos quite often programme his charming *Stornellatrice* as an encore but it has equals and indeed superiors here. *Tanto bella*, for example: ample grateful melody over a lilting accompaniment, with a haunting middle section. The *Canti all'antica* are fresh and very simple. But with the *Sei liriche* of 1912 we reach audible French influence and by 1917 and *Deità silvane* Respighi's smooth lines have become flexible and his idiomatic keyboard writing is now filled with vivid imagery. Reinild Mees is obviously as fond of *Deità silvane* as de Lisi is. Both are excellently recorded.

Silvestre Revueltas   Mexican 1899-1940

Revueltas studied in Mexico City, Austin and Chicago, his teachers including Tella and Borowski. From 1929 to 1935 he was assistant conductor of the Mexico SO, for which he composed rhythmically vigorous, boldly coloured pieces, most famously Sensemayá; (1938).   GROVEmusic

Orchestral Works

Revueltas Homenaje a Lorca. Planos. Ocho x Radio. El Renacuajo Paseador. Pieza para doce instrumentos. Sensemayá. Caminando. Este era un Rey. Hora de Junio **J Pomar** Preludio y Fuga ritmicos **Juan Carlos Tajes** spkr **Ebony Band, Amsterdam / Werner Herbers**
Channel Classics CD/SACD 🔊 CCSSA21104
(67' · DDD) Recorded live   Ⓕ

Revueltas recordings – those of the orchestral *Sensemayá* aside – have a tendency not to linger in the catalogue, a bizarre fact given his music's basic rhythmic and instrumental appeal. One such is the no longer available RCA Catalyst disc that encapsulates his highly coloured soundworld, 'The Night of the Mayas'.

The sheer verve and power of his music leads one to think of Revueltas as primarily an orchestral composer, but many of his works are written for relatively modest forces (or started out that way, like *Sensemayá*, given a spirited performance here). Often, it's the ferocity of his sound – and liberal use of percussion – that gives the music a bigger texture than its actual layout might suggest. Even so relatively modest a piece as the playful octet *Ocho x Radio* (1933) feels like a small orchestral score. Curiously, the early *Pieza para doce instrumentos* (1929; left untitled by Revueltas) seems much smaller in scale despite being longer. The four movements chart a gentle course in increasing tempi from *Lento* to *Allegro*. Here the burlesque and grotesque strains in his musical psyche were yet to be allowed full rein, but were unleashed in *El renacuajo paseador* ('The Wandering Tadpole', 1933), with its quotations and teasing allusions. The tiny suite describes how a tadpole meets an untimely end after going out for a drink with a mouse, the moral of which did not deter the composer from terminal alcoholism. *Caminando* (1937) is a real find.

One of the final projects Revueltas worked on was Luis Córdova's 'caustic satire on fascism', *Este era un Rey* ('Once there was a King', 1940). The *Preludio y Fuga ritmicos* by his close friend José Pomar completes a splendid disc – derived from concert performances – that deserves every success. Highly recommended.

Nicolay Rimsky-Korsakov
Russian 1844-1908

Apart from piano lessons, a love for the music of Glinka and a fascination with opera orchestras, Rimsky-Korsakov had little preparation for a musical career – he trained as a naval officer – until he met Balakirev (1861), who captivated him, encouraging his attempts at composition, performing his works and introducing him to Borodin, Dargomïzhsky, Cui and Mussorgsky. He wrote songs, orchestral works and an opera (The Maid of Pskov, 1873) before becoming professor at the St Petersburg Conservatory (1871) and inspector of naval bands (1873-84), teaching himself harmony and counterpoint, conducting at Balakirev's Free School and collecting folksongs. His next opera, May Night (1880), engaged his full creative powers with its blend of the fantastic and the comic (the realm in which he was to score most of his greatest successes), while Snow Maiden (1882) evoked a deeper world of nature-mysticism. Official duties at the imperial chapel (1883-91), work on the deceased Mussorgsky's and Borodin's manuscripts and advising for the publisher Belyayev interrupted composition, but he did produce the three colourful orchestral works by which he is best known, Sheherazade, the Spanish Capriccio and the Russian Easter Festival Overture, during 1887-8, after which he devoted himself to opera. Of the 12 dramatic works from Mlada (1892) to The Golden Cockerel (1909), Kitezh (1907) stands out for its mystical and psychological depths. Rimsky-Korsakov's operas far out-weigh in importance his other compositions, for both their brilliant scoring and fine vocal writing. If they lack dramatic power and strong characterisation, they nevertheless set delightful fantastic puppets in the context of musico-scenic fairy tales, using a dual musical language to delineate 'real' from 'unreal'. He transmitted his pellucid style to two generations of Russian composers, from Lyadov and Glazunov to Stravinsky and Prokofiev, all of whom were his pupils.   GROVEmusic

Scheherazade, Op 35

Rimsky-Korsakov Scheherazade, Op 35 **Balakirev** Islamey (arr Lyapunov) **Borodin** In the Steppes of Central Asia
Kirov Orchestra / Valery Gergiev
Philips 470 840-2PH (63' · DDD)   Ⓕ 🔊

for Presser, then in 1960 joined the faculty at the University of Pennsylvania. During the mid-1960s he began to work with quotations, drawing on music from Bach to the present, which seems to have led him to an overtly Romantic style in most of his music since the early 1970s. His works cover most genres and include five symphonies (1957-85), a Violin Concerto (1974), seven string quartets (1952-79) and other chamber and vocal music. GROVEmusic

Paganini Variations

50 Caprice Variations after Paganini
Peter Sheppard Skaerved vn
Metier Sound & Vision ② MSVCD92065 (91' · DDD)
⑤

The violin here is the 'Habeneck', put together by Stradivari in 1734 when he was 90, and formerly played by Ralph Holmes. Its wonderfully rich response makes a major sixth sound like a four-part chord. Peter Sheppard Skaerved was a pupil of Holmes and a worthy successor, as his playing here and elsewhere demonstrates. His CD booklet goes into detail about his connections with Rochberg when playing the *Caprice Variations*, written in 1970, shortly before the composer turned away from modernism in works like the Third Quartet. The prospect of 90 minutes of unaccompanied violin is intimidating but, since Rochberg is working within traditions from Bach to Mahler, the whole apparatus of tonality is in operation for 41 out of the 50 variations. There are connections with Beethoven, Brahms and Bach as well as Mahler and early Webern. For example, Variation 21 takes off from the finale of Beethoven's Seventh Symphony, of which Rochberg said: 'There is more sheer vitality per square measure...than in any number of pieces by major composers of our own time.' Then there's the Paganini theme itself, which has been the basis for variations by composers as different as Lutosławski and Andrew Lloyd Webber. We hear it briefly at the end and are left wondering if that was what the previous 90 minutes were about. In fact the previous five variations were dissonant, but the first 17 were blandly diatonic: 18 was a shock, with high shrieks which come back in 35. The performance is so compelling that interest never wavers; the recording is fine; and it doesn't matter where the music came from, since this magnificent instrument enjoys every note.

Joaquin Rodrigo   Spanish 1901-1999

Rodrigo, blind from the age of three, studied with Antich in Valencia and Dukas in Paris (from 1927), also receiving encouragement from Falla. His Concierto de Aranjuez for guitar and orchestra (1939) made his name and established his style of tuneful and smoothly colourful Hispanicism: his later works include similar concertos for violin, piano, cello, harp and flute as well as songs and small instrumental pieces, several for guitar.
GROVEmusic

Concertos (including 'de Aranjuez')

Concierto de Aranjuez[a]. Concierto andaluz[a].
Fantasía para un gentilhombre[b]
[a]**Ricardo Gallén** gtr [b]**EntreQuatre Quitar Quartet**
(Jesús Prieto, Roberto Martínez, Carlos Cuanda, Manuel Paz gtrs) **Asturias Symphony Orchestra / Maximiano Valdes**
Naxos 8 555841 (68' · DDD)   ⑤

Concierto en modo galante[b]. Canconeta[a].
Concierto como un Divertimento[b]. Concierto de estío[a]
[a]**Mikhail Ovrutsky** vn [b]**Asier Polo** vc **Castille and León Symphony Orchestra / Max Bragado-Darman**
Naxos 8 555840 (78' · DDD)   ⑤

Piano Concerto (Concierto heroico – ed Achúcarro)[a].
Juglares. Homenaje a la Tempranica. Música para un jardín
[a]**Daniel Ligorio Ferrándiz** pf **Castille and León Symphony Orchestra / Max Bragado-Darman**
Naxos 8 557101 (60' · DDD)   ⑤

The focus of these three volumes is on concertos, the most popular and arguably the best segment of Rodrigo's orchestral music. The best known are those for guitar and orchestra, of the very numerous recordings of which these are 'good enough to keep'. Lest anyone might think that the *Concierto para piano y orquesta* listed on Volume 4 is a previously overlooked work, it's in fact the *Concierto heroico* in modestly repackaged form. Achúcarro revised it with the composer's consent to make the work 'slightly more dynamic'. This is now the definitive form and performance of the concerto. The 'symphonic essay' *Juglares* (1923) was Rodrigo's first orchestral work, brief but characteristic of the music of Valencia, where he lived before going to Paris to study. It has no other current recording. All the remaining works on these three discs have alternative recordings but though one may prefer the warmer-sounding version of the *Concierto de estío* by Agustín León Ara, the composer's son-in-law, on the EMI set, these recordings are in every respect comparable with the 'opposition'.

Concierto de Aranjuez[a]. Three Piezas españolas[b].
Invocación y danza[c]. Fantasía para un gentilhombre[d]
Julian Bream gtr [a]**Chamber Orchestra of Europe / Sir John Eliot Gardiner;** [d]**RCA Victor Chamber Orchestra / Leo Brouwer**
RCA Victor 09026 61611-2 (69' · DDD) Recorded [abc]1982-83, [d]1987   Ⓜ●●●

In the early 1980s Bream had entered a phase when his musical and technical powers were at their height, which he too recognised and celebrated in this remarkable album. With it he confirmed that he's Segovia's truest and best successor, though in no sense his imitator, and established a benchmark in the history of the guitar on record.

Everything he touched turns to music, and is here recorded with the utmost reality. If anyone is wondering why he should here have taken his third bite at Aranjuez's cherry, it was in order to 'go digital' but in the event this proved a subsidiary *raison-d'être*. At the time the COE was no casual band assembled for a session, but a newly formed orchestra of young players from several countries, greeting the concerto as a fresh experience and playing it with splendid precision and vitality. John Eliot Gardiner's conducting is unfailingly idiomatic. Who catalysed whom is hard to say, but Bream certainly responded with the *Aranjuez* of his life, eloquently phrased and passionate; nothing is lost in the recording and the guitar is 'prestidigitalised' into unfailing audibility. This version of the concerto must remain the touchstone for a very long time, reaffirming the thoroughbred character of a warhorse that often sounds tired and overworked.

Leo Brouwer is a man of so many musical parts that the loss of one of them – his role as a virtuoso guitarist – has passed almost unnoticed; here he plays one of the others, that of conductor. What better than to provide the ammunition for others to fire, and to direct the campaign yourself? *Fantasía para un gentilhombre* has its own merits and demerits, with Bream stressing the musical rather than the virtuoso elements, adopting somewhat slower tempos than other interpreters in most of the movements – that of the final 'Canarios' is more in keeping with the character of the dance itself. Brouwer's splendid control of the orchestra reflects his experience of both sides of the concerto 'fence'. This disc is a must.

Rodrigo Concierto de Aranjuez **Castelnuovo-Tedesco** Guitar Concerto No 1 in D, Op 99 **Villa-Lobos** Guitar Concerto
Norbert Kraft *gtr* **Northern Chamber Orchestra / Nicholas Ward**
Naxos 8 550729 (60' · DDD) Recorded 1992 ⓢⵔ

The time has long passed when it was possible to point to any one recording of any of these concertos (the Rodrigo in particular) as 'The Best'; as with players, one can only discern a 'top bracket' within which choice depends finally on personal preference – or allegiance to your favourite performer, or indeed with the other works on the disc. Norbert Kraft's accounts of these concertos takes its place therein. In this recording Kraft is placed forwardly enough for every detail to be heard, but not to create an impression of artificiality. The Northern Chamber Orchestra plays with freshness and is alert to every detail and the beautifully clear recording catches it faithfully. At super-budget price this disc is a bargain.

Concierto de Aranjuez[ac]. Fantasía para un gentilhombre[ac]. Cançoneta[bc]. Invocacíon y danza[a]. Tres Pequeñas piezas[a]

[a]**Pepe Romero** *gtr* [b]**Augustín Léo Ara** *vn* [c]**Academy of St Martin in the Fields / Sir Neville Marriner**
Philips 438 016-2PH (64' · DDD) Recorded 1992Ⓕⵔⵔ

What we have here is simply one of the best: Pepe Romero, a close friend of Rodrigo, has the technique to do whatever he pleases, though his capacity for high speed doesn't tempt him to display it for its own sake. There's elegance and a certain nobility in his interpretations, though he lacks the warmth of Bream, and the 'flamenco steeliness' of his *rasgueados* does perhaps stand in uncomfortable contrast with the rest. The ASMF must know these scores by heart, but, perhaps stimulated by the presence of a soloist who's so completely in command of his material, its immaculate support bears no trace of staleness. The *Cançoneta* (1923) is one of Rodrigo's earliest works, a small (just under three minutes) island of peaceful romantic dreams in a sea of guitar music, sweetly played by Ara (Rodrigo's son-in-law) and ignored in the annotation. There's no better recording of the *Invocacíon y danza*, and only one other (also by Romero) of the *Tres Pequeñas piezas*, in the last of which the steely *rasgueados* are entirely in character. If you aren't already liberally provided with recordings of the two main items you may rightly be tempted by this outstanding recording.

Concierto de Aranjuez. Fantasía para un gentilhombre. Un tiempo fue Itálica famosa. Zarabanda lejana. Adela. Villancicos – Pastorcito Santo; Coplillas de Belén. Coplas del pastor enamorado
Manuel Barrueco *gtr* **Philharmonia Orchestra / Plácido Domingo** *ten*
EMI 556175-2 (67' · DDD) Texts and translation included Ⓕ

Concierto de Aranjuez. Fantasía para un gentilhombre. Concierto para una fiesta
David Russell *gtr* **Naples Philharmonic Orchestra (Florida) / Erich Kunzel**
Telarc CD80459 (72' · DDD) Ⓕⵔⵔ

Both discs are among the best recordings of the *Concierto de Aranjuez* and *Fantasia para un gentilhombre*. Barrueco and Russell are members of the guitar's top-drawer élite, giving performances of crystalline clarity, and they're both excellently supported by their orchestras. In both recordings the guitar is foregrounded to a greater extent than it ever is in the concert hall. You might regard this as a distortion, but as it more faithfully represents what was in the composer's inner ear it should be enjoyed in its own right. If you decide to add one of these recordings to your collection then your choice may depend on the other items they contain. In Russell's case it's the *Concierto para una fiesta*. The thought 'Where have I heard this before?' may cross your mind – in relation to both musical elements and the mode of orchestration. But you might find these familiar echoes lovably welcome. Barrueco adds two solos, neither one yet dulled by overfamiliarity. The *Zarabanda lejana* is given with the utmost expressivity, and *Un tiempo fue Itálica famosa* is delivered with panache. Barrueco has one more trump card to play – his partnership with Plácido Domingo in four songs, selected from those for which Rodrigo himself has made adaptations for the guitar of the original piano accompaniments. Both are longstanding devotees of Rodrigo's music. Domingo also conducts the orchestra, an exercise in which both parties demonstrate their happy meeting of minds.

Concierto madrigal

Concierto madrigal. Danza de la Amapola[a]. Evocaciones – Mañana en Trianae[a]. Gran marcha de los subsecretarios[a]. Piezas – Fandango del ventorrillo[a]. Serenata española[a]. Sonada de adiós, 'Hommage à Paul Dukas'[a]. Tonadilla ([a]arr Peter Katona, Zoltán Katona)
Peter Katona, Zoltán Katona gtrs **Rotterdam Chamber Orchestra / Conrad van Alphen**
Channel Classics CCS16698 (62' · DDD)   Ⓕ**O**

The best of the established guitar duos have consisted of players who are/were either married or blood-related – favourable conditions for in-built empathy. Presti-Lagoya set the pace in the 1960s, one which has still to be fully matched. Now we have the Hungarian duo of the Katona twins, possessed of a technique most others can only dream of. Their needle-sharp unanimity of thought and attack is such that listening 'blind' you might wonder how a player could possibly have so many digits. Rodrigo wrote only two works for two guitars, the *Tonadilla* and (with orchestra) the *Concierto madrigal*. Neither has been better recorded than here. In the latter the recorded balance often tips slightly in favour of the orchestra, but this is a minor quibble. In order to flesh out the aprogramme the Katonas have made admirable arrangements of six piano pieces written between 1931 and 1981, and these magnificently played versions for two guitars should keep Rodrigo aficionados happy enough. The Katonas have yet to parallel the emotional depth and warmth of Presti-Lagoya, but they have youth on their side and, being in total command of every other necessary 'tools', they may well become world-beaters. This is a stunning disc, to which the orchestra and recording engineers have made fitting contributions.

Concierto madrigal. Concierto para una fiesta
Ricardo Gallén, Joaquín Clerch gtrs **Asturias Symphony Orchestra / Maximiano Valdés**
Naxos 8 555842 (62' · DDD)   Ⓢ

The *Concierto madrigal* is, like the *Fantasía para un gentilhombre*, a tribute to times past though, since the first movement briefly tugs a forelock

to Monteverdi, and the madrigal *O felici occhi miei* plays a key role, it isn't an exclusively Spanish one. It's a fascinating work, with ten movements full of diversity and maybe the one of the 'family' that deserves a place on that distant desert island. As with the *Concierto para una fiesta*, this is a recording that can hold its own with any of its rivals – finely played with good sound from all concerned, excellently balanced and faithfully recorded. The *Concierto para una fiesta* was commissioned by a wealthy Texan as a present for the coming-out party of his daughters, admirers of Pepe Romero. He and the composer were reported at the time to be chuckling at the thought of listening (in Heaven) to others struggling to play it. Time passes, however, and there are now several good recordings of the work by others, of whom Ricardo Gallén is now one. Technical skills have been steadily on a rising curve for decades and, whether or not the curve is asymptotic, its highest point has yet to be attained indefinitely by one single guitarist. Around every corner there may be an equally fast or even faster 'gun'. It isn't the most riveting of Rodrigo's concertos for solo guitar, but it's notable for its slow movement, a clear souvenir of that of the *Concierto de Aranjuez*, and Gallén's performance certainly does it justice.

Per la flor del lliri blau

Per la flor del lliri blau. A la busca del más allá. Palillos y Panderetas. Dos danzas españolas[a]. Tres viejos aires de danza
[a]**Lucero Tena** castanets **Castilla y León Symphony Orchestra / Max Bragado Darman**
Naxos 8 555962 (69' · DDD)   Ⓢ

At the heart of this volume are two of Rodrigo's finest orchestral works – *Per la flor del lliri blau* (1934) and *A la busca del más allá* (1976). The former is a symphonic poem based on a Valencian legend in which the three sons of a dying king go in search of a blue lily whose magic powers can save their father. The outcome is successful but tragic, as clearly depicted as that of the eponym of Elgar's *Falstaff*. *A la busca del más allá* was commissioned by the Houston Symphony for the bicentennial celebrations in the US. Their choice of composer may seem curious, but it proved a wise one. Its title ('In search of what lies beyond') reflected Houston's status as the centre of space exploration. How would Rodrigo, who had until then devoted his attention to all things Spanish and was then 75, deal with such an unfamiliar demand? The answer was that he did so with skill and imagination, leaving little or no trace of Spanishry. The curtain rises and falls with a long roll on an undamped cymbal, and the principal motif of what separates these events contains a 'questioning' tritone. The performances of all the 'fillers' are exemplary but it's the two large works that make this recording indispensable to Rodrigo lovers.

Solo Piano Works

Complete Solo Piano Works
Sara Marianovich pf
Sony Classical ② S2K89828 (155' · DDD)   Ⓕ**O**

Rodrigo greatly valued his piano music and was disappointed that it was so seldom performed. His daughter tells us that Sarah Marianovich played this music for him and received his imprimatur. Understandably so, as she's very sensitive to its stylistic changes. In her hands, the innocent early *Suite* of 1923 has just the right simplicity, and she also catches the winning charm of the *Pastoral* (1926), a siciliana, and two delicate Berceuses, while the *Preludio al gallo mañero* glitters in the manner of Debussy. Much of Rodrigo's early music is eclectic in style, and the *Cinco Piezas del Siglio XVI* are arrangements for piano of pieces by Milán, Cabezón and Mudarra. But what character they have! The ambitious *Sonatas de Castilla con toccata a modo de pregón* (1950-51) brilliantly and hauntingly exploit the same basic material throughout, with each episode dedicated to a Spanish musician. Not surprisingly, the *Tres evocaciones* (remembering Turina) are the most atmospheric pieces of all, with the third, *Mañana en Triana* idealising Spanish dance rhythms with plenty of sparkling bravura. Rodrigo's final piano work (from 1987), the romantic *Preludio de Añoranza* ('Nostalgia'), is associated with Artur Rubinstein, and makes a magical postlude. Rodrigo could hardly have a more persuasive advocate. Highly recommended. ·

Piano Music, Volume 1

Al'ombre de Torre Bermeja. Air de Ballet sur le nom d'une Jeune Fille. Bagatela. Berceuse de Otoño. Berceuse de primavera. Cuatro Estampas andaluzas. Pastorale. Cincos Piezas del siglio XVI. Cuatro Piezas. Preludio de Añoranza. Serenata española. Sonata de adiós, 'Hommage à Paul Dukas'. Zarabanda lejana. Fantasía que contrahace la harpa de Ludovico
Artur Pizarro pf
Naxos 8 557272 (70' · DDD)   Ⓢ**OO**

Rodrigo's piano music appears infrequently in the recital room, though excellent two-CD surveys have appeared: Gregory Allen on Bridge and Sara Marianovich on Sony. Now comes a first-class collection from the perceptive and sympathetic Artur Pizarro, who opens brilliantly with Rodrigo's evocation of Albéniz, *A l'ombre de Torre Bermeja*, here, as elsewhere, bringing out its affinities with the guitar. *Cuatro Piezas* include a glittering 'Fandango' and a touchingly pensive 'Prayer of the Princess of Castille', while among the *Andalusian Pictures* (*Cuatro Estampas andaluzas*), 'Twilight over the Guadalquivir River' makes a reflective contrast with the quirky bravura of the devilish 'Seguidillas'. Among the simpler items, the nostalgic *Preludio*, and delicate *Pastorale*, the rip-

pling *Serenata española* and charming *Air de Ballet* are all highly beguiling. Pizarro captures the varying moods of this music very well. This generous collection is vividly recorded and with excellent booklet-notes by Graham Wade.

Philippe Rogier   Flemish 1561-1596

Rogier was a chorister at Philip II of Spain's chapel from 1572; he was ordained, becoming vice-maestro in 1584 and maestro de capilla in 1586. Of his large output (at least 250 works), only 16 motets (1595), five masses (1598) and a few chansons and other sacred works survive.   **GROVE**music

Missa Ego sum qui sum

Rogier Missa Ego sum qui sum. Laboravi in gemitu meo. Heu mihi Domine. Vias tuas. Taedet animam meam. Peccavi quid faciam tibi. Dominus regit me **Gombert** Ego sum qui sum
Magnificat / Philip Cave
Linn Records CKD109 (75' · DDD) Texts and translations included   Ⓕ**O**

So much first-rate 16th-century music still remains unrecorded, but here's a welcome addition. Philippe Rogier's death at the age of 35 in 1596 cut short a prolific stream of music. Worse was to come. In 1734 a fire destroyed the library of the Spanish royal chapel, which must have held a large number of his compositions (at the time of his death he was chief court musician to Philip II). How large a number can be gauged from the terrible earthquake that struck Lisbon in 1755, swallowing up the royal library along with 243 works. Today we're left with only 51, of which the present recital represents a sizeable proportion.

Rogier's music has Palestrina's imposing solidity and classical feel, but is more florid and freer in its use of dissonance. In this sense it looks forward to later Iberian music of the 17th century, achieving a sustained intensity in the motets. The Mass is a consummate demonstration, the skilful working out of a motet by Gombert, whose influence is very audible. The booklet-note rightly points out how Rogier develops his model in very different directions: the sequences that conclude most movements are persuasively managed, but sound utterly unlike Gombert.

Rogier's Mass *Domine Dominus noster* appears in a fine recording on Ricercar. But Magnificat's interpretation is of a different order. This is singing in the English tradition, but with greater warmth and richness than we're used to from mixed choirs of this kind. Given Rogier's predilection for fully scored writing, that richness pays dividends, as does the relatively large cast of 18 singers. Interpretation and music are well matched in more ways than one. Neither are strikingly original, but both make a striking impression.

Cipriano de Rore
Flemish 1515/16-1565

Rore was in Italy by the 1540s; he was associated with Willaert and others in Venice. He was established as a composer by 1547, when he was maestro di cappella at the Ferrarese court. In 1559 he moved to Brussels to serve Margaret of Parma, governor of the Netherlands, in 1561 to Parma, to enter Ottavio Farnese's service, and in 1563 to Venice, where he was briefly maestro di cappella at St Mark's. He returned to Parma in 1564. The most influential of the earlier madrigalists, he produced over 120 Italian madrigals (mainly in 10 bks, 1542-66), as well as c80 sacred motets (5 bks, 1544-63, 1595, and MSS), masses, a Passion, secular motets and chansons. His early madrigals, mainly serious in tone, show a masterly fusion of sophisticated Franco-Flemish polyphony and Italian lyricism, with controlled use of imagery, while his later ones include marked progressive elements; these were much admired by Monteverdi. **GROVE**music

Missa Praeter rerum seriem

Missa Praeter rerum seriem. Calami sonum ferentes. Mon petit cueur. Plange quasi virgo. Dissimulare etiam sperasti. Il secondo libro de madrigali – Mia benigna fortuna; Schiet'arbuscel. Il quarto libro de madrigali – Se ben il duol
Huelgas Ensemble / Paul van Nevel
Harmonia Mundi HMC90 1760 (65' · DDD) Texts and translations included ⓕ

The Huelgas Ensemble have recorded a masterly recital of works by Cipriano de Rore, subtitled 'Music, Mirror of the text'. That's an apt description of much of Rore's output, but the inspired and truly brilliant way in which he achieves his goal is what has left its mark upon future generations of composers. The major work of the collection is Rore's seven-part 'parody-cum-*cantus-firmus*' *Missa Praeter rerum seriem*, with its flowing melody and showers of taut little imitations. Based on a motet by Josquin and dedicated to Duke Ercole d'Este, in whose service Rore was enrolled in 1547, the composer hails his master by name in the tenor part of every movement. The remainder of the programme includes such widely different pieces as the charming little eight-part love-song *Mon petit cueur*, with its full canonic imitation and wonderful final cadence, and the slow-moving five-part responsary for Holy Saturday *Plange quasi virgo*. Another striking piece is the four-part madrigal *Calami sonum ferentes*, which exploits the lowest range of the basses in slowly rising chromatic scales. But possibly the most original and forward-looking of all are the last two pieces, in which Rore promotes his own, very personal technique of chordal homophony. The anguished experimental *Se ben il duol* is a small masterpiece, and so is the fully developed motet on a text from Virgil, *Dissimulare etiam sperasti*. Huelgas rises to the challenge of interpreting, with colour and genius, this amazing music describing Dido's despair.

Ned Rorem
American b1923

Rorem studied with Sowerby in Chicago (1938-9) and with Thomson (1944) and Diamond in New York, also attending the Curtis Institute (1943) and the Juilliard School. From 1949 to 1958 he was based in Paris, though spent two of those years in Morocco: his published diaries of this and later periods are flamboyantly candid. His large output includes symphonies, instrumental pieces and choral music, though he has been most productive and successful as a composer of songs. **GROVE**music

Chamber Works

Book of Hours[a]. Bright Music[b]. End of Summer[c]
The Fibonacci Sequence ([ab]Anna Noakes fl [c]Julin Farrell cl [a]Gillian Tingay hp [bc]Kathron Sturrock pf [bc]Jonathan Carney, [b]Ursula Gough vns [b]Michael Stirling vc)
Naxos American Classics 8 559128 (60' · DDD) Ⓢ○○

In Ned Rorem's *End of Summer* (1985) for clarinet, violin and piano, dramatic juxtapositions seem to be the work's organising principle. Without postmodern trickery, Rorem shows us that seemingly disparate elements can coexist quite happily. One hears a similar kind of musical détente going on in parts of *Bright Music* (1987) for flute, two violins, cello and piano – particularly in the opening Fandango, inspired by the image of a rat inside a rubbish bin. This is a substantial, delightful suite, centered on a brilliant *scherzo* movement ('Dance-Song-Dance') that enfolds one of Rorem's loveliest tunes. The slow movement (entitled 'Another Dance') is an expansive, aching song without words, and the whirlwind finale a clever and ultimately unsettling take on the last movement of Chopin's *Funeral March* Sonata. *Book of Hours* (1975), for flute and harp, is structured on the timetable of monastic prayer, beginning with Matins and continuing through Lauds all the way to Vespers and Compline. There are few sweet melodies here, though Rorem's language is always expressive. 'Sext (Noon)' is especially touching, with the flute's shakuhachi-like *glissandi* sighing over the harp's exquisitely fragile song. The performances by the Fibonacci Sequence are consistently polished and persuasive. Clear recording, too, though the instruments are placed very close to the microphones. Very strongly recommended.

Sun

Sun[a]. String Quartet No 3[b]
[a]**Lauren Flanigan** sop [b]**Mendelssohn Quartet** (Nicholas Eanet, Nicholas Mann vns Ulrich Eichenauer va Marcy Rosen vc) [a]**Manhattan School of Music Symphony / Glen Barton Cortese**
Newport Classic NPD85657 (52' · DDD) Texts included ⓕ○

Like the *concerto grosso*, *Sun* was composed in 1966, and this cycle for soprano and orchestra was intended by Rorem as a companion piece to his earlier *Poems of Love and the Rain*. 'The indicated need now seemed for songs of hate and the sun,' he quips in the introductory note. The opening song, based on an ancient Egyptian text gives way to more modern musings on sunrises and sleepless nights, and copious sounds of ticking clocks. Rorem seems to have been going through a Russian phase when he composed this, the sonorities and rhythms suggest Stravinsky and Prokofiev. It's a magnificent, large-scale enterprise to which those high sopranos who for years have made do with Strauss's *Four Last Songs* should look. Lauren Flanigan, who's fast becoming America's new *prima donna*, delivers it all with considerable aplomb. Rorem's Third String Quartet completes the CD. This is a much later work (1990) in five movements and, unusually for Rorem, who often refers to the 'serial killers', it opens with a movement based on a 12-note row. From this teasingly dissonant opening develops a luxuriously tuneful second movement called 'Scherzo-Sarabande-Scherzo'.

Songs

Santa Fé – No 2, Opus 101; No 4, Sonnet; No 8, The wintry mind; No 12, The sowers. Clouds. Early in the morning. The serpent. Now sleeps the crimson petal. I strolled across an open field. To a young girl. Jeanie with the light brown hair. Ode. For Poulenc. Little elegy. Alleluia. Look down, fair moon. O you whom I often and silently come. I will always love you. The tulip tree. I am rose. The Lordly Hudson. O do not love too long. Far far away. For Susan. A journey. Sometimes with one I love. Love. Orchids. Stopping by woods on a snowy evening. Do I love you more than a day? Ferry me across the water. That shadow, my likeness
Susan Graham sop **Malcolm Martineau** pf with **Ensemble Oriol** (Christiane Plath vn Sebastian Gottschick va Friedeman Ludwig vc)
Erato 8573-80222-2 (61' · DDD) Texts included Ⓕ**OO**

If Rorem's songs aren't as well known as those of Copland or Cole Porter it's probably because they're more difficult to sing. The earliest here is from 1947 (*The Lordly Hudson*, on a poem by Paul Goodman), the latest from 1983 (*That shadow, my likeness*, one of several Walt Whitman settings). Most of the others, though, were composed in the 1950s when Rorem was living in France. One could look for obvious French influences – Rorem was a close friend of Auric and Poulenc – but strangely it's the later songs, from the cycle *Santa Fé* on poems by Witter Bynner, that have a more Gallic sound, the piano and string trio accompaniment having that aching, nostalgic mood which Rorem himself describes as 'a period removed from Time and, like the act of love, [it] has no limits, no beginning nor end.' The only song in French is a poem by Ronsard, an ode to peace, but two songs are about Paris. *Early in the morning*, a poem by Robert Hillyer, is an evocation of a young poet in love in and with Paris, its accompaniment a homage to all the sad waltzes that murmur their recollections of the city from Satie to Kosma. *For Poulenc*, written especially by Frank O'Hara for Rorem to set as part of an album of songs in memory of Poulenc, describes all the city in mourning.

Rorem called his autobiography *Knowing when to stop*, and it's a wonderful description of his own songs. The strength and beauty of his settings lies in their directness and candour. He doesn't linger, the poem and song are one, the melody growing from the accompaniment into the vocal line, but just as you seem able to grasp it, it's gone. Martineau plays with an unfailing sensitivity, giving the tiny shifts of mood from exuberance to elegiac melancholy their exact weight.

Alleluia. Are you the new person?. As Adam early in the morning. Ask me no more. Early in the morning. Far-Far-Away. Full of life now. I am Rose. I strolled across an open field. Little Elegy. Love in a Life. Lullaby of the Woman of the Mountain. Memory. My Papa's Waltz. Nantucket. Night Crow. The Nightingale. Now sleeps the crimson petal. O you to whom I often and silently come. Orchids. Root Cellar. Sally's Smile. See how they love me. The Serpent. Snake. Spring. Stopping by Woods on a Snowy Evening. Such beauty as hurts to behold. Visits to St Elizabeth's. The Waking. What if some little pain… Youth, Day, Old Age and Night
Carole Farley sop **Ned Rorem** pf
Naxos 8 559084 (58' · DDD)   Ⓢ

Seventeen of these 32 songs aren't otherwise available on disc, and they include some of Rorem's finest and most haunting. The utter simplicity that weaves a magic spell in *Nantucket*, the beautiful paralleling of Gerard Manley Hopkins's ecstatic imagery in *Spring*, the bare but deeply eloquent *Such beauty as hurts to behold*, the amiable contemplation of old age and possible immortality in *Full of life now* – all these are warmly welcome, and it's good to have for the first time a complete recording of Rorem's nine settings of Theodore Roethke. Carole Farley's diction is so immaculate that you'll hardly need the booklet of texts, and her acute response to words must be one reason why Rorem so willingly collaborated with her on this recording. About the voice itself some might have a reservation. Although Farley fines her tone down for the most part effectively her sound is basically operatic. But rejecting this disc on that account would mean foregoing the infectious lilt of *The Nightingale*, the amply lyrical, movingly expressive *Love in a life*, the beautiful long lines of *Ask me no more* and all the others mentioned. No, admirers of Rorem's unique talent will simply have to have this collection. His piano-playing is beautifully supportive.

Six Songs for High Voice. Ariel[a]. Ode. Last Poems of Wallace Stevens[b]. Alleluia. Jack l'éventreur

Laura Aikin *sop* [a]Nicola Jürgensen *cl* [b]Gerhard
Zank *vc* Donald Sulzen *pf*
Orfeo C620 041A (66' · DDD · T)   Ⓕ

Interest continues in Ned Rorem's vocal music
– more than 300 solo songs and numerous song-
cycles. There's little duplication between Laura
Aikin's recital and those of Susan Graham
(Erato) and Carole Farley (Naxos). Since
Rorem often favours the mezzo voice, it's a surprise to find him in the high soprano strato-
sphere.

Jack l'éventreur ('Jack the Ripper') has lots of
odd imagery: the murderer is dressed in tweed,
with a rose between his teeth. The *Six Songs for
High Voice*, to poems by Dryden and Browning,
were scored originally for orchestra, but here
arranged for piano. Aikin relishes the coloratura
flourishes, but like all high sopranos isn't always
able to get the words across. The Wallace
Stevens settings, for voice, piano and cello, are
linked by two instrumental solos, accentuating
the sense of a journey through experience, a
growth of feeling and understanding. In *Ariel*,
on poems by Sylvia Plath, the clarinet takes over
as a third voice; Nicola Jürgensen provides a
spectacular obbligato to the slightly jazzy settings and here Aikin's words are splendidly
clear.

Donald Sulzen's accompaniments accentuate Rorem's sometimes severe, sometimes
complex keyboard writing. Aikin, whose repertory runs from Queen of the Night to Lulu, is a
singer to watch, and this is a major addition to
the discography.

Johann Rosenmüller
German c1619-1684

*Rosenmüller first worked as an organist and teacher
in Leipzig, but was imprisoned (on suspicion of
homosexuality) in 1655. From 1658 he was a trombonist at St Mark's, Venice, and in 1678-82 also
composer at the Ospedale della Pietà. Finally he
returned to Germany as court Kapellmeister at
Wolfenbüttel. A prolific composer, he was important
in transmitting Italian styles to Germany, where his
music was especially popular. He published four
instrumental collections (1645-82), which move
from simple dance suites to Italianate ensemble
sonatas; the 12 sonatas of 1682 include much fugal
writing. His sacred works number c200. The earliest
are mainly small German concertos (many were
published in two books, Kern-Sprüche, 1648 and
1652-3), but the later are mostly Latin, including
psalms, solo cantatas and music for the Mass; these
too show strong Italian features, and are notable for
their expressiveness, clarity of form and idiomatic
vocal writing.* GROVEmusic

Sacred Music

Weihnachtshistorie
Gloria in excelsis Deo. Lieber Herre Gott. Entsetze

dich, Natur. Es waren Hirten auf dem Felde bei den
Hürden. Nihil novum sub sole. Christus ist mein
Leben. Ich freue mich in dir. O nomen Jesu
**Cantus Cölln; Concerto Palatino / Konrad
Junghänel** *lte*
Harmonia Mundi HMC90 1861 (78' · DDD · T/t)   Ⓕ

After matriculating at Leipzig University in
1640, Johann Rosenmüller quickly became the
city's most prominent musician, but a promising early career was cut short in 1655 by accusations of pederasty. He escaped to Italy, which
must have been a natural destination: his poet
friend Caspar Ziegler had commented that any
visitor to Leipzig hearing Rosenmüller's church
music would be tricked into thinking that they
were in the heart of Venice.

Cantus Cölln has already championed Rosenmüller's Venetian music in a trail-blazing
recording of his Vespers, and now explore his
less familiar earlier period: almost all the featured music was created for Christmas at
Leipzig. *Es waren Hirten auf dem Felde bei den
Hürden* was composed 20 years before Schütz's
celebrated *Weihnachtshistorie*; it swells in scope
from a cluster of shepherds to a resplendent
heavenly host. Further to the flamboyance of
Rosenmüller's theatrical writing, there are
moments of sweet simplicity. He performed
Entsetze dich, Natur on Christmas Day 1649; it's
the most impressive piece on a disc full of treasures.

Cantus Cölln and Concerto Palatino give a
masterclass in sonorous contrasts between
finely shaded intimacy and colourful grandeur.
The singers and instrumentalists are technically
impeccable, and Konrad Junghänel directs with
his usual sensitivity and taste.

Gioachino Rossini   Italian 1792-1868

*Rossini's parents were musicians, his father a horn
player, his mother a singer. He learnt the horn and
singing, and as a boy sang in at least one opera in
Bologna, where the family lived. He studied there
and began his operatic career when, at 18, he wrote a
one-act comedy for Venice. Further commissions followed, from Bologna, Ferrara, Venice again and
Milan, where La pietra del paragone was a success at
La Scala in 1812. This was one of seven operas written in 16 months, all but one being comic.*

*This level of activity continued in the ensuing
years. His first operas to win international acclaim
come from 1813, written for different Venetian theatres: the serious Tancredi and the farcically comic
L'italiana in Algeri, the one showing a fusion of lyrical expression and dramatic needs, the other moving
easily between the sentimental, the patriotic, the
absurd and the sheer lunatic. Two operas for Milan
were less successful. In 1815 Rossini went to Naples
as musical and artistic director of the Teatro San
Carlo, which led to a concentration on serious opera.
But he was allowed to compose for other theatres, and
from this time date two of his supreme comedies,*

written for Rome, *Il barbiere di Siviglia* and *La Cenerentola*. The former has claims to be considered the greatest of all Italian comic operas, eternally fresh in its wit and its inventiveness. It dates from 1816; initially it was a failure, but quickly became the most loved of his comic works. The next year saw *La Cenerentola*, a charmingly sentimental tale in which the heroine moves from a touching folksy ditty as the scullery maid to brilliant coloratura apt to a royal maiden.

Rossini's most important operas in the period that followed were for Naples. The third act of his *Otello* (1816), with its strong unitary structure, marks his maturity as a musical dramatist. The Neapolitan operas, even though much dependent on solo singing of a highly florid kind, show an enormous expansion of musical means, with more and longer ensembles and the chorus an active participant; the accompanied recitative is more dramatic and the orchestra is given greater prominence. Rossini abandoned traditional overtures as well. In 1822 he married Naples' leading soprano Isabella Colbran, but it proved an ill match.

Among the masterpieces from this period are *Maometto II* (1820) and *Semiramide* (1823). In 1823 Rossini left for London and Paris where he took on the directorship of the Théâtre-Italien, composing for that theatre and the Opéra. Some of his Paris works are adaptations (*Le siège de Corinthe* and *Moïse et Pharaon*); the *opéra comique Le Comte Ory* is part-new, *Guillaume Tell* wholly. This last, widely regarded as his chef d'oeuvre, is a rich tapestry of his most inspired music, with elaborate orchestration, many ensembles, spectacular ballets and processions in the French tradition, opulent orchestral writing and a new harmonic boldness.

At 37, he retired from opera composition. He left Paris in 1837 to live in Italy, but suffered prolonged and painful illness there. Isabella died in 1845 and the next year he married Olympe Pélissier, with whom he had lived for 15 years. He composed hardly at all during this period (the *Stabat mater* belongs to his Paris years); but he went back to Paris in 1855, and his health, humour and urge to compose returned. He wrote a quantity of pieces for piano and voices, with wit and refinement, that he called *Péchés de vieillesse* ('Sins of Old Age'), including the graceful and economical *Petite messe solennelle* (1863). He died, universally honoured, in 1868.

GROVEmusic

Overtures etc

Discoveries
Robert Bruce – Overture (arr Niedermeyer). Péchés de Vieillesse, Book 3, 'Morceaux réservés' – Le chant des Titans. Grande Fanfare (Le Rendez-vous de chasse). Guillaume Tell – Final du Divertissement; Pas de deux. Ermione – Sinfonia. Moïse et Pharaon – Ouverture et Introduction[b]. La Siège de Corinthe – Ballabile-Galop. Inno alla pace, 'È foriera la Pace'[cd]. Hymne, 'De l'Italie et de la France'[ac]. Hymne à Napoléon III et à son vaillant peuple[b]
[a]Laura Giordano *sop* [b]Ildar Abdrazakov, [c]Michele Pertusi *bars* [d]Nelson Calzi *fp* Giuseppe Verdi Chorus and Symphony Orchestra, Milan / Riccardo Chailly

Decca 470 298-2DH (69' · DDD) Texts and translations included
Ⓕ**OO**

Philip Gossett calls this 'a Rossinian curio cabinet'. 'A banquet made with leftovers from the Rossini kitchen' would do as well. Whatever the analogy, the art is as much in the assembling of the materials as in the materials themselves. The most familiar music – gleanings from *Zelmira*, *Armida* and *La donna del lago* – is to be found in the very first item, the overture to the Rossinian pastiche *Robert Bruce*, assembled for the Paris Opéra in 1846 by the composer Louis Niedermeyer. The other orchestral items are all *echt*-Rossini. The splendid *Le Rendez-vous de chasse* for four hunting horns and orchestra dates from the time of the composition of *Guillaume Tell* and could almost be a pendant to it. But the pillars of the anthology are the splendid *Le Chant des Titans* and three of Rossini's grand but little-known occasional hymns. The earliest of these is *De l'Italie et de la France*, written in 1825 for Charles X's coronation; the latest, written in 1867 when Rossini was 75, is the grandiose *Hymne à Napoléon III à Son Vaillant Peuple*. It all goes with a tremendous swing and the cannon-and-church-bells end is spectacular. The voltage of Chailly's performances is unremitting high, as is the attention to shading and fine detail. This is conducting Toscanini or De Sabata would have been hard-pressed to better. The recordings, in Milan's new Auditorium di Milano, are also spectacularly good, vivid yet sensitive to the smallest detail.

String Sonatas

Rossini Sonate a quattro – No 1 in G; No 2 in A; No 3 in C; No 4 in B flat; No 5 in E flat; No 6 in D
Bellini Oboe Concerto in E flat **Cherubini** Horn Sonata in F **Donizetti** String Quartet in D (1828)
Roger Lord *ob* **Barry Tuckwell** *hn* **Academy of St Martin in the Fields / Sir Neville Marriner**
Double Decca ② 443 838-2DF2 (112' · ADD) Recorded 1964-68
Ⓜ**O**

Rossini's six string sonatas are usually heard performed by a string orchestra, although they were in fact composed for a quartet of two violins, cello and double bass. The sonatas, which display amazing musical dexterity and assurance, may date from as early as 1804. The world of 18th-century opera is never far away, with the first violin frequently taking the role of soprano soloist, particularly in the slow movements. Written for Rossini's friend Agostino Triosso, who was a keen double bass player, the sonata's bass parts are full of wit and suavity. There are other thoroughly recommendable modern digital versions, yet there's something very special about Marriner's Academy set, made for Argo in the late 1960s. The playing has an elegance and finesse, a sparkle and touch of humour that catches the full character and charm of these miraculous examples of the precocity of the 12-year-old composer. Among the substantial bonuses here are Donizetti's String Quartet, sounding elegant in its string-orchestra version, Bellini's Oboe Concerto, played stylishly by Roger Lord and Cherubini's mini-concerto for horn and strings is dispatched with aplomb by by Barry Tuckwell. Highly recommendable.

Petite messe solennelle

Petite messe solennelle
Daniella Dessì sop **Gloria Scalchi** mez **Giuseppe Sabbatini** ten **Michele Pertusi** bass **Chorus and Orchestra of the Teatro Comunale, Bologna / Riccardo Chailly**
Decca ② 444 134-2DX2 (82' · DDD) Recorded 1993.
Text and translation included　　　　　　Ⓜ**O**

A proper representative of the orchestrated version of the *Petite messe* has been long overdue. Chailly's performance is a glorious heart-warming affair. Not that you're likely to be convinced right away. To ears accustomed to the *Kyrie* in its original form, the texturing here is pure suet. Nor does the sound of the largish and here rather distantly placed choir seem especially well focused in the *Christe eleison*. Gradually, though, the ear adjusts, the musicians warm to their task, the performance gets into its stride. The Bologna Chorus sings the *Gloria* and *Credo* with passion, clarity and love. The tenor is adequate, the bass superb, the two girls absolutely fabulous. If the *Crucifixus* can never be as painful as it's in the sparer original version, this is amply offset by the sheer beauty of Daniella Dessì's singing and by the hair-raising force of the 'Et resurrexit' (superbly recorded) as Chailly and his choir realise it. By the end, after Gloria Scalchi's deeply affecting account of the *Agnus Dei*, you begin to wonder whether the orchestral version wasn't more than a match for the original. It isn't, but it's an indication of the cumulative eloquence of this utterly inspired performance that it comes to seem so.

Stabat mater

Stabat mater
Luba Orgonasova sop **Cecilia Bartoli** mez **Raúl Giménez** ten **Roberto Scandiuzzi** bass **Vienna State Opera Concert Choir; Vienna Philharmonic Orchestra / Myung-Whun Chung**
DG 449 178-2GH (59' · DDD) Text and translation included　　　　　　Ⓕ**O**

Chung's conducting of this work is somewhat Karajanesque: extremely beautiful orchestral playing; a choir which sings expressively but who yields something in focus and clarity of sound to the best rival English choirs; a strong dramatic sense with some unusual tempos that lead to the performance occasionally seeming mannered; and much fine solo singing, the singers encouraged to sing with great inwardness, with a special kind of quiet beauty. This is where the performance differs markedly from

Richard Hickox's account. There the soloists sing their solo numbers in far more open and extrovert manner. Between Della Jones (Hickox) and Cecilia Bartoli there's simply no comparison; for Jones and Hickox 'Fac ut portem' is a dramatic oration, for Bartoli and Chung it's a private meditation. The integration of singers, orchestra and acoustic isn't quite as well managed as on the Chandos recording, where we have a church acoustic as opposed to the more secular sounding Vienna Musikverein. Nor is Chung's reading as straightforward, as right-sounding as Hickox's. Nevertheless this recording can be regarded as first among equals.

Stabat mater　　　　　　　　　　　　　Ⓟ
Krassimira Stoyanova sop **Petra Lang** mez **Bruce Fowler** ten **Daniel Borowski** bass **RIAS Chamber Choir, Berlin; Academy for Ancient Music, Berlin / Marcus Creed**
Harmonia Mundi HMC90 1693 (57' · DDD) Text and translation included　　　　　　Ⓕ**O**

One of the first, and best, recordings of this splendid but interpretatively elusive work was made in Berlin in 1954 under the direction of Ferenc Fricsay. Like the present recording, it featured the RIAS (Berlin Radio) Chamber Choir, though in those days the fledgling choir was supplemented in the full choruses by the famous St Hedwig's Cathedral Choir. Now on its own, it acquits itself superbly in all movements and dimensions with its own conductor, the English-born Marcus Creed. That this recording uses period instruments might seem in so obviously 'vocal' a piece to be of no particular moment. In practice, the work's prevailingly dark orchestral colours are memorably realised by the instrumentalists of Berlin's Academy for Ancient Music. In the grand opening movement, the four soloists are recorded uncomfortably far forward; but if you can establish an agreeable level for this movement, the rest of the performance sounds very well indeed. Choir and orchestra are themselves unfailingly well balanced. Creed's reading is full of character: immensely strong but always sensitively paced. Rossini might have raised an eyebrow at Creed's fondness for romantically protracted codas; equally, he would have applauded his sensitive moulding of the accompaniments, matched shrewdly but never indulgently to the singers' (and the music's) needs. The soloists, highly talented, are excellent, more than a match for most rival teams.

Opera Arias

La donna del lago – Tanti affetti in tal momento. **Elisabetta, Regina d'Inghilterra** – Quant' è grato all'alma mia; Fellon, la penna avrai. **Maometto II** – Ah! che invan su questo ciglio; Giusto ciel, in tal periglio. **Le nozze di Teti e di Peleo** – Ah, non potrian reistere. **Semiramide** – Serenai vaghirai ... Bel raggio lusinghier. **Zelmira** – Riedi al soglio

Cecilia Bartoli *mez* **Chorus and Orchestra of the Teatro La Fenice, Venice / Ion Marin**
Decca 436 075-2DH (59' · DDD) Recorded 1991.
Texts and translations included   ⒻⒺ

This sparkling disc brings together a collection of arias Rossini composed for one of the great *prima donnas* of the 19th century, his wife, Isabella Colbran. It's tempting to wonder whether even she could match Cecilia Bartoli, one of the most luscious, most exciting voices in opera. All those dazzling chromatic runs, leaps, cadenzas and cascading coloraturas are handled with consummate ease. Throughout she sounds as if she's enjoying the music; there's always an engaging smile in the voice, although she's properly imperious in the extracts from *Elisabetta* and disarmingly simple in the prayerful 'Giusto ciel, in tal periglio' from *Maometto II*. The orchestral and choral forces provide a delightful intimacy, with some cheeky woodwind solos and fruity brass passages. The recording, produced at the Teatro La Fenice by Decca veteran Christopher Raeburn, favours the voices but gives it just enough distance to accommodate high Cs and astounding A flats at the bottom of the range. The orchestral perspective is changeable but satisfactory. For Rossini and Bartoli fans, this disc is a must.

Armida – Dove son io!�g. **Aureliano in Palmira** – Se tu m'ami, o mia reginaᵇ. **Bianca e Falliero** – Cielo, il mio labbro ispiraᶜ. **Elisabetta, Regina d'Inghilterra** – Qant'è grato all'alma miaᵃ. **Mosè in Egitto** – Mi manca la voceᵉ; Porgi la destra amataʰ. **Semiramide** – Se la vitaᶠ. **Vallace** – Viva Vallace! Vallace Vivaⁱ. **Zelmira** – Riedi al soglioᵈ
Nelly Miricioiu with ᵉʰⁱ**Patrizia Biccire** *sops* ᵇᶜ**Enkelejda Shkosa** *mez* ⁱ**Antonia Sotgiù** *voc* ᶜᵉᵍ**Bruce Ford,** ᵈᵉʰⁱ**Barry Banks,** ʰ**Dominic Natoli** *tens* ᶜᵈʰⁱ**Gary Magee,** ʰⁱ**Dean Robinson** *bars* ᶠ**Alastair Miles** *bass* ⁱ**Simon Bailey** *voc* ᵃᶜᵈʰⁱ**Geoffrey Mitchell Choir; Academy of St Martin in the Fields / David Parry**
Opera Rara ORR211 (67' · DDD) Texts and translations included   ⒻⒺ

Rossini is a difficult composer to anthologise. Callas and Walter Legge or Sutherland and Bonynge might have come up with something fascinating and fabulous had they been so minded. Caballé did: the eminently collectable *Rossini Rarities* disc she produced for the Rossini bicentenary in 1968. For the rest, successful recitals have been few and far between, indifferent singing or poor planning principally to blame. Not so Opera Rara's Rossini Gala. Patric Schmid's inventive programme focuses on Rossini's Naples period and the extraordinary array of roles he created for the great Spanish soprano Isabella Colbran. What distinguishes this recital is that it doesn't only anthologise set-piece arias. Rossini gave Colbran some grand entrances and some even grander exits, and there are examples of both here: Queen Elizabeth's arrival and Zelmira's final florid song of

thanksgiving. But there are also two wonderful quartets, two exquisite duets, a famous *coup de théâtre* (the Act 2 finale of *Mosè in Egitto* with its terrific lightning-strike), and one of Rossini's finest pieces of music-theatre: the scene near the start of Act 2 of *Semiramide* where the Queen and her lover, the adulterous regicide Assur, have rows worthy of the Macbeths over events which are beginning to overshadow them.

Miricioiu isn't a *bel canto* specialist; Santuzza is as much her territory as Semiramide. In neither role is the technique perfectly honed, but the effect is rarely less than compelling. Every one of the heroines presented here is vividly depicted, with a distinguished supporting cast helping to etch each scene into the imagination.

The gala ends with an intriguing rarity which has nothing to do with Colbran or Miricioiu. *Vallace* is a shortened, revised and relocated version of *Guillaume Tell* prepared for La Scala, Milan, in 1836-7. Austrian tyranny being an uncongenial subject to Milan's Austrian rulers, the libretto was recast to show English tyranny instead: Edward I's bloody crusade against the Scots, with William Wallace as a Scottish Tell. Rossini wasn't much involved in the adaptation, though he did agree to recast the finale scene so that the opera could end with a reprise of the overture's famous *pas redoublé*. It's that revised finale we have here, a travesty of Schiller (and Rossini), but great fun.

Playing, choral work and conducting for this Rossini Gala are all of a high order of excellence. As is the engineering (the lightning strike in *Mosè in Egitto* isn't for the faint-hearted). As always with Opera Rara, the accompanying 116-page booklet is superlatively informative. At the price of a single full-price CD, the disc is a terrific bargain, not least for the splendid hawk's-eye view the programme provides of 'serious' Rossini.

Il barbiere di Siviglia

Il barbiere di Siviglia
Roberto Servile *bar* Figaro **Sonia Ganassi** *mez* Rosina **Ramon Vargas** *ten* Count Almaviva **Angelo Romero** *bar* Bartolo **Franco de Grandis** *bass* Don Basilio **Ingrid Kertesi** *sop* Berta **Kázmér Sarkany** *bass* Fiorello **Hungarian Radio Chorus; Failoni Chamber Orchestra, Budapest / Will Humburg**
Naxos ③ 8 660027/9 (158' · DDD) Recorded 1992.
Notes and text included   ⓈⓈ ⓈⓄⓄ

Not everyone will approve, but there are ways in which this super-budget set of *Il barbiere di Siviglia* puts to shame just about every other version of the opera there has been. Those it may not please are specialist vocal collectors for whom *Il barbiere* is primarily a repository of vocal test pieces. If, however, you regard *Il barbiere* (Rossini, ex-Beaumarchais) as a gloriously subversive music drama – vibrant, scurrilous, vital – then this recording is guaranteed to give a great deal of pleasure.

'Performance' is the key word here. Humburg is described in the Naxos booklet as 'Conductor and Recitative Director', and for once the recitatives really are part of the larger drama. The result is a meticulously produced, often very funny, brilliantly integrated performance that you'll almost certainly find yourself listening to as a stage play. With a virtually all-Italian cast, the results are a revelation. The erotic allure of the duet 'Dunque io son' is striking. Similarly, Don Basilio's Calumny aria, superbly sung by Franco de Grandis, a black-browed bass from Turin who was singing for Karajan, Muti and Abbado while still in his twenties. This takes on added character and colour from the massive sense of panic created by de Grandis and the admirable Dr Bartolo of Angelo Romero when Basilio comes in with news of Almaviva's arrival in town.

The Overture is done with evident relish, the playing of the Failoni Chamber Orchestra is nothing if not articulate. Aided by a clear, forward recording, a *sine qua non* with musical comedy, the cast communicates the Rossini/Sterbini text with tremendous relish. They're never hustled by Humburg, nor are they spared: the *stretta* of the Act 1 finale is a model of hypertension and clarity. This *Il barbiere* jumps to the top of the pile.

Il barbiere di Siviglia
Thomas Allen bar Figaro **Agnes Baltsa** mez Rosina
Francisco Araiza ten Count Almaviva **Domenico Trimarchi** bar Dr Bartolo **Robert Lloyd** bass Don Basilio **Matthew Best** bass Fiorello **Sally Burgess** mez Berta **John Noble** bar Official **Ambrosian Opera Chorus; Academy of St Martin in the Fields / Sir Neville Marriner**
Decca Compact Opera Collection ② 470 434-2DOC2 (147' · ADD) Recorded 1982   Ⓜ**OO**

This was the most stylish and engaging account of *Il barbiere* to have appeared on record since the famous de los Angeles/Bruscantini set recorded by EMI with Glyndebourne forces in 1962. Here, making a rare but welcome appearance in an opera recording, is the stylish Academy of St Martin in the Fields. It's as pointed and sure-footed an account of the score as you could hope to hear, a reading which entirely belies the fact that this was Neville Marriner's operatic début on record. Quite how the producer, in duets, ensembles and recitatives, created so live a sense of theatre in so essentially unconvivial a place as Watford Town Hall, north-west of London, must for ever remain a mystery; here there's here a real and rare sense of the delighted interplay of character: a tribute, in the first place, to the degree to which Thomas Allen, Francisco Araiza, Domenico Trimarchi, Agnes Baltsa, Robert Lloyd and their fellows are inside their roles musically and dramatically. There's no vulgar horseplay in the recording; but equally there's nothing slavish or literal about the way in which Rossini's, and Beaumarchais's comic felicities have been realised. The

ROSSINI IL BARBIERE DI SIVIGLIA – IN BRIEF

Roberto Servile Figaro **Sonia Ganassi** Rosina **Ramón Vargas** Almaviva **Hungarian Radio Chorus; Failoni Chamber Orchestra / Will Humburg**
Naxos ③ 8 660027/9 (158' · DDD)   Ⓢ**OO**
Happily one of the best is also among the cheapest; fresh, full and brilliantly conducted, with a ripely Italianate cast including star-in-the-making Ramón Vargas.

Thomas Allen Figaro **Agnes Baltsa** Rosina **Francisco Araiza** Almaviva **Ambrosian Opera Chorus; ASMF / Sir Neville Marriner**
Decca ② 470 434-2DOC2 (148' · DDD)   Ⓜ**OO**
None the worse for international star quality. Marriner conducts a superlative, characterful cast with infectious sparkle and warmth, and first-rate recording.

Sesto Bruscantini Figaro **Victoria de los Angeles** Rosina **Luigi Alva** Almaviva **Glyndebourne Festival Chorus; Royal PO / Vittorio Gui**
EMI ② 567762-2 (141' · ADD)   Ⓜ**OOO**
Ⓖ A magical performance, not least because it derives from a much-loved Glyndebourne production. Gui's conducting is warm and affectionate, his stars more light-hearted and witty than brashly comic.

Tito Gobbi Figaro **Maria Callas** Rosina **Luigi Alva** Almaviva **Philharmonia Orchestra / Alceo Galliera**
EMI ② 556310-2 (132' · ADD)   Ⓕ
An inauthentic soprano Rosina is still a gain when it's Callas, with Gobbi's warmly robust Figaro as foil; she makes an enchanting spitfire, with some showy ornamentation. The experienced cast are splendid and Galliera's conducting wonderfully theatrical. One of the most thoroughly comic sets.

(In English) **Alan Opie** Figaro **Della Jones** Rosina **Bruce Ford** Almaviva **ENO Chorus and Orchestra / Gabriele Bellini**
Chandos ② CHAN7023/4 (149' · DDD)   Ⓕ
A cheerful English-language version with a likeable cast, especially Alan Opie's Figaro, Della Jones's mature but lively Rosina, and Peter Rose and Andrew Shore as magnificent *buffo* heavies. Only Bellini's rather lumpy conducting is a drawback.

Hermann Prey Figaro **Teresa Berganza** Rosina **Luigi Alva** Almaviva **Chorus and Orchestra of La Scala, Milan / Claudio Abbado**
DG 📀 073 021-9GH (142')   Ⓕ
A rather old-fashioned cinematic version in lip-sync, but still enjoyable and well worth considering for Abbado's rich but lively conducting and a very strong cast, even if Prey, though excellent, seems insufficiently Italianate, and Berganza is a shade mature.

text is Zedda, more or less. Robert Lloyd takes the Calumny aria in C (D is the 'authentic' key), rightly so, for his is a magnificent bass voice. It's a grand characterisation, very much in the Chaliapin style. Thomas Allen's Figaro and Francisco Araiza's Count bring out the opera's virility, its peculiarly masculine strength. Allen has a vivid sense of character and a brilliant technique. He also has a ripe sense of comedy.

Araiza is similarly compelling. Technically he's first rate. His divisions are unusually bright and clean, the top (including some flashy cadences) true, shaped in a way which is both musically vivid and dramatically right. Equally, Araiza can be confiding, and funny. His whining music-master is a delight, right down to an unscripted attempt at a reprise of 'Pace e gioia' at the end of the scene, cut off by a petulant 'Basta!' from the excellent Bartolo, Domenico Trimarchi. Baltsa's Rosina, too, is infected by the set's general liveliness: witness the delighted gurgle of joy which escapes from her at the news of the Count's intentions. Recitatives, edited down here and there, are very alert, theatrically pointed; and Nicholas Kraemer's accompaniments on a sweet-sounding fortepiano are an added pleasure. Philips preferred a dryish, intimate acoustic; the small-theatre atmosphere this confers is very likeable, the more so as it allows Marriner the opportunity to conduct with a tautness and vigour which a boomier, more open acoustic would disallow. With excellent choral work in the all important ensembles, and with a delightful Berta from Sally Burgess, this is undoubtedly one of the very best *Barbers* the gramophone has given us.

Il barbiere di Siviglia
Sesto Bruscantini bar Figaro **Victoria de los Angeles** sop Rosina **Luigi Alva** ten Count Almaviva **Ian Wallace** bass Dr Bartolo **Carlo Cava** bass Don Basilio **Duncan Robertson** ten Fiorello **Laura Sarti** mez Berta **Glyndebourne Festival Chorus; Royal Philharmonic Orchestra / Vittorio Gui**
EMI Great Recordings of the Century mono ②
567762-2 (141' · ADD) Recorded 1962. Notes, text and translation included   Ⓜ❍❍❍

Perhaps it's a shade misleading to refer to this classic EMI recording as a 'Glyndebourne' set. It has all the ingredients of a Glyndebourne production: notably the cast, the orchestra and chorus, and that doyen of Rossini conductors, Vittorio Gui. But as far as can be ascertained, there was no actual stage production of *Il barbiere* in 1962. Nor was the recording, for all its dryness and sharp-edged immediacy, actually made at Glyndebourne. It's a well-honed, conservatively staged stereophonic studio recording made by EMI in its Abbey Road Studio No 1. Gui's performance is so astutely paced that, while the music bubbles and boils, every word is crystal-clear. This is a wonderfully declaimed reading of the score, but also a beautifully timed one. Gui's steady tempos allow the music to show its

underlying toughness, and he secures characterful playing from the RPO, the wind players in particular. Where Victoria de los Angeles is so memorable is in the beauty of her singing and the originality of the reading. There has never been a Rosina who manages to be both as guileful and as charming as she. Team her up with the incomparable Sesto Bruscantini and, in something like the nodal Act 1 duet, 'Dunque io son', you have musical and dramatic perfection. Ian Wallace is a fine character actor, given plenty of space by Gui, allowing his portrait of Dr Bartolo to emerge as a classic compromise between the letter and the spirit of the part.

La Cenerentola

La Cenerentola
Teresa Berganza mez Angelina **Luigi Alva** ten Don Ramiro **Renato Capecchi** bar Dandini **Paolo Montarsolo** bar Don Magnifico **Margherita Guglielmi** sop Clorinda **Laura Zannini** contr Tisbe **Ugo Trama** bass Alidoro **Scottish Opera Chorus; London Symphony Orchestra / Claudio Abbado**
DG Double ② 459 448-2GTA2 (144' · ADD) Recorded 1971. Notes, text and translation included   Ⓜ❍

Rossini's Cinderella is a fairy-tale without a fairy, but no less bewitching for that. In fact the replacement of the winged godmother with the philanthropic Alidoro, a close friend and adviser of our prince, Don Ramiro, plus the lack of any glass slippers and the presence of a particularly unsympathetic father character, makes the whole story more plausible. La Cenerentola, Angelina, is more spunky than the average pantomime Cinders. She herself gives Don Ramiro one of her pair of bracelets, charging him to find the owner of the matching ornament, and thus taking control of her own destiny. Along the way, Don Ramiro and his valet Dandini change places, leading to plenty of satisfyingly operatic confusion and difficult situations.

This recording, when originally transferred to CD, was spread across three discs, but has now been comfortably fitted into two at mid-price. It gives a sparkling rendition of the score with a lovely light touch and well-judged tempos from Abbado and the LSO. Virtuoso vocal requirements are fully met by the cast. The chief delight is Teresa Berganza's Angelina, creamy in tone and as warm as she's precise. The supporting cast is full of character, with Luigi Alva a princely Don Ramiro, Margherita Guglielmi and Laura Zannini an affected and fussy pair of sisters, and Renato Capecchi, gleeful and mischievous as he takes on being prince for a day. The recording sounds more than usually well for its age.

Additional recommendation

Bartoli Angelina **Matteuzzi** Don Ramiro **Corbelli** Dandini **Bologna Teatro Comunale Chorus and Orchestra / Chailly**

Decca ② 436 902-2DH2 (148' · DDD) Ⓕ
For Bartoli fans, a cherishable set that doesn't quite match the sparkle of the Abbado. Matteuzzi sings well and there are some nicely drawn characters. Chailly directs with spirit.

Le Comte Ory

Le Comte Ory
Juan Diego Flórez ten Comte Ory **Stefania Bonfadelli** sop Adèle **Alastair Miles** bar Gouverneur **Marie-Ange** Todorovitch mez Isolier **Bruno Praticò** bar Raimbaud **Marina De Liso** mez Ragonde **Rossella Bevacqua** sop Alice **Prague Chamber Choir; Teatro Comunale Orchestra, Bologna / Jesús López-Cobos**
DG ② 477 5020 (130' · DDD) Recorded live at the Teatro Rossini, Pesaro, August 2003. Notes, libretto and translation included Ⓕ**OO**

Le Comte Ory is the first great French-language comic opera. A late work (Paris, 1828), sensuous, witty and exquisitely crafted, it's always been something of a connoisseur's piece.

The selling point here is the Ory, Juan Diego Flórez, and very striking he is, too. He has terrific presence, a well-nigh flawless technique, and a keen sense of the French vocal style. Jesús López-Cobos, an old Rossini hand, conducts robustly but with style. He overdrives the Act 1 ensemble in which the villagers come to Ory with their requests but paces to perfection the action within the celebrated nocturnal Trio in Act 2.

It would be nice to have a French Raimbaud, but Bruno Praticò, an old hand, knows how to ring the changes in a strophic patter-song. The only problematic *comprimario* role is that of Ory's Tutor. His Act 1 aria, a bespoke commission for the great French *basse chantante* Nicolas Levasseur, is a devil of a piece to bring off; López-Cobos races through the aria in a vain attempt to disguise the fact that Alastair Miles isn't entirely at ease with it.

The recprding has colour, life, dash, brio, and a measure of wit. It also has Juan Diego Flórez. Enough to be going on with? Absolutely. An *Ory* for the connoisseur? Not entirely.

Elisabetta, regina d'Inghilterra

Elisabetta, regina d'Inghilterra
Jennifer Larmore mez Elisabetta **Bruce Ford** ten Leicester **Majella Cullagh** sop Matilde **Manuela Custer** mez Enrico **Colin Lee** ten Guglielmo **Antonio Siragusa** ten Norfolk **Geoffrey Mitchell Choir; London Philharmonic Orchestra / Giuliano Carella**
Opera Rara/Peter Moores Foundation ③ ORC22 (147' · DDD) Notes, text and translation included Ⓕ

Rossini wrote *Elizabeth, Queen of England* for the star-studded San Carlo Opera in Naples in 1815. The plot is a verse reduction of a half-

remembered drama by an Italian advocate out of an entertaining but historically implausible English romance. Larmore makes a formidable Elizabeth; beautifully sung, her performance has presence, character, and a real sense of ingrained authority. The lovely *cantabile* duet for Elizabeth and Matilde at the start of Act 2 is sung to perfection by Caballé and Masterson on Philips' rival set but there's a greater depth of emotion, a grainier, gutsier feel to Larmore's performance with Majella Cullagh's equally characterful, if not at every point inch-perfect, Matilde. There's little to choose between Bruce Ford's Leicester and Carreras's for Philips – Carreras perhaps wins on points with a certain added youthful allure – but Opera Rara's Antonio Siragusa is a more compelling Norfolk than Ugo Benelli, who sings splendidly but without much menace. Siragusa is very fine. With such strong casting, it goes without saying that the great confrontations in the opera – Elizabeth and Norfolk, Leicester and Norfolk, and so on – all come vividly to life. The Opera Rara performance has a lovely rich, dark feel to it. This is partly to do with Carella's conducting and the London Philharmonic's playing; partly to do with the fact that orchestration is clearly different in places. For first-time buyers, this is the set to go for.

Guglielmo Tell

Guglielmo Tell
Sherrill Milnes bar Guglielmo Tell **Luciano Pavarotti** ten Arnoldo **Mirella Freni** sop Matilde **Della Jones** mez Jemmy **Elizabeth Connell** mez Edwige **Ferrucio Mazzoli** bass Gessler **Nicolai Ghiaurov** bass Gualtiero **John Tomlinson** bass Melchthal **Cesar Antonio Suarez** ten Un pescatore **Piero De Palma** ten Rodolfo **Richard Van Allan** bass Leutoldo **Ambrosian Opera Chorus; National Philharmonic Orchestra / Riccardo Chailly**
Decca ④ 417 154-2DH4 (235' · ADD) Recorded 1980. Notes, text and translation included Ⓕ**O**

If ever there was a case for armchair opera it's Rossini's *Guglielmo Tell*. The very limitations which have made it, so far, a non-repertory work, give space for the imagination to redress the balance: the short, Rousseau-esque scenes of life by Lake Lucerne, the distant entrances and exits of shepherds and huntsmen, the leisurely but perfectly balanced side-vignettes of fisherman, hunter, child.

Thanks to the clarity and liveliness of the recording itself and, above all, the shrewd casting, this set creates a vivid charivari of fathers, sons, lovers and patriots, all played out against some of Rossini's most delicately painted pastoral cameos. Chailly keeps up the undercurrent of tension between private love and public loyalty, as well as working hard the rustic jollity of the score. Tell himself could hardly have a better advocate than Sherrill Milnes. Arnoldo and Matilde, too, are cleverly cast. Pavarotti contains the coarse, direct impulsiveness of

Arnoldo's shepherd stock with the tenderness of love, in his characteristic charcoal *cantabile* and the numbness of his remorse. Freni, singing opposite him as the forbidden Princess Matilde, phrases with aristocratic poise, folding into every fragment of embryonic *bel canto* the fragile ardour of a young girl's love. The vocal chemistry between them in their Act 2 declaration of love is a lively incarnation of their roles. A similarly interesting patterning of vocal timbres is produced by the casting of Elizabeth Connell as Edwige, Tell's wife, and of Della Jones as Jemmy, their son. Their last-act Trio with Matilde is matched by the contrasting colours of the basses of Ghiaurov, Tomlinson and Van Allan: their roles may be small, but their characters are vividly stamped on an excellent ensemble performance.

L'inganno felice

L'inganno felice
Annick Massis *sop* Isabella **Raúl Giménez** *ten* Bertrando **Rodney Gilfry** *bar* Batone **Pietro Spagnoli** *bass* Tarabotto **Lorenzo Regazzo** *bar* Ormondo **Le Concert des Tuileries / Marc Minkowski**
Erato 0630-17579-2 (78' · DDD) Recorded live 1996. Notes, text and translation included   Ⓕ●

This is a fine and tremendously enjoyable recording of an exquisite early Rossini one-acter. The plot resembles that of a late Shakespearian comedy. Set in a seaside mining community, it's concerned with the discovery and rehabilitation of Isabella, Duke Bertrando's wronged and, so he thinks, long-dead wife. It's a work that's comic and serious, witty and sentimental; and there, perhaps, lies the rub. Rossini, especially early Rossini, is meant to be all teeth and smiles, yet *L'inganno felice* isn't quite like that. The very *mise-en-scène* is odd: 'seaside' and 'mining' being, in such a context, strangely contradictory concepts. This is a splendid performance, using a chamber ensemble of about 30 players. It's recorded with pleasing immediacy, which begins bullishly but settles to intimacy when the drama requires. The score is full of vocal pitfalls, not least for the tenor and for the baritone Batone. But Giménez and Gilfry cope more than adequately, with enough in reserve to produce moments of genuine ease and beauty. Annick Massis is a charming Isabella, good in her first aria, ravishing in her second. The final scene the work's finest sequence, is set at night amid the mining galleys and is beautifully performed.

L'italiana in Algeri

L'italiana in Algeri
Jennifer Larmore *mez* Isabella **Raúl Giménez** *ten* Lindoro **Alessandro Corbelli** *bar* Taddeo **John del Carlo** *bass* Mustafà **Darina Takova** *sop* Elvira **Laura Polverelli** *mez* Zulma **Carlos Chausson** *bass-bar*

Haly **Geneva Grand Theatre Chorus; Lausanne Chamber Orchestra / Jésus López-Cobos**
Teldec ② 0630-17130-2 (147' · DDD) Notes, text and translation included   Ⓕ●

This recording is hard to fault on any count. López-Cobos revels in all aspects of this dotty comedy, timing everything to perfection, enthusing his accomplished orchestra and cast to enjoy their collective self. First there's a magic moment as Isabella and Lindoro espy each other for the first time, and comment on the joy of reunion; then the main section gets under way to a perfectly sprung rhythm from the conductor, with all the passage's detail made manifest; finally the *stretta* is released with the kind of vitality that sets the feet tapping. Larmore obviously thoroughly enjoys the role and conveys that enjoyment in singing that matches warm, smiling tone to bravura execution of her *fioriture*. She's a mettlesome Isabella, who knows how to tease, then defy her would-be lover, Mustafà, and charm her real amour, Lindoro, her 'Per lui che adoro' sung with an immaculate line and sensuous tone, its repetition deftly embellished. Finally 'Pensa alla patria' evinces a touch of true *élan*. Lindoro is taken by that paragon among Rossini tenors, Raúl Giménez, who presents his credentials in 'Languir per una bella', honeyed tone succeeded by fleet runs. He's no less successful in his more heroic Cavatina in Act 2. Corbelli, another master-Rossinian, is witty as the put-upon Taddeo, his textual facility a marvel. The American bass-baritone John del Carlo is a characterful Mustafà, managing to suggest, as Rossini surely intended, a paradox of lovesick tyrant and ludicrous posturing without ever overstepping the mark into farce, and rolling Italian and his rotund roulades off his tongue with idiomatic assurance. The recording is up to Teldec's impeccably high standard.

L'italiana in Algeri
Marilyn Horne *mez* Isabella **Ernesto Palacio** *ten* Lindoro **Domenico Trimarchi** *bar* Taddeo **Samuel Ramey** *bass* Mustafà **Kathleen Battle** *sop* Elvira **Clara Foti** *mez* Zulma **Nicola Zaccaria** *bass* Haly **Prague Philharmonic Chorus; I Solisti Veneti / Claudio Scimone**
Erato Libretto ② 2292-45404-2 (140' · ADD) Recorded 1980. Notes and text included   Ⓜ

Written within the space of a month during the spring of 1813, and with help from another anonymous hand, Rossini's *L'italiana in Algeri* was an early success, and one which went on to receive many performances during the 19th century, with an increasingly corrupt text. A complete reconstruction was undertaken by Azio Corghi and published in 1981; this recording uses this edition which corresponds most closely to what was actually performed in Venice in 1813. *L'italiana* is one of Rossini's wittiest operas, featuring as did a number of his most successful works a bewitching central character, in this case Isabella, who makes fun of her various suitors, with the opera ending with a happy escape with her beloved, Lindoro, a typical *tenorino* role. This fine recording has plenty of vocal polish. Scimone's biggest asset is Marilyn Horne as Isabella: possibly the finest Rossini singer of her generation and a veteran in this role, she sings Rossini's demanding music with great virtuosity and polish. Her liquid tone and artful phrasing ensure that she's a continuous pleasure to listen to. She's strongly supported by the rest of the cast: Kathleen Battle is a beguiling Elvira, Domenico Trimarchi a most humorous Taddeo, and Samuel Ramey a sonorous Bey of Algiers. Ernesto Palacio's Lindoro, however, has patches of white tone and is correct rather than inspiring. Scimone's conducting is guaranteed to give considerable pleasure.

Semiramide

Semiramide
Dame Joan Sutherland *sop* Semiramide **Marilyn Horne** *mez* Arsace **Joseph Rouleau** *bass* Assur **John Serge** *ten* Idreno **Patricia Clark** *sop* Azema **Spiro Malas** *bass* Oroe **Michael Langdon** *bass* Ghost of Nino **Leslie Fryson** *ten* Mitrane **Ambrosian Opera Chorus; London Symphony Orchestra / Richard Bonynge**
Decca ③ 425 481-2DM3 (168' · ADD) Recorded 1966.
Notes, text and translation included Ⓜ**OO**

Wagner thought it represented all that was bad about Italian opera, and Kobbe's *Complete Opera Book* proclaimed that it had had its day – but then added that 'were a soprano and contralto to appear in conjunction in the firmament the opera might be successfully revived'. That was exactly what happened in the 1960s, when both Sutherland and Horne were in superlative voice and, with Richard Bonynge, were prominent in the reintroduction of so many 19th-century operas that the world thought it had outgrown. This recording brought a good deal of enlightenment in its time. For one thing, here was vocal music of such 'impossible' difficulty being sung with brilliance by the two principal women and with considerable skill by the men. Then it brought to many listeners the discovery that, so far from being a mere show-piece, the opera contained ensembles of quite compelling dramatic intensity. People who had heard of the duet 'Giorno d'orrore' were surprised to find it remarkably unshowy and even expressive of the ambiguous feelings of mother and son in their extraordinary predicament. It will probably be a long time before this recording is superseded.

Tancredi

Tancredi
Ewa Podles *contr* Tancredi **Sumi Jo** *sop* Amenaide **Stanford Olsen** *ten* Argirio **Pietro Spagnoli** *bar* Orbazzano **Anna Maria di Micco** *sop* Isaura **Lucretia**

Lendi *mez* Roggiero **Capella Brugensis; Collegium Instrumentale Brugense / Alberto Zedda**
Naxos ② 8 660037/8 (147' · DDD) Recorded 1994.
Notes and Italian text included Ⓢ**O**

Tancredi is a seminal work in the Rossini canon, mingling a new-found reach in the musical architecture with vocal and instrumental writing of rare wonderment and beauty. The singing is splendid throughout, with a cast that's unusually starry. Podles has sung the role of Tancredi to acclaim at La Scala, Milan; the Amenaide, Sumi Jo, is a touch cool at first, too much the pert coloratura but this isn't an impression that persists. Hers is a performance of wonderful vocal control and flowering sensibility.

Podles, a smoky-voiced Pole, likes to go her own way at times. In the event, though, she and Sumi Jo work well together, and they sound marvellous. Podles also manages, chameleon-like, to adjust to the purer, more obviously stylish Rossini manner of a singer who's very unlike herself, the American tenor Stanford Olsen. His portrait of the conscience-stricken father Argirio matches singing of grace and impetus with great fineness of dramatic sensibility. As a result, something like the scene of the signing of his daughter's death-warrant emerges here as the remarkable thing it is.

Alberto Zedda is lucky to have at his disposal another of those wonderfully stylish chamber orchestras and chamber choirs that Naxos seem able to conjure at will. The aqueously lovely preface to Tancredi's first entrance is a representative example of the players' ear for Rossini's delicately limned tone-painting. The recording itself is beautifully scaled.

Il turco in Italia

Il turco in Italia
Michele Pertusi *bass* Selim **Cecilia Bartoli** *mez* Fiorilla **Alessandro Corbelli** *bar* Don Geronio **Ramón Vargas** *ten* Don Narciso **Laura Polverelli** *mez* Zaida **Francesco Piccoli** *ten* Albazar **Roberto de Candia** *bar* Prosdocimo **Chorus and Orchestra of La Scala, Milan / Riccardo Chailly**
Decca ② 458 924-2DHO2 (142' · DDD) Notes, text and translation included Ⓕ**OOO**

Chailly, has recorded the work before, but in the years since, he's matured as a Rossini conductor, and the Scala orchestra has this music under its fingers; there's an energy and vitality to this playing that's infectious. For his earlier recording, Montserrat Caballé was an underpowered Fiorilla; but Cecilia Bartoli is full of fire and mettle here (her 'Sqallido veste bruna' is sensational). Michele Pertusi is a fine Selim whose performance seems to breathe stage experience – it's a characterisation that's as vocally fine as it's theatrically adept. Alessandro Corbelli, reinforcing his credentials as a Rossini singer of flair and panache, is a strongly characterised Geronio.

This is a recording that smacks of the theatre, and unlike so many so-called comic operas, has lost nothing in its transfer to disc. Under Chailly's baton it fizzes and crackles like few other sets – recitatives are dispatched with the assurance of native Italian speakers, and with a genuine feeling for the meaning of the text. Decca's recording is beautifully judged and the set makes a fine modern alternative to the now classic (but cut) 1954 recording under Gavazzeni with Maria Callas.

Nino Rota   Italian 1911-1979

Rota studied at the Milan Conservatory, privately with Pizzetti (1925-6), with Casella in Rome, and at the Curtis Institute (1931-2). In 1939 he joined the staff at the Bari Conservatory (director from 1950). He wrote fluently in a cool, direct style: his output includes operas (notably The Italian Straw Hat, 1955), three symphonies, concertos and instrumental pieces, besides numerous film scores (many for Fellini, Visconti and Zeffirelli). GROVEmusic

Piano Concertos

Piano Concertos – E minor; C
Massimo Palumbo *pf* **I Virtuosi Italiani / Marco Boni**
Chandos CHAN9681 (64' · DDD)   Ⓕ❍

Both these works are unashamedly Romantic and nostalgic in style. The E minor Piano Concerto was composed in 1960, at the same time as Rota's music for Fellini's film *La dolce vita*. As if in answer to the extreme cynicism of that and much of his other film music, the concerto seems to be a questioning exploration of the remaining possibilities in a modern, Romantic form. The opening *Allegro-tranquillo* movement begins with a dreamlike theme on the piano which is then taken up by the orchestra and developed as a sort of conversation – the orchestra insisting on a heroic, almost martial sound, while the piano and woodwind reiterate the original soft mood. The first movement is over 16 minutes: away from the rule of the film-editor's stop-watch Rota felt free to indulge himself. The same four-note figure that runs through the opening is taken up in the second movement, a quiet, slow section with a haunting intensity. The finale continues the awake-in-a-dream contrasts.

Rota composed four piano concertos, but the date of the one in C major seems to be in doubt. It's earlier than 1960, and is a sparer, jauntier work, in mood more reminiscent of the 1920s. It, too, presents a dialogue between the quest-like piano part and the orchestra asserting a darker mood.

Both concertos are played by Massimo Palumbo with brilliant technique; the recorded sound is excellent., and I Virtuosi Italiani under Marco Boni provide excellent support.

Symphonies

No 1 in G; No 2 in F, 'Tarantina – Anni di pellegrinaggio'
Norrköping Symphony Orchestra / Ole Kristian Ruud
BIS CD970 (63' · DDD)   Ⓕ

It's fascinating to encounter these early works by Nino Rota, written when he was in his twenties, after a period of study in the USA. Rota's early career was as a church musician, something to which he returned late in life, after decades composing for the screen and the theatre. The influences in the First Symphony (1935-9) include Sibelius and Stravinsky but perhaps more significantly Copland and Hindemith. It's clearly a youthful work, a bit long-winded, but showing Rota's already firm grasp of complicated and sophisticated orchestration. The last, fourth, movement especially seems to have a maturity that points towards future greatness.

The Second Symphony, which he began in 1937, while still at work on the First, is even more Coplandesque. What would this have sounded like to an audience in the 1930s? (It wasn't performed until 1970.) In one way it would have seemed conservative in the extreme, showing no tendency towards atonality or any influence of jazz. The score carries a subtitle, 'Tarantina – Anni di pellegrinaggio', referring to the period Rota spent in the extreme south of Italy, teaching in Taranto. It could be dismissed as 'light music', and the style wouldn't have offended the most sensitive ears, yet each movement is full of beautiful instrumental detail and constructed in a pleasing way. Rota had yet to find his unmistakable voice, one infused with irony and humour, which would make him the perfect match for Fellini. Devotees of his film music may find these symphonies bland, but anyone who enjoys the contemporary style of Alwyn or Coates in England will find them worth while. The orchestra plays both symphonies with a good sense of period manner, never overdoing the lush sound. Recommended for the adventurous.

Orchestral Works

Il Gattopardo – Dances. La Strada – Orchestral Suite. Concerto soirée[a]
[a]**Benedetto Lupo** *pf* **Granada City Orchestra / Josep Pons**
Harmonia Mundi HMC90 1846 (64' · DDD)   Ⓕ

This lavishly packaged CD – a hardback book runs to some 80 pages in four languages with three separate background pieces and a filmography – brings together two suites from Rota's most famous film scores plus a *concertante* piece for piano and orchestra which quotes from his film work.

There's a seven-movement suite from *La Strada* (1954) directed by Fellini, with whom

Rota collaborated frequently. The brilliant opening sets the scene for the raffish charms of the film's circus folk, depicted in colourful orchestration and with vibrant, tuneful music that conveys the atmosphere of life under the big top. His themes, both romantic and rhythmically infectious, are skilfully interwoven between movements.

Rota wrote the music for Visconti's *Il Gattopardo* ('The Leopard', 1963), before the film was shot. He probably knew that the set piece was to be a lavish ballroom sequence lasting over an hour in the original print. The sequence begins with a previously unpublished waltz by Verdi (in Visconti's private collection) and continues in a manner akin to Verdi's own ballet music. The intention was to give the impression of 'a modest ensemble hired for the occasion' and this is just the treatment it receives from the Granada City Orchestra under Josep Pons. Nothing is inflated or allowed to disturb the seamless flow of this delightful dance music.

Proportion and balance are just right, too, for the modest and endearing *Concerto soirée* in which the fetching piano writing, very much the centre of attention, is brilliantly performed by Benedetto Lupo and wittily executed by the orchestra. A most attractive disc.

Albert Roussel
French 1869-1937

After embarking on a naval career, in 1894 Roussel began studies with Gigout, moving on to train with d'Indy and others at the Schola Cantorum (1898-1908) where in 1902 he began teaching. In 1909 he made a tour of India and Indo-China, and he drew on that experience in writing his Hindu opera-ballet Padmâvatî; (1923), though other works, like the vocal-orchestral Evocations (1911) and ballet Le festin de l'araignée (1913), had already shown his ability to leaven d'Indyism with exotic material and Ravellian brilliance.

In the Symphony No 2 (1921), he moved on to an almost polytonal density, but in the 1920s his music (like Ravel's) became more spare and astringent, though still with a rhythmic vigour and motivic intensity that can be seen as a highly personal extension of Schola thinking. His later, neo-classical works, marked by wide-ranging regular themes and motoric rhythms, include the Symphonies Nos 3 and 4, the orchestral Suite in F, the Piano Concerto, the String Quartet and two ballets, Bacchus et Ariane and Aenéas. **GROVE**music

Bacchus et Ariane

Bacchus et Ariane, Op 43. Le festin de l'araignée, Op 17
BBC Philharmonic Orchestra / Yan Pascal Tortelier
Chandos CHAN9494 (68' · DDD) Ⓟ**OO**

Unlike his contemporary Dukas, Roussel has been somewhat sidelined as a 'connoisseur's composer'. That presumably means that he didn't write fat, lush tunes that could be exploited in television commercials, but produced works of vigorous ideas and more subtle quality. Record companies used to fight shy of his music – the Third and Fourth Symphonies have indeed maintained a foothold, but with the ballet *Bacchus et Ariane*, which is closely linked with the Third, we've mostly been given only its second half. Here are alert, rhythmically vital performances of Roussel's two most famous ballets, which even at the most exuberantly excited moments (like the 'Bacchanale' in *Bacchus*) preserve a truly Gallic lucidity, and which Tortelier marks by a captivating lightness of touch; and when it comes to quiet passages one could not ask for greater tenderness than in the beautiful end of Act 1 of *Bacchus*, when Bacchus puts Ariadne to sleep.

Le festin de l'araignée, written 18 years earlier, is in a quite different style. Where Bacchus's trenchant idiom at times makes one think of Stravinsky's *Apollon Musagète*, *Le festin* (which had the misfortune to be overshadowed by the *Rite of Spring*, produced only eight weeks later) is atmospheric and more impressionistic (in the same vein as Roussel's First Symphony). It's a score full of delicate invention, whose one weakness is that for its full appreciation a knowledge of its detailed programme is needed – and that's provided here in the booklet.

The BBC Philharmonic play it beautifully. If this is 'connoisseur's music', then be happy to be called a connoisseur: you'll find it delectable.

Miklós Rózsa
Hungarian/American 1907-1995

Raised in Budapest and on his father's rural estate, Rósza was exposed to Hungarian folk music from an early age. He studied piano with his mother (who was at the Budapest Academy with Bartók) and violin and viola with his uncle, a musician with the Royal Hungrian Opera. By the age of seven he was composing. In 1926 he was a student at the Leipzig Conservatory; by 1929 his chamber works were being performed and promoted throughout Europe. In 1931 moved to Paris where he finished his Theme, Variations and Finale, a work that soon gained international recognition. He was introduced to the film music genre through Honegger and from 1935-9 composed for London Films under Hungarian-born producer Alexander Korda. In 1940 he travelled with Korda to Hollywood to complete the score of The Thief of Baghdad and was soon in great demand as a freelance film composer and conductor. As a staff member at MGM (1948-62), he became one of the most highly regarded composers in the industry, writing music for over 100 films. The essence of his musical style springs from his early experiences with Hungarian peasant music. His works are also infused with the sentimental lyricism of the gypsy tradition. **GROVE**music

Concertos

Violin Concerto, Op 24[a]. Cello Concerto, Op 32[b].
Tema con variazioni, Op 29a[c]
[ac]**Robert McDuffie** vn [bc]**Lynn Harrell** vc **Atlanta Symphony Orchestra / Yoel Levi**
Telarc CD80518 (72' · DDD)   Ⓕ●

Rózsa completed his dashingly eloquent Cello Concerto in 1968 for János Starker. Not only is Telarc's engineering incomparably more vivid and realistic than that of its predecessors, the actual performance is the most irreproachably stylish and urgently impassioned of the bunch. Lynn Harrell brings all his commanding presence, customary swagger and cast-iron technique to Rózsa's strikingly idiomatic solo writing. Add a polished and enthusiastic response from the Atlanta Symphony under Yoel Levi's eagle-eyed direction, and the results are exhilarating. Written in 1953-4 for Jascha Heifetz, the irresistibly colourful and sublimely lyrical Violin Concerto remains perhaps the most popular of all Rózsa's 'serious' compositions. While Heifetz's inimitable 1956 recording enshrines one of the most treasurable specimens of his jaw-dropping virtuosity, this newcomer possesses many sterling strengths of its own. McDuffie makes a dauntingly accurate, sweet-toned soloist, producing the most radiant sonorities in the ravishing, Kodály-esque slow movement, while Levi and his Atlanta band once again prove model partners. Last but not least, McDuffie joins forces with Harrell for the engaging *Tema con variazioni* which originally began life as the centrepiece of the Op 29 *Sinfonia concertante* penned for Heifetz and cellist Piatigorsky. Again, the performance is utterly sympathetic and stands up perfectly well to that legendary Heifetz/Piatigorsky collaboration.

Edmund Rubbra   British 1901-1986

Rubbra, a pupil of Scott and of Holst and Morris at the Royal College of Music (1921-5), worked as a pianist, teacher and critic before his appointment as lecturer at Oxford (1947-68). His music took some while to develop independence from Ireland, Bax and Holst, but his First Symphony (1937) begins to show a characteristic style of rhapsodic growth tautened by thematic working and almost incessant polyphonic activity. His later works include 10 more symphonies, of which No 9 is an oratorio-like work (Sinfonia sacra, 1972), besides concertos for viola, piano and violin, four string quartets (1933-77), masses and motets (he became a Roman Catholic in 1948).
GROVEmusic

Symphonies

Symphony No 3, Op 49. Symphony No 7 in C, Op 88
BBC National Orchestra of Wales / Richard Hickox
Chandos CHAN9634 (71' · DDD)   Ⓕ●●

All 11 symphonies also available as boxed set, Chandos CHAN9944 (5 CDs for price of 4)

For some years the Third Symphony was a repertory piece, at least on BBC programmes, but it fell out of favour in the late 1950s. Commentators have noticed a certain Sibelian cut to its opening idea (with woodwind in thirds) but everything else strikes you as completely personal. There's a whiff of Elgarian fantasy in the fourth variation of the finale. It's been called the most genial and relaxed of Rubbra's symphonies but there's a pastoral feel to many of the ideas, bucolic even, in the same way that there is about the Brahms Second Symphony. Brahms springs to mind in the masterly variations and fugue of the finale, for not long before, Rubbra had orchestrated the Brahms *Handel* Variations.
Hickox and his players give a very persuasive and totally convincing account of the symphony. Anyone coming to the Seventh for the first time, particularly in this performance, will surely not fail to sense the elevated quality of its musical thought. Its opening paragraphs are among the most beautiful Rubbra ever penned, and it's evident throughout that this is music that speaks of deep and serious things. This performance speaks with great directness and power. The horn playing in the opening is eloquent and the orchestral playing throughout is of a uniformly high standard. These are magnificent and impressive accounts, and the recording is truthful and splendidly balanced.

Symphony No 4, Op 53. Symphony No 10, 'Sinfonia da camera', Op 145. Symphony No 11, Op 153
BBC National Orchestra of Wales / Richard Hickox
Chandos CHAN9401 (58' · DDD) Recorded 1993-4
Ⓕ●

Rubbra's music lacks the kind of surface allure that captivates the ear at first acquaintance, but he does have a sense of organic continuity that's both highly developed and immediately evident to the listener. Wilfrid Mellers put it in a nutshell when he said of the symphonies, there's 'nothing abstruse about their tonality and harmony', but they're difficult because 'the continuity of their melodic and polyphonic growth is logical and unremitting. The orchestration shows scarcely any concern for the possibilities of colour, nothing on which the senses can linger and the nerves relax. Second subjects are hardly ever contrasting ideas but rather evolutions from or transfigurations of the old.' The opening of the Fourth Symphony is one of the most beautiful things in the English music of our time. These pages are free from any artifice, and their serenity remains with the listener for a long time. The Fourth (1940-42) was a wartime work, though no one would ever guess so. The 10th and 11th Symphonies are from 1974 and 1979 respectively. Both are concentrated one-movement affairs that unfold with seeming inevitability and naturalness. This is music made to last. Richard Hickox has the measure of its breadth and serenity, and secures total commitment from his excellent players. The Chandos recording is in the best traditions of the house.

Symphony No 5 in B flat, Op 63. Symphony No 8, 'Hommage à Teilhard de Chardin', Op 132. Ode to the Queen, Op 83[a]
[a]**Susan Bickley** *mez* **BBC National Orchestra of Wales / Richard Hickox**
Chandos CHAN9714 (64' · DDD) Text included   Ⓕ

In the early 1950s Rubbra's Fifth Symphony was a repertory piece and broadcast frequently. Ten years later it had all but disappeared from programmes, and although a second recording was made by the late Hans-Hubert Schönzeler, this is its first digital recording, and the finest account of the Fifth ever. Part of the success of Hickox's series is his instinctive feeling for the tempo at which this music best comes to life and his scrupulous adherence to dynamic markings. Find the right tempo and everything falls into place; observe every dynamic nuance and the textures achieve the right degree of transparency. The quality of the recording also plays an important part: there's great detail, presence and warmth.

The Eighth Symphony (1966-8), subtitled *Hommage à Teilhard de Chardin*, was composed in a very different climate, for by the late 1960s Rubbra's music was out of fashion. The new symphony had to wait three years for its first performance in Liverpool. The thought of the Catholic philosopher Teilhard de Chardin had a great influence on Rubbra. The music's mystical feel and luminous texture are at times reminiscent of Holst. The Eighth speaks of deep and serious things and in this performance proves a powerful musical experience.

The Ode to the Queen is something of a discovery. Commissioned by the BBC to celebrate the Elizabeth II's Coronation, it's Rubbra's only song cycle with full orchestra. The songs are inspired and beautifully sung. A triumphant conclusion to Richard Hickox's Rubbra cycle.

Symphony No 9, 'Sinfonia sacra', Op 140. The Morning Watch, Op 55
Lynne Dawson *sop* **Della Jones** *mez* **Stephen Roberts** *bar* **BBC National Chorus and Orchestra of Wales / Richard Hickox**
Chandos CHAN9441 (57' · DDD) Recorded 1993. Texts included   ⒻⓄ

The Ninth (1973) is Rubbra's most visionary utterance, and its stature has so far gone unrecognised. (This is its only recording.) Its subtitle, *Sinfonia sacra*, gives a good idea of its character. It tells the story of the Resurrection very much as do the Bach Passions. There are three soloists: the contralto narrates from the New Testament, while the soprano takes the part of Mary Magdalen and the baritone that of Jesus. Other parts, those of disciples and angels, are taken by the chorus, which also functions

outside the action, in four settings of meditative Latin texts from the Roman liturgy or in Lutheran chorales to which Rubbra put verses by Bernard de Nevers. The symphonic dimension is reinforced by the opening motive, which pretty well dominates the work. Its argument unfolds with a seeming inevitability and naturalness that's the hallmark of a great symphony. Its depth and beauty call to mind only the most exalted of comparisons and it should be heard as often as *Gerontius* or the *War Requiem*. This is music of an inspired breadth and serenity and everyone connected with this magnificent performance conveys a sense of profound conviction. *The Morning Watch* is one of Rubbra's most eloquent choral pieces. It dates from 1946, and so comes roughly half-way between the Fourth and Fifth Symphonies. A setting of the 17th-century metaphysical poet, Henry Vaughan, it too is music of substance and its long and moving orchestral introduction is of the highest order of inspiration.

Additional recommendations

Symphonies Nos 3 and 4
Couplings. A Tribute for Ralph Vaughan Williams on his 70th Birthday. Resurgam Overture
Philharmonia Orchestra / Del Mar
Lyrita SRCD202 (73' · DDD)   Ⓕ
Dedicated performances of these superb symphonies under Norman Del Mar. The coupling, *Resurgam*, is a late work of great beauty.

Symphonies Nos 2 and 7
Coupled with: Festival Overture
London Philharmonic Orchestra / Boult; New Philharmonia Orchestra / Handley
Lyrita SRCD235 (78' · ADD)   Ⓕ
Fine performances, excellently transferred.

Sinfonia concertante

Sinfonia concertante, Op 38[a]. A Tribute, Op 56[d]. The Morning Watch, Op 55[b]. Ode to the Queen, Op 83[c]
[c]**Susan Bickley** *mez* [a]**Howard Shelley** *pf*
BBC National [b]**Chorus and Orchestra of Wales / Richard Hickox**
Chandos CHAN9966 (62' · DDD)   Ⓕ

A mouth-watering reissue comprising four outstandingly eloquent performances. The standout item here has to be Howard Shelley's imperious traversal of the big-boned *Sinfonia concertante* for piano and orchestra. Certainly, the opening 'Fantasia' exhibits an exhilarating thematic resource and craggy, almost Bartókian resilience. It's the finale, however, which contains the work's most rewarding, deeply felt inspiration: this is a prelude and fugue of grave nobility, economy and poise, whose elegiac countenance reflects Rubbra's sense of loss at the death of his teacher and good friend, Gustav Holst. Next comes an affectionate account of *A Tribute* (Rubbra's 70th-birthday tribute to

Vaughan Williams), followed by *The Morning Watch*, a noble choral setting of Henry Vaughan's mystic poem which possesses a power and radiance that can't fail to impress. Last, but not least, there's *Ode to the Queen* (1953); employing texts by three Tudor poets (Crashaw, D'Avenant and Campion), it's a charming, 13-minute creation, the two extrovert outer songs framing a *Poco adagio e tranquillo* setting of chaste beauty. Mezzo Susan Bickley is ideally cast, and Hickox tenders bright-eyed support. Superb sound throughout, enormously ripe and wide-ranging.

String Quartets

String Quartets – No 2, Op 73[a]; No 4, Op 150[b]. Lyric Movement, Op 24[c]. Meditations on a Byzantine Hymn, 'O Quando in Cruce', Op 117[ad]
[c]**Michael Dussek** pf [abc]**Dante Quartet** (Krysia Osostowicz vn/[d]va Declan Daly vn Judith Busbridge [d]va Alastair Blayden vc)
Dutton Laboratories Epoch CDLX7114 (59' · DDD)
Ⓜ**O**

Completed in 1951, the Second Quartet is a marvellously inventive piece, beautifully scored for the medium, unfailingly purposeful and full of beguilingly subtle rhythmic and harmonic resource. Bearing a dedication to Robert Simpson, the two-movement Fourth Quartet of 1975-7 was one of Rubbra's last major works. Probing and intensely poignant, it's another hugely eloquent, seamlessly evolving affair which repays repeated hearings. The Dante Quartet prove outstandingly sympathetic proponents of Rubbra's noble inspiration, their playing urgently expressive and tonally ingratiating. Pianist Michael Dussek joins proceedings for a stylish and delectably unforced account of the *Lyric Movement* of 1929, an expertly wrought essay for piano quintet which itself grew out of an earlier, discarded string quartet. Tony Faulkner's Maltings sound is excellent on the whole, if just a fraction too closely balanced. No matter, a wonderful disc.

String Quartets – No 1 in F minor, Op 35; No 3, Op 112. Cello Sonata, Op 60[a]. Improvisation for Unaccompanied Cello, Op 124.
[a]**Michael Dussek** pf **Dante Quartet** (Krysia Osostowicz, Matthew Truscott vns Judith Busbridge va [a]Pierre Doumenge vc)
Dutton Epoch CDLX7123 (72' · DDD)   Ⓜ**OO**

Rubbra originally conceived the first of his four string quartets in 1933. Thirteen years later, he overhauled his thoughts and added a new finale. Dedicated to Vaughan Williams and beautifully laid out for the medium, it's an invigorating and purposeful work, boasting a particularly memorable slow movement. The Third Quartet of 1963 is even finer; its seamlessly evolving structure demonstrates Rubbra's sebtle ear for harmony and counterpoint. The three movements play without a break, and once again the *Adagio*

centrepiece plumbs great depths.

It's good that the Dante Quartet have lost no time in completing their Rubbra cycle for Dutton. The previous coupling of Quartets Nos 2 and 4 was shortlisted for a *Gramophone* Award, and if anything this disc attains an even greater level of accomplishment and perception. These are eloquent readings that strike a perfect equilibrium between communication and rigour. Bouquets, too, for the Dante's young French cellist, Pierre Doumenge, who teams up with pianist Michael Dussek for a cogent and impassioned account of the 1946 Cello Sonata (more convincing than either comparative rival). Doumenge also shines in the unaccompanied *Improvisation* from 1964. The production values are exemplary. This is a most rewarding release.

Piano Trios

Piano Trios – No 1 'in one movement', Op 68[a]; No 2, Op 138[f]. Meditazioni sopra 'Coeurs désolés', Op 67[b]. Phantasy, Op 16[c]. Sonata for Oboe and Piano in C, Op 100[d]. The Buddah – Suite (arr Cruft)[e]. Duo, Op 156[g]
Endymion Ensemble ([e]Helen Keen fl [bdeg]Melinda Maxwell ob [acef]Krysia Osostowicz, [c]Catherine Manson vns [e]Catherine Manson va [aef]Jane Salmon vc [abcdfg]Michael Dussek pf)
Dutton Laboratories Epoch CDLX7106 (77' · DDD)
Ⓜ**O**

How wise to kick off with the Piano Trio No 1 of 1950 – a magnificent beast, brimful of doughty integrity and always evincing a breathtaking contrapuntal scope. It's cast in a single movement, comprising an initial *Andante moderato* of glorious, long-breathed eloquence, a perky *Episodio scherzando* and a concluding theme and three variations ('Meditazioni').

Like all Rubbra's finest music, the score unfolds with an intuitive purpose and questing spirituality as awesome as it's rewarding, an observation that extends to its scarcely less imposing two-movement successor of 20 years later. The mood here is darker, more rarefied, the opening *Tempo moderato e deliberato* distilling a lofty austerity that not even the jaunty, syncopated rhythms of the *Allegro scherzando* second movement can quite dispel.

The remaining five items span virtually the whole of Rubbra's career. Even in the early *Phantasy* for two violins and piano (1927) his burgeoning mastery of the flowing line and capacity for organic thought are already very much in evidence, the music's rapt, at times distinctly pastoral lyricism engagingly reminiscent of the young Herbert Howells's chamber offerings. It's a lovely work, as is the Suite for flute, oboe and string trio that Adrian Cruft prepared from Rubbra's incidental music to Clifford Bax's 1947 radio play, *The Buddha*. Of the two works for oboe, the appealing Sonata of 1958 impresses by dint of its quiet cogency, while the 1949 *Meditazioni sopra 'Coeurs désolés'* inhabits much the same gently ruminative landscape found in the last section of the Piano Trio No 1.

That just leaves the deeply felt Duo for cor anglais and piano (Rubbra's very last chamber work, completed six years before his death in 1986). Performances throughout are poised and dedicated; truthful sound and balance, too.

Violin Sonatas

Violin Sonatas[a] – No 1, Op 11; No 2, Op 31; No 3, Op 133. Four Pieces, Op 29[a]. Variations on a Phrygian Theme, Op 105
Krysia Osostowicz vn [a]**Michael Dussek** pf
Dutton Laboratories Epoch Series CDLX7101
(59' · DDD) Ⓜ○

Rubbra's First Violin Sonata is a notable achievement all round: its first two movements exhibit a bittersweet lyricism that will strike a chord with anyone who has ever responded to, say, John Ireland's glorious Second Violin Sonata or the chamber music of Howells. By contrast, the 'Fugal Rondo' finale intriguingly pursues an altogether more sturdy, determinedly neo-Classical mode of expression. Written six years later in 1931, the Second Sonata already reveals a wider emotional scope, as well as a striking use of progressive tonality that at least one contemporary critic found 'disturbing and unnecessary'. Championed by the great Albert Sammons, it will come as a substantial discovery to many: comprising an eventful, ever-evolving first movement, a strong, but never sentimental 'Lament' centrepiece, and a quasi-Bartókian finale, its wild exuberance seems to look forward across the decades to the last movement of this same figure's Violin Concerto of 1959. Framing that are the *Four Pieces* for beginners and the unaccompanied *Variations on a Phrygian Theme*, a work of compact resourcefulness. But even finer is the Third Sonata. It's a wondrous piece, its sense of purpose, rapt intuition and profound serenity irresistibly calling to mind Rubbra's Eighth Symphony, and it fully deserves the exalted advocacy it receives here. Indeed, Osostowicz and Dussek form an outstandingly sympathetic partnership.

Piano Works

Prelude and Fugue on a Theme of Cyril Scott, Op 69. Sonatina, Op 19. Introduction, Aria and Fugue, Op 104. Preludes, Op 131. Nemo Fugue. Studies, Op 139. Invention on the Name of Haydn, Op 160. Fantasy Fugue, Op 161. Teaching Pieces, Op 74[a]
Traditional (arr Rubbra) Fukagawa
Michael Dussek, [a]**Rachel Dussek** pfs
Dutton Laboratories Epoch CDLX7112 (62' · DDD) Ⓕ

Rubbra was an excellent pianist, and his output for the instrument spans pretty much his entire career. It's the earliest work here, the Sonatina of 1928-9, that proves by far the most technically demanding. Whereas the raptly lyrical first two movements have something of the outdoor tang of Vaughan Williams and Howells, the

finale seems to stand apart, its timeless, intuitive spirit and bracing contrapuntal mastery the hallmarks of Rubbra's mature voice. Other stand-out items include the noble *Introduction, Aria and Fugue*, the pithy Four Studies of 1970-71 and the Eight Preludes, Rubbra's most substantial piano offering, completed in 1966. The latter comprise a hugely rewarding sequence, the organic wholeness of Rubbra's luminous inspiration often calling to mind his masterly Eighth Symphony. Suffice it to say, Michael Dussek acquits himself extremely well throughout, and he has been sympathetically recorded.

Vocal Works

Missa Cantuariensis, Op 59[ab]. Magnificat and Nunc dimittis in A flat, Op 65[ab]. Missa in honorem Sancti Dominici, Op 66[a]. Prelude and Fugue on a Theme of Cyril Scott, Op 69 (arr Rose)[b]. Tenebrae, Op 72[a]. Meditation, Op 79[b]
[a]**St John's College Choir, Cambridge /**
Christopher Robinson [b]org
Naxos 8 555255 (71' · DDD) Texts and translations included Ⓢ Ⓢ○○

With this valuable Rubbra anthology Christopher Robinson and his St John's College Choir reinforce the favourable impression left by previous instalments in their English Choral Music series for Naxos. They prove especially eloquent, humane advocates of the eight-part *Missa Cantuariensis*. We've long needed a top-notch digital recording of this, the first of Rubbra's five Mass settings. Robinson and company rise to the challenge admirably, not least in the exuberant concluding *Gloria* with its lung-burstingly high tessitura. We also get a thoroughly idiomatic rendering of the taut and imposing *Magnificat* and *Nunc dimittis* in A flat that Rubbra wrote two years later.

In the glorious *Missa in honorem Sancti Dominici* from 1949 (inspired by Rubbra's own conversion to Roman Catholicism the previous year, on the feast day of St Dominic) our Cambridge group doesn't quite match the sumptuous blend, miraculous unanimity or spine-tingling fervour displayed by James O'Donnell's Westminster Cathedral Choir (to quote the composer: '...this is not austere music...red blood runs through its veins!'). On the other hand, these newcomers sound wholly captivated by the nine motets that make up the remarkable Op 72 *Tenebrae*. Boasting an infinitely subtle harmonic and contrapuntal resource, these timeless, wonderfully compassionate settings of the responsories used during Matins on Maundy Thursday show Rubbra very much at the height of his powers, encompassing an extraordinarily wide dramatic and expressive range. Robinson also gives us two instrumental bonuses in the rapt *Meditation* for organ, Op 79, and Bernard Rose's transcription of the more substantial *Prelude and Fugue on a Theme of Cyril Scott* (originally written for piano in 1950 to celebrate Scott's 70th birthday). Throw in Naxos's praiseworthy production, and you've a bargain of the first order.

Rubbra A Hymn to the Virgin, Op 13[ab]. Rosa mundi, Op 2[ab]. Fukagawa[b]. Pezzo ostinato, Op 102[b]. Songs, Op 4 – The Mystery[a]; Jesukin[ab]. Orpheus with his Lute, Op 8[ab]. Transformations, Op 141[b]. The Jade Mountain, Op 116[ab]. Improvisation, Op 124[c]. Discourse, Op 127[bc] **L Berkeley** Nocturne[b] **Howells** Prelude[b]
[a]**Tracey Chadwell** sop [b]**Danielle Perrett** hp [c]**Tim Gill** vc
ASV CDDCA1036 (67' · DDD) Texts included   Ⓕ

All but 10 minutes of this CD is devoted to Rubbra. Several works here are first recordings, including the impressive *Transformations* for harp, Op 141, and the early miniatures that open the disc, the *Hymn to the Virgin* and *Rosa mundi*. Both reflect the world of Holst and Scott. Many of the pieces also reflect the strong attraction Rubbra felt for the Orient, from the early *Fukagawa* arrangement (1929), to *The Jade Mountain* (1962), as well as the inspiring harp pieces: the *Pezzo ostinato* and the *Transformations*, the most extended (and perhaps the most exalted) piece on the disc. Both derive inspiration from the Indian *raga*. Perrett plays with finesse and sensitivity and her free, imaginative handling of the *Pezzo ostinato* is admirable. She brings authority to the *Improvisation*, Op 124 (1964). Chadwell proves an intelligent interpreter of the songs, although she appears more backwardly balanced and there's just a shade too much echo round her voice. But in general the recording is first-rate. The overall character of this music is meditative and readers should select a few pieces at a time. A must for Rubbra *aficionados*.

Poul Ruders
Danish b1949

Ruders studied piano and organ at the Odense Conservatory and graduated from the Royal Danish Conservatory in 1975. He worked initially as a church organist and freelance keyboard player. Although he had some lessons from Nørholm and orchestration from Kar Rasmussen, he describes himself as an essentially self-taught composer.

Ruders is widely recognised as the leading Danish composer of his generation. The large proportion of his works are for orchestra or large chamber ensemble; some of his scores use electronic keyboards and samplers. Ruders has developed a flexible musical language, organised only by his own 'homespun' systems; freely atonal but able to incorporate tonal references. His command of idiomatic instrumental and vocal writing, his strong sense of drama and his readiness to explore extremes of experience enable him to communicate directly and powerfully with audiences. **GROVE**music

Violin Concerto No 1

Violin Concerto No 1[a]. Etude and Ricercare[b]. The Bells[c]. The Christmas Gospel[d]
[c]**Lucy Shelton** sop [ab]**Rolf Schulte** vn [c]**Speculum Musicae** / **David Starobin** gtr [a]**Riverside Symphony Orchestra** / **George Rothman**; [d]**Malmö Symphony Orchestra** / **Ola Rudner**
Bridge BCD9057 (62' · DDD) Recorded 1994-5. Texts included   ⒻⓄ

Ruders' First Violin Concerto (1981) begins as routine minimalist auto-hypnosis. But it develops some wonderfully inventive ways of disrupting and reassembling itself. Admittedly the last movement, with its chaconne based on Vivaldi and Schubert, tiptoes on the border of sensationalism. Otherwise the work could join Schnittke's Fourth as one of the few contemporary violin concertos with a strong claim to standard-repertoire status. Schulte gives an intense account of the solo part; the Riverside orchestra is tight in discipline, the recording close. All these factors help to make the overall musical impression extremely vivid. Less persuasive is Ruders's vocal writing in *The Bells* (the same Edgar Allen Poe texts set by Rachmaninov), and there's something not quite convincing about the instrumental setting too – perhaps too uniform an intensity, too much frantic heterophony. *The Christmas Gospel*, tossed off in two weeks for a mixed animation and live-action film, is darkly impressive – necessarily simple and direct, but still rewarding, even when divorced from the visual images.

Corpus cum figuris

Four Dances in One Movement. Dramaphonia. Corpus cum figuris
Erik Kaltoft pf **Aarhus Sinfonietta** / **Søren Kinch Hansen**
BIS CD720 (70' · DDD)   Ⓕ

The name *Corpus cum figuris* ('body with figurations') comes from Thomas Mann's novel about a fictional German composer, *Dr Faustus*. There's no programmatic significance, says Ruders; it was the title itself that set his imagination working. At times the piece does sound like a grotesque, terrifying break-dance, full of jagged, joint-dismembering syncopations. But something of Mann's apocalyptic conception seems to have got into Ruders's music too – the smell of sulphur, the sense of prevailing desolation. It comes over well in this moody but very precise performance. So too does *Dramaphonia*, a one-movement piano concerto with an 'orchestra' of 11 instruments. This is more sombre still than *Corpus cum figuris*, the pace prevailingly slow and brooding. But Ruders knows how to hold the attention, even when very little seems to be happening. *Four Dances in One Movement* makes an excellent contrast. The darkness of the other two works isn't entirely absent from *Four Dances*, but the sweetly parodistic waltz tune of the second dance is delicious. Perhaps the performance could be a little more satirically stylish.

The Handmaid's Tale

The Handmaid's Tale
Marianne Rørholm *mez* Offred **Hanne Fischer** *mez* Double **Poul Elming** *ten* Luke **Ulla Kudsk Jensen** *mez* Offred's Mother **Anne Margrethe Dahl** *sop* Aunt Lydia **Dijna Mai-Mai** *sop* Moira **Lise-Lotte Nielsen** *sop* Janine **Annita Wadsholt** *contr* Moira's Aunt **Susanne Resmark** *contr* Serena Joy **Kari Hamnøy** *contr* Rita **Aage Haugland** *bass* Commander **Gert Henning-Jensen** *ten* Nick **Elsebeth Lund** *sop* Ofglen **Pia Hansen** *mez* New Ofglen **Bengl-Ola Morgny** *ten* Doctor **Elisabeth Halling** *mez* Warren's Wife **John Laursen** *ten* Commander X **Uffe Henriksen** *bass* First Eye and Guard **Morten Kramp** *bass* Second Eye and Guard **Royal Danish Opera Chorus and Orchestra / Michael Schønwandt**
Da Capo ② 8 224165/6 (144' · DDD) Recorded live 2000. Notes, text and translation included   Ⓕ**OO**

Ruders says of his vividly imaginative opera, based on Margaret Atwood's novel, that he composed it as though he were directing a film. Precisely: it's divided into 44 scenes, some very short, several incorporating flashbacks in which present and past sometimes appear simultaneously. The opera's 'present' is the not-too-distant future, a hideous fundamentalist autocracy in which women have no rights, not even to read and write, and those of them convicted of 'gender-treachery' (adultery, second marriage, contraception, abortion) are compelled to become 'Handmaids', ritually impregnated by the husbands of childess women. The central character, Offred (Of Fred – the name of the man whose property she now is), is portrayed by two singers: her present, brainwashed and imperfectly remembering self, and Offred as she was in 'Time Before', happily married (though as her husband's second wife a 'gender traitor' to the new order) with a five-year-old daughter. The opera depicts the brutal totalitarianism of 'Time Now', Offred's relationship with the Commander (Fred) and his alarming wife, her longing for her dimly remembered husband and child and her enlistment in a sort of resistance group. But it's in the very nature of the plot that we never learn her ultimate fate.

It's also in the plot's nature that it needs a great variety of types of music, as we move from past to present, from the grim rituals of Time Now to Offred's memories of Time Before. Ambiguous music, too, since in this shadowy, threatening world things are often not what they seem. Ruder's great achievement is to provide that variety and ambiguity from within the resources of his own style; in particular, he balances on the tightrope from tonality to atonality with great skill. The rituals of the Handmaids are accompanied by simple, chorale-like chants with 'minimalist' accompaniment. The most

striking passage to emerge from the score is a duet for the two Offreds in which both voices seem to be yearning for a tonal resolution, but can no more achieve it than two people 20 years apart in time can meet.

Ruders has been best known for his prodigiously resourceful orchestral writing, and he surpasses himself here: electronic keyboards, samplers and additional percussion are added to the large orchestra, but many of the strangest, most nightmarish or most radiant sounds are produced by normal instruments used with brilliant originality. Some of the more monstrous inhabitants of this nightmare world are portrayed in vocal lines that go to extremes, but far more often the writing for voices is idiomatically singable. The cast, among whom there isn't one single weak link, sing their hearts out, and Schønwandt conveys the kaleidoscopic colours of Ruder's score with a remarkable degree of clarity. The recording is first class.

John Rutter
British b1945

One of the most popular and widely performed composers of his generation, Rutter studied at Clare College, Cambridge, then taught at Southampton University, returning to Clare College as director of music in 1975. He left in 1979 to devote himself to composition and founded the Cambridge Singers with whom he has made many recordings of both his own and others' music. His works are predominately vocal; his musical style draws upon the British choral tradition – Holst, Vaughan Williams, Howells, Britten and Tippett – but also late 19th- early 20th-century European music, especially Fauré and Duruflé.   **GROVE**music

Requiem

Requiem[a]. Hymn to the Creator of Light. God be in my head. A Gaelic Blessing. Psalmfest – No 5, Cantate Domino. Open thou mine eyes[b]. A Prayer of St Patrick. A Choral Fanfare. Birthday Madrigals – No 2, Draw on, sweet night; No 4, My true love hath my heart. The Lord bless you and keep you
[a]**Rosa Mannion,** [b]**Libby Crabtree** *sops* **Polyphony; Bournemouth Sinfonietta / Stephen Layton**
Hyperion CDA66947 (69' · DDD) Texts and translations included   Ⓕ**O**

Here is music finely crafted, written with love for the art and an especial care for choral sound. It's melodious without being commonplace, harmonically rich without being sticky, modern in the graceful way of a child who grows up responsive to newness but not wanting to kick his elders in the teeth. He gives us the heart's desire. But he's on too familiar terms with our heart's desires, he doesn't extend them, or surprise us into realising that they were deeper and subtler than we thought. This is by way of cautiously savouring a remembered taste, which could readily be indulged without perceived need for an interval: one item leads to another and before we know it the pleasurable hour is over. The Requiem is the longest work; the other pieces vary from two to just over six minutes. Most are unaccompanied and show the choir of 25 voices as another of those expert groups of assured and gifted professionals that are among the principal adornments of modern musical life. Their capacity as a virtuoso choir is tested in the *Cantate Domino* and *Choral Fanfare*, but Rutter writes for real singers (not just singer-musicians) and their tone is unfailingly beautiful. The two soloists are excellent.

Additional recommendation

Coupled with: Advent anthem, 'Arise, shine'. Go forth into the world in peace. Toccata in seven. Variations on an Easter theme for organ duet. A Clare Benediction. Musica Dei donum. Come down, O Love divine.

Thomas sop **Jones** fl **Hooker** ob **Nicholas Rimmer, Collon** org **Dorey** vc **Clare College Choir, Cambridge; Members of the City of London Sinfonia / Brown**

Naxos 8 557130 (69' · DDD) Texts and translations included   Ⓢ Ⓢ ○○

> A fine selection of Rutter's work, recorded with the choir of Rutter's own Cambridge college. They're fresh and natural, thoroughly musical in feeling and professional in care. The version of the *Requiem* is the scoring for solo instruments and organ, rather than the full orchestral score heard on Hyperion.

Gloria

Gloria[abc]. Come down, O Love divine. Lord, make me an instrument of thy peace[b]. To everything there is a season. I my Best-beloved's am. Praise the Lord, O my Soul[ac]. I will lift up mine eyes[b]. As the bridegroom to his chosen[b]. A Clare Benediction. The Lord is my light and my salvation. Go forth into the world in peace. Thy perfect love[b]. Te Deum[ac]
Polyphony, [a]The Wallace Collection; [b]City of London Sinfonia / Stephen Layton with [c]Andrew Lumsden org
Hyperion CDA67259 (79' · DDD) Texts and translations included   Ⓕ

This superb disc contains a balanced cross-section of Rutter's sacred choral music, spanning over a quarter century and featuring several first recordings. Rutter's stylistic hallmarks are all here: an unfailing knack to get to the root of the text, exquisitely balanced vocal writing, melting harmonies, intensely sweet turns of phrase, short ecstatic climaxes, but also a willingness to be astringent, and rhythmically powerful. There are nods to pageantry, for example in the conclusion of the *Gloria* with its Waltonian swagger, some decliously *echt* Sullivan at the end of the *Te Deum* and, in *I my Best-beloved's am*, an occasional vision of the neo-Byzantine soundworld of his fellow Highgate School pupil, John Tavener. The artistry of the 25 full-bodied voices of Polyphony is beyond reproach, only suffering a deficit in sheer volume when pitted against the full fury of The Wallace Collection. Sumptuously recorded, all the forces involved play to perfection. Greatly enjoyable.

Five Traditional Songs

Rutter Five Traditional Songs **Vaughan Williams** Five English Folksongs **Traditional** (arr Rutter) I know where I'm going. Down by the sally gardens. The bold grenadier. The keel row. The cuckoo. She's like the swallow. Willow song. The willow tree. The miller of Dee. O can ye sew cushions? Afton water. The sprig of thyme. She moved through the fair (arr Runswick). The lark in the clear air (arr Carter) ·
Cambridge Singers; City of London Sinfonia / John Rutter
Collegium COLCD120 (66' · DDD) Recorded 1992 Texts included   Ⓕ ○

Pleasure in singing is almost the *raison d'être* of this disc. Rutter not only provides us with a healthy dollop of nostalgia, but gives these songs a whole new lease of life in some characteristically scrumptious arrangements. For some, though, there's always the danger that the superficial charms of Rutter's arrangements can smother the fundamental beauty of the original melody. But then one would argue that he doesn't attempt to follow in the footsteps of the great folksong arrangers (he pays tribute to this tradition by including Vaughan Williams's *Five English Folksongs*). His arrangements belong more to the light music tradition; what Messrs Binge, Coates and Tomlinson achieved with orchestral colours Rutter finds primarily through vocal ones – and it's significant that the very finest arrangements here (including a ravishing 'Golden Slumbers') are unaccompanied. The singers are outstanding.

Frederic Rzewski   American b1938

Rzewski was a pupil of Thompson and Spies at Harvard (1954-8) and of Wagner and Strunk at Princeton (1958-60). In 1962-4 he was associated with Stockhausen and in 1966-71 he was a member of Musica Elettronica Viva, based in Rome. During this period his music gained a socialist message (e.g. Coming Together, 1972) and he has explored folk and popular melodies; his works are characterized by drive and intensity.   GROVEmusic

---

Main Drag

Rzewski Main Drag. Coming together[b]. Attica[a]. Les Moutons de Panurge **Ielasi** Untitled (September 02) (original reworking of Attica) **Passarani** Left mouse button doesn't know what the right mouse button is doing (original remix of Les Moutons de Panurge) **Rimbaud** Dawnfire Mix (remix of Main Drag)

[a]**Frederic Rzewski,** [b]**Frankie HI NRG** *spkrs* **Alter Ego** (Manuel Zurria *fl* Poalo Ravaglia *cl* Francesco Peverini *vn* Francesco Dillon *vc* Oscar Pizzo *pf*) **Monica Lomero, Akane Makita** *kybds* **Gianluca Ruggeri** *perc* **Giuseppe Pistone** *elec gtr* **Massimo Ceccarelli** *bgtr*
Stradivarius STR33631 (70' · DDD)   Ⓕ●

Churning rhythm and seemingly minimalist, rigorously controlled melodic patterns characterise three of Frederic Rzewski's early works presented by the superbly accomplished Italian new-music ensemble Alter Ego.

Coming Together and *Attica* date from 1971-2, and were written in response to specific incidents in the wake of the 1971 prisoners' revolt at New York's Attica State Prison, an event that ended in violent, tragic consequences. Both works employ texts that are spoken with agonising deliberation, systematic repetition and long spaces between words. As a result, one senses, in *Coming Together*, the inner turmoil beneath the plain yet ambiguous language of a letter written by Sam Melville (one of the prisoners killed in the uprising).

For *Attica*, Rzewski's intense, raspy delivery of the line 'Attica is in front of me' effectively contrasts to the musicians' suave, lyrical interplay, quite different from Group 180's faster, harder-edged recording of the piece.

Rzewski's 1969 *Les Moutons de Panurge* encompasses a steadily accelerating unison line whose sequence of notes gradually accumulates and diminishes. In this concert performance, an added live electronic component by Marco Passarani starts with scattered handclaps and gradually escalates into massed crowd noises that only the enthusiastic audience response can possibly top.

Main Drag finds Rzewski revisiting these compositional techniques as phrases from an eight-note scale deftly ricochet from one instrument to the next like restless pinballs. This is followed by Passarani's driving, propulsive remix of the original by Robin Rimbaud, aka Scanner.

The disc also offers remixed interpretations of *Attica* and *Les Moutons de Panurge*. Both reveal how well Rzewski's methodology lends itself to the sound world of contemporary dance and ambient music. Robin Rimbaud compresses *Main Drag*'s single notes into murky chords that fly over a background of fleeting static. Giuseppe Ielasi gently crushes *Attica*'s lyrical lines into a canvas of B flat major jelly, with soft, insect-like blips dancing over it. Rzewski was doing similar stuff more than 30 years ago with Musica Elettronica Viva on far less sophisticated sound and recording equipment, but that's another story.

Kaija Saariaho   Finnish b1952

After studying with Paavo Haininen at the Sibelius Academy, Helsinki, she worked for Brian Ferneyhough and Klaus Huber at the Musikhochschule in *Freiburg (1981-2) and attended a computer music course at IRCAM in Paris in 1982. She is interested in enlarging the potential of traditional instruments and uses electronic instruments and computers to that end. For Lichtbogen (1985-6), for nine instruments and live electronics, a computer was used in the pre-compositional stage. She also makes use of extra-musical stimuli, such as texts or natural phenomena: Nymphéa (Jardin secret III) (1987), for string quartet and live electronics, employs models from nature for abstract musical composition.*

GROVEmusic

Flute Concerto

Flute Concerto, 'Aile du Songe'[d]. Laconisme de l'aile. Oiseaux[c] – French Version[a]; English Version[b]
Camilla Hoitenga *fl/*[b]*spkr* [a]**Amin Maalouf** *spkr* [c]**Kaija Saariaho** *elec* [d]**Finnish Radio Symphony Orchestra / Jukka-Pekka Saraste**
Montaigne MO782154 (60' · DDD) Text and translation included   Ⓕ●

Saariaho's Flute Concerto is beautiful and characteristically imaginative, an extended study of the flight and the movement of birds but also a very striking rethinking of the idea of 'concerto'. At the beginning the flute almost designs the orchestra, generating not only melodic ideas but timbres; in a later section (a brilliant virtuoso dance-*scherzo*) the soloist 'teaches' the orchestra the melodic and other ideas that this vividly coloured movement uses. Other instruments take flight and become kindred birds, the space between a hovering bird and its shadow on the motionless earth beneath is finely suggested, but this is no mere imitative piece. At the same time it's a meditation on the symbolism of birds suggested by the poems of Saint-John Perse, to whose imaginative world the solo flute piece *Laconisme de l'aile*, written at the very beginning of Saariaho's mature career, is also indebted. Indeed, in that piece the sounds of the flute, including multiphonics and other techniques, are generated by Perse's words, intoned by the flautist at the outset.

The disc is turned into an hommage to Perse by the inclusion of six of his poems. Each poem is equipped with a 'sonic environment' composed by Saariaho using fragments of birdsong and flute phrases manipulated by computer. This material fills rather more than half the disc, but it's the Concerto – one of Saariaho's major achievements – that makes this disc. It's splendidly played and both cleanly and spaciously recorded.

Château de l'âme

Graal Théâtre[a]. Château de l'âme[b]. Amers[c]
[b]**Dawn Upshaw** *sop* [a]**Gidon Kremer** *vn* [c]**Anssi Karttunen** *vc* [c]**Avanti Chamber Orchestra;** [a]**BBC Symphony Orchestra;** [b]**Finnish Radio Chamber Choir and Symphony Orchestra /** [abc]**Esa-Pekka Salonen**
Sony Classical SK60817 (72' · DDD)   Ⓕ●

An important recording, splendidly performed. *Château de l'âme* is a piece that demands to be heard; that these are spells, to awaken love, to protect and to heal, is sufficiently evident, even without the words. They are exquisitely sung, finely played and quite haunting. The cycle makes a fine introduction to Saariaho's music. *Graal Théâtre* is a two-movement, 28-minute violin concerto demanding rhetorical gestures and extraordinary feats of virtuosity from the soloist, responding to them with richly inventive orchestral landscapes. Quite apart from Saariaho's formidable ear it's obvious that she played the violin once, and is still in love with its flamboyant nature. *Amers* is a rather shorter two-movement cello concerto, a bit harder to grasp at first hearing because it's more concerned with colour and texture than with sustained line, but *Graal Théâtre* will lead you into its world, and it's no less formidably played. All three pieces are vividly recorded.

Sainte-Colombe   French c1630-c1701

Sainte-Colombe taught in Lyons in the late 1650s and went to Paris in 1660; an outstanding bass viol virtuoso, he was Marais's teacher. His most noted compositions are 67 Concerts for two viols.
GROVEmusic

Concerts for viols

Concerts à deux violes esgales – Le tendre; La conférence; Les Couplets; Air à boire (Les bonbon); Le Retrouve; Le Changé; L'Inccomparable; Le Badin; La Duchesse; La Pleureux; La Suppliant; L'Emporté; Le Sérieux Changeant; L'Importun; La Pierrotine; Le Craintif; Le Prompt; Les Bateries
Les Voix humaines (Susie Napper, Margaret Little *bass viols*)
ATMA Classique ACD22275 (115' · DDD)   Ⓕ

Marais Pièces de viole, Livre 2 – Suite in E minor; Suite in B minor **Sainte-Colombe** Les Six Suittes pour Basse de Viole seule
Jordi Savall *bass viol* **Rolf Lislevand, Xavier Díaz-Latorre** *theo/gtr* **Philippe Pierlot** *bass viol* **Pierre Hantaï** *hpd*
Alia Vox Ⓕ ③ AV9829A/C (161' · DDD)   Ⓕ

In spite of energetic research in recent years, little is known about the Sainte-Colombes, father and son. Marin Marais (briefly a pupil of the father and a contemporary of the son) and his music are better known. Both the elder Sainte-Colombe and Marais came into greater prominence as a result of the 1991 film *Tous les matins du monde*. However, neither the film nor the Pascal Quignard novel on which it's based refers to the existence of Sainte-Colombe *le fils*. We now know that the family was Protestant and the son seems to have sought refuge in Britain when Louis XIV revoked the Edict of Nantes, which granted religious and civil liberties to Protestants, in 1685. As a Catholic, Marais was free to make his way in Paris and at court as an opera composer and viol player. These recordings offer fascinating musical evidence of the ways in which the bass viol repertoire developed as a result.

Les Voix Humaines have issued the first of two CDs of the *concerts à deux violes esgales* of Sainte-Colombe *le père*. These are passionately committed performances, resonant and full of fresh insights, of a repertoire that often seems to occupy a world of its own. Napper and Little have momentarily penetrated the mists of time. Their ensemble in the unmeasured passages is like that of trapeze artists, trusting and perfectly timed. The range of Sainte-Colombe's expression is vividly portrayed, from the swaggering to the rhapsodic, infused along the way with delicate internal phrasing, moments of titillating two-finger vibrato further enhanced by changes of speed and growling, hellish-sounding notes from the low A string he was the first to employ.

Jordi Savall has served for many years as the supreme exponent of French viol playing. In the early days he infused his playing with his considerable personality; later he became more introspective and now he seems to have achieved a sublime equilibrium that suits Marais very well. His performances here may seem surprisingly unsentimental, but they reflect a deep engagement with the music.

The music of Sainte-Colombe *le fils* has been known for some time, but is rarely performed. Savall has remedied the situation by recording all that's known. His suites have moments of rhetorical power and range widely in their expression; they're more self-indulgent, more wayward than those of Marais. Like his father, he makes frequent use of the seventh string and chords, although they lack the grace of those of the other composers and the harmonic richness of Marais.

Camille Saint-Saëns   French 1835-1921

Saint-Saëns was a child prodigy and his dazzling gifts early won him the admiration of Gounod, Rossini, Berlioz and especially Liszt, who hailed him as the world's greatest organist. He was organist at the Madeleine, 1857-75, and a teacher at the Ecole Niedermeyer, 1861-5, where Fauré was among his devoted pupils. He also pursued a range of other activities, organising concerts of Liszt's symphonic poems (then a novelty), reviving interest in older music, writing on musical, scientific and historical topics, travelling often and widely and composing prolifically; on behalf of new French music he co-founded the Société Nationale de Musique (1871). A virtuoso pianist, he excelled in Mozart and was praised for the purity and grace of his playing. Similarly French characteristics of his conservative musical style – neat proportions, clarity, polished expression, elegant line – reside in his best compositions, the classically orientated sonatas (especially the first each for violin and cello), symphonies (No 3, the Organ) and concertos (No 4 for piano, No 3 for violin. He also wrote 'exotic', descriptive or dramatic works, including four symphonic poems, in a style influenced by Liszt, using thematic transformation, and 13 operas, of which only Samson et Dalila (1877), with its sound structures, clear declamation and strongly appealing scenes, has held the stage. Le carnaval des animaux (1886) is a witty frolic; he forbade performances in his lifetime, Le cygne apart. From the mid-1890s he adopted a more austere style, emphasising the classical aspect of his aesthetic which, perhaps more than the music itself, influenced Fauré and Ravel. **GROVE**music

Cello Concertos

No 1 in A minor, Op 33; **No 2** in D minor, Op 119

Cello Concerto No 1. Le carnaval des animaux – The swan[a]. Romance in F, Op 36[b]. Romance in D, Op 51[b]. Cello Sonata No 1 in C minor, Op 32[b]. Chant saphique in D, Op 91[b]. Gavotte in G minor, Op posth[b]. Allegro appassionato in B minor, Op 43[b]. Prière, Op 158
Steven Isserlis *vc* [a]**Dudley Moore,** [b]**Pascal Devoyon** *pfs* [c]**Francis Grier** *org* **London Symphony Orchestra / Michael Tilson Thomas**
RCA Victor Red Seal 09026 61678-2 (67' · DDD)
Recorded 1992 Ⓕ

'Concerto!' was a Channel Four TV series that showed participating soloists in rehearsal, in conversation with Dudley Moore and Michael Tilson Thomas and, ultimately, in performance, which resulted in several recordings, of which this is one. This disc is recommendable not so much for Steven Isserlis's Cello Concerto – smooth and intelligent as that is – as for the fill-ups. *The swan* has Moore and Tilson Thomas as joint accompanists, elegantly executed, but the items with Pascal Devoyon are especially valuable, the First Cello Sonata full of elegantly tailored drama, the two *Romances*, *Chant saphique* and *Gavotte* palpable charmers, tastefully played; and the headstrong, thematically memorable *Allegro appassionato*, one of the finest shorter pieces in the cellist's repertory. The disc is enhanced by the opportunity of hearing the rather affecting but relatively unfamiliar *Prière*, composed for André Hekking just two years before Saint-Saëns's death.

Cello Concerto No 2 in D minor, Op 119[c]. La muse et le poète, Op 132[ac]. Romance in E flat, Op 67[c] (orch cpsr). Cello Sonata No 2 in F, Op 123[b]
Steven Isserlis *vc* [a]**Joshua Bell** *vn* [b]**Pascal Devoyon** *pf* [c]**North German Radio Symphony Orchestra / Christoph Eschenbach**
RCA Red Seal 09026 63518-2 (76' · DDD) Ⓕ

Steven Isserlis follows up his earlier outstanding release of Saint-Saëns's cello music with another that's even more revelatory. This disc concentrates on the more neglected cello works

that Saint-Saëns wrote towards the end of his long career. It's true that neither Concerto nor Sonata quite matches its predecessor in memorable melody, but Isserlis, in powerful, imaginative performances, brings out other qualities to show how unjust their neglect is. That's particularly true of the Sonata, which, vividly supported by Pascal Devoyon, rivals Brahms's magnificent Second Cello Sonata in heroic power and scale. At 33 minutes, this is easily the longest of Saint-Saëns's cello works, its ambitious tone of voice instantly established (as it is in the Brahms) and then masterfully sustained throughout the first movement. The second-movement *scherzo*, almost as long and far more than just an interlude, is a sharply original set of variations, leading to a songful slow movement which in turn leads up to a passionate climax. Then in the surgingly energetic finale, both Isserlis and Devoyon articulate the rapid passagework with thrilling clarity.

The cello writing in the Second Concerto is rather less grateful, with its thorny passages of double-stopping, but the two-movement structure characteristic of Saint-Saëns works well, with each divided clearly in two, *Allegro* into *Andante*, *Scherzo* into cadenza and reprise of *Allegro*. Making light of technical problems, Isserlis is persuasive both in the bravura *Allegros* and in the hushed meditation of the slow section. Yet neither he nor Eschenbach can quite overcome the truncated feeling at the end, when the reprise of the opening material is so short.

The *Romance* is an adaptation of the slow fourth movement of the Cello Suite, Op 16, a charming piece which Saint-Saëns reworked several times. Yet best of all is the lyrical dialogue of *La muse et le poète*. Inspired by Alfred de Musset's poem, *La nuit de mai*, it opens with Saint-Saëns at his most luscious, reflecting de Musset's role as a hothouse romantic among French poets. It then moves seamlessly through contrasted episodes, with the violin (superbly played by Joshua Bell) representing the muse and the cello as the poet himself. A generous collection, warmly recorded.

Additional recommendation

Cello Concertos Nos 1 and 2
Coupled with: Suite, Op 16 (arr vc/orch). Allegro appassionato in B minor, Op 43. Le carnaval des animaux – The swan
Kliegel *vc* **Bournemouth Sinfonietta / Monnard**
Naxos 8 553039 (62' · DDD) Ⓢ
  Maria Kliegel performs the Second Cello Concerto with impressive panache and precision. The First, too, is well played, though not a first choice for the work.

Piano Concertos

No 1 in D, Op 17; **No 2** in G minor, Op 22;
No 3 in E flat Op 29; **No 4** in C minor, Op 44;
No 5 in F, Op 103, 'Egyptian'

Piano Concertos Nos 1-5. Wedding Cake, Op 76.
Rapsodie d'Auvergne, Op 73. Africa, Op 89. Allegro
appassionato, Op 70
Stephen Hough pf **City of Birmingham Symphony
Orchestra / Sakari Oramo**
Hyperion ② CDA67331/2 (155' · DDD) ℗ **OOO**

If Saint-Saëns's idiom once answered –
and maybe still does – to qualities fundamental to the French musical character, it must be said straight away that Hough
sounds the complete insider. He commands the
range of the big statements, whatever their
character, as well as sparkle and panache, a sense
of drama and seemingly inexhaustible stamina;
and he can charm. Yet perhaps most delightful
is the lightness and clarity of his decorative playing. It's a bonus for the virtuoso passages not
to sound hectic or overblown – for Saint-Saëns,
virtuosity always had an expressive potential.
There's an air of manufacture about the writing
sometimes, certainly, but as Hough knows,
there must be nothing mechanical in its delivery. Sweeping across the keyboard, dipping and
soaring through the teaming notes, he flies like
a bird. He manages to convey what makes these
pieces tick: fine workmanship, fantasy, colour,
and the various ways Saint-Saëns was so good at
combining piano and orchestra. The orchestra
has plenty to do. These scores are textbooks of
lean but firm orchestration from which at least
one major French composer learned (Ravel,
another eclectic, who must have seen the 'old
bear' as a kindred spirit). The days are past when
the CBSO under Louis Frémaux was considered Britain's 'French' orchestra, but with
Sakari Oramo it does splendidly here, playing
alertly with its inspiring soloist as he does with it
(another plus). The recording balances are fine,
with lovely piano sound and plenty of orchestral
detail in natural-sounding perspectives.

Saint-Saëns Piano Concerto No 2
Rachmaninov Piano Concerto No 3 in D minor, Op 30
Shostakovich Prelude and Fugue in D, Op 87 No 5
Emil Gilels pf **Paris Conservatoire Orchestra /
André Cluytens**
Testament mono SBT1029 (65' · ADD) Recorded
1954-6 ℗ **OO**

Gilels was a true king of pianists, and these
Paris- and New York-based recordings only
confirm his legendary status. Here, again, is that
superlative musicianship, that magisterial technique and, above all, that unforgettable sonority. What breadth and distinction he brings to
the first movement of the Saint-Saëns, from his
fulmination in the central octave uproar to his
uncanny stillness in the final pages. High jinks
are reserved for the second and third movements, the former tossed off with a teasing
lightness, the latter's whirling measures with
infinite brio. An approximate swipe at the
Scherzo's flashing double-note flourish, a false
entry and a wrong turning five minutes into the
finale offer amusing evidence of Gilels's high-

wire act. No performance of this concerto is
more 'live', and it's small wonder that Claudio
Arrau included it among his desert island
favourites.

Gilels's Rachmaninov is altogether more temperate yet, once more, this is among the few
truly great performances of this work. His
tempo is cool and rapid, and maintained with
scintillating ease through even the most formidable intricacy. The cadenza – the finer and
more transparent of the two – billows and
recedes in superbly musical style and the climax
is of awe-inspiring grandeur and the central
scherzando in the finale is as luminous as it's vivacious. The finale's *meno mosso* variation is
excluded and, it has to be said, Cluytens's partnership is distant and run of the mill. But the
recordings hardly show their age in such
admirably smooth transfers. Gilels's 'encore',
Shostakovich's Prelude and Fugue No 5 is like a
brilliant shaft of light after the Rachmaninov.
The performance is perfection, entirely justifying Artur Rubinstein's comment after hearing
him play in Russia: 'If that boy comes to the
West, I shall have to shut up shop'.

Saint-Saëns Piano Concerto No 4 in C minor,
Op 44[c]. Etude en forme de valse, Op 52 No 6[d]
Franck Symphonic Variations[a] **Ravel** Piano
Concertin D[b]
Alfred Cortot pf [a]**London Philharmonic Orchestra
/ Landon Ronald;** [b]**orchestra,** [c]**Paris Conservatoire
Orchestra /** [bc]**Charles Munch**
Naxos Historical 8 110613 (60' · ADD) Ⓢ Ⓢ **OO**

Here are performances of a timeless vitality and
validity. The exception is the Ravel Concerto,
which is wildly approximate and confused. Elsewhere, though, there's a super-abundance of wit
and charm – of Cortot at his most beguiling. His
capacity to be free and ecstatic, yet bracingly
unsentimental was one of his most exhilarating
qualities, and his *rubato* at the start of the Saint-
Saëns makes modern rivals such as Rogé
(Decca) and Collard (EMI) pale in comparison.
At 8'12" (*dolce tranquillo legato*) there's a classic
instance of the *cantabile* for which he was celebrated, and in the final pages of the same movement an inimitably limpid and delicate poetry.
Again, in the central *Allegro vivace*, his famous
or infamous scrambles and skirmishes are never
at the expense of the music's innate elegance
and style, and who else has spun off the Concerto's closing cascades with such glitter and
aplomb? Cortot's playing may not have been
note-perfect but there's no doubt that he was
every inch the virtuoso. As an encore, there's
Saint-Saëns's *Etude en forme de valse*, and while
the 1931 recording is by no means the equal of
the legendary 1919 disc, a performance that
prompted Horowitz's envy, it's gloriously alive
with Cortot's verve and magic. Mark Obert-
Thorn's transfers are exceptional and all lovers
of past but ever-present greatness will want this
second and final Naxos volume of Cortot's sadly
few concerto recordings.

Violin Concertos

No 1 in A, Op 20; No 2 in C, Op 58; No 3 in B minor, Op 61
Philippe Graffin vn **BBC Scottish Symphony Orchestra / Martyn Brabbins**
Hyperion CDA67074 (76' · DDD)   Ⓕ●

The first two violin concertos of Saint-Saëns were composed in reverse order. The Second is the longer and lesser-known of the two, but the First Concerto more resembles the thematic charm and concise design of the First Cello Concerto. Cast in a single short movement that falls into three distinct sections, it launches the soloist on his way right from the start, and features a delightful central section with some felicitous woodwind writing. Hyperion holds a trump card in Philippe Graffin, whose elegant, emotionally charged playing is strongly reminiscent of the young Menuhin, and whose understanding of the idiom is second to none – certainly among modern players.

Saint-Saëns's First Violin Concerto was composed in 1859, whereas his Second preceded it by a year. Unexpectedly, the first movement's thematic material has an almost Weberian slant. The orchestration is heavier than in the First, and the musical arguments are both more formal and more forcefully stated. It's a more overtly virtuoso work than the First Concerto, and perhaps rather less memorable, but again Graffin weaves a winsome solo line and Martyn Brabbins directs a strong account of the orchestral score, with prominently projected woodwinds. The relatively well-known Third Concerto (1880) is roughly the same length as the Second (around half an hour), but is more consistently interesting. The basic material is of higher quality, the key relations more telling and orchestration infinitely more delicate. No other recording liberates so much of the score's instrumental detail, probably because most of Graffin's predecessors have been balanced way in front of the orchestra.

Complete Symphonies

Symphonies – A; F, 'Urbs Roma'; No 1 in E flat, Op 2; No 2 in A minor, Op 55; No 3 in C minor, Op 78, 'Organ'
Bernard Gavoty org **French Radio National Orchestra / Jean Martinon**
EMI ② 569683-2 (156' · ADD) Recorded 1972-5   Ⓜ●

Saint-Saëns's four early symphonies have rather tended to be eclipsed by the popularity of his much later *Organ* Symphony. It's easy to see why the latter, with its rich invention, its colour and its immediate melodic appeal has managed to cast a spell over audiences, but there's much to be enjoyed in the earlier symphonies too.

The A major dates from 1850 when Saint-Saëns was just 15 years old and is a particularly attractive and charming work despite its debt to

Mendelssohn and Mozart. The Symphony in F major of 1856 was the winning entry in a competition but was immediately suppressed by the composer after its second performance. The pressures of writing for a competition no doubt contribute to its more mannered style, but it nevertheless contains some impressive moments, not least the enjoyable set of variations that form the final movement.

The Symphony No 1 proper was in fact written three years before the *Urbs Roma* and shares the same youthful freshness of the A major, only here the influences are closer to Schumann and Berlioz. The Second Symphony reveals the fully mature voice of Saint-Saëns and in recent years has achieved a certain amount of popularity which is almost certainly due in part to this particularly fine recording. Inevitably we arrive at the *Organ* Symphony, and if you don't already have a recording then you could do a lot worse than this marvellously flamboyant performance. Indeed, the performances on this generous set are persuasive and exemplary. A real bargain.

Symphony No 3, 'Organ'

Symphony No 3[a]. Samson et Dalila – Bacchanale[b].
Le déluge – Prélude[b]. Danse macabre[b]
[a]**Gaston Litaize** org [a]**Chicago Symphony Orchestra,**
[b]**Orchestre de Paris / Daniel Barenboim**
DG Galleria 415 847-2GGA (56' · ADD) Recorded 1976   Ⓜ

Daniel Barenboim's recording of the Third Symphony has dominated the catalogue since it first appeared on LP. In fact it's one of the most exciting, physically involving recordings ever made of this work. Barenboim secures not only fine ensemble from his Chicago players but conveys supremely well the mounting excitement of a live performance, without ever falling into hysteria. The organ part has been superimposed on the Chicago tape. It has Gaston Litaize at the organ of Chartres Cathedral, and though there may be objections in principle, the result is more sharply defined than on most rival recordings.

The reissue is generous in offering an exhilarating 'Bacchanale' from *Samson et Dalila*, a sparkling *Danse macabre* in which Luben Yordanoff plays his violin solo beautifully, if not especially diabolically, and the rather engaging and not too sentimental Prélude from *Le déluge*. The remastering has brought a brighter overall sound picture, with the bass response drier, and a very slight loss of bloom on the upper strings. At the famous organ entry in the finale the ear notices that the top is harder, but the spectacle remains, and retains its thrill.

Saint-Saëns Symphony No 3 **Debussy** La mer   Ⓗ
Ibert Escales
Berj Zamkochian org **Boston Symphony Orchestra / Charles Munch**

SAINT-SAËNS SYMPHONY NO 3, 'ORGAN' – IN BRIEF

Peter Hurford; Montreal SO / Charles Dutoit
Decca Ovation 430 702-2DM (58' · DDD) Ⓜ️Ⓞ
Spontaneity and sparkle are the hallmarks of Charles Dutoit's admirably prepared account, sumptuously engineered within the helpful acoustic of Montreal's Saint Eustache church.

Simon Preston; Berlin PO / James Levine
DG 419 617-2GH (49' · DDD) Ⓕ
One of the leading digital-era contenders. A performance of tingling drama, with the Berliners playing at full throttle for Levine, and an enormously vivid recording to match.

Berj Zamkochian; Boston SO / Charles Munch
RCA 09026 61500-2 (73' · ADD) Ⓜ️ⓄⓄ
A treat from the late 1950s: Munch's conception possesses sinewy propulsion and excitement, and the entry of the organ at the start of the finale still sounds magnificently spectacular.

Michael Matthes; Paris Opéra-Bastille Orchestra / Myung Whun Chung
DG 435 854-2GH (69' · DDD) Ⓕ
Chung's is a keenly pondered interpretation. With orchestral playing that's both agile and affectionate, the results are intensely refreshing, with no trace of empty posturing or flashy vulgarity.

Gaston Litaize; Chicago SO / Daniel Barenboim
DG Galleria 415 847-2GGA (56' · ADD) Ⓜ️Ⓞ
Barenboim's 1975 DG account is famous for its linear thrust and bracing vitality. Soloist Gaston Litaize employs the organ of Chartres Cathedral; his expertly dubbed contribution creates a massive impact.

Gillian Weir; Ulster Orchestra / Yan Pascal Tortelier
Chandos CHAN8822 (56' · DDD) Ⓜ️ⓄⓄ
One of Tortelier's happiest discs: bright-eyed orchestral playing and conducting of appealing zest. Chandos's exemplary Ulster Hall production triumphantly parades the benefits of an organ *in situ*, so to speak.

Bernard Gavoty; French Radio National Orchestra / Jean Martinon
EMI ② 569683-2 (156' · ADD) Ⓑ
Few grumbles here. Martinon's is a disarming, unmannered account that spells enjoyment from start to finish. Part of this maestro's delectable Saint-Saëns symphony cycle for EMI.

RCA Living Stereo 09026 61500-2 (73' · ADD) Ⓜ️ⓄⓄ
Recorded 1956-9

This famous recording was made in Symphony Hall, Boston. To combat the hall resonance the RCA engineers moved many of the seats from the body of the hall so that the orchestra could spread out, while the organ (situated behind the stage) was miked separately. The result was a wonderfully rich, sumptuous sound which also achieved internal clarity – one notices that in the *Scherzo* and the filigree passages for piano in the introduction to the finale. However, it's the spectacular moments that one remembrs: the rich bonding of organ and strings in the *Poco adagio* and the full-blooded organ entry from Berj Zamkochian in the finale. Munch's superb reading moves forward with a powerful lyrical impulse in a single sweep from the first note to the last. To make this issue even more enticing Munch's 1956 versions of Debussy's *La mer* and Ibert's *Escales* ('Port of call') have been included. There's some marvellous playing in both, especially from the lustrous Boston violins. Here, however, the original recordings were more closely balanced and the effect is less rich, the dynamic range less wide. The adrenalin runs high in both performances.

Symphony No 3[a]. Le carnaval des animaux[b]
Peter Hurford *org* **Pascal Rogé, Christina Ortiz** *pfs*
[a]**Montreal Symphony Orchestra;** [b]**London Sinfonietta / Charles Dutoit**
Decca Ovation 430 720-2DM (58' · DDD) Recorded 1980-82 Ⓜ️

In 1886 Saint-Saëns poured his considerable experience as an unequalled virtuoso of the organ, piano and practitioner of Lisztian unifying techniques into his *Organ* Symphony; it instantly put the French Symphony on the map, and provided a model for Franck and others. With its capacity for grand spectacle (aside from the organ and a large orchestra, its scoring includes two pianos) it has suffered inflationary tendencies from both conductors and recording engineers. Dutoit's (and Decca's) achievement is the restoration of its energy and vitality. The affectionate portraits in the 'zoological fantasy', *The carnival of the animals*, benefit from more intimate though no less spectacular sound, and a direct approach that avoids obvious clowning.

Additional recommendation

Coupled with: **Saint-Saëns** Le rouet d'Omphale, Op 31. Danse macabre, Op 40 **Poulenc** Organ Concerto in G minor
Alain *org* ORTF **National Orchestra / Martinon**
Apex 8573-89244-2 (71' · ADD) Ⓢ
Exciting and authoritative *Organ* Symphony that easily triumphs over the slightly harsh 1966 sound. Alain's is a distinguished presence both here and in the Poulenc. A vintage compilation well worth anyone's fiver.

The Carnival of the Animals

Le Carnaval des animaux[a]. Fantaisie, Op 124[b].
Prière, Op 158[c]. Romance, Op 36[d]. Septet, Op 65[e].
Samson et Dalila – Mon cœur s'ouvre à ta voix[f]
[a]**Emmanuel Pahud** fl [a]**Paul Meyer** cl [e]**David Guer-**
rier tpt [a]**Florent Jodelet** perc [acdef]**Frank Braley,**
[a]**Michel Dalberto** pfs [abe]**Renaud Capuçon,** [ae]**Béa-**
trice Muthelet, [ae]**Esther Hoppe** vns [acdef]**Gautier**
Capuçon vc [ae]**Janne Saksala** db [b]**Marie-Pierre**
Langlamet hp
Virgin Classics 545602-2 (63' · DDD) ⒻOO

'What hard things,' wrote Saint-Saëns, 'have
been said against virtuosity!… The fact must be
proclaimed from the house-tops – in art a difficulty overcome is a thing of beauty.' There are
many such beauties in *Le Carnaval des animaux*,
and their difficulties aren't for the faint-hearted
or the technically challenged, especially where
the two pianists are concerned. On this disc not
only are the difficulties overcome, but dispatched with tremendous verve and wit.

In the Septet the players rightly refuse to make
more of the music than is really there. This light
touch (first evident in the delicate give-and-take
of the fugal writing in the 'Préambule') allows
us to relish Saint-Saëns's professionalism: every
part in the texture has its own shape and colour
and, if there were compositional difficulties to
be overcome, you'd never know. The four
shorter pieces on this splendid disc include the
delicious *Fantaisie* for violin and harp, and three
arrangements for cello and piano taken from the
horn, organ and operatic repertoires.

Additional recommendation

Coupled with: **Ravel** Ma mère l'oye. Boléro **Bizet**
Jeux d'enfants. **Dukas** Sorcerer's Apprentice
Katin, Fowke pfs **Scottish National Orchestra /**
Gibson; Hallé Orchestra / Loughran
Classics for Pleasure 574 9472 (75' · DDD)　Ⓑ
A characterful and spontaneous reading with some
fine couplings at an attractive price.

Orchestral Works

Danse macabre in G minor, Op 40. Phaéton in C,
Op 39. Le rouet d'Omphale in A, Op 31. La Jeunesse
d'Hercule in E flat, Op 50. Marche héroïque in E flat,
Op 34. Introduction and Rondo capriccioso in A
minor, Op 28[a]. Havanaise in E, Op 83[a]
[a]**Kyung-Wha Chung** vn [a]**Royal Philharmonic**
Orchestra; Philharmonia Orch / Charles Dutoit
Decca 425 021-2DM (66' · ADD)　ⓂO

It's enough to make you weep – Saint-Saëns
wrote his first tune at the age of three, analysed
Mozart's *Don Giovanni* from the full score when
he was five, and at 10 claimed he could play all
Beethoven's 32 piano sonatas from memory.
There's some consolation that, according to a
contemporary, physically 'he strangely resem-
bled a parrot', and perhaps even his early brilliance was a curse rather than a blessing, as he

regressed from being a bold innovator to a dusty
reactionary. In his thirties (in the 1870s) he was
at the forefront of the Lisztian avant-garde. He
was the first Frenchman to attempt Liszt's new
genre, the 'symphonic poem', bringing to it a
typically French concision, elegance and grace.
Charles Dutoit has few peers in this kind of
music; here's playing of dramatic flair and classical refinement that exactly matches Saint-
Saëns intention and invention. Decca's sound
has depth, brilliance and richness.

Chamber Works

Bassoon Sonata, Op 168[a]. Caprice sur des airs
danois et russes, Op 79[b]. Clarinet Sonata, Op 167[c].
Oboe Sonata, Op 166[d]. Piano Quartet, Op 41[e].
Piano Quintet, Op 14[f]. Septet, Op 65[g]. Tarantelle,
Op 6[h]
Nash Ensemble ([bh]Philippa Davies fl [bd]Gareth
Hulse ob [bch]Richard Hosford cl [a]Ursula Leveaux bn
[g]Mark David tpt [efg]Marianne Thorsen, [g]David
Adams, [f]Benjamin Nabarro vns [efg]Lawrence Power
va [efg]Paul Watkins vc [g]Duncan McTier db Ian
Brown pf)
Hyperion ② CDA67431/2 (134' · DDD)　ⒻO

Saint-Saëns's chamber music fares better in the
concert hall than the recording studio, perhaps
because musicians tend to listen less to academic name-calling ('conservative', 'too prolific') than to the music itself. The three late
wind sonatas in particular have received far
fewer recordings than their status as repertoire
staples deserves. Try the kinky-Baroque first
movement of the Oboe Sonata, jauntily phrased
by Gareth Hulse, or the *animato* second of the
Clarinet Sonata, garbed in rich Mozartian cloth
by Richard Hosford. The Bassoon Sonata is
notable for its fresh and gentle wit and skirting
of cliché: Ursula Leveaux does it proud, with
especially luscious tone in the opening *Allegretto*.

Surprises are fewer in the earlier works, but
none is less than, 'finely put together' to echo
Ravel's assessment. Hummability quotient is
high in the Piano Quartet and Quintet, and off
the scale in the Septet. The late Lionel Salter
used to complain in *Gramophone* that recordings
of the Septet tend to sound like a trumpet concerto; not this one. If you employ hit artists like
Maurice André they will tend to hog the microphone but, happily, Mark David is a more sensitive soul who's fully imbibed the Nash's joyous
spirit of corporate music-making, and Hyperion's engineers have placed him at a respectable
distance. If anything it's Ian Brown's piano that
takes centre-stage, and that's no bad thing,
except in the extensive fugal finales to the Piano
Quartet and Quintet where Saint-Saëns, most
unusually, seems to over-run himself. The
Caprice and *Tarantelle*, for all Philippa Davies's
sparkling contributions, perhaps bear fewer
repetitions, but the set is really sheer delight:
let's hear it for imaginative conservatism.

Saint-Saëns Fantaisie, Op 124[a]. Fantaisie after
Weber's 'Oberon'. L'air de la pendule. Caprice brill-
ant **Chopin/Saint-Saëns** Nocturnes – No 16 in E flat,
Op 55 No 2; No 18 in E, Op 62 No 2 **Ysaÿe** Caprice
d'après l'Etude en forme de valse de Saint-Saëns
Chopin/Ysaÿe Ballade No 1 in G minor, Op 23. Waltz
No 14 in E minor, Op posth
Philippe Graffin vn [a]**Catherine Beynon** hp **Pascal
Devoyon** pf
Hyperion CDA67285 (77' · DDD)　　　　　Ⓕ○○

The 20th century decided, by and large, that
Saint-Saëns lacked passion and *Schwung*, perhaps taking a physical cue from the 'sharp little
man' Stravinsky spotted in the audience at the
première of *Le sacre*. And once performers are
led to believe that a composer is a purveyor of
sophisticated trifles, then they will tend to play
him that way. Now along comes Philippe Graffin to give us not only Saint-Saëns composer of
passion, but Saint-Saëns actor of genius. The
essence of acting is, some would say, to become
the character, and Saint-Saëns miraculously
'becomes' Chopin in his arrangements of two
Nocturnes for violin and piano. They are beautiful and effective pieces in their own right and
dispel all doubts as to the viability of the transcription process.

The end crowns the work, in the form of the
Fantaisie of 1907 for violin and harp. Graffin's
tone throughout is sweet and seductive, his
phrasing a thing of pure joy; but in this *Fantaisie*,
with delicate but prompt support from Catherine Beynon, he moves up a gear further still, to
reach the heart of this deeply moving piece. The
three Ysaÿe transcriptions are equally successful. A wonderful disc. Buy it.

Piano Trios

No 1 in F, Op 18; No 2 in E minor, Op 92
Joachim Trio (Rebecca Hirsch vn Caroline Dearnley
vc John Lenehan pf)
Naxos 8 550935 (65' · DDD) Recorded 1993　　Ⓢ

1863 and 1892 are the dates of these trios. No 1
was written by a composer not yet 30 but
already a confident master of his craft. Bland his
voice may be, but it's intelligent and agreeable:
a French Brahms without genius, one dares suggest, although Mendelssohn also comes to
mind. At the same time, there are passages
unlike either of these composers, such as the
bare and angular main theme of the A minor
slow movement in No 1, though Grieg might
have written it. Such music needs sympathetic,
unfussy interpretation; the skilful and sensitive
Joachim Trio gives it just that. The First Trio as
a whole is charming (try the fleet *Scherzo*); the
booklet-essay rightly notes the 'delicate brilliance' of the piano writing by a composer who
was also an expert player. The E minor Trio, a
more dramatic five-movement piece, is played
here with fine judgement, being warmly expressive without sentimentality or mannerism. The
recording is excellent.

Mélodies

Chanson (Nouvelle chanson sur un vieil air). Guitare.
Rêverie. L'attente. Le chant de ceux qui s'en vont sur
la mer. Le pas d'armes du Roi Jean. La coccinelle.
A quoi bon entendre. Si vous n'avez rien à me dire.
Dans ton coeur. Danse macabre. Mélodies persanes,
Op 26 – La brise; Sabre en main; Au cimetière;
Tournoiement. Marquise, vous souvenez-vous?.
La Cigale et la Fourmi. Chanson à boire du vieux
temps. Nocturne. Violons dans le soir. Guitares et
mandolines. Une flûte invisible. Suzette et Suzon.
Aimons-nous. Temps nouveau. Le vent dans la plaine.
Grasselette et Maigrelette
François Le Roux bar **Krysia Osostowicz** vn
Philippa Davies fl **Graham Johnson** pf
Hyperion CDA66856 (78' · DDD) Texts and
translations included　　　　　　　Ⓕ○

This is the most resounding blow yet to be
struck for the *mélodies* of Saint-Saëns. François
Le Roux, with his incisive diction and ability to
characterise each song, is a real champion for
the man, once so successful, who became, as
Graham Johnson puts it in the booklet, 'a foot-
note' rather than a chapter in the history of
French music.

Many of the poems that Saint-Saëns set were
used by other composers, for instance *Dans ton
coeur*, which became Duparc's *Chanson triste*, by
'Jean Lahor' (Henri Cazalis). The first song of
the *Mélodies persanes*, 'La brise', is full of eastern
promise, the second, 'Sabre en main' a rollicking bit of toy-soldier galloping away, but just as
you're beginning to think that Johnson is shooting himself in the foot by being so ironic about
the music they're performing comes the hauntingly beautiful fifth song, 'Au cimetière', with
its quietly rippling accompaniment and the languorous poem about the lovers sitting on a
marble tomb and picking the flowers. Le Roux
sings this with controlled, quiet intensity.

Johnson makes the point that it's of little
importance from which part of the composer's
life the songs come, he embodies that totally
French 19th-century style, sometimes anticipating Hahn and Massenet, sometimes harking
back to Boieldieu. If a setting of La Fontaine's
fable about the cicada and the ant is pure salon
charm, then the final 'Grasselette et Maigrelette' Ronsard *chanson*, composed when Saint-
Saëns was 85 in 1920, is a vivacious *café-concert*-
style evocation of old Paris.

Samson et Dalila

Samson et Dalila
Plácido Domingo ten Samson **Waltraud Meier** mez
Dalila **Alain Fondary** bar Priest **Jean-Philippe
Courtis** bass Abimelech **Samuel Ramey** bass Old
Hebrew **Christian Papis** ten Messenger **Daniel
Galvez-Vallejo** ten First Philistine **François
Harismendy** bass Second Philistine **Chorus and
Orchestra of the Bastille Opera, Paris / Myung-
Whun Chung**

EMI ② 754470-2 (124' · DDD) Recorded 1991. Notes, text and translation included Ⓕ**oo**

This is the most subtly and expertly conducted performance of this work to appear on CD, excellent as others have been in this respect, and also the best played and sung. Chung's achievement is to have welded the elements of pagan ruthlessness, erotic stimulation and Wagnerian harmony that comprise Saint-Saëns's masterpiece into a convincing whole. His success is based on the essentials of a firm sense of rhythm and timing allied to a realisation of the sensuousness and delicacy of the scoring. Whether in the lamenting of the Hebrews, the forceful music written for the High Priest, the heroics of Samson, the sensual outpourings of Dalila, or the empty rejoicing of the Bacchanale, he and his orchestra strike to the heart of the matter – and that orchestra plays with Gallic finesse, augmented by a dedicated discipline.

The choral singing, though too distantly recorded, is no less alert and refined, with a full range of dynamic contrast. Meier's Dalila is a fascinating portrayal of this equivocal antiheroine, seductive, wheedling, exerting her female wiles with the twin objects of sexual dominance and political command. All her sense of purpose comes out in her early greeting to the High Priest, 'Salut à mon père'; then she's meditative and expectant as Dalila ponders on her power at 'Se pourrait-il'. The set numbers are all sung with the vocal ease and long phrase of a singer at the zenith of her powers. She makes more of the text than Domingo who sings in his familiar, all-purpose style, admirable in itself, somewhat missing the particular accents brought to this music by the great French tenors of the past. They exist no more and one must salute the sterling and often eloquent tones of Domingo.

Fondary is superb as the High Priest, firm and rich in tone, commanding and vengeful in delivery: the most compelling interpreter of the part on disc, *tout court*. Ramey is luxury casting as the Old Hebrew, but as this is a part once sung by Pinza, Ramey probably felt he wasn't slumming it. After an unsteady start, he sings the small but important role with breadth and dignity. As Abimelech, Courtis makes much of little. Apart from the two reservations already made, the recording is admirable, with a wide and spacious sound, and the soloists forward, but well integrated. This must now be the outright recommendation for this work.

Additional recommendation

Vickers Samson **Gorr** Dalila **René Duclos Choir; Paris Opera Orchestra / Prêtre**
EMI Great Recordings of the Century ② 567598-2 (121' · ADD) Ⓜ
A classic recording with Rita Gorr's magnificent Dalila towering over the performance. Vickers, too, is superb. The sound isn't perfect but don't let that deter you.

Antonio Salieri
Italian 1750-1825

Salieri studied with Gassmann and others in Vienna, and also knew Gluck (who became his patron) and Metastasio. In 1774 he succeeded Gassmann as court composer and conductor of the Italian opera from 1788 he was also court Kapellmeister. He made his reputation as a stage composer, writing operas for Vienna from 1768 and presenting several in Italy, 1778-80. Later he dominated Parisian opera with three works of 1784-7; Tarare (1787), his greatest success, established him as Gluck's heir. In 1790 he gave up his duties at the Italian opera. As his style became old-fashioned his works lost favour, and he composed relatively little after 1804, but he remained a central and influential figure in Viennese musical life. His many pupils included Beethoven, Schubert and Liszt. There is little evidence of any intrigues against Mozart, still less of the charge of poisoning.

Salieri's c40 Italian operas are traditional in their emphasis on melodic expression, but they also show Gluck's influence, with dramatic choral writing, much accompanied recitative and careful declamation: some combine seria and buffa elements. In Tarare he came close to Gluck's dramatic ideals. Among his many other compositions are oratorios, church music, cantatas, arias, vocal ensembles, songs and orchestral and chamber works. GROVEmusic

Opera Arias

Armida – E non degg'io seguirla…Vieni a me. **La grotta di Trofonio** – La ra la. **Il ricco d'un giorno** – Dopo pranzo addormentata; Eccomi piu che mai. **La scuola de' gelosi** – Che dunque! **La secchia rapita** – Questo guajo mancava. **Palmira, Regina di Persia** – Voi luingate invano; Lungi da me. **La fiera di Venezia** – Vi sono sposa e amante. **La Cifra** – E voi da buon marito; Alfin son sola. **La finta scema** – Se lo dovessi vendere
Cecilia Bartoli *mez* **Orchestra of the Age of Enlightenment / Adám Fischer**
Decca 475 100-2DH (68' · DDD) Ⓕ

As the leading figure in Viennese operatic life for some three decades, and successful too in Venice and Paris, Antonio Salieri occupies no inconsiderable position in operatic history. This is a well-chosen selection of music from his Italian operas, in serious, comic and mixed genres. The purely comic pieces are perhaps the least interesting: his conception of comedy is, in the Italian tradition, quite literal and direct. But among the lighter items are a delightfully spirited little 'rustic' piece from *La finta scema* and a charming minuet from *La grotta di Trofonio*, very sharply and neatly characterised here.

That piece was written for Nancy Storace, the English soprano who created Mozart's Susanna. So is the beautiful slow aria from *La scuola de' gelosi*, preceded by a recitative sung with much feeling by Bartoli; the aria itself is a lament for lost love, deeply felt and affecting. So, too, is the rondo from *La cifra*, written for another Mozart singer, Adriana Ferrarese, the first Fiordiligi, again preceded by a forceful recitative, which is reminiscent of Mozart's 'Per pietà', written for Ferrarese shortly after, and which it surely influenced. This is a noble and powerful piece.

Others that demand to be mentioned here include a couple with spectacular orchestral writing: one from *La fiera di Venezia* with solo parts for flute and oboe, a real virtuoso piece, with lots of top Ds, and another from *La secchia rapita* with its dialogues with oboe and its arresting trumpet interventions.

Bartoli is an enormously accomplished artist: every note plumb in the middle, the words always carefully placed, naturally musical phrasing, and beauty and variety of tone. Musicianly and finely modulated playing from the Age of Enlightenment Orchestra set off the voice perfectly.

Aulis Sallinen
Finnish b1935

Sallinen was a pupil of Merikanto and Kokkonen at the Helsinki Academy (1955-60), where he returned to teach in 1970. In the late 1960s he began melding triads with avant-garde techniques; then in the 1970s he turned to opera, drawing on sources as diverse as Shostakovich, Janácek and Orff in The Horseman (1975), The Red Line (1978), The King Goes forth to France (1984) and Kullervo (1992). His concert works include four symphonies, five string quartets and concertos for violin and for cello. GROVEmusic

Orchestral Works

Variations for Orchestra, Op 8. Violin Concerto, Op 18. Some aspects of Peltoniemi Hintrik's funeral march, Op 19. The nocturnal dances of Don Juanquixote, Op 58
Eeva Koskinen *vn* **Torleif Thedéen** *vc* **Tapiola Sinfonietta / Osmo Vänskä**
BIS CD560 (63' · DDD) Recorded 1992 Ⓕ

Sallinen's operas and symphonies have stolen the limelight in recent years at the expense of other works fully worthy of attention, as this well-played and well-recorded disc proves. Whereas the Variations (1963) are somewhat anonymous if deftly written, the Violin Concerto (1968) is an altogether maturer work, unusually sombre for so bright a solo instrument, and perhaps the first piece to point to his later stature. His next published work was the Third String Quartet (1969), subtitled *Some aspects of Peltoniemi Hintrik's funeral march*, which, thanks to the Kronos Quartet's advocacy has become one of Sallinen's most heard works This arrangement for string orchestra dates from 1981. *The nocturnal dances of Don Juanquixote* is an extended fantasia for cello and strings, the title being the only parody of Strauss (although a solo violin enters late as Sancho Panza-leporello!). Sallinen is fond of playing games and all is never as it seems: one can

almost hear the collective thud of critics' jaws falling open at this Arnold-like spoof.

Songs of Life and Death, Op 69

Songs of Life and Death, Op 69. The Iron Age – Suite, Op 55b[a]
Margit Papunen *sop* **Jorma Hynninen** *bar* **Opera Festival Chorus;** [a]**East Helsinki Music Institute Choir; Helsinki Philharmonic Orch / Okko Kamu**
Ondine ODE844-2 (75' · DDD) Texts and translations included Ⓕ O

Listening to these two works by Aulis Sallinen is a bit like looking at two different photographs of the composer: the face is undeniably the same but not the perspective. *Songs of Life and Death* (1993-4) arose, rather by mischance, from a failed effort to compose a Requiem on verses by Lassi Nummi. Although title and outward form suggest Mahlerian associations, the conservative musical language brings Verdi to mind, and in a very real sense this cycle is a 20th-century equivalent of the latter's Requiem: both are symphonic in construction and operatic in idiom, composed from spiritual rather than religious standpoints, and make use of secular elements. There are differences, not least in scale and conception. And while Sallinen's songs are also very much songs of *life*, death isn't here perceived as a grim or tragic end, and this imparts to the whole a peculiarly late 20th-century aspect. Here at last is the choral-and-orchestral masterpiece Sibelius should have written, Finnish to the core yet international in appeal. It's one of the very finest compositions Sallinen has yet produced. Where in the *Songs of Life and Death* voices are the principal element, in the *Iron Age* Suite (1978-82) the focus is on the orchestra, the chorus being an important but more colouristic extra. The suite originated in music written for a series of prize-winning Finnish TV documentaries and in it the more familiar Sallinen of the symphonies and early operas is on display. Both works receive terrific performances.

Erik Satie
French 1866-1925

Satie entered the Paris Conservatoire in 1879, but his record was undistinguished. After leaving he wrote the triptychs of Sarabandes (1887), Gymnopédies (1888) and Gnossiennes (1890), of which the latter two sets are modal and almost eventless. In the 1890s he began to frequent Montmartre, to play at the café Chat Noir and to involve himself with fringe Christian sects. He also made the acquaintance of Debussy.

From 1905-8 he was a student again, at the Schola Cantorum. At last in 1911 his music began to be noticed, and this seems to have stimulated a large output of small pieces, mostly for solo piano and mostly perpetuating his earlier simplicity in pieces with ironic titles. Sports et divertissements (1914), published with illustrations by Charles Martin, contains 20 miniatures eccentrically and beautifully annotated by Satie. In 1915 he came to the attention of Cocteau, who seized on him as the ideal of the anti-Romantic composer and who facilitated the more ambitious works of his last years: the ballets Parade (1917), Mercure (1924) and Relâche (1924), and the cantata Socrate (1918). These have the same flatness as the smaller pieces and songs, achieved by means of directionless modal harmony, simple rhythm and structures made up through repetition or inconsequential dissimilarity. In different ways the style had an effect on French composers from Debussy and Ravel to Poulenc and Sauguet, as later on Cage. **GROVE**music

Piano Works

Six Gnossiennes. Ogives. Petite ouverture à danser. Sarabandes. Trois Gymnopédies
Reinbert de Leeuw pf
Philips 446 672-2PH (67' · DDD) Recorded 1992 Ⓕ**O**

Tender, solemn, droll, silly and occasionally plain boring, Satie's piano music has certainly proved its appeal for performers and record collectors, judging from the number of recitals devoted to it. But this one is out of the ordinary, for unlike the majority of artists, who offer a mixed bag of pieces, Reinbert de Leeuw has chosen music that's entirely solemn and even hieratic in utterance. He begins with the archaically beautiful *Gnossiennes*, taking the first of them unusually slowly but with compelling concentration. The composer's devotees will be thrilled, though you have to surrender completely to get the message of this repetitive, proto-minimalist music. The four *Ogives* derive their name from church architecture, and their unbarred, diatonically simple music has clear affinities with plainchant although, unlike chant, it's richly harmonised. Monotonous it may be, but that's part of its charm, if that term can apply to such a contemplative style. The very brief *Petite ouverture à danser* is a mere meandering sketch in lazy waltz-time, but all Satie is sacred to the converted and the writer of the booklet-essay accords it four lines, finding in it (as translated here) 'a suggestion of indifference, vacillating between a melancholy melody and indecisive harmony'. (Not exactly Beethoven, one might say.) The two pensively sad triptychs of *Sarabandes* and *Gymnopédies* – here very slow yet tonally most refined – complete this finely played and recorded disc, which offers nothing whatsoever of the bouncier *café-concert* Satie.

Alessandro Scarlatti Italian 1660-1725

When he was 12 Alessandro Scarlatti was sent to Rome, where he may have studied with Carissimi. He married in 1678 and later that year was

SATIE PIANO MUSIC – IN BRIEF

Reinbert de Leeuw
Philips 446 672-2PH Ⓕ**O**
A programme that focuses on the more solemn pieces in Satie's output, and offers playing of tremendous poise which merely adds to the power of the whole.

Peter Dickinson
RCA 09026 63976-2 Ⓜ
With first-rate recorded sound, Dickinson's 1989 recital from The Maltings, Snape, has great appeal and plenty of variety. He responds equally well to the quirkiness (*Poudre d'or* and *Le Piccadilly*) as to the more solemn works like the *Gymnopédies*.

Yitkin Seow
Hyperion CDA66344 Ⓕ**O**
A longtime favourite: classy playing that embraces many of Satie's most popular works. There's a winning freshness here that's most engaging.

Pascal Rogé
Decca 458 105-2 Ⓕ**OO**
Perhaps the classiest of modern Satie players, Rogé has made a number of collections of the music: this is a generous compilation entitled 'Piano Dreams' and shows the dreamier side of the composer. A fine disc if you're after just one Satie collection.

Michel Legrand
Apex 0927 41380-2 Ⓢ
A super-budget alternative demonstrating Legrand's affinity for his fellow composer. His approach is quirkily inconsistent veering between moment of quite superb playing to others when he seems slightly perplexed, something not helped by the rather fierce recording. But it's well worth considering if you're on a tight budget.

Anne Queffélec
Virgin 759296-2 Ⓜ
Queffélec is a stylish Satie player, full of character. This mid-price collection is very well recorded and nicely programmed, and is one of the most appealing available today.

appointed maestro di cappella of S Giacomo degli Incurabili (now 'in Augusta'). By then he had already composed at least one opera and a second, Gli equivoci nel sembiante, was a resounding success in 1679. It confirmed Scarlatti in his chosen career as an opera composer and attracted the attention of Queen Christina of Sweden, who made him her maestro di cappella.

In 1684 Scarlatti was appointed maestro di cappella at the vice-regal court of Naples, at the same time as his brother Francesco was made first violinist. It was alleged that they owed their appointments to the intrigues of one of their sisters (apparently Melchiorra) with two court officials, who were dismissed. For the next two decades over half the new operas given at Naples were by Scarlatti. Two of them, Il Pirro e Demetrio (1694) and La caduta dei Decemviri (1697), were especially successful, but by 1700 the War of the Spanish Succession was beginning to undermine the privileged status of the Neapolitan nobility, rendering Scarlatti's position insecure. In 1702 he left with his family for Florence, where he hoped to find employment for himself and his son Domenico with Prince Ferdinando de' Medici.

When these hopes failed, Scarlatti accepted the inferior position in Rome of assistant music director at S Maria Maggiore. With a papal ban imposed on public opera, he found an outlet for his talents in oratorio and in writing cantatas for his Roman patrons. In 1706 he was elected to the Arcadian Academy, along with Pasquini and Corelli. The following year he attempted to conquer Venice, the citadel of Italian opera, with Mitridate Eupatore and Il trionfo della libertà, but they both failed and Scarlatti was subsequently forced to return to Rome, where he was promoted to the senior post at S Maria Maggiore.

Scarlatti found little satisfaction in the life of a church musician, and towards the end of 1708 he accepted an invitation from the new Austrian viceroy to resume his position at Naples, where he remained for the rest of his life, though he maintained close contacts with his Roman patrons. It was probably in 1715 that he received a patent of nobility from Pope Clement XI. His final opera, La Griselda, was written for Rome in 1721, and he seems to have spent the final years of his life in Naples in semi-retirement.

Scarlatti's reputation as the founder of the Neapolitan school of 18th-century opera has been somewhat exaggerated. He was not influential or even very active as a teacher, nor was he the sole originator of the musical structures (da capo aria, Italian overture, accompanied recitative) with which his name is associated, although he did bring to these structures a level of skill and originality which surpassed those of his contemporaries. Some of his best music is in the chamber cantatas, too few of which are known today.　　　　　　　　　**GROVE**music

Vespers

The Cecilian Vespers. Salve regina. Audi filia, et inclina aurem. Nisi Dominus
Dominique Labelle, Susanne Rydén sops **Ryland Angel** counterten **Michael Slattery** ten **Neal Davies** bass **Philharmonia Chorale and Baroque Orchestra / Nicholas McGegan**

Avie ② CD/SACD 🔊 AV0048 (131' · DDD/DSD · T/t). Recorded live　　　　　　　Ⓕ

Scarlatti's Vespers were composed for a service at the Roman church of Santa Cecilia in Trastevere in 1721. He was in his sixties by then, his music out of fashion, and one can sense that with this friendly commission he was relishing the freedom to be himself, revisiting all his old skills in vocal brilliance, melodic charm, graceful counterpoint and succinctly effective word-setting. There are echoes of Handel and Vivaldi, though given Scarlatti's eminence in his own time it might be more appropriate to think of things the other way round. And if in the end it lacks either Handel's grandeur or Vivaldi's spark, it's palpably the work of a master. The performance is expertly shaped and paced by Nicholas McGegan.

Cain, overo il primo omicidio

Cain, overo il primo omicidio　　　　　　Ⓟ
Graciela Oddone, Dorothea Röschmann sops **Bernarda Fink** contr **Richard Croft** ten **Antonio Abete** bass **Academy for Ancient Music, Berlin / René Jacobs** counterten
Harmonia Mundi ② HMC90 1649/50 (138' · DDD) Text and translation included　　　Ⓕ**OOO**

This is a stunning performance of a remarkable work. It was classified at the time not as an oratorio but as a *trattenimento sacro* ('sacred entertainment'), which suggests that its first performance, in 1707 in Venice, took place in a private palace rather than a church. But Scarlatti brought to the work, besides his seemingly inexhaustible invention, all the dramatic instinct that had made him famous as a composer of operas (of which he had already written about 40). Anyone charged with extracting a 'highlights' selection from this would find themselves in a quandary, since almost every number could be considered a highlight, from the brilliant opening aria for Adam, to two remorseful arias, with affecting chromaticisms, for Eve, and Lucifer (with excited violins) tempting Cain.

Jacobs has assembled an absolutely outstanding cast whose technical accomplishment, dramatic commitment and stylish ornamentation could scarcely be bettered. Furthermore, the instrumental playing is first class.

Colpa, Pentimento e Grazia

Colpa, Pentimento e Grazia
María Espada sop **Lola Casariego** mez **Martín Oro** counterten **Seville Baroque Orchestra / Eduardo López Banzo**
Harmonia Mundi ② HMI98 7045/6 (83' · DDD) Text and translation included. Recorded live at the Ayamonte Festival, Spain, August 2003　　Ⓕ

Colpa, Pentimento e Grazia, an oratorio for Passiontide, isn't an account of the Passion story but rather an examination by the three allegorical characters of its title – Sin, Repentance and Grace – of their complex inter-relationship in the light of Christ's sacrifice. The libretto is by the great Roman patron Cardinal Ottoboni, who commissioned it for performance in his palace during Holy Week in 1708. It's is of the arcane sort that probably only a poetically inclined senior cleric could write, and includes paraphrases from the Lamentations of Jeremiah which Scarlatti sets in a rather haunting, plainchant-derived *arioso* style. But the composer's own seriousness of intent is evident in the rest of the music as well, not just in the high number of accompanied recitatives, but in the brilliantly sparing addition of trumpets and timpani to the string orchestra – notably to add menace to Sin's vision of the Last Judgement – and in the solemn but compelling tenor of the music as a whole, effortlessly sustained over the course of the work's 80 minutes.

Accounts of *Colpa*'s first performance describe a dramatically lit crucifix and the dropping of black wall hangings at appropriate moments, and one can well imagine it to have been a moving occasion. For his part, Scarlatti wrote with the confident imagination of an artist at the height of his powers.

The performance is directed with energy and intelligence by Eduardo López Banzo, and his soloists make strong dramatic contributions, with María Espada's clear-toned Grace just stealing the show. The recording is in a clearly evident church acoustic, though not an oppressive one. One could hardly ask for more, really, unless it be snappier gaps between numbers.

Oratorio per la Santissima Trinità

Oratorio per la Santissima Trinità   **P**
Véronique Gens, Roberta Invernizzi *sops* **Vivica Genaux** *contr* **Paul Agnew** *ten* **Roberto Abbondanza** *bass* **Europa Galante / Fabio Biondi**
Virgin Classics 545666-2 (67 minutes: DDD) Text and translation included   Ⓕ

One day we'll run out of Baroque music worth rediscovering, but for the moment there seems no reason to halt the digging, especially when a composer as talented and prolific as Alessandro Scarlatti remains so largely buried. *La Santissima Trinità*, one of his last oratorios, is thoroughly deserving of revival, despite its unpromising subject of five allegorical characters debating the existence of the Holy Trinity. Such high-flown dissertations were falling out of fashion by 1715, when the work was written, but Scarlatti was a past master at them, and in any case this particular oratorio has a notably lighter touch than, say, his *Colpa, Pentimento e Grazia*. It presents a simpler, more dramatically vital showdown between Faithlessness – who doesn't believe in the Trinity – and Faith, Divine Love, Time and Theology, who do.

Scarlatti responds with music that's pacy, varied and engaging. The format is conventional – recitatives alternate with arias, duets and occasional larger ensembles – but no single number lasts significantly longer than four minutes and the action never dawdles. Nor is there any danger of monotony, since the orchestra of strings and continuo is used with great resource; one duet is gorgeously adorned with solo violin birdsong and a cello for a river, and later two cellos conjure gently billowing waves.

The vocal writing, for a full range of voice-types, sparkles like summer wine. If, as seems possible, Scarlatti was composing for an off-duty operatic cast, it clearly inspired him to suitably extrovert and dramatically vivid heights. Likewise joyously inspired is the performance under the dedicated direction of Fabio Biondi, a Scarlatti interpreter of experience and flair who drives the work forward with unerring momentum, energy and care. Leading from the violin, he summons orchestral playing of vibrancy and energy, and is blessed with top-class Baroque singers, strongly communicative and evidently believing in the music. It's hard to imagine this work being better performed or presented.

Sedecia, re di Gerusalemme

Sedecia, re di Gerusalemme
Virginie Pochon *sop* **Philippe Jaroussky** *counterten*
Mark Padmore *ten* **Peter Harvey** *bass* **Il Seminario Musicale / Gérard Lesne** *counterten*
Virgin Veritas ② VC5 45452-2 (94' · DDD) Notes, texts and translations included   Ⓕ Ⓞ

Most of Alessandro Scarlatti's oratorios were written for Rome, where the genre had originated at the beginning of the 17th century, and where papal opposition to opera encouraged it to flourish. In practice the difference between opera and oratorio is more apparent than real, since they share many of the same formal elements. One of the finest of Scarlatti's oratorios, *Il primo omicidio* of 1707, was only relatively recently revealed as a masterpiece of great originality in René Jacobs's recording (Harmonia Mundi, reviewed above), and to this can now be added *Sedecia, re di Gerusalemme*, which was probably premièred in Rome during the composer's second period there in 1703-8. Full praise should go first to Gérard Lesne whose presence on this recording is the critical element in its undoubted success. This isn't just a question of his stylish singing, but of a vision of the dramatic articulation of the work as a whole. There are convincing portrayals from some of the other singers too, notably Virginie Pochon, who turns in an elegant performance distinguished by beautifully controlled passagework. Jaroussky's Ismael is a little erratic at times, particularly in the more bravura moments, but acan be most effective. Scarlatti's varied orchestral palette is sensitively explored by the instrumentalists. A rich and rewarding experience.

Cantatas

Il rosignolo (first version). Perchè tacete, regolati **P**
concenti?. Infirmata, vulnerata. Ombre tacite e sole.
Il genio di Mitilde mente non vè. O pace del mio cor
David Daniels counterten **Arcadian Academy /
Nicholas McGegan**
Conifer Classics 75605 51319-2 (74' · DDD) Texts and
translations included Ⓕ

The American countertenor David Daniels has
a fine, firmly produced voice, even throughout
its range; both his intonation and his enunciation are impeccable; he's exact in his handling of
florid passages; and his ornamentations are very
stylish. If there's one reservation, it's that for
too much of the time (except in *Infirmata, vulnerata*) he sings at one constant level of dynamics. It's possible the recording contributes to
this: it's certainly responsible for the harpsichord sounding much weaker in some cantatas
than in others.

By far the most substantial work here is the
earliest, *Perchè tacete*, probably dating from the
mid-1690s. It's the only one with a Venetian
opera-type overture, and the numerous movements include four arias, three of which are of
two strophes. At the other extreme is *Il rosignolo*,
scored only for continuo and consisting of just
two *da capo* arias joined by a recitative: the
nightingale's song, it emerges, is a lament for
love. Love is also the subject of *O pace del mio cor*
(the lover vainly seeking peace of mind) and the
1716 *Ombre tacite*, the despairing lament of a
deceived lover. In the recitatives of both of
these, Scarlatti underlines emotive words with
extraordinary harmonic progressions. The one
remaining work is something of an enigma:
though in Latin and printed as a 'sacred concerto', the words could be interpreted as referring either to divine love or to human (which is
presumably why McGegan includes it here).
The style is plainer than in the others except for
the vigorous ending: there are chromatic harmonies in the first aria, and a later aria is unusual
in being constructed on a seven-bar ground
bass. The disc demonstrates Scarlatti's range of
styles and the diversity of his scoring, even
within a single work.

La Griselda

La Griselda
Dorothea Röschmann sop Griselda **Lawrence
Zazzo** counterten Gualtiero **Veronica Cangemi** sop
Costanza **Bernarda Fink** mez Roberto **Silvia Tro
Santafé** mez Ottone **Kobie van Rensburg** ten
Corrado **Akademie für Alte Musik Berlin / René
Jacobs**
Harmonia Mundi ③ HMC90 1805/7 (182' · DDD)
Notes, libretto and translation included Ⓕ●

The opera *Griselda* was performed only once at
Rome's Teatro Capranica in 1721, towards the
end of Alessandro Scarlatti's career. It was probably sponsored by Prince Ruspoli, who'd been

Handel's major Roman patron 15 years earlier.
The libretto, adapted from the *Decameron*, portrays Gualtiero, King of Sicily, relentlessly testing his wife Griselda's fidelity. There's a lot of
recitative among the irony, deceptions and
intense passions, but the action progresses at a
compelling pace, and the concise arias are consistently inventive, unpredictable and attractive.
Dorothea Röschmann brings dignified integrity
to a dangerously subservient title-role, and
Lawrence Zazzo's lyrical singing is both sweet
and theatrical as the complex Gualtiero. Veronica Cangemi's steely voice is judiciously cast as
Griselda's daughter Costanza, and Bernarda
Fink is strong and stylish as her lover Roberto.
Silvia Tro Santafé is arrogant and dislikable as
Ottone, which is entirely right for the King's
malcontent villainous servant. Kobie van Rensburg displays marvellous assured coloratura that
flows smoothly, and it's good to hear a tenor of
such quality in this repertoire.

If *Griselda* represents one of Scarlatti's finest
artistic achievements, it's apt that this recording
accordingly shares a similarly privileged status
within René Jacobs' discography. The conductor is helped by the alert brilliance of the
Akademie für Alte Musik Berlin, which clearly
relishes the splendid score. Jacobs paces the
drama sensitively, and characterises the arias
with intelligence. His only sin is overly fussy
decisions about restless recitatives in which the
continuo is historically implausible and artistically intrusive. Yet whether you love or loathe
Jacobs, this is an immensely important achievement. Handel wasn't the only talented opera
composer working in the early 18th century, but
at long last we've a genuinely credible comparison on disc. This recording does much to
explain why Handel's librettist Charles Jennens
slyly remarked that the Saxon regularly pinched
musical ideas from Scarlatti.

Domenico Scarlatti Italian 1685-1757

*In 1701 Domenico Scarlatti was appointed organist
and composer of the vice-regal court at Naples, where
his father Alessandro was maestro di cappella. In
1705 his father sent him to find employment in
Venice where he may have first met Handel, with
whom he formed a strong attachment. By 1707,
however, he was in Rome, assisting his father at S
Maria Maggiore, and he remained in Rome for over
12 years, occupying posts as maestro to the dowager
Queen of Poland from 1711, to the Marquis de
Fontes from 1714, and at St Peter's (assistant maestro of the Cappella Giulia from November 1713,
maestro from December 1714).*

*In 1719 Scarlatti resigned his positions in Rome
and apparently spent some years in Palermo before
taking up his next post, as mestre of the Portuguese
court in Lisbon. The Lisbon earthquake of 1755
destroyed documents about his career there, but his
duties included giving keyboard lessons to John V's*

daughter, *Maria Barbara, and his younger brother, Don Antonio. When Maria Barbara married the Spanish crown prince in 1729 Scarlatti followed her to Seville and then, in 1733, to Madrid, where he spent the rest of his life. Although he continued to write vocal music, sacred and secular, the main works of his Iberian years are the remarkable series of keyboard sonatas, copied out in his last years and taken to Italy by his colleague, the castrato Farinelli.*

Scarlatti married twice: in 1728 a Roman, Maria Catarina Gentili, and in 1739 a Spaniard, Anastasia Maxarti Ximenes. None of his nine children became a musician. In 1738 King John V of Portugal knighted him: he responded by dedicating to the king a volume of Essercizi per gravicembalo, *the only music published during his lifetime under his supervision.*

The seven operas Scarlatti wrote in Rome for Queen Maria Casimira were by no means failures, and his church music and secular cantatas contain much admirable music. But his fame rightly rests on the hundreds of keyboard sonatas, nearly all in the same binary form, in which he gave free rein to his imagination, stimulated by the new sounds, sights and customs of Iberia and by the astonishing gifts of his royal pupil and patron. In these he explored new worlds of virtuoso technique, putting to new musical ends such devices as hand-crossing, rapidly repeated notes, wide leaps in both hands and countless other means of achieving a devastating brilliance of effect.
GROVEmusic

Keyboard Sonatas

Keyboard Sonatas Kk1, 3, 8, 9, 11, 17, 24, 25, 27, 29, 87, 96, 113, 141, 146, 173, 213, 214, 247, 259, 268, 283, 284, 380, 386, 387, 404, 443, 519, 520, 523
Mikhail Pletnev pf
Virgin Classics ② 561961-2 (140' · DDD) Recorded 1994 ⑤ Ⓑ ⓪⓪⓪

 Every so often a major pianist reclaims Scarlatti for the piano with an outstanding recording. As Ralph Kirkpatrick put it, Scarlatti's harpsichord, while supremely itself, is continually menacing a transformation into something else. True, the relation of the music to harpsichord sound could hardly be closer, and it wouldn't have been composed the way it is for a different instrument. Scarlatti is marvellous at suggesting imaginary orchestrations and stimulating the imagination. He makes us aware of different vantage points as the music passes before us, of the different tones of voice and rhetorical inflexions – as various in these sonatas as the events in them are unpredictable. There are dances, fiestas and processions here, serenades, laments, and evocations of everything from the rudest folk music to courtly entertainments and churchly polyphony; and as the kaleidoscope turns you marvel at the composer who could embrace such diversity, shape it and put it all on to the keyboard.

Pletnev's playing is strongly individual, and his free-ranging poetic licence may not be to your taste. Not that his spectacular virtuosity is likely to be controversial: this really is *hors de catégorie* and enormously enjoyable. And the evocations of the harpsichord are often very witty, but he doesn't shrink from using the full resources of the piano, sustaining pedal included, and if you baulk at the prospect, he may not be for you. The sustaining pedal is certainly dangerous in music that's almost wholly to do with lines, not washes of colour; it can make us see Scarlatti as if through Mendelssohn's eyes. Yet moments of such falsification are rare. Characterisation is everything, and though he can be coy in the reflective sonatas, he generally goes straight to the heart of the matter. The vigorous, full tone in the quick numbers is a joy, and most admirable is the way he makes sound immediately command character. Superb recorded sound.

Keyboard Sonatas Kk3, 54, 141, 145, 175, 162, 177, 185, 199, 208, 248, 249, 299, 310, 484, 492, 531, 535
Pierre Hantaï hpd
Mirare MIR9918 (68' · DDD) Ⓕ ⓪⓪

The first track (Kk535) is typical of the quick-moving sonatas that abound in this programme – an astonishing display of dexterity in which the harpsichord he uses (a 1999 copy of an anonymous Thuringian instrument of 1720) and the acoustic help in preserving total clarity. Even at maximum velocity (did Scarlatti and his pupil reach such speeds?) he manages to shape his phrases with micro-second dwellings.

It isn't only the speedy sonatas that are impressive; Kk208 exemplifies his skilful shifts to either side of the pulse in giving the lines a natural 'vocal' quality. It also illuminates Kk185, 310, 199 and 162, in the last of which it's more evident in the playful quicker 'interludes'. The irresistible disc is splendidly annotated by Hantaï and beautifully packaged.

Keyboard Sonatas Kk443, 444, 448, 450, 462, 466, 469, 474, 503, 504, 508, 516, 517, 526, 527, 531, 540, 541, 545, 548
Frédérick Haas hpd
Calliope CAL9330 (78' · DDD) Ⓕ

This is a stunning recording. There are some tough nuts here but Haas cracks them with ease and a sense of surging virtuosity. He plays on the warmly resonant but clear-sounding French harpsichord last used by Scott Ross. If you want to introduce Scarlatti to someone you couldn't do it better than by playing this disc. This appears to be a one-off recording but it offers strong temptation as a 'supplement' to anyone already embarked on an integral sonata collection.

Keyboard Sonatas, Kk3, 14, 20, 27, 32, 33, 39, 98, 109, 141, 146, 208, 209, 213, 322, 436, 481, 492, 517
Michael Lewin pf

Naxos 8 553067 (76' · DDD)　　　⑤●

Michael Lewin is an American pianist as dexterous and assured as he's audacious. Here there's no sense of 'studio' caution but only of liberating and dazzling music-making, live and on the wing. Kk492 in D could hardly provide a more brilliant curtain-raiser, and in Kk3 in A minor (the one where Scarlatti's impish humour offers the musical equivalent of someone slipping on a banana skin) Lewin's playing positively brims over with high spirits. The D major Sonata, Kk33, is all thrumbing guitars and bursts of sunlight and in Kk141, with its cascades of repeated notes, Lewin even gives Martha Argerich a run for her money. There's a no less appealing balm and musical quality in the more restrained numbers such as Kk32 in D minor and Kk208 in A, though the recital comes to a suitably ebullient conclusion with Kk517 in D minor which is here like a river in full spate.

The New York-based recordings are suitably lively. Not even the most persistent lover of Scarlatti on the harpsichord could accuse Michael Lewin of an absence of the necessary glitter, panache and stylistic awareness.

Keyboard Sonatas Kk20, 24, 27, 30, 87, 197, 365, 426, 427, 429, 435, 448, 455, 466, 487, 492, 545
Yevgeny Sudbin pf
BIS BIS-CD1508 (76' · DDD)　　　⑤●●

This generously packed CD is sheer delight from start to finish. Even with recorded selections available from the likes of Horowitz, Pletnev, Schiff and Pogorelich, the 25-year-old Russian pianist Yevgeny Sudbin makes his solo debut on disc with performances of a superlative vitality and super-fine sensitivity.

His choice of sonatas is richly enterprising, pinpointing their infinite variety, their abrupt changes of mood and direction, so that whether familiar or unfamiliar (and there are many unfamiliar numbers), each offering is a delectable surprise. Free from the nervous tension that can sometimes plague him in the concert hall, Sudbin relishes the way Scarlatti turns convention topsy-turvy, presenting him in both performance and his affectionate accompanying essay as one of music's most ardent and life-affirming adventurers. He's brilliant and incisive in Kk545, and makes every bar of the reflective Kk57 glisten with poetry. What thrumming guitars he evokes in Kk435 and 487, reminding us that Scarlatti forsook his native Italy and later Portugal for a heady addiction to all things Spanish.

There are spicy and witty imitations of changing registrations and some notably rumbustious closes to make every facet of these diamond-like sonatas spark and scintillate as if new-minted. This is, arguably, among the finest, certainly most enjoyable of all Scarlatti recitals. As a crowning touch Sudbin is heard in a beautifully warm and natural acoustic.

Keyboard Sonatas Kk1-30
Alain Planès pf
Harmonia Mundi ② HMC90 1838/9 (144' · DDD)　　⑤

It's a curious twist of fate that the classical music record industry has recently lavished more attention on Alessandro Scarlatti than his famous son. Nevertheless Domenico Scarlatti's adventurous and impressive keyboard music remains the acid test of any competent pianist. It isn't known when the *Essercizi* were created. After 1719, most of Scarlatti's career was in the service of Portuguese and Spanish royalty, but these pieces were first published in London during the late 1730s, headed by a preface by the composer: 'O Reader, whether you be dilettante or professor, do not expect from these compositions any profound understanding, but rather an ingenious jesting with art, to give you practice in achieving assurance on the harpsichord.'

This double-disc set contains 30 *Essercizi* played on a superb pianoforte of only six octaves, made by Johann Schantz in Vienna between 1795 and 1810. Alain Planès performs with magical dexterity, creates strong dynamic contrasts, and conjures an impression of textural variety. Considering Scarlatti's comment that these pieces provide something akin to a harpsichord masterclass, it initially seems an unusual choice not to use an earlier instrument. However, Planès's approach resonates with the significant influence Scarlatti had upon later 18th-century pianists including Haydn, Mozart, and Beethoven, yet still sounds approximate to the harpsichord. Definitely worth exploring.

Giacinto Scelsi　　　Italian 1905-1988

Of aristocratic birth, Scelsi had no formal training and ranged over many styles in his earlier works while remaining constant to an ideal of music as a link with the transcendental. That remained his conviction in works after the 1950s, in which he often used microtones, thin textures and extremely slow movement.　　　**GROVE**music

Choral Music

Complete Choral Works
Three Latin Prayers. Sauh – III; IV. Yliam. TKRDGa. Antifona sul nome Jesu. Tre Canti Populari. Tre Canti Sacri
[a]**Alan Thomas** gtr **New London Chamber Choir;**
[a]**Percussive Rotterdam** (Wilbert Grootenboer, Hans Leenders, Norman van Dartel perc) / **James Wood**
Accord 465 401-2 (72' · DDD)　　　Ⓜ

The best known music here is the *Tre Canti Sacri*, but just about everything is on a very high level of virtuosity and inspiration. The *Tre Canti Populari* are scarcely less inventive.

Scelsi's mysticism encompasses a fair degree of stylistic variety, but repeated listening tends to bring out what unites rather than the opposite. At the same time, he was capable of assuming strikingly different idioms more or less contemporaneously. The chant-inspired *Three Latin Prayers* and *Antifona* (the former seem like preparatory studies for the latter) both date from 1970, only two years after the *Canti Sacri*. 1968 also saw the composition of *TKRDG*, which incorporates the strongest Eastern influences, the only instrumental interventions (ably supplied by Percussive Rotterdam and guitarist Alan Thomas), and arguably the most radical aesthetic of this collection. The slightly earlier *Yliam* is marginally reminiscent of the choral music of Ligeti (and, indeed Xenakis) from the same period: the treatment of the super-high register is very effective, and admirably dispatched by the sopranos. That adjective describes these performance in the round (with perhaps the exception of the *Three Latin Prayers*, which sound a little tentative).

Scelsi's stature has grown steadily since his death in 1988 and this reissue only adds to his reputation. Within the contemporary choral repertory, it ought to be required listening.

Scharwenka, Franz Xaver
Polish-German 1850-1924

Scharwenka studied with Kullak in Berlin. A touring artist from 1874, he became increasingly active as a concert organizer and teacher in Berlin, founding his own conservatory in 1881 (the Klindworth-Scharwenka, with a New York branch in 1891). He was renowned as a Chopin interpreter. Among his best compositions are the Polish Dance op.3 no.1 and the Piano Concerto in B flat minor (1877). His brother Philipp (1847-1917) was a composer and teacher at the Scharwenka Conservatory.

Piano Concerto No 4

F X Scharwenka Concerto for Piano and Orchestra No 4 in F minor, Op. 82 **Sauer** Concerto for Piano and Orchestra No 1 in E minor
Stephen Hough pf **City of Birmingham Symphony Orchestra / Lawrence Foster**
Hyperion CDA66790 (70′ · DDD) Ⓔ❍❍❍

This jewel in the crown in Hyperion's Romantic Piano Concerto series marries flawlessly composer, performance, recording and presentation. Scharwenka's Piano Concerto No 4 is a far cry from his early, ubiquitous success, the E flat minor Polish Dance. Grand, Lisztian ambitions are fulfilled and embellished in writing of the most ferocious intricacy; the tarantella finale in particular throws everything at the pianist, seemingly simultaneously. It's therefore hardly surprising that after early triumphs the Fourth Concerto fell into neglect. At its second performance, given in 1910 with Scharwenka as soloist and Mahler as conductor, it was described as being

of a 'truly Dionysian and bewildering brilliancy', a phrase that encapsulates Stephen Hough's astonishing performance. For here is scintillating wit and ebullience. As magisterial as it's ear-tickling and affectionate, his playing glows with warmth in the third movement Lento, and pulses with the most nonchalant glitter in the finale; one guaranteed to strike down less intrepid and fluent spirits with St Vitus's dance.

Emil von Sauer's First Concerto has a style and content to make even the least susceptible listeners' heads nod and feet tap. The Cavatina is as luscious and enchanting as the finale is teasingly brief and light-hearted. Throughout, haunting melodies are embroidered with the finest pianistic tracery. Once again the performance is bewitching. In the Cavatina Hough's caressing, fine-spun tone and long-breathed phrasing are a model for singers as well as pianists, and in the finale there's a lightly deployed virtuosity that epitomizes his aristocratic style.

Though the spotlight falls unashamedly on the soloist in such music, the orchestra has no small part in the proceedings, and Lawrence Foster and the City of Birmingham Symphony Orchestra are superbly resilient and enthusiastic, with strings that sing their hearts out. Sound and balance are exemplary. Stephen Heliotis's accompanying notes deserve separate publication for their wit and perspicacity.

Samuel Scheidt
German 1587-1654

Scheidt was organist of the Moritzkirche, Halle, for several years, and studied with Sweelinck in Amsterdam before becoming Halle court organist in 1609. From 1619-20 he was also court Kapellmeister, but the musical establishment almost disbanded (because of the Thirty Years War) in 1625. In 1627-30 he was director of music in Halle, also composing for the Marktkirche. His duties as court Kapellmeister resumed in 1638. Scheidt was active as an organ expert and a teacher and knew both Schütz and Schein.

Scheidt distinguished himself in both keyboard and sacred vocal music, in which he combined traditional counterpoint with the new Italian concerto style. Contrapuntal chorale settings are important among his c150 keyboard pieces. Some appear in his three-volume Tabulatura nova (1624), the first German publication of keyboard music to be in open score rather than in German organ tablature or in two-staff format; the collection also contains variations and liturgical pieces. Scheidt left some 160 sacred vocal works. His first book, Cantiones sacrae (1620), consists of polychoral motets, some of them based on chorales, and his second (1620) of large concertos with obbligato instrumental parts. Small concertos for few voices make up the four volumes of Geistliche Concerte (1631-40). Scheidt also composed dances, canzonas, sinfonias etc and canons. **GROVE**music

Ludi Musici

Ludi Musici – Alamande a 4; Canzon ad   **P**
imitationem Bergamas angl a 5; Canzon super
Cantionem Gallicam a 5; Canzon super O Nachbar
Roland a 5; Five Courants a 4; Courant dolorosa a 4;
Two Galliards a 4; Galliard a 5; Galliard battaglia a 5;
Three Paduanas a 4
Hespèrion XX / Jordi Savall viol
Astrée Naïve ES9980 (62' · DDD)   Ⓜ

Scheidt's *Ludi Musici* reflects the fusion of English and German traditions in the emergent world of instrumental music in early 17th-century Germany and is a mouth-wateringly diverse and inventive mixture of dance, canzona and variation. These are works which brim over with character and nonchalantly brilliant craftsmanship. Scheidt has that rare knack, for the 1620s and 1630s, of sustaining an instrumental piece for more than two minutes without bombarding us with a new idea every 10 bars; the longer pieces such as the Paduanas and the brilliant Canzon a 5 *ad imitationem Bergamas angl*, with its thrilling close, convey admirable long-term direction amid a concentrated love of ephemeral effect. This is a cocktail which Hespèrion XX relishes. The Pavans are, as you would expect from Jordi Savall, eventful. There are moments when an indulgence from Savall's treble viol stifles the potential for a more reflective allusion, but the overriding effect is of a performer striving to find a meaningful discourse, not content just to 'let the music play itself'; the colour and shape he brings to line and texture is often beguiling (disarmingly poignant in the stillness of the final Paduana), at times too much of a good thing but always engaging.

Johann Hermann Schein
German 1586-1630

Schein trained as a soprano in the Dresden court chapel, studied at Schulpforta and Leipzig and later worked as music director and tutor to the children of Gottfried von Wolffersdorff, 1613-15. After a year as Kapellmeister at the Weimar court, he became Kantor of St Thomas's, Leipzig in 1616. He knew both Schütz, a close friend, and Scheidt. Primarily a composer for the voice, Schein was significant as one of the first composers to graft the modern Italian style on to the traditional elements of Lutheran church music. Much of his large sacred vocal output (nearly 400 works) is in five published volumes. The first part of Opella nova (1618) contains sacred concertos with continuo, clearly influenced by Viadana's but based (in most cases) on chorale melodies; the second part (1626), which uses fewer chorales, includes obbligato instrumental parts. His other sacred publications are a motet collection (1615), a book of sacred madrigals (1623) and the Cantional (1627), a hymnbook. Schein left some 90 secular vocal pieces, all to his own texts. Especially Italianate are the three-part settings in Musica boscareccia (1621-8)

and his German continuo madrigals (1624 – the first such works to be published). He also composed songs and occasional works. His main instrumental work is the Banchetto musicale (1617), containing 20 variation suites.   GROVEmusic

Israelis Brünnlein

Israelis Brünnlein
Ensemble Vocal Européen / Philippe Herreweghe
Harmonia Mundi HMX298 1574 (79' · DDD) Texts and
translations included   Ⓜ

Anyone who hears this sympathetic account of *Israelis Brünnlein* ('The Fountains of Israel' – 26 sacred madrigals in five and six parts with a *basso seguente*) from Ensemble Vocal Européen will be convinced that this is one of the great pillars of German Baroque music. It's fascinating not only as a demonstration of how the best German music incorporates foreign styles within indigenous techniques but also for Schein's discovery of his own unique expressive horizons. As in the *Lagrime di San Pietro* of Lassus (a composer whose poised contrapuntal craft is transmuted with profound respect by Schein), secular idioms successfully serve the sacred vision. Herreweghe, whose cool and collected reading of the Lassus masterpiece (see review under Lassus; refer to the Index) is vocally peerless, finds fresh priorities here. The exposed solo context draws out a greater sense of quasi-spontaneous attention, particularly in upbeat examples like 'Freue dich des Weibes' and the brilliance of 'Ist nicht Ephraim?'. Emotional intensity can, however, sound overmeasured in works like 'Die mit Tränen säen' and 'Was betrübst', where dramatic urgency is required above the restrained shapeliness that's Herreweghe's hallmark. There are some fine singers (underpinned by the splendid Peter Kooy), even if the tenor tuning isn't always beyond reproach; as an almost comprehensive – five pieces are left out – volume of 80-odd minutes, this further assures Schein's reputation as a master of exquisite characterisation.

Johann Heinrich Schmelzer
Austrian c1620/23-1680

Schmelzer was trained in Vienna and served in the court chapel from the mid-1630s, becoming a member of the orchestra in 1649 and vice-Kapellmeister in 1671. In 1679 he was made Kapellmeister. The leading Austrian composer of instrumental music before Biber, he wrote 150 ballet suites for court dramatic productions and over 100 sonatas. The former each have between two and nine dances, sometimes thematically related; some include elements of folk music. Notable among the sonatas are the six Sonatae unarum fidium (1664), the earliest published set for solo violin and continuo. Schmelzer's prolific output also includes sepolcri and other dramatic pieces, nearly 200 sacred works and some secular vocal music.   GROVEmusic

Sonatae unarum fidium

Schmelzer Sonatae unarum fidium – Nos 1-6. **P**
Sonata for Violin and Continuo in A minor, 'Il cucù'
Biber (arr A Schmelzer) Sonata for Violin and
Continuo, 'Victori der Christen'
Romanesca (Andrew Manze *vn* Nigel North *theorbo*
John Toll *hpd/org*)
Harmonia Mundi HMU90 7143 (67' · DDD) Also
includes a free sampler disc of Biber violin sonatas.
                                                    Ⓕ**O**

Coming to these recordings from Biber's extravagant and incomparably theatrical sonatas, one
is immediately struck by common stylistic
threads but also by Schmelzer's studied lyricism, a searing and disarming feel for melodic
progression (heard in the close of the *Cucù*
Sonata) and the sense of a man who, when he
isn't following his tail with ostinato basses, has
mastered the canzona-sonata mentality and
takes full advantage of its freedom. All Biberian
features certainly, but as Andrew Manze both
explains in his note and demonstrates in his
playing, there's less overall ostentation here;
while the extraordinary Sonata No 4 latterly
contains gloriously extended and potent outbursts, it's the patient arching direction of
Schmelzer's melodic frame which draws one in.
Manze and his accomplished continuo players
(the theorbo is exquisite and distinctive) are
wonderful exponents in this mesmerising
Baroque byway.

Schmelzer Sonatae unarum fidium[b] **Anonymous** **P**
Scordatura Violin Sonata[a] **Bertali** Chiaconna
John Holloway *vn* [ab]**Aloysia Assenbaum** *org*
[a]**Lars Ulrik Mortensen** *hpd/org*
ECM New Series 465 066-2 (63' · DDD)   Ⓕ**OO**

Johann Heinrich Schmelzer was the first home-
grown Kapellmeister to be appointed at the
Hapsburg Court in Vienna in 1679, following
generations of Italians hired for their *oltremon-
tani* flair and easy command of prevailing fashion. Schmelzer's six sonatas from 1664 are certainly Italianate, and not without freewheeling
virtuosity, but they also contain a type of
extended lyricism, and, as in the opening of the
Fourth Sonata, a sense of no-nonsense progression of comforting expectation. In fact, this
work, and that by his dynamic forebear, Antonio Bertali (whose own *Chiaconna* is quite a
party-piece) are typical 17th-century showcases
for the violin where intricate and fantastical
divisions unfold above a recurring bass pattern.
The playing in this technically demanding
repertoire is dazzling, and the intonation faultless. Yet equally impressive is John Holloway's
measured classicism and subtle poetical
restraint. Not every bar of Schmelzer's set is
compelling and he opts for a consistent clarity
of sound rather than milking every note as if it's
of earth-shattering importance; he uses *rubato*
discerningly, as in the introspective musings in
the Fifth Sonata where the narrative is
beautifully and elegantly articulated. The idea

of a double continuo of organ and harpsichord
is highly effective throughout.

The first recording of *Sonatae unarum* was
made by Romanesca (see above), and they too
opt for a counterpoint of continuos with organ
and theorbo. The sense of a rich consort-like
texture can only bring a much-needed breadth
to music which might otherwise test the concentration over the course of an hour. To
choose between these two fine recordings isn't
easy, save to say that Romanesca is more consistently adventurous and theatrical. Holloway
and his excellent keyboardists are less extrovert,
softer-grained and more inclined to hover with
sweet and restrained decorum. Both recordings
are exceptional in their way, revealing how
much interpretative leeway Schmelzer gives his
players.

Alfred Schnittke   USSR 1934-1998

*Schnittke was a pupil of Rakov and Golubev at the
Moscow Conservatory (1953-61), where he taught
until 1972. His works often use quotations, parodies
and stylistic imitations in a highly charged manner,
though some are more unified in expression. Textures are rich and complexly varied and string
instruments feature prominently in his output,
which, apart from four symphonies and various stage
works, includes five concerti grossi, four violin concertos, two violin sonatas and chamber music. He was
a prolific writer on Russian music.* GROVEmusic

Concerti grossi

Concerto grosso No 1[a]. Quasi una sonata[b].
Moz-Art à la Haydn[c]
Tatiana Grindenko *vn* **Yuri Smirnov** *hpd/prep pf/pf*
Chamber Orchestra of Europe / [a]**Heinrich Schiff,**
[bc]**Gidon Kremer** [a]*vn*
DG Masters 445 520-2GMA (75' · DDD) Recorded
live 1988   Ⓜ**O**

For a single representative of Alfred Schnittke's
work you could choose nothing better than the
first *Concerto grosso* of 1977. Here are the psy-
chedelic mélanges of Baroque and modern, the
drastic juxtapositions of pseudo-Vivaldi with
pseudo-Berg, producing an effect at once
aurally exciting and spiritually disturbing. The
piece has had many recordings, but never with
the panache of Kremer and friends and never
with the vivid immediacy of this live DG
recording (in fact the solo violins are rather too
closely miked for comfort, but that's only a tiny
drawback). *Quasi una sonata* was originally composed in 1968 for violin and piano and it was
something of a breakthrough piece for Schnittke as he emerged from what he called 'the
puberty rites of serialism', letting his imagination run riot for the first time. No one could call
it a disciplined piece, but if that worries you, you
should leave Schnittke alone anyway. The transcription for solo violin and string orchestra is

an ingenious one and Kremer again supplies all the requisite agonised intensity. *Moz-Art à la Haydn* is a very slight piece of work, and it really depends on visual theatricality to make its effect. Still, it complements the other two pieces, and the disc is an excellent introduction to this composer.

Schnittke Concerto grosso No 6ª. Violin Sonata **Takemitsu** Nostalgia **Weill** Concerto for Violin and Wind Orchestra, Op 12
Daniel Hope vn ªSimon Mulligan pf/hpd **English Symphony Orchestra / William Boughton**
Nimbus NI5582 (73' · DDD)   Ⓕ

Full marks to Nimbus for variety. The danger is that three such different composers, combined in a way you'd never expect in a concert, will cancel each other out. Fortunately, the performances are strong enough – even when heard in close succession – to justify the enterprise, and the recordings are no less successful in the way they capture the intimacy of tone characteristics of all four compositions.

A textual point of some interest emerges in the earlier of the Schnittke works, the Sonata. Usually, the harpsichord functions as the violinist's *alter ego* throughout, but Daniel Hope, with Schnittke's agreement, has the keyboardist move from harpsichord to piano from the final stages of the second movement onwards. The desiccated harpsichord sound may be preferable in the third movement, but the change is certainly justified in the finale, and adds an extra dimension to a commendably unexaggerated account of this turbulent score.

The early Weill Violin Concerto can easily sprawl and sound too earnest for its own good. Here there's an appropriate fluency; excessive gravity is avoided. Hope is able to project the required authority, especially in the cadenza, and although some might prefer a more forward placement for the soloist, the excellent qualities of his playing are no less appealing. As for Takemitsu's song of farewell for the film-maker Andrei Tarkovsky, the music is a model of how to balance emotional restraint and expressive warmth, and the performance does it justice.

Piano Quintet

Schnittke Piano Quintetª **Shostakovich** String Quartet No 15 in E flat minor, Op 144
ªAlexei Lubimov pf **Keller Quartet** (András Keller, János Pilz vns Zoltán Gál va Judit Szabó vc)
ECM New Series 461 815-2 (65' · DDD)   Ⓕ

Just as Schnittke's First Symphony picks up the threads from Shostakovich's last, so his Piano Quintet feels like the natural successor to Shostakovich's last string quartet; that makes ECM's coupling of the two chamber works an effective and thought-provoking one, the more so since both performances are of the highest quality.

This music is a good deal harder to bring off than it looks. The textures are emaciated, and the pain of emotional starvation needs to register with unremitting intensity. In Schnittke's solo piano opening, Alexei Lubimov shows the requisite temperament and control of sonority, and both he and the Kellers keep us inside the Quintet's world through the first movement's obsessive, quarter-tone-inflected bell-tolling, through the ghost-train-ride of the film-derived *Tempo di valse*, through the catatonic laments of the two succeeding slow movements, all the way to the anxious transfigurations of the finale.

Curiously, Lubimov goes against the score in the final phrase, where Schnittke asks for pitched notes to fade into the noise of fingertips tapping on the keys, echoing the pedal-knocking at the end of the first movement. But his carefully graded *diminuendo* is effective enough in its own way, and overall this is the only recorded performance to rival Ludmilla Berlinsky and the Borodins (reviewed above).

Single-disc versions of Shostakovich's valedictory quartet are surprisingly thin on the ground. Here, too, the Kellers can stand comparison with the very finest. Shostakovich's parched and starved textures can be made to sound even more discomforting, but the Kellers' tonal control brings out its own range of nuance. Recording quality is nicely judged, the players being set in a nicely unobtrusive perspective.

String Trio

String Trio. Violin Sonatas – No 1; No 2, 'Quasi una sonata'
Mateja Marinković vn **Paul Silverthorne** va **Timothy Hugh** vc **Linn Hendry** pf
ASV CDDCA868 (65' · DDD)   Ⓕ

Overall, this performance is extremely satisfying. It's atmospherically recorded, and convincingly reinforces the claims of the String Trio to be considered one of Schnittke's major works. The music is surely to be preferred in this original version, rather than as the 'Trio Sonata' of Yuri Bashmet's orchestral arrangement.

Dating from 1985, and written in response to a commission from the Alban Berg Society of Vienna, the Trio is notable for the extent to which its reminiscences and re-creations are far less contrived and self-indulgent than is often the case with this composer. They aren't merely backward-looking, nostalgic gestures, but suggest a blueprint for a new, romantically tinged post-modernism.

Whether or not you go along with this analysis, it's difficult to deny that the Trio puts the pair of early violin sonatas into the shade. They aren't negligible pieces, even so, and these performances have much to commend them. Mateja Marinković and Linn Hendry make a first-rate duo: even the most piano-bashing bits of the Second Sonata aren't deprived of all musical sense, and the urgent interplay between the instruments has an authentic intensity.

Suite in the Old Style

Suite in the Old Style. Moz-Art à la Haydn.
Praeludium in memoriam Dmitri Shostakovich. A
Paganini. Stille Musik. Stille Nacht. Madrigal in
Memoriam Oleg Kagan. Gratulations rondo
Mateja Marinkovič, Thomas Bowes vns **Timothy
Hugh** vc **Linn Hendry** pf
ASV CDDCA877 (68' · DDD) Recorded 1993   Ⓕ

At first glance, this disc presents a rather
scrappy impression. It contains no large-scale
pieces, and the largest work – the early *Suite in
the Old Style* – is for the most part an uneventful
exercise in dutiful imitation. It's what the *Suite*
only hints at that the other works realise more
fully. In the *Gratulations rondo* Schnittke again
wears the mask of conformity to an old, easygoing classicism. When the mask begins to slip, we
wonder what to think. Is this a serious lesson
about the potential banality of classicism's
familiar formulas? Are the distortions of those
formulas expressive of affection or hostility?

These issues come most fully into focus in
Stille Nacht, as Gruber's sweet little tune, with
its obediently basic harmony, is subjected to
quiet but ruthlessly dissonant deconstruction.
'Silent Night' acquires the connotations of
Rachel Carson's *Silent Spring*, suggesting an
environmental disaster rather than a cosy spirituality. Schnittke's ability to create memorable
musical laments is well displayed here, in the
Shostakovich and Kagan memorial pieces, in
Stille Musik and even in *A Paganini*, which traces
an absorbing contest between an apparent distaste for virtuosity and a celebration of it. The
impact of these compositions is the greater for
their relative concentration and Mateja
Marinkovič is a player of admirable technical
refinement. The recording is first class, and the
disc servse as an ideal introduction to Schnittke
for listeners who may have doubts about his
larger-scale works.

Violin Sonatas

Violin Sonatas – No 1; No 2, 'Quasi una Sonata'; No
3. Gratulations rondo. Stille Nacht. Suite in the Old
Style
Francesco d'Orazio vn **Giampaolo Nuti** pf
Stradivarius STR33675 (75' · DDD)   Ⓕ

Schnittke's music for violin and piano spans
most of his composing career, from the early
1960s, when Shostakovich's genius and Soviet
ideology both loomed large, to the mid-1990s, a
time of freedom and desperate illness. The
three sonatas and three other works chart
Schnittke's sad but heroic decline, as he confronted head-on the special 20th-century challenge of composing from the heart as well as
from a sense of history.

The First Sonata (1963) is probably the best of
the six compositions. There's already plenty of
that sardonic, to-hell-with-it manner he made
his own, but his willingness to grapple with the
possibilities of well-made instrumental design
and to admit a sense of pathos that didn't
exclude touches of understatement, make for a
memorable 15 minutes. By comparison, the
Second Sonata (1968) is more slapdash, not
polystylistic enough to engineer the surreal
confrontations of his most powerful exercises in
bringing old and new into collision, its climactic
bashings-out of a minor triad as dated as they
are annoying. In the third sonata (1994) the earlier energy hasn't totally drained away, and the
poignancy of a musical voice facing its own
imminent extinction still gets through. Hearing
this after the winsome pastiche of the *Suite in
Old Style*, the po-faced Mozartisms of the *Gratulations rondo*, and the crude but unfailingly
shudder-making deconstruction of *Stille Nacht*
is moving, with its hints of what might have
been had Schnittke lived in more stable times.
Francesco d'Orazio, as recorded here, doesn't
have the full-bodied tone and blazingly forthright rhetoric of a Russian violinist like Mark
Lubotsky, for whom Schnittke composed. But
he shapes the sonatas well, and has strong support from Giampaolo Nuti.

Concerto for Mixed Chorus

Concerto for Mixed Chorus. Minnesang. Voices of
Nature[a]
[a]**Rachel Gledhill** vibe **Holst Singers / Stephen
Layton**
Hyperion CDA67297 (65' · DDD)   Ⓕ

The rather anodyne title, Concerto for Mixed
Chorus (1984-5), actually conceals a work with
tremendous depths of faith and feeling, and a
masterpiece of choral writing building firmly on
the Russian sacred tradition. The text comes
from deeply penitential religious poetry by
Grigor Narekatsi, a 10th-century Armenian
monk, to which Schnittke responded with an
immediacy that makes this a colourful and considerably more approachable work than the
later Penitential Psalms. The Holst Singers
bring to its often stunningly rich textures not
only their previous experience with Russian
music, but also something of the English choral
tradition, which makes more striking those
moments that suggest the choral writing of, say,
Howells or Bax. The music can stand many different approaches, and this isn't only as convincing as any other version, but allows details
of the scoring to come through in a unique way.
The technical skill of the choir is truly impressive. It's the Concerto that provides the real
interest in this programme, and with a performance of this extraordinary quality it should earn
many new admirers.

12 Penitential Psalms

12 Penitential Psalms
Swedish Radio Choir / Tõnu Kaljuste
ECM New Series 453 513-2 (53' · DDD) Text and

translation included   Ⓕ**O**

Schnittke's 12 *Penitential Psalms* (1988) aren't biblical: Nos 1-11 use 16th-century Russian texts and No 12 is a wordless meditation which encapsulates the spirit and style of what precedes it. Though at times dark and despairing in tone, this is in no sense liturgical music. It's too expansive, and reaches towards the ecstatic too consistently, to qualify as ascetic or austere. Indeed, the warmly euphonious chorale-like textures with which several of the movements end are sumptuous enough for one to imagine a soulful saxophone weaving its way through them. As this suggests, the recording is extremely, and not inappropriately, resonant, and the performance is polished to a fault, the individual lines superbly controlled and the textures balanced with a fine feeling for their weight and diversity. Although some may find this issue a little too refined, it realises the work's expressive world with imposing and irresistible authenticity. In these works, Schnittke seems to be doing penance for the extravagant indulgences of pieces such as *Stille Nacht* and the Viola Concerto, abandoning modernism in general and expressionism in particular. The music nevertheless retains strong links with the images of lament and spiritual aspiration, and there's nothing in the least artificial or contrived about its emotional aura. It's difficult to imagine a more convincing or better recorded account of it than this one.

Othmar Schoeck   Swiss 1886-1957

Schoeck studied at the Zürich Conservatory and with Reger in Leipzig (1907-8), then worked in Zürich and St Gall as a conductor. He was one of the leading Swiss composers of his time. His numerous songs, usually setting German Romantic poetry, establish him among the foremost lieder composers, but he also wrote important operas: the dense and richly scored Penthesilea *(1927) and* Vom Fischer und syner Fru *(1930), which like other works is more folklike. The rest of his output includes choral and orchestral scores and a few chamber pieces.* GROVEmusic

Penthesilea

Penthesilea
Helga Dernesch sop Penthesilea **Jane Marsh** sop Prothoe **Mechtild Gessendorf** sop Meroe **Marjana Lipovšek** mez High Priestess **Gabriele Sima** sop Priestess **Theo Adam** bass-bar Achilles **Horst Hiestermann** ten Diomede **Peter Weber** bass Herold **Austrian Radio Chorus and Symphony Orchestra / Gerd Albrecht**
Orfeo C364941B (80' · ADD) Recorded live 1982.
Notes and text included   Ⓕ

Schoeck's one-act opera, *Penthesilea* is an astonishing and masterly score. It seems barely credible that a work so gripping in its dramatic intensity, and so powerful in atmosphere, should be so little known. It has the listener on the edge of the seat throughout its 80 short minutes and, like any great opera, it continues to cast a spell long after the music has ended. In the *Grove Dictionary of Opera*, Ronald Crichton wrote that 'at its most intense, the language of *Penthesilea* surpasses in ferocity Strauss's *Elektra*, a work with which it invites comparison'. In so far as it's a one-act work, set in the Ancient World, highly concentrated in feeling and with strongly delineated characters, it's difficult not to think of Strauss's masterpiece. Yet its sound world is quite distinctive. Though he's a lesser figure, Schoeck similarly renders the familiar language of Straussian opera entirely his own. The vocabulary isn't dissimilar yet the world is different. We are immediately plunged into a vivid and completely individual world, packed with dramatic incident: off-stage war cries and exciting, dissonant trumpet calls. There's an almost symphonic handling of pace, but the sonorities are unusual: for example, there's a strong wind section, some 10 clarinets at various pitches, while there are only a handful of violins; much use is made of two pianos in a way that at times almost anticipates Britten. This performance emanates from the 1982 Salzburg Festival; Helga Dernesch in the title-role commands the appropriate range of emotions as Penthesilea and the remainder of the cast, including the Achilles of Theo Adam, rise to the occasion. The important choral role and the orchestral playing under Gerd Albrecht are eminently committed and the recording is good. There's a useful essay and libretto, though in German, not English.

Arnold Schoenberg   Austro/Hungarian 1874-1951

Schoenberg began violin lessons when he was eight and almost immediately started composing, though he had no formal training until he was in his late teens, when Zemlinsky became his teacher and friend (in 1910 he married Zemlinsky's sister). His first acknowledged works date from the turn of the century and include the string sextet Verklärte Nacht *as well as some songs, all showing influences from Brahms, Wagner and Wolf. In 1901-3 he was in Berlin as a cabaret musician and teacher, and wrote the symphonic poem* Pelleas und Melisande, *pressing the Straussian model towards denser thematic argument and contrapuntal richness.*

He then returned to Vienna and began taking private pupils, Berg and Webern being among the first. He also moved rapidly forwards in his musical style. The large orchestra of Pelleas *and the* Gurrelieder *was replaced by an ensemble of 15 in Chamber Symphony No 1, but with greater harmonic strangeness, formal complexity and contrapuntal density. When atonality arrived in 1908, it was the inevitable outcome of a doomed attempt to accommodate ever more disruptive material. However, he found it possible a quarter-century later to return to something like his tonal style, as in the Suite in G for strings.*

That, however, was not possible immediately. The sense of key was left behind as Schoenberg set poems by George in the last two movements of String Quartet No 2 and in the cycle Das Buch der hängenden Gärten, and for the next few years he lived in the new, rarefied musical air. With tonality had gone thematicism and rhythmic constraint; works tended to be short statements of a single extreme musical state, justifying the term 'expressionist' (Five Orchestral Pieces; Three Pieces and Six Little Pieces for piano). The larger pieces of this period have some appropriate dramatic content: the rage and despair of a woman seaching for her lover (Erwartung), the bizarre stories, melancholia and jokes of a distintegrating personality (Pierrot lunaire, for reciter in Sprechgesang with mixed quintet), or the progress of the soul towards union with God (Die Jakobsleiter).

Gradually Schoenberg came to find the means for writing longer instrumental structures, in the 12-note serial method, and in the 1920s he returned to standard forms and genres, notably in the Suite for piano, String Quartet No 3, Orchestral Variations and several choral pieces. He also founded the Society for Private Musical Performances (1919-21), involving his pupils in the presentation of new music under favourable conditions. In 1923 his wife died (he remarried the next year), and in 1925 he moved to Berlin to take a master class at the Prussian Academy of Arts. While there he wrote much of his unfinished opera Moses und Aron which is concerned with the impossibility of communicating truth without some distortion in the telling.

In 1933 he was obliged as a Jew to leave Berlin: he went to Paris, and formally returned to the faith which he had deserted for Lutheranism in 1898. Later the same year he arrived in the USA, and he settled in Los Angeles in 1934. It was there that he returned to tonal composition, while developing serialism to make possible the more complex structures of the Violin Concerto and the String Quartet No 4. In 1936 he began teaching at UCLA and his output dwindled. After a heart attack in 1945, however, he gave up teaching and made some return to expressionism (A Survivor from Warsaw, String Trio), as well as writing religious choruses. **GROVE**music

Piano Concerto

Schoenberg Piano Concerto, Op 42ª. Drei Klavierstücke, Op 11. Sechs Klavierstücke, Op 19. **Berg** Sonata for Piano, Op 1. **Webern** Variations, Op 27
Mitsuko Uchida pf ªCleveland Orchestra / Pierre Boulez
Philips 468 033-2PH (63' · DDD)　　Ⓕ**OOO**

Uchida's distinctive musical personality and outstanding technique make her Schoenberg, Berg and Webern well worth hearing, however many other version of these works you have in your collection. She brings a marvellous spontaneity and sense of drama to the more overtly romantic compositions here – Berg's Sonata and Schoenberg's

Op 11 *Pieces*. This certainly isn't one of those accounts of the Berg where you question the composer's wisdom in marking the first section for repeat. As for the Schoenberg, never has one been more aware of this music's closeness in time and spirit to the cataclysmic world of the monodrama *Erwartung*. Uchida's earlier recording of Op 11 was warmly praised, and this one is no less accomplished. Elsewhere, her relish for strongly juxtaposed contrast risks occasional over-emphasis, as in the third of the Op 19 pieces, and the virtues of more sharply articulated playing in this repertory are demonstrated on Peter Hill's admirable super-bargain-price Naxos disc. His account of Webern's *Variations* is exemplary in its clarity and feeling for line; yet Uchida manages to suggest deeper links with more romantic perspectives without in any way traducing the music's inherent radicalism.

Links with romanticism are even more explicit in the texture and thematic character of Schoenberg's Concerto, and this performance places the work firmly in the tradition of Liszt and Brahms. Not even Pierre Boulez can bring ideal lucidity to the occasionally lumpy orchestral writing, but the performance as a whole, with excellent sound, has an attractive sweep and directness of utterance. Alfred Brendel's second recording (Philips) remains a fine achievment, but the orchestral playing is less refined than on the new disc, the recording drier, with a flatter perspective. Nor are Michael Gielen's readings of Schoenberg's two chamber symphonies as competitive as Uchidas's of the solo piano works.

Verklärte Nacht, Op 4

Verklärte Nacht, Pelleas und Melisande, Op 5
Berlin Philharmonic Orchestra / Herbert von Karajan
DG The Originals 457 721-2GOR (74' · ADD)
Recorded 1973-4　　Ⓜ

This is a very distinguished coupling, superbly played by the BPO – a truly 'legendary' reissue, quite unsurpassed on record. Karajan never approached contemporary music with the innate radicalism and inside knowledge of a composer-conductor like Boulez; yet he can't be accused of distorting reality by casting a pall of late-Romantic opulence and languor over these works. He's understandably most at home in the expansive and often openly tragic atmosphere of Schoenberg's early tone-poems *Verklärte Nacht* and *Pelleas und Melisande*. The richly blended playing of the BPO provides the ideal medium for Karajan's seamless projection of structure and expression. He remains especially sensitive to the music's lyricism, to the connections that to his ears override the contrasts. Although *Verklärte Nacht* has certainly been heard in performances less redolent of 19th-century tradition, as well as less calculated in its recorded acoustic, this remains a powerfully dramatic reading. One man's view, then: but, given the man, a notably fascinating one.

Schoenberg Verklärte Nacht, Op 4 (orig version) ⛒
Schubert String Quintet in C, D956
Alvin Dinkin va **Kurt Reher** vc **Hollywood Quartet**
(Felix Slatkin, Paul Shure vns Paul Robyn va Eleanor Aller vc)
Testament mono SBT1031 (73' · ADD) Recorded 1950-51   ⒡**OOO**

This was the first ever recording of *Verklärte Nacht* in its original sextet form and it remains unsurpassed. When it was first reviewed in *Gramophone*, the late Lionel Salter wrote of it as being 'beautifully played with the most careful attention to details of dynamics and phrasing, with unfailing finesse, with consistently sympathetic tone, and, most important, with a firm sense of the basic structure'. The Schubert too fully deserves its classic status. The tranquillity of the slow movement has never been conveyed with greater nobility or more perfect control. The Hollywood Quartet made music for the sheer love of it and as a relaxation from their duties in the film-studio orchestras, for which they were conspicuously over-qualified. They have incomparable ensemble and blend; and their impeccable technical address and consummate tonal refinement silence criticism. To add to the pleasure, the transfers could not be better.

Schoenberg Verklärte Nacht **Schubert** (arr Mahler) String Quartet No 14 in D minor, D810, 'Death and the Maiden'
Norwegian Chamber Orchestra / Iona Brown
Chandos CHAN9616 (69' · DDD) Recorded 1994 ⒡

Given the wrong sort of performance, *Verklärte Nacht* can drag on interminably – but not here. Iona Brown's reading with the Norwegian Chamber Orchestra lends every instrumental exchange the immediacy of live theatre: her lovers are voluble, unstinting and spontaneously communicative. There's colour in every bar: Schoenberg's ceaseless shifts in tone and tempo seem freshly credible, and the sum effect is extraordinarily compelling. The up-front recording further compounds a sense of urgency; only the closing pages seem a trifle uncomfortable with such close scrutiny.

Rivals, however, are plentiful. Among older alternatives, Karajan and the BPO are the most tonally alluring; but Brown runs it close, and her young Norwegian players are with her virtually every bar of the way. No digital rival is quite as good. The Schubert-Mahler also offers further confirmation of a genuine artistic alliance. Mahler's bolstered textures work least well in the second movement, something that even Brown's advocacy doesn't quite compensate for; but the rest is shot through with genuine passion and vitality. A memorable disc.

Five Orchestral Pieces, Op 16

Five Orchestral Pieces, Op 16. A Survivor from Warsaw, Op 46[cd]. Begleitmusik zu einer Lichtspielszene, Op 34. Herzgewächse, Op 20[a]. Serenade, Op 24[be]
[a]**Eileen Hulse** sop [b]**Stephen Varcoe** bar [c]**Simon Callow** narr [d]**London Voices;** [e]**Twentieth Century Classics Ensemble; London Symphony Orchestra / Robert Craft**
Koch International Classics 37263-2 (69' · DDD) Recorded 1994   ⒡

This is an absorbing issue, not least for the sheer variety of works that it contains. The two largest compositions, Op 16 and Op 24, define the disc's range. The *Five Orchestral Pieces*, in which expressionism can be heard emerging from the chrysalis of late romanticism, are played with supreme finesse by the LSO, and Robert Craft probes the richly diverse textures with exemplary concentration and precision. The downside is some loss of immediacy. There are also slight reservations about the balance in *A Survivor from Warsaw*, where Simon Callow is, one imagines, placed behind the orchestra, depriving this harrowing work of its visceral impact. A closer focus would have been preferable. *Herzgewächse* and *Begleitmusik zu einer Lichtspielszene* are both well performed, the latter with a recessed perspective, similar to that in Op 16, which ensures an extremely well-blended texture without loss of detail. Nevertheless, the finest performance here is that of the *Serenade*, Op 24, where the sound (recorded in New York, not in London) is cleaner, and the characterisation is superb from beginning to end. Stephen Varcoe is a rather breathy singer in the dauntingly angular and wide-ranging 'Sonnet', but the performance as a whole makes a convincing case for the work's high level of musical thought and purely technical mastery.

Variations for Orchestra, Op 31

Variations for Orchestra. Pelleas und Melisande
Chicago Symphony Orchestra / Pierre Boulez
Erato 2292-45827-2 (62' · DDD) Recorded 1991 ⒡**OO**

The two faces of Schoenberg could scarcely be more starkly juxtaposed than they are on this superbly performed and magnificently recorded disc – Boulez and the CSO at their formidable best. *Pelleas und Melisande* can be taken not only as Schoenberg's 'answer' to Debussy's opera (also based on Maeterlinck's play), but as his challenge to Richard Strauss's supremacy as a composer of symphonic poems. It's an intensely symphonic score in Schoenberg's early, late-Romantic vein, with an elaborate single-movement structure and a subtle network of thematic cross-references. Yet none of this is an end in itself, and the music is as gripping and immediate a representation of a tragic love story as anything in the German romantic tradition. To move from this to the abstraction of the 12-note

Variations, Op 31 may threaten extreme anticlimax. Yet from the delicate introduction of the
work's shapely theme to the turbulent good
humour of the extended finale Schoenberg
proves that his new compositional method did
not drain his musical language of expressive
vitality. The elaborate counterpoint may not
make for easy listening, but the combination of
exuberance and emotion is irresistible – at least
in a performance like this.

String Quartets

No 1 in D minor, Op 7 **No 2** in F sharp minor, Op 10
No 31 Op 30 **No 4** Op 37

String Quartets[a] – Nos 1-4. D. Verklärte Nacht,
Op 4[afg]. Chamber Symphony No 1 in E, Op 9 (arr
Webern)[ah]. Sechs Klavierstücke, Op 19[a]. Wind Quintet, Op 26 (both arr Guittart)[af]. Concerto for String
Quartet and Orchestra (after Handel's Concerto
grosso, Op 6 No 7)[ai]. Ode to Napoleon, Op 41[aeh].
String Trio, Op 45[b]. Phantasy, Op 47[bh]
[a]**Schoenberg Quartet** ([bc]Janneke van der Meer,
Wim de Jong vns [b]Henk Guittart va [b]Viola de Hoog
vc) with [d]**Susan Narucki** sop [e]**Michael Grandage**
spkr [f]**Jan Erik van Regteren** va [g]**Taco Kooistra** vc
[h]**Sepp Grotenhuis** pf [i]**Arnhem Philharmonic
Orchestra / Roberto Benzi**
Chandos ⑤ CHAN9939 (319' · DDD) Texts and
translations included　Ⓜ

The Schoenberg Quartet adopt an unashamedly Romantic approach in the early D
major Quartet, stressing its inheritance from
Brahms and Dvořák. This feels right in context,
and leads on seamlessly to a raptly expressive
reading of *Verklärte Nacht*. More restrained
than the Brandis and less overwrought than the
Juilliard recordings, it represents a modern
alternative to the fabled Hollywood Quartet,
and restores a sense of intimacy too often lost
now that the string orchestra transcription has
become the better known version.

Even more than in their earlier account of the
First Quartet, the Schoenbergs have found the
balance between highlighting salient detail and
the long-range cohesiveness that this intricately
structured work needs. Theirs is an engrossing
but never exhausting interpretation, the coda
suffused with a repose such as Schoenberg was
never again to attain so completely. If the First
Chamber Symphony makes effortless listening
in comparison, this is because Webern's skilful
'working reduction' removes the hectic confrontation of wind and strings, though this lucid
and animated performance is admittedly easier
on the ears than the Arditti's more highly pres-
surised reading. The Second Quartet is the one,
surprising disappointment here. The *scherzo*'s
malevolence is rather flaccidly conveyed, and
the music's pained transcendence eludes this
performance by a small but significant margin.

The Third Quartet, however, is superb. Years
of coaching from the late Jenö Lehner, second

violinist of the Kolisch Quartet, have enabled
the Schoenbergs to endow this often
intractable-seeming music with a grace and
rhythmic buoyancy unmatched since the Kolis-
ches themselves.

If the Fourth Quartet isn't quite as convincing, it packs a powerful emotional punch, and
scales heights of eloquence in the fervent *Largo*.
As with Bartók's Sixth Quartet, outward form is
radically redefined here by an inner expressive
force. The path to these mature and disquieting
masterpieces is laid with first recordings of
Henk Guittart's revelatory quartet transcription of the Op 19 *Piano Pieces* – Webernian in
size but not in expression – and his ambitious
rethink of the Wind Quintet for string quintet;
an altogether more ingratiating listen than the
original, and one which might just give this
unloved piece a new lease of life.

The String Trio is powerfully realised, suffusing this desperate masterpiece with a vision
that's never less than moving. Janneke van der
Meer ably realises the craggy eloquence of the
Phantasy, Schoenberg's final chamber work.

Cleanly recorded in a number of sympathetic
acoustics, this is a testament to 25 years of dedicated interpretative prowess by the Schoenberg
Quartet. This is music they care about with a
passion, and their performances amply convey
that belief. However well you think you know
this fascinating and often inspiring music, do
acquire this set.

String Quartets Nos 1-4
[a]**Dawn Upshaw** sop **Arditti Quartet** (Irvine Arditti,
David Alberman vns Garth Knox va Rohan de
Saram vc)
Auvidis Montaigne ② MO782135 (139' · DDD)
Recorded 1993　Ⓜ⒪

These recordings were made in London, in
collaboration with the BBC, and the sound is
consistently spacious, with a natural clarity and
an even balance; the details of Schoenberg's
complex counterpoint, as evident in No 1 as in
No 4, can be heard with a minimum of stress
and strain. Though one occasionally gets the
impression that the Arditti is relatively cool in
its response to this often fervent music, the
mood they create is far from anti-Romantic, and
they call on a wide range of dynamics and tone
colours. Even if every nuance in Schoenberg's
markings isn't followed, this is warmly expressive playing. Dawn Upshaw's contribution to
the Second Quartet helps to heighten the
drama, although she misses some of that mysterious, ecstatic quality which makes this music so
haunting. It's in the Third and Fourth Quartets
that the superior sound quality of the Auvidis
Montaigne issue pays greatest dividends. Textural clarity is vital here, and although even the
Arditti struggles to sustain the necessary lightness in the long second movement of No 4,
their wider dynamic range brings you close to
the toughly argued, emotionally expansive
essence of this music. Yet the performance of

No 3 is the finest achievement of the set: clarity of form and emotional conviction combine to create an absorbing account of a modern masterwork. It sets the seal on a most distinguished enterprise.

Choral Works

Friede auf Erden, Op 13. Kol nidre, Op 39. Drei Volkslieder, Op 49. Zwei Kanons – Wenn der schwer Gedrückte klagt; O dass der Sinnen doch so viele sind!. Drei Volkslieder (1929) – Es gingen zwei Gespielen gut; Herzlieblich Lieb, durch Scheiden; Schein uns, du liebe Sonne. Vier Stücke, Op 27. Drei Satiren, Op 28. Sechs Stücke, Op 35. Dreimal tausen Jahre, Op 50. De profundis (Psalm 130), Op 50b. Modern Psalm (Der erste Psalm), Op 50c. A Survivor from Warsaw, Op 46
John Shirley-Quirk, Günter Reich narrs **BBC Singers; BBC Chorus and Symphony Orchestra; London Sinfonietta / Pierre Boulez**
Sony Classical ② SM2K44571 (105' · DDD/ADD) Recorded 1976-86. Texts and translations included
Ⓑ🔾

Pierre Boulez's recordings of Schoenberg have been appearing at irregular intervals over many years. This two-disc compilation of choral works includes performances recorded on three separate occasions in 1982, 1984 and 1986, as well as transferring the 1976 recording of *A Survivor from Warsaw*, originally coupled on LP with three purely orchestral works. There's no lack of interpretative consistency in what we hear, however. By 1976 Boulez was a seasoned Wagner conductor, and while it may be simplistic to ascribe the weightiness and spaciousness of these Schoenberg performances to his experiences at Bayreuth, the generally recessed sound perspective strongly suggests a desire to turn the BBC's Maida Vale studios into a much larger and more resonant hall. This distancing is especially evident in John Shirley-Quirk's declamation of the text of *Kol nidre*, one of Schoenberg's later and more substantial sacred compositions. Once you adjust to the balance, the performance itself has an appropriately fervent atmosphere, as do the accounts of the other works involving narrator, chorus and orchestra, the unfinished *Modern Psalm* and *A Survivor from Warsaw*. Both are characteristically intense and exultant, the *Psalm* with some particularly telling orchestral interjections, *A Survivor from Warsaw* with its climactic choral hymn (sung in Hebrew, though the booklet fails to provide transliterations of the Hebrew text both for this and for Psalm 130). Günter Reich's memorably dramatic (but not melodramatic) narration in *A Survivor from Warsaw* benefits from his relatively forward placing.

Most of the music on the discs is for chamber choir, usually unaccompanied. Boulez's expressiveness tends to be fairly generalised, creating and sustaining an overall mood rather than responding to every nuance of the text. The BBC Singers are technically excellent, but the recording magnifies the collective vibrato,

the tonal fruitiness which can blur textural definition, especially in the close-knit part-writing of the six pieces for male choir, Op 35. Where the late-Romantic sheen Boulez casts over Schoenberg's harmony works best is in such beautifully turned exercises in nostalgia as the German folk-song arrangements, especially the ravishingly beautiful 'Schein uns, du liebe Sonne'. Fortunately the singers find the necessary incisiveness for the Opp 27 and 28 collections, even if a drier acoustic might have helped to clarify the convoluted lines of the problematic Op 27 No 4, 'Der Wunsch der Liebhabers'. A firm recommendation.

Gurrelieder

Gurrelieder
Susan Dunn sop **Brigitte Fassbaender** mez
Siegfried Jerusalem, Peter Haage tens **Hermann Becht** bass **Hans Hotter** narr **St Hedwig's Cathedral Choir, Berlin; Dusseldorf Musikverin Chorus; Berlin Radio Symphony Orchestra / Riccardo Chailly**
Double Decca ② 473 728-2 (101' · DDD) Recorded 1985. Text and translation included
Ⓜ🔾

This vast cantata, a direct descendant of Wagnerian music-drama, was for the turn-of-the-century musical scene the ultimate gorgeous sunset. Schoenberg's forces are, to put it mildly, extravagant. As well as the six soloists and two choruses, the orchestra sports such luxuries as four piccolos, ten horns and a percussion battery that includes iron chains; and so complex are some of the textures that, to achieve a satisfactory balance, a near miracle is required of conductor and recording engineers. Decca has never been mean with miracles where large-scale forces are concerned and this set is no exception. Chailly gives us a superbly theatrical presentation of the score. The casting of the soloists is near ideal. Susan Dunn's Tove has youth, freshness and purity on her side. So exquisitely does she float her lines that you readily sympathise with King Waldemar's rage at her demise. Siegfried Jerusalem has the occasional rough moment, but few previous Waldemars on disc have possessed his heroic ringing tones and range of expression. And Decca makes sure that its trump card, the inimitable Hans Hotter as the speaker in 'The wild hunt of the summer wind', is so tangibly projected that we miss not one vowel or consonant of his increasing animation and excitement at that final approaching sunrise.

Gurrelieder
Karita Mattila sop **Anne Sofie von Otter** mez
Thomas Moser ten **Philip Langridge** ten **Thomas Quasthoff** bass-bar **Berlin Radio Chorus; MDR Radio Chorus, Leipzig; Ernst Senff Choir; Berlin Philharmonic Orchestra / Sir Simon Rattle**
EMI ② 557303-2 (110' · DDD) Notes, texts and translations included
Ⓕ🔾🔾🔾

Apparently Rattle told the Berlin Phil-harmonic to play *Gurrelieder* 'as though it were *Daphnis et Chloé*', which sounds crazy until you listen to the result: indeed, the sonorities do rather often sound subtly and delicately French. It also seems obvious from this performance that he means it when he says that *Gurrelieder* is 'the world's largest string quartet'. It's only rarely that the full resources of Schoenberg's gargantuan orchestra are called for (all the more satisfyingly vast when they are). This has an effect on the soloists: none is required to force. Karita Mattila gains from this intimate approach, floating over exquisite orchestral textures in her first song and touching the second very lightly, though in the fourth she can manage both a splendid opening out and an ethereal close. Anne Sofie von Otter has a brighter voice than many exponents of the Wood Dove, better at quieter expressiveness than the wild, gutturally expressed grief of Brigitte Fassbaender, still unrivalled in this role in Riccardo Chailly's recording. Langridge is vividly characterful as Klaus-Narr, Thomas Quasthoff a fine Peasant and a vehement Speaker. The choral singing is first class, the orchestral playing superfine and the recording – a mixture of live and studio per-formances – both detailed and spacious. There are several fine accounts of *Gurrelieder* in the current catalogue, of which Chailly's has for a long while been a favourite; his soloists are at least as fine as Rattle's, but Rattle's control of *rubato*, his readiness to adopt more relaxed tempos and to allow silences to register are all tangible advantages. He now replaces Chailly at the head of the list.

Gurrelieder
Melanie Diener sop **Jennifer Lane** mez **Stephen O'Mara, Martyn Hill** tens **David Wilson-Johnson** báss **Ernst Haefliger** spkr **Simon Joly Chorale; Philharmonia Orchestra / Robert Craft**
Naxos ② 8 557518/9 (118' · DDD · N)   Ⓢ●

On the evidence of this superb performance we've quite clearly been underestimating Robert Craft. Precision and finely moulded detail are evident throughout, at least as clearly as in Chailly's and Rattle's accounts, but in Craft's case one is no less often aware of sumptuous richness, passionate eloquence and satisfying orchestral weight. He's also more prepared than rivals to adopt broad tempos and expressive *rubato*. Despite a few tiny reservations it a more thrilling account than either of the rivals mentioned above, and carries something of the excitement of a live performance.

Stephen O'Mara has the sort of voice you associate with Wagner's Siegmund, but with a fine sense of line and sufficient variety of dynamic to open out stirringly at climaxes. There have been more expressive Toves than Melanie Diener, but not many who are so firm-voiced and steady. Jennifer Lane is an excellent Wood Dove, dramatic and expressive, David

Wilson-Johnson a grippingly vehement Peasant, while anyone who thinks of Martyn Hill as a typically understating English tenor will be astonished by his Klaus-Narr, which is vividly acted and firm of voice. In his 83rd year Ernst Haefliger is an extraordinarily lively, urgent Speaker. The chorus are inspiritingly full-voiced, singing out like heroes.

Yet most of the memorable moments of this performance are Craft's and the Philharmonia's: the wonderfully glittering chamber textures of the penultimate scene, the passion and savagery of the orchestral interlude that heralds the death of Tove, the tumultuous power of the 'wild hunt'. *Gurrelieder* has been exceptionally fortunate on disc in recent years, but this recording (whose sound is often magnificently full and spacious) need fear none of its rivals.

Pierrot lunaire

Pierrot lunaire, Op 21. Herzgewächse, Op 20. Ode to Napoleon, Op 41
Christine Schäfer sop **David Pittman-Jennings** narr **Ensemble InterContemporain / Pierre Boulez**
DG 457 630-2GH (53' · DDD) Texts and translations included   Ⓟ●

Pierre Boulez's third recording of *Pierrot lunaire* is an intense yet intimate reading, in a recording that's positively anti-resonant, and which veers, like the music itself, between harshness and reticence. Boulez's second recording (for Sony Classical), with Yvonne Minton, has long been notorious as the 'sung' *Pierrot*, flouting the composer's specific instructions about recitation. This time Christine Schäfer is more speech-orientated, the few fully sung notes perfectly pitched, and although slidings-away from sustained sounds are on the whole avoided, the effect is superbly dramatic in the work's more expressionistic movements. The work's strange world, half-way between cabaret and concert hall, is admirably caught. In the *Ode to Napoleon* David Pittman-Jennings has a heavy voice, but he skilfully inflects the sketchily notated dynamics of the vocal part, and the instrumental backing is forceful and well nuanced. The sound may be clinically dry, but this is scarcely a serious drawback when the performance has such expressive immediacy. The disc is completed by the brief, exotic Maeterlinck setting from 1911, whose hugely demanding vocal line deters all but the hardiest. Christine Schäfer copes, while the accompaniment for celesta, harmonium and harp weaves its usual spell. A thoroughly memorable disc.

Songs

2 Balladen, Op 12 – Jane Grey[a]; Der verlorene Haufen[b]. Das Buch der hängenden Gärten, Op 15[a]. Lieder, Op 1 – Dank[b]. Lieder, Op 2[a]. Lieder, Op 3 – Die Aufgeregten[b]; Warnung[b]; Geübtes Herz[b].

Lieder, Op 6 – Lockung[a]; Traumleben[b]
[a]**Sarah Connolly** mez [b]**Roderick Williams** bar **Iain Burnside** pf
Black Box BBM1072 (65' · DDD) Texts and
translations included   Ⓕ**OO**

These performances were originally recorded
for BBC Radio 3's regular and imaginative
series, *Voices*. Roderick Williams's fine-grained
baritone copes well with some of the bigger
utterances here; only in the huge and awkward
intervals of 'Traumleben' is there any hint of
strain, and both baritone and pianist find real
power and drama in 'Der verlorene Haufen' and
in that quite repulsive (but fascinating) song
'Warnung'. The splendid, Brahmsian (but then
distinctly Wagnerian) 'Dank' opens the recital
most inspiritingly. The amount of work that
Burnside and Sarah Connolly put into preparing *Das Buch der hängenden Gärten* is obvious
throughout, in subtle phrasing and colouring,
intimacy of expression and scrupulous attention
to Stefan George's often obscure and feverish
words. A very fine reading, and Burnside is
throughout outstandingly imaginative. All the
songs here were recorded in as little as three
days, but all three musicians sound as though
they had lived with them for months at least. A
distinguished and absorbing recital, the recording admirably combining intimacy with space.

Moses und Aron

Moses und Aron
David Pittman-Jennings narr Moses **Chris Merritt**
ten Aron **László Polgár** bass Priest **Gabriele
Fontana** sop Young Girl, First Naked Woman
Yvonne Naef mez Invalid Woman **John Graham
Hall** ten Young Man, Naked Youth **Per Lindskog** ten
Youth **Henk de Vries** bar Young Man **Siegfried
Lorenz** bar Another Young Man **Chorus of the
Netherlands Opera; Royal Concertgebouw
Orchestra / Pierre Boulez**
DG ② 449 174-2GH2 (106' · DDD) Notes,text and
translation included   Ⓕ**O**

Moses und Aron is respected rather than loved,
with the reputation of being a tough assignment
for all concerned. One of the essays in the booklet accompanying this recording calls it a didactic opera. Pierre Boulez, however, is a conductor in whom didacticism is close to a passion,
and he's obviously passionate about this opera.
We take it for granted that, in any work to
which he feels close, every detail will be both
accurate and audible. But for Schoenberg *Moses
und Aron* was a warning as well as a homily, and
as much a confession of faith as either. Boulez,
often himself a Moses preaching against anti-
modern backsliding, is at one with Schoenberg
here.

Some such reason, surely, has led to this being
not only a performance of immaculate clarity,
but of intense and eloquent beauty and powerful
drama too. The recording was made during a
run of stage performances, but in the Concert-

gebouw in Amsterdam, not in the theatre. In the
beautiful acoustic of their own hall, the orchestra plays with ample richness and precision, and
the sometimes complex textures benefit enormously from a perceptible space around them.

The choral singing matches the orchestral
playing in quality: beautiful in tone, eloquently
urgent, vividly precise in the difficult spoken
passages. The soloists are all admirable, with no
weak links. Merritt in particular seems to have
all that the hugely taxing role of Aron demands:
a fine control of long line, intelligently expressive use of words, where necessary the dangerous demagogue's glamour. Pittman-Jennings is
a properly prophetic Moses, grand of voice.
This is one of Boulez's finest achievements and
a compelling argument for *Moses und Aron* as an
anything but coldly didactic opera.

Franz Schreker   Austrian 1878-1934

*Schreker studied with Fuchs at the Vienna Conser-
vatory (1892-1900) and won success with his ballet
Der Geburtstag der Infantin (1908) and still more
with his opera Der ferne Klang (1912), which established his mastery of a harmonically rich, luxuriantly eventful orchestral style, used to suggest the
surreal power of music over the characters. In 1908
he established the Philharmonic Choir, which performed many new works, and in 1912 was invited to
teach at the Music Academy in Vienna, from where
he moved in 1920 to the directorship of the Berlin
Musikhochschule: for the next 10 years his fame was
at its peak. Meanwhile the operas Die Gezeichneten
(1918) and Der Schatzgräber (1920) had shown a
more Wagnerian manner, though he returned to his
earlier style, influenced by the more expressionist
Strauss, in Irrelohe (1924). Der singende Teufel
(1928) and Der Schmied von Gent (1932) are more
neo-classical, but continue his abiding concern with
the metaphysics of artistic creation (he wrote all his
own librettos). Christophorus (1927), unperformed
in his lifetime and dedicated to Schoenberg, is the
most extraordinary expression of his existential
anguish and vision of voluptuousness. His few non-
operatic works include a Chamber Symphony (1916)
and songs.*   **GROVE**music

Overtures and Preludes

Prelude to a Drama. Valse lente. Ekkehard, Op 12.
Symphonic Interlude. Nachtstück. Fantastic
Overture, Op 15
BBC Philharmonic Orchestra / Vassily Sinaisky
Chandos CHAN9797 (78' · DDD)   Ⓕ**O**

Sumptuously performed and unflinchingly
recorded, this collection will be seized on by
Schreker enthusiasts, who will enjoy every massively scored climax, every gorgeously coloured,
embroidered and encrusted texture. Those who
are only Schreker enthusiasts north-north-west
may need to be warned that the climaxes are

pretty frequent and that the textures are in constant flux. Listening to this programme uninterrupted is recommended only to addicts; others may wonder whether Schreker isn't repeating himself. All are operatic preludes or entr'actes (from *Die Gezeichneten*, *Der Schatzgräber* and *Der ferne Klang* respectively), and all serve similar functions: to represent in a darkened auditorium erotic acts or emotions that could scarcely be represented on a stage. The *Valse lente* is balletic light music, softly and delicately scored. *Ekkehard* is a tone-poem about a monk who falls in love with a Duchess and goes to war to defend her: each of these aspects has its own theme, and they're turbulently developed before a peaceful conclusion on Ekkehard's 'monastic' melody over a palpable organ pedal. No programme is stated for the *Fantastic Overture*, but it approaches the three big dramatic pieces in richness. Not many composers demand quite so much of a vast orchestra as Schreker, and Sinaisky and his orchestra amply fulfil those demands.

Franz Schubert
Austrian 1797-1828

Schubert, son of a schoolmaster, showed an extraordinary childhood aptitude for music, studying the piano, violin, organ, singing and harmony and, while a chorister in the imperial court chapel, composition with Salieri (1808-13). By 1814 he had produced piano pieces, settings of Schiller and Metastasio, string quartets, his first symphony and a three-act opera. Although family pressure dictated that he teach in his father's school, he continued to compose prolifically; his huge output of 1814-15 includes Gretchen am Spinnrade and Erlkönig (both famous for their text-painting) among numerous songs, besides two more symphonies, three masses and four stage works. From this time he enjoyed the companionship of several friends: frequently gathering for domestic evenings of Schubert's music (later called 'Schubertiads'), this group more than represented the new phenomenon of an educated, musically aware middle class, it gave him an appreciative audience and influential contacts as well as the confidence, in 1818, to break with schoolteaching. More songs poured out, including Der Wanderer and Die Forelle, and instrumental pieces – inventive piano sonatas, some tuneful, Rossinian overtures, the Fifth and Sixth Symphonies – began to show increased harmonic subtlety.

In 1820-21 aristocratic patronage, further introductions and new friendships augured well. Schubert's admirers issued 20 of his songs by private subscription, and he and Schober collaborated on Alfonso und Estrella. Though full of outstanding music, it was rejected. Strained friendships, pressing financial need and serious illness – Schubert almost certainly contracted syphilis in late 1822 – made this a dark period, which however encompassed some remarkable creative work: the epic Wandererfantasie for piano, the passionate, two-movement Eighth Symphony (Unfinished), the exquisite Schöne Müllerin song cycle, Die Verschworenen and the opera Fierabras. In 1824 he turned to instrumental forms, producing the A minor and D minor (Death and the Maiden) string quartets and the lyrically expansive Octet for wind and strings; around this time he at least sketched the Great C major Symphony. With his reputation in Vienna now steadily growing Schubert entered a more assured phase. He wrote mature piano sonatas, notably the one in A minor, some magnificent songs and his last, highly characteristic String Quartet, in G. 1827-8 saw not only the production of Winterreise and two piano trios but a marked increase in press coverage of his music; and he was elected to the Vienna Gesellschaft der Musikfreunde. But though he gave a full-scale public concert in March 1828 and worked diligently to satisfy publishers – composing some of his greatest music in his last year, despite failing health – appreciation remained limited. At his death, aged 31, he was mourned not only for his achievement but for 'still fairer hopes'.

Schubert's fame was long limited to that of a songwriter, since the bulk of his large output was not even published, and some not even performed, until the late 19th century. Yet, beginning with the Fifth Symphony and the 'Trout' Quintet, he produced major instrumental masterpieces. These are marked by an intense lyricism, a spontaneous chromatic modulation that is surprising to the ear yet clearly purposeful and often beguilingly expressive, and, not least, an imagination that creates its own formal structures. His way with sonata form, whether in an unorthodox choice of key for secondary material (Symphony in B minor, 'Trout' Quintet) or of subsidiary ideas for the development, makes clear his maturity and individuality. The greatest of his chamber works is acknowledged to be the String Quintet in C, with its rich sonorities, intensity and lyricism, and in the slow movement depth of feeling engendered by the sustained outer sections embracing a central impassioned section in F minor. Among the piano sonatas, the last three represent another summit of achievement. His greatest orchestral masterpiece is the Great C major Symphony, with its remarkable formal synthesis, rhythmic vitality, felicitous orchestration and lyric beauty. Among the choral works, the partsongs and masses rely on homophonic texture and bold harmonic shifts for their effect; the masses in A flat and E flat are particularly successful.

Schubert effectively established the German Lied as a new art form in the 19th century. He was helped by the late 18th-century outburst of lyric poetry and the new possibilities for picturesque accompaniment offered by the piano, but his own genius is by far the most important factor. Reasons for their abiding popularity rest not only in the direct appeal of Schubert's melody and the general attractiveness of his idiom but also in his unfailing ability to capture musically both the spirit of a poem and much of its external detail. He uses harmony to represent emotional change (for example, magically shifting to a 3rd related key) and accompaniment figuration to illustrate poetic images (moving water, a church bell). Schubert's discovery of Wilhelm Müller's narrative lyrics gave rise to his further development of the

Lied by means of the song cycle. Again, his two mas-terpieces were almost without precedent and are unsurpassed. Both identify nature with human suf-fering, Die schöne Müllerin *evoking a pastoral sound-language, and* Winterreise *a more intensely Romantic, universal, profoundly tragic quality.*

GROVEmusic

Symphonies

No 1 in D, D82; **No 2** in B flat, D125; **No 3** in D, D200; **No 4** in C minor, D417, 'Tragic'; **No 5** in B flat, D485; **No 6** in C, D589; **No 8** in B minor, D759, 'Unfinished'; **No 9** in C, D944, 'Great'

Symphonies Nos 1-9
Berlin Philharmonic Orchestra / Karl Böhm
DG Collectors Edition ④ 471 307-2GB4 (250' · ADD)
Recorded 1963-71   Ⓑ

These are marvellous performances: vibrant, clear, characterful and effortlessly well played. The recordings, too, still seem new-minted, even the Ninth, the first of the symphonies to be recorded. The Berliners' art is the art that dis-guises art. Böhm never feels the need to do any-thing clever but just quietly sees to it that this superb orchestra plays at its best. Böhm's way with the two late symphonies is, in fact, highly sophisticated. The *Unfinished* begins in what seems to be a leisurely fashion but his perform-ance of the first movement catches Schubert's mix of lyricism and high drama with extraordi-nary acuity. Conversely, the second movement seems swift but brings the work full circle with an equally extraordinary sense of calm and catharsis in the final pages. The celebrated 1963 Ninth out-Furtwänglers Furtwängler in the myriad means it uses within a single grand design to capture the symphony's sense of dan-ger and derring-do in addition to its lyricism, nobility, and earthy Austrian charm.

In the early symphonies, Böhm's approach is simpler-seeming and more direct. Rhythms are so finely propelled, the pulse so effortlessly sus-tained, the music always lands on its feet. The zest comes from the stylish Berlin string-playing; melodically, it's the woodwinds (every one a Lieder singer) who catch the beauty of Schubert's melodies and the skirl of the atten-dant descants. You won't find yourself tiring of Böhm's approach; he doesn't give in to irritat-ing idiosyncrasies (à la Harnoncourt), but ensures that the Schubertian stream is always clear to the eye and sweet to the taste.

Symphonies Nos 1-6, 8 & 9
Royal Concertgebouw Orchestra / Nikolaus Harnoncourt
Teldec ④ 4509-91184-2 (284' · DDD) Recorded live 1992   Ⓜ❍

Harnoncourt, like Abbado on DG, has exam-ined Schubert's own manuscripts, and corrected many unauthentic amendments that found their

way into the printed editions of the symphonies, such as the eight bars later added to the Fourth Symphony's first movement exposition; but the differences between Harnoncourt's interpreta-tive Schubert and Abbado's are startling. The Ninth's finale, unlike Abbado's, a whirling, spinning *vivace* – is borne aloft on astonishingly precise articulation of its rhythms and accents, and a springy delivery of the triplets. Character-istics one has come to expect from a Harnon-court performance. Still, what a joy to hear this Allegro, and those of most of the earlier sym-phonies, seized with such bright and light-toned enthusiasm. Here's urgent, virile and vehement playing, never too forceful, overemphatic or burdened with excessive weight. What came as a surprise was the consistent drawing out of these scores' potential for sadness and restlessness. Harnoncourt doesn't set apart the first six sym-phonies as merely diverting; unlike Abbado: their bittersweet ambiguities and apparent affectations of anxiety here acquire a greater significance, and the cycle, as a whole, a greater continuity.

Up to a point, the darker, more serious Schu-bert that emerges here, derives from the type of sound Harnoncourt fashions from his orches-tra; not least, the lean string tone and incisive brass. And maybe, up to a point, from the cor-rections: Harnoncourt refers to the manuscripts as often being 'harsher and more abrupt in tone [than the printed editions], juxtaposing extreme dynamic contrasts', though you can't help feel-ing that contrasts in general have been given a helping hand. Trios are mostly much slower than the urgent minuets/scherzos that frame them (with pauses in between the two). And Schubert's less vigorous moments are very noticeable as such, and are inflected with vary-ing degrees of melancholy. It's uncanny how the string playing, in particular, often suggests a feeling of isolation (along with the sparing vibrato is an equally sparing use of that enliven-ing facility: *staccato*). The *Unfinished* Sym-phony's first movement is a stark, harrowing experience (yet it remains a well-tempered musical one: gestures are never exaggerated); the opening is as cold as the grave itself; the sec-ond subject knows its song is short-lived. In both movements, the elucidation and balance of texture can only be described as masterly: just listen to the trombones casting shadows in both codas. This, then, is as seriously pondered, coherent and penetrating a view of the complete cycle as we have had. Whether or not you feel Harnoncourt focuses too much on Schubert's darker side, you have to marvel at his ability to realise his vision. The recorded sound offers that inimitable Concertgebouw blend of the utmost clarity and wide open spaces.

Symphonies Nos 3, 5 & 6   🄷
Royal Philharmonic Orchestra / Sir Thomas Beecham
EMI Great Recordings of the Century 566984-2
(78' · ADD) Recorded 1955-9   Ⓜ❍❍❍

Beecham was well into his seventies when he made these recordings with the Royal Philharmonic, the orchestra he had founded in 1946. His lightness of touch, his delight in the beauty of the sound he was summoning, the directness of his approach to melody, and his general high spirits will all dominate our memory of these performances. But listening again, we may be reminded that Beecham could equally well dig deep into the darker moments of these works. Schubert's elation was rarely untroubled and the joy is often compounded by its contrast with pathos – Beecham had that balance off to a tee. It should be noted that he doesn't take all the marked repeats and he doctored some passages he considered over-repetitive. However, these recordings may also serve as a reminder of the wonderful heights of musicianship that his players achieved, as in the trio of the Third and effective plans they are, and how marvellous it has been to re-encounter Wand's sublimely wrought rubato); as does the conductor's views on repeats (taken in the Eighth's first movement, but not in the Ninth's outer movements).

It's pointless to speculate whether the small details that *have* changed (for example, the now truly *pianissimo* second subject of the Eighth's first movement) are due to Wand's further four years' thought on the works, or changes brought about by the Berlin orchestra's own musical collective, or just 'another time, another place'. Maybe a bit of all three. If you already own the Hamburg recordings, there's no need to rush out to buy this. If you don't, this set is an obvious choice. Wand's Schubert is informed by a very special devotion, wisdom and insight, and a very individual spirit of adventure.

Schubert Symphony No 8
Mendelssohn Symphony No 4
Philharmonia Orchestra / Giuseppe Sinopoli
DG Masters 445 514-2GMA (62' · DDD) Recorded 1983　　　　　　　　　　　　　　　Ⓕ**O**

Giuseppe Sinopoli made an auspicious choice of repertory for this, his first recording as Principal Conductor with the Philharmonia. It was this coupling which Guido Cantelli chose for one of his last recordings, made with the Philharmonia in the palmy days of the mid-fifties. Enough to say that Sinopoli could hardly have provided a sharper contrast in everything except the quality of the playing of the Philharmonia: this recording shines out as a superb example of Philharmonia refinement, responsiveness and virtuosity, a tribute not just to Sinopoli's own intensive work but to the standards he had built up largely with the help of his compatriot predecessor, Riccardo Muti.

In a sense with readings of both works so sharply individual as Sinopoli's no comparisons are strictly relevant. Where Cantelli for example made a glowing impact by his simple, natural way with every single movement, Sinopoli

SCHUBERT SYMPHONY NO 8, 'UNFINISHED' – IN BRIEF

Philharmonia Orchestra / Guido Cantelli
EMI 574801-2 (76' · ADD)　　　　　　　　Ⓜ
A deeply moving, much revered performance, which shares a disc with these same artists' towering versions of Schumann's Fourth Symphony and Mendelssohn's *Italian*.

Berlin PO / André Cluytens
Testament SBT1182 (68' · ADD)　　　　　　Ⓕ
Previously only released in France, Cluytens's remarkably trenchant *Unfinished* with the Berliners from 1960 is without a doubt one of the most gripping from the early stereo era.

Berlin PO / Wilhelm Furtwängler
DG ⑥ 474 030-2GOM6 (7 hr 15')　　•　　Ⓑ
A legendary partnership caught on the wing in an unforgettable concert relay from February 1952. Part of an unmissable six-CD survey of live Furtwängler recordings from 1944-53.

Cleveland Orchestra / George Szell
Sony SBK48268 (70' · ADD)　　　　　　　Ⓑ
Szell and his magnificent Ohio band offer as taut and stylish an *Unfinished* as any. With a majestic *Great* C major as the coupling, this budget-priced reissue represents superb value for money.

Philharmonia Orchestra / Sir Adrian Boult
BBC Legends BBCL 4039-2 (75' · ADD)　·　Ⓜ
Boult's radiant, touchingly unforced *Unfinished* emanates from a Royal Albert Hall Prom in July 1964. BBC Legends' valuable portrait of this great conductor also contains works by Bizet, Ravel and Sibelius.

Concertgebouw Orchestra / Leonard Bernstein
DG 427 645-2GH (57' · DDD)　　　　　　Ⓕ
Bernstein's is a deeply personal reading, surprisingly fleet in the opening *Allegro moderato*, provocatively unhurried in the *Andante con moto*. Fortunately, the Amsterdam orchestra is with him all the way.

Philharmonia Orchestra / Giuseppe Sinopoli
DG 445 514-2GMA (62' · DDD)　　　　　Ⓕ**O**
Sinopoli's début disc as the Philharmonia's principal conductor brought this individual and searching *Unfinished*, full of sharp contrasts and exquisitely played.

Berlin PO / Günter Wand
RCA 09026 68314-2 (85' · DDD)　　　　Ⓜ**O**
A penetrating and lofty *Unfinished* from a much-missed maestro. Recorded live in Berlin during March 1995, this is inspired music-making. The Berlin Philharmonic play like angels for their veteran guest conductor.

directs readings which in almost every bar call attention to unexpected points. Undoubtedly they will be controversial, both in the interpretative style and often in the very choice of speeds. What makes both performances intensely revealing, exhilarating and refreshing is the extraordinary intensity which compels attention from the very first note. Some may find the moulding of the great second subject theme on the cellos in the *Unfinished* too calculated. Others may feel that he moulds too much in the very slow account of the third movement of the *Italian*. Elsewhere the glow of commitment alongside such playing is intense.

Sinopoli's view of the *Unfinished*, from the menacing *pianissimo* of the opening motif onwards, makes the point strongly that this is a progress from darkness to light. The tragedy of the B minor first movement could hardly be contrasted more strongly against the ethereal glow of fulfilment in the second. The contrasting moods of the *Italian* Symphony are sharply etched too. In the first movement Sinopoli sets a dangerously fast speed, but unlike most rivals he sacrifices neither clarity, precision nor detail with delectable pointing in the rapid triplets and with subtle phrasing and shading of dynamic to match even Karajan (DG) at his slower speed. Both the middle two movements find Sinopoli adopting slow speeds and moulded phrasing, with the Pilgrims' March made weighty and melancholy in its beauty, the third movement bringing fairyland horn calls in the Trio. The final *Saltarello* is bitingly brilliant with Sinopoli at the end emphasising in a final thrust Mendelssohn's refusal to allow the minor key to resolve into the major, leaving a bitter tang.

Symphony No 9[a]. **Wagner** Siegfried Idyll[b]
Vienna Philharmonic Orchestra / Sir Georg Solti
Decca Legends 460 311-2DM (74' · DDD)
Recorded [b]1965 & [a]1981　　　　(M)**000**

Solti's Ninth is likely to bowl you over when you first hear it: you somehow don't expect him to be such a mellow and smiling Schubertian. The VPO playing has great vitality too. As a performance it's quite glorious and can hold its own with any of its rivals, and in terms of recorded sound it's amazing (one of Decca's very best, and in the demonstration class, still). In its LP format, it was notable for its wide-ranging dynamics, its warmth and real 'presence'. The sound is, indeed, full-bodied and well-defined. Yet the CD remaster is undoubtedly superior: the instruments seem positively tangible. Initially, you may wonder whether the higher transfer level of the CD is responsible for the greater sense of immediacy but adjusting the controls still leaves the CD sounding firmer, more 'present' and richer. Altogether a most impressive disc and though one might quibble about the balance (rather forward in the concert hall), there's no doubt that this is a winner.

Schubert Symphony No 9 in C, 'Great', D944[c]　　[H]
Cherubini Anacréon – Overture[a]
Cornelius The Barber of Baghdad – Overture[b]
[a]**Royal Philharmonic Orchestra;** [bc]**BBC Symphony Orchestra / Sir Adrian Boult**
BBC Legends/IMG Artists [b]mono BBCL4072-2
(72' · ADD) Recorded live [a]1963; [b]1954, [c]1969　　(F)

Schubert's *Great* C major Symphony was a work close to Boult's heart. He recorded it for the first time in 1934, for the last in 1972, and in between came countless performances. This one was at rather a noisy Prom in 1969, when he returned to the BBC Symphony Orchestra from which, he had been severed by the mercilessness of BBC bureaucracy.

Among much else, he was a supreme master of the orchestra, attentive to his players without ever losing sight of a work's architecture. In this performance there's his absolute security of tempo, which doesn't mean stiffness. The finale is steady without inflexibility; the *scherzo* drives along brightly; and the *Andante* moves inexorably towards its terrifying climax, with a movingly sad cello aftermath. This is vintage Boult. So, in their own ways, are the two overtures.

Symphony No 10 in D, D936a (realised Newbould). Symphonic fragments – D, D615; D, D708a (orch Newbould)
Scottish Chamber Orchestra / Sir Charles Mackerras
Hyperion CDA67000 (54' · DDD)　　　　(F)

Someone will have to find another name for Schubert's *Unfinished* Symphony (the B minor) before long. In fact there are six unfinished Schubert symphonies: there are two whole movement expositions for D615, torsos of three movements and a nearly complete *Scherzo* for D708a, and enough sketch material for Brian Newbould to attempt a complete conjectural reconstruction of D936a, the symphony Schubert began writing in the last weeks of his life. Inevitably some will ask, why bother? Well, apart from the increase in the sense of wonder at Schubert's sheer productivity, there's some wonderful music here, especially the slow movement of D936a, desolate and warmly consoling by turns. As a whole, D936a suggests that, even at this late stage, Schubert was still thinking in terms of new developments. The concluding third movement, contrapuntally fusing elements of scherzo and finale, is like nothing else in Schubert – or any other composer of the classical period. Newbould has had to do some guessing here, but the results are mostly strikingly authoritative. The performances carry conviction and the recordings are atmospheric yet detailed. Altogether a fascinating disc.

Additional recommendation

Complete Symphonies
Academy of St Martin in the Fields / Marriner

Philips ⑥ 470 886-2PB6 (367' · DDD)　　　⑤ⓑ

Marriner's Schubert is light on its feet, full of sprung rhythms and gracefully turned phrases. His set can be confidently recommended if you respond to a more agile, 'modern' (though not authentic) approach.

Octet in F, D803

Octet
Gaudier Ensemble (Richard Hosford *cl* Robin O'Neill *bn* Jonathan Williams *hn* Marieke Blankestijn, Lesley Hatfield *vns* Iris Juda *va* Christoph Marks *vc* Stephen Williams *db*)
Hyperion CDA67339 (60' · DDD)　　　Ⓕ⊙⊙

An intriguing point arises in the second movement. It's meant to be *Adagio* but the Gaudier pace it fairly swiftly, offering a reminder that one edition marks it *Andante un poco mosso*. The Vienna Octet of 1957 followed this instruction, but its 1990 counterpart preferred something slower. The Gaudier, though, are anything but perfunctory. Their line is curvaceous and malleable with a dynamic range that contains many shades of softness. Engineer Tony Faulkner has helped by using the ambience of the Henry Wood Hall to create both a blend and a distinctiveness of timbre. There's a glow to the sound that other versions don't have.

The Gaudier's control over the grading of tonal intensity draws attention to the many passages in this work that are written *piano* or *pianissimo*; and where leavened by hairpin accents, stabbing *sforzandos* and even *fortissimos* they supply necessary impact without being crude. If there's one movement that encapsulates all that's striking about this performance, then it's the fourth – an *Andante* with seven variations. Here's an example of how these musicians balance themselves, and how they've thought about the different facets of the music. Were he alive today, this recording might even persuade Schubert scholar Maurice JE Brown to change his mind about the seventh variation, which he described as 'a distasteful episode'.

Octet. Minuet and Finale in F, D72
Vienna Octet; Vienna Wind Soloists
Decca Eclipse 448 715-2DEC (72' · DDD) Recorded 1990　　　⑤ⓑ⊙⊙

Over the years Decca has made a speciality of recording the Schubert Octet in Vienna, and this budget-priced reissue by the Vienna Octet, captured in the glowing acoustics of the Mozartsaal of the Vienna Konzerthaus, and ideally balanced by Christopher Raeburn, is most winning. There's an enticing warmth to the opening *Adagio*, and the central movements – the *Scherzo* bustling with vitality and the deliciously played *Andante con variazioni* – are unforgettable. Then comes the lovingly Schubertian *Menuetto*, and after an arresting *tremolando* introduction, the joyfully bucolic finale rounds things off in sparkling fashion. At its price, this Vienna version is in a class of its own. As a bonus we're offered the *Minuet and Finale*, D72, two engaging miniatures from the composer's youth, nicely elegant in the hands of the Vienna Wind Soloists. The demonstration-standard recording makes this an unmissable bargain.

String Quintet in C, D956

Schubert String Quintet in C, D956 **Beethoven** Grosse Fuge in B flat, Op 133
Hagen Quartet (Lukas Hagen, Rainer Schmidt *vns* Veronika Hagen *va* Clemens Hagen *vc*) **Heinrich Schiff** *vc*
DG 439 774-2GH (68' · DDD) Recorded 1991[a] and 1993[b]　　　Ⓕ⊙⊙

By following Boccherini in using two cellos instead of two violas for his String Quintet, Schubert increased the potential for greater textural contrast. Moreover, the dichotomy between the tragic perspective and Viennese gaiety in the Quintet, so evident in much of Schubert's greatest music, generates an especially potent dramatic force.

The Hagen Quartet's performance of the first movement, which presents remarkably clear textural detail, is broad and expansive. The Hagen, unlike the Alban Berg Quartet, include the exposition repeat in a movement that lasts almost 20 minutes. Perhaps as a consequence, they play the *Adagio* second movement at an unusually fast tempo. However, through breathtaking dynamic control in the first section, passionate intensity in the second, and engaging spontaneity of the ornamentation in the final section, the Hagen achieve an expression that's powerfully compelling.

The second half of the Quintet is often treated as a period of emotional relief from the profound concentration of the first two movements. Startlingly, the Hagen maintain the tension with violent textural and dynamic contrast in the *Scherzo*, and distinctively varied registral sonority in the Trio. The finale, in which the Hagen effectively balance the music's charming Hungarian flavour with its more sinister touches, provides an arresting conclusion

The Hagen's account of Beethoven's *Grosse Fuge* is polished and sensitive and, though it may lack the raw excitement of the Alban Berg's live version, it vividly conveys the difference between Beethoven's and Schubert's compositional means. The Hagen's is an outstanding disc, in which exceptional performances, that challenge the finest alternatives, are complemented by superb recording.

String Quintet[a]. Symphony No 5[b]　　　Ⓗ
[a]Isaac Stern, [a]Alexander Schneider *vns* [a]Milton Katims *va* [a]Paul Tortelier *vc* [b]Prades Festival Orchestra / Pablo Casals [a]*vc*
Sony Classical Casals Edition mono SMK58992

(76' · ADD) Recorded 1952-3   Ⓜ**OOO**

⌘ This should have an in-built fail-safe against hasty consumption, in that their interpretative ingredients are so rich, varied and unpredictable that to experience it all at once is to invite mental and emotional exhaustion. Casals is the lynchpin. A charismatic presence, he embraces everything with the passion of a devoted horticulturist tending his most precious flowers, and that his love extended beyond the realms of music to mankind itself surely enriched his art even further. The most celebrated Prades recording ever is still the Stern/Casals/Tortelier reading of the C major Quintet, a masterful traversal graced with elastic tempos, songful phrasing, appropriate rhetorical emphases (especially in the first and second movements) and fabulous string playing. The coupling is a 'first release' of Schubert's Fifth Symphony, recorded in 1953 – a warm, keenly inflected performance, jaunty in the outer movements and with an adoring, broadly paced *Adagio*. One presumes that it has been held from previous view only because of a few minor executant mishaps. It's certainly well worth hearing. The transfer of the Quintet reveals itself as marginally warmer but occasionally less well-focused than previous incarnations. Still, the original was no sonic blockbuster to start with but this shouldn't deter you from hearing this disc.

String Quintet in C, D956
The Lindsays (Peter Cropper, Ronald Birks *vns* Roger Bigley *va* Bernard Gregor-Smith *vc*) **Douglas Cummings** *vc*
ASV CDDCA537 (58' · DDD) Recorded 1985   Ⓕ

Schubert's sublime C major Quintet is eminently well served on disc. With this version one is immediately struck by its naturalness. You are left with the impression that you're eavesdropping on music-making in the intimacy of a private home. Although there's plenty of vigour and power, there's nothing of the glamourised and beautified sonority that some great quartets give us. (The two cellos, incidentally, are both by the same maker, Francesco Rugeri of Cremona.) They observe the first-movement exposition repeat, and the effortlessness of their approach doesn't preclude intellectual strength. The first movement surely refutes the notion that Schubert possessed an incomplete grasp of sonata form, an idea prompted by the alleged discursiveness of some of the sonatas. This is surely an amazing achievement even by the exalted standards of his day, and The Lindsays do it justice, as indeed they do the ethereal *Adagio*. Here they effectively convey the sense of it appearing motionless, suspended as it were, between reality and dream, yet at the same time never allowing it to become static. The quartet sound isn't as full-bodied or richly burnished as that produced by many rivals, lacking quite the splendour or richness given to the best sound-

recordings, but they have what can only be called a compelling wisdom. Their reading must be placed at the top of the list and for many readers will be an obvious first choice.

Additional recommendations

Alban Berg Quartet with **Heinrich Schiff** *vc*
EMI Great Recordings of the Century 566890-2
(48' · ADD)   Ⓜ
  A classic recording that still takes some beating. The music floats effortlessly in the outside sections, and the effect is mesmeric, and in the finale the players find just the right combination of understatement and swagger.

Coupled with: Schoenberg Verklärte Nacht, Op 4 Ⓗ
(orig version) **Hollywood Quartet** (Felix Slatkin, Paul Shure *vns* Paul Robyn *va* Eleanor Aller *vc*) **Alvin Dinkin** *va* **Kurt Reher** *vc*
Testament mono SBT1031 (73' · ADD)   Ⓕ
  In the 1950s the authors of *The Record Guide* spoke of the Schubert as 'one of the best [LPs] in the discography of chamber music'; and so it remains. The Schoenberg, too, is superb.

Piano Quintet in A, 'Trout', D667

Piano Quintet in A, 'Trout'[a]. Quartet in G, D96[b]
[b]**Wolfgang Schulz** *fl* [a]**Gerhard Hetzel** *vn* **Wolfram Christ** *va* **Georg Faust** *vc* [a]**Alois Posch** *db* [b]**Göran Söllscher** *gtr* [a]**James Levine** *pf*
DG 431 783-2GH (65' · DDD) Recorded 1990   Ⓕ**O**

Schubert composed the *Trout* Quintet in his early twenties for a group of amateur musicians in the town of Steyr in Upper Austria, then noted for its fine fishing and keen fishermen. The Quintet, like all great occasional music, stands as strongly as ever today, with its freshly bubbling invention and sunny melodiousness. In the present version by James Levine and members of the Vienna Phil, the unity of ensemble and common sense of purpose are most compelling. Both acoustically and musically, their performance has an affecting intimacy. Particularly noticeable are the warmth of Faust's cello playing within the texture and the heavenly phrasing of the orchestra's leader, Gerhard Hetzel, who was tragically killed in a walking accident in 1993. The piano is attractively balanced as a member of the ensemble, rather than as a soloist, which makes the variation fourth movement unusually appealing. Like most of their rivals, this group doesn't repeat the exposition in the finale. A rarity has been included which ensures that any Schubertian will want this issue in their collection. The so-called Guitar Quartet, D96, is an arrangement of a trio by Wenzel Matiegka which Schubert made in 1814. It's a charming work, presumably intended for domestic use, whose grace and elegance are highly infectious in this delightful performance.

Piano Quintet in A, 'Trout', D667[a]. String Trios –
B flat, D581; B flat, D111a
Members of the **Leipzig Quartet** (Andreas Seidel vn
Ivo Bauer va Matthias Moosdorf vc) [a]**Christian
Zacharias** pf [a]**Christian Ockert** db
Dabringhaus und Grimm MDG307 0625-2
(66' · DDD)   Ⓕ❍❍

This *Trout* must surely be one of the very best
versions of this much-recorded work – the
sound is wonderfully natural, and so is the performance. You get the impression that here was
an occasion when everything 'clicked', giving
the playing a friendly, relaxed feeling that's just
right for this carefree piece. Zacharias has the
knack of making even the simplest phrase sound
expressive, and the strings, without any exaggeration, produce the most beautiful tonal shadings. All five players, too, have an impressive
sense of line; the phrasing and points of emphasis are balanced so that Schubert's expansive
designs are projected compellingly. If the *Trout*
shows a Schubertian spaciousness, his one completed String Trio is unusually compact.
Another distinguished feature is the florid,
Spohr-like elegance of much of the violin writing – Andreas Seidel is splendidly stylish and
confident. This is another very fine performance, emphasising the predominating gentle
lyricism, but with plenty of vigour and panache
when required. The String Trio fragment, less
than two minutes, continues the same, 'let's
hear everything' approach; it's a sketch for what
subsequently became the comparatively familiar
B flat Quartet, D112.

Schubert Piano Quintet in A, 'Trout'[a] **Mozart** Piano
Quartet in G minor, K478
Thomas Zehetmair vn **Tabea Zimmermann** va
Richard Duven vc [a]**Peter Riegelbauer** db **Alfred
Brendel** pf
Philips 446 001-2PH (75' · DDD) Recorded 1994
                                              Ⓕ❍❍

Brendel is the lynchpin here, and, as ever, balances heart and mind with innate good taste.
Time and again you find yourself overhearing
detail that might otherwise have passed for
nothing: every modulation tells; every phrase of
dialogue has been polished, pondered and carefully considered. And yet it *is* a dialogue, with
the loose-limbed Thomas Zehetmair leading
his supremely accomplished colleagues through
Schubert's delightful five-tier structure. The
Scherzo and *Allegro giusto* frolic within the
bounds of propriety (some will favour an extra
shot of animal vigour), whereas the first, second
and fourth movements are rich in subtle – as
opposed to fussy – observations. The recording,
too, is exceedingly warm, with only the occasional want of inner detail to bar unqualified
enthusiasm. Philips, as ever, achieves a well-
rounded, almost tangible piano tone.
    Mozart's G minor Quartet makes for an unex-
pected, though instructive, coupling, following
the *Trout*. Here again there's much to learn and
enjoy, especially in terms of phrasal dovetailing

SCHUBERT PIANO QUINTET, 'TROUT' – IN BRIEF

Christian Zacharias; Leipzig Quartet
Dabringhaus und Grimm MDG307 0625-2
(66' · DDD)   Ⓕ❍❍
Beautiful string tone and glistening piano
work are just the surface trappings of a fine,
musicianly account of Schubert's evergreen
masterpiece, caught in excellent sound.

Levine; Hetzel; Christ; Faust; Posch
DG 431 783-2GH (65' · DDD)   Ⓕ❍
A slightly more intense performance, but still
with plenty of charm, the fairly close-focus
sound placing the listener in among the
musicians. Its coupling with the rare Guitar
Quartet, D96, makes this an especially attractive issue.

Clifford Curzon; members of the Vienna Octet
Decca 417 59-2DM (71' · ADD)   Ⓜ❍
Curzon's genial piano playing and the sweet-
toned playing of Willi Boskovsky and his
colleagues ideally complement each other
in this classic recording. The dryish mono
sound adds to the intimate charm.

Ax; Frank; Young; Ma; Meyer
Sony Classical SK61964 (65' · DDD)   Ⓕ
A sprightly yet genial performance, bubbling
with energy. Though clearly individual
players, they evidently enjoy each other's
company and working as a team.

András Schiff; Hagen Quartet
Decca Ovation 458 608-2 (75' · DDD)   Ⓜ
After a tension-filled opening, this proves to
be another fresh reading, most delightful in
the bouncing lightness of the *scherzo*.

**Brendel; Zehetmair; Zimmermann; Duven;
Riegelbauer**
Philips 446 001-2PH (75' · DDD)   Ⓕ❍❍
Despite a rather languid start, the performance becomes quite forthright – serious
rather than relaxed – yet it's also persuasive
and engaging.

Jenö Jandó; Kodaly Quartet; Istvan Toth
Naxos 8 550658 (53' · DDD)   Ⓢ❍
Though the sound is not quite in the same
class as the full-price versions, with the piano
a touch prominent at the expense of the
strings, this is a charming performance and
excellent value at the price.

**Clifford Curzon; Amadeus Quartet; James
Edward Merrett**
BBC Legends BBCL4009-2 (82' · ADD)   Ⓜ
A joyous live performance which, despite one
or two slightly rough spots and a moment of
premature applause, rises to truly memorable
heights. Coupled with an inspired account of
the Brahms Piano Quintet.

SCHUBERT STRING QUINTET – IN BRIEF

Heinrich Schiff; Hagen Quartet
DG 439 774-2GH (68' · DDD)　　　Ⓕ**OO**
Coupled with the *Grosse Fuge*, the Hagen Quartet and Heinrich Schiff give a very fine reading, full of detail and sensitivity to texture. It's a performance that maintains a high level of intensity throughout. Very impressive.

Stern; Schneider; Katims; Tortelier; Casals
Sony Classical mono SMK58992 (76' · ADD)
　　　　　　　　　　　　　　Ⓜ**OOO**
☀ Recorded in 1952 at Casals' Prades Festival, this is one of the great Schubert Quintets, human, rich, varied and totally spontaneous. The sound is good for the age, but the sheer quality of playing soon sweeps any sonic reservations to one side. (Coupled with Schubert's Fifth Symphony conducted with charm by Casals.)

Douglas Cummings; Lindsay Quartet
ASV CDDCA537 (58' · DDD)　　　　　　Ⓕ
A fine, natural performance with an appealingly intimate sense of scale. There are some truly heavenly moments in this reading which fills the disc thanks to the first-movement repeat.

Heinrich Schiff; Alban Berg Quartet
EMI 566890-2 (48' · DDD)　　　　　　Ⓜ**OO**
Another recording featuring Heinrich Schiff and something of a modern classic. There is a wonderful ease about the playing that's very appealing. Rather short value though.

Kurt Reher; Hollywood Quartet
Testament mono SBT1031 (73' · ADD)　　Ⓕ**O**
A glorious and civilised reading from the 1950s. These musicians really get under the skin of the music and search out its passionate, beating heart. Generously coupled with Schoenberg's *Verklärte Nacht*.

Matt Haimowitz; Miró Quartet
Oxingale OX2006 (79' · DDD)　　　　　Ⓕ**O**
Coupled with Mendelssohn's last string quartet, this is a very fine modern version from one of the US's most imaginative and charismatic young cellists. Youth certainly does not preclude profundity, and these young musicians deliver a stunning performance.

Villa Musica Ensemble
Naxos 8 550388 (77' · DDD)　　　　　Ⓜ**O**
A fine, super-budget-price performance coupled with the B flat String Trio that offers some very classy chamber musicianship. Theirs is quite a dramatic reading with plenty of passion.

and elegant articulation (Brendel's opening flourish is a model of Mozartian phrase-shaping). Still, you may sometimes crave rather more in the way of *Sturm und Drang* – a fiercer, more muscular attack, most especially in the first movement. Yet there will be times when the conceptual unity and executive refinement of this performance – its articulate musicality – will more than fit the bill. Both works include their respective first movement repeats.

Piano Quintet in A, 'Trout'[a]. Adagio and Rondo concertante in F, D487
Kodály Quartet (Attila Falvay, Tamás Szabo *vns* Gábor Fias *va* János Devich *vc*) [a]**IstvánTóth** *db*
Jenö Jandó *pf*
Naxos 8 550658 (53' · DDD)　　　　Ⓢ**SO**

This disc is further proof of Naxos's impressive ability to produce outstanding recordings at an astonishingly low price. Jenö Jandó's recording of the Trout Quintet, in a version which is based on the first edition of 1829, is buoyant and vigorous. The string support from members of the Kodály Quartet and István Tóth, despite some rough edges, is generally sonorous and appropriate. Balance is good, with the piano agreeably highlighted. The result is a performance which is a most desirable acquisition. Although Schubert wrote no concertos, he did write a concertante work for piano and strings which is also included here. Notwithstanding limitations of thematic invention, the Adagio and Rondo makes an attractive coupling. Jandó's sheer enthusiasm for this music provides a compelling alternative to other full-price accounts.

Piano Quintet in A, 'Trout'[a]. Litanei, D343. Variations on 'Trockne Blumen', D802
Renaud Capueon *vn* [a]**Gérard Caussé** *va* [a]**Gautier Capueon** *vc* [a]**Alois Posch** *db* Frank Braley *pf*
Virgin Classics 545563-2 (59' · DDD)　　Ⓕ**OOO**

🌓 A memorable account of the *Trout* Quintet. This group may not project the warmth and bonhomie of the famous Curzon/Boskovsky recording, nor does it have the searching quality of the performance led by Alfred Brendel, but for verve and refinement it's hard to beat. The happy, carefree nature of the music is captured perfectly on a beautifully clear recording; it's especially notable how every detail of the double bass's very spirited contribution, is clearly heard yet with no sense that Alois Posch is 'bringing out' his part. Especially enjoyable is the *Scherzo* – a fast tempo, but finely poised, and with a subtle, effective relaxation of the trio – and the Variations. In Variation 2 Renaud Capuçon's figuration is so delicate that the viola melody can create a particularly strong expressive effect, and the following variation is just as magical – Frank Braley's demisemiquavers are quite brilliant, with a lovely, silvery tone, and the bass melody has, for once, nothing elephantine about it.

The elaborate, showy set of variations on 'Trockne Blumen' from *Die schöne Müllerin*, dating from 1824, is an unhackneyed choice of filler. It's curious that the current catalogue lists only two recordings, and one of these, like the present version, substitutes violin for the original flute. It certainly makes a virtuoso violin and piano piece, and played with the precision and delicacy that Capuçon and Braley bring to it is highly effective, though with only occasional touches of the melancholy we expect in late Schubert. After this extravagant music, the touching simplicity of the song arrangement is the more striking.

String Quartets

D18 in B flat; **D32** in C; **D36** in B flat; **D46** in C; **D68** in B flat; **D74** in D; **D87** in E flat; **D94** in D; **D103** in C minor (fragment); **D112** in B flat; **D173** in G minor; **D353** in E; **D703** in C minor (Quartettsatz); **D804** in A minor (Rosamunde); **D810** in D minor (Death and the Maiden); **D887** in G

String Quartets D87 & D804   **P**
Quatuor Mosaïques (Erich Höbarth, Andrea Bischof vns Anita Mitterer va Christophe Coin vc)
Auvidis Astrée E8580 (68' · DDD)   ⓕ**O**

This recording of the A minor Quartet, D804, was the first ever on period instruments. With unusually broad tempos, the Mosaïques consistently stresses the music's pathos, loneliness and fatalism. The Hungarian-flavoured finale is normally seen as a stoically cheerful reaction to the pain that has gone before. But here it steals in as if in a dream from the spectral close of the Minuet, the opening melody delicately floated, its off-beat accents barely flicked; where the Alban Berg brings a faintly military strut to the C sharp minor melody, the Mosaïques, suppressing any hint of swagger in the dotted rhythms, distils a doleful balletic grace.

In the *Andante* of the *Rosamunde* the Mosaïques, while slower than its rivals, never loses sight of the *gehende Bewegung*, the walking motion that underlies so many of Schubert's *andantes*. It matches its rivals in its tender, sentient phrasing, subtly flexing the pulse in response to harmonic movement. The Minuet, with its glassy, vibratoless *pianissimos*, is more eerily remote, less human in its desolation, than from the Alban Berg.

For the coupling the Mosaïques offers the early E flat Quartet, D87, written when Schubert was just 16. Not even this affectionate, considered advocacy can do much for the dull, harmonically stagnant opening movement. But the players relish the raw energy of the *Scherzo*, with its braying donkey evocations, and bring a delicious demure wit to the Rossinian second theme of the finale (0'58"). And, as in the absorbing, moving reading of the A minor Quartet, the delicacy of nuance and clarity of texture, easier

to obtain from the sparer-toned period instruments, is often revelatory. The recording is clean, vivid and immediate. An outstanding disc in every way.

String Quartets D87, D703 & D804
Belcea Quartet (Corina Belcea, Laura Samuel vns Krzysztof Chorzelski va Alasdair Tait vc)
EMI 557419-2 (73' · DDD)   ⓕ**OOO**

 'Schubert's Quartet has been performed, rather slowly in his opinion, but very purely and tenderly,' wrote Moritz von Schwind on the day D804 was premièred by the Schuppanzigh Quartet. The composer may well have reacted similarly on hearing the Belcea's first movement. It's a spacious tempo, certainly, causing some of the more energetic music – the last four bars for instance – to sound slightly ponderous. But purity and tenderness are certainly in evidence. Internal balance and intonation are exemplary, and in the songful melodic writing that dominates the whole work, Corina Belcea and her colleagues seem to have the knack of shaping each long phrase to perfection, knowing just when to intensify the vibrato or give a note extra emphasis, and when to allow the music to flow effortlessly onwards.

These fine qualities persist throughout. There may be more dramatic accounts of D703, but no other group presents its *cantabile* music in a more affecting way. The lesser work, D87, gets a charming, persuasive interpretation, but the profound and subtle way these young players engage with the later, greater music is the most impressive thing this group has done so far.

String Quartets D87[b] & D810[a]
Alban Berg Quartet (Günther Pichler, Gerhard Schulz vns Thomas Kakuska va Valentin Erben vc)
EMI 556470-2 (57' · DDD) Recorded live [a]1994, [b]1997
                                                   ⓕ
String Quartets D703 & D887
Alban Berg Quartet (Günther Pichler, Gerhard Schulz vns Thomas Kakuska va Valentin Erben vc)
EMI 556471-2 (60' · DDD) Recorded live 1997 ⓕ**OO**

The Alban Berg Quartet's policy of making recordings at concert performances certainly produces impressive results: interpretations that avoid any feeling of routine or of being overcareful. What impresses above all is the flexibility and sensitivity of these performances. In the first movement of D887 the Alban Berg, by subtly drawing our attention to the precise emotional colour of all Schubert's magical harmonic shifts, finds a touching, intimate quality within the grand design. And it's certainly an advantage for any group performing this quartet to be able to produce such a magnificent *tremolando* – whether it's the forest murmurs of the first movement or the Gothic shuddering of the *Andante*'s middle section.

The G major Quartet is the outstanding performance on these discs, but *Death and the Maiden* isn't far behind, particularly the *con fuoco Scherzo* and finale. There are a few places, where Schubert is straightforwardly tuneful (in D703 and in the outer movements of D87, especially) where one wishes Günther Pichler would play in a simpler, more direct manner. The Busch Quartet's 1930s recordings of D810 and D887 are smoother, less emphatic than that of modern groups, and this enables it to convey the emotional nuances, particularly of the D minor Quartet, in a more inward and profound way. And the two quartets are available (with some repeats missing) on a single CD. But it's a measure of the Alban Berg Quartet's exceptional quality to realise that it's in the same league, with the same sense of players totally absorbed in the music. The recorded sound is immeasurably more vivid and lifelike.

String Quartets D703[a], D804[b], D810[a] & D887[b]
Quartetto Italiano (Paolo Borciani, Elisa Pegreffi vns Piero Farulli va Franco Rossi vc)
Philips Duo ② 446 163-2PM2 (142' · ADD) Recorded [a]1965, [b]1976-7   Ⓜ

The Italians' playing has freshness, affection, firm control and above all authority to a degree that no relative newcomer can match. It's notable not only for the highest standards of ensemble, intonation and blend, but also for its imaginative insights; these attributes readily apply to the music-making on this Duo reissue, particularly in the slow movements. Indeed, the players' progress through the wonderful set of variations in the *Andante con moto*, which reveals the *Death and the Maiden* Quartet's association with the famous Schubert song of that name, has unforgettable intensity (it's a grand conception packed with memorable detail – the evocation of terror in the early stages of the first movement coda has never been bettered).

The comparable *Andante* of No 13, with its lovely *Rosamunde* theme – which is approached here in a relaxed, leisurely manner – is held together with a similar (almost imperceptible) sureness of touch. When this work was originally issued, the first-movement exposition repeat was cut in order to get the quartet complete on to a single LP side. Here it has been restored.

Finest of all is the great No 15, a work of epic scale. The first movement alone runs to nearly 23 minutes, and the players' masterly grip over the many incidents that make up the *Allegro molto moderato* is effortless. For an encore we're given No 12, a piece on a smaller scale, but here presented with a comparable hushed intensity of feeling. This, like No 14, was recorded in 1965 and the textures are leaner than on the others, with a fractional edge on *fortissimos*. Nevertheless, the ear soon adjusts when the playing is as remarkable as this. The other recordings have more body, and a fine presence. The CD transfers throughout are excellent.

Piano Trios

Piano Trios[a] – B flat, D28 (Sonata in one movement); B flat, D898; E flat, D929. Notturno in E flat, D897[b]. String Trios[b] – B flat, D471; B flat, D581
[a]**Beaux Arts Trio** (Menahem Pressler pf Daniel Guilet vn Bernard Greenhouse vc); [b]**Grumiaux Trio** (Arthur Grumiaux vn Georges Janzer va Eva Czako vc)
Philips Duo ② 438 700-2PM2 (127' · ADD) Recorded 1966-9   Ⓜ●

These performances are polished, yet the many solo contributions from each of the players emerge with a strong personality. The Beaux Arts cellist brings lovely phrasing and a true simplicity of line, so right for Schubert – memorably in the lovely slow movement melody of the Trio No 2 in E flat. In addition to the great piano trios (B flat, D898 and E flat, D929) the set includes the extremely personable, very early Sonata in B flat, D28, where the lyrical line already has the unmistakable character of its young composer. Also included is the *Notturno*, D897, a raptly emotive short piece played here with a remarkable depth of feeling that recalls the gentle intensity of the glorious slow movement of the String Quintet. The recording is naturally balanced, although a little dry in the treble. Of the two rarer string trios, also early works, the four-movement Trio, D581, is totally infectious, with that quality of innocence that makes Schubert's music stand apart. Such persuasive advocacy and vivid recording can't fail to give the listener great pleasure.

Piano Trios – B flat, D898; E flat, D929. Sonata in A minor, D821, 'Arpeggione'. Notturno in E flat, D897
Yuuko Shiokawa vn **Miklos Perényi** vc **András Schiff** pf
Teldec ② 0630-13151-2 (127' · DDD)   Ⓕ●●

This set begins with an outstanding performance of the *Arpeggione* Sonata. The recording is clear and spacious, and the outer movements have an effortless sense of momentum that isn't too inflexible to allow for some expressive rubato and pointing of the phrases. There's no hint in Perényi's playing that this is a difficult work for the cello, and he produces a most beautiful, warm, serene tone for the *Adagio*. Schiff's special feeling for Schubert is apparent even in the most subsidiary details of the piano part and particularly in the more dominating roles of the trios and the *Notturno*.

These three well-matched players find exactly the right tone and feeling. In the first Allegro of the B flat Trio the superior recording helps them to convey the music's grandeur and the following Andante is played with a flowing, evocative style. Shiokawa's clear-toned, elegant violin playing is certainly a great asset here. In the Notturno, too, a flowing tempo doesn't spoil the tranquillity of the opening melody, but allows the contrasting episode to emerge triumphantly.

Shiokawa and Perényi seem sometimes to be a

little polite and decorous in the monumental E flat Trio Schiff, but their interpretation certainly doesn't lack in vitality or variety. The finale in this performance lasts nearly 20 minutes: the players have gone back to the original version of the movement – Schubert made cuts when preparing the trio for publication. If you're an admirer of Schubert's 'heavenly length' then you'll hear it as the true culmination of one of his greatest instrumental works.

Piano Trio in E flat, D929
Florestan Trio (Susan Tomes pf Anthony Marwood vn Richard Lester vc)
Hyperion CDA67347 (58' · DDD)　　　Ⓕ**OO**

This profound, yet still often light-hearted, E flat Trio was written in the same month (November) that Schubert completed *Winterreise*. We are instantly reminded of this in the Florestan's eloquent and aptly paced account of the C minor *Andante con moto*, with what Richard Wigmore describes as its 'stoical trudging gait'. Its essential melancholy is gently caught, first by the cellist, Richard Lester, and then equally touchingly by the pianist, Susan Tomes. The dramatically rhythmic opening of the first movement could almost be by Beethoven, but once again these players show themselves to be completely within the Schubertian sensibility and catch perfectly the atmosphere of the more important lyrical motif, first heard on the cello (in bars 15 and 16), which is to dominate the movement alongside the engaging repeated-note figure (so delicately articulated by the piano).

They set a winningly jaunty mood for the finale, which is maintained whenever the main theme reappears, even though, as always with late Schubert, much happens to vary the music's mood and atmosphere. Another superb performance then from the Florestans, penetrating, yet full of spirited spontaneity, and in spite of the moments of sadness, much Schubertian bonhomie. The recording is completely lifelike and very well balanced.

Works for Piano Duet

Divertissements – à la hongroise, D818; sur des　　Ⓟ
motifs originaux français, D823
Andreas Staier, Alexei Lubimov fp duet
Teldec 0630-17113-2 (66' · DDD)　　　Ⓔ**OO**

Schubert's *Divertissement à la hongroise*, his most flamboyant essay in the Hungarian vernacular style, has always overshadowed the *Divertissement* on French themes. Yet the less favoured work is in some ways the more compelling. Its profoundly un-divertimento-like first movement has a haunting, quintessentially Schubertian second theme and one of the composer's most turbulent and tonally audacious developments. The *Andantino*, a set of variations on a glum little theme that sounds more plausibly

French than anything else in the work, is transfigured by its ravishing final variation in the major; and the finale is a sprawling, colourful rondo. Using a fine copy by Christopher Clarke of an 1826 Graf instrument, Staier and Lubimov give performances which, in poetry, *élan* and sheer relish have never been surpassed. One immediate advantage of a fortepiano in this music is the way it clarifies the textures, especially in the bass regions. Then there's the unique array of colours available through the use of no fewer than five pedals – the harp-like sonorities of the *una corda* pedal, for instance, or the 'bassoon' pedal, with its buzzing lower strings. The instrument's *coup de grâce* is its so-called Turkish pedal, attached to bass drum, bells and cymbals, which the players unleash with swashbuckling effect. If you're a sceptic about period performance, then these hugely enjoyable performances should convert you.

Sonata for Piano Duet in C, D812, 'Grand Duo'. Eight Variations in A flat, D813. Trois marches militaires, D733
Daniel Barenboim, Radu Lupu pf duet
Teldec 0630-17146-2 (77' · DDD) Recorded 1993　Ⓕ**O**

One might expect this combination of artists playing Schubert to produce winning results, and so it does. Rarely will you hear duet playing of such refined elegance and multicoloured animation. Here, the playing is vivid and glamorous; the dynamic and colouristic range of Barenboim's and Lupu's performances suggests a public environment. After the spirited brio of the familiar *Marches militaires*, the remainder of the disc contains music of greater seriousness and architectural breadth. The Variations in A flat are beautifully played, with subtle and discerning pianism. The largest work on this disc is the C major Sonata: here it runs to 43 minutes, longer than any of Schubert's solo sonatas. It can reasonably be classed alongside Schubert's two other late masterpieces in C, the *Great* Symphony and the String Quintet. The *Grand Duo* is symphonic in scope and expression, although the writing is innately pianistic. The fine detail of Barenboim's and Lupu's account, their diversity of colour and attack and their voicing of melodic and inner lines, suggests an image of suitably orchestral depth and variety. Furthermore, the surface gloss of these performances is underpinned by the most crystalline lucidity and poetry. The recording is excellent.

Piano Sonatas

D157 in E; D279 in C; D459 in E; D537 in A minor; D557 in A flat; D566 in E minor; D568 in E flat; D571 in F sharp minor; D575 in B; D613 in C; D625 in F minor; D664 in A; D784 in A minor; D840 in C (Relique); D845 in A minor; D850 in D; D894 in G; D958 in C minor; D959 in A; D960 in B flat

Piano Sonatas – E, D157; G, D894. Die schöne
Müllerin – Der Müller und der Bach (arr Liszt, S565)
Arcadi Volodos pf
Sony Classical SK89647 (64' · DDD)   Ⓕ**O**

Here is irrefutable proof of Arcadi Volodos's
genius and versatility. Naturally, lovers of long-
cherished recordings by Schubertians of the
stature of Schnabel, Kempff, Pollini and Brendel will hesitate, equating Volodos's sheen and
perfection with an external glory rather than an
interior poetic truth. But such witnesses for the
prosecution will find themselves silenced by an
empathy with Schubert's spirit so total that it
would be extraordinary in a pianist of any age,
let alone one still in his twenties.

The jubilant burst of scales and arpeggios that
launch the E major Sonata, D157, are given
with a deftness and unforced eloquence that are
pure Volodos, while the *Andante*'s sighing chromaticism and surprise modulations have a tonal
translucence that will make lesser mortals weep
with envy. But it's in the G major Sonata, D894,
that epitome of Schubertian lyricism, that Volodos erases all possible doubts. His opening has
an unforgettable stillness and mystery, his vel-
vet-tipped sonority and seamless *legato* a reminder that Schubert's vocal and instrumental
inspiration were for the most part one and the
same. For Volodos and for his listeners this is a
true dance of the gods. The recordings are as
flawless as the playing.

Piano Sonata in E flat, D568, Moments musicaux,
D780
Mitsuko Uchida pf
Philips 470 164-2PH (68' · DDD)   Ⓕ**O**

This is a magical re-creation of the E flat
Sonata, D568. Let's not make an exaggerated
claim for the piece: it comes near the beginning
of Schubert's 12 completed piano sonatas, and
the later ones are played more often because
they're greater. But this one is an enchantment,
and weighing in at 31 minutes, as it does here, it
sits proudly as the first of his grand four-movement sonatas, purposeful and confident in the
space it makes for itself. How characteristic of
Uchida to make you want to celebrate the music
first of all. She inhabits it completely, and her
preferred Steinway for Schubert, and this
recording of it – at the Musikverein in Vienna,
in the main auditorium – are at one with her
endeavour, perfectly judged in what they bring
to it, part of the focus. In the *Moments musicaux*,
however, it's possible to question the weight
with which almost every phrase and paragraph
is invested – perhaps some of the rhythmic freedom too – while being carried through by the
power of her vision and technical control. Carried through, yes, but borne along? This is magnificent playing, but to enjoy her to the full you
have to accept Uchida's slow tempos and a projection of the expression that's painstaking to
the point of laboriousness, especially with all the
repeats. No singer could push Schubert as far as

Uchida does – but so what? A stunning record
nonetheless, and perhaps one to feel quite pos-
sessive about.

Piano Sonatas – B, D575; F minor, D625; A, D664.
Moment musical in C, D780 No 1
Sviatoslav Richter pf
BBC Legends BBCL4010-2 (78' · ADD) Recorded live
1979   Ⓜ**OO**

Richter's Schubert is simply in a class of its own.
No pianist did more to overturn the traditional
view of the composer as a blithe, unreflecting
child of nature. And in this Festival Hall recital
three sonatas from 1817-19 unfold with a
grandeur of conception, a spirituality and a stoical timelessness that were unique to Richter.
The first two movements of the A major Sonata
are, on the face of it, implausibly slow: but with
his mesmeric, self-communing intensity Richter convinces you for the duration of the performance that no other way is admissible.
Phrases, paragraphs are shaped with calm inevitability, underpinned by the sublime, luminous simplicity of Richter's *cantabile*; and no
pianist is more sensitive to Schubert's magical
harmonic strokes or understands more surely
their place in the larger scheme. As Richter conceives them, the first two movements of the A
major, D664, foreshadow the rapt, philosophical contemplation of the late G major and B flat
Sonatas, D894 and D960; and even the finale,
projected with Richter's characteristic mastery
and subtlety of rhythm, has something rarefied
in its playfulness. Richter is equally lofty and
far-sighted in the two lesser-known sonatas.

The BBC recording, while perhaps a shade
bass-light, is warm, and does ample justice to
Richter's vast dynamic and tonal palette. A
bronchial March audience can intrude at the
start of tracks, especially in finales. But no matter. All but those terminally resistant to Richter's uniquely introspective, long-spanned view
of the composer should acquire as a matter of
urgency these visionary performances by one of
the greatest Schubertians of the century.

Piano Sonatas – A minor, D784; D, D850
Mitsuko Uchida pf
Philips 464 480-2PH (62' · DDD)   Ⓕ**OO**

Mitsuko Uchida's Schubert is never less than
wonderfully finished in pianistic terms, and as
an interpretation it's only occasionally a little
disappointing. In these two latest sonatas she's
close to her best. The D major, D850, a product
of the composer's extended summer tour in
Austria in 1825, is, as Misha Donat's essay
notes, 'among Schubert's sonatas…the most
brilliant and extrovert'. With her exceptional
finger technique Uchida takes its technical
demands in her stride (there are several
renowned Schubertians of whom this much
can't be said), yet she never allows physical
excitement to become the be-all-and-end-all.

She finds playfulness in the contrasting themes of the first movement, and handles the song-like writing of the second and fourth with the expertise of a great Lieder accompanist, each phrase being subtly inflected yet never to the detriment of the long line. However, the horn-call-based second theme in the slow movement sounds a little over-excited and more than a little over-pedalled. But when it and the main theme of the movement are superimposed on the final page, Uchida's tone is fabulously well graded. Most memorable of all are the half tones she deploys in the third movement *Trio* and the exceptional delicacy and refinement of her passagework in the finale.

In the A minor Sonata, D784, she brings out the world-weariness of the first movement, the fragile hopefulness of the *Andante*, and the finale's seething energy. The contrasting martial theme in the first movement again finds her a fraction over-excitable. Nor does the finale coda sweep all before it in the exultant way of a Richter.

Richter is on peak form in the D major sonata from Moscow in 1956 (Melodiya), and the A minor from Tokyo in 1979 (Olympia). Everything he does seems to have deeper roots and to be carried forward by an even stronger artistic imperative than Uchida's, so he doesn't need to resort to her occasionally rather calculated-seeming hesitations. But for an alternative in rich modern sound, Uchida remains a good bet. Once again the recordings, from the Vienna Musikverein, verge on the over-resonant; but detract hardly at all from the music or the playing.

Piano Sonatas – C, D613; A minor, D784; B flat, D960
Stephen Hough pf
Hyperion CDA67027 (76' · DDD)   Ⓕ**O**

Stephen Hough's moving performance of D960 is marked throughout by refined, discerning pianism and an uncommonly subtle ear for texture. In all four movements, he seeks out the music's inwardness and fragility, its ethereal, self-communing remoteness. The opening *Molto moderato*, unfolding in vast, calm spans, has a hypnotic inevitability; there are countless felicities of timing and colour, but always a vital sense of forward motion. Hough adopts a dangerously slow tempo in the *Andante* but sustains it through the breadth and concentration of his line, the subtlety of his tonal palette and his pointing of rhythmic detail. His rarefied grace and delicacy, his gentle probing of the music's vulnerability, are of a piece with his conception of the sonata as a whole.

As usual, Hyperion doesn't stint over playing time, offering another complete sonata in addition to the two-movement fragment, D613. D784, perhaps Schubert's most depressive instrumental work, is magnificently done. Hough distils an immense weight of suffering from the pervasive two-note motif that dominates the first movement like some massive, Wagnerian

pendulum; but, typically, the lyrical music is limpidly coloured and poignantly inflected, with an unusually precise observation of Schubert's accents. The *Andante* is flowing and long-arched, with some ravishing soft playing, and he a brings a superb rhythmic impulse to the eerily scudding counterpoint of the main subject and a piercing tenderness to the contrasting F major theme. The fragmentary C major Sonata, D613, one of numerous Schubert torsos from the years 1817-22, is no great shakes: two pleasant but uneventful movements, both incomplete. The recording is of exemplary clarity, warmth and truthfulness.

Piano Sonatas – A minor, D784; D, D850
Alfred Brendel pf
Philips 422 063-2PH (63' · DDD) Recorded 1987   Ⓕ**O**

There's an extraordinary amount of highly experimental writing in Schubert's piano sonatas. The essence of their structure is the contrasting of big heroic ideas with tender and inner thoughts; the first impresses the listener, the second woos him. The two works on this CD are in some ways on a varying scale. The D major, D850, lasts for 40 minutes, the A minor, D784, for around 23. However, it's the latter that contains the most symphonically inspired writing – it sounds as if it could easily be transposed for orchestra. Alfred Brendel presents the composer not so much as the master of Lieder-writing, but more as a man thinking in large forms. Although there are wonderful quiet moments when intimate asides are conveyed with an imaginative sensitivity one remembers more the urgency and the power behind the notes. The A minor, with its frequently recurring themes, is almost obsessive in character, while the big D major Sonata is rather lighter in its mood, especially in the outer movements. The recorded sound is very faithful to the pianist's tone, while generally avoiding that insistent quality that can mar his loudest playing.

Piano Sonatas – in C, D840 ; in G, D894
Mitsuko Uchida pf
Philips 454 453-2PH (70' · DDD)   Ⓕ

Schubert's G major Sonata, D894, is the ultimate *Frühlingstraum*. Pervading the entire work is that oscillation between light-filled dream and stark waking reality. These may be juxtaposed in dramatic motivic contrast, but they're, quintessentially, twin sides of a single consciousness; and it's Mitsuko Uchida's supreme achievement to understand and re-create precisely this quality. She creates a true opening *molto moderato* of profound stillness and long distances. Chords really resonate and breathe out, yet her quick intakes of breath as the second subject steps into dance are tempered with the more flexible, whimsical intimacy of a Schiff. Uchida's gentleness of touch is ballasted by a firmly delineated bass and a weight of rhythmic articulation. She finds an easy, instinctive pace for the *Andante*, creating compacted shocks in the ringing chords of its minor-key episodes. These chords announce a Menuetto in which the Trio slinks in as the merest spectre of a Ländler, and leads to a finale in which Uchida creates a dance of the spirit within a deep inner stillness. The *Relique* Sonata, D840, one of Schubert's great and tantalisingly unfinished works, sounds entire, fully achieved in Uchida's hands. She shares with Schiff a leisured playing-out of the first movement. And her *Andante* is no less intimate in its *bel canto* of minute nuance and inflexion, starker and bleaker still than Schiff's masterpiece.

Piano Sonata in A minor, D845. Impromptus, D946
Alfred Brendel pf
Philips 422 075-2PH (61' · DDD) ⒻⓄ

Though love of the music alone, as pianists know, isn't enough to master these pieces, it's essential, and in this big A minor Sonata Brendel presents us with a drama that's no less tense for being predominantly expressed in terms of shapely melody. There's a flexibility in this playing that reminds us of the pianist's own comment that in such music 'we feel not masters but victims of the situation': he allows us plenty of time to savour detail without ever losing sight of the overall shape of the music, and the long first movement and finale carry us compellingly forwards, as does the *Scherzo* with its urgent energy, while the *Andante* second movement, too, has the right kind of spaciousness. In the *Impromptus* which date from the composer's last months, Brendel is no less responsive or imaginative. Richly sonorous digital recording in a German location complements the distinction of the playing on this fine disc.

Piano Sonata in A minor, D845. Impromptus, D946 Ⓟ
Andreas Staier fp
Teldec Das Alte Werk 0630-11084-2 (62' · DDD) ⒻⓄ

Once again, it's Andreas Staier's imagination and insight as a musician, rather than Staier-as-fortepianist, which comes to the fore in this rich recital. In the Sonata, for instance, Staier sets up a wide gulf between the two poles of Schubert's musical material – the sustained and lyrical, and the percussive and propulsive – in metaphysical terms, if you like, between the inner and outer, the contemplative and active life of this movement. Then he starts to paint with the pedal: there's a choice of four on this 1825 Viennese Johann Fritz fortepiano, and his changing use of them as the hands wander through the development creates a wide landscape for the journey, reminiscent of some of the piano writing in *Winterreise*. Here, and in the even more far-reaching expressive palette of the E flat major *Impromptu*, Staier really does realise the truth of his own statement that this – unlike the multi-

purpose modern concert grand – is truly a 'specifically Romantic instrument'. In the slow movement's variations, the shifting balance between the hands are uniquely tailored to the resonating scale of the instrument, to uniquely revelatory effect. None of this could happen without Staier's own exceptionally sensitive imagination. At the start of the E flat minor *Impromptu* he creates a wide area of open space for the *Andante*, with the little, high, cadenza-like scalic figure appearing, as a sudden and wonderful bright light, as time is momentarily suspended.

Piano Sonata in C minor, D958. Impromptus, D899. Deutsche Tänze, D783
Imogen Cooper pf
Ottavo OTRC78923 (70' · DDD) Recorded 1989 ⒻⓄ

This is the last of Imogen Cooper's six-disc cycle of the piano music of Schubert's last six years, a cycle launched in 1988 hard on the heels of similar cycles given on the concert platform in both London and Amsterdam. Like its predecessors, it confirms her as a Schubert player of exceptional style and finesse. Intuitively perceptive phrasing and a willingness to let the music sing within a wholly Schubertian sound world are prime virtues. And though (like her erstwhile mentor, Alfred Brendel) she's no slave to the metronome when contrasting first and second subjects in sonata expositions, she still makes the music her own without the self-consciously mannered kind of interpretation heard from one or two more recent rivals in this strongly competitive field. Her urgent yet poised performance of the late C minor Sonata certainly confirms her admission that the comparatively clinical atmosphere of an audience-less recording venue worries her not at all. In London's Henry Wood Hall her Yamaha is as clearly and truthfully reproduced as most else in the series.

Piano Sonatas – C minor, D958; A, D959; B flat, D960 Ⓟ
Andreas Staier fp
Teldec Das Alte Werk ② 0630-13143-2 (119' · DDD) ⒻⓄ

The harpsichord has all but replaced the concert grand in Baroque keyboard music. But resistance to the fortepiano is still strong; that clattery tone, the lack of sustaining power in high registers – it just doesn't sing like a modern piano. However, there are many instances where the sound of the 1825 Johann Fritz piano, and especially Andreas Staier's handling of it, are simply revelatory. Staier uses the fortepiano's moderator pedals and the *una corda* pedal, which shifts the hammers so that they strike only one string each, to great effect. Staier's use of these tools never seem excessive or misplaced, and it's hard to believe that Schubert wouldn't have made similar use of them. It isn't only in the special effects department that the fortepiano scores. In the middle of the slow movement of D959 there's a remarkable, violent cadenza-like passage which is rarely effective on modern concert pianos. On the fortepiano you can strain and pound for all you're worth, and yet the *scale* of the sound feels absolutely right. The later recitative-like contrast of the *ffz* chords and short, pleading *piano* phrases at the climax of the second movement of D959 works wonderfully here. Similarly, Staier can play the *fzp* and *ffzp* accents in the trio section of D960's *Scherzo* with due emphasis without destroying the music's lightweight character. But it's Staier's handling of the instrument, not the instrument itself, that makes these recordings so exceptional. In tempo, phrasing and so on, his approach is thoroughly modern; in fact his performances would probably translate very effectively to a modern piano without any – or much – sense of incongruity.

Piano Sonata in B flat, D960. Drei Klavierstücke, D946
Mitsuko Uchida pf
Philips 456 572-2PH (71' · DDD)　　　　　Ⓕ**OO**

Uchida's concentration and inwardness are of a rare order in her absorbed, deeply poetic reading of the B flat Sonata. No pianist makes you so aware how much of the first two movements is marked *pp* or even *ppp*; and none conjures such subtlety of colour in the softest dynamics: listen, for instance, to her playing of the three unearthly C sharp minor chords that usher in the first-movement development, or her timing and colouring of the breathtaking sideslip from C sharp minor to C major in the *Andante*. Other pianists may find a stronger undercurrent of foreboding or desperation in these two movements – though Uchida builds the development of the initial *Molto moderato* superbly to its dramatic climax. But none probes more hauntingly the music's mysterious contemplative ecstasy or creates such a sense of inspired improvisation. And her limpid *cantabile* sonorities are always ravishing on the ear. She's equally attuned to the less rarefied world of the *Scherzo* and finale, the former a glistening, mercurial dance, *con delicatezza* indeed, the latter graceful and quixotic, with a hint of emotional ambiguity even in its ostensibly cheerful main theme and a tigerish ferocity in its sudden Beethovenian eruptions.

The coupling is generous: the three *Klavierstücke*, D946, composed, like the sonata, in Schubert's final year, 1828, and assembled by Brahms for publication. She brings a wonderfully impassioned sweep, with razor-sharp rhythms, to the opening of the E flat minor, No 1, and mesmerically floats its slow B major episode. She also restores the beguiling barcarolle-like episode in A flat that Schubert excised from his autograph manuscript. The recording finely captures Uchida's subtle, pellucid sound world. A revealing disc from a Schubertian of rare insight and spirituality.

SCHUBERT PIANO SONATA IN B FLAT, D960 – IN BRIEF

Sviatoslav Richter
Olympia OCD335 (78' · ADD)　　　　　　　Ⓕ
A slow-burning account, dark and brooding in the first two movements. Even the positively bubbling *scherzo* is undercut by a drily cynical trio section, and the recurring stentorian octave in the finale is given a very sinister ring indeed. Powerful stuff.

Mitsuko Uchida
Philips 456 572-2PH (71' · DDD)　　　　Ⓕ**OO**
There is a sense of wariness, even apprehension from the start, as if anticipating the ominous bass trill. This is a beautifully nuanced performance, with poignant lyricism and baleful menace revealed as complementary traits. Excellently recorded.

Alfred Brendel
Philips ② 456 573-2PM2 (138' · DDD)　　Ⓜ
Although in this live recording the listener is initially aware of Brendel's audience (in this respect the sound on the coupled works is better), such is the concentration of his playing that you're quickly absorbed. A truly dramatic account not to be missed.

Stephen Hough
Hyperion CDA67027 (76' · DDD)　　　　　Ⓕ**O**
Hough takes relatively slow speeds in his thoughtful and concentrated performance, his sensitivity to phrasing and pianistic colour compelling attention throughout.

Andras Staier
Teldec ② 0630 13143-2 (119' · DDD)　　　Ⓕ
A masterful performance on a fortepiano, whose different registers translate into quasi-orchestral contrasts in colour, so adding a further dimension to Schubert's masterpiece.

Stephen Kovacevich
EMI 562817-2 (72' · DDD)　　　　　　　　Ⓜ
A straightforward account which underplays the lyricism in favour of structural clarity, bringing the sonata closer to Beethoven in sound. The piano is sometimes a bit clangorous at the bass end.

Clifford Curzon
Decca ④ 475 084-2DC4 (304' · ADD)　　　Ⓜ**O**
A musicianly account which cuts to the core of Schubert's inspiration, yet overstates nothing: details are in place, but never at the expense of the overall musical structure.

Wilhelm Kempff
DG ② 459 412-2GTA2 (150' · ADD)　　　Ⓜ**OO**
A ravishingly beautiful account, though the sound is quite dated, and can often seem rather shallow.

Wandererfantasie, D760

Fantasie in C, D934[a]. Fantasy in C,
'Wandererfantasie', D760
[a]Yuuko Shiokawa vn András Schiff pf
ECM New Series 464 320-2 (50' · DDD)　　Ⓕ**O**

Nearly all Schubert's great instrumental works
maintain the Classical four-movement layout:
but he did turn occasionally to the fashionable,
looser, fantasia-style forms – in the case of the
Wandererfantasie, one of his most disturbing
works, he seems to be using his structural know-
how in order to subvert the expectations of
Classical form. András Schiff vividly brings out
the switches between Classical poise, intensely
Romantic mood-painting and near-expression-
istic disruption; the key lies in the way he does-
n't exaggerate any contrast, but makes each
detail tell, so that the full range of the piece can
be heard. One shouldn't underestimate the
technical achievement – the lead-in to the *adagio*
section is a perfect demonstration of a gradual
diminuendo, of energy falling away, and when
the *Adagio* arrives the chordal playing is superb
– the melodic line perfectly balanced by the
dark, melancholic colours in the bass.

Balance and lack of exaggeration inform the
D934 *Fantasie*, too. From the start, when
Shiokawa steals in above the piano *tremolando*,
there's an air of magic. Her fine, silvery tone
only rarely expands to a richer or more dramatic
utterance, but her care not to overplay actually
adds to the rich impression the performance
gives. Whereas Kremer and Afanassiev present
the central variation set as a brilliant showpiece,
Schiff and Shiokawa paint a noticeably more
varied picture – drama and virtuosity alternating with delicacy and touches of lyrical tenderness. In short, these are interpretations of rare
penetration and individuality: a must for the
Schubert section in your collection.

Schubert Fantasy in C, 'Wandererfantasie' D760
Schumann Fantasie in C, Op 17
Maurizio Pollini pf
DG The Originals 447 451-2GOR (52' · ADD)
Recorded 1973　　Ⓜ**OOO**

 The cover shows Caspar David
Friedrich's familiar *The Wanderer
above the Sea of Fog*. Pollini, on the
other hand, is a wanderer in a transparent ether
or crystalline light, and both these legendary
performances, recorded in 1973 and beautifully
remastered, are of a transcendental vision and
integrity. In the Schubert his magisterial, resolutely unvirtuoso approach allows everything
its time and place. Listen to his flawlessly
graded triple *piano* approach to the central *Adagio*, to his rock-steady octaves at 5'23" (where
Schubert's merciless demand is so often the
cause of confusion) or to the way the decorations in the *Adagio* are spun off with such rare
finesse, and you may well wonder when you've
heard playing of such an unadorned, unalloyed

glory. Pollini's Schumann is no less memorable.
Doubting Thomases on the alert for alternating
touches of imperiousness and sobriety will be
disappointed, for, again, Pollini's poise is unfaltering. The opening *Moderato* is *sempre energico*,
indeed, its central *Etwas langsamer* is so sensitively and precisely gauged that all possible criticism is silenced. The coda of the central march
(that *locus classicus* of the wrong note) is immaculate and in what someone once called the
finale's 'shifting sunset vapour' Pollini takes us
gently but firmly to the shores of Elysium. Here
is a record that should grace every musician's
shelf.

Impromptus

Impromptus – D899; D935. Drei Klavierstücke, D946
Allegretto in C minor, D915
Maria João Pires pf
DG ② 457 550-2GH2 (108' · DDD)　　Ⓕ**OOO**

 This is something very special. Pires's
characteristic impassioned absorption
in all she plays – that concentration
which makes the listener appear to be eavesdropping on secrets shared between friends –
could hardly find a truer soul mate than Schubert. Each *Impromptu* has a rare sense of integrity and entirety, born of acute observation and
long-pondered responses.

Pires's instinct for tempo and pacing brings a
sense of constant restraint, a true *molto moderato*
to the *Allegro* of the C minor work from D899,
created by a fusion of right-hand *tenuto* here
with momentary left-hand rubato there. Then
there's the clarity of contour within the most
subtly graded undertones of the G flat major of
D899 which re-creates it as a seemingly endless
song. Or an *Andante* just slow, just nonchalant
enough for the *Rosamunde* theme of the D935
B flat major to give each variation space and
breath enough to sing out its own sharply
defined character.

The *Allegretto*, D915 acts as a *Pause* between
the two discs, a resting place, as it were, for
reflection and inner assessment on this long
journey. Its end – which could as well be its
beginning – is in the *Drei Klavierstücke*, D946 of
1828. The first draws back from the fiery
impetuousness within the *Allegro assai*'s tautly
controlled rhythms, to an inner world with its
own time scale; the second, more transpired
than played, has an almost unbearable poignancy of simplicity. The paradox of these unselfregarding performances is how unmistakably
they speak and sing out Pires and her unique
musicianship. To draw comparisons here would
be not so much odious as to miss the point.

Piano Works

Andante in C, D29. Minuet in A minor, D277a.
Minuet in A, D334. 13 Variations in A minor on a
theme by Anselm Hüttenbrenner, D576. Andante in

A, D604. Fantasy in C, 'Grazer Fantasie', D605a.
Three Impromptus, D946
James Lisney pf
Olympia OCD479 (65' · DDD)   Ⓕ

An illuminating programme of lesser-known works, which demonstrates the composer's exploitation of tonal colour and keyboard sonority. After a sensitive performance of the enchanting C major *Andante*, D29, Lisney plays a group of pieces that exploit the expressive potential of A major/minor tonality. Two minuets establish the emotional contrast between these tonal colours: the A minor one is bold and defiant, with a tranquil F major trio, while the carefree, amiable A major work is balanced by a poignantly lyrical trio in E major. The *Variations on a theme by Anselm Hüttenbrenner* demonstrates a more complex and dramatic A major/minor dichotomy, which Lisney here presents beautifully with subtle control of the theme's different transformations and telling modal shifts. In addition, Lisney offers a thoroughly absorbing, searching account of the brooding, introspective A major *Andante* and a poetically romantic, finely conceived performance of the *Grazer Fantasie*.

To conclude, carefully observed interpretations of the three *Impromptus*, D946, while perhaps lacking the spontaneity of Brendel's reissued versions (on a two-disc set), nevertheless confirm Lisney as a thoughtful and perceptive Schubertian. This fascinating concert, which benefits from satisfyingly faithful recorded sound, should attract a wide audience.

Piano Transcriptions

Schubert/Godowsky Passacaglia. Die schöne Müllerin, D795 – No 8, Morgengruss. Winterreise, D911 – No 1, Gute Nacht **Schubert/Prokofiev** Waltzes Suite **Schubert/Busoni** Overture in the Italian style, D590 **Schubert/Liszt** Erlkönig, D328. Winterreise – No 5, Der Lindenbaum; No 17, Im Dorfe; No 18, Der stürmische Morgen
Antti Siirala pf
Naxos 8 555997 (63' · DDD)   Ⓢ●

This young Finnish prize-winning pianist makes his recorded début with a challenging and enterprising a programme of Schubert transcriptions by Liszt, Godowsky, Prokofiev and Busoni.

Schubert takes less kindly to arrangement than most; his profound simplicity is easily compromised. True Schubertians might well have winced at what Godowsky does to 'Morgengruss' from *Die schöne Müllerin*, where innocence is turned into experience and a tropical efflorescence. Yet if to some this is sacrilegious, others, will celebrate an act of engaging decadence. Liszt, for all his theatricality, is much more an ardent devotee than mischief-maker, often memorably true to both his own and Schubert's sharply opposed natures, whereas Prokofiev and Busoni's offerings are disap-

pointingly more deferential than genuinely re-creative.

Siirala's performances are masterly and warmly sympathetic throughout, and never more so than in Godowsky's horrendously demanding Passacaglia on Schubert's *Unfinished* Symphony. Even Horowitz balked before this challenge, complaining that you needed six hands to encompass such fearsome difficulties.

Masses

Mass No 5, D678. Deutsche Messe, D872   Ⓟ
Stefan Preyer treb **Thomas Weinhappel** counterten **Jörg Hering** ten **Harry van der Kamp** bass **Arno Hartmann** org **Vienna Boys' Choir; Chorus Viennensis; Orchestra of the Age of Enlightenment / Bruno Weil**
Sony Classical Vivarte SK53984 (60' · DDD) Recorded 1993. Texts and translations included   Ⓕ●

In the *Deutsche Messe* Bruno Weil makes no attempt to impose interpretative individuality on music designed purely for liturgical use: he's content merely to oversee neat ensemble and balance. The orchestra, consisting mainly of wind instruments, doubles the chorus parts and while its role might seem largely superfluous it does provide a comfortable cushion on which the choir can relax while making its way effortlessly through such unchallenging music. It's a different story with the sparkling A flat major Mass, but again Bruno Weil's understated direction results in an immensely satisfying performance. There's a youthful vigour and infectious enthusiasm here, much of which comes from the superb singing of the Vienna Boys' Choir. Their exuberant 'Hosanna's in the *Sanctus* and *Benedictus* are unashamedly joyful. The two boy soloists sing with a musical maturity way beyond their years. That isn't to belittle the splendid contribution from the adult voices nor the exquisite playing of the Orchestra of the Age of Enlightenment. Weil achieves the perfect tonal blend: nothing disturbs the open-hearted honesty of this genuinely sincere performance.

Sacred Choral Works

Stabat mater, D383. Magnificat in C, D486. Offertorium in B flat, D963
Sheila Armstrong sop **Hanna Schaer** mez **Alejandro Ramirez** ten **Philippe Huttenlocher** bar **Lausanne Vocal Ensemble; Lausanne Chamber Orchestra / Michel Corboz**
Erato 4509-96961-2 (59' · ADD) Recorded 1979 Ⓜ●

Schubert's strikingly fresh setting of the *Stabat mater* (in a German translation) was written in the composer's 19th year, yet it displays clear anticipations of his later music, especially in the terzetto (No 11) for soprano, tenor, baritone and chorus and the striking chorus 'Wer wird Zähren sanflen Mitleids' (No 5) with its superb horn writing. There's a beautiful tenor aria with oboe obbligato, in which Alejandro Ramirez is very stylish, while the bass aria 'Sohn des Vaters' is dark and strong. Here Philippe Huttenlocher may not be quite sombre enough, yet his contribution is still most enjoyable. The singing of the Lausanne Vocal Ensemble, with the Lausanne CO under Corboz, combines clarity of focus with a firm sonority, and Schubert's lively fugues have plenty of vigour. The two shorter pieces, the Magnificat (again with a fine contribution from Ramirez) and the Offertorium, are also given strong performances. The recording, though not crystal clear, has transferred vividly.

Part-songs

Psalm 23, D706. Im Gegenwärtigen Vergangenes, D710. Gesang der Geister über den Wassern, D714. Gondelfahrer, D809. Coronach, D836. Nachthelle, D892. Grab und Mond, D893. Nachtgesang im Walde, D913. Ständchen, D920. Die Nacht, D983c. Gott im Ungewitter, D985
Birgit Remmert contr **Werner Güra** ten **Philip Mayers** pf **Scharoun Ensemble; RIAS Chamber Choir, Berlin / Marcus Creed**
Harmonia Mundi HMC90 1669 (59' · DDD) Texts and translations included Ⓕ🔵

Most of the part-songs here evoke some aspect of night, whether benevolent, romantic, transfigured or sinister. Between them they give a fair conspectus of Schubert's achievement in the part-song genre, ranging from the mellifluous, Biedermeier *Die Nacht*, forerunner of many a Victorian glee, and the gently sensuous *Gondelfahrer* to the eerie, harmonically visionary *Grab und Mond* and the brooding *Gesang der Geister über den Wassern*. Other highlights here include the alfresco *Nachtgesang*, with its quartet of echoing horns, *Ständchen*, a delicious nocturnal serenade, the austere, bardic Scott setting *Coronach* and the serenely luminous *Nachthelle*. The RIAS Chamber Choir confirms its credentials as one of Europe's finest, most virtuosic ensembles. It sings with rounded, homogeneous tone, wellnigh perfect intonation and an excitingly wide dynamic range. Characterisation tends to be very vivid, whether in the ecstatic central climax in *Nachthelle*, sharp contrasts in *Gesang der Geister über den Wassern* or the great sense of awe – and palpable feeling for Schubert's strange modulations – in *Grab und Mond*.

Birgit Remmert, the alto soloist in *Ständchen* (sung, incidentally, in the version with women's voices), sings well enough but with insufficient lightness and sense of fun. But Werner Güra negotiates what one of Schubert's friends called 'the damnably high' tenor solo in *Nachthelle* gracefully and with no sense of strain. Philip Mayers is a serviceable rather than specially imaginative pianist, though the delicate, silvery treble of the early 19th-century instrument is enchantingly heard in *Psalm 23* and the shimmering high repeated notes of *Nachthelle*; and the other instrumentalists make their mark –

splendid rotund horns in *Nachtgesang im Walde*, sombrely intense strings in *Gesang der Geister*. The recorded sound is clear and warm, with a well-judged vocal-instrumental balance.

Secular Choral Works

Complete Secular Choral Works
Elisabeth Flechl, Ruth Ziesak sops **Martina Steffl, Angelika Kirchschlager** mezzos **Birgit Remmert** contr **Franz Leitner, Thomas Künne, Christoph Prégardien, Herbert Lippert** tens **Oliver Widmer** bar **Karl Heinz Lehner, Hiroyuki Ijichi, Edgard Loibl, Robert Holl** basses **Barbara Moser, András Schiff, Andreas Staier, Werner Schröckmayr** pfs **Arnold Schoenberg Choir; Vienna Konzertverein / Erwin Ortner**
Teldec ⑦ 4509-94546-2 (480' · DDD) Texts and translations included Ⓕ🔵

The scheme of presentation here is both sensible and imaginative. Each of the discs has a subject-heading and each has its share of the treasures. The first, 'Transience', opens with the setting of Goethe's *Gesang der Geister über den Wassern* for men's voices and string quartet (without violins), probably the supreme masterpiece of the whole collection. The fascinating contrapuntal treatment of Schiller's *Dreifach ist der Schritt der Zeit* in its male-voice setting, and the gentle melancholy of Scott's *Coronach* are also memorable. The love-songs on the second disc begin and end with the *Ständchen*, 'Zögernd leise', its second version, with male-voice chorus, being the more attractive in these performances.

Under the heading of 'Eternity' (third disc) comes much that has perhaps a questionable place in a secular anthology: good to have, never the less, the anthem known to British choristers as *Where Thou reignest* as *Schiksalslenker, blicke nieder*. The fourth disc has 'Heroism' as its theme, with *Mirjams Siegesgesang* as its lengthiest work. 'Nature' produces several masterpieces, including Kleist's *Gott in der Natur* and the magical *Nachthelle*. The sixth, devoted to 'Celebration', has some longer occasional pieces, none so delightful as the brief cantata written for his father's birthday in 1813, with guitar accompaniment. The last disc, 'Circle of Friends', begins, beguilingly, with *Der Tanz* and ends with *Zur guten Nacht*. Ortner's soloists do well, but it's in the choral singing that the great merit of these performances lies. The Arnold Schoenberg Choir is a fine body of musicians and here they show a virtually unflawed beauty and opulence of tone. The pianists, headed by András Schiff, are excellent.

Lieder

Abendstern, D806ª. Amalia, D195ª. Atys, D585ª. Auf dem See, D543ᵇ. Auflösung, D807ª. Augenlied, D297ª. Blumenlied, D431ᵇ. Die Entzückung an Laura, D390ª. Gondelfahrer, D808ᵇ. Die Götter

Griechenlands, D677 – Strophe[b]. Die junge Nonne, D828[b]. Der Jüngling am Bache, D30[a]. Der Jüngling und der Tod, D545[c]. Memnon, D541[a]. Der Musensohn, D764[a]. Das Rosenband, D280[b]. Schwestergruss, D762[c]. Sehnsucht, D636[a]. Der Sieg, D805[a]

Dame Janet Baker mez [a]**Geoffrey Parsons,** [b]**Graham Johnson,** [c]**Martin Isepp** pfs
BBC Legends BBCL4070-2 (73' · ADD) Live broadcasts from [c]1970, [b]1977, [a]1980 　　ⒻⓄ

The interpretation of Schubert's Lieder comes no better than this, a recital taken from three different broadcast sources, catching Dame Janet at the absolute peak of her powers. Most of the songs are by poets who moved the composer to his most noble inspiration. As several Schubert specialists have commented, for each he reserved a particular style, in response to their very different manner, and Baker catches the precise meaning of each.

Of the Schiller settings, the operatic expression of *Amalia* and the dreamy rapture of the praise of *Laura* (here the singer achieves one miraculous *pianissimo* effect) are perfectly caught. Best of all is that wonderful song, *Die Götter Griechenlands*, where longing is so movingly expressed. All seven Mayrhofer settings find Baker truly at one with the poet's high-minded self-communing on the meaning of life, and with his underlying fatalism. Most notable are the calm assurance and serenity she brings to *Der Sieg*, the resigned isolation found in *Abendstern*, and the holy fire of *Auflösung*, the last two masterpieces that the singer did so much to make popular.

As Gerald Moore once pointed out, Baker liked the stimulus of the different ideas she received from different pianists. Here Isepp, Parsons and the young Graham Johnson provide just that, completing pleasure in a recital that goes to the heart of the chosen material: as ever one realises that Baker was, above all, a singer of conviction. The absence of any texts or translations is the only blot on a superb issue.

Ave Maria, D839. Ganymed, D544. Kennst du das Land, D321. Heiss mich nicht reden, D877 No 2. So lasst mich scheinen, D877 No 3. Nur wer die Sehnsucht kennt, D877 No 4. Liebhaber in allen Gestalten, D558. Heidenröslein, D257. Nahe des Geliebten, D162. Die Forelle, D550. Auf dem Wasser zu singen, D774. Im Abendrot, D799. Ständchen, D889. Du bist die Ruh, D776. Gretchen am Spinnrade, D118. Gretchens Bitte, D564. Der Hirt auf dem Felsen, D965
Barbara Bonney sop **Sharon Kam** cl **Geoffrey Parsons** pf
Teldec 4509-90873-2 (73' · DDD) Recorded 1994.
Texts and translations included 　　ⒻⓄⓄ

Bonney's programme is most carefully planned. She begins with a substantial selection of Goethe settings, going to the heart of the matter in all the Mignon songs, singing *Ganymed* with exemplary *legato* and breath control. Then

she makes a well-varied selection from many of the better-known pieces. She crosses paths with Blochwitz only in *Die Forelle* and *Auf dem Wasser zu singen*. Both take the same time over each, but it's worth noting that Jansen, for Blochwitz, finds more variety and lift in the barcarolle-like accompaniment of the latter song than does Parsons. Vocally speaking, both versions are enjoyable in their natural accomplishments.

Bonney's line and breath are again remarkable in *Du bist die Ruh*, which also demonstrates, as do all the other offerings, the purity of her tone – more North American clear-aired than Viennese creamy – yet that's never allowed to exclude depth of feeling. Indeed, when she returns to the Goethe settings with *Gretchen am Spinnrade* she shows particular eloquence in the way that, at a deliberate pace, she builds the song unerringly to its climaxes and also catches the inwardness of Gretchen's state of mind. The recording is faultless.

Lied eines Schiffers an die Dioskuren, D360. Nachtstück, D672. Auf der Donau, D553. Abendstern, D806. Auflösung, D807. Geheimes, D719. Versunken, D715. Schäfers Klagelied, D121. An die Entfernte, D765. Am Flusse, D766. Willkommen und Abschied, D767. Die Götter Griechenlands, D677. An die Leier, D737. Am See, D746. Alinde, D904. Wehmut, D772. Über Wildemann, D884. Auf der Riesenkoppe, D611. Sei mir gegrüsst, D741. Dass sie hier gewesen, D775. Der Geistertanz, D116
Ian Bostridge ten **Julius Drake** pf
EMI 557141-2 (68' · DDD) 　　ⒻⓄⓄ

A truly memorable experience. The first half of the programme is divided between settings of Mayrhofer and Goethe, two poets who drew the very best out of Schubert. Bostridge responds to this inspiration with singing that's worthy of the pieces both in terms of silvery, poised tone and inflection of the text. Such musing songs as *Nachtstück*, *Abendstern*, *Geheimes*, *Versunken* and *An die Entfernte* are delivered in that peculiarly plangent tone of the tenor's which causes his audiences to tremble in admiration.

Using vibrato, verbal emphases, *pianissimos* and floated touches to quite magical yet seemingly spontaneous effect, these songs, and many others receive near-ideal performances. Only in the rough-hewn *Willkommen und Abschied* would perhaps a heavier voice, a baritone rather than a tenor, be preferable. Bostridge enthusiasts will lap up this wonderful issue; so ought all lovers of Schubert Lieder. Bostridge need fear no comparison with other great interpreters of these songs. The admirable recording catches voice and piano in ideal balance.

Auf der Bruck, D853. Fülle der Liebe, D854. Im Walde, 'Waldesnacht', D708. Der liebliche Stern, D861. Der Schmetterling, D633. Tiefes Leid, 'Im Jänner 1817', D876. Vom Mitleiden Mariä, D632. Der Wanderer, D649. Wiedersehn, D855. Piano

Sonata No 17 in D, D850
Ian Bostridge ten **Leif Ove Andsnes** pf
EMI 557509-2 (69' · DDD) Texts and translations
included   Ⓕ**OO**

EMI hit an inspired note when it invited Andsnes and Bostridge to complement the fomer's
series of Schubert's greatest sonatas with an
aptly chosen selection of songs. For here, surely,
are musical soul-mates, two artists who fuse to
become one and whose love of Schubert's variety and ambivalence is evident in every bar. In
Der liebliche Stern their range of nuance never
excludes naturalness and what concentrated
musical energy they discover in *Auf der Bruck*.
Each twist and turn of the narrative in *Fülle der
Liebe* is deftly caught and both artists find a cool,
attenuated, almost Gallic beauty in *Der Wanderer* with its final line 'froh ungeben, doch
alleine' ('there is joy all around, yet I am alone').
Again, in the concluding *Der Schmetterling* you
could hardly hope for a lighter touch or a
greater sense of enchantment and it's only in the
sonata that a few doubts arise.

Here it's Andsnes's naturalness that impresses
most. Everything is kept refreshingly on the
move and if there's an occasional impression of
more sense than sensibility the playing is never
less than musicianly. The hushed coda is
notable, but Andsnes's coolness and control
hardly make you forget long-cherished recordings by Schnabel, Kempff, Curzon, Brendel
and, perhaps most of all, Gilels.

Buy it for the inspired partnership with
Bostridge. The recorded sound is excellent, and
the translations of the songs are by Richard
Wigmore.

An den Mond, D193. Wandrers Nachtlied I, D224.
Der Fischer, D225. Erster Verlust, D226.
Heidenröslein, D257. Erlkönig, D328. Litanei auf das
Fest Allerseelen, D343. Seligkeit, D433. Ganymed,
D544. An die Musik, D547. Die Forelle, D550.
Frühlingsglaube, D686. Im Haine, D738. Der
Musensohn, D764. Wandrers Nachtlied II, D768.
Der Zwerg, D771. Auf dem Wasser zu singen, D774.
Du bist die Ruh, D776. Nacht und Träume, D827.
Fischerweise, D881. Im Frühling, D882. An Silvia,
D891
Ian Bostridge ten **Julius Drake** pf
EMI 556347-2 (69' · DDD) Texts and translations
included   Ⓕ**OO**

Bostridge's devoted admirers will once more
wonder at his famed engagement with the text
in hand and his innate ability both to sing each
piece in an entirely natural manner and at the
same time to search out its inner meaning,
everything achieved without a vocal or technical
mishap within hearing. His gift for finding the
right manner for each song is exemplified in the
contrast between the easy simplicity he brings
to such apparently artless pieces as *Fischerweise*,
Frühlingsglaube and the less familiar *Im Haine*
(this a wondrous performance of a song that's
the very epitome of Schubert the melodist) and

the depth of feeling found in *Erster Verlust* (a
properly intense reading), *Nacht und Traüme*,
Wandrers Nachtlied I and II, *Du bist die Ruh* (so
elevated in tone and style) and *Litanei*.

Bostridge also characterises spine-chillingly
the intense, immediate drama of *Erlkönig* and
Der Zwerg, though here some may prefer the
weight of a baritone. In the latter piece Drake is
particularly successful at bringing out the originality of the piano part, and in a much simpler
song, *An Sylvia*, he gives to the accompaniment
a specific lift and lilt that usually goes unheard.
In these songs, as in everything else, the ear
responds eagerly to the tenor's fresh, silvery
tone and his ever-eager response to words. The
recording and notes are faultless.

Lieder, Volumes 1-3 DG (21 discs)
437 214-2GX21 (1463' · ADD) Recorded 1966-72
                                    Ⓢ Ⓑ **OOO**

Volumes also available separately, as detailed below.
234 Lieder, written between 1811 and 1817
Dietrich Fischer-Dieskau bar **Gerald Moore** pf
DG ⑨ 437 215-2GX9 (404' · ADD) Recorded 1966-8 Ⓑ

171 Lieder, written between 1817 and 1828
Dietrich Fischer-Dieskau bar **Gerald Moore** pf
DG ⑨ 437 225-2GX9 (395' · ADD) Recorded 1969
                                         Ⓢ Ⓑ

Die schöne Müllerin, D795. Winterreise, D911. Schwa-
nengesang, D957
Dietrich Fischer-Dieskau bar **Gerald Moore** pf
DG ③ 437 235-2GX3 (184' · ADD) Recorded 1971-2
                                         Ⓢ Ⓑ

Twenty-one discs at under £100 bringing together two of this century's
greatest Lieder interpreters – it sounds
like a recipe for success, as indeed it is, fulfilling
the highest expectations. The recordings were
made when Dietrich Fischer-Dieskau was at his
peak and Gerald Moore could draw on a lifetime's experience and love of this repertoire.
Though the set makes no claims to completeness, most of the songs for male voice are
included here. The use of a single singer and
pianist gives the set a unity that allows the listener to gasp anew at the composer's wide-
ranging inspiration and imagination.

Fischer-Dieskau brings a unique understanding, an elegant line and a diction that renders
the text clear without resort to the written texts.
If occasionally he imparts an unnecessary
weightiness to the lighter songs, this quibble is
as nothing when his historic achievement is
taken as a whole. And though he made many
recordings of the song cycles these are perhaps
the finest, with Moore the ideal partner. Try for
example, the bleakness of 'Ihr Bild' from *Schwanengesang* or the hallucinatory happiness of 'Der
Lindenbaum' from *Winterreise*. The songs
themselves are basically in chronological order
(but with the three song cycles collected
together in the final box). It's unfortunate
there's no index – trying to find individual

songs can be frustrating. Also, the translations are distinctly quirky in places; better to use Richard Wigmore's excellent book *Schubert: The Complete Song Texts* (Gollancz: 1988) if you have a copy to hand.

An die Entfernte, D765ᵃ. Auf dem Wasser zu singen, D774ᵃ. Du bist die Ruh, D776ᵇ. Erlkönig, D328ᶜ. Die Forelle, D550ᵇ. Heidenröslein, D257ᵇ. Das Heimweh, D456ᵃ. Der Jüngling an der Quelle, D300ᵇ. Der Jüngling und der Tod, D545ᵃ. Das Lied im Grünen, D917ᵃ. Litanei auf das Fest aller Seelen, D343ᵃ. Nachtgesang, D314ᵃ. Der Schiffer, D536ᵃ. Sei mir gegrüsst, D741ᵇ. Ständchen, 'Horch! Horch! die Lerch', D889ᵇ. Der Strom, D565ᵃ. Der Tod und das Mädchen, D531ᵃ. Der Wanderer, D649ᵃ. Der Winterabend, D938ᵃ. Das Zügenglöcklein, D871ᵃ. Der zürnende Barde, D785ᵃ
Dietrich Fischer-Dieskau bar **Gerald Moore** pf
EMI Encore 574754-2 (69' · ADD) Recorded 1960, 1966   Ⓢ

Almost 70 minutes of Fischer-Dieskau singing Schubert in his absolute prime at super-bargain price can't be bad, in spite of the absence of texts. The songs chosen – some outright favourites, others fine pieces the baritone helped to rescue from obscurity – make up a most desirable programme. As regards interpretation, Fischer-Dieskau is at his most soft-grained and persuasive in the lyrical pieces, notably the rarely heard but most beautiful *Nachtgesang*, at his most melodramatic in the more forceful Lieder, culminating in a hair-raising account of *Erlkönig*.

Moore is both sensitive and positive as the great baritone's partner, and contributes meaningfully to all the performances. EMI's recording of the period was wholly successful in catching the full tone of its singers.

Heidenröslein, D257. Die Forelle, D550. An die Nachtigall, D497. Im Frühling, D882. Die junge Nonne, D828. Nacht und Träume, D827. Auf dem Wasser zu singen, D774. Ave Maria, D839. Frühlingsglaube, D686. Gretchen am Spinnrade, D118. Du bist die Ruh, D776. Der Tod und das Mädchen, D531. Viola, D786. Die Männer sind méchant, D866 No 3
Renée Fleming sop **Christoph Eschenbach** pf
Decca 455 294-2DH (66' · DDD) Texts and translations included   Ⓕ

When yet another recital of Schubert Lieder appears, composed in the main of well-known songs, one looks for some special attributes to set it off from what has gone before in such profusion. Renée Fleming frequently supplies just those touches of individual response and high art which the ear is seeking. Like Dame Margaret Price she brings considerable stage experience to bear on her readings in terms of dramatic immediacy. That's particularly true of *Die junge Nonne* and *Gretchen am Spinnrade*, both of which carry the charge of emotions

made manifest at the moment of recording. There's almost as much to enjoy and appreciate in the more reflective, inward pieces. *Im Frühling*, in both voice and piano, catches very precisely the sense of longing evoked by the spring, with Eschenbach pointing up the poignancy of alternating major-minor. In *An die Nachtigall*, Fleming's tone is poised, finely controlled, even more so in the more difficult *Du bist die Ruh*, where she shades the end of the final two couplets with a ravishing *piano*. *Nacht und Träume*, still harder to sustain, is as time-stopping as it should be. In the sadly neglected flower-ballad *Viola* the pair suggest a true partnership of thought and execution. At least three other songs, *Auf dem Wasser zu singen*, *Ave Maria* and *Frühlingsglaube* seem marginally too slow. Here, and sometimes elsewhere, a shade more rhythmic verve, a greater attention to consonants, would improve on what's already a formidable array of virtues, and Eschenbach's habit of indulging in *ritenutos* sometimes becomes a distraction. These small points apart, this is a Liederabend to savour and faultlessly recorded too.

Lieder, Volume 27
Lob der Tränen, D711. Lebensmelodien, D395. Sprache der Liebe, D410. Wiedersehn, D855. Sonett I, D628. Sonett II, D629. Sonett III, D630. Abendröte, D690. Die Berge, D634. Die Vögel, D691. Der Fluss, D693. Der Knabe, D692. Die Rose, D745. Der Schmetterling, D633. Der Wanderer, D649. Das Mädchen, D652. Die Sterne, D684. Die Gebüsche, D646. Blanka, D631. Der Schiffer, D694. Fülle der Liebe, D854. Im Walde, D708
Matthias Goerne bar **Christine Schäfer** sop
Graham Johnson pf
Hyperion CDJ33027 (78' · DDD) Texts and translations included   Ⓕ

Goerne's brief is Schubert's settings of the brothers Schlegel, whose volatile character and life are amply and fascinatingly described in Johnson's introduction to the booklet. As ever in this series, there are songs that we should curse ourselves for neglecting for so long. Among the few settings of August von Schlegel is the interesting *Lebensmelodien*, where the Swan and the Eagle engage in a colloquy – the one all tranquil, the other all disturbed – and are observed by doves on whom Schubert lavishes his most beautiful music. In the formal *Wiedersehn*, as Johnson avers, Schubert imitates the style of a Handelian aria. The second of three Petrarch translations prefigures, arrestingly, the mood of *Winterreise*.

When we come to brother Friedrich and the quasi-cycle *Abendröte* we're in an even more exalted world where *Der Fluss*, another of Schubert's miraculous water songs, *Der Knabe*, above all *Die Rose*, where the fading of the rose is a metaphor for lost virginity (this, movingly done by Schäfer), and *Der Wanderer* show just how willingly Schubert responded to Schlegel's imagery. About Goerne's singing as such, ably assisted by Johnson's playing, there are no reservations, particularly in the visionary *Die Sterne*, but as the CD progresses his interpretations can seem a shade soporific; one wonders if he has lived long enough with these songs to penetrate to their heart. His easily produced, slightly vibrant and mellifluous baritone and sense of Schubertian style make him a largely rewarding interpreter. The recording is superb.

Schubert Atys, D585. Einsamkeit, D620. Der Fluss, D693. Im Freien, D880. Die Gebüsche, D646. Die Götter Griechenlands, D677. Sehnsucht, D516
Hüttenbrenner Frühlingsliedchen. Der Hügel. Lerchenlied. Die Seefart. Seegras. Spinnerlied. Die Sterne
Gundula Janowitz *sop* **Irwin Gage** *pf*
Orfeo C592021B (72' · DDD) Recorded live 1972 ⓂO

This is an unusual and wholly absorbing recital by a soprano often, mistakenly, considered no more than a singer with a lovely voice. In 1972, at the height of her appreciable powers, Janowitz impressed her Salzburg audience with this, her first recital at the Festival. Her discerning choice comprises some notable songs by Schubert rarely heard in recital and ones by his contemporary Hüttenbrenner, which Janowitz sang from manuscript copies, seldom performed since the composer's day. These are surely their first recordings.

Has there ever been such a lovely, poised account of the great Schiller-inspired song, *Die Götter Griechenlands* or such an ingratiating one of *Sehnsucht*, the Mayrhofer setting? The first offering, *Im Freien*, has its winning cantilena filled with gloriously sustained, long-breathed tone. The programme ends with *Einsamkeit*. This grandly imaginative if slightly impersonal quasi-cantata, to a Mayrhofer text, a composition that Schubert himself thought so highly of, is a kind of a panorama of a life, ending in a wonderfully reposeful final section. Janowitz and her impressive partner perform it with total conviction, sustaining interest throughout. Although not in Schubert's class – who is? – Hüttenbrenner reveals a talent apparently well able to encompass the meaning of poems in fluent and often imaginative writing. Orfeo provide no texts, let alone translations, but the delightful *Spinnerlied* must be about spinning: it's an artlessly charming song. *Der Hügel* is obviously about more serious matters, and in its sad course comes closes to Schubert in depth of feeling. *Frühlingsliedchen* has a simple, spring-like joy to it, and an appealingly varied, strophic form. Janowitz takes the measure of them all, and adds to a gently vibrant tone many tints and touches of half-voice. They could not have a better advocate.

The recording catches the full glow of the singer's voice. The only drawback, that absence of texts, isn't serious enough to stop acquiring this issue, given that Janowitz virtually tells you in her utterance what the songs are about.

Heidenröslein, D257. Wonne der Wehmut, D260. Der Jüngling an der Quelle, D300. Erntelied, D434. Im Walde, D708. Geheimes, D719. Suleika I, D720. Dass sie hier gewesen, D775. Viola, D786. Im Abendrot, D799. Abendstern, D806. Ave Maria, D839. Totengräbers Heimweh, D842. Bei dir allein, D866 No 2. Der Wanderer an den Mond, D870. Im Frühling, D882. An Silvia, D891. Ständchen, D920
Anne Sofie von Otter *mez* **Bengt Forsberg** *pf* with **Swedish Radio Chorus**
DG 453 481-2GH (69' · DDD) Texts and translations included Ⓕ O

This is a recital alive with the delight of long-awaited encounter and the vocal security of choices well made. In songs such as *An Silvia* and *Geheimes* the wide-eyed wonder of her own discovery incarnates that of the songs' own subjects. Tiny moments of gentle emphasis, and a little spring on each note of its rising sequences adds to the wondering incredulity of *An Silvia*'s questionings. There are many epiphanies along the way for even the most experienced Schubertian. *Heidenröslein*, for example, is re-created as a sudden, elusive *Augenblick*, a passing moment in time in which pique and piquancy fuse without a hint of mere coyness. And listen to the way in which von Otter and the ever perceptive Bengt Forsberg bring a sense of wry self-awareness to *Der Wanderer an den Mond*.

The recital grows gradually darker, moving, by way of *Standchen*, D920 to the twilight of *Im Abendrot*. Here, long, firmly grounded vowels are backlit by the afterglow of Forsberg's piano line before some deep, passionate digging into the *Angst* of *Totengrabers Heimweh*, and a wonderfully breathless, intimately urgent imprecation of an *Ave Maria*.

Lieder, Volume 23
Der Tod Oscars, D375. Das Grab, D377[a]. Der Entfernten, D350. Pflügerlied, D392. Abschied von der Harfe, D406. Der Jüngling an der Quelle, D300. Abendlied, D382. Stimme der Liebe, D412. Romanze, D144. Geist der Liebe, D414. Klage, D415. Julius an Theone, D419. Der Leidende, D432. Der Leidende (second version), D432b. Die frühe Liebe, D430. Die Knabenzeit, D400. Edone, D445. Die Liebes-götter, D446. An Chloen, D363. Freude der Kinderjahre, D455. Wer sich der Einsamkeit ergibt, D478. Wer nie sein Brot mit Tränen ass, D480. An die Türen, D479. Der Hirt, D490. Am ersten Maimorgen, D344. Bei dem Grabe meines Vaters, D496. Mailied, D503. Zufriedenheit, D362. Skolie, D507
Christoph Prégardien *ten* [a]**London Schubert Chorale; Graham Johnson** *pf*
Hyperion CDJ33023 (78' · DDD) Recorded 1994. Texts and translations included O

When the Hyperion Schubert Edition is completed, this latest wondrous offering will rank among its most precious jewels. Prégardien is a prince among tenor interpreters of Lieder at present, on a par with Blochwitz in instinctive, natural and inevitably phrased readings. Johnson, besides finding exactly the right performers for these songs, surpasses even his own high standard of playing in this series. Then there's Schubert himself, the Schubert of 1816 by and large, who was, Johnson tentatively suggests in his notes, going through a phase of 'bringing himself under control'. That means, largely but far from entirely, writing gently lyrical strophic songs, most of them of ineffable beauty and simplicity, starkly contrasting with the Harfenspieler settings from *Wilhelm Meister*, two of which were written in 1816, the other in 1822.

In such an outright masterpiece as *Der Jüngling an der Quelle*, Prégardien and Johnson confirm the latter's view that this piece 'makes time stand still'. They emphasise, in *Stimme der Liebe*, how Schubert uses shifting harmonies to indicate romantic obsession. They show in the two similar but subtly different versions of *Der Leidende* ('The suffering one') what Johnson calls 'two sides of the same coin', with the tenor's plangent, tender singing, line and text held in perfect balance. The two Hölty songs that follow, *Die frühe Liebe* and *Die Knabenzeit*, evince a wonderful affinity with thoughts of childhood on the part of poet and composer, again ideally captured here. So is the 'chaste and wistful' mood of Klopstock's *Edone*. The recording is ideally balanced .

Der Alpenjäger, D524. Antigone und Oedip, D542. Atys, D585. Auf der Donau, D553. Auflösung, D807. Der entsühnte Orest, D699. Fahrt zum Hades, D526. Fragment aus dem Aeschylus, D450. Freiwilliges Versinken, D700. Gondelfahrer, D808. Lied eines Schiffers an die Dioskuren, D360. Memnon, D541. Nach einem Gewitter, D561. Nachtstück, D672. Nachtviolen, D752. Philoktet, D540. Der Schiffer, D536. Der Sieg, D805. Die Sternennächte, D670. Wie Ulfru fischt, D525. Der Zürnenden Diana, D707
Christoph Prégardien ten **Andreas Staier** fp
Teldec Das Alte Werk 8573-85556-2 (70' · DDD)
⑤⓿⓿

Prégardien and Staier, who have now been musical partners for more than 10 years, add to their laurels as interpreters of Lieder with this remarkably satisfying disc entirely devoted to Schubert's settings of Mayrhofer. Here singer and player are equally in sympathy with the mood of every Lied. Prégardien seems fully up to imparting the power expressed in such songs as *Fahrt zum Hades* and *Der Schiffer*, railing against fortune in the most imposing manner. Some of the songs devoted to classical subjects are among the hardest in the whole Schubert oeuvre for interpreter and listener to encompass, but with these artists as guides, they seem reasonably approachable, *Memnon* a particular success. It hardly needs saying that in the more lyrical songs, the pair are at their very best, the tenor's plaintive, seamless and eloquent singing supported by Staier's refined insights into the keyboard contributions, here played on a wonderfully translucent instrument. The rarely encountered *Abschied* is well worth unearthing when done so sympathetically. Best of all are pieces such as *Auf der Donau*, *Abendstern*,

Gondelfahrer and *Auflösung*, once seldom done but now regularly performed. These readings are as lovingly sung and convincingly phrased on both sides as any. Add an excellent recording, and this is a CD all Schubertians will want.

Im Frühling, D882. Die Blumensprache, D519. Die gefangenen Sänger, D712. Der Schmetterling, D633. An den Mond, D259. An den Mond, D296. Die Gebüsche, D646. Der Fluss, D693. Der Knabe, D692. Nacht und Träume, D827. Im Abendrot, D799. Glaube, Hoffnung und Liebe, D955. Vom Mitleiden Mariä, D632. Beim Winde, D669. Des Mädchens Klage, D6. Blanka, D631. Das Mädchen, D652. Die Rose, D745. Die junge Nonne, D828. Nähe des Geliebten, D162
Christine Schäfer sop **Irwin Gage** pf
Orfeo C450971A (79' · DDD) Texts and translations included
⑤⓿

What makes Schäfer such a special artist is the candid, plaintive, natural quality of her tone and her simplicity of phrasing. These are combined with clear, unaffected diction, and a sense of vulnerability in the timbre, to evoke the pure spirit of each song. Some, used to more vibrant, luscious voices, may find Schäfer's tone too narrow or they may be troubled by moments when she's deliberately on the flat side of a note but they're part of her vocal personality and perhaps nearer to what was heard in Schubert's day. Her attributes as a Schubertian are confirmed by her discerning choice of songs in this generously filled programme. Whether the pieces are grave or cheerful, Schäfer finds the right expression. The simplicity at the start of *An den Mond* (D296) is succeeded by heightened intensity at just the appropriate moment, in the fifth stanza. In that underrated Schlegel setting, *Der Fluss*, she adds special urgency to the last line. In better-known songs, such as *Nacht und Träume* and *Im Abendrot* the soprano refreshes the familiar through a new draught of feeling, simple yet inward, and that's the epithet that comes most readily to mind in those two melancholic songs, *Das Mädchen* and *Die Rose*, the one about an unloved girl, the other about a flower speaking of its mortality. To end she catches the perfect Schubert/Goethe accord of *Nähe des Geliebten*, where 'Ich denke dein' and 'Ich bin bei dir' are affirmations of a deep love. Irwin Gage partners his singer with many touches of subtle, finely shaded phrasing. Add a surely balanced recording and Lieder lovers are in for a generous treat.

An die Musik, D547. Im Frühling, D882. Wehmut, 🅷 D772. Ganymed, D544. Das Lied im Grünen, D917. Gretchen am Spinnrade, D118. Nähe des Geliebten, D162. Die junge Nonne, D828. An Silvia, D891. Auf dem Wasser zu singen, D774. Nachtviolen, D752. Der Musensohn, D764. Six moments musicaux, D780[a]
Elisabeth Schwarzkopf sop [a]**Edwin Fischer** pf
EMI Références mono 567494-2 (67' · ADD)
Recorded [a]1950, 1952
Ⓜ⓿

Many young and not-so-young singers can't abide Schwarkopf's interpretative style, which is strikingly at odds with the straightforward readings so often heard today. Playing devil's advocate, one can understand the nature of the complaints about her interventionist approach, her occasional distortion of vowel sounds and a general approach that William Mann once described as 'verschmuckt' (bejewelled). You may judge such views, for instance, in a song like *Auf dem Wasser*, where not a phrase is left to speak for itself; compare it with the natural and simple reading of her contemporary Irmgard Seefried (Testament), which is so much more appropriate to the song.

That said, the doubters should listen to this recital with Edwin Fischer, one of the greatest ever discs of Schubert singing. As so often in her recitals dating back to Oxford days in 1950, annoyance with the occasional mannerism soon gives way to wonder at such an amazingly eager response to every facet of a song and its setting. And truly inspired by Fischer, she throws caution utterly to the wind and astonishes us in accounts of *Die junge Nonne*, *Ganymed* and *Gretchen am Spinnrade* that have seldom if ever been surpassed for vocal consistency and concentration – though it's a pity the singer makes a break in the final, long phrase of *Ganymed*.

Fischer, one of the noblest Schubert interpreters of his or any time, is obviously a partner in a thousand, and on his own confirms his stature in the legendary 1950 recording of *Moments musicaux* better transferred here than ever before – as are the Lieder. So this is a CD no Schubertian can do without.

Lieder – Gruppe aus dem Tartarus, D583. Litanei auf das Fest Allerseelen, D343. Die Forelle, D550. An die Leier, D737. Lachen und Weinen, D777. Schwanengesang, D957 – Ständchen; Das Fischermädchen; Die Taubenpost. Meerestille, D216. Der Wanderer, D489 (formerly D493). Erlkönig, D328. Der Tod und das Mädchen, D531. Heidenröslein, D257. Wandrers Nachtlied II, D768. An die Musik, D547. Auf der Bruck, D853. Schäfers Klagelied, D121. An Silvia, D891. Du bist die Ruh', D776. An die Laute, D905. Rastlose Liebe, D138. Ganymed, D544. Der Musensohn, D764
Bryn Terfel bass-bar **Malcolm Martineau** pf
DG 445 294-2GH (69' · DDD) Recorded 1994. Texts and translations included   Ⓕ**ⓞⓞⓞ**

Ⓖ Terfel's gift is a generous, individual voice, a natural feeling for German and an inborn ability to go to the heart of what he attempts. His singing here is grand in scale – listen to any of the dramatic songs and the point is made – but like Hotter, whom he so often resembles, he's able to reduce his large voice to the needs of a sustained, quiet line, as in *Meerestille*. When the two come together as in *Der Wanderer*, the effect can be truly electrifying, even more so, perhaps, in *Erlkönig* where the four participants are superbly contrasted. Yet this is a voice that can also smile, as in *An die*

Laute and 'Die Taubenpost' or express wonder, as in *Ganymed*, a most exhilarating interpretation, or again explode in sheer anger as in the very first song, the strenuous *Gruppe aus dem Tartarus*. Terfel isn't afraid to employ rubato and vibrato to make his points and above all to take us right into his interpretations rather than leave us admiring them, as it were, from afar. Throughout, Martineau's at once vigorous and subtle playing is an apt support: his accompaniment in *Erlkönig* is arrestingly clear and precise.

Lieder, Volume 24
Schäfers Klagelied, D121. An Mignon, D161. Geistes-Gruss, D142 (two versions). Rastlose Liebe, D138. Der Gott und die Bajadere, D254. Tischlied, D234. Der Schatzgräber, D256. Der Rattenfänger, D255. Bundeslied, D258. Erlkönig, D328. Jägers Abendlied, D215. Jägers Abendlied, D368. Wer nie sein Brot mit Tränen ass, D480 (two versions). Nur wer die Sehnsucht kennt, D359. So lasst mich scheinen, D469a & D469b (two fragments). Nur wer die Sehnsucht kennt, D481. Nur wer die Sehnsucht kennt, D656. An Schwager Kronos, D369. Hoffnung, D295. Mahomets Gesang, D549 (cptd R. Van Hoorickx). Ganymed, D544. Der Goldschmiedsgesell, D560. Gesang der Geister über den Wassern, D484 (cptd R Van Hoorickx). Gesang der Geister über den Wassern, D705 (cptd E Asti).
Christine Schäfer sop **John Mark Ainsley** ten
Simon Keenlyside bar **Michael George** bass
Graham Johnson pf **London Schubert Chorale /**
Stephen Layton
Hyperion CDJ33024 (79' · DDD) Recorded 1993-4. Texts and translations included   Ⓕ

Renewed praise first of all for Graham Johnson. This volume is as cogent an example as any of his method, a masterly exposition, in written words and musical performance, of the crucial relationship between Goethe and Schubert upon which Johnson throws a good deal of new light. Not all here is notable Schubert, but the lesser songs serve to place in perspective the greater ones.

The CD begins with one of the latter, *Schäfers Klagelied*, in a finely honed, dramatic performance by Ainsley, who's heard later on the disc always to advantage. Good as Christine Schäfer is in the first version of *An Mignon*, she's better in the sadly neglected *Der Gott und die Bajadere*, as Johnson avers. This is the only song in the genre about prostitution, and a haunting one too, even though, throughout its appreciable length, it relies on just one melody, and Schäfer precisely catches its haunting atmosphere. But the climax of her contribution comes in *Ganymed* – with Johnson providing exactly the right rhythmic lilt at the piano, her voice conveys all the elation of poem and music.

Schäfer is the child in a three-voice rendering of *Erlkönig*, a manner of performing the piece that has the composer's blessing. Johnson has surely never surpassed his account here of the hair-raisingly difficult piano part. George, who perhaps has the least ingratiating songs to perform, sings with feeling and style but sometimes an excess of vibrato. An invaluable addition to the series.

Lieder, Volume 26

Der Einsame, D800. Des Sängers Habe, D832. Lied der Delphine, D857 No 1. Lied des Florio, D857 No 2. Mondenschein, D875. Nur wer die Sehnsucht kennt, D877 No 1. Heiss mich nicht reden, D877 No 2. So lasst mich scheinen, D877 No 3. Nur wer die Sehnsucht kennt, D877 No 4. Totengräberweise, D869. Das Echo, D990C. An Silvia, D891. Horch, horch! die Lerch', D889. Trinklied, D888. Wiegenlied, D867. Widerspruch, D865. Der Wanderer an den Mond, D870. Grab und Mond, D893. Nachthelle, D892. Abschied von der Erde, D829

Christine Schäfer *sop* **John Mark Ainsley** *ten* **Richard Jackson** *bar* **London Schubert Chorale; Graham Johnson** *pf*

Hyperion CDJ33026 (76' · DDD) Texts and translations included Ⓕ●●

It's hard to know where to begin in praise of this disc. It has several centres of excellence, the first being Schäfer's beseeching, urgent account of the Mignon settings from Goethe's *Wilhelm Meister* that make plain her pre-eminence today among sopranos in Lieder. Next comes Ainsley's winningly fresh account of *An Silvia*. You may be surprised at how wholly new-minted Ainsley's ardent tones and Johnson's elating piano manage to make of such a hackneyed song. Schäfer and Johnson do the same service for *Horch, horch! die Lerch'*. Then comes the extraordinary discovery of this volume. As a rule, Johnson has excluded unaccompanied vocal pieces from his project; happily, he has made an exception in the case of the astonishingly original Seidl setting *Grab und Mond*, which touches on eternal matters, or rather the permanence of death, a message starkly expressed in typically daring harmony. The London Schubert Chorale gives it a spellbinding interpretation and also contributes positively to a performance of another Seidl setting, the better-known *Nachthelle*, where the high-lying tenor lead provides no problems for Ainsley. There have to be reservations over the work of Richard Jackson; his tone is inadequate to the demands of *Der Einsame*, the unjustly neglected *Totengräberweise* and *Der Wanderer an den Mond*, which call for a richer sound-palette.

Throughout, Johnson's playing is a source of pleasure and enlightenment. The recording is well-nigh faultless.

Lieder, Volume 32

An die Sonne, D439. Beitrag zur fünfzigjährigen Jubelfeier des Herrn von Salieri, D407. Das war ich, D174a/D450a. Didone Abbandonata, D510a (both cptd Hoorickx). Der Entfernten, D331. Entzückung, D413. Der Geistertanz, D494. Gott der Weltschöpfer, D986. Gott im Ungewitter, D985. Grablied auf einen Soldaten, D454. Das Grosse Halleluja, D442. Des Mädchens Klage, D389. Licht und Liebe, D352. Naturgenuss, D422. Ritter Toggenburg, D397. Schlachtgesang, D443. Die verfehlte Stunde, D409. Der Wanderer, D489. Zufriedenheit, D501: Zum Punsche, D492

Lynne Dawson, Patricia Rozario, Christine Schäfer *sops* **Ann Murray, Catherine Wyn-Rogers** *mezzos* **Paul Agnew, John Mark Ainsley, Philip Langridge, Jamie MacDougall, Daniel Norman, Christoph Prégardien, Michael Schade, Toby Spence** *tens* **Simon Keenlyside, Maarten Koningsberger, Stephan Loges, Christopher Maltman, Stephen Varcoe** *bars* **Neal Davies, Michael George** *basses* **Graham Johnson** *pf* **London Schubert Chorale / Stephen Layton**

Hyperion CDJ33032 (78' · DDD) Notes, texts and translations included Ⓕ●

Like the previous Schubertiads in the Edition, this disc mixes solo songs and partsongs, familiar and unfamiliar. The only really famous work here is *Der Wanderer*, that archetypal expression of romantic alienation whose popularity in Schubert's lifetime was eclipsed only by that of *Erlkönig*. Some of the partsongs – *Zum Punsche*, *Naturgenuss* and *Schlachtgesang* – cultivate a vein of Biedermeier heartiness that wears a bit thin today. Nor will Schubert's consciously archaic tribute to his teacher Salieri have you itching for the repeat button – though, like several other numbers, it shows the 19-year-old composer rivalling Mozart in his gift for musical mimicry. To compensate, though, there are partsongs like the sensual *Der Entfernten*, with its delicious languid chromaticisms, and the colourful setting of *Gott im Ungewitter*. The slight but charming setting of *Das war ich* is appealingly done by the light-voiced Daniel Norman, and Ann Murray brings her usual charisma and dramatic conviction to the pathetic Italian scena *Didone Abbandonata*.

Christine Schäfer is equally charismatic in the unjustly neglected *Die verfehlte Stunde* (recorded here for the first time), catching perfectly the song's mingled yearning and ecstasy and negotiating the mercilessly high tessitura with ease. Other happy discoveries include Schubert's virtually unknown third setting of *Des Mädchens Klage*, with its soaring lines, a melancholy tale of courtly love, sung by Christoph Prégardien with as much drama and variety as the music allows, and the surging *Entzückung* ('music for an infant Lohengrin,' as Graham Johnson puts it), for which Toby Spence has both the flexibility and the necessary touch of metal in the tone. Doubts were fleetingly raised by Lynne Dawson's slight tremulousness in *Des Mädchens Klage*, and by Christopher Maltman's prominent vibrato at *forte* and above in an otherwise involving performance of *Der Wanderer*. But, these cavils apart, no complaints about the singing or Graham Johnson's vivid accompaniments.

Lieder, Volume 34

La pastorella al prato, D513[fjpt]. Frohsinn, D520[q]. Der Alpenjäger, D524[r]. Die Einsiedelei, D563[i]. Das

Grab, D569[u]. Atys, D585[o]. Der Kampf, D594[s]. Das Dörfchen, D598[f][j][p][t]. Die Geselligkeit, D609[c][d][g][t]. Sing-Übungen, D619[a][c] (ed Roblou). Das Abendrot, D627[s]. Abend, D645[h] (ed Brown). Das Mädchen, D652[e]. Cantate zum Geburtstag des Sängers Michael Vogl, D666[b][l][m]. Prometheus, D674[p]. Über allen Zauber Liebe, D682[k] (ed Hoorickx). Die gefangenen Sänger, D712[n]. Grenzen der Menschheit, D716[s]. Wandrers Nachtlied II, D768[r]
[a]Lorna Anderson, [b]Lynne Dawson, [c]Patricia Rozario *sops* [d]Catherine Denley, [e]Marjana Lipovšek *mezzos* [f]John Mark Ainsley, [g]Ian Bostridge, [h]Martyn Hill, [i]Philip Langridge, [j]Jamie MacDougall, [k]Daniel Norman, [l]Michael Schade *tens* [m]Gerald Finley, [n]Matthias Goerne, [o]Thomas Hampson, [p]Simon Keenlyside, [q]Stephan Loges, [r]Christopher Maltman *bars* [s]Neal Davies *bass-bar* [t]Michael George *bass* [u]London Schubert Chorale / Stephen Layton; Graham Johnson *pf*
Hyperion Schubert Edition CDJ33034 (79' · DDD)
Recorded 1991-9. Texts and translations included
Ⓕ Ⓞ

In his guise as a wizard of an impresario, Graham Johnson has gathered together four baritones and one bass-baritone (Neil Davies) to give us a feast of finely wrought, intelligent interpretations. Hampson's rendering of that outsider's lament, *Atys*, is at once an object-lesson in refined singing and a deeply felt out-pouring of sorrow. Keenlyside, singing with as much firm, mellow tone and feeling as his American coeval, gives a properly intense, ago-nised account of the great, Zeus-defying *Prometheus*, magnificently supported by Johnson. Goerne is assigned the seldom-heard Schlegel setting, *Die gefangenen Sänger*, and brings his gently vibrant tone, reminiscent of his noted predecessor Herbert Janssen, and his natural gift for phrasing to bear on this strange but captivating piece. Maltman, growing in stature as a Lieder artist, begins the programme with the extrovert *Der Alpenjäger* and ends it with the introverted *Wandrers Nachtlied* on which he lavishes the hushed concentration due to a page of rapt utterance, a suitable conclusion to the performance of Goethe settings in the whole edition.

Neil Davies erupts into the series with three absorbing interpretations: the declamatory Schiller setting *Der Kampf*, the flowing, glowing *Das Abendrot* and the awe-inspiring *Grenzen der Menschheit*. All three evince his real affinity for the German language and the world of Schubert. He also has the low notes the pieces call for. The one female solo brings back Lipovšek at her most beguiling in the poignant and unfor-gettable Schlegel setting *Das Mädchen*, already performed just as movingly by Christine Schäfer in Vol 27. This wonderful fare is inter-spersed with lighter, less demanding material, all done with pleasure by varying groups of singers, plus three tenor solos. Langridge is pre-dictably charming in *Die Einsiedelei*. Hill isn't quite at his best, and Norman's style is etiolated in their offerings. Piano playing both maintain Hyperion's usual high standard.

Lieder, Volume 37
Auf dem Strom, D943[c][d]. Herbst, D945[a]. Bei dir allein, D866/2[c]. Irdisches Glück, D866/4[c]. Lebensmut, D937[c]. Schwanengesang, D957 – No 1, Liebesbotschaft[a]; No 2, Kriegers Ahnung[a]; No 3, Frühlingssehnsucht[a]; No 4, Ständchen[a]; No 5, Aufenthalt[a]; No 6, In der Ferne[a]; No 7, Abschied[a]; No 8, Der Atlas[b]; No 9, Ihr Bild[b]; No 10, Das Fischermädchen[b]; No 11, Die Stadt[b]; No 12, Am Meer[b]; No 13, Der Doppelgänger[b]. Die Taubenpost, D965A[b]. Glaube, Hoffnung und Liebe, D955[a][b][c]
[a]John Mark Ainsley, [b]Anthony Rolfe Johnson, [c]Michael Schade *tens* [d]David Pyatt *hn* Graham Johnson *pf*
Hyperion Schubert Edition CDJ33037 (80' · DDD)
Texts and translations included
Ⓕ Ⓞ

This disc, the last in Hyperion's Schubert Edition, is in large part devoted to the performance of the non-cycle *Schwanengesang*, that extraordinary collection in which Schubert seems more original and more inclined even than in earlier Lieder to peer into the future. We usually encounter the work transposed for a baritone, though Schreier and Schiff have recorded it memorably for Decca. Johnson has astutely divided the songs between two voices. Ainsley is given the Rellstab settings, Rolfe Johnson the Heine, plus Seidl's *Die Taubenpost*, which so poignantly and airily closes the set.

Ainsley interprets his songs with the tonal beauty, fine-grained phrasing and care for words that are the hallmarks of his appreciable art, even if his voice sometimes lacks a difficult-to-define individuality of timbre. The over-exposed *Ständchen* is given a new spontaneity of utterance by both the singer and Graham Johnson. Anthony Rolfe Johnson brings all the appropriate intensity one would expect from him to the tremendous Heine settings. Some-times his tone hardens when he's depicting the deserted lover present in so many of these pieces, but that's hardly inappropriate to the depth of feeling being expressed.

Most of the other songs of 1828, which open the recital, are assigned to Schade, who sings them with refined tone and an innate feeling for sharing his enjoyment in performing them, nowhere more so than in the opening *Auf dem Strom*. Ainsley reads his sole offering here, *Bei dir allein*, with just the fiery passion it calls for.

This is a worthy, often inspired conclusion to the series, once more enhanced by Johnson's copious notes. It also has a complete index to the Edition. The recording is faultless.

Song cycles

Die schöne Müllerin, D795. **Schwanengesang**, D957. **Winterreise**, D911

Die schöne Müllerin[a]. Nacht und Träume, D827[b]. Ständchen, D889[b]. Du bist die Ruh, D776[b]. Erlkönig, D328[c]

Dietrich Fischer-Dieskau *bar* [a]Jörg Demus,
[bc]Gerald Moore *pfs*
DG 463 502-2GFD (75' · ADD) Recorded 1968,
[bc]1970   Ⓜ**OO**

Schwanengesang. Vollendung, D579. Die Erde,
D579*b*. An die Musik, D547. An Silvia, D891. Heiden-
röslein, D257. Im Abendrot, D799. Der Musensohn,
D764. Die Forelle, D550. Der Tod und das Mädchen,
D531
Dietrich Fischer-Dieskau *bar* Gerald Moore *pf*
DG 463 503-2GFD (73' · ADD)   Ⓜ**OOO**

 You wouldn't think that a recording by
Fischer-Dieskau, given his huge Schubert discography, could still offer an
exciting revelation – but that's what the 'new'
Die schöne Müllerin recording offers. Explana-
tions for its suppression vary. The singer seems
to think it has something to do with its technical
quality: the booklet-note, slightly more credibly, tells us that it was planned before DG
decided to include the cycle in its 'complete'
Schubert with the baritone and Gerald Moore,
which caused this performance to be put on the
back burner. Now we can enjoy a reading that's
absolutely spontaneous, daring in its dramatic
effects – bold extremes of dynamics, for instance
– and full of even more subtle detail than in Fischer-Dieskau's other recordings.

This approach owes not a little to Demus's
piano. As Alan Newcombe says in his notes:
'Aided by Demus's lightly pedalled, often
almost brusque *staccato* articulation, the result is
starker, more elemental, less comfortable [than
the reading with Moore], conceived on a larger
scale.' To that one should add that the singer is
at the absolute height of his powers; tone, line,
breath control and intuitive imagination are
most remarkable in the strophic songs that, in
lesser hands, can seem over-long. Another feature of this is the significant underlining he
gives to pertinent words. For instance, in *Pause*
note how 'gehängt', 'durchschauert' and
'Nachklang' receive this treatment. It's this
unique vision of the German language in music
that still marks out this baritone from his many
successors. Immediate, unvarnished sound
heightens the value of this extraordinary performance.

The singer's partnership with Gerald Moore
in Schubert is well represented by their second,
1972 recording of *Schwanengesang*. It was one of
the most rewarding fruits of their long collaboration and crowned their joint labours on the
composer's oeuvre. The extra nine, mostly popular songs only confirm the impression left by
the quasi-cycle: who could resist this pair in *Die
Forelle* and *An Silvia*?

Die schöne Müllerin, D795

Die schöne Müllerin
Jochen Kupfer *bar* **Susanne Giesa** *pf*
Channel Classics CCS18898 (66' · DDD) Text and
translation included   Ⓕ**OO**

This reading of Schubert's cycle is confirmation, as if that were needed, of Jochen Kupfer's
beautiful singing, and even more of his gifts as a
Lieder interpreter. Kupfer's voice and style is
highly reminiscent of Wolfgang Holzmair's,
but his technique is just that shade firmer and
his voice more youthful than the older baritone's with Imogen Cooper, recalling rather
Holzmair's first (1983) recording on Preiser.
Both artists have a tenor-like quality to their
voices, coming near to some ideal for the work.
Kupfer begins with the basic verities of immaculate line and imaginative phrasing, to which he
adds a complete identification with the youthful
lover's aspirations and eventual disappointment
and tragedy.

This lad sets out with a spring in his heels and
a smile in his voice, quite avoiding any sense of
despondency from the outset. All is going to be
well in his wooing. That's conveyed in the first
few songs with fresh immediacy as though the
poetic emotions and their setting were new-
minted. The arrival of the unwanted and
aggressive hunter provokes an almost breathless
jealousy and, in that arresting song, 'Die liebe
Farbe', an appropriately mesmeric, plaintive
approach. From there on the downward curve
of emotional feeling, so arrestingly depicted in
the words and music, finds in Kupfer and his
alert partner an answering mood of despair, the
raw and anguished passion in those final three
songs fully achieved. All the while you feel the
disillusionment and pathos in the texture and
verbal acuity of the interpretation.

With a finely balanced recording to add to
one's pleasure, this is a performance among
baritones to place very near the top of the pile, if
not at its apex, and it challenges even the prevailing tenor recommendations, the versions by
Ian Bostridge and Werner Güra.

Die schöne Müllerin
Werner Güra *ten* **Jan Schultsz** *pf*
Harmonia Mundi HMC90 1708 (63' · DDD) Text and
translation included   Ⓕ**OOO**

 An enthralling account of the cycle on
virtually every count that seriously
challenges the hegemony of the many
desirable versions already available. In the first
place Güra must have about the most beautiful
voice ever to have recorded the work in the
original keys (and that's not to overlook Wunderlich, a far less perceptive interpreter). Its
owner has a technique second to none, able to
vary his tone, sing a lovely *pianissimo* and/or a
long-breathed phrase with perfect control.
Then no musical or verbal subtlety seems to
escape him at any stage of the young man's dis-
illusioning journey from happiness to misery
and death.

The plaintive quality of his voice and its
youthful sap are precisely right for conveying
the protagonist's vulnerability and, where
needed, his self-pity. That great song 'Der
Neugierige' encapsulates these virtues, with the

final couplet of questioning the brook immaculately done, just as the *pp* at the close of the previous song is given a curious sense of uncertainty on the boy's part. The three strophic songs are finely varied: here, as throughout, the use of *rubato* is natural and inevitable and the integration of singer and pianist, who's happily playing a Bechstein, are at their most compelling.

'Mein' is properly eager, expectant, 'Pause' as plangent as it should be, especially at its end. The frenetic anger of the 14th and 15th songs is as over-heated as it should be, 'Die liebe Farbe' rightly hypnotic. In those great songs, 'Trockne Blumen' and 'Der Müller und der Bach', both artists go to the heart of the matter, and the final lullaby is soft-grained and consoling. Schultsz's contributions are sometimes controversial, always challenging. Güra surpasses even the *Gramophone* Award-winning Bostridge, simply because his voice is under even better control and because his German is more idiomatic. The Harmonia Mundi sound, in spite of some reverberance, catches voice and piano in ideal balance.

Die schöne Müllerin, with a reading of six poems not set by Schubert
Ian Bostridge ten **Dietrich Fischer-Dieskau** narr
Graham Johnson pf
Hyperion CDJ33025 (73' · DDD)
Recorded 1994-5. Text and translation included
Ⓕ**OOO**

The 20 songs of *Die schöne Müllerin* portray a Wordsworthian world of heightened emotion in the pantheistic riverside setting of the miller. The poet, Wilhelm Müller, tells of solitary longings, jealousies, fears and hopes as the river rushes by, driving the mill-wheel and refreshing the natural world. Ian Bostridge and Graham Johnson go to the heart of the matter, the young tenor in his aching tones and naturally affecting interpretation, the pianist in his perceptive, wholly apposite playing. The sum of their joint efforts is a deeply satisfying experience.

Bostridge has the right timbre for the protagonist and a straightforward approach, with an instinctive rightness of phrasing. His peculiarly beseeching voice enshrines the vulnerability, tender feeling and obsessive love of the youthful miller, projecting in turn the young lover's thwarted passions, self-delusions and, finally, inner tragedy. Nowhere does he stretch beyond the bounds of the possible, everything expressed in eager then doleful tones. Johnson suggests that 'Ungeduld' mustn't be 'masterful and insistent' or the youth would have won the girl, so that even in this superficially buoyant song the sense of a sensitive, sad, introverted youth is maintained. The daydreaming strophic songs have the smiling, innocent, intimate sound that suits them to perfection, the angry ones the touch of stronger metal that Bostridge can now add to his silver, the tragic ones, before the neutral 'Baches

Wiegenlied', an inner intensity that rends the heart as it should. An occasional moment of faulty German accenting matters not at all when the sense of every word is perceived.

As a bonus we have here a recitation of the Prologue and Epilogue and of the Müller poems not set by Schubert: Fischer-Dieskau graces it with his speaking voice. The ideal Hyperion recording catches everything in very present terms. In all musical matters, everything Johnson writes only enhances one's enjoyment, if that's the right word, of a soul-searching interpretation.

Die schöne Müllerin
Dietrich Fischer-Dieskau bar **Gerald Moore** pf
EMI Great Recordings of the Century 566907-2
(59' · ADD) Recorded 1961. Text and translation
included Ⓜ**OO**

This reissue is the best of Fischer-Dieskau's three recordings of this work, made at the height of his – and Moore's – powers. His interpretation is simply more idiomatic and natural. He and Moore are here more spontaneous than in 1951 (for EMI), less affected than in 1972 (reissued on a DG CD in 1985). The conglomeration of Fischer-Dieskau's subtleties and insights are almost overwhelming but here they're mostly subsumed in the immediacy of a highly individual, always alerting performance. But the difference between conscious interpretation and interior restraint can be felt if you compare Fischer-Dieskau and Patzak in the phrase 'sie mir gab' in 'Trockne Blumen'. Moore throughout offers a discerning and musically valid characterisation of the participating stream: nothing is overplayed yet all is made manifest. So the intending purchaser is embarrassed with riches in a work that almost always brings the best out of its interpreters. Whichever other interpretation you opt for, you'll certainly want Fischer-Dieskau for complete command and understanding of this glorious work.

Die schöne Müllerin
Christian Gerhaher bar **Gerold Huber** pf
Arte Nova 82876 53172-2 (66' · DDD) Ⓢ**O**

Christian Gerhaher's voice, reminiscent of Fischer-Dieskau's, also exhibits many of that master-singer's stylistic virtues. He brings a keen, palpitating sound to the false expectations of the earlier songs: 'Ungeduld' is a particular success. A sadder timbre colours those moments of doubt in the middle of the work, before a proper plangency to the songs of sorrow culminates in arrestingly beautiful accounts of those two outright masterpieces, 'Trockne Blumen' and 'Der Müller und der Bach'. This is interpretation of Lieder at the highest level.

In its reading, rather than vocal timbre, the performance recalls in many respects that of Wolfgang Holzmair in its sense of a vulnerable soul motivated by self-delusion pursued to its inevitable consequences. Gerold Huber, the baritone's regular partner, adds to the disc's merits by virtue of his wholly sympathetic playing, in ideal accord with Gerhaher's view of the work. The recording itself is faultless. Listeners who want to hear the cycle for the first time need have no fear that they are will get anything less than the best, in spite of the asking-price. It's a performance that will stand the test of time and repetition.

Die schöne Müllerin **H**
Julius Patzak ten **Michael Raucheisen** pf
Preiser mono 93128 (61' · AAD) Recorded 1943 Ⓕ

'Der Mensch hat so eine Stimme' ('The man has a tone of voice') says Rocco of Florestan, and it's always a phrase that seems particularly apt for the voice of the great Viennese tenor, Julius Patzak, who was an unsurpassed Florestan himself. The same plangent utterance that was so affecting in his portrayal of Beethoven's suffering hero informs his famous interpretation of Schubert's cycle about the lovelorn millerhand. Indeed, his account of 'Die liebe Farbe' is so subjectively intense as to be hardly bearable, and the whole reading, with its poignant diction and lambent tone, places it quite in a class of its own. None reaches to the heart of the matter with quite Patzak's unerring skill. The range of his tone colour and methods of expression are evident not only in 'Die liebe Farbe' but also in the two great songs that succeed it.

In 'Die liebe Farbe', such phrases as 'grüne Rasen' and 'hat's jagen so gern' carry an enormous weight of grief as does the piercing enunciation of 'tote liebe' in 'Trockne Blumen'. The end of this song is taken very fast, as if in a fever of unjustified hope. But in earlier, happier moments, Patzak is no less eloquent – try the third verse of 'Des Müllers Blumen' or the whole of 'Morgengruss', where he creates the illusion of actually talking to the girl, or hear the intimate articulation in 'Der Neugierige' while, by contrast, the words tumble out abruptly in the fierce hatred of 'Der Jäger' and the following song. This is an interpretation that's *hors concours*, and not perhaps an interpretation one would wish to hear every day – it's too despairing. It's immensely detailed and subjective, free and spontaneous seeming, never calculated and sophisticated. Raucheisen is at times revelatory at the piano, at times wayward.

The recording, though immediate, has the occasional distortion, and the piano is backward. But the greatness of the reading overrides any drawbacks.

Schwanengesang, D957

Schwanengesang. Sehnsucht, D879. Der Wanderer an den Mond, D870. Wiegenlied, D867. Am Fenster, D878. Herbst, D945
Brigitte Fassbaender mez **Aribert Reimann** pf

DG Gramophone Awards Collection 474 535-2 (68' · DDD) Recorded 1989-91. Texts and translations included ⓂOOO

 Fassbaender and Reimann offer something equally compelling but rather different in their account of *Schwanengesang*. Fassbaender's interpretation, idiosyncratic in every respect, pierces to the heart of the bleak songs with performances as daring and challenging as the playing of her partner. More than anyone, these two artists catch the fleeting moods of these mini-dramas, and their searing originality of concept. Even the lighter songs have a special individuality of utterance. This is a starkly immediate interpretation that leaves the listener shattered. The extra Seidl settings, rarely performed, are all worth hearing. Both of these notable partnerships are superb in their own ways.

Schubert Schwanengesang **Beethoven** An die ferne Geliebte
Matthias Goerne bar **Alfred Brendel** pf
Decca 475 6011DH (72' · DDD · T/t) Recorded live at Wigmore Hall, London, 5-7 November 2003 ⒻOOO

 As Misha Donat reminds us in outstanding booklet essays, *Schwanengesang* divides clearly into eight Rellstab and six Heine settings; 'Herbst' is here added to the Rellstab group, while the Seidl 'Die Taubenpost' is made into the encore of a wonderful recital.

Goerne and Brendel form one of the great Lieder partnerships of the day. The sympathy between them goes beyond skilful ensemble and shared enjoyment of the wealth of illustration in Schubert, into a deep understanding of the poetry as he composed it. It's no surprise that they should produce powerful performances of the most inward-looking Heine songs – the suffering power of 'Der Atlas', the misery from which the harmony allows no escape in 'Die Stadt', the terror of 'Der Doppelgänger'. But the lighter ones are scarcely less affecting. And their mutual understanding completely solves such a difficult song as 'Kriegers Ahnung'.

The Beethoven cycle moves in a steady progress not into the usual triumphant assertion but into a warmth of belief that song may truly join the parted lovers. This is music-making of genius.

Additional recommendations

Schwanengesang
Coupled with: 10 Lieder **H**
Hotter bar **Moore** pf
EMI Références 565196-2 (78' · ADD) Ⓜ
Hotter's pioneering 1954 recording is a deeply satisfying reading. The nobility and softness of voice, the refinement of his diction and profound understanding of the text remain touchstones in interpreting this 'cycle'.

SCHUBERT DIE WINTERREISE – IN BRIEF

Christoph Prégardien ten **Andreas Staier** fp
Teldec 0630 18824-2 (74' · DDD)   Ⓜ●●
Prégardien's tenor cycle lays bare the raw
pain at the heart of the verses, while Staier's
less usual fortepiano lends the accompaniments a starker edge.

Dietrich Fischer-Dieskau bar **Jörg Demus** pf
DG 427 421-2GOR (71' · ADD)   Ⓜ●●
Fischer-Dieskau's immensely detailed,
emphatic approach is less in fashion now,
but he's still deeply felt and often extremely
beautiful to hear, and this cycle, ably accompanied by Jörg Demus, catches him at his
vocal peak.

Peter Schreier ten **András Schiff** pf
Decca 436 122-2DH (72' · DDD)   Ⓕ●
Schreier's finely expressive tenor and Schiff's
strong accompaniment create an intense,
nervy yet extremely beautiful performance.

Bernd Weikl ten **Helmut Deutsch** pf
Nightingale NC070960-2 (70' · DDD)   Ⓕ
Weikl's rich, powerful baritone makes this
a strikingly flowing, melodic performance,
though not lacking in expression and colour,
and well supported by Deutsch.

Matthias Goerne ten **Alfred Brendel** pf
Decca 467 092-2DH (75' · DDD)   Ⓕ
A stunning new performance, recorded live.
Matthias Goerne's dark baritone takes on a
uniquely haunted, tormented quality, without
sacrificing any of its beauty, and Brendel's
piano is just as profoundly expressive.

Peter Pears ten **Benjamin Britten** pf
Decca ② 452 402-2DF2 (147' · ADD)   Ⓕ
A classic 1963 performance of refined but
unrelenting intensity. Pears's distinctive tone
conveys anguish without exaggeration, while
Britten's accompaniment is marvellously
responsive in its shadings.

Brigitte Fassbaender mez **Aribert Reimann** pf
EMI 574989-2 (69' · ADD)   Ⓜ
Another performance that sees a major composer in the role of pianist and, like Britten
for Pears, Reimann proves a hugely imaginative partner. This is a tremendously powerful
account, and one that certainly justifies a
woman interpreter in this male territory.

Ian Bostridge ten **Julius Drake** pf
NVC Arts 🄳🅅🄳 8573 83780-2 (124')   Ⓕ
Bostridge's interpretation is finely sung but
perhaps too overtly neurotic. Filmed by controversial producer David Alden as visions in
an abandoned asylum, the performance is in
danger of over-emphasis but remains an
interesting experiment.

Winterreise, D911

Winterreise   Ⓟ
Christoph Prégardien ten **Andreas Staier** fp
Teldec Das Alte Werk 0630-18824-2 (74' · DDD) Texts
and translations included   Ⓜ●●

Prégardien and Staier have something new and
important to offer. From the very first song,
we're in the presence of a sensitive, inward man
in fear of his fate. Something is actually happening to this sufferer's soul at the second 'des
ganzen Winters Eis'; indeed the whole final
verse of the second song expresses the youth's
anguish. Just as memorable are the stab of pain
in the repeated final line 'Da ist meiner Lieb-
stens Haus' at the end of 'Wasserflut', the introverted misery of the ice-carving of the loved-
one's name in 'Auf dem Flusse' and the almost
mesmeric feeling in the final verse as the torrent
rages in the protagonist's heart. This is what the
singing of this cycle is about: the exposing of
raw nerves.

Staier is just as revelatory. Using his fortepiano to maximum effect, he finds so many fresh
perceptions in his part, as in the precise weighting at the start of 'Einsamkeit' and, as important, ones that accord perfectly with those of his
regular partner. Here you've the sense of performers who have lived together with the cycle
and conceived a unified, thought-through
vision. For example, listen to the way the pair
mesh together to searing effect at the end of
'Irrlicht'. The ineffable sadness of 'Frühlingstraum' (the text ideally articulated, the close
properly trance-like), the raw blast of winter in
'Der stürmische Morgen', the tense weariness
of 'Der Weg-weiser', the weary half-voice of
'Das Wirtshaus' – these and so much else contribute to the impression of a truly great performance. The recording is very finely balanced.

Winterreise
Dietrich Fischer-Dieskau bar **Jörg Demus** pf
DG The Originals 447 421-2GOR (71' · ADD)
Recorded 1965. Text and translation included   Ⓜ●●

On the verge of his fifth decade, the singer was
in his absolute prime. Listening to his interpretation is like coming home to base after many
interesting encounters away from the familiar.
Indeed, it's possibly the finest of all in terms of
beauty of tone and ease of technique – and how
beautiful, how smooth and velvety was the baritone's voice at that time. This is the most interior, unadorned and undemonstrative of his
readings, perhaps because Demus, a discerning
musician and sure accompanist, is the most
reflective of all the singer's many partners in the
cycle. Demus never strikes out on his own, is
always there unobtrusively and subtly supportive, with the right colour and phrasing, literally
in hand.

Given an intimate, slightly dry recording,
finely remastered, the whole effect is of a pair
communing with each other and stating the sad,

distraught message of Schubert's bleak work in terms of a personal message to the listener in the home. A deeply rewarding performance. Certainly if you want Fischer-Dieskau in the cycle you need look no further.

Winterreise
Peter Schreier ten **András Schiff** pf
Decca 436 122-2DH (72' · DDD) Recorded 1991. Text
and translation included ⓅⓄ

Schreier, in his note in the accompanying booklet, refers to the unique density and spiritual concentration of the *Winterreise* songs; that, and their hallucinatory nature, inform this riveting performance from start to finish, nowhere more so than in 'Wasserflut' and 'Einsamkeit'. The latter is a paradigm of the whole searing, almost unbearable experience. If you can tolerate it you'll be engaged and surely moved by the whole. In this song, Schreier leans into the words and notes of 'Ach, das die Luft so ruhig!' suggesting the cry of a desperate, tormented soul – as does the emphatic enunciation of the single word 'Bergstroms' earlier, in 'Irricht'. Also arresting is the curiously daring way Schreier asks the question at the end of 'Die Post', as if it were a spontaneous afterthought. These make the moments of calm and repose all the more eerie. The sad delicacy of Schiff's playing at the start of 'Frühlingstraum' sets the scene of the imagined May to perfection, and the flowing lift of his left hand in 'Täuschung' is as deceptively friendly as the light described by the singer. 'Das Wirtshaus' is all false resignation: voice and piano tell us of the man's tired emptiness. Anger and defiance are registered in raw, chilling tone and phraseology.

The final songs taken simply, speak beautifully of acceptance. The recording is warm yet clear.

Winterreise
Bernd Weikl bar **Helmut Deutsch** pf
Nightingale Classics NC070960-2 (70' · DDD)
Recorded 1993. Text and translation included Ⓕ

For those who prefer a baritone, Weikl seriously challenges the hegemony, among lower-voiced singers, of the many available versions. Indeed, it's the absolute vocal security and evenness of Weikl's actual singing that so impresses even before one considers his view of the work. Nowhere is there any sign of strain, overemphasis, faltering in pitch, or failure of nerve in executing a phrase with a long breath, and as the singer has such a strong voice one feels throughout that there's always something held in reserve.

As a reading the Weikl unerringly keeps that balance between detachment and subjectivity. Tempos are perfectly judged – and here Deutsch's well-observed, well-balanced playing makes a real contribution – a wonderful frozen feeling in 'Auf dem Flusse', for instance. Weikl

displays many gradations of tone to enhance his thought-through reading – 'Gefrorne Tränen' is a good example – but he uses vocal emphases more sparingly, reserving his most pointed verbal accents for such things as 'Gras' in 'Erstarrung', 'Hähne' in 'Frühlingstraum' and 'Hunde' in 'Im Dorfe', but even these never upset the verities of line and firm tone, and the sheer beauty of the singing, as in 'Der Lindenbaum', is balm to the ear.

For those who find Fischer-Dieskau's more agonised readings too much to bear, or find his style too interventionist, Weikl is the obvious choice. A superb recording.

Additional recommendation

Winterreise
Fassbaender mez **Reimann** pf
EMI Encore 574989-2 (69' · DDD) Ⓑ
An account that plumbs the depths of emotional sorrow and despair. This is an arrestingly powerful and immediate interpretation of the cycle; some may find her treatment of *rubato* too idiosyncratic, others will find that the style breathes conviction.

Ervin Schulhoff · Bohemian 1894-1942

Schulhoff was a pupil of Reger in Leipzig (1908-10) and later in Germany (1919-23) he associated with Klee and the dadaists; back in Prague he was active as a pianist, in jazz and as an exponent of Hába's quarter-tone music. His works include stage pieces, six symphonies and two piano sonatas, displaying diverse styles. He died in a concentration camp.
GROVEmusic

Symphonies

Symphonies Nos 3 & 5
Prague Radio Symphony Orchestra / Vladimír Válek
Supraphon 11 2161-2 (53' · DDD) Recorded 1994 Ⓕ

Posthumous premières of these works in the 1950s aroused little interest, but Schulhoff has acquired quite a following in recent years and this latest addition to his discography shouldn't be overlooked. As always in music where there's no performance tradition to speak of, the range of interpretative possibilities is wide. On this showing, Vladimír Válek is the most deft and neo-classical of Schulhoff conductors, offering well-prepared, notably fluent accounts of both pieces; his aim seems to be to reconcile their blatant Communistic idiom with the lighter, Roaring Twenties manner of the composer's previous creative period. In Israel Yinon's recording of the Third Symphony, you sense that the music isn't just being given room to breathe; it can only be considered in the light of the composer's death in a Nazi concentration camp. Accordingly, Yinon adopts a much weightier tempo in the first movement, its ostinato unrelenting, its drums militantly thwacked. Albrecht's idea of *moderato* is yet more funereal, suggesting that it's the Czech conductor who's out of line. Nevertheless, Válek's account is arguably the most persuasive of the three, executed with commendable crispness. In the Fifth Symphony, risking some loss of *gravitas*, Válek is again nothing if not urgent. The music makes better sense in his hands, and any lack of clarity in the orchestral textures seems to derive from the score. Even the lack of a clinching melodic idea is made to appear less important. This is a valuable disc, well annotated.

Sextet

Sextet. String Quartet in G, Op 25. Duo[a]. Solo Violin Sonata[b]
Rainer Johannes Kimstedt *va* **Michael Sanderling** *vc* **Petersen Quartet** ([b]Conrad Muck, [a]Gernot Sussmuth *vns* Friedemann Weigle *va* [a]Hans-Jakob Eschenburg *vc*)
Capríccio 10 539 (77' · DDD) Recorded 1994 Ⓕ**O**

As Schulhoff enthusiasts will have come to expect, the works represented aren't at all uniform in style. The early quartet is prematurely neo-classical. It was conceived in 1918 when the composer was still serving in the Austrian Army. The German group certainly gives it their all. Taut and tough, they seem intent on radicalising the discourse whether through a heightened response to its finer points or a profound understanding of the Beethovenian models that lurk beneath the surface invention. As a result, the Quartet emerges as a witty, substantial piece.

The string Sextet was completed six years later but sounds quite different, its Schoenbergian first movement well integrated with the more eclectic idiom of the rest. Whatever the outward manner, Schulhoff's rhythmic phraseology is metrically conceived. Even if you already know the Sextet the Petersen makes a plausible first choice. The aggressive communication of their playing is emphasised by the bright, not quite top-heavy sound balance.

The Janáček-Bartók-Ravel axis of the *Duo* is equally well served. The Sonata for solo violin (1927) is at least as interesting as similar works by Hindemith. A thoroughly distinguished issue by an ensemble seemingly incapable of giving a dull performance.

String Quartet No 1

Schulhoff String Quartet No 1 **Hindemith** String Quartet No 3, Op 22 **Weill** String Quartet
Brandis Quartet (Thomas Brandis, Peter Brem *vns* Wilfried Strehle *va* Wolfgang Boettcher *vc*)
Nimbus NI5410 (60' · DDD) Recorded 1992 Ⓕ

All three works bear witness to a culture that, in terms of tempo and sensation, was in the process of excited transformation. The period covered is 1923-4, the time of rocketing German inflation, the establishment of the USSR, Rilke's *Duino Elegies* as well as major Kafka (who died in 1924), Mann, Musil, Cocteau and Bréton (his Surrealist manifesto). This music is full of it all. Hindemith's bold Third Quartet launches its explorations within a relatively formal framework, certainly in comparison with Schulhoff and Weill. Rich invention is tempered by a sense of outward propriety. Weill's Quartet opens with real expressive warmth, although it soon busies itself with a whole range of interesting ideas (the finale is particularly rich in incident), with a hoot of a *Scherzo* that suddenly swerves to a Reger-like March, then waltzes gently forth in a manner that suggests Shostakovich before embarking on further discursive episodes and scurrying off to a cheeky *diminuendo*. Granted, one feels that Weill is in search of something he never quite finds, but the very act of searching makes for an absorbing adventure.

Even more compelling, however, is Schulhoff's dazzling First Quartet, the last piece in the programme and a highly dramatic musical mystery tour. Urgency rules right from the opening bars, while Schulhoff's tonal palette is both wide-ranging and ingeniously employed: pizzicato, *col legno*, *sul ponticello*, harmonics (wonderfully effective in the finale), dense harmonic computations and a rhythmic vitality that recalls Bartók at full cry. The work's pale, equivocal coda recalls the parallel quartet mysteries of Schulhoff's fellow Holocaust victims Krása and Haas, while the work as a whole is far more than the sum of its restless and endlessly fascinating parts. A fine programme, lustrously recorded.

William Schuman   American 1910-1992

Schuman studied at Columbia University and under Harris at the Juilliard School. He came firmly to public notice with his Symphony no.3 (1941). He taught at Sarah Lawrence College, 1935-45, then became president of the Juilliard School, which he extensively reorganised. He was president of the Lincoln Center, 1962-9. He received many honours and awards. His symphonies (ten up to 1975) are central to his work; they embody vigorous drive, febrile rhythms and expansive musical and orchestral gestures, with a broad melodic line and a generally tonal idiom. Sometimes his music is layered, using different instrumental groups at different speeds. His chamber music includes four string quartets; he also composed, mainly after the mid-1970s, large-scale vocal pieces. GROVEmusic

Violin Concerto

Schuman Violin Concerto[a]. New England Triptych
Ives Variations on 'America' (orch Schuman)

aPhilip Quint vn Bournemouth Symphony
Orchestra / José Serebrier
Naxos 8 559083 (57' · DDD)   ⓢⓞ

The rediscovery here is the Violin Concerto. The work is in two substantial movements both showing Schuman's own kind of exuberant energy with brass and percussion as well as a special mystical stillness in soft music. The soloist plunges in right at the start of the first movement; there's an oasis of calm at and then a sprawling cadenza of nearly three minutes. The second movement has an aggressive start which clears the way for the delayed entry of the soloist. Again there's lyrical rapture as well as fireworks and – another Schuman fingerprint – a fugato. Philip Quint, the Russian-born American violinist, make his CD début here. It's a very capable performance in every way – look out for him again. Schuman's *New England Triptych*, based on three hymns by the first prominent American pioneer-composer, William Billings, is one of his most familiar pieces, well represented on CD. The *Variations on 'America'* – sending up the USA, royalty or both – ensures that this useful Schuman package ends with a good laugh.

example – Chopin's *Allegro de Concert* (his 'third' Concerto). The 'Romance''s rocking rhythm is touched with a startling degree of dissonance and decoration, and the final Polonaise dips into the most piquantly harmonised and varied introspection at 2'14", once again suggesting a wholly personal voice and character.

Hearing such music side by side with a tirelessly celebrated and performed masterpiece is a most intriguing experience particularly when the performances of both Concertos are so superb. Brigitte Engerer's resilience and affection would surely have delighted her great predecessor.

Even more remarkably, she plays Robert's Concerto with such fervour and mastery that it sounds new-minted, as if recreated on the spot. Absolutely nothing is taken for granted. The theme itself, whether in its major or minor key manifestation, is memorably poised and inflected and in the cascading *animato* sections her playing glows and surges with a Romantic sense of impetus and momentum.

Never for a moment does this sound like a studio performance and the youthful orchestra under Philippe Bender respond with a scarcely less tingling vitality.

Clara Schumann   German 1819-1896

Developed by her father, Friedrich, into a musician of consummate artistry, she won dazzling success as a touring piano virtuoso both before and after she married Robert Schumann (1840), being praised not only for her mastery of a progressive repertory (Chopin, Schumann and Brahms) but also for her thoughtful interpretations and singing tone. She taught privately in Dresden and Düsseldorf and at the conservatories in Leipzig and Frankfurt. As a composer she showed imagination and control, notably in the Piano Trio, Op 17 and the songs, Op 23, but her ambitions were not serious; she ceased composing in 1854, the year of Robert's collapse. She prepared a complete edition of his music, attended to family duties and maintained a close relationship with Brahms to the end of her life. GROVEmusic

Piano Concerto

C Schumann Piano Concerto in A minor, Op 7
R Schumann Piano Concerto in A minor, Op 54
Brigitte Engerer pf **Cannes Regional Orchestra /
Philippe Bender**
L'Emprinte Digitale ED13146 (53' · DDD)   Ⓕⓞ

Clara Schumann's Concerto, composed amazingly when she was 16 (though partly composed three years earlier), proves conclusively that she was a serious, most individual composer as well as a legendary pianist. The opening *Allegro maestoso* moves with a heavier Teutonic tread than Robert's, and the bravura, while Hummel-based at one level, is closely integrated, recalling in its strenuousness and difficulty – at 3'12", for

Robert Schumann   German 1810-1856

The son of a bookseller, Schumann early showed ability as a pianist and an interest in composing as well as literary leanings. He was also enthusiastic over the writings of 'Jean Paul' (JPF Richter), girl friends and drinking champagne, tastes he retained. In 1821 he went to Leipzig to study law but instead spent his time in musical, social and literary activities. He wrote some piano music and took lessons from Friedrich Wieck. After a spell in Heidelberg, ostensibly studying law but actually music, he persuaded his family that he should give up law in favour of a pianist's career, and in 1830 he went to live with Wieck at Leipzig. But he soon had trouble with hands (allegedly due to a machine to strengthen his fingers, but more likely through remedies for a syphilitic sore). Composition, however, continued; several piano works date from this period.

In 1834 Schumann founded a music journal, the Neue Zeitschrift für Musik; he was its editor and leading writer for ten years. He was a brilliant and perceptive critic: his writings embody the most progressive aspects of musical thinking in his time, and he drew attention to many promising young composers. Sometimes he wrote under pseudonyms, Eusebius (representing his lyrical, contemplative side) and Florestan (his fiery, impetuous one); he used these in his music, too. His compositions at this time were mainly for piano: they include variations on the name of one on his lady friends, Abegg (the musical notes A-B-E-G-G), the character-pieces Davidsbündlertänze ('Dances of the league of David', an imaginary association of those fighting the Philistines), Carnaval (pieces with literary or other allusive meanings, including one on the notes

A-S-C-H after the place another girl friend came from), Phantasiestücke (a collection of poetic pieces depicting moods), Kreisleriana (fantasy pieces around the character of a mad Kapellmeister) and Kinderszenen ('Scenes from Childhood'). Affairs of the heart played a large part in his life. By 1835 he was in love with Wieck's young daughter Clara, but Wieck did his best to separate them. They pledged themselves in 1837 but were much apart and Schumann went through deep depressions. In 1839 they took legal steps to make Wieck's consent unnecessary, and after many further trials they were able to marry in 1840.

Schumann, understandably, turned in that year to song; he wrote c150 songs, including most of his finest, at this time, among them several groups and cycles, the latter including Frauenliebe und -leben ('A Woman's Love and Life') and Dichterliebe ('A Poet's Love'), which tells (to verse by Heine) a tragic Romantic story of the flowering of love, its failure and poet's exclusion from joy and his longing for death. Schumann, as a pianist composer, made the piano partake fully in the expression of emotion in such songs, often giving it the most telling music when the voice had finished.

In 1841, however, Schumann turned to orchestral music: he wrote symphonies and a beautiful, poetic piece for piano and orchestra for Clara that he later reworked as the first movement of his Piano Concerto. Then in 1842, when Clara was away on a concert tour (he disliked being in her shadow and remained at home), he turned to chamber music, and wrote his three string quartets and three works with piano, of which the Piano Quintet has always been a favourite for the freshness and Romantic warmth of its ideas. After that, in 1843, he turned to choral music, working at a secular oratorio and at setting part of Goethe's Faust. He also took up a teaching post at the new conservatory in Leipzig of which Mendelssohn was director. But he was an ineffectual teacher; and he had limited success as a conductor too. He and Clara moved to Dresden in 1844, but his deep depressions continued, hampering his creativity. Not until 1847-8 was he again productive, writing his opera Genoveva (given in Leipzig in 1850 with moderate success) and chamber music and songs. In 1850 he took up a post in Düsseldorf as town musical director. He was at first happy and prolific, writing the eloquent Cello Concerto and the Rhenish Symphony (no.3: one movement depicts his impressions in Cologne Cathedral). But the post worked out badly because of his indifferent conducting. In 1852-3 his health and spirits deteriorated and he realised that he could not continue in his post. In 1854 he began to suffer hallucinations; he attempted suicide (he had always dreaded the possibility of madness) and entered an asylum, where he died in 1856, almost certainly of the effects of syphilis, cared for at the end by Clara and the young Brahms. GROVEmusic

Cello Concerto in A minor, Op 129

Schumann Cello Concerto. Adagio and Allegro in **P** A flat, Op 70. Fantasiestücke, Op 73. Fünf Stücke im Volkston, Op 102. Mass in C minor, Op 147 – Offertorium **Bargiel** Adagio in G, Op 38
Steven Isserlis vc **Dame Felicity Lott** sop David

King org **Deutsche Kammerphilharmonie / Christoph Eschenbach** pf
RCA Red Seal 09026 68800-2 (75' · DDD) Ⓕ

Only two of the works in this forwardly recorded anthology – the *Fünf Stücke im Volkston* of 1840 and the Cello Concerto of a year later – were originally inspired by the cello. But in closely attuned, super-sensitive partnership with Eschenbach as both conductor and pianist, Steven Isserlis somehow persuades us that no instrument better revealed 'the beloved dreamer whom we know as Schumann', as Tovey once put it. Helped by unhurried tempos and a lovely voiced c1745 Guadagnini cello, Isserlis draws out the rich, nostalgic poetry of the concerto's first two movements with the eloquence of speech. And with his buoyancy of heart and bow he silences all criticism of the finale – even its low-lying cadenza (this he subsequently plays again with the composer's surely less effective flourish for the soloist in the closing bars). The five engaging *Volkston* pieces with piano are vividly characterised and contrasted in mood. And the Op 73 and Op 70 miniatures lose nothing through transfer from clarinet and horn respectively to one of the composer's two optional alternatives.

The *Adagio and Allegro* for horn surely gains in expressive intimacy and vitality when bowed rather than blown. The *Offertorium* is sung by Felicity Lott with heart-easing beauty. The inclusion of a hitherto unrecorded, noble *Adagio* by Clara Schumann's gifted half-brother, Woldemar Bargiel, also helps to make this disc a collector's piece.

Piano Concerto in A minor, Op 54

Piano Concerto[a]. Piano Quintet in E flat, Op 44[b]
Maria João Pires pf [b]**Augustin Dumay**, [b]**Renaud Capuçon** vns [b]**Gérard Caussé** va [b]**Jian Wang** vc
[a]**Chamber Orchestra of Europe / Claudio Abbado**
DG 463 179-2GH (62' · DDD) Recorded [a]1997, [b]1999
Ⓕ**OO**

It makes an unusual and apt coupling to have the Schumann Piano Concerto alongside the most powerful of his chamber works. In both, Pires is inspired to give freely spontaneous performances, at once powerfully persuasive and poetic. In the Quintet the feeling of interplay between musicians is a delight; distinguished individually, they plainly enjoy working together. The warmth of the whole performance is reflected in the way that Pires leads the team to play with natural, unselfconscious *rubato* in all four movements, the speeds perfectly chosen and the structure firmly held together. The rhythmic spring of the playing is a constant delight, too. In the Concerto Pires is also at her most persuasive. Abbado has conducted several previous recordings of the work, notably for Perahia on Sony and Pollini on DG, yet here with the Chamber Orchestra of Europe he's able to match the volatile quality in Pires's performance with beautifully transparent accompaniment. So the hushed *Andante espressivo* section in the first movement finds the COE flute and clarinet fully matching their soloist in expressiveness. The central *Intermezzo* is light and fresh at a flowing *Andante grazioso*, free *rubato* making it sound like an improvisation. It leads to a sparkling account of the finale, which lightly emphasises the *scherzando* quality of the writing at a relatively relaxed speed. Two beautifully judged performances, both well recorded, make this an original coupling.

Piano Concerto[a]. Cello Concerto in A minor[b].
Introduction and Allegro appassionato, Op 92[a].
[a]**Daniel Barenboim** *pf* [b]**Jacqueline du Pré** *vc*
[a]**London Philharmonic Orchestra / Dietrich Fischer-Dieskau;** [b]**New Philharmonia Orchestra / Daniel Barenboim**
EMI Encore 574755-2 (74' · ADD) Recorded [a]1974, [b]1968   Ⓢ Ⓑ⚫

If ever a performance of Schumann's Piano Concerto stressed the principle of dialogue between soloist and conductor, then this is it. True, the Philharmonia's string ensemble isn't as water-tight under Fischer-Dieskau as it might have been under some other conductors; and poetry is invested at the premium of relatively low-level drama. Orchestral textures are absolutely right for Schumann – warm yet transparent, full-bodied yet never stodgy – and poetry is a major priority. Add Barenboim's compatible vision and keyboard finesse, and you indeed have a memorable reading. Despite the extensive competition, both Stephen Kovacevich and Leif Ove Andsnes remain the top recommendations for this work (both reviewed under Grieg) though.

The more discursive *Introduction and Allegro appassionato* has plenty of interest, but remembering that this isn't exactly top-drawer Schumann, the performance could be more arresting. The coupling is du Pré's Schumann Cello Concerto, the tear-laden quality in the slow movement more than matching that in her famous Elgar account. A rewarding disc.

Schumann Piano Concerto[a] **Beethoven** Piano Concerto No 4[b]
Hélène Grimaud *pf* [a]**Deutsches Symphony Orchestra, Berlin / David Zinman;** [b]**New York Philharmonic / Kurt Masur**
Warner Elatus 0927-49617-2 (DDD) Recorded [a]1995   Ⓜ⚫

Such is Grimaud's immediacy of response to every change of mood in the opening *Allegro affettuoso* of Schumann's concerto that some listeners may think it a little too excitable – at the expense of maturer composure and poise. But never in this movement, nor in a finale of unflagging vitality and *joie de vivre*, is there any hint of mere keyboard display. You could certainly never hope to hear the first movement's nostalgic main theme played with a more eloquent simplicity. Piano and orchestra are in exceptionally close accord throughout, and not least in the intimate conversational exchanges of the *Andantino grazioso*. Warner's sound is clear-cut rather than lusciously cushioned, but never hard-edged: it falls agreeably on the ear.

Piano Concerto. Introduction and Allegro appassionato in G, Op 92. Introduction and Allegro in D minor, Op 134
Murray Perahia pf **Berlin Philharmonic Orchestra / Claudio Abbado**
Sony Classical SK64577 (57' · DDD) Recorded 1994
Ⓕ**OO**

From Perahia and Abbado the Piano Concerto comes across with refreshing eagerness, as if Schumann could scarcely pause for breath in an uprush of inspiration. But unflagging strength of direction by no means excludes the personal. The first movement, in particular, brings intimately revealing nuances of phrasing from Perahia, with a finely shaped, richly expressive cadenza before a delectably light-fingered, effervescent coda. Free of coy cosseting the *Andante* has a natural, gracious flow. However, a more expansive melodic glow in the middle section would not have gone amiss, not least when the violins soar into the upper reaches (a masterstroke of orchestration) near its end. Piquantly crunched acciaccaturas at the start inject the finale with inexhaustible rhythmic buoyancy. Recorded in Berlin's Philharmonie, the sound quality is vibrantly full and forward.

Perahia adds Schumann's two later works for piano and orchestra as couplings, of which the sorely neglected last in D minor was part of a birthday present for Clara. Though less immediately ear-catching than the Mendelssohnian G major work , Schumann's farewell to the genre – as played here – is striking as by far the more intense of the two, with eventual major-key victory won after deeper internal struggle.

Additional recommendation

Piano Concerto
Coupled with: Introduction and Allegro appassionato in G. Concert-Allegro with Introduction in D minor
Lausanne Chamber Orchestra / Zacharias pf
Dabringhaus und Grimm MDG340 1033-2 (62' · DDD)   Ⓕ

Zacharias establishes his own distinctive view, as compelling in its way as that of Perahia and Abbado. The scale is Mozartian, allowing extra transparency of texture, with Zacharias's articulation a consistent joy. A refreshing alternative, bright and alert, to Perahia.

Violin Concerto, Op posth

Schumann Violin Concerto in D minor, Op posth
Wieniawski Légende, Op 17. Violin Concerto No 2 in D minor, Op 22
Juliette Kang vn **Vancouver Symphony Orchestra / Sergiu Comissiona**

CBC Records SMCD5197 (63' · DDD)   Ⓕ**O**

Juliette Kang here plays with quicksilver brilliance not only in the virtuosic Wieniawski concerto but in the rugged Schumann work, less grateful for the player. Yet, though she plays brilliantly, with dazzlingly clean articulation in bravura passages, these are comparatively small-scale readings. Where those virtuosos in the grand Romantic tradition are balanced relatively close, Kang is more naturally balanced in a slightly recessed acoustic. The impression is of a sweet, silvery violin tone that can't expand so fully; the orchestral strings, too, sound relatively small-scale. What matters is that the performances are all very persuasive. The Schumann, with its bravura double-stopping at the start, finds Kang fiery and impetuous, making up for barnstorming power, and when it comes to lyrical passages the poetry is beautifully caught. So too in the slow movement – introduced in a tender account of the brief opening cello solo – while the finale is taken at a speed which allows a delicious lilt in the dance-rhythms, yet not eccentrically slow as in the Kremer/Harnoncourt.

Similarly, in the Wieniawski Concerto, Kang is light and volatile in the rapid passagework, and relaxes sweetly into the songful beauty of the motto theme, playing with a natural, unexaggerated lyricism.

Those who insist on display as the first essential may not be completely satisfied, but deeper qualities amply make up for that. For those who want this unique coupling, this is a first-class recommendation.

Symphonies

No 1 in B flat, Op 38, 'Spring' **No 2** in C, Op 61 **No 3** in E flat, Op 97, 'Rhenish' **No 4** in D minor, Op 120

Symphonies Nos 1-4. Overture, Scherzo and Finale, Op 52
Staatskapelle Dresden / Wolfgang Sawallisch
EMI Great Recordings of the Century mono
② 567768-2 (148' · ADD) Recorded 1972   Ⓜ**OO**

Schumann's symphonies come in for criticism because of his supposed cloudy textures and unsubtle scoring, but in the hands of a conductor who's both skilful and sympathetic they're most engaging works. Sawallisch's recordings, brightly transferred, are a much admired set. His style, fresh and unforced, isn't as high powered as some other conductors but it's sensible, alert and very pleasing. He achieves great lightness in the First and Fourth Symphonies – there's always a sense of classical poise and control but never at the expense of the overall architecture of the pieces. The Second and Third Symphonies, larger and more far-reaching in their scope, again benefit from Sawallisch's approach. The playing of the Staatskapelle Dresden is superlative in every department, with a lovely veiled string sound and a real sense of ensemble. With the *Overture, Scherzo and Finale* thrown in for good measure, this isn't to be missed.

Symphonies Nos 1 & 2
Bavarian Radio Symphony Orchestra / Rafael Kubelík
Sony Classical Essential Classics SBK48269
(74' · ADD) Recorded 1978-9　　　Ⓢ Ⓑ●

Symphonies Nos 3 & 4. Manfred, Op 115 – Overture
Bavarian Radio Symphony Orchestra / Rafael Kubelík
Sony Classical Essential Classics SBK48270
(76' · ADD) Recorded 1978-9　　　Ⓑ

It's hard to understand why Kubelík's wonderful cycle failed to make an impact when it was first issued. His sensitivity to detail, his refusal to bully Schumann's vulnerable structures and his ability to penetrate occasional thickets of orchestration, make these especially memorable. Just listen to the cheeky bassoon backing clarinet, 1'44" into the *Spring* Symphony's fourth movement or the to-ing and fro-ing between first and second violins in the last movement of the Second. Only the first movement of the Fourth seems a little heavy-handed, but then the poetry of the *Romanze* and the exuberance of the finale more than make amends. First movement repeats are observed and the playing throughout is rich in felicitous turns of phrase. The sound, though, is a minor stumbling block: violins are thin, brass a little fuzzy and the whole production less focused than Sawallisch's set. But Kubelík's insights are too varied and meaningful to miss, and there's much pleasure to be derived from them. What with a stirring *Manfred* Overture added for good measure, they also constitute exceptional value for money.

Symphonies Nos 1-3; No 4 (1841 & 1851　　Ⓟ
G minor versions);WoO29, 'Zwickauer'. Overture,
Scherzo and Finale, Op 52. Konzertstück in F, Op 86
Roger Montgomery, Gavin Edwards, Susan Dent, Robert Maskell hns **Orchestre Révolutionnaire et Romantique / Sir John Eliot Gardiner**
Archiv Produktion ③ 457 591-2AH3 (202' · DDD) Ⓕ●

The first point to note is how much more comprehensive this is than previous cycles, even the outstanding RCA set of period performances from Roy Goodman and the Hanover Band. Gardiner offers both versions of Symphony No 4, 1841 and 1851, and his performances of them are very well geared to bringing out the contrasts. Still more fascinating is the inclusion of both the early, incomplete Symphony in G minor, and the *Konzertstück* of 1849 for four horns, with the ORR soloists breathtaking in their virtuosity in the outer movements, using horns with rotary valves crooked in F. Otherwise, except in three specified movements, natural horns are used, braying clearly through orchestration which always used to be condemned as too thick. In his note, Gardiner fairly points out the merits of the 1841 version in transparency and other qualities, suggesting, as others have, that the doublings in the later version make it safer and more commonplace. Paradoxically in performance, Gardiner is if anything even more electrifying in the later, more thickly upholstered version, as ever clarifying textures and building up to a thrilling conclusion. Even the *Zwickauer* Symphony of 1832 emerges as very distinctive of Schumann.

The contrasts between Gardiner and Goodman in their approach to the numbered works aren't as marked as expected, often as much a question of scale and recording quality as of interpretative differences, with Goodman's orchestra more intimate, and with the RCA sound a degree less brightly analytical. Both prefer fast speeds, with Goodman a shade more relaxed and Gardiner more incisive, pressing ahead harder, with syncopations – so important in Schumann – more sharply dramatic. One advantage that Gardiner has in his slightly bigger scale is that he brings out more light and shade, offering a wider dynamic range. Hence the solemn fourth movement of the *Rhenish* Symphony inspired by Cologne Cathedral – as with Goodman taken at a flowing speed – builds up more gradually in a bigger, far longer *crescendo*, in the end the more powerful for being held back at the start. Though the Goodman set still holds its place, Gardiner offers a conspectus of Schumann as symphonist that's all the richer and more illuminating for the inclusion of the extra rarities.

Symphonies Nos 1-4. Manfred, Op 115 – Overture Ⓗ
Cleveland Orchestra / George Szell
Sony Classical Masterworks Heritage ② 5160272
(135' · ADD) Recorded 1958-60　　　Ⓜ●

This famous set gives us the heart of George Szell, his feeling for style, for line and for Schumann's warming but fragile symphonic structures. Szell loved the Schumann symphonies, but readers should be warned that he attempts to correct – and here we quote Szell himself – 'minor lapses [in orchestration] due to inexperience' with 'remedies' that range from 'subtle adjustments of dynamic marks to the radical surgery of re-orchestrating whole stretches'. More often than not, the musical results serve Schumann handsomely. Szell sometimes takes *crescendo* to imply *accelerando*, but his insistence on watertight exchanges facilitates a snug fit between various instrumental choirs, the strings especially. Markings such as *Animato* (in the First Symphony's *Allegro molto vivace*) or *piano dolce* (in the same movement) are scrupulously observed, and so are most of Schumann's metronome markings. Playing standards are very high, but the close-set recordings occasionally undermine Szell's painstaking efforts to clarify Schumann's orchestration, the *Rhenish* being the worst offender.

The *Rhenish* again yields high musical dividends, with sensitively shaped central movements, but were we to single out just one track on the whole set, it would have to be the Second Symphony's *Adagio espressivo*, a performance of such warmth, nobility and elasticity (the latter not a quality normally associated with Szell) that it's tempting to grant it the accolade of 'best ever'. The *Manfred* Overture is given a wildly spontaneous performance, with extreme tempos and some brilliant playing. Sometimes you may feel that Szell was being overprotective towards the music and that the same interpretations played live might have thrown caution to the wind. Still, Szell should certainly be granted equal status with his bargain stablemates Kubelík and Sawallisch. Both are perhaps marginally more spontaneous in the First and Third Symphonies, but Szell's loving exegeses underline details in the music that you won't have heard on many other recordings. Transfers and presentation are superb.

Symphonies Nos 1-4
Tonhalle Orchestra, Zurich / David Zinman
Arte Nova ② 82876 57743-2 (123' · DDD)   Ⓢ

David Zinman has recorded Schumann's symphonies before, in Baltimore in the late 1980s, a set recently remarketed by Telarc at mid-price. The remake involves a radical change of orchestral sonority, more grainy, notably lighter, with the sort of sharpened dynamic profile and fine-tipped attenuation more associated with period instrument orchestras.

Zinman's second Schumann set also involves some minor textural novelties. Added ornaments and appoggiaturas appear in the *Adagio espressivo* of No 2, for example, and in the first movement of the *Rhenish*. For this latest project Zinman uses period brass and timpani: note the stopped horns for the pivotal four-note motive in the *Spring* Symphony's *Allegro molto vivace*. Tempos are in general swifter than before. The opening of the *Spring*'s *Scherzo*, for example, just about exceeds the prescribed metronome marking, whereas in Baltimore it was marginally slower. More significantly, the third-movement trio in No 4 is now virtually in tempo with the outer sections. Zinman provides a sort of Schumann slimming kit, useful for those who find the symphonies turgid and who crave more air between and around the notes.

Symphony No 2. Konzertstück in F, Op 86.
Manfred, Op 115 – Overture
Philharmonia Orchestra / Christian Thielemann
DG 453 482-2GH (76' · DDD)   ⒻⓄⓄ

This programme is brilliantly designed for continuous listening. Thielemann is his own man, making no stylistic concessions to 'historically informed' performance. The disc begins with the *Manfred* Overture: its opening three chords

are very smoothly delivered (they're usually incisive and strong), but they're justified by the spacious gravity and dignity of what follows. You may find this *Manfred* too ready to yield to introspective slower motion (a feature of the performance of the Second Symphony). Then *Manfred*'s interior world is blown away by 'something quite curious' as Schumann described his *Konzertstück* for four horns and orchestra. Replace 'curious' with 'dazzling', even 'reckless', and you might gain a better idea of the piece. Here is playing of great brilliance and bravado.

We've not had a performance of the Second Symphony as satisfying since Karajan's and Sawallisch's from the early 1970s. On first hearing, one occasionally feels that Thielemann had lost his sense of proportion, principally in the *Scherzo*, whose much slower Trios can sound self-conscious. But, more often than not, a few bars further on, and the nature of the expression released by that slower tempo makes clear the reason for its choice. And in the Symphony's outer *Allegros* Thielemann always ensures enough urgent propulsion and springing energy to make workable his many slowings. Never do you feel the tension sagging as a result of a slowing; on the contrary, the contrasts invariably intensify the drama. The Symphony's *Adagio* is the disc's principal glory: a wondrously sustained and shaped *cantabile*, with the essential bass-line well defined. It might be thought a risky business recording Schumann in a church, but the microphones are close and this ample sound offers a convincing focus and proportion.

Schumann Symphony No 4 **Schubert** Symphony No 4 in C minor, D417, 'Tragic' **Mendelssohn** Die schöne Melusine, Op 32
Berlin Philharmonic Orchestra / Nikolaus Harnoncourt
Teldec 4509-94543-2 (77' · DDD)   Ⓜ

'I think of it as one of the greatest symphonic poems,' Harnoncourt has said of *Die schöne Melusine*. A bold claim, but here indeed is a bold and beauteous performance. Beauty first, 'the beauty of calm waters' as Tovey described the opening: upwardly curling mother-of-pearl Berlin winds and strings. Then boldness: and here the strongly rhythmic second theme is subjected to such a dramatic *animato* that its definition may strike you as initially blurred (a momentary impression though, and the Overture as a whole benefits from Harnoncourt's tempo contrasts).

The Berliners' musical collective would appear to have had a profound (and positive) effect on Harnoncourt in the Schubert. Compare, for instance, the slow movement with his Concertgebouw recording: there, the *Andante*'s relatively detached period manners are here transformed (at a slower tempo, though still an *Andante*) into a very real beauty and eloquence of phrase and expression. Very startling, if you don't know Harnoncourt's Amsterdam recording, is the removal of eight bars (from the printed editions) in the first movement's exposition, and Harnoncourt's fateful half-tempo delivery of the finale's closing unison C chords.

Dramatic delaying tactics – whether tiny hesitations or huge fermatas – have always been a feature of Harnoncourt's conducting. Together with his insistent accentuation, sudden contrasts of dynamics, texture and tempo (for example, Scherzo/Trio tempos), you may feel that this Schumann Fourth (the familiar revision) sets out to contradict the symphony's apparent continuity, certainly compared to a performance like Wand's on RCA. But then, this is a performance that can catch fire spectacularly in a way that few others do, especially in the symphony's closing stages.

The Berliners' playing is magnificent, and the Philharmonie sound is both present and spacious.

Piano Quintet in E flat major, Op 44

Piano Quintet in E flat, Op 44. Andante and Variations, Op 46. Fantasiestücke, Op 73. Märchenbilder, Op 113.
Marie-Luise Neunecker hn **Dora Schwarzberg, Lucy Hall** vns **Nobuko Imai** va **Natalia Gutman, Mischa Maisky** vcs **Martha Argerich, Alexandre Rabinovitch** pf
EMI 557308-2 (75' · DDD) Recorded live 1994   Ⓕ

After 'one memorable day of rehearsal', as the introductory note puts it, Martha Argerich and a group of friends recorded this programme at a public concert in Holland 'with the enthusiasm and intimate inspiration of a house-party'. The rarity is the *Andante and Variations*, Op 46, here brought up with all the spontaneous freshness of new discovery in a performance as enjoyable for its self-generating continuity as its diversity. Argerich and her fellow pianist, Rabinovitch divide keyboard responsibilities in the remainder of the programme. Her own major triumph comes in the Quintet (with truly inspirational help from Maisky's cello). Every note tingles with life and colour in an arrestingly imaginative reading of exemplary textural transparency. In none of the more familiar works in the concert is that little extra stimulus of live as opposed to studio recording combined with more finesse and finish than here.

In the smaller pieces Argerich reaffirms herself as an artist of 'temperament', much given to the impulse of the moment. The recording itself is pleasingly natural. And there's heartening audience applause as a further reminder that we're at a live performance.

String Quartets, Op 41

No 1 in A minor No 2 in F No 3 in A

String Quartets, Op 41 – Nos 1 & 3
Zehetmair Quartet (Thomas Zehetmair, Matthias Metzger vns Ruth Killius va Françoise Groben vc)
ECM New Series 472.169-2 (50' · DDD)   Ⓕ**OOO**

 The Zehetmair Quartet's coupling focuses the music's alternating wildness and fragility with altogether unique perception. Theirs is an agitated, combustible and loving view of Schumann, a credible trip into his troubled world that reflects older playing styles not by exaggerating or abandoning vibrato but by constantly varying tone, tempo, bow pressure and modes of attack. Aspects of this trend are usefully exemplified by their handling of the pensive second section of the Third Quartet's third movement, and by the way they negotiate the sudden, bloodless *moderato* passage that forms the coda of the First Quartet's finale. In the less consistent but more challenging First Quartet, minute variations in pulse and emphasis are consistently engaging, ie they enjoy maximum freedom within the law of the page. Contrapuntal passages that other quartets present as dry or self-conscious – at 2'36" into the first movement of No 1, for example, where the viola takes the initial lead – assume new-found meaning. Indeed, their playing has similarities with Alfred Cortot in Schumann's piano music and Adolf Busch in his First Violin Sonata, both of whom focus the fantasy while keeping tabs on structure.

These aren't comfortable performances. They pass on cosmetic appeal and would rather grate and rail than pander to surface 'gloss'. So be warned. But they're profoundly beautiful in their truthful appropriation of music that can be both poignant and aggressive. Delicate, too, in places (Mendelssohn with added fibre); in fact more comprehensive as musical statements than most of us had previously suspected. That realisation is due almost entirely to the persuasive powers of these supremely accomplished, and realistically recorded, performances.

String Quartets, Op 41 – Nos 1 & 3
St Lawrence Quartet (Geoff Nuttall, Barry Shiffman vns Lesley Robertson va Marina Hoover vc)
EMI 556797-2 (59' · DDD)   Ⓕ

String Quartets, Op 41 – Nos 1-3   **Ⓟ**
Eroica Quartet (Peter Hanson, Lucy Howard vns Gustav Clarkson va David Watkin vc)
Harmonia Mundi HMU90 7270 (79' · DDD)   Ⓕ

The St Lawrence Quartet formed as a permanent group in 1989, and are now established as ensemble-in-residence at California's Stanford University. Here, in their début recording, studio discipline – plus respect for Schumann's own veering from wayward Romanticism towards a new Classical control – brings its rewards in performances of irresistible youthful immediacy and intensity while at the same time, through the individuality of each strand in the argument, opening your ears anew to the sheer skill of the craftsmanship. The full, forward succulence of the recorded tone will also play a large part in winning these works new admirers.

Whereas the St Lawrence's EMI coupling plays for just on an hour, the Eroica's Harmonia Mundi issue, lasting for some 80 minutes, offers all three works at the same full price. The recorded tone here is a little less voluptuous, a little more astringent. But the main difference lies in this group's avowed pursuit of 'period style'. This neither robs their playing of emotion in slow tempo, nor of vitality elsewhere. But the end result could be summarised as more objectively classical than that of the fervently committed, open-hearted, vibrato-full Canadians.

Their recourse to the autograph scores reveals a structural change of outstanding interest: that what we now know as the four-bar *stringendo* leading from the First Quartet's slow A minor introduction into the main *Allegro* (surprisingly in F major) was in fact originally conceived as an arresting start to the second F major Quartet itself. Other small changes of prime interest to this group would seem to lie in details of fingering and bowing possibly suggested by Ferdinand David (leader of Leipzig's Gewandhaus Orchestra) when the Quartets were first tried out at Clara's 23rd birthday party that September.

In the First Quartet's opening 6/8 *Allegro* one wonders if the Eroica's insistent second-main-beat accentuation slightly disrupts continuity of line (as again in the *Scherzo*'s central Intermezzo). Nor do they dispel the feeling that Schumann's intricate syncopation in the course of the Second Quartet's variation movement defeats its own ends as the average ear so soon translates compound triple rhythm into simple duple. But both these new arrivals are more than welcome companions for the Melos Quartet's DG trilogy of so many years ago.

Additional recommendation

String Quartets, Op 41 – Nos 1-3
Ysaÿe Quartet (Guillaume Sutre, Luc-Marie Aguera vns Miguel da Silva va François Salque vc)
Aeon F AECD0418 (79' · DDD)

All three quartets are included. And the performance of the Second Quartet is a fine one, stressing the first movement's soaring lyricism, the weird rhythmic dislocations in the *Scherzo*, and bringing out all the finale's fantastical contrasts.

Piano Trios

No 1 in D minor, Op 63 **No 2** in F, Op 80 **No 3** in G minor, Op110

Piano Trios Nos 1 & 2
Florestan Trio (Anthony Marwood vn Richard Lester vc Susan Tomes pf)
Hyperion CDA67063 (57' · DDD) ⓅⓄ**OOO**

For those who have always thought of Schumann's First Piano Trio as his finest chamber work after the Piano Quintet, the Florestan Trio may encourage you to think again about the Second Trio – a wonderful piece, full of poetic ideas. The artists make vigorous work of the first movement's urgent thematic interrelations but the real surprise is the third movement, a lilting barcarolle awash with significant counterpoint, although the heart of the Trio is its slow and deeply personal second movement. The differences in the trios are more marked than their similarities. The Second Trio is mellow, loving and conversational, but the First is troubled, tense, even tragic – save, perhaps, for its Mendelssohnian finale. The Florestan Trio realises the music's myriad perspectives, coaxing its arguments rather than confusing them. Marwood employs some subtle *portamento* and varies his use of vibrato, whereas Susan Tomes never forces her tone. Real teamwork, equally in evidence for the gently cantering *Scherzo* and the fine, elegiac slow movement.

Piano Trio No 3. Fantasiestücke, Op 88. Piano Quartet in E flat, Op 47[a]
[a]**Thomas Riebl** va **Florestan Trio** (Anthony Marwood vn Richard Lester vc Susan Tomes pf)
Hyperion CDA67175 (71' · DDD) ⒫**O**

After their 1999 *Gramophone* Award-winning disc of the first two piano trios, these players champion three works which are less frequently encountered in concert, proving once again how a revelatory interpretation can make us all think again.

The G minor Piano Trio (No 3) of 1851 suffers from over-repetitive, at times perfunctory, rhythmic patterning. But thanks to the mercurial vitality and the spontaneous response to every passing innuendo from all three interwoven voices, not a note here sounds unmotivated. The three fanciful 1842 miniatures for piano trio (revised under the title of *Fantasiestücke* in 1849) have long been criticised for the dominance of the keyboard in all but the third, entitled 'Duet'. Susan Tomes makes no attempt to disguise this.

Last but not least, the Piano Quartet of 1842, long overshadowed by the much-loved Piano Quintet. Misha Donat's appreciative note reminds us that even the loyal Clara waited some seven years before taking it into her repertory. The piano is rarely silent, and mustn't be allowed to dominate; so praise goes to Susan Tomes for a keen ear for balance. The *Scherzo* has a Mendelssohnian, elfin fleetness, and the finale (surely Schumann's *ne plus ultra* in exhilarating contrapuntal ingenuity) an exemplary textural clarity. The slow movement, played with touching simplicity, speaks as eloquently as any of the composer's Clara-inspired love-songs. Excellently recorded, this welcome disc should win all three works a new lease of life.

Schumann Piano Trio No 1^b　　　　　**H**
Mendelssohn Piano Trio in D minor, Op 94^a
Alfred Cortot pf **Jacques Thibaud** vn **Pablo Casals** vc
Naxos Historical mono 8 110185 (59' · ADD)
Recorded 1928/9　　　　　　　　　　　　Ⓢ

Tully Potter's introductory note reminds us that it was in Paris, in their later twenties, that these three legendary artists first made music together – just for pleasure. But international acclaim after a public début in 1907 soon led to their devoting a regular part of each year to this sphere for just over the next quarter-century. We're told that Schumann's No 1 was always one of their recital favourites. Here it's difficult to evaluate their playing in technical terms such as minute attention to expressive detail without loss of flow, impeccable ensemble, and last but not least, choice of tempo (slower than Schumann's suggestions in the searching *Langsam, mit inniger Empfindung*). The impression is more of intimately shared awareness of, and response to, the music's inner secrets – as if personally communicated to them by the composer himself. In reproduction you're at once aware of difficulty in doing justice to Thibaud's beguiling violin, notably in the higher reaches of Mendelssohn's agitated opening movement. Here it's outweighed by Casals' sumptuously ripe cello and Cortot's multi-voiced keyboard. But the immediacy and freshness of the playing wins the day in a beautifully nuanced *Andante*, a delectably mischievous *Scherzo*, and an unflaggingly urgent finale. Ward Marston's skilful engineering is at its truest and best here.

Violin Sonatas

No 1 in A minor, Op 105 **No 2** in D minor, Op 121
No 3 in A minor

Violin Sonatas Nos 1 & 2
Gidon Kremer vn **Martha Argerich** pf
DG 419 235-2GH (49' · DDD)　　　　　　　Ⓕ❹

These two violin sonatas are late works, dating from 1851, both were written quickly, apparently in four and six days respectively. This rapidity of composition is nowhere evident except perhaps in the vigour and enthusiasm of the music. Argerich and Kremer, both mercurial and emotionally charged performers, subtly balance the ardent Florestan and dreamily melancholic Eusebius elements of Schumann's creativity. This is even more striking in Sonata No 2, a greater work than its twin, thematically vigorous with a richness and scope that make it a striking as well as ideally structured work. Kremer and Argerich have established a close and exciting duo partnership and this fine recording shows what like minds can achieve in music so profoundly expressive as this.

Violin Sonatas Nos 1 & 2; No 3 – Intermezzo
Ilya Kaler vn **Boris Slutsky** pf
Naxos 8 550870 (51' · DDD) Recorded 1993　Ⓢ

These performances, powerfully recorded in Indiana by these two young Russian artists, are most enjoyable. The passion of their playing is perhaps not wholly Germanic, but every artist legitimately brings something of himself to the music he performs, and nothing here takes us out of touch with Schumann's world. There's an impressive intensity to this playing, although refinement and tenderness are rightly also present. Kaler and Slutsky mould these melodies well; it's a matter of timing as well as tone and dynamics, as the *Allegretto* of the A minor Sonata shows. The same movement also demonstrates how they follow Schumann naturally through his characteristically rapid changes of mood, while the finale that follows has power and purpose. The single movement from the composite 'FAE Sonata' dedicated to Joseph Joachim, in which Schumann collaborated with the young Brahms and Albert Dietrich, makes a useful bonus in a disc which would otherwise last under 50 minutes. The Naxos disc at super-bargain price represents fine value.

Davidsbündlertänze, Op 6

Davidsbündlertänze. Etudes symphoniques, Op 13 (1852 version). Arabeske in C, Op 18. Blumenstück in D flat, Op 19
András Schiff pf
Warner Elatus 0927-49612-2 (76' · DDD)　　Ⓜ

Schumann was a great rethinker, in Schiff's opinion not always for the better in later life – hence his choice of Schumann's original (1837) conception of the *Davidsbündlertänze* rather than its more usually heard 1851 revision. Except for a touch of mischief (subsequently removed) at the end of No 9, textual differences are slight. But Schiff prefers the fewer repeat markings in the first edition, so that ideas never lose their freshness. More importantly, the exceptional immediacy and vividness of his characterisation reminds us that Schumann initially signed nearly all these 18 'bridal thoughts' with an F (the impetuous Florestan) or an E (the introspective, visionary Eusebius) – or sometimes both – as well as including literary inscriptions (and one or two more colourful expression marks) as a clue to the mood of the moment.

Schiff laughs and teases, storms and yearns, as if the hopes and dreams of the youthful Robert, forbidden all contact with his distant beloved, were wholly his own – there and then. The impatient Florestan fares particularly well. For the much metamorphosed *Etudes symphoniques* Schiff chooses the generally used late version of 1852 with its admirably tautened finale. Here, his bold, firmly contoured approach reaffirms it as the most magisterially 'classical' work the young Schumann ever wrote. Schiff emphasises its continuity and unity as a whole. Even the five so-called supplementary variations emerge as more purposeful, less ruminative, than often heard. These Schiff wisely offers as an independent group at the end. The recital is completed by the *Arabeske* and *Blumenstück*, again played with a very strong sense of direction, even if Schiff isn't yet Richter's equal in disguising the repetitiveness of the latter. Nothing but praise for the naturalness of the reproduction.

Davidsbündlertänze. Etudes symphoniques, Ⓗ
Op 13. Carnaval, Op 9. Kreisleriana, Op 16.
Papillons, Op 2. Kinderszenen, Op 15.
Fantasiestücke, Op 12 – No 1, Des Abends.
Waldszenen, Op 82 – No 7, Vogel als Prophet
Alfred Cortot *pf*
Music & Arts mono ② CD-4858 (131' · ADD)
Recorded 1928-48   Ⓜ●

It's good to have this sharply focused issue of Cortot's evergreen, ever-fresh performances on a well-presented two-CD set. These recordings have been reissued many times before. How many artists, today, one wonders, could hope to garner such tribute? So here, again, is that magically floated *cantabile* tugging at the heartstrings in 'Des Abends' (how one longs for the rest of the cycle) yet maintained with the flawless line and impetus of a great singer. In the *Davidsbündlertänze*, one of Cortot's most poetically potent if battle-scarred recordings, his confusion in Florestan's *schneller* in No 3 or in the vaulting leaps of No 12 is, perhaps, not quite what the composer had in mind in his instruction, *Mit Humor*. Yet who can resist his *dolce cantando* in No 14, the gem of his 'Schumann, alive with a rich polyphonic pianistic tradition that Alfred Brendel so sadly claims has virtually vanished from the music scene.

In *Kinderszenen* the 'poet' of the epilogue is at once Schumann and Cortot, creator and re-creator, and in the *Etudes symphoniques* the gold-dust scattering of the posthumous studies throughout the main work is done with such passion and inwardness that only a Beckmesser could possibly object. Playing like this seems light years away from today's style or standard. But *pace* Cortot, his idiosyncrasy, his pell-mell virtuosity and poetic ecstasy may strike a foreign and even alien note in our more puritan times yet, as Yvonne Lefebure so eloquently put it, 'even his wrong notes were those of a god'.

Davidsbündlertänze. Papillons, Op 2. Carnaval, Op 9.
Etudes symphoniques, Op 13. Kinderszenen, Op 15.
Kreisleriana, Op 16. Fantasie in C, Op 17. Arabeske in
C, Op 18. Humoreske in B flat, Op 20. Piano Sonata
No 2 in G minor, Op 22. Vier Nachtstücke, Op 23.
Drei Romanzen, Op 28. Waldszenen, Op 82. Bunte
Blätter, Op 99 – No 9, Novelette
Wilhelm Kempff *pf*
DG Collectors Edition ④ 471 312-2GB4 (297' · ADD)
Recorded 1967-75   Ⓜ●●

Davidsbündlertänze, Papillons and Carnaval also available on DG Eloquence 469 765-2 Ⓑ Kinderszenen, Drei Romanzen, Waldszenen and Papillons also available on DG Eloquence 469 645-2 Ⓑ

A collection that will give great pleasure. Sample it anywhere and there can be no mistaking who this is – you know great pianists by their sound. Kempff was one of the most distinguished German pianists of the last century, blossoming through two decades in the Austro-German repertory after the death of Schnabel and Edwin Fischer, but he never carried the flame quite as they did. Performing bravura pieces didn't interest him, so the Toccata, the *Concert-Studies after Paganini*, Op 10, and the *Abegg* Variations aren't here. Nevertheless it's a good selection, lacking only the Fantasy Pieces, Op 12, to give a rounded picture of the phenomenal explosion of Schumann's creativity for the piano that took place between the ages of 20 and 29.

Kempff's special quality seems to be a songfulness and *cantabile* style which is in danger of becoming a forgotten art nowadays. Listening to him in Schumann, it's as if a wind is blowing through, rising and falling, sweeping incident along and carrying everything forward: song, dance, stories, poems, moods, portraits, parades of characters, visions of landscape, recollections. Few players have matched his infallible touch with the way the music holds together.

As pianism his *Carnaval* may not leave you astonished, but it's immaculately characterised: festive, buoyant, irresistible in movement, the comings and goings of the masked personages and the guest appearances of 'Chopin' and 'Paganini' all spot on. There's no single right way to play this masterpiece, but his is vivid.

When he made the earliest of these recordings he was already 71; the last are from his 78th year. In the later ones you notice more weight on the keys and perhaps a reduced inclination to be volatile; but he has kept his technique in trim, and continues to sound at ease with the instrument. The difficult numbers in the *Davidsbündlertänze* are hard for every pianist, but Kempff doesn't see them as virtuoso challenges to be confronted and dispatched. Always the music is paramount, and beautiful sound, and a control of voices under the fingers that seem to be following Schumann instinctively in the exploration of the piano's potential. The opening of *Kreisleriana* hangs fire as if he were feeling his way into it but the rest is magnificent and thrillingly projected, in a huge picture.

When at his best you have the impression his insights aren't only musical but brought to bear on every area of Schumann's imagination. All the big works have this definition and can be counted among the best on record. The *Fantasy* comes high on the list, perhaps top, as does the undervalued *Humoreske*. He's a guide to Schumann you should not be without, authoritative and companionable, balanced and most human.

Additional recommendation

Davidsbündlertänze
Coupled with: Fantasiestücke, Op 12
Frith pf
Naxos 8 550493 (63' · DDD) Recorded 1991   Ⓢ
Frith summons his excellent technique here for
some exciting pianism. Recommended not just for
the budget-conscious but for those who enjoy
youthful pianistic exuberance.

Fantasiestücke, Op 12

Fantasiestücke. Kinderszenen, Op 15. Humoreske,
Op 20
Philippe Cassard pf
Ambroisie AMB9961 (74' · DDD)   ⒻⓄ

Here's a disc of fine Schumann playing,
superbly recorded and on a beautifully voiced
piano. To undertake a critical nit-pick of each of
the 27 short pieces that make up these three
works would seem invidious and, besides, not
reflect the spirit in which the music is offered. In
the *Fantasiestücke* some might feel that Cassard
uses too much pedal here, or takes such-and-
such too fast or too slow there; others might justifiably counter by saying that Richter in his
famous 1956 selection uses too little pedal, and
strives for effect, compared with Cassard's more
relaxed approach in infinitely better sound.

Kinderszenen, likewise, is distinguished by its
simplicity, its tenderness and unexaggerated
rubato, nowhere more apparent than in the final
'Der Dichter spricht'. Perhaps Argerich finds
more impish delight in the extrovert titles, but
that again must be a matter of personal preference.

Humoreske – 42 pages almost all in B flat major
or G minor – is one of Schumann's works that
might have been more satisfactory had he let it
mature in the cellar for a while before drinking.
It's difficult to overcome the problems presented by a continuous flow of fragments of
such varying musical interest. Cassard almost
succeeds if only because his mellifluous tone
and subtle phrasing are such a pleasure to hear.
Both Ashkenazy (1972) and Horowitz (1979) in
their very different ways find more character in
the details, the latter's pacing of Schumann's
meandering 'Conclusion' more convincing than
Cassard. But that's quite the wrong note on
which to conclude a review of a recital that merits the highest praise.

Kreisleriana, Op 16

Kreisleriana. Humoreske in B flat, Op 20
Kinderszenen, Op 15.
Radu Lupu pf
Decca 440 496-2DH (75' · DDD) Recorded 1993
   ⒻⓄⓄ
As piano playing this disc has an aristocratic dis-
tinction reminiscent of Lipatti. As music-

making it's underpinned by unselfconscious
intuition, making you feel you're discovering
the truth of the matter for the first time. It's difficult to recall a more revealing performance of
Schumann's *Humoreske*. Lupu captures all the
unpredictability of its swift-changing moods
while at the same time imparting a sense of
inevitability to the sequence as a whole. Florestan's caprice is as piquant as Eusebius's tenderness is melting.Yet there's an underlying
unity in the diversity from Lupu, enhanced by
most beautifully timed and shaded 'links'.
Goodness knows how long this work has been in
his repertory. But here it emerges with the keen
edge of new love. Next, *Kinderszenen*: simplicity
is its keynote. To begin with (as notably in the
opening 'Von fremden Ländern und Menschen') you wonder if, in rejection of sentimentality, he might not be allowing himself enough
time for wide-eyed wonderment. But you're
soon won over by his limpid tonal palette and
the sheer purity of his phrasing. Each piece tells
its own magical little tale without the slightest
trace of special pleading. Such pristine grace
will never pall, however often heard. *Kreisleriana* in its turn offers rich contrasts of desperation, dedication and Hoffmannesque drollery.
And except, perhaps, in the impetuous No 7
(taken dangerously fast), it brings further
reminders that we're in the presence of a master
pianist – among so much else able to rejoice
in this work's endless dialogues between left
hand and right with his opulent bass and
gleaming treble. Reproduction is totally faithful
throughout.

Kreisleriana. Allegro in B minor, Op 8. Gesänge der
Frühe, Op 133.
Maurizio Pollini pf
DG 471 370-2GH (48' · DDD)   ⒻⓄⓄ

There's no one to touch Pollini these days in
Schumann. Formerly perhaps only Richter
would have equalled him, and once or twice one
is reminded of him here, not because of a similarity of character but rather because of that rare
territory you glimpse where only the greatest of
virtuosos and musical minds meet. Though
Pollini may seem plain or his stance over-objec-
tive to some, you couldn't call him cold. He's
impassioned, poetic, sometimes almost violent
(a quality apt to parts of *Kreisleriana*) yet always
airborne, and everything has been lived
through. Above all he gives you Schumann in
wonderful sound and with electrifying rhythmic
grip. This is a *Kreisleriana* to put with the best
ever: rounded out to the extremes of its expression and engaged with the core of the music, not
with ideas about the music. And there's an
enterprising choice of items to complement this
masterpiece. The rarely played B minor *Allegro*
of 1831 comes from the source of free, imaginative sonata-type first movements quarried
around the time when Schumann projected
more big sonatas than he eventually achieved.
The five *Gesänge der Frühe* ('Dawn Songs') are

SCHUMANN KINDERSZENEN & KREISLERIANA – IN BRIEF

Radu Lupu
Decca 440 496-2DH (75' · DDD)   Ⓕ**OO**
Lupu's characteristically limpid and purposeful playing effortlessly holds attention, revealing the character and charm of each vignette in *Kinderszenen*. Just as effortlessly, he hurls his listener into the quite different world of *Kreisleriana*, capturing its emotional turmoil and its dazzling contrasts.

Vladimir Horowitz
Sony SMK90443 (61' · ADD)   Ⓜ**O**
A classic account of *Kreisleriana*, demonstrating profound understanding of Schumann's idiom and projected with extraordinary clarity, most impressively in the final movement where several themes weave together symphonically.

Alfred Cortot
Music & Arts ② CD858 (131' · ADD)   Ⓕ
Here's a style of piano-playing all but non-existent today, yet one which still compels attention with its combination of rhetoric and limpid musicality. Both as narrator and protagonist, Cortot is an engaging artist, fully identifying with the emotional tenor of Schumann's music.

Martha Argerich
DG 410 653-2GH (52' · DDD)   Ⓕ**O**
By turns affectionate and vigorous, these are never tame performances. Argerich's vivid characterisations in *Kinderszenen* may be a bit extreme for some tastes, but will delight those who dislike more salon-friendly performances.

Wilhelm Kempff
DG ④ 471 312-2GB4 (317' · ADD)   Ⓜ
Kempff made these recordings in his seventies; though he doesn't, or possibly can't, play up the virtuosity of *Kreisleriana*, he projects the music compellingly. His laconic style, however, is perhaps not ideal for Schumann's fervid Romanticism.

Maurizio Pollini (*Kreisleriana* only)
DG 471 370-2GH (48' · DDD)   Ⓕ**OO**
Despite rather close and clangorous sound, Pollini's artistry shines through in a performance which may seen a touch detached from the emotional drama, but has a steady burn that becomes irresistible.

Mitsuko Uchida (*Kreisleriana* only)
Philips 442 777-2PH (67' · DDD)   Ⓕ
A virtuoso and brilliantly executed account, that may yet strike some as rather detached from Schumann's drama. Nonetheless the music's sometimes quite strange beauty shines through.

from the other end of his career (1853), when his final mental derangement was only months away; they're full in sound, complicated and sometimes overwritten. But the first, in particular, is wondrously strange, and all are to be enjoyed here as perhaps never before. Wonderful sound but, sadly, not wonderful recorded sound. Though in itself balanced and at a suitable distance, it's a shade too open and diffuse.

Kreisleriana. Kinderszenen, Op 15
Martha Argerich *pf*
DG 410 653-2GH (52' · DDD) Recorded 1984   Ⓕ**O**

'A positively wild love is in some of the movements' so Schumann wrote to *Kreisleriana*'s only begetter, Clara Wieck. Martha Argerich's pianistically brilliant, highly charged recording makes that fact very clear. She's also at pains to emphasise the vein of caprice, even eccentricity, stemming from ETA Hoffmann, whose Kapellmeister Kreisler gave Schumann his title. Also, she's deeply appreciative of the searching introspective intensity of the slow numbers.

There's an enormous amount to admire and enjoy from this uncommonly individual artist, who always makes you listen to everything with new ears. Argerich's fast tempo is very fast – provocatively so in No 1 (especially the central episode in the major) and dangerously so in No 7 (where the fugal episode scarcely makes sense because it's so gabbled). As for the Hoffmannesque caprice, her No 8 is wholly winning. In the slow numbers the intensity of her involvement now and again finds outlet in impulsive little surges, alike of pace and dynamics, that can only be described as *echt* Argerich.

Argerich's *Kinderszenen* is a performance all children will love because of the vividness of the story-telling – not least in the whirlwind 'Catch me if you can', the dare-devil 'Knight of the Hobby-Horse', the eerie 'Frightening' and the deep drowsiness of 'Child falling asleep'. Adults, on the other hand, might find the reading over impressionable. Some may certainly prefer a rubato that draws less attention to itself.

Kreisleriana. Arabeske, Op 18. Davidsbündlertänze, Op 6. Fantasiestücke, Op 12. Frühlingsnacht (arr Liszt). Papillons, Op 2. Waldszenen, Op 82. Widmung (arr Liszt)
Leon McCawley *pf*
Avie ② AV0029 (143' · DDD)   Ⓜ

This two-CD album celebrates a richly inclusive cross-section ranging from Schumann's Opp 2 to 82, from early ardour to later introspection, and *vice versa*. For whatever the opus, Schumann's ultra-Romantic genius – his rapid shifts from pain to solace, from tears to laughter – is paramount. Above all, it's in his wide-eyed wonder, his naivety, that Leon McCawley shines and makes his mark.

True, a certain politeness inhibits him from relishing to the full every shift of the kaleidoscopic imagination in, say, *Papillons*, but else-where – in the closing, enchanted reminiscence of *Davidsbündlertänze* or in the 'exquisite bird song in an ominous setting' (the 'Prophet Bird' from Op 82) – he's at his very best. In the *Fantasiestücke* he delights in the cross-accentuation, kittenish by-play of 'Fabel' and provides an attractive alternative to more hectic perform-ances of 'Träumes Wirren'.

The *Arabesque* is another notable success (par-ticularly in the glowing retrospective coda). Most of all, he's finely sensitive to the inner promptings and recesses of *Kreisleriana*: the *sehr langsam* and *Bewegt* of No 4, the central mock-polyphonic whirl of No 7 or the alternately gen-tle and explosive whimsy of No 8 all testify to his winning ease and sensitivity. Excellent record-ing, first-class accompanying essay and lavish presentation.

Additional recommendation

Kreisleriana, Op 16
Coupled with: **Bach/Busoni** Chaconne. **Beethoven** Rondo, Op 51 No2 and Rondo capriccio, Op 129
Kissin pf
RCA Victor Red Seal 09026 68911-2 (63' · DDD) Ⓕ
The fantastic side of *Kreisleriana* isn't always in focus here. That said, this is still a very enjoyable performance.

Fantasie in C, Op 17

Fantasie in C. Faschingsschwank ausWien, Op 26. Papillons, Op 2
Sviatoslav Richter pf
EMI Encore 575233-2 (67' · ADD/DDD) Recorded 1961-2 🅢 Ⓢ ❍❍❍

 There can surely be no doubt as to Richter's current status as elder states-man of the piano world. And collectors now have a bewildering array of his recent, mainly live performances and reissues to choose from. Richter's Schumann is unequalled. The *Fantasia* is arguably Schumann's keyboard mas-terpiece. And Richter plays it better than other pianists. Nobody can phrase as beautifully as he can, or produce those marvellously soft accom-paniments beneath quietly singing tunes or toss off the middle movement with such speed and brilliance. There's astonishing poetry in his playing. It almost amounts to a rediscovery of the work.

And the same could be said of *Faschings-schwank aus Wien* and *Papillons*. (The way he plays the main theme of the latter should make you buy this disc if nothing else does – he seems to add stature to the work.) His assets in all these works are, first, an unusually musical sense of phrasing. Secondly, he can reduce an accompa-niment to a mere murmur without any loss of evenness so that a tune above it can sing even when it's soft. Thirdly, he uses a great deal of rubato, but always with impeccable taste; his

rubato in slow passages has a mesmeric quality only partly due to the fact that he usually plays such passages much slower than other pianists. Fourthly, he has faultless technique. His superi-ority is apparent throughout. The recording is magnificent for its date. Classic performances which no pianophile should be without.

Fantasie in C. Piano Sonata No 1, Op 11
Maurizio Pollini pf
DG 423 134-2GH (63' · ADD) Ⓟ ❍❍

These works grew from Schumann's love and longing for his future wife Clara. Pollini's per-formances are superb, not least because they're so truthful to the letter of the score. By eschew-ing all unspecified rubato in the *Fantasie*, he reminds us that the young Schumann never wrote a more finely proportioned large-scale work; this feeling for structure, coupled with exceptional emotional intensity, confirms it as one of the greatest love-poems ever written for the piano. His richly characterised account of the Sonata is refreshingly unmannered. Cer-tainly the familiar charges of protracted pat-terning in the faster flanking movements are at once dispelled by his rhythmic *élan*, his crys-talline texture and his ear for colour. The CD transfer is most successful.

Novelletten, Op 21

Novelletten. Allegro in B minor, Op 8. Drei Fantasiestücke, Op 111. Gesänge der Frühe, Op 133
Ronald Brautigam pf
Olympia OCD436 (79' · DDD) Recorded 1993 Ⓕ

The note reminds us that even the eight *Novel-letten* chosen as the centrepiece here aren't often heard in sequence as a set. Brautigam prefaces them with the early (1831-2) B minor *Allegro* originally intended as the first movement of a sonata to be dedicated to Moscheles. They're followed by the last two suites Schumann ever wrote for the piano – the *Gesänge der Frühe* only a year before his final breakdown.

Most enjoyable is Brautigam's vitality – of imagination no less than of fingers. You're immediately gripped by his plunge into the Op 8 *Allegro*, with its arresting octave motto. His mercurial fancy and ear for hidden melodic strands in the ensuing stream makes nonsense of hasty dismissal of this work as mere old-style virtuoso note-spinning. Moreover, such is his unflagging impulse in the eight *Novelletten* that you're never tempted to accuse Schumann of over-repetitively patterned figuration.

Potently characterised and contrasted as are the three *Fantasiestücke*, Op 111 of 1851, Brautigam leaves no doubt as to their unity as a set – as he does again in the more elusive spiritual world of the five *Gesänge der Frühe*. The bright, clear tonal reproduction is accept-able enough.

Piano Sonatas

No 1 in F sharp minor, Op 11 **No 2** in G minor, Op 22 **No 3** in F minor, Op 14

Piano Sonatas Nos 1 & 3
Bernd Glemser pf
Naxos 8 554275 (65' · DDD)　　　🅢 Ⓢ ⦿⦿

Bernd Glemser's playing here is an exceptionally arresting experience in its graphic immediacy and freshness. With his prodigious technique, underpinned by exuberant imaginative vitality, it was no surprise to learn that in a wideranging repertory, he feels particularly drawn to the later Romantic virtuoso school. Some listeners might well think his approach to Schumann's F sharp minor Sonata (written at the age of 25) too overtly Lisztian in expression to be truly stylish. Sure, the more classically disciplined Clara, for example, would never have allowed herself such extreme changes of tempo in contrasting Florestan's turbulence with Eusebius's idyllic lyricism in the two spacious outer movements. Yet with his innate musicality Glemser somehow allows the argument to cohere. His challenging rhythm in the *Scherzo* (and the richly savoured burlesque of its trio), like the *senza passione ma espressivo* of the slow movement's intimate song, are all finely judged. The F minor Sonata comes in Schumann's 1853 revision, restoring the second of the two *Scherzos* omitted when the work was first published 17 years earlier, as a three-movement *Concert sans orchestre*. With Naxos's tonal reproduction at its best, this disc comes recommended as a true 'super-bargain' not to be missed – despite the catalogue's formidable list of rivals.

Szenen aus Goethes Faust

Szenen aus Goethes Faust
Karita Mattila, Barbara Bonney, Brigitte Poschner-Klebel, Susan Graham sops **Iris Vermillion** mez **Endrik Wottrich, Hans-Peter Blochwitz** tens **Bryn Terfel** bass-bar **Jan-Hendrik Rootering, Harry Peeters** basses **Tölz Boys' Choir; Swedish Radio Chorus; Berlin Philharmonic Orch / Claudio Abbado**
Sony Classical ② S2K66308 (115' · DDD) Recorded live 1994. Notes, text and translation included Ⓕ ⦿⦿

No one before Schumann had ever attempted to set Goethe's mystical closing scene, which he finished in time for the Goethe centenary in 1849. What eventually emerged as his own Parts 1 and 2 (in turn portraits of Gretchen and the by now repentant Faust) followed later, after his move from a Mendelssohn-dominated Leipzig to a Wagner-ruled Dresden, hence the striking difference in style. Nothing Schumann ever wrote is more dramatic than Faust's blinding and death in the course of Part 2. The Berlin Philharmonic is very forwardly recorded – occasionally perhaps a little too much so for certain

voices. But never in the case of Bryn Terfel in the title-role. Any advance fears that he might disappoint were immediately banished not only by the generosity and flow of his warm, round tone but also the total commitment and conviction of his characterisation. Moreover as Dr Marianus in Part 3 he offers some wonderfully sustained *mezza* and *sotto voce*. Karita Mattila's Gretchen is always sympathetically pure-toned, clean-lined and assured. At times, as positioned, the other male soloists seem a little outweighed by the orchestra. No praise can be too high for the Four Grey Sisters (so tellingly contrasted in vocal colour) led by Barbara Bonney: their midnight encounter with Faust and his eventual blinding is brilliantly done. And there's splendidly characterful choral singing thoughout from both adult and youthful choirs. In the more operatically conceived Parts 1 and 2 and the visionary Part 3, Abbado himself takes the music to heart and what he draws from his orchestra makes nonesense of the charge that Schumann was an inept scorer. This is worth every penny of its full-price.

Der Rose Pilgerfahrt, Op 112

Der Rose Pilgerfahrt
Inga Nielsen, Helle Hinz sops **Annemarie Møller, Elizabeth Halling** mezzos **Deon van der Walt** ten **Guido Päevatalu** bar **Christian Christiansen** bass **Danish National Radio Choir and Symphony Orchestra / Gustav Kuhn**
Chandos CHAN9350 (62' · DDD) Recorded 1993. Text included　　　Ⓕ ⦿

Amidst today's great upsurgence of interest in Schumann's later choral undertakings, the work's long neglect is no doubt due to its all-too-naive tale of a rose who, after an eagerly sought transformation into a maiden to experience human love, chooses to sacrifice herself for her baby. Schumann's own ready response to Moritz Horn's poem can best be explained by its underlying moral message together with a strain of German rusticity then equally close to the composer's heart. Having said that, how grateful Schumann lovers should be to Chandos for at last introducing the work to the English catalogue in so sympathetic yet discreet a performance from this predominantly Danish cast. All credit to the conductor, Gustav Kuhn, for revealing so much fancy in fairyland, so much brio in peasant merriment, and so much charm in more tender lyricism without ever making heavy weather of this essentially *gemütlich* little score. No praise can be too high for the Danish National Radio Choir: such immediacy of response leaves no doubt as to their professional status. Nor do the soloists or orchestra disappoint. Tonal reproduction is agreeably natural.

Liederkreis, Op 24

Liederkreis. Myrthen, Op 25 – No 7, Die Lotosblume;

No 21, Was will die einsame Träne?; No 24, Du bist wie eine Blume. Romanzen und Balladen – Op 45: No 3, Abends am Strand; Op 49: No 1, Die beiden Grenadiere; No 2, Die feindlichen Brüder; Op 53: No 3, Der arme Peter; Op 64: No 3, Tragödie. Belsatzar, Op 57. Lieder und Gesänge, Op 127 – No 2, Dein Angesicht; No 3, Es leuchtet meine Liebe. Gesänge, Op 142 – No 2, Lehn deine Wang; No 4, Mein Wagen rollet langsam
Stephan Genz bar **Christoph Genz** ten **Claar ter Horst** pf
Claves CD50-9708 (59' · DDD) Texts and translations included   ⒡**O**

This is a recital of promise and fulfilment. Stephan Genz's voice and style are as wide-ranging as his mode of expression. He lives every moment of Op 24, entering into all aspects of Schumann's settings and Heine's originals yet never overstepping the mark in his verbal painting. The other Heine settings receive no less than their due. The sensuous and plaintive qualities in Genz's tone are well suited to the three Heine poems in *Myrthen*. In contrast he rises to the histrionic challenges of *Die beiden Grenadiere, Belsatzar* · and the rarely encountered *Die feindlichen Brüder*, performances that are felt as immediately as if at the moment of composition. In *Abends am Strand* the voice follows to the full the song's romantic import. In the third song of Op 64, *Tragödie*, the baritone is joined by his talented tenor brother: their voices naturally blend well. Finally, Genz is inspired by that amazingly original song, *Mein Wagen rollet langsam*, to give of his absolute best. Here, as throughout, Claar ter Horst matches the perceptions of her partner, and both are caught in an amenable acoustic.

Frauenliebe und -leben, Op 42

Frauenliebe und -leben. Gesänge, Op 31 – No 1, Die Löwenbraut; No 2, Die Kartenlegerin. Gedichte, Op 35 – No 1, Lust der Sturmnacht; No 8, Stille Liebe. Rose, Meer und Sonne, Op 37 No 9. Fünf Lieder, Op 40. Der Schatzgräber, Op 45 No 1. Volksliedchen, Op 51 No 2. Die Soldatenbraut, Op 64 No 1. Lieder-Album für die Jugend, Op 79 – No 5, Vom Schlaraffenland; No 22, Des Sennen Abscheid; No 26, Schneeglöcken. Mein schöner Stern!, Op 101 No 4. Abendlied, Op 107 No 6. Die Meerfee, Op 125 No 1. Dein Angesicht, Op 127 No 2
Anne Sofie von Otter mez **Bengt Forsberg** pf
DG 445 881-2GH (79' · DDD) Recorded 1993 Texts and translations included   ⒡**O**

This is one of those records where the promise of something exceptional in the first phrases is fully borne out by all that follows. The *Frauen-liebe* cycle is sung by a character, as vividly defined as any Fiordiligi, Senta or Mimì in opera. Von Otter is one of those rare artists who can adapt the voice and yet be true to its natural identity. In these songs of Schumann (not only in the *Frauenliebe*) she seems, unselfconsciously, to find a new voice-personality for each and still

to confine herself to what lies naturally within her scope, forcing nothing and falsifying nothing. The woman of the 'life and love' starts out as a girl. 'Seit ich ihn gesehen' has a shy, private rapture which then grows bold for 'Er, der Her-rlichste von allen', frank in its enthusiasm, radiant as the voice rises to its highest notes. 'Ich kann's nicht fassen, nicht glauben' is fully outgoing, an expression of utter commitment, and the smile is always in the voice. The engagement-ring induces maturity, the girl now a woman. The wedding-day preparations, confiding of motherhood, and then the emptiness of life at the husband's death: all are caught as in reality and in character. It's a completely absorbed and absorbing performance.

The generous selection of songs which follows works its spell partly by contrasts. In these and in all else von Otter lights upon the right tone, and the right shades of that tone. The programme is well planned, too, rounded off with 'Rose, Meer und Sonne', sketching the melodies of *Frauenliebe und -leben* with which the recital began. Occasionally the piano is recorded too heavily or too prominently for the voice. But generally the sympathy of singer and pianist are all that could be desired – as is the recital *in toto*. This will be a much-prized addition to your shelves.

Frauenliebe und -leben. Sieben Lieder, Op 104. Gedichte der Königen Maria Stuart, Op 135. Lieder und Gesänge – I, Op 27: No 1, Sag an, o lieber Vogel; No 4, Jasminenstrauch; III, Op 77: No 3, Geisternähe; No 4, Stiller Vorwurf; IV, Op 96: No 4, Gesungen!; No 5, Himmel und Erde. Romanzen und Balladen – III, Op 53: No 1, Blondels Lied; No 2, Loreley; IV, Op 64: No 1, Die Soldatenbraut. Die Kartenlegerin, Op 31 No 2
Juliane Banse sop **Graham Johnson** pf
Hyperion CDJ33103 (74' · DDD) Texts and translations included Includes readings of 'Traum der eignen Tage' and 'Nachschrift'.   ⒡**O**

This offering places Banse and Johnson among the most thoughtful and convincing of Schumann interpreters in the history of recording the composer's Lieder. From start to finish, in well-loved pieces and in others that will be new discoveries to many, the pair at once work in close concord and get to the heart of Schumann's very particular genius. The pair wholly dispel the oft-repeated view that Schumann's later songs are by and large failures: it's simply that the older man wrote differently from his younger, Romantically exuberant self. Thus the 1852 settings of Mary Stuart unerringly capture the soul of the troubled Queen's predicaments through the most concise means. Not a florid or untoward gesture is allowed to destroy the mood of sustained concentration and intimate musings. Banse brings to the songs just the right sense of a person sharing her innermost thoughts with us, the mezzo-like warmth of her lower voice gainfully employed, Johnson's piano communing in consort with the voice.

Schumann showed himself equally in sympathy with the poems of Elisabeth Kulmann (Op 104), a susceptible girl who died at the age of 17, his writing here simple and apparently artless. The composer, amazingly, thinks himself into the thoughts of the imaginative, fanciful young poetess; so does his interpreter, Banse, here using a lighter, more palpitating tone.

The faultless recording completes one's pleasure in a very special issue.

Frauenliebe und -leben. Liederkreis, Op 39
Soile Isokoski sop **Marita Viitasalo** pf
Finlandia 0630-10924-2 (49' · DDD) Recorded 1993-5.
Texts and translations included   Ⓕ**O**

This interpretation from this young Finnish soprano can stand comparison with the best. In her wonderfully straightforward and musical performance, she marries a sincere spontaneity with a warming sense of line and phrase, a style well learnt yet put to her own, positive purpose. Before you is the rapturous bride-to-be in all her moods, then the young woman struck almost dumb by unexpected grief. Nothing in her portrayal is forced or in the least contrived yet everything, felt from the heart, goes to it. And the voice itself? Well, reminders of Flagstad's richness, Ameling's naturalness and Price's precision are here to be heard and enjoyed. She's just as imaginative in Op 39 as in Op 42, giving a very central, unaffected account of the *Liederkreis* encompassing all its varied moods and one that makes its points unobtrusively and, as with Op 42, with the emphasis on long-breathed phrasing and rock-steady tone. The partnership with Viitasalo is obviously a fruitful one. The two artists think and 'breathe' alike though in Op 42 he's just occasionally too prominent, at least as recorded.

Frauenliebe und -leben, Op 42. Myrthen, Op 25 – No 3, Der Nussbaum; No 7, Die Lotosblume. Die Kartenlegerin, Op 31 No 2. Ständchen, Op 36 No 2. Das verlassne Mägdlein, Op 64 No 2. Aufträge, Op 77 No 5. Lieder-album für die Jugend, Op 79 – No 13, Der Sandmann; No 29, Mignon. Lieder, Op 90. Nachtlied, Op 96 No 1
Bernarda Fink mez **Roger Vignoles** pf
Harmonia Mundi HMC90 1753 (60' · DDD) Notes, texts and translations included   Ⓕ**O**

Bernarda Fink proves conclusively here that she can be just as compelling in German song as she is in Baroque works. For a start few accounts of any of these pieces have been quite so beautifully and effortlessly sung. Not a note in this recital is ugly or mishandled; everything is projected on a stream of perfectly produced, mellow mezzo tone. In itself, that's almost enough to recommend the disc. But Fink has so much more to offer. Her interpretation of the oft-recorded *Frauenliebe* cycle isn't one with the kind of overwhelming emotional tug evinced by Baker and von Otter, yet in her slightly more

reticent way Fink conveys just as much feeling as her rivals. Her sweet, reflective, slightly vibrant tone very much calls to mind Seefried's and Isokoski's equally artless style among soprano versions. With Roger Vignoles as a sympathetic and positive partner, Fink's version deserves to be equated with those of her distinguished predecessors. There's no anti-climax in the other performances. The very familiar 'Nussbaum' and 'Aufträge' are as delightfully eager and spontaneous as they ought to be. Those ineffably Schumannesque pieces, 'Die Lotosblume' and, in the Op 90 settings of Lenau, 'Meine Rose', receive treatment, in timbre and line and verbal assurance that would be hard to better. The recording has the singer blessedly forward so one catches the true flavour of her voice and words. A joy from start to finish.

Dichterliebe, Op 48

Dichterliebe. Liederkreis, Op 24. Belsatzar, Op 57. Abends am Strand, Op 45 No 3. Die beiden Grenadiere, Op 49 No 1. Lieder und Gesänge, Op 127 – No 2, Dein Angesicht; No 3, Es leuchtet meine Liebe. Vier Gesänge, Op 142 – No 2, Lehn deine Wang; No 4, Mein Wagen rollet langsam
Ian Bostridge ten **Julius Drake** pf
EMI 556575-2 (69' · DDD) Texts and translations included   Ⓕ**OOO**

Bostridge makes you think anew about the music in hand, interpreting all these songs as much through the mind of the poet as that of the composer, and, being youthful himself, getting inside the head of the vulnerable poet in his many moods. Quite apart from his obvious gifts as a singer and musician, that's what raises Bostridge above most of his contemporaries, who so often fail to live the words they're singing. Every one of the magnificent Op 24 songs has some moment of illumination, whether it's the terror conveyed so immediately in 'Schöne Wiege', the breathtaking beauty and sorrow of 'Anfang wollt ich' or the breadth and intensity of 'Mit Myrten und Rosen'. In between the two cycles comes a group of the 1840 Leipzig settings that adumbrates every aspect of Bostridge's attributes, as well as those of his equally perceptive partner.

The vivid word-painting in *Belsatzar* brings the Old Testament scene arrestingly before us. Perhaps best of all is the unjustly neglected *Es leuchtet meine Liebe*, a melodrama here perfectly enacted by both performers. *Mein Wagen rollet langsam* forms a perfect introduction, in its lyrical freedom, to *Dichterliebe*, an interpretation to rank with the best available in terms of the sheer beauty of the singing and acute response to its sustained inspiration. Listen to the wonder brought to the discovery of the flowers and angels in 'Im Rhein', the contained anger of 'Ich grolle nicht', the sense of bereavement in 'Hör ist das Liedchen' and you'll judge this is an interpretation of profundity and emotional identification, the whole cycle crowned by the sensitivity of Drake's playing of the summarising postlude. To complete one's pleasure EMI has provided an exemplary and forward recording balance.

Dichterliebe. Liederkreis, Op 39
Werner Güra ten **Jan Schultsz** pf
Harmonia Mundi HMC901766 (56' · DDD) Texts and translations included ⓕ**OO**

Güra delivers *Dichterliebe* with impeccable line and tone, and in a style following the best traditions of German tenors in the work. Only in 'Ich will meine Seele tauchen' does he stray from grace, choosing an oddly dragging tempo, slower than any other singers in this song. Although Bostridge's singing for EMI (with Julius Drake at the piano) is slightly softer-grained, he opts for a more dramatic approach than Güra, distinctly underlining certain words, even syllables, to press home the import of Heine's and Schumann's inspiration. This may be found a shade mannered on repeated hearing. The contrast is most marked in 'Ich hab' im Traum geweinet'. Güra sings this in a dreamy *legato*, as if in a trance; Bostridge often breaks the shape of a phrase in order to give it a more histrionic edge. His very personal approach is underlined by a more intimate recording than Güra receives. Both pianists seem wholly in consort with their respective singer.

Bostridge adds to his disc more Heine, Op 24, and separate songs to texts by the same poet, a consistent policy, and it also has more music over all; but Güra's choice of Op 39 is entirely justified by his quite beautiful rendering of this haunting work. His classically wrought, plangent-voiced reading goes, without too much interpretative intervention, to the heart of Eichendorff, and to Schumann's imaginative response to the poems. Listen to such masterpieces as 'Die Stille', 'Mondnacht' (a perfect *legato* here again) and 'Wehmut' and you'll hear him at his most eloquent, pianist Jan Schultsz adding his own insights to the tenor's reading. This simpler, unsophisticated version goes to the heart of the matter, and deserves a place among the élite.

Dichterliebe. Die Lotosblume, Op 25 No 7. Die Minnesänger, Op 33 No 2. Romanzen und Balladen – II, Op 49: No 1, Die beiden Grenadiere; III, Op 53: No 3, Der arme Peter; IV, Op 64: No 3, Tragödie. Belsatzar, Op 57. Lieder und Gesänge – Op 127: No 2, Dein Angesicht; No 3, Es leuchtet meine Liebe. Gesänge, Op 142 – No 2, Lehn deine Wang; No 4, Mein Wagen rollet langsam **C Schumann** Lieder, Op 13 – No 1, Ich stand in dunklen Träumen; No 2, Sie liebten sich beide. Loreley. Volkslied
Christopher Maltman bar **Graham Johnson** pf
Hyperion CDJ33105 (77' · DDD) Texts and translations included ⓕ**OO**

With this superbly executed recital Maltman

SCHUMANN DICHTERLIEBE – IN BRIEF

Werner Güra; Jan Schultsz
Harmonia Mundi HMC90 1766 ⓕ**OO**
An interpretation of impeccable credentials: beautifully phrased by tenor Werner Güra with an exquisite sense of line, this is a very impressive modern version. Jan Schultz is a fine accompanist.

Ian Bostridge; Julius Drake
EMI 556575-2 ⓕ**OOO**
☼ This won a well-deserved *Gramophone* Award in 1998. Tenor Ian Bostridge's reading is very personal, and emotionally charged, with lots of drama. *Dichterliebe* is coupled with more songs to texts by Heine; again Julius Drake is the stylish accompanist.

Christopher Maltman; Graham Johnson
Hyperion CDJ33105 ⓕ**OO**
A splendid programme that inspires Maltman to considerable heights of interpretative insights. His baritone is of a perfect weight and flexibility for these songs, and Johnson is the ever-impeccable companion.

Christian Gerhaher; Gerold Huber
RCA 82876 58995-2 ⓕ**OO**
A superb account by this outstanding young baritone. He enters fully into the melancholic world of Heine's imaginings, portraying the rejected lover with perfect poise and characterisation. His dynamic range, too, is most impressively handled, from the quietest whisper to the most full-throated cry.

Dietrich Fischer-Dieskau; Christoph Eschenbach
DG 415 190-2
A recording from the 1970s that finds the great German baritone in the excellent company of Christoph Eschenbach. There's an appealing warmth in Fischer-Dieskau's voice that makes this a most attractive performance.

Fritz Wunderlich; Hubert Giesen
DG 449 747-2
Wunderlich's pliant, sappy tenor voice is heard to wonderful effect here. Giesen is no more than an adequate partner, but with singing like this that's a small price to pay.

leaps in a single bound into the front rank of Lieder interpreters today. Seemingly inspired by the wonderful programme, he executes it with bitingly intense tone and an innate feeling for the German language, his high baritone easily encompassing every test placed on it. There are so many deeply satisfying performances here of mostly familiar songs that it's difficult to know which to alight on for special praise, but the last two groups – the sad, frightening tale of the near-deranged Peter and the great *Dichterliebe* cycle – undoubtedly form the climax of the recital.

Maltman's and Johnson's account of the cycle reminds one of the underrated version made long ago by Waechter and Brendel: it has the same immediacy, the same perceptions, with the singer's voice on each occasion being of the ideal weight and tessitura, and in its absolute prime. All the inner melancholy of words and notes, all their variety of texture are adumbrated. And here we have the added advantage of Johnson's inspired exegesis of the work in his accompanying notes.

Johnson also points out the foretaste of Mahler in the third of the Peter songs, a piece Maltman sings with just the right touch of vulnerability. He's just as sensitive in such well-known pieces as *Die Lotusblume* and *Dein Angesicht*, and brings tremendous impulse of drama to the familiar *Die beiden Grenadiere*, here sounding new-minted. The songs by Clara are a pleasing bonus, but the difference between talent and genius is apparent in comparing her setting of 'Es fiel ein Reif' (from Heine's *Volkslied*) with Schumann's. A perfectly balanced recording adds to one's pleasure in listening to this generously filled CD, which is up to the high standard of this series to date.

Dichterliebe. Sechs Gedichte und Requiem.
Belsatzar. Die Löwenbraut. Der arme Peter
Christian Gerhaher *bar* **Gerold Huber** *pf*
RCA Red Seal 82876 58995-2 (66' · DDD · T/t) Ⓕ**OO**

With this recital Christian Gerhaher confirms his pre-eminence in Lieder, and bids fair to equal or surpass his fellow baritones by dint of his attractively warm, firm tone and his complete understanding of the songs. In *Dichterliebe* he fully enters into the melancholic, romantic world of the rejected lover, projecting the love and sorrow in a committed yet unexaggerated manner. It's hard to imagine a reading by a voice of his kind that could possibly surpass his inspired performance – and that includes even the legendary Fischer-Dieskau.

He makes as good a case as possible for the *Six Poems* and *Requiem*, though it's hard to breathe life into the broken-backed ballad that is *Die Löwenbraut*. On the other hand, Gerhaher arrestingly enacts the melodrama of *Belsatzar*, biting consonants to the fore; the sadness of *Der arme Peter* benefits from the same thoughtful approach as *Dichterliebe*. Huber supports his partner with finely honed playing. The record-

ing could not be better balanced or more immediate. This is, in every respect, a winner.

Lieder Recitals

Liebesfrühling, Op 37 – No 1, Der Himmel hat ein Träne geweint; No 5, Ich hab' in mich gesogen. Myrthen, Op 25 – No 1, Widmung; No 2, Freisinn; No 3, Der Nussbaum; No 5, Lied aus dem Schenkenbuch im Divan I; No 6, Lied aus dem Schenkenbuch im Divan II; No 17, Venetianisches Lied I; No 18, Venetianisches Lied II; No 26, Zum Schluss **C Schumann** Liebeszauber. Liebst du um Schönheit, Op 12 No 2. Lieder, Op 13 – No 2, Sie liebten sich beide; No 6, Die stille Lotusblume. Lieder aus Jucunde, Op 23 – No 2, An einem lichten Morgen; No 3, Geheimes Flüstern; No 6, O Lust, o Lust
Wolfgang Holzmair *bar* **Imogen Cooper** *pf*
Philips 462 610-2PH (67' · DDD) Notes, texts and translations included Ⓕ**O**

This welcome disc has something extra to offer in the wonderful rapport between Wolfgang Holzmair and Imogen Cooper. Singer and pianist work together almost by instinct in thinking themselves into the very heart of these songs. Anything of extrovert display or seeking the limelight is quite foreign to their natures. Each song is approached from within, so that the results are like being a witness at their communion with both composers. Holzmair's plangent, very Viennese voice bespeaks the vulnerability that lies at the soul of Robert's Eusebius side, heard to mesmeric effect in the great, slower songs of Op 35, but he's just as capable of tramping the ways with Schumann when he's in his Florestan mood. In his other songs, Holzmair is equally mesmeric in the Venetian song, so intimately done, almost whispered and the old favourite *Der Nussbaum* receives as delicate a reading as one could wish.

Clara Schumann is well represented, especially by an inspired setting of a sad poem by Heine, *Sie liebten sich beide*, and it's interesting to hear what she does with Rückert's *Liebst du um Schönheit*, which Mahler set very differently a half century later. Clara doesn't pale by the comparison. Cooper is as wholly in sympathy with Clara's pianistic style as she is, needless to say, with Robert's. Her playing throughout the programme is at once supportive of her partner and individual in itself. The recording is faultless.

Complete Lieder, Volume 2

Drei Gedichte, Op 30. Die Löwenbraut, Op 31 No 1. 12 Gedichte, Op 35. Lieder und Gesänge aus Wilhelm Meister, Op 98a – No 2, Ballade des Harfners; No 4, Wer nie sein Brot mit Tränen ass; No 6, Wer sich der Einsamkeit ergibt; No 8, An die Türen will ich schleichen. Vier Husarenlieder, Op 117
Simon Keenlyside *bar* **Graham Johnson** *pf*
Hyperion CDJ33102 (70' · DDD) Texts and translations included Ⓕ**OO**

In his notes Graham Johnson says that what we have always lacked is a convincing way of performing late Schumann songs, often spare in texture and elusive in style. Well, he and Keenlyside seem to have found one here in their wholly admirable versions of the very different Opp 98*a* and 117. The Op 98*a* settings of the Harper's outpourings from *Wilhelm Meister* have always stood in the shade of those by Schubert and Wolf. This pair show incontrovertibly that there's much to be said for Schumann's versions, capturing the essence of the old man's sad musings, as set by the composer in an imaginative, free way, alert to every nuance in the texts.

The extroverted Lenau *Husarenlieder* could hardly be more different. Keenlyside identifies in turn with the bravado of the first, the cynicism of the second, and the eerie, death-dominated mood of the fourth. The pair enter into the open-hearted mood called for by the *Knabenhorn* settings, most of all in the irresistible 'Der Hidalgo'. Keenlyside is just as forthright in *Die Löwenbraut* and in those of Op 35, the well-known Kerner settings, and he brings impressive control to the Eusebius ones, not least the all-enveloping 'Stille Tränen'. The interpretation of this quasi-cycle is convincing and unerringly paced. The recording and Johnson's persuasive playing are superb.

Lieder, Op 40[a]. Spanisches Liederspiel, Op 74[b]. Spanische Liebeslieder, Op 138[c] **C Schumann** Lieder aus Jucunde, Op 23[d]
[bcd]**Geraldine McGreevy** sop [bc]**Stella Doufexis** mez [bc]**Adrian Thompson** ten [abc]**Stephan Loges** bar **Graham Johnson**, [c]**Stephen Hough** pfs
Hyperion CDJ33106 (76' · DDD) Notes and texts included   Ⓕⵔ

This disc is a delight from start to finish. Songs and interpretations are on a high level of achievement, in this case all the more welcome as these groups, for various reasons, don't figure that often in recitals. Both the Spanish sets are of the highest order of composition, though not often acknowledged as such. The Op 74 set is notable for many mood changes and its touches of fantasy, melded with a typically Schumannesque pull on the emotions. Alone or together, all four singers revel in their chances for expressive singing, none more than McGreevy, now a Lieder singer of major calibre, in 'Melancholie'. McGreevy also stands out in the wistful duet 'In der Nacht' with the sensitive Thompson, a poem set quite differently, as are some others, by Wolf later in the century. Loges contributes to concerted pieces with his expected artistry and has fun with 'Die Contrabandiste'.

The Op 138 set is even fuller of variety of mood and composition. All four singers seize their chances eagerly, with faultlessly sculpted readings under the tutelage of Johnson, who's joined here by no less a pianist than Stephen Hough in the two-piano accompaniments. The Andersen settings (Op 40) are fascinating songs delivered by Stephan Loges with refined tone

and diction to which he adds a sure insight into their meaning in performances that compel one to place the set among Schumann's masterpieces in the genre. Add the naturally balanced recording and Johnson's extensive notes and this issue is treasure indeed.

Myrthen, Op 25[a]. Four Duets, Op 34[a]. Four Duets, Op 78[a]. John Anderson, Op 145 No 4[b]
[a]**Dorothea Röschmann** sop [a]**Ian Bostridge** ten **Graham Johnson** pf [b]**Polyphony / Stephen Layton**
Hyperion CDJ33107 (78' · DDD)   Ⓕⵔⵔ

Hyperion's Schumann song series has already produced some profoundly satisfying discs, but none quite to equal the pleasures found on this volume. Its centrepiece, *Myrthen* – the cycle of love songs celebrating the union of Clara and Robert – is framed by eight duets to form a wonderfully balanced offering, and one that could hardly be surpassed in execution, through the understanding and skills of the three participants.

If one has to be singled out for particular praise, it must be Dorothea Röschmann. In tones at once fresh, warm and communicative, she sings all her contributions with an ideal balance between word and note. To such a familiar and lovely song as 'Der Nussbaum' she brings a heartfelt sense of anticipated pleasure that bears comparison with any of the heap of noted performances from the past, occasional vibrato used to arresting effect, as in all her readings. And 'Lied der Suleika' has its intensity underlined by the palpitating intimacy of her singing.

Not to be outdone, Bostridge presents deeply considered accounts of all his songs, combining his silvery, lightly tremulous tone with his customary feeling for words, most notably in the song 'Aus den hebräischen Gesängen' and the two Venetian Songs. Even better is his sensitive enactment of the marvellous setting of Heine, 'Was will die einsame Träne', which reveals his complete understanding of the idiom, and of the popular 'Du bist wie eine Blume', where his half-voice is skilfully deployed.

Johnson is on his most alert and empathetic form at the piano throughout. In the two sets of duets, full of Schumann at his most easeful, the voices intertwine effortlessly. Some oldsters will recall the famous, endearingly romantic Lehmann/Melchior recordings of some of these: Röschmann and Bostridge are just as persuasive. With one of Hyperion's best recordings to complement the performances, voices nicely forward, this disc is definitely one to have.

Complete Lieder, Volume 1
Das verlassene Mägdlein, Op 64 No 2. Melancholie, Op 74 No 6. Aufträge, Op 77 No 5. Op 79 – No 7a, Zigeunerliedchen I; No 7b, Zigeunerliedchen II; No 23, Er ist's!. Die Blume der Ergebung, Op 83 No 2. Röslein, Röslein!, Op 89 No 6. Sechs Gedichte und Requiem, Op 90. Op 96 – No 1, Nachtlied; No 3 Ihre Stimme. Lieder und Gesänge aus Wilhelm Meister,

Op 98a – No 1, Kennst du das Land?; No 3, Nur wer
die Sehnsucht kennt; No 5, Heiss' mich nicht reden;
No 7, Singet nicht in Trauertönen; No 9, So lasst
mich scheinen. Sechs Gesänge, Op 107. Warnung,
Op 119 No 2. Die Meerfee, Op 125 No 1. Sängers
Trost, Op 127 No 1. Mädchen-Schwermut, Op 142
No 3
Christine Schäfer sop **Graham Johnson** pf
Hyperion CDJ33101 (75' · DDD) Texts and translations
included   ⓕ❍❍❍

This disc launches Hyperion's Schumann Lieder project as auspiciously as
Dame Janet Baker's recital opened
their Complete Schubert Edition. As ever, Graham Johnson shows an unerring gift for matching singer and song. These are almost all late
pieces, written between 1849 and 1852 under
the shadow of depression and sickness; and their
intense chromaticism can all too easily seem
tortuous. However, imaginatively supported by
Johnson, Christine Schäfer illuminates each of
these songs with her pure, lucent timbre, her
grace and breadth of phrase and her unselfconscious feeling for verbal meaning and nuance.
The voice is an expressive, flexible lyric-col-
oratura; she can spin a scrupulously even *legato*,
integrates the high notes of, say, 'Er ist's' perfectly within the melodic line, and has the
breath control to sustain the long phrases of
'Requiem' with apparent ease.

Aided by Johnson's lucid textures and subtle
feel for *rubato* and harmonic direction, Schäfer
avoids any hint of mawkishness in songs like
'Meine Rose', Op 90 No 2, 'Mädchen-Schwermut' and 'Abendlied. Several songs here have
been overshadowed or eclipsed by the settings
by Schubert, Wolf or Brahms, and Schäfer and
Johnson do much to rehabilitate them.

Schäfer brings an exquisite wondering stillness to the Goethe 'Nachtlied', more disturbed
and earthbound than Schubert's sublime setting, but here, at least, scarcely less poignant.
She also has the dramatic flair to bring off the
difficult Mignon songs, especially the volatile,
quasi-operatic 'Heiss' mich nicht reden' and
'Kennst du das Land', where the final verse,
evoking Mignon's terrifying passage across the
Alps, builds to a climax of desperate, almost
demented yearning. At the other end of the
emotional spectrum, Schäfer brings a guileful,
knowing touch to the first of the *Zigeunerliedchen*; the Mendelssohnian 'Die Meerfee'
glistens and glances and 'Aufträge' has a winning eagerness and charm, with a delicious
sense of flirtation between voice and keyboard.
A delectable, often revelatory recital. The
recording is natural and well balanced, while
Graham Johnson provides typically searching
commentaries.

Genoveva, Op 81

Genoveva
Ruth Ziesak sop Genoveva **Deon van der Walt** ten
Golo **Rodney Gilfry** bar Hidulfus **Oliver Widmer** bar

Siegfried **Marjana Lipovšek** mez Margaretha
Thomas Quasthoff bar Drago **Hiroyuki Ijichi** bass
Balthasar **Josef Krenmair** bar Caspar **Arnold
Schoenberg Choir; Chamber Orchestra of Europe
/ Nikolaus Harnoncourt**
Teldec ② 0630-13144-2 (129' · DDD) Recorded live
1996. Notes, text and translation included   ⓕ❍

For most listeners Schumann's only opera is still
a relatively unknown quantity, but lovers of his
music will celebrate a work that's intimate,
thought-provoking and melodious. The libretto (by Schumann himself, after Tieck and
Hebbel) deals with secret passion and suspected
adultery, while the music mirrors emotional
turmoil with great subtlety, and sometimes with
astonishing imagination. Copious foretastes are
provided in the familiar overture, and thereafter, discoveries abound. Sample, for example,
the jagged counter-motif that shudders as Genoveva's husband Siegfried entreats Golo (his
own *alter ego*) to guard his wife while he's away
at war; or the off-stage forces representing
drunken servants; or the almost expressionist
writing at 4'00" into track 10, where Golo
responds with seething hatred to Genoveva's
vengeance. The entreaties of Drago's ghost
(track 4, 6'10") aren't too far removed from
Siegmund's 'Nothung!' in Act 1 of *Die Walküre*,
and Genoveva's singing from 'a desolate, rocky
place' (track 5, first minute or so), sounds prophetic of Isolde (who was as yet unborn, so to
speak). Harnoncourt suspects that *Genoveva* was
a 'counterblast' to Wagner, and though Wagner
apparently thought the opera 'bizarre', there
remains a vague suspicion of sneaking regard,
even a smidgen of influence.

Teldec's balancing is mostly judicious, and
the musical direction suggestive of burning conviction. The worthy though relatively conventional Gerd Albrecht (in Orfeo's mellow 1992
recording) only serves to underline the leaner,
more inflected and more urgently voiced profile
of Harnoncourt's interpretation. As to the two
sets of singers, most preferences rest with the
latter's line-up. Stage effects are well handled;
the sum effect is of a top-drawer Schumann set
within an unexpected structural context.

Heinrich Schütz   German 1585-1672

*In 1590 Schütz moved with his family to Weis-
senfels. In 1598 Landgrave Moritz, impressed by his
musical accomplishments, took him to Kassel, where
he served as a choirboy and studied music with the
court Kapellmeister, Georg Otto. In 1609 Schütz
proceeded to the University of Marburg to study law,
but Landgrave Moritz advised him to abandon his
university studies and to go to Venice as a pupil of G
Gabrieli; moreover, the landgrave provided the
financial means to do this. Schütz remained in
Venice for over three years, returning to Moritz's
court at Kassel in 1613. The following year he was*

seconded to serve for two months at the electoral court in Dresden, and in 1615 the Elector Johann Georg I requested his services for a further two years. Moritz reluctantly agreed, and was obliged, for political reasons, to comply when the elector insisted on retaining Schütz in his permanent employ.

As Kapellmeister at Dresden, Schütz was responsible for providing music for major court ceremonies, whether religious or political. He also had to keep the Kapelle adequately staffed and supervise the musical education of the choirboys. His pupils during the following decades included the composers Bernhard, Theile and Weckmann. In 1619 Schütz published his first collection of sacred music, the Psalmen Davids, dedicated to the elector, and later that year he married Magdalena Wildeck. She died in 1625, leaving Schütz with two daughters whom he placed in the care of their maternal grandmother; he never remarried.

Schütz was often absent from Dresden on his own or the elector's business, and in 1627 he was at Torgau, where his Dafne (the first German opera) was performed for the wedding of the elector's daughter Sophia Eleonora. Visits to Mühlhausen and possibly Gera were undertaken later in the year. Towards the end of the 1620s economic pressures of the Thirty Years War began to affect the electoral court. Musicians wages fell into arrears, and in 1628 Schütz decided on a second visit to Venice, where he was able to study developments in dramatic music under Monteverdi's guidance. He returned to Dresden in 1629, but two years later Saxony entered the war and musical activities at court soon came to a virtual halt. Schütz then accepted an invitation to direct the music at the wedding of Crown Prince Christian of Denmark. He arrived in Copenhagen in December 1633 and was paid a salary as Kapellmeister by King Christian IV until his return to Dresden in May 1635.

From Michaelmas 1639 Schütz was again absent from Dresden, this time for about 15 months in the service of Georg of Calenberg. On his return he found the Kapelle further depleted and its members living in penury, and for most of 1642-4 he was again employed at the Danish court. After a year in and around Brunswick he went into semi-retirement, spending much of his time in Weissenfels, though he retained the title and responsibilities of Kapellmeister at Dresden. The end of the Thirty Years War had little immediate effect on musical conditions and in 1651 Schütz renewed an earlier plea for release from his duties and the granting of a pension. This and later petitions were ignored and Schütz obtained his release only on the elector's death in 1656. He was far from inactive during his remaining 15 years. He continued to supply music for occasions at Dresden, frequently travelled and worked on the masterpieces of his last years – the Christmas History, the three Passions and the settings of Psalms cxix and c.

Schütz was the greatest German composer of the 17th century and the first of international stature. His output was almost exclusively sacred; he set mainly biblical texts and wrote little chorale-based music. His early works explore a variety of styles and genres: the polychoral Psalmen Davids (1619) are notable for their contrasting textures and sonorities,

while the Cantiones sacrae (1625) present a wide range of motet settings, from the polyphonic to the concertato. Later, he exploited the Italian concertato idiom to the full, notably in the three books of Symphoniae sacrae (1629, 1647, 1650), which give equal weight to voices and instruments. His two sets of Kleine geistliche Concerte (1636, 1639), written after the Thirty Years War and for limited forces, emphasise the meaning of the text, combining principles of monody and counterpoint to create powerful and expressive declamation. Schütz's late works are dominated by the oratorical pieces and by the three unaccompanied 'dramatic' Passions, said to be the last great examples of the genre. His music, largely to German texts, constitutes the ultimate realisation of Luther's endeavours to establish the vernacular as a literary and liturgical language, and embodies the Protestant and humanistic concept of musica poetica in perhaps its most perfect form. **GROVE**music

Motets

Ich hab mein Sach Gott heimgestellt, SWV305. Ich **P** will dem Herren loben allezeit, SWV306. Was hast du verwirket, SWV307. O Jesu, nomen dulce, SWV308. O misericordissime Jesu, SWV309. Ich leige und schlafe, SWV310. Habe deine Lust an dem Herren, SWV311. Herr, ich hoffe darauf, SWV312. Bone Jesu, verbum Patris, SWV313. Verbum caro factum est, SWV314. Hodie Christus natus est, SWV315. Wann unsre Augen schlafen ein, SWV316. Meister, wir haben die ganze Nacht gearbeitet, SWV317. Die Furcht des Herren, SWV318. Ich beuge meine Knie, SWV319. Ich bin jung gewesen, SWV320. Herr, wann ich nur dich habe, SWV321. Rorate coeli desuper, SWV322. Joseph, du Sohn David, SWV323. Ich bin die Auferstehung, SWV324
Tölz Boys' Choir / Gerhard Schmidt-Gaden with **Roman Summereder** org
Capriccio 10 388 (77' · DDD) Recorded 1989-90.
Texts and translations included   Ⓕ

Getting music published evidently encountered economic difficulties during the Thirty Years' War, for Heinrich Schütz had to issue his *Kleiner geistlichen Concerten* ('Little Sacred Concertos') – short motets for vocal soloists and continuo – in two parts in, respectively, 1636 and 1639. The voices of the soloists here are typically very individual and characterful, and all are remarkably adroit and stylish, so the personal witness that's so pronounced in the text is particularly well portrayed. These are performers well used to the subtleties of Baroque word-setting and they highlight all the ingenuity that Schütz lavished on these seemingly simple texts. There's an evident delight in the way the composer deployed his limited resources, constantly ringing the changes on traditional formulas to produce a richness of ideas that it took a Bach or Handel to emulate. The rather close recording allows all these intricacies to emerge undiminished and although the resonance of the acoustic seems restrained, this is no bad thing for repertoire that, despite its title, has the feel of chamber music.

Psalms of David

Psalmen Davids sampt etlichen Moteten und
Concerten, SWV22-47
Cantus Cölln (Elisabeth Scholl, Annette Labusch
sops Elisabeth Popien mez Stratton Bull counterten
Gerd Türk, Wilfried Jochens, Jörn Lindemann tens
Stephan Schreckenberger, Stephan MacLeod
basses) **Concerto Palatino / Konrad Junghänel**
Harmonia Mundi ② HMC90 1652/3 (143' · DDD)
Texts and translations included   Ⓕ❍

Here's something to get excited about: a new
recording, at last, of Schütz's first monumental
publication of sacred music. Whether anything
can be worth waiting for that long is a moot
point, but Cantus Cölln and Concerto Palatino
give us an interpretation that's unlikely to be
surpassed. With eight singers and no fewer than
two dozen instrumentalists, the scale is little
short of symphonic. For sheer splendour, who
can top *Danket dem Herren* (SWV45) or the next
piece in the collection, *Zion spricht*?

It's easy enough to single out the most opulent
pieces, but as Peter Wollny remarks in his
admirable booklet-notes, the whole point of the
Psalmen Davids is its variety in the treatment of a
medium whose potential for cliché is very great.
The musicians respond to Schütz's demands
with verve and perception and the sort of confidence that would carry any music aloft in triumph. The sound recording does them full justice. You'll almost certainly listen, enthralled, to
the entire collection – nearly two-and-a-half
hours – in one sitting.

Symphoniae sacrae

Symphoniae sacrae, SWV341-67
Emma Kirkby, Suzie Le Blanc sops **James**   Ⓟ
Bowman counterten **Nigel Rogers, Charles Daniels**
tens **Stephen Varcoe, Richard Wistreich** basses
Jeremy West, Nicholas Perry cornets **Purcell**
Quartet (Catherine Mackintosh, Catherine Weiss vns
Richard Boothby va da gamba Robert Woolley hpd)
Chandos Chaconne ② CHAN0566/7 (139' · DDD)
Recorded 1993-4. Text and translation included   Ⓕ❍

These discs are in various ways revelatory.
Schütz's collection is difficult to get through in
one sitting, but each item is a jewel. This is
church music on a small scale in terms of physical resources, but of enormous invention and
beauty. Sometimes the Purcell Quartet do not
push the music along quite enough. In general,
however, the instrumentalists respond with
enthusiasm and great understanding of the style
of these rather recondite works. It takes considerable sensitivity to bring out the rich textures
of *Meine Seele erhebt den Herren* or *Der Herr ist
meine Stärke* without enjoying such moments at
the expense of the vocal soloist. The relatively
well-known bass solo *Herr, nun lässest du deinen
Diener* is another example of a perfect match
between voice and instruments.

Emma Kirkby brings all her customary charm

and precision to her two solo arias. Both tenors
are in their element, if sometimes a little understated, and Stephen Varcoe and Richard
Wistreich really understand and communicate
the glowing black and gold colours of Schütz's
writing for the bass voice.

Schütz's debt to Monteverdi is very much evident in *Der Herr ist mein Licht* and even more so
in *Es steh Gott auf*, but Schütz's natural reluctance to 'deck out my work with foreign
plumage' means that his own voice as a composer is always in evidence. This reconciliation
of Italian *stile concertato* with Schütz's northern
reticence is one of the challenges in performing
his music, and one to which this recording rises
magnificently.

Secular Works

Freue dich des Weibes deiner Jugend, SWV453.
Liebster, sagt in süssem Schmerzen, SWV441.
Nachdem ich lag in meinem öder Bette, SWV451.
Glück zu dem Helikon, SWV96. Haus und Güter
erbat man von Eltern, SWV21. Tugend ist der beste
Freund, SWV442. Teutoniam dudum belli atra
pericla, SWV338. Wie wenn der Adler, SWV434.
Siehe, wie fein und lieblich ists, SWV48. Vier
Hirtinnen, gleich jung, gleich schön, SWVAnh1. Lässt
Salomon sein Bette nicht umgeben, SWV452. Die
Erde trinkt für sich, SWV438. Wohl dem, der ein
Tugendsam Weib hat, SWV20. Itzt blicken durch des
Himmels Saal, SWV460. Syncharma musicum, SWV49
Weser-Renaissance Bremen / Manfred Cordes
CPO CPO999 518-2 (71' · DDD) Texts and
translations included   Ⓑ❍

Here's a discovery of several unrecorded byways
of Schütz's miscellaneous secular music. The
17th century being what it is, secular and sacred
are deliberately dovetailed into a cultural pea
soup: these works are embedded in the literary
morality of the age and aren't entirely profane.
There's a pleasing lightness of touch from the
soloists (especially the soprano) and the instrumental consort doesn't attempt, as is so mistakenly regarded these days as the ideal, to ape the
vocal lines at every turn in a wash of homogeneity; there are many distinctive virtuosic commentaries, as in *Tugend ist der beste Freund*,
which Cordes (enhanced by the excellent
recorded sound) allows to breathe naturally.
Noble intensity and harmonious accord are the
order of the day in the splendidly uplifting concerto *Teutoniam dudum*, which through its
extraordinary structural clarity immediately
delights the listener with a celebration of the
cessation of hostilities after the miserable
Thirty Years War. Most impressive, though, is
the sympathetic and gentle treatment of the
words from Weser-Renaissance, beautifully
complemented by the soft articulation of the
winds, especially in *Siehe, wie fein* and the
domestic charm of *Wohl dem, der ein Tugendsam*.
This is chamber music-making from the heart,
tempered convincingly by the intellect and
affectionately delivered.

Alexander Scriabin   Russian 1872-1915

Scriabin was a fellow pupil of Rachmaninov's in Zverev's class from 1884 and at the Moscow Conservatory (1888-92), where his teachers were Taneyev, Arensky and Safonov. From 1894 his career as a pianist was managed by Belyayev, who arranged his European tours and also published his works: at this stage they were almost exclusively for solo piano, and deeply influenced by Chopin (most are preludes and mazurkas), though in the late 1890s he began to write for orchestra. In 1903 he left Russia and his family to live in western Europe for six years with a young female admirer, and his musical style became more intensely personal, developing a profusion of decoration in harmony becalmed by unresolved dominant chords or whole-tone elements. The major works of this period include the Divine Poem and again numerous piano pieces.

In 1905 he encountered Madame Blavatsky's theosophy, which soon ousted the enthusiasm for Nietschean superhumanism that had underlain the immediately preceding works. The static and ecstatic tendencies in his music were encouraged, being expressed notably in the Poem of Ecstasy and Prometheus, the latter intended to be performed with a play of coloured light. Still more ambitious were the plans for the Mysterium, a quasi-religious act which would have united all the arts, and for the composition of which the exclusively piano works of 1910-15 were intended to be preparatory, this journey into mystical hysteria going along with a voyage beyond tonality to a floating dissonance often based on the 'mystic chord' (C-F sharp-B flat-E-A-D).

GROVEmusic

Piano Concerto

Scriabin Piano Concerto in F sharp minor, Op 20
Tchaikovsky Piano Concerto No 1 in B flat minor, Op 23
Nikolai Demidenko *pf* **BBC Symphony Orchestra / Alexander Lazarev**
Hyperion CDA66680 (65' · DDD) Recorded 1993   Ⓕ

The chief attraction here is the unusual coupling which pairs two sharply opposed examples of Russian Romanticism, and although the reasons for the neglect of Scriabin's Piano Concerto aren't hard to fathom (its lyrical and decorative flights are essentially inward-looking), its haunting, bittersweet beauty, particularly in the central *Andante*, is hard to resist. Demidenko's own comments, quoted in the accompanying booklet, are scarcely less intense and individual than his performance: 'in the ambience, phrasing and cadence of his music we meet with a world almost without skin, a world of nerve-ends where the slightest contact can bring pain.' His playing soars quickly to meet the music's early passion head on, and in the first *più mosso scherzando* he accelerates to produce a brilliant lightening of mood. His flashing *fortes* in the *Andante*'s second variation are as volatile as his *pianissimos* are starry and refined in the finale's period reminiscence, and although he might

seem more tight-lipped, less expansive than Ashkenazy on Decca, he's arguably more dramatic and characterful. Demidenko's Tchaikovsky, too, finds him ferreting out and sifting through every texture, forever aiming at optimum clarity. While this is hardly among the greatest Tchaikovsky Firsts on record, it's often gripping and mesmeric. The recorded balance isn't always ideal and the piano sound is sometimes uncomfortably taut.

Symphonies

No 1 in E, Op 26 **No 2** in C minor, Op 29 **No 3** in C minor, Op 43 'Divin poème'.

Symphonies – Nos 1[a], 2 & 3. Le poème de l'extase, Op 54[b]. Prometheus, Op 60, 'Le poème du feu'[c]
[a]**Stefania Toczyska** *mez* [a]**Michael Myers** *ten* [c]**Dmitri Alexeev** *pf* [b]**Frank Kaderabek** *tpt* [a]**Westminster Choir**; [c]**Philadelphia Choral Arts Society; Philadelphia Orchestra / Riccardo Muti**
EMI ③ 567720-2 (188' · DDD) Recorded 1985-90. Text and translation included   Ⓜ**OO**

There can be few more thrilling sounds on disc (and no more compelling reason for a totally sound-proofed listening room) than the climax to Muti's *Poème de l'extase*. The clamour of bells here (both literal and imitative) reveals an essentially Russian heart at the core of this most cosmopolitan of Russian composers, and the *maestoso* proclamation of the theme of self assertion has the raised Philadelphia horns in crucially sharp focus. As in the corresponding climax in *Prometheus* (at 18'21"), this 'éclat sublime' is filled out with a floor-shaking contribution from the organ. Like the organ, the wordless chorus at this point in *Prometheus* registers more as a device for enriching and exalting the texture, rather than as a striking new presence.

Muti's *Prometheus* is, arguably, the most complete realisation of the mind-boggling demands of this score ever to have been recorded. The inert opening ('Original chaos' – lovely *pp* bass drum!) and mysterious awakening have rarely sounded so atmospheric. Alexeev's first entry isn't as strong willed as some, but he seems to be saving a more imperious attack for the same point in the recapitulation. Muti builds the work superbly: the imposing clash of states in the development (and the changes of tempo) charted with mighty assurance. And thereafter *Prometheus* is airborne, with Alexeev both agile and articulate in the 'Dance of Life'.

Throughout the cycle, the tonal allure of the Philadelphia Orchestra is fully in evidence. Only in the Third Symphony, *Divin poème*, do Muti and the EMI team seem to be on less than their indomitable form. Compared with some versions, the tempo relationships in the first movement don't fully convince. However, this cycle is unlikely to be seriously challenged for many a year. As a whole it immeasurably enhances Scriabin's stature as a symphonist and offers the kind of playing and recording which, as recently as two decades ago, Scriabin enthusiasts could only have imagined in their dreams.

Prometheus

Scriabin Prometheus **Stravinsky** The Firebird
Alexander Toradze pf **Kirov Opera Chorus and Orchestra** / **Valery Gergiev**
Philips 446 715-2PH (72' · DDD)   ℗**O**

Stravinsky and the short-lived Scriabin were almost contemporaries; of these two exactly contemporary works (1909-10), *Prometheus*, as Oliver Knussen has put it, is 'so much more than a period piece; pregnant with possibilities for the future', whereas *The Firebird*, aside from its 'Infernal Dance', rarely does anything more startling than pick up from where Rimsky-Korsakov left off – indeed, in certain sections, it shows that Stravinsky also knew his Scriabin rather well (for example, the Firebird's 'Dance of Supplication'). Gergiev's *Firebird* is certainly a startling performance. All manner of things contribute to the impression of distinction, among them the fact that this is that rare thing on record, an all-Russian complete *Firebird*.

The music-making seems alive with a special presence: the orchestra is fairly close, though there's a real sense of the hall, never more so than when a heart-stopping crack is let loose from the drums on Kashchey's appearance. But the primary presence here (obvious enough, but it needs saying) is of a man of the theatre, maybe too audibly (for some) breathing life into the proceedings, moving from one section of the ballet to the next with the transitional mastery of a Furtwängler, and taking risks with tempo (do hear the end of the 'Infernal Dance'). The darkness to light of the ballet's last few minutes is nothing less than mesmeric.

Prometheus is equally compelling. Toradze's solo contribution is slightly less the centre of the piece's universe than Argerich in the sensational Abbado recording, in terms of both imaginative daring and recorded scale, though it never lacks character. The only reservation about the Abbado is the relatively fined down impression of Scriabin's huge orchestra. Yet with the more imposing-sounding Russian team you really know about it. Gergiev's is also a much broader view of the piece, but it never sounds overly languid, indeed it enables him and Toradze, unlike Argerich and Abbado, to achieve a dizzying *accelerando prestissimo* in the final bars that's faster than anything that has preceded it.

Etudes

Etude in C sharp minor, Op 2 No 1. 12 Etudes, Op 8.
Etudes, Op 42. Etude in E flat, Op 49 No 1. Etude,
Op 56 No 4. Three Etudes, Op 65
Piers Lane pf Hyperion CDA66607 (56' · DDD)
Recorded 1992   ℗**O**

Although Scriabin's *études* do not fall into two neatly packaged sets in the same way as Chopin's celebrated contributions, nevertheless there's a strong feeling of continuity and development running throughout the 26 examples produced between the years 1887 and 1912. This is admirably demonstrated in this excellent issue from Hyperion, which, far from being an indigestible anthology proves to be an intriguing and pleasurable hour's worth of listening charting Scriabin's progression from late-romantic adolescence to harmonically advanced mystical poet. Indeed, although these studies can be counted as amongst the most digitally taxing and hazardous of their kind, Scriabin also saw them as important sketches and studies for his larger works, and as experiments in his gradually evolving harmonic language and mystical vision.

Piers Lane attains the perfect balance of virtuoso display and poetic interpretation. Expressive detail and subtle nuance are finely brought out, and he's more than receptive to Scriabin's sometimes highly idiosyncratic sound world; rarely, for instance, has the famous 'Mosquito' Etude (Op 42 No 3) been captured with such delicate fragility as here, and in No 1 of the three fiendishly difficult *Etudes*, Op 65 the tremulous, ghostly flutterings are tellingly delivered with a gossamer-light touch and a sense of eerie mystery. The clear, spacious recording is exemplary.

Mazurkas

10 Mazurkas, Op 3. Nine Mazurkas, Op 25.
Two Mazurkas, Op 40
Gordon Fergus-Thompson pf
ASV CDDCA1086 (80' · DDD)   ℗**O**

Volume 4 of Gordon Fergus-Thompson's Scriabin series for ASV is of the complete *Mazurkas*. The *Mazurka* remains an intransigently indigenous dance genre, and Chopin's incomparable example is more than a hard act to follow. However, Scriabin was among the few who accepted such a challenge wholeheartedly and, while his gratitude to his beloved Polish master is obvious, so too is the skill with which he takes Chopin's Slavonicism on a journey through bittersweet nostalgia into a more convoluted idiom and, finally, into a pensive and hallucinatory shadowland. The elusive character of these fascinating and neglected works could hardly be presented more vividly and insinuatingly than by Fergus-Thompson.

How well he understands the way Scriabin's momentary high spirits (in, say, No 4) collapse into morbid introspection in No 5 – into a close-knit chromaticism later refined still further by dark and obsessive intervals and patterning. The balletic leaps of No 6 are deftly contrasted with its sinuous central melody, and, however circuitous the route, Fergus-Thompson travels it with a special clarity and romantic fervour. The two confidential Op 40 *Mazurkas* are a notable success, and the recordings are crystalline and immediate.

Preludes

Complete Preludes – Op 2 No 2; Op 9 No 1; Opp 11, 13, 15-17, 22, 27, 31, 33, 35, 37, 39; Op 45 No 3; Op 48; Op 49 No 2; Op 51 No 2; Op 56 No 1; Op 59 No 2; Opp 67 & 74
Piers Lane pf
Hyperion ② CDA67057/8 (127' · DDD)   ⒻⓄⓄ

Everything about this two-disc set is ideal. Beautifully packaged and recorded, superbly played, there's the added bonus of an outstanding essay by Simon Nicholls, in which acute musical analysis is presented within the wider context of Scriabin's bewildering genius. Nicholls sees Scriabin as 'a musical Fabergé', a composer who contrasted his love of the ambitious epic with an even greater love of miniatures that could be 'short as a sparrow's beak or a bear's tail'. And throughout the extraordinary journey from Op 2 No 2 to Op 74, where the memories of Chopin are subdued by 'scarifying documents of individual and social catastrophe', you're tossed abruptly from a serene or bitter introspection to a crazed violence and exuberance, encouraged by idiosyncratic directions such as *patetico, con stravaganza, vagamente, irato impetuoso, sauvage belliqueux*.

The demands on the pianist are fierce, but it would be hard to imagine a more focused or immaculate reading than that offered by Piers Lane. Few pianists could show more sympathy and affection for such volatile romanticism, or display greater stylistic consistency. He underlines the despondency of the left-hand Prelude, Op 9 No 1 (here separated from its celebrated Nocturne companion); and in, for example, Op 11 No 3 the fleeting melodic outline is always kept intact amid so much whirling activity. The turbulence of No 14 is caught just as surely, and as an instance of how his scrupulousness is combined with the most vivid imagination, he gives us No 16 in an agitated and freely expressive style rather than opting for a more conventional, stricter tempo, creating a novel and nightmarish dimension. He takes No 2 at a true *Allegro* (as marked) and is never tempted into the sort of virtuoso skirmish offered by lesser players. Indeed, his gift for clarifying even the most tortuous utterances with an exemplary poise and assurance is among his finest qualities. The machine-gun fire of Op 31 No 3 and the menacing tread of Op 33 No 4 are fully realised, and Lane ably taps the darkest regions of the imagination in the final Op 74 Preludes.

These discs complement Piers Lane's earlier Hyperion recording of the complete Scriabin Etudes, and although competition is strong in this repertoire, especially from Evgeny Zarafiants and from Gordon Fergus-Thompson in his ongoing series, this new set of the Preludes should be in any serious record collection.

Preludes – Op 22; Op 27; Op 31; Op 33; Op 35; Op 37; Op 39; Op 48; Op 67; Op 74. Prelude in E flat, Op 45 No 3. Prelude in F, Op 49 No 2. Prelude in A minor, Op 51 No 2. Prelude in E flat minor, Op 56 No 1. Prelude, Op 59 No 2 **J Scriabin** Prelude in C, Op 2. Preludes, Op 3 – No 1 in B; No 2. Prelude in D flat
Evgeny Zarafiants pf
Naxos 8 554145 (65' · DDD)   ⓈⓈⓄ

With this second volume Evgeny Zarafiants completes his superb survey of Scriabin's 86 Preludes, adding four Preludes by Julian Scriabin, the composer's precociously gifted son, as encores. Listening to music of such morbid and refined intricacy played with the finest musical poise and commitment returns us to Stravinsky's bemused question, 'Scriabin, where does he come from, and who are his followers?' Is the angst and angry convolution of, say, Op 27 No 1 a slavonic memory of Brahms's Op 118 No 1? Does the explosive whimsy of Op 35 No 3 take its cue from the *Scherzo* of Beethoven's Op 26 Sonata? The hair-raising *presto* of Op 67 No 2 recalls the menace and enigma of the finale from Chopin's Op 35 Sonata, while the terse and belligerent Op 33 No 3 looks ahead to Stravinsky's sharpest modernist utterances. Yet if there are countless examples of reflection and prophecy, there are still more of the most startling originality. Scriabin is always Scriabin, and as he journeys from Op 22 to Op 74 into the darkest reaches of the imagination you're reminded that this is hardly music for the fainthearted.

Once again, Zarafiants is equal to each and every vivid occasion. Whether in the fragrant *grazioso* of Op 22 No 2, where the line twists and turns like so much honeysuckle, in the toppling argument of Op 31 No 3, or in the *sauvage belliqueux* of Op 59 No 2, he's richly responsive, his playing alive with a rare pianistic skill and imaginative brio. The Brandon Hill recordings are resonant and full-blooded.

Complete Piano Sonatas

No 1 in F minor, Op 6 **No 2** in G sharp minor (Sonata-fantasy), Op 19 **No 3** in F sharp minor, Op 23 **No 4** in F sharp, Op 30 **No 5** in F sharp, Op 53 **No 6** in G, Op 62; **No 7** in F sharp (White Mass), Op 64 **No 8** in A, Op 66 **No 9** in F (Black Mass), Op 68 **No 10** in C, Op 70

Piano Sonatas Nos 1-10. Fantasie in B minor, Op 28. Sonata-fantaisie in G sharp minor
Marc-André Hamelin pf
Hyperion ② CDA67131/2 (146' · DDD) Recorded 1989-90   ⒻⓄⓄ

Scriabin was an ambitious composer. A romantic alchemist, he saw his music as a transmuting agent. Through its influence pain would become happiness and hate become love, culminating in a phoenix-like rebirth of the universe.

-With Shakespearian agility he would change the world's dross into 'something rich and strange'. Not surprisingly, given Scriabin's early prowess as a pianist, the 10 sonatas resonate with exoticism, ranging through the First Sonata's cries of despair, to the Second Sonata's Baltic Sea inspiration, the Third Sonata's 'states of being', the 'flight to a distant star' (No 4) and 'the emergence of mysterious forces' (No 5). Nos 7 and 9 are *White* and *Black Mass* Sonatas respectively, and the final sonatas blaze with trills symbolising an extra-terrestrial joy and incandescence.

Such music makes ferocious demands on the pianist's physical stamina and imaginative resource. However, Marc-André Hamelin takes everything in his stride. Blessed with rapier reflexes he nonchalantly resolves even the most outlandish difficulties. He launches the First Sonata's opening outcry like some gleaming trajectory and, throughout, his whistle-stop virtuosity is seemingly infallible.

You might, however, miss a greater sense of the music's Slavonic intensity, its colour and character; a finer awareness, for example, of the delirious poetry at the heart of the Second Sonata's whirling finale. Hamelin's sonority is most elegantly and precisely gauged but time and again his fluency (admittedly breathtaking) erases too much of the work's originality and regenerative force. However, he shows a greater sense of freedom in the Fifth Sonata, and in the opalescent fantasy of the later sonatas, he responds with more evocative skill to subjective terms, as well as to moments where Scriabin's brooding introspection is lit by sudden flashes of summer lightning.

The recordings are a little tight and airless in the bass and middle register, but the set does includes a superb essay on Scriabin.

The Early Scriabin
Piano Sonata in E flat minor. Sonate-fantaisie. Allegro appassionato, Op 4. Canon in D minor. Etude No 12 in D sharp minor, Op 8. Fugue. Nocturne in A flat. Two Nocturnes, Op 5. Two Pieces for the left hand, Op 9. Mazurkas – in B minor; in F. Valses – Op 1; Op 6, No 1; No 2. Variations on a theme by Mlle Egorova
Stephen Coombs pf
Hyperion CDA67149 (74' · DDD)   Ⓔ

Stephen Coombs's 'The Early Scriabin' is a programme of fascinating rarities played with touching sensitivity and affection. Coombs's booklet essay, a mine of information and research, tells the history of such oddities as the sombre D minor Canon and E minor Fugue (their titles essentially alien to Scriabin's precociously romantic and far-reaching sensibility) or the complex provenance of the masterly E flat minor Sonata. He also tells us that Scriabin's genius received short shrift from the academic *ancien régime*; allowing him to graduate in piano but not in composition. Coombs's performances are, for the most part, what painters call 'low in tone', and even when you wish for greater voltage in, say, the nightmarish eques-

trian finale of the Sonata you can hardly wish for more gently persuasive accounts of the Waltzes or the A flat Nocturne. He's much less dazzling and rhetorical than, for example, Leon Fleisher in the Prelude and Nocturne for the left hand but, conversely his playing suggests a subtly characterful and communing alternative. He does, though, make a full-blooded but finely graded assault on the cadenza just before the return of the principle idea in the *Allegro appassionato*. This record is a most impressive achievement, as beautiful in sound as it's endlessly thought-provoking.

Peter Sculthorpe   Australian b1929

Sculthorpe studied at Melbourne University and with Rubbra and Wellesz at Oxford (1958-61) and in 1963 he began teaching at Sydney University. His music features an expressive brilliance of colour and vigorous use of ostinato, sometimes reflecting his interest in Balinese music. His works include the opera Rites of Passage (1974), orchestral and vocal pieces (including the series Sun Music) and a sequence of nine string quartets.   GROVEmusic

Piano Concerto

Piano Concerto. Little Nourlangie. Music for Japan. The song of Tailitnama
Kirsti Harms mez **Mark Atkins** didjeridu **Tamara Anna Cislowska** pf **David Drury** org **Sydney Symphony Orchestra / Edo de Waart**
ABC Classics 8 770030 (53' · DDD) Text included   Ⓕ

Sculthorpe has long been preoccupied with the music from other countries situated in and around the Pacific – and Japanese music in particular, elements of which he has incorporated into other works such as the present Piano Concerto of 1983. Sculthorpe's Piano Concerto is an imposing creation, less indigenous-sounding and 'pictorial' than many of his other compositions, including *The song of Tailitnama* (1974). Conceived for high voice, six cellos and percussion, this haunting piece was in fact written for a TV documentary.

Little Nourlangie dates from 1990. It takes its name from a small outcrop of rocks in Australia's Kakadu National Park on which can be found the Aboriginal Blue Paintings, depicting fish, boats and ancestral figures and which inspired the composer. *Little Nourlangie* is a characteristically striking creation, scored with much imaginative flair. It shares its diatonic main theme with that of Sculthorpe's 1989 guitar concerto, *Nourlangie*, and comprises four-and-a-half minutes of 'straightforward, joyful music' (to quote the composer). By contrast, *Music for Japan* exhibits a much more uncompromising demeanour, and according to annotator Graeme Skinner, is at once 'his most abstract and modernist orchestral score'.

Edo de Waart presides over a set of performances that exhibit great commitment and exemplary finish. The recording is excellent too.

Cello Dreaming

Irkanda I[a]. Irkanda IV[ac]. Lament for strings[c]. Sonata for Strings No 2[c]. Cello Dreaming[bc]. Djilile[c]
[b]Emma-Jane Murphy vc [c]Australian Chamber Orchestra / Richard Tognetti [a]vn
Chandos CHAN10063 (66' · DDD)   Ⓕ

The Australian Chamber Orchestra has consistently championed the music of its countryman Peter Sculthorpe. *Cello Dreaming*, premièred by Steven Isserlis and the BBC Philharmonic during the 1998 Manchester Cello Festival, is inspired by the sights, sounds and diverse cultural mix of Australia's northern coastline. It's a beguiling evocation, boasting nature music of imagination and local colour; Emma-Jane Murphy is an impressive soloist. The Aboriginal melody known as 'Djilile' was first used by Sculthorpe as far back as 1950 in his Fourth String Quartet. This transcription for strings is one in a series of reworkings of a tune that has haunted the composer for over 50 years. No less appealing is the substantial Second String Sonata (1988), an arrangement of the Ninth Quartet of 1975.

Shrewd programming frames the threnodic *Irkanda IV* for solo violin, strings and percussion (Sculthorpe's first real breakthrough from 1961, named after the Aboriginal word for a remote and lonely place) between *Irkanda I* for solo violin from 1955 (a beautifully proportioned essay which provides the first glimpse of the mature composer in its rapt identification with Australia's landscape and wildlife) and the moving 1976 Lament for strings. It isn't hard to detect a kinship, so naturally does each piece emerge from its predecessor.

Three tracks here (*Irkanda IV, Lament* and the Second Sonata) overlap with a rival ABC Classics release featuring these same artists. There's little to choose between the two in terms of performance (those earlier accounts are a degree more restrained), but Chandos's sound has the edge, possessing breathtaking definition and range. A very fine issue.

Earth Cry

Earth Cry[a]. Kakadu. Piano Concerto[b]. Memento Mori. From Oceania
[a]William Barton didg [b]Tamara Anna Cislowska pf
New Zealand Symphony Orchestra / James Judd
Naxos 8 557382 (71' · DDD)   Ⓢ

Earth Cry. Kakadu. Mangrove. Songs of Sea and Sky. From Ubirr
William Barton didg Queensland Orchestra / Michael Christie
ABC Classics ABC476 1921 (71' · DDD)   Ⓕ

Earth Cry (1986), previously recorded in 1989 by Stuart Challender, is one of Sculthorpe's major utterances, music at once approachable and elusive. These aspects are extraordinarily heightened by a recently added didgeridoo part. The two recordings here use this new version sound quite different. Judd revels in a harsher orchestral sound, spotlighting each detail, while Christie conjures a more rounded tone, though edgy and laden with menace. William Barton's haunting didgeridoo playing is quite different on each.

Kakadu (1988), another shared item, finds both Judd and Christie alive to every nervy detail, though Christie responds more naturally to its mercurial changes. It's Challender, however, who finds the sheer joy: his interpretation is unsurpassed. He's also unbeatable in *Mangrove*, another heavyweight score that repays further investigation, though Christie summons a shining performance and shows a fine understanding of every nuance of the intricate orchestration.

Christie's disc includes another work revised to include didgeridoo: *From Ubirr*, which is conceptually and audibly related to *Earth Cry*. Sculthorpe wrote it for Kronos, and Christie has arranged it for larger forces. The orchestra finds greater sonic depth and the didgeridoo emphasises the earthy quality of the music. *Songs of Sea and Sky*, originally for clarinet and piano, also benefits from expansion from its original chamber format.

The mesmerising Piano Concerto, dating from 1983, is one of Sculthorpe's finest creations. Tamara Anna Cislowska has already recorded it with Edo de Waart, a relaxed performance with 'impressionistic' orchestral sound; this Naxos recording is sharper. Judd also includes a work from Sculthorpe's 'sun music' period, *From Oceania* (1970/2003), more ostentatiously bright and more 'foreign' than later works, as well as the affecting and straightforward *Memento Mori* (1993).

Sculthorpe lovers will want both these recordings, but for a one-disc showcase of his work the programme and performances of the Queensland Orchestra have the edge.

John Sheppard   British c1515-1559/60

Sheppard was at Magdalen College, Oxford, 1543-8, and by 1552 was a Gentleman of the Chapel Royal. Most of his extant music for the Latin rite probably dates from Mary's reign. The six-voice Magnificat, for example with its florid counterpoint and lack of imitation, belongs to the tradition of the Eton Choirbook composers. Among his more modern works are the four-voice Magnificat, the Missa 'Cantate' and the Mass 'The Western Wynde'. He was at his best when writing vigorous counterpoint around a plainchant. The English works, which include 15 anthems and service music, seem to date from Edward's reign. **GROVE**music

Western Wynde Mass

Western Wynde Mass. Gaude, gaude, gaude Maria;
Dum transisset Sabbatum I; Spiritus Sanctus
procedens II; In manus tuas II; Audivi vocem de
coelo; Libera nos, salva nos II; Beata nobis gaudia;
Impetum fecerunt unanimes; Sancte Dei preciose;
Sacris solemniis; Aeterne Rex altissime; Dum
transisset sabbatum II; Hostes Herodes impie; In
manus tuas III; Te Deum laudamus.
The Sixteen / Harry Christophers
Hyperion Dyad ② CDD22022 (DDD) Recorded 1992
Texts and translations included   Ⓜ●

This set centres round one of Sheppard's best-
known four-part Masses, *The Western Wynde*.
Though largely syllabic in style, in accordance
with liturgical prescriptions at a time when taste
in church music was turning towards ever
greater emphasis on the text, this Mass still has
moments that recapture the earlier visionary
style in all its wonder. The section 'Et incarnatus est', coming after an amazing cadence at
'descendit de coelis' in the *Credo*, is a case in
point. 'Pleni sunt coeli' is another, and also the
opening of the *Benedictus*, where the melody
unfolds unhurriedly over the delicate counterpoint of the mean and the bass. In such passages
The Sixteen is in its element, each singer relating to the others with the intimacy and mutual
understanding of performers of chamber music.
The supporting programme includes *alternatim* hymn settings, responsories and a *Te Deum*.
In all these the chant is sung with excellent
phrasing and a smooth *legato*. Some subtle
repercussions in the intonation to *Dum transisset
Sabbatum* are particularly pleasing.

In all five pieces, though, the tempo of the
chant sections bore little relationship to the
polyphony – the least far removed being that of
the hymn *Aeterne Rex altissime*, where the individual chant notes had roughly the duration of a
half-beat of the polyphony. The English *Magnificat and Nunc dimittis* reveal Sheppard fully conforming to the later syllabic style in a rich and
joyful texture. Here, and in the Latin *Te Deum*
The Sixteen display to the full their glowing
vocal qualities. This is wonderful singing, with a
sense of freedom and flow that's almost overpowering.

The Second Service

The Lord's Prayer. The Second Service – Magnificat;
Nunc dimittis. Gaude, gaude, gaude Maria. Filie
Ierusalem. Reges Tharsis et insulae. Spiritus sanctus
procedens. Laudem dicite Deo nostro. Hec dies.
Impetum fecerunt unanimes. Libera nos, salva nos
**Choir of Christ Church Cathedral, Oxford /
Stephen Darlington**
Nimbus NI5480 (67' · DDD) Texts and translations
included   Ⓕ

This enjoyable recording opens with two works
in English which were probably written within
days of John Sheppard's early death, as Roger

Bowers's introductory essay explains. The
hypothesis is an intriguing one, for *The Lord's
Prayer* and the Second Service largely lack the
wayward dissonances that play an integral (and
controversial) part in this composer's style.
Whether the difference is due to the switch to
the vernacular is a moot point, for the Latin
Responds that make up most of the disc show
off the older style more conspicuously. The
most impressive of these is the elaborate *Gaude,
gaude, gaude Maria*, but the piece that most
clearly enunciates its composer's idiosyncrasies
has to be the concluding *Libera nos*. (Sheppard
wrote two identically scored settings of this text,
but neither the programme details nor Bowers's
essay makes clear which one is performed here.)
Sheppard's special predilection for high voices
makes the participation of boy trebles here particularly appropriate. In such traditional choral
establishments, unanimity of ensemble is crucial. From that standpoint this choir is difficult
to fault, although towards the end of the recital
a certain tiredness is just perceptible. If anything, the sound is a shade top-heavy at times (as
in *Filie Ierusalem*), but a couple of the Responds
dispense with trebles altogether, providing a
welcome contrast.

Dmitry Shostakovich
Russian/USSR 1906-1975

*He studied with his mother, a professional pianist,
and then with Shteynberg at the Petrograd Conservatory (1919-25): his graduation piece was his
Symphony no.1, which brought him early international attention. His creative development, however,
was determined more by events at home. Like many
Soviet composers of his generation, he tried to reconcile the musical revolutions of his time with the urge
to give a voice to revolutionary socialism, most conspicuously in his next two symphonies, no.2 ('To
October') and no.3 ('The First of May'), both with
choral finales. At the same time he used what he
knew of contemporary Western music (perhaps
Prokofiev and Krenek mostly) to give a sharp
grotesqueness and mechanical movement to his operatic satire The Nose, while expressing a similar keen
irony in major works for the ballet (The Age of Gold,
The Bolt) and the cinema (New Babylon). But the
culminating achievement of these quick-witted,
nervy years was his second opera The Lady Macbeth
of the Mtsensk District, where high emotion and acid
parody are brought together in a score of immense
brilliance.*

*Lady Macbeth was received with acclaim in Rus-
sia, western Europe and the USA, and might have
seemed to confirm Shostakovich as essentially a dramatic composer: by the time he was 30, in 1936, he
was known for two operas and three full-length ballets, besides numerous scores for the theatre and
films, whereas only one purely orchestral symphony
had been performed, and one string quartet. However, in that same year Lady Macbeth was fiercely
attacked in Pravda, and he set aside his completed*

Symphony no.4 (it was not performed until 1961), no doubt fearing that its Mahlerian intensity and complexity would spur further criticism. Instead he began a new symphony, no.5, much more conventional in its form and tunefulness – though there is a case for hearing the finale as an internal send-up of the heroic style. This was received favourably, by the state and indeed by Shostakovich's international public, and seems to have turned him from the theatre to the concert hall. There were to be no more operas or ballets, excepting a comedy and a revision of Lady Macbeth; instead he devoted himself to symphonies, concertos, quartets and songs (as well as heroic, exhortatory cantatas during the war years).

Of the next four symphonies, no.7 is an epic with an uplifting war-victory programme (it was begun in besieged Leningrad), while the others display more openly a dichotomy between optimism and introspective doubt, expressed with varying shades of irony. It has been easy to explain this in terms of Shostakovich's position as a public artist in the USSR during the age of socialist realism, but the divisions and ironies in his music go back to his earliest works and seem inseparable from the very nature of his harmony, characterised by a severely weakened sense of key. Even so, his position in official Soviet music certainly was difficult. In 1948 he was condemned again, and for five years he wrote little besides patriotic cantatas and private music (quartets, the 24 Preludes and Fugues which constitute his outstanding piano work).

Stalin's death in 1953 opened the way to a less rigid aesthetic, and Shostakovich returned to the symphony triumphantly with no.10. Nos.11 and 12 are both programme works on crucial years in revolutionary history (1905 and 1917), but then no.13 was his most outspokenly critical work, incorporating a setting of words that attack anti-semitism. The last two symphonies and the last four quartets, as well as other chamber pieces and songs, belong to a late period of spare texture, slowness and gravity, often used explicitly in images of death: Symphony no.14 is a song cycle on mortality, though no.15 remains more enigmatic in its open quotations from Rossini and Wagner. GROVEmusic

Cello Concertos

No 1 in E flat, Op 107; No 2 in G, Op 126

Cello Concertos Nos 1 & 2
Mischa Maisky vc **London Symphony Orchestra / Michael Tilson Thomas**
DG 445 821-2GH (65' · DDD) Recorded 1993 · Ⓕⓞ

The Second Cello Concerto is one of the major concertos of the post-war period – as potent a representative of the composer's later style as the last three symphonies, be it through irony (second movement), poetry (first and third) or anger (beginning of the third). Few cellists have tended the *piano espressivo* of the *Largo*'s opening bars as lovingly as Mischa Maisky does, while the rapt quality of his soft playing and the expressive eloquence of his double-stopping wring the most from Shostakovich's extended

soliloquy. Michael Tilson Thomas points and articulates with his usual skill. Only the opening of that movement (with its furious whoop horns) seems marginally underprojected, although the main climax later on is both immensely powerful and extraordinarily clear. The First Concerto harbours fewer mysteries than the Second and yet remains a pivotal work. Maisky phrases beautifully, while Tilson Thomas and the LSO again come up trumps, even though 1'33" into the finale the dramatic switch to 6/8 sounds less spontaneous than it does under, say, Maxim Shostakovich. In other respects, however, this is a forceful and fairly outgoing interpretation, beautifully recorded and a suitable coupling for the disc's star act – the finest available studio recording of the Second Concerto. In fact, this CD is now the prime recommendation for the two concertos coupled together.

Piano Concertos

No 1 C minor for Piano, Trumpet and Strings, Op 35; No 2 in F, Op 102

Piano Concertos Nos 1 & 2. The Unforgettable Year 1919, Op 89 – The assault on beautiful Gorky
Dmitri Alexeev pf **Philip Jones** tpt **English Chamber Orchestra / Jerzy Maksymiuk**
Classics for Pleasure 7625562 (48' · DDD) Ⓑⓞ

Shostakovich's piano concertos were written under very different circumstances, yet together they contain some of the composer's most cheerful and enlivening music. The First, with its wealth of perky, memorable tunes, has the addition of a brilliantly conceived solo trumpet part (delightfully done here by Philip Jones) that also contributes to the work's characteristic stamp. The Second Concerto was written not long after Shostakovich had released a number of the intense works he had concealed during the depths of the Stalin era. It came as a sharp contrast, reflecting as it did the optimism and sense of freedom that followed the death of the Russian dictator. The beauty of the slow movement is ideally balanced by the vigour of the first, and the madcap high spirits of the last. The poignant movement for piano and orchestra from the Suite from the 1951 film *The Unforgettable Year 1919*, 'The assault on beautiful Gorky', provides an excellent addition to this disc of perceptive and zestful performances by Alexeev. He's most capably supported by the ECO under Maksymiuk, and the engineers have done them proud with a recording of great clarity and finesse. A joyous issue.

Shostakovich Piano Concertos Nos 1 & 2
Shchedrin Piano Concerto No 2
Marc-André Hamelin pf [a]**Mark O'Keefe** tpt **BBC Scottish Symphony Orchestra / Andrew Litton**
Hyperion CD/SACD hybrid 🔊 SACDA67425 (63' · DDD) Ⓕ

For a virtuoso as consummate as Marc-André Hamelin, Shostakovich's piano concertos might seem like a stroll in the park. On the other hand, their mercurial shifts of mood might easily elude him. Neither suspicion is confirmed by this fine recording. The Canadian's technical command is as exciting as ever, but that doesn't mean that he's insensitive to the music's many quieter tones of voice. The clearest example of this is his expansive treatment of the slow movements – that of No 2 may even be a shade too languid for some tastes. In fact he never launches into a new idea without carefully weighing its character in relation to its context and in the process coming up with something fresh and engaging.

Shchedrin's Second Concerto is one of the most inventive examples of early Soviet polystylism, holding a balance between 12-note techniques, a dash of Polish aleatory and a twist of jazz. Hamelin gives a full-blooded reading, and the BBC Scottish show lots of idiomatic flair.

Hyperion scores well for its natural-sounding balance and acoustic.

Violin Concertos

No 1 in A minor, Op 99; **No 2** in C sharp minor, Op 129

Violin Concertos Nos 1 & 2
Lydia Mordkovitch *vn* **Scottish National Orchestra / Neeme Järvi**
Chandos CHAN8820 (69' · DDD) Recorded 1989
Ⓕ**OOO**

This coupling completely explodes the idea of the Second Violin Concerto being a disappointment after the dramatic originality of No 1. Certainly No 2, completed in 1967, a year after the very comparable Cello Concerto No 2, has never won the allegiance of violin virtuosos as the earlier work has done, but here Lydia Mordkovitch confirms what has become increasingly clear, that the spareness of late Shostakovich marks no diminution of his creative spark, maybe even the opposite. In that she's greatly helped by the equal commitment of Neeme Järvi in drawing such purposeful, warmly expressive playing from the Scottish National Orchestra. With such spare textures the first two movements can be difficult to hold together, but here from the start, where Mordkovitch plays the lyrical first theme in a hushed, beautifully withdrawn way, the concentration is consistent.

The première recording of the work from David Oistrakh (on Chant du Monde but currently out of the catalogue), dedicatee of No 2 as of No 1, has remained unchallenged for a generation, and Mordkovitch doesn't always quite match her mentor in the commanding incisiveness of the playing in bravura passages. But there's no lack of power, and the more vital element in this work is the dark reflectiveness of the lyrical themes of the first two movements.

It isn't just that Mordkovitch has the benefit of far fuller recording and a less close recording balance, but that her playing has an even wider range of colouring and dynamic than Oistrakh's. She conveys more of the mystery of the work and is perfectly matched by the orchestra. As in the First Concerto the principal horn has a vital role, here crowning each of the first two movements with a solo of ecstatic beauty in the coda. The Russian player on the Chant du Monde version is first-rate, no Slavonic whiner, but the SNO principal is far richer still, with his expressiveness enhanced by the wider dynamic and tonal range of the recording. The range of the recording helps too in the finale, where the *Allegro* has a satisfyingly barbaric bite, while the *scherzando* element is delectably pointed, as it is in the first movement too.

In the First Concerto Mordkovitch is hardly less impressive. As in Concerto No 2 one of her strengths lies in the meditative intensity which she brings to the darkly lyrical writing of the first and third movements. Here, too, she has never sounded quite so full and warm of tone on record before. In the brilliant second and fourth movements she may not play with quite the demonic bravura of Oistrakh, but again there's no lack of power, and in place of demonry she gives rustic jollity to the dance rhythms, faithfully reflecting the title of the finale, *Burlesque*. She's helped by recorded sound far fuller than Oistrakh's. This is a superb disc.

Shostakovich Violin Concertos Nos 1 & 2
Maxim Vengerov *vn*; **London Symphony Orchestra / Mstislav Rostropovich**
Warner Elatus 0927 46742-2 (73' · DDD) Recorded 1994-5
Ⓜ**OOO**

There's an astonishing emotional maturity in Vengerov's Shostakovich. He uses Heifetz's bow, but it's to David Oistrakh that he's often compared. His vibrato is wider, his manners less consistently refined, and yet the comparison is well founded. Oistrakh made three commercial recordings of the Shostakovich and one can guess that Vengerov has been listening to those earlier Oistrakh renditions, as there's nothing radically novel about his interpretation. Some may find Vengerov's impassioned climaxes a shade forced by comparison. Yet he achieves a nobility and poise worlds away from the superficial accomplishment of most modern rivals. He can fine down his tone to the barest whisper; nor is he afraid to make a scorching, ugly sound. While his sometimes slashing quality of articulation is particularly appropriate to the faster movements, the brooding, silver-grey 'Nocturne' comes off superbly too, though it seems perverse that the engineers mute the low tam-tam strokes. Rostropovich has the lower strings dig into the third movement's passacaglia theme with his usual enthusiasm. Indeed the orchestral playing is very nearly beyond reproach.

This is an exceptionally fine peformance of

the Second, the desperate bleakness perfectly realised. There has been no finer account since that of the dedicatee, David Oistrakh (Chant du Monde). With Rostropovich rather than Kondrashin on the podium, tempos are comparatively deliberate in the first two movements, but there's no lack of intensity in the solo playing and rather more in the way of light and shade. In the stratospheric writing of the *Adagio*, Vengerov is technically superb, while the all-pervading atmosphere of desolation has never been more potently conveyed. The finale is more extrovert than some will like, the fireworks irresistible, and yet you do not lose the disquieting sense of a composer at the end of his tether, seemingly contemptuous of his own material. This is an extraordinary disc.

Shostakovich Violin Concerto No 1 **Prokofiev** Violin Concerto No 2 in G minor, Op 63
Vadim Repin *vn* **Hallé Orchestra / Kent Nagano**
Erato 0630-10696-2 (59' · DDD)   ⓕ**OO**

Vadim Repin's interpretation of the Shostakovich comes across as less quintessentially Russian than Vengerov's in its avoidance of rhetorical overkill. Without underplaying the bravura passages (the *Scherzo* is taken at an incredible speed), he stresses rather the chamber-like intimacy of the score. Rather surprising, perhaps, is the flowing tempo for the slow third movement, but, thanks also to Nagano and the Hallé, we do actually hear the music as a passacaglia. The tam-tam is perfectly caught in the 'Nocturne'.

Given Repin's dazzling achievement in the Shostakovich, his Prokofiev is a shade disappointing. His violin is less sweetly caught and he sometimes makes the kind of uningratiating noises which imply some impatience with the straightforward *Romeo and Juliet*-style lyricism of the work. The finale sounds spontaneous but the lovely slow movement could do with more space to indulge its sweetly singing lines. However, if the coupling appeals, Repin represents a clear first choice; anyone who cares about the Shostakovich will want to hear this disc.

Shostakovich Violin Concerto No 1[a] **Mendelssohn** Violin Concerto in E minor, Op 64[b]
Hilary Hahn *vn* **Oslo Philharmonic Orchestra /** [b]**Hugh Wolff,** [a]**Marek Janowski**
Sony Classical SK89921 (64' · DDD)   ⓕ**O**

Years ago the merest mention of Shostakovich's First Violin Concerto brought just two key stylistic templates to mind: David Oistrakh and, a little later, Leonid Kogan. Oistrakh in particular had fashioned such a warm and intimate reading of the piece that it became almost impossible to imagine a credible alternative. And yet the passing years have brought many, not least Perlman, Mullova, Vengerov and Repin, to name some of the best.

Hilary Hahn is certainly in their league, though different again. She's a lean, athletic player, utterly still at the muted centre of the Concerto's first movement, and with elfin agility in the *Scherzo*. Hahn is to be preferred, primarily because her sweetness-and-steel tone, with its expressive but narrow vibrato, lends a fresh perspective to the work but also because of Marek Janowski's fine conducting.

Some might find Hahn's approach a trifle cool, especially in the cadenza. Hahn is a very clean player, colour-conscious but never dangerous in the manner of her most rival, Ilya Gringolts, though she does engage in some active dialogue with individual soloists. Only the finale seems a little short on what one might call ambiguous sparks – where sudden ignition could be taken either as celebration or protest – but as fiddle-playing per se, it really does cut the mustard. Among digital rivals Vengerov and Repin (especially) are still tops, though as Hahn is nearer than they are to the honeyed tones of pre-war players some collectors might favour her on that count alone.

As to the coupling, Hahn gives a swift, resilient, bright-toned reading, tender-hearted in the *Andante* and very fast in the finale. Too fast perhaps for true composure. Still, it's a fine display, and this is a thoroughly fine disc, confirming Hilary Hahn as among the most gifted and individual players on the concert circuit.

Symphonies

No 1 in F minor, Op 10; No 2 in B, Op 14, 'To October'; No 3 in E flat, Op 20, 'The first of May'; No 4 in C minor, Op 43; No 5 in D minor, Op 47; No 6 in B minor, Op 54; No 7 in C, Op 60, 'Leningrad'; No 8 in C minor, Op 65; No 9 in E flat, Op 70; No 10 in E minor, Op 93; No 11 in G minor, Op 103, 'The year 1905'; No 12 in D minor, Op 112, 'The year 1917'; No 13 in B flat minor, Op 113, 'Babiy Yar'; No 14, Op 135; No 15 in A, Op 141

Complete Symphonies

Symphony Nos 5[a] & 9[b]
[a]**Concertgebouw Orchestra;** [b]**London Philharmonic Orchestra / Bernard Haitink**
Decca London 425 066-2DM (76' · ADD/DDD)
Recorded 1981. Texts and translations included
          Ⓜ**OOO**

Symphony Nos 6 & 12
Concertgebouw Orchestra / Bernard Haitink
Decca London 425 067-2DM (74' · ADD/DDD)
Recorded 1983. Texts and translations included   Ⓜ

Symphony No 7
London Philharmonic Orchestra / Bernard Haitink
Decca London 425 068-2DM (79' · ADD/DDD)
Recorded 1979. Texts and translations included   Ⓜ

Symphony No 8
Concertgebouw Orchestra / Bernard Haitink
Decca London 425 071-2DM (62' · ADD/DDD)
Recorded 1982. Texts and translations included   Ⓜ

Symphony No 13
Marius Rintzler *bass* **Concertgebouw Choir and**

Orchestra / Bernard Haitink
Decca London 425 073-2DM (64' · ADD/DDD)
Recorded 1982. Texts and translations included Ⓜ**O**

Symphony No 15[a]. From Jewish Folk Poetry, Op 79[b]
Elisabeth Söderström *sop* **Ortrun Wenkel** *contr*
Ryszard Karczykowski *ten* [a]**London Philharmonic
Orchestra;** [b]**Concertgebouw Orchestra / Bernard
Haitink**
Decca London 425 069-2DM (73' · ADD/DDD)
Recorded 1978. Texts and translations included Ⓜ

The cycle is also available as an 11-disc set:
444 430-2LC11   Ⓢ Ⓑ

This, the first complete Western cycle of the
symphonies, conducted by Bernard Haitink,
returns to the catalogue at mid-price, Decca
having jettisoned a few minor works and decou-
pled several major ones. It's hard to argue with
this presentation when it includes modern
annotations and full recording data. Concerned
for tradition, and with the need to challenge it,
the young Shostakovich could be classical and
modern, polemical and prankish by turns.
Haitink, not entirely po-faced, turns in a thoroughly decent account of the First Symphony,
missing just a little of the element of pastiche.
The recoupling with the Third does strike
sparks, the language of the later music variously
foreshadowed in divergent contexts. In the
Fourth, Haitink offers no stupendous revelations, content to bring out the dignity of the
writing in a piece where we have come to expect
something more sensational, less perfectly controlled. His outer movements are helpfully split,
by additional cues – but his literalness and
sobriety fall short of the ideal, as, marginally,
does the playing.

Haitink's Fifth, deeply considered and almost
indecently well upholstered, isn't easy to assess.
Originally greeted with extreme reverence, it's
an earnest attempt to make structural sense of
the music's grand symphonic aspirations. It's
only because the orchestral playing is generally
so immaculate that one registers the curious
glitch 2'13" into the *Largo*. That movement is
less affecting than it can be, yet the preceding
Allegretto is triumphantly brought off as a
heavy-footed Mahlerian ländler. Then again,
the first movement's long-limbed second subject chugs along reluctantly, dourly unphrased,
with none of the easeful balm found in other
interpretations. Haitink's Fifth is now generously paired with his solid, untrivial but scarcely
earth-shattering Ninth. His Sixth and 12th are
characterised by playing of *gravitas* and tonal
splendour. This 12th could be seen as the 'best'
modern version.

The *Leningrad* is another matter. It has rightly
been praised for its symphonic integrity and
splendid sound. Haitink's stoical view of the
Eighth is highly impressive, though not very
varied in mood. Curiously, the finale is mis-
cued. Kurt Sanderling's reading (Berlin Classics) is also highly impressive. The 10th has
always seemed less dependent on a conductor
steeped in the Russian tradition, and the only

drawback of Haitink's well-played, well-
recorded account is his unsubtle, over-
confident tone in the enigmatic third movement
Allegretto. There's real demonic abandon in the
Scherzo. Karajan's 10th (DG) is very desirable
but he offers no makeweight. Haitink offers a
well-prepared account of No 2, where the
choral contribution has the odd awkward
moment but the overall effect is very arresting.
His 11th too has such weight and precision that
his customary detachment is mostly less noticeable than his phenomenal control. Haitink's
13th boasts another of Decca's huge, reverberant recordings, of such 'cinematic' brilliance
and range that it threatens to dwarf the music-
making. The chorus and orchestra are on
terrific form and the soloist, Marius Rintzler,
would seem to be at one with Haitink's brooding approach (reviewed further on).

As one of the first of Shostakovich's late scores
to be taken seriously in the West, it's odd that
the 14th should have been so poorly represented in the CD catalogue. Haitink's polyglot
reading doesn't really represent a viable solution – too much vital and specific tone colour is
lost along with the original note-values. To
make matters worse, Fischer-Dieskau is in hectoring mode and both soloists' proximity to the
microphones makes for uncomfortable listening, though the orchestral contribution is excellent. Barshai (Russian Disc) can lay claim to
absolute authenticity. It's a fascinating document, as he and Vishnevskaya rage against the
dying of the light in every song, slicing seconds
(sometimes minutes) off the timings of the
Western account. Generally speaking the sound
is close and crude, by no means intolerable but
sufficiently prone to distortion to inhibit a general recommendation. In its way, however, this
disc is indispensable.

Haitink's 15th has always been highly
regarded, despite some less than needle-sharp
contributions from the percussion where it matters most. At medium price, and with a rather
high-level transfer of its coupling (whose historical significance is ably outlined in the insert-
note), this merits a place at or near the top of
anyone's list. To sum up: Haitink's set, superbly
engineered, is nothing if not reliable. For those
who prize technical finesse over raw passion,
Haitink remains a plausible first choice.

Symphony No 1

Symphonies Nos 1 & 6
Scottish National Orchestra / Neeme Järvi
Chandos CHAN8411 (64' · DDD) Recorded 1984-5 Ⓕ

The First Symphony, the 19-year-old composer's graduation piece from the then Leningrad Conservatory in 1925, may be indebted to
Stravinsky, Prokofiev, Tchaikovsky and even
Scriabin. But it rarely sounds like anything
other than pure Shostakovich. The sophisticated mask of its first movement is drawn aside
for a slow movement of Slav melancholy and

foreboding, and the finale brilliantly stage-manages a way out. The Sixth (1939) takes the familiar Shostakovichian extremes of explosive activity and uneasy contemplation (that the composer reconciles in the finale of the First) and separates them into individual movements. Two swift movements (a mercurial but menacing *Scherzo*, and a real knees-up of a finale) follow on from an opening *Largo* whose slow lyrical declamations eventually all but freeze into immobility. Järvi has a will (and Chandos, the engineering) to explore the extremes of pace, mood and dynamics of both symphonies; his account of the First Symphony convinces precisely because those extremes intensify as the work progresses. Some may crave a fuller, firmer string sound, but the passionate intensity of the playing (in all departments) is never in doubt.

Symphony No 4

Shostakovich Symphony No 4 **Britten** Russian Funeral
City of Birmingham Symphony Orchestra / Sir Simon Rattle
EMI 555476-2 (68' · DDD) Recorded 1994   Ⓕ●

This could just be the most important Western recording of the Fourth since the long-deleted Ormandy and Previn versions. Naturally, it complements rather than replaces Kondrashin's reading (Chant du Monde), taped shortly after the work's belated unveiling in December 1961: papery strings and lurid brass can't disguise that conductor's unique authority even when Shostakovich's colouristic effects are muted by rudimentary Soviet sound engineering. In his recording, Rattle's approach is more obviously calculated, supremely brilliant but just a little cold. A certain firmness and self-confidence is obvious from the first. The restrained Hindemithian episode is relatively square, the first climax superbly built. The second group unfolds seamlessly with the glorious *espressivo* of the strings not much threatened by the not very mysterious intrusions of harp and bass clarinet. Tension builds again, some way into the development, with the lacerating intensity of the strings' *moto perpetuo fugato* passage.

Six miraculously terraced discords herald the two-faced recapitulation. Kondrashin and Järvi (Chandos) find more emotional inevitability in Shostakovich's destabilising tactics hereabouts. Rattle doesn't quite locate a compensating irony, although his closing bars are convincingly icy, with nicely audible gong. Even in Rattle's experienced hands, the finale isn't all plain sailing. The initial quasi-Mahlerian march is underpinned by disappointingly fuzzy timpani strokes which lose the point of their own lopsidedness. But then the section's mock-solemn climax is simply tremendous (and tremendously loud). The incisive *Allegro* is launched with (deliberate?) abruptness at an unbelievably fast tempo and, even if the music doesn't always

make sense at this pace, the results are breathtaking. The denouement is approached with real flair. A superbly characterised trombone solo, hushed expectant strings and the most ambiguous of all Shostakovich perorations is unleashed with devastating force. The coda is mightily impressive too.

After this, the Britten encore risks seeming beside the point; this really is emotional play-acting. Neither Kondrashin's nor Järvi's more direct emotional involvement is easily passed over. On the other hand, Rattle does give us a thrilling example of what a relatively objective, thoroughly 'modern' approach has to offer today. With its huge dynamic range and uncompromising, analytical style, EMI's recording pulls no punches, and the awesome precision of the CBSO's playing makes for an unforgettable experience.

Additional recommendation

Symphony No 4
Coupled with: Symphony No 8
National Symphony Orchestra / Rostropovich
Warners Ultima ② 8573-87799-2 (DDD) Recorded 1992   Ⓢ Ⓑ

Rostropovich's Fourth is an extremely fine reading, verging on self-recommendation; the Eighth isn't quite so good but at this price no one's going to complain!

Symphony No 5

Symphony No 5. Ballet Suite No 5, Op 27*a*
Royal Scottish National Orchestra / Neeme Järvi
Chandos CHAN8650 (76' · DDD) Recorded 1988   Ⓕ

There are more Shostakovich Fifths than you can shake a stick at in the catalogue, and several are very good. Järvi's makes perhaps the safest recommendation: it has a generous coupling (which can't be said of many of its rivals), it has no drawbacks (save, for some tastes, a slight touch of heart-on-sleeve in the slow movement) and a number of distinct advantages. A deep seriousness, for one thing, and an absolute sureness about the nature of the finale, which many conductors feel the need to exaggerate, either as brassy optimism or as bitter irony. Järvi takes it perfectly straight, denying neither option, and the progression from slow movement (the overtness of its emotion finely justified) to finale seems more natural, less of a jolt than usual.

The RSNO can't rival the sheerly massive sound of some of the Continental orchestras who have recorded this work, but you'd hardly notice the lack, so urgent and polished is the playing. A very natural recording, too, and the lengthy Suite (eight movements from Shostakovich's early ballet *The Bolt*, forming an exuberantly entertaining essay on the various modes that his sense of humour could take) makes much more than a mere fill-up.

SHOSTAKOVICH SYMPHONY NO 5 – IN BRIEF

Philadelphia Orchestra / Leopold Stokowski
Dutton CDAX 8017 (79' · ADD) Ⓜ
Stokowski's 1939 world premiere recording continues to thrill to the marrow in its searing intensity and overwhelming emotional clout.

Czech PO / Karel Ančerl
Supraphon SU3699-2 (74' · ADD) Ⓜ
There's no missing the tingle-factor on this vintage display from Prague. Ančerl's lucid conception has tremendous sweep and ardour, while the playing of the Czech PO is predictably superb.

Concertgebouw Orchestra / Bernard Haitink
Decca 467 478-2 (76' · DDD) ⒷO
In sheer sonic splendour, Haitink's 1981 Decca recording has no equals. The performance unfolds in typically noble, unmannered fashion and won't disappoint this maestro's many admirers.

London SO / André Previn
RCA 82876 55493-2 (76' · ADD) Ⓑ
Previn's much-loved 1965 recording with the LSO has come up as fresh as new paint in its latest remastering. Serebrier's lively account of the suite from Shostakovich's *Hamlet* incidental music makes a generous fill-up.

Royal Scotish National Orchestra / Neeme Järvi
Chandos CHAN8650 (76' · DDD) ⒻO
Interpretatively, Järvi doesn't put a foot wrong. Although the RSNO's hard-working strings are not always absolutely secure, this account replicates the buzz of Järvi's Shostakovich in the concert hall.

New York PO / Leonard Bernstein
Sony SMK66937 (77' · DDD) Ⓜ
An no-holds-barred performance from Lenny and his beloved New Yorkers, recorded live on tour in Japan during the summer of 1979.

Vienna PO / Mariss Jansons
EMI 556442-2 (71' · DDD) Ⓕ
Another live recording, this time from January 1997, and Jansons' second recording of the Fifth for EMI. Although not entirely free of self-regarding gesture, it's a painstakingly prepared performance that communicates urgently.

BBC NOW / Mark Wigglesworth
BIS ② BIS-CD973/4 (140' · DDD) ⒻO
Wigglesworth is nothing if not individual. Often daringly broad and pungently characterised, this Fifth serves up plenty of ear-tickling observation and sumptuous food for thought.

Symphony No 5. Chamber Symphony, Op. 110*a*
Vienna Philharmonic Orchestra / Mariss Jansons
EMI 556442-2 (71' · DDD) Ⓕ

Setting a course somewhere between Sanderling's grey-faced stoicism and Bernstein's relentless exposure of nerve-endings, Jansons exercises tight technical control, imparting rather less in the way of inner character. As usual he goes for maximal rhythmic clarity, smooth legato lines and extreme dynamic contrasts. Inevitably, some will feel that the luscious string sound only gets in the way and there are a few agogic touches. Isn't there something unnatural about the shift up a gear in the first-movement development (around 8'00"), the cliff-edge dynamics of the slow movement, the self-conscious pacing of the start of the finale?

More positively, there are some wonderfully sustained *pianissimos* from both strings and winds – try the return of the first movement's second subject (from 12'26"). EMI's recording isn't quite ideal, cavernous and a little occluded in the bass; the presence of an audience is never betrayed, and doesn't seem to have influenced the character of the music-making. The Chamber Symphony is distinguished by its unique atmosphere. If the magnificent Vienna strings are arguably too suave, it's also the conductor's coolly calculated conception that lacks the last ounce of brutality.

Additional recommendation

London Symphony Orchestra / Previn
RCA 74321 24212-2 (76' · ADD) ⓈⓈ
André Previn's classic 1960s recording of the Fifth still figures among the very finest accounts, and at this price it represents a superb bargain.

Symphony No 6

Symphonies Nos 6 & 10
Dallas Symphony Orchestra / Andrew Litton
Delos ② DE3283 (83' · DDD) Ⓕ

Apparently far more difficult to bring off than the 10th Symphony, the Sixth here receives a performance of profound insight, and with no extraneous fuss. From the first phrase of his beautifully shaped opening *Largo*, Litton is right inside the idiom. And he stays there through the *scherzo*, following its phantasmagorical progress like a boy going goggle-eyed from one grotesque circus-act to another. Virtually matching Mravinsky for intensity, he drives the manic finale as though there's something behind the musicians that won't bite so long as they don't turn round to look at it.

Litton's latest version of the 10th (he's recorded it once before for Virgin) still doesn't cut the mustard, however. Though the Dallas Symphony players pull out all the stops, once again the performance is marred by applied nuances that speak of careful rehearsal rather than true conviction. Overall, the 10th offers no serious challenge to Karajan's classic account. But a truly great performance of the Sixth.

Symphony No 7

Symphonies Nos 1 & 7
Chicago Symphony Orchestra / Leonard Bernstein
DG ② 427 632-2GH2 (120' · DDD) Recorded live
1988   Ⓕ⚫⚫

The *Leningrad* Symphony was composed in haste as the Nazis sieged and bombarded the city (in 1941). It caused an immediate sensation, but posterity has been less enthusiastic. What business has the first movement's unrelated long central 'invasion' episode doing in a symphonic movement? Is the material of the finale really distinctive enough for its protracted treatment? Michael Oliver, in his original *Gramophone* review, wrote that in this performance 'the symphony sounds most convincingly like a symphony, and one needing no programme to justify it'. Added to which the work's epic and cinematic manner has surely never been more powerfully realised. These are live recordings, with occasional noise from the audience (and the conductor), but the Chicago Orchestra has rarely sounded more polished or committed. The strings are superb in the First Symphony, full and weightily present, and Bernstein's manner here is comparably bold and theatrical of gesture. A word of caution: set your volume control carefully for the *Leningrad* Symphony's start; it's scored for six of both trumpets and trombones and no other recording has reproduced them so clearly, and to such devastating effect.

Symphony No 7 in C, 'Leningrad', Op 60
Cologne Radio Symphony Orchestra / Rudolf Barshai
Regis Records RRC1074 (72' · DDD) Recorded live
1992   Ⓑ⚫

With the disappearance of the Melodiya catalogue (at least in the UK), seekers after truth – or at least some measure of authenticity – in their Shostakovich symphonies will have to look elsewhere. One option is to investigate the recordings made outside Russia by musicians closely associated with the composer. Rudolf Barshai certainly qualifies for inclusion in this select group. Certain musicians seem to have found him more pernickety than inspirational, but Sviatoslav Richter for one praised his honesty and professionalism. Now, belatedly, cult status has arrived, thanks in part to the 'underground' success of a live account of Mahler's Fifth Symphony.

It's idle to pretend that the players of Bernstein's Chicago Symphony need look to their laurels. Nor does Barshai feel the need to go for broke (and bombast?) in the Bernstein manner. That said, his first movement is both 'felt' and

fluent, the main material presented with convincing elegance and lucidity at a flowing pace. Barshai's slow movement glows with (rather than oozes) compassion, and it's principally in the finale that the conducting doesn't always succeed in disguising the fact that Shostakovich was, of necessity, composing on automatic pilot. Even here, timps are well tuned, and Barshai's diligence is always readily apparent in the detailed phrasing of his strings. The recorded sound has been well managed too, the crystalline textures obtained by the conductor and the attractively spacious acoustic compensating for a relatively constricted dynamic range and limited bass response. This disc is a clear winner in its price range: it's vastly superior to Ladislav Slovák's bargain basement alternative on Naxos. Expect a few fluffs and some audience noise and you won't be disappointed.

Symphony No 8

Symphony No 8
London Symphony Orchestra / André Previn
HMV Classics HMV5 74370-2 (61' · ADD) Recorded
1973   Ⓢ Ⓑ⚫⚫

The Eighth Symphony, written in 1943, two years after the *Leningrad*, offers a wiser, more bitterly disillusioned Shostakovich. The heroic peroration of the Seventh's finale is here replaced by numbed whimsy and eventual uneasy calm. André Previn has since re-recorded the Eighth (DG) but this youthful account serves to remind us that the music is the product of a young man's imagination. The remake has greater breadth in every sense and, note for note, the orchestral playing is often finer. Even so the urgency of this earlier version is to be preferred. At that time, Previn seemed content to add a patina of mid-Atlantic gloss, and a good deal of subtlety, to the raw expressivity of the earlier Soviet recordings; he had not yet adopted the self-consciously epic manner thought appropriate today. With Sanderling among the few who know how to bring off the symphony as a gloomy and spiritless *in memoriam*, the lithe freshness of the Previn remains a compelling alternative. EMI's transfer is punchy and focused, but the orchestra seems smaller than before, drier and cleaner in the bass.

Shostakovich Symphony No 8
Mozart Symphony No 33 in B flat, K319
Leningrad Philharmonic Orchestra / Evgeny Mravinsky
BBC Legends/IMG Artists ② BBCL4002-2 (82' · ADD)
Recorded live 1960   Ⓜ⚫

There was a time when Mravinsky's greatness had to be taken on trust, such was the paucity of his representation in the record catalogues. The situation has been transformed in recent years; hence this version of the Shostakovich has to find its niche in a market-place documenting the orchestra's prowess in the piece from the 1940s to the 1980s. In a variety of different transfers (and at a variety of different pitches) Mravinsky's March 1982 concert performance is widely known. But in 1960, when the orchestra made an epochal visit to these shores with Rostropovich, Rozhdestvensky and Shostakovich himself in tow, the work had never been heard here and was unavailable on disc. Small wonder the event was such a sensation, with the November 1960 *Gramophone* leading the call for new recordings of the Soviet repertoire played on the tour.

Mravinsky was a conductor in the Karajan mould both in his undemonstrative, albeit politically ratified, exercise of authority and the way in which his interpretations remained broadly consistent from one decade to the next. The authentic timbre of the Leningrad Philharmonic is there for all to hear – the winds tearing into their phrases like scalded cats, the string sound huge and inimitable, dominating the sound-stage and yet never fat or complacent. In almost every respect, Mravinsky's London performance lives up to its legendary status, and the sound has been reprocessed to yield excellent results. Unfortunately the listeners in the hall are surprisingly restless. The first movement is patiently built, stoic, even bleaker than usual from this source, and with only minor technical imperfections: the problem is the barrage of coughing. The power and control of the second and third movements is awesome by any standards and here the audience is less intrusive. In the finale, Mravinsky keeps a tight rein on his players, adopting marginally slower tempos and securing finer results than he did in 1982. The climax is cataclysmic with the paying public at last stunned into silence during the magical coda. Shostakovich dedicated the symphony to Mravinsky, and it's for this work that most people will want to acquire the set.

Symphony No 10

Shostakovich Symphonies Nos 1[a] & 10[b].
Concerto for Piano, Trumpet and Strings, Op 35[c]
Mussorgsky[b] (orch Shostakovich) Songs and Dances of Death
[b]**Robert Lloyd** *bass* [c]**Mikhail Rudy** *pf* [c]**Ole Edvard Antonsen** *tpt* [ac]**Berlin Philharmonic Orchestra;** [b]**Philadelphia Orchestra / Mariss Jansons**
EMI Double Forte ② 575178-2 (DDD) [ab]Recorded 1994   Ⓜ

In the West the 10th Symphony is now widely regarded as the finest of the cycle of 15, not just for its sheer depth of personal feeling, but because it finds the purest and subtlest musical representation of that feeling. Perhaps this is why it's less dependent than some of Shostakovich's major works on a conductor steeped in the Russian idiom. Anyone expecting a welter of hairpin *diminuendos* and expressive nudges will be disappointed by Jansons's Shostakovich –

solid, sturdy and rhythmically taut rather than overly individualistic. Jansons's first movement is basically brisk, with thrustful strings and conscientiously Soviet-style woodwind. It's a cogent enough view and yet the sense of underlying desolation is lacking, despite the conductor's vocal exhortations. The *Scherzo* is brilliantly articulated – even if the relatively leisurely pace robs the music of its potential to intimidate. The 'difficult' third movement is more convincing. The main body of the finale is launched with precise rhythmic clarity rather than irrepressible enthusiasm. In short, this is an excellent, sometimes dazzling choice among modern versions but it may strike seasoned listeners as slightly sterile. There's more passion in the Mussorgsky. Robert Lloyd is curiously under-represented on CD in the Russian repertoire that suits him so well. His admirers are bound to want this performance, which is very impressive as sheer singing. Throughout the disc, the close focus of the recording exposes a few instances of less than perfect synchronisation but with playing so spectacularly accomplished, this must be counted an outstanding achievement in its way.

Symphony No 10
Berlin Philharmonic Orchestra / Herbert von Karajan
DG 439 036-2GHS (52' · DDD) Recorded 1981   Ⓕ Ⓞ

Few works give a deeper insight into the interior landscape of the Russian soul than Shostakovich's 10th, and this is a powerful and gripping account of what's, by general consent, his masterpiece. Karajan has the measure of its dramatic sweep and brooding atmosphere, as well as its desolation and sense of tragedy. Haitink's is nowhere near so intense or, for that matter, so well played, though the recording has impressive transparency of detail. There are many things here (the opening of the finale, for example) which are even more succesful than in Karajan's 1966 recording, though the main body of the finale still feels too fast – however, at crotchet=176, it's what the composer asked for. His earlier account of the first movement is for some more moving – particularly the poignant coda. However, the differences aren't significant and this is hardly less impressive. The CD deserves a strong recommendation.

Additional recommendation

Berlin Philharmonic Orchestra / Karajan
DG Galleria 429 713-2GGA (51' · ADD)   Ⓜ
  Karajan's powerful 1966 recording is a steal at mid price.

Symphony No 11

Symphony No 11 in G minor, 'The Year 1905', Op 103
London Symphony Orchestra / Mstislav Rostropovich

LSO Live LSO0030 (72' · DDD)　　⑤ⓈⓄⓄⓄ

 The critical reputation of Shostakovich's cinematic evocation of the first Russian Revolution of 1905 has been rising of late. Not that our supposed ability to 'decode' a subtext has led inexorably to readings of superior insight.

Rostropovich clearly has something unique to say about this work, transcending any doubts about his conducting technique per se. On its initial appearance nearly a decade ago, his studio recording had some negative press, but there was real atmosphere in it and an epic breadth from which so many performers have shied away. That conception remains basically unchanged here, and the buzz of a special event is felt from the start in the eerie, almost inaudible breath of sound with which the strings conjure up the frozen hush and epic breadth of Mother Russia. While there are few notes on the page – at Rostropovich's tempo, they seem fewer than ever – the atmosphere is potent indeed. His reading is surprisingly objective until the build up to the 'Bloody Sunday' massacre. Here, you can't miss the trombones' astonishing, leering *glissandi*. Nor the bizarre, highly personal nuancing at the very height of the clamour, something which must surely pall on repetition.

The opening paragraph of the finale is articulated with tremendous cut and thrust, the sheer heft of the strings mightily impressive. So, too, in a quite different way, is the evocative cor anglais solo from track 4, 9'42".

This is one of the strongest releases yet from LSO Live: the production team seem to have come to terms with the 'improved' Barbican Hall; there's more depth and distance now, with instruments more convincingly 'placed' and string sonorities realistically full. At the price, this sweeps the board. Play loud or not at all.

Symphony No 13

Symphony No 13
Marius Rintzler bass **Concertgebouw Orchestra Choir** (male voices) **Concertgebouw Orchestra / Bernard Haitink**
Decca 425 073-2DM (64' · DDD) Recorded 1984.
Notes, texts and translations included　　ⓂⓄⓄ

With one single reservation Haitink's account of *Babiy Yar* is superb. The reservation is that Marius Rintzler, although he has all the necessary blackness and gravity and is in amply sonorous voice, responds to the anger and the irony and the flaming denunciations of Yevtushenko's text with scarcely a trace of the histrionic fervour they cry out for. The excellent chorus, though, is very expressive and it makes up for a lot, as does the powerful and sustained drama of Haitink's direction. He has solved the difficult problems of pacing a symphony with three slow movements (one is gripped throughout) and the atmosphere of each movement is vividly evoked, with a particular care for the subtleties of Shostakovich's orchestration. The orchestral sound, indeed, is magnificent: one can readily believe that the huge forces called for in the score were actually provided, but this doesn't necessitate any unnatural focusing on (say) the celeste in order that it shall register. The perspective is very natural throughout, and there's an excellent sense of the performance taking place in a believable space.

Symphony No 14

Symphony No 14. Two Pieces for String Quartet (arr Sikorski)
Margareta Haverinen sop **Petteri Salomaa** bass **Tapiola Sinfonietta / Joseph Swensen**
Ondine ODE845-2 (59' · DDD) Text and translation included　　ⒻⓄ

The multilingual version of the 14th Symphony was sanctioned by the composer but it remains a rarity on disc; some vital and specific tone colour is lost along with the original note values, and the 'three lilies' adorn the grave of 'The Suicide' more elegantly in the Russian. Haitink may not agree. He elected to use the multilingual text in his 1980 recording and now Joseph Swensen presents this compelling alternative. We tend to take sonic excellence for granted these days but this is a true state-of-the-art recording with the soloists more naturally placed than in the rival Decca issue and an orchestral sound combining great clarity with just enough hall resonance. The performance has character too, if lacking the pervasive chill of the earliest Soviet accounts. The conductor secures excellent results from the Tapiola Sinfonietta.

Of the soloists, the bass-baritone Petteri Salomaa is particularly impressive: his is a voice of rare tonal beauty, a Billy Budd rather than a Boris. His pronunciation is a little odd at times, but you may not see this as a problem. Tempos are perceptibly more 'extreme' than Haitink's, with the opening 'De profundis' dangerously slow in the modern manner and a strikingly well-characterised instrumental contribution to 'A la Santé' ('In the Santé Prison'). The fillers, larger than life, brilliantly dispatched and curiously inappropriate, are based on original quartet pieces which only came to light in the mid-1980s. The first shares material with *Lady Macbeth of Mtsensk*; the second appears as the polka from *The Age of Gold*! This is nevertheless a more rewarding, more probingly conducted disc than most of the current Shostakovich crop.

Symphony No 15

Symphonies Nos 1 & 15
Cincinnati Symphony Orchestra / Jesús López-Cobos
Telarc CD80572 (77' · DDD)　　Ⓕ

These are extremely well played and cleanly recorded performances, and in a field surprisingly lacking in strong contenders they deserve serious consideration. By dint of careful preparation López-Cobos brings exceptional clarity to the First Symphony, forcing you to admire afresh the sheer inventiveness of the teenage Shostakovich's counterpoint. His Cincinnati players are suave, without ever sounding emotionally complacent, and they seem to appreciate better than most Western orchestras the extraordinary depth of feeling at the heart of the finale. That said, there's little of the bite and sheer recklessness that make Kondrashin's interpretation so special, though sadly that classic version is hampered by poor recording quality, and the Moscow Philharmonic's first oboe in the slow movement is excruciating.

López-Cobos's account of Symphony No 15 lacks a fanatical edge in the fast movements, a sense of mystery in the slow ones and of strangeness throughout, but this Cincinnati version is as good as anything currently available, and certainly better than the over-praised Haitink, Rostropovich or Sanderling. López-Cobos plays the symphony straight and keeps the stylistically competing elements in balance. He negotiates the treacherous finale successfully, building the passacaglia to a properly passionate climax.

The Golden Age, Op 22

The Golden Age
**Royal Stockholm Philharmonic Orchestra /
Gennadi Rozhdestvensky**
Chandos ② CHAN9251/2 (134' · DDD) Recorded
1993   Ⓕ

The ballet *The Golden Age* (1930) depicts an industrial exhibition organised in a capitalist country, at which a group of Soviet sportsmen have been invited to compete. The general idea of the music is to differentiate between goodies and baddies by assigning them respectively healthy-folk and decadent-bourgeois idioms. The trouble was that Shostakovich couldn't stop himself enjoying being decadent.

Not all the 37 movements stand up independently of the stage-action. But the finales and the whole of Act 3 are top-notch stuff, at times surprisingly threatening in tone and symphonic in continuity; and there are several movements which could undoubtedly be promoted alongside the four in the familiar concert suite (the Tap Dance of Act 2 is especially appealing, for instance). Those who know that Shostakovich will be constantly intrigued by foretastes of *Lady Macbeth*, the Fourth Symphony and the *Hamlet* music, and by the appearance of Shostakovich's 'Tea for Two' arrangement as an Interlude in Act 2.

This first complete recording is a major coup for Chandos. Admittedly not even their flattering engineering can disguise a certain lack of confidence and idiomatic flair on the part of the Royal Stockholm Philharmonic Orchestra.

But don't let that deter anyone with the least interest in Shostakovich, or ballet music, or Soviet music, or indeed Soviet culture as a whole, from investigating this weird and intermittently wonderful score. A really fascinating disc.

Film Music

The Film Album
The Counterplan, Op 33 – Presto; Andante (with **Alexander Kerr** vn); The Song of the Counterplan. Alone, Op 26 – March; Galop; Barrel Organ; March; Altai; In Kuzmina's hut; School children; Storm Scene. The Tale of the Silly Little Mouse, Op 56 (arr Cornall). Hamlet, Op 116 – Introduction; Palace Music; Ball at the Castle; Ball; In the Garden; Military Music; Scene of the Poisoning. The Great Citizen, Op 55 – Funeral March. Sofia Perovskaya, Op 132 – Waltz. Pirogov, Op 76a (arr Atovmian) – Scherzo; Finale. The Gadfly, Op 97 – Romance (Kerr)
Royal Concertgebouw Orchestra / Riccardo Chailly
Decca 460 792-2DH (78' · DDD)   Ⓕ Ⓞ

Only ardent film buffs and die-hard Shostakovich completists will cavil at this selection of Chailly's rather offbeat collection, cutting across as it does several more serious-minded projects. He gives us some genuine novelties too. 'The Song of the Counterplan' (track 3) was transmogrified into an MGM production number in the 1940s for the film *Thousands Cheer*. The 'Funeral March' from *The Great Citizen* turns up again in the 11th Symphony (track 22). And the much later 'Waltz' from *Sofia Perovskaya* is also unfamiliar. Less committed listeners should perhaps sample track 11 for Shostakovich's take on the spooky weirdness of the theremin, and track 25 for the ubiquitous 'Romance' from *The Gadfly*.

There may be no great music here – some of the darker numbers from *Hamlet* come closest with their echoes of *Stepan Razin* and the 13th Symphony – but with music-making of this quality it scarcely matters. Chailly has rarely sounded so unbuttoned in the studio and the selection is generous, if random. Only the final chord of the 'Finale' from *Pirogov* is a bit of a puzzle. Given the top-notch Decca production values on display, what sounds here like a dropout or similar technical fault could be either the conductor executing a tricksy hairpin *diminuendo* or Shostakovich perpetrating a Mahler 7-type joke. Warmly recommended in any event.

Light Music

The Dance Album
Moscow-Cheryomushki, Op 105 – concert suite (ed Cornall). The Bolt – ballet suite, Op 27a (1934 version). The Gadfly, Op 97 – Overture; The Cliff; Youth; Box on the Ear; Barrel Organ; Contredanse; Galop; At the Market Place; The Rout; The Passage

of Montanelli; Finale; The Austrians; Gemma's Room
Philadelphia Orchestra / Riccardo Chailly
Decca 452 597-2DH (73' · DDD)　　　　Ⓕ**O**

Although entitled 'The Dance Album', interestingly only one of the items on this disc (*The Bolt*) is actually derived from music conceived specifically for dance. However, what the disc reveals is that Shostakovich's fondness for dance forms frequently found expression in his other theatrical/film projects. The world première recording of a suite of four episodes from the 1959 operetta *Moscow-Cheryomushki* will be of particular interest to Shostakovich devotees. Despite the somewhat mundane plot, the score produces some surprisingly attractive and entertaining numbers, most notably perhaps the invigorating 'A spin through Moscow' and the 'Waltz'. For the suite from the ballet *The Bolt* Chailly brings us the less frequently heard 1934 version in which the composer dropped two of the eight numbers and changed some of the titles in order to deflect from the story-line of the ballet. Lots of parody and plenty of Shostakovich with his tongue planted firmly in his cheek is what we get, and if this aspect of the composer's output appeals then you'll certainly enjoy Chailly's and his players' spirited and colourfully buoyant performances of this energetic score. Less familiar light is also shed on the music from the film *The Gadfly* which is heard here in a version which brings together 13 of the score's episodes and preserves Shostakovich's original orchestration, as opposed to the suite prepared and reorchestrated by Levin Atovmyan. All the performances on the disc are superbly delivered and the recorded sound is excellent.

The Jazz Album
Jazz Suites Nos 1 & 2. Taiti trot, Op 16. Concerto for
Piano, Trumpet and Strings in C minor, Op 35
[a]**Peter Masseurs** *tpt* [a]**Ronald Brautigam** *pf*
**Royal Concertgebouw Orchestra / Riccardo
Chailly**
Decca 433 702-2DH (59' · DDD)　　　　Ⓕ**OO**

Shostakovich's lively and endearing forays into the popular music of his time were just that, and light years away from the work of real jazz masters such as, say Jelly Roll Morton or Duke Ellington And yet they do say something significant about Shostakovich's experience of jazz, as a comparison of these colourful, Chaplinesque *Jazz* Suites with roughly contemporaneous music by Gershwin, Milhaud, Martinu, Roussel and others will prove. Shostakovich engaged in a particularly brittle almost Mahlerian form of parody – his concert works are full of it – and that's what comes across most powerfully here. Besides, and as annotator Elizabeth Wilson rightly observes, 'real' jazz was treated with suspicion in Soviet Russia and Shostakovich's exposure to it was therefore limited.

The two *Jazz* Suites were composed in the 1930s, the First in response to a competition to

'raise the level of Soviet jazz from popular cafe music to music with a professional status', the Second at the request of the then-newly formed State Orchestra for Jazz (!). The First will make you chuckle, but it's the Second (subtitled 'Suite for Promenade Orchestra') that contains the best music, especially its achingly nostalgic Second *Waltz*. The instrumentation is light (the saxophone and accordion add a touch of spice to a generally bland recipe), while the playing is quite superb. In fact, there's little to be said about Chailly's direction other than that it's good-humoured, affectionate and utterly professional, his Royal Concertgebouw players sound at home in every bar and the recording (Grotezaal, Concertgebouw) is both clean and ambient.

Taiti trot came to life when Nikolai Malko challenged Shostakovich to score Vincent Youmans's *Tea for Two* in an hour, or less – which he did, as a sort of mini-concerto for orchestra, each refrain being dealt to different instrumental forces. Fun that it is, its charm is terminal. Which leaves the Piano Concerto, music that for sophistication and inventive ingenuity is actually closer to what we now think of as jazz than the *Jazz* Suites. (Sample the freewheeling, improvisatory opening to the last movement, on track 7.)

Ronald Brautigam's instrument is twangy at the bass end, which mightn't seem too inappropriate, but as it was recorded two years before the other items on the disc (1988), I doubt that that was the intention. Still, it's a lively and fairly intense reading, neatly supported by Chailly and trumpeter Peter Masseurs, but ultimately less memorable than Alexeev (HMV Classics) or Jablonski or the composer himself.

Piano Quintet in G minor, Op 57

Piano Quintet in G minor, Op 57[a]. Piano Trio No 2
in E minor, Op 67. String Quartets Nos 1 & 15
Elisabeth Leonskaja *pf* **Borodin Quartet** (Mikhail
Kopelman, [a]Andrei Abramenkov *vns* [a]Dmitri
Shebalin *va* Valentin Berlinsky *vc*)
Warners Ultima ② 8573 87820-2 (DDD)　　　Ⓢ Ⓑ**O**

The Piano Quintet is almost symphonic in its proportions, lasting some 35 minutes, and has been popular with audiences ever since its first performance in 1940. Much of its popularity stems from Shostakovich's highly memorable material, particularly in the boisterous and genial *Scherzo* and finale movements. Because of the presence of a piano and of the powerful emotions expressed in them, the Quintet and Trio are commonly given very big performances. Those on this recording are by no means small, but they're chamber music, and that seems to be the view of the pianist as well as the string players. The finale of the Piano Trio actually gains in power from this, the greatest weight of tone being reserved for the true climax, and half the intensity of the Quintet, in this reading, comes from a remarkably wide and masterfully controlled range of sonority and dynamic. Leonskaja is a superb partner in both works. The Quartets Nos 1 and 15 make a superb coupling (the playing style mirroring the richness of the one and the austerity of the other). The recordings are very fine, with the balance just right. A bargain.

String Quartets

No 1 in C, Op 49 No 2 in A, Op 68 No 3 in F, Op 73 No 4 in D, Op 83 No 5 in B flat, Op 92 No 6 in G, Op 101 No 7 in F sharp minor, Op 108 No 8 in C minor, Op 110 No 9 in E flat, Op 117 No 10 in A flat, Op 118 No 11 in F minor, Op 122 No 12 in D flat, Op 133 No 13 in B flat minor, Op 138 No 14 in F sharp minor, Op 142 No 15 in E flat minor, Op 144

String Quartets Nos 1-15
Fitzwilliam Quartet (Christopher Rowland, Jonathan Sparey vns Alan George va Ioan Davies vc)
Decca ⑥ 455 776-2LC6 (377' · ADD)
Recorded 1975-7   Ⓢ Ⓑ ❍❍❍

If Shostakovich's cycle of 15 symphonies can be said to represent a musical thread passing through the whole of the composer's public life, then it can be argued that his cycle of 15 string quartets represents the private persona of the man behind the mask, from the beginning of his personal anguish in the late 1930s, until his death in 1975. At the time of his First Quartet, composed in 1938, he was already an experienced and respected composer with five symphonies to his credit as well as much music for stage and film. Thenceforth his symphonic music inscrutably presented the emotions – albeit largely ironically – that the State expected from its leading composer, while the quartets provided an outlet for the emotions within and for his personal responses to the events taking place in the world around him. If the music is rich in irony, then the language the composer uses is straightforward, with a defined tonality, simple melodies, uncluttered rhythms and clear textures. There's only one possible composer, so recognisably individual is the voice.

The Fitzwilliam Quartet originally recorded its cycle in the mid-1970s, shortly after a concentrated period of study with the composer. Despite being recorded in analogue, the sound quality is still remarkably good. The group has a remarkable understanding of the idiom and of the music's underlying motivation. In the First Quartet it captures the uneasy mood (reminiscent of the Fifth Symphony) behind the seemingly placid surface. In the Fourth Quartet, it gives the Jewish idioms – a metaphor for the oppressed artist – a more deliberate, and thus more natural-sounding, tempo. Probably the best known of the quartets is No 8, composed in Dresden in 1960 and dedicated to the victims of Fascism and of the War, and in view of the constant use of the DSCH motif and the quotations

from several of his own pieces, there can be little doubt that Shostakovich considered himself among their number. It's a grim, often macabre, work and once again the Fitzwilliam captures the loneliness of the composer. So often, his solo melodies, set against a stark and sombre accompaniment, sound like a voice crying in the wilderness. The quartets are well worth getting to know and the performances by the Fitzwilliam Quartet, despite their age, still seem to reach the heart of the composer's intentions.

String Quartets – Nos 1-5; 6-10; 11-15 Two Pieces[b]
Emerson Quartet (Eugene Drucker, Philip Setzer vns Lawrence Dutton va David Finckel vc)
DG ⑤ 463 284-2GH5 (360' · DDD)   Ⓕ ❍❍❍

The Emerson Quartet have played Shostakovich all over the world, and this long-pondered *intégrale* sets the seal on a process that has brought the quartets to the very centre of the repertoire – the ensemble's and ours. Operating here out of Aspen, Colorado, several geopolitical worlds away from the old Soviet Union, the Americans outpace the classic Borodin recordings in almost every movement, their virtuosity powerfully evident in the many *scherzos* and toccata-like passages. While some listeners will miss the intangible element of emotional specificity and sheer Russianness that once lurked behind the notes, the playing is undeniably committed in its coolness, exposing nerve endings with cruel clarity. The hard, diamond-like timbre of the two violins (the leader's role is shared democratically) is far removed from the breadth of tone one might associate with a David Oistrakh, just as cellist David Finckel is no Rostropovich. But these recordings reveal surprising new facets of a body of work that isn't going to stand still. The Fourth Quartet is a case in point, more delicate than most rivals with the finale relatively pressed, less insistently Jewish. The Fifth sometimes seems closer to Ustvolskaya or American minimalism than the mid-century Soviet symphonic utterance we're used to; the Emerson's almost hectoring mode of address and unfluctuating tempo are maintained for as long as (in)humanly possible. The very vehemence of, say, the finale of the Ninth tends to blunt the harmonic sense of the music, leaving something more visceral and rosiny than the argument can stand. To get the unique feel of this set, sample one of the encore pieces, the 'Polka' from *The Age of Gold*. Little humanity and wit, but can you resist the explosive brilliance of the technique?

DG's recording is exceptionally vivid if somewhat airless, the separation of the instruments being achieved at the expense of tonal blend. Given that all the quartets were taped live with only remedial patching, the audience is commendably silent: their enthusiastic applause is retained for Nos 1, 2, 9 and 12 only. This is a Shostakovich cycle for the 21st century.

String Quartets Nos 2, 5 & 7
Shostakovich Quartet
Olympia OCD532 (78' · ADD) Recorded 1978-85 Ⓕ**O**

String Quartets Nos 6, 8 & 9
Shostakovich Quartet
Olympia OCD533 (74' · ADD) Recorded 1978-85   Ⓕ

String Quartets Nos 10, 11 & 15
Shostakovich Quartet   Ⓕ**OO**
Olympia OCD534 (78' · ADD) Recorded 1978-85

String Quartets Nos 12-14
Shostakovich Quartet
Olympia OCD535 (73' · ADD) Recorded 1978-85 Ⓕ**O**

Any attempt to rank these players in relation to their more widely acclaimed opposite numbers in the Borodin Quartet seems pointless at this level of dedication; both teams have lived through this most extraordinary of 20th-century quartet-cycles many times. If any general observation about the two can be made, it's that the Borodin finds more corporate subtleties and passing shades in some of the earlier quartets, while the individual members of the Shostakovich Quartet make even stronger, more vibrant soloists. In the context of Shostakovich's many, very vocal solos and recitatives, it hardly seems invidious to single out the first violinist, Andrei Shishlov – dark, powerful and flawless of intonation throughout. Listen to his sleight-of-hand freedom in the unaccompanied melody of No 6's finale: the Borodin's Mikhail Kopelman doesn't begin to touch imagination like that.

These players also teach us to hold in equal awe the more classically contained quartets – No 6 and the outer movements of No 10 have a special grace – and all the slow movements are impressively unfolded with a steady fluency (notable in the passacaglias). As for the last rites of No 15, not even the Borodin finds such implicit human warmth in the still *fugato* of the Elegy. In tandem with the impassioned solos of the later movements, it's an impressive summing-up of this team's best intentions. Balances in the earlier recordings are less than kind to second fiddle, and cellist and are uncomfortably boxy. You'll also have to adjust the volume-level for consecutive listening. If you seek only a single-disc token of the achievement, that with Nos 10, 11 and 15 is the one to have.

Piano Trios

No 1 in C minor, Op 8 **No 2** in E minor, Op 67

Shostakovich Piano Trios Nos 1 & 2 **Schnittke** Trio
Vienna Piano Trio (Wolfgang Redik *vn* Marcus Trefny
Stefan Mendl *pf*)
Nimbus NI5572 (69' · DDD)   Ⓕ**O**

Shostakovich's adolescent First Trio's ramshackle structure seems to matter less than its surprisingly Gallic-sounding, passionately late-romantic invention. The Vienna Piano Trio

offers a rich-toned and meticulously prepared account. The tricky cello opening to the Second Trio is wonderfully ethereal here, and the even more tricky accumulating tempo over the entire movement is steady and logical, though this and the main tempo for the *Scherzo* are both more reined in than in the composer's own account (once available on Supraphon). The passacaglia and finale are properly intense and none the worse for being kept within the bounds of euphony, though the ideal performance, yet to be realised on CD, would be one which drained bitterer dregs of sorrow and took excitement closer to the point of hyperventilation.

Schnittke's Trio is more than an interesting makeweight. The String Trio original dates from 1985, the fateful year of the composer's first stroke and a period when he seemed to have a direct line to a kind of other-worldly inspiration. True, the two longish movements occasionally seem at a loss, but overall this is one of Schnittke's most economical and restrained scores, and one of his finest. At every turn the Vienna Piano Trio is sensitive to the character and flow of this haunting music. A fine disc, then – imaginative programming, accomplished performances, and rich, well-balanced recording.

24 Preludes and Fugues, Op 87

No 1 in C **No 2** in A minor **No 3** in G **No 4** in E minor **No 5** in D **No 6** in B minor **No 7** in A **No 8** in F sharp minor **No 9** in E **No 10** in C sharp minor **No 11** in B **No 12** in G sharp minor **No 13** in F sharp **No 14** in E flat minor **No 15** in D flat **No 16** in B flat minor **No 17** in A flat **No 18** in F minor **No 19** in E flat **No 20** in C minor **No 21** in B flat **No 22** in G minor **No 23** in F **No 24** in D minor

Preludes and Fugues Nos 1-24
Vladimir Ashkenazy *pf*
Decca ② 466 066-2DH2 (142' · DDD)   Ⓕ**O**

Here's a Shostakovich Preludes and Fugues cycle to be reckoned with. It starts none too promisingly, with (by the highest standards) a rhythmically stiff, tonally lumpy C major prelude and some overpedalling in the fugue. However, the neo-Baroque figuration of the A minor prelude and its spiky fugue, on the other hand, presents his true credentials. On form and well prepared, as here, Ashkenazy remains a formidably fluent pianist, and the clarity and energy he brings to the faster, denser pieces is surpassed only by Richter (Philips). The sound itself is quite 'pingy', with a generous ambience behind it. That serves to heighten the impact of the more demonstrative pieces, but makes it difficult for Ashkenazy to sustain the atmosphere of the more meditative ones. Or maybe he simply doesn't feel the music that way. In the final D minor Fugue (No 24), where you can almost hear Shostakovich's 10th Symphony being born, Ashkenazy fails to build the texture as mightily as the early stages lead you to expect. Nikolaieva surpasses him here, and in general she reveals both subtler and grander perspectives, especially in her tauter, more drily recorded 1987 Melodiya set. Even so the balance-sheet for Ashkenazy comes out comfortably in the black. For consistency of pianism, straightforward integrity of interpretation and high quality of recording, his set can be warmly recommended.

Shostakovich Preludes and Fugues Nos 1, 5, 6, 7, 11, 12, 13, 17, 18, 19, 23, 24 in D minor **Bach** The Well-Tempered Clavier, Book I – C minor, C sharp, C sharp minor, E flat minor, E, E minor, F sharp minor, G, G minor, A minor, B flat, B flat minor
Olli Mustonen pf
Ondine ② ODE1033-2D (105' · DDD)   Ⓕ

The first volume of Olli Mustonen's thoughtfully melded sequence of Bach's '48' (Book 1) and Shostakovich's '24' Preludes and Fugues appeared on RCA, the sequence there based on chromatically ascending keys. Here, the pattern is planned according to the circle of fifths, especially fascinating for listeners who are sensitive to the contrasting colours of individual key signatures. Consistent to both is the sometimes bewildering extremism of Mustonen's own playing.

Our first port of call is a winning performance of Shostakovich's C major Prelude, with its light, sensual touch, and gently rhapsodised phrasing. Then in bounces the A minor Prelude from Bach's Book 1, brittle and jabbing with dramatic dynamic oscillations, especially in the succeeding fugue where even at speed individual notes either fade to near-inaudibility or virtually poke your eyes out. This seems unlikely to be tolerable for long, but, by the end, one's gripped.

Yes, there are affectations, such as the prettily arpeggiated flourish at the start of Bach's E minor Prelude, and the way the succeeding line bobs like a buoy at sea. But then there are such things as the ravishing delicate arpeggios at the start of Shostakovich's D major Prelude, or the shaded spectres in the beautifully played B minor Fugue.

Two very different views of counterpoint then: Bach the consummate master of abstract patterns, Shostakovich more the dramatic tone poet donning Bachian garb. Whatever the ultimate judgement on Mustonen's interpretations, you can't deny either the brilliance or imagination of his playing, or the consistency of his approach.

From Jewish Folk Poetry, Op 79

From Jewish Folk Poetry, Op 79. The New Babylon – suite (arr Rozhdestvensky)
Tatyana Sharova sop **Ludmila Kuznetsova** mez
Alexei Martynov ten **Russian State Symphony Orchestra / Valéry Polyansky**

Chandos CHAN9600 (70' · DDD) Text and translation included   ⒻⓄ

This recording of Shostakovich's song cycle *From Jewish Folk Poetry* is first-rate. For a start Polyansky's three vocal soloists are uncommonly well chosen: the light, youthful, slightly vulnerable soprano, the rich, world-weary mezzo and the ardent but unheroic tenor are ideally suited to the texts Shostakovich cunningly chose to convey his solidarity with mass suffering. Polyansky sets spacious tempos which allow every nuance of that suffering to register, and his orchestra is responsive and idiomatic in colouring. The recording, by Russian engineers, feels almost too good to be true in its excessive warmth; otherwise this version is preferable to the rival Rozhdestvensky on RCA. Polyansky's choice of the first of Shostakovich's 35 or so film scores makes for a more than welcome coupling. Polyansky offers an admirably idiomatic version of the Suite. He's especially adept at choosing timbres to reflect mood and situation. Even if you don't know the story-line the music was designed to accompany, this performance is so vividly characterised it can hardly fail to engage you.

Songs

Complete Songs, Volume 1
Four Monologues on Poems by Alexander Pushkin, Op 91[d]. Spanish Songs, Op 100[c]. Five Romances, 'Songs of Our Days', Op 98[d]. Two Romances to Lyrics by Lermontov, Op 84[b]. Four Songs to Lyrics by Dolmatovsky, Op 86[a]. Four Greek Songs[c]
[a]**Victoria Evtodieva** sop [b]**Natalia Biryukova** mez [c]**Mikhail Lukonin** bar [d]**Fyodor Kuznetsov** bass **Yury Serov** pf
Delos DE3304 (71' · DDD) Texts and translations included   ⒻⓄⓄ

Complete Songs, Volume 2
Four Verses of Captain Lebyadkin, Op 146[c]. Seven Romances on Verses by Alexander Blok, Op 127[a]. Six Marina Tsvetayeva Poems, Op 143[b]. Preface to the Complete Edition of my Works and a Brief Reflection apropos of this Preface, Op 123[c]. Five Romances, Op 121[c]
[a]**Victoria Evtodieva** sop [b]**Liubov Sokolova** mez [c]**Fyodor Kuznetsov** bass [a]**Lidia Kovalenko** vn [a]**Irina Molokina** vc **Yury Serov** pf
Delos DE3307 (70' · DDD) Texts and translations included   ⒻⓄⓄ

Here are two CDs dedicated to some of the finest and most under-recorded song repertoire of the 20th century. Yury Serov is the presiding spirit; his sharply characterised piano playing radiating musical and cultural understanding, and his singers are first-rate.

The first volume is dedicated to the 1950s and contains several first recordings; few, if any, of the songs have ever appeared on CD before. Much of his music from this time is marked by various nuances of cheerfulness (tentative, determined, over-stated, but never as brattish as in his first maturity). Often these seem rather to belie his true nature. Indeed, only the four *Pushkin Monologues*, with their topics of suffering, sorrow, imprisonment and resistance, are easily recognisable as the voice of Shostakovich, the Chronicler and Conscience of his Times. Fyodor Kuznetsov is slightly unsteady of voice here, but he still manages to convey a quality of wise, noble weariness that rings absolutely true.

It's to the enormous credit of all four singers that most of the remaining songs come across not as mere sops to authority but as genuine attempts to take on new artistic challenges. Was it still possible to do something worthwhile with the homespun, soft-centred verses of Yevgeny Dolmatovsky? Many of Shostakovich's countrymen certainly thought he had done so, at least in respect of 'The Homeland is Listening' (first of the Op 86 Songs), since this was taken up as a signature tune for All-Union Radio and was actually sung by Yuri Gagarin during the first manned space-flight. Seemingly looking back to the tradition of Tchaikovsky, Rimsky-Korsakov and Rachmaninov, Shostakovich's two *Lermontov Romances* are gorgeously atmospheric and tender. By contrast his earthier *Greek* and *Spanish Songs* reflect his long-standing interest in poetry from other national traditions. Was his heart in them? Again you wouldn't find it hard to think so after hearing these fine performances.

Volume 2 gathers together the cycles from the last decade of Shostakovich's life, with the exception of his massive *Suite on Verses by Michelangelo*. While this repertoire isn't quite so rare as that on Volume 1, the performances are just as fine. In the Blok cycle – surely the finest songs on the disc – Evtodieva may not be the last word in subtlety, but she's still far preferable to the crude hectoring of Natalia Gerasimova on Chant du Monde. Given that the *Four Verses of Captain Lebyadkin* are otherwise unavailable, and the extraordinarily elusive *Six Marina Tsvetayeva Poems* can currently be obtained only in the composer's orchestrated version, this disc is again pretty well self-recommending.

Altogether this enterprise is a winner. The recording quality is good, though there's a slight 'pinginess' to the piano sound.

Lady Macbeth of Mtsensk, Op 29

Lady Macbeth of the Mtsensk District
Galina Vishnevskaya *sop* Katerina Izmailova **Nicolai Gedda** *ten* Sergey Dubrovin **Dimiter Petkov** *bass* Boris Izmailov **Werner Krenn** *ten* Zinovy Borisovich Izmailov **Robert Tear** *ten* Russian peasant **Taru Valjakka** *sop* Aksinya **Martyn Hill** *ten* Teacher **Leonard Mroz** *bass* Priest **Aage Haugland** *bass* Police Sergeant **Birgit Finnila** *mez* Sonyetka **Alexander Malta** *bass* Old convict **Leslie Fyson** *ten* Milhand, Officer **Steven Emmerson** *bass* Porter **John Noble** *bar* Steward **Colin Appleton** *ten* Coachman, First foreman **Alan Byers** *bar* Second foreman **James Lewington** *ten* Third foreman **Oliver**

Broome *bass* Policeman **Edgar Fleet** *ten* Drunken Guest **David Beaven** *bass* Sentry **Lynda Richardson** *mez* Female convict **Ambrosian Opera Chorus; London Philharmonic Orchestra / Mstislav Rostropovich**
EMI Great Recordings of the Century ② 567776-2 (155' · ADD) Notes text and translation included ⓂⓄ

Rostropovich's cast has no weak links to it. More importantly, he gives a full-blooded projection of the poignant lyricism that underlies the opera's brutality. Vishnevskaya's portrayal of Katerina is at times a bit too three-dimensional, you might think, especially when the recording, which favours the singers in any case, seems (because of her bright and forceful tone) to place her rather closer to you than the rest of the cast. But there's no doubt in her performance that Katerina is the opera's heroine, not just its focal character, and in any case Gedda's genially rapacious Sergey, Petkov's grippingly acted Boris, Krenn's weedy Zinovy, Mroz's sonorous Priest, and even Valjakka in the tiny role of Aksinya, all refuse to be upstaged.

The 'minor' parts are luxuriously cast from artists who may not have had the advantage of singing their roles on stage but have clearly relished building them into vivid portraits. The close focusing on the voices and the relative distancing of the orchestra into a warmer, more ample acoustic is a bit more noticeable on CD than it was on LP.

Lady Macbeth of the Mtsensk District
Maria Ewing *sop* Katerina Izmailova **Sergei Larin** *ten* Sergey **Aage Haugland** *bass* Boris Izmailov **Philip Langridge** *ten* Zinovi Izmailov **Heinz Zednik** *ten* Shabby Peasant **Kristine Ciesinski** *sop* Aksinya **Ilya Levinsky** *ten* Teacher **Romuald Tesarowicz** *bass* Priest **Anatoly Kotcherga** *bass* Police Sergeant **Elena Zaremba** *mez* Sonyetka **Kurt Moll** *bass* Old Convict **Grigory Gritziuk** *bar* Millhand **Carlos Alvarez** *bass* Officer **Guillaume Petitot** *bass* Porter **Jean-Pierre Mazaloubaud** *bass* Steward **Alan Woodrow** *ten* Coachman **Jean-Claude Costa, Jean Savignol, Jose Ochagavia** *tens* First, Second and Third Foremen **Philippe Duminy** *bass* Policeman **Mario Agnetti** *ten* Drunken Guest **Johann Tilli** *bass* Sentry **Margaret Jane Wray** *sop* Woman Convict **Chorus and Orchestra of the Opera-Bastille, Paris / Myung-Whun Chung**
DG ② 437 511-2GH2 (156' · DDD) Notes, text and translation included Ⓕ

The main flaws in Rostropovich's historic recording of this opera with Galina Vishnevskaya in the title-role (reviewed above) are its very close focus on the solo voices and the at times distracting use of dramatising effects. Both are corrected in this new account, which has a very natural balance between voices and orchestra, and allows a cast of pungent singer-actors to do their own dramatising.

Rostropovich's version is luxuriously cast; Chung's cast may be less familiar, but it's no less distinguished: Larin is less characterful than

Gedda but a real Russian tenor with impressive line and care for words, Haugland is a formidable bully of a Boris, Tesarowicz and Kotcherga are vivid in their roles, Zaremba a Carmen-like bitch of a Sonyetka while Kurt Moll as the Old Convict contributes much more than a cameo: he adds a whole tragic dimension to Act 3 that Alexander Malta, for Rostropovich, can't approach. Maria Ewing's voice is nowhere near as commanding as Vishnevskaya's, and the recorded focus emphasises this. There are times when you can hardly hear her above the orchestra; others indeed where you certainly can't, and she's an unequal partner in the duet scenes with Larin and Haugland. This goes with such an intensely dramatic utterance, swooping up to and away from notes, that her singing and her *parlando* (her *Sprechstimme*, indeed) are sometimes hard to distinguish. The crucial test of her style of interpretation is the tragic 'aria' in Act 3 where Katerina realises the worthlessness of the man for whom she has murdered and suffered both humiliation and a destruction of all hope. Ewing is graphically expressive, every word placed in poignant relief, but at times you need to guess at what notes she's sketching and the whole passage is taken at about half its marked speed. Time standing still at such a moment is effective and not inappropriate; you only have to turn to Vishnevskaya and Rostropovich to realise that the passage can be lyrically sung and given a sense of forward movement without any loss of pathos.

Chung is a first-rate Shostakovich conductor, and he gets a warmer, fuller sound from his spaciously recorded Paris players than the no doubt intentionally leaner quality that Rostropovich asks of the LPO. Oddly enough the extra brass players that the score calls for make more impact in the slightly drier older recording, and there are sufficient pages on which Rostropovich finds a touch more hysterical energy or lurid colour to prefer his account even if Ewing had been a closer match for the imperious, but for that very reason more moving, Vishnevskaya.

Jean Sibelius
Finnish 1865-1957

Sibelius studied in Helsinki from 1886 with Wegelius, also gaining stimulus there from Busoni, though at the same time he fostered ambitions as a violinist. In 1889 he went to Berlin to continue his composition studies with Becker, then after a year to Vienna under Goldmark and Fuchs. He returned to Helsinki in 1891 and immediately made a mark with his choral symphony Kullervo, though it took him another decade to establish a wholly consistent style and to emerge from the powerful influence of Tchaikovsky: important stages on the journey were marked by the Karelia suite, the set of four tone poems on the legendary hero Lemminkäinen (including The Swan of Tuonela), the grandiose Finlandia and the first two symphonies.

As these titles suggest, he was encouraged by the Finnish nationalist movement (until 1917 Finland was a grand duchy in the Russian empire), by his readings of Finnish mythology (Kullervo and Lemminkäinen are both characters from the Kalevala, which was to be the source also for subjects of later symphonic poems) and in some degree by the folk music of Karelia. But the most important stimulus would seem to have been purely musical: a drive towards continuous growth achieved by means of steady thematic transformation, and facilitated by supporting the main line very often with highly diversified ostinato textures instead of counterpoints. The singleness of purpose also has to do with the frequently modal character of Sibelius's harmony.

The Violin Concerto of 1903 was effectively a farewell to 19th-century Romanticism, followed by a pure, classical expression of the new style in the Symphony No 3. This was also a period of change in his personal life. In 1904 he bought a plot of land outside Helsinki and built a house where he spent the rest of his life with his wife and daughters, removed from the city where he had been prone to bouts of heavy drinking. Also, his music gained a large international following, and he visited England (four times in 1905-12) and the USA (1914). Symphony No 4, with its conspicuous use of the tritone and its austere textures, took his music into its darkest areas; No 5 brought a return to the heroic mould, developing the process of continuous change to the extent that the first movement evolves into the scherzo. But that work took him some time to get right (written in 1915, it was revised in 1916 and again in 1919), and after World War I he produced only four major works: the brilliant and elusive Symphony No 6; No 7, which takes continuity to the ultimate in its unbroken unfolding of symphonic development; the incidental music for The Tempest; and the bleak symphonic poem Tapiola. He lived for another three decades, but published only a few minor pieces; an eighth symphony may possibly have been completed and destroyed. His reputation, however, continued to grow, and his influence has been profound, especially on Scandinavian, English and American composers, reflecting both the traditionalism and the radical elements in his symphonic thinking. **GROVE**music

Violin Concerto in D minor, Op 47

Violin Concerto (original 1903-4 version and final 1905 version)
Leonidas Kavakos vn **Lahti Symphony Orchestra / Osmo Vänskä**
BIS BISCD500 (75' · DDD) Recorded 1991 Ⓕ❶❶❶

It's difficult to conceive of a masterpiece in any other form than it is. The impression the listener receives from Sibelius's Fifth Symphony – or *The Rite of Spring* or *La mer* – must convey what Schoenberg called the illusion of spontaneous vision. It's as if the artist had caught a glimpse of something that's been going on all the time, and has stretched out and effortlessly captured it. One of Sibelius's letters written to his friend Axel Carpelan in the autumn of 1914 puts it perfectly: 'God opens his door for a moment, and his orchestra is playing Sym 5'. But life isn't like that, and Sibelius worked for seven years (1912-19) before the Fifth Symphony reached its final form. He was nothing if not self-critical, and a number of his works underwent their birth-pangs in public. The main theme came to him much earlier than 1903, and he recognised it for what it was, an inspired idea which remained unchanged. After its first performance in Helsinki in 1904 Sibelius decided to overhaul it. He realised the necessity to purify it, to remove unnecessary detail that impedes the realisation of a cogent structure. In its finished form, it was given in Berlin with Karl Halir as soloist and Richard Strauss conducting.

Listening to Sibelius's first thoughts played with great virtuosity and excellent taste by Leonidas Kavakos and the superb Lahti orches-tra is an absorbing experience. Although it's a great pity that many interesting details had to go, there's no doubt that the movement gains structural coherence. The fewest changes are in the slow movement, which remains at the same length. As in the case of the Fifth Symphony, where the revision is far more extensive than it is here, the finished work tells us a great deal about the quality of Sibelius's artistic judge-ment, which is what makes him such a great composer.

This disc offers an invaluable insight ino the workings of Sibelius's mind. Kavakos and the Lahti orchestra play splendidly throughout, and the familiar concerto which was struggling to get out of the 1903–4 version emerges equally safely in their hands. The BIS team have put us greatly in their debt by making the two versions available for study side by side.

Sibelius Violin Concerto **Tchaikovsky** Violin Concerto in D, Op 35
Kyung-Wha Chung vn **London Symphony Orchestra / André Previn**
The Classic Sound 425 080-2DCS (66' · ADD)
Recorded 1970   Ⓜ️Ⓞ

If the vital test for a recording is that a perform-ance should establish itself as a genuine one, not a mere studio run-through, Chung's remains a disc where both works leap out at you for their concentration and vitality, not just through the soloist's weight and gravity, expressed as though spontaneously, but through the playing of the LSO under Previn at a vintage period. The great melodies of the first two movements of the Sibelius are given an inner heartfelt intensity rarely matched, and with the finale skirting dan-ger with thrilling abandon. Chung's later Mon-treal version of the Tchaikovsky (also Decca) is rather fuller-toned with the tiny statutory cuts restored in the finale. Yet the very hint of vul-nerability amid daring, a key element in Chung's magnetic, volatile personality, here adds an extra sense of spontaneity. This remains breathtaking playing, and the central slow movement, made to flow without a hint of sen-timentality, has an extra poignancy. The Kings-

way Hall sound, full and sharply focused, gives a sense of presence to match or outshine today's digital recordings.

Violin Concerto[a]. Symphony No 2 in D, Op 43[b]   Ⓗ
[a]**Ginette Neveu** vn [a]**Philharmonia Orchestra / Walter Susskind;** [b]**New York Philharmonic Symphony Orchestra / Sir John Barbirolli**
Dutton mono CDBP9733 (71' · ADD) Recorded 1940-46   Ⓢ️Ⓢ️ⓄⓄ

In Ginette Neveu's fêted account of Sibelius's Violin Concerto, the strength, passion and stamina of the solo playing is particularly admirable, though Walter Susskind's Philhar-monia accompaniment is rather foursquare, especially in the finale. Heifetz and Beecham triumph every time. Still, EMI's famous record-ing is a fine memento of a fiery interpretation, and the solo line comes across with miraculous immediacy in Mike Dutton's transfer – better, in fact, than the orchestra, which tends to retreat under a veil whenever the music qui-etens. Barbirolli's impulsive New York record-ing of the Second Symphony burns bright and fast, but there are countless minor imprecisions that may irritate on repetition. A handful of slow but distant swishes suggests that Dutton's generally excellent refurbishment might have been based on an early LP transfer.

Additional recommendations

Violin Concerto

Coupled with: **Tchaikovsky** Violin Concerto   Ⓗ
Glazunov Violin Concerto
Heifetz vn **London Philharmonic Orchestra / Beecham; Barbirolli**
EMI Références mono 764030-2 (80' · AAD)   Ⓜ️
A masterly interpretation from 1935 – Heifetz's virtuosic, cool approach is more than matched by Beecham, an ideal Sibelian.

Coupled with: Two Serenades, Op 69[a]. Six Humoresques, Opp 87/89[b]. Suite in D minor
Fried [a]**J Kuusisto,** [b]**Kavakos** vns
Helsinki Philharmonic Orchestra / Kamu
Warner Apex 0927-40606-2 (79' · DDD)   Ⓢ️
An extremely useful compilation of Sibelius's complete music for violin and orchestra. The concerto is beautifully played and conducted, if not a first choice; it's the couplings that make this a really very competitive library choice.

Coupled with: **Nielsen** Violin Concerto
Lin vn **Philharmonia; Swedish Radio Symphony Orchestra / Salonen**
Sony Classical SMK89748 (69' · DDD)   Ⓕ
A *Gramophone* Award-winning coupling. Beautiful playing from the ever-sensitive Cho-Liang Lin.

Coupled with: **Tchaikovsky** Violin Concerto
Repin vn **London Symphony Orchestra / Krivine**
Erato 4509 98537-2 (67' · DDD)   Ⓜ️

SIBELIUS VIOLIN CONCERTO – IN BRIEF

Ginette Neveu; Philharmonia Orchestra / Walter Susskind
Dutton CDEA5016 (71' · ADD)　　　Ⓢ**OO**
Among the pantheon of great fiddlers who have recorded Sibelius's Concerto, the tragically short-lived Ginette Neveu continues to occupy a special place of honour.

Jascha Heifetz; Chicago SO / Walter Haendl
RCA 09026 61744-2 (69' · ADD)　　　Ⓜ**O**
As jaw-droppingly brilliant a display as you would expect from this giant of the violin. Heifetz's pioneering 1935 mono recording with Beecham is also definitely worth seeking out.

David Oistrakh; Stockholm PO / Sixten Ehrling
Testament SBT1032 (75' · ADD)　　　Ⓜ
The composer himself professed admiration for Oistrakh's wonderfully poised and serene interpretation. Sibelians and violin fanciers alike needn't hesitate.

Salvatore Accardo; London SO / Sir Colin Davis
Philips ② 446 160-2PM2 (146' · ADD)　　　Ⓜ
Accardo plays with great taste and assurance. Part of an all-Sibelius twofer which includes Sir Colin Davis's magnificent Boston accounts of Symphonies Nos 3, 6 and 7.

Kyung Wha Chung; London SO / André Previn
Decca 425 080-2DCS (66' · ADD)　　　Ⓜ**O**
Chung was at the outset of her career when she set down this touching, spontaneous-sounding recording, which is balanced to perfection by Decca's late-lamented Kenneth Wilkinson.

Cho-Liang Lin; Philharmonia Orchestra / Esa-Pekka Salonen
Sony SMK89748 (65' · DDD)　　　Ⓜ**OO**
Lin's immaculate, silk-spun version is second to none, and Salonen conducts with great sympathy both here and in the Nielsen Concerto which acts as a coupling.

Viktoria Mullova; Boston SO / Seiji Ozawa
Philips 464 741-2PM (66' · DDD)　　　Ⓜ
The Russian virtuoso's first disc heralded a formidable violinistic talent. Powerfully supported by Ozawa, Mullova gives a performance of intrepid expressive scope.

Sergey Khachatryan; Sinfonia Varsovia / Emmanuel Krivine
Naïve V4959 (70' · DDD)　　　Ⓕ
Armenian Sergey Khachatryan was just 15 when, in 2000, he became the youngest ever winner of the Sibelius Competition. He's already an exceptionally gifted musician, and this, his début concerto recording, has to be be heard.

Another fine coupling of this popular pair. Vadim Repin shows great imagination and technical flair.

Coupled with: Karelia Suite. Belshazzer's Feast.
Kuusisto vn **Helsinki Philharmonic Orchestra / Segerstam**
Ondine ODE878-2 (65' · DDD)　　　Ⓕ
There's nothing like the Helsinki orchestra in Sibelius – a performance with great character.

Symphonies

No 1 in E minor, Op 39 No 2 in D, Op 43 No 3 in C, Op 52 No 4 in A minor, Op 63 No 5 in E flat, Op 82 No 6 in D minor, Op 104 No 7 in C, Op 105

Complete Symphonies

Symphonies Nos 1-7. The Oceanides. Kuolema – Scene with cranes. Nightride and Sunrise[a]
City of Birmingham Symphony Orchestra, [a]Philharmonia Orchestra / Sir Simon Rattle
EMI ④ 764118-2 (267' · DDD)　　　Ⓜ**O**

Symphonies Nos 1-4 & 6 are also available on HMV Classics: HMV5 740602; HMV5 72319-2; HMV5 73048-2　　　Ⓑ

Simon Rattle's reissued Sibelius cycle is now accommodated on four mid-price CDs (as opposed to five full-priced ones), losing among the fill-ups only Kennedy's well-played account of the concerto. The first movement of Symphony No 1 is impressive; its epic quality is splendidly conveyed. You may be less taken with the slow movement: the rather mannered closing bars, not particularly acceptable in the concert hall, are distinctly worrying on disc. The measured tempo of the *Scherzo* is also a problem: it's slower than the metronome marking and the movement lacks fire. However, *The Oceanides* is the finest on disc. In the Second Symphony, Rattle's first movement is again on the slow side and the Trio section of the *Scherzo* is pulled about. The Fourth and Seventh find him at his finest and the magnificent EMI recording is very richly detailed and well defined.

The Fourth distils a powerful atmosphere in its opening pages; one is completely transported to its dark landscape with its seemingly limitless horizons. Only Beecham has surpassed Rattle in the slow movement.

Rattle's version of the Sixth is still among the best around, with tremendous grip and concentration. In both the Third and the Fifth he's equally impressive, although his handling of the celebrated transition in the first movement of the Fifth in his Philharmonia version is preferable (reviewed further on).

However, the inducement of *The Oceanides*, *Nightride and Sunrise* and an evocative account of the 'Scene with cranes' from *Kuolema* tips the scales in Rattle's favour.

Symphonies Nos 1-7
Philharmonia Orchestra / Vladimir Ashkenazy
Double Decca ② 455 402-2DF2 & ② 455 405-2DF2
(144' & 150' · ADD/DDD) Recorded 1980-96   Ⓜ**OO**

Of all the cycles of Sibelius's symphonies recorded in recent years this is one of the most consistently successful. Ashkenazy so well understands the thought processes that lie behind Sibelius's symphonic composition just as he's aware, and makes us aware, of the development between the Second and Third Symphonies. His attention to tempo is particularly acute and invariably he strikes just the right balance between romantic languor and urgency. The Philharmonia plays for all it's worth and possesses a fine body of sound. The recordings are remarkably consistent in quality and effectively complement the composer's original sound world.

Symphonies – selected

Symphonies Nos 1, 2 & 4. Karelia Suite. Finlandia
Philharmonia / Vladimir Ashkenazy
Double Decca ② 455 402-2DF2 (144' · DDD)
Recorded 1979, 1980, 1984   Ⓜ**O**

Vladimir Ashkenazy's account of the First Symphony is a strong one, arguably as successful artistically as it is in terms of recorded sound. It's well held together and finely shaped: it's every bit as committed as Simon Rattle's with his Birmingham orchestra but free from the occasional mannerism that disfigured that account. Ashkenazy is exactly on target in the *Scherzo* (dotted minim = 104), fractionally faster than Karajan and much more so than Rattle, who's far too measured here. The resultant sense of momentum is exhilarating.

The opening of the work is strongly projected and boldly contrasted with the movement which grows out of it. In fact, this movement has real grip – and a powerful sense of its own architecture. But throughout, the sheer physical excitement this score engenders is tempered by admirable control. Only at the end of the slow movement might you feel that Ashkenazy could have given it greater emotional restraint.

The playing of the Philharmonia is superb. The Fourth rather disappoints – one is left with a feeling that Ashkenazy could have wrung more from the desolate woodwind solos of the *Largo*. However, his *Karelia* and *Finlandia* are very good indeed. This set will give you hours of listening pleasure.

Symphony Nos 1 & 7
Helsinki Philharmonic Orchestra / Leif Segerstam
Ondine ODE1007-2 (59' · DDD)   Ⓕ**O**

This is an issue to rank alongside Segerstam's outstanding Helsinki PO coupling of the *Legends* and *Tapiola* (Ondine) in its pungent character and re-creative spark.

Segerstam's Seventh is well paced and keenly phrased, hitting real heights in the darkly boiling maelstrom beginning at 13 bars before fig L (9'53") and awe-inspiring culmination at fig Z (18'06"). His orchestra responds with zest and no mean poise. In fact, despite what sounds suspiciously like an edit at 15'50", this Seventh is one of the most imposing and highly charged of recent years. Bracing drama and a bold emotional scope are the keynotes to Segerstam's deeply pondered reading of the First Symphony. Assisted by alert and enthusiastic playing from his Helsinki band, he uncovers much illuminating detail within Sibelius' meticulous canvas, yet seldom to the detriment of the grander scheme. You may not agree with every interpretative decision, but Segerstam never sells the music short, revelling in its passion and often daring originality (sample the untamed fury of the *Allegro molto* material in the finale – nature red in tooth and claw). If Segerstam's strikingly pliable account lacks the thrust of, say, Vänskä's exhilarating Lahti SO performance, his Helsinki strings generate greater lyrical breadth.

True, the recording is very good rather than exceptional, but Segerstam is never dull and makes you listen.

Symphony No 2. Pohjola's Daughter, Op 49.   Ⓗ
Legends – No 2, The Swan of Tuonela; No 4,
Lemminkäinen's return. Finlandia
NBC Symphony Orchestra / Arturo Toscanini
Naxos Historical mono 8 110810 (76' · ADD)
Recorded live 1940   Ⓢ

As the symphony's finale builds to its apotheosis, you'll have to contend with trumpets that sound as if they more usually play at wedding parties for *The Godfather*. This is presumably how Toscanini liked his trumpets (and woodwinds and strings) to sound when singing, just as he liked them to deliver more forceful, rhythmical figures with a vengeance – the 'vengeance' perhaps a result of close microphones and/or little evidence of a hall acoustic. This means that if your notions of Nordic nobility in the symphony are gathered across the decades from recordings by Kajanus, Collins, Koussevitzky and Karajan, you should probably give Toscanini a wide berth. But then you'd be depriving yourself of perhaps the most dramatically intense and physically exciting performances of the symphony and *Pohjola's Daughter* ever recorded.

Symphonies Nos 2 & 3
Lahti Symphony Orchestra / Osmo Vänskä
BIS BISCD862 (76' · DDD)   Ⓕ

The first issue in the Sibelius cycle by Osmo Vänskä and the Lahti orchestra (Symphonies Nos 1 and 4) made a strong impression. Indeed it holds its own against the most exalted competition. The present set doesn't disappoint either: these artists are right inside this music.

First, the Second Symphony where competition is stiffest, with Karajan, Barbirolli and Colin Davis leading a field that includes Szell (Philips), Kletzki (EMI) and Ormandy (Sony). Admittedly it would have been preferable if Vänskä had set a slightly brisker tempo at the very opening, though he's not alone in the pace he adopts. Karajan and Sir Colin are equally measured. Kajanus took 8'14" over this movement and Sibelius's first biographer, the scholar-critic Erik Furuhjhelm, records that the composer took it even faster! Perhaps the briskest of all modern performances is Neeme Järvi and the Gothenburg Symphony Orchestra. Vänskä's reading is both powerfully wrought and well thought-out though there are some self-conscious touches. He pulls back a little too much at the *tranquillo* marking in the first movement (track 1, 4'31"), of which one becomes too aware. Elsewhere he makes one think afresh about the score. The F sharp major tune on the strings in the slow movement marked *ppp* is played as a barely audible whisper (track 2, 4'40") and so exaggerated does it seem that the wind four bars later sound (and are) much louder than the marked *pianissimo*. But these are minor matters in a performance marked by feeling and eloquence.

It's good to see the Third Symphony doing so well on record. Vänskä sets the right tempo for the first movement and gets the right atmosphere. The opening bars do not build up as powerfully as they do in the hands of the LSO and Sir Colin, and it's possible to feel a certain want of momentum in the slow movement by their side and in comparison with Kajanus's pioneering set. On the whole, however, this is a very good performance, well paced and full of perceptive touches. The sound is excellent and, exceptionally wide-ranging.

Symphonies Nos 2[a], 5[a] & 7[b]. Swanwhite[c] – **H**
The maidens with roses. Tapiola[d]. Pohjola's
Daughter[c]
[acd]**Boston Symphony Orchestra;**
[b]**BBC Symphony Orchestra / Koussevitzky**
Pearl ② GEMMCDS9408 (125' · ADD) Recorded
[b]1933 (live), [a]1935, [c]1936, [d]1939   Ⓕ**OOO**

 Among the great conductors closely identified in the public mind with Sibelius (Kajanus, Beecham and Karajan), ·Koussevitzky is the one whose star has faded. But if he hasn't acquired cult status, his claims on our allegiance is every bit as strong. In the 1930s and 1940s his reputation as a great Sibelius conductor was second to none. Less well known is that he was a relatively late convert to his cause: not until the mid-1920s was his enthusiasm really fired. In 1926, two years after he'd come to Boston, he presented the Seventh Symphony, and his celebrated recording was made seven years later, during his guest appearances with the BBC Symphony Orchestra. It remains the most electrifying performance ever

committed to disc, an account of extraordinary intensity and concentration. This new transfer gives it an exhilarating body and presence.

Koussevitzky recorded the Second Symphony in Boston two years later, in 1935, and then again in 1950. The present version of the work was the second to appear – Kajanus's pioneering account had been made in 1930 for Columbia. Koussevitzky's, however, is very different: the opening *allegretto* is far more measured and has the greater breadth, though one suspects that Kajanus was closer to Sibelius's intentions. The orchestral playing of the Boston Symphony is vastly superior, particularly the strings, which positively glow. Throughout this Boston performance there's a sustained feeling for line, a *tenuto* of remarkable quality and a sense of direction and power that are altogether exceptional. Koussevitzky's account of the Fifth Symphony has been surpassed in dramatic fire only by Toscanini, and *Pohjola's daughter* has the same wonderful sense of line Koussevitzky achieved in the Symphonies Nos 2 and 7.

The wonderfully concentrated and thrilling account of *Tapiola* is among the pantheon of great performances on record; such is its intensity that one wonders whether it has ever been surpassed, even by Beecham and Karajan. In Koussevitzky's hands the forests seem to howl in some kind of primaeval agony. His performance of 'The Maidens with roses' from *Swanwhite* is equally seductive. A marvellous set, superbly transferred.

Symphonies Nos 2 & 6
London Symphony Orchestra / Sir Colin Davis
RCA Victor Red Seal 09026 68218-2 (73' · DDD)
Recorded 1994   Ⓕ**OO**

The eloquent polyphony, purity of utterance and harmony of spirit give the Sixth Symphony a special place in the canon. Sibelius's mastery enables him to move with a freedom so complete that the musical events are dictated by their own inner necessity. And in Davis's hands this music unfolds with a freedom and naturalness that are totally convincing. As Sibelius said of the Fourth Symphony, this is music 'with nothing of the circus about it', and in this reading there's no playing to the gallery.

There's no playing to the gallery either in Sir Colin's account of the Second. He views the work as a whole and doesn't invest detail with undue expressive vehemence at its expense, but strikes just the right balance between the nationalist-romantic inheritance on the one side and the classical power of Sibelius's thinking on the other. The first movement has dignity and breadth, and as with Karajan (EMI), the pacing of climaxes is magisterial. The recording has splendid presence and space.

Symphonies[a] Nos 3 & 5.   **H**
March of the Finnish Jaeger Battalion, Op 91 No 1[b]
[a]**London Symphony Orchestra;** [b]**Helsinki**

Philharmonic Orchestra / Robert Kajanus
Koch Historic mono 37133-2 (62' · ADD) Recorded
1928-33 Ⓜ️Ⓞ

Finlandia has already reissued all Kajanus's
London recordings on a three-disc set. That
edition contains transfers made by Anthony
Griffith for World Records, issued in the 1970s,
and they still sound very good indeed. Griffith
had the advantage of working from original
masters: Koch's Mark Obert-Thorn has been
obliged to use commercial pressings and while
he has obtained good sound, there's inevitably
more background noise and an unevenness in
the quality which isn't present in Finlandia's
transfers. However, Koch has scored an important point by including Kajanus's only Sibelius
recording with his own Helsinki orchestra. The
piece itself is perhaps the composer's weakest,
but the performance has great historical importance, for it's played by an orchestra with which
Sibelius had close links, and under a conductor
who was his chosen interpreter. We can hear
clearly just why Sibelius admired Kajanus so
much in the two symphonies here. At the age of
76 he was still able to generate a good deal of
tension and energy in the London Symphony
Orchestra's playing, yet there's a particular
sense of balanced, logical music-making, a
seemingly natural authority in the phrasing and
an apparent inevitability in the way he unfolds
the composer's symphonic argument. Everything seems perfectly in place, and the music
speaks to us in a very direct and compelling
fashion.

Symphonies Nos 4 & 7. Kuolema – Valse triste
**Berlin Philharmonic Orchestra / Herbert von
Karajan**
DG Galleria 439 527-2GGA (66' · ADD) Recorded
1965-7 Ⓜ️ⓄⓄ

Karajan recorded the Fourth Symphony three
times, once in the 1950s with the Philharmonia
and twice with the Berlin Philharmonic. The
work obviously meant a great deal to him. He
insisted on its inclusion in his very first concert
on his appointment at the Berlin Philharmonic
in the early 1960s at a time when Sibelius's cause
had few champions in Germany, so keen was he
to stake its claim as one of the great symphonies
of the day. Karajan's account has withstood the
test of time as one of the most searching, profound and concentrated performances of this
masterpiece, and its reappearance at mid price
was very welcome. The Seventh is finer than his
earlier Philharmonia version but doesn't enjoy
quite the same classic status. Karajan's *Valse
triste* is wonderfully seductive. Indispensable!

Symphonies Nos 4 & 7ᵃ.
Pelléas et Mélisande, Op 46. Swanwhite, Op 54.
Tempest – Dance of the Nymphs. Tapiola, Op 112
**Royal Philharmonic Orchestra / Sir Thomas
Beecham** Ⓗ

BBC Legends/IMG Artists ② BBCL4041-2
(139' · ADD) Recorded live ᵃ1954, 1955. Includes
Beecham on Sibelius, broadcast 1955 Ⓜ️Ⓞ

In a broadcast concert to mark Sibelius's 90th
birthday on December 8, 1955, the RPO under
Sir Thomas Beecham (friend of the composer
for nearly 50 years and one of his doughtiest
champions) played to a capacity Royal Festival
Hall. The inclusion here of the British and
Finnish national anthems, both stirringly done,
recreates the necessary sense of occasion. In the
delightful, too rarely encountered *Swanwhite*
suite, from which Beecham omits the powerfully sombre fifth movement ('The Prince
alone'), one may at first miss his characteristic
concentration and charisma, but his leisurely,
affectionate rendering grows on one. Orchestral
discipline takes a dip with the Fourth Symphony, but far more disconcerting is the all-pervading air of loose-limbed impatience: the
opening *Tempo molto moderato, quasi adagio* is
wayward and fussy. There are glimpses of greatness in the third movement (the strings at the
climax have a refulgent warmth about them), as
well as some effective dynamic emendations in
the finale, but overall it's a curiously uninvolv-
ing display.

Only in the concert's second half does this legendary partnership really begin to show what
it's capable of. The *Pelléas* suite distils a poetic
enchantment (try the ineffably touching
'Mélisande') and tingling sense of atmosphere
that not only make you forget about the maddeningly bronchial audience, but also act as a
timely reminder that these artists' glorious studio recording dates from exactly the same
period (EMI – unavailable at present). *Tapiola* is
even finer, a performance of giant authority,
devastating emotional candour and towering
humanity – indeed Beecham's most powerful
Tapiola currently available. As an encore, the
fetching 'Dance of the Nymphs' from *The Tempest* is delectably done. As a substantial bonus
there's a radiantly moving Sibelius Seventh
from the 1954 Proms, and a personable, at times
entertainingly scatty talk on Sibelius and his
music by the inimitable maestro recorded for
the BBC's Third Programme two weeks before
that 90th-birthday concert. A mandatory purchase for the frequently spellbinding contents
of disc 2 alone.

Symphony No 5 (original 1915 version). En saga
(original 1892 version)
Lahti Symphony Orchestra / Osmo Vänskä
BIS BISCD800 (58' · DDD) Ⓕ ⓄⓄⓄ

 Every so often a CD appears which, by
means of some interpretative insight,
changes our view of a piece of music.
This disc changes our whole perspective in a
wholly different sense, for it gives us a glimpse
of two familiar masterpieces in the making.
Sibelius struggled with the Fifth Symphony for
almost seven years from about 1912 until it

SIBELIUS'S SYMPHONY NO 5 – IN BRIEF

London SO / Robert Kajanus
Koch Historic 37133-2 (62' · ADD)　　　Ⓜ●
Kajanus was one of the composer's favourite interpreters of his music. What this pioneering 1932 recording may lack in refinement is more than made up for by the subtlety and electric charge of the conductor's purposeful direction.

Boston SO / Serge Koussevitzky
Naxos Historical 8 110170 (71' · ADD)　　　Ⓢ
A performance of boundless integrity and pedigree, notable for its painstaking attention to detail and astonishing depth of string tone. The 1936 recording has impressive body and bloom in this new transfer.

Berlin PO / Herbert von Karajan
DG ② 457 748-2GOR2 (149' · ADD)　　　Ⓜ●●
Karajan always had the measure of this great symphony and this famous 1965 recording for DG is by common consent one of the pinnacles of his recorded legacy.

Philharmonia Orchestra / Vladimir Ashkenazy
Decca ② 455 405-2DF2 (150' · DDD)　　　Ⓜ
By no means a first choice artistically, but Decca's Kingsway Hall sound is just stunning. Excellently played, Ashkenazy's fresh-faced performance gives little cause for complaint.

Philharmonia Orchestra / Sir Simon Rattle
EMI 764737-2 (78' · DDD)　　　Ⓜ●●
Rattle was still in his mid-twenties when he taped this unerringly paced and finely disciplined account of the Fifth. With its substantial Nielsen couplings, here's an enormously attractive reissue.

City of Birmingham SO / Sir Simon Rattle
EMI 749717-2 (62' · DDD)　　　Ⓕ
Rattle's Birmingham remake is fascinatingly different from his 1982 predecessor in its fleeter, more animated manners. Coupled with Rattle's invigorating 1987 account of the Sibelius Concerto with Nigel Kennedy.

Lahti SO / Osmo Vänskä
BIS BIS-CD800 (58' · DDD)　　　Ⓕ●●●
✷ This BIS issue is a model of rewarding enterprise, coupling the Fifth in the second of its three versions from 1915 with *En Saga* in its original 1892 guise. Exemplary performances and production values.

Iceland SO / Petri Sakari
Naxos 8 554377 (69' · DDD)　　　Ⓢ
If the pennies are in short supply, then this likeable account from Reykjavík should prove just the ticket. Alert and enthusiastic playing from the Iceland SO under Petri Sakari, and very good sound to boot.

reached its definitive form in 1919. Although the finished score of the first version doesn't survive, the orchestral material does, so it was not difficult to reconstruct the score.

To study how the two scores differ is to learn something important about the creative process and it's this mystery that makes this disc imperative listening – and not just for Sibelians. The four-movement 1915 score has a more complex harmonic language than the final score and so it provides a missing link, as it were, between the Fourth Symphony and the definitive Fifth. The opening horn motive has yet to emerge, and the finale's coda has yet to acquire its hammer-blow chords. And in between you'll find that the various themes, some distinctly recognisable, others taking off in totally unexpected directions and charting unknown regions.

The version of *En saga* with we're familiar with doesn't come between the *Kullervo* Symphony and the *Karelia* music, but from 1901, between the First and Second Symphonies and was made for Busoni.

The original offers fascinating material for comparison: there's a brief glimpse of Bruckner, whose work he had encountered in Vienna a year or two earlier, and the orchestral writing, though not always as polished as in the later version, still has flair. Praise to the Lahti orchestra and their fine conductor, and the excellent and natural balance.

Symphonies Nos 6 & 7. Tapiola, Op 112
Lahti Symphony Orchestra / Osmo Vänskä
BIS BISCD864 (68' · DDD)　　　Ⓕ●●

The Lahti orchestra bring total dedication to these great scores, and Osmo Vänskä is a Sibelian of substance. With this account of the Sixth and Seventh he brings his survey to a triumphant conclusion. Indeed this is every bit as impressive as the First and Fourth. To the Sixth Symphony he brings total concentration: a serene slow movement but a very fast Scherzo and tautly held-together finale. The Seventh is finely conceived and paced and though the Lahti orchestra aren't the equal of the Finnish RSO for Saraste or the Helsinki PO for Berglund (both conductors fine Sibelians), directed by Vänskä they give the more compelling and convincing performances. *Tapiola* is thrilling: atmospheric and powerfully built up and though it doesn't displace Karajan, Koussevitzky or Beecham, it's a measure of its splendour and power – and the terror it evokes – that it invites only the most exalted comparisons. In the Sixth Symphony one wouldn't want to be without either Sir Colin Davis, the Beecham or any of the Karajan versions, and for the Seventh the roll-call must certainly include Koussevitzky's seminal account, as well as both Sir Colin's Boston and LSO accounts. This is an impressive issue. The recorded sound is in the first flight, and there are excellent notes by Andrew Barnett.

Symphonies Nos 6 & 7. The Tempest – Suite No 2,
Op 109
Iceland Symphony Orchestra / Petri Sakari
Naxos 8 554387 (71' · DDD)   Ⓢ

A most enjoyable conclusion to Petri Sakari's
Sibelius symphony cycle. Sakari's Sixth
impresses by dint of its unpretentious honesty
and quiet cogency. As on previous instalments
within this series, the Icelanders respond with a
keen fervour as contagious as it's heartwarming.
Their woodwind roster comprises an especially
personable bunch, and if the strings inevitably
lack that very last ounce of tonal clout and sheer
composure provided by, say, Karajan's Berlin
Philharmonic or the San Francisco Symphony
under Blomstedt – to name but two of the
strongest rivals – there's no missing the touching expressive warmth they bring to the work's
transcendental closing pages. In Sakari's hands
both outer movements develop real fire and
purpose, and he uncovers plenty of happy detail
along the way – the distinctive colouring of the
bass clarinet being one of this performance's
chief pleasures.

Sakari's Seventh, too, is very good indeed,
patient and imaginative in the manner of
Vänskä, or Sanderling's much underrated, irresistibly sinewy 1974 recording with the Berlin
Symphony Orchestra. Perhaps the Iceland
Symphony's principal trombonist could have
been just a touch more assertive for that heroic
initial solo six bars after fig C, and the timpanist
appears to enter a bar late just before fig E, but
the only sizeable niggle concerns Sakari's not-
quite-seamless handling of that tricky *Poco a poco
affrettando* transition passage into the *Vivacissimo* section beginning at fig J, itself not entirely
free of a certain breathless fluster. All this means
that Sakari's conception as a whole isn't as
thrillingly inevitable an experience as Koussevitzky's, Maazel's (a magnificent reading,
sounding fresher than ever on a new Decca Legends compilation) or Boult's masterly 1963 concert relay with the RPO. That said, Sakari
builds the shattering *Largamente* climax at fig Z
superbly, and the closing bars are exceptionally
fine. Not a front-runner, perhaps, but no mean
achievement all the same. Well worth investigating at Naxos price.

Additional recommendations

Symphonies Nos 1-4
Helsinki Philharmonic Orchestra / Berglund
EMI Double Forte ② 568643-2 (140' · DDD)   Ⓜ
Berglund's Sibelius is always worth listening to;
few conductors have such experience in this music.
Quite a bargain!

Symphonies No 5-7
Coupled with: The Oceanides. Finlandia. Tapiola
Helsinki Philharmonic Orchestra / Berglund
EMI Double Forte ② 568646-2 (112' · DDD)   Ⓜ
The other half of Berglund's 1980s Sibelius cycle.
Notable for its rugged intensity.

Symphony No 7
Coupled with: **Schubert** Symphony No 8. **Bizet** Jeux
d'enfants – excerpts. **Ravel** Daphnis et Chloé
Royal Philharmonic Orchestra / Boult
BBC Music Legends/IMG Artists BBCL4039-2
(75' · ADD)   Ⓜ
Boult iasn't a conductor you'd immediately
associate with Sibelius, but this honest reading
forms part of a highly enticing concert.

Symphonies Nos 1, 2, 4 & 5
Boston Symphony Orchestra / C Davis
Philips Duo ② 446 157-2PM2 (154' · ADD)   Ⓜ
Davis's late-1970s Boston Sibelius cycle has many
admirers, and should entrance a new generation of
music-lovers in this competitive reissue.

Symphonies Nos 3, 6 & 7
Coupled with: Violin Concerto. Finlandia. Tapiola.
Legends, 'Lemminkäinen Suite', Op 22
Accardo vn **Boston Symphony Orchestra; London
Symphony Orchestra / C Davis**
Philips Duo 446 160-2PM2 ② (146' · ADD)   Ⓜ
The second half of the cycle. The symphonies
have a wonderful sheen and the couplings are
particularly generous.

Symphonies Nos 2, 3 & 5
Coupled with: Valse Triste. Andante festivo.
Oslo Philharmonic Orchestra / Jansons
EMI Double Forte ② 575 673-2 (DDD)   Ⓜ
A beautiful performance of the Second Symphony,
full of incidental detail and given a majestic, aristo-
cratic sweep. The Third is just as fine – masses of
detail and some superb playing.

Symphony No 2
Coupled with: Romance for Strings
Gothenburg Symphony Orchestra / Järvi
BIS CD252 (DDD)   Ⓕ
This is a performance full of sinew and fire. Fast
and vigorous in the first movement, the orchestra
play with tremendous commitment.

Symphonies Nos 4-7.
Coupled with: The Swan of Tuonela. Tapiola
Berlin Philharmonic Orchestra / Karajan
DG The Originals ② 457 748-2GOR2 (ADD)   Ⓜ

Symphonies Nos 5 & 6
Coupled with: Legends, 'Lemminkäinen Suite', Op 22
Berlin Philharmonic Orchestra / Karajan
DG Galleria 439 982-2GGA (69' · ADD)   Ⓜ
Karajan's glorious account of the Sixth remains,
for some, unsurpassed. His DG Berlin Fifth is also
very fine and indisputably the best of his four
accounts.

Symphonies Nos 1 & 3
Iceland Symphony Orchestra / Sakari
Naxos 8 554102 (68' · DDD)   Ⓢ
Well worth considering for those on a budget.
Good, committed playing from the Iceland SO.

Symphonies Nos 6 & 7
Coupled with: Nightride and Sunrise
Berlin Symphony Orchestra / Sanderling
Berlin Classics 0092 812BC (70' · DDD)   Ⓜ
A coupling that enjoys quite a following among
informed Sibelians. By no means mainstream but
worth exploring.

En saga, Op 9

En saga, Op 9. Night Ride and Sunrise, Op 55. The
Dryad, Op 45 No 1. Dance-Intermezzo, Op 45 No 2.
Pohjola's Daughter, Op 49. The Bard, Op 64. The
Oceanides, Op 73
Lahti Symphony Orchestra / Osmo Vänskä
BIS BIS-CD1225 (76' · DDD)   Ⓕ**OOO**

 Anyone who has already encountered
the Lahti/Vänskä partnership in
Sibelius will know to expect performances of great vitality and freshness. And the
expectation is fully met – perhaps even surpassed; in these tone poems he simply allows his
profound grasp of musical inner workings to
dictate the course of events. The trenchant
Lahti strings, the ecstatically floating woodwind
and the rasping brass all play their part. But
while their contributions are gripping in their
own right, they're the more impressive for
being so precisely placed at the service of the
music's larger-scale unfolding.

Each of the longer works feels as though composer and performers alike have imagined them
in one huge mental breath. Vänskä knows
exactly when and how much to hold back, when
to push on, and, crucially, when simply to stand
back and let the music tick over to the beat of
some higher rhythm. The same sense of
inevitability informs the more compact masterpieces – *The Dryad* and the extraordinarily cryptic *The Bard*. Only the *Dance-Intermezzo*, companion piece to *The Dryad*, is in any way
negligible.

All the other tone poems have been recorded
many times over, but rarely with such a consistent feeling of idiomatic rightness. (Vänskä
himself has recorded the 1892 original version
of *En Saga* as well – coupled with the original
Fifth Symphony on a *Gramophone* Award-winning set, reviewed under Symphony No 5 – and
a fascinating contrast it makes with the more
compact 1902 revision offered here.) BIS's
recording is of demonstration quality. An outstanding release.

Additional recommendations

En Saga

Coupled with: Tapiola. Spring Song. Scenes with
Cranes. Canzonetta. Valse romantique. The Bard.
Valse triste
Claesson *cl* **Gothenburg Symphony Orchestra /
Järvi**
DG 457 654-2GH (71' · DDD)   Ⓕ
You're always in safe musical hands with Neeme
Järvi, and his Sibelius never fails to please. The
Gothenburgers plays these short pieces with great
charm and panache.

Coupled with: Tapiola. The Bard. The Oceanides.
Pohjola's Daughter
Iceland Symphony Orchestra / Sakari
Naxos 8 555299 (70' · DDD: rec c2001)   Ⓢ

En Saga unfolds with enviable naturalness and
vigour, yet the dusky mystery of the coda is also
very well conveyed. *Tapiola*, too, receives a
stimulating interpretation, with a gripping climax
to its famous storm.

Karelia Suite, Op 11

Karelia Suite. Incidental music – King Christian II;
Pelleas and Melisande (all original versions)
Anna-Lisa Jakobsson *mez* **Raimo Laukka** *bar* **Lahti
Symphony Orchestra / Osmo Vänskä**
BIS CD918 (78' · DDD) Texts and translations included
                                                    Ⓕ

Sibelius supplied four numbers for the February
1898 Helsinki première of Adolf Paul's historical drama *King Christian II* – the 'Minuet', 'The
Fool's Song', 'Elegy' and 'Musette' – and these
eventually took their place in the five-movement concert suite alongside the 'Nocturne',
'Serenade' and 'Ballade' which the composer
completed the same summer. The street music
of the 'Musette' is simply delightful in its original garb without added strings, and in both the
'Serenade' and 'Ballade' Vänskä uncovers
strong thematic and stylistic links with the
almost exactly contemporaneous First Symphony. The defiant quality these fine artists
bring to 'The Fool's Song' (eloquently delivered by Raimo Laukka) is also very likeable.
Music-making of refreshing perception and
meticulous sensitivity similarly illuminates this
first complete recording of Sibelius's original
incidental music for a 1905 production of
Maeterlinck's symbolist play (the venue was
again Helsinki's Swedish Theatre). There are
10 numbers in all.

The performance of the *Karelia Suite* in its
original scoring (which acts as a splendid curtain-raiser here) has been compiled from Vänskä's complete recording of the original *Karelia*
music. Both outer movements have a real sense
of pageantry about them (Vänskä directs with
exhilaratingly clean-limbed swagger), though
there are certain reservations about his
occasional predilection for exaggerated and
affected *pianopianissimos*. Thus, at around 3'30"
in the central 'Ballade' (track 2), the dynamic
level drops almost below the threshold of audibility and has you rushing to boost the volume
control (Vänskä repeats this trick twice in the
King Christian II 'Elegy', and towards the end of
the final number in *Pelléas*). For optimum
results, therefore, playback needs to be higher
than many listeners may think reasonable. That
said, the engineering is quite spectacularly
truthful throughout and there's no doubt that
this is an unusually absorbing collection.

The Wood Nymph, Op 15

The Wood Nymph, Op 15. The Wood Nymph
(melodrama). A lonely ski-trail. Swanwhite, Op 54 –
incidental music (original version)
Lasse Pöysti *narr* **Lahti Symphony Orchestra /**

Osmo Vänskä
BIS CD815 (62' · DDD).   ⒡●

Although most Sibelians will know of the tone-poem, *The Wood Nymph*, they won't have heard it, as the score has remained in Helsinki University Library. It opens very much in *Karelia* mode, and as one might expect, inhabits much the same world as the Lemminkäinen *Legends*. Though it's less developed than the 1892 *En saga*, let alone the *Legends* in their definitive form, it still bears the characteristic Sibelian hallmarks. This disc gives us an opportunity to put it alongside the melodrama of the same name, scored for speaker, horn, strings and piano. This is a setting of the mainland-Swedish poet, Viktor Rydberg, best known in the Sibelius context for *Autumn Evening* ('Höstkväll').

Not content with these interesting novelties, the CD also gives us two other works new to the catalogue, another short melodrama, *A lonely ski-trail* to words by Bertel Gripenberg, which in its piano form dates from 1925 and which Sibelius scored for harp and strings as late as 1948, a short, slight and atmospheric piece; and above all, the complete incidental music to Strindberg's *Swanwhite*. The score runs to some 30 minutes and is full of that special light and sense of space characteristic of *Pelleas and Melisande*. The playing of the Lahti orchestra under Osmo Vänskä is excellent and the recording, too, is very fine: spacious and refined.

Legends (Lemminkäinen Suite), Op 22

Legends. En Saga, Op 9
Swedish Radio Symphony Orchestra / Mikko Franck
Ondine ODE953-2 (74' · DDD)   ⒡●●

Mikko Franck presides over the most intrepidly individual and pungently characterful performance of the Lemminkäinen *Legends* since Leif Segerstam's 1995 Helsinki PO account for this same label. Clocking in at an eyebrow-raising 53'48" overall, Franck's conception evinces an unhurried authority, a generous expressive scope and a richly stocked imagination remarkable in one so young.

Lemminkäinen and the Maidens of the Island unfolds in especially gripping fashion here. Even more than Segerstam, Franck takes an extraordinarily long-breathed, flexible view of this heady tableau, imparting an unashamedly sensual voluptuousness to the secondary material in particular. It's a risky, impulsive approach, but one that pays high dividends in terms of intoxicating sweep, brazen ardour and, well, sheer daring. Both *The Swan of Tuonela* (which, in a refreshing change from the norm these days, Franck places second, according to Sibelius's final wishes) and *Lemminkäinen in Tuonela* combine dark-hued grandeur with tingling atmosphere, the latter's haunting A minor

central episode handled with particular perception. True, *Lemminkäinen's Return* lacks something in animal excitement, but its unruffled sense of purpose, rhythmic spring and sinewy, clean-cut textures serve up plenty of food for thought none the less.

The *Legends* are preceded by an uncommonly fresh *En Saga*, brimming with watchful sensitivity and interpretative flair, and once again studded with revelatory detail. Throughout, the Swedish RSO responds with heartwarming application and genuine enthusiasm, audibly galvanised by Franck's fervent, always invigorating direction. The engineering, too, is very good, without perhaps being absolutely in the top flight.

An auspicious recording début, then, from a young artist of clearly prodigious potential.

Legends. Karelia Suite, Op 11. Finlandia, Op 26
Iceland Symphony Orchestra / Petri Sakari
Naxos 8 554265 (73' · DDD)   Ⓢ Ⓢ●

Most impressive. In its keen intelligence, fiery snap and thrust, Petri Sakari's account of the four *Legends* proves more than a match for the finest. The Iceland SO may not be world-beaters, but they respond to their thoughtful young Finnish maestro's illuminating direction with clean-limbed zest and commitment to the cause (their winds are an especially personable bunch).

Perhaps the highlight of the new set is *Lemminkäinen in Tuonela*, which, like Segerstam and Salonen before him, Sakari places second (reverting to the composer's original scheme), and where he distils a relentless concentration and pin-sharp focus (only Segerstam is more gripping in this brooding essay). No one should miss out on the heady opulence of Ormandy's magnificent Philadelphia strings in those glorious singing lines of *Lemminkäinen and the maidens of the island*, but the Icelanders play their hearts out, and anyway Sakari gives a dramatic reading of bold contrasts and strong symphonic cohesion. No grumbles, either, about *The Swan of Tuonela* or *Lemminkäinen's Homeward Journey* which is firmly controlled, dashingly detailed and genuinely exciting (as opposed to merely excitable).

Sakari's rewarding *Legends* comes very near the top of the heap alongside (though, ultimately, not ahead of) Segerstam, Saraste and Ormandy. In the popular couplings, Sakari's unhackneyed approach once again pays dividends, though his unusually brisk (and ever-so-slightly hectic) tempo for the main portion of the *Karelia* Suite's opening Intermezzo isn't always convincing . None the less, this is quite a bargain. Eminently pleasing sound, too: free of gimmickry and tonally very true.

Legends. Tapiola, Op 112
Helsinki Philharmonic Orchestra / Leif Segerstam
Ondine ODE852-2 (70' · DDD)   ⒡●

SIBELIUS TAPIOLA – IN BRIEF

Helsinki PO / Leif Segerstam
Ondine ODE852-2   Ⓕ
The Helsinki orchestra have just the perfect
sound for Sibelius, and naturally they play
with a total grasp of the idiom. Segerstam can
be a willful Sibelian, but he unfurls this glorious piece with a winning simplicity.

**Royal Philharmonic Orchestra / Sir Thomas
Beecham**
BBC Legends BBCL4041-2   ⒻO
Recorded in 1955 this shows what a great
Sibelian Beecham was: this is his finest
version of *Tapiola*, an interpretation of
colossal emotional weight and scope.

Lahti Symphony Orchestra / Osmo Vänskä
BIS BIS-CD864   ⒻOO
Joining the Sixth and Seventh Symphonies,
Vanska's *Tapiola* receives an extraordinarily
intense performance with fine playing from
his loyal Lahti band. Top-class BIS sound.

Philharmonia Orchestra / Vladimir Ashkenazy
Decca 452 576-2DF2   ⓂO
A really tremendous performance that gives
this atmospheric work a colossal emotional
charge. Ashkenazy has clearly absorbed much
of the Finnish spirit oin his many visits to the
country and it certainy shows in this powerful
vision of *Tapiola*.

Boston SO / Sir Colin Davis
Philips 446 160-2PM2   Ⓜ
Paired with Symphonies Nos 5 and 6, this is
Sibelius playing with a strong and loyal following: the Boston orchestra have a really
alluring sound in this music and Davis is
totally in his element.

**Berlin Philharmonic Orchestra /
Herbert von Karajan**
DG 457 748-2GOR2   ⓂOO
Coupled with Symphonies Nos 4-7 (includ-
ing a magnificent No 6), this *Tapiola* from the
mid-1960s remains for many unsurpassed
evoking the mood of the Nordic forests.
Glorious, rich tone from the BPO

Gothenburg SO / Neeme Järvi
DG 475 634-2GH   Ⓕ
Neeme Järvi is an excellent guide in the
music of Sibelius, and with his superb
Gothenburg orchestra on fine form, this is an
impressive performance.

Iceland Symphony Orchestra / Petri Sakari
Naxos 8 555299   Ⓢ
A fine collection of shorter Sibelius works
contains this excellent performance of *Tapiola*, with a particularly gripping account as
the storm reaches its powerful climax.

The four *Legends* first began to surface in
Sibelius's mind in 1893, at the same time as he
was working on his *Kalevala* opera, *The Building
of the Boat*, the prelude to which became *The
swan of Tuonela*. It isn't the only thing from the
opera that found its way into the *Legends*. The
lovely A minor idea for muted strings in the
middle section of *Lemminkäinen in Tuonela* is
also among the sketches, where Sibelius scrib-
bled over it the words, 'the Maiden of Death'. In
the opera she would have rowed Väinämöinen
across the river to Tuonela. In the tone-poem
she symbolises the very opposite, the loving
mother whose ministrations return Lemminkäinen to life. In 1954 Sibelius reversed the order
of the inner movements so that *The swan* preceded *Lemminkäinen in Tuonela*. Segerstam disregards the composer's wishes and places them
in the old order; there's a case for this – you otherwise have two highly dramatic pieces
(*Lemminkäinen in Tuonela* and *Lemminkäinen's
Homeward Journey*) placed alongside each other.
Segerstam gets very good results from the
Helsinki orchestra, which responds with a keen
enthusiasm that's inspiriting. The performance
is free from excessive mannerisms, and his
account of *Tapiola* is very impressive. He
tellingly evokes the chilling terrors and awesome majesty of the Nordic forest.

Finlandia, Op 26

Finlandia, Op 26ᵃ. Karelia Suite, Op 11ᵃ. Tapiola, Op
112ᵃ. En Sagaᵃ. Luonnotar, Op 70ᵃ. Pohjola's
Daughter, Op 49ᵇ. Nightride and Sunrise, Op 55ᵇ.
Legends, 'Lemminkäinen Suite', Op 22ᵇ
ᵃPhilharmonia Orchestra / Vladimir Ashkenazy;
ᵇOrchestra de la Suisse Romande / Horst Stein
Double Decca ② 452 576-2DF2 (DDD/ADD)
ᵃRecorded 1980-85   ⓂO

Ashkenazy makes a superb job of *Finlandia*,
which boasts some of the most vibrant, powerful
brass sounds on disc.
  More than 30 years separate *En Saga* and *Tapiola*, yet both works are quintessential Sibelius.
The latter is often praised for the way Sibelius
avoided 'exotic' instruments, preferring instead
to draw new and inhuman sounds from the
more standard ones; and the former is, in many
ways, just as striking in the way the orchestration evokes wind, strange lights, vast expanses
and solitude. Both works suggest a dream-like
journey: *En Saga* non-specific, though derived
from Nordic legend; *Tapiola* more of an airborne nightmare in, above and around the
mighty giants of the Northern forests inhabited
by the Green Man of the Kalevala, the forest
god Tapio (the final amen of slow, bright major
chords brings a blessed release!). Ashkenazy's
judgement of long-term pacing is very acute;
the silences and shadows are as potent here as
the wildest hurricane. And Decca's sound allows
you to visualise both the wood and the trees;
every detail of Sibelius's sound world is caught
with uncanny presence, yet the overall orchestral image is coherent and natural.

Humoresques, Opp 87 and 89

Humoresques Nos 1-6, Opp 87 & 89. Two Serenades,
Op 69. Two Pieces, Op 77. Overture in E. Ballet
scene
Dong-Suk Kang vn **Gothenburg Symphony
Orchestra / Neeme Järvi**
BIS CD472 (62' · DDD) Recorded 1989   ⒻO

The music for violin and orchestra here is marvellously rewarding and gloriously played. The
six *Humoresques*, Opp 87 and 89 come from the
same period as the Fifth Symphony, at a time
when Sibelius was toying with the idea of a second violin concerto, and some of the material of
the *Humoresques* was possibly conceived with a
concerto in mind. Sibelius wrote that these radiant pieces convey something of 'the anguish of
existence, fitfully lit up by the sun', and behind
their outward elegance and charm, there's an
all-pervasive sadness. This is even more intense
in the *Serenades*, which are glorious pieces and
quintessential Sibelius. Dong-Suk Kang is an
outstanding player. His impeccable technique
and natural musical instinct serve this repertoire
well and he seems to have established an excellent rapport with Järvi and the Gothenburg
orchestra. The two fill-ups are juvenilia and are
only intermittently characteristic. The Overture is very much in his *Karelia* idiom, though
they're of undoubted interest to all Sibelians.
The recording up to BIS's usual high quality.

Pelleas and Melisande, Op 46

Cassazione, Op 6. Pelleas and Melisande, Op 46.
Suite mignonne, Op 98a. Suite champêtre, Op 98b.
Suite caractéristique, Op 100. Presto
Tapiola Sinfonietta / Tuomas Ollila
Ondine ODE952-2 (56' · DDD)   Ⓕ

Don't let the low opus number hoodwink you:
Cassazione dates from 1904 and was first given
under Sibelius's baton at the same Helsinki concert as the première of the first version of the
Violin Concerto. Revised the following year but
never published, it's well worth hearing, containing as it does echoes of both *Pelleas and
Melisande* and the Second Symphony's finale.
The dashing *Presto* began life as the third movement of Sibelius's Op 4 String Quartet in B flat
of 1889-90, and was subsequently transcribed
for string orchestra in 1894. The three suites
date from 1921-2. True, the *Suite caractéristique*
serves up a pretty thin brew, but both the *Suite
mignonne* and *Suite champêtre* contain their fair
share of felicities and are delightfully scored.

These performances from Tuomas Ollila and
the Tapiola Sinfonietta evince a bracing, unsentimental thrust and high degree of technical finish, though some will crave more in the way of
affectionate charm and tingling atmosphere.
However, it's in the *Pelleas and Melisande* incidental music that these newcomers truly throw
down the gauntlet. There's no hint of the customary portentous grandeur in Ollila's 'At the

Castle Gate', a nervy urgency that resurfaces
with a vengeance in 'Melisande at the Spinning
Wheel' and the ensuing 'Entr'acte'. Elsewhere,
those screaming winds and *sul ponticello* strings
at the heart of 'At the Seashore' set one's teeth
on edge, while textures throughout are uncommonly transparent. What's missing is any real
sense of poignancy or pathos: 'The Death of
Melisande' is very cool, the characteristically
bleached string timbre emphasising the disconcertingly pristine, self-conscious mood. An
intriguing and intelligent re-think, then, but
not to all tastes (anyone brought up on, say,
Beecham will be in for a shock). Crystal-clear,
slightly clinical sound.

Swanwhite, Op 54

Swanwhite, Op 54. Scènes historiques – Suite No 1,
Op 25; Suite No 2, Op 66. Belshazzar's Feast,
Op 51 – Suite
Norwegian Radio Orchestra / Ari Rasilainen
Finlandia 0927-41935-2 (74' · DDD)   ⒻO

Here we have a particularly generous selection
of Sibelius's extensive output of incidental
music, played with a rather special freshness and
sensitivity that makes each of the 17 movements
feel like a miniature masterpiece.

Sibelius derived the first set of *Scènes historiques* from his *Press Celebrations Music* of 1899,
the series of tableaux that concluded with 'Finland Awakes', later to be turned into *Finlandia*.
The second set is a very different affair, consisting of original pieces added in 1912, more
abstract in feeling than the first set and strongly
connected to the Fourth Symphony of the previous year and to the symphonies still to come.
Belshazzar's Feast was a play by Hjalmar Procopé, mounted in Helsinki in November 1906.
The 11 numbers of Sibelius's score have been
recorded in their entirety (superbly by Osmo
Vänskä on BIS), but the four-movement concert suite here recorded picks out the shiniest
gems. Shortly afterwards Sibelius supplied 14
musical numbers for Strindberg's *Swanwhite*, a
kind of *Pelleas and Melisande* with a happy ending. This is one of his most powerful theatre
scores, marvellously economical yet telling in
each tiniest gesture.

Throughout this excellently recorded CD the
playing is precise and idiomatic, with that elusive blend of transparency and warmth that still
comes most naturally to Nordic orchestras and
conductors. If the coupling suits, or if you're
looking for just one disc as a sampler of
Sibelius's music for the theatre, you shouldn't
hesitate.

Violin Works

Five Pieces, Op 81. Novelette, Op 102. Five Danses
champêtres, Op 106. Four Pieces, Op 115. Three
Pieces, Op 116
Nils-Erik Sparf vn **Bengt Forsberg** pf

Sibelius Vocal

BIS CD625 (57' · DDD) Recorded 1993 Ⓕ Ⓞ

No one listening to this music would doubt that Sibelius had a special feeling for the violin. Whether he's composing lighter music such as the captivating 'Rondino' from the Op 81 set or the more substantial later pieces, such as the first of the *Danses champêtres*, which comes close to the world of *The Tempest*. Neither the Op 115 nor the Op 116 set contains great music but they're much finer than they have been given credit for. Both 'On the heath' and the 'Ballade', Nos 1 and 2 of Op 115, have an innocence that calls to mind the wonderful *Humoresques* for violin and orchestra. In particular 'The Bells', Op 115 No 4 is a rather cryptic miniature and the 'Scène de danse' of Op 116, with its striking tonal juxtapositions, is a kind of Finnish equivalent of the Bartók *Romanian Dances*. Nils-Erik Sparf and Bengt Forsberg are dedicated and sensitive exponents who make the most of the opportunities this repertoire provides. One small reservation: the piano tone sounds a little thick at the bottom end, and the violin is by no means the dominant partner. Enthusiastically recommended.

Choral Songs

Partsongs, Op 18ᵃ – No 1, The Broken Voice; No 3, The Boat Journey of Väinämöinen; No 4, Fire on the Island; No 6, The Song of my Heart. Busy as a Thrushᵃ. Play, Beautiful Girlᵃ. Rakastava, Op 14ᵃ. The Thrush's Toilingᵃ. Festive Marchᵃ. Cantata for the Helsinki University Ceremonies of 1897, Op 23ᵃ. To Thérèse Hahlᵃ. Nostalgiaᶜ. Not with Griefᵃ. Wonderful Giftsᶜ. March of the Finnish Jaeger Battalion, Op 91 No 1. Three Runeberg Songsᵃ. Awaken!ᵃ. Choir of the Winds. Balladᵃ. The Son's Bride. Men from Plain and Sea, Op 65aᵃ. Dreamsᵃ. Christmas Songᵃ. Give Me No Splendour, Op 1 No 4ᵃ. Bell Melody of Berghaill Church, Op 65bᵃ. Three Introductory Antiphons, Op 107b. Ode, Op 113 No 11ᵃ. Carminaliaᵇᶜ. Primary School Children's Marchᶜ. In the Morning Mistᶜ. Hail, O Princessᵃ. The Landscape Breathes, Op 30ᵃ. Three American School Songs. The Way to Schoolᵃ. School Songᵃ. March of the Labourersᵃ. The World Song, Op 91b. Song of the Athenians, Op 31 No 3ᵇᶜ. To the Fatherlandᵃ. Song for the People of Uusimaaᵃ. Finlandiaᵃ
ᵃTapiola Chamber Choir; ᵇFriends of Sibelius / Hannu Norjanen; ᶜTapiola Choir / Kari Ala-Pöllänen with Ilmo Ranta pf Johanna Torikka org/harm
Finlandia 0630-19054-2 ② (147' · DDD) Texts and translations included   Ⓕ

This survey of Sibelius's complete choral songs is important – and irresistible – for both its consistently fine performance and its historical context. The two-disc set begins where – in the mythology of Finnish oral tradition – all music began: with the life-giving song of Väinämöinen from the *Kalevala*'s compilation of folk poetry; the verse which tuned Sibelius's ear to the musicality of the Finnish language (at a time

when he and his social class still spoke Swedish) also inspired his first distinctive song settings. Here, excellent production most sensitively captures the division and shifting of the finely blended voices of the Tapiola Chamber Choir, as solo and ensemble voices trace the asymmetrical metres and modal cadences of works such as 'The Boat Journey' from Op 18 and 'The Lover'. References to the *Kalevala* return in the group of songs for ceremonies and festivities in which solo exhortations are pitted against shifting choral harmonies, as images of journey, hope and freedom are expressed in the supple melodies of 10 songs for a university degree ceremony from 1897 (Op 23).

A fervent and optimistic tribute to Finland's great Romantic painter Albert Edelfelt sets works by Sibelius's beloved Swedish-language poet, Rüneberg: and his 'Autumn Evening' could be an aural re-creation of one of the painter's own canvases. Sibelius's music pierces dark, close harmonies with high lines of anguish, presaging the imaginative virtuosity of later masterpieces such as 'Men from Plain and Sea' and 'Dreams' with their sense of the wandering and yearning of the human spirit. The second disc follows three simple Christmas carols with the composer's sacred and liturgical pieces. The songs for children range from uninspired English-language commissions for American schools, to a tiny and perfect setting of 'The Landscape Breathes', in which the girls' voices slowly and chromatically thaw from their unison freeze. Finland's and Sibelius's unjingoistic patriotism returns at the end with gently yet distinctively harmonised hymns to specific regions of the motherland and, finally, with the great *Finlandia* hymn.

Kullervo, Op 7

Kullervo
Lilli Paasikivi *mez* Raimo Laukka *bar* Helsinki University Chorus; Lahti Symphony Orchestra / Osmo Vänskä
BIS CD1215 (81' · DDD) Text and translation included   Ⓕ Ⓞ Ⓞ

Vänskä is undoubtedly a Sibelian of strong instinct, and his *Kullervo* enshrines an interpretation of extraordinary grandeur and slumbering, runic mystery. After an ideally paced opening *Allegro moderato* (the Lahti strings lacking just a touch in sheer muscle), 'Kullervo's Youth' lasts an eyebrow-raising 19'18", well over three minutes longer than any predecessor. Courageously, Vänskä sticks to his guns, the music's unnervingly tragic portents distilled with mournful gravity. It's in the big central *scena* that BIS's sumptuously realistic and wide-ranging production really comes into its own. Vänskä directs with keen observation and tingling narrative flair, not missing the wondrous poetry of the nature music accompanying the lament of Kullervo's sister. What's more, his soloists and chorus are first-rate, though baritone Raimo Laukka isn't quite as fresh-voiced here as he was for Segerstam's in 1994. Following a splendidly lusty 'Kullervo goes to War', Vänskä crowns proceedings with a thrillingly grim and inevitable 'Kullervo's Death', with eloquent contributions from the men of the Helsinki University Chorus. As should be clear by now, this recording must feature high on any short list. The recent reappearance on EMI Double Forte of Berglund's pioneering Bournemouth version is certainly welcome, though the deletion of that conductor's Helsinki digital remake (also for EMI) is disappointing. Despite one or two eccentricities, both Segerstam and Paavo Järvi quarry the staggering originality of Sibelius's youthful vision to often riveting effect. The fleeter Saraste, too, gives a humane, thoroughly likeable performance, whereas Salonen's stunningly articulate realisation with the Los Angeles PO perhaps is marginally too slick for comfort. Only Sir Colin Davis adopts as daringly expansive a view as Vänskä, but his hard-working LSO forces simply don't sound as wholly attuned to the idiom as their Finnish rivals. Whether Vänskä's epic conception as a whole 'stacks up' with quite the same cumulative majesty as, say, the digital Berglund is debatable, but its insights are legion and for many it will be a natural first choice.

Karelia

Incidental Music – Karelia; Kuolema. Valse triste, Op 44 No 1 (1904 versions)
Heikki Laitinen, Taito Hoffren sngrs **Kirsi Tiihonen** sop **Raimo Laukka** bar **Lahti Symphony Orchestra / Osmo Vänskä**
BIS CD915 (76' · DDD) Texts and translations included
Ⓕ

This is a disc which will be of great interest to Sibelians. The original score of the *Karelia* music was discovered in the conductor Kajanus's library after his death in 1933 and his widow returned it to Sibelius three years later. The music extended to eight tableaux which portrayed various episodes in Karelian history. In the 1940s Sibelius destroyed the score, about which he had had second thoughts since its première in 1893, sparing only the overture, the movements familiar from the suite and the first number, 'A Karelian Home – News of War'. Fortunately for posterity, a set of orchestral parts came to light, albeit incomplete, and were put into shape by Kalevi Kuoso. It was these that the composer Kalevi Aho used in preparing the edition on which this recording is based.

In all there are some 40 minutes of music, over half of which is new. Those familiar with the 'Ballade' from the Op 11 Suite will no doubt be slightly disconcerted to hear the familiar cor anglais melody taken by a baritone and will find the piece too long in its original form. The opening of the fifth tableau, 'Pontus de la Gardie at the gates of Käkisalmi [Kexholm Castle] in 1580', is highly effective and leads into the famous 'Alla marcia'. It's fascinating to hear what the piece is like, and what Sibelius was

prepared to lose. Listening to this reaffirms and illumines both the sureness of his artistic judgement and the vitality of his creative imagination. Sibelius's incidental music to *Kuolema*, the play by his brother-in-law, Arvid Järnefelt, dates from 1903. The most familiar music from it is the *Valse triste*, which Sibelius revised the following year, adding flute, clarinet, horns and timpani and making it altogether more sophisticated harmonically and melodically. Osmo Vänskä and his Lahti players prove reliable and responsive guides in this atmospheric music and it's hard to imagine their performances being improved on. Wide-ranging and expertly balanced recorded sound.

Everyman, Op 83

Incidental Music – Everyman, Op 83; Belshazzar's Feast, Op 51. The Countess's Portrait, Op posth
Lilli Paasikivi mez **Petri Lehto** ten **Sauli Tiilikainen** bar **Pauli Pietiläinen** org **Leena Saarenpaä** pf **Lahti Chamber Choir; Lahti Symphony Orchestra / Osmo Vänskä**
BIS CD735 (65' · DDD) Texts and translations included
ⒻⓄ

These are all first recordings, and interest centres on the score Sibelius wrote for Hofmannsthal's morality play, *Jedermann* ('Everyman') in 1916. The final score comprises 16 numbers and runs to some 40 minutes. Some of the music is fragmentary and hardly makes sense out of context, though most is atmospheric and it's all characteristic. The sustained *Largo* section for muted, divided strings (track 11), is among the most searching music Sibelius ever wrote for theatre and, artistically, is fit to keep company with *The Tempest* music. Overall the material doesn't lend itself to being turned into a suite in the same way as *Belshazzar's Feast* but this recording rescues from obscurity some strangely haunting and at times really inspired music – the last 25 minutes are very powerful.

By all accounts Hjalmar Procopé's *Belshazzar's Feast* was a feeble play and when it first appeared, one newspaper cartoon showed the playwright being borne aloft in the composer's arms. There seems little doubt that his name wouldn't be alive if it weren't for Sibelius's music. The latter certainly makes an expert job of creating an effective and (in the case of the 'Notturno') a moving concert suite. *The Countess's Portrait* (1906) is a wistful, pensive and charming piece for strings, which was published only recently. Obviously this is a self-recommending issue of exceptional interest.

The Tempest, Op 109

The Tempest
Kirsi Tiihonen sop **Lilli Paasikivi** mez **Anssi Hirvonen, Paavo Kerola** tens **Heikki Keinonen** bar **Lahti Opera Chorus and Symphony Orchestra / Osmo Vänskä**

BIS CD581 (68' · DDD) Recorded 1992. Text and translation included   Ⓕ**O**

A first recording of the full score! Sibelius's music for *The Tempest*, his last and greatest work in its genre, was the result of a commission for a particularly lavish production at the Royal Theatre, Copenhagen in 1926. The score is far more extensive than the two suites and consists of 34 musical numbers for soloists, mixed choir, harmonium and large orchestra. Readers will be brought up with a start by the music for the 'Berceuse', the second item, which uses a harmonium rather than the strings we're familiar with from the two suites. Although it's still more magical in the familiar orchestral suite, the original has an other-worldly quality all its own. The music is played in the order in which it was used in the 1927 production of the play and there are ample and excellent explanatory notes. The 'Chorus of the Winds' is also different but no less magical in effect. Taken out of the theatrical context, not everything comes off, but even if the invention isn't consistent in quality, at its best it's quite wonderful. The singers and chorus all rise to the occasion and Osmo Vänskä succeeds in casting a powerful spell in the 'Intermezzo', which opens Act 4. The recording is marvellously atmospheric, though a little recessed. For Sibelians this issue recommends itself.

Additional recommendation

Viljakainen *sop* Groop *mez* Silvasti *ten* Hynninen, Tilikainen *bars* Finnish Opera Festival Chorus; Finnish Radio Symphony Orchestra/Saraste
Ondine ODE813-2 (60' · DDD)   Ⓕ
  A fine alternative version with idiomatic singing and playing from these Finnish performers.

Songs

King Christian II, Op 27 – Fool's Song of the Spider. Five Christmas Songs, Op 1. Eight Songs, Op 57. Hymn to Thaïs. Six Songs, Op 72 – No 3, The kiss; No 4, The echo nymph; No 5, Der Wanderer und der Bach; No 6, A hundred ways. Six Songs, Op 86. The small girls
Monica Groop *mez* **Love Derwinger** *pf*
BIS CD657 (66' · DDD) Recorded 1994. Texts and translations included   Ⓕ

Monica Groop, following her success in the Cardiff Singer of the World Competition, has built up a busy career. Communication is her strength, and unevenness of line a relative weakness. Sibelius's songs are a rich and still undervalued part of the song repertoire. Still only four or five are really well known, and none of those is included here. Not all are of very special quality: the title is probably the best thing about the 'Fool's Song of the Spider' (from *King Christian II*), and the *Hymn to Thaïs* gains interest

through being Sibelius's only song in English rather than through intrinsic merit. Yet there are many delights here, including the closing waltz-song, *The small girls*. The acoustic is perhaps somewhat too reverberant but has plenty of presence.

Songs, Volume 3. Seven Songs, Op 13. Six Songs, Op 50. Six Songs, Op 90. The Wood Nymph. Belshazzar's Feast – The Jewish Girl's Song. Resemblance. A Song. Serenade. The Thought[a]
Anne Sofie von Otter, [a]**Monica Groop** *mezzos*
Bengt Forsberg *pf*
BIS CD757 (67' · DDD) Recorded 1994-5. Texts and translations included   Ⓕ**O**

The vast majority of Sibelius's songs are in Swedish, the language with which he grew up as a child, and here they're given by a distinguished native Swedish partnership. The *Seven Songs*, Op 13, are all Runeberg settings and come from the composer's early years (1891-2). Best known, perhaps, are 'Spring is flying' and 'The dream', but there are others, such as 'The young hunter', that are no less delightful and characterful. The other Runeberg settings here, the *Six Songs*, Op 90, come towards the end of Sibelius's career as a song composer (1917-18). 'The north', as in all the nature poetry of Runeberg, touches a very special vein of inspiration. Along with 'Die stille Nacht', Op 50 No 5, which is equally affectingly given by these two artists – it's among his finest songs. Interest naturally focuses on the rarities.

The Wood Nymph, not to be confused with the melodrama or the tone-poem, is recorded here for the first time. As well as *A Song*, there are two other early Runeberg settings, the 1888 *Serenade* and *Resemblance*, both of them also première recordings. 'The Jewish Girl's Song' will be familiar from the incidental music to *Belshazzar's Feast*, and is affecting in this form – particularly sung as it is here. Given the artistry and insight of this splendid partnership, and the interest and beauty of the repertoire, this is a self-recommending issue.

To evening, Op 17 No 6. Six Songs, Op 36. Five Songs, Op 37. Six Songs, Op 50. Belshazzar's Feast, Op 51 – The Jewish Girl's Song. I am a tree, Op 57 No 5. The Elf-King, Op 57 No 8. The North, Op 90 No 1. Who has brought you here?, Op 90 No 6. Under the fir-trees, Op 13 No 1. Spring is flying, Op 13 No 4
Katarina Karnéus *mez* **Julius Drake** *pf*
Hyperion CDA67318 (65' · DDD) Notes, texts and translations included   Ⓕ**O**

Sibelius's songs have taken a long time to come in from the cold. After all, the few that are relatively well-known (*Black roses* and Op 37 No 5, 'The Tryst') are passionate enough to have come from Italian opera, and others which over the years have found a place in the repertoire have a span of phrase and a melodic surge that encourage the voice to rise thrillingly, as in 'The

Tryst's' predecessor, 'Was it a dream?'. The tingle of a Nordic chill in among this is in fact a further excitement of the blood. Given a voice that can combine the sparkle of sunlight on snow with the dark splendour which lies at the heart of those black roses, an entire programme of Sibelius's songs offers not an austere pleasure but almost a rich indulgence.

But from both singer and pianist there must also be a ready supply of imagination. Katarina Karnéus and Julius Drake answer these calls magnificently. The voice is firm and resonant, purest in quality in the upper D-to-F region and of ample range. In Julius Drake she has a pianist who extends the normal field of vision, and the two work together to great effect.

In the opening song, *To evening* ('Illalle'), Karnéus and Drake 'build' the verses with such effective graduations of power and intensity that everything is enhanced – the vocal line, the piano's *tremolando*s, words, mood, the poem-as-painting, the song as miniature epic.

In some others – 'Little Lasse' in Op 37 and the remarkable 'Tennis in Trianon' of Op 36 are examples – von Otter and Bengt Forsberg bring a further sophistication, more rightfully placed in the second example than the first. But if you want a single disc of 25 to to represent Sibelius's output of roughly 100 songs then this disc must take first choice.

Sibelius Arioso, Op 3. Luonnotar, Op 70. And I questioned them no further, Op 17 No 1. Dawn, Op 37 No 3. Autumn evening, Op 38 No 1. Belshazzar's Feast, Op 51 – The Jewish Girl's Song. Spring rushes by, Op 13 No 4. Sancta Maria ('The Maiden in the Tower') **Grieg** The first meeting, Op 21 No 1: A swan, Op 25 No 2. Last Spring, Op 33 No 2. From Monte Pincio, Op 39 No 1. Peer Gynt – Solveig's Song; Solveig's Cradle Song
Karita Mattila sop **City of Birmingham Symphony Orchestra / Sakari Oramo**
Warner Classics 8573 80243-2 (58' · DDD)　　ⒻⓄ

Karita Mattila's voice has grown to be the most imposing lyric soprano of our day, and this disc of Grieg and Sibelius songs will be a welcome bonus for collectors keen to hear her outside her operatic repertoire.

The six Grieg songs form the more modest part of the programme, though the finest of them give us Mattila in her best voice. There's a Northern-lights gleam to her singing of Solveig's two songs that couldn't be any other Straussian soprano today. It's there, too, in her expansively lyrical performance of *The first meeting*. The Sibelius selection ranges widely from the lyrical Op 3 *Arioso* to the high drama of the *The Maiden in the Tower*, where Mattila tries on her Wagnerian helmet for size. She sings with much sensitivity and brings the words alive.

Sakari Oramo and the CBSO give the singer the spacious and romantically coloured accompaniments she needs, confirming the high reputation they won with their Sibelius cycle.

Valentin Sil'vestrov　　Ukrainian b1937

Sil'vestrov was a pupil of Lyatosyns'ky at the Kiev Conservatory (1958–64). Influenced at first by his teacher and by Shostakovich, he came in the early 1960s to use serialism, aleatory forms and other avant-garde techniques and in the 1970s to work with a plurality of styles, new and old. His works include symphonies, chamber music, piano pieces, songs, characterized by an individual, expressive lyricism.　　GROVEmusic

Requiem for Larissa

Requiem for Larissa
National Choir of Ukraine, 'Dumka'; National Symphony Orchestra of Ukraine / Volodymyr Sirenko
ECM New Series 472 112-2 (53' · DDD) Text included
　　ⒻⓄ

Much of Sil'vestrov's music since the mid-1970s has been a requiem in all but name – a rite of regret and consolation for music and for the hopes and dreams of modern consciousness. So it's no surprise that he should join Schnittke, Denisov, Tishchenko and others of the post-Shostakovich generation in composing a work of that name. The external stimulus was the sudden death in 1996 of his musicologist wife Larissa Bondarenko, his staunch supporter through trials of the kind virtually all modernist composers in the former USSR had to face.

He completed the work three years later, having built into the 'Tuba Mirum' section the fractured but passionate textures of his First Symphony of 1963, and having arranged the second *Agnus Dei* around his Mozartian piano piece, *The Messenger*. At the heart of the Requiem is his Taras Shevchenko setting, 'The Dream', as breathtakingly moving here as in its original place in the cycle *Silent Songs*. Otherwise he fragments the Requiem text and disposes its incomplete phrases across seven mostly slow movements; only the 'Lacrimosa' survives intact. The choir features a *basso profundo* section and three soloists who gently ease in and out of the texture. The classical-size orchestra is augmented by synthesizer, first heard in the celestial harmonies succeeding the first *Agnus Dei*.

Whether or not you know the fragile, haunting sound world of Ukraine's senior composer, this is a disc you should try.

Robert Simpson　　British 1921-1997

Simpson, a pupil of Howells (1942–6), worked for the BBC (1951–80). His main achievement was his cycles of nine symphonies and eight string quartets, both begun in 1951 and both displaying a dynamic tonality quite individual in its energy and purposefulness, encouraged more than influenced by his admiration for Beethoven, Bruckner and Nielsen (on whom he published studies).　　GROVEmusic

Symphonies

Symphonies Nos 1 & 8
Royal Philharmonic Orchestra / Vernon Handley
Hyperion CDA66890 (73' · DDD)   Ⓕ

Here's an inspiring encounter with music whose surface affinities (the dynamism of Beethoven, the registral awareness of Berlioz, the obsessional drive of Bartók and so on) fade from the mind as its unique blend of unquenchable energy and alert meditation takes you over. Like a number of composers, Simpson seems to have responded to the power of late Beethoven and thought, 'I can do that'; like very few, he can.

The First's construction on the basis of proportionally related tempos enables it to be simultaneously part of the world of conflict and feeling and yet at the same time somehow soaring above it. The Eighth, by contrast, seems to embody some colossal inner rage. Each partial untying of its knotted psyche unleashes apocalyptic fury, and the quietus of harmonic resolution is denied until the very last moment.

The Eighth had an unhappy première performance in 1982. For this recording Vernon Handley has clearly devoted a labour of love to it, and he seems to have persuaded the Royal Philharmonic to do the same.

Symphonies Nos 2 & 4
Bournemouth Symphony Orchestra / Vernon Handley
Hyperion CDA66505 (75' · DDD) Recorded 1992   Ⓕ

The opening of the Second Symphony is breathtaking – an 'active but mysterious' idea, utterly distinctive in its silvery harmonic colouring, it holds the key to a world where wistfulness can transmute into energy and where energy itself occasionally has to be rescued from the obsessional corners it drives itself into. The slow movement is no less characteristic of its composer in its gentle restorative quality, probing unfamiliar areas of the mind and conjuring them to life. For the finale it's doubtful if there's any parallel in Simpson's output; the rhythmic drive and grittiness of Beethoven's Seventh Symphony is there in the background, but there's an almost irresponsible rollicking character similar to the Hindemith of the *Symphonic Metamorphoses*.

The Fourth Symphony contains perhaps the most remarkable and certainly the most instantly communicative of Simpson's Beethoven paraphrases. The model here is the scherzo of the *Choral* Symphony, with a Haydn quotation supplying material for the Trio section. To stay so close to the structure of the original and yet to create such an entirely new and individual experience is a feat of genuine compositional virtuosity. It's like Icarus and the sun all over again, except that Simpson gets away with it.

Some may find the following slow movement featureless. But experience suggests that a mind-stretching power will eventually disclose itself. In the meantime there are the constantly renewing horizons of the first movement to savour, with that special combination of transparent texture, blunt rhythms and polytonal shadings that gives Simpson's musical paragraphs their forward-looking momentum. And finally there are the massively energising shouts which crown the work. All this gives Handley and his orchestra plenty to get their teeth into, and their response is as splendid as in their *Gramophone* Award-winning account of Simpson's Ninth.

Symphonies Nos 3 & 5
Royal Philharmonic Orchestra / Vernon Handley
Hyperion CDA66728 (71' · DDD) Recorded 1994
                                        ⒻOO

The Third Symphony is Simpson's best-known work and Vernon Handley play the symphony like the repertoire piece it deserves to be, and Hyperion's recording reveals a wealth of unsuspected detail and beauty. The Beethovenian impulse still comes across, and the abrasive edge is only slightly softened. But what has been gained is clarity, blend and perspective, plus a sense of dialogue (Simpson's polyphony never ceases to amaze) and an altogether subtler realisation of the luminosity of Simpson's scoring. The long accumulating second movement is absorbingly poetic, witty in its dialogue, and inevitable in its conclusion.

The Fifth Symphony is surely one of Simpson's most vivid pieces. Moods of terror, anger, anxious probing and fierce determination are right on the surface, and there's a feeling of terrific will-power being exerted to transmute those moods into a symphonic experience. This is one of the great symphonies of the post-war era, magnificently realised by all concerned.

Symphonies Nos 6 & 7
Royal Liverpool Philharmonic Orchestra / Vernon Handley
Hyperion CDA66280 (60' · DDD) Recorded 1987   Ⓕ

The first performances of these symphonies had shown many characteristic and admirable qualities, but there was a suspicion of some tentativeness a lowering of sights even, after the explosive Fifth Symphony. One should have guessed that closer acquaintance and more expert performance would show this to be more a matter of concentration of ideas and of conscious change of direction. The Royal Liverpool Philharmonic Orchestra and Vernon Handley show the Sixth to be a work of immense inner power, and if the Seventh is a more cryptic statement, this recording certainly brings it into a clearer focus than previously.

Whereas Tippett (in the same year) wrote a birth-to-death symphony (No 4) Simpson's Sixth shifts the process one stage back – from conception to prime of life. Intense expectancy gives way to a memorable downward-stalking unison figure, the fertilised seed which becomes the most active force in the early stages of the work. From here to the irresistible energy of the final pages Simpson's control of musical momentum can only be marvelled at; and if you don't marvel at it, that may be because you're worrying about the apparent restriction on colour and lyricism, and thus missing the point.

As yet the final D major outcome still refuses to register as a natural outcome, although presumably there's any amount of logical justification for it. The neutral, non-triadic conclusion to the Seventh rings truer, though in this work the processes before it are more inscrutable – not in the technical sense, but simply in terms of what the techniques are driving at. But anyone who has puzzled over, and then clicked with, say, Sibelius's Fourth or Shostakovich's 15th, will know how dangerous it is to jump to conclusions. And even if the click never happens, one probable masterpiece is surely enough to be getting on with.

Symphony No 9
Bournemouth Symphony Orchestra / Vernon Handley
Hyperion CDA66299 (68' · DDD) Recorded 1988.
Includes an illustrated talk by the composer Ⓕ**❍❍❍**

 If you know that feeling of expectancy, of vast potential energy, at the outset of a great symphony, you'll surely respond to the opening of Simpson's Ninth – and be wholly engrossed. You'll be led through shifting pedal-points and wedge-shaped themes encompassing a specific harmonic universe; through waves of energy pulsating fit to burst, until burst they do into a titanic scherzo; through slow, disembodied traceries of string lines, through awe-inspiring climaxes to a no less awe-inspiring hushed coda. And as rising scales pass through the coda's pedal-points into the final glacial sonority you'll know that you've heard one of the finest symphonies of the post-war era.

The composer adds an explanatory 18-minute talk. Here are laid bare some of the salient constructional features of the work – the opening's basis in chorale prelude procedures (a fairly cosmic rethinking thereof!), the single underlying pulse of the entire work (a recurrent feature in Simpson's output, but never before applied on this scale), the palindromic variations in the second half, the debts to Bach, Beethoven and Bruckner. To which one might add that the rigorous processes described in this talk suggest a somewhat unlikely kinship with Bartók at his most abstract (as in the first movement of *Music for strings, percussion and celesta*).

Bartók, it's safe to say, has as little to do with this work's symphonic instincts as any other 'big name' of the last 50 years or so. Simpson stands not at any fixed pole of today's music, but rather at a kind of magnetic north, free from attempts of musical cartographers to pin down his position, spiritually allied to composers of any age

and style who have penetrated to the essence of music's motion in time. A totally absorbing symphony and the performance and recording are surely the best possible tribute to all concerned.

String Quartets

String Quartets Nos 7 & 8
Delme Quartet (Galina Solodchin, Jeremy Williams vns John Underwood va Stephen Orton vc)
Hyperion CDA66117 (51' · AAD) Recorded 1983 Ⓕ**❍❍**

String Quartet No 9
Delme Quartet (Galina Solodchin, Jeremy Williams vns John Underwood va Stephen Orton vc)
Hyperion CDA66127 (58' · AAD) Recorded 1984 Ⓕ

Quiet music with a sense of purpose and forward-looking destiny; slow music which bears the promise of a controlled release of energy, these are rare and treasurable qualities in music of our time, and they make their presence felt at the beginnings of Simpson's Seventh and Eighth Quartets. How he progresses through subdued scherzo to vehement climax is something to reflect on at length, and with further acquaintance comes the Beethovenian thrill of hearing the music think. But at first these things just steal up on you and take the breath away.

The Seventh Quartet is dedicated to Susi Jeans, widow of astronomer and mathematidan Sir James Jeans, the Eighth is dedicated to entomologist David Gillett and his wife. Both works draw on the kind of motion suggested by those areas of sdentific enquiry. On the other hand the Ninth calls up what would seem to be the bitterest enemy of forward movement – the palindrome; 32 variations and a fugue, in fact, on the minuet from Haydn's Symphony No 47 and all of them, like the original theme, palindromic. If Simpson's powers of invention falter at any stage in this hour-long tour de force you would be hard pushed to discover where. But then this music so completely absorbing that the necessary critical detachment is difficult to achieve. The only reservation that did register was over recording quality, which for the Ninth Quartet is disappointingly boxy – sensuous appeal isn't what this music is about, but a more ingratiating acoustic wouldn't do it any harm – and to hear the Seventh without the distraction, however faint, of traffic noise would be preferable.

The Delme Quartet's performances are outstandingly dedicated. The Ninth Quartet was composed for their 20th anniversary and they prove themselves entirely worthy of the honour.

String Quartet No 13. String Quintet No 2. Clarinet Quintet
Thea King cl **Christopher van Kampen** vc **Delmé Quartet** (Galina Solodchin, John Trusler vns John Underwood va Jonathan Williams vc)
Hyperion CDA66905 (64' · DDD) Ⓕ**❍**

An invigorating and thought-provoking disc. In the Clarinet Quintet of 1968 the wind partner is treated as an equal of the strings, which makes the linear and contrapuntal inventiveness all the more remarkable and absorbing, though for some it may make the music seem no more than monochrome. Like late Beethoven, Simpson seems to begin by charting a realm just out of emotional reach yet somehow crucial to one's psychic well-being. The mental energy gained then spills over into actual fast music, even into an engaging jigginess. The Quintet feels as though it could go on much longer than its actual 31 minutes without the inventive resources drying up. The rarefied conclusion is all the more moving for its steadiness of gaze. The 13th Quartet (1989) retains many familiar Simpson hallmarks. It opens with a sinewy, deceptively triadic theme which soon gives way to spidery, triplety counterpoint. It's all very ascetic and self-denying and the second and fourth movements go into an interior, attenuated world in which it's difficult to feel entirely at home.

The even more recent String Quintet No 2 keeps its cards just as close to its chest. Again the design alternates austere, lyrical music with a knotty *Allegro*, initially short-lived but gradually expanding, while the slower sections are more or less constant in duration. The impression is less of conflict and resolution than of a stand-off between the two tempo-types, eyeing one another in mutual suspicion; the conclusion is bleak-Sibelian. The Delmé is a longstanding Simpson advocate and it seems to have the ideal sound for him – crystalline, alert and focused, as though beyond obvious human expressiveness in a realm of higher wisdom. The same goes for their admirable partners, Thea King and Christopher van Kampen. This may be one of the less immediately accessible Simpson programmes, but it's still richly rewarding.

Vocal Works

Canzona[a]. Media morte in vita sumus[b]. Tempi[c]. Eppur si muove[d]
[d]Iain Quinn *org* [ab]**Corydon Brass Ensemble;** [bc]**Corydon Singers / Matthew Best**
Hyperion CDA67016 (68' · DDD) Texts included   Ⓕ❍

Simpson would never have claimed that choral music was his *métier*. Yet for lovers of his music there's something especially revealing about the two pieces recorded here. In *Media morte in vita sumus* ('In the midst of death we are in life') he deliberately reverses the scriptural motto in order to articulate his personal 'anti-pessimist' creed. The musical setting for chorus, brass and timpani is appropriately austere, and Simpson's words are translated into Latin for the sake of universality. *Tempi* for a cappella chorus is a *jeu d'esprit*, the text consisting entirely of Italian tempo and character markings. The Corydon Singers offers superbly confident performances, as does the Corydon Brass Ensemble which also

shines in the comparatively well-known *Canzona*. It's impossible to avoid comparisons with Nielsen when it comes to the 31-minute *Eppur si muove* ('But it does move') for organ. This 12-minute *ricercare* followed by a 19-minute passacaglia sets its jaw squarely against conventional organ-loft grandiosity. Its intellectual monumentality is clearly in the *Commotio* mould, though it's considerably tougher going than Nielsen's late masterpiece. Iain Quinn joins the long line of dedicated performers who have made Hyperion's Simpson series such a consistent triumph. Recording quality leaves nothing to be desired.

Nikos Skalkottas   Greek 1904-1949

Skalkottas studied as a violinist at the Athens Conservatory and as a composer in Berlin with Juon, Kahn, Jarnach (1925-7), Weill (1928-9) and Schoenberg (1927-31). In 1933 he returned to Athens, where he worked as a back-desk violinist. His Berlin works are relatively compact and high-spirited, being almost exclusively instrumental and following the neo-classicism of his teachers (in 1927 his music became atonal, but not yet serial). But the bulk of his music dates from 1935-45, when the genres remained traditional but the forms were greatly expanded to contain a deep complexity of serial thematic working: major works of this period include the Third Piano Concerto (1939), the Fourth Quartet (1940) and the overture The Return of Odysseus (1943); he wrote several concertos, chamber and vocal music. He also produced tonal works, including a collection of 36 Greek Dances for orchestra (1936).
GROVEmusic

Piano Concerto No 1, AK16

Piano Concerto No 1, AK16[a]. The Maiden and Death – Ballet Suite, AK12. Ouvertüre concertante, AK46
[a]**Geoffrey Douglas Madge** *pf* **Iceland Symphony Orchestra / Nikos Christodoulou**
BIS CD1014 (56' · DDD)   Ⓕ❍

BIS's Skalkottas cycle started very well and gets better with each release. The First Piano Concerto's characteristic use of a family of note-rows, rather than just one, may have ignited the rift between the apprentice composer and his teacher, Schoenberg. The neo-classical elements can't have been to the latter's liking, either. Geoffrey Douglas Madge gives a barnstorming performance and the accompaniment is electrifying. The orchestra is heard at its best and in its own right in the suite from the folk-ballet *The Maiden and Death* (1938). Here Skalkottas's brilliant orchestration shines through in what's much more than a pre-run of *The Mayday Spell*. The idiom is less fragmentary than the latter; indeed, it suggests a Greek *Miraculous Mandarin*, if less overtly spectacular in sound or scandalous in plot.

The disc concludes with a further movement

from the unfinished Second Symphonic Suite (1944-5; compare the *Largo sinfonico* on the first disc). This *Ouvertüre concertante* is pretty much what the title leads you to expect it to be, a superbly scored sonata-derivative, employing the composer's note-row-complex manner in a most attractive fashion.

Violin Concerto, AK22

Violin Concerto, AK22[a]. Largo Sinfonico, AK4a.
Greek Dances, AK11 – Epirotikos; Kretikos; Tsamikos; Thessalikos; Mariori mou-Mariori mou; Arkadikos; Kleftikos (arr cpsr)
[a]**Georgios Demertzis** vn **Malmö Symphony Orchestra / Nikos Christodoulou**
BIS CD904 (78' · DDD)   ⓕ〇

From Skalkottas's earliest works, a personal idiom was clearly in evidence, combining European modernism with the rhythmic dynamism of Greek traditional music, and characterised by a tensile strength and translucency of sound. Like Bartók, Skalkottas wrote 'popular' music without compromise. The *Greek Dances* are ideal encore pieces, not least in these suave arrangements for strings.

The Violin Concerto of 1937 is among his major works, with a solo part that's demanding yet integral to the symphonic nature of the score – something that Georgios Demertzis's vital account readily conveys here. The close of the *Andante* possesses true lyrical repose, before the finale provides fireworks as well as clinching the musical design.

The *Largo Sinfonico*, completed in 1944, embodies some of Skalkottas's most personal music; a seamless fusion of variation and sonata forms, it's as satisfying formally as it is emotionally. Nikos Christodoulou's accompanying notes speak of a private musical universe, yet the plangency of the cello theme and the remorseless tread of the central climaxes betray an unease that must surely be inseparable from the time of composition. The final bars, with the thematic material recast as a series of unearthly chords, feel as much a stoic acceptance of reality as they are a 'harmony of the spheres'. With the Malmö orchestra fully attuned to the idiom, Christodoulou's powerfully shaped reading makes for a compelling experience.

String Quartets

String Quartets – No 3, AK34; No 4, AK35
New Hellenic Quartet (Georgios Demertzis, Dimitris Chandrakis vns Paris Anastasiades va Apostolos Chandrakis vc)
BIS CD1074 (58' · DDD)   ⓕ

Make no mistake about it, BIS's Skalkottas cycle is among the most stimulating recording projects of recent years, and the present disc further enhances its status. The Third Quartet (1935) marked his full return to composition after four years of depression and likely stylistic uncertainty, and the contrasts in idiom evident from his Berlin years are replaced by a tight integration of form and content. The alternate harmonic and melodic presentation of material throughout the opening movement is paralleled by the modal cadential idea which increasingly pervades the *Andante*, in turn governing the tonal outcome of the finale. What appears an overtly classical structure takes on a unity akin to Bartók's Third Quartet.

In terms of musicianship, the New Hellenic Quartet are significantly superior to rivals' accounts, while their dedication establishes the previously unrecorded Fourth Quartet as the missing masterwork in the 'golden age' of inter-war quartet writing.

In his booklet-note, Kostis Demertzis speculates that the work may have been originally planned as a symphony for strings, but the rhythmic velocity of the first movement and *Scherzo* is such that few larger ensembles would be able to do it justice. Formally, the work has intriguing parallels with Beethoven's Op 127 quartet, not least the variation sequence comprising the lengthy second movement; and the fantasia-like third variation seems almost a thematic nucleus for the whole work. Quartet No 4 needs repeated listening for its myriad subtleties to come through, but the New Hellenic ensure that this is as pleasurable as it is enthralling. Natural recorded sound, with a realistic dynamic range, sets the seal on this most rewarding disc.

Violin Sonatinas

Violin Sonatinas[a] – No 1, AK46; No 2, AK47; No 3, AK48; No 4, AK49. March of the Little Soldiers, AK53[a]. Rondo, AK54[a]. Nocturne, AK55[a]. Little Chorale and Fugue, AK56[a]. Gavotte, AK57[a]. Scherzo and Menuetto Cantato, AK58[a]. Solo Violin Sonata, AK69
Georgios Demertzis vn [a]**Maria Asteriadou** pf
BIS CD1024 (66' · DDD)   ⓕ〇

Here's a window onto Skalkottas's music for his own instrument, itself a microcosm of his development. There's nothing stylistically tentative about the early Solo Violin Sonata (1925). Written with a Bachian economy of manner, the composer draws in references to jazz and popular music; the finale serves notice of his technical skill with an arching four-part fugue, reaching maximum intensity at the point where it returns to the prelude. The sense of a still-emerging personality is reinforced by the first two *Sonatinas* (both 1929, the *Andantino* is all that survives from No 1). Skalkottas's rhythmic incisiveness owes something to Stravinsky and even Bartók, but the tang of the harmonic writing is his alone. With the Third and Fourth *Sonatinas* (both 1935), the Skalkottas idiom, sinuous and expressive, is in place. The thematic integration of No 3 is breathtaking, as is the variety of tone with which the violin sustains continuity in the *Andante*. If the Fourth *Sonatina* is almost too diverse in mood, its *Adagio* is one of Skalkottas's finest: a threnody unfolding in three waves of mounting intensity, it looks forward to the expansive slow movements of the composer's last decade.

The miniatures are anything but trifles. *March of the Little Soldiers* is a savage take on militarism, while *Nocturne* reinterprets the expressive vocabulary of the 'song without words' for the 20th century. There could be no more sympathetic advocate than Georgios Demertzis. As in his recording of the Violin Concerto (BIS), he gets to the heart of Skalkottas's demanding but deeply felt music, with Maria Asteriadou an attentive partner. Inquiring listeners shouldn't hesitate to acquire this disc.

Piano Works

Musik für Klavier: 32 Piano Pieces, AK70. Suite No 1, AK71. Four Etudes, AK74
Nikolaos Samaltanos *pf*
BIS ② BIS-CD1133/4 (119' · DDD)　　　　Ⓕ❍

Over 60 years after its completion, Skalkottas's *Musik für Klavier* – the overall title of his 32 Piano Pieces – can assume its place among the major piano cycles of the 20th century. Formidably difficult technically, its apparently disparate content – there isn't the conceptual focus of, say, Messiaen's *Vingt regards sur l'enfant Jésus* – may have militated against its wider recognition. So it's a tribute to Nikolaos Samaltanos, in this first complete recording, that he projects the work as an integral entity, and as the compendium of mid-century pianism that the composer intended.

Achieving equal conviction across such diversity is a tall order, given the absence of a performing tradition against which to assess an interpretation. His playing of individual pieces may be open to question but Samaltanos has the measure of the cycle and the way that its groupings of pieces interconnect. The powerful rhetoric of the 'Passacaglia' and sombre poetry of 'Nachtstück', a double-apex on all levels, are impressively wrought, while the relative nonchalance of the closing *divertissement* is dispatched with élan. Other recordings will surely follow but rivals will be hard pressed to match the scintillating virtuosity of Samaltanos in 'Katastrophe' or the 'Etüde phantastique'.

Wide-ranging sound, lacking only the last degree of clarity in the more heavily chorded pieces, and detailed notes from Christophe Sirodeau. Urgently recommended.

Songs

16 Songs. 15 Little Variations. Sonatina. Müsik für Klavier – Berceuse. Echo
Angelica Cathariou *mez* **Nikolaos Samaltanos** *pf*
BIS BIS-CD1464 (60' · DDD · T/t)　　　　　Ⓕ

Not known primarily for vocal music, Skalkot-

tas made an important contribution with the *16 Songs*. Written in 1941, to texts by Hrissos Evelpidis, the cycle is inspired by Schoenberg's *Das Buch der hängenden Gärten*.

The plaintive first song, 'Perfection', typifies the subject-matter of the cycle – the ceaseless motion of wind and wave, travel as an existential journey into oblivion. The vocal part is an unfolding melodic line, with which the piano engages in a flow of imitative gestures and motivic offshoots.

The songs makes formidable demands on stamina; Angelica Cathariou is well equipped to deal with them, even if greater expressive nuance would have been welcome. Pianist Nikolaos Samaltanos impresses with his clarity and focus.

Of the solo piano couplings, the *15 Little Variations* packs a diverse range of moods into its relatively modest dimensions, while the Sonatina (both 1927) surrounds a wistful *Siciliano* with toccata-like movements which suggest more than passing acquaintance with Prokofiev. Samaltanos supplies a succinct but useful booklet-note and, despite piano sound which lacks a little definition, the disc can be warmly recommended for illuminating a hitherto unexplored facet of a protean creative force.

Bedřich Smetana   Bohemian 1824-1884

Smetana took music lessons from his father, a keen violinist, and from several local teachers. In his teens he attended the Academic Gymnasium in Prague, but neglected school work to attend concerts (including some by Liszt, with whom he became friendly) and to write string quartets for friends, until his father sent him to the Premonstratensian Gymnasium at Plzen. At first he earned a precarious living as a teacher in Prague until, in January 1884, he was appointed resident piano teacher to Count Leopold Thun's family, which provided him with the means to study harmony, counterpoint and composition with Josef Proksch. When he failed in an attempt to launch a career as a concert pianist in 1847, Smetana decided to found a school of music in Prague. This showed little profit, but he was able to earn something by teaching privately and by playing regularly to the deposed Emperor Ferdinand, and in 1849 he was able to marry Katerina Kolárová, whom he had known since his Plzen days.

Smetana's financial situation improved little in the years that followed, and political uncertainty and domestic tragedy only added to his unrest: three of his four daughters died between 1854 and 1856. When he heard there was an opening for a piano teacher at Göteborg he jumped at the chance. In Sweden his prospects improved, and he was in demand as a pianist, teacher and conductor. Inspired by Liszt's example, he composed his first symphonic poems. His wife's health forced him to return to Bohemia with her in 1859, but she died at Dresden on the way home. After two further summers in Göteborg, between which he found a second wife in Bettina

Ferdinandová, Smetana felt the need to return permanently to Prague in order to play an active role in the reawakening of Czech culture that followed the Austrian defeat by Napoleon III at Magenta and Soferino.

He was disappointed to find himself no more successful in Prague than he had been before. It was not until his first opera, The Brandenburgers in Bohemia, was enthusiastically received in January 1866 that his prospects there improved. His second, The Bartered Bride, was speedily put into production and soon found favour, though (as with his other operas) foreign performances long remained rarities. As principal conductor of the Provisional Theatre, 1866-74, Smetana added 42 operas to the repertory, including his own Dalibor (on a heroic national theme) and The Two Widows. Dalibor and Libuše (performed at the opening of the National Theatre in Prague in 1881) are Smetana's two most nationalistic operas; when completing the latter he also planned a vast orchestral monument to his nation which became the cycle of symphonic poems entitled Má vlast ('My fatherland'), including the evocative and stirring Vltava, a picture of the river that flows through Prague.

In 1874 the first signs of the syphilis appeared that was to result in Smetana's deafness. The String Quartet From my Life (1876) suggests in its last movement the piercing whistling that haunted his every evening, making work almost impossible. He somehow managed to complete two more operas, a second string quartet and several other works, but by 1883 his mental equilibrium was seriously disturbed. In April 1884 he was taken to the Prague lunatic asylum, where he died the following month.

Smetana was the first major nationalist composer of Bohemia. He gave his people a new musical identity and self-confidence by his technical assurance and originality in handling national subjects. In his operas and symphonic poems he drew on his country's legends, history, characters, scenery and ideas, presenting them with a freshness and colour which owe little to indigenous folksong but much to a highly original and essentially dramatic musical style.

GROVEmusic

Má vlast

Má vlast
Czech Philharmonic Orchestra / Rafael Kubelík
Supraphon 11 1208-2 (78' · DDD) Recorded live 1990
Ⓕ**OO**

Smetana's great cycle of six tone-poems, Má vlast, celebrates the countryside and legendary heroes and heroines of Bohemia. It's a work of immense national significance encapsulating many of the ideals and hopes of that country. What a triumphant occasion it was when Rafael Kubelík returned to his native Czechoslovakia and to his old orchestra after an absence of 42 years and conducted Má vlast at the 1990 Prague Spring Festival. Supraphon's disc captures that live performance – not perfectly, since the sound is efficient rather than opulent – but well enough to show off what's arguably the finest performance on record since Talich's early LP set.

SMETANA MÁ VLAST – IN BRIEF

Czech PO / Václav Talich
Supraphon 11 1896-2 (74' · ADD) Ⓜ**OOO**
☼ Inifintely flexible, warm-hearted and full of chest-swelling pride, the great Václav Talich's third and final recording from 1954 has the very stamp of greatness in every bar.

Czech PO / Karel Ančerl
Supraphon SU3661-2 (75' · ADD) Ⓜ
Ančerl's 1961 recording sounds far richer on CD than it ever did on LP. It's an exciting, always purposeful account, marvellously well played.

Czech PO / Rafael Kubelík
Supraphon 11 1208-2 (78' · DDD) Ⓕ**OO**
Returning to his homeland after an absence of nearly 42 years, Rafael Kubelík launched the 1990 Prague Spring Festival with this unforgettable performance of Smetana's patriotic cycle.

Bavarian RSO / Rafael Kubelík
Orfeo C115842A (77' · DDD) Ⓕ**OO**
Kubelík again, this time at the helm of his beloved Munich band in arguably the most spellbinding, subtly moulded version of all.

Royal Liverpool PO / Libor Pešek
Virgin 561223-2 (76' · DDD) Ⓜ
An enjoyable Má vlast from Merseyside, always shapely and refreshingly free of bombast. Agile and affectionate work from the RLPO; first-rate engineering.

Concertgebouw Orchestra / Antál Dorati
Philips 442 641-2PM (79' · DDD) Ⓜ
The airy Concertgebouw acoustic lends a lovely bloom and richness to Dorati's strongly characterised performance. The Amsterdam orchestra respond with praiseworthy composure and dedication.

Polish National RSO / Antoni Wit
Naxos 8 550931 (80' · DDD) Ⓢ
A distinctive account from Katowice. Wit opts for unusually lesiurely tempi, but there's no lack of momentum or atmosphere. Worth snapping up as a supplement to Talich and Kubelík.

Czech PO / Sir Charles Mackerras
Supraphon SU3456-2 (74' · DDD) Ⓕ
Another memorable Prague Spring Festival concert, this time from May 1999 and featuring a maestro whose lifelong experience and wisdom in Slavonic repertoire require no further comment.

You'd never imagine that Kubelík had emerged from five years of retirement and a recent serious illness, such is the power and eloquence of his conducting. He takes a lyrical rather than a dramatic view of the cycle, and if there's strength enough in more heroic sections there's also a refreshing lack of bombast. Kubelík's intimate knowledge of the score shows time and time again in the most subtle touches. Even the weakest parts of the work are most artfully brought to life, and seem of much greater stature than is usually the case. 'Vltava' flows beautifully, with the most imaginative flecks of detail, and in 'From Bohemia's Woods and Fields' there are vivid visions of wide, open spaces. The orchestra rewards its former director with superb playing.

Má vlast   **H**
Czech Philharmonic Orchestra / Václav Talich
Supraphon mono 11 1896-2 (74' · AAD) Recorded
1954   **F⃝OOO**

Try listening from just before six minutes into 'From Bohemia's Woods and Fields' and you reach the very heart of this great performance. The CPO brass lunges towards the main melody with unconstrained eagerness, their impact much aided by smiling *glissandos*. And as Talich and his players climb aboard Smetana's homespun melody, everything assumes a sunny glow: it's almost as if the entire work thus far had prepared for that one magical moment. But there are countless additional splendours: the luminous mobility of 'Vltava', the grimness of 'Sárka' (so different here to the excitable Kubelík), the sense of foreboding in 'Tábor' and the chest-swelling patriotism of 'Blaník'. The strings retain more than a hint of the *portamentos* that were such a distinctive feature of Talich's 1929 recording, but the woodwinds are notably superior and the basically excellent sound releases more of the music's dynamism than was easily audible on 78s.

The transfer makes a warmer case for the original tapes than did the old LPs, and generally serves Talich well – except in one maddening respect. A couple of bars have dropped from 'Tábor', thus utterly ruining the contour of a major climax. The offending cut was not present on the original recording. If you can write off the missing bars as 'historical wear and tear', then expect a *Má vlast* that's way above average, an inspired affirmation of national pride by a wonderful people who had only recently escaped one form of tyranny, and would subsequently fall prey to another.

Additional recommendation

Má vlast
Czech Philharmonic Orchestra / Mackerras
Supraphon SU3465-2 (76' · DDD)
   A live recording from the Rudolfinum in Prague

finds the West's leading Czech music specialist utterly at home with the music and the orchestra. The sound is excellent.

Piano Works

Three Poetic Polkas, B95. Three Salon Polkas, B94. Polkas – E; G minor; A; F minor. Two Souvenirs of Bohemia in the form of Polkas, B115. Two Souvenirs of Bohemia in the form of Polkas, B116
András Schiff pf
Teldec 3984-21261-2 (57' · DDD)   **F⃝O**

The E flat *Allegro, tempo rubato* from the *Souvenirs of Bohemia in the form of Polkas*, Op 13 presents a blend of yearning chromaticism typical of the composer, with additional elements drawn from Chopin. The work was composed during Smetana's Swedish sojourn and suggests aching homesickness expressed in musical terms. Op 12 is also Chopinesque, though the expansive *moderato* second movement (the longest piece on the programme) has a folk-like melodic slant, harmonic richness and sense of narrative that are entirely Smetana's own. The three *Salon* (or 'Drawing Room') *Polkas*, Op 7, dedicated to Smetana's first wife, are among the most charming, especially the first piece. Much of this music was written in the wake of great loss (annotator Graham Melville-Mason suggests the second of the three *Poetic Polkas* could reflect the illness and death of Smetana's second daughter, but its cheerful demeanour spells courage and optimism.

Perhaps the most immediately appealing piece on the disc is the delightful A major *Polka* that in some bizarre way anticipates the Waltz from Bernstein's 1980 *Divertimento*. Schiff's programme is of varying levels of technical difficulty but the same interpretative virtues are common throughout: a marked liking for inner voices, a lilt to the rhythms (notably in the second Op 13 piece), crisp fingerwork and a natural approach to rubato. Comparing Schiff to the excellent Jan Novotný on Supraphon (which programmes the majority of pieces included here) shows that while the Hungarian is more prone to employ colouristic effects, the Czech more likely to lay equal stresses on all voices (which is useful for underlining Smetana's often sombre harmonies).

Both players are undeniably masterful, although Schiff's delicious brand of pianistic sorcery will probably win this music the largest audiences, and Teldec's recording is marginally the better of the two.

The Bartered Bride

The Bartered Bride   **H**
Ada Nordenova sop Marenka **Otta Horáková** sop
Esmeralda **Marie Pixová** sop Ludmila **Marta
Krásová** mez Háta **Vladimir Toms** ten Jeník **Jaroslav
Gleich** ten Vasek **Karel Hruska** ten Circus Master **Jan
Konstantin** bar Krusina **Emil Pollert** bass Kecal
Zdenek Otava bass Micha **Václav Marek** bass Indian
Prague National Opera Company Chorus; Prague

National Opera Company Orchestra/Otakar Ostrčil
Naxos CD ② 8 110098/9 (118 minutes) Recorded 1933

Ⓢ

This is the first ever recording of Smetana's most popular opera, performed by a team steeped in the tradition of interpreting the work in Prague. Otakar Ostrčil gives a rhythmically exhilarating, suitably expectant account of the overture, directs the dances with just the right amount of brio tempered by lightness, and gives thoughtful support to his singers. The whole cast is Czech, so the recitative flows with a natural feeling for speech rhythms and accentuation. Nordenova as Mařenka has a sweet, unaffected timbre that's exactly right for her part, and she employs portamento in a way that would not be tolerated today; so much the worse for today. Her Jeník has a plangent tone and intimate delivery nearideal for the role, though some may be surprised at hearing such a light voice in a part now assigned to heavier tenors. The somewhat confined recording has been miraculously restored to obviate most of the drawbacks of the original. At the asking price, anyone interested in the early traditions of interpreting this work will enjoy a welcome bargain.

Libuše

Libuše
Gabriela Beňačková *sop* Libuše **Václav Zítek** *ten*
Přemysl **Antonín Svorc** *bass* Chrudoš **Leo Marian**
Vodička *ten* Stáhlav **Karel Průša** *bass* Lubtor **René**
Tuček *bar* Radovan **Eva Děpoltová** *sop* Krasava **Věra**
Soukupová *mez* Radmila **Prague National Theatre**
Chorus and Orchestra / Zdeněk Košler
Supraphon ③ 11 1276-2 (166' · DDD) Recorded live 1983. Notes, text and translation included

Ⓕ●

Libuše is a patriotic pageant, static and celebratory, with such plot as there's concerning the mythical founder of Prague, Libuše, and her marriage to the peasant Přemysl, founder of the first Czech dynasty. Václav Zítek makes a fine, heroic Přemysl; but the triumphant performance comes, as it must, from Gabriela Beňačková. The opera concludes with a series of tableaux in which Libuše prophesies the future kings and heroes who will assure the stability and greatness of the nation. At the end of a long performance her voice is undimmed in its ringing splendour; and earlier, as near the very start, the beauty of her tone and line seeks out all the warmth, character and humanity which she proves to be latent in Smetana's spacious but seemingly plain vocal writing. *Libuše* is scarcely Smetana's greatest opera, as he liked to claim, but especially in so splendid a performance from Beňačková, and under the grave but impassioned direction of Zdeněk Košler, it makes compelling listening. The live recording does include some applause, but there's little else in the way of distraction.

Fernando Sor
Spanish 1778-1839

After leaving Spain, Spanish composer and guitarist Fernando Sor lived in Paris (1813-15 and from 1826) and London (1815-26) and visited Russia (1823). He was a famous concert performer and wrote over 60 guitar works (sonatas, studies, variations etc) and an important method (1830). His guitar music is notable for its part-writing. He was also admired for his songs and eight ballets (1821-8); other works include an opera (1797) and chamber and keyboard pieces. **GROVE**music

Guitar Works

Fantaisies – No 12, Op 58; No 13, Op 59, 'Fantaisie élégiaque'. Studies, Op 60
Nicholas Goluses *gtr*
Naxos 8 553342 (65' · DDD) Recorded 1994

Ⓢ

Sor's guitar music forms a body of work that's perhaps the most consistent in quality, and most manageable in quantity of any major guitar composer of the period. While he was born and died later than Beethoven Sor's language was closer to that of Mozart, barely on the edge of romanticism.

He was a polished, elegant composer, whose works have more quiet emotional content and expressiveness than those of his contemporaries, and though he often calls for technical virtuosity he doesn't lean too heavily on it. The *Fantaisie*, Op 58 isn't one of Sor's more riveting works. Goluses plays it in a somewhat matter-of-fact way. The *Fantaisie élégiaque*, arguably Sor's finest single work, elicits a very different response, a deeply sensitive and dignified reading in which the moments of silent grief are given the breathing-space they call for. Sor devoted five opus numbers to his 97 studies, of which Op 60 was the last. Each has a clear technical and/or musical purpose and even the simplest is lovingly crafted music – which is how Goluses treats it, with lots of care lavished on it.

The guitar of Sor's time differed from today's in construction, stringing and sound, and Sor played without using the right-hand nails. Goluses uses a modern instrument and plays with nails, which inevitably leads to differences in sound and, to some extent, interpretation. Accepting the differences, Goluses sets a benchmark for present-day guitarists.

Grand Sonatas – C, Op 22; C, Op 25. Divertissement, Op 23. Eight Short Pieces, Op 24
Adam Holzman *gtr*
Naxos 8 553340 (75' · DDD) Recorded 1994

Ⓢ

The major works in Holzman's programme are the two sonatas, each with four movements. Of these Op 25 is by far the finer – and the best work of its kind from the period; the last movement is a Minuet, a final lightening of atmosphere that was not then uncommon. The *Divertissement*, Op 23 contains 10 pieces – *Valses*,

Allegrettos, *Andantes*, a *Minuetto* and an *Allemande*. With a few exceptions they're more likely to be of interest to guitarists than to the general listener. Holzman plays very well, with a softer sound than Goluses (see above), and in a tighter acoustic. At slower tempos he exercises a pleasing degree of rubato and commendable dynamic shading; one wishes he had done likewise in the quicker ones, which incline to the metronomic. These are two discs that should, both in their own right and at super-budget price, be irresistible to guitarists.

Introduction and Variations on 'Que ne suis-je la fougère!', Op 26. Introduction and Variations on 'Gentil Housard', Op 27. Introduction and Variations on 'Malbroug', Op 28. 12 Studies, Op 29. Fantaisie et Variations brillantes, Op 30
Jeffrey McFadden gtr
Naxos 8 553451 (62' · DDD)　　　　　　Ⓢ Ⓢ ●●

This contribution to Naxos's integral archive of Sor's guitar music consists neatly of the last works he published with Meissonnier, before transferring to Pacini. Sets of variations, whether *per se* or framed in the *Fantaisie*, Op 30, abound. The *12 Studies*, Op 29 are described as 'Book 2', those of Op 6 being 'Book 1', and are here given as Nos 13-24, as they were in the original edition of 1827. Jeffrey McFadden is a very musical player, with the clear and three-dimensional tone for which his fingers are admirably suited. No composer for the guitar of the time wrote studies that were more truly expressive than those of Sor; McFadden plays them, and everything else here, with humanity and respect. An outstanding disc.

Kaikhosru Sorabji   English 1892–1988

Sorabji was of Spanish-Sicilian-Parsi parentage. Largely self-taught, he became known in the 1920s for luxuriant and polyphonic piano works in a style relatable to Szymanowski and Busoni, and sometimes of enormous duration: the Opus clavicembalisticum (1930) plays for nearly three hours. But soon after writing it he withdrew from public activity and placed an embargo on his music, though he continued to compose immense piano and symphonic works, many incorporating Eastern influences. Only in 1976 did he allow performances to recommence. He was a biting critic of flashing wit, who often praised composers who only later became fashionable; his two books contain many of those essays. **GROVE**music

Piano Works

Legendary Works for Piano
Fantaisie espagnole. Fantasiettina. Gulistän. Le jardin parfumé. Nocturne. Three Pastiches. Opus clavicembalisticum – Introito and Preludio-Corale. Prelude, Interlude and Fugue. Quaere reliqua hujus materiei inter secretiora. St Bertrand de Comminges, 'He was laughing in the tower'. Two Pieces. Valse-Fantaisie. Fragment for Harold Rutland **Habermann** A la manière de Sorabji: 'Au clair de la lune'
Michael Habermann pf
British Music Society ③ 3-for-the-price-of-2
BMS427/9CD (197' · ADD/DDD)　　　　　　Ⓕ

The music of Sorabji acquired mythic status long before his death in 1988 at the age of 96, not least through the ban on public performances imposed by him in 1938. When the ban was lifted in 1976 Michael Habermann was among the first pianists to take up Sorabji in earnest. The fruits of his devotion – technically and conceptually – to some of the most demanding music yet conceived for piano can be heard on these recordings, made over a 15-year period.

Spanning mainly the period 1918-41, the set covers the first half of Sorabji's career, dominated by the vast *Opus clavicembalisticum*, later championed by John Ogdon and Geoffrey Douglas Madge, and represented here by a swift and eventful rendition of its first two sections. 'In the Hothouse' and *Fantaisie espagnole* will appeal to anyone who enjoys the more demonstrative output of Scriabin or Szymanowski, while the pastiches show that Sorabji's music wasn't without humour.

The second disc comprises a trio of nocturnes: pieces whose rhapsodic unfolding belies their intricacy of construction. If the harmonic profile of *Le jardin parfumé* draws in resonances of Delius and pre-echoes of Messiaen, that of *Djâmî* represents a sublimation of means to wholly original ends – and is the undoubted masterpiece of this collection. Aficionados would no doubt make even greater claims for *Gulistän*, but here the very complexity of texture seems designed to conceal rather than intensify expression.

As to the performances, there can be no doubting the extent of Habermann's sympathies, nor his depth of insight. The sound as remastered here has considerably more tonal depth than the selection which ASV reissued some years ago). The release comes with informative notes by Habermann, and can be cordially recommended to those keen to immerse themselves in a composer whose singularity of expression is sometimes matched by the conviction of his achievement.

Louis Spohr   German 1784-1859

Spohr gained his first important experience as a chamber musician at the Brunswick court, soon becoming a virtuoso violinist and touring throughout Germany; his playing was influenced particularly by his admiration for Rode. As Konzertmeister in Gotha (1805-12) he took up conducting (with a baton) and had some of his own works performed

but was most successful as a touring artist (1807-21) with his wife, the harpist Dorette Scheidler. Operatic conducting posts at Vienna (1813-15) and Frankfurt (1817-19) coincided with significant bursts of composing activity, yielding chamber music and the successful operas Faust (1813) and Zemire und Azor (1819). He settled down as Kapellmeister at Kassel in 1822, where the premières of Jessonda (1823; his greatest operatic success), the oratorio Die letzten Dinge (1826) and the Symphony No 4 (1832) were major achievements; here too he contributed to the cultivation of interest in both Bach and Wagner. A favourite in England, he received international honours and became Generalmusikdirektor at Kassel (1847), but by the 1850s he was an aging, middle-class representative of a rather sober tradition, and after his death his works were largely forgotten. Spohr's early Romantic origins and his devotion to Mozart largely determined his style, with its careful craftsmanship and adherence to classical forms but also its freely expressive elements (much chromaticism and a fondness for the elegiac). Among his instrumental works (15 violin and 10 other concertos, ten symphonies, virtuoso solo works, scores of chamber works, including a series of double quartets), the four clarinet concertos, the string quartets, the Violin Concerto No 8 ('In the form of a vocal scene') and the Octet and Nonet for wind and strings are noteworthy. His operas anticipate Wagner in being through-composed and in their use of leitmotif.
GROVEmusic

Violin Concertos

Violin Concertos – No 1 in A, Op 1; No 14 in A minor, Op 110, 'Sonst und Jetzt'; No 15 in E minor, Op 128
Ulf Hoelscher vn **Berlin Radio Symphony Orchestra / Christian Fröhlich**
CPO CPO999 403-2 (66' · DDD)　　　Ⓑ

Hoelscher has the elegance and almost vocal quality with which Spohr's violin writing is associated, but he can also master the virtuosity which is needed for the oddest work here, entitled *Sonst und Jetzt*, or 'Then and Now'. There's something of an in-joke for violinists here. Irritated by the playing of the Norwegian virtuoso, Ole Bull, whom Schumann regarded as the equal of Paganini, Spohr wrote this piece contrasting the lyrical qualities of the violin (in an expansive re-creation of the Minuet) with a hectic *Tarantella* embodying all he disliked in the showy 'modern' style. The idea falls flat as a piece of music criticism, simply because Spohr produces rather a good *Tarantella* and integrates it ingeniously and not contentiously with his more lyrical music. Hoelscher could have made the point by playing the two kinds of music in more extreme fashion; but, if it's true that nothing is colder than the ashes of dead controversies, the more musical course is to play the work as he does, warmly and without *partipris*. The Concerto No 15 is a rather more weary piece, in which Spohr goes through the motions expertly but without his full creative attention. Op 1 is a juvenile work (he was 18), obviously close to his beloved Mozart in spirit

but also heavily influenced by Kreutzer, Rode and especially Viotti. The best movement is the delightful *Siciliano*, which Spohr embellishes lovingly.

Piano Trios

Piano Trios – No 3 in A minor, Op 124; No 4 in B flat, Op 133
Borodin Trio (Rostislav Dubinsky vn Laszlo Varga vc Luba Edlina pf)
Chandos CHAN9372 (66' · DDD) Recorded 1994　　Ⓕ

Spohr's late piano trios are virtuoso works, in every sense. They are ingeniously composed and are difficult to balance with true effect; above all they demand great technical dexterity, and the dexterity to allow many extremely difficult passages to play a secondary or supporting role. In particular No 3 in A minor places demands on the players who need virtuosity of the kind which the Borodin Trio are well able to provide. Their skills need no recommendation; here, they also have a subtlety and quickness of response that come from a proper sympathy with Spohr's idiom. They rise to the occasion with, for instance, the racing piano fingerwork in the Variations of No 3; they also respond with the flexibility of tempo the music needs for its full expressive effect. Moreover, in places where Spohr seems to have lost concentration for a moment – his capacity to meander down beguiling but distracting chromatic paths, his habit of striking a cliché chord like a dramatic attitude, his gear-changing modulations – the Borodin hold faith and make the music come off effectively. The A minor Trio is the more worthwhile piece, and deserves all this interpretative concentration; but the rather less well invented work in B flat, apparently here receiving a first recording, is worth having for some recreational music.

The recording team can't always have had an easy task with balance; it all works excellently.

Sir John Stainer　　　British 1840-1901

English organist, scholar and composer Stainer, after appointments at St Michael's College, Tenbury, and Oxford University, became organist at St Paul's Cathedral (1872-88), reforming the musical service there, increasing the number of musicians and expanding the repertory. He soon became a pre-eminent church musician, scholar and composer, helping found the Musical Association, and becoming professor at Oxford University. He was knighted in 1888. As a scholar he made valuable editions of music before Palestrina and Tallis (Early Bodleian Music, 1901). His services and anthems were fashionable during his lifetime and his hymn tunes are still used; his oratorio The Crucifixion (1887) is one of his best-known works. GROVEmusic

The Crucifixion

Martyn Hill ten **Michael George** bass **BBC Singers; Leith Hill Festival Singers / Brian Kay** with **Margaret Phillips** org
Chandos CHAN9551 (71' · DDD) Text included Ⓕ🅞

Stainer's *Crucifixion* unfolds with a seamless ease, never jolting the listener with gratuitous theatricality or the type of rhetorical intensity which the English find mildly embarrassing. The emotional engagement here is about an unintrusive sobriety, affected by a glowing sentimental identification with the Saviour's plight. One has to admire Stainer for writing a challenging work of sensible length which, without an orchestra, is achievable and satisfying for a capable parish choir: Stainer's *Crucifixion* is a celebration of amateurism, that cherished English virtue. Brian Kay has worked a great deal with committed amateurs, in this case the Leith Hill Festival Singers, the festival of which he's director. There's an underlying freshness of expression here, of singers with eyes and ears on stalks and a real sense of purpose. They are fortified by the excellent BBC Singers. Margaret Phillips's imaginative, genial registrations, not to mention her skilful accompaniment, provide notable support to the fine contributions of the soloists. An unselfregarding and genuine performance.

Sir Charles Villiers Stanford

Irish/British 1852-1924

Stanford was educated at Cambridge (1880-84), where he was appointed organist of Trinity College in 1873 and professor in 1887; from 1883 he also taught at the RCM (his own education had been completed under Reinecke in Leipzig, 1874-5, and Kiel in Berlin, 1876). A demanding and highly influential teacher, he also demanded much of himself in living up to the great tradition, though the weight of academic responsibility could be leavened by his Irish heritage of folksong and mysticism and by his keen feeling for English words. Yet, apart from his Anglican cathedral music, little of his large output (nearly 200 opus numbers) has remained in performance. His works include ten operas (notably Shamus O'Brien, 1896; Much Ado about Nothing, 1901; and The Travelling Companion, given posthumously,1926), a quantity of choral music and songs (his B flat Service of 1879 is still used, and some of his sensitive partsongs are remembered, particularly The Blue Bird), seven symphonies and other orchestral scores (Clarinet Concerto, 1902, and a series of Irish Rhapsodies), eight string quartets, and organ and piano music. GROVEmusic

Violin Concerto

Violin Concerto in D, Op 74. Suite for Violin and Orchestra, Op 32
Anthony Marwood vn **BBC Scottish Symphony Orchestra / Martyn Brabbins**
Hyperion CDA67208 (67' · DDD) Ⓕ🅞

This is a discovery of major importance. Hubert Parry (no mean critic) regarded Stanford's Violin Concerto as one of his finest works, yet it has been played rarely, if at all, since his death in 1924. One preliminary word of warning though: despite Stanford's reputation as a disciple of Brahms, don't listen to this concerto expecting it to sound Brahmsian. Often enough it does, but when it doesn't it isn't because Stanford has failed to match the quality of his 'model'; far more often it's because he's going his own way, speaking with his own and not a derivative voice.

The very opening of the concerto is a case in point: the soloist's melody is accompanied by a beautifully delicate texture of plucked strings and rippling woodwind. There's nothing quite like it in Brahms; nor is Brahms always so generous with his thematic material as Stanford is in this movement. After that 'first subject' and an extensive and varied 'second subject group', a big and dramatic orchestral *tutti* leads not to the expected development but to a new and quite splendid theme. There's plenty of room for virtuosity, but very often the display is modified by a pensive quality, a reticence, that's seemingly Stanford's own, and most attractive.

The slow movement is also notable for its individual scoring (very spare at the outset; a magical return of the melancholy opening melody at the end over murmuring *tremolando* strings) and for its melodic distinction. The sadness of the first theme is again reticent, adding greatly to the eloquence of the heartfelt *tutti* that leads to the finest theme in the entire work, upon which Stanford lavishes rhapsodic figuration of great beauty.

There's not a player better suited to bringing this concerto back to life than Anthony Marwood. He easily surmounts its technical demands, but his distinction as a chamber musician enables him to seek out all its quieter subtleties and pensive asides. The Suite is a lesser but still highly entertaining work, an exercise in neo-Baroque designed as a warmly affectionate tribute to Joseph Joachim. Its sheer ingenuity (the first movement, for example, is a combination of sonata form and two sets of interlocked variations) saves it from being a mere exercise, and its melodic freshness from being a mere makeweight to the masterly concerto. First-class orchestral playing, sympathetically conducted, and a recording that's both clean and spacious.

Symphony No 3 in F minor, 'Irish'

Stanford Symphony No 3 in F minor, 'Irish', Op 28
Elgar Scenes from the Bavarian Highlands, Op 27
Bournemouth Symphony Chorus; Bournemouth Sinfonietta / Norman Del Mar
EMI British Composers 565129-2 (70' · ADD) Recorded 1981-2. Text included Ⓑ🅞

A valuable addition to the catalogue on its initial appearance, Norman Del Mar's characteristically enterprising 1982 recording of Stanford's Irish Symphony re-emerges in splendidly vital fashion on this beautifully presented release. Compared with Vernon Handley and the excellent Ulster Orchestra on Chandos, Del Mar is perhaps just a touch lacking in charm and it's undoubtedly the former who more effectively minimises the element of dutiful convention which occasionally afflicts both outer movements (Handley is nearly three minutes quicker in the opening *Allegro moderato*, yet there's no feeling of undue haste). However, Del Mar draws the threads together most satisfyingly for the symphony's ample peroration, and his Bournemouth band responds with commendable vigour throughout. Preceding the Stanford is the orchestral version of Elgar's *Scenes from the Bavarian Highlands* getting a rare outing. This six-movement choral suite shows Elgar at his most carefree and joyous, qualities savoured to the full in Del Mar's exuberant performance.

Piano Quartet No 1

Piano Quartet No 1, Op 15[a]. Piano Trio No 1, Op 35
[a]Philip Dukes *va* Pirasti Trio (Nicholas Miller *vn* Alison Wells *vc* Jeffrey Sharkey *pf*)
ASV CDDCA1056 (59' · DDD)   Ⓕ

Stanford was 26 when he completed his First Piano Quartet in April 1879. It's a delightful discovery in every way, whose purposeful, driving outer movements frame a delectably clean-cut, skipping *scherzo* and an autumnal, at times very Brahmsian *Poco adagio* of burnished lyrical beauty. In the similarly assured First Piano Trio of 10 years later, Brahms's shadow looms more intimidatingly over the landscape and there's perhaps not quite the same youthful, carefree quality to Stanford's sturdy inspiration. All the same, there are a few surprises in store, not least the extended *Tempo di menuetto ma molto moderato* third movement with its two trio sections – and the way the winsome second movement coquettishly dallies between the home key of G minor and relative major of B flat.

The Pirasti Trio prove eloquent, unfailingly stylish advocates throughout. For the Piano Quartet, they're joined by that admirable violist, Philip Dukes. Boasting truthful sound and pleasing balance, this exemplary coupling earns a firm recommendation.

String Quartets

String Quartets – No 1; No 2. Fantasy[a]
RTÉ Vanbrugh Quartet (Gregory Ellis, Keith Pascoe *vns* Simon Aspell *va* Christopher Marwood *vc*) with [a]Stephen Stirling *hn*
Hyperion CDA67434 (68' · DDD)   Ⓕ

Stanford wrote the first two of his eight string quartets within just six weeks during the sum-

mer of 1891. Cast in four movements and impeccably laid out for the medium, the G major First Quartet launches with an impressive *Allegro assai*, whose considerable intellectual and expressive resource is quarried to the full by the Vanbrughs. Both the *Scherzo* and finale smile as they should, while these fine players bring a rare eloquence to the deeply felt slow movement. Superior craftsmanship is also a trademark of its A minor companion. The first movement's ruminative main theme is developed further still in the *Andante espressivo* slow movement. In between comes a dashing *Prestissimo scherzo*. The work concludes with an irresistible *Allegro molto* (whose cheeky initial idea brings with it more than a whiff of Hungarian paprika).

The A minor Fantasy for horn and string quartet (1922), a companion piece to the Two Fantasy Pieces for clarinet quintet completed not long before, shares that diptych's formal integration (its four sections are interlinked) and technical flair. Stephen Stirling audibly relishes the superbly judged horn writing and generates a most satisfying rapport with the Vanbrughs.

These exemplary first recordings make the best possible case for all this rare material; sound and balance are first-class, too.

Requiem, Op 63

Requiem. The Veiled Prophet of Khorassan – Overture; Ballet music No 1; There's a bower of roses; Ballet music No 2
Virginia Kerr, Frances Lucey *sops* **Colette McGahon** *mez* **Peter Kerr** *ten* **Nigel Leeson-Williams** *bass-bar* **RTÉ Philharmonic Choir and National Symphony Orchestra of Ireland / Adrian Leaper, Colman Pearce**
Naxos ② 8 555201/2 (105' · DDD · T)   Ⓢ

This resissue of a late-Victorian masterpiece gains the well-deserved chance of wider circulation on the popular Naxos label. The Requiem was written in 1896 in memory of Lord Leighton. Scored for the usual forces of solo quartet, chorus and orchestra, it strikes a familiar balance between grief and condolence; its manner is essentially lyrical, its form determined by that of the Mass and by its well-defined musical climaxes. Yet the composer's individuality is everywhere unobtrusively evident, as is the warmth of his feeling. If these things were indeed too unobtrusive to gain recognition in their own time and the largely unsympathetic century that followed, they should win it now.

The performance is admirable, with good work by all four soloists. A special word of appreciation is due to the delightful soprano, Frances Lucey. The choir needs more presence in the recorded sound, which in general is none too sharply defined. The excerpts from *The Veiled Prophet*, another rarity, provide a well-chosen bonus.

Stabat mater, Op 96

Stabat mater, Op 96. Te Deum, Op 10 No 1.
Six Bible Songs, Op 113
Ingrid Attrot sop **Pamela Helen Stephen** mez **Nigel Robson** ten **Stephen Varcoe** bar **Ian Watson** org
Leeds Philharmonic Chorus; BBC Philharmonic Orchestra / Richard Hickox
Chandos CHAN9548 (74' · DDD) Texts and
translations included Ⓕ⊙

Writing of his old teacher in 1952, Vaughan Williams foretold that his time would come round again: 'With the next generation the inevitable reaction will set in and Stanford will come into his own.' It has taken more than a generation, but at last it does begin to look as though he was right. This recording of a 'symphonic cantata', the *Stabat mater*, strong in ideas, deeply felt and structurally assured, will certainly strengthen the steadily growing appreciation of his worth. The Prelude, impressive as it is, is almost *too* soundly constructed, and the first choral movement, rich in its Verdi-like foreground of soloists, signs off with a slightly self-conscious repetition of the opening words by the soprano. Stanford is never abashed by the prospect of melodic commitment, and the orchestral Intermezzo comes out boldly with what promises to be a good, old-fashioned Grand Tune; but then he seems to remember where he is, and the piece ends with murky explorations that seem not quite to find what they may be seeking. The work itself ends, as Lewis Foreman suggests in his useful notes, in Eternity: 'we seem to reach the crest of a hill only to find the path stretching onward and upward to another.' The performance carries conviction, with Hickox exercising that natural rightness of his so that in a work such as this, without predecessors on record, a listener will feel that this is how it should 'go'.

Fine orchestral playing and choral singing give pleasure throughout. The solo quartet is led by Ingrid Attrot's colourful but none too evenly produced soprano, and in the *Bible Songs* Stephen Varcoe sings sensitively to the judiciously registered organ accompaniment of Ian Watson. The most tuneful of *Te Deum*s follows, blithe and buoyant in its orchestrated version.

Morning and Evening Services

Morning and Evening Services in B flat, Op 10[a].
Evening Services – A, Op 12[a]; F, Op 36[a]; E flat[b]. Two Anthems, Op 37[b]. Three Motets, Op 38. Pater noster. The Lord is my Shepherd[a]
Winchester Cathedral Choir / David Hill with [a]**Stephen Farr,** [b]**Christopher Monks** org
Hyperion CDA66964 (78' · DDD) Texts included Ⓕ⊙

The *Magnificat and Nunc dimittis* in E flat major dates back to 1873 isn't with any certainty known even to have been performed. Perhaps this is because both settings are almost inde-

cently tuneful: an apocalyptic 'scattered the proud', a broadly melodious 'to be a light' and a 'Gloria' as catchy as a comic opera. As for the B flat major settings written six years later, these (both Morning and Evening services) have long owed their popularity to a melodic gift that's almost Schubertian and a correspondingly deft mastery of construction.

Winchester Cathedral Choir is surely one of the best in the UK. Under David Hill, the trebles have some of the bright, distinctive tone of the Westminster Cathedral boys. The men are excellent, and all sound as though they're singing for the joy of it. Several of these works involve more than the customary four parts, and the eight-part *Pater noster*, recorded for the first time, has splendid richness, with the choir forming massive pillars of sound in the powerful climax. Stanford's writing for the organ is also a delight, and at times we might wish that the fine playing of both organists had been brought into sharper focus. The choir we hear with rare clarity.

Evening Service in G, Op 81. Services in C, Op 115.
Six Short Preludes and Postludes: Set 2, Op 105 –
No 3, Prelude in G; No 6, Postlude in D minor. For lo,
I raise up, Op 145. Three Motets, Op 38.
St John's College Choir, Cambridge / Christopher Robinson org
Naxos 8 555794 (72' · DDD) ⑤Ⓢ⊙

The mean old saying, 'Those who can, do, and those who can't, teach', would have withered in the presence of Stanford; and no doubt one of the reasons why he was such a great teacher is that he could and did, and so set an example. His C major services (Morning, Evening and Communion, all included in this programme) are so eminently the works of a master who knows how to get from here to there in one move, to keep always something in reserve for later use but never to write without a good clear melodic idea in the first place. Everything in this programme has freshness and well-founded assurance. It's music with clarity of purpose: it knows where it's going and doesn't put a foot wrong.

Under Christopher Robinson, the choir has enjoyed a period in which the distinguishing mark has been a renewed vitality of style. It's well caught in this CD. The start of the first track, the C major Te Deum, has it straightaway – the praise carries spirit and conviction. The final track opens still more strikingly. This is *For lo, I will raise up*, for which Stanford, writing in 1914, set his imagination free to bestir the choir-stalls into an almost fiercely dramatic life. The St John's choir bite into the words with relish, while the acoustic and their well-judged tempo reinforce the rhythmic energy of the passage.

Even in the best-stocked collection this would prove a welcome addition, and for those who have as yet nothing of the master, it should provide a lively introduction.

Songs

Tragödie, Op 14 No 5. Op 19 – No 2, A Lullaby; No 5,
To the Rose. Windy Nights, Op 30 No 4. Clown's
Songs from 'Twelfth Night', Op 65. The Fairy Lough,
Op 77 No 2. Songs of the Sea, Op 91. Songs of Faith,
Op 97 – No 4, 'To the Soul'; No 6, 'Joy, Shipmate,
Joy'. Phoebe, Op 125. A Fire of Turf, Op 139. The
Pibroch, Op 157 No 1. For Ever Mine. Tom Lemmin
Stephen Varcoe bar **Clifford Benson** pf
Hyperion CDA67124 (77' · DDD) Texts and
translations included   Ⓕ◐

Stanford's *Songs of the Sea* have kept the British
baritone afloat for the best part of a century.
Drake's hammock and the barnacles of The Old
Superb used to be familiar in parlours and draw-
ing-rooms throughout the land. The cries of
Captain Keats and his crew ('"Ship ahoy!" a
hundred times a day'), the alliterative mysteries
of 'Fetter and Faith … Faggot and Father' and
the assurance that Drake even now was 'ware
and waking' were assimilated almost as the
words of folksongs, while the music seemed part
of our flesh and blood. They are splendid songs,
and the set of five constitutes a small masterpiece. Sceptical readers should try them again in
this new recording. Stephen Varcoe and Clifford Benson give a most sensitive performance,
not emasculated but treating them thoughtfully.
The two quieter songs, 'Outward Bound' and
'Homeward Bound', become more central, better integrated, than usual, and the very fact that
this is the solo version, without the male-voice
chorus added later, makes it easier to hear them
(the whole set) as a personal utterance. With
'Drake's Drum', for instance, Varcoe is very
intent upon seeing sense, where others have
often sought for little beyond a generalised
patriotic earnestness. These, perhaps, are *The
Songs of the Sea* as Captain Edward Fairfax Vere
might have sung them.

In reviewing the first volume, Michael Oliver
wrote of the difficulty of reconciling the Irishman and the Brahmsian in Stanford: the
melodic vein of the one seemed at odds with the
harmonic language of the other. The occasions
here when a dichotomy of style does cause trouble are found in the *Songs of Faith*. Whitman's
auto-intoxication incites Stanford to indulge in
grandiose gestures that aren't natural to him at
all. He's much more at home with Shakespeare
and Dekker, or, for that matter, with Quiller-
Couch and Winifred M Letts, whose *A Fire of
Turf* provides him with poems for some masterly settings. All are beautifully performed by
these excellent artists.

Wilhelm Stenhammar

Swedish 1871-1929

*Brought up in a cultivated and musical family,
Stenhammar composed from childhood and had little
formal training. His earlier music is in a late
Romantic style showing influences from Wagner,*

*Liszt and Brahms, but from 1910 he moved towards
a more classical manner, stimulated by contrapuntal
studies and a profound concern with Beethoven.
Much of his music has a Nordic colour, though he did
not use folk material. His works include two symphonies (1903, 1915), two piano concertos, a Serenade (1913), cantatas (Sången, 1921), six string
quartets (1894-1916) and songs. An admired
pianist, he was also conductor of the Göteborgs
Orkesterförening (1906-22), making the city a
musical rival to Stockholm.*   GROVEmusic

Piano Concerto No 1 in B flat, Op 1

Piano Concerto No 1. Symphony No 3 (fragment)
**Mats Widlund Royal Stockholm Philharmonic
Orchestra / Gennady Rozhdestvensky**
Chandos CHAN9074 (51' · DDD)   Ⓕ

The First Piano Concerto comes from 1893,
when Stenhammar was 22, a year after he'd
made his triumphant pianistic debut in Stockholm with the Brahms D minor Concerto. Both
the autograph and the orchestral parts were
destroyed during the Second World War but
the piano score and a short score survived, and
Kurt Atterburg, who'd heard Stenhammar play
the work several times, reconstructed the
orchestral part from memory. Dr Allen Ho discovered a copy of the full score in the Library of
Congress. It had apparently been bought from a
second-hand dealer in Berlin in 1904, and had
probably been made for the American premiere.
In general the scoring is thicker, more Germanic, and the wind and brass more active than
in the Atterberg reconstruction. Mats Widlund
brings colour and subtlety to the solo part and
Rozhdestvenasky proves an imaginative partner.

As a coupling Chandos offers the fragment
from the Symphony No 3 in C, on which Stenhammar embarked in 1918-19, prepared by
Tommy Andersson. There is a sturdy and exhilarating opening, and some characteristic
touches elsewhere, but some other ideas
(including the fanfare figures) don't cohere in a
fully convincing way.

Symphony No 2, Op 34

Excelsior! Symphony No 2
**Royal Scottish National Orchestra / Petter
Sundkvist**
Naxos 8 553888 (58' · DDD)   Ⓢ

This is the first recording of Stenhammar's
G minor Symphony to be made by a non-
Swedish orchestra; Petter Sundkvist, a young
Swedish conductor, draws very good results
from the Royal Scottish National Orchestra and
conducts this work with evident feeling.

This symphony grows more glorious with
every hearing and this time is no exception.
Sundkvist realizes its moments of poetry with a
natural ardour and eloquence and without the
slightest expressive self-indulgence. He builds

up the architecture of the symphony impressively.

The exhilarating *Excelsior!* overture can more than hold its own with any rival, even if the recording doesn't. The acoustic is a shade on the dryish side. Notwithstanding this caveat, the quality of the performance is such as to deserve a strong recommendation.

Alessandro Stradella   Italian 1644-1682

Stradella spent most of his career in Rome, where he lived independently but composed many works to commissions from Queen Christina of Sweden, the Colonna family and others. Most of his stage works there were prologues and intermezzos, notably for operas by Cavalli and Cesti revived at the new Tordinona Theatre in 1671-2. His life included many scandals and amorous adventures. He left Rome in 1677 after a dispute, and went by way of Venice and Turin (escaping an attempt on his life) to Genoa (1678). His only comic opera, Il Trespolo tutore, was given there in c 1677; later he presented several other operas, including Il Corispero. He was killed there in 1682, again a consequence of an amorous intrigue.

Stradella was one of the leading composers in Italy in his day and one of the most versatile. His music was widely admired, even as far afield as England. Most of it is clearly tonal, and counterpoint features prominently. His vocal output includes c 30 stage works, several oratorios and Latin church works and some 200 cantatas (most for solo voice). In his operas the orchestra consists of two violin parts and continuo, but some other works, such as the oratorio S Giovanni Battista (1675, Rome), follow the Roman principal of concerto grosso instrumentation. There is a clear differentiation between aria and recitative (which sometimes includes arioso writing), but their succession is still fluid; various aria forms are used. Stradella's 27 surviving instrumental works are mostly of the sonata da chiesa type. **GROVE**music

Cantatas

Ah! troppo è ver. Si apra al riso ogni labro. Sonata di viole
Lavinia Bertotti, Emanuela Galli, Barbara Zanichelli sops **Roberto Balconi** counterten
Maurizio Sciuto ten **Carlo Lepore** bass **Orchestra Barocca della Civica Scuola di Musica di Milano / Enrico Gatti**
Arcana A79 (67' · DDD) Texts included   Ⓕ

This disc features two Christmas cantatas, *Si apra al riso* for three mixed solo voices, two violins and continuo, and the larger *Ah! troppo è ver* for mixed solo voices, with a concertino of violin, cello and continuo, and *ripieno* strings supplying the *concerto grosso*. The disc also contains a Sonata consisting of concertino and ripieno elements, a *concerto grosso*, in fact, of which form Stradella was a pioneer. Gatti and his almost all-Italian ensemble of singers and instrumentalists enliven this music, his imagination responding unfailingly to Stradella's often individual, at times, quirky style, and his feeling for texture and declamation most impressive. These and other qualities may be sensed at once in the splendid, larger-than-life account of *Ah! troppo è ver*. The performances have rough patches, but they convey with fervour the spirit and atmosphere of the music.

San Giovanni Battista

San Giovanni Battista   Ⓟ
Catherine Bott, Christine Batty sops **Gérard Lesne** counterten **Richard Edgar-Wilson** ten **Philippe Huttenlocher** bar **Les Musiciens du Louvre / Marc Minkowski**
Erato 2292-45739-2 (61' · DDD) Recorded live 1991.
Notes, text and translation included   Ⓜ❍❍❍

Although an outstanding oratorio composer, Stradella was considered in his time foremost as a composer for the theatre, and he treated the New Testament story of the imprisonment and murder of John the Baptist with real dramatic force. San Giovanni Battista was first performed in Rome in 1657. The librettist, a Sicilian priest, Girardo Ansaldi, dispensed with a testo or narrator, concerning himself more directly with the exchanges between Herod and John the Baptist. Stradella portrays this relationship with great subtlety, as he does equally that between Herod, his wife Herodias and their daughter Salome.

The work is in two parts. Events in Part 1 are presented in three stages. After a Sinfonia comes a pastoral scene where John bids farewell to the countryside as he prepares to travel to Herod's court. Then the scene moves to the court, where the king's birthday festivities are in full swing. Stage three is marked by the arrival of John who interrupts proceedings, commanding Herod to give up his brother's wife. Herod is enraged and orders John to be thrown into prison. Part 2 contains the well-known events leading to the beheading of John, and concludes with a masterly duet in which the contrasting emotions of foreboding and joy are expressed by Herod and Salome.

Marc Minkowski has assembled a strong team of soloists with Gérard Lesne in the title-role. Additionally there are three brief sections allotted to a chorus fulfilling various functions in the first part of the oratorio. Minkowski paces the music well, making the most of Stradella's admirably effective contrasts of texture and mood. Lesne's portrayal of John the Baptist is affecting, and his warm tone and subdued vocal colour suit the music in Part 2 especially well. Herodias and Salome both come over well though neither singer succeeds in concealing the difficulties presented by Stradella's wide tessitura. Catherine Bott gives a virtuoso performance of her aria 'Sù, coronatemi' and Huttenlocher's Herod is splendid.

This animated and imaginative approach to a masterly score does the work justice. Minkowski realises the inherent richness of invention and the sheer beauty of the music with insight, affection and a lively awareness of its dramatic intent. The recording is excellent.

Eduard Strauss
Austrian 1835-1916

Johann Strauss I
Austrian 1804-1849

Josef Strauss
Austrian 1827-1870

Johann Strauss II
Austrian 1825-1899

This Austrian family of dance musicians and composers gave the Viennese waltz its classic expression. Johann senior, a violinist in Josef Lanner's dance orchestra, formed a band in 1825 which became famous for its open-air concerts with his original dance music and paraphrases on the symphonic and operatic music of the day, all performed with exquisite precision. He took the band on European tours from 1833, creating a sensation with the fire and finesse of his conducting, violin in hand. His music, its Austrian folk flavour refined by a characteristic rhythmic piquancy (cross-rhythms, syncopations, pauses and rests), includes over 150 sets of waltzes, besides galops, quadrilles (which he introduced to Vienna), marches (notably the Radetzky-Marsch Op 228), polkas and potpourris.

Johann had three sons who were composer-conductors. Johann II, also a violinist and the most eminent member of the family, directed his own orchestra, 1844-9, in rivalry with his father's; after 1849 the two Strauss bands were merged into one. Vienna's imperial-royal music director for balls, 1863-71, and Austria's best-known ambassador (the 'king of the waltz'), he was acclaimed by swarms of admirers, especially on European tours, 1856-86, and in the USA (1872). In form, his waltzes resemble his father's – slow introduction, five waltzes and coda – but the sections are longer and more organic; the melodies, often inspired, are wide and sweeping, the harmonic and orchestral details richer and more subtle, even Wagnerian in places. Among his most celebrated waltz masterpieces, dating from the 1860s and early 1870s, are Accellerationen Op 234, Wiener Bonbons Op 307, An die schönen, blauen Donau ('The Blue Danube') Op 314, Wein, Weib und Gesang Op 333 and Wiener Blut Op 354. Of his 17 operettas, the sparkling Die Fledermaus (1874) and the colourful Die Zigeunerbaron (1885) deservedly claim a central place in the repertory.

His brother Josef was a melancholy introvert, shared the direction of the family orchestra in the 1850s and 1860s, and composed waltzes in a more serious, Romantic vein, as well as polkas, quadrilles and marches. The younger brother Eduard, Vienna's imperial-royal music director for balls, 1872-1901, became the best conductor of the family and was much sought after by orchestras throughout Europe. **GROVE**music

Dance Music

Ein Straussfest II
E Strauss Ohne Aufenthalt, Op 112 **Josef Strauss** Plappermäulchen, Op 245. Sphären-Klänge, Op 235. Jockey, Op 278 **J Strauss I** Chinese Galop, Op 20 **J Strauss II** Ägyptischer Marsch, Op 335a. Künstler-Quadrille, Op 71. Kaiser-Walzer, Op 437. Freikugeln, Op 326. Jubelfest-Marsch, Op 396. Tritsch-Tratsch-Polka, Op 214. Geisselhiebe, Op 60. Klipp Klapp, Op 466. Wein, Weib und Gesang, Op 333. Perpetuum mobile, Op 257
Cincinnati Pops Chorale and Orchestra / Erich Kunzel
Telarc CD80314 (68' · DDD) Recorded 1991-92 ℗○

This collection sets out to adorn popular Strauss pieces with sound effects to outdo anything one hears at a Vienna New Year Concert. It starts with Eduard Strauss's *Ohne Aufenthalt*, which is accompanied by steam railway effects, has bullets flying mercilessly in the *Freikugeln* Polka, and includes neighing nags and swishing whips in the *Jockey* Polka. The fun is increased by the inclusion of the *Künstler-Quadrille*, a sort of 1850s 'Hooked on Classics' that begins with Mendelssohn's 'Wedding March' and continues through the likes of Mozart's Symphony No 40 and Chopin's 'Funeral March' Sonata to Beethoven's *Ruins of Athens* and *Kreutzer* Sonata. If the Viennese lilt is just a shade lacking in the waltzes, the playing is nevertheless excellent throughout. The Strausses themselves would have approved.

Additional recommendation

Waltzes
Vienna Johann Strauss Orchestra / Boskovsky
EMI Encore 575239-2 (77' · DDD) ⑤ⓑ○
 There have been no finer recordings of Johann Strauss than those by Willi Boskovsky. If you've no waltzes in your collection, this disc is a must.

New Year's Day Concerts

New Year's Day Concert 2000
E Strauss Mit Extrapost, Op 259. Gruss an Prag, Op 144 **J Strauss I** Radetzky March, Op 228 **J Strauss II** Lagunen-Walzer, Op 411. Hellenen-Polka, Op 203. Albion-Polka, Op 102. Liebeslieder, Op 114. Ritter Pasman – Csárdás. Wein, Weib und Gesang, Op 333. Persischer Marsch, Op 289. Process, Op 294. Eljen a Magyar!, Op 332. Vom Donaustrande, Op 356. An der schönen, blauen Donau, Op 314 **Josef Strauss** Die Libelle, Op 204. Künstlergruss, Op 274. Marien-Klänge, Op 214 **Suppé** Ein Morgen, ein Mittag, ein Abend in Wien – Overture
Vienna Philharmonic Orchestra / Riccardo Muti
EMI ② 567323-2 (92' · DDD) Ⓜ○

The title *Mit Extrapost* ('By Special Post') of the final item in the first half of this New Year's Concert might just as readily apply to the remarkable way in which record companies these days get out the finished article within 10 days or so of the actual performance. The only trace of corners being cut is in the absence of track timings. Otherwise the result is perfection itself – a polished presentation of a concert that seemed exhilarating and stylish on television on New Year's Day and does so no less now. The balance between familiar and unfamiliar in the programme is as well judged as ever. The latter includes a fair homage to various nationalities – to the Greeks in the *Hellenen-Polka*, the British in the *Albion-Polka*, the Czechs in *Gruss an Prag* – to complement the more familiar *Persischer-Marsch* and *Eljen a Magyar!* Utterly delightful is another piece that, surprisingly, received its first performance at these concerts – Josef's *Marien-Klänge* Waltz, which confirms the second brother's unique sensitivity and refinement. Among the more familiar items, Muti also takes the right option in giving the full version of the *Wein, Weib und Gesang* Waltz, which is too often played with its introduction abridged. Most importantly, the music throughout flows along as naturally and beguilingly as the Danube itself. Nobody who has enjoyed any previous Vienna New Year Concert should be disappointed with this new one.

New Year's Day Concert 2002
J Hellmesberger II Danse diabolique **J Strauss I**
Radetzky-Marsch **J Strauss II** Die Fledermaus – Overture. Hünstlerleben. Zivio! Eisen-Polka. Wiener Blut. Tik-Tak. An der schönen, blaüen Donau **Josef Strauss** Die Schwätzerin. Vorwärts! Aquarellen. Die Libelle. Plappermäulchen!
Vienna Philharmonic Orchestra / Seiji Ozawa
Philips 468 999-2PH (79' · DDD)   Ⓕ❍

Ozawa, always happy in balletic music, which in effect Strauss's waltzes and polkas are, draws the most refined playing from the Vienna Philharmonic. If there were some raised eyebrows at the choice of Ozawa, plainly there's complete rapport between players and conductor.

Fully at home in the idiom, Ozawa dares to exaggerate the Viennese lilt in waltzes, encouraging the orchestra to indulge in a habit, once more marked than it usually is now, of anticipating the second beat of the bar. Certainly, Harnoncourt in 2001's concert (Teldec), though Viennese in his background, took a more purist attitude. As it is, the waltzes *Artist's Life*, *Aquarellen*, *Vienna Blood* and the traditional encore, *The Blue Danube*, have a coaxing persuasiveness impossible to resist, and the recording isn't just ripe in the way one expects of the venue, but clearer on detail than it sometimes has been. If one quality marks out the whole concert, it's the daring of Ozawa's control of *rubato*, aided by the unfailing responsiveness of the VPO. A truly Viennese experience.

New Year's Day Concert, 2003
Brahms Hungarian Dances – No 5 in G minor; No 6 in D (orch Reichert) J Strauss I Chineser Galopp. Radetzky-Marsch **J Strauss II** Kaiser-Franz-Joseph I

Rettungs-Jubel-Marsch. Der Zigeunerbaron – Schatzwalzer. Niko-Polka. Scherz-Polka. Secunden. Hellenen-Polka. Kaiser-Walzer. Bauern-Polka. Lob der Frauen. Leichtes Blut. Krönungslieder. Furioso-Polka. An der schönen blauen Donau Josef Strauss Delirien. Pêle-mêle Weber Invitation to the Dance, J260 (orch Berlioz)
Vienna Philharmonic Orchestra / Nikolaus Harnoncourt
DG ② 474 250-2GH2 (107' · DDD)   Ⓜ❍

Unusually in 2003's New Year's Day concert there's nothing by the supporting cast of Viennese dance composers such as Hellmesberger, Komzák or Ziehrer. Instead, Weber, as arranged by Berlioz (in his bicentenary year), and Brahms get to show their dance steps, not to mention Brahms's orchestrator here, Friedrich D Reichert. Otherwise it's all Strauss.

The now customary international touch is provided most obviously by the *Hellenen-Polka*, marking the accession of Greece to the EU presidency in 2003. By contrast, the international scene of the Strausses' time is recalled by the waltz *Krönungslieder*, composed for the coronation of Tsar Alexander II in 1856, and the sprightly *Niko-Polka*.

The Vienna Philharmonic is unmatched in this repertory. With a native conductor such as Harnoncourt, with an instinctive feel for the music, even familiar numbers such as Johann's *Kaiser-Walzer* and Josef's glorious *Delirien* waltz receive outstanding performances. Not least, the *Furioso-Polka* provides an absolutely exhilarating conclusion.

Graceful and fiery by turns, and always supremely polished, this must rank among the very best of Vienna New Year Concerts.

Vocal Music

A Tribute to Johann Strauss
J Strauss II Schwipslied[a]. Die Fledermaus – Overture; Spiel' ich die Unschuld[a]. Frühlingsstimmen, Op 410[a]. Im Krapfenwald'l, Op 336. Liebeslieder, Op 114[a]. Eine Nacht in Venedig – Frutti di mare!...Seht, oh seht![a]. Pesther Csárdás, Op 23. Pizzicato Polka. Die Tänzerin Fanny Elssler – Draussen in Sievering[a] (arr Stalla). Wiener Blut – Wiener Blut[a] (arr Müller). Wienerwald Lerchen[a] (arr Schönherr). Wo die Zitronen blüh'n, Op 364[a] (arr Genée)
[a]**Sumi Jo** sop **Vienna Volksoper Orchestra / Rudolf Bibl**
Erato 3984-25500-2 (58' · DDD) Texts and translations included   Ⓕ❍

Here is an imaginatively conceived and brilliantly executed collection of vocal Johann Strauss numbers. In an exciting performance of the original soprano solo version of *Frühlingsstimmen*, Sumi Jo's luxurious coloratura soars gloriously over the orchestra. The vocal arrangement of the *Liebeslieder-Walzer* and Richard Genée's show-piece adaptation of *Wo die Zitronen blüh'n* are no less thrilling. But it's by no means just the coloratura pieces in which Sumi Jo excels. The characterisation she gives to the contrasted parts of the audition song from *Die Fledermaus* makes it as compelling an interpretation as any. The fish-selling song from *Eine Nacht in Venedig* comes up with equal freshness. Add the way she skips from note to note in 'Draussen in Sievering' and the gentle hiccup at the end of the 'Tipsy Song' (an adaptation of the *Annen-Polka*), and one has an uncommonly well-thought-out and superbly varied collection. The participation of the Vienna Volksoper players under veteran conductor Rudolf Bibl ensures the authentic style not only in the vocal items but also in the short linking orchestral pieces. There was no need, though, for yet another *Fledermaus* Overture. It's a pity, too, that Michael Rot's excellently scholarly notes are sadly mangled in their English translation. Nothing, though, can diminish the exquisite quality of Sumi Jo's singing.

Die Fledermaus

Die Fledermaus
Julia Varady *sop* Rosalinde **Lucia Popp** *sop* Adele
Hermann Prey *ten* Eisenstein **René Kollo** *ten* Alfred
Bernd Weikl *bar* Doctor Falke **Ivan Rebroff**
bass/mez Prince Orlofsky **Benno Kusche** *bar* Frank
Ferry Gruber *ten* Blind **Evi List** *sop* Ida **Franz**
Muzeneder *bass* Frosch **Bavarian State Opera Chorus and Orchestra / Carlos Kleiber**
DG The Originals ② 457 765-2GOR2 (107' · ADD)
Recorded 1975. Notes, text and translation included
Ⓜ️**OO**

Twenty-five years after its original release there's still no recording of *Die Fledermaus* that, for many collectors, matches this one for the compelling freshness of its conductor's interpretation – the attention to every nuance of the score and the ability to bring out some new detail, all allied to extreme precision of vocal and instrumental ensemble. The ladies, too, as so often seems to be the case in recordings of *Die Fledermaus*, are quite superlatively good, with ideally characterised and projected singing. If the men are generally less outstandingly good, one can have no more than minor quibbles with the Eisenstein of Hermann Prey or the Alfred of René Kollo. But it's less easy to accept Ivan Rebroff singing the role of Orlofsky falsetto. Some collectors find that his contribution quite ruins the whole set, but most will find it tolerable enough for the glories to be found elsewhere on the recording. DG remastered the set to make it sound as though it were recorded only yesterday; but it continues to provoke puzzlement by the break between discs, which occurs during the Act 2 finale. If a split into such uneven lengths is to be made, why not have it between Acts 1 and 2? Enough of minor quibbles – this set is a 'must buy'.

Die Fledermaus   Ⓗ
Elisabeth Schwarzkopf *sop* Rosalinde **Rita Streich**

JOHANN STRAUSS II
DIE FLEDERMAUS – IN BRIEF

Julia Varady *Rosalinde* **Lucia Popp** *Adele*
Hermann Prey *Eisenstein* **Bavarian State Opera Chorus and Orchestra / Carlos Kleiber**
DG ② 457 765-2GOR2 (107' · ADD)   Ⓜ️**OO**
Kleiber's mercurial, translucent conducting and a superb cast make this a marvellous performance – except, sadly, for popular singer Ivan Rebroff's weird falsetto Orlofsky.

Elisabeth Schwarzkopf *Rosalinde* **Rita Streich**
Adele **Nicolai Gedda** *Eisenstein* **Philharmonia Chorus and Orchestra / Herbert von Karajan**
EMI ② 567074-2 (110' · AAD)   Ⓜ️**OO**
A 1955 mono recording, but with a wonderfully idiomatic cast and Karajan's urbane conducting it still sounds engaging.

Kiri Te Kanawa *Rosalinde* **Edita Gruberová**
Adele **Wolfgang Brendel** *Eisenstein* **Vienna State Opera Chorus, Vienna PO / André Previn**
Philips ② 464 031-2PM2 (112' · DDD)   Ⓜ️
Previn's reading is warmer than the above, but still with plenty of sparkle and another splendid cast, especially Kiri Te Kanawa as Rosalind. Some may find the dubbed-in 'party buzz' in Act 2 off-putting.

Hilde Gueden *Rosalinde* **Erika Köth** *Adele*
Waldemar Kmentt *Eisenstein* **Vienna State Opera Chorus, Vienna PO / Herbert von Karajan**
Decca ② 421 046-2DH2 (143' · ADD)   Ⓕ**O**
A 1960 stereo classic, with one of the most characterfully Viennese casts and Karajan in almost as fine form. A huge star-studded gala scene featuring the likes of Del Monaco, Nilsson and Sutherland will appeal to many.

Hilde Gueden *Rosalinde* **Erika Köth** *Adele*
Waldemar Kmentt *Eisenstein* **Vienna Volksoper Chorus, Vienna SO / Willi Boskovsky**
HMV ② HMVD573407-2 (110' · ADD)   Ⓢ
A bubbly but pleasantly unexaggerated performance from the archetypal Viennese Straussian, with a strikingly distinguished cast including Dietrich Fischer-Dieskau and the young Brigitte Fassbaender's marvellous Orlofsky.

Kiri Te Kanawa *Rosalinde* **Hildegard Heichele**
Adele **Hermann Prey** *Eisenstein* **Chorus and Orchestra of the Royal Opera House / Plácido Domingo**
NVC Arts 📀 4509 99216-2 (177')   Ⓕ
Domingo on the podium can't match Kleiber's *Schwung*, but remains lively and serviceable for Covent Garden's splendidly batty multi-lingual production, in richly authentic sets with fine principals, including Dennis O'Neill's hilariously Italianate Alfred, and authentic Viennoiserie from Josef Meinrad's beanpole Frosch.

sop Adele **Nicolai Gedda** *ten* Eisenstein **Helmut Krebs** *ten* Alfred **Erich Kunz** *bar* Doctor Falke **Rudolf Christ** *ten* Prince Orlofsky **Karl Dönch** *bar* Frank **Erich Majkut** *ten* Doctor Blind **Luise Martini** *sop* Ida **Franz Böheim** buffo Frosch **Philharmonia Chorus and Orchestra / Herbert von Karajan**
EMI Great Recordings of the Century mono ②
567074-2 (110' · ADD) Recorded 1955. Notes, text and translation included ⓂⓄⓄ

This classic set is the aptest of candidates for EMI's Great Recordings of the Century. Such is the CD transfer that one completely forgets that this is in mono, not stereo, and the extra sense of presence and space makes for a clearer separation of the voices, well forward in the manner of EMI's recordings in the mid-1950s. In his note, Richard Osborne quotes Schwarzkopf on what Karajan (and her husband, Walter Legge, as producer) were seeking to bring out: 'grit, dash, pep'. That may sound as though the result is serious rather than comic, but it isn't so. What's most striking is the animation of the production. The dialogue is so strongly characterised and so brilliantly acted, with each character so sharply defined, that even the most determined non-German-speaker will not only follow but be charmed by it. Legge's editing down of the dialogue was very much part of his concept, alongside the immaculate, inspired casting of soloists. The very first confrontation between Streich as the parlourmaid, Adele, and Schwarzkopf as Rosalinde, her mistress, is delicious, with the characters so vividly heightened. So it is throughout the set.

One may question the choice of a tenor Orlofsky, but Karajan and Legge were following the example of Max Reinhardt in his famous Berlin production of 1929, and Rudolf Christ in cabaret style presents a wonderfully convincing portrait of an effete, slightly tipsy nobleman. As for the others, it would be hard to imagine more compelling portraits than these, consistently reflecting Legge's genius in assembling his team. The musical performance, like the deft speaking of the dialogue, is both polished and exuberant. It's astonishing what precision Karajan achieves in his moulding of Viennese rubato, not only from his singers but from the Philharmonia players. The dialogue is tracked separately, but few will want to omit it when it adds so much to the total joy of the experience.

Der Zigeunerbaron

Der Zigeunerbaron
Pamela Coburn *sop* Saffi **Herbert Lippert** *ten* Barinkay **Wolfgang Holzmair** *bar* Homonay **Rudolf Schasching** *ten* Zsupán **Christiane Oelze** *sop* Arsena **Júlia Hamari** *mez* Czipra **Elisabeth von Magnus** *contr* Mirabella **Jürgen Flimm** *bar* Carnero **Robert Florianschutz** *bass* Pali **Hans-Jürgen Lazar** *ten* Ottokar **Arnold Schoenberg Choir; Vienna Symphony Orchestra / Nikolaus Harnoncourt**
Teldec ② 4509-94555-2 (150' · DDD) Recorded live

1994. Notes, text and translation included ⒻⓄ

This is an uncommonly interesting and enjoyable release. The extra music comes because Harnoncourt and Johann Strauss specialist Norbert Linke have sought to restore *Der Zigeunerbaron* to the form it had before Strauss made various cuts. The real merits of the set lie elsewhere. Not least, Harnoncourt has stripped away generations of Viennese *Schmaltz* and performing tradition.

This is the first recording to include every number of the published score, and for once the music is sung at its original pitch, without the usual downward transpositions for Zsupán and Homonay. Most particularly Harnoncourt has completely rethought the style of the performance. *Der Zigeunerbaron* is a long work, described as 'Komische Oper' rather than 'Operette', and much of its music is unusually solid for Strauss. Harnoncourt gives the major numbers their full weight, phrasing them beautifully, and drawing refined singing from the soloists, among whom Herbert Lippert and Pamela Coburn combine beautifully in the duet 'Wer uns getraut?', and Christiane Oelze is a delectably sweet Arsena.

The necessary light relief comes not only from Zsupán (Rudolf Schasching in fine voice) but from usually omitted subsidiary numbers. Elisabeth von Magnus sings Mirabella's 'Just sind es vierundzwanzig Jahre' with exhilarating comic zest, and joins with Jürgen Flimm (more actor than singer) to make the trio 'Nur keusch und rein' an irresistible delight. The live recording comes with some audience laughter and coughs but with the applause suppressed. This deserves to win new admirers both for Harnoncourt and for Strauss's masterly score.

Richard Strauss   German 1864-1949

Strauss's father, a professional horn player, gave him a musical grounding exclusively in the classics, and he composed copiously from the age of six. He went briefly to university, but had no formal tuition in composition. He had several works given in Munich, including a symphony, when he was 17, and the next year a wind serenade in Dresden and a violin concerto in Vienna. At 20, a second symphony was given in New York and he conducted the Meiningen Orchestra in a suite for wind. In 1885 he became conductor of that orchestra, but soon left and visited Italy. He had been influenced by Lisztian and Wagnerian thinking; one result was Aus Italien, which caused controversy on its première in 1887. By then Strauss was a junior conductor at the Munich Opera.

Other tone poems followed: Macbeth, Don Juan and Tod und Verklärung come from the late 1880s. It is Don Juan that, with its orchestral brilliance, its formal command and its vivid evocation of passionate ardour (he was in love with the singer Pauline von Ahna, his future wife), shows his maturity and indeed virtuosity as a composer. With its première, at Weimar (he had moved to a post at the opera house there), he was recognised as the leading progressive composer in Germany. He was ill during 1891-3 but wrote his first opera, Guntram, which was a modest success but a failure later in Munich. His conducting career developed; he directed many major operas, including Wagner at Bayreuth, and returned to Munich in 1896 as chief conductor at the opera. To the late 1890s belong the witty and colourful Till Eulenspiegel, a portrait of a disrespectful rogue with whom Strauss clearly had a good deal of sympathy, the graphic yet also poetic and psychologically subtle Don Quixote (cast respectively in rondo and varia-tion forms) and Ein Heldenleben, 'a hero's life', where Strauss himself is the hero and his adversaries the music critics. There is more autobiography in the Symphonia domestica of 1903; he conducted its pre-mière during his first visit to the USA, in 1904.

Strauss was now moving towards opera. His Feuersnot was given in 1901; in 1904 Salome was begun, after Wilde's play. It was given at Dresden in 1905. Regarded as blasphemous and salacious, it ran into censorship trouble but was given at 50 opera houses in the next two years. This and Elektra (given in 1909) follow up the tone poems in their evocation of atmosphere and their thematic structure; both deal with female obsessions of a disordered, macabre kind, with violent climaxes involving gruesome deaths and impassioned dancing, with elements of abnormal sex-uality and corruption, exploiting the female voice pressed to dramatic extremes.

Strauss did not pursue that path. After the violence and dissonance of the previous operas, and their harsh psychological realism, Strauss and his librettist Hofmannsthal turned to period comedy, set in the Vienna of Maria Theresa, for Der Rosenkavalier; the score is no less rich in inner detail, but it is applied to the evocation of tenderness, nostalgia and humour, helped by sentimental Viennese waltzes. Again the female voice – but this time its radiance and warmth – is exploited, in the three great roles of the Marschallin, Octavian and Sophie. It was given at Dresden in 1911 with huge success and was soon pro-duced in numerous other opera houses. Strauss fol-lowed it with Ariadne auf Naxos, at first linked with a Molière play, later revised as prologue (behind the scenes at a private theatre) and opera, mixing com-media dell'arte and classical tragedy to a delicate, chamber orchestral accompaniment. The two ver-sions were given in 1912 and (in Vienna) 1916. Strauss had been conducting in Berlin, the court and opera orchestras, since 1908; in 1919 he took up a post as joint director of the Vienna Staatsoper, where his latest collaboration with Hofmannsthal, Die Frau ohne Schatten, was given that year: a work embodying much symbolism and psychology, opu-lently but finely scored, and regarded by some as one of Strauss's noblest achievements. His busy, interna-tional conducting career continued in the inter-war years; there were visits to North and South America as well as to most parts of Europe in the 1920s, which also saw the premières of two more operas, both at Dresden, the autobiographical, domestic comedy Intermezzo and Die ägyptische Helena. His last Hofmannsthal opera, Arabella, an appealing re-cre-ation of some of the atmosphere of Rosenkavalier, fol-

lowed in 1933. Of his remaining operas, Capriccio (1942), a 'conversation-piece' in a single act set in the 18th century and dealing with the amorous and artistic rivalries of a poet and a musician, is the most successful, with its witty, graceful, serene score.

During the 1930s Strauss, seeking a smooth and quiet life, had allowed himself to accept – without facing up to their full import – the circumstances cre-ated in Germany by the Nazis. For a time he was head of the State Music Bureau and he once oblig-ingly conducted at Bayreuth when Toscanini had withdrawn. But he was frustrated at being unable to work with his Jewish librettist, Stefan Zweig (Hof-mannsthal had been part-Jewish), and he protected his Jewish daughter-in-law; during the war years, when he mainly lived in Vienna, he and the Nazi authorities lived in no more than mutual toleration. When Germany was defeated, and her opera houses destroyed, Strauss wrote an intense lament, Meta-morphosen, for 23 solo strings; this is one of several products of a golden 'Indian summer', which include an oboe concerto and the Four Last Songs, works in a ripe, mellow idiom, executed with a grace worthy of his beloved Mozart. GROVEmusic

Concertos

Horn Concertos Nos 1 & 2. Duett-Concertino, AV147. Serenade, Op 7
David Pyatt hn **Joy Farrall** cl **Julie Andrews** bn
Britten Sinfonia / Nicholas Cleobury
Classics for Pleasure 573 513-2 (66' · DDD) Recorded 1994   Ⓢ Ⓑ ⚫⚫⚫

David Pyatt won the BBC's 'Young Musician of the Year' Competition back in 1988. Since then the fledgling has well and truly flown. This is sensationally good horn playing, with a noble legato and a beautiful sound, full, even and unclouded. He's sparing with the brassy timbres, holding them in reserve for dramatic effect, for such times as the instrument's well-rounded jocularity must take on a brazen, huntsmen-like air, or rise to shining heroics – like the challenging motto theme of the First Concerto. He shapes the big phrases with ease and authority, but his person-ality is equally conveyed in the rhythmic articu-lation: a dashing, Jack-be-nimble mischievous-ness in Strauss's athletic allegros. Most of all, though – and this is rare – he loves to play really quietly. He's a master of those dreamy, far-away departures – twilit forest-murmurings: mysteri-ous, unreal.

The recording helps with a beautifully inte-grated balance. The sound of the early *Serenade*, Op 7, is particularly fine with ripe, euphonious *tuttis* and room enough for individual personal-ities to open up. And that's the most remarkable aspect of the piece, the utterly natural way it blends and contrasts across the whole spectrum of wind voices. Two of them take centre-stage in the delightful *Duett-Concertino*. Joy Farrall's clarinet and Julie Andrews's bassoon are like Octavian and the Baron Ochs in this gentle but spirited opus. This is a spendid disc, then, and sympathetically directed, too.

Horn Concertos[a]   **H**
Coupled with: **Hindemith** Horn Concerto[b]. Concert Music for Brass and Strings[c]
Brain hn **Philharmonia Orchestra /** [a]**Sawallisch,** [bc]**Hindemith**
EMI Great Recordings of the Century [b]mono
567782-2 (65' · ADD) Recorded 1957-9   **M**OO

Brain relishes the Straussian bravura in the First Concerto, and the coda is stunning – wonderfully nimble. The frocklicking *Rondo* finale of the Second is another highlight, played with a deliciously light *spiccato* by Brain. Sawallisch proves himself a natural Straussian, and his account of the *Concert Music for Brass* is marvellously played – an outstanding bonus.

Eine Alpensinfonie, Op 64

Eine Alpensinfonie
Berlin Philharmonic Orchestra / Herbert von Karajan
DG Karajan Gold 439 017-2GHS (51' · DDD) Recorded 1980   Ⓕ OO

The *Alpensinfonie* is no longer a rarity on disc, but there are still grounds for preferring the famous Karajan version to subsequent digital rivals, especially in this successful remastering. Karajan's sureness of line is always impressive in Strauss and, while the Berlin Philharmonic Orchestra isn't at its immaculate best, some playing is magnificent here. The sound remains rather fierce, but several passages have been substantially remixed, and the effect is certainly less constricted overall. Perhaps it doesn't matter that the horn theme that floats in with the (still blinding) 'Sonnenaufgang' isn't quite aligned with the strings. More worrying is the subtle transformation of the opening phrase of 'Der Anstieg': whereas we used to experience it 'from the bottom up' with the balance favouring the basses, we hear more cellos now—and most of them fluff the B flat! That said, the breadth and majesty of Karajan's conception is indisputable.

Eine Alpensinfonie. Der Rosenkavalier – Suite for Orchestra
Vienna Philharmonic Orchestra / Christian Thielemann
DG 469 519-2GH (77' · DDD)   Ⓕ OO

'I shall call my *Alpine Symphony* the *Anti-Christian*, because in it there's moral purification by means of one's own strength, liberation through work, worship of glorious, eternal nature.' In the end, Strauss shied away from the inflammatory subtitle, yet the quotation is instructive. With more on his mind than a day's hike, Strauss originally intended the work to convey a Nietzschean vitalism. (Is it coincidence that the trombones announce the summit in grandiloquent Zarathustrian fifths?)

Thielemann's is, by a considerable margin, the finest account we have had since Karajan's, and is rather better played. The performers' emotional commitment is stamped on every bar. The VPO is on top form: the brass is electrifying throughout, no mean achievement since this disc was recorded live. If you wish to sample the performance at its formidable best, you might start 'on the glacier' (track 9) – the perilously high trumpet writing more confidently negotiated than for Karajan – and continue until you're 'on the summit'. On the way up, 'Dangerous moments' (track 10) is superb, Thielemann and the orchestra alive to every flickering nuance of accent and dynamic. The oboe's awestruck contemplation of the surrounding vistas is outstanding, the *rubato* exactly conveying the climber's physical breathlessness and spiritual exaltation. Thereafter, Strauss's ecstatic tumult is given full rein. No one holds back, no one plays safe.

Which isn't to imply anything unsubtle: you hear the close kinship between 'Rising mists' (track 13) and the passage where the Captain and Doctor contemplate the lake in which Berg's Wozzeck has just drowned himself, so clearly does Thielemann articulate the disparate strands. In principle, you might object to some of Thielemann's bizarrely slow tempos and his tendency to linger over phrase endings, but here at least is someone who believes in the music and has something to say about it.

The various *Rosenkavalier* 'suites' usually seem insubstantial, but this one is both a generous filler and an effective wind-down after the main work.

Captured in a recording at once lushly upholstered and thrillingly visceral, this is unquestionably Thielemann's finest release to date. Ozawa and even Previn with the same orchestra are effectively superseded, though some will still prefer Karajan's narrower range of tempos and absolute sense of where the music is going.

Coupled with: Till Eulenspiegels lustige streiche. Also sprach Zarathustra. Don Juan. Ein Heldenleben.
Bavarian Radio Symphony Orchestra Chicago Symphony Orchestra, Vienna Philharmonic Orchestra; / Solti
Decca Double ② 440 618-2DF2 (152' · ADD) Recorded 1970s   **M**O

The formidable power of Solti's personality dominates all these brilliant performances. *Eine Alpensinfonie* has the most glorious tone (especially the brass). Such is the amplitude of the sound and the warm commitment of the playing that it counteracts the conductor's tendency to press forward. Even if other performances of Strauss's music have more subtlety of feeling, Solti's admirers will count this anthology a great bargain.

Symphonia domestica, Op 53

Symphonia domestica. Josephslegende – Suite
Seattle Symphony Orchestra / Gerard Schwarz

Delos DE3082 (777' · DDD) Recorded 1988   Ⓕ

Schwarz and his orchestra give an extremely fine account of the *Symphonia domestica*, far finer in fact than Zubin Mehta and the Berlin Philharmonic on Sony. The Berliners may be superior players but the Seattle Symphony sound to be enjoying themselves much more and to be appreciating the wit, fun and sentiment of the music. Schwarz's achievement is that the work becomes a real symphony under his baton. The playing is relaxed and warm and often very tender. At strenuous moments, though, the sound inclines to be a little unflattering to the strings but otherwise it's clear and spacious.

Why don't more orchestras include *Josephslegende* – such a tuneful, colourful score – in their repertoires? Schwarz clearly believes in it, and his excellent orchestra, with a pliant string section and lively woodwind, respond enthusiastically to his lead. Recommended.

Also sprach Zarathustra, Op 30

Also sprach Zarathustra. Ein Heldenleben, Op 40 Ⓗ
Chicago Symphony Orchestra / Fritz Reiner
RCA Living Stereo 09026 61494-2 (76' · ADD)
Recorded 1954   ⓂOO

It's astonishing that this recording of *Also sprach Zarathustra* was made in 1954, in stereo when Toscanini was still (just) recording in low-fi in New York's Carnegie Hall. The sound may be tonally fierce by current standards, but the balance is fully acceptable, with the first and second violins set close to the listener on either side of the podium, and the basses hard left.

Reiner's *Also sprach* is intense and extrovert. In his second year with the Chicago Symphony Orchestra, the conductor was already getting a thrilling response from the strings, though woodwind intonation could be a problem. Confident and well played as it is, the spectacular opening sunrise inevitably lacks the impact of modern recordings. Instead there's a measure of raw passion and forward thrust unequalled on disc. In the reflective passages, conductor and engineers display some reluctance to achieve a real *pianissimo*, but as the tempo builds Reiner invariably creates great excitement. His reading of *Ein Heldenleben* has humanity as well as virtuosity.

Also sprach Zarathustra. Don Juan, Op 20
Berlin Philharmonic Orchestra / Herbert von Karajan
DG 439 016-2GHS (54' · DDD) Recorded 1983   ⒻO

Also sprach Zarathustra, Op 30. Don Juan, Op 20.
Till Eulenspiegels lustige Streiche. Salome – Dance of the Seven Veils
Berlin Philharmonic Orchestra / Herbert von Karajan
DG The Originals 447 441-2GOR (79' · ADD)
Recorded 1973   ⓂOOO

RICHARD STRAUSS'S ALSO SPRACH ZARATHUSTRA – IN BRIEF

Chicago SO / Fritz Reiner
RCA 09026 61494-2 (76' · ADD)   ⓂOO
Reiner's incandescent 1954 account is the stuff of which legends are made. Impossible to believe that the stereo tapes are half a century old.

Berlin PO / Herbert von Karajan
DG 447 441-2GOR (79' · ADD)   ⓂOOO
☀ Arguably the most imposing of Karajan's three recordings. An interpretation of tremendous stature and aplomb; fabulous playing from the Berliners.

Concertgebouw Orchestra / Bernard Haitink
Philips ② 442 281-2PM2 (152' · ADD/DDD)   Ⓜ
Bernard Haitink's distinguished 1973 account appeared at roughly the same time as the above-mentioned Karajan. Some might even prefer it for its extra nobility and opulence.

Boston SO / Serge Koussevitzky
Biddulph WHL054 (65' · ADD)   Ⓜ
Koussevitzky was an exciting and dedicated Straussian, and his pioneering 1935 recording of *Zarathustra* remains a 'must hear'.

Vienna PO / Clemens Krauss
Testament SBT1183 (76' · ADD)   Ⓕ
Once you've adjusted to the rather acidulous string timbre, Clemens Krauss's authoritative 1950 reading with the VPO displays a glowing perception that never loosens its hold on the listener.

Staatskapelle Dresden / Rudolf Kempe
EMI 574756-2 (79' · ADD)   ⓈO
A somewhat lightweight introduction apart, Kempe secures a performance of treasurable flexibility and comprehensive understanding. What a great Straussian he was!

Zurich Tonhalle Orchestra / David Zinman
Arte Nova 74321 87071-2 (76' · DDD)   Ⓢ
Anyone wanting a bargain-basement *Zarathustra* in realistic, up-to-date sound could do a lot worse than invest in this characterful and sympathetic account from Zurich.

Boston SO / William Steinberg
DG 463 627-2GOR (76' · ADD)   Ⓜ
The opening sunrise (of *2001: A Space Odyssey* fame) creates an all-engulfing impact in Steinberg's energetic Boston account from March 1971. An often thrilling performance, marvellously played.

The playing of the Berlin Philharmonic Orchestra on both sets is as glorious as ever; its virtuosity can be taken for granted along with its sumptuous tonal refinement, and in Strauss Karajan has no peer. As a recording the 1983 disc is very good indeed, though it doesn't offer the spectacular definition and transparency of detail of the Dorati, but the playing is in a different league. The famous opening has greater intensity in the 1973 version, and you may prefer its marginally greater warmth and glow of the strings. The DG engineers adopt a slightly closer balance on this newcomer, which has greater range and impressive detail, particularly in the bass. Both *Don Juan*s are fine performances, too. To sum up, Karajan's classic 1973 account holds sway.

Don Quixote, Op 35

Don Quixote. Lieder – Morgen, Op 27 No 4; Der Rosenband, Op 36 No 1; Wiegenlied, Op 41 No 1; Freundliche Vision, Op 48 No 1; Waldseligkeit, Op 49 No 1; Die heiligen drei Könige, Op 56 No 6
Dame Felicity Lott *sop* **André Vauquet** *va* **François Guye** *vc* **Suisse Romande Orchestra / Armin Jordan**
Mediaphon MED72 165 (69' · DDD)   Ⓜ●

This disc is notable for taking advantage of the superlative acoustic of the Victoria Hall in Geneva, home of the Suisse Romande Orchestra, thus giving us the most impressively recorded *Don Quixote* yet, in sound terms. The detail of the brilliant scoring is clearly delineated, while the whole picture is one of amazing warmth and resplendence. Jordan and his orchestra offer a performance worthy of both the place and the production. Guye brings out all Quixote's endearing and aggravating qualities without a hint of exaggeration, his tone always full and poised.

The songs are more than a makeweight. Lott, the leading Straussian soprano of the day, knows how to make the most of six of the composer's best-loved songs with ethereal, fine-grained tone and line. Jordan presents the music without any excess of sentiment. So what a great pity, then, that texts and translations aren't provided, the only blot on a disc that's certain to give much pleasure and satisfaction.

Additional recommendation

Don Quixote
Coupled with: Cello Sonata in F. Romanze in F
Isserlis *vc* **Hough** *pf* **Bavarian Radio Symphony Orchestra / Maazel**

RCA Red Seal 74321 75398-2 (76' · DDD)   Ⓕ
Isserlis has all the imagination and variety of tone colour the work needs, plus the necessary sense of humour. He's especially good in the more eloquent passages, helped along by Maazel's affectionate moulding of detail.

Ein Heldenleben, Op 40

Ein Heldenleben[a] Don Juan, Op 20[b]. Till   Ⓗ
Eulenspiegels lustige Streiche, Op 28[a]
[a]**Philadelphia Orchestra / Eugene Ormandy;**
[b]**Cleveland Orchestra / George Szell**
Sony Classical Essential Classics SBK48272
(75' · ADD) Recorded 1957-60   Ⓑ●

In *Heldenleben* Ormandy's hero is a transatlantic with a fat cigar in his mouth; it's obvious from the start that he's out to impress. He employs glamorous representatives, too: slick brass and percussion, smartly ordered winds and a plush, generous army of strings. Yet, he isn't without soul, as his 'Works of Peace' and 'Retirement from the World and the Fulfilment of his Life' ably illustrate. In fact, his having *been* fulfilled earlier on in the score only goes to underline his profound change of heart. And with solo violinist Ansel Brusilow an eloquent commentator, and truthful if rather opaque sound, the hero's 'Indian summer' is most eloquently portrayed. Turn then to Szell, and the contrast is quite startling. Szell used to play his own piano-solo arrangement of *Till Eulenspiegel* to Strauss, and his recording of the work reveals the depth of his perception. No hint of brashness here, just wit, myriad detail and astonishing orchestral virtuosity. There can't be many better *Don Juan*s on CD. The transfers from fair-to-middling originals are absolutely first rate.

Ein Heldenleben. Tod und Verklärung, Op 24.
Salome – Dance of the Seven Veils
Staatskapelle Dresden / Rudolf Kempe
EMI Great Recordings of the Century 567891-2
(75' · DDD) Recorded 1972   Ⓜ●●●

 Kempe gives a superb reading of *Ein Heldenleben*, marginally lighter in tone than familiar modern rivals'. As ever, his music-making is unfailingly civilised, but for those accustomed to Karajan's sensational power and opulence, it may seem that he lets the hero's critics off rather lightly and disdains to raise the roof for the hero's deeds of war. But Kempe shows such sympathy that wonder and delight are really the only justifiable reactions. These performances have a deftness of touch and never sound heavy or over-blown. Recommended.

Ein Heldenleben, Op 40. Metamorphosen
West German Radio Symphony Orchestra, Cologne / Semyon Bychkov
Avie AV0017 (75' · DDD)   Ⓕ●

Semyon Bychkov's Op 40 'Hero' is the sort you could happily live with: he knows his worth but doesn't thrust his exploits in your face. The opening self-portrait more or less says it all, a confident exposition (warm strings, strong brass, crystal-clear timps), well paced, sonorous but never over-forceful. Strauss's cackling adversaries are more chuckled over than caricatured, and violinist Kyoko Shikata makes for an affectionately playful companion, thankfully not the manic cadenza that's sometimes visited on us. In *Metamorphosen* the line remains fluid but constant, urged on (though never hampered) by genuine warmth of feeling. You sense that the notes and their emotional subtext are being granted an equal footing. Avie's recording has impressive amplitude and, in *Heldenleben*, credible presence. This is a unusual coupling – any rival would need to do a lot to upstage this sympathetic production. Recommended.

R Strauss Ein Heldenleben **Mozart** Symphony No 36 in C, 'Linz', K425
London Symphony Orchestra / Sir John Barbirolli
BBC Legends/IMG Artists BBCL4055-2 (73' · ADD)
Recorded live 1969 Ⓜ●

Barbirolli's studio recording of *Ein Heldenleben* appeared posthumously, and seemed to sum up a lifetime's achievement – 'a hero's life' for the conductor as much as the composer. It can be argued that this live performance is even more remarkable than the familiar studio version. It's a degree faster and a shade tougher, although this impression has something to do with the vivid but shrill acoustics of the venue. There's more electricity in the playing, less subtlety and richness in the sound. No doubt the actual remastering has been carefully done, and the accompanying documentation is excellent.

Like Bernstein in his last years, Barbirolli could be an uninhibited reshaper of the music he loved. The opening passage is grand to be sure, even a bit loose in places, but then the interpretation doesn't offer too much too soon. Things are tauter in the Royal Festival Hall. The leader, John Georgiadis, copes heroically with the beloved's (and the conductor's) demands. Michael Kennedy's authoritative note explains that they looked through the part together in exhaustive detail. The battle scene has breadth and dignity, by no means slower than Karajan was wont to take it in his last days. For once there's no sense of disappointment when the ringing climax gives way to the hero's works of peace. As in the studio, so here, the pot-pourri of motifs from the composer's back-catalogue has a particularly emotive quality: Barbirolli, painfully aware of his mortality, lavishes every ounce of affection and sensibility on these allusions to music he would not live to conduct again. The Elgarian nobility of the closing stages is again striking. This release is warmly recommended.

Additional recommendation

Ein Heldenleben
Coupled with: **Strauss** Don Juan Ⓗ
Wagenaar Cyrano de Bergerac
Concertgebouw Orchestra; New York Philharmonic Symphony Orchestra / Mengelberg

Pearl mono GEMMCD0008 (71' · ADD) Recorded
1928-42 Ⓜ●
The perfect set for anyone remotely interested in Strauss or in the history of recording. By the time this disc was made Mengelberg had nearly three decades of the piece under his belt – this is the definitive *Heldenleben*. Given its age, the transfer is little short of miraculous.

Metamorphosen

Metamorphosen. Tod und Verklärung, Op 24
Berlin Philharmonic Orchestra / Herbert von Karajan
DG Gramophone Awards Collection 474 8892
(52' · DDD) Recorded 1982 Ⓜ●●●

 These are a clear first-choice in both works. Karajan's *Metamorphosen* has almost unbearable intensity and great emotional urgency – it's a gripping and involving account. The sound is marginally more forward and cleaner than is ideal, though the rich ambience is very appealing. *Tod und Verklärung* isn't as spectacularly recorded as some more modern versions, but it's a greater performance that just about any other, and finer than any of Karajan's earlier versions. It's electrifying, with superb playing and a life-and-death intensity to the climaxes. It's more vividly recorded than his most recent previous version, and the performance is tauter and more powerful. The quality of the recording gives no cause for reproach.

Violin Sonata in E flat, Op 18

R Strauss Violin Sonata in E flat, Op 18 **Bartók** (arr Székely) Six Romanian Folkdances, Sz56 **Stravinsky** (arr Stravinsky/Dushkin) Divertimento
Vadim Repin *vn* **Boris Berezovsky** *pf*
Erato 8573-85769-2 (53' · DDD) Ⓕ●

Stylistically, Strauss's lyrical Op 18 (1887) sits poised somewhere between Brahms's chivalrous song cycle *Die schöne Magelone* and Strauss's own *Don Juan* of the following year. The finale is rich in heroics though not before a seductive 'Improvisation' and the appearance of one of Strauss's loveliest melodies. Anyone familiar with Heifetz's three recordings – his second, the first of two with the late Brooks Smith, is probably the most comprehensively expressive – will have a job adapting to anyone else. No one draws a sweeter, more tender opening phrase, though Vadim Repin, like Gidon Kremer, more or less matches Heifetz in terms of repose.

Repin's feline violin faces leonine support from Boris Berezovsky, whose outsize musical personality draws maximum mileage from Strauss's virtuoso piano writing, though he too is capable of relaxing. His elegant fingerwork is nicely demonstrated in the decorative figurations that dominate the third section of the second movement. Kremer and Oleg Maisenberg are also excellent, but Repin's engagement with the music's lyrical element just about gives him the edge . Heifetz is more 'accompanied' by Brooks Smith than partnered by him.

Echoes of Strauss return for the *Adagio* from Stravinsky's *Fairy's Kiss* re-run, a witty *Divertimento* prepared in collaboration with violinist Samuel Dushkin. Repin's strongest current rival is Perlman, though his reading is perhaps less subtly characterised and, again, Berezovsky's strong-arm pianism strengthens the frame. Bartók's ubiquitous *Romanian Folkdances* are rather less spicy here than you would expect from someone who has fiddled in gypsy style with Lakatos, but Repin's harmonics in the 'Pe loc' third movement are admirably clean and the final dances are suitably dashing. The sound is very well balanced.

Choral Works

Deutsche Motette, Op 62[a]. Gesänge, Op 34. An den Baum Daphne (epilogue to 'Daphne'), AV137[b].
Die Göttin im Putzzimmer, AV120
[a]Tina Kiberg, [b]Marianne Lund *sops* [b]Christian Lisdorf *treb* [a]Randi Stene *contr* [a]Gert Henning-Jensen *ten* [a]Ulrik Cold *bass* [b]Copenhagen Boys' Choir; Danish National Radio Choir / Stefan Parkman
Chandos CHAN9223 (57' · DDD) Recorded 1993. Texts and translations included ⒡**O**

Under Stefan Parkman the Danish National Radio Choir has established a reputation second to none. Parkman handles his singers as if they were a fully fledged symphony orchestra; which isn't at all inappropriate in this programme by the supreme master of orchestral colour. From the heart of the 16 chorus parts of the *Deutsche Motette* a further seven are projected by solo voices emerging imperceptibly from the midst of a dense, luxuriant texture. The depth of colour and range of emotions are every bit as extensive in these works as in the great orchestral tone-poems; indeed few orchestral tone-poems evoke dusk and sunset so vividly as in 'Der Abend', the first of the 1897 *Zwei Gesänge*. There's a wonderfully luminous soundscape here; a combination of superb compositional skill, sensitive musical direction, superlative choral singing and a warm, full-bodied recording.

Four Last Songs, AV150 (Op posth)

Four Last Songs. Das Rosenband, Op 36 No 1. Lieder, Op 68 – Ich wollt ein Sträusslein binden; Säusle, liebe Myrte; Als mir dein Lied erklang. Befreit, Op 39 No 4. Lieder, Op 27 – Ruhe, meine Seele!; Morgen. Wiegenlied, Op 41 No 1. Meinem Kinde, Op 37 No 3. Zueignung, Op 10 No 1. Die heiligen drei Könige aus Morgenland, Op 56 No 6
Soile Isokoski *sop* Berlin Radio Symphony

Orchestra / Marek Janowski
Ondine ODE982-2 (64' · DDD) Notes, texts and translations included ⒡**OOO**

Strauss singing doesn't come much better than this. No doubt the composer himself, with his love of the soprano voice, would have been enthralled by Isokoski's glorious singing. He might also have approved of Janowski's straightforward, quite brisk conducting as he was never one to sentimentalise his own music. With a combination of free, unfettered tone, not a hint of strain in high-lying passages, a fine legato and an amazingly long breath, Isokoski fulfils every demand of her chosen songs. To those attributes she adds just a hint of quick vibrato, which she uses unerringly to expressive purpose throughout. Add the depth of feeling she brings to inwardly emotional pieces such as *Befreit*, *Ruhe meine Seele!* and, above all, *Morgen!*, a perfect realisation of this oft-recorded piece, and you have performances to rival any of the greats of the past.

She reminds one most of Lisa della Casa, the first soprano to record the *Four Last Songs*, and Sena Jurinac. She has the same smiling timbre, the same natural style, the same avoidance of wallowing in music that contains its own proportion of sentiment. Try the ecstatic execution of the final verse of 'Beim Schlafengehen' and you'll understand. If, on the other hand, you prefer a more leisurely approach, there are always Janowitz and Karajan.

Janowski is obviously at one with his soprano, not only here but also in *Zueignung*. Refined playing from the Berlin Radio Symphony and an open recording complete the pleasure.

Four Last Songs[a]. Capriccio – Morgen mittag um elf! ... Kein andres[b]. Tod und Verklärung[c]
[ab]Gundula Janowitz *sop* [a]Berlin Philharmonic Orchestra / Herbert von Karajan; [b]Bavarian Radio Symphony Orchestra, [c]Staatskapelle Dresden / Karl Böhm
DG Classikon 439 467-2GCL (65' · ADD) Recorded 1971-2 Ⓜ**OO**

Here's a feast of glorious Strauss at bargain price, though the performances are anything but bargain in quality. In spite of strong challenges from far and wide, the singing of them by Gundula Janowitz has, arguably, still not been surpassed for Straussian opulence and tenderness – we emphasise 'arguably', for people feel passionately about interpretations of this work! – and Karajan conducts a near-ideal account of the orchestral score. Janowitz, in glorious voice, sings the *Four Last Songs* flowingly. The recording is more hazy than on the other two exemplary performances. The fashion of the moment to denigrate Böhm is incomprehensible when you encounter readings as splendid as his two contributions here, in which he again proves himself an ideal Straussian.

The live account of *Tod und Verklärung* caught

at the 1972 Salzburg Festival but not released until 1988 (in memoriam) builds naturally to its various incandescent climaxes, and the music is never allowed to drag or descend into sentimentality. The playing of the Dresden orchestra is lithe and warm. The final scene of *Capriccio* comes from the complete set recorded in Munich in 1971. Once more Böhm judges tempos and texture to a nicety, the music always moving forward in perfect balance to its end.

R Strauss Four Last Songs **Wagner** Wesendonk Lieder. Tristan und Isolde – Prelude and Liebestod
Cheryl Studer *sop* **Dresden Staatskapelle / Giuseppe Sinopoli**
DG 439 865-2GH (61' · DDD) Notes, texts and translations included ⑤●

In the Strauss, Cheryl Studer's voice, lyrical yet with dramatic overtones, seems near-ideal for Strauss and for this work in particular, quite apart from the sheer beauty and technical accomplishment of her singing. In the first two songs there's the necessary ecstasy and longing in her singing as Strauss reviews, elegiacally, his musical credo. For example, one could cite the loving treatment in 'September' of the phrases beginning 'Langsam tut er', the singer's tone poised, the shading of the line perfectly natural. It's the seamless legato and lovely voice that again make 'Beim Schlafengehen' so rewarding, while in the final song Studer is suitably hushed and reflective. Sinopoli and the Staatskapelle Dresden provide ideal support for their singer with the playing in all these works as lyrically expressive as the singing above it.

Similar praise can be given to the reading of the Wesendonk Lieder. Here, once again, one notes Studer's amazing combination of vocal mastery and interpretative insight. Every dynamic and expressive mark is scrupulously followed (listen to the piano at 'Luft' and 'Duft' in the second song) in the pursuit of seamless phrasing and a due attention to the text. The richness of her singing, the thorough mastery of German diction and phraseology, make this another special performance. Sinopoli's reading of the Prelude to Tristan is flowing, intense and spontaneous and the playing is predictably superb, all adding to the disc's worth. The recordings are for the most part happily spacious and well focused.

Additional recommendation

Coupled with: **Wagner** Wesendonk Lieder
Norman *sop* **Leipzig Gewandhaus Orchestra / Masur** Ⓜ
Philips 50 Great Recordings 464 742-2PM (48' · DDD)
Norman's glorious performance of Strauss's poignant swansong gained her 1984's *Gramophone* solo vocal award. If you're a Janowitz or Schwarzkopf advocate you'll find it too languorous. For anyone else it's unmissable, despite the short running time.

RICHARD STRAUSS'S FOUR LAST SONGS IN BRIEF

Soile Isokoski; Berlin RSO / Marek Janowski
Ondine ODE982-2 (64' · DDD) ⑤●○○○
Perfectly realised interpretations with which Isokoski proves herself a radiant Straussian yet avoids any trace of sentimentality with relatively brisk tempos. Ideally clean and luminous recording helps.

Gundula Janowitz; Berlin PO / Herbert von Karajan
DG 439 467-2GCL (65' · ADD) Ⓜ○○
A more measured, rich-textured approach from a soprano and conductor at one in their pursuit of tonal beauty and sureness of line in 1973.

Cheryl Studer; Staatskapelle Dresden / Giuseppe Sinopoli
DG 439 865-2GH (61' · DDD) ⑤●
Cheryl Studer in her prime has the vocal equipment to deliver Strauss's long lines with complete assurance. Her blazing combination of the lyrical and the dramatic is carried over into the coupling, Wagner rather than the usual Strauss.

René Fleming; Houston SO / Christoph Eschenbach
RCA 82876 59408-2 (69' · DDD) Ⓜ
Renée Fleming in 1995 opts for generally spacious tempos that showcase her mature honeyed tone and free, ringing top.

Jessye Norman; Leipzig Gewandhaus / Kurt Masur
Philips 464 742-2 (48' · DDD) Ⓜ●
As set down in 1982, the most commanding of all recordings, and probably the slowest. The original disc won the solo vocal category of the 1984 *Gramophone* Record Awards, but Wagner's Wesendonk-Lieder have since replaced the Strauss songs formerly included. Simply glorious even so.

Elisabeth Schwarzkopf; Berlin RSO / George Szell
EMI 566908-2 (65' · ADD) Ⓜ○○○
Elisabeth Schwarzkopf's several recordings combine beauty of sound with unequalled feeling for the words. This final version under George Szell, with its very special autumnal quality, has acquired classic status. The current reissue generously augments the programme, with additional Strauss culled from subsequent sessions with Szell and the LSO. The sound belies its 1960s vintage.

Songs

The Complete Songs – 1

Acht Gedichte aus Letzte Blätter, Op 10 – No 1,
Zueignung; No 4, Die Georgine; No 8, Allerseelen.
Sechs Lieder aus Lotusblättern, Op 19 – No 2, Breit
über mein Haupt dein schwarzes Haar; No 4, Wie
sollten wir geheim sie halten. Sechs Lieder, Op 37 –
No 1, Glückes genug; No 2, Ich liebe dich; No 6,
Hochzeitlich Lied. Fünf Lieder, Op 39 – No 1, Leises
Lied; No 4, Befreit. Fünf Lieder, Op 41 – No 1,
Wiegenlied; No 2, In der Campagna. Sechs Lieder,
Op 56 – No 5, Frühlingsfeier; No 6, Die heiligen drei
Könige aus Morgenland. Gesänge des Orients,
Op 77
Christine Brewer sop **Roger Vignoles** pf
Hyperion CDA67488 (61' · DDD · T/t)   ⓕ**OO**

This is the first volume of a projected Richard
Strauss edition, something to be devoutly hoped
for: he was a great Lieder composer but only a
small fraction of his 200-plus songs are at all
well known. Admittedly, his taste in poetry
wasn't always as elevated as that of his fellow
composers, yet his music can transform rather
ordinary verses. And the major poets do get a
look-in. This disc includes two Heine settings,
one of which, 'Frühlingsfeier', came a year after
Salome and echoes the operatic score. This is
where Christine Brewer, whose repertory
includes the title-roles in *Ariadne auf Naxos*
and *Die ägyptische Helena*, might be expected
to be most comfortable: her big, gleaming
soprano sweeps through impressively. If at first
her voice seems less than ideally flexible as a
Lieder instrument, especially in the earlier
songs, it would be ungrateful not to marvel at
what she does ultimately bring to these performances.

Opening with 'Zueignung', which Strauss
never intended to be relegated to encore status,
Brewer sounds glorious if a little staid. But
she quickly lightens up, catching the palpita-
tions of 'Wie sollten wir geheim sie halten' and
the gem-like intimacy of 'Leises Lied'. She
positively blazes in the sunlight-evoking 'In
der Campagna', where Vignoles's piano captures the splash of a Straussian orchestra. Both
artists bring something fresh to the chestnuts
'Allerseelen' and 'Wiegenlied', in which Brewer
floats a beautiful line over the rippling accompaniment. Having the high tessitura demanded
in the rarely heard *Gesänge des Orients*, she
clinches any remaining argument magnificently.

Lieder aus Letzte Blätter, Op 10 – No 1, Zueignung;
No 8, Allerseelen. Ständchen, Op 17 No 2. Lieder,
Op 27 – No 1, Ruhe meine Seele; No 3, Heimliche
Aufforderung; No 4, Morgen. Traum durch die Däm-
merung, Op 29 No 1. Lieder, Op 32– No 1, Ich trage
meine Minne; No 3, Liebeshymnus. Verführung, Op
33 No 1. Das Rosenband, Op 36 No 1. Befreit, Op 39
No 4. Wiegenlied, Op 41 No 1. Waldseligkeit, Op 49
No 1. Die heiligen drei Könige aus Morgenland Op
56 No 6. Capriccio, Op 85 – Interlude, 'Moonlight

Music'. Der Rosenkavalier, Op 59 – Second Waltz
Suite
Steve Davislim ten **State Orchestra of Victoria /
Simone Young**
Melba Recordings 301081 (71' · DDD) Notes, texts
and translations included   ⓕ

Here's a solo recital to warm the hearts of all
lovers of attractive, well-contoured singing and
engaging interpretation. Steve Davislim, a
Zurich-based Australian tenor, who has already
pleased Covent Garden audiences with his Fenton and Zurich ones with his Tamino, is worth
being spoken of in the same breath as his
notable predecessors of similar voice – Peter
Anders and Fritz Wunderlich – and praise can
hardly be higher than that. Possessor of a well-
produced, sappy, lyrical tenor, he has the ideal
instrument with which to sing Strauss.

There's little or nothing to criticise in these
youthfully ardent, finely phrased performances.
Like all the best Strauss tenors of the past he
knows just when to sing full out, when to reduce
his tone to a refined piano, also how to employ
rubato. Add to that German that sounds wholly
idiomatic and you have the ingredients for a
winner. Simone Young and her orchestra provide sensitive support to this outstanding talent.

Opera Arias

Der Rosenkavalier[a] – Da geht er hin; Ach, du bist
wieder da!; Die Zeit, die ist ein sonderbar Ding; Ich
hab ihn nicht einmal geküsst; Marie Theres!…Hab'
mir's gelobt; Ist ein Traum. **Arabella**[b] – Ich danke,
Fräulein. **Capriccio**[c] – Interlude; Wo ist mein Bruder?
Renée Fleming sop with [ab]**Barbara Bonney** sop
[a]**Susan Graham** mez [a]**Johannes Chum** ten [ac]**Walter
Berry** bass-bar **Vienna Philharmonic Orchestra /
Christoph Eschenbach**
Decca 466 314-2DH (78' · DDD) Texts and translations
included   ⓕ**OO**

This is a happily chosen Strauss showcase for
Fleming. Her creamy, full-toned, vibrant voice
is about the ideal instrument not only for the
Marschallin but also for the other parts she
attempts here. She has mastered the phraseology and verbal inflexions needed for all three
roles, and imparts to them a quick intelligence
to second the vocal glories. Sometimes her performance as the Marschallin or Countess
Madeleine recalls, almost uncannily, those of
Schwarzkopf, leaving one in no doubt that she
has studied the readings of her distinguished
predecessor. If Schwarzkopf with a slightly
slimmer tone has the finer line and quicker
responses, her successor provides the richer
tone. Fleming need fear no comparisons with
more recent interpreters such as Te Kanawa,
Tomowa-Sintow and, as Madeleine only,
Janowitz. Indeed, Fleming's account of the closing scene of *Capriccio* is just about ideal. Her
deluxe team of co-stars includes Susan Graham,
who makes an ardent suitor in *Rosenkavalier*'s
Act 1 duets; her timbre is so similar to Fleming's

that it's hard to tell them apart, though she isn't as verbally acute as her partner. And Barbara Bonney finally commits an extract of her enchanting Sophie, the best since Lucia Popp's; she also joins Fleming in the Arabella-Zdenka duet. Even the cameo appearances of a lackey at the close of Act 1 of *Der Rosenkavalier*, of Fani-nal after the Act 3 trio, and the major-domo in the closing scene from *Capriccio*, are filled by the veteran Walter Berry. Under Eschenbach, the VPO plays immaculately – the horn solo in the Moonlight music is pure magic – and the sound quality is outstandingly life-like. A treat for Straussians.

Strauss: Ariadne auf Naxos – Ein schönes war; Es gibt ein Reich. **Arabella** – Mein Elemer! **Wagner: Die Walküre** – Der Männer Sippe; Du bist der Lenz. **Lohengrin** – Einsam in trüben Tagen. **Tannhäuser** – Dich teure Halle; Allmächt'ge Jungfrau. **Der fliegende Holländer** – Joho hoe! ... Traft ihr das Schiff. **Tristan und Isolde** – Mild und leise
Elisabeth Meyer-Topsøe sop **Copenhagen Philharmonic Orchestra / Hans Norbert Bihlmaier**
Kontrapunkt 32249 (60' · DDD) Texts included   ⒻOO

There are few, if any, sopranos today who can sing this repertory more securely than Meyer-Topsøe. A pupil of Nilsson, she sings with her teacher's ringing confidence, tone and technique solid and unblemished. It's heartening to hear once more a Scandinavian interpreter of Wagner with such a thrilling sound, one for whom the challenge of Senta, Elsa, Elisabeth and Isolde are as nothing. All that said, there's as yet room in some items for more dramatic involvement. Studio restrictions and/or a somewhat careful conductor may not be a help in that respect. An exception to this stricture is the Liebestod, where Meyer-Topsøe sounds a Nilsson-like touch of transfiguration.

Her Straussian credentials have already been revealed in the *Four Last Songs* . They are amply confirmed here in her Ariadne and Arabella. Here's evidence, most of all in a gloriously outgoing 'Es gibt ein Reich', of identification with a given role. Her Arabella is hardly less engrossing as she ponders on her 'Fremde Mann', the soprano's even, youthful timbre exactly right for the eager yet thoughtful girl.

The recording rightly has the singer centre-stage, the exciting voice caught in a natural acoustic. Only German texts are provided, no translations, and it's slight pity that the tracks have not been arranged in chronological order. But, that shouldn't deter connoisseurs of the voice heroic from acquiring this CD.

Salome – Ach! du wolltest mich nicht deinen Mund küssen lassen. **Ariadne auf Naxos** – Overture; Ein Schönes war; Es gibt ein Reich. **Die Liebe der Danae** – Wie umgibst du mich mit Frieden; Interlude, Act 3. **Capriccio** – Interlude; Wo ist mein Bruder?; Kein andres, das mir so im Herzen loht[a]
Julia Varady sop **Bamberg Symphony Orchestra /**

Dietrich Fischer-Dieskau [a]bar
Orfeo C511991A (62' · DDD)   ⒻO

After giving choice recitals of Verdi and Wagner, Varady turned her attention to Strauss, and once again the results are for the most part rewarding. The final scene of Salome, under the watchful eye of Varady's husband, Fischer-Dieskau, has the perfection of pitch and phrase one expects of this singer, as well as an expected acuity for the meaning of the text. Perhaps, away from the theatre in a part she never undertook on stage, the absolute conviction of such great interpreters as Cebotari, Welitsch and Rysanek is absent, but not by much. The two almost consecutive solos of Ariadne benefit from shapely, poised singing, ever obedient to the score, although occasionally one misses the creamier tones that Lisa della Casa (DG) and Gundula Janowitz (DG video, and EMI) brought to the part. As Danae, Varady seems a shade tentative and vocally out of sorts. There need be no reservations about the final scene of Capriccio, in which she catches ideally Countess Madeleine's emotional perplexity as she tries (unsuccessfully) to choose between her poet and musician admirers. Both her identification with the role and her execution of Strauss's operatic farewell to his beloved soprano voice are near-ideal. Fischer-Dieskau, endearingly, sings the short part of the Haushofmeister. However, his conducting, although sensibly paced, sometimes errs on the side of caution. As a whole, this CD nicely complements Fleming's Strauss concert on Decca, the two discs offering a compendium of the composer's writing for the soprano voice he loved so much.

Arabella, Op 79

Arabella
Julia Varady sop Arabella **Helen Donath** sop Zdenka **Dietrich Fischer-Dieskau** bar Mandryka **Walter Berry** bass Waldner **Helga Schmidt** mez Adelaide **Elfriede Höbarth** sop Fiakermilli **Adolf Dallapozza** ten Matteo **Hermann Winkler** ten Elemer **Klaus-Jürgen Küper** bar Dominik **Hermann Becht** bar Lamoral **Doris Soffel** mez Fortune Teller **Arno Lemberg** spkr Welko **Bavarian State Opera Chorus; Bavarian State Orchestra / Wolfgang Sawallisch**
Orfeo ② C169882H (144' · DDD) Recorded 1981. Notes, text and translation included   ⒻO

Complete except for a brief cut in Matteo's part in Act 3, Sawallisch's 1981 Orfeo recording of *Arabella* has been easily fitted onto two CDs. Sawallisch is the most experienced conductor of Strauss's operas alive today and at his best in this one, his tempos exactly right, his appreciation of its flavour (sometimes sentimental, at others gently ironic and detached) unequalled. Helen Donath's delightful Zdenka is a perfect foil for Varady's Arabella. Varady's singing of the title-role is characterful and intelligent. One should be left with ambivalent feelings about this heroine; is she lovable or a chilling opportunist? Or both? And while Fischer-Dieskau's singing of Mandryka has not the total security of his earlier DG recording of the role with Keilberth, he remains the best Mandryka heard since the war.

Ariadne auf Naxos, Op 60

Ariadne auf Naxos
Dame Elisabeth Schwarzkopf sop Ariadne **Irmgard Seefried** sop Composer **Rita Streich** sop Zerbinetta **Rudolf Schock** ten Bacchus **Karl Dönch** bar Music-Master **Hermann Prey** bar Harlequin **Fritz Ollendorff** bass Truffaldino **Helmut Krebs** ten Brighella **Gerhard Unger** ten Scaramuccio **Lisa Otto** sop Naiad **Grace Hoffman** mez Dryad **Anny Felbermayer** sop Echo **Hugues Cuénod** ten Dancing Master **Alfred Neugebauer** spkr Major-Domo **Philharmonia Orchestra / Herbert von Karajan**
EMI Great Recordings of the Century mono ② 567077-2 (128' · ADD/mono) Recorded 1954 Ⓜ❍❍❍

Karajan's *Ariadne* is perfectly cast, magnificently performed, and very well recorded. The scoring, for a small orchestra, demands virtuoso playing from what, in effect, is a group of soloists; the members of the Philharmonia Orchestra rise brilliantly to the occasion. There's a warmth and beauty of tone, a sweep of phrase, that gives lively promise of the wonderful playing we hear throughout the opera. Karajan's genius has never been more apparent than in his treatment of the Bacchus-Ariadne scene, where he makes the score glow with a Dionysiac ardour and in which, at the tremendous climax when Bacchus enters and is greeted by Ariadne as the herald of Death, he gets an ample volume of tone from his players.

Every character is vividly brought to life – Karl Dönch's harassed music master is offset by the cynical dancing master of Hugues Cuénod, and Alfred Neugebauer, in his speaking role, conveys with a superbly calm pomposity his contempt for both sets of artists. The way he enunciates his words is superb. The other small parts, all sung by experienced artists, are wholly in the picture. Rita Streich sings the lyrical phrases of Zerbinetta beautifully. Technical difficulties do not appear to exist for her and all she does is musical. Irmgard Seefried, as the Composer, has less beauty of tone but more variety. The ineffably lovely trio for the Naiad, Dryad and Echo is exquisitely sung by Lisa Otto, Grace Hoffman and Anny Felbermayer, paralleled by the equally beautiful singing of the other trios. They are simply ravishing and, like all the concerted music, have a perfect ensemble. The *commedia dell'arte* characters are all very good, especially Hermann Prey: and their ensembles between themselves and with Zerbinetta are a great delight. After an awkward start, Elisabeth Schwarzkopf, as Ariadne, brings the dark tone that's needed, to Ariadne's sorrows, and gives us much lovely singing thereafter, and also all the rapture called for at the end of her great address to the herald of Death and in her

greeting to Bacchus. Rudolf Schock sings the latter with heroic tone and sufficient nuance to make one believe in the youthful god.

The general impression is of a truly magnificent performance and recording in which all concerned have, under Karajan's superb direction, been inspired to give of their best.

Ariadne auf Naxos
Gundula Janowitz sop Ariadne **Teresa Zylis-Gara** sop Composer **Sylvia Geszty** sop Zerbinetta **James King** ten Bacchus **Theo Adam** bass-bar Music Master **Hermann Prey** bar Harlequin **Siegfried Vogel** bass Truffaldino **Hans Joachim Rotzsch** ten Brighella **Peter Schreier** ten Scaramuccio, Dancing Master **Erika Wustmann** sop Naiad **Annelies Burmeister** mez Dryad **Adele Stolte** sop Echo **Erich-Alexander Winds** spkr Major-Domo **Staatskapelle Dresden / Rudolf Kempe**
EMI Opera ② 764159-2 (118' · ADD) Recorded 1968. Notes, text and translation included Ⓜ❍❍

At mid-price this classic set can't be recommended too highly. Nobody knew more about how to pace Strauss's operas than Kempe, and he was at his best when working with the Staatskapelle Dresden, a group of players who have Strauss in their veins. This reading brings out all the sentiment and high spirits of this delightful work, and the results are beautifully recorded. Janowitz's golden tones were ideal for the title-role, which she sings with poise and inner feeling, though she makes little of the text. Zylis-Gara is a suitably impetuous Composer in the engaging Prologue where 'he' meets and has a gently erotic encounter with the charming but flighty Zerbinetta, a role here taken with brilliant accomplishment by Sylvia Geszty, who made it her own in the 1960s. James King is a forthright though none too flexible Bacchus. The smaller parts are also well taken.

Capriccio, Op 85

Capriccio
Elisabeth Schwarzkopf sop The Countess **Eberhard Waechter** bar The Count **Nicolai Gedda** ten Flamand **Dietrich Fischer-Dieskau** bar Olivier **Hans Hotter** bass-bar La Roche **Christa Ludwig** mez Clairon **Rudolf Christ** ten Monsieur Taupe **Anna Moffo** sop Italian Soprano **Dermot Troy** ten Italian Tenor **Karl Schmitt-Walter** bar Major-domo **Philharmonia Orchestra / Wolfgang Sawallisch**
EMI Great Recordings of the Century mono ② 567394-2 (135' · ADD) Recorded 1957. Notes, text and translation included Ⓜ❍❍❍

 Not only is *Capriccio* a source of constant and none-too-demanding delight but its performance and recording, especially in this CD reincarnation, are well-nigh faultless. Walter Legge assembled for the recording in 1957 what was almost his house cast, each singer virtually ideal for his or her part. Some might say that no role she recorded suited Schwarzkopf's particular talents more snugly than Countess Madeleine. Her ability to mould words and music into one can be heard here to absolute advantage. Then the charming, flirtatious, sophisticated, slightly artificial character, with the surface attraction hiding deeper feelings revealed in the closing scene (quite beautifully sung), suit her to the life. She, like her colleagues, is superbly adept at the quick repartee so important an element in this work.

As her brother, the light-hearted, libidinous Count, the young Eberhard Waechter is in his element. So are the equally young Nicolai Gedda as the composer Flamand, the Sonnet so gently yet ardently delivered, and Fischer-Dieskau as the more fiery poet Olivier. Christa Ludwig is nicely intimate, conversational and cynical as the actress Clairon, handling her affairs, waning with Olivier, waxing with the Count, expertly. Above all towers the dominating presence of Hotter as the theatre director La Roche, impassioned in his defence of the theatre's conventions, dismissive of new and untried methods, yet himself not above a trivial flirtation – and how delicately Hotter manages his remarks about his latest protegee as she dances for the assembled company.

Even with so many distinguished singers gathered together, it's the closeness of the ensemble, the sense of a real as distinct from a manufactured performance that's so strongly conveyed. And Legge did not neglect the smaller roles: Rudolf Christ makes an endearingly eccentric Monsieur Taupe, the veteran Schmitt-Walter a concerned Major-domo. Anna Moffo and Dermot Troy sing the music of the Italian soprano and tenor with almost too much sensitivity.

Crowning the performance is the musical direction of Wolfgang Sawallisch, always keeping the score on the move, yet fully aware of its sensuous and its witty qualities: Krauss's amusing libretto has much to do with the work's fascination. Both the extended Prelude and the interludes are gloriously played by the vintage Philharmonia Orchestra, who are throughout alert to the old wizard's deft scoring, as refined here as in any of his earlier operas. The recording might possibly have given a little more prominence to the instruments; in every other respect, although it's in mono, it hardly shows its age. This is a jewel in the industry's crown and it will be a source of enduring pleasure to those familiar or unfamiliar with Strauss's inspired swansong.

Additional recommendation

Janowitz Countess **Fischer-Dieskau** Count **Schreier** Flamand **Prey** Olivier **Bavarian Radio Symphony Orchestra / Böhm**
DG ② 445 347-2GX2 (142 minutes)　　Ⓜ
Karl Böhm's 1971 *Capriccio* stands on a par with Sawallisch's, but is better recorded. It captures the glorious Janowitz voice in its prime. Her lovely Countess Madeleine is admirably supported by a fine cast.

Elektra, Op 58

Elektra　　　　　　　　　　　　　　　Ⓗ
Astrid Varnay sop Elektra **Res Fischer** contr
Klytemnestra **Leonie Rysanek** sop Chrysothemis
Helmut Melchert ten Aegisthus **Hans Hotter** bassbar Orestes **Heiner Horn** bass Tutor **Gertie Charlent** sop Confidante **Helene Petrich** sop Trainbearer
Hasso Eschert ten Young Servant **Arno Reinhardt** bass Old Servant **Käthe Retzmann** sop Overseer **Ilsa Ihme-Sabisch** contr First Maidservant **Trude Roesler** mez Second Maidservant **Marianne Schröder** mez Third Maidservant **Marlies Siemling** sop Fourth Maidservant **Käthe Möller-Siepermann** sop Fifth Maidservant **Cologne Radio Chorus and Symphony Orchestra / Richard Kraus**
Koch Schwann mono ② 31643-2 (100' · ADD)
Recorded live 1953. Notes included　　　　Ⓕ Ⓞ

Hard to realise that in 1953, when this *Elektra* was broadcast from Cologne, no recording of the work existed, probably because it was considered too daring for the public to buy in the required numbers. This version, appearing officially for the first time, would have caused quite a stir had it been issued at the time. Obviously rehearsed with care, it fulfils all the work's exigent demands. It features Varnay at the peak of her career in an *annus mirabilis* for her, when she had been acclaimed at Bayreuth for her Brünnhilde and Isolde. As with those roles, she brings to her interpretation a response perfectly suited to it, adapting her tone to its special needs in terms of nuance and phrase. Her voice, in far better fettle than when she sang the part at the 1964 Salzburg Festival under Karajan, is fully equal to Strauss's inordinate demands: she's a true *Hochdramatische* of a kind hard to find today, even if her tone hardens a little under pressure at the top.

Rysanek, who sang Chrysothemis in London in the early 1950s to arresting effect, was the leading interpreter of the part over many years. Here, in her early prime, her truly Straussian voice soars easily over the orchestra, seeming to take on further sheen the higher she goes. As in all her parts, she gives her whole self to projecting the emotions of the moment. Res Fischer's Klytemnestra is a securely sung, clearly declaimed reading which eschews the histrionics often heard in the part. In a radio studio, she and Varnay turn the mother-daughter confrontation into an intimate conversation with all sorts of undertones. Then there's Hotter, as Orestes, in a heroic role that might have been written for him: his noble utterance and (on this occasion) wholly steady voice impart true stature to this small but important part, his enunciation of the text, as ever, having a Liedersinger's acuity. Melchert brings variety and an appropriately sharp-edged tone to Aegisthus.

Kraus, who did much sterling work for Cologne Opera and Radio, conducts a precise, finely shaped and well-timed reading, avoiding all excess except that which is implicit in the score. In this of all operas you miss a more sumptuous recording of the score, but by and large this is a performance that affords the listener with real satisfaction.

Elektra
Birgit Nilsson sop Elektra **Regina Resnik** mez
Klytemnestra **Marie Collier** sop Chrysothemis
Gerhard Stolze ten Aegisthus **Tom Krause** bar
Orestes **Pauline Tinsley** sop Overseer **Helen Watts**
contr **Maureen Lehane, Yvonne Minton** mezzos
Jane Cook, Felicia Weathers sops First, Second,
Third, Fourth and Fifth Maidservants **Tugomir Franc**
bass Tutor **Vienna Philharmonic Orchestra /
Sir Georg Solti**
Decca ② 417 345-2DH2 (108' · ADD) Recorded 1966-7.
Notes, text and translation included　　　Ⓕ**OOO**

 Elektra is the most consistently inspired of all Strauss's operas and derives from Greek mythology, with the ghost of Agamemnon, so unerringly delineated in the opening bars, hovering over the whole work. The invention and the intensity of mood are sustained throughout the opera's one-act length, and the characterisation is both subtle and pointed. It's a work peculiarly well suited to Solti's gifts and it's his best recording in the studios. He successfully maintains the nervous tension throughout the unbroken drama and conveys all the power and tension in Strauss's enormously complex score which is, for once, given complete. The recording captures the excellent singers and the Vienna Philharmonic in a warm, spacious acoustic marred only by some questionable electronic effects. Notwithstanding the latter, this is undoubtedly one of the greatest performances on record and sounds even more terrifyingly realistic on this magnificent transfer.

Elektra　　　　　　　　　　　　　　Ⓗ
Inge Borkh sop Elektra **Jean Madeira** mez
Klytemnestra **Lisa della Casa** sop Chrysothemis **Max
Lorenz** ten Aegisthus **Kurt Böhme** bass Orestes
Alois Pernerstorfer bass-bar Tutor **Anny
Felbermayer** sop Confidante **Karol Loraine** mez
Trainbearer **Erich Majkut** ten Young Servant **György
Littasy** bass Old Servant **Audrey Gerber** sop
Overseer **Kerstin Meyer, Sonja Draksler, Sieglinde
Wagner, Marilyn Horne** mezzos **Lisa Otto** sop First,
Second, Third, Fourth and Fifth Maidservants **Vienna
State Opera Chorus; Vienna Philharmonic
Orchestra / Dimitri Mitropoulos**
Orfeo mono ② C456972I (107' · ADD) Recorded live
1957　　　　　　　　　　　　　　　Ⓜ**OO**

This is an enthralling performance. Mitropoulos made a speciality of the score, his most important contribution to opera interpretation. Souvenirs exist of his performances at the Met in 1949 and at the Maggio Musicale in Florence in 1950, but his Salzburg reading is the one to have. No other conductor, not even Böhm or Solti in the studio, quite matches the *frisson* of this overwhelming account. And it confirms that Inge Borkh is indeed the most comprehen-

sively equipped soprano for the title-role, vocally secure – high C apart – and emotionally capable of fulfilling every demand of the strenuous part. In the great scene with Orestes she first expresses ineffably the sorrow at his supposed death, the 'tausendmal' and 'nie wiederkommt' passage done with such a searing sense of loss; then comes the great release of recognition – sung with immense warmth – followed by another almost silvery voice as Elektra recalls her lost beauty. It's a passage of singing to return to repeatedly for its many insights. Chrysothemis finds in della Casa an unusual interpreter, wonderfully ecstatic and pure of voice if not as emotionally involving as some. Madeira is a formidable Klytemnestra, her nightmarish thoughts expressed in a firm voice, accurately deployed. Böhme, a real bass, presents an implacable, angry Orestes, not as subtle or as sympathetic as Krause for Solti. Lorenz's fading *Heldentenor* is ideal to express Aegisthus's fatuity. And the maids have never, surely, been cast with such secure voices.

Inevitably, cuts are made as is almost always the case in the theatre where, otherwise, Elektra might be left voiceless by the end. If you want the complete score, the famous Solti set will do very nicely. If you want Borkh, you must choose between the Böhm in stereo (DG) or this unique experience.

Die Frau ohne Schatten, Op 65

Die Frau ohne Schatten
Julia Varady sop Empress **Plácido Domingo** ten
Emperor **Hildegard Behrens** sop Dyer's Wife **José
van Dam** bar Barak the Dyer **Reinhild Runkel** contr
Nurse **Albert Dohmen** bar Spirit-Messenger **Sumi
Jo** sop Voice of the Falcon **Robert Gambill** ten
Apparition of a Young Man **Elzbieta Ardam** mez
Voice from Above **Eva Lind** sop Guardian of the
Threshold **Gottfried Hornik** bar One-eyed Brother
Hans Franzen bass One-armed Brother **Wilfried
Gahmlich** ten Hunchback Brother **Vienna Boys'
Choir; Vienna State Opera Chorus; Vienna
Philharmonic Orchestra / Sir Georg Solti**
Decca ③ 436 243-2DHO3 (195' · DDD) Recorded
1989-91. Notes, text and translation included
　　　　　　　　　　　　　　　　Ⓕ**OOO**

 This was the most ambitious project on which Strauss and his librettist Hugo von Hofmannsthal collaborated. It's both fairy tale and allegory with a score that's Wagnerian in its scale and breadth. This Solti version presents the score absolutely complete in an opulent recording that encompasses every detail of the work's multi-faceted orchestration. Nothing escapes his keen eye and ear or that of the Decca engineers. The cast boasts splendid exponents of the two soprano roles. Behrens's vocal acting suggests complete identification with the unsatisfied plight of the Dyer's Wife and her singing has a depth of character to compensate for some tonal wear. Varady gives an intense, poignant account of the Empress's taxing music. The others, though never less than adequate, leave something to be desired. Domingo sings the Emperor with vigour and strength but evinces little sense of the music's idiom. José van Dam is likewise a vocally impeccable Barak but never penetrates the Dyer's soul. Runkel is a mean, malign Nurse as she should be, though she could be a little more interesting in this part. It benefits from glorious, dedicated playing by the VPO.

Guntram, Op 25

Guntram
Alan Woodrow ten Guntram **Andrea Martin** bar
The Old Duke **Elisabeth Wachutka** sop Freihild **Ivan Konsulov** bar Robert **Hans-Peter Scheidegger** bar Freihold **Enrico Facini** ten The Duke's Fool **Thomas Kaluzny** bar Messenger, Young Man, Minnesinger **Jin-Ho Choi** bar Old Man, Minnesinger **Ute Trekel-Burkhardt** mez Old Woman **Manfred Bittner** ten Young Man, Minnesinger **Matthias Heubusch** voc Minnesinger **Werdenfelser Male Chorus; Marchigiana Philharmonic Orchestra / Gustav Kuhn**
Arte Nova Classics ② 74321 61339-2 (100' · DDD)
Recorded live 1998. Text included   Ⓢ

However much influenced by Wagner this, Strauss's first opera, may have been, it already shows him moving off in his own melodic and harmonic direction. It contains much attractive, well-crafted music, but from the start it was lamed by the composer's own prolix libretto and hesitant dramaturgy. The story of the brave, libertarian knight Guntram's adventures in 13th-century Germany and his love for the heroine Freihild, daughter of the local ruler, whose husband Duke Robert is a sort of villain and opponent of peace, is really one about individual responsibility being more important than religious orthodoxy, something that offended Strauss's strict Catholic mentor, Alexander Ritter. This live performance under the experienced Straussian Gustav Kuhn gives a fair idea of its virtues and defects. His direction is vigorous, forward moving, strongly limned with a proper advocacy of the score's more original features, with resplendent playing from his orchestra. The performance is well served by its two principals. In the title-role, the ENO tenor Alan Woodrow here makes a more-than-passable Heldentenor in the first of many roles for that voice calling for strong, virile, penetrative tone. Woodrow produces just that, plus much of the romantic fervour Guntram's role calls for. Elisabeth Wachutka is reasonably successful as the object of Guntram's desires. Though her tone can be edgy, she rises finely to the challenge of her extended monologue in Act 2. The rest, who don't have much to do, are so-so. The recording is clear and well balanced. At the price, this is worth sampling to hear Strauss's apprentice effort in the operatic field he was so soon to grace with many masterpieces.

Der Rosenkavalier, Op 59

Der Rosenkavalier   Ⓗ
Dame Elisabeth Schwarzkopf sop Die Feldmarschallin **Christa Ludwig** mez Octavian **Otto Edelmann** bass Baron Ochs **Teresa Stich-Randall** sop Sophie **Eberhard Waechter** bar Faninal **Nicolai Gedda** ten Italian Tenor **Kerstin Meyer** contr Annina **Paul Kuen** ten Valzacchi **Ljuba Welitsch** sop Duenna **Anny Felbermayer** sop Milliner **Harald Pröghlöf** bar Notary **Franz Bierbach** bass Police Commissioner **Erich Majkut** ten Feldmarschallin's Major-domo **Gerhard Unger** ten Faninal's Major-domo, Animal Seller **Karl Friedrich** ten Landlord **Loughton High School for Girls and Bancroft's School Choirs; Philharmonia Chorus and Orchestra / Herbert von Karajan**
EMI Great Recordings of the Century mono ③
567605-2 (191' · ADD) Recorded 1956. Notes, text and translation included   Ⓜ❍❍❍

Der Rosenkavalier concerns the transferring of love of the young headstrong aristocrat Octavian from the older Marschallin (with whom he's having an affair) to the young Sophie, a girl of *nouveau riche* origins who's of his generation. The portrayal of the different levels of passion is masterly and the Marschallin's resigned surrender of her ardent young lover gives opera one of its most cherishable scenes. The comic side of the plot concerns the vulgar machinations of the rustic Baron Ochs and his attempts to seduce the disguised Octavian (girl playing boy playing girl!). The musical richness of the score is almost indescribable, with streams of endless melody, and the final trio which brings the three soprano roles together is the crowning glory of a masterpiece of the 20th century.

This magnificent recording, conducted with genius by Karajan, and with a dream cast, is unlikely to be challenged for many a year. The Philharmonia play like angels, and Schwarzkopf as the Marschallin gives one of her greatest performances. The recording, lovingly remastered, is outstanding. In 1956 stereo was new to the commercial recording world, and, unwilling to gamble everything on the new medium, producer Water Legge arranged for the sessions to be captured in both mono and stereo, using separate microphone layouts and separate balance engineers. This is the mono recording's first issue on CD; one's immediately struck by its warmer, closer balance: for example, Schwarzkopf is a significantly more rounded, fuller and essentially dominant presence, never in danger of being overwhelmed by the orchestra. The detail and transparency of the overall canvas on the stereo recording is more naturally convincing, but the mono will make a special appeal to those who prefer intimate access to these great singers. The dilemma is that each recording is impressive in its way and yet so very different. Students of the voice will almost certainly favour the mono set; devotees of the opera itself may well prefer the stereo.

RICHARD STRAUSS'S DER ROSENKAVALIER – IN BRIEF

Elisabeth Schwarzkopf *Die Feldmarschalin*
Christa Ludwig *Octavian* **Otto Edelmann** *Baron Ochs* **Philharmonia Chorus and Orchestra /**
Herbert von Karajan
EMI ③ 567605-2 (182' · ADD)　　Ⓜ●○○

☀ Taped as long ago as 1956, Karajan tends to linger over the work's purple passages, but, for most commentators, this is *the* classic, thanks not least to the casting of Schwarzkopf, Ludwig and Stich-Randall. Polished yet passionate and often intensely beautiful.

Maria Reining *Die Feldmarschalin* **Sena Jurinac** *Octavian* **Ludwig Weber** *Baron Ochs* **Vienna State Opera Chorus; Vienna PO / Erich Kleiber**
Decca ③ 467 111-2DMO3 (197' · ADD)　　Ⓜ●○

Recorded in 1954 in mono only, Kleiber's *echt* Viennese set is still top-rated by connoisseurs who welcome its opening out of the small stage cuts sanctioned by the composer and followed by Karajan.

Yvonne Kenny *Die Feldmarschalin* **Diana Montague** *Octavian* **John Tomlinson** *Baron Ochs* **London PO / David Parry**
Chandos CHAN3022 (80' · DDD)　　Ⓕ○

A delightful highlights disc with several principals familiar from English-language ENO productions, who are at least as distinguished as their counterparts on the more recent original-language recordings.

Lotte Lehman *Die Feldmarschalin* **Maria Olszewska** *Octavian* **Richard Mayr** *Baron Ochs* **Vienna State Opera Chorus; Vienna PO / Robert Heger**
Naxos ② 8 110191/2 (142' · ADD)　　Ⓢ

A famous Vienna State Opera set of extended excerpts or 'selected passages' made in September 1933.

Kiri Te Kanawa *Die Feldmarschalin* **Anne Sofie von Otter** *Octavian* **Kurt Rydl** *Baron Ochs* **Dresden State Opera Chorus; Staatskapelle Dresden / Bernard Haitink**
EMI ③ 754259-2 (223' · DDD)　　Ⓕ

Warmly played and sung, Haitink's Dresden recording is the finest audio-only account of the digital era. Te Kanawa's Marschallin is the most beautiful of recent years.

Régine Crespin *Die Feldmarschalin* **Yvonne Minton** *Octavian* **Manfred Jungwirth** *Baron Ochs* **Vienna State Opera Chorus; Vienna PO / Sir Georg Solti**
Decca ③ 417 493-2DH3 (200' · ADD)　　Ⓕ

Solti's 1968 set has high production values and an all-star casting of minor roles. He avoids the over-affectionate approach, but takes the climactic moments very broadly.

Der Rosenkavalier　　Ⓗ

Maria Reining *sop* Die Feldmarschallin **Sena Jurinac** *sop* Octavian **Ludwig Weber** *bass* Baron Ochs **Hilde Gueden** *sop* Sophie **Alfred Poell** *bar* Faninal **Anton Dermota** *ten* Italian Tenor **Hilde Rössl-Majdan** *mez* Annina **Peter Klein** *ten* Valzacchi **Judith Hellweg** *sop* Leitmetzerin **Berta Seidl** *sop* Milliner **Walter Berry** *bass* Police Commissioner **Harald Pröglhöf** *bass* Feldmarschallin's Major-domo **August Jaresch** *ten* Faninal's Major-domo **Erich Majkut** *ten* Animal Seller, Landlord **Franz Bierbach** *bass* Notary **Vienna State Opera Chorus; Vienna Philharmonic Orchestra / Erich Kleiber**
Decca Legends ③ 467 111-2DMO3 (197' · ADD)
Recorded 1954. Notes, text and translation included
Ⓜ●○

Decca has done wonders in cleaning the sound on this reissued classic recording. It seems warmer and more spacious than in any of its LP guises. The bloom on the playing of the Vienna Philharmonic is grateful to the ear, and the voices stand ideally in relation to the instruments. That's doubly heartening given that Kleiber's interpretation still stands above that of any of his successors. His innate deep understanding of the score and his instinctive feeling for the Viennese idiom remain unsurpassed; so does his convincing treatment of the score's weaker pages. Above all, he never makes the mistake of lingering too long over the work's purple passage, nor does he overheat its more active ones: the key to his reading is a combination of lightness, line and incandescence.

The vocal glory of the set remains Sena Jurinac's Octavian. Here in more refulgent voice perhaps than anywhere else on disc, she gives the performance of one's dreams. How gleaming yet how warm is her voice, how naturally impetuous and intense her colloquies with her elders. Jurinac carefully denotes Octavian's growing fascination with Sophie. Then, as the maudlin Mariandl of Act 3, she changes her tone subtly, never exaggerating. Finally, her voice soars gloriously in the trio and duet that crown the work. Without question it's a definitive interpretation, and will surely remain so.

Maria Reining's Marschallin has been badly underrated. Her approach is natural, stylish and very moving in its simplicity and obedience to the score. Not a trace of self-consciousness or arch phrasing spoils the patent honesty of her portrayal. The voice sounds a little tremulous at the start, and it never quite gains the warmth other Marschallins achieve, but the unmannered yet absolutely idiomatic enunciation of the text is compensation enough, and her partnership with Jurinac's Octavian is often memorable. Hilde Gueden's singing may be a shade sophisticated for Sophie, but the accuracy and firm focus of her singing count for much. Ludwig Weber's Ochs is a ripe, assured assumption sung with total command of the text and in an authentic Viennese accent. All the singers are versed in that essential command of Strauss's *parlando* style, so that Hofmannsthal's racy, keenly fashioned libretto is given wit and point. Although the admiration for Karajan remains undiminished, Kleiber is the performance to take to your desert island.

Der Rosenkavalier
Yvonne Kenny sop Marschallin **Diana Montague** mez Octavian **John Tomlinson** bass Baron Ochs **Rosemary Joshua** sop Sophie **Andrew Shore** bar Faninal **Jennifer Rhys-Davies** sop Marianne **Elizabeth Vaughan** mez Annina **Peter Kay** Children's Choir; Geoffrey Mitchell Choir; London Philharmonic Orchestra / David Parry Chandos Opera in English CHAN3022 (80' · DDD) Sung in English ⒻⓄ

This is a delightful disc, with a cast of principals that need fear little from comparison with international singers on original-language recordings. One can only regret that Chandos and the Peter Moores Foundation, which so faithfully underwrites this admirable venture, haven't been bold enough to record the whole work. In particular one would like much more of Tomlinson's Ochs, well known from the ENO production. In the close of Act 2 he shows us just how much can be made of the text, using a translation sensibly tailored to his own needs, and projects with enormous relish in a role that suits his vocal acting to perfection.

Yvonne Kenny sings of the joys and sorrows of love with beautiful tone and shapely phrasing, her voice of an ideal weight for the part. Like Tomlinson she's keen with her words. By her side is Diana Montague's eager, ardent Octavian, the two singers matching each other in evincing strong emotions. With Rosemary Joshua, another singer repeating her ENO role, as a mettlesome Sophie, easing naturally into her high lines, the trio is the climax of Act 3 that it should be. Andrew Shore makes much of little as Faninal. Only Elizabeth Vaughan's harsh, overdone Annina is a drawback. David Parry nicely catches both the serious and comic sides of things, and his pacing of everything but the final scene, which is a shade too hesitant, is admirable. He persuades the LPO to play at the top of its bent for him, so that the score sounds as warm and rich-hued as it should in a typically spacious Chandos recording.

Additional recommendation

Crespin Marschallin **Minton** Octavian **Jungwirth** Ochs **Donath** Sophie **Vienna Philharmonic Orchestra / Solti** Decca 417 493-2DH3 (200' · DDD) Ⓕ For those craving good sound and a reading of great charm – Crespin's rather Gallic Marschallin is wondrously sung – Solti's 1968 set is worth considering. Many collectors rate this even more highly than the classic Karajan.

Salome, Op 54

Salome
Birgit Nilsson sop Salome **Eberhard Waechter** bar

Jokanaan **Gerhard Stolze** ten Herod **Grace Hoffman** mez Herodias **Waldemar Kmentt** ten Narraboth **Josephine Veasey** mez Page **Tom Krause** bar First Nazarene **Nigel Douglas** ten Second Nazarene **Zenon Koznowski** bass First Soldier **Heinz Holecek** bass Second Soldier **Theodore Kirschbichler** bass Cappadocian Vienna Philharmonic Orchestra / Sir Georg Solti Decca ② 414 414-2DH2 (99' · ADD) Recorded 1961. Notes, text and translation included ⒻⓄⓄⓄ

Solti's *Salome* was one of Decca's notable Sonic-stage successes and still beats most of its competitors in terms of sound alone. There's a real sense here of a theatrical performance, as produced by John Culshaw, with an imaginative use of movement. The vivid, nervous energy of Strauss has always been Solti's territory, and this is an overwhelming account of Strauss's sensual piece, sometimes a little too hard-hitting: there are places where the tension might be relaxed just a shade, but throughout, the VPO answers Solti's extreme demands with its most aristocratic playing. With only a single break, the sense of mounting fever is felt all the more. Birgit Nilsson's account of the title-role is another towering monument to her tireless singing. Here, more even than as Brünnhilde, one notices just how she could fine away her tone to a sweet and fully supported *pianissimo*, and her whole interpretation wants nothing of the erotic suggestiveness of sopranos more familiar with the role on stage. Gerhard Stolze's Herod is properly wheedling, worried and, in the final resort, crazed, but there are times, particularly towards the end of his contribution, when exaggeration takes over from characterisation. Other interpretations show how effects can be created without distortion of the vocal line. Eberhard Waechter is an aggressive rather than a visionary Jokanaan. Grace Hoffman is a suitably gloating Herodias. Much better than any of these, Nilsson apart, is Waldemar Kmentt's wonderfully ardent Narraboth. Hardly any of the rivals since 1961 has managed a true challenge to this simply outstanding recording.

Salome
Cheryl Studer sop Salome **Bryn Terfel** bar Jokanaan **Horst Hiestermann** ten Herod **Leonie Rysanek** sop Herodias **Clemens Bieber** ten Narraboth **Marianne Rørholm** contr Page **Friedrich Molsberger** bass First Nazarene **Ralf Lukas** bass Second Nazarene **William Murray** bass First Soldier **Bengt Rundgren** bass Second Soldier **Klaus Lang** bar Cappadocian **Orchestra of the Deutsche Oper, Berlin / Giuseppe Sinopoli** DG ② 431 810-2GH2 (102' · DDD) Recorded 1990. Notes, text and translation included ⒻⓄⓄ

Strauss's setting of a German translation of Oscar Wilde's play is original and erotically explicit. It caused a sensation in its day and even now stimulates controversy. Sinopoli's recording is a magnificent achievement, mainly because of Cheryl Studer's representation of the spoilt Princess who demands and eventually gets the head of Jokanaan (John the Baptist) on a platter as a reward for her striptease ('Dance of the Seven Veils'). Studer, her voice fresh, vibrant and sensuous, conveys exactly Salome's growing fascination, infatuation and eventual obsession with Jokanaan, which ends in the arresting necrophilia of the final scene. She expresses Salome's wheedling, spoilt nature, strong will and ecstasy in tones that are apt for every aspect of the strenuous role.

She's supported to the hilt by Sinopoli's incandescent conducting and by Bryn Terfel's convincing Jokanaan, unflaggingly delivered, by Hiestermann's neurotic Herod, who makes a suitably fevered, unhinged sound as the near-crazed Herod, and Rysanek's wilful Herodias. The playing is excellent and the recording has breadth and warmth. This is eminently recommendable. For a newcomer to the work, Studer's superb portrayal may just tip the balance in favour of Sinopoli, though Solti's famous version is in a class of its own, with a gloriously sung Salome and the ravishingly beautiful playing of the Vienna Phil.

Salome
Inga Nielsen sop Salome **Robert Hale** bass-bar Jokanaan **Reiner Goldberg** ten Herod **Anja Silja** sop Herodias **Deon van der Walt** ten Narraboth **Marianne Rørholm** contr Page **Bent Norup** bar First Nazarene **Morten Frank Larsen** bar Second Nazarene **Per Høyer** bar First Soldier **Stephen Milling** bass Second Soldier **Anders Jokobsson** bass Cappadocian **Henriette Bonde Hansen** sop Slave **Danish National Radio Symphony Orchestra / Michael Schønwandt**
Chandos ② CHAN9611 (99' · DDD) Notes, text and translation included   Ⓕⓞ

Inga Nielsen is a Salome of quite exceptional talent, even inspiration. Better than any of her predecessors she creates a princess who sounds credibly teenaged with surely just the pearl-like yet needle-sharp tone Strauss intended. Nobody has so convincingly conveyed the impression of a spoilt, petulant innocent with the will and determination to get her way – and then exploited her manipulative character to frightening effect as, sexually awakened, Salome becomes obsessed with the body of Jokanaan. In a performance that's vocally stunning from Salome's first entrance, Nielsen fashions her reading with supreme intelligence in her response to words and notes. Throughout she sings keenly, even maliciously off the text. While still having nothing but praise for Studer's beautifully sung portrayal on the Sinopoli set – her tone is more refulgent, less narrow than Nielsen's but she isn't so much inside the role – or for Nilsson's vocally overwhelming portrayal for Solti, Nielsen simply seems a Salome by nature, made for the part. Happily Nielsen's riveting interpretation receives suitable support. Schønwandt yields to

none of his illustrious predecessors in impressing on us the still-extraordinary originality, fascination and tense horror of Strauss's score. From start to finish, including an electrifying account of the Dance, his is a fiery direct, highly charged yet never vulgar reading. Hale, who has partnered Nielsen in this work at the Brussels Opera, is a noble-sounding, resolute Jokanaan of long experience. Although he doesn't attempt the larger-than-life, tremendous performance of Terfel for Sinopoli, and his tone isn't as steady, his reading is surely more of a piece with the opera as a whole. Goldberg is just right as the degraded, superstitious, lecherous Herod, vocally astute and characterful. Silja is a well-routined, if sometimes over-the-top Herodias.

Chandos provides a recording of extraordinary range and breadth, yet one that makes sure that the singers take stage front. Anyone who already has the highly regarded Sinopoli version will probably not feel the need to invest in this set, but newcomers are urged to hear it. Even though other elements are well taken care of on earlier versions, Nielsen is really unmissable.

Additional recommendation

Salome   Ⓗ
Goltz Salome **Braun** Jokanaan **Patzak** Herod **Kenney** Herodias **Dermota** Narraboth **Vienna Philharmonic Orchestra / Clemens Krauss**
Decca Original Masters ② mono 475 6087DC2 (102' · ADD)   Ⓑ
Why Strauss considered Clemens Krauss to be his favourite interpreter is amply demonstrated by this set, at last generally available on CD. His magnificently taut, powerful yet translucent way with is obvious from start to finish. As far as was possible in mono, Decca caught a riveting reading in well-balanced, spacious sound. Christel Goltz was the leading Salome of the day, and Patzak as Herod remains unsurpassed. This version is well worth anyone's money.

Die schweigsame Frau, Op 80

Die schweigsame Frau
Kurt Böhme bass Sir Morosus **Martha Mödl** mez Housekeeper **Barry McDaniel** bar Barber **Donald Grobe** ten Henry Morosus **Reri Grist** sop Aminta **Lotte Schädle** sop Isotta **Glenys Loulis** mez Carlotta **Albrecht Peter** bar Morbio **Benno Kusche** bar Vanuzzi **Max Proebstl** bass Farfallo **Bavarian State Opera Chorus and Orchestra / Wolfgang Sawallisch**
Orfeo d'or ② C516992I ('126' · ADD) Recorded 1971   Ⓕ

That ardent and devoted Straussian, William Mann, slated this production (in Opera) when he saw it at its première in Munich in 1971 because the score was 'cut to ribbons', declaring that it was therefore, in Strauss's home city, 'a national disgrace'. Notwithstanding this objection, all the liveliness and spirit of the Munich event is conveyed in this recording from the archives of

Bavarian Radio to the extent that you hear a lot of stage noises. Sawallisch wholly enters into the spirit of the Ben Jonson comedy as adapted for his libretto by Stefan Zweig. The cast, excellent all round, easily get their collective tongues around the profusion of words. Kurt Böhme, near the end of his long career, is, as he was in the flesh, a magnificently rotund Morosus, with real 'face' in his singing and possessing all the bass notes that Hotter (DG) and Adam (on the absolutely complete EMI version) don't quite possess, being bass-baritones. The then-young American singers, who all spent most of their careers in Germany, cast as Aminta, Henry and the Barber, all possess good German. Grist is a delightfully fresh and pleasing Aminta and Barry McDaniel an inventive Barber, though his rivals on the other sets are even better. As Henry, Grobe isn't quite the equal of Wunderlich – who can be? Mödl enjoys herself hugely as the Housekeeper.

Sawallisch, in 1971 newly appointed Music Director in Munich and destined to do so much there for the cause of Strauss, manages to keep clear all the many strands in Strauss's score; so do Böhm and Janowski. This version, in stereo, has that advantage over the DG, but the singing on the latter is, by a small margin, superior. If you want every note you must have Janowski – three CDs, but at mid-price.

Further listening

Daphne
Gueden Daphne **King** Apollo **Schoeffler** Peneios
Wunderlich Leukippos
Vienna State Opera Chorus; Vienna Symphony Orchestra / Bohm
DG ② 445 322-2GX2 (94' · ADD)   Ⓜ
Live recording

Daphne isn't perhaps as involving as Strauss's later operas, but it contains some typically beautiful writing for the soprano voice in the title-role. A fine performance.

Die Liebe der Danae
Kupper Danae **Schöffler** Jupiter **Traxel** Mercury Ⓗ
Vienna State Opera Chorus, Vienna Philharmonic Orchestra / Krauss
Orfeo mono ③ C292923D (164' · ADD) Live recording
from the Salzburg Festival   Ⓕ

Despite a number of pages in Strauss's most appealing, late autumnal vein, this is a deeply flawed work, not least because of the wordy and rather empty libretto. For Strauss completists, though, this 1952 recording is the one to have.

Igor Stravinsky
Russian/French/American 1882-1971

Stravinsky was the son of a leading bass at the Mariinsky Théatre in St Petersburg, he studied with Rimsky-Korsakov (1902-8), who was an influence

on his early music, though so were Tchaikovsky, Borodin, Glazunov and (from 1907-8) Debussy and Dukas. This colourful mixture of sources lies behind The Firebird (1910), commissioned by Dyagilev for his Ballets Russes. Stravinsky went with the company to Paris in 1910 and spent much of his time in France from then onwards, continuing his association with Dyagilev in Petrushka (1911) and The Rite of Spring (1913).

These scores show an extraordinary development. Both use folktunes, but not in any symphonic manner: Stravinsky's forms are additive rather than symphonic, created from placing blocks of material together without disguising the joins. The binding energy is much more rhythmic than harmonic, and the driving pulsations of The Rite marked a crucial change in the nature of Western music. Stravinsky, however, left it to others to use that change in the most obvious manner. He himself, after completing his Chinese opera The Nightingale, turned aside from large resources to concentrate on chamber forces and the piano.

Partly this was a result of World War I, which disrupted the activities of the Ballets Russes and caused Stravinsky to seek refuge in Switzerland. He was not to return to Russia until 1962, though his works of 1914-18 are almost exclusively concerned with Russian folk tales and songs: they include the choral ballet Les noces ('The Wedding'), the smaller sung and danced fable Renard, a short play doubly formalised with spoken narration and instrumental music (The Soldier's Tale) and several groups of songs. In The Wedding, where block form is geared to highly mechanical rhythm to give an objective ceremonial effect, it took him some while to find an appropriately objective instrumentation; he eventually set it with pianos and percussion. Meanwhile, for the revived Ballets Russes, he produced a startling transformation of 18th-century Italian music (ascribed to Pergolesi) in Pulcinella (1920), which opened the way to a long period of 'neo-classicism', or re-exploring past forms, styles and gestures with the irony of non-developmental material being placed in developmental moulds. The Symphonies of Wind Instruments, an apotheosis of the wartime 'Russian' style, was thus followed by the short number-opera Mavra, the Octet for wind, and three works he wrote to help him earn his living as a pianist: the Piano Concerto, the Sonata and the Serenade in A.

During this period of the early 1920s he avoided string instruments because of their expressive nuances, preferring the clear articulation of wind, percussion, piano and even pianola. But he returned to the full orchestra to achieve the starkly presented Handel-Verdi imagery of the opera-oratorio Oedipus rex, and then wrote for strings alone in Apollon musagète (1928), the last of his works to be presented by Dyagilev. All this while he was living in France, and Apollon, with its Lullian echoes, suggests an identification with French classicism which also marks the Duo concertant for violin and piano and the stage work on which he collaborated with Gide: Perséphone, a classical rite of spring. However, his Russianness remained deep. He orchestrated pieces by Tchaikovsky, now established as his chosen ancestor, to make the ballet Le baiser de la fée, and in 1926 he rejoined the Orthodox Church. The Symphony of

Psalms was the first major work in which his ritual music engaged with the Christian tradition.

The other important works of the 1930s, apart from Perséphone, are all instrumental, and include the Violin Concerto, the Concerto for two pianos, the post-Brandenburg 'Dumbarton Oaks' Concerto and the Symphony in C, which disrupts diatonic normality on its home ground. It was during the composition of this work, in 1939, that Stravinsky moved to the USA, followed by Vera Sudeikina, whom he had loved since 1921 and who was to be his second wife (his first wife and his mother had both died earlier the same year). In 1940 they settled in Hollywood, which was henceforth their home. Various film projects ensued, though all foundered, perhaps inevitably: the Hollywood cinema of the period demanded grand continuity; Stravinsky's patterned discontinuities were much better suited to dancing. He had a more suitable collaborator in Balanchine, with whom he had worked since Apollon, and for whom in America he composed Orpheus and Agon. Meanwhile music intended for films went into orchestral pieces, including the Symphony in Three Movements (1945).

The later 1940s were devoted to The Rake's Progress, a parable using the conventions of Mozart's mature comedies and composed to a libretto by Auden and Kallman. Early in its composition, in 1948, Stravinsky met Robert Craft, who soon became a member of his household and whose enthusiasm for Schoenberg and Webern (as well as Stravinsky) probably helped make possible the gradual achievement of a highly personal serial style after The Rake. The process was completed in 1953 during the composition of the brilliant, tightly patterned Agon, though most of the serial works are religious or commemorative, being sacred cantatas (Canticum sacrum, Threni, Requiem Canticles) or elegies (In memoriam Dylan Thomas, Elegy for JFK). All these were written after Stravinsky's 70th birthday, and he continued to compose into his mid-80s, also conducting concerts and making many gramophone records of his music. During this period, too, he and Craft published several volumes of conversations.

GROVEmusic

three great ballets. It's fascinating to chart his development from the 1908 *Scherzo fantastique* with its orchestral colours scintillating in the best Rimsky-Korsakovian manner, to the wholly original language of *Les noces* with its almost exclusively metrical patterns and monochrome scoring (soloists, chorus, pianos and percussion) begun only six years later. The links are there: witness the Rimskian bumble-bee that flies through the *Scherzo* to find its winged counterpart two years on in *The Firebird*; and the primitive rhythmic force of Kastchei's 'Infernal dance' in *The Firebird* finding its fullest expression, another three years later, in *The Rite of Spring*; and so on. Each work is a logical, if time-lapse progression from the previous one. Like *Les noces*, the animal rites of the farmyard opera-cum-burlesque *Renard* (1916) and *L'histoire du soldat* (1918), a morality play designed for a small touring theatre company (the Suite included here omits the speaking roles) leave behind the lavish orchestra of *The Rite* for small and unusual instrumental and vocal combinations.

To have the composer at the helm, and a consistent approach to the way the music is recorded, ensures that those links are clearly established. The orchestra that takes the lion's share of the task, the Columbia Symphony, was assembled by CBS to include many of the finest players in America. One could criticise the recordings for close balances and spotlighting, but many modern contenders will more often than not deprive you of adequate articulation of the music's linear and rhythmic ingenuity. On the whole these recordings reproduce with good tone, range, openness and presence. As to Stravinsky the conductor, only *Les noces* finds him at less than his usual rhythmically incisive self. This *Petrushka* is more representative: it pulsates with inner life and vitality – incidentally, he uses his leaner, clearer 1947 revision, not the original 1911 score as the booklet claims.

Complete Stravinsky Edition

The Complete Edition, Volume 1   **H**

The Firebird[a]. Scherzo à la russe[a]. Scherzo fantastique[b]. Fireworks[a]. Petrushka[a]. The Rite of Spring[a]. Renard[c]. L'histoire du soldat – Suite[c]. Les noces[d]

Mildred Allen *sop* Regina Sarfaty *mez* Loren Driscoll, George Shirley *tens* William Murphy *bar* Richard Oliver, Donald Gramm *basses* Toni Koves *cimbalom* Samuel Barber, Aaron Copland, Lukas Foss, Roger Sessions *pfs* [d]American Concert Choir; [d]Columbia Percussion Ensemble; [a]Columbia Symphony Orchestra; [b]CBC Symphony Orchestra; [c]Columbia Chamber Ensemble / Igor Stravinsky

Sony Classical ③ SM3K46291 (194' · ADD) Recorded 1959-63   Ⓜ**O**

This set contains virtually all the music from Stravinsky's 'Russian' period, including the

The Complete Edition, Volume 2

Apollo[a]. Agon[b]. Jeu de cartes[c]. Scènes de ballet[d]. Bluebird – Pas de deux[a]. Le baiser de la fée[a]. Pulcinella[a]. Orpheus[e]

Irene Jordan *sop* George Shirley *ten* Donald Gramm *bass* [a]Columbia Symphony Orchestra; [b]Los Angeles Festival Symphony Orchestra; [c]Cleveland Orchestra; [d]CBC Symphony Orchestra; [e]Chicago Symphony Orchestra / Igor Stravinsky

Sony Classical ③ SM3K46292 (210' · ADD) Recorded 1963-5   Ⓜ

Volume 2 comprises ballets written between 1919 and 1957. *Pulcinella* was based on music originally thought to have been written by Pergolesi, but now known to be the work of various 18th-century composers. In 1919 Stravinsky hadn't long embraced neo-classical style, but here was a brilliant example of old wine in new bottles, with the melodies sounding as if they come from the pen of Stravinsky himself. The composer conducts a lively, sharply accented account of the score. 1928 saw the production of two Stravinsky ballets. *Apollo*, a mainly quiet, contemplative score, written for string orchestra, has many passages of great beauty. Stravinsky the conductor doesn't linger over these but allows the work's cool classical elegance to speak for itself. In *Le baiser de la fée* Stravinsky used themes by Tchaikovsky as the basis for his score. Once again, the music seems quite transformed, and the result is a most captivating work. Stravinsky's watchful, affectionate performance is perfectly proportioned. His arrangement of the 'Pas de deux' from Tchaikovsky's *Sleeping Beauty* is no more than a reduction for small pit orchestra, however, and a mere curiosity. In *Jeu de cartes*, which dates from 1936, Stravinsky used music by Rossini and others, but here the references are only fleeting and merely enhance the humour of this robust, outgoing score. His performance brings out all the work's vigour and personality very effectively, but here and there rhythms become slightly unstuck, and a slightly hectic quality manifests itself.

Scènes de ballet was written in 1944 and possesses a slightly terse quality in the main, though there are some more lyrical passages. Stravinsky does nothing to soften the work's edges in his performance, and it emerges as a strong, highly impressive piece. *Orpheus* was completed in 1947 and shows Stravinsky's neo-classical style at its most highly developed. Much of the music is quiet, after the manner of *Apollo*, but then the orchestra suddenly erupts into a passage of quite savage violence. Stravinsky conducts this passage with amazing energy for a man in his eighties, and elsewhere his performance has characteristic clarity and a very direct means of expression typical of a composer performance.

Finally *Agon*, written in 1957, attracts the listener with its colourful opening fanfares and then pursues an increasingly complex serial path in such a brilliant and highly rhythmical fashion that one is hardly aware that the technique is being used. This work, brilliantly conducted by Stravinsky, is an ideal introduction to his late style and to the serial technique itself. Remastering has been carried out with the greatest skill, and all the recordings in this set sound very well indeed for their age.

The Complete Edition, Volume 4
Symphonies – No 1 in E flat[a]. Stravinsky in rehearsal. Stravinsky in his own words. Symphony in Three Movements[b]. Symphony in C[c]. Symphony of Psalms[d]
Toronto Festival Singers; [ad]Columbia Symphony Orchestra; [b]Columbia Symphony Orchestra; [c]CBC Symphony Orchestra / Igor Stravinsky
Sony Classical ② SM2K46294 (143' · ADD) Recorded 1961-6　　Ⓜ

The word 'symphony' appears in the title of each work on these two discs, but this term covers some very diverse material. Stravinsky was in his mid-twenties when he wrote his Symphony in E flat, and the score is very much in the style of his teacher Rimsky-Korsakov. It has genuine colour and flair, however, and the octogenarian conductor brings paternalistic affection and a good deal of vigour to his performance. The *Symphony in C* dates from 1940, when Stravinsky was in his neo-classical phase. The work has many beautiful pages, as well as much pungent wit. In this performance Stravinsky drives the music much harder than he did in his 1952 mono recording with the Cleveland Orchestra, and although there are some exciting moments the music does tend to lose its elements of grace and charm.

The performance of the *Symphony in Three Movements* is also characterised by the use of fastish tempos. But this violent work, written in 1945, and inspired by events in the Second World War, responds more readily to a strongly driven interpretation. Stravinsky wrote his *Symphony of Psalms* in 1930, and this composition reflects his deep religious convictions in varied settings from the Book of Psalms. His use of a chorus is interestingly combined with an orchestra which lacks upper strings. Stravinsky conducts a fervent, serious, beautifully balanced performance.

All the 1960s recordings in this set sound very well in their CD transfers. In some quarters the elderly Stravinsky has been wrongly portrayed as a frail, inadequate figure who only took over performances when works had been thoroughly rehearsed for him. Nothing could prove more clearly that this was not true than the rehearsal excerpts in this set, which show a vigorous, alert octogenarian very much in control, and rehearsing passages in some detail.

Agon

Stravinsky Circus Polka. Ode. Scherzo à la Russe. Scènes de ballet. Concertino. Agon. Greeting Prelude 'Happy Birthday to You'. Canon on a Russian Popular Tune. Variations 'Aldous Huxley in memoriam' **Stafford Smith/Key** (arr Stravinsky) The Star-Spangled Banner
London Symphony Orchestra / Michael Tilson Thomas
RCA Red Seal 09026 68865-2 (76' · DDD)　　ⒻⓄⓄ

This CD has been absorbingly programmed to chart the progress from Stravinsky's early years in America, awkwardly coming to terms with a new language, a new and rather harsh economic climate and a musical public that welcomed him warmly enough but was at the same time welcoming scores of other refugee musicians. Acutely conscious of money and the absence of it, he attempted in vain to obtain film music commissions from Hollywood and tried to write pop songs and to make money in the relatively prosperous world of jazz. But the *Scherzo à la Russe*, originally for jazz band (played here in its orchestral version), sounds like a rejected movement from *Petrushka*. Rather more shrewdly he wrote the *Scènes de ballet* for a Broadway revue and was rewarded with a respectable run of performances. The *Concertino*, written for string quartet long before his arrival in America, arranged there for a chamber orchestra of 12 instruments, is a neat demonstration of how much of his late style was already present in his earlier work. The proto-serial *Agon* and the super-serial *Variations* both represent Stravinsky's relief and sheer exuberance, not so much at finding serialism as at realising that he had been writing quasi-serially all his life and that he could exploit its techniques while remaining himself.

What makes this hugely entertaining as well as instructive is the infectious zest of the performances. The enjoyable racket of the *Circus Polka*, the gorgeous trumpet tune in *Scènes de ballet*, the delight in inventing entrancing new sonorities that's central to *Agon*, the more arcane but none the less obvious pleasure in the *Aldous Huxley* Variations of constructing perfect, crystalline mechanisms – all these are conveyed with exemplary precision. The recordings are brilliant.

Apollon musagète

Apollon musagète (1947 version). ªThe Rite of Spring. The Firebird – Suite. Jeu de cartes. Petrushka.
Royal Concertgebouw Orchestra, ªCleveland Orchestra / Riccardo Chailly
Double Decca ② 473 731-2DF2 (149' · DDD)
Recorded 1993-2002   Ⓜ**OO**

This is a great little set, coupling a ravishing *Apollon musagète* with a truly stunning *Rite of Spring*. The *Petrushka* is equally fine. The fact that Stravinsky's revision of *Apollon* dispensed with 'half the woodwind, two of the three harps, glockenspiel and celesta from the original scoring' hardly constitutes the bleaching process that a less colour-sensitive performance might have allowed. Part of the effect comes from a remarkably fine recording where clarity and tonal bloom are complementary, but Chailly must take the credit for laying all Stravinsky's cards on the table rather than holding this or that detail to his chest. Everything tells, much as it does in the *Scherzo fantastique* – whether the euphonious winds and brass at 3'52", the motorised repeated notes later on or the ornamental swirlings that, in stylistic terms, dance us all the way from Rimsky's Arabian Nights to the unmistakably Russian world of *The Firebird*.

Apollon musagète is something else again, and Chailly takes the lyrical line, pointing without punching and allowing his excellent strings their head. The coda is jaunty, the 'Apothéose' suitably mysterious, and 'Variation d'Apollon' features fine solo work from the orchestra's leader, Jaap van Zweden. Viable alternatives include leaner, more ascetic readings, but Chailly balances gracefulness with tonal substance and the sound is glorious.

Le baiser de la fée

Le baiser de la fée. Faun and Shepherdess, Op 2. Ode
Lucy Shelton *sop* **Cleveland Orchestra / Oliver Knussen**
DG 449 205-2GH (64' · DDD) Text and translation included   Ⓕ**OO**

Oliver Knussen offers us the best-played, best-recorded and most sensitively interpreted account of *Le baiser de la fée* that we have had so far on CD, with meticulous attention to Stravinsky's dynamic markings and delicate instrumental pointing. Stravinsky's subtle Tchaikovsky orchestrations (the musical 'grid' of *Le baiser*) inspire a reading that exhibits delicate sensibilities and quick reflexes, and Knussen's fill-ups respond equally well to those same qualities. The mildly erotic *Faun and Shepherdess* is seductively played, with soprano Lucy Shelton sounding agile and vocally appealing. The tripartite *Ode* is a quietly eventful memorial for Natalie Koussevitzky. Even Stravinsky's own 1965 Columbia Symphony Orchestra recording, although full of lovely things and of great historical interest, is outclassed here.

The Firebird

The Firebird – Suite (1945). Jeu de cartes
Granada City Orchestra / Josep Pons
Harmonia Mundi HMC90 1728 (58' · DDD)   Ⓕ**O**

Stravinsky doesn't specify the number of strings to be used for the 1945 *Firebird* suite, but the wind forces are exactly the same as in *Jeu de cartes*, where he asks for strings in the proportion 12, 10, 8, 6, 6. The Granada City Orchestra provide 11, 10, 7, 6, 4, which seems a better balance. In *Firebird*, Pons and his players quite convince you that we're missing something when it's played by a full-size symphony orchestra. Real quiet and delicacy of detail are easier for a 'large chamber' group, especially when the conductor seems to be urging them to play like chamber musicians, listening intently to each other and giving real character to solo passages. Solo strings are allowed *portamento* from time to time, and one reason why Pons chose a magically slow speed for the outset of the finale was surely that he knew his first horn would sound wonderful at that tempo. Speeds are often a touch on the slow side, not to make life easier for the players but because they and their conductor have obviously enjoyed working on subtle phrasings and *rubato*. Yet they can play fast too and with a big tone without congestion. But above all one is reminded how full this score is of quiet, delicate colour.

There are some slowish tempos in *Jeu de cartes* too, but not at the expense of crispness of detail and lightness of touch. This isn't a coupling in which you marvel that the Granada City Orchestra can put up a respectable showing, but one in which you salute with respect an ensemble of pronounced character and a conductor who understands that moderately small can be very beautiful.

Stravinsky The Firebird (Original version 1910). Symphonies of Wind Instruments
London Symphony Orchestra / Kent Nagano
Virgin Classics The Classics 561848-2 (59' · DDD)
Recorded 1991-2   Ⓢ Ⓑ **OO**

The reissue of Kent Nagano's vividly detailed LSO recording of the original Stravinsky *Firebird* score must go right to the top of the recommended list. From the very opening the clearly delineated kaleidoscope of orchestral colour reminds one of Dorati's famous Mercury recording, but the new Virgin sound balance is even finer, slightly softer-grained, richer, but with hardly less impact. At the opening the playing generates slightly less tension than with Dorati, but the concentration steadily increases, the orchestral colour glows radiantly, and the big set pieces – the spectacular 'Danse infernale' of Kashchei, the lovely 'Princesses' Round Dance' and the 'Berceuse' – are all superbly played. The final climax expands gloriously. Nagano also uses the original 1920 score of the *Symphonies of Wind Instruments* and the result is ear-tickling in the best sense, with sonorities juxtaposed most skilfully, textures keenly balanced, and a well-maintained onward flow.

The Firebird. The Rite of Spring. Perséphone
Stephanie Cosserat narr **Stuart Neill** ten **Ragazzi,
The Peninsula Boys Chorus; San Francisco Girl's
Chorus; San Francisco Symphony Chorus and
Orchestra / Michael Tilson Thomas**
RCA Red Seal (special price) ③ 09026 68898-2
(119' · DDD) Recorded live 1996-8. Text and
translation included   Ⓕ **O**

On the face of it, an odd compilation. Why issue one of Stravinsky's least-known ballets in harness with two of his most popular? The answer lies partly in *Perséphone*'s revisiting, 20 years on, of the theme of *The Rite* (earth and rebirth) with Homer's Greece replacing pagan Russia in a neo-classical piece described by Elliott Carter as 'a humanist *Rite of Spring*'. Rather more difficult to explain is the presence of *The Firebird* (the complete 1910 score plus a piano), but a performance as good as this is its own justification. We have no idea how much post-concert 'patching' there was after the two live recordings (*The Firebird* and *The Rite*), but the playing is superbly 'finished'. Possibly, the ballet's ending was better on that particular night than any of the others; certainly, Tilson Thomas's timing and shading of the last minutes' darkness-to-light is spellbinding, the management of the *crescendo* on the final chord, even more so. Perfumes are distinctly French, with the *Firebird*'s 'supplication' as seductive as any on disc. The general exuberance of the playing in *The Rite* might also be thought French, though the virtu-

oso delivery and flamboyance are recognisably American. It isn't a *Rite* that investigates the score's radicalism; rather it's one to send you home from the concert hall exhilarated.

You'd be lucky to catch *Perséphone* in the concert hall. Rather baffling given the quality of a piece which shares with *Oedipus Rex* an inspired blend of distancing and direct appeal, and with *Apollo* and *Orpheus*, an archaic beauty and limpidity. The singers rise to that challenge with superb choral work. Stravinsky called *Perséphone* a 'melodrama', referring to the spoken title-role. And as Persephone *is* Spring, RCA has cast an aptly youthful-sounding actress in the part, very good at eagerness, passion and compassion. It may be that the voice is too young for *gravitas*; it may equally be that, as recorded there was no need to project in the same way, and stage projection might have helped create an element of *gravitas*. It's a small point, and her relative immediacy is always appealing. In all other respects, RCA's balance can't be criticised.

The Firebird (trans Stravinsky)
Idil Biret pf
Naxos 8 555999 (55' · DDD)   Ⓢ

So popular was *The Firebird* when first performed in 1910 that Stravinsky published three concert suites from it in 1911, 1919 and 1945. His piano transcription dates from 1910, too, but it remains far less familiar than Guido Agosti's celebrated three-movement virtuoso transcription of the closing numbers. Here, everything is included, and the result is a glittering tapestry played with tireless resource by the intrepid Idil Biret. Such enterprise notwithstanding, there are surely too many moments when this transcription remains a transcription. Too often the original score's colour and vibrancy is reduced to a black-and-white alternative, with many stock devices (notably growling or murmuring *tremolandi*) doing duty for a truer evocation. And it's in this sense that this arrangement hardly equals the success of Stravinsky's transcription of *Petrushka*, where you could almost confuse the finished product with an original masterpiece. Biret's playing can be more dependable than spine-tingling, but at her best she's stylish and dextrous in resolving a fearsome array of difficulties, and she's been excellently recorded.

Petrushka

Petrushka. The Firebird – Suite. Scherzo à la Russe
Cincinnati Symphony Orchestra / Paavo Järvi
Telarc CD80587 (60' · DDD)   Ⓕ **O**

Paavo Järvi's Telarc coupling of *Petrushka* and *The Firebird* Suite is outstanding in every way. *Petrushka* is so arresting that it invites comparison with the famous pioneering Ansermet account. It should be noted that Ansermet uses the original 1911 score, and Järvi the 1947 version. Switching between the two accounts, the surprise is the closeness of the two interpretations, with Ansermet pressing forward at one moment, Järvi the next, each relishing every detail of Stravinsky's sparkling orchestral palette, yet each completely individual. The more natural concert hall-balance in the superb acoustics of Cincinnati's Music Hall, adds ambient warmth and atmosphere, giving a translucent glow to the woodwind (yet still achieving wonderful detail), a rich patina to the strings, and filling out the brass sonorities without loss of bite. The important piano roulades, too, brilliantly played by Michael Chertock, glitter irridescently. Järvi's reading certainly doesn't lack histrionic qualities, yet it has added pathos, particularly the scene in the Moor's Room, and at the very end of the ballet. With Ansermet, Petrushka's ghost reappears fiercely, even demonically; Järvi chooses a distanced effect and creates a haunting atmosphere of desolate melancholy.

The Firebird Suite is equally memorable. Again the wonderful Rimskyan colouring is conveyed in lusciously translucent detail, but the spectacular entry of Kashchei will surely make you jump, and the finale expands gloriously. Jack Renner, Telarc's outstanding chief recording engineer, produces the best bass drum in the business, and those thwacks as Järvi builds his final climax are riveting, as is the amplitude of the overall sound.

So this CD not only offers truly memorable performances, splendidly played, but demonstration sound that audiophiles will relish.

Petrushka (1947 version). Pulcinella
Peter Donohoe pf **City of Birmingham Symphony Orchestra / Sir Simon Rattle**
HMV Classics HMV5 73551-2 (74' · DDD) Recorded 1986   Ⓢ Ⓑ ●

Rattle's performance of *Petrushka* is most notable for its fresh look at details of scoring and balance, with pianist Peter Donohoe making a strong impression. The results are robust and persuasive, though one sometimes has the impression that the characters are being left to fend for themselves. The atmospheric sound with its generous middle and bass is certainly very natural. The symphony, too, is eminently recommendable, sounding more high-spirited than it sometimes has, with Rattle particularly relishing the jazzy bits.

Petrushka. Apollon musagète (1947 version). ªThe Rite of Spring. The Firebird – Suite. Jeu de cartes
Royal Concertgebouw Orchestra, ª**Cleveland Orchestra / Riccardo Chailly**
Double Decca ② 473 731-2DF2 (149' · DDD) Recorded 1993-2002   Ⓜ ●●

In *Petrushka* Chailly has his players characterise even the smallest detail. Note the tongue-in-cheek lead-in to the 'Russian Dance' and the carefree 'squeeze-box' character of the dance itself (with dynamic crossfire between wind and brass and some excellent piano playing). 'Petrushka' (second tableau) is played *con amore*, with much humanity and not entirely without malice: perhaps the anger and frustration aren't as blatant as they might be; but the pain and humiliation certainly are. It's a performance that breathes, that sings and neither rushes its fences nor loses sight of the score's very specific rhythmic profile. As for the recording, given top-ranking engineers – who could rightly expect anything less than exceptional? The couplings, too, are equally fine.

Pulcinella

Pulcinellaᶜ. Danses concertantesª. Petrushkaᵇ. The Rite of Springᵈ. Two Suitesᵉ
ᶜ**Yvonne Kenny** sop ᶜ**Robert Tear** ten ᶜ**Robert Lloyd** bass ᶜᵉ**Academy of St Martin in the Fields;** ª**Los Angeles Chamber Orchestra / Sir Neville Marriner;** ᵇᵈ**Philadelphia Orchestra / Riccardo Muti**
EMI Double Forte ② 574305-2 (136' · DDD/ADD) Recorded 1968-82   Ⓜ

A very reliable coupling for anyone wanting these six pieces. Marriner's *Pulcinella* is a joy from first bar to last; how the players enjoy the quirkiness of Stravinsky's scoring, and you can almost see jaws dropping as Robert Tear, in the second movement, does precisely what the score asks and sustains a held B flat for 13 seconds. The wit of the two Suites has a deliciously light touch and the good humour as well as the balletic grace of *Danses concertantes* are finely caught. Muti's *Rite of Spring* provokes one or two slight reservations (he over-marks dynamics quite often and his 'Sacrificial Dance' is impressively efficient rather than terrifying or exciting), but the playing is superb – an extraordinarily virtuosic 'Games of the Rival Tribes' – and detail is crystal-clear.

No quibbles about the slightly later *Petrushka*, which is vividly coloured and characterised. All the remasterings sound very well indeed.

The Rite of Spring

Stravinsky The Rite of Spring **Scriabin** Le poème de l'extase
Kirov Orchestra / Valery Gergiev
Philips Classics 468 035-2PH (55' · DDD)   Ⓕ ●●

This is probably the most extraordinary *Rite of Spring* to have been dreamt up since Stravinsky's own final (and finest) 1960 recording. Stravinsky himself said, in so many words, that *The Rite* was born from his unconscious. And although now isn't the time or place to ponder to what extent his – and our – unconscious minds are capable (if at all) of harbouring any memories of pre-Christian ritual, suffice it so say that an exceptional performance of *The Rite* should at least have us thinking about it as a possibility…and about why we respond to *The Rite* in the way that we do.

Among modern interpreters, there isn't anyone better than Gergiev at the important dual roles of showman and shaman. So many of the score's darker workings have a striking profile here – tubas bellowing strange moans, the bass drum sending shock waves around the performance space, the lower strings in 'Spring Rounds' almost 'exhaling' their notes, and, for once, giving a proper foundation to that most significant of quiet chords – the one where the Sage kisses the earth. Indeed, 'Earth' and the 'elemental' seem not so much cultivated in this performance, as an inherent part of it.

Either Gergiev has really pondered the 'sound stuff' of the *Rite*, or it just comes naturally to him and his players. Though whether nature or nurture, the end results make for a marginally more compelling overall listen than all the finest recorded *Rites* of the last four decades. More controversial is some of the timing of 'events', especially the delay of the ascent to the final chord, though when it arrives, you wonder if its shocking make-up has ever been as effectively exposed. The delaying tactics – theatrical pauses and suspensions – proved a little more problematic in the second half of Scriabin's *Poem of Ecstasy* – along with Gergiev's extremes of tempo in the piece. But should one even be thinking these thoughts when offered a *Poem* which openly embraces the extravagant wonders of the piece as this one does? Better to marvel at all the mysterious curves, the fabulous dark rushes of sound, the celebratory splendours, and the final resolution (dissolution?) into an uncomplicated glory of C major. Here, as in *The Rite*, the recording is superb.

The Rite of Spring (two versions) **H**
Philharmonia Orchestra / Igor Markevitch
Testament mono/stereo SBT1076
(67' · ADD) Mono version recorded 1951, stereo 1959
Ⓕ**OO**
Markevitch's 1959 stereo *Rite* is in a league of its own. This is a model of how to balance the score (and of how to create the illusion of a wide dynamic range within more restricted parameters). Markevitch would have been totally familiar with every note of the piece (in 1949 he sent Stravinsky a list of mistakes he had noticed in the recently revised edition), and by 1959 he clearly knew what it needed in performance, including how to keep its shock-value alive. There are 'improprieties' here, such as the slowing for the 'Evocation of the Ancestors' (making the most of those timpani volleys), but nothing serious. As it happens, Markevitch's 'Introduction' to Part 2 is unusually fast, but he's able to take in the following small marked variations of tempo, providing valuable contrasts. And in any case, the playing is so alive, alert and reactive, whatever the dynamic levels: listen to the incisive clarinets' entry in the 'Mystic Circles' and the *frisson* imparted to the following *pianissimo*

STRAVINSKY'S THE RITE OF SPRING – IN BRIEF

Columbia SO / Igor Stravinsky
Sony SMK60011 (65' · ADD) Ⓜ
Stravinsky's own interpretation exhibits an innate musicality, rhythmic bounce and satisfying transparency that really hits the mark. The 1960 recording still packs a pleasing wallop.

Cleveland Orchestra / Pierre Boulez
Sony SMK64109 (69' · ADD) Ⓜ**O**
Boulez's 1969 performance remains intensely compelling in its cumulative drive, seismic power and irreproachable precision. Very fine sound, too.

CBSO / Sir Simon Rattle
EMI 749636-2 (65' · DDD) Ⓕ**OO**
A refreshingly thoughtful, immaculately honed *Rite* from Rattle. Rhythm and ensemble are consistently tight; nor is there any lack of primitivistic fervour.

Concertgebouw Orchestra / Sir Colin Davis
Philips ② 464 744-2PM2 (142' · ADD) Ⓜ
Davis's *Rite* has an irresistible poise, choreographic flair and giddy sense of drama, all captured with unflinching splendour by the Philips engineers.

San Francisco SO / Michael Tilson Thomas
RCA ③ 09026 68898-2 (119' · DDD) Ⓜ
A superbly balanced live recording from Davies Symphony Hall in San Francisco. Thomas's *Rite* is as copiously detailed and exhilarating as any that have appeared in many a moon.

Philadelphia Orchestra / Riccardo Muti
EMI 574581-2 (64' · ADD) Ⓢ
Muti puts his virtuoso Philadelphia band through their paces to flamboyant, often startling effect. As bargain-basement *Rites* go, you won't do better than this.

Philharmonia Orchestra / Igor Markevitch
Testament SBT1076 (67' · ADD) Ⓕ**OO**
Testament allows us the opportunity to compare and contrast Markevitch's 1951 recording and his stereo remake of eight years later. Both are little short of stunning in their immaculate co-ordination and volcanic force.

Kirov Orchestra / Valery Gergiev
Philips 468 035-2PH (55' · DDD) Ⓕ**OO**
Gergiev has the happy knack of making you listen with fresh ears. Here's a searingly powerful *Rite*, full of elemental fury and fierce abandon.

tremolando from the strings.

We could fill the rest of the page with similar highlights and other features unique to the performance, but that would be to spoil the fun of discovery (or rediscovery – and what a transfer of the original!). This is a great *Rite* for lots of reasons, not the least of which is that the sessions were obviously electric. As a fascinating bonus, Testament also offers a 1951 mono recording of a great *Rite* in the making. The differences aren't radical, but enough to justify the idea.

The Rite of Spring. Apollon musagète •
City of Birmingham Symphony Orchestra / Sir Simon Rattle
EMI 749636-2 (65' · DDD) Recorded 1987-8   Ⓕ**OO**

Recordings of *The Rite of Spring* are legion, but it's rare to find Stravinsky's most explosive ballet score coupled with *Apollon musagète*, his most serene. The result is a lesson in creative versatility, confirming that Stravinsky could be equally convincing as expressionist and neo-classicist. Yet talk of lessons might suggest that sheer enjoyment is of lesser importance, and it's perfectly possible to relish this disc simply for that personal blend of the authoritative and the enlivening that Simon Rattle's CBSO recordings for EMI so consistently achieve. Rattle never rushes things, and the apparent deliberation of *The Rite*'s concluding 'Sacrificial Dance' may initially surprise, but in this context it proves an entirely appropriate, absolutely convincing conclusion. Rattle sees the work as a whole, without striving for a spurious symphonic integration, and there's never for a moment any hint of a routine reading of what's now a classic of the modern orchestral repertoire.

The account of *Apollon* has comparable depth, with elegance transformed into eloquence and the CBSO strings confirming that they have nothing to fear from comparison with the best in Europe or America. The recordings are faithful to the intensity and expressiveness of Rattle's Stravinsky, interpretations fit to set beside those of the composer himself.

Additional recommendation

Rite of Spring
Coupled with: **Debussy** La mer **Boulez** Notations VII
Chicago Symphony Orchestra / Barenboim
Teldec 8573-81702-2 (69' · DDD)   Ⓕ**O**

Gergiev's reading may be too theatrical for some, while Barenboim's is a formidable but never mechanical *Rite*. Coupled with a truly superb *La mer* – the emotional force and intellectual grasp of his reading puts it on a par with Karajan's.

L'histoire du soldat

L'histoire du soldat (in English)[a]. Concerto in E flat, 'Dumbarton Oaks'

[a]David Timson, [a]Benjamin Soames, [a]Jonathan Keeble *spkrs* **Northern Chamber Orchestra / Nicholas Ward**
Naxos 8 553662 (76' · DDD)   Ⓢ

In this full-length *The Soldier's Tale* (the English translation by Michael Flanders and Kitty Black), the actors have the full measure of their parts, and the musicians, taken as a group, about two-thirds the measure of theirs. The notes are there, but not always the will to make something of them. Perhaps one shouldn't expect violin- and trumpet-playing of the flair and feature of Manoug Parikian and Maurice André in the classic 1962 Markevitch recording (now part of a two-disc set on Philips, and spoken in the original French). On the other hand Nicholas Cox's always fully responsive clarinet-playing on the Naxos recording is a vast improvement on Markevitch's narrow-toned and quavery clarinettist. If Nicholas Cox seems to do a little better out of the Naxos balance than some of his musical colleagues, it's probably because of his more consistent projection of character.

In general, it's a very natural balance that welds the years and miles between the separately recorded actors and musicians into a reasonably convincing illusion of a single-stage whole (with the actors placed in front of the musicians), though it's less convincing than the Markevitch, where the same acoustic was used by both actors and musicians (and where Jean Cocteau's narrator can become almost submerged). The generous bonus here is Stravinsky's modernised 'Brandenburg Concerto', *Dumbarton Oaks*, marginally more presently recorded than the musical contributions to the main work, but with the same mixture of determination to put it across (a wonderful strutting *marcato* at the start of the finale) and lapses into a competent neutral. So, should you be interested at the price? If you only know *The Soldier's Tale* through the Concert Suite (most of the music; none of the words), and can sample before purchasing this complete recording, try two 'low points' – the very opening ('The soldier's march'), and the close ('The devil's triumphal dance') – and if the proceedings don't strike you as tame and lacking vitality, this could be a very rewarding use of a fiver.

Les noces

Les noces[a]. Mass[b]
Anny Mory *sop* **Patricia Parker** *mez* **John Mitchinson** *ten* **Paul Hudson** *bass* **English Bach Festival Chorus; Trinity Boys' Choir; Martha Argerich, Krystian Zimerman, Cyprien Katsaris, Homero Francesch** *pfs* [a]**English Bach Festival Percussion Ensemble;** [b]**members of the English Bach Festival Orchestra / Leonard Bernstein**
DG 20th Century Classics 423 251-2GC (44' · ADD)
Texts and translations included   Ⓜ**O**

Les noces
Traditional Russian Village Wedding Songs Play,

Skomoroshek. River. Trumpet. Cosmas and Demian.
The Drinker. Green Forest. God bless, Jesus. My
White Peas. Steambath. Berry. Black Beaver. In the
House. Bunny with Short Legs. The Bed. Birch Tree
Pokrovsky Ensemble / Dmitri Pokrovsky
Nonesuch 7559-79335-2 (54' · DDD) English texts
included   Ⓕ

You might look askance at the short timing
here. However, these are top-drawer Bernstein
performances, excellently recorded. *Les noces*
sports an impressive array of pianists; but that
needn't be a decisive factor, since rhythmic precision and good balance are far more at a premium than individual flair or power – fortunately these individuals are equally fine
ensemble players. It's even more important that
the choir should be meticulously prepared
(which they are), that the vocal soloists should
be precise and full-blooded (which they are) and
that the conductor should impart a sense of the
profundity of the whole conception (which
Bernstein emphatically does). The Mass is an
ideal coupling for *Les noces*, not just because of
the shared importance of the chorus, but
because it, too, displays a fundamental ritual
experience, in this case the sacrament of worship rather than marriage, with archetypal clarity. Bernstein's reading has all the calm devotion of the composer's own, even if the soloists
are rather variable. Highly recommended.

For the Nonesuch recording Dmitri
Pokrovsky and the singers in his ensemble travelled to southern and western Russia in search
of melodies and texts related to *Les noces*; and
they found rich pickings. True, the melodic
similarities aren't as tangible as the folk sources
for *Petrushka*, but the 15 songs, recorded with
immense flair and enjoyment to a variety of
instrumental accompaniments, will be a revelation to all listeners. Be prepared for some acerbic sounds. Authentic Russian folk polyphony is
an extraordinarily modern-sounding experience, as is authentic open-throated singing. The
value of the disc is multiplied by the fact that the
singers have carried over the style and expressive content of the folksongs into their performance of *Les noces* itself, bringing it to life in a way
that must surely be unprecedented and uniquely
illuminating. Not only that, but Pokrovsky had
the inspired idea of recreating the instrumental
parts on a computer, thus continuing Stravinsky's search for the ideal mechanical realisation.

Oedipus Rex

Oedipus Rex. Symphony of Psalms   Ⓗ
Ivo Zídek *ten* Oedipus **Věra Soukupová** *mez*
Jocasta **Karel Berman** *bass* Créon **Eduard Haken**
bass Tiresias **Antonin Zlesák** *ten* Shepherd **Zdeněk**
Kroupa *bar* Messenger **Jean Desailly** *narr* **Czech**
Philharmonic Chorus and Orchestra / Karel Ančerl
Supraphon Historical SU3674-2 (73' · AAD) Recorded
1964-6   Ⓜ**OO**

Oedipus Rex, to words by Jean Cocteau, is one of

Stravinsky's most compelling theatre pieces, a
powerful drama that re-enacts the full force of a
glorious high spot in ancient culture. The
fusion of words and music in *Oedipus* is masterly,
and arrests the attention consistently, from the
animated severity of the opening narration,
through the calculated tension of its musical
argument, to the tragic restraint of its closing
pages. Karel Ančerl was one of Stravinsky's
most committed exponents. This particular
recording was taped in the Dvořák Hall of the
House of Artists, Prague, and earned itself at
least three major awards. Ančerl traces and
intensifies salient points in the tragedy yet
maintains a precise, sensitive touch. His vocal
collaborators include the noble Karel Berman
(Créon) who, like Ančerl himself, suffered considerably during the Nazi occupation of
Czechoslovakia. Věra Soukupová is a fine
Jocasta and the convincing but occasionally
unsteady Ivo Zídek sings the part of Oedipus.
Both here and in the *Symphony of Psalms* – one
of the most serenely perceptive recorded performances of the work – the Czech Philharmonic Chorus excel, while Supraphon's 1960s
engineering (not the DDD suggested on the
box) has an appealing brightness.

Perséphone

Stravinsky Perséphone[a] Dukas Polyeucte[b]
[a]**Nicole Tibbels** *sop* [a]**Paul Groves** *ten* [a]**Trinity**
Boys' Choir; [a]**Cantate Youth Choir; BBC**
Symphony [a]**Chorus and Orchestra /** [a]**Sir Andrew**
Davis, [b]**Yan Pascal Tortelier**
Warner Classics 2564 61548-2 (67' · DDD) Recorded
live at the Royal Albert Hall, London, during the BBC
Proms, [a]10 & [b]19 August 2003. Text and translation
included   Ⓜ

Stravinsky's recordings of his own music always
have a certain indispensable something. But it's
surprising what performers under his baton
were sometimes allowed to get away with. In his
recording of *Perséphone* it's the French language
that suffers, notably at the hands of Vera Zorina
in the title role, whose French was probably
close to Stravinsky's own.

Happily, Nicole Tibbels, Paul Groves and the
three choruses employed here have changed all
that. Tibbels's narration is particularly impressive. Her French diction is full of variety in
speed and tone, and always alive to the drama.
Her placing of the narrative in relation to the
music is also intelligent. Groves is quite simply
one of the best tenors around, and his singing
here is clean, powerful and practically faultless
in pitching the sometimes awkward melodic
lines. The orchestra and choruses live up to
these high standards in every respect to produce
a treasurable recording of this extraordinarily
haunting piece.

The Dukas overture makes an odd coupling,
but it's one of the best things he ever wrote, with
its Wagnerisms surprisingly well digested for a

26-year-old. Yan Pascal Tortelier produces a more sinewy, contrapuntally aware reading than David Zinman, but also one that breathes more expansively.

Symphony of Psalms

Symphony of Psalms[a]. Les noces[b]. Threni[c]
[b]**Alison Wells**, [c]**Julie Moffat** sops [b]**Susan Bickley**, [c]**Jennifer Lane** mezs [bc]**Martyn Hill**, [c]**Joseph Cornwell** tens [b]**Alan Ewing**, [c]**David Wilson-Johnson**, [c]**Martin Robson** basses [a]**Simon Joly Chorale** [b]**International Piano Quartet** (Elizabeth Bergmann, Marcel Bergmann, Jeroen Van Veen, Maarten Van Veen pfs) [b]**Tristan Fry Percussion Ensemble;** [a]**Philharmonia Orchestra /** [abc]**Robert Craft**
Koch International Classics KICCD7514 (75' · DDD)
Texts and translations included Ⓕⵔ

Craft meticulously observes the markings in the *Symphony of Psalms*, and invariably makes sense of them. On a spot check of six or seven performances he gets closer than any other conductor (closer than Stravinsky himself) to what the score specifies for those abrupt rappings from horns and bassoons that begin the fast section of the finale: *staccato* but *piano*, only the first of each group carrying an accent and a *sforzato*. There are more fervent accounts of this score – in particular Bernstein's – but few that demonstrate how precise Stravinsky's ear was.

In this hugely enjoyable account of *Les noces* the singers are all British but they obviously worked hard on sounding as authentically full-voicedly Russian as possible. It's hard to believe that Alan Ewing isn't dressed in priestly robes (with a flask of vodka concealed beneath his cassock) and that Alison Wells isn't a Russian bride in a ceremonial costume rigid with embroidery. The remarkably Slavonic sound points up both the joyful exuberance of the piece and its sense of ancient ritual; its rhythmic life never for one moment sags, and the ending is magical and moving.

As Robert Craft says in his notes *Threni* is 'little known after almost 50 years', though it's 'among Stravinsky's greatest works'. With its leaping atonal vocal lines, however, it's also one of his most difficult, and yet no allowances need be made here: it's beautifully sung. The choral singing is very fine, the soloists sound absolutely secure, and Martyn Hill in particular makes his awkward intervals sound perfectly idiomatic.

The Rake's Progress

The Rake's Progress
Jerry Hadley ten Tom Rakewell **Dawn Upshaw** sop Anne **Samuel Ramey** bass Nick Shadow **Grace Bumbry** mez Baba the Turk **Steven Cole** ten Sellem Anne **Collins** contr Mother Goose **Robert Lloyd** bass Trulove **Roderick Earle** bass Keeper **Chorus and Orchestra of Opéra de Lyon / Kent Nagano**
Erato ② 0630-12715-2 (138' · DDD) Ⓜⵔ

Any number of the world's opera houses would have given their eye teeth for the privilege of presenting the première of Stravinsky's only true opera, but he, intensely money-conscious though he was (and he had worked on the piece for three years without a commission fee), insisted on La Fenice in Venice – because he was fond of the city, but also because *The Rake's Progress* is a chamber opera. And this is a chamber performance of it, with a fairly small orchestra, much singing of almost *parlando* quality and crystal-clear words. It's also intimate, with a strong sense of the stage, of characters reacting to each other. With Nagano's on the whole brisk tempos, it gives the impression of a real performance, and a gripping one. Upshaw's isn't the purest soprano voice to have attempted the role of Anne, and there have been more spectacular high Cs than hers, but she's movingly vulnerable, totally believable.

So is Hadley, acting at times almost too vividly for the music's line: as he occasionally demonstrates he has a wonderfully beautiful head voice. He isn't, therefore, quite the touchingly likeable 'shuttle-headed lad' that Alexander Young portrayed so unforgettably in the composer's own recording, but no other Tom Rakewell surpasses him. Ramey's is a bigger voice than most of the others here – firm and superbly produced. Collins and Lloyd are both first-class as Mother Goose and Trulove, Cole an unusually light-voiced, confidingly conspiratorial Sellem. If any, Bumbry is the disappointment of the cast, somewhat over-loud and baritonal almost throughout, but the French chorus sing nimbly and in admirable English. Stravinsky's own recording is still to be cherished, but of modern recordings of *The Rake's Progress* this is a hugely, if not the most, enjoyable one.

The Rake's Progress
Ian Bostridge ten Tom Rakewell **Deborah York** sop Anne **Bryn Terfel** bass-bar Nick Shadow **Anne Sofie von Otter** mez Baba the Turk **Peter Bronder** ten Sellem **Anne Howells** mez Mother Goose **Martin Robson** bass Trulove **Julian Clarkson** bass Keeper of the Madhouse **Monteverdi Choir; London Symphony Orchestra / Sir John Eliot Gardiner**
DG ② 459 648-2GH2 (134' · DDD) Notes, text and translation included Ⓕⵔⵔ

Gardiner's *Rake's Progress*, in all but one respect, easily withstands comparison with its five rivals, and in several it surpasses them; if you're happy with Terfel's Nick Shadow, it can be set alongside Stravinsky's own 1964 recording as the finest available. Gardiner is conscious throughout that this is a chamber opera, and the orchestral textures are outstandingly clean and transparent, the rhythmic pointing crisp but airy. This enables his cast to give a fast-moving, conversational account of the text, with every word crystal-clear (including those from the chorus) and no need for any voice to force.

This benefits the soprano and tenor especially. Deborah York, sounds a very young and touchingly vulnerable Anne; her voice may seem a little pale, but there's pathos as well as brilliance in her Act 1 aria, and the desolation of her reaction to Tom's marriage to Baba the Turk ('I see, then: it was I who was unworthy') is moving. Ian Bostridge is the best Tom Rakewell since Alexander Young in Stravinsky's recording: he too sounds likeably youthful, sings with intelligence and sweetness of tone and acts very well.

Howells is an unexaggerated Mother Goose, and von Otter's economy of comic gesture is a marvel. 'Finish, if you please, whatever business is detaining you with this person' receives the full Lady Bracknell treatment from most mezzos; von Otter gives it the vocal equivalent of a nose wrinkled in well-bred disdain. Terfel often demonstrates that he can fine his big voice down to the subtlety of the other principals, and when he does he's a formidably dangerous, insinuating Shadow. But almost as often he not only lets the voice rip but indulges in histrionics quite uncharacteristic of the performance as a whole. You may not mind: why after all should the Devil restrainedly under-act? At times, though, he sounds bigger than the orchestra. The recording is close but theatrically atmospheric. There are a few sound effects, though some may find the raucous owl in the graveyard scene distracting.

Josef Suk
Bohemian 1874-1935

Suk studied at the Prague Conservatory, 1885-92, where he was Dvořák's favourite pupil, and in 1898 married his daughter. Dvořák was, too, the dominant influence on his early music, as in the Serenade for strings (1892) and the Fairy Tale suite (1900); later, most notably in the vast symphony Asrael (1906) – written under the impact of the deaths of his wife and his father-in-law – he developed a more personal style comparable with Mahler's in structural mastery and emotional force. He drew little on folk music. Other works include two published quartets (he was second violinist in the Czech Quartet for most of his life and played in over 4000 concerts), piano pieces (Things lived and Dreamed, 1909) and a group of symphonic poems, A Summer's Tale (1909), The Ripening (1917) and the choral-orchestral Epilog (1929). From 1922 he directed a master class in composition at the Prague Conservatory.
GROVEmusic

Asrael, Op 27

Asrael
Bavarian Radio Symphony Orchestra / Rafael Kubelík
Panton 81 1101-2 (64' · ADD) Recorded 1981 Ⓕ**OO**

To use large-scale symphonic form for the purging of deep personal grief carries the danger that the result will seriously lack discipline. In 1904-5 Suk's world was shattered by two visits from Asrael (the Angel of Death in Muslim

mythology): he lost his father-in-law (and revered teacher) Dvořák, and his beloved wife, Otylka. Forgivably, Suk does perhaps linger a little too long in the fourth movement's gentle, mainly lyrical portrait of Otylka, but elsewhere the progress is as satisfying psychologically as it is symphonically. Much of the music has a concentrated dream-like quality; at the extremes, spectral nightmare visions merge with compensatory surges of lyrical ardour. Set Kubelík's reading alongside any of the other modern versions and one is immediately aware of a wholly compelling imaginative intensity and interpretative flair that betoken a true poet of the rostrum. Kubelík's control throughout is awesome and he conjures up playing of enormous expressive subtlety from his fine Munich orchestra. No other recorded performance – not even Václav Talich's legendary 1952 Supraphon account – succeeds in conveying the intensely personal nature of this music with such devastating emotional candour. Technically, too, one need have no qualms about this Panton disc – the Bavarian Radio engineers secure most truthful results.

Chamber Works

Chamber works, Volumes 1-3
Supraphon ③ 11 1874-2 (aas: 208' · ADD/DDD) Recorded 1966-92 Ⓜ

String Quartets – No 1 in B flat, Op 11[a]; No 2, Op 31[b]. Tempo di menuetto[b]. Meditation on an Old Czech Hymn, Op 35a[b]. Quartet movement in B flat[a]
Suk Quartet ([a]Antonín Novák, [b]Ivan Straus, Vojtěch Jouza vns Karel Rehák va Jan Stros vc)
Supraphon 11 1531-2 (71' · ADD/DDD) Ⓜ**O**

Piano Trio in C minor, Op 2. Elégie, Op 23. Piano Quartet in A minor, Op 1. Piano Quintet in G minor, Op 8
Josef Suk vn **Jan Talich** va **Michaela Fukačová** vc **Pavel Stěpán** pf **Suk Trio** (Josef Suk vn Josef Chuchro vc Josef Hála, Jan Panenka pfs) **Suk Quartet** (Antonín Novák, Vojtěch Jouza vns Karel Rehák va Jan Stros vc)
Supraphon 11 1532-2 (74' · ADD/DDD) Ⓜ

Mélodie. Minuet. Balada in D minor. Four Pieces, Op 17. Ballade in D minor, Op 3 No 1. Serenade in A, Op 3 No 2. Bagatelle, 'Carrying a Bouquet'. Barcarolle in B flat. Balada in D minor. Elégie, Op 23. Sousedská
Jiří Válek fl **Josef Suk, Jitka Nováková, Ludmila Vybíralová, Miroslav Kosina, Jaroslav Krištůfek, Zdeněk Mann** vns **Marek Jerie, František Host, Ivo Laniar** vcs **Tomáš Josífko** db **Renata Kodadová** hp **Josef Hála** pf/harm **Jan Panenka, Iván Klánský** pfs **Josef Fousek, Libor Kubánek** perc **Suk Quartet**
Supraphon 11 1533-2 (63' · ADD/DDD) Ⓜ

A treasure-trove of heartfelt music performed with refinement and flair. Volume 1 concentrates on Suk's string quartet output (Suk himself was the second violinist in the great Czech

Quartet for 40 years). If the First Quartet (1896) doesn't quite show the same freshness or entrancing melodic vein of the String Serenade of four years earlier, it remains a delightfully unassuming creation with the genial presence of Suk's teacher Dvořák looming large over the proceedings. It's followed by a rare hearing for the alternative finale Suk composed some 19 years later in 1915. By this time the composer had already found his own strongly personal voice. Both the resourceful Second Quartet of 1911 (an ambitious one-movement essay of nearly 28 minutes' duration and considerable emotional variety) and the deeply felt *Meditation on an Old Czech Hymn* (1914) are works of some substance well worth exploring, and these passionate accounts enjoy excellent sound. The remaining two volumes perhaps contain more to interest Suk aficionados than newcomers, though the adorable *Four Pieces* for violin and piano, Op 17, have always remained great favourites.

Volume 2 features youthful offerings: the Piano Trio, the Piano Quartet, the likeable, if rather garrulous, Piano Quintet of 1893 and the touching *Elégie* for piano, violin and cello from 1902, written to celebrate the anniversary of the death of the poet and dramatist, Julius Zeyer. Apart from the *Four Pieces* already mentioned, the third and final volume also contains, amongst much else, the *Elégie* in its original guise for violin, cello, string quartet, harmonium and harp, no fewer than three different *Ballades* in D minor conceived for various instrumental combinations during Suk's days at the Conservatory, the 'Barcarolle' slow movement of a very early String Quartet from 1888, as well as the composer's last completed piece from 1935, the engaging *Sousedská*. Recording dates range from 1966 to 1992 (most of the material is designated as AAD), but the quality is consistently praiseworthy and the volumes are available either separately or gathered together within an attractive slipcase.

Sir Arthur Sullivan   British 1842-1900

Sullivan, a Chapel Royal chorister, became a pupil of Sterndale Bennett at the Royal Academy of Music (1856) and studied at the Leipzig Conservatory (1858-61). The promise shown by his incidental music for The Tempest (1861) and other early concert works led to festival commissions and conducting posts, which he complemented with work as organist, teacher and song and hymn tune writer; from 1866, he also dabbled in comic opera. His increasing success in this last field – with CF Burnand in Cox and Box and then WS Gilbert in Trial by Jury – culminated in the formation by Richard D'Oyly Carte of a company expressly for the performance of Gilbert and Sullivan works. With HMS Pinafore the collaborators became an institution. Their works, produced at the Savoy Theatre from 1881 (the most popular 'Savoy Operas' were The Mikado and The Gondo-

liers), won a favour with English-speaking audiences that has never waned. Sullivan was knighted in 1883 and continued to conduct, notably the Leeds Festival and the Philharmonic Society concerts, but his serious ouput dwindled. A breach with Gilbert (1890), recurring ill-health and the relative failure of his last works clouded his final years.

Sullivan was essentially an eclectic, drawing on elements from opera, ballads, choral and church music, by composers from Hander to Bizet. Some lack of emotional depth and an unsure grasp of large-scale structure have limited the success of his more serious music (Golden Legend, Ivanhoe). It was in Gilbert's satirical subjects and witty verses that his talents found their happiest, most consistent inspiration, underpinned as they are by a highly professional compositional technique. Here his inventive melodies fit perfectly the sense and accentuation of the words, while lively choruses underscore traits of particular groups and deft instrumentation points up character. His clever parodies of serious music and use of 'tune combination' increase the fun.   GROVEmusic

Symphony in E, 'Irish'

Symphony in E, 'Irish'. The Tempest – Suite. Overture in C, 'In Memoriam'
BBC Philharmonic Orchestra / Richard Hickox
Chandos CHAN9859 (75' · DDD)   Ⓕ❍

Plaudits all round to Richard Hickox and his excellent Manchester band (and the Chandos production team) for at last granting Sullivan's *Irish* symphony the first wholly recommendable digital recording it so richly deserves. And what a charmer of a work it is! Mendelssohn (and his *Reformation* Symphony above all) provides the dominant stylistic template, but the work is soundly constructed, effectively scored, and the *scherzo*'s irresistibly perky oboe tune, in particular, already reveals a very real melodic gift. Like Owain Arwell Hughes before him, Hickox observes the first-movement repeat, but his direction is infinitely more imaginative (at the hushed heart of the development section, sample the tingling atmosphere he conjures during those magical bars beginning at 9'13") and he never allows tensions to sag. What's more, the playing of the BBC Philharmonic ideally combines bright-eyed affection, keen vigour and nimble polish.

Following the symphony's successful March 1866 première under August Manns, Sullivan was asked to provide a work for that same year's Norwich Festival. The sudden death of his father just a few weeks before the festival proper jolted Sullivan into penning the likeable overture, *In Memoriam*. Written within 10 days and first given in Norwich on October 30 under Julius Benedict, the work soon won great popularity, though in terms of inventive freshness and orchestral scope it's rather trumped by the astonishingly confident incidental music for Shakespeare's *The Tempest* that Sullivan had written nearly six years earlier while still a student at the Leipzig Conservatory. Indeed, it comes as no surprise to learn that the British première of *The Tempest* in April 1862 made the 19-year-old a celebrity overnight, and the present suite draws upon seven of the original 12 numbers. Again, Hickox and company do plentiful justice to Sullivan's precocious inspiration, not least the powerfully moody 'Introduction', delectable 'Overture to Act IV' and the exquisite skip of the 'Dance of Nymphs and Reapers' (appealing echoes in the last-named of Schumann's *Spring* Symphony). A thoroughly enjoyable collection, then, accorded sound of glowing realism in the finest Chandos tradition.

Sullivan Cello Concerto in D[a] (reconstr Mackerras and Mackie). Symphony in E, 'Irish'[b]. Overture di ballo[b] **Elgar** Romance, Op 62[a] (arr vc)
[a]**Julian Lloyd Webber** vc [a]**London Symphony Orchestra / Sir Charles Mackerras;** [b]**Royal Liverpool Philharmonic Orchestra / Sir Charles Groves**
EMI British Composers 764726-2 (71' · ADD/DDD)
Recorded [a]1986, [b]1968   Ⓢ Ⓑ Ⓞ

Sir Charles Groves's sturdy yet affectionate reading of Arthur Sullivan's wholly charming *Irish* Symphony was always one of the best of his EMI offerings with the RLPO, and the 1968 recording remains vivid. In the sparkling *Overture di ballo*, again, Groves conducts with plenty of character. There are also first-rate performances of Sullivan's undemanding Cello Concerto from 1866 (in a fine reconstruction by Sir Charles Mackerras – the manuscript was destroyed in Chappell's fire of 1964) as well as Elgar's wistful little *Romance* (originally for bassoon). This is a thoroughly attractive and rewarding mid-price reissue.

Overtures

Overtures – Cox and Box; The Sorcerer; HMS Pinafore; The Pirates of Penzance; Patience; Iolanthe; Princess Ida; The Mikado; Ruddigore (arr Toye); The Yeomen of the Guard; The Gondoliers; The Grand Duke
Royal Ballet Sinfonia / Andrew Penny
Naxos 8 554165 (70' · DDD)   Ⓢ Ⓖ Ⓞ

The first thing that sets this apart from other collections of Sullivan overtures is that – for the first time – it covers the entire Gilbert and Sullivan output. The only works that are missing are *Thespis*, *Trial by Jury* and *Utopia Limited*, none of which had overtures as such. The sensible addition of the overture to *Cox and Box* means that all the Sullivan comic operas likely to be of interest to the general collector are here. An even more intelligent feature is that they're presented in chronological order, so that one can chart the progression of Sullivan's comic opera style from the very French-sounding ending of *Cox and Box* and the equally French-sounding opening of *The Sorcerer* through to more distinctively Sullivanesque sounds of the later pieces. None of this would count for much if the per-

formances weren't up to scratch. Happily they're models of their kind. Andrew Penny has an agreeably light touch, alternatively reflective and sparkling, and gets graceful phrasing from the Royal Ballet Sinfonia – ideal performers of light music. Nobody wanting a collection of Sullivan's comic opera overtures need look elsewhere.

The Gondoliers

The Gondoliers. Overture di ballo (1870 version)
Richard Suart bar Duke of Plaza-Toro **Philip Creasey** ten Luiz **John Rath** bass Don Alhambra **David Fieldsend** ten Marco **Alan Oke** bar Giuseppe **Tim Morgan** bar Antonio **David Cavendish** ten Francesco **Toby Barrett** bass Giorgio **Jill Pert** contr Duchess of Plaza-Toro **Elizabeth Woollett** sop Casilda **Lesley Echo Ross** sop Gianetta **Regina Hanley** mez Tessa **Yvonne Patrick** sop Fiametta **Pamela Baxter** mez Vittoria **Elizabeth Elliott** sop Giulia **Claire Kelly** contr Inez **D'Oyly Carte Opera Chorus and Orchestra / John Pryce-Jones**
TER ② CDTER2 1187 (109' · DDD) Recorded 1991   Ⓕ

This is one of a series of recordings by the new D'Oyly Carte Opera Company that offers a vastly better quality of sound than any of its ageing competitors. Orchestral detail is the most immediate beneficiary, and the overture serves to demonstrate John Pryce-Jones's lively tempos and lightness of touch. Outstanding among the singers are perhaps John Rath, who gives Don Alhambra's 'I stole the prince' and 'There lived a king' real presence, and Jill Pert, a formidable Duchess of Plaza-Toro. Richard Suart not only provides the leading comedy roles with exceptionally clear articulation and musicality, but also adds considerable character to his portrayals. David Fieldsend and Alan Oke provide attractive portrayals of the two gondoliers, and Lesley Echo Ross and Regina Hanley are also most agreeable.

Seasoned listeners may note numerous changes of detail as a result of the purging of the performance material of changes made to the parts around the time of the 1920s Savoy Theatre revivals. There's no dialogue, but added value is provided by Sullivan's sunniest comic opera score being accompanied by the sparkling *Overture di ballo*, played in its original version with some traditional cuts opened up.

Additional recommendation

The Gondoliers
Coupled with: Cello Concerto in D[a]
Evans Duke of Plaza-Toro **Young** Luiz **Brannigan** Don Alhambra **Lewis** Marco **Cameron** Giuseppe **Glyndebourne Festival Chorus; Pro Arte Orchestra / Sargent;** [a]**Lloyd Webber** vc [a]**London Symphony Orchesta /** [a]**Mackerras**   Ⓑ
HMV Classics ② HMVD5 73672-2 (114' · ADD/DDD)
A really beautiful 'Pair of sparkling eyes' from Lewis.

HMS Pinafore

HMS Pinafore
Richard Suart bass Sir Joseph Porter **Felicity Palmer**
mez Little Buttercup **Rebecca Evans** sop Josephine
Thomas Allen bar Captain Corcoran **Michael
Schade** ten Ralph Rackstraw **Donald Adams** bass
Dick Deadeye **Valerie Seymour** sop Hebe **Richard
Van Allan** bass Bill Bobstay **John King, Philip Lloyd-
Evans** bars Bob Becket **Welsh National Opera
Chorus and Orchestra / Sir Charles Mackerras**
Telarc CD80374 (74' · DDD) Recorded 1994. Notes
and text included ⓕ**OO**

As always, Mackerras keeps the livelier numbers
moving along comfortably without ever a hint
of rushing, while giving full weight to the tender
moments and, above all, caressing all the details
of Sullivan's delicious orchestration.

Right from the overture, with its beautifully
shaped *Andante* section, this is music-making to
perfection. Of the singers, Felicity Palmer's
Buttercup truly oozes plumpness and pleasure,
while Thomas Allen's Captain doesn't just do
the crew of the *Pinafore* proud, but all of us.
If Rebecca Evans's Josephine is a shade lacking
in colour, Mackerras has found in Michael
Schade's Ralph Rackstraw a most elegant addition to his G&S team. As for Richard Suart's Sir
Joseph Porter, this is surely as stylish a demonstration of patter singing as one can find anywhere on disc, while Donald Adams's Dick
Deadeye is no worse for his 40-odd years
singing the role.

Add orchestral playing of refinement, choral
work whose perfection extends from the formal
numbers to the varied inflexions of 'What nevers?', plus a recording that brings out the instrumental detail to perfection, and one has a
Pinafore that's unadulterated delight from first
note to last.

Additional recommendation

Coupled with: Trial by Jury
Baker Sir Joseph Porter **Cameron** Captain Corcoran
Lewis Ralph Rackstraw **Brannigan** Dick Deadeye **Sin-
clair** Little Buttercup **Milligan** Bill Bobstay **Glynde-
bourne Festival Chorus; Pro Arte Orchestra /
Sargent**
HMV Classics ② HMVD5 73056-2 (101' · ADD)   Ⓑ
A sensitive reading of *HMS Pinafore* and a super
coupling: George Baker is superb as the judge in
Trial by Jury.

The Mikado

The Mikado
John Holmes bass The Mikado **John Wakefield** ten
Nanki-Poo **Clive Revill** bar Ko-Ko **Denis Dowling**
bar Pooh-Bah **John Heddle Nash** bar Pish-Tush
Marion Studholme sop Yum-Yum **Patricia Kern** mez
Pitti-Sing **Dorothy Nash** sop Peep-Bo **Jean Allister**
mez Katisha. Iolanthe – excerpts **Elizabeth
Harwood, Elizabeth Robson, Cynthia Morey** sops

Heather Begg, Patricia Kern mezzos **Stanley
Bevan** ten **Eric Shilling, Denis Dowling, Julian
Moyle** bars **Leon Greene** bass **Sadler's Wells
Opera Chorus and Orchestra / Alexander Faris**
Classics for Pleasure ② 5759902 (135' · ADD)
Recorded 1962   Ⓢ Ⓑ **OO**

At the core of these performances are some of
the finest British singers of 30 years ago, who
were all chosen not just for their singing but for
their sense of the theatricality and humour of
Gilbert and Sullivan. Just listen, for instance, to
how John Heddle Nash gives full expression to
every word of Pish-Tush's 'Our great Mikado'.
Here, too, is Marion Studholme's delicious
Yum-Yum and Elizabeth Harwood's joyous
Phyllis. If one singles out Clive Revill for special
mention, it's because his Ko-Ko is uniquely well
judged and imaginative, combining superb
comic timing, verbal clarity and vocal dexterity.
His 'little list' is hilarious, and you can almost
feel your hand gripped at the words 'shake
hands with you *like that*'. At the helm in both
works is Alexander Faris who knew supremely
well how to capture the lightness and sparkle of
operetta. The new Overture put together for
The Mikado may come as a surprise, but it's apt
and cleverly done. The sound is inevitably dated
when compared with more recent recordings,
but it scarcely mars the enjoyment.

Additional recommendation

Adams The Mikado **Rolfe Johnson** Nanki-Poo **Suart**
Ko-Ko **Van Allen** Pooh-Bah **McLaughlin** Yum-Yum
Howells Pitti-Sing **Palmer** Katisha **Welsh National
Opera Chorus and Orchestra / Mackerras**
Telarc CD80284 (79' · ADD)   Ⓕ
A delicious Nanki-Poo and a magnificent Katisha.

The Pirates of Penzance

The Pirates of Penzance
Eric Roberts bar Major-General Stanley **Malcolm
Rivers** bar Pirate King **Gareth Jones** bar Samuel
Philip Creasy ten Frederic **Simon Masterton-Smith**
bass Sargeant of Police **Marilyn Hill Smith** sop
Mabel **Patricia Cameron** sop Edith **Pauline Birchall**
mez Kate **Susan Gorton** contr Ruth **D'Oyly Carte
Opera Chorus and Orchestra / John Pryce-Jones**
TER ② CDTER2 1177 (85' · DDD) Recorded 1990   Ⓕ

The revival of the D'Oyly Carte Opera Company produced the first digital recordings of
complete Gilbert and Sullivan scores, and this
TER set is a very happy example. Philip Creasy
is an engaging and vocally secure Frederic, and
Marilyn Hill Smith trips through 'Poor wandering one' with a delectable display of vocal ability
and agility. The couple's interplay with the chorus in 'How beautifully blue the sky' is quite
enchanting, and their exchanges in 'Stay, Frederic, stay' splendidly convincing. Eric Roberts
makes the Major-General a thoroughly engaging personality, and the dotty exchanges

between Simon Masterson-Smith's Sergeant of Police and his police force are sheer joy. Even such details as the girls' screams at the appearance of the pirates in Act 1 have a rare effectiveness. John Pryce-Jones keeps the score dancing along. Those who want the dialogue as well as the music must look elsewhere, but this is certainly to be recommended.

Additional recommendation

Coupled with: Overture In C, 'In Memoriam'. The Sorcerer. Cox & Box. Princess Ida
Baker Major-General Stanley **Milligan** Pirate King **Lewis** Frederic **Brannigan** Sergeant of Police **Morison** Mabel **Glyndebourne Festival Chorus; Pro Arte Orchestra / Sargent**
HMV Classics ② HMVD5 730622 (113' · ADD) Ⓑ
A glorious 'Paradox' trio, and the lovely duet for Mabel and Frederic beautifully sung by Morison and Lewis.

The Yeomen of the Guard / Trial by Jury

The Yeomen of the Guard
Peter Savidge bar Sir Richard Cholmondeley **Neill Archer** ten Colonel Fairfax **Donald Adams** bass Sergeant Meryll **Peter Hoare** ten Leonard **Richard Suart** bar Jack Point **Donald Maxwell** bar Shadbolt **Alwyn Mellor** sop Elsie **Pamela Helen Stephen** mez Phoebe **Felicity Palmer** mez Dame Carruthers **Clare O'Neill** sop Kate **Ralph Mason** ten First Yeoman **Peter Lloyd Evans** bar Second Yeoman

Trial by Jury
Rebecca Evans sop Plaintiff **Barry Banks** ten Defendant **Richard Suart** bar Judge **Peter Savidge** bar Counsel **Donald Adams** bass Usher **Gareth Rhys-Davies** bar Foreman **Welsh National Opera Chorus and Orchestra / Sir Charles Mackerras**
Telarc ② CD80404 (121' · DDD) Notes and texts included Ⓕⓞ

Between them, *The Yeomen of the Guard* and *Trial by Jury* contain all that's best in Sullivan's music for the theatre. In the former there's some of his more serious and ambitious writing, in the latter some of his most consistently light-hearted and engaging. All of this is brought out in Telarc's series of recordings with Welsh National Opera. As always, Sir Charles Mackerras paces the music impeccably, and he has assured contributions from such stalwarts as Donald Adams, Felicity Palmer and Richard Suart. The last-named may be a shade light-voiced compared with some of the more comic performers of Jack Point and the Learned Judge; but in *The Yeomen* it's surely his performance that stands out. His handling of the dialogue after 'Here's a man of jollity' is masterly, and his 'Oh, a private buffoon' is as winning as any, with impeccable clarity of diction and a perfectly judged French accent for 'jests ... imported from France'. Neill Archer and Alwyn Mellor are admirable as Fairfax and Elsie; but

Pamela Helen Stephen could have displayed more of the minx in Phoebe Meryll's personality, while in *Trial by Jury* Barry Banks has too small a voice to convince as the Defendant. Recommended, especially if you want both works on the same set.

Further listening

Iolanthe
Coupled with: Overture di Ballo[a]
Baker The Lord Chancellor **Wallace** Earl of Mountararat **Young** Earl Tolloller **Brannigan** Private Willis
Glyndebourne Festival Chorus; Pro Arte Orchestra; [a]**BBC Symphony Orchestra / Sargent**
HMV Classics ② HMVD5 73675-2 (106' · ADD) Ⓑ
Sargent's affectionate handling of the score contributes to the great success of this issue.

Ruddigore
Coupled with: The Merchant of Venice – Suite[a]
Baker Sir Ruthven Murgatroyd **Lewis** Dauntless **Brannigan** Sir Despard Murgatroyd **Glyndebourne Festival Chorus; Pro Arte Orchestra / Sargent;** [a]**City of Birmingham Symphony Orchestra /** [a]**Dunn**
HMV Classics ② HMVD5 73681-2 (97' · ADD) Ⓑ
Lacking nothing in the way of humour and drama, this is a hugely musical performance.

Jan Pieterszoon Sweelinck
Dutch 1562-1621

Sweelinck studied with his father, organist of the Oude Kerk, Amsterdam, succeeding him in or before 1580. He remained in this post all his life, with a few excursions to inspect new organs in other cities. Among the most influential and sought-after teachers of his time, he included Germans among his pupils, notably Scheidt, Jacob Praetorius and Scheidemann. He wrote over 250 vocal works, including a complete French psalter (1604-21), motets (1619), chansons (1594, 1612) and Italian madrigals (1612). But he is best known for his c70 keyboard works, which include monumental fugal fantasias, concise toccatas and well-ordered variation sets. He perfected forms derived from, among others, the English virginalists and greatly influenced 17th-century north German keyboard music, becoming one of the leading composers of his day. His son Dirck (1591-1652), who succeeded him at the Oude Kerk in 1621, edited a popular song collection (1644) and also composed songs and keyboard music.

GROVEmusic

Complete Keyboard Works

Complete Keyboard Works
Freddy Eichelberger, Liuwe Tamminga, Leo van Doeselaar, Pieter van Dijk, Bernard Winsemius, Reinhard Jaud, Stef Tuinstra, Bert Matter, Vincent van de Laar orgs **Glen Wilson, Siebe Henstra,**

Sweelinck Instrumental

Menno van Delft, Pieter Dirksen, Bob van Asperen, Pieter-Jan Belder *hpds*
NM Classics ⑨ 92119 (10 hours, 29' · DDD)   Ⓑ

The fact that no fewer than 15 musicians (nearly all Sweelinck's countrymen) have contributed to this complete keyboard project in no way lessens the impressiveness of what has been achieved here. Led by Pieter Dirksen and Pieter van Dijk, they get through nearly 90 pieces (some of which are heard more than once on organ and on harpsichord). This complete edition rests on sound and fresh scholarship, and is laid out in an engaging and informative manner. Each artist contributes a recital intended to stand on its own, usually on the same instrument.

Fourteen organs from the 16th and 17th centuries, and three harpsichords, are heard over the course of ten-and-a-half hours. The harpsichords are an original by Johannes Ruckers, and two recent copies of other instruments also by him. But it's the organs that steal the show: spread across three countries, several still close to original condition, their individual characteristics and the acoustics of their respective churches make for endlessly absorbing listening. As an anthology of great early organs this set would be worth recommending. The fact that here they're pressed into serving music of such sustained quality only increases their impact. For there's no doubting Sweelinck's variety, charm and infinite resource. He touched all the significant genres of the keyboard repertory of his day (toccatas, fantasias, dance movements, variation sets, ricercars).

Of all these genres, the fantasia furnishes Sweelinck with perhaps his most congenial medium: simple subjects serve as the basis for wide-ranging explorations, stretching out over many minutes without ever losing the thread – indeed, frequently his conclusions have an awe-inspiring power. Sweelinck needs no advocacy beyond the performances themselves; rather, it's the consistency of these performances that concerns us here. That consistency would be impressive had it originated with a single interpreter, but given the number of participants it's equally remarkable. It's all very impressive. What more could one want?

Organ Works

Toccata in C. Ballo del granduca. Ricercar.Malle Sijmen. Mein junges Leben hat ein End'. Aeolian Echo Fantasia. Onder een linde groen. Toccata in A minor I. Erbarm dich mein, o Herre Gott. Poolsche dans
James David Christie *org*
Naxos 8 550904 (64' · DDD) Recorded 1993 Played on the C B Fisk Organ, Houghton Chapel, Wellesley College, USA   Ⓢ❶

The Houghton Chapel is nowhere near as resonantly spacious as the Oude Kerk in Amsterdam, but its relative intimacy doesn't rob the organ of its natural resonance and tonal beauty. James David Christie presents what's in effect a most satisfactory re-creation of one of Sweelinck's organ recitals, given daily between 1580 and 1621, for the burghers of Amsterdam. One hopes they were appreciative of the most consistently witty and generous-spirited keyboard music before the era of Buxtehude, Couperin and Bach.

While Christie may not possess the lyricism of a Leonhardt, the humane warmth of a Piet Kee or the mercurial whimsy of a Koopman, he is, in his own right, a bold, stylish, unhasty player, clearly thoroughly versed in early performance practice, with an incisive technique disclosing musical intelligence and common sense. He's particularly successful in the five major variation sets here, relishing the variety of decorative motifs but still conveying an impression of structural coherence and unity. Just occasionally his articulation might have worked better in a somewhat larger acoustic: at times a more obviously singing touch might have suggested greater tenderness in quieter moments and more ample majesty in louder ones.

Nevertheless, with appealing registrations, an almost ideal choice of programme and undistractingly natural recording this is recommended.

Choral Works

Ab Oriente. Angelus ad pastores ait. Beati omnes. Beati pauperes. Cantate Domino. De profundis. Diligam te Domine. Domine Deus meus. Ecce nunc benedicite. Ecce prandium. Ecce virgo concipiet. Euge serve bone. Gaudeate omnes. Gaude et laetare. Hodie beata Virgo Mariae. Hodie Christus natus est. In illo tempore. In te Domine speravi. Iusti autem. Laudate Dominum. Magnificat. Non omnis. O Domine Jesu Christe. O quam beata lancea. O sacrum convivium. Paraclectus autem. Petite et accipietis. Qui vult venire post me. Regina coeli. Tanto tempore. Te Deum laudamus. Timor Domini. Ubi duo vel tres. Venite, exultemus Domino. Vide homo. Videte manus meas. Viri Galilaei
Clare College Choir, Cambridge / Timothy Brown
with **James Grossmith, Andrew Henderson** *org*
Etcetera ② KTC2025 (141' · DDD) Notes,texts and translations included   Ⓕ❶

That Sweelinck is a true doyen of sacred vocal music is emphatically confirmed in an important and invigorating world première recording of the complete 1619 *Cantiones sacrae*. This collection of 37 motets in five-voices demonstrates the quality of his aesthetic, in which textual representation and pure contrapuntal pleasure converge with effortless mastery; you need only hear the first minute of the first track, a quasi-introit, 'Gaudete', of infectious energy, to dance to its buoyant rhythms and bask in the clarity of the harmonic conception. *Cantiones sacrae* projects a distinctive containment, both in scale and emotional judgement, which should appeal to choirs of all shapes and sizes – and listeners too.

These performances by the young voices of Clare College Choir are impressive. Brown expertly circumnavigates his disciplined larger forces of about 26 voices around music that's both introspective and ecstatic. The smaller-scale consort is perhaps less polished, the tuning of the sopranos has a tendency to 'dip' intermittently, and there's an occasional 'piping kettle' quality to the timbre. Generally, too, the lack of colorific range and resonance betrays the youthful membership of the choir; this can be telling in some of the slower music. These are small gripes in a project which stands out for a pioneering place in the catalogue and its fine advocacy of Sweelinck's seemingly unlimited resource.

Karol Szymanowski   Polish 1882-1937

Szymanowski was born into an artistic family of the Polish landed gentry and began his musical education with his father. At 13, in Vienna, he was powerfully impressed by hearing Wagner for the first time. He then had formal tuition from Zawirski and Noskowski in Warsaw (1901-4), and during the next decade began to make an international reputation for music in the German tradition, relating to Wagner, Strauss and Reger: the main works of this period include the Symphony No 2 (1910), Piano Sonata No 2 (1911) and the opera Hagith (1913).

During these years he visited Italy, Sicily and north Africa he also encountered Pelléas, The Firebird and Petrushka, and all these enriching influences were remembered in his abundant output of 1914-17, when he was confined by the war to Russia. Works of this period are typically classical or oriental in inspiration, and ornately figured in a manner relating to Skryabin or Debussy. They include the choral Symphony No 3 (1916), Violin Concerto No 1 (1916), Myths for violin and piano (1915) and the piano triptychs Metopes (1915) and Masques (1916). He then used this new, highly sensuous language to tackle the theme of The Bacchae in his opera King Roger (1926), set in the orientalised Norman kingdom of Sicily. In 1919 he settled in Warsaw, now the capital of an independent Poland; and he began while completing King Roger to compose in a nationalist style, drawing on folk music in his choral orchestral Stabat mater (1926), ballet Harnasie (1935) and other works. He accepted the directorship of the Warsaw Conservatory (1927-32), but his last years were dogged by ill health, and he wrote nothing after his Violin Concerto No 2 (1933) and a pair of piano mazurkas, adding to a set of 20 dating from 1924-5. Other works include two quartets, songs, folksong arrangements and cantatas. GROVEmusic

Violin Concertos

No 1 Op 35 **No 2** Op 61

Violin Concertos Nos 1 & 2. Three Paganini Caprices, Op 40. Romance in D, Op 23
Thomas Zehetmair vn **Silke Avenhaus** pf **City of Birmingham Symphony Orchestra / Sir Simon Rattle**
EMI 555607-2 (65' · DDD)   Ⓕ**○○○**

They make an admirable coupling, the two Szymanowski violin concertos, but a demanding one for the soloist. They are both so beautiful that it must be tempting to embellish both with a similarly glowing tone. They inhabit quite different worlds (they were written 16 years apart) and Zehetmair shows how well they respond to quite different approaches.

In the First, after a rapt solo entry, he uses for the most part a lovely but delicate tone, expanding to athletic incisiveness but not often to lushness. It all fits very well with Rattle's handling of the orchestra: occasionally full and rich but mostly a sequence of exquisitely balanced chamber ensembles. Generous but finely controlled *rubato* from both soloist and conductor allows the concerto's improvisatory fantasy to flower; and the quiet close even has a touch of wit to it.

Zehetmair's sound is immediately less ethereal, more robust, for the opening melody of the Second Concerto. This is the sort of tone, you suspect, that he would use in Bartók's Second Concerto, and it points up a vein of Bartókian strength to this work's longer and firmer lines. Rattle, too, seeks out bolder and more dense colours.

The *Paganini Caprices* were equipped by Szymanowski not with deferential accompaniments but with independent and quite freely composed piano parts. They change Paganini, even where the violin part is unmodified, into a late Romantic virtuoso, with a hint of Lisztian poetry alongside the expertly pointed-up fireworks of the Twenty-Fourth *Caprice*; even here Zehetmair is a listening violinist, not one to upstage his excellent pianist. The *Romance*, the warmest and most luscious piece here, is beautifully done but with a touch of restraint to prevent it cloying. A first-class coupling, and a recording that makes the most of the superb acoustic of Symphony Hall in Birmingham.

Additional recommendation

Violin Concertos 1 & 2
Coupled with: Demeter. Mandragora. Stabat mater. Litany to the Virgin Mary. Górecki Three Pieces in the Old Style **Baird** Colas Breugnon Suite
Kulka vn **Polish Radio Chorus of Krakow; Polish National Radio Symphony Orchestra / Maksymiuk, Wit**
EMI Double Forte ② 575670-2 (142' · ADD/DDD)   Ⓜ
A fine introduction to Szymanowski's sound world; great performances, all authentically Polish. Kulka's recordings of the concertos are particularly appealing – rich-timbred and committed. Both conductors have the measure of the composer's lush, heavily scented world.

Symphonies

No 1 in F minor, Op 15 No 2 in B flat, Op 19 No 3
(The Song of the Night), Op 27 No 4 (Symphonie
concertante), Op 60

Symphony No 2 in B flat, Op 19. Concert Overture in
E, Op 12. Wordsong, Op 46[a]. Songs of the
Infatuated Muezzin, Op 42[a]
[a]**Zofia Kilanowicz** sop **London Philharmonic
Orchestra / Leon Botstein**
Telarc CD80567 (68' · DDD)   Ⓕ●

The *Concert Overture* is a hugely gifted young
composer's homage to Richard Strauss, and
fully worthy of its model in impetuousness, rich
sonority and close-woven polyphony. The Second Symphony is no less rich but more disciplined, with Reger's influence added to (and
modifying) that of Strauss, and with Szymanowski's own high colouring, sinuous
melody and tonal adventurousness now in their
first maturity. The *Infatuated Muezzin* songs are
a high point of his middle period, Debussian
harmony and florid orientalising arabesques
fusing to an aching voluptuousness, colour now
applied with the refinement of a miniaturist.
Leon Botstein is fully aware of the quite different palettes these pieces use, and the orchestra
play splendidly.
   Wordsong (Telarc's translation for *Słopiewnie*)
is the key to Szymanowski's final phase, a setting
of five poems in an artificial language, using
Slavonic roots to suggest a sort of 'pre-Polish'.
Szymanowski responded to the poems' asso-
nances, rhythms and alliterations (he couldn't
resist 'słodzik słowi słowisienkie'), finding for
them a fusion of folk elements, archaisms and
melodies that retain something of the discarded
middle period's exoticism.
   You sense the influence of Stravinsky (*Les noces*
in particular) and hear already both the folk
vigour and the ritual purity of Szymanowski's
late style (in the third song, too, there's a startling pre-echo of the slow movement of
Górecki's Third). There's a slight, attractive
tremor to Kilanowicz's voice, but she has both
the almost white purity and the flexible coloratura the songs need. It's very hard to make a
single adverse comment about this important
addition to the discography.

Piano Works

Piano Sonata No 1 in C minor, Op 8. Mazurkas, Op 50
– No 13, Moderato; No 14, Animato; No 15, Alle-
gretto dolce; No 16, Allegramente – vigoroso.
Etudes, Op 33. Four Polish Dances, Op 47. Prelude
and Fugue in C sharp minor
Martin Roscoe pf
Naxos 8 553867 (69' · DDD)   Ⓢ

This volume three concludes Martin Roscoe's
cycle of Szymanowski's piano music (a pity,
then, that we won't get to hear his account of

the Third Sonata and the remaining six
Mazurkas). It offers a cross-section of Szymanowski's styles as a composer for the keyboard, from the early First Sonata (always
described as post-Chopin and post-Scriabin
but, Roscoe convincingly demonstrates, no less
importantly post-Liszt as well) to the pungent
Mazurkas, with their flavour of Bartók as well as
of late Grieg.
   The *Prelude and Fugue* is an interesting link
between that early Sonata and the Op 33 *Etudes*
which are usually referred to as representing
Szymanowski's 'impressionist' phase. Again,
Roscoe makes you question this conventional
description: yes, the harmonies look rather
Debussian but they don't often sound that way.
These very brief pieces (just over a minute on
average) are studies in the conventional sense,
written by one fine pianist for another, Alfred
Cortot, but they're also exercises in harmonic
subtlety and rich in Szymanowski's personal
fantasy. The *Four Polish Dances* inhabit the same
world as the *Mazurkas*, and it's obvious that
Roscoe enjoys open fifths and flat sevenths as
much as Szymanowski did.
   A warm recommendation, then, although one
tinged with regret. Given the omission of the
Third Sonata and the remaining *Mazurkas* one
could supplement Roscoe's three volumes with
Pavel Kamasa's superb recording of the complete *Mazurkas* (Koch Schwann) and Raymond
Clarke's of the Third Sonata (Athene). Naxos's
piano sound is excellent.

Stabat mater, Op 53

Stabat mater, Op 53. Litany to the Virgin Mary,
Op 59. Symphony No 3, Op 27, 'The song of the
night'
Elzbieta Szmytka sop **Florence Quivar** contr
Jon Garrison ten **John Connell** bass **City of
Birmingham Symphony Orchestra and Chorus /
Sir Simon Rattle**
EMI 555121-2 (56' · DDD) Texts and translations
included   Ⓕ●●●

The first impression here is that Rattle
is relatively new to Szymanowski.
There's a huge enthusiasm here, a mis-
sionary quality that bespeaks the recent convert.
On the other hand the care over matters of balance, the knowledge of just those points where
Szymanowski's complexity needs very careful
handling if it isn't simply to blur into opacity,
suggest a conductor who has been there before
and knows the dangers. You get the feeling that
a conscious decision was made to delay recording this music until the circumstances were
right.
   The CBSO Chorus sound thoroughly at
home not only in the music but in the language
too. In Elzbieta Szmytka, Rattle has a soprano
who might have been born to sing Szymanowski's pure, floated and very high-lying
soprano lines. The result is very fine: one of the
most beautiful Szymanowski recordings ever

made. And yet 'beautiful Szymanowski' isn't all that hard if the orchestra's good enough and the conductor capable. Rattle's insistence that all the music be heard, its urgency and passion as well as its deliquescent loveliness, makes for uncommonly gripping Szymanowski as well. He reminds one of how much more there is to the Third Symphony than voluptuous yearning.

The choice of soloists for the *Stabat mater* is interesting: alongside Szmytka's radiant purity are Quivar's throaty vibrancy and Connell's weighty darkness. Not a matching trio, but the contrast is appealing. Garrison in the symphony is a touch hard and strenuous, less enraptured than one or two of the Polish tenors (and sopranos) who've recorded it, but he's a musicianly and likeable singer. The recording is outstanding: lucid, rich and spacious.

Songs

Complete Songs for Voice and Piano
Juliana Gondek, Iwona Sobotka sops **Urszula Kryger** mez **Piotr Beczala** ten **Reinild Mees** pf
Channel Classics ④ CCS19398 (264' · DDD · T/t) Ⓜ

This set proposes a kind of luxury musical package-tour for the jet-set age – today expressionist Austria, tomorrow Slavic fantasy, the day after high-romanticism in Germany, and then away for a weekend in the exotic realms of the Near East. The different locales materialise out of thin air, colourful, fully formed, without a moment for the traveller to get bored on the way. Szymanowski's song output is doubly intriguing – first, for those far-flung contrasts of style; second, because it's so little known. Though the Polish language is an issue, this admirable set reminds us that there are also songs in German and even a James Joyce cycle in English.

Four singers take part, one to each disc. Piotr Beczala is a light, poetic young tenor with some passion up his sleeve. He's dreamily captivating in the early Six Songs of Op 2, where Fauré and Rachmaninov seem to be whispering ideas alternately over Szymanowski's shoulders; catches well the change of tone to religious concentration in the *Three Fragments by Jan Kasprowicz*; and brings lyric beauty to the Schoenberg-inspired Op 13 settings.

The voice of soprano Juliana Gondek is a touch brittle for the sultry mood Szymanowski must have had in mind for the *Songs of the Infatuated Muezzin*, and a bit more could be made of the words in the Joyce cycle; yet there's still much to enjoy.

The sensitive singing of mezzo Urszula Kryger plunges straight into the swirling Tristanesque ecstasy of the Wagnerian Op 20 set. The glinting lights of the Orient return in *Des Hafis Liebeslieder*, another set of paraphrases by Hans Bethge to place beside *Das Lied von der Erde*, and the four songs of Op 41 take us forward into more ambiguous and experimental terrain.

The familiar *Songs of the Fairy Princess* promise a magical opening to the fourth disc in a winning performance by young Iwona Sobotka. Here's a pure, steady, light soprano who can flit up into the ledger lines without a hint of shrillness. She's also interesting in the antique Polish songs of the *Słopiewnie*, Op 46, and makes a lively job of the miniature *Children's Rhymes* of Op 49, even if a few go rather a long way.

The pianist, Reinild Mees, exhibits a faultless sense of atmosphere throughout, whether delicately conjuring Oriental mystery or thundering up and down Lisztian octaves. The adventurous traveller need look no further.

King Roger, Op 46

King Roger
Thomas Hampson bar Roger II **Elzbieta Szmytka** sop Roxana **Ryszard Minkiewicz** ten Shepherd
Robert Gierlach bar Archbishop **Jadwiga Rappé** contr Deaconess **Philip Langridge** ten Edrisi **City of Birmingham Symphony Youth Chorus; City of Birmingham Symphony Chorus**

Symphony No 4, 'Symphonie concertante', Op 60
Leif Ove Andsnes pf **City of Birmingham Symphony Orchestra / Sir Simon Rattle**
EMI ② 556823-2 (112' · DDD) Notes text and translation included Ⓕ**ⓞⓞⓞ**

King Roger is a ravishingly beautiful opera, but a very fragile one. With a shrill soprano or a less than ideally cast tenor it would be fatally flawed. Minkiewicz's Dionysiac Shepherd betrays a slight hardness and a touch of stress in full voice, but he has both the allure and the mystery that the role imperatively demands. Almost his first words are 'My God is as beautiful as I', and he should vocally suggest that he is indeed radiantly beautiful. His voice shades to a croon at times, but he never sounds epicene.

Szmytka is a wonderful Roxana, with beautifully pure high notes and bell-like coloratura. At the end of Act 2 her florid aria is repeated (in Szymanowski's concert version), at just the point where you might well have replayed the earlier track for the pleasure of listening to her again. The use of distinguished singers in the smaller roles is no extravagance: Langridge evokes the exotic strangeness of the Arab sage Edrisi, while Rappé and Gierlach add to the hieratic gravity of the opening scene. Hampson in the central role is in fine voice, easily conveying Roger's authority, his angry but bewildered rejection of the Shepherd's new religion. He's even finer, however, in Act 5, where the King is painfully torn between Dionysus and Apollo. The ambiguity of the final scene remains, as it must. Is Roger accepting the Shepherd in place of Roxana? Or, since Roxana herself immediately succumbs to the Shepherd's glamour, is Roger achieving wholeness by at last acknowledging feminine intuitions within himself? That these questions remain resonant and provoking at the end of the performance is a tribute both to the work itself, and also to Rattle's handling of it. The orchestral textures are voluptuously rich and subtly coloured, aided by a spacious recording (the vast Byzantine basilica of the opening scene is magnificently evoked) and orchestral playing of a very high order indeed. This is the finest recording of *King Roger* that has so far appeared.

The Fourth Symphony, in Szymanowski's later, folk-derived and harder-edged style, is a huge contrast: quite a shock after the opera's radiant conclusion. Andsnes's powerfully athletic playing points up the music's affinities with Prokofiev, and both he and Rattle emphasise the new vigour that Szymanowski was drawing from the fiddle music of the Tatra region.

King Roger
Wojciech Drabowicz bar Roger ‖ **Olga Pasiecznik** sop Roxana **Krzysztof Szmyt** ten Edrisi **Piotr Beczala** ten Shepherd **Romuald Tesarowicz** bass Archbishop **Stefania Toczyska** mez Deaconess **Alla Polacca Youth Choir; Polish National Opera Chorus and Orchestra / Jacek Kaspszyk**
CD Accord ACD131-2 (80' · DDD · S/T/t/N)   Ⓕ

The opening of King Roger, an evocation of religious ritual in Byzantine Palermo, is an operatic one-off. And if no other composer has ever conceived quite such an atmospheric curtain-raiser, no other recording of Szymanowski's 1926 masterpiece has ever conveyed it as thrillingly as this new release from the Polish National Opera on that country's excellent CD Accord label. Simon Rattle's fine recording set a new standard over earlier and rougher Polish versions, but this one surpasses them all. The sound is more vivid, allowing these completely idiomatic performers maximum impact. Where Rattle was characteristically high-gloss, Jacek Kaspszyk uses the experience of live performance to dig deeper into this ambiguous work. The same can be said for the respective castings of the title role, with the polished Thomas Hampson versus the more questing Wojciech Drabowicz.

This compact work makes a mesmerizing impression under Kaspszyk. Drabowicz sings Roger with darksome magnificence; his queen, Roxana, is sung in glowing, easy tone by Olga Pasiecznik; Piotr Beczala is lyrically insinuating as the Shepherd, who unsettles everyone when he's revealed as the personification of Dionysus. This is a recording of authentic depth.

Toru Takemitsu   Japanese 1930-1996

Takemitsu was a pupil of Kiyose from 1948. Influenced by Webern, Debussy and Messiaen, he has reflected what is most oriental in these composers: a concern with timbre and elegant sound and with the precision of the moment rather than with pattern

and development. His music often gives the impression of spatial experience and of materials evolving freely of their own accord; silence is fully organised. Some of his works use Japanese instruments, but most are for Western orchestral and chamber media. Among the best known are Requiem for strings (1957), November Steps for biwa, shakuhachi and orchestra (1967), A Flock Descends into the Pentagonal Garden (1977) and From me flows what you call Time (1990) for percussion quintet and orchestra.   **GROVE**music

Quotation of Dream

Day Signal. From Heaven. Quotation of Dream[a]. How Slow the Wind. Twill by Twilight. Archipelago S. Dream/Window. Night Signal
[a]**Paul Crossley**, [a]**Peter Serkin** pfs **London Sinfonietta / Oliver Knussen**
DG Gramophone Awards Collection 453 495-2 (71' · DDD)   Ⓜ**OOO**

'Dream', 'Slow', 'Twilight': these are the kind of words that give the key to Takemitsu's later style, and all the works on this disc were written between 1985 and 1993. The Debussy connection is easy to hear, but, simply because of that, Takemitsu's own personal blend of the flowing and the disjunctive, against a harmonic background consistently more dense than Debussy's, stands out as one of the most significant late 20th-century responses to an early 20th century master. Second-hand impressionism it isn't.

Oliver Knussen's performances are models of balance and clarity, with the music's purely colouristic qualities not excessively indulged. Also crucial here is the excellent quality of the DG recording, extremely well-designed for the way most of these pieces alternate so subtly between soloistic writing and fuller yet no less richly imagined textures. *Dream/Window* sets the tone for the kind of restrained yet eloquent ceremonies that can also be heard in the tribute to Feldman, *Twill by Twilight* and the two beautifully constructed works, *How Slow the Wind*, and *Quotation of Dream*. It's extremely tempting to say that this is the best single CD of Takemitsu's music so far issued.

I Hear the Water Dreaming

I Hear the Water Dreaming[d]. Toward the Sea I[a]. Le fils des étoiles[b]. Toward the Sea II[bd]. And then I knew 'twas Wind[bc]. Toward the Sea III[b]. Air
Patrick Gallois fl [a]**Göran Söllscher** gtr [b]**Fabrice Pierre** hp [c]**Pierre-Henri Xuereb** va [d]**BBC Symphony Orchestra / Sir Andrew Davis**
DG 20/21 453 459-2GH (67' · DDD)   Ⓕ**OO**

This disc is a follow-up to Oliver Knussen's selection of orchestral works on the Gramophone Award-winning 'Quotation of Dream', and is in one sense at least a far bolder concept, risking the inclusion of three different versions of the same work, Toward the Sea, which in duration amount to about half of the total playing time.

Yet the risk is justified. The three short but beautifully fashioned movements of Toward the Sea, inspired by Melville's great novel Moby Dick, are vintage Takemitsu in their spell-binding evocativeness and economy, and throughout these performances Patrick Gallois' range of tone colour and sensitivity to line are of exceptional quality. Even if you finally conclude that the original version with guitar is, after all, the best, the variations of texture and atmosphere which the different instrumentations provide make for absorbing listening.

The rest of the programme easily sustains this level, although And then I knew 'twas Wind (citing a poem by Emily Dickinson) is more loosely constructed than its companions, underlining just how rarely the pejorative term 'improvisatory' can be applied to Takemitsu's refined and understated art. Gallois and his colleagues don't have the field to themselves in this repertory, and some listeners will rightly value Aurèle Nicolet's accounts for Philips of And then I knew 'twas Wind, Toward the Sea III and Air. But the superb technical quality of the recording and the subtle yet alert responsiveness of the interpretations make this an outstanding release. It's a dream of a disc.

I Hear the Water Dreaming[a]. riverrun[b]. A String around Autumn[c]. A Way A Lone II
[a]**Sharon Bezaly** fl [c]**Philip Dukes** va [b]**Noriko Ogawa** pf **BBC National Orchestra of Wales / Tadaaki Otaka**
BIS BIS-CD1300 (60' · DDD)   Ⓕ**OOO**

 Since Takemitsu's evolution into self-confessed Romantic, virtually every major label has released something by him, so Otaka has stiff competition, notably Patrick Gallois's fine reading of Water Dreaming. A Way A Lone II is included on Rudolf Werthen's admirable survey of Takemitsu's film and concert music. Aided effectively by the soloists, Otaka's interpretations compare well.

In riverrun Takemitsu approached closer to the conventional soloist-ensemble than usual. Noriko Ogawa, who has recorded the complete piano solos for BIS, judges the balance sensitively, preparing the ground for that moment when the orchestra leaves the piano to decorate the silence with a few farewell notes.

riverrun and A Way A Lone draw inspiration from Finnegans Wake. Leif Hasselgren notes a parallel between the circular structure of Joyce's novel and the way Takemitsu's music seems to 'start from nowhere and disappear into the same nowhere'. For all his acknowledged debt to French Impressionism, and to Japanese traditions, his early interest in electronic music – where sounds appear and fade like headlights on the horizon or plants flowering in a time-lapse film – has undoubtedly had a strong influence.

Sharon Bezaly's flute playing intensifies the feeling that Water Dreaming is a perfect crash-course in later Takemitsu, full of references to his influences yet identifiable at any moment as pure, individual and personal Takemitsu, and always bewitching.

Air

Air[a]. And then I knew 'twas Wind[b]. Bryce[c]. Itinerant[d]. Rain Spell[e]. Rain Tree[f]. Toward the Sea[g]. Voice[h]
New Music Concerts Ensemble ([e]Joaquin Valdepeñas cl [e]David Swan pf [ce]Robin Engelman mari/vib [c]John Wyre, [f]Bob Becker, [f]Russell Hartenberger, [f]Ryan Scott percs [g]Norbert Kraft gtr [bce]Erica Goodman, [c]Sanya Eng hps [b]Steven Dann va) / [abcdegh]**Robert Aitken** fl
Naxos 8 555859 (72' · DDD)   Ⓢ**O**

Takemitsu's work in the final decade of his life was gentle, full of tenderness, sentiment and sighs. But he never entirely discarded the starker beauty of his earlier work. Air distills much of the spirit of his music, evoking the French Impressionists, modernist asceticism and the pared-down elegance of Japanese traditional music and gardens. It was written for flautist Aurèle Nicolet and first played in public by Yasukazu Uemura, but it's hard to imagine Robert Aitken's performance being bettered.

Aitken invited Takemitsu to Canada in 1975 and 1983. From these visits grew a special relationship with the musicians featured on this outstanding album. They performed most of these works for the composer, so we can assume that the interpretations bear the hallmark of authenticity: they sound utterly convincing, with their perfect balance of the technical and the emotional. Itinerant (1989) is a case in point: Takemitsu pictures a garden where vegetable and mineral, motion and stability mingle in precisely designed harmony, yet each visitor's perspective discovers a fresh view.

The programming is as admirable as the playing, surveying Takemitsu's music for small forces from 1971 (Voice, with its references to Noh theatre) to 1995 (Air). From the pastoral, slightly eerie trio for flute, viola and harp And Then I Knew – devised as a companion-piece to Debussy's 1915 Sonata for the same instruments – and the shimmering, celestial Rain Tree, to Rain Spell, brooding and turbulent in turns, this is yet another excellent 20th-century showcase from Naxos.

Thomas Tallis   British c1505-1585

Tallis was organist of the Benedictine Priory of Dover in 1532, then probably organist at St Mary-at-Hill, London (1537-8). About 1538 he moved to Waltham Abbey where, at the dissolution (1540), he was a senior lay clerk. In 1541-2 he was a lay clerk at Canterbury Cathedral, and in 1543 became a Gentleman of the Chapel Royal; he remained in the royal household until his death acting as organist, though he was not so designated until after 1570. In 1575 Elizabeth I granted him a licence, with Byrd, to print and publish music, as a result of which the Cantiones sacrae, *an anthology of Latin motets by both composers, appeared later that year.*

*His earliest surviving works are probably three votive antiphons (*Salve intemerata virgo, Ave rosa sine spinis *and* Ave Dei patris filia*) in the traditional structure common up to c1530: division into two halves, with sections in reduced and full textures. Other early works include the Magnificat and another votive antiphon,* Sancte Deus, *both for men's voices. Two of his most sumptuous works, the six-voice antiphon* Gaude gloriosa Dei mater *and the seven-voice Mass '* Puer natus est nobis *', date from Mary Tudor's brief reign (1553-8), the former featuring musical imagery and melismatic writing, the latter expert handling of current techniques of structural imitation and choral antiphony. He also composed six Latin responsories and seven Office hymns for the Sarum rite and large-scale Latin psalm motets early in Elizabeth's reign. The 40-voice motet,* Spem in alium, *an astonishing technical achievement, may have been composed in 1573.*

Tallis was one of the first to write for the new Anglican liturgy of 1547-53. Much of this music, including If ye love me *and* Hear the voice and prayer, *is in four parts with clear syllabic word-setting and represents the prototype of the early English anthem. His Dorian Service is in a similar style. Among his Elizabethan vernacular music are nine four-voice psalm tunes (1567) and various English adaptations of Latin motets (e.g.* Absterge Domine*); the Latin Lamentations and paired five-voice Magnificat and Nunc dimittis also date from this period. His instrumental works include keyboard arrangements of four partsongs and many cantus firmus settings and a small but distinguished contribution to the repertory of consort music which includes two fine* In Nomines. *Tallis's early music is relatively undistinguished, with neither Taverner's mastery of the festal style nor Tye's modernisms. But much of his later work is among the finest in Europe, ranging from the artless perfection of his short anthems to the restrained pathos of the Lamentations.* GROVEmusic

Beati immaculati

Beati immaculati. Puer natus est nobis. Mass 'Puer natus est nobis'. Viderunt omnes. Dies sanctificatus. Celeste organum. Viderunt omnes. Suscipe quaeso Dominus. Gaude gloriosa Dei mater
Chapelle du Roi / Alistair Dixon
Signum Records SIGCD003 (65' · DDD) Texts and translations included ⓕ

The illuminating insert-notes place Mary's short reign within the bewilderingly stormy context of the 16th century with a calm understanding that enables the listener to see how this Latin music came to be written. Incidentally, the first piece was originally an English setting of *Beatus vir*. Sandon says it falls naturally into place with its Latin text. But the verses in the booklet don't exactly correspond to what's

being sung, which raises an unnecessary question mark. Sandon's edition of the Proper Salisbury chants for the Third Mass of Christmas are performed between the polyphonic items. Meticulously researched, they serve as a foil to the sumptuous settings of the Ordinary.

If only they had been sung with more solemnity and gusto, omitting those irritating little bursts of volume on the high notes! All these chants would have sounded more authentic at a slower tempo with the occasional semi-metrical dactyl: as it is, they comes across rather as a poor relation beside the magnificence of Tallis's seven-part polyphony. The polyphonic singing is exemplary, the clarity of the individual parts and the rhythmic interplay well under control. The singers enter into the spirit of the liturgical texts, in particular in the third section of the *Agnus Dei*. Their interpretation of the final motet, *Gaude gloriosa*, at times almost touches the visionary.

Lamentations of Jeremiah

Lamentations of Jeremiah. Motets – Absterge Domine; Derelinquat impius; Mihi autem nimis; O sacrum convivium; In jejunio et fletu; O salutaris hostia; In manus tuas; O nata lux de lumine. Salve intemerata virgo
The Tallis Scholars / Peter Phillips
Gimell CDGIM025 (68' · DDD) Texts and translations included ⓕ⦿

This, the third volume of the survey by The Tallis Scholars of the music of the Tudor composer, Thomas Tallis, contains the well-known *Lamentations*, eight motets, and the extended motet *Salve intemerata virgo*. The *Lamentations* and motets are typical of the style of late Renaissance English composers. The overall mood is one of considerable austerity and their simplicity is indicative of the probability of their having been written for the private use of loyal Catholics rather than for formal ritual. *Salve intemerata virgo*, on the other hand, looks back to the glories of the late 15th century. In particular, Tallis's use of the phrygian mode gives the work as a whole a strong sense of the medieval. Despite this disparity of styles the Tallis Scholars acquit themselves, as always, with great distinction. In the *Lamentations* and motets they achieve an appropriate sense of intimacy, while in *Salve intermerata virgo* they rise fully to the challenges of one of the more extended and demanding examples of Tudor choral composition. In addition the formidable challenges which this latter work sets for the conductor, such as the sense of pace, variation of dynamics, and overall architecture of the work, are all extremely well handled by Peter Phillips. The recording is very fine.

Complete Works – 8, Lamentations and Contrafacta

Sing and glorify heaven's high majesty. Lamentations

of Jeremiah – I; II. Blessed are those that be
undefiled. I call and cry to thee. Wipe away my sins.
Forgive me, Lord, my sin. Arise, O Lord, and hear.
With all our hearts. O sacred and holy banquet.
When Jesus went into Simon the Pharisee's house.
Blessed be thy name. O praise the Lord (2nd version)
Chapelle du Roi / Alistair Dixon
Signum Records SIGCD036 (64' · DDD) Texts and
translations included   Ⓕ

Two of the Biblical lessons for Maundy Thursday show Tallis at his most creative and imaginative. 'Incipit lamentatio…' the rising fourth,
followed by a descending minor scale, imitated
in turn by each of the other voices, sets the tone
of sorrowful lamenting. Chapelle du Roi capture this mood with calm perfection. The flowing melodies of the introductory Hebrew letters, the clear articulation of the homophonic
sections, each element is performed with understanding, due restraint, and never overdone.

The Latin motets that lie behind the English
contrafacta have been recorded on Volume 7 of
this series. It's remarkable how well the English
texts, not necessarily translations or paraphrases, are made to fit the originals. Much
interesting research lies behind the notes to
Volumes 7 and 8: the identification of the original sources throws additional light on the religious and political struggles of Tallis's working
life, and offers glimpses of domesticity. Dixon's
choice between two possible groupings of five
voices, the lower male-voice group and a higher
one to include the ladies of the house, makes
perfect sense.

Sing and glorify is a *contrafactum* of Tallis's
monumental *Spem in alium*, intended for a joyful royal investiture a quarter of a century after
his death. The motet was recast in an entirely
different mould: to wish long life to the young
Prince of Wales was a far cry from a desperate
appeal to God for mercy: even Dixon's faster
tempo can't alter that, but what a fine performance his singers give of it.

Additional recommendation

Lamentations of Jeremiah
Coupled with: **Brumel** Lamentations **A Ferrabosco I**
De lamentatione Ieremiae prophetae **Palestrina**
Lamentations for Holy Saturday **Tallis** Lamentations
of Jeremiah **White** Lamentations of Jeremiah
The Tallis Scholars / Peter Phillips

Gimell CDGIM996 (73' · DDD) Texts and translations
included   Ⓕ

A compilation of 16th-century Tenebrae music for
Holy Week. The Lamentations texts set are quite
different, but all show an intensity and a devotional
power that work cumulatively to produce a
remarkably satisfying disc.

Spem in alium

Te lucis ante terminum. Salvator mundi. Spem in
alium. In jejunio et fletu. O salutaris hostia. Lamenta-

---

tions I & II. Miserere. Mass for four voices
Magnificat / Philip Cave
Linn Records CKD233 (67' · DDD) Texts and
translations included   Ⓕ**OOO**

 This is quite simply the best performance of Tallis's 40-part *Spem in alium*
to date. Sung by a constellation of
singers, many of them familiar names from
other well-established choral groups, it's a gripping realisation. The effect of the slowly moving harmonies is enhanced by a well-conceived
and very positive use of dynamics. Precise
entries, gently undulating rhythms that are
wonderfully supple, and then those firm
antiphonal phrases – one group of choirs
answered by another at 'Creator coeli et terra' –
raise the tension, until we twice almost miss a
heart-beat at the well-placed rest before
'Respice …'.

That great motet, so central to the whole programme, is well supported by the four-part
Mass and the delightful group of other pieces
for various combinations of voices. The hymn
Te lucis with its alternating chant strophes
sounding so very English (almost too perfect for
what was, after all, just run-of-the-mill everyday
chant!) has the tempo relationship of the chant
to the polyphony just right, which is a tremendous plus, rarely achieved.

Spem in alium. Salvator mundi (I, II). Sancte Deus,
sancte fortis. Gaude gloriosa Dei mater. Miserere
nostri. Loquebantur variis linguis
The Tallis Scholars / Peter Phillips
Gimell CDGIM006 (43' · DDD) Recorded 1984   Ⓕ**OO**

For the 1985 quatercentenary of Tallis's death,
Peter Phillips and The Tallis Scholars produced
this version of *Spem in alium*; in many respects
it's clearly the most successful ever recorded.
Not only is the choir superb and the interpretation an intelligent one; this is also the only
recording in which the eight choirs seem genuinely to sing from different positions in the
stereo spread, a technical achievement that
leads to some thrilling antiphonal exchanges.
Above all, Phillips's reading is a confident and
assertive one. The effect is more that of a plea
than a prayer, and the overall shaping is most
characterful. Inevitably there are problems of
balance, both at the top of the texture (several of
the trebles are given rather too much prominence) and in the middle, where in full sections
the music of the inner voices sometimes blends
too readily into rich chords rather than emerging as a complex web of counterpoint. But these
are relatively small complaints to be made
against an outstanding achievement. This is a
Spem in alium to be cherished.

No one who cares for Tudor choral music
should be without this disc.

Complete Works – 7, Music for Queen Elizabeth
Spem in alium. Absterge Domine. Derelinquat

TALLIS SPEM IN ALIUM
IN BRIEF

Tallis Scholars / Peter Phillips
Gimell ② CDGIM203 (159' · DDD) ⓂⓄⓄ
Gimell CDGIM006 (43' · DDD) ⒻⓄⓄ
The punchy, no-holds-barred sonorities and spot-on tuning of The Tallis Scholars make for exhilarating listening. The recording – crucial when it comes to delineating 40 separate lines – doesn't wrap around the listener, but offers a tightly focused experience. It's available both with the original couplings of Latin motets or as the starter for The Scholars' complete recordings of Tallis.

Magnificat / Philip Cave
Linn CKD075 (67' · DDD) ⒻⓄⓄⓄ
☀ Demonstration-quality openness and balance makes this quite spacious version one to treasure. Lots of young British voices bring an unchurchy, dynamic panorama to Tallis's elaborate testament of faith – *My hope is founded in the Lord* – and demonstration of compositional skill.

Clerkes of Oxenford / David Wulstan
Classics for Pleasure 575982-2 (69' · ADD) Ⓑ
A pioneering 'new' early-music choir in the 1970s combining modern scholarship (and female voices) with roots in the English choral tradition. The result is unhurried and effortlessly conveys the scale of Tallis's conception. Fine couplings of church music.

Chapelle du Roi / Alistair Dixon
Signum SIGCD047 (20' · DDD) Ⓑ
If you only want *Spem*, this is the one to have. The second track is the first recording of the English version of the motet, *Sing and glorify*. Carefully sung and balanced.

The Sixteen / Harry Christophers
Coro ⦿ CORSACD16016 / 📀 CO5RDVD1 (72' · DDD) Ⓕ
Spem is literally a surround-sound piece, so this recording, the first to use the latest technology in new audio formats, gets closer than most. The Sixteen (enlarged to the requisite 40) have a suitably festive air for this, their 25th anniversary recording.

Choir of Winchester Cathedral / David Hill
Hyperion CDA20400 (59' · DDD) Ⓕ
A definite first choice for those who want to hear the boys' voices that Tallis would have composed for. A wide, open recording within Winchester's vast space still captures all the intricate detail to touching effect.

Kronos Quartet
Nonesuch 7559 79242-2 (62' · DDD) Ⓕ
For something a bit different: the avant-garde string quartet, multi-tracked with sometimes revelatory clarity.

impius. Domine quis habitat. In ieiunio et fletu. In manus tuas. Laudate Dominum. Mihi autem nimis. Miserere nostri. O nata lux de lumine. O sacrum convivium. O salutaris hostia. Salvator mundi, salva nos – I & II
Chapelle du Roi / Alistair Dixon
Signum Records SIGCD029 (63' · DDD) Texts and translations included ⒻⓄⓄ

Volume 7 of Chapelle du Roi's complete series of Tallis recordings, is a further witness to the composer's consummate command of his art, in whatever religious or political situation he found himself at each changing period of his life. It might seem puzzling that Elizabeth, in 1575, should sanction the publication of Tallis's and Byrd's *Cantiones sacrae*, but she apparently enjoyed hearing Latin-texted music in her private chapel, and many of the prayers would have been familiar from her childhood.

Dixon makes a number of interesting points. He demonstrates Tallis's use of older material: for example, the Latin *Absterge Domine*, side by side with its later English contrafactum *Discomfort them, O Lord*. He shows how five-voice scoring might be used for an all-male ensemble, or privately in, say, a recusant family situation, with ladies on the top line (*In ieiunio et fletu*). Tallis's craftsmanship is further revealed in his two through-composed psalms, *Domine, quis habitabit* and *Laudate Dominum*, which, while adhering to 16th-century principles of syllabic word-setting, are varied enough to relieve the inevitable tedium. We hear finally, Dixon's masterly interpretation of *Spem in alium* 'in the round' – or 'in horseshoe formation' – possibly the Chapelle's highest achievement to date.

Tan Dun Chinese/America b1957

Growing up during the Cutural Revolution, Tan Dun received no early musical training. After working as a violinist, at the age of 19 he entered the composition department of Beijing's reopened Central Conservatory of Music. There he encountered Western music and was stimulated by visits of guest composers Goehr, Crumb and Takemitsu. He moved to New York in 1986. GROVEmusic

Yi²

Tan Dun Yi² **Rouse** Concert de Gaudí
Sharon Isbin gtr **Gulbenkian Orchestra / Mu Hai Tang**
Teldec 8573-81830-2 (57' · DDD) ⒻⓄⓄⓄ

☀ These two concertos will come as a shock to anyone who believes that guitar music is about Spanishry and tunes to carry away in memory's pocket, but if approached with open ears the shock should benefit both them and the guitar. Chrisopher Rouse's tribute to Gaudí is as spectacular and unconventional as its eponym's cathedral in

Barcelona – and it's at least finished! The strummed opening seems to herald another *Concierto de Aranjuez* but it's utterly deceptive; any connection with traditional Spanish music is soon submerged in a polychromatic succession of episodes.

Tan Dun's *Yi*[2] recalls the shamanistic rituals that accompanied burials near his childhood home, but 'does not relate to the death of any one person'. Intense orchestral passages represent 'the weeping and wailing by everyone present – a part of the ritual'. The Chinese lute, the pipa, was in his mind but here he fuses Chinese traditions with elements of flamenco. The music has been described as 'flamenco meets Stravinsky in the Hard Rock Café', which leaves out only the Chinese element that pervades the whole of this astonishing fabric of strange sounds and fluctuating emotions. It's perhaps the most remarkable work yet written for guitar and orchestra. No superlative would be excessive in describing Sharon Isbin's performances in this vivid recording. Her work on behalf of the guitar's present and future remains unparalleled, a continuation of that of Segovia and Julian Bream, supported by skill, musicality and seemingly boundless energy.

Sergey Taneyev · Russian 1856-1915

At the Moscow Conservatory Taneyev studied with Nikolay Rubinstein (piano) and Tchaikovsky (composition), whose friend he became, giving the Moscow première of Tchaikovsky's Piano Concerto no.1 (1875) and succeeding him as teacher at the conservatory (1878). He eventually became director (1885-9) though it was as a teacher that he had the greater influence (his pupils included Skryabin, Rakhmaninov and Glier). An eclectic and conservative at heart, he was early drawn to the music of Bach and the Renaissance contrapuntists; these studies, allied to his diligence in formal planning, gave him a compositional skill unsurpassed by his Russian contemporaries. His most successful works are the large-scale instrumental pieces, particularly the fluent sonata structures, as in the C minor Symphony (1898) and the First String Quintet (1901), his craftsmanship and contrapuntalism lend uncommon precision and polish to the musical argument. But his unoriginality and rejection of the indigenous Russian tradition resulted in conventional melodies and wooden musical characterisation, for example in his ambitious opera The Oresteia (1887-94). Apart from the important chamber works (11 string quartets, three quintets), Taneyev wrote choruses and many songs (some in Esperanto); his last work, the cantata At the Reading of a Psalm (1915), was acclaimed and considered by some his masterpiece. He wrote books on counterpoint and on canon.

GROVEmusic

Symphonies

Symphonies – No 2 in B flat minor; No 4 in C minor,

Op 12
Russian State Symphony Orchestra / Valeri Polyansky
Chandos CHAN9998 (75' · DDD)　　　　　Ⓕ

Polyansky provides a splendidly passionate and invigorating introduction to music that we really should know better in the West. The Fourth Symphony has always been the most popular of Taneyev's symphonies, and with good reason. He writes a powerful opening *Allegro* and a well-built finale, but for all his symphonic skills here, it's in the middle two movements that the most personal music is to be found. The *scherzo* dances along with the vitality that many a Russian composer has brought to comparable movements, and with the rhythmic quirks that he liked so much; but it's in the *Adagio* that something more is discovered. Taneyev has routinely been reproached for lacking melodic distinction, sometimes with reason, but this superb movement comes close to the manner of Bruckner, or sometimes Mahler. For English ears, the sense of 'stately sorrow' serves as a reminder that the phrase was coined of his own music by Elgar.

Conductor and players make of this fine music a tragic statement, and it's here that they're at their most intense. Polyansky also produces a strong case for the Second Symphony, his sense of structure holding the rather oddly organised opening movement together, as a powerful chorale passage has to be integrated with a sonata *Allegro*. He doesn't play down the suggestions of Dvořák, whom Taneyev clearly found sympathetic. This is a striking, and very well-recorded, pair of performances, well worth the attention of lovers of Russian music.

Giuseppe Tartini · Italian 1692-1770

After abandoning plans for a monastic career Tartini studied in Assisi (probably with Cernohorsk‡) and by 1714 had joined the orchestra at Ancona. He later spent time in Venice and Padua, where he settled in 1721 as principal violinist at the basilica of S Antonio. He worked there until 1765 except for a period in Prague (1723-6). Besides performing with success, he founded in 1727-8 a 'school' of violin instruction; his many pupils included JG Graun, Nardini and Naumann.

Tartini was one of the foremost Italian instrumental composers, writing over 400 works: these include violin concertos and sonatas (many with virtuoso solo parts), trio sonatas and sonatas for string ensemble. Most have three movements, ordered slow-fast-fast (sonatas) or fast-slow-fast (concertos). His later works in particular approach Classical structures and display galant features, including regular four-bar melodic phrases. Elaborate cadence formulae are especially characteristic. He also composed some sacred music. Noteworthy among his writings are a work on violin playing and ornamentation, Traité des agréments de la musique – published only in 1771 but thought to have been written earlier (L Mozart, in 1756, is thought to have borrowed from it, but it may be the other way round) – and two treatises on the acoustical foundations of harmony (1754, 1767), in which his discovery of the Difference tone phenomenon is discussed.

GROVEmusic

Violin Concertos

Violin Concertos – D, D15; G, D78; B flat, D123; G, D80; A minor, D115
Gordan Nikolitch vn **Auvergne Orchestra / Arie van Beek**
Olympia OCD475 (76' · DDD)   Ⓜ

The Auvergne Orchestra isn't a period instrument ensemble but it demonstrates a lively and playful rapport with late Baroque music. The performances are full of vitality and caprice. Nikolitch is a sensitive player who's constantly aware of the underlying poetry in Tartini's music, above all in slow movements. In these Tartini sometimes appended poetic mottoes, often in secret code, mainly drawn from Tasso and Metastasio. These established the mood of the movement in question and, more and more, became the focal point of the work. Sometimes, too, Tartini would provide a concerto with an alternative slow movement, one of which he might regard as definitive. One such instance is included in this programme (in the G major Concerto, D80) where, happily, Nikolitch gives us both slow movements. The dance-like character of many of the outer movements is an attractive feature of Tartini's concertos. Bright and clear recorded sound.

Violin Concertos – C, D4ª; E minor, D56ᵇ;   Ⓟ
F, D63ᶜ; G, D75ᵈ
ᵃᵈ**Federico Guglielmo,** ᶜ**Carlo Lazari** vns **L'Arte dell'Arco /** ᵇ**Giovanni Guglielmo** vn
Dynamic CDS220 (64' · DDD)   Ⓕ

The works in this fourth volume of Tartini's violin concertos all supposedly belong to the composer's earliest period, the years between *c*1720 and 1735. One of them, in E minor, has long been popular with soloists and has often been recorded. The remaining three, however, are less familiar and, it's claimed, here make their first appearance on disc. The C major piece sounds as if it might be the earliest concerto here, though many of the distinctive hallmarks of Tartini's style are firmly in place – little chromaticisms and short-lived, playful melodic patterns in the outer movements, and wistfully lyrical solo cantilenas in the tenderly expressive slow one. The author of the accompanying note erroneously claims the tonal plan is more imaginative than in Vivaldi's concertos. Tartini simply avails himself of a more advanced pool of stylistic knowledge, in no sense improving on the art of his forebears – especially Vivaldi.

An enjoyable programme with engaging solo

contributions from Guglielmo. Listeners will notice the acid quality of the *tutti* playing, and a recorded sound that does little to ameliorate it, though they will quickly adjust to both.

Violin Sonatas

Tartini Violin Sonata in G minor, 'Devil's Trill' (arr Kreisler) Corelli Violin Sonata in D minor, 'La Folia', Op 5 No 12 (arr Kreisler) Nardini Sonata (arr Flesch) Vitali Chaconne (arr David)
Ida Haendel vn **Geoffrey Parsons** pf
Testament SBT1258 (59' · ADD) Recorded 1970s.
From HMV ASD3352.   ⒻⓄ

This is a genuinely great fiddle record, one to place alongside those in which Heifetz, Szigeti or Elman (to name but three) tackle similar repertoire. Indeed, if it's possible to make this music sound so beautiful, why does the 'historic performing' lobby kick up so much noisy opposition? One understands all the counter-arguments; and, yes, these are arrangements – which is different. But to take just one small example, at around 2'02" into the opening *Adagio* of Nardini's Sonata, Haendel suddenly dips from *mezzo-forte* to *piano*, as if she's switching from a serene smile to a questioning glance. The effect is both subtle and dramatic. Corelli's *La Folia* and Tartini's *The Devil's Trill* Sonata are similarly expressive. As for Vitali's *Chaconne*, Haendel admits that she was knocked out when she heard Heifetz play the piece and in some ways her impassioned performance resembles Heifetz's interpretatively spectacular 1950 recording (of Respighi's arrangement; Haendel plays David's more comprehensive alternative). Always there's that ecstatic control of melodic line, holding fast to the harmonic thread – musically, patiently and with the touch of a true craftsman. The recording is superb, and the partnership with Geoffrey Parsons is beautifully balanced. A truly wonderful CD.

Violin Sonatas – G minor, 'Devil's Trill', B:g5;   Ⓟ
A minor, B:a3. Variations on a Gavotte by Corelli, B:F11 – excerpts. Pastorale in A, B:A16 (all arr Manze)
Andrew Manze vn
Harmonia Mundi HMU90 7213 (69' · DDD)   ⒻⓄ

The romantic connotations of Tartini's Violin Sonata in G minor, the *Devil's Trill*, deriving from the composer's account of an appearance by the devil in a dream, have contributed towards making it one of the great *morceaux favoris* of the 19th and 20th centuries. Furthermore, it's just about the only remaining piece of Baroque music where a piano accompaniment can still be countenanced without raised eyebrows. Some traditions die hard. But Tartini never intended anything of the kind; in fact, he probably never envisaged a keyboard continuo part at all, since none of his surviving autographs contains a figured bass for keyboard realisation. Most include unfigured bass parts, though these were often provided as an afterthought, for reasons of convention. Andrew Manze sees this as a justification for playing all the pieces in his programme without bass accompaniment. On the whole the experiment works well, since the expressive content and structural power of the music lies foremost in Tartini's melodic line. There are moments, however, where harmonic support from the bass is required, and at such times, above all in the *Devil's Trill* Sonata, Manze has had to introduce chords in the violin part to compensate for the absence of a cello. His athletic technique, his musical sensibility and perhaps, too, his engaging sense of fun, ensure fascination and entertainment in equal measure. None will regret the passing of the piano in this context. A stimulating release, beautifully recorded, and rich in fantasy.

Sir John Tavener
British b1944-

Tavener studied with Berkeley and Lumsdaine at the Royal Academy of Music (1961-5). Most of his music is explicitly religious, influenced by late Stravinsky but containing strong, bold images from a variety of other sources; his biblical cantata The Whale (1966) enjoyed a vogue. An early leaning towards Catholic devotion reached a consummation in the Crucifixion meditation Ultimos ritos (1972) and the opera Thérèse (1979). In 1976 he converted to the Russian Orthodox faith, composing in a simpler, luminous style (Liturgy of St John Chrysostom for unaccompanied chorus, 1978; Protecting Veil for cello and orchestra, 1989). **GROVE**music

The Protecting Veil

Tavener The Protecting Veil. Thrinos **Britten** Solo Cello Suite No 3
Steven Isserlis vc **London Symphony Orchestra /
Gennadi Rozhdestvensky**
Virgin Classics 561849-2
(74' · DDD) Recorded 1991   Ⓜ**❍❍❍**

 First impressions of *The Protecting Veil* are of a consonant, major-key sweetness that could portend a pastoral after the style of Samuel Barber. Yet it soon becomes evident that this isn't neo-Romantic music. The religious aura of this Hymn to the Mother of God explains its style – moving between simple contemplativeness and heartfelt lament – but not the enthusiasm with which audiences have greeted it. One suspects that its most telling effect – the return of the opening idea with heightened eloquence at the end, which then dissolves into potent images of grief – is one major reason for its impact. Many listeners will also welcome Tavener's total rejection of contemporary complexity, though there's a price to pay for this in occasional passages where the musical thought grows dangerously desultory. But this performance, well recorded, is ideal in

every way, with a soloist who shapes the long, simple lines effortlessly, and a conductor who's never tempted to push the music on beyond its natural pace.

Isserlis also plays Britten's Third Suite with free expression and fine control. After the Tavener this is the music of a troubled, doubting mind, and a feeling of dramatic tension replaces his meditative ritual. As with *The Protecting Veil*, the recording is superbly natural and immediate.

Akathist of Thanksgiving

Akathist of Thanksgiving
James Bowman, Timothy Wilson *countertens*
Martin Baker *org* **Westminster Abbey Choir; BBC Singers; BBC Symphony Orchestra / Martin Neary**
Arc of Light SK64446 (78' · DDD) Recorded live 1994
Text and translation included   Ⓕ

With the success of the ecstatic *Protecting Veil* it has perhaps been easy to forget how rigorous and austere Tavener's music was only a few years previously. In 1986, his music had reached an extreme of 'inner silence'. *Eis Thanaton* was the work which broke through the barrier, moving painfully from darkness to light, but nevertheless the blaze of light of pieces such as the *Akathist* was hardly to be predicted. An *akathistos* is a long hymn used in the Orthodox rite, prescribed liturgically in the modern Russian use to be sung at Matins on the Saturday in the fifth week of Great Lent. The prototype *akathist* (others were written later) is addressed to the Mother of God and was written during the seventh century. The text Tavener sets was written strictly according to liturgical structure by Archpriest Gregory Petrov in a Siberian prison camp shortly before his death in the 1940s. The poetry is remarkable, for the quality and variety of its life-affirming imagery as much as for the fact that it was written at all in circumstances of such adversity.

The danger in setting such poetry is that the music will be correspondingly diverse and lack structure. Alhough Tavener doesn't entirely succeed in generating a real harmonic structure for the work, the score is a catalogue of riches. The dark-hued, quasi Bulgarian male-voice sections, the sparkling countertenor duets, the variety of the scoring and the deeply moving recurring 'Amin', and the unexpected quiet climax in the ninth *kontakion* sung by a solo countertenor, are all extraordinarily powerful. They are very well sung indeed on this live recording (though the tenors have trouble maintaining control when in the higher registers); in particular the trebles are beyond reproach, and the duets by Bowman and Wilson wonderfully sensitive.

Eternity's Sunrise

Eternity's Sunrise[a]. Funeral Canticle[b]. Petra: A Ritual

Dream^c. Sappho: Lyrical Fragments^d. Song of the Angel^e
^ade**Patricia Rozario**, ^d**Julia Gooding** sops
^bc**George Mosley** bar ^e**Andrew Manze** vn
Academy of Ancient Music ^bc**Chorus and Orchestra / Paul Goodwin**
Harmonia Mundi HMU90 7231 (65' · DDD). Notes, texts and translations included   Ⓕ

Once upon a time we dreamt of breaking down musical barriers, but nowadays we can happily recount how many have been broken. This particular venture reconciles genres and generations on various fronts – between father and son, religious denominations, old and new musical modes, poetry and liturgy, and old instruments newly employed. The title-piece, *Eternity's Sunrise*, was born in the wake of loss. Tavener's late father was its prompting inspiration, and Diana, Princess of Wales its dedicatee. The tonal structure is simple: earth is represented by the solo soprano, angels by hand bells and heaven by a modest instrumental ensemble. It's a deceptively simple work, and rendered especially appealing in this context by Harmonia Mundi's vivid recording. Tavener devotees will love it. The brief and warmly harmonised *Song of the Angel* for soprano and solo violin is set at a further distance but works well. *Petra: A Ritual Dream* calls on the Greek poet Giorgios Seferis to help reinvent the transcendent (represented, in terms of music, by violin harmonics). George Mosley intones the text, backed by a small chorus. Some of Tavener's word setting is fairly dramatic, and there's a folkloric slant to selected melodic lines. Tavener's *Sappho: Lyrical Fragments* (1981), the earliest work on the programme, is set for two sopranos with brief instrumental interludes between sections. Mysterious yet gripping, the *Fragments* owe something to Stravinsky (of, say, *Apollo*) whereas the last and longest piece on the disc – the *Funeral Canticle* for Tavener's father – cradles its texts between disparate styles, from plainchant to a reassuring variation on the Bach-style chorale. Could this be the son holding the father's hand, or vice versa? Whatever the unconscious subtext, *Funeral Canticle* is probably the most durable piece here.

Innocence

Innocence. The Lamb. The Tiger. The Annunciation. Hymn to the Mother of God. Hymn for the Dormition of the Mother of God. Little Requiem for Father Malachy Lynch. Song for Athene.
Patricia Rozario sop **Leigh Nixon** ten **Graham Titus** bass **Alice Neary** vc **Charles Fullbrook** bells **Martin Baker** org **Westminster Abbey Choir; English Chamber Orchestra / Martin Neary**
Sony Classical SK66613 (64' · DDD) Recorded 1994-95. Texts included   ⒻＯ

This is recommended as a single disc to convince anyone of the mastery of John Tavener. As well as the superb new work, *Innocence*, spe-cially written for Westminster Abbey – encapsulating in 25 minutes what many of his more expansive pieces have told us – we have a rich and rewarding selection of other shorter choral pieces. They include not just the established favourites like the two intense Blake settings, *The Lamb* and *The Tiger*, and the two hymns for the Mother of God – here more openly passionate than in previous recordings – but the bald and direct *Little Requiem for Father Malachy Lynch*, the sharply terraced *Annunciation* and the *Song for Athene*, all among Tavener's most beautiful and touching inspirations. The theme of *Innocents* is Innocent Victims, which prompted Tavener to compose a ritual built on texts from varied sources, Christian, Jewish, Islamic and Hindu. The result is both moving and atmospheric, with the climax introducing one element after another in rich *crescendo*, to provide a resolution very comparable to Britten's in the *War Requiem*.

Neary draws intensely committed singing from his choir, with the principal soloists, Patricia Rozario and Graham Titus, both excellent, as well as the tenor, Leigh Nixon All the performances have a warmth of expressiveness which defies any idea of ecclesiastical detachment. The discs of shorter Tavener works from both The Sixteen (Collins) and St George's Chapel Choir (Hyperion) offer excellent performances of the four shortest and best-known works, but they seem relatively cool next to Neary's, whose reading of the *Hymn to the Mother of God* is overwhelmingly powerful within its three-minute span.

The recording vividly captures Westminster Abbey's acoustic with extreme dynamics used impressively to convey space and distance.

Lamentations and Praises

Lamentations and Praises
Chanticleer; Handel and Haydn Society of Boston Ensemble / Joseph Jennings
Teldec 0927-41342-2 (69' · DDD) Notes and texts included   ⒻＯ

At a first listening, this work would seem to defy analysis. Is it a masterpiece or a self-indulgent extravaganza? It's been labelled a 'liturgical drama'. We're led through a series of powerful scenes depicting the death and resurrection of Christ. The few quiet notes of the opening theme, which reappear, transformed, at the close are a pointer to what follows, much of which is of great beauty, tenderness and drama.

You notice at once the almost constant incongruous use of an English text, sung with voices carefully groomed by a Greek *psalmista* to produce the ornaments and microtones of a non-Western tradition, normally reserved for Greek or Church Slavonic. Further unusual borrowings include the moving threefold Greek threnody with its lamenting descending scale passages for solo voices, the bass at one point reaching a softly fading, incredibly low C sharp.

In direct contrast, the chorus sings a slow rhythmic hymn of praise. The procession into Hades is dramatic and tragic. Christ's trampling down by death is portrayed by the crashing percussion with heavenly and earthly choirs uniting to proclaim 'Risen! Risen! Risen!'.

Drama, tragedy, final victory – but don't be misled: this is poles apart from the ethos of the holy Orthodox liturgy. With all its Eastern trappings, it remains one man's personal insight and interpretation. A masterpiece, or a very personal extravaganza? It's for you, the listener, to decide.

Svyati

God is With Us. Song for Athene. The Lamb. The Tiger. Magnificat and Nunc dimittis. Funeral Ikos. Two Hymns to the Mother of God. Love Bade Me Welcome. As One Who Has Slept. The Lord's Prayer. Svyati[a]
[a]**Tim Hugh** vc **St John's College Choir, Cambridge / Christopher Robinson**
Naxos 8 555256 (70' · DDD)　　　Ⓢ Ⓢ**OO**

If John Tavener's reputation were to rest solely on his unaccompanied choral music and nothing else, then his stature as one of the most striking and original composers working today would be just as high. Much of Tavener's creativity is founded on the traditions of his Orthodox faith and of Orthodox chant, and yet curiously, intentionally or unintentionally, he has also, through works such as those presented here, extended the tradition of English choral music. Through their popularity *The Lamb*, *The Tiger* and *Song for Athene* have become immovably imbedded in our choral tradition, but one need only listen to the splendid *Magnificat and Nunc dimittis*, for instance, to find a unique symbiosis of Eastern and Western traditions at work.

Many of the works presented on this CD have enjoyed wide circulation on numerous Tavener-only and compilation discs, but the performances here from the Choir of St John's College, Cambridge, under the direction of Christopher Robinson, have much to recommend them and the super-budget price makes this issue especially desirable for those seeking a survey of Tavener's choral music for the first time.

Svyati for solo cello and choir, with echoes of *The Protecting Veil*, opens a window on Tavener's more overtly Eastern/ Orthodox-inspired music. Tim Hugh's serenely beautiful account of the solo cello part is a winner from beginning to end. The recording, made in St John's College Chapel, is resplendently atmospheric.

Total Eclipse

Agraphon[a]. Total Eclipse[b]
[a]**Patricia Rozario** sop [b]**Max Jones** treb

[b]**Christopher Robson** counterten [b]**James Gilchrist** ten [b]**John Harle** sax [b]**New College Choir, Oxford; Academy of Ancient Music / Paul Goodwin**
Harmonia Mundi HMU90 7271 (62' · DDD) Texts and translations included　　　Ⓕ**OO**

Tavener's ability to arrest the listener's ear is nowhere more apparent than in the extraordinary opening pages of *Total Eclipse*. The work, Tavener tells us, is an esoteric contemplation on the word *metanoia* – meaning 'change of mind' or 'conversion' – and Tavener uses the conversion of St Paul on the road to Damascus to give the work structure and meaning. Ideally, *Total Eclipse*, premièred in 2000, needs to be experienced *in situ*: the spatial separation of instrumental groups and the space in which the work should be performed are essential components combined to create a transcendental, metaphysical experience. A high, sustained ison (drone) on strings, the rolling of multiple antiphonal timpani and the anarchic, terrifying 'alarm' calls of the solo soprano saxophone (a symbolic representation of St Paul) create a visceral effect on the listener, and the subsequent descending choral sequences on the word *Stavroménos* (Crucified) and Christ's calling of Saul are equally striking.

The recording can only hint at the spatial effects that Tavener envisaged, but it has nevertheless been exceptionally well committed to disc. Paul Goodwin and his team have no problems coping with Tavener's demands, and John Harle's stunning account of the solo saxophone part, together with Christopher Robson's and James Gilchrist's vocal contributions, make this extraordinary work a must for all Tavener fans.

Agraphon, for soprano, timpani and strings (1995), is no less extraordinary. Here Tavener chooses as his text a powerful set of verses by the Greek poet Angelos Sikelianos that were penned during the German occupation of Athens in 1941. The work places extraordinary intonational and stylistic demands upon the soprano: indeed Patricia Rozario, whose voice the work is specifically written for, spent several months in India studying and perfecting the techniques that Tavener calls for. The effort must have been worthwhile, for Rozario produces a compelling performance of exceptional intensity.

Choral Works

As One Who Has Slept. The Bridegroom. Birthday Sleep. Butterfly Dreams. The Second Cominga. Schuon Hymnen. Shûnya. Exhortation and Kohima **Polyphony / Stephen Layton** with [a]**Christopher Bowers-Broadbent** org
Hyperion CDA67475 (75' · DDD) Texts and translations included　　　Ⓕ**OOO**

 As One Who Has Slept, the earliest work here, represents Tavener's most musically ascetic period, which, by 1996 was drawing to a close. The mesmeric use of drone-like chords behind and beyond the melodic lines reassures and comforts the listener during this portrait of Christ's harrowing of hell. He soon returned to a warmer palette and a wider range of techniques. In *Birthday Sleep* and *The Bridal Chamber* (1999) hymn-like tunes still predominate, but the voices move more independently, the harmonies are richer.

The 2001 setting of Yeats's *The Second Coming* is full of skilfully realised, dramatically startling gestures, but the mood is quizzical where it should describe fear-threaded apprehension, bombastic where it should be aghast with dismay.

Finally, a group of pieces completed in 2003. In *Butterfly Dreams*, a set of miniatures, form and content are better matched. Parts of *Schuon Hymnen*, especially the writing for solo soprano (a glittering, heart-lifting performance by Amy Haworth) suggests music from 1950s sci-fi films: as with those films, it's easy to see how the effects are achieved, yet somehow the magic survives. *Exhortation and Kohima* achieves a Tudoresque splendour, while *Shûnya* adds elements of Buddhist ritual to the mix.

The Veil of the Temple

The Veil of the Temple (short version)
Patricia Rozario *sop* **Simon Wall, Nathan Vale** *tens*
Adrian Peacock, Jeremy Birchall *basses* **Temple Choir / Stephen Layton**
RCA Red Seal ⓈⒶ ② 82876 66154-2 (149' · DDD/
DSD · T/t)   Ⓕ**OO**

Ravi Shankar teases European audiences about their short attention span, condescending to limit improvisations to under an hour rather than the much longer performances expected at an Indian concert. Tavener's original conception for *The Veil of the Temple* was as an all-night vigil, lasting some seven hours. It moves through eight cycles, intensifying in structural complexity and emotional depth, each cycle reflecting the mood of the hour of the night in which it's heard, like a time-specific *rāg*.

Tavener believes that tired audiences are more likely to open up to the deepest spiritual levels of the music. Since the Renaissance Western art has been about promoting artists' individuality. Eastern art is more concerned with tapping into a collective ideal: icons are to be meditated on, not dissected.

He always intended to distil a concert version of *The Veil*, lasting around two-and-a-half hours. This handsomely presented set draws on three of the earliest performances of the complete vigil at the Temple Church in London. Even at around one-third of its full length, *The Veil*, with its rich mix of Orthodox, Indian and English devotional gestures, is a mesmerising experience, a convincing journey from dusk to dawn.

Patricia Rozario is at her heart-stoppingly beautiful best, and there are marvellous contributions from tenor soloists Simon Wall and

Nathan Vale and basses Adrian Peacock and Jeremy Birchall. As the ritual moves towards the final revelations, Stephen Layton deftly marshals the swirling chorales and increasingly elemental brass and percussion, keeping everything in sharp focus through to the closing celebratory hymn.

As the piece was devised to be seen as well as heard and, indeed, smelt – live performances incorporate lighting effects, candles and incense – and as the audience should be immersed in the experience, listening to a CD is inevitably a somewhat pale reflection of the whole. However, these recordings do a creditable job of evoking the atmosphere. For those without SACD surround-sound capability, listening on headphones is recommended to get the best impression of positioning and movements.

Akhmatova Songs

Akhmatova Songs[a]. Diódia[b]. Many Years[c].
The World[d]
[acd]**Patricia Rozario** *sop* **Vanbrugh Quartet**
(Gregory Ellis, Elizabeth Charleson *vns* Simon Aspell *va* Christopher Marwood *vc*)
Hyperion CDA67217 (63' · DDD)   Ⓕ**OO**

The centrepiece of this disc is *Diódia*, the third and latest of Tavener's string quartets. He appears to have reserved the string quartet medium almost exclusively as a vessel into which to pour the distillations of some of his largest and most important compositions. His first quartet, *The Hidden Treasure* (1989), drew material from the large-scale choral piece *The Resurrection*, and the second, *The Last Sleep of the Virgin* (1991), from the choral work *The Apocalypse*. Similarly, *Diódia* (1995) grew out of material from *The Toll Houses*, a large-scale choral work that deals with the concept of 'the posthumous states of being of the soul, where it's decided whether the soul spends a certain amount of time in hell and a certain time in heaven'. Tavener describes *Diódia* as 'liquid metaphysics', and it's wonderfully meditative and haunting music. As with all his work, it eschews traditional form, but instead unfolds as a series of episodes that alternate with each other in almost mantric fashion. The overall atmosphere is contemplative, with passages of luminous beauty, but these are interrupted at various points by more energetic, worldly episodes. A particularly haunting passage featuring a rhythmic drum figure makes several appearances and brings this extraordinary work to a close. The Vanbrugh Quartet's intense and committed performance is of the highest calibre.

The remaining items all feature music for soprano and string quartet, beautifully performed by Patricia Rozario, for whom Tavener has composed many pieces. *The World* is a movingly intense setting of an astonishing poem by Kathleen Raine, makes a welcome addition to the catalogue, as does the austerely beautiful

Akhmatova Songs, originally composed for soprano and cello, but heard here arranged for soprano and string quartet. An indispensable and thoroughly recommendable disc.

... Depart in Peace

... Depart in Peace. My Gaze Is Ever Upon You. Tears of the Angels
Patricia Rozario sop **Matthew Rooke** tambura
BT Scottish Ensemble / Clio Gould vn
Linn Records CKD085 (59' · DDD)   Ⓟ**OO**

The most immediately striking work on this disc is the meditative, extremely beautiful ... *Depart in Peace*, for soprano, violin, tambura and strings. Dedicated to the memory of Tavener's father, it's a setting of the *Nunc dimittis*, interspersed with Alliuatic antiphons. The work follows a hypnotic sequence of repeating segments – an ecstatic string sequence with soprano (the first Alliuatic antiphon); the Song of Simeon (soprano, solo violin, tambura and cellos); an exquisitely beautiful, hymn-like sequence (the second Alliuatic antiphon) and finally an ecstatic Middle-Eastern sounding chant (the third Alliuatic antiphon). As the work progresses the antiphons lengthen on each repetition – the effect, over 25 minutes, is spellbinding and stunning.

Tavener describes *My Gaze Is Ever Upon You* as 'a series of sixteen gazes, moments and ecstatic breaths, written in Trinitarian guise' for solo violin, with taped violin and string bass drone. Although less obviously immediate to the ear than ...*Depart in Peace*, it nevertheless weaves a magical spell, as does *Tears of the Angels* for solo violin and strings, which Tavener asks to be played 'at the extreme breaking point of tenderness'. All is performed with great authority, conviction and beauty, and Patricia Rozario's singing in ...*Depart in Peace* is extraordinarily fine. A beautiful disc.

John Taverner   British c1490-1545

The earliest unequivocal references to Taverner occur in 1524-5, when he was a lay clerk at the collegiate church of Tatershall. In 1526 he accepted the post of instructor of the choristers at Cardinal College (now Christ Church), Oxford, and c1530 became a lay clerk (and probably instructor of the choristers) at the parish church of St Botolph, Boston. By 1537 he had retired from full-time employment as a church musician. Although he was embroiled in an outbreak of Lutheran heresy at Cardinal College (in 1528) there is no evidence, contrary to popular opinion, that his views were seriously in conflict with Catholicism or that he ceased composing on leaving Oxford.

Most of his extant works, which include eight masses, three Magnificats, numerous motets and votive antiphons and a few consort pieces and fragmentary secular partsongs, probably date from the

1520s. The three six-voice masses use cantus firmi, sectional structure, huge spans of melisma and skilful counterpoint; of the smaller-scale masses ' Western Wynde ' is based on a secular tune and in a less expansive, more Lutheran style. Characteristic of his writing is the development of a melodic or rhythmic fragment in imitation or canon or as an ostinato figure. The Magnificats are large-scale, florid works in the English tradition, also using cantus firmi. Two of his antiphons, however, Mater Christi sanctissima and Christe Jesu, pastor bone, clearly show Josquin's influence. His four-voice In Nomine, the prototype of this English genre, is simply a transcription of the 'In nomine Domine' section of his Missa 'Gloria tibi Trinitas'.

Taverner was pre-eminent among English musicians of his day: he enriched and transformed the English florid style by drawing on its best qualities, as well as on some continental techniques, and produced simpler works of great poise and refinement.

GROVEmusic

Missa Mater Christi sanctissima

Hodie nobis caelorum Rex. Mater Christi   Ⓟ
sanctissima. Magnificat sexti toni. Nesciens mater.
Quemadmodum a 6. Missa Mater Christi sanctissima.
In nomine a 4
Fretwork (Wendy Gillespie, Richard Campbell treble viols Susanna Pell, Julia Hodgson, Richard Boothby bass viols William Hunt great bass viol) **The Sixteen / Harry Christophers**
Hyperion Helios CDH55053 (65' · DDD) Recorded 1992. Texts and translations included   Ⓑ**O**

The Sixteen offer an impressive account of Taverner's five-part *Missa Mater Christi sanctissima*, based on his votive anthem of the same name. It's a lively and vigorous work, beautifully crafted, and this performance amply matches its craftsmanship. Harry Christophers attempts no liturgical reconstruction, concentrating instead upon sheer musical quality. Three female sopranos replace the boy trebles. The music is pitched up a tone, which has the effect of adding brilliance to every climax. He demonstrates the good acoustic of St Jude's in Hampstead – an acoustic of space and definition, ideal for the interweaving of the strands of early Tudor polyphony; indeed, clarity and a sense of space are hallmarks of the recording. The supporting programme of the Christmas responsory, *Hodie*, the votive anthem *Mater Christi* and a four-part *Magnificat* is completed – unexpectedly but most delightfully – by two pieces for viols.

Missa Corona spinea

Taverner Missa Corona spinea. Audivi vocem **Byrd** Laetentur coeli. Tristitia et anxietas
London King's College Choir / David Trendell
Proudsound PROUCD149 (61' · DDD)   Ⓕ

These 28 singers from King's College London have successfully tackled an ambitious polyphonic programme: Taverner's monumental six-part *Missa Corona spinea* and a handful of motets by Byrd and Taverner, none of which is without its stern individual demands. The Mass was possibly intended for Wolsey's Cardinal College in Oxford, to which Taverner was appointed *Informator choristarum* in 1526. This may explain the abundance of exuberant writing for the high voices, sopranos here though intended for trebles by Taverner. The youthful first entry of the London students steadies itself as the music proceeds, settling into determinedly purposeful strength and flow in the abundance of almost unending melismata of the early Tudor style.

The choir have done us a service in bringing this marvellously varied music to our ears, varied through its ever-changing use of differing timbres and combinations of voices, which move imperceptibly from texture to texture.

Missa Sancti Wilhelmi

Missa Sancti Wilhelmi. Motets – O Wilhelme, pastor bone; Dum transisset Sabbatum; Ex eius tumba
The Sixteen / Harry Christophers
Hyperion Helios CDH55055 (52' · DDD) Recorded 1990 Texts and translations included   Ⓑ

The *Missa Sancti Wilhelmi* isn't one of Taverner's best known works, but there's no reason why this should be the case. Though it doesn't have the sometimes rather wild melodic beauty of the six-voice Masses, it's nevertheless an impressive work in a more modern imitative style, in keeping with its model *O Wilhelme, pastor bone*. The Sixteen perform with their customary clarity and precision, and convey enthusiasm even in the somewhat syllabic *Gloria* and *Credo* movements of the Mass, something which isn't always easy to do. While both the 'Wilhelm' works and *Dum transisset Sabbatum* are among Taverner's later works, there's no doubt at all that *Ex eius tumba* is one of the earliest. It's firmly late medieval in style, and the intricate tracery of its construction makes a thought-provoking contrast to the pieces in a more 'continental' imitative style. At 15 minutes this is a substantial composition, and one can only be surprised that it's so little known. *Dum transisset Sabbatum* is, however, the high point of the disc, and if The Sixteen do not quite attain the ecstatic heights achieved in the recording by The Tallis Scholars, neither do they fail to rise to Taverner's inspiration.

Pyotr Ill'yich Tchaikovsky
Russian 1840-1893

Tchaikovsky began piano studies at five and soon showed remarkable gifts; his childhood was also affected by an abnormal sensitivity. At 10 he was sent to the School of Jurisprudence at St Petersburg, where the family lived for some time. His parting from his mother was painful; further, she died when he was 14 – an event that may have stimulated him to compose. At 19 he took a post at the Ministry of Justice, where he remained for four years despite a long journey to western Europe and increasing involvement in music. In 1863 he entered the Conservatory, also undertaking private teaching. Three years later he moved to Moscow with a professorship of harmony at the new conservatory. Little of his music so far had pleased the conservative musical establishment or the more nationalist group, but his First Symphony had a good public reception when heard in Moscow in 1868.

Rather less successful was his first opera, The Voyevoda, given at the Bol'shoy in Moscow in 1869; Tchaikovsky later abandoned it and re-used material from it in his next, The Oprichnik. A severe critic was Balakirev, who suggested that he wrote a work on Romeo and Juliet: this was the Fantasy-Overture, several times rewritten to meet Balakirev's criticisms; Tchaikovsky's tendency to juxtapose blocks of material rather than provide organic transitions serves better in this programmatic piece than in a symphony as each theme stands for a character in the drama. Its expressive, well-defined themes and their vigorous treatment produced the first of his works in the regular repertory.

The Oprichnik won some success at St Petersburg in 1874, by when Tchaikovsky had won acclaim with his Second Symphony (which incorporates Ukrainian folktunes); he had also composed two string quartets (the first the source of the famous Andante cantabile), most of his next opera, Vakula the Smith, and of his First Piano Concerto, where contrasts of the heroic and the lyrical, between soloist and orchestra, clearly fired him. Originally intended for Nikolay Rubinstein, the head of Moscow Conservatory, who had much encouraged Tchaikovsky, it was dedicated to Hans von Bülow (who gave its première, in Boston) when Rubinstein rejected it as ill-composed and unplayable (he later recanted and became a distinguished interpreter of it). In 1875 came the carefully written Third Symphony and Swan Lake, commissioned by Moscow Opera. The next year a journey west took in Carmen in Paris, a cure at Vichy and the first complete Ring at Bayreuth; although deeply depressed when he reached home – he could not accept his homosexuality – he wrote the fantasia Francesca da Rimini and (an escape into the 18th century) the Rococo Variations for cello and orchestra. Vakula, which had won a competition, had its première that autumn. At the end of the year he was contacted by a wealthy widow, Nadezhda von Meck, who admired his music and was eager to give him financial security; they corresponded intimately for 14 years but never met.

Tchaikovsky, however, saw marriage as a possible solution to his sexual problems; and when contacted by a young woman who admired his music he offered (after first rejecting her) immediate marriage. It was a disaster: he escaped from her almost at once, in a state of nervous collapse, attempted suicide and went abroad. This was however the time of two of his greatest works, the Fourth Symphony and Eugene Onegin. The symphony embodies a 'fate' motif that recurs at various points, clarifying the structure; the first movement is one of Tchaikovsky's most individ-

ual with its hesitant, melancholy waltz-like main theme and its ingenious and appealing combination of this with the secondary ideas; there is a lyrical, intermezzo-like second movement and an ingenious third in which pizzicato strings play a main role, while the finale is impassioned if loose and melodramatic, with a folk theme pressed into service as second subject. Eugene Onegin, after Pushkin, tells of a girl's rejected approach to a man who fascinates her (the parallel with Tchaikovsky's situation is obvious) and his later remorse: the heroine Tatyana is warmly and appealingly drawn, and Onegin's hauteur is deftly conveyed too, all against a rural Russian setting which incorporates spectacular ball scenes, an ironic background to the private tragedies. The brilliant Violin Concerto also comes from the late 1870s.

The period 1878-84, however, represents a creative trough. He resigned from the conservatory and, tortured by his sexuality, could produce no music of real emotional force (the Piano Trio, written on Rubinstein's death, is a single exception). He spent some time abroad. But in 1884, stimulated by Balakirev, he produced his Manfred symphony, after Byron. He continued to travel widely, and conduct; and he was much honoured. In 1888 the Fifth Symphony, similar in plan to the Fourth (though the motto theme is heard in each movement), was finished; a note of hysteria in the finale was recognised by Tchaikovsky himself. The next three years saw the composition of two ballets, the finely characterised Sleeping Beauty and the more decorative Nutcracker, and the opera The Queen of Spades, with its ingenious atmospheric use of Rococo music (it is set in Catherine the Great's Russia) within a work of high emotional tension. Its theatrical qualities ensured its success when given at St Petersburg in late 1890. The next year Tchaikovsky visited the USA; in 1892 he heard Mahler conduct Eugene Onegin at Hamburg. In 1893 he worked on his Sixth Symphony, to a plan – the first movement was to be concerned with activity and passion; the second, love; the third, disappointment; and the finale, death. It is a profoundly pessimistic work, formally unorthodox, with the finale haunted by descending melodic ideas clothed in anguished harmonies. It was performed on October 28. He died nine days later: traditionally, and officially, of cholera, but recently verbal evidence has been put forward that he underwent a 'trial' from a court of honour from his old school regarding his sexual behaviour and it was decreed that he commit suicide. Which is true must remain uncertain.

GROVEmusic

Piano Concertos

No 1 in B flat minor; **No 2** in G, Op 44; **No 3** in E flat, Op 75

Piano Concerto No 1[a]. The Nutcracker – Suite, Op 71a (arr Economou)[b]
Martha Argerich, [b]**Nicolas Economou** pfs [a]**Berlin Philharmonic Orchestra / Claudio Abbado**
DG 449 816-2GH (53' · DDD) Recorded [b]1983, live [a]1994   Ⓕ●

Tchaikovsky's First Concerto has already appeared twice on disc from Martha Argerich in complementary performances: live and helter-skelter on Philips with Kondrashin (reviewed under Rachmaninov), studio and magisterial with Dutoit on DG. Now, finely recorded, here's a third, live recording with the BPO and Claudio Abbado surpassing even those earlier and legendary performances. Argerich has never sounded on better terms with the piano, more virtuoso yet engagingly human. Lyrical and insinuating, to a degree her performance seems to be made of the tumultuous elements themselves, of fire and ice, rain and sunshine. The Russians may claim this concerto for themselves, but even they will surely listen in disbelief, awed and – dare one say it – a trifle piqued. Listen to Argerich's *Allegro con spirito*, as the concerto gets under way, where her darting *crescendos* and *diminuendos* make the triplet rhythm speak with the rarest vitality and caprice. Her nervous reaching out towards further pianistic frays in the heart-easing second subject is pure Argerich and so are the octave storms in both the first and third movements that will have everyone, particularly her partners, tightening their seat belts. The cadenza is spun off with a hypnotic brilliance, the central *Prestissimo* from the *Andantino* becomes a true 'scherzo of fireflies', and the finale seems to dance off the page; a far cry from more emphatic Ukranian point-making and brutality.

For encores DG has reissued Argerich's 1983 performance of *The Nutcracker* where she's partnered by Nicolas Economou in his own arrangement, a marvel of scintillating pianistic prowess, imagination and finesse.

Piano Concertos[a] Nos 1-3. Violin Concerto[b]
Victoria Postnikova pf **Kyung-Wha Chung** vn [a]**Vienna Symphony Orchestra / Gennadi Rozhdestvensky;** [b]**Montreal Symphony Orchestra / Charles Dutoit**
Double Decca ② 448 107-2DF2 (142' · DDD) Recorded 1981-2   Ⓜ

Victoria Postnikova commands a handsome tone and there's no lack here of pianistic thunder. The First Concerto is revealing in the sense that dialogue between soloist and orchestra is particularly sensitive; listen, for example, to the delicately voiced woodwinds at 6'38" (in the first movement), to Postnikova's subsequent response and, most especially, to the pianist's free yet nimble handling of the second movement's treacherous *valse-prestissimo* (4'05"). As Tchaikovsky Firsts go, this is among the most searching, personal and individual available, though one can already hear a loud opposition: '*too* slow, *too* mannered, *too* indulgent, *too* soft-grained, orchestrally'.

Again, in the Second and Third Concertos Postnikova plumbs the depths. Her handling of Tchaikovsky's epic cadenzas is second to none; at times the solo writing is so massive in scale that you temporarily forget the mute presence

TCHAIKOVSKY PIANO CONCERTO NO 1 – IN BRIEF

Vladimir Horowitz; NBC SO / Arturo Toscanini
Naxos 8 110671 (74' · ADD)   Ⓢ○
Horowitz's celebrated live 1941 Carnegie Hall recording with his father-in-law Toscanini serves up a potent mix of adrenalin-fuelled vigour and jaw-dropping virtuosity.

Solomon; Philharmonia Orch / Issay Dobrowen
Testament SBT1232 (60' · ADD)   Ⓕ
A high-voltage yet nourishing reading from this incomparable British pianist. Definitely one to hear, as is Solomon's earlier 1929 recording with Harty and the Hallé (now refurbished on Naxos 8 110680).

Emil Gilels; Chicago SO / Fritz Reiner
RCA 09026 68530-2 (74' · ADD)   Ⓜ
The work with which Gilels made his belated American début in October 1955. Later that same month, RCA shrewdly took the opportunity to preserve his by turns dazzling and poetic interpretation for posterity.

Earl Wild; RPO / Anatole Fistoulari
Chesky CD13 (60' · ADD)   Ⓕ
Originally made for Reader's Digest and engineered by Decca's Kenneth Wilkinson, Earl Wild's coruscating 1962 account yields to no rival in terms of keyboard dexterity. Partnered with a terrific performance of Dohnányi's *Nursery Song* Variations.

Martha Argerich; Berlin PO / Claudio Abbado
DG 449 816-2GH (53' · DDD)   Ⓕ○
Martha Argerich's smouldering pianism silences criticism and sparks off a hugely eloquent reponse from the Berliners under Claudio Abbado.

Mikhail Pletnev; Philharmonia Orchestra / Vladimir Fedoseyev
Virgin ② 561463-2 (112' · DDD)   Ⓢ
Pletnev's imperious account represents tempting value, coming as it does with this same team's laudable survey of all of Tchaikovsky's output for piano and orchestra.

Lang Lang; Chicago SO / Daniel Barenboim
DG 474 291-2GH (59' · DDD)   Ⓕ
Lang Lang's 2003 Proms performance was a big hit with the public, so this glittering and dapper studio recording should find a wide, appreciative audience.

Nikolai Lugansky; Russian National Orchestra / Kent Nagano
Pentatone PTC5186022 (68' · DDD)   Ⓕ
Lugansky, winner of the 1994 Tchaikovsky Competition, possesses quicksilver reflexes and a dark, burnished tone. A thoughtful performance, but with a passionate edge, too.

of an orchestra. Rozhdestvensky views Tchaikovsky's orchestral architecture with a fine sense of perspective. This is *real* interpretation and presents a powerful case for a much maligned work (torso though it is). True, there's still room for critical controversy (the Second Concerto's first movement is hardly *Allegro brillante*), but Postnikova and Rozhdestvensky have so much to say about the music.

Decca also offers a poised and elegantly phrased account of the Tchaikovsky Violin Concerto, where a rather edgy-sounding Kyung-Wha Chung is offered blandly 'regular' support by the Montreal Symphony Orchestra under Dutoit. Not a world-beater by any means, but a sensible makeweight, very well recorded. As indeed is the rest of the set, although the Vienna Symphony strings will strike some as rather thin in tone. An altogether riveting reissue and a genuine bargain as well.

Tchaikovsky Piano Concerto No 1 **Mendelssohn** Piano Concerto No 1
Lang Lang pf **Chicago Symphony Orchestra / Daniel Barenboim**
DG 474 291-2 (59' · DDD)   Ⓕ

Lang Lang's performances here bear out glowing reports of his youthful brilliance and sensitivity. He's helped by sympathetic accompaniment from this high-powered orchestra under a conductor who as a soloist has been a brilliant interpreter of such showpieces. On this showing he isn't a pianist intent on breaking speed records. Though, with breathtaking virtuosity, he's totally at ease in the bravura passages of the Tchaikovsky, his tempos tend to be broader than the classic recordings of Ashkenazy and Argerich, made when they too were in their twenties.

The opening of the Tchaikovsky establishes this as a big-scale performance, strongly rhythmic and sharply accented, with high dynamic contrasts. When the music relaxes into the second subject, Lang Lang shows his preference for broadening in lyrical passages; the result sounds a little self-conscious, though he's masterly in control of freely expressive *rubato*. The tempo he chooses for the *Andantino semplice* is dangerously slow even if he's very persuasive. The central *Prestissimo* sparkles. In the finale Barenboim may have encouraged his soloist to vary the tempo rather more than usual. What matters is the conviction of the playing.

Though the dynamics are less extreme in the Mendelssohn, the close balance of the piano again establishes this as a big-scale performance. In the slow movement Lang Lang opts for a tempo markedly slower than Hough, who turns it more clearly into a 'Song Without Words'; but he tends to remind you of the main melody's closeness to a Victorian hymn. Even so, with such sparkling playing – Lang Lang erupting into a winningly joyful account of the finale – this makes a rare and attractive coupling for the distinctive account of the Tchaikovsky.

Violin Concerto in D, Op 35

Tchaikovsky Violin Concerto **Sibelius** Violin
Concerto
Kyung-Wha Chung *vn* **London Symphony
Orchestra / André Previn**
Decca The Classic Sound 425 080-2DCS (66' · ADD)
Recorded 1970   Ⓜ●

If the vital test for a recording is that a performance should establish itself as a genuine one, not
a mere studio run-through, Chung's remains a
disc where both works leap out at you for their
concentration and vitality, not just through the
soloist's weight and gravity, expressed as though
spontaneously, but through the playing of the
LSO under Previn at a vintage period.
   Chung's 1982 Montreal version of the Tchaikovsky is rather fuller-toned, with the tiny
statutory cuts restored in the finale. Yet the very
hint of vulnerability amid daring, a key element
in Chung's magnetic, volatile personality, here
adds an extra sense of spontaneity. This remains
breathtaking playing, and the central slow
movement, made to flow without a hint of sentimentality, has an extra poignancy.
   The great melodies of the first two movements of the Sibelius are given an inner heartfelt
intensity rarely matched, and with the finale
skirting danger with thrilling abandon. The
Kingsway Hall sound, full and sharply focused,
gives a sense of presence to match or outshine
today's digital recordings.

Tchaikovsky Violin Concerto **Brahms** (arr Joachim)
Hungarian Dances – No 1 in G minor; No 2 in D
minor; No 4 in B minor; No 7 in A
Sarah Chang *vn* **Jonathan Feldman** *pf* **London
Symphony Orchestra / Sir Colin Davis**
EMI 754753-2 (49' · DDD) Recorded 1992-3   Ⓕ●

The range of dynamic truthfulness conveyed in
Sarah Chang's performance, helped by a clear,
full, naturally balanced recording, brings not
just momentary delight in individual phrases
but cumulative gain, in a reading that strongly
hangs together. Not only does she play with
exceptionally pure tone, avoiding heavy coloration, but her individual artistry doesn't
demand the wayward pulling-about often found
in this work. She's enormously helped by the
fresh, bright and dramatic accompaniment of
the LSO under Sir Colin Davis. In the outer
movements she conveys wit along with the
power and poetry, and the intonation is immaculate. Brahms's *Hungarian Dances* are delectable, marked by the sort of naughty pointing of
phrase and rhythm that tickles your musical
funny-bone just as Kreisler always did. Here's a
young artist who really does live up to the claims
of the publicists.

Violin Concerto. Piano Concerto No 1
ᵃ**Christian Tetzlaff** *vn* ᵇ**Nikolai Lugansky** *pf* **Russian
National Orchestra / Kent Nagano**

TCHAIKOVSKY VIOLIN CONCERTO –
IN BRIEF

Jascha Heifetz; Chicago SO / Fritz Reiner
RCA 09026 61495-2 (64' · ADD)   Ⓜ●
A performance of outsize personality from
Heifetz and Reiner. Coupled with this same
partnership's sovereign account of the
Brahms Concerto.

**David Oistrakh; Staatskapelle Dresden /
Franz Konwitschny**
DG ② 447 427-2GOR2 (142' · ADD)   Ⓜ●●
Oistrakh at his sublimely musical and involving best in a work that stood at the centre of
his extensive concerto repertoire. DG's 1954
mono recording retains its remarkable sense
of presence.

**Leonid Kogan; Paris Conservatoire Orchestra /
Constantin Silvestri**
EMI Encore 574757-2 (69' · ADD)   Ⓢ
Yet another fabulous Russian fiddler, this
time Leonid Kogan, who plays with a muscular panache and unruffled security that rivet
the attention. Silverstri lends splendidly
feisty support.

Viktoria Mullova; Boston SO / Seiji Ozawa
Philips 464 741-2PM (66' · DDD)   Ⓜ
Mullova's début on disc caused quite a
splash on its initial release back in 1986 – and
no wonder, for she displays abundant
musicality and surmounts every technical
hurdle with ease.

Kyung Wha Chung; London SO / André Previn
Decca 425 080-2DCS (66' · ADD)   Ⓜ●
Chung's engagingly svelte and warm-hearted
account has barely aged at all. A long-
standing favourite, this, with Previn and the
LSO also on top form.

Sarah Chang; London SO / Sir Colin Davis
EMI 754753-2 (49' · DDD)   Ⓕ●
For once the hype didn't mislead: soloist
Sarah Chang was only 11 when she made this
recording, and her vibrant tone and absolute
technical security betoken a very special
talent.

Vadim Repin; Kirov Orchestra / Valery Gergiev
Philips 473 343-2PM (72' · DDD)   Ⓕ
Enterprisingly coupled with Miaskovsky's
lovely Concerto, Repin's remake of the
Tchaikovsky proves even more masterly and
engrossing than his Erato predecessor.

**Christian Tetzlaff; Russian National Orchestra /
Kent Nagano**
Pentatone PTC5186022 (68' · DDD)   Ⓕ
Tetzlaff and Nagano take a gentler, more
restained approach than is customary, but
there's no want of brilliance or brazen intensity.

Pentatone CD/SACD 🅢 PTC5186 022 (68' · DDD) Ⓕ

These are stimulating versions of two favourite concertos, which take a fresh interpretative approach. Nikolai Lugansky's conception is spacious, with pianist and conductor taking time to relish the music's puissance. The opening is broad and weighty. Then, although the first subject of the *Allegro* has a vividly Russian rhythmic character, in both the exposition and recapitulation much is made of the beauty of lyrical secondary material and the Romantic link with Tchaikovsky's *Romeo and Juliet*. The exquisitely delicate central *Andantino* is followed by a scintillating *Scherzando*. The finale bursts forth with irrepressible dash and virtuosity. When, near the close, the tempo broadens massively to make a hugely positive climax some forward impetus is lost, but Lugansky's bravura is thrilling.

Tchaikovsky's friendly opening for his Violin Concerto is shaped by Nagano in a mood of disarming simplicity, and the two main themes are invested with lyrical warmth. Tetzlaff bounces his bow with engaging lightness in the key passage (7'03") that Hanslick described as 'beating the violin black and blue', while the cadenza is played with such affectionate detail that it becomes a highlight of the work. Tetzlaff's playing throughout is polished and secure.

In both concertos the recording has the orchestra placed naturally within a warm concert hall acoustic.

Symphonies

No 1 in G minor (Winter Daydreams), Op 13 **No 2** in C minor (Little Russian), Op 17 **No 3** in D (Polish), Op 29; **No 4** in F minor, Op 36; **No 5** in E minor, Op 64; **No 6** in B minor (Pathétique), Op 74

Complete Symphonies

Symphonies Nos 1-6. Violin Concerto in D, Op 35[a]. Piano Concerto No 1 in B flat minor, Op 23de. 1812 Overture, Op 49. Capriccio italien, Op 45. Eugene Onegin – Polonaise; Waltz. Marche slave, Op 31. The Nutcracker – Suite, Op 71[a]. Romeo and Juliet Fantasy Overture. Serenade in C, Op 48. The Sleeping Beauty – Suite. Swan Lake – Suite. Variations on a Rococo Theme, Op 33[c]
[a]**Christian Ferras**, [b]**Michel Schwalbé** vns [c]**Mstislav Rostropovich** vc [d]**Sviatoslav Richter** pf **Berlin Philharmonic Orchestra**, [e]**Vienna Symphony Orchestra / Herbert von Karajan**
DG Ⓑ 463 774-2GB8 (531' · ADD/DDD) Recorded 1962-80   🅢Ⓑ🅾🅾

Karajan was unquestionably a great Tchaikovsky conductor. Yet although he recorded the last three symphonies many times, he did not turn to the first three until the end of the 1970s, and then proved an outstanding advocate. In the Mendelssohnian opening movement of the First, the tempo may be brisk, but the music's full charm is displayed and the melancholy of the Andante is touchingly caught. Again at the opening of the Little Russian (No 2), horn and bassoon capture that special Russian colouring, as they do in the engaging Andantino marziale, and the crisp articulation in the first movement allegro is bracing. The sheer refinement of the orchestral playing in the scherzos of all three symphonies is a delight, and finales have great zest with splendid bite and precision in the fugato passages and a convincing closing peroration.

The so-called *Polish* Symphony (No 3) is the least tractable of the canon, but again Karajan's apt tempos and the precision of ensemble makes the first movement a resounding success. The *Alla tedesca* brings a hint of Brahms, but the Slavic dolour of the *Andante elegiaco* is unmistakeable and its climax blooms rapturously. No doubt the reason these early symphonies sound so fresh is because the Berlin orchestra was not over-familiar with them, and clearly enjoyed playing them. The sound throughout is excellent. It gets noticeably fiercer in the Fourth Symphony, recorded a decade earlier, but is still well balanced. The first movement has a compulsive forward thrust, and the breakneck finale is viscerally thrilling. The slow movement is beautifully played but just a trifle bland. Overall, though, this is impressive and satisfying, especially the riveting close.

DG has chosen the 1965 recording of the Fifth, rather than the mid-'70s version, and they were right to do so. It's marvellously recorded (in the Jesus-Christus Kirche): the sound has all the richness and depth one could ask and the performance too is one of Karajan's very finest. There's some indulgence of the second-subject string melody of the first movement. But the slow movement is gloriously played from the horn solo onwards, and the second re-entry of the Fate theme is so dramatic that it almost makes one jump. The delightful Waltz brings the kind of elegant warmth and detail from the violins that's a BPO speciality, and the finale, while not rushed Mravinsky fashion, still carries all before it and has power and dignity at the close.

The *Pathétique* was a very special work for Karajan (as it was for the Berlin Philharmonic) and his 1964 performance is one of his greatest recordings. The reading as a whole avoids hysteria, yet the resolution of the passionate climax of the first movement sends shivers down the spine, while the finale has a comparable eloquence, and the March/*Scherzo*, with ensemble wonderfully crisp and biting, brings an almost demonic power to the coda. Again the sound is excellent, full-bodied in the strings and with plenty of sonority for the trombones.

The *String Serenade* is digital, brightly recorded in the Philharmonie in 1980, but naturally balanced. Marvellous playing. The Waltz, with a most felicitous control of *rubato*, is the highlight, and the *Elégie* is certainly ardent; and if the first movement could have been more neatly articulated, the finale has tremendous bustle and energy. As for the *concertante* works, the account of the glorious *Rococo* Variations with Rostropovich is another classic of the gramophone, even though it uses the truncated score. The First Piano Concerto is a disappointment, with Richter and Karajan failing to strike sparks as a partnership. In spite of brilliant solo playing, the first movement lacks supporting tension in the orchestra, and in the finale you can sense Richter wanting to press forward, while Karajan seems to hold back: the coda itself hangs fire in the orchestra. Similarly Ferras was not an ideal choice for the Violin Concerto. Not all will take to his somewhat febrile timbre, with its touches of near-schmaltz. But the performance as a whole works better than the Piano Concerto.

Romeo and Juliet is finely done, passionate and dramatic, if not quite so spontaneously inspired as Karajan's early VPO version for Decca, especially at the opening. But *Marche slave*, ideally paced, is very successful, sombre and exciting by turns. *Capriccio italien* and *1812* are both brilliantly played, and the triptych of ballet suites can be recommended almost without reservation, with the *Sleeping Beauty* suite memorable for some very exciting climaxes.

Even with the reservations about the two concertos, this bargain box is a fine investment, and certainly value for money. The documentation is excellent.

Symphonies Nos. 1-6
Berlin Philharmonic Orchestra / Herbert von Karajan
DG Symphony Edition ④ 429 675-2GSE4
(264' · ADD) Recorded 1975-9   Ⓜ**O**

Symphonies Nos 1-3 also available on
DG ② 459 518-2GTA2 (plus Marche slave &
Capriccio italien)   Ⓜ
Symphonies Nos 4-6 also available on
DG ② 453 088-2GTA2   Ⓜ

Those who are looking for an outstanding bargain, need go no further than this Karajan set. All six numbered symphonies are squeezed onto only four CDs, selling at mid-price. The minor snag is that Nos 2 and 5 are broken between discs. Karajan's discography reveals no fewer than seven versions of the *Pathétique* and six each of Nos 4 and 5, but the ones here, dating from 1975 and 1976, are in almost every way, both for sound and as interpretations, the finest he did, and far preferable to the more recent DG series made with the Vienna Philharmonic. Symphonies Nos 1, 2 and 3, dating from 1979 are Karajan's only recordings of those earlier works, but ones which saw him at his very finest, combining high polish with freshness and lyrical spontaneity. There are points where he's clearly preferable even to Jansons, as in the superb building of the final climax on the horn theme in the slow movement of No 1. Many will also prefer Karajan's faster speed in the first movement of No 2, where for once Jansons

takes an unusually measured, if finely pointed, view.

Though in the opening of No 4 with Karajan, the digital transfer makes the brassy motto theme a little too fierce, generally these are among the best of his 1970s recordings from Berlin, fuller and more detailed than the digital sound on his Vienna versions of Nos 4-6.

Symphonies – Nos 1-6. Manfred Symphony, Op 58. Capriccio Italien, Op 45. Serenade in C, Op 48. The Tempest, Op 18. Romeo and Juliet. Eugene Onegin – Polonaise
Bournemouth Symphony Orchestra / Andrew Litton
Virgin Classics ⑥ 561893-2 (420' · DDD) Recorded 1989-93   Ⓢ Ⓢ**OO**

Here's another of those extraordinary Virgin bargain boxes, offered at an astonishingly low price. These Tchaikovsky performances would be highly recommendable if they cost twice as much, while the recordings – realistically set back in a concert hall acoustic – are superb, full-bodied, and wide ranging and brilliant. The playing of the Bournemouth Orchestra may not always be quite as polished as, say, the Berlin Philharmonic for Karajan, but it's still very, very good indeed: ensemble is as keen as it's passionately responsive. Moreover Litton has a natural ear for Tchaikovskian detail – time and again he draws the listener to revel in those delightful orchestral touches with which Tchaikovsky embroiders his melodies.

Litton gets off to an outstanding start with Nos 1 and 2, where the atmosphere is imbued with bonhomie and high spirits; he readily disguises the structural flaws of the *Polish* Symphony with his geniality and a clever ebb and flow of tempos; in No 4 you're more aware of the slight distancing of the sound, which he matches by his spacious tempo in the first movement; the same broad approach works less well in No 5, where you need more impetus in the outer movements; but he's back on form in No 6. There the phrasing of the first movement's secondary theme is ravishing, and the climax is as powerful as the cumulative peak of the *scherzo*/march. In *Manfred* his emphasis is on its programmatic basis, with tenderly delicate splendidly dramatic moments.

The extra items are all enjoyably spontaneous, the *Capriccio italien* has visceral thrills and panache, the *String Serenade* is warmly romantic; and both *Romeo and Juliet*, matching romantic pathos with passion, and the underrated but masterly Shakespearean *Tempest* are among the highlights. Even if you have much of this repertoire already, this set remains very enticing.

Symphonies Nos 1-6. Manfred Symphony, Op 58. Romeo and Juliet – Fantasy Overture. Capriccio italien, Op 45. 1812 Overture, Op 49. Marche slave, Op 31. Francesca da Rimini, Op 32. The Storm, Op 76

Concertgebouw Orchestra / Bernard Haitink
Philips Bernard Haitink Symphony Edition ⑥
442 061-2PB6 (423' · ADD) Recorded 1961-79   Ⓜ

It's clear that Haitink is more at home with symphonic substance than with the shorter colourful showpieces. This set documents his development as a conductor (and a Tchaikovskian) – the shorter pieces were recorded 1961-72, the symphonies 1974-9. The exception is the student Tchaikovsky's overture, *The Storm*, recorded with the symphonies, whose performance is so masterful, colourful and exciting that you might think it a more mature work. As the symphonies comprise 80 per cent of the contents of this package, let's deal briefly with the rest. You might wonder if Haitink had ever heard an Italian singing an Italian song, as anything less capricious or Italian would be hard to imagine. There are moments in the feud music of *Romeo and Juliet* that suggest his resolve, and his communication of that resolve, wasn't what it was shortly to become. From eight years later, we have the brilliantly realised letter of the score in *Francesca*, the *1812* Overture and *Marche slave*.

On to the symphonies: as a symphonic cycle, it remains temperate, considered and patient, living mostly at a fair distance from the edge, with rarely a hint of exaggeration or overemphasis – sterling qualities indeed. Haitink's grand and dignified manner is immensely stirring and satisfying. Throughout the symphonies, tempos and dynamics are chosen to guarantee impeccable articulation, beauty of tone production, flawless instrumental balances and a typical awareness of the important climactic moment. The recordings of the symphonies have all been available on CD before, with the exception of *Manfred* which was long overdue for reissue. Its pastoral and orgy (third and fourth movements) encapsulate what's both most frustrating and most formidable in Haitink's Tchaikovsky. Philips's Concertgebouw engineering broke new ground with the symphonies. The *tuttis* here reproduce with a clarity and epic splendour that have rarely, if ever, been bettered.

Symphonies Nos 1-6
Russian National Orchestra / Mikhail Pletnev
DG ⑤ 449 967-2GH5 (263' · DDD)   Ⓕ

The very opening of the First Symphony's first movement, the 'Daydreams on a wintry road', is initially very dreamy at a tempo a lot slower than you might be used to. You wonder, though, if the shape of the first theme is best served by a tempo this slow. The spirit of the dance also seems loath to visit the finale: very impressive indeed is the holding back of the heavies so that *tutti* force is more evenly balanced than usual with ensuing fugal vigour, but mightn't the wind band have been persuaded to kick a little higher in the second subject?

It may be that you have to try to forget the various familiar Russian ways with these symphonies, as Pletnev seems keener to focus

attention on Tchaikovsky's other cosmopolitan, Classical self. He avoids the time-honoured unmarked dynamic and tempo adjustments that virtually all other interpreters feel to be essential props for varying repetitions and building climaxes. And his orchestra's cultured tones seem ever more fitted for the job: there's a choir-like blend and evenness of tone from top to bottom of the orchestra (brass contributions, in particular, are rounded and sonorous); and it's a very Russian-sounding 'choir' in that, time after time, your attention is caught by the colour, richness and definition of the orchestra's basses, whether bass trombone, tuba, bassoon or string basses. All this is heard to great effect in the Second Symphony's finale, lightly dispatched with relish as outsize Haydn.

In the Second Symphony's finale, ideals and actual performance come together. On other occasions though, the seriousness of intention can preclude real performance tensions. You listens with a certain detached fascination to the Fourth's first movement, admiring such things as the steady continuity rather than contrast between the two subject groups and the tamed 'fate' fanfares in the brass. But will it ever deliver? Perhaps it does in the coda, where these magnificent strings give out the last statement of the first *moderato* theme. A refusal to overstate the case again ennobles much of the Fifth Symphony, but for Pletnev, the *Pathétique*, seems to stand apart from the other symphonies, as this interpretation throws moderation to the winds. Compared with his 1991 début recording on Virgin Classics, the first movement *Allegro* is a degree more moderate, but the *Scherzo*/March is no less immoderate. Here the finale is broader tragedy with darker colourings; the strings sing with greater intensity and there's no stinting on blistering trumpet tone at the top of the climactic scale. The trumpets' *fff* outburst in the first movement's development is equally powerful, though you can now hear more of the surrounding activity. And that's a tribute to the DG recording; more open, clearer and more present than the Virgin recording, and one that perhaps conveys a greater sense of occasion.

Symphonies – selected

Symphony No 1
Oslo Philharmonic Orchestra / Mariss Jansons
Chandos CHAN8402 (44' · DDD)   Ⓕ●

Symphony No 2. Capriccio italien, Op 45
Oslo Philharmonic Orchestra / Mariss Jansons
Chandos CHAN8460 (48' · DDD) Recorded 1985 Ⓕ●

The composer gave the work the title *Winter Daydreams*, and also named the first two movements. The opening *Allegro tranquillo* he subtitled 'Dreams of a winter journey', while the *Adagio* bears the inscription 'Land of desolation, land of mists'. A *Scherzo* and finale round off a conventional four-movement symphonic structure. In the slow movement Jansons inspires a performance of expressive warmth and tenderness, while the *Scherzo* is managed with great delicacy and sensitivity. Both the opening movement and finale are invested with vigour and passion, and everywhere the orchestral playing is marvellously confident and disciplined.

Jansons also has the full measure of the Second Symphony. It's a direct performance – the first movement *allegro* is relatively steady, but never sounds too slow, because of crisp rhythmic pointing – and the second movement goes for charm and felicity of colour. The finale is properly exuberant, with the secondary theme full of character, and there's a fine surge of adrenalin at the end. The *Capriccio italien*, a holiday piece in which the composer set out to be entertaining, is also played with great flair and the hint of vulgarity in the Neapolitan tune isn't shirked. Again the closing pages produce a sudden spurt of excitement which is particularly satisfying. The recording here is just short of Chandos's finest – the massed violins could be sweeter on top, but the hall resonance is right for this music, and there's a proper feeling of spectacle.

Symphony No 4
Oslo Philharmonic Orchestra / Mariss Jansons
Chandos CHAN8361 (42' · DDD)　　　　Ⓕ**O**

A high emotional charge runs through Jansons's performance of the Fourth, yet this rarely seems to be an end in itself. There's always a balancing concern for the superb craftsmanship of Tchaikovsky's writing: the shapeliness of the phrasing; the superb orchestration, scintillating and subtle by turns; and most of all Tchaikovsky's marvellous sense of dramatic pace. Rarely has the first movement possessed such a strong sense of tragic inevitability, or the return of the 'fate' theme in the finale sounded so logical. The playing of the Oslo Philharmonic Orchestra is first rate: there are some gorgeous woodwind solos and the brass achieve a truly Tchaikovskian intensity. Recordings are excellent.

Symphonies Nos 4-6
Leningrad Philharmonic Orchestra / Evgeny Mravinsky
DG ② 419 745-2GH2 (129' · ADD) Recorded 1960
　　　　　　　　　　　　　　　　Ⓕ**OOO**

These recordings are landmarks not just of Tchaikovsky interpretation but of recorded orchestral performances in general. The Leningrad Philharmonic plays like a wild stallion only just held in check by the willpower of its master. Every smallest movement is placed with fierce pride; at any moment it may break into such a frenzied gallop that you hardly know whether to feel exhilarated or terrified. The whipping up of excitement towards the fateful outbursts in Symphony No 4 is astonishing – not just for the discipline of the

---

TCHAIKOVSKY'S SYMPHONIES NOS 4-6 – IN BRIEF

Berlin PO / Herbert von Karajan
DG ② 453 088-2GD2 (139' · ADD)　　Ⓜ**O**
Of Karajan's countless recordings of Tchaikovsky's three last symphonies, this set from the mid-1970s is probably the finest. With excellent playing by the BPO it certainly makes a safe recommendation, neither over-emotional nor cool. (His 1960s set is also available on a budget-price DG set, but it's worth going for this one at much the same price.)

Philharmonia / Vladimir Ashkenazy
Decca ② 443 844-2DF2 (136' · DDD)　　Ⓜ
Among Ashkenazy's earliest recordings as a conductor, this trilogy demonstrates his effectiveness of the podium. There's a really refreshing feeling here, with the Philharmonia playing superbly.

Leningrad PO / Kurt Sanderling (No 4),
Evgeny Mravinsky
DG mono ② 447 423-2GDO2 (133' · ADD)　　Ⓜ
Staggering performancs from the great St Petersburg orchestra. Everything is held on a very tight rein, but the passion and intensity comes through with incredible force. The *Pathétique* leaves you absolutely shattered.

Leningrad PO / Evgeny Mravinsky
DG ② 419 745-2GH2 (129' · DDD)　　Ⓕ**OOO**
🌑 Mravinsky re-recorded Nos 5 and 6 when on tour in the UK, and also set down No 4 – in stereo. It may lack the visceral thrill of the mono set but here we're talking high-intensity performances, way above the norm. These are stunning, with playing of astounding virtuosity.

London SO / Igor Markevitch
Philips ② 438 335-2PM2 (132' · DDD)　　Ⓕ
A very exciting trio from the great Igor Markevitch – No 4 is the highlight here, and like Mravinsky he doesn't overlay any emotional baggage onto the music but lets it emerge from within.

Oslo PO / Mariss Jansons
Chandos ② CHAN8361, CHAN8351, CHAN8446
(42', 43' & 44' · DDD)　　　　　　Ⓜ
The three individual Chandos CDs from Jansons's cycle are included here simply because they are so fine, and deserve to be considered in any discussion of the last three Tchaikovsky symphonies. The Fifth is earth-shattering; the other two scarcely less involving. And, given the extraordinarily high standard of sound Chandos achieved here, these are major performances – it's a shame Chandos has yet to box them up more economically.

stringendos themselves, but for the pull of psychological forces within them. Symphony No 5 is also mercilessly driven, and pre-echoes of Shostakovichian hysteria are particularly strong in the coda's knife-edge of triumph and despair. No less powerfully evoked is the stricken tragedy of the *Pathétique*. Rarely, if ever, can the prodigious rhythmical inventiveness of these scores have been so brilliantly demonstrated.

The fanatical discipline isn't something one would want to see casually emulated but it's applied in a way which sees far into the soul of the music and never violates its spirit. Strictly speaking there's no real comparison with Mariss Jansons's Chandos issues, despite the fact that Jansons had for long been Mravinsky's assistant in Leningrad. His approach is warmer, less detailed, more classical, and in its way very satisfying. Not surprisingly there are deeper perspectives in the Chandos recordings, but DG's refurbishing has been most successful, enhancing the immediacy of sound so appropriate to the lacerating intensity of the interpretations.

Symphony No 5
Oslo Philharmonic Orchestra / Mariss Jansons
Chandos CHAN8351 (43' · DDD) Recorded 1984 Ⓕ❍

With speeds which are fast but never breathless and with the most vivid recording imaginable, this is as exciting an account as we have had of this symphony. In no way does this performance suggest anything but a metropolitan orchestra, and Jansons keeps reminding one of his background in Leningrad in the great years of Mravinsky and the Philharmonic. Nowhere does the link with Mravinsky emerge more clearly than in the finale, where he adopts a tempo very nearly as hectic as Mravinsky's on his classic DG recording. In the first movement he resists any temptation to linger, preferring to press the music on, and the result sounds totally idiomatic. In the slow movement Jansons again prefers a steady tempo, but treats the second theme with delicate rubato and builds the climaxes steadily, not rushing his fences, building the final one even bigger than the first. In the finale it's striking that he follows Tchaikovsky's notated slowings rather than allowing extra *rallentandos* – the bravura of the performance finds its natural culmination.

The Oslo string ensemble is fresh, bright and superbly disciplined, while the wind soloists are generally excellent. The Chandos sound is very specific and well focused despite a warm reverberation, real-sounding and three-dimensional with more clarity in *tuttis* than the rivals.

Symphony No 5 in E minor, Op 64. Romeo and Juliet
Royal Philharmonic Orchestra / Daniele Gatti
Harmonia Mundi HMU90 7381 (66' · DDD)　　Ⓕ❍

In Daniele Gatti's performance of Tchaikovsky's Fifth the detail of the wind scoring is continually and vividly revealed, helped by

some superb playing from the RPO's soloists. Tempos are close to the composer's metronome markings, somewhat faster than usually heard. The result in the first movement is invigorating, the forward thrust carrying from beginning to end. The primary secondary theme is graceful and Romantic, rather than ardently passionate in a Slavic manner. The great climaxes of the slow movement are spacious but not viscerally overwhelming, and the powerful interruptions of the motto theme are less theatrical than usual. The Abbey Road recording is first class, full-bodied, with resplendent brass, and glowing woodwind and horns. Perhaps the massed violins lack a little weight, but the overall sonority has the necessary depth and amplitude for Tchaikovsky.

Gatti's acount of *Romeo and Juliet* is superbly characterised. It opens chillingly, then introduces the great love theme very gently, followed by the most delicate moonlight sequence. The central climax, with the reintroduction of the Friar Lawrence theme, is terrific, and the love theme blooms gloriously in a great curving sweep of violins. What more can you ask?

Symphony No 6. Marche slave, Op 31. The Seasons, Op 37b. Six morceaux composés sur un seul thème, Op 21· The Sleeping Beauty (arr Pletnev) – excerpts
Russian National Orchestra / Mikhail Pletnev pf
Virgin Classics ② 561636-2 (138' · DDD) Recorded 1989-94　　Ⓢ Ⓑ❍❍❍

Ⓖ　There's no denying that Russian orchestras bring a special intensity to Tchaikovsky, and to this Symphony in particular. But, in the past, we have had to contend with lethal, vibrato-laden brass and variable Soviet engineering. Not any more. Pianist Mikhail Pletnev formed this orchestra in 1990 from the front ranks of the major Soviet orchestras, and the result here is now regarded as a classic. The brass still retain their penetrating power, and an extraordinary richness and solemnity before the Symphony's coda; the woodwind make a very melancholy choir; and the strings possess not only the agility to cope with Pletnev's aptly death-defying speed for the third movement march, but beauty of tone for Tchaikovsky's yearning *cantabiles*. Pletnev exerts the same control over his players as he does over his fingers, to superb effect. The dynamic range is huge and comfortably reproduced with clarity, natural perspectives, a sense of instruments playing in a believable acoustic space, and a necessarily higher volume setting than usual. *Marche slave*'s final blaze of triumph, in the circumstances, seems apt.

Pletnev finds colours and depths in *The Seasons* that few others have found even intermittently. Schumann is revealed as a major influence, not only on the outward features of the style but on the whole expressive mood and manner. And as a display of pianism the whole set is outstanding, all the more so because his brilliance isn't purely egoistic. Even when he does something unmarked – like attaching the hunting fanfares of 'September' to the final unison of 'August' – he's so persuasive that you could believe that this is somehow inherent in the material. This is all exceptional playing, and the recording is ideally attuned to all its moods and colours.

Manfred Symphony, Op 58

Manfred Symphony. The Tempest, Op 18
Russian National Orchestra / Mikhail Pletnev
DG 439 891-2GH (76' · DDD) Recorded 1993　Ⓕⓞ

There are no cheap thrills in Pletnev's *Manfred*. Percussion and brass are very carefully modulated, their brilliance and power reserved quite noticeably for what Pletnev sees as the few crucial climactic passages in the outer movements. Timpani in particular provide support rather than make a show – it's the lower strings that course through Manfred's outburst in the second movement (from 5'50"), not the almost standard spurious timpani swells. It's the strong, dark woodwind, not the more usual stuttering horns, that you initially hear in the first movement's concluding *Andante con duolo* (from 13'09"). The deep satisfaction to be had from this account comes from the superlative strings, and from Pletnev's pacing which takes notice of Tchaikovsky's tempo indications, most obviously in the properly flowing third movement's pastoral, and in the successful bonding of the finale's episodic structure (the magniloquent Muti's Achilles' heel).

More eccentric is Pletnev's drop in tempo for those rising unison scales on strings at the start of the bacchanale, but it's less troubling than Toscanini's and Jansons's speeding up for those hammering chords before Astarte returns; and, mercifully, there are none of the cuts made by Toscanini. *The Tempest*, a generous coupling, brings much the same priorities and equal rewards – no more need be said, except to observe that the horns receive a better deal from the balance than in the symphony. As to the recording generally, the timpani are probably less focused than Pletnev would have wanted; in other respects, the sound does justice to the riches of his orchestra and seriousness of his intent.

Additional recommendation

Manfred Symphony
Coupled with: **Chabrier** España **Debussy** La mer **Glinka** A Life for the Tsar – Sinfonia; Polonaise; Krakowiak; Waltz **Ravel** Daphnis et Chloé – Suite No 2 **R Strauss** Till Eulenspiegels lustige Streiche **Verdi** La forza del destino – Overture
London Symphony Orchestra; various other orchestras / Markevitch
EMI/IMG Artists ② 575124-2 (153' · ADD) Recorded 1959-67　Ⓜⓞⓞ
　Markevitch's *Manfred* must be experienced. With the LSO on peak form, this is a reading that will

grip you from first to last bar in its unsentimental thrust and fresh-faced ardour. The 1963 sound is remarkably vivid. The couplings are a mixed bag – the *La mer* lacking a little magic, but the *España* has real fire in its belly.

Swan Lake, Op 20

Swan Lake
Montreal Symphony Orchestra / Charles Dutoit
Decca ② 436 212-2DH2 (154' · DDD) Recorded 1991
　　　　　　　　　　　　　　　　　　　Ⓕⓞ

No one wrote more beautiful and danceable ballet music than Tchaikovsky, and this account of *Swan Lake* is a delight throughout. This isn't only because of the quality of the music, which is here played including additions the composer made after the première, but also thanks to the richly idiomatic playing of Charles Dutoit and his Montreal orchestra in the superb and celebrated location of St Eustache's Church in that city. Maybe some conductors have made the music even more earthily Russian, but the Russian ballet tradition in Tchaikovsky's time was chiefly French and the most influential early production of this ballet, in 1895, was choreographed by the Frenchman Marius Petipa. Indeed, the symbiosis of French and Russian elements in this music (and story) is one of its great strengths, the refinement of the one being superbly allied to the vigour of the other, notably in such music as the 'Russian Dance' with its expressive violin solo. This is a profoundly romantic reading of the score, and the great set pieces such as the Waltz in Act 1 and the marvellous scene of the swans on a moonlit lake that opens Act 2 are wonderfully evocative; yet they do not overshadow the other music, which supports them as gentler hills and valleys might surround and enhance magnificent, awe-inspiring peaks, the one being indispensable to the other. You do not have to be a ballet aficionado to fall under the spell of this wonderful music, which here receives a performance that blends passion with an aristocratic refinement and is glowingly recorded.

Additional recommendation

Swan Lake
Russian State Symphony Orchestra / Yablonsky
Naxos ② 8 555873/4 (148' · DDD)　　　　　Ⓢ
　This complete *Swan Lake* is thoroughly recommendable and most enjoyable, both as a performance and as a recording. The Orchestra is obviously utterly at home, as is their excellent conductor, whose tempi can hardly be faulted. This is an obligatory bargain buy.

The Sleeping Beauty, Op 66

The Sleeping Beauty
Czecho-Slovak State Philharmonic Orchestra / Andrew Mogrelia Naxos ③ 8 550490/92 (174' · DDD) Recorded 1991　　　　Ⓢ Ⓢⓞ

Andrew Mogrelia is clearly a ballet conductor to his fingertips. His account of *The Sleeping Beauty* isn't only dramatic, when called for, but graceful and full of that affectionate warmth and detail which readily conjure up the stage imagery. Moreover, the House of Arts in Košice seems to have just the right acoustics for this work. If the sound is too brilliant the louder passages of Tchaikovsky's score can easily hector the ear; if the effect is too mellow, the result can become bland. Neither happens here – the ear is seduced throughout and Mogrelia leads the listener on from number to number with an easy spontaneity. The woodwind playing is delightful (try track 9 with its 'singing canaries' – so like Delibes in its scoring). At the end of Act 1 the Lilac Fairy's tune is given a spacious, *frisson*-creating apotheosis. The alert Introduction to Acts 2 and 3 brings crisp brass and busy strings on the one hand, arresting hunting horns on the other, and what sparkling zest there is in the strings for the following 'Blind-man's buff' sequence, while the famous Act 2 Waltz has splendid rhythmic lift. Act 3 is essentially a great extended *Divertissement*, with Tchaikovsky's imagination at full stretch through some two dozen characterful dance numbers of every balletic flavour, are all played here with fine style. Irrespective of price, this vies with Gergiev as a first choice among current recordings of the score, and you get two and a half hours of music. The value is even more remarkable when the excellent notes clearly relate the ballet's action to each of the 65 separate cues.

The Sleeping Beauty
BBC Symphony Orchestra / Gennadi Rozhdestvensky
BBC Legends/IMG Artists ② BBCL4091-2
(141' · ADD) Recorded live 1979   Ⓜ**OO**

David Brown, Tchaikovsky's eminent biographer, thought that on balance *The Sleeping Beauty* was the finest of the three great ballet scores. But as Diaghilev found to his cost when he mounted it in London in 1921, it's a very extended work and suffers from a storyline in which not a great deal happens. Performing it is as a complete orchestral work in the concert hall is probably not the best way to approach the work but, if it's to be performed in this way, Rozhdestvensky is just the man for it. In this recording he shows just how to hold together Tchaikovsky's remarkably diverse score as a symphonic entity by creating a consistent narrative momentum without ever over-driving.

The very opening is enormously dramatic and arresting, and then the petite Lilac Fairy appears in her delectably delicate orchestral apparel. Rozhdestvensky is a master of this kind of contrast. Sample the daintiness of string texture at the opening of the 'Pas de six' (track 3), the delicious piccolo and *pizzicato*s for the 'Singing canary' (track 8), so reminiscent of Delibes, followed by the sheer energy of track 9 ('Violente').

The ballet ends grandiloquently, but with great majesty, and one is left in wonder: there isn't a single number in which Tchaikovsky's imagination fails him.

Several other versions of this ballet are available on CD, including a superb set by the Russian National Orchestra under Pletnev. But Rozhdestvensky is even finer, and the BBC recording is remarkably good, with plenty of amplitude, a warm string patina, glowing woodwind and a natural concert-hall balance. Highly recommended.

The Sleeping Beauty
Russian National Orchestra / Mikhail Pletnev
DG ② 457 634-2GH2 (159' · DDD)   Ⓕ**O**

That Pletnev knows and loves this score was already obvious from his own piano arrangements of parts of it, and their recordings. And if ever proof was needed of the pianist's ability to transfer completely intact to the orchestra his own special brand of fantasy and superfine articulacy, this is it. Hardly a minute passes without your ear being enchanted by an affective gesture of the utmost precision, poise and sensitivity (all the various solos are superbly done); and significantly, the now-familiar Pletnev ideal of the tactfully and revealingly balanced *tutti* doesn't result in anticlimax, as it did in some of the symphonies.

If you need convincing, try the last 10 minutes of Act 2 – a symphonic impression of the 100-year sleep, owing not a little to Wagner in its methods and to something of the magical workings of Tchaikovsky's own sea music for *The Tempest* – and ask yourself if you've ever heard it as atmospherically shaded, the subtle glints of Tchaikovsky's wonderful orchestration as well caught, or the transition from static contemplation, through the kiss, to genuinely joyful activity as well gauged.

A very special combination of all the right choices is made as regards dynamics, tempo and differentiation of mood and, like so much else in this performance, a scene whose potential is rarely as fully realised as it is here. The DG sound is as vibrant as you could wish, with deeper perspectives and a superbly managed ambience, with the 'magical' scenes bathed in the appropriate enchanted halo, yet the textures kept clear in the active, louder sections of the score. It's a fractionally more brilliant sound than DG supplied in the symphonies (at last, the timpani are fully in focus!) and if the cellos are occasionally obviously spotlit and the violins inclined to a very slight steeliness in their upper reaches, there's no denying the expert matching of tone and body of these divided fiddles. Good to hear the formidable partnership once again firing on all cylinders.

1812 Overture, Op 49

Tchaikovsky 1812 Overture[a]. Capriccio italien,   Ⓗ

Op 45^b **Beethoven** Wellingtons Sieg, 'Die Schlacht
bei Vittoria', Op 91^c
^a**University of Minnesota Brass Band;**
^{ab}**Minneapolis Symphony Orchestra;** ^c**London
Symphony Orchestra / Antál Dorati**
Mercury Living Presence 434 360-2MM (66' · ADD)
Recorded 1955-60. Includes commentary on making
the recordings   Ⓜ**OO**

Both battle pieces incorporate cannon fire
recorded at West Point, with *Wellington's Victory* adding antiphonal muskets and *1812*, the
University of Minnesota Brass Band and the
bells of the Laura Spelman Rockefeller carillon.
In a recorded commentary on the *1812* sessions,
Deems Taylor explains how, prior to 'battle',
roads were blocked and an ambulance crew put
on standby. The actual weapons used were chosen both for their historical authenticity (period
instruments of destruction) and their sonic
impact, the latter proving formidable even
today. In fact, the crackle and thunder of *Wellington's Victory* could easily carry a DDD
endorsement; perhaps we should, for the occasion, invent a legend of Daring, Deafening and
potentially Deadly. Dorati's conducting is brisk,
incisive and dramatic. *1812* in particular suggests a rare spontaneity, with a fiery account of
the main 'conflict' and a tub-thumping peroration where bells, band, guns and orchestra conspire to produce one of the most riotous key-
clashes in gramophone history.

Capriccio italien was recorded some three years
earlier (1955, would you believe) and sounds
virtually as impressive. Again, the approach is
crisp and balletic, whereas the 1960 LSO Beethoven recording triumphs by dint of its energy
and orchestral discipline. As 'fun' CDs go, this
must be one of the best – provided you can
divorce Mercury's aural militia from the terrifying spectre of real conflict. Wilma Cozart Fine
has masterminded an astonishingly effective
refurbishment, while the documentation – both
written and recorded – is very comprehensive.

Fantasy Overtures

Hamlet, Op 67. The Tempest, Op 18. Romeo and
Juliet.
Bamberg Symphony Orchestra / José Serebrier
BIS BIS-CD1073 (62' · DDD)   Ⓕ**OO**

What a good idea to couple Tchaikovsky's three
fantasy overtures inspired by Shakespeare. José
Serebrier writes an illuminating note on the
genesis of each of the three, together with an
analysis of their structure. He notes that once
Tchaikovsky had established his concept of the
fantasy overture in the first version of *Romeo and
Juliet* in 1869 – slow introduction leading to
alternating fast and slow sections, with slow
coda – he used it again both in the *1812 Overture*
and *Hamlet. The Tempest* (1873) has similarly
contrasting sections, but begins and ends with a
gently evocative seascape, with shimmering
arpeggios from strings divided in 13 parts.

It's typical of Serebrier's performance that he
makes that effect sound so fresh and original. In
many ways, early as it is, this is stylistically the
most radical of the three overtures here, with
sharp echoes of Berlioz in some of the woodwind effects. The clarity of Serebrier's performance, both in texture and in structure, helps to
bring that out, as does a warm and analytical BIS
recording.

Hamlet, dating from much later, is treated to a
similarly fresh and dramatic reading, with Serebrier bringing out the yearningly Russian
flavour of the lovely oboe theme representing
Ophelia. He may not quite match the thrusting
power of his mentor, Stokowski, but he's not far
short, and brings out far more detail.

Serebrier is also meticulous in seeking to
observe the dynamic markings in each score.
Those in *The Tempest* are nothing if not extravagant – up to a *fortissimo* of five *f*s in the final
statement of the love theme – yet Serebrier
graduates the extremes with great care. Highly
recommended.

Hamlet, Op 67. Francesca da Rimini, Op 32   Ⓗ
New York Stadium Orchestra / Leopold Stokowski
dell'Arte CDDA9006 (43' · ADD) Recorded 1958 Ⓕ**O**

Stokowski's inspired performance of *Hamlet* is
still far, far superior to any other recorded version. *Francesca* is nearly as fine and generates
enormous tension at the sequence just before
the lovers are discovered where their passion is
encompassed in polyphonic string textures of
the greatest intensity. Then, after the dramatic
moment of their death, they're consigned to the
whirlwinds of Dante's Inferno, which rage fren-
ziedly until the riveting final climax, where the
gong isn't allowed to drown the nemesis of bold
orchestral dissonances at the last few bars.
Stokowski's reading is equally memorable for
the beguiling wind solos in the romantic middle
section – depicting the idyll of the lovers –
shaped with characteristic magic.

Hamlet is sensational. It's also even better
recorded than *Francesca*, and the sonority of the
lower strings is particularly telling at the electrifying opening, while at the big climax the
weight of the trombones and tuba is splendidly
caught. But perhaps the most spectacular
moment is the foreboding march-like sequence,
dominated by the side-drum, which is sinisterly
dramatic each time it appears: this device anticipates Shostakovich at the climax of the first
movement of the Fifth Symphony, and the
emotional character of the playing is very Russian in its fervour. The desolation of mood of the
coda is intensely moving, with a power of
melancholy to equal that at the close of the
Pathétique Symphony.

If you're wondering about the identity of the
New York Stadium Orchestra, Bert Whyte, the
brilliant engineer of this recording and also one
of the founders of the Everest label, has
affirmed that it's the New York Philharmonic
under a pseudonym. This was the pre-Bernstein

era and the ensemble isn't always immaculate, but the tremendous commitment of the playing more than compensates. It's unclear whether Bryan Crimp's remastered version is used for the CD, but certainly the sound is cleaner than originally. During the closing years of his life Stokowski said, 'When I get to Heaven I shall shake Tchaikovsky by the hand and thank him for all the wonderful music he has given us'.

Francesca da Rimini, Op 32[a]. 1812 Overture, Op 49[a]. Marche slave, Op 31[a]. Romeo and Juliet[a]. Eugene Onegin – Tatyana's Letter Scene[b]
[b]**Eilene Hannan** sop [a]**Royal Liverpool Philharmonic Orchestra;** [b]**London Philharmonic Orchestra / Sian Edwards** Classics for Pleasure 575567-2 (79' · DDD) Recorded 1989-91 Ⓢ Ⓑ ⓞⓞ

This is surely one of the finest Tchaikovsky collections in the catalogue, irrespective of price. The orchestral introduction to the Letter Scene brings a rich surge of ardour in the orchestra, revealing Sian Edwards to be a natural Tchaikovskian, while in *Romeo and Juliet* the very different introduction of the sombre Friar Lawrence theme on the woodwind against *pizzicato* strings has admirable simplicity, yet the underlying tension is unmistakable. The love theme arrives naturally and the delicacy of the 'moonlight' sequence is touchingly tender. In the thrilling development, the vibrant clash of swords is matched by the passion of the lovers, while the coda has a genuine sense of tragedy.

By contrast, *Marche slave* is joyously high spirited – no doleful Russian melancholy here – with a piquantly coloured middle section and a fast, exhilarating coda. But it's in *Francesca da Rimini* that Sian Edwards most tellingly displays her Tchaikovskian credentials. After the resonating doom-laden warning of the opening, she moves forward swiftly and fierily into the inferno whirlwinds, but Francesca's entry is portrayed with a most delectably gentle clarinet solo, and Tchaikovsky's richly scored variants on her lovely melody are beautifully played by woodwind and strings. One thinks of Beecham here, and of Stokowski in the gathering intensity of the mutual passion of Francesca and Paolo, and their discovery and murder, which are thrillingly evoked; the frantic desperation of the coda leads to a tumultuous finale cadence.

The *1812 Overture* is sheer joy: the climax is as sensational as any on record. And the fusillade of canon and carillon can't drown the sheer orchestral exuberance.

Credit must be given to Andrew Keener and Mike Clements for achieving some of the most spectacular and wide-ranging Tchaikovsky sonorities on CD – this is truly a demonstration disc, with a specially rich bass response.

Variations on a Rococo Theme, Op 33

Variations on a Rococo Theme. Nocturne No 4,

Op 19. (arr Tchaikovsky). Pezzo capriccioso, Op 62. When Jesus Christ was but a child No 5, Op 54. Was I not a little blade of grass? No 7, Op 47 (both orch Tchaikovsky). Andante cantabile, Op 11 (arr Tchaikovsky)
Raphael Wallfisch *vc* **English Chamber Orchestra / Geoffrey Simon**
Chandos CHAN8347 (48' · DDD) Recorded 1984 Ⓢ Ⓢ ⓞ

This account of the *Rococo* Variations is the one to have: it presents Tchaikovsky's variations as he wrote them, in the order he devised, and including the *allegretto moderato con anima* that the work's first interpreter, 'loathsome Fitzenhagen', so high-handedly jettisoned. (See also the review under Dvořák where Rostropovich uses the published score rather than the original version.) The first advantage is as great as the second: how necessary the brief cadenza and the *andante* that it introduces now seem, as an upbeat to the central sequence of quick variations (Fitzenhagen moved both cadenza and *andante* to the end). And the other, shorter cadenza now makes a satisfying transition from that sequence to the balancing *andante sostenuto*, from which the long-suppressed eighth variation is an obvious build-up to the coda – why, the piece has a form, after all! Raphael Wallfisch's fine performance keeps the qualifying adjective 'rococo' in mind – it isn't indulgently over-romantic – but it has warmth and beauty of tone in abundance. The shorter pieces are well worth having: the baritone voice of the cello suits the *Andante cantabile* and the Tatyana-like melody of the *Nocturne* surprisingly aptly. The sound is first-class.

Serenade in C, Op 48

Serenade in C. Souvenir de Florence, Op 70
Vienna Chamber Orchestra / Philippe Entremont
Naxos 8 550404 (65' · DDD) Recorded 1990 Ⓢ Ⓢ ⓞⓞ

This is one of the many CDs now on the market that dispel the myth once and for all that only full-price recordings contain really outstanding performances. The Naxos label is just about as 'bargain' as you can get, and here they have given us superlative performances of two of Tchaikovsky's most endearing works. The Serenade in C contains a wealth of memorable and haunting music, beautifully and inventively scored and guaranteed to bring immense pleasure and delight to those dipping their toes in to the world of classical music for the first time. Philippe Entremont and the Vienna Chamber Orchestra give a marvellously polished and finely poised performance full of warmth, affection and high spirits, and the famous second movement Waltz in particular is played with much elegance and grace. The *Souvenir de Florence*, originally written for string sextet, makes a welcome appearance here in Tchaikovsky's own arrangement for string orchestra. This is a delightfully sunny performance, full of suavity, exuberance and romantic dash, but always alert to the subtleties of Tchaikovsky's skilful, intricate part-writing. The *Adagio cantabile* is particularly notable for some extremely fine and poetic solo playing from the violin and cello principals of the VPO. The beautifully spacious recording does ample justice to the performances.

Suite No 2, Op 53

Suite No 2. The Tempest
Detroit Symphony Orchestra / Neeme Järvi
Chandos CHAN9454 (64' · DDD) Recorded 1994-5 Ⓕ

Tchaikovsky's elusive blend of instrumental precision and free-flowing thematic fantasy in the Second Suite meets its match in the Detroit/Järvi partnership: the conductor's imagination works alongside the lean, clean Detroit sound with interesting results. The strings aren't always the ideal: the lush chordings and central fugal energy of the opening movement, 'Jeu de sons', cry out for a richer, Russian tone. But the semiquaver patter is beautifully done, the lower lines clear and personable. Keen articulation and driving force go hand-in-glove as Järvi prepares for the entry of the four accordions in the virile 'Rondo-Burlesque', sweeping on to the folk-song of the central section with characteristic aplomb. It's in the Schumannesque phrases and the subtly shifting moods of the most poetic movement, 'Rêves d'enfant', that Järvi really comes into his own; the short-lived, other-worldly radiance at the heart of the movement seems more than ever like a preliminary study for the transformation scenes of *The Nutcracker*, just as the woodwind choruses look forward to that and *Sleeping Beauty*.

The magical haze surrounding Prospero's island in *The Tempest* doesn't quite come off; here it's Pletnev (reviewed above) who surprises us with the true magician's touch, but then his Russian horns, and later his trumpeter, cast their incantations more impressively. Järvi is no more successful than any other conductor in stitching together Tchaikovsky's strong impressions of the play, though a little more forward movement in the love-music might have helped.

Souvenir de Florence, Op 70

Tchaikovsky Souvenir de Florence. **Dvořák** String
Sextet in A, B80
Sarah Chang, Bernhard Hartog vns **Wolfram
Christ, Tanjia Christ** vas **Georg Faust, Olaf
Maninger** vcs
EMI 557243-2 (68' · DDD) Ⓕ**OO**

Two of the finest string sextets ever written by Slavonic composers make an excellent coupling, particularly with such a starry line-up of musicians. Sarah Chang's warmly individual artistry is superbly matched by players drawn from the Berlin Philharmonic, past and present. These are players who not only respond to each other's artistry, but do so with the most polished ensemble and a rare clarity of inner texture, not easy with a sextet.

Souvenir de Florence is given the most exuberantly joyful performance. Written just after he had left Florence, having completed his opera, *The Queen of Spades*, Tchaikovsky was prompted to compose one of his happiest works, one which for once gave him enormous pleasure. The opening movement's bouncy rhythms in compound time set the pattern, with the second subject hauntingly seductive in its winning relaxation, a magic moment here (track 1, 1'28").

The *Adagio cantabile* second movement is tenderly beautiful, with the central section sharply contrasted, while the folk-dance rhythms of the last two movements are sprung with sparkling lightness. There are now dozens of versions of this winning work in the catalogue, both for sextet and string orchestra, but none is more delectable than this.

Equally, the subtlety as well as the energy of Dvořák's Sextet is consistently brought out by Chang and her partners, with the players using a huge dynamic range down to the gentlest *pianissimo*. Here, too, it just outshines the competition.

String Quartets

No 1 in D, Op 11 **No 2** in F, Op 22 **No 3** in E flat minor, Op 30

String Quartets Nos 1-3. Quartet Movement in B flat.
Souvenir de Florence, Op 70
Yuri Yurov va **Mikhail Milman** vc **Borodin Quartet**
(Mikhail Kopelman, Andrei Abramenkov vns Dmitri
Shebalin va Valentin Berlinsky vc)
Teldec ② 4509-90422-2 (151' · DDD) Recorded 1993
Ⓕ**OOO**

Who could fail to recognise the highly characteristic urgency and thematic strength of the F major Quartet's first movement development section, or miss premonitions of later masterpieces in the Third Quartet's *Andante funèbre*? None of these works is 'late' (the last of them pre-dates the Fourth Symphony by a couple of years), yet their rigorous arguments and sweeping melodies anticipate the orchestral masterpieces of Tchaikovsky's full maturity. So why the neglect of all but the First Quartet? The most likely reason is our habitual expectation of orchestral colour in Tchaikovsky, a situation that doesn't really affect our appreciation of the early, almost Schubertian D major Quartet (the one with the *Andante cantabile* that moved Tolstoy to tears). The Second and Third Quartets are noticeably more symphonic and particularly rich in the kinds of harmonic clashes and sequences that Tchaikovsky normally gave to the orchestra. Even minor details, like the quick-fire exchanges near the beginning of No 3's *Allegretto*, instantly suggest 'woodwinds' (you can almost hear oboes, flutes and clarinets jostle in play), while both finales could quite easily have been transposed among the pages of the early symphonies. But if these and other parallels are to register with any conviction, then performers need to locate them, and that's a challenge the Borodins meet with the ease of seasoned Tchaikovskians.

They are natural and spontaneous, most noticeably in the first movement of the exuberant *Souvenir de Florence* sextet, and in that wonderful passage from the Second Quartet's first movement where the lead violin calms from agitated virtuosity to a magical recapitulation of the principal theme – an unforgettable moment, superbly paced here. Additionally we get a 15-minute B flat Quartet movement – an appealing torso imbued with the spirit of Russian folksong.

Piano Trio

Tchaikovsky Piano Trio in A minor, Op 50
Rachmaninov Trio élégiaque in G minor (1892)
Kempf Trio (Pierre Bensaid *vn* Alexander Chaushian *vc* Freddy Kempf *pf*)
BIS BIS-CD1302 (69' · DDD)   Ⓕ**OO**

Understandably, remembering its dedicatee, Nikolai Rubinstein, Tchaikovsky's Trio is dominated by the piano part, which has moments of intrepid (sometimes repetitive) rhetoric, which must ring out triumphantly yet not be allowed to usurp the work's underlying elegiac feeling. In many respects this performance carries all before it. Freddy Kempf leads with great conviction, yet can pull back whenever his colleagues are in the ascendant. The very opening is lyrically seductive, and the closing pages, with a moving reprise of the opening theme in the *Lugubre* finale, are most sensitively managed. But before that the kaleidoscopic variations of the second movement, which begins so serenely, have been presented with sparkling panache: the delightful pianistic roulades of Variation 3 and the exquisite music-box effect of Var 5 both show Kempf as delectably light-fingered, yet he finds real swagger for Var 7, and a Chopinesque rhythmic delicacy for the *Tempo di mazurka* of Var 10. And in the lovely *Andante flebile* (Var 9) violinist Pierre Bensaid and cellist Alexander Chaushian share a ravishing delicate duet.

While Tchaikovsky's Piano Trio is ambitiously epic in scale; Rachmaninov's, although obviously drawing on the inspiration of the Tchaikovsky model, with the piano still taking a leading role, is in a single movement. Its mood is tinged with melancholy throughout, surging to moments of passion less extrovert than with Tchaikovsky, but with that characteristic ebb and flow of expressive feeling captured most naturally by these players; they find a touching gentleness for the wistfully sad closing bars.

The performance comes into competition with that by the superb Borodin Trio on Chandos, whose coupling is more logical (the first *Trio élégiaque*, Op 8); but on performance grounds Kempf and his colleagues are by no means second best.

The recording is very well balanced, and the acoustic seems equally suitable for both works. Altogether this is a splendid disc.

Piano Works

Piano Sonata in G, Op 37. Dumka, Op 59. Valse in F sharp minor, Op 40 No 9. Méditation in D, Op 72 No 5. Deux Morceaux, Op 10. Valse-scherzo No 1 in A, Op 7. The Nutcracker, Op 71a – Andante maestoso (arr Pletnev)
Ayako Uehara *pf*
EMI 557719-2 (68' · DDD)   Ⓟ**OO**

Ayako Uehara isn't only the first woman to win the Tchaikovsky International Piano Competition, but also the first Japanese pianist to win one of the more widely publicised competitions. Her in her beautifully planned and enterprising selection of Tchaikovsky provides irrefutable evidence of her calibre. In Pletnev's arrangement of the *Andante maestoso* from the *Nutcracker* Suite there are some magically singing lines and a rich vein of full-blooded fantasy. The *Scherzo* from the Op 37 Sonata brims over with concentrated wit and zest. Had the composer heard these performances he might well have revised his characteristically gloomy view of his piano music as so many 'musical pancakes' quickly tossed and served. Here's a pianist who, unlike most young competition winners, is already a world-class artist. EMI's sound is immaculate.

Tchaikovsky 18 Morceaux, Op 72 **Chopin** Nocturne No 20 in C sharp minor, Op posth
Mikhail Pletnev *pf*
DG 477 5378GH (70' · DDD) Recorded live at the Tonhalle, Zurich, June 2004   Ⓕ**OOO**

 Mikhail Pletnev's persuasive 1986 recording of Tchaikovsky's *18 Morceaux* for Melodiya (nla) was unfortunately hampered by strident sound and an ill-tuned piano. Happily, a state-of-the-art situation prevails in this new live recording for Deutsche Grammophon, extending, of course, to Pletnev's own contributions. His caring, characterful and technically transcendent way with this cycle casts each piece in a three-dimensional perspective that honours the composer's letter and spirit beyond the music's 'salon' reputation, while making the most of its pianistic potential. The results are revelatory, akin to, say, Ignaz Friedman's illuminating re-creations of Mendelssohn's *Songs Without Words*.

The Fifth *Morceau*, 'Meditation', demonstrates the Pletnev-Tchaikovsky chemistry at its most sublime. The melodies are firmly projected yet flexibly arched over the bar-lines, as if emerging from different instruments, culminating in a febrile central climax that gently dissipates into some of the most ravishing trills on record. In No 8, 'Dialogue', Pletnev elevates Tchaikovsky's *quasi parlando* with the type of off-hand skill and pinpoint timing of a master actor who knows just which lines to throw away.

Note, too, the deliciously pointed scales and music-box colorations in No 13, 'Echo rustique'. Shades of Liszt's Third *Liebestraum* seep into No 14, 'Chant élégiaque', in what amounts to a masterclass in how to sustain long melodies against sweeping accompaniments. A stricter basic pulse throughout No 9, 'Un poco di Schumann', might have made the dotted rhythms and two strategically placed *ritenutos* more obviously Schumannesque, yet there's no denying the inner logic the looser treatment communicates.

There's extraordinary virtuosity behind the musical insights. For example, the interlocking octaves in the coda to No 7, 'Polacca de concert', are unleashed with Horowitz-like ferocity and not a trace of banging. The rapid, vertigo-inducing triplet runs in No 10, 'Scherzo-fantaisie', could scarcely be more even and controlled. Pletnev is all over the final, unbuttoned *trepak* in grand style, and he certainly makes the glissandos swing. A fresh, unfettered account of Chopin's C sharp minor Nocturne is offered as an encore to this urgently recommended recital.

Liturgy of St John Chrysostom, Op 41

Liturgy of St John Chrysostom. Nine Sacred Pieces. An Angel Crying
Corydon Singers / Matthew Best
Hyperion CDA66948 (75' · DDD) Texts and translations included Ⓕ⬤

Tchaikovsky's liturgical settings have never quite caught the popular imagination which has followed Rachmaninov's (his All-Night Vigil, at any rate). They are generally more inward, less concerned with the drama that marks Orthodox celebration than with the reflective centre which is another aspect. Rachmaninov can invite worship with a blaze of delight, setting 'Pridite'; Tchaikovsky approaches the mystery more quietly. Yet there's a range of emotion which emerges vividly in this admirable record of the Liturgy together with a group of the minor liturgical settings which he made at various times in his life. His ear for timbre never fails him. It's at its most appealing, perhaps, in the lovely 'Da ispravitsya' for female trio and answering choir, beautifully sung here; he can also respond to the Orthodox tradition of rapid vocalisation, as in the Liturgy's Creed and in the final 'Blagosloven grady' (in the West, the Benedictus). Anyone who still supposes that irregular, rapidly shifting rhythms were invented by Stravinsky should give an ear to his

Russian sources, in folk poetry and music but also in the music of the Church.

Matthew Best's Corydon Singers are old hands at Orthodox music, and present these beautiful settings with a keen ear for their texture and 'orchestration'. The recording was made in an (unnamed) ecclesiastical acoustic of suitable resonance, and sounds well.

The Snow Maiden

The Snow Maiden
Irina Mishura-Lekhtman *mez* **Vladimir Grishko** *ten*
Michigan University Musical Society Choral Union;
Detroit Symphony Orchestra / Neeme Järvi
Chandos CHAN9324 (79' · ADD) Recorded 1994.
Text and translation included Ⓕ

Tchaikovsky wrote his incidental music for Ostrovsky's *Snow Maiden* in 1873, and though he accepted it was not his best, he retained an affection for it and was upset when Rimsky-Korsakov came along with his full-length opera on the subject. The tale of love frustrated had its appeal for Tchaikovsky, even though he was not to make as much as Rimsky did of the failed marriage between Man and Nature. But though he did not normally interest himself much in descriptions of the natural world, there are charming pieces that any lover of Tchaikovsky's music will surely be delighted to encounter. A strong sense of a Russian folk celebration, and of the interaction of the natural and supernatural worlds, also comes through, especially in the earlier part of the work. There's a delightful dance and chorus for the birds, and a powerful monologue for Winter; Vladimir Grishko, placed further back, sounds magical.

Natalia Erassova (for Chistiakov's recording on CdM) gets round the rapid enunciation of Lel's second song without much difficulty, but doesn't quite bring the character to life; Mishura-Lekhtman has a brighter sparkle. Chistiakov's Shrove Tuesday procession goes at a much steadier pace than Järvi's, and is thus the more celebratory and ritual where the other is a straightforward piece of merriment. Both performances have much to recommend them, and it isn't by a great deal that Järvi's is preferable. Chandos provides transliteration and an English translation.

Additional recommendation

Arias from The Enchantress, Eugene Onegin, The Maid of Orleans, Mazeppa and Queen of Spades
Varady *sop* **Evangelatos** *mez*

Munich Radio Orchestra / Kofman
Orfeo C540011A (78' · DDD) Ⓕ
Varady is truly a phenomenon; recording in her 59th year she shows no signs of age and brings to these arias her innate gift for going to the heart of the matter.

TCHAIKOVSKY'S EUGENE ONEGIN – IN BRIEF

Dmitri Hvorostovsky *Eugene Onegin*
Nuccia Focile *Tatyana* **Neil Schicoff** *Lensky*
St Petersburg Chamber Choir; Orchestre de
Paris / Semyon Bychkov
Philips ② 438 235-2PH2 (141' · DDD) ⓕO

A fleetfooted, vividly conducted performance
with two highly convincing stars in Dmitri
Hvorostovsky's warm-voiced Onegin and
Nuccia Focile's Tatyana, fresh and youthful.
Neil Schicoff's plangent Lensky heads a fine
supporting cast, and the recording is excellent.

Bernd Weikl *Eugene Onegin* **Teresa Kubiak**
Tatyana **Stuart Burrows** *Lensky*
John Alldis Choir; Orchestra of the Royal
Opera House / Sir Georg Solti
Decca ② 417 413-2DH2 (143' · ADD) ⓕ

A polished old warhorse, conducted by Solti
with superlative warmth, and international
principals. The theatrical energy is there but,
despite orchestral gloss and some superb
singing, especially Stuart Burrows's Lensky,
it never quite attains the idiomatic feeling of
more Slavic versions.

(In English) **Thomas Hampson** *Eugene Onegin*
Kiri Te Kanawa *Tatyana* **Neil Rosenshein** *Lensky*
WNO Chorus and Orchestra / Sir Charles
Mackerras
Chandos ② CHAN3042 (142' · DDD) ⓕ

This English-language recording is not the
best, but with Thomas Hampson's strong
Onegin and Mackerras's propulsive, atmospheric conducting it's still enjoyable; and for
non-Russian listeners the English does make
this intimate drama much more immediate.

Panteleimon Nortsov *Eugene Onegin* **Yelena
Kruglikova** *Tatyana* **Ivan Kozlovsky** *Lensky*
Bolshoi Theatre Chorus and Orchestra /
Alexander Orlov
Naxos ② 8 110216/7 (136' · AAD) ⓢO

The first Bolshoi version of 1937, in early but
reasonable sound and still fascinating, particularly for its principals, Nortsov's resonant
Onegin, Kruglikova's sensitive, touching
Tatyana, and the great Ivan Koslovsky's
plangent Lensky.

Bernd Weikl *Eugene Onegin* **Teresa Kubiak**
Tatyana **Stuart Burrows** *Lensky*
John Alldis Choir; Orchestra of the Royal
Opera House / Sir Georg Solti
Decca 🟡 071 124-9DH (117') ⓕ

Enterprising director Petr Weigl has created
this cinematic version, using, as he often does,
actors miming to a recording, in this case
Solti's (see above). It looks marvellous, with
lustrous production values; but chunks are cut,
especially half the opening scene, and though
the actors convince, the lip-sync may not.

Iolanta, Op 69

Iolanta
Galina Gorchakova *sop* Iolanta **Gegam Grigorian**
ten Vaudémont **Dmitri Hvorostovsky** *bar* Robert
Sergei Alexashkin *bass* King René **Nikolai Putilin**
bar Ibn-Hakia **Larissa Diadkova** *mez* Martha **Nikolai
Gassiev** *ten* Alméric **Tatiana Kravtsova** *sop* Brigitta
Olga Korzhenskaya *mez* Laura **Gennadi
Bezzubenkov** *bar* Bertrand Chorus and Orchestra
of the Kirov Opera, St Petersburg / Valery Gergiev
Philips ② 442 796-2PH2 (96' · DDD) Recorded 1994.
Notes, text and translation included ⓕ

Iolanta, the touching little princess, blind and
virginal, into whose darkness and isolation there
eventually shines the 'bright angel' of Duke
Robert, is delightfully sung by Galina Gorchakova. There's a freshness and sense of vulnerability here, especially in the opening scenes
with Martha in the garden as she sings wistfully
of something that appears to be lacking in her
life: the *Arioso* is done charmingly and without
sentimentality. Gegam Grigorian sometimes
sounds pinched and under strain, even in the
Romance. He's also overshadowed by Hvorostovsky who's at his best here: warm and with a
somewhat dusky tone. The King, Provence's
'bon roi René', is benignly if a little throatily
sung by Sergei Alexashkin, and he has at hand a
sturdy-voiced Ibn-Hakia in Nikolai Putilin.
Valery Gergiev conducts a sensitive performance, responding constructively to the unusual
scoring, and not overplaying the more demonstrative elements in a score that gains most
through some understatement.

The Queen of Spades, Op 68

The Queen of Spades
Gegam Grigorian *ten* Herman **Maria Gulegina** *sop*
Lisa **Irina Arkhipova** *mez* Countess **Nikolai Putilin**
bar Count Tomsky **Vladimir Chernov** *bar* Prince
Yeletsky **Olga Borodina** *mez* Pauline **Vladimir
Solodovnikov** *ten* Chekalinsky **Sergei Alexashkin**
bass Surin **Evgeni Boitsov** *ten* Chaplitsky **Nikolai
Gassiev** *ten* Major-domo **Gennadi Bezzubenkov**
bass Narumov **Ludmila Filatova** *mez* Governess
Tatiana Filimonova *sop* Masha Kirov Theatre
Chorus and Orchestra / Valery Gergiev
Philips ③ 438 141-2PH3 (166' · DDD) Recorded 1992.
Notes, text and translation included ⓕO

There are major problems with all the current
sets of *The Queen of Spades*, but Valery Gergiev,
one of the outstanding Tchaikovskians of the
day, here coaxes from a thoroughly Western-
sounding Kirov Theatre Orchestra what's
surely the most refined account of the score yet
recorded, and one that's never lacking energy or
full-blooded attack. His isn't so much a compromise approach as one which stresses fatalism
and underlying sadness. The recording was
made in the Kirov Theatre itself, and there's
admittedly some constriction to the orchestral
sound picture; but for many the atmosphere of a

real stage-venue will be a plus, and the all-important balance between voices and orchestra is just right. If the spine still fails to tingle as often as it should, that's mainly a reflection of the respectable but unexciting singing.

Alexander Tcherepnin
USSR/French/American 1899-1977

An American composer of Russian origin, Tcherepnin's father Nikolay Nikolayevich (1873-1945) was a pupil of Rimsky-Korsakov who wrote ballets for Dyagilev (Le pavillon d'Armide, 1908) and settled in Paris in 1921. Alexander completed his studies there and became associated with Martinu and Beck, experimenting with new scales in a Franco-Russian neo-classical style (including one sometimes known by his name: C-D flat-E flat-E-F-G-A flat-A-B-C). In 1934-7 he travelled in the Far East, which brought about additions to his range of materials. In 1950 he settled in the USA. His large output, spirited in style and cosmopolitan in manner, includes ballets, four symphonies (1927-57), six piano concertos (1919-65), chamber and keyboard music.
GROVEmusic

Narcisse et Echo, Op 40

Narcisse et Echo
The Hague Chamber Choir; The Hague Residentie Orchestra / Gennadi Rozhdestvensky
Chandos CHAN9670 (53' · DDD)   Ⓕ **O**

Tcherepnin's *Narcisse et Echo* was one of the first of Diaghilev's Paris ballets, produced in 1911 and hence anticipating Ravel's *Daphnis et Chloé* by a year. Tcherepnin's ear is a match for Ravel's in orchestral subtlety, and his skill in scoring for his large orchestra decorates the ballet with some ravishing sounds. The work was reproached at the time for being static, which it could hardly help being when Narcissus spends the last quarter of an hour gazing adoringly at his reflection in a pool. Not even Nijinsky could do much with that, even with Tcherepnin's most sensuous music twining itself lovingly around him. There's also a dance for Narcissus with the hapless Echo, and some set pieces for a group of Boeotians. Neither of these generates much musical exhilaration, nor, despite a flurry of rhythmic complexity, does the arrival of a troop of depressingly sober Bacchantes. Tcherepnin gives them all lovely sounds, but there's nothing of Ravel's intoxicating energy, let alone his exquisite melodic invention. But as aural sensation it's captivating, especially when played as beautifully as it is here.

Georg Philipp Telemann
German 1681-1767

Telemann was one of the most prolific composers ever. At 10 he could play four instruments and had

written arias, motets and instrumental works. His parents discouraged musical studies, but he gravitated back to them. At Leipzig University he founded a collegium musicum; at 21 he became musical director of the Leipzig Opera at 23 he took on a post as church organist. The next year he moved to Žáry, as court Kapellmeister, where he wrote French-style dance suites, sometimes tinged by local Polish and Moravian folk music, and cantatas. In 1708 he went in the same capacity to the Eisenach court and in 1712 to Frankfurt as city music director. As Kapellmeister of a church there, he wrote at least five cantata cycles and works for civic occasions, while his duties as director of a collegium musicum drew from him instrumental works and oratorios.

He was offered various other positions, but moved only in 1721, when he was invited to Hamburg as director of music at the five main churches and Kantor at the Johanneum. Here he had to write two cantatas each Sunday, with extra ones for special church and civic occasions, as well as an annual Passion, oratorio and serenata. In his spare time he directed a collegium musicum and wrote for the opera house; the city councillors waived their objections to the latter when he indicated that he would otherwise accept an invitation to Leipzig. He directed the Hamburg Opera from 1722 until its closure in 1738. In 1737 he paid a visit to Paris, appearing at court and the Concert Spirituel. From 1740 he devoted more time to musical theory, but from 1755 he turned to the oratorio. He published much of his music, notably a set of 72 cantatas and the three sets of Musique de table (1733), his best-known works, each including a concerto, a suite and several chamber pieces. He was eager to foster the spread of music and active in publishing several didactic works, for example on figured bass and ornamentation. He was by far the most famous composer in Germany; in a contemporary dictionary he is assigned four times as much space as J. S. Bach.

Telemann composed in all the forms and styles current in his day; he wrote Italian-style concertos and sonatas, French-style overture-suites and quartets, German fugues, cantatas, Passions and songs. Some of his chamber works, for example the quartets in the Musique de table, are in a conversational, dialogue-like manner that is lucid in texture and elegant in diction. Whatever style he used, Telemann's music is easily recognisable as his own, with its clear periodic structure, its clarity and its ready fluency. Though four years senior to Bach and Handel, he used an idiom more forward-looking than theirs and in several genres can be seen as a forerunner of the Classical style.
GROVEmusic

Flute Concertos

Concerto for Flute, Strings and Continuo in D, TWV51:D2. Concerto for Flute, Strings and Continuo in G, TWV51:G2. Concerto for 2 Flutes, Violone, Strings and Continuo in A minor, TWV53:A1[a]. Concerto for Flute, Violin, Cello, Strings and Continuo in A, TWV53:A2. Concerto for Flute, Oboe d'amore, Viola d'amore, Strings and Continuo in E, TWV53:E1
Emmanuel Pahud, [a]**Jacques Zoon** fls **Berlin Baroque Soloists** (Wolfram Christ vad Georg Faust

vc Klaus Stoll *violone* Albrecht Mayer *obd)* / **Rainer Kussmaul** *vn*
EMI 557397-2 (66' · DDD)   Ⓕ●

You'll rarely hear such personality in a Baroque-concerto soloist as the extraordinary Emmanuel Pahud exhibits here. Berlin Baroque Soloists acclimatise effortlessly to an 18th-century palette, and distinguished colleagues they make for Pahud. The flautist sets out his stall from the *Andante* of the succinct G major concerto (completed from a damaged source and therefore making its recording début) whose startling resemblance to the slow movement of Bach's F minor Concerto, BWV1056, seems to inspire Pahud to a lyricism of understated elegance which one often hears in the best performances of the Bach work. Indeed, it's his sensitivity to Telemann's gestural implications and ability to colour the music at every turn which makes Pahud's playing so enchanting in all five concertos.

Telemann performance on a modern flute will inevitably lead to some recoiling, but one never feels deprived of the gentle and beguiling articulation of a 'period' instrument or its capacity for soft dynamic and purity of sound. One only has to hear the lithe performance of the A major Triple Concerto, from Part 1 of Telemann's famous banquet publication of 1733, *Tafelmusik*, where character abounds through Pahud's concern with first principles. Joyous exchange and textural delights abound in the Triple Concerto in E major, where Wolfram Christ's viola d'amore and Albrecht Mayer's oboe d'amore combine with the flautist in a ravishingly blended montage. The Flute Concerto in D confirms everything about Pahud's exquisite taste and mesmerising sound. A real winner.

Horn Concertos

Concerto for Three Horns, Violin and Orchestra   Ⓟ
in D major. Overture-Suites – C, TWV55:C5, 'La bouffonne'; F, TWV55:F11, 'Alster Echo'. Concerto in G, 'Grillen-Symphonie'
Anthony Halstead, Christian Rutherford, Raul Diaz hns **Collegium Musicum 90 / Simon Standage** *vn*
Chandos Chaconne CHAN0547 (70' · DDD)
Recorded 1993   Ⓕ●

This release shows Telemann at his most irrepressibly good-humoured and imaginative. There's a concerto for three rattling horns and a solo violin (a splendid sound, with the horns recorded at what seems like the ideal distance), and an elegant suite for strings which sounds like Handel, Bach and a few French composers all thrown in together. More striking, though, is the most substantial piece on the disc, the *Alster Echo* Overture-Suite, a nine-movement work for strings, oboes and horns full of tricks and surprises occasioned by a host of representative titles. Thus 'Hamburg Carillons' brings us horns imitating bells, 'Concerto of Frogs and Crows' has some mischievously scrunchy wrong

notes, and in 'Alster Echo' there's a complex network of echoes between oboes and horns. But the show-stealer is the *Grillen-Symphonie* ('Cricket Symphony'). This is a work for the gloriously silly scoring of piccolo, alto chalumeau, oboe, violins, viola, and two double basses, a somewhat Stravinskian combination that you're unlikely to encounter every day. But it's not just the instrumentation that's irresistibly odd. There's a slow movement with curious, melancholy woodwind interventions a little reminiscent of *Harold in Italy*, and a finale which is quite a hoot.

String Concertos

Concerto for 4 Violins and Strings in A, TWV54:A1. Ⓟ Concertos for 4 Violins without Continuo – in G, TWV40:201; in D, TWV40:202; in C, TWV40:203. Violin Concerto in A, 'Die Relinge', TWV51:A4. Sinfonia Spirituosa in D, TWV44:1. Symphony in D, TWVAnh50:1. Overture in D, TWV55:D6[a]
[a]**Jaap ter Linden** va da gamba **Musica Antiqua Köln / Reinhard Goebel** *vn*
Archiv Produktion 471 492-2AH (74' · DDD)   Ⓕ

With works and performances of such bristling vitality and colour, no excuses need be made for Telemann. The programme begins with the emphatically dynamic *Sinfonia spirituosa*, more often heard with its ad lib trumpet part but arguably better off without it; the second movement (which looks a slight entity on paper) is shaped with all the poise and elegance of Goebel at his most cultivated. So, too, the Overture in D, where the opening *saccadé* ('jerked') rhythms receive an arrow-like precision of ensemble, although *concertante* cellist Jaap ter Linden – returning to his alma mater for a guest appearance – appears perhaps slightly less comfortable than one might have imagined.

Between such opulent generosity, Goebel interleaves three 'concertos' for four solo violins, *sui generis* pieces providing transparent delicacies of the sort Telemann offers in his 12 Fantasias for solo violin. They are life-loving vignettes, interchanging poignant twists with sparkling extroversion. Even less conventional, and just as innovative, is the Concerto in A, *Die Relinge*, a work which explores a testingly high tessitura for a 'violine principale' above three further violin parts, viola and continuo. The final minuet manages to keep everyone happy. This is where Telemann could not be in better hands. Goebel and his thrusting virtuoso band have the measure of almost everything that this mercurial composer throws at them. A vitally conceived new release, especially for those who think Telemann is a poor man's Bach.

Overture-Suites

Overture-Suite in A minor[a]. Concerto in E minor Ⓟ for Recorder and Flute[b]. Viola Concerto No 1 in G[c].
Ouverture des nations anciennes et modernes for

Strings and Continuo, TWV55
[b]**Franz Verster** fl **Paul Doctor** va [a]**South-West German Chamber Orchestra / Friedrich Tilegant;**
[b]**Amsterdam Chamber Orchestra / André Rieu;**
[c]**Concerto Amsterdam / Frans Brüggen** rec
Apex 0927-40843-2 (69' · ADD) Recorded 1967-8

Ⓢ Ⓢ🅾🅾

Four performances of the highest calibre, marvellously recorded in the 1960s and now sounding as fresh as the day they were made. Two of them feature the distinguished recorder player Frans Brüggen. He's at his inimitable finest, and this is very fine indeed, in the masterly Suite in A minor for recorder and strings (every bit as fine a work as the Bach B minor Suite for the same instrumentation) and the E minor Concerto for recorder, transverse flute and strings with its attractive interplay of solo texture. Here he's joined by Franz Verster. Brüggen then moves to the conductor's podium to direct the Concerto Amsterdam, joined by a superb viola player, Paul Doctor, in the famous G major Viola Concerto. The *Ouverture des nations anciennes et modernes* is another suite, full of the composer's most felicitous invention. The music is played with great character and the CD transfer is exemplary.

La Bizarre
Overture-Suites – in B flat, 'Les Nations', TWV55: Ⓟ B5; in D, TWV55: D18; in G, 'La Bizarre', TWV55: G2. Violin Concerto in A, 'Les Rainettes', TWV51: A2[a]
[a]**Midori Seiler** vn **Akademie für Alte Musik, Berlin**
Harmonia Mundi HMC90 1744 (71' · DDD) Ⓕ🅾

More entrancing Telemann suites. Here we have *La Bizarre*, rather excitedly named after some textural oddities in the overture; a trumpet suite with no title but including an amusing depiction of a postillion; and *Les Nations*, a whizz through the national characteristics by turns of the Turks (coarse and direct), the Swiss (calm and dignified), the Muscovites (represented by their church bells) and the Portuguese (exuberant dancing). This is music of unremitting good humour, with plenty of jokes for musicians and listeners alike, in which the ideas never stop flowing and the craftsmanship never falters. The Berlin Academy of Early Music could have been made for these works. All it takes to bring them off, after all, is to play with Tiggerish energy, virtuoso precision of ensemble and a huge smile in your heart, and this they do with a group spirit that's all the more remarkable for the fact that they operate without a director. True, they may lack some of the clarity and grace shown by Collegium Musicum 90 under Simon Standage in their account of *Les Nations* on Chandos, but their strength of commitment more than compensates. The result is a joy from start to finish.

Overture-Suites – G minor, TWV55:g4; A minor, Ⓟ
TWV55:a2; C, TWV55:C6; D, TWV55:D15; D minor,
TWV55:d3; F minor, TWV55:f1

Vienna Concentus Musicus / Nikolaus Harnoncourt
Warners Ultima @ 0927-41403-2 (148' · ADD)
Recorded 1978

Ⓢ Ⓑ🅾

Harnoncourt is nowhere more at home than in the aesthetic world of this music. The Overtures of the ravishing G minor Suite and the bolder C major work show him to be a master of noble gesture and purposeful articulation. There's a robust, biting energy about Harnoncourt which is infectious; often, as in the Bourée *en trompette* of the C major work, one imagines that the exaggerated contrasts and deliberate accentuations would appear mannered if executed by anyone other than Harnoncourt. Throughout, he conjures up subtle rhythmic deviations, each paragraph flexibly shaped but still controlled and naturally breathed. If pliancy of this kind is an answer to making sense of Baroque phrasing, then texture speaks volumes too: Telemann's oboe writing in particular, and its place within a string body, is exceptionally skilled; his scoring of three oboes is especially effective and the oboists play with irresistible *esprit*. The D major Suite is full of instances where their performances brim with personality, contributing greatly to that fruity and ever so musty nose which characterises Concentus Musicus on vintage form. The recorded sound is full of presence. With Harnoncourt one can imagine few exponents better suited to this colourful repertoire. This release is full of many unique delights.

Overture-Suite in G, 'Burlesque de Don Quichotte',
TWV55:G10. Overture-Suite in D minor, WV55:d3.
Overture-Suite in E flat, 'La Lyra', TWV55: Es3
Northern Chamber Orchestra / Nicholas Ward
Naxos 8 554019 (57' · DDD) Ⓢ

Overture-Suite in G, 'Burlesque de Don Quichotte',
TWV55:G10. Overture-Suite in B minor, TWV55:h1.
Concerto for Two Violins, Bassoon and Strings in D.
Overture-Suite in G
Collegium Musicum 90 / Simon Standage
Chandos Chaconne CHAN0700 (66' · DDD) Ⓕ

Telemann is never more irresistible than when he's in light-hearted pictorial mode, and both these new releases feature one of the most entertainingly evocative of all his overture-suites for strings, the *Burlesque de Quixote*. Taking episodes from the Cervantes novel as its inspiration, it provides us with a memorable sequence of cameos, from the deluded Don tilting at windmills and sighing with love, to Sancho Panza tossed high in a blanket, to portrayals of the pair's respective steeds. Telemann achieves all this with such humour and descriptive precision that, when you hear it, you'll surely laugh in delighted recognition. What a good film composer he would have been!

Both performances strike an appropriate tongue-in-cheek attitude. Northern Chamber Orchestra show good style and a pleasingly light and clear texture, unclouded by excessive vibrato or over-egged string tone. Only at the bass end does the sound occasionally become a little thick, but this is really quibbling when what we actually have is a good demonstration of how to perform Baroque music on modern strings. It still makes quite a contrast with Collegium Musicum 90, however, whose period instruments, recorded more intimately, sound slighter and sparkier. Having already recorded so much of Telemann's music, they sound more at home and have that extra ounce of freedom to enjoy themselves.

The couplings of the Chandos disc are more interesting. For all that the NCO offer another attractive string suite, *La Lyra*, containing a typically realistic and beguiling hurdy-gurdy impersonation, the D major Overture isn't especially memorable; CM90 have found more colourful stuff in the strikingly French-accented G major Overture and a thoroughly charming Concerto for two violins, bassoon and strings. A pair of bassoons also makes a delightful appearance in the second Minuet of the Overture in B minor.

Musique de Table / Tafelmusik

Tafelmusik, Part 1 – Overture: Suite in E minor;
Quartet in G; Trio in E flat; Conclusion in E minor;
Part 2 – Quartet in D minor
Florilegium (Ashley Solomon, Andrew Crawford *fls*
Walter van Hauwe *rec* Alexandra Bellamy *ob* Kati
Debretzeni, Rodolfo Richter *vns* Jane Rogers *va*
Jennifer Morsches *vc* Robert Nairn *db* David Miller
lte James Johnstone *hpd*)
Channel Classics CCS19198 (75' · DDD)   ⒻO
Also available on SACD CCSSA19002

No dogma here from Florilegium. They have jettisoned authoritarian 'authenticity' and taken responsibility for considering options – which is what interpretation is about. So, no double dotting in the introduction of the French-style *Overture*. It's played as written, but not stolidly, because crisp attack is allied to a flowing but pliant treatment of the basic pulse. This is a pointer to how these artists recreate music that doesn't contain many pointers to how it might be recreated.

Florilegium don't put a foot wrong in their decisions about tempo, articulation, phrasing and dynamics. Nor do they ignore that elusive quality called content. Try the *Loure* (track 4) where, through the appropriate weighting of accents and evocative shaping of lines, the melancholia also woven into this slow jig is captured. Rhythms are shaped too, by slight changes in the stressing of note patterns. This way, a seemingly unvaried design (as in the first movement of the D minor Quartet), reveals different facets to its makeup.

Intelligent thinking also comes from another period instrument group, the Orchestra of the Golden Age (reviewed here). As yet, they lack the ultimate in technical refinement; but their recordings offer spaciousness and perspective

that's only discerned on the current release if the volume is cut to curb a ridiculously high output level that coarsens tone and flattens the image. Musically, though, an outstanding disc.

Musique de Table, 'Tafelmusik', Part 3 – Concerto for
Two Horns and Strings in E flat; Overture in B flat;
Quartet in E minor; Sonata for Oboe and Continuo
in G minor; Trio in D; Conclusion in B flat
Orchestra of the Golden Age
Naxos 8 553732 (73' · DDD)   Ⓢ

The Orchestra of the Golden Age bring expressive warmth to this evergreen repertoire. The present disc contains the third of the three 'Productions' that make up Telemann's most comprehensive orchestral/instrumental publication. It's the shortest of the three and so can be accommodated comfortably on a single disc. Like its predecessors, the Third consists of an orchestral Suite, Quartet, Concerto, Trio, Sonata for melody instrument with figured bass and an orchestral 'Conclusion'. Telemann had already generously provided for transverse flute, trumpet and solo violins in the previous 'Productions' while maintaining the flute profile (Quartet and Trio) in the third anthology; he gives pride of place to oboe(s) in the Suite, Sonata and Conclusion, and a pair of horns in the Concerto.

One might feel that a slightly augmented string section would have been justified for the orchestral suites and concertos. But, in this instance the players realise the innate nobility of the French overture character with a justly 'occasional' tempo. In the Concerto, which comes over well, if perhaps a shade rigidly in its rhythm, the horn players Roger Montgomery and Gavin Edwards sustain an evenly balanced and tonally secure partnership. That also goes for the lightly articulated flute partnership of Edwina Smith and Felicity Bryson in the Trio. The lovely G minor Oboe Sonata is played with warmth and expressive intimacy by Heather Foxwell. Telemann brings all to a vigorous close with a little three-section orchestral coda, marked *Furioso*. This is a set which makes rather more of Telemann's inflective *délicatesse* than others at twice or even three times the price.

Chamber Works

Sonates Corellisantes – No 1 in F, TWV42:F2.   Ⓟ
Paris Quartets, 'Nouveaux quatuors en Six Suites' –
No 6 in E minor, TWV43:e4. Essercizii Musici – Trio
No 8 in B flat, TWV42:B4. Quartets – A minor,
TWV43:a3; G minor, TWV43:g4
Florilegium Ensemble
Channel Classics CCS5093 (53' · DDD) Recorded
1992   ⒻOO

The rarity here is the *Sonata Corellisante* for two violins and continuo in which Telemann pays tribute to Corelli. The remaining works are the sixth and perhaps finest of the 1738 *Nouveaux*

Quatuors or *Paris Quartets* as they have become known, a little *Quartet* (or *Quadro*) in G minor, a B flat Trio from the *Essercizii Musici* collection (*c*1739) and a fine Concerto da camera (Quartet) in A minor, very much along the lines of Vivaldi's pieces of the same kind in which each instrument other than the continuo has an obbligato role. The finest work is the *Paris Quartet*, which consists of a Prelude, a sequence of dance-orientated movements and an elegiac Chaconne that lingers long in the memory. The performance is full of vitality and probes beneath the music's superficialities. Throughout the programme there's an intensity and a youthful spontaneity about this playing which has considerable appeal.

Paris Quartets, Volume 2 **P**
Quartets – in D, TWV43: D3; in A minor, TWV43: a2; in G, TWV43: G4. Six Concerts and Six Suites – Suite No 1 in G, TWV42: G4
Florilegium (Ashley Solomon *fl* Kati Debretzini *vn* Reiko Ichise *bvio*
Jennifer Morsches *vc* James Johnstone *hpd*)
Channel Classics CD/SACD 🎵 CCSSA20604 (71' · DDD)   Ⓕ

Printed in Paris by Le Clerc without Telemann's permission in 1736 but composed in Hamburg in 1730, the first six of these quartets called 'Quadri' were such a success that the composer himself was able to have printed – through a 'Privilege du Roi' – another six, the *Nouveaux quatours en suites*, in 1738. That set, too, had originated in the German city but also went down a treat with the Parisians.

Both groups are written for flute, violin, viola da gamba (with an alternative part for cello) and basso continuo, and comprise the composer's total output for this set of instruments. But confusingly, he divided 'Quadri' into pairs titled concertos, sonatas and suites; and in Concerto Primo, Florilegium use the cello while sticking with the gamba for the remaining pieces.

As before, James Johnstone is the right sort of continuo player, an inventive and expressive presence, not an intrusion. His colleagues are of a similar persuasion and their responses to both the robustness and delicacy of the music is exemplified in the first movement ('Allègrement') of the A minor quartet and second movement ('Légèrement') of the G major quartet. These interpretations are of very high calibre, though a selection from Trio Sonnerie (Virgin Classics, nla) is also valuable, and worth seeking out.

On CD playback, the image is on the close side and the lines are a little crowded; a reduction in volume helps separate them and convey more clearly the nuances in the playing.

Kleine Cammer-Music – Partita No 2 in G, **P**
TWV41: G2. Essercizii Musici – Solo No 5 in B flat, TWV41: B6; Solo No 11 in E minor, TWV41: e6; Trio No 12 in E flat, TWV42: Es3. Der getreue Music-

Meister – Sonata in A minor, TWV41: a3. Der Harmonische Gottesdienst – No 26, Am Sonntage Jubilate in C minor, TWV1: 356[a]; No 31, Am ersten Pfingstfeiertage in G, TWV1: 1732[a]
Paul Goodwin *ob* **Nigel North** *lte/theorbo* Susan Sheppard, [a]Lynden Cranham *vcs* John Toll *hpd*
Harmonia Mundi HMU90 7152 (65' · DDD)   Ⓕⵔ

Paul Goodwin is surely one of the finest Baroque oboists of the moment, so when he turns his mind to such a master of agreeable and skilfully composed chamber music as Telemann, it must be worth our while listening in. Every piece has its own character and charms: here's a seven-movement Partita from the *Kleine Cammer-Music* of 1716, then a couple of Solos and a quirky Trio involving an obbligato harpsichord from the *Essercizii Musici* of 1739, while a Lesson from the giant 1720s part-work, *Der getreue Music-Meister*, sits alongside movements with oboe obbligato from the slightly earlier sacred cantata collection *Der harmonische Gottesdienst*. The variety of form and nomenclature is more than matched on this disc by that of accompaniments which, as so many of the best continuo teams do these days, make an indispensable creative contribution to the success of the performance as a whole.

With the boisterous and inspired Romanesca pair of Nigel North and John Toll on board this is no surprise. A cello also takes the original vocal line in the cantata movements. As for Goodwin himself, his playing is bold and bright with solid, versatile technique and fluid phrasing, and his interpretations are detailed and intelligent while losing nothing in spontaneity. The recorded sound for all instruments is perhaps rather aggressive over the space of an hour's listening, but then these are performances which by their very refusal to be timid demand full attention from the listener.

Trio Sonatas – F, TWV42: F10; G minor, TWV42: g7. **P**
Quartets – C, TWV43: C2; B minor, TWV43: b3; G, TWV43: G12
Limoges Baroque Ensemble (Maria-Tecla Andreotti *fl* Sergio Azzolini *bn* Gilles Colliard *vn* Vittorio Ghielmi *va da gamba* Bruno Cocset *vc/violone* Willem Jansen *hpd*) / **Christophe Coin** *va da gamba*
Auvidis Astrée E8632 (56' · DDD)   Ⓕⵔⵔ

This discerningly assembled programme of chamber music with viola da gamba shows off the composer in some of his finest and most varied colours. Each piece is of sustained musical interest and expressive charm. Christophe Coin, who plays viola da gamba and directs the ensemble, is one of the most interesting minds at work in this period, and his performances are full of rhythmic energy, expressive fervour and technical expertise. Coin has always been keen to highlight Telemann's sensibility towards colour and texture, a feature that becomes strikingly apparent in the Quartet in B minor. It's scored for flute, viola da gamba, bassoon and continuo and, like its companion in C major, conforms with an Italian *concerto a quattro*. The two slow movements of the B minor work are enormously expressive, the one tinged with melancholy, the other more conventionally lyrical. More startling than either of these, though, is the exotic finale with its central European folk-dance rhythmic inflexions, so beloved by the composer.

The remaining pieces are all delightful, especially the Quartet in G major, scored for flute, two violas da gamba and harpsichord. Why is the companion piece always ignored? It's on a comparable inspirational level.

This is a first-rate release and one of the most invigorating discs of Telemann's chamber music available. The recorded sound is outstanding.

---

12 Fantaisies for Violin without Continuo, TWV40: **P** 14-25. Der getreue Music-Meister – 'Gulliver' Suite in D, TWV40:108
Andrew Manze, Caroline Balding vns
Harmonia Mundi HMU90 7137 (78' · DDD) Recorded 1994 Ⓕ

Andrew Manze brings a very distinctive angle to the 12 *Fantaisies*. We have learnt to take virtuosity for granted with Manze – his remarkable feats allow the most prejudiced to forget that he's playing a Baroque fiddle. But without such an instrument he could barely create such a biting astringency in the more self-effacing and tortured moments (*Fantaisie* No 6) or a cultivated assurance and definition in articulation to the recognisably regular sections, such as *Fantaisie* No 10, where Telemann is working in established forms – particularly in the latter works in the set where dance forms predominate. If characterisation is the key, Manze is arguably more persuasive than any of his rivals. He grows through phrases in the Gigue of the Fourth *Fantaisie* in a fashion which gives the work a peculiarly stoical strength, purrs through the contrapuntally conceived *Fantaisies* with nonchalant disdain for their extreme technical demands and leaves sighs and pauses hanging with supreme eloquence. With sheer lucidity, imagination and colour, he most acutely captures the sense of a famous public figure ensconced in a private world against the backdrop of a musical world in a state of flux. To add spice to an already outstanding release, we have the short and delightful *Gulliver* Suite for two violins.

---

12 Sonate metodiche **P**
Barthold Kuijken fl **Wieland Kuijken** va da gamba
Robert Kohnen hpd
Accent ② ACC94104/5D (140' · DDD) Recorded 1994 Ⓕ**OO**

No, the title is hardly an incentive to part with your pocket-money. But with Telemann we should know better than to be taken in by such packaging details. These are, in fact, 12 skilfully written and entertaining sonatas, published in two sets of six and issued in 1728 and 1732. Telemann seems, right from the start, to have had two instruments in mind: flute or violin, and though Barthold Kuijken has elected to them play all on a Baroque flute, he does so with such technical mastery that there's little cause for regret. He savours the many playful ideas contained in the faster movements and realises a touching sense of melancholy in several of the slow ones. Among the most impressive of the sonatas is that in B minor, which Kuijken plays with sensitivity and technical panache. The interpretation is on a sufficiently elevated level to warrant unqualified praise. The recorded sound is first rate.

Die Donner-Ode, TWV6:3

Der Herr ist König, TWV8:6. Die Donner-Ode, **P** TWV6:3
Ann Monoyios, Barbara Schlick sops **Axel Köhler** counterten **Wilfried Jochens** ten **Harry van der Kamp, Hans-Georg Wimmer, Stephan Schreckenberger** basses **Rheinische Kantorei; Das Kleine Konzert / Hermann Max**
Capriccio 10 556 (65' · DDD) Recorded 1990-92. Texts and translations included Ⓕ

The *Donner-Ode* was one of Telemann's biggest public successes during his lifetime and is a striking piece in its own right, a vivid reaction to the Lisbon earthquake of 1755. The shock caused to the international community by this dreadful event (in which some 60,000 people were killed) was enormous, and in Hamburg a special day of penitence was the occasion for this 'Thunder Ode', though it does perhaps suggest a rather smug satisfaction that such a disaster didn't befall northern Germany. 'The voice of God makes the proud mountains collapse', the text proclaims, 'Give thanks to Him in His temple!' The music, too, both in its mood and in that extraordinarily up-to-date style of Telemann's later years, frequently conjures the benign, entertainingly song-like pictorial mood of a Haydn Mass or oratorio. Entertaining is the word, though, especially in this energetic performance under Hermann Max. He's fleet-footed and buoyantly athletic, benefiting from what's becoming his customary excellent team of German soloists.

For the coupling Max chooses another German work, the cheerful cantata *Der Herr ist König*, written much earlier in the composer's life and more Bach-like in character and form (though it's worth pointing out that since it survives partly in Bach's hand, we ought perhaps to conclude that Telemann was the one wielding the influence here). As in the *Ode*, choir, soloists and orchestra are bright, tight-knit and well recorded, making this release an enjoyable one.

Die Hirten an der Krippe zu Bethlehem

Die Hirten an der Krippe zu Bethlehem, **P**

*TWV1:797. Siehe, ich verkündige Euch, TWV1:1334.
Der Herr hat offenbaret, TWV1:262
Constanze Backes sop **Mechthild Georg** contr
Andreas Post ten **Klaus Mertens** bass **Michaelstein
Chamber Choir; Telemann Chamber Orchestra /
Ludger Rémy**
CPO CPO999 419-2 (65' · DDD) Texts and
translations included ⒻＯ

The tenderly expressive and ingenuous character of German Protestant Christmas music of
the Baroque seldom fails to exert its magic.
Though the greatest achievements in this tradition greatly diminished after Bach, there were
exceptions. One of them is Telemann's intimate
and imaginative oratorio *Die Hirten an der
Krippe zu Bethlehem* ('The Shepherds at the Crib
in Bethlehem'). The text is by the Berlin poet,
Ramler and though Ramler's taste for classical
forms sometimes makes his work stiff and austere, nothing could be further removed from
this than his intimate account and celebration of
Christ's birth. Certainly, it touched a chord in
Telemann, who responded with music of
expressive warmth and irresistible charm.
   This isn't at all the world of Bach's *Christmas
Oratorio*. Indeed, it's only approximately a sixth
of the length of Bach's masterpiece. Telemann's
concept is one rather of noble simplicity, a
sought-after goal in post-Bach church music
which, in this respect, at least, provided a perfect foil to Ramler's text. Every reader will
recognise the melody of the opening number as
belonging to the Latin carol *In dulci jubilo*. Telemann's harmonisation of the 16th-century tune
sets the scene concisely and intimately. Thereafter, follows one delight after another. Of outstanding beauty are the 'Shepherd's Song' and
the bass aria, 'Hirten aus den goldnen Zeiten'.
This is an extremely pleasurable, well-filled,
disc with a pervasive charm. The remaining two
items are both Christmas cantatas, of 1761 and
1762 respectively, and contain music of enormous appeal. Performances are excellent, with
outstanding singing by Klaus Mertens and
Mechthild Georg. Both choir and orchestra rise
to the occasion under the sensitive and stylish
direction of Ludger Rémy. Three hitherto
unrecorded pieces in performances of such
vitality make this a very strong issue.

Cantatas

Lobet den Herrn, alle seine Heerscharen, TWV1:061.
Wer nur den lieben Gott lässt walten, TWV1:593. Der
Tod ist verschlungen in den Sieg, TWV1:320
Dorothee Fries sop **Mechthild Georg** contr
Andreas Post ten **Albert Pöhl** bass **Friedemann
Immer Trumpet Consort** (Friedemann Immer, Klaus
Osterloh, Ute Hübner tpts Stefan Gawlik timp) **Bach
Collegium Vocale, Siegen; Hanover Hofkapelle /
Ulrich Stötzel**
Hänssler Classic CD98 179 (56' · DDD) Texts and
translations included Ⓕ

While Telemann's concertos, suites, instru-

mental chamber music and oratorios have been
well explored by performers, his large-scale
cantatas, comparatively speaking, have not. Part
of the problem is that there's a truly daunting
number of them. And, it need hardly be said, the
quality is variable. But few are utterly devoid of
inspiration and the three pieces contained in
this programme rise well beyond that category.
Until now they have remained very possibly
unperformed, but certainly unrecorded. These
aren't domestic pieces of the kind which characterise his well-known Hamburg anthology, *Der
harmonische Gottes-dienst*, but generously, sometimes colourfully orchestrated works with choruses, recitatives, arias and chorales. The
format, in short, is Bach-like, though with nothing remotely comparable to the great opening
choral fantasies of which Bach was the master.
Telemann usually treats his hymn melodies
simply, this approach lending them a distinctive, ingenuous charm.
   The three cantatas offer strong contrasts of
colour and of mood. The New Year piece, *Lobet
den Herrn* has glittering trumpet parts with timpani and Telemann's deployment of them is
deft and effective. The Neumeister setting, on
the other hand, with an orchestra confined to
strings and woodwind, is quietly spoken and
more reflective. Performances are stylish, and
the director, Ulrich Stötzel, has a lively feeling
for Telemann's frequent use of dance rhythms.
The soloists are expressive, notably Mechthild
Georg, who offers a lyrical account of her aria
with oboe in the Easter cantata, *Der Tod ist verschlungen in den Sieg*. In short, this is a release
which should interest and delight all readers
with a taste for the music of this imaginative,
prolific and seemingly indefatigable composer,
whose fecundity too often prompts generalisations that are as unwelcome as they're unjustified.

Orpheus

Orpheus
Roman Trekel bar Orpheus **Ruth Ziesak** sop Eurydice
Dorothea Röschmann sop Orasia **Werner Güra** ten
Eurimedes **Maria Cristina Kiehr** sop Ismene **Hanno
Müller-Brachmann** bar Pluto **Isabelle Poulenard** sop
Cephisa, Priestess **Axel Köhler** counterten Ascalax
**RIAS Chamber Choir, Berlin; Academy for Ancient
Music, Berlin / René Jacobs**
Harmonia Mundi ② HMC90 1618/9 (159' · DDD)
Notes, text and translation included ⒻＯ

This is the first performance on disc of an opera
that was recognised as being the product of
Telemann's pen only some 20 years ago. The
original libretto was by a Frenchman, Michel du
Boullay. Telemann seems to have adapted the
text to suit Hamburg taste, but though the
libretto has survived virtually complete, a small
part of the score is lost. For the edition used
here, Peter Huth – who has also contributed a
useful essay – Jakob Peters-Messer and René
Jacobs have filled the lacunae with music from

other Telemann sources. Telemann's *Orpheus* has an additional dimension to the standard version of the legend in the person of Orasia, widowed Queen of Thrace. She occupies a key position in the drama, first as murderess of Eurydice of whose love for Orpheus she's jealous, then of Orpheus himself, since he, understandably, rejects her advances. The plot develops effectively, contributing greatly to the dramatic coherence and overall satisfaction provided by text and music alike. In common with a great many operas for the Hamburg stage, *Orpheus* contains arias sung in languages other than the German vernacular. Italian was the usual alternative, but here there are airs in French, too, and Telemann, on these occasions, lends emphasis to the 'mixed style' aesthetic, in which he was an ardent believer, by retaining the distinctive stylistic character of each country. But the German arias are often both the most interesting and the most varied, since it's the Lied and the *arioso*, as developed in the Passion-Oratorio settings, that provide those additional ingredients which vitalise, refresh and give distinction to his music.

The cast is first-rate. Dorothea Röschmann projects a passionate and temperamental Orasia for whom Telemann has provided several strongly characterised arias. Orpheus is sung by Roman Trekel, Eurydice by Ruth Ziesak. Telemann adorns both roles with an affecting blend of lyricism and pathos. Eurydice's part in the drama is, perforce, relatively small but her music is often alluring and nowhere more so, perhaps, than when she welcomes the shades, who gather to prevent an opportunity for the lovers to look upon one another during the rescue scene. There are some forward-looking harmonies here which foreshadow later developments in opera. Orpheus's music is, appropriately, captivating more often than not; and it's strikingly varied in character.

The other major beneficiary of Telemann's musical largesse is Orpheus's friend, Eurimedes, a tenor role expressively sung by Werner Güra. Pluto, a bass-baritone role sung with resonance and authority by Hanno Müller-Brachmann, appears in Act 1 only; but he has some splendid music. The remaining roles are small, but, of these, Ismene, one of Orasia's ladies-in-waiting, deserves mention for the aria, 'Bitter und süss sind Rachgier und Liebe'. This double-edged piece is ravishingly sung by Maria Cristina Kiehr. And another, for Pluto's servant Ascalax, contains moments of vivid word-painting fluently if, perhaps, tamely handled by Axel Köhler. In choosing a soprano of the calibre of Isabelle Poulenard to sing the minor role of Cephisa, a nymph, Jacobs showed shrewd judgement, since Telemann wrote a virtuoso aria for her which Poulenard sings with brilliance and technical skill. Cephisa also shares some delightful music with a chorus of nymphs.

There are several fine choruses, lightly and articulately sung by the RIAS Chamber Choir and a handful of invigorating instrumental numbers. Jacobs and his musicians deserve congratulations, and so does Harmonia Mundi for the first-rate recording. This is an important and hugely enjoyable release.

Sir Michael Tippett   British 1905-1998

Tippett studied with C Wood and Kitson at the RCM (1923-8), then settled in Oxted, Surrey, where he taught, conducted a choir and began to compose. However, dissatisfaction with his technique led him to take further lessons with Morris (1930-32), and he published nothing until he was into his mid-30s. By then he was conducting at Morley College, of which he became music director in 1940; there he performed his oratorio A Child of our Time (1941), which uses a story of Nazi atrocity but draws no simple moral from it, concluding rather that we must recognise within ourselves both good and evil. Earlier works, like the String Quartet No 1 and the Concerto for double string orchestra, had married Stravinskian neo-classicism with a bounding rhythm that came from the English madrigal, but the oratorio added to these a Baroque concept of form and black spirituals to replace the chorales of a Protestant Passion. It also made clear Tippett's willingness to exert himself in the public world, which he did again as a conscientious objector in 1943 in accepting imprisonment rather than conscription.

A Child of our Time seems further to have released creative energy that went into a series of works – two more quartets, the cantata for tenor and piano Boyhood's End and the Symphony No 1 – leading to the composition of the opera The Midsummer Marriage in the years 1946-52. This, at once a pastoral, a modern morality and a mystery play of psychic growth, called for a further extension of resources: luminous static harmony, orchestral brilliance, a bold command of large spans of time, and a lively variety of rhythm in the largely danced middle act. The message is again that of the oratorio: before marriage the central characters must each accept the wedding within their personalities of intellect and carnality. The theme relates to The Magic Flute, and Tippett's sources for his own libretto also include Shaw, Yeats and Eliot.

The opera's musical exuberance spilt over into succeeding works, including the Fantasia concertante on a Theme of Corelli for strings and the Piano Concerto, but then through the Symphony No 2 (1957) came a clearing and hardening of style towards the vivid block forms and declamatory vocal style of the opera King Priam, composed in 1958-61, which concerns the problem of free will. Once more an opera had its offshoots; notably in the Piano Sonata No 2 and the Concerto for Orchestra, with its distinct gestures and circular formal schemes, but followed by a new, ecstatic continuity in the cantata The Vision of St Augustine (1965). Here the baritone's central narrative is subverted by huge choral parentheses, representing the density of thought and feeling embracing the simple account of the circumstances leading up to the vision. In his opera The Knot Garden (1970) he concentrates on the emotional substance of clashes of personality and their outcome.

His unusually candid if stylised presentation of raw human relationships and of the need to make a success of the seemingly incompatible ones produce a score of lapidary compression, notable for its metallic sonorities, its use of a 12-note theme (though not serial technique) to represent fractured relationships and its revival of blues and boogie-woogie in a manner analogous to his use of spirituals in A Child of our Time.

Symphony No 3 continues to explore the seemingly inexhaustible flow of invention stimulated by the 'light' and the 'shadow'; the abstract musical argument of the first part is answered by the overtly human involvement of the second, where blues again express a basic human predicament and Beethoven's music provides archetypal gestures. The range of reference is wider in the opera The Ice Break, where again the blues stand for human warmth in a time of uncertainty but where the composer alludes to diverse strands of high and popular culture in a work that depicts and transfigures clashes of age, race and milieu. Again, the opera is composed of fragmentary scenes in which archetypal characters confront one another, but now in a context of global discord; the musical style is even more jaggedly kaleidoscopic, as it is also in Symphony No 4, which abandons the vocal solution of the Third but finds in purely musical development a metaphor of physical birth, growth and dissolution. Other late works include the oratorio The Mask of Time (1982), a grand restatement of Tippett's musical and philosophical concerns, as well as a Concerto for string trio and orchestra.

GROVEmusic

Concerto for Double String Orchestra

Concerto for Double String Orchestra. Fantasia concertante on a Theme of Corelli. The Midsummer Marriage – Ritual Dances
BBC Symphony Chorus and Orchestra / Sir Andrew Davis
Warner Apex 8573-89098-2 (64' · DDD) Recorded 1993. Text and translation included ⓢ

Sir Andrew Davis's formidable Tippettian credentials shine through in every bar of this outstanding anthology. Aided by realistic, firmly focused sound, the *Concerto for Double String Orchestra* sounds glorious here. Davis directs a performance of enormous humanity, intelligence and dedication – even Sir Neville Marriner's excellent EMI remake now seems a little matter-of-fact by comparison. In the slow movement Davis secures a rapt response from his BBC strings (the exquisite closing bars are drawn with ineffable tenderness), while the finale bounds along with irrepressible vigour and fine rhythmic panache. Davis's *Fantasia concertante* is an even more remarkable achievement. This is another inspirational display: sensitive and fervent, yet marvellously lucid and concentrated too. Once again, the BBC strings are on radiant form, and the lyrical intensity of their playing during the central climax has to be heard to be believed. Davis's identification with this sublime music is total. Much the same applies, for that matter, to the committed and

incisive account of the 'Ritual Dances' from *The Midsummer Marriage*, a veritable tour de force to which the BBC Symphony Chorus contributes thrillingly in the final dance.

Divertimento on Sellinger's Round. Little Music for Strings. The Heart's Assurance (orch Bowen). Concerto for Double String Orchestra
John Mark Ainsley ten **City of London Sinfonia / Richard Hickox**
Chandos CHAN9409 (71' · DDD) Text included Ⓕ

Chandos has here secured the first recording of the orchestral version of Tippett's major song cycle *The Heart's Assurance*. The *Concerto for Double String Orchestra* is Tippett's first masterwork, and it's marvellous to have a recording that does justice to all those antiphonal textural subtleties. One might wish for a touch more brio in the first movement and a richer, stronger tone in places, but this is still a very satisfying performance, not least because the finale comes across with such a winning blend of vitality and eloquence. Meirion Bowen's orchestration of *The Heart's Assurance* had Tippett's approval, and it's undoubtedly a resourceful piece of work. What makes the effect so different from the voice and piano original is that the all-important doublings of voice and instrument seem so much more prominent when the instrument can sustain the sound for as long as the voice itself. For this reason the original may be preferable, and in addition, despite John Mark Ainsley's excellent contribution to this recording, the final song doesn't build to its overwhelming climax as inexorably as it should. However, this is a valuable Tippett disc, and the recording is satisfyingly rich in detail.

Symphonies

Symphony No 1. Piano Concerto
Howard Shelley pf **Bournemouth Symphony Orchestra / Richard Hickox**
Chandos CHAN9333 (72' · DDD) Recorded 1994 ⒻⓄ

The riot of proliferating counterpoint that is Tippett's Symphony No 1 presents enough problems of orchestral balance to give recording teams nightmares. Chandos has managed creditable degrees of containment and clarity, without loss of realism, and the impact, when the last movement finally settles on to its long-prepared harmonic goal, is powerful and convincing. Doubts as to whether initial impetus is sufficient to keep the complex structures on course prove groundless. This is a fine account, well balanced between lively rhythmic articulation and broad melodic sweep. The performance of the Piano Concerto is no less notable for the inexorable way in which its mighty design unfolds. There may be too much decorum, too little passion, in certain episodes, yet Howard Shelley makes persuasive sense of the *con bravura* marking in the finale, and his shaping of the first movement's long, dreamingly decorative lines is as alert and sensitive as his control of the second movement's more dynamic discourse. This is a truly symphonic concerto, with a wealth of invention, remarkable textural ingenuity and a particularly imaginative use of the orchestra to complement the bright colours of the solo instrument. The recording is faultless.

Symphony No 2. New Year – Suite
Bournemouth Symphony Orchestra / Richard Hickox
Chandos CHAN9299 (65' · DDD) Recorded 1994 Ⓕ

The balance Hickox achieves between attention to detail and large-scale symphonic sweep is exemplary, and especially impressive in the tricky finale, where he conveys the essential ambiguity of an ending which strives to recapture the optimistic *élan* of the work's opening without ever quite managing it. The Chandos recording, too, gives us much more of the symphony's contrapuntal detail. The first recording of music from Tippett's latest opera *New Year*, premièred in 1989, is thoroughly welcome. The music of this suite may seem over-emphatic to anyone who hasn't experienced the opera in the theatre, and the recording relishes the booming electric guitars and wailing saxophones, as well as the taped spaceship effects. Yet there are many imaginative moments, like the use of the 'paradise garden' sarabande borrowed from *The Mask of Time*, and the exotic arrangement of *Auld Lang Syne* near the end. This is Tippett firing on all cylinders, with a performance and recording to match.

Praeludium. Symphony No 3
Faye Robinson *sop* **Bournemouth Symphony Orchestra / Richard Hickox**
Chandos CHAN9276 (64' · DDD) Recorded 1993.
Text included Ⓕ**OO**

The Third Symphony is one of Tippett's most complex and highly charged attempts to create a convincing structure from the collision between strongly contrasted musical characteristics. It evolves from a purely orchestral drama – fast first movement, slow second movement, both large-scale, followed by a shorter *Scherzo* – to a less extended but also tripartite sequence of blues settings, the whole capped by a huge, climactic coda in which the soprano voice finally yields the last word to the orchestra. The first two movements remain a considerable technical challenge, especially to the strings, but this performance manages to sustain an appropriate level of tension without sounding merely effortful, and without skimping on the opportunities for eloquence of phrasing. It could well be that Tippett has over-indulged the percussion in the slow movement, but this vivid and well-balanced recording lets us hear ample detail without exaggerating the bright colours and hyper-resonant textures. The later stages have the

advantage of a superbly characterful singer in Faye Robinson. She has the power, the edge, and also the radiance, to make the progression from idiosyncratic blues to Beethoven-quoting peroration utterly convincing. The work ends, famously, on a question-mark, dismissing the unrestrained affirmation of Beethoven's *Choral* finale in favour of the unresolved opposition of loud brass and soft strings. Will that 'new compassionate power/To heal, to love' which the text 'senses' actually be achieved? Nearly thirty years on, the jury is still out on Tippett's great humanist challenge. Meanwhile, there can be no questioning the achievement of this performance and recording, coupled strikingly with the highly characteristic *Praeludium* for brass, bells and percussion of 1962.

Additional recommendation

Symphonies Nos 1-3
Coupled with: Suite in D[a]
LSO / Colin Davis; CSO / [a]Georg Solti
Decca British Music Collection ② 473 092-2 (140' · ADD/DDD) Ⓜ
Davis and the LSO provide intensely committed performances that interrogate the increasing complexity of the music to telling effect. Essential, benchmark readings to set alongside Hickox's Chandos cycle.

The Rose Lake

The Rose Lake[a]. The Vision of St Augustine[b]
[b]**John Shirley-Quirk** *bar* **London Symphony Chorus and Orchestra / [a]Sir Colin Davis, [b]Sir Michael Tippett**
Conifer Classics 75605 51304-2 (68' · [b]ADD/[a]DDD)
Recorded [a]1997, [b]1971. Text and translation included Ⓕ**OO**

Although Tippett let it be known that *The Rose Lake* would be his last orchestral work, it doesn't sound valedictory. It's based on the profound impression made on him, during a holiday in Senegal, of a small lake which at midday was transformed from whitish green to translucent pink. Tippett imagines the lake singing and frames the five verses of its song with glittering ostinatos and bright toccatas, with much tuned percussion including three octaves of the rototoms that he used so effectively in *Byzantium*. It's a simple, satisfying, rondo-like structure, with the lake first awakening (calm, woodland horns), its song then echoing from the sky (woodwind and string counterpoint) and reaching 'full song' (a long, eloquent string line underpinned by drums) at the centre. The latter half of the work isn't a literal mirror-image of the first, but a series of poetic and ingenious 'doubles' of what went before, ending with magical horn calls recalling those in *The Midsummer Marriage*, a quiet rattle of xylophone and rototoms and, as a surprising coda, an abrupt sequence of *staccato* wind chords. It's a lovely and a moving piece, brimming with characteristically Tippettian melody. Almost as important, it's of just the right length to couple with the composer's own recording of one of his greatest but least often performed masterpieces. *The Vision of St Augustine* is hideously difficult to perform, but the choral singing here is quite heroic, and Shirley-Quirk's account of the taxing solo part nothing short of superb. On further acquaintance it reveals itself as truly visionary and profoundly moving. Davis's account of *The Rose Lake* is as urgently communicative as Tippett's own of the cantata, and the older recording is by no means put in the shade by the newer: both are excellent.

String Quartets

String Quartets – No 1ª; No 2 in Fª; No 3ª; No 4ᵇ; No 5ᶜ
The Lindsays (Peter Cropper, Ronald Birks *vns* ªRoger Bigley, ᵇᶜRobin Ireland *vas* Bernard Gregor-Smith *vc*)
ASV ② CDDCS231 (123' · ADD/DDD) Recorded 1975-92   Ⓕ◐

Tippett coached the The Lindsays for these recordings of his first three quartets, and wrote the other two for the quartet. In a note written for their 25th anniversary in 1992 he said that in these recordings they were 'concerned to establish good precedents in matters of style, so that succeeding generations of interpreters start at an advantage'. In fact one of the most enjoyable things about these readings is that they're so very characteristic of the The Lindsays. A number of the qualities you might call 'characteristic' are uncommonly well suited to Tippett's earlier quartets: big tone, vigour of attack and an infectious enjoyment of his lithe sprung rhythms. These performances are excellent precedents for later interpreters. They establish a style – big-scaled, urgently communicative – that's presumably 'authentic' and yet they challenge listeners as well as other performers to imagine how else they might be done. They also affirm the aching absence of a quartet between the Third and the Fourth (Tippett intended to write one in the late 1940s or early 1950s but got side-tracked by *The Midsummer Marriage*) and make one wonder what the rejected two movements of the First Quartet might be like. It's wonderful, though, to hear the five as a sequence in such authoritative readings. The recordings sound very well, but have been transferred at an exceptionally high level.

Tippett String Quartet No 5 **Brown** Fanfare to welcome Sir Michael Tippett **Purcell** Fantasias – F, Z737; E minor, Z741; G, Z742 **Morris** Canzoni Ricertati – No 1, Risoluto; No 6, Lento sostenuto **C Wood** String Quartet in A minor
The Lindsays (Peter Cropper, Ronald Birks *vns* Robin Ireland *va* Bernard Gregor-Smith *vc*)
ASV CDDCA879 (76' · DDD) Recorded 1992   Ⓕ◐

This is a precise re-creation of the concert at which Tippett's Fifth String Quartet had its first performance. Music by two of his teachers and one of his great inspirers is preceded by a greeting prelude that quotes both Purcell and Tippett himself. Tippett's Quartet is quite typical of him, both in its exquisitely singing lyricism and in the fact that it's by no means a mere looking back towards his earlier lyrical phases. Here intensification of expression is often achieved by distillation, towards such a simplicity of utterance that at crucial moments the music thins sometimes to one, often to no more than two, of the quartet's voices. RO Morris's *Canzoni Ricertati* subject faintly folk-like melodies to ingenious fugal and canonic treatment. In Charles Wood's quartet, the ingenious interplay of short motives in his *Scherzo* is something that might have caught the young Tippett's ear, and his finale dresses up the Irish folk-song *The lark in the clear air* in its best Sunday clothes. The Purcell *Fantasias* point up Tippett's Purcell ancestry rather touchingly as does Christopher Brown's miniature *Fanfare*. The Lindsays' beautiful performances are cleanly but not clinically recorded.

Piano Sonatas

Piano Sonatas Nos 1-3
Nicholas Unwin *pf*
Chandos CHAN9468 (55' · DDD)   Ⓕ◐

These are very big performances indeed, giving a clear and infectious impression of how satisfying these sonatas must be when your technique is as commanding as Nicholas Unwin's. The tireless toccata vein in Tippett's piano writing, the abrupt grandeur of some of his juxtapositions, what one might call the 'Beethoven-plus' element (angular dotted figures not far from the *Grosse Fuge*, a buoyant humour closely related to the late *Bagatelles*) – all these are finely conveyed. Possibly missing is the blithely springy lightness of touch that some other pianists have found, especially in the First Sonata. Unwin is capable of light, transparent textures and of fluid lyricism, so he provides pretty well 90 per cent or more of what these sonatas require. No one has supplied more, though it might have been a different 90 per cent: these are works that can take a variety of interpretations and gain from them. The recordings match the performances well, offering a commandingly big piano sound, but there's also no lack of more sober colour.

Choral Works

The Windhover. The Source. Magnificat and Nunc dimittis, 'Collegium Sancti Johannis Cantabrigiense'. Lullaby. Four Songs from the British Isles. Dance, Clarion Air. A Child of Our Time – Five Negro Spirituals. Plebs angelica. The Weeping Babe
Finzi Singers / Paul Spicer with **Andrew**

Lumsden org
Chandos CHAN9265 (55' · DDD) Recorded 1994.
Texts included ⓕⓞ

The Finzi Singers are eloquent in the Spirituals, and polished in the *British Songs* (especially the beguiling 'Early One Morning'). However, it's especially good to have the works which represent early sightings of Tippett's later, less lusciously lyrical style – the *Lullaby* (with countertenor, reminding us that it was written for the Deller Consort) and the *Magnificat* and *Nunc dimittis*: here not only are the intonation and phrasing of the tricky lines supremely confident, but the accompanying organ is recorded with exemplary naturalness. The vocal sound throughout is generally no less successful. There may be almost too full and rich a texture for the linear intricacies of *Plebs angelica* and *The Weeping Babe* to make their maximum effect, but there's no lack of exuberance in *Dance, Clarion Air* and the other secular pieces.

A Child of our Time

A Child of our Time
Faye Robinson sop **Sarah Walker** mez **Jon Garrison** ten **John Cheek** bass **City of Birmingham Symphony Chorus and Orchestra / Sir Michael Tippett**
Naxos 8 557570 (70' · DDD) Ⓢ

The centenary of Sir Michael Tippett's birth saw a fair amount of critical agonising about whether he was, any longer, a composer for our time, or whether his time had passed. It's difficult to find much substance in that viewpoint when confronted with a work, first performed in 1944, which seems to have more in common with John Adams's much-admired *El Niño* of 2000 than with *Belshazzar's Feast*, or even *War Requiem*. The starkness of the confrontations in *A Child of our Time* between politics and psychology, between a high-art style rooted in Bach and a more popular, folk-tinged manner (the tango, Negro Spirituals), remains vivid, as does the sense of a composer doggedly carving out a viably personal idiom while not shirking matters of burning social and spiritual relevance. Maybe the focus wavers in places but the accumulated dramatic power, and its double release, first in a magical vision of spring, then in a more anxious, uncertain cry for peace and reconciliation, isn't something a bumbling amateur could have brought off.

Tippett was 87 when this recording was made, and neither its rhythmic momentum nor its textural clarity are ideal. But the composer's own lovingly crafted reading has a special place in the discography of this still-modern masterpiece.

Songs

Tippett Music. Songs for Ariel. Songs for Achilles.

Boyhood's End. The Heart's Assurance **Purcell** If music be the food of love, Z379/2. The Fairy Queen – Thrice happy lovers. The Fatal hour comes on apace, Z421. Bess of Bedlam, Z370. Pausanias – Sweeter than roses
Martyn Hill ten **Craig Ogden** gtr **Andrew Ball** pf
Hyperion CDA66749 (70' · DDD) Recorded 1994.
Texts included ⓕⓞ

The two longest works – the cantata *Boyhood's End* and song cycle *The Heart's Assurance* – challenge the musicianship and sensitivity of both singer and pianist alike. *Boyhood's End* (1943), a setting of prose that's never prosaic, shows the ecstasy of *Midsummer Marriage* to be already within the system, and the profusion of notes has to be mastered so that the dance shall seem as delicate and natural as graceful improvisation. In *The Heart's Assurance* (1951) the spirit's similar, although the technical accomplishment of all concerned, composer and performers, is heightened. For the singer, in addition to the quite fearsome difficulties of pitch and rhythm, there's also likely to be some problem of tessitura, particularly in the third of the songs, 'Compassion'. For the pianist, concentration has to be divided between the virtuoso writing of his own part and responsiveness to the singer, his notes, words and expression. Martyn Hill and Andrew Ball are wonderfully at one in all this, and the balancing of voice and piano has been finely achieved. The *Songs for Achilles*, with guitar, also convey a real sense of ardent improvisation, and the voice rings out freely. The *Songs for Ariel* here work their natural magic. Tippett's affinities with Purcell are felt at one time or another in most of these compositions, starting with the opening of the programme, the setting of Shelley's *Sleep*. The disc was issued to mark the composer's 90th birthday, and serves as a touching and eloquent tribute.

Boris Tishchenko   Russian b1939

Tishchenko studied at the Leningrad Conservatory and with Shostakovich (1962-5). He is an outstanding representative of a generation that reinvigorated Russian music in the 1960s. His richly inventive works include symphonies, concertos, string quartets, piano sonatas, and children's stage pieces.
                                          GROVEmusic

Symphony No 7, Op 119

Symphony No 7
Moscow Philharmonic Orchestra / Dmitry Yablonsky
Naxos 8 557013 (53' · DDD) Ⓢ

Not very much of Boris Tishchenko's substantial list of works has so far appeared on record. It includes ten piano sonatas, five string quartets and a cello concerto for Rostropovich, which

Shostakovich himself took the trouble to rescore for more conventional forces than the original. Like so many composers of his generation he's been much influenced by Shostakovich, with whom he studied for a while. The influence shows in this symphony, even though it's for the most part thoroughly absorbed and makes for a quirky but fascinating work.

Tishchenko doesn't give his movements titles or even tempo indications. The first is an unusual but convincing symphonic exposition, based on an obsessive use of a simple figure. The second makes much play with ragtime clichés, merry enough on the face of it though with a deliberately forced atmosphere creeping in. The third is a forlorn, dirge-like piece, with a bleak climax. The fourth begins gracefully enough with what one may perhaps describe as a frightened waltz. Like the other movements, including the finale, it has a restrained lyricism that seems vulnerable to attack, and indeed is attacked by dissonant and alarming orchestral climaxes, after which the music ends on an equivocal note.

Tishchenko scores imaginatively, with chamber music textures and single instruments unusually handled – xylophone, bass clarinet, piano, tom-toms. The Moscow players respond skilfully, and though the recording is sometimes over-anxious to single out individual instrumental contributions, it seems to give a fair representation of the imaginative scoring. This is a piece well worth hearing.

Thomas Tomkins   British 1572-1656

Tomkins, from a musical family, claimed Byrd as his teacher. He divided his time between Worcester Cathedral (organist from 1596) and London, becoming a Gentleman in Ordinary of the Chapel Royal by 1620, assistant organist from 1621 and senior organist from 1625; that year he wrote music for Charles I's coronation. He left Worcester in 1654. A prolific and respected successor of Byrd, he composed church music, including over 100 anthems (Musica Deo sacra, 1668), madrigals (1622, among them When David heard, a moving, polyphonic setting of a powerful text), over 50 keyboard pieces and a few highly original fantasias, pavans and galliards for viol consort. His half-brothers John, Giles and Robert and his son Nathaniel were also musicians.
                                                    GROVEmusic

Keyboard Works

Barafostus' Dream. Fantasia. Fancy. Fancy for two to play. Fortune my foe. A Ground. A Grounde. In Nomine, 'Gloria tibi Trinitas'. The Lady Folliott's Galliard. Miserere. Pavan. Pavan and Galliard, 'Earl Strafford'. Pavan and Galliard of Three Parts. A sad pavan for these distracted times. Toy, 'Made at Poole Court'. What if a day. Worster Braules
Carole Cerasi hpd **James Johnstone** virg/bhpd
Metronome METCD1049 (74' · DDD)   Ⓕ**OO**

Forming a mental picture of Thomas Tomkins isn't difficult. Most of the pieces here were composed in the 1640s and 50s, yet adopt the style of three or four decades earlier, when composers like Gibbons, Bull and Tomkins's own teacher Byrd were alive. A contemporary of these men, Tomkins had survived them through the execution of Charles I and the destruction during the Civil War of the organ at Worcester Cathedral, where he had presided since 1596. Now, in later life, he had retired to live with his family and quietly compose plainsong settings, variation sets, fancies, grounds and pavans 'for these distracted times'. But though about as fashionable as a 'Welcome home, Walter Raleigh' hat, these pieces have a quality to them – showing by turns something of the exuberance of Bull and the eloquence of Byrd – that's more than enough to maintain their currency today. This disillusioned early version of a *Daily Telegraph* reader was nothing less than the last representative of that great school of keyboard composers known as the English virginalists, and more than 350 years·on, it matters not a bean to the listener which decade he was writing in.

Cerasi's selection of about a third of Tomkins's extant keyboard pieces showcases all the genres in which he composed, as well as demonstrating the excellence and range of her own technique. Few listeners will fail to be impressed by the fearless accuracy and panache with which she throws off Tomkins's torrential passagework and finger-breaking double thirds, but she's sensitive, too, in the slower pavans and fancies. Like Leonhardt, she achieves a supreme eloquence in such pieces by the sheer precision and control with which she places each note, and it's a pleasure just to hear her playing. An outstanding disc.

Prelude. Fancy. Three In Nomines. Voluntary.   Ⓟ
Pavan and Galliard of Three Parts. Fancy (arr cpsr).
Toy, 'Made at Poole Court'. Pavan. Robin Hood. Two
Pavans. Ground
Bernhard Klapprott hpd/virg
Dabringhaus und Grimm MDG607 0704-2 (72' · DDD)
                                                    Ⓕ

Tomkins is perhaps best known as a later representative of the school of English madrigalists, and one of Byrd's most talented pupils; yet he composed in all the genres available to him, and left a substantial quantity of keyboard music. Tomkins is at his best when unfettered by pre-ordained conceits, and while he can't match his great mentor's grasp of form or his knack for writing instantly memorable tunes, the best pieces here aren't without charm (the little *Toy*, for example). Bernhard Klapprott plays mostly on a harpsichord, and more rarely on a much softer virginal, which seems the more effective instrument for conveying the music's unaffected delicacy. He strives to find the right expression for each piece; rubato is applied differently from one work to the next according to each piece's character, rather than exclusively by genre. Tempos could have been equally varied: they're uniformly on the slow side, even where greater agility would at least be warranted (as in the Galliard). The choice of instrument may have something to do with this: the virginal's softer sound encourages more rapid runs, whereas the harpsichord's seems to do the opposite. Still, a pleasing disc: Klapprott's advocacy of Tomkins reminds us how much of this first golden age of the keyboard remains unexplored.

Choral Works

Third Service. O Lord, let me know mine end. O that the salvation were given. Know you not. In Nomine (1648). In Nomine (1652). Voluntaries – G; C; A minor
New College Choir, Oxford / Edward Higginbottom with **David Burchell** org
CRD CRD3467 (62' · DDD) Recorded 1990 Texts included   Ⓕ

This is a well-balanced programme of sacred music by Thomas Tomkins. The four movements of the Third, or Great Service, together with the three anthems are spaced out with five organ pieces – two *In Nomines* and three voluntaries – chosen and arranged in such a way that the resulting key sequence has a satisfying natural flow. After an unassuming intonation, the truly royal *Te Deum* of the Great Service takes off with great verve and vigour, the rich 10-part texture of the full sections contrasting well with the lighter scoring of the verses. This energy and these contrasts are characteristic of the performances as a whole. There's some delightful solo singing in the verse anthems, in particular the alto solo in *O Lord, let me know mine end*. The two solo trebles are kept busy: they have a rather distinctive but complementary tone-quality, which makes up for a slight imbalance in volume. In general, however, the balance is good and the ensemble excellent. The trebles are a confident group with good articulation; they soar up to their top B flats with ease.

Tomás de Torrejón y Velasco
Spanish 1644-1728

Torrejón y Velasco went to Peru in 1667 when his employer was appointed viceroy there. He held administrative (non-musical) posts until 1676 when he became maestro de capilla of Lima Cathedral. He was admired for his villancicos, some of them polychoral; he also wrote liturgical music (notably vespers for Charles II) and an opera La púrpura de la rosa (after Calderón) celebrating Philip V's 18th birthday in 1701; it is the earliest surviving opera from the New World. **GROVE**music

La púrpura de la rosa

La púrpura de la rosa (ed Stein/Lawrence-King)
Ellen Hargis sop Caliope, Adonis **Judith Malafronte**

mez Terpsicore, Venus **María del Mar Fernández Doval** *sop* Urania, Marte **Josep Cabré** *bar* El Tiempo, Desengaño **Gloria Banditelli** *mez* España, Dragón **Päivi Järviö** *mez* Belona **Douglas Nasrawi** *ten* Chato **Nancy Mayer** *mez* Celfa **Johanna Almark** *sop* Amor **Santina Tomasello** *sop* Flora, Envidia **Gabriela de Geanx** *sop* Cintia, Temor **Catríona O'Leary** *sop* Clori, Sospecha **Jennie Cassidy** *mez* Libia, Ira **chorus; The Harp Consort / Andrew Lawrence-King** *hp/hpd/org*
Deutsche Harmonia Mundi ② 05472 77355-2 (137' · DDD) Text and translation included   Ⓕ●

In 1701 Torrejón y Velasco was commissioned to compose an opera to honour the new king, Philip V, on his 18th birthday: it was the first opera produced in the New World whose music is extant. Preceded by a *loa* in which allegorical figures hail the arrival of a new star, *La púrpura de la rosa* ('The blood of the rose') is a one-act opera on a text by Calderón. It deals with the myth of Venus and the initially hesitant Adonis and the jealousy of Mars, who's goaded on by his sister Bellona; inserted into it are popular dances, low-life characters and some personifications of human emotions.

The work's quite individual style differs markedly from contemporary Italian Baroque opera: recitatives are replaced by strophic *ariosos*; all the characters but two are allotted to actresses, so the tessitura throughout is high, and the three main characters are each provided with a theme that serves to identify them at the start of a scene.

The prevalence of women's voices makes it almost impossible to know who everyone is, and what's going on, unless you keep a firm eye on the libretto. It's somewhat bewildering that Mars is the most feminine-sounding; but all the singers are good, particularly Ellen Hargis in the demanding part of Adonis.

Concerted voices tend to be overloud (abetted by the acoustics of the recording venue); and it isn't until well into the second half that much attempt is made to underline the work's dramatic course – for example, off-stage placing, frequently called for, is totally ignored. This often results in long, repetitious strophic sequences. But the dramatic high spot – the battle between Mars, who seeks to wreak revenge on Adonis, and Venus, who implores Jupiter to intervene with his thunderbolts – is stirring, and occurs to the rhythm of a *xácara*. Predictably, the most moving music is at the death of Adonis and Venus's lament for him. After the play itself, the mournful mood is rudely dispelled with a rowdy kind of *vaudeville* on a peasant's lot.

All the performers, and DHM's enterprise in making this rare work known, are to be warmly applauded. There's much here to enjoy.

La púrpura de la rosa
Isabel Alvarez *sop* Amor **Alicia Borges** *mez* Belona **Graciela Oddone** *sop* Adonis **Adriana Fernández** *sop* Celfa **Marcello Lippi** *bar* Chato **Elisabetta**

Riatsch *mez* Cintia **Nadia Ortega** *sop* Clori **Furio Zanasi** *bar* Desengaño **Susanna Moncayo** *mez* Dragón **Fabián Schofrin** *counterten* Envidia **Sandrah Silvio** *sop* Flora **Sandra Galiano** *sop* Ira **Eliana Bayón** *sop* Libia **Mariana Rewerski** *sop* Sospecha **Isabel Monar** *mez* Venus **Cecilia Diáz** *mez* Marte **Madrid Zarzuela Theatre Orchestra and Chorus; Elyma Ensemble / Gabriel Garrido**
K617 ② K6171082 (129' · DDD) Texts and English notes included Ⓕ●

Following the Harp Consort recording of Torrejón y Velasco's *La púrpura de la rosa* for DHM, here is another version, based on a production mounted in opera houses in Geneva and Madrid under the musical direction of Gabriel Garrido. The textual problems of both words and music give rise to some marked differences between this version and that by the Harp Consort. Both versions introduce additional items, and show considerable ingenuity in the realisation of the score. The great strength of the new recording by Garrido is the way in which it conveys the dramatic nature of the piece. It helps that it was performed on stage before being taken into the recording studio, but there's also a fundamental difference in approach: not only is Garrido's dramatic pacing more revealing, but his interpretation is far more text-based. And what a text! This is powerful, evocative writing, full of poetry, universal resonances and deep human emotions. Garrido's singers, more operatically trained than most of those on the Harp Consort version, and more at home with the language, use the music to enhance the text, singing the dialogues and soliloquies with real meaning so that the tragic tale of Venus and her beautiful but doomed Adonis unfolds with great immediacy. If the Harp Consort's roses – the symbol of Adonis's blood and the flower into which he's finally transformed – are of red satin, sensual and enveloping, Garrido's have the scent – and the thorns – of the real thing.

Given that the recordings are so different, one can only recommend that you have both. Torrejón y Velasco isn't Monteverdi or Cavalli, not Lully or Purcell, but with this one work he shows himself to have been an instinctive opera composer writing in a highly distinctive idiom with its roots in Spanish tradition.

Charles Tournemire French 1870-1939

Tournemire was a pupil of Widor at the Paris Conservatoire and of Franck, whose place as organist at Ste Clotilde he inherited in 1898; from 1919 he also taught at the Conservatoire. His works include operas, oratorios and eight symphonies (1900-24), often on religious and esoteric subjects. But he is remembered for the monumental L'orgue mystique (1932), 51 organ masses using plainsong melodies appropriate to a particular Sunday, for the liturgical year, in a mystical style between Franck and Messiaen. **GROVE**music

Symphonies

Symphonies – No 5 in F minor, Op 47; No 8 in G minor, 'Le triomphe de la mort', Op 51
Liège Philharmonic Orchestra / Pierre Bartholomée
Astrée Naïve V4793 (69' · DDD) Ⓕ

The Liège Philharmonic may not be a world-class orchestra, but it plays with wholehearted commitment and sensitive dynamics, and is directed by a conductor who's clearly in sympathy with the Franckian school, so that these performances offer a very satisfactory presentation of this deeply felt, passionate music. Tournemire, one of Franck's successors at Ste Clotilde, could best be described as a Romantic mystic: unlike some other enormously prolific composers, his ideas have quality and his treatment of them is both original and extremely effective. Those wishing to sample his style are recommended to start with the beatific *Pastorale* of the Fifth Symphony, a work written in 1913-14 and inspired by Alpine scenery which produced in him a poetic mood of exaltation. The Eighth Symphony of a decade later, which employs a gigantic orchestra in virtuoso and varied fashion and is somewhat bolder in harmonic idiom, is subtitled *Triumph over Death* and was written on the death of the composer's dearly loved wife. Without doubt, a remarkably individual and gripping voice that demands to be heard.

L'Orgue mystique

L'Orgue mystique – Office 2, Postlude; Office 3, Paraphrase; Office 7, Fantaisie; Office 11, Diptyque; Office 27, Fantaisie paraphrase; Office 29, Alleluia No 1; Office 30, Alleluia No 2; Office 31, Alleluia No 3; Office 32, Alleluia No 4; Office 33, Alleluia No 5; Office 35, Paraphrase and Carillon; Office 43, Choral alleluiatique No 1; Office 51, Fantaisie sur le Te Deum et Guirlandes Alleluiatiques Office 44, Choral alleluiatique No 2; Office 45, Choral alleluiatique No 3; Office 46, Choral alleluiatique No 4; Office 47, Choral alleluiatique No 5
Marie-Bernadette Dufourcet-Hakim *org*
Priory ② PRCD669AB (134' · DDD) Recorded 1990, 1995. Played on the organs of La Sainte Trinité, Paris and La Basilique du Sacré-Cœur de Montmartre, Paris. Ⓢ

This two-CD set makes an excellent introduction to the sprawling, theatrical, sometimes hysterically neo-Gothic and spontaneous world of *L'Orgue mystique*, the magnum opus of Charles Tournemire. Until 1927 his compositional output was directed mostly at secular music, orchestral symphonies, string quartets and opera. Over the next five years he renewed French liturgical organ music, writing 51 suites (one for each Sunday of the year) based on 300 Gregorian plainchants. Mme Dufourcet-Hakim's 17-track selection consists of postludes, 11 of them drawn from the 13 suites for Sundays during Pentecost, thereby duplicating the excellent recording of the complete Pentecostal suites made by Georges Delvallée in St Sernin, Toulouse (on Accord). She captures brilliantly the improvisatory fleetingness and impressionistic mysticism inherent in Tournemire's music. She steers committedly and seemingly effortlessly around this often turbulent organistic assault course, helped by the generous acoustics of La Sainte Trinité (Messiaen's church), and, in two tracks, the Basilica of Sacré-Coeur in Montmartre, the latter more out of tune than the former. For anyone intrigued by the roots of Messiaen's radical organ writing these recordings will provide clear answers. These sizzling performances strongly recommended.

Suite évocatrice, Op 74

Tournemire Suite évocatrice, Op 74 **Vierne** Symphony No 3, Op 28 **Widor** Symphonie Gothique, Op 70
Jeremy Filsell org
Herald HAVPCD145 (71' · DDD) Recorded 1991 on the Harrison & Harrison organ of Ely Cathedral ℗**OO**

Compared with, say, the symphonies of Tchaikovsky or Sibelius the organ symphonies of Widor and his pupil Vierne aren't particularly long. But in terms of organ music they're among the longest single works in the repertory. Within their five-movement form the composers set out to exploit the full expressive range of the organ, and it was no coincidence that the organ symphony developed in turn of the century France. The great French organ builder Aristide Cavaillé-Coll was then producing instruments capable of hitherto undreamt-of colour and expression. Both Widor at St Sulpice and Vierne at Notre Dame had at their disposal the finest instruments in Paris and they indulged themselves fully in their symphonies. The subtitle of Widor's Ninth (*Gothic*) says it all. The structure is vast, intricately detailed, and almost forbidding in its grandness. Vierne's Third also presents an awesome spectacle, full of complex music and technically demanding writing, while Tournemire's neo-Classical Suite gives a moment almost of light relief in such heavyweight company. Jeremy Filsell is an outstanding virtuoso player with a gift for musical communication, and the Ely Cathedral organ produces the range of the great French instruments, but within an altogether clearer acoustic. These are performances and recordings of exceptional quality.

Eduard Tubin   Estonian 1905-1982

Tubin was a pupil of Eller at the Tartu Academy (1924-30); in 1944 he moved to Sweden. His music often combines propulsive rhythm with expansive melody, orchestrated in an expressive manner; he wrote ten symphonies (1934-73). **GROVE**music

Symphonies

Symphonies – No 1 in C minor[a]; No 2, 'The Legendary'[b]; No 3 in D minor[c]; No 4 in A, 'Sinfonia lirica'[d]; No 5 in B minor[e]; No 6[b]; No 7[f]; No 8[c]; No 9, 'Sinfonia semplice'[g]; No 10[h]. Kratt – Ballet Suite[e]. Toccata[g]
[abc]Swedish Radio Symphony Orchestra; [d]Bergen Philharmonic Orchestra; [e]Bamberg Symphony Orchestra; [fgh]Gothenburg Symphony Orchestra / Neeme Järvi
BIS ⑤ CD1402/4 (331' · DDD) Recorded late 1980s
Ⓜ**OO**

Vividly scored and dynamically expressive, Tubin's symphonies span almost his entire creative career. The First, only his third orchestral score, dates from 1931-4, and the single-movement Tenth from 1973, while at his death nine years later an Eleventh lay unfinished on his desk. Even without the Eleventh, the BIS set has much to commend it. The performances, variable in acoustic, are remarkably consistent in approach and quality of execution. Järvi's commitment to and understanding of the music is total and its quality shines through in every bar, whether in the early symphonies where Tubin was still moving towards his mature style, or Nos 5 to 8 with their absolute mastery of form. OK, even Järvi can't avoid the Third's peroration sounding like *The Pines of Tallinn*, but there's no doubt of the work's or its creator's stature. Although repackaged from the original issues, BIS avoids laying out the symphonies in chronological sequence. The recordings still sound wonderful, though occasionally perhaps too spacious. Järvi never sounds rushed, allowing the Eighth's opening *Andante quasi Adagio* to build into an impressive-sounding edifice. He's unmatched in the deeply felt finale. Overall, Järvi remains first choice, especially at this price.

Symphonies – No 4, 'Sinfonia lirico'; No 7
Estonian National Symphony Orchestra / Arvo Volmer
Alba ABCD155 (63' · DDD)   Ⓕ

Tubin's Fourth is quite different in character to works such as Nos 5-8, or even the Third. Its lyrical, pastoral melodies often have a modal feel that brings Vaughan Williams or even Rubbra to mind, while – especially in the *scherzo* – there's more than a hint of 1930s Hilding Rosenberg. There are fleeting concurrences of style with other figures of the period, but Tubin was his own man and in this performance the Fourth Symphony comes alive in a way that Järvi's account doesn't. The Seventh (1955-8) is more typical of Tubin's later style, thematically chromatic and harmonically more astringent (with a higher norm of dissonance) within a freely tonal and more concise expressive idiom. The lyrical impulse is still present, however, and Volmer gives the music a lean, Classical-style balance. He takes a more measured view of tempos than Järvi, missing some of his rival's headlong excitement but still whipping up a rather Simpson-like storm in the finale. Honours between the two versions are equal – the interpretative gains in the one offset by the virtuosity of the other. If you like your symphonies coupled, Alba's is self-recommending: BIS's couplings are of smaller orchestral works and the Piano Concerto.

Joaquín Turina   Spanish 1882-1949

Turina trained in Seville, Madrid and Paris (at the Schola Cantorum), and was associated with Falla, with whom he returned to Spain in 1914; he remained there, working as a teacher, critic and composer. His Schola experience gave him a command of the grand scale, moderated by Sevillian grace and wit. His works include operas, orchestral works (he was the only leading Spaniard of his generation to compose a symphony), chamber music, guitar music, songs and numerous piano pieces, including many colourful and effective character and genre pieces as well as some larger-scale works.

GROVEmusic

Orchestral Works

Sinfoniá sevillana. Danzas fantásticas. Ritmos (Fantasía coreográfica). La procesión del Rocío
Castilla y León Symphony Orchestra / Max Bragado Darman
Naxos Spanish Classics 8 555955 (62' · DDD) Ⓢ Ⓢ Ⓞ

Turina was a gentle man who, like Segovia, placed high value on beauty and clarity of thought, and responded to 'programmatic' images; the portrayal of profound tragedy had no place in his music. Although he tried harder than his contemporaries to write in the conventional musical forms, his *Sinfonía sevillana* is a poetic and colourful tone poem rather than a symphony, a French-influenced depiction of aspects of the city of his birth.

Ritmos was conceived as a ballet but was never performed as such – present-day choreographers please note! The *Danzas fantásticas* range from the quietly poetic to the energetic, and relate to quotations from José Más's novel *La orgía*. Two dances, the Aragonese *jota* and the Andalusian *farruca*, frame a dream-like evocation of elements of Andalusian melody and dance rhythm of the Basque *zortziko*. More specifically focused is *La procesión del Rocío*, a charming picture of the annual festival procession in the village of El Rocío.

Turina's skill and sensitivity in the art of orchestration shines throughout this programme, as does that of the Castilla y Léon Symphony Orchestra in extracting every good feature the music offers. The recording is clear, with a believably spacious acoustic. There are other recordings of these works, but none that brings them all together – or exceeds the quality of these performances. An outstanding issue.

Mark-Anthony Turnage   British b1960

Turnage studied at the Royal College of Music, with Oliver Knussen and John Lambert. He gained wide attention with his first orchestral score Night Dances (1981) which won the Guinness Prize and revealed the eclectic nature of his style, drawing on a wide range of early 20th-century sources and the inflections of jazz and blues harmonies. An even wider stylistic net informs On All Fours for 13 instruments (1986), in which Baroque dance forms, refracted through the model of Stravinsky's Agon, provide the rhythmic impulsion. He attracted wide attention with his opera Greek (1988, Munich).

GROVEmusic

Blood on the Floor

Blood on the Floor[a]. Dispelling the Fears[b]. Night Dances[c]. Some Days[d]. Your Rockaby[e]
[d]**Cynthia Clarey** sop [ae]**Martin Robertson** sax [b]**Håkan Hardenberger**, [b]**John Scofield** egtr [a]**Peter Erskine** drum kit [d]**Chicago SO** / **Bernard Haitink**; [e]**BBC SO** / **Sir Andrew Davis**; [c]**London Sinfonietta** / **Oliver Knussen**; [b]**Philharmonia O** / **Daniel Harding**; [a]**Ensemble Modern** / **Peter Rundel**
Decca ② 468 814-2DM (139' · DDD) [a]Recorded live 1996 Ⓜ Ⓞ Ⓞ

Turnage's sound world attempts to form a central amalgam between jazz and associated black music, and the avant-garde concert hall; these recorded performances draw on top musicians from both spheres. The earliest work here, *Night Dances* (1981), is an ear-tickling, transluscent sequence of exotic sounds, using a chamber solo group plus string quintet, orchestra and a wide range of percussion. The song cycle *Some Days* also expresses despair, its awkward vocal lines powerfully projected by Cynthia Clarey and accompanied with conviction by Bernard Haitink. Here, as with Birtwistle, you're often struck by its unexpected affinities with Stravinsky's dance-inspired *Rite of Spring*.

But it's in the ambitious *Blood on the Floor* that Turnage's different stylistic patterns coalesce most readily into a satisfying whole, with jazz influences made especially potent by the hand-picked cast of player-soloists. Turnage's opening movement combines vibrant *moto perpetuo* minimalism with something approaching a jam session, and the following sections range from the bluesy, melodically memorable 'Junior addict' to an extended finale. This is an abbreviated version of the earlier, thornily complex work for two virtuoso trumpets and orchestra, *Dispelling the Fears*. Whether it was wise to use it here again is open to question. Turnage obviously intended a a remarkably compelling coda and it does make a convincing resolution. But even when added in abbreviated form, it outbalances the rest of the work, and takes the overall length of *Blood on the Floor* to nearly 69 minutes. Performance and recording are superb.

Coupled with: Dispelling the Fears. Night Dances.
Some Days. Your Rockaby.
Various artists, orchestras and conductors
Decca British Music Collection 468 814-2DM
(139' · DDD)   Ⓜ

An excellent collection for newcomers to Turnage.
Performances and recording are superb.

An Invention on Solitude

Two Memorials[a]. An Invention on Solitude[b]. Sleep
on[c]. Cortège for Chris[d]. Two Elegies Framing a
Shout[e]. Three Farewells[f]. Tune for Toru[g]
Nash Ensemble ([f]Philippa Davies *fl* [bdf]Richard Hosford cl [bf]Marianne Thorsen, [bf]Elizabeth Wexler vns
[bf]Lawrence Power va [bcdf]Paul Watkins vc [f]Skaila
Kanga hp [cde]Ian Brown pf [ce]Richard Hosford cl
[ae]Martin Robertson *sop sax*)
Black Box BBM1065 (58' · DDD)   Ⓕ

An effective showcase for the composer's small-
ensemble music of the 1990s, this album might
have been entitled 'Another Side of…Mark-
Anthony Turnage'. Where, in some of his
major orchestral works, Turnage's idiom has
seemed quintessentially urban, indebted (via
Tippett and Britten) to Stravinsky and Berg,
here we come surprisingly close to the much-
derided English pastoral tradition. The jazz element is evident too, as you might expect, but
there's little trace of the composer's penchant
for rock and raunch; the mood is more wistful
than confrontational. Anyone who thinks that
contemporary music and memorable melodic
writing are somehow incompatible should audition this disc without delay. From the plangent
solo sax of the *Two Memorials* to the intensely
evocative solo piano version of *Tune for Toru*,
there's little to frighten the horses and much
that touches the heart. The biggest utterance is
the clarinet quintet, *An Invention on Solitude*,
composed, like much of this music, during Turnage's work on the score of his opera *The Silver
Tassie*. The Nash Ensemble are no strangers to
Turnage and their unsentimental playing is well
served by the boldly immediate recording.

Erkki-Sven Tüür   Estonia b1959

*Drawing on both his immediate classical heritage
and aspects of jazz and rock, Tüür came to prominence with the Architectonic series of nine ensemble
pieces (1990-93), each with an atmospheric and
open-minded approach to instrumental writing.
This timbral sensitivity has been continued in such
recent works as the Third Symphony (1997), whose
formal subtlety and thematic resource is a promising
continuation of the Nordic tradition.* GROVEmusic

Symphony No 3

Symphony No 3. Cello Concerto[a]. Lighthouse
[a]**David Geringas** vc **Vienna Radio Symphony**

Orchestra / Dennis Russell Davies
ECM New Series 465 134-2 (64' · DDD)   Ⓕ Ⓞ

Among the younger generation of would-be
symphonists, Erkki-Sven Tüür is one of the
most hope-inspiring. The first movement of his
Third Symphony builds impressive momentum
from the contrast of two types of music: one
dogged and metronomic, the other free and
apparently tempo-less. These eventually collide, producing an electrifying climax. The second movement has wildly diffuse elements –
from Lutosławskian modernism to quasi-
Bachian chorale tune and lush tonal romanticism. This is music of strong personality,
integrity and confidence, with warmth as well as
acerbity, directness as well as ingenuity. The
same could equally be said for the string fantasy
Lighthouse, and still more for the Cello
Concerto, though here the transition from
modernism to Romantic lyricism is easier to follow and harder to resist. Also appealing is the
vigour of much of the writing, especially for the
strings, occasionally recalling the great string
works of Tippett. Like the Finnish symphonist
Kalevi Aho, Tüür is plainly worth taking very
seriously, and it's good to report that the performers on this disc do just that. Excellent
recordings too.

Crystallisatio

Architectonics VI. Passion. Illusion. Crystallisatio.
Requiem
**Estonian Philharmonic Chamber Choir; Tallinn
Chamber Orchestra / Tõnu Kaljuste**
ECM New Series 449 459-2 (64' · DDD) Recorded
1994-5. Text and translation included   Ⓕ

Architectonics VI (1992) sounds like one of those
titles that are too good to resist, and it's to the
credit of Erkki-Sven Tüür that he admits as
much in the brief interview in the booklet to this
beguiling disc. Tüür's piece isn't especially
architectonic in construction, but it's well put
together and effective on its own terms. *Passion*
and *Illusion*, both for string orchestra and composed in 1993, are closer in spirit to the prevailing 'New Simplicity' of current East Baltic composition. *Passion*, indeed, is occasionally
reminiscent of Tüür's better-known compatriot, Arvo Pärt, although the brief *Illusion* has a
curiously English feel to it. The title track, *Crystallisatio* (1995), is scored for three flutes, bells,
string orchestra and live electronics and is
somewhat more demanding in scope. It's here
that Tüür's synthesis of minimalism with serial
techniques is heard most eloquently; not wholly
achieved, perhaps, but fascinating in application. By far the biggest piece is the Requiem
(1992-3), in memory of the conductor Peeter
Lilje. It's a deeply felt, half-hour-long setting of
the Mass for the Dead, and is of markedly different character to the other pieces here. This is
a handsomely produced, thought-provoking
release. If you want to hear up-to-the-minute

new music that won't sear the ears off your head, do try it.

Geirr Tveitt
Norwegian 1908-1981

Tveitt studied at the Leipzig Conservatory and in Vienna and Paris. His often rhythmic, dynamic music derives from Norwegian folk music and he wrote two concertos for the Hardanger fiddle. He was heard as the soloist in his six piano concertos.
GROVEmusic

Hardanger Fiddle Concertos

Hardanger Fiddle Concertos[a] – No 1, Op 163; No 2, 'Three Fjords', Op 252. The Water Sprite, Op 187
[a]**Arve Moen Bergset** hard **Stavanger Symphony Orchestra / Ole Kristian Ruud**
BIS BIS-CD1207 (65' · DDD)   Ⓕ

The Hardanger fiddle of western Norway probably originated in the mid-17th century, possibly – as Reidar Storaas suggests in his notes – as a hybrid of earlier folk fiddles and the viola d'amore. Its tone is smaller than the violin and, with its four sympathetic strings, sounds not unlike a treble viol. Local boy Geirr Tveitt has produced these two marvellous concertos for the instrument. The First dates from 1955, and its première at the Bergen Festival the following year was a triumph for the composer. It isn't hard to hear why: the idiom is Tveitt's best folksy manner, the orchestration expert and bright, with a virtuoso solo part. The opening movement is relatively gentle, succeeded by a wonderfully atmospheric if wistful *Andante* and a lively finale reminiscent of Malcolm Arnold. The Second followed ten years later, and replicates the same basic design, yet is a more personal utterance, the structure more concisely realised, the inspiration drawn from the three fjords of his native region. Arve Moen Bergset is a prize-winning folk player and plays with commendable feeling and technical assurance. He's ably supported by Ruud and the splendid Stavanger orchestra, who also provide an excellent performance of *The Water Sprite* ('Nykken', 1956), a tone-poem relating how the sprite snares a boy by disguising itself as a horse. Beautifully clear as usual from BIS.

Piano Concerto No 4

Piano Concerto No 4, 'Aurora Borealis'. Variations on a Folksong from Hardanger[a]
Håvard Gimse, [a]**Gunilla Süssmann** pfs **Royal Scottish National Orchestra / Bjarte Engeset**
Naxos 8 555761 (61' · DDD)   Ⓢ**OO**

There are many musical depictions of the Northern Lights, but few if any on quite so lush and expansive a scale as Tveitt's Fourth Piano Concerto (1947). A paean to this extraordinary natural phenomenon, it's conceived on a Baxian scale following a seasonal cycle with its kaleidoscopic first movement, 'The Northern Lights awakening above the autumn colours', running to almost 31 of the whole 51-minute length. The slower central span, 'Glittering in the winter heavens, and…' is more straightforward and the swifter final movement ('Fading away in the bright night of spring') acts as an epilogue. The manuscript of the Fourth Concerto was lost in the calamitous 1970 fire that destroyed Tveitt's home and 80 per cent of his output. Christian Eggen was able to reconstruct it from the orchestral parts and a two-piano reduction, leaving the Third to be issued (Nos 2 and 6 are irretrievably lost). The coupling here is the delightful *Variations on a Folksong from Hardanger* for two pianos and orchestra, written in 1939 for Tveitt to play with his first wife, a highly diverse late-Romantic effusion and a real winner. The performances are superb, Gimse totally in the Tveitt style with exemplary support from the RSNO and Bjarte Engeset; Gunilla Süssmann makes a splendid second soloist in the *Variations*. Excellent sound and a marvellous disc.

A Hundred Hardanger Tunes

A Hundred Hardanger Tunes, Op 151 – Suite No 2, 'Fifteen Mountain Songs'; Suite No 5, 'Troll-tunes'
Royal Scottish National Orchestra / Bjarte Engeset
Naxos 8 555770 (72' · DDD)   Ⓢ

Only four of Geirr Tveitt's suites from his unique, folk-inspired collection, *A Hundred Hardanger Tunes*, survive. The two presented here exhibit the same principal characteristics as Nos 1 and 4 (also on Naxos), although without the quasi-narrative structure of No 4, *Wedding Suite*. The Second Suite is largely a pastoral affair, though with moments of rugged grandeur befitting its subject, the mountains of Hardanger in western Norway. They are brilliantly orchestrated, as one now expects from Tveitt, the final six exceptionally so. The scoring of the Fifth Suite is richer still, like a kind of concerto for orchestra. The trolls here aren't the moronic ogres of *Harry Potter* or *The Fellowship of the Ring*, nor even the subterranean imps of *Peer Gynt*, but rather all the 'netherworld' peoples, whose music is as dazzling as they were legendarily beguiling. The Royal Scottish orchestra sound as if they thoroughly enjoyed themselves in this music, as well they should have. A splendid and enjoyable disc, beautifully played and recorded. Strongly recommended.

Marco Uccellini
Italian c1603-1680

Uccellini became head of instrumental musica at the Modena court in 1641 and maestro di cappella at Modena Cathedral in 1647. From 1665 he was court maestro di cappella at Parma. He composed instrumental music, stage works and vocal pieces; his solo and ensemble sonatas (1639-49) are notable for their thematic unity, chromaticism and advanced violin technique. **GROVE**music

Sonatas

Sonatas – Op 4 No 2; Op 5 Nos 3, 4, 9, 12; Op 7 Nos 1, 3, 11; Op 9 No 1. Arias, Op 4 – Nos 2, 3, 9. Sonata over Toccata No 5. Correntes – Nos 4, 9, 20
Romanesca (Andrew Manze vn Nigel North archlte/Baroque gtr/theorbo John Toll hpd/org)
Harmonia Mundi HMU90 7196 (65' · DDD) Ⓕ**O**

Uccellini, along with Marini, Fontana, Turini and several others, developed an idiomatic, virtuoso approach to violin writing which aspired to emulate the expressive range of the human voice. With their imaginative exploration of the violin's technical potential and in the pioneering spirit of the time, these composers made significant and lasting contributions both to technique and form. Thus in Uccellini's music we're made aware of a distinctively exploratory, improvisatory idiom in which there's a highly developed sense of fantasy. It's one of Andrew Manze's many strengths that he unfailingly responds to the technical and interpretative challenges of this repertoire with curiosity, stylistic propriety and playful imagination. Expressive delicacy, engaging inflexions and a discerning love of detail are all of the greatest assistance in bringing these pieces to life. In each department Romanesca succeeds admirably, enlivening Uccellini's extravagant gestures with demonstrative panache and rhythmic vigour, the more introspective ones with affectionate warmth. The gamut of his expressive range, and Romanesca's realisation of it, are vividly displayed in the fine Sonata No 1 from the composer's Op 7 (1660). The instrumental sonorities are rewarding, and this aspect of the performance has been very well captured by the sympathetic recorded sound.

Edgard Varèse French/American 1883-1965

Varèse studied with d'Indy at the Schola Cantorum (1903-5) and Widor at the Paris Conservatoire (1905-7), then moved to Berlin, where he met Strauss and Busoni. In 1913 he returned to Paris, but in 1915 he emigrated to New York; nearly all his compositions disappeared at this stage, with the exception of a single published song and an orchestral score, Bourgogne (1908), which he took with him but destroyed towards the end of his life. His creative output therefore effectively begins with Amériques for large orchestra (1921), which, for all its echoes of Debussy and of Stravinsky's early ballets, sets out to discover new worlds of sound: fiercely dissonant chords, rhythmically complex polyphonies for percussion and/or wind, forms in continuous evolution with no large-scale recurrence.

In 1921 he and Carlos Salzedo founded the International Composers Guild, who gave the first performances of several of his works for small ensemble, these prominently featuring wind and percussion, and presenting the innovations of Amériques in pure, compact form: Hyperprism (1923), Octandre (1923) and Intégrales (1925). Arcana (1927), which returns to the large orchestra and extended form with perfected technique, brought this most productive period to an end.

There followed a long stay in Paris (1928-33), during which he wrote Ionisation for percussion orchestra (1931), the first European work to dispense almost entirely with pitched sounds, which enter only in the coda. He also took an interest in the electronic instruments being developed (he had been calling for electronic means since his arrival in the USA), and wrote for two theremins or ondes martenot in Ecuatorial for bass, brass, keyboards and percussion (1934). The flute solo Density 21.5 (1936) was then his last completed work for nearly two decades.

During this time he taught sporadically and also made plans for Espace, which was to have involved simultaneous radio broadcasts from around the globe; an Etude pour Espace for chorus, pianos and percussion was performed in 1947. Then, with electronic music at last a real possibility owing to the development of the tape recorder, he produced Déserts for wind, percussion and tape (1954) and a Poème électronique (1957-8), devised to be diffused in the Philips pavilion at the Brussels Exposition of 1958. His last years were devoted to projects on themes of night and death, including the unfinished Nocturnal for voices and chamber orchestra (1961).

GROVEmusic

Complete Works

Tuning Up. Amériques. Poème électronique. Arcana. Nocturnal. Un grand sommeil noir (orig version/orch Beaumont). Offrandes. Hyperprism. Octandre. Intégrales. Ecuatorial. Ionisation. Densité 21.5. Déserts. Dance for Burgess
Sarah Leonard, Mireille Delunsch *sops* **Kevin Deas** *bass* **Jacques Zoon** *fl* **François Kerdoncuff** *pf* **Edgard Varèse** *electronics* **Prague Philharmonic Choir; ASKO Ensemble; Royal Concertgebouw Orchestra / Riccardo Chailly**
Decca ② 460 208-2DH2 (151 minutes: DDD) Texts and translations included Ⓕ**OOO**

This set is announced as 'The Complete Works' of Edgard Varèse. 'Complete' requires clarification. Excluded are *La procession du Vergès*, the electronic interlude from the 1955 film *Around and About Joan Mirò*, as well as the 1947 *Etude* Varèse wrote as preparation for his unrealised *Espace* project.

Works such as *Octandre* and *Intégrales* require scrupulous attention to balance if they're to sound more than crudely aggressive: Chailly secures this without sacrificing physical impact – witness the explosive *Hyperprism*. He brings out some exquisite harmonic subtleties in *Offrandes*, Sarah Leonard projecting the surreal imagery of the texts with admirable poise. The fugitive opening bars of *Ionisation* sound slightly muted in the recorded ambience, though not the cascading tuned percussion towards the close.

The instrumentational problems of *Ecuatorial* are at last vindicated, allowing Varèse's inspired mix of brass and electronic keyboards to register with awesome power. Chailly opts for the solo bass, but a unison chorus would have heightened the dramatic impact still further. *Amériques*, the true intersection of romanticism and modernism, is performed in the original 1921 version, with its even more extravagant orchestral demands and bizarre reminiscences of *The Rite of Spring* and Schoenberg's *Five Orchestral Pieces*, understandably replaced in the revision. *Arcana* was recorded in 1992, Chailly probing beyond the work's vast dynamic contours more deeply than any other rival on disc.

No one but Varèse has drawn such sustained eloquence from an ensemble of wind and percussion, or invested such emotional power in the primitive electronic medium of the early 1950s. *Déserts* juxtaposes them in a score which marks the culmination of his search for new means of expression. The opening now seems a poignant evocation of humanity in the atomic age, the ending is resigned but not bitter. The tape interludes in Chailly's performance have a startling clarity, as does the *Poème électronique*, Varèse's untypical but exhilarating contribution to the 1958 Brussels World Fair. The unfinished *Nocturnal*, with its vocal stylisations and belated return of string timbre, demonstrates a continuing vitality that only time could extinguish. Varèse has had a significant impact on post-war musical culture, with figures as diverse as Stockhausen, Charlie Parker and Frank Zappa acknowledging his influence. Chailly's recordings demonstrate, in unequivocal terms, why this music will continue to provoke and inspire future generations.

Peteris Vasks
Latvian b1952

Peteris Vasks was born in Aizpute, Latvia, and trained as a double-bass player. In 1970 he joined the Latvian National Opera orchestra, the Latvian Symphony Orchestra and chamber orchestra. In 1978, after graduating from the Latvian State Conservatory's Composition Class, Vasks began his teaching career, and many of his pupils are now noted Latvian composers. His initial compositional forays were noted for their unconventionality but by the 1980s he had found his uniquely Latvian voice in string, brass and piano music. GROVEmusic

Symphony No 2

Symphony No 2ᵃ Violin Concerto, 'Distant Light'ᵇ
ᵃTampere Philharmonic Orchestra / ᵇJohn Storgårds vn ᵇOstrobothnian Chamber Orchestra / Juha Kangas
Ondine ODE1005-2 (73' · DDD) Ⓕ❍

Peteris Vasks has been winning himself something of a cult following over the past decade. On the evidence of this blistering première recording, his Second Symphony of 1998-9 seems set to repeat the popular and critical success of *Voices*, its hugely effective 1991 predecessor for string orchestra.

A single-movement canvas of nearly 40 minutes' duration, it traverses emotions from barefaced rage and serene contemplation to icy despair, achieving a vast, uneasy quietude at the close ('a sense of light-filled sorrow,' in the composer's words). Stylistic echoes are plentiful: Shostakovich, Kancheli, Górecki and Pärt; folk-music, birdsong and hymnody are further ingredients in this approachable cocktail. Fortunately, Vasks's compassionate inspiration eschews any hint of New Age pretentiousness or designer chic, conveying instead a strength of conviction, unflinching honesty and profound sense of wonder that easily hold the listener in its thrall. All of which is also testament to the formidable interpretative skills of conductor John Storgårds, who secures exemplary results from the Tampere Philharmonic. The sound is splendidly ample and detailed to match.

For the coupling, Storgårds gives a heartfelt performance of Vasks's Violin Concerto (*Distant Light*). Written in 1996-7 at the behest of Gidon Kremer and his then recently formed Kremerata Baltica, this is another single-movement, readily assimilable essay, though its at times enigmatically disparate elements are here perhaps less convincingly fused into a satisfying whole. Nevertheless, this enterprising release deserves every success.

Ralph Vaughan Williams
British 1872-1958

Vaughan Williams studied with Parry, Wood and Stanford at the Royal College of Music and Cambridge, then had further lessons with Bruch in Berlin (1897) and Ravel in Paris (1908). It was only after this that he began to write with sureness in larger forms, even though some songs had had success in the early years of the century. That success, and the ensuing maturity, depended very much on his work with folksong, which he had begun to collect in 1903; this opened the way to the lyrical freshness of the Housman cycle On Wenlock Edge and to the modally inflected tonality of the symphonic cycle that began with A Sea Symphony. But he learnt the same lessons in studying earlier English music in his task as editor of the English Hymnal (1906) – work which bore fruit in his Fantasia on a Theme by Tallis for strings, whose majestic unrelated consonances provided a new sound and a new way into large-scale form. The sound, with its sense of natural objects seen in a transfigured light, placed Vaughan Williams in a powerfully English visionary tradition, and made very plausible his association of his music with Blake (in the ballet Job) and Bunyan (in the opera The Pilgrim's Progress). Meanwhile the new command of form made possible a first symphony, A London Symphony), where characterful detail is worked into the scheme. A first opera, Hugh the Drover, made direct use of folksongs, which Vaughan Williams normally did not do in orchestral works.

His study of folksong, however, certainly facilitated the pastoral tone of The Lark Ascending, for violin and orchestra, and then of the Pastoral Symphony. At the beginning of the 1920s there followed a group of religious works continuing the visionary manner: the unaccompanied Mass in G minor, the Revelation oratorio Sancta civitas and the 'pastoral episode' The Shepherds of the Delectable Mountains, later incorporated in The Pilgrim's Progress. But if the glowing serenity of pastoral and vision were to remain central during the decades of work on that magnum opus, works of the later 1920s show a widening of scope, towards the comedy of the operas Sir John in Love (after The Merry Wives of Windsor) and The Poisoned Kiss, and towards the angularity of Satan's music in Job and of the Fourth Symphony. The quite different Fifth Symphony has more connection with The Pilgrim's Progress, and was the central work of a period that also included the cantata Dona nobis pacem, the opulent Serenade to Music for 16 singers and orchestra, and the A minor string quartet, the finest of Vaughan Williams's rather few chamber works.

A final period opened with the desolate, pessimistic Sixth Symphony, after which Vaughan Williams found a focus in the natural world for such bleakness when he was asked to write the music for the film Scott of the Antarctic : out of that world came his Seventh Symphony, the Sinfonia antartica, whose pitched percussion colouring he used more ebulliently in the Eighth Symphony, the Ninth returning to the contemplative world of The Pilgrim's Progress.

GROVEmusic

Piano Concerto

Vaughan Williams Piano Concerto in C
Foulds Dynamic Triptych, Op 88
Howard Shelley *pf* **Royal Philharmonic Orchestra / Vernon Handley**
Lyrita SRCD211 (57' · DDD) Recorded early 1980s Ⓕ Ⓞ

There are four unequivocal masterpieces for piano and orchestra in English 20th-century music: Bax's *Winter Legends*, Frank Bridge's *Phantasm* and the two works recorded here. Until the appearance of this recording the VW Concerto had been more frequently presented in its revised 1946 version for two pianos and orchestra – one that did no favours in revealing the masterpiece of his original inspiration. The exceptionally taxing solo part, and the power required by the soloist to project over an extremely large orchestra, almost certainly inhibited the original version's ingress into the repertoire. However, when heard under the guiding hand of a pianist of Howard Shelley's calibre, we're allowed once more to discover the work in its true glory.

It's easy to see why the piece was so admired by Bartók when it received its German première under Hermann Scherchen and the concerto's dedicatee Harriet Cohen, for this is surely one of the most cogent and tautly constructed examples of its genre to have emerged from English music of the period. John Fould's *Dynamic Triptych* is scarcely less impressive. Though it lacks the conciseness of the Vaughan Williams, this is a work and a performance to treasure.

Additional recommendations

Coupled with: **Foulds** Dynamic Triptych
Shelley *pf* **Royal Philharmonic Orchestra / Handley**
Lyrita SRCD211 (57' · DDD)   Ⓕ
    A vital reading of the one-piano version by
    Howard Shelley, aided by one of the most searching of Vaughan Williams conductors.

Coupled with: **Finzi** Eclogue. **Delius** Piano Concerto
Lane *pf* **Royal Liverpool Philharmonic Orchestra / Handley**
EMI 5759832 (61' · DDD)   Ⓜ
    Piers Lane brings an exhilarating dash and bravura to Vaughan Williams's craggy concerto, aided by Handley's lucid, watchful direction.

Symphonies

No **1**, 'A Sea Symphony'; No **2**, 'A London Symphony'; No **3**, 'A Pastoral Symphony'; No **4** in F minor; No **5** in D; No **6** in E minor; No **7**, 'Sinfonia antartica'; No **8** in D minor; No **9** in E minor

Complete Symphonies

Symphony No 1, 'A Sea Symphony'
Joan Rodgers *sop* **William Shimell** *bar* **Royal Liverpool Philharmonic Choir and Orchestra / Vernon Handley**
Classics for Pleasure 575 3082 (DDD)   Ⓑ

Symphonies – No 2, 'A London Symphony'; No 8
Royal Liverpool Philharmonic Orchestra / Handley
Classics for Pleasure 575 3092 (DDD)   Ⓑ

Symphonies – No 3, 'A Pastoral Symphony'; No 4
English Folksong Suite
Alison Barlow *sop* **Royal Liverpool Philharmonic Orchestra / Handley**
Classics for Pleasure 575 3102 (DDD)   Ⓑ

Symphony No 5. Flos campi. Oboe Concerto
Christopher Balmer *va* **Jonathan Small** *ob* **Royal Liverpool Philharmonic Choir and Orchestra / Handley**
Classics for Pleasure 575 3112 (DDD)   Ⓑ

Symphonies – Nos 6 & 9. Fantasia on Greensleeves
Royal Liverpool Philharmonic Orchestra / Handley
Classics for Pleasure 575 3122 (DDD)   Ⓑ

Symphony No 7, 'Sinfonia antartica'. Serenade to Music. Partita for Double String Orchestra
Alison Hargan *sop* **Royal Liverpool Philharmonic Choir and Orchestra / Handley**
Classics for Pleasure 575 3132 (DDD)   Ⓢ Ⓑ ⊙⊙

Handley's performances can withstand comparison with the very best. The first to appear was the Fifth Symphony. Rightly acclaimed on its initial release, this remains a gloriously rapt, yet formidably lucid realisation. The coupling, a supremely dedicated rendering of the exquisite *Flos campi*, is just as distinguished. Handley's masterly pacing is a compelling feature of both the *Sea Symphony* and *Sinfonia antartica*, but, while it's difficult to fault either performance on artistic grounds, here more than elsewhere one notes the limitations of the slightly cramped acoustic of Liverpool's Philharmonic Hall.

There are no technical shortcomings about the intense Third or the Fourth, with its unbridled ferocity and orchestral virtuosity. The Second and Eighth bring outstandingly perceptive, marvellously communicative music-making, with both scores emerging as fresh as the day they were conceived. Handley's interpretation of the Sixth Symphony is a model of cogency and long-term control. Don't be deceived by the element of slight reserve in the opening movement. It soon transpires that Handley already has his eyes firmly set on the work's terrifying apex, namely the baleful climax of the succeeding *Moderato*. Handley's *Scherzo* teems with busy detail, its feverish contrapuntal workings laid out before us with maximum clarity and force. In the desolate, inconsolable landscape of the finale Handley achieves a truly awesome hush and concentration.

And what of the Ninth, VW's other 'E minor'? Few interpreters on disc have probed much beneath the surface of this elusive, craggy masterpiece. Handley captures the music's mordant wit, while allowing the listener to revel afresh in the astonishing vitality and startlingly original sonorities of VW's ever-imaginative inspiration. The overriding impression left is one of supreme sensitivity and utter dedication to the cause. In the visionary finale, whose monumental, block-like structure gradually takes shape before our eyes like Stonehenge itself, Handley's conception just has the edge over his rivals in terms of elemental power and effortless inevitability. The recordings are admirably natural.

Additional recommendations

Symphonies Nos 1-9   Ⓗ
Baillie, Ritchie *sops* **Cameron** *bar* **Gielgud** *narr* **London Philharmonic Choir and Orchestra / Boult**
Decca British Music Collection ⑤ 473 241-2DC5 (353' · ADD) Recorded 1952-8   Ⓜ
Music-making of the highest calibre throughout. The mono engineering is always vivid, often stunningly so – especially in *A Sea Symphony* and *Sinfonia antartica*.

Symphonies Nos 1-9
Coupled with: Fantasia on a Theme by Thomas Tallis. The Wasps. Serenade to Music. In the Fen Country. Norfolk Rhapsody No 1. The Lark Ascending. English Folk Song Suite. Fantasia on 'Greensleeves'. Con-

certo for Two Pianos and Orchestra. Job
Armstrong, Burrowes, Price *sops* **Case** *bar* **London Philharmonic Choir and Orchestra; New Philharmonia / Boult; various artists**
EMI ⑧ 573924-2 (534' · ADD)   Ⓑ
An ideal supplement to Belart's super-bargain box of Boult's mono VW cycle for Decca.

Symphonies No 1-9. Tallis Fantasia. In the Fen Country. The Lark Ascending. Norfolk Rhapsody No 1. On Wenlock Edge
Soloists; London Philharmonic Choir and Orchestra / Bernard Haitink
EMI ⑦ 586026-2 (474' · DDD · T)   Ⓢ
Haitink's majestic VW symphony cycle was recorded with the LPO over 13 years. His eloquent and illuminatingly intense interpretations serve up a feast of stimulating listening. The fillups are mostly marvellous, too; both *On Wenlock Edge* (with Ian Bostridge) and *In the Fen Country* receive sublime advocacy. An outstanding bargain.

Symphonies – selected

Symphony No 1   Ⓗ
Dame Isobel Baillie *sop* **John Cameron** *bar* **London Philharmonic Choir and Orchestra / Sir Adrian Boult**
Belart mono 450 144-2 (68' · ADD) Recorded 1952
                                           Ⓢ Ⓢ ○○○

'Classic recording of Symphony No 1' proclaims the sleeve of this superbudget Belart CD. That assessment is absolutely spot-on. Fine as is Boult's own 1968 stereo remake (available on an EMI reissue), this Decca performance surpasses it for sheer fervour and concentration: no one before or since has held the finale together with quite such effortless mastery. Vaughan Williams himself lent his supervision to the sessions, and the mono sound remains remarkably fullblooded, if inevitably rather lacking in range. No Vaughan Williams enthusiast can afford to overlook the present reissue. The singular lack of texts is, however, an irritating oversight.

Vaughan Williams Symphony No 2 (original version, 1913) **Butterworth** The Banks of Green Willow
London Symphony Orchestra / Richard Hickox
Chandos CHAN9902 (68' · DDD)   Ⓕ ○○○

It was during the summer of 1911 that George Butterworth, whose enchanting 1913 idyll, *The Banks of Green Willow*, comprises the achingly poignant curtain-raiser here, first suggested to Vaughan Williams that he should write a purely orchestral symphony. VW dug out some sketches h'd made for a symphonic poem about London, while at the same time deriving fruitful inspiration from HG Wells's 1908 novel, *Tono-Bungay*. Geoffrey Toye gave the successful Queen's Hall première in March 1914, and VW subsequently dedicated the score to Butterworth's memory. Over the next two decades or so, the work underwent three revisions (including much judicious pruning) and was published twice (in 1920 and 1936). In his compelling 1941 recording with the Cincinnati SO, Eugene Goossens employed the 1920 version, which adds about three minutes of music to that definitive 1936 'revised edition'. Now Richard Hickox at long last gives us the chance to hear VW's original, hour-long canvas – and riveting listening it makes too!

Whereas the opening movement is as we know it today, the ensuing, expanded *Lento* acquires an intriguingly mournful, even world-weary demeanour. Unnervingly, the ecstatic full flowering of that glorious E major *Largamente* idea, first heard at fig F in the final revision, never materialises, and the skies glower menacingly thereafter. Towards the end of the *Scherzo* comes a haunting episode that Arnold Bax was particularly sad to see cut ('a mysterious passage of strange and fascinating cacophony' was how he described it). The finale, too, contains a wealth of additional material, most strikingly a liturgical theme of wondrous lyrical beauty, and, in the epilogue, a gripping paragraph that looks back to the work's introduction as well as forward to the first movement of *A Pastoral Symphony*. Sprawling it may be, but this epic conception evinces a prodigal inventiveness, poetry, mystery and vitality that do not pall with repeated hearings. Hickox and the LSO respond with an unquenchable spirit, generous flexibility and tender affection that suit VW's ambitious inspiration to a T, and Chandos's sound is big and bold to match. An essential purchase for anyone remotely interested in British music.

Symphonies Nos 4[a] & 5[b]　　　　　　　　[H]
[a]**BBC Symphony Orchestra / Ralph Vaughan Williams;** [b]**Hallé Orchestra / Sir John Barbirolli**
Dutton mono BP9731 (66' · ADD) Recorded [a]1937, [b]1944　　　Ⓢ Ⓢ ❍❍❍

No performance on record of Vaughan Williams's Fourth Symphony has ever quite matched this very first one, recorded under the composer's baton in October 1937. As Michael Kennedy says in his note for this reissue, it's 'taken at a daredevil pace', and more importantly has a bite and energy beyond any rival. If early listeners to this violent work were shocked by the composer's new boldness, here his conducting demonstrates the passionate emotion behind the piece. The remastered sound is so vivid and immediate, so full of presence, that in places one almost has the illusion of stereo before its time.

Barbirolli's première recording of the Fifth Symphony, made in February 1944 eight months after the first performance, is hardly less remarkable. This, too, has never been matched since for the stirring passion of the great climaxes in the first and third movements, with Barbirolli in each carefully grading the intensity between exposition and recapitulation. It's also a revelation to find him taking the triple-time of

the Passacaglia finale much faster than latter-day rivals, relating it more closely than usual to the great example of the finale of Brahms's Fourth Symphony, making it no pastoral amble but a searing argument. Here again hiss has been virtually eliminated, but that has left the high violins sounding rather papery. Even so, there's no lack of weight in the big climaxes, with brass and wind atmospherically caught.

An outstanding issue for all lovers of this composer's music, not just those who specialise in historic recordings.

Symphony No 5[a]. Valiant-for-truth[b]. The Pilgrim Pavement[c]. Psalm 23 (arr Churchill)[b]. Hymn-tune Prelude on 'Song 13' by Orlando Gibbons (arr Glatz)[a]. Prelude and Fugue in C minor[a]
[c]**Ian Watson** org [bc]**Richard Hickox Singers;** [a]**London Symphony Orchestra / Richard Hickox**
Chandos CHAN9666 (71' · DDD) Texts included
Ⓕ ❍❍

This is an exceptionally powerful yet deeply moving account of the Fifth. Aided by glowing, wide-ranging engineering, Hickox's is an urgently communicative reading. The first and third movements in particular emerge with an effortless architectural splendour and rapt authority, the climaxes built and resolved with mastery. The *Scherzo* is as good a place as any to sample the lustrous refinement of the LSO's response. Hickox ensures that the symphony's concluding bars positively glow with gentle ecstasy: here's a Fifth that can surely hold its own in the most exalted company.

Material from *The Pilgrim's Progress* made its way into the Fifth Symphony and two of the five enterprising couplings here provide further links with John Bunyan's timeless allegory: the 1940 motet for mixed voices with organ, *Valiant-for-truth* and John Churchill's 1953 arrangement for soprano and mixed chorus of Psalm 23 (originally sung by The Voice of a Bird in Act 4 of *The Pilgrim's Progress*). The latter receives its finely prepared recorded début on this occasion, as do both *The Pilgrim Pavement* (a 1934 processional for soprano, chorus and organ) and Helen Glatz's string-orchestra arrangement of the solo-piano *Hymn-tune Prelude on 'Song 13'* by Gibbons. Which just leaves the Prelude and Fugue, originally written for organ in 1921, but heard here in a sumptuous orchestration.

Symphony No 6 in E minor[a]. The Lark Ascending[b]. A Song of Thanksgiving[c]
[c]**Betty Dolemore** sop [c]**Robert Speaight** narr [c]**Harry Grab** org [b]**Jean Pougnet** vn [c]**Luton Choral Society;** [a]**London Symphony Orchestra,** [bc]**London Philharmonic Orchestra / Sir Adrian Boult**
Dutton Laboratories mono CDBP9703 (69' · ADD) Recorded 1949-52　　　Ⓢ Ⓑ ❍❍

Although it was Boult who premièred VW's awesome Sixth Symphony, his white-hot February 1949 account with the LSO wasn't in fact the work's début recording – that honour fell to Stokowski and the New York Philharmonic (who pipped their British counterparts to the post by just two days). The return to the catalogue of Boult's legendary version – last available on an identically programmed Great Recordings of the Century anthology (EMI) – is a cause for celebration, especially in such a vivid transfer (if fractionally hollow in the bass), and so modestly priced to boot. Like Stokowski's scarcely less thrilling realisation, the performance offers us the opportunity to hear VW's original *Scherzo*. This has been allotted a separate track at the end of the symphony, its place taken by the same team's February 1950 recording of the composer's revision (not an ideal arrangement, perhaps). Whether the performance as a whole entirely displaces Sir Adrian's marvellous 1953 Decca version with the LPO (available in a disappointingly rough transfer on Belart) is open to debate, but both interpretations comprehensively outflank Sir Adrian's New Philharmonia stereo remake for EMI in terms of fiery concentration and sheer guts.

Written in response to a commission from the BBC in 1943 for a work to celebrate the defeat of Hitler's Germany, *A Song of Thanksgiving* was first broadcast shortly after VE Day. This commercial recording followed in December 1951. The work (which is scored for soprano, narrator, chorus and orchestra) has a smattering of decent invention (including, from around 4'30", fleeting echoes of the Sixth's second movement), but overall it's hardly representative of VW at his most inspired.

Last, and certainly not least, comes a wholly cherishable account (from October 1952) of *The Lark Ascending*, with Jean Pougnet a wonderfully silky toned, humane soloist. Boult's accompaniment, too, is a model of selfless dedication and intuitive rapture. For some, it remains, quite simply, the most tenderly unaffected and profoundly moving *Lark* on disc, though the string timbre on that earlier EMI restoration is much preferable to this overprocessed newcomer. None the less, a most valuable VW reissue.

Symphony No 6. Fantasia on a Theme by Thomas Tallis. The Lark Ascending
Tasmin Little *vn* **BBC Symphony Orchestra / Sir Andrew Davis**
Warner Apex 0927 49584-2 (62' · DDD) Recorded 1990
Ⓢ Ⓢ Ⓞ

Sir Andrew Davis clearly thought long and hard before committing this enigmatic and tragic symphony to disc, and the result is one of the most spontaneous and electrifying accounts of the Sixth Symphony available. The urgency and vigour of the first and third movements is astonishing, leaving one with the impression that the work might have been recorded in one take. His treatment of the second subject's reprise in the closing pages of the first movement is more underplayed and remote than the beautifully sheened approach of some recordings, but is

**VAUGHAN WILLIAMS
SYMPHONY NO 5 – IN BRIEF**

Royal Liverpool PO / Vernon Handley
Classics for Pleasure 575 3112   ⒷⓄⓄ
A magnificent performance, the first to be recorded in Handley's cycle, and a thing of incandescent beauty. The Liverpool band plays superbly and the recorded is very fine.

Hallé Orchestra / John Barbirolli
Dutton mono BP9731   ⓈⓄⓄⓄ
☀ Recorded in February 1944, the work's first recording has that extraordinary quality that seems to radiant from so many creator's recordings. Barbirolli conducts with incredible passion and fire. A fine transfer, too.

London SO / Richard Hickox
Chandos CHAN9666   ⒻⓄⓄ
With stunning playing by the LSO, this is a powerful and moving account of VW's Fifth. Hickox builds the piece with remarkable assurance ending the work on a note of incandescent poise. A highlight of his VW series.

Bournemouth SO / Kees Bakels
Naxos 8 550738   Ⓢ
Despite a slightly tentative opening, this is a vivid, nicely characterised performance. As a performance it must give way to the superior interpretations of Boult, Barbirolli and Handley, but it's well worth hearing.

London PO / Sir Adrian Boult
Decca 473 241-2   ⒷⓄ
From Boult's first VW cycle (1952-8), a performance of commanding assurance and sympathy. The mono sound is more than adequate. The LPO play with a real feeling for the idiom.

London PO / Bernard Haitink
EMI 586026-2   ⒷⓄⓄ
A rare performance by a non-British conductor, but what sympathy for this music Haitink shows: lucidity, power and a palpable integrity. Part of a complete VW cycle that's one of EMI's most enticing bargains.

Vaughan Williams Orchestral

arguably more nostalgic for being so. The feverish, nightmare world of the *Scherzo* is a real tour de force in the hands of an inspired BBC Symphony Orchestra, and the desolate wasteland of the eerie final movement has rarely achieved such quiescence and nadir as here. Davis's searchingly intense *Tallis Fantasia* is finely poised with a beautifully spacious acoustic. The disc concludes on a quietly elevated note with Tasmin Little's serene and gently introspective reading of *The Lark Ascending*. The recording is excellent.

Symphony No 9. Piano Concerto in C
Howard Shelley *pf* **London Symphony Orchestra / Bryden Thomson**
Chandos CHAN8941 (57' · DDD) Recorded 1990 Ⓕ**O**

Alongside the scorching account of the apocalyptic Fourth Symphony, this clear-headed, perceptive traversal of the enigmatic Ninth has fair claims to be regarded as the best thing in Bryden Thomson's underrated VW cycle for Chandos. Thomson's urgent conception of the opening *Moderato maestoso* in particular has a sweep and momentum one might not have previously associated with this movement, yet the gain in terms of sheer concentration and symphonic stature is irrefutable. Granted, some may find the outer sections of the succeeding *Andante sostenuto* just a little too lacking in evocative magic, but there's no gainsaying the effectiveness of gallumphing woodwind in the oafish *Scherzo*; certainly, the LSO's saxophone trio seems to be enjoying its day out hugely. In the finale, too, Thomson's approach is more boldly assertive than usual – not the way one would always want to hear this music, perhaps, but a thoroughly valid and convincing performance all the same. The coupling, Howard Shelley's distinguished remake of the same composer's craggily elusive Piano Concerto, is both imaginative and desirable. A highly recommendable disc: the LSO is in fine fettle, while the glowing sound is close to ideal.

Additional recommendation

Symphony No 4
Couplings : Violin Concerto, 'Concerto accademico'.
Sillito *vn* **London Symphony Orchestra / Thomson**
Chandos CHAN8633 (50' · DDD)   Ⓕ
  Thomson approaches the work as a magnificent piece of symphonic argument – exuberant, full of rumbustious humour and spiced with exquisite passages of lyricism.

Film Music

The Film Music of Ralph Vaughan Williams, Volume 2
49th Parallel – Suite[a]. The Dim Little Island[b]. The England of Elizabeth – Suite[c]. (all ed Hogger)
[a]**Emily Gray** *sop* [b]**Martin Hindmarsh** *ten*
[c]**Chetham's Chamber Choir; BBC Philharmonic**

Orchestra / Rumon Gamba
Chandos CHAN10244 (71' · DDD)   Ⓕ**O**

Directed by Michael Powell and written by Emeric Pressburger and Rodney Ackland, *49th Parallel* (1941) was the Ministry of Information's only feature film, its plot of five stranded Nazi U-boat crewmen journeying through Canada to the haven of the then neutral United States – designed, in Powell's words, 'to scare the pants off the Americans and bring them into the war'. Vaughan Williams's film score was the first of 11 he wrote between 1941 and 1958.

It was a challenge that evidently stoked his imagination, for inspiration runs high throughout this 39-minute sequence fashioned by Stephen Hogger. The unforgettable, nobly flowing 'Prelude' accompanies both the opening and closing titles, and enthusiasts will enjoy spotting thematic and stylistic links with masterworks to come (including Symphonies Nos 5-7 and Second String Quartet).

The present suite from *The England of Elizabeth* (written in the autumn of 1955 for a British Transport Commission documentary) adds eight minutes to Mathieson's three-movement adaptation (familiar to many from Previn's 1968 LSO account). It is, as annotator Michael Kennedy observes, a splendidly vital and inventive achievement. In the section depicting Tintern Vaughan Williams quotes a theme from his unpublished tone-poem of 1906, *The Solent* (the tune also crops up in his first and last symphonies), and it's soon followed by a haunting passage for choir alone.

Sandwiched between these two is a partial reconstruction of VW's amiable 1949 score for *The Dim Little Island*, a 10-minute short commissioned by the Central Office of Information (which also featured the composer in the role of narrator). It borrows heavily from VW's own *Five Variants of Dives and Lazarus* and even incorporates a verse of that self-same melody sung by a solo tenor.

Rumon Gamba draws a polished and wholehearted response from all involved. The Chandos recording has striking body and lustre; exemplary presentation, too. Very strongly recommended.

String Quartets

String Quartets – No 1 in G minor; No 2 in A minor.
Phantasy Quintet[a]
[a]**Garfield Jackson** *va* **Maggini Quartet**
Naxos 8 555300 (66' · DDD)   Ⓢ Ⓢ**OOO**

 Why isn't Vaughan Williams's Second Quartet part of the international chamber repertory? Played as eloquently as this it seems unarguably a masterpiece, one specifically of its time: 1942-3. Its first movement and deeply fraught *Scherzo* are as troubled as Shostakovich (whose music at moments, like a sudden stab of violence in that first *allegro*, it passingly resembles), while the misleadingly titled slow 'Romance' is haunted and haunting. It's tranquil but not at peace. It achieves an impassioned nobility and approaches serenity at the end, but something ghostly (it walks again in the Epilogue to the Sixth Symphony) refuses to be exorcised until the beautiful calm finale.

What these players do with the two much earlier pieces is no less remarkable. In them Vaughan Williams's style is audibly emerging from the influences (notably Ravel, briefly his teacher) that helped form it. In the First Quartet's opening movement an arching, lyrical melody that sounds like Vaughan Williams speaking with a French accent (and is it a French lark that ascends a little later?) has shed the accent by its return; something similar happens in the finale. But it was not an immature composer (he was 36, after all) who in the slow movement recognised a kinship with Fauré. And the *Phantasy Quintet* is audibly by the composer of the *Tallis* Fantasia, grateful to Ravel for giving him access to a deft rhythmic flexibility, but exploring his own unmistakable territory in the serenity tinged with poignancy of the slow movement. The Magginis and Garfield Jackson clearly love this music deeply; they play it with great beauty of tone and variety of colour and with passionate expressiveness. The ample recording allows both grand gestures and quiet intimacy.

Dona nobis pacem

Dona nobis pacem[a]. Sancta civitas[b]
[a]**Yvonne Kenny** sop [b]**Philip Langridge** ten **Bryn Terfel** bass-bar [b]**St Paul's Cathedral Choir; London Symphony Chorus and Orchestra / Richard Hickox**
EMI British Composers 754788-2 (63' · DDD)
Recorded 1992. Texts included　　Ⓢ Ⓑ ⦿⦿

This is a generous and inspiring coupling of two of Vaughan Williams's most important choral utterances. Hickox coaxes magnificent sounds from the LSO throughout: in *Dona nobis pacem*, for example, the sense of orchestral spectacle during 'Beat! Beat! drums!' is riveting in its physical impact. The London Symphony Chorus combines full-throated discipline and sensitivity to nuance, and Hickox's trio of soloists is excellent, with Terfel outstandingly eloquent. *Sancta civitas* is a work whose multi-layered scoring places great demands on both conductor and production team alike: suffice it to report, it's difficult to see Hickox's inspirational account of this still-underrated score being surpassed for years to come. EMI's clean, wide-ranging sound is admirable.

Additional recommendations

Coupled with: Five Mystical Songs
Wiens sop **Rayner Cook** bar **London Philharmonic Choir and Orchestra / Thomson**
Chandos CHAN8590 (57' · DDD)　　　　Ⓕ

A strong, convincing, well-paced interpretation. Brian Rayner Cook could scarcely be bettered.

Coupled with: Four Hymns. Toward the Unknown Region. O clap your hands. Lord, thou hast been our Refuge
Howarth sop **Ainsley** ten **Allen** bar
Corydon Singers and Orchestra / Best
Hyperion CDA66655 (76' · DDD)　　　　Ⓕ
An enticing VW collection enhanced by the late Christopher Palmer's typically illuminating notes.

Further listening

Vaughan Williams Magnificat
Coupled with: Song of Thanksgiving, Choral Hymns, Shepherds of the Delectable Mountains, Old 100th
Dawson sop **Wyn-Rogers** contr **Ainsley** ten **Terfel** bar **Corydon Singers, CLS / Best**
Hyperion CDA66569 (73' · DDD)　　　　Ⓕ
The only version available of the sensuous *Magnificat*.

Mass in G minor

Vaughan Williams Mass in G minor. Te Deum in G
Howells Requiem. Take him, earth, for cherishing
Mary Seers sop **Michael Chance** counterten **Philip Salmon** ten **Jonathan Best** bass **Corydon Singers / Matthew Best** with **Thomas Trotter** org
Hyperion CDA66076 (60' · ADD) Texts included
　　　　　　　　　　　　　　　　　Ⓕ⦿⦿

Vaughan Williams's unaccompanied Mass in G minor manages to combine the common manner of Elizabethan liturgical music with those elements of his own folk-music heritage that make his music so distinctive, and in so doing arrives at something individual and new. The work falls into five movements and its mood is one of heartfelt, if restrained, rejoicing. Howells's Requiem dates from 1936, a year after the death of his only son. The work was not released in his lifetime but was reconstructed and published in 1980 from his manuscripts. It's a most hauntingly beautiful work of an intensely personal nature. *Take him, earth, for cherishing* was composed to commemorate the assassination of J F Kennedy. The text is an English translation of Prudentius's 4th-century poem, *Hymnus circa Exsequias Defuncti*. Again it shows the great strength of Howells's choral writing, with a clear outline and affecting yet unimposing harmonic twists. The Corydon Singers give marvellous performances and the sound is very fine.

Mass in G minor. Lord, thou hast been our refuge. Prayer to the Father of Heaven. O vos omnes. O clap your hands. O taste and see. O how amiable. The Christian Year. Come down, O Love divine
Thomas Fitches org **Elora Festival Singers / Noel Edison**
Naxos 8 554826 (57' · DDD)　　　　Ⓢ Ⓢ⦿

This fine Canadian choir perform very beautifully in a style which seems natural and right.

The Elora Festival Singers have much in common with King's College, Cambridge under Willcocks; relaxed and habituated, they offer the welcome loveliness of a choral tone where the blend and match of voices produce a sound that's eminently 'at unity with itself'. There's no shortage of good recordings of the Mass in G minor, the one that stands out as being open-eyed and adventurous in spirit being the version on Meridian by the Choir of New College, Oxford. They favour a sharper tone, a quicker tempo in the *Credo* and a brighter acoustic. The choice between women's and boys' voices may prove the deciding factor when it comes to which version; the Elora Singers' female voices seem to give this music precisely what's required. Yet more decisive may be the coupling. The two recordings by the college choirs couple music by other composers. The Canadians stay with Vaughan Williams, in a mood which assorts well with the Mass. Particularly apt is *O vos omnes*, also written for Sir Richard Terry and the Choir of Westminster Cathedral. The Skelton setting, *Prayer to the Father of Heaven*, from 1948 – a comparative rarity and sensitively performed – has a chill which is partly medieval, partly perhaps from the Antarctica of VW's Seventh Symphony. *Down Ampney* ('Come down, O Love divine') brings the warmth and cheer of a settled major tonality at the close.

Serenade to Music

Serenade to Music[cd]. The Poisoned Kiss Overture. Old King Cole[cd]. Five Mystical Songs[ad]. Prelude on an Old Carol Tune. The Running Set. 49th Parallel – Prelude. Sea Songs. The Lark Ascending[c]. Two Hymn-Tune Preludes. Oboe Concerto in A minor[b]. Fantasia on 'Greensleeves'. Preludes on Welsh Hymn-Tunes – No 2, Rhosymedre; No 3, Hyfrydol (orch Foster). Violin Concerto in D minor, 'Concerto accademico'[c]Five Variants of 'Dives and Lazarus'
[a]**Stephen Roberts** bar [b]**Roger Winfield** ob
[c]**Bradley Creswick** vn [d]**Northern Sinfonia Chorus; Northern Sinfonia / Richard Hickox**
EMI British Composers ② 573986-2 (157' · DDD)
Recorded 1983-7   Ⓢ Ⓑ OO

This release comprises the contents of nearly three exemplary VW collections from the 1980s (the only casualty being a fine *Flos campi* – a work that Hickox has anyway since re-recorded with violist Philip Dukes and these same Tyneside forces on Chandos). Outstanding items include swaggeringly affectionate performances of the lovely 1929 overture to *The Poisoned Kiss* and that delightful 1923 ballet *Old King Cole* (the latter featuring a splendidly lusty contribution from the Sinfonia Chorus). Hickox also directs a most sensitive account of the glorious *Five Mystical Songs* (though baritone Stephen Roberts's timbre lacks something in bloom). Bradley Creswick surpasses himself in the Violin Concerto and *The Lark Ascending* (irreproachably poised and sensitive realisations, both). Roger

Winfield isn't quite as agile or quick-witted a soloist in the Oboe Concerto as some of his rivals, but he's a supremely touching presence all the same, and Hickox's typically warmhearted, pliant accompaniment is quite masterly. Even old chestnuts like the *Fantasia on 'Greensleeves'* and *Five Variants of 'Dives and Lazarus'* come up as fresh as the day they were created, and there's also an agreeable clutch of relatively unfamiliar offerings to enjoy, not least the stirring prelude to the 1941 film *49th Parallel* and those two generously sung *Hymn-Tune Preludes* (listen to 'Hyfrydol' for a pungent example of VW's penetrating modality).

Serenade to Music. Flos campi. Five mystical songs[a]. Fantasia on Christmas carols[a]
Elizabeth Connell, Linda Kitchen, Anne Dawson, Amanda Roocroft sops **Sarah Walker, Jean Rigby, Diana Montague** mezzos **Catherine Wyn-Rogers** contr **John Mark Ainsley, Martyn Hill, Arthur Davies, Maldwyn Davies** tens [a]**Thomas Allen, Alan Opie** bars **Gwynne Howell, John Connell** basses **Nobuko Imai** va **Corydon Singers; English Chamber Orchestra / Matthew Best**
Hyperion CDA66420 (68' · DDD) Recorded 1990.
Texts included   ⒻO

In 1938 Sir Henry Wood celebrated his 50 years as a professional conductor with a concert. Vaughan Williams composed a work for the occasion, the *Serenade to Music*, in which he set words by Shakespeare from Act 5 of *The Merchant of Venice*. Sixteen star vocalists of the age were gathered together for the performance and Vaughan Williams customised the vocal parts to show off the best qualities of the singers. The work turned out to be one of the composer's most sybaritic creations, turning each of its subsequent performances into aspecial event. Hyperion has gathered stars of our own age for this outstanding issue and Best has perceptively managed to give each their head, while melding them into a cohesive ensemble. A mellow, spacious recording has allowed the work to emerge on disc with a veracity never achieved before.

The coupled vocal pieces are given to equal effect and the disc is completed by Nobuko Imai's tautly poignant account of *Flos campi*, in which the disturbing tension between solo viola and wordless chorus heighten the cryptic nature of the work.

Additional recommendations

Serenade to Music

Coupled with: The Wasps Overture. Symphony No 2. Fantasia on 'Greensleeves'
Sols inc **Baillie, Suddaby** sops **Nash** ten **Henderson** bar **BBC Symphony Orchestra; Queen's Hall Orchestra / Wood**
Dutton Laboratories CDBP9707 (63' · ADD)   Ⓜ
This performance with the 16 original soloists possesses a very special beauty and atmosphere.

Coupled with: English Folk Song Suite. Fantasia on a theme by Thomas Tallis. Fantasia on 'Greensleeves'. The Lark Ascending. Wasps (excerpts)
Sols inc **Burrowes** sop **Partridge** ten **Noble** bass
London Philharmonic Orch / Boult; various artists
HMV5 72162-2 (66' · ADD)   Ⓑ
A well-matched group of soloists, with a passionate commitment in the climaxes unmatched since Sir Henry Wood.

Five Tudor Portraits

Five Tudor Portraits. Five Variants of 'Dives and Lazarus'
Jean Rigby mez **John Shirley-Quirk** bar **London Symphony Chorus and Orchestra / Richard Hickox**
Chandos CHAN9593 (55' · DDD) Text included   Ⓕ**O**

First heard at the 1936 Norwich Festival, Vaughan Williams's *Five Tudor Portraits* find the composer at his most dazzlingly inventive, the resourceful and witty writing fitting Skelton's words like a glove. Moreover, an irresistible humanity illuminates the most ambitious of the settings, 'Jane Scroop (Her Lament for Philip Sparrow)', which contains music as compassionate as Vaughan Williams ever conceived. It's a life-enhancing creation and well deserving of this first-rate recording. Aided by disciplined orchestral support, the London Symphony Chorus launches itself in lusty fashion into the ale-soaked narrative of 'The Tunning of Elinor Rumming', though the resonant acoustic rather precludes ideal clarity of diction. Hickox is exuberant in this sparkling tableau, while Jean Rigby's characterful contribution should raise a smile. John Shirley-Quirk's is a touching presence in 'My Pretty Bess', and the mordant, black humour of 'Epitaph of John Jayberd of Diss' is effectively captured. Jane Scroop's lament in the fourth (and surely best) movement finds these fine artists at their most perceptive. How ravishingly Hickox moulds his strings in the hushed passage following 'It was proper and prest!' where the music movingly anticipates the poignancy of the closing section. Listen out, too, for the wealth of exquisitely observed woodwind detail in the enchanting funeral processional. The concluding 'Jolly Rutterkin' goes with a swing, though Shirley-Quirk is a mite unsteady at the top of his range.
The coupling is a heart-warming *Dives and Lazarus*, with the LSO strings producing their most lustrous tone.

A Cotswold Romance

A Cotswold Romance. Death of Tintagiles
Rosa Mannion sop **Thomas Randle** ten **Matthew Brook** bar **London Philharmonic Choir; London Symphony Orchestra / Richard Hickox**
Chandos CHAN9646 (54' · DDD) Text included   Ⓕ

A Cotswold Romance is a gift from Vaughan Williams to those who hold the music of *Hugh*

the Drover in deep affection but who, under torture, would probably have to admit that the opera itself is less than perfect. *Hugh*, first produced in 1924, enjoyed sufficient immediate success for a set of records to be produced with the original cast. It then had to wait till 1979 for a complete recording on LP (reissued on EMI), and till 1994 for a new one on CD. The adaptation as a dramatic cantata came out in 1951, reducing the two-act opera to 10 numbers and rescoring some of the music to allow a larger part for the chorus. The addition of wordless chorus is delightful, not least when the chorus sings the first part of Hugh's song of the road and re-enters with delicious harmonies at 'All the scented night'. Thomas Randle, who has the voice of a man of the road and a lover, is admirably cast. Rosa Mannion, with a slight hint of turning tremulous under pressure, is otherwise an ideal Mary, and the chorus is excellent. Hickox conducts with brio and with due feeling for the romance. *Death of Tintagiles* is incidental music written for a play by Maeterlinck, performed without much success in 1913. In his interesting notes, Stephen Connock associates it with *Riders to the Sea* and the *Sinfonia antartica*; and it's true that there are sternly impressive moments, of menace and darkness. Though it hardly seems viable as an orchestral suite, it's good to have on this disc, nevertheless.

On Wenlock Edge

On Wenlock Edge. Merciless Beauty. Two English Folksongs. Ten Blake Songs. Along the Field
John Mark Ainsley ten **The Nash Ensemble** (Gareth Hulse ob Leo Phillips, Elizabeth Wexler vns Roger Chase va Paul Watkins vc Ian Brown pf)
Hyperion CDA67168 (69' · DDD) Texts included   Ⓕ**O**

The programme here has an identity of its own and as such is without competitors. Its 'theme' is to collect those of Vaughan Williams's songs which have something other than piano accompaniment. *On Wenlock Edge* (1909) is for voice, piano and string quartet, *Merciless Beauty* (1921) with string trio, *Along the Field* (1927) and *Two English Folksongs* (published 1935 but of earlier date) voice and violin, and the Blake songs (1957) with oboe. Eligible for inclusion might have been *Four Hymns* (1914) with piano and viola, and perhaps *The Willow Whistle* (1939) for voice and pipe. The *Three Vocalises* of 1958, with clarinet, are specifically for soprano, but show the composer's continuing taste for such combinations right into the last year of his life. John Mark Ainsley sings with the sense of a civilised personal utterance, refined and restrained, yet capable of full-bodied tone and a ringing *forte* when needed: the cry 'O noisy bells, be dumb' is as emotional as an operatic climax and all the more effective for the exceptional frankness of its release. These are highly demanding pieces, the voice unremittingly exposed. He brings to them a fine poise, in breathing, phrasing, expression and the even emission of quite beautiful tone. He has also the considerable advantage of exceptional players to work with. Individually admirable, they combine in *On Wenlock Edge* to give an unusually imaginative performance.

Songs of Travel

Vaughan Williams Songs of Travel **Butterworth** Bredon Hill and other songs. A Shropshire Lad **Finzi** Let us garlands bring, Op 18 **Ireland** Sea Fever. The Vagabond. The Bells of San Marie
Bryn Terfel *bass-bar* **Malcolm Martineau** *pf*
DG 445 946-2GH (77' · DDD) Texts included   Ⓕ**OO**

There's a touch of genius about Bryn Terfel. To those who've known most of these songs since childhood and heard them well performed innumerable times, it will come not quite as a revelation but more as the fulfilment of a deeply felt wish, instinctive rather than consciously formed. As in all the best Lieder singing, everything is specific: 'Fly away, breath' we recite, thinking nothing of it, but with this singer it's visual – we see it in flight, just as in *Sea Fever* we know in the very tiniest of gaps that in that second he has *heard* 'the seagulls crying'. As in all the best singing of songs, whatever the nationality, there's strong, vivid communication: he'll sometimes sing so softly that if he'd secured anything less than total involvement he'd lose us. There's breadth of phrase, variety of tone, alertness of rhythm. All the musical virtues are there; and yet that seems to go only a little way towards accounting for what's special.One after another, these songs are brought to full life. There's a boldness about Terfel's art that could be perilous, but which, as exercised here, is marvellously well guided by musicianship, intelligence and the genuine flash of inspiration. Malcolm Martineau's playing is also a delight: his touch is as sure and illuminating as the singer's.

Vaughan Williams Songs of Travel[a]. On Wenlock Edge[a] **Butterworth** Love blows as the wind blows[b] **Elgar** Pleading, Op 48 No 1[b]. Song Cycle, Op 59[b]. Two Songs, Op 60[b]
Robert Tear *ten* **Thomas Allen** *bar* **City of Birmingham Symphony Orchestra** / [a]**Sir Simon Rattle**, [b]**Vernon Handley**
EMI British Composers 764731-2 (69' · DDD/ADD) Recorded 1979-83. Texts included   Ⓢ Ⓑ**O**

Neither of Vaughan Williams's song cycles was originally written with orchestral accompaniment. *On Wenlock Edge* was scored for accompaniment of piano and string quartet, while the *Songs of Travel* were written with piano. Both lose a little when sung with orchestra but the gain seems to considerably outweigh any loss, especially when three such superb artists are involved. Tear's singing is notable for some wonderfully long phrases (as also is Allen's in the other cycle) together with the other Tear qualities, of clarity of words and such matters.

The CBSO plays especially well for Rattle – superb performances that do justice to Vaughan Williams's imagination, his care for words and orchestration. The Tear/Handley Elgar and Butterworth items are rarities and all première recordings. Throughout, Tear sings with sensitivity and the CBSO under Handley gives irreproachably alert imaginative support. The recording is vivid and well balanced.

The Pilgrim's Progress

The Pilgrim's Progress
Gerald Finley *bar* Pilgrim **Peter Coleman-Wright** *bar* John Bunyan **Jeremy White** *bass* Evangelist, Envy, Third Shepherd **Donaldson Bell** *bar* Pontius Pilate **Gidon Saks** *bass* Apollyon, Lord Hate-Good, Mistrust **Richard Coxon** *ten* Pliable, Mister By-Ends **Francis Egerton** *ten* Timorous, Usher **Roderick Williams** *bar* Obstinate, Watchful, First Shepherd **Adrian Thompson** *ten* Lord Lechery, Celestial Messenger **Rebecca Evans** *sop* Madam Wanton, Shining One **Pamela Helen Stephen** *mez* Madam Bubble, Shining One, Heavenly Being II **Anne-Marie Owens** *mez* Madam By-Ends, Pickthank **Christopher Keyte** *bass* Simon Magus **John Kerr** *bass* Judas Iscariot **Susan Gritton** *sop* Malice, Bird, Shining One, Heavenly Being I **Neil Gillespie** *ten* Worldly Glory **Jonathan Fisher** *bar* Demas **Mark Padmore** *ten* Interpreter, Superstition, Second Shepherd **Robert Hayward** *bar* Herald **Mica Penniman** *sop* Woodcutter's Boy **Chorus and Orchestra of the Royal Opera House, Covent Garden** / **Richard Hickox**
Chandos ② CHAN9625 (130' · DDD) Notes and text included   Ⓕ**O**

It's a matter of choosing here between Hickox's excellent version and the classic Boult (reviewed below). Both have strong soloists, though voice for voice Boult fares better than Hickox, though with a crucial exception. John Noble was a fine Pilgrim on the earlier recording, but Gerald Finley brings not only a voice that's as good and well suited but also a dramatic quality that is more colourful and intense. But Boult's cast is very strong, with several of the short parts, such as the Herald (Terence Sharpe) better sung than as here (Robert Hayward). In the Valley of Humiliation the voice of Apollyon comes as an amplified sound from off-stage, but on record the trick is to catch an overpowering terror, and this they manage better on EMI, partly by virtue of having Robert Lloyd to strike it, and also by the producer's decision to bring it closer. Nor, in the comparison, is there any sense of a confrontation of 'bright young feller' and 'grand old fuddy-duddy'. Boult doesn't *sound* like an old man, any more than Hickox sounds like a youngster. The Boult recording, finely remastered, is a strong survivor. Hickox has a bigger canvas for the recorded sound, and achieves a clearer texture. The newer version also has Gerald Finley, and is a fine performance anyway.

The Pilgrim's Progress
John Noble *bar* Pilgrim **Raimund Herincx** *bass*
John Bunyan, Lord Hate-Good **John Carol Case** *bar*
Evangelist **Wynford Evans** *ten* Pliable **Christopher
Keyte** *bass* Obstinate, Judas Escariot, Pontius Pilate
Geoffrey Shaw *bass* Mistrust, Demas **Bernard
Dickerson** *ten* Timorous, Usher **Sheila Armstrong**
sop Shining One 1 **Marie Hayward Segal** *sop*
Shining One 2, Madam Wanton **Gloria Jennings**
mez Shining One 3, Madam By-Ends **Ian Partridge**
ten Interpreter, Superstition **John Shirley-Quirk** *bar*
Watchful **Terence Sharpe** *bar* Herald **Robert Lloyd**
bass Apollyon **Norma Burrowes** *sop* Branchbearer,
Malice **Alfreda Hodgson** *contr* Cupbearer,
Pickthank **Joseph Ward** *bar* Lord Lechery **Richard
Angas** *bass* Simon Magus, Envy **John Elwes** *ten*
Worldly Glory **Delia Wallis** *mez* Madam Bubble
Wendy Eathorne *sop* Woodcutter's Boy **Gerald
English** *ten* Mister By-Ends **London Philharmonic
Choir and Orchestra / Sir Adrian Boult**
EMI British Composers ② 764212-2 (153 mintues:
ADD) Recorded 1970-71. Notes and texts included
Ⓢ Ⓑ ●

When this glowing performance of one of
Vaughan Williams's most raptly beautiful
works first appeared in 1972 as a centenary
offering to the composer, it was hoped that the
record would lead to more stage performances
on both sides of the Atlantic. That hope, alas,
wasn't fulfilled. That Vaughan Williams drew
from a whole series of Bunyan inspirations over
30 years has made for meatiness of material and
little or no inconsistency of style. 'They won't
like it,' predicted the composer after the first
performance at Covent Garden. 'They don't
want an opera with no heroine and no love duets
– and I don't care. It's what I meant, and there it
is.' Though he described the work as a 'morality', he was aggressively concerned that it
should be treated as an opera, not as an oratorio.
One can see what he meant. He wanted the
work's strength and cohesion brought out, not
just its piety, but in truth precious little is lost
from not having it staged, and the format of
recording might well be counted as ideal, allowing the listener to picture his own staging.

Sir Adrian's portrait, marvellously characterful, stands as one of the very finest of his many
records of Vaughan Williams's music, beautifully paced and textured with the fascinating
references to the symphonies – not just No 5
which took material from the previously written
Act 1 but (at least by implication) Nos 3, 4 and 7
as well, not to mention the *Serenade to Music*.
In every way Vaughan Williams's Bunyan inspirations permeated his music, and this opera
stands as their centre-point. John Noble, who as
a very young singer scored a great success in the
1954 Cambridge production, may not have
the richest or most characterful baritone, but
his dedication and understanding make for
compelling results. Outstanding among the
others are such singers as Sheila Armstrong, Ian
Partridge, Norma Burrowes and John Shirley-
Quirk. The chorus sings with fervour, and the
sound – using the always helpful London
Kingsway Hall – remains first rate.

The Poisoned Kiss

The Poisoned Kiss
Neal Davies *bar* Dipsacus **Janice Watson** *sop*
Tormentilla **Pamela Helen Stephen** *mez* Angelica
James Gilchrist *ten* Amaryllus **Roderick Williams**
bar Gallanthus **Gail Pearson** *sop* First Medium
Helen Williams *sop* Second Medium **Emer
McGilloway** *sop* Third Medium **Anne Collins**
contr Empress Persicaria **John Graham-Hall** *ten*
Hob **Richard Suart** *bar* Gob **Mark Richardson**
bass Lob **Adrian Partington Singers; BBC
National Orchestra of Wales / Richard Hickox**
Chandos ② CHAN10120; CD/SACD hybrid
CHSA5020 (116' · DDD) Notes and libretto
included Ⓕ ●

Written in the late 1920s when he was at the
height of his powers, *The Poisoned Kiss* is
Vaughan Williams's forgotten opera: this is the
first complete recording. The composer chose
his friend Evelyn Sharp to write a libretto based
on a short story by Richard Garnett about a
beautiful princess who lives on poison. But the
verse treatment is deplorable. Though the pair
had in mind the operettas of Gilbert and Sullivan, the result is coy and self-conscious, never
witty or pointed in a Gilbertian way. Vaughan
Williams made revisions in 1936 and 1955, but
there are still too many embarrassingly unfunny
lines. This recording helps to rehabilitate the
opera by eliminating virtually all the spoken
dialogue.

Neither Vaughan Williams nor Sharp could
work out the right balance between comedy and
the central romance – the love between Prince
Amaryllus and Tormentilla, brought up on poison by her magician father, Dipsacus.

Though planned as a light opera, the music
has substance. The score is rich in ideas; each
number is beautifully tailored, never outstaying
its welcome. At almost two hours of music, it has
to be said that the opera is too long (and it would
be even longer with dialogue), but the inspiration never flags.

Charm predominates, with tender melodies
like that in the Act 1 duet of Amaryllus and Tormentilla, 'Blue larkspur in a garden', and a surging emotional climax in the ensemble which
crowns Act 2, when their love leads to the passionate poisoned kiss. There are direct echoes
of Sullivan in the multi-layered ensembles and
patter numbers, which come closest to achieving the lightness aimed at.

Whatever the shortcomings of the piece, no
lover of Vaughan Williams's music should miss
hearing this wonderful set, with a strong and
characterful cast superbly led by Richard
Hickox, and with atmospheric sound enhancing
the musical delights. Janice Watson as Tormentilla sings with sweetness and warmth,
while giving point to the poisonous side of the
character, and James Gilchrist makes an ardent
Amaryllus. Pamela Helen Stephen and Roderick Williams are totally affecting in their love
music, and Neal Davies is firm and strong as the
magician Dipsacus.

Sir John in Love

Sir John in Love
Adrian Thompson ten Shallow/Dr Caius **Stephan
Loges** bar Shallow/Host **Stephen Varcoe** bass Sir
Hugh Evans **Daniel Norman** ten Slender **Henry
Moss** ten Peter Simple **Roderick Williams** bar Page
Donald Maxwell bar Sir John Falstaff **John Bowen**
ten Bardolph **Richard Lloyd-Morgan** bass Nym
Brian Bannatyne-Scott bass Pistol **Susan Gritton**
sop Anne Page **Laura Claycomb** sop Mrs Page
Sarah Connolly mez Mrs Ford **Mark Padmore** ten
Fenton **Mark Richardson** bass Rugby **Anne-Marie
Owens** mez Mrs Quickly **Matthew Best** bass Ford
**The Sinfonia Chorus; Northern Sinfonia / Richard
Hickox**
Chandos ② CHAN9928 (137' · DDD) Notes and text
included   Ⓕ

There's no lack of glorious melody in *Sir John
in Love*, and not just folksong cunningly interwoven. Musically, what comes over strongly,
more richly than ever before in this magnificent
recording from Richard Hickox, is the way
that the writing anticipates later Vaughan
Williams, not just the radiant composer of the
Fifth Symphony and *Serenade to Music*, with
key-changes of heartstopping beauty, but the
composer's darker side, with sharply rhythmic
writing.

The work's title, *Sir John in Love*, points to
Vaughan Williams's different approach to the
central character. With him Shakespeare's fat
knight isn't just comic but a believable lover,
more genial and expansive than in Boito's portrait, yet hardly a noble figure such as Elgar portrayed in his big symphonic study. Donald
Maxwell makes a splendid Falstaff, relishing the
comedy without making it a caricature. Above
all, his full, dark voice is satisfyingly fat-sound-
ing. On the only previous recording, the vintage
EMI set of 1974, Raimund Herincx gave a finely
detailed performance, but lacked that important
quality. The 1974 set certainly stands the test
of time remarkably well, but the extra fullness
and richness of the Chandos sound coupled
with as keen a concern for the atmospheric
beauties of the score, notably in offstage effects,
gives the new set an obvious advantage. Interpretatively, Hickox is just as incisive as Meredith Davies on EMI in bringing out the sharper
side of the score, though he's more warmly
expressive, a degree more affectionate in drawing out the glowing lyricism.

Chandos's casting is satisfyingly consistent,
with no weak link. Matthew Best may be rather
gruff at times as Ford, but that's very much in
character, when, if anything, he's more venomous here than in Verdi, until at the start of
Act 3 Vaughan Williams allows a wonderful
duet of reconciliation with Mrs Ford, 'Pardon
me, wife'.

As Ursula Vaughan Williams has reported,
her husband wrote *Sir John in Love* 'entirely for
his own enjoyment', because he was in love with
the subject. And from first to last this new set
reflects that.

Giuseppe Verdi   Italian 1813-1901

*Born into a family of small landowners and tavern-
ers, at 12 Verdi was studying with the local church
organist at the main church in nearby Busseto, whose
assistant he became in 1829. In 1832 he was sent to
Milan, but was refused a place at the conservatory
and studied with Vincenzo Lavigna, composer and
former La Scala musician. He returned to Busseto,
where he was passed over as maestro di cappella but
became town music master in 1836 and married
Margherita Barezzi, his patron's daughter (their
two children died in infancy).*

*Verdi had begun an opera, and tried to arrange a
performance in Parma or Milan; he was unsuccessful
but had some songs published and decided to settle in
Milan in 1839, where his Oberto was accepted at La
Scala and further operas commissioned. It was well
received but his next, Un giorno di regno, failed
totally; and his wife died during its composition.
Verdi nearly gave up, but was fired by the libretto of
Nabucco and in 1842 saw its successful production,
which carried his reputation across Italy, Europe and
the New World over the next five years. It was followed by another opera also with marked political
overtones, I lombardi alla prima crociata, again well
received. Verdi's gift for stirring melody and tragic
and heroic situations struck a chord in an Italy struggling for freedom and unity, causes with which he
was sympathetic; but much opera of this period has
political themes and the involvement of Verdi's
operas in politics is easily exaggerated.*

*The period Verdi later called his 'years in the gal-
leys' now began, with a long and demanding series of
operas to compose and (usually) direct, in the main
Italian centres and abroad: they include Ernani,
Macbeth, Luisa Miller and eight others in 1844-50,
in Paris and London as well as Rome, Milan, Naples,
Venice, Florence and Trieste (with a pause in 1846
when his health gave way). Features of these works
include strong, sombre stories, a vigorous, almost
crude orchestral style that gradually grew fuller and
richer forceful vocal writing including broad lines in
9/8 and 12/8 metre and above all a seriousness in his
determination to convey the full force of the drama.
His models included late Rossini, Mercadante and
Donizetti. He took great care over the choice of topics
and about the detailed planning of his librettos. He
established his basic vocal types early, in Ernani: the
vigorous, determined baritone, the ardent, courageous but sometimes despairing tenor, the severe bass;
among the women there is more variation.*

*The 'galley years' have their climax in the three
great, popular operas of 1851-3. Rigoletto, produced
in Venice (after trouble with the censors, a recurring
theme in Verdi), was a huge success, as its richly varied and unprecedentedly dramatic music amply justifies. No less successful, in Rome, was the more direct
Il trovatore, at the beginning of 1853; but six weeks
later La traviata, the most personal and intimate of
Verdi's operas, was a failure in Venice – though with
some revisions it was favourably received in 1854 at
a different Venetian theatre. With the dark drama
of the one, the heroics of the second and the grace and
pathos of the third, Verdi had shown how extraordinarily wide was his expressive range. Later in 1853*

he went – with Giuseppina Strepponi, the soprano with whom he had been living for several years, and whom he married in 1859 – to Paris, to prepare Les vêpres siciliennes for the Opéra, where it was given in 1855 with modest success. Verdi remained there for a time to defend his rights in face of the piracies of the Théâtre des Italiens and to deal with translations of some of his operas. The next new one was the sombre Simon Boccanegra, a drama about love and politics in medieval Genoa, given in Venice. Plans for Un ballo in maschera, about the assassination of a Swedish king, in Naples were called off because of the censors and it was given instead in Rome (1859). Verdi was involved himself in political activity at this time, as representative of Busseto (where he lived) in the provincial parliament; later, pressed by Cavour, he was elected to the national parliament, and ultimately he was a senator. In 1862 La forza del destino had its première at St Petersburg. A revised Macbeth was given in Paris in 1865, but his most important work for the French capital was Don Carlos, a grand opera after Schiller in which personal dramas of love, comradeship and liberty are set against the persecutions of the Inquisition and the Spanish monarchy. It was given in 1867 and several times revised for Italian revivals. Verdi returned to Italy, to live at Genoa. In 1870 he began work on Aida, given at Cairo Opera House at the end of 1871 to mark the opening of the Suez Canal: again in the grand opera tradition, and more taut in structure than Don Carlos. Verdi was ready to give up opera; his works of 1873 are a string quartet and the vivid, appealing Requiem in honour of the poet Manzoni, given in 1874-5, in Milan, Paris, London and Vienna. In 1879 composer-poet Boito and publisher Ricordi prevailed upon Verdi to write another opera, Otello; Verdi, working slowly and much occupied with revisions of earlier operas, completed it only in 1886. This, his most powerful tragic work, a study in evil and jealousy, had its première in Milan in 1887; it is notable for the increasing richness of allusive detail in the orchestral writing and the approach to a more continuous musical texture, though Verdi, with his faith in the expressive force of the human voice, did not abandon the 'set piece' (aria, duet etc) even if he integrated it more fully into its context – above all in his last opera. This was another Shakespeare work, Falstaff, on which he embarked two years later – his first comedy since the beginning of his career, with a score whose wit and lightness betray the hand of a serene master, was given in 1893. His final work was a set of Quattro pezzi sacri (although he was a non-believer). He spent his last years in Milan, rich, authoritarian but charitable, much visited, revered and honoured. For his funeral 28,000 people lined the streets.

GROVEmusic

Overtures and Preludes

Overtures and Preludes – Oberto; Un giorno di regno; Nabucco; Ernani; Giovanna d'Arco; Alzira; Attila; I masnadieri; Macbeth; Il corsaro; La battaglia di Legnano; Luisa Miller; Rigoletto; La traviata; I vespri siciliani; Un ballo in maschera; La forza del destino; Aida **Berlin Philharmonic Orchestra /Herbert von Karajan**

DG @453 058-2GTA2 (113' · ADD) Recorded 1975

Ⓜ︎Ⓞ

Karajan was one of the most adaptable and sensitive of dramatic conductors. His repertoire in the theatre is extraordinarily wide, and he's at home equally in Verdi, Wagner, Richard Strauss and Puccini. In this celebrated 1975 collection of all Verdi's overtures, he gives us some fine insights into the composer's skill as an orchestrator, dramatist and poet. Though Karajan had only recorded Aida complete his dramatic instincts bring some fine performances of the lesser-known preludes. The earliest, Nabucco from 1842 (the collection is arranged chronologically), already shows a mastercraftsman at work, with a slow introduction promising much. La traviata shows a quite different skill – the delicate creation of a sensitive poet working in filigree. The final four preludes are great works fully worthy of this individual presentation. Even the lesser-known preludes are enhanced by Karajan's dramatic instincts. Good recordings, though less than outstanding.

Overtures and Preludes – Oberto; Nabucco; Giovanna d'Arco; Alzira; La battaglia di Legnano; Attila; I masnadieri; Il corsaro; Un giorno di regno; Ernani; I due Foscari; Macbeth. Ballet Music – Macbeth **BBC Philharmonic Orchestra / Sir Edward Downes** Chandos CHAN9510 (76' · DDD) Ⓕ︎Ⓞ

These performances from an experienced British operatic stalwart have dignity (witness the brass in Nabucco), panache and splendidly colourful orchestral playing, including real string virtuosity, using the widest dynamic range. The crescendo at the opening of Giovanna d'Arco is most compelling. Some of the shorter preludes are full of atmosphere. The brief Macbeth Prelude is particularly potent, and the ballet music is both dramatic and rumbustious while I masnadieri closes with a swooning cello solo. La battaglia di Legnano, which ends the programme, has plenty of full-blooded brass at the opening and close. The recording is spectacular.

Messa da Requiem

Verdi Messa da Requiem[b]. Overture 'I vespri siciliani'[c] **Schubert** Mass No 6 in E flat, D950[a] [a]**Anne Pashley**, [b]**Amy Shuard** sops [a]**Sybil Michelow**, [b]**Anna Reynolds** mezzos [a]**David Hughes**, [b]**Richard Lewis**, [a]**Duncan Robertson** tens [a]**William McCue**, [b]**David Ward** basses [a]**Scottish Festival Chorus**, [a]**New Philharmonia Orchestra**; **Philharmonia** [b]**Chorus and** [b][c]**Orchestra / Carlo Maria Giulini** BBC Legends/IMG Artists BBCL4029-2 (153' · ADD) Recorded live [b][c]1963, [a]1968 Ⓜ︎ⓄⓄⓄ

 In Great Britain in the 1960s, the art of large-scale choral singing reached what was arguably its apogee with the work of the two choruses featured here: the

Philharmonia Chorus, directed by Wilhelm Pitz, and the Edinburgh Festival Chorus, directed by Arthur Oldham. Even allowing for the fact that this Prom performance of the Verdi *Requiem* was given around the time of an intensive period of rehearsal during which the EMI studio recording was also being made, the Philharmonia Chorus's singing is stunningly good: first-rate diction, impeccable intonation, fine dynamic control and absolute involvement in the music as Giulini relays it to them.

In the Schubert Mass the Edinburgh Festival Chorus acquits itself magnificently. Giulini's reading is powerful and reverential, one in which the chorus comes to speak with the single voice of an individual believer.

The Verdi is superbly recorded. The un-named BBC team working live in the Royal Albert Hall produce sound that's focused yet open, clear but warm. Giulini's reading of the *Requiem*, thrilling yet humane, is precisely the one we hear on EMI's recording, with the Philharmonia Chorus and Orchestra as expert live as they are on record (the orchestral playing is well-nigh flawless). Of the solo singers, the youngest, Anna Reynolds, could have gone straight into the EMI recording, so well does she sing. Richard Lewis, nearing the end of his career, is less gorgeous of voice than EMI's Nicolai Gedda, but the bass, David Ward, here at the height of his powers, is more than a match for the younger Nicolai Ghiaurov. Amy Shuard and EMI's Elisabeth Schwarzkopf are complementary. Shuard is technically fine; very much the real thing dramatically and absolutely right for the live performance. In short, this is an indispensable set.

Messa da Requiem
Angela Gheorghiu *sop* **Daniela Barcellona** *mez*
Roberto Alagna *ten* **Julian Konstantinov** *bass* **Eric Ericson Chamber Choir; Swedish Radio Chorus; Berlin Philharmonic Orchestra / Claudio Abbado**
EMI ② 557168-2 (84' · DDD) Recorded live 2001. Also available on DVD ⓅⓄ

EMI was quite right to be on hand to record this performance in Berlin at a time when Abbado had arisen from his sick-bed to show just how much this work meant to him in the circumstances. It's conveyed in spades through the tremendous concentration and emotional thrust felt throughout this shattering interpretation. This performance has something extra that you find in Fricsay's live, 1960 account, and both come close to the spiritual element in the music. Abbado has at his bidding a superb group of specialist choirs who combine effortlessly into a cohesive whole, singing with commendable breadth, accuracy and involvement, few if any better on disc. They find fit counterparts in the players of Abbado's Berlin Philharmonic who seem individually, in solos, and collectively intent on giving of their appreciable best for their chief. So all the big choral moments, *Dies Irae*, *Rex tremendae*, *Sanctus*, *Libera me* fugue are

superbly achieved. EMI's recording is wide-ranging and immediate, the equal of any the work has yet received.

If the solo singing can't be given such an unqualified encomium, much of it is impressive, especially that of the young mezzo Daniela Barcellona, even in tone and beseeching in manner. Gheorghiu does so much so well: she sings throughout in that rich, warm tone of hers and offers many long, arching phrases. She's also as dramatic as one could wish in the *Libera me*, but she doesn't really do the ethereal moments as well as many of her predecessors. Alagna has his uneven moments and can't compare with Pavarotti on Muti's version (reviewed below) for sheer effulgence, but he sings with a deal of passion and authority. The disappointment is the youthful Bulgarian bass Julian Konstantinov, whose singing is lamed by several untidy moments and by ill-tuned pitching.

In terms of fidelity to Verdi, Toscanini, Serafin, Giulini (in the BBC Legends version), Muti (though the live EMI recording at La Scala isn't so successful as this one in Berlin) and Gardiner, in his individually authentic way, are indispensable, but the new Abbado, given its superlative sound and special circumstances, is an important addition to the work's discography.

Messa da Requiem
Cheryl Studer *sop* **Dolora Zajick** *mez* **Luciano Pavarotti** *ten* **Samuel Ramey** *bass* **Chorus and Orchestra of La Scala, Milan / Riccardo Muti**
EMI digital ② 749390-2 (88' · DDD) Recorded live 198. Text and translation included ⒻⓄ

Muti's tempos, both in his 1979 EMI version and here, are substantially faster (*Sanctus*) or slower (opening *Kyrie*, 'Rex tremendae', 'Lacrymosa') than Verdi indicates and permits far more *rallentandos* than are marked. Nobody wants slavish adherence to what may be accounted only as suggestions on the composer's part, but Muti does sometimes lose the overall view of a movement by overplaying his hand as an interpreter. That's the main criticism of a performance that's certainly positive in terms of its dramatic strength, deriving from Muti's close rapport with his Scala forces.

Here he has a very different chorus from the much smaller professional British group on his earlier set (on EMI Double Forte). That has advantages and disadvantages. The sound here is grander, more specifically operatic in scale as one would expect, with some arrestingly histrionic effects such as the bold, black-browed singing at 'Rex tremendae' and the awed *senza misura* incantation at the start of the 'Libera me'. But there isn't quite the bright, incisive quality found on the former recording.

The performance starts hesitantly, particularly where the soloists are concerned. Cheryl Studer initially seems a shade tentative and over-awed, but as the evening develops she confirms what a fine *lirico-spinto* soprano she is.

The final phrase of the 'Offertorio' is perfectly accomplished and the whole of the 'Libera me' is delivered with strong, firm tone and a deal of passion. Her slightly resinous tone blends very well with Zajick's in the 'Recordare' and the *Agnus Dei*, one of the set's most successful movements. On her own Zajick also improves from an anonymous start to reach heights of eloquence at the start of the 'Lux aeterna'. The dark grain of her chest register contrasts with a degree of brilliance at the top.

Many will probably buy the recording for Pavarotti. He's in his best, most persuasive form, more individual and subtle in utterance than for Solti (Decca), even if the voice has lost a little of its old opulence. He's also more considerate of his colleagues in the unaccompanied passages, which here are as carefully blended as on any recording, much helped by Ramey's solid bottom line. Ramey trumps even Pavarotti at 'Hostias' in the 'Domine Jesu', his dolcissimo singing here full of inward feeling. 'Oro supplex', taken up to Verdi's tempo rather than being dragged as it can be by heavier basses, is firmly and securely phrased. Others have sung the bass part with more character, few – except Pinza – with such security and musicality.

The recording is rather recessed with the character of the soloists' voices hard to discern. However, where the chorus and orchestra are concerned, the new Muti certainly achieves a theatrical perspective, catching the atmosphere of La Scala, and the choral recording obviously has a bigger range than on his old set.

Messa da Requiem[a] . Quattro pezzi sacri[b]　　**P**
[a]**Luba Orgonášová**, [b]**Donna Brown** sops **Anne Sofie von Otter** mez **Luca Canonici** ten **Alastair Miles** bass **Monteverdi Choir; Orchestre Révolutionnaire et Romantique /Sir John Eliot Gardiner**
Philips ② 442 142-2PH2 (120' · DDD) Recorded 1992
Notes, texts and translations included　　Ⓕ**O**

Gardiner's Verdi *Requiem* is in a class of its own. His are readings that combine a positive view and interpretative integrity from start to finish, something possible only in the context of the superb professionalism of the (augmented) Monteverdi Choir, which sings with a burnished and steady tone throughout and suggests, rightly, a corporate act of worship. Its contribution is beyond praise.

He might also have been surprised and delighted to ear the soloists' contribution sung with such precision by such a finely integrated quartet, who perform the important unaccompanied passages with special grace and sensitivity. Instead of the usual jostle of vibratos, here the four voices are firm and true. Individually they're also distinguished. Pride of place must go to Orgonášová who gives the performance of her life. The exactly placed high B in the 'Quid sum miser' section of the 'Dies irae', the perfect blending with von Otter at 'Dominum', the whole of the Andante section of the 'Libera me',

---

VERDI MESSA DA REQUIEM – IN BRIEF

Philharmonia Orchestra / Carlo Maria Giulini
BBC Legends ② BBCL4029-2 (153' · ADD)
Ⓜ**OOO**

☀ Of the several performances by Giulini currently in circulation, this one arguably has the most atmosphere and the best sound. It's a live relay of a concert he gave at the Royal Albert Hall with British soloists in the run up to his starrier studio recording.

Berlin PO / Claudio Abbado
EMI ② 557168-2 (84' · DDD)　　Ⓕ**O**
A live recording, also available on DVD, to mark the occasion of the 100th anniversary of the composer's death. The conductor's searing intensity reflects his own recent brush with mortality. The soloists, Angela Gheorghiu in particular, are excellent too.

La Scala Chorus and Orchestra / Riccardo Muti
EMI ② 749390-2 (88' · DDD)　　Ⓕ**O**
Muti's second recording is an authentically Italian affair on a big operatic scale, with sometimes histrionic extremes of tempo and Pavarotti in the line-up of soloists. The recorded sound conveys the spaciousness of the venue at some expense of detail.

Orchestre Révolutionnaire et Romantique / Sir John Eliot Gardiner
Philips ② 442 142-2PH2 (120' · DDD)　　Ⓕ**O**
Gardiner's historically aware set has many assets: uncommonly accurate choral singing, a cleaned-up text, the widest dynamic range and traditionally broad tempos. The makeweight is an unbeatable *Four Sacred Pieces*.

Hungarian State Opera / Pier Giorgio Morandi
Naxos ② 8 550944/5 (126' · DDD)　　Ⓢ**O**
A super-budget account with youthful sounding soloists and effective, if not ideally focused choral forces.

Kirov Orchestra / Valery Gergiev
Philips ② 468 079-2 (DDD)　　Ⓕ
Gergiev conducts one of the latest, most theatrical (and certainly the most hyped) account of the *Messa da Requiem* in the current catalogue; his Kirov forces are joined by the 'dream team' line-up of Renée Fleming, Olga Borodina, Andrea Bocelli and Ildebrando d'Arcangelo

NBC SO / Arturo Toscanini
RCA mono ② 74321 72373-2 (141' · ADD)　　Ⓜ
Toscanini's searingly intense LP version of 1951 is considered a classic of the gramophone; his singers are Herva Nelli, Fedora Barbieri, Giuseppe di Stefano and Cesare Siepi.

sung with ethereal tone and a long breath, make the heart stop in amazement.

In 'Oro supplex' Gardiner follows Verdi's tempo marking. More often he follows tradition, with slower speeds than those suggested, and he allows more licence than the score, or conductors like Toscanini. But as his liberties all seem so convincing in the context of the whole, who should complain? In the *Pezzi sacri*, Gardiner gives the most thrilling account yet to appear.

The recording, made in Westminster Cathedral, has a huge range which may cause problems in confined spaces. You're liable to be overwhelmed, for instance, by the 'Dies irae'.

Messa da Requiem. Quattro pezzi sacri
Elena Filipova sop **Gloria Scalchi** mez **César Hernández** ten **Carlo Colombara** bass **Hungarian State Opera Choir and Orchestra / Pier Giorgio Morandi**
Naxos ② 8 550944/5 (126' · DDD) Texts and translations included ⑤❍

Morandi brings to his interpretation a youthful, Italian energy and generosity of expression. Given a judicious choice of young soloists, all up to their exigent tasks, an excellent chorus (a shattering 'Dies irae', an alert, not too drilled *Sanctus*, a disciplined 'Libera me' fugue) and a well-fashioned recording, this set makes a compelling case for recommendation as an alternative to Gardiner's period-performance set. Try track 7, the 'Rex tremendae', where you can hear how Morandi builds a movement unerringly to an appropriately tremendous climax.

The soloists show how involved they are in the work, form a good ensemble and individually exhibit the intelligence to sing quietly as needed. Filipova and Scalchi combine into a rich-toned duo in 'Liber scriptus', spoilt a little by moments of indeterminate pitch from the soprano. Hernández, with his warm, baritonal, Spanish-style tenor, sings a sensitive 'Ingemisco' (a touch of insecurity at the start excepted), succeeded by Colombara's truly magisterial conjuring of the flames of hell at 'Confutatis maledictis'. Filipova's floated entry at 'huic ergo' in the succeeding trio and the sheer intensity of the whole 'Lacrymosa' bring the 'Dies irae' to a fitting close.

The rest of the work's performance is on an equivalent level of achievement, Morandi always judging speeds to a nicety. The fill-up to this large-scale reading is a fine performance of the *Quattro pezzi sacri*.

Additional recommendations

Messa da Requiem

Caniglia sop **Stignani** mez **Gigli** ten **Pinza** bass 🅷
Rome Opera Chorus and Orchestra / Serafin
EMI Références mono 567486-2 (72' · ADD) Text and translation included Ⓜ
Also available on Naxos Historical 8110159 Ⓢ

Serafin's 1939 *Requiem* recording is something of a classic, with Ebe Stignani and Ezio Pinza ideal for their parts and Maria Caniglia and Beniamino Gigli almost as good. Note, there are small cuts.

Coupled with: Te Deum. Aida –Sinfonia. La forza 🅷 del destino – Sinfonia. Luisa Miller – Sinfonia. La traviata – Preludes: Act I & II. I vespri siciliani – Sinfonia
Tebaldi sop **Elmo** mez **Prandelli** ten **Siepi** bass **Westminster Choir; Chorus and Orchestra of La Scala, Milan; NBC Symphony Orchestra / Toscanini**
Istituto Discografico Italiano mono ② IDIS345/46 (135' · ADD) Recorded 1940-43, 1945; live 1950 Ⓜ❍
The huge plus of this set is the young Tebaldi in radiant voice; not many soloists have come so close to fulfilling all this work demands. All the other soloists are good if not outstanding; the chorus is a shade unruly, but Toscanini himself is at his best, combining dramatic force with lyrical warmth.

Milanov sop **Thorborg** mez **Rosvaenge** ten 🅷 **Moscona** bass **BBC Symphony Chorus and Orchestra / Arturo Toscanini**
Testament mono ② SBT21362 (89' · ADD · N/T/t). Recorded live at the Queen's Hall, London, 27 May 1938 Ⓜ
Skilfully remastered from BBC originals, this is a superior performance to Toscanini's familiar RCA version of 1951 simply because he gives the music more time to breathe. He imposes a unified and beseeching style on all his charges, impressing on them his own awe before Verdi's score.

Opera Choruses

Un ballo in maschera – Posa in pace. **Don Carlos** – Spuntato ecco il dì. Aida – Gloria all' Egitto. **I Lombardi** – Gerusalem!; O Signore, dal tetto natio. **Macbeth** – Tre volte miagola; Patria oppressa. **I masnadieri** – Le rube, gli stupri. **Nabucco** – Gli arredi festivi giù cadano infranti; Va, pensiero, sull'ali dorate. **Otello** – Fuoco di gioia. **Rigoletto** – Zitti zitti. **La traviata**[a] – Noi siamo zingarelle … Di Madride nio siam mattadori. **Il trovatore** – Vedi! Le fosche notturne spoglie; Squilli, echeggi la tromba guerriera. **Requiem** – Sanctus
[a]**Marsha Waxman** mez [a]**David Huneryager**, [a]**Richard Cohn** basses **Chicago Symphony Chorus and Orchestra / Sir Georg Solti**
Decca 430 226-2DH (70' · DDD) Recorded 1989. Texts and translations included Ⓕ❍

Verdi's opera choruses are invariably redblooded and usually make a simple dramatic statement with great impact. The arresting 'Chorus of the Hebrew Slaves' from *Nabucco* is probably the best-known and most popular chorus in the entire operatic repertoire, immediately tugging at the heart-strings with its gentle opening cantilena, soon swelling out to a great climax. Solti shows just how to shape the noble melodic line, which soars with firm control, yet retaining the urgency and electricity in every bar. The dramatic contrasts at the opening of 'Gerusalem!' from *I Lombardi* are equally powerfully projected, and the brass again makes a riveting effect in 'Patria oppressa' from *Macbeth*. Bu not all Verdi choruses offer blood and thunder: the volatile 'Fire chorus' from *Otello* flickers with an almost visual fantasy, while the wicked robbers in *I masnadieri* celebrate their excesses gleefully, and with such rhythmic jauntiness that you can't quite take them seriously. The 'Gypsies' chorus' from *La traviata* has a nice touch of elegance, and the scherzo-like 'Sanctus', from the *Requiem* is full of joy. But it's the impact of the dramatic moments that's most memorable, not least the big triumphal scene from *Aida*, complete with the ballet music, to provide a diverse interlude in the middle. The recording is in the demonstration class.

cabaletta all light eagerness on both sides. Then there's plangent singing on both sides in the sad little piece from *Vespri*, though it's a pity they did not attempt this in the original French. Here and throughout Alagna is his customary self, assured (a few over-pressed high notes, some unwritten, apart), impassioned, thoughtful and accurate in his phraseology, nowhere more so than in the parts he's unlikely as yet to take on stage – Radames and Otello. Even more important in so many passages, Alagna finds the right *mezzo-piano*, where heavier tenors have to sing forte , notably in the closing phrases where Otello wafts his love of Desdemona on to the night air – a moment of sheer magic.

Abbado and the Berlin Philharmonic Orchestra are at their peak of achievement and the recording catches these voices in their full glory, making this a most desirable issue.

Opera Duets

Aida[a] – La fatal pietra; Morir si pura e bella; O terra addio[b]. **Don Carlo** – E dessa!...Un detto, un sol; Vago sogno m'arrise; Ma lassù cí vedremo. **I Lombardi**[a] – Oh belle, a questa misera; All' armi! **I masnadieri** – Qual mare, qual terra; Qui nel bosco?; Lassù risplendere. **Otello** – Già nella notte densa; Venga la morte!. **Rigoletto** – Ah! veglia, o donna; Signor ne principe; T'amo! T'amo; E il sol dell' anima; Addio, addio[c]. **Simon Boccanegra** – Cielo di stelle orbato; Vieni a mirar la cerula. **La traviata**[a] – Libiamo, ne' lieti calici. **Il trovatore**[a] – Miserere ...Ah, che la morte ognora. **I vespri siciliani** – Pensando a me!
Angela Gheorghiu *sop* **Roberto Alagna** *ten* [bc]**Sara Mingardo** *mez* [c]**Brian Parsons,** [c]**Rodney Gibson** *tens* [ab]**London Voices; Berlin Philharmonic Orchestra /Claudio Abbado**
EMI 556656-2 (70' · DDD) Texts and translations included ⓕ**OO**

This long, fascinating, highly ambitious recital is nothing less than a conspectus of Verdi's soprano-tenor duets, and is executed with distinction on all sides. Gheorghiu deserves particular plaudits. It seems that nothing in Verdi (and indeed in much else) is beyond her capabilities. Her singing here, especially as Gilda, Aida and Desdemona, is so exquisite, the tone so warm and limpid, the phrasing so shapely as surely to melt any heart. Take, for example, Gilda's touching exchanges with Giovanna, herself sung by the superb mezzo Sara Mingardo, the whole of Aida's solo beginning 'Presago il core', with the soprano's warm lower register coming into play and that ultimate test, Desdemona's poised 'Amen'. Throughout, both musically and interpretatively, she simply can't be faulted.

Neither she nor her husband is backward in coming forward with less hackneyed pieces, those from the early operas – try the section starting 'Ma un' iri di pace' in the *Masnadieri* duet, the two voices in ideal blend, phrases and tone sweetly shaded with the following

Opera Arias

Aida – Qui Radames verrà; O patria mia. **Un ballo in maschera** – Morrò, ma prima in grazia. **Don Carlo** – Tu che le vanità. **La forza del destino** – Pace, pace, mio Dio. **Otello**[a] – Era più calmo?; Mia madre aveva; Piangea cantando; Ave Maria. **Rigoletto** – Gualtier Maldè ...Caro nome. **Simon Boccanegra** – Come in quest'ora bruna. **Il trovatore**[b] – Che più t'arresti?... Tacea la notte placida ...Di tale amor. **I vespri siciliani** – Mercè, dilette amiche
Angela Gheorghiu *sop* [a]**Laura Polverelli,** [b]**Tiziana Tramonti** *mezzos* **Giuseppe Verdi Symphony Orchesra, Milan/Riccardo Chailly**
Decca 466 952-2DH (67' · DDD) Texts and translations included ⓕ**OOO**

So much is enthralling in this superbly executed recital that it's hard to know where to begin. In some respects Elisabetta's long scene from *Don Carlo* is a template for everything. There you hear the spinto sound that's just about ideal for the big-breathed phrases at the start; the floated tone and *voce portando* in the remembrances of happier days in France; finally, in the agitated section, comes the glottal attack so reminiscent of great Verdi sopranos from the past. As important as any of these attributes is Gheorghiu's ability to think herself from nowhere into a new character. All Elisabetta's torment of the soul is there. Callas is an obvious influence at certain key moments, and the reading need fear nothing by comparison. Montserrat Caballé in the complete *Don Carlo* (EMI) is another great singer recollected, but Gheorghiu, as sensitive as the Spanish soprano, as the more appropriate voice.

'O patria mia' is again just about ideal, with the difficult close nicely encompassed. One notices here, too, the acuity with words, the wonderful control of breath, the poise of line. Throughout the programme, Chailly gives not only considerate support but also helps by establishing tempos that never drag. Each aria flows easily and naturally, effects all the better for being made within a firmly set context. Gheorghiu's warmth of feeling and tone informs the *Boccanegra* Amelia's sea-influenced thoughts, but here, and possibly for Gilda, a slightly brighter timbre would be preferable. The prayer of that other Amelia, the erring wife of King Gustavus in *Ballo*, adumbrates all her desperation. Better still are the even more desperate thoughts of the *Forza* Leonora *in extremis*, an interpretation to rank with the most compelling on disc.

At last, sated with so much sure artistry, we reach Desdemona. The Willow song flows beautifully in voice and orchestra, and with so many shades and colourings used the 'Ave Maria' has a beseeching, inward quality. Scotto or de los Angeles finds even more pathos in the scena, but none sings with quite the same degree of security and natural ease. The Milan recordings, at two sessions and venues, are excellent.

Un ballo in maschera – Ecco l'orrido campo ... Ma dall'arido stelo divulsa ... Morrò, ma prima in grazia. **La forza del destino** – Pace, pace, mio Dio. **Nabucco** – Ben io t'invenni ... Anch'io dischiuso un giorno. **La traviata** – E strano!... Ah, fors'è lui ... Follie! Sempre libera[a]; Teneste la promessa ... Addio del passato. **Il trovatore** – Tacea la notte placida ... Di tale amor; Timor di me? ... D'amor sull'ali rosee
Julia Varady sop [a]**Lothar Odinius** ten **Bavarian State Orchestra / Dietrich Fischer-Dieskau**
Orfeo C186951 (51' · DDD)   ⓕ❍

Varady endows these arias we have heard hundreds of times, and of which we all have our favourite memories and recordings, with renewed life through an art which is fully responsive, highly fastidious, lovely in the quality of its sound and individual in its timbre and inflection. The beauty of tone is evident first of all in its well-preserved purity (and Varady, born in 1941, is of an age when normally allowances have to be made). Hers isn't a full-bodied, rich Ponselle-like voice, but she makes wonderfully effective use of her resources, which include a surprisingly strong lower register and an upward range that (as we hear) easily encompasses the high D flat and has an E flat available. She's dramatic in style yet also thoroughly accomplished in her scales, trills and other fioriture. Her first *Trovatore* aria, for instance, includes the cabaletta with its full complement of technical brilliances. The musical instinct seems almost infallible – a 'wrong' portamento or rubato always irritates and here everything seems just right. A remarkable sensitivity is at work throughout.

The orchestra is conducted by Fischer-Dieskau, Varady's husband, and here too is a fine example of a positive, non-routine collaboration, the pacing and shading of the orchestral parts so frequently having something specific to offer (for example, in the letter passage from *La traviata*). The recording is well balanced.

Aida

Aida   Ⓗ
Maria Callas sop Aida **Fedora Barbieri** mez Amneris **Richard Tucker** ten Radames **Tito Gobbi** bar Amonasro **Giuseppe Modesti** bass Ramphis **Nicola Zaccaria** bass King of Egypt **Elvira Galassi** sop Priestess **Franco Ricciardi** ten Messenger **Chorus and Orchestra of La Scala, Milan / Tullio Serafin**
EMI Callas Edition mono ② 556316-2 (144' · ADD) Recorded 1955. Notes, text and translation included   ⓕ❍❍

Aida, the daughter of the Ethiopian king, is a prisoner at the Egyptian court where she falls in love with Radames, an Egyptian captain of the guard; Amneris, the Egyptian princess, also loves him. The tensions between these characters are rivetingly portrayed and explored, and the gradual build-up to Aida's and Radames's union in death is paced with the sureness of a master composer.

Callas's Aida is an assumption of total understanding and conviction; the growth from a slave-girl torn between love for her homeland and Radames, to a woman whose feelings transcend life itself represents one of the greatest operatic undertakings ever committed to disc. Alongside her is Fedora Barbieri, an Amneris palpable in her agonised mixture of love and jealousy – proud yet human. Tucker's Radames is powerful and Gobbi's Amonasro quite superb – a portrayal of comparable understanding to set alongside Callas's Aida.

Tullio Serafin's reading is in the central Italian tradition of 50 years ago. That's to say, it's unobtrusively right in matters of tempo, emphasis and phrasing, while occasionally passing indifferent ensemble in the choral and orchestral contribution. Although the recording can't compete with modern versions (it was never, in fact, a model of clarity), nowhere can it dim the brilliance of the creations conjured up by this classic cast.

Aida
Birgit Nilsson sop Aida **Grace Bumbry** mez Amneris **Franco Corelli** ten Radames **Mario Sereni** bar Amonasro **Bonaldo Giaiotti** bass Ramfis **Ferruccio Mazzoli** bass King **Piero de Palma** ten Messenger **Mirella Fiorentini** mez Priestess **Chorus and Orchestra of Rome Opera / Zubin Mehta**
HMV Classics ② HMVD5 73410-2 (141' · ADD) Recorded 1966   Ⓢ Ⓑ ❍

In the 1950s and 1960s EMI made a series of what have become classics with Rome Opera forces that have Verdi in their blood. This *Aida*, greeted with reservations then, now seems like manna from heaven in a world starved of true Verdian voices. Above all there's Corelli's truly *spinto* tenor, a thrilling sound in itself, and used, as Radames (one of the most exciting on disc), with far more sensitivity than is usually allowed for. Nilsson matches Corelli in vocal bite and gets inside the character, even if she's a touch unwieldy at times. As on stage, Bumbry is an imposing, spirited Amneris, Sereni makes an above-average Amonasro and Giaiotti sounds like Pinza as Ramfis – praise can't be higher. The young Zubin Mehta conducts with a deal of dramatic verve. The recording is excellent.

Aida
Anna Tomowa-Sintow sop Aida **Brigitte Fassbaender** mez Amneris **Plácido Domingo** ten Radames **Siegmund Nimsgern** bar Amonasro **Robert Lloyd** bass Ramfis **Nikolaus Hillebrand** bass King **Norbert Orth** ten Messenger **Marianne Seibel** sop Priestess; Bavarian State Opera Chorus and Orchestra / **Riccardo Muti**
Orfeo d'Or ② C583 022I (143' · ADD) Recorded live at the National Theatre, Munich in 1979 Notes included   Ⓕ◐

Riccardo Muti's 1974 studio recording on EMI, with Caballé, Cossotto and Domingo, has been one of the steady recommendations for this work on CD. This live account from 1979 in many, but not all ways, surpasses the studio performance. In the first place, Muti's reading has matured to the extent of being less wilful – for instance, his tempo for the closing scene's 'O terra addio' is the better for being more orthodox – and even more persuasive in terms of fulfilling Verdi's exacting demands on all concerned. Seldom can the full panoply and subtlety of the composer's scoring, especially the wonderful wind writing, have been so clearly expounded. The chorus is also commendable in every respect.

Domingo, fine enough on EMI, here gives possibly his most responsive and exciting Radames on disc and that's saying something. In tremendous voice, he produces magic towards the end of 'Celeste Aida' with the triple *pianissimo* Verdi asks for but seldom gets, and throughout he make every effort to fulfil Verdi's demand for *dolce* and *pp* effects. It hardly needs saying that he was at the time at the peak of his amazing powers.

Tomowa-Sintow provides most of the heft combined with sensibility that the title part calls for. Although she can't manage Caballé's many exquisite moments when she floats her tone on high, she has the firmer, stronger voice to ride the orchestra at climactic moments. You don't quite feel the strong identification with the part that Fassbaender undoubtedly gives to her first Amneris. Fassbaender is very much her idiosyncratic, wholly compelling self, rising to heights of music-drama in Amneris's great Act 4 scene, the repeated 'io stessa… lo getta' rending the heart. This is an interpretation to savour.

The recording, although the voices are sometimes a little distanced, catches the high excitement of a first night in the opera house. Applause is never intrusive, scenery change only once so. This is as gripping an account of the piece of any on disc.

VERDI AIDA – IN BRIEF

Anna Tomowa-Sintow Aida **Brigitte Fassbaender** Amneris **Siegmund Nimsgern** Amonasro **Bavarian State Opera Chorus and Orchestra / Riccardo Muti**
Orfeo ② C583022I (143' · ADD)   Ⓜ◐
Under Riccardo Muti's vivid direction an already special cast gains greatly from the excitement of a live recording, worth the very few flaws in voice and recording.

Maria Callas Aida **Fedora Barbieri** Amneris **Tito Gobbi** Amonasro **Chorus and Orchestra of La Scala, Milan / Tulio Serafin**
EMI ② 556316-2 (144' · AAD)   Ⓕ◐◐
Maria Callas's blazing yet vulnerable Aida heads a cast of great names, conducted with real grandeur by Serafin. Only the mono recording is any drawback.

Birgit Nilsson Aida **Grace Bumbry** Amneris **Mario Sereni** Amonasro **Rome Opera Chorus and Orchestra / Zubin Mehta**
HMV ② HMVD573410-2 (141' · ADD)   Ⓑ◐
Nilsson and Corelli are a vocally towering pair of lovers, along with Bumbry's rich Amneris the main attractions of a cast that otherwise ranges from excellent to acceptable.

Leontyne Price Aida **Rita Gorr** Amneris **Robert Merrill** Amonasro **Rome Opera Chorus and Orchestra / Sir Georg Solti**
Decca ② 460 765-2DF2 (152' · ADD)   Ⓜ
Two superlative voices, Leontyne Price a sensuous, dark-toned Aida, and Vickers a steely yet tormented Radames, with strong support from Rita Gorr's Amneris and Robert Merrill's bluff Amonasro. Solti's conducting is electrifyingly dramatic.

Adina Aaron Aida **Kate Aldrich** Amneris **Giuseppe Garra** Amonasro **Arturo Toscanini Foundation Chorus and Orchestra / Massimiliano Stefaneli**
TDK **DVD** DV-AIDDB (188')   Ⓕ
Aida works unexpectedly well in the smaller scale, in a good-looking 'traditional' staging by Franco Zeffirelli with a non-starry but immensely vital young cast, in the theatre at Verdi's birthplace Busetto.

Aprile Millo Aida **Dolora Zajick** Amneris **Sherrill Milnes** Amonasro **Metropolitan Opera Chorus and Orchestra / James Levine**
DG **DVD** 073 001-9 (158')   Ⓕ
The Met's staging is on a suitably Pharaonic scale, although the spectacularly authentic sets aren't matched by the rather silly costumes. Domingo, though below his best, is a splendid Radames, and, while local girl Millo isn't as expressive as some, she's still involving. Levine conducts with epic grandeur but too little *brio*.

Verdi Opera

Additional recommendation

Aida
Caballé Aida **Domingo** Radames **Cossotto** Amneris
Chorus of the Royal Opera House, Covent Garden;
New Philharmonia Orchestra;Trumpeters of the
Royal Military School of Music, Kneller Hall / **Muti**
EMI Great Recordings of the Century ③ 567613-2
(148' · ADD)   Ⓜ
Highlights available on EMI Encore Ⓑ 574759-2

Montserrat Caballé gives her most successful
Verdi performance on record, full of those vocal
subtleties and beauties that inform her best
singing, while Riccardo Muti gives an impassioned
account of the score.

Un ballo in maschera

Un ballo in maschera   Ⓗ
Maria Callas sop Amelia **Giuseppe di Stefano** ten
Riccardo **Ettore Bastianini** bar Renato **Eugenia
Ratti** sop Oscar **Giulietta Simionato** contr Ulrica
Antonio Cassinelli bass Sam **Marco Stefanoni** bass
Tom **Giuseppe Morresi** bar Silvano **Angelo
Mercuriali** ten Judge **La Scala, Milan Chorus and
Orchestra / Gianandrea Gavazzeni**
EMI mono ② 567918-2 (131' · ADD) Recorded live
1957. Notes, text and translation included   Ⓜ**OO**

This set comes from live performances at La
Scala in the mid-1950s when the diva was at the
height of her powers. Callas gives here an even
more vital performance than on her studio
recorded set. It was Callas's particular genius to
find exactly the appropriate mode of expression
for every role she tackled. Here we have Callas
the tormented, guilty wife. But she also gives us
a hundred different individual inflections to
reflect the emotion of the moment: indeed, as
John Steane points out in one of his illuminating notes, it's often a small aside that reveals as
much about the character she's portraying s a
big set-piece.

The context of an evening in the theatre
makes this a more arresting, vivid interpretation
on all sides than its studio counterpart of a year
earlier, with Gianandrea Gavazzeni galvanising
his fine cast to great things. As the late John
Ardoin put it in his study of Callas's recordings:
'The La Scala performance is sung with more
vivid colours, with accents more etched and a
general intensification of Verdi's drama.' Here
the sound picture is appreciably superior to that
on earlier live sets which capture Callas in other
roles at La Scala. The irresistible Di Stefano is
the soul of vital declamation as Riccardo. Ettore
Bastianini's forthright Renato, the only role he
sang in London and one of his best in an all too
short career, and Giulietta Simionato's classic
Ulrica are also huge assets. Other roles are filled
with house singers of the day. An unbeatable set.

Un ballo in maschera   Ⓗ
Giuseppe di Stefano ten Riccardo **Tito Gobbi** bar
Renato **Maria Callas** sop Amelia **Fedora Barbieri**
mez Ulrica **Eugenia Ratti** sop Oscar **Ezio Giordano**
bass Silvano **Silvio Maionica** bass Samuel **Nicola**

Zaccaria bass Tom **Renato Ercolani** ten Judge
**Chorus and Orchestra of La Scala, Milan /
Antonino Votto**
EMI Callas Edition mono ② 556320-2
(130' · ADD) Recorded 1956. Notes, text and
translation included   Ⓕ**OO**

Ballo manages to encompass a vein of light-
hearted frivolity (represented by the page,
Oscar) within the confines of a serious drama of
love, infidelity, noble and ignoble sentiments.
None of the more recent recordings has quite
caught the opera's true spirit so truly as this one
under Votto's unerring direction. Callas has not
been surpassed in delineating Amelia's conflict
of feelings and loyalties, nor has di Stefano been
equalled in the sheer ardour of his singing as
Riccardo. Add to that no less a singer than Tito
Gobbi as Renato, at first eloquent in his friendship to his ruler, then implacable in his revenge
when he thinks Riccardo has stolen his wife.
Fedora Barbieri is full of character as the sooth-
sayer Ulrica, Eugenia Ratti a sparky Oscar. It's
an unbeatable line-up.

Un ballo in maschera
Plácido Domingo ten Riccardo **Piero Cappuccilli**
bar Renato **Martina Arroyo** sop Amelia **Fiorenza
Cossotto** mez Ulrica **Reri Grist** sop Oscar **Giorgio
Giorgetti** bass Silvano **Gwynne Howell** bass Samuel
Richard Van Allan bass Tom **Kenneth Collins** ten
Judge **David Barrett** bar Servant **Haberdashers'
Aske's School Girls' Choir; New Philharmonia
Orchestra; Chorus of the Royal Opera House,
Covent Garden / Riccardo Muti**
EMI 566510-2 (127' · ADD) Recorded 1975 Notes, text
and translation included   Ⓜ**O**

This is the *Ballo* which, above all else, glories in
Muti as an exuberant man of the theatre. The
impetus with which he whips up the constituent
parts of an ensemble into the vortex, and the
juxtaposition of blasting *tutti* with slim, sweetly
phrased woodwind detail, so typical of this
opera, hits the ear more thrillingly than ever. So
does the equally characteristic tugging undercurrent of the *ballo* against the intrigue of the
maschera, activated by Muti with such acute perception and *élan*.

He provides pliant, springing support for all
his singers too: Domingo, a warm, generous
Riccardo, is every bit as happy with Muti as with
Abbado. The same can't be said of Martina
Arroyo, the weak link on this recording. Dramatically forceful, but curiously cool and
detached from the expressive nuancing of her
part, she has little of the vulnerability of a Ricciarelli (Abbado), or the individuality of a Price
(Solti). But, although this mid-price recording
may not offer the most consistently luxurious
vocal banquet, none the less, with Cossotto's
stentorian Ulrica and Cappuccilli's staunch,
resilient Renato, its strong sense of theatrical
presence and its dramatic integrity will make it
the chosen version for many new collectors.

Additional recommendation

Un ballo in maschera
Ricciarelli Amelia **Domingo** Riccardo **Bruson** Renato
Chorus and Orchestra of La Scala, Milan / Abbado
DG ② 453 148-2GTA2 (127' · ADD) Notes included Ⓜ
A satisfying and unified performance, largely
because Abbado and his La Scala forces give us the
sense of a real theatrical experience. Ricciarelli
and Domingo give involved and expressive
performances.

Don Carlos

Don Carlos
Plácido Domingo ten Don Carlo **Montserrat
Caballé** sop Elisabetta di Valois **Shirley Verrett** mez
Eboli **Sherrill Milnes** bar Rodrigo **Ruggero
Raimondi** bass Filippo II **Giovanni Foiani** bass
Grand Inquisitor **Simon Estes** bass-bar Monk **Delia
Wallis** mez Tebaldo **Ryland Davies** ten Conte di
Lerma **John Noble** bar Herald **Maria-Rosa del
Campo** sop Voice from Heaven **Ambrosian Opera
Chorus; Royal Opera House Orchestra, Covent
Garden /Carlo Maria Giulini**
EMI Great Recordings of the Century ③ 567401-2
(209' · ADD) Recorded 1970. Text and translation
included   Ⓜ❶❶❶

From the day that Giulini conducted
the now legendary production of *Don
Carlo* at Covent Garden in 1958, a
recording of the opera by him looked a must. In
fact, it was to be 12 years before EMI took the
plunge, but the set was worth waiting for: it's
the five-act version in Italian, without the cuts
made at the Royal Opera, and well recorded and
handsomely cast. Giulini himself had slowed
down since the live performances, but the blend
of majesty and lyric beauty that he brings to the
opera is hard to resist. The music glows warmly
in his hands, as befits one of Verdi's most
human dramas.

His cast gathers together five of the leading
singers of the 1970s. In particular, the trio of
Caballé, Domingo and Milnes seemed to be
rather predictably the names on almost every
Italian opera recording at the time, but how
glad we would be to have young singers like
them today. Caballé, though occasionally
sounding blowsy, is exquisite whenever quiet
singing is called for, and Domingo is at his
golden best throughout. Their murmured
farewells at the monastery of San Giusto in Act
5 have never been surpassed. Verrett is a fiery
Eboli (although it's a shame Giulini did not give
her more pace in 'O don fatale'), and Milnes
provides generous-hearted singing as Rodrigo.
It's good to have an Italian bass as Philip II, but
Raimondi lacks the black tone and fearsome
presence of his notable predecessor in the role,
Boris Christoff. Lovers of the opera will want to
investigate the four-act version under Santini
and also the five-act version in French under
Pappano, both on EMI (which has more or less
cornered the market for this opera). Otherwise,
30 years on, Giulini's splendid performance is as
satisfying as any, probably still the number one
recommendation.

Don Carlos
Roberto Alagna ten Don Carlos **Karita Mattila** sop
Elisabeth **Waltraud Meier** mez Eboli **Thomas Hampson** bar Rodrigue **José van Dam** bass-bar Philippe II
Eric Halfvarson bass Grand Inquisitor **Csaba Airizer**
bass Monk **Anat Efraty** sop Thibault **Scot Weir** ten
Comte de Lerme, Herald **Donna Brown** sop Voice
from Heaven **Chorus of the Théâtre du Châtelet;
Orchestre de Paris / Antonio Pappano**
EMI ③ 556152-2 (206' · DDD) Recorded live 1996.
Notes, text and translation included   Ⓕ❶❶

This is an eloquent and inspiriting performance
of Verdi's singular music-drama depicting private tragedy within public conflict, and a
recording of the French version. With regard to
the text, Pappano excludes the opening scene
for the chorus at Fontainebleau, cut by the composer before the first night; he includes the
important dress-changing scene at the start of
Act 3 (which explains Carlos's ardour towards
the 'wrong' woman), a snippet of the Elisabeth-
Eboli duet in Act 4, and the whole of the Carlos-
Philippe duet after Posa's death (the theme of
which was reused in the Requiem). Pappano
also chooses some of the alternative settings,
notably in the Rodrigue-Philippe duet in Act 2
and the farewell encounter of Elisabeth and
Carlos in Act 5, amendments that Verdi made
for the neglected 1872 Naples revision. Neither
seems an improvement.

Pappano's is a subtly shaped, superbly paced
and vital interpretation from start to finish. He's
as able to encompass the delicacies of the Veil
song and the succeeding exchanges as he is to
purvey the grand, tragic passion of Elisabeth
and Carlos in Act 2, the intricacies and changes
of feeling in the colloquy between Rodrigue and
Philippe, the terrible menace of the Grand
Inquisitor. The orchestra supports him with
playing of dedication and sensitivity. Giulini's
noble conducting of the Italian version
(reviewed above) comes to mind when listening
to Pappano and his players. Praise can't be
higher.

By and large he has singers who can sustain his
vision. Mattila sings a lovely Elisabeth. Her
soft-grained yet strong tone and exquisite
phrasing in all her solos and duets are balm to
the ear. By Mattila's side Alagna offers an
equally involving Carlos, presenting a more vulnerable picture of the unbalanced infante. His is
a fully rounded portrayal that will please his
many admirers, the difficult tessitura seldom
troubling him and his French is impeccable. As
Rodrigue, Marquis de Posa, Hampson also has
idiomatic French. His mellifluous baritone well
suits this French version and he provides many
moments of vocal beauty. Arguably, the death
needs a more imposing voice but the added
decibels can easily be borne to appreciate
Hampson's intelligence. Van Dam nicely balances the exterior authority and interior agony

of Philippe, everywhere in command of line, language, phrase.

The recording catches the *frisson* of the theatrical experience; everything is clear and in its place, and the balance with the pit sounds natural. This is a landmark in the *Don Carlos* discography.

Christoff makes more of the text.

Mitropoulos sanctions a few regrettable cuts not tolerated by Muti. In other respects there's little to choose between these two live performances. For its age the sound on this 'new' version is remarkably good and well worth investigating at mid-price.

Ernani

Ernani   H
Mario Del Monaco ten Ernani **Anita Cerquetti** sop Elvira **Ettore Bastianini** bar Don Carlo **Boris Christoff** bass De Silva **Luciana Boni** sop Giovanna **Athos Cesarini** ten Don Riccardo **Aurelian Neagu** bass Iago **Maggio Musicale Fiorentino Chorus and Orchestra / Dimitri Mitropoulos**
Bel Canto mono ② BCS5011 (118' · ADD) Recorded live 1957. Notes included   Ⓜ●

This is a performance to delight Verdians, Florence seriously challenging its La Scala rival on EMI. The calibre and strength of the singing is a reminder of how often today we put up with third-best. All four principals not only have voices of essential power but also have Verdian style as part of their interpretative make-up. Furthermore they're led by the legendary Mitropoulos, such a force for good at the Maggio Musicale until his untimely death. He easily encompasses the cut and thrust, the rudimentary fervour of one of Verdi's earliest successes, combining at once rude rhythms with lyrical breadth of phrase in supporting is admirable cast and firmly controlling the many ensembles, and his orchestra responds with eagerness to is positive beat.

Cerquetti, whose brief but distinguished career came to an abrupt end not long after this performance took place, had an evenly projected *spinto* soprano and used it with such command that she was at the time spoken of as Tebaldi's equal. She encompasses with confidence her taxing aria and cabaletta at the beginning of the work and makes the most of what little the composer offers his soprano thereafter, shining particularly in the final trio, where Verdi is at his most inspired. As the eponymous hero, Del Monaco shows conclusively that he was more than the stentorian tenor he was often portrayed as being in his day, combining, in the lovers' brief moment of repose in Act 2, with Cerquetti's Elvira in a quietly reflective way. Where the supposed bandit breathes fire, Del Monaco is there with the appropriately flashing tone that made him so popular.

Verdi gives his baritone, Don Carlo, the meatiest music. Bastianini, then at the height of his powers, sings all his solos with resplendent and keen tone. Although he doesn't provide all the subtleties of line and colour Bruson achieves for Muti, Bastianini touches a real note of eloquence at 'O sommo Carlo' in Act 3. As old Silva, Christoff is his imposing self, rivalling his younger Bulgarian colleague, Ghiaurov, on the version from La Scala: both are excellent, but

Ernani
Plácido Domingo ten Ernani **Mirella Freni** sop Elvira **Renato Bruson** bar Don Carlo **Nicolai Ghiaurov** bass De Silva **Jolanda Michieli** sop Giovanna **Gianfranco Manganotti** ten Don Riccardo **Alfredo Giacomotti** bass Iago **Chorus and Orchestra of La Scala, Milan / Riccardo Muti**
EMI ② 747083-8 (128' · DDD) Recorded live 1982. Notes, text and translation included   Ⓕ

Renato Bruson's Don Carlo is an assumption that's as gripping dramatically as it is vocally. In his portrayal more than anywhere, the musical tension of *Ernani* becomes manifest, and everywhere Bruson offers superb Verdi singing. Domingo's Ernani is hardly less impressive and he benefits from being caught live on stage. His opening aria and cabaletta are full of delicate touches and obedience to the dynamic marks. In the last act, his recitative, 'Tutto ora tace d'intorno', has great pathos, and his contributions to the final trio an overwhelming eloquence. Here, too, Freni achieves most, the etching in of 'Il riso del tuo volto fa ch' io veda', a brief utterance of happiness, most affecting, and her desperate appeals to Silva for mercy sung with brio.

In her opening aria and cabaletta, the famous 'Ernani, Ernani', too much is asked of a voice not really meant by nature for this kind of heavy duty, but none can quite match the sorrow and heartbreak of Elvira's predicament that Freni manages in the theatre. Ghiaurov, rusty as his voice had become, creates a great impression of dignity and implacable strength, and many of those qualities are carried over into his singing. 'Infelice' is delivered with mature nobility, 'Ah, io l'amo' is intensely moving. Ghiaurov is denied Silva's probably spurious cabaletta. Otherwise the work is given complete.

Muti conducts the score in exemplary manner. He has learnt when to allow his singers licence to phrase with meaning and when to press on. The La Scala chorus gives us the genuine sound of Italian voices in full flight, sounding much more inside their various assumptions than their rivals. The audience is occasionally in evidence, as are the on-stage effects, but the atmosphere of being in an opera house and taking part, as it were, in a real occasion has all the advantages over the aseptic feeling of a studio.

Falstaff

Falstaff   H
Tito Gobbi bar Falstaff **Rolando Panerai** bar Ford **Elisabeth Schwarzkopf** sop Alice Ford **Anna Moffo** sop Nannetta **Luigi Alva** ten Fenton **Fedora**

Barbieri *mez* Mistress Quickly **Nan Merriman** *mez*
Meg Page **Tomaso Spataro** *ten* Dr Caius **Renato
Ercolani** *ten* Bardolph **Nicola Zaccaria** *bass* Pistol
**Philharmonia Chorus and Orchestra / Herbert von
Karajan**
EMI Great Recordings of the Century ② 567083-2
(120' · ADD) Recorded 1956. Notes, text and
translation included Ⓜ❍❍❍

 This *Falstaff* still stands (with Toscanini) peerless in the catalogue. At its
centre stands Tito Gobbi, and his is a
presence large enough to encompass both the
lord and the jester, the sensuous and the sensual,
and the deep seriousness as well as the deep
absurdity of his vision. Few Falstaffs have such a
measure of the simplicity of his first monosylla-
bles in the bustle around him; few find the poise
as well as the confusion within his music. Karajan's recording is incomparable in its quartet of
merry wives. Schwarzkopf's Alice radiates both
the 'gioia nell'aria' and the 'gioia nel' cor' of
Verdi's writing, Fedora Barbieri's redoubtable
Mistress Quickly, with her stentorian cries of
'Povera donna!', puts other readings in the
shade; Anna Moffo's Nannetta, perfectly
matched in timbre and agility with Luigi Alva's
Fenton, is a constant delight. Above all, it's their
corporate presence that works at such a distinctively higher level. Rolando Panerai is a magnificent Ford; his 'E sogno? o realtà?' is a high
point of the performance.

This 1956 recording has been discreetly and
skilfully doctored, but a little background hiss
does remain. But one doesn't actually end up
hearing it. This great recording is a-flutter with
pungent solo detail, realising, with Nannetta,
that the world is 'tutto deliro, sospiro e riso'.
The episodes of the opera, its exits and
entrances, its subjects and counter-subjects,
pass with the unique sensibility of Verdi's final
great exuberant fugue of life.

Falstaff
Bryn Terfel *bass-bar* Falstaff **Thomas Hampson** *bar*
Ford **Adrianne Pieczonka** *sop* Alice Ford **Dorothea
Röschmann** *sop* Nannetta **Daniil Shtoda** *ten* Fenton
Larissa Diadkova *mez* Mistress Quickly **Stella
Doufexis** *mez* Meg Page **Enrico Facini** *ten* Doctor
Caius **Anthony Mee** *ten* Bardolph **Anatoli
Kotscherga** *bass* Pistol Berlin Radio Chorus; Berlin
Philharmonic Orchestra / Claudio Abbado
DG ② 471 194-2GH2 (113' · DDD) Notes, text and
translation included Ⓕ

In the event, Terfel's portrayal of the title-role
doesn't quite live up to expectations; though the
singing is extremely fine, this perhaps is really a
Falstaff for Terfel fans only. Somehow he's too
knowing and too self-conscious; in the two
monologues, for instance, he sometimes allows
us to see him, as it were, without the make-up.
But such moments pass and there's plenty else
to listen to. This is a well-cast recording (much
better than the recent one under Gardiner with
its vocally ill-focused Falstaff). The wives are

excellent, especially Larissa Diadkova as
Quickly, and the Nannetta, Dorothea Röschmann, is among the best of all. Thomas Hampson as Ford is perhaps not such a good idea – his
voice doesn't have a mean streak in it. But the
comics do well and the interesting Daniil
Shtoda is a distinctive Fenton. This array of talent is recorded with little sense of presence
compared to their predecessors, most notably
those of the Karajan/Gobbi set of 1956 and the
Solti/Evans of 1963. The aural vision is clear
enough; it's just rather reduced and remote.

Falstaff is a musical score of the rarest quality.
You won't hear it much better sung and played
than it is here. Abbado conducts with a full
appreciation of the wit and tenderness, energy
and refinement, all justly balanced. But in this of
all operas it's essential to 'see' the stage. The
characters must be there before the ears which
are your eyes. Otherwise (among other consequences) you don't get the fun of it – and if it's
fun you want there's always Toscanini!

Falstaff Ⓗ
Giuseppe Valdengo *bar* Falstaff **Frank Guarrera** *bar*
Ford **Herva Nelli** *sop* Alice Ford **Teresa Stich-
Randall** *sop* Nannetta **Antonio Madasi** *ten* Fenton
Cloe Elmo *contr* Mistress Quickly **Nan Merriman**
mez Meg Page **Gabor Carelli** *ten* Dr Caius **John
Carmen Rossi** *ten* Bardolph **Norman Scott** *bass*
Pistol **Robert Shaw Chorale; NBC Symphony
Orchestra /Arturo Toscanini**
RCA Gold Seal mono ② 74321 72372-2 (117' · ADD)
Recorded 1950. Notes, text and translation
included Ⓜ❍❍❍

 This *Falstaff* remains, as it always has
been, one of the half a dozen greatest
opera sets ever recorded. It's a miracle
in every respect. How Toscanini loved Verdi
and how he strained every sinew to fulfil this
amazing score's variety in line, feeling and
colour. Whether it's the clarity and discipline of
the ensembles, the extraordinary care taken
over orchestral detail or the alert control of
dynamics, Toscanini is supreme, yet nothing is
done for effect's sake; everything seems natural,
inevitable, unforced, as though the score was
being created anew before us with chamber-
music finesse – and the atmosphere of a live performance adds to the feeling of immediacy.
Nobody dares, or seems to want, to interrupt
the magic being laid before him. Toscanini in
his old age is matching the subtlety and vitality
of the composer's own Indian summer – or one
might be tempted to say spring, so delicate and
effervescent does the scoring sound.

If, vocally, the main glory is the wonderful
sense of ensemble gained through hours of hard
rehearsals, individual contributions are almost
all rewarding. Indeed, Valdengo's Falstaff,
under Toscanini's tutelage, has not been surpassed on disc even by Gobbi. Flexibility,
charm, exactness, refinement inform his beautifully and wisely sung portrayal. He's no less
pointed and subtle in his encounter with Frank

Guarrera's imposing Ford. Another great joy of the set is the women's ensemble, their contribution the very epitome of smiling chatter. The Alice, Meg and Nannetta (Stich-Randall – none better), all sound, as they were, fresh and youthful. Herva Nelli is a lively and delightful Alice and Cloe Elmo's Quickly is as rich and ripe of voice and diction as any on disc, though a trifle coarse at times. The Fenton is sweet and Italianate in tone, but not as stylish as others. The smaller roles are all very much part of the team.

This set should certainly be a source of delightful revelation to a new generation of collectors who may have a wrong-headed view of what Toscanini was about. The remastering gives it clearer, more immediate sound than ever heard before from the originals.

Falstaff
Michele Pertusi bar Sir John Falstaff **Carlos Alvarez** bar Ford **Ana Ibarra** sop Alice Ford **Maria José Moreno** sop Nannetta **Bülent Bezdüz** ten Fenton **Jane Henschel** contr Mistress Quickly **Marina Domashenko** mez Meg Page **Alasdair Elliott** ten Dr Caius **Peter Hoare** ten Bardolph **Darren Jeffrey** bass Pistol **London Symphony Chorus and Orchestra / Sir Colin Davis**
LSO Live ② LSO0055 Ⓢ; .🎵. ② LSO0528 (119' · DSD/DDD · T/S/t/N) Recorded live Ⓜ**OO**

By all accounts the performances at the Barbican were among the most enjoyable of their kind in London for a long time, and certainly the enjoyment comes across on disc. The 'how' of it isn't so easily defined. It isn't the applause and occasional chuckles, though they help (comedy abhors a vacuum). It isn't even that, despite this being a concert rather than a staged event, the cast are performing entirely in character, and that they're doing so with zest and humorous intelligence. Rather it's as though a spirit of fun is in the air, breathed in by everyone, including the orchestra, who see the score's jokes and respond to its wit with the speed of light. Much of this must emanate from the maestro, who has every right to take pride in a brilliant achievement.

Michele Pertusi as Falstaff may lack Tito Gobbi's expressive resources, but he nevertheless has plenty of variety to offer. The grotesque acolytes and preposterous doctor play up well, and the lovers, Nannetta and Fenton, are a charming couple, convincingly young in voice and lyrical in style. Jane Henschel is a strong Mistress Quickly, better integrated into the ensemble than the riper plum-pudding dames who get the big laughs.

Falstaff has been well served on records ever since Toscanini set the standard high in 1950, but in few versions can the orchestra have played with more evident appreciation of the comedy on stage – it's almost as though the members of the LSO know the libretto by heart. This bids to become a firm favourite.

Additional recommendation

Falstaff
Trimarchi Falstaff **Servile** Ford **Faulkner** Alice Ford **Dilbèr** Nannetta **Comencini** Fenton **Chorus and Orchestra of Hungarian State Opera / Humburg**
Naxos ② 8 660050/1 (120' · DDD) Notes and synopsis included Ⓢ Ⓢ

Naxos's set does a good job at challenging the best in the field. Humburg strikes just the right balance between the high spirits and the delicacy in Verdi's score. Trimarchi as Falstaff gives a reading full of ripe understanding; his voice lies, as the role requires, ideally poised between baritone and bass. A very lovable portrait. This is a *Falstaff* to savour and one that will bear repetition.

La forza del destino

La forza del destino   Ⓗ
Maria Caniglia sop Leonora **Galliano Masini** ten Don Alvaro **Carlo Tagliabue** bar Don Carlo **Tancredi Pasero** bass Padre Guardiano **Ebe Stignani** mez Preziosilla **Saturno Meletti** bar Fra Melitone **Ernesto Dominici** bass Marquis of Calatrava **Giuseppe Nessi** ten Trabuco **Liana Avogadro** mez Curra **Italian Broadcasting Authority Chorus and Orchestra / Gino Marinuzzi**
Naxos Historical mono ② 8 110206/7(154' · ADD) Recorded 1941. Notes included Ⓢ

This is a fascinating, unmissable set both in historic and musical terms. Marinuzzi, a Toscanini coeval at La Scala, was chosen as conductor, and it's his only complete recording of an opera. The recording took place in May 1941 and was issued on 78rpm discs by Cetra. After the war Parlophone, which was then in charge of Cetra recordings in Britain, issued – in desultory fashion – a few separate discs. Sadly the whole version has never had the currency its great merits deserve, not at least as the first complete set (bar one traditionally cut scene) of the work and one with an entirely Italian cast. Now we have it to enjoy at super-budget price and in admirable transfers from original Cetra pressings, by Ward Marston.

For the recording Marinuzzi had assembled a vintage cast of Italian singers of the day. Caniglia herself rightly considered her Leonora here as one of her finest recordings: one can hear why in her committed, vibrant and often very sensitive singing: she even attempts some of the refined *pianissimo*s that graced the reading of this role by her near-contemporary, Zinka Milanov. It's a performance imbued with spiritual yearning – exactly what's wanted. By her side Masini's Alvaro is obviously a man of action with his blade-like, *spinto* tenor and sense of desperation at Alvaro's plight. If he's occasionally too lachrymose that's only a sign of his empathy with his role. As Alvaro's implacable antagonist, Don Carlo, Tagliabue provides dependable tone and an authentically styled interpretation of a kind seldom heard today. The pair's final and fatal encounter is one of the score's and the set's highlights.

Stignani, in her absolute prime, is a formidable Preziosilla, full in tone and clear in her passage-work, exemplary in every way. Marston has made the recording as amenable as is possible. In any case it would be worth suffering much worse sound than this for such a satisfying traversal on all sides of this inspired score.

La forza del destino   🄷
Stella Roman sop Leonora **Frederick Jagel** ten Don Alvaro **Lawrence Tibbett** bar Don Carlo **Ezio Pinza** bass Padre Guardiano **Irra Petina** mez Preziosilla **Salvatore Baccaloni** bass Melitone **Louis d'Angelo** bass Marquese **Thelma Votipka** mez Curra **Alessio de Paolis** ten Trabuco **Lorenzo Alvary** bass Mayor **John Gurney** bass Surgeon **Metropolitan Opera Chorus and Orchestra, New York / Bruno Walter**
Naxos Historical mono ③ 8 110038/40 (168' · AAD) Recorded live 1943   🄢

There has never been quite so electrifying a *Forza* as Walter's vital, brilliantly executed reading, which encapsulates the essence of the forthcoming drama. It confirms what few may know today, that Walter was a superb interpreter of Verdi. Yet this was the first time he had conducted *Forza*, so his lithe, finely honed reading is all the more remarkable. The other revelation is the Leonora of Stella Roman, a greatly underrated soprano brought to the Met in 1941, who yields few points to such notable interpreters of the part as Ponselle, Milanov and Tebaldi. They apart, you would go far to hear a Leonora so well equipped for the role, and so committed to it, one who uses her warm, generous voice to unerring effect in projecting the woman's dire predicament.

Padre Guardiano appears in the guise of Pinza, none better, and sounding, one uncertain high E apart, secure, concerned and authoritative. Jagel as Don Alvaro passes easily the test of the taxing aria of sad recollection at the start of Act 3. Tibbett as Don Carlo compels attention at every entry with his distinctive timbre and faultless style, but truth to tell the glorious tone had dulled since his great days in the 1930s and at times he sounds stretched by the part. Both his arias suffer cuts. Carlo's second (of three) duets with Alvaro is also excised as was then the custom, and strettas throughout are foreshortened. Baccaloni enjoys himself hugely as Melitone and obviously relishes his encounters with his superior, the Padre Guardiano, the two Italians revelling in the text. Petina is a lively but lightweight Preziosilla.

The sound is a bit crackly and restricted but good enough to enjoy an absorbing account of the score. This vivid version has much to commend it at the price.

La forza del destino
Martina Arroyo sop Leonora **Carlo Bergonzi** ten Don Alvaro **Piero Cappuccilli** bar Don Carlo

Ruggero Raimondi bass Padre Guardiano **Biancamaria Casoni** mez Preziosilla **Geraint Evans** bar Melitone **Antonio Zerbini** bass Marchese **Florindo Andreolli** ten Trabuco **Mila Cova** mez Curra **Virgilio Carbonari** bar Mayor **Derek Hammond-Stroud** bar Surgeon **Ambrosian Opera Chorus; Royal Philharmonic Orchestra / Lamberto Gardelli**
EMI Opera ③ 567124-2 (168' · ADD) Recorded 1969 Notes, text and translation included   🄜🅞

This opera demands an array of principal singers who need to be skilled in an unusually wide range of vocal and dramatic skills. It's a 'chase' opera, in which Carlo pursues Alvaro and Leonora through two countries, through cloister and convent, through scenes popular and martial, all treated on the most expansive scale. It's dominated by its series of magnificent duets that are composed so that the music marches with the development of situation and character. All the work's qualities are made manifest in this magnificent performance.

Gardelli's reissue is an excellent mid-price buy. It features Bergonzi, that prince among Verdi tenors, as an exemplary and appealing Alvaro, and Piero Cappuccilli – like Bergonzi at the peak of his powers when this set was made – as a full-blooded and Italianate Carlo. In the three all-important duets, their voices blend ideally. Leonora was the most successful of Arroyo's recorded roles, and she sings here with a feeling and urgency appropriate to Leonora's desperate situation. Casoni's vital Preziosilla, Raimondi's grave but over-lugubrious Padre Guardiano and Sir Geraint's keenly characterised Melitone all complete a well-chosen cast. Over all presides Gardelli, a Verdi conductor with an instinctive feeling for the ebb and flow of his music.

The recording, through subtle movements of the singers, convincingly suggests a stage performance.

Additional recommendations

La forza del destino

Price Leonora **Domingo** Don Alvaro **Milnes** Don Carlo **John Alldis Choir; London Symphony Orchestra /Levine**
RCA ③ 74321 39502-2 (171' · DDD) Notes, text and translation included   🄜

A well-cast set and a strong recommendation. Leontyne Price followers will be tempted no doubt, but note she's past her prime here. The recording is uncut.

Callas Leonora **Tucker** Don Alvaro **Tagliabue**   🄷
Don Carlo **Chorus and Orchestra of La Scala, Milan / Serafin**
EMI ③ 556323-2 (164' · ADD) Notes, text and translation included   Ⓕ

Callas is superb as Leonora and, Tagliabue aside, the rest of the cast turn in fine performances. Serafin does, however, make some cuts.

I Lombardi alla prima crociata

I Lombardi alla prima crociata
June Anderson sop Giselda **Luciano Pavarotti** ten
Oronte **Samuel Ramey** bass Pagano **Richard Leech**
ten Arvino **Ildebrando d'Arcangelo** bass Pirro **Yanni
Yannissis** bass Acciano **Jane Shaulis** mez Sofia
Anthony Dean Griffey ten Prior **Patricia Racette**
mez Viclinda **Chorus and Orchestra of the
Metropolitan Opera, New York /James Levine**
Decca ② 455 287-2DHO2 (129' · DDD) Notes, text
and translation included   Ⓕ

Pavarotti appeared in the Metropolitan Opera
production of *I Lombardi* in 1993: this recording
is the delayed result. He's in good voice and
sings Oronte's aria with fine legato, binding the
decorative turns of the cabaletta beautifully into
the vocal line and throwing in a respectable top
C to show us he still can. I Lombardi is a visc-
ally exciting opera. The first complete recording, conducted by Lamberto Gardelli (Philips),
set a good benchmark in 1972, but that need not
deter us from welcoming this lively newcomer.
The Met Opera Orchestra plays with splendid
precision and, as Turks and Crusaders, women
of the harem and virgins, the Met Chorus has a
high old time on both sides of *I Lombardi*'s war-
zone. Levine himself has improved beyond
recognition as a Verdian; this studio recording
is well paced and has a good sense of theatre.
Everything is swift and crisp on the surface.

The best role goes to the soprano Giselda,
specially tailored for the delicate skills of
Erminia Frezzolini. Among the current crop of
Verdi sopranos, June Anderson is probably as
plausible a modern Frezzolini as any. There's
some lovely, pure-toned singing in her big
scene at the end of Act 2 and her coloratura is
shining bright, both in this cabaletta and later in
'In fondo all' alma'. Samuel Ramey makes a relatively lightweight Pagano, who alone decorates
his second verses. In the second tenor role
Richard Leech holds his own, although his
voice doesn't take well to the microphone. Ildebrando d'Arcangelo proudly represents the
younger generation of Italian singers in the
small role of Pirro, and Patricia Racette sings
brightly as Viclinda.

Gardelli's crusading first recording has a
rough Italianate vigour that lovers of early
Verdi will enjoy, but Levine and his forces more
than hold their ground with pace and brilliance,
and a bright, modern recording with on balance
a better cast and the voices well forward.

Luisa Miller

Luisa Miller
Montserrat Caballé sop Luisa **Luciano Pavarotti** ten
Rodolfo **Sherrill Milnes** bar Miller **Bonaldo Giaiotti**
bass Count Walter **Anna Reynolds** mez Federica
Richard Van Allan bass Wurm **Annette Celine** mez
Laura **Fernando Pavarotti** ten Peasant **London
Opera Chorus; National Philharmonic Orchestra /
Peter Maag**

Double Decca ② 473 365-2 (144' · ADD) Recorded
1970s. Notes, text and translation included   Ⓜ Ⓞ

This transitional work shows Verdi enhancing
his skills and refining is musical style. The plot,
based on a Schiller drama, involves the tragedy
and death of Luisa and her beloved Rodolfo
brought about by the evil Wurm, apt predecessor of Verdi's Iago. The title-role could not find
a more appealing interpreter than Caballé, who
spins a fine line and is highly responsive to
Luisa's sad situation. She's partnered by
Pavarotti at the height of his powers as Rodolfo.
He excels in 'Quando le sere al lacido', the
work's most famous aria. As Luisa's equivocal
father, Miller, Milnes gives one of is best performances on disc and Van Allan is a properly
snarling Wurm.

Maag, an underrated conductor, directs a
strong, well-proportioned performance. He
gives the impression of being in love with this
opera and he goes right to the heart of the score,
finding its seriousness as well as its fire. The last
act is specially fine, containing what are
regarded as among the gramophone classics, the
two duets of Luisa, first with her father, then
with Rodolfo. The production is unobtrusively
effective in creation of atmosphere and is spaciously recorded.

Additional recommendation

Luisa Miller
Ricciarelli Luisa **Domingo** Rodolfo **Chorus and
Orchestra of the Royal Opera House, Covent
Garden / Maazel**
DG ② 459 481-2GTA2 (133' · ADD) Notes, text and
translation included   Ⓜ
Finely sung performances, and a close rival to
Decca's set, though Maazel's handling of the score
is rather prosaic by comparison with Maag's.

Macbeth

Macbeth
Piero Cappuccilli bar Macbeth **Shirley Verrett** mez
Lady Macbeth **Nicolai Ghiaurov** bass Banquo
Plácido Domingo ten Macduff **Antonio Savastano**
ten Malcolm **Carlo Zardo** bass Doctor **Giovanni
Foiani** bass Servant **Sergio Fontana** bass Herald
Alfredo Mariotti bass Assassin **Stefania Malagú**
mez Lady-in-waiting **Chorus and Orchestra of
La Scala, Milan / Claudio Abbado**
DG The Originals ② 449 732-2GOR2 (154' · ADD)
Recorded 1976. Notes, text and translation included
                                                    Ⓜ Ⓞ

Verdi's lifelong admiration for Shakespeare
resulted in only three operas based on his plays.
Macbeth, the first, originally written in 1847,
was extensively revised in 1865. Without losing
the direct force of the original, Verdi added
greater depth to is first ideas. Once derided as
being un-Shakespearian, it's now recognised as
a masterpiece for its psychological penetration
as much as for its subtle melodic inspiration.

Abbado captures perfectly the atmosphere of dark deeds and personal ambition leading to tragedy, projected by Verdi, and his reading holds the opera's disparate elements in the score under firm control, catching its interior tensions. He's well supported by his Scala forces. Shirley Verrett may not be ideally incisive or Italianate in accent as Lady Macbeth, but she peers into the character's soul most convincingly. As ever, truly inspired by Abbado, Cappuccilli is a suitably daunted and introverted Macbeth who sings a secure and unwavering legato. Domingo's upright Macduff and Ghiaurov's doom-laden Banquo are both admirable in their respective roles.

Macbeth

Peter Glossop bar Macbeth **Rita Hunter** sop Lady Macbeth **John Tomlinson** bass Banquo **Kenneth Collins** ten Macduff **Richard Greager** ten Malcolm **Christian du Plessis** bass Doctor **Michael George** bass Servant **Roger Heath** bass Assassin **Ludmilla Andrew** mez Lady-in-Waiting **BBC Singers; BBC Concert Orchestra / John Matheson**
Opera Rara/Peter Moores Foundation Opera
② ORCV301 (132' · DDD) Recorded 1979   Ⓕ**OO**

This recording starts project engendered by the Verdi specialist Julian Budden in the more adventurous days of Radio 3 to perform a number of Verdi operas in their original versions. Although Verdi's revisions of his first Shakespearian opera are mostly improvements, several aspects of the original score are worth reviving. Inevitably it's a more consistent whole, since the later amendments are in a changed and improved style. Lady Macbeth's second aria, 'Trionfai', is more basic and showy than its subtle successor, 'La luce langue'. The cabaletta to Macbeth's Act 3 aria is rousing and unusual, and was dropped in favour of another duet for Macbeth and his Lady. The chorus at the start of Act 4, replaced by a more distinctive piece, is in its own right a fine example of Risorgimento ardour, and the final scene, besides having Macbeth's effective aria as he lies mortally wounded is tauter, if more blatant, than its successor.

What makes this issue most worthwhile, however, is the superb performance. John Matheson directs a vital, finely timed and well-integrated account of the score that catches all its astonishing originality. Rita Hunter is as accomplished and appropriate a Lady Macbeth as any on disc, bar the unique Callas for De Sabata. Peter Glossop's Verdian style is faultless, and his understanding of the part complete. Kenneth Collins delivers 'Ah, la paterno mano' in exemplary voice and style. John Tomlinson, then in pristine voice, is an imposing Banquo. Chorus and orchestra are hard to fault. The recording, slightly bass-heavy, has been transferred at rather a low level, but its balance is as good as you'd expect, given its origins. This is definitely an experience convinced Verdians should not miss.

Additional recommendation

Macbeth   Ⓗ
Mascherini Macbeth **Callas** Lady Macbeth **Tajo** Banquo **Chorus and Orchestra of La Scala, Milan / de Sabata**
EMI mono ② 566447-2 (139' · ADD) Notes, text and translation included Live recording   Ⓜ
Callas's portrayal of Lady Macbeth is definitive and Victor de Sabata's conducting electrifying. However, the rest of the cast aren't up to much, and the recorded sound is poor. A set for Callas fans only.

Nabucco

Nabucco
Tito Gobbi bar Nabucco **Bruno Prevedi** ten Ismaele **Carlo Cava** bass Zaccaria **Elena Suliotis** sop Abigaille **Dora Carral** sop Fenena **Anna d'Auria** sop Anna **Giovanni Foiani** bass High Priest of Baal **Walter Krautler** ten Abdallo **Vienna Opera Orchestra; Vienna State Opera Chorus / Lamberto Gardelli**
Decca ② 417 407-2DH2 (121' · ADD) Recorded 1965. Notes, text and translation included   Ⓕ**O**

The years have hardly lessened the excitement of listening to this vigorous, closely knit performance. One realises why we were all amazed by Suliotis's account of the role of Abigaille. Her singing seizes you by the throat through its raw depiction of malice and through its youthful, uninhibited power. With the benefit of hindsight one can ear how a voice treated so carelessly and unstintingly could not last long, and so it was to be; but we should be glad for the brightness of the meteor while it flashed all too briefly through the operatic firmament. As an interpretation, her Abigaille seems a little coarse set beside the refinements shown by Scotto for Muti on EMI. However, Suliotis can manage by nature what Scotto has to conjure up by art, and she's certainly a subtler artist than Dimitrova on the wayward Sinopoli/DG version.

Gobbi, nearing the end of his illustrious career in 1965, remains the most convincing interpreter on record of the crazed king. The voice may have become a shade hard and ungratiating, but his use of Italian and his colouring of his tone, finally his pathos, are certainly not rivalled by Cappuccilli (Sinopoli). Carlo Cava exudes implacable fury as old Zaccaria, but he's inclined to go through his tone at forte . Prevedi is more than adequate as Ismaele, Carral less than adequate as Fenena (here DG score with Valentini Terrani).

One of the main assets of the Decca remains Gardelli's prompt, unfussy, and yet thrillingly delivered interpretation, clearly conveyed to his excellent Viennese forces. It's much more steadily and convincingly paced than Sinopoli's reading. The recording is forward and has plenty of presence, but it now sounds a little boxy beside the greater spaciousness of the DG. But the panache of the Decca enterprise silences criticism (except when the minute cuts in Nabucco's part are conceived). It's a pleasure to hear the bold inspiration of Verdi's first triumph conveyed with such conviction.

VERDI OTELLO – IN BRIEF

Plácido Domingo Otello **Cheryl Studer**
Desdemona **Sergei Leiferkus** Iago **Bastille Opera**
Chorus and Orchestra / Myung-Whun Chung
DG ② 439 805-2GH2 (132' · DDD)   Ⓕ**OO**

Chung's high-octane conducting sets the standard for a marvellous set, with Domingo at his peak of vocal power and expression and Sergei Leiferkus a smooth-voiced, subtle Iago.

Ramon Vinay Otello **Herva Nelli** Desdemona
Giuseppe Valdengo Iago **NBC Symphony**
Orchestra / Arturo Toscanini
RCA mono ② GD60302 (125' · AAD)   Ⓜ**O**

A historic 1947 performance by which others are still judged, even if Herva Nelli's Desdemona is no match for the darkly stentorian Ramon Vinay and Giuseppe Valdengo's resonantly malign Iago. The sound, however, is too restricted to make this a first choice.

Jon Vickers Otello **Leonie Rysanek** Desdemona
Tito Gobbi Iago **Rome Opera Chorus and**
Orchestra / Tullio Serafin
RCA ② 09026 63180-2 (144' · ADD)   Ⓜ**O**

Jon Vickers is a heroically anguished Moor in his first recording, with Gobbi a marvellously rich and malevolent Iago, and Rysanek a large-voiced but vulnerable Desdemona. Serafin's conducting is splendidly powerful.

Jon Vickers Otello **Mirella Freni** Desdemona
Peter Glossop Iago **Berlin Deutsche Oper**
Chorus; Berlin PO / Herbert von Karajan
EMI ② 769308-2 (140' · ADD)   Ⓜ

Karajan's recording comes up better on his spectacular film version, but since this isn't presently available the CD is still recommendable at mid-price, with Freni's deeply touching Desdemona and Peter Glossop's characterfully nasty Iago.

Plácido Domingo Otello **Barbara Frittoli**
Desdemona **Leo Nucci** Iago **Chorus and**
Orchestra of La Scala, Milan / Riccardo Muti
TDK 📀 DV-OPOTEL (140')   Ⓕ**O**

In this well-staged 2001 recording Domingo is in drier voice than he was in his younger selves, but is still overwhelming. Barbara Frittoli is a deeply felt Desdemona. Muti conducts with spirit.

Plácido Domingo Otello **Renée Fleming**
Desdemona **James Morris** Iago **Metropolitan**
Opera Chorus and Orchestra / James Levine
DG 📀 073 092-2GH (142')   Ⓕ

A fine 1995 stage version from the Met, with Domingo a commanding Moor, Renée Fleming a beautiful Desdemona and James Morris, though not the most menacing Iago, credible and richly sung. Levine's conducting, while not as lively as Muti's, is still enjoyable.

criticism (except when the minute cuts in Nabucco's part are conceived). It's a pleasure to hear the bold inspiration of Verdi's first triumph conveyed with such conviction.

Listen to the Act 1 finale and you're sure to be won over to the set as an entity.

Otello

Otello
Plácido Domingo ten Otello **Cheryl Studer** sop
Desdemona **Sergei Leiferkus** bar Iago **Ramón**
Vargas ten Cassio **Michael Schade** ten Roderigo
Denyce Graves mez Emilia **Ildebrando d'Arcangelo**
bass Lodovico **Giacomo Prestia** bass Montano
Philippe Duminy bass Herald **Hauts-de-Seine**
Maîtrise; Chorus and Orchestra of the Opéra-
Bastille, Paris / Myung-Whun Chung
DG ② 439 805-2GH2 (132' · DDD) Recorded 1993.
Notes, text and translation included   Ⓕ**OO**

Just as *Othello* is a difficult play to bring off in the theatre, so *Otello* is a difficult opera to bring off out of it. For some years now, Domingo has been, on stage, the greatest Otello of our age. On record, though, he has had less success. Leiferkus and Domingo have worked closely together in the theatre; and it shows in scene after scene –nowhere more so than in the crucial sequence in Act 2 where · Otello so rapidly ingests Iago's lethal poison. By bringing into the recording studio the feel and experience of a stage performance – meticulous study subtly modified by the improvised charge of the moment – both singers help defy the jinx that so often afflicts Otello on record. The skill of Leiferkus's performance is rooted in voice and technique: clear diction, a very disciplined rhythmic sense and a mastery of all ornament down to the most mordant of mordents. Above all, he's always there (usually stage right in this recording), steely-voiced, rabbiting on obsessively. We even hear his crucial interventions in the great Act 3 *concertato*.

Domingo is in superb voice; the sound seems golden as never before. Yet at the same time, it's a voice that's being more astutely deployed. To take that cruellest of all challenges to a studio-bound Otello, the great Act 3 soliloquy 'Dio! mi potevi', Domingo's performance is now simpler, more inward, more intense. It helps that his voice has darkened, winning back some of its russet baritonal colourings.

Chung's conducting is almost disarmingly vital. Verdi's scoring is more Gallic than Germanic. The score sounds very brilliant in the hands of the excellent Opéra-Bastille orchestra, and, in Act 4, very beautiful. Maybe Chung is wary of the emotional depths and, occasionally, the rhythmic infrastructure is muddled and unclear. And yet, the freshness is all gain. He's already a master of the big ensemble and the line of an act. Tension rarely slackens. On the rare occasions when it does, the mixing and matching of takes is probably to blame.

Studer's is a carefully drawn portrait of a chaste and sober-suited lady. Perhaps Verdi had a sweeter-voiced singer in mind for this paragon of 'goodness, resignation, and self-sacrifice' (Verdi's words, not Shakespeare's). Studer's oboe tones keep us at a certain distance, yet you'll look in vain for a better Desdemona. What's more, Studer is a singer who can single-mindedly focus the drama afresh, as she does more than once in Act 3. DG's recording is clear and unfussy and satisfyingly varied; Studer, in particular, is much helped by the beautifully open acoustic the engineers provide for the closing act. This is undoubtedly the best *Otello* on record since the early 1960s. It also happens to be the first time on disc that a great Otello at the height of his powers has been successfully caught in the context of a recording that can itself be generally considered worthy of the event, musically and technically.

Otello
Giuseppe Giacomini *ten* Otello **Dame Margaret Price** *sop* Desdemona **Matteo Manuguerra** *bar* Iago **Dino di Domenico** *ten* Cassio **Alain Gabriel** *ten* Roderigo **Martine Mahé** *mez* Emilia **Luigi Roni** *bass* Lodovico **Vincent le Texier** *bass-bar* Montano **Anton Kúrňava** *bass* Herald **Slovak Philharmonic Chorus; Les Petits Chanteurs de Bordeaux; Orchestre National de Bordeaux Aquitaine / Alain Lombard**
Forlane ② UCD216774/75 (128' · DDD) Recorded live 1991. Notes, text and translation included   Ⓕ●

On the evidence of this Otello, and much else, Giacomini is more viscerally exciting than any of the famous Three. Certainly no tenor in this role since Del Monaco in his prime had the ele-mental, almost frightening power evinced by Giacomini's reading, but his talents go well beyond the possession of a real tenore robusto. His dark, louring tone and agonised delivery of the text exactly match the passion and jealousy of the Moor, alternately achingly sorrowful as he imagines his wife's infidelities, and fiercely tormented as he rants and raves at her supposed wrongdoing. There's much to study in this sear-ing interpretation, which is on a par with Vinay's for Toscanini and sung in the same dark-grained, tormented fashion.

Giacomini's overwhelming portrayal is well supported. Dame Margaret Price provides rounded, cleanly produced tone, even if there are a few signs of wear, and her interpretation – in response to a real occasion – is emotionally compelling. In the Act 3 duet, she brings to the passage beginning 'Mi guarda!' and the line 'E son io l'innocente' the depth of Desdemona's heart-stricken soul as she tries to defend herself against Otello's accusations, and her Act 4 scene is shaped and executed with the expected sense of impending doom.

Matteo Manuguerra, an experienced and sym-pathetic Verdian, was already in his mid-sixties when this performance took place and there are times when his voice has to be husbanded, but he shows much intelligence in portraying the

subtlety of Iago's evil. The smaller roles are decently if not exceptionally cast.

Alain Lombard keeps the performance consis-tently on the boil. He handles the public scenes, most notably the Act 3 ensemble (given uncut), with the urgency and large scale they call for. His chorus and orchestra, while not quite in the highest class, perform with keen awareness of the score's pithy quality. This set may not entirely challenge the hegemony of the 1947 Toscanini and Serafin sets, but it's histrionically exciting, largely because of the live ambience and there's a straightforward honesty about it that has eluded more glamorous recordings. Stage noise is seldom in evidence. The record-ing is at times over-resonant, but catches the excitement of the occasion. With Giacomini giving such an authentically vivid account of the title-role, most Verdians will want to own it.

Additional recommendations

Otello

Domingo Otello **Scotto** Desdemona **Milnes** Iago **National Philharmonic Orchestra; Ambrosian Opera Chorus / Levine**
RCA ② 74321 39501-2 (134' · ADD)   Ⓜ●
For some this is the finest of Domingo's several recorded Otellos. Also, Scotto's Desdemona is one of the most moving on disc. At mid price this set is a real winner.

Vickers Otello **Rysanek** Desdemona **Gobbi** Iago **Rome Opera Chorus and Orchestra / Serafin**
RCA ② 09026 63180-2 (144' · ADD)   Ⓜ
Tito Gobbi's Iago remains irreplaceable (except possibly for Giuseppe Valdengo's for Toscanini), and Jon Vickers is a superb Otello, more metallic and heroic than Domingo though not necessarily more sensitive.

Rigoletto

Rigoletto   Ⓗ
Leonard Warren *bar* Rigoletto **Bidú Sayão** *sop* Gilda **Jussi Björling** *ten* Duke **Norman Cordon** *bass* Sparafucile **Martha Lipton** *contr* Maddalena **William Hargrave** *bass* Monterone **Thelma Altman** *sop* Giovanna **Richard Manning** *ten* Borsa **George Cehanovsky** *bar* Marullo **Maxine Stellman** *mez* Countess Ceprano **John Baker** *bass* Count Ceprano **Metropolitan Opera Chorus and Orchestra, New York / Cesare Sodero**
Naxos Historical ② 8 110051/2 (116' · ADD) Recorded live 1945   Ⓢ Ⓢ●●

This performance marked the return of Björ-ling to the Met after a wartime break of four years spent mostly in his native Sweden. And what a return it was: at 34 he was at the absolute peak of his powers and sings a Duke of Mantua imbued with supreme confidence and tremen-dous brio – just try the start of the Quartet. He and the house clearly revel in his display of tenor strength, yet that power is always tempered by

VERDI RIGOLETTO – IN BRIEF

Leonard Warren *Rigoletto* **Bidù Sayão** *Gilda*
Jussi Björling *Duke* **Metropolitan Opera Chorus
and Orchestra / Cesare Sodero**
Naxos mono ② 8 110051/2 (116' · AAD) ⑤〇〇
A superb performance live from the New
York Met in this bargain-price 1945 set,
although the sound wouldn't make it every-
one's first choice.

Tito Gobbi *Rigoletto* **Maria Callas** *Gilda*
Giuseppe di Stefano *Duke* **Chorus and
Orchestra of La Scala, Milan / Tullio Serafin**
EMI mono ② 556327-2 (118' · AAD) - Ⓕ〇〇
Equally historic but in much finer sound,
though still mono, this 1955 version has the
great trio of principals with Serafin's dynamic
conducting.

Renato Bruson *Rigoletto* **Edita Gruberová** *Gilda*
Neil Shicoff *Duke* **Santa Cecilia Academy
Chorus and Orchestra / Giuseppe Sinopoli**
Philips ② 462 158-2PM2 (128' · DDD) Ⓕ
Renato Bruson and Edita Gruberová head a
good cast in a fine modern version, though
Neil Shicoff's Duke is sometimes rather
forced. Sinopoli's exciting reading is less
eccentric in its tempi than usual.

Piero Cappuccilli *Rigoletto* **Ileana Cortrubas**
Gilda **Plácido Domingo** *Duke* **Vienna State
Opera Chorus; Vienna PO / Carlo Maria Giulini**
DG ② 457 753-2GOR2 (128' · DDD) Ⓜ〇
Giulini's graceful, detailed conducting has
plenty of drama, still more so a strong cast
headed by Plácido Domingo, Piero Cappuccilli's restrained jester and Ileana Cotrubas's
meltingly vulnerable Gilda.

Robert Merrill *Rigoletto* **Anna Moffo** *Gilda*
Alfredo Kraus *Duke* **RCA Italiana Opera Chorus
and Orchestra / Sir Georg Solti**
RCA ② GD86506 (113' · ADD) Ⓜ
The 1960s Solti at high voltage may not suit
everyone, but this is an exciting and splendidly
cast set – Alfredo Kraus in his elegant prime,
Anna Moffo a beautifully girlish Gilda, Robert
Merrill's rich-voiced jester, uncharacteristically expressive, and for once, among the
supporting cast, the commanding Monterone
that Verdi required.

Paolo Gavanelli *Rigoletto* **Christine Schäfer** *Gilda*
Marcelo Álvarez *Duke* **Chorus and Orchestra of
the Royal Opera House / Edward Downes**
BBC Opus Arte 📀 OA0829D (169') Ⓕ
This highly modern but recognisable Covent
Garden staging, splendidly conducted by
Sir Edward Downes, stands out among
DVDs. Paolo Gavanelli is a magnificent
jester, Marcello Alvarez a swaggering Duke
and Christine Schäfer's clear-voiced Gilda
detailed and moving.

innate artistry. If not a subtle interpreter, he's
always a thoughtful one, and never indulges
himself or his audience.

Similarly, Warren was, at the time, at the
zenith of his career. Vocally he's in total command of the role and the house. His reading,
although slightly extroverted in some areas,
evinces a firm tone, a secure line and many
shades of colour. He's at is very best in his two
duets with Gilda (sadly and heinously cut about)
and no wonder, given the beautiful, plangent
singing of Sayão, whose 'Caro nome' is so delicately phrased, touching and keenly articulated.
'Tutte le feste' is still better, prompting Paul
Jackson (who in general is unjustifiably hard on
the performance in *Saturday Afternoons at the old
Met*, Duckworth:1992) to comment that Sayão's
'lovely, pliant, fully rounded tones are immediately affecting'. Indeed, in spite of the merits of
the two male principals, it's her truly memorable interpretation that makes this set essential
listening.

All round, there are few recordings that match
this one for vocal distinction – perhaps the
Serafin-Callas-Gobbi on EMI and the Giulini-
Cotrubas-Cappuccilli on DG. They are much
more expensive but boast superior sound. Björling and Warren both made later studio sets, but
neither matches his live contribution here, off
the stage.

The final virtue of this absorbing experience is
the conducting of the little-known Sodero. His
moderate – but never sluggish – tempos allow
for almost ideal articulation on all sides, and his
insistence on letting us hear the score so clearly
makes one regret even more all those excisions
then common in the opera house and the
studios. This is a set worth £10 or so of any
Verdian's money.

Rigoletto Ⓗ
Tito Gobbi *bar* Rigoletto **Maria Callas** *sop* Gilda
Giuseppe di Stefano *ten* Duke **Nicola Zaccaria**
bass Sparafucile **Adriana Lazzarini** *mez* Maddalena
Plinio Clabassi *bass* Monterone **Giuse Gerbino** *mez*
Giovanna **Renato Ercolani** *ten* Borsa **William Dickie**
bar Marullo **Elvira Galassi** *sop* Countess Ceprano
Carlo Forti *bass* Count Ceprano **Chorus and
Orchestra of La Scala, Milan /Tullio Serafin**
EMI mono ② 556327-2 (118' · ADD) Recorded 1955
Notes, text and translation included Ⓕ〇〇

That one recording should continue to hold
sway over many other attractive comers after 45
years is simply a tribute to Callas, Gobbi, Serafin and Walter Legge. Whatever the merits of
its successors, and they are many, no Rigoletto
has surpassed Gobbi in tonal variety, line, projection of character and understanding of what
Rigoletto is about; no Gilda has come anywhere
near Callas in meaningful phrasing – listen to
'Caro nome' or 'Tutte le feste' on any other set
if you're disbelieving – nor achieved such a careful differentiation of timbre before and after
her seduction; no conductor matches Serafin
in judging tempo and instrumental detail on a

nicety; nor benefited from a chorus and orchestra bred in the tradition of La Scala; no producer has equalled Legge in recording voices rather than the space round them. And di Stefano? Well, he may not be so stylish a Duke as some others, but the 'face' he gives his singing, and the sheer physical presence he conveys, not to mention his forward diction, are also unique in this opera. Nothing in this world is perfect, and so there are some small drawbacks here. Serafin sadly makes small cuts in the first Gilda-Rigoletto duet and omits entirely the Duke's cabaletta as used to be practice in the theatre. Gobbi could be said not to have quite the weight of voice ideally called for by a Verdi baritone role. Finally, the recording, although immeasurably improved from previous issues of the set, still has one or two places of distortion obviously present on the original tape. In every other way, this remains the classic performance on record, and one that should be on the shelf of every self-respecting Verdi collector.

Simon Boccanegra

Simon Boccanegra
Piero Cappuccilli bar Simon Boccanegra **Mirella Freni** sop Amelia **José Carreras** ten Gabriele **Nicolai Ghiaurov** bass Fiesco **José van Dam** bass-bar Paolo **Giovanni Foiani** bass Pietro **Antonio Savastano** ten Captain **Maria Fausta Gallamini** sop Maid **Chorus and Orchestra of La Scala, Milan / Claudio Abbado**
DG The Originals ② 449 752-2GOR2 (136' · ADD)
Recorded 1977. Notes, text and translation included
Ⓜ**OO**

This famous recording has become a classic, a studio performance following a series of performances at La Scala in the Strehler staging. The close, slightly claustrophobic recording exactly mirrors the mood of nefarious activities and intrigues following Boccanegra's rise to be Doge of Genoa, he and his lovely daughter victims of the dark deeds round them. In his plebeian being, clement exercise of authority and warm, fatherly love, Simon Boccanegra is made for Cappuccilli, who, under Abbado's tutelage, sings it not only con amore but with exemplary, delicately tinted tone and unbelievably long-breathed phrasing. As his daughter Amelia, Freni was just entering her quasi-spinto phase and expands her lyric voice easily into the greater demands of this more dramatic role. Similarly heavier duties hadn't yet tarnished the youthful ardour and sap in the tone of the 30-year-old Carreras. As the implacable Fiesco, Ghiaurov exudes vengeful command, and van Dam evil machinations as the villain Paolo. Over all presides Abbado in what remains one of his greatest recordings, alert to every facet of the wondrous score, timing every scene, in an opera tricky to pace, to near-perfection, and bringing theatrical drama into the home. This set should be essential to any reputable collection of Verdi.

Simon Boccanegra　　　　　　　　　Ⓗ
Tito Gobbi bar Simon Boccanegra **Victoria de los Angeles** sop Amelia **Giuseppe Campora** ten Gabriele **Boris Christoff** bass Fiesco **Walter Monachesi** bar Paolo **Paolo Dari** bar Pietro **Paolo Caroli** ten Captain **Silvia Bertona** mez Maid **Chorus and Orchestra of the Rome Opera House / Gabriele Santini**
EMI Références mono ② 567483-2 (119' · ADD)
Recorded 1957. Notes, text and translations included
Ⓜ**O**

Although the sound of this version, even in its refurbished state, is indifferent, as it was even for the standards of its day, it simply can't be over-looked because it preserves two interpretations that are now of historic importance – Gobbi's Boccanegra and Christoff's Fiesco, the brothers-in-law (in real life) rivalling each other in projecting dramatic conviction. Even with Cappuccilli's superb reading in mind (he recorded Boccanegra both for Gavazzeni and Abbado), Gobbi's still remains definitive. Through his sensitive diction and fine gradations of tone he portrays unforgettably the Doge's changes of character, so unerringly delineated by Verdi himself, from unruly pirate to commanding Doge to loving father and, after the poisoning, to tragic hero. The weary acceptance and sad accents of the final scene match those of Cappuccilli in his equally moving interpretations, especially that on the Abbado set. Gobbi at the time was at the height of his vocal powers so that the often high tessitura bothers him little, though it's certainly true that Cappuccilli has still greater resources to call on.

Christoff may not have quite the vocal amplitude of Ghiaurov (DG), but his reading has more vocal character. His pungent, crisply articulated singing is ideally suited to the proud, implacable patrician Fiesco. His singing shades into deeply felt remorse in the final, conciliatory meeting with Boccanegra. De los Angeles is an Amelia very much in the mould of Ricciarelli (RCA), vulnerable in character, gentle and elegiac in voice with just a suggestion of strain in the highest register. Los Angeles's tone is actually clearer, more girlish than that of either of her rivals, and she's more adept than either of them at suggesting passion for Gabriele and a daughter's love for her father through her sensitive painting of words. She's quite exquisite in the downward runs in the final ensemble. Campora makes a likeable, fiery Gabriele more in the mould of Carreras (DG) than Domingo (RCA). Monachesi is an imposing Paolo.

Neither Santini's conducting nor the playing of the Rome Opera Orchestra matches that of their La Scala counterparts (DG). Abbado's realisation of this work is unlikely to be surpassed, though Gavazzeni's reading has much to commend it. The voices in this mono recording are more fairly caught than the chorus and orchestra, but there's a persistent though hardly disturbing tape hiss. Even if they may regret the needless cuts, this is a set those interested in great recordings of Verdi operas must have.

La traviata

La traviata

Maria Callas *sop* Violetta Valéry **Alfredo Kraus** ☐
ten Alfredo Germont **Mario Sereni** *bar* Giorgio
Germont **Laura Zanini** *mez* Flora Bervoix **Piero De
Palma** *ten* Gastone **Alvaro Malta** *bar* Baron
Douphol **Maria Cristina de Castro** *sop* Annina
Alessandro Maddalena *bass* Doctor Grenvil **Vito
Susca** *bass* Marquis D'Obigny **Manuel Leitao** *ten*
Messenger **Chorus and Orchestra of the Teatro
Nacional de San Carlos, Lisbon /Franco Ghione**
EMI mono ② 556330-2 (123' · ADD) Recorded live
1958
Ⓜ ⊙⊙

Callas caught live is preferable to Callas
recorded in the studio, and Violetta was perhaps
her supreme role. The former Covent Garden
producer Ande Anderson pointedly commented
that, whereas other sopranos made you cry in
the final act of *Traviata*, Callas also made you
cry in the second, and one hears here what he
meant, as Callas's Violetta comes to the stark
realisation that she's going to have to give up
her one and only true beloved seemingly for
ever. The desperation that enters her voice at
'Non sapete' is surpassed only by the sorrow and
emptiness in the lead-in to 'Dite alla giovine',
then the fatalism of 'morro! la mia memoria',
which John Steane in his note that accompanies
this essential CD reissue describes as being sung
with such 'fullness of heart and voice'.

The final act is almost unbearable in its
poignancy of expression:the reading of the letter so natural in its feeling of emptiness, the
realisation that the doctor is lying so truthful,
the sense of hollowness at what's possibly the
opera's most moving moment, 'Ma se tornando
...': 'If in returning you haven't saved my life,
then nothing can save it.' All this and so much
else suggests that Callas understood better than
anyone else what this role is truly about.

But there's more to it even than that. Alfredo
Kraus's Alfredo as heard here is as appealing as
any on record. His Schipa-like tone at that stage
in his career, his refinement of phrasing, especially in the duets with Callas, and his elegant
yet ardent manner are exactly what the role
requires. Mario Sereni may not quite be in the
class of his colleagues but his Germont père is
securely, sincerely and often perceptively sung
and more acutely characterised than in his
account of the part with de los Angeles. Almost
as important, contrary to what you may read in
some earlier reviews, Franco Ghione is an
expert, knowledgeable conductor of this score,
yielding to his singers yet prompt and dramatic
when need be, and able to draw singing string
tone from his excellent orchestra in the two
preludes. So are there any drawbacks? Yes
indeed; the prompter is all too audible, the audience coughs intrusively, particularly during the
recitative at the start of Act 3, and the score is
extensively cut in the manner traditional to pre-
authentic days. Nevertheless, if it's to be but one
Traviata in your collection, it must be this one.

La traviata

Valerie Masterson *sop* Violetta **John Brecknock** *ten*
Alfredo **Christian du Plessis** *bar* Germont **Della
Jones** *mez* Flora **Shelagh Squires** *mez* Annina
Geoffrey Pogson *ten* Gastone **John Gibbs** *bar*
Baron **Denis Dowling** *bar* Marquis **Roderick Earle**
bass Doctor **Edward Byles** *ten* Giuseppe **John
Kitchiner** *bar* Messenger **Chorus and Orchestra of
English National Opera /Sir Charles Mackerras**
Chandos/Peter Moores Foundation Opera in English
Series ② CHAN3023 (119' · ADD) Recorded 1980
Sung in English. Text included
Ⓕ ⊙

Each new encounter with this increases both
respect and affection – not just for the recording
but for the opera itself. This is partly an effect of
opera-in-English, at any rate in such a very
human opera as *Traviata*, and Edmund Tracey's
translation also improves on reacquaintance ('I
wonder' used to seem a terrible substitute for 'E
strano' but it now seems natural enough in context). It's also partly a testimony to the imaginative freshness with which all details of the performance have been approached. The choruses,
which usually sound like so much well-
rehearsed routine, are alive with intelligent
responsiveness. Similarly, Mackerras doesn't
allow the orchestra to take anything for granted.

Valerie Masterson's Violetta is infinitely
touching, not only through her expressiveness
but perhaps primarily because the music is so
scrupulously sung. Her staccatos, triplets and
arpeggios in the first duet are so cleanly placed;
her gradations of tone in the great solo are so
finely judged; her control of the soft high notes
in the last Act's farewell is so clearly that of a
singer who knows that, whatever the fashionable cant to the contrary, singing comes first.
Sensitivity and study have added the rest, and
the result is simply one of the most satisfying
accounts of the role on record. If there's a limitation it lies in the want of richer tonal
resources, and this is true also of the Alfredo,
John Brecknock. Christian du Plessis as the
father sounds not quite so firm and even in his
production; good, however, in rounding off the
two verses of his famous song. Della Jones and
Denis Dowling bring their minor roles to life,
and indeed there isn't much by way of weakness
in the whole of this heart-warming production.

La traviata

Tiziana Fabriccini *sop* Violetta **Roberto Alagna** *ten*
Alfredo **Paolo Coni** *bar* Germont **Nicoletta Curiel**
mez Flora **Antonella Trevisan** *mez* Annina **Enrico
Cossutta** *ten* Gastone **Orazio Mori** *bar* Baron **Enzo
Capuano** *bass* Marquis **Francesco Musinu** *bass*
Doctor **Ernesto Gavazzi** *ten* Giuseppe **Ernesto
Panariello** *bass* Servant **Silvestro Sammaritano** *bass*
Messenger **Chorus and Orchestra of La Scala,
Milan /Riccardo Muti**
Sony Classical ② S2K52486 (136' · DDD) Recorded
live 1992. Notes, text and translation included
Ⓕ ⊙

An exciting and eloquent reading on all
sides, this version must now be rated with the

established front-runners – but, as with some of those, most notably any of Callas's versions, it isn't for the fainthearted, or for those who like their Violettas to have full, equally produced voices. Fabriccini is evidently not an Act 1 Violetta. But even without assured coloratura and with problems at the *passaggio*, she's one who's going to hold our attention and move us. In Act 2 so much bespeaks not only complete identification with Violetta's predicament but also vocal acumen of an exceptional kind, often based on the seemingly lost art of *portamento*.

The final tragedy is still better, very much modelled on Callas. The voice, more settled now than anywhere in the performance, manages her role with long-breathed phrasing and pathetic accents, the result of a true understanding of Verdian style yet never self-conscious – this is great singing and interpretation.

The death is deeply moving. Alagna, in the role that brought him to attention, is just the Alfredo for this Violetta; youthfully ardent, with keen-edged tone, finely attuned to the *legato* essential in Verdi.

The recording is taken from four performances, given at La Scala, and is a theatrical view full of electricity, vitally executed by the forces of La Scala, as vital as any in the recorded history of the work. Don't miss it.

La traviata
Angela Gheorghiu *sop* Violetta **Frank Lopardo** *ten* Alfredo **Leo Nucci** *bar* Germont **Leah-Marian Jones** *mez* Flora **Gillian Knight** *mez* Annina **Robin Leggate** *ten* Gaston **Richard Van Allan** *bass* Baron **Roderick Earle** *bass* Marquis **Mark Beesley** *bass* Doctor **Neil Griffiths** *ten* Giuseppe **Bryan Secombe** *bass* Messenger **Rodney Gibson** *ten* Servant **Chorus and Orchestra of the Royal Opera House, Covent Garden /Sir Georg Solti**
Decca ② 448 119-2DHO2 (127' · DDD) Recorded live 1994 . Notes, text and translation included   Ⓕ**o**

For Angela Gheorghiu, Violetta was the right role at the right time. The whole drama is there in her voice, every expression in the eyes and beat of the heart reflected in the way she shapes and colours Verdi's vocal lines. Her quiet singing is particularly lovely, affording subtle variations of tenderness and inner anxiety. When she does choose to make a point with force, as in her sudden warmth of feeling towards Giorgio Germont at 'Qual figlia m'abbracciate' or her chilling cry of 'Morro!', accompanied by a loud thump on the table, her ideas always hit home. A few moments of vocal weakness are accentuated by the microphone, mainly a tendency to go sharp and some hardness at the top of the voice that was not troublesome in the theatre. Otherwise she's the most complete and moving Violetta we have had since her compatriot, Ileana Cotrubas.

These live performances were the first time that Sir Georg Solti, at the age of 82, had conducted a staged *La traviata* and he wanted two young singers who were also coming fresh to

---

VERDI LA TRAVIATA – IN BRIEF

Maria Callas *Violetta* **Alfredo Kraus** *Alfredo*
Mario Sereni *Germont* **San Carlos Theatre Lisbon Chorus and Orchestra / Franco Ghione**
EMI ② 556330-2 (124' · AAD)   Ⓜ**oo**
Callas incarnates the doomed Violetta unlike any rival, with Alfredo Kraus a poised, plangent Alfredo, even if Ghione is not quite their equal, the traditional cuts are made and the live recording is not brilliant.

Ileana Cotrubas *Violetta* **Plácido Domingo** *Alfredo* **Sherrill Milnes** *Germont* **Bavarian State Opera Chorus and Orchestra / Carlos Kleiber**
DG ② 415 132-2GH2 (106' · ADD)   Ⓕ**o**
Cotrubas makes a more touching heroine than Callas, vocally glorious and ardently supported by Plácido Domingo's Alfredo and Kleiber's tautly dramatic conducting. Despite traditional cuts, a deeply moving performance.

(In English) **Valerie Masterson** *Violetta* **John Brecknock** *Alfredo* **Christian du Plesses** *Germont* **ENO Chorus and Orchestra / Sir Charles Mackerras**
Chandos ② CHAN3023 (119' · DDD)   Ⓕ**o**
The only English language version. Valerie Masterson's clear-voiced, elegant Violetta and John Brecknock's elegant Alfredo can hold their own among the finest, still more so the vividly theatrical Mackerras.

Tiziana Fabbricini *Violetta* **Roberto Alagna** *Alfredo* **Paolo Coni** *Germont* **Chorus and Orchestra of La Scala, Milan / Riccardo Muti**
Sony ② S2K52486 (136' · DDD)   Ⓕ**o**
Fabbricini's vocally taxed but passionately involving heroine, Alagna's youthful Alfredo and Muti's theatrical verve make this live recording well worth considering.

Angela Gheorghiu *Violetta* **Frank Lopardo** *Alfredo* **Leo Nucci** *Germont* **Chorus and Orchestra of the Royal Opera House / Sir Georg Solti**
Decca ② 448 119-2DHO2 (127' · DDD)   Ⓕ**o**
The famous performance that marked Gheorghiu's début appearance and one of Solti's last. Splendidly recorded and alive – but do consider the DVD.

Angela Gheorghiu *Violetta* **Frank Lopardo** *Alfredo* **Leo Nucci** *Germont* **Chorus and Orchestra of the Royal Opera House / Sir Georg Solti**
Decca 📀 071 431-9DH (135')   Ⓕ**o**
TV schedules were unprecedentedly cleared for this broadcast, such was the excitement over Gheorghiu's brilliantly sung and nervily beautiful Violetta, a good match for Solti's dramatic reading. Lopardo is rather stiff physically, and the production lively but unexceptional, with a decent supporting cast, but it's still immensely involving.

the opera. What was so spellbinding in the theatre was the touching intimacy they brought to their scenes together. Instead of the duets for Violetta and Alfredo turning into standard Italian operatic bawling, they became lovers' whispers. The effect comes across here in the cadenzas, where Gheorghiu and Frank Lopardo really seem to be listening to each other. Elsewhere, one is more aware than in the theatre that Lopardo's light tenor is far from being an idiomatic Italian voice. His idiosyncratic tone quality and un-Italian vowels can be problematical, as is some ungainly lifting up into notes. Leo Nucci, Decca's resident Verdi baritone at the time, makes a standard Giorgio Germont, not more, and apart from Leah-Marian Jones's energetic Flora, the smaller roles don't say a great deal for the Royal Opera's depth of casting.

Solti insisted that the opera be performed complete. But there's nothing studied about his conducting: the performance is fresh and alive from the first note to the last, the result of a lifetime's experience of how to pace a drama in the opera house . With the increasing number of live opera sets, a recommendation for *La traviata* is likely to be based on whether one is prepared to accept noises-off or not. Decca's recording is well balanced and vivid, dancing feet and banging doors included. Among the live sets, Giulini and Callas at La Scala in 1955 must be *hors concours*, but in rather awful sound. Muti's more recent La Scala set, in which he has to wrestle with Tiziana Fabbricini's wayward talents as Violetta, is the nearest comparison.

Additional recommendations

La traviata
Callas Violetta **di Stefano** Alfredo **Bastianini**   🅗
Germont **Chorus and Orchestra of La Scala, Milan**
/Giulini
EMI mono ② 566450-2 (124' · ADD) Recorded 1955 Ⓜ
> Surely the most famous recording of *Traviata*, with Callas an incomparable Violetta. The big let down, though, is Bastianini's Germont and the poor recorded sound.

De los Angeles Violetta **del Monte** Alfredo   🅗
Sereni Germont **Rome Opera Chorus and**
Orchestra / Serafin
EMI Double Forte ② 573824-2 (119' · ADD)   Ⓜ
Also available on HMV Classics HMVD5 728082-2   Ⓑ
> Alfredo and Germont are both well portrayed, but de los Angeles's Violetta is quite unforgettable.

Il trovatore

Il trovatore   🅗
Maria Callas sop Leonora **Giuseppe di Stefano** ten
Manrico **Rolando Panerai** bar Count di Luna **Fedora**
Barbieri mez Azucena **Nicola Zaccaria** bass
Ferrando **Luisa Villa** mez Ines **Renato Ercolani** ten
Ruiz, Messenger **Giulio Mauri** bass Old Gipsy
Chorus and Orchestra of La Scala, Milan / Herbert

von Karajan
EMI ② 556333-2 (129' · ADD) Recorded 1956. Notes,
text and translation included   ⒻⓄⓄ

Callas and Karajan took the world by the ears in the 1950s with this *Il trovatore*. Leonora was one of Callas's finest stage roles, and this recording is wonderfully intense, with a dark concentrated loveliness of sound in the principal arias that puts one in mind of Muzio or Ponselle at their best. Walter Legge always managed to team Callas with the right conductor for the work in question. Often it was Serafin, but Karajan in *Il trovatore* is utterly compelling. This opera, like Beethoven's Seventh Symphony and Stravinsky's *The Rite of Spring*, is one of music's great essays in sustained rhythmic intensity; dramatically it deals powerfully in human archetypes. All this is realised by the young Karajan with that almost insolent mastery of score and orchestra which made him such a phenomenon at this period of is career. There are some cuts, but, equally, some welcome inclusions (such as the second verse of 'Di quella pira', sung by di Stefano with his own unique kind of *slancio*).

Although the EMI sound is very good, one or two climaxes suggest that in the heat of the moment, the engineer, Robert Beckett, let the needle run into the red and you might care to play the set in mono to restore that peculiar clarity and homogeneity of sound which are the mark of Legge's finest productions of the mono era. But whatever you do don't miss this set.

Il trovatore
Plácido Domingo ten Manrico **Leontyne Price** sop
Leonora **Sherrill Milnes** bar Count di Luna **Fiorenza**
Cossotto mez Azucena **Bonaldo Giaiotti** bass
Ferrando **Elizabeth Bainbridge** mez Ines **Ryland**
Davies ten Ruiz **Stanley Riley** bass Old Gipsy
Neilson Taylor bar Messenger **Ambrosian Opera**
Chorus; New Philharmonia Orchestra / Zubin
Mehta
RCA Red Seal ② 74321 39504-2 (137' · ADD)
Recorded 1969. Notes, text and translation included
  ⓂⓄ

The Leonora of Leontyne Price is the high point of the Mehta recording: her velvety, sensuous articulation of what's certainly an 'immenso, eterno amor' is entirely dignified and dramatically astute. The New Philharmonia is a no less ardent exponent. Mehta's pacing may be uneven, his accompanying breathless, but he draws robust playing in bold primary colours to which the recording gives vivid presence. The acoustic serves Manrico less well: he seems to be singing in the bath when we first overhear him. This, though, is a younger, simpler Domingo than the one we encounter elsewhere, and there are passages of wonderfully sustained intensity. Cossotto's Azucena is disappointing. All the vocal tricks and techniques are there, but it's very much a concert performance, and we're never entirely engaged.

Il trovatore
Franco Corelli ten Manrico **Gabriella Tucci** sop
Leonora **Robert Merrill** bar Count di Luna **Giulietta
Simionato** mez Azucena **Ferruccio Mazzoli** bass
Ferrando **Luciana Moneta** mez Ines **Angelo
Mercuriali** ten Ruiz, Messenger **Mario Rinaudo** bass
Old Gipsy **Chorus and Orchestra of Rome Opera /
Thomas Schippers**
HMV Classics ② HMVD5 73413-2 (123' · ADD)
Recorded 1964   Ⓑ

In the 1950s and 1960s EMI made a series of
what have become classics with Rome Opera
forces that have Verdi in their blood. These two
recordings, greeted with reservations then, now
seem like manna from heaven in a world starved
of true Verdian voices. Above all there's
Corelli's truly spinto tenor, a thrilling sound in
itself, and used, both as Radames (one of the
most exciting on disc) and as Manrico, with far
more sensitivity than is usually allowed for.
Tucci is a Leonora in the Tebaldi mould, with a
strong voice and natural phrasing. Simionato, a
shade past her best, remains an affecting,
idiomatic Azucena. Robert Merrill is a Verdi
baritone of poise and style. Schippers conducts
with verve.

Additional recommendation

Il trovatore
Price Leonora **Corelli** Manrico **Simionato** Azucena
DG mono ② 447 659-2GX2 (139' · ADD)   Ⓜ
Leontyne Price, at the height of her powers, gives
a vital performance, and Corelli is an exciting
Manrico. The most compelling reason for hearing
this set, though, is Giulietta Simionato's deeply
felt, wondrously sung Azucena.

I vespri siciliani

I vespri siciliani
Cheryl Studer sop Elena **Chris Merritt** ten Arrigo
Giorgio Zancanaro bar Monforte **Ferruccio
Furlanetto** bass Procida **Gloria Banditelli** contr
Ninetta **Enzo Capuano** bass De Bethune **Francesco
Musinu** bass Vaudemont **Ernesto Gavazzi** ten
Danieli **Paolo Barbacini** ten Tebaldo **Marco
Chingari** bass Roberto **Ferrero Poggi** ten Manfredo
**Chorus and Orchestra of La Scala, Milan /
Riccardo Muti**
EMI ③ 754043-2 (199' · DDD) Recorded live 1989-90.
Notes, text and translation included   Ⓕ

Vespri is one of the most difficult of Verdi's
operas to bring off. Scribe's libretto, true to
Parisian taste nurtured on Auber and Meyerbeer, is a somewhat superficial, broken-backed
affair; Verdi's attempt to fulfil Parisian tastes,
long ballet and all, isn't at all times convincing,
yet for the most part the composer rose above
the demands for show and grandeur to disclose
the real feelings of his characters, none of
whom is a particularly lovable creature. Andrew
Porter, when reviewing Levine's RCA set on LP
back in 1974, commented that the opera 'is a

VERDI IL TROVATORE – IN BRIEF

Giuseppe di Stefano Manrico **Maria Callas**
Leonora **Fedora Barbieri** Azucena **Chorus and
Orchestra of La Scala, Milan / Herbert von
Karajan**
EMI mono ② 556333-2 (129' · AAD)   ⒻⓄⓄ
A 1957 mono recording shouldn't put you off
this, with its thrilling combination of Maria
Callas and Giuseppe di Stefano in top form.
Karajan is at his most dramatic, with the
rest of the cast, notably Fedora Barbieri's
Azucena, to match.

Plácido Domingo Manrico **Leontyne Price**
Leonora **Fiorenza Cossotto** Azucena **Ambrosian
Opera Chorus, New Philharmonia Orchestra /
Zubin Mehta**
RCA ② 74321 39504-2 (136' · AAD)   ⓂⓄ
This is probably the best among several
excellent modern recordings, with no weak
links in its stellar cast. Mehta is more galvanic
than usual. A rich, vivid recording.

Franco Corelli Manrico **Gabriella Tucci** Leonora
Giulietta Simionato Azucena **Rome Opera
Chorus and Orchestra / Thomas Schippers**
HMV ② HMVD573413-2 (123' · ADD)   Ⓢ
Vivid, fast-moving conducting and a less
conventional cast – apart from its stars – give
this a real sense of drama.

Plácido Domingo Manrico **Aprile Millo** Leonora
Dolora Zajick Azucena **Metropolitan Opera
Chorus and Orchestra / James Levine**
Sony ② S2K48070 (129' · DDD)   Ⓕ
The real heavyweight, with Levine's massively
dramatic reading, rich orchestral playing and a
typically luxurious Metropolitan Opera cast,
although Aprile Millo doesn't quite match her
rivals, nor Domingo his younger selves.

Jussi Björling Manrico **Zinka Milanov** Leonora
Fedora Barbieri Azucena **Robert Shaw Chorale,
RCA Victor Orchestra / Renato Cellini**
RCA ② GD86643 (107' · AAD)   Ⓜ
A 1952 mono recording that still carries
plenty of excitement, with two quite extra-
ordinary voices in Jussi Björling and the
Met's great Verdi baritone Leonard Warren.
Zinka Milanov is slightly less compelling, but
Barbieri is a fine Azucena, and Cellini is more
vital than many better-known interpreters.

Plácido Domingo Manrico **Rosalind Plowright**
Leonora **Brigitte Fassbaender** Azucena **Santa
Cecilia Academy Chorus and Orchestra /
Carlo Maria Giulini**
DG ② 423 858-2GH2 (140' · DDD)   Ⓕ
'The thinking man's *Trovatore*', beautifully
judged and detailed in both conducting and
singing – yet intensely Italianate, with a cast
conceding nothing to other versions.

structure involving large ensembles, elaborate spectacle … intricate and novel orchestral effects, a big ballet, and virtuoso singers pushed to the limits of their technique'.

Muti realises all these assets with unperturbed ease and easily overcomes any drawbacks, real or imagined. He rouses his forces, solo and concerted, with all his old gifts for energising rhythms and shaping a Verdian line. He yields where wanted to the needs of his singers, presses on when the drama or a dull page demands it, and draws the best out of what's generally considered Verdi's most telling ballet music. He's less impulsive, and more ready to take his time than Levine.

The set is graced by some superb singing – at least in the two most important and interesting roles, those of Elena and Monforte. Cheryl Studer confirmed her ebullient form in *Attila* as a lirico-spinto with full control of coloratura, thus placing her in the royal line of Ponselle, Callas, Sutherland and Caballé (the last two of whom encouraged Studer to undertake this kind of repertory). In her first appearance, as she instils the Sicilians with courage, 'Coraggio, su coraggio', she immediately shows her mettle with confident, inspiriting attack, the tone vibrant, the diction fiery. In the duet with Arrigo in Act 4, her long solo 'Arrigo! ah, parli ad un core', a passage made famous by Callas, she floats her tone most appealingly, the accents delicate, affecting. In the Bolero she rivals any of her predecessors in delicacy, a real smile in the voice, the phrasing long breathed, the coloratura not quite perfect, but near it. Taken with her soaring contributions to the ensembles, this is great singing by any standards, past or present.

To find Zancanaro in equally impressive form is an added blessing. Monforte is the work's most interesting character, the French governor of Sicily, father of the Sicilian Arrigo, who's his sworn enemy. In his great scene at the start of Act 3, Zancanaro finds deeper strains of feeling than we have heard from him in any other role, and then sings the subtly written aria 'In braccio alle dovizie' with a refinement of line and variety of dynamics that enhance the strength of voice and clarity of diction we have always admired in his singing. He's just as eloquent in the ensuing duet with Arrigo, taken here by Chris Merritt, another singer inspired by the occasion or the work to surpass himself: Merritt delivers all his music with such conviction and such a belief in himself that past criticism of his voice is almost silenced. Which leaves, of the principals, Furlanetto. Heard to such advantage in Mozart and Rossini, he here sounds overparted. 'O tu Palermo' lacks the weight and authority of a Pinza, Pasero or Christoff but he improves immeasurably after that, pronouncing his anathemas on the French with a verve that compensates for any failings in vocal power.

Those who want their orchestras to be big and resonant may be disappointed by the confined sound heard here. However, the voices are, on the whole, caught well in a true theatre perspec-

tive. A few coughs and some applause will worry only those who must have complete silence.

The RCA set has much to commend it, most of all Domingo's full-flooded Arrigo, though he gives points to Merritt in Act 5. On balance it's more convincingly cast and conducted. It won't please those who are longing to hear the piece in the original, but Verdi did approve of the Italian version and certainly would have approved of its vital execution here.

Johannes Verhulst   Dutch 1816-1891

Verhulst became a close friend of Schumann in Leipzig, where he conducted programmes of progressive music. Holding conducting posts in Rotterdam, The Hague and Amsterdam, he virtually controlled Dutch musical life until 1886. His compositions, strongly influenced by Schumann and Mendelssohn, include choral works, songs, overtures and piano pieces. GROVEmusic

Mass, Op 20

Mass, Op 20
Nienke Oostenrijk sop **Margriet Van Reisen** contr
Marcel Reijans ten **Hubert Claessens** bass
Netherlands Concert Choir; Hague Residentie Orchestra / Matthias Bamert
Chandos CHAN10020 (65' · DDD) Text and
translation included   Ⓕ

We read that Verhulst was a pupil of Mendelssohn, but that much is self-evident from this extended setting of the Mass. Composed in 1879 for the Golden Jubilee of the Netherlands' Foundation of the Promotion of Music, Verhulst's Mass was the longest sacred choral work written up to that time by a Dutch composer. Certainly with its wealth of charming melodies, elegant orchestral accompaniments and lavish writing for chorus, it gives us a fair idea of what Mendelssohn himself might have come up with had he ever written a Mass on this scale. The eighth in a series of discs exploring Dutch music of the past 200 years marking 2004's centenary of the Residentie Orchestra, it has to be said that the focus here is, both musically and so far as the recorded sound is concerned, very much on the 15-year-old 100-voice Netherlands Concert Choir. While they sing with great clarity and precision, there's a somewhat lightweight quality about their sound which undermines the climaxes, not least the potentially thrilling moment of resurrection described in the *Credo*. Nevertheless, Bamert's taut reading draws some particularly impressive dynamic control from them, especially in the highly charged opening section of the *Sanctus*. It's left to the excellent quartet of soloists, however, to produce the most captivating music-making here. Supported by gracious obbligato solo cello and clarinet, their performance of the charming *Benedictus* is a moment of pure delight.

Tomás Luis de Victoria
Spanish 1548-1611

Victoria was a choirboy at Avil Cathedral; when his voice broke he was sent to the Jesuit Collegio Germanico, Rome (c1565), where he may have studied under Palestrina. He was a singer and organist at S Maria di Monserrato (1569-at least 1574) and from 1571 to 1576-7 he taught at the Collegio Germanico (maestro from 1575). He became a priest and joined the Oratory of S Filippo Neri. In the 1580s he returned to Spain as chaplain to Philip II's sister the Dowager Empress Maria, at the Descalzas Reales convent, Madrid, from 1587 until her death in 1603; he remained there as organist until his death, apart from a visit to Rome (1592-5), when he attended Palestrina's funeral. The greatest Spanish Renaissance composer, and among the greatest in Europe in his day, he wrote exclusively Latin sacred music. Most was printed in his lifetime; in 1600 a sumptuous collection of 32 of his most popular masses, Magnificats, psalms and motets appeared in Madrid. Though his output ranged widely through the liturgy, he is chiefly remembered for his masses and motets, which include well-known pieces (Missa Ave regina caelorum, Missa pro victoria, O magnum mysterium, O quam gloriosum, O vos omnes). Like Palestrina, he wrote in a serious, devotional style, often responding emotionally to the texts with dramatic word-painting. Some of his more poignant pieces are characterised by a religious, almost mystical fervour. **GROVE**music

Masses

Missa Gaudeamus. Missa pro Victoria (both ed Dixon). Motets –Cum beatus Ignatius; Descendit angelus Domini; Doctor bonus amicus Dei Andreas; Ecce sacerdos magnus; Estote fortes in bello; Hic vir despiciens mundum; O decus apostolicum; Tu es Petrus; Veni, sponsa Christi (all ed Skinner)
The Cardinall's Musick /Andrew Carwood
ASV Gaudeamus CDGAU198 (78' · DDD) Texts and translations included Ⓕ**OO**

There have been some fine recordings of Victoria's music in recent years, but none finer than this one at its best. The Cardinall's Musick has become known for its CDs of English renaissance polyphony, but its approach, which joint directors Andrew Carwood and David Skinner describe as 'open and soloistic', works extremely well here, too. The two contrasted Mass settings are given the same highly expressive treatment as the motets, which, sung one to a part, have a madrigalian quality bringing out beautifully the natural, unforced rhetoric of Victoria's idiom.

The *Missa Gaudeamus*, based on a Morales motet, is scored for six voices. Performed with only two singers on each part, it sounds as rich and dark as the strongest chocolate; the overall blend is superb, clear and strikingly well balanced. With only two female voices on the upper part, the polyphonic texture isn't, as is so

often the case, top-heavy; each strand carries equal weight, just as the densely contrapuntal writing demands. The final canonic *Agnus Dei* is sublime, and throughout – even in the longer movements – Carwood's sure-footed pacing allows the polyphony to ebb and flow like the swell of the sea.

The *Missa pro Victoria*, based on Janequin's chanson, *La guerre*, could hardly be more different in its forward-looking polychoral idiom. Here the writing is more condensed, more economical, but nevertheless highly dramatic. The ending of the *Gloria* is breathtaking, as is the magical opening of the Sanctus and the final 'dona nobis pacems' of the *Agnus Dei*. The clarion calls of the second *Kyrie* are equally striking. There are so many high spots on this disc that it's simply impossible to mention them all, and this is perhaps still more to the group's credit given that, as explained in the notes, a bout of flu among the singers can't have made for the easiest of recording sessions.

Officium defunctorum

Officium defunctorum
Gabrieli Consort /Paul McCreesh
Archiv Produktion 447 095-2AH (60' · DDD) Recorded 1994, Text and translation included Ⓕ**OO**

This is a remarkable recording. In some ways it's like a rediscovery, for here's an approach not too far from Pro Cantione Antiqua at its best and yet that group never recorded the work. The Gabrieli Consort adds chant to the Requiem Mass itself, thus creating more of a context for Victoria's magisterial work.

We have therefore the Epistle and preceding prayer, the Tract, Sequence, Gospel, Preface, Lord's Prayer and Postcommunion in addition to the polyphony; this also means, for example, that the *Kyrie* is sung nine-fold with alternating chant instead of simply three-fold only in polyphony. We can presume that the chant was taken from a suitable Spanish source by Luis Lozano Virumbrales, who's an expert in this field and the author of the insert-notes together with Paul McCreesh.

The performance itself is stately and imposing, with a tremendous homogeneity of sound: the use of an all-male choir, together with the added chant, lends it a tangibly monastic feel, though it would have been a fortunate monastery indeed that had falsettists of this quality. About the performance of the chant there are two points of interest: first, that it's doubled, like the polyphony, by a shawm, common Spanish practice at this period, and second, that McCreesh isn't afraid to have the falsettists singing the chant too.

The pace of the polyphony often seems unhurried, but never feels slow, and Westminster Cathedral Choir is faced with the hugely reverberant acoustics of its home building. From the beginning the singing is involving and incarnate, but the real magic comes nearer the end: from the *Agnus Dei* onwards one feels that the Gabrieli Consort have really got the measure of the music and is allowing it to speak through them. The final great responsory, the 'Libera me', is performed with heart stopping power and conviction. McCreesh's approach shows how the Mass would have fitted into and complemented the liturgical framework without ever losing its own internal power and drama. A revelatory disc.

Missa O quam gloriosum. Missa Ave maris stella. Motet – O quam gloriosum
Westminster Cathedral Choir / David Hill
Hyperion CDA66114 (57' · DDD) Recorded 1983
Ⓟ**OOO**

 This is likely to become one of your most cherished discs. It's notable for its spacious depth of sound, volatile unpredictability of interpretation, and above all the soaring sostenuto of the boy trebles, with their forward and slightly nasal tone quality. With their magnificently controlled legato lines, the Westminster boys treat Victoria's music as though it were some vast plainchant, with a passion that excites and uplifts. The choir is recorded in the exceptionally resonant Westminster Cathedral, at a distance and with great atmosphere.

Ave maris stella isn't one of Victoria's familiar Masses, quite simply because no music publisher has made it available to choirs in a good, cheap edition. To have it rescued from obscurity is laudable in itself, but to have it sung with such poise and sensitivity is an unexpected double treat. Unlike *O quam gloriosum*, this is a work that thrills with echoes of Victoria's Spanish upbringing, of Morales and his predecessors, even of Josquin Desprez, whose own *Ave maris stella* Mass was brought to the cathedrals of the Iberian peninsula earlier in the century. The plainchant melody, familiar through Monteverdi's setting in the 1610 Vespers, completely dominates Victoria's music, for it's placed most often in huge treble lines that wheel high above the general texture. Magnificent as the early parts of the work are, nothing quite matches the final five-part *Agnus Dei*, sung here with admirable support and exquisitely shaped by David Hill. Recommended without reservation.

Veni Sancte Spiritus. Dum complerentur. Missa Dum complerentur. Popule meus. Vexilla Regis. Veni Creator Spiritus. Pange lingua gloriosi. Lauda Sion
Westminster Cathedral Choir /James O'Donnell
with **Joseph Cullen** org
Hyperion CDA66886 (70' · DDD) Texts and translations included
Ⓕ**OO**

Westminster Cathedral Choir here makes a special contribution to the music of Tomás Luis de Victoria. The *Missa Dum complerentur*, for Pentecost, is based on Victoria's own motet; he adds an extra voice in the parody Mass setting

and draws much on the opening material of the motet as well as its distinctive 'Alleluia' sections which ring out like a peal of bells – especially in this excellent performance. Indeed, the motet is finely conceived, with Victoria characteristically responding to the imagery of the text with changes of texture and pacing within the essentially contrapuntal idiom: a true master.

The choir, with its full-bodied sound and well-sustained vocal lines, has, over long years of tradition in singing this particular part of the repertory, achieved an almost intuitive feel for the flow of the music, which is perhaps as near as we'll ever get today to the authentic situation of professional church singers in Rome or the Spanish cathedrals in the 16th century. What we'll never know is whether the sonority – in particular the timbre of the boys' voices – resembles anything Victoria might have heard, that distinctive focus and intensity of tone well illustrated by the two Holy Week settings on the disc: the homophonic Popule meus and the hymn *Vexilla Regis*. This, and the two Pentecost hymns, are performed in alternatim with alternate verses in plainchant and polyphony. This is a superb and compelling disc that adds to our knowledge and appreciation of Victoria's art.

Motets

Et Jesum
Alma redemptoris mater. Domine non sum dignus. Duo seraphim clamabant. Missa O magnum mysterium – Sanctus; Benedictus; Agnus Dei. Ne timeas, Maria. O magnum mysterium. O quam gloriosum. Salve regina – Et Jesum, benedictum fructum. Senex puerum portabat. O decus apostolicum. Pueri hebraeorum vestimenta. Missa Gaudeamus – Pleni sunt; Domine Deus. Doctor bonus amicus Dei Andreas. Estote fortes in bello. Missa Quam pulchri sunt – Domine; Crucifixus. Iste sanctus pro lege. Magi viderunt stellam
Carlos Mena counterten **Francisco Rubio Gallego** cort **Juan Carlos Rivera** alte/vihu
Harmonia Mundi HMI98 7042 (65' · DDD) Texts and translations included Ⓕ

In Victoria's time, intabulations – an arrangement for plucked instrument of a choral piece – were a way for music lovers to experience their favourite music for themselves. Adding a soloist radically changes the dynamic: sacred choral music becomes domestic chamber music. This is the transformation envisioned by Carlos Mena. All the transcriptions used here are drawn from prints of the period; so, for all the surprises in store, Victoria would have been familiar with the style of these performances.

The recording provides a forceful answer to those who would question the present-day value of such intabulations. Victoria's music is transfigured. It's remarkable just how much of the original polyphony is retained in transcription, and its song-like qualities are enhanced by the focus on a particular voice. The comparison with chamber music is made explicit in several selections for which the voice and lute are joined by a cornet. The lovely *Duo Seraphim*, with its treble-dominated texture, seems ideally suited to this treatment.

Most of the credit belongs to the performers. It needs a special voice to focus the attention so clearly on itself, and Mena's fits the bill. He has an extraordinary range: the break in the lower register is virtually imperceptible, and in *Iste Sanctus* he takes the alto line completely convincingly. In the middle and upper ranges his tone is very rounded, full and clear, with no hint of strain; rather like a cornet, in fact. His use of ornamentation is discreet and just sufficient to spring the occasional surprise on those who know the music well. Juan Carlos Rivera is a fine accompanist when he needs to be, but elsewhere he can let Mena take centre stage without himself disappearing from the texture. His own solos are mostly drawn from intabulations of Victoria's Mass music: yet more evidence of its versatility.

This particular incarnation of Victoria has great charm; those who dislike the 'churchy' aspect of the music will find it revelatory.

Heitor Villa-Lobos   Brazilian 1887-1959

Villa-Lobos was taught to play the cello by his father, and in his teens he performed with popular musicians in the city. He then travelled widely, returning to Rio in his mid-20s for a few formal lessons. From 1923 to 1930 he was in Paris, where he wrote several works in his Chôros series, giving Brazilian impressions a luxuriant scoring: Messiaen and others were impressed. He returned to Brazil, where he did valuable work in reforming musical education. In 1945 he founded the Brazilian Academy of Music in Rio de Janeiro. Also during this period he produced the cycle of nine Bachianas brasileiras for diverse combinations (1930-45), marrying the spirit of Brazilian folk music with that of Bach; the two for eight cellos (one with soprano) have been especially successful. His gigantic output includes operas, 12 symphonies (1916-57), 17 string quartets (1915-57), numerous songs and much piano music.

GROVEmusic

Chôros

Introduction to the Chôrosa. Chôros – No 1[a]; No 2[b]; No 3, 'Picapau'[c]; No 4; No 5, 'Alma brasileira'[d]; No 6; No 7, 'Settiminio'
[b]Johanne-Valérie Gélinas *fl* [b]Radovan Cavallin *cl* [a]Carlos Oramas *gtr* [d]Sergio Alonso *pf* Gran Canaria Philharmonic [c]Chorus and Orchestra / Adrian Leaper
ASV CDDCA1150 (70' · DDD)   Ⓕ

The word 'Chôro' derives from the verb *chôrar* (to weep), a reflection of the vein of melancholy never far below the surface of even the more cheerful Brazilian popular music – a dichotomy

in the national character, inherited via the Portuguese *fado*. The 14 *Chôros* of Villa-Lobos are remarkable fusions of the multi-faceted music of Brazil with that of Europe, written in the 1920s, long before the induction of American popular music gave birth to *bossa nova*.

After completing the cycle in 1929 Villa-Lobos added a trailer-like 'Introduction' in which he refers to themes that have yet to be heard in the various *Chôros*. To an orchestra of epic size and variety he adds a guitar, the instrument to which the first *Chôro* is entrusted; its thematic material, however, isn't that of the *Chôro*, rather is it related to the opening of his then-unwritten Guitar Concerto.

No two works call for the same instrumentation. No 2 is a dance-rhythmic flute/clarinet duet. No 3, for male chorus and wind, is based on an Indian song, Villa-Lobos's earliest depiction of rainforest Brazil. No 4, for three horns and trombone, is portentous, contrapuntal and amusing by turns. No 5, *Alma brasileira* ('Brazil's soul'), encapsulates the melancholy/cheerful dichotomy. No 6, for full orchestra, returns to the landscape of Brazil, a kaleidoscopic 'tour' of its vast size and variety. There's nothing specifically Brazilian about No 7 (for eight-part chamber ensemble) save some fleeting dance rhythms and its unmistakable character, but it's essentially cheerful with a romantic core.

No other corpus of his works offers greater access to the imaginative and colourful world of Villa-Lobos, and the catalogue lists no currently available of the *Chôros* in their entirety. The remaining seven are scheduled to follow on a second disc. These splendid performances do full justice to every piece and are as well recorded as might be hoped for. They are both listener-friendly and unique in the 20th-century world of music; they're strongly recommended.

Chôros No 11
Ralf Gothóni *pf* **Finnish Radio Symphony Orchestra / Sakari Oramo**
Ondine ODE916-2 (62' · DDD)   ⒻО

Villa-Lobos wrote five piano concertos as well as other works for piano and orchestra with less concertante titles, such as *Momoprecoce* and the third of the *Bachianas Brasileiras*: in fact *Chôros* No 11 is the largest-scale of them all, though despite its ferociously demanding solo part it has been described rather as a 'mammoth concerto grosso'. If that term conjures up for you an image of a neat neo-classical work, forget it: this is Villa-Lobos in his usual excitably coloured, hyper-exuberant style, writing in a grandiose loose form that – since few of its vast proliferation of themes are developed – defies analysis but whose overall effect is strangely riveting. Every so often lyrical passages occur among the manic busyness, and the linked second movement, profligately overscored as it is, is really romantic, with three related but not identical melodic ideas (and a big cadenza). The finale, which begins with a *fugato*, is thematically more integrated than the rest (for a time, at least) and consequently could be considered the most successful movement.

The sound is vivid, Ralf Gothóni contributes prodigious feats of virtuosity and the Finnish orchestra displays total commitment to this quite extraordinary work.

Bachianas Brasileiras

Bachianas Brasileiras Nos 2, 4 & 8
Cincinnati Symphony Orchestra / Jesús López-Cobos
Telarc CD80393 (70' · DDD)   Ⓕ**O**

If any parallels existed between Bach and Brazilian idioms, they were largely in Villa-Lobos's mind – even the Fugue in No 8 of these *Bachianas Brasileiras* is totally un-Bach-like; so anyone coming fresh to these exotically coloured, rather sprawling works should not be misled by false expectations. But they're fascinating, indeed haunting, in a highly individual way. In view of the composer's sublime indifference to instrumental practicalities (as, for instance, the feasible length of a trombone glissando), his carelessness over detail in his scores, his Micawber-like trust that problems of balance he had created would be sorted out in performance, the chaotic state of the printed scores and orchestral parts of his music (littered as they are with wrong notes), and numerous misreadings in past performances, the only half-way reliable yardstick for conductors or critics is the composer's own recordings, made in the 1950s and now preserved in a six-CD box on EMI.

Compared to them, the present issue shows a number of differences. Chief of these is the warmer, more generalised sound, with less emphasis on clarity of detail. This works reasonably well in the Preludio of No 8, where concentration on the melodic line and the adoption of a slower tempo aid the movement's lyricism (likewise the more sentimental approach to the Aria of No 2). The Aria of No 8 is unquestionably more poetic and the Dansa of No 4 lighter; but in the most famous movement, the hilarious and ingenious 'Little train of the Caipira' of No 2, the rasps near the start and the clatter of wheels on the track (evoked by the fiendishly difficult piano part) are far too subdued in favour of the 'big tune'.

López-Cobos deals persuasively with knotty questions of balance, such as in the middle section of No 3's Toccata, and brings to the fore the bell-like araponga bird's cry in No 4's Coral, but makes less of that movement's jungle screeches. He makes clear the thematic link between the sections of No 4's Aria, and seeks to overcome the repetitious pattern of its Preludio by taking a faster speed rather than by the wealth of tonal nuance the composer imself introduced. Perhaps such detailed comparisons are superfluous: enjoy, enjoy!

Bachianas Brasileiras – Nos 4, 5, 7 & 9. Chôros No 10, 'Rasga o coração'
Renée Fleming *sop* **BBC Singers; New World Symphony /Michael Tilson Thomas**
RCA Red Seal 09026 68538-2 (78' · DDD)   Ⓕ**O**

In his booklet-note, the commentator here calls *Chôros* No 10 the masterpiece of that quintessentially Brazilian series. It's certainly the most ambitious, with very large orchestral and choral forces in a complex mélange of urban street song (a popular schottisch by Medeiros), chattering native Indian chants and bird-song twitterings, of mysterious jungle atmosphere, compulsive ostinato rhythms and virtuoso orchestral effects. The present performance is excellent. The couplings here are illuminating, consisting as they do of more Villa-Lobos – four of his highly individual tributes to Bach's influence. By far the best known of the *Bachianas Brasileiras* is No 5, whose Aria demonstrates the composer's ability to spin a haunting long-flowing melody. Renée Fleming is the sweet-toned soloist with the cello section of this accomplished orchestra of young graduates from American conservatoires: warmly lyrical as she is, however, and brilliantly exact in the dartings of the Dansa, her words aren't very distinct even in the slow-moving Aria.

By his deeply expressive shaping of No 4's Preludio Tilson Thomas avoids any satiety with its extreme monothematicism, and in the second movement secures coherent continuity despite the (rather loud) insistent interventions of the araponga bird's repeated note. He produces a beautifully poetic tranquillity in the brief Prelude of No 9 and complete lucidity and rhythmic buoyancy in its Fugue. If that's the most Bachian of the series, the much more substantial No 7 also has its moments of homage: its first movement has a fine breadth, and its finale is an impressive and serious-minded large-scale fugue that begins quietly and culminates in a grandiose blaze of sound; but the busy Toccata is characteristically and challengingly Brazilian, and the first part of its Giga (before it goes all Hollywood) is delightfully fresh in this invigorating performance.

Solo Piano Works

As três Marias. Prole do bebê, Books I & II. Rudepoêma
Marc-André Hamelin *pf*
Hyperion CDA67176 (64' · DDD)   Ⓕ

Music for Children
Carnaval das crianças. Guia pratico, Volumes 1-6
Caio Pagano *pf* Glissando 779 009-2 (65' · DDD) Ⓕ**O**

Here are two invaluable raids on Villa-Lobos's rich and exotic store of piano music. First and foremost is Marc-André Hamelin, whose transcendental sheen and facility bless everything he plays. He makes *As três Marias* ('The three stars') wink and scintillate with an inimitable verve before continuing with both books of *Prole do bebê*, registering the change from affection to savagery with an impeccable degree of mastery and insight. In Book 1 the tolling bells which are at the heart of the enchanting 'Caboclinha'ring out fortissimo and ben marcato, while the fleetness that Hamelin delivers in 'O Polichinello' leaves all others standing.

Yet such delectable charm is virtually erased by the increasingly astringent and percussive Book 2. Here the insect and animal world has graduated from innocence to experience with a vengeance. The 'Little Wooden Horse', eyes dilating and nostrils flaring, gallops away from danger and the paper cockroach sounds disillusioned with its lot. Red Riding Hood, too, would surely have fled in terror, not deceived for a moment, from Villa-Lobos's jaw-snapping, not-so-little 'Glass Wolf'. Finally, there's *Rudepoêma*, the composer's supposed masterpiece. Rubinstein was understandably disconcerted by a portrait of such roughness. Hoping for a more genial offering with which to delight his adoring public he quickly abandoned *Rudepoêma*. True, there are brief moments of bittersweet accessibility, but elsewhere the assault is relentless, and even Hamelin's superb and unflagging brio hardly reconciles you to the music's length and bombast. Hyperion's production is as immaculate as ever.

Caio Pagano's brilliant and more amiable recital is devoted to music for children and includes six of the 11 volumes entitled *Guia pratico*. Here one enters a magical world quite without the adult pain and nostalgia that colour Schumann's *Kinderszenen* and Debussy's *Children's Corner*. A nun waltzes as she gives a child a necklace and Garibaldi goes to Mass with a real spring in his step. Two doves sing of their love, safe from all possible harm, while a wandering troubadour presses his claims on a countess with much vehemence. A widow looking for a husband is no less eagle-eyed and determined, and virtually all these pieces, performed by Pagano with the liveliest of engagement, are so witty and touching that you're left longing for Volumes 7-11. *Carnaval das crianças* is a more ornate celebration of colour and brio, and even when you miss the percussion and offbeat drum strokes from the finale of the piano and orchestra version you can only delight in Pagano's relish, his crisp and stylish playing. He's excellently recorded.

Prole do bebê No 1. Cirandas. Hommage à Chopin
Sonia Rubinsky *pf*
Naxos 8 554489 (65' · DDD) Recorded 1994　　Ⓢ❍

Villa-Lobos's claim that his music was 'the fruit of an immense, ardent and generous land' at once disarms familiar criticism of extravagance and formlessness. To regard such largesse through the blinkered eyes of someone exclusively nurtured on a more restrained and economical diet is unacceptable. There may be

tares among the wheat but such strictures hardly apply to the music in this Vol 1 which commences with the enchanting *Prole do bebê*, Book 1 (the Second Book is a tougher, altogether more astringent and percussive experience, while a Third Book is sadly lost). Intimately associated with Artur Rubinstein (who rearranged Villa-Lobos's miniatures, omitting some and ending 'O Polichinello' with an unmarked rip-roaring *glissando*), *Prole do bebê* is here played complete. Sonia Rubinsky makes light of a teasing rhythmic mix in 'Morenhina' (No 2) and in 'Caboclinha'(No 3) she relishes Villa-Lobos's audacity; his way of making his seductive melody and rhythm surface through a peal of church bells. Again, despite strong competition from Alma Petchersky on ASV in the no less delightful *Cirandas*, Rubinsky scores an unequivocal success, ideally attuned to the central and beguiling melody of 'Terezinha de Jesus' (No 1) with its *forte e canto* instruction, and allowing the fight between the carnation and the rose (No 4) to melt into a delicious love duet. Much celebrated in her native Brazil and also in America, Sonia Rubinsky is excellently recorded.

Choral Works

Missa São Sebastião. Bendita sabedoria. Praesepe[a]. Cor dulce, cor amabile. Panis angelicus. Sub tuum praesidium. Ave Maria a 5. Ave Maria a 6. Pater noster. Magnificat-alleluia[b]
[a]**Ansy Boothroyd**, [b]**Elizabeth McCormack** *mez*
Corydon Singers and Orchestra /Matthew Best
Hyperion CDA66638 (77' · DDD) Recorded 1992-3
Texts and translations included　　Ⓕ

Asked to identify the composer of all these religious works except the Mass one would be most unlikely to think of Villa-Lobos. That larger-than-life exotic, that extravagantly experimental and boisterous figure, the composer of such chastely restrained music, the sweetly gentle *Cor dulce*, the controlled fervour of the *Pater noster*? Even the impressive and grandiose *Magnificat-alleluia* gives no hint of its country of origin. The one clue here might be that, of the two *Ave Marias*, the (earlier) five-part setting is in Portuguese. It's only the Mass that reveals all. Amid its austere style and purely diatonic, contrapuntal idiom the *Sanctus* suddenly seems to come from a different background: then one remembers that Sebastian is the patron saint of Rio de Janeiro; and looking into the score one finds that the liturgical heading of each movement is followed by a local one, the final *Agnus Dei* bearing the subtitle 'Sebastian, protector of Brazil'.

This programme, all of unaccompanied music except for the *Magnificat-alleluia*, should not be listened to as a continuity if some feeling of sameness is to be avoided: the Corydon Singers are most efficient in all they do, but the outstanding performance is of the Mass.

Antonio Vivaldi

Italian 1678-1741

Vivaldi was the son of a professional violinist who played at St Mark's and may have been involved in operatic management. Vivaldi was trained for the priesthood and ordained in 1703 but soon after his ordination ceased to say Mass; he claimed this was because of his unsure health (he is known to have suffered from chest complaints, possibly asthma or angina). In 1703 he was appointed maestro di violino at the Ospedale della Pietà, one of the Venetian girls' orphanages; he remained there until 1709, and held the post again, 1711-16; he then became maestro de' concerti. Later, when he was away from Venice, he retained his connection with the Pietà (at one period he sent two concertos by post each month). He became maestro di capella, 1735-8; even after then he supplied concertos and directed performances on special occasions. Vivaldi's reputation had begun to grow with his first publications: trio sonatas (probably 1703-5), violin sonatas (1709) and especially his 12 concertos L'estro armonico op. 3 (1711). These, containing some of his finest concertos, were issued in Amsterdam and widely circulated in northern Europe; this prompted visiting musicians to seek him out in Venice and in some cases commission works from him (notably for the Dresden court). Bach transcribed five op. 3 concertos for keyboard, and many German composers imitated his style. He published two further sets of sonatas and seven more of concertos, including 'La stravaganza' op 4 (c1712), Il cimento dell'armonia e dell'inventione (c1725, including 'The Four Seasons') and La cetra (1727).

It is in the concerto that Vivaldi's chief importance lies. He was the first composer to use ritornello form regularly in fast movements, and his use of it became a model; the same is true of his three-movement plan (fast-slow-fast). His methods of securing greater thematic unity were widely copied, especially the integration of solo and ritornello material; his vigorous rhythmic patterns, his violinistic figuration and his use of sequence were also much imitated. Of his c550 concertos, c350 are for solo instrument (more than 230 for violin); there are c40 double concertos, more than 30 for multiple soloists and nearly 60 for orchestra without solo, while more than 20 are chamber concertos for a small group of solo instruments without orchestra (the 'tutti' element is provided by the instruments all playing together). Vivaldi was an enterprising orchestrator, writing several concertos for unusual combinations like viola d'amore and lute, or for ensembles including chalumeaux, clarinets, horns and other rarities. There are also many solo concertos for bassoon, cello, oboe and flute. Some of his concertos are programmatic, for example 'La tempesta di mare' ((the title of three concertos). Into this category also fall 'The Four Seasons', with their representation of seasonal activities and conditions accommodated within a standard ritornello form – these are described in the appended sonnets, which he may have written himself. Vivaldi was also much engaged in vocal music. He wrote a quantity of sacred works, chiefly for the Pietà girls, using a vigorous style in which the influence of the concerto is often marked. He was also involved in opera and spent much time travelling to promote his works. His earliest known opera was given in Vicenza in 1713; later he worked at theatres in Venice, Mantua (1718-20), Rome (probably 1723-5), possibly Vienna and Prague (around 1730), Ferrara (1737), Amsterdam (1738) and possibly Vienna during his last visit.

He was by most accounts a difficult man; in 1738 he was forbidden entry to Ferrara ostensibly because of his refusal to say Mass and his relationship with the singer Anna Giraud, a pupil of his with whom he travelled. More than 20 of his operas survive; those that have been revived include music of vitality and imagination as well as more routine items. But Vivaldi's importance lies above all in his concertos, for their boldness and originality and for their central place in the history of concerto form.

GROVEmusic

Cello Concertos

Cello Concertos – in D minor, RV407; in E flat, RV408; in F, RV411; in A minor, RV420; in A minor, RV421. Concerto for Multiple Instruments in C, RV561[ab]. Concerto for Violin, Cello and Strings, 'Il Proteo o sia il mondo al rovescio', RV544[a]
Ensemble Explorations ([a]Christine Busch, Dirk Vandaele vns Frans Vos va [b]Richte van der Meer vc Love Persson db Mike Fentross theo/gtr Attilio Cremonesi hpd/org) / **Roel Dieltiens** vc
Harmonia Mundi HMC90 1745 (71' · DDD)

Roel Dieltiens is a Baroque cellist *par excellence* and the modest size of Ensemble Explorations (seven players including continuo) suits these works admirably. Vivaldi poured some of his finest music into his numerous concertos for bassoon and cello, both dual-register instruments for which he had obvious affection – to which the affecting slow movements richly testify. Dieltiens' superb bow control and his natural empathy with style and emotional aura make these memorable musical experiences. His 'vocal' nuancing of volume and addition of exquisite embellishment comfortably reach the benchmark set by Pleeth and Bylsma in their 1977 recording of the G minor Double Concerto, RV531 (L'Oiseau Lyre). Listen to the *Largo* of the E flat Concerto, RV408, and prepare to tug a grateful forelock. These qualities enhance the quicker movements, albeit at a less intimate level.

The smaller ripieno is especially apt to the sonata-related concertos such as that in A minor, RV420, and in those in which it plays a more prominent role the ensemble provides ample weight to ensure contrast; their incisiveness, energy and audible enthusiasm are infectious. The quality of the recording calls for another tug of the forelock. A truly superb disc which will hold your attention from beginning to end.

Cello Concertos – in C minor, RV401; in B flat, RV423. Violin Concerto in F minor, 'Winter', RV297. Double Concerto in G minor, RV519. Double Concerto, RV540[a]. Gloria, RV589 – Laudamus te[a]g. Juditha

Triumphans, RV645[a] – Noli ò cara, te adorantis[b]; Quanto magis generosa[f]. La Fida ninfa, RV714[a] – Così sugl'occhi miei[bde]; Dite oihime[gh]. Il Giustino, RV717 – La gloria del mio sangue[abc] ([a]arr Koopman) **Yo-Yo Ma** *bqvc* with [b]**Alfredo Bernardini,** [c]**Michel Henry** *obs* [d]**Wouter Verschuren** *bn* [e]**Margaret Faultless** *bqvn* [f]**Katherine McGillivray** *vad* [g]**Jonathan Manson** *bqvc* [h]**Mike Fentross** *lte* **Amsterdam Baroque Orchestra / Ton Koopman** *hpd/org* Sony Classical SK90916 (68 minutes: DDD)   Ⓕ

It was only a matter of time before Yo-Yo Ma turned to Vivaldi, the first of the great composers to take the cello seriously as a soloist. Strange to relate, however, in this cheery get-together with Ton Koopman and the Amsterdam Baroque Orchestra only three of its 11 pieces – the Double Concerto RV531, and the two solo concertos RV401 and 423 – were written for the cello. The others are all arrangements, from the appropriation of the slow movement of 'Winter', to the recasting of vocal numbers for colourful combinations of winds and strings, to the transformation of the beautiful Concerto for viola d'amore and lute, RV540, into a slightly less magical concerto for cello and organ.

Koopman, whose arrangements these are, claims that no one in Vivaldi's day would have thought twice about such things. Maybe he's right. RV540 apart, they're perfectly convincing, and you'd have to be a sour old grouch to object to them for long when they are played as expertly, as joyously and as lovingly as they are here. And, superb though Ma is on his 'baroqued' 1712 Stradivarius, each of the musicians, with special mentions going to Katherine McGillivray's exquisite viola d'amore and Jonathan Manson's cello, matching Ma all the way in RV531 and 'Laudamus te'.

An uncomplicated joy all round then, for its music, its performances and its recording, too, save only for the sometimes maddening prominence of the keyboard continuo.

Flute Concertos

Flute Concertos, Op 10. Flute Concerto in C minor, RV441 **Nicolaus Esterházy Sinfonia / Béla Drahos** *fl* Naxos 8 553101 (59' · DDD)   ⓈⓄ

Vivaldi's flute concertos have certainly not been neglected on disc, and there's a wide choice of 'authentic' and middle-of-the-road versions played on both tranverse flute and recorder; this present selection is in the MOR vein and faces numerous competitors. In the flute concertos Béla Drahos is a superb soloist, as smooth as silk and agile as a kitten, and whose flights of fanciful embellishment might have won Vivaldi's approval. The Esterházy Sinfonia sounds a little beefy at times in its opening statements, but in the presence of the soloist its touch is appropriately light, and the third Largo ('Il sonno'), of

Op 10 No 2, 'La notte', is impressively hushed. The outer movements of the bonus concerto, R441, dance on the lightest of feet; the work was originally written for the recorder, but on whichever instrument it's played, you wonder why it has no other currently listed recording. This present one would carry a warm recommendation even if it were not at bargain price.

Oboe Concertos

Oboe Concertos –C, RV447; C, RV450; D, RV453; A minor, RV461; A minor, RV463. Concerto for Violin and Oboe in B flat, RV548 **Douglas Boyd** *ob* **Marieke Blankestijn** *vn* **Chamber Orchestra of Europe** DG 435 873-2GH (59' · DDD) Recorded 1991   ⒻⓄ

Vivaldi wrote 17 solo oboe concertos, three for two oboes and another for oboe and violin. In this virtuoso programme the oboist, Douglas Boyd, has chosen five of the solo oboe concertos together with the more modestly conceived but no less captivating Concerto in B flat for oboe and violin. The oboe concertos have been selected discerningly, not only for their musical interest but also, it would seem, with an eye to their rarity value on the concert platform. Boyd, playing a modern oboe, gives fluent, sensitively shaped performances and is supported in a lively manner by the strings of the COE. Boyd is expressive in slow movements – they almost invariably possess considerable lyrical appeal – and athletic in faster ones; and he needs to be, for Vivaldi seldom showed mercy on his soloists. From among the many beautiful movements here the Larghetto of the Concerto in A minor (RV461) stands out and may be ranked among Vivaldi's happiest creations for the oboe. Fine recorded sound.

Double Concerto for Two Oboes and Strings in D Ⓟ minor, RV535. Concertos for Multiple Instruments – A, RV552, 'per eco in lontano'; D, RV562; F, RV568; F, RV569; G minor, RV577, 'per l'orchestra di Dresda' **Philharmonia Baroque Orchestra / Nicholas McGegan** Reference Recordings RRCD77 (72' · DDD)   ⒻⓄ

Here is Vivaldi-playing with a commendably light, athletic touch. It's so easy to make a meal out of his orchestral *tuttis* yet these performances inspire the music with expressive delicacy and rhythmic vitality. The programme is a colourful one of concertos for a variety of instruments, wind and strings, in various combinations. Apart from occasional instances of predictable passagework, present above all in some of the wind writing, this music is engaging on many different levels. Slow movements such as the wonderfully free violin fantasy of RV562 reveal the exhilarating flights of fancy of which Vivaldi was capable, while the profusion of alluring inflexions present in fast and slow movements alike makes strong appeal to the senses. Vivaldi was no stranger to the art of parody and, in the opening movement of RV568, we find him introducing sensuous, sighing quaver motifs present in the finale of the Concerto a due cori per la Santissima Assenzione di Maria Vergine (RV535). This kind of approach to Vivaldi's music greatly enlivens and refreshes its innate character. The disc is superbly recorded, allowing us to revel in every sonorous detail of solo and continuo playing alike.

Recorder Concertos

Recorder Concertos[d] – in C minor, RV441[b]; in F, RV442[a]; in C, RV443[b]; in C, RV444[b]; in A minor, RV445[b]. Chamber Concerto in D, 'La Pastorella', RV95[bc]
[a]László Czidra,[b]László Kecskeméti recs [c]Béla Horváth ob [c]István Hartenstein bn [c]Tamás Zalay vn [c]György Eder vc [c]Borbála Dobozy hpd
[d]Nicolaus Esterházy Sinfonia
Naxos 8 553829 (64' · DDD)   Ⓢ

This is claimed to be a recording of the 'complete' recorder concertos of Vivaldi (RV441-5) and there's no other listed version of RV441 it has that field to itself. Such archival primacy would be of little significance if the performances were sub-standard – but here they're high quality on all counts.

Kecskeméti bears the bulk of the soloist's burden, while Czidra appears only in RV442 (for treble recorder). Kecskeméti acquits himself on the same instrument with no less distinction in RV441 and, with no reflection on Czidra's manifest abilities, he could surely have made a clean sweep. Kecskeméti has the greatest 'showcase' opportunities, and he makes the most of them. His speed and clarity of articulation (as clean as a whistle, as it were) in the flanking movements are breathtaking and in some scale passages his sure-tongued choice of separate articulation gives life and variety – listen to the *Allegro molto* of RV443 and marvel! He adds embellishment where appropriate and in good taste. The basic five concertos alone would leave a disc somewhat under-filled and the choice of RV95, in which the recorder is featured, as a filler is a happy one. The Nicolaus Esterházy Sinfonia's contributions are happily light-footed. Excellent recording quality and bargain price are just extra reasons why this disc is a must-buy.

Vivaldi Recorder Concertos – in C minor, RV441;   🄿
in G, RV443; in C, RV444 **Sammartini** Recorder Concerto in F **Telemann** Suite in A minor, TWV55:a2
Pamela Thorby recs **Sonnerie** (Monica Huggett, Emilia Benjamin vns Katherine McGillivray va Alison McGillivray vc Sarah Groser vion Mathew Halls hpd/org)
Linn Records CKD217 (69' · DDD)   🄟🄞

Pamela Thorby's work with the Palladian Ensemble has alone been sufficient to establish her as a world class performer, and the reputa-

tion of Sonnerie has long been sky-high. Their coming together offers a delightful prospect and though, as any sports-person knows, teams assembled from star players don't always work happily, this one lives up to its promise. Their material has a familiar look but their delivery of it is of rare quality and fully justifies this journey along oft-trodden paths.

The music trips off Thorby's tongue with the utmost fluency, cleanly articulated, and without any trace of the distressing sagging or wavering of pitch on long notes that haunts too many otherwise laudable performances by some others. No less notable is her enhancing embellishment, particularly though not exclusively in the slow movements. Sonnerie provide the perfect substrate for Thorby's excursions: stylish, precise and ideally balanced in the Linn recording.

Throughout, one has the impression of a single mind in control of two 'hands', soloist and *ripieno*. This recording is sheer pleasure and comes highly recommended.

Violin Concertos, Op 4 – La stravaganza

Violin Concertos 'La stravaganza', Op 4 – No 1 in B flat, RV383 a; No 2 in E minor, RV279; No 3 in G, RV301; No 4 in A minor, RV357; No 5 in A, RV347; No 6 in G minor, RV316a
Andrew Watkinson vn **City of London Sinfonia / Nicholas Kraemer**
Naxos 8 553323 (52' · DDD)   Ⓢ

Violin Concertos, 'La stravaganza', Op 4 – No 7 in C, RV185; No 8 in D minor, RV249; No 9 in F, RV284; No 10 in C minor, RV196; No 11 in D minor, RV204; No 12 in G, RV298
Andrew Watkinson vn **City of London Sinfonia / Nicholas Kraemer**
Naxos 8 553324 (46' · DDD)   Ⓢ

La stravaganza is the second of the sets of concertos published during Vivaldi's lifetime. It was issued in about 1714 as the composer's Op 4 and, as with the greater number of his printed collections, contains 12 works. They are essentially violin concertos, although, to a much lesser extent than *L'estro armonico*, Vivaldi also provides on occasion solo parts for an additional violin or cello. These concertos have long been favourites, above all, perhaps, for the profusion of lyrically affecting slow movements, of which those belonging to Concertos Nos 1, 4, 5 and 12 are notably fine examples: in this music there's delicate nuance, poetic fantasy and sheer originality lying beneath the immediately recognisable hallmarks of the composer's outward style. Nicholas Kraemer is no stranger to this repertory having already recorded two of Vivaldi's other printed sets, Opp 8 and 9. Those, however, were with his period-instrument Raglan Baroque Players, whereas *La stravaganza* is played on instruments tuned to today's standard pitch. This, paradoxically, may be closer to the pitch which Vivaldi himself used rather than the lower Baroque pitch.

Listening to this music, so full of vitality, invention and expressive tenderness, leaves one feeling exhilarated. Andrew Watkinson plays with virtuosic flair, but senses the highly developed fantasy present in every one of the concertos. His embellishments are tasteful and restrained and his melodic line always clearly articulated. Tempos, for the most part, are effectively judged, though the almost unbearably beautiful *Largo* of the First Concerto, with its emotionally highly charged modulation towards the close, is perhaps a shade too slow.

The strings of the City of London Sinfonia sound tonally bright and unfailingly alert. Only in the *Adagio* of No 8 does the balance of the recording falter; the harpsichord's arpeggios (notably in the *Adagio molto* of 'Autumn') might have been allowed a little more prominence.

Violin Concertos 'La stravaganza', Op 4 – Nos 1-12 🄿
Arte dei Suonatori / Rachel Podger *vn*
Channel Classics ② CCS19598 (103' · DDD) Also
available on SACD CCSSA19503   🄕🅞🅞🅞

By the standards of the average Vivaldi violin concerto, the *La stravaganza* set is quite extravagant stuff, full of fantasy and experiment – novel sounds, ingenious textures, exploratory melodic lines, original types of figuration, unorthodox forms. It's heady music, and listening to its 12 concertos at a sitting, isn't a mode of listening one would recommend.

Still less so in performances as high in voltage as the present ones. There's a current trend in Baroque performance to get away from the coolness and objectivity which for a long time were supposed (on the whole, mistakenly) to be a part of performing practice of the time, but possibly the pendulum has swung a little wildly the other way. Perhaps here it's intended to reflect Vivaldi's own notorious freedom of performance. But anyone who's admired earlier recordings with period instruments may find these a little extravagant and hard-hitting. And they aren't helped by the resonant acoustic of the church in Poland used for the recording, which produces a full and bright sound but a boomy bass and less clear a texture than might be ideal.

That said, however, these performances by Rachel Podger are crackling with vitality and executed with consistent brilliance as well as a kind of relish in virtuosity that catches the showy spirit, the self-conscious extravagance, of this particular set of works. There are plenty of movements here where her sheer digital dexterity is astonishing – for instance, the finale of No 6, with its scurrying figures, the second movement of No 7 or the finale of No 2 with its repetitive figures and leaping arpeggios. But perhaps even more enjoyable is the exquisitely fine detail of some of the slow movements. No 8 in D minor is perhaps the wildest concerto of the lot, with its extraordinary lines in the first movement, the passionate, mysterious outer

sections in the second and the powerful and original figuration in the finale: that one has a performance to leave you breathless.

Another thing Podger is specially good at is the shaping of those numerous passages of Vivaldian sequences, which can be drearily predictable, but aren't so here because she knows just how to control the rhythmic tension and time the climax and resolution with logic and force. This set is certainly recommended as a fine example of a modern view of Baroque performance – and it sounds even better on SACD.

Violin Concertos, Op 8 (The Four Seasons)

Violin Concertos, Op 8 – Nos 1-4, 'The Four Seasons': No 1 in E, 'Spring', RV269; No 2 in G minor, 'Summer', RV315; No 3 in F, 'Autumn', RV293; No 4 in F minor, 'Winter', RV297; **No 5** in E flat, RV253, **'La tempesta di mare'; No 6** in C, RV180, **'Il piacere'; No 7** in D minor, RV242; **No 8** in G minor, RV332; **No 9** in D minor, RV236; **No 10** in B flat, RV362, **'La caccia'; No 11** in D, RV210; **No 12** in C (two versions, RV178 & RV449)

Violin Concertos, Op 8 – Nos 1-4   🄿
(The Four Seasons). Violin Concertos in E flat, RV257;
in B flat, RV376; in D, RV211
Giuliano Carmignola *vn* **Venice Baroque Orchestra
/ Andrea Marcon**
Sony Classical SK51352 (72' · DDD)   🄕🅞🅞

Vivaldi's Four Seasons, like nature's, come and go in their various moods and meteorological vicissitudes. We've had ochre sunsets from Louis Kaufmann, Harnoncourt's Breughel-style rusticity and the provocative Nigel Kennedy, to mention but a scant few. Giuliano Carmignola's primary claim on our attentions (this is his second shot at the piece) is, aside from a delightfully woody-sounding Baroque instrument, a keen narrative flair. He knows the musical period, understands principles of embellishment and doesn't hesitate to enrich his performances with added colour and with rhythmic thrust. 'Spring' arrives in rude high spirits, toying with birdsong (slowly at first then speeding up) and with thunder thrashing between violin desks. The violas' 'barking dog' is worryingly prominent (if you don't like dogs) and the finale contrasts a swelling *legato* against sparkly solo passagework. The 'impetuous weather of summer' has power enough to keep the National Grid up and running, and the diverse winds of the multi-faceted opening *Allegro* of 'Autumn' and the way the harpsichord holds its own in the second and third movements are wonderful. The cruel weathers of 'Winter' inspire the expected bursts of virtuosity while the *Largo*'s raindrops unexpectedly seep through to the busy bass line (most versions don't allow for the leak). Varieties of plucked continuo help fill out textures and Carmignola himself plays with immense brilliance. The three additional violin concertos are

VIVALDI FOUR SEASONS – IN BRIEF

Concerto Italiano / Rinaldo Alessandrini
Opus 111 ② OP30363 (103' · DDD)   Ⓕ**OO**
A stunning new version of the *Four Seasons*,
each season granted its own soloist. Theatricality and discipline are ideally combined in
this unforgetable performance.

Enrico Onofri; Il Giardino Armonico
Teldec 4509-96158-2 (61' · DDD)   Ⓕ**OO**
Though a relatively small group, Il Giardino
Armonico give as much vigour and sonority
as you might wish, while allowing telling
contributions from their continuo section,
including delightful theorbo playing.

**Giuliano Carmignola; Venice Baroque
Orchestra / Andrea Marcon**
Sony Classical SK51352 (72' · DDD)   Ⓕ**OO**
Here's a violinist of extraordinary technique
and attractive tone married to a truly imaginative interpretation. He's aided by the equally
inventive playing of the orchestra, and the
result is one of the most highly charged and
characterful performances.

**Gottfried von der Goltz; Freiburg Baroque
Orchestra, Harp Consort**
Deutsche Harmonia Mundi 05472 77384-2
(66' · DDD)   Ⓕ
An imaginative performance which draws
from a rich but tastefully used palette of
continuo instruments – a lirone, Baroque
lute, cittern, archlute, guitar, theorbo,
arch-cittern, harp and psaltry, together with
harpsichord, organ and regal!

**Andrew Manze; Amsterdam Baroque
Orchestra / Ton Koopman**
Elatus 0927 46726-2 (57' · DDD)   Ⓕ
An 'authentic' performance for those who
don't want their performance too spiced up.
A straightforward account with subtle but
telling individual touches by Manze.

**Anthony Marwood; Scottish CO /
Nicholas McGegan**
BMG 75605 570452 (67' · DDD)   Ⓜ
An excellent performance on modern instruments, but with the briskness and lightness of
Baroque practice. Real thought has gone into
the characterisation of each season, and this
is easily one of the most invigorating and
uplifting accounts you can hope to find.

Mariana Sirbu; I Musici
Philips 446 699-2PH (60' · DDD)   Ⓕ**O**
A safe choice for those who prefer modern
instruments to highly embellished 'authenticity', with some truly delightful lute playing
as well as harpsichord in the continuo.

all said to be first recordings and reveal a rather
different aspect of Vivaldi's style. Generally
speaking, they sound more formal than the *Four
Seasons*, almost pre-classical in RV257's opening
Andante molto e quasi allegro and with sideways
glances at Rameau in the opening of RV211
(which also includes a brief first-movement
cadenza). Dance rhythms again predominate.

Great sound, full and forward and with every
instrumental strand given its proper due.
Thinking in terms only of the *Four Seasons*,
good rivals are so plentiful that comparative discussion becomes less a question of 'who gets it
right' than how you like your birds and storms.
There are countless period-instrument options
and almost as many that use modern instruments, but take heed of period performing practice. Up to now, the period favourites have been
Il Giardino Armonico (reviewed below) and
Harnoncourt's Concentus Musicus Wien, and
there's no reason why this new version should-
n't join their hallowed ranks.

Violin Concertos, Op 8 Nos 1-4 (The Four   Ⓟ
Seasons), 8 & 9
Enrico Onofri vn **Paolo Grazzi** ob **Il Giardino
Armonico / Giovanni Antonini**
Teldec 4509-96158-2 (61' · DDD) Recorded 1993
Ⓕ**OO**
Il Giardino Armonico doesn't do anything
extraordinary; it's more a matter of demonstrating what can be achieved with small forces:
5-1-2-1 plus soloist and continuo. Here, small is
flexible and it highlights the differences in
colour achieved by varying the continuo – bassoon, cello, organ, harpsichord and theorbo,
unobscured by the *ripieno*, all have their
moments. Numbers of 'chamber' dimensions
also favour unanimity of attack and changes of
dynamics and pace, all vividly accomplished.
The dog barks harshly in 'Spring' but without
disturbing the shepherd's peaceful dreams, and
the chill of 'Autumn' in the *Adagio molto* is conveyed by the ethereal strings with the harpsichord firmly relegated to a supporting role.
Onofri is as good a soloist as may be met in a
long march, pitch-perfect, incisive but not
'edgy', and effortlessly alert to every nuance.

All the foregoing good things are also to be
found in the other two concertos from Op 8,
together with Grazzi's liquid-toned and agile
oboe playing in that in D minor, attractively
supported in the *Largo* by theorbo and bassoon.
A tasty addition to any collection.

Violin Concertos, Op 8 – Nos 1-4 (The Four
Seasons)[a]

Includes bonus disc of – 'Concerto Italiano – Portrait'
Bach Concerto in the Italian style in G, 'Italian
Concerto', BWV971 (arr Alessandrini)[b] **Handel** Il
Trionfo del Tempo e del Disinganno, HWV46a –
Voglio Tempo[c] **Marenzio** Madrigals, Book 2: Il
secondo libro de madrigali – E s'io doglio, Amor[d]
Monteverdi Scherzi musicali – Damigella tutta

bella[e] **Rossini** Il Barbiere di Siviglia – Overture[f].
Tancredi – No che il morir non è[g] **A Scarlatti**
Magnificat à 5 voci[h] – Magnificat anima mea;
Et exultavit **D Scarlatti** Stabat mater – stabat mater
dolorosa[i] **Vivaldi** L'Olimpiade[j] – Overture; Mentre
dormi, Amor fomenti; E troppo spietato il barbaro
fato. La Senna Festeggiante, RV693 – Sinfonia[k].
Concerto grosso in D minor, RV565[l]
[g]**María Bayo**, [c]**Deborah York**, [c]**Gemma
Bertagnolli, Elisabetta Tiso** sops **Anna Simboli,**
[j]**Sonia Prina**, [c]**Sara Mingardo** contrs **Paolo Costa**
counterten [c]**Nicholas Sears, Gianluca Ferrarini** tens
Sergio Foresti bass [a]**Stefania Azzaro**, [a]**Mauro
Lopes Ferreira**, [l]**Riccardo Minasi**, [al]**Antonio De
Secondi**, [ab]**Francesca Vicari** vns [al]**Luca Peverini** vc
Concerto Italiano / Rinaldo Alessandrini
Opus 111 ② (2-for-the-price-of-1) OP30363
(103' · DDD)   Ⓕ**OO**

Of the huge number of recordings of the *Four
Seasons*, none sounds such a clear 'wake up' call
as this one. No matter how many you may
already have, you should add this one to their
number. If you have none, go straight for it.

These are appropriately 'Italian' performances, but the flanking movements aren't
rushed; indeed, 'Summer' begins at an unusually leisurely pace and no season is noticeably
hurried to its conclusion. The central movements are taken somewhat more slowly than in
other recordings, but so beguilingly that one
barely notices it – and never in a pejorative way.
What's striking is the sharply defined characterisation of the *frisson*-making chill of 'Autumn'
and the furious 'Summer' storm that sends the
mind running for imaginary cover.

In a unique display of their strength in depth,
Concerto Italiano assign a different soloist to
each concerto. Their approaches to embellishment are both personal and refreshingly free
from clichés. The most up-front is Francesca
Vicari, who enthusiastically applies it also to the
final movement of 'Winter' (where others
haven't ventured to tread) with a controlled
ferocity that keeps you on the edge of your seat.
The knife-edge unanimity of attack, tone and
dynamics of the 14 members of Concerto Italiano is remarkable, and the recording is crystal
clear, luculent and perfectly balanced. They
don't merely play the score, they live it. Some
may regard the performances as 'theatrical' and
so they are, but they are acted with total commitment and in good style and taste.

The *Four Seasons* alone don't add up to a well-
filled disc, but there's a bonus CD, a showcase
sampler with tracks from existing recordings
and others not previously issued. Concerto
Italiano's high reputation has rested on their
recordings of Baroque music (instrumental and
vocal), but the final Rossini tracks signal a
rewarding venture into pastures new.

Violin Concertos, Op 8 – Nos 1-4 (The Four   Ⓟ
Seasons)Oboe Concertos, Op 7 – No 1 in B flat,
RV465; No 5 in F, RV285a
Andrew Manze vn **Marcel Ponseele** ob **Amsterdam**

Baroque Orchestra / Ton Koopman
Warner Elatus 0927-46726-2 (56' · DDD) Recorded
1993-4   Ⓜ**O**

This is a splendid set, valid for a lifetime of
pleasure. Little differences in attention to detail
soon begin to show, first at 0'17"of the first
movement of 'Spring', where the chords that
are usually hit hard are here given a happy little
squeeze. Amsterdam Baroque (consisting here
of 13 instrumentalists) play with the unanimity
of one mind and body, with extreme changes of
volume that never sound theatrically contrived,
as concerned with the fate of every note as with
the shaping of each phrase. Manze's bow
breathes vocal life into his strings; in the slow
movements many notes whisper their way into
being, and his *fortissimo* whiplashes have rasp-
free edges. There are many delightful little personal touches – his slurred resolution of the
sighing appoggiatura at 2'50" in the third movement of 'Spring', and the way he nudges his way
up the ladder of trills in the first movement of
'Autumn' are just two.

The remaining works come from Op 7, in the
first of which (RV465) the oboe is the soloist; its
transcribed role in No 5 (RV285a) accords with
Baroque practice. Both are charming works
with a high level of inspiration, played with no
less affection than the Seasons.

Violin Concertos, Op 8 – Nos 5-7, 9-11 & 12 (two   Ⓟ
versions)
Enrico Onofri vn **Paolo Grazzi** ob **Il Giardino
Armonico / Giovanni Antonini**
Teldec Das Alte Werk 4509-94566-2 (74' · DDD)
Recorded 1994-5   Ⓕ**O**

In the completion disc of Il Giardino Armonico's Op 8, as two of the concertos exist in alternative forms, for oboe or violin (RV236 = 454,
RV178 = 449), they're given in both versions –
with negligible differences in tempo. The
virtues of Il Giardino Armonico are, if anything,
even more vividly apparent in this recording.
Onofri is spellbinding in his imaginative use of a
varied continuo, here highlighted in the *Adagio*
of RV362 (*La caccia*) played only by violin and
theorbo. One complaint: if there's logic behind
the order in which the concertos are presented,
it isn't apparent. The first volume has six concertos (61 minutes), Vol 2 has eight (74 minutes), whereas to place Nos 1-6 and RV454 on
one disc, and Nos 7-12 and RV449 on the other
would have created no apparent problem. However, you'd need a far more compelling reason
not to make a beeline for the nearest CD store
for these magical and finely recorded discs.

Violin Concertos – Miscellaneous

Dresden Concertos – D, RV213; D, RV219; D, RV224;
D minor, RV240; E flat, RV260; A, RV344; B minor,
RV388

Cristiano Rossi vn Accademia I Filarmonici /
Alberto Martini
Naxos 8 554310 (67' · DDD) Ⓢ

The Dresden link was forged by Vivaldi's friend
and one-time pupil Johann Georg Pisendel.
Pisendel visited Venice in 1716 when he appears
to have struck up a warm friendship with
Vivaldi, who dedicated several sonatas and concertos to him. The seven violin concertos on
this disc have survived in manuscripts preserved
in the Dresden Sächsische Landesbibliothek.
Much of this music will be entirely new to most
collectors. By and large these are pieces which
do not wear their hearts on their sleeves. There
are few extravagant flourishes and perhaps less
than we might expect in the way of extrovert
gesture. But there's no lack of brilliance in the
solo violin writing – Pisendel's reputation as a
virtuoso was hardly less than Vivaldi's –and, as
ever, the music contains a profusion of effective
rhythmic ideas. The solo violin parts are
entrusted to Cristiano Rossi, who often, though
not always, discovers the fantasy in Vivaldi's
solo writing. The bowing is graceful and relaxed
even if intonation is occasionally awry. The A
major Concerto, RV344 affords a good instance
of soloist and orchestra at their most persuasive.
But the lyrically expressive violin melody
against a dotted rhythm continuo of the *Largo* of
RV224 is unquestionably the most alluring.

The more you hear this music, the more
you're likely to be captivated by it. The
recorded sound seems a little boxy and confined, but textures come through clearly all the
same.

Violin Concertos – in C, RV177; in C, RV191; in D, ℗
RV222; in E minor RV273; in F RV295; in B flat RV375
Giuliano Carmignola vn **Venice Baroque Orchestra**
/ Andrea Marcon hpd
Sony Classical SK89362 (75' · DDD) Ⓕ

The point of this release is that these relatively
unfamiliar violin concertos, probably composed
in the 1730s, come from late in Vivaldi's career
and therefore have a style of their own. Vivaldi
stopped publishing his concertos after his Op 12
set of 1729, having come to the conclusion that
he could make more money from selling them
singly in manuscript to the many wealthy music
lovers who visited Venice on the Grand Tour
and preferred a work by Vivaldi to a Canaletto
painting as their souvenir. The result is that
today these concertos are virtually unknown,
and so, too, is the notion of a late Vivaldi style.
But it's there, and this disc demonstrates it well.
Here, the regularity and succinctness of the better-known concertos are replaced by an altogether more discursive kind of inspiration, in
which Vivaldi takes more time, thickens the textures, investigates a few more corners. There's
less raw energy than before, but more grace and
richness and still plenty of memorable
moments. The performances are first-rate.
Giuliano Carmignola, a relatively recent con-

vert from the modern violin, is a highly accomplished soloist, able to negotiate Vivaldi's complex lines with great assurance and a wide variety of attacks and articulations, though always
with the smoothness and easy elegance that one
ought to expect from a pupil of Milstein and
Szeryng. The Venice Baroque Orchestra are
lithe and alert, and produce a marvellously full
sound, with bass notes positively thundering out
into the recording's ample acoustic.

Violin Concertos – in D minor, RV235; in E flat, ℗
RV251; in E flat, RV258; in F, RV296; in B minor, RV386;
B minor, RV389
Giuliano Carmignola vn **Venice Baroque Orchestra**
/ Andrea Marcon
Sony Classical SK87733 (72' · DDD) Ⓕ

A whole facet of Vivaldi's work has long been
under-appreciated, which is a pity because compared to the pithy energy of the earlier published concertos these works are richer, more
ruminative, perhaps simply more beautiful. The
first movement of RV258 has a distinctly pre-
Classical sound to it, while its second movement
shows an operatic concentration of emotion.
Yet the old violinist trickery is still there, even if
it's more attuned to the overall tenor of the
music. This may be the Red Priest with pipe and
slippers, but he can still make the notes jump
when the bow is in his hand.

As we have come to expect from this soloist
and orchestra, these are performances of
immense accomplishment and poise. Giuliano
Carmignola is a silky player whom Vivaldi's
most difficult violin-writing can't perturb, but
he's more than just a technician who can whizz
through scales and arpeggios in his sleep;
throughout, his playing displays a sweetly nourished tone and a fine poetic sense which is
entirely in keeping with the music's relaxed
beauty. The sensitively attentive strings of the
Venice Baroque Orchestra, superbly recorded
as ever, make the perfect match. Exquisite stuff.

Concertos for the Emperor
Violin Concertos – in C, RV189; in C minor, RV202; in
F, 'Concerto per la solennità di San Lorenzo', RV286;
in C, RV183; in E, 'L'amoroso', RV271; in E minor, 'Il
favorito', RV277
The English Concert / Andrew Manze vn
Harmonia Mundi HMU90 7332 (79' · DDD) Ⓕ

Vivaldi published his Op 9 concertos, *La cetra*
('The Lyre'), in 1727. Soon after, he presented
Charles VI, the Habsburg emperor, with a manuscript set of concertos, also called *La cetra*. It
was long supposed that these were the same
concertos until someone looked at them more
carefully, and noticed that 11 of the 12 were
entirely different works. Vivaldi had simply
used the same name again for a set of pieces he
thought particularly well suited to the needs of
the Viennese court. No one seems to have gathered them together for performance as a group

until now. The six presented here show Vivaldi in his grandest and most magnificent vein, and exceptionally varied in mood.

The first item (No 2 of the set) is a dashing C major piece, with vigorous scales to catch the attention, then more contemplative minor-key music with much brilliant high writing for the soloist; there's a quietly eloquent slow movement, again with violin reaching its upper reaches; and in the finale, a lively, playful piece, the cadenza is positively stratospheric.

The second concerto (No 10) is entirely different, soft-toned, with a lovely E major glow, and a tenderness to the musical ideas untypical of Vivaldi. Then comes a big C minor work (No 7) with large gestures in its outer movements; in the finale there's a huge *crescendo* that makes the later Mannheim ones sound tame by comparison, with some elaborate violin coloratura.

The final concerto, in F major (No 4), is a big, ceremonial, stately piece, originally composed 'per la solennità di San Lorenzo', but it serves Charles VI pretty well, too, with a virtuoso finale to round it off. Perhaps the most powerful of the concertos, however, is No 11, full of nervous energy in its first movement, with an improvisatory violin line in its second above soft chords, and a strong reminiscence of the *Four Seasons* (not the only one here) in the finale.

This is an immensely enjoyable disc: the music very characteristic, but much freer of cliché than Vivaldi sometimes is. The violin-playing from Andrew Manze is of an extremely high order: rhythms beautifully springy, articulation clear and precise, intonation perfect, great refinement in the shaping of phrases, and a real command of the logic of the music. The orchestral support is strong and energetic, the recorded quality first-rate. An outstanding CD in every way.

Double and Triple Concertos

Concertos – for Two Cellos in G minor, RV531; for Violin and Cello in F, RV544, 'Il Proteo ò sia il mondo rovescio'; for Three Violins in F, RV551; for Two Violins in A, RV552, 'Per eco in lontano'; for Violin, Two Cellos in C, RV561; for Two Violins, Two and Cellos in D, RV564
Christophe Coin vc **Il Giardino Armonico /
Giovanni Antonini**
Teldec Das Alte Werk 4509-94552-2 (64' · DDD)
Recorded 1994　　　　　　　　Ⓕ**ⒶⒶⒶ**

This is a strong programme which almost unfailingly presents the Venetian composer in his most colourful clothing. Though Vivaldi often wrote imaginatively for pairs of wind instruments, his musical ideas were of necessity confined by their technical limitations. With violins and cellos, on the other hand, he was better able to extend his creative faculties, which resulted in music of more sustained interest. This is certainly true of the two concertos which he wrote for two violins,

two cellos and strings, one of them (RV564) included here. Making an even rarer appearance on disc is a Concerto in F major for violin and cello (RV544), the least well known of three such works from Vivaldi's pen. Two versions of this concerto exist, the other (RV572) containing additional parts for pairs of flutes and oboes. Both carry the engaging title *Il Proteo ò sia il mondo al rovescio*. Infrequently performed, too, is a C major piece for violin, two cellos and strings (RV561), though the characteristically Vivaldian ritornello of the opening movement may recall other contexts in the minds of listeners. The three remaining works are fairly mainstream Vivaldi: the G minor Concerto for two cellos (RV531), the F major Concerto for three violins (RV551) and the A major Concerto for two violins, one of them functioning as an echo, the *violine per eco in lontano* (RV552). From this, readers will infer a pleasing variety of texture and, within the limits of a purely string programme, colour. Il Giardino Armonico has thought carefully about the latter, ringing the changes in the keyboard continuo between organ and harpsichord, and introducing a theorbo, too. But what makes this disc a real winner is the exhilarating character of the playing, both solo and ripieno. Playing of vitality and lyricism brings Vivaldi's music to life in a thrilling manner. Indeed, the integrity and musicianly character of these performances is in no small measure heightened by the presence of Christophe Coin. An outstanding issue.

Concertos – for Two Cellos in G minor, RV531;　Ⓟ
for Two Violins, Two and Cellos in D, RV564; for Recorder – A minor, RV108; G, RV436. Trio Sonatas – D minor, 'La follia', RV63; C minor, RV83
Musica Alta Ripa
Dabringhaus und Grimm MDG309 0927-2 (56' · DDD)
　　　　　　　　　　　　　　　　　Ⓕ**Ⓐ**

None of the pieces is new to the catalogue, but the playing is of a calibre that might entice readers to consider these alternative versions. The two largest works are the Concerto for two cellos and strings in G minor, and another, in D major, for two violins, two cellos and strings. Both fare well in the hands of sensitive performers such as these, and especially enjoyable is the beautifully inflected playing of the two solo cellists in the G minor work.

Albert Brüggen is an excellent cellist, and here (alongside partner Juris Teichmanis) he fulfils expectation raised by previous discs. Vivaldi wrote two concertos for pairs of solo violins and cellos; the other is RV575 – and both are satisfying pieces with beguiling slow movements. Melodically, this one gives pride of place to a solo violin in its centrally placed Largo, but one should nevertheless be allowed to hear more of the solo cello than is granted by this performance. The rhythmic élan of the finale is quite exhilarating. The two remaining concertos feature a recorder. One, RV436, is scored for transverse flute with strings, though a descant recorder has been substituted here. The other,

RV108, is a chamber concerto for treble recorder, two violins and continuo. The soloist in each is Danya Segal, who brings the music to life with fluency and unpretentious eloquence. An attractive menu is completed by two strongly contrasting sonatas which, in their quite different ways, demonstrate Vivaldi's craftsmanship and invention in the medium.

This disc makes rewarding listening. The pieces have been chosen with real discernment and are played with virtuosity and an effective understanding of style.

Concerto for Multiple Instruments in C, RV557 **P**
Double Concertos – 2 Oboes in D minor, RV535; Oboe and Bassoon in G, RV545; 2 Trumpets in C, RV537; 2 Horns in F, RV538. Oboe Concerto in A minor, RV461. Bassoon Concerto in E minor, RV484
Ensemble Zefiro /Alfredo Bernardini
Astrée Naïve E8679 (64' · DDD)   Ⓕ**OO**

Ensemble Zefiro is one of the most remarkable Baroque bands to emerge during the last decade or so, though we hear of it less often than it deserves. Its specialised front line is its battery of exceptionally gifted wind players, but the support troops of strings and continuo are no less worthy of commendation. In all technical and musical respects they think, breathe and act as one. Their dynamic range (from sotto voce whisper to as many *f*s as you regard as adding up to 'issimo') is put to vivid and impressive use, whether terraced in *crescendo*s or *diminuendo*s, or in the finely judged squeezing of notes. The Allegros are crisp, animated, joyously propulsive and full of Italian sunshine, and the eloquent music-making of the oboe and bassoon soloists effortlessly conceals Vivaldi's severe technical demands. It's perhaps the slow movements that make the deepest impression: how many times have we heard the same harmonic progressions but marvelled at Vivaldi's ability to invest them with constantly new charm and depth? There are appealing conversations in those of RV545 (oboe and bassoon), RV535 (two oboes), RV557 (two recorders, whose players aren't among the declared personnel in the booklet!) and RV538 (two cellos). They are all marked by stylish embellishment, and the last was an irresistible reminder of the benchmark recording of the two-cello Concerto RV531 by Pleeth and Bylsma with the AAM (L'Oiseau Lyre). Nicholas Anderson has rightly described Alberto Grazzi as 'the poet of the bassoon'; in this recording we have a veritable eisteddfod. This is a faultless and marvellous recording.

Concertos[a] – D, 'L'inquietudine', RV234; E, **P**
'Il riposo, per il Santissimo Natale', RV270. Recorder Concerto No 2 in G minor, 'La notte', RV439[b]. Concerto for 2 Cellos in G minor, RV531[c]. Concertos for Multiple Instruments – A, 'Per eco in lontano', RV552; F, 'La tempesta di mare', RV570; B flat, 'Concerto funèbre', RV579
[b]**Lorenzo Cavasanti** rec [c]**Maurizio Naddeo**,

[c]**Antonio Fantinuoli** vcs **Europa Galante / Fabio Biondi**[a] vn
Virgin Veritas 545424-2 (64' · DDD)   Ⓕ**O**

There's a real lickety-split opening to this colourful disc of Vivaldi concertos: the violin concerto *L'inquietudine*, not one of its composer's best-known, really earns its title with a restlessly virtuosic solo part, dispatched with taut, nervous energy by Fabio Biondi. In truth there's some scintillating music here, as well as performances which mix suitable inspiration with scrupulous but unfussy attention to detail. The nearest we get to well-trodden ground here are the vigorous *La tempesta di mare* and the fantastical *La notte* (played here in their later 'flute' revisions, but on recorder), and both are performed with tightly controlled virtuosity, and with plenty of surprises – the giant off-beat accents in both concertos' finales, for instance. Elsewhere we get a creamy account of the charming (but perhaps slightly long) *Concerto per eco in lontano*, a strong-boned concerto for two violins, and an exquisite, muted-string Christmas concerto entitled *Il riposo*. If the sombre *Concerto funèbre* for multiple soloists is a slight disappointment, it's only because Concerto Italiano (for Erato) have recently taken it to another level of dark theatricality. Overall, though, this is another disc to add to the growing pile of wonderfully refreshing and enlightening Vivaldi recordings to have come out of Italy in recent years.

Concertos for Multiple Instruments – C, 'Per la Solennità di S Lorenzo', RV556[b] ; C, RV554; B flat, 'Concerto funèbre', RV579[b]. Concerto for Strings in E flat, 'Sonata al Santo Sepolcro', RV130[b]. Clarae stellae, RV625[a]. Stabat mater in F minor, RV621[ab]
[a]**Sara Mingardo** contr **Concerto Italiano / Rinaldo Alessandrini** [b]hpd
Opus 111 OP30367 (71' · DDD) Texts and translations included   Ⓕ**O**

'Rediscover the feminine vocal world of the Red Priest in Venice' state the cover notes to this release. In fact, only two of the six pieces offered here are vocal, of which the star work, the *Stabat mater*, is one of the few by Vivaldi thought to have been written for a male alto. In both the motet *Clarae stellae* and the *Stabat mater*, Mingardo's singing is firm and richly coloured, moving easily through a range that includes the kind of rock-solid low notes that few male altos seem able to produce. In the *Stabat mater*, furthermore, she demonstrates exemplary control in some notably slow tempos. Where well-regarded recordings of the piece from Andreas Scholl and Robin Blaze have scored through sheer vocal beauty, Mingardo and Alessandrini present a dejectedly emotional and drawn-out reading which, without resorting to hysterics, reaches several levels deeper into the text. This is something quite special, and it's only a pity that the voice is somewhat recessed in the balance.

The instrumental pieces on the disc make a fascinating selection, ranging from two of Vivaldi's kaleidoscopic 'multi-instrument' concertos to the tiny *Sonata al Santo Sepolcro*, and all are performed crisply and with plenty of thoughtful and original detail by Alessandrini and his band. Most striking is the *Concerto funèbre*, a consolatory piece full of unusual instrumental colours – including parts for a chalumeau and three viole all'inglese (a 'lost' instrument substituted here by violas d'amore) – which in its introductory slow movement even manages to take on a rather Beethovenian hue. Elsewhere, the San Lorenzo Concerto sees gaily bubbling outer movements framing a memorable slow one in which a typically serene solo violin line is accompanied by a gently prodding C clarinet. It's an extraordinary sound, but only one of the many delights and surprises of this inspiriting disc, which is in almost all respects a most satisfying Vivaldi release.

Concertos – for Viola d'amore and Lute in D minor, **P** RV540; for Cello in G, RV413; for Flute in G minor, 'La notte', RV439; for Oboe in D minor, RV454; for Two Horns in F, RV539; for Multiple Instruments – in D minor, RV566; in F, 'Il Proteo ò sia il mondo rovescio', RV572. Chamber Concerto in G minor, RV107.
Orchestra of the Age of Enlightenment
Linn Records CKD151 (74' · DDD)   (F)O

It's a nice idea for the Orchestra of the Age of Enlightenment to record a disc of such varied Vivaldian fare. The young women of the orchestra which Vivaldi directed at the Ospedale della Pietà in Venice were as renowned for the range of instruments they could wield as for their virtuosity; so it seems neatly apposite that the OAE, so full of capable soloists itself, should use this music to celebrate its members' own star qualities. And the mixture is a wide one:three solo concertos; a rare Concerto for two horns; the deservedly popular Concerto for lute and viola d'amore, two concertos for typically extravagant Vivaldian multiple line-ups; and one of those chamber concertos in which all the players are soloists. The OAE play with great expertise and good taste throughout. Judging by the list in the booklet, they use a relatively large body of strings, but, although this is noticeable, there's no feeling of heaviness, and indeed the use of two double basses gives the sound a substantial foundation which is at the same time deliciously light on its feet. There's a total of 16 soloists listed: among the highlights are David Watkin's habitually assured and intensely musical playing of the Cello Concerto; Lisa Beznosiuk, sensitive as ever in *La notte* (though struggling a bit against the string sound); Andrew Clark and Roger Montgomery, treading securely and confidently through the Concerto for two horns; Anthony Robson, a little under the note sometimes but showing good breath control and phrasing in the Oboe Concerto; and a fairy-light performance of the Concerto for lute and viola d'amore

from Elizabeth Kenny and Catherine Mackintosh. The performances are all directorless, and there was the odd place where a guiding hand might have pepped things up (or stopped the theorbo from twiddling so much in the slow movement of the Cello Concerto), but in general this is a relaxed and convivial Vivaldi programme that one can simply sit back and enjoy.

Concertos, Op 3 – L'estro armonico

L'estro armonico   **P**
Europa Galante / Fabio Biondi vn
Virgin Classics Veritas ② 545315-2 (100' · DDD) (F)OO

No other set of Vivaldi's concertos contains the sheer variety on display in *L'estro armonico*. The catalogue has seldom been without a decent recording of these ceaselessly fascinating works, though none begins to approach this version in respect of fantasy and exuberance. Fabio Biondi and his Italian ensemble, Europa Galante, bring something entirely fresh and vital to oft-performed repertoire, illuminating well-trodden paths with affective articulation and eloquently voiced inflexions. Not all of their extravagant, Mediterranean gestures, perhaps, will find favour with listeners; indeed, some of Biondi's own embellishments can be a little inapposite. Tempos are well chosen, by and large, and ensemble is clear-textured and evenly balanced. The continuo group, which includes harpsichord, organ, archlute and Baroque guitar, makes an important contribution to the overall success.

This music is wonderful stuff, rejuvenating and immensely satisfying.

String Concertos

String Concertos – in C, RV110; in C, 'Ripieno', RV115; in C minor, RV118; in D minor, 'Madrigalesco', RV129; in E minor, RV134; in F, RV142; in G, RV145; in G, 'Alla rustica', RV151; in G minor, RV156; in A, 'Ripieno', RV158; in A minor, RV161; in B flat, RV166; in B flat, RV167
Collegium Musicum 90 / Simon Standage vn
Chandos Chaconne CHAN0687 (62' · DDD)   (F)O

This third volume of Collegium Musicum 90's survey of Vivaldi's string concertos offers a varied selection of works which bears testament to their composer's untiring imagination. Vivaldi composed more than 40 of these sparky little miniatures, united by an (almost) uniform adoption of a three-movement format and by the lack anywhere of any kind of soloist; for this reason they're also sometimes known either as 'concertos for orchestra' or 'ripieno concertos'. None lasts longer than eight minutes, and most come in under five.

CM90 perform with accomplished ease, attempting nothing outrageous but maintaining a relaxed bonhomie and clear-cut eloquence entirely suited to the music's modest aspirations. Theirs isn't the taut Vivaldi sound we have become used to hearing from other ensembles, but they have no difficulty serving up lyrical sweetness or joyous energy as required. Realistically and lucidly recorded, the disc leaves little to be desired.

String Concertos – D minor, RV129, 'Concerto   **P**
madrigalesco'; E flat, RV130, 'Sonata al santo
sepolcro'; C minor, RV202; G minor, RV517; B flat,
RV547; C minor, RV761. Sinfonia in B minor, RV169,
'Sinfonia al santo sepolcro'. Double Concerto in
G minor, RV517
Adrian Chamorro vn **Maurizio Naddeo** vc **Europa
Galante / Fabio Biondi** vn
Opus 111 OP309004 (52' · DDD) Recorded 1990   Ⓕ❍
Also available (coupled with RV281, 133, 541, 286,
511 & 531) on Opus 111 ② OP20009   Ⓜ

This invigorating programme contains both well-known and less well-known concertos by Vivaldi. The performances sparkle with life and possess an irresistible spontaneity. The Concertos for one and two violins (RV761 and RV202) are comparative rarities and are played with agility and insight by the soloist director Fabio Biondi and his alert and responsive ensemble. Biondi himself is capable of light and articulate bowing and has a natural feeling for graceful turns of phrase. Vivaldi's virtuoso writing occasionally finds chinks in his armour, but with enlightened music-making of this order it matters little. Everywhere Vivaldi's infectious rhythms are tautly controlled and the music interpreted with character and conviction. Perhaps the highlight of the disc is the Concerto in B flat for violin and cello. Outer movements are crisply articulated and played with almost startling energy while the poignant lyricism of the *Andante* is touchingly captured. A refreshing and illuminating disc; the recorded sound is clear and ideally resonant.

String Concertos – in C, RV115; in C minor, RV120; in
D, RV121; in D, RV123; in D minor, 'Madrigalesco',
RV129; in F, RV141; in F minor, RV143; in G minor,
RV153; in G minor, RV154; in G minor, RV156; in A,
RV158; in A, RV159
Concerto Italiano / Rinaldo Alessandrini hpd
Opus 111 OP30377 (66' · DDD)   Ⓕ

Vivaldi's concertos for string orchestra without soloist were long an underconsidered area. With no concerto lasting much more than six minutes and no single movement more than three, this music has a slight look to it; in fact it's probable that some were opera sinfonias, and some may even have been orchestral training material. But there a good deal of variety and interest here; indeed, more than might be found in an average disc of violin concertos. Without a soloist to dominate proceedings, Vivaldi's thrown back on his musical resources in a way that's warmingly direct and revealing.

The music is unmistakably his, but ranges from brilliant violin figuration to creamy slow-drawn chords, and from vocal transcriptions to enjoyable short fugues. The cumulative effect is like visiting a workshop and finding examples of all the things an artist might do when freed from the public's demands.

Concerto Italiano's performances can't be faulted. Alessandrini has a knack for vital and exciting music-making that's utterly straightforward and free from overworked mannerism.

Chamber Concertos

Chamber Concertos –D, RV93; D, RV94;   **P**
F, RV98, 'La tempesta di mare'; G minor, RV104, 'La
notte'; G minor, RV107; A minor, RV108; F, RV442. Trio
Sonata in D minor, RV63 **Il Giardino Armonico**
Teldec 4509-91852-2 (67' · DDD) Recorded 1990-92
  Ⓕ❍

There are Baroque groups that are dull, and there are others on whom stylistic felicity sits naturally and gracefully. Il Giardino Armonico, an 11-strong group of young Italians, is one of the best. the group is as Italian as the music itself – brightly coloured, individualistic, confident, stylish, arrestingly decorated and bubbling with enthusiasm. The only un-Italian thing about them is their collective unanimity! Set these performances against any others in the catalogue and, with no detriment to the others, the differences are likely to deal you a blow to the solar plexus. Any sneaking fear that such unbridled *élan* leads to a uniformly vigorous approach is unfounded; equally 'Italian' is their wide dynamic range, dramatically exploited in RV104 and RV63, and all calls for serenity are answered. The recording is bright and clear.

Trio Sonatas

12 Trio Sonatas for Two Violins and Continuo, Op 1.
Sonata for Cello and Continuo in A minor, RV43. Trio
Sonatas for Two Violins and Continuo – C, RV60; F,
RV70; G minor, RV72. Trio Sonata for Violin, Cello and
Continuo in C minor, RV83
Sonnerie (Emilia Benjamin, Monica Huggett vns
Alison McGillivray vc Gary Cooper hpd) with **William
Carter** gtr/lte/theorb
CPO ② CPO999 511-2 (143' · DDD)   Ⓕ❍

Good recordings of Vivaldi's Op 1 are hard to come by. The set lacks the distinctive imprint of what we understand and recognise as Vivaldian, yet the pieces have great charm if handled sensitively and imaginatively. These have long been virtuous features in Monica Huggett's playing: her gently inflected approach to the music, shared by the other members of Sonnerie, is a constant pleasure, and is heard to great advantage in the many beguiling slow movements. In addition to the Op 1 Trio Sonatas, Sonnerie plays two further trios, a Sonata for two violins, a Sonata for violin, cello and continuo and one of Vivaldi's nine cello sonatas. These miscellaneous additions to Sonnerie's programme are in all but one instance more immediately identifiable as products of Vivaldi's pen than the Op 1 pieces. The G minor Sonata hints at other of Vivaldi's chamber works, while the Sonata in F major (RV70), in its two-violin writing, brings to mind Vivaldi's double concertos. The writing is essentially unaccompanied, but in this performance a discreet plucked string instrument is included.

The Trio Sonata in C major (RV60) is the least Vivaldian of the appended group and its authenticity was questioned until fairly recently. Yet its spirited *Allegro* finale seems at times to foreshadow passages in the concertos of *L'estro armonico* (Op 3).

Alison McGillivray plays the Cello Sonata with a feeling for the music's declamatory content as well as for its lyrical properties. She ornaments freely but with restraint and her intonation is excellent. The remaining Sonata, for violin and cello (RV83), is a worthy companion piece to the better-known Sonata for treble recorder and bassoon (RV86). Even more than RV70, the supple, virtuoso dialogue between treble and bass is concerto-like and is sustained with even balance and expressive sensibility by Huggett and McGillivray.

This is a first-rate release which comfortably outclasses any rival versions of Vivaldi's Op 1, as well as providing us with a rare opportunity of hearing several other uncommonly encountered pieces. Strongly recommended.

Cello Sonatas

Cello Sonatas – E flat, RV39; E minor, RV40;　　　　Ⓟ
G minor, RV42; A minor, RV44; B flat, RV45; B flat,
RV46
Pieter Wispelwey vc **Florilegium Ensemble**
(Elizabeth Kenny, William Carter ltes/theorboes/gtrs
Daniel Yeadon vc Neal Peres da Costa hpd/org)
Channel Classics CCS6294 (66' · DDD) Recorded　　Ⓕ**O**
1994

Vivaldi wrote with great imagination for the cello, and the sonatas, like the concertos, are plentifully endowed with affecting melodies – the third movement of the E minor Sonata is a superb example –and virtuoso gestures. It would seem, on the strength of these pieces, that Vivaldi possessed a rare sensibility to the expressive *cantabile* possibilities in writing for the cello. Certainly, few Baroque composers other than Bach and perhaps Geminiani realised the instrument's solo potential better than he. Wispelwey is a sensitive player who draws a warm if at times under-assertive sound from his instrument. Fast movements are clearly articulated, slow ones lyrically played with some feeling for the poetry of the music. The performances are thoughtful and enlightened, with a continuo group that includes organ, harpsichord, cello, archlutes, theorboes and guitars in a variety of combinations. The quality of the recorded sound is fine.

Violin Sonatas

12 Violin Sonatas, Op 2 – No 1 in G minor, RV27;
No 2 in A, RV31; No 3 in D minor, RV14; No 4 in F,
RV20; No 5 in B minor, RV36; No 6 in C, RV1
Elizabeth Wallfisch vn **Richard Tunnicliffe** vc
Malcolm Proud hpd
Hyperion CDA67467 (59' · DDD)　　　　　　　　Ⓕ

Vivaldi's 12 violin sonatas, Op 2 were originally released in an edition by the Venetian music publisher Antonio Bortoli in 1709. They were highly regarded enough for Estienne Roger to publish his own edition in Amsterdam three years later, quickly followed by a pirated edition by John Walsh in London. Listening to this impressive new recording it's easy to understand why they were so appealing. Each of the six included here is packed with musical treasure. Elizabeth Wallfisch's delivery of the fast movements is dazzling, and her animated and witty playing in the Giga towards the end of the second sonata is stunning. More memorable still is her clean and lyrical expression in the simpler melodic movements. The slower *Andantes* that introduce each sonata are sensuously played, and suggest Vivaldi could articulate emotional depth beyond his Corellian model.

Richard Tunnicliffe and Malcolm Proud form an ideally sympathetic continuo section. In Bortoli's 1709 printed edition these sonatas were described as for violin and cello, without mention of a keyboard instrument. Following this clue, the third sonata is performed as a fabulous sinewy duet.

This magnificent disc is complemented by an authoritative essay by Michael Talbot.

12 Violin Sonatas, 'Manchester Sonatas'　　　　　Ⓟ
HMU90 7089: No 1 in C, RV3; No 2 in D minor, RV12;
No 3 in G minor, RV757; No 4 in D, RV755; No 5 in B
flat, RV759; No 6 in A, RV758 HMU90 7090: No 7 in C
minor, RV6; No 8 in G, RV22; No 9 in E minor, RV17 a;
No 10 in A minor, RV760; No 11 in E flat; RV756; No
12 in C, RV754
Romanesca (Andrew Manze vn **Nigel North** lte/the-
orbo/gtr John Toll hpd)
Harmonia Mundi ② HMX2907342/43 (73' & 72' ·
DDD) Recorded 1992　　　　　　　　　　　　　Ⓜ**O**

Vivaldi is so well known for his concertos that we're apt to overlook his admittedly much smaller output of sonatas. This set of 12 for violin and continuo was discovered in Manchester's Central Music Library during the 1970s, though five of them exist in versions which have been known for much longer. It's probable that they all date from the early to mid-1720s when Vivaldi assembled them to present to Cardinal Ottoboni on the occasion of his visit to Venice, the city of his birth, in 1726. The violinist Andrew Manze has an appealing rapport with this music and is expressive in his shaping of phrases. He reveals sensibility towards Vivaldi's pleasing melodic contours. Indeed, this is a quality in which these sonatas abound, not only in the varied Preludes with which each Sonata begins but also in the brisker, sometimes very brisk allemandes and correntes. He ornaments the music with an effective blend of fantasy and good taste and he dispenses with bowed continuo instruments, preferring the lighter textures provided by harpsichord, arch-lute, theorbo or guitar. This is music of great beauty and vitality which will delight most if not all lovers of the late Baroque; and it's sympathetically interpreted and warmly recorded.

Gloria in excelsis Deo, RV588

Gloria in excelsis Deo, RV588abcd Laetatus sum, RV607d. Laudate pueri, RV601b. Vestro principi divino, RV633c. Jubilate, o amoeni chori, RV639abcd. aSusan Gritton, bCarolyn Sampson sops cNathalie Stutzmann contr aCharles Daniels ten The King's Consort and dChoir / Robert King
Hyperion CDA66819 (69' · DDD) Notes, texts and translations included   Ⓕ

Volume 6 of this series was a *Gramophone* Award nominee in 2001 and this one is just as good: it contains some very fine and largely unfamiliar music, in splendid performances. The principal work is the 'other' *Gloria* – RV588, not the popular 589, which, however, by no means outshines it. This setting, in fact, begins particularly fascinatingly, as the choral climax to a short, introductory solo motet *Jubilate, o amoeni chori*; the motet elides, as it were, into the choral *Gloria* in an attractive and lively movement. Then follows a poetic, choral 'Et in terra pax', rich in texture and especially in harmony, and several further movements scarcely less appealing than their counterparts in RV589.

The disc starts a shade unpromisingly, with what seems rather a routine *Laetatus sum*, in solid block choral writing against orchestral figuration. But the *Laudate pueri* is quite another matter, a highly demanding solo motet which Carolyn Sampson sings with great precision and brilliance – Vivaldi often writes for the solo voice as if it has the agility of a violin, but this clearly doesn't disturb her. There's a lot of original and imaginative writing here.

The short motet *Vestro principi divino* was probably written for a weak contralto, in which case the use of Nathalie Stutzmann is an inspired piece of miscasting: she sings this entertaining piece with great power and accuracy, and goes on to do the motet introducing the *Gloria* in virtuoso fashion. The other soloists, Susan Gritton and Charles Daniels, have less to sing but do it with no less distinction. And Robert King directs his choir and orchestra with sensitive feeling for tempo, nuance and style. One could hardly ask for more.

Gloria, RV588. Dixit Dominus, RV595. Jubilate o amoeni chori. Nulla in mundo pax
Jane Archibald, Michele de Boer sops **Anita**

Krause *mez* **Peter Mahon** *counterten* **Nils Brown** ten **Giles Tomkins** *bass-bar* **Aradia Ensemble / Kevin Mallon**
Naxos Ⓢ 8 557445; G M 5 110064; ⚟ Ⓜ 6 110064 (69' · DDD · T/t)

In 1713 Vivaldi, teacher of the violin at the school of the Ospedale della Pietà in Venice, found himself taking on the responsibility for composing music for the Pietà's all-female choir. Here, in the first of a new series of recordings of all his sacred music on Naxos, are three works from around 1715: none is well known, but all are extremely attractive.

Dixit Dominus only came to light in the 1960s. Visitors came from all over Europe to hear the girls' singing and playing, and in 'Tecum principium', for two sopranos and two cellos, we can imagine their delight. The puzzle is how the 'male' parts were sung. Was the bass-line taken at pitch by deep-voiced women, or transposed upwards? The Aradia Chorus goes for the conventional lay-out, with a mixed alto line, and sings with admirable clarity and vigour.

Jane Archibald, who copes fearlessly with the coloratura of 'Dominus a dextris tuis', does equally well in the 'Alleluia' of *Nulla in mundo*, and tastefully decorates the reprise of the *da capo* siciliana with which the motet begins.

The oddity here is Vivaldi's integration of the alto motet, *Jubilate, o amoeni chori*, with a setting of the Gloria, RV588. Anita Krause is up against stiff competition from the throaty contralto of Nathalie Stutzmann on Hyperion, but more than holds her own, especially in the lilting 'Qui sedes'. Kevin Mallon is rather dogged in the Gloria's 'Et in terra pax', but elsewhere he conducts with a sure sense of style.

Gloria in D, RV589

Gloria in D, RV589. Magnificat in G minor, RV611 Ⓟ Concerto for Strings in D minor, RV243. Concerto for Oboe, Trumpet and Strings in D, RV563
Deborah York, Patrizia Biccire sops **Sara Mingardo** contr **Andrea Mioh** ob **Gabriele Cassone** tpt **Akademia; Concerto Italiano / Rinaldo Alessandrini**
Opus 111 OP30195 (60' · DDD) Texts and translations included   Ⓕ

Once you recover from the shock of hearing the opening chorus of Vivaldi's *Gloria* sung at what initially seems a breakneck tempo, you'll quickly begin to enter into the vital spirit of Alessandrini's performance. In fact it isn't only this introductory movement that's thought-provoking, but also the carefully considered tempos of several other sections of the work, some of them much slower than we've become used to. He lays far greater emphasis than many of his rivals on the meaning of the Latin text. The two supplicatory sections, 'Domine Deus, Rex caelestis' and 'Domini Deus, Agnus Dei', are both sensitively handled with affective dynamic shading; in the first of them he avails himself of Vivaldi's option for a violin solo rather than the more customary oboe. The piece is lyrically sung by Deborah York with a beautifully sustained violin accompaniment. The soloist in the second of these movements, Sara Mingardo, also makes a favourable impression. The other sacred vocal work in this release is the latest of several adaptations Vivaldi made of a Magnificat he had originally written for the Pietà. A principal difference between this version and the earlier ones lies in five effectively contrasted arias for named singers among the *figlie di coro* of the Pietà. In this performance the solos are distributed among three rather than five artists, but it hardly matters, since each is sung with distinctive character and accomplished technique. Two concertos of contrasting aspect and instrumentation complete this very attractive programme. Both have been recorded previously, though, in the case of RV563, not quite in the way it's performed here, with a natural trumpet and oboe in the outer movements. In the slow movement the trumpet is tacet, the oboe assuming a solo role with scalewise passages of a somewhat vacuous character. Never mind, this is a rewarding issue, above all for the expressive performance of the Magnificat.

Vivaldi Gloria in D, RV589[b]. Ostro picta, RV642[c]. Nisi Dominus, RV803[d] **Ruggieri** Gloria, RV ANH 23[a] [ab]**Joanne Lunn, Carolyn Sampson** *sops* [ab]**Joyce DiDonato,** [ad]**Tuva Semmingsen** *mezs* [abd]**Hilary Summers** *contr* [a]**Robin Blaze** *counterten* **The King's Consort Choir; The King's Consort / Robert King** Hyperion CDA66849 (77' · DDD) Texts and translations included ⓕ

Robert King had the good fortune that a lost Vivaldi *Nisi Dominus* turned up just as his project to record the composer's complete sacred music reached its 10th and final volume. This is its première recording. As the work's authenticator, Michael Talbot, has pointed out, only Vivaldi would have dared to include solos for chalumeau, violin 'in tromba marina', viola d'amore, organ and cello in a single multi-sectional work. If, as it seems, this is one of the great colouristic experimenter's last sacred compositions, he certainly goes out with a bang. An atmospheric and loving performance gives a perfect start to its new life.

The other major work for this final volume is the famous *Gloria*, a fitting crown to the series. So much is good in it – boldness, brightness, expressive depth, melodic beauty – and it all comes through in this carefully judged interpretation. Carolyn Sampson is excellent in the short solo motet *Ostro picta*, a final reminder that high-quality solo singing has been one of the principal pleasures of this series. But King gives the final word to the members of his choir, who ably sing the stand-out solos in the intriguing *Gloria* by Giovanni Maria Ruggieri from which Vivaldi pinched his own concluding

'Cum Sancto Spiritu' fugue. With its bold strokes of originality and colour, it's easy to see how it could have impressed Vivaldi.

Psalms

Dixit Dominus in D, RV595[ab]. Domine ad ⓟ adiuvandum me, RV593[a]. Credidi propter quod, RV605. Beatus vir in B flat, RV598[ab]. Beatus vir in C, RV597[abc] [a]**Susan Gritton,** [b]**Catrin Wyn-Davies** *sops* [b]**Catherine Denley** *mez* [c]**Charles Daniels** *ten* [c]**Neal Davies** *bass* [c]**Michael George** *bass* **Choir of The King's Consort; The King's Consort / Robert King** Hyperion CDA66789 (70' · DDD) Texts and translations included ⓕ

Here are two of Vivaldi's most extended and impressive psalm settings. These are the single-choir *Dixit Dominus*, RV595 (Psalm 110), and double-choir *Beatus vir*, RV597 (Psalm 112). Vivaldi set both psalms more than once, and King's programme also includes the single-movement *Beatus vir*, RV598, as well as the response, *Domine ad adiuvandum me*, RV593, and the conservatively styled Vesper psalm, *Credidi propter quod*, RV605. The King's Consort Choir make a lively and warm-textured contribution; the solo line-up is also strong; with Susan Gritton and Catrin Wyn-Davies providing an evenly matched, lightly articulated partnership in their two duets. Neal Davies and Michael George are splendidly robust in their vigorous 'Potens in terra' duet from *Beatus vir* (RV597). Catherine Denley gives an appropriately strongly inflected account of 'Judicabit in nationibus' but is intimate and tender in her beautiful 'De torrente in via bibet' (from *Dixit*). The remaining soloist, Charles Daniels, delivers the virtuoso 'Peccator videbit' (*Beatus vir*, RV597) with lightness and comfortable agility. Although consisting of only three movements, the G major *Domine ad adiuvandum me*, is easily on a level with the larger-scale pieces, its expressive warmth irresistible. This is a rewarding issue, spaciously recorded.

Dixit Dominus in D, RV594[e]. Lauda Jerusalem in ⓟ E minor, RV609[b]. Magnificat in G minor, RV610[a]. Kyrie in G minor, RV587[c]. Credo in E minor, RV591[d] [abe]**Susan Gritton,** [abe]**Lisa Milne** *sops* [ae]**Catherine Denley** *mez* [ae]**Lynton Atkinson** *ten* [e]**David Wilson-Johnson** *bar* **The King's Consort Choristers and Choir; The King's Consort / Robert King** Hyperion CDA66769 (63' · DDD) Recorded 1994. Texts and translations included ⓕ

King's 'super-group' featuring choristers drawn from seven English cathedral and collegiate choirs sounds better than ever – technically reliable, with a good, full sound – and are a credit to King's vision in bringing them together. This volume has five typically uplifting works, three of which – *Lauda Jerusalem*, *Dixit Dominus* and the G minor *Kyrie* – offer the opulent sound of double choir and orchestra. *Dixit Dominus* is the most substantial, a colourful 23-minute sequence of varied solos and choruses, with trumpets, oboes and two organs all chipping in, most notably in an awe-inspiring depiction of the Day of Judgement. The other two are perhaps less striking, though *Lauda Jerusalem* is certainly charming in its two-soprano interchanges. Highlights of the single-chorus works include another exquisite soprano duet and a fiery 'Fecit potentiam' in the *Magnificat*, and an extraordinary 'Crucifixus' in the *Credo* which departs from the pain-wracked norm by seemingly depicting with lugubrious slow tread Christ's walk to Calvary. King manages very well in capturing the essence of Vivaldi's bold, sometimes disarmingly straightforward style. These tidy performances are driven with just the right amount of springy energy – neither too much nor too little – and are well recorded in the warm resonance of St Jude's Church, Hampstead in London.

Motets

Laudate pueri Dominum, RV600[a].
Salve Regina, RV616[c]. Sanctorum meritis, RV620[a].
Sum in medio tempestatum, R632[b]. Cur sagittas, cur tela, RV637[c]
[a]**Susan Gritton** *sop* [b]**Tuva Semmingsen** *mez*
[c]**Nathalie Stutzmann** *contr* **The King's Consort /
Robert King**
Hyperion CDA66829 (68' · DDD) Texts and
translations included   Ⓕ

The best-known item here is the *Salve Regina*, a piece which has been recorded on several occasions before, usually by countertenors. Vivaldi intended it for a woman, however, and here Nathalie Stutzmann is given the chance to show off the depth and dark nobility of her contralto voice. She strikes a suitably reverential tone, one which King's orchestral accompaniment matches perfectly – the opening *ritornelli* of the first and last sections are both exquisitely done.

The psalm *Laudate pueri* presents 23 minutes of attractive music without really doing much to set the pulse racing. More interesting are *Cur sagittas, cur tela* – which shows the soul maintaining stoical faith in the face of attack by 'the soldiers of hell' (with violins exuberantly chucking the arrows of the title), before enjoying the protected world of the believer – and the disc's star find, *Sum in medio tempestatum*. This is a bright, unashamedly operatic number, opening with a classic simile aria comparing the troubled soul to a storm-tossed ship, and going on to depict the safe haven that hoves into view when one has turned to Jesus. The virtuoso vocal writing is negotiated with stunning agility and lightness by mezzo Tuva Semmingsen.

Another well-executed Vivaldi disc, then, from King. The recorded sound is also just right.

Salve regina in C minor, RV616. Introduzione al   Ⓟ
Miserere, RV641. Introduzione al Gloria, RV637. Salve
regina in G minor, RV618. Concerto for Violin and
Strings in C, RV581 ('Per la Santissima Assenzione di
Maria Vergine')
Gérard Lesne *counterten* **Fabio Biondi** *vn*
Il Seminario Musicale
Virgin Classics Veritas 759232-2 (77' · DDD) Recorded
1991. Texts and translations included   ⒻⓄ

The principal works here are two settings of the Marian antiphon Salve regina, but the French countertenor Gérard Lesne follows this with an extended Introduzione to a *Miserere*, one of two by Vivaldi, and an Introduzione to a *Gloria*; and by way of making up a programme, he divides the four vocal pieces into two groups inserting a Violin Concerto between them. The main bias of this music is contemplative, often deeply so, as is the case with the darkly expressive, sorrowful introduction to the *Miserere non in pratis*. Lesne approaches the music with style. Indeed, a stronger advocate for these affecting compositions is hard to imagine since he's technically almost faultless.

Then there's the Concerto in C major (*in due cori*), a splendid example of Vivaldi's skill in this medium, admirably played by the violinist Fabio Biondi with Lesne's own group Il Seminario Musicale. Vivaldi enthusiasts will require no further proof of this disc's merit, but readers in general should also find much to enjoy here, both in the singing and playing. The recorded sound is pleasantly resonant, serving the best interests of Lesne's voice and of the instruments too. A fine release.

Stabat mater in F minor, RV621[c]. Confitebor tibi   Ⓟ
Domine, RV596[a]. Deus tuorum militum, RV612[b].
In turbato mare, RV627[d]. O qui coeli terraeque
serenitas, RV631[d]. Non in pratis aut in hortis, RV641[e]
[d]**Susan Gritton** *sop* [abe]**Jean Rigby** *mez* [c]**Robin
Blaze** *counterten* [ab]**Charles Daniels** *ten* [a]**Neal
Davies** *bass* **The King's Consort / Robert King**
Hyperion CDA66799 (78' · DDD) Texts and
translations included   ⒻⓄ

This release in Robert King's complete cycle of Vivaldi's church music mainly features works unconnected with the Ospedale della Pietà, including a motet written in Rome and the famous *Stabat mater* composed for a church in Brescia. All are for solo voice or voices and orchestra, and for the most part they all carry the typical Vivaldi trademarks: boisterous energy alongside a tender if angular lyricism; a vivid and excitable responsiveness to verbal imagery; and what the insert-notes describe as 'a shocking radicalism: a willingness to strip music down to its core and reconstitute it from these simplest elements'. The best works on this disc are the first three. *In turbato mare* is a rip-roaring 'simile' motet which makes use of the old operatic device of comparing a troubled soul to a storm-tossed ship finding peace in port. The noble *Non in pratis aut in hortis* is an *introduzione*, a short motet designed to precede a performance of a lost *Miserere*; since it ends on a half-close, it's followed here (with musical if not liturgical logic) by the *Stabat mater*. All are excellently sung; few recordings exist of the first two, but it's hard to imagine the ebulliently virtuosic Susan Gritton and the movingly firm-voiced Jean Rigby being significantly bettered. By contrast, the *Stabat mater* is well-trodden territory, but the warmly mellifluous Robin Blaze easily matches his rivals on disc. The King's Consort is a little raw in the string department, but in general it shows bright and lively form and is well served by an acoustic perfectly suited to the occasion. Under King's direction, too, they capture splendidly the spirit of this uncomplicated but atmospheric music.

Stabat mater, RV621. Domine ad adiuvandum me, Ⓟ
RV593. Beatus vir, RV597. Magnificat, RV610ᵃ
**Ex Cathedra Chamber Choir and Baroque
Orchestra / Jeffrey Skidmore**
ASV Gaudeamus CDGAU137 (70' · DDD) Recorded
1991 Texts and translations included   Ⓕ

This is an interesting and mainly successful attempt to place a handful of Vivaldi's sacred pieces in a liturgical context. The best-known work here is the *Stabat mater* for alto voice and strings, but the others deserve to be heard more often. Ex Cathedra Chamber Choir is a well-disciplined, youthful sounding ensemble whose contribution is first-rate. And it's from the choir that solo voices emerge as required, giving the performances a homogeneity of sound and intent. The instrumentalists, too, make a strong contribution and together with the voices project interpretations which are full of vitality.

There are rival versions on disc of all the music sung here, but on the strength of the thoughtful way it has been presented by the director of Ex Cathedra, Jeffrey Skidmore, this is perhaps the most affecting of them. Few will be disappointed, for example, by the gently inflected, poignant account of the *Stabat mater* by the countertenor Nigel Short. Hardly a detail has been overlooked, even to the extent of allowing the listener to hear a distant bell during the opening Versicle.

Stabat mater, RV621. Cessate, omai cessate, Ⓟ
RV684. Filiae mestae Jerusalem, RV638. String
Concertos – C, RV114; E flat, RV130, 'Sonata al Santo
Sepolcro'
Andreas Scholl *counterten* **Ensemble 415 / Chiara
Banchini** *vn*
Harmonia Mundi HMC90 1571 (52' · DDD) Texts and
translations included   ⒻⓄⓄⓄ

Here's a very attractively prepared menu whose main course is the *Stabat mater* for countertenor and strings. Hors-d'oeuvres and side-dishes consist of a *ripieno* concerto (RV114), a chamber cantata for countertenor and strings (RV684), a string

sonata in E flat (RV130) and an introductory motet to a lost *Miserere* (RV638). Taken together, the pieces demonstrate something of Vivaldi's diverse style as a composer.

The chamber cantata, if closely related to the two sacred vocal items on the disc in respect of tonal colour, differs from them in character. Conforming with the standard Italian cantata pattern at the time of two pairs of alternating recitative and da capo aria Vivaldi enlivens his pastoral idyll with two particularly affecting arias, the first with a palpitating *pizzicato* violin, the second a virtuoso vocal tour de force illustrating the plight of the forsaken lover. Andreas Scholl brings the whole thing off superbly with only a moment's faulty intonation at the close of the first aria. Unlike settings of the *Stabat mater* by Pergolesi and others, Vivaldi used only the first 10 of the 20 stanzas of the poem. His deeply expressive setting of the poem will be familiar to many readers, but few will have heard such an affecting performance as Scholl achieves here. The lyrical prayer of human yearning for faith contained in the 'Fac ut ardeat' movement is tenderly sung and here, as throughout the programme, sympathetically supported by Ensemble 415 under Chiara Banchini's experienced direction.

In furore gustissimae irae, RV626. Longe mala, Ⓟ
umbrae, terrores, RV629. Clarae stellae, scintillate,
RV625. Canta in prato, ride in monte, RV623. Filiae
mestae Jerusalem, RV638. Nulla in mundo pax,
RV630 **Deborah York** *sop* **Catherine Denley** *mez*
James Bowman *counterten* **The King's Consort /
Robert King**
Hyperion CDA66779 (69' · DDD) Texts and
translations included   ⒻⓄ

This volume in Robert King's exploration of Vivaldi's sacred music offers five of his motets for solo voice and strings, together with RV623, one of the Introduzioni he composed to precede his liturgical choral pieces. As ever with Vivaldi, they're completely beguiling pieces of music, impossible to dislike and easy to be beguiled by. Their Latin texts – which usually allow for two arias separated by a recitative and followed by an 'Alleluia' – are about as profound as the sonnets which accompany *The Four Seasons*, but they inspire in Vivaldi just the same kind of charmingly uncomplicated reaction. Nightingales, scenes of general Arcadian bliss, the storms of God's wrath and the touching sorrow of the mournful daughters of Jerusalem before the Cross – all bring forth what you might be tempted to call stock responses if it weren't for the fact that the music is always so instantly recognisable as being by Vivaldi. Vivaldi's singers must have been good to judge from these pieces, which show a brand of virtuosity more at home in the instrumental concerto than the aria. James Bowman and Catherine Denley are both on good form (the latter having a particularly taxing number to sing), but the star of the disc is Deborah York, yet another of the many outstanding young sopranos to have arrived on the scene in recent years. Her *In furore iustissimae irae* is a tour de force of vocal power and agility with a teasing little top C at the end of the first aria; while the deceptive beauties of *Nulla in mundo pax sincera* are artfully conjured by sly portamentos.

The string accompaniments throughout are buoyant but beefy, aided by an excellent recorded sound, and tempos seem well judged.

Vespers

Vespri Solenni per la Festa dell'Assunzione di Maria Vergine (ed Alessandrini/Delaméa) – Violin Concerto in C, RV581^g; Concerto for 2 Violins and 2 Organs in F, RV584^h; Domine ad adiuvandum me festina in G, RV593^b; Introduzione al Dixit, RV635^b; Dixit Dominus in D, RV594^{abdef}; Laudate pueri in C minor, RV600^a; Laetatus sum, RV607; Nisi Dominus in G minor, RV608^d; Lauda Jerusalem in E minor, RV609^{ab}; Magnificat in G minor, RV610a^{abdef}; Salve Regina in C minor, RV616^d; Antiphons^c
^a**Gemma Bertagnolli,** ^b**Roberta Invernizzi,** ^c**Anna Simboli** sops ^d**Sara Mingardo** contr ^e**Gianluca Ferrarini** ten ^f**Matteo Bellotto** bar ^g**Antonio De Secondi,** ^h**Mauro Lopes Ferreira,** ^h**Francesca Vicari** vns ^h**Francesco Moi,** ^h**Ignazio Schifani** orgs **Concerto Italiano / Rinaldo Alessandrini**
Opus 111 ② OP30383 (153' · DDD) Texts and translations included ⓕ**OOO**

 This isn't the 'Vivaldi Vespers', or even a reconstruction of a specific event, but a kind of 'sacred concert' in Vespers form, of the sort that Venetian churches in Vivaldi's time would mount in the name of worship. Whether he ever supplied all the music for any such occasion isn't clear, but he certainly set plenty of Vespers texts, enough at any rate for Rinaldo Alessandrini and scholar Frédéric Delaméa to put together this rich programme.

So this is music for a Vespers for the Feast of the Assumption as it might have been heard in one of Venice's more important churches, made up of Vivaldi's settings of the five Vespers psalms, a *Magnificat*, a *Salve Regina*, a solo motet (*Ascende in laeta*) and a couple of orchestral concertos. Unmistakably Vivaldian in almost every bar, these pieces nevertheless show considerable variety; the psalms range from the opulence of *Dixit Dominus* for five soloists, two choirs and two choirs, to the expressive solo settings of *Laudate pueri* and *Nisi Dominus*, to the breezily functional choral treatments of *Laetatus sum* and *Lauda Jerusalem*; *Ascende in laeta* is a virtuoso showpiece for soprano, and the *Salve Regina* a sombre vehicle for contralto. The liturgical thread is supplied by plainchant antiphons, prettily rendered in a fascinating conjectural imitation of the 18th century's 'corrupt' manner, which is to say, with organ accompaniment and unabashed ornamentation.

Alessandrini's reading has an energy which is both forthright and controlled. His solo singers

are of high quality; Roberta Invernizzi and Sara Mingardo are from the front rank of Italian Baroque singers, capable of expressive lyricism and thrilling virtuosity, but Gemma Bertagnolli is no less effective. The orchestra plays with inspiriting precision and life, but the choir could be improved on, and is poorly favoured in the recorded balance. Indeed, the recorded sound as a whole is a bit noisy, in places suffering a distant mechanical whir. Still, the overall effect is what counts most in a recording like this: the music has a vital sense of direction, resulting in two and a half hours of invigorating listening.

Juditha triumphans, RV644

Juditha triumphans, RV645   ⓟ
Magdalena Kožená mezzo **Anke Herrmann** sop **Maria José Trullu, Marina Comparato, Tiziana Carraro** mezs **Coro di Camera Accademia Nazionale di Santa Cecilia; Academia Montis Regalis / Alessandro de Marchi**
Opus 111 ② OP30314 (105' · DDD) Text and translation included   ⓕ**OO**

Vivaldi's only surviving oratorio, *Juditha triumphans* (1716), with its strongly characterised roles and luxuriant orchestration, is a true Baroque masterpiece. Alessandro de Marchi has departed from other recent interpreters by daring to transpose the tenor and bass choral parts up an octave, as is widely believed was done by Vivaldi himself to accommodate the choir of the Ospedale della Pietà. The effect is breathtaking: the compressed, female choral textures positively gleam. From his superb cast of female soloists, de Marchi coaxes remarkable and dramatically convincing male vocal timbres. Maria José Trullu projects the various sides of Holofernes, who's depicted not merely as a monster but as capable of dignity and charm, even if ultimately incautious; she infuses her tone with a warmth and richness that countertenors might envy.

Magdalena Kožená, the Bethulian widow Judith, casts a spell on those who only hear her: as well as Holofernes. She sings with poise almost throughout, as she enters the enemy camp, meets and seduces Holofernes, reflects on the transitoriness of life and prays for peace and strength before murdering the sleeping Holofernes. Only then, as she carries out her heroic – if horrific – mission does she fully convey her emotion.

The instrumentation offers a treasure trove of unusual and evocative instruments, even for the time: a pair of clarinets to characterise the dissolute Assyrian soldiers, recorders for 'nocturnal breezes' and a quartet of theorbos to depict the preparation of the feast. These and the more common obbligato and continuo instruments of the day are affectingly played by the musicians of the Academia Montis Regalis. At every turn there's ample evidence of the care de Marchi has lavished on this performance, and Robert

King's by comparison seems less full-blooded and relatively static. Congratulations all round for an outstanding recording.

Chamber Cantatas

Cantatas – Alla caccia, alla caccia, RV670; Care selve amici prati, RV671; Elvira, anima mia, RV654. Chamber Concertos – in F, RV97; in G minor, 'La notte', RV104; in G minor, RV105.
Laura Polverelli *mez* **L'Astrée Ensemble**
Opus 111 OP30358 (55' · DDD) Texts and translations included ℗○

Whether Vivaldi wrote these cantatas for an exceptionally talented singer or just decided to give others a mischievously hard time isn't known; the fact remains that they're tough assignments. If Polverelli finds them so, she gives no sign of it. She's a mezzo with a cloudless upper register and a full-throated lower one, a wide and subtly nuanced range of volume, supple and pitch-perfect. These three chamber cantatas deal with various unhappy aspects of love, and she projects them without resorting to 'grand-operatic' excess. These are performances to treasure.

The chamber concertos show Vivaldi at his most happily inventive. All those on this disc have alternative versions, and if RV97 and 105 lack something of the verve of those by Giardino Armonico they're no less infectious.

The recording is clear and very well balanced, and the vocal texts are given in three languages, including English. A thoroughly enjoyable disc.

Opera Arias & Sinfonias

Opera Arias and Sinfonias: **Griselda** – Sinfonia; Ⓟ
Ombre vane, ingiusti orrori; Agitata da due venti.
Tito Manlio – Non ti lusinghi la crudeltade. **Ottone in Villa** – Sinfonia; Gelosia, tu già rendi l'alma mia; L'ombre, l'aure, e ancora il rioᵃ. **L'Atenaide** – Ferma, Teodosio. **Bajazet** – Sinfonia. **L'Incoronazione di Dario** – Non mi lusinga vana speranza. **Catone in Utica** – Se mai senti spirarti sul volto; Se in campo armato
Emma Kirkby, ᵃ**Liliana Mazzarri** *sops*
The Brandenburg Consort / Roy Goodman
Hyperion CDA66745 (75' · DDD) Recorded 1994.
Texts and translations included ℗○

This is an entertaining programme. The arias have been chosen with discernment, thoughtfully grouped and effectively interspersed with three of Vivaldi's opera sinfonias. The formula proves so successful that it even occurs to you that this was maybe the happiest solution to reviving at least the more problematic of Vivaldi's operas. Emma Kirkby's voice is still maturing, filling out, and she's able to achieve an ever increasing variety of colour. 'Ombre vane, ingiusti orrori', a ravishing piece from Griselda (1735), is beautifully and effortlessly

controlled, delicately shaded and rhythmically vital; and her feeling for apposite embellishment comes across with pleasing spontaneity and stylistic assurance. The voice is supported and highlighted by the sympathetic partnership of The Brandenburg Consort conducted by Roy Goodman. This disc will delight Vivaldi enthusiasts. Excellent recorded sound.

Bajazet

Bajazet Ⓟ
Ildebrando D'Arcangelo *bass-bar* Bajazet **Patrizia Ciofi** *sop* Idaspe **David Daniels** *counterten* Tamerlano **Elina Garanca** *mez* Andronico **Vivica Genaux** *mez* Irene **Marijana Mijanovic** *mez* Asteria **Europa Galante / Fabio Biondi** *vn*
Virgin Classics ② 545676-2 (147' · DDD · S/T/t/N)
℗○○○

Vivaldi's *Bajazet*, based on the same libretto as Handel's *Tamerlano*, tells the story of the Tartar emperor Tamerlano and the Ottoman sultan Bajazet whom he's defeated. Vivaldi responds with sound dramatic sense. His recitatives especially show a conversational realism that allows them to be more than just a functional advancement of the plot; indeed, Bajazet's biggest moment is a powerful accompanied recitative.

Vivaldi works hard at characterisation, if by unusual means: *Bajazet* is partly a *pasticcio*, which is to say that it borrows and adapts arias from other operas written in the fashionable and suave Neapolitan style by composers such as Hasse and Giacomelli, who by the 1730s were beginning to dominate the operatic world. Vivaldi chose well. He'd have appreciated the crowd-pleasing virtuosity of an aria such as 'Qual guerriero in campo armato', originally written for Farinelli by his brother Riccardo Broschi; here it aptly expresses Irene's near-deranged indignation at being dumped by Tamerlano. Clever choices such as this make *Bajazet* a real opera, not just a hotch-potch.

The same can be said for the performers here. The cast has hardly a weak link: David Daniels is in typically beautiful voice as Tamerlano, yet at the same time manages enough hardness to suggest the spiteful anger of the man; Elina Garanca conveys a suitable measure of weakness as the indecisive Andronico; and Marijana Mijanovic's moving and dignified Asteria never looks like losing her moral high ground. Vivica Genaux gives a show-stopping display as Irene, and Patrizia Ciofi proves no less equal to the tough technical challenges set by the role of Andronico's friend Idaspe. Only Ildebrando D'Arcangelo as Bajazet disappoints slightly, failing to reach to the Sultan's defiant heart.

The orchestra's contribution, on the other hand, is a major bonus. Fabio Biondi has never been one to miss details, and he and his players bring out countless nuances in the score with their usual array of interpretative devices ranging from gentle cello chords in recitative to sparky off-beat accents and *pizzicati*, and even some acid *sul ponticello*. There could hardly be a better way to bring this opera to life.

L'Olimpiade

L'Olimpiade, RV725 (ed Alessandrini)   **P**
Sara Mingardo *contr* Licida; **Roberta Invernizzi** *sop*
Megacle; **Sonia Prina** *mez* Aristea; **Marianna
Kulikova** *mez* Argene; **Laura Giordano** *sop* Aminta;
Riccardo Novaro *bar* Clistene; **Sergio Foresti** *bass*
Alcandro; **Concerto Italiano / Rinaldo Alessandrini**
Opus 111 ③ OP30316 (175' · DDD) Notes, libretto
and translation included   Ⓕ**OO**

More than 50 composers set Pietro Metastasio's libretto *L'Olimpiade* between 1733 and 1815, starting with Caldara and including along the way such names as Pergolesi, Galuppi, Cimarosa, Cherubini and Paisiello. The booklet note for this new recording suggests that Vivaldi was trying to take on the newly fashionable Neapolitan composers at their own game, not only by setting a poem by their favourite librettist, but also by adopting some of their musical mannerisms. Maybe so, but there can be few composers with a more deeply ingrained personal style than our friend the Red Priest, and it's an unmistakably Vivaldian flavour which is the strongest in this thoroughly agreeable work.

Despite the public context – the story is played out against the backdrop of the Olympic Games– this is a drama which focuses on the personal predicaments of the principal characters, each of whom faces an interesting conflict between head and heart somewhere along the line. This is more apparent from Metastasio's words than from Vivaldi's music, to be honest, but that isn't to say that the composer has been unresponsive. The most effective and intimate moments occur in the recitatives, which are fluidly conversational and full of realistic interruptions, questions and exclamations, all of which Vivaldi handles with considerable (and, some might say, surprising) dramatic skill.

Rinaldo Alessandrini's direction is typically unfussy and to the point, ever alert to the music's dramatic intent but without imposing himself on it unduly. The finest vocal performances come from Sara Mingardo, Roberta Invernizzi and Sonia Prina, but in truth no one is a weak link. The recitatives are effectively done, the arias thrown off with dash and aplomb, and everyone sounds as if they believe in the work.

Orlando finto pazzo

Orlando finto pazzo   **P**
Antonio Abete *bass* Orlando **Gemma Bertagnolli**
sop Ersilla **Marina Comparato** *mez* Tigrinda **Sonia
Prina** *contr* Origille **Manuela Custer** *mez* Argillano
Martín Oro *counterten* Grifone **Marianna Pizzolato**
mez Brandimarte **Teatro Regio Chorus, Turin;
Academia Montis Regalis / Alessandro de Marchi**
Opus 111 ③ OP30392 (207' · DDD) Notes, synopsis
and libretto included   Ⓕ**O**

Opus 111's Vivaldi series continues to expand at bewildering pace, as indeed it needs to if its aim of recording the 450 Vivaldi manuscripts in the National Library in Turin is ever to reach completion. *Orlando finto pazzo* ('Orlando feigns madness') was the second of his numerous operas, and his first for the Venetian stage. The story of Orlando's madness is taken not from the usual source, Ariosto's poem *Orlando furioso*, but Boiardo's earlier *Orlando innamorato*, a similarly tragicomic mix of love, intrigue and magic. In Ariosto's poem Orlando's madness is real, but here he pretends it for no obvious reason; in fact it's no more than a couple of episodes in a convoluted and unengaging plot built around a love-pentangle (no less), and further complicated by various disguises and rampant dissembling.

As it happens, Vivaldi doesn't on this evidence appear to have been a natural musical dramatist. Yet what makes this music worth hearing is his evident desire to make an operatic splash at his first major attempt: there's music of irrepressible zest and personality; this early attempt deploys all the fiery and ebullient energy of his concertos and allies it to vocal music of neck-tingling excitement. Like Haydn, Vivaldi may not have been a great opera composer, but he did write operas full of great music.

Alessandro de Marchi's joyous recording brings together a typical Italian Baroque cast for a performance and recording of skill and enthusiasm.

Orlando furioso

Orlando furioso   **P**
Marie-Nicole Lemieux *contr* Orlando **Jennifer
Larmore** *mez* Alcina **Veronica Cangemi** *sop*
Angelica **Philippe Jaroussky** *counterten* Ruggiero
Lorenzo Regazzo *bass-bar* Astolfo **Ann Hallenberg**
mez Bradamante **Blandine Staskiewicz** *mez* Medoro
**Les Eléments; Ensemble Matheus / Jean-
Christophe Spinosi**
Naive/Opus 111 ③ OP30393 (183' · DDD ·
S/T/t/N)   Ⓕ**OO**

Vivaldi's opera combines magic, heroism and comedy to tell of a seductive sorceress, a noble knight driven insane by love, a feisty fiancée who disguises herself as a man to rescue her bewitched lover, and a magic ring that helps ensure everything ends happily ever after. This recording bears the fruit of Vivaldi scholar Frédéric Delaméa's painstaking reconstruction of the original 1727 version. In contrast to the 15 arias on the rival Erato recording, here we have 27, and each is a gem.

Marie-Nicole Lemieux's delivery of Orlando's anguished and often unhinged recitative is astonishingly good, full of conviction, passionate, and vocally brilliant. When his sanity is restored, she achieves a tangible lucidity that makes the drama wholly satisfying. Jennifer Larmore's sorceress Alcina is devious, vivacious, and venomous. Philippe Jaroussky's Ruggerio is adept at both delicacy and heroism and Ann Hallenberg is excellent as his fiancée Bradamante.

Ensemble Matheus provide bright *ritornelli* and intelligent accompaniments. The playing is often abrasive and intentionally percussive in fast music, but the performers also excel at the softer moments. Spinosi's direction is vividly theatrical, and recitatives are declaimed with aplomb, although sometimes it sounds as if characters cannot wait to interrupt with their next line.

Vivaldi's score has a dramatic stature greater than most of his other operas. He rarely devoted much attention to accompanied recitatives, but here he composed several that are unusually extensive and adventurous. This is a magnificent achievement: if Vivaldi needed a champion to establish his credentials as an opera composer, then this recording is it.

Ottone in Villa

Ottone in Villa   Ⓟ
Monica Groop *mez* Ottone **Nancy Argenta** *sop*
Caio Silio **Susan Gritton** *sop* Cleonilla **Sophie Daneman** *sop* Tullia **Mark Padmore** *ten* Decio
Collegium Musicum 90 /Richard Hickox
Chandos Chaconne ② CHAN0614 (145' · DDD)
Notes, text and translation included   Ⓕ

This, Vivaldi's very first opera, was premièred in Vicenza in 1713 and was an instant hit. The story is a relatively uncomplicated one by the standards of Baroque opera, of amatory pretences and misunderstandings: it has been admirably summarised by Eric Cross (who has edited the work) as a 'light-weight, amoral entertainment in which the flirtatious Cleonilla consistently has the upper hand, and gullible Emperor Ottone (a far from heroic figure) never discovers the truth about the way he has been deceived'. The score proceeds in a succession of secco recitatives (with just a very occasional accompagnato) and da capo arias – which the present cast ornament very stylishly. There are no duets or ensembles except for a perfunctory final chorus in which the characters merely sing in unison; but there's an abundance of tuneful arias, and when Vivaldi can be bothered to write proper accompaniments to them – he often merely has violins doubling the voice, plus a bass line – he can provide interesting imitative counterpoint. Several arias employ only the upper strings without cello and bass except in ritornellos. The small Vicenza theatre couldn't afford star singers, so only limited opportunities were provided for vocal virtuosity; but the present cast makes the most of its opportunities, both in display and in meditative mood. It isn't always easy to tell the three sopranos apart, but Susan Gritton well suggests the scheming minx Cleonilla; Nancy Argenta with her bright voice has the castrato role that includes several fine arias, and displays a *messa di voce* in an echo aria;

and Sophie Daneman, in a breeches role, produces a wide range of colour. Monica Groop slightly undercharacterises Ottone except when roused to dismiss Rome's anxiety at his dalliance. It's quite a relief to ear one male voice, and Mark Padmore is excellent. Richard Hickox keeps a firm rhythmic hand on everything and delivers quite the best and neatest Vivaldi operatic recording yet.

Sebastián de Vivanco
Spanish c1551-1622

Vivanco was maestro di capilla of the cathedrals of Lerida (until 1576), Segovia, Avila (1588-1602) and Salamanca, where he was also university music professor. A leading composer of his age, erudite and harmonically bold, he published masses (1608), Magnificats (1607) and motets (1610).
GROVEmusic

Sacred Music

In Manus Tuas – Mass, Magnifcat and Motets
Missa, 'In manus tuas'. In manus tuas. Christus factus est. Circumdederunt me dolores mortis. Ecce sacerdos magnus. Versa est in luctum. Caritas Pater est. Quis dabit capiti meo. Assumpta est Maria. O quam suavis est. Magnificat Quarti toni. Cantate Domino
vocal ensemble; Orchestra of the Renaissance / Richard Cheetham, Michael Noone
Glossa GCD921405 (64' · DDD) Texts and translations included   Ⓕ

Vivanco is a composer who has received only periodic and limited exposure on record, in spite of the pioneering transcription work of the American musicologist Dean L Nuernberger. This disc should help to place him among the stars in the firmament of the Siglo de Oro, for he was a composer of singular talent.

The Orchestra of the Renaissance give a splendid mass, based on Vivanco's own miniature *In manus tuas* and transcribed by Nuernberger, and a selection of motets for various occasions, as well as a *Magnificat*. These show tremendous craftsmanship and the variety of his sonic imagination to the full. *Caritas Pater est*, using three choirs to symbolise the Trinity, is particularly noteworthy; also impressive are the modern *Cantate Domino* and the shining *Assumpta est Maria*.

Although some of the decisions concerning scoring are curious in terms of instrumental-vocal balance, and the textures can become a little top-heavy (notably in the *Sanctus* of the Mass), there's some extraordinarily beautiful singing and playing. The *Sanctus* is, in fact, one of the most striking sections of a work that consistently impresses as being of the highest quality. Vivanco, like Victoria, was a sublime melodist, and he deserves to take his place alongside the better-known master.

Richard Wagner

Wagner was the son either of the police actuary Friedrich Wagner, who died soon after his birth, or of his mother's friend the painter, actor and poet Ludwig Geyer, whom she married in August 1814. He went to school in Dresden and then Leipzig; at 15 he wrote a play, at 16 his first compositions. In 1831 he went to Leipzig University, also studying music with the Thomaskantor, CT Weinlig; a symphony was written and successfully performed in 1832. In 1833 he became chorus master at the Würzburg theatre and wrote the text and music of his first opera, Die Feen; this remained unheard, but his next, Das Liebesverbot, written in 1833, was staged in 1836. By then he had made his début as an opera conductor with a small company which, however, went bankrupt soon after performing his opera. He married the singer Minna Planer in 1836 and went with her to Königsberg, where he became musical director at the theatre, but he soon left and took a similar post in Riga, where he began his next opera, Rienzi, and did much conducting, especially of Beethoven. In 1839 they slipped away from creditors in Riga, by ship to London and then to Paris, where he was befriended by Meyerbeer and did hack-work for publishers and theatres. He also worked on the text and music of an opera on the 'Flying Dutchman' legend; but in 1842 Rienzi, a large-scale opera with a political theme set in imperial Rome, was accepted for Dresden and Wagner went there for its highly successful première. Its theme reflects something of Wagner's own politics (he was involved in the semi-revolutionary, intellectual 'Young Germany' movement). Die fliegende Holländer ('The Flying Dutchman'), given the next year, was less well received, though a much tauter musical drama, beginning to move away from the 'number opera' tradition and strong in its evocation of atmosphere, especially the supernatural and the raging seas (inspired by the stormy trip from Riga). Wagner was now appointed joint Kapellmeister at the Dresden court.

The theme of redemption through a woman's love, in the Dutchman, recurs in Wagner's operas (and perhaps his life). In 1845 Tannhäuser was completed and performed and Lohengrin begun. In both Wagner moves towards a more continuous texture with semi-melodic narrative and a supporting orchestral fabric helping convey its sense. In 1848 he was caught up in the revolutionary fervour and the next year fled to Weimar (where Liszt helped him) and then Switzerland (there was also a spell in France); politically suspect, he was unable to enter Germany for 11 years. In Zürich, he wrote in 1850-51 his ferociously anti-semitic Jewishness in Music (some of it an attack on Meyerbeer) and his basic statement on musical theatre, Opera and Drama; he also began sketching the text and music of a series of operas on the Nordic and Germanic sagas. By 1853 the text for this four-night cycle (to be The Nibelung's Ring) was written, printed and read to friends – who included a generous patron, Otto Wesendonck, and his wife Mathilde, who loved him, wrote poems that he set, and inspired Tristan und Isolde – conceived in 1854 and completed five years later, by which time more than half of The Ring was written. In 1855 he con-

ducted in London; tension with Minna led to his going to Paris in 1858-9. 1860 saw them both in Paris, where the next year he revived Tannhäuser in revised form for French taste, but it was literally shouted down, partly for political reasons. In 1862 he was allowed freely into Germany; that year he and the ill and childless Minna parted (she died in 1866). In 1863 he gave concerts in Vienna, Russia etc; the next year King Ludwig II invited him to settle in Bavaria, near Munich, discharging his debts and providing him with money.

Wagner did not stay long in Bavaria, because of opposition at Ludwig's court, especially when it was known that he was having an affair with Cosima, the wife of the conductor Hans van Bülow (she was Liszt's daughter); Bülow (who condoned it) directed the Tristan première in 1865. Here Wagner, in depicting every shade of sexual love, developed a style richer and more chromatic than anyone had previously attempted, using dissonance and its urge for resolution in a continuing pattern to build up tension and a sense of profound yearning; Act 2 is virtually a continuous love duet, touching every emotion from the tenderest to the most passionately erotic. Before returning to the Ring, Wagner wrote, during the mid-1860s, The Mastersingers of Nuremberg: this is in a quite different vein, a comedy set in 16th-century Nuremberg, in which a noble poet-musician wins, through his victory in a music contest – a victory over pedants who stick to the foolish old rules – the hand of his beloved, fame and riches. (The analogy with Wagner's view of himself is obvious.) The music is less chromatic than that of Tristan, warm and good-humoured, often contrapuntal; unlike the mythological figures of his other operas the characters here have real humanity. The opera was given, under Bülow, in 1868; Wagner had been living at Tribschen, near Lucerne, ince 1866, and that year Cosima formally joined him; they had two children when in 1870 they married. The first two Ring operas, Das Rheingold and Die Walküre, were given in Munich, on Ludwig's insistence, in 1869 and 1870; Wagner, however, was anxious to have a special festival opera house for the complete cycle and spent much energy trying to raise money for it. Eventually, when he had almost despaired, Ludwig came to the rescue and in 1874 – the year the fourth opera, Götterdämmerung, was finished – provided the necessary support. The house was built at Bayreuth, designed by Wagner as the home for his concept of the Gesamtkunstwerk ('total art work' – an alliance of music, poetry, the visual arts, dance etc). The first festival, an artistic triumph but a financial disaster – was held there in 1876, when the complete Ring was given. The Ring is about 18 hours' music, held together by an immensely detailed network of themes, or leitmotifs, each of which has some allusive meaning: a character, a concept, an object etc. They change and develop as the ideas within the opera develop. They are heard in the orchestra, not merely as 'labels' but carrying the action, sometimes informing the listener of connections of ideas or the thoughts of those on the stage. There are no 'numbers' in the Ring; the musical texture is made up of narrative and dialogue, in which the orchestra partakes. The work is not merely a story about gods, humans and dwarfs but embodies reflections on every aspect of the human condition. It has been interpreted as socialist, fascist, Jungian, prophetic, as a parable about industrial society, and much more.

In 1877 Wagner conducted in London, hoping to recoup Bayreuth losses; later in the year he began a new opera, Parsifal. He continued his musical and polemic writings, concentrating on 'racial purity'. He spent most of 1880 in Italy. Parsifal, a sacred festival drama, again treating redemption but through the acts of communion and renunciation on the stage, was given at the Bayreuth Festival in 1882. He went to Venice for the winter, and died there in February of the heart trouble that had been with him for some years. His body was returned by gondola and train for burial at Bayreuth. Wagner did more than any other composer to change music, and indeed to change art and thinking about it. His life and his music arouse passions like no other composer's. His works are hated as much as they are worshipped; but no-one denies their greatness.

GROVEmusic

Orchestral Excerpts from Operas

Lohengrin – Prelude. Tannhäuser – Overture   Ⓗ
Siegfried Idyll. Götterdämmerung – Siegfried's Rhine Journey; Siegfried's Funeral March
Lucerne Festival Orchestra; Vienna Philharmonic Orchestra / Wilhelm Furtwängler
Testament mono SBT1141 (61' · ADD) Recorded late 1940s   ⒻO

This is, as they say, something else. The *Lohengrin* Act 1 Prelude opens the disc of studio recordings, the only item of five with the Lucerne Festival Orchestra. The way the Swiss brass *crescendo*s on the upbeat to the climactic delivery of the hymn must rate as among the most elating of all Furtwängler moments. Why this and the *Tannhäuser* Overture have never been issued before remains a mystery, as probably do all the reasons why, in the latter piece, the Vienna Philharmonic sounds on fire for Furtwängler and on duty for, say, Knappertsbusch in 1953 (once available on a Decca LP). Siegfried's Rhine Journey evolves in one seamless sweep, barring the split-second but disconcerting rhythmic hiatus at the moment of take-off (4'51"). And mercifully, Furtwängler doesn't tag on the trite concert ending (as did Reiner and Toscanini), giving a chance to wonder at the uniquely resonant low brass sounds of the VPO. Then on to the Funeral March, every dark sound fully charting the depths, every phrase carrying special import, and, as in the *Siegfried Idyll*, the occasional passage reminding us of standards of tuning of the day. The latter account, Furtwängler's only recording of the piece, engages rather than diverts and charms, with Vienna string-playing typically sweet and rapturous, and 'Siegfried, Hope of the World' tensely built to an almost delirious climax. Depth, presence and a naturally achieved clarity characterise all these recordings, and 78 sources only occasionally make their presence felt.

Tannhäuser – Overture and Venusberg Music.
Die Meistersinger von Nürnberg – Prelude, Act 3.
Tristan und Isolde – Prelude and Liebestod
Berlin Philharmonic Orchestra / Herbert von Karajan DG Karajan
Gold 439 022-2GHS (50' · DDD) Recorded 1984.
Also available (plus Lohengrin Prelude/Flying Dutchman Oveture) on EMI DVD-Audio
DVC4 92397-9)   ⒻOO

What's so special about Karajan's digital recordings that they're reissued at full price and, ungenerously in this case, with only their original programme?

The answer might be another question: when, in modern times, have you heard from Berlin (or anywhere else) such long-drawn, ripe, intense, characterful, perfectly formed and supremely controlled Wagner playing? Not from some other sources with the *Tannhäuser* Overture, whose Pilgrims are less solemn and grand and whose revellers produce less of Karajan's joyous éclat.

Moving on a few minutes, and the passage where Karajan's Venus succeeds in quelling the riot finds him effecting a spellbinding sudden diminuendo (from 4'41", track 2), leaving us with the enchanted eddying of the orchestra. It must surely qualify as one of Karajan's 'greatest moments', if the seemingly unstoppable tidal wave that preceded it hadn't already done so.

The true keeper of Berlin's 'Wagner on record' has latterly been Daniel Barenboim. His *Tristan* Prelude is more conventionally paced (i.e. faster) than Karajan's, with the phrasing just as steeply raked, and the balance and control, in some respects, even more accomplished. But the breadth of Karajan's conception is matched by his concentration (it never feels too slow), the playing is achingly intense, the whole superbly built, and the reserves of tone he's able to draw on for the climax seem limitless (the tone is never forced).

Tristan und Isolde – Love Music (arr Stokowski).
Die Walküre – Ride of the Valkyries; Wotan's Farewell and Magic Fire Music. Götterdämmerung – Siegfried's Death and Funeral March (both arr Gerhardt). Siegfried Idyll
National Philharmonic Orchestra / Charles Gerhardt
Chesky CD161 (78' · DDD) Recorded 1985-95   ⒻO

Charles Gerhardt opens with Stokowski's unashamedly indulgent synthesis of the themes from *Tristan und Isolde*, with the vocal parts seamlessly welded into the orchestration, beginning at the Introduction to Act 2, including the Love Music from the same act and the Liebestod. Gerhardt moves naturally from yearning and languishing to real passion, following Stokowski in using divided strings, employing 16 first violins, 10 second violins, 12 violas and 12 double basses. The off-stage six-part hunting-horn episode (at 1'35") sounds glorious with the expansion to ten horns weighted with a bass trombone, Wotan's infinitely touching Farewell to his daughter, Brünnhilde, in *Die Walküre*, and the following truly magical Fire Music. Even without the voices the tremendously committed string playing is very moving indeed, and the recording is superb. The *Siegfried Idyll* is also beautifully played and makes a flowing, gentle interlude. Gerhardt lets the tension slip a little in the middle but gathers the themes together magnetically in the involving closing section. He then begins Siegfried's Death and Funeral March earlier than Stokowski, at the moment when Hagen kills Siegfried. The result is very direct and powerful with fine brass playing. The Valkyries then ride, or rather gallop in at breakneck speed to finish the concert exuberantly. The recordings were made in Walthamstow (*Tristan*, 1985), All Saint's, Petersham (*Die Walküre*, 1994 – the best sound of all), Air Studios (*Siegfried Idyll*, 1995), and St John's, Smith Square (*Götterdämmerung*, 1990), and the Valkyries bring another clear, bright studio offering (1995).

This is a record for hi-fi buffs, and on really discerning equipment it's fascinating to compare the ways in which the five different engineers have coped with the widely varying ambience effects here, with their positioning of the microphone.

Tannhäuser – Overture. Siegfried Idyll. Tristan und Isolde – Prelude and Liebestod
Jessye Norman sop Vienna Philharmonic Orchestra / Herbert von Karajan
DG 423 613-2GH (54' · DDD) Recorded live 1987. Text and translation included ⓕ

For the Wagner specialist who has a complete *Tannhäuser* and *Tristan* on the shelves, this disc involves some duplication. Even so, it isn't hard to make room for such performances as are heard here. For the non-specialist, the programme provides a good opportunity for a meeting halfway, the common ground between Master and general music-lover being the *Siegfried Idyll*. This offers 20 minutes of delight in the play of musical ideas, structured and yet impulsive, within a sustained mood of gentle affection. The orchestration is something of a miracle, and it can rarely have been heard to better advantage than in this recording, where the ever-changing textures are so clearly displayed and where from every section of the orchestra the sound is of such great loveliness. It comes as a welcome contrast to the *Tannhäuser* Overture, with its big tunes and fortissimos, the whole orchestra surging in a frank simulation of physical passion. A further contrast is to follow in the *Tristan* Prelude, where again Karajan and his players are at their best in their feeling for texture and their control of pulse. Jessye Norman, singing the Liebestod with tenderness and vibrant opulence of tone, brings the recital to an end. There's scarcely a single reminder that it was recorded live.

Wesendonk Lieder

Wesendonk Lieder. Tristan und Isolde – Prelude, Act 1; Mild und leise. Götterdämmerung – Dawn and Siegfried's Rhine Journey; Starke Scheite
Julia Varady sop **Deutsches Symphony Orchestra, Berlin /Dietrich Fischer-Dieskau**
Orfeo C467981A (71' · DDD) Texts and translations included ⓕⓞⓞ

This is a truly riveting recital of Wagner from Varady (magnificent singing) and Fischer-Dieskau. Varady's reading of the *Wesendonk Lieder* is remarkable, enthralling. There's nothing here of the slow, wallowing approach often favoured today. The feeling of the words is one of very present emotions. Try the final section of 'Stehe still!' starting 'Die Lippe verstummt' or the emphasis on the single word 'Smaragd' in 'Im Treibhaus' or the whole of a most beautifully etched 'Träume'. She's helped here by Fischer-Dieskau's refusal to indulge the music.

There have been few such warmly and intelligently sung versions of the Immolation. Maybe on stage Brünnhilde might have been beyond Varady; here there's not a sign of strain as she rides the orchestra, sympathetically supported by her husband. But what makes it stand out from performances by possibly better-endowed sopranos is her deep understanding of the text: again and again, nowhere more so than at 'Ruhe, ruhe, du Gott', where Varady's vibrating lower register is so effective, you feel the tingle factor coming to the fore. In the more heroic final sections, this Brünnhilde is like a woman transfigured. And transfiguration is a feature of Varady's concentrated, urgent Liebestod, her complete absorption with the text as much as with the music an object-lesson in great Wagner singing. The players of Fischer-Dieskau's Berlin orchestra cover themselves in glory. The recording is exemplary.

Opera Duets

Love Duets

Siegfried – Act 3 scene 3.. Tristan und Isolde[a] – Act 2 scene 2 (concert version from 'O sink hernieder')
Deborah Voigt sop [a]**Violeta Urmana** mez **Plácido Domingo** ten Royal Opera House Orchestra, Covent Garden / Antonio Pappano
EMI 557004-2 (57' · DDD) Texts and translations included ⓕⓞ

It appears that in 1862, three years before *Tristan and Isolde*'s première, Wagner hoped that the Schnorrs, his original Tristan and Isolde, would give part of the Love duet in a concert performance. This never took place, and nothing was known about the musical preparations Wagner made for the event until 1950; even then it seems the material remained unexamined, and certainly unused, until very recently. Omitting the first 15 minutes or so, the duet was to start at 'O sink hernieder' and continue to the end, including in it the interpolations of Brangäne. The question which forms in the listener's mind as the end approaches is how that's to be managed. This supreme expression of eroticism in music culminates in erotic catastrophe. It's hard to imagine a concert performance ending with the rude abruptness of the score, but worse to think of its possible closure (as in some early recordings) on a glib and alien major chord. However, without giving the game away, the solution constitutes a stroke of genius; it has that kind of simplicity and rightness that evokes a cry of 'But of course!', almost as though one had thought of it oneself – which assuredly one had not. Unfortunately the booklet-notes provide no information on the genesis of this ending. Amazing as it is to relate, Domingo's voice, after all these years and all this unsparing usage, is still the most beautiful – the most richly firm and even – on recordings of this music. He's exact and lyrical in his reading of the music and is largely, if not invariably, imaginative and convincing in his dramatic commitment. Voigt impresses as being less successfully 'in character', especially as the Siegfried Brünnhilde, whose exaltation and wonder lack the majesty of her godly state as they do the excitement of her humanity. The fresh and vibrant tones are good to hear even so, as is the firm-voiced mezzo of Violeta Urmana's Brangäne. The Covent Garden orchestra play for Pappano with fine attentiveness and exhilaration, and he seems to bring a renewing spirit to everything he touches.

Der fliegende Holländer

Der fliegende Holländer
Falk Struckmann bar Holländer **Jane Eaglen** sop
Senta **Robert Holl** bass Daland **Peter Seiffert** ten
Erik **Felicity Palmer** contr Mary **Rolando Villazon**
ten Steersman **Berlin State Opera Chorus; Berlin
Staatskapelle / Daniel Barenboim**
Teldec ② 8573-88063-2 (135' · DDD) Notes, text and
translation included   ⓕ**OO**

Barenboim delivers a traversal of the storm-tossed score that, as far as his conducting is concerned, almost equals the best among previous readings. At once big-boned and intensely dramatic, it has a driving force, at rather faster speeds than many sets, that's commanding in its control of detail and structure. With his own Berlin State Opera forces offering faithful and acutely accented support – the chorus, so important here, in particularly fine form – this is a version that catches much of the theatrical excitement found on most of the recordings emanating from Bayreuth.

He chooses to perform the original Dresden version while incorporating the instrumental improvements Wagner made later in his career. He sometimes is so caught up with the drama that his groans become audible. Unfortunately, not all the singing attains a similar standard. Falk Struckmann is certainly a Dutchman to be reckoned alongside the most convincing por-

trayals on disc. His voice, reminiscent of Theo Adam's grainy, tense tone on the Klemperer set, matches all the role's appreciable demands. His monologue has all the anguish and poignancy one could wish for, with the text really made to tell, and his departure is properly desperate. Only at the beginning of the love duet, 'Wie aus der Ferne', does he miss something of the haunted quality called for, eschewing the hushed tones of the most convincing interpreters as this point. He may not have been inspired by Jane Eaglen's middling Senta – listen to Adam and Silja under Klemperer to hear just how arresting this music can sound.

Much of Eaglen's reading of her part has sensitivity and even inwardness, and she catches some of the girl's single-minded desperation. But in the part's more strenuous moments, especially in the higher registers of her voice, her singing sounds strained and unacceptably threadbare. As Daland, Robert Holl offers some sturdy singing but his tone has become sadly dulled and grey, particularly as compared with that of, say, Weber (Keilberth) or Talvela (Klemperer) in this role. As on the sure-footed Steinberg set, Seiffert is a more-than-capable Erik, but his voice isn't quite as pleasing to the ear as it was 10 years ago. The Steersman of Villazon, a new young Mexican tenor with a potentially glorious voice, and Felicity Palmer's vital Mary are both excellent.

Among modern sets, this is to be ranked above the Dohnányi (Decca) by virtue of its extra sense of the theatre. But Klemperer's more measured, grander reading (EMI Great Recordings of the Century), is far better cast all-round – particularly Silja as Senta. Still, if you can overlook some vocal vagaries, Barenboim's considered performance is a force to be reckoned with.

Der fliegende Holländer
Theo Adam bass-bar Holländer **Anja Silja** sop Senta
Martti Talvela bass Daland **Ernst Kozub** ten Erik
Annelies Burmeister mez Mary **Gerhard Unger** ten
Steuermann **BBC Chorus; New Philharmonia
Orchestra / Otto Klemperer**
EMI Great Recordings of the Century ② 567408-2
(152' · ADD) Recorded 1968 Notes, text and
translation included   Ⓜ**O**

Klemperer's magisterial interpretation of this work was unavailable in any form for far too long so that its reissue was most welcome. As ever, Klemperer by and large justifies some moderate tempos by the way in which he sustains line and emphasises detail. Only once or twice – in the Spinning and Sailors' choruses – do you sense a lack of propulsion. Otherwise throughout there's a blazing intensity to the reading that brooks no denial. The storm and sea music in the Overture and thereafter is given stunning power, and the Dutchman's torture and passion is evoked in the orchestra. Indeed, the playing of the New Philharmonia is a bonus throughout. Klemperer catches as convincingly as anyone the elemental feeling of the work – the sense of the sea, basic passions and the interplay of character unerringly adumbrated.

There have been few baritones before or since Theo Adam who have sustained the line of the Dutchman so well and so intelligently reached the heart of the matter where the text is concerned. Silja's bright, sometimes piercing timbre isn't to everyone's taste, but hers is a most moving portrayal of trust and loyalty and love unto death, the interpretation of an outstanding singing-actress. Martti Talvela, singing magnificently and suggesting a formidable presence, is a bluff, burly Daland. Ernst Kozub's Erik has its clumsy moments, but one admires the shining tone. Gerhard Unger offers an ardent, cleanly articulated Sailor. Annelies Burmeister is a ripe Mary. The overall sound is a shade on the dry side but doesn't detract from the enjoyment.

Additional recommendation

Hotter Holländer **Varnay** Senta **Glaz** Mary **H**
Haysward Steersman **Svanholm** Erik **Nilsson** Daland
Metropolitan Opera Chorus and Orchestra, New York / Reiner
Naxos Historical mono ② 8 110189/90 (128' · ADD)
Recorded live at the Met, New York 1950. Notes and synopsis included **⑤O**

This performance marked the Met house début of Hans Hotter, and what a début! Varnay and Hotter seem to inspire each other to astonishing feats of musical and dramatic truth. Among historic recordings, this deserves a place up there with the Clemens Krauss. Those who want to hear Hotter in his prime will surely want this issue. The sound is excellent.

Götterdämmerung

Götterdämmerung **H**
Astrid Varnay sop Brünnhilde **Bernd Aldenhoff** ten
Siegfried **Ludwig Weber** bass Hagen **Heinrich Pflanzl** bass Alberich **Hermann Uhde** bar Gunther
Martha Mödl sop Gutrune, Third Norn **Elisabeth Höngen** mez Waltraute **Elisabeth Schwarzkopf** sop
Woglinde **Hanna Ludwig** sop Wellgunde **Hertha Töpper** mez Flosshilde **Ruth Siewert** mez First Norn
Ira Malaniuk mez Second Norn **Chorus and Orchestra of the Bayreuth Festival /Hans Knappertsbusch**
Testament mono ⊙ ⑥ SBTLP6175; ④ SBT4175
(281' · ADD) Recorded live 1951. Notes, text and translation included **ⒻOOO**

Testament awakened this sleeping Brünnhilde after half a century in Decca's vaults, held there because of an age-old dispute over rights between that company and EMI. This is a fitting memorial, alongside the exactly contemporaneous Parsifal (Teldec), to the phoenix-like reincarnation of Bayreuth post-war and to Wieland Wagner's genius as a producer and gatherer of all the talents to the Green Hill. The other hero of the occasion, as with Parsifal, is Knappertsbusch.

From the first bars of the Prologue he takes us right into the work, as concerned as three notable Norns (Mödl the most arresting of the three when prophesying the conflagration to come) with the inevitability of the tragic events portrayed within. He then takes us from Stygian gloom to mountain-top ecstasy with a masterly touch few equal. There we meet Varnay's youthful, vibrant, womanly heroine. Beside her is Aldenhoff's not-so-lovely Siegfried, yet once you become accustomed to his aggrandising, extrovert moments you hear a Heldentenor in the old mould, alive to every word and communicating with his audience. Later, arriving at Gibichung Hall, you meet the most forthright, articulate Gunther in Uhde. His greeting to Siegfried, 'Begrüsse froh, O Held', makes one realise why Uhde is pre-eminent in this role. Beside him is Weber's louring, gloating, ambitious Hagen. What intelligence there is in every bar he sings (try 'Ein Weib weiss ich' or the whole of the Watch). As Gutrune, Mödl isn't your usual sweet-toned milksop but a women not afraid to show her deep emotions. The great mezzo Höngen as Waltraute conveys with amazing immediacy Wotan's despair, and, with a shudder in her tone at 'Da brach sich sein Blick', the tenderness of his thoughts on his beloved Brünnhilde, making one feel it to be the most moving moment in the whole *Ring* and consoling us for occasionally grainy tone.

Throughout Act 2, Knappertsbusch is trenchant in characterising the tremendous conflicts depicted therein. Weber rouses the vassals with vigorous enthusiasm. Varnay is tremendous in her denunciations of Siegfried, Aldenhoff as vivid in his replies. Such immediacy can only be found in the opera house – damn the momentary lapses in ensemble, the few distractions when scenery is being moved or the audience coughs. In Act 3 the Rhine Maidens, led by Schwarzkopf, are too backwardly placed, the sole blot on the sound picture. In Siegfried's Narration, Aldenhoff captures the vitality of his earlier exploits, supported by gloriously rippling strings, and sings a fulsome death-song. Knappertsbusch, eagerly supported by Bayreuth's hand-picked orchestra (all individually named in the accompanying booklet), unleashes all the tremendous import of the Funeral March. Finally Varnay carries all before her, in better voice than later at Bayreuth, in a visionary account of the Immolation that rightly crowns a noble interpretation of her role and the whole work. The recording is superior even to that of the 1951 *Parsifal*, with only a few passages of uncertain balance to fault it, supporting an experience nobody ought to miss.

Lohengrin

Lohengrin
Jess Thomas ten Lohengrin **Elisabeth Grümmer** sop
Elsa **Christa Ludwig** mez Ortrud **Dietrich Fischer-Dieskau** bar Telramund **Gottlob Frick** bass King
Henry **Otto Wiener** bass Herald **Vienna State**

Opera Chorus; Vienna Philharmonic Orchestra / Rudolf Kempe
EMI Great Recordings of the Century ③ 567415-2 (217' · ADD) Recorded 1963-4. Text and translation included ⓂOO

EMI's sound may have less presence and a narrower perspective than other versions, but neither the 'studio' ambience – the recording was made in the Theater an der Wien – nor the occasionally excessive prominence of the voices prevents Kempe's reading from projecting a strongly theatrical quality. However, it's the all-round excellence of the cast, plus the bonus of an uncut Act 3, which makes this the leading mid-price recommendation.

Jess Thomas combines ardour and anguish as well as any, and with Fischer-Dieskau a formidable (but never over-emphatic) antagonist, and Gottlob Frick a majestic King Henry, the drama of the opera's central conflict remains supremely immediate and powerful. As Elsa and Ortrud, Elisabeth Grümmer and Christa Ludwig are ideal opposites, the former radiant yet quite without the simpering overtones that afflict some Elsas, the latter as potent in seductive insinuation as in demonic ferocity. Not even Ludwig can surpass the visceral intensity of Astrid Varnay in the 1953 Bayreuth set under Keilberth, and Keilberth's Telramund and Elsa (Hermann Uhde and Eleanor Steber) are also outstanding: yet Wolfgang Windgassen's Lohengrin isn't as distinguished, nor as distinctive, as Jess Thomas's here. Even more importantly, Keilberth's reading lacks the visionary quality that Kempe finds in the score. Ultimately, it's the power of that vision which raises this performance above its rivals.

Lohengrin
James King ten Lohengrin **Gundula Janowitz** sop Elsa **Gwyneth Jones** sop Ortrud **Thomas Stewart** bar Telramund **Karl Ridderbusch** bass King Henry **Gerd Nienstedt** bass Herald **Bavarian Radio Chorus and Symphony Orchestra / Rafael Kubelík**
DG ③ 449 591-2GX3 (222' · ADD) Recorded 1971. Notes, text and translation included ⓂO

The attributes of Kubelík's *Lohengrin* have been underestimated. It will hold your interest from first to last, not least thanks to Kubelík's masterly overview. Not only does he successfully hold together all the disparate strands of the sprawling work, he also imparts to them a sense of inner excitement through his close attention to the small notes and phrases that so often delineate character in this score and through his vital control of the large ensembles. He's helped inestimably by the Bavarian Radio forces – gloriously singing strings, characterful winds, trenchant, involving chorus – of which he was, in 1971, a beloved chief. There's never a dull moment in his vivid, theatrical *Lohengrin*. The recording imparts a suitably spacious atmosphere to the piece but also places the principals up front where they should be except when distancing is required – as at Lohengrin's first appearance and at the moment when Elsa appears on the balcony to address the night breezes. Janowitz's Elsa is one of the set's major assets. Pure in tone, imaginative in phrasing, she catches the ear from her first entry, very much suggesting Elsa's vulnerability. Later she eloquently conveys her deep feelings in the love duet, followed by her voicing of all the doubts that beset her character. King's Lohengrin is more ordinary; today we would be grateful for such solid, musical and well-judged singing. Few if any Lohengrins can sing the passage starting 'Höchstes Vertraun' (third disc, track 5) with anything like King's true tone and powerful conviction. Though not as detailed or subtle in is colouring of the text as some, Thomas Stewart sings a sturdy Telramund, managing the high tessitura with consummate ease. Gwyneth Jones's portrayal, taken all-round, is reasonably convincing despite turning a vibrato that might flatteringly be called opulent into something more objectionable. Her Ortrud registers high on the scale of vicious malevolence in the part. The difficulty, as it always has been with this intelligent artist, is that the subtlety evinced in quiet passages is vitiated when the tone comes under pressure.

The chorus are nothing short of superb. So, this makes an irresistible bid for recommendation. It's well recorded, sounding wholly resplendent and as cogently conducted as any of its rivals.

Lohengrin
Peter Seiffert ten Lohengrin **Emily Magee** sop Elsa **Deborah Polaski** sop Ortrud **Falk Struckmann** bar Telramund **René Pape** bass King Henry **Roman Trekel** bar Herald **Chorus of the Deutsche Oper, Berlin; Staatskapelle Berlin / Daniel Barenboim**
Teldec ③ 3984-21484-2 (211' · DDD) Notes, texts and translations included Ⓕ

This recording is based on the cast with which Barenboim performed the opera at the Berlin State Opera in 1996, although the tenor taking the title-role is different. The chorus, so important in this work, sings with refinement, discipline and enthusiasm in its many roles while all departments of the orchestra play the score to the hilt. Barenboim himself manages to give an overriding unity to a work that can, in lesser hands, sprawl. That's particularly true as regards Act 2, which can test a listener's concentration; not here when the conductor so unerringly weaves the disparate elements into a coherent, forward-moving whole. He's also to be commended for playing Act 3 complete, restoring not only the theatre cuts often made in recording but also the second verse of Lohengrin's Grail narration, cut by Wagner before the first night. In the opera house it's sensibly omitted because it lengthens the act unduly. The only reservation concerns the famous Prelude to Act 3, which seems too brash and too fast. All the singers, with one exception, are regulars at the Berlin State Opera. The exception is Seiffert as Lohengrin, who in tone, phrasing and sheer lyrical ardour makes a near-ideal white knight. His Elsa is Emily Magee, her tone full and refulgent, her interpretation deeply felt. The one worry is that her voice is so much like that of Polaski that they're hard to tell apart in their long confrontation in Act 2. Polaski makes a splendidly forceful and articulate Ortrud, only very occasionally sounding taxed by heavier passages, most worryingly in her closing imprecations. Struckmann's Telramund isn't as tortured as Fischer-Dieskau's in Kempe's set, but these vital, involving interpretations have their own validity. Pape is a model King Henry, pouring out his concerns in golden tone. Trekel is a strong Herald. The set is enhanced by a perfectly balanced and warm recording.

Die Meistersinger von Nürnberg

Die Meistersinger von Nürnberg
Thomas Stewart bar Hans Sachs **Sándor Kónya** ten Walther **Gundula Janowitz** sop Eva **Franz Crass** bass Pogner **Thomas Hemsley** bar Beckmesser **Gerhard Unger** ten David **Brigitte Fassbaender** mez Magdalene **Kieth Engen** bass Kothner **Horst Wilhelm** ten Vogelgesang **Richard Kogel** bass Nachtigall **Manfred Schmidt** ten Zorn **Friedrich Lenz** ten Eisslinger **Peter Baillie** ten Moser **Anton Diakov** bass Ortel **Karl Christian Kohn** bass Schwartz **Dieter Slembeck** bass Foltz **Raimund Grumbach** bass Nightwatchman **Bavarian Radio Chorus and Symphony Orchestra / Rafael Kubelík**
Calig ④ CAL50971/4 (272' · ADD) Recorded 1967
Ⓕ⦿⦿

There could be no more fitting memorial to Kubelík than the appearance of this, probably the most all-round satisfying *Meistersinger* in the era of stereo. It was recorded in 1967 by Bavarian Radio to mark the work's centenary the following year. Kubelík conducts an unforced, loving interpretation, showing a gratifying grasp of overall structure. As a whole the reading has an unobtrusive cohesion achieved within flexible tempos and dynamics. Everything proceeds at an even, well-judged pace with just the right surge of emotion at the climaxes. All this is conveyed unerringly to his own Bavarian Radio Symphony forces.

Stewart's Sachs is certainly his most successful performance on disc. He offers a finely moulded, deeply considered reading that relies on firm, evenly produced, mostly warm tone to create a darkish, philosophical poet-cobbler. Kónya is simply the most winning Walther on any set, superseding Sawallisch's excellent Heppner by virtue of a greater ardour in his delivery. Kónya pours out consistently warm, clear tone, his tenor hovering ideally between the lyric and the heroic. Nor are there many better Evas than the young Janowitz, certainly none with a lovelier voice. Franz Crass, a less pompous Pogner than some, sings his part effortlessly, with noble feeling. Hemsley, though singing his first Beckmesser, evinces a close affinity with the

Town Clerk's mean-mindedness, and his German is faultless. Unger is a paragon among Davids, so eager in his responses and finding just the right timbre for the role. His Magdalene, again perfect casting, is the young Fassbaender. With a characterful Kothner in Engen, the requirements for a near-ideal *Meistersinger* ensemble are in place. As the recording doesn't betray its age this would undoubtedly be the first choice among stereo versions.

Die Meistersinger von Nürnberg
Bernd Weikl bar Hans Sachs **Ben Heppner** ten Walther **Cheryl Studer** sop Eva **Kurt Moll** bass Pogner **Siegfried Lorenz** bar Beckmesser **Deon van der Walt** ten David **Cornelia Kallisch** contr Magdalene **Hans-Joachim Ketelsen** bass Kothner **Michael Schade** ten Vogelgesang **Hans Wilbrink** bar Nachtigall **Ulrich Ress** ten Zorn **Hermann Sapell** bar Eisslinger **Roland Wagenführer** ten Moser **Rainer Büse** bass Ortel **Guido Götzen** bass Schwarz **Friedmann Kunder** bass Foltz **René Pape** bass Nightwatchman **Bavarian State Opera Chorus; Bavarian State Orchestra / Wolfgang Sawallisch**
EMI ④ 555142-2 (257' · DDD) Recorded 1993 Notes, text and translation included
Ⓕ⦿

Sawallisch's *Meistersinger* is very much a version for today – profoundly musical, as it was bound to be under him, sung with a consistent beauty of sound, and recorded truthfully and spaciously. Anybody coming to the work for the first time, and wanting a version backed by modern sound, will find it a sensible choice, a performance for the most part measuring up to the score's many demands on its interpreters. Sawallisch obtains singing and playing on the highest level of achievement, observant of detail, rich in texture, sure in pacing and – very important in this score – anxious to move forward where there's any danger of the music seeming over-extended, as in the recital of the tones and the Act 2 episode of Beckmesser's courting. Sawallisch's reading also catches the warmth that pervades the whole opera, yet is also successful in deftly projecting its comedy.

It must be said, however, that with Sawallisch the earth doesn't move, the spirit is seldom lifted as it should be. On the other hand, nobody is better than Sawallisch at characterising the disputes among the Masters in Act 1, or the pointed humour of the Act 2 Sachs-Beckmesser scene, and much else of that nature is unobtrusively right.

Where the recording itself is concerned, great care has been taken over the placing of the singers in relation to one another and the correct distancing of the voices where called for. The balance in relation to the orchestra seems just about ideal. Sawallisch takes an honoured place in the illustrious company of interpreters. His reading is full of thoughtful aperçus and natural flow, and displays a sensible overview of the score. Vocally it will satisfy all but those with the most demanding tastes in and/or long experience in Wagnerian interpretation.

Parsifal

Parsifal
Jess Thomas ten Parsifal **George London** bass-bar
Amfortas **Hans Hotter** bass-bar Gurnemanz **Irene
Dalis** mez Kundry **Gustav Neidlinger** bass-bar
Klingsor **Martti Talvela** bass Titurel **Niels Møller** ten
First Knight **Gerd Nienstedt** bass Second Knight
Sona Cervená mez First Squire Sixth Flower Maiden
Ursula Boese mez Second Squire **Gerhard Stolze**
ten Third Squire **Georg Paskuda** ten Fourth Squire
**Rita Bartos, Gundula Janowitz, Anja Silja, Elsa-
Margrete Gardelli, Dorothea Siebert** sops Flower
Maidens; **Bayreuth Festival Chorus and Orchestra
/ Hans Knappertsbusch**
Philips 50 Great Recordings ④ 464 756-2PM4
(250' · ADD) Recorded live 1962. Notes, text and
translation included   Ⓜ️❍❍❍

This isn't merely one of Philips's Great
Recordings but also one of the greatest
sets of all time. Every time one returns
to it, its inspiration and distinction seem to have
been enhanced. There have been many fine
recordings of this great Eastertide opera, but
none has so magnificently managed to capture
the power, the spiritual grandeur, the human
frailty and the almost unbearable beauty of the
work as Hans Knappertsbusch. This live
recording has a cast that has few equals. Hotter
is superb, fleshing out Gurnemanz with a depth
of insight that has never been surpassed. London's Amfortas captures the frightening sense
of impotence and anguish with painful directness, while Thomas's Parsifal grows as the performance progresses and is no mean achievement. Dalis may lack that final degree of
sensuousness but she provides a fine interpretation nevertheless. Throughout the work, Knappertsbusch exercises a quite un-equalled control
over the proceedings; it's a fine testament to a
great conductor. The Bayreuth acoustic is well
reproduced, and this record is a profound and
moving experience.

Parsifal
Peter Hofmann ten Parsifal **José van Dam** bass-bar
Amfortas **Kurt Moll** bass Gurnemanz **Dunja Vejzovic**
mez Kundry **Siegmund Nimsgern** bass Klingsor
Victor von Halem bass Titurel **Claes Hakon Ahnsjö**
ten First Knight **Kurt Rydl** bass Second Knight
Marjon Lambriks, Anne Gjevang mezzos **Heiner
Hopfner** ten **Georg Tichy** bass Squires **Barbara
Hendricks, Janet Perry, Inga Nielsen** sops **Audrey
Michael** mez **Doris Soffel, Rohângiz Yachmi Caucig**
contrs Flower Maidens **Hanna Schwarz** mez Voice
from above **Berlin Deutsche Opera Chorus; Berlin
Philharmonic Orchestra / Herbert von Karajan**
DG ④ 413 347-2GH4 (256' · ADD) Recorded 1979-80
Notes, text and translation included   Ⓕ❍❍❍

Karajan's *Parsifal* seems to grow in
stature as an interpretation on each
rehearing; on its CD transfer it appears
to have acquired a new depth, in terms of sound,
because of the greater range of the recording

and the greater presence of both singers and
orchestra. As in practically all cases, CD offers a
more immediate experience. Karajan's reading,
a trifle stodgy in Act 1, grows in intensity and
feeling with the work itself, reaching an almost
terrifying force in the Prelude to Act 3 which is
sustained to the end of the opera. Moll's Gurnemanz is a deeply expressive, softly moulded performance of notable beauty. Vejzovic, carefully
nurtured by Karajan, gives the performance of
her life as Kundry. Hofmann's tone isn't at all
times as steady as a Parsifal's should be, but he
depicts the character's anguish and eventual
serenity in his sincere, inward interpretation.
Van Dam is a trifle too placid as Amfortas, but
his singing exhibits admirable power and fine
steadiness. Nimsgern is the epitome of malice as
Klingsor. The choral singing doesn't have quite
the confidence of the superb orchestral playing,
which has both qualities of Keats's imagining of
beauty and truth in abundance.

Das Rheingold / Die Walküre

Das Rheingold
John Tomlinson bass Wotan **Linda Finnie** mez
Fricka **Graham Clark** ten Loge **Helmut Pampuch**
ten Mime **Günter von Kannen** bar Alberich **Eva
Johansson** sop Freia **Kurt Schreibmayer** ten Froh
Bodo Brinkmann bar Donner **Birgitta Svendén** mez
Erda **Matthias Hölle** bass Fasolt **Philip Kang** bass
Fafner **Hilde Leidland** sop Woglinde **Annette
Küttenbaum** mez Wellgunde **Jane Turner** mez
Flosshilde **Bayreuth Festival Orchestra / Daniel
Barenboim**
Teldec ② 4509-91185-2 (149' · DDD) Recorded live
1991. Notes, text and translation included   Ⓕ❍❍

Die Walküre
Poul Elming ten Siegmund **Nadine Secunde** sop
Sieglinde **Anne Evans** sop Brünnhilde **John
Tomlinson** bass Wotan **Linda Finnie** mez Fricka,
Siegrune **Matthias Hölle** bass Hunding **Eva
Johansson** sop Gerhilde **Eva-Maria Bundschuh** sop
Helmwige **Ruth Floeren** sop Ortlinde **Shirley Close**
mez Waltraute **Hebe Dijkstra** mez Rossweisse
Birgitta Svendén mez Grimgerde **Hitomi Katagiri**
mez Schwertleite **Bayreuth Festival Orchestra /
Daniel Barenboim**
Teldec ④ 4509-91186-2 (233' · DDD) Recorded live
1992. Notes, text and translation included   Ⓕ❍❍

These are enthralling performances. Tomlinson's volatile Wotan is the most potent reading
here. He manages to sing every word with insistent meaning and forceful declamation while
maintaining a firm *legato*. His German is so
idiomatic that he might have been speaking the
language his whole life and he brings breadth
and distinction of phrase to his solos at the close
of both operas. Anne Evans as a single, important advantage over other recent Brünnhildes in
that her voice is wholly free from wobble and
she never makes an ugly sound. Hers is a light,
girlish, honest portrayal, sung with unfailing
musicality if not with the ultimate insights.

Linda Finnie is an articulate, sharp-edged Fricka, and Graham Clark a sparky, incisive Loge. Nadine Secunde's impassioned Sieglinde is matched by the vital, exciting Siegmund of Poul Elming, and Matthias Hölle as both Hunding and Fasolt is another of those black basses of which Germany seems to have an inexhaustible supply. The whole is magnificently conducted by Barenboim, a more expansive Wagnerian than Böhm. By 1991 he had the full measure of its many facets, bringing immense authority and power to building its huge climaxes, yet finding all the lightness of touch for the mercurial and/or diaphanous aspects of the score. He has the inestimable advantage of a Bayreuth orchestra at the peak of its form, surpassing – and this says much – even the Metropolitan orchestra for Levine. Similar qualities inform his interpretation of *Die Walküre*. Barenboim has now learnt how to match the epic stature of Wagner's mature works, how to pace them with an overview of the whole, and there's an incandescent, metaphysical feeling of a Furtwänglerian kind in is treatment of such passages as Wotan's anger and the Valkyrie ride. The orchestra is superb. It's backed by a recording of startling presence and depth, amply capturing the Bayreuth acoustic.

Rienzi

Rienzi
René Kollo *ten* Cola Rienzi **Siv Wennberg** *sop* Irene
Janis Martin *sop* Adriano **Theo Adam** *bass* Paolo
Orsini **Nikolaus Hillebrand** *bass* Steffano Colonna
Siegfried Vogel *bass* Raimondo **Peter Schreier** *ten*
Baroncelli **Günther Leib** *bass* Cecco del Vecchio
Ingeborg Springer *sop* Messenger of Peace **Leipzig
Radio Chorus; Dresden State Opera Chorus;
Staatskapelle Dresden / Heinrich Hollreiser**
EMI ③ 567131-2 (225' · ADD) Recorded 1974-6
Notes, text and translation included ⓜ

Rienzi is grand opera with a vengeance. Political imperatives count for more than mere human feelings, and politics means ceremony as well as warfare: marches, ballet music and extended choruses are much in evidence in this work, while even the solo arias often have the rhetorical punch of political harangues. It could all be an enormous bore. Yet the young Wagner, basing his work on Bulwer Lytton's story of the tragic Roman tribune, did manage to move beyond mere tub-thumping into a degree of intensity that – for those with ears to hear – prefigures the mature genius to come. In the end, Rienzi himself is more than just a political animal, and the existential anguish of Tannhäuser, Tristan and even Amfortas can be found glimmering in the distance. This performance isn't ideal in every respect, either musically, or as a recording. But its virtues outweigh its weaknesses by a considerable margin. Siv Wennberg was not in best voice at the time, but the other principals, notably René Kollo and Janis Mar-

tin, bring commendable stamina and conviction to their demanding roles. Above all Heinrich Hollreiser prevents the more routine material from sounding merely mechanical, and ensures that *Rienzi* has a truly Wagnerian sweep and fervour.

Introduction to The Ring

Der Ring des Nibelungen – spoken introduction with 193 musical examples
Deryck Cooke *narr* **various singers; Vienna Philharmonic Orchestra / Sir Georg Solti**
Decca The Classic Sound ② 443 581-2DCS2
(141' · ADD) Recorded 1967. Booklet of musical illustrations included ⓜ

Deryck Cooke died, prematurely, in 1976 before he completed his comprehensive study on *The Ring*. Fortunately, in 1967, Decca had had the foresight to invite him to record this introduction to the cycle. In this he developed at length his ideas on its leitmotifs, using 193 examples, most of them taken from the Solti recording, and a few made specifically to illustrate a point Cooke was making.

Wagner, as he avers, described the motifs as 'melodic moments of feeling', not signposts or tags. He also adds that their psychological significance and development are of the essence in comprehending *The Ring*, and divides them into four groups – character, objects, events, emotions – then proceeds to describe, in simple, pungent language, how they're deployed throughout the work. His straightforward, unfussy method and delivery, so typical of a man quite without egotistical pretension, enhances one's understanding and, more important, enjoyment of this mighty work. An essential adjunct to any cycle.

The Complete Ring Cycle

Das Rheingold   Ⓗ
George London *bass-bar* Wotan **Kirsten Flagstad**
sop Fricka **Set Svanholm** *ten* Loge **Paul Kuen** *ten*
Mime **Gustav Neidlinger** *bass-bar* Alberich **Claire
Watson** *sop* Freia **Waldemar Kmentt** *ten* Froh
Eberhard Waechter *bar* Donner **Jean Madeira**
contr Erda **Walter Kreppel** *bass* Fasolt **Kurt Böhme**
bass Fafner **Oda Balsborg** *sop* Woglinde **Hetty
Plümacher** *mez* Wellgunde **Ira Malaniuk** *mez*
Flosshilde

Die Walküre   Ⓗ
James King *ten* Siegmund **Régine Crespin** *sop*
Sieglinde **Birgit Nilsson** *sop* Brünnhilde; **Hans
Hotter** *bass-bar* Wotan **Christa Ludwig** *mez* Fricka
Gottlob Frick *bass* Hunding **Vera Schlosser** *sop*
Gerhilde **Berit Lindholm** *sop* Helmwige **Helga
Dernesch** *sop* Ortlinde **Brigitte Fassbaender** *mez*
Waltraute **Claudia Hellmann** *sop* Rossweisse **Vera
Little** *contr* Siegrune **Marilyn Tyler** *sop* Grimgerde
Helen Watts *contr* Schwertleite

Siegfried　　　　　　　　　　　　　　　　🄷
Wolfgang Windgassen *ten* Siegfried **Hans Hotter**
bass-bar Wanderer **Birgit Nilsson** *sop* Brünnhilde
Gerhard Stolze *ten* Mime **Gustav Neidlinger** *bass-bar* Alberich **Marga Höffgen** *contr* Erda **Kurt Böhme** *bass* Fafner **Joan Sutherland** *sop* Woodbird

Götterdämmerung　　　　　　　　　　　　🄷
Birgit Nilsson *sop* Brünnhilde **Wolfgang Windgassen** *ten* Siegfried **Gottlob Frick** *bass* Hagen **Gustav Neidlinger** *bass-bar* Alberich **Dietrich Fischer-Dieskau** *bar* Gunther **Claire Watson** *sop* Gutrune **Christa Ludwig** *mez* Waltraute **Gwyneth Jones** *sop* Wellgunde **Lucia Popp** *sop* Woglinde **Maureen Guy** *mez* Flosshilde **Helen Watts** *contr* First Norn **Grace Hoffman** *mez* Second Norn **Anita Välkki** *sop* Third Norn
Vienna State Opera Chorus; Vienna Philharmonic Orchestra / Georg Solti
Decca ⑭ 455 555-2DMO14 (876' · ADD) Recorded 1958-65. Notes, texts and translations included Also available separately　　　　　　　　Ⓜ**OO**

As perspectives on the Solti/Culshaw enterprise lengthen, and critical reactions are kept alert by the regular appearance of new, or newly issued, and very different recordings, it may seem increasingly ironic that of all conductors the ultra-theatrical Solti should have been denied a live performance. There are indeed episodes in this recording that convey more of the mechanics of the studio than of the electricity of the opera house – the opening of *Die Walküre*, Act 2, and the closing scenes of *Siegfried* and *Götterdämmerung*, for example. Yet, in general, dramatic impetus and atmosphere are strongly established and well sustained, sometimes more powerfully than is usually managed in the theatre. As just one example one would instance the superb control with which the intensity of Donner's summoning up of the thunder in *Das Rheingold* is maintained across Froh's greeting to the rainbow bridge into Wotan's own great salutation. At the majestic climax of this scene the power of feeling conveyed by George London's fine performance counts for more than any 'artificiality' in the way the voice is balanced against the orchestra.

Equally memorable in a totally different context is Solti's management of the long transition in *Götterdämmerung* between Hagen's Watch and the appearance of Waltraute. Nothing could be less mannered or unnatural than Solti's grasp of perspective and feeling for the life of each phrase in this music. On CD the clarity of instrumental detail is consistently remarkable, and while not all the singers sound as if they're constantly in danger of being overwhelmed there are some vital episodes, especially those involving Windgassen and Nilsson. Awareness of what these artists achieved in other recordings strengthens the suspicion that they may have been giving more than we actually get here. Windgassen isn't allowed to dominate the sound picture in the way his part demands, and Nilsson can seem all-too relaxed within the comforting cocoon of the orchestral texture.

Factors like these, coupled with those distinctive Soltian confrontations between the hard-driven and the hammily protracted, have prevented the cycle from decisively seeing off its rivals over the years. It's questionable nevertheless whether any studio recording of *The Ring* could reasonably be expected to be more atmospheric, exciting or better performed than this one. The VPO isn't merely prominent, but excellent, and such interpretations as Svanholm's Loge, Neidlinger's Alberich and Frick's Hagen remain very impressive.

Above all, there's Hotter, whose incomparably authoritative, unfailingly alert and responsive Wotan stands up well when compared to his earlier Bayreuth accounts. Nowhere is he more commanding than in *Siegfried*, Act 1, where one even welcomes Stolze's mannerisms as Mime for the sparks they strike off the great bass-baritone. Earlier in this act the interplay of equally balanced instruments and voices in relatively intimate conversational phrases displays the Culshaw concept at its most convincing. He would have been astonished to hear what his successors have achieved in renewing his production through digital remastering. One now realises how much of the original sound was lost on the old pressings. In comparison with the 1980 Janowski/RCA version, the approaches are so different they almost seem like different experiences. Culshaw was intent on creating a theatre on record with all the well-known stage effects; the rival version eschews all such manifestations. In general, Janowski presents a much more intimate view of the work than Solti's.

However many other *Ring*s you may have, though, you'll need this one.

Das Rheingold[a]
Theo Adam *bass-bar* Wotan **Yvonne Minton** *mez* Fricka **Peter Schreier** *ten* Loge **Christian Vogel** *ten* Mime **Siegmund Nimsgern** *bass-bar* Alberich **Marita Napier** *sop* Freia **Eberhard Büchner** *ten* Froh **Karl-Heinz Stryczek** *bass* Donner **Ortrun Wenkel** *contr* Erda **Roland Bracht** *bass* Fasolt **Matti Salminen** *bass* Fafner **Lucia Popp** *sop* Woglinde **Uta Priew** *mez* Wellgunde **Hanna Schwarz** *contr* Flosshilde

Die Walküre[b]
Siegfried Jerusalem *ten* Siegmund **Jessye Norman** *sop* Sieglinde **Jeannine Altmeyer** *sop* Brünnhilde **Theo Adam** *bass-bar* Wotan **Yvonne Minton** *mez* Fricka **Kurt Moll** *bass* Hunding **Eva-Maria Bundschuh** *sop* Gerhilde **Ruth Falcon** *sop* Helmwige **Cheryl Studer** *sop* Ortlinde **Ortrun Wenkel** *contr* Waltraute **Uta Priew** *mez* Rossweisse **Christel Borchers** *mez* Siegrune **Kathleen Kuhlmann** *contr* Grimgerde **Anne Gjevang** *contr* Schwertleite

Siegfried[c]
René Kollo *ten* Siegfried **Theo Adam** *bass-bar* Wanderer **Jeannine Altmeyer** *sop* Brünnhilde **Peter Schreier** *ten* Mime **Siegmund Nimsgern** *bass-bar* Alberich **Ortrun Wenkel** *contr* Erda **Norma Sharp** *sop* Woodbird **Matti Salminen** *bass* Fafner

WAGNER'S RING CYCLE – IN BRIEF

Birgit Nilsson *Brünnhilde* **Wolfgang Windgassen**
Siegfried **Hans Hotter, George London** *Wotan*
Vienna PO / Sir Georg Solti
Decca ⑭ 455 555-2DMO14 (14 hr 36' · ADD)
                                                    Ⓜ️OO

The first complete cycle is still the most
clearly recommendable. Even if Solti's blazingly dynamic conducting isn't everyone's
ideal, he unites the most consistently superb
casting with John Culshaw's still magnificent
recording. A classic of the recording era.

Birgit Nilsson *Brünnhilde* **Wolfgang
Windgassen** *Siegfried* **Theo Adam** *Wotan*
Bayreuth Festival Orchestra / Karl Böhm
Philips ⑭ 412 475/478/483/488-2 (13 hr 39' · ADD)
                                                    ⒻOOO

☀ This 1967 recording offers the immediacy of live Bayreuth, though with stage
noises and some rough edges. Böhm whips
up excitement at some cost in detail, but
draws vivid performances from a cast very
similar to Solti's, handicapped chiefly by
Theo Adam's harsh, unsteady Wotan.

Jeannine Altmeyer *Brünnhilde* **René Kollo**
Siegfried **Theo Adam** *Wotan*
Staatskapelle Dresden / Marek Janowski
RCA ⑭ 74321 45416-2 (13 hr 59' · DDD)   ⒷOO
Janowski makes this first digital version fresh,
fast and straightforward, with several fine
voices such as Jessye Norman and Peter
Schreier, but also, unfortunately, Adam's
now desiccated Wotan, and a rather studio-
bound recording.

Rita Hunter *Brünnhilde* **Alberto Remedios**
Siegfried **Norman Bailey** *Wotan* **ENO /
Sir Reginald Goodall**
Chandos ⑯ CHAN3038/45/54/60 (16 hr 31' · DDD)
                                                    ⒷOO
Goodall's famously massive reading may
shock some with its slowness, but it's beautifully detailed, with the immediacy of English,
and offers some truly world-class performances. Recorded live, mostly in winter, hence
some obtrusive coughing.

Helga Dernesch *Brünnhilde* **Helge Brilloth**
Siegfried **Dietrich Fischer-Dieskau** *Wotan*
Berlin PO / Herbert von Karajan
DG ⑭ 457 780-2GOR14 (14 hr 58' · ADD)   ⒷO
An underrated version, largely because
Karajan's emphasis on orchestral and vocal
beauty sometimes sounds mannered, and
encompasses inconsistent and occasionally
inadequate casting – particularly Siegfried.
Nevertheless this is a well recorded and
often magical set.

Götterdämmerung[d]
Jeannine Altmeyer *sop* Brünnhilde **René Kollo** *ten*
Siegfried **Matti Salminen** *bass* Hagen **Siegmund
Nimsgern** *bass-bar* Alberich **Hans Günter Nöcker**
bar Gunther **Norma Sharp** *sop* Gutrune **Ortrun
Wenkel** *contr* Waltraute **Uta Priew** *mez* Wellgunde
Lucia Popp *sop* Woglinde **Hanna Schwarz** *contr*
Flosshilde **Anne Gjevang** *contr* First Norn **Daphne
Evangelatos** *mez* Second Norn **Ruth Falcon** *sop*
Third Norn **Men's Voices of the Leipzig State
Opera; Dresden State Opera Chorus;
Staatskapelle Dresden / Marek Janowski**
RCA Red Seal ⑭ 74321 45417-2 (839' · DDD)
Recorded [a]1980, [b]1981, [c]1982, [d]1983. Notes, texts
and translations included   ⒷOO

Here's a desirable bargain. This, the first digitally recorded cycle to appear on CD, has always
had a great deal to commend it, and at budget
price it becomes even more attractive. One of its
most telling assets is the recording itself, still the
most natural, clear and most sensitively balanced available. Then it has the Dresden
Staatskapelle playing with the utmost beauty
from start to finish and with lean power when
that's called for. Voices and players are in an
ideal relationship. Which isn't to say that such
purple passages as the Magic Fire Music, Ride
of the Valkyries, Rhine Journey and Funeral
March want anything in visceral excitement.
Janowski conducts a direct, dramatic interpretation, concerned throughout with forward
movement. His clear-sighted conducting conveys theatrical excitement from start to finish
without fuss or attempts at portentous readings.
All this makes it an ideal introduction to the
Ring for any young collector, who can later go
on to more philosophically inclined interpretations. The casts are by and large excellent. *Das
Rheingold* is dominated by three central performances – Nimsgern's vibrant, articulate
Alberich, Schreier's wonderfully vital, strikingly
intelligent and articulate Loge and Adam's
experienced Wotan. But Fricka, Giants and
Rhinemaidens are all well cast, and the whole
performance grips one's attention from start to
finish as the kaleidoscopic drama unfolds. *Die
Walküre* introduces us to Norman's involving if
not wholly idiomatic Sieglinde and, even better,
the youthful Jerusalem's near-ideal Siegmund,
forthright and sincere, not forgetting Moll's
granite Hunding. Adam is so authoritative, so
keen with the text, so inside his part that an
occasional unsteadiness can be overlooked.
With Altmeyer's Brünnhilde we come to the
one drawback of the set. Though in this and the
succeeding operas, we're thankful for such
clear, clean and youthful tone, her reading is
unformed and one-dimensional, lacking the
essential insights of a Varnay or Behrens. In the
title-role in *Siegfried* Kollo gives one of is most
attractive portrayals on disc, full of thoughtful
diction poised on clear-cut tone. Schreier
misses nothing in his interpretation of the dissembling, wily Mime, Adam is at is very best
as the wise, old Wanderer, and the smaller parts
are well catered for. In *Götterdämmerung*,

Salminen is a commanding, often subtle Hagen, though inclined to bark in his call, Nöcker a splendid Gunther. This set is particularly recommended to anyone wanting a reasonably priced introduction to the cycle. Even at a higher level, it has much going for it in comparison with supposedly more prestigious recordings.

The Complete Ring Cycle in English

The Valkyrie (sung in English)
Alberto Remedios ten Siegmund **Margaret Curphey** sop Sieglinde **Rita Hunter** sop Brünnhilde **Norman Bailey** bar Wotan **Ann Howard** contr Fricka **Clifford Grant** bass Hunding **Katie Clarke** sop Gerhilde **Anne Evans** sop Helmwige **Ann Conoley** sop Ortlinde **Elizabeth Connell** sop Waltraute **Anne Collins** contr Rossweisse **Sarah Walker** mez Siegrune **Shelagh Squires** mez Grimgerde **Helen Attfield** sop Schwertleite **English National Opera Orchestra / Reginald Goodall**
Chandos Opera in English Series ④ CHAN3038 (249' · ADD) Recorded live 1976.Notes and English translation included   Ⓕ●

Siegfried (sung in English)
Alberto Remedios ten Siegfried **Norman Bailey** bass-bar Wanderer **Rita Hunter** sop Brünnhilde **Gregory Dempsey** ten Mime **Derek Hammond-Stroud** bar Alberich **Anne Collins** contr Erda **Clifford Grant** bass Fafner **Maurine London** sop Woodbird **Sadler's Wells Opera Orchestra / Reginald Goodall**
Chandos ④ CHAN3045 (279' · ADD) Recorded live 1973. English text included   Ⓕ●●

The Rhinegold (sung in English)
Norman Bailey bar Wotan **Katherine Pring** mez Fricka **Emile Belcourt** ten Loge **Gregory Dempsey** ten Mime **Derek Hammond-Stroud** bar Alberich **Lois McDonall** sop Freia **Robert Ferguson** ten Froh **Norman Welsby** bar Donner **Anne Collins** contr Erda **Robert Lloyd** bass Fasolt **Clifford Grant** bass Fafner **Valerie Masterson** sop Woglinde **Shelagh Squires** mez Wellgunde **Helen Attfield** sop Flosshilde **English National Opera Orchestra / Reginald Goodall**
Chandos Opera in English Series ③ CHAN3054 (174' · ADD) Recorded live 1975. Notes and English text included   Ⓕ●

Twilight of the Gods (sung in English)
Alberto Remedios ten Siegfried **Norman Welsby** bar Gunther **Aage Haugland** bass Hagen **Derek Hammond-Stroud** bar Alberich **Rita Hunter** sop Brünnhilde **Margaret Curphey** sop Gutrune **Katherine Pring** mez Waltraute **Anne Collins** contr First Norn **Gillian Knight** mez Second Norn **Anne Evans** sop Third Norn **Valerie Masterson** sop Woglinde **Shelagh Squires** mez Wellgunde **Helen Attfield** contr Flosshilde **English National Opera Orchestra and Chorus / Reginald Goodall**
Chandos Opera in English CHAN3060 (312' · ADD) Recorded live 1977. Notes and English text included   Ⓕ●

Valkyrie: There's something inevitable, even eternal about Goodall's long-breathed, full-toned, often ideally articulated reading. The ENO management's faith in him was handsomely repaid in his ability to convey his life-time vision to is regular cast and eventually to his audiences. On paper, tempos may look unacceptably slow; in practice there are very few places – perhaps Siegmund's Spring song and Sieglinde's reply – where they seem too tardy. That's largely due to his ability to find the *Hauptstimme* for every paragraph of the music, indeed for a whole act and, perhaps even more, to his ability to persuade players and singers alike to sustain a long line. Listeners familiar only with the Solti cycle will hardly recognise this as the same work.

By 1976 all his singers were entirely inside their respective roles and so able to project a feeling of familiarity with their music that's evident in every bar. Like all the most satisfying sets of the *Ring*, it benefits enormously from being heard live in a theatre acoustic, and here no compromises have to be made, so superb are producer John Mordler's and his team's skills. You seem to be seated in centre stalls imbibing the performance. Rita Hunter bestrides the role of Brünnhilde in a confident manner achieved in relatively modern times only by Birgit Nilsson, whose bright tone and effortless top Hunter's so much resembles. She's also a thoughtful, very human interpreter of the role, keen with her words and investing them with the right import. By her side Bailey confirms that he's as excellent a Wotan as any since Hans Hotter. His reading of the taxing part is virtually tireless and his interpretation combines authority with fatherly concern. Remedios's Siegmund remains one of the most sweetly sung and appealing on disc. If Curphey isn't quite in his class vocally, she offers a deeply felt and sympathetic Sieglinde. Ann Howard is, rightly, a termagant of a Fricka, with a touch of asperity in her tone. Clifford Grant is a sonorous, towering Hunding. The Valkyries, comprising many of the most promising female singers of the day (among them Elizabeth Connell and Anne Evans), acquit themselves very well. All the cast benefit from Andrew Porter's carefully wrought, very singable translation. Overall, a hearty welcome back to a great recording.

Siegfried: That Reginald Goodall idolised Klemperer and Knappertsbusch is evident in every aspect of this weighty, consistently thought-through interpretation; indeed it consoles us for the cycle Klemperer never recorded. The performance is also a reminder of what those then in charge of the ENO – Stephen Arlen, Lord Harewood and Edmund Tracey – had the sense to realise: that here was a unique opportunity to let a seasoned Wagnerian have his head in terms of the time and trouble to prepare a cycle in his own long time-scale. The results are there for all to hear in the total involvement of every member of the orchestra, the lyrical lines of the singers, the superb enunciation of the faultless translation.

Remedios's fresh, lyrical singing is a joy from start to finish; nobody since has equalled him as Siegfried. Dempsey's Mime is at once subtle, funny yet menacing. Those who so praise Tomlinson as Wotan/Wanderer can't have heard Bailey's better sung, articulate and eloquent assumption, another reading not since surpassed. To crown the performance we have Rita Hunter's glorious Brünnhilde, so luminously and keenly sung, just about on a par with Nilsson in the role. They are all wonderfully supported by Goodall and his players. Only in some of Siegfried's Act 1 forging and his struggle with Fafner might one ask for a shade more physical energy, but that's a small price to pay for such understanding of Wagnerian structure. *Rhinegold* and *Twilight of the Gods*: After more than 25 years, these recordings remain gripping for reasons similar to those applying to the other sections of the English Ring reissued by Chandos. In spite of speeds that in other hands would seem often unreasonably slow, or to an extent because of them, Goodall's interpretation has an unerring sense of lyrical and dramatic concentration, every paragraph, phrase and bar carefully considered and executed with loving care by singers and players alike, all so closely coached by their veteran conductor. Above all there's the refined legato observed by all the singers. And the sense of real-life occasion, the theatre's acoustic clearly felt throughout. Andrew Porter's wonderfully lucid translation is given its full due by all the soloists, who once more sound an utterly convincing team. In *Rhinegold* the main honours are carried off by Emile Belcourt's plausible, witty and articulate Loge, Hammond-Stroud's imposing, strongly sung Alberich, Robert Lloyd's sympathetic Fasolt and Bailey's ever-authoritative Wotan. With a pleasing trio of Rhinemaidens headed by Masterson's gleaming Woglinde, Clifford Grant's gloomy, louring Fafner and Anne Collins's deep-throated Erda, the strength of the ENO roster at the time is there for all to hear. In *Twilight*, Hunter and Remedios excel themselves as a more heroic than tragic pair, their singing steady, keen with words and very much in character following so many performances, by 1977, of the complete cycle. The recently departed Aage Haugland offers a welcome souvenir of his career as a louring Hagen. Welsby uncovers the right touches of weak will for Gunther while Curphey is suitably alluring as sister Gutrune. Pring offers an appropriately urgent and strongly sung Waltraute. The Norns could hardly be more strongly cast. By and large, the playing of the ENO Orchestra is of an equally consistent nature, responding to Goodall's long-breathed conducting with playing of beauty and strength adding up to a formidable traversal of the score. The recording, masterminded by John Mordler, need not fear comparison with anything more recent. Indeed the absence of unwanted reverberation and excessive sound effects is most welcome. What we get is the music unvarnished and truthful, for which many thanks again to the foresight of the

ENO directors of the day and to Peter Moores for providing the wherewithal to execute it. Anyone wanting the work in the vernacular, who hasn't already acquired it in its previous incarnations, need not hesitate.

Der Ring des Nibelungen – abridged [H]
Sopranos – **Florence Austral, Noel Eadie, Florence Easton, Tilly de Garmo, Nora Gruhn, Genia Guszalewicz, Frida Leider, Göta Ljüngberg, Elsie Suddaby, Louise Trenton** Mezzos – **Evelyn Arden, Lydia Kindermann, Elfriede Marherr-Wagner, Maartje Offers, Maria Olczewska** Contraltos – **Emmi Leisner, Gladys Palmer, Nellie Walker** Tenors – **Waldemar Henke, Rudolf Laubenthal, Kennedy McKenna, Lauritz Melchior, Albert Reiss, Heinrich Tessmer, Walter Widdop** Baritones – **Howard Fry, Emil Schipper, Deszö Zádor** Bass-baritones – **Rudolf Bockelmann, Friedrich Schorr** Basses – **Ivar Andrésen, Frederick Collier, Arthur Fear, Eduard Habich, Emanuel List** Orchestras – **Berlin State Opera, London Symphony, Vienna State Opera** Conductors – **Karl Alwin, John Barbirolli, Leo Blech, Albert Coates, Lawrance Collingwood, Robert Heger, Karl Muck**
Pearl mono ⑦ GEMMCDS9137 (500 minutes)
Recorded 1926-32   Ⓜ Ⓞ

Here we have, in its entirety, what one might term the Old Testament of *The Ring* recordings, the discs made in the late 1920s and early 1930s in London and Berlin. The operas given the major share are *Die Walküre* and *Siegfried*. The four extracts from *Das Rheingold* are notable only for Friedrich Schorr's magisterial 'Abendlich strahlt'. *Götterdämmerung* suffers most from being reduced to brief extracts, although the passages have been well chosen to give a substantial flavour of the vast work. Coates and the slightly less admirable Blech share the conducting with a few incursions from Heger, the young Barbirolli and others. The playing, mostly by the LSO of the day and the Berlin State Opera Orchestra, is remarkable for its sweep, also for its care over detail, much of which has astonishing clarity considering the dates of the recordings. Coates is particularly successful in projecting the ardour of the *Walküre* love duet and the forging of the sword in *Siegfried*. His speeds are always on the swift side. The singing is the most treasurable aspect of the whole enterprise. Encountering Leider again one realises anew that few, if any, have equalled her combination of vocal security, close-knit line and phrasing, and that matching of feeling with a goddess's natural dignity. Her Brünnhilde is an assumption all aspiring heroic sopranos should closely study (but they don't!). Fledgling Heldentenors would be unwise to listen to Melchior, for they might be inclined to suicide. The sheer élan, strength and verbal acuity of his singing are, and will surely remain, unique. For these reasons alone he's unsurpassable as Siegfried, a role that ideally suited his remarkable attributes. Schorr's Wotan is just as remarkable. Once again tone, technique and text are in perfect accord as his noble bass-baritone fills every passage grandly, movingly.

The sound is vivid throughout these seven (for the price of five), generously filled CDs. The voices are recorded more successfully than in most modern versions of these works, and their relationship with the orchestra is more natural than that favoured in studios today. This is a set no enquiring Wagnerian should be without.

Tannhäuser

Tannhäuser
Peter Seiffert ten Tannhäuser **Jane Eaglen** sop
Elisabeth **Thomas Hampson** bar Wolfram **Waltraud Meier** mez Venus **René Pape** bass Hermann
Gunnar Gudbjörnsson ten Walther **Hanno Müller-Brachmann** bass-bar Biterolf **Stephan Rügamer** ten
Heinrich **Alfred Reiter** bass Reinmar **Dorothea Röschmann** sop Shepherd **Berlin State Opera Chorus; Berlin Staatskapelle / Daniel Barenboim**
Teldec ③ 8573-88064-2 (195' · DDD) Notes, texts and translations included   Ⓕ❍

This must be one of the most opulent recordings made of any opera. The truly remarkable range, perspective and balance of the sound is most appropriate for a work conceived on the grandest scale, yet it retains its focus in the more intimate scenes. The achievement of Barenboim's Berlin chorus, so important in this opera, and orchestra could hardly be bettered. The results are, if nothing else, an audio treat, surpassing the DG version's rather hit-and-miss engineering and the now slightly dated feel of the Decca. Indeed it's Konwitschny's 40-year-old set (EMI) that comes closest to the Teldec in terms of sonic breadth.

Domingo recorded Tannhäuser for DG but shied away from it on stage. The title-role, as many tenors admit, is a real killer. Seiffert is probably its most telling exponent: his performance that combines vocal assurance and emotional involvement to create a vivid portrait of the hero torn between sacred and profane love. The objects of Tannhäuser's attention are impressively portrayed by Waltraud Meier and Jane Eaglen. Meier makes the most of the bigger opportunities and brings her customary tense expression to bear on Venus's utterance, while not quite effacing Christa Ludwig's voluptuous reading for Solti. Eaglen launches herself into the Hall of Song with a rather squally 'Dich teure Halle'; thereafter she sings with much of the inner feeling and prayerful dignity predicated by Wagner for his Elisabeth.

Hermann is a gift of a role for most German basses and René Pape takes his chances with his accustomed feeling for notes and text. Thomas Hampson delivers Wolfram's solos with the expected blend of mellifluous tone and verbal acuity, but his manner is a touch set apart and self-conscious, as if he has had to record these at separate sessions. One reservation about this Teldec set: Barenboim's penchant in meditative passages for very slow speeds. But he paces the

Prelude, the huge ensemble at the end of Act 2 and all the Pilgrim's music with unerring skill.

It's unlikely that we shall ever hear a totally convincing account of what was, after all, Wagner's problem child among his mature works, but this new one has about as much going for it as any in recent times. If you want the Dresden version unaltered by later revisions, and there's something to be said for that choice, the Konwitschny has much to offer in terms of its conductor, sound and much of the solo work.

Tannhäuser (Paris version)
Plácido Domingo ten Tannhäuser **Cheryl Studer** sop Elisabeth **Andreas Schmidt** bar Wolfram **Agnes Baltsa** mez Venus **Matti Salminen** bass Hermann
William Pell ten Walther **Kurt Rydl** bass Biterolf
Clemens Biber ten Heinrich **Oskar Hillebrandt** bass
Reinmar **Barbara Bonney** sop Shepherd Boy **Chorus of the Royal Opera House, Covent Garden; Philharmonia Orchestra / Giuseppe Sinopoli**
DG ③ 427 625-2GH3 (176' · DDD) Notes, text and translation included   Ⓕ❍

Domingo's Tannhäuser is a success in almost every respect. He evokes the erotic passion of the Venusberg scene and brings to it just the right touch of nervous energy. This is boldly contrasted with the desperation and bitterness of the Rome Narration after the hero's fruitless visit to the Pope seeking forgiveness:Domingo's description of how Tannhäuser avoided every earthly delight on his pilgrimage is delivered with total conviction. In between he berates the slightly prissy attitude of his fellow knights on the Wartburg with the dangerous conceit of someone who knows a secret delight that they will never enjoy in their measured complacency. His tenor must be the steadiest and most resplendent ever to have tackled the part, although his German is far from idiomatic. Baltsa also has problems with her German, but she has the range and attack for an awkwardly lying part. It's obviously Sinopoli's concern throughout to bring out every last ounce of the drama in the piece, both in terms of orchestral detail and in his awareness in this opera of the longer line, often sustained by the upper strings. The Philharmonia's violins respond with their most eloquent playing. The kind of *frisson* Sinopoli offers is evident in the anticipatory excitement at the start of Act 2 and the iron control he maintains in the big ensemble later in the same act. Cheryl Studer's secure, beautiful voice has no difficulty coping with Sinopoli's deliberate tempos. She takes her part with total conviction, both vocal and interpretative, phrasing with constant intelligence. Andreas Schmidt is a mellifluous, concerned Wolfram, Salminen a rugged, characterful Landgrave and Barbara Bonney an ideally fresh Shepherd Boy.

The Covent Garden Chorus sings with consistent beauty of sound, and has been sensibly balanced with the orchestra. Domingo and Studer make this version a winner.

Tannhäuser   H
Wolfgang Windgassen ten Tannhäuser **Gré Brouwenstijn** sop Elisabeth **Dietrich Fischer-Dieskau** bar Wolfram **Herta Wilfert** mez Venus **Josef Greindl** bass Hermann **Josef Traxel** ten Walther **Bayreuth Festival Chorus and Orchestra / André Cluytens**
Orfeo d'Or mono ③ C643043D (198' · ADD)
Recorded live at the Festspielhaus, Bayreuth, 9 August 1955   M

This is a revelatory interpretation of a work which isn't easy to bring off. André Cluytens had taken over the musical direction from Eugen Jochum at short notice, and he seems energised by the challenge. Contemporary reviews spoke of the bright, shining strings and the luminous texture of the orchestra, and of the 'intoxicating magic' of the whole concept – all of which is confirmed by this first release. It comes from the second year of what is still considered one of Wieland Wagner's most elevating productions, and the photos in the booklet show us its moving simplicity and sense of dedication.

Director and conductor seem to have persuaded a fine cast to give of their very best. Wolfgang Windgassen, who also takes the title-role in Wolfgang Sawallisch's 1962 recording from Bayreuth, is here in fresher voice and is even more alternately elated and anguished in his delivery than seven years later. His paean to Venus in Act 1 is as heroically fervent as his narration in Act 3, telling of the Pope's rejection of his appeal for pardon, and expressing his own terrible torment of the spirit.

His true love, Elisabeth, is sung with total commitment and vibrant, outgoing voice by Gré Brouwenstijn. Her radiance in 'Dich teure Halle' and her reverence in her Act 3 Prayer could hardly be better done, equalling if not surpassing Anja Silja's rather different but just as valid approach in 1962. The young Fischer-Dieskau is a model Wolfram with a heart of gold and tone to match, each phrase benefiting from his eloquent approach. Josef Greindl, if you can excuse variable intonation, is an imposing Landgraf. Herta Wilfert, a little-known mezzo, is competent but perhaps a little staid as Venus.

Wieland, as later in 1962, opts for the Paris version in Act 1, the Dresden in Act 2. The latter restores Walther's solo, a definite plus when it is sung with such beauty by Josef Traxel. The choral singing is up to the superb standard of Wilhelm Pitz during his long reign as Bayreuth's chorus-master, and Cluytens draws playing of tremendous élan from what sounds like a vintage Bayreuth band. The mono sound is so good that you soon forget any limitations. This set enters the pantheon of great Bayreuth performances on disc.

Tristan und Isolde

Tristan und Isolde   H
Lauritz Melchior ten Tristan **Kirsten Flagstad** sop Isolde **Sabine Kalter** contr Brangäne **Emanuel List**

bass King Marke **Herbert Janssen** bar Kurwenal **Frank Sale** ten Melot **Octave Dua** ten Shepherd **Leslie Horsman** bar Steersman **Roy Devereux** ten Young Sailor **Royal Opera House Chorus, Covent Garden; London Philharmonic Orchestra / Fritz Reiner**
Naxos Historical mono ③ 8 110068/70 (209' · ADD)
Recorded live 1936   S O

This is an improved remastering by Ward Marston of a VAI set which received a warm welcome for preserving the rewarding partnership of Flagstad and Melchior, some would say unsurpassed in their respective roles and here on great form. The soprano, though at the start of her career in the part, is already a fully formed Isolde, and one marvels at Melchior, confirming his stature as the greatest Wagner tenor of all time. The rest of the cast are nothing special. Reiner, after a slow start, provides the right breadth and vitality to the work even when the playing leaves a little to be desired. The then-customary cuts are made in Acts 2 and 3. At super-bargain price (the VAI was at full price) this is an essential purchase for Wagnerians.

Tristan und Isolde
Wolfgang Windgassen ten Tristan **Birgit Nilsson** sop Isolde **Christa Ludwig** mez Brangäne **Martti Talvela** bass King Marke **Eberhard Waechter** bar Kurwenal **Claude Heater** ten Melot **Erwin Wohlfahrt** ten Shepherd **Gerd Nienstedt** bass Helmsman **Peter Schreier** ten Sailor **Bayreuth Festival Chorus and Orchestra / Karl Böhm**
DG The Originals ③ 449 772-2GOR3 (219' · ADD)
Recorded live 1966. Notes, text and translation included   M O O O

Siegfried Jerusalem ten Tristan **Waltraud Meier** mez Isolde **Marjana Lipovšek** mez Brangäne **Matti Salminen** bass King Marke **Falk Struckmann** bar Kurwenal **Johan Botha** ten Melot **Peter Maus** ten Shepherd **Roman Trekel** bar Helmsman **Uwe Heilmann** ten Sailor **Berlin State Opera Chorus; Berlin State Opera Orchestra / Daniel Barenboim**
Teldec ④ 4509-94568-2 (235' · DDD) Recorded 1994. Notes, text and translation included   F O

Böhm's recording is a live Bayreuth performance of distinction, for on stage are the most admired Tristan and Isolde of their time, and in the pit the 72-year-old conductor directs a performance which is unflagging in its passion and energy. He has a striking way in the Prelude and Liebestod of making the swell of passion seem like the movement of a great sea, sometimes with gentle motion, sometimes with the breaking of the mightiest of waves. Nilsson characterises strongly, and her voice with its cleaving-power can also soften beautifully. Windgassen's heroic performance in Act 3 is in some ways the crown of his achievements on record, even though the voice has dried and aged a little. Christa Ludwig is the ideal Brangäne, Waechter a suitably forthright Kurwenal and Talvela an expressive, noble-voiced Marke.

Orchestra and chorus are at their finest.

Over several seasons of conducting the work at Bayreuth, Barenboim has thoroughly mastered the pacing and shaping of the score as a unified entity. Even more important, he has peered into the depths of both its construction and meaning, emerging with answers that satisfy on almost all counts, most tellingly so in the melancholic adumbration of Isolde's thoughts during her narration, in the sadly eloquent counterpoint of bass clarinet, lower strings and cor anglais underpinning King Marke's lament, and in the searingly tense support to Tristan's second hallucination. These are but the most salient moments in a reading that thoughtfully and unerringly reveals the inner parts of this astounding score. The obverse of this caring manner is a certain want of spontaneity, and a tendency to become a shade self-regarding. You occasionally miss the overwhelming force of Furtwängler's metaphysical account or the immediacy and excitement of Böhm's famous live Bayreuth reading. But the very mention of those conductors suggests that Barenboim can live in their world and survive the comparisons with his own perfectly valid interpretation. Besides, he has the most gloriously spacious yet well-focused recording so far of this opera, and an orchestra not only familiar with his ways but ready to execute them in a disciplined and sensitive manner. The recording also takes account of spatial questions, in particular the placing of the horns offstage at the start of Act 2.

Salminen delivers a classic account of Marke's anguished reproaches to Tristan, his singing at once sonorous, dignified and reaching to the heart, a reading on a par with that of his fellow countryman Talvela for Böhm. Meier's Isolde is a vitally wrought, verbally alert reading, which catches much of the venom of Act 1, the visceral excitement of Act 2, the lambent utterance of the Liebestod. Nothing she does is unmusical; everything is keenly intelligent, yet possibly her tone is too narrow for the role. Lipovšek's Brangäne tends to slide and swim in an ungainly fashion, sounding at times definitely overparted. Listening to Ludwig (Böhm) only serves to emphasise Lipovšek's deficiencies. Then it's often hard on the newer set to tell Isolde and Brangäne apart, so alike can be their timbre. As with her partner, Jerusalem sings his role with immaculate musicality; indeed, he may be the most accurate Tristan on disc where note values are concerned, one also consistently attentive to dynamics and long-breathed phrasing. On the other hand, although he puts a deal of feeling into his interpretation, he hasn't quite the intensity of utterance of either Windgassen (Böhm) or, even more, Suthaus (Furtwängler). His timbre is dry and occasionally rasping: in vocal terms alone Suthaus is in a class of his own. Yet, even with reservations about the Isolde and Tristan, this is a version that will undoubtedly hold a high place in any survey of this work, for which one performance can never hope to tell the whole story.

WAGNER TRISTAN UND ISOLDE – IN BRIEF

Lauritz Melchior *Tristan* **Kirsten Flagstad** *Isolde* **Sabine Kalter** *Brangäne* **Chorus of the Royal Opera House; London PO / Fritz Reiner** Naxos ③ 8 110068/70 (209' · AAD)　　Ⓢ●
A 1936 live recording from Covent Garden, chiefly memorable for preserving the classic Melchior/Flagstad team in Reiner's broad reading. Some cuts, and only reasonable sound.

Wolfgang Windgassen *Tristan* **Birgit Nilsson** *Isolde* **Christa Ludwig** *Brangäne* **Bayreuth Festival Chorus and Orchestra / Karl Böhm** DG ③ 449 772-2GOR3 (219' · ADD)　　Ⓜ●●●
✸ A 1966 live recording from Wieland Wagner's legendary Bayreuth production, with Bohm's fast-moving, dramatic conducting and Nilsson's searing, dominant Isolde, Windgassen's restrained Tristan, and Talvela's warm Marke heading a good cast.

Siegfried Jerusalem *Tristan* **Waltraud Meier** *Isolde* **Marjana Lipovšek** *Brangäne* **Berlin State Opera Chorus; Berlin PO / Daniel Barenboim** Teldec ④ 4509 94568-2 (235' · DDD)　　Ⓟ●
Excellent modern studio recording captures Barenboim's warm, balanced reading and a good cast, with the two lovers less vocally resplendent than most rivals, but youngersounding and no less committed.

René Kollo *Tristan* **Margaret Price** *Isolde* **Brigitte Fassbaender** *Brangäne* **Leipzig Radio Chorus; Staatskapelle Dresden/ Carlos Kleiber** DG ③ 477 5355GOR3 (235' · DDD)　　Ⓜ
Kleiber's quicksilver reading makes full use of studio recording to create a lighter-voiced, less effortful performance, Margaret Price's cut-glass Isolde in particular. Finely cast, very beautiful, but somewhat artificial.

Ludwig Suthaus *Tristan* **Kirsten Flagstad** *Isolde* **Blanche Thebom** *Brangäne* **Chorus of the Royal Opera House; Philharmonia Orchestra / Wilhelm Furtwängler** EMI ④ 585873-2 (255' · AAD)　　Ⓑ●
Unarguably a classic, with Furtwangler's richly flowing reading, even if Flagstad sounds rather matronly (with a couple of high notes provided by Elisabeth Schwarzkopf) and Suthaus is more dependable than exciting.

Jon Vickers *Tristan* **Helga Dernesch** *Isolde* **Christa Ludwig** *Brangäne* **Berlin Deutsche Oper Chorus; Berlin PO / Herbert von Karajan** EMI ④ 769319-2 (246' · ADD)　　Ⓜ
Despite peculiar recorded perspectives, at mid-price Karajan's sleekly beautiful version is worth considering, with a fine cast headed by Vickers's toweringly tragic Tristan and Dernesch's most feminine Isolde.

Additional recommendation

Tristan und Isolde
Mödl Isolde **Vinay** Tristan **Hotter** Kurwenal **Weber**
King Mark **Bayreuth Festival Orchestra / Karajan**
Urania ③ URN22.218 (231' · ADD) Recorded live
1952   Ⓜ

This set is a must – a reading far superior to
Karajan's studio effort; in improved sound it
houses psychological studies of the lovers from
Mödl and Vinay both at the height of their vocal
powers, and given ideal support from Karajan.

Sir William Walton   British 1902-1983

*Walton was educated at Oxford, and was a member
of the Sitwells circle from the beginning of the 1920s.
His first important work was Façade, setting poems
by Edith Sitwell for reciter and sextet and evidently
modelled on Pierrot lunaire while looking more to
Les Six in its wit and jazziness. The next works
again showed Parisian connections: with Stravinsky
and Honegger in the overture Portsmouth Point,
with Prokofiev in the Viola Concerto. Then, without
losing the vividness of his harmony and orchestration, he responded to the English Handelian tradition in Belshazzar's Feast and to Sibelius in his First
Symphony, though here Elgar too is invoked, as in
much of his later music. The Violin Concerto (1939)
confirmed this homecoming. The next decade was
comparatively unproductive, except in film music
(Henry V, Hamlet). At the end of it he married and
moved to Ischia, where all his later works were composed. These include the opera Troilus and Cressida,
found theatrically effective if conservative in
approach when given at Covent Garden in 1954,
and his one-act opera The Bear, a parodistic
Chekhovian extravaganza, given at Aldeburgh in
1967. Among the late orchestral works are a Cello
Concerto, cooler and more serene than the earlier
concertos, a Second Symphony and miscellaneous
pieces including a finely worked set of Hindemith
Variations, which shows an improvisatory character
typical of his late music.*   GROVEmusic

Concertos, Symphonies, etc

Centenary Edition
Cello Concerto[el]. Viola Concerto[dl]. Violin
Concerto[cl]. Symphonies – No 1 in B flat minor[al];
No 2[bl]. Scapino[fl]. Variations on a Theme by
Hindemith[hl]. Crown Imperial[jn]. Orb and Sceptre[k].
Henry V – Suite[m]. Facade Suites[gl] – No 1; No 2.
Coronation Te Deum[i]. Belshazzar's Feast[ln]
[n]**Bryn Terfel** bass-bar [c]**Tasmin Little** vn [d]**Paul
Neubauer** va [e]**Robert Cohen** vc [i]**Timothy Byram-
Wigfield** org [n]**L'inviti;** [in]**Waynflete Singers;**
[i]**Winchester Cathedral Choir; Bournemouth
Symphony Orchestra and** [n]**Chorus /** [l]**Andrew
Litton,** [ik]**David Hill**
Decca ④ 470 508-2DC4 (298' · DDD) Recorded
1992-6. [dgh]Also available separately as Decca
470 200-2   Ⓜ ●●

Decca's four-disc Walton Edition offers consistently fine versions of all the composer's most
important orchestral works, some of them
unsurpassed, in full, brilliant sound. Andrew
Litton, the conductor of all but two minor
items, is central to the success of the whole. Like
his compatriot, André Previn, he's idiomatic,
with a natural feeling for the jazzy syncopations
at the heart of so much of Walton's music.

This issue brings together the three Litton
discs previously issued, with important additions. The third disc was issued separately, and
contains outstanding versions, never previously
released, of the Viola Concerto and *Hindemith
Variations* plus the two *Façade* Suites. Where
most latterday interpreters of the Viola Concerto have taken a very expansive view of the
lyrical first movement, Paul Neubauer comes
nearer than anyone else to the original interpreters on disc, Frederick Riddle and William
Primrose.

With Neubauer – his tone firm and precise,
clean rather than fruity – the result is more persuasive than other modern versions, with no
suspicion of expressive self-indulgence. The
brisker passages are taken faster than is now
usual; the impact is tauter and stronger without
losing romantic warmth. He relaxes seductively
for the hauntingly beautiful epilogue, using the
widest dynamic range. Litton encourages wide
contrasts in the orchestra, the big *tutti*s bringing
an element of wildness in the brassy syncopations, the ensemble kept crisp and incisive. The
Hindemith Variations also brings a taut and purposeful performance with contrasts in both
dynamic and speed heightened to extremes.
Façade is predictably fun, though there's some
danger of the warm acoustic softening some of
the sharpness of these witty parodies.

Two of the other discs remain the same as with
their original release, with Tasmin Little's
heartfelt reading of the Violin Concerto coupled with Litton's outstanding account of the
Second Symphony, the finest digital version yet,
as well as *Scapino*, while Robert Cohen's
thoughtful reading of the Cello Concerto is
coupled with the richly recorded First Symphony. Litton's powerful account of *Belshazzar's Feast* with Bryn Terfel brings fresh, cleanly
focused choral sound in an atmospheric acoustic
that clearly lets you appreciate the terracing
between the different groupings of voices. That
aptly comes with the coronation music – and the
Henry V Suite, with David Hill, chorus-master
in *Belshazzar*, ably standing in for Litton in the
Coronation Te Deum and *Orb and Sceptre*.

Cello Concerto

Cello Concerto. Symphony No 1 in B minor
Lynn Harrell vc **City of Birmingham Symphony
Orchestra / Sir Simon Rattle**
HMV Classics HMV5 74320-2 (74' · DDD) Recorded
1990-91   Ⓢ Ⓑ ●●

Simon Rattle's version of Walton's First Symphony is as intelligent and dynamic a traversal as one would expect from this talented figure. Texturally speaking, the inner workings of Walton's score are laid bare as never before, aided by what sounds like a meticulously prepared CBSO. Some may find a touch of contrivance about Rattle's control of dynamics in the scorching first movement, but there's absolutely no gainsaying the underlying tension or cumulative power of the whole. Under Rattle the Scherzo darts menacingly (the most convincing account of this music since the classic 1966 Previn account), while the slow movement is an unusually nervy, anxious affair. Certainly, the finale is superbly athletic and lithe, though by now one is beginning to register that EMI's sound is, for all its transparency and natural perspective, perhaps a little lightweight for such enormously red-blooded inspiration. Overall, though, Rattle's is a very strong account and his disc's claims are enhanced by the coupling, a wholly admirable performance of the same composer's luxuriant Cello Concerto. Here Rattle and Lynn Harrell form an inspired partnership, totally dedicated and achieving utter concentration throughout – no mean feat in this of all works which demand so much from both performers and listeners.

Cello Concerto[a] Violin Concerto[b]
[a]**Tim Hugh** vc [b]**Dong-Suk Kang** vn **English Northern Philharmonia / Paul Daniel**
Naxos 8 554325 (60' · DDD)　　　Ⓢ Ⓢ Ⓞ

Tim Hugh, outstanding in every way, gives a reading of the Concerto that's the most searching yet. More than direct rivals he finds a thoughtfulness, a sense of mystery, of inner meditation in Walton's great lyrical ideas – notably the main themes of the outer movements and the yearning melody of the central section of the second movement Scherzo. Most strikingly his *pianissimos* are more extreme. The openings of both the outer movements are more hushed than ever heard before on disc, with Hugh in inner intensity opting for broader speeds than usual. Not that he dawdles, as the overall timings of each movement make plain, and the bravura writing finds him equally concentrated, always sounding strong and spontaneous in the face of any technical challenges.

In the Violin Concerto Dong-Suk Kang plays immaculately with fresh, clean-cut tone, pure and true above the stave. If this isn't quite so warmly Romantic an approach as that of Kyung-Wha Chung or Tasmin Little, there's nothing cold or unsympathetic about his reading, with the *rubato* in the Neapolitan second theme of the Scherzo delectably pointed. Many will also applaud the way that Kang opts for speeds rather faster and more flowing than have latterly been favoured. That follows the example of Heifetz as the original interpreter, and Kang similarly relishes the bravura writing, not least in diamond-sharp articulation in the Scherzo.

As in their previous Walton recordings, Paul Daniel and the English Northern Philharmonia play with equal flair and sympathy, so that the all-important syncopations always sound idiomatic. But though the recorded textures are commendably clear, the strings are too distantly balanced, lacking weight, so that moments where the violins are required to surge up warmly sound thin – hardly the fault of the players. An excellent coupling, though, with the Cello Concerto offering new depths of insight.

Viola Concerto in A minor

Viola Concerto in A minor. Symphony No 2. Johannesburg Festival Overture
Lars Anders Tomter va **English Northern Philharmonia / Paul Daniel**
Naxos 8 553402 (61' · DDD)　　　Ⓢ

This disc opens with one of the wittiest, most exuberant performances of the *Johannesburg Festival Overture*: Daniel encourages the orchestra's virtuoso wind and brass soloists to point the jazz rhythms idiomatically, making the music sparkle. The Viola Concerto is just as delectably pointed, the whole performance magnetic. Tomter's tone, with its rapid flicker-vibrato, lacks the warmth of Kennedy's (reviewed below), but the vibrato is only obtrusive in that upper-middle register and his intonation is immaculate, his attack consistently clean, to match the crisp ensemble of the orchestra. Although he adopts relatively measured speeds both for the Scherzo and the jaunty opening theme of the finale, the rhythmic lift brings out the scherzando jollity of the latter all the more.

Daniel's keen observance of dynamic markings is again brought out in the stuttering fanfare theme of the Scherzo, with muted trumpets and trombones for once played *pianissimo* as marked. The close of the slow epilogue has never been recorded with such a profound hush as here, subsiding in darkness, and the recording team is to be complimented on getting such beautiful sound, clean with plenty of bloom. Paul Daniel adopts a relatively broad tempo in the Symphony's first movement, which makes less impact than in Andrew Litton's powerful Decca version, and the flowing tempo for the central slow movement makes for a lighter, less passionate result too. The finale, with its brassy first statement of the Passacaglia theme, brings fine dynamic contrasts, but again Litton and others produce a fatter, weightier sound, which on balance is preferable. Yet Daniel's view is a very valid one, to round off most convincingly an invaluable addition to the Walton discography.

Walton Viola Concerto[a] **Bruch** Violin and Viola Concerto in E minor, Op 88[b]. Romance, Op 85[c] Kol Nidrei, Op 47[c]
Yuri Bashmet va [b]**Viktor Tretyakov** vn London

Symphony Orchestra /[a]André Previn, [bc]Neeme Järvi
RCA Red Seal 09026 63292-2 (64' · DDD) Recorded 1994, 1996   Ⓕ**OO**

Presumably, this outstanding version of the Walton Viola Concerto from Yuri Bashmet, warm and intense, recorded in 1994, was held up for lack of a suitable coupling. Having the three Bruch works may seem odd, but with the passionate Bashmet the mixture works well. After all, both composers are at their most richly lyrical, and though in style they're worlds apart, the Bruch Double Concerto and the Walton Concerto date from successive decades, written respectively in 1911 and 1929. In the Walton, Bashmet adopts a very slow speed for the opening Andante, but is fast and incisive in the vigorous third subject, and the central Scherzo brings a dazzling display of virtuosity. In the finale, Bashmet finds plenty of fun in Walton's scherzando writing, but then draws out the epilogue at a very slow speed, beautifully sustained, not just by him but by Previn and the orchestra, the ideal accompanists.

The rarely played Bruch Double Concerto is better known in the version for clarinet and viola. As performed here by Bashmet with his pure-toned violinist colleague, Viktor Tretyakov, it gains in sensuousness from having the solo instruments closely allied rather than sharply contrasted. It's amazing what a fund of melodic invention Bruch kept into his seventies, not just in this concerto but in the glorious Romance for viola and orchestra of 1912. Bashmet again gives a heartfelt performance, as he does of *Kol Nidrei*.

With Bashmet at his finest, and the LSO playing beautifully for both conductors, this is a disc to recommend to anyone with a taste for romantic viola music.

Violin Concerto

Violin Concerto. Sonata for Violin and Piano (orch. Palmer). Two Pieces (orch. Palmer)
Lydia Mordkovitch vn **London Philharmonic Orchestra / Jan Latham-Koenig**
Chandos CHAN9073 (69' · DDD) Recorded 1991   Ⓕ**O**

Lydia Mordkovitch gives the most expansive account of the Walton concerto on disc, sustaining spacious speeds warmly and persuasively. The very opening finds her deeply meditative in the soaring melody of the first theme, yet her double-stopping in the bravura passages designed for Heifetz is irresistibly purposeful, never sounding too slow or laboured. Latham-Koenig may not have quite the spark that Previn brings to the orchestral writing in both the Chung (Decca) and Kennedy (EMI) versions, but he's keenly idiomatic both in his feeling for sharply syncopated rhythms and in flexible rubato for Walton's Romantic melodies. In the central *Presto Scherzo*, above all a virtuoso display piece, the speed is no slower than that

chosen by most rivals, while the Spanish dance-rhythm of the first contrasting interlude couldn't sound more aptly slinky, whether from soloist or orchestra. The characteristically warm Chandos recording is a help, too.

The unique coupling makes this version particularly attractive to Walton devotees, since Christopher Palmer's arrangements of the Sonata and the two short pieces are full of Waltonian fingerprints. Recommended.

Sinfonia concertante

Walton Sinfonia concertante[a]. Façade – Suites Nos 1-3[a]. Siesta[b]. Portsmouth Point[a] **Arnold** Popular Birthday[a]
Eric Parkin pf **London Philharmonic Orchestra / [a]Jan Latham-König, [b]Bryden Thomson**
Chandos CHAN9148 (59' · DDD) Recorded 1990-92 Ⓕ

The *Sinfonia concertante* (1926-7), with its sharply memorable ideas in each movement and characteristically high voltage, has never had the attention it deserves, and that's all the more regrettable when there's such a dearth of attractive British piano concertos. The soloist, Eric Parkin, is perfectly attuned to the idiom, warmly melodic as well as jazzily syncopated. He points rhythms infectiously and shapes melodies persuasively, though the recording sets the piano a little backwardly, no doubt to reflect the idea that this isn't a full concerto.

Jan Latham-König proves most understanding of the composer's 1920s idiom, giving the witty *Façade* movements just the degree of jazzy freedom they need. The Third Suite, devised and arranged by Christopher Palmer, draws on three apt movements from the *Façade* entertainment, ending riotously with the rag-music of 'something lies beyond the scene'. That's a first recording, as is Constant Lambert's arrangement of the overture *Portsmouth Point*. *Siesta* is given an aptly cool performance under Thomson, and the *Popular Birthday* is Malcolm Arnold's fragmentary linking of 'Happy Birthday to You' with the 'Popular Song' from *Façade*, originally written for Walton's 70th birthday. The impact of some of the pieces, notably in *Façade*, would have been even sharper had the recording placed the orchestra a fraction closer.

Symphonies

Symphony No 1. Partita
English Northern Philharmonia / Paul Daniel
Naxos 8 553180 (64' · DDD) Recorded 1994   Ⓢ Ⓢ**OO**

Daniel demonstrates clearly here his natural affinity with Walton's music. In the sustained paragraphs of the First Symphony he knows unerringly how to build up tension to breaking point, before resolving it, and then building again – a quality vital above all in the first and third movements. He's freer than many in his use of *rubato* too, again often a question of building and resolving tension, as well as in the degree of elbow-room he allows for jazzy syncopations, always idiomatic. This symphony, with its heavy orchestration, would certainly have benefited from rather drier sound, but well-judged microphone balance allows ample detail through. Only occasionally do you feel a slight lack of body in high violin tone, a tiny reservation. Daniel's reading of the *Partita* brings out above all the work's joyfulness. It may not be quite as crisp in its ensemble as that of the dedicatees (Szell and the Cleveland Orchestra), but the degree of wildness, with dissonances underlined, proves a positive advantage in conveying enjoyment. In the slow movement Daniel at a relatively slow speed is markedly more expressive than those brilliant models, again a point which makes the performance more endearing.

Irrespective of price, this is a version of the much-recorded symphony that competes with the finest ever, and outshines most.

Symphony No 1 in B flat minor[a]. Violin Concerto[b]. Viola Concerto[c]. Cello Concerto[d]. Sinfonia concertante[e]

[b]**Jascha Heifetz** vn [c]**Yuri Bashmet** va [d]**Gregor Piatigorsky** vc [e]**Kathryn Stott** pf [ac]**London Symphony Orchestra / [a]André Previn, [c]Neeme Järvi; [b]Philharmonia Orchestra / William Walton; [d]Boston Symphony Orchestra / Charles Munch; [e]Royal Philharmonic Orchestra / Vernon Handley**
RCA Red Seal [b]mono ② 74321 92575-2 (145' · ADD/[ce]DDD) Recorded [a]1966, [c]1998, [d]1959, [b]1950, [e]1989
Ⓜ**OO**

RCA's two-disc collection includes the première recording of the Cello Concerto with Piatigorsky – who commissioned the work – and the Boston Symphony under Charles Munch. Here is a high-powered reading, given an upfront recording, commendably full and open for 1959. Similarly Heifetz, who commissioned the Violin Concerto, remains supreme as an interpreter of that work, urgent beyond any rival as well as passionate. Here he plays with the composer conducting the Philharmonia. The 1950 mono recording has been nicely opened up, putting more air around the sound, making the absence of stereo a minimal drawback. The other two concertante works come in digital versions: Kathryn Stott, originally for Conifer, adventurously going back to the original more elaborate version of the *Sinfonia concertante*, and Yuri Bashmet bringing his yearningly Slavonic temperament and masterly virtuosity to the Viola Concerto.

Bashmet's partners are the ideal combination of Previn and the LSO, and it's Previn's vintage version of the First Symphony with the LSO of an earlier generation that sets the seal on the whole package. Previn has never been matched, let alone surpassed. Also remarkable is the clarity, definition and sense of presence of the 1966 recording, with the stereo spectrum more sharply focused than in the digital recordings.

Symphony No 2[c]. Variations on a Theme by Hindemith[d]. Partita[c]. Violin Concerto[b]. Johannesburg Festival Overture[e]. Capriccio burlesco[e]. Belshazzar's Feast[a]

[a]**Walter Cassel** bar [b]**Zino Francescatti** vn [a]**Rutgers University Choir; [cd]Cleveland Orchestra / George Szell; [ab]Philadelphia Orchestra / Eugene Ormandy; [e]New York Philharmonic Orchestra / André Kostelanetz**
Sony ② SB2K 89934 (143' · ADD) Recorded 1959-73Ⓑ

Sony's two-disc Essential Classics collection brings together major offerings from three previous Walton CDs, all of them American. Outstanding are the vintage Szell performances with the Cleveland Orchestra, in sheer brilliance never likely to be outshone. The composer himself was bowled over by Szell's 1961 Second Symphony, a work till then rather discounted, which drew an interpretation not just brilliant but passionate. In Szell's high-powered reading the *Hindemith Variations*, too, hang together superbly, and the *Partita*, a Cleveland commission, is scintillating from first to last.

André Kostelanetz turns the *Capriccio burlesco* into a sparkling comedy overture, a work he was the first to conduct, and the *Johannesburg Festival Overture* is made to sparkle too, arguably the finest of the Walton overtures. Both the Violin Concerto and *Belshazzar's Feast* are given expressive performances by Ormandy conducting the Philadelphia Orchestra. In the Concerto Zino Francescatti is powerful and passionate with his rapid, slightly nervy vibrato, while in *Belshazzar* choir and soloist are as committed as any British performers, even if their pronunciation of 'Isaiah' is pure American, the second syllable rhyming with 'day'. The sound is typically up-front and not as warm as it might be, though with plenty of atmosphere. Buy it for Szell's Second – an account Walton described as 'fantastic and stupendous'.

Short Orchestral Works

Overtures – Johannesburg Festival; Portsmouth Point; Scapino. Capriccio burlesco. The First Shoot (orch Palmer). Granada Prelude. Prologo e Fantasia. Music for Children. Galop final (orch Palmer)
London Philharmonic Orchestra / Bryden Thomson
Chandos CHAN8968 (70' · DDD)　　　　Ⓕ**O**

Enthusiasts for Walton's music may justifiably complain that there isn't enough of it, but usually concede that what there is is readily available in good recorded performances. However, thanks to the dedicated and skilful work of Christopher Palmer, still more is now coming to light. How many people have ever heard *The First Shoot*, a miniature ballet written for a C B Cochran show in 1935, the *Granada Prelude* devised for that television company in the 1960s, or the *Prologo e Fantasia*, which was Walton's last work, written for Rostropovich and his National Symphony Orchestra of Washington? Such fresh and welcome items as these appear along with familiar material such as the splendidly open-air, nautical overture *Portsmouth Point* that Walton wrote nearly 40 years earlier, at the very start of his career. The Cochran piece, as orchestrated by Palmer, has five little sections that are delightfully jazzy in a way that recalls *Façade*; the only thing to regret is that there isn't more of it. All this music is in the excellent hands of Bryden Thomson and the LPO. The recording is richly toned, taking some edge off the composer's characteristically sharp scoring.

Spitfire Prelude and Fugue. Sinfonia concertante[a].
Variations on a Theme by Hindemith. March – The
History of the English Speaking Peoples
[a]**Peter Donohoe** *pf* **English Northern Philharmonia
/ Paul Daniel**
Naxos 8 553869 (53' · DDD)　　　　　　Ⓢ**OO**

Naxos opts for the original version of the *Sinfonia concertante* rather than Walton's revision, with piano writing and orchestration slimmed down. Walton himself, before he died, suggested such a return. As soloist Peter Donohoe plays with power and flamboyance, brought home the more when the piano is very forwardly balanced, too much so for a work which doesn't aim to be a full concerto, leaving the orchestra a little pale behind. Even so, hopefully this account, broad in the first movement, flowing in the central *Andante*, will persuade others to take it up, young man's music built on striking, colourful ideas, used with crisp concision.

Paul Daniel is splendid at interpreting the jazzy syncopations with the right degree of freedom, and in the *Spitfire Prelude and Fugue* he adds to the impact by taking the big march tune faster than many, similarly demonstrating that *The History of the English Speaking Peoples March*, buried for rather too long, is a match for Walton's other ceremonial marches. Best of all is the performance of the *Hindemith Variations*, given here with winning panache. The strings of the English Northern Philharmonia may not be as weighty as in some rival versions, but the articulation is brilliant, and the complex textures are all the more transparent. The fire and energy of the performance has never been surpassed on disc.

Façade

Walton Façade – An Entertainment[a] **Lambert**
Salome – Suite
[a]**Eleanor Bron,** [a]**Richard Stilgoe** *spkrs* **Nash
Ensemble** (Paul Watkins *vc*, Philippa Davies *fl*,
Richard Hosford *clar*, John Wallace *tpt*, Martin
Robertson [a]*sax*, Simon Lembrick *perc*) / **David
Lloyd-Jones**
Hyperion CDA67239 (72' · DDD) Texts included　Ⓕ**O**

The *Façade* entertainment – poems by Edith Sitwell to music by the then-unknown William Walton – was an amorphous creation, a collection of over 40 poems and settings built up over the years between 1922 and 1928.

Pamela Hunter in her disc on the Koch Discovery label did a marvellous job collecting all the surviving settings, adding recitations of the poems for which the music had been lost. The difference is that, instead of being recited on the disc, the texts of those extra poems are printed in the booklet, with revealing comments. Also, David Lloyd-Jones has devised an order for the 34 items (including the opening fanfare) which is arguably the best yet, avoiding the anticlimactic effect of *Façade 2* being separated. Eleanor Bron and Richard Stilgoe make an excellent pair of reciters, and the recording in a natural acoustic balances them well – not too close. They inflect the words more than Edith Sitwell and early interpreters did, but still keep a stylised manner, meticulously obeying the rhythms specified in the score. Not everyone will like the way Stilgoe adopts accents – Mummerset for 'Mariner Man' and 'Country Dance', Scots for 'Scotch Rhapsody', and something like southern-state American for the jazz rhythms of 'Old Sir Faulk' – but he's the most fluent *Façade* reciter on disc so far, with phenomenally clear articulation. Eleanor Bron is also meticulous over rhythm, in slower poems adopting a trance-like manner, which is effective and in style.

Under David Lloyd-Jones the brilliant sextet of players from the Nash Ensemble couldn't be more idiomatic.

Walton Façade[c]　　　　　　　　　　Ⓗ
Britten Serenade, Op 31[a]. Folksongs[b] – The Bonny
Earl o' Moray; Avenging and Bright; The Last Rose of
Summer; Sally in our Alley
[abc]**Peter Pears** *ten/spkr* [c]**Dame Edith Sitwell** *spkr*
[a]**Dennis Brain** *hn* [b]**Benjamin Britten** *pf* [a]**Boyd Neel
String Orchestra / Benjamin Britten;** [c]**English
Opera Group Ensemble / Anthony Collins**
Decca 468 801-2DM (74' · ADD/DDD) Recorded
1953-54　　　　　　　　　　　　　　Ⓜ**O**

This recording of *Façade* was a consummate technical and artistic miracle of Decca's mono era. Edith Sitwell and Pears deliver the engagingly preposterous words with bravura insouciance, Collins conducting the English Opera Group Ensemble with matching wit and flair, and even today the 1953 recording sounds almost like stereo. It's coupled with one of the great highlights of the whole Britten discography, that first magical recording of the *Serenade*, with Pears in fresh, youthful voice and Dennis Brain's marvellous horn obbligatos. What playing! The transfer is faithful; but why didn't Decca remove the surface rustle and, above all, the clicks?

Piano Quartet

Piano Quartet[a]. Violin Sonata[b]. Anon in love[c].
Passacaglia[d]. Façade – Valse[e]

^c**John Mark Ainsley** *ten* ^c**Craig Ogden** *gtr*
^a**Nash Ensemble** (^bMarianne Thorsen *vn* Lawrence Power *va* ^dPaul Watkins *vc* ^{be}Ian Brown *pf*)
Hyperion CDA67340 (76' · DDD) Text included Ⓕ**OO**

This excellent Hyperion issue brings together a wide-ranging group of Walton's chamber works, from his earliest major work, the Piano Quartet, originally written when he was 16, to his last instrumental piece, the *Passacaglia*, which he composed for Rostropovich when he was nearly 80. As a substantial bonus there's the little song cycle for tenor and guitar, *Anon in Love*, as well as the two shorter pieces.

That gives an immediate advantage to this issue over the Chandos Walton Edition, and though some will prefer the weightier readings of those two major works on Chandos, the Nash versions are very winning; they're generally more volatile and spontaneous-sounding, no doubt reflecting the players' experience of performing them in concert.

Helped by a not quite so immediate recording, the extra lightness and clarity brings an element of fantasy into such a movement as the *Scherzo* of the Piano Quartet and an extra tenderness into the lovely slow movement. Nowhere else does Walton so enthusiastically use modal thematic material, starting with the mysterious opening theme, which the Nash players take very reflectively at a speed much slower than the movement's main tempo, *Allegramente*. It's an astonishingly confident work for so young a composer, with adventurous writing for the strings that belies the fact that Walton was no string-player.

The Violin Sonata, a more elusive work, long underestimated, is given an equally persuasive performance, with Marianne Thorsen, accompanied by Ian Brown, freely expressive. John Mark Ainsley is totally undaunted by the taxing vocal writing of *Anon in Love*, originally designed for Peter Pears. And Craig Ogden is an ideal accompanist, totally idiomatic, adding sparkle to the vigorous songs in this offbeat collection. Though Ian Brown gives a slightly sluggish account of *Façade*'s 'Valse' – in the awkward piano transcription ascribed to Walton himself – cellist Paul Watkins crowns the disc with a fine reading of the solo *Passacaglia*.

String Quartets

Piano Quartet in D minor^a. String Quartet in A minor
^a**Peter Donohoe** *pf* **Maggini Quartet** (Laurence Jackson, David Angel *vns* Martin Outram *va* Michal Kaznowski *vc*)
Naxos 8 554646 (58' · DDD) Ⓢ**OO**

The Maggini Quartet give refined and powerful performances in this Naxos release. The opening of the 1947 String Quartet is presented in hushed intimacy, making the contrast all the greater when Walton's richly lyrical writing emerges in full power. There's a tender, wistful quality here, which culminates in a rapt, intense

account of the slow movement, where the world of late Beethoven comes much closer than most interpreters have appreciated. The poignancy of those two longer movements is then set against the clean bite of the second movement Scherzo and the brief hectic finale, with their clear and transparent textures. With Peter Donohoe a powerful and incisive presence, and the Maggini Quartet again playing most persuasively, the early Piano Quartet – an astonishing achievement for a teenage composer – is also given a performance of high contrasts, enhanced by a refined recording which conveys genuine pianissimos that are free from highlighting. If, in the first three movements, the pentatonic writing gives little idea of the mature Walton to come, some characteristic rhythmic and other devices are already apparent. Even the pentatonicry suggests that the boy had been looking at the Howells Piano Quartet rather than any Vaughan Williams. It's in the finale that one gets the strongest Waltonian flavour in vigorously purposeful argument, though there the echoes are different, and Stravinsky's *Petrushka* is an obvious influence. The only reservation is that, refined as the recording is, the piano is rather too forwardly balanced.

String Quartets – 1922; A minor
Emperor Quartet (Martin Burgess, Clare Hayes *vns* Fiona Bonds *va* William Schofield *vc*)
Black Box BBM1035 (58' · DDD) Ⓕ**O**

The Emperor Quartet are very good indeed, and their account of the extraordinary First Quartet is especially convincing. Here we have the very young Walton under the influence of Bartók's first two quartets, flirting with Bergian rather than Schoenbergian atonality and having the admirable cheek to write a finale consisting of a slow and a fast fugue, the latter making clear reference to Beethoven's *Grosse Fuge*. But genuine Waltonian lyricism also emerges – and here the Emperor are more ardent and sweeter-toned than the Gabrieli (on Chandos) – alongside strong implications that if he had followed either of these 'wrong turnings' he would have become a pretty formidable member of Bartók's or Berg's 'school'.

Some of the evidence for that is in the rich palette of string colour that the Emperor draw from the central *scherzo* and in the far greater urgency they bring to the two fugues. In the A minor Quartet there's less to choose between the two groups, but the Emperor's rhythmic alertness and their relaxation into the 'serenade with guitar accompaniment' of the slow movement is especially winning. An excellent recording, too. You should hear the Emperor Quartet even if you aren't especially interested in Walton: they could persuade you otherwise.

Belshazzar's Feast

Belshazzar's Feast^a. Coronation Te Deum. Gloria^b

[b]Ameral Gunson *contr* [b]Neil Mackie *ten* [a]Gwynne
Howell, [b]Stephen Roberts *bars* Bach Choir;
Philharmonia Orchestra / Sir David Willcocks
Chandos CHAN8760 (62' · DDD) Recorded 1989.
Texts included   Ⓕ○

With Sir David Willcocks in charge of the choir
which he has directed since 1960, one needn't
fear that the composer's many near-impossible
demands of the chorus in all three of these masterpieces won't be met with elegance and poise.
In *Belshazzar* there's also a predictably fine balance of the forces to ensure that as much detail
as possible is heard from both chorus and
orchestra, even when Walton is bombarding us
from all corners of the universe with extra brass
bands and all manner of clamorous percussion
in praise of pagan gods. Such supremely musical
concerns bring their own rewards in a work that
can often seem vulgar. The revelation here is
the sustained degree of dramatic thrust, exhilaration and what Herbert Howells called 'animal
joy' in the proceedings. How marvellous, too, to
hear the work paced and scaled to avoid the
impression of reduced voltage after the big
moments. Gwynne Howell is the magnificently
steady, firm and dark toned baritone. The *Gloria* and *Coronation Te Deum* are informed with
the same concerns: accuracy and professional
polish are rarely allowed to hinder these vital
contributions to the British choral tradition.
The recording's cathedral-like acoustic is as
ideal for the *Te Deum*'s ethereal antiphonal
effects, as it is for *Belshazzar*'s glorious spectacle; and Chandos matches Willcocks's care for
balance, bar by bar.

Belshazzar's Feast[b]. Viola Concerto[a].   Ⓗ
Facade – Suite No 1[c]; Suite No 2[d]
[b]Dennis Noble *bar* [a]Frederick Riddle *va*
[b]Huddersfield Choral Society; [a]London
Symphony Orchestra; [b]Liverpool Philharmonic
Orchestra; [cd]London Philharmonic Orchestra /
William Walton
Pearl mono GEM0171 (76' · ADD) Recorded [b]1943,
[c]1936, [d]1938   Ⓜ○○

A fine CD transfer of Walton's own première
recording of *Belshazzar's Feast* is coupled here
with two other important first recordings of his.
In some ways these have never been surpassed
musically. That applies especially to the *Belshazzar* performance, made with lavish resources
at the height of the war. The recording was
made over two weekends in 1943, in sessions
supervised by Walter Legge. The challenge of a
work then regarded as difficult for an amateur
choir was superbly taken, with Walton's conducting even more electric and impulsive than
in his later stereo version, and with Dennis
Noble unsurpassed as the baritone soloist. The
'writing on the wall' sequence has never
sounded creepier, despite the limitations of
mono sound, and the choral and brass sounds
are full and immediate, with the words of the
chorus commendably clear.

The *Facade Suites* in their orchestral form
stand among the demonstration recordings of
the period, while the première recording of the
Viola Concerto just as strikingly makes its
claims against any version recorded since. Even
more than William Primrose in his subsequent
recordings, Riddle brings expressive warmth as
well as tautness. There's an outstanding CD
transfer on Dutton – a fraction fuller-bodied
than this with a little less hiss – but no one will
be disappointed with the sound on Pearl.

Additional recommendation

Coupled with: Job
Terfel *bass-bar;* BBC Singers; BBC Symphony
Orchestra / A Davis
Warner Apex 0927-44394-2 (78' · DDD)   Ⓑ
  Bryn Terfel makes an electrifying soloist in Davis's
  recommendable version of *Belshazzar*, and brings
  the important solo utterances vividly before us.
  Walton's rarely performed ballet is equally fine.

Coronation Te Deum

Coronation Te Deum. A Litany: Drop, drop slow tears.
Magnificat and Nunc Dimittis. Where does the
uttered music go? Jubilate Deo. Henry V – Touch her
soft lips and part; Passacaglia. Cantico del Sole. The
Twelve.Set me as a seal upon thy heart. Antiphon.
Missa Brevis
Christopher Whitton *org* St John's College Choir,
Cambridge / Christopher Robinson
Naxos 8 555793 (66' · DDD)   Ⓢ○○

This latest addition to Naxos's English Church
Music series isn't just a first-rate bargain but
provides a distinctive alternative to the Finzi
Singers in the Chandos Walton Edition, in its
use of boy trebles. The presence of boys' voices
consistently brings extra freshness to the St
John's Choir's performances, giving them the
sort of bite one can imagine the composer having in mind, with Waltonian syncopations wonderfully idiomatic in their crisp articulation.
Smaller in scale, with the organ set behind the
choir, these more intimate readings also convey
more clearly the impression of church performances, a clear advantage in the liturgical items
above all, not just the delightful *Missa brevis*, but
the *Jubilate*, and the *Magnificat and Nunc dimittis*. You might argue that this collegiate choir is
on the small side for the big ceremonial *Te
Deum* written for the Queen's Coronation in
1953, but there, more than ever, the freshness
and bite make for extra clarity hard to achieve
with bigger forces. With Robinson and the St
John's Choir the words aren't just sharply
defined but are given life, with subtle *rubato* and
fine shading of dynamic.

Coronation Te Deum[ab]. A Queen's Fanfare[b].
A Litany (three versions). The Twelve[a]. Set me as
a seal upon thine heart. Magnificat and Nunc
Dimittis[a]. Where does the uttered music go?

Jubilate Deo[a]. Missa Brevis[a]. Cantico del sole. Make
we joy now in this fest. King Herod and the cock.
All this time. What cheer? Antiphon[ab]
[a]**James Vivian** org **Polyphony;** [b]**The Wallace
Collection / Stephen Layton**
Hyperion CDA67330 (77' · DDD) Notes and texts
included ⓕⓞ

This disc has important bonuses that all Walton
devotees will value. The inclusion of The Wallace Collection brings an immediate advantage
in the first choral item, the *Coronation Te Deum*,
when the extra bite of brass adds greatly to the
impact of a piece originally designed for very
large forces in Westminster Abbey. Brass also
adds to the impact of the final item, *Antiphon*,
one of Walton's very last works, setting George
Herbert's hymn *Let all the world in every corner
sing*. The new disc also includes Walton's four
carols, which makes this as comprehensive a
collection of Walton's shorter choral pieces as
could be imagined. As for the performances and
recording, the professional group, Polyphony,
with sopranos very boyish, have many of the
advantages that the St John's Choir offer on
Naxos in bright choral sound set in an ecclesiastical atmosphere. The acoustic of Hereford
Cathedral is a little washy in places, and the balance of some of the solo voices is odd at times,
yet the merits of these performances far outweigh any slight reservations, with the professional singers a degree more warmly expressive
than the all-male St John's Choir.

The Bear

The Bear
Della Jones mez Madame Popova **Alan Opie** bar
Smirnov **John Shirley-Quirk** bar Luka **Northern
Sinfonia /Richard Hickox**
Chandos CHAN9245 (53' · DDD) Recorded 1993. Text
included ⓕⓞ

If Walton's sense of humour was firmly established from the start in *Façade*, his one-acter,
The Bear, among his later works brings out very
clearly how strong that quality remained
throughout his life. In this Chekhov tale, Walton times the melodramatic moments marvellously – notably the climactic duel between the
mourning widow and her husband's creditor
(the bear of the title) – and Hickox brings that
out most effectively. Walton also deftly heightens the farcical element by introducing dozens
of parodies and tongue-in-cheek musical references, starting cheekily with echoes of Britten's
Midsummer Night's Dream. Hickox brings out
the richness of the piece as well as its wit, helped
by the opulent Chandos recording, which still
allows words to be heard clearly. The casting of
the three characters is as near ideal as could be.
Della Jones is commanding as the affronted
widow, consistently relishing the melodrama
like a young Edith Evans. Alan Opie as
Smirnov, 'the bear' is clean-cut and incisive,
powerfully bringing out the irate creditor's

changing emotions, while John Shirley-Quirk,
still rich and resonant, is very well cast as the old
retainer, Luka.

Troilus and Cressida

Troilus and Cressida
Judith Howarth sop Cressida **Arthur Davies** ten
Troilus **Clive Bayley** bass Calkas **Nigel Robson** ten
Pandarus **Alan Opie** bar Diomede **James Thornton**
bar Antenor **David Owen-Lewis** bass Horaste
Yvonne Howard mez Evadne **Peter Bodenham** ten
Priest **Keith Mills** ten Soldier **Bruce Budd** bass First
Watchman **Stephen Dowson** bass Second
Watchman **Brian Cookson** ten Third Watchman
**Chorus of Opera North; English Northern
Philharmonia / Richard Hickox**
Chandos ② CHAN9370/1 (133' · DDD) Notes and
text included ⓕⓞⓞⓞ

Ⓖ *Troilus and Cressida* is here powerfully
presented as an opera for the central
repertory, traditional in its red-
blooded treatment of a big classical subject. Few
operas since Puccini's have such a rich store of
instantly memorable tunes as this. Walton
wrote the piece in the wake of the first great
operatic success of his rival, Benjamin Britten.
What more natural than for Walton, by this
time no longer an *enfant terrible* of British music
but an Establishment figure, to turn his back on
operas devoted like Britten's to offbeat subjects
and to go back to an older tradition using a classical love story, based on Chaucer (not Shakespeare). Though he was praised for this by critics in 1954, he was quickly attacked for being
old-fashioned. Even in the tautened version of
the score offered for the 1976 Covent Garden
revival – with the role of the heroine adapted for
the mezzo voice of Dame Janet Baker – the
piece was described by one critic as a dodo. Yet
as Richard Hickox suggests, fashion after 40
years matters little, and the success of the Opera
North production in January 1995 indicated
that at last the time had come for a big, warmly
Romantic, sharply dramatic work to be appreciated on its own terms. This recording was made
under studio conditions during the run of the
opera in Leeds. The discs confirm what the live
performances suggested, that Walton's taut-
ening of the score, coupled with a restoration of
the original soprano register for Cressida,
proved entirely successful.

Hickox conducts a performance that's magnetic from beginning to end. The scene is
atmospherically set in Act 1 by the chorus, initially off-stage, but then with the incisive Opera
North chorus snapping out thrilling cries of
'We are accurs'd!'. The first soloist one hears is
the High Priest, Calkas, Cressida's father, about
to defect to the Greeks, and the role is superbly
taken by the firm, dark-toned Clive Bayley.
Troilus's entry and his declaration of love for
Cressida bring Waltonian sensuousness and the
first statements of the soaring Cressida theme.
Arthur Davies isn't afraid of using his head voice

for *pianissimos*, so contrasting the more dramatically with the big outbursts and his ringing top notes. This is a young-sounding hero, Italianate of tone. Similarly, Judith Howarth's Cressida is quite girlish, and she brings out the vulnerability of the character along with sweetness and warmth. After Calkas has defected to the Greeks, her cry of 'He has deserted us and Troy!' conveys genuine fear, with her will undermined. All told, although some fine music has been cut, the tautened version is far more effective both musically and dramatically, with no longueurs. The role of Diomede, Cressida's Greek suitor, can seem one-dimensional, but Alan Opie in one of his finest performances on record sharpens the focus, making him a genuine threat, with the element of nobility fully allowed. As Antenor, James Thornton sings strongly but is less steady than the others, while Yvonne Howard is superb in the mezzo role of Evadne, Cressida's treacherous servant and confidante. Not just the chorus but the orchestra of Opera North, the English Northern Philharmonia, respond with fervour.

Naturally and idiomatically they observe the Waltonian *rubato* and the lifting of jazzily syncopated rhythms which Hickox as a dedicated Waltonian instils, echoing the composer's own example. As for the recorded sound, the bloom of the acoustic enhances the score, helped by the wide dynamic range.

Peter Warlock   British 1894-1930

Warlock was self-taught, though he was in contact with Delius from 1910, and was a friend of Van Dieren, Moeran and Lambert. Under his original name of Heseltine he wrote on music and edited English works of the Elizabethan era. As Warlock he produced a large output of songs, some dark, desolate and bleakly intense (The Curlew for tenor and sextet, 1922), others rumbustious, amorous or charming, but all informed by an exceptional sensitivity to words and high technical skill. He also wrote choral music and a few instrumental pieces (notably Capriol Suite for strings, 1926, based on 16th-century dances).   **GROVE**music

Choral Works

Warlock A Cornish Carol. I saw a fair maiden. Benedicamus Domino. The Full Heart. The Rich Cavalcade. Corpus Christi. All the flowers of the spring. As Dewe in Aprylle. Bethlehem Down. Cornish Christmas Carol **Moeran** Songs of Springtime. Phyllida and Corydon
Finzi Singers / Paul Spicer
Chandos CHAN9182 (76' · DDD) Recorded 1992.
Texts included   Ⓕ**O**

The Peter Warlock of the evergreen *Capriol Suite* and the boisterous songs seems a world away from the introverted and intense artist of these unaccompanied choral carols. Perhaps

Warlock's real genius was an ability to create profound expression in short musical structures, but even the more outgoing pieces – the joyful *Benedicamus Domino* and the *Cornish Christmas Carol*, with its gentle hint at 'The First Nowell' – have an artistic integrity which raises them high above the level of the syrup of modern-day carol settings. Given performances as openly sincere and sensitive as these, few could be unmoved. In the two Moeran madrigal suites there's an indefinable Englishness – the result of a deep awareness of tradition and love of the countryside. The Finzi Singers' warm-toned, richly expressive voices capture the very essence of this uniquely lovely music.

Songs

The Wind from the West. To the Memory of a   F
Great Singer. Take, o take those lips away. As ever I saw. The bayley berith the bell away. There is a lady. Lullaby. Sweet content. Late summer. The Singer. Rest sweet nymphs. Sleep. A Sad Song. In an arbour green. Autumn Twilight. I held love's head. Thou gav'st me leave to kiss. Yarmouth Fair. Pretty Ring Time. A Prayer to St Anthony. The Sick Heart. Robin Goodfellow. Jillian of Berry. Fair and True. Ha'nacker Mill. The Night. My Own Country. The First Mercy. The Lover's Maze. Cradle Song. Sigh no more, ladies. Passing by. The Contented Lover. The Fox
John Mark Ainsley ten **Roger Vignoles** pf
Hyperion CDA66736 (69' · DDD) Recorded 1994.
Texts included   Ⓕ**O**

Philip Heseltine, so strangely renamed, didn't facilitate either the singing or the playing of his songs. For the voice they have a way of passing awkwardly between registers, and, though the high notes aren't very high, they tend to be uncomfortably placed. The pianist, caught for long in a pool of chromatics, suddenly finds his hands flying in both directions. Yet, for the singer with the control of breath and command of voice that John Mark Ainsley so splendidly employs, and for a pianist with Roger Vignoles's sureness of touch and insight, they must be wonderfully satisfying, for there's such a love of song implicit in them and they speak with such a personal voice. The programme here is arranged chronologically, 1911-30. Favourite sources are early and Elizabethan poems, and the verse of contemporaries such as Belloc, Symons and Bruce Blunt. Even the earliest setting, *The Wind from the West*, has the characteristic touch of a lyrical impulse, directly responsive to words, and a fastidious avoidance of strophic or harmonic banality. Often a private unease works within the chromaticism, as in the *Cradle Song*, yet nothing could be more wholehearted in gaiety when he's in the mood (*In an arbour green, Robin Goodfellow, Jillian of Berry*). Ainsley sings with fine reserves of power as well as softness; he phrases beautifully, and all the nuance that's so essential for these songs (in 'Sleep,' say) is most sensitively judged. Vignoles is entirely at one with singer and composer.

Carl Maria von Weber
German 1786-1826

Weber studied in Salzburg (with Michael Haydn), Munich (JN Kalcher)and Vienna (Abbé Vogler), becoming Kapellmeister at Breslau (1804) and working for a time at Württemberg (1806) and Stuttgart (1807). With help from Franz Danzi, intellectual stimulation from his friends Gänsbacher, Meyerbeer, Gottfried Weber and Alexander von Dusch and the encouragement of concert and operatic successes in Munich (especially Abu Hassan), Prague and Berlin, he settled down as opera director in Prague (1813-16). There he systematically reorganised the theatre's operations and built up the nucleus of a German company, concentrating on works, mostly French, that offered an example for the development of a German operatic tradition. But his searching reforms (extending to scenery, lighting, orchestral seating, rehearsal schedules and salaries) led to resentment. Not until his appointment as Royal Saxon Kapellmeister at Dresden (1817)and the unpre-cedented triumph of Der Freischütz (1821) in Berlin and throughout Germany did his championship of a true German opera win popular support. Official opposition continued, both from the Italian opera establishment in Dresden and from Spontini in Berlin; Weber answered critics with the grand heroic opera Euryanthe (1823, Vienna). His rapidly deteriorating health and his concern to provide for his family induced him to accept the invitation to write an English opera for London; he produced Oberon at Covent Garden in April 1826. Despite an enthusiastic English reception and every care for his health, this last journey hastened his decline; he died from tuberculosis, at 39.

Weber's Romantic leanings can be een in the novel emotional flavour of his music and its relevance to emergent German nationalism, his delicate receptivity to nature and to literary and pictorial impressions, his parallel activities as critic, virtuoso pianist and Kapellmeister, his dedication to the evolution of a new kind of opera uniting all the arts and above all his wish to communicate feeling. His role as a father-figure of musical Romanticism was acknowledged by those who succeeded him in the movement, from Berlioz and Wagner to Debussy and Mahler. His melodic and harmonic style is rooted in classical principles, but as he matured he experimented with chromaticism (the diminished 7th chord was a particular favourite). He also was among the subtlest of orchestrators, writing for unusual but dramatically apt and vivid instrumental combinations. All his most successful music, including the songs and concertos, is to some degree dramatically inspired.

Weber won his widest audience with Freischütz, outwardly a Singspiel celebrating German folklore and country life, using an idiom touched by German folksong. Through his skilful use of motifs and his careful harmonic, visual and instrumental designs notably for the Wolf's Glen scene, the outstanding example in music of the early Romantic treatment of the sinister and the supernatural – he gave this work a new creative status. Euryanthe, despite a weak libretto, further advances the unity of harmonic and formal structures, moving towards continuous, freely

composed opera. In Oberon Weber reverted to separate numbers to suit English taste, yet the work retains his characteristically subtle motivic handling and depiction of both natural and supernatural elements. Of his other works, some of the German songs, the colouristic Konzertstück for piano and orchestra, the dramatic clarinet and bassoon concertos and the virtuoso Grand duo concertant for clarinet and piano deserve special mention.

GROVEmusic

Clarinet Concertos

Clarinet Concertos – No 1 in F minor, J114; No 2 in E flat, J118. Grand duo concertant, J204
Sharon Kam *cl* **Itamar Golan** *pf* **Leipzig Gewandhaus Orchestra / Kurt Masur**
Warner Elatus 0927-46744-2 (64' · DDD)   Ⓜ●

Teldec provides a good programme in having the two Weber clarinet concertos coupled with a work which is virtually another concerto but with piano accompaniment, the *Grand duo concertant*. Sharon Kam is a young Israeli whom Kurt Masur heard in her home country, immediately inviting her back to Leipzig to play concertos. She was contracted by Teldec in 1994, but this is the first disc entirely devoted to her playing, revealing her as a most imaginative and individual artist, using the widest tonal and dynamic range, and with a very sure technique, with every note cleanly in place. As the opening movement of the First Concerto demonstrates, she has the gift of magicking a phrase, and one mark of her magnetism and flair is the way she can hold tension over an exaggerated pause or tenuto. Most remarkable of all is the dark intensity of Kam's account of the slow minor-key *Romanza* of the Second Concerto, with the soloist clearly the one insisting on a very measured tempo, when Masur's preference is always towards flowing *Andantes*. She's similarly impressive in the *Grand duo concertant*, though there the piano tone of Itamar Golan is on the shallow side.

Clarinet Concertos – Nos 1 & 2. Clarinet Concertino in E flat, J109. Clarinet Quintet in B flat, J182
Kari Kriikku *cl* **New Helsinki Quartet** (Jan Söderblom, Petri Aarnio *vns* Ilari Angervo *va* Jan-Erik Gustafsson *vc*) **Finnish Radio Symphony Orchestra / Sakari Oramo**
Ondine ODE895-2 (76' · DDD)   Ⓕ●

Kari Kriikku's are brilliant performances of works that more or less reinvented the clarinet as an instrument of brilliance, at any rate in the hands and under the flashing fingers of Weber's friend Heinrich Bärmann. The formidable difficulties hold no terrors for Kriikku; indeed, wonderfully fluent as his playing is in, for instance, the fireworks music that ends the Second Concerto and the Quintet, one almost wants there to be more sense of difficulties overcome as witness of the virtuoso as hero. But that would be to quibble, especially when Kriikku has such a wide range of expression and such an intelligent approach to the music. He plays the First Concerto as a slightly tense, witty work, giving the Adagio a long-breathed lyricism and the finale humour as well as wit. The only questionable element is his own over-long cadenza to the first movement. The Second Concerto is treated as a more lyrical and dramatic work, with an elegant *polacca* finale, and there's a beautiful length of phrasing in the *Andante*, as there is in the 'Fantasia' movement of the Quintet. Kriikku neatly touches off the mock-sinister intervention in the Quintet's finale, refusing to take it seriously. He's well accompanied throughout.

Grand duo concertant

Grand duo concertant, J204[b]. Clarinet Quintet in B flat, J182[a]. Seven Variations on a Theme from 'Silvana', J128[b]
Pascal Moraguès *cl* [b]**Mari Izuha** *pf* [a]**Pražák Quartet** (Vaclav Remes, Vlastimil Holek *vns* Josef Klusoň *va* Michal Kaňka *vc*)
Praga Digitals PRD250164 (61' · DDD)   Ⓕ

In his note Pierre Barbier comments that the *Grand duo concertant* 'can be understood as a concerto without orchestra'. It would be fairer to say 'double concerto without orchestra', and it's certainly no sonata. In no other recording do the two soloists so fully respond to each other, in subtlety of *rubato*, in swift and witty changes of mood, in delicacy of balance between the instruments. It's a work that really needs the timbre of a contemporary piano, especially in the *con molto affetto* section of the finale, with its churning piano tremolos, but the players have such an attentive ear for one another (as well as a dashing individuality that can make them seem enthusiastic rivals), that it all comes out as brilliantly as Weber must have intended when he wrote the piece for himself and his cavalier friend Heinrich Bärmann.

The Quintet is rather less successful than this piece or the lighthearted *Silvana* variations. Pascal Moraguès's clear, bright tone, attractively as he phrases and irresistibly as he brings off the cascading music of the closing section, can lack something of the warmth Weber admired in Bärmann's playing. David Shifrin (on Delos) also couples these three works. While he's excellent in the Quintet he can't, with David Golub, match this scintillating performance of the *Grand duo concertant*.

Piano Sonatas

Piano Sonatas –No 1 in C, J138; No 2 in A flat, J199. Rondo brillante in E flat, J252, 'La gaité'. Invitation to the Dance, J260
Hamish Milne *pf*
CRD CRD3485 (76' · DDD) Recorded 1991   Ⓜ⒪

Weber's piano music, once played by most pianists, has since suffered neglect and even the famous *Invitation to the Dance* is now more often heard in its orchestral form. Since he was a renowned pianist as well as a major composer, the neglect seems odd, particularly when other pianist composers such as Chopin and Liszt are at the centre of the concert repertory; but part of the trouble may lie in the difficulty of the music, reflecting his own huge hands and his tendency to write what the booklet-essay calls 'chords unplayable by others'. Hamish Milne makes out a real case for this music, and his playing of the two sonatas is idiomatic and resourceful, even if one can't banish the feeling that Weber all too readily used the melodic and harmonic formulae of 18th-century galanterie and simply dressed them up in 19th-century salon virtuosity. From this point of view, a comparison with Chopin's mature sonatas or Liszt's magnificent single essay in the form reveals Weber as a lightweight. A hearing of the first movement in the First Sonata will quickly tell you if this is how you may react, while in its Presto finale you may praise a Mendelssohnian lightness but also note a pomposity foreign to that composer. Leaving aside the musical quality of these sonatas, this is stylish playing which should win them friends. The *Rondo brillante* and *Invitation to the Dance* make no claim to be other than scintillating salon music, and are captivating in Milne's shapely and skilful performances. The recording is truthful and satisfying.

Lieder

Meine Lieder, meine Sänge, J73. Klage, J63. Der Kleine Fritz an seine jungen Freunde, J74. Was zieht zu deinem Zauberkreise, J86. Ich sah ein Röschen am Wege stehn, J67., Er an Sie, J57. Meine Farben, J62. Liebe-Glühen, J140. Über die Berge mit ungestüm, Op 25 No 2. Es stürmt auf der Flur, J161. Minnelied, J160. Reigen, J159. Sind es Schmerzen, J156. Mein Verlangen, J196. Wenn ich ein Vöglein war', J233. Mein Schatzerl ist hübsch, J234. Liebesgruss aus der Ferne, J257. Herzchen, mein Schätzchen, J258. Das Veilchen im Thale, J217. Ich denke dein, J48. Horch'!, Leise horch', Geliebte, J56. Elle était simple et gentilette, J292
Dietrich Fischer-Dieskau *bar* **Hartmut Höll** *pf* Claves CD50-9118 (52' · DDD) Recorded 1991. Texts and translations included   ⒻⓄ

'In my opinion the first and most sacred duty of a song-writer is to observe the maximum of fidelity to the prosody of the text that he is setting.' Weber was writing in defence of a number he composed for an obscure play, but his words can stand as an apologia for his 90-odd songs. His contribution to German song has been underrated, for his ideas were different from those of his contemporaries. Fischer-Dieskau used to resist suggestions that he might take up Weber's songs, and it's good that he has now done so, even late in his career. Always sensitive to words, he now responds with the subtlety of understanding that comes from many years of closeness to German poetry. Only very occasionally is there the powerful emphasis on the single expressive word that sometimes used to mar his interpretations, keeping them too near the surface of the poetry. He can still use individual colour marvellously: the tonal painting of 'blue', 'white' and 'brown' in *Meine Farben* is exquisitely done. But more remarkable, here and in other songs, is the manner in which he follows the novel melodic lines which Weber has contrived out of the poetry.

Ein steter Kampf is a masterly example; so is *Was zieht zu deinem Zauberkreise*, one of the few songs in which Weber enters Schubertian territory; so are *Es türmt auf der Flur* and *Liebesgruss aus der Ferne*. Not even Fischer-Dieskau can quite bring off the coy *Der Kleine Fritz* by slightly sending it up (the only hope), and there's something a bit hefty about *Reigen*, a very funny wedding song full of 'Heissa, lustig!' and 'Dudel, didel!', though Hartmut Höll does wonders with the clanking accompaniment. Höll varies his tone so much here from the warmth and depth of his touch elsewhere that one wonders if the engineers did not take a small hand: why not? These are charming, touching, witty, colourful verses, often by minor figures of Weber's circle, and they drew from him music that eightens their point. Fischer-Dieskau's intelligent artistry could not more eloquently support the praise for Weber from Wilhelm Müller, poet of *Die schöne Müllerin* and *Winterreise*, as 'master of German song'.

Der Freischütz

Der Freischütz
Peter Schreier *ten* Max (Hans Jörn Weber) **Gundula Janowitz** *sop* Agathe (Regina Jeske) **Edith Mathis** *sop* Aennchen (Ingrid Hille) **Theo Adam** *bass* Caspar (Gerhard Paul) **Bernd Weikl** *bar* Ottokar (Otto Mellies) **Siegfried Vogel** *bass* Cuno (Gerd Biewer) **Franz Crass** *bass* Hermit **Gerhard Paul** *spkr* Samiel **Günther Leib** *bar* Kilian (Peter Hölzel) **Leipzig Radio Chorus; Staatskapelle Dresden / Carlos Kleiber**
DG The Originals ② 457 736-2GOR2 (130' · ADD)
Recorded 1973. Notes, text and translation included
Ⓕ **OO**

Carlos Kleiber's fine set of *Der Freischütz* earns reissue on CD for a number of reasons. One is the excellence of the actual recorded sound with a score that profits greatly from such attention. Weber's famous attention to details of orchestration is lovingly explored by a conductor who has taken the trouble to go back to the score in manuscript and observe the differences between that and most of the published versions. So not only do we hear the eerie sound of low flute thirds and the subtle contrast of unmuted viola with four-part muted violins in Agathe's 'Leise, leise', among much else, with a new freshness and point, but all the diabolical effects in the Wolf's Glen come up with a greater sense of

depth, down to the grisliest detail. The beginning of the Overture, and the opening of the Wolf's Glen scene, steal upon us out of a primeval silence, as they should. All this would be of little point were the performance itself not of such interest. There's a good deal to argue about but this is because the performance is so interesting. Even if some of Kleiber's tempos are possibly unwise, they spring from a careful, thoughtful and musical mind. The singing cast is excellent, with Gundula Janowitz an outstanding Agathe to a somewhat reflective Max from Peter Schreier, at his best when the hero is brought low by the devilish machinations; Edith Mathis is a pretty Aennchen, Theo Adam a fine, murky Caspar. The dialogue, spoken by actors, is slightly abbreviated and occasionally amended. Kleiber's reading produces much new insight to a magical old score.

Additional recommendation

Grümmer Agathe **Hopf** Max **Streich** Aennchen Ⓗ **Proebstl** Caspar **Poell** Ottokar **Böhme** Hermit **Cologne Radio Symphony Orchestra and Chorus / E Kleiber**
Koch Schwann mono ② 316422 (125' · ADD)
Recorded 1955   Ⓕ
Grümmer is in superb form here, and Streich a model Aennchen. Under Kleiber's inspired direction they make out a good case for this profoundly satisfying performance, different from but just as valid as son Carlos's later version on DG. One of the most desirable on disc – it sounds as if it might have been recorded yesterday.

Anton Webern   Austrian 1883-1945

Webern studied at Vienna University under Adler (1902-6), taking the doctorate for work on Isaac; in composition he was one of Schoenberg's first pupils (1904-8), along with Berg. Like Berg, he developed rapidly under Schoenberg's guidance, achieving a fusion of Brahms, Reger and tonal Schoenberg in his orchestral Passacaglia, already highly characteristic in its modest dynamic level and its brevity. But he was closer than Berg in following Schoenberg into atonality, even choosing verses by the same poet, George, to take the step in songs of 1908-9. His other step was into a conducting career which he began with modest provincial engagements before World War I.

After the war he settled close to Schoenberg in Mödling and took charge of the Vienna Workers Symphony Concerts (1922-34). Meanwhile he had continued his atonal style, mostly in songs:the relatively few instrumental pieces of 1909-14 had grown ever shorter, ostensibly because of the lack of any means of formal extension in a language without key or theme. However, the songs of 1910-25 show a reintroduction of traditional formal patterns even before the arrival of serialism (especially canonic patterns, no doubt stimulated, as was the instrumenta-

tion of many of these songs, by Pierrot lunaire), to the extent that the eventual adoption of the 12-note method in the Three Traditional Rhymes (1925) seems almost incidental, making little change to a musical style that was already systematised by strict counterpoint. However, Webern soon recognised that the 12-note principle sanctioned a severity and virtuosity of polyphony that he could compare with that of the Renaissance masters he had studied. Unlike Schoenberg, he never again sought to compose in any other way. Rather, the highly controlled, pure style of his Symphony appears to have represented an ideal which later works could only repeat, showing different facets. His use of the series as a source of similar motifs, especially in instrumental works, merely emphasises the almost geometrical perfection of this music, for which he found literary stimulus in Goethe and, more nearly, in the poetry of his friend and neighbour Hildegard Jone, whose words he set exclusively during his last dozen years. With Schoenberg gone, Berg dead and himself deprived of his posts, Webern saw Jone as one of his few allies during World War II. He was shot in error by a soldier after the end of hostilities, leaving a total acknowledged output of about three hours' duration..

GROVEmusic

Complete works, Opp 1-31

Passacaglia, Op 1 (**London Symphony Orchestra / Pierre Boulez**). Entflieht auf leichten Kähnen, Op 2 (**John Alldis Choir / Boulez**). Five Songs from 'Der siebente Ring', Op 3. Five Songs, Op 4 (**Heather Harper** sop **Charles Rosen** pf). Five Movements, Op 5 (**Juilliard Quartet**). Six Pieces, Op 6 (**LSO / Boulez**). Four Pieces, Op 7 (**Isaac Stern** vn **Rosen** pf). Two Songs, Op 8 (**Harper** sop **chamber ensemble / Boulez**). Six Bagatelles, Op 9 (**Juilliard Qt**). Five Pieces, Op 10 (**LSO / Boulez**). Three Little Pieces, Op 11 (**Gregor Piatigorsky** vc **Rosen** pf). Four Songs, Op 12 (**Harper** sop **Rosen** pf). Four Songs, Op 13. Six Songs, Op 14 (**Harper** sop **chamber ens / Boulez**). Five Sacred Songs, Op 15. Five Canons on Latin Texts, Op 16 (**Halina Lukomska** sop **chamber ens / Boulez**). Three Songs, Op 18 (**Lukomska** sop **John Williams** gtr **Colin Bradbury** cl **/ Boulez**). Two Songs, Op 19 (**John Alldis Ch, members LSO / Boulez**). String Trio, Op 20 (**members Juilliard Qt**). Symphony, Op 21 (**LSO / Boulez**). Quartet, Op 22 (**Robert Marcellus** cl **Abraham Weinstein** sax **Daniel Majeske** vn **Rosen** pf **/ Boulez**). Three Songs from 'Viae inviae', Op 23 (**Lukomska** sop **Rosen** pf). Concerto, Op 24 (**members LSO / Boulez**). Three Songs, Op 25 (**Lukomska** sop **Rosen** pf). Das Augenlicht, Op 26 (**John Alldis Ch, LSO / Boulez**). Piano Variations, Op 27 (**Rosen** pf). String Quartet, Op 28 (**Juilliard Qt**). Cantata No 1, Op 29 (**Lukomska** sop **John Alldis Ch; LSO / Boulez**). Variations, Op 30 (**LSO / Boulez**). Cantata No 2, Op 31 (**Lukomska** sop **Barry McDaniel** bar **John Alldis Ch; LSO / Boulez**). Five Movements, Op 5 –orchestral version (**LSO / Boulez**) Bach (orch Webern) Musikalischen Opfer, BWV1079 – Fuga (Ricercata) No 2 (orch Webern) Deutsche Tänze, D820 (**Frankfurt Radio Orchestra / Anton Webern**) (recorded live 1932) **Various artists**

Sony Classical ③ SM3K45845 (223' · ADD). Recorded 1967-72. Notes, texts and translations included

Ⓜ●○○

Webern is as 'classic' to Boulez as Mozart or Brahms are to most other conductors, and when he's able to persuade performers to share his view the results can be remarkable – lucid in texture, responsive in expression. There are many sides to Webern, despite his well-nigh exclusive concern with miniature forms, and although this set isn't equally successful in realising them all, it leaves you in no doubt about the music's variety and emotional power, whether the piece is an ingenious canon-by-inversion or a simple, folk-like Lied. From a long list of performers one could single out Heather Harper and the Juilliard Quartet for special commendation; and the smooth confidence of the John Alldis Choir is also notable. The recordings were made over a five-year period, and have the typical CBS dryness of that time. Even so, in the finest performances which Boulez himself directs, that remarkable radiance of spirit so special to Webern is vividly conveyed. It's a fascinating bonus to hear Webern imself conducting his Schubert arrangements – music from another world, yet with an economy and emotional poise that Webern in his own way sought to emulate.

Passacaglia, Op 1

Webern Passacaglia, Op 1. Six Pieces, Op 6. Five Pieces, Op 10. Variations, Op 30 **Bach** (arr Webern) Musikalisches Opfer, BWV1079 –Ricercar a 6 **Schoenberg** A Survivor from Warsaw, Op 46 **Gottfried Hornik** narr **Vienna State Opera Chorus; Vienna Philharmonic Orchestra / Claudio Abbado** DG 431 774-2GH (50' · DDD) Recorded 1989-92. Text and translation included

Ⓕ●

This is a fine reading of the rarely heard and forcefully dramatic *Variations*, Op 30. Abbado and the VPO respond to the romantic intensity of the early *Passacaglia*, and the sets of expressionist miniatures are even more convincing in their blend of delicacy and power. The fourth piece from Op 6, the closest Webern came to concentrating the essence of a Mahlerian funeral march, and ending with an ear-splitting percussion *crescendo*, is all the more effective for Abbado's refusal to set a self-indulgently slow tempo. Technically, these recordings outshine the competition, though there are other memorable interpreters – Boulez especially in Op 30. Given the evident rapport between Webern and Abbado it seems odd that the disc doesn't include more of Webern's music. The Bach arrangement is nevertheless an ear-opening exercise in passing Baroque counterpoint through a kaleidoscope of expressionist tone colours, and Schoenberg's *A Survivor from Warsaw* retains its special power to move and disturb.

Webern Passacaglia, Op 1. Five Pieces, Op 5. Six Pieces, Op 6. Im Sommerwind **Bach** (orch Webern) Musikalisches Opfer, BWV1079 –Ricercar a 6 **Schubert** (orch Webern) Deutsche Tänze, D820 **Berlin Philharmonic Orchestra / Pierre Boulez**
DG 447 099-2GH (67' · DDD) Recorded 1993-4 Ⓕ〇

With the exception of the Bach and Schubert arrangements, this is all relatively early, pre-serial Webern, yet Boulez devotes as much care and as much affection to the D minor *Passacaglia* and to the undeniably immature but irresistibly luscious *Im Sommerwind* as to the far more characteristic Op 5 and Op 6 pieces. Boulez doesn't imply that the mature Webern is present here in embryo; but he does perhaps make us ask how much of that later music is, like this, inspired by nature.

To be reminded of Brahms by the *Passacaglia* is no less appropriate. This is a Janus of a piece, looking back not only to Brahms's Fourth Symphony but beyond, and at the same time moving onwards from the delicate chamber passages in *Im Sommerwind* towards the 'orchestral chamber music' of Op 5 and Op 6. Boulez looks both ways too, with rich orchestral amplitude and expressive phrasing (very broad *rubato*) but he also notices Webern's already marked liking for transparent textures, quiet subtleties of string colour and the sound of the muted trumpet. And yes: heard in this context the shorter pieces are a logical progression. They are intensely expressive, with a wide range of emotion often within a few bars; no wonder Boulez prefers the earlier, richer scoring of Op 6. He obviously loves their Mahler-derived dissolution of the boundary between orchestral and chamber music, and encourages the orchestra to play with great tonal beauty. Those qualities recur in the Bach and Schubert arrangements. The recordings are warm and clean.

Five Pieces, Op 5

Webern String Quartet (arr Poppen). Five Pieces, Op 5. **Bach** Musical Offering, BWV1079 – Ricercar a 6 (orch Webern). Cantata No 4, Christ lag in Todesbanden, BWV4[a]
[a]**Hilliard Ensemble; Munich Chamber Orchestra / Christoph Poppen**
ECM New Series 461 912-2 (69' · DDD) Ⓕ〇〇〇

Symmetry, the cyclic evolution of a musical germ and the idea of birth in the midst of death: all are fundamental to this disc. Webern's motivically determined orchestration of the Ricercar from Bach's late *The Musical Offering*, where single lines change colour by the bar, opens and closes the programme. Christoph Poppen's orchestration of Webern's 1905 String Quartet soars and surges with an ardour that befits this early but significant masterpiece. Like Webern in Bach, Poppen knows how and where to taper his forces, while his players respond with obvious dedication. Bach's Cantata *Christ lag in Todesbanden*

grows, as Herbert Glossner reminds us, from a 'primordial cell' of a single semitone motive. Eight stanzas each end with a 'Halleluja', as unalike in shade and meaning as the strands of Webern's 'Ricercar', so magnificent is the young Bach's handling of the texts. Like Joshua Rifkin and more recently Paul McCreesh, Poppen performs choral Bach with single voices; he also encourages a string playing style that largely dispenses with vibrato, so that when you cross from Webern's Quartet to Bach's BWV4 you could as well be switching to a period performance. The Hilliards sing beautifully, both solo and in ensemble, and the balance between voices and instruments is impeccable.

Some might balk at the sudden eruption of Webern's violent 'Heftig betwegt' on the heels of Bach's closing 'Halleluja', but the musical sense of having five 'symmetrical' Movements for String Quartet fall within the greater symmetry of the programme as a whole overrides any initial discomfort. Again, Poppen's finely tooled reading focuses in precise detail the mood and texture of each miniature so that the eventual return of Bach-Webern is indeed like a profound thought revisited by a changed mind. This is a disc you'll want to return to again and again – surely recommendation enough.

Kurt Weill German/American 1900-1950

Weill was a pupil of Humperdinck, Busoni and Jarnach in Berlin (1918-23); their teaching informed his early music, including the choral Recordare (1923)and the Concerto for violin and wind (1924), the latter also influenced by Stravinsky. But the deeper influence of Stravinsky, coupled with an increased consciousness of music as a social force, led him to a rediscovery in the mid-1920s of tonal and vernacular elements, notably from jazz, in his cantata Der neue Orpheus and one-act stage piece Royal Palace, written between two collaborations with the expressionist playwright Georg Kaiser: Der Protagonist and Der Zar lässt sich photographieren. In 1926 he married the singer Lotte Lenya, who was to be the finest interpreter of his music.

His next collaborator was Brecht, with whom he worked on The Threepenny Opera (1928), The Rise and Fall of the City of Mahagonny (1929) and Happy End (1929), all of which use the corrupted, enfeebled diatonicism of commercial music as a weapon of social criticism, though paradoxically they have beome the epitome of the pre-war culture they sought to despise. Yet this is done within the context of a new harmonic consistency and focus. These works have also drawn attention from the theatre works in which Weill developed without Brecht during the early 1930s, Die Bürgschaft and Der Silbersee (with Kaiser again).

In 1933 he left Germany for Paris, where he worked with Brecht again on the sung ballet The Seven Deadly Sins. Then in 1935 he moved to the

USA, *where he cut loose from the European art-music tradition and devoted himself wholeheartedly to composing for the Broadway stage, intentionally subordinating aesthetic criteria to pragmatic and populist ones. Yet these works are still informed by his cultivated sense of character and theatrical form.*
GROVEmusic

Songs

Ute Lemper sings Kurt Weill

Der Silbersee – Ich bin eine arme Verwandte (Fennimores-Lied); Rom war eine Stadt (Cäsars Tod); Lied des Lotterieagenten. Die Dreigroschenoper – Die Moritat von Mackie Messer; Salomon-Song; Die Ballade von der sexuellen Hörigkeit. Das Berliner Requiem – Zu Potsdam unter den Eichen (arr Hazell). Nannas-Lied. Aufstieg und Fall der Stadt Mahagonny – Alabama Song; Wie man sich bettet. Je ne t'aime pas. One Touch of Venus – I'm a stranger here myself; Westwind; Speak low
Ute Lemper sop **Berlin Radio Ensemble / John Mauceri**
Decca New Line 425 204-2DNL (50' · DDD) Texts and translations included   Ⓕ**OO**

The songs in this collection are mostly from the major works Weill composed between 1928 and 1933, but also included are one from his years in France and three items from the 1943 Broadway musical *One Touch of Venus*. By comparison with the husky, growling delivery often accorded Weill's songs in the manner of his widow Lotte Lenya, Ute Lemper has a voice of clarity and warmth. What distinguishes her singing, though, is the way in which these attributes are allied to an irresistible dramatic intensity. Her 'Song of the Lottery Agent' is an absolute tour de force, apt to leave the listener emotionally drained, and her Je ne t'aime pas is almost equally overwhelming. Not least in the three numbers from *One Touch of Venus*, she displays a commanding musical theatre presence. This is, one feels, how Weill's songs were meant to be heard.

The Seven Deadly Sins

Die sieben Todsünden[a]. Symphony No 2[b]
Teresa Stratas, Nora Kimball sops **Frank Kelley, Howard Haskin** tens **Herbert Perry, Peter Rose** basses **Chorus and Orchestra of the Opéra National de Lyon / Kent Nagano**
Erato 0630-17068-2 (65' · DDD) Recorded [a]1993; [b]1996. Text and translation included   Ⓕ**O**

Weill and Brecht's Seven Deadly Sins, written in haste just after their flight from Hitler's Germany, was their last major collaboration. The question of its interpretation will always be bound up with the memory of Lotte Lenya, who created the role of Anna I. This performance of Sins was recorded at the same time that Stratas performed it for Peter Sellars's film of the work (available on video from Decca). There's a certain amount of stage noise in this recording,

especially in 'Lust' – the heart of the work. Stratas's singing isn't pretty, but then it's not meant to be; she projects text and music in such a dramatic and heartfelt way that it puts this version immediately in the front rank. Nagano's conducting begins with a very slow introduction, which may sound off-putting to those familiar with the much sprightlier Rattle or Masur versions, which also have soprano soloists. As the performance progresses though, Nagano's control of the drama seems just right. The recorded sound of the symphony is noticeably better than that of Sins. As Weill's only major orchestral work, it has never really caught on, though the orchestral writing is as sophisticated as anything in his operas. With so many versions of Die sieben Todsünden, preferences for voice and coupling are important. Fassbaender and von Otter both have a selection of Weill songs and arias, Réaux with Masur has the Lulu suite, Ross with Rattle, Stravinsky's Pulcinella. For first-time Weill buyers, we're inclined to recommend this version over all the others.

Street Scene

Street Scene
Kristine Ciesinski sop Anna Maurrant **Richard Van Allan** bass Frank Maurrant **Janis Kelly** sop Rose Maurrant **Bonaventura Bottone** ten Sam Kaplan **Terry Jenkins** ten Abraham Kaplan **Meriel Dickinson** mez Emma Jones **Angela Hickey** mez Olga Olsen **Claire Daniels** sop Jennie Hildebrand **Fiametta Doria** sop First Nursemaid **Judith Douglas** mez Second Nursemaid **English National Opera Chorus and Orchestra / Carl Davis**
TER Classics ② CDTER21185 (146' · DDD) Recorded 1989   Ⓕ

Street Scene is the most ambitious product of Weill's American years. It's something of a *Porgy and Bess* transferred from Catfish Row to the slum tenements of New York. Where *Porgy and Bess* is through-composed with recitatives, though, *Street Scene* offers a mixture of set musical numbers, straight dialogue, and dialogue over musical underscoring. The musical numbers themselves range from operatic arias and ensembles to rousing 1940s dance numbers. It's consistently well sung, particularly where style is concerned. Weill described the work as a 'Broadway opera', and it demands a vernacular rather than a classical operatic singing style. This it duly gets from Kristine Ciesinski as Anna Maurrant, while Janis Kelly's beautifully clear but natural enunciation and her sense of emotional involvement make daughter Rose's 'What good would the moon be?' a performance of real beauty. Praiseworthy, too, is Richard Van Allan as the murderous husband, his 'Let things be like they always was' creating a suitably sinister effect. Among the subsidiary attractions is the appearance of Catherine Zeta Jones, performing the swinging dance number 'Moon-faced, starry-eyed'.

Silvius Leopold Weiss
German 1686-1750

Weiss, a lutenist and composer, served in Breslau, then spent 1708-14 in Italy where he worked with the Scarlattis in Rome. By 1717 he had joined the Saxon court chapel at Dresden. He performed in cities including London, Vienna and Leipzig (where he met Bach in 1739). He was both the greatest of all lutenists and the most prolific of solo lute composers, writing nearly 600 pieces. Most are grouped in dance suites (often starting with an unbarred prelude); they are mainly late Baroque in style, but later works show more galant features. He also wrote sonatas and concertos for lute with other instruments. GROVEmusic

Lute Sonatas

Lute Sonatas – No 7; No 23; No 45
Robert Barto *lte*
Naxos 8 555722 (75' · DDD)   Ⓢ

Silvius Weiss, a contemporary of JS Bach, was a virtuoso lutenist of a high order. He spent most of his career as a court chamber musician at Dresden, but he was much in demand as a composer-performer and travelled widely in Europe, meeting Corelli and the Scarlattis in Italy, and Quantz and Graun in Prague. In 1739 he was a celebrated guest of Bach in Leipzig, who subsequently arranged his A major Sonata for violin and harpsichord (BWV1025). He's undoubtedly the most important Baroque composer for the lute and wrote hundreds of pieces for his instrument.

At the core of his output lie a substantial number of suites, of which 34 have survived in manuscripts held in Dresden and London. Their layout is very much like the keyboard suites and partitas of Bach, usually beginning with a prelude, followed with a group of dance movements: allemande, courante, bourrée, sarabande, minuet and gigue. The music is of remarkably high quality and invariably through-composed, so that each movement is inter-related while having an independent thematic existence.

The disc spans the range of Weiss's career with the early C minor Sonata (No 7) actually dated 1706 by the young composer in pencil on the manuscript; the writing has a youthful precosity. Sonata No 23 in B flat probably dates from around 1720, and is unusual in having a pair each of bourrées, gavottes and minuets, of which the second in each case is rather more demanding of virtuosity than the first. Apart from the stately Sarabande, the Sonata is a light-hearted work, ending with a jaunty Saltarella. The A major Sonata (No 45) is a late work from the 1740s. Instead of a prelude it has an *Introduzzione* in the form of a French overture which introduces a theme a little like Handel's *Harmonious Blacksmith*. The rest of the Sonata shows the composer at his most ambi-

tious. Canadian-born Robert Barto is in the process of recording all of these Suites for Naxos; the present issue is Volume 6. Barto gives first-class performances on a beautifully recorded period lute. With such enjoyable music this is a disc and series well worth exploring, for Weiss is always highly inventive.

Egon Wellesz
Austrian 1885-1974

Wellesz was a pupil of Schoenberg and Adler like his close friend Webern. Unlike Webern, though, he continued to pursue both creative and scholarly activities, before and after his move to England in 1938, where he lectured at Oxford from 1943. He did important, far-reaching work on Venetian opera, Viennese Baroque music and Byzantine chant, especially notation and hymnography; his compositions cover many genres and extend from a Schoenbergian style towards Bruckner (especially in the nine symphonies 1945-71, his major works in England), BartÙk (in his chamber music, which includes a fine octet, 1949, a Clarinet Quintet, 1959, nine string quartets, 1912-66) or Strauss (in the operas, notably Alkestis, 1924, Die Bakchantinnen, 1931, and Incognita, 1951). GROVEmusic

Symphonies

Symphonies – No 4, 'Sinfonia Austriaca', Op 70; No 6, Op 95; No 7, 'Contra torrentem', Op 102
Vienna Radio Symphony Orchestra / Gottfried Rabl
CPO CPO999 808-2 (71' · DDD)   Ⓕ

Had he been less of an individualist, Wellesz's name might nowadays be uttered in the same breath as Berg and Webern as a cornerstone of the Second Viennese School. As it was, he extricated himself from Schoenberg's circle early on to forge his own career, embracing subjects as diverse as grand opera, orchestral and chamber music, a biography of his former teacher, and musicological research into Byzantine music.

Like his near-contemporaries Ernst Toch and Havergal Brian, Wellesz came late to the symphony, composing his first (1945), inspired by memories of Austria, at the age of 60. No 4 (1951-53) had similar inspiration and bears the soubriquet *Sinfonia Austriaca*. Although Wellesz used atonality or serialism throughout his life, he also used tonality if he felt it appropriate, mixing the disciplines as his expressive purposes demanded. No 4 is a case in point, essentially a pastoral (albeit vigorously so) tonal symphony employing varying degrees of 'free tonality' throughout, especially in the intense *Adagio*.

Wellesz's later symphonies employ a slow-fast-slow design, the slow outer spans tending to be varied in pulse, encasing vigorous central *scherzi*. No 6 (1965) is perhaps his best known, having been broadcast a few times over the years. A riveting work, it's one of his finest utterances, showcasing his mastery of symphonic cogency, formal construction and orchestration. As in the late symphonies of Vaughan Williams, Wellesz was constantly refining and exploring his sound world: if the harmonic language of the Fourth is the most accessible to general listeners, the orchestration of the terser Seventh (1967) makes the earlier work seem pallid by comparison.

Gottfried Rabl (who provides an additional note on the problems with Wellesz's manuscripts) and the Vienna RSO give excellently prepared accounts. CPO's sound is fine, albeit a touch studio-bound. Very strongly recommended.

Symphonies – No 2, 'The English', Op 65; No 9, Op 111
Vienna Radio Symphony Orchestra / Gottfried Rabl
CPO CPO999 997-2 (75' · DDD)   Ⓕ

The Second Symphony (1947-8) may come as a big surprise to those who know Wellesz only from his later Expressionist, atonal idiom. Here is a large-scale symphony in the grand Austrian tradition, albeit neither of Brucknerian length nor Mahlerian hysteria. Tonality is the dominating force of its harmonic language, even going so far in the *Adagio* third movement to suggest English folk song (hence, perhaps, its soubriquet), although in truth its character is Austrian through and through.

If this was a 'compositional re-orientation', as annotator Hannes Heher suggests, prompted by a need to communicate with the more conservative audience of his adopted country, Wellesz didn't dumb down any more than his teacher Schoenberg did in the US. Listen behind the classical façade of this magnificently warm-hearted music and you'll discern clearly the structural mastery, as keenly realised as in any work of Schubert or Bruckner, and considerably more cogent than Mahler. The *Scherzo* is a pure joy, while the sonata-derived outer movements are vividly dramatic.

The Ninth (1970-71), his symphonic swansong, is altogether different. The increasing concentration of form and expression evident from the Sixth onwards, reached its ultimate form here, though always perfectly realised within his own sound-world. Ironically, the atonal Ninth appears to owe more – at least superficially – to contemporaneous British symphonism than the 'English' Second ever did, due largely to the increased cosmopolitanism of younger British composers than any idiomatic *volte-face* by the emigré Wellesz.

Gottfried Rabl's keen study of Wellesz has once again produced superb performances.

Orchestral Songs

Leben, Traum und Tod, Op 55[b]. Lied der Welt, Op 54[a]. Ode an die Musik, Op 92[b]. Sonnette der Elizabeth Barrett Browning, Op 52[a]. Symphonic

Epilogue, Op 108. Vision, Op 99[a]. Vorfrühling, Op 12
[a]**Regina Klepper** sop [b]**Sophie Koch** mez
Deutsches Symphony Orchestra, Berlin / Roger Epple
Capriccio 67 077 (70' · DDD) Texts and translations included   Ⓕ

The revival of interest in the music of Egon Wellesz continues apace. Even more encouraging, as with CPO's continuing symphonic cycle, is the fine quality of the performances – here expertly directed by Roger Epple – and Capriccio's sound, crystal-clear and rich yet without being overheated.

The vocal items come from two distinct periods, the mid-1930s and 1965-6. In setting the five *Sonnets of Elizabeth Barrett Browning* (1934) Wellesz used Rilke's translations, which he felt improved on 'the beauty of the originals'. The landscape is atonal, the textures Schoenbergian, but the cycle builds with impeccable harmonic logic to the intense final.

The Hofmannsthal settings from the 1930s, *Leben, Traum und Tod* ('Life, Dream and Death') – actually a pair of Lieder – and *Lied der Welt* ('Song of the World'), aren't as expansive but feel like operatic scenas. By contrast, *Ode an die Musik* (1965) and *Vision* (1966) are more abstract and freer in form, not unlike Dallapiccola's late vocal works, albeit less aphoristic.

The leaner, more dissonant nature of their idiom is more manifest in the purely orchestral *Symphonic Epilogue* (1969), a compelling example of Wellesz's last style. It makes a terrific contrast to the opening item, the neo-impressionistic soundscape *Vorfrühling* ('The Dawn of Spring') of 1912, with its gorgeous late-Romantic harmonies. Strongly recommended.

Henryk Wieniawski   Polish 1835-1880

After studying at the Paris Conservatoire Wieniawski embarked on the career of a travelling virtuoso, giving concerts in Russia, Germany, Paris and London. At the bidding of Anton Rubinstein he settled in St Petersburg (1860-72) and exerted a decisive influence on the growth of the Russian violin school. Meanwhile he composed his best works including the demanding Etudes-caprices op.18, the Polonaise brillante op.21 and his masterpiece, the Second Violin Concerto in D minor op.22. Further world travels, notably to the USA and Russia, and a period as violin professor at the Brussels Conservatory (1875-7) contributed to the breakdown of his health. One of the most important violinists of the generation after Paganini, he was known for the emotional quality of his tone. As a composer he combined the technical advances of Paganini with Romantic imagination and Slavonic colouring, showing Polish nationalism in his mazurkas and polonaises. His brother Józef (1837-1912) was an accomplished pianist who taught in Moscow, Warsaw and Brussels; their nephew Adam (1879-1950) was a director of the Chopin Music School in Warsaw. **GROVE**music

Violin Concerto No 1

Wieniawski Violin Concerto No 1 in F sharp minor,
Op 14[b] Beach Romance, Op 23[a] Debussy Préludes –
La fille aux cheveux de lin (arr A Hartmann)[a] Elgar
Chanson de nuit, Op 15 No 1[a] Kreisler La Gitana[a]
Poldini Marionnettes – Poupée valsante (arr
Kreisler)[a] Prokofiev Tales of an Old Grandmother,
Op 31 (arr Milstein)[a] – Andantino; Andante assai
Midori vn [a]**Robert McDonald** pf [b]**St Louis**
Symphony Orchestra / Leonard Slatkin
Sony Classical SK89700 (52' · DDD) [b]Recorded live
1988 and 2001   Ⓕ●

Wieniawski's First Violin Concerto has never
matched No 2 in popularity, but Midori's
involving performance makes one wonder why.
Put it alongside Perlman's EMI version with the
LPO under Ozawa, and – perhaps not surprisingly – her live account sounds more volatile
and more freely expressive, with even the conventional passage-work given an extra sparkle.
She also chooses a more flowing *Larghetto* for
the central 'Preghiera' (Prayer) slow movement,
which brings out the songful lyricism more persuasively, with her first entry magically hushed,
full of natural gravity. The dotted rhythms of
the Rondo finale are then even more playful.
The radio recording is full and forwardly balanced, but the range of dynamic and expression
in Midori's playing is never compromised.

In the encore pieces, the range of dynamic is
again remarkable. She plays the opening item,
Hartmann's arrangement of Debussy's 'La fille
aux cheveux de lin', with such delicacy she seems
simply to be musing to herself, and her simple
gravity in Elgar's *Chanson de nuit*, the last item,
taken steadily, turns it into a sort of prayer. Such
an approach could easily have lapsed into sentimentality, but emphatically not so here.

A thoroughly enjoyable disc.

Johann Wilms   German 1772-1847

Symphonies

Symphonies – No 6 in D minor, Op 58; No 7 in
C minor
Concerto Köln / Werner Ehrhardt vn
Archiv Produktion 474 508-2AH (61' · DDD) Ⓕ●●●

Johann Wilhelm Wilms was a German
who made his home in Amsterdam,
where he was a pianist, organist,
orchestral flautist and teacher. His Sixth Symphony won a prize in Ghent in 1820, and was
published by Breitkopf & Härtel; the Seventh
dates from the early 1830s, but wasn't performed in its entirety until Concerto Köln disinterred it in 2002.

If his work is almost completely forgotten
today, it's our loss. These are the works of a man
who knew the music of his more famous con-

temporaries. The *Adagio* opening to No 6 starts
with a solemn unison statement in the manner
of Haydn's Symphony, No 104: this is developed sequentially before leading into an *Allegro*
exposition that contrasts the fierce opening with
a gentle theme on the woodwind and a closing
passage led by the solo horn. The muscular
vigour of the movement recalls the tread of
Mozart's Commendatore. There's little relaxation in the *Scherzo* and the Rondo finale,
despite a turn to the major. The second movement, a flowing *Andante quasi allegretto* in triple
time, provides welcome balm.

No 7 is even finer. There's another solemn
opening, *Andante* and *piano*, followed by a
fugato, and the *Allegro* begins with a unison figure that is combined later with the second subject. The rest of the symphony, the spirit of
Beethoven looming large, is equally satisfying.

The playing of Concerto Köln is first class,
and their advocacy should do wonders for the
reputation of this unknown master.

Hugo Wolf   Austrian 1860-1903

Wolf played the violin, piano and organ as a child
and studied briefly at the Vienna Conservatory
(1875-7, meeting his idol Wagner) but, lacking dis-
cipline and direction, he had to rely on friends and
cultured benefactors for help and introductions. His
first important works, the songs of 1877-8, arose
from the effects of his sexual initiation and first
romantic attachment. Some are bright, others ago-
nised, reflecting his depression and illness from a
syphilitic infection. Though in 1880 this cloud
seemed to abate, a pattern of cyclic mood swing and
sporadic creativity was already established. Holidays,
studies of Wagner and radiant song settings alter-
nated with personal estrangements and a dark, dra-
matic strain in his music. For three years (1884-6),
he wrote trenchant musical criticism for the Wiener
Salonblatt, siding with Wagner and against
Brahms, meanwhile working on Penthesilea
(1883-5) and the D minor Quartet (1878-84)and
beginning a secret love affair with Melanie Köchert.
Compositional mastery and a sense of purpose came
only in the late 1880s, when he turned from subjec-
tivity to imaginative literature as a stimulus. In
1888 Eichendorff's poetry and in particular
Mörike's inspired a sudden flowering of song music
that in profusion and variety matched Schubert and
Schumann. His acclaimed public performances won
new converts, and in February 1889 he finished the
51 songs of the Goethe songbook, in April 1890 the
44 Spanish songs. Publication and critical recogni-
tion turned his thoughts to opera but from 1891
physical exhaustion and depressive phases stemmed
the flow of original music. In 1895 he composed his
only completed opera, Der Corregidor, but it was
unsuccessful; in 1897 he composed his last songs and
had the mental breakdown that led to his terminal
illness.

Wolf's strength was the compression of large-scale
forms and ideas – the essences of grand opera, tone

*poem and dramatic symphony – into song. Combin-
ing expressive techniques in the piano part with an
independent vocal line, and using an array of rhythmic and harmonic devices to depict textual imagery,
illustrate mood and create musical structure, he continued and extended the lied tradition of Schubert
and Schumann. Yet he was original in his conception
of the songbook as the larger dramatic form; each one
seems to have been planned in advance to represent a
poet or source. Folk music, nature studies, humorous
songs and ballads peopled by soldiers, sailors, students
or musicians recur in the German settings, while
religious or erotic themes dominate the Spanish and
Italian songbooks.* **GROVE**music

Goethe Lieder

Goethe Lieder – Harfenspieler: I, Wer sich der **H**
Einsamkeit ergibt; II, An die Türen; III, Wer nie sein
Brot; Cophtisches Lied I & II; Anakreons Grab;
Ob der Koran von Ewigkeit sei?; So lang man
nüchtern ist; Prometheus; Grenzen der Menschheit.
Italienisches Liederbuch – Ein Ständchen Euch
zu bringen; Schon streckt' ich aus; Geselle, woll'n
wir uns in Kutten hüllen. Drei Gedichte von
Michelangelo. Eichendorff Lieder – Der Musikant..
Mörike Lieder – Der Tambour; Nimmersatte Liebe;
Fussreise; Verborgenheit
Hans Hotter bass-bar **Gerald Moore** pf
Testament mono SBT1197 (70' · ADD) Recorded
1951, 1953 & 1957. Texts and translations included
Ⓕ**OO**

At last: a reissue of Hotter's 1953 Hugo Wolf
recital, which forms the centrepiece of this
release, and it's in far better, more immediate
sound than on the original LP. Hotter's interpretations of *Prometheus, Grenzen der Menschheit*, the gloomy *Harfenspieler* Lieder and
resigned Michelangelo settings – Wolf at his
greatest – remain virtually unsurpassed. They
were surely written with a bass-baritone of Hotter's calibre in mind and, quite apart from his
vocal prowess, his verbal insights are once again
remarkable, while the account of the naughty
monks' exploits from the *Italian Songbook*
remind us of Hotter the humorist. The earlier
and later items that complete the CD disclose
similar gifts, notably the delightful *Der Tambour*
– and *Anakreons Grab*, which, both in 1951 and
1957, matches the *Innigkeit* of Goethe's poem
and Wolf's setting. Moore is a masterly partner
in music that severely taxes the pianist. This disc
is a must for Wolf enthusiasts.

Goethe Lieder – Mignon – I, Heiss mich nicht reden;
II, Nur wer die Sehnsucht kennt; III, So lasst mich
scheinen. Philine. Mignon, 'Kennst du das Land?'.
Gutmann und Gutweib. Epiphanias. St Nepomuks
Vorabend. Der Schäfer. Blumengruss. Gleich und
Gleich. Die Spröde. Die Bekehrte. Frühling übers
Jahr. Anakreons Grab. Dank des Paria. Phänomen.
So lang man nüchtern ist. Hoch beglückt in deiner
Liebe. Als ich auf dem Euphrat schiffte. Nimmer will
ich dich verlieren! Ganymed. Gretchen vor dem

Andachtsbild der Mater Dolorosa. Wanderers
Nachtlied
Geraldine McGreevy sop **Graham Johnson** pf
Hyperion CDA67130 (76' · DDD) Texts and
translations included Ⓕ

The first and abiding impression made by this
recital is of air and grace. Graham Johnson's
piano-playing is delightfully free yet exact.
McGreevy's voice has a warmth in its still
youthful glow; she also has the art of making it
smile. In the first two Mignon songs she intensifies tone and emotion quite movingly; in
Kennst du das Land? she may be not quite *seeing*
the mountain and caves of the third verse or
feeling the awesome power of the 'Flut', and in
Philine she lacks the naughty zest for it. Yet
always there are lovely things – as when she
catches the expression of the statues as they put
to Mignon their piteous question. She's also
good (as are they both) at the boisterous *Gutmann und Gutweib*: a rarity that's lucky to find in
Johnson so persuasive an advocate.

Italienisches Liederbuch

Italienisches Liederbuch
Christiane Oelze sop **Hans Peter Blochwitz** ten
Rudolf Jansen pf
Berlin Classics Ⓕ 0017482BC (78' · DDD) Texts
included **O**

These three excellent artists sensibly understate
rather than overstate the songs' emotional content and where – about midway through the collection – the feelings become more immediate,
the performers come forth with just the right
amount of added intensity.

Christiane Oelze's fine-grained soprano, spirited readings and incisive diction fulfil just
about every side of the songs assigned to her –
from mocking, jealousy and anger to true love –
and she wholly avoids the archness that afflicts
some interpreters. Hans Peter Blochwitz,
always a discerning Lieder singer, may have lost
a little of his sweet tenor's bloom but compensates with a true understanding of the lyrical
impulse that suffuses those wonderful love
songs given to the male interpreter, especially
the three successive, outright masterpieces
beginning with 'Sterb' ich, so hüllt in Blumen'.

Rudolf Jansen deserves a notice to himself for
his unravelling of all the intricacies of the often
independent piano parts and for his outright
mastery in giving the keyboard its due without
ever stealing the thunder of the singers; his
instrument is ideally balanced with the voices in
a truthful recording. These songs are so
remarkable that there will never be one definitive way of singing them. On the only other disc
featuring a tenor, Schreier is a fuller-voiced,
more 'interventionist' interpreter than Blochwitz: that pays huge dividends in some songs,
less in others. In the end, the choice depends on
a preference for one singer over another: Oelze
and Blochwitz are probably favourite.

Mörike Lieder

Mörike Lieder –Der Genesene an die Hoffnung; Ein Stündlein wohl vor Tag; Der Tambour; Nimmersatte Liebe; Fussreise; Verborgenheit; Im Frühling; Auf einer Wanderung; Der Gärtner; In der Frühe; Gebet; Neue Liebe; Wo find' ich Trost?; Frage und Antwort; Lebe wohl; Heimweh; Denk' es, o Seele!; Der Jäger; Storchenbotschaft; Bei einer Trauung; Selbstgeständis; Abschied
Peter Schreier ten **Karl Engel** pf
Orfeo C142981A (60' · DDD) Texts and translations included   Ⓕ🔘

Peter Schreier's ever-supple tenor, honed by keen-eyed intelligence and a verbal palate sharp enough to taste and try every last word, makes him a Wolf interpreter of the highest order. In this meticulously shaped programme of 22 of Wolf's eager settings of Mörike, one wonder appears after another. Schreier and his ever-sentient pianist, Karl Engel, move from a gentle awakening of love, which grows in intensity towards the innermost core of songs of doubt and fear, and on through a gallery of wonderfully dry, wry tableaux to the final farewell and the kicking of the critic downstairs. The first song here, *Im Frühling*, epitomises the equilibrium, security and entirety of performances which have grown from long-pondered consideration. The long, drowsy vowels, and Schreier's sensitivity to the high-register placing of crucial words of longing all fuse into the slow-walking movement of cloud, wing, river, breeze, as language becomes expanded and enriched by tone. Schreier's remarkable steadiness of line in *Verborgenheit* reveals the song's secrets only reluctantly: the fierce intensity of sudden illumination is all the more searing. Grotesquerie and poignancy coexist in *Bei einer Trauung*, and we feel every catch of the voice as Schreier turns weird and whimsical tale-teller in Storchenbotschaft.

Mörike Lieder – Der Genesene an die Hoffnung; Er ist's; Begegnung; Fussreise; Verborgenheit; Im Frühling; Auf einer Wanderung; Um Mitternacht; Auf ein altes Bild; In der Frühe; Wo find' ich Trost?; An die Geliebte; Peregrina I; Peregrina II; Lebe wohl; Heimweh; Denk' es, o Seele!; Der Feuerreiter; Die Geister am Mummelsee; Storchenbotschaft; Auftrag; Abschied
Roman Trekel bar **Oliver Pohl** pf
Oehms OC305 (68' · DDD)Text included   Ⓕ

There can be no better advocate of Hugo Wolf than Roman Trekel, now at the peak of his career as a Lieder interpreter, who presents this deeply satisfying recital of the best of the *Mörike Lieder*. These inspired songs need, above all, the kind of intense expression and intimate, detailed treatment that Trekel brings them. Performed as convincingly as they are here, they offer a particular *frisson* of individual accent that no other composer in the genre, whatever their other merits, quite equals: words and music

seem as though they were written at one and the same time

Trekel achieves an ideal fusion of tonal security, sense of line and word-painting. In a comparatively long and complex Lied such as 'Im Frühling', he and the admirable Oliver Pohl traverse all the points of the expressive compass, and all the nuances of dynamics that belong to them. In that surpassingly sincere and beautiful love-song 'An die Geliebte' they build to the climax from 'Von Tiefe dann zu Tiefen' with a confidence that bespeaks long familiarity with the piece. Even better is the heartache they bring to 'Peregrina II' and 'Lebe wohl', where Wolf seems to enter into all the poet's suffering at the hands of a beloved. They also find the inner spirituality of the religion-inspired settings, such as 'Auf ein altes Bild' and 'Denk' es o Seele', the latter so compelling for saying so much in such a short time. In a quite different vein, they rise marvellously to the frenzied melodrama of 'Der Feuerreiter', always a challenge to singer and pianist and one that's surely met here.

A truthful recording adds to the disc's merits. Not so the notes, which omit any exposition of the songs and also English translations. Even so, this is a recital that ought to convert even Wolf heretics to the cause.

Additional recommendation

Mörike Lieder
Frauke May mez **Bernhard Renzikowski** pf
Arte Nova ② 74321 97127-2 (160' · DDD). Text included   Ⓢ
Wolf's 53 Mörike settings call for a variety of voices, male and female. Frauke May tackles the whole lot, paying no attention to the gender of the protagonist. Her rich expressive mezzo and keen intellect substantially match the challenge she's set herself. This accomplished if not wholly convincing interpretation is a real bargain.

Lieder

An * ('O wag es nicht'). Frage nicht. Herbst. Herbstentschlus. Nächtliche Wanderung. Traurige Wege. Liederstrauss – Sie haben heut' abend Gesellschaft; Ich stand in dunkeln Träumen; Das ist ein Brausen und Heulen; Aus meinen grossen Schmerzen; Mir träumte von einem Königskind; Mein Liebchen, wir sassen beisammen; Es blasen die blauen Husaren; Du bist wie eine Blume; Wenn ich in deine Augen seh'; Mädchen mit dem roten Mündchen; Wo ich bin, mich rings umdunkelt; Es war ein alter König; Mit schwarzen Segeln; Spätherbstnebel; Ernst ist der Frühling; Wie des Mondes Abbild zittert; Sterne mit den gold'nen Füsschen; Wo wird einst des Wandermüden.
Stephan Genz bar **Roger Vignoles** pf
Hyperion CDA67343 (67' · DDD)   Ⓕ🔘

This is a fascinating recital. Wolf's mature songs are generally reckoned to date from *Mörike Lieder* of 1888. One of the songs here ('Wo wird einst des Wandermüden') is from that year; the rest were written in 1876-80, when Wolf was 20. In these early songs, unpublished in his lifetime, he's by no means distinctively and identifiably 'Wolf'. Yet neither, for all the manifold influences at work on him (most notably Beethoven, Schubert and Schumann), is he anything but an independent composer with imagination, passion, a feeling for voice and words, and, even more remarkably, for the piano in combination with them – the outstanding absence being a gift for memorable melody.

Genz and Vignoles do him such service as would have done the young man's heart a world of good if he could have heard them. Most delightful in the quieter, *legato* songs such as 'Ich stand in dunkeln Träumen' and 'Ernst ist der Frühling', the baritone is also masterly in expression, finding ample resources of coloration for *Abendbilder*. Roger Vignoles is equally responsive, and turns his hands with skill and flair to both the grand Romantic style of *Nächtliche Wanderung* and the nimble merriment of 'Mädchen mit dem roten Mündchen'.

Hugo Wolf Society Edition   Ⓗ
Mörike Lieder – excerpts. Spanisches Liederbuch – excerpts. Italienisches Liederbuch – excerpts. Eichendorff Lieder – excerpts. Goethe Lieder – excerpts. Drei Gedichte von Michelangelo. Gedichte von Scheffel, Mörike, Goethe und Kerner – excerpts. Gedichte von Richard Reinick – excerpts. Gedichte nach Heine, Shakespeare und Lord Byron – excerpts **Marta Fuchs, Ria Ginster, Tiana Lemnitz, Elisabeth Rethberg, Alexandra Trianti** sops **Elena Gerhardt** mez **Karl Erb, John McCormack, Helge Roswaenge** tens **Herbert Janssen, Gerhard Hüsch** bars **Friedrich Schorr** bass-bar **Alexander Kipnis, Ludwig Weber** basses with various pianists
EMI mono 566640-2 (375' · ADD) Recorded 1931-8. Texts and translations included   ⓂⓄⓄⓄ

The old Hugo Wolf Society recordings hold their place not only as regards the distinction of the readings but as evidence of the pioneering work done by Ernest Newman and Walter Legge in the promulgation of the composer's highly original style. Six volumes were issued on 78rpm discs between 1931 and 1938, but a planned seventh was not released as a set (because of the war intervening) until the LP reissue came out in 1981. Here a further six titles have been unearthed from the EMI archives. This is a cornucopia of delights for the Lieder lover. Gerhardt had the whole of the first volume to herself, and launches the project with a typical honesty of approach. Her slightly grand voice and inimitable style may not be to modern tastes but persist and you'll surely respond to the generosity of her singing. The next volumes are dominated by Hüsch, Janssen and Kipnis, to whom Legge assigned exactly the right pieces for their respective styles. All are deeply rewarding, but Hüsch in love-songs from the *Spanish Songbook* and Kipnis in the *Michelangelo Songs* and so much else make particularly memorable

contributions. Among the women, the much underrated Greek soprano Alexandra Trianti brings just the right lightness of touch to some of the teasing, airy pieces from the *Italian Songbook*. Elisabeth Rethberg encompasses the grander passions of the *Italian Songbook* and is unsurpassed in the sorrowful abasement of 'Mühvoll komm' ich und beladen' from the *Spanish Songbook*. To round things off Gerhardt is heard again, in a newly issued version of a rarely heard, grief-laden song, 'Über Nacht', on which she lavishes all her love for Wolf. The pianists from Bos to Moore are uniformly excellent, but it's Wolf and the singers who make this one of the great enterprises of the pre-war gramophone.

Spanisches Liederbuch
Anne Sofie von Otter mez **Olaf Bär** bar **Geoffrey Parsons** pf
EMI Double Forte ② 575181-2 (109' · DDD) Recorded 1992-4. Texts and translations included   ⓂⓄ

The songs are performed not in the published order but in one devised by Bär for several recitals of the set given by this trio, and now carried over into the recording studio. For the 10 religious songs the reordering works well. In any case here the two singers show a deep and rewarding comprehension of the agony and ecstasy of poems and music. Listen, too, to von Otter's sense of smiling wonder in 'Ach, des Knaben Augen' as the holy mother looks into her son's eyes. By contrast in 'Mühvoll komm' ich und beladen' she changes to a searing, soul-searching manner that captures completely the woman's remorse, magnificently so at the climactic 'Nimm mich an'. Bär is as tense and inward in the great 'Herr, was trägt der Boden hier', capturing the voices of penitent and Christ to perfection. Note, too, Parsons's deliberately heavy gait in 'Die du Gott gebarst'. There are problems, however, in the secular songs.

With von Otter, apart from downward transpositions that make the piano parts sound unduly dark and Parsons consequently a shade heavy-handed, there's little to quarrel with. She teases, flirts, falls in love with the best of them, alert with her words, but never overdoing the archness. Bär, though, isn't only up against the perhaps more formidable challenge of Fischer-Dieskau (on DG) but also against his own reordering. He doesn't have the immense tonal range and emotional charge of the older baritone. 'Herz, verzage nicht geschwind' is broader, more biting in Fischer-Dieskau's reading, for instance, 'Ach im Maien' that much more mellifluous, but you could say that Bär's more contained, but by no means reticent approach has its own, Wolfian justification. But it's entirely Bär's fault that songs Nos 21 and 24, which should be sung as a group, lose some of their force when separated as here, thoughtfully as Bär sings each in its turn. However, the readings as a whole are worthy of the collection.

There's more space around the voices than on the closer-miked DG set, where Fischer-Dieskau is very much a presence in the room with you. This newer version doesn't replace the old, but those who want another, fresh, valid view of the *Spanisches Liederbuch* or just want to hear von Otter in her element will wish to acquire these two absorbing discs.

Iannis Xenakis   Greek/French 1922-2001

Xenakis was a French composer of Greek parentage and Romanian birth. In 1932 his family returned to Greece, and he was educated on Spetsai and at the Athens Polytechnic, where he studied engineering. In 1947 he arrived in Paris, where he became a member of Le Corbusier's architectural team, producing his first musical work, Metastasis, only in 1954, based on the design for the surfaces of the Philips pavilion to be built for the Brussels Exposition of 1958. This, with its divided strings and mass effects, had an enormous influence; but in ensuing works he moved on to find mathematical and computer means of handling large numbers of events, drawing on (for example) Gaussian distribution (ST/10, Atrées), Markovian chains (Analogiques) and game theory (Duel, Stratégie). Other interests were in electronic music (Bohor, 1962), ancient Greek drama (used in several settings) and instrumental virtuosity (Herma for piano, 1964; Nomos alpha for cello, 1966). His later output, chiefly of orchestral and instrumental pieces, is large, many works from the mid-1970s onwards striking back from modernist complexity to ostinatos and modes suggestive of folk music.   **GROVE**music

Knephas

A Colone. Nuits. Serment. Knephas. Medea
New London Chamber Choir; Critical Band / James Wood
Hyperion CDA66980 (58' · DDD) Texts and
translations included   Ⓕ**ooo**

This enterprising release is a great success, showing just how varied – and unintimidating – Xenakis's music can be. The performances are nothing short of phenomenal in their technical assurance and emotional power, and the recording is also something special, giving the singers just the right degree of space and resonance to project the often complex textures with all the necessary precision. The earliest works offer different angles on the composer's ultra-expressionist idiom, with *Nuits* (1967) adopting a very direct way of representing its anguished lament for the martyrs of Greece's struggle for freedom after 1945. *Medea* (also 1967) uses much more text, and its chant-like style has affinities with Stravinsky's *Les noces*, but the overall effect is much harsher, with abrasive yet imaginative instrumental writing. *A Colone* (1977) also has Stravinskian affinities, and the text (Sophocles's

description of the delights of Colonus) prompts music which is uninhibitedly exuberant. This warmer, more celebratory side of Xenakis is carried over into *Serment* (1980), a short setting of a text derived from the Hippocratic Oath and not, one suspects, an entirely serious effort, though there's nothing trivial about it either. Finally, the superb *Knephas* ('Darkness') of 1990 begins in an appropriately unsparing manner, but ends with a hymnic apotheosis which recalls Messiaen in its harmonic character and warmth of atmosphere. Here is one of the 20th century's most important musical voices, and this recording does it full justice.

Eugene Ysaÿe   Belgian 1858-1931

Ysaÿe studied under Wieniawski at Brussels and Vieuxtemps at Paris, forming close ties with Franck, Chausson, d'Indy, Fauré, Saint-Saëns and Debussy. As professor at the Brussels Conservatory (1887-99) he initiated the Concerts Ysaÿe, appearing as violinist and conductor in contemporary French and Belgian music, meanwhile becoming renowned throughout Europe and in the USA (conductor of the Cincinnati SO, 1918-22); the shift to a conducting career was necessitated by his increasingly unsteady bowing arm. Idolized by a generation of violinists for his intense but poetic playing, he also composed with expertise in a post-Romantic style, notably for the violin (Six Sonatas op.27, eight concertos, Poème élégiaque, Caprice Saint-Saëns).   **GROVE**music

Violin Sonatas

Solo Violin Sonatas, Nos 1-6
Thomas Zehetmair vn
ECM New Series 472 687-2 (66' · DDD)   Ⓕ**oo**

By tailoring his solo sonatas to fit the styles of six very different violinists Eugène Ysaÿe may have been acting as the ultimate critic, describing his subjects with musical illustrations rather than mere words. For example, there are the winking appoggiaturas in the finale of No 4, dedicated to Kreisler, which Thomas Zehetmair throws off with a mere flick of the wrist, or the rich chord structures of No 1, whose dedicatee, Joseph Szigeti, was a great Bach player. Bach is a particularly strong presence there, the key (G minor) and language so reminiscent of his first solo sonata. Again, the Jacques Thibaud piece, No 2 in A minor, has obsessive repetitions of the Prelude from Bach's E major Partita, played initially by Zehetmair with the lightest touch, though later repetitions gain in intensity. The sinister melding of Bach with the 'Dies irae' chant has to be one of the canniest masterstrokes of the period. There are stylistic parallels between No 2 and No 4, just as there were similarities between the players themselves.

The spicy Sixth Sonata recalls the Spanish fiddler Manuel Quiroga and takes on Latin influences, initially suggesting Ravel's *Tzigane* (composed at around the same time, though the similarity is probably coincidental) before shifting, a little later, to *habañera* mode.

As the ultimate thinking virtuoso, Zehetmair is an ideal interpreter of these pieces, delving between the notes, coaxing a wealth of colour, inflection and dynamic shading from each score, always with acute imagination. He is both explorer and demonstrator, his modes of attack as varied as his tone colouring. This is the best possible showcase for some marvellous if still undervalued music.

Jan Dismas Zelenka
Bohemian 1679-1745

After serving Count Hartig in Prague, Zelenka became a double bass player in the royal orchestra at Dresden in 1710. He studied with Fux in Vienna and Lotti in Venice, 1715-16; from 1719 he remained in Dresden, except for a visit to Prague in 1723. Having gradually taken over the duties of the ailing Kapellmeister, Heinichen, he was made only church music composer (1735); Hasse was the new Kapellmeister. He composed mainly sacred works, among them three oratorios, 12 masses, and many other pieces; his output also includes a festival opera (1723, Prague), six chamber sonatas for oboes (c 1715) and other instrumental pieces. His music, like that of Bach (whom he knew), is notable for its adventurousness, its contrapuntal mastery and its harmonic invention. GROVEmusic

Capriccios

Capriccios – No 2 in G; No 3 in F.   P
Concerto a 8 in G. Hipocondrie a 7 in A
Das Neu-Eröffnete Orchestre /Jürgen Sonnentheil
CPO CPO999 458-2 (61' · DDD)   F

This disc contains two of Zelenka's five *Capriccios*, a Concerto for eight instruments and the intriguingly titled *Hipocondrie*, which is something between suite and concerto. Zelenka was skilled in the art of combining instruments of differing colours, ordering them about in a way that makes us wonder if he had a grudge against players. The horn-writing in the *Capriccios* is merciless, with uncommonly high parts often emerging in exposed moments in the texture. His melodic facility, rhythmic imagination and instinctive feeling for effective instrumental ranges and colours sustain the interest. There's an inventive freshness about his music which contains surprises at almost every turn. Sometimes, however, as in the finale of the Concerto *a 8*, sequential patterns are overworked, giving the movement a somewhat amorphous, unsatisfying shape. Initial rather good ideas, almost always arresting, are less well sustained than, say, Telemann's, even if they're sometimes bolder and more adventurous. Sonnentheil achieves spirited, amiable performances from Das Neu-Eröffnete Orchestre. The two horns

are excellent, and, if oboes and strings sound a shade unrefined occasionally, this does little to spoil enjoyment of an entertaining programme.

Trio Sonatas

Trio Sonatas –No 2 in G minor, No 5 in F;   P
No 6 in C minor
Ensemble Zefiro (Paolo Grazzi, Alfredo Bernardini *obs* Alberto Grazzi *bn* Roberto Sensi *db* Rolf Lislevand *theorbo* Rinaldo Alessandrini *hpd/org*)
Astrée Naïve E8511 (52' · DDD) Recorded 1993   F O

For sheer élan and spirit the Baroque instrumental players on this disc take some beating. Zelenka's six sonatas for two oboes, bassoon and continuo are among the most rewarding and at times most difficult pieces of Baroque chamber music in the oboe repertory. Indeed, pieces demanding such virtuosity from these instruments were probably without precedent at the time (1715). The writing is often such as to make us wonder if they were destined for friends or for enemies of the composer. Here, then, we're treated to some splendidly invigorating playing of music which offers a great deal beyond face value. The sounds of the solo instruments themselves, together with an effective continuo group of double bass, harpsichord/organ and theorbo are admirably captured in the recording.

The Lamentations of Jeremiah

The Lamentations of Jeremiah   P
Michael Chance *counterten* **John Mark Ainsley** *ten* **Michael George** *bass* **Chandos Baroque Players**
Hyperion Helios CDH55106 (73' · DDD) Recorded 1990. Texts and translations included   B

Between the incomparable settings by Thomas Tallis and the extremely austere one by Stravinsky (which he called *Threni*) the *Lamentations of Jeremiah* have attracted surprisingly few composers. Perhaps the predominantly sombre tone, without even the dramatic opportunities presented by the *Dies irae* in a *Requiem*, is off-putting. Be that as it may, Zelenka showed remarkable resourcefulness in his 1722 setting for the electoral chapel at Dresden, where he was Kapellmeister. His musical language is in many ways similar to that of JS Bach but there are also daring turns of phrase which are entirely personal. The six *Lamentations* feature each singer twice; this performance is intimate, slightly spacious in tempo and with a resonant acoustic.

Sub olea pacis et palma virtutis

Sub olea pacis et palma virtutis   P
Noémi Kiss, Anna Hlavenková *sops* **Markus Forster** *counterten* **Jaroslav Březina, Adam**

Zdunikowski *tens* Aleš Procházka *bass* Czech Boys'
Choir; Musica Florea; Musica Aeterna; Ensemble
Philidor / Marek Štryncl
Supraphon ② SU3520-2 (94' · DDD) Text and
translation included ⓕ

From obsequiousness comes greatness. Coupled to an allegorical play, designed to laud not
only a Habsburg emperor (Charles VI) at his
coronation in Prague in 1723 but also his predecessors who had controlled the Czech lands
since 1526, is Italianate music of vigour,
grandeur and tenderness. It simply needs to be
experienced. *Sub olea pacis* is one of only four
Latin plays with music, out of hundreds, to survive complete and is the only one which identifies the composer; Zelenka seems to have written most of the music in a hurry; the libretto
mentions the presence of dancers but the score
contains no dance interludes, so what they did
or what they represented is unknown. Sensibly,
the play itself has been omitted in this recording. Zelenka's contribution is operatic and, after
a three-part Overture, matches the drama with a
prologue, three acts and epilogue. There are
recitatives, choruses and arias. Let's now dispense with an irritating technical flaw. First and
second violins are placed on either side of the
podium (as they should be) but the firsts aren't
always stable. They tend to move within their
own area, sometimes merging with the seconds
on the right. Otherwise the recording is very
good: spacious with no gimmicky close-ups to
give the period instruments a bad sound and the
solo singers an artificial presence.

Throughout the performance, Stryncl's pacing of the music and balancing of dynamics
show concern not only for his colleagues but
also for making sense of the words themselves.
His ability to float a flexible rhythm is keen,
though, occasionally, he veers towards rigidity.
Look out for those remarkable arias that pit solo
instruments against singers, particularly No 22
where a chalumeau (precursor of the clarinet,
here played by Christian Leitherer) duets with a
soprano. So there you have it, a magnificent
work. And Zelenka, anticipating Haydn, signed
off with the words 'Laus Deo'. Most appropriate – which is another way of saying that this
set is a significant addition to the recorded
repertoire. Do listen and delight in what it has
to offer.

Alexander Zemlinsky
Austrian 1871-1942

*Zemlinsky was a pupil of Fuchs at the Vienna Con-
servatory (1890-92). In 1895 he became a close
friend of Schoenberg's; he also had encouragement
from Mahler, who presented his opera Es war einmal at the Hofoper in 1900. His orchestral fantasy
Die Seejungfrau dates from these years. By this time
he was working as a theatre conductor in Vienna his
later appointments were at the German theatre in*

*Prague (1911-27) and the Kroll Opera in Berlin
(1927-31). In 1933 he fled to Vienna, and then in
1938 to the USA. From the same background as
Schoenberg, and similarly influenced by Mahler and
Strauss, he developed an impassioned style in such
works as his Second Quartet (1914), one-act operas
Eine florentinische Tragödie (1917) and Der Zwerg
(1922), and Lyric Symphony (1923). Later works,
including the opera Der Kreidekreis (1932), the
Sinfonietta (1934) and the Fourth Quartet (1936),
are influenced more by Weill and German neo-
classicism.* GROVEmusic

Eine lyrische Symphonie, Op 18

Zemlinsky Eine lyrische Symphonie, Op 18[b] 🅢
Berg Lyric Suite (arr cpsr). Fünf Orchesterlieder nach
Ansichtskartentexten von Peter Altenberg, Op 4[a]
[ab]Vlatka Orsanić *sop* [b]James Johnson *bar*
South West German Radio Symphony Orchestra /
Michael Gielen
Arte Nova 74321 27768-2 (67' · DDD) Recorded 1994
Ⓢ🅞

A first-class bargain, let down by the fact that
the words of the vocal pieces aren't provided
and a slightly but not disagreeably lean orchestral sound. Gielen has the reputation of a specialist in contemporary music, of 'advanced'
contemporary music in particular, and that
might imply that he will take a coolish view of
Zemlinsky. In fact he responds with a beautiful
sense of long, lyrical line, and although his
orchestra lacks the last degree of sumptuousness, his accuracy and clarity of detail reveal
more of the subtle beauties of the score than
some more opulent readings, as well as bolder
vehemence. His control of tempo and his readiness to slow the music to breathless stillness are
both admirable. These virtues would count for a
lot less if the soloists were merely competent.
Both are more than that. Orsanic is clean and
accurate; although she doesn't hover as ecstatically as she might in the fourth song, she
responds to the solo string writing at its opening
with an imaginative fining-down of tone. Even
so, she sounds rather more at home in the Berg
Altenberg Lieder, where she reacts intelligently
to the texts and opens out to lyrical vehemence
at the end of the cycle. Johnson is still better, a
fine lyric baritone with dignity, clear diction
and admirable phrasing. The pieces from the
Lyric Suite are exceptionally well done, richness
of texture combining with excellent precision of
attack, fine solo playing and warm expressiveness. Gielen's reading of the Zemlinsky will not
disappoint any admirer of the work, regardless
of their bank balance.

Additional recommendation

Eine lyrische Symphonie, Op 18
Voigt *sop* **Terfel** *bass-bar* **Vienna Philharmonic
Orchestra / Sinopoli**
DG 449 179-2GH (49' · DDD) ⓕ
A sumptuous performance from Sinopoli and the
Vienna Phil, with both soloists on superb form.

Eine florentinische Tragödie

Eine florentinische Tragödie[a]. Eine lyrische
Symphonie, Op 18[b]. Symphonische Gesänge[c].
3 Psalms
[a]Iris Vermillion *mez* Bianca [a]Heinz Kruse *ten*
Guido Bardi [a]Albert Dohmen *bar* Simone
[b]Alessandra Marc *sop* [b]Håkan Hagegård *bar*
[c]Willard White *bass* Royal Concertgebouw
Orchestra / Riccardo Chailly
Double Decca ② 473 734-2DF2 (156' · DDD) Ⓜ︎Ⓞ●

A Florentine Tragedy is a disturbing, shocking
piece, but to make its fullest impact it also needs
to sound ravishingly beautiful. Zemlinsky's
sumptuous scoring often demands an orchestra
of the Royal Concertgebouw's stature, and in
this reading it sounds quite magnificent. But the
score needs a conductor of subtlety and shrewd-
ness to point up the two passages of contrasting
serene lyricism, one where Simone's wife
Bianca assures Count Bardi of her eternal love
and another when husband and wife rediscover
their love for each other. Vermillion is very fine
at both these points, her mezzo timbre adding
warmth to her line. Kruse is admirable too, fin-
ing down his ringing tenor in that duet scene,
and, as Simone, Dohmen is forceful and dangerous. But Chailly is the real star, pacing the opera
so well that it seems over in no time, drawing
richly complex but never muddy textures from
his remarkable orchestra.

Again, exquisitely though Vermillion sings the
orchestrated Alma Mahler songs, Chailly must
take at least half the credit. Each is taken faster
than in most recordings with piano, and every
one of them gains from it in impulsive urgency.
The recording leaves nothing to be desired: the
colours are rich and clean.

Additional recommendation

Eine florentinische Tragödie
Vermillion Bianca Lutsiuk Bardi Dohmen Simone
French Radio Philharmonic Orchestra / Armin Jordan
Naïve V4987 (60' · DDD · T/t/N) Recorded live at the
Olivier Messiaen Hall, Paris, 13 September 2003 Ⓕ
A fine performance, not as classy as the Chailly,
but if you should want just the opera this new
Naïve disc offers a splendid alternative.

Der König Kandaules

Der König Kandaules
James O'Neal *ten* König Kandaules **Monte
Pederson** *bar* Gyges **Nina Warren** *sop* Nyssia **Klaus
Häger** *bass* Phedros **Peter Galliard** *ten* Syphax
Mariusz Kwiecien *bar* Nicomedes **Kurt Gysen** *bass*
Pharnaces **Simon Yang** *bass* Philebos **Ferdinand
Seiler** *ten* Sebas **Guido Jentjens** *bar* Archelaos
Hamburg State Philharmonic Orchestra / Gerd
Albrecht
Capriccio ② 60 071/2 (128' · DDD) Recorded live
1996 Notes, text and translation included Ⓕ

Der König Kandaules, based on a play by André
Gide, was Zemlinsky's last opera, written during the Nazis' rise to power and complete in
short score when he fled to America in 1938. He
showed it to his pupil Artur Bodanzky, then a
principal conductor at the Met, who seems to
have warned him that the libretto would not be
acceptable. It concerns Kandaules, king of
Lydia, who befriends Gyges, a fisherman, and
persuades him to use a magic ring to become
invisible and see his queen, Nyssia, naked. After
they spend a night of passion together Nyssia
orders Gyges to kill Kandaules and seize power.

Zemlinsky never completed the orchestration
but left a large number of indications of scoring.
Antony Beaumont's orchestration sounds perfectly convincing. When two excerpts from the
score were performed and recorded in 1994 it
already looked as though a major work was
about to be revealed. And that's the case: a marvellous and quite characteristic score, but in
some ways a dismaying one. All the orchestral
richness and the voluptuously singing lines are
there, but wedded to a plot that seems all too
accurately to reflect the disorder and disillusion
of the times in which it was written.

The performance is a fine one, O'Neal lacking
only the last touch of heroic vocal stature for
Kandaules, Warren only a little stretched by the
Ariadne-like role of Nyssia, Pederson first class
(a moment or two of suspect intonation aside) as
Gyges. Albrecht is perfectly at home in this sort
of music, the orchestra's admirable richness of
tone doesn't obscure detail, and the recording is
atmospheric (stage business audible) but clear.
Zemlinsky's reputation can only be enhanced by
this ravishing, richly complex, disturbing opera.

COLLECTIONS

THE CLASSICAL
GOOD
CD&DVD
GUIDE
2006

ORCHESTRAL

Cello Concertos

Boccherini (arr Grützmacher) Cello Concerto in B flat, G48 **Bruch** Kol Nidrei, Op 47 **Elgar** Cello Concerto in E minor, Op 85 **Haydn** (arr Gevaërt) Cello Concerto No 2 in D, HobVIIb/2 – Allegro moderato; Adagio
Pablo Casals vc **London Symphony Orchestra / Sir Landon Ronald; BBC Symphony Orchestra / Sir Adrian Boult**
Biddulph mono LAB144 (79' · ADD) Recorded 1936-46 **Ⓜ︎O**

The leonine growl that prefaces Elgar's most introspective orchestral masterpiece is played here with uncompromising defiance, whereas the weary solo ascent that follows can rarely – if ever – have conveyed a deeper sense of disorientation. Casals' handling of the solo line is wistful, sometimes wilful, and profoundly personal. No other performance is quite as successful in contrasting the 'brave front' of Elgar's bolder *tuttis* with the ineffable sadness of his solo writing. Occasional hiccups in the cello line go for nothing, and Casals' distant groaning merely serves to compound an impression of total commitment.

Biddulph's annotation relates how a changing critical climate gradually became sympathetic to Casals's account of the Elgar Concerto (initial reactions were fairly hostile), and how Britain's handling of the Franco situation in Spain deeply offended Casals. Projected sessions never materialised, and the Haydn Concerto recording that's issued here for the first time (it was set down the day after the Elgar) remained incomplete. What we do have, however, is very well recorded, typically eloquent and full of interpretative incident, with sundry expressive subtleties and an especially memorable account of the *Adagio*. *Kol Nidrei* is given one of the slowest, purest and most deeply felt readings imaginable, perfectly reflecting the pain, resolution and quiet victory that mark the three stages of repentance. Transfers are excellent. If you're in search of 'The Quintessential Casals' then you need look no further.

Jacqueline du Pré: Les introuvables
Bach Cello Suites – No 1 in G, BWV1007; No 2 in D minor, BWV1008 (rec live 1962) **Beethoven** 12 Variations on Handel's 'See the conqu'ring hero comes', Wo045[i]. Seven Variations in E flat on Mozart's 'Bei Männern, welche Liebe fühlen', Wo046[i]. 12 Variations in F on 'Ein Mädchen oder Weibchen', Op 66[i] (recorded live 1970). Cello Sonatas[c] – No 3 in A, Op 69; No 5 in D, Op 105 No 2 **Bruch** Kol Nidrei, Op 47[a] **Chopin** Cello Sonata, Op 65[i] **Delius** Cello Concerto[e] **Dvořák** Cello Concerto in B minor, B1919. Silent woods, B182[g] **Elgar** Cello Concerto in E minor, Op 85[d] **Fauré** Elégie, Op 24[a] **Franck** Violin Sonata in A[i] (arr vc/pf) **Handel** Oboe Concerto in G minor,

HWV287[b] (arr vc/pf Slatter. rec live 1961) **Haydn** Cello Concertos – No 1 in C[h]; No 2 in D[d] **Monn** (arr Schoenberg) Cello Concerto in G minor[d] **Saint-Saëns** Cello Concerto No 1 in A minor, Op 33[f] **Schumann** Cello Concerto in A minor, Op 129[f]
Jacqueline du Pré vc [a]**Gerald Moore**, [b]**Ernest Lush**, [c]**Stephen Kovacevich** pfs [d]**London Symphony Orchestra / Sir John Barbirolli;** [e]**Royal Philharmonic Orchestra / Sir Malcolm Sargent;** [f]**New Philharmonia Orchestra;** [g]**Chicago Symphony Orchestra,** [h]**English Chamber Orchestra / Daniel Barenboim** [i]pf
EMI ⑥ 568132-2 (857' · ADD) **Ⓢ︎ Ⓑ︎OO**

As the title suggests, this fine six-disc retrospective of Jacqueline du Pré's recording career – a mere 10 years long – was masterminded by French EMI. The wonder was that right from the start Jacqueline du Pré was mature in her artistry, and it's good that from the period even before the first official EMI sessions the collection includes three BBC recordings: Bach's Cello Suites Nos 1 and 2 and a Handel sonata arranged from the Oboe Concerto in G minor. Those early BBC recordings are inevitably flawed, but the sheer scale of the artistry is never in doubt. Of the handful of items recorded by EMI in July 1962 with Gerald Moore accompanying, only Bruch's *Kol Nidrei* is included.

The Delius was du Pré's first concerto recording, and she wasn't nearly as much at ease as she came to be later. The CD transfers don't minimise any of the flaws in the original recordings, notably the disappointing sound given to her Chicago recording of the Dvořák Concerto. Not only does the orchestra sound coarse and thin with a lot of background hiss, the cello is balanced far too close. Even so, the wide dynamic range of du Pré's playing is clearly represented, down to a whispered *pianissimo*. It was right to include it and also the cello sonata recordings of Chopin and Franck, the last she ever made, in December 1971. The tone may not have been quite so even, but the fire and warmth are undiminished. All the concerto recordings are welcome, with the tear-laden quality in the slow movement of the Schumann matching that in the Elgar. It's good that her supreme Beethoven sonata recordings with Stephen Bishop (later Kovacevich) are included, both sparkling and darkly intense. From the Beethoven series recorded at the 1970 Edinburgh Festival by the BBC only the three sets of variations are included. A must for anyone who was ever magnetised by du Pré's playing.

Mstislav Rostropovich: Mastercellist
Chopin Introduction and Polonaise brillante in C, Op 3[a] **Dvořák** Cello Concerto in B minor, B191[b] **Glazunov** Chant du ménéstrel, Op 71[c] **Rachmaninov** Cello Sonata in G minor, Op 19[d]. Vocalise, Op 34 No 14[a] **Schubert** Impromptu in G flat, D899 No 3 (arr Heifetz/Rostropovich)[a] **Schumann** Cello Concerto in A minor, Op 129[e]. Träumerei, Op 15 No 7[a] **Tchaikovsky** Andante cantabile[f]
[ad]**Alexander Dedyukhin** pf [e]**Leningrad**

Philharmonic Orchestra / Gennadi Rozhdestvensky; ^cBoston Symphony Orchestra / Seiji Ozawa; ^{bf}Berlin Philharmonic Orchestra / ^bHerbert von Karajan, ^fMstislav Rostropovich vc
DG ^{ad}mono ② 471 620-2GM2 (134' · ADD) Recorded 1959-79 Ⓜ

Of the two major celebratory collections which appeared simultaneously to celebrate the great Russian musician's 75th birthday, the DG two-disc package is a clear first choice, unless you already have his famous and unsurpassed 1969 recording of the Dvořák Concerto with Karajan, or indeed the hardly less imaginative account of the Schumann Concerto, which reaches out to the listener equally compellingly.

The slighter, touchingly nostalgic Glazunov *Chant du ménéstrel* is exquisitely sung, and Rostropovich equally readily communicates his affection for the pair of warmly lyrical Tchaikovsky melodies which form the *Andante cantabile*. But what makes this compilation quite indispensable are the works with piano. These pieces, recorded in Poland in 1956, show a youthful Rostropovich, and include a fresh and inspirational reading of Rachmaninov's Cello Sonata, a characteristically intense work with its richly burgeoning lyrical melodies. Rostropovich plays raptly with a rare delicacy of feeling, his timbre in the upper range sweetly refined, his melismatic line slightly more restrained than in later years, and always echoed by the poetic Alexander Dedyukhin. The encores are played affectionately and the mono recording is faithful and well balanced.

Kabalevsky Cello Concerto No 2 in G, Op 77^a
Prokofiev Symphony-Concerto in E minor, Op 125^b
Tsintsadze Five Pieces on Folk Themes^c
Daniil Shafran vc ^cNina Musinyan pf ^aLeningrad Philharmonic Orchestra / Dimitry Kabalevsky; ^bUSSR State Symphony Orchestra / Gennady Rozhdestvensky
Cello Classics CC1008 (78' · DDD) ^b Recorded live at the Great Hall of the Moscow Conservatoire 1961, ^a1967, ^c1957 Ⓕ

This is an important cello release that no aficionado of great string playing can afford to ignore. As a relative youngster Daniil Shafran shared important competition prizes with Rostropovich; but his appearances outside Russia were rare, and most of his recordings remained all but unknown beyond specialist circles. Kabalevsky's Second Cello Concerto (1964) is a fairly big work, mostly serious in tone, with demanding cadenzas and a wink or two in the direction of Prokofiev's *Symphony-Concerto*. Kabalevsky himself was hugely impressed by Shafran's playing, with its sensual tone, its agility in faster music and unerring concentration. Shafran's sound is very different from Rostropovich's, more prone to building vibrato on the note – starting 'cold' then gradually intensifying the vibration – or alternating notes with, or without, vibrato. Others bent on similar ploys

can sound mannered, but not Shafran, whose seamless bowing and widened dynamics, not to mention his extraordinary deftness, have inspired accolades bordering on a cult. Where in the Prokofiev Rostropovich is earnest but suave, Shafran is more colourful but unremittingly intense. The Kabalevsky alone is in stereo and there's some excellent annotation by Isserlis and Andrew Stewart.

The Swan – Classic Works for Cello and Orchestra
Bruch Ave Maria, Op 61 **Dvořák** Silent Woods, B182 **Fauré** (arr Hazell) Sicilienne, Op 78. Après un rêve, Op 7 No 1 **Glazunov** Chant du ménéstrel, Op 71 **LJ Kim** (orch R Panufnik) Korean Elegy **Rachmaninov** (arr Hazell) Vocalise, Op 34 No 14 **Respighi** Adagio con variazioni **Saint-Saëns** (arr Hazell) Le cygne **Tchaikovsky** Nocturne, Op 11
Han-Na Chang vc Philharmonia Orchestra / Leonard Slatkin
EMI 557052-2 (63' · DDD) Ⓕ**OO**

The phenomenally gifted Han-Na Chang's first CD (which included a glorious account of Tchaikovsky's *Rococo* Variations) to which Rostropovich – who also conducted it – gave his enthusiastic imprimatur – received the highest praise. She was 13 then; now she's 18, but that wonderfully spontaneous musicality which is hers by natural instinct (one thinks of the young Menuhin) has flowered with maturity. Her line is marginally firmer, and her ardour and sensibility bring phrasing which simply breathes with the music. The opening Fauré *Après un rêve* begins with winning delicacy – its ardour never over-emotes, while *Sicilienne* is utterly delightful. But it's perhaps in Rachmaninov's *Vocalise* that her singing line and subtle colouring touch the heartstrings most poignantly, although the much less familiar Respighi *Adagio*, Dvořák's *Klid* and the Kim *Elegy* all have a disarmingly simple eloquence. Saint-Saëns' famous *Swan* has never glided by more guilelessly (yet there's a subtle dynamic control) and, not surprisingly, the Slavic dolour of Tchaikovsky's *Nocturne* is perfectly caught. 'You can see that I am in love with all these pieces,' Chang says in the notes, and her passionate advocacy of Bruch's *Ave Maria*, 'full of inner conflicts', makes for a splendid coda to a highly enjoyable disc, with Slatkin a warmly supportive accompanist. Chris Hazell's arrangements of about half the items are superb. As Chang notes in the booklet: 'I think they reflect in a very honest way what the composers had in mind.' The recording is beautiful, and has an 'old-fashioned' mellow EMI analogue-style ambience, but with the cello set forward and caught with total digital realism.

Guitar solos with orchestra

Iberia
Albéniz Iberia (arr Gray) – El Albaicín; Triana; Rondeña **Granados** Valses poéticos (trans Williams) **Rodrigo** Invocación y Danza. En los trigales

Anonymous (arr Llobet). Ten Catalan Folksongs
John Williams *gtr* **London Symphony Orchestra /
Paul Daniels**
Sony Classical SK48480 (71' · DDD) Recorded 1989-91
Ⓕⓞ

The amalgam of technical guitaristic perfection
in the face of daunting demands, fluid musicality
and exemplary tone-production, caught in this
exceptionally lifelike recording, represents a
landmark in the instrument's march towards
true parity with other instruments. Granados's
Valses are unabridged, Rodrigo's moody *Invocación y Danza* comes in its original and more
effective form, and two of the charming settings
of Catalan folk-songs arranged by Llobet have
no other recording. Nothing in Albéniz's virtuoso *Iberia* is accessible to the solo guitar, but
with the aid of the LSO and Gray's enchantingly
evocative arrangements, Williams shows three
of its movements in a new and colourful light.
To anyone with the slightest interest in the guitar or Spanish romantic music, this disc is a
required purchase.

Oboe Concertos

English Oboe Concertos
Elgar Soliloquy (orch Jacob) **Goossens** Oboe
Concerto **Holst** A Fugal Concerto[a] **Jacob** Oboe
Concerto **Vaughan Williams** Oboe Concerto
[a]**Kate Hill** *fl* **Ruth Bolister** *ob* **Elgar Chamber
Orchestra / Stephen Bell**
ASV CDDCA1173 (67' · DDD)   Ⓕ

This is an immensely enjoyable collection. Ruth
Bolister's refined phrasing and elegance of articulation are captivating, especially in Elgar's delicate *Soliloquy* (a fragment of an Oboe Suite,
scored by Gordon Jacob). Jacob's own First
Concerto is the most substantial work, and
given its recording première here. It was written
for Evelyn Rothwell, although Leon Goossens
then purloined it and gave the première in partnership with Beecham. In Ruth Bolister's hands,
the neo-Classical first movement is most divert-
ingly presented and the wistfully yearning
Andante is quite lovely, followed by a more characteristically pastoral closing Rondo.

Flautist Kate Hill's contribution is equally
delightful in the Holst Fugal Concerto; the
opening *Moderato* brings a felicitous interplay,
and the *Adagio*, with its flowing line reminding
one of Bach, has surely never been more beautifully played on record. The Goossens Concerto
is succinctly structured with spicy and unpredictable moments of astringency; the piece has a
sombre lyrical core, yet ends genially. The closing work by Vaughan Williams then makes a
perfect foil, its pastoral feeling naturally caught.

Stephen Bell's accompaniments with the
excellent Elgar Chamber Orchestra could not
be more stylish, the string playing neat and polished, the lustrous recording, warm, natural,
transparent and very much in the demonstration
bracket. Very highly recommended.

Piano Concertos

Beethoven Piano Concerto No 4 in G **Franck**
Symphonic Variations **Ravel** Piano Concerto in G
Ivan Moravec *pf*
Prague Philharmonia / Jiří Bělohlávek
Supraphon SU3714-2 (70' · DDD)   Ⓕⓞ

The coupling may seem odd, but the distinctive
artistry of pianist and conductor results in an
attractive consistency, with each work illuminating the others on this consistently refreshing
disc. What makes Moravec's playing so magnetic is his extraordinary clarity of articulation,
which is well caught in a recording which has the
piano to the fore, if not obtrusively so.

Moravec's crisp enunciation of each note
makes for sparkling results in the first movement of the Beethoven: the delicate tracery of
the piano part in the recapitulation (10'22"
onwards) is wonderfully clear. With incisive
support from Bělohlávek and the Prague Philharmonia, there's no lack of muscular strength
either. Here and in a meditative slow movement
Moravec draws on a wide tonal range. In the
finale Bělohlávek matches his soloist in drawing
from the orchestra comparably transparent textures. The reading is unexaggerated yet fresh
and resilient, often tenderly expressive.

That ability to convey expressive warmth
without exaggeration is also evident in Franck's
Symphonic Variations. The improvisatory writing for the soloist sounds completely natural and
spontaneous as Moravec lavishes rubato on his
part. The faster variations beget bright, clear
textures in both piano part and the orchestral
writing too.

Such lightness and clarity brings out the neo-
classical element in the Ravel Concerto. In the
first movement the contrast is heightened
between the rapid passagework of the main *Allegro* sections and the lyricism of the *Andante* passages, with Bělohlávek colourfully touching in
the jazz influences. The slow movement is
poised, rapt and poetic, the more moving for its
degree of understatement; Moravec characteristically manages a velvety *legato* with only the
lightest use of the pedal. In the reprise of the
main melody the cor anglais is then far too backward when it takes up the theme, an inconsistency that hardly detracts from the effect of the
whole.

Trumpet Concertos

The Trumpet Shall Sound
Handel Trumpet Concertos[a] – in B flat, HWV301;
in B flat, HWV302a; in G minor, HWV287. Messiah,
HWV56 – The trumpet shall sound[b] **Haydn** Trumpet
Concerto in E flat, HobVIIe/1[c] **M Haydn** Trumpet
Concerto in D, MH104[c] **FX Richter** Trumpet
Concerto in D[d] **A Scarlatti** Sinfonia No 2 in D[e]
Stölzel Trumpet Concerto in D[f] **Telemann** Trumpet
Concertos[a] – in E minor, TWV51: e1; in G,
TWVAnh51: G1; in C minor, TWV51: c1. Concerto
Sonata in D, TWV44: 1[f] **Torelli** Trumpet Concerto

No 2 in D^f **Vivaldi** Double Concerto for 2 Trumpets and Strings in C, RV537^f **Viviani** Capricci armonici da chiesa e da camera, Op 4 – Sonata Prima in C^g
Maurice André tpt ^b**Franz Crass** bass ^e**Hans-Martin Linde** fl **Hedwig Bilgram** ^gorg/^a hpd ^f**Maurits Sillem**, ^b**Hilde Noe** hpds ^ab**Munich Bach Orchestra / Karl Richter;** ^cd**Munich Chamber Orchestra / Hans Stadlmair;** ^e**Zurich Collegium Musicum / Paul Sacher;** ^f**English Chamber Orchestra / Sir Charles Mackerras**
DG ② 474 331-2GM2 (155' · ADD) From DG and Archiv Produktion originals, recorded 1965-77　Ⓜ

The first true modern-day classical trumpet soloist, Maurice André is still an icon for many who reckon his unmistakable qualities remain unsurpassed. To celebrate his 70th year DG has compressed his solo work for them onto two full CDs. After his famous win in the Munich Competition of 1963 he went on to become the father of modern playing. He established his instrument as a serious solo vehicle, promulgating new repertoire, either in transcriptions or commissions. He tended to gravitate to the easy juxtaposition of intricate *passagi* and seamless lyricism of the Baroque, almost as if he were an opera singer. His effortless soaring top notes, cultivated vibrato and a soft-tongued articulation were his stock-in-trade. This is a welcome celebration of André's art, but only a snapshot, since he recorded relatively little for DG, the majority from the early years. Erato has previously released collections but with too little discrimination between discs of André in full flow and those made in a mist of Gallic nonchalance.

Sergei Nakariakov – No Limit
Bruch Canzone in B, Op 55^a **Gershwin** (arr Dokshitser) Rhapsody in Blue^b **Massenet** Thaïs – Méditation^a **Saint-Saëns** Introduction and Rondo capriccioso in A minor, Op 28^b **Tchaikovsky** Andante cantabile, Op 11^a. Variations on a Rococo Theme in A, Op 33^a (all arrangements by Mikhail Nakariakov unless otherwise indicated)
Sergei Nakariakov ^aflugelhn/^btpt **Philharmonia Orchestra / Vladimir Ashkenazy**
Teldec 8573-80651-2 (62' · DDD)　Ⓕ〇

What a wonderful trumpeter the young Sergei Nakariakov is! So beautiful is his tone, so naturally musical is his phrasing, so astonishing is his easy virtuosity, that he almost reconciles you to these arrangements. Certainly to the Saint-Saëns, which comes off with splendid panache – and that hair-raisingly fast tonguing at the end is extraordinary. (Is it single- or double-tonguing? It's so clean that it's impossible to tell.) The disc is worth considering for this piece alone.

But for all the warmth of line and tasteful vibrato, Tchaikovsky's Andante cantabile on the flugelhorn just doesn't work. The Rococo Variations fare rather better, with the melodic line at times lying higher up. It really is a lyrical (Variation 3 is beautifully phrased) and bravura tour de force, but still sounds far better on a cello. Max Bruch's Canzone emerges unscathed, and

Massenet's 'Méditation' is romantically stylish if inevitably carrying a whiff of the bandstand. Certainly flugelhorn playing of this calibre is rare.

Nakariakov is undoubtedly in his element in Gershwin, where he returns to the trumpet. He clearly enjoys himself and it's a sparkling performance, with a nice jazzy inflection, and here the trumpet's middle and lower range is used to good effect, with a touch of humour when the bassoon briefly takes over. The big tune is introduced delicately and beguilingly with a mute; but in the following string tutti the saxes fail to shine through.

Throughout, Ashkenazy provides good support; these are very much accompaniments, and the recording balance reflects that priority. But that Gershwin opening should have been left to the clarinet (it was apparently Benny Goodman's idea in the first place).

British Piano Concertos, Volume 3
Darnton Piano Concertino **Ferguson** Piano Concerto, Op 12 **Gerhard** Piano Concerto **Rowley** Piano Concerto No 1
Northern Sinfonia / Peter Donohoe pf
Naxos 8 557290 (78' · DDD)　Ⓢ〇

This third volume in Naxos's British Piano Concerto series is a rewarding survey in which Peter Donohoe maintains the auspicious standards he set in previous anthologies devoted to Rawsthorne and Bliss.

Christian Darnton (1905-81) was a pupil of Charles Wood at Cambridge University who subsequently studied at the RCM and in Berlin. His Concertino for piano and strings dates from 1948; its three compact movements employing an enjoyably astringent, neo-classical language reminiscent of Stravinsky, while offering the soloist plenty of opportunities for display.

A decade earlier, Alec Rowley (1892-1958) completed his First Concerto for piano, strings and percussion. Like the Darnton it's an enjoyable find which never outstays its welcome. Not only is the writing zestful and melodious, the work's centrepiece, a winsome miniature waltz marked *Andante naif*, has all the trappings for widespread popular appeal.

Howard Ferguson (1980-1999) wrote his Concerto for the Festival of Britain in 1951. It's a deeply lovable creation full of the most captivating invention, not least in the haunting theme and variations that form the slow movement. Try the ravishing fifth variation, where Ferguson lays bare his Irish roots, or that profoundly touching final backward glance just before the concerto's joyous conclusion.

Roberto Gerhard's First Concerto, also from 1951, is a more challenging proposition but its fearsome technical demands hold no terrors for Donohoe and Co., who drive an urgent course through the toccata-like opening *Allegro* and 'frenzied, carnival-folly atmosphere' (to quote the composer) of the finale. In the elegiac slow movement a set of variations is woven around a

Catalan religious song and also incorporates elements of the *Dies irae*.

Directing from the keyboard, Donohoe obtains first-class results from the Northern Sinfonia and displays his customarily superior brand of pianism throughout. A superb release and remarkable value for money.

Violin Concertos

Heifetz the Supreme Ⓗ
Bach Violin Partita No 2 in D minor, BWV1004 – Chaconne **Brahms** Violin Concerto in D, Op 77[a]
Bruch Scottish Fantasy, Op 46[b] **Gershwin** (arr Heifetz) Three Preludes[c] **Glazunov** Violin Concerto in A minor, Op 82[d] **Sibelius** Violin Concerto in D minor, Op 47[e] **Tchaikovsky** Violin Concerto in D, Op 35[f]
Jascha Heifetz *vn* [c]Brooks Smith *pf* [aef]Chicago Symphony Orchestra / [af]Fritz Reiner; [b]New Symphony Orchestra / [b]Sir Malcolm Sargent; [d]RCA Victor Symphony Orchestra / [de]Walter Hendl
RCA Red Seal ② 74321 63470-2 (154' · ADD)
Recorded 1955-65 Ⓜ

For once a record company's hype is totally justified. Heifetz was and is supreme. He plays the Bach 'Chaconne', with an extraordinary range of dynamic and feeling, and a total grip on the structure. The subtlety of his bowing is a thing to marvel at. This is a superb anthology, excellently accompanied. How persuasively Reiner shapes the opening of the Brahms, and Sargent the *Scottish Fantasy*; how tenderly Heifetz plays the 'Canzonetta' of the Tchaikovsky, and then astonishes us with his quicksilver brilliance in the finale. Heifetz's first entry in the Sibelius is quite Elysian, and his tone in the slow movement sends shivers down the spine. He discovered all the romantic charm in the Glazunov concerto, and virtually made it his own. And how good that the selection ends with Gershwin, sparklingly syncopated and bluesy by turns: nothing else here better shows the flexibility of the Heifetz bow arm, even if the microphones are too close.

Brahms Violin Concerto in D, Op 77[b] **Hindemith** Violin Sonata in E flat, Op 11[a] **Schnittke** Quasi una Sonata[a] **Schumann** Violin Concerto in D minor, Op posth[c] **Sibelius** Violin Concerto in D minor, Op 47[c] **Weber** Grand duo concertant, J204[a]
Gidon Kremer *vn* [a]**Andrei Gavrilov** *pf* [b]**Berlin Philharmonic Orchestra / Herbert von Karajan;** [c]**Philharmonia Orchestra / Riccardo Muti**
EMI Double Forte ② 569334-2 (151' · ADD) Recorded 1976-82 Ⓜ

This is a fine showcase for Kremer's talent. The Schumann has been a benchmark performance for some years, strong and purposeful in the outer movements, hushed and dedicated in the central slow movement. With Muti a challenging yet sympathetic partner, the Sibelius is also remarkable, not just for Kremer's expressive

warmth, but for his inner intensity in the great opening melodies of the first two movements, each played as a hushed meditation, but with the first flowing freely, fanciful and poetic, not too slow for an *Allegro moderato*. The finale is fast and volatile. His glowing account of the Brahms Concerto was his first collaboration with Karajan and plainly inspired them both. The slow movement has poise and purity, leading to a beautifully sprung account of the finale, with dance rhythms brought out. The analogue recording is comparably spacious. In the three new items Gavrilov proves a comparably inspired partner, with the Weber so winningly characterised – fiery in the first movement, dedicated in the *Andante* and exuberant in the finale – that one almost forgets the original clarinet version, so satisfying is the transformation. The early Hindemith Sonata can rarely have been played with such warmth and intensity, and the Schnittke, full of extended, pregnant pauses, is superbly held together by the concentrated interplay of the performers, an astonishing 20-minute tapestry.

Itzhak Perlman: A la carte
Glazunov Mazurka-Oberek in D. Meditation, Op 32 **Kreisler** The Old Refrain. Schön Rosmarin **Massenet** Thaïs – Méditation **Rachmaninov** Vocalise, Op 34 No 14 **Rimsky-Korsakov** (arr Kreisler) Fantasia on Two Russian Themes, Op 33 **Sarasate** Zigeunerweisen, Op 20. Introduction and Tarantella, Op 43 **Tchaikovsky** (orch Glazunov) Scherzo in C minor, Op 42 No 2 **Wieniawski** Légende, Op 17. Zigeunerweisen
Itzhak Perlman *vn* **Abbey Road Ensemble / Lawrence Foster**
EMI 555475-2 (63' · DDD) ⒻⓄ

A most enjoyable programme. Perlman approximates the 'old school' with something of an actor's skill: he feels the period, not as a first-hand witness (even at 50, he's far too young for that), but as a respectful recipient of a great tradition. His 'Méditation' is an elevated 'easy listen', sensitively accompanied. The Glazunov *Mazurka-Oberek* should be at least as popular as Saint-Saëns's concert pieces for violin and orchestra, and Perlman does it proud. The initial pages of Rachmaninov's *Vocalise* are a little over-sweet (too many well-oiled slides), but its latter half achieves genuine expressive eloquence. Glazunov's *Meditation* is suitably honeyed, and the Kreisler-Rimsky *Fantasia* (where Goldmark's A minor Concerto hovers around the main theme) is given a truly splendid performance. Of the rest, the two Kreisler pieces are exceptional, *Schön Rosmarin* especially, while Lawrence Foster's expert Abbey Road Ensemble provides a discreet but flavoursome orchestral base.

Miscellaneous Orchestral

Haydn Symphony No 83 in G minor, 'La Poule' **Lehár**

Gold und Silber, Op 79 **J Strauss II** Die Fledermaus – Overture. Kaiser-Walzer, Op 437. Perpetuum mobile, Op 257. Tritsch-Tratsch-Polka, Op 214 **R Strauss** Der Rosenkavalier Suite
Hallé Orchestra / Sir John Barbirolli
BBC Legends/IMG Artists BBCL4038-2 (76' · ADD)
Recorded live 1969   ⓂⓄⓄ

Among all the treasures rediscovered in the BBC archives, this disc of a Barbirolli Prom Concert of 1969 is among the most enticing. He opens with one of his favourite Haydn symphonies, and only Beecham can match his delightful characterisation of *The Hen* (dainty violins, plus gently clucking oboe) which Haydn makes sure we hear several times in the course of a most appealing first movement. As shaped by JB the *Andante* combines an Elysian simplicity with classical beauty of line, and the *Minuet* and finale similarly match grace with exuberance. There's surely no finer performance on disc.

Then comes the Johann Strauss section, with Sir John himself vocalising in the Overture's glorious waltz theme. But the highlight is a richly contoured, magical account of the *Emperor Waltz*, with all the mellow nobility of line one associates with Bruno Walter, plus an added touch of Barbirolli's Italianate sunshine. The reprise is so lovely it would melt the hardest heart. Then follows a fun performance of the *Tritsch-Tratsch-Polka*, with outrageous agogic tempo distortions and sudden pauses which bring a couple of great bursts of laughter from the Promenaders. But the best is yet to come.

With the *Rosenkavalier* suite the Hallé strings and horns surpass themselves. The suite may be no more than a comparatively inept pot-pourri, but Sir John invests each section of the score with such loving detail that you can only regret that he never recorded the whole opera. The Prelude, with its sexy, whooping horns, and a great passionate *tenuto* on the key moment of the lovers' passionate embrace (behind the curtain), then leads on to a wonderful feeling of tenderness as their ardour gently subsides. Later the Presentation of the Rose scene, with exquisite oboe playing, is meltingly beautiful. After the great surge of the Viennese waltz sequence, the closing section and the softly sensuous duet that sees Octavian and Sophie raptly departing together is wonderfully affectionate, rudely interrupted by the explosive coda.

The encore is Lehár's *Gold and Silver*. Sir John encourages his Promenaders to hum along gently so as not to overwhelm its famous lyrical melody; he even manages to entice them into a *pianississimo* when it's reprised. Prommers in the late 1960s were just as appreciative but more self-disciplined than they are today, and there's no hint of vulgarity and much warmth in their response. Sir John cuts the coda to make time for his own witty little speech in appreciation of their contribution, continuing with a warmly expressed wish to return with his orchestra; this alone is worth the price of an unforgettable disc, recorded with great warmth and atmosphere.

The Beecham Collection – Delius   Ⓗ
An Arabesk[dfh]. A Mass of Life – Part 2 No 3: Prelude[h]. Songs of Sunset – Parts 1-7[bdfh]; Part 8[cegi]. I-Brasil[ah]. Le ciel est pardessus le toit[ej]. Cradle Song[ej]. Irmelin Rose[ej]. Klein Venevil[eh]. The Nightingale[ej]. Twilight Fancies[ej]. The Violet[eh]. The Violet[ej]. Whither[eh]
[a]**Dora Labbette** *sop* [b]**Olga Haley,** [c]**Nancy Evans** *mezzos* [d]**Roy Henderson,** [e]**Redvers Llewellyn** *bars* [f]**London Select Choir;** [g]**BBC Chorus;** [h]**London Philharmonic Orchestra;** [i]**Royal Philharmonic Orchestra / Sir Thomas Beecham** [j]*pf*
Somm Recordings mono SOMM-BEECHAM8
(74' · ADD) Recorded 1929-46   ⓂⓄ

The Beecham Collection – Handel   Ⓗ
Piano Concerto in A (arr Beecham)[a]. The Gods Go a'Begging[b] – Introduction; Minuet; Hornpipe; Musette; Tambourine; Gavotte; Sarabande; Fugato. The Gods Go a'Begging[c] – Introduction; Larghetto; Gavotte; Allegro; Ensemble; Bourrée The Origin of Design[d]
[a]**Lady Betty Humby Beecham** *pf* [abd]**London Philharmonic Orchestra;** [c]**Royal Philharmonic Orchestra / Sir Thomas Beecham**
Somm Recordings mono SOMM-BEECHAM7
(75' · ADD) Recorded 1932-49   Ⓜ

Thanks to Shirley, Lady Beecham, we have here a splendid range of recordings from Sir Thomas's personal archive, most never issued before. The great treasure is the live recording of Delius's orchestral song-cycle to words by Ernest Dowson, *Songs of Sunset*. The performance has been described as 'achingly beautiful', and that's no exaggeration. Recorded at the Leeds Festival in 1934, it presents a strikingly different view of the work from that of other interpreters on disc. Beecham conveys a virile thrust and energy in the writing, partly opting for faster speeds. Thanks to his magnetism, arguments have a tautness that can otherwise seem to ramble. Both in this, with its seven linked sections, and in the single span of *An Arabesk*, a setting of Jens Peter Jacobsen in Philip Heseltine's translation, the line of the argument is clarified. Roy Henderson is the clean-cut, sensitive baritone soloist in both, sounding very English, with Olga Haley a fresh, bright mezzo soloist in the *Songs of Sunset*. What prevented this inspired reading of the *Songs of Sunset* from being issued before is that the test pressing of the final climactic section is missing. To complete the work, that final ensemble for soloists and chorus together is taken from the studio recording Beecham made for HMV in 1946, but which he rejected. With Nancy Evans and Redvers Llewellyn as soloists, it makes an excellent conclusion, with the chorus more clearly focused than its predecessor in 1934. What matters is that the choral sound in both has ample weight. There's some noise at the ends of 78 sides, but the full-bodied nature of the transfer makes that flaw easy to ignore.

Dora Labbette is the enchanting soprano soloist in all the separate songs, bright and silvery, attacking even the most exposed high notes with astonishing purity and precision, producing magical *pianissimos*. Four of the ten come in the beautiful orchestral versions, with the rest accompanied at the piano by Beecham himself. He may not have been the most accomplished pianist, but his natural magnetism still shines out, not least in the striking early song, longer than the rest, *Twilight Fancies*.

The disc of his arrangements of Handel is just as distinctive, always elegant and warmly expressive. He defies latterday taste if anything even more radically than Stokowski in his arrangements of Bach, yet is similarly winning. The ten movements from the ballet *The Origin of Design* come from the very first recording sessions of Beecham's newly founded London Philharmonic in December 1932. The following month he re-recorded three of the movements, but this far bigger selection of movements was never issued – brilliantly performed, with the players on their toes, not least the soloist Leon Goossens. Sadly the 78 side containing the 'Serenade' is so damaged that the opening of the movement is omitted.

Seven of the movements from the later ballet *The Gods Go a'Begging*, made between 1933 and 1938, did get published, but all the rest, including the six movements from the same ballet recorded with the RPO in 1949, have never appeared in any format.

The oddity is the four-movement Piano Concerto that Beecham cobbled together from various Handel movements for his wife, the pianist Betty Humby. The result makes a curious confection, starting with a nine-minute 'Chaconne' in which grandly spacious sections punctuate energetic chaconne variations. The result is energetic, sounding less like Handel than 20th-century pastiche, with keyboard figuration and pianistic tricks unashamedly reflecting the romantic concerto tradition. As in the Delius disc, transfers bring satisfyingly full-bodied sound, if with obvious limitations. What's clear throughout is the Beecham magic – wonderful control of phrasing and rhythm in performances that are light of touch and full of fun.

Sir Thomas Beecham: The RPO Legacy,   🄷
Volume 5
Berlioz King Lear, Op 4 – Overture **Delius** Summer Evening (ed & arr Beecham) **Dvořák** The Golden Spinning Wheel, Op 109 **Handel-Beecham** The Great Elopement (excerpts) **Haydn** Symphonies – No 40 in F; No 102 in B flat **Liszt** Symphonic Poem, Orpheus, S98 **Massenet** La Vierge – Le dernier sommeil de la Vierge **Méhul** Les deux aveugles de Tolède – Overture **Mendelssohn** Octet, Op 20 – Scherzo. Die schöne Melusine, Op 32 – Overture **Paisiello** Nina, o sia la pazza per amore – Overture **Saint-Saëns** Le rouet d'Omphale in A, Op 31
Royal Philharmonic Orchestra / Sir Thomas Beecham
Dutton Laboratories ② 2CDEA 5026 (151' · ADD)
Recorded 1947-51   Ⓢ ⑬●

Older readers who collected Beecham 78s in the late 1940s, will remember all these recordings. The overtures by Méhul and Paisiello show the great maestro with a twinkle in his eye, but it's the Dvořák *Golden Spinning Wheel* that you never forget and rightly remember for its vividness. In this new Dutton transfer the sound is remarkably wide-ranging, delivering astonishingly crisp percussion and bright violins which offset the truly golden horns, and it comes up almost like a modern recording. The performance, too, of what's essentially an episodic piece, is wonderfully alive and spontaneous.

Fair Melusina was another favourite, and to end the first disc Dennis Brain leads the RPO horns with superb confidence in the spectacular *Trio* of the Minuet of Beecham's pioneering recording of Haydn's 40th, F major Symphony. The performance of No 102 is marvellous: what grace and vitality there is here. The Mendelssohn *Scherzo* is as light as thistledown, and only Martinon (Decca) approached Beecham's exquisite touch in *Le rouet d'Omphale*. *Orpheus*, too, sounds especially beautiful in Beecham's hands, while Handel-Beecham is like Bach-Stokowski: its unique qualities (here an affectionate elegance and a true feeling for Baroque colour) certainly counter any charges of anachronism. This is altogether an unmissable collection; and the Dutton transfers are fresh, clear and full-bodied like the old 78s were (even on modest equipment). The notes, as usual, are by Lyndon Jenkins, and they're as informative as ever.

Beethoven Leonore Overture No 2, Op 72[b]   🄷
Brahms Tragic Overture, Op 81[b]. Symphony No 2 in D, Op 73[d] **Haydn** Sinfonia concertante in B flat, Hob I:105[ab] **Mendelssohn** Symphony No 4 in A, 'Italian', Op 90[b] **Mozart** Symphony No 36 in C, 'Linz', K425[b] **R Strauss** Don Juan, Op 20[c] **Weber** Der Freischütz – Overture[b]
[a]**Waldemar Wolsing** ob [a]**Carl Bloch** bn [a]**Leo Hansen** vn [a]**Alberto Medici** vc [b]**Danish State Radio Symphony Orchestra;** [c]**London Philharmonic Orchestra / Fritz Busch**
EMI/IMG Artists mono ② 575103-2 (157' · ADD)
[ab]Recorded 1947-51, [c]1936, [d]1950   Ⓜ

Those who think of Fritz Busch simply as a Mozartian, the great musical architect of opera at Glyndebourne from 1934 onwards, will find it a revelation that he conveys such authority in this wide range of works in the central orchestral repertory. They are superbly played by the Danish orchestra he did so much to bring up to a standard; in many ways, it put British orchestras at that time to shame. Not only is the playing refined and polished in a way that after the war only the newly founded Philharmonia and RPO were beginning to match, but every one of these performances conveys high voltage intensity.

Except for the 1936 account of Strauss's *Don Juan* with the LPO, searingly dramatic though recorded in boxy sound, all these recordings were made with the Danish State Radio Orchestra between 1947 and 1951 in the hall built by

Danish Radio – a wonderfully helpful acoustic. It seems irrelevant that these are all mono recordings, so full and atmospheric is the sound.

Busch's 1947 recording of Brahms's Second Symphony is a recording long cherished by collectors, and this new transfer rekindles the thrill of the performance. At speeds that are fast as well as steady, it brings out the dramatic thrust of a work often regarded as lyrical above all.

The Weber Overture and Mozart *Linz* Symphony are just as compelling, with bite and energy given higher priority than charm. The recordings of *Leonore* No 2, Brahms's *Tragic Overture* and Mendelssohn's *Italian* Symphony are all taken from live radio recordings, which unlike some from that immediate post-war period are as vivid in sound as the commercial recordings of EMI, though the Weber recording has relatively high surface hiss.

Glazunov Symphony No 6 in C minor, Op 58 [H]
Liszt Orpheus, S98. Héroïde funèbre, S102. Mazeppa, S100. Festklänge, S101. Prometheus, S99
Mendelssohn A Midsummer Night's Dream – Overture; Scherzo **Tchaikovsky** 1812 Overture, Op 49
Moscow Radio Symphony Orchestra / Nicolai Golovanov
EMI/IMG Artists mono ② 575112-2 (148' · ADD). From Melodiya originals recorded 1948-53 Ⓜ

Nicolai Golovanov was one of the outstanding Russian conductors of the generation before Mravinsky. Hounded from his post as chief conductor at the Bolshoi Theatre in 1952, he died the following year, but not before making some recordings that richly deserve their place in this series. Unlike Mravinsky, he evidently did not rehearse familiar repertoire to death, being more prepared to tolerate rough edges in the interests of the live re-creative act. So while these performances may not make first choices, they're all inspiring in one way or another.

The Glazunov Sixth Symphony will startle those inclined to consider his musical invention rather slack. Everything here tingles with life and passion, as though the music were being composed in front of our very eyes. As with the great Furtwängler, incandescence and revelation are the words that come to mind. Intensity is sustained across all four movements, and Golovanov even makes the finale seem less of a stop-start affair than usual.

Of the remaining performances, Tchaikovsky's *1812* – recorded only three years after the end of the Great Patriotic War, and with the 'Slava' chorus from Glinka's *A Life for the Tsar* grafted on to the Tsarist hymn at the end – appears to be the most valuable. Recording quality is surprisingly clean for this vintage and provenance. True, the end of the first movement of the Glazunov suddenly changes perspective, while *Prometheus* suffers quite badly from distortion. But the communicative force of Golovanov's conducting triumphs over such shortcomings.

Beethoven Symphony No 5 in C minor, Op 67[a] [H]
Harris Symphony No 3[b] **Liszt** Mephisto Waltz No 1, S110 No 2[c] **Rachmaninov** The Isle of the Dead, Op 29[d] **Sibelius** Symphony No 7 in C, Op 105[e]
Tchaikovsky Symphony No 5 in E minor, Op 64[f]
[bcdf]**Boston Symphony Orchestra;** [e]**BBC Symphony Orchestra;** [a]**London Philharmonic Orchestra / Serge Koussevitzky**
EMI Classics/IMG Artists mono ② 575118-2 (149' · ADD) Recorded [a]1933, [b]1942, [c]1936, [e]live 1933, [f]1944, [d]1945 Ⓜ⬤

This set provides the perfect entrée into Serge Koussevitzky's world. There are no weak links; even the Beethoven, a little self-consciously grandiloquent in style, is by no means uninteresting or lacking in fervour. Transfers are vivid and full, notwithstanding some unavoidably crumbly moments in the Harris. Only don't expect too wide a dynamic range – it isn't there in the original source material.

The conductor's instrument of choice was the Boston Symphony Orchestra, which he led from 1924 until 1949. Their music-making is distinguished by a peculiar intensity allied to a depth of sonority and care over finish unequalled until Karajan's Berlin years. EMI's programme starts with a famously white-hot version of Tchaikovsky's Fifth. The conductor's considerable liberties matter not a jot, given the urgently communicative nature of the music-making: it would be a cold-hearted music-lover who could not respond to such a performance. Curiously perhaps, the reading's marked freedom of nuance isn't a feature of the Rachmaninov symphonic poem, let alone the Roy Harris Third Symphony. Again though, it's impossible to imagine either work being performed with greater electricity.

The Sibelius is something else again: Koussevitzky guest conducting in what was then very unfamiliar music and with a very new orchestra – the BBC Symphony. For some listeners, the extraordinary tension of this performance, captured live in 1933, is too much of a good thing, and one has heard carping criticism of the conductor's departures from the score. The truth is that no metronome marks having yet been printed, Koussevitzky had no choice but to go his own way. What matters is that such priceless documents remain in circulation to show us what these disconcertingly astute dinosaurs were capable of. Strongly recommended.

Constant Lambert – The Last Recordings [H]
Chabrier Pièces posthumes – Ballabile (orch Lambert)[a] **Suppé** Ein Morgen, ein Mittag, ein Abend in Wien – Overture[b]. Pique Dame – Overture[c]
Waldteufel Estudiantina, Op 191[d]. Les Patineurs, Op 183[e]. Pomone, Op 155[f]. Sur la plage, Op 234[g]
Walton Façade[h] – Suite No 1; Suite No 2
Philharmonia Orchestra / Constant Lambert
Somm Céleste Series mono SOMMCD023 (73' · ADD) Recorded 1949-50 Ⓜ

Constant Lambert was a flamboyant, sparkling

figure who thrived on colourful music like this, so it's sad that he died just before the advent of stereo. That all his recordings are in mono has had the effect, at least until recently, of deterring those who might resurrect them in whatever format. This charming disc, a generous and very well-transferred collection, fills an important gap. Lambert's flair as a ballet conductor is reflected in all the items here. Consistently whether in Waldteufel waltzes, Suppé overtures or the orchestral *Façade* pieces – source of a highly successful ballet – Lambert is masterly at giving a spring to the dance-rhythms, while never indulging excessively in *rubato* unhelpful to dancers. The idiomatic Viennese-style hesitations in the waltzes, notably the *Skaters' Waltz* and the Suppé Viennese overture, are exquisitely judged, never too obtrusive, just nudging you enough, while Lambert rivals even the composer himself in bringing out the fun of *Façade*. He was, after all, almost its surrogate creator, the friend of Walton who alongside him discovered the joys of jazz and syncopated rhythms in the early 1920s.

It's remarkable, too, that even with the limitations of mono recording of 1950 Lambert keeps textures ideally clear and transparent, helped by the refined playing of the Philharmonia Orchestra, not least the string section, adding to the freshness of all these performances. A delightful disc.

American Tapestry
Griffes The White Peacock **Hovhaness** Symphony No 2, 'Mysterious Mountain', Op 132 **Ives** Orchestral Set No 1, 'Three Places in New England' **Piston** Suite, The Incredible Flutist **Schuman** New England Triptych
Dallas Symphony Orchestra / Andrew Litton
Dorian DOR90224 (73' · DDD)　　Ⓕ🅾🅾

A dazzling calling-card for the formidable technical and interpretative skills of the Litton/Dallas Symphony partnership, featuring five American masters at their most approachable; an ideal introduction for anyone yet to dip a toe into the vast range of repertoire beyond Gershwin, Copland and Barber. We kick off in exhilarating style with William Schuman's marvellous *New England Triptych* of 1956. Taking its cue from hymn tunes by Schuman's countryman William Billings (1746-1800), the work comprises two bustling tableaux framing a central meditation ('When Jesus wept') of exalted beauty and compassion. Next comes Charles Griffes's gorgeous *The White Peacock* – a transatlantic cousin to Debussy's *Prélude à l'après-midi d'un faune*. With the first of Ives's *Three Places in New England*, for all its fastidious refinement, Litton's direction remains oddly earthbound and short on atmosphere. Otherwise, all goes swimmingly, the giddy, increasingly hilarious din of the central 'Putnam's Camp' dashingly well conveyed. No grumbles, either, about Litton's clean-limbed, purposeful way with Alan Hovhaness's *Mysterious Mountain* (his Second Symphony, composed

in 1955 for Stokowski and the Houston Symphony), a serene yet agreeably sturdy score. Last there's the crowd-pleasing concert suite that Walter Piston fashioned from his 1938 ballet score *The Incredible Flutist*. It's a delectably tuneful and witty confection, crammed with indelible invention. Litton and his terrific band do it proud. The glorious acoustic of Dallas's Eugene McDermott Hall lends an glow to a sound picture of bewitching tonal naturalness and stunning range (bass-drum fanciers will have a field-day in both outer movements of the Schuman). A classy collection.

Entente Cordiale
Franck Chorale No 2 in B minor (arr Phelps)[b]
J Gabriel-Marie Miréio, Suite Provençal **Hope** Four French Dances **Jongen** Two Pieces, Op 53a (arr Lane)[a] **Lecocq** Liline et Valentin – Overture (arr Nelson) **P Lewis** À Paris **Smyth** Entente cordiale – Interlude (Two Interlinked French Melodies) **Warlock** Capriol Suite
[a]**Verity Butler** *cl* **City of Prague Philharmonic Orchestra / Gavin Sutherland,** [b]**Christopher Phelps**
ASV White Line CDWHL2147 (70' · DDD)　　Ⓜ

ASV White Line has an enviable catalogue of lighter music; but this offering is one of the best. It begins on familiar territory with Warlock's *Capriol Suite*, played in its orchestral version in a spirited interpretation, and ends on less familiar ground with Christopher Phelps's orchestral transcription of the second of César Franck's organ Chorales. In between come more transcriptions of organ pieces by a Belgian in two short and contrasted impressionist pieces by Joseph Jongen, orchestrated by the CD's producer, Philip Lane. The brief but engaging Ethel Smyth piece comes from her light opera *Entente cordiale*, while that by Charles Lecocq is from his 1864 operetta *Liline et Valentin*. Refurbished more than 100 years later by Havelock Nelson, it's at once the earliest, briefest and jolliest piece here. Beyond that, the French tributes of Peter Hope and Paul Lewis again show what accomplished and appealing music present-day British light music composers have to offer.

Most impressive of all, perhaps, is the suite of six movements from a 1930 dramatisation of *Miréio*, Frédéric Mistral's Provençal epic poem from which came Gounod's opera *Mireille*. Its Marseilles-based composer, Jean Gabriel-Marie, was the son of Gabriel-Marie, whose delightful miniature *La Cinquantaine* is still enjoyed. Steeped in Provençal atmosphere, the *Miréio* music breathes the air of Bizet's *L'Arlésienne* as it vividly evokes day-to-day life, customs, and celebrations.

Admirably played and recorded, the programme has a freshness and variety that makes delightful listening from beginning to end.

New World Jazz
J Adams Lollapalooza **Antheil** A Jazz Symphony

Bernstein Prelude, Fugue and Riffs **Gershwin**
Rhapsody in Blue **Hindemith** Ragtime **Milhaud** La
création du monde **Raksin** The Bad and the Beautiful
– main theme **Stravinsky** Ebony Concerto
Tad Calcara, Jerome Simas cls **New World**
Symphony / Michael Tilson Thomas pf
RCA Red Seal 09026 68798-2 (68' · DDD) Ⓕ**OO**

The Ultimate Jazz Album, this, imaginatively
programmed and impeccably realised by all
involved. We kick off with the dazzling world
première recording of John Adams' *Lollapalooza*
(1995), whose infectiously rhythmic, post-modern cavortings are relished to the full by Tilson
Thomas and his superb young band. This *Rhapsody in Blue* evinces an improvisatory fantasy and
edge-of-seat, theatrical fervour to make one
appreciate anew the extraordinary boldness,
reckless danger even, of Gershwin's ground-
breaking inspiration. Bernstein's exhilarating
Prelude, Fugue and Riffs receives the outing of
a lifetime, a gloriously idiomatic, stunningly
assured display which, like the wonderfully
poised reading of Stravinsky's *Ebony Concerto*,
invites and fully withstands comparison with the
best rivals. We also get a singularly deft and
atmospheric performance of Milhaud's 1923
ballet masterpiece, *La création du monde*, whose
striking pre-echoes of Gershwin have never
seemed more potent. All of which leaves Hindemith's 'well-tempered' *Ragtime*, a mischievous
reworking from 1921 of the C minor Fugue
from Book 1 of the *48* (and dispatched on this
occasion with a gleeful exuberance), George
Antheil's endearingly outrageous *A Jazz Symphony* and David Raksin's gorgeous main title for
Vincente Minnelli's *The Bad and the Beautiful*
(1952). Thrillingly realistic sound throughout.
Not to be missed!

Tortelier's French Bonbons
Adam Si j'étais roi – Overture **Auber** Le cheval de
bronze – Overture **Chabrier** Habanera. Joyeuse
marche **Gounod** Marche funèbre d'une marionnette
Hérold Zampa – Overture **Maillart** Les dragons de
Villars – Overture **Massenet** Les Erinnyes – Tristesse
du soir. Thaïs – Méditation[a][c]. Mélodie – Elégie (arr
Mouton)[b]. La Vierge – Le dernier sommeil de la
Vierge **Offenbach** La belle Hélène – Overture (arr
Haensch). Les contes d'Hoffmann – Entr'acte et
Barcarolle[c]. **Thomas** Mignon – Overture; Me voici
dans son boudoir
[a]**Yuri Torchinsky** vn [b]**Peter Dixon** vc [c]**Royal**
Liverpool Philharmonic Choir; BBC Philharmonic
Orchestra / Yan Pascal Tortelier
Chandos CHAN9765 (75' · DDD) Ⓕ

This splendid collection is a worthy successor to
many nostalgically remembered LPs by Paul
Paray and others. The concert opens in the
bandstand with gusto and style; and after
Hérold's *Zampa* comes Gounod's whimsical little *Marche funèbre d'une marionnette*, beloved of
Alfred Hitchcock. The succession of wind (and
harp) solos at the opening of *Mignon* is beautifully played (there's plenty of warm romantic

feeling throughout the disc) and Adam's *Si j'étais
roi* is delectably pointed, as is the exhilarating
closing galop of Auber's *Cheval de bronze*. Maillart's grandiose, very French military piece is
vigorously projected, Chabrier lilts, and the
gentler evocations by Massenet make seductive
interludes. But it's the overall zest one remembers. Tortelier doesn't push anything too hard,
yet gives the rhythms plenty of lift, and his codas
fizz nicely. The BBC Philharmonic is on top
form and the Chandos recording is top-drawer,
vivid, resonant and glowing. All in all, a programme to cheer you up on a bleak winter's day.
Just try *La belle Hélène* and you'll be won over.

Martucci Song of Remembrance[a] **Schumann** Ⓗ
Symphony No 2 in C, Op 61 **Tommasini** Il carnevale a
Venezia **Wagner** A Faust Overture
[a]**Bruna Castagna** mez **NBC Symphony Orchestra /**
Arturo Toscanini
Naxos Historical ② 8 110836/7 (89' · ADD) Recorded
1941   Ⓢ

Schubert Symphony No 2 in B flat, D125 **Wagner**
Parsifal – Prelude; Good Friday music (concert
version); Klingsor's Garden (concert version)
NBC Symphony Orchestra / Arturo Toscanini
Naxos Historical 8 110838 (73' · ADD) Recorded 1940
Ⓢ**O**

The success of any Toscanini broadcast series
depends largely on the quality of available
source material, and on that count alone,
Naxos's enterprise seems notably superior to
most that have preceded it.

Martucci's lyrical *La canzone dei ricordi* (or
'The Song of Remembrance') was orchestrated
by the composer in 1900 and is vaguely reminiscent of Debussy's *La damoiselle élue*. Bruna
Castagna's seamless mezzo is well employed,
and so are the tender-toned NBC strings.
Debussy's muse also haunts Tommasini's
colourful *Carnival of Venice* Variations where
Toscanini's characteristic interpretative priorities are textural clarity, singing lines and driving
rhythms. Neither work strikes one as especially
memorable; perhaps the Martucci just edges it.
Both sound adequate, though the opening bars
of *La canzone* are prone to crumble.

The tension of the opening pages of the 1941
account of Wagner's Faust Overture, the
swelling Brucknerian curve of the broadened
principal theme and the finely tensed delivery of
the main argument, all are exceptional. So is the
playing, though it's not as demonstrably spectacular as the second movement of Schumann's
Second Symphony. Aside from staccato-style
phrasing at great speed, the switch between the
main motive and two successive trios witnesses a
degree of dynamic elasticity that any soloist
would view as a severe challenge. Here, the
entire band swings from one episode to the next
like a single player. It's simply stunning.

Turning to the 1940 concert, Schubert's Second is again up against a Toscanini rival, from
1938 this time. But while the 1946 Schumann
Second does at least have a spot of extra clarity

on its side, the 1938 Schubert Two (the two performances are usefully coupled together on Dell'Arte) sounds bad-tempered and relentless virtually for the duration. Two years later, Toscanini let the air in – and he also encouraged his players to sing. True, the mood is still high-octane and speeds are pretty nifty (a pitch rise in the second movement further intensifies a sense of haste). But those who know only the earlier broadcast will note how this second version accommodates added perspectives, as well as extra flexibility and countless tiny crescendos that were barely hinted at before. It's a far more musical reading, better balanced as sound though not as viscerally 'immediate'.

The Parsifal selection is fascinating, though the 'acid top' that grated on the old Music & Arts LPs is still sometimes in evidence. Generally, though, the sound is improved and the performances are, for the most part, extraordinarily gripping. The Prelude is the exception, which Toscanini played with greater intensity on other occasions, though here the closing pages are beautifully sustained. Naxos advises us that, in addition to the Prelude and Good Friday Music, we should expect 24 minutes of Klingsor's Garden. Not so. The general intention seems to have been to counter the static aura of the previous excerpts with a healthy quota of music drama. What we actually hear is the Prelude to Act 2, followed by the Third Act Prelude, the animated lead-up to Klingsor's Magic Garden, the Garden itself and then an orchestrated version of the opera's serene closing pages. Why Toscanini didn't insert the Good Friday Music between the Klingsor's Garden and the finale is anyone's guess, but as a makeshift 'synthesis' it works well, and most of the playing is fabulous. It offers a tantalising glimpse of what Toscanini's Parsifal might have sounded like in the theatre, though tempos are rather faster than we have been led to expect.

CHAMBER

String Quartets

Black Angels
Crumb Black Angels **Tallis** (arr Kronos Qt) Spem in alium **Marta** Doom. A sigh **Ives** (arr Kronos Qt/Geist) They are there! **Shostakovich** String Quartet No 8 in C minor, Op 110
Kronos Quartet (David Harrington, John Sherba vns Hank Dutt va Joan Jeanrenaud vc)
Nonesuch 7559-79242-2 (62' · DDD) Ⓕ**OO**

This is very much the sort of imaginative programming we've come to expect from this talented young American quartet. With an overall theme of war and persecution the disc opens with George Crumb's *Black Angels*, for electric string quartet. This work was inspired by the Vietnam War and bears two inscriptions to that

effect – *in tempore belli* (in time of war) and 'Finished on Friday the 13th of March, 1970', and it's described by Crumb as 'a kind of parable on our troubled contemporary world'. The work is divided into three sections which represent the three stages of the voyage of the soul – fall from grace, spiritual annihilation and redemption.

As with most of his works he calls on his instrumentalists to perform on a variety of instruments other than their own – here that ranges from gongs, maracas and crystal glasses to vocal sounds such as whistling, chanting and whispering. *Doom. A sigh* is the young Hungarian composer István Marta's disturbing portrait of a Romanian village as they desperately fight to retain their sense of identity in the face of dictatorship and persecution.

Marta's atmospheric blend of electronic sound, string quartet and recorded folk-songs leave one with a powerful and moving impression. At first sight Tallis's *Spem in alium* may seem oddly out of place considering the overall theme of this disc, but as the insert-notes point out the text was probably taken from the story of Judith, in which King Nebuchadnezzar's general Holofernes besieged the Jewish fortress of Bethulia. Kronos's own arrangement of this 40-part motet (involving some multi-tracking) certainly makes a fascinating alternative to the original.

A particularly fine account of Shostakovich's Eighth String Quartet (dedicated to the victims of fascism and war) brings this thought-provoking and imaginative recital to a close. Performances throughout are outstanding, and the recording first-class.

LifeMusic
D'Rivera The Village Street Quartet **Pann** Love Letters **Puts** Dark Vigil of Youth **Torke** Corner in Manhattan
Ying Quartet (Timothy Ying, Janet Ying vns Phillip Ying va David Ying vc)
Quartz QTZ2003 (76' · DDD) Ⓕ**O**

Dark Vigil, written just after the Columbine High School shootings, is a meditation on the emotional turmoil of adolescence and its increasing expression through violence. It's a controlled piece in one 20-minute movement, cast in late-Romantic/early-Modern mould and proving there is still something fresh to be said within 'the great tradition'. Kevin Puts achieves a number of marvellous textural effects, occasionally evoking Bartók and Shostakovich. While there are passages of intense grief, he never succumbs to melodrama, potentially a major trap with a subject as emotionally fraught and bewildering as this.

Carter Pann, too, inspired by Janáček's *Intimate Letters*, draws heavily on Romanticism, but also throws in other stylistic references right up to contemporary pop. These are, however, so well integrated that there is no sense of Po-Mo chicanery. Indeed, one of the most pleasing aspects of this CD is how the composers work within the classic quartet tradition, in contrast to so many contemporary exponents who resort to obtrusive tricks of technique and additional instruments. The Yings respond with exemplary performances.

Torke and D'Rivera set out to celebrate the rhythms of Lower Manhattan life, with particular reference to Greenwich Village. It's a tall order, and probably neither composer fulfils it. D'Rivera employs various styles to depict the Village's multi-ethnic character. Torke sticks to his usual schtick to create an entertaining kaleidoscope of activity morning, noon and night on the streets that intersect outside his apartment, with some unexpectedly languorous writing in the slow movement.

String trios

Forbidden Music
Klein Trio[ab]. Duo[b] **Krása** Tanec[ab]. Passacaglia and Fugue[ab] **Ravel** Kaddish (arr Hope) **Schulhoff** Duo[b]. Solo Violin Sonata
Daniel Hope vn [a]**Philip Dukes** va [b]**Paul Watkins** vc
Nimbus NI5702 (67' · DDD)   Ⓕ

Divorcing 'forbidden art' from the tragic circumstances of its targeted creators is a painfully difficult task. Yet the crucial question remains: how might posterity have viewed Gideon Klein, Hans Krása and Ervín Schulhoff had they lived on to pursue a regular composing career? Possibly much as it has viewed (for example) Bloch, Martinů and Milhaud, strong voices gratefully heard, even musically significant.

At 25 Klein was the youngest to fall, his gritty String Trio of 1944 having been completed days before he was transported from Theresienstadt (promoted by the Nazis as a 'self-ruling' Jewish community) to Auschwitz. His early Duo for violin and cello lay uncompleted, a pity given that its second movement *Lento* – played here as Klein left it – was venturing into deep waters.

All this music is vital, intelligent, heartfelt and unsentimental. On occasion, humorous too. Time and again there are strange and unexpected things, such as echoes of Wagner. The folk element is strong throughout, most forcefully in Schulhoff's 1922 Sonata for solo violin, and ingeniously in Krása's five-minute *Tanec* for string trio, a dazzling mini-masterpiece.

It would be all too easy to lavish praise on this programme more out of compassion than as a result of objective appraisal, but happily that isn't necessary. Hope, Dukes and Watkins play their hearts out. The disc ends with a touching solo rendition of Ravel's *Kaddish*, the Jewish prayer for the dead. A magnificent CD.

Piano Trios

Beaux Arts Trio – Philips Recordings 1967-74
Chopin Piano Trio in G minor, Op 8 **Ives** Piano Trio

Mendelssohn Piano Trios[a] – No 1 in D minor, Op 49; No 2 in C minor, Op 66 **C Schumann** Piano Trio in G minor, Op 17 **Schumann** Piano Trios – No 1 in D minor, Op 63; No 2 in F, Op 80; No 3 in G minor, Op 110 **Shostakovich** Piano Trio No 2 in E minor, Op 67 **Smetana** Piano Trio in G minor, B104 **Tchaikovsky** Piano Trio in A minor, Op 50
Beaux Arts Trio (Menahem Pressler *pf* Isidore Cohen, [a]Daniel Guilet *vns* Bernard Greenhouse *vc*)
Philips Original Masters ④ 475 171-2PC4 (308' · ADD)
From Philips originals, recorded 1967-74   Ⓑ

This bumper selection from the Beaux Arts' vast discography reminds you of their ability to encompass every aspect of Romantic music.

The two Mendelssohn trios feature their original line-up, with Daniel Guilet's elegant, clear-toned violin playing. In the outer movements of the D minor Trio the many passages of continuous piano passagework are given shape through Menahem Pressler's uncommonly expressive touch, resulting in performances that are unusually dramatic. The *scherzos* in both trios are marvels of delicacy and precision, with Guilet and Greenhouse demonstrating sparkling, carefree *spiccato* bowing.

Pressler is similarly idiomatic and persuasive with Schumann and Chopin, playing the virtuoso episodes in the Chopin fluently, with beautifully balanced tone, reserving a harder, more brittle sound for a few climactic moments.

Schumann's style of trio writing, favouring warm, blended sonorities, benefits from the sound of Isidore Cohen's violin, with its more soft-edged quality. It's a revelation to hear such a splendid account of the Clara Schumann, a work that's more classical in outlook than Robert's chamber music, but full of original, romantic touches.

The trio embrace wholeheartedly the direct, uninhibited emotional expression of Smetana's early masterpiece, written as an elegy after the death of his young daughter. The players avoid crudely melodramatic sounds and gestures; more intimate passages have a warm, heart-on-sleeve expressiveness that's deeply touching.

Tchaikovsky pushes the boundaries of chamber music further than Smetana, demanding large-scale, concerto-style projection. This version tends to emphasise intimate detail above grand, pseudo-orchestral effects. The climaxes are played for all they're worth, but with refinement, so that even in the most intense passages we're aware of small inflexions and changing tones of voice.

The Ives is extremely persuasive, even if some of the jagged edges in the first and last movements are smoothed over. The middle movement, 'T.S.I.A.J.' (explained as 'This Scherzo Is A Joke'), done with amazing panache and exactness, is a masterpiece of surreal comedy.

The Shostakovich isn't an entirely idiomatic account (they don't always manage to tone down their habitual warmth), but has some extraordinary moments – a ferociously fast second movement, and a climax in the finale that's built up with a gradual, inexorable rise in tension.

Duos

Duos for Violin and Cello

Bach Two-Part Invention No 6 in E, BWV777
Handel/Halvorsen (arr Press) Passacaglia **Kodály**
Duo, Op 7 **Ravel** Sonata for Violin and Cello
Kennedy vn **Lynn Harrell** vc
EMI 556963-2 (58' · ADD)   Ⓕ

Here's a brilliant expiation for those crusty old curmudgeons who would tell you that Kennedy's musical priorities are rather to shock than to please. He plays into Lynn Harrell's hands as if they had once shared a single umbilical chord. Ravel's rarely heard Sonata for Violin and Cello finds them locked in earnest dialogue (as in the first movement) or sparring furiously (in the second), alternating sundry dramatic effects, such as slammed cello *pizzicatos* and lacerating bowed *fortissimos* (a Kennedy speciality). They also alternate harmonics (2'40" into the *Très vif* second movement), then bring a veiled brand of poetry to the slow movement (marked *Lent* and a sure recollection of the Piano Trio's *Passacaille*, composed some six years earlier). It's an amazing piece, mostly characteristic but with fleeting suggestions of various contemporaries. One imagines that Kennedy's interest in various indigenous musics fuels his enthusiasm for Kodály's earthy Op 7. You can almost see him chuckle at the tipsy folk-tune at 4'32" into the last movement – even more so when it makes a humorous return – and Harrell's playing mirrors the mood exactly.

In the Handel-Halvorsen *Passacaglia* Kennedy and Harrell employ a very individual brand of fire – teasing, grappling, racing or duetting as if they were playing jazz. Wonderful fun and an urgent candidate for the Replay button, that's if you reach it before the Bach Two-part Invention has started. If it has, you'll end the listening session with a mood of sublime simplicity. You can't really go wrong, either way.

Violin Fantasies

Ernst Fantaisie brillante…sur Otello de Rossini,
Op 11 **Schoenberg** Phantasy, Op 47 **Schubert** Fantasie in C, D934 **Waxman** Carmen Fantasia
Frank Huang vn **Dina Vainstein** pf
Naxos 8 557121 (57' · DDD)   Ⓢ

Frank Huang is a winner of many international prizes, culminating in his triumph in the 2003 Naumburg competition, America's oldest and most prestigious. His silken virtuosity makes light of the most outlandish difficulties in the Ernst and Waxman items, and glows with an unfaltering musicianship throughout.

His opening fantasy, D934 – sufficiently novel to provoke a walk-out at its first performance – is as fine-toned and vivacious as the most ardent Schubertian could wish, played with enviably translucent poetry. Ernst's Fantaisie demands, as the excellent accompanying notes tell us, 'all the technical command of a Paganini', and Huang is more than alert to its qualifying *bril-*

lante marking, spinning off the coda with nonchalant finesse. Schoenberg's Phantasy could hardly be given more persuasively. Huang's playing in Waxman's *Carmen Fantasia* is a marvel of technical finish and poetic allure. He's more than ably partnered by Dina Vainstein, who's clearly a fine pianist in her own right. Sound and balance are exemplary; this is an outstanding addition to the Naxos Laureate Series.

Devil's Dance

Bazzini La ronde des lutins, Op 25 **Bolcom** Graceful
Ghost **Brahms** Walpurgisnacht, Op 75 No 4 **Grieg**
(arr Achron) Puck, Op 71 No 3 **Korngold** (arr Révay)
Caprice fantastique, 'Wichtelmännchen'
Mendelssohn Hexenlied, Op 8 No 8 **Morris** Young
Frankenstein – A Transylvanian Lullaby **Paganini** (arr
Schumann) Caprice No 13 in B flat **Saint-Saëns** (arr
cpsr) Danse macabre, Op 40 **Sarasate** Concert
Fantasy on Gounod's 'Faust' **Tartini** (arr Kreisler)
Violin Sonata in G minor, 'Devil's Trill' **Williams** (arr
cpsr) The Witches of Eastwick – The Devil's Dance
Ysaÿe Solo Violin Sonata in A minor, Op 27 No 2 –
first movement
Gil Shaham vn **Jonathan Feldman** pf
DG 463 483-2GH (69' · DDD)   Ⓕⵔ

According to the prominent red caution notice provided, you approaches the opening track on this CD at your peril. But as it happens John Williams's title-piece, ingenious as it is, is less devilish than the closing excerpt from Ysaÿe's Solo Violin Sonata, Op 27 No 2, which, after a whiff of unaccompanied Bach, offers the *Dies irae* as a demonic *cantus firmus* (always clear) for Gil Shaham's dazzlingly fiendish decorations. Tartini's *Devil's Trill* Sonata (supposedly inspired in a dream by the Prince of Darkness himself), heard in Kreisler's arrangement, opens with a disarmingly mellow warmth. Shaham makes light of the once much-feared trills and here totally civilises the satanic influence. If you need to be petrified by this piece, you have to turn to Andrew Manze's recording. Nevertheless, overall this is a most engaging collection, imaginatively devised, played with panache, and given demonstration sound quality – not a scratch can be heard.

There are quite a few finds too, notably Grieg's delicious 'Puck', a sparkling *scherzando*, and Korngold's impish *Wichtelmännchen*, with its quirky coda, while Mendelssohn's *Hexenlied* has a 'sprite'-ly charm . Bazzini's *La ronde des lutins* , one of the most hair-raising of all violinistic showpieces, is taken here at a fair old lick, and with much aplomb, while William Bolcom's elegantly *Graceful Ghost* brings a wraith-like halcyon interlude. Paganini himself couldn't have presented this programme with more diabolically easy bravura, and certainly not with such a consistent sense of style.

Virtuoso

Bazzini La ronde des lutins, Op 25 **Bloch** Baal shem –
Nigun **Kreisler** Schön Rosmarin. Tambourin chinois.

Caprice viennois **Messiaen** Thème et Variations
Paganini I palpiti, Op 13 **Sarasate** Caprice basque,
Op 24 **Tchaikovsky** Souvenir d'un lieu cher, Op 42 –
No 2, Scherzo in C minor; No 3, Mélodie in E flat
Wieniawski Polonaise No 1 in D, Op 4. Légende,
Op 17
Maxim Vengerov vn **Itamar Golan** pf
Teldec 9031-77351-2 (67' · DDD) Recorded 1993 ⓂⓄ

Maxim Vengerov is such a masterful musician
that everything he touches turns to gold. First,
his intonation is impeccable. The purity and
steadiness of Paganini's *I palpiti* is such that one
never has the impression of his being under any
strain. The double-stopping episodes in Wieniawski's *Légende* appear to come as naturally to
him as single notes. He captures the mawkish
Slavonic melancholy with real intensity. In the
Kreisler selection Vengerov is gentle and generous-spirited, charmingly pure in *Schön Rosmarin*
and idiomatic for the tongue-in-cheek *Tambourin chinois*. The Bazzini has terrific attack,
though it might have been more impish. The
piece is undeniably inconsequential, but one is
left gawping at the phenomenal accuracy and
confidence of the left-hand *pizzicato* section at
the end. In conclusion it must be said that rarely
if ever does one hear the Tchaikovsky *Mélodie*
played with more eloquence or refined tone
colour.

Kreisler Liebesfreud. Liebesleid **Paganini** Cantabile
Rachmaninov Rhapsody on a Theme of Paganini –
Variation 18 (arr Kreisler). Vocalise (arr Press) **Sarasate**
Introduction and Tarantella, Op 43 **Wieniawski**
Polonaises – No 1; No 2. Scherzo-tarantelle.
Variations on an Original Theme **JT Williams**
Schindler's List – Theme **Ysaÿe** Caprice d'après
l'Etude en forme de valse de Saint-Saëns
Maxim Vengerov vn **Ian Brown** pf
EMI 557916-2 (72' · DDD) ⒻⓄ

This mixture of fireworks and sweetmeats
perfectly suits the showmanship of Maxim
Vengerov. Though there are many favourites
included here, such as the two Kreisler charmers, the selection is unusual in centring on four
items by Wieniawski. Two, the first of the Polonaises and the *Scherzo-tarantelle*, are among the
favourites, too, but it's good to have the second
and much longer Polonaise – not quite so striking but with opportunities for Vengerov to use
his charm as well as his brilliance – and the
longest item of all, the *Variations on an Original
Theme*, with which the recital starts. It's true that
after the showy introduction the arrival of the
chirpy, banal theme is a slight disappointment,
but many great sets of variations have been written on trivial themes. Like all the Wieniawski
items, it exudes the composer's joy in his
prowess as a virtuoso violinist.

The Paganini is firmly among the sweetmeats
rather than the fireworks, and even the Sarasate
for half its length is sweetly lyrical, before the
tarantella proper. The Press arrangement of the
Rachmaninov *Vocalise* sounds curiously different

from the original, but Kreisler's arrangement of
the celebrated 18th variation from Rachmaninov's *Paganini* set is admirably straightforward.

John Williams's haunting theme for *Schindler's
List* works rather well in this context, even if the
melody comes round once too often, while the
rare Ysaÿe *Caprice* ends the recital. It's an attractive ragbag of a piece which again reflects the
love of the composer as well as of the artist for
the expressive range of the violin.

Vengerov's brilliance, even in the most hair-
raising writing, goes without saying, and, with
Ian Brown an ever-sympathetic accompanist, he
heightens the effect of the lyrical pieces using
daring dynamic extremes, often producing the
sweetest, gentlest threads of sound.

Devil's Trill
Gluck Orfeo ed Euridice – Dance of the Blessed
Spirits **Leclair** Sonatas for Violin and Continuo – D,
Op 8 No 2; C minor, Op 5 No 6 **Tartini** Sonata for
Violin and Continuo in G minor, 'Devil's Trill' **Vivaldi**
(arr Respighi) Sonata for Violin and Continuo in D,
Op 2 No 11
Yuval Yaron vn **Jeremy Denk** pf
Naim Audio NAIMCD018 (48' · DDD) ⒻⓄ

This is truly beautiful violin playing, elegant in
the opening *Larghetto* of Tartini's *The Devil's
Trill* Sonata and with the truest intonation later
on. The cadenza, too, is extremely brilliant,
though never 'showy'. Both sonatas by the 18th-
century dancer-turned-composer Jean Leclair
find Yaron in fine fettle, with a winsome tone
and tastefully controlled vibrato. Respighi's
naughty-but-nice reworking of a sonata that
Vivaldi dedicated to Frederick IV of Norway
and Denmark features some delicious piano harmonies beneath the solo line, and you would be
hard put to find a more eloquent voicing of the
Gluck/Kreisler 'Mélodie'. So who, you may ask,
is Yuval Yaron? Violin *aficionados* may already
have encountered him, but the more general
reader might like to know that he won First
Prize at the 1975 Sibelius Competition in
Helsinki, studied with Gingold and at Heifetz's
masterclasses and is currently Professor of Violin at the Indiana University School of Music in
Bloomington, where his excellent pianist
Jeremy Denk also serves and where Naim's
recordings were. The timing is stingy but, as
already suggested, Yaron's playing is a joy.

Dvořák Romantic Pieces, B150[a]. Violin Sonatina in G,
B183[a]. Humoresque in B flat minor, B187 No 8[b].
Violin Sonata[a] **Smetana** From the homeland, T128[a]
James Ehnes [a]vn/[b]pf [a]**Eduard Laurel** pf
Analekta fleurs de lys FL23191 (68' · DDD). Includes
bonus Analekta sampler disc ⒻⓄ

The Canadian violinist James Ehnes has made a
number of outstanding recordings, mainly for
the Canadian company Analekta, all of them displaying his flawless technique and immaculate
intonation. In many ways this delightful disc

outshines them all. The collection of violin and piano music by the three greatest Czech composers inspires him and his pianist to performances that bring out the best winning qualities of each work with rare understanding .

Sympathetic as Itzhak Perlman and Samuel Sanders are, their readings of Dvořák and Smetana are more generalised, with Perlman loading on the vibrato, less attentive to the specifically Czech qualities of these works. Ehnes and Laurel are freer in their use of rubato while using a wider tonal range.

Ehnes and Laurel also bring a welcome spontaneity to Dvořák's four Romantic Pieces, with an extra swagger to the second, marked *Allegro maestoso*. Laurel's phenomenally clean articulation is a delight here, as it is throughout the disc. The gravity of the final *Larghetto*, twice as long the others, is magnetically caught. The Sonatina, a product of Dvořák's American years, brings delectably sprung performances, with the *Scherzo* bounding even more crisply than it does in Perlman's performance, and the finale with its syncopations and melodic shapes typical of the 'American' Dvořák sounding like a cross between a Slavonic dance and a hoe-down.

As a charming coda to his performance of Janáček's elusive Sonata, Ehnes switches to the piano for a slightly wayward reading of Dvořák's *Humoresque*. Analekta supplement the disc with a sampler including Ehnes's Kreisler collection, an intriguing chamber arrangement of Saint-Saëns's *Danse macabre* and a sparkling account of the finale of Beethoven's Piano Trio Op 1 No 1, counterbalanced by a rather dull finale to Brahms's F major Cello Sonata.

Ligeti Viola Sonata **Prokofiev** Romeo and Juliet, Op 64 (arr Borisowsky)[a] – La danse des chevaliers; Juliette enfant; Mercutio; Montagues et Capulets; La mort de Juliette **Roslavets** Viola Sonata No 1[a] **Takemitsu** A Bird came down the Walk[a]
Lawrence Power va [a]**Simon Crawford-Phillips** pf
Harmonia Mundi Les Nouveaux Musiciens
HMN91 1756 (61' · DDD)   Ⓑ〇

Though still in his early 20s prize-winning violist Lawrence Power has concertised, broadcast and toured with encouraging regularity. His keen reflexes, supple bowing and acute sense of style suggest a definite star in the ascendant. His opening selection is a tightly knit Viola Sonata that Nicolai Roslavets composed in 1926, music that weaves a complex web of ideas based on 'synthetic chords'. The musical language seems to meld elements of Scriabin, Berg and early Schoenberg and the gritty piano writing finds a sympathetic advocate in Simon Crawford-Phillips. Power himself fronts this highly dramatic performance with fervour and perception. Ligeti's 1995 Sonata for unaccompanied viola opens uncompromisingly on the C string only, toying with pitch much as Britten does (on the horn) at the start of his *Serenade* – though at one point Ligeti seems to be quoting Mahler 10. Its six variegated movements incorporate a jagged

Presto and a haughty 'Chaconne chromatique' to close. Toru Takemitsu's *A Bird came down the Walk* (1994) sounds more grateful to play – its repertoire of gestures edge nearer the soul of the instrument, or seems to – and Power makes the most of its wide range of tone colours. But for many the highlight of the disc will be the sequence of four pieces that WW Borisowsky arranged from Prokofiev's *Romeo and Juliet*. Here Power and Crawford-Phillips collaborate for some vivid character painting. The performances are masterly and the sound is first-rate.

From Jewish Life
Bernstein Three Meditations from 'Mass' – Meditation 1; Meditation 2 **Bloch** Baal Shem – Nigun. Méditation hébraïque. From Jewish Life – Prayer; Supplication; Jewish Song. Cello Sonata **Bruch** Kol Nidrei, Op 47 **Shchedrin** Cardil **Stutschewsky** Kinah **Traditional** Avremi, the pickpocket. Chanukah Oy Chanukah. Dona, Dona
Paul Marleyn vc **John Lenehan** pf
Signum Two SIGCD505 (73' · DDD)   Ⓕ

Although it takes in a wide range of Jewish repertoire, composed and traditional, this collection centres on the music of Ernest Bloch. The programme opens with Max Bruch's well-known *Kol Nidrei*, which the pianist John Lenehan introduces with gentle sensitivity before Paul Marleyn takes up the passionate soliloquy, with its memorably warm *Adagio* main theme. Bloch's contribution includes a fine early (1897) Cello Sonata, a straightforward cyclic work in which the principal ideas only slightly anticipate his mature Hebrew melodic style. But it's freshly enjoyable when given such committed advocacy. Bloch is heard at his most passionate in the *Méditation hébraïque*, played with engulfing ardour, and if the three pieces *From Jewish Life* ('Prayer', 'Supplication' and 'Jewish Song') are more restrained, they are no less heartfelt.

The Bernstein *Meditations*, written for Rostropovich, and improvisational in feeling, occupy a more rarified soundworld. They're placed as interludes in his Mass, and act similarly here. Stutschewsky's heartfelt lament *Kinah* has much in common with the characteristic traditional numbers, as has Shchedrin's *Cardil*, which mix Hebrew irony and nostalgia with sudden *accelerandi* into cheerful dance music. The penultimate popular song, *Chanukah Oy Chankah*, celebrates a family festival of candles, presents, joy and love, and gathers momentum infectiously The closing Bloch 'Nigun' taken from *Baal Shem* makes an eloquent, sombre coda. It was written for violin and piano, but Marleyn's cello sings the fervent melodic line with deep lyrical feeling to make the transcription completely convincing.

The playing of both artists is totally idiomatic throughout, and the recording, too, is vivid and present within an attractive acoustic. A most rewarding concert if you enjoy the special melodic flavour of Hebrew music.

Paris French Flute Sonatas **Dutilleux** Sonatine **Ibert** Jeux. Aria **Jolivet** Chant de Linos **Messiaen** Le merle noir **Milhaud** Sonatina for Flute and Piano, Op 76 **Poulenc** Flute Sonata **Sancan** Sonatine
Emmanuel Pahud fl **Eric Le Sage** pf
EMI 556488-2 (66' · DDD)   Ⓕ⊙

Examinations are usually viewed with aversion and some suspicion, but the Paris Conservatoire's custom of commissioning new works for its final examinations has valuably enriched the repertoire for wind instruments: three of the works on this disc – the *Sonatinas* (of 1943 and 1946 respectively) of the exact contemporaries Dutilleux and Sancan, and Messiaen's *Le merle noir* – owe their origin to these competitive exams. By their nature they lay stress on technical virtuosity, as indeed do nearly all the works here, which though differing widely in idiom share a certain Gallic style recognisable by its 'clarity, refinement and lightness of touch', as the insert-note puts it. These qualities are also characteristic of the playing of the Swiss-born Emmanuel Pahud, Principal Flute of the Berlin Philharmonic, who has a lighter tone than some of his distinguished predecessors. All the items here have been recorded before, however. Excellent partnered by Eric Le Sage, Pahud's brilliant and sensitive performances are outstanding. Exhilaratingly skittish in the brief *scherzando* finale of the Sancan and that of the Poulenc, intense in the Jolivet, mysteriously atmospheric in the first movement of the Dutilleux (a work undervalued by its composer), tender in the Ibert *Aria* and powerfully athletic at the end of the Messiaen, this disc is a winner.

Pastoral
Bax Clarinet Sonata[a] **Bliss** Pastoral (posth)[a]. Two Nursery Rhymes[b] **Ireland** Fantasy-Sonata in E flat[a] **Stanford** Clarinet Sonata, Op 129[a] **Vaughan Williams** Six Studies in English folk song[a]. Three Vocalises for Soprano Voice and Clarinet[b]
Emma Johnson cl [b]**Judith Howarth** sop [a]**Malcolm Martineau** pf
ASV CDDCA891 (74' · DDD)   Ⓕ⊙

A lovely programme, radiantly performed and most judiciously chosen. Things get under way in fine style with John Ireland's marvellous *Fantasy-Sonata*: beautifully written, passionately argued and encompassing (for Ireland) a wide range of moods; it's certainly a work that shows this underrated figure at the height of his powers. The Clarinet Sonata by Ireland's teacher, Stanford, is one of that composer's most successful works: formally elegant and most idiomatically laid out, it boasts a central *Adagio* (entitled 'Caoine' – an Irish lament) of considerable eloquence. Johnson is a gloriously mellifluous exponent in both Vaughan Williams's *Six Studies* and the Bax Sonata, and in the first movement of the latter she manages to convey a slumbering mystery that's somehow almost orchestral in its imaginative scope. Judith Howarth joins Johnson for the haunting *Three*

Vocalises (one of Vaughan Williams's very last utterances from his final year) and makes an equally agile showing in Bliss's delightful *Two Nursery Rhymes* and touching *Pastoral*. A real pleasure, then, from start to finish and Malcolm Martineau proffers superb accompaniments.

Carmen Fantasy: Virtuoso Music for Trumpet
Arban Variations on a theme from Bellini's 'Norma'[a]. Variations on a Tyrolean Theme[a] **W Brandt** Concert Piece No 2 **Falla** La vida breve – Danse espagnole[b] **Fauré** Le réveil[b] **Paganini** Caprice in E flat, Op 1 No 17[b]. Moto perpetuo in C, Op 11[b] **Saint-Saëns** Le carnaval des animaux – The swan[b] **Sarasate** Zigeunerweisen, Op 20[c] **Tchaikovsky** Valse-scherzo in C, Op 34[b] **Waxman** Carmen Fantasia[a] (Items marked [a] arr Markovich, [b]Nakariakov, [c]Dokshitzer)
Sergei Nakariakov tpt **Alexander Markovich** pf
Teldec 4509-94554-2 (59' · DDD) Recorded 1994   Ⓕ⊙

Sergei Nakariakov is an extraordinary talent. It's one thing to be able to play the violin at the age of 17 with the technical aplomb of one's elders but a brass instrument – on a purely physical level – requires a strength and maturity which can be accelerated only so fast. His prowess as a trumpeter lies not only in the sphere of technical wizardry, which he has in super-abundance, but in a security of tone and interpretational vision: the subtle tuning in this selection of mainly transcribed violin pieces and the gypsyish *portamento*s are astute and accomplished. The Russian-ness of his playing is fascinating; he has that intensity of tone that Westerners find so hard to emulate without sounding corny or chastened. Nakariakov has a focused but fat, epic sound (though no doubt it will get even more wholesome with age) and a total security and command in all registers. His technique is particularly admirable in the lower reaches where he seems rarely to need the air at his disposal to progress through phrases. Nakariakov's slow playing is fluid, especially in *Le réveil*.

Abbott Alla caccia **Beethoven** Horn Sonata in F, Op 17 **Damase** Pavane variée. Berceuse, Op 19 **Koechlin** Horn Sonata, Op 70 **Hindemith** Horn Sonata **Schumann** Adagio and Allegro in A flat, Op 70 F **Strauss** Nocturno, Op 7
David Pyatt hn **Martin Jones** pf
Erato 3984-21632-2 (66' · DDD)   Ⓕ⊙

Beethoven's Horn Sonata – premièred in its day premièred by the Bohemian virtuoso, Punto – is nevertheless written rather clumsily for the horn (the composer suggested the cello as an alternative), and even Dennis Brain had problems with it. David Pyatt – *Gramophone*'s Young Artist of the Year in 1996 – sails off into the work with aplomb and gives it one of the finest performances on or off record. He makes it seem to sit easily on the instrument and provides just the right kind of timbre and buoyant lyrical flow – indeed it sounds like a masterpiece, which it very nearly is. He's helped by a first-rate partnership with Martin Jones and an excellently balanced recording. The second piece here is an attractive novelty by Franz Strauss, father of Richard, and another famous player who advised Wagner on the format of Siegfried's horn call. Koechlin's Sonata has a rather fine *Andante très tranquille*, and another Frenchman, Jean-Michel Damase, provides two short but memorable occasional pieces. The Hindemith Sonata is wayward: it never seems quite sure where it's progressing harmonically, but Pyatt and Jones are so naturally and spontaneously attuned to the work that it becomes readily assimilable. Abbott's *Alla caccia* is an endearing lollipop while Schumann's *Adagio and Allegro* here emerges flowing almost as easily as if it had been written by Mozart – who knew just what a horn could manage without sounding effortful. Altogether this is a splendid recital that will give much pleasure to any lover of this highly rewarding instrument.

Double Dream
Alperin Ostinato. Prelude and Vivace. Procession **Bach** French Suite No 2 in C minor, BWV813 **Chopin** Mazurka No 13 in A minor, Op 17 No 4 **Debussy** 12 Etudes – Pour les huits doigts **Janáček** On an Overgrown Path – Procession **Mozart** Adagio in C, K356/ K617a **Prokofiev** Toccata in C, Op 11. Visions fugitives, Op 22 – No 10, Ridiculosamente **Saeverud** Tunes and Dances from Siljustøl: Suite No 2, Op 22 – Digitalis Purpurea (Revebjølle) **Schumann** Waldszenen, Op 82 – **Schumann/Tristano** Vogel als Prophet/Requiem **Scriabin** Danse languide in G, Op 51 No 4. Two Poèmes, Op 63 – Etrangeté. Deux Preludes, Op 67 (all arr Alperin / Rudy)
Misha Alperin, Mikhail Rudy pfs
EMI 557769-2 (53' · DDD)   Ⓕ

Here's a record to startle and delight those listeners who enjoy breaking free of ties previously considered sacred. For Misha Alperin and Mikhail Rudy, the music of Bach, Mozart, Schumann and Debussy *et al* can represent a starting- rather than a finishing-point, and their improvisations are a teasing and sophisticated mix of the urbane and elegiac. Inspired by the experimental jazz pianist Lenny Tristano, they extend Schumann's *Vogel als Prophet* into a requiem, for Rudy 'like a journey through a forest of crystal'. And if Schumann's original brevity is the soul of wit, this elaboration is both a serious and intriguing response to his inimitable and seemingly complete poetry.

Elsewhere, Debussy's *Etude pour les huit doigts* is embellished with flashing asides. Chopin's wistfulness in his early A minor Mazurka is transformed into a hypnotic funeral tread. Prokofiev is subjected to high jinks that would surely have won even his hard-won approval. Scriabin's exotic and far-reaching idiom is combined with free-wheeling jazz elements. The sexy ache of Alperin's Prelude from his *Prelude and Vivace* is hard to resist and so, like two adults determined to disobey a 'keep-off-the-grass' sign these two intrepid explorers 'enter harbour's scene for the first time'. This disc is,

above all, an act of warmth and sincerity rather than mere cleverness or presumption. The recordings are excellent. The notes include moving essays by both pianists.

Fantaisie for Flute and Harp
L Boulanger Nocturne **Caplet** Rêverie **Fauré** Fantaisie, Op 79. Après un rêve, Op 7 No 1. Sicilienne, Op 78. Pièce **Piazzolla** Histoire du Tango **Ravel** Pavane pour une infante défunte **Saint-Saëns** Romance, Op 37 **Traditional** El diablo suelto. La partida. Spanish Love Song (trans Galway). Urpila. Bailecito de procesión **Villa-Lobos** Modinha. Bachianas Brasileiras No 5
Anna Noakes fl **Gillian Tingay** hp
ASV White Line CDWHL2101 (76' · DDD)   Ⓜ

This lightweight but entertaining collection happily juxtaposes French insouciance with Latin American sparkle. The pair of South American folksongs which opens the programme are real lollipops; then comes some lilting Villa-Lobos; first the sultry rhythmic *Modinha*, nudged with a nice rhythmic subtlety, and then the famous (soprano/cello) *Bachianas Brasileiras* No 5, which sounds seductive enough on the flute. The disc includes flowing, coolly beautiful Fauré and a gentle, haunting *Nocturne* by Lili Boulanger (meltingly phrased by Anna Noakes), followed by a romantic *morceau* by Saint-Saëns. One of the most enticing later pieces is the chimerical *Rêverie* of André Caplet and the recital ends with a highly individual and immediately arresting suite of four strongly flavoured miniatures by Astor Piazzolla called *Histoire du Tango*, bewitching in their combination of Latin rhythmic inflexions with a smoky Parisian night-club atmosphere. They are presented with much *élan* and sparkle and given added lift by various uninhibited percussive thwacks from both players. Although the harp sounds somewhat recessed, it always provides a glowing web of sound.

Wind Ensembles

Beethoven Quintet for Piano and Wind in E flat,   ⊞
Op 16ᵃ **Brahms** Trio for Horn, Violin and Piano in E flat, Op 40ᵇ **Dukas** Villanelleᶜ **Marais** Le Basqueᵈ (arr hn & pf) **Mozart** Quintet for Horn and Strings in E flat, K407/K386ᵉ
Dennis Brain hn ᵇ**Max Salpeter** vn ᶜᵈ**Wilfrid Parry,** ᵇ**Cyril Preedy** pfs ᵃ**Dennis Brain Wind Ensemble;** ᵉ**English String Quartet**
BBC Legends/IMG Artists BBCL4048-2 (72' · ADD)
Recorded 1957   Ⓜ ⓿⓿⓿

This is a marvellous record that does the fullest justice to the art of Dennis Brain, whom Boyd Neel called 'the finest Mozart player of his generation on any instrument'. This 1957 recording of the Mozart Horn Quintet surely bears that out. Brain has warm support from the English String Quartet, particularly in the lovely slow movement, but here his playing consistently dominates the ensemble lyrically, while the closing *Rondo* is sheer joy. So is Marais's delectable *Le Basque*. James Galway has subsequently made this piece his own on record, but Brain uses it as a witty encore, without showing off. Needless to say, the performance of the Brahms Horn Trio is very fine indeed. The infinitely sad, withdrawn atmosphere of the slow movement created by Brain's gentle soliloquy is unforgettable; and the infectious hunting-horn whooping of the finale carries all before it. The recording is distanced in a resonant acoustic and isn't ideally clear, but one soon forgets this.

The Dukas *Villanelle* is an arch-Romantic piece which all horn players feature for the want of something better, and Brain's ardour all but convinces us that it's fine music. But the highlight of the programme is the Beethoven piano and wind quintet, in which Brain shows himself the perfect chamber music partner. Without wishing to dominate, he can't help making his mark at every entry. And his colleagues join him to make a superb team. The recording is astonishingly real. The blending is so perfect, and Parry's pianism isn't only the bedrock of the performance – the playing itself is very beautiful indeed.

In short, this is the performance against which all others must now be judged.

Miscellaneous Chamber Groups

Journey to the Amazon
L Almeida Historia do Luar[a] **Barrios** Waltz, Op 8 No 4. Julia Florida **Brouwer** Canción de cuna, 'Berceuse'[a] (arr Grenet) **Canonico** Aire de Joropo[a] (arr Lauro/Diaz) **Lauro** Seis por derecho[a]. El marabino. Valses venezolanos – No 3, Natalia[a] **Montaña** Porro[a] **Savio** Batucada[a] **Thiago de Mello** A Hug for Pixingha[a]. Chants for the Chief[ab] – No 1, A Chamada dos ventos/Canção Nocturna; No 2, Uirapurú do Amazonas (both arr cpsr). Lago de Janaucá. A Hug for Tiberio[a]. Cavaleiro sem Armadura[ab] (arr Wolff) **Vianna** Cochichando[a] (arr Barbosa-Lima)
Sharon Isbin gtr with [a]**Gaudencio Thiago de Mello** perc [b]**Paul Winter** sax
Teldec 0630-19899-2 (55' · DDD)   Ⓕ ⊙

No one is currently doing more to free the guitar from its rent-a-programme image than Sharon Isbin. She's not South American, nor does the Amazon flow through Cuba, Colombia, Venezuela or Paraguay, but none of this matters in the least. Others before her have hitched rides with specialists in particular areas and sounded like uncomfortable passengers, but Isbin has loved and felt this music for over a quarter of a century and in the company of Thiago de Mello and Paul Winter is entirely at home. One might fear the addition of assorted percussive sounds and 'rain-forest' noises to be intrusive, especially in the familiar items, but they're atmospherically enhancing, handled with great discretion (delightfully in Grenet's

arrangement of Brouwer's *Canción de cuna*) and often rhythmically uplifting. Lauro's setting of the traditional *Seis por derecho* has never sounded more full of vitality. The guitar has a wide range of tone colour, which Isbin exploits with skill and taste in traversing the gamut from tenderness to joyously rhythmic energy. Recording is beautifully clear and well balanced. Waste no time in getting your hands on this disc.

Mnemosyne
Anonymous Alleluia nativitatis. Eagle Dance. Fayrfax Africanus. Novus novus. Russian Psalm **Athenaeus** Delphic Paean **Billings** When Jesus Wept **Brumel** Agnus Dei **Dufay** Gloria **Garbarek** Loiterando. Strophe and Counter-Strophe **Guillaume le Rouge** Se je fayz dueil **Hildegard of Bingen** O ignis Spiritus Paracliti **Mesomedes** Hymn to the Sun **Tallis** O Lord, in Thee is all my trust **Tormis** Estonian Lullaby **Traditional** Mascarades. Quechua Song. Remember me, my dear (all arr Hilliard Ensemble)
Jan Garbarek saxes **The Hilliard Ensemble**
ECM New Series ② 465 122-2 (105' · DDD) Texts and translations included   Ⓕ

'A sign we are, inexplicable without pain...' The words are by the 19th-century German poet Friedrich Hölderlin, taken from *Mnemosyne*, one of the cryptic hymns that he wrote before descending into madness. ECM publishes the entire first strophe as a sort of legend, and the reference is telling. 'Mnemosyne' was the mother of the muses, and the word also means 'memory'. For Hölderlin, song was an 'abandoned, flowing nature', a description that fits this album beautifully. Memory, ecstasy, pain, joy, reconciliation: all are, at one time or another, signalled in the present programme.

Garbarek spices the English 13th-century *Alleluia nativitatis* that opens the second disc with some unexpectedly Eastern-sounding modulations. The *Delphic Paean* that follows dives headlong among some absorbing dissonances, whereas Garbarek's own *Strophe and Counter-Strophe* enjoys a more sophisticated harmonic climate. Add Basque folk-song fragments warmed by the breathy aural contours of Garbarek's saxophone, and you've a characteristic sampling of a sequence that lasts, in total, for one-and-three-quarter hours. Both discs feature twilit Estonian lullabies (placed third on disc 1, and sixth on disc 2). Dufay's *Gloria* (sung *sans* Garbarek) ends on a desolate, protracted Amen, with Fayrfax Africanus marking an exultant point of contrast. Brumel's *Agnus Dei* allows Garbarek to temporarily monopolise the main melody line, but perhaps the most striking collaboration of all is for Hildegard's *O ignis Spiritus* which reaches spine-tingling levels of ecstasy.

The second CD includes a Russian Psalm where Garbarek adopts a resonant bass presence, an up-tempo Iroquois and Padleirmiut Eagle dance and, to close, works by William Billings and Mesomedes that complete the musical arch with something close to perfection.

It's a difficult disc to categorise. Maybe we should view it as a collaborative original composition which balances ancient and modern, sacred and profane, body and soul.

Debussy Syrinx[a]. Chansons de Bilitis (arr Lenski)[b]. La plus que lente[c] **Prokofiev** Flute Sonata in D, Op 94[b] **Ravel** Trois chansons madécasses[d]
[d]**Katarina Karnéus** mez [abd]**Emmanuel Pahud** fl
[d]**Truls Mørk** vc [bcd]**Stephen Kovacevich** pf
EMI 556982-2 (61' · DDD)   Ⓕ❂

Pahud's range of tone colour is amazing – no one listening to the Prokofiev Sonata is likely to feel short-changed by not hearing it in its familiar violin transcription, and in 'Aoua!', the central song of Ravel's *Chansons madécasses*, Pahud gets closer than most flautists to playing, as the composer directs, 'like a trumpet'. His dynamic range is still more startling, but there's never any sense of him extending the instrument beyond its nature, of forcing it to do un-flute-like things. Katarina Karnéus's clean French diction and wide range are well suited to the Ravel (the *Chansons madécasses* ideally demand a mezzo who's also a soprano, or *vice versa*).

The *Chansons de Bilitis* recorded here aren't Debussy's set of three songs nor, strictly speaking, his incidental music for a stage entertainment based on Pierre Louÿs's poems. It's the *Six épigraphes antiques* (for piano duet or two pianos) that Debussy based on that stage music which have been transcribed for flute and piano by Karl Lenski. The flute is either evoked or deliberately imitated throughout the *Epigraphes*, so, especially when played this beautifully, it seems an appropriate addition to the flautist's repertoire. In which the Prokofiev Sonata is central: Pahud gives it a big, bold and vivid reading, but with nothing overstated in the lyrical dialogues of the opening movement or the warmly expressive Andante. The recording is a little close, but richly colourful.

Continental Britons – The Emigré Composers
Gál Violin Sonata, Op 17[b]. Funf Melodien, Op 33[a]
Goldschmidt Mediterranean Songs – The Old Ships[a]. Fantasy[d] **Gellhorn** Intermezzo[b] **Rankl** War[a] – They; Böhmisches Rekrutenlied. The Whim, Op 6 No 6[a] **Reizenstein** Wind Quintet, Op 5[d] **Seiber** Violin Sonata[b] **Spinner** Zwei Kleine Stücke[b] **Tausky** Coventry[d] **Wellesz** Octet, Op 67[d]. Geistilches Lied[abc]. Kirschblütenlieder[a]
[a]**Christian M Immler** bar [b]**Nurit Pacht** vn [c]**Paul Silverthorne** va [a]**Erik Levi**, [b]**Konstantin Lifschitz** pfs [d]**Ensemble Modern**
Nimbus ② NI5730/1 (153' · DDD)   Ⓜ❂❂

The humbling cover photograph shows a hat, an overcoat and a violin case resting on top of some baggage. You might say that the concept of 'baggage' underpins this whole enterprise, the baggage of history, of conscience, and of compassion for the persecuted. How could anyone hope to evaluate these exiled composers without bringing the potentially extenuating circumstances of the Holocaust into the equation? Michael Haas's booklet-note certainly throws down the gauntlet: 'At the time of Hitler's rise in 1933,' he writes, 'Jewish musicians were perhaps Germany's most important living cultural assets.' A strong and compassionate claim, with an understandably defiant tone – though Wilhelm Furtwängler, Walter Gieseking, Franz Lehár, Hans Pfitzner, Richard Strauss and a whole host of personages 'from the other side' (so to speak) inevitably suggest an alternative viewpoint. Ultimately one has to ask whether the works themselves will withstand posterity's natural selection process; the evidence presented here is often impressive.

Hans Gál, for example, who landed on British shores in 1938, is a fine, communicative composer; his tightly knit, lyrical, Violin Sonata of 1920 is redolent of Strauss and Brahms, even Fauré. It's played here with the expressive shifts and tone production that reflect playing styles of the period. Nurit Pacht and Konstantin Lifschitz make an admirable partnership, as do baritone Christian Immler and Erik Levi, pianist, professor and expert on the whole complex business of music in the Third Reich. It would be difficult to surpass Immler and Levi in Gál's subtle *Fünf Melodien*, their worlds running parallel with Strauss and early Berg, or Egon Wellesz's equally imaginative *Kirschblütenlieder*, 'Cherry Blossom Songs'.

Wellesz's Octet of 1948 was commissioned by the Vienna Octet for a piece to programme alongside Schubert's Octet and melds elements of musical flashback with more than a hint of Schoenberg's First Chamber Symphony. Throughout this set there's an wide variety of texture, style, and musical mood. Franz Reizenstein's 1934 Wind Quintet is both formally strong (echoes of Hindemith) and pleasing to the ear. Matyás Seiber's Violin Sonata is a tougher beast, knotty but often serene, and Berthold Goldschmidt's Fantasy for oboe, cello and harp is quietly questioning; both are late works. Then there's Vilem Tausky's heartfelt quartet *Coventry* – 'a meditation' on the bombing of that city – and the variously shaded shorter work of Peter Gelhorn, Karl Rankl and Leopold Spinner, all of which attest to a chorus of individual voices that could, and did, add significant ingredients to the UK's musical heritage.

Playing standards are consistently high, the sound quality realistically reflects the sympathetic Wigmore Hall acoustic and Nimbus's annotations are comprehensive.

INSTRUMENTAL

Pierre-Laurent Aimard *piano*

At Carnegie Hall
Beethoven Piano Sonata No 23 in F minor,
'Appassionata', Op 57 **Berg** Piano Sonata, Op 1
Debussy Etudes – Pour les huit doigts. Images –
Reflets dans l'eau; Poissons d'or **Ligeti** Etudes, Book
1 – Cordes à vide; Automne à Varsovie; Book 2 – Der
Zauberlehrling **Liszt** Deux Légendes – St François de
Paule marchant sur les flots, S175 No 2 **Messiaen**
Vingt Regards sur l'enfant Jésus – Première
Communion de la Vierge
Pierre-Laurent Aimard *pf*
Teldec 0927-43088-2 (76' · DDD)   Ⓕ**OO**

There can be no justice in this world if this document of a 2001 recital at Carnegie Hall doesn't
establish Pierre-Laurent Aimard as a major
artist on the international stage. The range of
his carefully composed programme may astonish. So, surely, will his excellence in all departments – pianistic, musical, intellectual and
imaginative. The highest qualities in these
domains are constantly in play and in balance,
without lapse, and there's a temperament, a
warmth and a freshness of vision here that make
everything wondrous and delightful.

The Berg and the Beethoven, the first half of
the recital, are thoughtfully counterpointed –
the Berg, a pivotal work, suggesting 'a reflection
on what the sonata has been and might become'
(Aimard's own annotation) and instructive when
placed as a preface to the *Appassionata*. Admire
this pianist's formal strength and perfectly
judged rhetoric in both, and a reading of the
Beethoven not just as tragedy, still less as a succession of extreme contrasts, but as a completely
characterised poetic drama.

Throughout the programme Aimard makes
everything speak – the continuity to be understood only in musical terms, naturally, but as if
there were narrative in the way one thing follows another. Then Debussy, played like a composer, the spaces wondrously inhabited. Of the
Ligeti Etudes one needs say only that he's
Ligeti's preferred exponent, so these three are
self-recommending. Exciting playing and, once
again, drawing attention only to the music.

Carnegie Hall cheered to the rafters,
applauded lots everywhere and kept commendably quiet during the music. Aimard says he did
barely half an hour of retouches afterwards,
mostly to cover the coughs. If he isn't yet known
to you, hold back no longer.

Piotr Anderszewski *piano*

Bach English Suite No 6 in D minor, BWV811
Beethoven Piano Sonata in D minor No 31, Op 110
Webern Variations, Op 27
Piotr Anderszewski *pf*
Virgin Classics 545632-2 (61' · DDD)   Ⓕ**OO**

In an age when great, good, bad and indifferent
recordings rub shoulders in a chaotic market-
place, Piotr Anderszewski's playing stands out
like a beacon of light and quality. His is the most
powerful and distinctive of musical voices, a rare
combination of purity and adventure. In Bach's
Sixth *English Suite* his intelligence is as razor-
sharp as his technique is immaculate. What an
endless play of light and shade he brings to the
Prelude, what buoyancy to the First Gavotte!
His varied registration in the Second Gavotte is
central to a deeply imaginative response to
Bach; so too is the uncanny stillness he evokes in
the Sarabande or the sinister momentum of the
final nail-biting, fiercely chromatic Gigue.

In Beethoven's Op 110 he gives us a scrupulously modern equivalent of legendary recordings of the past (by Solomon and Myra Hess, for
example), reawakening our sense of the other-
worldly, the speculative and mystical in this late
masterpiece. His poise and tonal translucency in
the opening *Moderato* are enviable, and so is his
explosive sense of contrast in the following *Allegro molto*. And if for some his attention to detail
will seem microscopic and over-refined, others
will surely rejoice in a concentration and
integrity that are at once exhausting and exhilarating.

Exceptionally self-critical, Anderszewski once
left the stage during a performance of the
Webern Variations at the Leeds Piano Competition, unhappy and disgruntled with his playing. Here, even he must have felt a sense of
achievement, with his precise and deeply sensitive performance.

Leif Ove Andsnes *piano*

A Portrait
Brahms Intermezzo in B flat minor, Op 117 No 2
Grieg Piano Concerto in A minor, Op 16. Lyric
Pieces, Op 43 – No 1, Butterfly; No 6, To the Spring;
Op 65 – No 6, Wedding Day at Troldhaugen **Haydn**
Piano Concerto, HobXVIII/11. Piano Sonata,
HobXVI/32 **Janáček** Sonata 1.X.1905, 'From the
Street' **Johansen** Portraits, Op 5 – The Little Stone
God; Reindeer; Towards the Father's Mountain **Liszt**
Mephisto Waltz No 1, S514 **Nielsen** Humoresque
Bagatelles, FS22 **Rachmaninov** Etudes-tableaux in C,
Op 33 No 2 **Sæverud** Ballad of Revolt, Op 22 No 2
Schumann Fantasie, Op 17 **Shostakovich** Concerto
for Piano, Trumpet and Strings, Op 35 **Tveitt** Fifty
Folk-tunes from Hardanger, Op 150 – A-wooing;
Langeleik tune; The Long, Long Winter Night
Leif Ove Andsnes *pf* **Bergen Philharmonic Orches-
tra / Dmitri Kitaienko; City of Birmingham Sym-
phony Orchestra / Paavo Järvi; Norwegian Cham-
ber Orchestra**
EMI Classics 574789-2 (151' · DDD) Recorded 1991-9
Ⓜ

This two-disc selection taken from Andsnes's
previous discography offers many examples of
his unassuming and superlative artistry. Never
for a moment is there even a whiff of narcissism,
or a hint of the sort of pianist with an eye for special effects or for tints and underlinings achieved

at the expense of the composer. All these performances are quietly resolute with an imperious yet effortless command and a rare poetic candour and simplicity.

His Grieg Concerto is among the finest of all recordings of this evergreen masterpiece. He's subtly and gently communing in the principle theme, and brilliantly alert in the *animato e molto leggiero* cascades or in the final *presto* sprint to the exultant close. Throughout, you could never confuse his simplicity with plainness; time and again you're made aware of the sort of musicianship which can only be encouraged rather than taught. Even when he seems a trifle remote from Brahms's autumnal glow and rapture in the Second Intermezzo from Op 117, his musicianship is unfailing and on home ground in Grieg (three of the *Lyric Pieces*), while he evinces a deeply moving poetic empathy with lesser-known composers such as Tveitt, Johansen and Saeverud. He shows a frightening affinity for the heart-stopping violence and desolation of the Janáček Sonata, and his *Gramophone*-award-winning Haydn is a marvel of dexterity and sustained musical radiance.

So here's a very special tribute designed for those few listeners still not fully aware of this artist's calibre.

Martha Argerich
piano

Début Recital

Brahms Two Rhapsodies, Op 79 **Chopin** Scherzo No 3 in C sharp minor, Op 39. Barcarolle in F sharp, Op 60 **Liszt** Hungarian Rhapsody No 6 in D flat. Piano Sonata in B minor, S178 **Prokofiev** Toccata in D minor, Op 11 **Ravel** Jeux d'eau
Martha Argerich pf
DG The Originals 447 430-2GOR (71' · ADD)
Recorded 1960-71　　　　　　　　　Ⓜ❍❍❍

 Here, on this richly filled CD, is a positive cornucopia of musical genius. Martha Argerich's 1961 disc remains among the most spectacular of all recorded débuts, an impression reinforced by an outsize addition and encore: her 1972 Liszt Sonata. True, there are occasional reminders of her pianism at its most fraught and capricious (Chopin's *Barcarolle*) as well as tiny scatterings of inaccuracies, yet her playing always blazes with a unique incandescence and character.

The Brahms *Rhapsodies* are as glowingly interior as they're fleet. No more mercurial Chopin *Scherzo* exists on record and if its savagery becomes flighty and skittish (with the chorale's decorations sounding like manic bursts of laughter), Argerich's fine-toned fluency will make other, lesser pianists weep with envy. Ravel's *Jeux d'eau* is gloriously indolent and scintillating and the Prokofiev *Toccata* is spun off in a manner that understandably provoked Horowitz's awe and enthusiasm. Liszt's Sixth *Hungarian Rhapsody* is a marvel of wit and daring and the B minor Sonata is among the most dazzling ever perpetuated on disc. The

recordings have worn remarkably well and the transfers have been expertly done.

Alessio Bax
piano

Baroque Reflections

Bach Concerto in D minor, BWV974 **Bach/Busoni** Toccata and Fugue in D minor **Bach/Hess** Jesu, joy of man's desiring **Bach/Rachmaninov** Violin Partita No 3 Bach/Siloti **Prelude** in B minor **Liszt** Sarabande and Chaconne from Handel's Almira **Rachmaninov** Corelli Variations **Sgambati** Mélodie d'Orfeo de Gluck
Alessio Bax pf
Warner Classics 2564 61695-2 (69' · DDD)　　Ⓕ❍❍

Alessio Bax, a young Italian-born, American-based pianist who has had a number of notable successes in international competitions, here makes a début recital of a special quality and enterprise. The Baroque style is seen through richly varied perspectives, ranging from the audacious to the devotional, from the intimate to the heaven-storming. Bax launches the Bach-Busoni Toccata and Fugue with a superbly crisp and articulate call to attention. Favouring brilliance over effulgence he keeps everything clinically clean, and his playing in the *Adagio* from Bach's D minor Concerto is memorably acute and fastidious. His way with the Bach-Siloti Prelude (the work with which Gilels used to end his recitals; a romantically troubled benediction) is brightly lit but lovingly etched, and his Handel-Liszt is of an unfaltering virtuosity and poetic inwardness. The Bach-Rachmaninov and *Corelli* Variations, too, are of the most concentrated wit and individuality: Variation 9 is particularly introspective, and in the insinuating waltz of Variation 15 and the desolating coda (where emotion is recollected in pain rather than tranquillity) his playing quivers with an almost hypnotic intensity. Sound and instrument are ultra-bright.

Julian Bream
guitar

Falla Homenaje, 'Le tombeau de Claude Debussy' **Moreno Torroba** Prelude. Sonatina. Burgalesa **Sor** Estudios – No 5 in B minor; No 12 in A. Fantasia Op 7 No 2. Guitar Sonata in C, Op 22 – Minuetto: Allegro; Rondo: Allegretto. Studies in A minor, Op 31 No 20. Andante largo, Op 5 **Turina** Fandanguillo, Op 36. Hommage à Tárrega, Op 69. Ráfaga, Op 53 **Villa-Lobos** Preludes (1940)
Julian Bream gtr
DG Westminster Legacy mono 471 236-2GWM (75' · ADD) Recorded 1955-6　　　　　Ⓜ

Albéniz Córdoba, Op 232 No 4. Mallorca, Op 202. Suite española, Op 47 No 1 **Granados** Dedicatoria, Op 1. Danzas españolas, Op 37 – No 4, 'Villanesca'; No 5, 'Andaluza'. Tonadillas al estilo antiguo – La maja de goya. **Malats** Serenata española **Pujol** Tango española. Guajira
Julian Bream gtr

RCA Redseal 74321 68016-2 (75' · DDD) Recorded 1982, 1991 Ⓢ

Julian Bream is probably the most universal guitarist of the 20th century. The Westminster recordings, made during the 21st and 22nd years of his life, signalled the emergence of the first truly significant English guitarist in history, potentially capable of becoming worthy of mention in the same breath as Segovia – a status he indeed achieved. Segovia not only brought new life to the 19th-century repertory of the guitar, he also extended it by 'borrowing' suitable music originally written for the lute and the early guitar, and by persuading then-contemporary composers to write for him. Julian Bream has done likewise but, with the benefit of later scholarship, in greater depth. On the one hand he has played a major role in the revival of the lute itself and the Elizabethan consort; on the other he has received works from an impressive list of famous composers – unrestricted by Segovia's innate conservatism. All in all, it's a unique achievement.

The Westminster recordings reveal the astonishing maturity Bream displayed at this early stage. The combination of infectious freshness and instinctive understanding of what lies behind the written notes is redolent of the early Segovia – but without the latter's idiosyncratically free approach to *rubato*. He's also less devoted to 'orchestrating' the music via a wide variety of tone colour, but his sound is no less 'three-dimensional' and he's no less conscious of the function and character of every note. The re-mastering of the recording *per se* is spectacularly successful in conveying the crystal clarity of every aspect of these wonderful performances. The RCA disc is a compilation drawn from recordings of Bream in his full maturity, and is of particular interest to those who have not invested in RCA's full 28-CD archive. A splendid issue.

Alfred Brendel   *piano*

Beethoven Rondo for Piano and Orchestra in B flat, WoO6[a]. Quintet for Piano and Wind in E flat, Op 16[b]. Piano Sonatas – No 17 in D minor, 'Tempest', Op 31 No 2; No 26 in E flat, 'Les adieux', Op 81a; No 30 in E, Op 109. 11 Bagatelles, Op 119. 15 Variations and Fugue on an Original Theme in E flat, 'Eroica', Op 35. Seven Variations in F on Winter's 'Kind, willst du ruhig schlafen', WoO75. Fantasia in G minor, Op 77. Rondo in G, Op 51 No 2 **Dvořák** Slavonic Dances[c] – B78: No 1 in C; No 2 in E minor; No 6 in A flat; No 8 in G minor; B145: No 1 in B; No 2 in E minor; No 4 in D flat; No 6 in B flat; No 7 in A **Haydn** Piano Concerto in D, HobXVIII/11[d] **Liszt** Années de pèlerinage – Deuxième année, Italie, S161: Sonetto 47 del Petrarca; Sonetto 104 del Petrarca. Harmonies poétiques et réligieuses, S173 – No 3, Bénédiction de Dieu dans la solitude; No 7, Funérailles; No 10, Cantique d'amour. Etudes d'exécution transcendante d'après Paganini, S140 – E flat; A flat minor. Hungarian Rhapsody in A minor,

S244 No 11. Mephisto Waltz No 1, S514. Opera Transcriptions – Oberon, S574; Il trovatore, S433; Tristan und Isolde, S447 **Mozart** Piano Concerto No 27 in B flat, K595[e] Rondo for Piano and Orchestra in D, K382[e] **Prokofiev** Piano Concerto No 5 in G minor, Op 55[f] **Schoenberg** Piano Concerto, Op 429. **Schubert** Fantasy in C, 'Wanderer', D760. Drei Klavierstücke, D946 **Stravinsky** Three Movements from Petrushka

Alfred Brendel *pf* with [c]**Walter Klien** *pf* [b]**members of the Hungarian Wind Quintet;** [a]**Vienna Volksoper Orchestra / Wilfried Boettcher;** [d]**Vienna Chamber Orchestra,** [e]**Vienna Pro Musica Orchestra / Paul Angerer;** [f]**Vienna State Opera Orchestra / Jonathan Sternberg;** [g]**South West German Radio Symphony Orchestra, Baden-Baden / Michael Gielen**

Vox ⑥ CD6X3601 (453' · ADD) Recorded 1955-66 ⑧●

Writing with superb authority, Alfred Brendel once answered his own rhetorical question. 'What is piano playing of genius? Playing which is at once correct and bold. Its correctness tells us that's how it has to be. Its boldness presents us with a surprising and overwhelming realisation: what we had thought impossible becomes true.' Heard at his greatest, as in these Vox and Regis reissues of recordings from 1955-67, Brendel makes criticism fall silent. Wherever you turn, you won't hear a dishonest note or phrase, anything less than profoundly considered. Even Prokofiev's Fifth Concerto, music Brendel despises and which he recorded when his career was still not fully launched, comes up fresh, its extravagance illuminated by a pin-point wit and delicacy.

True, most great artists regard their early recordings with suspicion. Yet even Brendel, with his intimidating scrutiny, must have periodically delighted in his early candour and assurance, his effortless resolving of complexity into simplicity, in the absolute 'rightness' of his interpretations and their untrammelled virtuosity. His later work for Philips may be more speculative but his early freshness, even sang-froid, is something to marvel at. Here, he wears his profound insights with the lightest of touches. Thought-provoking and personal to the last, his performance of Mozart's final Concerto captures exactly music of a clouded radiance and a momentary burst of anger at 3'22" in the finale, a 'do not go gentle into that good night' reminder of Mozart's lack of resignation. The selection, too, of Beethoven's Sonatas abounds with unselfconscious slants and angles unknown to lesser artists. And you'll rarely hear a more internal or communing performance of Schubert's Wanderer, almost as if Brendel is telling us that such outwardly uncharacteristic music hardly goes against the grain but remains an organic part of Schubert's oeuvre. In Liszt's Cantique d'amour you can sense him caught in the breathless central elaboration, yet he never allows his playing to degenerate into conversational salon elegance or flashy rhetoric. His inwardness, too, in the central blessing of the 'Bénédiction' is a marvel of poetic insight.

Brendel may be celebrated for his intellectual probity, yet, as this memorable album shows, his warmth and humanity are supported by an unfaultering virtuosity. Here, surely, is an incomparable marriage of heart and mind.

David Briggs   *organ*

Great European Organs, Volume 57
Brewer Marche héroïque **Bridge** Adagio in E, H63
No 3 **Faulkes** Grand choeur in D **Harris** Caprice
Macpherson Fantasy-Prelude **Mendelssohn** (arr
Best) Athalie – War March of the Priests **Parry**
Chorale Preludes, Set 2 – Eventide **Stanford** Organ
Sonata No 3 in D minor, 'Britannica', Op 152
David Briggs *org*
Priory PRCD680 (68' · DDD) Played on the Lewis
organ of St John the Evangelist, Upper Norwood,
London.   Ⓕ❍

Perhaps a more appropriate title would be 'Great British Organ', as this CD is a celebration of home-grown artistry: Victorian and Edwardian music played on a vintage late 19th-century instrument by one of Britain's finest organists. Although this Lewis organ may not be in a prestigious venue like a cathedral, city hall or concert hall, this doesn't mean it's an instrument of lesser quality. On the contrary, it has all the colour and brilliance heard on the larger organs Lewis built for Southwark Cathedral and the Kelvingrove Art Gallery, Glasgow (these latter instruments can be heard on previous 'Great European Organs' CDs).

Briggs's programme is ideally suited to the organ, too, and he gives splendid performances. You can tell from the finely judged *rubato* and judicious choice of tempos that he's an experienced choral and orchestral conductor as well as a very fine soloist. This all makes for eminently satisfying music-making, and his imaginative use of the organ means that we hear all its available tone colours.

Priory's production is of the highest order – the recording is excellent and the insert-notes informative. Inevitably as the century progresses this organ will show signs of wear and tear, so it's good to have a recording made so soon after the recent restoration by Harrisons. Lovers of the late 19th-century British organ will be indebted to Briggs and Priory for committing its magnificent sound to CD.

Shura Cherkassky   *piano*

Liadov A musical snuffbox, Op 32 **Liszt** Piano   Ⓗ
Concerto No 1 in E flat, S124ᵃ. Liebestraum in A flat,
S541 No 3. Réminiscences de Don Juan (Mozart),
S418. Hungarian Rhapsody No 13 in A minor, S244.
Faust (Gounod) – Waltz, S407 **Saint-Saëns** Le
carnaval des animaux – Le cygne
Shura Cherkassky *pf* ᵃ**Philharmonia Orchestra /
Anatole Fistoulari**
Testament mono SBT1033 (62' · ADD) Recorded
1952-8   Ⓕ❍

Here, in excellent transfers of HMV recordings dating from the 1950s, is a vintage Cherkassky recital. Mercurial and hypnotic, his way with Liszt's E flat Concerto reminds us in every nook and cranny that he has always been able to enliven and transform even the most over-familiar score. True, there are moments – such as the start of the *Allegro vivace* – where he's less than ideally poised or balletic (one of those instances where his elfin caprice can seem close to uncertainty and where he leads Fistoulari and the Philharmonia a Puckish dance: now you hear me, now you don't), yet his sparkle and charm are inimitable. Again, in Variation 1 of the *Don Juan* Fantasy he's perhaps more flustered than *elegantamente*, but even when his virtuosity is less than watertight, his playing is infinitely more fascinating and imaginatively varied. Cherkassky can be garrulous or somnolent, his phrasing languorous or choppy, yet in the ecstatic, long-breathed descent just before the coda of the *Liebestraum* No 3 and in all the *Hungarian Rhapsody* No 13 and the *Faust* Waltz, his mastery has seldom, if ever, sounded more effortless or unalloyed. Finally, an encore of *friandises*: Godowsky's fine-spun elaboration of Saint-Saëns's 'Le cygne'.

Clifford Curzon   *piano*

Haydn Andante and Variations in F minor, HobXVII:6
Liszt Sonetto 104 del Petrarca, S161 No 5. Berceuse,
S174 (2nd version). Valse oubliée, S215 No 1. Piano
Sonata in B minor, S178 **Schubert** Impromptus, D899
– No 2 in E flat; No 3 in G flat; No 4 in A flat
Sir Clifford Curzon *pf*
BBC Legends/IMG Artists mono BBCL4078-2 0
(67' · ADD) Recorded live 1961   Ⓕ❍

Curzon was always reluctant to work in the recording studio, and so one treasures a compilation such as this of live performances, flawed on detail though they can be. Anyone who wants to count the occasional slips of finger in his account of the Liszt Sonata, for example, will obviously reject it in favour of the more studied, less spontaneous studio version he recorded for Decca two years later. Yet the impulsive energy of this live account is invaluable in letting us appreciate a side of Curzon's genius rarely revealed in his official recordings – the daring of the virtuoso. As for the other Liszt items, they reveal his magic at its most intense, so that in the *Petrarch Sonnet* his velvet *legato* has one imagining a voice singing the words, and equally the improvisational quality he brings to his playing of Liszt is again magnetic in the *Valse oubliée*.

In the Haydn Variations, he similarly finds sparkle and fantasy in a performance recorded for the BBC, and the Schubert Impromptus – for him core repertory – find him at his happiest, though his breathtakingly fast tempo for No 2 with its rippling scales in triplets may initially seem disconcerting. The mono sound from the early 60s may be limited, but undistractingly lets you enjoy the performances.

Evgeni Finkelstein   *guitar*

The Fall of Birds – Russian Guitar Music
Beljaev Prelude and Three Valses **Koshkin** Andante
quasi passacaglia and toccata, 'The fall of birds'.
Suite, 'Elves'. Variations on a theme by Štěpán Rak,
'The Porcelain Tower' **Rudnev** Variations on a Russian
Folk Song
Evgeni Finkelstein *gtr*
Acoustic Music Records 319 1273 2 (50' · DDD)   Ⓕ

Nikita Koshkin arrived on the contemporary
guitar scene in the early 1980s with his ground-
breaking suite *The Prince's Toys*; he remains
Russia's most famous composer for the instrument. Two of his works on this disc, *The fall of
birds* and *Variations on a theme of Štěpán Rak*, are
among the most remarkable in the guitar's contemporary repertory, absorbing products of a
powerful imagination. The former is 'symbolic
of the end of the world', the latter came at a time
when he was fascinated by Chinese art. The
Elves are whimsicalities from his love of fairy-
tales. Sergei Rudnev's more conservative Variations closely follow the structure of the song in a
variety of imaginative textures, the most magical
evoking a distant balalaika. Gennady Beljaev's
Prelude and Three Waltzes are well written.

Evgeni Finkelstein is a formidable performer,
possessing every quality required by this music,
and the validity of his interpretations of
Koshkin's music derives from his close association with the composer. This is a thrilling disc
that should be on the shelves of anyone who has
the slightest interest in the guitar.

Annie Fischer   *piano*

Bartók 15 Hungarian Peasant Songs, Sz71 **Brahms**
Piano Sonata No 3 in F minor, Op 5 **Dohnányi**
Rhapsody in C, No 3 Op 11 **Liszt** Three Concert
Studies, S144 – No 3, Un sospiro. Grandes études de
Paganini, S141 – No 6, Quasi Presto
Annie Fischer *pf*
BBC Legends/IMG Artists mono BBCL4054-2
(64' · ADD) Recorded live 1961   Ⓜ●

Few pianists have found a more direct path to
poetic truth than Annie Fischer. Blessedly free
of all attitudinising or exaggeration, her finest
performances burned with a fierce clarity and
vision, and her London appearances, both in
recital and with Otto Klemperer during the 60s,
became the stuff of musical legends. Like, say,
Schnabel and Myra Hess, Annie Fischer felt
inhibited in the studios, and the story of her
endlessly protracted Hungaroton recording of
the complete Beethoven Piano Sonatas testifies
to her discomfort. So all credit to those who rescued this magnificent recital taken live from the
1961 Edinburgh Festival. How characteristic is
that mix of brio and poetry in the Brahms F
minor Sonata. Others, such as Radu Lupu, may
be more romantically inclined but few have
played this early masterpiece with such sweep
and panache. Her assault on the notorious

octave swirl commencing the first-movement
development may be more fearless than impeccable, but the final pages of the *Andante* are truly
molto appassionato and *fortissimo*, and how typical
is that forthright – not merely vague or impressionistic – end to the Intermezzo, with its muffled timpani strokes. In such hands the finale is
an epic waltz indeed, and she reveals the glory of
one daunting rhetorical gesture after another.

Her Bartók is wonderfully free-wheeling and
idiomatic, and in Liszt's *Un sospiro* the directness
of her playing suggests heroic rather than sentimental passion. Her way with the Dohnányi
Rhapsody, too, reminds us of her versatility, her
joy in unbounded virtuosity as well as her dedication to the great masterpieces of the repertoire. The recordings faithfully reflect a special
sense of occasion, and the excellent notes offer
an apt reminder that Annie Fischer lived before
a time when 'genuine musical interest was often
squeezed to the margins'.

Leon Fleisher   *piano*

Two Hands
Bach Jesu, Joy of Man's desiring (arr Hess). Sheep
may safely graze (arr E Petri) **Chopin** Mazurka No 32.
Nocturne No 8, Op 27 No 2 **Debussy** Suite
bergamasque – Clair de lune **D Scarlatti** Keyboard
Sonata in E, Kk380 **Schubert** Piano Sonata No 21
Leon Fleisher *pf*
Vanguard Classics ATMCD1551 (74' · DDD)   Ⓕ●●

This verges on the unbelievable. Leon Fleisher,
now 75, who for more than 35 years couldn't use
his right hand because of dystonia (a neurologi-
cal disease 'characterised by involuntary muscle
contractions which force certain parts of the
body into abnormal, sometimes painful movements or positions'), recovers fully after treatment with botulinum toxin (more familiarly
known as Botox). And he plays as if he'd never
been incapacitated. Dexterity and dynamics are
effortlessly controlled. Tone is evenly spread;
bass lines aren't weak, chords are cleanly articulated and inner voices have their place. Best of
all, technique is coupled to an imaginative intellect that portrays the language of each composer
in deep terms.

Schubert's sonata is very personal, running a
gamut of feelings from resignation to gaiety but
Fleisher (who repeats the first-movement exposition) also finds an undercurrent of toughness
which he allows to burst forth in the finale. Yet
there's a place for ease, for moments of stillness
in the transcriptions of Bach; and it''s gratifying
to hear Chopin hauntingly dark and shorn of
glitter. Perhaps some glitter would have enlivened Scarlatti's sonata but Fleisher finds a
contemplative side to the music that is often
overlooked.

Good sound, though the piano is close and
recorded level is higher in the Schubert. There
are also breathing noises. No matter. This is a
proud comeback for which allowances aren't
necessary.

Ignaz Friedman *piano*

Ignaz Friedman Plays Mendelssohn, Chopin and Liszt H

Chopin Ballade No 3 in A flat, Op 53. Impromptu No 2 in F sharp, Op 36. Mazurkas – No 5 in B flat, Op 7 No 1; No 6 in A minor, Op 7 No 2; No 7 in F minor, Op 7 No 3; No 17 in B flat minor, Op 24 No 4; No 23 in D, Op 33 No 2; No 25 in B minor, Op 33 No 4; No 26 in C sharp minor, Op 41 No 1; No 31 in A flat, Op 50 No 2; No 41 in C sharp minor, Op 63 No 3; No 44 in C, Op 67 No 3; No 45 in A minor, Op 67 No 4; No 47 in A minor, Op 68 No 2. Nocturne No 16 in E flat, Op 55 No 2 Liszt Hungarian Rhapsody No 2 in C sharp minor, S244 No 2 Mendelssohn Songs without Words – A, 'Hunting Song', Op 19 No 3; G minor, 'Venetian Gondola Song', Op 19 No 6; F sharp minor, 'Venetian Gondola Song', Op 30 No 6; C minor, Op 38 No 2; A flat, 'Duetto', Op 38 No 6; E flat, Op 53 No 2; F, Op 53 No 4; F sharp minor, Op 67 No 2; A, 'Kinderstück', Op 102 No 5

Ignaz Friedman pf
Biddulph LHW044 (77' · ADD) Recorded 1930-36 Ⓜ

If many modern pianists can be dismissed with damning brevity, Ignaz Friedman's elegance and aplomb demand a book rather than a review. In his tantalising selection of Chopin *Mazurkas* his inimitable brio allows for both a sense of peasant origins (that slight lift on the second beat, that light or emphatic – according to context – stress on the third) and the rarest sense of fantasy and idealisation. His rapid tempo in, say, Op 24 No 4 offers him, paradoxically, time for one enchanting felicity or passing piquancy after another, and an airborne lightness and freedom. His *legato* and *cantabile* make notes melt together rather than merely join or elide with another. Who would have thought that Op 67 No 3, a relatively slight work, could be spun off with such vivacious idiosyncrasy or that the Third *Ballade* could emerge free from all constraint? True, Friedman can play free and easy with the score. Taken at such a speed the Second *Impromptu*'s final *leggiero* scales turn into an unapologetic display, their innate beauty compromised by an extravagant flurry. But in the E flat *Nocturne*, Op 55 No 2, with its subtle prophecy of Fauréan radiance, Friedman spins the most magical of lines. Seemingly as natural as breathing, his artistry is quite without (disfiguring) archness, leaving younger pianists to wonder at such insouciance, at such effortless transcending of received wisdom. The transfers are admirable, and Allan Evans's notes are good enough to survive some careless proof-reading.

Marc-André Hamelin *piano*

Blanchet Au jardin du vieux sérail Blumenfeld Etude for the left hand, Op 36 Casella Deux contrastes, Op 33 Glazunov The Seasons, Op 67 – Autumn: Petit adagio Godowsky Triakontameron – Alt Wien Hamelin Etudes – No 3 (d'après Paganini-Liszt); No 6: Essercizio per pianoforte (Omaggio a D Scarlatti)

Hofmann Kaleidoskop, Op 40. Nocturne, 'Complaint' Kapustin Toccatina Lourié Gigue Massenet Valse folle Michalowski Etude d'après l'Impromptu in A flat by Chopin Moszkowski Etude A flat minor, Op 72 No 13 Offenbach Concert Paraphrase of 'The Song of the Soldiers of the Sea' Poulenc Intermezzo in A flat Rachmaninov Polka de W R Vallier Toccatina EB Woods Valse phantastique

Marc-André Hamelin pf
Hyperion CDA67275 (67' · DDD) Ⓕ

Whatever enchants, teases and outrages is offered here in a cornucopia of encores tailor-made to delight those who revel in music's byways. No other pianist could have brought off a recital of this kind with such wit, assurance and boundless dexterity. Hamelin even gives such champions of the Rachmaninov Polka as Horowitz, Cherkassky and the composer himself, with their more personalised bravura, a run for their money, while his own étude on *La campanella* makes Liszt's original seem like a beginner's piece. Like some phenomenal juggler he makes you aware, so to speak, of an ever-widening pattern of glittering clubs and balls as he enlarges and refines the scope of his *légerdemain*. His take-off of Scarlatti is wickedly inventive, parodying every aspect of his musical character; his Hofmann Nocturne (with its warm memory of Chopin) as beguiling as it's accomplished. He plays John Vallier's *Toccatina* more explosively than Moiseiwitsch in his famously suave recording, and if Kapustin's identically entitled piece reminds us that he was fond of writing a tale twice or, indeed, many times told, Hamelin's performances are a wonder of brilliance and refinement. The recordings are superb, Jeremy Nicholas's notes a mine of informative tit-bits. In Marc-André Hamelin Hyperion clearly has a pianist to turn other record companies green with envy.

The Composer-Pianists
Alkan Esquisses, Op 63 – No 46, Le premier billet-doux; No 47, Scherzetto Bach/Feinberg Kommst du nun, Jesu, vom Himmel herunter BWV650 Busoni Fantasia after J. S. Bach Feinberg Berceuse, Op 19a Godowsky Toccata in G flat, Op 13 Hamelin Etudes – No 9, 'd'après Rossini'; No 10, 'd'après Chopin'; No 12 (Prelude and Fugue) Haydn/Alkan Symphony No 94 in G, 'Surprise' – Andante Medtner Improvisation in B flat minor, Op 31 No 1 Rachmaninov Moment musical in E flat minor, Op 16 No 2. Etude-tableau in E flat, Op 33 No 4 Scriabin Poème tragique in B flat, Op 34. Deux Poèmes, Op 71 Sorabji Pastiche on Hindu Song from Rimsky-Korsakov's 'Sadko'

Marc-André Hamelin pf
Hyperion CDA67050 (68' · DDD) ⒻOO

Here is a cunning and potent mix of every conceivable form of pianistic and musical intricacy (it excludes the merely decorative, salon or ephemeral). Everything is of the most absorbing interest; everything is impeccably performed. Hamelin's richly inclusive programme ranges from Godowsky's *Toccata*, music of the most wicked, labyrinthine complexity, to three of his own projected cycle of 12 *Etudes*, among them a ferociously witty and demanding Prelude and Fugue and a reworking of Chopin's Op 10 No 5, full of black thoughts as well as black notes. Then there's Alkan's sinister absorption of the *Andante* from Haydn's *Surprise* Symphony (loyal to Haydn, Alkan's teasing perversity also makes such music peculiarly his own); a *Berceuse* by Samuel Feinberg that prompts Francis Pott, in his brilliantly illuminating notes, to question what sort of child would be lulled by such strangeness; some superb Medtner and Scriabin and a cloudy, profoundly expressive *Fantasia after J. S. Bach* by Busoni. Clearly among the most remarkable pianists of our time, Hamelin makes light of every technical and musical difficulty, easing his way through Godowsky's intricacy with yards to spare, registering every sly modulation of Alkan's 'Le premier billet-doux' and generating a white-hot intensity in Rachmaninov's admirably revised version of his Second *Moment musical*. Here, Hamelin's maintenance of a 'line' set within a hectically whirling complexity is something to marvel at. Taut, sinewy and impassioned, this performance is a worthy successor to Rachmaninov's own legendary disc. Every phrase and note is coolly appraised within its overall context and the results are audacious and immaculate as required. Hyperion's sound is superb.

Christopher Herrick · *organ*

Organ Fireworks VI
Cocker Tuba tune **Elgar** Organ Sonata No 1 in G, Op 28 **Hollins** A Trumpet Minuet **CS Lang** Tuba tune **Lemare** Concertstück in the form of a Polonaise, Op 80 **Spicer** Kiwi Fireworks – Variations on 'God defend New Zealand' **Sumsion** Introduction and Theme **Wagner** (trans Lemare, arr Westbrook and Herrick) Die Meistersinger von Nürnberg – Prelude, Act 1
Christopher Herrick *org*
Hyperion CDA66778 (76' · DDD) Recorded on the Norman and Beard organ in the Town Hall, Wellington, New Zealand, 1995　　　　ⒻⓄ

This series turned into something of a world tour for Christopher Herrick and the 'Organ Fireworks' team, and here they travel to New Zealand. They've come up with one genuine piece of 'home-grown' music (although CS Lang left New Zealand for England almost before he could tell a nappy from a nazard) and a connection with Edwin Lemare; he played this organ three months after its completion in 1906. However, the starting-point for this programme is the tradition of civic organ concerts that was exported from the town halls of Edwardian England to such far-flung corners of the British Empire. The Wellington Town Hall organ is typical of a large turn-of-the-century English symphonic organ; it might seem a little extravagant to go half-way round the world to find such

a thing, but, following its 1985-6 restoration, it's rare in being substantially unaltered and in excellent working condition. Full organ is gloriously meaty, the flue tone beautifully blended and the solo reeds a joy to behold – a silvery Tromba perfect for Hollins's elegant Minuet; a gutsy Tuba ideal for both Cocker and Lang. As ever, Herrick's performances have both musical integrity and great communicative flair: his is a matchless performance of the Elgar Sonata, in which the composer's strangely awkward use of the organ, in places treating it almost orchestrally, is immaculately managed.

Organ Fireworks IX
Bach (arr Reger) Chromatic Fantasia and Fugue in D minor, BWV903 **Bartók** (arr Herrick) Six Romanian Folkdances, Sz56 **Eftestøl** Seven Allegorical Pictures **Gowers** An Occasional Trumpet Voluntary **Langlais** Trois paraphrases grégoriennes, Op 5 **N Rawsthorne** Dance Suite – Line Dance **Widor** Symphony No 5 in F minor, Op 42 No 1 – Toccata **Wolstenholme** Bohemesque
Christopher Herrick *org*
Hyperion CDA67228 (72' · DDD) Played on the organ of Berner Münster, Switzerland　　　　Ⓕ

Beyond a fascinating and varied mix of familiar and unfamiliar repertoire, the strengths of Hyperion's spectacular 'Organ Fireworks' series lie in consistently first-rate recordings of some of the world's most aurally stunning instruments (of which this 57-stop organ in Berne is a classic example), and Herrick's playing, which can only be described as unfailingly brilliant. There are surely few players around who in the same breath, as it were, could plunge into the emotional intensity of Langlais' *Paraphrases grégoriennes*, glide over the glib figurations of Widor's *Toccata*, dance with agility through a masterly transcription (by Herrick himself) of Bartók's *Romanian Folkdances*, and delve into the surprising rhythmic intricacies of Wolstenholme's *Bohemesque*, with its peculiarly disturbing 15/8 time-signature. Herrick is a musician with a powerful urge to communicate. And communicate he does, drawing on his enormous technical and intellectual resources to turn out performances which sometimes amaze, often astound but never fail to stimulate.

Organ Dreams, Volume 2
Barber (arr Strickland) Adagio, Op 11 **Dubois** In paradisum **Bridge** Adagio in E, H63 No 2 **Elgar** 11 Vesper Voluntaries, Op 14 **Guilmant** Sonata No 7 in F, Op 89 – Rêve **Howells** Siciliano for a High Ceremony **Liszt** Evocation à la Chapelle Sixtine, S658 **Schumann** Study in A flat, Op 56 No 4 **S Wesley** Short Pieces with Voluntary – No 5 in A minor; No 8 in F; No 9 in F; No 11 in D
Christopher Herrick *org*
Hyperion CDA67146 (73' · DDD)　　　　ⒻⓄ

Following eight highly acclaimed discs of 'Organ Fireworks', the winning combination of

Christopher Herrick and Hyperion turn their attention towards the calmer and more reflective repertory grouped under the title 'Organ Dreams'. Volume 2 consists mostly of original organ music spanning the period 1815-1952, all of which fits the instrument in Ripon Cathedral like a well-tailored glove.

Not every title reflects a dream-like state, though the disc's opening track – Dubois' *In paradisum* creates an aura of calm. Frank Bridge's oft-played *Adagio in E* is also smoothly shaped, with its grand climax carefully controlled. Guilmant's 'Rêve' of 1902 is delicious, its impressionistic perfume wafting effortlessly.

With a running time of 19 minutes, Elgar's rarely heard *Vesper Voluntaries* of 1889 form the centrepiece of Herrick's programme. What charmers they are: mostly *mezzopiano* in dynamic, with occasional fuller-bodied outbursts, none of them outstays its welcome. They are followed by Howells' rambling *Siciliano* (the most recent piece on the disc), which Herrick keeps moving. However, he does allow himself plenty of time for William Strickland's convincing arrangement of Barber's *Adagio*.

The Liszt is a shameless piece of kitsch which borrows freely from Allegri's *Miserere* and Mozart's *Ave verum corpus*. More worthwhile are Schumann's *Study* and a quartet of miniatures by Samuel Wesley. The only fault with the whole package is that the portrait purporting to be that of Wesley senior is, in fact, that of his natural son, Samuel Sebastian.

In summary, this thoroughly enjoyable disc is sensitively and affectionately played, and works well at a single hearing.

Vladimir Horowitz   *piano*

The Solo European Recordings, 1930-36,   Ⓗ
Volumes 1 and 2
APR5516 – **Chopin** Etudes – C sharp minor, Op 10
No 4; G flat, 'Black Keys', Op 10 No 5; F, Op 10 No 8;
F, Op 25 No 3 (recorded 1934). Mazurkas – F minor,
Op 7 No 3; E minor, Op 41 No 2; C sharp minor, Op
50 No 3. Scherzo No 4 in E, Op 54. Piano Sonata No
2 in B flat minor, 'Funeral March', Op 35 – Grave ...
doppio movimento (rec 1936) **Liszt** Funérailles, S173
No 7. Piano Sonata in B minor, S178   **OO**

APR5517 – **Bach/Busoni** Nun freut euch, lieben
Christen gmein, BWV734 **Beethoven** 32 Variations on
an Original Theme in C minor, WoO80 **Debussy**
Etude No 11 'Pour les arpèges composés' **Haydn**
Keyboard Sonata in E flat, HobXVI/52 **Poulenc**
Pastourelle. Toccata **Prokofiev** Toccata in D minor,
Op 11 (rec 1930) **Rachmaninov** Prelude in G minor,
Op 23 No 5 **Rimsky-Korsakov/Rachmaninov** The
tale of Tsar Saltan – Flight of the bumble-bee
D Scarlatti Keyboard Sonatas – B minor, Kk87; G,
Kk125 **Schumann** Presto passionato in G minor (rec
1932). Arabeske in C, Op 18. Traumes Wirren, Op 12
No 7. Toccata in C, Op 7 **Stravinsky** Petrushka –
Russian dance (rec 1932)
Vladimir Horowitz pf   Ⓜ**OO**
APR mono ② APR5516/7 (oas: 69' & 71' · ADD)

Horowitz's 1930-36 European recordings are beyond price, and so it's more than gratifying to have them permanently enshrined on APR rather than fleetingly available elsewhere. This is notably true of Horowitz's legendary, forever spine-tingling 1932 recording of the Liszt Sonata. Here, once more, is that uniquely teasing and heroic sorcery with octaves and passage-work that blaze and skitter with a manic force and projection; an open defiance of all known musical and pianistic convention. Horowitz's virtuosity, particularly in his early days, remains a phenomenon, and hearing, for example, the *vivamente* elaboration of the principal theme or the octave uproar preceding the glassy, retrospective coda is to be reminded of qualities above and beyond the explicable. His way with the Chopin *Mazurkas* unites their outer dance elements and interior poetry with a mercurial brilliance and idiosyncrasy, and who but Horowitz could use his transcendental pianism to conjure a *commedia dell'arte* vision of such wit and caprice in Debussy's *Etude, Pour les arpèges composés*? Of the previously unpublished recordings, the first movement from Chopin's Second Sonata is as macabre and tricky as ever, with a steady, oddly menacing tempo. Prokofiev's *Toccata*, on the other hand, is tossed off at a nail-biting speed, and not even a small but irritating cut, a wild, approximate flailing at the end and an added chord by way of compensation, can qualify the impact of such wizardry. In Rachmaninov's G minor Prelude, however, Horowitz's volatility gets the better of him. If Horowitz, in common with virtually every other pianist, was not equally convincing in every composer and was even 'a master of distortion' for some, he was a Merlin figure of an indelible, necromantic brio for all others.

Though expertly transferred, they do show their age somewhat, but nothing can lessen the impact of Horowitz's early charisma.

Debussy Children's Corner – Serenade for a doll.   Ⓗ
Etudes – Pour les cinq doigts; Pour les sixtes; Pour
les huits doigts **Kabalevsky** Piano Sonata No 2 in E
flat, Op 45. Preludes, Op 38 – No 1 in C; No 3 in G;
No 8 in F sharp minor; No 10 in C sharp minor; No 16
in B flat minor; No 17 in A flat; No 22 in G minor; No
24 in D minor **Moszkowski** Etincelles, Op 36 No 6.
Etudes de virtuosité, Op 72 – in F; in A flat **Prokofiev**
Three Pieces from Cinderella, Op 95 – No 2, Gavotte;
No 3, Valse lente
Vladimir Horowitz pf
Urania mono SP4206 (61' · ADD) Recorded live
1947-51   Ⓕ

If anyone needs a sharp reminder of Horowitz's greatness in certain repertoire, then this is it. Who else could show such a teasing and phenomenal mastery of tone in his tantalisingly brief selection of Debussy *Etudes*, biting and acerbic when not suave and luxuriant, their fantasy unfolded with all the cunning and artifice at his command? His 'Serenade for a Doll,' as on so many other occasions, is more speculative than coquettish, remembering, like Debussy himself, a long-vanished world of childhood innocence. Who but Horowitz could make Kabalevsky sound so indelibly Russian, rather than frivolous? He casts an aura of rare distinction over the eight Preludes he chooses from Op 38, conjuring a memory of Mussorgsky's 'Gnomus' (*Pictures at an Exhibition*) in No 10, and whirling us through the *moto perpetuo* of No 3 with aplomb. His long-favoured Moszkowski encores are tossed off with nonchalance and demonism. His mischievous charm and ravishing *cantabile* in Prokofiev's 'Gavotte' and 'Valse lente' from *Cinderella* close a recital of live New York performances from 1947-51, when he was at the height of his powers. Such playing has you by the throat, roaring and whispering its audacity through every page. This reissue brilliantly captures Horowitz's instrument with its resonating bass and splintering treble.

Rediscovered – Carnegie Hall Recital, November 16, 1975
Chopin Scherzo No 1 in B minor, Op 20. Waltz No 3 in A minor, Op 34 No 2 **Debussy** Children's Corner – Serenade for a doll **Liszt** Au bord d'une source, S160 No 4. Valse oubliées in F sharp, S215 No 1 **Moszkowski** Etincelles, Op 36 No 6 **Rachmaninov** Etudes-tableaux, Op 39 – No 5 in E flat minor; No 9 in D. Prelude in G, Op 32 No 5 **Schumann** Blumenstück in D flat, Op 19. Träumerei, Op 15 No 7. Piano Sonata No 3 in F minor, Op 14
Vladimir Horowitz *pf*
RCA Red Seal ② 82876 50754-2 (87' · ADD) **Ⓜ❍❍❍**

 Aged 72 at the time of this 1975 Carnegie Hall recital, this musical Merlin plays with all his compulsive, mesmerising magic. Mischievous, egotistical, lavishly tinted and tilted very much towards the performer rather than the composer it may be, but the illusion that theirs is the only possible way still holds in a concert issued on disc for the first time.

Schumann was always at the heart of Horowitz's repertoire, the *Blumenstück* a speciality with which he loved to tease and cajole his audience, its arched and inflected phrases declaring his identity in every coaxing note and nuance. His performance of the Third Sonata, too, is of an astonishing intricacy. Everything is on the wild side, a mix of raging passions and whispered confidences.

Such playing isn't for those who feel that music should be allowed its own voice, that the zenith of artistry lies in the selfless subordination of re-creator to creator. His performance of Chopin's A minor Waltz, for example, is at once outrageous and inimitable, sighing and crooning shamelessly to the gallery.

RCA faithfully capture the sound of Horowitz's piano, its glassy treble and resonating bass making Neville Cardus's description of 'the greatest pianist dead or alive' a vivid and persuasive possibility, rather than mere hyperbole.

Stephen Hough   *piano*

English Piano Album
Bantock Song to the Seals (arr Hough) **Bowen** Rêverie d'amour, Op 20 No 2. Serious Dance Op 51 No 2. The Way to Polden, Op 76 **Bridge** The Dew Fairy. Heart's Ease **Elgar** In Smyrna **Hough** Valse énigmatique – No 1; No 2 **Leighton** Study Variations, Op 56 Rawsthorne Bagatelles **Reynolds** Two Poems in Homage to Delius. Two Poems in Homage to Fauré
Stephen Hough *pf*
Hyperion CDA67267 (74' · DDD) .   Ⓕ

The very opening item, Rawsthorne's four *Bagatelles*, instantly makes it clear that this latest recital disc from Stephen Hough has a different aim from his previous collections of charmers. Gritty and tough, in Hough's hands sounding wonderfully pianistic, these miniatures are thoughtful and intense, balanced at the end of the disc by the final item, also by far the longest, Kenneth Leighton's *Study Variations*. These do not make for easy listening either, but they inspire Hough to superb pianism over six sharply characterised pieces, at times echoing Bartók in their angry energy, at others full of fantasy. What all these very varied pieces demonstrate is Hough's profound love of keyboard sound and textures, and his rare gift of bringing out the full tonal beauty.

It's evidence, too, of Hough's wizardry that he makes the Elgar piece, *In Smyrna*, sound so magical. In his hands it's like an improvisation with echoes of the lovely solo viola serenade in the overture, *In the South*. The three Bowen works are simple and song-like using an almost cabaret-style of piano writing. In all these pieces Hough's magic is presented in full, clear Hyperion sound. Thoroughly recommended.

Stephen Hough's New Piano Album
Chaminade Autrefois, Op 87 No 4. Pierrette, Op 41 **Godowsky** Triakontameron – Alt Wien **Hough** Etude de Concert. Musical Jewellery Box **Kálmán** Was weiss ein nie geküsster Rosenmund (arr Hough) **Liszt** Soirée de Vienne in A minor, S427 No 6 **Moszkowski** Etincelles, Op 36 No 6 **Pabst** Paraphrase on 'Sleeping Beauty' (arr Hough) **Paderewski** Mélodie in G flat, Op 16 No 2 **Rachmaninov** Humoresque in G, Op 10 No 5. Mélodie in E, Op 3 No 3 (1940 vers) **Rodgers** Carousel – The Carousel Waltz. The King and I – Hello, Young Lovers (all arr Hough) **Schubert** Moment musical in F minor, D780 No 3. Die schöne Müllerin, D795 – No 8, Morgengruss (all arr Godowsky) **Tchaikovsky** Dumka, Op 59. Humoresque in E minor, Op 10 No 2. Swan Lake, Op 20 – Pas de quatre (arr Wild) **Traditional** The Londonderry Air (arr Hough)
Stephen Hough *pf*
Hyperion CDA67043 (78' · DDD)   Ⓕ

Stephen Hough fashions a viable programme culled from a bottomless piano bench of transcriptions, encores and other sundry ear-ticklers. Indeed, Hough proves that one can make a well-balanced meal using only desserts. Modern pianists, to be sure, are more calorie conscious than their forebears, and Hough is no exception. It's not his way to emphasise inner voices or linger over juicy modulatory patterns, *à la* Hofmann, Moiseiwitsch, Horowitz, Cortot or Cherkassky. If Hough prefers to bind Godowsky's garish counterpoints with skimmed milk rather than double cream, he's cheeky (and smart!) enough to insert his own *ossias* into Moskowski's *Etincelles*, or to retool the Tchaikovsky/Pabst *Sleeping Beauty* Paraphrase to more brilliant pianistic effect. As in his previous 'Piano Albums', Hough serves up his own Rodgers & Hammerstein transcriptions. If the decorative note-spinning in 'Hello, Young Lovers' distracts from rather than enhances the eloquent original, the pianist's giddy romp through 'The Carousel Waltz' is a tour de force that brilliantly recaptures both the tender and tough-minded qualities inherent in the musical's book. Hough's own *Etude de Concert* gets plenty of finger-twisting mileage out of a rather un-memorable theme, harmonised, however, with clever Gershwinisms. The unadorned Rachmaninov and Tchaikovsky selections are played with heartfelt simplicity and a lean yet singing sonority.

Julius Katchen   *piano*

Balakirev Islamey **Brahms** Piano Sonata No 3 in F minor, Op 5. Variations on an original theme in D, Op 21 No 1. Hungarian Dances **Chopin** Ballade No 3 in A flat, Op 47. Fantasie in F minor, Op 49 **Franck** Prélude, choral et fugue **Liszt** Hungarian Rhapsody No 12 in C sharp minor, S244 **Mendelssohn** Prelude and Fugue in E minor/E, Op 35. Introduction and rondo capriccioso, Op 14 **Rorem** Piano Sonata No 2
Julius Katchen pf
Philips Great Pianists of the 20th Century ② 456 856-2PM2 (157' · ADD) Recorded 1949-62 Ⓜ**OO**

The booklet-essay claims that Katchen's 1949 Brahms F minor Sonata was the first ever piano LP. You're likely to be totally bowled over by it now. Katchen plays each of the five movements as to the manner born, calling to mind Schumann's eulogy: 'We heard the most genial playing, which made an orchestra out of the piano. There were sonatas, more like disguised symphonies...'. You begin to wonder if this colossal performance will spoil the rest of the programme. It all has immense character, but apart from the Brahms at the end nothing quite reaches the same heights.

Katchen certainly makes a good case for Ned Rorem's Sonata, a pastiche-Gallic affair which in less temperamental and skilful hands would almost certainly sound merely insipid. The Mendelssohn *Prelude and Fugue* eventually tips over into Wagnerian hyperbole, while the *Introduction and rondo capriccioso* is treated as a pretext for flash-fingered display, as is, more justifiably, the Liszt *Rhapsody*.

Not many pianists would dare to deliver

Islamey with such delirious abandon, and the central section is fabulously atmospheric. Whether the last few pages come off depends on personal tolerance levels, however; at these tempos they're inevitably something of a smash and grab affair. The Franck *Prélude* is unfolded patiently and with marvellously natural rhetorical presence, and the two Chopin pieces have the feeling of one-off, showstopping encores designed to bring the house down, rather than considered interpretations for repeated listening.

In these particular instances the recording quality must be partly to blame, because the Brahms Variations sound immediately warmer and less concerned with effect. They are all the better for Katchen's letting the climaxes grow organically rather than screaming them out. And the *Hungarian Dances* are pure joy. Katchen played music on his own terms rather than the composer's. He was a big enough artist to get away with that most of the time, and when the temperamental affinity was particularly strong, as with early Brahms, the results were well-nigh incomparable.

Wilhelm Kempff   *piano*

Bach Chromatic Fantasia and Fugue in D minor, BWV903 **Beethoven** Piano Sonata No 22 in F, Op 54 **Schubert** Piano Sonata No 12 in F minor, D625. Drei Klavierstücke, D946. Impromptus, D899 – No 3 in G flat; No 4 in A flat
Wilhelm Kempff pf
BBC Legends/IMG Artists BBCL4045-2 (77' · ADD) Recorded live 1969 Ⓜ**OOO**

 Kempff's art was at its apogee at the time of his 70th birthday in the autumn of 1965; rigour and fantasy held in perfect poise. Bryce Morrison, who has provided the notes for this BBC Legends release, and who was present at this concert – and indeed many other legendary recitals, recalls: 'If I were to single out one musical experience that transcended all others, it would have to be Wilhelm Kempff's 1969 Queen Elizabeth Hall recital. At his greatest, as he undoubtedly was on this occasion, Kempff's playing seemed bathed in a numinous light or halo of sound, his choice of music by Bach, Beethoven, and Schubert seemingly improvised on the spot.'

Alfred Brendel has said of Kempff, 'he was an Aeolian harp, ever ready to respond to whatever interesting wind blew his way'. It's a remark that applies especially well to Kempff's Schubert. He has said that in his early years Schubert's music was a book with seven seals. He played Schubert Lieder, but it was not until much later, after the First World War, that he entered the private world of the piano sonatas. For him, Schubert's 'heavenly length' was never lengthy if seen in proportion to the larger experience. 'If length becomes evident as longueur,' Kempff has written, 'the fault lies with the interpreter (I speak from my own experience ...).'

Not here. The reading is wonderfully taut yet touched with a rare ease of utterance. The enigmatic end is perfectly judged (and well 'heard' by an audience whose applause merely stutters into life). After the 'disconsolate lyricism' (BM's phrase) of the sonata, the *Drei Klavierstücke* offer more or less unalloyed pleasure, Kempff winging the music into life. The playing has charm, dash and magic. He once said of Schubert's piano music: 'It ought not to be subjected to the glaring lights of the concert halls, as it's the confession of an extremely vulnerable spirit. Schubert reveals his innermost secrets to us *piano-pianissimo*.' We hear this wonderfully well in Kempff's playing of the first of his two encores, the Impromptu in G flat, where his fabled *cantabile* comes even more mesmerisingly into its own. An Aeolian harp indeed!

At the start of the recital, Kempff provides a shrewdly voiced and somewhat Mendelssohnian account of Bach's *Chromatic Fantasia and Fugue*. It's a performance to free the fingers and light the way ahead, the great work assuming the role of warm-up man with as good a grace as can be expected.

Rare Recordings, 1936-1945 ⊞

Bach Chromatic Fantasia and Fugue in D minor, BWV903. Cantata No 147, Herz und Mund und Tat und Leben – Choral: Wohl mir, dass ich Jesum habe (arr Kempff) **Beethoven** Piano Concerto No 5 in E flat, 'Emperor', Op 73ᵃ **Chopin** Berceuse in D flat, Op 57. Mazurkas – No 7 in F minor, Op 7 No 3; No 34 in C, Op 56 No 2. Fantaisie-impromptu in C sharp minor, Op 66 **Fauré** Nocturne No 6 in D flat, Op 63 **Mozart** Piano Concerto No 21 in C, K467ᵇ **Liszt** Ánnées de pèlerinage – Première année, S160: Au lac de Wallenstadt; Au bord d'une source; Eglogue; Deuxième année, S161: Il penseroso; Sonetto 123 del Petrarca. Venezia e Napoli, S162 – No 1, Gondoliera

Wilhelm Kempff *pf* ᵃ**Berlin Philharmonic Orchestra / Peter Raabe;** ᵇ**Leipzig Symphony Orchestra / Hans Weisbach**

Music & Arts ② CD1071 (134' · AAD) Recorded 1936-45   ℗**OO**

Here is musical treasure confirming that Wilhelm Kempff was a unique artist, whose miraculous pianism expressed a poetry as deep as it was natural. His early teacher, Heinrich Barth, is quoted in the sleeve-note as saying, 'Boy, what I cannot give you must come from heaven,' to which one can only retort that Kempff's gifts were, indeed, heaven-sent. A more modest teacher, Marguerite Long, listened in astonishment to Kempff's performance of Fauré's Sixth Nocturne (a work she had played to the composer and taught to successive generations of French pianists), chastened and feeling that she was hearing this rapturous piece for the first time.

How to explain the start of the central section, with its idealised birdsong emerging in a *pianissimo* so delicate and luminous that it seems to come from another world? Above all, the play-

ing has an improvisatory freedom that can never be taught; ironically, considering Kempff's nationality, this may well be the most magically re-creative performance of a Fauré piano work ever to appear on record. Kempff's Chopin, too, is a marvel of poise and economy, a classic instance of his style and under-statement, and his Liszt, taken from the gentler, more picturesque side of his genius, is evocative in a manner unthinkable from any other pianist. Who else could confide the opening of the 'Sonetto 123 del Petrarca' with such a sense of its *lento placido*, *dolcissimo* and *espressivo* or close with a more beatific or glowing memory of the poet's words, 'I saw on earth angelic grace.' Again, his Bach is light-years away from other more pedantic or 'correct' versions, freely and unapologetically romantic in the *Chromatic Fantasia*, light, buoyant and inimitably voiced in the *Fugue*.

Then there are two live performances of concertos where the supposed division between Mozart's Appollonian and Beethoven's Dionysian genius seems to melt at a touch. Here's the most radiant, least hectoring of *Emperor* Concertos, with a rapt sense of poetry beneath the outer tumult that not even the dim 1936 recording can hide. The Mozart is introduced as played by 'Professor Kempff', but the performance is so filled with light and air, a spirit of adventure and, in the finale, a transcendental fleetness, that the title seems comically ponderous and inept. Kempff's cadenzas, which include a quote from the C minor Fantasia, K475, offer further instances of his inventiveness, his wit and solemnity. Most of the recordings, when you stop to consider them, have come up remarkably well and those who thirst for true musical genius should invest in this double album without delay. These are rare recordings in every sense.

Zoltán Kocsis   *piano*

Bartók Six Romanian Folkdances, Sz56 **Debussy** Deux arabesques. D'un cahier d'esquisses. L'isle joyeuse. Estampes. Fantaisieᵃ **Dohnányi** Variations on a Nursery Song, Op 25ᵃ **Grieg** Lyric Pieces, Book 3, Op 43 **Liszt** Années de pèlerinage, troisième année, S163 – Les jeux d'eau à la Villa d'Este **Rachmaninov** Piano Concerto No 4 in G minor, Op 40ᵇ. Prelude in C sharp minor, Op 3 No 2. Vocalise, Op 34 No 14 (arr Kocsis)

Zoltán Kocsis *pf* ᵃ**Budapest Festival Orchestra / Ivan Fischer;** ᵇ**San Francisco Symphony Orchestra / Edo de Waart**

Philips Great Pianists of the 20th Century ② 456 874-2PM2 (153' · DDD) Recorded 1982-95 Ⓜ**OO**

As a pianist, Zoltán Kocsis (also a conductor, composer and musicologist) is at once fastidious, interpretatively innovative and profoundly respectful of the recorded legacies left by major artists of the past – most notably those of Bartók and Rachmaninov. His recording of Rachmaninov's Fourth Concerto reawakens memories of the composer's own.

Edo de Waart and his San Francisco players are with him every single bar of the way, heightening the drama of the outer movements, end tenderising the wistful *Largo*. The solo playing is agile and quick-witted, with amazing finger velocity and a distinctive brand of *rubato*. One might imagine that Kocsis's arrangement of the *Vocalise* would subscribe to the same taut, trimly tailored pianistic aesthetic: but what we hear is malleable almost to excess and, towards the end of the piece, extravagantly decorated. The C sharp minor Prelude is given a far more central reading, and a brilliant one at that. Memories of Rachmaninov also inform Kocsis's approach to Grieg's Op 43 *Lyric Pieces*, particularly the chirruping 'Vöglein' and of 'Erotik' which – unlike the *Vocalise* – allows for phrasal freedom while holding fast to the musical line. Control is a very Kocsisian attribute, and helps to forge aural sculpture out of Debussy's two early *Arabesques*. The *Suite bergamasque* is scarcely less accomplished while *Estampes* and *D'un cabier d'esquisses* balance sensuality and spontaneity. Kocsis brings a winning lilt to *L'isle joyeuse*, although his fingerwork remains extraordinarily clear throughout.

The *Fantaisie* for piano and orchestra is given a fine performance which centres more on clarity than atmosphere, while the *Nursery* Variations combines fun with pianistic finesse: both works are superbly accompanied by Fischer and the Budapest Festival Orchestra (which Fischer and Kocsis co-founded). Liszt's ochre-tinted fountain is viewed with the hindsight of Bartók (or so it seems): Kocsis's performance attends rather more to the music's harmonic constituents than to its virtuoso aspect. And then there are Bartók's *Romanian Folkdances*, idiomatic and musically satisfying. The recorded sound has great presence.

Dinu Lipatti   *piano*

The Last Recital
Bach Partita in B flat, BWV825 **Chopin** Waltzes – Nos 1 & 3-14 **Mozart** Piano Sonata No 8 in A minor, K310/K300d **Schubert** Impromptus, D899 – No 2 in E flat; No 3 in G flat
Dinu Lipatti *pf*
EMI mono 5628192 (73' · ADD) Recorded live 1950
Ⓜ❍❍❍

 Apart from the two Schubert *Impromptus*, the programme of Lipatti's last recital consisted of works he had recorded only some 10 weeks earlier for EMI, in a Geneva studio, while enjoying a miraculous cortisone-wrought new lease of life. However, when honouring this Besançon Festival engagement on September 16, 1950, against the advice of his doctors, leukaemia had once more gained the upper hand. Less than three months later he was dead, aged only 33. As those of us who have long cherished the original LPs already know, the only evidence of weakness was the omission of the last of the concluding Chopin *Waltzes* (in his own favoured sequence, that in A flat major,

Op 34 No 2). For the rest, the recital stands as 'one of the great musical and human statements, a testimony to his [Lipatti's] transcendental powers, an almost frightening assertion of mind over matter', as the sympathetic introductory note puts it in the insert-booklet. One has to marvel at the clarity of articulation and part-playing in the Bach Partita, at once so attentive to craftsmanly cunning yet so arrestingly unpedagogic and alive. For Mozart he finds a wonderfully translucent sound world, rich in subtleties of colouring – not least in the slow movement's laden song. And as in the two Schubert *Impromptus*, the musical message is all the more affecting for its totally selfless simplicity and purity of expression. Even if just one or two of the *Waltzes* might be thought too fast, with over-swift internal tempo changes for contrasting episodes, his gossamer lightness of touch and mercurial imaginative fancy explain why his way with them has now acquired legendary status.

The only small regret is that this excellently remastered mid-price CD deprives us of the endearingly spontaneous extended arpeggio with which Lipatti prefaced the opening Partita, as if in greeting to his instrument, and likewise the improvisatory modulation with which he carried his Besançon listeners from Bach's B flat major to Mozart's A minor.

Tasmin Little   *violin*

Tchaikovskiana
Brahms Scherzo in C minor, 'FAE Sonata', WoO2.
Hungarian Dance No 2 in D minor (arr Joachim)
Delius Légende in E flat **Elgar** Salut d'amour,
'Liebesgrüss', Op 12 **Heuberger** Der Opernball –
Im chambre separée (arr Kreisler) **Janáček** Dumka
Kreisler La Gitana. Liebesleid. Tambourin chinois,
Op 3 **Lenehan/Little** Tchaikovskiana **Monti** Csárdás
(arr Little/Lenehan) **Ponce** Estrellita (arr Heifetz) **Ravel**
Pièce en forme de habanera **L Sainsbury** Cuban
Dance No 2
Tasmin Little *vn* John Lenehan *pf*
Classics for Pleasure 585615-2 (67' · DDD)   Ⓑ❍

We've heard Tasmin Little at the peak of her form in her masterly Prom of the formidable Violin Concerto by Ligeti. Though this collection of lollipops represents the opposite end of her repertory, it's beautifully constructed to make a satisfying, well-contrasted programme.

It might be unique for a violin disc to start with a virtuoso flourish from the accompanist, but that is how *Tchaikovskiana* opens: it's a fantasy on Tchaikovsky themes, mainly from *Swan Lake*. Originally improvised by the two performers in recitals, here it's given in a more formalised version. It harks back endearingly to the virtuoso pot-pourris so beloved of performers in the late 19th and early 20th centuries, full of display and with a sense of fun.

Elgar's *Salut d'amour* is expressive yet not sentimental, with breathtaking *pianissimos*. The dynamic range of Little's playing is remarkable throughout: the rare *Légende* by Delius provides a fine example, with high contrasts of dynamic, expression and tone. There's weight, too, in a tough, animated performance of the *Scherzo* that Brahms contributed to the *FAE* Sonata, jointly composed with Schumann and Albert Dietrich. The Ravel is seductively slinky, as is the unpretentious little salon piece by Lionel Sainsbury, and the three Kreisler items are ideally chosen. Kreisler is the arranger of Heuberger's most famous theme, 'Im chambre separée', labelling it *Midnight Bells*. Heifetz's delicious arrangement of Ponce's *Estrellita* brings more seduction. The Janáček *Dumka* is an attractive rarity. Little and Lenehan reserve for the end their flamboyant arrangement of an old warhorse, Monti's *Csárdás*. The joy of the performers on this disc makes you share in it.

Joanna McGregor — *piano*

Messiaen Quatuor pour la fin du temps – Louange à l'éternité de Jésus[a] **Pärt** Cantus in memory of Benjamin Britten[b] Urban Prophecies[d] **Sawhney** Neural Circuits[c]. **Schnittke** Piano Concerto[e] **Traditional** Siwe Bell Music[f]. Nyive Iwa[f] [bce]**Joanna MacGregor** [ce]pf [d]**Aref Durvesh** *tabl* [a]**Christopher van Kampen** *vc* [cdf]**Bash Ensemble** (Chris Brannick, Joby Burgess, Steve Hiscock, Andrew Martin *perc*); [bce]**Britten Sinfonia**; [d]**Play Ensemble** (Emma-Louise Hible *fl* Timothy Sidford, George King, Jakob Lindbirk, Nick Hougham *kybds/synts* Henry Baldwin, Patrick King, Owen Gunnell, Sam Staunton *perc*) / [d]**Cameron Sinclair, Joanna McGregor**
SoundCircus SC008 (56' · DDD) ⓕ**O**

This would be a highly covetable album if it merely introduced Sawhney's *Neural Circuits*, but the programming is admirable throughout, creating a network of contextualising links: the 'found sound' techniques evoke Reich's *City Life* and *The Cave* (and there are also hints of free-jazz pianist Cecil Taylor's *Unit Structures* and Stockhausen's *Hymnen*); the traditional Ghanaian pieces remind us how Reich's African studies informed minimalism and, consequently, much subsequent composition; while Schnittke, as ever, alludes disconcertingly to any period or style of music which takes his fancy – witness the references to Russian Church music, which the piano attempts to shout down, or the episode of strolling jazz bass.

This account of Pärt's *Cantus* comprises MacGregor's recorded début as conductor. Despite the competition (notably Russell Davies on ECM) she manages to throw fresh light on this now-familiar but still strikingly beautiful piece, and the merging of the final bell resonances into the opening sounds of the lithe and luminous Ghanaian pieces is magical. *Urban Prophecies* is another riveting and thought-provoking Sawhney construct. Not as stunning as *Neural Circuits* (there's nothing with the power of the ferocious piano part and the increasingly prominent vibraphone figures), its

web of interlocking compound time-signatures and snatches of news bulletins on apocalyptic events still impresses. The CD ends with a ravishing performance of Messiaen's cooler contemplation of the end of time.

Yehudi Menuhin — *violin*

Menuhin in Japan Ⓗ
Bach Solo Violin Sonatas – No 1 in G minor, BWV1001; No 2 in D minor, BWV1002 – Sarabande. Solo Violin Partita No 3 in E, BWV1006 **Bartók** Six Romanian Folkdances, Sz56[a] (arr Székely) **Beethoven** Sonatas for Violin and Piano[a] – No 5 in F, 'Spring', Op 24; No 9 in A, 'Kreutzer', Op 47 **Brahms** Hungarian Dance No 1 in G minor[a] (arr Joachim) **Dvořák** (arr Kreisler) Slavonic Dance in E minor, B78 No 2[a]. Symphony No 9 in E minor, 'From the New World', B178[a] – Largo **Granados** (arr Kreisler) 12 Danzas españolas, Op 37[a] **Kreisler** Caprice viennois, Op 2[a] **Nováček** Perpetuum mobile, Op 5 No 4[a] **Ravel** (arr Catherine) Pièce en forme de habanera[a] **Sarasate** Danzas españolas[a] – Malagueña; Habanera; Romanza andaluza, Op 22 No 1 **Tartini** (arr Kreisler) Sonata for Violin and Continuo in G minor, 'Devil's Trill'[a] **Wieniawski** Scherzo-tarantelle in G minor, Op 16[a]
Yehudi Menuhin *vn* with [a]**Adolf Baller** *pf*
Biddulph mono ② LAB162/3 (146' · ADD) Recorded 1951 Ⓜ**O**

Here's a fully fired-up Menuhin, high on adrenalin and relishing the thrill of the moment. The circumstances were a Japanese tour, a punishing concert schedule and a two-day sequence of sessions which, on the evidence of the manifest results, probably involved a minimum of 'takes'. There were technical audio problems, most of them concerning substandard shellac and a rough-sounding end product. Surface levels are unusually high for 1951 commercial releases, but the recorded balance is adequate. What really surprises is the raging intensity and burnished tone quality of Menuhin's playing, especially when considering that his commercial recordings from the same period were prone to roughness. Even close scrutiny, though, suggests it isn't a question of those 'rough edges' being camouflaged by a blanket of surface noise. It seems that this playing really is as good as it sounds! The *Kreutzer* Sonata throws caution to the wind (a little too much perhaps in first movement's central section) with a compensating spontaneity that recalls Menuhin's audacious youth and those fabulous records from the 1930s. Adolf Baller is no mere accompanist, but an immensely strong player in his own right, with plenty of individual ideas.

The Bach solo sonatas are truly home territory for Menuhin, and these particular readings show greater maturity than his pre-war recordings and a surer technical command than the two complete sets that he made a few years later. In his notes Erik Wen rightly suggests that the Japanese performances 'project an expressive, almost improvisatory, freedom while maintaining an eloquent pacing throughout', though the sound on the pre-war set is better. The heat remains full on for Tartini's *Devil's Trill*, again notably superior to Menuhin's earlier commercial recording. The 'encores' breathe fire and passion by the second: Brahms's First *Hungarian Dance* is super-fast and the Dvořák 'Negro Spiritual Melody' (ie the principal theme from the *New World* Symphony's *Largo*) witnesses a veritable flood of tone. Occasionally in these shorter pieces the tempo is pushed too far, but the excitement is almost tangible. A marvellous release.

Arturo Benedetti Michelangeli   *piano*

Chopin Fantasie in F minor, Op 49. Ballade No 1 **H** in G minor, Op 23. Waltz in E flat, Op posth **Debussy** Images – Reflets dans l'eau; Hommage à Rameau; Cloches à travers les feuilles; Et la lune descend sur le temple qui fût **Schumann** Carnaval, Op 9. Faschingsschwank aus Wien, Op 26 **Mompou** Cançons i danses No 6 – Canción
Arturo Benedetti Michelangeli pf
Testament mono ② SBT2088 (130' · ADD) Includes a half-hour rehearsal sequence. Recorded live 1957   Ⓕ

Readers who are familiar with Michelangeli's 1971 DG recording of Debussy's *Images* will be astonished at this highly mobile 1957 concert performance of 'Cloches à travers les feuilles', which is almost a full minute faster than its stereo successor; or 'Reflets dans l'eau', which glides across the water's surface with such swiftness and ease that the more considered DG alternative – glorious though it is – sounds studied by comparison. 'Hommage à Rameau' is shaped with the utmost finesse and 'Et la lune descend sur le temple qui fût' coloured by exquisitely graded nuances. The performance of Schumann's *Carnaval* is a choice gallery of aural sculpture, whether in the minutely calculated responses of 'Pierrot', the teasing rubato of 'Coquette', the energy and attack of 'Papillons', the effortless flow of 'Chopin' or the ecstatic lingerings in 'Aveu'. Michelangeli's 'Eusebius' is tender but unsentimental, whereas his 'Florestan' has enough 'reflective' ingredients to suggest that the two characters are closer in spirit than we often think. *Faschingsschwank aus Wien* contrasts muscular assertiveness (the opening *Allegro*) with the most amazing control (in the 'Romanze'), while the 'Intermezzo' promotes a virtually orchestral surge of dynamics. Michelangeli's Chopin has a rare nobility, the *Fantasie* especially which, at a rather faster tempo than usual, holds together as a narrative entity. Then there's the imposing First *Ballade* and the encores – a sunny posthumous E flat *Waltz* (a regular extra on Michelangeli's concert programmes) and Mompou's sad but tender 'Canción'. This disc leaves you humbled by, and grateful for, some wonderful piano playing. Michelangeli's art is both rare and elusive, his expressive vocabulary finely distilled and

unlikely to impress those who listen only for technical mastery. So it's ironic that those who criticise Michelangeli for 'coldness' or 'aloofness' are often the very commentators who are so dazzled by his virtuosity that they can't hear beyond it. Testament's transfers are superb.

Maurizio Pollini   *piano*

Boulez Piano Sonata No 2 **Prokofiev** Piano Sonata No 7 in B flat, Op 83 **Stravinsky** Petrushka – three movements **Webern** Piano Variations, Op 27
Maurizio Pollini pf
DG The Originals 447 431-2GOR (68' · ADD) Recorded 1971-6   ⓂＯＯＯ

Perfection needs to be pursued so that you can forget about it. Pollini's *Petrushka* movements are almost inhumanly accurate and fast; but what comes across is an exhilarating sense of abandon, plus an extraordinary cumulative excitement. The Prokofiev Seventh Sonata remains a benchmark recording not only for the athleticism of its outer movements but for the epic remorselessness of the central *Andante*. The Webern Variations are a magical fusion of intellectual passion and poetry, and the Boulez Sonata vividly reminds us why the European avant-garde was such a powerful force in the 1950s. These recordings are a monument to what it's possible for two hands to achieve on one musical instrument. The 'original-image bit-processing' has given a bit more brilliance and presence, as claimed, and another gain is the retention of atmosphere between movements.

Sviatoslav Richter   *piano*

Chopin Etude in E, Op 10 No 3 **Liszt** Valses **H** oubliées, S215 – No 1; No 2. Etudes d'exécution transcendante, S139 – No 5, Feux follets; No 11, Harmonies du soir **Mussorgsky** Pictures at an Exhibition **Rachmaninov** Prelude in G sharp minor, Op 32 No 12 **Schubert** Moment musical No 1 in C, D780. Impromptus, D899 – No 2 in E flat; No 4 in A flat
Sviatoslav Richter pf
Philips 50 Great Recordings 464 734-2PM (74' · ADD) Recorded live 1958   ⓂＯＯ

Even at the height of his powers Richter could be an erratic player, but on this occasion the force was with him from first note until last. Not only did the recital help to spread the Richter 'legend' in the months leading up to his much-hyped London and New York débuts in 1960, his Mussorgsky *Pictures* made a decisive contribution to the rehabilitation of that piece as a staple of the piano repertoire. Here is virtuosity entirely at the service of the music, defying anyone to say a word against Mussorgsky's pianistic imagination or to want to hear Ravel's orchestral make-over ever again. The rest of the recital displays Richter's view of the romantic repertoire at its first mature flowering, after a period of occasionally experimental overstatement and before its rigidification. His Schubert, Chopin and Liszt share a common core of determined resistance to buffeting emotions. Yet on the surface his Schubert is as beautiful and refined as anyone's; the possibly disconcerting intensity of his Chopin is built strictly around the composer's expression markings; and as all collectors of recorded piano music already know, his Liszt *Feux follets* remains a benchmark performance to this day. It's impossible to say for sure if the Prokofiev sonatas presented here are the absolute best available, though one suspects they are. He was in at the birth, or nearly so, of all three pieces, and his identification with their expressive worlds is complete. Defiance and unstoppable momentum are at the heart of the matter, and virtuosity of the highest order is pressed into the service of those core values. It's doubtful whether anyone has taken the *Scherzo* of the Sixth Sonata more convincingly at this tempo (the fast end of *allegretto*), for instance, or found more wide-ranging yet integrated drama in all three movements of the Eighth. You could certainly wish for more refined recording quality on the first disc, though the Prokofiev sonatas are well enough recorded, especially the Eighth. Overall it's difficult to imagine a truer encapsulation of the Richter phenomenon. If by any chance you've missed these recordings in past incarnations you now have an opportunity not to be passed up.

Richter Rediscovered
Chopin Ballade No 3 in A flat, Op 47. Etudes, Op 10 – No 10 in A flat; No 12 in C minor, 'Revolutionary'. Mazurka in C, Op 24 No 2. Scherzo No 4 in E, Op 54 **Debussy** Préludes, Book 1 – No 5, 'Les collines d'Anacapri' **Haydn** Keyboard Sonata No 60 in C, HobXVI/50 **Prokofiev** Gavotte, Op 95 No 2. Piano Sonata No 6, Op 82. Visions fugitives, Op 22 – No 3, Allegretto; No 4, Animato (two recordings); No 5, Molto giocoso; No 6, Con eleganza; No 8, Commodo; No 9, Allegretto tranquillo; No 11, Con vivacità; No 14, Feroce; No 15, Inquieto; No 18, Con una dolce lentezza **Rachmaninov** Preludes – F sharp minor, Op 23 No 1; A, Op 32 No 9; G sharp minor, Op 32 No 12 **Ravel** Jeux d'eau. Miroirs – La vallée des cloches
Sviatoslav Richter pf
RCA Red Seal ② 09026 63844-2 (113' · ADD)
Recorded live 1960   Ⓕ Ⓞ

'Richter Rediscovered' is a two-disc album celebrating a unique pianist in much of his early glory. The producer's note tells us that 'virtually none of the recordings on these CDs have been heard since their actual performance of over 40 years ago.' He also tells us that the reasons for this remain unclear, though knowing Richter's fluctuating attitudes to his own performances, it isn't difficult to deduce why these recitals have remained in limbo for so long. True there are gaucheries and confusions, inaccuracies and memory lapses, but never for a second do you doubt that you're listening to one of the greatest

of all pianists. Both recitals date from 1960 and were given with an almost palpable tension, a discomfort that has you on the edge of your seat in both an enthralling and bad sense; the playing is phenomenal at one level, strange and nerve-wracking at another.

He courses his way through the first movement of Haydn's C major Sonata, hiding behind an incontestable but inscrutable mastery, is teasingly whimsical in Chopin's Fourth *Scherzo* and much given to sudden sprints and skirmishes in the Third Ballade (try him at the capricious flight commencing at 4'10"). He chivies Ravel's delicious indolence and sparkle in *Jeux d'eau* virtually out of existence but is unforgettable in the chiming bells of *La vallée des cloches*. He's at his most awe-inspiring on home territory, plumbing the very depths of despair in Rachmaninov's great B minor Prelude before storming through its central carillon of Moscow bells in a style all his own. Prokofiev's Sixth Sonata is launched with a punishing venom and articulacy, its extremes of stillness and hyperactivity miraculously unified, and how he tantalises his adoring audience with his incomparably played selection from the *Visions fugitives*! Chopin's Etude Op 10 No 10 is spun off with a grace and rapidity that must have left all aspiring pianists weak at the knees.

The recordings have come up trumps. All in all, these records create an ever-astonishing portrait of a pianist of bewildering fantasy and caprice, urgency and commitment.

Andreas Staier   *harpsichord*

Variaciones del Fandango español
Albero Recercata, Fuga and Sonata – G; D **Boccherini** Guitar Quintet in D, G341 – Fandango (arr Staier/Schornsheim)[a] **Ferrer** Adagio and Andantino in G minor **Gallés** Keyboard Sonatas – No 9 in C minor; No 16 in F minor; No 17 in C minor **López** Variaciones del Fandango español **Soler** Fandango
Andreas Staier hpd with [a]**Christine Schornsheim** hpd [a]**Adela Gonzáles Cámpa** castanets
Teldec 3984-21468-2 (65' · DDD)   Ⓕ Ⓞ

The heyday of the fandango dance was in the 18th century (Mozart introduced a form of it in *Figaro*, following Gluck's *Don Juan*). It was danced by a single couple who didn't touch but whose movements were highly erotic; and there were several local varieties of it, including the malagueña, the granadina, the rondeña and the murciana. Despite the disc's title, Andreas Staier doesn't confine himself to the fandango rhythm or to the key of D minor which was so prevalent for it. He kicks off with stunning virtuosity with Soler's famous piece (if it really *was* by him), with its exciting build-up and fearsome hand-crossings. After the initial *tiento* (which he pulls about with violent changes of speed), he tears at a most un-fandango-like breakneck pace into the dance, whirling breathlessly to the end and employing a free range of registrations on his

German-type instrument. He doesn't make the mistakes of spoiling the cumulative effect by rubatos and changes of speed or tacking on a reprise which wrongly ends the work on the tonic instead of the dominant. He adopts the same fast pace for the very similar but shorter variations on the fandango by López (which he discovered), who was an organist in the royal chapel in Madrid under Charles III and IV. It's a distinct relief to find a more authentic speed adopted in a free arrangement for two harpsichords of a fandango from a Boccherini quintet, which is enlivened by (obbligato) castanets. Albero's *recercatas* and gigantic fugues are every bit as astonishing in their chromaticisms and eccentric key-shifts as Bach's *Chromatic Fantasia and Fugue* – in fact, more outlandish. The *recercatas* resemble the older lute *préludes non-mesurés*; the lively sprawling fugues (that in D minor a gigue) call forth brilliantly virtuoso playing and splendidly rhythmic stamina; and each work closes with a binary sonata movement which contains Scarlattian chordal scrunches. Of the other non-fandango works here, the most interesting is an F minor Sonata by Josep Gallés, a Catalan whose other sonatas disclose a somewhat disorganised musical mind.

Antal Szalai · *violin*

Bach Partita No 2 in D minor, BWV1004 **Kreisler** Recitative and scherzo-caprice, Op 6 **Ysaÿe** Solo Violin Sonata in D minor (Ballade), Op 27 No 3
Petrovics Rhapsody No 1
Antal Szalai vn
BMC BMCCD047 (55' · DDD)   🅕**O**

Bach's spirit is everywhere. Szalai opens his programme with a patient and warm-hearted account of the D minor *Partita* where the crowning Chaconne takes 15'24" to unfold, a good overall timing, unhurried but mobile enough to avoid sluggishness. Emil Petrovics' First Rhapsody is an ingenious study in aural perspectives that opens like a ticking clock and ends – as violin rhapsodies usually do – with faster, folk-like material.

Kreisler's comparatively unfamiliar *Recitativo and Scherzo-Caprice* is brilliant without being showy, and a fine example of Szalai's richness on the lower strings. Ysaÿe's Sonata, the one dedicated to Enescu, is deeply expressive music but technically very demanding, a minefield of potential disaster when it comes to intonation which Szalai surveys with considerable skill and accuracy. Szalai's sound is pleasingly full bodied, his vibrato intense but unobtrusive, his double-stops evenly gauged and his bowing mostly immaculate.

The close-miked recording captures the full lustre of his tone. Many lesser players would have us suffer a repertoire of off-bow noises, but not Szalai, whose smooth delivery never precludes a rare level of musicianship. This is a very fine violin CD.

Simon Trpčeski · *piano*

Scriabin Piano Sonata No 5 in F sharp, Op 53
Stravinsky Three movements from Petrushka
Prokofiev Piano Sonata No 6 in A, Op 82
Tchaikovsky The Nutcracker – Suite, Op 71a (arr Pletnev)
Simon Trpčeski pf
EMI Debut 575202-2 (73' · DDD)   💲 ⓈOOO

 The minute Trpčeski opens Pletnev's Concert Suite from Tchaikovsky's *Nutcracker*, you hear a master of rhythmic precision and, later, a capacity to shoulder fierce challenges with unflinching aplomb and authority. Everything is musically and ardently inflected and while Trpčeski's virtuoso voltage in the final pages of the *Andante maestoso* is awe-inspiring, his unfailing musicianship is even more remarkable. Again, in Scriabin you sense a pianist who, for all his compelling mastery, sounds still in the first flush of love for the composer's vividness and idiosyncrasy. The *accelerando* into the first *Presto con allegrezza* is steep and thrilling and Trpčeski's sense of Scriabin's towering rhetoric at 7'20" is masterly.

In *Petrushka*, Trpčeski rejoices in virtuosity tailor-made for Artur Rubinstein, but also remembers the music's balletic origins. Time and again he fills a score too often treated as a vehicle for black and white ferocity with a wealth of colour and character.

There are more pulverising accounts of Prokofiev's Sixth Sonata (notably from Richter, Kissin and, most recently, the formidably lean and articulate François-Frédéric Guy) but few more musical. Trpčeski's quality is unfailing, and he has been recorded with a fine mix of clarity and resonance.

Fredrik Ullén · *piano*

Got a Minute?
Brahms Study after Chopin's Etude, Op 25 No 2
Chopin Waltz in D flat, 'Minute', Op 64 No 1 **Cortot** Adagio after Chopin's Cello Sonata, Op 65 **Ferrata** Second Study after Chopin's Waltz, Op 64 No 1 **Furst** Showpan Boogie **Godowsky** Waltz after Chopin's Op 64 No 1 **Gruenberg** Jazz Masks, Op 30a **Joseffy** Two Concert Studies after Chopin **Michałowski** Paraphrase on Chopin's Waltz, Op 64 No 1 **Moszkowski** Waltz after Chopin's Op 64 No 1 **Philipp** Two Concert Studies after Chopin's Op 64 **Reger** Five Special Studies after Chopin **Rosenthal** Study after Chopin's Waltz, Op 64 No 1 **Sorabji** Pastiche on Chopin's Waltz, Op 64 No 1. Pasticcio capriccioso sopra l'op 64 no 1 del Chopin
Fredrik Ullén pf
BIS CD1083 (77' · DDD)   🅕**O**

This is a treasure trove for those with a sweet tooth. Godowsky's infamous reworkings of Chopin's Etudes will be familiar, but few are aware of the diversity of Chopin arrangements conjured by Godowsky's peers. This collection concentrates on the surprising range of treatments of the *Minute* Waltz, from virtuoso enhancements à la Moszkowski or Rosenthal to the wild and fantastical pastiches of Sorabji. True, the usual understanding of transcription – the idiomatic recasting of music from one medium to another – may be stretched by this sort of super-pianistic amplification, but the wit and invention of these ear-tickling fantasies have their own authentic rewards.

Musically, the most daring works are by Reger and Sorabji, who treat Chopin's structures as springboards for their own imaginative adventures. Try Reger's transformation of Chopin's Etude in thirds (Op 25 No 6), cruelly recast in sixths, or the wealth of subsidiary thematic embellishment in his elegant gloss on the C sharp minor Waltz (Op 64 No 2). The Polish Chopin specialist Aleksander Michałowski wrote numerous Chopin elaborations, and his version of the *Minute* Waltz is as dazzling as it's demanding. Rosenthal, Joseffy and Ferrata were all Liszt pupils, and their treatments, although varied, exhibit familiar traits: doubling in thirds, and a saturation of filigree embroidery and polyphonic enrichment. It's all good harmless fun, and Chopin – like Bach – can easily withstand the treatment without suffering irrevocable damage to the identity and purity of the originals. As if to prove the point, Ullén ends his exploration with the original D flat Waltz, and makes the astute observation that 'our perception of a piece depends as much on our knowledge of its descendants as of its precursors'.

Ullén performs these treacherous pieces with astonishing clarity and dexterity, dispatching the torrents of notes and intricate detail with unruffled aplomb. Anyone who plays Ligeti's *Etudes* must have mental agility and a fearless technique, but Ullén also shows a refinement of nuance and musical shape, making music of even the most over-written material. The principal caveat is his tendency to keep the embellishing figuration too much in the foreground, at the expense of depth of sonority in the melodic line; there are also places that cry out for bolder primary colours, rather than his pastel shades. But this is a remarkable achievement, and should be snapped up by all piano enthusiasts. The recorded sound is rather glassy, but crystal clear.

Maxim Vengerov *violin*

Bach Toccata and Fugue in D minor, BWV565 **Shchedrin** Echo Sonata. Balalaika[a] **Ysaÿe** Solo Violin Sonatas, Op 27 – No 2 in A minor; No 3 in D minor (Ballade); No 4 in E minor; No 6 in E
Maxim Vengerov vn
EMI 557384-2 (67' · DDD)　　　　　Ⓕ**OO**

This solo violin recital offers a masterly demonstration of the artistry as well as the virtuoso prowess of Maxim Vengerov. It culminates in the two items which will obviously win the widest popular appeal, a thrilling solo violin transcription of Bach's D minor Toccata and Fugue and Shchedrin's *Balalaika*, written in

1997, which Vengerov uses as a party-piece encore, dispensing with his bow and playing the violin *pizzicato* as though it's a balalaika, to the great amusement of the audience.

Vengerov makes Bach's Toccata and Fugue into a formidable showpiece, something that in its sustained power can well stand comparison even with the great Chaconne of the D minor Partita, with Vengerov thrillingly bringing out the dramatic and dynamic contrasts.

Vengerov lifts off with Ysaÿe's Sonata No 2, the one in A minor dedicated to Jacques Thibaud, which opens with surreal fragments of the Preludio to the Third Partita. Vengerov is in total command emotionally and technically of this demanding piece, and his readings of the four Ysaÿe Sonatas are similarly passionate. His red-blooded approach provides a striking contrast with Frank Peter Zimmermann's finely disciplined studio performances also on EMI.

Vengerov is warmer, more volatile and spontaneous in romantic style. He almost seems to improvise; he's also the more immediately persuasive, emphatically bringing out the Dies Irae quotations in No 2 and deftly in the Sarabande of No 4 bringing out the melody implied in the pizzicato line. This is a solo violin recital, which, unlike many, in its magnetism and variety, its power and passion, runs no risk of monotony.

Jason Vieaux *guitar*

Barrios Waltzes, Op 8 – Nos 3 & 4. Julia Florida – Barcarola **Bustamente** (arr Morel) Misionera **Krouse** Variations on a Moldavian Hora. Merlin Suite del recuerdo. Morel Chôro. Danza Brasileira. Danza in E minor **Orbón** Preludio y Danza **Pujol** Preludios – Nos 2, 3 & 5
Jason Vieaux gtr
Naxos 8 553449 (64' · DDD)　　　　　Ⓢ Ⓢ**O**

This is the début recording by an artist of great talent. His technical prowess is impressive to say the least, as near flawless as one may get, and his tone is as clear and expressive as his musical thinking. There are now many finger-perfect guitarists on tap, but those of Vieaux's natural musicality are rare indeed; everything in the moulding of the phrases comes from within – you just can't *programme* sensitivity of this kind. The main thrust of the music is Latin-American, a nice juxtaposition of the well known (Morel, Barrios, Pujol and Bustamente) with some unfamiliar but substantial (of their kind) pieces by Merlin and Orbón. The apparent 'misfit' is the work by Krouse, far removed from Latin America, but why should music of this quality be excluded, for whatever reason? It's included for the best of reasons, because the performer loves it and is right to do so. The theme is Moldavian and the language of the imaginative and technically punishing variations convincingly matches it. Vieaux plays everything with chameleon-like felicity of style and feeling. Superb recording and excellent notes complete an issue of the greatest distinction.

Arcadi Volodos _piano_

Piano Transcriptions
Horowitz Variations on a Theme from Bizet's
'Carmen' **Rachmaninov** Morning, Op 4 No 2.
Melody, Op 21 No 9 (all arr Volodos) **Liszt** Hungarian
Rhapsody No 2 in C sharp minor, S244 (arr Horowitz).
Litanei, S562 No 1. Schwanengesang, S560 – No 3,
Aufenthalt; No 10, Liebesbotschaft **Rimsky-Korsakov**
The tale of Tsar Saltan – Flight of the bumble-bee
(arr Cziffra) **Prokofiev** Pieces from Cinderella –
Gavotte, Op 95 No 2; Oriental dance, Op 97 No 6;
Grand waltz, Op 107 No 1 **Tchaikovsky** Symphony
No 6 in B minor, Op 74, 'Pathétique' – Allegro molto
vivace (arr Feinberg) **Bach** Trio Sonata No 5 in C,
BWV529 – Largo (arr Feinberg) **Volodos** Concert
Paraphrase on Mozart's 'Turkish March'
Arcadi Volodos pf
Sony Classical SK62691 (61' · DDD) Ⓕ**OO**

Arcadi Volodos, Russian-born but Spanish-
based, here declares himself both as elegant lyri-
cist and spectacular virtuoso; his playing is as
tactful as it's audacious, the work, surely, of a
Romantic pianist for our times. His tributes to
Horowitz (the ultimate Russian virtuoso icon)
and Cziffra (the _ne plus ultra_ of pianistic necromancy) are as coolly masterful as they're personally engaging, and are wholly devoid of wilful-
ness or undue idiosyncrasy. Those anxious for
Horowitz's splintering treble and thundering
bass or for Cziffra's manic explosions and accelerations will listen in vain. Mercifully, Volodos
remains his own man, tempering some heart-
stopping octaves and _glissandos_ at the close of
Feinberg's transcription of the _Scherzo_ from
Tchaikovsky's _Pathétique_ Symphony with a
touch of nonchalance, and in Feinberg's other
arrangement, guiding Bach gently but firmly
into the 19th century. Volodos is no less beguiling in his own Rachmaninov song transcriptions; here's that dreamed-of vocal 'line', luscious _cantabile_ and aristocratic rather than
ostentatious voicing and texturing. Last but far
from least, his elaboration of Mozart's 'Turkish
March' seasons the most decadent and epi-
curean taste with a teasing wit and insouciance.
Sony's sound is superlative and this delectable
recital makes one long for more substantial as
well as glittering fare from a pianist who, as his
producer puts it, 'never loosens the reins of his
guiding intellect'.

Arcadi Volodos at Carnegie Hall
Liszt Hungarian Rhapsody No 15 in A minor, S244,
'Rákóczy'. A Midsummer Night's Dream – Wedding
March, S410 (both arr Horowitz) **Rachmaninov**
Fragment in A flat. Etudes-tableaux – No 8 in D
minor, Op 39; C minor, Op posth **Schumann** Bunte
Blätter, Op 99 **Scriabin** Piano Sonata No 10 in C, Op
70. Enigma, Op 52 No 2. Caresse dansée, Op 57 No
2. Prelude in B, Op 2 No 2
Arcadi Volodos pf
Sony Classical SK60893 (72' · DDD) Ⓕ**OO**

This recording from Volodos's Carnegie Hall

début recital at the age of 26 confirms a daunting legend. He's unquestionably among the
world's master pianists, a virtuoso for whom
even the most fiercely applied difficulties simply
do not exist. At the same time, everything is
given with an unfaltering sense of equilibrium;
as fast as you marvel at one thing it's immediately counterpointed by another. His technique
in, say, the Liszt _Rhapsody_ and _Wedding March_
Variations is stupendous but never at the
expense of musical quality. His sonority can be
as delicate as it's thunderous and full-blooded.
His accuracy and taste are impeccable so that
instead of celebrating something self-serving or
rip-roaring you find yourself conscious of
higher virtues, of rhythm that can be magically
free or held in a vice-like grip, as well as an
unequalled fluency and aplomb. In Scriabin's
Tenth Sonata he's faithful to the composer's
obsessive and opalescent vision at every point,
more than equal to even the most decadent and
esoteric directions. Volodos's Rachmaninov, in
this brief but enterprising selection, is played
with the same magical sense of flux and clarity.
Yet if one had to choose just one item from this
recital for a desert island, it would have to be
Schumann's _Bunte Blätter_, an audacious gathering with a graphic shift from the lighter to the
darker side of Romanticism (Nos 1-8 and 9-14
respectively). Sony's sound triumphs over difficult circumstances, and if a teasing touch of
enigma remains, both in performance and
choice of repertoire, with an artist of this calibre
you can hardly say that the golden age of
pianism is dead.

Gillian Weir _organ_

Organ Master Series – Volume 1
Hindemith Organ Sonata No 1 **Jongen** Sonata
Eroica, Op 94 **Reubke** Sonata on the 94th Psalm in C
minor **Willan** Introduction, Passacaglia and Fugue,
B149
Gillian Weir org
Priory PRCD751 (74' · DDD) Played on the Aeolian-
Skinner Organ of The First Church of Christ, Scientist,
Boston, Massachusetts Ⓕ**OO**

A mouth-watering programme, containing four
of the finest romantic works for organ. Hindemith's is probably the only name widely known,
but if anyone thinks of him as a rather dry composer they should listen to Weir's outstanding
performance of his Sonata No 1. As she says in
her programme notes, this is the most Romantic
of Hindemith's three sonatas, but it gives her the
opportunity to bring to the fore the more classical sounds of the Aeolian-Skinner organ.

This instrument was designed by Dame
Gillian's husband, Lawrence Phelps, and is one
of the largest in the USA. It has a thrilling _tutti_
and a huge range of lovely colours which Dame
Gillian exploits with complete mastery. It
receives a fine, natural recording from Priory,
and organ buffs will be well satisfied with the
detailed notes about the instrument.

Dame Gillian's virtuoso playing vividly communicates itself to the listener, and at all times she performs with clarity of articulation and flexibility of tempo. Perhaps there's a little too much *rubato* in the Willan, and one may prefer the more natural flow of Francis Jackson's inspired 1964 recording. However, the Jongen and Reubke sonatas receive strong, dramatic performances which are amongst the finest ever recorded. In sum, an irresistible combination of great music, great playing and a spectacular instrument.

The Grand Organ of The Royal Albert Hall
Cook Fanfare **Elgar** Variations on an Original Theme, 'Enigma' – Nimrod. Pomp and Circumstance March No 1 **Howells** Rhapsody, Op 17 No 3 **Lanquetuit** Toccata **Liszt** Fantasia and Fugue, 'Ad nos, ad salutarem undam'. St Francis de Paule walking on the water **Parry** Toccata and Fugue, 'The Wanderer' **Gillian Weir** org
Priory PRCD859 (78' · DDD) Played on the grand organ of the Royal Albert Hall, London   Ⓕ

The sight and sound of the Royal Albert Hall organ are familiar to Proms-goers, but for those who regard it as merely a noisy backdrop to the orchestral works of Elgar, Mahler, Strauss and others, this CD will come as a revelation. There's a wealth of colourful quiet registers on the newly restored instrument which are fully exploited by Dame Gillian Weir, including a soft percussion Carillon stop heard during Liszt's *Ad nos Fantasia*.

She gives this giant composition a truly authentic 19th-century Romantic-style performance, with an unhurried approach to the slow middle movement and rhythmic virtuosity in the rapid outer sections. The vast *tutti* of the organ makes the C major conclusion even more glorious than usual and her account of this piece is one of the most spectacular you'll ever hear.

The other solo works are equally successful. Howells's Rhapsody is passionate and eloquent, and Parry's Toccata and Fugue has a dignified flow. In comparison, Cook and Lanquetuit's pieces may seem lightweight, but the former has some attractive jazzy elements and the latter is as dazzling a French toccata as you'd hear from Dupré, Widor *et al.* Meanwhile, the transcriptions of Elgar and Liszt are entirely convincing thanks to Weir's skill as a colourist.

Priory has done the RAH organ proud with an excellent recording and a comprehensive booklet. One must salute the endurance of Weir and engineer Paul Crichton for making this disc during the hall's only available hours – 1am to 6am. This is an exceptionally fine CD that should become a landmark recording.

Pieter Wispelwey   *cello*

Britten Cello Sonata in C, Op 65
Prokofiev Cello Sonata in C, Op 119
Shostakovich Cello Sonata in D minor, Op 40

Pieter Wispelwey vc **Dejan Lazić** pf
Channel Classics CCS20098 (70' · DDD)   Ⓕ
Also available on SACD CCSSA20003

We're not short of first-rate accounts of the Sonata Britten wrote for Rostropovich in 1960-61. Pieter Wispelwey and Dejan Lazíc immediately throw down the gauntlet with a provocatively mobile, nervy reading of the opening 'Dialogo'. They're well over a minute swifter than both comparative rivals. It's a lean, lithe and sparky view that proves symptomatic of the whole. Traditionalists may find it all perhaps a bit too cunning for comfort, but there's no denying the intellect, emotional scope and questing spirit on show. Wispelwey's mellow, distinctively 'vocal' tone-projection is heard to particular advantage in the flowing lyrical lines that are such a feature of first and third movements of the Shostakovich Sonata. If ultimately not quite as selfless or humane as Rostropovich's 1964 Aldeburgh alliance with Britten, here's a rapt and characterful reading that never loses sight of the Classical sensibility beneath this music's by turns troubled and slyly humorous surface. These quick-witted newcomers give Prokofiev's seductive Sonata another articulate and poetic display, with results that are more personable and subtly variegated than the beefier Chang/Pappano version.

Boasting vividly truthful sound and admirable balance (audiophiles should make a bee-line to the SACD equivalent), this classy Channel Classics release should afforded heaps of stimulation and pleasure.

Sophie Yates   *harpsichord*

French Baroque Harpsichord   Ⓟ
D'Anglebert Pièces de Clavecin – Suite in G minor; Tombeau de M. de Chambonnières **F Couperin** L'Art de toucher le clavecin – Prélude in D minor. Livre de clavecin, Deuxième ordre – Seconde Courante; Sarabande, 'La Prude'; Les Idées heureuses; La Voluptueuse **Forqueray** La Rameau; La Boisson; La Sylva; Jupiter **Rameau** L'enharmonique. L'Egyptienne. La Dauphine **Sophie Yates** hpd
Chandos Chaconne CHAN0545 (71' · DDD)
Recorded 1993   ⒻⓄ

Sophie Yates has a real understanding of the French style – so difficult to capture, with its special conventions and elaborate ornamentation. Her phrasing is subtle as well as musical; and she proves herself capable of the flexibility proper to this music without risk to the underlying pulse or to continuity. Her reading of *La Dauphine*, Rameau's last harpsichord piece, is justifiably free and improvisatory, since it's thought to be a transcription of Rameau's extemporisation at the wedding of the Dauphin in 1747. She savours Rameau's bold enharmonics, too, shows drive and energy in his *L'Egyptienne*, impressive dignity in Forqueray's tribute to his great contemporary and in a d'Anglebert sarabande, expressiveness in Forqueray's *La Sylva* and a sense of enjoyment in the trenchant drama of the flashing thunderbolts of his *Jupiter*. Yates also has the advantage of admirable recording of a particularly beautiful and rich-sounding instrument (a copy of a Goujon).

Evan Ziporyn   *clarinet*

This is not a clarinet
D Lang Press Release[a] **Tenzer** Three Island Duos[b]
Ziporyn Four Impersonations[b]. Partial Truths[a]
Evan Ziporyn [a]*bass cl/bcl*
Cantaloupe Music CA21002 (53' · DDD)   Ⓕ**OO**

This is no ordinary clarinet recital, and Ziporyn, truly a phenomenon in American music, can't simply be understood as a clarinettist. For a start, there are moments in his composition *Partial Truths* where it's hard to believe that this is a clarinet record. 'Are these pan-pipes? Or Didgeridoos?' was one typical response from one poor unsuspecting listener.

Ziporyn's clarinet sound is so individual, so raunchy, that it would be hard to imagine any other player making this record. But it may yet turn out that the big Z's most lasting contribution to American music is to be found in his own compositions. In many ways he makes music like a traveller who trades between continents. His *Four Impersonations* captures the sounds of Japanese *gagaku*, Balinese music and Nairobi guitar music. The precision with which he hears subtle nuances of tuning and phrasing is spellbinding. The fact that this is all achieved through the medium of a solo clarinet is beyond belief. The recital is rounded off with another *tour de force*, a masterly rendition of David Lang's *Press Release*, one of the clarinet's great modern classics.

Nikolaj Znaider   *violin*

Bravo!
Achron Hebrew Melody, Op 33 (arr Auer)[a]**Chopin**
Nocturnes[a] – No 8, Op 27 No 2 (in D – originally D
flat – trans Wilhelmj); No 16 in E flat, Op 55 No 2
(trans Heifetz) **Kreisler** Recitativo and Scherzo-
Caprice, Op 6 **Ponce** Estrellita (arr Heifetz)[a]
Rachmaninov Vocalise, Op 34 No 14 (trans Press)[a]
Sarasate Danzas españolas – Romanza Andaluza,
Op 22 No 1[a] Wieniawski Polonaise No 1 in D, Op 4[a].
Variations on an Original Theme, Op 15[a] **Ysaÿe** Solo
Sonata, 'Ballade', Op 27 No 3
Nikolaj Znaider *vn* [a]**Daniel Gortler** *pf*
RCA Red Seal 82876 50470-2 (60' · DDD)   Ⓕ**OO**

Violin buffs with good memories or sizeable record collections will already know many of these pieces from old 78s. Nikolaj Znaider's performances are more acts of homage than of imitation, even in cases where his finest recorded predecessors – Heifetz mostly, but also Elman and perhaps Szeryng – provided formidable benchmarks.

Znaider already has a very distinctive style, with quick-reflex bowing, a colourful range of dynamics, a fast and fairly narrow vibrato, phrasing that's thought through virtually by the bar, clean multiple stops and an interpretative take on each piece that's invariably more thoughtful than flashy. Wieniawski's *Polonaise* is full of individual incident, exuberant but finely detailed. Much the same goes for the less familiar *Variations on an Original Theme*, but some of the most overtly brilliant playing is in the two unaccompanied pieces, especially Ysaÿe's Third Sonata, music that toys with the close of Bach's 'Chaconne'.

Much to delight the ear, then, the sort of fare that was once commonplace but that nowadays graces our CD players all too rarely. This kind of repertoire stands or falls on the strengths or weaknesses of its interpreters and Znaider vies with the best in recent years for strengths. With good sound and intelligent accompaniments, you won't be disappointed.

Organ Music

EMI Great Cathedral Organ Series, Volume 1
Gigout 10 Organ Pieces – No 4, Toccata[f] **Howells**
Rhapsody, Op 17 No 1[e] **Karg-Elert** Pastel in F sharp,
Op 92 No 3[d] **Parry** Choral Fantasy No 1, Old 100th[e]
Reubke Sonata on the 94th Psalm in C minor[b]
Saint-Saëns Fantaisie in D flat, Op 101[a] **Statham**
Lament[d] **S S Wesley** Choral Song and Fugue[e]
Whitlock Four Extemporizations – No 4, Fanfare[c]
[a]**Christopher Dearnley** *Salisbury Cathedral* [b]**Roger
Fisher** *Chester Cathedral* [c]**Noel Rawsthorne**
Liverpool Anglican Cathedral [d]**Heathcote Statham**
Norwich Cathedral [e]**Herbert Sumsion** *Gloucester
Cathedral* [f]**Arthur Wills** *Ely Cathedral*
Amphion Recordings PHICD160 (76' · ADD)
Recorded 1963-70   Ⓕ**O**

The 19 LPs of EMI's 'Great Cathedral Organs' series released between 1963 and 1971 constituted one of the most important recording projects in the history of the English organ. The brainchild of producer Brian Culverhouse (whose booklet-essay provides some fascinating anecdotes), it featured organs of impeccably English lineage and organists steeped in the centuries' old traditions of English cathedral music. Since most of these organs have long since been replaced or modified in an attempt to give them a more European flavour, and many modern-day English cathedral organists belong to a more cosmopolitan musical generation, these recordings have assumed particular historical significance. They recorded, quite literally, the end of an era. The CD transfers vary from the disappointing (Ely) to the outstanding. Interestingly enough, the oldest recordings, those made on Liverpool's vast Willis organ, have come out with simply staggering presence – but all present vivid aural pictures of these uniformly wonderful organs set within generous helpings of the gloriously atmospheric acoustics of their respective cathedrals. The men who oversee the day-to-day running of the music in a great cathedral don't necessarily make the best solo performers on disc, and many of these performances wouldn't bear close scrutiny beside other available versions. But Roger Fisher's stunning and breath-takingly exciting account of the Reubke, despite the pervasive hiss, is a performance in a million, and Noel Rawsthorne elicits awed admiration with his brilliantly communicative playing.

Great European Organs, Volume 48
Commette Scherzo **Dallier** Cinq Invocations
Guilmant Marche funèbre et chant séraphique,
Op 17 No 3 **Ibert** Trois Pièces **Philip** Toccata and
Fugue in A minor
Gerard Brooks org
Priory PRCD558 (79' · DDD) Recorded on the
Cavaillé-Coll organ in the Abbey Church of St Ouen,
Rouen 1995   Ⓕ

Here we have a magnificent recording of one of the truly Great European Organs. In Gerard Brooks, Priory has found a player as eager to reveal the glories and subtleties of one of Cavaillé-Coll's greatest creations as his own impressive virtuosity. Widor's description of this as a 'Michelangelo of an organ' seems singularly apt in the light of a disc which displays the instrument so vividly. A simple reading of the track list might imply that such opulent resources are being squandered on a collection of oddities drawn from the ample dark recesses of French organ literature. If Guilmant is the only familiar name (so far as organists are concerned, Ibert is an obscure figure), the music of the others is as familiar as a new Andrew Lloyd Webber score – we're sure we've heard it all before but can't quite remember where.

Edouard Commette's *Scherzo* is clearly first cousin to Henri Mulet's famous *Carillon sortie*, Achille Philip's *Toccata* comes from the same stable as that from Boëllman's *Suite gothique*, while Henri Dallier's *Invocations* inspired by Latin Marian texts could easily pass for Vierne, especially the glittering final Toccata. But if the idioms are familiar and the ideas derivative, the musical quality in both intellectual and emotional terms is undeniable. Simply put, this is a programme of immensely enjoyable music, all of which bears repeated listening and is certainly deserving of a place on the shelves of lovers of good organ music.

Great European Organs, Volume 51
Bach Pastorale in F, BWV590 **G Böhm** Vater unser im
Himmelreich, WKii138 **Buxtehude** Prelude, Fugue
and Chaconne in C, BuxWV137 **Eben** Homage to
Dietrich Buxtehude **Guridi** Triptico del Buen Pastor.
Liszt (trans Schaab) Orpheus, S98 **Saint-Saëns**
Fantaisie in D flat, Op 101
Peter King org
Priory PRCD618 (78' · DDD) Recorded on the Klais
organ of Bath Abbey 1997   Ⓕ Ⓞ

This seems rather a peculiar programme with a focus on Buxtehude and the North German Baroque and with a few other disparate pieces thrown in to spice up the menu. Peculiar or not, it works superbly. The new Bath Abbey instrument is adorable – a complete rejection of the argument often propounded that, on purely musical terms, an organ built outside the British Isles is inappropriate for a major English ecclesiastical building – and it makes everything here sound convincing and impressive. This sumptuous instrument is well served by a beautifully proportioned recording. For those interested in the music rather than the instrument, Peter King's performances range from the solid (Buxtehude's *Praeludium* in G minor) to the near-inspired (Bach's *Pastorale*). Eben's *Homage* is based on material from the two Buxtehude pieces on the disc and uses Buxtehudian structures and figurations in a typically astute Eben manner. The inclusion of the Liszt and Saint-Saëns is obviously inspired by King's deep fondness for these pieces – it shows in every bar of these lovingly nurtured performances – while the Guridi has moments which allow us to hear the organ's more atmospheric qualities. Not everybody will be immediately attracted to this disc by the music, but for the sheer pleasure of hearing a truly wonderful, modern instrument, this release can't be recommended too highly.

Twelve Organs of Edinburgh
Bach Concerto in G, BWV592[be] **Bridge** Adagio in E,
H63 No 2[df] **Bruhns** Praeludium in E minor[cg]
Buxtehude Prelude, Fugue and Chaconne in C,
BuxWV137[bh]. Praeludium in D minor, BuxWV140[di]
Couperin Messe pour les paroisses – Tierce en
taille[bh] **Handel** Il pastor fido – Overture[dj]. Ode for St
Cecilia's Day, HWV76 – March[df] **Hesse** Variations on
an original theme, Op 34[ck] **Hollins** Concert Overture
No 3 in F minor[be] **Høvland** Toccata – Now thank we
all our God[df] **Humperdinck** (arr Lemare) Hänsel und
Gretel – Angel scene[bl] **Krebs** O König, dessen
Majestät[cg] **Leighton** Prelude, Scherzo and
Passacaglia, Op 41[cm] **Mendelssohn** Organ Sonata in
B flat, Op 65 No 4[an] **Pachelbel** Alle Menschen
müssen sterben[di] **Saint-Saëns** Fantaisie in E flat[ao]
Sweelinck Ballo del granduca[ao] **Tomkins** Voluntary[ap]
Walond Voluntary in D[ap]
[a]**Peter Backhouse,** [b]**Timothy Byram-Wigfield,**
[c]**Michael Harris,** [d]**John Kitchen** orgs
Priory ② PRCD700AB (153' · DDD) Played on the
organs of [e]St Cuthbert's Church, [f]McEwan Hall,
[g]Canongate Kirk, [h]Greyfriars Kirk, [i]Reid Concert Hall,
[j]St Cecilia's Hall, [k]St Andrew's and St George's Church,
[l]St Mary's Episcopal Cathedral, [m]St Giles Cathedral,
[n]Broughton St Mary's Church, [o]St Stephen's Church
Centre, [p]Lodge Canongate, Kilwinning   Ⓕ Ⓞ

The instruments on these CDs span three centuries and originate in Britain, Northern Ireland, Denmark and Austria. From the 18th century, we hear two surviving British organs with an exquisite, singing tone. The 19th century brought greater power and variety of orchestral colour, well illustrated by Byram-Wigfield's performance of the Humperdinck at St Mary's Cathedral. The 20th century has seen a return to a clearer, more 'Baroque' type of organ-building, together with the use of computer technology to improve playing aids and the design of the mechanism and casework. The Rieger organ at St Giles Cathedral is a supreme example of an outstanding contemporary instrument.

The pieces on these discs have been brilliantly selected to display the essential character of each organ, and this alone is a considerable achievement. It's always interesting to see and hear an artistic partnership developing between the player and the organ, and all four performers strike up a fruitful and happy relationship with their instruments. Some of the pairings could be described as a match made in heaven, and into this category falls Byram-Wigfield's colourful performances of Hollins and Humperdinck, and Kitchen's spontaneous, stylish performances of Buxtehude, Handel and Pachelbel. Harris's playing of Leighton's masterpiece is quite stunning, and this track is an awesome monument to 20th-century organ-building and composition at the highest level.

Priory's recordings and production are, as always, truly excellent.

CHORAL

Ampleforth Schola Cantorum

Carols from Ampleforth
Traditional O come, all ye faithful. Once in Royal David's city. Unto us is born a son. The Sussex Carol. God rest you merry, gentlemen. Hark! the herald angels sing (all arr Willcocks). Personent hodie (arr Holst). Good King Wenceslas (arr Jacques). Adam lay y-bounden (arr Warlock). Angel tidings (arr Rutter). Past three o'clock. Ding dong! merrily on high (both arr Wood). It came upon a midnight clear. Come with torches. Silent Night (all arr Little). Still, still, still (arr Ledger). The Infant King (arr Pettman). The First Nowell (arr Stainer/Willcocks) **H C Stewart** On this day earth shall ring **M Praetorius** A great and mighty wonder **Mathias** Sir Christemas
Ampleforth Schola Cantorum / Ian Little with **Simon Wright** org
Ampleforth Compact Discs AARCD1 (58' · DDD)   Ⓕ

Here is a programme of carols as traditional as turkey and plum pudding, and as wholesome. You don't have to groan at the approach of *Have yourself a merry little Christmas* or any other feeble compromise with the changing times; there's not even a bleat from John Tavener and William Blake's unprofitably questioned little lamb. Musically, the programme is in the first place a triumph for Anon, and then for Sir David Willcocks whose arrangements are rich in sea-

sonable splendour and knowledge of how to get the best out of choir and organ. Other arrangers have done good work too, including the choir's director, Ian Little, who provides inspired embellishments in the last verse of *It came upon a midnight clear* but may just possibly have gone a little over the top towards the end of Silent Night. He has also trained a splendid choir. Forthright tone from the trebles, ample tone from the men, combine to live up to the name of their foundation. The organist, Simon Wright, does an excellent job, varying the might of his invincible reeds and implacable pedals with a scattering of two-foot spangle-dust, light and bright as a Christmas-tree fairy. The building itself is aurally spacious, the harmonies of *Ding dong! merrily on high* engaging in merry argument with their echo. There will doubtless be homes in which a playing of this disc will constitute the Christmas Day reveille, and if the rest of the day goes as well they can count themselves lucky.

Cambridge Singers

Feel the Spirit
Carmichael Skylark (arr Rutter) **Rutter** Feel the Spirit[ad]. Birthday Madrigals[bc] **Shearing** Songs and Sonnets from Shakespeare[bc] **Rutter** The Heavenly Aeroplane **Traditional** Lord of the Dance (arr Rutter)
[a]**Melanie Marshall** mez [b]**Malcolm Creese** db [c]
[c]**Wayne Marshall** pf **Cambridge Singers**; [d]**BBC Concert Orchestra / John Rutter**
Collegium COLCD128 (75' · DDD) Texts included   Ⓕ

This disc's Anglo-American thread pays homage to three of John Rutter's favourite musical traditions – the spiritual, the madrigal and American song. The most substantial work here is the new half-hour-long cycle of spirituals *Feel the Spirit*, which received its première in Carnegie Hall in June 2001. These luscious arrangements bear repeated listening: orchestrally colourful and playfully witty. In their exuberant moments they lie somewhere between *Porgy and Bess* and George Mitchell's brand of close-harmony minstrelsy. Melanie Marshall's voice is engagingly honeyed, especially in the Vaughan Williams-flavoured 'Sometimes I feel like a motherless child'. The Cambridge Singers and BBC Concert Orchestra are on top form throughout.

Rutter's *Birthday Madrigals* were completed in 1995 to celebrate George Shearing's 75th birthday. Drawing on texts from the Elizabethan era, they feature the superb bass-playing of Malcolm Creese and some sympathetic pianistic embellishments from Wayne Marshall, and are juxtaposed by Shearing's own beautiful *Songs and Sonnets* (1999), a follow-up Shakespearean cycle to *Music to Hear* (1985).

The fillers offer a triple bonus and include a full French impressionist treatment of Hoagy Carmichael's exquisite *Skylark*. A delightful disc. Strongly recommended.

Hail, Gladdening Light
J Amner Come, let's rejoice **Anonymous** Rejoice in the Lord **Bairstow** I sat down under his shadow **Dering** Factum est silentium **Elgar** They are at rest **J Goss** These are they that follow the lamb **WH Harris** Bring us, O Lord God **Howells** Nunc dimittis **Morley** Nolo mortem peccatoris **Philips** O beatum et sacrosanctum diem **Purcell** Remember not, Lord, our offences, Z50 **Rutter** Loving shepherd of Thy sheep **J Sheppard** In manus tuas **Stanford** Justorum animae, Op 38 No 1 **R Stone** The Lord's Prayer **Tallis** O nata lux **Tavener** A hymn to the mother of God. Hymn for the dormition of the mother of God **Taverner** Christe Jesu, pastor bone **Tomkins** When David heard **Vaughan Williams** O vos omnes **Walton** A litany **C Wood** Hail, gladdening light
Cambridge Singers / John Rutter
Collegium COLCD113 (72' · DDD) Texts and translations included ⒻⓄ

This has the subtitle 'Music of the English Church' and it's arranged under four main headings: anthems and introits (these count as one), Latin motets, settings of hymns and other poetry, and prayer-settings. Each of them is well represented in a programme that varies delightfully in period and style, and in performances which are remarkably consistent in quality. Some of the items will come as discoveries to most listeners: for example, the anthem *Come, let's rejoice*, a splendid, madrigal-like piece written by John Amner, organist from 1610 to 1641 at Ely Cathedral where these recordings were made. Others are equally impressive in their present performance: a deep quietness attends the opening of Richard Dering's *Factum est silentium*, which ends with rhythmic Alleluias set dancing with subdued excitement. Among the hymn-settings is one by a 16-year-old called William Walton. Included in the prayers is the choirmaster's own setting, characteristically made for pleasure, of *Loving shepherd of Thy sheep*. All are unaccompanied, and thus very exactingly test the choir's blend of voices, its precision, articulation and feeling for rhythm. In all respects it does exceptionally well; the tone is fresh, the attack unanimous, the expression clear and sensitive, the rhythm on its toes. These are young, gifted singers, formed with disciplined enthusiasm into a choir with a distinctive style – recorded with admirable results by a family firm.

Sing, ye Heavens
Anonymous Pange lingua. Veni Creator Spiritus. Vexilla Regis **Croft** (arr Rutter) O God, our help in ages past **Gibbons** Drop, drop slow tears **Luther** (arr Rutter) A mighty fortress **Miller** (arr Rutter) When I survey the wondrous Cross **Monk** (arr Rutter) All things bright and beautiful. Christ the Lord is risen today **RH Prichard** (arr Rutter) Love divine, all love excelling **Purcell** (arr Rutter) Christ is made the sure Foundation **Rutter** Eternal God **Scholefield** (arr Rutter) The day thou gavest, Lord, is ended **Schulz** (arr Rutter) We plough the fields and scatter **Tallis**

Glory to thee, my God **Traditional** (arr Rutter) Amazing Grace. Be thou my vision. The King of love my Shepherd is. Let all mortal flesh keep silence. Lo! he comes with clouds descending. Morning has broken
Thelma Owen *hp* **John Scott** *org* **Cambridge Singers; City of London Sinfonia Brass / John Rutter**
Collegium COLCD126 (77' · DDD) Texts and translations included ⒻⓄ

The Service was the Lord's; anthem, canticles, psalms and responsories were the choir's; and the hymns were anybody's. That (roughly) is how one remembers it. Of course, the best hymns were acknowledged as having dignity, strength and other appeals to heart and head; and with descants and special harmonies by Vaughan Williams or David Willcocks they could join in musical character and interest. But it seems to be a relatively recent development that their performance has become something of an art form.

The art lies in knowing how much to arrange and how much to leave be. On the whole John Rutter has it right. In *Love divine*, for instance, the first verse has the voices in unison and the harmonies 'straight', verse 2 has the choir in standard four-part harmony, and verse 3 has a descant and new harmonies, both of which are emboldened to acquire a richer life towards the end. Most are accompanied by the organ, some by organ and brass, a few by harp. These include the group described as 'folk hymns' ending with *We plough the fields and scatter*, taken at a brisk pace and sounding almost Haydnesque. Gibbons's *Drop, drop slow tears* is sung unaccompanied throughout, with no 'improvements'. Tallis's *Glory to thee, my God* has verse 4 in double canon. And Rutter provides a hymn of his own, *Eternal God*, written in 1999 'with the aim of augmenting the meagre stock of hymns which make mention of music'.

Generally, the selection is fine, both words and music. In performance, the plainsong hymns are rather too 'barred', and the somewhat garish stained-glass ending of *Let all mortal flesh keep silence* will not be to everyone's taste. But this, as we know, is an excellent choir; they're fortified by some splendid players; and presentation and recorded sound (apart from recessing the choir too much in the hymns with brass) are admirable also.

Additional recommendations

A cappella – works by Debussy, Ravel and Poulenc
Cambridge Singers / Rutter
Collegium CSCD509 (63' · DDD) Recorded 1980s Ⓜ
  A very attractive programme, with a most touching and expert pastiche madrigal, *Lay a Garland* by RL Pearsall.

There is Sweet Music – works by Vaughan Williams, Britten, Grainger, Holst and Moeran
Cambridge Singers / Rutter

Collegium CSCD505 (56' · DDD) Recorded 1980s Ⓜ
A delectable disc, packed full of your favourite
choral pieces, sung by a choir that John Rutter
made into one of the best in the country.

Clare College, Cambridge

Blessed Spirit – Music of the soul's journey
Anonymous Requiem aeternam. Kontakion of the
Dead. Domine Jesu Christe. O quanta qualia. In
paradisum **Byrd** Iustorum animae **Harris** Faire is the
Heaven **Hildegard of Bingen** O felix anima **Holst**
The Evening Watch, H159 **Parry** Songs of Farewell –
No 4, There is an old belief **Schütz** Selig sind die
Toten **Sheppard** Audivi vocem de caelo **Tavener**
Funeral Ikos **Tchaikovsky** Blessed are they
Traditional Steal Away (arr Brown). Deep River (arr
Luboff) **Victoria** O quam gloriosum **Walford-Davies**
Psalm No 121 and Requiem aeternam
Clare College Choir, Cambridge / Timothy Brown
Collegium COLCD127 (71' · DDD) Texts and
translations included   Ⓕ●

There can be nothing but praise for the excellence of these performances, for the quality and
choice of the music itself and, most of all, for the
gorgeous sound quality of these recordings
made in Ely Cathedral. Add to this some eminently readable booklet-notes and we have a real
winner, even if the overall aural effect bears a
striking resemblance to those ubiquitous inof-
fensive compilation discs played in hotel lobbies
the world over.

Within the basic theme of death and the soul's
subsequent journey to paradise the music juxtaposes chunks of plainsong and standard cathedral choir repertoire with some rather more esoteric choral pieces. Whether it's the ancient
plainchant *In paradisum*, Psalm 121 sung to
Walford Davies's fine Anglican chant, William
Harris's richly textured anthem *Faire is the
Heaven* or the almost erotically indulgent
arrangement by Timothy Brown of *Steal Away*,
Clare College Choir distinguish it all with finely
crafted and beautifully shaped performances
that aren't just note-perfect but intensely perceptive as well. There's no hint of the sickliness
we sometimes experience when church music is
exposed to such slick professionalism on disc –
rather a real sense of wonder and awe at the
timeless beauty of the programme.

It's difficult to listen to the disc in its entirety
without falling into some kind of soporific
trance, but taken individually each piece is, in its
own way, as dramatic and earth-shaking as the
garish blue cover leads us to suspect.

Illumina
Anonymous Lumen ad revelationem **Byrd** O lux,
beata Trinitas **Grechaninov** The seven Days of the
Passion, Op 58 – O gladsome light **Harris** Bring us,
O Lord God **Hildegard of Bingen** O choruscans
stellarum **Holst** Nunc dimittis, H127 **Josquin
Desprez** Nunc dimittis **Ligeti** Lux aeterna **Palestrina**
Christe, qui lux es et dies. Lucis Creator optime

Rachmaninov Vespers, Op 37 – Nunc dimittis
Rautavaara Vigilia – Evening Hymn **Rutter** Hymn to
the Creator of Light **Tallis** O nata lux de lumine. Te
lucis ante terminum **Tchaikovsky** Vesper Service, Op
52 – Hail, gladdening Light **Whyte** Christe, qui lux es
et dies **Wood** Hail, gladdening light
Clare College Choir, Cambridge / Timothy Brown
Collegium COLCD125 (76' · DDD) Texts and
translations included   Ⓕ●

Retrospectively the disc's final item, Ligeti's
Lux aeterna, dominates the recital. Not only
does it make an indelible impression, but it also
casts its light over the entire programme and
style of singing. To a listener who has not heard
it before (a slightly smaller category than might
be thought, as the piece was used in the film
2001: A Space Odyssey) it may even come as the
light on the road to Damascus, a blinding revelation of unknown choral sonorities. An extraordinary sound-world is opening up, with long,
finely ruled streams of light, a spectrum of
colours wide as the distance from heaven to
earth, and all mingling eventually within the
cavern of a great bell. The challenge to singers
(even when assisted by the reverberance of Ely
Cathedral's Lady Chapel) is formidable indeed,
and these young voices (with lungs and ears
involved also) do marvellously well. And so they
do throughout. The quality of choral tone here
is remarkable: no thready sopranos, none of
those bone-dry basses, but a sound that, though
strictly disciplined in the matter of vibrato, is
still fresh and natural. They achieve wonders of
crescendo, as in William Harris's *Bring us, O Lord
God*, and their opening chords (in Tallis's *O nata
lux* for instance) are as if cut by the sharpest
slicer ever made. Even so, this smooth, flawless
beauty of sound is, in some contexts, like the
modern beauty of the face of a heroine in some
televised piece of period-drama. Josquin
Desprez's *Nunc dimittis* is an example: the
singing is extremely beautiful, but conceptually
(and not just in the women's voices) seems
anachronistic. It's as though they have worked
on their programme with the precept 'All choral
music aspires to the condition of Ligeti'. A wondrous record, all the same.

Dresden Kreuzchor

Musica Divina
Bach Der Geist hilft unsrer Schwachheit, BWV226
Brahms Motets, Op 29 – Schaffe in mir, Gott, ein
reines Herz **Bruckner** Os justi **Draeseke** Psalm 93,
Op 56 **Duda** Friede über Israel, Op 25 **Hessenberg**
O Herr, mache mich zum Werkzeug deines Friedens,
Op37 No 1 **Homilius** Domine, ad adiuvandum me.
Herr, wenn Trübsal da ist **Mendelssohn** Jauchzet
dem Herrn alle Welt **Reger** Nachtlied, Op 138 No 3
Schein Psalm 116 **Schütz** Die Himmel erzählen die
Ehre Gottes, SWV386. Das ist je gewisslich wahr,
SWV388
Dresden Kreuzchor / Roderich Kreile
DG 453 484-2GH (76' · DDD) Texts and translations
included   Ⓕ●

The choir is in quite splendid form here: fine in blend, balance and tone, scrupulously precise, alert and responsive to the direction of its still relatively new conductor, Roderich Kreile, appointed 28th Kantor in 1997. The very opening phrases tell us what we want to know in embarking on a recital of this kind: it's a choir that has the life of the music within it. The opening of Schütz's *Das ist je gewisslich wahr* ('This is a faithful saying ... that Christ Jesus came into the world to save sinners') is choralelike in form, but has an underlying rhythmic vitality which a duller choir could easily miss but which here carries the rich promise of a wonderful piece of work about to unfold. And so it does, and still more so the Creation motet (*Die Himmel erzählen*) which follows.

And then comes the work which alone would give sufficient reason for drawing special attention to the recital. Johann Schein's 'Das ist mir lieb', one of a collection dating from 1616 when a certain Burchhard Grossmann thought to celebrate his return to health by commissioning 16 composers to set Psalm 116 to music (all can be heard on a three-disc set on CPO). Schein's contribution is vivid as a picture-book, with tears that flow and feet that slide to illustrate the text, sometimes also as effective in natural speech-rhythms as a good dramatic monologue. It's a magnificently resourceful piece of writing, and ends with a funfair of Hallelujas.

But everything here is worth hearing. Some of the motets are of recent composition, one of them, Kurt Hessenberg's prayer to 'make me an agent of your peace' a quietly intense plea for reconciliation, doubly moving in the context of this recital and coming from this place. Bach is the master at the centre of all – practically every later composer pays some implicit tribute. *Der Geist hilft unsrer Schwachheit* is the second of the Six Motets, inexhaustible in its development of ideas, harmonic and contrapuntal. It also seems to assume similar tirelessness in its singers; and as far as this choir is concerned, the confidence is well placed, for their vitality fully meets the challenge. It's an excellent record, and (to go a little further) an inspiring one.

Ely Cathedral

Magnificat and Nunc dimittis, Vol 14
Bairstow Evening Service in G **Blow** Evening Service in G **Bullock** Evening Service in D **Child** Evening Service in E minor **Cruft** Collegium Regale **Greene** Evening Service in C **Orr** Short Service **Rose** Evening Service in C minor **Wills** Evening Service on Plainsong tones **C Wood** Evening Service in G
Ely Cathedral Choir / Paul Trepte with **David Price** *org*
Priory PRCD592 (71' · DDD)   Ⓕ❍

All the items here are worthy of the series, and each has its distinctive flavour. Ernest Bullock's *Magnificat*, which opens the recital, is a good example of Anglican unpredictability. Gentle and lyrical in mood and manner, it develops with

what seems to be an almost rhapsodic freedom, the organ part moving with a fluent independence, and as intimate as a piano accompaniment. Bernard Rose, in his Service for trebles, approaches the canticle in similar mood but with entirely different results, making much of the resonance of boys' voices in thirds, and giving full rein to his invention in his writing for the organ. Robin Orr is another who puts much of his more creatively adventurous self into the organ part, and his settings aren't made for comfort: the first *Gloria* for instance strikes an awed note, with its rather severe minor tonality. Adrian Cruft, most modern of these composers, in both date and style, writes boldly, with skill in the deployment of the voices in his men-only settings, which, the notes tell us, were originally for accompaniment by wind instruments as an alternative to accompaniment by the organ. From the 17th century there are masterly settings by John Blow and William Child; from the 18th, Maurice Greene; nothing from the 19th (unless it be said that Bullock, Wills, Wood and Bairstow were all children of the 19th). With fine work by the organist, David Price, and with the choir showing itself a confident, spirited master of its business, the performances are to be relished.

King's College, Cambridge

Best Loved Hymns
Bain Brother James's Air[a] (arr Johns) **Bourgeois** Praise to the Lord, the Almighty[b] **Gibbons** Drop, drop slow tears **Goss** Praise my soul, the King of Heaven[b] **Handel** Thine be the glory, risen, conquering Son[b] (arr Cleobury) **W Harris** O what their joy and their glory must be[b] **Howells** All my hope on God is founded[bc] **Ireland** My song is love unknown[b] **Luther** A mighty fortress is our God[bc] (arr Rutter) **Miller** When I survey the wondrous cross[b] **Parry** Dear Lord and Father of Mankind[b] **Rutter** Be thou my vision[a] **Scholefield** The day thou gavest, Lord, is ended[b] **Taylor** Glorious things of Thee are spoken[b] **Traditional** All people that on earth do dwell[bc] (arr Vaughan Williams). Morning has broken[a] (arr Rutter). Let all mortal flesh[b] (arr Jackson) **Vaughan Williams** Come down, O Love Divine[b]
[a]**Sioned Williams** *hp* [b]**Benjamin Bayl, Thomas Williamson** *orgs* **King's College Choir, Cambridge;** [c]**The Wallace Collection / Stephen Cleobury**
EMI Classics 557026-2 (69' · DDD)   Ⓕ❍

Here is the high art of hymnody. No tentative playover on the stopped diapason while kneejoints crack and fingers fumble for collection money. No intrusive notes from the congregation with members who pride themselves on 'singing seconds' (presumably, as Harvey Grace remarked, because the interval almost exclusively used is that of a third). These are musical performances, as surely as if they were the canticles and anthems featured here, and in some instances the form is indeed that of the hymn-anthem. The hymns themselves, as the title proclaims, are 'best loved', but are presented with elaborations for brass, organ, harp and descanting trebles. Dressed up in Sunday best, they're thrilling in majesty, exquisite in contemplative piety, but very largely cordoned off amid notices that say 'Do not join in.'

The selection probably reflects modern, conservative good taste quite faithfully. At the popular end, *Brother James's Air* and *Morning has broken* are admitted; at the mystical other, *Let all mortal flesh keep silence* preserves the ancient tune but swathed in subtly abrasive harmonies. Of things grandly Victorian, *The day Thou gavest* is in, but *Lead, kindly light* and *Abide with me* are out. Some would have found a place among any 'top 10' chosen 50 years ago – *Dear Lord and Father of Mankind, When I survey the wondrous Cross* and *Praise, my soul, the King of Heaven* for example. Some such as *All my hope on God is founded* and *Be thou my vision* are relatively new to the lists. Two – *A mighty fortress* and the *Old Hundredth* – seem timeless.

The famous choir sing well (though their uncovered 'ee' sounds nag somewhat, as does an oddly unyielding element somewhere in the men's voices). The accompaniments are skilfully played, colourfully arranged and spaciously recorded. Excellent annotations are provided by Alan Luff, who comes up with a fund of information such as the identity of Brother James (a Christian Scientist, James Leith Macbeth Bain) and the origin of the tune *Abbot's Leigh*, which was composed in 1941 when BBC listeners were complaining that *Glorious Things of Thee are Spoken* was still being sung to the old German national anthem.

A Festival of Nine Lessons and Carols
Adès The Fayrfax Carol Bach In dulci jubilo **Darke** In the bleak mid-winter **Goldschmidt** A tender Shoot **Ord** Adam lay ybounden **Rutter** Dormi, Jesu **Tavener** The Lamb **Traditional** Once in Royal David's city. Up! good Christen folk. The Truth from Above. Sussex Carol. In dulci jubilo. God rest you merry, gentlemen. Gabriel's Message. Joys Seven. Riu, riu, chiu. While Shepherd's watched. I saw three ships. O come, all ye faithful. Hark! the herald angels sing **Weir** Illuminare, Jerusalem
King's College Choir, Cambridge / Stephen Cleobury
EMI ② 573693-2 (83' · DDD)   Ⓜ**OO**

Surprising as it may seem, this is the first complete commercial recording of this celebrated event. Happily, little has changed down the years to rob the service of its sense of serenity and quiet joy. On the present recording, the readings are all skilfully done, and the carols, in Stephen Cleobury's felicitous phrase, are 'the handmaid' of Milner-White's liturgy. Since 1918, the repertory has evolved, quietly, almost imperceptibly. Indeed, one of the pleasures of this recording is its chronicling of the care and imagination with which successive organists and choir-masters have selected and arranged the music down the years. The choir's performance style, too, has changed at a pleasingly slow rate,

though rather a lot has changed since the (abridged) service was last recorded. The present choir's music-making is lighter toned, the diction cleaner, the pacing altogether more urgent. This is a lustier, merrier style of carol singing. Their fresher, less consciously beautiful style both suits and reflects the performing preferences of our age; yet out there, amid the secularised mass markets toward which releases like this are unerringly aimed, there's a palpable hankering after mystery. Does this explain the recording itself? Unlike its analogue predecessors, this spectacularly engineered digital affair puts not the choir, but the famous King's acoustic centre-stage. The choir as always is self-evidently 'there', the trebles very much so; and although the congregational version of God rest you merry, gentlemen is something of a muddle, the hymns generally sound well: the descants in great barnstorming perorations of O come, all ye faithful and Hark! the herald angels sing thrillingly caught. Above all is the thrill of having this great event complete on record for the first time. The philosopher George Santayana has said: 'Fixity of tradition, of custom, of language is perhaps a prerequisite to complete harmony in life and mind.' That may not be a fashionable view in fin de siècle Britain, but it's why, each Christmas, this Festival of Nine Lessons and Carols sends a beam out into the world of special luminescence and beauty.

Laudibus

All in the April evening
Bennet All creatures now **Byrd** Ave verum corpus **Campion** Never weather-beaten saile more willing bent to shore (arr Parry) **Elgar** As torrents in summer. My love dwelt in a northern land, Op 18 No 3. Grant Crimond (arr Ross) **Morley** Fyer, fyer **Roberton** All in the April evening **Stanford** The bluebird, Op 119 No 3 **Sullivan** The long day closes **Traditional** O can ye sew cushions? (arr Bantock). Ca' the Yowes. The turtle Dove (both arr Vaughan Williams). All through the night. The banks o' Doon. Dream Angus. Drink to me only with thine eyes. An Eriskay love lilt. Wee Cooper o'Fife (all arr Roberton) **Vaughan Williams** Three Shakespeare Songs **Warlock** Corpus Christi
Laudibus / Michael Brewer
Hyperion CDA67076 (69' · DDD)   Ⓕ**O**

How Sir Hugh Roberton would have loved these fresh young voices. 'Soo gracious, soo musical', he used to murmur when the audience leant their uncertain voices to a rehearsal of *Crimond*. The new choir under Michael Brewer may not be quite so expert in the choral *portamento* as the Glasgow Orpheus used to be, but they sing in that tradition, the first requirement of which is beautiful sound, in tone and blend. Sir Hugh's arrangements of Scottish folk-songs find a natural home here, the melodies sweet and strong, the hummed accompaniments gentle and affectionate. Those by Vaughan Williams have a more distinctive flavour, and this, too, is well brought out, with feeling for the characteristic rise-and-fall, the sadness lurking close to the heart. The programme takes a natural half-time break after some more of Sir Hugh, and wakes us from an interval-nap with Morley's *Fyer, fyer* and John Bennet's *All creatures now*: they make us feel that, compared with the first Elizabethans, we're never really more than half-awake anyway. The effect of having a choir (even if a relatively small one), rather than single voices, isn't what we're used to in these things, but Laudibus have the rhythm of them in their bones and the sense of the words in their heads. Then there are some of the masterpieces among our later part-songs: Elgar's *My love dwelt in a northern land* (lovely to hear that magical third verse so well done), Stanford's *The bluebird* (with the smoothest of textures and a charming soloist), Warlock's *Corpus Christi* and Vaughan Williams's *Tempest* settings. And then, in spirit if not in truth, back to Sir Hugh for *The long day closes*, Sullivan's patent eye-moistener. A delightful disc.

New College Choir, Oxford

Agnus Dei I and II
Allegri Adagio in G minor[a]. Miserere mei **Bach** Cantata No 147, Herz und Mund und Tat und Leben – Jesu, bleibet meine Freude[a]. St John Passion, BWV245 – Ruht wohl **Barber** Agnus Dei, Op 11 **Bizet** Agnus Dei **Brahms** Geistliches Lied, Op 30[a] **Bruckner** Christus factus est[a] **Byrd** Ave verum corpus **Elgar** (arr Cameron) Variations on an original theme, 'Enigma', Op 36 – Lux aeterna **Fauré** Ave verum, Op 65 No 1 (both arr Higginbottom)[a]. Cantique de Jean Racine, Op 11 (arr Rutter)[a]. Requiem, Op 48[a] – In paradisum; Pie Jesu; Libera me **Górecki** Totus tuus, Op 60 **Lotti** Crucifixus a 8 **Martin** Mass for Double Choir – Agnus Dei **Mendelssohn** Hear my prayer **Monteverdi** Selva morale e spirituale – Beatus vir[a] **Mozart** Ave verum corpus, K618[a] **Palestrina** Missa Papae Marcelli – Kyrie **Purcell** Hear my prayer, O Lord, Z15 **Rachmaninov** Vespers, Op 37 – No 6, Ave Maria **Schubert** Psalm 23, D706 (all arr Cameron)[a] **Tavener** The Lamb
New College Choir, Oxford; [a]Capricorn / Edward Higginbottom
Erato 3984-29588-2 (139' · DDD) **Ⓜ Ⓞ**

This issue combines the two popular choral compilations 'Agnus Dei I' and 'Agnus Dei II'. From the original first disc the Allegri, Bach, Fauré and Mendelssohn are clear favourites. When we realise that Barber's *Agnus Dei* is an arrangement of his famous *Adagio* and that Elgar's *Lux aeterna* is 'Nimrod' with a halo, then those must be added too.

The performances are delightful, with the single exception of 'Jesu, bleibet meine Freude' ('Jesu, joy of man's desiring') where each of the choir's minims has its swell and *diminuendo* so that they bounce along before us like so many faintly ridiculous balloons. Thomas Herford is the excellent soloist in *Hear my prayer* and a capital exponent of the high C in the Allegri. The

quality of choral sound is very fine: also the warmth of the acoustic, not usually associated with New College Chapel, is ideal.

From the original second disc, the performance of the famous *Adagio* ascribed to Albinoni, courtesy of Remo Giazotti, and set here by John Cameron to a text, in Latin, from the New Testament, is deserving of as much success as Barber's *Adagio*. The other items from that issue are taken at rather faster speeds than usual. Lotti's *Crucifixus*, Schubert's 23rd Psalm and Martin's *Agnus Dei* from the Mass for Double Choir are examples, and they all benefit, especially in this context. The choir itself has long been one of the best in its normal repertoire of church music, and these excursions have emboldened it in coloration and expressive scope. Purcell's *Hear my prayer*, for instance, is sung with exceptional intensity. Some of the arrangements may be questionable. Albinoni is fair game, but Brahms's lovely Op 30 forfeits the spiritual quietness of church when deprived of its organ accompaniment, and Schubert isn't really in need of strings and harp. For all that, though, it remains a delightful compilation, and not to be dismissed by 'serious' musicians on account of its wider appeal.

St Paul's Cathedral

Advent at St Paul's
Anonymous Laudes Regiae. Angelus ad Virginem (arr Willcocks)[a]. O come, O come, Emmanuel (arr Carter)[a]. Rejoice in the Lord alway **Britten** A Hymn of St Columba[a] **Bruckner** Virga Jesse floruit **Byrd** Laetentur coeli **A Carter** Toccata on Veni Emmanuel[b] **Gibbons** This is the record of John[a] **Handl** Ecce concipies[c] **R Lloyd** Drop down, ye heavens[a] **Palestrina** Matins Responsory. Vesper Responsory **Parsons** Ave Maria **Peerson** Blow out the trumpet[a] **Rutter** Hymn to the Creator of Light **Weelkes** Hosanna to the Son of David **Wilby** Echo Carol[a]
St Paul's Cathedral Choir / John Scott [b]org with [a]Andrew Lucas org
Hyperion CDA66994 (71' · DDD) Text and translations included **Ⓕ**

As in the seasonal calendar a single window opens first, so in this Advent recital a solo voice sings in the distance; and by the end, all windows alight, the great Cathedral is filled with the organ's *fortissimo* from deepest pedal sub-bass to brightest trumpet and topmost piccolo. The programme begins with some plainsong dating back to the first millennium of the era. The end, more plainsong but not so plain now, has *O come, O come, Emmanuel* audaciously arranged, then to become the subject of an organ toccata with sufficient energy to propel the hymn, the Cathedral and all into the new age. In between comes a satisfying alternation of ancient and modern. Particularly splendid is Martin Peerson's *Blow out the trumpet*, an anthem strong in rhythm and colour. Robert Parsons's five-part *Ave Maria* is also a joy. The modern works include an interesting, deeply felt piece by John Rutter, *Hymn to the Creator of Light*: its first section, less ingratiating (but not therefore less good) than his more characteristic style, is followed by an angular refulgence of praise in preparation for a chorale-melody sung quietly in octaves amid an affectionate interweave of gentle polyphony – the effect is lovely.

The choir is on top form. Britten's *Hymn of St Columba* is especially well performed, probably making the strongest impression of all. Andrew Lucas is the remorselessly exercised organist in this, and John Scott takes over for the Toccata: both are excellent.

Epiphany at St Paul's

Bingham Epiphany **Byrd** Praise our Lord all ye Gentiles. Senex puerem portabat **Cornelius** Weihnachtslieder, Op 8 – Die Könige **Crotch** Lo! Star-led chiefs **Dearnley** The growing limbs of God the Son **Eccard** When to the temple Mary went **Handl** Omnes de Saba venient **Holst** Nunc dimittis, H127 **Howells** Here is the little door **Marenzio** Tribus miraculis **Mendelssohn** Christus, Op 97 – When Jesus our Lord **Ouseley** From the rising of the sun **Surplice** Brightest and best of the sons of the morning **Traditional** Coventry Carol. O worship the Lord **SS Wesley** Ascribe unto the Lord
St Paul's Cathedral Choir / John Scott
with **Huw Williams** *org*
Hyperion CDA67269 (72' · DDD) Notes and texts included   Ⓕ ⦿

'As with gladness men of old did the guiding star behold': the best-known of Epiphany hymns isn't in this recital, which nevertheless is luminous with a sense of goodness and well-being, brightest and best of choral records for some time. It ranges widely over the centuries, from the 16th onwards. Eighteenth-century elegance is embodied in Crotch's Lo, star-led chiefs. The 19th century does well with tuneful Ouseley and a masterpiece, Ascribe unto the Lord, from SS Wesley. The most recent work is Judith Bingham's *Epiphany*, written for Winchester Cathedral in 1995. Impressively eventful, it develops from a quiet, rather mystical opening to a dramatic and powerful *fortissimo* conclusion. But probably the most sublime moment in the recital comes from the other end of the 20th century with the opening of Holst's eight-part Nunc dimittis of 1915. This, through to the almost carol-like rejoicing of the Gloria and its exultant 'Amen', casts a glow over the whole programme. And that programme is one which could hardly have been better performed, anywhere or at any time. The Cathedral choir are on top form, opulent in tone, tasteful in style; Huw Williams accompanies with skill and imagination. In short, a distinguished record: inspiring and not in the least 'inspirational'.

Hear my Prayer

Allegri Miserere mei[a][b][d][i][j] **B Rose** Feast Song for St Cecilia[a][c][f] **Brahms** Ein deutsches Requiem – Ich hab'

nun Traurigkeit[a][j] **Britten** Festival Te Deum, Op 32[a][j] **Harvey** Come, Holy Ghost[a][e][g] **Mendelssohn** Hear my prayer[a][j] **Stanford** Evening Canticles in G[a][i][j] **Tavener** I will lift up mine eyes **Wise** The ways of Zion do mourn[a][h][j]
[a]**Jeremy Budd**, [b]**Nicholas Thompson** *trebs* [c]**Simon Hill**, [d]**Wilfred Swansborough** *countertens* [e]**Andrew Burden**, [f]**Alan Green** *tens* [g]**Nigel Beaven**, [h]**Charles Gibbs**, [i]**Timothy Jones** *basses* St Paul's Cathedral Choir / John Scott with [j]**Andrew Lucas** *org*
Hyperion CDA66439 (76' · DDD) Recorded 1990. Texts and translations included   Ⓕ

The special distinction of this disc is the work of the treble soloist, Jeremy Budd. He sings in a programme which is very much the choirboy's equivalent of an operatic soprano's 'Casta diva' and more of that sort. As it is, he crowns the Allegri *Miserere* with its five top Cs, spot-on, each of them (rather like Melba singing 'Amor' at the end of Act 1 in *La bohème* five times over). He commands the breath, the long line and the purity of tone necessary for the solo in Brahms's Requiem and copes with the difficult modern idiom of Jonathan Harvey's *Come, Holy Ghost* with an apparent ease that to an older generation may well seem uncanny. Other modern works are included. John Tavener's *I will lift up mine eyes*, written for St Paul's in 1990, has its characteristic compound of richness and austerity; and in this, the words penetrate the mist of echoes more successfully than do those of the *Feast Song for St Cecilia*, written by Gregory Rose and set to some very beautiful music by his father Bernard. It's good, as ever, to hear Stanford's Evening Service in G, with its almost Fauré-like accompaniment finely played by the excellent Andrew Lucas; and for a morning canticle there's Britten's *Te Deum* with its effective build-up to 'Lord God of Sabaoth' and its faint pre-echo of *The Turn of the Screw* at 'O Lord, save Thy people'. There's also a melancholy anthem by Michael Wise, whose fate it was to be knocked on the head and killed by the watchman to whom he was cheeky one night in 1687.

Psalms for St Paul's Volume 9

Bairstow Psalm 107 **Hurford** Psalm 108 **Jacobs** Psalm 112 **Ouseley** Psalm 105 **Stewart** Psalm 106 **Turle** Psalm 109. **Vann** Psalm 110 **Vann** Psalm 113 **Woodward** Psalm 111
Huw Williams *org* **St Paul's Cathedral Choir / John Scott**
Hyperion CDP11009 (63' · DDD) Texts included   Ⓕ ⦿⦿

Psalms for St Paul's Volume 12

Bertalot Psalm 141 **Camidge** Psalm 140 **Day** Psalm 139 **Hanforth** Psalm 145 **Hervey** Psalm 143 **Monk** Psalm 144. Psalm 146 **Rose** Psalm 121 **Scott** Easter Anthem **Stanford** Psalms 147, 149 & 150 **Stewart** Psalm 142 **Talbot** Psalm 150 **Willcocks** Psalm 148
Huw Williams *org* **St Paul's Cathedral Choir / John Scott**
Hyperion CDP11012 (64' · DDD) Texts included Ⓕ ⦿⦿

The phrase 'fearfully and wonderfully made',

coined some 3000 years ago by the Psalmist for his 139th Psalm, perfectly describes these final releases in Hyperion's series, Psalms from St Paul's. Over the course of 12 discs all 150 Psalms have been presented in the traditional Anglican grouping covering Matins and Evensong for every day of a 30-day month. After weeks in which we have been subjected to wounds which 'stink and are corrupt through my foolishness' (8th morning), heathen who 'grin like a dog and run about through the city' (11th evening), 'all manner of flies and lice' (21st morning), not to mention the shedding of innocent blood, 'even the blood of their sons and of their daughters' (21st evening), the unrestrained joy of the 30th evening, especially Psalm 150, comes as a welcome relief. And to mark the end of the monthly cycle Psalm 150 is sung to an appropriately celebratory chant (unique in having its own built-in descant) by Stanford which also provides a fitting conclusion to an exceptionally inspiring and captivating – not to say enchanting – series.

The intense pleasure and satisfaction to be gleaned from these discs is hard to explain to the uninitiated, who will seek in vain for any intrinsically musical interest. But while the 20 simple chords of a typical Anglican chant might appear a preposterously miniscule structure to those weaned on Bach cantatas or Mahler symphonies, for the true aficionado the framework of a chant offers infinite scope for expressive creativity. James Turle (1802-82) conjured up real pathos in his lovely chant for Psalm 109 while the Revd Sir Frederick Arthur Ouseley (1825-89) achieved an air of total contentment for Psalm 105. In more recent times Barry Rose shamelessly milks the St Paul's acoustic with his delicious chant to Psalm 121 (included as an appendix to the final disc), John Bertalot gives us a tantalisingly bittersweet chant for Psalm 141 while Sir David Willcocks depicts true majesty for Psalm 148.

Huw Williams' accompaniments are models of sensitivity and discretion, although not without occasional touches of humour ('ye dragons and all deeps' seems to shake the very foundations in Psalm 148 while his 'right hand' certainly provides generous support for Psalm 139), and John Scott's relaxed direction, lovingly caressing these timeless words and phrases, ensures that the leisurely pace, which might from less inspired choral directors induce its hearers to a state of suspended animation, here creates an aura of mystery and sanctity; an aura fully enhanced by this spacious and warmly atmospheric recording. Here, surely, is the very apogee of English Psalm singing.

Portsmouth Cathedral

Magnificat and Nunc Dimittis, Volume 4
Andrews Evening Service in G **Bairstow** Evening Service in D **Brewer** Evening Service in E flat **Darke** Evening Service in F **Howells** Evening Service in E. Evening Service in B minor **Lassus** Magnificat quarto toni **R Shephard** Salisbury Service **Stanford** Evening Service in C, Op 115 **Victoria** Nunc dimittis **Weelkes** Evening Service for Trebles – Magnificat; Nunc dimittis
Portsmouth Cathedral Choir / Adrian Lucas with **David Thorne** org
Priory PRCD527 (79' · DDD) Texts included ⒫❶

One good thing after another; it almost surprises that a succession of *Mags* and *Nuncs* can be so varied, satisfying and enjoyable. The programmes in this excellent series allow for a fair variety of styles and centuries, but in this instance a particularly generous share of the credit must go to the performances. Forthright and invigorating, they give rise to a distinct suspicion that the whole business may be a pleasure: that the choristers have some rhythm in their bones and at certain points might even have a smile on their faces. It's there right from the start, with Brewer in E flat (and how undeservedly stodgy that can sound in performance) bright with energy and encouraging a conviction that there genuinely is something in which to rejoice. This extends to Lassus, Victoria and Weelkes, where, instead of the more usual formal reading of notes, there's a common effort of understanding and imagination, lifting the notes off the page and sometimes, with a little judicious semi-*staccato*, setting them a-dance. Nor is there any lack of sensitive shading or of repose in the right places – a fine feeling for mood in the lovely and little-known B minor setting of Howells, for example. A splendid recital, with a fine choice of repertoire, and consistently admirable playing by the organist.

Robert Shaw Festival Singers

O Magnum Mysterium
Górecki Totus tuus, Op 60[a] **Lauridsen** O Magnum Mysterium[b] **Poulenc** Quatre motets de Noël – O magnum mysterium[a] **Rachmaninov** Vespers, Op 37 – Praise the name of the Lord[a] **Schubert** Der Entfernten, D331[b] **Tallis** If ye love me[ac]. A new commandment[ac] **Traditional** Amazing Grace[a]. Sometimes I feel like a moanin' dove[a]. Wondrous Love[a] **Victoria** O vos omnes, qui transitis per viam[ac]. O magnum mysterium[ac]
[a]**Robert Shaw Festival Singers,** [b]**Robert Shaw Chamber Singers / Robert Shaw**
Telarc CD80531 (57' · DDD) Recorded 1992, 1994, 1997, [c]live 1989 ⒫❶❶

This compilation of unaccompanied choral music is a tribute to Robert Shaw, one of the world's great choir trainers. He quickly established that reputation back in the 1940s, when Toscanini chose the Robert Shaw Chorale for major choral recordings with the NBC Symphony Orchestra. Later, over two decades as music director of the Atlanta Symphony, Shaw was diverted more towards the orchestral repertory, his choral recordings then usually involving the orchestra too.

After retiring from that post in 1988 he once

again found time for unaccompanied choral music, establishing in 1989 a summer festival of choral concerts and workshops at Quercy in south-central France, using a choir of students from American universities chosen by competitive audition. Between then and 1994 he made a series of recordings for Telarc with that festival choir. They provide most of the items here, atmospherically recorded in St Pierre at Gramat.

The four opening items on the disc, the Tallis and Victoria motets, were recorded in that first year, 1989, with the intention of including them with similar repertory on a full disc. In the event, they now appear on disc for the first time, immaculate performances from a relatively large choir, which demonstrate the consistent refinement of matching and balance characteristic of Shaw's choral work.

The Poulenc and Rachmaninov items also date from 1989, the movement from the Rachmaninov *Vespers* demonstrating the fervour that Shaw could draw from his singers. The two American hymns and one spiritual item are from the 1992 Festival, with Shaw's own arrangements exploiting the sort of elaborate choral effects he relished in other music. The last and longest item on the disc, the Górecki motet, recorded in 1994, brings a performance which concentratedly sustains a very slow speed and extremes of *pianissimo* that are both rapt and dreamlike.

At under an hour the compilation might have been more generous, but that's a tiny criticism to set against the outstanding quality of singing and recording.

The Sixteen

Renaissance: music of inner peace
Allegri Miserere mei **Anonymous** Veni creator spiritus. Ubi caritas. Te lucis ante terminum. In paradisum **Barber** Agnus Dei **Blow** Salvator mundi **Bruckner** Locus iste **Byrd** Ave verum corpus. Gradualia, Vol 1/i: Feast of All Saints – Offertory: Iustorum animae. Mass for four voices – Agnus Dei **F Guerrero** Ave virgo sanctissima. Duo Seraphim **G Gabrieli** Exultet jam angelica turba **Gibbons** Hosanna to the Son of David **Górecki** Totus tuus **Josquin** Ave Maria **Lassus** Ave regina coelorum. Timor et tremor **Lotti** Crucifixus a 8 **Melgás** Salve Regina **Monteverdi** Christe, adoramus te **Mouton** Nesciens mater virgo virum **Palestrina** Missa Papae Marcelli – Kyrie. Sicut cervus desiderat **Parsons** Ave Maria **Poulenc** Salve Regina **Purcell** Beati omnes qui timent Dominum. Hear my prayer, O Lord **Sheppard** Libera nos, salva nos I **Tallis** If ye love me. O nata lux de lumine. Salvator mundi Domine. Adesto nunc proprius **Tavener** The Lamb **Tomkins** When David heard **Victoria** Salve regina **Weelkes** Hosanna to the Son of David
The Sixteen / Harry Christophers
Universal Classics and Jazz ② 986 6737 (150' · DDD)
Ⓜ❍❍

This splendid two-disc set features works from

The Sixteen's repertory. Over a quarter of a century, under the direction of Harry Christophers, group has never done anything that wasn't totally compelling in its musicianship and technical assurance.

Even the most casual collector is likely to have at least some of these pieces on disc already, but you'd have to look very hard to find performances to match any here. For example, they give us an electrifying account of Guerrero's *Duo seraphim*, while that great English Tudor classic, Weelkes' *Hosanna to the Son of David* can rarely have been recorded with such fiery zeal. That mainstay of any half-decent church choir's repertoire, *Locus iste*, comes across here as freshly and as intensely moving as it must have sounded in 1869 when Bruckner wrote it. As for modern repertory, the subtlety brought to pieces by Górecki and Tavener elevates these already established choral classics.

For some this pair of discs will serve as conclusive proof that The Sixteen is the finest small choral group in existence. For others this matchless music-making will provide a source of endless satisfaction and enrichment.

Tenebrae

Mother and Child
RR Bennett Sermons and Devotions – The seasons of his mercies **Dove** See Him that Maketh the Seven Stars **Filsell** O be joyful in the Lord **L'Estrange** Lute-Book lullaby **Pott** The Soul of the Righteous. My song is love unknown **Swayne** Magnificat, Op 33 **Tavener** Mother and Child
Jeremy Filsell *org* **Tenebrae / Nigel Short**
Signum Two SIGCD501 (63' · DDD) Texts and translations included
Ⓕ

The chamber choir Tenebrae aims to create 'an ethereal mood of contemplation' in concerts of medieval, Renaissance and contemporary devotional music. They commissioned Tavener's *Mother and Child*, a setting of a poem by Brian Keeble that uses images of light and flame to symbolise love. In its development from the contemplative chant-like opening minutes, through a blazing climax augmented by organ and gong, to the final, restrained 'Hail Mary', Tavener demonstrates his mastery of radiance and pellucidity where most composers can only do brilliance and brightness.

Richard Rodney Bennett was one of the first composers to move with understanding and facility between 'serious music', jazz, film scores and 'quality pop'. The path he helped beat is now trodden as a matter of routine. L'Estrange, one of those who followed his example, works as a jazz instrumentalist, classical chorister and composer of stage musicals. His *Lullaby* dresses the somewhat arcane octotonic scale in attractive and accessible melodies. Bennett and L'Estrange avoid the most common pitfall of this contemporary eclecticism, which tends to import from popular music a certain saccharine quality in harmonies and intervals. It crops up in the majority of the other pieces, but not enough to mar enjoyment. A well-balanced programme, impeccably performed.

Wells Cathedral Choir

Hills of the North, rejoice
Anonymous On Jordan's bank the Baptist's cry. When I survey the wondrous cross. Come, Holy Ghost, our souls inspire **A Brown** Come, ye faithful, raise the strain **Crüger** Ah! holy Jesu **W Davies** O little town of Bethlehem **Dykes** Holy! Holy! Holy! **Evans** For the beauty of the earth **Ferguson** From the Eastern mountains **Gauntlett** Ye choirs of new Jerusalem **Gibbons** Drop, drop slow tears **G Ives** Gracious Spirit, Holy Ghost **Maclagan** Palms of glory, raiment bright **Schulz** We plough the fields and scatter **Shaw** Hills of the North, rejoice **Stanford** For all the Saints **Stainer** Lord Jesus think on me **Thrupp** Brightest and best of the sons of the morning **Traditional** Of the Father's heart begotten. Forty days and forty nights. I bind unto myself today **Vaughan Williams** It is a thing most wonderful **R Williams** Hail the day that sees him rise
Wells Cathedral Choir / Malcolm Archer with **Rupert Gough** org
Hyperion CDP12103 (76' · DDD) Texts included Ⓕ●

In this recital the voices are magnificent; likewise the organ. Records from Wells always have a healthy glow about them. The choir, who are as well-disciplined musically as any in the country, sing as though for the joy of it. The men ('gentlemen' is the approved term) are excellent: distinctive pleasures lie in the easy resonance of their unison verses and the fine balance of well-matching tones in the verses arranged for alto, tenor and bass.

The programme follows the Church year, from Advent to All Saints, with something good for every season. At Christmas, what Alan Luff in his notes describes as 'the fine rolling tune' *Divinum mysterium* swings us from verse to verse of *Of the Father's heart begotten* as apparently it has done since the 11th century. At Passiontide, *When I survey the wondrous Cross* has the altos fluting a delicious obbligato, and Ascension inspires the organist to seek out rare harmonies and inject a fresh rhythmic energy in the last verse of *Hail the day that sees him rise*. The whole record is a delight, and if one hymn collection is to be chosen, then this should be it.

Worcester Cathedral

Great Cathedral Anthems – XI
Beach Let this mind be in you **Dirksen** Songs of Isaiah – Arise, shine **Friedell** Draw us in the Spirit's tether **Hancock** Earthquake, Wind and Fire **Hoiby** The Lord is King **Macfarlane** Open our eyes **Neswick**

Happy are they that fear the Lord **Parker** Jam sol recedit igneus **Rorem** Exaltabo te, Domine **Sowerby** I was glad
Judith Hancock org **Choir of Saint Thomas Church, Fifth Avenue / Gerre Hancock**
Priory PRCD629 (64'·· DDD) Texts included Ⓕ●

Great Cathedral Anthems – XII
Atkins Abide with me. If ye then be risen with Christ. There is none that can resist thy voice **Day** Turn back O Man. When I survey the wondrous cross **Elgar** Light out of darkness. O hearken thou **Guest** For the Fallen **Lucas** Sacerdotes Domini **Tomkins** O sing unto the Lord. When David heard that Absolom was slain **Willcocks** My heart is fixed, O God
Adrian Lucas org **Worcester Cathedral Choir / Sir David Willcocks**
Priory PRCD750 (61'· DDD) Ⓕ●

To conclude its 12-disc series of Great Cathedral Anthems, Priory celebrates the work, not of a major church music composer, but of one of the best-known and most respected choral directors of our time. Sir David Willcocks goes back to Worcester, where he was Master of the Choristers 1950-57. The in the 1950s would have been a very different-sounding body from their 21st-century successor, and perhaps it's unfair to criticise the occasional raggedness of blend and ensemble, while the over-bright boys' tone seems a world apart from the smooth 'coo' that became Willcocks' hallmark at King's College, Cambridge. But he never made recordings with his Worcester Choir. So the chance to hear such Worcester gems as *When I survey* by Edgar Day, and *If ye then be risen* by Willcocks's predecessor at Worcester, not to mention rarely heard anthems by the greatest Worcesterian of them all, Elgar, the combination of a legendary choral director, a keen and enthusiastic choir and Adrian Lucas's resourceful and vivid organ accompaniments, makes this a fitting conclusion to a rewarding series.

Volume 11 of the series gives British church music aficionados a rare chance to sample American anthems. Few of those included here will be familiar to English ears and only Harold Friedell's charming *Draw us in the Spirit's tether* could be mistaken for the genuine English product. But the unfettered drama, vivid musical imagery and sheer Technicolor opulence of these anthems make a refreshing change from the restrained emotions and tight-lipped charm of their English counterparts. Under Gerre Hancock, himself something of a legend in church music circles, the choir of St Thomas's New York prove themselves to be one of the best cathedral choirs on either side of the Atlantic and Judith Hancock's polished and imaginative organ accompaniments add a fine touch of distinction. Priory's recording achieves the perfect balance between atmosphere (which in this location is most generous) and clarity.

VOCAL

Sir Thomas Allen
baritone

More Songs My Father Taught Me

Barri The old brigade **Clay** I'll sing thee songs of
Araby **Coates** The green hills o' Somerset. I heard
you singing. Star of God **d'Hardelot** Because **Z Elliot**
There's a long, long trail a-winding **AF Harrison** In the
gloaming **Hatton** Simon the Cellarer **H Hughes**
Down by the Salley Gardens. The Star of the County
Down **Jacobs-Bond** Just a-wearying for you. A perfect day **Molloy** Love's old sweet song **Murray** Will
you go with me **Olcott** Mother Machree **Sanderson**
Friend o'mine. Time to go **Sheldon** O men from the
fields **Somerset** A song of sleep. Echo **Squire** Mountain Lovers **Sterndale Bennett** The songs of today
Sullivan Orpheus with his lute **Traditional** The water
of Tyne. She moved through the fair **Wallace** Yes, let
me like a soldier fall **Haydn Wood** Roses of Picardy
Woodforde-Finden Four Indian Love Lyrics – Pale
hands I loved beside the Shalimar (Kashmiri Song)
Sir Thomas Allen bar **Malcolm Martineau** pf
Hyperion CDA67374 (79' · DDD) Texts included ⒡❍

Sir Thomas dedicated the first volume to the
memory of his father, who had these songs
always at hand ready to be sung by family and
friends on musical evenings around the piano at
home. Now comes a second series. Many of us
who were brought up in a similar culture tended
rather to dissociate ourselves from it, cultivating
a taste for more developed musical forms and
more complex modes of expression. Such 'high-
brow' disdain dated back certainly to the early
1900s, when these songs were in their heyday.
But now their time seems to have come around
again. A musically knowledgeable audience may
feel free to enjoy them. Their limitations can be
recognised, but we now seem to feel open to the
attractions of such frankly melodic music and
such unabashed kindliness of feeling.

Allen's voice, which is still amazingly beautiful
in quality and still under such masterly control,
is so 'central' in character, and his own appearance and manner are so eminently likeable, that
he embodies the ideal drawing-room visitor for
such an evening. Malcolm Martineau's accompaniments are always alert to whatever harmony, rhythm or melodic counterpoint enlivens
the plain-looking scores, usually revealing more
than you might think.

Victoria de los Angeles
soprano

Berlioz Les nuits d'été, Op 7ᵃ – Villanelle;
Le spectre de la rose; L'île inconnue **Brahms** Meine
Liebe ist grün, Op 63 No 5. Nachtigall, Op 97 No 1
Delibes Bonjour, Suzon! **Halffter** Dos Canciones
Handel Judas Maccabaeus, HWV63 – So shall the
lute and harp awake **Nin** Cantos populares españolas
– Montañesa; Paño murciano **Obradors** Chiquitita la
novia **Ravel** Vocalise en forme de habanera **A Scar-
latti** Le Violette **Schubert** Mein!, D795 No 11 **Schu-**
mann Widmung, Op 25 No 1 **Stravinsky** Pastorale
Valverde Clavelitos **Vives** Canciones epigramáticas –
La presumida; El ritrato de Isabela
Victoria de los Angeles sop **Gerald Moore** pf
ᵃ**BBC Symphony Orchestra / Rudolf Schwarz**
BBC Legends/IMG Artists mono BBCL4101-2
(62' · ADD) Recorded live 1957 ⒡❍❍

When Victoria de los Angeles appeared at the
Edinburgh Festival in 1957, she was in her
prime, the voice as supple and sensitive as it was
beautiful. Everything she tackled seemed to be
touched by the magic of her attractive presence
and glorious singing.

Good as her account of Schumann's *Widmung*
may be, it's when she gets to Brahms, perhaps
her favourite composer in this genre, that she's
wholly at home, the wistful sense of pain in
Nachtigall caught to perfection. In the wordless
pieces by Stravinsky and Ravel she floats that
warm yet ethereal tone of hers with consummate ease, and the long-breathed phrasing and
excellent French in Duparc's *mélodie* are
enhanced by this artist's innate skill in word-
painting. For all that, audiences were always
impatient for her to get to the Spanish part of
her programme, for in this field she was unsurpassed as a singer and interpreter. Many of these
songs were also recorded by her in the studio,
but the live occasion gives these performances
an extra *frisson*. The encores are even better. An
account of *Clavelitos* is a superior reading even to
those famous ones available elsewhere. That's
complemented by a delightfully insouciant
account of the Delibes song that she didn't
attempt on any other recorded occasion.

Gerald Moore, as was his wont, manages to
change idioms in his familiar virtuosity. As a
whole, this is an invaluable addition to the
singer's extensive discography.

Songs of Spain – traditional and early; medieval; ⒣
Renaissance; Baroque. Medieval and Renaissance
songs of Andalusia. Renaissance songs. 19th- and
20th-century arrangements and art songs by
Barrera/Calleja, Falla, Granados, Guridi, Halffter,
Lorca, Mompou, Montsalvatge, Nin, Rodrigo, Toldrá,
Vals and Valverde. Opera arias – Goyescas, La
Tempranica (Giménez) and La vida breve
Victoria de los Angeles sop with various artists
EMI mono/stereo ④ 566937-2 (301' · ADD/DDD)
Recorded 1950-92. Texts and translations included
Ⓜ❍

Nothing could be more appropriate in celebrating Victoria de los Angeles's 75th birthday than
this extensive conspectus of her recordings of
Spanish song over 40 years. We begin with her
1950 set of traditional songs arranged by Gra-
ciano Tarragó, evocative of an era and a style
preserved amazingly in various collections. She
isn't as outgoing or communicative as she was
soon to become, perhaps a shade intimidated by
this early encounter with the microphone.
There's a certain sameness to her approach, but
the voice of the young artist, so refulgent, is a
delight. The Renaissance and Baroque pieces

that fill the rest of the first disc are another matter. Not only is the music more accessible but she performs it with a winning charm. The second disc is devoted entirely to medieval and Renaissance songs recorded in 1960 and 1967 with the Ars Musicae de Barcelona.

The last two discs bring us to 19th- and 20th-century arrangements of traditional material and original compositions. Among the former, Lorca's set, *Canciones populares españolas*, are absolutely irresistible both in themselves and as performed by the unflagging Victoria in 1970. These imaginative re-creations, full of sentiment, verve and fun, release every aspect of the singer's genius – eager, forward tone, vital enunciation of the texts and unfettered joy in the simple act of communication.

The remainder of the songs, which all featured frequently in her recitals, maintain this high standard. We're also given what was perhaps her signature-tune, Valverde's 'Clavelitos' – not the early 78rpm version, but the 1960 stereo remake – a sure-fire encore at most of her recitals.

The final CD includes her unrivalled recordings of Granados's *Tonadillas*, and his *Tres majas dolorosa*, suffering love epitomised in music and interpretation, as it is in Salud's arias from Falla's *La vida breve*. Then, dating from a live recital at Hunter College, NY, in 1971 with her close contemporary Alicia de Larrocha at the piano, we have Granados's *Canciones amatorias*, another favourite item of the singer's, and her dark-grained, intense account of Falla's *Seven Spanish Popular Songs*, with exuberant, subtly shaped support from Larrocha. Catching the bird on the wing, as it were, adds a further dimension of immediacy to our appreciation of this much loved artist. Andrew Walter's transfers are impeccable.

Songs and Arias by Brahms   Ⓗ
Falla, Fusté, Granados, Guridi, Handel, Nin, Respighi, Schumann, Toldrá, Turina, Valverde and Vives
Victoria de los Angeles *sop* with various artists
Testament mono SBT1087 (75' · ADD) Recorded 1942-53   Ⓕ

The two Respighi songs are magical performances – *Stornellatrice*, with the golden voice at its richest and *E se un giorno tornasse*, a study in subtle shading of tone, a dialogue between a mother and her dying, jilted daughter. For those two brief items alone, superbly transferred, this collection is an essential for all admirers of this singer, but there's much more. Handel's 'O had I Jubal's lyre' in German rather than English may be odd, but the performance sparkles and among the Lieder it's good to have not just 'Der Nussbaum' – the Schumann song which was always special to her – but two previously unpublished, 'Widmung' from the Myrthe songs and 'Ich grolle nicht' from *Dichterliebe*.

Through the whole collection the superb transfers capture the full-throated glory of los Angeles's voice at the beginning of her career. The 1942 recordings of two Hungarian folk-

songs, previously unpublished, may be rough and limited – made when the singer was only 18 – but they amply demonstrate that already the voice was fully developed in its beauty. No fewer than 18 of the 27 items are of Spanish songs, and though in one or two instances los Angeles was destined to make even more idiomatic readings later with a Spanish accompanist, these ones with Gerald Moore as her partner have a freshness and brilliance that has rarely been matched in this repertory. In particular it's good to have her first recording of the encore number which she made her own, *Clavelitos*.

Arleen Auger   *soprano*

Liederabend
Includes **Beethoven** Marmotte, Op 52 No 7. Wonne der Wehmut, Op 83 No 1. Zärtliche Liebe, WoO123 **Gluck** Einem Bach der fliesst **Haydn** Lieder für das Clavier, HobXXVIa – No 4, Eine sehr gewöhnliche Geschichte; No 21, Das Leben ist ein Traum. Canzonettas, HobXXVIa – No 34, She never told her love; No 35, Piercing eyes **Mozart** Wie unglücklich bin ich nit, K147/K125g. Oiseaux, si tous les ans, K307/K284d. Der Zauberer, K472. Die Zufriedenheit, K473. Das Veilchen, K476. Die Alte, K517. Im Frühlingsanfang, K597. Das Kinderspiel, K598 **Schubert** Nähe des Geliebten, D162b. Claudine von Villa Bella – Liebe schwärmt auf allen Wegen. Heidenröslein, D257. Seligkeit, D433. Geheimes, D719
Arleen Auger *sop* **Erik Werba** *fp*
Orfeo d'Or C509011B (70' · ADD) Broadcast performance 1978   Ⓕ

When this recital was given in the spring of 1978, Auger was at the absolute height of her powers and obviously in fabulous voice. And given the irresistible repertory she offers here, this is a disc to treasure. Her tone and its management were ideal for her utterly apt choice of Lieder. Whether the mood is grave or gay, she captures it perfectly and her effortless command of German means that the text is always given its full due. Sad and/or intimate pieces, such as Haydn's *She never told her love*, Mozart's *Als Luise die Briefe*, Beethoven's *Wonne der Wehmut* and Schubert's *Nähe des Geliebten* are given the benefit of Auger's full, appropriately plangent timbre. Then in cheerful songs, such as Mozart's *Der Zauberer*, Beethoven's *Marmotte*, Schubert's *Heidenröslein* and *Seligkeit*, Auger adopts a suitably smiling tone.

In all, her treatment is natural and unaffected, proving her the true successor to Irmgard Seefried in this repertory. Nothing should deter anyone from acquiring this delightful recital.

Dame Isobel Baillie & Kathleen Ferrier

To Music   Ⓗ
Songs, Arias and Duets by [a]Arne, [ab]Brahms, [b]Elgar, [b]Gluck, [b]Greene, [a]Grieg, [b]Handel, [ab]Mendelssohn, [ab]Purcell, [a]Schubert and [a]Scott

[a]**Dame Isobel Baillie** sop [b]**Kathleen Ferrier** contr
Gerald Moore pf
APR mono APR5544 (69' · ADD) Recorded 1941-5. All
items sung in English   Ⓜ

This is a delightful disc, with a happily chosen
programme and well-matched contributions
from both singers. Even so, it has to be admitted
that the first thought concerns date. The piano
arrangements of Purcell duets and Handel arias
are definitely of the period; nothing could be
more remote from the modern style which was
even then coming into vogue. But 'dated' in a
much better way is the quality of the singing
itself. Would you today find the runs in Purcell
and Handel sung with at once such clear articulation and such smoothness? Dame Isobel is
sometimes a little pipey but mostly charming.
Ferrier is royal. The transfers are excellent.

Dame Janet Baker   mezzo-soprano

Scottish and English Folksongs

Arne The Tempest – Where the bee sucks[a]
Beethoven Scottish Songs, Op 108[b] – No 5, The
sweetest lad was Jamie; No 7, Bonnie laddie,
highland laddie; No 20, Faithfu' Johnie; WoO156[b] –
Cease your funning; Polly Stewart **Boyce** Tell me
lovely shepherd[c] Third Booke of Ayres[d] – If
thou long'st so much to learne; Never love unlesse
you can; Oft have I sigh'd for him that heares me not.
Fourth Booke of Ayres[d] – Faine would I wed a faire
young man **Dowland** The First Book of Songs or
Ayres – Come againe[d] **Haydn** Scottish Folksong
Arrangements[e] – I'm o'er young to marry yet; John
Anderson; O can ye sew cushions; Sleepy Bodie; Up
in the morning early; The White Cockade; The brisk
young lad; O bonny lass; Duncan Gray; My boy
Tammy; Shepherds, I have lost my love; Green grow
the rashes; Love will find out the way; The birks of
Abergeldie; My ain kind dearie; Cumbernauld
House; Jamie come try me; The Flower of Edinburgh
Monro My lovely Celia[c] **Purcell** Lord, what is man?,
Z192[c]. Sleep, Adam, sleep and take thy rest, Z195[c]
Dame Janet Baker mez [a]**Douglas Whittaker** fl
[be]**Yehudi Menuhin** vn [b]**Ross Pople** vc [ac]**Ambrose
Gauntlett** vada [d]**Robert Spencer** lte George
Malcolm [b]hpd/[e]pf [ac]**Martin Isepp** hpd
Testament SBT1241 (70' · ADD) Recorded 1967, 1975.
Texts and translations included   Ⓟ**OOO**

'A Pageant of English Song' was
Baker's first solo LP for EMI. Side 1, in
which she's accompanied by Martin
Isepp and Robert Spencer, is reissued on this
CD. Side 2, with Gerald Moore at the piano, can
be heard on a double CD on EMI. Dame Janet
was at the beginning of the high summer of her
career when this was recorded in 1967. Every
recital, concert appearance or opera role was an
event. In the first song, Dowland's 'Come
againe', each word is given the perfect weight,
with beautiful touches on the repeated 'I sit, I
sigh, I weep, I faint, I die'. The jolly 'Never love
unlesse you can', the melancholy 'Oft have I
sigh'd' and the coquettish 'Faine would I wed'

each has its own 'face', Baker finding just the
right expression in her voice. The Scottish songs
arranged by Haydn, recorded eight years later,
seem rather slight in comparison. Nineteen of
these arrangements one after another seem
rather too much of a good thing. The five
Beethoven Scottish arrangements are the best
part of the 1975 session. 'Fathfu' Johnnie' is a
setting to place beside any great song of the
same period. The recording seems to favour the
instrumentalists somewhat, whereas in the 1967
selections, Baker's voice is always fresh and forward.

Haydn Arianna a Naxos, HobXXVIb/2[a] **Schubert** Der
Blinde Knabe, D833[b]. Totengräberweise, D869[b]
Schumann Frauenliebe und -leben, Op 42[c]. Der
Page, Op 30 No 2[b]. Meine Rose, Op 90 No 2[b]
R Strauss Vier Lieder, Op 27[b] – No 3, Heimliche
Aufforderung; No 4, Morgen. Befreit, Op 39 No 4[b]
Wolf Spanisches Liederbuch[b] – Die ihr schwebet
um diese Palmen; Geh' Geliebter
Dame Janet Baker mez [a]**John Constable,** [b]**Paul
Hamburger,** [c]**Geoffrey Parsons** pfs
BBC Music Legends/IMG Artists BBCL4049-2 (80' ·
ADD) Recorded live [ab]1968, [c]1971   Ⓜ**OO**

Although recorded on three separate occasions,
and with different accompanists, this programme is fairly typical of the recitals that Dame
Janet gave in the late 1960s and early 70s when
she was at the absolute peak of her form. She
probably wouldn't have opened with the Haydn,
reserving it usually as the final item in the first
half, an operatic climax to work towards. She
recorded it later with Raymond Leppard, but
this live version has a wonderful sense of intimacy. The recording is first rate, with marvellous presence; Baker has that ability to invest a
simple phrase in the first recitative such as 'la
face splenda del nostro amor' with unforgettable
poignancy. In the second part, as Ariadne rails
against her fate, she allows herself an almost
verismo-like outburst at 'ei qui lascia in abbandono'. This cantata can sometimes seem a bit
heavyweight on a recital programme, but as
Baker sings it seems to grows in beauty and
intensity.

Frauenliebe und -leben was the work that
brought Baker early fame as a recording artist, in
her recital for Saga. Later she recorded it again
for EMI with Barenboim. This recording from
1968, accompanied by Geoffrey Parsons, finds
her in luxurious full voice, revelling in each successive melody. It isn't preferable to the earlier
Saga version with Isepp, but here she lets herself
go more at certain key moments such as 'O lass
im Traüme' in the third song. This cycle
belonged to Janet Baker, and with the single
exception of Sena Jurinac, there just isn't a
singer to equal her in it.

The songs recorded in the studio with Paul
Hamburger include two by Wolf, not available
anywhere else in Baker's discography. 'Geh'
Geliebter' is sung with typical ardour. The two
Schubert and Schumann songs are fresh and

lively, but it's the Strauss group that has the highest voltage. *Heimliche Aufforderung* doesn't really suit her, with its intoxicated ardour, but *Morgen* is a superb example of that hushed, rapt quality that was one of the characteristic joys of Baker's art. The final song, *Befreit*, achieves a dramatic thrust that suggests the theatre in the best possible sense. Admirers who already possess Baker's other versions of this material shouldn't be deterred – this is a splendid souvenir of her in the full glory of her prime. Newcomers to Baker's singing – there can't be many people under 30 who heard her live – are in for a treat.

Brahms Vier ernste Gesänge, Op 121ᵈ. Lieder, Op 91e. Four Duets, Op 28ᶠ **Chausson** Poème de l'amour et de la mer, Op 19ᵇ **Duparc** Phidyléᵇ. La vie antérieureᵇ. Le manoir de Rosemondeᵇ. Au pays où se fait la guerreᵇ. L'Invitation au voyageᵇ **Ravel** Shéhérazadeª **Schumann** Frauenliebe und-leben, Op 42ᶜ
Dame Janet Baker *mez* ᶠ**Dietrich Fischer-Dieskau** *bar* ᵉ**Cecil Aronowitz** *va* ᶜᶠ**Daniel Barenboim** *pf* ª**New Philharmonia Orchestra / Sir John Barbirolli;** ᵇ**London Symphony Orchestra /** ᵈᵉ**André Previn** *pf*
EMI ② 568667-2 (134' · ADD) Recorded 1967-77   Ⓜ

There comes a time in each great singer's career when they're at the peak of their form: artistry, voice, confidence, everything is at the maximum. Where Dame Janet Baker is concerned, that happy coincidence was in the years from 1967 to 1971. On the opera stage, her Dido in *Les troyens*, her Lucretia, Octavian, Dorabella and finally Diana in *Calisto* showed us her range of dramatic and comic skills. On the concert platform, working with Barbirolli, Szell, Giulini, Boult, Boulez and Barenboim, everything she did seemed well-nigh perfect. This two-CD selection from her EMI recordings opens with her famous performance of Ravel's *Shéhérazade* under Barbirolli, recorded in 1967. Of the song-cycles they recorded, this is perhaps the least regarded – Baker's voice never had quite the sensuous quality one is hoping for in this piece; but the security, the joy in the sound of her voice as she sings of Asia, and the right pace, all add up to a very fine recording. What's missing can be noted in the final line, about the beautiful boy walking past, with his feminine movements. One waits for a hint of irony, a slight smile of regret in the voice, but it isn't there. Baker was not given to innuendo; her humour was more robust. The succeeding Chausson *Poème de l'amour et de la mer* and then the group of songs by Duparc, recorded nearly 10 years later, show up a marked deterioration in her voice. Where once all had been steady, there's a beat that becomes intrusive, a sense of strain on some of the high notes, even here and there a slight worry over the pitch. *Le manoir de Rosemonde* is the best performance, the high drama bringing out the best in her.
The performance of Schumann's *Frauenliebe und -leben* dates from 1975. Although at the time many people thought this outshone if not eclipsed Baker's earlier, justly famous Saga disc, this is debatable. The sound is certainly better on EMI and in the mid-1960s she had the ability to convey both the hushed, girlish quality of the earlier songs and the mature, and then even tragic, tones for the last three. The extra verbal clarity of this later performance doesn't make up for the slight sense of strain. There are no reservations whatsoever about the Brahms songs, with Previn. The extra darkness in Baker's voice by 1977 makes these the highlight of the whole selection. In the *Vier ernste Gesänge*, and then the two Op 91 songs with piano and viola, Baker, Previn and Cecil Aronowitz achieve the perfect balance. As an encore we get four Brahms duets with Dietrich Fischer-Dieskau. Everything Dame Janet recorded is worth hearing, and this pair of discs gives an unusual cross-section of her repertory.

Cecilia Bartoli   *soprano*

An Italian Songbook
Bellini Vaga luna che inargenti. L'abbandono. Malinconia, ninfa gentile. Il fervido desiderio. Torna, vezzosa Fillide. Vanne, o rosa fortunata. Dolente imagine di figlia mia. La farfalleta. Per pietà, bell'idol mio **Donizetti** Il barcaiolo. Ah, rammenta, o bella Irene. Amore e morte. La conocchia. Me voglio fa'na casa **Rossini** Péchés de vieillesse – Book 3: L'esule; Book 11: A ma belle mère; Aragonese. La passeggiata. Mi lagnerò tacendo – Boléro. Soirées musicales – La danza
Cecilia Bartoli *mez* **James Levine** *pf*
Decca 455 513-2DH (67' · DDD) Texts and translations included   Ⓕ

The transforming power of imagination is rarely shown so clearly. On record and in recital these songs and their like have so often appeared as tepid little exercises, cautious investigations of the voice, the acoustic, the audience. But now, behold, they burgeon. Life abundant lies within the vocal line, and even the silly old accompaniments sound well. Such is the effect of the Bartoli-Levine combination. From the very first bars it feels that something special among Bartoli's many fine recordings have come into being here with these two distinguished artists in association. These are thoughtful, passionate and colourful performances, which outshine all previous versions of the more familiar songs. Among the less familiar items, Bellini's *Torna, vezzosa Fillide* may come as the most engaging discovery. Rossini's miniature Requiem for his mother-in-law seems not to be a joke, whereas the *Aragonese* (a setting in the style of Aragon of *Mi lagnerò tacendo*) surely must be. There might have been something to say here and now about intrusive 'h's and that other intrusion, a breathy quality sometimes cultivated in the interests of expression or intimacy, but they aren't gross or prohibitive features of the singing here, and the lovely voice and lively art make ample amends.

Arie Antiche

Anonymous O leggiadri occhi belli **Caccini** Tu ch'hai le penne, amore. Amarilli **Caldara** Selve amiche. Sebben, crudele **Carissimi** Vittoria, vittoria! **Cavalli** Delìzie contente **Cesti** Intorno all'idol mio **Giordani** Caro mio ben **Lotti** Pur dicesti, o bocca bella **Marcello** Quella fiamma che m'accende **Paisiello** Nel cor più non mi sento. Il mio ben quando verrà. Chi vuol la zingarella **Parisotti** Se tu m'ami **A Scarlatti** Già il sole dal Gange. Son tutta duolo. Se Florindo è fedele. O cessate di piagarmi. Spesso vibra per suo gioco **Vivaldi** Sposa son disprezzata **Cecilia Bartoli** *mez* **György Fischer** *pf* Decca 436 267-2DH (66' · DDD) Texts and translations included Recorded 1990-91 Ⓔ➊

With Scarlatti and Vivaldi among the composers, these *arie antiche* aren't necessarily very old. Italian singers have long been accustomed to lumping together all songs earlier than Mozart (or perhaps Haydn) under this heading, piously including them at the start of a recital so as to establish a classical tone and give them time to try out their voices before entering on the more strenuous and popular part of their programme. Bartoli here devotes a whole disc to them, as things delightful in themselves, varied in mood and style, and calling in turn on almost all the essential arts of a good singer. No one can come away with a feeling of having been shortchanged at the end of this. Her voice is ideal, both silken and chaste, finely controlled, cleanly produced. With a simple, direct song such as the famous *Caro mio ben* she will never fuss or show off; with Vivaldi's *Sposa son disprezzata* she exploits the most deliciously languishing tone and sometimes one more frankly passionate and 'operatic'. Most of the items are gems, and to all of them György Fischer brings the touch of the expert jeweller, knowing exactly how best to set off the beauties of voice and melody.

Chant d'amour

Berlioz Tristia, Op 18 – La mort d'Ophélie. Zaïde, Op 19 No 1 **Bizet** Chant d'amour. Ouvre ton coeur. Adieux de l'hôtesse arabe. Tarantelle. La Coccinelle **Delibes** Les filles de Cadix **Ravel** Chants populaires – Chanson française; Chanson espagnole; Chanson italienne; Chanson hébraïque. Vocalise en forme de Habanera. Deux mélodies hébraïques. Tripatos **Viardot-Garcia** Hai luli!. Havanaise. Les filles de Cadix **Cecilia Bartoli** *mez* **Myung-Whun Chung** *pf* Decca 452 667-2DH (68' · DDD) Texts and translations included Ⓔ➊

Cecilia Bartoli goes from strength to strength. Taking on the French repertory in this delightful disc, she also gives us some great rarities. The opening Bizet group includes two of his best-known songs, *Ouvre ton coeur* and *Adieux de l'hôtesse arabe*. In the first, one perhaps might ask for more of a smile in the voice. In the pessimistic Hugo poem about the Arab girl bidding farewell to the handsome traveller, Bartoli relishes the muezzin-like vocalise on 'Hélas, adieu,

souviens-toi'. This is one of the best performances of this mini-drama since Conchita Supervia's orchestral-accompanied version. In this, and the succeeding *Tarantelle*, 'tra-la-la's and froth, one is prompted to wonder if there will one day be a Bartoli *Carmen*. *La Coccinelle* ('The ladybird') is a little salon gem, with a fast waltz motif. Bartoli uses a croaky little voice to act out the Ladybird.

Delibes's *Les filles de Cadix*, all trills and sunshine, is contrasted with an equally demanding setting of the same poem by Pauline Viardot. *Hai luli!* with words by Xavier de Maistre is a sad second-cousin to the Willow Song from Rossini's *Otello*. *Havanaise* is a real curiosity: the first and last stanzas, sung in Spanish, frame a middle section in French which breaks into a Rossinian flight of coloratura before returning to the swaying movements of the dance. Evenings *chez* Viardot must have been enlivened considerably by such songs. The narration of Ophelia's death, words by Ernest Legouvé, vaguely based on Shakespeare, ends with a wordless melody which Bartoli sings in a hushed, beautiful tone. In *Zaïde* she plays the castanets with skill; if this song is less interesting than the evocations of Spain by Bizet, Delibes and Viardot, that's Berlioz's fault, not Bartoli's. In the concluding Ravel group, an interesting contrast can be made between Viardot's *Havanaise* of the 1840s and Ravel's *Habanera* of 1907. In the four popular songs, Bartoli is especially effective in the Hebrew number as well as the two other *Mélodies hébraïques*, 'Kaddish' and 'L'énigme éternelle'. All these Ravel songs have often been recorded, so one can't help wishing that Bartoli and Chung had stayed with the 19th-century French salon repertory to uncover more rarities. Still, this is one of the most satisfying recitals by one of the great singers of our time. First-rate recording and sensitive accompaniment throughout.

Italian Songs

Beethoven La Partenza, WoO124. Four Ariettas, Op 82. In questa tomba oscura, WoO133 **Haydn** Arianna a Naxos, HobXXVIb/2 **Mozart** Ridente la calma, K152/K210*a* **Schubert** Didone abbandonata, D510. Im Haine, D738. An die Leier, D737. La pastorella al Prato, D528. Vier Canzonen, D688. Pensa, che questo istante, D76. Willkommen und Abschied, D767 **Cecilia Bartoli** *mez* **András Schiff** *pf* Decca 440 297-2DH (68' · DDD) Recorded 1992. Texts and translations included Ⓔ

It's good to be reminded of these composers' responses to the Italian muse in this particularly well-cast recital. Central Europe, in the person of András Schiff, meets Italy, in Cecilia Bartoli, to delightful, often revelatory effect. The simple form and undemanding vocal line of Beethoven's little *La Partenza* makes for a truthfulness of expression which Bartoli's clear, light-filled enunciation re-creates to the full. With her warm breath gently supporting the voice's lively, supple inflexion, she reveals Beethoven's own skill in word-setting both here and in two fascinatingly contrasted settings of 'L'amante impaziente' in the *Ariettas*, Op 82. Schubert's 10 *Canzone* selected here show a wide range of treatment, from the compressed lyric drama of Dido's lament 'Vedi quanto adoro', in which Bartoli's lives intensely from second to second, to the honeyed Goldoni *pastorella* and the thrumming, pulsating serenade of 'Guarda, che bianca luna', D688 No 2. A gently, fragrantly shaped Mozart *Ridente la calma*, and a Haydn *Arianna a Naxos* of movingly immediate and youthful response complete this unexpectedly and unusually satisfying recital.

Live in Italy
Bellini Malinconia, ninfa gentile. Ma rendi pur contento **Berlioz** Zaïde, Op 19 No 1 **Bizet** Carmen – Près des remparts de Séville **Caccini** Nuove musiche e nuova maniera di scriverle – Al fonte al prato; Tu ch'hai le penne. Amarilli mia bella **Donizetti** La conocchia. Me voglio fa'na casa **T Giordani** Caro mio ben **Handel** Il trionfo del Tempo e del Disinganno –. Lascia la spina **Montsalvatge** Canto negro **Mozart** Oiseaux, si tous les ans, K307/K284d. Le nozze di Figaro – Voi che sapete **Rossini** Mi lagnerò tacendo, Book 1 – No 2 in D; No 3 in D minor, 'Sorzico'; No 4 in E, 'Il risentimento'. L'orpheline du Tyrola. Zelmira – Riedi al soglio. Canzonetta spagnuola **Schubert** La pastorella al Prato, D528 **Viardot** Havanaise. Hai luli! **Vivaldi** Griselda – Agitata da due venti
Cecilia Bartoli *mez* **Jean-Yves Thibaudet** *pf*
Sonatori de la Gioiosa Marca
Decca 455 981-2DH (77' · DDD) Texts and translations included   Ⓕ

Bartoli's voice is still in lovely, almost unflawed condition. If one wishes to take stock of her growth as an artist, the second item in her programme, Caccini's *Amarilli*, affords an opportunity. She recorded it first in 1990 in a touching performance, beautiful as sound and sensitive in mood (available on Decca). But the mood was set, and she was singing a song written and remembered. In the newer recording she's living and seemingly inventing it. Thus the development of feeling at 'Credilo pur' brings a fresh impulse, a more urgent appeal, and the repetitions of the beloved name acquire a musing, improvisatory quality. All of this (and much more of its kind) is sheer enrichment. Nevertheless, if the vocal equivalent of a selective weed-killer could be employed, it might make short work of two other fast-growing products of this fair field. One, the persistent aspirating of runs, is probably too deep-rooted by now; the other, more insidious, is of comparatively recent cultivation, a breathy winsomeness, an exhalation of pretty pathos or girlish wide-eyed intimacy. If this were reserved for occasional use it might be acceptable and effective, but in the present recital it's habitual. As for the technique used in passagework such as abounds in the Vivaldi aria, it does facilitate rapid movement and helps to ensure clear articulation. Everything is height-

ened in these performances – the rich depth of contralto tone, languor and vivacity in the Viardot songs, the panache of the Berlioz, and smouldering promise and fiery fulfilment of Rossini's *Canzonetta spagnuola*. The variety of accompaniments is another attraction, all delightfully played. With the live atmosphere and the sense of freedom around the voice, this is surely the most faithful and revealing of all Bartoli's records to date.

María Bayo   *soprano*

Baroque Zarzuela Arias
Boccherini Clementina – Overture; Almas que amor sujetó **Hita** La Briseida – Amor, sólo tu encanto; Deydad que las venganzas **Martín y Soler** La madrileña – Overture; Inocentita y niña **Nebra** Amor aumenta el valor – Triste cáecel oscura…¡Ay, amor! ¡Ay, Clelia mia!; Adios, prenda de mi amor; Más fácil será al viento. Para obsequio a la deydad – Overture; Liega ninguno intente; Piedad, Señor
María Bayo *sop* **Les Talens Lyriques / Christophe Rousset**
Naïve E8885 (70' · DDD)   ⒻⓄⓄ

Rediscovery of the Baroque Spanish zarzuela has gained impetus in recent years. The name of José Melchor de Nebra Blasco (1702-68) is known particularly through his *Viento es la dicha de amor*, and his further output provides six of the items here. From his early *Amor aumenta el valor* comes the aria '¡Ay, amor! ¡Ay, Clelia mia!', sung here to riveting effect, with splendid interplay between coloratura and flutes.

María Bayo applies her beautifully clear, warm and intelligent coloratura to music from her own country. In her notes she likens the emotional content of these basically Italian-style arias to that aroused by Handel, Gluck and Mozart, while highlighting the distinctive Spanish features. These are most obvious in Violante's captivating seguidilla, 'Inocentita y niña', from Vicente Martín y Soler *La madrileña*, composer of the much cited (and, by Mozart, quoted) *Una cosa rara*.

The two items from Antonio Rodriguez de Hita's *La Briseida* of 1768 represent another key work of the 18th-century zarzuela, composed to words by the distinguished poet Ramón de la Cruz. So, too, was Boccherini's witty 1786 *Clementina*, from which the heroine's cavatina 'Almas que amor sujetó' is another delight.

The fresh, crisp and invigorating playing of Les Talens Lyriques under Christophe Rousset contributes to a wonderfully enterprising, impeccably performed, and altogether magical statement of the delights of Baroque zarzuela.

Stephanie Blythe   *mezzo-soprano*

Bach St John Passion, BWV245 – Von den Stricken; Es ist vollbracht!. Mass, BWV232 – Agnus Dei. St Matthew Passion, BWV244 – Erbarme dich; Können Tränen meiner Wangen **Handel** Hercules, HWV60 –

Where shall I fly?. Giulio Cesare, HWV17 – Priva
son d'ogni conforto; Son nata a lagrimar;
Al lampo dell'armi; Dall'ondoso periglio;
Aure, deh, per pietà; Madre!. Semele, HWV58 –
Awake, Saturnia; Iris, hence away. Serse, HWV40 –
Ombra mai fu; Frondi tenere
Stephanie Blythe mez with **David Daniels**
counterten **Jérôme Hantaï** va da gamba
Martin Isepp, Emanuelle Haïm hpds
Paris Ensemble Orchestra / John Nelson
Virgin Classics 545475-2 (72' · DDD) Texts and
translations included   Ⓕ

A new Marilyn Horne perhaps? This is Stephanie Blythe's solo début recording. Her tone
and timbre call strongly to mind the work of her
distinguished fellow-American predecessor. She
too possesses a rich, firm, characterful mezzo,
particularly solid in the lowest register, and also
seems to have Horne's technical fluency. In
Handel here, she dispatches Dejanira's desperate imprecations and Juno's anger as to the manner born, diction clear, attention paid to the dramatic situation in each. She encompasses
martial and pensive Caesar with equal aplomb.
Then she switches, with due versatility, to
despairing Cornelia, aria and duet. In the latter
she's joined by David Daniels as Sesto. The
duet, in particular, is delivered on both sides
with understanding and feeling.

Her Bach is only a mite less compelling. Again
the vocal and technical accomplishment aren't
in question, but the interpretations are on the
cool side, 'Es ist vollbracht!' excepted. Never
mind, this is a well-recordeddisc that marks the
arrival of an auspicious talent.

Barbara Bonney   mezzo-soprano

The Radiant Voice
Includes **Bach** Cantata No 211, 'Coffee Cantata' –
Heute noch, lieber Vater, tut es doch **Donizetti**
L'elisir d'amore – Chiedi all'aura lusinghiera **Grieg**
Peer Gynt – Solveig's Song **Lloyd Webber** Requiem
– Pie Jesuf **Mozart** Exsultate, jubilate, K165 –
Alleluia. Vespers, K339 – Laudate Dominum. Le nozze
di Figaro – Deh, vieni, non tardar. Die Zauberflöte –
Ach, ich fühl's **Pergolesi** Stabat Mater – Stabat Mater
Dolorosa **Purcell** Dido and Aeneas – When I am laid
in earth **Schumann** Liederkreis, Op 39 – Mondnacht
R Strauss Morgen, Op 27 No 4. Der Rosenkavalier –
Mir ist die Ehre widerfahren
Barbara Bonney sop **Various performers,
orchestras and conductors**
Decca 468 818-2DH (76' · DDD) Recorded 1988-2000
                                                    Ⓕ
'The Radiant Voice.' And, it might be added,
the exquisite art. The excellent programme
selection is arranged chronologically, starting
with John Dowland and ending with André
Previn, whose *Vocalise* for voice, cello and piano
provides a thoughtful, sensitively chosen final
number. In between there's some delightful
Bach and Mozart, with Lieder by Schumann and
Strauss, songs by Grieg and Sibelius and,
among other items, two excerpts from opera.

The *Rosenkavalier* duet is '[wie] himmlisch'
indeed, Bonney's Sophie heard in ideal partnership with Susan Graham as Octavian. The earliest recordings – 'Solveig's Song' and Susanna's
'Deh, vieni' – come from 1988. Very slightly,
these and others from the early 1990s are perceptibly more youthful in sound, and among the
latest it's possible to identify an added depth and
fullness. But most remarkable is the consistency,
the consistency too of pleasure given throughout the anthology.

Ian Bostridge   tenor

The English Songbook
Britten The Salley gardens[a] **WCD Brown** To
Gratiana dancing and singing[a] **Delius** Twilight
Fancies[a] **Dunhill** The Cloths of Heaven, Op 30 No 3[a]
Finzi The dance continued, Op 14 No 10[a]. Since we
loved, Op 13 No 7[a] **German** Orpheus with his lute[a]
Grainger Bold William Taylor, BFMS43[a]. Brigg Fair,
BFMS7[b] **Gurney** Sleep[a] **Parry** No longer mourn for
me[a] **Quilter** Come away, death, Op 6 No 1[a]. I will go
with my father a-ploughing[a]. Now sleeps the crimson
petal, Op 3 No 2[a] **Somervell** To Lucasta, on going to
the wars[a] **Stanford** La belle dame sans merci[a]
Traditional The death of Queen Jane[a]. The little
turtle dove[a]. My love's an arbutus (arr. Stanford)[a]
Vaughan Williams Linden Lea[a]. Silent Noon[a]
Warlock Cradle Song[a]. Jillian of Berry[a]. Rest, sweet
nymphs[a]
Ian Bostridge ten [a]**Julius Drake** pf [b]**Polyphony /
Stephen Layton**
EMI 556830-2 (69' · DDD) Texts included   Ⓕ●

The recital begins with Keats and ends with
Shakespeare: that can't be bad. But it also begins
with Stanford and ends with Parry; what would
the modernists of their time have thought about
that? They would probably not have believed
that those two pillars of the old musical establishment would still be standing by in 1999. And
in fact how well very nearly all these composers
stand! Quilter's mild drawing-room manners
might have been expected to doom him, but the
three songs here – the affectionate, easy grace of
his Tennyson setting, the restrained passion of
his Come away, death and the infectious zest of
I will go with my father a-ploughing – endear
him afresh and demonstrate once again the
wisdom of artists who recognise their own small
area of 'personal truth' and refuse to betray it in
exchange for a more fashionable 'originality'.
Likewise Finzi, whose feeling for Hardy's
poems is so modestly affirmed in The dance
continued. Does that song, incidentally, make
deliberate reference, at 'those songs we sang
when we went gipsying', to Jillian of Berry by
Warlock (whose originality speaks for itself)?
Jillian of Berry itself perhaps calls for more full-
bodied, less refined tones than Bostridge's. One
could do with a ruddier glow and more rotund
fruitiness in the voice. Yet for most of the programme he isn't merely a well-suited singer but
an artist who brings complete responsiveness
to words and music. The haunted desolation of

Delius's Twilight Fancies is perfectly caught in the pale hue of the voice which can nevertheless give body and intensity to the frank cry of desire, calming then to pianissimo for the last phrase amid the dim echoes of hunting horns in the piano part. Julius Drake plays with strength of imagination and technical control to match Bostridge's own.

Maria Callas   *soprano*

Bellini Norma – Casta diva **Bizet** Carmen – ☐Ⓗ
L'amour est un oiseau rebelle; Près des remparts de Séville; Les tringles des sistres **Catalani** La Wally – Ebben? … Ne andrò lontana **Donizetti** Lucia di Lammermoor – Spargi d'amaro pianto **Giordano** Andrea Chénier – La mamma morta **Gluck** Orphée et Eurydice – J'ai perdu mon Eurydice **Puccini** Gianni Schicchi – O mio babbino caro. La bohème – Sì, mi chiamano Mimì; Donde lieta uscì. Madama Butterfly – Un bel dì vedremo. Tosca – Vissi d'arte **Rossini** Il barbiere di Siviglia – Una voce poco fa **Saint-Saëns** Samson et Dalila – Mon coeur s'ouvre à ta voix **Verdi** La traviata – Ah, fors'è lui; Addio del passato
Maria Callas *sop* with **various artists**
EMI Classics 557050-2 (74' · ADD) Texts and translations included   Ⓕ**OO**

Bellini Norma – Casta diva. La sonnambula – ☐Ⓗ
Ah! non credea mirarti **Bizet** Carmen – L'amour est un oiseau rebelle; Près des remparts de Séville; Les tringles des sistres **Catalani** La Wally – Ebben? … Ne andrò lontana **G Charpentier** Louise – Depuis le jour **Cilea** Adriana Lecouvreur – Io son l'umile ancella **Donizetti** Anna Bolena – Al dolce guidami. Lucia di Lammermoor – Spargi d'amaro pianto **Giordano** Andrea Chénier – La mamma morta **Gluck** Orphée et Eurydice – J'ai perdu mon Eurydice **Gounod** Roméo et Juliette – Je veux vivre **Massenet** Le cid – De cet affreux combat; Pleurez, mes yeux. Manon – Adieu, notre petite table **Meyerbeer** Dinorah – Ombre légère **Mozart** Le nozze di Figaro – Porgi, amor **Puccini** La bohème – Sì, mi chiamano Mimì; Donde lieta uscì. Gianni Schicchi – O mio babbino caro. Madama Butterfly – Un bel dì vedremo. Manon Lescaut – In quelle trine morbide. Tosca – Vissi d'arte. Turandot – Signore, ascolta!; Tu, che di gel sei cinta **Rossini** Il barbiere di Siviglia – Una voce poco fa **Saint-Saëns** Samson et Dalila – Printemps qui commence; Mon coeur s'ouvre à ta voix **Spontini** La vestale – O Nume, tutelar degli infelici **Verdi** Otello – Ave Maria. Rigoletto – Gualtier Maldè; Caro nome. La traviata – Ah, fors'è lui; Addio del passato. Il trovatore – D'amor sull'ali rosee
Maria Callas *sop* with **various artists**
EMI Classics ② 557062-2 (148' · ADD)   Ⓕ**OO**

The single disc here would seem to come with the subtitle 'Callas sings film', as half the items have been chosen to link with film soundtracks. It may be interesting to learn that 'Vissi d'arte' was used in a film called *Copycat* or that the Habanera from *Carmen* now has three film credits to its name, but that's unlikely to sway the confirmed opera-lover. The more important factors will be the generous length of the CD at

74 minutes and its full-price tag, which is optimistic for what's in effect a sampler designed to encourage purchasers to investigate Callas's recordings further.

There's nothing cut-price about the performances. The 17 tracks on this disc are taken from recordings that made operatic history in the second half of the 20th century. It's particularly heartening to find items from the 1954 Puccini recital disc that Callas made with Serafin, where the singing is perfectly schooled in every detail. The two extracts from the live performance of *La traviata* in Lisbon are welcome for showing that Callas was as impressive live as on disc, though it's a shame that 'Ah, fors' è lui' is shorn of both its recitative and cabaletta.

Purchasers of the two-disc compilation get all these tracks and about the same number again. With Callas this also means double the range of experience, which would not be the case with every singer: the smouldering sexuality of Dalila's 'Printemps qui commence' is unlike anything on the single disc and so is the virginal purity of Gilda's 'Caro nome' from *Rigoletto*. Hearing early and late recordings mixed up sometimes means a jolt in the quality of voice we hear, as when the impeccable young Callas of Dinorah's 'Ombra leggiera' gives way to the unsteady Waltz song from Gounod's *Roméo et Juliette*. But whatever Callas sang, there were moments that she brought to life unlike anybody else. We may have technically less fallible singers today, but we do not have personalities like hers, and that's ultimately to the music's loss. To judge from the high percentage of French operas represented here and the Paris-centric notes, the set was planned primarily for French buyers. Any compilation of Callas, however, will appeal to everybody.

Joseph Calleja   *tenor*

Tenor Arias
Cilea Adriana Lecouvreur – La dolcissima effigie. L'Arlesiana – E la solita storia (Lamento) **Donizetti** L'elisir d'amore – Quanto è bella. Lucia di Lammermoor[a] – Tombe degli avi miei… Fra poco a me ricovero; Oh meschina; Tu che a Dio spiegasti l'ali **Puccini** Madama Butterfly – Addio fiorito asil **Verdi** Macbeth – O figli, o figli miei!… Ah, la paterna mano. Rigoletto – Questa o quella; Ella mi fu rapita… Parmi veder le lagrime; Duca, duca!; Possente amor mi chiama; La donna è mobile. La traviata[b] – Lunge da lei… De' miei bollenti spiriti; O mio rimorso
Joseph Calleja *ten* with [b]**Lydia Easley** *mez* [a]**Giovanni Battista Parodi** *bar* **Giuseppe Verdi Chorus and Symphony Orchestra, Milan / Riccardo Chailly**
Decca 475 250-2DH (53' · DDD) Texts and translations included   Ⓕ**OO**

You wait for years for a good new tenor and then two arrive at once. Just after Rolando Villazón burst on to the scene with his first recital disc for Virgin Classics, Joseph Calleja is planting his flag on the same artistic territory. All but two of the operas Calleja sings from are also chosen by Villazón, so the opera world will be buzzing with comparisons.

How different these two young tenors turn out to be. At the age of 26, Calleja sounds slighter of voice, with a technique that doesn't like being pushed to extremes – some of the soft singing in the aria from *L'arlesiana* is worryingly shallow of tone and the high D that ends the *Rigoletto* scene was not a good idea. His very fast *vibrato* may disturb those who are unfamiliar with tenors of a bygone era, such as De Lucia or Bonci.

This is where the comparisons get interesting. Calleja is said to have an interest in the great tenors of the past and that must be what inspires the *bel canto* elegance of his singing. In *La traviata* Villazón is firm, musical, decisive, but Calleja goes further, inflecting the music with light and shade, catching the joy of the recitative, the intimacy at 'Qui presso a lei', the tenderness of the *pianissimi*.

The hand of Riccardo Chailly is evident everywhere, from the first-rate playing to the detail he demands from Calleja, lifting the performances to a higher level of artistry.

Emma Calvé   *soprano*

The Complete 1902 G&T, 1920 Pathé   ⊞
and 'Mapleson Cylinder' Recordings

Opera arias – Amadis de Gaulle, Carmen, Cavalleria rusticana, Les contes d'Hoffmann, Le domino noir, Faust, Galathée, Hamlet, Manon, Mignon, Mireille, Norma, Le nozze di Figaro, Le pardon de Ploëmel, La perle du Brésil, La périchole, Philémon et Baucis, Pré aux clercs, Roméo et Juliette, Sapho and La vivandière; songs by **Beethoven, Bland, De Lara, Foster, Gounod, Hahn, Key, Massenet, Thomas** and **Traditional**
Emma Calvé, Cécille Merguillier *sops* with various artists
Marston mono ② 52013-2 (139' · ADD) Recorded 1902-20   Ⓕ

In the alphabetical index of great singers, Calvé follows Callas, and the sequence is suggestive. Both were actress-singers who brought revelations of opera-as-theatre to the audiences of their time; both acted with the voice (as contemporary accounts of Calvé tell and as we know to be so with Callas); and both were strong personalities among the most famous women in the world. One sad and striking difference is that Callas's recordings testify amply to this, while Calvé's are inadequate in repertoire as well as technical conditions to do her justice. Yet much is caught, right from those extraordinary cylinders made at performances in the Metropolitan in 1902 where, among all that's lost, her highnotes can be heard ringing out well into the house above the orchestra, with a tone sufficiently distinctive for us to associate it with the studio recordings made later that same year. They in turn are reinforced by the amazingly vivid series made for Pathé in 1920, by which year the singer was in her early 60s. The quality

of copies used and results obtained is fine. There's a second singer here and her presence adds greatly to its attractions. Cécile Merguillier recorded for Pathé and Edison in 1904 and 1905 when virtually in retirement though only in her early 40s, and still singing with fresh voice, assured technique and captivating style. A light soprano, she was singing Philine in *Mignon* in 1887, the night the old Opéra-Comique burnt down. Her solos from *Mireille* and *Philémon et Baucis* are especially delightful, and as far as can be ascertained, this is the first time a full sequence of her records has been collected on disc.

Enrico Caruso   *tenor*

Complete Recordings, Volume 5, 1908-1910   ⊞
Franchetti Germania – Studenti udite; Non, non chiuder gli occhi vaghi **Geehl** For you alone **Gounod** Faust – O merveille!ª; Seigneur Dieu, que vois-je!ᵇ; Eh! quoi! toujours seule?ᵇ; Il se fait tard!ᶜ; O nuit d'amourᶜ; Mon coeur est pénétré d'épouvante!ᶜ; Attends! Voici la rueᶜ; Que voulez-vous, messieurs?ᵈ; Alerte! alerte!ᵉ **Leoncavallo** Pagliacci – No, Pagliaccio non son **Mascagni** Cavalleria rusticanaᵍ – O Lola ch'ai di latti fior di spino **Ponchielli** La Gioconda – Cielo e mar! **Puccini** Madama Butterfly – Amore o grillo; Non ve l'avevo detto?ᶠ **Tosti** Addio **Verdi** Il trovatore – Mal reggendoʰ; Se m'ami ancorʰ. Aida – Già i sacerdotiʰ; Misero appien mi festiʰ
ᵇᶜᵉ**Geraldine Farrar** *sop* ᵇ**Gabrielle Gilibert** *mez* ʰ**Louise Homer** *contr* **Enrico Caruso** *ten* ᵈᶠ**Antonio Scotti** *bar* ᵃᵇᵈᵉ**Marcel Journet** *bass* ᵍ**Francis Lapitino** *hp* **Victor Orchestra**
Naxos Historical 8 110720 (79' · AAD) Recorded 1910   Ⓢ

'O merveille!' as Caruso sings in the first phrase of all. And what a miracle it is, after all. To take that opening phrase for a start: so gentle, beautifully rounded and expressive (the consonants made to work, the *portamento* like a sigh of wonder). And then in the quartet how well he shows himself as an artist mindful of others in ensemble. How shapely his phrases in the Prison scene, how incisive his tones in the Duel trio! Also a major pleasure is to hear again his colleagues Farrar and Journet, both of them singing with a distinction worthy of their great partner. The 1910 sessions (none of them date back to 1908, notwithstanding the album title) also included the solo from *Otello*, deeply felt as though he had it already worked into the system. Lovely also to hear the 'Cielo e mar' and the *Germania* solos still preserving so much of his younger, less weighty and heroic self. The sound generally is a degree fuller and smoother than on the rival Pearl set. Another advantage is that the excerpts are separately tracked.

Caruso in Opera, Volume 2   ⊞
Arias – L'Africaine, Andrea Chenier, La bohème (Leoncavallo and Puccini), Carmen, Cavalleria rusticana, Don Pasquale, Eugene Onegin, La favorita, Les Huguenots, Macbeth, Martha, Nero, La reine de

Saba, Rigoletto, Tosca & Il trovatore
Enrico Caruso ten with various artists
Nimbus Prima Voce mono NI7866 (79' · ADD)
Recorded 1905-20 ⑤

The 1906 recording of 'M'apparì' from *Martha* comes first, and it introduces an aspect of Caruso's singing that rarely finds a place in the critical commentaries: his subtlety. Partly, it's rhythmic. The move-on and pull-back seems such an instinctive process that we hardly notice it (though no doubt a modern conductor would – and check it immediately). It makes all the difference to the emotional life of the piece, the feeling of involvement and spontaneous development. Then there's the phrasing, marvellously achieved at the melody's reprise. The play of louder and softer tones, too, has every delicacy of fine graduation; and just as masterly is the more technical covering and (rare) opening of notes at the *passaggio*. An edition of the score which brought out all these features of Caruso's singing would be a densely annotated document. It would, even so, be a simplification, for accompanying all this is the dramatic and musical feeling, which defies analysis – and, of course, the voice. That voice! You may feel you know all these records and hardly need to play them, yet there's scarcely an occasion when the beauty of it doesn't thrill with a sensation both old and new (the first 'Ah!' is one of recognition, the second of fresh wonder). So it is with the items here: excepting the *Eugene Onegin* aria, which remains external, and the late *L'Africaine* recording, with its saddening evidence of deterioration. The transfers are excellent.

Tracey Chadwell   *soprano*

Tracey Chadwell's Song Book
RR Bennett A Garland for Marjory Fleming[a]
Cresswell Words for Music[a] **Farquhar** Six Songs of Women[a] **Joubert** The Turning Wheel, Op 95[a]
Lefanu I am Bread[a]. A Penny for a Song[a] **Lilburn** Three Songs[a] **Lumsdaine** A Norfolk Songbook[b]
Maconchy Sun, Moon and Stars[a]. Three Songs[a]
Whitehead Awa Herea[a]
Tracey Chadwell sop [a]Pamela Lidiard pf [b]John Turner recs
British Music Society ② BMS420/1CD (141' · ADD)
Recorded 1988-94. Texts included ⑤

Tracey Chadwell, a soprano of exceptional gifts and intelligence, died in her mid-30s early in 1996 after a long and courageous battle with leukaemia. Nicola Lefanu, who contributes an affectionate note to this anthology of recordings from the BBC archives, was at her last concert, three weeks before her death, and says that 'she looked and sounded ravishing'. She always did, and apart from its value as a memorial to a much loved and deeply missed artist and as a collection of fine songs (many of them written for her), this pair of discs could stand as a model to other singers in the expert management of a voice, in fearless vocal resource and joyful adventurous-

ness in choice of repertory. She had admirable taste: there's no music here that needs special pleading, and her advocacy of it is compelling. Most of it's unfamiliar, much of it not recorded before, so it's probably helpful to single out a few particular pleasures: Lefanu's haunting, intimate and subtle *I am Bread* easily sustaining its seven-minute duration, not least because of Chadwell's care over line and florid detail; the elegant talent of David Farquhar, making a simple but memorable thing of Sir Philip Sidney's 'My true love hath my heart and I have his'; the strong drama and toughly strong melody of Gillian Whitehead's *Awa Herea*, using texts in Maori and English, and making huge demands of the singer's technique as well as her imagination; Richard Rodney Bennett's beautiful settings of the poems of a child who died at eight years old (Chadwell's tender line in 'Sweet Isabell' is deeply moving here). She brings a wonderfully pure tone and limpid line to Elizabeth Maconchy's Thomas Traherne settings. Pamela Lidiard, her regular accompanist, is an ideally sensitive partner and the recordings are excellent.

Alice Coote   *mezzo-soprano*

Haydn Arianna a Naxos, HobXXVIb/2
Mahler Lieder aus 'Des Knaben Wunderhorn' – Das irdische Leben; Rheinlegendchen; Urlicht. Funf Rückert-Lieder – Liebst du um Schönheit; Ich atmet' einen linden Duft; Um Mitternacht; Ich bin der Welt abhanden gekommen **Schumann** Frauenliebe und leben, Op 42
Alice Coote mez **Julius Drake** pf
EMI Debut 585559-2 (75' · DDD) ⑧**OO**

Alice Coote justifies her fast-growing reputation in this profoundly satisfying recital in which two groups of Mahler frame items by Haydn and Schumann. Everywhere she shows her attractively warm timbre, innate musicianship and interpretative intelligence. Her rich tones ring out with youthful sap in them. Hers is an individual voice, both literally and metaphorically.

To Haydn's *Arianna* cantata she brings a considerable feeling for Italian and for projecting the deserted heroine's thoughts in recitative and aria alike. Though less dramatic, she isn't at all put in the shade by comparisons with Janet Baker or Cecilia Bartoli in the same music; she achieves a great deal in a more restrained manner, saving histrionic immediacy for Ariadne's most tormented outburst in the second half of the work.

In the Schumann, her intimate tone and accomplishment of the protagonist's ingenuous feelings is always apt, and care is taken over details of verbal acuity and dynamic shading. Tempos are just a shade on the deliberate side. Sung in idiomatic German, it's already a lovely interpretation, one to which pianist Julius Drake contributes much. Her Mahler readings are up there with the best. There's charm and a smile in the voice for the lighter songs, deep eloquence for 'Ich bin der Welt', earth-goddess tones for 'Urlicht' and outgoing affirmation for 'Um Mitternacht'. No marks at all for EMI's exclusion of texts and translations, really essential here.

Régine Crespin   *soprano*

Berlioz Les nuits d'été **Ravel** Shéhérazade[a] **Debussy** Trois chansons de Bilitis[b] **Poulenc** Banalités[b] – Chansons d'Orkenise; Hôtel. La courte paille[b] – Le carafon; La reine de coeur. Chansons villageoises[b] – Les gars qui vont à la fête. Deux poèmes de Louis Aragon[b]
Régine Crespin *sop* [b]**John Wustman** *pf* [a]**Suisse Romande Orchestra / Ernest Ansermet**
Decca Legends 460 973-2DM (68' · ADD) Recorded 1963-7. Texts and translations included   Ⓕ

Some recordings withstand the test of time and become acknowledged classics. This is one of them. Régine Crespin's voluptuous tone, her naturally accented French and her feeling for the inner meaning of the songs in the Berlioz and Ravel cycles are everywhere evident. Better than most single interpreters of the Berlioz, she manages to fulfil the demands of the very different songs, always alive to verbal nuances. In the Ravel, she's gorgeously sensuous, not to say sensual, with the right timbre for Ravel's enigmatic writing. The Debussy and Poulenc songs on this disc enhance its worth. Crespin offers an extremely evocative, perfumed account of the Debussy pieces and is ideally suited to her choice of Poulenc, of which her interpretation of 'Hôtel' is a classic. Ansermet and his orchestra, though not quite note-perfect, are right in timbre and colour for these rewarding cycles. The sound is reasonable given the age of the recording.

David Daniels   *countertenor*

Sento amor
Gluck Telemaco – Se parentro alla nera foresta. Orfeo ed Euridice – Che puro ciel!; Ahimè! Dove trascorsi? … Che farò senza Euridice? **Handel** Tolomeo – Inumano fratel … Stille amare. Partenope – Rosmira, oh! Dio! … Sento amor; ch'io parta?; Furibondo spira il vento **Mozart** Ascanio in Alba – Ah di sì nobil alma. Mitridate, re di Ponto – Venga pur, minacci; Vadasi … oh ciel …Già dagli occhi. Ombra felice! … Io ti lascio, K255
David Daniels *counterten* **Orchestra of the Age of Enlightenment / Harry Bicket**
Virgin Classics Veritas 545365-2 (62' · DDD) Texts and translations included   Ⓕ●

Curiously, the music on this disc is presented in reverse chronological order. Any slight reservations that one might feel at the beginning or in the middle are swept away when it comes to the end, for David Daniels is a magnificent interpreter of Handel and sings these arias with a freedom, a passion and a beauty of tone that he doesn't quite achieve in the later music. The

dramatic recitative 'Inumano fratel', from Tolomeo, is declaimed with great force; Daniels uses the words as well as the notes to produce a performance of due rhetorical power, and both here and in the lamenting aria that follows his tone is ringing and finely focused. In the first of the Partenope arias the detail of Handel's complex line is etched with exemplary clarity; the second, another song of despair (as the hero Arsace thinks himself abandoned by his beloved), is done softly, with much expressive intensity; and the third is a tour de force, an angry piece full of rapid semiquavers thrown off with vitality and precision. This is model Handel singing, at one with the idiom and its expressive language. Much of the continuo accompaniment is assigned, happily, to a lute. Gluck's 'Che farò' is finely sung, full and warm in tone, and with some very sweet legato, but is perhaps a shade objective and sober for a character allegedly in desperation. The wonderment of 'Che puro ciel!' is better caught by both Daniels and the orchestra. Of the Mozart pieces, the Ascanio in Alba aria is done with due vigour. In the concert aria one might wish for a rather sharper attack than a countertenor can readily provide, but something of the excitement of this piece is certainly caught. The two arias for Farnace from Mitridate that begin the disc are cleanly sung, with some happy touches of phrasing (particularly at the little ornamental figures in 'Venga pur', done with a nice hint of wit), delicate, warm tone and sensible, effective cadenzas, but the total result does seem slightly pallid for Mozart. But this is in sum a very enjoyable recital, of appealing music, done by one of the most distinguished countertenors.

A Quiet Thing
Anchieta Con amores, la mi madre **Anonymous** Shenandoah **Arlen** My shining hour **Bach/Gounod** Ave Maria **Bellini** Vaga luna, che inargenti. Malinconia, ninfa gentile. Ma rendi pur contento **Bernstein** Mass – A simple song. So pretty **Dowland** Come again, sweet love **Foster** Beautiful dreamer **Kander** A quiet thing **Martini** Plasir d'amour **Mena** A la caza **Purcell** Music for a while **Schubert** Ave Maria, D839 **Torre** Pámpano verde **Wilder** Blackberry winter
David Daniels *counterten* **Craig Ogden** *gtr*
Virgin Classics 545601-2 (64' · DDD)   Ⓕ●●●

 David Daniels has been wandering farther and farther from the Baroque fare at the heart of a countertenor's repertoire. 'Serenade', his previous song recital album, placed songs by Beethoven, Schubert, Vaughan Williams and Poulenc alongside those of Cesti, Purcell and Gluck. This new recital disc adds songs from the American musical theatre to the mix, in a programme with guitar accompaniment.

Daniels lavishes the same tightly bound *legato* and careful dynamic shading on the Broadway numbers as he does on three Bellini songs. Which isn't to suggest stylistic insensitivity. The Bellini songs are suffused with a lilting sweetness, and he imaginatively differentiates between the sensuous heat of a set of Renaissance Spanish *canciones* and the contemplative intensity of a pair of Dowland songs. Stylistic distinction is also made through differences in tone colour. In Stephen Foster's *Beautiful Dreamer* his bright sound projects the ardour of a starry-eyed youth, while in the folk song *Shenandoah* he darkens his voice to suggest an adult experiencing the pleasurable pain of nostalgic longing. Guitarist Craig Ogden is a similarly sensitive interpreter, giving the Renaissance songs and the Dowland a drier and more delicate, lute-like pluck and shaping the Bellini accompaniments with fluid elegance.

Half the songs were recorded at the Academy of Arts & Letters in New York, and half at the Arsenal de Metz in France, yet Virgin's engineers have created a fairly consistent acoustic of warm coziness. The intimate atmosphere allows Daniels' pure-toned, occasionally penetrating voice to be heard in thrillingly close proximity.

Geraldine Farrar   *soprano*

Geraldine Farrar in French Opera   Ⓗ
Opera Arias and Duets – Carmen, Les contes d'Hoffmann, Manon, Mignon, Roméo et Juliette & Thaïs
Geraldine Farrar sop with various artists
Nimbus Prima Voce mono NI7872 (79' · ADD)
Recorded 1908-21   Ⓢ

This is a lovely addition to the Prima Voce series. Farrar's Carmen appears as a model of effectiveness within the restraints of good musical and dramatic behaviour. The 'Séguedille' is sheer enchantment (irresistible promise in that breathed 'je l'aimerai' and the dreamily provocative reprise of 'Près des remparts'), while in the 'Chanson bohème' we catch the energy of her personality as well as the carrying power of her by no means robust lyric soprano. These are all cherishable records, of the kind that on some pleasant desultory evening with the gramophone one will feel a prompting to take down from the shelves. Seasoned collectors should not necessarily assume that they already have everything on the disc: for instance, there's the unpublished 'Je veux vivre' (*Roméo et Juliette*) from 1911, a performance of surprising delicacy and charm. The Prelude to Act 4 is there, too, in a recording from 1921 said to be by the orchestra of La Scala conducted by Toscanini, one of those legendary sessions which put him off the gramophone for a decade. If he had heard the results as cleanly defined as they are here, he might have thought again.

Montserrat Figueras   *soprano*

Ninna Nanna
Anonymous My little sweet darling[b]. Mareta, no'm faces plorar[bc] **Byrd** Come, pretty babe[b] **Falla** Siete canciones populares españolas – Nana[b] **Lorca** Can-

ciones españolas antiguas – Nana de Sevill[ab] **Merula** Hor ch'è tempo di dormire[b] **Milhaud** Berceuse, Op 86 No 3[a] **Mussorgsky** The Nursery – With the doll[a] **Pärt** Christmas Lullaby[b]. Kuus, kuus kallike[bc] **Reger** Maria Wiegenlied, Op 76 No 52[a] **Reichardt** Chanson d'une malheureuse mère – Dors mon enfant[b] **Traditional** Nani, nani[b]. José embala o menino[b]. Sleep, my baby[b]. Amazigh lullaby[b]. Noumi noumi yaldati[b]. La mare de Déu[b]
Montserrat Figueras sop [c]**Arianna Savall** sop [a]**Paul Badura-Skoda** pf [b]**Hespèrion XXI**
Alia Vox AV9826 (77' · DDD) Texts and translations included   Ⓕ

There have been anthologies of lullabies before, but few that have ranged as widely as this. In geographical terms the programme stretches from Portugal to Greece, Russia to Morocco; and, in the roughly chronological order in which they are presented, the songs start back in the medieval era and end with a pair of specially composed lullabies by Arvo Pärt. The accompaniments field a small army of specialists, including Jordi Savall leading the viols, Andrew Lawrence-King on harp, Paul Badura-Skoda for the piano accompaniments, and other players on flutes, guitars, bells and non-Western instruments.

The two Pärt lullabies – one in Russian, the other a duet in Estonian – are scored for a consort of viols with psaltery and are in tuneful diatonic mode, both attractive. The Catalan lullaby, *Mareta, mareta, no'm faces plorar*, performed as a duet, is a welcome discovery. Milhaud's *Dors, dors* uses harmonies judiciously and to piquant effect. Jordi Savall has produced performing versions of some of the items, including the well-known 'Nana' from Falla's *Seven Popular Spanish Songs*, which comes out three times the usual length and having gained a viola da gamba obbligato.

Renée Fleming   *soprano*

The Beautiful Voice
Dvořák Songs my mother taught me, B104 No 4 **Cano** Luna – Epilogo **Canteloube** Chants d'Auvergne – Baïlèro **Charpentier** Louise – Depuis le jour **Flotow** Martha – 'Tis the last rose of summer **Gounod** Faust – O Dieu! que de bijoux! … Ah! je ris **Korngold** Die tote Stadt – Glück, das mir verblieb **Lehár** Die lustige Witwe – Es lebt eine Vilja **Massenet** Manon – Obéissons quand leur voix appelle **Orff** Carmina Burana – In trutina **Puccini** La rondine – Chi il bel sogno di Doretta **Rachmaninov** Vocalise, Op 34 No 14 (arr Braden) **J Strauss II** Die Fledermaus – Klänge der Heimat **R Strauss** Morgen, Op 27 No 4
Renée Fleming sop **English Chamber Orchestra / Jeffrey Tate**
Decca 458 858-2DH (70' · DDD) Texts and translations included   Ⓕ Ⓞ

Sweet tooth, prepare for action. What does Lamb say in his *Chapter on Ears*? Something about piling honey upon sugar and sugar upon honey. The programme capitulates in stages. It begins well, sharpening the palate with Marguerite's Jewel Song after Louise's erotic musings. Soon we're swaying dreamily with the 'Viljalied' and then reclining in the drowsy sunshine and languid trickle of Canteloube's 'Baïlèro'. Louise, in this performance, cares for words and feelings as well as tone, Marguerite relishes her new role of 'coquette', and Manon plays lovingly with the consciousness of her own beauty. Throughout, the singing provides pleasures that are *not* simply those of 'the beautiful voice', as the title has it. Occasionally, it's true, one wishes for a more athletic style (the creamy Caballé-Te Kanawa associations spiced with a dash of Ninon Vallin perhaps). But this *is* 'the beautiful voice', no doubt about that, exercised with skill and heard in what will appeal widely as a programme of captivatingly beautiful music.

Great Opera Scenes
Britten Peter Grimes – Embroidery in childhood[b] **Dvořák** Rusalka – O silver moon **Mozart** Le nozze di Figaro – Porgi, amor; E Susanna non vien! … Dove sono **R Strauss** Daphne – Ich komme, grünende Brüder **Tchaikovsky** Eugene Onegin – Letter scene[a] **Verdi** Otello – Era più calmo? … Mia madre aveva … Piangea cantando … Ave Maria[a]
Renée Fleming sop [a]**Larissa Diadkova** mez [b]**Jonathan Summers** bar **London Symphony Orchestra / Sir Georg Solti**
Decca 455 760-2DH (72' · DDD) Texts and translations included   Ⓕ

Here's a singer who's reached complete maturity as an artist, revelling in her vocal and interpretative powers. To the warm and vibrant voice is added an imagination that places her in the first rank of today's lyric sopranos. The eclectic, ambitious programme lets us hear every aspect of her art. She's exactly the impulsive Tatyana, the girl's unreasoned ardour pouring out here in a stream of richly varied tone and feeling. Desdemona's Willow song is full of foreboding, also full of lovely singing, the repeated 'Cantiamo' voiced with precision of tone and timing, notes fined away with the utmost sensitivity. Ellen Orford's Embroidery aria is sung beautifully, the high B flat and A flat on 'Now' taken perfectly *pianissimo* after the *forte* A. These scenes benefit enormously from being placed in context, allowing Fleming to fit into the relevant situation. Diadkova is an idiomatic, responsive Filipyevna, and she makes the most of Emilia's few phrases. Summers is a wise and experienced Balstrode. All in all, Fleming lays claim here to Te Kanawa territory, and proves a worthy successor. More than Dame Kiri, she identifies with each character and moulds her voice to the woman in question. For Sir Georg this is obviously a labour of love, nowhere more so than in the postlude to *Daphne*, most sensuously done; he and the LSO provide worthy support for their superb soloist. The recording is faultless, capturing voice and orchestra in ideal balance.

I Want Magic
Barber Vanessa – He has come…Do not utter a word, Anatol **Bernstein** Candide – Glitter and be gay **Floyd** Susannah – Ain't it a pretty night; The trees on the mountains **Gershwin** Porgy and Bess – Summertime; My man's gone now **Herrmann** Wuthering Heights – I have dreamt **Menotti** The Medium – Monica's Waltz **D Moore** The Ballad of Baby Doe – The Letter Song **Previn** A Streetcar Named Desire – I want magic! **Stravinsky** The Rake's Progress – No word from Tom…I go to him
Renée Fleming sop **Metropolitan Opera Orchestra, New York / James Levine**
Decca 460 567-2DH (58' · DDD) Texts and translations included   Ⓕ**ⓄⓄⓄ**

 This survey of operas old and new reinforces the feeling that the current generation of star singers in the USA is making an effort to explore home-grown repertory. Fleming's voice is sumptuous, her lower register especially sounds so warmly resonant that it's reminiscent of Leontyne Price in her glory days. Fleming shows herself equal to every mood; only at the end of 'Glitter and be gay' is there a false moment when she rather overdoes the brittle laughter. What beautiful tunes there are here, including the waltz song from *The Medium* and 'Ain't it a pretty night' from *Susannah*. This was recorded before Fleming took part in the world première of André Previn's *A Streetcar Named Desire* in San Francisco and her programme ends with a sneak preview of that. 'I want magic!' is Blanche's philosophy of life, justifying her flights of fancy. Among the other items, Fleming makes the extract from *Wuthering Heights* sound positively Mahleresque, and Anne's great aria from *The Rake's Progress* – 'officially' an American opera, Stravinsky, Auden and Kallman at least all being resident there when it was written – suits her surprisingly well. Levine and the Met Orchestra provide idiomatic accompaniment.

Juan Diego Flórez   tenor

Una furtiva lagrima
Bellini I Capuleti e i Montecchi[bc] – O, di Capellio generosi amici; E serbato a questo acciaro; L'amo tanto e m'è si cara. I Puritani – A te, o cara[abc]. La sonnambula[a] – Vedi, o madre; Tutto è sciolto; Pasci il guardo; Ah! perche non posso odiarti **Donizetti** Don Pasquale – Povero Ernesto!; Cercherò lontana terra; Com' è gentil. Elisabetta – Ah non sogno!; Disperato amante afflitto. L'elisir d'amore – Una furtiva lagrima. Rita – Allegro io son. La fille du régiment[b] – Ah! mes amis; Pour mon âme quel destin!
Juan Diego Flórez ten [a]**Ermonela Jaho** sop [b]**Nikola Mijalovic** bar [c]**Nicola Ulivieri** bass **Giuseppe Verdi Chorus and Symphony Orchestra, Milan / Riccardo Frizza**
Decca 473 440-2DH (64' · DDD) Texts and translations included   Ⓕ**Ⓞ**

This is a well-thought-out programme showing

the continuing development in this singer's art. The opening number, a light-hearted waltz song from Donizetti's rarely heard one-act comedy *Rita* is balanced by the finale, which is the by-now celebrated solo for Tonio in *La fille du régiment* with its nine top Cs that at one time seemed to be the unique possession of Luciano Pavarotti. Such convivialities contrast with the more elegiac mood of Ernesto's 'Cercherò lontana terra' in *Don Pasquale*, and that in turn with the turbulent excerpt from *Elisabetta*. Items which call for the participation of other soloists and/or chorus are well supplied, to most lovely effect in *I puritani*.

It's altogether an attractive record, introduced with a lively and informative note by Tom Sutcliffe. A slight cause for regret is the lack of a sentence or two putting each extract briefly into dramatic context. As for Flórez, the grace and accomplishment with which he uses his clear, resonant voice are beyond praise; the next stage in his career should see a growth of imagination and a deepening of feeling.

Cimarosa Il matromonio segreto – Pria che spunti un ciel l'aurora **Donizetti** La figlia del reggimento – Eccomi finalmente... Feste? Pompe? Lucrezia Borgia – Com'è soave quest'ora...Anch'io provai le tenere smanie d'un puro amore **Gluck** Orphée et Euridice – J'ai perdu mon Euridice **Halévy** La Juive – Loin de son amie vivre sans plaisirs **Puccini** Gianni Schicchi – Avete torto!... Firenze è come un albero fiorito **Rossini** Semiramide – La speranza più soave. L'Italiana in Algeri – Languir per una bella **Verdi** Un giorno di Regno – Pietoso al lungo pianto...Deh! lasciate. Rigoletto – La donna è mobile
Juan Diego Flórez ten **Milan Giuseppe Verdi Symphony Orchestra and Chorus / Carlo Rizzi**
Decca 475 6187 (58' · DDD · T/t) Ⓕ**❍❍❍**

 In this engaging recital, the best he's recorded so far, Juan Diego Flórez goes from Gluck's *Orphée* (1774) to Puccini's *Gianni Schicchi* (1918) via some rarities.

He brings some sense of fun to the aria from Verdi's early comedy *Un giorno di Regno*, but gets down to business with the big scene for Idreno in Rossini's *Semiramide*. Most theatres, having engaged the two prima-donnas and bass needed for this opera are left without a star tenor. Flórez makes the aria sound like one of the highlights of the score. Rizzi urges the cabaletta on, and once past this, the whole programme seems to take off. The solo from *Lucrezia Borgia* (never recorded before) has one of those typical tear-soaked Donizetti melodies, with a terrific flourish at the end. Here Flórez shows off a fuller tone than we've heard from him before. The lightness and brilliance he brings to the lovely aria from *Il matrimonio segreto* as he sings of the quiet elopement 'dalla porta del giardino' is especially alluring.

SACD postscript: Recorded in the Auditorium di Milano, Milan, in 2003, this has a very persuasive, comfortable atmosphere. The image is plausibly distanced and there's a life-like

depth and character to the sound-stage. Flórez is refreshingly well integrated, modestly a part of the orchestral canvas.

Bruce Ford   *tenor*

Three Rossini Tenors
Rossini La donna del lago – Alla ragion deh rieda; Qual pena in me. Otello – No, no temer, serena; Non m'inganno, al mio rivale; Ah! vieni, nel tuo sangue ...; Ahimè fermate ... Che fiero punto è questo. Ricciardo e Zoraide – Donala a questo core. Armida – Come l'aurette placide; In quale aspetto imbelle
Nelly Miricioiu sop **Paul Austin Kelly, Bruce Ford, William Matteuzzi** tens **Geoffrey Mitchell Choir; Philharmonia Orchestra, Academy of St Martin in the Fields / David Parry**
Opera Rara ORR204 (70' · DDD) Texts and translations included   Ⓕ

'Only *three*?' Rossini might have remarked. During the years 1815-22, which this recital so thrillingly celebrates, Rossini had four, possibly five, world-class tenors at his disposal. Still, it's a good marketing ploy, with Opera Rara's three tenors turning in bravura performances in repertoire which *the* three tenors have only occasionally flirted with. It says much for Rossini's guile, and the guile of the programming, that one comes away from this recital, not bored or sated, but thrilled and satisfied. Amusingly, there's no actual trio for tenors until the last track, the astonishingly beautiful scene in *Armida* where Carlo and Ubaldo hold the adamantine shield up to Rinaldo's gaze and, in so doing, confront him with an image of his own baseness. Rossini's leading heroic tenor was Andrea Nozzari. Bruce Ford sings the Nozzari roles here, with Paul Austin Kelly and William Matteuzzi taking turn and turn about with the more purely brilliant roles (Uberto, Rodrigo, Ricciardo) Rossini wrote for the celebrated *tenore contraltino* in the Naples company, Giovanni David. All three acquit themselves superbly. To have Nelly Miricioiu on hand to sing Elena and Desdemona is an added bonus. David Parry and the Philharmonia Orchestra give performances of great dash and beauty. The recording places the orchestra rather obviously to the rear of the singers, but that's no bad thing. Slightly more distracting is the fact that the Rossini tenor is clearly a difficult creature for the microphone to decipher and absorb, particularly *en masse*. Thus, while Matteuzzi and Kelly are allowed to coo into the microphones like a pair of sucking doves, Bruce Ford is cast more in the role of the blackguard outsider, never quite as well forward, the sound never quite as 'clean'. The insert-notes are altogether excellent.

Inessa Galante   *soprano*

Verdi Galante
Verdi Aida – Ritorna vincitor; O patria mia. Un ballo in maschera – Ma dall' arido stelo divulsa; Morro, ma

prima in grazia. Don Carlo – Tu che le vanità. Falstaff – Sul fil d'un soffio etesio. La forza del destino – Le Vergine degli angeli; Pace, pace, mio Dio. Otello – Piangea cantando (Willow song); Ave Maria. Messa da Requiem – Libera me
Inessa Galante sop **Stockholm School of Economics Choir, Riga; Latvian National Symphony Orchestra / Terje Mikkelson**
Campion RRCD1349 (73' · DDD) Notes included Ⓕ

Here, in a taxing selection of extracts from Verdi's later works, Inessa Galante shows the merits of her well-formed, rich-hued *spinto* voice and uses it with the utmost feeling for style. She demonstrates this through her vibrant tone, firm, well-sustained line, long-breathed phrasing and, above all, by the way she seems to get inside the troubled minds of the characters portrayed. One other important asset in which she surpasses almost all her peers in this repertory is her ability to float the most effortless *pianissimo* high notes, as at the tricky close of 'O patria mia', the final phrase of Desdemona's Ave Maria and the climactic note of the *Andante* section in the 'Libera me' from the Requiem. This is Verdian singing of the highest class.

Cristina Gallardo-Domâs   *soprano*

Bel Sogno – Italian Arias and Scenes
Bellini I Capuleti e i Montecchi – Eccomi in lieta vesta; Oh! quante volte **Catalani** La Wally – Ebben?…Nè andrò lontana **Cilèa** Adriana Lecouvreur – Ecco…Io son l'umile ancella **Donizetti** Anna Bolena – Piangete voi?; Al dolce guidami **Puccini** Madama Butterfly – Un bel dì vedremo. La bohème – Sì, mi chiamino Mimì; Donde lieta uscì. Manon Lescaut – In quelle trine morbide. Suor Angelica – Senza mamma. Gianni Schicchi – O mio babbino caro **Verdi** La traviata – È strano!…Ah, fors'è lui…Sempre libera[a]; Teneste la promessa; Addio, del passato. Simon Boccanegra – Come in quest'ora bruna. Otello – Ave Maria
Cristina Gallardo-Domâs sop [a]**Jonas Kaufmann** ten **Munich Radio Orchestra / Maurizio Barbacini**
Teldec 8573-86440-2 (78' · DDD) Ⓕ●

Gallardo-Domâs, in a wide-ranging recital, proves that she needn't fear comparison with any of her contemporaries and little from the best of her predecessors. By dint of her unimpeachable musicality, the sheer beauty of her truly Italianate tone and her exemplary way with words, she makes every track on this generously filled recital an individual experience to treasure – and of how few singers can that be said? As Butterfly she's suitably intense and lonely, her Mimì is at once fragile and determined – phrase after phrase of both her solos seems to achieve some kind of ideal. Manon's 'In quelle trine morbide' has all the necessary attention to detail, equalling an unforgettable performance by the young Tebaldi, and 'O mio babbino caro' is just the charming, unaffected solo it ought to be. In Verdi, the singer has been rightly admired as Violetta, one of her calling-cards, in many

noted houses, and shows why by her identification with the woman's plight. There's an intensity of utterance combined with a care over phrasing and dynamic that's very special. With good orchestral support and a faithful, well-balanced recording, this CD is surely going to please even the most fastidious admirer of the soprano voice.

Amelita Galli-Curci   *soprano*

Opera Arias and Songs   Ⓗ
Arias from Il barbiere di Siviglia, Dinorah, Don Pasquale, Lakmé, Lucia di Lammermoor, Manon Lescaut (Auber), Martha, Le nozze di Figaro, I Puritani, Rigoletto, Roméo et Juliette, La sonnambula and La traviata; songs by **Alvarez**, **Benedict**, **Bishop**, **Buzzi-Peccia**, **David**, **Delibes**, **Giordani**, **Grieg**, **Massenet**, **Proch**, **Samuels**, **Seppilli**
Amelita Galli-Curci sop with various artists
Romophone mono ② 81003-2 (159' · ADD) Recorded 1916-20   Ⓕ

The editor of *Gramophone* in 1923 wrote: 'One of the most solid grounds I have for facing the coming of old age with equanimity is the reasonable hope that I shall spend it listening to as many records of *la diva* Galli-Curci's voice as there are of Caruso's'. The purity of her voice was certainly a delight; it was at that time firm and even throughout its wide compass; and her fluency in scalework, precision in *staccato*, and ability to swell and diminish on a long-held high note were exceptional. She was an artist who could phrase and nuance exquisitely and who, within the boundaries of a more or less pretty joy and sadness, could be quite poignantly expressive. In the years of her greatest fame and success, roughly the decade from 1916 to 1926, her operatic repertoire was the standard one for the 'coloratura' soprano, and it's well represented by her records. What they also have, making them treasurable beyond anything that such a summary might suggest, is a personal flavour, a caress, a way of making words sound like water purling gently on a summer's afternoon, a dreaminess that can awaken to fun and affection though she could also flatten rather sadly in pitch. The transfers on this release, which concentrates on her recordings up to 1920, are of fine quality and make for a most enjoyable disc.

Lesley Garrett   *soprano*

Soprano in Red
Chabrier L'étoile – O petite étoile; Je suis Lazuli! **Coward** Bitter Sweet – If love were all **Heuberger** Der Opernball – Im chambre séparée **Lehár** Zigeunerliebe – Hör' ich Cymbalklänge. Friederike – Warum hast du mich wachgeküsst? Die lustige Witwe – Es lebt eine Vilja, ein Waldmägdelein[a] **Novello** Perchance to dream – We'll gather lilacs. The Dancing Years – Waltz of my heart **Offenbach** La belle Hélène – On me nomme Hélène la Blonde.

Orphée aux enfers – J'ai vu le Dieu Bacchus[a]; Ce bal est original[a] **Romberg** The New Moon – Softly, as in a morning sunrise; Lover, come back to me **J Strauss II** (arr Benatzky) Casanova – Nuns' Chorus and Laura's Song[a] **Sullivan** The Contrabandista – Only the night wind sighs alone
Lesley Garrett sop [a]**Crouch End Festival Chorus; Royal Philharmonic Concert Orchestra / James Holmes**
Silva Screen Classics SILKTVCD1 (60' · DDD) All items sung in English.   Ⓕ

Lesley Garrett has won herself a huge following of those who respond to her straightforward, unaffected vocalising, to the clarity and bright-ness of her voice and its ringing top notes. What also appeals about Garrett's recordings is the attention paid to less familiar material and the quest for authenticity of period style. Both facets are fully evident in this collection. The eager entreaties of Laura's Song from *Casanova*, the bright expressiveness of 'If love were all' and the sheer joyfulness of 'Waltz of my heart' (com-plete with piano contribution) are highlights. Especially gratifying, though, are the rarities. In the pedlar Lazuli's two numbers from Chab-rier's *L'étoile*, Garrett's clarity of diction shows off Jeremy Sams's lyrics to fine effect and she should certainly win over the Sullivan faction with the first ever recording of an engaging little number from the pre-Gilbert operetta *The Contrabandista*. In Novello's 'We'll gather lilacs' double tracking permits Garrett to duet with herself. Ensemble and momentum go curiously adrift at the choral entries in Offenbach's 'Hymn to Bacchus', but this detracts only a little from another delightful Garrett collection.

Angela Gheorghiu   *soprano*

Casta Diva
Bellini Norma – Casta Diva[a]; Ah! bello, a me ritorna[a]. I puritani – Qui la voce sua soave… Ah! rendetemi la speme; Vien, diletto. La sonnambula – Ah! non cre-dea mirarti **Donizetti** Anna Bolena – Piangete voi?[a]… Al dolce guidami castel natio. Lucia di Lammermoor – Regnava nel silenzio; Quando rapito in estasi **Rossini** Guglielmo Tell – S'allontanano alfine!…Selva opaca. Il barbiere di Siviglia – Una voce poco fa…Io sono docile. L'assedio di Corinto – L'ora fatal s'ap-pressa…Giusto ciel! in tal periglio[a]
Angela Gheorghiu sop [a]**Chorus of the Royal Opera, Covent Garden; London Symphony Orchestra / Evelino Pidò**
EMI 557163-2 (61' · DDD) Texts and translations included   ⒻOO

Once again we have to count our blessings. As with the recent recital by Karita Mattila (Erato – reviewed further on), we're a lucky generation, in this respect at least, that here we have sopra-nos with such purity of tone, evenness of pro-duction and scrupulous musicianship; and with Gheorghiu's recital it's rare that ghost-voices of singers from the past enter the listening mind clamouring to be brought out for comparison. If

they do so at all it's in the solos from *Il barbiere di Siviglia* and *Lucia di Lammermoor*. Gheorghiu, one could say, isn't a Rosina: in the famous cavatina she catches the determination of those 'lo giurai's and 'vincerò's but not the fun-loving trickster behind them. As Lucia, more surpris-ingly, she simply fails to make it clear that this is a ghost story with blood in it.

Otherwise we're in the land of heart's desire. In 'Casta diva' and the other Bellini solos, Gheorghiu finds (better than most) the right balance between purity of line and the inflec-tions needful for expression. In the aria from *I puritani* the phrases are finely bound yet mov-ingly 'inner'; and then, with 'Vien, diletto', comes a marvellously vivid change, the face lighting up with eagerness located in the bright vowels and pointed rhythms. The scales, trills and ornaments are also a delight, whether as sheer technical accomplishment or as heighten-ers of emotion. Perhaps listeners should be warned that, although Lucia's cabaletta sports a high D and Elvira's an E flat, these aren't (as they would be with Sutherland) crowning events: the 'event', so to speak, is the whole per-formance.

Angela Gheorghiu & Roberto Alagna

Opera Arias and Duets
Berlioz Les troyens – Nuit d'ivresse![ab] **Bernstein** West Side Story – Only You … Tonight, it all began tonight[ab] **G Charpentier** Louise – Depuis le jour[a] **Donizetti** Anna Bolena – Al dolce guidami[a]. Don Pasquale – Tornami a dir[ab] **Gounod** Faust – Il se fait tard! … O nuit d'amour[ab] **Mascagni** L'amico Fritz – Suzel, buon di … Tutto tace[ab] **Massenet** Manon – Je suis seul! … Ah! fuyez, douce image[b]; Toi! Vous! … N'est-ce plus ma main[ab] **Offenbach** La belle Hélène – Au mont Ida[b] **Puccini** La bohème – O soave fanciulla[ab]
[a]**Angela Gheorghiu** sop [b]**Roberto Alagna** ten **Orchestra of the Royal Opera House, Covent Garden / Richard Armstrong**
EMI 556117-2 (61' · DDD) Texts and translations included   ⒻO

Ideally matched, the two young lyric artists of our day who have most taken the hearts and hopes of public and critics sing here in a pro-gramme that's both aptly and imaginatively selected. It ranges quite widely over the French and Italian repertoires, always combining instant satisfaction with a wish for more. The Cherry duet from *L'amico Fritz* comes first, and the voices have just the right freshness for it, the soprano warm-toned, the tenor elegant and cleanly defined; the style too is charming, natu-ral and mutually responsive. Then with the excerpts from *Manon* they aren't only well suited but show already a real dramatic impulse in their duet, again with its developments so well felt and understood. The Garden scene works unusual magic. The solos provide welcome opportunities: Gheorghiu, delightful in 'Depuis le jour', is even more so in the aria from *Anna*

Bolena, exquisitely phrased and shaded as though it were the slow movement of a sonata by Mozart. 'Ah! fuyez, douce image' opens with the softness associated from long ago with Smirnov and Muratore; Alagna never forgets what he's singing about, is thrilling on his high B flats and finely controlled in the concluding *diminuendo*. His Mount Ida song from *La belle Hélène* has panache and humour, a deliciously promising *pianissimo* start to the last verse and a good robust C thrown in before he finishes. And then, inspiration on somebody's part, there's *West Side Story*. 'Tonight' has never been better sung, and it also brings us to the other element in this recital – the playing of the Covent Garden orchestra under Richard Armstrong. In this, they make us realise afresh how distinctively flavoured (in harmony and orchestration) is Bernstein's marvellous score: the duet is intensely moving, yet the rhythm is kept strong and there's no sugar-coating or melting into slush. Repeatedly, in Gounod and Bernstein as in Mascagni and Puccini, one reacts with an 'I'd never noticed that before' or simply a smile or sigh of pleasure in the sound.

Beniamino Gigli   *tenor*

The Complete HMV Recordings, 1918-32   🅷

Opera arias and duets – L'amico Fritz, La bohème, Cavalleria rusticana, Faust, La favorita, Fedora, La Gioconda, Iris, Lodoletta, Mefistofele, Les pêcheurs de perles, Stabat mater (Rossini), Tosca; songs by **Cannio**, de Curtis, **Niedermeyer**, **Schubert**, **Sullivan** and **Tosti**

Beniamino Gigli *ten* with various artists
Romophone mono ② 82011-2 (139' · ADD) Recorded 1918-19 and 1931-2   Ⓜ️Ⓞ

The first of these two CDs enshrines the golden youth of Gigli, and therefore some of the most beautiful tenor sounds ever committed to disc. Listen to the three extracts from *La Gioconda* – the Act 1 encounter with Barnaba, 'Cielo e mar' and the love duet with Laura made at the first sessions in Milan in 1918 – and imagine yourself with the audiences when the singer had one of his earliest successes as Enzo; also enjoy the honeyed, mellifluous timbre, the homogeneous tone, the fluid delivery, the enthusiastic attack that must have enthralled Gigli's contemporaries. The ease and naturalness of the sound still have the power to amaze the ear, as they do in such a dreamy, sweet account of 'Apri la tua finestra' from Mascagni's *Iris*. Then in 'Spirto gentil' (*La favorita*), the subtle, suave way Gigli moves into the reprise has surely never been equalled, let alone surpassed. Pieces that he repeated later – the arias of Cavaradossi and *Faust*, the Act 1 duet from *La bohème*, for instance – are here done with fewer of the maddening if endearing traits that informed the later recordings. Faust was not yet in his repertory, but the aria and even more the Garden Duet with the estimable Maria Zamboni are filled with the kind of immediate, open-hearted pas-

sion that's the hallmark of all Gigli's records. A pity he has such an acid-toned partner in the Cherry Duet from *L'amico Fritz* because he's perfectly suited by the role of the shy Korbus.

Six tracks into the second disc we're carried forward 12 years to 1931, when Gigli returned to HMV from his spell with Victor. This is the fully fledged Gigli with which collectors will be most familiar, the voice more mature, the style a deal coarsened. Yet who can resist Tosti's *Addio* or Sullivan's *The Lost Chord* (conducted by Barbirolli), both sung in delightfully accented English, or even his outrageously self-indulgent account of the Dream from *Manon*, in Italian? The 1931 coupling of the arias from *Faust* and *La bohème* must have been Gigli's best-selling operatic 78s: both pieces are sung in score pitch, the tenor's high C now firmly in place. Neither reading is a model of style, but both are emotionally overwhelming, the boyish charm, use of *portamento* and verbal detailing of his Rodolfo especially winning. In a famous account of the *Cavalleria* duet, he's partnered by an impassioned Giannini: both artists exhibit an authentic *spinto* style now severely in jeopardy. At the end come a wonderfully forthright account of 'Cujus animam' from Rossini's *Stabat mater* (though he abjures the high D flat) and two soulful Neapolitan songs by de Curtis, perfect Gigli territory. The transfers of the electrics are faultless; the sound of the acoustics, poor recordings in themselves, is less amenable.

Alma Gluck   *soprano*

Anonymous (words by Ben Jonson) Have you seen but a white lily grow? **Bellini** La sonnambula – Ah! non credea mirarti **Bishop** Lo, here the gentle lark **Bizet** Carmen – Je dis que rien ne m'épouvante **Charpentier** Louise – Depuis le jour **Godard** Jocelyn – Oh! ne t'éveille pas encore **Hahn** Chansons grises – L'heure exquise **Handel** Atalanta – Care selve, ombre beate. Theodora – Angels, ever bright and fair **Humperdinck** Hänsel und Gretel – Suse, liebe, Suse **Loewe** War schöner als der schönste Tag **Massenet** Elégie **Puccini** La bohème – Quando m'en vo' soletta; Donde lieta uscì **Rameau** Hippolyte et Aricie – Rossignols amoureux **Rimsky-Korsakov** Snow Maiden – Going berrying; Lel's Third Song. Sadko – Song of the Indian Guest. The Tsar's Bride – Haste thee, mother mine **Saint-Saëns** Le timbre d'argent – Le bonheur est chose légère **Smetana** The Kiss – Cradle song **Tosti** La serenata
Alma Gluck *sop* with various artists
Nimbus Prima Voce NI7904 (77' · ADD) Recorded 1911-17   Ⓢ

In 1915 WJ Henderson called Gluck 'the most beautiful lyric soprano before the public'. Her record of Carry me back to old Virginy was the first celebrity disc in America to sell over a million copies. Yet her career lasted little beyond a decade; less, if one counts time out for re-training. It was a delicate voice and, as she soon found, any sort of operatic hurly-burly endangered it. There still must have been something wrong in its training or usage. Her records remain a precious memento, and the best of her recorded art can be very happily sampled here. The Nimbus transfer process suits Gluck well. Otherwise it might be a foregone conclusion that with Marston's two-CD volume still available, readers would be referred back to the more comprehensive selection. As it is, Nimbus has three items not included by Marston, all good, and one of them, the famous solo from Jocelyn, surely quintessential. Gluck had the most lovely soft tones, perhaps of all, in the upper part of the voice; and in this lullaby ('Angels guard thee' in the English version) the precise take and pure quality of the upper notes are heavenly. In Musetta's song from La bohème (also absent from Marston) she gives a lesson to all screaming Musettas, singing (as Nigel Douglas observes in his booklet-note) con molta grazia ed eleganza as Puccini recommended. Lo, here the gentle lark, the third bonus item, matters less and isn't one of the showier versions abounding in alts; resourcefully sung, even so. Included are most of the gems – the Rameau, Loewe's canzonetta, Hahn's L'heure exquise and Have you seen but a white lily grow? for instance.

Susan Graham   *mezzo-soprano*

French Operetta Arias
Hahn Brummell – Air de la Lettre. Ciboulette – C'est pas Paris, c'est sa banlieue. Mozart – Etre adoré. O mon bel inconnu! – O mon bel inconnu; C'est très vilain d'être infidèle **Honegger** Les aventures du roi Pausole, H76 – Si vous saviez **Messager** L'amour masqué – J'ai deux amants; Mon rêve. Coups de roulis – Les hommes sont biens tous les mêmes. Fortunio – Je ne vois rien. Passionément – L'amour est un oiseau rebelle. La petite fonctionnaire – Je regrette mon Pressigny. Les p'tites Michu – Vois-tu, je m'en veux. Les dragons de l'impératrice – Amour, amour, quel est donc ton pouvoir **Simons** Toi c'est moi – C'est ça la vie; Vagabonde **Yvain** Yes – Yes
Susan Graham *mez* **City of Birmingham Symphony Orchestra / Yves Abel**
Erato 0927-42106-2 (59' · DDD) Notes, texts and translations included   Ⓕ**OO**

This is a scrumptious album of bonbons – mostly from the latter end of the golden age of French operetta – to which Susan Graham brings her lovely soprano-ish mezzo very much à la Parisienne. She opens and closes the programme with two numbers from Moïse Simons' *Toi c'est moi*. The first, 'C'est ça la vie, c'est ça l'amour', is a flamboyant tribute to Bizet's *Carmen*, full of Latin-American rhythmic bravado. Graham sings it with a wicked I-can-be-Carmen-too twinkle in her sly, sexy delivery without sounding too knowing. She's in her element, too, with the closing 'Vagabonde', a vivacious waltz-song.

In between Graham takes us on a delectable Paris-by-night tour of latish French operetta, mostly dating from the era when Sacha Guitry and his wife Yvonne Printemps were the romantic leads. Of the 17 numbers she selects, only two come from works that have remained in the consciousness of today's music-lovers.

This is the musical equivalent of an expensive box of scrummy chocolates. The perfect treat for the music lover.

Il tenero momento
Gluck Paride ed Elena – O del mio dolce ardor. Iphigénie en Tauride – O toi qui prolongeas mes jours; O malheureuse Iphigénie!; Non, cet affreux devoir … Je t'implore et je tremble. Orphée et Eurydice – Qu'entends-je? Qu'a-t-il dit?; J'ai perdu mon Eurydice **Mozart** Le nozze di Figaro – Non so più cosa son; Voi che sapete. La clemenza di Tito – Parto, parto, ma tu, ben mio[a]; Deh per questo istante. Idomeneo – Non ho colpa, e mi codanni. Lucio Silla – Dunque sperar poss'io … Il tenero momento
Susan Graham *mez* [a]**Antony Pay** *bscl* **Orchestra of the Age of Enlightenment / Harry Bicket**
Erato 8573-85768-2 (63' · DDD)   Ⓕ**OO**

This is an unusually satisfying operatic recital by a modern singer. Graham, now at the apex of her career, displays her skills as singer and interpreter in a sensibly planned and executed programme, comprised of arias from roles she's sung on stage. In consequence she sounds entirely inside all her music and dispenses it with a confidence and truly amazing attack, but the refulgent, vibrant voice and faultless technique – except perhaps in a virtuoso cadenza at the end of Orfeo's Act 2 showpiece (from the Viardot 1869 edition of Gluck's work) – are wholly at the service of the music, the mezzo showing a sensitive empathy with the emotions of every character she portrays. Vulnerable Iphigénie, insecure Sesto, palpitating Cherubino, forlorn Orfeo (in 'J'ai perdu'), lovelorn Paris and Cecilio (*Lucio Silla*) all come before us in lifelike form by virtue of Graham's exemplary use of words, themselves enhanced by firm consonants. Beyond that there's her understanding of the Baroque verities and her idiomatic command of Italian and French.

If you need to be convinced to buy this disc – and you can sample before buying – then listen to Sesto's two arias. They are templates of the rest in the ideal moulding of phrase, evenness of tone throughout a wide tessitura and exemplary coloratura allied to an identification with the youth's plight. The moment to savour most is the reprise, in the second piece, of the words 'Deh, per questo istante solo' where Graham employs a quite magical *mezza voce*.

To complete one's pleasure in a treasurable CD, there are the wholly stylish playing of the alert orchestra under the command of Harry Bicket, who's a specialist in this kind of music, and a perfect balance in the recording between voice and instruments.

Susan Graham at Carnegie Hall

Berg Seven Early Songs **Brahms** Zigeunerlieder, Op 103 – No 1, He, Zigeuner, greife; No 2, Hochgetürmte Rimaflut; No 3, Wisst ihr, wann mein Kindchen; No 4, Lieber Gott, du weisst; No 5, Brauner Bursche führt zum Tanze; No 6, Röslein dreie in der Reihe; No 7, Kommt dir manchmal; No 11, Rote Abendwolken ziehn **Debussy** Proses lyriques. Fantoches, L21 **Hahn** A Chloris **Mahler** Rückert-Lieder – No 2, Liebst du um Schönheit **Messager** L'amour masqué – J'ai deux amants. Les P'tites Michu – Vois-tu, je m'en veux **B Moore** Sexy Lady **Poulenc** Quatre poèmes de Guillaume Apollinaire **Simons** C'est ça la vie, c'est ça l'amour
Susan Graham mez **Malcolm Martineau** pf
Warner Classics 2564 60293-2 (75' · DDD)
Texts and translations included ⓕOO

Through her recital discs Susan Graham has been revealing different facets of her character. Now we get a rounded portrait: this live recording of 14 April 2003 ranges from the high seriousness of German Lieder to a final encore where she lets her hair down.

The recital opens with the Brahms *Zigeunerlieder*, as Leontyne Price did for her Carnegie Hall recital début. Her voice catches a restless fast vibrato in the early part of the programme, but that's receding by the time she reaches Berg's *Seven Early Songs*. Malcolm Martineau's playing is a boon here, setting speeds at which the sense of the music flows in paragraphs. The singing is light and clean, quick with intelligence. Anne Sofie von Otter's DG disc is the closest mezzo competition in the catalogue, delving deeper into the late-Romantic, hot-house atmosphere, but at the price of heavy-handed accompaniments from Bengt Forsberg.

As might be expected, the French side of the recital is a delight. Graham's mezzo has the light touch for the French repertoire, and Martineau is in his element, lighting on the subtlest of colours. They allow themselves some space in Debussy's *Proses lyriques*, but don't abuse it. In 'Dè greve' the skittish, girly playfulness of the waves and the darkness of the gathering storm are held in a judicious balance. The mood of the Poulenc group is nicely urbane. The two Messager solos revisit familiar ground with happy results. After all this the audience demanded four encores. The Hahn and Debussy are delicious, the Mahler is super-sensitive, and Ben Moore's wicked *Sexy Lady*, a high-camp cabaret number about mezzos in trouser roles, brings the house down.

Elisabeth Grümmer   *soprano*

Great Singers of the Century

Mendelssohn Lieder, Op 71 – No 2, Frühlingslied; No 6, Nachtlied. Auf Flügeln des Gesanges, Op 34 No 2. Scheidend, Op 9 No 6. Neue Liebe, Op 19a No 4 **Schoeck** Lieder, Op 10 – Erinnerung; Die Einsame. Lieder, Op 20 – Auf meines Kindes Tod; Nachruf. Ergebung, Op 30 No 6. Motto, Op 51 No 2. Das holde Bescheiden, Op 62 – Auf der Teck; Im

Park; Nachts **Schumann** Frauenliebe und -leben, Op 42 **Wolf** Spanisches Liederbuch – In dem Schatten meiner Locken; Mögen alle bösen Zungen; Bedeckt mich mit Blumen; Sie blasen zum Abmarsch
Elisabeth Grümmer sop **Aribert Reimann** pf
Orfeo C506001B (68' · ADD) Recorded 1963, 1966, 1968   ⓕOO

Elisabeth Grümmer was disgracefully under-recorded, in particular in relation to her recital repertory. The central interpretation here, the Schumann cycle, discloses all this sincere, warm soprano's many virtues, above all her ability to sing the music in exemplary style with unaffected, straightforward feeling, entirely free from gloss and mannerisms and, where appropriate, a charming glint in her voice. In that sense she's a throwback to some of her great pre-war predecessors such as Lehmann and Lemnitz, but she's a better technician than either of those revered artists. She's the deferential, happy, wondering girl of the first songs to the life, then the eager bride and grateful mother, finally the desolate widow. Word and note are in perfect alliance; everything is clear, filled with meaning yet nothing is exaggerated or portentous, and the tone itself is amazingly fresh for a singer in her mid-50s.

Mendelssohn's *Auf Flügeln des Gesanges* and *Neue Liebe* are sung with the same fresh spontaneity. So are some interesting settings of Eichendorff and Mörike by Schoeck. The four masterpieces from Wolf's *Spanish Songbook* are still better: *Bedeckt mich mit Blumen* has just the right erotic languour, *In dem Schatten meiner Locken* just the right sense of fun without any of the archness that can ruin its irresistibly loving message. Reimann, here and throughout, is a finely imaginative partner and the recording could not be bettered. This is a CD for all connoisseurs of Lieder singing at its very best.

Nathan Gunn   *baritone*

American Anthem – from Ragtime to Art Song

Barber Songs, Op 13 – No 3, Sure on this shining night; No 4, Nocturne **Bolcom** Cabaret Songs – Over the piano; Fur (Murray the Furrier); Song of Black Max **Copland** Old American Songs, Set 1 – Long time ago. Old American Songs, Set 2 – At the river **Gorney** Americana – Brother, Can You Spare a Dime? **Hoiby** The lamb **Ives** General William Booth Enters into Heaven. Slugging a vampire. Two little flowers **Musto** Recuerdo **Niles** The lass from the Low Countree **Rorem** Early in the morning. The lordly Hudson **Scheer** Lean Away (arr Thomas). American Anthem. At Howard Hanks' House. Holding each other (all arr Musiker) **Traditional** I wonder as I wander (arr Niles/Horton). Shenandoah (arr Musiker)
Nathan Gunn bar **Kevin Murphy** pf
EMI Debut 573160-2 (68' · DDD)   Ⓑ

Nathan Gunn is a protégé of the Met in New York and this is an exceptional début. As the title of the collection implies, there's a wide range of styles united simply through being American music, and Gunn wanted to illustrate the rich diversity of his inheritance. He has plenty of classics at his disposal. Of the three by Ives, *Slugging a vampire* is swashbuckling; *General William Booth* is delivered with complete confidence; and *Two little flowers* is suitably charming. Copland's arrangements of *Long time ago* and *At the river* are dead right and particularly moving in Gunn's smooth and steady delivery. The two Barber songs show the same effortless command. When Gunn moves towards the vernacular he chooses three hilarious character sketches from William Bolcom's *Cabaret Songs*, which are done with perfect rhythmic control in partnership with Kevin Murphy at the piano. In the traditional tunes and the real pop songs by Scheer they're just as effective as a team. Gunn's flexible, lyrical baritone often resembles Thomas Hampson and he brings the same intelligence to a wide range of Americana. Well recorded, if slightly harsh at times. A real discovery.

Roy Henderson   *baritone*

Centenary Recital
Songs – **T Arne**, **Boyce**, **G Butterworth**, **Dale**, **Hatton**, **Purcell**, **Short**, **Stanford**, **Tchaikovsky**, **Vaughan Williams** and **Warlock**
Roy Henderson *bar* with various artists
Dutton Laboratories mono CDLX7038 (72' · ADD)
Recorded 1925-45   Ⓑ

Roy Henderson was one of the country's most distinguished baritones during the interwar years. He sang Count Almaviva at Glyndebourne's inaugural season in 1934, was an outstanding Elijah and for many years virtually monopolised the all-important baritone solo in Delius's *A Mass of Life* and *Sea Drift* until he retired in 1952. He was also a noted recitalist, and to celebrate his centenary Dutton has had the excellent idea of reissuing his most significant 78rpm discs of British song, very few previously available either on LP or CD. We start with his 1940s Decca recordings of Butterworth's *A Shropshire Lad* and a tranche of Warlock, Vaughan Williams and Stanford songs. The transferred sound is clarity itself, matching the same attribute in Henderson's approach to words. Indeed, he's quoted by Tully Potter in his notes as saying: 'It is the words that count, and determine the pace, the variations and the time.' He observes his dictum in his eloquently shaped and subtly inflected readings, notable for the true half-voice he employs on many occasions, especially in 'Is my team ploughing?' in the Butterworth cycle. Other delights are his warm tone and fine *legato* in Vaughan Williams's lovely *Orpheus with his lute* and the sheer élan in Boyce's *Song of Momus to Mars*, a Dryden setting. The Vocalions and Columbias, dating from the 1920s, disclose a firmer, meatier tone, although the sensitivity is already there in Ireland's *Sea Fever*, a Henderson favourite – he re-recorded it for Decca. He also offers varied and amusing accounts of Hatton's *Simon the Cellarer*

and the traditional *O no, John!* Finally, a 1929 account of Tchaikovsky's *To the forest* shows that Henderson was just as successful in non-British song. Gerald Moore, Ivor Newton and Eric Gritton provide excellent support in this generously filled, rewarding tribute.

Hans Hotter   *bass-baritone*

Opera Monologues, 1957-62   Ⓗ
Mussorgsky Boris Godunov – I have attained the highest power; Your Majesty, I make obeisance; Farewell, my son, I am dying **Rossini** Il barbiere di Siviglia – La calunnia è un venticello **R Strauss** Die schweigsame Frau – Wie schön ist doch die Musik **Verdi** Don Carlo – Ella giammai m'amò **Wagner** Der fliegende Holländer – Die Frist ist um. Die Meistersinger von Nürnberg – Was duftet doch der Flieder; Wahn! Wahn! Uberall Wahn!
Hans Hotter *bass-bar* Dorothea Siebert *sop* Lorenz Fehenberger *ten* Bavarian Radio Chorus and Symphony Orchestra / Meinhard von Zallinger, Rudolf Alberth, Eugen Jochum
Orfeo d'Or C501991B (67' · ADD) Recorded 1957-62.
All items sung in German   ⓂⓄⓄ

Too many collectors today know Hotter only as a Wagnerian (then usually in the Solti *Ring* where he was past his best) or as a fine interpreter of Lieder. In fact he was also renowned in Austria and Germany in other repertory, and even as an accomplished comedian, singing his roles, as was then the custom, in the vernacular. These tracks, drawn from Bavarian Radio archives, tell us something of that other Hotter. In *Don Carlos* he sang both King Philip and, more often, the Grand Inquisitor. He gives us a haunted yet commanding Philip, sung in a commendable *legato*. His amusing Don Basilio couldn't be a greater contrast. A video exists showing Hotter's giant, scheming, faintly ridiculous prelate, commanding the scene, as he commands the aria here. He's equally in character in Sir Morosus's monologue – the old man at last contented and at peace. But the revelation here is his Boris Godunov. He sang the role on stage just once, at Hamburg in 1937, but 20 years later Bavarian Radio mounted a studio production under Jochum with Hotter in the title-role. In both Act 2 monologues, the scene with Shuisky (the subtle, wily Fehenberger) and Boris's death, Hotter presents a frightened, superstitious yet still authoritative and curiously sympathetic Tsar. All are sung with a wealth of inner meaning and fidelity to dynamic marks while avoiding histrionics that aren't in the notes. Here, at the peak of his powers, Hotter is as superb as he is in his 1960 account of the Dutchman's monologue, a benchmark reading.

Equally setting standards for others to emulate are his versions of Sachs's monologues, so refined and thoughtful. As in all Hotter's performances, it's the interior meaning conveyed through a deep understanding of the text, allied to warmth and beauty of the voice, that remains so telling; here's the singing actor *par excellence*.

Maria Ivogün   *soprano*

Opera Arias and Songs   🅷
Anonymous O du liebs Angeli[a]. Z'Lauterbach han
i'mein Strumpf verlor'n[a]. Gsätzli. Maria auf dem
Berge[a] **Bishop** Lo, here the gentle lark[b] **Chopin**
Nocturne in E flat, Op 9 No 2[b] (arr sop/orch) **Handel**
L'allegro, il penseroso ed il moderato, HWV55 –
Sweet bird[b] (recorded 1925) **Donizetti** Don Pasquale
– Ah! un foco insolito[b] (rec 1924). Lucia di
Lammermoor – Ardon gl'incensi[b] (rec 1917) **Kreisler**
Liebesfreud[b] **Meyerbeer** Les Huguenots – Une
dame noble et sage[b] (German) **Nicolai** Die lustigen
Weiber von Windsor – Nun eilt herbei[b] (all rec 1917)
Rossini Il barbiere di Siviglia – Una voce poco fa[b]
(rec 1925) **Schubert** Ständchen (Horch! die
Lerch), D899[b]. Winterreise, D911 – Die Post[b]
J Strauss II Frühlingsstimmen, Op 410[b] (rec 1924).
G'schichten aus dem Wienerwald, Op 325[b]. An die
schönen, blauen Donau, Op 314[c]. Die Fledermaus –
Klänge der Heimat[c] **Verdi** La traviata – E strano …
Ah, fors'è lui … Sempre libera[b] (sung in German, rec
1916)
Maria Ivogün sop [a]**Michael Raucheisen** pf
[b]**orchestra**; [c]**Berlin State Opera Orchestra / Leo
Blech**
Nimbus Prima Voce NI7832 (78' · ADD) Recorded
1916-32   Ⓢ

Somewhere or other, after much searching of
the memory, ransacking of the catalogues and
phoning around among connoisseurs, it might
be possible to discover a more delightful example of the coloratura's art than that of Maria
Ivogün as displayed in her recording of
Kreisler's *Liebesfreud*, made in 1924: if so, one
such doesn't spring to mind now. With the most
pure and delicate of tones, nothing shrill or
piercing about them, she sings way above a normal mortal's reach, ease and accuracy in the
purely technical feats going along with a lilt and
feeling for the idiomatic give-and-take of waltz
rhythm that are a joy musically.
    Turn to Handel, with the solo from *Il
penseroso*, and the same art is put to lovely use in
a different idiom. Her *Traviata* aria has warmth
and spontaneity; her Frau Fluth in *Die lustigen
Weiber von Windsor* is a woman of charm and
energy; and the 1934 recording of the Czardas
in *Die Fledermaus* shines as bright in spirit as in
clarity of timbre. From the same period comes
the set of four songs, Swiss and German, that
show most touchingly her command of the art
to be simple.
    This is an admirable introduction to a most
lovely singer, and it represents the Prima Voce
series at its best.

Sumi Jo   *soprano*

La Promessa
Bellini Malinconia, ninfa gentile. Per pietà, bell'idol
mio **Benedict** La capinera **Caldara** Alma del core
Cesti Intorno all'idol mio **Donaudy** O del mio amato
ben. Vaghissima sembianza **G Giordani** Caro mio
ben **Gluck** Paride ed Elena – O del mio dolce ardor

Handel Rinaldo – Lascia ch'io pianga. Giulio Cesare
– V'adoro, pupille **Mozart** Ridente la calma,
K152/K210a **Paisiello** L'amor contrastato – Nel cor
più non mi sento **Rosa** Star vicino **Rossini** Soirées
musicales – La promessa **Sarti** Giulio Sabino – Lungi
dal caro ben (arr Parenti) **A Scarlatti** Se Florindo è
fedele **D Scarlatti** Qual farfalletta amante **Tosti** Non
t'amo più! **Verdi** Ad una stella
Sumi Jo sop **Vincenzo Scalera** pf
Erato 3984-23300-2 (68' · DDD) Texts and translations
included   Ⓕ

Here is one of the most delightful singers of our
time heard in a programme that extends her
repertoire on record and, being apt and congenial in itself, brings a double refreshment.
There's a delicious coolness about the Korean
soprano's singing: an 18th-century elegance.
And not the slightest coldness about it; simply a
humanity and a civilisation where the heart isn't
worn on the sleeve. Interestingly, this is so even
in the songs which often excite a more overtly
passionate style of performance, Tosti's *Non
t'amo più!* and the two by Stefano Donaudy.
Similarly, such light-hearted 19th-century
pieces as Rossini's 'La promessa' and Benedict's
La capinera carry their gaiety with poise and
refinement.
    It's partly that they benefit from the company
of Handel and Mozart, partly that the clear
voice and graceful style bring out the Classicism
in which their composers were educated rather
than the thicker Romanticism to which their age
was tending. Voice and style here are as one, and
the opening *Caro mio ben* is a fine example of
both. The tone remains unequivocally that of a
high lyric soprano but now with a mature and
reassuring warmth in the lower notes. The
phrases are beautifully sustained and are shaded
with respect for the unity of line. The quickening pace of the middle section is well judged, as
is the modestly decorated 'tanto rigor' leading
back to the principal melody. Sumi Jo is responsive to the urgency of Bellini's *Malinconia* and
the lightness of Scarlatti's *Farfalletta*. Vincenzo
Scalera accompanies tastefully, and recorded
sound is fine.

Sumi Jo at Carnegie Hall
Adam Le toréador – Ah, vous dirai-je, maman **Bellini**
I Puritani – Son vergin vezzosa; Qui la voce … Vien,
diletto **Benedict** The Gipsy and the Bird **Bernstein**
Candide – Glitter and be gay **Bishop** Lo, here the
gentle lark **Cho** Seonguja **Herbert** Naughty Marietta
– Italian Street Song **Hong** Springtime of home
Kim I shall live in the Blue Mountains **Mozart** Vorre
spiegarvi, oh Dio, K418 **Offenbach** Les contes
d'Hoffmann – Les oiseaux dans la charmille **J Strauss
II** Die Fledermaus – Mein Herr Marquis (arr Rauber)
Sumi Jo sop **Orchestra of St Luke's / Richard
Bonynge**
Erato 3984-21630-2 (64' · DDD)   Ⓕ⬤

This sounds like a good night out at Carnegie
Hall, and not one whose memory is spoilt when
heard again, transferred to disc. Apart from a

little wear on the upper register at a *forte*, the voice remains pure, firm and lovely, its tone rather fuller than when we first knew it, the technique secure, its accomplishments impressively displayed. Expressiveness is perhaps not a prime requisite here, and indeed one might wish for a programme that did require a little more than a pretty smile shaded off now and again into a pretty pathos; but all goes well and the audience's evident enthusiasm is well justified. The only item which doesn't really succeed is Adam's variations on the nursery tune, *Ah, vous dirai-je, maman*, usually thought of simply as a display piece. The air is a wistful little thing, sung by a girl feeling the first torments of love and finding consolation in the tender, softly rocking melody of a song. That feeling is absent in Sumi Jo's technically admirable performance. Happily, in the very next item, 'Qui la voce' from *I Puritani*, Sumi Jo's singing has just the right degree of emotion for a concert performance, with Bonynge and his players responding sensitively to the quickening of pulse and its sad relaxation. This and the Polonaise, sung later in the programme, find the singer at her delightful best, as does the Mozart with which the recital so enchantingly opens. The three songs said to be of Korean origin sound thoroughly western, and application to the booklet-notes gains no further enlightenment. Still, this isn't the kind of occasion for queries and complaints. Here is a delectable singer amidst an appreciative public, and we're fortunate to have the opportunity of sharing their enjoyment.

Virtuoso Arias

Bellini La sonnambula – Ah! non credea mirarti … Ah! non giunge[a] **Bernstein** Candide – Glitter and be gay[a] **Delibes** Lakmé – Où va la jeune indoue … Là-bas dans la forêt plus sombre[a] **Donizetti** Lucia di Lammermoor – Mad scene[a] **Meyerbeer** Dinorah – Ombre légère[a] **Mozart** Die Zauberflöte – Der Hölle Rache[b] **Rossini** Il barbiere di Siviglia – Una voce poco fa … Io son docile[a] **R Strauss** Ariadne auf Naxos – Noch glaub' ich dem einen ganz … So war es mit Pagliazzo … Als ein Gott kam jeder gegangen[a] **Verdi** Rigoletto – Gualtier Maldè … Caro nome[a] **Yoon** (arr. Constant) Barley Field[a]
Sumi Jo *sop* [a]Monte-Carlo Philharmonic Orchestra / Paolo Olmi; [b]Paris Orchestral Ensemble / Armin Jordan
Erato 4509-97239-2 (74' · DDD) Recorded 1994. Texts included   Ⓕ

Many listeners, well disposed towards most kinds of vocal recital, still tend to approach a new 'coloratura' programme with misgivings – all of which would seem to be obviated here. The emotional range of the music goes well beyond mere prettiness, whether of girlish glee or wilting pathos. The florid passages are assumed by the singer to have an expressive purpose, which she then seeks out and fulfils. Her tone is bright but not piercing, her style clean but not cold; she understands perfectly well that, though these arias are famous for their high

notes, far more of the singer's time is spent in the middle register, where a scrawny or breathy tone and flawed *legato* will not be excused on account of a few brilliances *in alt*. Intelligence is clearly at work from the start, in the enunciation of the words. 'Una voce poco fa qui nel cuor mi risuono': the 'qui' ('here') is the 'gesture-word', the one that makes it actual and individual. 'La vincerò' is determined, but not doubly underlined or given that arch, over-confident touch which may gain a point but, in doing so, forfeits likeableness. In *La sonnambula* sympathy is actually *strengthened* by the cleaning-up of all those downward portamentos that have threatened to become inseparable from the music since Callas and Sutherland introduced them. Similarly, the Mad scene from *Lucia di Lammermoor* is enacted as a genuinely dramatic piece but with a fresh realisation, rather than from a mind loaded with memories of those illustrious predecessors. The only way in which Jo appears at a disadvantage is in the relative hardness of some high notes.

Vesselina Kasarova   *mezzo-soprano*

A Portrait

Handel Rinaldo – Or la tromba in suon festante **Gluck** Orfeo ed Euridice – Che farò senza Euridice? **Mozart** Le nozze di Figaro – Voi che sapete. Don Giovanni – Batti, batti, o bel Masetto **Rossini** La Cenerentola – Nacqui all'affano[abdeg]. Il barbiere di Siviglia – Una voce poco fa. L'Italiana in Algeri – Pronti abbiamo e ferri e mani … Amici in ogni evento … Pensa alla patria[g] **Donizetti** Anna Bolena – Sposa a Percy … Per questa fiamma indomita … Ah! pensate che rivolti[cfg]. La favorita – Fia dunque vero … O mio Fernando! **Bellini** I Capuleti e i Montecchi – Se Romeo t'uccise un figlio … La tremenda ultrice spada[cfg]
Vesselina Kasarova *mez* [a]Isolde Mitternacht-Geissendörfer *sop* [b]Barbara Müller *contr* [c]Andreas Schulist, [d]Dankwart Siegele *ten* [e]Tim Hennis *bass* [f]Leonid Savitzky *bass* [g]Bavarian Radio Chorus; Munich Radio Orchestra / Friedrich Haider
RCA Red Seal 09026 68522-2 (64' · DDD)Texts and translations included   Ⓕ

This is the stuff of legends: it's difficult to imagine a début opera recital that could give so much pleasure. The vibrant richness of Kasarova's tone allied to her totally uninhibited manner before the microphone allows her to bring to astonishing life each of the characters portrayed within. She begins as she continues, with tremendous panache as Rinaldo invokes trumpets to great deeds, and Kasarova proves the warrior-lover to the life, Handel's complex coloratura used as an engine to express youthful fire. Then immediately she becomes the tender, lamenting Orpheus, real grieving in the plush, well-controlled tone. The two Mozart pieces disclose different timbres in the voice – bright and palpitating as befits Cherubino, soft-grained and sensuous as suits Zerlina. Kasarova is a fabulous Rossinian. In the three pieces here she combines vitality, verbal acuity and dispatch of *fioriture*. It's wonderful how she starts in mild, forgiving manner, caressing the start of 'Non più mesta', then lets fly in viscerally exciting manner for the roulades.

Even the well-trodden path of 'Una voce' sounds newly minted as you seem to hear Rosina's varied thoughts passing through her mind, the text freshly inflected. As Isabella inspires her followers in 'Pensa alla patria', one notes the subtle accents on 'il tenero amor' and 'Caro, ti parli in petto', evincing all Isabella's inner feelings for her beloved Lindoro. Then it's off on another invigorating display at 'Fra pochi istanti'. From here Kasarova moves on to so-called *bel canto* territory. With 'O mio Fernando!' it's again the judgement of tonal colour, here sensual, heartstopping, while Jane Seymour's resistance to Henry VIII shows yet another 'face', dignified and noble. But in both Leonora's and Romeo's cabaletta, 'La tremenda ultrice spada', a little less might mean so much more: there's too much emphasis, too many breaths. But that's part of the style of a singer who's making no concessions to the studio, and is rather living out every moment of the given dramas.

Yvonne Kenny   *soprano*

Bizet The Pearl Fishers – I'm all alone here…As once before; Leïla! Leïla!…Your heart was never tuned to mine[b] **Boughton** The Immortal Hour – How beautiful they are **Catalani** La Wally – I'll float into the distance **Donizetti** Linda di Chamounix – Linda! Linda![b] **Handel** Joshua – O had I Jubal's lyre. Rinaldo – Hear thou my weeping **Mozart** Idomeneo – Gentle zephyrs, soft caressing. Nehmt meinen Dank, ihr holden Gönner, K383 **Porter** Kiss Me, Kate – So in love am I **Puccini** Gianni Schicchi – Oh, my beloved father **Purcell** The Indian Queen – I attempt from love's sickness. King Arthur – Fairest isle **Rossini** Semiramide – Dark day of dread![a]. William Tell – Dark, sombre wood **Stravinsky** The Rake's Progress – Gently, little boat[c] **Sullivan** The Mikado – The sun, whose rays **Zeller** The Bird Catcher' – When you're sent roses in this land
Yvonne Kenny sop [a]**Della Jones** mez [b]**Barry Banks** ten [c]**Geoffrey Mitchell Choir; Philharmonia Orchestra / David Parry**
Chandos/Peter Moores Foundation Opera in English Series CHAN3035 (76' · DDD) Texts included Ⓕ**OO**

Lovely, lovely record, and that wretched, inevitable little word 'but' had better be admitted immediately and sent on its way. The 'but' concerns tone-quality when, at a certain volume and a certain height, a bright, metallic tinkle of wear or overtones obtrudes and momentarily compromises the purity of sound. It has long been a feature of Kenny's voice and makes only intermittent appearance here (in the *Pearl Fishers* duet, for example), but it has to be mentioned. That aside, delight is more or less continuous from start to finish.

Taking a look at the programme, one might at first think its order haphazard and likely to be

too fragmentary and inconsequential: not so in practice. The disc opens with Lauretta's plea to her daddy ('daddy' surely, not 'father') and is quite happily followed by Ilia's invocation to the breezes, then back to Purcell and on to Handel and Donizetti and so forth. The jumps aren't ones to break a leg over though. Perhaps this is because everything here, from Purcell to Cole Porter, is treated in a spirit of thinking the best – and finding it. All concerned seem united in this – the singer, the players and their admirable conductor. When a refined musical spirit is brought to it, the music responds. Handel's 'Jubal's lyre' responds as we no doubt expected it to, but when Rossini's 'Dark day of dread!' follows, instead of the heavyweight posturing suggested by the title, we find a blissfully scored duet, an idyll of love-birds in thirds with orchestral *pizzicatos*; and when this is followed by the famous solo from *La Wally*, that too is heard as an utterance almost refined in its passion, the song of a heartbroken girl rather than an aria for the spotlighted diva.

Delightful throughout is the cleanness of style: intervals, intonation, phrasing, the handling of words. Perhaps the characters need more differentiation, but then again perhaps not (this isn't Mimì turning into Tosca, or Violetta into one of the Leonoras). As for the oddities – *The Mikado*, *Kiss me Kate* and so on – they all earn their welcome. And the odd notion of ending a lyric-soprano recital with what's properly a tenor solo (the Faery song from *The Immortal Hour*) proves to make for an inspired and magical coda.

Emma Kirkby   *soprano*

Classical Kirkby
Blow Sappho to the Goddess of Beauty. Sappho to the Goddess of Love **Boyce** An answer to Orpheus and Euridice. When Orpheus went down to the Regions below **Campion** When to her lute Corinna sings **Eccles** Corinna now you'r young and gay **Ferrabosco** So beautie on the waters stood **Greene** Orpheus with his Lute **Lanier** Hero and Leander **H Lawes** At dead low ebb of night. Ayres and Dialogues – Anacreon's Ode, call'd The Lute; Away, Away, Anacreon; Legousin hai gunaikes (Anacreon). Orpheus's Hymn to God. **Weldon** Stop, O ye waves **Wilson** Horace's Odes – Diffugere nives; Integer vitae
Emma Kirkby sop **Anthony Rooley** theo/lte
BIS BIS-CD1435 (54' · DDD) Texts and translations included Ⓕ**O**

'Classical Kirkby' is a delightful programme of English 17th- and 18th-century song with an uncommon and charming provenance. As a former Oxford classics scholar, Emma Kirkby was invited to become President of the Classical Association, and baulking at the idea of having to give the obligatory inaugural lecture offered to sing instead. The offer was accepted, and this is the outcome, a nicely varied and unusual recital of songs on classical texts and subjects, some serious, some humorous, some dramatic and some simply pretty. Perhaps the rarest items are those setting words by classical poets themselves: two of Anacreon's poems appear in their original Greek, set by Henry Lawes, while two of Horace's Odes are heard in delicate settings by John Wilson. Other highlights include Nicholas Lanier's powerful depiction of Hero watching her beloved Leander drown, a rather sweet Shakespeare setting by Maurice Greene, and two jokey accounts by William Boyce of the Orpheus legend, seen from respective male and female viewpoints. All are sung with Kirkby's customary radiance of voice, technical agility and interpretative intelligence. This really is the kind of intimate programme that this great singer does best; this isn't just 'classical Kirkby' but 'classic', too.

Magadalena Kožená   *soprano*

Gluck La clemenza di Tito – Se mai senti spirarti sul volto. Paride ed Elena – Le belle immagini d'un dolce amore; O del mio dolce ardor bramato oggetto! **Mozart** La clemenza di Tito – Parto, ma tu, ben mio; Deh, per questo istante solo. La finta giardiniera – Va' pure ad altri in braccio. Idomeneo – Il padre adorato. Lucio Silla – Il tenero momento. Le nozze di Figaro – Voi che sapete è amor **Mysliveček** Abramo ed Isacco – Deh, parlate, che forse tacendo. Antigona – Sarò qual è il torrente. L'Olimpiade – Che non mi disse un di!; Più non si trovano
Magdalena Kožená *mez* **Prague Philharmonia / Michel Swierczewski**
DG 471 334-2GH (68' · DDD) Notes, texts and translations included   Ⓕ**O**

On this CD there's some of the most compelling singing of late 18th-century operatic music that you're likely to encounter. Magdalena Kožená shows she possesses a full, firm, creamy voice, ideal for Classical-period music, and a keen sense of how to characterise it dramatically.

Mysliveček was highly gifted, successful throughout Italy, and was admired by the Mozarts. The aria from his oratorio *Abramo ed Isacco*, sung by Sarah when she believes Abraham has sacrificed their son, is an intense, impassioned piece, preceded by a vivid recitative, giving Kožená ample scope for expressive singing and incisive articulation. She draws beautifully long lines in Gluck's 'Le belle immagini', but it's the famous 'O del mio dolce ardor', Paris's first declaration of his love for Helen, where she catches the air of haunting oriental mystery so beautifully, that's especially affecting. But the best things naturally come in the big serious arias – in Mozart's two *Tito* arias for Sextus she shines above all, making Sextus's dilemmas, torn between love and duty, real with her colouring of the words, her variation of tone between firm resolution and soft tenderness (but always with a clear ringing sound), the warmth of her phrasing. Altogether a splendid disc, with first-rate support from Swierczewski and the Prague orchestra.

Britten A Charm of Lullabies, Op 4[a] **Ravel** Trois Chansons madécasses[b] **Respighi** Il tramonto[c] **Schulhoff** Drei Stimmungsbilder, Op 12[d] **Shostakovich** Five Satires, Op 109[e]
Magdalena Kožená *mez* [c]**Henschel Quartet** ([d]Christoph Henschel, Markus Henschel *vns* Monika Henschel-Schwind *va* Matthias D Beyer-Karlshøj *vc*) [b]**Paul Edmund-Davies** *fl* [b]**Jiří Bárta** *vc* [a][b][d][e]
Malcolm Martineau *pf*
DG 471 581-2GH (64' · DDD)   Ⓕ**OO**

Magdalena Kožená has shown an admirable determination to push at the boundaries of her artistry. On stage, she's gone from a picture of archetypal femininity as Zerlina at Salzburg to the gritty realism of an Idamante in battle fatigues at Glyndebourne; while her recitals have ranged across many languages and styles, including the five contrasting composers assembled here.

The one constant feature is vocal beauty. Her mezzo is a young gazelle of a voice, soaring up into soprano territory as easily as Anne Sofie von Otter or Susan Graham, and it takes very kindly to the recording process. There isn't a moment on this disc where the tone sounds strained or its beauty manufactured.

Kožená and the Henschel Quartet hold at bay the temptation to wallow in Respighi's super-romantic *Il tramonto*, while giving the music the sunset glow it craves. The Schulhoff songs inhabit a similar hothouse atmosphere, and again she's sensitive and subtle. Ravel's *Chansons madécasses* are less successful: the fine line that these songs tread between an imaginary world and the harshness of reality is obcured by a soft-focus gauze.

The Shostakovich and Britten cycles work on a different level. The playful sparkle Kožená and Malcolm Martineau bring to the Shostakovich *Satires* has a sly undercutting edge. Britten's *Charm of Lullabies* has attracted surprisingly few singers and they deserve thanks for bringing it to notice.

French Arias

Auber Le Domino noir – Je suis sauvée enfin!; Flamme vengeresse **Berlioz** La Damnation de Faust, Op 24 – Autrefois un roi de Thulé **Bizet** Carmen – Les tringles des sistres **Boïeldieu** La Dame blanche – D'ici voyez ce beau domaine **Gounod** Cinq Mars – Par quel trouble; Nuit resplendissante. Roméo et Juliette – Depuis hier je cherche en vain mon maître!; Que faites-tu, blanc tourterelle. Sapho – Où suis-je?; O ma lyre immortelle **Massenet** Cendrillon – Ah! Que mes sœurs sont heureuses! Cléopâtre – J'ai versé le poison. Don Quichotte – Par fortune!; Alza! Alza! Ne pensons qu'au plaisir d'aimer **Offenbach** Les Contes d'Hoffmann – Pardieu! j'étais bien sûr; Voyez-la sous son éventail **Ravel** L'Heure espagnole – Oh! la pitoyable aventure **A Thomas** Mignon – Connais-tu le pays? **Verdi** Don Carlos – Sous ces bois; Au palais des fées
Magdalena Kožená *mez* **Chœur des Musiciens du Louvre; Mahler Chamber Orchestra / Marc Minkowski**

DG 474 214-2GH (79' · DDD) Ⓕ**OOO**

Kožená performs here a mixture of French arias for soprano and mezzo. The recital opens with the dotty aria from *Le Domino noir*, in which the rowdy nun has found herself locked out of the convent; Kožená has the spirit, and the coloratura, for this decidedly soprano role. The three Gounod arias are contrasted in mood, ranging from sensuality to pathos. Of the Massenet items, *Cléopatre*'s 'J'ai versé le poison', with its insinuating clarinet obbligato, seems made for her. Eboli's Veil song is something of a stunt, notwithstanding its panache; you really can't imagine Kožená in *Don Carlos*. The major rarity here is an aria from *Les Contes d'Hoffmann* never performed before. It's a reconstruction from Offenbach's sketches, skilfully orchestrated by Jean-Christophe Keck. It was meant to have been sung by Nicklausse in the Olympia act and begins with yet another outburst of yearning, all about dreams and love, before Nicklausse warns Hoffmann against Olympia in a merry, fast waltz.

This is a fascinating disc from one of the most promising voices today. Minkowski conducts the Mahler Chamber Orchestra with a fine sense of the shifting moods and styles, from 1825 (*La Dame blanche*) to 1914 (*Cléopatre*).

Alfredo Kraus   *tenor*

Alfredo Kraus con el Corazón
Bonfa/Maria Canción de Orfeo[b] **Chapí** El milagro de la Virgen – Flores purísimas[a] **Chaplin** Eternally[a] **Fain** Love is a many splendored thing[a] **Guerrero** El huésped del sevillano – Mujer de los ojos negros[b] **Guridi** El caserío – Yo no sé que veo en Ana María[a]. La meiga – Yo te vi pasar[b] **Jiménez** Corazón, corazón[c] **Kosma** Les feuilles mortes[b] **Lara** Noche de Ronda[a] **Luna** La pícara molinera – Paxarín, tu que vuelas[b] **Maggio/Ferilli** Un amore così grande[a] **Monnot** Hymne à l'amour[a] **Esparza Oteo** Rondalla[c] **Porter** You do something to me[a] **Ramírez** Alfonsina y el mar[a] **Serrano** La dolorosa – La roca fría del Calvario[a]. Los claveles – Mujeres[a]. La alegría del batallón – Al mismo rey del moro[b]. Alma de Dios – Canción del vagabundo[b] **Sorozábal** La tabernera del puerto – No puede ser[b] **Pérez Soriano** El guitarrico – Jota[a] **Soutullo/Vert** El último romántico – Bella enamorada[b] **Moreno Torroba** Luisa Fernanda – De este apacible rincón de Madrid[b] **Trenet/Lasry** La mer[b] **Vives** Doña Francisquita – Por el humo se sabe[a] (Song arrangements by Peter Hope and Joan Albert Amargós)
Alfredo Kraus ten [a]**Tenerife Symphony Orchestra / Víctor Pablo Pérez;** [b]**Gran Canaria Philharmonic Orchestra / Carlos Riazuelo;** [c]**Madrid Complutense University Orchestra / Santiago López**
RCA Victor ② 74321 72246-2 (101' · DDD)   Ⓕ**O**

The real glory of the two CDs lies in the seven zarzuela numbers that each contains. Some have been recorded by Kraus on previous occasions,

but others (such as the two Guridi numbers and the Chapí rarity) probably have not. Either way, no tenor has ever created the *frisson* that Kraus does in this glorious music. Has anyone, for instance, shaped and caressed the phrases of 'Mujeres' from *Los claveles* as lovingly and sweetly as he does? Has anybody made the romance from *El caserío* such a tender realisation of affection for a woman who has too often been taken for granted? And, among the many performances of the aria from *Doña Francisquita*, has anyone balanced the passion, reflection and finely shaped line as he does?

The second CD ends with a further two songs performed to the accompaniment of an orchestra of mandolins, lutes and guitars. They make a glorious noise, and Kraus sounds thoroughly at home. But the zarzuela numbers are the real glory of this invaluable souvenir of a wonderful singer.

Erich Kunz   *baritone*

Opera Arias   Ⓗ
Don Giovanni, Der lustige Krieg, Eine Nacht in Venedig, Le nozze di Figaro, Der Vogelhändler, Der Waffenschmied, Der Wildschütz, Zar und Zimmermann, Die Zauberflöte and Der Zigeunerbaron; Viennese songs by various composers
Erich Kunz bar with various artists
Testament mono SBT1059 (79' · ADD) Recorded 1947-53   Ⓕ

Here is Kunz in his absolute prime, moving his agreeable voice around Figaro's, Leporello's and Papageno's music with the confidence derived from experience in the roles in Vienna, but without the slightest sense of routine. It should not be forgotten that he was one of the first German-speaking singers to learn his Da Ponte roles in Italian: his diction and accent in them, as we find here, are virtually perfect. Under Karajan, in Figaro's 'Non più andrai' he's disciplined by a fast tempo, while Ackermann is more yielding in Leporello's 'Madamina'. Karajan also conducts the Giovanni/Zerlina duet (with the incomparable Seefried). It's a wonderful souvenir of two artists, whose voices blending ideally, who sang so often together in that notable ensemble in Vienna. Kunz was also loved in his home city for his assumption of *buffo* parts in Lortzing's operas, and he brings to their arias, again with Ackermann in sympathetic support, a rich vein of comic characterisation without ever resorting to caricature – Kunz was, above all, a sensitive musician. The second half of this issue is devoted to operetta items and Viennese songs. In the former it may be complained that he was often adopting, and transposing down, music written originally for a tenor: four songs from *Ein Nacht in Venedig*, in the Korngold rescension, rather suffer in that respect, yet Kunz's wholly idiomatic approach almost makes us forget the anomaly. In what are mostly Heurigen songs, he's absolutely in his element; only his older, tenor colleague, Julius Patzak was his peer in these. The accompanying Schrammel Ensemble are wholly authentic. Try, if you can, *Da draussen in der Wachau*, so beguiling in tone and style, and you won't be able to resist the rest.

Lotte Lehmann   *soprano*

Songs – **Balogh, Beethoven, Brahms,**   Ⓗ
Cimara, Franz, Gounod, Grechaninov, Hahn,
Jensen, Marx, Mozart, Pfitzner, Sadero, Schubert,
Schumann, Sjöberg, Wolf and **Worth**
Lotte Lehmann *sop* with various artists
Romophone mono ② 81013-2 (157' · ADD) Recorded
1935-40   Ⓕ

Lotte Lehmann was at the height of her powers as a song interpreter in the late 1930s: the bloom of youth is still in the tone, now enhanced by the experience of many years of stage interpretation. Thus, her characters *in extremis* become something of a talisman of suffering women. Her impassioned Gretchen in Schubert's great song is sister to, and inhabits the same world as, Lehmann's Leonore and Sieglinde. The searing intensity of 'Was hör ich alte Laute?' in Schumann's *Alte Laute* goes through you, becomes etched in the mind, just as do certain phrases in her operatic portrayals. Yet while the passions are felt on a large scale throughout these songs, the intimate mould of Lieder singing is never breached. The readings are generous and free, never dull, careful or limited, or by another token overladen with detailed word-painting in the Schwarzkopf manner. Unlike many of her contemporaries Lehmann ranged wide in her choice of repertory. She digs out Jensen's *Lehn' diene Wang' an meine Wange* and makes you believe this little sentimental song is a masterpiece. However, it's for the Schubert (including 12 songs from *Winterreise*, so immediate in effect, no holds barred), Schumann, Brahms and Wolf, that the myriad admirers of this artist will want these two lavishly filled CDs. The transfers are clean and clear, but at times impart a slight glare to Lehmann's tone. This offering is an essential addition to the Lehmann discography.

Dame Felicity Lott   *soprano*

Chausson Poème de l'amour et de la mer, Op 19
Duparc Chanson triste. L'Invitation au voyage.
Phidylé **Ravel** Shéhérazade
Dame Felicity Lott *sop* **Suisse Romande Orchestra**
/ Armin Jordan
Aeon AECD0314 (60' · DDD) Texts and translations
included   Ⓕ

What sort of style really suits Ravel's *Shéhérazade*? It's been recorded so often by large voices, heroic sopranos or powerful mezzos, that one forgets that the sort of sound Ravel had in mind was probably a silvery, typically French soprano. The two shorter songs, 'La flute

enchantée' and 'L'indifférent', are given delicate performances here by Felicity Lott. Bit the opening song, 'Asie', is perhaps better suited to the fuller tone of, say, Heather Harper. The Chausson *Poème de l'amour et de la mer* suits her much better.

For those concerned principally with repertory, this coupling of the two cycles is unusual: the Ravel is so often paired with Berlioz's *Les nuits d'été*. The three Duparc songs make a good finish to the programme, the restful mood of *Phidylé* offsetting the angst of *Chanson triste*, and Verlaine's enigmatic *L'invitation au voyage*, perhaps the poem most closely associated with Felicity Lott; she has twice recorded Chabrier's alternative setting of it.

Giovanni Martinelli   *tenor*

Opera Arias and Duets   Ⓗ
Giordano Andrea Chenier – Un dì all'azzurro spazio[e];
Come un bel dì di maggio[f]. Fedora[e] – Amor ti vieta;
Mia madre, la mia vecchia madre **Mascagni**
Cavalleria rusticana[f] – O Lola; Mamma, quel vino è
generoso **Leoncavallo** Pagliacci – Recitar!...Vesti la
giubba[f]; Per la morte! smettiamo...No, Pagliaccio
non sona[d]. Zazà – E un riso gentil[f] **Puccini** La
bohème – Che gelida manina[e]. Tosca – E lucevan le
stelle[e] **Verdi** Rigoletto – La donna è mobile. Il
trovatore – Quale d'armi fragor...Di quella pira[ad]. La
forza del destino[b] – Oh, tu che in seno; Invano
Alvaro...Le minacciei fieri accenti. Aida – Se quel
guerrier io fossi...Celeste Aida[e]; Nume, custode e
vindici[c]
Giovanni Martinelli *ten* [a]**Grace Anthony** *sop*
[b]**Giuseppe de Luca** *bar* [c]**Ezio Pinza** *bass*
[d]**Metropolitan Opera Chorus and Orchestra /**
Giulio Setti, [e]**Josef Pasternack,** [c]**Rosario Bourdon**
Preiser Lebendige Vergangenheit mono 89062
(68' · AAD) Recorded 1926-7   Ⓕ

Here is one of the most fascinating of singers. He can also be one of the most thrilling, his voice having at its best a beauty unlike any other, his art noble in breadth of phrase and concentration of tone. It also has to be said that his records hardly make easy or restful listening, but what at first may even repel soon becomes compulsive, the intensity of expression and individuality of timbre impressing themselves upon the memory with extraordinary vividness. Martinelli's career was centred on the Metropolitan, New York, where he sang first at the height of the Caruso era, inheriting Caruso's more dramatic roles in 1921. This selection makes an unrepresentative start with 'La donna è mobile', but the excerpts from *Il trovatore* and *La forza del destino* have the very essence of the man, masterly in his shaping and shading of recitative, or in the long curves of his melodic line and the tension of his utterance. There are also superb performances of solos from *Andrea Chénier* and *Pagliacci*, the involvement of his 'No, Pagliaccio non son' unequalled before or since. These are recordings from 1926 and 1927, the period in which his vocal and artistic qualities were probably best matched.

The transfers are fine apart from the song from Leoncavallo's *Zazà* which plays below pitch.

Karita Mattila   *soprano*

Arias and Scenes
Janáček Jenůfa – Jenůfa's Prayer **Lehár** Die lustige Witwe – Es lebt eine Vilja, ein Waldmägdelein **Puccini** Manon Lescaut – In quelle trine morbide **R Strauss** Elektra – Ich kann nicht sitzen und ins Dunkel starren **Tchaikovsky** The Queen of Spades – It is close on midnight already; What am I crying for? **Verdi** Simon Boccanegra – Come in quest'ora bruna **Wagner** Lohengrin – Einsam in trüben Tagen; Euch Lüften, die mein Klagen. Die Walküre – Der Männer Sippe; Du bist der Lenz
Karita Mattila sop **London Philharmonic Orchestra / Yutaka Sado**
Erato 8573 85785-2 (56' · DDD) Texts and translations included   Ⓕ Ⓞ

We are surely a favoured generation that has three singers – Renée Fleming, Angela Gheorghiu and Karita Mattila (and perhaps more that don't come quite so easily to mind) – who satisfy so pre-eminently the taste for a soprano voice that has these sensuous virtues of richness, smoothness, firmness and purity.

On their own, and number by number, the performances are delightful. You couldn't wish for a lovelier voice, and it suits all these operatic characters in turn, for all, whatever the nationality and present mood, presuppose a lyric soprano with powers of generous expansion, a warmth of tone in the essential middle register, and resources on high that can match the excitements of an emotional climax with a voice rich in its reserves of range and volume. Mattila has all of that, and the mastery to turn from Russian to Italian, German to Czech, Puccini to Janáček, Wagner to Lehár. She phrases well (hear the start of 'In quelle trine morbide'), commands a mature tone and manner (try Sieglinde's narrative) and is scrupulous over matters of detail (getting the climax of Lisa's 'midnight' aria right, for instance, where many don't).

If that's enough – and it's certainly a great deal – then this recital (well recorded and with admirable orchestral work) will give unspoilt pleasure. If something additional is wanting – and those who are accustomed to read between the lines will probably sense that there is – it's at least not so urgently wanting that its absence should spoil the pleasure of what is present.

John McCormack   *tenor*

Opera and Operetta Arias   Ⓗ
Il barbiere di Siviglia, Barry of Ballymore, La bohème, Carmen, L'elisir d'amore, Faust, La fille du régiment, La Gioconda, In a Persian garden, Lakmé, Lucia di Lammermoor, Naughty Marietta, Les pêcheurs de perles, Rigoletto and La traviata; songs by **Balfe**, **Barker**, **Blumenthal**, **Cherry**, **Claribel**, **Crouch**, **MacMurrough**, **Marshall**, **Parelli**, **Rossini** and

Traditional
John McCormack ten with various artists
Romophone mono ② 82006-2 (155' · ADD) Recorded 1910-11   Ⓕ

You think, at the start of this journey through the recordings of two years, that here's McCormack at his absolute best, in the first of the *Lucia di Lammermoor* solos; but no, for the second one ('Tu che a Dio spiegasti l'ali'), made two months later, is better still, a perfection of lyrical singing, the music lying ideally within his voice as it was at that time, and with the heart and imagination more evidently involved. A little later comes 'Una furtiva lagrima', where the modulation into D flat major ('m'ama') brings surely some of the most beautiful, most unflawed tenor singing ever recorded. This album, from 1910 and 1911, presents him in finest voice. He was only 25 at the outset: in the first flush of his operatic success and already the partner of Melba and Tetrazzini. His favourite baritone partner was Mario Sammarco, who turns up as a blustery Figaro to his elegant Almaviva, retiring to a more discreet distance behind the recording horn in the duet from *Les pêcheurs de perles* (the deservedly rare version included here along with the more familiar 10 inch). They also join in the *gondolieri*-like harmonies of Rossini's *Li marinari* (splendid high Bs from McCormack) and give each other a run for their money in a full-bodied, exciting account of the duet from *La Gioconda*. McCormack, it's true, had still to develop eloquence as a singer of songs, but his eventual mastery is clearly foretold in the old Irish song, *She is far from the land*, a haunting and heartfelt piece of tender nostalgia. The transfers are excellent.

Lauritz Melchior   *tenor*

Complete MGM Recordings 1946-47   Ⓗ
F Andersen I det frie[b] **Bach/Gounod** Ave Maria **Bizet** Agnus Dei[b]; Cantique de Noël **Bond** I Love You Truly **De Curtis** Torna a Surriento **De Koven** O Promise Me **Geehl** For You Alone **Heuberger** The Kiss in Your Eyes **Hildach** Der Lenz **Kern** The Song is You **Lehár** You Are my Heart's Delight **Leoncavallo** Mattinata. Pagliacci[c] – Vesti la giubba; No, Pagliaccio non son **Nevin** The Rosary **Porter** Easy to Love[b] **Puccini** Tosca[c] – Recondita armonia; E lucevan le stelle **Rotter** Spring Came Back to Vienna **Schubert** Who is Silvia?, D891 **J Strauss** Il Kaiser, Op 437 **Stravinsky** Summer Moon (arr Klenner) **Traditional** All mein Gedanken[a]; Helan går[b]; Silent Night **Youmans** Without a Song
Lauritz Melchior ten [a]**Lou Raderman** vn [a]**Albert Sendry** org **MGM Studio Orchestra** and [b]**Chorus / Georgie Stoll** [a]pf; [c]**Giocomo Spadoni**
Romophone mono ② 82019-2 (78' · ADD) Recorded 1946-7   Ⓕ Ⓞ

In the years just after the war, two of the 20th-century's greatest singers, Pinza and Melchior, moved from the opera house into a world of more popular music. They were castigated for their pains because they were considered to be lowering the standards of their art. Today we take a more tolerant attitude to these things; indeed, it's frequently encouraged, especially by record companies. Melchior's move into films and the like was a success with the general public, and MGM signed him up for a series of recordings, made in 1946-7, when he was 56. They're presented here in their entirety.

The legendary Danish Heldentenor, still at the time singing Wagner at the Metropolitan, tackles a good deal of dross but turns more or less everything into gold by dint of his dignified artistry. A few of the songs are beyond even him to save, but he sings Schubert's *Who is Sylvia?*, Italian songs (in the original), Viennese operetta (in English) and Christmas songs – Bizet's *Cantique de Noël* a particular success – with total conviction. In a Danish children's song (this item comes from a film soundtrack) and a Swedish drinking song, both introduced by his own speech, his disarming honesty of approach is its own justification. The latter is an absolutely delightful and jovial end to the whole project, with a cry of 'Skol' to round it off!

That his voice had lost virtually nothing of its operatic opulence is proved in Cavaradossi's two arias, not wholly idiomatic in style, and Canio's two jealous outbursts, all recorded at the final session on December 26, 1947, by which time he was 57. As Canio, his impassioned utterance is full of the requisite pathos and power, yet avoiding the extravagant effects of some Italian tenors, a fitting end to his distinguished career in the studio recording the heavier tenor repertory. The transfers, by Mark Obert-Thorn, are exemplary.

although the first disc above, a brave disc of Italian chamber vocal music, isn't for the faint-hearted. Nevertheless, any collaboration between Sara Mingardo and Rinaldo Alessandrini is destined to be special.

Merula's *Hor ch'è tempo di dormire* is a poignant and personal expression of Mary's grief over the crucified Christ. In the haunting and introspective performance of Salvatore's pastoral cantata *Allor che Tirsi udia*, Mingardo's hushed evocation of a dying lover's final moments is worth the price of the disc alone. Monica Bacelli has been drafted in for Monteverdi's duet 'Vorrei baciarti', and Alessandrini has composed several instrumental realisations to flesh out the continuo skeleton of a few pieces. Alongside precious rarities by famous masters, Mingardo gives spellbinding performances of intimate works by Carissimi and Legrenzi. An extended scene from Cavalli's *La Calisto* is the ideal demonstration of how the Baroque singer's art ought to be both gorgeous and intense, and Handel's seldom-recorded cantata *Lungi da me pensier tiranno* is wonderful, with magnificent continuo from Alessandrini and cellist Luca Peverini. It almost goes without saying that Mingardo's Vivaldi is superb.

The delectable sampler 'Contralto' features extracts from Mingardo's previous recordings with Concerto Italiano. Her excellence shines through at every moment: eloquent poignancy in three moving settings of the *Stabat mater*, the colourful and extrovert emotion in Vivaldi's *Cessate, omai cessate*, and the charismatic beauty of Handel's first oratorio. 'Mentre dormi', from Vivaldi's *L'Olimpiade*, is a ravishing delight.

Lovers of Baroque singing should not miss these performances.

Sara Mingardo   *contralto*

Carissimi Deh memoria e che più chiedi **Cavalli** La Calisto – Erme e solighe cime **Handel** Lungi da me pensier tiranno **Legrenzi** Costei ch'in mezzo al volto scritt'ha il mio cor **Merlua** Hor ch'è tempo di dormire **Monteverdi** Se i languidi miei sguardi. Vorrei baciarti, O Filli[a] **Salvatore** Allor che Tirsi udia **Vivaldi** Pianti, sospiri
Sara Mingardo *contr* [a]Monica Bacelli *sop* **Concerto Italiano / Rinaldo Alessandrini**
Naïve Opus 111 OP30395 (72' · DDD · T/t) Ⓟ**ⓞⓞⓞ**

Contralto

Extracts from **Handel** Il Trionfo del Tempo e del Disinganno **Pergolesi** Stabat mater[a] **A Scarlatti** Stabat mater **Vivaldi** Concerto for Strings in C, RV117. Cessate, omai cessate. Gloria, RV589[b]. Magnificat, RV611[b]. Stabat mater. L'Olimpiade – Mentre dormi
Sara Mingardo *contr* with [a]**Gemma Bertagnolli** *sop* [b]**Akademia; Concerto Italiano / Rinaldo Alessandrini**
Naïve Opus 111 OP30373 (66' · DDD) Ⓕ

 Opus 111 has carved out a distinctive niche by producing first-class recordings of unusual Italian Baroque gems,

Diana Montague   *mezzo-soprano*

Great Operatic Arias, Volume 2
Berlioz La damnation de Faust, Op 24 – D'amour l'ardente flamme **Delibes** Lakmé – Viens Mallika; Dôme épais le jasmin ... Sous le dôme épais (Flower duet) **Donizetti** La favorite – Fia dunque vero? ... O mio Fernando **Gluck** Orfeo ed Euridice – Che farò senza Euridice? **Gounod** Faust – Faites-lui mes aveux **Offenbach** La périchole – O mon cher amant, je te jure; Ah! quel dîner je viens de faire!; Tu n'es pas beau, tu n'es pas riche **Rossini** Le comte Ory – A la faveur de cette nuit obscure **Saint-Saëns** Samson et Dalila – Printemps qui commence; Amour! viens aider ma faiblesse!; Mon coeur s'ouvre à ta voix **A Thomas** Mignon – Connais-tu le pays?; Me voici dans son boudoir
Diana Montague *mez* **Mary Plazas** *sop* **Bruce Ford** *ten* **Philharmonia Orchestra / David Parry**
Chandos/Peter Moores Foundation Opera in English Series CHAN3010 (76' · DDD) English texts included
Ⓕ

Montague, our leading interpreter of what the French call the *Falcon* repertory (after a singer of this special character), has been far too little celebrated, at least on disc, so this superbly executed programme of French opera arias, with one exception, sung in the vernacular with impeccable diction and full of dramatic import, must be reckoned the jewel so far in the Chandos Opera in English series. Her distinctive timbre, sense of the correct style and complete identification with each character in turn make the recital so thrilling, exciting and pleasing.

An account of Orfeo's 'What is life?' that equals if not surpasses Ferrier's, a Delilah to die for, each of her arias given a different character as required, a Marguerite (Berlioz's) who yearns with the best on disc (Montague's low tones here so eloquent, the climax given all its due before the intense reprise), a Mignon who's suitably mysterious ('Have you heard of the land?' so full of longing for a lost ideal with a marvellous lift at the words 'my home') and a Donizetti Léonore who 'speaks' so tenderly of her love for her Fernando, with a cabaletta, including repeat, to show off the singer's forceful attack, all these emotional states are contained within a line and tone that respect vocal verities.

Montague has often been called upon to take breeches roles on stage so it's good to be reminded of her lighter touch, not only as Siebel and Frédéric, but also as Isolier, a part she sang to critical approval at Glyndebourne in 1997: the trio from *Comte Ory* is graced by Bruce Ford's elegant Ory and Plazas as the Countess Adèle. Plazas also partners Montague in a nicely flowing account of *that* duet from *Lakmé*. Finally we have Montague the witty comedienne in three deliciously articulated numbers of *Périchole*. Parry and the Philharmonia provide euphonious accompaniments and, where needed, true passion. The recording keeps a nice balance between voice and orchestra. This is a triumph for Diana Montague.

Claudia Muzio   *soprano*

Opera Arias   H
Aida, Un ballo in maschera, La bohème, Carmen, Cavalleria rusticana, Les contes d'Hoffmann, Ernani, La forza del destino, Gianni Schicchi, La Gioconda, Guillaume Tell, Louise, Madama Butterfly, Madame Sans-Gêne, Manon, Manon Lescaut, Mefistofele, Mignon, Otello, Pagliacci, Il segreto di Susanna, Suor Angelica, Tosca, La traviata, Il trovatore, I vespri siciliani & La Wally; songs by **Braga, Burleigh, Buzzi-Peccia, Delibes, Donaudy, Giordano, Mascheroni, Olivieri, Roxas** and **Sanderson**
Claudia Muzio *sop* with various artists
Romophone mono ② 81010-2 (140' · ADD) Recorded 1917-25   Ⓕ

Romophone has put us in its debt by issuing the 1917-25 Pathés and adding four unpublished and fascinating Edison titles. Inevitably there's some overlapping with the first set (reviewed below) but it's surprising how many titles were not remade by the soprano. Here we have, on the first disc, an impassioned and nicely shaded 'Suicidio!' in a reading that's amazingly accomplished, given that Muzio was just 28 at the time. 'O patria mia' and 'Un bel dì' adumbrate the

sheer beauty of the voice of the young *spinto*: strength is there, but also refinement and feeling, although the technical command, as often with this singer, isn't always faultless. Above all, we catch an echo over the years of what Muzio must have been like: deeply affecting, in these roles, confirming contemporary comment.

The songs are irresistible. Buzzi-Peccia's *Baciarmi* is poised sensuously on a skein of gossamer tone. In another song, Burleigh's *Jean*, we can delight in Muzio's excellent and clear English and also in the better sound. Then come the four 'new' Edisons, which include Donaudy's *O del mio amato ben*, later repeated in 1935 for Columbia: the performance is just as plangent. Even more tenderly accented is a little-known and unattributed song, *Torna amore*, and the even more evocative traditional *Mon jardin*.

Opera Arias and Duets   H
Adriana Lecouvreur, Andrea Chénier, L'Arlesiana, La bohème, Cavalleria rusticana, Cecilia, La forza del destino, Mefistofele, Norma, Otello, La sonnambula, Tosca, La traviata & Il trovatore; songs by **Buzzi-Peccia, Debussy, Delibes, Donaudy, Parisotti, Refice** and **Reger**. Also contains part of Tosca, Act 1, recorded live 1932
Claudia Muzio *sop* with various artists
Romophone mono ② 81015-2 (155' · ADD) Recorded 1934-5   Ⓕ

This set completes Romophone's comprehensive survey of all Muzio's records, masterminded by Ward Marston. Since their first release, Muzio's Columbias of 1934-5 have always been her most accessible discs, but they have never, even on previous CD reissues, sounded as present and clear as here. This most eloquent of divas seems to be in the room with us, and the music in hand is delivered with such sincere passion, such total conviction, that tears are brought to the eyes. Not for a moment can one be anything but enthralled by these readings. Since there isn't enough material to fill two CDs, Romophone have added a substantial extract from Act 1 of a 1932 San Francisco *Tosca*, primitively recorded and so far known only to a few Muzio fanatics. However, this is an essential issue for anyone wanting to know about the art of one of the most lovable and vital interpreters.

Opera Arias and Songs   H
Adriana Lecouvreur, L'Africaine, L'amico Fritz, Andrea Chénier, Bianca e Fernando, La bohème, Carmen, Les contes d'Hoffmann, Eugene Onegin, La forza del destino, Hérodiade, I Lombardi, Loreley, Madame Sans-Gêne, Mefistofele, Pagliacci, Paride e Elena, Rinaldo, Salvator Rosa, La traviata, Il trovatore, I vespri siciliani, La Wally & Zazà; songs by **Bachelet, Buzzi-Peccia, Chopin, Guagni-Benvenuti, Herbert, Mascheroni, Monahan, Pergolesi, Rossini** and **Sodero**
Claudia Muzio *sop* with various artists
Romophone mono ② 81005-2 (153' · ADD) Recorded 1911-25   Ⓕ

The crackles and surface noise that usually afflict Edison reproduction have all but been eliminated, so that we can hear Muzio's voice in its absolute prime without, as it were, the effort of listening through a sea of interference. The sheer beauty of the soprano's voice and her wonderful intensity of expression can now be experienced with astonishing immediacy. All the Muzio gifts, including that of refined, exquisite phrasing combined with that peculiarly heart-rending intensity that was hers alone, are heard in that enchanting song by Bachelet, *Chère nuit* (first disc, track 8). If your dealer will let you hear that, even if you're sceptical about singers of the past, you're sure to make off home with this set, eager to hear the rest. A feast of captivating interpretations await the listener.

Anna Netrebko   *soprano*

Bellini La sonnambula – Care compagne, e voi, teneri amici...Come per me sereno **Berlioz** Benvenuto Cellini – Les belles fleurs!...Quand j'aurai votre âge **Donizetti** Lucia di Lammermoor[a] – Ancor non giunse!... Regnava nel silenzio **Dvořák** Rusalka – O, moon high up in the deep, deep sky **Gounod** Faust – Les grands seigneurs ont seuls des airs si résolus...Ah! je ris (Jewel Song) **Massenet** Manon – Suis-je gentille ainsi?...Je marche sur tous les chemins...Obéissons, quand leur voix appelle **Mozart** Don Giovanni – Crudele? Ah no, mio bene!... Non mi dir, bell'idol mio. Idomeneo – Quando avran fine omai...Padre, germani, addio! **Puccini** La bohème – Quando m'en vo'
Anna Netrebko *sop* [a]**Elina Garanca** *mez* **Vienna State Opera Chorus; Vienna Philharmonic Orchestra / Gianandrea Noseda**
DG 474 240-2GH (63' · DDD) Texts and translations included ⓕⓞ

Also available on SACD 474 240-2

In the past few years Anna Netrebko has become one of the most admired young lyric sopranos the world over. So this first solo recital disc comes not before time, though it's saddening to read in the biographical introductory notes that she 'does not consider herself a particularly persuasive champion of Russian opera' and prefers to devote herself to French and Italian.

The selection is good: everything suits the voice, including Donna Anna's 'Non mi dir'. In Bellini and Donizetti she shows the primary strength of drawing a firm, even melodic line, and when she rises above the stave it's without that tendency to hardening and shrillness which has so often beset Italian sopranos. In the French repertory the free, glistening high notes are a great asset to her Manon, and the *Benvenuto Cellini* aria is a joy.

Occasionally some feature of pronunciation reminds us that she isn't a native speaker of these languages, and there are times when greater clarity would not come amiss. Yet the limitation lies more in that elusive quality we call, for short, the personal touch. Here is one of the best

of the younger generation, faithfully recorded and notably well accompanied by the VPO under Noseda.

Anne Sofie von Otter   *mezzo-soprano*

Lamenti
Bertali Lamento della Regina d'Inghilterra[abd]
Legrenzi Il ballo del Gran Duca, Op 16 – Corrente nona[de] **Monteverdi** Madrigals, Book 7 – Con che soavità[ade]. Lamento d'Arianna[ac] **Piccinini** Ciaccona[c] **Purcell** Incassum, Lesbia, rogas, Z383[ad]. O Solitude! my sweetest choice, Z406[ac] **Vivaldi** Cessate, omai cessate, RV684[ad]
[a]**Anne Sofie von Otter** *mez* [b]**Franz-Josef Selig** *bass* [c]**Jakob Lindberg** *theorbo* [d]**Musica Antiqua Köln / Reinhard Goebel** [e]*vn*
Archiv Produktion 457 617-2AH (60' · DDD) Texts and translations included ⓕⓞ

Anne Sofie von Otter adds to her laurels with this issue, which belies any doom and gloom suggested by its title with singing of an intensity of expression, subtlety of nuance and rich palette of vocal colour that leave one full of admiration. Whether lamenting a stony-hearted lover (*Cessate, omai cessate*) or a faithless one (in *Arianna*, all that remains of a lost Monteverdi opera), a queen of Arcadia (*Incassum, Lesbia, rogas*) or the husband of an English queen (presumably Charles I, in view of the frenzied cries for revenge), von Otter fills every word with vivid meaning while still preserving the musical line. Vengeance is also the passionate response of the lover in the Vivaldi cantata (no stranger to the record catalogue), superbly performed here, with full-blooded instrumental backing by Musica Antiqua Köln. At the opposite end of the emotional spectrum, another highlight of the disc is Purcell's sad, touching *Incassum, Lesbia*. His *O Solitude!* is built on a ground bass, as is the little piece for solo theorbo by Piccinini, as well as the Legrenzi *Corrente* – neither of which, in fact, suggests lamenting. The most varied instrumentation occurs in Monteverdi's sectional *Con che soavità*, with its changeable tempos and ornamental vocal line. The contribution by an admirable bass, Franz-Josef Selig, in two brief but low-lying narrations in the Bertali (a work largely in recitative, but with interludes for three violas) shouldn't be overlooked. Altogether an outstanding disc.

Watercolours
Alfvén Peonies. Take my heart **Aulin** And the knight rode to the Holy Land. To a rose. Winter in my heart. What do I want? The Judgment **Frumerie** Songs of the heart, Op 27. Aftonland – A summer morning **Larsson** Nine Songs, Op 35 – Kiss of the wind. Grass sings under wandering feet. The cloud, the flower and the lark **Linde** Four Songs. Two Songs **Nordqvist** Three Songs **Nystroem** Three Songs **Rangström** Ond Dance. A moment in time. Serenade. The Amazon
Anne Sofie von Otter *mez* **Bengt Forsberg** *pf*

DG 474 700-2GH (73' · DDD) Texts and translations
included Ⓕ**ⓞⓞⓞ**

 'Watercolours' is an evocative description of this collection of pastel-tinted
Swedish songs. Here's a world of suggestive half-lights, aqueous textures and rippling arpeggios reminiscent of Debussy – reflections of nature, shaded by the melancholy gloom
of the North. The period covered is from about
1910 to the 1950s, but the musical language
rarely ventures into modernist idioms. Many of
the composers went to study abroad, but it's the
Swedish national character and the rhythms of
the language, occasionally fortified by folksong, that were the inspiration for their music.

Von Otter sweeps the listener thrillingly along
in Larsson's stormy *Kiss of the wind*, and
Nordqvist's grandly romantic *On the sea*. But
these are the odd ones out, and in the many
near-Impressionist songs it's the keen sensitivity
of her singing that counts, matched by more delicacy than we usually hear from her accompanist, Bengt Forsberg. The gentle Nordic melancholy of this music lingers well after the final
track has played.

Music for a while
Caccini Dovro dunque morire? **Dowland** In
darknesse let mee dwell. The Third and Last Book of
Songs or Aires – What if I never speede?; Weepe you
no more sad fountaines. Can she excuse my wrongs
Ferrari Musiche varie, Book III – Amanti, io vi so dire
(ciaccona) **Frescobaldi** Se l'aura spira **R Johnson II**
Fantasia **Kapsberger** Libro IV d'intavolatura di
chitarrone – Capona: Sferraina L'Arpeggiata
Monteverdi Scherzi musicali – Ecco di dolci raggi;
Quel sguardo sdegnosetto. L'incoronazione di
Poppea – Adagiati, Poppea **Purcell** Sarabande with
Division. An Evening Hymn on a Ground, 'Now that
the sun hath veil'd his light'. Oedipus – Music for a
while. Pausanias – Sweeter than roses. Rule a Wife
and Have a Wife – There's not a swain. The Tempest
– Dear pretty youth **Storace** Ciaccona **Strozzi** Udite,
udite Amanti L'eraclito Amoroso
Anne Sofie von Otter *mez* **Jacob Lindberg**
gtr/lte/theo **Anders Ericson** *theo* **Jory Vinikour** *hpd*
Archiv Produktion 477 5114 (68' · DDD · T/t) Ⓕ**ⓞⓞ**

'Music for a while' demonstrates that Anne Sofie
von Otter remains committed to exploring the
Baroque repertoire that established her reputation. Monteverdi's 'Ecco di dolci raggi', accompanied only by harpsichordist Jory Vinikour,
shows von Otter's coloratura and timbre are still
marvellous if riding in the right vehicle. Her
gentle 'Adagiati, Poppea' demonstrates that her
attention to detail, especially words, is as sharply
perceptive as it ever was. Frescobaldi's pastoral
evocation of the breeze is sensitively accompanied by Anders Ericson and Jakob Lindberg,
and her delicately poetic slow singing shines in
an assured performance of Caccini's *Dovrò
dunque morire?*
Vinikour's harpsichord solos avoid the danger
of a cruel jolt to the intense melancholy of songs

by Purcell and Dowland. 'Music for a while' is
attractive, but lacks the profound eroticism that
most other singers find in it. 'An Evening
Hymn' is unusually jaunty, and like a theatre
song. Von Otter keeps things sincere and simple
in four songs by Dowland, and her partnership
with Jakob Lindberg's subtle lute reaps massive
rewards in a mesmerizing performance of 'In
darkness let me dwell'. The Dowland selection
is the finest aspect of this disc, and shows one of
our greatest modern singers still at the peak of
her art.

Mark Padmore *tenor*

Britten Six Hölderlin Fragments. Um Mitternacht.
Who are these children? **Finzi** A Young Man's
Exhortation **Tippett** Boyhood's End
Mark Padmore *ten* **Roger Vignoles** *pf*
Hyperion CDA67459 (78' · DDD · T/t) Ⓕ**ⓞⓞ**

Padmore comes to his first recorded recital in
control of his voice more completely than he
was just a few years ago – there are still occasionally high notes without resonance (in the
familiar English fashion) and a trifle backward in
production, but this is still a voice of youthful
freshness, commanded with skill and assurance.
The programme tests his musicianship very
thoroughly, and it reveals also considerable
powers of expressiveness, both forthright and
subtle.

In Tippett's cantata and Britten's songs we can
hardly help think of Peter Pears, for whom they
were written. But Padmore does not evoke
memories of that voice or manner: he sings
more in the way of Martyn Hill, who recorded
Boyhood's End for the composer's 95th birthday.
Finzi's Hardy settings also had Hill as their
singer some years ago, and the new performances should commend them to a new generation. They, on the other hand, may be interested
primarily on account of Britten's *Who are these
children?*, an unjustly neglected work, never
recorded commercially by Britten and Pears. It
collects short, often enigmatic, poems by the
Scot William Suter, and the settings are strong
and haunting. In all these, Vignoles is marvellously clear in notes (often fiendishly difficult)
and rhythm, and he contributes an excellent
essay.

Adelina Patti *soprano*

Opera Arias and Songs Ⓗ
Adelina Patti *sop* with Mario Ancona, Mattia
Battistini, Emma Calvé, Fernando De Lucia, Edouard
de Reszke, Emma Eames, Lucien Fugère, Wilhelm
Hesch, Lilli Lehmann, Félia Litvinne, Francesco
Marconi, Victor Maurel, Dame Nellie Melba, Lillian
Nordica, Adelina Patti, Pol Plançon, Maurice Renaud,
Sir Charles Santley, Marcella Sembrich, Francesco
Tamagno and Francesco Viñas
Nimbus Prima Voce mono ② NI7840/1 (120' · ADD)
Recorded 1902-28 Ⓜ

This is a 'historical' issue for straightforward enjoyment. Although the originals were made in the very earliest years of recording, they're reproduced here with a vividness that calls for very little in the way of making allowances. It starts in party mood with the first Falstaff of all, Victor Maurel, singing to a bunch of cronies in the studio of 1907 the 'Quand'ero paggio' which he sang at La Scala in the première of 1893. They cheer and call for an encore, which he gives them, then again, this time in French. The record has been transferred many times, but never has it been so easy for the listener to 'see' it and feel part of it.

The magnificent bass Pol Plançon follows with King Philip's solo from *Don Carlos*, beautifully even in production and deeply absorbed in the character and his emotions. The hauntingly pure, well-rounded soprano of Emma Eames in Tosti's *Dopo*, and then the miraculously spry and elegant 80-year-old Lucien Fugère lead to the first of the Patti records: the one her husband thought unladylike and asked to be withdrawn from the catalogue, *La calesera*, and the most joyous she ever made. Tamagno, Melba, Nordica, Renaud: they're all here, and on thrillingly good form.

Rosa Ponselle   *soprano*

Rosa Ponselle On the Air, Volume 1, 1934-36 Ⓗ
Bartlett A Dream **Bizet** Carmen – Danse bohémienne; Habanera; Seguédille; Mêlons! Coupons!. Ouvre ton coeur. **Bond** I Love You Truly **Brahms** Volks-Kinderlieder – Wiegenlied **Charles** When I Have Sung My Songs **Del Riego** Homing **Dvořák** Humoresques, B187 – No 7 in G flat **Eden** What's In The Air **Gluck** Alceste – Divinités du Styx **Grosvenor** I Carry You In My Pocket **Kountz** The Sleigh Kreisler The Old Refrain **Lehár** Die lustige Witwe – Waltz Song **Lockhart** In the Luxembourg Gardens **Mana-Zucca** The Big Brown Bear[a] **Mascagni** Cavalleria rusticana – Voi lo sapete; Ave Maria (arr from Intermezzo by Weatherly) **Mozart** Don Giovanni – Batti, batti **Nevin** The Rosary **Padilla** La violetera Ponce Estrellita **Reger** Schlichte Weisen, Op 76 – Maria Wiegenlied **Romani** Fedra – O divina Afrodite **Saint-Saëns** Samson et Dalila – Printemps qui commence **Sandoval** Ave Maria **Schaefer** The Cuckoo Clock **Schubert** Erlkönig, D328 **Serradell** La golondrina **Spross** Will-o'-the-Wisp **J Strauss II** An der schönen, blauen Donau, Op 314 **O Straus** Der tapfere Soldat – Mein Held! **Tchaikovsky** Songs, Op 6 – Nun wer die Sehnsucht kennt **Tosti** Goodbye. L'ultima canzone **Traditional** The Last Rose of Summer. Danny Boy. Comin' thro' the Rye **Valverde** Clavelitos
Rosa Ponselle sop [a]**Charles Henderson** pf **orchestra / André Kostelanetz**
Marston ② 52012-2 (145' · ADD) Recorded 1934-6. Ⓕ

In the 1930s, at the height of the Depression, the Americans weren't going to the opera very much – the Met was regularly half empty. Nor were they buying many records; they were, however, smoking. Chesterfield's, one of the leading tobacco manufacturers, sponsored a weekly radio programme, and a frequent guest on it was Rosa Ponselle. Ponselle herself said that these off-the-air recordings were a more accurate record of her singing than her studio-made discs. The sound is variable, there's a good deal of hiss and some distortion, but the familiar Ponselle style comes across loud and clear. It seems quite extraordinary now, but Ponselle made no commercial discs between 1930 (when she was at the very peak of her career) and 1939, when, just after her marriage, she was about to retire. Her singing is generous, emotive, a bit over the top sometimes in slight songs such as Ponce's *Estrellita* or Serradell's *La golondrina*. She has no difficulty crossing over to operetta, with *Der tapfere Soldat* ('The Chocolate Soldier') and *The Merry Widow*, since her stage career had begun in vaudeville. The only opera extracts here from roles she sang on stage are from *Carmen*, *Cavalleria rusticana* and Romani's *Fedra*.

The strength of her voice posed problems for the engineers, but by moving the broadcast microphone away from the orchestra, they were able to capture something of the energy and power of Ponselle's singing that she felt was absent from her earlier 78s. A lot of the material is ephemeral, but in a trifle like *The Sleigh* by Kountz one gets a vivid glimpse of her agility – it was one of the thrills of Ponselle's singing that such a huge voice had such a facility with coloratura passages, and that she could fine down the tone to wonderful *pianissimos*.

The sentimentality of many of these songs, such as Bartlett's *A Dream* or Bond's *I Love You Truly* would be completely beyond the scope of most modern singers, but Ponselle's directness lifts them above kitsch. It's sad that she didn't include arias from some of the operas she was singing at the Met at the same time – *Luisa Miller* or *Andrea Chénier*. As it is, this collection offers a fascinating souvenir of this great singer in her prime.

Leontyne Price   *soprano*

Historic Performances, 1938 and 1953 Ⓗ
CPE Bach Nonnelied[b] **Barber** Hermit Songs[a]. Nuvoletta[a]. The Daisies[a]. Sleep now[a]. Nocturne[a] **Brahms** Der Gang zum Liebchen[b]. Der Tod, das ist die kühle Nacht[b] **Fauré** Au bord de l'eau[a] **Mendelssohn** Frage[b] **Poulenc** Trois Métamorphoses – C'est ainsi que tu es[a]. Ce doux petit visage[a]. Main dominée par le cœur[a]. Miroirs brûlants[a] **Sauguet** La Voyante[a] **Schubert** Der Jüngling an der Quelle[b] **Schumann** In der Fremde[b] **Traditional** Batti, batti[b]. O waly waly[b]. Chi ti ci fa venir[b]. O brother Greene, O come to me[b]. Old woman, old woman, will you go a-shearing?[b] Zu dir zieht's mi hin[b]
[a]**Leontyne Price** sop **Samuel Barber** bbar/pf
Bridge mono BRIDGE9156 (80' · DDD · T) [a]Recorded live at the Library of Congress, Washington in October 1953
Ⓕ**OO**

Leontyne Price was on the threshold of her international career when she and Samuel

Barber gave their first recital together, in Washington in October 1953. The main item was the world première of Barber's *Hermit Songs*, based on Celtic texts from the 8th-12th centuries. The cycle, and the four other Barber songs, have been issued before (RCA), but the other tracks are new to the catalogue.

Price's pristine voice (she was 26), combined with Barber's sensitive accompaniment, make the songs flow with the mystery and humour that the poems demand. They made a studio recording of the cycle the following year, but there's an added excitement about hearing this first performance. She recorded all but one of the Poulenc mélodies later with David Garvey (RCA), but Sauguet's cycle *La Voyante* is an addition to her discography; the songs suit her soaring soprano. Although the voice sometimes overwhelms the microphone, the sound is excellent for a 51-year-old live event.

The 12 songs recorded by Barber, accompanying himself, in 1938 are quite a surprise. He had a beautiful voice, a sort of American Pierre Bernac. The sound here is variable, but there's more than just curiosity value. The two Tuscan folk songs are especially charming.

Dame Margaret Price   *soprano*

The Romantic Lied
Cornelius Trauer und Trost, Op 3 **Liszt** Freudvoll und leidvoll, S280. Über allen Gipfeln ist Ruh, S306. Mignons Lied, S275. Der du von dem Himmel bist, S279 **Wagner** Wesendonk Lieder **Wolf** Mörike Lieder – Er ist's; Begegnung; Der Gärtner; In der Frühe; Lebe wohl; Heimweh; Gesang Weylas; Bei einer Trauung
Dame Margaret Price *sop* **Graham Johnson** *pf*
Forlane UCD16728 (71' · DDD) Recorded 1993
Texts and translations included   Ⓕ

Price and Johnson have done it again. He has chosen a programme for her that exactly suits her talents and style, and she (with his inestimable help) has executed it with commitment and understanding. The programme in itself is fascinating, comparing and contrasting composers of roughly the same generation and period. The cross-fertilisation of musical ideas is apparent, yet each emerges as an artist with something highly individual to say. Wolf isn't a composer with whom Price has been very much associated until now, but in a group of the Mörike settings, she proves herself at one with the poems and their music, catching in particular the restless ardour of *Begegnung*, the timeless mystery of *Gesang Weylas*, and the peculiarly Wolfian charm of the lighter pieces. Liszt is even more to her liking. She and Johnson choose the later, longer version of *Freudvoll und leidvoll* and make a grand romantic statement of it that's just right. The interpretation of the *Wesendonk Lieder* is the crowning glory of this wonderful recital. A virtually faultless reading, speeds (no unwanted lingering), phrasing, line and tone ideally adapted to the words and music.

Graham Johnson places the piano part in perfect relationship with the voice, helped by the exemplary recording of both.

Thomas Quasthoff   *bass-baritone*

Evening Star
Lortzing Zar und Zimmermann – O sancta justitia! Ich möchte rasen; Den hohen Herrscher würdig zu empfangen; Sonst spielt ich mit Zepter, mit Krone und Stern. Der Wildschütz – Fünftausend Taler! Träum oder wach ich?; Lass Er doch hören!...Bei diesem schlimmen Fall[a]; Wie freundlich strahlt die holde Morgensonne **R Strauss** Die schweigsame Frau – Wie schön ist doch die Musik **Wagner** Tannhäuser – Gar viel und schön ward hier in dieser Halle; Wie Todesahnung Dämmrung deckt die Lande; O du, mein holder Abendstern
Weber Euryanthe – Wo berg ich mich?; Schweigt, glühenden Sehnes
Thomas Quasthoff *bass-bar* [a]**Christiane Oelze** *sop*
Chorus and Orchestra of the Deutsche Oper, Berlin / Christian Thielemann
DG 471 493-2GH (67' · DDD) Notes, texts and translations included   Ⓕ◉

Once more Thomas Quasthoff puts us in his debt with a recital wholly out of the ordinary, executed confidently in singing of such strength and beauty as to almost silence criticism. Surveying German Romantic opera from the now-neglected Lortzing to Richard Strauss, he ranges easily through roles usually assigned to either a specifically baritone or bass voice.

In the lengthy extracts from *Zar und Zimmermann* he portrays both the pompous, amusingly portrayed mayor Van Bett and the upright figure of the Tsar, whose Act 3 aria he sings with refined tone and elegiac feeling. In *Der Wildschütz* he's funny as the schoolmaster Baculus, a *buffo* bass figure whose 'Fünftausend Taler' used to be a staple of a German bass's repertory; then he sings Graf Eberbach's lovely solo in a mellow baritone. It's good to be reminded in such a positive way of Lortzing's merits.

In the *Tannhäuser* pieces he projects the address of the benevolent Landgrave with complete authority and then sings Wolfram's Evening Star aria, from which the CD takes its title, with perfection of tone and line. Finally he catches finely old Morosus's restored peace after all the disturbing events of *Die schweigsame Frau* have finally come to an end.

Thielemann, and his Berlin orchestra and chorus, are at one with their soloist throughout, and the recording catches everything in a clear, warm perspective.

Rosa Raisa   *soprano*

The Complete Recordings, 1917-26   Ⓗ
Opera arias and duets – L'Africaine, Aida, Andrea Chénier, Cavalleria rusticana, Don Giovanni, Ernani, La forza del destino, La Gioconda, Madama Butterfly, Mefistofele, Norma, Otello, Tosca, Il trovatore and I

vespri siciliani; songs by **Tchaikovsky** and **Yradier**
Rosa Raisa sop with various artists
Marston mono ③ 53001-2 (227' · ADD) Recorded
1917-26 ⓂⓄ

'I would listen to them, and then break them
into pieces' wrote Raisa in 1962, explaining why
she possessed none of her own records. It's a pity
she could not have heard them in these fine
transfers and reproduced on modern equipment. Her objection was that they failed to show
the volume of her voice, and that's very probably
true. The impression they give is that of an
ample lyric soprano with a dramatic style rather
than a full dramatic voice. What they preserve is
a sound of exceptional beauty and in several
instances singing of equally exceptional skill.
Outstanding is the single previously unpublished item, the cabaletta 'Ah! bello a me ritorna'
from *Norma*, recorded for Brunswick in 1929. A
superb demonstration of vocal mastery, it seems
totally unaware of difficulties. The semiquaver
passagework, the bold intervals, the matching of
rhythmic energy with lyric grace, all are mastered with apparent ease. It's sad to think that
this is all that remains of a Norma often
reported as having been the finest of all in this
century, at any rate up to Callas's time.

There are many other lovely things here.
Raisa's chequered career as a recording artist
began with the aria from *Andrea Chénier*, 'La
mamma morta', on Pathé in 1917, and this was
also the subject of her last recording, in 1933.
Despite the difference in tempo (the later version being more expansive), they're very alike in
style and affectionate in feeling. Similarly with
the six (no less) versions of 'Voi lo sapete'. Her
'Un bel dì' is unexpectedly touching and intimate, the manner delicate and girlish, till the
'per non morir', when the girl becomes woman.
The duets with her baritone husband, Giacomo
Rimini, include one (clear-voiced and dramatic
against a scrunchy background) from *Il trovatore*
on a Vitaphone soundtrack. Then the third disc
ends with an interview, not especially illuminating but nice to have, given in 1962 and in lively
style, a year before her death. Raisa was one of
the great singers of her time, and among them
perhaps the most outstanding example of neglect by the major record companies. The
Marston catalogue is enriched by this release.

Elisabeth Rethberg   *soprano*

Opera Arias   Ⓗ
Aida, Andrea Chénier, La bohème, Der Freischütz,
Lohengrin, Madama Butterfly, Le nozze di Figaro,
Otello, Serse, Sosarme, Tannhäuser, Tosca & Die
Zauberflöte; songs by **Bishop**, **Braga**, **Cadman**,
Densmore, **Flies**, **Gounod**, **Grieg**, **Griffes**, **Hildach**,
Jensen, **Korschat**, **Lassen**, **Loewe**, **Massenet**,
Mendelssohn, **Rubinstein**, **Schubert**, **Schumann**,
Taubert and **Tchaikovsky**
Elisabeth Rethberg sop with various artists
Romophone mono ② 81012-2 (158' · ADD)
Recorded 1924-9 Ⓕ

They're very collectable, these Romophone
complete editions. Up they go on the shelves,
and you know that there's another small but
quite important area in the history of singing on
records properly covered, ready for reference at
any time, and reference that will be a pleasure
because the standard of transfer is so reliable.
In this instance it's the Rethberg Brunswicks:
records which capture the voice in its lovely
prime. Purely as a singer, Rethberg was surely
the most gifted and accomplished lyric soprano
of her age. The essential gift was a voice of
exquisite quality, and her upbringing contributed to the purity of intonation and a feeling
for musical style. Her production was even
and fluent; on all these records there's scarcely
a note or a phrase that isn't delightful purely
as singing. Some of the later records show it also
as a voice capable of considerable expansion in
volume. In Aida's 'O patria mia' Rethberg is
celestial, ample in volume, sensitive in feeling,
phrasing beautifully, taking the C softly and
in a broad single sweep. Equally lovely is her
Mimì, and then in the *Andrea Chénier* aria
there's such an unpressured beauty of utterance
that it almost becomes a different composition.
A previously unpublished delight is a blissful
performance of Eugen Hildach's *Der Spielmann*,
and among the less familiar songs is a charmer
by Carl Taubert, *Es steht ein Baum in jenem
Tal*.

Opera Arias and Duets   Ⓗ
L'Africaine, Andrea Chénier, The Bartered Bride,
La bohème, Carmen, Madama Butterfly, Le nozze di
Figaro, Tosca, Die Zauberflöte & Der Zigeunerbaron;
songs by **Bizet**, **Mozart**, **Pataky** and **R Strauss**
Elisabeth Rethberg sop with various artists
Preiser Lebendige Vergangenheit mono 89051
(71' · AAD) Recorded 1920-25 Ⓕ

Elisabeth Rethberg died in 1976, when little
notice was taken of the passing of a singer once
voted the world's most perfect. The year 1994
was the centenary of her birth, so this fine selection of her early recordings was well timed. The
earliest catch her at the charming age of 26 (the
voice settled, but still that of a young woman),
and the last of them, made in 1925, find her just
into her 30s, mature in timbre, feeling and
artistry. It's doubtful whether a judicious listener would at any point cry 'Ah, it's an Aida
voice!', but Aida was the part for which she
became most famous. In Countess Almaviva's
first aria, her *legato* is the next thing to perfection; in Pamina's 'Ach, ich fühl's' the head tones
are beautifully in place, the portamentos finely
judged, emotion always implicit in the singing.
The duets with Richard Tauber include the
music of Micaëla and Don José sung with unrivalled grace and intimacy, Rethberg shading off
the end of her solo most elegantly, Tauber softening in his so as to welcome and not overwhelm
the soprano's entry. The songs are equally
delightful.

Opera Arias and Ensembles 🅗
L'Africaine, Aida, Attila, Un ballo in maschera,
Boccaccio, Carmen, Cavalleria rusticana, Don
Giovanni, Faust, Die Fledermaus, Der fliegende
Holländer, Lohengrin, I Lombardi, Madama
Butterfly, Die Meistersinger von Nürnberg, Le nozze
di Figaro, Otello, Il rè pastore, Tannhäuser & Der
Zigeunerbaron; songs by **Brahms**, **Mendelssohn** and
Wolf
Elisabeth Rethberg sop with various artists
Romophone mono ② 81014-2 (155' · ADD) Recorded
1927-34   Ⓕ

To the older collector of vocal recordings it's to
be feared that not many of these records will
come as new. Attention can be directed, however, to the last three. These were made in 1932
in the Bell Telephone Laboratories as part of an
experiment in improved recording methods.
They were recorded at 33rpm, and they
achieved startling results. The quality of the
voice is captured to perfection, but most impressive is the freedom of emission, no longer confined within the studio but able to ring and
expand, the contrasts of loud and soft tones
being effective and often as exquisite as they
would have been in the flesh. Most revealing is
Elisabeth's Greeting from *Tannhäuser*, sung
with piano accompaniment but with a dramatic
conviction and enthusiasm far more vivid than
that of the earlier orchestral version. Other new
items are unpublished takes of the two Verdi
trios with Gigli and Pinza, differing slightly in
balance, but very little in style. The six electric
Parlophones include the tender Micaëla's aria
and the solo from *L'Africaine* with its haunting
unaccompanied introduction. Supreme among
the Victors is the second *Un ballo in maschera*
aria, the *Meistersinger* duet with Schorr running
it close. It's also good to have the complete Nile
scene from *Aida*, with Lauri-Volpi in his prime,
de Luca a bit past his. Transfers are of the usual
high standard, and with the first volume, this is
clearly the primary source of a comprehensive
Rethberg collection on disc.

Aksel Schiøtz   tenor

The Complete Recordings 1933-46, Volume 1 🅗
Opéra and Oratorio Arias – Così fan tutte, Die
Entführung aus dem Serail, Eugene Onegin, Don
Giovanni, Faust, Die Zauberflöte, Acis and Galatea,
Christmas Oratorio, Messiah, St Matthew Passion,
Die Schöpfung & Solomon; songs by **Dowland** and
Was mich auf dieser Welt betrübt (**Buxtehude**)
Aksel Schiøtz ten with various artists
Danacord mono DACOCD451 (75' · ADD) Recorded
1933-46   Ⓕ

Schiøtz's singing was always the very epitome of
silvery elegance. His attributes in Handel,
Haydn and Mozart are amply confirmed in this,
the first disc of Danacord's comprehensive 10-
disc survey of all his recorded output. Sadly his
career was cut short by a brain tumour in 1946,
but for the 10 years of his prime, he was rightly

fêted for his beautiful singing and masterly sense
of style. Long before period-instrument performances were current, Schiøtz and Wöldike
were seeking an authentic style of performing
Handel and Bach, as exemplified here in the
poised, unaffected account of the opening solos
from *Messiah*, and arias from the *St Matthew Passion* and *Christmas Oratorio*. 'Frohe Hirten' from
the latter and the lovely aria by Buxtehude
sound even better now that they have been
released from the scratch on the originals, the
transfers expertly done by EMI's Andrew Walter. Also in the oratorio field the aria from *Die
Schöpfung* demonstrates perfectly the singer's
delicately etched line and pure tone.

There are few more fine-grained versions of
Tamino's 'Portrait' aria, Ottavio's arias nor of
Pedrillo's Serenade, but 'Un aur'amorosa' suffers from an uncomfortably fast speed. Schiøtz is
also among the most elegiac of Lenskys in that
character's lament (slightly cut), the most sweet-
toned of Fausts, the top C taken in the head as is
the case with other tenors of his type. It seems
hardly to matter that these pieces are sung in
Danish. The Dowland, like the Handel, is given
authentically, though a guitar rather than a lute
is used for the accompaniments.

As a bonus there are rehearsal performances of
Acis's 'Love sounds the alarm', minus *da capo*,
and 'Sacred raptures' from *Solomon*, the former
impeccable, the latter showing an un-accus-
tomed fallibility in the runs. The booklet is full
of interesting photos and articles.

The Complete Recordings, 1933-46, Volume 2 🅗
Grieg Melodies of the Heart, Op 5[b] – No 1, Two
brown eyes; No 3, I love but thee. Songs, Op 33 –
No 2, Last Spring[b]; No 9, At Rondane[c]. Songs and
Ballads, Op 9 – No 4, Outward Bound[c] **Schubert** Die
schöne Müllerin, D795[a]
Aksel Schiøtz ten [a]**Gerald Moore**, [bc]**Folmer
Jensen** pfs
Danacord mono DACOCD452 (75' · ADD) Texts and
translations included   ⒻⓄ

The Complete Recordings, 1933-46, Volume 3 🅗
Bellman Fredman's Epistles – Dearest brothers,
sisters and friends; Old age is with me; Sit down
around the spring here. Fredman's Songs – Hear
bells give out a frightful boom; So tipsy we are taking
leave; Joachim lived in Babylon **Brahms** Die
Mainacht, Op 43 No 2. Sonntag, Op 47 No 3.
Ständchen, Op 106 No 1 **Buxtehude** Aperite mihi
portas justitiae, BuxWV7 **Grieg** Songs, Op 49 – No 3,
Kind greetings, fair ladies; No 6, Spring showers. The
Poet's farewell, Op 18 No 3 **Schumann** Dichterliebe,
Op 48
Aksel Schiøtz ten with various artists
Danacord mono DACOCD453 (69' · ADD) Texts and
translations included   ⒻⓄ

The years 1945-6 were particularly fruitful ones
for Schiøtz in relation to recording. With Walter Legge's eager support the Danish tenor
could at last come to London to resume his
recording career with *Die schöne Müllerin*, which

takes up the lion's share of Vol 2. The Danacord transfer of this sensitive reading is now the one to go for: not only is the sound marginally superior to Preiser's earlier transfer but added to it are five wonderful readings of Grieg songs, these actually recorded for the composer's centenary in 1943. In particular the popular *I love but thee* and the gloriously ardent *Last Spring* find in Schiøtz an ideal interpreter, a singer whose style so effortlessly and unassumingly goes to the heart of the matter. He's just as convincing in the three lesser-known songs by Grieg in Vol 3, devoted to six months of recording activity at the start of 1946.

Yet another facet of his art is revealed in the Bellman songs, aptly recorded in Sweden, Schiøtz disclosing his sense of humour in the bawdy songs of the 18th century, pleasure-loving Bellman. In *So tipsy we are taking leave*, he captures to perfection the devil-may-care, bawdy mood and in all these attractive pieces finds a willing partner in Ulrik Neumann's guitar. But this third volume is most valuable for giving us Schiøtz's marvellous *Dichterliebe*, perhaps his finest achievement of all on disc.

Then come three Brahms songs, never issued on 78s, that are also near ideal, especially the delicately floated line of *Die Mainacht*. Gerald Moore, as ever, fits his playing intuitively to the singer he's partnering. Then, after the Grieg and Bellman, comes more evidence of the tenor's and Wöldike's championship of Buxtehude, then a neglected figure, which again benefits from Schiøtz's innate sense of the right style for the music in hand. It also allows us to hear a pleasing mezzo (Elsa Sigfuss) and bass (Holger Nørgaard). Andrew Walter's re-mastering of all this disparate material at Abbey Road is faultless.

The Complete Recordings, 1933-46, Volume 4 H
Hartmann Tell me, star of night, Op 63. Little Christine – Sverkel's romance **Lange-Müller** Once Upon a Time – Serenade; Midsummer song **Mozart** Per pietà, non ricercate, K420 **Riisager** Mother Denmark **Schubert** Die schöne Müllerin, D795 – No 1, Das Wandern; No 6, Der Neugierige; No 7, Ungeduld; No 8, Morgengruss; No 10, Tränenregen; No 11, Mein; No 15, Eifersucht und Stolz; No 17, Die böse Farbe; No 19, Der Müller und der Bach; No 20, Des Baches Wiegenlied **Schubert/Berté** Das Dreimäderlhaus – excerpts **Weyse** Angel of Light, go in splendour. In distant steeples.
The Sleeping-Draught – Fair lady, open your window
Aksel Schiøtz ten with various artists
Danacord mono DACOCD454 (72' · ADD) Texts and translations included ⒻO

'Hidden Treasure' is the appropriate subtitle for this volume of the complete Schiøtz recordings. It begins with the 10 songs from what ought to have been a complete *Schöne Müllerin*, two songs recorded in London in 1939, eight with Hermann D. Koppel, who took over from Moore, in Denmark in 1939-40. The cycle was never finished, because – it seems – Koppel as a Jew had

to flee his country when the Nazis occupied it. Schiøtz's voice, when he was 33, was even fresher, his reading even more spontaneous in suggesting the vulnerable youth's love and its loss, most poignant in an account of 'Der Müller und der Bach' that surpasses in forlorn expression other famed tenor interpreters such as Patzak, Pears, Schreier and Bostridge, but the whole sequence is a pleasure to hear for the plangency of Schiøtz's singing. There follows part of the Mozart aria *Per pietà* that the tenor sang as test for EMI in 1938, interesting as a rarity but not special. By contrast all the Danish items are desirable, among them the two Hartmann offerings: *Tell me, star of night*, a haunting song, is given ideal voicing by Schiøtz as is 'Sverkel's romance' from a romantic work, *Little Christine*, based on an Andersen fable.

The two items by Lange-Müller, written as incidental music for a play called *Once Upon a Time*, are even better, in particular the magical 'Midsummer song'. The note-writer tells how wonderful was Schiøtz's singing of this item in an open-air performance in 1941. His recordings had made Schiøtz famous and he also appeared the same year playing the role of Schubert in *Lilac Time*, of which we hear an amusing pot-pourri (a photo in the booklet shows him in the part). That Schiøtz was not averse to popular items is confirmed by Riisager's *Mother Denmark*, which he brought to London for that first session in May 1939. It's a song written for a *diseuse* about the delights of the homeland, and Schiøtz delivers it with the intimacy it calls for. Again, the transfers are faultless and this example of Anglo-Danish co-operation is highly recommendable.

Tito Schipa   *tenor*

Opera Arias H
L'Arlesiana, Il barbiere di Siviglia, La bohème, Don Giovanni, Don Pasquale, L'elisir d'amore, La favorita, Lakmé, Luisa Miller, Manon, Martha, Pagliacci, Rigoletto, La traviata and Werther
Tito Schipa ten with various artists
Preiser Lebendige Vergangenheit mono 89160 (77' · AAD) Recorded 1925-8 ⒻO

The Master. And yes: he surely is, and never more so than in the recordings of this period. Schipa was then at the height of his fame and fortune, the voice approaching the end of its very best days (a thrill and a freshness which began to diminish in the early 1930s) and with the art having developed just about as far as it would go. Lovely examples are: 'Sogno soave' (*Don Pasquale*), 'Questa o quella' and 'E il sol dell'anima' (*Rigoletto*), the *Traviata* duets, the *Lakmé* and *Werther* solos, Harlequin's Serenade (*Pagliacci*), 'E la solita storia' (*L'Arlesiana*) and the finale of *La bohème* with the exquisite Bori. But if 'The Master', then one whose mastery was exercised within severe limitations. Today's tenors in the repertoire cultivate an extensive upper range, whereas Schipa sings here nothing above a B flat, transposing 'La donna è mobile', and even lowering 'M'apparì' so that the B flat becomes an A. His modern successors attempt and often attain a brilliance of bravura which can make Schipa sound tame and cautious (his 'Ecco ridente' is fine but lacks the brilliance of true virtuosity, and his 'Il mio tesoro' is essentially a bit of artful dodging). There are other limitations too, but these are enough for the present: and enough remains to place him among the unforgettables and the irreplaceables. Any of the recommendations mentioned will show why, and there's the added, vital and elusive quality of voice-personality.

This collection comprises a complete run of Schipa's operatic records made electrically for the Victor company. Transfers are faithful, with the sound well defined. Among all the many CDs currently devoted to him this would be a very suitable first choice.

The Complete Victor Recordings, 1922-25 Ⓗ

Opera arias and duets – L'africaine, Il barbiere di Siviglia, La bohème, La corte del amor (Padilla), Don Pasquale, L'elisir d'amore, Emígranyes (Barrera), Lakmé, Lucia di Lammermoor, Manon, Marta, Mignon, Pagliacci, Rigoletto, La sonnambula, La traviata and Werther; songs by **Barthélemy, Buzzi-Peccia, Costa, di Crescenzo, de Feuntes, di Capua, Huarte, Lakacios, Oteo, Paladilhe, Perez-Freire, Ponce, Roig, Schipa** and **Silvestri**
Tito Schipa ten with various artists.
Romophone mono ② 82014-2 (150' · ADD) Recorded
1922-5 Ⓕ

Tito Schipa is utterly special. Whether by art or personality (not always readily separable) he's one of those singers who instantly establish themselves in mind, memory and affections. He had a voice that could ring out strongly as well as commanding the style and delicacy for which he was renowned. He also had the skill, taste and personal magnetism to make something magical out of some very third-rate music (a faculty that contributed to the restriction of his artistic growth), and there are plenty of examples here – such as one called *Quiéreme mucho*, which veterans will recognise as a wartime hit over here called *Yours*. Alan Blyth's introductory essay points out that the acoustic Victors have been the least commonly reissued of Schipa's recordings, and that, while this is perhaps understandable (because the most popular of the titles were remade electrically a year or two later), they also catch him at the peak of his career and in his prime. Sometimes, indeed, the earlier recordings are marginally preferable to the more familiar remakes: the Dream song from *Manon* is rather more elegant, the *Pagliacci* serenade a shade more charming, and in the *Traviata* duets his partner, Amelita Galli-Curci, enjoys better vocal health. More importantly, some of the best items were never re-recorded, including the delightful *Sonnambula* duet and *Mignon* arias. Some of the songs, too, are charming,

Pesca d'amore for example and the tiny tarantella by Vicenzo di Crescenzo called *Ce steve 'na vota*. 1925 saw the advent of electrical recording, and roughly a dozen of Schipa's first electricals are included. These are more ingratiating in the quality of the singing than in that of the recorded sound: one sympathises with those who complained at the time that the microphone added an unnatural harshness; it's also true that the shellac used just then often produced a particularly high and gritty surface-noise. Whatever has been done to mitigate them, these are still features that limit pleasure in listening here to the recordings of that period. Better quality came in with some of the very latest, and among these are the solos from *Werther* and *Lakmé* and the Death scene from *La bohème* with Lucrezia Bori, all among Schipa's very best. All who love singing will value Schipa's art, and all who value his art will want these records.

Andreas Scholl *countertenor*

German Baroque Cantatas
Albertini Sonata quarto in C minor **J Christoph Bach** Ach, das ich Wassers g'nug hätte **Buxtehude** Fried- und Freudenreiche Hinfahrt, BuxWV76 – Muss der Tod denn auch entbinden (Klag-Lied), Jubilate Domino, omnis terra, BuxWV64 **Erlebach** Wer sich dem Himmel übergeben **Legrenzi** Libro quarto di sonate, La cetra' – Sonata quinta **Rovetta** Salve mi Jesu **Schütz** Kleiner geistlichen Concerten, SWV306-37 – Was hast du verwirket, SWV307; O Jesu, nomen dulcem, SWV308. Symphoniae sacrae, SWV341-67 – Herzlich lieb hab ich dich, o Herr, SWV348 **Tunder** Ach, Herr lass deine lieben Engelein
Andreas Scholl counterten **Concerto di Viole** (Brian Franklin, Friederike Heumann, Brigitte Gasser, Arno Jochem de la Rosée); **Basle Consort** (Pablo Valetti, Stephanie Pfister vns Karl Ernst Schröder lte Markus Märkl hpd/org)
Harmonia Mundi HMC90 1651 (72' · DDD)
Texts and translations included Ⓕ

Expressively versatile though Scholl unquestionably can be, it's perhaps in the sphere of elegy and plaint that his art can be heard to strongest advantage. Two pieces of outstanding merit fall into this category and are sung here with tonal beauty, stylistic assurance and expressive *puissance*. One of them is Johann Christoph Bach's lament *Ach, das ich Wassers g'nug hätte*. This member of the family worked during the second half of the 17th century and was greatly admired by J S Bach, who described him as 'profound'. The lament, in *da capo* form, is scored for countertenor, violin, three violas da gamba, cello and organ. The other is the much better-known strophic 'Klag-Lied' from the longer *Fried- und Freudenreiche Hinfahrt* by Buxtehude, written in memory of his father who had died early in 1674. Scholl does great justice to each of these intimate pieces, attending as much to the spirit and utterance of the texts as to the sorrowful and at times searing inflections of the music.

These performances alone would be sufficient enticement to acquire the disc but, happily, there's much else in the programme to touch our sensibilities. Schütz is well represented with three tenderly expressive pieces, two of them from the *Kleiner geistlichen Concerten* and a third from the *Symphoniae sacrae* (1647); and Franz Tunder by a declamatory and rhythmically graceful setting of a verse of the hymn *Herzlich lieb hab ich dir, o Herr*. This piece is one of two whose composers have been wrongly exchanged on the track listing: the other is *Salve mi Jesu* which, though preserved in a Tunder manuscript, is probably the work of the Venetian, Giovanni Rovetta. Sensibly, the order of events is punctuated by two works for instrumental ensemble, one of them by Ignazio Albertini, the other by Legrenzi, whose position in the history of recording seems still to be that of occasional stand-in. He deserves better, and doubtless will come into his own one day. The playing of the two groups, Concerto di Viole and the Basle Consort, is accomplished and refined, both in ensemble and tuning, providing sensitive support in the vocal pieces and affecting insights to the instrumental ones. Despite the fanciful (if ingenious) packaging, which is brittle, inconvenient and impractical, this release is strongly recommended.

Heroes

Gluck Orfeo ed Euridice – Che farò senza Euridice. Telemaco – Ah non turbi **Handel** Serse – Fronde tenere...Ombra mai fù. Semele – Where'er you walk. Saul – O Lord, whose mercies; Such haughty beauties. Rodelinda – Con rauco mormorio; Vivi tiranno!. Giulio Cesare – Dall' ondoso periglio...Aure deh, per pietà **Hasse** Artaserse – Palido il sole **Mozart** Ascanio in Alba – Al mio ben. Mitridate, Re di Ponto – Venga pur, minacci
Andreas Scholl *counterten* **Orchestra of the Age of Enlightenment / Sir Roger Norrington**
Decca 466 196-2OH (58' · DDD) Texts and translations included   Ⓕ Ⓞ

Heroes indeed! This is some of the finest heroic singing around, and in a countertenor voice – often supposed to be weakly or effeminate. There's heroism here in both love and war. Andreas Scholl's countertenor is formidable in every sense and transmits sturdy, masculine emotion just as forcefully as the softer sorts called for in, for example, what are probably the two most famous of the arias here: 'Ombra mai fù' (Handel's 'Largo'), which opens the recital, and 'Che farò' from *Orfeo*. The first of these discloses a wonderfully ample, creamy voice, beautifully even and controlled, capable of a poignantly soft top F and firm in profile in the lower register; the latter elicits an outpouring, a passionate one, of lovely tone, with a line of the chastity and purity that exactly captures Gluck's vision of his semi-divine hero. In 'Where'er you walk' – a tenor piece, transposed – he seems tonally more constrained, yet it's an uncommonly smooth and flowing performance. Of the

other Handel items, particular mention should be made of the *Saul* aria 'O Lord, whose mercies', one of the loveliest Handel ever wrote, sung with great intensity of tone; the *Rodelinda* arias, one of them full of rapid *fioritura*, riskily but faultlessly delivered, and a peaceful one about a murmuring stream which, if perhaps taken rather quickly, nevertheless is a fine, serene piece of singing. The Hasse item is strong and impassioned, giving scope to Scholl's full bottom register; and of the two Mozart arias the one from *Mitridate* is a noble, powerful statement of defiance, done strongly and directly. Norrington provides generally sympathetic accompaniments.

This is an exceptional recital in which one of today's most beautiful and imaginatively used voices is heard at its finest.

A Musicall Banquet

Anonymous Go, my flock, go get you hence. O bella più. O dear life, when shall it be? Passava Amor su arco desarmado. Sta notte mi sognava. Vuestros ojos tienen d'Amor **Batchelar** To plead my faith **Caccini** Amarilli mia bella. Dovrò dunque morire? **Dowland** Far from triumphing court. In darkness let me dwell. Lady, if you so spite me. Sir Robert Sydney His Galliard **Guédron** Ce penser qui sans fin tirannise ma vie. Si le parler et le silence. Vous que le bonheur rappelle **Hales** O eyes, leave off your weeping **Holborne** My heavy sprite **Martin** Change thy mind since she doth change **Megli** Se di farmi morire? **Tessier** In a grove most rich of shade
Andreas Scholl *counterten* **Edin Karamazov** *ltes/gtr/orph* **Christophe Coin** *bass viol* **Markus Märkl** *hpd*
Decca 466 917-2DH (67' · DDD) Texts and translations included   Ⓕ

Like his *Varietie of Lute Lessons*, also published in 1610, Robert Dowland's *A Musicall Banquet* is an odd and interestingly innovative collection. It includes works by his famous father as well as by several otherwise unknown English composers alongside four pieces with French texts, two with Spanish texts, and four in Italian. There are timeless masterpieces like John Dowland's *In darkness let me dwell* and Caccini's *Amarilli mia bella*; but there's also a pioneering attempt to bring a truly international repertory to England.

The complete volume has been recorded twice before, in the late 1970s: Nigel Rogers did a splendid version with the inspired partnership of Anthony Bailes and Jordi Savall; and the Consort of Musicke, as part of their complete John Dowland set, presented a version – with four excellent singers and Anthony Rooley on particularly eloquent form on the lute – coming a little closer to the source in the use of a voice on some of the generally texted bass lines. But it was high time for a new version; and, with music in four languages, there could hardly be a better collection to show the qualities of Andreas Scholl. He has that ability to float a line marvellously without compromising the clarity of the text; and if some listeners feel that greater variety of colour is possible, he more than compensates with his unwavering, faultless control.

Edin Karamazov carries the bulk of the accompaniment with a range of plucked instruments and performing styles: he shows particular success in the cruelly exposed and slow lines of *In darkness let me dwell* and in the more jaunty Spanish songs. Markus Märkl is a spirited harpsichordist in five pieces, and the wonderful Christophe Coin shows an astonishing range of colours and techniques on the bass viol.

This recording may not supersede the two earlier versions, but it offers many interesting alternatives, including a good reconstruction of the thoroughly garbled Italian that Dowland printed for *Sta notte*. Nobody will be disappointed.

Arcadia

Bencini Introduzione **Corelli** Concertino **Gasparini** Destati, Lidia Mia. Ecco, che alfin ritorno **B Marcello** Quando penso agl'affanni **B Pasquini** Sinfonia. Navicella, ove tin vai **A Scarlatti** Ferma omai, fugace e bella

Andreas Scholl *counterten*
Accademia Bizantina / Ottavio Dantone

Decca 470 296-2DH (78' · DDD) Texts and translations included   Ⓕ

The disc's title signifies not just that these five secular cantatas are on pastoral subjects, but that they're all by composers who belonged to the Accademia dell'Arcadia, the literary club in which Roman sophisticates got together in the years around 1700 to explore the ideals of rural love and longing. For a musician to be admitted was a special honour, and Francesco Gasparini, Bernardo Pasquini, Alessandro Scarlatti and Benedetto Marcello were four of the most respected Italian composers of the time. Their cantata texts are subtly shaded depictions of love (alas, almost always unreturned) between shepherds and shepherdesses, to which the music responds with both elegance and resourceful attention to detail.

Scarlatti is the most familiar of them today, and the late cantata offered here typifies his natural skills in word-setting. The other three composers are probably little more than names, even to Baroque music-lovers, yet their vocal works are clearly well worthy of investigation. Marcello's piece is gracefully composed yet also offers a muscly depiction of the 'wild beast' Love, while Pasquini writes in a touching strophic style reminiscent of his 17th-century predecessors. It's Gasparini, however, who's the happiest discovery : his two cantatas mixing sure skills in vocal writing with an assured expressiveness helped along by telling orchestral details.

Scholl sings with his customary expertise and sheer vocal loveliness. He's excellently partnered by the period strings of the Accademia Bizantina; three well-performed orchestral pieces, including a rare 'concertino' by Corelli (another 'Arcadian'), prove that they haven't just come to support the main act.

Elisabeth Schwarzkopf *soprano*

Unpublished Lieder and Songs 1957-64   Ⓗ
Bizet Pastorale[a] **Brahms** Von ewiger Liebe, Op 43 No 1[a]. Deutsche Volkslieder – In stiller Nacht[a]. Volks-Kinderlieder – Sandmännchen[a]. Wiegenlied, Op 49 No 4[a] **Flies** Wiegenlied[a] **Mozart** Un moto di gioia, K579[b]. Warnung, K433a[a] **Parisotti** Se tu m'ami, C xxii, 68[a] **Schubert** Claudine von Villa Bella – Liebe schwärmt auf allen Wegen[a]. Lachen und Weinen, D777[a]. Die Vögel, D691[a]. Der Jüngling an der Quelle, D300[a]. Du bist die Ruh, D776[a]. Wiegenlied, D498[a]. Die Forelle, D550[a] **Schumann** Widmung, Op 25 No 1[a] **R Strauss** Ruhe, meine Seele, Op 27 No 1[a]. Zueignung, Op 10 No 1[a]. Wiegenlied, Op 41 No 1[a] **Wagner** Wesendonk Lieder – Träume[a] **Wolf** Eichendorff Lieder[a] – Die Zigeunerin; Nachtzauber. Alte Weisen[a] – Tretet ein, hoher Krieger; Das Köhlerweib ist trunken

Elisabeth Schwarzkopf *sop* [a]**Gerald Moore**,
[b]**Walter Gieseking** *pfs*

Testament SBT1206 (72' · ADD) Recorded 1957-64
                                                                                 ⓂⓄ

'Unpublished' is a word to warm the hearts and imaginations of collectors, and many of these recordings, though originally passed for issue, aren't even listed in official discographies. The first track here is a case in point – the aria from Schubert's *Claudine von Villa Bella* was a favourite with Schwarzkopf, but if one compares this recording from 1961 with the one eventually issued, made four years later, the 1965 version is more relaxed, having more of a sense of the surging lover's declaration. Persevere, though, and there are gems to be found.

Wolf's 'Die Zigeunerin' was one of Schwarzkopf's standbys. Perhaps you recall her singing it at the end of the first half of her last Royal Festival Hall concert in 1975. This was often a great moment in a Schwarzkopf recital – all nerves by then banished, the voice under control, she would play with the acoustic of the hall, using little echo effects that are caught on this recording. Maybe the reason it wasn't used, as in several other cases on the CD, is that the voice is a little too far forward, the pianist seeming to be banished to halfway back in the studio; but this gives a lovely sense of presence. In other cases the songs were discarded probably because there simply wasn't room on the LP. One of these is the single track which isn't accompanied by Gerald Moore, *Un moto di gioia*, part of her famous Mozart programme accompanied by Walter Gieseking. It's a joy, as is *Warnung*. The other 'encore' pieces by Flies, Bizet and Parisotti must surely have been intended for the LP called *Songs You Love*, a Cook's Tour through song. In *Se tu m'ami* there's a slight fluff on one of the little laughs which perhaps led to its exclusion, but in every other way it's as charming and beguiling as any light-hearted song Schwarzkopf ever recorded.

The Brahms group is compelling. This was the beginning of a project to record a whole LP of Brahms songs with which she continued into the 1970s, though only a few songs were ever released (on the fourth and final 'Songbook'

LP). Strauss's *Zueignung* seems awfully slow, and less involved than one would expect.

Wagner's 'Träume' is the one instance of the unpublished take being preferable to that issued. Again, one can see why the later recording is a more dramatic reading, but here the voice is poised with such lightness and it's so intimate – if you're in doubt about the prospect of this CD, listen to that followed by the Bizet *Pastorale* and then 'Die Zigeunerin'. At once one is in the presence of the great singer, a perfectionist in everything she did, as hard on herself when judging her records as she sometimes could be on her students. She would shake her head after some lovely piece of pure vocalism and murmur, 'Ah, but that's the easy part'.

The Unpublished EMI Recordings (1946-52) ⊞
Opera arias – La bohème, La traviata and Die Zauberflöte (sung in English); songs and sacred works by Bach, Gounod, T Arne, Morley, Mozart, Schubert, R Strauss and Wolf
Elisabeth Schwarzkopf *sop* with various artists
Testament mono ② SBT2172 (134' · ADD) Recorded 1946-52. Texts and translations included   Ⓕ●

What need for more Schwarzkopf when there's already a heap of her recordings available? Well, there's a very good reason why Testament – and Schwarzkopf herself – thought this unissued material worth unearthing from the copious EMI archive. It may be heretical in the record world to say so, but Walter Legge had an Achilles' heel: he demanded perfection, and it was just occasionally bought at the expense of spontaneity. In the case of the commercial recordings included here, he thought his wife could perform the pieces better on a later occasion, but now we may judge that these earlier interpretations have that much more eager freshness than the previously published versions.

That's particularly so in the case of Bach's *Jauchzet Gott* and Mozart's *Exsultate, jubilate*. With Schwarzkopf in pristine, youthful voice, her production at its easiest, her breath long, both works shine forth as joyful things to hear – tone, line, runs, all in perfect accord. The remainder of the first CD, bar the final track, is a conspectus of the work the soprano was doing at the time, in the late 1940s, at Covent Garden where she was for a while a member of the resident company. Her Violetta, in English, and her Mimì, in Italian, both show her care over the words, which are inflected with heartfelt meaning in both cases. But the gem is Schwarzkopf's private recording of all Pamina's role sung at home in English to piano accompaniment in order that she might learn the role properly in the vernacular. So here we have an invaluable souvenir of a quite beautifully sung performance of 51 years ago. Schwarzkopf introduces this delightful oddity herself, a further bonus for posterity. The very last item on this CD brings a discovery of a very different kind. Legge apparently thought the Bach-Gounod *Ave Maria*

wasn't musically worthy of the partnership, so the performance was never issued. How wrong he was: it turns out to be one of those occasions when a great artist can convert dross into gold.

On the second disc we have another addition to the singer's recorded legacy in a charming account of Morley's *It was a lover and his lass*. For the rest, it's all discarded takes of Lieder issued in later performances. None is as compelling as the 1948 *Gretchen am Spinnrade*, a performance of concentrated feeling urgently executed, and an irresistible account of *Der Musensohn* is preferable to issued versions because of its verve. Two versions of Wolf's *Storchenbotschaft* are included; the first from 1948 the simpler, more natural, the second from 1951 a shade over-elaborated. Of the remaining Wolf songs, all recorded in 1951, three songs demand mention: *Bedeckt mich mit Blumen*, always a favourite with the singer, for its dreamy eroticism ideally adumbrated and sung with just the vibrancy called for, a reading of *Im Frühling*, filled with spring's yearning, and *Wiegenlied im Sommer*, in which Schwarzkopf's soothing, tender tones would persuade any child to untroubled sleep. Throughout, Gerald Moore is the soprano's faithful, supportive partner, and EMI's clean recording adds to profound pleasure in an issue lovingly performed and lovingly prepared, with evocative photos and full texts and translations.

Irmgard Seefried   *soprano*

Lieder by **Brahms, Flies, Mozart, Schubert** ⊞
and **Wolf**
Irmgard Seefried *sop* with various artists
Testament mono SBT1026 (74' · ADD) Recorded 1946-53   Ⓕ

Another 'must' for anyone who loves Seefried. In these wonderfully immediate and faithful transfers of performances made in Vienna and London, Seefried is heard at the peak of her powers, when her voice was at its freshest and easiest. In the Mozart, whether the mood is happy, reflective or tragic, Seefried goes unerringly to the core of the matter. Here we have the archness of *Die kleine Spinnerin*, the naughty exuberance of *Warnung*, the deep emotion of *Abendempfindung* and *Unglückliche Liebe*. We are offered five Schubert songs, including an unsurpassed *Auf dem Wasser zu singen*, so airy and natural; a pure, elevated *Du bist die Ruh* and a poised, ravishing *Nacht und Träume*. The lullabies of Flies, Schubert and Brahms are all vintage Seefried. The Wolf items are a real treasure trove: a sorrowful, plangent account of *Das verlassene Mägdelein* (perhaps the most compelling interpretation of all here; unutterably moving), an enchanting, spontaneous *Elfenlied* (with Gerald Moore marvellously delicate here). For the most part, Moore is in attendance to complete one's pleasure in an irresistible and generously filled disc.

Amy Shuard   *soprano*

Giordano Andrea Chénier – La mamma morta[a]
Mascagni Cavalleria rusticana – Voi lo sapete[a]
Puccini Turandot – In questa Reggia[a]. Gianni
Schicchi – O mio babbino caro[a]. Tosca – Vissi
d'arte[a]. La bohème – Quando m'en vo' soletta[a]
Tchaikovsky Eugene Onegin – Tatyana's Letter
Scene, Act 1[b] **Verdi** Aida[a] – Ritorna vincitor; L'insana
parola; Qui Radames verrà; O patria mia. Un ballo in
maschera – Morrò, ma prima in grazia[a]
Amy Shuard *sop* [a]Royal Opera House Orchestra,
Covent Garden / Sir Edward Downes; [b]Royal
Philharmonic Orchestra / George Weldon
Dutton Laboratories CDCLP4006 (56' · DDD)
Recorded 1961-2   Ⓜ

'Where has this voice been all my life?' people
will be saying as they come upon it for the first
time in this disc. Indeed, others who knew it will
wonder whether they appreciated it properly
when it was part of more or less day-to-day
experience. The impression is magnificent: a
tone as beautiful as, say, mid-period Tebaldi and
a volume comparable to that of Shuard's great
teacher, Dame Eva Turner. The first phrase of
all, the opening of 'Ritorna vincitor', could
almost be mistaken for Dame Eva's, every 'r' so
resolutely rolled, and an expression severely that
of the princess rather than the slave-girl. She
softens in manner and volume for 'Numi, pietà',
but on the whole this is an Aida in the heroic
mould, and even in 'O patria mia' the mood is
firmly regulated, the nostalgia kept within
bounds. Turandot is also Tureneresque, formidable in vocal demeanour, indomitable on high.
Plenty of critical opinion can be adduced to
confirm from live experience the superb impression created by these records, though some will
not remember it quite so. Nevertheless, she was
a genuinely distinguished operatic artist, and in
international casts clearly earned her place.
Of the negative elements, the record recalls
her somewhat unvarying countenance and a
sense of limited responsiveness (she knows when
to soften, as she does, beautifully, in Tatyana's
Letter scene, but doesn't enter into the development of feeling towards that point). However, it
also revives a memory of her warm, moving and
very accomplished singing of the *Ballo* aria, and
it kindles a wish that we could have heard her in
Andrea Chénier. The gift and accomplishment
put on record here remain outstanding, as is the
quality of transfer.

Gérard Souzay   *baritone*

Songs of Many Lands   Ⓗ
Songs by Brahms, Buratti, Canteloube, Dørums-
gaard, Durante, Ginastera, Grieg, Guarnieri,
Hughes, Kilpinen, Liszt, Massenet, Mendelssohn,
Mussorgsky, Nin, Ovalle, Respighi, Roussel,
Sfakianakis, Villa-Lobos, Vuillermoz
Gérard Souzay *bar* Dalton Baldwin *pf*
Testament SBT1207 (79' · ADD) Recorded 1958, 1959,
1978 , 1979   Ⓕ

The gems Souzay offers here should be cause for
extraordinary celebration. The songs that particularly catch the imagination include the
Jägerleben, with its witty evocation of Schubert's
'Der Musensohn', Villa-Lobos's song of the
noisy ox-cart driver, and *I'm goin' away*, which
copies Paul Robeson's tone to the life. Also the
haunting Moravian song, *Preletel Slavicel*, the
Venetian *La barcheta* (ascribed here to one
Buratti, but it must be Reynaldo Hahn), and the
audience's favourite, the song of the blue bird,
Azualaò, from Brazil. All these, and more,
Souzay sings with rich, vibrant tone, resourceful
art and plenty of character. The remastering is
excellent. An enterprising edition, offering the
privilege of extended encore-time with a great
singer in his prime.

Chausson Sept mélodies, Op 2 – Nanny;   Ⓗ
Le Charme; Les Papillons; Sérénade italienne; Le
Colibri. Deux mélodies, Op 36 – Cantique à
l'épouse. Poème de l'amour et de la mer, Op. 19.
Debussy Trois ballades de François Villon – Ballade
que Villon feit à la requeste de sa mè Mandoline. Le
Promenoir des deux amants – La Grotte **Duparc**
Chanson triste. Élégie. L'Invitation au voyage.
Lamento. Le Manoir de Rosemonde. Phidylé.
Sérénade florentine. Soupir. Testament. La Vague et
la cloche. La Vie antérieure. **Ravel** Don Quichotte à
Dulcinée
Gérard Souzay *bar* Jacqueline Bonneau *pf* Paris
Conservatoire Orchestra/Edouard Lindenberg
Testament CD SBT1312 (80' · ADD)   Ⓕ**OOO**

Can a voice be 'too beautiful'? That
was the charge laid against Souzay by
Roland Barthes in his book *Mythologies*
(Seuil, 1970). He's remarkable for the smoothness of his tone, and the fluid way he can pass
from the lower register to a head voice of a delicacy that few male singers ever achieve.
The producers at Decca in the early 1950s
obviously considered Souzay to be their answer
to EMI's Fischer-Dieskau, and recorded a series
of LPs. Decca has reissued a number of these
recordings on CD over the years. This all-
French programme opens with Ravel's *Don Quichotte à Dulcinée*, the only time Souzay recorded
this with orchestra, and one of the splendours of
his discography. Edouard Lindenberg conducts
with the exact pace and lightness of approach
that the three songs need. This recording has
never been surpassed.
The three Debussy songs that follow, two
orchestrated by Louis Beydts, are also among
the supreme examples of Souzay's singing: the
Villon *Ballade* has an intensity reminiscent of his
best role in opera, Golaud. Like Claire Croiza,
one of his teachers, he's never afraid to give
plenty of voice where it's needed. The Chausson
group is also just right; so many of Chausson's
songs are gloomy, but the balance between
the nostalgia of *Le Colibri* is balanced with the
mystery of *Cantique a l'épouse* and the yearning
of *Le temps des lilas*. When it comes to the

Duparc settings, the contrast with his subsequent recordings on Philips and EMI, both with Dalton Baldwin, is more extreme. There are points where the later, grittier interpretations take precedence.

Giuseppe Di Stefano — tenor

Opera Arias Ⓗ
L'amico Fritz, L'Arlesiana, L'elisir d'amore, La fanciulla del West, La forza del destino, Gianni Schicchi, Manon, Mignon, Tosca & Turandot; songs by Bixio, **Tagliaferri**; Sicilian folk-songs
Giuseppe Di Stefano ten with various artists
Testament mono SBT1096 (79' · ADD) Recorded 1944-56 Ⓕ

Very moving it is to hear this voice again in its absolute prime. It's hardly possible to hear those Swiss recordings of 1944, with piano, and be untouched by the thought, as well as the sound, of this 22-year-old, singing his heart out, with so much voice and, already, with so much art. The 'Una furtiva lagrima' is perhaps not the fully polished article, but what Forster called the Italian 'instinct for beauty' is there, with lovely shading and phrasing. It's good to have the two Bixio songs (*Se vuoi goder la vita* and *Mamma*), previously unpublished, heartfelt, open-throated performances in the national tradition that used to get mocked and is now so missed. Indeed, thinking of that sequence of recordings, one could well wish this disc had given priority to reproducing them all: there's an amazingly good 'Pourquoi me réveiller?', for instance, and (till the end) a beautifully restrained *Musica proibita*. Still, what we have here fulfils exactly the promise of the label's name: it's a testament, and a testament of youth. The later operatic recordings, from 1955, find the tenor with some signs of wear and with a recklessly open way of taking his high As and B flats, but there's real passion, and imagination with it. In the latest recording, a commonplace song called *Passione* from 1956, one almost looks up at the speakers to see the face there: it seems so very clear and lifelike. Some of the sound (recording or transfer) seems overbright – the second *Manon* solo is a prime example – but it's always vivid and compelling. In the booklet-listing a translation of the song-titles would have been welcome. It would also have been useful if Peter Hutchinson's notes had related the excerpts to Di Stefano's career (did he for instance ever sing Dick Johnson, Rinuccio and Calaf on stage?).

Elsie Suddaby — soprano

Songs and Arias by M Arne, T Arne, Bach, Besly, Ⓗ Carey, Denza, Ford, German, Handel, Haydn, Jackson, MacCunn, Mendelssohn, Morley, Mozart, Purcell, Schubert, Somervell, Stanford, Warlock
Elsie Suddaby sop with various artists
Amphion mono PHICD134 (80' · ADD) Recorded 1924-52 Ⓜ

Elsie Suddaby (1893-1980) was a close contemporary of Isobel Baillie and Dora Labbette and in many ways she evinces the strongest personality of the three, and has a distinctive timbre very much her own. That can be heard in the first item, Michael Arne's *The lass with the delicate air*, a piece she virtually appropriated as her signature tune. She sings it with such variety of tone and, yes, such delicacy of accent, that one capitulates at once to so graceful an artist. In Dido's Lament, the singular quality of being able, simply and naturally, to move the listener is there: adding appoggiaturas to the recitative and discreetly employing *portamento* in the Lament itself she goes to the heart of the matter. There's also the joyfully affirmative side of her art, shown in a fresh account of 'Rejoice greatly' from *Messiah* and 'Endless pleasure', as Semele wallows in her conquest of Jupiter. Better still is a version of 'Let the bright Seraphim' (*Samson*) that rings the rafters with its zealous delivery. Runs in all these Handel pieces are keenly accomplished, though not quite with Baillie's assurance. These HMV recordings catch Suddaby in her prime, when she was in her 30s, yet on a Decca 10-inch of 1941 of Thomas Arne's *Where the bee sucks* and Morley's *It was a lover and his lass*, there's no diminution of her powers, and even the Warlock songs and Mozart's *Agnus Dei*, when Suddaby was in her late 50s, find the tone almost as fresh as ever and wholly free of wobble. The CD is a generous offering, the transfers mostly well done and the booklet obviously a labour of love.

Dame Joan Sutherland — soprano

La Stupenda
Opera Arias – The Bohemian Girl , Beatrice di tenda, Norma`, I Puritani, La sonnambula, Home, sweet home, Adriana Lecouvreur, Operette, Lakmé, La fille du régiment, Linda di Chamounix, Lucia di Lammermoor, Alcina, Esclarmonde, Die Zauberflöte, Les contes d'Hoffmann, Turandot, The Boys from Syracuse, Semiramide, Casanova, Attila, Rigoletto, La traviata, Tristan und Isolde. **Glière** Concerto for Coloratura Soprano, Op 82
Joan Sutherland sop with various artists
Decca ② 470 026-2DM2 (154' · ADD) Recorded 1959-90 Ⓜ

An excellent selection, and a well-ordered one. The proof is that it can be played quite happily from start to finish, all 154 minutes of it, in one session, and still leave you wanting more. This is a tribute to the singer, who's stupendous by virtue of several qualities, variety not notably being one of them. Roughly 20 operatic characters are represented in these excerpts, but it's hardly a portrait-gallery we enter: much the same face looks out from each of them, the most distinctive being the bride of Lammermoor's. And though they aren't inexpressive, the nature of the expression, whether sad or happy, tends to be usually rather mild: even Turandot sounds like a nice woman, certainly not one who has been out in the cold so long as to need melting. The recording process has also reduced somewhat the impact of a feature which truly was stupendous in the opera-house – namely the sheer size of the voice. The early recordings especially might well give an impression that at the time of her famous triumph as Lucia her voice was still quite light, whereas the wonder of it lay in the combination of purity, agility and range with such ample house-filling power.

Anyway, there's plenty to feast upon here. Highlights include the aria from *Linda di Chamounix*, the polonaise from *I puritani* and the early 'Casta diva'. Among the less expected items it's good to find Glière's Concerto and the jolly song from *The Boys of Syracuse*. Two lesser tracks are 'I dreamt I dwelt in marble halls' and 'Home, sweet home' where vowels, consonants and the melodic line all seem to go into meltdown. Otherwise superb.

The Art of the Prima Donna
Opera Arias – Artaxerxes, Die Entführung aus dem Serail, Faust, Hamlet, Les Huguenots, Lakmé, Norma[a], Otello, I Puritani, Rigoletto[a], Roméo et Juliette, Samson, Semiramide[a], La sonnambula & La traviata
Dame Joan Sutherland *sop* [a]**Chorus and Orchestra of the Royal Opera House, Covent Garden / Francesco Molinari-Pradelli**
Decca Legends ② 467 115-2DL2 (109' · ADD)
Recorded 1960. Texts and translations included
Ⓜ❍❍❍

 'The Art of the Prima Donna', hardly out of the catalogue since 1960, is now remastered for Classic Sound. There can't be many admirers who haven't already got this, so for newcomers to Sutherland on disc one can only say – listen and wonder. Her voice, even throughout its range right up to the high E, always keeping its natural quality, is heard at its early fullness. Perhaps the best tracks of all are 'The soldier tir'd' from *Artaxerxes* and 'Let the bright seraphim' from *Samson*, but every track is beautiful. 'Casta Diva' – her earliest attempt at it – is her most limpid recording of this prayer, 'Bel raggio' from *Semiramide* has sparkling decorations, quite different from the ones she sang on the complete recording six years later, and the whole thing ends with the Jewel Song from *Faust*. It was a big voice and sounded at its best in larger theatres; listening to 'O beau pays' from *Les Huguenots*, you can see Sutherland in your mind's eye, in pale blue silk, as Marguerite de Valois at the Royal Albert Hall in 1968. It's difficult to imagine anyone, coming to it for the first time, being disappointed.

Richard Tauber *tenor*

Opera Arias and Duets Ⓗ
Aida, Il barbiere di Siviglia, The Bartered Bride, La bohème, Carmen, Don Giovanni, Eugene Onegin, Der Evangelimann, La forza del destino, Fra Diavolo, I gioielli della Madonna, Der Kuhreigen, Madama

Butterfly, Martha, Mignon, Der Rosenkavalier, Tosca, Die tote Stadt, La traviata, Il trovatore, Die Walküre & Die Zauberflöte
Richard Tauber *ten* with various artists
Preiser Lebendige Vergangenheit mono ② 89219 (143' · AAD) Recorded 1919-26 Ⓕ

Das Deutsche Volkslied Ⓗ
Opera Arias – Don Giovanni & Die tote Stadt; songs by **Heymann** and **R Strauss**
Richard Tauber *ten* with various artists
Claremont mono CDGSE78-50-64 (67' · ADD)
Recorded 1924-39 Ⓜ

These two issues present a neatly complementary view of Tauber's career. The Preiser set gives us a picture of the young tenor in his days almost exclusively as an opera artist in German-speaking lands singing in the vernacular. It evinces the golden, sappy, honeyed tone of Tauber in his prime. The style at this stage is wholly disciplined, but already we hear that outgoing, spontaneous exuberance that was soon to bring him world-wide fame in operetta. Few if any tenors have sung Mozart quite as beautifully as Tauber at this point in his career: the 1922 Bildnis aria is a model of its kind, preferable to his later version, and an object-lesson in phrasing for any aspiring tenor. His interpretations of Lensky's aria, the famous piece from *Der Evangelimann*, José's Flower Song, Jenik's aria (a glorious 1919 version) and Wilhelm Meister's farewell to Mignon show the plangent, almost melancholy timbre with which he could invest such repertory. Then for pure singing his readings of the Italian Tenor's aria, Siegmund's Spring Song, Alfredo's aria and Pinkerton's outpouring of remorse are hard to beat. Add to this the many duets he never repeated in electric versions and you've a most desirable issue. In the company of regular colleagues of that time, such as Rethberg, Bettendorf, Sabine Kalter and, best of all perhaps, Lotte Lehmann, his contributions reveal his generosity of both voice and manner. This is free-ranging, rich-hued singing marred only by most of the music being sung in the 'wrong' language. There are a few downward transpositions in the solos, but that was common practice at the time. Otherwise there's little to criticise here in the performances and none in the excellent transfers. The more intimate side of Tauber's art comes in the series of *Volkslieder* he recorded for Parlophone in 1926, nicely transferred by Claremont. Here one admires the very personal way in which he caresses these charmingly unassuming pieces. Four Strauss songs from 1932 sessions follow, notable for the passion in the tone. What a pity the CD wasn't completed with more Lieder rather than operatic items already available in numerous transfers, including the less-than-satisfactory Ottavio arias of 1939. But at the end there's a gem: 'Kennst du das kleine Haus am Michigansee?' where Tauber lavishes on a trifle all the magic of his incredible technique and heady tone, including those *pianissimos* conjured from nowhere. The transfers are excellent.

Renata Tebaldi   *soprano*

Opera Arias – Mefistofele, La Wally, Adriana Lecouvreur, Andrea Chénier, Die lustige Witwe, La Gioconda, La bohème, Gianni Schicchi, Manon Lescaut, Suor Angelica, Il tabarro, Tosca, Turandot, Madama Butterfly, La fanciulla del West, La regata veneziana, Aida, Un ballo in maschera, Don Carlo, La forza del destino, Otello, La traviata, Il trovatore **Renata Tebaldi** *sop* various artists including **Grace Bumbry** *mez* **Carlo Bergonzi, Gianni Poggi, Mario del Monaco** *tens* **Cornell MacNeil, Robert Merrill** *bars* **Cesare Siepi, Nicolai Ghiaurov** *basses;* orchestras including **Rome Santa Cecilia Academy Orchestra and Chorus; Royal Opera House Orchestra, Covent Garden; Vienna Philharmonic Orchestra;** conductors including **Herbert von Karajan; Tullio Serafin; Richard Bonynge; Sir Georg Solti**
Decca ② 470 280-2DX2 (149' · ADD) Recorded 1949-69   Ⓜ

Renata Tebaldi has often said that she found recording a very difficult experience. She missed the stimulation of an audience, and in the early days the engineers used to insist that she turn her head away from the microphone at each climactic note; this was because her voice was so powerful that the equipment couldn't deal with it. It's all the more impressive then, given the power of her voice, how consistent it remained throughout the 20 years this collection covers. Like every singer, she had her vocal problems from time to time, but she maintained the wonderfully even tone, and smooth *legato*, even at the moments of high drama.

This is an extremely satisfying survey. The items have been chosen to demonstrate Tebaldi's range as singer and actress. The closing scene from *Adriana*, the tense game of poker from *Fanciulla*, and the horrific last moment of *Il tabarro* show off Tebaldi the *verismo* specialist. All the Puccini items are very fine, culminating in the aria and duet from the end of Act 1 of *La bohème*, with Bergonzi as Rodolfo. Although the *Don Carlo*, *Ballo* and *Gioconda* scenes all come from the mid-1960s, the period after Tebaldi 'remade' her voice aiming to create a darker sound, in no way does it appear to have deteriorated. And the Rossini songs bring a lovely sense of fun, which was one of the characteristics of Tebaldi the recitalist.

Tebaldi once said that she would never have been able to appear in *Suor Angelica* on stage, for even when recording the part she cried so much she could hardly get through it. It's this total commitment and sincerity that shines through all Tebaldi's work. It's easy to hear how much she loved singing, and relished the Italian language. For those who never heard her, this is a fine 80th birthday celebration.

Bryn Terfel   *bass-baritone*

Some Enchanted Evening
Berlin White Christmas Lane On a Clear Day You Can See Forever – She wasn't you **Loewe** Camelot – If ever I would leave you; How to handle a woman. My Fair Lady – On the street where you live; Get me to the church on time. Brigadoon – There but for you go I. Paint Your Wagon – I was born under a wand'rin' star; They call the wind Maria. The Little Prince – Little Prince **Rodgers** South Pacific – Some enchanted evening; Younger than springtime; There is nothing like a dam. Carousel – If I loved you; You'll never walk alone. Oklahoma! – Oh, what a beautiful morning. The King and I – Something wonderful; I have dreamed. Allegro – Come home; A fellow needs a girl. The Sound of Music – Edelweiss **Weill** Love Life – Here I'll stay
Bryn Terfel *bar* with Stephen Briggs, Keith Mills *tens* Maurice Bowen, Stephen Dowson *basses* **Opera North Chorus; English Northern Philharmonia / Paul Daniel**
DG 471 425-2GH (77' · DDD) Notes and texts included   Ⓕ

As an example of an opera singer putting his special gifts to the service of popular music, this is altogether one of the happiest. Indeed these marvellous songs have never been so consistently beautifully performed.

It helps that 'Some Enchanted Evening' was written for an operatic bass-baritone. Yet other numbers such as 'Oh, what a beautiful morning', so closely associated with Gordon MacRae, come across equally well. Terfel even performs those written for actors or female singers so convincingly as to make them completely his own. True, there's little attempt at a Cockney accent in 'Get me to the church on time'; but there's characterisation in the lead-up to 'On the street where you live', and for the most part he gives us just the sort of vernacular, non-operatic performances these numbers need. His command of *pianissimo* is used to marvellous effect, and the way the voice swells at 'He is wonderful' is quite thrilling. Sensitive conducting and authentic orchestrations play their full part in creating a totally absorbing effect.

Opera Arias
Borodin Prince Igor – No sleep, no rest
Donizetti Don Pasquale – Bella siccome un angelo
Gounod Faust – Vous qui faîtes l'endormie
Mozart Le nozze di Figaro – Non più andrai. Don Giovanni – Madamina, il catalogo è questo; Deh! vieni alla finestra. Così fan tutte – Rivolgete a lui lo sguardo. Die Zauberflöte – Der Vogelfänger bin ich ja **Offenbach** Les contes d'Hoffmann – Allez! … Pour te livrer combat…Scintille, diamant
Rossini La Cenerentola – Miei rampolli femminini **Verdi** Macbeth – Perfidi! All'angelo contra me v'unite!…Pietà, rispetto, amore. Falstaff – Ehi! paggio! …L'Onore! Ladri! **Wagner** Tannhäuser – Wie Todesahnung…O du mein holder Abendstern. Der fliegende Holländer – Die Frist ist um
Bryn Terfel *bass-bar* **Orchestra of the Metropolitan Opera, New York / James Levine**
DG 445 866-2GH (71' · DDD) Texts and translations included   Ⓕ 🔴🔴

In a careless moment we might describe Bryn Terfel as a very physical singer, and it would be true up to a point. His physical presence is much in evidence when he sings, or for that matter when he talks or just breathes. Having seen him 'in the flesh', one seems to see him while hearing the sound of his voice on records. But the crowning distinction of Terfel's art (granted the voice, the technique and the general musicianship) is its intelligence. As with words, so with characters: each is a specific, sharp-minded creation, and none is a stereotype. This Leporello exhibits his master's catalogue with pride; it's the book of life and not to be taken lightly. This Don Magnifico recounts his dream in all good faith (he doesn't *know* that he's a complete idiot, and doesn't deliberately set himself up to sound like one). No less impressive, as an aspect of intelligence, is the linguistic command, and still more so the use he makes of it: the sheer mental concentration of his Dutchman carries intense conviction and an ever-specific understanding. In short, a magnificent recital.

Silent Noon
Britten The Salley Gardens. Oliver Cromwell. The foggy, foggy dew **Drofnatzki (Stanford)** The Aquiline Snub. The Compleat Virtuoso **Dunhill** The Cloths of Heaven **Elwyn-Edwards** The Cloths of Heaven **Gurney** Sleep Head The Lord's Prayer. Money O! **Keel** Trade Winds. Port of many Ships. Mother Carey **Parry** Love is a bable **Quilter** Weep you no more. Come Away Death. O Mistress mine Blow, Blow, thou winter wind. Now sleeps the crimson petal. Go, lovely rose **Somervell** A Shropshire Lad **Vaughan Williams** Silent Noon. Linden Lea **Warlock** Captain Stratton's Fancy
Bryn Terfel bass-bar **Malcolm Martineau** pf
DG 474 2192 (74' · DDD) Ⓕ**OOO**

 As in 'The Vagabond', predecessor and companion-volume to this new recital, Bryn Terfel and Malcolm Martineau combine to persuade their listeners that these are the best songs in the world. Which may be true, except perhaps for Somervell's obtuse setting of *A Shropshire Lad*. The performances are both old and sensitive, expert in accomplishment and judgement. The exception is *The foggy, foggy dew*, which has too much nudging and underlining by Terfel, though Martineau's easy-rider accompaniment, with its crafty low bass, is delightful. But the two settings of Yeats's *The Cloths of Heaven* are exquisite. Lovely, too, is Ivor Gurney's *Sleep*, with that striving, head-above-water, cry of 'O, let my joys have some abiding'. The Terfel-Martineau English Songbook Volume 2 deserves every welcome.

Luisa Tetrazzini *soprano*

Opera Arias Ⓗ
Un ballo in maschera, Il barbiere di Siviglia, Carmen, Dinorah, La forza del destino, Las hijas del Zebedeo, Lakmé, Linda di Chamounix, Lucia di Lammermoor, Mignon, La perle du Brésil, Rigoletto, Roméo et Juliette, Rosalinda, La sonnambula, La traviata, Il trovatore, I vespri siciliani & Die Zauberflöte; songs by **Benedict, Brahms, Cowen, De Koven, Eckert, Gilbert, Grieg, Moore, Pergolesi, Proch** and **Venzano**
Luisa Tetrazzini sop with various artists
Romophone mono ② 81025-2 (150' · ADD) Recorded 1904-20　　　　　　　　　　　　　　Ⓕ

Though Tetrazzini was one of the most prized and assiduously collected of recording artists in her time, her career on record was not really very satisfactory. As was true of several others she repeated the same items in several versions, whereas, especially in those days of such restricted recording-time, an extension to the repertoire would have been so much more welcome. The repertoire itself relied heavily on the familiar *chevaux de bataille*, the Mad scenes, Bell song, Shadow song and so forth, and often when something out of the way comes along, either, like the 'Pastorale' from Veracini's *Rosalinda*, it isn't well suited, or, as with Proch's vapid variations, it was not worth doing in the first place.

There must also have been difficulties in successfully catching a voice which combined such brilliance and power with what could all too often emerge on record as a colourless and even infantile quality. Of the Victors reproduced here the best and most essential is the 1911 'Ah, non giunge' (*La sonnambula*). The cabaletta, 'Di tale amor', following 'Tacea la notte' (*Il trovatore*), is also a joy. The *Lucia di Lammermoor* sextet and *Rigoletto* quartet are also prime attractions, fine performances in many (but not all) ways and remarkably clear and lifelike as recorded sound.

Maggie Teyte *soprano*

Chansons by **Berlioz, Debussy, Duparc, Fauré** Ⓗ
Dame Maggie Teyte sop with various artists
Pearl mono GEMMCD9134 (74' · ADD) Recorded 1936-41　　　　　　　　　　　　　　Ⓜ

There was some sort of magic in the air at the EMI Abbey Road Studios in London on March 12 and 13, 1936. Maggie Teyte, just short of her 48th birthday, and Alfred Cortot, both of whom had been well acquainted with Claude Debussy, recorded 14 of his *mélodies*. This is no studio-bound recital but a performance, the passion and beauty of tone matched stroke for stroke by pianist and singer. These records, and the later ones Teyte made with Gerald Moore, are among the jewels of Debussy singing and playing. No one with an interest in French song should hesitate to acquire them, for they provide a lesson, not just in pronunciation of the French language (though, like her contemporary and supposed rival, Mary Garden, Teyte sang with a pronounced English accent – something that entranced the French in the *belle époque*, when all things English were *à la mode*).

The beauty of Teyte's tone, the freshness and

girlish quality of her high notes – something which never deserted her, and she continued to sing for another 20 years after this recording – are constantly astonishing. So, too, is the passion she puts into phrases such as 'Qu'il était bleu, le ciel, et grand l'espoir!' in 'Colloque sentimental' from the second book of *Fêtes galantes*, or the decidedly dark-hued 'Il me dit: 'Les satyres sont morts,' in 'Le tombeau des Naïdes' from *Chansons de Bilitis*.

Those who already have some of the other reissues of Teyte's Debussy recordings will find that this Pearl disc has a rather higher surface noise, perhaps the price one has to pay for getting the voice more forward. One wonders why Pearl have called the disc 'Chansons', the correct term for these settings is *Mélodies* – or there's the good old English word 'song'.

Dawn Upshaw   *soprano*

Goethe Lieder
Mozart Das Veilchen, K476 **Schubert** Rastlose Liebe, D138. Gretchen am Spinnrade, D118. Mignons Gesang, D877 No 4. Suleika I, D720. Versunken, D715. Wanderers Nachtlied II, D768. Ganymed, D544. An den Mond, D296 **Schumann** Liebeslied, Op 51 No 5. Nachtlied, Op 96 No 1. Lieder und Gesänge aus Wilhelm Meister, Op 98*a* – No 1, Mignon; No 5, Heiss mich nicht reden; No 7, Singet nicht in Trauertönen **Wolf** Blumengruss. Die Bekehrte. Die Spröde. Frühling übers Jahr
Dawn Upshaw *sop* **Richard Goode** *pf*
Nonesuch 7559-79317-2 (53' · DDD) Texts and translations included. Recorded 1993   Ⓟ❍

Upshaw and Goode are a musical marriage made in heaven, each a highly individual, probing and sincere artist prepared to challenge received views on a song. Thus their *Gretchen am Spinnrade* in this programme of all-Goethe settings is an outburst of a desperate and infinitely perturbed woman breaking conventional bonds. To emphasise the point Upshaw leans into the first syllable of 'nimmer' at each repetition with added feeling and times the climax of the great song at the word 'Kuss' in an overwhelming way, only such a similarly involving (although very different) interpreter as Lotte Lehmann could. Goode's playing simply underlines and reinforces the singer's intense utterance.

The Schumann settings are filled with just as much spontaneous emotion and direct imagination. The pair make as strong a case as is possible for Schumann's setting of Mignon's *Kennst du das Land* being superior even to Wolf's, the repeated 'Kennst du das wohl?' carrying an extraordinary charge. The singer's voice is also ideally fitted for Wolf's teasingly sensual *Die Spröde* and *Die Bekehrte* and the pair bring the lightest touch to *Blumengruss*. Finally they give Mozart's *Das Veilchen* a deeper meaning than almost any interpreters. The recording is ideally balanced, forward yet spacious.

I wish it so
Bernstein West Side Story – I feel pretty. Candide – Glitter and be gay. The Madwoman of Central Park West – My new friends **Blitzstein** Juno – I wish it so. No for an Answer – In the clear. Reuben, Reuben – Never get lost **Sondheim** Anyone Can Whistle – There won't be trumpets. Saturday Night – What more do I need? The Girls of Summer – The Girls of Summer. Merrily We Roll Along – Like it was. Evening Primrose – Take me to the world **Weill** One Touch of Venus – That's him. Lady in the Dark – The saga of Jenny; My ship. Lost in the Stars – Stay well
Dawn Upshaw *sop* **orchestra / Eric Stern**
Nonesuch 7559-79345-2 (45' · DDD) Texts included. Recorded 1993   Ⓜ❍❍❍

Bernstein, Blitzstein, Sondheim and Weill are a good quartet to explore in a recital and Dawn Upshaw's clear soprano is well suited to nearly all these songs. The Blitzstein numbers will only be familiar to specialists. 'I wish it so' from Blitzstein's adaptation of O'Casey's *Juno* seems to herald the mood of the whole disc, songs of longing, some optimistic, some resigned. 'In the clear' is one of the songs from *No for an Answer*, Blitzstein's follow-up to *The Cradle Will Rock*; it was first given in 1940, the same week that saw the first night of Weill's *Lady in the Dark*. In the Blitzstein, Eric Stern's arrangement with a solo cello part played by Matthias Niegele turns the song into a melancholy lullaby. This and a brilliant performance of 'Glitter and be gay' from *Candide* show off Upshaw's impressive range – from the coloratura of the Bernstein to mezzo-ish moodiness for the Blitzstein. Of the Weill songs, 'Stay well' from *Lost in the Stars* is especially successful, and 'That's him' from *One Touch of Venus* is playful. The two numbers from *Lady in the Dark* are given the most extensive overhaul, the melody of 'The saga of Jenny', such as it is, disappears beneath Larry Wilcox's rearrangement and although Upshaw sings 'My ship' quite beautifully, again Daniel Troob has made an arrangement that pulls it about. All in all, this is a very attractive foray into the Broadway territory.

Voices of Light
Debussy Trois Chansons de Bilitis **Fauré** La chanson d'Eve **Golijov** Lúa descolorida **Messiaen** Chants de terre et de ciel – Résurrection. Harawi – L'escalier redit, gestes du soleil; Amour oiseau d'étoile. Poèmes pour Mi – Le collier; Prière exaucée
Dawn Upshaw *sop* **Gilbert Kalish** *pf*
Nonesuch 7559 79812-2 (62' · DDD · T/t)   Ⓕ❍❍❍

Here Dawn Upshaw uses the Messiaen songs to act as a counterpoint to the two song cycles, opposites as they are, Fauré's settings of Charles Van Lerberghe's evocation of paradise in *La chanson d'Eve*, and Debussy's delicate and mysterious *Chansons de Bilitis*, to the poems of that arch-sensualist, Pierre Louÿs. Upshaw writes that, as a student, she was inspired by Frederica Von Stade's recording (Sony, nla) of the Debussy songs, yet their approaches are quite different. Upshaw characterises them with precise detail, the false innocence of 'La flute de Pan', the *Pelléas*-like languor of 'La chevelure', and then the sense of loss in 'Le tombeau des naïdes'. Gilbert Kalish's accompaniment in these is warm without being precious.

We're accustomed to hearing a darker voice, such as that of Sarah Walker, in Fauré's *La chanson d'Eve*. In this, quite rightly, there's only the feeling of quiet purity: this is Eve before the serpent arrives. The five Messiaen songs are separated by the other works, and offer an even greater expressive challenge. In particular the passionate urgency of 'L'escalier redit, gestes du soleil', (1945), is an ode to joy, even in the face of death. From the same year, 'L'oiseau d'étoile' begins in an ecstatic flood of love, but ends with a sort of question mark – how can the artist really come to terms with such beauty? It's placed before a song composed for and dedicated to Upshaw by Osvaldo Golijov, *Lúa descolorida*, a setting of words by the 19th-century Galician poet Rosalía de Castro, which has since become part of Golijov's *Pasión según San Marcos*. It makes a gently beautiful punctuation between the songs by the great composers from the last century. A fascinating disc, exploring extremes of tenderness and wonder at life and love.

Julia Varady   *soprano*

Mozart La clemenza di Tito – Ecco il punto... Non più di fiori vaghe catene. Idomeneo – Chi mai del mio provò... Idol mio se ritroso **R Strauss** Arabella – Mein Elemer; Das war sehr gut **Verdi** La forza del destino – Son giunta! grazie... Madre, pietosa Vergine; Or siam soli. Nabucco – Ben io t'invenni... Anch'io dischiuso un giorno. Il trovatore – Vanne! Lasciami... D'amour sull'ali rosee **Wagner** Der fliegende Holländer – Joho hoe! Traft ihr das Schiff. Die Meistersinger von Nürnberg – Selig wie die Sonne (Quintet)
Julia Varady sop with various artists **Bavarian State Opera / various conductors**
Orfeo d'Or C579 041A (76' · ADD) Recorded live 1975-92   Ⓕ**OOO**

 Julia Varady can lay claim to be the most versatile, committed and technically assured lyric-dramatic soprano of the 20th century's final quarter. Here are more invaluable examples of her live portrayals from the Bavarian State Opera, where she sang no fewer than 400 times.

Elettra's one happy aria in *Idomeneo* is evidence of her vocal beauty pure and simple, sweet in tone, firmly vibrant in line. In Vitellia's grand Act 2 scene from *Clemenza* she accomplishes the coloratura and wide range with certainty. She captures all Leonora's mental anguish in the big aria from Act 2 of *Forza*, and the duet outside the monastery is even better. With Kurt Moll as an imposing, warm Padre Guardiano, this is a track

to treasure, Verdi singing of the highest level. The excerpts from *Arabella* are well worth including as a reminder of Varady's deeply moving, perfectly sung account of the final scene, with her husband Dietrich Fischer-Dieskau as her partner and Sawallisch so idiomatic in support.

In all these excerpts there's a palpable sense of the superb acoustics of the Munich Nationaltheater.

Rolando Villazón   *tenor*

Italian Opera Arias
Cilea L'Arlesiana – E la solita storia (Lamento) **Donizetti** Il Duca d'Alba – Inosservato, penetrava; Angelo casto e bel. L'elisir d'amore – Quanto è bella; Una furtiva lagrima. Lucia di Lammermoor – Tombe degl'avi miei; Fra poco a me ricovero **Mascagni** L'amico Fritz – Ed anchè Beppe amò; O Amore, o bella luce. Nerone – Vergini, Muse; Quando al soave anelito **Puccini** La bohème – Che gelida manina. Tosca – E lucevan le stelle **Verdi** Don Carlo – Io la vidi. I Lombardi – La mia letizia infondere. Macbeth – O figli, o figli miei!; Ah, la paterna mano. Rigoletto – Ella mi fu rapita!; Parmi veder le lagrime; La donna è mobile. La traviata – Lunge da lei; De' miei bollenti spiriti ... O mio romorso!
Rolando Villazón ten
Munich Radio Orchestra / Marcello Viotti
Virgin Classics 545626-2 (62' · DDD) Texts and translations included   Ⓕ**OO**

Here comes the new tenor on the block. Rolando Villazón's first disc on Virgin Classics might have been expected to provide a souvenir snapshot, but it doesn't quite. A voice that sounds slim, lithe, intently focused in the theatre is more resilient here, and comes with a grainy quality that isn't unpleasant, but certainly sets it aside from the purity of any native Italian.

The short aria from *I Lombardi*, briskly dispatched by Viotti, shows the singer's quick reflexes as he deftly catches expressive details on the wing. The *L'elisir d'amore* and *La traviata* arias have some similar nuances, but could do with more. Even in the helpful ambience of Glyndebourne his Rodolfo in *La bohème* only scraped by with just enough depth of tone, but here he sounds made for the role.

This Mexican newcomer has no single knock-out gift, but his strengths are many and varied – a healthy, youthful tenor, decent sense of line, and a young man's ardour and energy. He's well served by the recording. The booklet comes with texts and translations, but not a word about the singer himself. Maybe Virgin Classics felt that the best of Villazón's biography lies in the future.

Norman Walker   *bass*

A Portrait of Norman Walker   Ⓗ
Opera and Oratorio Arias – Acis and Galatea, The Children of Don, The Creation, The Dream of

Gerontius, Dylan, Die Entführung aus dem Serail, Faust, Judas Maccabaeus, Messiah, La morte d'Orfeo, Le quattro stagioni (**B Marcello**) & Die Zauberflöte; songs by **Capel**, **Haynes**, **Lane Wilson**, **Purcell** and **Storace**
Norman Walker bass with various artists
Dutton Laboratories mono CDLX7021 (71' · ADD)
Recorded 1928-54   Ⓑ

Norman Walker was one of our leading basses for some 17 years from 1937 when he sang as the Commendatore and the Speaker at Glyndebourne and King Mark (with Dame Eva Turner as Isolde) at Covent Garden. From then on he balanced his career nicely between the stage and the concert hall. This welcome reissue opens resplendently with Walker singing Handel and Haydn in the classic manner: steady, burnished tone, every run in its place and diction exemplary. Then comes Walker's unsurpassed account of the Angel of the Agony's solo from Gerontius, so urgent, so sympathetic, here allowed to run on to let us hear Heddle Nash sing 'I go before my judge' so movingly. Of Walker's opera repertory we hear a student account of 'O Isis und Osiris', which gives some evidence of what was to follow, and a test made in 1944 for Walter Legge of Osmin's aria, which suggests he might have been a good interpreter of that role. The extracts indicate Walker's dramatic prowess (though his Italian is far from idiomatic) – as does his brief contribution to the closing trio from Faust, with Joan Cross a suitably distraught Marguerite. More valuable than these, however, because they display so unerringly Walker's gifts as a conviction-singer, are the four British songs made at one session in 1952 with Gerald Moore. They are exemplified in the bass's confident tone, unobtrusive word-painting and subtle use of rubato. Indeed the singer, in these faultless transfers, seems to be in the room with us. Malcolm Walker provides a warm, personal cameo of his father in his notes.

Dolora Zajick   *mezzo-soprano*

The Dramatic Soprano Voice
Cilea Adriana Lecouvreur – Acerba voluttà **Gluck** Orphée et Eurydice – J'ai perdu mon Eurydice. Alceste – Divinités du Styx **Mascagni** Cavalleria rusticana – Voi lo sapete **Mussorgsky** Khovanshchina – Sily potalnye **Rossini** Semiramide – Ah! quel giorno ognor rammento **Saint-Saëns** Samson et Dalila – Mon coeur s'ouvre à ta voix **Tchaikovsky** The Maid of Orleans – Prostite vy kholhv **Verdi** Don Carlo – O don fatale. Macbeth – La luce langue; Una macchia è qui tuttora. Il trovatore – Condotta ell'era in ceppi
Dolora Zajick mez **Royal Philharmonic Orchestra / Charles Rosekrans**
Telarc CD80557 (69' · DDD)   Ⓕ

Zajick, widely known as one of the leading operatic mezzo-sopranos of the day, is introduced here as a soprano, though neither the voice nor repertoire seems greatly to have changed. The addition of Lady Macbeth to the list of roles is interesting but not surprising, for it has been sung quite often by mezzos (on records, for instance, by Cossotto, Höngen and Verrett). It isn't clear what purpose is served by apportioning the voice and (presumably) the repertoire to a different vocal category; the case is perhaps made out in the booklet, which was not included in the review copy, but it would have to be remarkably strong to convince us that Gluck's Orpheus, Verdi's Azucena and Mussorgsky's Marfa are roles for a soprano, however dramatic.

The voice is certainly one of exceptional quality and power. In spite of some 20 years of hard usage (she had been singing professionally for some time before winning her Tchaikovsky prize in 1982), the surface remains to a large extent unworn, its high and low notes particularly thrilling in thrust and opulence. The limitation lies in something which, if not exactly Slavonic wobble (Zajick is American by birth), is 'operatic vibrato', a condition common to many powerful voices where sustained notes, especially at a *forte*, may be perfectly firm while losing evenness and definition elsewhere. This affects the pleasure of her 'J'ai perdu mon Eurydice' more than that of 'Divinités du Styx' and of her Rossini rather more than her Cilea. In Verdi her richness of tone and assurance of dramatic authority carry the day.

Best is probably the *Don Carlos*: a towering performance of Eboli's great solo, impresssive on record, overwhelming in the effect one can imagine it having in the theatre. The deep, baleful phrases of Azucena in *Il trovatore* have the authentic quality, too. In *Semiramide* it is good to hear her singing the runs without aspirates. In *Khovanshchina* she catches well the awe of Marfa's invocation and the humanity of her prophetic utterance. As Lady Macbeth she's not imaginative in colouring or in verbal expressiveness but rises triumphantly to the climaxes, both the loud and the soft. With no other solo recital to her name in the current catalogue, Zajick is certainly welcome to the opportunities afforded by this one, in which she's well supported by the RPO and its sympathetic conductor.

Various Artists

Singers of Imperial Russia,   Ⓗ
Volumes 1-4
GEMMCDS9997/9: recorded 1900-11: *Soprano* – **Medea Mei-Figner**; *Tenors* – **Ivan Ershov, Nikolai Figner, Leonid Sobinov**; *Baritone* – **Ioakim Tartakov**; *Basses* – **Adamo Didur, Vasili Sharonov**

GEMMCDS9001/03: 1901-11: *Sopranos* – **Natalia Ermolenko-Juzhina, Maria Michailova**; *Mezzo-soprano* – **Antonina Panina**; *Tenors* – **David Juzhin, Andrei Labinsky, Gavril Morskoi**; *Baritones* – **Oskar Kamionsky, Polikarp Orlov**; *Basses* – **Dmitri Bukhtoyarov, Vladimir Kastorsky, Vasili Sharonov, Lev Sibiriakov**

GEMMCDS9004/06: 1901-24: *Sopranos* – **Irena Bohuss, Anna El-Tour, Janina Korolewicz-Wayda,**

Maria Kuznetsova, Lydia Lipkowska, Nadezhda Zabela-Vrubel; *Contralto* – Evgenia Zbrueva; *Tenors* – Dmitri Smirnov, Eugene Witting; *Bass* – KE Kaidanov

GEMMCD9007/09: 1901-14: *Sopranos* – **Maria Michailova, Antonia Nezhdanova;** *Mezzo-soprano* – **Galina Nikitina;** *Contralto* – **Evgenia Zbrueva;** *Tenors* – **Alexandr Alexandrovich, Alexandr Bogdanovich, Alexandr Davidov, Andrei Labinsky, Eugene Witting;** *Baritone* – **Nikolai Shevelev. Basses** – **Vladimir Kastorsky, Lev Sibiriakov**

Pearl mono 4x ③ GEMMCDS9997/9, 9001/3, 9004/6, 9007/9 (oas: 207′, 209′, 222′ & 221′ · AAD)   Ⓜ**OOO**

This is the equivalent of one of those exhibitions for which queues form long and deep and daily outside the Tate Gallery or the Royal Academy: in fact, if a similar exhibition of paintings, furniture and porcelain from the Tsar's palaces were mounted in London it would surely be a sell-out. Quite simply, there has never been a published collection to match this, both in the quality of the items and in its extensiveness. Of the singers of Imperial Russia, the world came to know Chaliapin, who eclipsed the rest. He isn't among the artists presented here, but we have, among the basses, two who at least for vocal splendour are his equal: Adamo Didur, the Pole who was New York's first Boris Godunov (preceding Chaliapin there), and Lev Sibiriakov, another giant of a man with a magnificently produced voice to match. The tenors include Smirnov and Sobinov, a kind of collector's Tweedledum and Tweedledee, though in fact very unalike indeed. New to most listeners will be Ivan Ershov, heard in Siegfried's Forging Song from St Petersburg, 1903, with piano and anvil accompaniment: an astonishing voice and most accomplished in technique. Evgenia Zbrueva the contralto, sopranos Nezhdanova, Ermolenko-Jushina, Mei-Figner and the superbly recorded Korolewicz-Wayda are also plentifully represented. Most amazing of all, perhaps, is the vividness of sound. These are some of the world's rarest recordings and they're almost all in pristine condition.

The Reopening of La Scala Concert
Boito Mefistofele[a] – Prologue **Puccini** Manon Lescaut – Intermezzo; Act 3[b] **Rossini** La gazza ladra – Overture. Guillaume Tell – Passo a sei; Wedding Chorus[c]; Soldier's Dance. Mosè in Egitto – Dal tuo stellato soglio[d] **Verdi** Nabucco – Overture; Va pensiero[e]. I vespri siciliani – Overture. Quattro pezzi sacri[f] – Te Deum
[bc]**Mafalda Favero,** [d]**Renata Tebaldi** *sops* [cd]**Jolanda Gardino** *mez* [bcd]**Giovanni Malipiero,** [b]**Giuseppe Nessi** *tens* [b]**Mariano Stabile** *bar* [b]**Carlo**

Forti, [acd]**Tancredi Pasero** *basses* [abcef]**Chorus and Symphony Orchestra of La Scala, Milan / Arturo Toscanini**
Naxos Historical mono ② 8 110821/2 (108′ · AAD)
Recorded from a broadcast performance 1946   Ⓢ

The war over, the Milanese set about the immediate rebuilding of the bombed La Scala. By 1946 the work was complete in time for Toscanini to return – by public demand – to his old house to direct the opening concert. This legendary occasion features on CD in tolerable enough sound to enjoy its many virtues. Chief among them are the old maestro's inimitable, indeed unique way of inspiriting singers and orchestra to perform Rossini and Verdi as perhaps never before or since. Nobody else combines the ability to give these composers musical precision and make the music sing as does Toscanini (try the cello melody in the Vespri Overture, or, for his exactness of execution, the following staccato passage). Those attributes are evident in all the overtures presented here, giving the music that quality of Italianità of which Toscanini was an absolute master. Or try the three piercing chords just before the chorus enters in 'Va, pensiero' to judge the conductor's interpretative genius. Then, who (except perhaps Beecham) would be able to invest the dances from William Tell with such a light, exuberant touch? And, still on the first CD, there's the utterly heart-warming feeling in the Prayer from Mosè in Egitto with the very young Tebaldi glorious on the soprano line and the veteran Pasero intoning, as only an Italian bass can intone, the bass-line.

The Verdi *Te Deum* that opens the second disc displays that special quality found in Italian choral singing, and all the chorus members sing their hearts out for their old master, even when there are some less than steady moments which reveal that the war's exigencies haven't yet quite been overcome. Then we hear something of Toscanini's affection for two of his other operatic loves, Puccini and Boito. The Intermezzo to *Manon Lescaut* is a searing experience, followed by a performance of Act 3 given by three of La Scala's stars of the pre-war and wartime era, plus the inimitable *comprimario* Giuseppe Nessi as the Lamplighter. Favero and Malipiero, with their clear diction and ability to sing off the words with agility, show what Puccini interpretation has lost in authenticity in these days of international homogenised performance. Toscanini is again in his element, while in the Prologue to *Mefistofele* he shows an affinity with this eccentric score. Pasero has a high old time in the title-role. Only the inadequate notes, which keep on repeating the same information in different articles and say nothing whatsoever about the performances, mar a most important issue, surely a must for opera collectors.

EARLY MUSIC –
ENSEMBLE & INSTRUMENTAL

Bell' Arte Antiqua

The Italian Connection　　　　　　　　　Ⓟ
Corelli Trio Sonata in A minor, Op 3 No 12[ab]
Geminiani Sonatas for 2 Violins and Continuo[ab] – in
D 'Bush aboon Traquair'; in F 'The last time I came
o'er the moor'. Sonata for Violin and Continuo in D
minor, Op 1 No 2[ab] **Lonati** Sonata for Violin and
Continuo in G minor[a] **Matteis** Divisions on a Ground
in D minor[a] **Veracini** Sonata in A, Op 2 No 9[a] **Vivaldi**
Trio Sonata for 2 Violins and Continuo in D minor,
RV64[ab]
Bell' Arte Antiqua ([a]Lucy van Dael, [b]Jacqueline
Ross vns William Hunt va da gamba Terence
Charlston hpd)
ASV Gaudeamus CDGAU199 (60' · DDD)　　　ⒻⓄ

If the Bell' Arte Antiqua isn't yet a household
name with Baroque music lovers, it soon could
be. Lucy van Dael and William Hunt, already
members of more than one high-profile early
music ensemble, join forces here with Jacqueline Ross and Terence Charlston to breathe
fresh life into the Italian duo and trio sonata
repertory.

Corelli is represented by a Roman *sonata da
chiesa* of great vitality and breadth that demonstrates the high level of technical and musical
rapport already established between van Dael
and Ross. Van Dael performs a sonata by
Corelli's lesser-known Neapolitan contemporary, Lonati, with equal amounts of verve and
sensitivity, bringing to it a superb command of
period ornamentation. She infuses Matteis's virtuoso variations on *La Folia* with the immediacy
of an unfolding drama that will encourage listeners to make comparisons with Corelli's set.
Elements of the personal styles of Corelli and
Lonati come together in the trio sonatas of their
student, Geminiani, in the idiomatic ornamentation of the *Andante* of the D major Sonata, the
seemingly demure opening *Grave* of the D
minor Sonata (deftly characterised by van Dael
and Ross with musical gestures akin to raised
eyebrows and fluttering eyelashes) and the compelling dialogue between the violins and the bass
viol in the *Grave* of the F major Sonata.

The D minor Trio Sonata of Vivaldi is nicely
understated. The members of Bell' Arte Antiqua
draw attention to the thematic links between the
rhythmically contrasting Preludio and Corrente; then, in the succeeding *Grave*, stretch and
sustain their individual lines while inviting listeners to luxuriate in the glorious suspensions
that result.

Veracini's Sonata completes the picture. Like
his fellow expatriate Geminiani he used British
folksongs as inspiration for instrumental pieces:
Veracini's *Aria scozzese con variazione* would
impress even the best Scottish folk fiddler, and it
may come as a happy surprise that the opening

Andante of Geminiani's F major Sonata was
inspired by *The last time I came o'er the moor*.

These are stylish performances. There are no
gimmicks, just good music, beautifully played.

Brook Street Band

Handel's Oxford Water Music
Corelli Trio Sonatas – in C, Op No 7; in G, Op 2
No 12 **Geminiani** Violin Sonatas in A minor, Op 4
No 5 **Handel** Water Music, HWV348-350 (ed Theo) –
Suite in F; Suite in G minor; Suite in D. Trio Sonatas,
Op 2 – No 2 in G minor, HWV387; No 3 in B flat,
HWV388 **Leclair** Première Récréation de musique in
D, Op 6
Brook Street Band (Hannah McLaughlin ob
Marianna Szücs, Katalin Kertész vns Tatty Theo vc
Carolyn Gibley hpd)
Avie AV0028 (78' · DDD)　　　　　　　　　Ⓕ

The Brook Street Band is a young group of
Baroque specialists whose name proclaims their
primary allegiance to Handel, sonatas by whom
frame their programme here. They bring a
delightful freshness and lack of affectation to all
these trio sonatas, playing in a vivacious style,
with quickish tempos, that makes it very clear
that they're enjoying themselves.

They differentiate nicely between styles:
Corelli is done with high dignity and poise; the
more overtly dramatic element in Geminiani is
well caught, with some delicate nuance; and the
gracefully French accent that Leclair brings to
this Italian form is captured in the hints of the
plaintive in the Forlane and the Sarabande, the
quirkiness in the Gracieusement and the subtle
shading of the Gavotte.

Handel's '*Oxford*' *Water Music* is a version
from an Oxford manuscript that presents parts
of the *Water Music* in chamber-music form. The
music is much lighter and perkier than in its
orchestral disposition, especially such movements as the F major minuet and the bourrées.

In the trio sonatas the playing is very alert. The
opening of Op 5 No 4 is beautifully springy and
in its Passacaille there's a distinct Purcellian
flavour to the *minore* section; in Op 2 No 4 the
opening *Andante* is nicely poised and the shaping of the *Allegro* gives the whole a sense of
direction. Excellent interplay by the violins, and
a shapely bass-line: all very clearly audible in a
recording that's slightly clinical and dry, but
happily catches the spirit of the performances.

Europa Galante

Italian Violin Sonatas
Geminiani Violin Sonata in A minor, Op 4 No 5
Locatelli Violin Sonata in D minor, Op 6 No 12
Mascitti Psyché, Op 5 No 12 **Tartini** Violin Sonata
in G minor, Op 2 No 1 **Veracini** Violin Sonata in
G minor, Op 1 No 1
Europa Galante (Sergio Ciomei hpd/org/clav
Giangiacomo Pinardi theo/gtr/citt Maurizio
Naddeo vc) / **Fabio Biondi** vn

Virgin Classics Veritas 545562-2 (70' · DDD) Ⓕ

The world of the violin sonata in the first half of the 18th century, between Corelli and Mozart, is an underexplored one, even though it's populated by some important and interesting figures. Principal among them, Francesco Maria Veracini, Pietro Locatelli, Francesco Geminiani and Giuseppe Tartini, four of the great Italian violinist-composers of the age, have been sparsely represented on disc, and then usually by their orchestral music. Elizabeth Wallfisch's Locatelli Trio has done sterling work in this area, but often in single-composer packages, so this release, which offers a sample sonata by each of the above named, is a welcome and enticing arrival.

Here we have music by the nervy, ever-so-slightly unhinged Veracini, the elegantly virtuoso Locatelli, the energetic Corelli pupil Geminiani, and the later, *galant*-tinged but far-from-empty-headed Tartini. As an extra treat there's a semi-programmatic suite, full of typical French operatic gestures, by the little-known Michele Mascitti, a favourite Italian in Paris.

Fabio Biondi's bustling virtuosity and highly personal mix of the quirky and the controlled is ideally suited to bringing out the best in these extrovert yet solidly constructed pieces, where he seems thoroughly at home. With a sweet but keenly produced tone, he peppers things up with sparky ornamentations and the odd fleeting *spiccato*, a favourite gesture of his.

The continuo players of Europa Galante clearly enjoy the music as much as he does, and contribute much to its visceral excitement. Although a wide range of instruments is listed, they are used sensitively and imaginatively by just three players (four if you count the double-tracked harpsichord and organ in the Mascitti, where the steely jangling of a cittern and the wobbly twang of a clavichord are further happy inspirations). It's hard to imagine this deserving music being more enchantingly presented.

Fretwork

Agricola De tous biens playne. Si dedero Ⓟ Tandernaken **Anonymous** Dit le Bourguygnon. Fortuna desperata. Je suis d'Alemagne. Numqua fue pena major. Se congie pris. La Spagna **Brumel** Fors seulement **Busnois** Le Serviteur **Caron** Helas que pourra devenir **Ghiselin** Favus distillans. Fors seulement **Hayne van Ghizeghem** De tous biens plaine **Isaac** J'ay pris amours. La morra. Tartara **Japart** Vray dieu d'amours **Josquin Desprez** Adieu mes amours. Baisez moy, ma doulce amye. La Bernardina. De tous biens playne **Lapicida** Tandernaken **Obrecht** Fors seulement. J'ay pris amours. Orto Ave Maria. Si sumpsero. Tsat een meskin **Pinarol** Fortuna desperata **Stappen** Beati pacifici/De tous biens plaine **Stokem** Brunette **Fretwork** (Richard Boothby, Richard Campbell, Wendy Gillespie, Julia Hodgson, William Hunt, Susanna Pell *viols*)
Harmonia Mundi HMU90 7291 (76' · DDD) Ⓕ●

Few better compliments can be paid than returning to a recording again and again, for sheer pleasure. The occasion of Fretwork's collection is the anniversary of the establishment in Venice more than 500 years ago of the first music-printing presses. This is certainly the most stylish of several recordings made in connection with Ottaviano Petrucci's epoch-making achievement.

To present a recital of these song arrangements and 'purely' instrumental pieces exclusively on viols is a novelty worth commenting on. Most other recordings of this repertory use a mixed consort; part of the charm of this disc is that it seduces you into the belief that the music was actually intended for viols. Fretwork's single-mindedness is further emphasised by their eschewal of a guest singer, an option that would have guaranteed more variety on the surface level, and allowed them perhaps a greater range of options. That they have not done so is admirable.

Another strength of the recital is programming. Sheer generosity aside (there are 32 tracks), it's a treat to have so many favourite pieces here. The 15th century's hit-parade is also reflected, with no fewer than four settings of *De tous biens plaine*, three of *Fors seulement*, and two each of *Fortuna desperata*, *J'ay pris amours* and *Tandernaken*. There are lesser-known pieces too, but always, it seems, the viols' advocacy of the music (and of their suitability to it) is uppermost. Lovers of polyphony of all sorts, in all its abstraction and all its sensuousness, have something special in store. And lovers of chamber music of later periods will find themselves on surprisingly similar territory.

The Harp Consort

Spanish Gypsies – Celtic and Spanish Ⓟ
Music in Shakespeare's England
Anonymous Rowallan Manuscript – The Gypsy Lilt; Gregory Walker: Quadran Pavan; Buffins; Hay de Gie. Irish Ho-Hoane. Trenchmore. Rownde Scottishe tune. Lady Louthians Lilt **Byrd** Gypsy's Round, BK80 **Farnaby** Spagnioletta. Mal Sims **Holborne** Muy linda **Hume** Captaine Humes Poeticall Musicke – A Spanish Humour **R Johnson** Gypies Metamorphosed – The Gypsies Song **Playford** The English Dancing Master – Part 1: The Wherligig; The Spanish Jeepsie; Pakington's Pound; Part 2: The Punks Delight; Lulle me beyond thee; Scotch Cap; Appendix: A new Scotch Jig. Musick's Hande-Maide – An Ayre called Corke; Sarabande to Corke **Harp Consort / Andrew Lawrence-King** *hp*
Deutsche Harmonia Mundi 05472 77516-2 (71' · DDD)
Ⓕ●●

The subtitle of this album says more about its content than does the main one. There's much titular reference to Spain and to gypsies, but only in 'The Spanish Jeepsies' do the two come together. It seems that in Shakespeare's time Spanish popular tunes were perceived as being of gypsy origin. More to the point, the programme is skilfully devoted to showing the influence of Celtic and Spanish idioms on English popular music.

Charles I's Consorte opened the way for courtly instruments to 'fraternise' with humbler ones, creating a variety of new sounds, and the Harp Consort take full advantage of this 'social' freedom. The eight players form a kaleidoscope of broken consorts drawn from the 18 instruments (plucked, bowed, blown and percussed) at their disposal, producing a remarkable spectrum of sound from the ethereal ('Lady Louthians Lilt') to the downright boisterous ('The Wherligig'). Only five of the 23 items last for more than four minutes but one never has the impression of a trayful of canapés deputising for a good meal.

When it comes to putting together a coherent and well-researched programme of assorted small-scale items, only Peter Holman springs to mind as Andrew Lawrence-King's peer. Excellent recording is the icing on this delectable cake, one that takes 71 minutes to enjoy.

much so that they feel able to add fairly substantial fantasies of their own. These work well enough, though they share a feature which is much apparent elsewhere on the recording – the process of accumulating more and more diverse instruments as each piece progresses. This colourful sound-world – one that finds its apotheosis in the extended variations on the ballad *Conde claros* and the multi-tracked realisation of Henestrosa's 40-part fugue on *Unum colle Deum* – is fantastic, both in the sense of very attractive but also in that of departing, at least to some extent, from reality.

The most compelling items are those for harp alone, or a reduced line-up of instruments. Here the glosses sound genuinely improvised rather than semi-composed, and, especially in more contrapuntal textures, the underlying musical logic can be followed without being distracted by a kaleidoscope of instrumental colour. Nevertheless, this is an infectiously enjoyable CD, abounding in superb playing.

El Arte de Fantasía
Anonymous Ave Maris Stella **Cabezón** Ave maris stella a 2. Diferencias sobre la Gallarda Milanesa. Tres glosas sobre la Alta. Tiento XVIII **Mudarra** Tres libros de musica en cifras para vihuela – Tiento para harpa y organo **Narváez/Josquin** La cancion del Emperador, 'Mille regres'. Paseávase el rey moro. Baxa de contrapunto **Palero** Paseávase el rey moro **Valderrábano** Silva de Sirenas – Para discanto; Soneto a manera de dança; Tiento sobre: la Pavana real **Vasquez** De los álamos vengo **Venegas de Henestrosa** Libro de cifra nueva – Entrada; Canción: Je vous; Pavana con su glosa; Canción: Mundo, qué me puedes dar?; Fuga a 40: Unum colle Deum; Canción: Míralo cómo llora; Final; Diferencias sobre: Guárdame las vacas (Narváez); Canción: Demandez vous (Crequillon); Diferencias sobre: Conde claros (Valderrábano); Ave Maris Stella a 3 (Cabezón); Ave Maris Stella: Himno a 4 (Cabezón); Ave Maris Stella: Himno de canto llano (Cabezón)
Harp Consort (Hille Perl *va da gamba* Lee Santana *vihu/citt* Steven Player *gtr/perc* Helen Coombs *org/hpd*) / **Andrew Lawrence-King** *hp/org/hpd/psal*
Harmonia Mundi HMU90 7316 (69' · DDD)　　Ⓕ⊙

This is a compilation of works from instrumental collections published in mid-16th-century Spain. In his informative booklet notes Andrew Lawrence-King points up the importance and unjustified neglect of a volume published in 1557 by Luis Venegas de Henestrosa. The *Book of new tablature for keyboard, harp and vihuela* provides a fascinating snapshot of musical life at the court of Emperor Charles V. It's probably because the collection consists largely of arrangements that it's been neglected on CD up till now, so to present these pieces music under the banner of the 'Art of Fantasy' is cunning; so too their suite-like groupings under headings such as 'Entrada' and 'A manera de dança'.

So much for the packaging; what of the music-making? The musicians have really tried to get under the skin of the music and make it theirs, so

Jacob Heringman　　　　　　　　· *lute*

The Art of the Lute Player
Bakfark Un Gay Bergier. Si grand è la pietà. Non accedat ad te malum, secunda pars. Fantasia No 9 Desprez[d] Adieu mes amours. Ave Maria. Benedicta es, caelorum regina. Christe Fili Dei[b]. Mille regretz[b] Gerle Scaramella Holborne Heres paternus. A Horn pype[a]. Responce. Galliard, 'The Fairie-round' Milán Fantasías[b] – XII; XXIV; XXXI. Pavanas[b] – I; VI. Tento IV[b] Mudarra Tres libros de musica en Cifras para vihuela – Fantasia que contrahaze la harpa en la manera de Ludovico[b]; Fantasia del primer tono[b]; Fantasia del segundo tono[b]; Tiento del segundo tono[b]; Fantasia del quinto tono[c] Waissel Polish Dances – I; II; III; IV; V [d]Intabulations by Ripa
Jacob Heringman *lte/[a]citt/[b]vihu/[c]gtr*
Avie AV0011 (79' · DDD)　　　　　　　Ⓕ

Despite its title this isn't merely another programme of lute music. Jacob Heringman, a distinguished lutenist, here shows his considerable technical and musical skills on three lutes, vihuela, cittern and renaissance guitar. His choice of repertoire springs from his particular love of 16th-century music and it includes many items by neglected composers, most of which have not been recorded before.

There's an abundance of dances and fantasias, the staple diet of most lutenists, but Heringman also focuses on the important but generally overlooked area of intabulations, adaptations of vocal works for the lute and vihuela. Since the plucked-string instruments lack the sustaining power of the human voice the vocal lines were kept 'alive' by adding embellishments.

This disc offers a unique variety of music, some of it rescued from undeserved oblivion, played on a matching variety of instruments and superbly recorded. The supple expressivity of the performances reflects Heringman's love of the music. Buy it without delay.

Hespèrion XX / XXI

Ostinato   P

Anonymous Greensleeve to a Ground **Correa de Arauxo** Tres Glosas sobre 'Todo el mundo en general' **Ortiz** Quinta pars IX. Ricercadas – II; V; VII **Falconieri** Ciaccona. Il Primo libro di canzone – Passacalle **Marini** Passacaglia **Merula** Ciaccona. Ruggiero **Pachelbel** Canon and Gigue **Purcell** Fantasia upon a Ground, Z731. Sonatas in Four Parts, Z802-11 – No 5 in G minor **Rossi** Sonata sopra l'Aria di Ruggiero **Traditional** Canarios **Valente** Gaillarda Napolitana
Hespèrion XXI / Jordi Savall va da gamba
Alia Vox AV9820 (73' · DDD)   F○

Here the group re-create the improvisatory world of instrumental music of the 16th and 17th centuries. Repeated bass or harmonic patterns – the basso ostinato – are the linking factor while each composer from Ortiz to Purcell displays amazing skill at combining the restriction of harmonic repetition with freedom of inventiveness, discipline stimulating creativity with brilliant result. The players' disciplined virtuosity brings out the improvisatory background of much of this music in a dazzling display that enthralls the listener.

Despite the constant of the ostinato, the variety in texture and instrumental colour is such that there's never a dull moment: Jordi Savall on viols ranging from bass to treble is completely at one with the music of Diego Ortiz – never has it been more convincingly performed. The continuo team, mostly plucked strings in the earlier repertory and keyboard (harpsichord or organ) with theorbo in the later works, is superb: inventive and as virtuoso as the soloists they accompany.

These elaborated versions of improvisatory techniques are in many ways parallel to the best recordings of jazz, capturing for posterity an inspiration of the moment.

Elizabethan Consort Music

Alberti Pavin of Alberti. Gallyard **Anonymous** In Nomine a 5. Desperada. Gallyard I-III. Allemande. Ronda. La represa I & II. Allemana d'amor. Dance I & II. Pavana I & II. Brandeberges **Daman** Di sei soprani **W Mundy** O mater mundi **Parsons** In Nomines a 7 – IV; V. The Songe called Trumpetts **Strogers** In Nomines – III a 5; IV a 6 **Taverner** Quemadmodum. **R White** In Nomine V **Woodcock** Browning my dere. In Nomines a 5 – II; III
Hespèrion XX / Jordi Savall va da gamba
Alia Vox AV9804 (66' · DDD)   F

Jordi Savall and Hespèrion XX in this recording of Elizabethan consort musichave committed the contents of a rare manuscript collection to CD. The manuscript, in the British Library, dates from the 1570s and 1580s, and contains dances, transcriptions of chansons and motets and fantasies, intended for performance at court by the queen's musicians. These performances are highly sonorous and imaginatively realised.

Savall orchestrates the repeats of the dances and chansons, usually beginning with a drum, a solo treble viol or lute and then building up the layers of sound with each restatement. The manuscript contains a fascinating array of pieces: numerous In Nomines which climax in the astonishingly rich seven-part settings by Robert Parsons contrast with transcriptions of bawdy chansons, the evergreen *Browning my dere*, an ethereal fantasy by William Daman for six treble viols (surely a collectors' item), William Mundy's eponymous *O mater mundi* and the sublimity of John Taverner's *Quemadmodum*. This is music fit for a courtly Sunday Elizabethan banquet, with a bit of dancing thrown in, should you wish to entertain in that style. The recording does offer a wonderful glimpse of the variety of music enjoyed at the court of Elizabeth I; it's a one-off and should be treasured as such.

Barthold Kuijken   *flute*

Bach Partita in A minor, BWV1013 **CPE Bach** Solo Flute Sonata, H562 Wq132 **Hotteterre** Brunette, 'L'autre jour ma Cloris'. Air de Mr Lambert, 'Je suis aimé de celle que j'adore'. Air de Mr Bousset, 'Vous qui faites votre modèle de la constante tourterelle' **Vivaldi** 'Le Printemps', RV269 (arr Rousseau) **Weiss** French Suite in G
Barthold Kuijken fl
Accent ACC20144 (75' · DDD)   F

An entire disc of 18th-century solo flute may look like a bit of a daunting prospect, but then not everyone plays the instrument like Barthold Kuijken. Throughout his recital this experienced Baroque musician caresses our ears with playing of supreme ease and natural fluidity, producing not a single shrill or rasping note and displaying at all times an exquisite and gentle musicianship. The music includes the Baroque period's two greatest solo flute works, the Partita by JS Bach and the Sonata by his son CPE, alongside some of Hotteterre's poignant arrangements and elaborations of French *airs de cours*. Kuijken's style isn't to shock or surprise, but simply to play as beautifully and tastefully as he can. The results here are utterly beguiling, above all in the slow music of the Hotteterre pieces, with their haunting, plaintive urgency, and the sarabandes of Bach and Weiss, both executed with faultless poise and grace. Elsewhere, he shows sure-footed virtuosity and balance, not only making light of the leaps, runs and arpeggios but doing so with sufficient control to drop in some fleet dynamic contrasts, as in the first-movement bird-calls of the Vivaldi. Principally a disc for flute fans, but lovers of good Baroque music-making should find plenty to admire, too.

Andrew Lawrence-King   *harp*

His Majesty's Harper

Anonymous Scott's Lament **Byrd** Alman in G. La coranto. Fantasia. A gigg. Praeludium to Ye Fancie

Fantasia. Rowland (arr Dowland) **Dowland** Awake, sweet loue, thou art return'd. Can she excuse. A fancy. Farwell. Fine knacks for Ladies. Frogg galliard. Go cristall teares. Mrs Winter's Jump. My dear Adieu, my sweet love farewell. My Lady Hunsdons Puffe. My thoughts are wingd with hopes. Pavana lacrima. Robin. Semper Dowland semper dolens. Suzanna Galliard. Tarleton's Jigge. Tarletones Riserrectione **le Flelle** The Queens Maske **Macdermott** Allmane. Cormacke. Mr Cormake Allman. Schoc.a.torum Cormacke
Andrew Lawrence-King hp
Deutsche Harmonia Mundi 05472 77504-2 (65' · DDD)
ⒻⓄ

Andrew Lawrence-King's resourceful plundering of the harpsichord and lute books in search of an elusive early harp repertoire takes him here to music from 16th-century England. With some of the best instrumental music of the time on offer, much of it displaying that irresistible folk-like charm and melancholy peculiar to English melody, he can't go far wrong. Here, making delightful appearances, are Dowland's *Pavana lacrima* and *Semper Dowland semper dolens*, some of his shorter catchy dance-songs, and more dances and contrapuntal pieces by Byrd. All transfer to the harp superbly in Lawrence-King's hands, which once again manage to find in his instrument the subtleties of the lute together with the power and agility of the harpsichord. More importantly, it's hard to imagine this music being played with a greater or more honest expressiveness. Most of the pieces here are played on a gut-string Italian triple harp – gentle and mellow of tone but powerful and macho when it needs to be – but there are also some intriguing contributions from the brass-strung Irish *cláirseach*, which Lawrence-King uses in the anonymous *Scott's Lament* and four pieces by Cormack Macdermott, harpist at the court of James I. It's an instrument which, if you haven't come across it before, is almost certain to confound your expectations with its rippling, metallic sound. This is a thoroughly enjoyable disc, the kind which touches you with its sound alone; the music seems as if it could have been intended for the harp all along, a simple effectiveness which makes it all the more strange that so little real harp music from this time survives.

Gustav Leonhardt   harpsichord/organ

Bach Aria variata in A minor, BWV989. Partite diverse sopra, 'O Gott, du frommer Gott', BWV767. Fantasia in C minor, BWV1121 **J Christoph Bach** Prelude and Fugue in E flat – Prelude **Bull** Dr Bull's Goodnight **Byrd** The Queen's Alman, BK10. A Ground, BK43. Corranto, BK45 **Gibbons** Fantasia in A minor, MBXX/10 **H Hassler** Canzon **Pachelbel** Toccata In G. Fantasia **C Ritter** Allemanda **Strogers** Fantasia
Gustav Leonhardt hpd, claviorg
Alpha ALPHA042 (70' · DDD)
ⒻⓄ

On this disc Gustav Leonhardt uses a reproduction of a German harpsichord (School of Silbermann, *c*1735, by Anthony Sidey) and a claviorganum. The latter, though a great rarity today, was already in use in Europe by the beginning of the 16th century and continued until the late 18th century; the last surviving harpsichord made in England was part of a claviorganum. It consisted of a one- or two-manual keyboard instrument with a chamber organ beneath it. The reconstructed instrument used here has a one-manual harpsichord (after Aelpido Gregori) and a chest-like chamber organ with two stops. The harpsichord and organ may be used separately or together.

Although no music is known to have been specifically intended for the claviorganum, the catch-all use of the word 'keyboard' leaves the door open for its use. The sound of the two keyboards combined is fascinating, but Leonhardt uses it sparingly, as solo voice in the items by Hassler, Strogers and Byrd (*Queen's Alman*) and to add a pedal bass to Pachelbel's brief *Toccata* – how he does this is unclear! The organ has its solo day in Gibbons's Fantasia II. The remaining items are played as harpsichord solos. The otherwise admirable inlay booklet doesn't indicate what is played on what.

The programme includes some rarities and Leonhardt is at his mature best. The warmth and flexibility of his phrasing belie the severity of his personal appearance. This recording is a must for all aspects of the performances – and the arguably overdue reappearance of the claviorganum.

London Baroque

The Trio Sonata in 17th-Century England
Blow Ground in G minor. Sonata in A **Coprario** Eight Fantasia-suites – in C **Gibbons** Nine Fantasias a 3 – No 6; No 8; No 9 **Jenkins** Fantasia and Ayre. Fantasia a 3 **Lawes** Eight Fantasia-Suites – Sett No 1 in G minor **Locke** Little Consort: Ten Suites – in D minor **Purcell** Sonatas in Four Parts – in D **Simpson** Pavan. Almaine. Courante. Air. Courante. Air
London Baroque (Ingrid Seifert, Richard Gwilt vns Charles Medlam bass viol Terence Charlston hpd/org)
BIS BIS-CD1455 (70' · DDD)   Ⓕ

Having over the years recorded the core trio sonata repertoire in the usual format of single-composer CDs, London Baroque have change dtack with this release, the first in an eight-disc series exploring the development of the trio sonata throughout Europe. Although names such as Corelli, Purcell, Vivaldi, Leclair and Handel will inevitably be revisited, quite a few rarer but still deserving ones get a look-in, too. Such is the case with this first release, which traces the emergence of the trio sonata in England. Only two of the works presented actually call themselves sonatas, so it's probably more accurate to say that what's on offer here are English examples of trio style.

This is how a viol-consort man like Gibbons can sneak in, a group of his three-part fantasias being deemed near enough to the characteristic trio sonata texture of two treble instruments and bass to serve as a starting-point; from there the fantasias and suites follow a satisfying transition to the recognisable violinistic trio style of Blow and Purcell. Along the way are other 'consort-thinking' composers such as the bold and lively John Coprario, the emotionally intense William Lawes and the elegant John Jenkins, as well as the more European-inspired Matthew Locke and Christopher Simpson.

London Baroque has a distinctive fluid and vibrant string sound that's mainly heard in high-Baroque repertoire. It isn't what we're used to for the earlier pieces on this disc. No wispy Englishness here; instead gutsy bowing and forthright expression that brings intensity and sonic weight to the pieces. You need to like it, though; London Baroque rarely relent, and the rather reverberant sound means that some listeners may find it a little rich after a while. But even if you only feel able to sample this disc in smallish doses, it should always be a pleasure to hear such an expert ensemble at work in this repertoire.

Nigel North   *lute*

A Varietie of Lute Lessons
Anonymous Fantasie No 2. Volt **Ballard** Coranto No 1. Volt No 2 **Bacheler** Monsieur's Almaine. Pavan No 4 **Cato** Fantasie No 1 **Dowland** Sir John Smith's Almain, P47. The King of Denmark's Galliard, P40. The Earl of Essex's Galliard, P42a. My Ladie Riches Galyerd, P43a. The Right Hon Ferdinando Earle of Darby's Galliard, P44. Lady Clifton's Spirit. Queen Elizabeth's Galliard. Sir Henry Guilforde's Almaine **A Ferrabosco II** Fantasia No 5. Pavan No 6 **Huwet** Fantasie No 6 **Holborne** Pavan No 2. **Laurencini di Roma** Fantasie No 4 **Moritz** Pavan **Morley** Pavan No 3 **Perrichon** Coranto No 2 **Saman** Coranto No 4 **Nigel North** *lte*
Linn Records CKD097 (78' · DDD)   Ⓕ

A Varietie of Lute Lessons, compiled by Robert Dowland, was the last book of lute tablature to be published (1610) in England, and it's important both for the internationality and high quality of the music it contains. Six genres are represented, each by seven pieces: fantasies, pavans, galliards, almaines, corantos and voltes. Several items lack attribution in the original book, but the authors of *Sir John Smith's Almain* and *Volt No 2* have been identified, and the named composer of *Fantasie No 4*, 'The Knight of the Lute', is revealed as Laurencini di Roma. In making his selection, North has wisely passed over some of the 'pops' in favour of less well-known pieces, including: the magnificent *Pavan No 1* dedicated to John Dowland and quoting from *Lachrymae*; the beautiful *Fantasie No 4* of Laurencini, with its joyous chain of suspensions at the climax; and Bacheler's unusually structured variations on *Monsieur's Almaine* – long, but worth every minute. North's performances are full of warmth, unfailingly musical and stylish, and are recorded with clarity.

Go From My Window

Anonymous Greensleeves. Variations on 'John Come Kiss Me Now'. Robyn **Bacheler** Une Jeune Fillette, P93 **Byrd** Lord Willobies welcome home, BK7 The woods so wild, BK85. **Collard** Go from my window **Danyel** Mistress Anne Grene her leaves be greene **Dowland** Settings of Ballads and Other Popular Tunes – Go from my window, P64; Lord Willoughby's welcome home; Walsingham, P67; Loth to departe, P69 **A Holborne** Tinternell (Short Almain) **J Johnson** The carmans whistle. Walsingham. The old medley **Robinson** The Spanish pavan
Nigel North *lte*
Linn Records CKD176 (67' · DDD) SACD hybrid disc
                                                  Ⓕ

An entire disc of Renaissance lute music, especially one that includes no fantasias, can easily be the aural equivalent of a fast-changing kaleidoscope. Nigel North avoids this risk with high-quality items: only four of the 17 last for less than three minutes, and two play for over six minutes. He juxtaposes settings of three popular songs of the day by two different composers, of whom Dowland is one in each case. The contrasts between his settings of *My Lord Willoughby's Welcome Home* with that of Byrd, of *Walsingham* with Johnson's, and with Collard's *Go From My Window* are striking; the less well known 'others' deserve better recognition.

Not only is the programme sagely chosen, it's magnificently played. There are many lutenists who perform this music in correct style but few who present it in such 'human' fashion. With his lines shaped by finely controlled rubato and subtly shaded dynamics, North deserves his place among the finest living lutenists. The recording captures his splendid, 'three-dimensional' tone and his avoidance of unwanted ghostly sounds from the movements of his fingers on the fretboard, and his annotation is a model of its kind. If you should wish to instill a love of lute music in a friend, you could not do better than by beginning with this lovely recording.

Paul O'Dette   *lute*

Alla Venetiana
Anonymous Laudate Dio **Capirola** Spagna seconda. Non ti spiaqua l'ascoltar. Padoana belissima. Ricercari I, II, V & XIII. Tientalora. La Villanella **Cara** O mia cieca de dura sorte **Dalza** Calata ala Spagnola. Pavana alla ferrarese. Pavana alla venetiana. Piva I-III. Recercar. Recercar dietro. Saltarello **Ghizeghem** De tous bien playne (arr O'Dette). De tu biens plaene (arr Capirola) **Josquin Desprez** Adieu mes amours. Et in terra pax. Qui tolis pechata mundi **Martini** Malor mi bat **Pesenti** Che farala, che dirala **Spinacino** Recercare I & II
Paul O'Dette *lte*
Harmonia Mundi HMU90 7215 (73' · DDD)   ⒻO

When lutenists began to use the fingers of their right hands to pluck the strings, the instrument made a quantum leap forward. Three- and four-part counterpoint was suddenly on the agenda and the expanded range of the repertory made the lute popular even in Italian court circles. O'Dette focuses on two of the earliest printed books of tablature by Spinacino (1507), Dalza (1508), and the handwritten book of music by Capirola (c1520). Whoever it was who wrote the last of these, his student 'Vidal' or Capriola himself, touchingly showed his human fallibility; in a book written with much tender loving care and lavishly adorned with paintings, he had to insert the missing 'a' in 'Pado(a)na' with a caret! The selected items cover the basic genres of *tastar de corde*, *recercare*, dances and intabulations of vocal music by non-lutenist composers. In the last of these a lutenist demonstrated his skill in adapting and embellishing the original, as O'Dette does in his own intabulation of van Ghizegem's *De tous bien playne*. What comes through clearly is the joyous freshness of this music and the quickly acquired ingenuity in bringing more complex counterpoint to the fingerboard, as though the right-hand fingers had uncorked a bottle and released an inspirational genie. O'Dette has many talents, and an unusual ability to bring this music to life is one of them. A disc to lift the spirits and first-class recording too.

Palladian Ensemble

A Choice Collection
Anonymous Old Simon the King **Baltzar** John come kiss me now **J Banister** Divisions on a Ground **Blow** Ground in G minor **Butler** Variations on Callino Casturame **Locke** Broken Consorts – D; C **Matteis** Setts of Ayres – Book 2: No 10, Preludio in ostinatione; No 12, Andamento malincolico; Book 3: No 7, Preludio-Prestissimo; No 8, Sarabanda-Adagio; No 9, Gavotta con divisioni; Book 4: No 27, Bizzararrie sopra un basso malinconico; No 28, Aria amorosa-Adagio **Weldon** Sett of Ayres in D
Palladian Ensemble (Pamela Thorby *rec* Rachel Podger *vn* Susanne Heinrich *va da gamba* William Carter *gtr/theorbo*)
Linn Records CKD041 (66' · DDD)   Ⓕ❍

The 'choice collection' of 'music of Purcell's London' is of items such as might have been heard at the concerts of then contemporary music held on the premises of Thomas Britton, the 'small coal man', surely one of the most unlikely patrons in the history of music. It complements the ensemble's earlier disc ('An Excess of Pleasure', Linn CKD010), with another liberal helping of Nicola Matteis's various and sometimes agreeably bizarre *Ayres* and two more of Locke's *Broken Consorts*, which we find absorbing rather than confusing – as Charles II did. With this release John Weldon and Henry Butler are newcomers to the catalogue, the former with what amounts to an irregularly ordered suite, and the latter with splendid variations on *Callino Casturame*, in which Susanne Heinrich plays most expressively, and proves that chords played on the viola da gamba don't have to sound like teeth being pulled. *Old Simon the King* couldn't have been heard in Purcell's own time in this anonymous setting from *The*

division flute of 1706, but the tune was printed as early as 1652. If you aren't already aware of the high quality of the instrumental playing, stylish musicality and imaginative approach of the Palladian Ensemble, then this disc provides a good chance to find out what you've been missing.

Held by the Ears
Anonymous *Straloch Lute Book* – Canaries; A Scots Tune; Gallus Tom; Whip my Toudie; Hench Me Mallie Gray. *Rowallan manuscript* – Gypsies Lilt. Divisions on a Ground in G. Roger of Coverly Divisions in D minor **Matteis** Sett of Ayres. Sett of Ayres in D. Sett of Ayres in D minor. Sett of Ayres in G. Sett of Ayres for the Guitar. Aria ad Imitatione della Trombetta **Traditional** The lass of Peatie's Mill. Dumbarton's Drums. Bonny Christie. When she came Ben she bobed. Gilliam Callum. A new Tune
Palladian Ensemble (Pamela Thorby *rec* Rachel Podger *vn* Susanne Heinrich *va da gamba* William Carter *gtr/lte/theorbo*)
Linn Records CKD126 (73' · DDD)   Ⓕ❍

The Palladian Ensemble's very first recording featured a number of pieces by Nicola Matteis. Now they have drawn more items from his huge ragbag of short pieces for two melody instruments and continuo and made them the main subject of their latest disc, borrowing its title from Roger North's description of Matteis's playing: 'flaming as I have seen him, in a good humour he hath held the company by the ears…for more than an hour together'.

But acknowledging that Matteis's inspiration is a little hit-and-miss for a whole disc, they have mixed them with a few anonymous instrumental solos of the time and, most intriguingly, their own arrangements of Scottish folk tunes. In his insert-note Palladian lutenist William Carter admits that the connection between Matteis and musical matters Caledonian is 'indefinable', but the ear picks it up all right, and the combination works well. Not the least enjoyable feature is the convincingly folkish accent with which the Scottish tunes are performed; Pamela Thorby's soulful bends and grace notes are like an echo of the glens, while Rachel Podger's violin playing is as lithe as a fly-fisher's rod. As for Matteis, well, he's no genius, but his music can be fun, and besides, it doesn't seem to take much to get these players' imaginations going. After all, the Palladian Ensemble are a group whose quick-witted inventiveness and almost supernatural internal rapport never fail to delight, whatever the music.

Paolo Pandolfo   *viola da gamba*

A Solo
Abel Arpeggiata. Adagio. Allegro **Anonymous** Aria della Monicha (arr Pandolfo) **Bach** Solo Cello Suite No 4 in E flat BWV1010 **Corkine** The Punckes delight. Come live with me **Hume** Captaine Humes Musicall Humors – A Pavane **Machy** Prélude **Marais** Pièces de viole – Les voix humaines; Le badinage **Ortiz**

Trattado de glosas – Pass'emezzo antico;
Pass'emezzo moderno **Pandolfo** A Solo
Sainte-Colombe le fils Aire en rondeau **Sumarte**
Daphne. Whoope doe me no harm
Paolo Pandolfo viol/va da gamba
Glossa GCD920403 (77' · DDD)   ⓕ**OO**

Seventy-seven minutes of music for unaccompanied viola da gamba? Yes, and every second is a
pleasure in the company of one of the most brilliant of the instrument's exponents. Using three
different instruments Paolo Pandolfo takes us
on a well-planned journey through gamba-
playing Europe, starting with Italy and proceeding through early 17th-century England, mid-
Baroque France, 18th-century Germany and
the brink of the classical style, and finally back to
Italy for a composition of his own. Throughout,
not a single accompanying instrument is heard,
a feat Pandolfo makes light of by the simple
expedient of dispensing with continuo parts
where they exist and by exploiting to the full the
gamba's ability to play chords. Surely few listeners will be prepared, however, for the variety of
rich sonorities and colourings to be encountered
in this recital, or for Pandolfo's expressive versatility; the Italian pieces are virtuoso and vigorous, the French ones refined and deeply personal, and the bold transcription of Bach's
Fourth Solo Cello Suite, though it loses out in
cleanness to cello performances, full of strength
and energy. Most striking of all, however, is the
English group: the soldier-musician, Tobias
Hume has never sounded so touching as in the
spread *pizzicato*s which open his Pavan, while
Richard Sumarte's *Daphne* has a hauntingly
wistful folk quality which comes as an almost
eerie surprise. Pandolfo has put a lot of himself
into this recording, not least in his own piece,
which carries a touching personal dedication.
The result is a beautiful and moving recital.

Parley of Instruments

A High-Priz'd Noise – Violin Music for Charles I ℗
A **Ferrabosco II** Pavan and Alman **R Johnson II** The
Prince's Alman and Coranto. Air in G minor. The
Temporiser a 4. The Witty Wanton. Fantasia in G
minor **W Lawes** Alman in D 'for the Violins of Two
Trebles'. Airs for consort **Nau** Suite in F. Ballet in F.
Pavan and Galliard in D minor **Notari** Variations on
the 'Ruggiero' **Webster** Four Consort pieces
**Parley of Instruments Renaissance Violin Band /
Peter Holman**
Hyperion CDA66806 (67' · DDD)   ⓕ**O**

This recording is less concerned with musical
monuments, such as Lawes's large consorts,
than in rejuvenating a repertoire which might
have accompanied the King's re-creation, or
been the actual means for it. Most of the works
are written in dance forms, though we can be
reasonably certain that the majority wouldn't
have been conceived for accompanying dance.
The violin's specific association with active
dance music – except of a more base and popular

kind – goes only so far, as the 17th century progresses. Of the courtly violin bands it's the more
expansive one in the Presence Chamber (performing for public rather than private space at
court) which has the most instantly appealing
repertory – the opening set of works by Robert
Johnson and the wonderful *Pavan and Alman* by
Alphonso Ferrabosco II; the latter composition,
although timeless in its exquisite part-writing, is
given new life with a period violin band. Both
pieces gleam with an engaging transparency, a
compelling sound for those who have yet to hear
this ensemble. The *Pavan* is magically forthcoming in its gracious lines with just a hint of
melancholy, a poignant fragility which gives way
to the noble rapture of the *Alman*. The Parley's
14-strong group of four violins, six violas and
four bass violins is marshalled with a degree of
characterisation that gleefully extricates this
music from dusty library shelves.

Hille Perl   *viola da gamba*

Doulce Memoire – Glosas, Passeggiati   ℗
and Diminutions around 1600
Bonnizzi Jouissance **Dalla Casa** Doulce memoire
Monteverdi Sinfonia **Notari** Ben qui si mostra il ciel
Ortiz Passamezzo antico. Recercada de canto llano.
Recercada sobre tenore. Recercada quarta sobre
Doulce memoire. Doulce memoire **Rogniono** Susanne
ung jour. Anchor che c'ol partire **Rore** Ben qui si
mostra il ciel **Selma** Vestiva hi colli **Terzi** Jouissance
Trabaci Ancidetemi pur **Willaert** Jouissance vous
donneray
Hille Perl va da gamba with **Robert Sagasser,
Martina Rothbauer, Paulina van Laarhoven** va da
gambas **Matthias Müller** va da gamba/violone
Andrew Lawrence-King double hp **Lee Santana**
lte/gtr/chittarone
Deutsche Harmonia Mundi 05472 77502-2
(63' · DDD)   ⓕ**O**

Viol watchers will know what to expect from a
disc with this subtitle. In particular, they will be
anticipating a selection of Diego Ortiz's *recercadas* from his *Trattado de glosas*, in which he
demonstrated the many and various ways in
which an instrumental player can improvise on
existing dance tunes and contrapuntal vocal
compositions. Less predictable is the rest of this
beautifully planned and executed CD, on which
Hille Perl and her friends from two of the
groups in which she plays – The Harp Consort
and Sirius Viols – play instrumental arrangements and derivations from works by some of
the great names of late Renaissance vocal music.
The practices employed range from simply
playing a madrigal on viols (as in Rore's *Ben qui
si mostra*) to one viol playing an elaborate, newly
composed part while a lute plays the rest straight
(Selma's version of Palestrina's *Vestiva hi colli*),
to the 'alla bastarda' method in which the viol
plays florid decorations on as many parts as it
can as it leaps from one to the other (Notari's
version of the Rore).
    If this sounds like it might be a vehicle for

empty instrumental virtuosity, think again. Perl and Co. perform all these pieces from the heart, feeling every note and never losing touch with the music's origins. Helped by a warm and lovingly nurtured tone, Perl's playing is wonderfully expressive without ever losing its poise or subtlety, while her accompanists are impeccably sensitive and supportive. For good measure, Andrew Lawrence-King's solo, a Trabaci madrigal arrangement, is a perfect demonstration of the unique eloquence of the Baroque harp. As is her wont, Perl provides her own quirky booklet-notes which, while not terrifically informative, are guaranteed to raise a smile and add to the disc's glow of amity. A richly civilising release – exquisitely played, handsomely recorded and elegantly presented – but then that's no more than you would expect from someone who shares her family home with music, cats and chickens, now is it?

Phantasm

Four Temperaments

Byrd Pavan and Galliard a 6, BE17/15. Mass for four voices. Prelude and Ground, 'The Queen's Goodnight' **A Ferrabosco** I In Nomine a 5 – No 1; No 2; No 3. Fantasia a 4. Fantasia a 6. Pavan a 5 **Parsons** In Nomine a 5. A Song called Trumpets. Ut re me fa sol la. De la Court. A Song of Mr Robert Parsons **Tallis** In Nomine a 4 – No 1; No 2. A Solfaing Song

Phantasm (Laurence Dreyfuss, Wendy Gillespie, Jonathan Manson, Marrku Luolajan-Mikkola *viols*) with **Emilia Benjamin, Asako Morikawa** *viols*
Avie AV2054 (72' · DDD)   Ⓕ**ⓄⓄⓄ**

The 'Four Temperaments' of the title refer back to the ancient theory of the four humours, or bodily fluids, responsible for conditions of the body and so, by extension, for personalities. Laurence Dreyfus suggests that each composer represented personifies one of these 'temperaments': Parsons the choleric, Alfonso Ferrabosco the Elder the calm phlegmatic, Tallis the sanguine, and Byrd the passionate melancholic.

Admitting, however, that personalities are far more complex than that, what this recording really demonstrates is the vast variety of colour and mood represented not only by each composer individually but also by the skill and beauty of the consort's interpretation. The stately patterning of the pavans contrasts with the sprightly tossing, by one player to another, of small melodic fragments in other pieces.

The arrangement of the programme, too, is carefully planned: pitches, sometimes even themes, follow naturally one after another. A fine example is Ferrabosco's *In nomine I*, with its theme of a rising minor scale, followed by the same scale in Byrd's *Sanctus*. The ingenious interspersing of movements from Byrd's four-part Mass is justifiable by his description of some of his works as suitable for 'voices or viols', though the plangent descending final phrases of

the *Agnus Dei* call for the sung text to fulfil their ultimate purpose.

The players' contribution to the painting and mixing of humours is outstanding. They bring to life the importance of the viol consort in Elizabethan society, in teaching as well as entertainment for old and young. Did Parsons have in mind the children of the Chapel Royal with his *Ut re mi fa sol la*? Or Tallis with his *Solfaing Song*, or in the settings of familiar tunes, both sacred – the Ferrabosco, Tallis or Parsons *In nomine*s – and secular, for example Parsons's brilliant *Song called Trumpets*? For insight as well as enjoyment, this recording is highly recommended.

Jordi Savall   *viola da gamba*

La Folia, 1490-1701

Anonymous Folia: Rodrigo Martínez **Cabezón** Folia: Para quien crié cabellos **Corelli** Violin Sonata in D minor, Op 5 No 12, 'La folia' **Enzina** Folia: Hoy comamos y bebamos **Marais** Deuxième Livre de Pièces de viole – Couplets de folies **Martín y Coll** Diferencias sobre las folias **Ortiz** Ricercadas sobre la Folia – IV; VIII

Jordi Savall *va da gamba/viol* **Rolf Lislevand** *gtr/theorbo/vilhuela* **Michael Behringer** *org/hpd* **Arianna Savall** *triple hp* **Bruno Cocset** *vc* **Pedro Estevan** *perc* **Adela Gonzalez-Campa** *castanets*
Alia Vox AV9805 (55' · DDD)   Ⓕ

This release charts two centuries of musical madness in the shape of the *folia* (which can mean anything from 'wild amusement' to 'insanity'). The earliest references to the *folia* are to a Portuguese dance of popular origin that by the end of the 15th century had become still more popular in court circles. Its distinctively minimalist harmonic patterns, but on only four different chords, make it a perfect vehicle for instrumental jam sessions in the Renaissance and this improvisatory tradition is explored by Savall and his team. Virtuosity is a *sine qua non* in the *folia* business and Savall is an established virtuoso. Allied to this, is his ability to make the music seem as spontaneous and full of fantasy as the improvisatory practice from which the endless chameleon-like variations by Corelli and Marais sprang.

These works are well known to all aficionados of Baroque music; less familiar is the set of *diferencias* by the Spanish composer Antonio Martín y Coll, although he's almost equally inventive. Here Savall chooses to emphasise the Iberian origin of the *folia* with an accompaniment of triple harp, Baroque guitar and castanets which he describes as being 'in keeping with the characteristic Iberian sound of the period.' Such a sound world may well have more to do with late 20th-century preconceptions than historical fact and the castanets seem lost and uncertain in these elaborate, sophisticated variations.

Savall's re-creations of the early *folia* are much freer still; and, his version of *Rodrigo Martínez*, a dance-song from the *Cancionero Musical de Palacio*, is almost outrageously exuberant in its percussionisation. Still, Savall's attempt to trace an important improvisatory tradition is fascinating and it's a tribute to his musical imagination that the ear never tires of those four chords in almost an hour's music. Recommended – despite Savall's improvised humming!

Scaramouche

Henry Purcell and his Time $\boxed{P}$
Baltzar Divisions on 'John Come Kiss me Now'[b]
Jenkins Fantasia in three parts **W Lawes** Fantasia-Suite No 7 in D minor **Locke** The Broken Consort – Suites Nos 3[b] & 4 **Purcell** Pavans – B flat, Z750; G minor, Z752[a]. Fantasia upon a Ground, Z731[ab]
C Simpson Prelude. Divisions on a Ground[b]
Scaramouche (Andrew Manze, Caroline Balding vns Jaap ter Linden bass viol Ulrike Wild hpd/org)
[a]**Foskien Kooistra** vn [b]**Konrad Junghänel** theorbo
Channel Classics CCS4792 (60' · DDD) Recorded 1992
    $\boxed{F}$

Scaramouche's recording of 17th-century English chamber music offers a homogeneous selection of music and instrumental combinations. The innocent charm of other selections of this nature is largely replaced by the weightier, more sober pronouncements of Lawes, Locke and Purcell, but also by a bold interpretative vigour that makes it just as lively a listen in its own way.

Jaap ter Linden's rendition of his Simpson piece is suitably poetic, while Andrew Manze's version of *John Come Kiss me Now* has a Turkey-in-the-Straw ending that will certainly make you chuckle.

This may be a slightly less polished and fluent recording than some others, but in the end, moments such as these – as well as the fact that there's lastingly rewarding music to be heard here – will make you want to play this disc again and again.

By the way, the disc advertises itself as offering the music of 'Henry Purcell and His Time'. Yet Lawes, for one, died over a decade before Purcell was born. The dubious history is eloquently symbolised by a portrait of an unmistakably Elizabethan lady on the front of the box!

Sinfonye

Red Iris – Instrumental music from $\boxed{P}$
14th-century Italy
Istampite – Trotto; Tre Fontane; Principio di virtu; La manfredina and la rotta; Chominciamento di gioa; Palamento; Two Salterellos; Belicha
Sinfonye (Jim Denley, Pedro Estevan perc) / **Stevie Wishart** medieval fiddle/hurdy-gurdy/dir
Glossa GCD920701 (53' · DDD) Interactive CD $\boxed{F}$ **O**

Many people have recorded the 14th-century instrumental dances that appear only in a single manuscript now in London. Apart from some pieces apparently for keyboard, they're almost the only known early works for a solo melody instrument. The nine pieces (out of a total of 15) presented here offer no novelty of repertoire.

What's new is the way Stevie Wishart plays them. She views the shorter pieces as dances, to be performed with percussion accompaniment. This is common enough, though they're done extremely well, with Jim Denley and Pedro Estevan producing a stunning range of sounds from their various percussion instruments. But the longer ones are treated as elaborate and weaving instrumental solos, without any accompaniment. Wishart plays them on the vielle and, in one case, on the hurdy-gurdy, never rushing, never tempted to gloss over the many unexpected details in the lines. This approach stresses the quality and inventiveness of the melodies, and it perhaps aligns them with their true historical context, the repertory of long monophonic *lais* from the 14th century. That in its turn makes the pieces far more than virtuoso showpieces. But it says much for the power of Wishart's playing that she keeps the music constantly interesting and is invariably persuasive. The disc comes with a CD-ROM track that portrays, among other things, frescoes of the time, the instruments and the manuscript. But even without that this is a superbly convincing performance, recorded with a nice full sound and giving relatively familiar music an added intellectual depth.

EARLY MUSIC –
CHORAL & VOCAL

Al Ayre Español

Spanish Baroque, Volume 1 $\boxed{P}$
Anonymous Canción a dos tiples. Two Pasacalles
C Galán Al espejo que retrata. Humano ardor **F de Iribarren** Quién nos dira de una flor. Viendo que Jil, hizo raya **Literes** Ah del rustico pastor **J de Torres** Más no puedo ser. Al clamor **F Valls** En un noble, sagrado firmamento
Al Ayre Español / Eduardo López Banzo
Deutsche Harmonia Mundi 05472 77325-2
(70' · DDD) Recorded 1994. Texts and translations included $\boxed{F}$ **O**

López Banzo could well be set to achieve for the Spanish Baroque what William Christie and Les Arts Florissants have done for French music of the 17th and 18th centuries. There are many parallels between English and Spanish musical cultures in the Baroque: French and Italian stylistic and structural elements are incorporated into a musical language that's nevertheless as clearly Spanish as the Purcell idiom is English.

The melodiousness characteristic of the Spanish repertory and its rhythmic patterns are immediately apparent. The *villancicos* and *cantadas* by Torres, Literes, Iribarren and Valls are all sectional works that alternate recitative and arias in the manner of the Italian cantata, but they also introduce minuets, elegant slow movements, lively refrains and even Spanish dances of popular origin such as the *jácara*. Indeed, the disc ends with one of those foot-tapping pieces (performed in cathedrals and chapels on such joyous feasts as Christmas) by Iribarren who was chapelmaster at Malaga Cathedral.

The performances are very fine. The instrumentalists seem to be completely at home with the style and point up the idiomatic syncopations with just the right degree of emphasis. Under the secure direction of López Banzo, they generally serve the music extremely well. The singers are Spanish, which is probably essential, at least at this stage in our knowledge of the repertory. They, too, are excellent. The soprano Marta Almajano's voice is agile and well focused with a hint of that dark, enriching quality – like velvet-clad steel – that seems to characterise the Spanish voice (think of Victoria de los Angeles or even Plácido Domingo). As the music demands, she's expressive or virtuoso, lyrical or brilliant, and always has a superb sense of line.

Anonymous Canción a dos tiples. Dos pasacalles **Durón** Veneno es de amor la envidia – Ondas riscos, pezes, mares. El impossible mayor en amor le venze Amor – Donde vas; Danae, cuya belleza; Oye, escucha, aguarda, espera **Galán** Al espejo que retrata. Humano ardor **Iribarrén** Quién nos dira de una flor. Viendo que Jil, hizo raya.**Literes** Ah del rústico pastor. Azis y Galatea – Seguidillas; Confiado gilguerillo; Monstruo, en quien ha sobrado; Pues del culto mi piedad; Coplas. Los elementos – Deydades que en el monte; Ay amor; Mas si fuese la planta fugitiva. El estrago en la fineza, o Jupiter y Semele – Pues soy abejuela; Yo he de enmudecer; Ven dulcissimo bien. **Martín y Coll** (arr anon) Flores de música – Ruede la Vola; Canción franzesa; Diferencias sobre la gayta **San Juan** Una noche que los reyes **Torres** Más no puedo ser. Al clamor. Arpón que glorioso. **Valls** En un noble, sagrado firmamento **Marta Almajano** *sop* **Al Ayre Español / Eduardo López Banzo** *hpd/org*
RCA Red Seal ② 74321 84586-2 (142' · DDD) Recorded 1994-9   Ⓜ

You don't have to be a Spanish specialist to take pleasure in these wonderful recordings. Credit for this goes primarily to the performances, directed with unstinting commitment and energy by Eduardo López Banzo. The irresistible rhythmic vitality which he brings to this music is the first thing you notice, but he also finds a more reflective quality when it's needed, and the music-making is never less than highly polished. All these qualities come together, too, in the set's star performer, soprano Marta Almajano, a singer who's been described as 'the Spanish Emma Kirkby' – which isn't to say that she sounds similar (on the contrary, she has a distinctive Spanish darkness to her voice) but that she's an artist of great interpretative intelligence and technique, and most early-music groups in Spain want her to sing with them. Why she has not become better known internationally is a mystery.

As for the music, composers such as Durón, Literes and Torres may not be household names either, but their music gives enormous enjoyment. Immediate favourites from this well-made selection of predominantly vocal music for chamber and stage include Durón's haunting *Ondas riscos, pezes, mares*, Torres' wistful *Al clamor*, and Iribarrén's foot-inspiring *Viendo que Jil, hizo raya*. Only the careless omission of the original issues' excellent documentation spoils the enjoyment of seeing these infectious recordings reappear at mid-price.

A batallar estrellas
Cabanilles Pasacalles – Pasacalles IV. Tientos – Tientos de primer tono; Tiento de falsas I **Comes** A la sombra estáis **Durón** Salve de ecos. A batallar estrellas. Lamentación primera, del Miércoles **Galán** Oygan los dulzes ecos **Patiño** Maria, Mater Dei. In Devotione **Samaniego Ruiz** De esplendor se doran los ayres
Al Ayre Español / Eduardo Lopéz Banzo
Harmonia Mundi HMI98 7053 (64' · DDD · T/t)   ⒻⓄ

As Eduardo López Banzo, director of Al Ayre Español, points out in the booklet-notes to their most recent recording, the cathedral music of 17th-century Spain for the most part remains untouched in dusty archives. Dusted down and scored up for the vocal and instrumental forces of Al Ayre Español, these works, with their mix of Spanish and Italianate features, are well worth hearing. There's a large repertory of polychoral music out there that's both impressive and effective in performance, as for example Patiño's motet *In devotione*, a sonorous and well put-together piece; his *Maria mater dei* presents a string of affective suspensions. Of similarly high quality is Durón's setting of the *Lamentations* which combines progressive elements from theatre music (and it's given a very theatrical performance here!), madrigalian effects as well as wonderfully expressive counterpoint. These Latin works are set alongside *villancicos* in the vernacular in the lively idiom familiar from Al Ayre Español's previous recordings. These are interpreted with tremendous energy, and if this sometimes results in a sense of headlong, even precipitous, rushing, there is utter conviction behind such choices of tempi. String arrangements of organ pieces by Cabanilles work very well by way of contrast and in their own right. The whole is enhanced by the rich sound achieved by Harmonia Mundi in the new Auditorio in Zaragoza, though the foregrounding of the various plucked continuo instruments results in a somewhat artificial (if very attractive) balance. Another superb achievement for Al Ayre Español.

Alia Musica

El canto espiritual judeoespañol
Anonymous (arr Sánchez) Albinu malkenu. Yede rašim. Nostalgia y alabanza de Jerusalén. `Et ša'aré

rašón. Yirú `enenu. Los siete hijos de Hana. Hodú
l'Adonay. Yašen al teradam. El mélej. Noche de aljad.
Ki ešmerá šabat. La fragua del estudio. Dodí yarad
leganó. La ketubá de la ley
Alia Musica / Miguel Sánchez *voc*
Harmonia Mundi HMI98 7015 (62' · DDD) Texts and
translations included   Ⓕ

This is a recital of sacred music, liturgical and
paraliturgical, from the Judeo-Spanish or Sephardic tradition, where ancient Jewish psalmody
and cantillation have assimilated many of the
musical characteristics and compositional techniques of Muslim Spain and the Ottoman
empire. One doesn't listen for long before hearing the augmented second, the typical ornamentation, the voice-production with its Middle
Eastern flavour, the interplay of free rhythm,
Arabic metrical, and also what Solange Corbin
has described as 'rythme unaire'. Then there are
all those characteristic Turkish instruments:
kanun, 'ud, ney, kaval and kamanya, each with
its own delightfully unusual timbre. Alia Musica
is an ensemble of eight singers and players, all
male with one exception, three of them being
both players and singers. The leader, Miguel
Sánchez, sings his solos with remarkable ease
and flexibility. The contralto, Albina Cuadrado,
has a powerful, yet tender voice, well suited to
her highly elaborate lament for the seven sons of
Hannah, sung in 'ladino' (Jewish-Spanish); and
also to the Sabbath evening *Noche de aljad* inter-
cessions. One striking example of the interplay
of styles is the 12th-century Hebrew poem by
Yehudá aben Abbas, `Et ša'aré rašón`, with its
abundant ornamentation in the dramatic slow-
beat solo cantillation, contrasting with a measured chorus with drone, and a vigorously animated rhythmic finale. This is a splendid
achievement.

Anonymous 4

**1000: A Mass for the End of Time – Medieval
Chant and Polyphony for the Ascension**
Anonymous Judicii signum. Quem creditis super
astra/Viri galilei. Celestis terrestrisque. Prudentia
prudentium. Dominus in sina. Ascendens cristus.
Salvator mundi/Rex omnipotens die hodierna.
Elevatus est rex fortis/Viri galilei. Ante secula.
Omnipotens eterne. Corpus quod nunc/Psallite
domino. Apocalypse 21:1-5. Regnantem sempiterna.
Cives celestis patrie
Anonymous 4 (Marsha Genensky, Susan Hellauer,
Jacqueline Horner, Johanna Rose *sngrs*)
Harmonia Mundi HMU90 7224 (72' · DDD) Texts and
translations included   Ⓕ

For their tenth recording and their first of the
new millennium, Anonymous 4 have decided to
go apocalyptic. Not that it shows in the customary purity and calmness of their chanting, but
for this CD they have taken as their theme the
Last Judgment as evoked in a liturgical reconstruction of a Mass for Ascension Day from

about the year 1000. The fears of what would
happen at the end of the first millennium were
genuine and widespread: Mankind would be
judged and found wanting, Satan would appear
and reap destruction.

Much of the music on this CD comes from
manuscripts of chant and early polyphony from
around 1000, mostly from the abbey of St Martial in Limoges, but with two pieces from the
Winchester Troper. A lot of the chant, then, is
Aquitanian in origin, and it can sound quite different to the now more familiar Gregorian tradition, with melodies that have a sweep and
range not commonly encountered there.
Indeed, Anonymous 4 make the most of these
steeper melodic curves, notably in the troped
Offertory *Elevatus est rex fortis/Viri galilei*, which
gives them something to get their teeth into;
elsewhere the chanting can sound a little tentative or even become rather static. Generally,
though, the flow is good, and the different ways
of embellishing the chant are convincingly done
and provide welcome contrast. The embellishments range from the addition of other vocal
lines which move in parallel or contrary motion
to the chant, or simply serve as a sustained drone
(a kind of harmonic trope of the melody), to the
introduction of various types of ornament:
repeated notes, simple turns, or Eastern-sounding slides. These are used sparingly and are executed with great precision.

The insert-notes make commendably clear
which pieces have been elaborated poly-
phonically by the group, so alerting the listener
to this further element of reconstruction. Leading chant scholars have been consulted about
certain aspects of interpretation, and the recording is on the whole as exemplary in its thoughtful presentation as in the scrupulous performances they offer. If at times their singing is
over-careful and unspontaneous, their fans will
not be disappointed by this, the latest impressive
contribution to little-known corners of the very
early musical repertory by the 'fab four of
medieval music' as *The New Yorker* has described
them.

Darkness into Light
Anonymous Christe, qui lux es. Inventor rutili. Jube
Domine/In principio. Leccio libri apokalipsis. Lectio
yasye prophete/Surge illuminare. Medie noctis
tempus est. O lux beata trinitas. Quinque prudentes
virgines **Tavener** As one who has slept[a]. The
Bridegroom[a]. Come and do Your will in me[a].
The Lord's Prayer
Anonymous 4 (Marsha Genensky, Susan Hellauer,
Johanna Rose, Jacqueline Horner *sngrs*);
[a]**Chilingirian Quartet** (Levon Chilingirian, Charles
Sewart *vn* Asdis Valdimarsdottir *va* Philip de
Groote *vc*)
Harmonia Mundi HMU90 7274 (64' · DDD) Texts and
translations included   ⒻⓄⓄ

There are those who consider Anonymous 4's
style just too impeccable and pure, and though
elements of their repertoire might benefit from

a more maculate approach, just a few bars of their luminous singing of *O lux*, radiantly recorded, will seduce you from such wicked thoughts. The group's celestial perfection is right for this beautiful devotional music, and they're as utterly beguiling in Tavener's compositions as in the medieval pieces.

The Bridegroom, inspired by the parable of the wise and foolish virgins, is the last piece in a triptych commissioned for the Chilingirian Quartet. The other Tavener works were originally written for, respectively, the Chester and Winchester Cathedral Choirs and The Tallis Scholars. Various recordings of the original versions of *The Lord's Prayer* and *As one who has slept* are currently in catalogue, but the clarity and focus of these one-voice-to-a-part performances more than compensate for the loss of the choral fullness. The astringency of the strings is an effective complement to the sweetness of the voices, all blending into a bright yearning which Tavener characterises as 'a kind of Divine eros'. Anonymous 4 sound as marvellous as ever.

Star in the East
Medieval Hungarian Christmas Music
Anonymous 4 (Ruth Cunningham, Marsha Genensky, Susan Hellauer, Johanna Rose *sngrs*)
Harmonia Mundi HCX3957139 (68' · ADD) Texts and translations included Ⓑ

This disc is a selection of liturgical and paraliturgical Christmas pieces, taken from medieval Hungarian sources. Most are monophonic, but there's a modest sprinkling of simple polyphonic pieces for two, three and four voices. The charm of the performance lies in its unpretentious, almost childlike simplicity – suggested, maybe, by the delightful extracts from the Christmas story as quoted in the notes. The classic liturgical pieces, which include the Introit *Dum medium silentium*, the splendid Gradual *Speciosa forma*, and others, are heard in a version which tends to use the pentatonic scale, thus avoiding both B natural and B flat. The sung readings are impressive with their polyphonic settings. The rich Genealogy (*Liber generationis*) with its beautifully constructed melody are most enjoyable. Some of the vernacular pieces, as well as the Latin song for New Year's Day, have a regular ternary rhythm. The Hungarian *Te Deum* offers an interesting alternative for the concluding verses: it simply transposes the original theme up a fourth. The booklet is a marvel.

The Binchois Consort

Marriage of England and Burgundy
Anonymous O pulcherrima mulierum/Girum coeli circuivi. Incomprehensibilia firme/Praeter rerum ordinem **Busnois** Regina coeli I. Regina coeli II **Frye** Missa Sine Nomine. Missa Summe trinitati
The Binchois Consort / Andrew Kirkman
Hyperion CDA67129 (75' · DDD) ⒻⓄⓄ

This is another disc to derive inspiration from the marriage in 1468 of Charles the Bold, Duke of Burgundy, and Margaret of York, sister of Edward IV and Richard III. The event fascinates performer-scholars because a manuscript of polyphony survives that can be very plausibly linked to these wedding celebrations (it's now kept in the Royal Library of Belgium in Brussels). After the Ferrara Ensemble's CD of mostly secular music came the Clerks' Group's mix of Masses from the manuscript (including Walter Frye's *Flos regalis* and Plummer's three-voice setting) and secular English songs. Now, with last year's Early Music Award-winners, the Binchois Consort, offering an all-sacred programme, four out of the five so-called 'Brussels' Masses (all in fact by English composers) are now available in fine performances.

It would be easy to insist on the fact that this programme is led by recent research. The attribution to Walter Frye of the anonymous three-voice Mass that opens this recording was made by Andrew Kirkman himself, and those of the two motets that conclude it to Busnois were proposed by Sean Gallagher (*O pulcherrima/ Girum coeli*) and Rob Wegman (*Incomprehensibilia firme/Praeter rerum ordinem*), all young scholars with impeccable credentials. Kirkman's notes are informative and detailed, but he's as concerned as his singers to drive home the music's purely aesthetic, chamber-musical qualities. As to Kirkman's attribution there's no doubt: listen to the sustained duets of the *Sanctus* and *Agnus Dei*, and there can be no doubt that the Mass is by a composer of the first rank; one has to agree that Wegman's attribution of *Incomprehensibilia* cries 'Busnois' out of the speakers: it could hardly be by anyone else. Rightly Kirkman gently expresses doubts concerning *O pulcherrima/ Girum coeli*, – in fact it puts one very firmly in mind of late Dufay, and of his motet *Ave regina coelorum* in particular.

In some these are faultlessly judged and engaging performances. The music's nuances and details are very sensitively rendered, but so is the sense of larger-scale architecture and pacing; and Kirkman's long-standing commit-ment to Frye is particularly evident. The performances of Busnois' motets (both conjecturally attributed and firmly ascribed) are, at their best, equally exciting; but just occasionally there's the hint of strain in the higher voices' upper reaches and in the intricate tracery of *O pulcherrima* and *Incomprehensibilia* (particularly the latter, whose many sections do not quite flow together), and of the singers bracing themselves for the cross-rhythms of *Regina coeli I*. But these are details, and it's difficult to imagine more lucid or elegant performances. In a very short time, the Binchois Consort have established themselves as one of the very finest ensembles in the field.

Robin Blaze *countertenor*

English Lute Songs
Anonymous The Last of the Queenes Maskes

Banister The Tempest[a] – Come unto these yellow sands; Where the bee sucks; Dry those eyes; Full fathom five. Give me my lute[a] **Blow** Lovely Selina, innocent and free[a] **Campion** Faire if you expect admiring[a] **Danyel** Can doleful notes[a] **Dowland** In darknesse let mee dwell[a]. The Third and Last Book of Songs or Aires[a] – Time stands still; Behold a wonder heere **R Johnson II** The Tempest[a] – Full fathom five; Where the bee sucks; Fantasia **W Lawes** Why soe pall and wan, fond lover[a]. He that will not love[a]. To the Sycamore[a]. Gather ye rosebuds while you may[a] **Locke** Psyche – The delights of the bottle[a] **Purcell** The Second Part of Musick's Hand-maid – Rigadoon in C, Z653; Song Tune in C, Z T694; A New Irish Tune in G, Z646; Sefauchi's Farewell in D minor, Z656. St Cecilia's Day Ode, Z328 – Tis Nature's voice[a]. Welcome Song, Z324 – Be welcome then, great Sir[a]. The History of Dioclesian – Still I'm wishing[a]. Birthday Ode, Z332 – By beauteous softness[a] **Reggio** Arise, ye subterranean winds[a]
[a]**Robin Blaze** counterten **Elizabeth Kenny** lte
Hyperion CDA67126 (71' · DDD) Texts included
Ⓕ**OO**

Seventy minutes of countertenor may not be everyone's idea of fun, but Robin Blaze has the special ingredients to transcend any latent prejudice, especially in a recital as wide-ranging and intelligently programmed as this. Opening with Johnson's *Tempest* Songs, Blaze and his fine accompanist, Elizabeth Kenny, mellifluously shift from the melancholic Dowland to the less ubiquitous theatre songs of William Lawes, as they move inexorably to the great Orpheus, Henry Purcell – via several by-waters of English 17th-century song. Blaze has always had a natural and unforced instrument, but its hovering sweetness, which he employs to pretty effect throughout, can now ripen on cue, as in *In darknesse let mee dwell*. This is perhaps the most elusive quality in a countertenor and Blaze has the means to colour his texts, not just with superior diction, but timbral variation to keep the listener hearing each song afresh. In a recital of 15 so-called lute songs and 15 Restoration pieces there are too many highlights to list. One is Danyel's *Can doleful notes*, a superb Jacobean example of pleasuring in a particular conceit (in this case, whether art can truly express grief). Blaze moves from embedded cynicism to tender faith in music's power. There's an impressive and buoyant security in the Banister songs and around some exquisite solo lute numbers Blaze appears as ever the natural heir to James Bowman in *Be welcome then, great Sir*. It's wonderfully gauged, as is John Blow's delectable *Lovely Selina*, even if some may find him occasionally sitting a little high on the note. Another fine achievement from two of Britain's brightest and best.

Cambridge Taverner Choir

Music from Renaissance Portugal
Anonymous Si pie Domine **Carreira** Stabat mater
P de Cristo Magnificat. Ave Maria. Sanctissimi quinque mar tires. De profundis. Lachrimans sitivit anima mea. Ave Regina caelorum **A Fernandez**
Libera me Domine. Alma redemptoris mater **D Lôbo** Missa pro defunctis
Cambridge Taverner Choir / Owen Rees
Herald HAVPCD155 (69' · DDD) Recorded 1992. Texts and translations included
Ⓕ**OO**

This is one of those rare examples of scholarship and musicianship combining to result in performances that are both impressive and immediately attractive to the listener in excellent music. There's a wonderful glow about this recording that reflects the skilful engineering on the part of Herald as well as the imagination of the sonority on Rees's part. The striking feature of his approach is the emphasis on the meaning of the words. This choir sings of the Day of Judgement or the rejoicing due to the Virgin as if it really means it: Rees isn't afraid to shape phrases, to use dynamics, to vary the intensity of the sound in the service of the words which, though even more familiar to the monks and chapel singers who originally performed these pieces at the monastery of Santa Cruz in Coimbra, would have had an immediacy and a reality for them that it's hard to recapture today. How graphic those texts, in fact, are, and how well this choir brings them to life.

Canterbury Cathedral

Gregorian Chant
Mass for the Feast of St Thomas of Canterbury.
The Office of Matins for St Thomas of Canterbury.
St Dunstan's Kyrie
Lay Clerks of Canterbury Cathedral Choir / David Flood
Metronome METCD1003 (74' · DDD) Recorded 1994.
Texts and translations included
Ⓕ

A recording of music for the Feast of St Thomas à Becket by the Lay Clerks of Canterbury Cathedral is a delightful idea. The music for this feast in the Salisbury rite is rich and memorable, particularly that for the Offices. In this case the selection from Matins includes five magnificent responsories and two antiphons, as well as the hymn *Martyr Dei* and the Invitatory, *Assunt Thomas Martyris*. This last item is particularly valuable, since though the Invitatory has generally not found much favour in recordings and concerts (either as chant or set polyphonically), the cumulative effect of the form is, quite simply, extraordinary. This anthology also includes the Mass for the Feast of St Thomas (in which the Sequence, *Solemne canticum*, is especially impressive) and the *Kyrie, Rex splendens*, attributed to St Dunstan. The singing is restrained and sober and somewhat lacking in colour. The problem seems to be that there's little response to the words on the part of the singers: the chant somehow doesn't sound 'organic', as though it were sung liturgically. This is a difficult problem to solve, but there's no doubt that the quality of the singing itself is very high. Certainly no one with an interest in Western chant should hesitate to buy this very worthwhile recording.

La Capella Reial de Catalunya

El Cançoner del Duc de Calabria

Almodar Ah, Pelayo que desmayo! **Anonymous** Ay luna que reluzes. Dizen a mi que los amores he. Gózate, Virgen sagrada. Si de vos mi bien. Un niño nos es nacido. Con qué la lavaré. Ojos garços ha la niña. Si la noche haze escura (attrib. F. Guerrero). Estas noches à tan largas. Vella, de vós som amorós (attrib. M. Flechaa). Yo me soy la morenica. Falai, meus olhos **Carceres** Soleta so jo ací **Flecha** Que farem del pobre Joan! Teresica hermana **Morales** Si n'os hubiera mirado

La Capella Reial de Catalunya / Jordi Savall
Astrée Naïve ES9960 (68' · DDD) Texts and translations included   Ⓜ

This is vintage Capella Reial. The singing and playing are superb, and the repertory – melodious and dancey by turn – of the Cançoner del Duc de Calabria is right up its alley. Amazingly, this is the first commercial recording dedicated to this songbook from the Valencian court of the Duke of Calabria – surprising because of the accessibility and quality of the music. Several items from the book have become well known (notably the ubiquitous *Riu, riu, chiu*, which, thankfully, isn't included here), but up till now it has been difficult to gain an appreciation of the collection as a whole. Published in Venice in 1556, it records an earlier repertory, dating from the first decade of the 16th century through the 1530s and, possibly, 1540s. The Valencian court was one of the major cultural centres of the Iberian peninsula at this period, and the court culture was heavily influenced by the latest humanistic trends from Italy. In musical terms, the repertory of the *Cançoner* reflects this mix of imported and indigenous elements; most of the songs conform to the fixed-form *villancico* of the later 15th century, but within the essential refrain-and-verse structure much of the writing reveals a more madrigalian idiom. Indeed, popular-style refrains are often succeeded by madrigalian verses, and Capella Reial reinforce this through the scoring adopted; popular songs and refrains attract full-blown 'orchestrations' (the *tutti* ensemble of viols, winds, plucked instruments and percussion so characteristic of the Capella ensemble), or at least varied combinations of instruments, while the more imitative sections blend voices, viols and harp or vihuela. The songs are well chosen and nicely varied in poetic content and interpretation; it's particularly good to have the relatively few Catalan items from the songbook, which when sung by Jordi Savall's excellent team of native singers, are lent a distinctly dark flavour – thanks to the covered vowel sounds of the language. This outstanding disc brings to light another unjustly neglected corner of the repertory in performances that reveal Capella Reial at their best.

Capilla Flamenca

The A-La-Mi-Re Manuscripts

Anonymous Plus oultre. Salve Regina (on Myn Hert) **Alamire** Tandernaken op den Rijn **Gascogne** Missa Myn hert – Kyrie **Isaac** Maudit soyt **Josquin** Proch dolor/Pie Jhesu. Plaine de duel **Marbianus de Orto** Dulces exuviae **Moulu** Mater floreat **Mouton/Févin** Celeste beneficium/ Adiutorium nostrum **Newseider** Myn hert altyt heeft verlanghen **De la Rue** Autant en emporte. Jam sauche. Myn hert altyt heeft verlanghen. Soubz ce tumbel **Rigo** Celle que j'ay **Willaert** Missa super Benedicta es – Agnus Dei
Capilla Flamenca
Naxos 8 554744 (62' · DDD) Texts and translations included   ⓈⓄ

Petrus Alamire – without the curious hyphens of this disc's title – was the head of a thriving workshop of music-copyists connected with the Netherlands court in the early 16th century. His beautiful manuscripts were sent to princes, popes and the super-rich across Europe, and contained music by the greatest composers of the age.

The works recorded here are a minute sampling of what was produced, in some ways an unrepresentative one: the majority of these manuscripts contained not songs, but sacred music, especially masses. Yet in another way this recit beautifully captures the tone and ambience of the Netherlands court: grave, serious, sometimes cerebral music, but richly and densely involving. Josquin is represented by the songs of his old age, and de la Rue, the star composer of the court chapel, by pieces written for his patron, Margaret of Austria, aunt of Charles V. They are exactly suited to the rich, warm and expressive tone of Capilla Flamenca, which records on Naxos for the first time. The group is complemented here by the instrumental consort La Caccia which provides light relief and occasional accompaniment. This alliance is well judged and satisfying: it isn't often one hears a crumhorn consort in full flood. Some decisions seem to make light of the music's potential (Josquin's *Plaine de duel*, for example, taken at somewhat too brisk a pace), but on the whole there's much fine music-making to savour: especially enjoyable is the countertenor Marnix de Cat's delivery of de la Rue's *Soubz ce tumbel* (a distant precursor of Telemann's *Canary Cantata*), a lament on Margaret's favourite pet. The accompanying notes give an informative account of Alamire's colourful life, and the value of his enterprise. As to a final recommendation, it would be silly to pretend that cost is irrelevant: this is excellent value for money.

Missa Alleluia – Music at the Burgundian Court

Works include **La Rue** Missa Alleluia **Òbrecht** Salve regina **Josquin Desprez** Huc me sydereo
Capilla Flamenca
Eufoda CDEUF1232 (60' · DDD)   Ⓕ

Here is classically full-throated, rich Flemish singing. The motets are hardly new to the catalogue, but these readings more than hold their own. Worth noting is the use of choirboys, notably in Obrecht's six-voice *Salve regina*, and

Josquin's *Huc me sydereo*, here in its six-voice version. But the centrepiece is unquestionably the Mass by Pierre de la Rue. The singing is mostly very stylish, with a sound image to wallow in. Strongly recommended.

Capriccio Stravagante

Anonymous Amarilli mijn schone. Ay, luna que [P] reluzes. En Belén están mis amores. Gagliarda gamba e le forze d'Hercole. Pass'e mezo antico primo e secondo. Pastorçico, non te aduermas **Arcadelt** Il primo libro de Madrigali – O felici occhi miei **Azzaiolo** Il primo libro de villotte – Tanto sai fare **Caccini** Le nuove musiche – Amarilli mia bella **Encina** Ay triste, que vengo **Frescobaldi** Arie musicali per cantarsi, primo libro – Così me disprezzate; Dunque dovrò; Se l'aura spira **Lambardi** Aria di Cupido **Malvezzi** Sinfonia **Marini** Sonate, symphonie…e retornelli – Sonata terza, Variata **Ortiz** Recercadas – II; IV **Philips** Amarilli di Giulio Romano **Sanz** Instrución de música sobre la guitarra española, Book 1 – Canarios **Scandello** Vorria che tu cantass' **Vecchi** Gitene, Ninfe
Guillemette Laurens *mez* **Capriccio Stravagante / Skip Sempé** *hpd*
Astrée Naïve E8870 (64' · DDD) Notes, texts and translations included   [P][O]

This disc aims to conjure the flavour of the Mediterranean region with the music of 16th- and 17th-century Italy and Spain. It contains a thoroughly attractive mixture of short vocal and instrumental pieces, ranging from Italian arias and Spanish villancicos to a violin sonata by Marini to pieces for viol consort and solos for harpsichord, harp and lute. The voice is the common link, however, for almost all the instrumental pieces have vocal origins: a recorder will play the voice part in a villancico, for instance, or a viol consort will play an arrangement of Caccini's *Amarilli mia bella* which leads to Peter Philips's florid keyboard elaboration of the same piece. It's the kind of clever sequencing that Skip Sempé is especially good at, and it results here in a programme which maintains its interest from beginning to end. The performances themselves are keen and alert, striking a well-judged balance between tonal beauty and expressive vigour, so that, while contrasts in tempo and dynamic can be strong, they're never overdone.

La Columbina Ensemble

Canciones, Romances and Sonetos
Encina Triste España sin ventura! Antonilla es desposada. Tan buen ganadico. Mi libertad en sosiego. Pues que tú, Reina del cielo. Cucú, cucú, cucú **Guerrero** Niño Dios, d'amor herido. Prado verde y florido. Huyd, huyd. Si tu penas no pruevo. Todo quanto pudo dar **Romero** A quién contaré mis quejas. En Belén están mis amores. Como suele el blanco zisne. Soberana María. Las voces del fuego **Vásquez** A, hermosa, abrime cara de rosa. Con qué

la lavaré. Torna, Mingo, a namorarte. Si no os uviera mirado. En la fuente del rosel. Soledad tengo de tí. Buscad buen amor. O dulce contemplación. De los álamos vengo
La Columbina Ensemble (Mariá Cristina Kiehr *sop* Claudio Cavina *counterten* Josep Benet *ten* Josep Cabré *bass*)
Accent ACC95111D (56' · DDD) Texts and translations included   [F]

In this survey of Spanish song in the 16th- and 17th-centuries the pieces chosen admirably reflect the consistency of idiom and quality during the period. Distinctive to the repertory is the blend of popular and *culto* elements, in both text and music. Madrigalian elements gradually infiltrate the simple, homophonic idiom cultivated by Encina and are thoroughly mastered by Juan Vásquez, the genius of Spanish song of the first half of the 16th century, and subsequently by Francisco Guerrero. All these developments are further consolidated by Romero, a near contemporary of Monteverdi, the two- and three-part songs selected here reflecting the 16th-century continuum that dominates the early Spanish Baroque. Apart from some *stile concitato* effects in the battle-cry refrains to *En Belén están mis amores* and *Las voces del fuego*, these technically highly accomplished but effective pieces are still predominantly in the Renaissance polyphonic idiom. None of the songs is more than about four minutes long, and most last around two, so that La Colombina's carefully chosen groupings of works by the same composer help to make a larger structure, and they very successfully juxtapose the more familiar with the less well known while giving a good insight into the range of the repertory. Their interpretations are always expressive and sensitive to the imagery of the text, and the blend and accuracy of ensemble are exemplary. These are utterly convincing performances without any need whatsoever for the 'orchestrated' approach so familiar from, say, Hespèrion XX. Here the madrigalian writing so apparent within Spanish forms such as the *villancico*, *romance* and *soneto* finally comes into its own for about the first time on CD.

Doulce Mémoire

Viva Napoli – Canzoni Villanesche   [P]
Azzaiolo Il primo libro de villotte – Al di dolce ben mio; Chi passa per 'sta strada. Il secondo libro de villotte – Girometta senza te **Bendusi** Pass'e mezzo della paganina, gagliarda. Pass'e mezzo ditto il romano, Pass'mezzo ditto il compasso **Caroso** Il ballarino – Chiarenzana **Festa** Madonna io sono un medico perfetto **Lassus** Madonna mia pietà. La cortesia voi donne predicate. Tu sai, madonna mia, ch'io t'amo e voglio **Nasco** Il primo libro di canzone villanesche alla napolitana – Vorria che tu cantassi **Negri** Le gratie d'amore – Bizzarria d'amore **Nola** Chi la gagliarda **Valente** Intavolatura di cimbalo – Gaillarda Napolitana; Tenore grande alla Napolitana **Willaert** Vecchie letrose non valete niente. O bene

mio. Madonna mia fa **Zanetti** Il scolaro – La bella Pedrina; Saltarello
Ensemble Doulce Mémoire / Denis Raisin-Dadre *fl*
Astrée Naïve E8648 (63' · DDD) Texts and
translations included   Ⓕ**O**

To date, Ensemble Doulce Mémoire's discography has been fairly evenly divided between French and Italian repertories. Here the group associates itself more firmly still with a specific location and repertory, that of Naples in the mid-16th century. One finds here the usual suspects of the popularising trend with which Naples is associated: Gian Domenico da Nola, Adrian Willaert (represented by his infamous *Vecchie letrose* and the delightful *Madonna mia fa*) and the young Lassus, on whom the city's popular musical culture clearly made a lasting impression. Indeed, the imaginative and entertaining programme notes invite us to imagine Lassus masterminding an evening's entertainment at the home of his Neapolitan employer, of which this is the programme. Some recent releases have shown that such re-creations are by no means easy to carry off convincingly; but Denis Raisin-Dadre and his ensemble do just that.

Similarly, this disc's other theme, the villanella and its more learned polyphonic offshoots, has been generously treated by native Italian ensembles (notably on the Opus 111 label); it's a great compliment to these French musicians that they can hold their own in their Italian masquers' outfits. There's hardly a track that fails to convince; the diminutions in *Madonna mia pietà*, in common with the instrumental contributions in general, are skilfully done (even if they place more rhythmic constraints on the voices than one would like), and *Vecchie letrose* is as nasty as it ought to be. Even when the improvisatory licence is occasionally exceeded, the general tenor of this recital is strong enough to be convincing. The ensemble takes great care to present the booklet-notes as integral to the disc's conception; and after an hour's entertainment, a little unscripted surprise awaits.

This repertory is slowly gaining decent representation on disc, but it's doubtful that there's a better-judged recital than this one.

Early Music Consort of London

The Art of the Netherlands
A **Agricola** De tous biens plaine (two versions). Fortuna desparata **Anonymous** Fortuna desparata. Mijn morken gaf mij een jonck wijff **Barbireau** Een wrolick wesen **Brumel** Du tout plongiet/Fors seulement. Missa 'Et ecce terrae motus' **Busnois** Fortuna disperata **Compère** O bone Jesu **Ghiselin** Ghy syt die wertste boven al **Hayne Van Ghizeghem** De tous biens plaine. De tous biens plaine (arr Josquin) **Hofhaimer** Ein fröhlich wesen **Isaac** Donna di dentro dalla tua casa. Missa 'La bassadanza' **Josquin Desprez** Scaramella va alla guerra. Allégez moy, doulce pleasant brunette. Allégez moy, doulce

pleasant brunette (anonymous arrangement for two lutes). El grillo è buon cantore. De profundis clamavi a 5. Benedicta es, caelorum regina. Credo 'De tous biens playne'. Guillaume se va chauffeur. Adieu mes amours. Adieu mes amours (16th-century anonymous arrangement for organ). Inviolata, integra et casta es, Maria **Mouton** Nesciens mater virgo virum **Obrecht** Ein fröhlich wesen. Haec Deum caeli. Laudemus nunc Dominum **Ockeghem** Prenez sur moi vostre exemple. Ma bouche rit. Intemerata Dei mater **La Rue** Missa 'Ave sanctissima Maria'. Ave sanctissima Maria **Tinctoris** Missa sine nomine
Early Music Consort of London / David Munrow
Virgin Classics Veritas ② 561334-2 (132' · ADD) Texts and translations included Recorded 1975   Ⓜ**OOO**

This is arguably Munrow's most consistent and most polished collection, devoted to the sacred and secular polyphony of the mid- to late-15th century. These recordings remain marvellously fresh and vital – even in the case of pieces that have since had more polished or more clearly recorded interpretations. That's especially true of the sacred music, recorded entirely vocally and (in most cases) one to a part. It would be a challenge to name a more tempestuous reading of Brumel's 'Earthquake Mass', a more sombre, self-absorbed *Intemerata Dei mater*, or more luminously clear canons (in *Ave sanctissima Maria* and *Nesciens mater*). In the recordings of secular music, the passage of time is rather more obvious. But idiosyncratic though it may now appear, the choice of instruments always combines flair and verve. In the songs, tempos are rather more languorous than we're now used to, but Munrow's finest inspirations still strike very deep.

The phrase 'essential listening' is often used (perhaps too often), but it surely applies to 'The Art of the Netherlands'. A word of warning: the contents of the three original LPs aren't reproduced exactly. The entire instrumental portion, some 20 minutes of music, is cut. This is one of the most influential recordings of early music ever made.

Ensemble Cantilena Antiqua

Canticum Canticorum
The sacred symbol of love in the medieval musical tradition
Ensemble Cantilena Antiqua / Stefano Albarello
counterten
Symphonia SY95135 (72' · DDD)   Ⓕ

This intriguing collection of music on the Song of Solomon includes not only 12th- and 13th-century Western monody and polyphony, but also Hebrew, Sephardic and Maronite melodies. The performances blend voices and instruments in a manner much favoured by Italian ensembles today; there's some fine singing, that of the countertenor Stefano Albarello being particularly striking. Text and documentation are intelligently and stylishly presented.

Ensemble Clément Janequin

Les Plaisirs du Palais
Anonymous C'est tout abus. Si vous n'avez madame. Triquedon daine **Appenzeller** Je pers espoir. Musae Jovis **Barbion** Pour quelque paine que j'endure **Baston** Ung souvenir me conforte **Certon** En languissant avoir secours j'attens. Que n'est-elle auprès de moy **Clemens non Papa** Priere devant le repas, O souverain Pasteur **Dambert** Secouez moy **Decarella** En Tour la feste Saint Martin **Gombert** La chasse au lièvre **Hesdin** Ung vray musicien **Le Heurteur** Mirelaridon **Mittantier** Laissons amour **Le Roy** Alemande du pied de cheval. Bransle de Champaigne. Bransles de Poictou **Sermisy** Aupres de vous a 2 voix. Aupres de vous a 4 voix. Hau, hau, hau le boys! **Susato** Priere apres le repas, Pere esternel
Ensemble Clément Janequin / Dominique Visse
Harmonia Mundi HMC90 1729 (61' · DDD)　Ⓕ🔴

This is a feast. Ensemble Clément Janequin often hold their concerts seated round a table, and the theme of feasting recurs in their discography as well (remember their superb 'Une fête chez Rabelais'). Here the menu boasts a greater preponderance than usual of anonymous and lesser-known *chanson* composers, alongside masters like Certon and Sermisy. But the programme's exoticism extends to the greatest composers of the time: Gombert's *La chasse au lièvre* could be described as a pastiche in the style of Janequin's representative songs (*La chasse* being the obvious model). In Gombert's narrative, however, the hunters end up round a table. Dominique Visse and his gang were bound to perform this piece sooner or later. Here it's the centrepiece of their recital, and like the whole, finds them at their best.

That said, you needs to be familiar with their discography to appreciate this new offering to the full. Around Gombert's hunt the disc is arranged palindromically, topped and tailed with prayers before and after the meal; but Clemens non Papa's exhortation to partake in moderation seemingly goes unheeded. There follows the familiar miscellany of love-songs, of ribaldry and drink, of voices and instruments. But there are new twists, and real gems, in the more out-of-the-way selections, like Mittantier's *Laissons amour*. Appenzeller's well-known *deploration* on Josquin is a fitting pendant to his *Je pers espoir*, itself modelled on Josquin's *Mille regretz*. Another new departure is the use of just one voice accompanied by viols (Bruno Boterf in Certon's *En languissant* and Visse in Sermisy's *Aupres de vous*).

You also needs to be familiar with the French *chanson* repertory in general; and certainly you must understand the texts, without which certain interpretative tricks may disconcert. (A pity, then, that some of the translations are wildly off base – a recurring problem with Harmonia Mundi, and crucial to put right with an idiom as exotic as this).

So this is a connoisseur's feast, but it grows in stature with repeated hearing.

Ex Cathedra

New World Symphonies: Baroque Music from Latin America
Anonymous Hanacpachap Cussicuinin **Araujo** Los coflades de la estleya. Ut queant laxis **G Fernandes** Xicochi conetzintle **H Franco** Salve Regina a 5 **Lobo** Versa est in luctum **Padilla** Missa, 'Ego flos campi' **Traditional** Symbolo Catholico Indiano – Capac eterno Dios (Creed) **Zéspedes** Convidando est la noche **Zipoli** Missa San Ignacio – Kyrie; Gloria
Ex Cathedra / Jeffrey Skidmore
Hyperion CDA67380 (70' · DDD)　Ⓕ🔴🔴

Ex Cathedra's survey of Baroque music from Latin America ranges from a double-choir mass to homophonic settings of texts in Quechua (the language of the Incas) and Nahuatl (that of the Aztecs) to *villancicos* infiltrated with the colourful African rhythms still very apparent in Cuban music. Given the richness of this mix, and the excellence of the performances, it's probably unfair to point out that the one piece of genius on the recording – Lobo's *Versa est in luctum* – is by a Spanish composer who never travelled to the New World. However, it was performed at the funeral exequies held for Philip II (*d*1598) in various centres of his vast colonial empire. This richly rewarding CD would be worth acquiring for the superbly intense and dramatic reading of this miniature masterpiece alone, but there are other gems here.

Juan Gutiérrez de Padilla's mass based on the otherwise unknown motet *Ego flos campi* abounds in interesting detail, and the climactic moments, such as at the end of the *Credo*, are sumptuously realised with a varied panoply of voices and instruments. As in many concert performances these days, the movements of the mass are separated by other items. The performers clearly enjoy the cross-rhythms of Juan de Araujo's *Los coflades de la estleya*, a lively *villancico* in which voices and instruments again join to good effect; it's foot-tapping stuff. At the other end of the spectrum the simple homophony of Gaspar Fernandes's *Xicochi conetzintle* has its own magic. The late Italian Baroque reached the New World when Domenico Zipoli travelled in 1718 as part of a Jesuit mission to Paraguay. His music was highly influential in many parts of South America, and his mass in honour of St Ignatius Loyola is an attractive work performed with tremendous conviction.

I Fagiolini

All the King's Horses
Anonymous Basses danses: Par fin despit; La volunté. Bransle gay: Mari je songerois. Der Hundt. Saltarello el francosin **Arcadelt** O felic'occhi miei **Cara** Mentre io vo per questi boschi **Certon** La, la, la, je ne l'ose dire **Finck** In Gottes Namen faren wir **Isaac** J'ay pris amours **Janequin** Frère Thibault. Le chant des oyseaulx **Othmayr** Der Winter kalt. Ich weiss mir ein Maidlein **Patavino** Dillà da l'aqua **Rore** Or che'l ciel e la terra **Ruffo** La gamba. El travagliato

Sandrin Puisque vivre en servitude. La volunté **Senfl** Ach Elslein. Sich hat ein' neue Sach' aufdraht. Ich weiss nit. Wiewohl viel Herter Orden sind **Sermisy** Au pres de vous
I Fagiolini; Concordia / Mark Levy *viol*
Metronome METCD1013 (67' · DDD) Texts and translations included ⓕ

We travel here to France, Germany and Italy. The results are most appealing: these spirited performances articulate both text and music in a clear and attractive manner. In the French repertory I Fagiolini successfully takes up the challenge of emulating the Ensemble Clément Janequin's masterful approach to text-projection, and its softer sound and slightly more relaxed approach (try *Frère Thibault*) will please those who find the French ensemble too rough. Even in such a well-known piece as *Le chant des oyseaulx* it finds new, delightful inflexions. The German selections are rather less well known (or at any rate less often recorded) than the French, but just as convincingly dispatched: the pieces by Senfl, Othmayr and Isaac are well worth discovering. Isaac's arrangement of *J'ay pris amours* (performed here by Concordia) reminds us just how much of a virtuoso contrapuntalist he was.

The aim here is to represent the diversity of early 16th-century secular music: diversity of mood and content, and of possible relations between voices and instruments. This anthological ambition is the set's most conspicuous success, and carries matters forward even when individual items or details appear to miss the mark (the concluding madrigal by Rore is too slow, and more generally the Italian selection is the least satisfying of the three). The sound-recording, immediate and close, is well up to Metronome's usual standard, and the booklet is well laid-out and presented.

Ferrara Ensemble

Balades a III chans ⓟ
Anonymous Adieu vous di, tres doulce compaynie. Lamech Judith et Rachel de plourer. Le mont Aon de Thrace **Antonius de Civitate** Io vegio per stasone **Cordier** Tout par compas suy composés **Grimace** Se Zephirus, Phebus et leur lignie **Matteo da Perugia** Rondeau-refrain. Pres du soloil deduissant s'esbanoye **Trebor** Helas pitié envers moy dort si fort. Si Alexandre et Hector fussent en vie
Ferrara Ensemble / Crawford Young
Arcana A32 (59' · DDD) Recorded 1994. Texts and translations included ⓕ**OO**

The *ballade*, that noblest form (in every sense) of 14th-century secular music, was meant to honour the dukes and counts who did so much to foster the fine arts while war, famine and plague raged round them. Their musical protégés were by all accounts a slightly surreal bunch, dedicated seekers-out of weirdness, addicted to the bottle – possibly even to hashish. Small wonder that so much of their music seems hopelessly

capricious on the page. Crawford Young's special achievement is to demonstrate what many enthusiasts of *Ars subtilior* have felt all along. In performance, that wilful strangeness can suddenly come across with astonishing naturalness: all it takes is the right singers, and here they are. Or perhaps that last sentence should read: 'here she is'. It's no slight on the other members of the Ferrara Ensemble to say that the mezzo-soprano, Lena Susanne Norin, steals the show. Her singing can only be described as luscious. True, the quality of these performances is partly a matter of direction. Tempo is of the first importance because it determines the specific gravity of the dissonances. Beyond that, however, the sensitivity to these details is down to Norin herself. This fierce-looking music, once tamed, becomes almost unbelievably sensuous. The tone of the accompanying string instruments is perfectly judged, the sound-recording outstanding – warm and glowing. The presen-tation of *ballades* is a tricky business: to perform all three stanzas can take well over 10 minutes. In the past, singers have tended to confine themselves to just one or two stanzas. That has the advantage of fitting more music into a recital, but aesthetically it makes about as much sense as trimming the tail of a peacock. A glorious recital.

The Whyte Rose
Anonymous Ballo de love (arr Young). Danse de Cleves. Fayre and discrete fresche wommanly figure. Love wolle I withoute eny variaunce/T'Andernacken al op den Rijn. My wofull hert of all gladnesse baryeyne. My herte ys so plungit yn greffe. Thus ye compleyne my grevous hevynesse **Busnois** Anima liquefacta est/Stirps Jesse. Je ne puis vivre ainsi **Frye** Alas, alas is my chief song. Salve virgo mater pya. Sospitati dedit **Molinet** Tart ara mon cuer sa plaisance **Morton** Le souvenir de vous me tue **Ockeghem** Quant de vous seul **Robertus d'Anglia** El mal foco arda quella falsa lingua
Ferrara Ensemble / Crawford Young *lte*
Arcana A301 (66' · DDD) Texts and translations included ⓕ**OO**

The emphasis here is on secular music, but motets are represented as well. As for the repertory, it includes such prominent names as Busnois, Ockeghem, Morton and Frye (to whom one may attribute *Alas, alas, alas*, here listed as anonymous), but there's a fair sprinkling of first-rate songs by lesser-known or anonymous composers, and instrumental dances favoured as light relief on some of this ensemble's previous recordings. The sound is strikingly warm, vivid and clear, and captures the almost sensuous interplay of lines whatever the distribution.

In the English music the almost weightless approach to rhythm works wonderfully: Frye's music lays very little agogic stress on the strong beat. But in the pieces by Busnois, whose music draws so much more from rhythmic impetus, this approach is less effective and leads to the very few solecisms on the disc (such as the perceptible slowing of the pulse in the first phrase of *Je ne puis vivre*, or the occasional lack of direction in *Anima mea liquefacta est*). Yet even here there are moments that can only be described as gorgeous, and elsewhere the combination of sound-image and interpretative nous is as admirable as anything the group has achieved: one can mention, almost at random, *Alas, alas, Quant de vous seul, Le souvenir, Tart ara*.

Florilegium

In the Name of Bach
GC Bach Siehe, wie fein und lieblich (Geburtstagkantate)[a] **JE Bach** Violin Sonata in F minor. Sammlung auserlesener Fabeln I – Die ungleichen Freunde[b]; Die Unzufriedenheit[b]; Der Affe und die Schäferin[b]; Der Hund[b] **WF Bach** Adagio and Fugue in D minor, F65. Duetto for Two Flutes in E minor, F54 **JC Bach** Sonata for Keyboard, Violin and Cello in G, T313/1 (Op 2 No 2) **JB Bach** Overture in D – Passepieds Nos 1 & 2; La Joye [b]**Catherine Bott** *sop* [a]**Julian Podger**, [a]**Robert Evans** *tens* [a]**Michael McCarthy** *bass* **Florilegium**
Channel Classics CCS9096 (75' · DDD) Notes and texts included ⒻⒻ

Here's a Bach family anthology featuring three members of the clan whose music seldom finds its way into record catalogues. The earliest representative is Georg Christoph, one of Sebastian Bach's uncles. He was, for a time, town Kantor at Schweinfurt in Franconia where in 1684 he received a visit on his birthday from his two brothers. Georg Christoph was so delighted that, shortly afterwards, he wrote a cantata to record the event, *Siehe, wie fein und lieblich* ('Behold, how good and how pleasant it is for brethren to dwell together in unity'). Tenors Julian Podger and Robert Evans, with bass Michael McCarthy, provide a well-focused and evenly balanced ensemble seemingly to savour the spirit in which the piece was written. Next in the family chronology comes Johann Bernhard Bach, a cousin of JSB. Not a great deal of his music survives, but among that which does are four orchestral suites which may well have resulted from his exposure to those of Telemann who was already a fluent master of the form. It's a pity that Florilegium saw fit to include only three short dances from the Fourth Suite in D major. The music is well worth performing without omission. The highly gifted but emotionally complex Wilhelm Friedemann is represented by the long-admired, poignant and oft-recorded *Adagio and Fugue* in D minor for two flutes and strings, and by one of his several *Duettos* for two flutes, this one in E minor. Florilegium, corporately and individually, plays the music with heartfelt expression and a sensibility that mirrors the stylistic idiom.

It's the music of J S Bach's nephew and pupil, Johann Ernst, which occupies the greater part of the programme. This member of the family seems wholeheartedly to have embraced the early classical idiom, further demonstrating, both in the Violin Sonata in F minor and in the four songs selected from his *Sammlung auserlesener Fabeln*, that he was a composer with a distinctive and affecting musical vocabulary at his disposal. Catherine Bott gives warmly expressive performances, savouring the considerable lyrical content of a little-known area of Bach family industry. The prodigious talent of this dynasty again reaches a peak in Florilegium's programme with a Quartet in G major by Johann Christian, the 'London Bach'. Musically speaking, the expansive opening movement is especially engaging but the entire work is played with elegance and charm by these artists. In summary, this is varied and enjoyable entertainment, well off the beaten track. Although the absence of any translation from the German of the texts of the four songs is regrettable, it doesn't prevent a warm recommendation.

Jean-Paul Fouchécourt   *tenor*

Air(s) de cour – French songs from the 16th to 18th centuries
Anonymous Ma belle si ton ame[a] **Attaingnant** Chansons et danses[a] – Tant que vivrai **Bataille** Airs de différents autheurs, mis en tablature de luth[a] – Un satire cornu; Ma bergère non légère **Brassens** Marquise[c] **Chabanceau de la Barre** Si c'est un bien que l'esperance[b] **Couperin** Doux liens de mon coeur[d]. Qu'on ne me dise[d]. Zéphire[b] **Du Buisson** Plainte sur la mort de M Lambert[e] **M Lambert** Airs de cour[b] – Trouver sur l'herbette; Par mes chants tristes et touchants; Ma bergère est tendre et fidelle; Pour jouir d'un bonheur; Vous ne sçauriez mes yeux; Vos mespris **Lully** Récit de la beauté[b] **Moulinié** Paisible et ténébreuse nuit[a]. Puisque Doris[a]. Amis environs nous[a] **Richard** Ruisseau qui cours apres toy-mesme
Jean-Paul Fouchécourt *ten* **Eric Bellocq** [a]*lte*/[b]*theo*/[c]*gtr* [b]**Nicolas Mazzoleni, Simon Heyerick** *vns* [bd]**Christine Plubeau** *va da gamba* **Olivier Baumont** [e]*org*/[bd]*hpd*
Glissando 779 013-2 (69' · DDD) Notes, texts and translations included ⒻⓄⓄ

This anthology traverses 150 years of the *air de cour* repertory, from its beginnings in the 'Parisian' chanson to the time of François Couperin. So it's probably the most comprehensive survey of the genre, and it certainly bids fair to be one of the finest. Fouchécourt chooses wisely and well: the earlier repertory has been fairly well served, but much of what he offers will be new to most. His light tenor is well known from the opera repertoire, but he manages just fine on his own. The opening 'Tant que vivray' seems rather low-pitched for his voice, but the following pieces allow him to stretch his vocal chords languorously, wittily or eloquently in turns.

His lyricism speaks for itself, but the drinking song *Amis environs nous* is robust and suitably breathless, and his portrayal of the hapless protagonist in 'Un satire cornu' has irony tinged with compassion. Is it that Fouchécourt is French? No disrespect intended to Nigel

Rogers, Charles Daniels and other fine practitioners of the genre, but the Gallic ease with which Fouchécourt characterises these different situations is quite distinctive. And it could only occur to a Frenchman to connect this genre to the modern song-writer Georges Brassens, whose (slightly revised) setting of a text by Corneille nicely divides the programme into two halves. The later period is, if anything, more limited and conventionalised in its expressive scope, but Fouchécourt's sense of line and ornamentation keep things moving along.

Gabrieli Consort

Venetian Vespers Ⓟ

Gabrieli (ed Roberts) Intonazione[a]. Versicle and response: Deus in adiutorium; Domine ad adiuvandum **Rigatti** Dixit Dominus **Grandi** O intemerata. Antiphon: Beata es Maria **Monteverdi** Laudate pueri **Banchieri** Suonata prima[a]. Antiphon: Beatam me dicent **Monteverdi** Laetatus sum **Finetti** O Maria, quae rapis corda hominum. Antiphon: Haec est quae nescavit **Rigatti** Nisi Dominus **Banchieri** Dialogo secondo[a]. Antiphon: Ante thronum **Cavalli** Lauda Jerusalem **Grandi** O quam tu pulchra es **Anonymous** Praeambulum[a]. Chapter: Ecce virgo **Monteverdi** Deus qui mundum crimine iacentem. Versicle and response. Ave Maria; Dominus tecum. Antiphon. Spiritus Sanctus **Rigatti** Magnificat **Marini** Sonata con tre violini in eco. Collect: Dominus vobiscum – Deus, qui de beatae Mariae. Dismissal: Dominus vobiscum – Benedicamus Domino **Monteverdi** Laudate Dominum **Fasolo** (ed Roberts) Intonazione – excerpts[a] **Rigatti** Salve regina ·
Gabrieli Consort and Players / Paul McCreesh with [a]**Timothy Roberts** org
Archiv Produktion ② 459 457-2ATA2 (96' · DDD)
Recorded 1990. Texts and translations included
Ⓑ ⓢ ❍❍❍

Paul McCreesh's sense of adventure made quite an impact with his reconstruction of Doge Grimani's Coronation in 1595. This follow-up recording takes as its starting point a Vespers service 'as it might have been celebrated in St Mark's, Venice 1643', and it's no less striking a speculation. McCreesh is wisely not attempting to re-create a historical event but to provide a rejuvenating context for some more wonderful Venetian church music. There can be little doubt that listening to psalm settings within a liturgical framework illuminates the theatricality and significance of the works in a unique way, barely possible in an ordinary format where one work simply follows another. Yet the quality of the music is what really counts, and this is where McCreesh deserves the greatest praise. He has skilfully blended a range of diverse concerted works with equally innovative and expressive solo motets, each one offset by ornate organ interludes and home-spun plainchant.

Monteverdi is well represented, as you'd expect, but by introducing resident composers regularly employed by the great basilica a strong Venetian sensibility prevails in all these works,

despite the many contrasting styles of the new Baroque age. The little-known Rigatti is arguably the sensation of this release with his highly dramatic and richly extravagant sonorities. The settings of *Dixit Dominus* and *Magnificat* are almost operatic at times, though they maintain the spatial elements inspired by St Mark's.

The Gabrieli Consort and Players is a group with an extraordinary homogeneity of sound and focused energy: Monteverdi's *Laetatus sum* is one of the many examples where it reaches new heights in early 17th-century performance. The solo performances are deliciously executed too, particularly those involving the falsettists. This two-disc set is an achievement of the highest order.

A Venetian Coronation, 1595 Ⓟ

G Gabrieli Intonazioni – ottavo tono; terzo e quarto toni; quinto tono alla quarta bassa[a]. Canzonas – XIII a 12; XVI a 15; IX a 10. Sonata VI a 8 pian e forte. Deus qui beatum Marcum a 10[c]. Omnes gentes a 16[c] **A Gabrieli** Intonazioni – primo tono[a]; settimo tono[b]. Mass Movements[c] – Kyrie a 5-12; Gloria a 16; Sanctus a 12; Benedictus a 12. O sacrum convivium a 5[c]. Benedictus Dominus Deus sabbaoth[ab] (arr Roberts) **Bendinelli** Sonata XXX-XXXIII. Sarasinett[a] **M Thomsen** Toccata I
[a]James O'Donnell, [b]Timothy Roberts orgs
Gabrieli Consort and Players / Paul McCreesh
HMV Classics HMV575606-2 (71' · DDD) Texts and translations included
Ⓑ❍❍❍

The coronation of a new Doge of Venice was always a special occasion, and never more so than when Marino Grimani (1532-1605) was elected to that office. We don't know what music was played then, but the whole ceremony is notionally and credibly reconstructed in this recording by Paul McCreesh and his cohorts. The recording was made in Brinkburn Priory, a church whose acoustic (aided by deft manipulation of the recording controls) is spacious enough to evoke that of the Basilica of St Mark, the site of the original event. Space *per se* is vital to the music of the Gabrielis, who excelled in using it by placing instrumental and vocal groups in different parts of the building – which thereby became an integral part of the music. A fine selection of music that *could* have been played then is enhanced by the opening tolling of a bell, a *crescendo* marking the leisurely approach of the ducal procession, and the impression of architectural space created by changing stereo focus. It would be difficult to speak too highly of the performances, supplemented by first-class annotation, in this memorable recording. A trip to Venice would cost a lot more than this disc but, though you could visit the real St Mark's, it would not buy you this superb musical experience.

Cabezón Beati omnes. Confitebor tibi. Magnificat a 12. Tiento para arpa. Tiento para órgano **Gombert** Mon seul a 7 **Guerrero** Beatus es et bene tibi. Lauda

Jerusalem. Nobis datus a 4. Verbum caro **Lobo** O quam suavis est, Domine. Ego flos campi a 4 **Rogier** Credidi. Regina caeli laetare/Resurrexi. Cancion a 5 **Romero** Dixit Dominus a 16 **Urrede** Tiento para órgano. Panga lingua a 5 **Victoria** Magnificat a 12. Salve Regina a 8. Tu es Petrus a 6. Plus additional anonymous liturgical works
Gabrieli Consort and Players / Paul McCreesh
Archiv ② 471 694-2AH2 (112' · DDD) Texts and translations included ⓕ**OO**

Francisco Gómez de Sandoval y Rojas, Duke of Lerma, was the powerful favourite, or *valido*, of Philip III of Spain, who dominated Spanish politics at the beginning of the 17th century and, many believe, singlehandedly brought about the beginning of that country's decline as a major European and colonial power. His credentials as a patron of the arts, however, can't be disputed. To this day the small town of Lerma is dominated by the collegiate church built by the Duke and it was there that the Gabrieli Consort and Players recorded these two impressive CDs of music that can be closely associated with the liturgical ceremonies held there during the Duke's lifetime.

The first disc re-creates a vespers service as it might have been celebrated during a royal visit such as that in October 1617; the second focuses on the music for the 'Salve' service, a well-established tradition in all the major cathedrals and churches of Spain which was generally solemnified by polyphonic or concerted music.

The selection of pieces and the manner of their performance will take some listeners by surprise. The importance of the role of purely instrumental music in Spanish churches is becoming ever clearer through recent research, but it isn't, perhaps, until you hear the documentary and source evidence realised in sound that this aspect of the late Renaissance sound-world is re-created for our ears.

Paul McCreesh and Kirk present the sequence of antiphons and psalms that comprise the vespers service with plainchant alternating with different instrumental combinations. There's evidence for this from Guerrero's instructions to the instrumentalists of Seville Cathedral, though at that time he doesn't mention stringed instruments – which clearly did form part of the Lerma *capilla* – and it's less clear that there would have been verses played on solo harp, for example. The Gabrieli Consort are thus given the opportunity to show their considerable skills to the full, and the playing is of the highest standards enhanced by the excellent sound quality.

After this extended alternation of chant and instrumental verses, the large-scale vocal pieces make a tremendous impact: Victoria's 12-voice *Magnificat* makes a dramatic intervention and is performed with compelling conviction, and the same can be said for his eight-voice setting of the *Salve Regina* on the second disc, the voices here being doubled by instruments.

This CD offers an experience anyone interested in or attracted by Renaissance music will want to share.

Gothic Voices

The Marriage of Heaven and Hell – 13th-Century French Motets and Songs
Anonymous Je ne chant pas. Talens m'est pris. Trois sereurs/Trois sereurs/Trois sereurs. Plus bele que flors/Quant revient/L'autrier jouer. Par un martinet/Hé, sire!/Hé, bergier! De la virge Katerine/Quant froidure/Agmina milicie. Ave parens/Ad gratie. Super te Jerusalem/Sed fulsit virginitas. A vous douce debonnaire. Mout souvent/Mout ai esté en doulour. Quant voi l'aloete/Dieux! je ne m'en partiré ja. En non Dieu/Quant voi la rose. Je m'en vois/Tels a mout. Festa januaria **Bernart de Ventadorn** Can vei la lauzeta mover **Blondel de Nesle** En tous tans que vente bise **Colin Muset** Trop volontiers chanteroie. **Gautier de Dargies** Autre que je ne seuill fas
Gothic Voices / Christopher Page
Hyperion CDA66423 (46' · DDD) Texts and translations included ⓕ**OO**

The reasons for the dazzling success of Gothic Voices both in the recording studio and the concert hall are once again evident in this collection. It's both an entertaining and well-planned recital and, if one chooses to take it that way, reading Christopher Page's insert-notes while listening, a detailed lecture-recital. The music, all French and dating from the 13th century, is that seemingly impenetrable repertoire of poly-textual motets, unexpectedly compared and contrasted with monophonic trouvère songs. The comparison is illuminating, and the performances of both genres of music are up to Gothic Voices' usual high standards. The clever juxtaposition of the trouvère Bernart de Ventadorn's *Can vei la lauzeta mover* with the triple-texted motet *Quant voi l'aloete/Dieux! je ne m'en partiré ja/NEUMA* encapsulates the thinking behind this recording: a compelling musical experience and a provocative intellectual one.

The Spirits of England and France, Volume 4
Anonymous Missa Caput (ed Curtis). The story of the Salve regina. Salve regina. Jesu for thy mercy[a]. Clangat tuba. Alma redemptoris mater. Old Hall Manuscript – Agnus Dei **Smert** Jesu fili Dei[a] **Traditional** Make we merry[a]. Nowell, nowell, nowell [a]**Shirley Rumsey**, [a]**Christopher Wilson** *Ites* **Gothic Voices / Christopher Page** [a]*Ite*
Hyperion CDA66857 (66' · DDD) Texts and translations included ⓕ

This recording broke new ground for Gothic Voices in terms of repertory. For the first time, the group tackled a large-scale multi-movement work. You could hardly imagine a more appropriate Mass for their début in the genre than the anonymous English *Caput* cycle. Composed *c*1440 and long thought to be by Dufay, it lays fair claim to being the single most influential work of the 15th century. Its most innovative technical features were widely copied by Continental composers, but on this recording we can at last begin to appreciate what all the fuss was about: few on the Continent at the time were capable of writing music of such breathtaking confidence. You can feel the impact, the delighted surprise of contemporary listeners on hearing that very first burst of four-note writing in the *Kyrie*. It's sobering to think that the identity of this supremely influential composer may forever remain a mystery.

That phrase 'breathtaking confidence' aptly describes Gothic Voices, who are at the top of their form here. At first the briskness of this performance seems surprising, but there's little sign of hurry even in the most demandingly athletic places. Although the declamation of the text is kept fairly low-key, the sense of phrase and line, of the notes taking their place amid a kaleidoscope of changing sounds, is all beautifully judged. And with intonation and ensemble of this consistency, it's possible to revel in sheer sonority. The accompanying items make for lighter listening and a nicely balanced programme. This is a disc that grows in stature with each hearing.

The Spirits of England and France, Volume 5
Anonymous Missa, 'Veterem hominem'. Jesu, fili virginis. Doleo super te. Gaude Maria virgo. Deus creator omnium. Jesu salvator. A solis ortus. Salvator mundi. Christe, qui lux es. To many a well. Sancta Maria virgo. Mater ora filium. Ave maris stella. Pange lingua **Dunstable** Beata mater
Gothic Voices / Christopher Page
Hyperion CDA66919 (65' · DDD) Texts and translations included ⒡

Gothic Voices' peculiar brand of extrovert dynamism puts a new spin on the performance of 15th-century Mass music; more than just a Mass, what we have here is a glimpse into the very mind of a medieval composer. Music as contemplation, certainly, but active, not passive; music in which each single voice conveys weight, number, proportion. Thus, the recurring head-motif at the beginning of each movement of the *Veterem hominem* Mass cycle is experienced not so much as a structural device as a manifestation of divine immutability. In a similar spirit, the same tempos are retained in all the movements; this hasn't been attempted very often, but far from being unrelenting, the result suits both pieces very well. If Page and friends let rip in the Mass and in the carols (delivered with exhilarating brashness), they deliberately adopt a more placid approach for some of the smaller Marian pieces. As to the chants that intersperse the polyphony, they provide contrast; but can it be that the 15th-century singers who polished off their polyphony with such gusto, took their 'daily bread' of plainsong with so little salt?

Harp Consort

The Play of Daniel
Douglas Nasrawi ten Daniel **Jeremy Birchall** bass Habacuc **Harry van der Kamp** bass King Baltassar

Ian Honeyman ten King Darius **Barbara Borden** sop Queen **Caitríona O'Leary** voc Child
The Harp Consort / Andrew Lawrence-King
hp/psaltery/org
Deutsche Harmonia Mundi 05472 77395-2 (78' · DDD)
Notes, text and translation included ⒡

Andrew Lawrence-King has assembled a thoughtful and attractive rendering of *The Play of Daniel*. The rhythmic interpretation of the unmeasured pitches is sensitively varied. A single pitch-standard is retained throughout – which seems to be the best approach, though there are plenty of good reasons for thinking otherwise. And, most important of all, the drama works well because careful and original thought has been given to the meaning of the words: as one example among many, Daniel's final speech is prefaced with a grand organ introduction that actively frames it as a prophecy well apart from the story. In fact the entire flow of the closing scenes is particularly effectively caught.

Douglas Nasrawi is an excellent Daniel, managing to encompass the wide range of musical styles in the role without losing the strong character; and he gives a wonderfully expressive reading of the great lament as Daniel enters the lions' den. Ian Honeyman may well be the first Darius on record to portray him fully as a thoroughly nice but weak man: somehow the music invites a bolder approach at the moment when Darius usurps Belshazzar, but plainly the present interpretation works better. Harry van der Kamp is a splendidly strong Belshazzar; and all the smaller roles are well characterised. Alongside this is a superbly skilled instrumental ensemble. There are many different ways of doing *The Play of Daniel*, but this one is thoroughly viable throughout.

Henry's Eight

Missa cum iucunditate
Clemens non Papa Pater peccavi. Ego flos campi
Josquin Desprez Absolve, quaesumus, Domine
Ockeghem Ave Maria **Pierre de la Rue** Missa cum iucunditate **Willaert** O crux splendidior
Henry's Eight / Jonathan Brown bass
Etcetera KTC1214 (60' · DDD) Texts and translations included ⒡ⓞⓞ

The *Missa cum iucunditate* is one of Pierre de la Rue's most widely circulated settings, and hearing it sung as zestfully as it's here, one understands why. It's pervaded by the 'jollity' of the title, and belies de la Rue's rather dour reputation. In a previous recording The Hilliard Ensemble sang it one-to-a-part and sounded as though they were nearing the end of a long recording session; Henry's Eight involves all its members, so that the addition of a second countertenor in the *Credo* is neither contrived nor artificial, but an extension of what precedes it. The ensemble seems also to have allowed itself time to locate the music's rhetorical peaks: each movement has something new and fresh to offer, but the 'Osanna' stands out especially, demonstrating their ability to 'sing out' in an unrestrained manner, while still sounding unmistakably English. The selection of motets complements the Mass handsomely, and shows off some of the Eight's other emotional registers. The gems here are the performances of Ockeghem's *Ave Maria* (perhaps the finest available, contemplative and tensile: witness the final descent of the top line) and of Josquin's funeral motet, *Absolve, quaesumus, Domine*.

The Virgin and Christ Child
Anonymous Alma redemptoris mater. Alleluia – Now well may we mirthes make. Ave Maria. Gregorian Chant for Advent – Ave Maria **Arcadelt** Missa Noe, Noe **Isaac** Virgo prudentissima **Mouton** Nesciens mater virgo virum. Noe, Noe **Traditional** There is no rose of such virtue
Henry's Eight (Declan Costello, William Towers *countertens* Duncan Byrne, Nicholas Todd, Toby Watkin *tens* Robert-Jan Temmink, Giles Underwood *basses*) / **Jonathan Brown** *bass*
Etcetera KTC1213 (64' · DDD) Texts and translations included   Ⓕ**O**

The most substantial work is the Mass by Arcadelt based on a motet by Jean Mouton. Henry's Eight have often championed neglected composers in the past, and Arcadelt is better known for his madrigals than for his sacred music. One is struck by the music's sheer quality, for which Henry's Eight are once again persuasive advocates. At times, the subtly varying degrees of vibrato between singers tend to draw too much attention to this aspect of their technique, but there will be those who welcome a more relaxed approach. The disc is rounded off with English carols, and two Marian motets by Isaac and Mouton. Isaac's *Virgo prudentissima*, composed for the coronation of Isaac's patron Maximilian as Holy Roman Emperor, is festal in scoring and design. In relation to rival recordings (from David Munrow and Paul Hillier for Mouton, and from The Tallis Scholars for Isaac) Henry's Eight do more than hold their own (barring the odd fluffed entry, as at the start of the second half of *Virgo prudentissima*). Yet more might have been made of certain special moments: the rich suspensions of the eight-voice *Nesciens mater*, or the thrilling climax of *Virgo prudentissima*. Against the broad canvas provided by these expansive works, the English carols seem out of place, especially with the modern English pronunciation adopted here. That aside, this is first-rate music in performances of real commitment.

Hespèrion XX / XXI

Music for the Spanish Kings
Crecquillon Pour un plaisir. Un gay bergier. Diferencias sobre 'Las vacas' **Francisco de la Torre** Il Re di Spagna **Ghizeghem** De tous bien playne

Giovane da Nola O Dio se vede chiaro. Cingari siamo venit'a giocare **Gombert** Dezilde al caballero **Guglielmo Ebreo da Pesaro** Collinetto **Ortiz** Fantasia I & II 'Salve Regina' **Spagna** Tres glosas sobre la Alta **Valente** Intavolatura di Cimbalo – Gaillarda Napolitana **Willaert** Vecchie letrose non valete niente. Je fille quant dieu me donne de qouy
Montserrat Figueras *sop* **Hespèrion XX** / **Jordi Savall**
Virgin Veritas ② VBD 561875-2 (103' · DDD) Recorded 1980s   Ⓜ**O**

No group has done more to create a sound world for Spanish music of this period than Hespèrion XXI, and, while both these CDs, reissued under the heading 'Music for the Spanish Kings', are classic examples of their colourfully instrumented and imaginative interpretations, they also represent the range of the degrees of musical 'otherness' that their performances can convey. The first CD, of secular music from the Aragonese court in Naples and from that of Charles V, is full of characteristic kaleidoscopic instrumentation, in which percussive instruments such as drums of various kinds and tambourines add a distinct flavour, whether strictly 'Spanish' or not.

The second CD of the arrangements of Antonio de Cabezón, the famous blind organist of Charles V and Philip II, generally sounds much less overtly 'Spanish' and the music, and the interpretations of it, which alternate wind band, viol consort and solo keyboard or lute/vihuela, fit much more squarely into a pan-European musical tradition. Here again the quality and panache of the playing make this a recording to treasure. This is vintage Hespèrion XXI – you'll be amazed by these recordings' freshness and originality.

Diáspora Sefardí
Alejandría Las estrellas de los cielos **Esmirna** El Rey de Francia[a]. Yo era niña de casa alta **Jerusalén** Hermoza muchachica **Marruecos** Nani, nani[a] **Rhodes** El moro de Antequera[a]. La guirnalda de rosas[a] **Salónica** Levantose el Conde Niño[a]. Axerico de quinze años **Sarajevo** Por que llorax blanca niña[a]. A la una yo nací. Paxarico tu te llamas **Sofía** El rey que tanto madruga[a]. En la santa Helena. Longe de mi tu estarás **Turquía** Por allí pasó un cavallero[a].
Two Improvisations
[a]**Montserrat Figueras** *sop* **Hespèrion XXI** / **Jordi Savall** *viol/lira/rebab*
Alia Vox ② AV9809 (130' · DDD) Texts and translations included   Ⓕ**OO**

It's perhaps ironic that the Inquisition should have helped to preserve and enrich the musical tradition of the Sephardic Jews. Inquisitorial records provide an important source of information on musical practice in the Jewish community that until the diaspora of 1492 resided in the Iberian peninsula. The *conversos* who remained in Spain regularly came under suspicion for singing their own songs – taken as evidence of reversion to their own faith – while those who were expelled fanned out through northern Africa, eastern Europe and the Middle East. Thus, although the Sephardic tradition had its roots in medieval Hispanic culture, it was subsequently open to and enriched by multiple and diverse musical influences. Hespèrion XXI's recreation of this repertory casts its net wide, drawing on material from late medieval Spain, but also adapting living ballad traditions in Greece and incorporating Balkan-Turkish elements. It's important to emphasise the *creativity* of the musical process at work: the oral tradition of the Sephardic Jews is all but lost, and we know little enough about actual performance practice in previous centuries. No matter: the result is beautiful, exotic, fantastical and at times profoundly moving. Montserrat Figueras's distinctive voice seems ideally suited to the long-breathed, meandering melodies, punctuated by those sinuous, fluttering, Eastern-sounding ornaments at which she excels. And even if the mix of languages makes it impossible to follow the story-line without recourse to the booklet-notes, she conveys a strong narrative sense: try the extended ballad *Por que llorax blanca niña* or the strangely mesmeric lullaby *Nani, nani*.

The instrumental accompaniment of plucked and bowed strings, recorders and percussion, comes across as genuinely improvisatory (although a good deal must surely have been worked out in advance), and this is also true of the purely instrumental creations on the second CD, some of which are simply called improvisations. The playing of the instrumentalists is superb, and it all makes for compelling listening.

Battaglie & Lamenti 1600-1660
Anonymous Sarabande italienne[g] **Chilese** Canzon in Echo[gi] **Falconiero** Battaglia de Barbaso, yerno de Satanás[g] **Fontei** Pianto d'Erinna[afhi] **G Gabrieli** Canzon III a 6[g] **Guami** Canzon sopra la Battaglia[g] **Monteverdi** Lamento d'Arianna[abdefj] **Peri** Uccidimi, dolore[afi] **Rossi** Fantasia, 'Les pleurs d'Orphée'[g] **Scheidt** Pavane[g]. Galliard Battaglia[g] **Strozzi** Sul Rodano severo[acfhi]
[a]**Montserrat Figueras** *sop* [b]**Rolf Lislevand,** [c]**Robert Clancy** *theorbos* [d]**Paolo Pandolfo** *viol* [e]**Lorenz Duftschmid** *violone* [f]**Ton Koopman** *hpd* [g]**Hespèrion XXI / Jordi Savall** *va da gamba/*[h]*viol* [i]
Alia Vox AV9815 (76' · ADD/DDD) Recorded 1981, 1989, 1999. Texts and translations included   Ⓕ**O**

This release brings together laments and battle pieces from the 17th century. This might at first glance seem an odd thematic coupling, but it makes for a good sense of contrast (all battles, or all laments would be too much), and the two are in some ways linked: both were set pieces of the early Baroque, genres with a clearly defined frame of reference for composer and listener alike.

The laments here were originally recorded for the most part in 1981, while the instrumental battle pieces and canzonas date from much more recently. It's good to have the chance to appreciate the singing of Montserrat Figueras from 20

years ago, when her voice was probably at its finest: still fresh, yet with the added depth of maturity and experience. Indeed, comparing the laments by Peri, Fontei and Strozzi she recorded in 1981 and the version of Monteverdi's famous *Lamento d'Arianna* which she made in 1989 is interesting. The Monteverdi is interpreted in a powerfully expressive way, and the plangent quality inherent in her voice makes it in many ways ideally suited. Yet, for example, the Peri, a lament by Iole for Hercules, was more moving, largely because the voice has the bloom of a singer at the height of her powers: there's more warmth, more flexibility, and thus the intensity of the complaint is maintained with greater ease.

Not all the instrumental items are battle pieces; in fact, one of the most striking and original works is the *Fantasia on 'Les pleurs d'Orphée'* by Luigi Rossi. This is a shortish piece, but so full of chromaticism and dense string writing that it makes an immediate impact. Savall and his team play it beautifully, the performance as crafted and intimate as that of a great string quartet; you get the sense (quite rare on disc) that the players are all listening intently to each other, and this helps to draw the listener in too. The battle pieces, by Scheidt, Guami and Falconiero, offer all the virtuosity you could hope to hear from strings and wind alike. Strongly recommended.

Isabel I, Reina de Castilla
Anonymous Muy crueles bozes dan. Sanctus. Exultet. Turkish March. Toccata. Lavava y suspirava. Canción en ritmo Quddan de la Nuba Gribt Al Hussein de Marruecos **Cornago** Kyrie: Ayo visto lo mappamundi. Patres nostri peccaverunt **Dufay** Je ne vis onques la pareille **Enzina** Romances and Villancicos – Levanta, Pascual; Triste España sin ventura; El que rige y el regido Pavana, 'Pues que jamás olvidaros' **Escobar** Missa pro defunctis – Requiem aeternam **Francisco de la Torre** La Spagna **Narváez** Paseávase al rey moro **Tordesillas** Franceses, por qué 'rrazón? **Triana** Dinos, madre del donsel **Verardi** Viva el gran Re Don Fernando
Montserrat Figueras, Arianna Savall *sops* **Andrew Lawrence-King** *hp* **La Capella Reial de Catalunya; Hespèrion XXI / Jordi Savall**
Alia Vox 🔊 AVSA9838 (78' · DDD/DSD · T/t) Ⓕ**OO**

As the musicologist Rui Vieira Nery points out in his excellent notes to this album of music from the time of Isabel I (1451-1504), this CD could be seen 'as a sort of soundtrack ... to a historical film dedicated to the fascinating figure of the Catholic Queen'. This is a sequence of pieces by composers of the latter part of the 15th century presented in association with specific, and dated, events such as the taking of Granada or the death of Isabel's only son and heir, Prince Juan. Other occasions are rather less clearly fixed in music: the discovery of the New World, or the expulsion of the unconverted Muslims in 1502. The danger is that there's precious little evidence for fixing these items to such a chronological time-line.

The musical interpretations, too, are highly imaginative, with added fanfares or instrumental introductions and interjections. The lavish combinations of instruments and voices, punctuated or defined by a colourful palette of percussive sounds, suggests a film score.

A good range of musical styles and idioms from the period is on offer here, though it's an open question whether these wonderfully rich and sonorous interpretations – performances of great virtuosity, verve and expressiveness as required – would sound familiar to Isabel's ears. Hespèrion XXI certainly know how to make this music attractive and compelling, and perhaps that's ultimately more important than musicological quibbles. Add this CD to your collection and enjoy.

Villancicos y Danzas Criollas
Anonymous Jota. Cachua **Arañés** Chacona: A la vida bona **Bocanegra** Hanapachap cussicuinin **Cererols** Seráfin que con dulce harmoniá **G Fernandez** Tleycantimo choquiliya **Flecha** San Sabeya gugurumbé **P Guerrero** Dì, perra mora **Hidalgo** Ay, que me río de Amor **Madre de Deus** Antonya, Flaciquia, Gasipà **Martín y Coll** Flores de música – Danza del hacha **Padilla** A siolo flasiquiyo **Torrejón y Velasco** Desvelado dueño mio **Torres y Portugal** Un juguetico de fuego quierò cantar **Zéspedes** Convidando est la noche. Ay que me abraso
La Capella Reial de Catalunya; Hespèrion XXI / Jordi Savall va da gamba
Alia Vox AV9834 (77' · DDD · T/t) Ⓕ

There's no mistaking it as the product of Hespèrion XXI: the soundworld, with a wide range of instruments and featuring percussion, the distinctive voice of Figueras and the distinguished viol-playing of Savall. And as the stimulating booklet-notes by Rui Vieira Nery suggest, what we glimpse here is the persistence of various cultures within a multicultural, multilingual context and 'the permanent interplay between all social levels of artistic movements'. So the popular, of whatever cultural tradition – European, African, Amerindian – rubs shoulders with the more cultivated.

The mix of musical elements in these (mostly 17th-century) pieces from Latin America and the Iberian Peninsula is fascinating. Dance rhythms pervade much of this vocal music, the texts of which are rich in imagery or dynamic in their dialogue format. Particularly enjoyable are the semi-improvised *cachua* which, though featuring viol and plucked strings, could well be imagined on panpipes, and Torrejón y Velasco's beautiful Christmas *villancico* in the form of a lullaby, *Desvelado dueño mio*, performed with finely judged expressivity: touching but unsentimentalised.

Cererols's eight-part *villancico* based on the popular melody of the otherwise quite racy Marizápolos melody is similarly affecting. No percussion in these two items, but plenty elsewhere. Some of the texts, particularly that of the five-voice *negro Antonya, Flaciquia, Gasipà* by the

Portuguese Filipe da Madre de Deus, are not only racy but racist by today's standards. It's all interesting and really original.

The Hilliard Ensemble

Officium
Includes Plainchant, Notre Dame polyphony and motets by Dufay, de la Rue and Morales – with saxophone
Jan Garbarek sax **The Hilliard Ensemble** (David James counterten Rogers Covey-Crump, John Potter tens Gordon Jones bar)
ECM New Series 445 369-2 (78' · DDD) Recorded 1993. Latin texts included Ⓕ

The play between ancient chant and structured jazz-style improvisation creates a sort of spiritual time warp where past and present happily co-exist on the basis of shared musical goals. For no matter how one views so-called crossover, or the relative lack of wisdom in sticking to rigid musical boundaries, the evidence is conclusive: 'Officium' transcends any limitations imposed by time and style. If you've any doubts, then play either the opening or closing tracks, both of which find Jan Garbarek (a master of apposite extemporisation) easing around Christóbal de Morales's polyphonic 'Pace mihi domine' (from the *Officium defunctorum*) as if it were his own creation. The effect is enchanting, and when, eight tracks later, the same piece is presented without Garbarek's saxophone, we somehow miss the commentary. If the success of this album has prompted certain jazz fans and early music specialists to commiserate over their invaded territories, or cynics to align Garbarek and the Hilliards with Górecki and the Monks, then take heart: we're still listening to Respighi's ancient masters, Stravinsky's 'Pergolesi', Tchaikovsky's Mozart and Loussier's Bach, not to mention Ellington's Tchaikovsky. Stylistic cross-pollination makes for a healthy creative environment, and this CD is one of its happiest symptoms. Recordings, documentation and presentation are exemplary.

Spain and the New World
Alba Stabat mater **Alonso** La tricotea **Anonymous** Tierra içielos se quexavan. Di, por que mueres en cruz. Dindirin, dindirin. Si la noche haze escura **Encina** Triste España sin ventura!. Cucú, cucú, cucú. Hoy comamos y be bamos. Mas vale trocar **Escobar** Clamabat autem mulier. Pásame por Dios barquero. Salve regina **Franco** In ilhuicac cihuapille (attrib). Memento mei, Deus. Dios itlazo nantzine (attrib) **Guerrero** Ave Virgo sanctissima **Lienas** Salve regina **Lobo** O quam suavis est, Domine **Luchas** A la caça, sus, a caça **Millán** O dulce y triste memoria **Mondéjar** Ave rex noster **Morales** Pater noster. Parce mihi, Domine. Magnificat a 6 **Padilla** Transfige, dulcissime Domine **Peñalosa** Inter vestibulum et altare. Magnificat quarti toni **Rivafrecha** Vox dilecti mei **Urreda** Nunca fué pena ma yor
The Hilliard Ensemble (David James, Ashley Stafford

countertens Rogers Covey-Crump, John Potter, Mark Padmore *tens* Gordon Jones *bar*)
Virgin Classics Veritas ② 561394-2 (126' · DDD)
Recorded 1990-91. Texts and translations included Ⓑ

Originally released in late 1991, this two-CD set was The Hilliard Ensemble's contribution to the Columbus commemorations of the following year. It was also their first recording after Paul Hillier's departure from the group. In keeping with the Columbus theme, the collection includes music composed both in the Old World and in the New. The languages used are Latin for the sacred music and Spanish for the secular – but in addition there are two small pieces in Nahuatl, the tongue of the Aztecs.

With well over two hours of music, there's time for The Hilliard to dwell on many composers and genres, most of whom have but a small representation on disc. Spanish polyphony has a marked tendency to asperity in its treatment of dissonance, and generally eschews the more complex forms of polyphony adopted by Franco-Flemish composers: that makes for sobriety in its sacred music, and directness in the secular. This is best heard in the music of Encina and Peñalosa in the early 16th century; the closest Spain comes to a home-grown exponent of the international style is Morales, one of whose splendid *Magnificat*s stands out as a high point.

The ensemble is more at ease with sacred music than secular. Pieces in the latter category come across either as forced, or as insufficiently defined. The collection as a whole, however, is a distinctive one, and offers a convincing picture of a country whose polyphonic tradition has often passed for a poor relation of the mainstream Continental idiom.

Paul Hillier   *baritone*

Chansons de Trouvères
Anonymous Volez vous que je vous chant. Quant voi la flor nouvele **Colin Muset** En mai, quant li rossignolez **Gace Brulé** Les oxelés de mon païx. A la douçor de la bele seson **Moniot d'Arras** Ce fu en mai **Thibault de Champagne** Aussi conme unicorne sui. Deus est ensi conme li pellicanz. Chançon ferai, que talenz m'en est pris
Paul Hillier *voc* **Andrew Lawrence-King**
psaltery/hp/org
Harmonia Mundi Classical Express HCX3957184
(70' · DDD) Texts and translations included Ⓢ Ⓑ O

The repertoire of *trouvère* songs is one 'we are only now beginning to explore', writes Margaret Switten. This is an enlightened and well-chosen selection, sensitively presented and delightfully sung by Paul Hillier with insight and feeling. The main object of the poets' attention is *fin'amor*, but other themes, including the return of spring, make their joyful appearance, and there's one piece in a completely different vein, a serious piece of religious polemics: *Deus est ensi conme li pellicanz*. The melodies, simple and stanzaic, are of great beauty. Outstanding in this

respect is Gace Brulé's *A la douçor de la bele seson*. Many are modal (Dorian) and a few share a well-known opening phrase with a Gregorian *melodie-type* that Andrew Lawrence-King has made much use of in his accompaniments. His own contribution is momentous: if the manner in which these songs were originally performed still remains a mystery for the singer, it's even more of an enigma for the accompanist. But Lawrence-King has taken the word *trouvère* to heart: he's a true 'finder'. His empathy with text, music and singer is total: he 'invents' with a sure touch, and it isn't going too far to say it's a touch of genius.

Maria Cristina Kiehr   *soprano*

Canta la Maddelena
Agneletti Gloria[ab] **Bernabei** Heu me miseram et infelicem[ab] **Ferrari** Queste pungenti spine[ab] **Frescobaldi** Arie musicali per cantarsi[ab] – primo libro: A pie della gran croce; secondo libro: Dove, dove sparir. Toccata[c]. Canzona[c] **Gratiani** Dominus illuminatio mea[ab] **Kapsberger** Toccata arpeggiata[c] **Mazzocchi** Dialoghi, e sonetti[ab] – Lagrime amare; Dunque ove tu Signor; Homai le luci erranti **L Rossi** Pender non prima vide sopra vil tronco[ab] **M Rossi** Toccata settima[c]
[a]**Maria Cristina Kiehr** *sop* [b]**Concerto Soave** (Matthias Spaeter *archlte/cittarrone* Sylvie Moquet *bass viol* Mara Galassi *hp*) / **Jean-Marc Aymes** *org/*[c]*hpd*
Harmonia Mundi HMC90 1698 (72' · DDD) Texts and translations included Ⓕ OO

Much skill has gone into this programme celebrating the popular 17th-century emblem of Mary Magdalene's lamentation and deploration at the foot of the Cross. Framed by two exquisite and largely unknown works, one by Agneletti and a fine cantata by Ferrari, Maria Cristina Kiehr spins a shapely, instinctive line, nuanced rather than overwhelmed by expressive ardour. (How often vapid over-indulgence by undernourished voices rips the heart out of this music.) Kiehr shows admirable judgement in how she sustains the intensity of the most sectional work, Rossi's *Pender non prima* (taking as its model Monteverdi's *Lamento d'Arianna*). A noble and graciously covered mezzo register is the conduit for Kiehr's profound sensuality, heard delightfully in the Gratiani work, where her gleaming and accurate upper register shuns the piping angel and portrays a 'faithful grieving Lover' in a state of extreme emotion. The high tessitura isn't the prettiest nor the most controlled, and it underlines her limited tonal range in works such as Bernabei's *Heu me miseram* where excitement results in some shrillness. She often makes up for this in the subtlety of her accentuation and inflexion. The Frescobaldi works fit her like a glove – paragraphed declamatory songs, beautifully formed and succinctly expressed. In 'A pie della gran croce', she shows a feeling for the text which lifts superficial narrative into heart-felt supplication.

With some evocative and breezy instrumental contributions, the disc which tackles this music with distinction. These are mature readings of works whose performance too often misses the mark. Thumbs up, nearly all round.

The King's Consort

Lo Sposalizio – The Wedding of Venice to the Sea
Anonymous Fanfares – Rotta; Imperiale prima; Imperiale seconda. Sursum corda. Variazoni sopra 'La Ciaccona' **A Gabrieli** Vieni, vieni Himeneo. Cantiam de Dio **Canzona** La Battaglia. Intonationi – Primo tono; Settimo tono. Gloria a 16 **G Gabrieli** Lieto godea sedendo. Udite, chiari et generosi figli. Kyrie a 12. Sanctus a 12. Sonata XX **Guami** Canzona XXIV **Gussago** Canzon XIX, 'La Leona' **Kapsberger** Kapsberger **Massaino** Canzon per otto tromboni **Monteverdi** Christe, adoramus te **Piccinini** Variazoni sopra 'La Folia' **Viadana** Canzona, 'La Veneziana'
The King's Consort Choir; The King's Consort / Robert King
Hyperion ② CDA67048 (89' · DDD) Texts and translations included ⓂⓄ

This mouth-watering celebration of Venice is devised with considerable expertise in ritual, contextual aspects and the imaginative allocation of music to, in this particular instance, the processions and journey across the lagoon and the subsequent solemn Mass held in San Nicolò. Robert King explains in the note, with his inimitable enthusiasm and clarity, how, from the 11th century, mariners congregated annually to ask for St Nicholas's protection. The festival became, over the centuries, an important social event in the calendar as the symbolic 'fertility rite': the marriage between Venice and her blessed Adriatic, prayerfully celebrated on Ascension Day. The central act was when the Doge would toss a gold ring into the sea from his resplendently ornate galley (rowed by 400 hapless slaves). He would then move amongst the flotilla, with glorious music wafting over the calm ripples of the lagoon, his progress punctuated by various stop-offs for blessings and further ceremonial. The musical journey across to the Lido is principally a secular exercise and we're treated to some delectable madrigals by both Gabrielis. Although some listeners may find the ensemble a touch undernourished in the first madrigal, *Vieni, vieni Himeneo*, it soon transpires that sweetness and balance are the essential ingredients for King; the result in the exquisite instrumental numbers is a sensitivity to matching timbre which is an unusual delight both in the Guami *Canzona XXIV a 8* and the imploring counterpoint that acts as a foil to the fencing in Andrea Gabrieli's *Battaglia*.

Indeed, what shines through with great dignity is the sense of an unfolding procession with a seemingly effortless choreography, the musical highlight of which is Giovanni Gabrieli's eight-part madrigal *Lieto godea sedendo*, set here with two falsettists and strings, portraying 'the disturbance of spring' in all its poignant and fleeting glory. The intimate and affectionate duetting of James Bowman and Robin Blaze, so beautifully rendered on this disc, is something of a landmark as the inimitable mentor shares the reins with the pick of the younger generation of countertenors.

The depth of quality and the control within individual voices of the vocal consort is a match for anyone in the magisterial 16-part Gabrieli piece *Udite, chiari et generosi*, though the acoustic of St Jude's, Hampstead – and the pragmatic recording techniques required for such an undertaking – demand that *tutti* work is clearly defined and that a strong interpretative angle is projected. This is where the Gabrieli Mass movements for San Nicolò, which constitute the second disc, are far more successfully realised than in *Cantiam de Dio*: this is the only multi-voiced work where the performance appears prosaic compared with the poised elegance that informs the vocal and instrumental dialogue of the *Kyrie* and *Sanctus a 12*. This is a small gripe in an otherwise exceptional recording. Running through the veins of nearly all the pieces are the ingredients of commitment, immediacy and spontaneous musicianship which allow one to view this ravishing music on its own terms, rather than losing sight of it with endless speculative reconstruction for its own sake. A very fine achievement all round.

The King's Noyse

Pavaniglia – Dances and Madrigals from 17th-Century Italy Ⓟ
Douglass Tarantella[b] **Corbetta** Follia[c]. Ciaconna[c] **Farina** Pavana Terza[b] **Gesualdo** Tall' or sano desio[b]. Moro, lasso, al mio duolo[b] **Monteverdi** Voglio di vita uscir[ab]. Ohimè ch'io cado[ab] **Pesenti** Quanto t'inganni Amor[ab] **Rossi** Orfeo – Lasciate Averno, o pene, e me seguite![ab]. Passacaille del seigneur Luigi[b] (arr Douglass). Prima Canzon 'Scipione Stella'[d] **Sances** Lagrimosa beltà[b] **Zanetti** Il scolaro[b] – Intrata e Balletto del Marchese di Caravazzo con la sua Gagliarda; Pas è mezzo sù Chiave Maestro; Saltarello della pas è mezzo; Saltarello detto il Genovesino; Pavaniglia; La Sartorella; Il Gabonano; La Balloria; La Montagnura; Saltarello della Battagli
The King's Noyse (aEllen Hargis *sop* bDavid Douglass, bRobert Mealy *vns* bScott Metcalfe, bMargriet Tindemans *vas* bEmily Walhout *vc*) cPaul O'Dette *gtr/chit* dAndrew Lawrence-King *hp*
Harmonia Mundi HMU90 7246 (74' · DDD) Texts and translations included Ⓕ

This is a very engaging and well-constructed programme, containing some better-known pieces, but concentrating for the most part on Italian dance music: a pavan, a tarantella, a chaconne, a follia, to name only four. Some of the most refreshing selections are to be found among the 12 minutes' worth of dances from Zanetti's *Il scolaro*: the sound of two violins playing the top line in a string consort is extraordinarily evocative, and on this recording one readily understands why such string bands caught on so rapidly. The ensemble conveys such spontaneity that even the arranged pieces – such as Sances's *Lagrimosa beltà* – sound as though they were written specially for it. Only the Gesualdo madrigals – performed, again, with just strings – seem to not quite fit the medium, despite the superb polish of the performances. The individual contributions are impressive as well: Andrew Lawrence-King and Paul O'Dette each boast very effective solos, and Ellen Hargis is persuasive as always, especially in the livelier pieces, where her richness and her flexibility of tone are impressively combined.

The King's Noyse set great store by the improvisatory, spontaneous character of the early Italian Baroque, and by the flexibility with which music could be adapted to suit given ensembles. This disc bears out such notions, and also feeds the hope that they might push them further still in future. Many would argue that the word 'authenticity' is now best left alone; but if one wishes to define it – one of many possible definitions – as facilitating the suspension of disbelief (the illusion of actually 'being there'), then the King's Noyse succeed brilliantly.

Gérard Lesne   *countertenor*

Dans un bois solitaire
Bernier Aminte et Lucrine **Clérambault** Pirame et Tisbé **Courbois** L'Amant timide **Du Buisson** Plainte sur la mort de Monsieur Lambert **Stuck** Les Festes bolonnoises
Gérard Lesne *counterten* **Il Seminario Musicale**
Virgin Classics Veritas 545303-2 (63' · DDD) Texts and translation included   Ⓕ●

A fascinating and still largely untapped corner of the repertoire, the *cantate française* was a popular form of home music-making in the early years of the 18th century, offering amateurs a chance, as the lexicographer Brossard put it, 'to soften the sorrows of solitude, without all the trouble expense and paraphernalia of an opera.' The reference to opera is significant, because these pieces – usually about a quarter-of-an-hour in length – really are like miniaturised operatic episodes, serving up a variety of moods and, in the best cases, capable of conveying considerable emotional power. The best works in this selection are *Aminte et Lucrine* by the French cantata's most prolific exponent, Nicolas Bernier, and *Pirame et Tisbé* by perhaps its most skilled master, Louis-Nicolas Clérambault. Hearing the impressively sonorous pronouncements of the Oracle of Diana in the former, or the roaring of the (continuo) lion in the latter, you begin to wonder why these two didn't compose any operas themselves, unless it be that they were justifiably quite happy with what they had already achieved here. All the works on the disc, however, have something to offer both dramatically and lyrically, and the lack of familiarity of the composers' names shouldn't be allowed to put anyone off. Gérard Lesne's singing is a constant pleasure. His distinctively rich and manly alto voice is a reliable and even-toned instrument, while his musical intelligence and excellent projection of words is insurance against the slightest hint of blandness. His continuo group is a little heavy-handed in places, though it's good to hear them being unafraid to enter into the dramatic spirit.

Monteverdi Choir

Santiago a cappella
Anonymous Mariam matrem Virginem **Cardoso** Non mortui **Guerrero** Ave virgo sanctissima. Duo Seraphim **João IV** Crux fidelis **Lobo** Versa est in luctum. Lamentationes – Ieremiae Prophetae **Rogier** Salva nos Domine **Victoria** O vos omnes, qui transitis per viam. O lux et decus Hispaniae
Monteverdi Choir / Sir John Eliot Gardiner
Emarcy 986 7305 (67' · DDD · T/t)   Ⓕ●●●

This impressive collection is the Monteverdi Choir going back, in a sense, to their roots, or even beyond them. After so many years in which it's concentrated on later styles, that John Eliot Gardiner's choir have their origins in earlier repertoire. They return to it here with gusto, illustrating their habitual superb choral blend, and a sense of pace and drama that the prize-strewn path of Bach and Mozart recordings hasn't in any way dampened.

Among the highlights are the taut rendition of Alonso Lobo's monumental *Lamentations* and the blaze of glory that is the same composer's *Versa est in luctum*, but Gardiner shows himself extremely sensitive to this late Iberian Renaissance style in general.

The only piece that actually has to do with the pilgrim route to Santiago de Compostela is the earliest, the lovely *Maria matrem* from the *Llibre Vermell*. This is mainly an excuse to assemble a marvellous collection of Iberian polyphony from a rather later period, and the collection is outstanding and the programme well conceived. Recommended.

Musica Antiqua of London

The Triumph of Maximilian – Songs and Instrumental Music from 16th-Century Germany
Anonymous Elslein **Aich** Ein frolky wesen. Elslein à 3. Der Hundt **Barbireau** Ein frolky wesen **Busnois** Fortuna disperata **Dietrich** Elslein à 3 **Finck** Ich stünd an einem Morgen **Ghiselin** Ein frolyk wesen **Isaac** Fortuna disperata. Der Hundt. Ich stünd an einem Morgen **Josquin Desprez** Fortuna à 3. Missa pange lingua – Pleni sunt coeli (Quis seperabit) **Othmayr** Entlaubet ist der Walde **Rhau** Elslein à 2. Ich stünd an einem Morgen **Senfl** Es taget vor dem Walde. Es taget à 4. Es taget: Elslein à 4. Exemplum. Es taget. Entlaubet ist der Walde à 4. Entlaubet ist der Walde. Ich stünd an einem Morgen à 3. Ich stünd an einem Morgen à 5. Ich stünd an einem Morgen à 4. Ich stünd an einem Morgen … Es taget … Kein Adler. Pacientia muss ich han. Quattour. Will niemand singen **Senfl/Gerle**

Elslein à 4 **Stolzer** Entlaubet ist der Waldea
Musica Antiqua of London / Philip Thorby with
John Potter ten
Signum Records SIGCD004 (69' · DDD) Recorded
1993   Ⓕ

Ludwig Senfl hasn't yet received the recognition that he deserves; and as this issue demonstrates, he's one of the most fascinating composers of the early 16th century. He combines
an astonishing contrapuntal skill with a range of
moods and formal control that make his German song settings among the finest of their century. One reason why he's little heard is that the
music is hard to sing: for most of it you need a
tenor with an extreme lightness of touch. But in
John Potter they seem to have the perfect
singer, perhaps the best ever heard in this repertory. He floats the lines with effortless grace and
with an uncannily sensitive projection of the
texts. Just listen to his control in the longest and
most serious song on the disc, Senfl's *Pacientia
muss ich han*. But he's also superbly supported by
the viols and recorders of Musica Antiqua of
London. Its playing, too, is apparently effortless. Some listeners may feel that the recorders
are occasionally allowed to run too fast, giving
less than full measure to the real substance of the
music; but the playing is undeniably wonderful,
and superbly recorded. For the viol playing, no
praise is too high: they do everything with a
pleasingly light touch and always with a real sensitivity to the music. There's another reason
why we hear less Senfl than we should: that his
best work needs to be understood within the
broader context of the German *Tenorlied* repertory. To cope with this, the disc puts Senfl
alongside settings of the same material by other
composers of the time.

The Newberry Consort

Il Solazzo   Ⓟ
Anonymous La Badessa. Bel fiore danza. Nova stella.
Cominciamento di gioia. Trotto. Principe di virtu
Bartolino da Padova Alba columba **Ciconia** O rosa
bella. Ligiadra donna **Jacopo da Bologna** Non al
suo amante **Landini** La bionda treccia. Dolcie
signorie. Donna, s'i, t'o fallito. El gran disio **Zacharo
de Teramo** Rosetta. Un fior gentil
The Newberry Consort / Mary Springfels
Harmonia Mundi HCX3957038 (62' · DDD)   Texts and
translation included Recorded 1990   Ⓑ

If medieval Italian music pales somewhat in
comparison to the glories of opera from the 19th
century onwards, there are still riches to be discovered in this collection of *trecento* vocal and
instrumental works. The Chicago-based ensemble, The Newberry Consort, use a mere five
performers to provide over an hour of entertainment. This was the era of writers such as Dante,
Petrarch, Boccaccio, but also of Simone Pro-
denzani – the author of a cycle of sonnets entitled *Il Solazzo*, many of which were later set to
music. While some of the *Solazzo* texts are pre-

sented here in musical form (the scurrilous *La
Badessa* is one), Italian ballata from leading composers of the time are also represented – Ciconia's *O rosa bella* and Landini's *La bionda treccia*,
for example. The vocal numbers are all taken by
mezzo Judith Malafronte and countertenor
Drew Minter who clear the hurdles of tricky
pronunciation and flamboyantly complex vocal
lines to give a thoroughly communicative performance of this wonderful music. Mary
Springfels provides elegant and musical direction as well as that essential ingredient to a disc
such as this – the informative booklet. If the
prospect of an hour of early Italian song sounds
daunting, fear not, for the instrumental dances
on the disc (especially the anonymous *Cominciamento di gioia*) are played with a vitality that will
make you want to jump up and join in! Explorers
of the riches from Italian times long gone by
need have no qualms when sampling from this
lively, superbly performed disc.

Villon to Rabelais
Anonymous Amours m'ont fait. L'autrier quant je
chevauchoys. La belle se siet. Belles tenés moy. Bon
vin. En amours n'a si non bien. En douleur et
tristesse. Faisons bonne chère. Héllas! Mon coeur
n'est pas à moy. J'aimeray mon amy. My, my. Puis
qu'autrement ne puis avoir. Petit fleur. Quant je suis
seullecte. Réveillez-vous, Piccars. Rolet ara la
tricoton. Suite of Bransles. Danse de Cleves (arr
Duffin). La gelosia (arr Duffin). Petit vriens (arr
Duffin) **Busnois** Vostre beauté **Févin** Faulte d'argent. Il fait
bon aimer l'oyselet. Soubz les branches **Marot**
Jouissance vous donneray **Stockhem** Je suis
d'Alemagne. Marchez là dureau
The Newberry Consort (Drew Minter *counterten*
William Hite *ten* Tom Zajac *bar/hp/recs/perc* David
Douglass *vielle*) **/ Mary Springfels** *vielle/rebec*
Harmonia Mundi HMU90 7226 (72' · DDD) Texts and
translations included   Ⓕ

Rarely does an Anglo-Saxon early music ensemble declaim French quite so convincingly. This
recital from The Newberry Consort takes in the
huge variety of expressive registers in secular
music from the late 15th and early 16th centuries, including dance music. Part of the attraction is that most of this music was previously
neglected on disc because it was anonymous:
this includes works better known among scholars than by the general public, but whose musical worth transcends purely historical considerations. If the disc shows any bias, it's towards
pieces of popular inspiration, often through the
use of rustic texts, sometimes combined with
more artful poems (as in *Puis qu'autrement/
Marchez là dureau* or *Vostre beauté/Vous marchez
du bout du pie*, or the settings of *La tricotée*). This
is the only evident connection between Villon
and Rabelais and the pieces recorded here.
(None of them set texts by either writer.) The
projection and enunciation of texts has
been given careful thought, and is clearly executed, so recourse to the booklet is only when
several texts are declaimed at once. Drew

Minter's contribution is worth mentioning in this regard, and the ensemble as a whole sings out even when the effect turns to slapstick (as in the drinking-song *Bon vin*).

It's become a truism that secular repertories are too often treated as also-rans in the discography of this period; a recital like this helps redress that imbalance. Fittingly, it's dedicated to the memory of the scholar Howard Mayer Brown, who did so much to further the understanding of instruments and their participation in Renaissance music. It's a worthy tribute.

Orlando Consort

Rare 15th Century English Church Music
Anonymous Ave regina caelorum. Gaude virgo mater Christi. O pulcherrima mulierum. O sanctissime presul. Sanctus. Stella caeli. Audivi vocem **Benet** Gloria. Credo **Dunstable** Salva scema sanctitatis **Forest** Tota pulcra es **Frye** Ave regina celorum **Lambe** Stella caeli **Mowere** Beata Dei genitrix **Plummer** Anna mater matris Christi. Tota pulchra es **Pyamour** Quam pulchra es **Trouluffe** Nesciens mater
Orlando Consort (Robert Harre-Jones *counterten* Angus Smith, Charles Daniels *tens* Donald Grieg *bar*) Harmonia Mundi HMU90 7297 (71' · DDD) Texts and translations included ⓕⓞ

The Orlando appear to improve with each recording. They've honed their distinctive, richly plummy sound to near-perfection, and their interpretative intelligence shows no sign of letting up. Be it one of the period's best-known pieces (like Frye's *Ave regina celorum*) or an otherwise unheard work (like the striking, anonymous *Stella caeli* that opens the disc), their ability to communicate something of a sense of discovery in each piece is remarkable.

And what glorious music it is! With the help of Gareth Curtis, one of the foremost specialists of this period, the Orlando have assembled a remarkably varied programme. Anthologies of 15th-century English sacred music often focus on one or other of two surviving sources, the Old Hall manuscript from the beginning of the century (represented here by Forest and John Pyamour), and the Eton Choirbook near the end (here, Walter Lambe's intricate *Stella caeli*). Between these poles there lie fragments, shards of a wonderful history. The great strength of this disc is its account of this contingent repertory. Every piece is involving in some vital way; so often one wonders, 'How come I've not heard *that* before?' Acknowledged 'masterpieces' like Frye's *Ave regina* or Dunstable's isorhythmic motet *Salve scema* rub shoulders with works by near-complete unknowns such as Richard Mowere and John Trouluffe.

But whatever the name (or indeed the absence of one), invention is sustained at a high level. Even connoisseurs of this 'rare' repertory have surprises in store for them here. This is simply one of the finest recordings of this repertoire.

Food, Wine and Song   ℗
Adam de la Halle Prenés l'abre/Hé resveille toi Robin **Anonymous** Montpellier Codex – Chançonette/Ainc voir/A la cheminee/Par verité. Apparuerunt apostolis. Si quis amat. Canto de' cardoni. Canto di donne maestre di far cacio. La plus grant chière. Cancionero musical de Palacio – La Tricotea. Quem tem farelos. Trinkt und singt **Binchois** Je ne vis onques **Compère** Sile fragor **Dufay** Adieu ces bons vins de Lannoys **Encina** Oy comamos y bebamos **Greiter** Von Eyren **Isaac** Donna di dentro/Dammene un pocho/Fortuna d'un gran tempo **Ponce** Ave color vini clari **Machaut** Nes que on porroit **Senfl** Von edler Art **Smert** Nowell, Nowell: The boarës head **Zachara da Teramo** Cacciando per gustar
Orlando Consort (Robert Harre-Jones *counterten* Charles Daniels, Angus Smith *tens* Donald Grieg *bar*) Harmonia Mundi HMU90 7314 (74' · DDD) Texts and translations included ⓕⓞ

Many music lovers are also foodies; this is aimed mainly at them. It isn't so much a CD as an elegantly designed, hard-cover 120-page booklet with a CD slipped into the back. There's a large selection of recipes from various luminaries of the food world. Most are based on medieval sources, but adapted so that the ingredients are those available from any supermarket. But the music is wonderfully presented, too. First, it's an anthology from the 12th century to the 16th, all of works that mention (or at least imply) food. Alongside a small number of favourites, there's a large number of extremely rare and wonderful pieces. They add up to a highly attractive and instructive sweep through music of the Middle Ages.

The Orlando Consort are on their very best form. Indeed, it may be their best CD yet, which is high praise indeed. A foolproof Christmas present – for any lover of medieval music with even a slight interest in food, for any lover of unusual food with even a slight interest in medieval music, for anyone who loves good singing, and probably for anyone with an interest in the unusual or the beautiful.

Passion
Compère Crux triumphans **Dufay** Victimae paschali laudes. Vexilla regis prodeunt **Josquin Desprez** Victimae paschali laudes **Isaac** Easter Mass Proper **Obrecht** Salve cru **Tinctoris** Lamentationes Jeremiex
Orlando Consort (Robert Harre-Jones *counterten* Charles Daniels, Angus Smith *tens* Donald Grieg, Robert Macdonald *basses*)
Metronome METCD1015 (62' · DDD) Texts and translations included ⓕ

This is an attractive programme of Holy Week and Easter pieces, some by unlikely composers such as Tinctoris, the 15th-century musical theorist. It's centred around Isaac's four-part *Easter Mass*, with its polytextual structure. Isaac sets all the pieces of the Proper, with the exception of the Offertory, and he interweaves three popular Easter tunes. The end product is a wonderfully joyful and festive Mass, the nearest modern equivalent that comes to mind being Honegger's Christmas cantata with its carol sequence. Isaac's Mass is flanked by Tinctoris's moving *Lamentation*, two settings of the *Victimae paschali laudes*, and three fine pieces honouring the Cross.

The Orlando Consort do full justice to this splendid programme. The singing is superb, the individual parts easily identifiable yet marvellously blended. Listeners may be slightly foxed by the pronunciation of the Latin, particularly by the nasal French vowels. Much care has gone into this search for authenticity.

Worcester Fragments
English Sacred Music of the Late Middle Ages
Orlando Consort (Robert Harre-Jones *counterten*
Charles Daniels, Angus Smith *tens* Donald Grieg *bar*)
Amon Ra CD-SAR59 (58' · DDD) Recorded 1992.
Texts and translations included   Ⓕ

In this recording the Orlando Consort provides the listener with the chance to gain an overall impression of how music developed in England during the 13th and early 14th centuries – a development distinguished by its intriguing variety, creativity and undoubted beauty, its peculiar sweetness being marked by the constant harmonic use of the interval of a third. The consort manages to achieve a balance between the type of buzzing vocal timbre, believed to have been that of the Middle Ages with its roughness of approach, and their own good solid modern standards of professional musicianship. It also attempts to reproduce what scholars believe to have been the way in which ecclesiastical Latin was pronounced in medieval England.

Le Poème Harmonique

Nova Metamorfosi
Anonymous Psalm 110, 'Dixit Dominus'. Confitemini Domino **Monteverdi** Secondo libro della musica – O infelix recessus. Terzo libro della musica – Anima miseranda; O gloriose martyr; O Jesu, mea vita; O stellae coruscantes **Ruffo** Kyrie eleison. Gloria. Credo. Sanctus. Agnus Dei
Le Poème Harmonique / Vincent Dumestre
Alpha ALPHA039 (61' · DDD) Texts and translations included   Ⓕ

Erudite as this programme may appear, Vincent Dumestre has cooked up a ravishing, if partly speculative dish of late 16th-century church music. Its premise is explored in the opulent booklet, which analyses Agnolo Bronzino's painting *The Holy Family with St Anne and the Infant St John*. This pits simplicity of expression against the complexity of emblems typical of High Renaissance mannerists.

The glory of the paradox is what governs the framing *faux-bourdon* psalms of this disc, where the unadulterated *cantus firmus* is recited, and a 'false bass' of supposedly simple polyphony makes its own mark. The result can be exotic,

even dissonant; this is music which only plays the game up to a point. Ruffo's *Kyrie* is a dutiful example of Counter-Reformation homophony but it explores new expressive territory within the set limits. Similarly, the Monteverdi examples are recognisable madrigals from Books 4 and 5, but presented as *contrafacta*, where the original secular text is replaced by a sacred one.

The performances are often remarkable; spontaneous mosaics of refined divisions, impassioned appogiatura, dissonance and textural imagination. Monteverdi's *O infelix recessus* with cornetto and viols is a gem of extraordinarily fine musical judgement. The musicians of Le Poème Harmonique reveal how composers circumnavigated the loss of free-range polyphony through glorious melodic extravagance – the 'new metamorphosis' that kicked the Council of Trent's dichotomy into touch.

Pomerium

Carolus Maximus – Music in the life of Charles V
Crecquillon Carolus magnus erat. Quis te victorem **Josquin Desprez** Mille regretz **Gombert** Missa a la Incoronation, 'Sur tous regrets' – Kyrie; Gloria. Mille regretz. Qui colis Ausoniam **Lassus** Heroum soboles. Si qua tibi obtulerint **Morales** Missa, 'L'homme armé' – Credo. Jubilate Deo omnis terra. Missa, 'Mille regretz' – Sanctus. Missa pro defunctis – Agnus Dei. Circumdederunt me **Narváez** La canción el Emperador, 'Mille regres'[a]. Fantasia del octavo tono[a]
[a]**Dolores Costoyas** *vihuela* **Pomerium / Alexander Blachly**
· Glissando 779008-2 (73' · DDD) Texts and translations included   Ⓕ

'Music in the life of Charles V', produced to accompany a major exhibition on the 500th anniversary of his birth, brings together some of the many pieces dedicated to or closely associated with the emperor. Charles was a great musical enthusiast, gaining his first music lessons at the age of seven, and, almost 50 years later, after his retreat to the Jeronymite monastery at Yuste, priding himself on his musical discernment when presented with a Mass by Guerrero. His European profile is reflected in the selection of works offered here by French, Flemish and Spanish composers: only the northern composers served in his celebrated Flemish chapel, though the vihuelist Luys de Narváez was master of the choirboys in the chapel of his son Philip. Morales, the leading Spanish composer of his time, never found favour at the royal court even though he dedicated several works to Charles. An interesting programme, then, from favourites such as Josquin's chanson *Mille regretz* (known as the 'Song of the Emperor' and also presented in Narváez's version for vihuela) to less familiar repertory by Gombert and Crecquillon.

Gombert's *Missa 'Sur tous regrets'* is characteristically dense, but it nevertheless re-creates something of the highly developed ceremonial of Charles's chapel. The motets by Crecquillon, an underrated composer, are very fine. Pomerium's performances, recorded in the resonant acoustic of the Ascension Roman Catholic Church in New York, are measured and generally well balanced, allowing the closely woven polyphonic textures to speak for themselves. While Alexander Blachly's direction isn't insensitive to phrasing, more attention could be given to overall shaping and, especially in the motets, the musical rhetoric. For all the vocal energy behind these interpretations, they occasionally come across as bland. That said, the disc affords a fascinating insight into the repertory of Charles's chapel and, to a lesser extent, chamber: well worth adding to any self-respecting collection of Renaissance polyphony.

Renaissance Camerata of Caracas

Baroque Music of Latin America
Anonymous El día de corpus. Esta noche yo baila **Araujo** Recordad jilguerillos. A recoger pasiones inhumanas **Bocanegra** Hanapachap cussicuinin **Cascante** Villancico al nascimiento **Castellanos** Ausente del alma mía. Si de rosa el nombre **Araujo Ceruti** A cantar un villancico **Fernandes** Tleycantimo choquilya. Dame albricia Mano Anton. Mano Fasiquiyo **J Herrera** A la fuente de bienes **J Mathias** Quien sale aqueste día disfraçado **De la Mota** Dios y Josef apuestan **Torrejón y Velasco** Cuando el bien que adoro. A este sol peregrino. Desvelado dueño mío **Velásquez** Niño mío
The Renaissance Camerata of Caracas / Isabel Palacios
Dorian DOR93199 (65' · DDD) Recorded 1992 Texts and translations included ⓕ

This is a reissue of a recording made in 1992, but previously available only on a very limited basis: Dorian has performed a sterling service in making it available to a wider public. Most of the music is barely known, even among specialists, and it certainly can't be described as over-recorded. The Camerata is a group that reinforces the stereotypical idea that Latin American musicians are more successful when working with lively, rhythmical music, and less so when they're required to sing sustained melodic lines. A number of the pieces come across as somewhat bland because of this limitation, as in the somewhat undercharacterised *Ausente del alma* by Rafael Antonio Castellanos, but in general the group has the measure of the style. Mathias's sarabande-like *Quien sale aqueste* and Castellanos's *Si de rosa el nombre* prove this amply, and the performance of Torrejón y Velasco's justly renowned *A este sol peregrino* is quite lovely.

The rather oddly Baroque performance of the Quechua hymn *Hanapachap cussicuinin* heralds a change in a section balanced in favour of earlier repertoire, specifically villancicos by Gaspar Fernandes, an extraordinarily original composer of Portuguese origin who worked in Guatemala and Mexico. The Camerata give us three works

by him, all done idiomatically (especially the slinky rendition of *Mano Fasiquiyo*), though *Dame albricia Mano Anton* is just a little too fast, however expert the singers are in getting their tongues round the text at that speed. The programme finishes with a brilliant rendition of the anonymous *Esta noche yo baila*, which will remind you of nothing so much as mambo. Recommended, but don't forget your dancing shoes.

La Reverdie

Legenda Aurea
Anonymous Facciam laude a tuc'ti i sancti. Sia laudato San Francesco. San Domenico beato. Ciascun ke fede sente. Santa Agnese da Dio amata. Novel canto/Sia laudato San Vito. Laudiam 'li gioriosi martiri. Pastor principe beato. Magdalena degna da laudare. Spiritu Sancto dolçe amore. Benedicti e llaudati
La Reverdie
Arcana A304 (70' · DDD) Texts and translations included ⓕ❶

La Reverdie has focused on *laude* in the past, specifically of the Marian variety. Here they concentrate on the praise of other saints. Some of them are well known such as *Sia laudato San Francesco*, but others are less so. This ensemble has always mixed voices and instruments in highly imaged and striking ways. In the case of the *laude* repertory, recent research by the American scholar Blake Wilson into the Laudesi societies that abounded in Italy confirms a richly documented variety of approaches to performance of this intrinsically popular genre, ranging from voices alone to an array of hired instrumentalists of all sorts. In the longer pieces comprising many stanzas, La Reverdie improvises added counterpoints, both vocal and instrumental, and individual singers step into the limelight, sometimes declaiming the text without the benefit of music. Regarding the relationship of text to music, La Reverdie advocates a metrical interpretation of the notation's unmeasured neumes. This makes intuitive sense, given the formal markers of a genre destined for a congregation singing in the vernacular. Just as the variety of performance options must have been welcome to congregations of the time, so it is on this CD: there's something to suit every taste. The core quartet of female vocalists has a pleasing quality, and are matched by an equal number of equally striking male singers. The unspecified soloist on the opening track, *Facciam laude a tuc'ti i sancti*, rings the changes most compellingly. There's now a considerable number of *laude* recordings in the discography; this is one of the finest.

La Romanesca

Al alva venid – Spanish secular music of the ⓟ
15th and 16th centuries
Anonymous Al alva venid. L'amor, dona, ch'io te

porto. Rodrigo Martines. A los maitines era. Nina y vina **Encina** Más vale trocar. Si abrá en este baldrés! Qu'es de ti, desconsolado? Hoy comamos y bevamos **Mudarra** Tres libros de musica – Si me llaman a mi; Ysabel, perdiste la tu faxa; Guárdame las vacas **Narváez** Paseavase el rey moro. Lós Seys libros del delphin – Diferencias de Guardame las vacas **D Ortiz** Trattado de glosas – Recercarda segunda sobre el passamezzo moderno; Recercada tercera para viola de gamba sola; Recercada quarta sobre la folia; Recercada quinta sobre el passamezzo antiguo; Recercada settima sobre la Romanesca **Pisador** Libro de música – En la fuente del rosel; La manana de Sant Juan **Vásquez** Orphenica lyra – De los álamos vengo; Con qué la lavaré; Glosa sobre Tan que vivray; De Antequera sale el moro
La Romanesca (Marta Almajano *sop* Paolo Pandolfo *va da gamba* Juan Carlos de Mulder *vihuela/gtr* Pedro Estevan *perc*) / **José Miguel Moreno** *vihuela*
Glossa GCD920203 (60' · DDD) Texts and translations included ⓕⓞⓞ

Many of these pieces – songs and vihuela music from 16th-century Spain – have been recorded before, but this CD takes pride of place in this repertory. La Romanesca performs' with true *fantasía* but without any of the mannerisms – the excesses and the understatements – of many of its predecessors and rivals: it seem to hit it just right. It has mostly selected songs with a strong popular flavour – precisely those songs that have attracted most attention because they're simply so attractive – but their realisations are re-strained in terms of instrumental accompani-ment (plucked strings, viol and a smattering of percussion), but full of musical vitality – in other words, the emphasis is, justly, on the music and not the 'orchestrated' arrangement of it. The players, led by José Miguel Moreno, are bril-liant, and the singer, Marta Almajano shines in this repertory. She brings out perfectly the lyri-cism inherent in the popular-inspired court song tradition – take, for example, Vásquez's lovely *De los álamos vengo*: these songs demand an elusive blend of sophistication and simplicity. Take this disc with you wherever you go, and especially to that desert island.

The Scholars of London

French Chansons
Arcadelt En ce mois délicieux; Margot, labourez les vignes; De temps que j'estois amoureux; Sa grand beauté **Bertrand** De nuit, le bien **Clemens Non Papa** Prière devant le repas; Action des Graces **Costeley** Arrête un peu mon coeur **Gombert** Aime qui vouldra; Quand je suis aupres **Janequin** Le chant des oiseaux. Or vien ça, vien, m'amye **Josquin Desprez** Faulte d'argent. Mille regretz **Lassus** Beau le cristal. Bon jour mon coeur. Un jeune moine. La nuict froide et sombre. Si je suis brun **Le Jeune** Ce n'est que fiel. **Passereau** Il est bel et bon **Sandrin** Je ne le croy **Sermisy** Tant que vivray en eage florissant. Venez, regrets. La, la Maistre Pierre **Tabourot** Belle qui tiens ma vie **Vassal** Vray Dieu
The Scholars of London

Naxos 8 550880 (60' · DDD) Recorded 1993. Texts and translations included Ⓢ

Listening to this carefully crafted selection, one is struck by the flexibility of a style that accom-modates so many distinctive temperaments – the verve of Janequin, the suavity of Sermisy, the gravity of Gombert. It's a democratic genre in the truest sense, appealing to the great (Josquin and Lassus) while permitting lesser figures to shine as well. The term 'democratic' also describes the *chanson*'s appeal, then as now: here are some of the most beguiling tunes of any period. To call these performances unobtrusive is to do them no injustice. The Scholars of Lon-don capture the wistful elegance of the courtlier pieces – for example, Le Jeune's *Ce n'est que fiel*. In some of the more scurrilous songs there's a Gallic rambunctiousness but at times the tem-pos are a shade too brisk for comfort, and the choice of pitch-standard in Janequin's famous *Chant des oiseaux* (sung here in its through-com-posed version) sets a strain on the singers' accus-tomed agility. But such details merely affect the odd piece. This is a disc that gives great pleas-ure: like ephemera trapped in amber, the music in this collection bears modest yet touching tes-timony to a period that produced much 'great' music. Its smaller creations are no less admirable.

Andreas Scholl   *countertenor*

English Folksongs and Lute Songs
Anonymous King Henry. Kemp's jig. Go from my window **Campion** I care not for these ladies. My love hath vow'd. My sweetest Lesbia **Dowland** The First Booke of Songs or Ayres – Can she excuse my wrongs?; All ye, whom love or fortune. The Second Booke of Songs or Ayres – I saw my Lady weepe; Flow my teares fall from your springs; Sorrow sorrow stay, lend true repentant tears. The Third and Last Booke of Songs or Ayres – Behold a wonder heere; Me, me and none but me; Say, loue, if euer thou did'st find. The Lady Russell's pavan. Go from my window **Traditional** The three ravens. O waly, waly. I will give my love an apple. Barbara Allen. Lord Rendall
Andreas Scholl *counterten* **Andreas Martin** *lte*
Harmonia Mundi HMC90 1603 (69' · DDD) Texts included Ⓕ

'Interval' isn't a word that has ever been inserted into a song recital on CD, but it would be quite a good idea if it were. In this instance the stop-ping-point hardly needs to be marked, as it's so natural and obvious; and that's one of the many attractions of this well-designed programme. A group of songs by Dowland, followed by a piece for lute, makes a substantial first section; then come two folk-songs, another couple by 'Anon.' and a lively, well-contrasted selection of songs by Campion. The second half starts with more Dowland, a satisfyingly representative sequence constituting the heart of the programme, with more folk-songs to conclude. The mixture is a charming one and delightfully well ordered.

The performances are equally pleasing. Perhaps it's inevitable that an English listener should still think of Alfred Deller in this repertoire, but here the name comes to mind also because of a distinct similarity of timbre. At the resonant centre of Scholl's voice is a passage of lower middle notes where the vibrancy is strong and rich in a way very comparable to Deller's. Stylistically, on the other hand, Scholl has developed an art that's quite independent of his great original: his manner is more forthright, less responsive to the spiritual intensity of *Sorrow sorrow stay*, though still capable of introducing that 'poisoned' intonation which Deller and his successors would bring to *All ye, whom love or fortune hath betrayed*. As regards balance, the lute is placed as the accompanying instrument rather than as one of an equal, intimate partnership; still, all is clear, and the lute solos are played with fine technical skill.

Sequentia

Edda – Myths from medieval Iceland

Baldur's Dreams. The End of the Gods. Havamal – Odin's Rune-verses. In Memory of Baldur. The Song of Fire and Ice. The Song of the Mill. The Tale of Thrym. Völuspa I-III, 'The Prophecy of the Sybil'
Sequentia (Barbara Thornton, Lena Susanne Norin *vocs* Elizabeth Gaver *vn* Benjamin Bagby *voc/lyre*)
Deutsche Harmonia Mundi 05472 77381-2
(77' · DDD)   Ⓕ**O**

Sequentia has amazed and delighted even native Icelanders with the curiosity, imagination and dedication with which it has been bringing to life some of the island's earliest music. The Cologne-based Sequentia, specialists in the northern European oral song tradition, have worked painstakingly on Iceland's great store of *rímur* – the medieval sung poetry, possibly related to the early *chanson de geste*, and whose strains can still be detected in children's playground songs in Reykjavík today. Sequentia has applied its research into the performance of *rímur* to re-creating sung texts from the *Elder* or *Poetic Edda*. We have no way of knowing how this music really did sound; but listening to Benjamin Bagby and his colleagues, you'll find yourself compelled by the vigour, eloquence and integrity of their own re-created authenticity. Isolation has at least ensured that living Icelandic offers pretty good indications for the pronunciation of Old Norse – and Bagby has listened with a keen ear. The late Barbara Thornton's copper-bright soprano is heard alone and with her colleagues in three 'panels' from the apocalyptic *Prophecy of the Sybil*, 'Völuspá'. They form the real set-pieces of this recital. In between, spirited fiddle pieces are played by Elizabeth Gaver; Bagby gives a virtuoso performance of *The Tale of Thrym*; and the voices entwine in the haunting *In Memory of Baldur*. It's a wonderful disc.

Singphoniker

Officium

Anonymous Officium Beatae Mariae Virginis.
Ad Vesperas. In Conceptione Beatae Mariae Virginis
Singphoniker / Godehard Joppich
Glissando 779007-2 (75' · DDD) Texts and translations
included   Ⓕ**O**

Don't let the jokey name fool you: these gentlemen are serious about their plainchant. Directed by the scholar Godehard Joppich, these six German singers present an interpretation of plainchant very different from the more speculative attitudes of such ensembles as the French Organum and the Spanish Alia Musica. While they describe their approach as one of 'scholarly reinterpretation', they avoid the ornaments and embellishments favoured by their more experimental counterparts. Some may see it as a more conservative approach, but the result is very satisfying. That's partly to do with the sound quality and recording, both of which are full-bodied and solid. Clearly these are professional singers and not monks, but there's none of the 'churchy' tameness that too often bedevils plainchant performances.

Another positive aspect is the programming, which reveals aspects of liturgical structure in a way that makes musical sense to a modern listener: thus the main item here is the full Marian Vespers. Each of the five psalms is coupled with its antiphon, which both precedes and follows the psalm itself. In the source used here (a late 14th- or early 15th-century manuscript from Hamburg), all five antiphons are drawn from the *Song of Solomon*, which imparts a satisfying sense of coherence and of – dare one use the word? – logic.

The series also includes two of the most famous Marian pieces, the *Regina celi* and *Alma redemptoris mater*. Presented as an unbroken sequence of continuous music, the 'experience' of plainsong has an aesthetic impact which popular plainchant compilations simply can't match. Following the full Vespers is a selection from the rhymed office of another Hamburg manuscript from the late 15th century. So many plain-chant interpretations inserted into liturgical reconstructions are simply bland, however these give unalloyed pleasure to the listener. It's a pity that Joppich's insert-notes don't spell out his conception of performance. To the knowledgeable audience which such a recording clearly deserves to attract, the continuing debate over plainchant interpretation would surely be worth pursuing.

The Sixteen

Music for Monarchs and Magnates

Byrd Deus, venerunt gentes **Gibbons** Great King of Gods. O all true faithful hearts **Tallis** Spem in alium. Te Deum. Sing and glorify heaven's high majesty **Tomkins** Be strong and of a good courage. Know you not. O God, the heathen are come

The Sixteen / Harry Christophers
Coro CD/SACD hybrid ⊛ CORSACD16016
(72' · DDD). Texts and translations included ⓕ

This CD was planned as a bumper recording for The Sixteen's Siver Jubilee. Their numbers were augmented for Tallis's 40-part motet, and a further 20 instrumentalists, sackbutts and cornetts, viols and organ brought in. The monarchs and magnates of the title were chiefly James I and his eldest son, Henry, though the time-scale takes us back to Elizabethan times, and forward to the Civil War.

Spem in alium introduces the programme (with top As much in evidence) and its contrafactum *Sing and glorify* (only up to Gs this time) brings it to a close. There is much variety in between, with Byrd's subtle use of several verses of a Latin psalm in *Deus venerunt gentes* to highlight and mourn the execution in 1581 of Edmund Campion, followed by *Know you not* by Thomas Tomkins, a moving English verse anthem lamenting the death of Prince Henry in 1612, with parts added by Harry Christophers for sackbutts and cornetts. These splendid instruments make their appearance in several items, notably in *Great King of Gods* by Orlando Gibbons, sung during James I's state progress to Edinburgh in 1617. A highlight is *O God, the heathen are come*, newly reconstructed by John Milsom and brilliantly sung with accompaniment of viols.

Surround sound is the perfect vehicle for *Spem*, although all these pieces profit by its enhanced spatial definition. Not as transparent as some SACD recordings, it is nevertheless most impressive. *Spem* was recorded with the performers circling the microphones (surround sound in every sense). Its 1610 revival, heard here with instruments and two chamber organs as well as voices, is quite overwhelming – with glorious textures and 'weight'.

Les Voix Humaines

The Spirite of Musicke
Coprario Songs of Mourning – 'Tis now dead night; To the World **A Ferrabosco II** Like hermit poore. So Beautie on the waters stood (all arr Little/Napper) **Hume** Captaine Humes Poeticall Musicke – What greater grief; Sweet ayre; Cease leaden slumber. The First Part of Ayres – Touch me sweetly; The Spirite of Musicke **Jenkins** Suite in A minor **C Simpson** Divisions on a Ground – F; G
Suzie Le Blanc sop **Les Voix Humaines** (Susie Napper, Margaret Little vas da gamba)
ATMA ACD22136 (63' · DDD) Texts included ⓕ

Over the years they have been playing together as Les Voix Humaines, the bass viol players Susie Napper and Margaret Little have developed a command of their repertory and a rapport that few other ensembles have approached. They express themselves clearly as individuals but play together with perfect precision. In Tobias Hume's flirtatious *Touch me sweetly* they banter playfully, their control of articulation and dynamics superb; so too in Hume's evocation of a bandora by two bass viols in *The Spirite of Musicke*. To Simpson's divisions for two bass viols they bring a depth of expression not often heard, but they seem especially in their element in John Jenkins's sublimely crafted Suite in A minor. Not content with the existing music for their instruments, they have taken inspiration from Hume, who composed the deeply affecting *Cease leaden slumber* and *What greater grief* for voice and two bass viols, and arranged the lute accompaniment of songs by the Jacobean violists Giovanni Coprario and Alfonso Ferrabosco II for two viols. The result is most often ravishing, although the melancholic simplicity of the vocal line of Coprario's *'Tis now dead night* is overpowered by busy viols. Elsewhere, in Coprario's *To the World* and Ferrabosco's *So Beautie on the waters stood*, their arrangements are more successful. They are joined on this recording by Suzie Le Blanc whose clear, bell-like upper register suits the music ideally. She seems completely at one with the texts and their settings, investing just the right emotional weight. The viol players rely perhaps too much for this repertory on a swelled bow stroke which can add too much colour to a delicate accompaniment or unsteady a dance. All in all, though, this is an appealing recording which you'll want to listen to again and again.

THE CLASSICAL
GOOD
CD&DVD
GUIDE
2006

COMPOSERS

Adams

El Niño
Dawn Upshaw sop **Lorraine Hunt Lieberson** mez
Willard White bar **Maîtrise de Paris Children's
Choir; London Voices; Theatre of Voices;
Deutsches Symphony Orchestra, Berlin / Kent
Nagano** Stage director **Peter Sellars** Video director
Peter Maniura
ArtHaus DVD 100 220 (147' · 16:9 · 2.0 · 0) Includes
'Making Of' documentary. Notes included   Ⓕ⊙

'An opera by John Adams' says the packaging. Not quite. This is the composer's multi-cultural, post-feminist, quasi-minimalist take on Handel's *Messiah*, drawing on sources ranging from the pre-Christian prophets to 20th-century Hispanic women writers. While designed to allow fully staged productions, the concept and its musical realisation bring us closer to oratorio. Adams's musical language is predictably inclusive. There's a prominent role for three Brittenish countertenors, Broadway and popular idioms are more or less willingly embraced, and the use of repetition is sometimes reminiscent of Philip Glass in his heyday. *El Niño's* sound world is delicate and lustrous, and, although Part 1 can seem a mite static with a surfeit of vocal recitative, there are fewer longueurs in Part 2. If not perhaps the unqualified masterpiece acclaimed by some critics, this is an effective and often truly affecting score: derivative, to be sure, yet obstinately fresh.

The performance as such is pretty much beyond criticism. The main characters are on top form, combining absolute vocal assurance with dramatic flair – and none more so than Lorraine Hunt Lieberson. The crisp DVD images certainly help explain the sensational impact of the European première, a multimedia extravaganza from Peter Sellars' top drawer in which dance and film interact quirkily with the

exertions of chorus and soloists. If you haven't yet acquired a player, the remarkable success of *El Niño* is as good a reason as any to take the plunge. Strongly recommended.

The Death of Klinghoffer
Sanford Sylvan bar Klinghoffer **Christopher
Maltman** bar Captain **Yvonne Howard** mez Marilyn
Klinghoffer **Tom Randle** ten Molqi **Kamel Boutros**
bar Mamoud **Leigh Melrose** bar Rambo **Emil Marwa**
act Omar (sung by **Susan Bickley** mez) **London
Symphony Chorus and Orchestra / John Adams**
Video director **Penny Woolcock**
Decca DVD 074 189-9 (166' · DDD; NTSC · 16:9 ·
PCM stereo & 5.1 · 0) Includes a 'Making of…'
documentary   Ⓕ

Klinghoffer has yet to be performed in the US, and Penny Woolcock's live-action film, shot on location, won't do much to quieten the controversies that have kept it off the stage. She fleshes out the opera's philosophies, inasmuch as the composer conducted and discussed production details with Woolcock, and was thereby at least complicit in the choice of images. *Klinghoffer* is more an oratorio than an opera, and she uses the choruses and non-dramatic stretches to fill out the characters with flashbacks to 1940s Palestine and even historical footage of Nazi Germany.

This is Adams's slowest stage piece, and Woolcock's close, hand-held camerawork tests severely the singers' acting, particularly when they aren't singing. The singers were actually recorded live during the on-location filming, after the orchestra was recorded. The payoff is immense: synchronisation is perfect, and what we hear goes believably with what we see. Even in these trying circumstances, the vocalism and acting are outstanding.

So, does the film show librettist Alice Goodman and stage director Peter Sellars's scenario to be anti-Semitic and sympathetic to terrorism, as some of its American critics claim? The film does round out the terrorists' characters, but there's a balanced portrayal, showing the good and the bad of both Jews and Palestinians. The terrorists show regret after the killing, but there is also a stoning where a Palestinian mob gets drunk on its own brutality. Some of the Jewish tourists are parodies early on, but Marilyn Klinghoffer comes to take on towering dignity and strength. Most of those who've criticised the politics are responding to what they want to see in the opera than what's actually there.

Woolcock has turned *Klinghoffer* into a fairly gripping visual drama; but her success shows up the musical deficiencies: encountered as an opera rather than a film, it may be of no more than topical interest.

Albéniz

Merlin
David Wilson-Johnson bar Merlin **Eva Marton** sop
Morgan le Fay **Stuart Skelton** ten King Arthur **Carol**

Vaness *sop* Nivian **Ángel Ódena** *bar* Mordred **Victor Garcia Sierra** *bass* King Lot of Orkney **Ángel Rodriguez** *ten* Gawain **Juan Tomás Martinez** *bar* Sir Ector de Maris **Federico Gallar** *bar* Sir Pellinore **Eduardo Santamaria** *ten* Kay **Stephen Morscheck** *bass* Archbishop of Canterbury **Madrid Community Children's Choir Madrid Symphony Chorus and Orchestra** / José De Eusebio *Stage director* **John Dew** *Video director* **Toni Bargalló**
BBC/Opus Arte ② 𝐃𝐕𝐃 OA0888D (184' · 16:9 · 2.0 & 5.1 · 0) Recorded live at the Teatro Real, Madrid, 9 June 2003. Includes interviews with José de Eusebio, Eva Marton and David Wilson-Johnson. Notes included Ⓕ ●

Decca's release of its outstanding recording of Albéniz's *Merlin* marked a turning-point in our appreciation of this Spanish composer, best known for his colourful nationalistic piano music. José de Eusebio, conductor and force behind that project, followed it with a full staging of the opera in Madrid; this DVD is the result.

The staging certainly adds to one's involvement. When you can see the young Arthur drawing Excalibur from the stone, the Wagnerian echoes become clearer, even if Albéniz is much more diatonic. John Dew's direction sets out the story clearly, and the stylised sets and costumes are medieval enough to create the right atmosphere, but with a touch of science fiction.

Though the cast isn't as starry as that on disc (with Plácido Domingo as King Arthur), there's obvious benefit in having English speakers in three of the principal parts, David Wilson-Johnson commanding and noble as Merlin, with the American tenor, Stuart Skelton as Arthur, powerful rather than subtle, and Carol Vaness, also American, as Nivian. The big snag is the singer who might have been counted the star, Eva Marton as the evil Morgan le Fay. The unsteadiness of her voice, so extreme that one can hardly tell what pitch she's aiming at, may convey the wickedness of the character. She acts convincingly, but is painful on the ear. Ángel Odena characterises her son Mordred well but also has bouts of unsteadiness; Victor Garcia Sierra, as King Lot of Orkney, is another wobbler.

Happily, the chorus work is first-rate, and Eusebio draws warmly committed playing from the Madrid Symphony Orchestra. With so rare an opera it's a pity that the booklet contains no synopsis, though there's compensation in having English subtitles available, even if that underlines the banality and incomprehensibility of the doggerel verses of Francis Burdett Money-Coutts's libretto. Outweighing any flaws, though, what shines out is the richness and variety of Albéniz's musical inspiration.

JS Bach

Das wohltemperierte Klavier, BWV846-893 – Book 1: Nos 1-12[a]; Nos 13-24[b]; Book 2: Nos 1-12[c]; Nos 13-24[d]
[a]**Andrei Gavrilov**, [b]**Joanna MacGregor**, [c]**Nikolai Demidenko**, [d]**Angela Hewitt** *Video directors*

[ab]**Karen Whiteside**, [cd]**Peter Mumford**
Euroarts ② 𝐃𝐕𝐃 205 0309 (260' · 16:9 · PCM stereo & 5.1 · 0) Ⓕ

In February 2000 BBC Wales and Euroarts Music co-produced Bach's complete *Well-Tempered Clavier* for television, dividing the work between four very different pianists filmed in four visually distinct venues. Rather than impart a concert performance continuity between the pieces, the directors treat each Prelude and Fugue as a separate entity in terms of lighting, camera angles, placement of the piano, extramusical imagery (kept to a minimum), as well as the pianists' wardrobe and hairstyles.

Collectors familiar with Andrei Gavrilov's romantically tinged, pianistic Bach *French* Suites won't register much surprise as to how he treats Book 1's first 12 Preludes and Fugues. Contrapuntal rigour takes a back seat to melodic nuance and tone colour in his languid, slightly sedate way. It's interesting how his pianism contrasts with the stark visual impact of Walsall's Art Gallery. Conversely, the gothic, shadowy detail Whiteside conveys in Barcelona's Güell Palace differs from Joanna McGregor's leaner propulsion throughout the rest of Book 1.

While she and Gavrilov use the printed score, Nikolai Demidenko and Angela Hewitt play Book 2 from memory. The plangent clarity of Demidenko's Fazioli concert grand stands out in Nos 1-12 (the other pianists perform on Steinways). Several tempo choices are wayward, such as an over-fast and flippant F minor Prelude. However, his linear clarity in the difficult-to-balance C sharp major Prelude and rhythmic swagger in the D major Prelude greatly impress.

Of the four pianists, Angela Hewitt commands the widest variety of articulations and inner dynamics, together with her finely honed ability to follow Bach's lines through to their final destination without sounding the least bit studied. Cogent examples include the long-lined refinement of the G sharp minor Prelude and Fugue, the G major Prelude's lilting, conversational trajectory, and the B major Prelude's delicate yet firmly centred fingerwork. In the B flat minor Prelude the camera zooms in on Hewitt from above, allowing one to observe how she achieves her superior *legato* through fingers and hand balance alone. Aside from optional titles, the menu offers no bells and whistles to supplement the programme, but the audio engineering boasts ample warmth and presence.

St John Passion, BWV245
Gerd Türk *ten* Evangelist **Stephen MacLeod** *bass* Christus **Midori Suzuki** *sop* **Robin Blaze** *counterten* **Chiyuki Urano** *bass-bar*; **Bach Collegium Japan** / **Masaaki Suzuki** *Video director* **Shokichi Amano**
TDK 𝐃𝐕𝐃 DV-BAJPN (120' · 16:9 · 2.0 · 0) Ⓕ

With his outstanding series of choral recordings for BIS, Masaaki Suzuki has rightly established a high reputation for stylish interpretations of Bach. As he explains in a brief interview which comes as a supplement on this DVD, he had intensive training in period performance in Holland. Certainly, his vigour and sensitivity in Bach defies any idea that Japanese culture has been a barrier in authentically interpreting Bach. Suzuki recorded the *St John Passion* for BIS back in 1998. This DVD version marks a special performance recorded on the anniversary on 28 July 2000 of Bach's birth 250 years earlier. In essence the interpretation remains the same, with fresh, light textures and generally brisk speeds which yet allow for depth of feeling, and the sense of occasion is irresistible.

Gerd Türk gives an achingly beautiful performance, with his profound involvement all the more evident when seen as well as heard. Türk also sings the tenor arias, and the other soloists also have double roles, singing in the 16-strong choir before stepping forward when needed as soloists: Stephen MacLeod singing Christus as well as the bass arias, Chiyuki Urano singing Pilate and other incidental solos, Robin Blaze a superb alto soloist and the ravishing Midori Suzuki in the two soprano arias.

First-rate sound too. The leaflet offers minimal information and no text, though one can plumb into subtitles, either the original German or the English translation, but not both together.

Beethoven

Fidelio
Gabriela Beňačková *sop* Leonore **Josef Protschka** *ten* Florestan **Monte Pederson** *bar* Don Pizarro **Robert Lloyd** *bass* Rocco **Marie McLaughlin** *sop* Marzelline **Neill Archer** *ten* Jaquino **Hans Tschammer** *bass-bar* Don Fernando **Lynton Atkinson** *ten* First Prisoner **Mark Beesley** *bar* Second Prisoner **Royal Opera House Chorus and Orchestra, Covent Garden** / **Christoph von Dohnányi** *Video director* **Derek Bailey** *Stage director* **Adolf Dresen**
ArtHaus Musik 💿 100 074 (129' · Regions 2 & 5) Ⓕ⊙

'Triumph! Triumph! Triumph!' as nasty Pizarro exultantly cries. He's in for a disappointment, of course. Not so the listener and viewer of this performance, which is caught in fine sound and skilfully filmed. Pizarro will, for instance, have no place in the great festival of light that is the finale. Here the rejoicing is so powerful that we switch off the DVD player and go to bed with the surge and sequence of inspired creation fully in possession, convinced that in the whole of opera there's nothing to match it. That's the sign of a great *Fidelio*, and it means that, throughout, the proportions, structure and balance of the work have been rendered with clarity and conviction. That in turn means that the opening scene – the Marzelline-Jaquino duet and the solos which might seem to be from some other opera – has been integrated, so that the work is a journey from light into the blackest tunnel and out again into an infinitely greater light.

A prime contribution to the success of this process is made by the portrayal of Rocco, the gaoler. Instead of the bumbling, coarse-grained character of convention, Robert Lloyd presents a full human being, a man with a rueful-realistic twinkle, and above all a loving father. This of itself guards against the alien introduction of comic opera, and helps to fashion the role so that even here our concern is with real humanity. Leonore is the radiant Beňačková, and she presents a problem. The camera reveals unsparingly a disguise which just possibly might pass in the theatre. It says much for her singing, and for something in the spirit of her performance, that the willing suspension of disbelief can prevail as well as it does. In all other respects (except perhaps in the pointless speculation as to why the date of these events should have been advanced by about a century) the visual element satisfies well; and musically, under Dohnányi's direction, this is a memorable and moving *Fidelio*.

Fidelio
Camilla Nylund *sop* Leonore **Jonas Kaufmann** *ten* Florestan **Alfred Muff** *bass* Don Pizarro **László Polgár** *bass* Rocco **Elizabeth Magnuson** *sop* Marzelline **Christoph Strehl** *ten* Jaquino **Günther Groissböck** *bass* Don Fernando **Bogusław Bidzinski** *ten* First Prisoner **Gabriel Bermúdez** *bass* Second Prisoner **Zurich Opera House Chorus and Orchestra** / **Nikolaus Harnoncourt** *Stage director* **Jürgen Flimm** *Video director* **Felix Breisach**
TDK 💿 DV-OPFID (134' · 16:9 · PCM stereo, 5.1 & DTS 5.1 · 0). Recorded live at the Opernhaus, Zürich, 15 February 2004 Ⓕ

Harnoncourt's predominantly light but dramatic reading harks back to the 18th century rather than forward to the 19th, with romantic feeling at a premium. The orchestra foretells the rest in its crisply accented rhythms, clean sound and sense of the impending drama: they play splendidly. However, the thrust of Beethoven's universal message sometimes goes missing by comparison with the Dohnányi version on DVD from Covent Garden.

The simple, somewhat geometric sets, sensitively lit, house a direction that's sometimes fussy in detail. Jürgen Flimm offers a fairly minimalist production concentrating on the characters of the principals. Marzelline (the bright-voiced Elizabeth Magnuson) and Jaquino are preparing guns and ammunition for the troops. She is bossy, he slightly sadistic. By contrast, Rocco – a wonderfully moving, warm and eloquent performance from László Polgár – is kindly, cowed by his surroundings, and alert to every nuance of feeling in those around him. His body language and his eyes tell us everything about the jailer's torment.

Leonore, in the arresting figure of Camilla Nylund, is slim and appealing, truly believable as a young man. Her singing, in the modern way, is lighter than one would have expected of yore. Every note is well placed, united into a real *legato* projected on a compact, firm tone. Jonas

Kaufmann's Florestan, also a more youthful portrayal than usual, sings with accuracy and feeling, though he may find more in the words and notes in years to come. He and Nylund make 'O namenlose Freude', taken at an extraordinarily slow tempo, more an inward expression of release than the usual excited one. Alfred Muff's Pizarro, more conventional, is always a hateful presence, as he should be.

The sound could be a bit more immediate; the video direction is for the most part perceptive.

Bellini

Norma

Montserrat Caballé sop Norma; **Josephine Veasey** sop Adalgisa **Jon Vickers** ten Pollione **Agostino Ferrin** bass Oroveso **Gino Sinimberghi** ten Flavio **Marisa Zotti** mez Clotilde **Teatro Regio di Torino Chorus and Orchestra / Giuseppe Patanè** Stage director **Sandro Sequi** Video director **Pierre Jourdan**
Hardy Classic Video 📀 HCD4003 (161' · 4:3 · 1.0 · 0)
Recorded live 1974   Ⓕ**OOO**

Here in Orange, France, on a wind-swept, night in 1974, they had great-ness itself. Pierre Jourdan's film of the event is a priceless document, first of all, in the history of the opera. Stage-settings of *Norma* are usually hopeless: an offence to the eye, a chafing confutation of the spirit by gross matter. The ancient Roman amphitheatre is at any rate wor-thy and appropriate, and the Mistral, which threatened to close down the whole show and turn away an audience estimated at 10,000, adds a fine reminder of the power of Nature as it sets the druidical robes billowing and attacks the microphones.

The vastness of the stage provides a further challenge to the man in charge, and although conductor Giuseppe Patanè's star is somewhat eclipsed in the general view of things, he deserves congratulation for two contrary achievements – holding the ensemble together and giving the soloists freedom. But it's their night, and particularly Caballé's. She called it the greatest single performance of her career. In certain passages it's hard to think of any voice we've known that could sound more lovely; but, more than that, the great role is sung and acted with such well-founded assurance that for once it fulfils its own legend, the embodiment of musical-dramatic sublimity in 19th-century opera. Of the others in the cast it must for now suffice to say that they're worthy partners.

Berg

Wozzeck

Franz Grundheber bar Wozzeck **Hildegard Behrens** sop Marie **Walter Raffeiner** ten Drum Major **Philip Langridge** ten Andres **Heinz Zednik** ten Captain **Aage Haugland** bass Doctor **Anna Gonda** contr Margret **Alfred Sramek** bass Apprentice I

Alexander Maly bar Apprentice II **Peter Jelosits** ten Madman **Vienna State Opera Chorus and Orchestra / Claudio Abbado**
Video director **Brian Large** Stage director **Adolf Dresen**
ArtHaus Musik 📀 100 256 (97' · 4:3, 2.0 · 2 & 5)   Ⓕ

Coarse conducting and highly approximate singing have been so readily excused in 'difficult' idioms such as Wozzeck's that they became almost expected, obscuring the music's beauty and emotional intensity. Not so, in this welcome DVD appearance of an appropriately Viennese production long unavailable except on laserdisc. Abbado recognises the late Romantic lyricism that unifies the score, but emphasises translu-cent textures rather than Teutonic density, while still unleashing Berg's nascent Expres-sionist snarls with vividly theatrical force. The singers, too, treat the vocal line with greater respect than was once the norm, especially Grundheber's memorable Wozzeck. Behrens sings Marie's anguished, tender lines with intense beauty and keen characterisation, sug-gesting a sluttishness almost sanctified by her capacity for love. Zednik's steely-toned, neu-rotic Captain becomes unusually sinister, a sort of hellish Laurel to the late Aage Haugland's Hardy. Adolf Dresen, sometimes a dull pro-ducer, here creates a quite effective world whose derelict interiors and expansively desolate marshlands reflect its alienation of human feel-ing. Sliding sets keep the short scenes moving crisply, but lowering the curtain during inter-ludes leaves Brian Large's excellent visual direc-tion with only conductor and orchestra, to the detriment of tension. Striking and involving none the less, with no competition on DVD.

Lulu

Christine Schäfer sop Lulu **Wolfgang Schöne** bar Dr Schön, Jack the Ripper **David Kuebler** ten Alwa **Kathryn Harries** mez Countess Geschwitz **Stephan Drakulich** ten Painter, Negro **Norman Bailey** bass Schigolch **Jonathan Veira** bass Professor of Medicine, Banker, Theatre Manager **Donald Maxwell** bass Animal tamer, Athlete **Neil Jenkins** ten Prince, Manservant, Marquis **Patricia Bardon** contr Dresser, High-School Boy, Groom **London Philharmonic Orchestra / Sir Andrew Davis** Stage director **Graham Vick** Video director **Humphrey Burton**
Warner Music Vision/NVC Arts 📀 0630 15533-2 (183' · NTSC · 4:3 · PCM stereo · 2-6)   Ⓕ**OO**

Warner has reissued Glyndebourne's 1996 stag-ing of all three acts of *Lulu*, a much-lauded affair that won the *Gramophone* Award for Best Video in 1997. Graham Vick's direction is admirable not only for what it achieves but also for what it avoids. With its redbrick interior, upward-curv-ing staircase and minimal furnishings, the stage-set has a spartan air, enlivened by a central hole in the floor through which characters disappear and emerge according to the needs of the drama. Costumes have a generalised present-day feel, and the recourse to mobile phones was a pre-scient touch. Crucially, this staging doesn't encumber the opera with a specious extra-musical concept or smother it with designer cleverness. The filmed interlude in Act 2 is both a pragmatic realisation of Berg's concept and faithful to the spirit of his intentions: a triumph of dramatic common sense.

Schäfer's Lulu is the best sung and most beau-tifully voiced yet recorded: diffident, even dis-tanced at the outset, yet assuredly in control as she closes down Dr Schön's emotional space at the end of Act 1 and evincing real expressive pain at her degradation in Acts 2 and 3. Wolf-gang Schöne has the right hollow authority for Dr Schön, and brings an appropriately Mr Hyde-like demeanour to his Jack the Ripper *alter ego*, while David Kuebler's fantasising Alwa is the most complete rendition since Kenneth Riegel's for Boulez. Aloof in her initial emo-tional exchanges, Kathryn Harries goes on to to find quiet strength and nobility in Countess Geschwitz. Stephan Drakulich's seedy-looking Painter is unusually accurate, Donald Maxwell's Athlete over-acted to the point of caricature, while Norman Bailey's Schigolch has a wiliness that makes the part more substantial than usual.

Davis conducts with a sure awareness of short-term incident and long-term tension. His sense of dramatic pace makes the best case yet for the first scene of Act 3, its mosaic-like succession of exchanges throwing the the second scene's seamless intensity into greater relief. Friedrich Cerha's realisation of this act has come in for its share of criticism, but makes for a musical and dramatic whole such as Berg is unlikely to have altered appreciably had he lived to complete the work.

As directed for video, Humphrey Burton goes to town on facial asides and long-range stares. The picture reproduces with the expected sharpness of focus, though the sound throws the orchestra a little too far forward – giving voices a slightly distanced, though never unfocused quality. Subtitles are clear and to the point, and the 33 chapter selections well-placed for ease of access. On DVD this performance is now a clear first choice.

Berlioz

La-damnation de Faust, Op 24
Vesselina Kasarova *mez* **Paul Groves** *ten* **Willard White** *bass* **Andreas Macco** *bass* San Sebastian People's Choral Society; Tölz Boys' Choir; Staatskapelle Berlin / **Sylvain Cambreling** *Stage directors* **Alex Olle, Carlos Pedrissa** *Video director* **Alexandre Tarta**
ArtHaus Musik ▬ 100 003 (146' · DDD)   Ⓕ**OOO**

This production was the sensation of the 1999 Salzburg Festival, and this riveting DVD captures most of the excitement that must have been felt at the time in the evocative Felsenreitschule. The staging is a joint venture. The spectacular scenic realisa-tion of Berlioz's 'Légende dramatique' origi-nated with the Spanish theatre troupe La Fura dels Baus; the staging itself is the work of Olle and Pedrissa. The sets and costumes were con-ceived by the Spanish sculptor Jaume Piensa.

The results were described in the press as 'extreme theatre' – and one can see why when viewing the virtuoso treatment of the vast stage area. It's dominated by a transparent cylinder which serves all sorts of purposes, depicting in particular the soul-searching struggles of Faust and Méphistophélès; while the complex choral movements and an elaborate lighting plot are all carried out without a hint of a hitch.

The producer certainly managed to inspire all the participants to heights of interpretative skill. Cambreling and the Berlin Staatskapelle per-form with discipline and fire, wanting only that extra dedicated vision evinced by Colin Davis and the LSO on CD. Kasarova and Willard White, stage beings to their fingertips, sing and act with total conviction. Kasarova is the vulner-able, insecure, beautiful Marguerite to the life, every gesture and facial expression supporting her intense reading of the glorious music Berlioz wrote for her. Her vision of the great Romance is idiosyncratic to say the least, but a triumph of erotic communication on its own account, a cross between Callas and Ewing at their most individual. White is commanding throughout – at once demonic, cynical, relaxed and satirical, his huge voice absolutely in command of the role. Groves isn't quite on his colleagues' level of accomplishment, but acts and sings with the awe and sense of identity-seeking which this production requires of its Faust. The sound, as on most DVDs, is exemplary. Highly recom-mended.

Les Troyens
Susan Graham *mez* Dido **Gregory Kunde** *ten* Aeneas **Anna Caterina Antonacci** *sop* Cassandra **Ludovic Tezier** *bar* Choroebus **Renata Pokupic** *contr* Anna **Laurent Naouri** *bass* Narbal **Nicolas Testé** *bass* Pantheus **Stéphanie d'Oustrac** *mez* Ascanius **Mark Padmore** *ten* Iopas **Topi Lehtipuu** *ten* Hylas, Helenus **Monteverdi Choir; Théâtre du Châtelet Chorus, Paris; Orchestre Révolutionnaire et Romantique / Sir John Eliot Gardiner** *Stage director* **Yannis Kokkos** *Video director* **Peter Maniura**
BBC/Opus Arte ③ ▬ OA0900D (312' · NTSC · S/s/N · 16:9 · PCM Stereo, DTS 5.1 · 0) Recorded live. Includes documentary, cast gallery   Ⓕ**OO**

Les Troyens hasn't fared well on DVD, but this superb authentic-instrument performance of October 2003 from the Théâtre du Châtelet, Paris, equals Sir Colin Davis's pioneering origi-nal. Orchestrally it's everything we've come to expect from Gardiner's Berlioz, his tempi swift and dynamic, sharing the composer's delight in complex rhythmic interplay, yet always pro-pelling the drama. Passages like Andromache's entrance and Hector's ghost nevertheless have their proper gravitas and sombre hues against the brighter shades of Carthage. Colour is the great gift of the period instruments, revealing a wide range of sonorities, and creating a sense of freshness and discovery. The effect is sometimes rawer, sometimes more classical, but almost always more complex and dramatic than the homogenised modern sound.

Gardiner's singers, too, could hardly be more committed. Anna Caterina Antonacci is a fiery Cassandra, superbly classical-looking, so wrung and tormented that some moments of strain scarcely matter. Gregory Kunde tackles Aeneas with ringing tone, looks and acts pretty well, and brings a welcome *bel canto* touch to the gorgeous duet. Susan Graham, though, needs no caveats: a radiant Dido, queenly yet youthful, lyrical and lighter-toned than Janet Baker, but in her final despair no less tragically moving. Other roles are generally excellent. The mostly youthful chorus sounds marvellous, and is a constant force in Yannis Kokkos's moderately modern production.

The stage is plain and bare, capped by a reflector in which most of the décor appears: an Italian Renaissance cityscape for Troy, and the Horse only as a menacing head. Carthage is a classical vision of white walls and blue sea with stylised ships. The Trojans wear the inescapable greatcoats the brutal Greeks, inevitably, American combat gear, and the Carthaginians vaguely North African whites and pastels. This is a mostly straightforward, lively staging which lets characters and drama speak for themselves, and so works well on screen. The magnificent high-definition recording does it ample sonic and visual justice.

For anyone who loves *Les Troyens*, this is a revelatory and essential performance.

Bernstein

West Side Story – The Making of the Recording
Kiri Te Kanawa *sop* Tatiana Troyanos *mez* José Carreras *ten* Kurt Ollman *bar* orchestra and chorus / Leonard Bernstein *Film director* Christopher Swann
DG **DVD** 073 017-9GH (89' · NTSC · 4:3 · 2.0 · 0)
Filmed during the recording sessions in 1984 ⓕⓞ

This is the famous – or notorious – documentary about the 'operatic' recording of Bernstein's best-loved work, a considerable popular and critical success that overrode the rather silly crossover controversy it aroused. Seeing it again in this excellent DVD transfer emphasises both the strengths and weaknesses of Bernstein's approach. Unquestionably the music is fine enough to stand the weight of the operatic treatment, and it's a pleasure to watch him rejuvenated by rediscovering his own score. However, the visual element shows that, despite his denials, even the youngest and freshest trained voices do add an extra layer of artificiality. Kurt Ollmann and the other Jets sound altogether too mannered, for all the heavy accents, and the chattering teenyboppers more like housewives.

Te Kanawa, with her popular background, is at least at home in the idiom, and her songs benefit from the richer colour and *legato*; but Troyanos, for all her authentically comic West-Sidese, sounds inescapably middle-aged and blowsy for a girlish role. And Carreras is ludicrously condemned to play the all-American boy. This miscasting causes him painful struggles with diction and tempo, especially in the fiendishly difficult 'Something's Coming!' number, and Bernstein's refusal to allow for this clearly provokes the ugly scenes in which the composer petulantly humiliates him – not his finest moment. But Carreras and the others obviously love the music so much that, while they can't obscure these handicaps, they largely transcend them. A fascinating record of a great composer/conductor.

Bizet

Carmen
Maria Ewing *mez* Carmen **Jacques Trussell** *ten* Don José **Miriam Gauci** *sop* Micaëla **Rosemary Ashe** *sop* Frasquita **Ludmilla Andrew** *sop* Mercédès **Alain Fondary** *bar* Escamillo **Emile Belcourt** *ten* Remendado **David Hamilton** *bar* Dancaïre **Rodney McCann** *bass-bar* Zuniga **Christopher Blades** *bass* Moralès **Ambrosian Opera Chorus; National Philharmonic Orchestra / Jacques Delacôte** *Stage director* **Steven Pimlott** *Video director* **Gavin Taylor**
Stax Entertainment **DVD** MAWA131 (165' · 4:3 · 5.1 · 0) Recorded live 1989 ⓕⓞⓞ

This DVD derives from a television relay from Earl's Court in June 1989, an unexpectedly successful staging in the barn-like venue. The triumph of the event was almost entirely due to Steven Pimlott's highly imaginative use of the huge space, presenting the work in the round on a large dais with a kind of moving platform surrounding it.

Maria Ewing's Carmen, as on her other two video interpretations of the role (Glyndebourne and Covent Garden, neither yet on DVD), is an earthily mesmeric, wholly sensual and elemental gypsy, conceived perfectly for her own character yet marching with Bizet's concept. She's in wonderful voice, with many subtle emphases of word and tone to bring her solos to life. Trussell is a good foil, at once fiery, vulnerable, tetchy, and he sings with a combination of plangency and power. Fondary delivers his native French and the character of Escamillo with unerringly economic strength as to the manner born. Gauci is a limpid, lyrical, properly ingenuous Micaëla.

Delacôte is a near-ideal conductor of this score, an elegant, sensitive, vibrant reading that hits all the right spots. The work is played superbly by the National Philharmonic, who are heard to far better effect here than in the original venue. The sound-enhancement occasionally produces odd effects, but they hardly detract from enjoyment of the riveting performance. Subtitles are provided, but in the last two acts they're out of synch with the action. With neither the Rosi film nor the Glyndebourne/ Peter Hall production yet available on DVD, this has the field to itself among recommendable versions.

Britten

The Turn of the Screw
Helen Field sop Governess **Menai Davies** mez Mrs Grose **Richard Greager** ten Peter Quint / Prologue **Phyllis Cannan** sop Miss Jessel **Machiko Obata** sop Flora **Samuel Linay** treb Miles **Stuttgart Radio Symphony Orchestra / Steuart Bedford** Stage director **Michael Hampe** Video director **Claus Viller** ArtHaus Musik **DVD** 100 198 (114' · 4:3 · 2.0 · 2-8) Recorded live 1990   Ⓕ

Michael Hampe clearly places the audience in the expected quandary as to whether the ghosts are 'real' or a product of the Governess's vivid imagination. The concept is underlined by Helen Field, who makes the role very much her own by her intelligent acting and fine singing of it. The young Samuel Linay could hardly be bettered as Miles, suggesting the boy's innocence and his devilment while singing purely and accurately. Menai Davies brings out all Mrs Grose's generous character and her slight befuddlement at events beyond her ken. Phyllis Cannan is at once a menacing and unearthly Miss Jessel. Richard Greager sings splendidly as Quint but rather misses out on the character's menace. The Flora, as so often with this part, looks too mature. The instrumental playing is superb. The sound balance and video direction faultless. With the only potential rival version – Petr Weigl's dubbed film, filmed outdoors or on location – not yet on DVD, this excellent issue has the field to itself.

The Turn of the Screw
Mark Padmore ten Peter Quint **Lisa Milne** sop Governess **Catrin Wyn-Davies** sop Miss Jessel **Diana Montague** sop Mrs Grose **Nicholas Kirby Johnson** treb Miles **Caroline Wise** sop Flora **City of London Sinfonia / Richard Hickox** Video director **Katie Mitchell** BBC/Opus Arte **DVD** OA0907D (117' · 16:9 · PCM stereo · 0) Extra features include Synopsis and Cast Gallery   ⒻⓄⓄⓄ

This film was much lauded when shown on BBC2. Katie Mitchell's arresting production opens up the story, taking it into the countryside and producing spooky and louring images to create the mysterious and dangerous aura of Bly, which does no harm to the intentions of Henry James and Benjamin Britten. Mitchell allows the characters' interior monologues to be heard while the singers' mouths remain closed – especially apt for the role of the Governess.

For about two-thirds of the work the director keeps within the boundaries stipulated by Britten and librettist Myfanwy Piper, making us fully aware of the ambiguities of the participants and their relationships. But in the third part she rather allows her ideas to get out of hand, the nightmarish images becoming too surreal, especially for the ghosts and the children, although she recovers in time to make the final struggle between the Governess and Quint for Miles's soul an arresting close. We're left, as we should be, uncertain at the state of the Governess's mind and the exact powers of the ghosts.

Richard Hickox commands every aspect of the tricky score, lovingly executed by members of his City of London Sinfonia, even if the balance with the singers sometimes goes awry. The cast is splendid. Nicholas Kirby Johnson as Miles achieves just the right balance between innocence and knowingness. His singing is fluent and pointed, as is that of Caroline Wise, a teenage Flora with a lively presence, expressive eyes and a malleable voice. Lisa Milne, unflatteringly garbed, is rather too confident of voice and mien as the Governess. Although she sings with her customary clarity of line and word, she doesn't suggest the nervous vulnerability of Jennifer Vyvyan, who created the role. Diana Montague is a gratifyingly sympathetic Mrs Grose, using body language to convey just the right feeling of apprehension and concern over the fate of her charges. Mark Padmore is among the best of Quints, vocally and histrionically. Catryn Wyn-Davies is a properly wild and scary Miss Jessel. All in all, this is the version to have.

Owen Wingrave
Gerald Finley bar Owen Wingrave **Peter Savidge** bar Spencer Coyle **Hilton Marlton** ten Lechmere **Josephine Barstow** sop Miss Wingrave **Anne Dawson** sop Mrs Coyle **Elizabeth Gale** sop Mrs Julian **Charlotte Hellekant** mez Kate **Martyn Hill** ten Sir Philip Wingrave **Andrew Burden** nar **Deutsches Symphony Orchestra, Berlin / Kent Nagano** Video director Margaret Williams ArtHaus Musik **DVD** 100 372 (150' · 16:9 · PCM stereo · 2 & 5) Includes 'Benjamin Britten: The Hidden Heart' – a film directed by Teresa Griffiths   ⒻⓄⓄ

Britten's penultimate opera was planned to be equally effective on television or in the opera house, but it was its first stage production at Covent Garden that made the bigger impact,. Now this film version, imaginatively directed by Margaret Williams and tautly conducted by Kent Nagano, helps swing the balance the other way.

There's almost nothing stagey about the opera here. The camera roams freely indoors and out, using cleverly executed angles to follow members of the fearsome Wingrave family at their ancestral home, and throwing in flashbacks and voice-overs wherever they might be apposite – much as one might expect of an adaptation of a literary classic. In fact, the period has been updated to the 1950s, which necessitates some minor changes to Myfanwy Piper's libretto (no need to escort the ladies to their bedchambers by candlelight any more) but this handsome version in all other respects stays close to Britten's intentions.

Gerald Finley is a tower of strength as Owen Wingrave, completely believable as the sturdy but sensitive scion of an upper-crust family. The other singers are well cast, and play expertly to the camera.

The 'special feature' on the disc, Teresa Griffiths's three-part biographical film, *Benjamin Britten: The Hidden Heart*, lasts as long as the opera. It focuses on three major works – *Peter Grimes*, the *War Requiem* and *Death in Venice* – and, while its message is somewhat diffuse and the editorial style jumps irritatingly from image to image as if afraid to let the camera come to rest, it does include a wealth of fleeting extracts showing Britten and Pears in performance. Those alone are enough to make it a desirable collector's item.

Byrd

Playing Elizabeth's Tune

Byrd Ave verum corpus. Great Service – Magnificat. Mass for five voices. Mass for four voices. Mass for three voices. Ne irascaris Domine. O Lord make thy servant. Prevent us, O lord. Tristitia et anxietas. Vigilate. Tribue, Domine. Diffusa est gratia. Nunc dimittis servum tuum

The Tallis Scholars / Peter Phillips *Video directors* **Philip George, Rhodri Huw**

Gimell 🔟 GIMDP901 (184' · 16:9 · PCM stereo & 5.0 · 0). Includes a documentary about the life and music of Byrd, presented by Charles Hazlewood Ⓕ

In 2002 The Tallis Scholars recorded an audio-visual Byrd-fest in three parts: a concert-format sequence of some of his sacred music in the atmospheric setting of Tewkesbury Abbey; a documentary of his life and his relationship to his powerful patroness, Queen Elizabeth I; and, as an 'audio bonus', another outing for the Scholars' outstanding version of the three Byrd Masses, recorded in Merton College Chapel.

Charles Hazlewood fronts the documentary; Casually attired and casually unshaven, he has a degree of ease, if not exactly charm, in front of the camera. He traces adeptly and fluently the different phases of Byrd's career, with stunning visuals of Lincoln Cathedral, the Chapel Royal and Ingatestone Hall as impressive backdrops. The whole is lent authority through the erudite but accessible contributions of experts on Reformation England (Christopher Haigh) and Byrd's music (David Skinner). Hazlewood sums up by talking about the hidden depths of passion in Byrd's music, and its range, though given that the documentary is slanted towards his development as a composer of church music, we get only background snippets of his keyboard and consort music. Nevertheless, the tale is well told, not least with added visual elements such as shots of 16th-century documentation, the original printed editions of Byrd's music and his own beautifully penned autograph.

As to the performances, it's interesting to hear

Peter Phillips emphasize the passionate nature of Byrd's sacred music, when this aspect is fairly understated in The Tallis Scholars' performances. This isn't to say that they don't have a high degree of intensity at times: on the whole: they capture the ebb and flow of the music well, but there's a sense of distance. Phillips talks of getting right inside, of 'ticking along with the music', and that's what he does above all: he keeps the tactus of the music while the singers allow 'the words to wrap the music' exactly as he describes in his interview with Hazlewood. This may not be the only way to perform Byrd's music but it's still very impressive in the ethereal clarity of the overall sound, and in the total commitment and rare understanding resulting from these musicians' years of experience.

Debussy

Pelléas et Mélisande

Neill Archer *bar* Pelléas **Alison Hagley** *sop* Mélisande **Donald Maxwell** *bar* Golaud **Kenneth Cox** *bass* Arkel **Penelope Walker** *contr* Geneviève **Samuel Burkey** *treb* Yniold **Peter Massocchi** *bar* Doctor, Shepherd **Welsh National Opera Chorus and Orchestra / Pierre Boulez** *Stage and Video director* **Peter Stein**

DG ② 🔟 073 030-9GH2 (158' · NTSC · 4:3 · 2.0, 5.1 & DTS 5.1 · 0) Includes picture gallery, 'Pelléas at Welsh National Opera'. Notes included Recorded live 1992 Ⓕ❍❍❍

 This is, in every respect, a model of what a DVD ought to be, a perfect realisation in picture and sound of Debussy's sole and inspired opera. Peter Stein staged the work for Welsh National Opera in 1992 and won universal praise, as did Pierre Boulez for his conducting.

Within austere, wholly appropriate sets, beautifully lit by Jean Kalman, Stein catches the very essence of this singular and elusive piece. Each of the 15 scenes is given its own distinctive décor in which the action is played out on several levels – high for the tower scenes, low for the eerie, subterranean grottoes, for instance. A masterstroke is the subtle evolution from one scene to another in view of the audience, offering a visual counterpoint to the interludes.

Stein sees that Debussy's instructions are scrupulously observed. In fact, as a whole, this is an object-lesson in modern staging. Stein and his collaborators reflect the ebb and flow of crude realism and fragile dream-life that permeate the score, which Boulez has identified as lying at its heart. Director and conductor worked closely with each other over a six-week rehearsal period, something unlikely to occur today, so Boulez's interpretation is in complete accord with the staging, his musical direction at once direct and luminous, timbres finely balanced one with the other.

The cast also benefited from the long gestation. Alison Hagley catches ideally the paradox that is Mélisande, candour married to duplicity, and sings the enigmatic character with an acute ear for French syllables. Neill Archer, though not quite as responsive to the French language, is a poetic, youthfully ardent Pelléas. Donald Maxwell's Golaud rightly stands at the centre of the production, conveying guilt, jealousy and self-torment in tellingly intense tones. Kenneth Cox is a grave, world-weary Arkel, Penelope Walker a properly dignified, compassionate Geneviève. The treble singing Yniold is remarkably assured.

The picture and sound are even better than on their VHS and Laserdisc counterparts. This is a riveting experience.

Additional recommendation

Pelléas et Mélisande
Le Roux Pelléas **Alliot-Lugaz** Mélisande **Van Dam** Golaud **Chorus and Orchestra of the Lyon Opera / Gardiner** Stage director **Pierre Strosser** Video director **Jean-François Jung**
ArtHaus Musik *DVD* 100 100 (147' · Regions 2 & 5)
Recorded 1987   Ⓕ**OO**

On DVD, with superb lighting and camerawork, the results are even more convincing than in the theatre. Gardiner conducts a translucent, firmly shaped account. His interpretation brings the piece even more clearly into a post-Wagnerian world of sound, and the Lyon Orchestra play up to the hilt. The entirely French cast is one of the best to record the work, challenging the hegemony of the audio-only versions conducted by Desormière (EMI) and the earlier Ansermet set (Decca).

Delius

Song of Summer
Max Adrian Frederick Delius **Maureen Pryor** Jelka Delius **Christopher Gable** Eric Fenby **David Collings** Percy Grainger **Geraldine Sherman** Girl next door **Elizabeth Ercy** Maid **Roger Worrod** Bruder Film director **Ken Russell**
BFI *DVD* BFIVD518 (72' · 4:3 · 1.0 · 0) Made for the BBC in 1968. Includes director's commentary and on-screen biography.   Ⓕ

Ken Russell's extraordinarily compelling and intensely moving *Song of Summer* remains, quite simply, a joy from start to finish, arguably the controversial director's finest achievement to date and a landmark in the history of British television. Based on Eric Fenby's 1936 memoir *Delius as I knew him* (Faber & Faber: 1981), *Song of Summer* tells of Delius's syphilis-wracked final years and the remarkable relationship that develops between the blind, crippled composer and his gifted, tirelessly devoted amanuensis. The screenplay (by Russell and Fenby) fairly teems with intelligent observation, darkly mischievous humour and compassionate warmth. Indeed, the film's chief fascination lies in its subtle exploration of the profoundly contradictory nature of Delius's life and art ('I can't reconcile such hardness with such lovely music,' says Fenby, just after Delius's wife, Jelka, has filled

him in on her unfaithful husband's wanton sexual exploits from years past).

Memorable characterisations abound. As the by-turns irascible yet vulnerable composer, Max Adrian gives a performance of towering eloquence. Christopher Gable, too, is totally believable in the role of Fenby, while Maureen Pryor makes a touching Jelka. There's also a boisterous cameo from David Collings as Percy Grainger. Dick Best's luminous black-and-white photography comes up with pristine freshness, and Russell himself provides a typically candid and personable commentary. All told, a real treat.

Donizetti

L'elisir d'amore
Angela Gheorghiu sop Adina **Roberto Alagna** ten Nemorino **Roberto Scaltriti** bar Belcore **Simone Alaimo** bass Dulcamara **Elena Dan** sop Giannetta **Lyon National Opera Chorus and Orchestra / Evelino Pidò** Stage director **Frank Dunlop** Video director **Brian Large**
Decca *DVD* 074 103-9DH (177' · 16:9 · 2.0 & 5.1 · 0) Includes documentary 'Love Potion', a behind-the-scenes look at the making of the production   Ⓕ

Frank Dunlop's witty, unvarnished view of Donizetti's country comedy, updated to the 1930s, is delightful to see, wondrous to hear. Gheorghiu and Alagna make an ideal partnership as capricious girl and shy bumpkin. They both act and sing their roles to near perfection in a staging that exposes the heart and heartlessness as much as the fun of this work.

Singing with every care for tone and nuance, Gheorghiu presents Adina as by turns, haughty, flighty, concerned, annoyed when the other girls paw him, and finally tender when love at last triumphs, and she finds the vocal equivalent for each mood. Not so versatile vocally, but always tidy and responsive to the text, Alagna makes an attractively naive, emotionally vulnerable Nemorino. Scaltriti's Belcore is made deliberately unsympathetic by Dunlop and at times he seems to be overblowing his basically attractive voice. There need be no reservations about Alaimo's witty yet genial Dulcamara: all the *buffo* elements of the part are there but never exaggerated. Evelino Pidò conducts a trim account of the score, his often fast speeds justified by the way his singers enjoy them in terms of athletic delivery. Brian Large's video direction is predictably exemplary. The sound and widescreen picture make us feel present at an obviously enjoyable night at the opera.

Dvořák

Deo Gratias – A documentary on the life of Antonín Dvořák
Written and directed by Martin Suchánek
Includes movements from Symphony No 9, Piano Concerto, Cello Concerto, Slavonic Dances, String

Serenade, 'American' Quartet, Biblical Songs, Te
Deum
Artists include **Gustav Rivinius** vc **Martin Kasik** pf
**Skampa Qt; Czech PO / Kout, Košler, Neumann;
Prague Philharmonic / Bělohlávek; Prague SO /
Delogu** Video directors **Jan Bonaventura, Adam
Rezek**
Supraphon DVD SU7007-9 (142' · NTSC · 16:9 · PCM
stereo & 2.0 · 0)   Ⓕ

'Deo Gratias' ('Thanks be to God'), Dvořák's
final comment on his life, is an admirably direct
and informative documentary, with plenty of
illustrations of people and places, complemented by historic film.

The opening, shots of the 1969 moon landing,
are a surprise, though we learn that, aptly, the
New World Symphony was playing on Neil
Armstrong's headphones as he stepped onto the
lunar surface. Other points are less surprising
but more revealing: reports from Dvořák's first
music school were unflattering, for example,
and his New York salary as director of the Conservatoire was 30 times higher than what he was
getting at home.

The film contrasts the rapturous reception he
received in England, and later in the United
States, with the relative indifference and even
hostility that greeted him in Germany, and covers the composition of key works, giving us an
engaging portrait.

It's a pity that the musical items are single
movements rather than complete works, but the
selection is fair. The New World finale and the
first movement of the Cello Concerto, with
soloist Gustav Rivinius, are vintage recordings,
but the brilliantly played Piano Concerto finale
is recent.

Elgar

Elgar – A film by Ken Russell
Peter Brett Mr Elgar **Rowena Gregory** Mrs Elgar
George McGrath Sir Edward Elgar **Ken Russell**
Himself
British Film Institute DVD BFIVD524 (71' · 4:3 Black &
White · 1.0 · 2) Includes commentary by Ken Russell
and Michael Kennedy, historical footage and photo
gallery   Ⓕ❍❍❍

Originally screened in November 1962
as the 100th programme within the
BBC's ground-breaking *Monitor* series,
Ken Russell's 'Elgar' has lost none of its power
to entrance, stimulate and provoke. If you never
caught the film on television, prepare to be
bowled over by the perfect marriage of music
and pictures, especially during the scenes shot
on and around Elgar's beloved Malvern Hills
(against which the purposeful stride of the *Introduction and Allegro* for strings acts as a marvellously apt backdrop). Any minor factual anom-
alies along the way pale into insignificance when
set against film-making of such poetry, wit and
imagination. Pioneering, too, in as much as it
was made at a time when Elgar's reputation was

at a comparatively low ebb. Indelible images
come thick and fast: Elgar's burgeoning love for
Alice is exquisitely conveyed by the delicate
interplay of four hands on the keyboard performing the piano-duet arrangement of *Salut
d'amour*; the jaw-dropping transformation of
Worcestershire Beacon into the cross-topped
hill at Calvary (to the strains of 'Sanctus fortis'
from *Gerontius*); or the composer on his bicycle
rushing through the dappled woodland and
heather. The result is an undisputed classic of
British television.

Extras include rare home-film footage of the
Three Choirs Festivals of 1929, 1930 and 1932
(during which we also see Elgar relaxing at
home), as well as a November 1931 Pathétone
movie-reel of the 74-year-old composer conducting the LSO in *Land of Hope and Glory*. Not
to be missed.

Elgar Enigma Variations
BBC Symphony Orchestra / Sir Andrew Davis
Video director **Diana Hill**
BBC/Opus Arte DVD OA0917D (85' · 16:9 · PCM
stereo & DTS 5.1 · 0) Includes documentary, 'A
Hidden Portrait'   Ⓕ

Sir Andrew Davis's warmly committed performance of the *Enigma* Variations, atmospherically recorded in Worcester Cathedral, introduces a highly enjoyable documentary about the
work and the 'friends pictured within'. Davis
suggests that each variation, as well as reflecting
the character of a particular friend, reveals much
about Elgar himself, 'like an actor playing many
roles'. Each section is illustrated with archive
material and period reconstructions, happily
with no dialogue, only Davis's narration. He
describes and analyses nine of the 14 variations
with orchestral clips and illustrations played on
the piano.

So the first variation, 'CAE', depicting Elgar's
wife Alice, concentrating on the central major-
key section of the theme, includes a brief, passionate climax, 'showing his depth of feeling'.
'RBT', subject of the third variation, was the
treasurer of the local golf club, who got Elgar
accepted as a member even though his social
class was against him. We're shown what used to
be the clubhouse, now set in waste land. 'Nimrod' depicts the publisher August Jaeger and
Elgar walking together, and Davis points to
echoes of the slow movement from Beethoven's
Pathétique Sonata. The intermezzo, 'Dorabella',
brings a good portrait of the young Dora Penny,
but after a reference to her cycling, ends absurdly on shots of a modern couple roller-
blading – an example of fussy and intrusive
visual illustration. Fairly enough, Davis favours
the idea that the 13th variation, 'Romanza', represents not Lady Mary Lygon, as has generally
been thought, but his first love, Helen Weaver,
who emigrated to New Zealand. Irritating are
the accompanying shots of a soulful modern
teenager on Lambeth Bridge looking at a launch
bearing his girlfriend away.

The performance itself has no unwanted intrusions – just a sepia photo of the subject as each variation begins – and is a fine one.

Giordano

Andrea Chénier
Franco Corelli ten Andrea Chénier **Celestina Casapietra** sop Maddalena **Piero Cappuccilli** bar Carlo Gérard **Ermanno Lorenzi** ten Incredibile **Gabriella Carturan** mez Contessa de Coigny **Giovanna di Rocco** mez Bersi **Luigi Roni** bass Roucher **Leonardo Monreale** bass Pietro Fléville **Mario Chiappi** bass Fouquier Tinville **Renzo Gonzales** bass Schmidt **Florindo Andreolli** ten Abate **Cristina Anghelakova** mez Madelon **Giorgio Giorgetti** bar Mathieu **Milan RAI Chorus and Orchestra / Bruno Bartoletti** Stage director **Vaclav Kaslik**
Hardy Classic Video 📀 HCD4008 (110' · NTSC · 4:3 · 1.0 · 0) Recorded at RAI-TV Studios, Milan 1973   Ⓕ

This is something of a find – a production produced in Milan's television studios in 1973 that does more than justice to Giordano's verismo work about personal conflicts at the time of the French Revolution. It's directed, with considerable imagination, by the Czech Vaclav Kaslik, at the top of his profession in the 70s. In realistic period sets he unerringly creates the milieu of a degenerate aristocracy in Act 1 and of the raw mob-rule of the Revolution in the succeeding acts. The only drawback is the poor lip-synch.

Conductor Bruno Bartoletti makes certain we're unaware of the score's weaker moments and releases all the romantic passion in Giordano's highly charged writing for his principals. Chénier was one of Corelli's most notable roles so it's good that his splendid portrayal has been preserved for posterity. He doesn't disappoint with his excitingly trumpet-like tones and finely moulded phrasing of the composer's grateful writing for his tenor hero, and – although already 52 – he still looks the part of the glamorous, challenging poet.

Cappuccilli was famous for his Gérard and here – at the height of his powers – he projects all the man's conflicting feelings with enormous conviction on a stream of burnished tone. Celestina Casapietra, a generally underrated soprano from Genoa, is just what Maddalena should be, and sings with a nice combination of tenderness and intense feeling. She and Corelli do full justice to their duets. The RAI orchestra plays well, but unfortunately it's too backwardly placed as regards the singers.

Gounod

Roméo et Juliette
Roberto Alagna ten Roméo **Angela Gheorghiu** sop Juliette **Frantisek Zahradnicek** bass Frère Laurent **Vratislav Kríz** bar Mercutio **Ales Hendrych** bass Capulet **Zdenek Harvánek** bar Paris **Kühn Mixed Choir; Czech Philharmonic Chamber Orchestra /**

Anton Guadagno Film director **Barbara Willis Sweete**
ArtHaus Musik 📀 100 706 (90' · 16:9 · 2.0, 5.1 & DTS 5.1 · 0) Filmed on location in Zvikov Castle, Czech Republic, 2002   Ⓕ

Gounod's opera has been described as a love duet with interruptions; here the interruptions are much reduced. Other characters do indeed appear and sing a phrase or two from time to time, but Mercutio has no Queen Mab, Capulet no 'jeunes gens', the Friar none of those solos one calls less easily to mind, and Stephano the page is eliminated altogether.

Events are similarly compressed. Important news items such as Romeo's banishment and Juliet's impending marriage are relegated. Adjustments are made to such of the interruptions as remain (for instance, Romeo doesn't take part in the mourning, 'O jour de deuil', for Mercutio, but is seen walking away with Juliet who has watched the unfortunate events from her balcony and quite understands).

Indeed, there's a great deal of walking in this production. Juliet walks home after her first love duet and Romeo sings an abbreviated aria while walking towards the second. He walks up a staircase to the balcony, in fact a nice long gallery good for a gentle stroll. 'Ah, ne fuis pas encore' is also sung on the move and when we meet Romeo again, at dawn, he's still walking. The motif persists right up to the ambulatory death scene.

On the other hand, the countryside, the river, the castle and the weather are all so beautiful that it would be a sin to stay indoors, and as long as one takes this film for what it is (which isn't Gounod's five-act opera) there's much pleasure to be gained. Gheorghiu sings feelingly and with tone to match the natural beauties of earth and sky around her. Alagna, but for his habit of 'lifting' to notes, gives a stylish, sensitive performance and is in good voice. The love duets can rarely have been better sung, and that's what it's really all about.

Handel

Agrippina
Véronique Gens sop Agrippina **Philippe Jaroussky** counterten Nero **Ingrid Perruche** sop Poppea **Nigel Smith** bar Claudius **Thierry Grégoire** counterten Otho **Bernard Deletré** bass Pallas **Fabrice Di Falco** counterten Narcissus **Alain Buet** bass Lesbo **La Grande Ecurie et La Chambre du Roy / Jean-Claude Malgoire** Stage director **Frédéric Fisbach** Video director **Tiziano Mancini**
Dynamic ② 📀 DV33431 (172' · NTSC · 4:3 · PCM stereo, 5.1 & DTS 5.1 ● 0). Recorded live at the Théâtre Municipal, Tourcoing, March 2003   Ⓕ

Frédéric Fisbach's production of *Agrippina* gives an amusing account, respectful yet inventive, of librettist Vincenzo Grimani's look at the shenanigans of ancient Rome. *Agrippina* shares three characters with *L'incoronazione di Poppea*, but at an earlier stage of the story, Poppea here being pursued by Otho, Nero and the emperor Claudius. Agrippina, Claudius's wife, spends the opera scheming to discredit Otho and to get Nero, her son by a previous marriage, designated as the next emperor.

The mood is light and ironic, but with a darker side as well. Against a minimalist set, above which French surtitles are, disconcertingly, sometimes visible, the costumes are exaggeratedly 18th-century. Poppea's yards of chiffon conceal two suitors simultaneously in a scene that anticipates *L'heure espagnole*. Nero, with rouged cheeks, sports an aubergine wig; the wigs of the other characters include various degrees of red, with a striking raspberry shade for Poppea. Otho wears no wig, perhaps to distinguish his genuine emotions from the buffoonery of Nero, Pallas and Narcissus.

In the accompanied recitative 'Otton, Otton' and the aria 'Voi che udite il mio lamento', with its aching suspensions in the strings, Thierry Grégoire gives moving expression to Otho's melancholy. As Claudius, Nigel Smith looks comically put out as Poppea fails to notice his preening, but strikes the right lyrical note with 'Vieni o cara'. To decorate the opening of 'Cade il mondo' and leave the *da capo* penny plain is surely to get things the wrong way round.

In the castrato role of Nero, Philippe Jaroussky shows an astonishing agility at soprano pitch. The penultimate aria, 'Come nube', is a *tour de force* with solo violins, cellos and oboes. Ingrid Perruche has a nice lightness of touch for Poppea, as do Bernard Deletré as Pallas and Fabrice Di Falco as a mincing Narcissus. To Véronique Gens fall two of this delightful opera's best numbers: the heartfelt 'Pensieri' and the jaunty 'Ogni vento'. If she doesn't quite plumb the depths of the first, her performance overall is sharp and amusing.

Ariodante

Ann Murray *mez* Ariodante **Joan Rodgers** *sop* Ginevra **Lesley Garrett** *sop* Dalinda **Christopher Robson** *counterten* Polinesso **Paul Nilon** *ten* Lurcanio **Gwynne Howell** *bass* King of Scotland **Mark Le Brocq** *ten* Odoardo **English National Opera Chorus and Orchestra / Ivor Bolton** *Stage director* **David Alden** *Video director* **Kriss Rusmanis**
Arthaus Musik ⏣ 100 064 (178' · Regions 2, 3, 5)
ⒻⓄ

David Alden's staging of *Ariodante* was generally praised when it was first staged by WNO, a joint venture with ENO. This DVD is a recording of the much-admired revival at the ENO in 1996. Its appearance confirms the extraordinary perspicacity of Alden's production, which explains, from an almost Freudian viewpoint, the loves, hates, fears and fantasies of the principal characters so unerringly and deeply delineated in Handel's masterly score, in which aria after aria exposes new layers of emotional thrust and instability. Ann Murray gives a committed performance as the unhinged Ariodante and displays a physical and vocal virtuosity only occa-

sionally vitiated by a harsh tone. The great arias, 'Scherza infida' and 'Dopo notte' are just the climactic moments they should be. Joan Rodgers as Ginevra is hardly less impressive in her portrayal of the myriad feelings suggested by Handel and Alden.

Christopher Robson, as the villain Polinesso, is the very incarnation of evil lasciviousness, for which his edgy countertenor isn't inappropriate. Lesley Garrett gives Dalinda just the right touch of vulnerability as she submits to Polinesso's wiles while being sexually captivated by him. Gwynne Howell is the upright King to the life. Ivor Bolton conducts a vital, well-played account of the score with modern strings sounding very much like their period counterparts. Almost three hours of gripping music-drama pass in a trice, helped by the unbroken sequence of DVD. The sound is commendable, the picture superb.

Giulio Cesare (sung in English)
Janet Baker *mez* Giulio Cesare **Valerie Masterson** *sop* Cleopatra **Sarah Walker** *mez* Cornelia **Della Jones** *mez* Sextus **James Bowman** *counterten* Ptolemy **John Tomlinson** *bass* Achilles **Brian Casey** *sngr* Pothinus **John Kitchiner** *bar* Curio **Tom Emlyn Williams** *counterten* Nirenus **English National Opera Chorus and Orchestra / Sir Charles Mackerras** *Stage director* **John Copley** *Video director* **John Michael Phillips**
ArtHaus Musik ⏣ 100 308 (180' · 4:3 · 2.0 · 2 & 5)
Recorded 1984. Notes included
ⒻⓄ

This is a 1984 studio re-creation, with the original cast, of John Copley's ENO production. Mackerras' performing edition is by no means literally 'authentic'; arias are removed, including much of Sextus's role, recitatives are trimmed, and much of Caesar's role is transposed – inevitably, since it was written for the exceptionally low contralto castrato Senesino. The result is no travesty, however: it's fast-moving and dramatically satisfying, and conducted by Mackerras in the same spirit.

Copley also strives to avoid tedium, for instance backing *da capo* passages with stage activity – sometimes rather obviously. However, his staging, combining John Pascoe's warm-hued, vaguely 18th-century designs with more naturalistic acting, translates quite well to the screen – not least because the singers are so committed. Janet Baker displays great Handelian affinity. She not only delivers these difficult, florid arias with fiery élan and appropriate ornament, but infuses them with a real emotional intensity that sweeps one over the credibility gap.

Sarah Walker makes the lachrymose Cornelia almost as intense, and Valerie Masterson carries off Cleopatra's gorgeous music with admirable if slightly self-conscious virtuosity and a kittenish seductiveness reminiscent of Vivien Leigh. Della Jones is a splendid Sextus, and John Tomlinson a thunderously melodramatic Achilles. Though James Bowman's hooting tone is rather obtrusive, he plays Ptolemy as a petulantly Farouk-ish villain to fine comic effect.

The main video alternative, Decca's Dresden recording is more complete musically but an inferior performance, marred by a fidgety modern production; so this is definitely the one to enjoy.

Giulio Cesare

Graham Pushee *counterten* Giulio Cesare **Yvonne Kenny** *sop* Cleopatra **Rosemary Gunn** *mez* Cornelia **Elizabeth Campbell** *mez* Sesto **Andrew Dalton** *counterten* Tolomeo **Stephen Bennett** *bass* Achillas **Richard Alexander** *bass* Curio **Rodney Gilchrist** *counterten* Nireno **Australian Opera and Ballet Orchestra / Richard Hickox** *Stage director* **Francisco Negrin** *Video director* **Peter Butler** Euroarts ② 🎦 205 3599 (208' · 4:3 · PCM stereo, 5.1 & DTS 5.1 · 0). Recorded live at the Opera House, Sydney, June 1994 Ⓕ

Francisco Negrin's production of *Giulio Cesare* is remarkably satisfying. Richard Hickox's musical direction is exemplary, with timing, tempi and phrasing that never go awry. The modern-instrument orchestra plays without a trace of soggy over-indulgence. The singing is less uniformly ideal: Yvonne Kenny's gutsy coloratura is undone by wobbly intonation, and Elizabeth Campbell's Sesto inclines towards shrillness. Rosemary Gunn's Cornelia isn't a convincing drop-dead gorgeous icon who could initiate the doom of lusting Egyptians, and her heavy vibrato obscures the melodic beauty of 'Priva son d'ogni conforto'. Stephen Bennett delivers a wonderful 'Tu sei il cor' which suggests that Achillas is capable of greater eloquence and sincerity than we'd suspected. Graham Pushee's lyrical Cesare is consistently marvellous: his superbly acted role as an enlightened ruler perfectly fits Negrin's concept of him as representing ideal kingship, which is how such figures were supposed to be interpreted by Handel's Haymarket audience.

This is by no means a historical Baroque staging, but Negrin ensures that each strand of the plot is faithful to both libretto and Handel's music. He takes some daring risks with staging while doing nothing to subvert the musical rhetoric or the purity of the narrative. He intelligently allows the soliloquy convention to be respected. Unlike so many directors who do not understand Handel's dramatic power, he ensures that Cleopatra sings 'Piangerò' alone; the lack of distractions magnifies an intensely emotional moment. The production nevertheless features plenty of clever stagecraft. The most significant liberty reaps handsome dividends: the role of Nireno is incidental in the score, yet the director imagines that he pulls all the strings behind the scenes to ensure that all the plot-strands resolve happily. It's common to admire a Handel opera performance for its singing while deploring the staging; here, though, is a precious rare example of a production that's a joy.

Tamerlano, HWV18

Monica Bacelli *mez* Tamerlano **Thomas Randle** *ten* Bajazet **Elizabeth Norberg-Schulz** *sop* Asteria **Graham Pushee** *counterten* Andronicus **Anna Bonitatibus** *sop* Irene **Antonio Abete** *bass* Leone **The English Concert / Trevor Pinnock** *Stage director* **Jonathan Miller** *Video director* **Helga Dubnyicsek** ArtHaus Musik ② 🎦 100 702 (323' · 16:9 · 2.0 & 5.1 · 0) Includes documentaries and interviews. Notes included Ⓕ

This is an uncommonly interesting examination of how a great Handel opera may be performed without insisting that only Baroque specialists need apply. Some of the singers here aren't obvious Handelians: Elizabeth Norberg-Schulz has something of the attack and occasionally the cutting edge of a lyric-dramatic soprano, while Thomas Randle quite often puts his voice under pressure in response to the extreme demands of Handel's first and most intensely dramatic major tenor role. And yet one hardly ever wishes for more 'authentic' voices. Both singers are very musical, well aware of the requirements of Handel's style; both, especially Randle, are highly accomplished actors – it's a minor but significant point that when either of them was on screen I neither watched nor needed the subtitles. Both, not wholly irrelevantly, are strikingly handsome.

That they can be so effective is largely due to Jonathan Miller's very plain but highly intelligent production, to Trevor Pinnock's alert and sympathetic direction and to the wonderfully intimate theatre at Bad Lauchstadt where the opera was filmed as part of the 50th Halle Handel Festival in 2001. The set is basic – a few mottled gold panels – the costumes are sumptuous, but in a theatre this size everyone in the audience can see facial expressions and the slightest gestures, and Miller has concentrated his direction on this. The result, at such a moment as when Bajazet and his daughter Asteria resolve on suicide rather than further humiliation by Tamerlano is intensely moving, as is the exquisite duet in which Asteria and her lover Andronico vow that their love will even survive her death.

Handelian voices or no, it is in short an utterly Handelian performance. The orchestra is splendid and Pinnock's pacing of the drama ideal.

Theodora

Dawn Upshaw, Lorraine Hunt *sops* **David Daniels** *counterten* **Richard Croft** *ten* **Frode Olsen** *bass* **Orchestra of the Age of Enlightenment / William Christie** *Stage and video director* **Peter Sellars** Warner Music Vision/NVC Arts 🎦 0630 15481-2 (207' · NTSC · 4:3 · 2.0 · 2-6) Recorded live at Glyndebourne Opera House, 1996 Ⓕ

What a paradox it is that one of the great opera productions of our time should be of a work not intended for the stage. If you're repelled by the thought of Roman soldiers in US army uniforms and a Roman governor glad-handing like a US president, then think again. The score is of a matchless beauty, the production riveting, the individual performances flawless. Unmissable.

Haydn

Die Schöpfung, HobXXI/2
Edith Mathis sop **Christoph Prégardien** ten **René Pape** bass **Lucerne Festival Chorus; Scottish Chamber Orchestra / Peter Schreier** Video Director **Elisabeth Birke-Malzer**
ArtHaus Musik 🔲 100 040 (109' · Region 0)   Ⓕ

This enjoyable performance of Haydn's supreme choral masterpiece was recorded at the Lucerne Festival of 1992. It takes place in the appropriate setting of an evocative baroque church, which isn't identified either on screen or in the (inadequate) supporting booklet. The small choir sings with attentive enthusiasm, and is weak only in the tenor department. The Scottish Chamber Orchestra players cover themselves in glory both as an ensemble and individually, and they're adept at imposing period practice on modern instruments. Schreier's direction is relaxed and benevolent, yet his keen ear for rhythmic precision and flexibility in phrasing is constantly felt.

The soloists are all Swiss. The veteran Mathis remains a paragon of classical style, phrasing her arias and contributions to the ensembles with firm tone and finely honed phrasing. Prégardien's liquid, silvery tenor and sensitive way with words is just what the tenor part calls for. The young Pape's sonorous bass and confident delivery are ideal; he and Mathis make an appealing Adam and Eve in Part 3.

The video direction is discreet, and prompt in homing in on the right performer at the right time. The sound picture is as spacious and well defined as one expects from the new medium, which allows us to hear the whole, long work without a break.

Henze

Documentary: Memoirs of an Outsider
Includes performances by **Oliver Tobias** spkr **Ian Bostridge** ten **Michaela Kaune** mez **Julius Drake** pf **Frankfurt Radio Symphony Orchestra / Markus Stenz; City of Birmingham Symphony Orchestra / Sir Simon Rattle**
Requiem
Håkan Hardenberger tpt **Ueli Wiget** pf **Ensemble Modern / Ingo Metzmacher** Video director **Barrie Gavin**
ArtHaus Musik 🔲 100 360 (160' · 16:9 · 2.0 · 0) Notes included   Ⓕ

Memoirs of an Outsider was first shown on BBC2 in 2001 to mark the composer's 75th birthday. It's a beautifully photographed, almost lyrical documentary of aspects of Henze's life and work. Barrie Gavin's film is an interleaved series of interviews, in English and German (so make sure you turn on the subtitles) with Henze himself and Oliver Knussen, Sir Simon Rattle and Markus Stenz. There are entertaining vignettes, such as of Walton, Ashton, Ingeborg Bachmann and the first meeting of the composer with his life partner, Fausto Moroni, but the omissions are curious, too: little or nothing of Henze's relationships and collaborations with, for example, Auden, Treichel or Visconti, or the scandal of the première of *The Raft of the Medusa*.

Gavin has also cannily selected the musical illustrations, some archival, some specially recorded, so the succeeding film of a complete performance of the nine 'sacred concertos' that comprise the *Requiem* provides a quite different, and much needed, vista of the music itself. The performance is excellent, though the sound, while very good, seems less well focused than the newly recorded snippets in the documentary. It's stunning, nonetheless, and fully merits Henze's onstage thumbs-up at the end – held as the final image of the film.

Der Prinz von Homburg
William Cochran ten Elector of Brandenburg **Helga Dernesch** sop Electress of Brandenburg **MariAnne Häggander** sop Princess Natalie **François Le Roux** bar Prince Friedrich von Homburg **Claes-Håkan Ahnsjö** ten Count Hohenzollern **Hans Günter Nöcker** bass-bar Field Marshal Dörfling **Bavarian State Orchestra / Wolfgang Sawallisch** Stage director **Nikolaus Lehnhoff** Video director **Eckhart Schmidt**
ArtHaus Musik 🔲 100 164 (105' · 16:9 · 2.0 · 2 & 5) Recorded live 1994   ⒻOO

Der Prinz von Homburg (1958-60) was composed at a time of burgeoning acclaim for Henze. The librettist, Ingeborg Bachmann, fashioned a splendid reduction of Kleist's famous drama of the dreamy aristocrat who, distracted by love into disobeying orders in battle, is given the choice of escaping condemnation if he feels the verdict unjust. Only when he accepts the inevitability of his sentence, and walks out to face execution, is he pardoned.

Henze's crisp and vital music is a remarkable, natural-sounding fusion (controversially for the time) of the influences of Schoenberg and Stravinsky. And Eckhart Schmidt's film is a most faithful record of Lehnhoff's 1994 production. Le Roux is almost ideal as the lovestruck dreamer Prince, alternately distracted and impetuous. His chemistry with MariAnne Häggander – who sings beautifully – is tangible, essential for a successful production, though it's William Cochran, rich-voiced and expressively stern as the severe but not unbending Elector, who steals the show. Sawallisch directs the Bavarian State Orchestra impeccably, the sound spacious and clear. *Der Prinz von Homburg* may not be as spectacular as *König Hirsch* or *The Bassarids*, or as directly popular as *Der junge Lord*, but it remains one of Henze's most completely achieved and important operas. Its appearance on DVD (there's no CD equivalent) is unequivocal cause for celebration.

L'Upupa und der Triumph der Sohnesliebe
Laura Aikin sop Badi'at **Matthias Goerne** bar al Kasim **John Mark Ainsley** ten Demon **Alfred Muff** bar Old Man **Hanna Schwarz** mez Malik **Günther Missenhardt** bar Dijab **Axel Köhler** counterten Adschib **Anton Scharinger** bbar Gharib **Vienna State Opera Concert Choir; Vienna Philharmonic Orchestra / Markus Stenz** Stage director **Dieter Dorn** Video director **Brian Large** Euroarts [DVD] 2053929 (143' · NTSC · 16:9 · PCM stereo, 5.1 & DTS 5.1 · 0). Recorded live at the Salzburg Festival, August 2003　　　　Ⓕ**OO**

The title of Henze's 'German comedy in 11 tableaux based on the Arabic' translates as 'The Hoopoe and the Triumph of Filial Love'. Setting his own libretto, and regarding the work as his farewell to the lyric stage, the composer casts a wryly retrospective eye on the magic and absurdity of the medium. This parable of the good son, al Kasim, who embarks on a dangerous quest for the beautiful, exotic hoopoe bird lost and longed for by his father, follows many time-honoured operatic precedents as the hero undergoes various trials and tribulations before finding true love and returning home safely, to be greeted by his grateful and loving father.

During al Kasim's quest for the hoopoe, his main companion and helper is a gently comic 'demon' who's more a fallen guardian angel than a Mephistopheles. The composer's affection seems centred on this character, portrayed by John Mark Ainsley with a restraint that makes the element of pathos the more effective. During this final 10 minutes the music is purely orchestral, its poetic blend of eloquence and regret as touching in its distinctive way as Strauss's valedictory epilogue for *Capriccio*.

This recording from the Salzburg premiere is in most respects a delight for both eye and ear. It's no great weakness that the young lovers, well sung and acted by Matthias Goerne and Laura Aikin, seem relatively one-dimensional alongside Ainsley's helpful, bewildered demon, and the stage production fits the work's knowingly light-hearted tone without overdoing the comic exoticism. With strong support from such seasoned character-singers as Hanna Schwarz and Alfred Muff, the only weak link is the rather pallid countertenor of Axel Köhler.

Technically, Brian Large is well practised in the art of avoiding excessive nudging of the viewer with obtrusively prolonged close-ups, and Markus Stenz is the ideal conductor to bring out the essential threads of Henze's richly diffuse musical weave.

Janáček

The Cunning Little Vixen
Eva Jenis sop Vixen **Thomas Allen** bar Forester **Hana Minutillo** contr Fox **Libuše Márová** mez

Forester's Wife, Owl **Josef Hajna** ten Schoolmaster, Mosquito **Richard Novák** bass Parson, Badger **Ivan Kusnjer** bar Harašta **Jean-Philippe Marlière** bass Innkeeper, Dog **Sarah Connolly** mez Innkeeper's Wife, Cock, Jay **Florence Bonnafous** sop Hen **François Martinaud** sop Woodpecker **Châtelet Choir; Hautes-de-Seine Maîtrise; Orchestre de Paris / Sir Charles Mackerras** Stage director **Nicholas Hytner** Video director **Brian Large** ArtHaus Musik [DVD] 100 240 (98' · 16:9 · 2.0 · 2 & 5)　　　　Ⓕ**O**

Mackerras conducts with all the vibrancy of his landmark CD recording (Decca), plus the immediacy of live performance, and if the Orchestre de Paris has leaner strings and less secure brass than the VPO, it still responds well. Hytner's production was an instant hit at the time, with good reason. The forest scenes rely heavily on dance, as Janáček's notes suggest, so the set is a ballet-style level stage with hanging flats; but within those constraints it comes alive with clever imagery and gaudy colour.

Eva Jenis is a vivacious, characterful Vixen, though not as creamy as Popp on the CD. Janáček's vocal casting isn't observed consistently; Hana Minutillo makes a fine contralto Fox, but there's a case for giving the role to a male voice, as the Dog is here. Richard Novák and Josef Hajna, in the important animal/human roles, and Ivan Kusnjer's roughneck Poacher provide firmly idiomatic support, but Allen's grizzled Forester remains the lynchpin. If his voice is slightly less rich than when he first sang the role at Glyndebourne in the 1970s, its expression has deepened, and he sounds quite at ease in Czech. His final paean to the renewing force of Nature, with Mackerras in full lyrical flow, is magical. A strong recommendation.

Jenůfa
Roberta Alexander sop Jenůfa **Anja Silja** sop Kostelnička **Philip Langridge** ten Laca **Mark Baker** ten Števa **Menai Davies** contr Grandmother Buryja **Robert Poulton** bar Foreman of the Mill **Gordon Sandison** bar Mayor **Linda Ormiston** mez Mayor's Wife **Alison Hagley** sop Karolka **Sarah Pring** sop Barena **Lynne Davies** sop Jano **Glyndebourne Festival Chorus; London Philharmonic Orchestra / Sir Andrew Davis** Stage director **Nikolaus Lehnhoff** Video director **Derek Bailey** ArtHaus Musik [DVD] 100 208 (118' · 4:3 · 2.0 · 2 & 5) Recorded live in 1989　　　　Ⓕ**O**

Nikolaus Lehnhoff's acclaimed 1989 Glyndebourne production makes a welcome appearance on DVD, the picture a touch grainy but still a dramatic improvement over the videotape, the sound still more so. Andrew Davis's conducting emphasises the score's lyricism without diminishing its rhythmic vigour and folk resonances. The staging, in Czech despite its Anglophone cast, is just as idiomatic. If Act 1's mill looks somewhat cramped on the old Glyndebourne stage, the indoor scenes gain a natural, sometimes claustrophobic, intimacy, well captured in Derek Bailey's direction.

The performers display the same naturalness. Roberta Alexander's heroine is sung with a warmth and fervour that exactly captures Jenůfa's open and loving nature. Langridge is a rather mature Laca, but his sinewy tenor and twisted, hungry demeanour render the character's distorting jealousy and inner decency equally credible and sympathetic. Lehnhoff and Silja play the Kostelnička as the traditional black-clad puritan rather than the less sophisticated old peddler woman, pious and desperate, whom Janáček drew from the original play. But her steely tones and incisive diction movingly illuminate the fiercely proud and loving nature, warped (as a restored solo reveals) by marital abuse, which makes her so fanatically protective of Jenůfa; her murderous Act 2 soliloquy and conscience-stricken terror are harrowing.

Kát'a Kabanová

Nancy Gustafson sop Kát'a Kabanová **Barry McCauley** ten Boris **Felicity Palmer** mez Kabanicha **Donald Adams** bass Dikoj **Ryland Davies** ten Tichon **John Graham-Hall** ten Kudrjáš **Louise Winter** mez Varvara **Robert Poulton** bar Kuligin **Christine Bunning** mez Glaša **Linda Ormiston** mez Fekluša **Rachael Hallawell** mez Woman **Christopher Ventris** ten Bystander **Festival Chorus and Orchestra / Sir Andrew Davis** Stage director **Nikolaus Lehnhoff** Video director **Derek Bailey**
ArtHaus Musik **DVD** 100 158 (99' · Regions 2 & 5)
Recorded live in 1988   (F)

This transfer to DVD of a 1988 Virgin VHS houses an entirely recommendable staging by Lehnhoff for Glyndebourne. He directs his excellent cast with an astonishing ability to delineate their inner feelings, receiving the most positive response from Nancy Gustafson in the title-role. She presents, from her initial entry, an overwrought, highly impressionable girl frustrated beyond endurance by the casual attentions of her husband Tichon, and longing for the erotic charge offered by the attractive Boris. When she finally capitulates to his advances, she mirrors the sense of release tinged with guilt evinced in the music. Her singing is firm, soaring, vibrant. Palmer is the very picture of buttoned-up severity as Kabanicha. Her command over Káta and Tichon is terrible to behold. Davies suggests Tichon's lack of backbone. McCauley's Boris conveys the man's ability to infatuate the repressed Káta. His tenor is keen, though under strain in the upper register. Andrew Davis brings out all the passion and anguish in the wonderful score. Tobias Hoheisel's sets derive from Russian art of the period of the story's genesis. Picture and sound are an improvement on the VHS counterpart.

Mendelssohn

Symphony No 3 in A minor, 'Scottish', Op 56. Violin Concerto in E minor, Op 64[a]. A Midsummer Night's Dream – Overture; Wedding March

[a]**Frank-Michael Erben** vn **Leipzig Gewandhaus Orchestra / Kurt Masur** Video director **Bob Coles**
Arthaus Musik **DVD** 100 030 (82' · Region 0)   (F)

This concert's visual interest rests squarely on the players and conductor; its setting is the anodyne modern Gewandhaus auditorium. Fortunately the director doesn't resort to Karajan-esque gimmickry to compensate. Masur is a pleasure to watch as he shapes his interpretations, underpinned by the orchestra's clear, airy textures, which come over with proper clarity in the Dolby Digital Stereo soundtrack. His *Dream* Overture has plenty of fleet-footed magic, and needs only more of a smile. Erben, the orchestra's leader, is a fluent, committed but unspectacular soloist in the concerto, and is none the worse for that; it's refreshing to hear Mendelssohn speaking for himself. The *Scottish* Symphony is a fine performance, capturing the first movement's melancholy with great grace, and there's plenty of energy in the *Scherzo* and final movement. Only the Wedding March seems rather short of vitality. Visually natural if not especially exciting, it's an engaging programme, and represents a decent body of music for the money.

Meyerbeer

L'Africaine

Shirley Verrett mez Sélika **Plácido Domingo** ten Vasco da Gama **Ruth Ann Swenson** sop Inès **Justino Diaz** bass Nélusko **Michael Devlin** bass-bar Don Pédro **Philip Skinner** bass Don Diégo **Joseph Rouleau** bass Grand Inquisitor **Kevin Anderson** ten Don Alvar **Patricia Spence** mez Anna **Mark Delavan** bar High Priest of Brahma **San Francisco Opera Ballet, Chorus and Orch / Maurizio Arena** Stage director **Lotfi Mansouri** Video director **Brian Large**
ArtHaus Musik ② **DVD** 100 216 (194' · 4:3 · 2.0 · 2 & 5)
Recorded live 1988   (F)

Handsomely staged and sumptuously costumed, this famous 1972 production makes good viewing; and the DVD sound is a distinct improvement on the original video. The singers benefit as much as the orchestra; Shirley Verrett in particular is heard to advantage, her high notes shining out with ease and purity, while Justino Diaz has body and warmth of tone as well as the command and panache for his exhilarating role. Domingo's voice is caught with the metal revealed rather at the expense of its characteristic richness, but there's a glorious thrust and passion in his singing and acting. A voice that sounds equally well in video and DVD is that of the young Ruth Ann Swenson, whose freshness and refinement are memorable and touching. Meyerbeer's last opera exhibits the mastery of a lifetime in high places. It has the required ingredients in due proportion, with a moving individuality in its quiet ending, where Verrett's imaginative portrayal makes a strong contribution. Maurizio Arena, treats the score appreciatively, with care and precision.

Monteverdi

Banquet of the Senses
Longe, mi Jesu. Madrigals, Book 4 (Il quarto libro de madrigali) – Ah dolente partita; Io mi son giovinetta; Ohimè, se tanto amate; Piange e sospira; Quel augellin che canta; Sfogava con le stelle; Si ch'io vorrei morire. Madrigals, Book 7 (Concerto: settimo libro de madrigali) – Parlo, miser'o taccio?
Consort of Musicke (Emma Kirkby, Evelyn Tubb *sops* Mary Nichols *contr* Andrew King, Joseph Cornwell *tens* Simon Grant *bass* Gabriele Micheli *org*) /
Anthony Rooley *lte*
Brilliant Classics 🔵 99784 (48' · 16:9 · 5.1 · 0)
Recorded at the Palazzo Te, Mantua. From Musica Oscura/Columns Classics VHS 211063   Ⓜ

This programme, released on VHS by the Consort's own label Musica Oscura in 1993, has now reappeared on DVD, and deserves attention both for its fine music-making and adventurous conception.

The performances are recorded in the banqueting apartments of the Gonzaga dukes of Mantua, for whose entertainment many of these madrigals were created. In this intriguing setting, beneath the famously sensuous Mantuan frescoes, the Consort make a brave stab at recreating those original performances, minimasques almost, with costume and dance. Rooley links them with an amiably informative commentary. The result is a welcome reminder of just how much of this music's magic we lose in the customary stuffed-shirt recital. Nevertheless, it isn't a total success. There's still something ineffably polite about it all, the wholesome 'G&S' jollity that tends to creep in when the English middle-classes aspire to the orgiastic. In the languishing *Parlo, miser'o*, the appearance of Mesdames Kirkby, Tubb and Nichols in diaphanous *deshabillé* could not be less than stirring, but can't quite shed the aura of a merry Roedean dorm party.

All the same, this is an engaging and original programme, and founded on first-rate performances. It isn't long, but it isn't expensive either, and well worth investigating.

L'Incoronazione di Poppea
Maria Ewing *sop* Poppea **Dennis Bailey** *ten* Nerone **Cynthia Clarey** *sop* Ottavia **Dale Duesing** *bar* Ottone **Robert Lloyd** *bass* Seneca **Elizabeth Gale** *sop* Drusilla **Glyndebourne Chorus; London Philharmonic Orchestra / Raymond Leppard** *Stage director* **Peter Hall** *Video directors* **Peter Hall, Robin Lough**
Warner Music Vision/NVC Arts 🔵 0630 16914-2 (155' · NTSC · 4:3 · PCM stereo · 2-6) Recorded live at the Glyndebourne Festival, 1984   Ⓕ**O**

Raymond Leppard's edition of *Poppea*, first staged at Glyndebourne in 1962, opened many people's eyes and ears to Monteverdi for the first time. By 1984, though, when Glyndebourne mounted this new production, his Respighi-isation of Monteverdi's sparse original was dis-

tinctly old hat. The allegorical prologue was restored; but as well as the lush string textures there remained the downward transposition of castrato roles and the squeezing of three acts into two. Yet only the most fanatical devotee of historically informed performance could fail to respond to this wonderful production with sumptuous designs by John Bury.

Peter Hall's production is, quite properly, dominated by Poppea. Maria Ewing is the personification of sensuousness, singing with rich tone throughout. She brilliantly conveys Poppea's ruthless ambition, her steely determination to become empress at all costs. By the end you feel that Poppea and Nero richly deserve each other, and the empress Ottavia is well shot of her husband. Hall frequently has his singers addressing the camera: a bold move, but one that forces the viewer to become involved in the fate of these mainly rather unappealing characters.

The drawbacks of Leppard's edition notwithstanding, this is a great theatrical experience.

Il Ritorno d'Ulisse in Patria
Dietrich Henschel *bar* Ulisse, Humana fragilità **Vesselina Kasarova** *sop* Penelope **Jonas Kaufmann** *ten* Telemaco **Boguslaw Bidzinski** *ten* Eurimaco **Anton Scharinger** *ten* Giove **Reinhard Mayr** *bass* Antinoo **Martin Zysset** *ten* Pisandro **Martin Oro** *counterten* Anfinomo **Isabel Rey** *sop* Minerva, Amore **Thomas Mohr** *ten* Eumete **Pavel Daniluk** *bass* Nettuno **Giuseppe Scorsin** *bass* Time **Martina Janková** *sop* Fortune **Giunone Cornelia Kallisch** *mez* Ericlea **Malin Hartelius** *sop* Melanto **Rudolf Schasching** *ten* Iro **La Scintilla Orchestra, Zurich / Nikolaus Harnoncourt** *Stage director* **Klaus-Michael Grüber** *Video director* **Felix Breisach**
ArtHaus Musik 🔵 100 352 (155' · 16:9 · 2.0 & 5.1 · 0)
Notes included   Ⓕ

The renowned collaborations between Zurich Opera and Nikolaus Harnoncourt in the 1970s and early 80s were crucial milestones in projecting historically aware performance away from historicism-for-its-own-sake, towards vitally conceived productions for contemporary audiences. *Il Ritorno* enjoyed great success in 1977 in Jean-Pierre Ponnelle's imaginative staging: Harnoncourt's opulent instrumental palette lifted the hearts of many, though only the eyebrows of the purists. In this musical 'revival' to celebrate 25 years of the swashbuckling original, Harnoncourt allows the nobility of the score to roll unimpeded by the driven intensity of the older recorded account on Teldec from 1971.

The vocal contributions are more eloquent than ever, with outstanding contributions from Vesselina Kasarova and Dietrich Henschel. Can Monteverdi have ever heard this opera sung with such an extraordinary range of vocal beauty and immediacy of expression? This extends to all the characters.

Of the two caveats here, the durability of Harnoncourt's big-band score with its bold instrumental canvas is likely to be a source of debate. Monteverdi left only a shell of his musical genius and, as convention dictated, the performers filled in the rest. The logic of using the greatest array of coloration to suit the context of characterisation and emotional states is highly plausible for all those who value music drama – and Monteverdi, more to the point – in pastels rather than charcoal. Yet there are moments when the spirit of realisation enters the realm of transcription, especially in the richly endowed brass ensembles used for divine intervention. A later baroque soundworld occasionally prevails, and the luminosity of the moment is lost. However, the warm glow of assured fidelity in 'Hor di parlar e tempo' – where Ulysses's *accompagnato* recitative lends authenticity to the composer's primal communicative instincts – is ravishing and persuasive. The DVD production is flawed only by some poor dubbing in Act 2.

Il Ritorno d'Ulisse in Patria
Krešimir Spicer *ten* Ulisse **Marijana Mijanović** *mez* Penelope **Cyril Auvity** *ten* Telemaco **Zachary Stains** *ten* Eurimaco **Eric Raffard** *ten* Giove **Rebecca Ockenden** *sop* Giunone **Bertrand Bontoux** *bass* Antinoo **Christophe Laporte** *ten* Pisandro **Andreas Gisler** *counterten* Anfinomo **Olga Pitarch** *sop* Minerva, Amore **Joseph Cornwell** *ten* Eumete **Paul-Henry Vila** *bass* Nettuno, Il Tempo **Rachid Ben Abdeslam** *counterten* L'Umana Fragilità **Geneviève Kaemmerlen** *mez* Ericlea **Katalin Károlyi** *mez* Fortuna, Melanto **Robert Burt** *ten* Iro **Les Arts Florissants / William Christie** *Stage director* **Adrian Noble** *Video director* **Humphrey Burton**
Virgin Classics 🄳🅅🄳 490612-9 (174′ · 16:9 · PCM stereo, 5.1 · 0) Includes an interview with William Christie   Ⓕ

William Christie has said that, until the right director comes along, he's not interested in mounting 'period' productions of operas, with scenery, costumes and deportment of the characters as a visual counterpart to the historically informed sounds emanating from the pit. This policy, understandable in its way, has resulted in occasional stinkers like Les Arts Florissants' production of Gluck's *Les pèlerins de la Mecque*. But this version of Monteverdi is very fine. Within the simplest of settings – bare walls, a few pots on one side – Adrian Noble secures performances of great emotional range from his young cast, from puppyish cavortings to a heart-stopping stillness.

The principals are magnificent. Marijana Mijanović, dark-haired and in a black dress, conveys all Penelope's anguish and loneliness; later she shows real anger at Telemaco's praise of Helen of Troy, and restrained ecstasy when reunited with her husband to the words 'Hor si ti riconosco'. Krešimir Spicer, despite a less than heroic appearance and looking the same age as his son, makes a worthy partner, a few strained top notes being a small price to pay for acting of such conviction. In the smaller roles, Katalin Károlyi and Zachary Stains provide a welcome erotic charge; Joseph Cornwell makes much of

the loyal Eumete, and Robert Burt nearly steals the show as the gluttonous Iro. The many felicities of Adrian Noble's direction include having Minerva mouth the words of Penelope's challenge to the suitors, Penelope herself being in a trance as she sings them.

William Christie directs his small band with unobtrusive skill; equally adept is the video direction of Humphrey Burton, despite a few faces in shadow now and then.

Mozart

La clemenza di Tito
Philip Langridge *ten* Tito **Ashley Putnam** *sop* Vitellia **Diana Montague** *mez* Sesto **Martine Mahé** *mez* Annio **Elzbieta Szmytka** *sop* Servilia **Peter Rose** *bass* Publio **Glyndebourne Festival Chorus; London Philharmonic Orchestra / Sir Andrew Davis** *Stage director* **Nicholas Hytner** *Video director* **Robin Lough**
ArtHaus Musik 🄳🅅🄳 100 406 (143′ · 4:3 · 2.0 · 2 & 5)
Recorded live at Glyndebourne 1991   Ⓕ⊙

This performance shows Glyndebourne at its peak in terms of preparatory work and ensemble playing. Add Andrew Davis's superbly taut and perceptive conducting and it's no wonder that here you feel *Tito* to be very near the top of the Mozartian operatic canon, a very different opinion from that which was current for so many years.

At the heart of the performance on stage are Philip Langridge as the clement yet tormented emperor of the title, acting – especially with his eyes – and singing with extreme eloquence, and Diana Montague's equally committed account of Sesto's part, a character so obviously torn, almost fatally, between his erotic love for Vitellia and his deep friendship for Tito. Montague also acts movingly with her eyes, and her singing is noble, warm and technically flawless. As the scheming Vitellia, Ashley Putnam somehow manages to enact both the character's classical origins while suggesting a soap-opera villainess. Vocally she's always willing, but sometimes the flesh is weak, particularly in the higher reaches.

Martine Mahé keeps up the high standard with her urgently sung and acted Annio. So does Peter Rose as the upright and concerned Publio. Only Elzbieta Szmytka, as Servilia, seems to be operating on a more conventional level of operatic expression. The LPO is on its best form. Robin Lough's video direction is spot on. The sound balance is faultless. Even so, main credit for this arresting event goes to Hytner.

Così fan tutte
Amanda Roocroft *sop* Fiordiligi **Rosa Mannion** *sop* Dorabella **Eirian James** *mez* Despina **Rainer Trost** *ten* Ferrando **Rodney Gilfry** *ten* Guglielmo **Claudio Nicolai** *bass* Don Alfonso **Monteverdi Choir; English Baroque Soloists / Sir John Eliot Gardiner** *Stage director* **Sir John Eliot Gardiner** *Video director* **Peter Mumford**

Archiv ② **DVD** 073 026-9AH2 (193' · 16:9 · 5.1 · 0)
Recorded live at the Théâtre du Châtelet, Paris 1992
ⓅⓄ

When this staging was presented in 1992, in various theatres, Gardiner decided to be his own director because he didn't trust any available alternative to be faithful to Da Ponte's and Mozart's original. In the circumstances his was a sensible decision because his deeply discerning stage interpretation perfectly seconds his own musically perceptive reading. His keen understanding of what this endlessly fascinating work is about is made plain in his absorbing essay in the booklet.

The first advantage of this film of the opera is Carlo Tommasi's ravishing décor that accords with what the libretto predicates, conjuring before our eyes 18th-century Naples overlooked by Vesuvius. Then Gardiner's direction makes all-too-clear the emotional turmoil engineered by Don Alfonso's cynical plans to test the ladies' constancy. At all times it's responsive to the music, except when members of the cast march through the stalls and when certain scenes are more sexually explicit than would have been contemplated in Mozart's age.

Amanda Roocroft's Fiordiligi is intrepidly sung, her tone always firm and gleaming, and she acts expressively. She's partnered, as originally intended, by a soprano Dorabella. Rosa Mannion proves an apt foil for her sister, and is deliciously flighty when falling for her 'Albanian' lover. Rainer Trost is the young, fluent, eager Ferrando who makes the most of his taxing music, although his second aria, 'Ah! lo veggio', is here excluded. His vulnerable portrayal is a nice contrast to Rodney Gilfry's macho Guglielmo. The four voices blend well in the many ensembles.

In the pit, Gardiner's direct, big-scale yet sensitive conducting is the engine-room of the performance, superbly sustained by his period-instrument band. Peter Mumford's video direction is faultless; so is the sound picture. All in all, it would be amazing if any successor surpasses this DVD's achievements on all sides. Recommended without reservation.

Così fan tutte
Daniela Dessì sop Fiordiligi **Delores Ziegler** mez Dorabella **Adelina Scarabelli** sop Despina **Josef Kundlak** ten Ferrando **Alessandro Corbelli** bar Guglielmo **Claudio Desderi** bass Don Alfonso **La Scala Chorus and Orchestra, Milan / Riccardo Muti** Stage director **Michael Hampe** Video director **Ilio Catani**
Opus Arte **DVD** OALS3006D (187' · S/T · 4:3 · 2.0 · 0)
Recorded live
Ⓕ

La Scala's *Così fan tutte* from 1989 enshrines a straightforward, witty production by Michael Hampe. Riccardo Muti draws ravishing effects from his disciplined orchestra, and paces the work with a nice blend of brio and subtlety, once or twice driving the music too briskly.

Daniela Dessì is the main beneficiary of Muti's caring attitude towards his singers, singing with steady, warm and pliable tone throughout, and Dolores Ziegler makes a fresh, eager contrast as Dorabella, though her voice is a touch heavy for the part. Josef Kundlak, denied his second aria, is a forthright yet sensitive Ferrando, Alessandro Corbelli a persuasive, personable Guglielmo. Adelina Scarabelli's truly Italianate Despina is neatly sung and acted. Claudio Desderi, as was his wont, easily commands the stage. Sound and picture are excellent.

Don Giovanni
Sir Thomas Allen bar Don Giovanni **Carolyn James** sop Donna Anna **Carol Vaness** sop Donna Elvira **Kjell Magnus Sandve** ten Don Ottavio **Ferruccio Furlanetto** bass Leporello **Andrea Rost** sop Zerlina **Reinhard Dorn** bass Masetto **Matthias Hölle** bass Commendatore **Cologne Opera Chorus; Cologne Gürzenich Orch / James Conlon** Stage director **Michael Hampe** Video director **José Montes-Bequer**
ArtHaus Musik **DVD** 100 020 (173' · Region 0)
Recorded live 1991
ⓅⓄ

If you're tired of and/or irritated by modern, psychological stagings of *Don Giovanni*, this traditional yet highly intelligent Cologne production will come as a blessed relief. In Michael Hampe's own dark-hued, spare and consistent sets, the drama moves swiftly to its appointed end, and the only disappointment is his failure to make Giovanni's descent into Hell at all threatening. Hampe is adept at giving his characters just enough to do without taking them beyond the bounds of the feasible in terms of acting while singing. In the title-role Allen probably needed no coaching at all, as by 1991 he was acknowledged as the leading Giovanni of his day, perhaps any day. He confirms that reputation here in an interpretation that blends in about equal measures magnetism, single-minded seductive purpose and cruelty. His murderous intents towards the Commendatore and Masetto, and his beating and threatening of Leporello all exhibit the idea of the Don as near-psychopath. Allen sings the role with total command of every nuance in aria, ensemble and recitative. It's a riveting performance, finely seconded by Furlanetto's Leporello, also alive to every aspect of his part's text and movement.

Nobody else in the cast achieves quite that level of distinction, although Carol Vaness, hitherto an Anna, sings Elvira with spirit and acts convincingly within a given convention. Her warm, firm soprano is equal to all the demands Mozart places on it. Carolyn James is a properly distraught Anna and sings with some flair, but her largish voice hardens uncomfortably under pressure. The Ottavio is adequate, no more, as is true of the Masetto and Commendatore, but Rost's youthful, appealing Zerlina is worth watching and hearing, especially in her encounter with Giovanni, where she exactly evinces the girl's uncertain, vulnerable reactions.

Conlon conducts a direct, unfussy reading at sensible speeds, very much in agreement with the action taking place above him, and his orchestra plays with grace and drive as required. The picture and sound are exemplary.

Die Entführung aus dem Serail
Eva Mei sop Konstanze **Patrizia Ciofi** sop Blonde
Rainer Trost ten Belmonte **Mehrzad Montazeri** ten
Pedrillo **Kurt Rydl** bass Osmin **Markus John** spkr
Pasha Selim **Chorus and Orchestra of Maggio
Musicale Fiorentino / Zubin Mehta** Stage director
Eike Gramss Video director **George Blume**
TDK Mediactive *DVD* DV-OPEADS (136' · 16:9 · 2.0,
5.1 & DTS 5.1 · 0)   ℉◯

What a pleasure it is to come upon this *Seraglio*, freshly recorded in Florence's beautiful Teatro della Pergola. It's straightforward without being staid, a crisp, witty, fast-moving production – and in Christoph Wagenknecht's colourful set, a seascape fronted with swiftly sliding panels in Turkish patterns, visually delightful as well.

Musically, too, it holds its end up. Zubin Mehta isn't an ideal Mozartian, but he conducts with affectionate warmth and theatrical verve, and he has a first-rate cast. Eva Mei, a passionate (if disconcertingly Turkish-looking) Konstanze, sings with a fiery virtuosity that makes 'Marten aller Arten' genuinely expressive and no mere showpiece. Rainer Trost, technically adept if occasionally reedy, copes elegantly even with the fiendish 'Ich baue ganz', but plays Belmonte as rather a ninny, leaving the real heroism to Mehrzad Montazeri's livewire, fresh-voiced Pedrillo. Patrizia Ciofi's Blonde is a truly terrifying little spitfire with a penetrating, glassy voice that unfortunately splinters around high E, but she strikes comic sparks off Kurt Rydl's magnificent Osmin. He sings with irresistible gusto, lacking only that last ounce of *buffo* richness, and thankfully plays not some proto-Ayatollah, but the baffled, vulnerable bully the music depicts. Young viewers may appreciate his pet watch-crocodile.

This performance is very satisfying – and entirely recommendable.

Idomeneo
Philip Langridge ten Idomeneo **Jerry Hadley** ten
Idamante **Yvonne Kenny** sop Ilia **Carol Vaness** sop
Elettra **Thomas Hemsley** bar Arbace **Anthony
Roden** ten High Priest **Roderick Kennedy** bass Voice
of Neptune **Glyndebourne Chorus; London
Philharmonic Orchestra / Bernard Haitink** Stage
director **Trevor Nunn** Video director **Christopher
Swann**
Warner Music Vision/NVC Arts *DVD* 5050467
3922-2-9 (181' · NTSC · 4:3 · 2.0 · 2-6) Recorded live
                                          Ⓢ

Trevor Nunn produced his first opera, *Idomeneo*, Glyndebourne in 1983, with felicitous results. John Napier's designs imaginatively evoke the Cretan milieu, supported by restrained, dignified costumes and lighting. The spare setting now seems a model beside what usually passes for decor today. Within it Nunn directs his principals and chorus with economic yet pointed care.

Philip Langridge is a compellingly distraught and haunted Idomeneo, singing with his customary feeling for word-painting. He easily encompasses the longer version of 'Fuor del mar'. Carol Vaness offers a fiery, richly contoured Elettra. Yvonne Kenny's beautifully sung Ilia is more conventional and Jerry Hadley is a fresh, pleasing Idamante. Bernard Haitink conducts a lithe, forward-moving account of the score, though you'll need a high volume setting to get the best out of the sound.

Die Zauberflöte
Ulrike Sonntag sop Pamina **Deon van der Walt** ten
Tamino **Cornelius Hauptmann** bass Sarastro **Andrea
Frei** sop Queen of Night **Thomas Mohr** bar
Papageno **Patricia Rozario** sop Papagena **Sebastian
Holecek** bass-bar Speaker **Kevin Connors** ten
Monostatos **Elizabeth Whitehouse** sop First Lady
Helene Schneiderman mez Second Lady **Renée
Morloc** mez Third Lady **Ludwigsburg Festival Choir
and Orchestra / Wolfgang Gönnenwein** Stage
director **Axel Manthey** Video director **Ruth Kärch**
ArtHaus Musik *DVD* 100 188 (147' · 4:3 · 2:0 · 0)   ℉◯

This is one of the most wondrous and simple stagings of Mozart's elevated *Singspiel* yet. As its musical attributes are almost as excellent, it's an experience no one with DVD should miss. The action is choreographed in a manner precisely fitting the mood of the moment, serious or comic. Details, such as the dragon, animals responding to Tamino's flute, the arrival of the three Boys, the evocation of fire and water and several others, often invitations to director's *bêtises*, all march here with the thought-through and pleasing-to-look-at concept. How happy that it should be preserved on video, though a pity it's in 4:3 rather than in widescreen format.

Gönnenwein conducts a reading that fits perfectly with what's happening on stage in terms of unaffected, rhythmically firm and keenly articulated playing from his fine orchestra. Deon van der Walt's Tamino is a well-known quantity but he surpasses himself here in strong tone and finely moulded phrasing. He has a fit partner in Ulrike Sonntag's pure-voiced, moving Pamina. Thomas Mohr, though unflatteringly attired, is a nicely unfussy and gently amusing Papageno. Good and evil, at bottom and top of the range, aren't so happily done. Hauptmann's visually impressive Sarastro lacks vocal presence and tends to unsteadiness. Similarly Frei's formidable figure as Queen of Night produces an edgy, uncontrolled sound. Ladies and Boys are all admirable.

The video direction is sensitive; the sound, for the most part clear and well balanced, suffers from occasional moments of distortion. But that shouldn't detract from your enjoyment of this life-enhancing experience.

Le nozze di Figaro
Knut Skram bass Figaro **Ileana Cotrubas** sop
Susanna **Benjamin Luxon** bar Count Almaviva **Kiri Te
Kanawa** sop Countess Almaviva **Frederica von
Stade** mez Cherubino **Nucci Condò** sop Marcellina
Marius Rintzler bass Bartolo **Glyndebourne Chorus;
London Philharmonic Orchestra / John Pritchard**
Stage director **Peter Hall** Video director **Dave
Heather**
ArtHaus Musik 🎦 101 089 (185' · NTSC · 4:3 · PCM
stereo · 0) Recorded live   Ⓕ

Peter Hall's Glyndebourne *Figaro* of 1973 was
his memorable first effort at staging Mozart, and
was much praised at the time. His unfussy production is set in John Bury's lived-in, warmly
coloured decor and combines well with John
Pritchard's unassumingly stylish conducting.
Dave Heather's TV direction is worthy of the
original, and the picture looks as if it might have
been filmed yesterday. The sound, however,
lacks a little in clarity and range.

The cast that season was choice. Kiri Te
Kanawa, youthful of mien, glowing of voice,
sings the Countess. It is a wonderful memento
of her great promise and appreciable achievement at the time. Her admirably priapic Count
is Benjamin Luxon, singing with firm, velvet
tone and a fine line. The participants below
stairs are of equal stature. Ileana Cotrubas is an
alert, cool-headed and warm-hearted Susanna,
and she sings faultlessly. Knut Skram, her
Figaro, isn't such a definite character, but is
unobtrusively right. The young Frederica von
Stade's Cherubino is sparky and wide-eyed if
vocally a little thin. It's a cast welded into a true
and rewarding ensemble.

Mussorgsky

Boris Godunov (complete version, 1872)
Robert Lloyd bass Boris Godunov **Alexei
Steblianko** ten Grigory **Olga Borodina** mez Marina
Alexander Morosov bass Pimen **Vladimir
Ognovenko** bass Varlaam **Yevgeny Boitsov** ten
Shuisky **Igor Yan** ten Missail **Sergei Leiferkus** bass
Rangoni **Larissa Dyadkova** mez Feodor **Olga
Kondina** sop Xenia **Yevgenia Perlassova** mez Nurse
Ludmila Filatova mez Hostess **Vladimir
Solodovnikov** ten Simpleton **Mikhail Kit** bar
Shchelkalov **Yevgeny Fedotov** bass Nikitich **Grigory
Karasyov** bass Mityukha **Kirov Opera Chorus and
Orchestra / Valery Gergiev** Stage directors **Andrei
Tarkovsky, Stephen Lawless** Video director
Humphrey Burton
Philips ② 🎦 075 089-9PH2 (221' · NTSC · 4:3 · 2.0,
DTS 5.1 · 0) Recorded live at the Mariinsky Theatre,
St Petersburg 1990   Ⓕ

Film director Andrei Tarkovsky, famous for
science-fiction classics *Solaris* and *Stalker* and
the historical epic *Andrei Rublev*, was a master of
symbolic effect – the gigantic pendulum, the
grotesquely faceless Idiot, living statuary, the
angelic murdered child amid falling snow. But
against such stylisation the action, vividly cap-

tured by video director Humphrey Burton,
comes correspondingly alive, no stiff Bolshoi
pageant; chorus and soloists act their hearts out.

Borodina is an ideal Marina, beautiful and burnished of tone but chillingly self-absorbed; perhaps rightly, she strikes more sparks with
Leiferkus's vampiric, honey-toned Rangoni
than with Steblianko's stolid but lyrical Pre-
tender. Ognovenko's Varlaam is somewhat
young and baritonal, but foreshadows stardom,
as does Dyadkova's superbly touching, plangent
Feodor. Boitsov's Shuisky, Morosov's noble
Pimen and Solodovnikov's Idiot are less outstanding but still excellent. The only outsider is
at the centre. Robert Lloyd's Boris first appears
(reflecting contemporary portraits) moustached
but beardless; the customary hedge appears in
later acts, neatly marking the passing years. His
finely shaded *basso cantante* has been criticised
for being too light, but such doubts fade before
his idiomatic-sounding Russian and magnificent
characterisation, culminating in a truly harrowing death scene.

Gergiev's reading is less brilliant than his
recent dual recording, often rather soft-centred;
but he still brings out the sheer anguished
beauty of the score. The excellent stereo soundtrack has also been remastered into DTS surround-sound, and very airy and ambient this
sounds, from the opening wave of applause
sweeping across the auditorium. However,
many systems – some of today's surround-sound
televisions, for example – can't decode DTS, so
it's advisable to check.

Khovanshchina
Nicolai Ghiaurov bass Ivan Khovansky **Vladimir
Atlantov** ten Andrey Khovansky **Yuri Marusin** ten
Golitsïn **Anatoly Kocherga** bar Shaklovity **Paata
Burchuladze** bass Dosifei **Ludmila Semtschuk** mez
Marfa **Brigitte Poschner-Klebel** sop Susanna **Heinz
Zednik** ten Scribe **Joanna Borowska** sop Emma
Péter Köves bass Varsonofiev **Wilfried Gahmlich** bar
Kuzka **Timothy Breese** ten Strezhnev **Wilfried
Gahmlich** bass First Strelets **Goran Simic** bass
Second Strelets **Vienna Boys' Choir; Slovak
Philharmonic Chorus; Vienna State Opera Chorus
and Orchestra / Claudio Abbado** Stage director
Alfred Kirchner Video director **Brian Large**
ArtHaus Musik 🎦 100 310 (188' · 4:3 · PCM stereo ·
2 & 5)   Ⓕ

The Vienna *Khovanshchina* is justly famed for
the quality of the orchestral and chorus work
under Abbado's passionate conducting. It's
uncut and in Shostakovich's orchestration
(Mussorgsky having left almost the entire opera
in short score) except for the last scene, where
Stravinsky's 1913 working for Diaghilev is used
– this is now generally regarded as being truer to
the composer's intentions. Alfred Kirchner's
direction is solidly realistic without being
cliché-ridden, straying into gratuitous silliness
only with the scene of the condemnation and
reprieve of the Strel'tsï in Act 4. Erich Wonder's
sets are effective too. An added touch of sym-

bolic interpretation comes with the pile of skulls projected onto the curtain at nodal points. But this is by no means inappropriate, since the self-immolation of the Old Believers is the trajectory of the drama as a whole; though its appearance during the orchestral prologue would have been still more effective had it been placed a few seconds later, when the music itself darkens.

The cast is not entirely the same as on Abbado's CD set (DG). However, all the solo roles, from the most imposing to the most modest, are taken with distinction. Khovanshchina is more about historical issues than personal interaction, and the voices and stage presences are accordingly statuesque. ArtHaus's documentation includes an adequate synopsis and background essay, and there are decent subtitles.

Offenbach

La belle Hélène   **P**
Dame Felicity Lott sop Hélène **Yann Beuron** ten p Paris **Michel Sénéchal** ten Ménélas **Laurent Naouri** bar Agamemnon **François Le Roux** bar Calchas **Marie-Ange Torodovitch** mez Oreste **Eric Huchet** bar Achille **Alain Gabriel** ten Ajax I **Laurent Alvaro** bar Ajax II **Hjördis Thébault** sop Bacchis **Stéphanie d'Oustrac** sop Leoena **Magali Léger** sop Parthoenis **Choeur des Musiciens du Louvre; Les Musiciens du Louvre** / **Marc Minkowski** Stage director **Laurent Pelly** Video director **Ross MacGibbon**
TDK 📀 DV-OPLBH (153' · 16:9 · 2.0, 5.0 & DTS 5.0 · 2) Includes documentary, 'Behind the Scenes'
   Ⓕ●

Minkowski triumphs here – this is the most idiomatic Offenbach conducting since René Leibowitz. DVD reveals how deftly he propels Pelly's splendidly loopy production. The alarmingly tinny opening bars come from a bedside TV, before which a frustrated housewife dozes. As the music proper starts, her dreams become the production, full of glamorous magazine imagery – royalty, travel, sun-kissed Greek beaches – without ever quite leaving the bedroom. It's properly surreal, satirical and sexy. Dame Felicity fits this perfectly, a soprano Helen as opposed to Harnoncourt's mezzo Vesselina Kasarova (on ArtHaus Musik, reviewed below), slightly more mature but no less alluring and displaying greater comic talent. She wafts dizzily through the action in a hilarious haze of newly liberated lubricity, her delightful Franglais enhancing the comedy. Beuron sings Paris with uncommonly melting tone, even in his fiendish yodelling song, and radiates fresh-faced toyboy charm. Menelaus is the veteran Sénéchal, beaming with complacent idiocy; with Le Roux's manic Calchas and Naouri's stiff-necked Agamemnon their Patriotic Trio is a gem. Todorovitch's Orestes is delightful, as are 'his' floozies Leoena and Parthoenis, and the lesser kings. There isn't a weak link, the fresh-voiced chorus and dancers mingling roles and costumes with manic energy. One of the best DVDs yet.

La belle Hélène
Vesselina Kasarova mez Hélène **Steve Davislim** ten Achille **Deon van der Walt** ten Paris **Oliver Widmer** bar Agamemnon **Ruben Amoretti** ten Ajax I **Cheyne Davidson** bar Ajax II **Ruth Rohner** sop Bacchis **Carlos Chausson** bar Calchas **Volker Vogel** ten Ménélas **Liliana Nichiteanu** mez Oreste **Jakob Baumann** bar Slave **Zurich Opera House Chorus and Orchestra** / **Nikolaus Harnoncourt** Stage director **Helmut Lohner** Video director **Hartmut Schottler**
Arthaus Musik 📀 100 086 (124' · Region 0) Recorded live 1997
   Ⓕ●

This Zurich production from 1997 fully enters into the spirit of Offenbach's satirical romp, hardly ever stepping over into farce. Everything is at once disciplined, contained and at the same time appropriately zany under the observant stage direction of Helmut Lohner.

In the pit is Harnoncourt to ensure that the musical values are as exemplary as the visual ones. His Zurich band is of a suitably small enough size to allow for all the instrumental detail to be clearly delineated. Strings use little vibrato. The composer's innate wit is to the fore. In sum, the score sounds fresh-minted.

The polyglot cast, speaking and singing excellent French, enjoys its collective self, headed by Kasarova's languidly erotic Helen. She sings her music in a suitably suggestive manner, flaunting her vocal as much as her physical attributes. Deon van der Walt, a lively Paris, sings with the sweetness and sensitivity of the best French tenors of the past in this genre. The comic roles are all enthusiastically taken, but among the lesser parts Liliana Nichiteanu steals the honours with her cheeky Oreste, sung in a firmly projected, attractive mezzo and with a glint in her eye – surely a star in the making.

Add perceptive video direction by Hartmut Schottler and superb sound and you have what amounts to an outright winner.

Orphée aux enfers
Yann Beuron ten Orpheus **Natalie Dessay** sop Eurydice **Jean-Paul Fouchécourt** ten Aristeus-Pluto **Laurent Naouri** bar Jupiter **Lydie Pruvot** mez Juno **Martine Olmeda** mez Public Opinion **Steven Cole** ten John Styx **Maryline Fallot** sop Venus **Cassandre Berthon** sop Cupid **Virginie Pochon** sop Diane **Etienne Lescroart** ten Mercury **Alketa Cela** sop Minerva **Grenoble Chamber Orchestra; Lyon Opera Chorus and Orchestra** / **Marc Minkowski** Stage director **Laurent Pelly** Video director **Jean-Pierre Brossmann**
TDK Mediactive 📀 DV-OPOAE(123' · 16:9 · PCM Stereo, 5.1 & DTS 5.1 · 0)
   Ⓕ

Before their acclaimed La belle Hélène, Laurent Pelly and Marc Minkowski staged Offenbach's first great success for Lyon Opera in the same pleasantly outrageous manner. Minkowski's conducting again recalls Leibowitz's classic recordings – bone-dry, sprightly and slightly manic. Certain quirks in the CD version, in particular the destructive speed of Eurydice's sensuous 'Bacchus Hymn', are explained if not excused by Pelly's production – as manic and as refreshing, in his clever use of dancers, surreal sight gags, and cheerfully unfettered sex. His 'backstage' settings make less sense than *Hélène*'s, but the Cloud-Cushion-Land Olympus is inspired.

The hard-worked cast respond superbly, notably Natalie Dessay's modern Parisienne Eurydice, dressy, leggy, and neurotic, delivering zinging coloratura while bouncing on a sofa or perched high on a stage lift.

Minkowski occasionally forces the pace, and Pelly's high camp sometimes tips over into shrill vulgarity. The remastered surround-sound is rather stagey, occasionally losing voices in unfriendly perspectives. It's still treasurable, and vastly superior to its only DVD rival, a dismal Brussels staging. Avoid that; buy this; rejoice.

Merrick, delivered with shriek-and-squeak parody by Magali Léger. But it's the Elephant Man's own phrases, eloquent with pent-up anguish, that really stick in the mind. Petitgirard gives the title-role, rather unexpectedly, to a contralto. Jana Sykorová, who took the part in the Prague stage premiere, makes it a restrained *tour de force*, singing with haunting feeling and clear French despite the burden of her grotesque whole-body suit – obviously artificial on camera, but, like the rest of the staging, still touching. Producer Daniel Mesguich has an avant-gardist reputation but this is entirely straightforward, stylized but atmospherically Victorian. Petitgirard himself conducts, and the Nice chorus and orchestra respond with credit.

This is a work that doesn't posture or assume profundity; it has an emotional directness that makes watching it more than an intellectual exercise.

Petitgirard

Joseph Merrick, The Elephant Man
Jana Sykorová *contr* Joseph Merrick **Nicolas Rivenq** *ten* Le Docteur Treves **Robert Breault** *ten* Tom Norman **Valérie Condoluci** *sop* Mary **Elsa Maurus** *mez* Eva Lückes **Nicolas Courjal** *bass* Carr Gomm **Magali Léger** *sop* La Coloratura **Nice Opera Chorus; Nice Philharmonic Orchestra / Laurent Petitgirard** *Stage director* **Daniel Mesguich** *Video director* **Jean-David Curtis**
Marco Polo *DVD* 2 220001 (167' · NTSC · 16:9 · 2.0 · 0)   Ⓕ

This is a contemporary opera that's neither musically leaden nor dramatically pretentious, but lyrical and as accessible as anything in the repertory. Laurent Petitgirard is a distinguished composer and conductor, with a best-selling Mozart Requiem to his credit. The tragic story of Joseph Merrick, the appallingly deformed 'Elephant Man' of Victorian London, is well known from David Lynch's film. Here the sensitive Merrick is depicted as a victim mishandled by society – high-minded doctors as much as jeering fairground crowds.

There are resonances with *Peter Grimes*, though with a gentler, more elegiac character. It's also slower-moving because Petitgirard sets parts of the dialogue in *Sprechgesang*. Worst in this respect are the solemn musings of Dr Treves – finely sung by baritone Nicolas Rivenq, all stiff neck and sidewhiskers – and the complacent hospital chairman Carr Gomm, wheeled about on bits of set. Elsewhere, though, there's livelier vocal writing, as in the showman's bravura spiel, zestfully delivered by Robert Breault, and more that's genuinely moving, especially for Merrick's angelic nurse, sweetly sung by Valérie Condoluci, and Elsa Maurus's compassionate matron.

Petitgirard, unafraid of traditional forms, creates some impressive choruses. At the other extreme is an extraordinary coloratura aria for the publicity-seeking actress who flirts with

Poulenc

Les dialogues des Carmélites
Didier Henry *bar* Marquis de la Force **Anne Sophie Schmidt** *sop* Blanche de la Force **Laurence Dale** *ten* Chevalier de la Force **Léonard Pezzino** *ten* L'Aumônier **Christophe Fel** *bass* Le geôlier **Nadine Denize** *mez* Madame de Croissy **Valérie Millot** *sop* Madame Lidoine **Hedwig Fassbender** *mez* Mère Marie **Patricia Petibon** *sop* Soeur Constance **Michèle Besse** *contr* Mère Jeanne **Allison Elaine Cook** *mez* Soeur Mathilde **Ivan Ludlow** *ten* L'Officier **Vincent de Rooster** *ten* First Commissaire **Merih Kazbek** *bass* Second Commissaire **Yves Ernst** *bar* Thierry **Jenz Kiertzner** *bar* Javelinot **Rhine National Opera Chorus; Strasbourg Philharmonic Orchestra / Jan Latham-König** *Stage director* **Marthe Keller** *Video director* **Don Kent**
ArtHaus Musik *DVD* 100 004 (149' · Region 0)   Ⓕⵔ

Marthe Keller's staging of Poulenc's austere, deeply eloquent opera about the martyrdom of a group of nuns during the French Revolution was produced at the Opéra du Rhin early in 1999. Keller's simple ideas march precisely with the intentions of the original, the plain sets and economy of movement mirroring the direct simplicity of Poulenc's beautiful score.

Every artist here performs in a wholly dedicated fashion as part of a well-tutored ensemble, no one more so than Anne Sophie Schmidt in depicting the psychological struggle and vulnerability of the central character, Blanche de la Force. With her greatly expressive features and her refined voice, Schmidt's portrayal is starkly moving. In complete contrast is Petibon's bright, radiant, perfectly sung Constance. Among the older members of the Convent community, Nadine Denize plays her two scenes as the Old Prioress with the authority and concentration they call for, going to her death as she loses her faith in an agonising bout of self-understanding. Hedwig Fassbender is all stern authority as Mother Marie, although one senses sympathy behind the harsh exterior, which is how this part should be. Valérie Millot is outwardly more sympathetic and warm as the new Prioress, Madame Lidoine, who instils courage in her charges when it comes to the crunch and, one by one, they go to the guillotine.

Video direction, sound and picture quality are admirable. This is one of the most worthwhile opera performances yet to appear on DVD.

Previn

A Streetcar Named Desire
Renée Fleming sop Blanche Dubois **Elizabeth Futral** sop Stella Kowalski **Rodney Gilfry** bar Stanley Kowalski **Anthony Dean Griffey** ten Mitch **Judith Forst** mez Eunice Hubbell **San Francisco Opera Orchestra / André Previn** Stage director **Colin Graham** Video director **Kirk Browning**
ArtHaus Musik 📀 100 138 (167' · 16:9 · 2.0 · 2, 5) Ⓕ

The success of André Previn's first opera has been remarkable. The importance of a composer and subject that are so widely known is clear, but Previn also demonstrates the value of a musical language that can be appreciated by the ordinary music-loving public.

Perhaps the most convincing portrayal is that of Rodney Gilfrey as the rough worker Stanley, perpetually chewing, smoking or drinking, periodically exploding into violence, but with beefy baritone always beautifully produced. Anthony Dean Griffey is almost equally good as the naive, mother-loving Mitch, so cruelly deceived by Blanche; while Elizabeth Futral does quite wonderfully well as the tender Stella. For all the beauty of her arias and her high notes throughout, perhaps the least convincing is Renée Fleming herself. Partly, this is because Previn too often pushes the voice into its higher reaches irrespective of natural speech patterns. It's almost as though he was determined to emphasise that this is opera, not musical theatre. In addition, though, Fleming's starry presence requires some suspension of belief to accept the full extent of Blanche's mental deterioration. But overall the work makes gripping listening and viewing, and the DVD is a marvellous memento of what was surely a significant landmark in operatic history.

Prokofiev

The Love for Three Oranges (sung in French)
Gabriel Bacquier bar King of Clubs **Jean-Luc Viala** ten Prince **Hélène Perraguin** mez Princess Clarissa **Vincent le Texier** bass-bar Leandro **Georges Gautier** ten Truffaldino **Didier Henry** bar Pantaloon Farfarello **Gregory Reinhart** bass Tchelio **Michèle Lagrange** sop Fata Morgana **Consuelo Caroli** mez Linetta **Brigitte Fournier** sop Nicoletta **Catherine Dubosc** sop Ninetta **Jules Bastin** bass Cook **Béatrice Uria-Monzon** mez Smeraldina **Lyon Opera Orchestra and Chorus / Kent Nagano** Stage director **Louis Erlo** Video director **Jean-François Jung**

ArtHaus Musik 📀 100 404 (106' · 16:9 · 2.0 · 2 & 5)
Recorded live 1989 Ⓕ●

Yet another classic opera video reappears refreshed on DVD and is all the more valuable since the *Gramophone* Award-winning CD set is currently deleted. The DVD, though, metaphorically flicks a light-switch to reveal that the fresh, fluent conducting and singing are only elements in a splendidly lively, witty and thoroughly integrated production.

As the production's pace demands, the singers are mostly young, although old stagers Jules Bastin and Gabriel Bacquier provide resonant ballast. Jean-Luc Viala's chubby, light-toned Prince, Georges Gautier's amiable wide-boy Truffaldino, Vincent le Texier's reptilian Leandro, Michèle Lagrange's Wagnerian Fata Morgana, Catherine Dubosc's delicate Ninetta – they're all excellent, but the real star is the ensemble, with no weak links and the benefit of natural French. Whether or not this is the 'original' language, Prokofiev approved it; more viewers will understand it; and it fits the vocal line at least as well as the Russian. The DVD transfer refreshes the original recording but also reveals its limitations: slightly thin sound and some grain in the picture. But you'll enjoy yourself too much to care.

Puccini

La bohème
Mirella Freni sop Mimì **Gianni Raimondi** ten Rodolfo **Adriana Martino** sop Musetta **Rolando Panerai** bar Marcello **Gianni Maffeo** bar Schaunard **Ivo Vinco** bass Colline **Carlo Badioli** bass Benoit **Carlo Badioli** bass Alcindoro **Franco Ricciardi** ten Parpignol **Giuseppe Morresi** bass Sergeant **Carlo Forti** bass Customs Official **Chorus and Orchestra of La Scala, Milan / Herbert von Karajan** Stage director **Franco Zeffirelli** Video director **Wilhelm Semmelroth**
DG 📀 073 027-9GH (111' · 4:3 · 2.0 · 0) Recorded 1965 Ⓕ●●

Dating from 1965, this is a thoroughly old-fashioned opera film. As was often Karajan's practice, the singers mime to their own pre-recording, not always in perfect synchronisation, and to see an ample *fortissimo* phrase launched with apparently no effort at all is disconcerting. Zeffirelli's La Scala sets have been reproduced but amplified for the purpose of filming, and the joins between 'real' and painted fence in the Barrière d'Enfer scene, for example, are very obvious. The lighting is often most unconvincing when the action is so would-be naturalistic: a single candle can fill the stage with light, and the proverbial blind man with half an eye would have no difficulty in finding Mimì's dropped key.

And yet it's as near an ideal *Bohème* as you could hope to find. Firstly because there are no 'guest artists' – this is La Scala's *Bohème* cast of the period; all are at home in this production and with each other – and all are believably young or youngish Bohemians. Mirella Freni was near the beginning of her international career, her voice at its freshest, and her acting is all the more affecting for its restraint: a downcast glance, a shy smile. Gianni Raimondi partners her very well and sings with elegance and ardour. Rolando Panerai is an immensely likeable and finely sung Marcello, Gianni Maffeo hardly his inferior as Schaunard and Ivo Vinco is a tow-haired, cheroot-smoking young philosopher. Adriana Martino's Musetta is, if you like, conventionally tarty in her vivid scarlet décolleté gown, but she sings charmingly. Karajan sounds as though he's enjoying himself thoroughly, never pressing the music or his singers too hard, quite often indulging both with a *rubato* that encourages long and eloquent line. The recorded balance is at times peculiar: Rodolfo's friends are evidently in the street below when they urge him to hurry, but they must have climbed the fire escape to comment ironically that he has 'found his poetry' in Mimì. The lovers sound properly off-stage at the end of Act 1 but they're quite visibly on it, in the doorway. But even these little flaws are oddly endearing; this is definitely a *Bohème* to live with.

La bohème

Mirella Freni sop Mimì **Luciano Pavarotti** ten Rodolfo **Sandra Pacetti** sop Musetta **Gino Quilico** bar Marcello **Nicolai Ghiaurov** bass Colline **Stephen Dickson** bar Schaunard **Italo Tajo** bass Benoit, Alcindoro **Chorus and Orchestra of the San Francisco Opera / Tiziano Severini**
Stage Director **Francesca Zambello**. *Video Director* **Brian Large**
ArtHaus Musik 📀 100 046 (116' · Region 0) Recorded live 1988   Ⓕ●

This recording received a complimentary review from John Steane when it appeared in LaserDisc format back in May 1993. One can share his enthusiasm for the restraint and experience of Freni and Pavarotti, who (even in 1988, when the performance took place) didn't look like the young lovers predicated by the libretto, but who made up for it with the 'rich humanity' (JBS's words) of their portrayals, although both evinced the occasional moment of strain that confirms they were no longer in the full flush of vocal youth. Ghiaurov, at 59, remains a tower of strength as Colline, although his voice sounds a shade rusty. These veterans tend to show up the relatively casual, upfront performances of the remaining singers. The conductor is sympathetic to the needs of singers and score.

The staging is traditional in the best sense, even if it can't rival the great Zeffirelli/La Scala production, also with Freni (reviewed above). Brian Large has his cameras in the right place at the right time, with a fine balance of distant and close-up shots. The sound has plenty of atmosphere, but, as with many LaserDiscs and DVDs, the voices aren't given enough prominence.

La bohème

Cristina Gallardo-Domâs sop Mimì **Marcelo Álvarez** ten Rodolfo **Hei-Kyung Hong** sop Musetta **Roberto Servile** bar Marcello **Natale de Carolis** bar Schaunard **Giovanni Battista Parodi** bass Colline **Matteo Peirone** bass Benoit **Giuseppe Verdi Chorus, Milan; Children's Choir, Chorus and Orchestra of La Scala, Milan / Bruno Bartoletti**
Stage director **Franco Zeffirelli** *Video director* **Carlo Battistoni**
TDK 📀 DV-OPBOH (134' · 16:9 · PCM stereo, 5.1 & DTS 5.1 · 0) Recorded live at La Scala, Milan, February 2003   Ⓕ●

This La Scala production is particularly good at capturing the Christmas spirit in the Latin Quarter and the snows of a wintry dawn at the Barrière d'Enfer. But that's Zeffirelli. In such operas, he runs the theatre of the heart's desire. No doctrinaire imposition of misery on the audience; on the contrary, wherever you look on stage there's something to gladden the eye. In the current orthodoxy of operatic production, this is revolutionary. It's beautiful to look at, meticulous in detail, and true to the score and the book.

Vocally we're, let's say, a little lower than the angels. Marcelo Álvarez sings a thoroughly competent Rodolfo: his voice has warmth, it's evenly produced and is sensitively used. The frailty of Cristina Gallardo-Domâs's Mimì extends too much to the voice itself: often its limitations can be overlooked, or accepted as part of a very touching portrayal, but there are times where a more substantial and firmly placed tone is wanted. The Musetta, Hei-Kyung Hong, is delightful in all respects; and a woman with so much life in her deserves a more animated Marcello – Roberto Servile's voice being no more varied or expressive than his face.

But nothing seriously spoils the joy of this. The sound is fine, team-working among the Bohemians has the combination of precision and apparent spontaneity which betokens inspired and thorough rehearsal. The orchestral playing under Bruno Bartoletti carries an assurance that never lapses into mere routine.

La fanciulla del West

Mara Zampieri sop Minnie **Plácido Domingo** ten Dick Johnson **Juan Pons** bar Jack Rance **Sergio Bertocchi** ten Nick **Luigi Roni** bass Ashby **Mario Chingari** bar Jake Wallace **Aldo Bramante** bass Billy Jackrabbit **Nella Verri** mez Wowkle **Antonio Salvadori** bar Sonora **Ernesto Gavazzi** ten Trin **Giovanni Savoiardo** bar Sid **Orazio Mori** bar Bello **Francesco Memeo** ten Harry **Aldo Bottion** ten Joe **Ernesto Panariello** bar Happy **Pietro Spagnoli** bass Larkens **Claudio Giombi** bass José Castro **La Scala Chorus and Orchestra, Milan / Lorin Maazel** *Stage director* **Jonathan Miller** *Video director* **John Michael Phillips**
Opus Arte 📀 OALS3004D (144' · 4:3 · 2.0 · 0) Recorded live at Teatro alla Scala, Milan, 1991. Synopsis and libretto included   Ⓜ

Recorded live by RAI for Italian television in January 1991, this DVD of *La fanciulla del West* presents Jonathan Miller's atmospheric production for La Scala, with sets by Stefanos Lazaridis and costumes by Sue Blane. The cast is strong, and Lorin Maazel proves a warmer, more idiomatic Puccinian here than he generally was in his audio recordings for Sony. His direction makes one marvel afresh at the imagination and colour in this score, distinct from other Puccini operas in its obsession with the whole-tone scale.

Miller's production takes the melodrama seriously, with realistic sets and period costumes. It even manages to bring off the improbable scene in Act 2 when Sherriff Rance finds Dick Johnson's blood dripping down from the loft of Minnie's cabin, leading to the game of poker when Minnie blatantly cheats. Though at the end Dick and Minnie get no further than the back of the stage instead of riding off into the sunset, the authentic gulp of emotion is well caught in this rare Puccini happy ending.

Plácido Domingo is in superb voice, and wins ovations for each of his big solos. Juan Pons is wonderfully firm and dark of tone as Jack Rance. Though Mara Zampieri as Minnie sings with clear focus and no suspicion of a wobble, the result is often near to hooting – a strong performance, nonetheless.

Camerawork is a little fussy but not too distracting. Not only is the documentation fuller than usual in DVD booklets, with a facsimile of the opera-house's cast-list on the back, it also contains a complete (if minuscule) libretto and translation.

Madama Butterfly

Raina Kabaivanska *sop* Madama Butterfly **Nazzareno Antinori** *ten* Pinkerton **Lorenzo Saccomani** *bar* Sharpless **Eleonora Jankovic** *mez* Suzuki **Mario Ferrara** *ten* Goro **Giuseppe Zecchillo** *bass* Prince Yamadori **Gianni Brunelli** *bass* The Bonze **Bruno Grella** *bar* Yakuside **Carlo Meliciani** *bar* Imperial Commissioner **Bruno Tessari** *bass* Registrar **Lina Rossi** *mez* Madama Butterfly's Mother **Annalia Bazzani** *sop* The Aunt **Sandra Zamuner** *sop* The Cousin **Verona Arena Chorus and Orchestra /** **Maurizio Arena** *Stage director* **Brian Large** Warner Music Vision/NVC Arts 💿 4509 99220-2 (144' · PAL 4:3 · 2.0 · 2-6) Recorded live 1983 ⓕ

If you want to know the difference between a star and a mere talent look no further. In this 1983 film Raina Kabaivanska has every disadvantage stacked against her: she's tall, obviously not 15 years old, and she's singing in the Arena at Verona, whose sheer vastness calls for ample gestures. A good deal of mopping and mowing is required of her by the stage director, and sweeping movements of the arms to show off her floor-length sleeves. Like nature, Verona abhors a vacuum, so Butterfly can't merely sit still watching for the dawn during the humming chorus: she must walk pensively through her garden and stand in vigil at the uppermost point

of it. And yet Kabaivanska surmounts all this (and a tenor who shows no trace of emotion on his flabby features until Sharpless scolds him in the final scene) by sheer ample glamour of voice and the sort of acting that you'll never see anywhere except on the operatic stage, and rarely enough there. A great and moving performance. The Pinkerton sings well enough, the Sharpless and Suzuki are fine, but this is Kabaivanska's *Butterfly*.

Tosca

Maria Guleghina *sop* Tosca **Salvatore Licitra** *ten* Cavaradossi **Leo Nucci** *bar* Scarpia **Giovanni Battista Parodi** *bass* Angelotti **Ernesto Gavazzi** *ten* Spoletta **Alfredo Mariotti** *bass* Sacristan **Silvestro Sammaritano** *bass* Sciarrone **Ernesto Panariello** *bass* Gaoler **Virginia Barchi** *treb* Shepherd Boy **Chorus and Orchestra of La Scala, Milan /** **Riccardo Muti** *Stage director* **Luca Ronconi** *Video director* **Pierre Cavasillas** TDK Mediactive 💿 DV-OPTOS (121' · 16:9 · 2.0, 5.1 & DTS 5.1 · 0) Notes included ⓕ

In March 2000 Muti conducted a staged performance of *Tosca* for the first time, only the second Puccini opera he'd conducted at La Scala. As this live-recorded DVD powerfully reveals, he emerged as the hero of a great occasion. The high-voltage electricity is unflagging, with the drama timed to perfection, the whole magnetically compelling from first to last. It makes one regret that he's so rarely turned to Puccini. But as the music director at La Scala since 1986, he knows unerringly how to pace his singers, letting them phrase expansively where needed, yet holding the structure firmly together.

Maria Guleghina makes a formidable Tosca, very believable in her jealousy, using a rich tonal range, with just a touch of vinegar at the top. She's at her finest in the great scene with Scarpia in Act 2, leading up to a radiant account of 'Vissi d'arte' and a chilling murder, even though the very ordinary dinner-knife she uses looks an unlikely weapon. The veteran Leo Nucci, tall, thin and mean, is most compelling as the police chief, at times a smiling villain, though the voice has its occasional roughness. As Cavaradossi, Salvatore Licitra may be an unromantic figure, and he's heavy-handed at the start in 'Recondita armonia', but he develops from there, and in Act 3 he sings superbly with fine shading of tone for 'E lucevan le stelle' and the duet with Tosca.

Luca Ronconi's production, well-directed for television by Pierre Cavasillas, consistently heightens the dramatic conflicts. The sets of Margherita Palli, as redesigned by Lorenza Cantini, bring a surreal contradiction between realism and fantasy, looking like conventional sets that have been hit by an earthquake, with uprights at all angles. Sections of scenery are retained from act to act, with an increasing pile of debris left behind. That makes the battlements of the Castel Sant'Angelo look like a bomb-site, which Tosca has to climb before flinging herself to her death. The idea, presumably, is to reflect the distorted mind of Scarpia, though in this *verismo* opera pure realism might be said to work best of all.

Tosca

Renata Tebaldi *sop* Tosca **Eugene Tobin** *ten* Cavaradossi **George London** *bar* Scarpia **Gustav Grefe** *bass* Angelotti **Hubert Buchta** *ten* Spoletta **Heinz Cramer** *bass* Sacristan **Siegfried Fischer-Sandt** *bass* Sciarrone **Wilhelm Baur** *bass* Gaoler **Claudia Hellmann** *treb* Shepherd Boy **Stuttgart State Opera Chorus and Orchestra / Franco Patanè** *Stage and Film directors* Uncredited Video Artists International ⦿ VAIDVD4217 (126' · 4:3 Black & White · 1.0 · 0) Recorded live at the Stuttgart Staatsoper, 1961   Ⓕ

Coming to this historic video recording after Muti's La Scala version is to register a quite different operatic world. Recorded in black and white at a performance in the Stuttgart Staatsoper in June 1961, it offers a sound, conventional production with in-period costumes and realistic if symmetrical sets by Max Fritzsche. The film direction too is highly conventional.

This DVD is specially valuable for Renata Tebaldi's assumption of the title-role. So dominant in our memories has Maria Callas's characterisation become, that we tend to forget that the role of Tosca was just as central in the repertory of her great rival of the time, Tebaldi, whose firm, creamy tones, perfectly controlled, could hardly be more sharply contrasted with the thrillingly individual, if at times flawed, singing of Callas. Tebaldi seemed to represent the essence of the *prima donna*, grand in a traditional way, and who better to play the role of Tosca?

There's ample evidence here of that commanding security in the role, with Tebaldi in 1961 still at her peak. Yet as recorded in limited mono sound, with voices well forward of the orchestra, at times there's an untypical edge on the creamy tone at the top. True to form, Tebaldi rises magnificently to the challenge of 'Vissi d'arte' in Act 2, with fine shading of tone and flawless *legato* in that moment of repose. That said, one has to note that in her acting this Tosca isn't so much passionate as stately.

Eugene Tobin as Cavaradossi, like many tenors, starts lustily, and then gets more expressive as he goes along, never betraying signs of strain. George London makes a handsome Scarpia, imperious and vehement both in his acting and in his singing. Yet as so often in recordings, his pitching is often vague. Franco Patanè as conductor is at times over-emphatic, again presenting a conventional view, and rarely conveying the sort of magnetism that makes the Muti performance so gripping.

Worth buying to hear Tebaldi in her prime.

Tosca

Magda Olivero *sop* Tosca **Alvinio Misciano** *ten* Cavaradossi **Giulio Fioravanti** *bar* Scarpia **Giovanni**

Foiani *bass* Angelotti **RAI Chorus and Orchestra, Turin / Fulvio Vernizzi** *Stage director* **Mario Lanfranchini**
With documentary, 'A tu per tu con Magda Olivero, artista e donna', including arias by Alfano, Cilea, Franck, Gounod, Handel, Mascagni, Puccini and Verdi
Hardy Classic Video ② ⦿ HCD4011 (208' · NTSC · 4:3 · 1.0 · 0)   Ⓕ

The production of *Tosca* dates from 1960. Ah, those naïve times when people believed it was set in Scarpia's Rome (not in Mussolini's, for example). The date is 1800 and the Battle of Marengo is news. And the scenery is for real. You could nose your way around Sant'Andrea della Valle, and feel quite at home in the Palazzo Farnese.

As for the *prima donna*, Magda Olivero (born 1910, debut 1932) has thought out every move, every expression, creating the conviction of living the whole role afresh here and now. She also sings with distinction. Try her in phrases like 'le voce delle cose' for delicacy and the great two-octave lunge of 'Io quella lama piantai nel cor' for power. Her Scarpia isn't so very far inferior to Gobbi: suave and brutal by turns, with fine resonance. Cavaradossi is likeable, both vocally and dramatically; Angelotti, for his brief operatic life, is outstanding.

The documentary of 2003 puts 1960 in perspective. It includes glimpses of Olivero singing in Milan the previous year, marking the 25th anniversary of Callas's death. It's a weirdly ethereal sound, sometimes very flat, but flat in a beautiful way. She sings *Panis angelicus*, and at a late stage is joined by her tenor pupil Danilo Formaggio. In interviews Olivero tells of the tenors in her career, from Schipa to Domingo, including a long story about appeasing Gigli. But the best things are three excerpts filmed in 1965: a delicately acted scene from *Iris*, authentic voice and style for Alfano's *Risurrezione*, and the great solo from Act 1 of *La traviata*. The last is astonishing in every way: the 'Ah, fors' è lui' muses privately; the 'Follies' are sudden, impetuous; the 'vortici' brilliant with nervous energy; top Cs that swell and diminish as you thought they did only in text-books; and a top E flat which you hadn't thought would be in her voice at all. And this is a youngster of 55.

It's a pity we don't get a taste of her pre-war recordings: that would have deepened the perspective. Seeing her at 92 leaves us with admiration and wonder for this extraordinary woman and her unquenchable devotion to her art.

Il Trittico

Il tabarro

Piero Cappuccilli *bar* Michele **Sylvia Sass** *sop* Giorgetta **Nicola Martinucci** *ten* Luigi **Sergio Bertocchi** *ten* Tinca **Aldo Bramante** *bass* Talpa **Eleonora Jankovic** *mez* Frugola **Ernesto Gavazzi** *ten* Ballad-seller **Anna Baldasserini** *sngr* Lover I **Bruno Brando** *sngr* Lover II

Suor Angelica
Rosalind Plowright sop Suor Angelica **Dunja
Vejzovic** contr Princess **Maria Garcia Allegri** mez
Abbess **Nella Verri** mez Mistress of the Novices
Giovanna Santelli sop Sister Genovieffa **Maria Dalla
Spezia** sop Sister Osmina **Midela d'Amico** sop Sister
Dolcina

Gianni Schicchi
Juan Pons bar Gianni Schicchi **Cecilia Gasdia** sop
Lauretta **Yuri Marusin** ten Rinuccio **Eleonora
Jankovic** contr Zita **Ferrero Poggi** ten Gherardo
Anna Baldasserini sop Nella **Alessandra Cesareo**
contr Gherardino **Franco Boscolo** bass Betto di
Signa **Mario Luperi** bass Simone **Giorgio Taddeo**
bar Marco **Nella Verri** mez La Ciesca **Claudio
Giombi** bass Spinelloccio **Virgilio Carbonari** bar
Notary **Pio Bonfanti** bass Pinellino **Ruggero
Altavilla** bass Guccio

**Orchestra and Chorus of La Scala, Milan /
Gianandrea Gavazzeni** Stage director **Sylvano
Bussotti** Video director **Brian Large**
Warner Music Vison/NVC Arts 🔘 5050467-0943-2-1
(161' · NTSC · 4:3· PCM stereo · 2-6) Recorded at La
Scala, Milan, 1983   Ⓕ

This Warner DVD offers idiomatic performances from La Scala of Puccini's trilogy. The
productions are broadly traditional, with an
ultra-realistic set for the grand guignol of *Il
tabarro* and rather more stylised settings for *Suor
Angelica* and *Gianni Schicchi*.

Casting is strong in *Il tabarro*, with Piero Cappuccilli in his prime as Michele, the cuckolded
bargemaster. His appeal to Giorgetta, his
estranged wife, is so passionate and tender that
his climactic solo has your total sympathy. Sylvia
Sass as Giorgetta tends to overact; the steely
edge in her voice helps keep your sympathies
with Michele. As Luigi, Nicola Martinucci is
powerful and unstrained. Outstanding among
the others is Eleonora Jankovic as La Frugola,
firm of voice and characterful without overacting. The staging of the murder and Michele's
revealing of the body under his cloak, always
tricky to bring off, is neatly managed.

The stylised set for *Suor Angelica* is unobjec-
tionable. What dominates, as it should, is Rosalind Plowright's moving performance of the
title role. Next to her, Dunja Vejzovic is disappointing, not so much vocally as in appearance
and personality; she seems too young and lightweight; hardly the unforgiving Princess. The
nuns are nicely touched in, and the chorus is
impressive. Brian Large's direction sidesteps the
final and sentimental vision of Angelica's dead
child.

Gianni Schicchi is placed in an enormous apartment with a panoramic view over Florence. The
claustrophobia that can add point to the comic
story is entirely absent, but the set is undistract-
ing. Eleonora Jankovic again stands out among
the incidental characters as the old woman, Zita,
and Yuri Marusin as Rinuccio copes well with
his big aria. Lauretta, his lover, is strongly cast,
with Cecilia Gasdia luxuriantly drawing out 'O

mio babbino caro' in finely shaded phrases, to
the delight of the Scala audience. Juan Pons is a
firm and commanding Schicchi, taking centre-
stage from his first entry.

Rameau

Les Boréades
Barbara Bonney sop Alphise **Paul Agnew** ten
Abaris **Toby Spence** ten Calisis **Laurent Naouri** bar
Borée **Stéphane Degout** bar Borilée **Nicolas Rivenq**
bar Adamas, Apollon **Anna Maria Panzarella** sop
Sémire **Jaël Azzaretti** sop Nymphe
**Paris National Opera Chorus; Les Arts Florissants
/ William Christie** Stage director **Robert Carsen**
Video director **Thomas Grimm**
BBC/Opus Arte ② 🔘 OA0899D (218' · 16:9 · PCM
stereo & 5.1 · 0) Recorded live at the Palais Garnier,
Paris, April 2003. Includes 'The Triumph of Love':
interviews with Robert Carsen, William Christie,
Barbara Bonney, Paul Agnew and Laurent Naouri.
Notes, synopsis and libretto included   Ⓕ

Les Boréades, a strange but fascinating piece,
seems not to have been performed in Rameau's
lifetime. Cast in the traditional five acts, it's
about the mutual love amid trials of Alphise,
queen of Bactria, and Abaris, a foreigner of
unknown origin who's been brought up by the
high priest of Apollo. The music is top-drawer
Rameau, with exquisite airs, vigorous choruses
and lots of ballet. The writing for orchestra is
outstanding: horn-calls from the overture permeate the first scene, a weird prelude of disjointed phrases announces the entrance of
Borée, and there's a cracking storm, the 'Suite
des Vents', to connect Acts 3 and 4 – except it
doesn't because, unbelievably, that's where the
break between discs occurs.

As with Les Arts Florissants' earlier productions, this is no bewigged homage to the *ancien
régime*. Instead, Robert Carsen has divided
Rameau's chorus of Bactrian subjects into two:
the severe Boreads, buttoned up in trench coats,
and scantily clad, let-it-all-hang-out Apolloni-
ans. Most of the action takes place in near
monochrome, symbolising the chill world of the
north wind, with flowers and blue sky at the end
representing all the connotations of spring.

Carsen's is well served by his cast. Barbara
Bonney is touching as the queen who prefers to
abdicate rather than give up her love. She's riveting in her first air, 'Un horizon serein', with its
graphic depiction of the wind whipping up the
sea. Paul Agnew is nowhere finer than in the
desolate landscape of Act 4, producing a beautiful *mezza voce* at 'Je vole, amour, où tu m'ap-
pelles'. Toby Spence and Stéphane Degout
make a properly creepy pair of suitors.

William Christie conducts with all his customary dedication. The sheer exhilaration of the
chorus in Act 3 has to be seen to be believed,
with Agnew and Spence shooting the coloratura
across like something out of Rossini. For some
the manic semaphoring of a dance group called
La La La Human Steps (*sic*) may be something
to be endured, not enjoyed. The subtitles are a

ghastly mixture of Olde Englishe and eccentricity. This is a serious attempt at interpreting Rameau in modern terms; unreconstructed traditionalists will be happier with the John Eliot Gardiner CD recording on Erato.

Rossini

Il barbiere di Siviglia
Manuel Lanza bar Figaro **Vesselina Kasarova** mez Rosina **Reinaldo Macias** ten Count Almaviva **Elizabeth Magnuson** mez Berta **Carlos Chausson** bar Doctor Bartolo **Valery Murga** bar Officer **Nicolai Ghiaurov** bass Don Basilio **Kenneth Roberson** bass Ambrogio **Zurich Opera House Chorus and Orchestra / Nello Santi** Stage director **Grischa Asagaroff** Video director **Felix Breisach**
TDK Euro Arts ② 🅓🅥🅓 DV-OPBDS (161' · 16:9 · DTS 5.1 & 2.0 · 0)   Ⓕ

This set offers a novel but never outlandish view of a familiar work. It's most distinguished by Luigi Perego's utterly delightful décor, which places the action in the art deco period. The gimmicky first scene has Almaviva arriving on a motor-cycle with sidecar and Figaro on a bicycle, but once indoors Asagaroff's direction proves witty, eschewing slapstick, making the characters larger than life, as perhaps they should be, but never to the point of exaggeration. He's helped by a youthful cast. Although rather young-looking, Carlos Chausson's fine observation of Bartolo's quirks are in the best tradition of the role, and his singing of his virtuoso aria is masterly. Manuel Lanza's slightly too laid-back and modern Figaro, and Reinaldo Macias's subtly acted, adequately sung Almaviva form part of a true ensemble. At its centre is Vesselina Kasarova's Rosina; she gives a typically individual performance, full in tone, clean in *fioriture*, but a bit too dramatically calculated. Nicolai Ghiaurov, though his voice is a shadow of its former self, makes a genial Basilio. Veteran conductor Nello Santi's reading of the score is clean-cut, never drawing attention to itself, always aware of Rossini's irresistible orchestration. A thoroughly enjoyable performance.

Il barbiere di Siviglia
Hermann Prey bar Figaro **Teresa Berganza** mez Rosina **Luigi Alva** ten Almaviva **Enzo Dara** bar Doctor Bartolo **Paolo Montarsolo** bass Don Basilio **Stefania Malagù** mez Berta **Renato Cesari** bass Fiorello **Luigi Roni** bar Officer **Hans Kraemmer** bass Ambrogio **Milan La Scala Orchestra and Chorus / Claudio Abbado** Stage director **Jean-Pierre Ponnelle** Video director **Ernst Wild**
DG 🅓🅥🅓 073 021-9GH (142' · 4:3 ·2.0 · 0)   Ⓕ

Claudio Abbado's youthful Beatle-cut marks the age of this film, still one of the better screen *Barbier*es if not absolutely the best. Jean-Pierre Ponnelle based it on his Scala stagings, but filmed it, as he always preferred, in studio with lip-sync, more successfully than most. As a result, it looks

and sounds very much fresher on DVD than contemporary videotapes.

The very strong cast reproduces that of Abbado's 1972 CD recording, but with La Scala forces. Teresa Berganza, often rather unexciting in sound alone, reveals a charming presence here, only a shade mature for a role she'd sung since the 1950s. In the manner of that era her Rosina is coquette rather than minx, but her slightly resinous tone and sensuous delivery makes 'Contro il cor' irresistible. You'd never guess Luigi Alva had been singing Almaviva for just as long, still youthful-looking, honeyed and elegant, even if his heavily aspirated ornament – the 'ha-ha' effect – wouldn't be acceptable today. Hermann Prey has everything a good Figaro needs, but despite his warmly incisive baritone and cheerfully egocentric, athletic characterisation he simply isn't idiomatic enough. Enzo Dara's pompous, foppish Bartolo is amusingly observed and richly sung, but he suffers unduly from the film's major drawback, the direction.

Ponnelle feels obliged to reinforce the comedy with a barrage of ingenious but spurious business, such as Basilio's alchemical explosions, and choppy editing. The effect is enjoyable but overdone.

Il barbiere di Siviglia
David Malis bar Figaro **Jennifer Larmore** mez Rosina **Richard Croft** ten Almaviva **Renato Capecchi** bar Doctor Bartolo **Simone Alaimo** bass Don Basilio **Leonie Schoon** mez Berta **Roger Smeets** bass Fiorello, Officer **Netherlands Opera Chorus; Netherlands Chamber Orchestra / Alberto Zedda** Stage director **Dario Fo** Video director **Hans Hulscher**
ArtHaus Musik 🅓🅥🅓 100 412 (154' · 4:3 · PCM stereo · 2 & 5) Recorded 1991   Ⓕ

We've cursed modern producers and their productions often enough, but here's a delight. The conductor, working with his own edition of the opera, is Alberto Zedda. But when the director and designer, Dario Fo, takes the last, climatic bow, he deserves every cheer he gets.

The performance was filmed at the Netherlands Opera in 1991, but the production dates back to 1987, and was Fo's first for the operatic stage. Employing a group of mime artists, he places the action in a *commedia dell'arte* setting and opens with a brilliant pantomime-accompaniment to the overture. The ideas match the music, and the visual style suits the elegance of Zedda's orchestral players. Throughout the opening solos, chorus and duet, a delightful ingenuity of movement plays along with the singers, who have the youth and elasticity of voice, limb and spirit to cope with the thousand-and-one tasks thrown at them. There's very little sense of distraction or overloading; just a feast of melody, wit and energy.

The tenor Robert Croft impresses most: his tone is clear; his scales are fluent and evenly articulated, and he can apply vocal decoration with panache and delicacy. The Figaro, another American, David Malis, has personality and bright high notes. Jennifer Larmore's Rosina, better when seen than merely heard, is strong-voiced and technically accomplished. Renato Capecchi is a memorable Bartolo, distinct from the potbellied bumbler of convention.

In the theatre the production might be found too restless, but, expertly filmed, it's just about the most enjoyable comic opera production available on DVD.

L'italiana in Algeri
Nuccia Focile sop Elvira **Rudolf Hartmann** bass Haly **Doris Soffel** mez Isabella **Robert Gambill** ten Lindoro **Günter von Kannen** bass Mustafà **Enric Serra** bar Taddeo **Susan McLean** mez Zulma **Bulgarian Male Chorus, Sofia; Stuttgart Radio Symphony Orchestra / Ralf Weikert** Stage director **Michael Hampe.** Video director **Claus Viller**
Arthaus Musik 🔲 100 120 (117' · Region 0)
Recorded live 1987   Ⓕ⚫

Bravi tutti! For a start, the house and stage: just the right size. And then, comprehensively, the whole team, with every aspect of the production delightfully cared for. Ralf Weikert conducts with zestful elegance, and the excellent players respond. The chorus is alert and precise, the camera catching never a lifeless face and several very funny ones. Each of the soloists fits the part, working both as individuals and as an ensemble. The comic roles are played amusingly without clowning. Doris Soffel as Isabella has charm and dignity. The range and runs are well managed, though she's probably best in the lyrical phrases of the cavatina 'Per lui che adoro' and the aristocracy of her bearing in 'Pensa alla patria'. The Mustafà, Günter von Kannen, specialises in comic roles but probably not in rapid passagework, of which there's much here; nevertheless, his sonorous voice establishes character, and his expressive mouth and eyes do the rest.

But for once the producer deserves top billing: he does his rightful job extremely well and doesn't exceed it. All the staging is effective, graceful and confident. With sets and costumes that are a distinct pleasure to look at, Michael Hampe's production is never short of good ideas and never imposes 'concepts'.

Tancredi
Bernadette Manca di Nissa contr Tancredi **María Bayo** sop Amenaide **Raúl Giménez** ten Argirio **Ildebrando D'Arcangelo** bass Orbazzano **Katarzyna Bak** mez Isaura **Maria Pia Piscitelli** sop Roggiero **Richard Baker** hpd **South German Radio Chorus; Stuttgart Radio Symphony Orchestra / Gianluigi Gelmetti** Stage director **Pier Luigi Pizzi** Video director **Claus Viller**
ArtHaus Musik 🔲 100 206 (166' · 4:3 · 2.0 · 2-8)
Recorded live 1992   Ⓕ

Today, although there are a few decent CD

recordings, stagings of *Tancredi* are rare, so it's good to have this crisply recorded DVD from the 1992 Schwetzingen Festival.

Visually, Pizzi's vaguely 18th-century, neoclassical pastiche staging is sumptuous. If the action is rather static, the opera's conventional structure is largely to blame; the individual performances are spirited enough. Musically, too, this can stand comparison with its CD rivals. Gelmetti's conducting is lively and serviceable, supporting some excellent singing, not least from Giménez as Argirio. Bayo, as his slandered daughter, is equally impressive, pure of voice yet intensely expressive and committed. As her jiltee and false accuser, D'Arcangelo combines a well-focused *basso cantante* with a youthfully malevolent presence. Singing-contest winners Bak and Piscitelli are excellent *comprimarii*.

Only the title-role is a problem. Even by operatic standards Manca di Nissa doesn't remotely resemble Tasso's tragic knight – more like Mistress Quickly *en travesti*. Vocally, though, she's splendidly rich-toned and heroic. This is especially welcome when, after the tragic finale true to Tasso and Voltaire she's resurrected for the more popular happy ending Rossini later provided, a welcome coda to a enjoyable and valuable performance.

Schubert

Die schöne Müllerin
Dietrich Fischer-Dieskau bar **András Schiff** pf Video director **Fritz Jurmann**
TDK 🔲 DV-CODSM (83' · 4:3 · PCM stereo · 0).
Recorded live at the Montforthaus, Feldkirch, on June 20, 1991. Includes 1985 interview with Dietrich Fischer-Dieskau   Ⓕ⚫⚫

To celebrate Fischer-Dieskau's 80th birthday Austrian Television issued this film made at the 1991 Schubertiade. It marked the return, after a 20-year break, of the great baritone, aged 66, to Schubert's first cycle. In restudying the work, the singer comments that he tried, really for the first time, to sing these songs 'not so much by feeling as by narrative, not so much concentrating on the vocal line as responding with curiosity and openness to the wealth of colour and expression in the piano part – which calls for a pianist as sensitive as Schiff'.

He's as good as his word, singing the cycle even more off the words than he had in the past, giving his audience a kind of mini-drama, underlined by some movement on the platform and a wealth of facial expression. At this late stage in his career his voice inevitably shows some decline in tonal body, but in almost every other respect he retains the famed qualities of his prime: astonishing breath-control, an arresting command of wide-ranging dynamics and total control in putting his ideas into action. The hypnotic reading reaches its proper moment of epiphany in the two penultimate, tragic songs, delivered with all the varied resources the performers can offer them.

As a bonus there's a 20-minute portrait of the singer, assembled at the 1985 Schubertiade. It includes a couple more valuable examples of his singing and a fascinating interview, in which he tells us a lot about himself and his approach to his art, something that will be invaluable in years to come.

Winterreise, D911

Ian Bostridge ten **Julius Drake** pf Stage director **David Alden** Video director **Peter West**
NVC Arts ⬛ 8573-83780-2 (124' · Regions 2-6)
Includes documentary on the making of the film Ⓕ●

Winterreise lives on its own without any staging. The initially dubious Bostridge and Drake make that point at the start of the feature, their faces filling with dismay as Alden describes his seemingly hare-brained ideas to turn it into a melodrama about a crazed protagonist. It's implied in what follows that singer and pianist gained confidence in what Alden had in mind, while the director came to respect Bostridge's intelligence and dramatic gifts. Indeed, the project would have collapsed had not the tenor the ability to sear the soul as much visually as aurally. His piercing eyes, striking looks and age make him an ideal candidate for such an experiment.

Inspired by a disused mental asylum in north London, Alden and his designer create a huge, empty space, as desolate as the abandoned asylum itself, in which the beginning and end of the cycle are enacted. In-between, Bostridge is projected on to a white background, arrestingly so in the case of 'Die Krähe', where the singer is viewed from above by the crow with Bostridge spread-eagled on the floor below, an astonishing image, mirroring the bird's menace. Among the unforgettable shots are the picture of the forlorn shattered figure in 'Die Nebensonnen', which Alden and Bostridge agree has a mystic, religious aura to it, the lone protagonist seen at a distance in 'Das Wirtshaus', the singer seated back to back with the pianist in 'Mut'. Doubts arise only with the introduction during two songs of the unfaithful girl and her family, disturbing the vision of the lonely sufferer.

At the heart of the video lies Bostridge's silvery tone, special, highly individual intensity of utterance and identification with the man's desperate plight. Drake supports him with playing of equal insight. The sound, fairly closely miked, is excellent; the camerawork highly imaginative.

Schumann

Schumann Dichterliebe, Op 48[a] Schoenberg Pierrot lunaire, Op 21[b]
Christine Schäfer sop [a]**Natascha Osterkorn** pf [b]**Ensemble InterContemporain, Paris / Pierre Boulez** Film director **Oliver Herrmann**
ArtHaus Musik ⬛ 100 330 (126' · 16:9 · 2.0 · 0) Ⓕ●

Schäfer's virtuosity as a singing actress is exploited to the full in this highly imaginative

double-bill. In the Schumann, work and artists are placed in a new and controversial context, with the production of the film intermingled with the performance of the cycle. In an intimate, sparsely lit nightclub in Berlin-Mitte, recreating the salon atmosphere of a performance in the composer's time, the cycle is sung by the soprano in a tight-fitting black outfit while moving around the room in sympathy with evocations of each song's mood. The idea is to make the emotions of the work part of everyday life. Schäfer's reading of the songs is at once simple and intense, devoid entirely of sentimentality. She's supported in the performance and rehearsal by the equally fascinating personality of the pianist Natascha Osterkorn.

As far as one can tell, the singer isn't dubbed here. But in the 'staging' of *Pierrot lunaire*, she's undoubtedly miming to her own *Sprechgesang*. With clown-like make-up, Schäfer wanders Kafka-like, through a kaleidoscopic range of situations and venues – including an abattoir, railway station and a medical lecture theatre – vaguely appropriate to the texts. In this, one of the soprano's best-known roles, she excels in declaiming the text with meaning, assisted by that past master of the genre, Pierre Boulez.

As a bonus, there's a 45-minute interview with the singer. This whole issue extends the boundaries of interpreting vocal works on DVD. A riveting experience.

Shostakovich

Lady Macbeth of the Mtsensk district
Galina Vishnevskaya sop **Katerina** Izmailova **Nicolai Gedda** ten Sergei **Dimiter Petkov** bass Boris Izmailov **Werner Krenn** ten Zinovi Izmailov **Robert Tear** ten Shabby Peasant **Taru Valjakka** sop Aksinya **Martyn Hill** ten Teacher **Leonard Andrzej Mróz** bass Priest **Aage Haugland** bass Police Sergeant **Birgit Finnilä** mez Sonyetka **Alexander Malta** bass Old Convict **Leslie Fyson** ten Millhand, Officer **Scott Emerson** ten Porter **John Noble** bar Steward **Colin Appleton** ten Coachman, Foreman I **Alan Byers** ten Foreman II **James Lewington** ten Foreman III **Oliver Broome** bass Policeman **Edgar Fleet** ten Drunken Guest **David Beavan** bass Sentry **Linda Richardson** mez Woman Convict **Ambrosian Opera Chorus; London Philharmonic Orchestra / Mstislav Rostropovich** Film director **Petr Weigl**
Carlton Entertainment ⬛ ID5655CLDVD (100' · Region 1) Ⓕ●

Petr Weigl returns to form with this remarkable realisation of Shostakovich's scarifying drama. Filming in his native Czech Republic, as usual with actors lip-synching singers, he nevertheless brings its nasty and brutish setting to vivid life. Only the Siberian trek looks a little milder than traditional depictions, but it's accurate enough. The atmospheric photography of the Izmailov farm's barren, lamplit rooms and bathhouse adds a *verismo* dimension to the music's quasi-expressionist force. You really feel a place like this would breed adultery and impulsive murder. The soundtrack is the classic Rostropovich recording, generally preferable to Myung-Whun Chung's more recent version with Maria Ewing (DG).

Its splendid pace and vivid playing suit the film, as do its lively effects, though it's substantially cut. The generally excellent actors do their best with the limitations of lip-synch, no doubt assisted by Czech's kinship with Russian. The Katerina is youngish, nervy and intense, tragically ripe pickings for Sergei's – and indeed her own – passion, but Vishnevskaya's maturely resonant dramatic soprano sits uneasily on her. The Sergei melds better with Gedda's bright tones to suggest the ruthless predator beneath the boyish charm, and Aksinya, old Izmailov and the Old Convict are splendidly portrayed. The studio acoustic is too evident, especially with the clarity of DVD mastering, to make the outdoor scenes convincing. But they achieve their effect through the music none the less. Highly recommended.

J Strauss II

New Year's Concert, 2002
Hellmesberger II Danse diabolique **J Strauss** Beliebte Annen-Polka, Op 137. Radetzky March, Op 228 **J Strauss II** Zivio!, Op 456. Carnevalsbotschafter, Op 270. Künsterleben, Op 316. Die Fledermaus – Overture. Perpetuum mobile, Op 257. Elisen-Polka, Op 151. Wiener Blut, Op 354. Tik-Tak Polka, Op 365. An der schönen blauen Donau, Op 314 **Josef Strauss** Die Schwätzerin, Op 144. Vorwärts!, Op 127. Arm in Arm, Op 215. Aquarellen-Polka, Op 258. Die Libelle, Op 204. Plappermäulchen, Op 245. Im Fluge, Op 230
Vienna Philharmonic Orchestra / Seiji Ozawa
Video director **Brian Large**
TDK Mediactive 📀 DV-WPNK02 (141' · 16:9 · 2.0, 5.0 & DTS 5.0 · 0) Ⓕ

What an advantage DVD provides in comparison with the Philips CD of this concert. Quite apart from the bonus of visual presentation, the DVD offers five numbers omitted from the CD – two of them by Josef Strauss celebrating his 175th anniversary, the polkas *Arm in Arm* and *Im Pfluge* and three Johann Strauss numbers, the *Carnevalsbotschafter* waltz, the *Beliebte Annen* polka and *Perpetuum mobile*.

Ozawa is at his most relaxed, naturally idiomatic in his often extreme use of idiomatic pauses and of warm *rubato*, reflected in his decision not to use a baton, relying instead on the inborn expressiveness of the Viennese players to mould in perfect time. In the *Fledermaus* Overture, for example, the switches of tempo and rhythm and the affectionate phrasing are immaculately achieved with a mere flutter of the fingers from the conductor.

Even by the standards of this celebratory occasion this was an unusually warm and happy event thanks to Ozawa. And more than anyone since Karajan in his one New Year concert, Ozawa controls the clapping of the audience, limiting it

to the proper passages in the final *Radetzky* March. The direction can't be faulted.

Die Fledermaus[a].
Bishop Home, sweet home[b]. **Cilea** L'arlesiana[c] – E la solita storia. **Rossini** Semiramide[d] – Serbami ognor sì fido. **Saint-Saëns** Samson et Dalila[e] – Mon coeur s'ouvre à ta voix **Verdi** La traviata[f] – Parigi, o cara [a]**Nancy Gustafson** *sop* Rosalinde [a]**Judith Howarth** *sop* Adele [a]**Louis Otey** *bar* Eisenstein [a]**Bonaventura Bottone** *ten* Alfred [a]**Anthony Michaels-Moore** *bar* Doctor Falke [a]**Jochen Kowalski** *counterten* Prince Orlofsky [a]**Eric Garrett** *bar* Frank [a]**John Dobson** *ten* Doctor Blind [a]**Glenys Groves** *sop* Ida [a]**John Sessions** *spkr* Frosch [a]**Peter Archer** *spkr* Ivan [bdf]**Dame Joan Sutherland** *sop* [cf]**Luciano Pavarotti** *ten* [de]**Marilyn Horne** *mez* **Royal Opera House Chorus and Orchestra, Covent Garden / Richard Bonynge** *Stage director* **John Cox** *Video director* **Humphrey Burton** ArtHaus Musik ② 📀 100 134 (197' · Region 2 & 5) Recorded live 1990 Ⓕ⬤

'Oh, what a night!' sings everybody on stage as Prince Orlofsky's ballroom takes leave of its earthly confines and sails for the happy isles borne on a tide of waltzes and a sea of champagne. It's always a good moment in *Die Fledermaus*, and this particular night was special. Most of those present at Covent Garden had seen a few New Year's Eves in their time, but never a one like this on December 31, 1990. And never, surely, has a *prima donna* been treated to such a stage party for her farewell. Dame Joan Sutherland sang that night for the last time in the house where she had made her début in 1952. Somebody had a brainwave when they thought of this as the occasion for what might otherwise have been a rather tearful event: Joan and two of her most illustrious partners of many performances would themselves be guests at Orlofsky's party in Act 2. Husband Richard Bonynge would conduct, so the party would therefore be complete. The guests slot in nicely at the moment when the revels are at their height. And there was New Year's Eve to celebrate. If the plan had a drawback it was one that concerned the opera itself. Act 3 of *Fledermaus* is always something of an anticlimax, and, with a celebrity recital thrown in, the middle act could seem to end with chords that cried 'Follow that!'. Happily, the production has a good move in store when, for the Finale, the backdrop for the prison scene goes up to reveal Orlofsky's ballroom aglow and once more ready to receive its guests. As for Act 1, it's extremely probable that the audiences at home will spend at least a part of it marvelling at the quality of sound and sight offered by the new medium of DVD.

Without in the least dominating, the orchestra here are present with a quite remarkable immediacy and naturalness. The outstanding voices among the cast were (in respect of pure tone) those of Judith Howarth and Anthony Michaels-Moore. Among the three celebrities, gallantly as both ladies sang, it was (and is on the film) Pavarotti whose voice had retained its quality. There's also plenty to watch, and with enjoyment. All on stage, including the chorus, act well. Humphrey Burton has supervised the filming so that the home viewer has the most privileged seat of all.

R Strauss

Elektra
Eva Marton *sop* Elektra **Brigitte Fassbaender** *mez* Klytemnestra **Cheryl Studer** *sop* Chrysothemis **Franz Grundheber** *bar* Orestes **James King** *ten* Aegisthus **Goran Simic** *bass* Tutor **Waltraud Winsauer** *mez* Confidante **Noriko Sasaki** *sop* Trainbearer **Wilfried Gahmlich** *ten* Young Servant **Claudio Otelli** *bass-bar* Old Servant **Gabriele Lechner** *sop* Overseer **Margarita Lilowa, Gabriele Sima, Margareta Hintermeier, Brigitte Poschner-Klebel, Joanna Borowska** Maidservants **Vienna State Opera Chorus and Orchestra / Claudio Abbado** Stage director **Harry Kupfer** Video director **Brian Large**
ArtHaus Musik *DVD* 100 048 (109' · DDD) Recorded live 1989 Ⓕ〇〇

This is an enjoyable performance, if that's the right word for *Elektra*'s gruesome drama, of Strauss's opera (taken from the first night of a new production at the Vienna State Opera in 1989), still one of the most sensational scores of the last century. Harry Kupfer may have conceived the work in even more lurid terms than its creators Hofmannsthal and Strauss intended, but the principals' psychotic behaviour is so convincingly enacted that we're carried into the soul of all their personal tortures of the mind. Elektra herself is a determined, raddled, single-minded harridan, lording it over sister and mother, a portrayal Eva Marton carries out with a deal of conviction, once one accepts the judder in her voice. Chrysothemis becomes a writhing, overwrought, frustrated figure, at one stage seeming to fake an orgasm, all of which Studer conveys with much emphasis on physical contact with her sister. She sings the taxing role with opulent tone and soaring phraseology.

Physicality is also of the essence in Fassbaender's study of guilt and inner disintegration as a Klytemnestra of intriguing complexity, yet she still somehow manages to suggest the character's feminine attraction. This portrayal alone makes this DVD essential viewing. Grundheber is the avenging Orestes to the life, with savagely piercing eyes and implacable tone. King is a properly futile paramour. In the activity of the extras, and such episodes as the butchering of Aegisthus and Chrysothemis wallowing in his blood-stained cloak, very little is left to the imagination. This is an enclosed world where licence and human sacrifices, unbridled in their ferocity, have taken over from order and humanity, and that was surely Kupfer's intention, so that Orestes' arrival has even more of a cleansing effect than usual.

In the pit, Abbado conducts with a single-minded intensity, constantly aware of the score's brutal and tragic aspects, and he procures playing of tremendous concentration from the Vienna Philharmonic. Although the staging takes place in Stygian gloom, you can discern more of its detail in this reincarnation on DVD, which has the added advantage of containing the whole opera on a single disc.

This is a version to buy for its absorbing, fully integrated view of Strauss's masterpiece.

Tan Dun

Concerto for Cello, Video and Orchestra, 'The Map' – A multimedia event in rural Chinaa. Includes the documentary, 'Rediscovering the Map'[b]
Anssi Karttunen *vc* **Shanghai Symphony Orchestra / Tan Dun** [a]*Aural and visual imaging* **Davey Frankel** *Video directors* [a]**Sheng Boji,** [a]**Wang Ping,** [b]**Uri Gal-Ed**
DG 20/21 *DVD* 073 4009GH (73' · NTSC · 4:3 · PCM stereo, 5.1 & DTS 5.1 · 0) Ⓕ〇

The Map is Tan Dun's quest to find the shamanistic 'stone man' he once heard in his youth. Armed with a commission from Yo-Yo Ma and the Boston Symphony Orchestra, he returned to Hunan with a camera crew to document village musical life and the non-Han minority peoples in particular. Once back in New York, he became a sort of Bartók for the media age, spinning ethnic traditional material into an abstract modernism while simultaneously preserving its roots on screen. The results are sprawling, to say the least. At times, such as the polyphonic tongue-singing of a group of Dong women, the orchestra merely frames the film footage. Elsewhere Tan's orchestral writing cheekily adapts the techniques of the village practitioners on a grand scale, such as having the entire percussion section enter into a dialogue with a group of Tujia cymbal players, or the winds and brass playing their reeds and mouthpieces in response to a village leaf-blower. The most creative touch comes in a *feige*, traditionally an antiphonal courtship song sung across mountains and valleys, but here featuring a Miao girl on screen performing with a live cello soloist, transcending entirely new boundaries of time and space.

Grasping the dimensions of this piece in a home format obviously requires a video recording; fortunately Hunan television was on hand when Tan brought the *The Map* to the village that inspired it. That broadcast, carefully edited and remixed here, is paired with a short film documenting that production, as well as Tan's original writing process.

Much of these musical traditions, it must be said, remain as exotic to most Chinese listeners as a Navajo chant would in the West. The most obvious weakness of *The Map* is that sometimes Tan seems all too content to play tourist, filming music that villagers play for outsiders rather than what they perform for themselves. Still, since his stated goal was not to document those cultures but to bring their rustic vitality into counterpoint with the slick urban world, *The Map* succeeds not in spite of its messiness but because of it.

Tavener

Fall and Resurrection
Patricia Rozario sop **Michael Chance** counterten **Martyn Hill** ten **Stephen Richardson** bass BBC Singers; St Paul's Cathedral Choir; City of London Sinfonia / **Richard Hickox** Video Director **David Kremer**
Etcetera 🄓🅥🄓 KTCD102 (96' · Region 0, in PAL & NTSC versions) Recorded live in 2000   🄕🅞

This could be called Tavener's *Creation*, an oratorio-like account of the Biblical tale beginning with a representation of primordial Chaos. It takes the story much further than Haydn, through Adam's fall to the Incarnation, ending in a 'Cosmic Dance of the Resurrection'. But, like Haydn's, this is a warmly mature work, epitomising its composer's style and personality.

The première at St Paul's Cathedral in January 2000, recorded here, was broadcast on TV and radio and released on CD by Chandos soon after. The disc was hailed in *Gramophone* as 'a wonderful document of an extraordinary evening of music'. There's little cause to disagree. Tavener's richly exotic textures, all founded on variations of an austere Byzantine chant and leavened with arcane instruments such as the shofar, or ram's horn, Tibetan temple bowls and Arabic kaval flutes, are beautifully evoked by Hickox and his forces, especially the vocal soloists.

The main question is whether DVD adds anything; and we believe it does. Visually, St Paul's, with its muted Byzantine influences, makes a splendid backdrop for this piece, which is infused with dramatic instrumental conflicts and clashes. Director David Kremer exploits the cathedral's spectacular aspects and perspectives, with discreet *chiaroscuro* lighting to underline these, and the Dolby 5.1 surround soundtrack accordingly strengthens the sense of spaciousness without seeming unduly unnatural. If you like Tavener, you need not hesitate.

Tchaikovsky

Queen of Spades
Yuri Marusin ten Herman **Nancy Gustafson** sop Lisa **Felicity Palmer** mez Countess **Sergei Leiferkus** bar Count Tomsky **Dimitri Kharitonov** bar Prince Yeletsky **Marie-Ange Todorovitch** contr Pauline **Graeme Matheson-Bruce** ten Chekalinsky **Andrew Slater** bass Surin **Robert Burt** ten Chaplitsky **Geoffrey Pogson** ten Major-Domo **Christopher Thornton-Holmes** bass Narumov **Enid Hartle** mez Governess **Rachel Tovey** sop Masha **Glyndebourne Festival Chorus; London Philharmonic Orchestra / Sir Andrew Davis** Stage director **Graham Vick** Film director **Peter Maniura**
ArtHaus Musik 🄓🅥🄓 100 272 (170' · 4:3 · 2.0 · 0)   🄕

Graham Vick's 1992 staging is worthy of this extraordinary score. He reflects exactly the highly charged emotions and sense of brooding menace pervading the composer's re-enactment of Pushkin's story, thus creating a compelling psychodrama that compels both eye and ear. Davis catches most, if not all, of the score's romantic sweep and inner, dislocating turbulence, although the impassioned undercurrents are better achieved in the Kirov video, conducted by Gergiev, not yet on DVD. Yuri Marusin is the crazed Herman incarnate. Whether or not you can accept his often off-pitch singing is a personal matter. As his Lisa, Nancy Gustafson, offers a portrayal of an impressionable girl driven to distraction and suicide by the unhinged behaviour of her lover. She sings the part in warm, passionate tones.

Peter Maniura's video direction catches every facial expression of both characters and of Felicity Palmer's electrifying Countess. Sergei Leiferkus is elegant and commanding as the free-loving Tomsky. Dimitri Kharitonov is the soul of rectitude as Yeletsky and brings a bronzed tone to his lovely aria. Marie-Ange Todorovitch is an attractively palpitating Pauline. Picture and sound are exemplary.

Additional recommendation

Queen of Spades
Grigorian ten Hermann **Guleghina** sop Lisa **Filatova** mez Countess **Leiferkus** bar Count Tomsky **Gergalov** bar Prince Yeletsky **Borodina** contr Pauline **Kirov Opera Chorus and Orchestra / Gergiev** Stage director **Temirkanov** Video director **Large**
Philips 🄓🅥🄓 070 434-9PH (179' · NTSC · 16:9 · 2.0 & DTS 5.1 · 0)   🄕🅞

This production from the Mariinsky Theatre, St Petersburg, and contemporaneous with the Glyndebourne production reviewed above, is a much more conventional but equally valid approach. The staging is always apt, and in terms of cast, the Kirov holds the edge over its rival. The young Guleghina is the intense, vibrant Lisa to the life. The video direction is exemplary, though the sound leaves something to be desired; there's a deal of distortion at the vocal climaxes.

Vecchi

L'Amfiparnaso
Simon Callow narr **Matthew Brook** bar Doctor Gratiano, Captain Cardon, Pedrolino, Frulla, Jew **Carys Lane** sop Hortensia, Francatrippa, Isabella **Rachel Elliott** sop Nisa **Richard Wyn Roberts** counterten Julian **Podger**, Nicholas **Mulroy** tens **Giles Underwood** bass Eligio Quinteiro **Ite Steven Devine** hpd I Fagiolini / **Robert Hollingworth** Pentalone; Lelio; Zanni; Jew. Stage director **Peter Wilson** Video director **Greg Browning**
Chandos Chaconne 🄓🅥🄓 CHDVD5029 (58' · 4:3 · 5.0 · 0) Extra features include an introduction by Robert Hollingworth; 'Working with singers'; character profiles and picture gallery. Notes, libretto and translation included   🄕

Performing a cohesive piece of 16th-century musical comedy is always a challenge. It's especially tough when the narrative is carried by a madrigal group of five voices (not like opera with a single voice per character), and the story embraces the serious and the delightful, a series of contemporary conceits, in-jokes, local dialects and puns impossibly embedded in the physiognomy of a world long gone. Add to this all the local knowledge, tricks and formulae that define the essentially improvisatory nature of *commedia dell'arte* and you have an arcane cocktail. But I Fagiolini turn a silk purse into one beaded with gold.

Vecchi's structure of 14 madrigal *scenas* sets out to evoke a vision of intense human observation, sensibility and foible, without action, a 'spectacle of the mind'. Robert Hollingworth has superimposed a level of invigorating *dell'arte* pastiche. Set in the grounds of Dartington, the 'Twin Peaks of Parnassus' play on the extremes of musical profundity and incorrigible slapstick. The action is taken from a live concert in the Hall; the singers sit discreetly to the side while the exhibitionists in the ensemble mime the action and dialogue. This includes sending up the stereotypes of the period – the rich and deluded merchant, the trading Jew and so on. Generally, the comedy is conceived with imagination and flair. Alongside the badinage Vecchi weaves in the elevated world of the mannerists, namely the delicious juxtaposition of love and tragic loss between Isabella and Lucio. The narrator, Simon Callow, doesn't actually act, but provides the deft facial expression and taut delivery to illuminate Timothy Knapman's snappy and suggestive verse.

A highly enjoyable production which celebrates the immediacy, relevance and enjoyment to be found in a 400-year old musical.

Verdi

Requiem
Angela Gheorghiu *sop* **Daniela Barcellona** *mez*
Roberto Alagna *ten* **Julian Konstantinov** *bass*
Swedish Radio Chorus; Berlin Philharmonic
Orchestra / Claudio Abbado *Video director* **Bob Coles**
EMI 🅓🅥🅓 DVB4 92693-9 (89' · 16:9, · 2.0, 5.1 &
DTS 5.1 · 0)   Ⓕⵔ

Seeing makes a deal of difference here. Though the CD issue of this performance at the Philharmonie, Berlin, in January 2001 was hugely enjoyable, this DVD enables one actually to see how the recently sick Abbado conducts the work as if it might be the last thing he does (happily not the case). He looks gaunt and tense: that translates into a heaven-seeking, searing account of the work, one to which everyone taking part readily responds. All the singers and players perform as though their lives depended on the outcome, and the results are simply electrifying. Praise can't be too high for the two professional choirs or for the Berlin Philharmonic

who, technically and emotionally, give their all. The soloists also seem on a devotional high, singing with appropriately spiritual fervour so that incidental criticisms seem of no importance. Bob Coles's video direction is always in the right place at the right time, and the sound perspective is as excellent as on the CD.

Aida
Adina Aaron *sop* Aida **Kate Aldrich** *mez* Amneris
Scott Piper *ten* Radames **Giuseppe Garra** *bar*
Amonasro **Enrico Giuseppe Iori** *bass* Ramfis **Paolo Pecchioli** *bass* King **Stefano Pisani** *ten* Messenger
Micaela Patriarca *sop* Priestess **Arturo Toscanini Foundation Chorus and Orchestra / Massimiliano Stefanelli** *Stage and video director* **Franco Zeffirelli**
TDK ② 🅓🅥🅓 DV-AIDDB (188' · 4:3 · 2.0 & 5.1 · 0)
Includes documentary, 'The Making of Aida'   Ⓕⵔ

Who would have imagined that this performance, which took place at Verdi's birthplace, Busseto, in January 2001 to mark the centenary of the composer's death, would carry such an emotional charge and evince such dramatic truthfulness? The performers are young singers gathered together under the auspices of the Toscanini Foundation and under the artistic direction of tenor Carlo Bergonzi, and of Franco Zeffirelli who directs the performance. It took place in the small gem of a 19th-century theatre at Busseto, not the most likely venue for such a grand opera, yet the very confinement of the surroundings forces everyone to re-think the work on a more intimate scale and in doing so they manage to go to the heart of the matter.

Adina Aaron is already a complete Aida. Every gesture, every movement, every note seems to come from the very soul of her being and her naturally shaped singing and sheer beauty of tone bespeak an auspicious future. As moving an Aida in fact since the young Leontyne Price.

Kate Aldrich as Amneris is very nearly as impressive. Possessor of a strikingly beautiful mezzo and the wherewithal to project it, she conveys every facet of the tormented Princess's predicament with total conviction. As Amonasro, Giuseppe Garra discloses a strong, vibrant baritone in the best traditions of his kind and he, like everyone else, acts with complete conviction. If the Radames, Scott Piper, another singer keen to obey Verdi's markings – witness a *pp* high B flat at the end of 'Celeste Aida' – was slightly less impressive, it's only because his voice is at present one size too small for the role. The orchestra plays with every fibre of its collective being for its committed conductor. Zeffirelli directs stage and film alike with all the experience at his command. The sound is a shade boxy, surely due to the small size of the venue. But that shouldn't be enough to stop anyone enjoying this riveting occasion.

Don Carlos
Roberto Alagna *ten* Don Carlos **Karita Mattila** *sop*
Elisabeth de Valois **Waltraud Meier** *mez* Eboli

Thomas Hampson *bar* Rodrigue **José van Dam**
bass-bar Philippe II **Eric Halfvarson** *bass-bar* Grand
Inquisitor **Csaba Airizer** *bass* Monk **Anat Efraty** *sop*
Thibault **Scot Weir** *ten* Comte de Lerme, Herald
Donna Brown *sop* Voice from Heaven **Chorus of the
Théâtre du Châtelet, Paris; Orchestre de Paris /
Antonio Pappano** *Stage director* Luc Bondy *Video
director* Yves André Hubert
NVC Arts 🅭 0630-16318-2 (211' · 2-6)   Ⓕ**OO**

This performance appeared on VHS back in
March 1997. On a new, wide-screen television,
it makes a far more arresting effect (on VHS the
top and bottom of the picture were cut off
because of the wide-screen format). The action
seems to be happening in the room with you.
That's due not only to the format but also to
director Luc Bondy's wish to portray the personal relationships, the characters' trials and
tribulations in the most intimate manner. In
contrast to most stagings of Verdi's epic, this
one turns all but the outdoor scenes, mainly the
Inquisition, into almost a domestic drama.

For better or worse, the principals seem very
modern. José van Dam, a magnificent and moving Philippe II, does sometimes remind one of
an out-of-sorts bank manager rather than a ruler
of an empire, with his troubled wife, in the
attractive person and voice of Mattila, as worka-
day Queen. Charisma is excluded by this interpretation. The relationship of Carlos and
Rodrigue, obviously a very close one, is a
touchy-feely affair, one that Alagna, in a sincere,
beautifully sung assumption, and a palpitating
Thomas Hampson, execute with flair.

As ever, Meier isn't content with conventional
acting: her Eboli is a scheming and seductive
presence, consoling us with the intensity of her
singing with a voice a shade light for her part.
Indeed, on re-appraising the musical side of the
performance, which was recorded live at the
Châtelet in Paris, it strikes you that all the voices
are a degree lighter than we're used to in the
piece, but that suits the French text, giving an
ease and fluidity to the vocal line that is, in truth,
its own justification.

Even more impressive on rehearing is Pappano's conducting, alive to every nuance of the
long work yet aware of its overall structure. In
the new medium the clarity and immediacy of
the picture is arresting. The sound, though a
shade soft in focus, is a great improvement on its
'ordinary' video counterpart. Owners of DVD
players who want to add this unforgettable work
to their collection need not hesitate – provided
they can see it on a wide screen.

Don Carlo
Luciano Pavarotti *ten* Don Carlo **Daniella Dessì** *sop*
Elisabetta di Valois **Luciana d'Intino** *mez* Eboli **Paolo
Coni** *bar* Rodrigo **Samuel Ramey** *bass* Filippo II
Alexander Anisimov *bass* Grand Inquisitor **Andrea
Silvestrelli** *bass* Monk **Marilena Laurenza** *sop*
Tebaldo **Orfeo Zanetti** *ten* Conte di Lerma **Mario
Bolognesi** *ten* Herald **Nuccia Focile** *sop* Voice from
Heaven **Chorus and Orchestra of La Scala, Milan /**

Riccardo Muti *Stage and video director* **Franco
Zeffirelli**
EMI 🅭 599442-9 (182' · NTSC · 4:3 · PCM Stereo
5.1 & DTS 5.1 · 0) Recorded live at Teatro alla Scala,
Milan, December 1992   Ⓕ

If you want the edition of the work revised in
Italian by Verdi, first performed in 1884, this is
your only choice to date on DVD – and it
proves, as it did on VHS, a satisfying experience.
The work in this form is tauter and more direct
than the five-act French original caught on the
DVD of the Châtelet production conducted by
Pappano. Those who know Zeffirelli's style
won't be surprised by the conventionally lavish
production, but it effectively evokes the atmosphere of religious oppression and personal
antagonisms Verdi so unerringly depicts.

The dark-hued, threatening setting fits Muti's
energetic, rhythmically vital conception. He
quickens the emotions in a peculiarly Italianate
way, and throughout evinces a feeling for the
colouring of the score. His reading is in turn a
good background for some thoughtful and
idiomatic singing.

Pavarotti delivers Carlo's music in a typically
fervent manner, words ideally placed on the
voice and his tone consistently firm and pliable.
His girth makes him unconvincing as the small,
lean, nervous Carlo of history, but his simple,
sincere acting is its own advocate. Daniella
Dessì looks the very image of the wronged, sympathetic Elisabetta and sings with feeling and
good phrasing. Paolo Coni offers a concerned,
upright Rodrigo, sung in warm tones though he
sometimes loses focus under pressure.

Zeffirelli's video direction is well fashioned
and the sound picture catches the aural ambience of La Scala. As a whole, this is a vivid experience.

Falstaff
Ambrogio Maestri *bass-bar* Falstaff **Roberto
Frontali** *bar* Ford **Barbara Frittoli** *sop* Alice Ford
Inva Mula *sop* Nannetta **Juan Diego Flórez** *ten*
Fenton **Bernadette Manca di Nissa** *contr* Mistress
Quickly **Anna Caterina Antonacci** *mez* Meg Page
Ernesto Gavazzi *ten* Doctor Caius **Paolo Barbacini**
ten Bardolph **Luigi Roni** *bass* Pistol **Chorus and
Orchestra of La Scala, Milan / Riccardo Muti** *Stage
director* **Ruggero Cappuccio** *Video director* **Pierre
Cavasillas**
TDK Mediactive 🅭 DV-OPFAL (118' · 16:9 · 2.0 &
5.1 · 0) Notes included   Ⓕ**OO**

This performance derives from a special production of *Falstaff* at Verdi's birthplace to mark
the centenary of his death. It's a replica of staging given in the same theatre, the Teatro Verdi,
under Toscanini, in 1913, using facsimiles of the
original sets. Some may find the small stage and
traditional sets simply old-fashioned, but given a
superb cast perceptively directed by Ruggero
Cappuccio, what we see and hear is Verdi's
masterpiece presented in the most natural,
unforced way, with everyone on stage enjoying

themselves. The result is a warm-hearted, unforced reading that makes the rival Graham Vick production at Covent Garden look, by its side, forced and contrived, not to mention the inadequacies of the anti-Verdian Aix production also on DVD. Muti's masterly traversal of the score – at once prompt yet relaxed – adds to the pleasure.

The cast is headed by Ambrogio Maestri, 31 at the time, in the title part who in vocal and physical size is Italy's answer to Bryn Terfel, Haitink's Falstaff, and as with Terfel is a youngish man playing the ageing Knight; but Maestri is very much a member of an ensemble, not a star giving his interpretation. He portrays the Fat Knight as still youthful in his outlook and quite nimble afoot. He performs it entirely without Terfel's (or Vick's) attempts at vulgar exaggeration: everything emerges from the text and music, and the singing itself is finely modulated and easy on the ear.

He's surrounded by a group of Merry Wives as ebullient and resourceful as any on audio or video versions. Barbara Frittoli's scheming Alice is nicely set of against Anna Caterina Antonacci's witty Meg, while Bernadette Manca di Nissa sings and acts Quickly truly, without the traditional guying of the part. Roberto Frontali's Ford is much more in character than on the rival version and he parleys perfectly with Maestri's Falstaff. Juan Diego Flórez and Inva Mula as sweet-voiced and handsome-looking lovers and excellent *comprimarios* are all part of this highly recommendable DVD. Video direction and sound picture are exemplary. Don't miss its many delights.

Falstaff

José Van Dam *bar* Falstaff **William Stone** *bar* Ford **Barbara Madra** *sop* Alice Ford **Elzbieta Szmytka** *sop* Nannetta **Laurence Dale** *ten* Fenton **Livia Budai** *mez* Mistress Quickly **Benedetta Pecchioli** *mez* Meg Page **Mario Luperi** *bass* Pistol **Ugo Benelli** *ten* Dr Caius **Théâtre de la Monnaie Chorus and Orchestra, Brussels / Sylvain Cambreling** *Stage director* **Lluis Pasqual** *Video director* **André Flédérick**
Warner Music Vision/NVC Arts 🆅 5050467 4469-2-2 (130′ · NTSC · 4:3 · 2.0 · 2-6) Recorded live at the Aix-en-Provence Festival, 1987 Ⓕ

There can seldom have been so wholly satisfactory a traversal of Verdi's closing masterpiece, on both dramatic and musical grounds, as this 1987 staging at Aix. Director Lluis Pasqual goes to the heart of the matter in sets by Fabia Puigserver that are at once minimalist yet highly evocative in terms of milieu, and happily coloured by sepia tints, subtly lit. Within them, Pasqual directs his principals with an eye for natural yet cleverly pointed movement.

He's lucky to have José Van Dam, at the height of his powers in 1987. This Falstaff is wholly believable as a mature lover and true knight, one who never plays the fool. At every point Van Dam allows him to arise from the text and the

music, which he sings with firm and well-moulded tone. He's surrounded by a cast on a similarly high level, headed by Barbara Madra's lively, quick-witted, beautifully sung Alice. Benedetta Pecchioli makes more of Meg than most mezzos, and also looks her part. Livia Budai is a witty, pert Quickly who sings the role rather than mugging it. William Stone projects Ford's jealousy convincingly on a flood of strong, firm tone. Mario Luperi is a nicely lugubrious Pistol, Ugo Benelli a characterful Dr Caius. The lovers may not be the most fluent ever heard, but they're worthy members of a distinguished ensemble.

Cambreling conducts a scrupulously prepared account of the score. The autumnal colours mean that sometimes the facial expressions aren't as clear as they might be, but by and large the video direction is excellent, as is the sound. This version is preferable to the admirable Muti one, which suffers from the rather restricting confines of the small theatre at Busseto.

La forza del destino

Renata Tebaldi *sop* Leonora **Franco Corelli** *ten* Don Alvaro **Ettore Bastianini** *bar* Don Carlo **Boris Christoff** *bass* Padre Guardiano **Oralia Dominguez** *mez* Preziosilla **Renato Capecchi** *bar* Fra Melitone **Jorge Algorta** *bass* Marquis of Calatrava **Mariano Caruso** *ten* Trabuco *mez* Curra **Anna di Stasio** *mez* Curra **Giuseppe Forgione** *bass* Mayor **Gianni Bardi** *bass* Surgeon **Naples San Carlo Opera Chorus and Orchestra / Francesco Molinari-Pradelli**
Hardy Classic Video 🆅 HCD4002 (160′ · NTSC · 4:3 · 1.0 · 0) Recorded live at the San Carlo Theatre, Naples 1958 Includes interview with Renata Tebaldi Ⓕ

Why is it that this performance in low-fi and indifferent black-and-white picture, and in a distinctly old-fashioned staging, has become a legend among collectors of opera on video to the extent of becoming a VHS best-seller? The answer lies in the quality of execution of a once-in-a-lifetime cast, supported by idiomatic conducting and playing at the San Carlo in Naples back in 1958.

Tebaldi had already proved at the Maggio Musicale at Florence in 1953 under Mitropoulos that Leonora was to be among her most successful roles, and here she confirms the fact in spades with her lustrous, effortlessly shaped and eloquent traversal of the role.

By her side she has the incomparable Corelli, singing his first Don Alvaro, and revealing that his brilliant, exciting yet plangent tone is precisely the right instrument to project Alvaro's loves and sorrows. At this stage of his career his thrilling upper register and incisive delivery of the text were at their most potent, as he makes abundantly clear in aria and duet. As his antagonist, Bastianini sings with the kind of Verdian élan seemingly now extinct among his breed. He may not be the most subtle of Verdian baritones, but here his macho approach ideally suits Don Carlo's vengeful imprecations.

If that weren't enough vocal splendour for one

occasion, there's Christoff – yet another member of the cast at the peak of his career – intoning Padre Guardiano's dignified utterances in that unique if not always entirely Italianate manner of his. Renato Capecchi for long made the part of Melitone his own: one can see and hear why here in his amusing yet never overstated sense of the role's comic possibilities. The voices are caught with very little distortion in goodish sound. The original film has suffered some deterioration over the years, but its recent restoration yields far better results than was once the case on dim VHS copies: this DVD derives from RAI's original master copy. Pleasure is completed by the bonus of a recent interview with Tebaldi.

Macbeth
Thomas Hampson bar Macbeth **Paoletta Marrocu** sop Lady Macbeth **Roberto Scandiuzzi** bass Banquo **Luis Lima** ten Macduff **Miroslav Christoff** ten Malcolm **Mihály Kálmándi** bass Doctor **Liuba Chuchrova** mez Lady-in-Waiting **Zurich Opera House Chorus and Orchestra / Franz Welser-Möst** Stage director **David Pountney** Video director **Thomas Grimm**
TDK Mediactive 📀 DV-OPMAC (186' · 16:9 · 2.0, 5.1 & DTS 5.1 · 2) Recorded live at the Opera House, Zurich 2001. Includes special feature, 'Macbeth – an Introduction'. Ⓕ**OO**

Here's yet another challenging and well-executed staging from the Zurich Opera, this one dating from 2001. David Pountney, in at least his third attempt at the work, presents the Shakespearian drama in predictably unorthodox manner, irritating in its overuse of distracting symbols, extras and props, but revelatory in its pointed treatment of the principal pair of characters. The production is at its most bizarre in the Witches' scenes, where a pack of maddened women disport themselves in an orgy of man-hating, but even when the effects are at their most outrageous a sense of a guiding hand is there to lend some sort of dramatic cohesion to the whole.

Pountney bases his concept on the erotic relationship, vividly delineated, between Macbeth and his spouse; their sex-dominated marriage is obviously the spur to their overweening ambition, with she – as ever – leading the way. Paoletta Marrocu, a Sardinian soprano with a growing reputation, throws caution to the winds in her energetic, purposeful, fierce attack on Lady Macbeth. From first to last it's a truly stunning performance both histrionically and vocally. Few sopranos, Callas undoubtedly is one, have sung the part so confidently and incisively in a powerful, lean yet strong voice unflinchingly projected. By her side Hampson's haunted Macbeth is a striking portrait of a man pushed to the limits in the cause of getting to the top. His voice may not be truly Italianate in timbre, but he uses it here with such intelligence and force that one can overlook the want of a certain bite in his tone.

Welser-Möst presides over everything with an acute ear for the work's *tinta* and judges his speeds to a nicety, with admirable support from his own house's chorus and orchestra. The 1987 Berlin version on ArtHaus Musik, finely conducted by Sinopoli, seems tame beside this one.

Otello
Mario Del Monaco ten Otello **Rosanna Carteri** sop Desdemona **Renato Capecchi** bar Iago **Gino Mattera** ten Cassio **Athos Cesarini** ten Roderigo **Luisella Ciaffi** mez Emilia **Plinio Clabassi** bass Lodovico **Nestore Catalani** bass Montano **Bruno Cioni** bass Herald **Chorus and Orchestra of RAI, Milan / Tullio Serafin** Film director **Franco Enriquez**
Hardy Classic Video 📀 HCD4004 (136' · NTSC · 4:3 Black & White · 1.0 · 0) Recorded 1958 Notes included Ⓕ

This film of *Otello* isn't to be overlooked, in spite of its age, because of the quality of the performance. It formed part of Italian television's pioneering series of productions employing the top rank of native singers when such a group still existed. On this occasion a well-known opera director, Franco Enriquez, was employed to achieve as much as was possible in terms of dramatic fluidity within the technical restrictions then applicable in the studio. The acting of minor characters may be a bit stilted, but the principals, who come under face-to-face scrutiny, stand up well to Enriquez's methods.

So preserved here is a native account of Verdi's masterpiece that would be hard to equal today. Mario Del Monaco was then at the height of his powers, the reigning Otello of the time, and one of the role's most powerful exponents ever. His portrayal had developed by the late 1950s into a psychological study of some depth and intensity, released on a stream of taut, exciting tone. By his side, Renato Capecchi sings a strongly voiced, highly articulate, intelligently shaped and believable Iago. But perhaps the most compelling performance of all is Rosanna Carteri's Desdemona. Love, fidelity and sincerity are conveyed in her eyes, indeed her whole being, and in her faultless vocal traversal of the role. Over all presides Serafin, conducting an unobtrusively correct and vital performance of a score he knew so well.

There are downsides. The lip-synch, especially in the case of Capecchi, leaves much to be desired. The sound is confined and occasionally wayward, and the film is obviously a shade worn, but all that's easily forgotten when you're caught up in such a convincing performance.

Otello
Plácido Domingo ten Otello **Barbara Frittoli** sop Desdemona **Leo Nucci** bar Iago **Cesare Catani** ten Cassio **Antonello Ceron** ten Roderigo **Rossana Rinaldi** mez Emilia **Giovanni Battista Parodi** bass Lodovico **Cesare Lana** bass Montano **Ernesto Panariello** bass Herald **Giuseppe Verdi**

Conservatory Children's Choir, Milan; La Scala
Children's Choir, Chorus and Orchestra, Milan /
Riccardo **Muti** *Stage director* Graham **Vick** *Video
director* Carlo **Battistoni**
TDK Mediactive 📀 DV-OPOTEL (140' · 16:9 · PCM
Stereo, 5.1 & DTS 5.1· 0) Notes and synopsis
included   Ⓕ**OO**

This is one of Graham Vick's most intelligent,
detailed and involving productions housed in
Ezio Frigero's superbly crafted and atmospheric
set and clothed by Franca Squarciapino's traditional, beautifully wrought costumes. Here's
proof, if proof were needed, that setting an
opera in its period still works best provided you
have such sensitive hands in control.

The thoughtful, often revelatory, handling of
the principals often lends a new dimension to
the work, especially with such eloquent singing
actors as Plácido Domingo and Barbara Frittoli;
remarkable is the strength of passion engendered by the fated lovers – blissful in Act 1, desperately tormented in Act 3.

At this late stage in his career Domingo was
able to compensate for a voice that doesn't
always obey his exemplary instincts with a moving portrayal of the Moor. His projection of his
own near-disbelief in his agony and jealousy in
Act 3, and again before the murder, is deeply
affecting. So are Frittoli's facial expressions and
body language, yielding and erotic in Act 1,
making her Act 3 and final disillusion that much
more terrifying to behold. Vocally Domingo
sings with even more variety of dynamic and
timbre than before. His pent-up fury in the big
ensemble is truly frightening. Frittoli sings with
many shades of tone and exquisite phrasing
throughout, not least in her Act 4 solos, which
she enacts with searing emotion. Leo Nucci's
penny-plain, dully sung Iago isn't in the same
league, and the young tenor taking Cassio lacks
the requisite sweetness in the voice. The Emilia
is admirable, as are the two basses. Muti leads
the drama to its dreadful conclusion with his
customary brio and care for incidentals.

The video direction and the sound picture
leave nothing to be desired. This is the only
modern-day DVD-Video of *Otello* worth having
at present.

Rigoletto
Paolo **Gavanelli** *bar* Rigoletto Christine **Schäfer** *sop*
Gilda Marcelo **Álvarez** *ten* Duke Eric **Halfvarson**
bass Sparafucile Graciela **Araya** *contr* Maddalena
Giovanni Battista **Parodi** *bass* Monterone Elizabeth
Sikora *sop* Giovanna Peter **Auty** *ten* Borsa Quentin
Hayes *bar* Marullo Dervla **Ramsay** *mez* Countess
Ceprano Graeme **Broadbent** *bass* Count Ceprano
Andrea **Hazell** *mez* Page Nigel **Cliffe** *bass* Usher
Royal Opera House Orchestra and Chorus, Covent
Garden / Edward **Downes** *Stage director* David
McVicar *Film director* Sue **Judd**
BBC/Opus Arte Media 📀 OA0829D (169' · 16:9 ·
5.1 · 0)   Ⓕ**O**

David McVicar's engrossing 2001 production of

Rigoletto at Covent Garden caused something of
a stir because of the frank licentiousness of the
opening scene, including sex of all varieties. It's
a bold and sensational beginning to the staging,
depicting the Duke of Mantua as a libidinous
and strident ruler of his ill-disciplined domain.
Given that picture of the court, the contrast of
Rigoletto's almost obsessive love for his daughter is all the more poignant.

That's the background to a performance of
thrilling commitment on all sides, at whose centre is the arresting portrayal of Rigoletto from
Paolo Gavanelli, probably the best acted and
most sensitively sung, in terms of variety and
colouring of tone, since Tito Gobbi essayed the
role in the same house 35 years ago (even if he
has an occasional tendency to lose pitch).

By comparison, Christine Schäfer's Gilda is a
trifle cool at the start, but once ravished she
comes to emotional life and is particularly moving in the final act. Her singing, though not Italianate in colour, is musically shaped and technically flawless. Marcelo Álvarez is the epitome of
a selfish, macho ruler, and Eric Halfvarson a
suitably sinister Sparafucile. Downes conducts a
well-nigh faultless account. The only reservation concerns the sound. Too frequently the
voices are too backwardly placed in relation to
the orchestra, but that shouldn't deter you from
being part of a very special occasion.

Additional recommendation

La traviata
Bonfadelli Violetta **Piper** Alfredo **Bruson** Germont
**Arturo Toscanini Foundation Chorus and
Orchestra / Domingo** *Stage director* **Zeffirelli**
TDK Mediactive ② 📀 DV-OPLTR (205' · 16:9 · 2.0,
5.1 & DTS 5.1 · 0) Includes documentary, 'Making of
La traviata' and interviews. Notes included   Ⓕ
    Lovingly directed and designed by the then 78-
    year-old Zeffirelli. Bonfadelli makes a very fine
    Violetta – it's a reading that demands to be seen
    and heard. Sound quality is beyond reproach, and
    though it may not surpass the Solti DVD
    (reviewed above) it deserves to stand alongside it
    as a recommendation.

Il trovatore
Kenneth **Collins** *ten* Manrico Joan **Sutherland** *sop*
Leonora Jonathan **Summers** *bar* Count di Luna
Lauris **Elms** *mez* Azucena Donald **Shanks** *bass*
Ferrando Cynthia **Johnston** *sop* Ines Robin **Donald**
ten Ruiz John **Durham** *bass* Old Gypsy **Australian
Opera Chorus; Elizabethan Sydney Orchestra /
Richard Bonynge** *Stage director* Elijah **Moshinsky**
Video director Riccardo **Pellizzeri**
ArtHaus Musik 📀 100 276 (142' · 4:3 · 2.0 · 2 & 5)
Recorded live at the Sydney Opera House, 1983.
Notes included   Ⓕ

This performance of Sutherland finds her on
something like her best form, not always the
case in the Australian performances recorded
late in her career. With large evocative gauzes

by Sidney Nolan, used as backcloths, appealing 19th-century costumes by Lucian Arrighi, and Moshinsky's animated, effectively spotlit tableaux, the eye is well-served. In this milieu Moshinsky directs his principals with his usual discernment.

He couldn't attempt anything unconventional with his *prima donna*, but Sutherland does convention uncommonly well, expressing emotion through minimal gestures and expressive eyes. She could have had a worthy career devoting herself to Verdi, but chose otherwise. It's good to hear her realising the music Verdi wrote for his heroine with full tone, grand phrasing and, where called for, much of her well-known skill as regards technique and coloratura – her last-act aria gives the best evidence of that. If the diva's lower voice was by her late fifties rather threadbare, the top here rings firmly and truly.

As her troubadour she has that sterling English tenor Kenneth Collins, singing with the innate strength and honesty that were always his hallmarks in early and mid-Verdi. Nothing in Manrico's role is shirked, everything is idiomatically phrased. His stage presence leaves something to be desired but that can be overlooked given the true *spinto* sound of his voice.

The more convincing pair are, however, Jonathan Summers as Luna and Lauris Elms as Azucena, both at different times much admired in this country. Bonynge is in energetic form in the pit, and always aware of how to give his singers room to phrase with feeling. The sound leaves something to be desired: it's fuzzy from time to time. The video direction is also a bit hit-and-miss. Neither reservation lessens the strength of this recommendation.

Il trovatore
Plácido Domingo ten Manrico **Raina Kabaivanska** sop Leonora **Piero Cappuccilli** bar Count di Luna **Fiorenza Cossotto** mez Azucena **José Van Dam** bass Ferrando **Vienna State Opera Chorus and Orchestra / Herbert von Karajan** Stage director **Herbert von Karajan** Video director **Günther Schneider-Siemssen**
TDK ② 🅳🅥🅳 DV-CLOPIT (151' · 4:3 · PCM stereo, 5.1 & DTS 5.1 · 0) Recorded live at the Staatsoper, Vienna, 1 May 1978   Ⓕ**OO**

Never available before, this marvellous performance marked Karajan's long-awaited return to the Vienna State Opera in 1978. It was also the notorious occasion when Franco Bonisolli threw a tantrum and walked out of the dress rehearsal. He was replaced at the eleventh hour by Domingo, who thereby completed a cast that has hardly been bettered. Inspired no doubt by the reception he receives on first entering the pit, Karajan is at his most proactive, and the singers react with real conviction to complement their exemplary singing.

The staging, Karajan's own, and the sets are pretty conventional, but who cares when the score is projected with such confidence and the voices are of such rare quality? The youngish

Domingo is the feisty troubadour of the title to the life, and he sings Manrico's taxing music as if that were the easiest thing in the world. As his adversary, Count di Luna, Piero Cappuccilli is in firm, supple voice, giving a faultless account of 'Il balen' and fierily dramatic in the ensembles. Fiorenza Cossotto offers her appreciable all to Azucena, a role she made very much her own and one in which she's yet to be surpassed. As Ferrando, José Van Dam launches the opera with tremendous authority. Raina Kabaivanska, the Leonora, may not have had a typically Verdian voice, but what she does with her resources is remarkable, combining a classic style – some beautifully etched phrasing – with a poise as a vocal and dramatic actress that's second to none, except perhaps Callas.

So it's one vocal treat after another, culminating in a superlative Act 4. Sound, picture and direction are exemplary. This absorbing issue is highly recommended to all admirers of Verdi and great singing.

Wagner

Die Meistersinger von Nürnberg
Wolfgang Brendel bass-bar Hans Sachs **Gösta Winbergh** ten Walther **Eva Johansson** sop Eva **Victor von Halem** bass Pogner **Elke Wilm Schulte** bar Beckmesser **Uwe Peper** ten David **Ute Walther** mez Magdalene **Lenus Carlson** bass Kothner **David Griffith** ten Vogelgesang **Barry McDaniel** bar Nachtigall **Volker Horn** ten Zorn **Peter Maus** ten Eisslinger **Otto Heuer** ten Moser **Ivan Sardi** bass Schwarz **Friedrich Molsberger** bass Foltz **Peter Edelmann** bass Nightwatchman **Berlin Opera Orchestra and Chorus / Rafael Frühbeck de Burgos** Stage director **Götz Friedrich** Video director **Brian Large**
Arthaus Musik ② 🅳🅥🅳 100 152 (266' · Region 0) Ⓕ**OO**

This has to be one of the most engrossing and satisfactory performances of *Die Meistersinger* in memory. Pleasure derives as much as anything from the sense of a complete intregration of music and action in a staging that has been scrupulously rehearsed on all sides. This is a 1995 revival with the same cast as the 1993 original, and it's clear how keen the response of the singers to each other is. The credit for one's profound enjoyment undoubtably goes to the late, lamented Götz Friedrich. Renowned for his handling of characters and their interaction on stage, his skills in that sphere have seldom if ever been more fruitfully displayed. The action and reaction of the masters in their Act 1 disputations, the subtle relationship between Sachs and Eva, the ebb and flow of the arguments between Sachs and Beckmesser, and the friendly interplay between Walther and Sachs, the disciple eagerly learning from the teacher in Act 1 scene 3, are all revelatory. In these and other scenes, more of the characters' humanity is expressed than has ever been shown before. This is operatic acting on the highest level of achievement.

Frühbeck de Burgos enhances the director's approach with his chamber-like treatment of the orchestra, allowing the singers' clear enunciation to be heard at all times. He's also to be commended for the discerning ebb and flow of his reading as a whole, which is at once lively and unforced. Wolfgang Brendel presents an affectionate, sympathetic, somewhat laid-back, ruminative Sachs, his voice lacking in warmth only at the bottom of his register, the sound more baritone than bass-orientated. As we know from Covent Garden, Winbergh is a well-nigh ideal Walther, singing his role with unwonted ease and lyrical breadth, responsive always to the text's meaning. Johansson is a knowing, flirtatious Eva, forthcoming in voice and mien; her earthbound start of the Quintet comes as a disappointment after her gloriously outgoing 'O Sachs, mein Freund'. Schulte sings and acts Beckmesser to perfection, never resorting to caricature in depicting the self-important, didactic town clerk and giving the role a wealth of nuance, always keeping to the notes. Peper is a well-routined, likeable David, Von Halem an imposing, properly fatherly Pogner.

As a whole, this is a performance to treasure. It has admirably balanced sound and perceptive video direction by the ultra-experienced Brian Large. Highly recommended.

Die Meistersinger von Nürnberg
James Morris bass Hans Sachs **Ben Heppner** ten
Walther **Karita Mattila** sop Eva **René Pape**
bass Pogner **Sir Thomas Allen** bass Beckmesser
Matthew Polenzani ten David **Jill Grove** mez
Magdalene **John Del Carlo** bass Kothner
**Metropolitan Opera Chorus and Orchestra, New
York / James Levine** Stage director Video director
Brian Large
DG ② 📀 0730949-2GH2 (292' · NTSC · 16:9 ·
PCM stereo, 5.1 & DTS 5.1 · 0) Recorded live at the
Metropolitan Opera, New York, December 2001.
Extras include picture gallery Ⓕ**OO**

This most humane and intimate of all Wagner's operas is a natural for DVD, but we haven't yet had a wholly satisfactory version. However, this Met version, superbly recorded in widescreen, boasting a mouthwatering cast, largely fulfils the considerable expectations it raises.

Conducting and staging are solidly uncontroversial. Levine's rich, weighty Wagner style seems to suit *Meistersinger* better than *The Ring*. There are still some unexpected gear changes, but better integrated into a fluent, warm reading. Otto Schenk's production is almost aggressively traditional – lively enough, but one longs for some subtler spark of originality or insight, in the sets especially. A properly bustling Act 3 'Festweise' is welcome, instead of dull grandstands, but the Act 2 brawl is sadly shirked.

The singers are the best on DVD. With his clear, unbaritonal lyric Heldentenor, Ben Heppner is a convincingly poetic Walther; but the bulky face and frame lose credibility in Brian Large's vivid camera direction. Even the beauti-

ful Karita Mattila's girlish antics look less appropriate, but she remains a stunning Eva, dramatic in power but with reserves of crystalline lyricism. René Pape's Pogner looks no older than his 'daughter', a minor blemish on a finely resonant performance, but a blow to dramatic involvement. Sir Thomas Allen's minutely characterised, acidulous Beckmesser is properly malevolent yet unexpectedly mellifluous, hilarious without vocal distortions. James Morris's Sachs is warm-hearted, quintessentially American and none the worse for that. His voice is more sinewy now and less steady, losing some of its rich tone and silken *legato*, but gaining in character. He's still not ideally expressive, though, making less of the cobbler-poet's visionary and temperamental side, and more telling as Eva and Walther's genial mentor than in the monologues. His fellow Mastersingers are well portrayed, though John Del Carlo could make more of Kothner, but the chorus and apprentices can't quite match Bayreuth's.

This amiable, large-scale performance is highly recommendable.

Der Ring des Nibelungen
**Chorus and Orchestra of the Metropolitan Opera,
New York / James Levine** Stage director **Otto
Schenk** Video director **Brian Large**
DG ⑦ 📀 073 043-9GH7 (941' · 4:3 · 2.0 & 5.1* · 0)
*Dolby digital & dts. Recorded live at the
Metropolitan Opera House 1989-90. Notes included
Ⓕ
Also available separately as below

Das Rheingold
James Morris bass Wotan **Christa Ludwig** mez
Fricka **Siegfried Jerusalem** ten Loge **Heinz Zednik**
ten Mime **Ekkehard Wlaschiha** bass Alberich **Mari
Anne Häggander** sop Freia **Mark Baker** ten Froh
Alan Held bar Donner **Birgitta Svendén** mez Erda
Jan-Hendrik Rootering bass Fasolt **Matti Salminen**
bass Fafner **Kaaren Erickson** sop Woglinde **Diane
Kesling** mez Wellgunde **Meredith Parsons** contr
Flosshilde
DG 📀 073 036-9GH (163') Ⓕ

Die Walküre
Gary Lakes ten Siegmund **Jessye Norman** sop
Sieglinde **Hildegard Behrens** sop Brünnhilde **James
Morris** bass Wotan **Christa Ludwig** mez Fricka **Kurt
Moll** bass Hunding **Pyramid Sellers** sop Gerhilde
Katarina Ikonomu sop Helmwige **Martha Thigpen**
sop Ortlinde **Joyce Castle** mez Waltraute **Jacalyn
Bower** mez Rossweise **Diane Kesling** mez Siegrune
Wendy Hillhouse mez Grimgerde **Sondra Kelly**
contr Schwertleite
DG ② 📀 073 049-9GH2 (241') Ⓕ

Siegfried
Siegfried Jerusalem ten Siegfried **James Morris**
bass Wanderer **Hildegard Behrens** sop Brünnhilde
Heinz Zednik ten Mime **Ekkehard Wlaschiha** bass
Alberich **Birgitta Svendén** mez Erda **Fritz Hübner**
bass Fafner **Dawn Upshaw** sop Woodbird
DG ② 📀 073 037-9GH2 (253') Ⓕ

Götterdämmerung
Hildegard Behrens sop Brünnhilde **Siegfried
Jerusalem** ten Siegfried **Matti Salminen** bass Hagen
Ekkehard Wlaschiha bass Alberich **Anthony Raffell**
bass Gunther **Hanna Lisowska** sop Gutrune **Christa
Ludwig** mez Waltraute **Kaaren Erickson** sop
Woglinde **Diane Kesling** mez Wellgunde **Meredith
Parsons** contr Flosshilde **Gweneth Bean** contr First
Norn **Joyce Castle** mez Second Norn **Andrea
Gruber** sop Third Norn
DG ② 📀 073 040-9GH2 (281') Ⓟ**OO**

None of the four video-recorded versions can be
called ideal; but this Met cycle has plenty of
strong points. It's the only one Wagner would
have recognised – no small consideration. It's
frequently assumed these days that he chose
myth primarily to convey political allegory, but
this is misleading. Myth inspired Wagner as
directly as it did, say, Sibelius; and producers
who ignore or mock this, like Patrice Chéreau
on Pierre Boulez's rival set, miss a vital dimension. Here, Otto Schenk and designer Gunther
Schneider-Siemssen preserve the Romantic
imagery, often beautifully, as Brian Large's
cameras reveal; but also unimaginatively, with
too many tired compromises. Some, such as the
Rhinemaidens' non-swimming contortions and
the feeble dragon, are embarrassing, and the
costumes often look poor on screen. Individual
performances, too, sometimes don't fit into a
satisfactory ensemble.

This set can also claim musical superiority; but
again, not conclusively. Boulez mistakes speed
for energy, drying out the richness of the score;
Levine, with the magnificent Met orchestra,
tends to wallow in it, especially in a disappointing *Rheingold*. Matters improve from *Walküre*
onward, but he's prone to sudden wheelspin-
ning accelerations, sometimes wrongfooting his
singers. Boulez remains invisible at Bayreuth;
Levine is too much with us, to the detriment of
atmosphere. Nevertheless, his monumental
approach does bring out *The Ring*'s sheer beauty
and grandeur, where Boulez simply seems glib.

Levine's cast is superior, too, although the pivotal roles are the closest. Both Brünnhildes are
splendid, spirited and deeply moving, but
Boulez's Gwyneth Jones has the fuller voice;
Hildegard Behrens, lithe and nervy, must force
an essentially lyric instrument – quite successfully, but the effort shows. James Morris, aspiring to be a *bel canto* Wotan, has a richer voice
than Boulez's Donald MacIntyre, but his diction
and his acting are less incisive – partly the producer's fault in *Rheingold*; he improves thereafter. Siegfried Jerusalem, though, eclipses
Boulez's inadequate Manfred Jung. More lyrical
and vocally more heroic, he's a finer musician,
less liable to strain and distort the line, and an
impressive stage figure.

Jerusalem's surprisingly characterful Loge,
despite his galia melon headgear, is probably the
best thing in *Rheingold*. It's rewarding to hear
the 'Narration' in this kind of voice. Otherwise
this is lacklustre. A superb Rhinemaiden trio is
left earthbound, writhing unconvincingly round

Ekkehard Wlaschiha's buffoonish Alberich,
short on menace until the final curse. Christa
Ludwig's once definitive Fricka looks and
sounds tired. Levine's tempi in *Rheingold* rival
those of Reginald Goodall, but without his
structure and pacing; the Giants' entrance is
marked *molto pesante*, not funereal. They, the
Rhinemaidens and the lesser gods – especially
Birgitta Svendén's keen-voiced Erda – outclass
their betters.

Levine handles *Walküre* more successfully. Act
1, though, isn't a success. Gary Lakes' massive
but rather lean-toned Siegmund is ill-matched
with Jessye Norman, whose vocally searing
Sieglinde is subverted by her *grande dame* manner, robbing the love scenes of any real involvement. Behrens, however, injects Act 2 with life,
and though Ludwig's Fricka still sounds tired,
Morris begins to make an impact, singing rather
than declaiming the Narration. With a ringingly
athletic Valkyrie band, Levine rushes the Ride,
but brings the act to a moving Farewell.

Siegfried is visually and musically the best, with
Levine at his liveliest, and a Romantic forest out
of Altdorfer or von Schwind. Jerusalem's ardent
hero may lack Heldentenor heft, and suffer
some constraint at the top, but he carries off the
forging and lyrical scenes with credit. The Wanderer often suits basses' range and personae, and
Morris's commanding, world-weary god dominates Zednik's veteran Mime (mercifully not
Chéreau's cute victim), Wlaschiha's now mordant Alberich; and Svendén's eerie Erda.
Levine's protracted 'Awakening' stretches
Behrens, but she and Jerusalem infuse the love
duet with appealing life.

Levine's expansiveness suits *Götterdämmerung*,
which opens with a powerful trio of Norns and a
radiant Dawn duet. Chez Gibichung, though,
the temperature drops, with Anthony Raffell (a
fine Wotan) a miscast, bumbling Gunther, and
Gutrune sadly unseductive. Matti Salminen's
brutish Hagen, though richly sung, lacks the
essential supernatural undertones. Ludwig is
much better as Waltraute, but Jerusalem and
especially Behrens carry the performance with
involving intensity. The Immolation strains her
voice, but remains satisfyingly cathartic, aided
by appropriate stage spectacle, though Valhalla's downfall is disappointing.

All told, while this set may be less stimulating
than the Boulez, it's also less distracting – without, as an eminent colleague once remarked,
someone forever shouting in your ear. As well as
the original digital stereo, remixed surround-
sound tracks convincingly evoke extra ambiance
and detail. The image also remasters well,
although you may want to turn up the colour.
Until Barenboim's set reaches DVD, this
remains the best; and many may still prefer it.

Das Rheingold
Falk Struckmann bass-bar Wotan **Lioba Braun**
mez Fricka **Graham Clark** ten Loge **Francisco Vas**
ten Mime **Günter von Kannen** bar Alberich
Elisabete Matos sop Freia **Jeffrey Dowd** ten Froh

Wolfgang Rauch *bar* Donner **Andrea Bönig**
contr Erda **Kwangchul Youn** *bass* Fasolt **Matthias**
Hölle *bass* Fafner **Cristina Obregón** *sop* Woglinde
Ana Ibarra *sop* Wellgunde **Francisca Beaumont**
mez Flosshilde **Liceu Grand Theatre Symphony**
Orchestra, Barcelona / Bertrand de Billy *Stage*
director **Harry Kupfer**
Opus Arte ② 𝐃𝐕𝐃 OA0910D (159' · NTSC · 16:9 ·
PCM stereo & DTS 5.1 · 0) Recorded live at the Gran
Teatre del Liceu, Barcelona, 1 & 7 June 2004   Ⓕ**O**

We still don't have a really good DVD *Ring*.
Here's a promising beginning to a cycle, in an
up-to-date recording from Barcelona: it's the
most recommendable *Rheingold* so far. Harry
Kupfer's Bayreuth staging was Teutonically
technological and ugly, but despite some dramatic silliness it actually heeded Wagner's stage
directions. So does this one, created originally
for Berlin, but it's a lot more attractive, and
rightly attentive to the *Ring*'s mythological core.
Its centrepiece, towering above a black mirrored
stage surface, is the massive World-Ash tree,
from which we see Wotan tearing his spear, and
around whose roots the Rhinemaidens gambol
and climb; the action moves up and down the
trunk with the aid of the Liceu's splendid new
machinery. Sillinesses – recurring suitcases, the
gods' premature entrances and over-extended
dance finale, the serpent reduced to feeble claws
– aren't crippling.

Bertrand de Billy's warm, slowish reading is
likeable, but doesn't generate enough shape and
dramatic drive. Falk Struckmann's Wotan is a
strong-voiced dynamic presence, but his tone is
harsh and vibrant, and his characterisation arro-
gantly unsympathetic. Günter von Kannen is
now a rather portly Alberich, and, despite a
wonderfully malign glare, short on vocal and
dramatic bite. Not so Graham Clark's Loge,
incisively sung, even if his character tenor
underplays the part's more lyrical side. Lioba
Braun, Elisabete Matos and Andrea Bönig are
worthy goddesses, Jeffrey Dowd a strong if not
ideally mellifluous Froh, and Wolfgang Rauch
an unusually impressive Donner. Veteran
Matthias Hölle and rising star Kwangchul Youn
are excellent Giants, android-like figures more
effective than Bayreuth's dehumanised monstrous puppets. That goes, too, for the romantic
rather than tarty Rhinemaidens.

So we have a decent modern staging on DVD,
recorded in vivid surround-sound and clear if
somewhat stygian vision. It does, though, have
one infuriating disadvantage: unlike any other
Rheingold it's spread over two discs; the side-
break isn't well chosen, and you have to go
through the whole menu rigmarole before the
second side.

The Golden Ring
BBC documentary on the making of Sir Georg Solti's
recording of Der Ring des Nibelungen. Filmed
during the recording of Götterdämmerung in 1964
Sir Georg Solti with various artists including **Dietrich**
Fischer-Dieskau, Gottlob Frick, Birgit Nilsson,

Claire Watson, Wolfgang Windgassen
Film director/Narrator **Humphrey Burton**
Decca 𝐃𝐕𝐃 Black & White. 071 153-9DH (157' ·
NTSC · 4:3 · 1.0 · 0) Includes bonus selection of audio
highlights from the complete studio recording in
5.1 surround sound. Notes, text and translation
included   Ⓕ**O**

One of the classic music documentaries comes
to DVD – classic, both in itself and in its subject.
Alec Robertson in *Gramophone* hailed Decca's
1964 *Götterdämmerung* recording as 'the greatest achievement in gramophone history yet', a
judgement the years have largely endorsed. Producer John Culshaw set out to make it a historic
event with 'the kind of dream cast…unlikely to
be encountered in the theatre', and we can only
be grateful that the BBC then had the vision to
capture its creation so effectively.

The programme's fascination lies not only in
seeing so many now-legendary performers, but
in the way director Humphrey Burton conveys
the 'rough magic' of the recording process.
Bravely, given the intrusive cameras and lighting of the time, Culshaw and Burton agreed that
nothing should be specially staged, and only one
or two 'now what are you chaps doing?'
sequences seem less than natural. Burton had
immense problems cutting more than 20 hours
of material, especially because of Solti's then-
unfashionable preference for long takes. What
remains brilliantly captures the white heat of
this immense collaboration – almost literally so,
as Solti dominates the floor of Vienna's Sofiensaal with crackling energy and edgy perfectionism. It contrasts tellingly with the determined
calm of Culshaw and engineers Gordon Parry
and James Brown in the control room.

The ultimate fascination, though, is seeing
Solti directing the glorious Vienna players, and
the era's greatest Wagnerian voices, Nilsson,
Windgassen, Frick and Fischer-Dieskau, shuf-
fling their music stands around Decca's famous
chequerboard stage.

The monochrome and monaural original is
well remastered. Decca wisely insisted only their
music tracks be used, and they come up splendidly (as does a deafening jet engine).

Walton

At the Haunted End of the Day – A Film by Tony Palmer
Includes performances by **Julian Bream, Iona**
Brown, Yvonne Kenny, Ralph Kirshbaum, Yehudi
Menuhin, Simon Preston, Simon Rattle, John
Shirley-Quirk *Film director* **Tony Palmer**
Decca 𝐃𝐕𝐃 074 150-9DH (99' · NTSC · 4:3 · 2.0 · 0)
Originally broadcast 1981   Ⓕ**O**

This extended television profile of William
Walton is among the most moving ever made of
a composer and makes a very welcome commercial appearance on DVD. The approach is both
direct and evocative, starting with Walton himself nearing 80 and plainly rather frail musing at

the keyboard of the piano in his work room. That brings several of the wrily humorous *obiter dicta* from him with which the film is delightfully dotted, prompting also an immediate and heartfelt tribute to both the man and his music from Laurence Olivier, for whom he wrote his finest film music.

The story of his career, with its extraordinary sequence of lucky breaks, is then told for the most part chronologically. We get evocative shots of his home town Oldham and the house where he was born, Oxford, and later London and Amalfi in Italy. The impact of *Belshazzar's Feast* is fully brought out, not least thanks to Simon Rattle's conducting of excerpts in his first major television contribution, though Walton himself dismisses the very first performance in Leeds in 1931 as 'pretty bloody'.

The film was made within a couple of years of Walton's death in 1983, and reflects in places his melancholy thoughts on death and how little he felt he had achieved. Even so, the impact of the film is anything but depressing, with the effervescent personality of Susana taking over towards the end who, as she says, 'was produced specially to take care of William'. A unique career, vividly re-created.

Weill

Aufstieg und Fall der Stadt Mahagonny
Dame Gwyneth Jones *sop* Leokadja Begbick **Roy Cornelius Smith** *ten* Fatty **Wilbur Pauley** *bass* Trinity Moses **Catherine Malfitano** *sop* Jenny Smith **Jerry Hadley** *ten* Jimmy Mahoney **Udo Holdorf** *ten* Jake Schmidt **Dale Duesing** *bar* Pennybank Bill **Harry Peeters** *bass* Alaska Wolf Joe **Toby Spence** *ten* Tobby Higgins **Vienna State Opera Chorus; Vienna Radio Symphony Orchestra / Dennis Russell Davies** *Stage director* **Peter Zadek** *Video director* **Brian Large**
ArtHaus Musik **DVD** 100 092 (160' · 16:9 · 2.0 · 2, 5) Ⓕ

Peter Zadek's production of Weill, and Brecht's largest-scale opera, was much criticised in 1998. It's possible to see in this DVD version that the Salzburg stage is really too big for the work, and that there's rather a lot of unnecessary action, much coming and going, walking about, and movement of furniture. However, Brian Large's filmed production makes such good use of close-ups that much of this is bypassed.

What makes this unmissable is Jerry Hadley's performance as Jim. From every point of view, dramatic, vocal and emotional, he encompasses the part so completely that you're totally gripped. The tension in his pose, his burning eyes, the physical daring of the interpretation command attention at every turn. At the end of Act 2, when Jenny sings 'Denn wie man sich bettet', Catherine Malfitano declaims the first verse as she's carried on Hadley's shoulders. Although the camera and the microphone are both harsh where Malfitano is concerned, she too gives such an involved and committed reading of the part that one has to forgive everything.

At no moment in her career would Gwyneth Jones's voice have been suitable for the role of the Widow Begbick, but she too is fascinating to watch, under-playing most of the time, so that when the trial scene arrives, the extra cruel edge she gives to gesture and song tells all the more. The other tremendous performance comes from Wilbur Pauley as a totally repellent Trinity Moses – his pose, Christ-like, after he's killed Joe in the boxing scene is horrific.

Dennis Russell Davies conducts a searing account of the score from the pit. The balance between voices and orchestra is sometimes very echoey, but this is inevitable on a stage as cavernous as Salzburg's.

Street Scene
Ashley Putnam *sop* Anna Maurrant **Marc Embree** *bar* Frank Maurrant **Teri Hansen** *sop* Rose Maurrant **Kip Wilborn** *ten* Sam Kaplan **Claudia Ashley** *sop* Nursemaid 1 **Muriel Costa-Greenspon** *mez* Nursemaid 2 **Yvette Bonner** *sop* Jennie Hildebrand **David Rae Smith** *ten* Abraham Kaplan **Janice Felty** *mez* Emma Jones **Heidi Eisenberg** *mez* Olga Olsen **Anthony Mee** *ten* Lippo Fiorentino **Ludwigshafen Theatre Chorus; Rhineland Palatinate State Philharmonic Orchestra / James Holmes** *Stage director* **Francesca Zambello** *Film director* **José Montes-Baquer**
ArtHaus Musik **DVD** 100 098 (143' · 16:9 · 2.0 · 2 & 5)
Recorded 1994 Ⓕ

Street Scene was the most ambitious product of Weill's American years. It'S a kind of *Porgy and Bess* transferred to the slum tenements of New York during the Depression, mixing genuine operatic writing with unashamedly popular numbers. It's essentially a team opera, with many roles, portraying the ups and downs of urban life, including childbirth and death.

Ashley Putnam is visually too young for the role of Anna, perhaps, but vocally outstanding in her solo numbers. Teri Hansen initially sounds a shade constricted as her daughter Rose, but she's tender enough in her duet with Kip Wilborn as her lover Sam. Marc Embree is suitably menacing as husband Frank, Janice Felty a strong Emma, and Anthony Mee a delightful roly-poly Neapolitan. An undoubted star of the production is designer Adrienne Lobel, against whose magnificently solid and realistic set the action unfolds. Another is James Holmes, who brings out the score's darker, dramatic moments as much as its unashamed romanticism and jazz-inflected numbers.

This production reveals what a wonderful work it is – convincing both for its extended operatic writing and its marvellous tunes.

BA Zimmermann

Die Soldaten
Mark Munkittrick *bass* Wesener **Nancy Shade** *sop* Marie **Milagro Vargas** *contr* Charlotte **Grace Hoffman** *mez* Wesener's Mother **Michael Ebbecke**

bar Stolzius **Elsie Maurer** *contr* Stolzius' Mother
Alois Treml *bass* Obrist **William Cochran** *ten*
Desportes **Guy Renard** *ten* Pirzel **Karl-Friedrich**
Dürr *bar* Eisenhardt **Klaus Hirte** *bar* Haudy
Raymond Wolansky *bar* Major Mary **Johannes**
Eidloth, Helmut Holzapfel, Robert Wörle *tens*
Young Officers **Ursula Koszut** *sop* Countess de la
Roche **Jerrold van der Schaaf** *sngr* Young Count
Stuttgart State Opera Chorus and Orchestra /
Bernhard Kontarsky *Stage director* **Harry Kupfer**
Video director **Hans Hulscher**
ArtHaus Musik ⚊ 100 270 (111' · 4:3 · 2.0 · 2 & 5)
Recorded live at State Opera House, Stuttgart 1989
Ⓕ

Bernhard Kontarsky's shaping of the alternately
coruscating and black dramatic score is splendid
and there are no weak links in the cast. In the
central role of Marie, Nancy Shade is sweetly
flighty in the first two acts, showing off her vocal
mettle in the agitated solo at the end of Act 1.
After romping with Desportes – a nicely turned
characterisation of the strutting womaniser by
William Cochran – her descent into the gutter
reduces her role almost to that of a prop, as Stolzius, her erstwhile fiancé, and others take over.

All the characters, major and minor, are finely
drawn, although necessarily some seem more
like caricatures: Mark Munkittrick's Wesener,
Marie's father, whose ambiguous attitude towards her suitors Desportes and Stolzius sets up
the tragedy; Michael Ebbecke as the simpering,
lovelorn Stolzius, who turns into the suicidal
avenger of Marie's ruin; Klaus Hirte as the
grotesque Haudy; and Ursula Koszut as the
Countess, who vainly offers Marie a chance of
escape – and the opera's only truly lyrical
episode – in a radiant trio with Marie and her
sister Charlotte (the excellent Milagro Vargas).

The Stuttgart production is extremely well
shot, Kupfer's fast moving, split-stage realisation brilliantly captured by Hans Hulscher's
film. Kupfer's lighting of this dark tale was a
crucial element, and the more nightmarish
scenes take place in semi-darkness: this doesn't
always translate well on-screen. *Die Soldaten*
cries out for cinematic reproduction visually,
but this film is a tremendous record of a stunning, if deeply disturbing, theatrical experience.

CONDUCTORS

Abbado · Barbirolli · Reiner · Stravinsky ·
Szell

Abbado in Lucerne
Debussy La mer[a]. Le Martyre de Saint Sébastien –
Suite[b]
[b]**Eteri Gvazava,** [b]**Rachel Harnisch** *sops*
Swiss Chamber Choir; Lucerne Festival Orchestra
/ Claudio Abbado *Video director* **Michael Beyer**
Euroarts ⚊ 205 3469 (64' · NTSC · 16:9 · PCM
stereo, 5.1 & DTS 5.1 · 0) [ab]Recorded live at the
Lucerne Festival in 2003. Includes the documentary

'From Toscanini to Abbado' – The History of the
Lucerne Festival Orchestra, written and directed by
Arthur Spirk   Ⓕ**O**

Sir John Barbirolli in rehearsal and performance
Haydn Oboe Concerto in C, HobVIIg/C1
Evelyn Rothwell *ob* **Vancouver Symphony**
Orchestra / Sir John Barbirolli
Video Artists International ⚊ VAIDVD4293 (60' · 4:3
b/w · PCM mono · 0)   Ⓕ**O**

George Szell – One Man's Triumph
Beethoven Symphony No 5
Berg Violin Concerto (in rehearsal)[a]
Brahms Academic Festival Overture (in rehearsal)
[a]**Rafael Druian** *vn* **Cleveland Orchestra / George**
Szell
Video Artists International ⚊ VAIDVD4271 (55' · 4:3
· PCM mono · 0) 1966 Bell Telephone Hour
documentary   Ⓕ**OO**

Fritz Reiner
Bach/Weiner Toccata, Adagio and Fugue in C,
BWV564[b] **Beethoven** Symphony No 2[b] **Debussy**
Petite Suite[a] **Mozart** Symphony No 39[a] **Tchaikovsky**
The Nutcracker – Waltz of the flowers[a]. The Sleeping
Beauty – Valse[a]
Chicago Symphony Orchestra / Fritz Reiner
Video Artists International ⚊ VAIDVD4287 (97' · 4:3
b/w · PCM mono · 0)   Ⓕ**OO**

Stravinsky
featuring interviews and recording sequences of the
Symphony of Psalms
Toronto Festival Singers; CBC Symphony
Orchestra / Igor Stravinsky *Directors* **Wolf Koenig,**
Roman Kroitor
Video Artists International ⚊ VAIDVD4290 (50' · 4:3
b/w · PCM mono · 0) 1965 documentary   Ⓕ**O**

For some the main attraction of *Abbado in*
Lucerne will be the great Italian maestro conducting Debussy at the 2003 Lucerne Festival.
For others it's the documentary, with its footage
of some of the last century's greatest conductors
in action: every brief glimpse adds flesh and
bones to the names that adorn the labels of
treasured discs by Ansermet, Fricsay, Kempe
Furtwängler and de Sabata. The film is confusingly structured, however, and though it
confronts admirably Karajan's ruthless use of
Lucerne to reinvent himself after his denazifica-
tion, the commentary sounds like something
written by the Swiss Tourist Board.

Barbirolli is filmed in Vancouver rehearsing
the Haydn-attributed Oboe Concerto with his
wife as soloist, who, as in her 1957 recording
with the Hallé, plays her own cadenzas. All eyes
are on JB (indeed, it's some time before we're
aware that the soloist is at the rehearsal at all)
but there is one lovely exchange when Rothwell
suggests that they start again from the repeat of
the second subject. 'Well, I don't know what the
second subject is,' retorts her husband. 'That's
for programme annotators.'

George Szell, who died in the same year as
Barbirolli (1970), was, by contrast, unpopular

and despotic. The colour film profiles – but does not explore or question – his extraordinary 24-year relationship with the Cleveland Orchestra. With his lupine smile and fearsome presence, he tries to play the role of regular guy: rehearsal and performance sequences are riveting, with fascinating footage of him instructing three young conductors (James Levine one of them) on how to kick-start *Don Juan* and Beethoven's Fifth.

With the hooded eyes of a falcon and his sour mien, Szell's fellow Hungarian, Fritz Reiner looks as unpleasant as his reputation conducting the Chicago Symphony in 1953-4 at the start of his celebrated nine-year association with the orchestra. These black-and-white transmissions (sometimes more black than white) of one of the truly great conductors are of immense importance, and include one work (the Bach-Weiner) that Reiner did not record commercially. The DVD preserves Francis Coughlin's hopelessly unprepared in-vision linking commentary: every faultering sentence makes you thank God for the invention of the autocue.

The Stravinsky documentary features the famous (and equally toe-curling) encounter between the young Julian Bream and the elderly composer. Just as Stravinsky is about to start recording his *Symphony of Psalms*, Bream is introduced, sits down and plays a pavane on the lute ... all the way through. As a conductor, Stravinsky is an uninspiring, baton-less time-beater, but the exchanges filmed simultaneously in the control room make for an unusually vivid sequence. Most revealing, though, is Stravinsky's conversation with his friend Nicholas Nabokov, filmed in Hamburg over a glass of whisky. Here, one of music's geniuses appears touchingly vulnerable and human. VAI may be a no-frills merchant but such treasure needs no fancy packaging. Its priceless contents speak for themselves.

Sir Thomas Beecham

Beecham in Chicago 1
Haydn Symphony No 102 in B flat **Mozart** Symphony No 38 in D, 'Prague', K504
Chicago Symphony Orchestra / Sir Thomas Beecham
NVC Arts ⊡ 8573-84095-3 (49' · ADD) Recorded live 1960 ⓕⓞ

Beecham in Chicago 2
Delius Florida Suite – By the River **Handel** Love in Bath – Suite **Mendelssohn** The Hebrides, Op 26 **Saint-Saëns** Le rouet d'Omphale, Op 31
Chicago Symphony Orchestra / Sir Thomas Beecham
NVC Arts ⊡ 8573-84096-3 (48' · ADD) Recorded live 1960 ⓕⓞ

Here's a rare quarry of film footage that can hardly fail to delight anyone who's interested in Beecham, the Chicago Symphony, or even the music itself. The concerts were specially staged

for television in the Grand Ballroom of the Sheraton Towers in Chicago in March 1960. It was Beecham's last visit to the United States (he died the following March). He was in his 80th year, not in the best of health but seemingly in fine fettle. He conducts without a score, mostly standing, though after an electrifying performance of the first movement of Mozart's *Prague* Symphony, he draws up a chair from where he presides as only he could preside over an exquisite account of the slow movement. The videos are billed as being the only extant footage of Beecham 'in colour'. This seems a sceptical selling-point until you see the videos. The fact is, black-and-white is fine for film, but TV concerts aren't films, they're reportage; and black-and-white reportage has a nasty habit of making relatively recent events seem strangely distant in time. This colour footage makes Beecham seem like our contemporary.

The actual picture quality is no more than fair. The original two-inch Kinescope tapes disappeared after someone dubbed them onto one-inch analogue tape in the 1980s. But it's perfectly watchable; expertly re-engineered, with good colour rendition and excellent sound. The non-concert hall staging also means that we have some tolerably enterprising camera-work, with Beecham himself, the Chicago strings, and two of the principal wind players, oboist Ray Still and flautist Donald Peck, getting the lion's share of the director's attention.

What a phenomenal ensemble the Chicago Symphony was in 1960! It's fascinating to watch the players at work here, connoisseurs of their craft in the presence of a Connoisseur-in-Chief. As the first violins bow their repeated Ds at the start of the *Prague* Symphony's *Allegro*, the camera catches a Humphrey Bogart look-alike on the second desk eyeing Beecham and gazing across the assembled banks of fiddles with a look that says 'Hey guys, listen to us!'. Later, as the coda kicks in with a typically Beechamesque blend of elegance and drive, the same player shoots a huge grin across to his neighbour.

Fritz Reiner was Chicago's principal conductor at the time, he of the bull-frog gaze and minuscule beat. Beecham has a rather larger beat, unerringly precise, almost never legato, and with a habit of galvanising the rhythm with a movement of the stick which is often a millisecond quicker than expected. The left hand is sparingly used, though the left fist, raised and briefly brandished, is always impressive. Even in his 80th year, Beecham's stance is erect, almost bandmasterish, his hands and body moving in a way that's delicate and exact. His other principal weapon is his eyes: dark eyes emitting a gaze that's sometimes roguish, occasionally Mephistophelean, always penetrating and intent.

Both programmes are more or less equally enjoyable. The 'fun' programme is just that. The readings will be familiar to seasoned collectors of 78s and LPs but the performances are new-minted: the *Hebrides* Overture clear, alert and full of fantasy, the Saint-Saëns incisive and exquisitely polished, Love in Bath, as always, outrageously enjoyable. (What leading conductor nowadays would dare conduct *Le rouet d'Omphale* in public or draw up his own arrangement of the music of some much-revered baroque master?) Merely to watch Beecham's eyes while listening to his unfolding of music from Delius's Florida Suite is to understand why (and in what ways) this music was so precious to him.

Beecham usually travelled with his own meticulously annotated orchestral parts. *Love in Bath* would certainly have been played from his parts. And by the look of pleasure on the wind players' faces during these superlative performances of Haydn's Symphony No 102 and Mozart's *Prague*, these might have been, too.

A joyous discovery, then, which goes some way beyond the 'unique concerts in colour' tag. It's doubtful if there are better images anywhere of the old sorcerer at work than the ones here.

Pierre Boulez

Pierre Boulez with The Vienna Philharmonic Orchestra – In Rehearsal
Berg Three Orchestral Pieces, Op 6 **Boulez** Notations I-IV
Vienna Philharmonic Orchestra / Pierre Boulez
Video director **Felix Breisach**
ArtHaus Musik 100 290 (57' · 4:3 · 2.0· 2 & 5)   Ⓕ

Several of Boulez's live performances have appeared on VHS and DVD-Video, but, until now, no official rehearsal footage. This new release focuses on two central items from his repertoire, with the Berg *Three Orchestral Pieces* an appropriate choice for the Vienna Philharmonic. It might seem perverse that the length of the rehearsal sequences are in inverse proportion to the length and complexity of the actual pieces, but this allows for a complete run-through of 'Präludium', followed by a refinement process in which Boulez's ear for orchestral balance and textural clarification is demonstrated at length. The interspersed interview clips are an effective complement.

That Boulez can play straight through his *Notations* says much about the VPO's more inclusive attitude to repertoire in recent years. The tonal allure and sensitivity of its response is impressive. By a combination of patience, informality and even-handed coercion he overcomes passing doubts of individual players as to his technical demands, and gets the results required. Again, pithy and relevant interview material.

Director Felix Breisach had ensured a smooth follow-through between shots of the conductor in action and close-ups of the players as they quizzically but good-naturedly sort out various sticking-points (Boulez's German appears to fail him only over the 'straight mute'!). Both sound and picture reproduction are fine, with subtitles provided in four languages. Aficionados of Boulez and the 'art' of conducting will need to have this often revealing documentary.

Sir Andrew Davis

Last Night of the Proms
Arne Rule, Britannia! (arr Sargent)[a] **Bach** Fantasia and fugue in C minor, BWV537 (arr Elgar). Violin Sonata No 1 in G minor, BWV1001[c] **Delius** The Walk to the Paradise Garden **Elgar** Pomp and Circumstance March No 1 in D, Op 39 **Grainger** Tribute to Foster[b] **Mozart** Violin Concerto No 4 in D, K218[a] **Parry** Jerusalem (arr Elgar) **Shostakovich** Jazz Suite No 2 (arr McBurney) **R Strauss** Salome – Dance of the Seven Veils; Final Scene[a] **Wood** Fantasia on British Sea-Songs
[a]**Jane Eaglen,** [b]**Janice Watson** sops [b]**Ann Murray** mez [b]**Toby Spence,** [b]**Robert Tear** tens [b]**Neal Davies** bass [c]**Hilary Hahn** vn **BBC Symphony Chorus and Orchestra / Sir Andrew Davis**
BBC 📀 WMDVD8001-9 (167' · 4:3 · 5.1 · 0) Includes interviews with Sir Andrew Davis, Jane Eaglen and Hilary Hahn   Ⓕ

Watching an old Last Night of the Proms programme on DVD might seem like eating half-warmed-up soup, but the year 2000 had some special claims – not just marking the Millennium but in saying goodbye to Sir Andrew Davis as chief conductor of the BBC Symphony Orchestra. Jane Eaglen is the soprano, producing the most opulent tone in the final scene from *Salome*, a commanding figure in every way. Needless to say, she also rises magnificently to the challenge of *Rule Britannia* in the final junketing, resplendent in a gown of royal blue and crimson with tiara to match, studded – as the camera reveals – with a diamanté Union Jack.

If that's far less showy than the gowns worn by some of her predecessors, or even Bryn Terfel's rugby jersey, the point follows that the patriotic flag-waving and the final items are less a demonstration of jingoism than plain exuberance over music-making as represented in this greatest of the world's music festivals.

Special facilities on the DVD consist of options on subtitles and an ability to limit the playing to music only, without introductions.

Carlo Maria Giulini

Bruckner Symphony No 9
Stuttgart Radio Symphony Orchestra / Carlo Maria Giulini *Video director* **Agnes Meth**
ArtHaus Musik 📀 101 065 (123' · 4:3 · PCM stereo · 0)   Ⓕ

'My intention always has been to arrive at human contact without enforcing authority … The great mystery of music-making requires real friendship among those who work together.' So said Carlo Maria Giulini, now living in seclusion in Milan. From the first few moments of the rehearsal, you know that he practises what he preaches, a gracious, spiritual presence whose stature doesn't preclude him from apologising at one point to the solo horn for suggesting a misleading dynamic: 'Sorry, that is my mistake – it sounds too much like

Debussy.' If you're unfamiliar with Bruckner's Ninth (the one he left incomplete at his death), then this absorbing hour-long sequence will prove a stimulating, unmissable introduction; for aspiring conductors and Brucknerphiles, this and the live concert performance as an essential purchase for repeated viewing.

Sir Simon Rattle

Adès Asyla **Mahler** Symphony No 5
Berlin Philharmonic Orchestra / Simon Rattle
Video director Bob Coles
EMI ② 𝓓𝓥𝓓 490325-9 (125' · 16:9, · 2.0, 5.1 &
DTS 5.1 · 0) Includes feature 'Simon Rattle in conver-
sation with Bob Coles'   Ⓕ**OO**

Sir Simon Rattle marked his formal assumption of the music directorship of the Berlin Philharmonic with a series of remarkable concerts in September 2002, including Mahler's Fifth. EMI's original audio-only release contained just the Mahler, captured over several days in Berlin and shorn of the final bravos; the performance has been reissued since in a limited edition that takes in a bonus CD of orchestral miniatures plus a revealing conversation with Nicholas Kenyon. But here you'll find the Berliners' brave stab at contemporary British music.

Rattle's performance of the Mahler is well known. In the Scherzo the DVD format makes it easier to accept the front-stage placement of the obbligato horn – not a whim of Rattle's but a decision based on precedent and scholarship. As sceptics like Klemperer and Scherchen might have observed, it doesn't make the movement any shorter, yet Rattle feels he's cracked it after the initial doubts candidly discussed in the accompanying talk.

Nor is there any doubting the energetic brilliance of Adès's *Asyla* (the plural of 'asylum' used in both its meanings, as a place of refuge and of madness). For the uninitiated/unconvinced, it should help that the zany percussion effects can be seen as well as heard. The Berliners are encouraged to loosen up for its vernacular element, without perhaps plunging in quite as wholeheartedly as the audio-only CBSO.

If you don't instinctively recoil from the prospect of additional noises off and some rather insistent close-ups of the participants, a great occasion is well represented here. Surprisingly perhaps, the director doesn't zero in on the brass for their climactic chorale, giving us the orchestra in long-shot before the precipitate dash to the finishing line. The sound, not quite as clear as it might be in such densely scored passages, is still eminently acceptable; the images are wonderfully crisp.

Sir Georg Solti

The Making of a Maestro
Video director **Peter Maniura**
ArtHaus Musik 𝓓𝓥𝓓 100 238 (93' · 16:9 · 2.0 · 2 & 5)   Ⓕ

Peter Maniura's beautifully photographed *Omnibus* documentary, completed only days before Solti's death in 1997, makes no attempt at critical assessment, but nor is it mere hagiography. Wisely, Maniura charts Solti's remarkable story, often allowing him literally to speak for himself; and the result is all the more impressive. There's little actual performance footage, but many rehearsal sequences from his postwar Munich days to his last concerts, with the occasional tantalising glimpse of his heavily marked scores; his recordings permeate the soundtrack. What comes through most clearly is that the dynamism which, for better or worse, drove both his career and his interpretations – 'like playing for Mephisto,' as one Chicago player admiringly puts it – stemmed not from mere showmanship but from an extraordinarily passionate love and knowledge of music. His initial unpopularity at Covent Garden isn't glossed over (although the anti-semitism which sometimes fuelled it is); but his achievement in raising the house to genuinely international standards is properly acknowledged. So, alongside his starry profile-raising for the Chicago Symphony, are both his daunting perfectionism and the kindness and humanity, especially towards young artists, it often concealed. Documentaries are often hard to recommend for repeated viewing. Not this one.

Various Artists

The Art of Conducting – Great Conductors of the Past
Sir John Barbirolli, Sir Thomas Beecham, Leonard Bernstein, Fritz Busch, Wilhelm Furtwängler, Herbert von Karajan, Otto Klemperer, Serge Koussevitzky, Arthur Nikisch, Fritz Reiner, Leopold Stokowski, Richard Strauss, George Szell, Arturo Toscanini, Bruno Walter, Felix Weingartner in
rehearsal and performance
Teldec/Warner Music Vision 𝓓𝓥𝓓 0927-42667-2
(164' · 4:3 · 2.0· 2-6)   Ⓕ**OO**

When the first instalment of 'The Art of Conducting', based on a BBC television series, originally appeared on VHS and LaserDisc it was rightly acclaimed as a revelation. Not surprisingly, it won many prizes, including the 1995 *Gramophone* Award for Video. It may not have solved the mystery of exactly how great conductors communicate to players, often despite flawed techniques, but seeing the differences between Klemperer, Furtwängler, Toscanini, Stokowski and Koussevitzky in quick succession made for a thrilling experience. On DVD the experience is even more intense, and quite apart from being more convenient to access, it offers added material.

In addition to the illuminating commentaries from a wide range of artists, there are now more extended interviews with four artists, offered as a supplement to the main menu: Elisabeth Schwarzkopf, Hugh Bean, Suvi Raj Grubb (EMI recording producer for Klemperer and others) and Isaac Stern.

The very opening launches into the sequence with a fascinating kaleidoscope of brief clips of four conductors tackling the first movement of Beethoven's Fifth Symphony – Toscanini, Karajan, Klemperer and Szell, with instant commentary from John Eliot Gardiner, Isaac Stern and Jack Brymer. After that the clips tend to be a little more extended. The oldest is from 1913, a silent film of Arthur Nikisch conducting unidentified music, with Oliver Knussen noting how he holds his arms high so that the players have to see his eyes. Longer excerpts are very much the exception, notably Felix Weingartner in Paris in 1932 conducting Weber's *Die Freischütz* overture and Fritz Busch in the same year in Dresden conducting the second half of Wagner's *Tannhäuser* overture.

Those are both fascinating, with the economy of Weingartner's technique matching his refreshing directness as an interpreter, but inevitably it's frustrating when the camera switches to the players for extended periods instead of concentrating on the conductor.

A really compelling issue.

INSTRUMENTALISTS

Alfred Brendel *piano*

Haydn Piano Sonata in E flat, HobXVI/49 **Mozart** Piano Sonata No 14 in C minor, K457 **Schubert** Impromptu in G flat, D899 No 3
Alfred Brendel pf
Opus Arte/BBC ② **DVD** ⓄA0811D (155' · 16:9 · 2.0 · 0) Includes documentary 'Man and Mask', conversations with Sir Simon Rattle and poetry readings   Ⓕⓞ

The main element in this double-disc tribute is the 70-minute portrait, 'Man and Mask', directed for television by Mark Kidel. This takes the great pianist to many of the haunts of his early life, as well as showing him relaxing at home in Hampstead. His first recital came in Graz in 1948, and received glowing notices, when he concentrated on works with fugues, including the Brahms *Handel Variations* and a sonata of his own which boasted a double-fugue at the end. In Vienna he recalls making his first recording for Vox, a coupling of Balakirev's *Islamey*, Mussorgsky's *Pictures at an Exhibition* and Stravinsky's *Petrushka* suite. Later, on the day after his début at Queen Elizabeth Hall, he had offers of recording contracts from three major companies. All this is amplified by clips from archive performances and a separate half-hour conversation with Sir Simon Rattle in rehearsal for Beethoven's Piano Concertos Nos 2 and 4, offering fascinating revelations from both pianist and conductor.

On the second disc comes a recital recorded at

The Maltings, Snape, crowning this revealing issue with masterly performances of three of Brendel's favourite works.

Pierre Cochereau *organ*

Cochereau
A documentary commemorating the 20th anniversary of his death. Includes archive footage and interviews
A film by **Yvette Carbou**
Solstice **DVD** SODVD01 (120' · NTSC · 4:3 · PCM stereo/mono · 0)   Ⓕ

The great organist Pierre Cochereau was acknowledged as one of the finest improvisers in the history of the instrument. He was organist at Notre-Dame from 1955, arguably the most prestigious organ post in France and, with it, the most important of all Cavaillé-Coll's instruments. This release marks the 20th anniversary of his sudden death in 1984 at the age of 59.

The bulk of the film is of snappily edited single-camera head-shot interviews with his son, daughter, former students, close friends and musicians. It's an absorbing, revealing and by no means hagiographic portrait of general interest, but essential viewing for organ buffs. The section where Cochereau is filmed teaching a student the art of improvisation is particularly valuable.

But there are a number of cavils. Repeatedly, archive extracts are cut off or faded out in favour of the newly filmed interviews. There is Cochereau in grainy black-and-white thrillingly thundering out the opening of the *allegro* of Vierne's Second Symphony only to be cross-faded after 30 seconds. Later a detached interlocutor hands him a theme on which to improvise: the same thing happens. What made Cochereau's improvisations so impressive were their forms and structures: we need to hear them in their entirety.

The booklet, in French and English, is a transcript of the interviews, this despite the excellent English subtitles. This seems to be the first film portrait of an organist's career and life, and as such it's warmly welcome and highly recommended.

Jacqueline du Pré *cello*

In Portrait
Includes performances of **Elgar** Cello Concerto in E minor, Op 85[a] **Beethoven** Piano Trio No 5 in D, 'Ghost', Op 70 No 1[b]
Jacqueline du Pré vc [b]**Pinchas Zukerman** vn [a]**New Philharmonia Orchestra / Daniel Barenboim** [b]pf
Film director **Christopher Nupen**
BBC/Opus Arte/Allegro Films **DVD** OACN0902D (155' · 4:3 · PCM stereo & mono · 0). Extra features include talks by Christopher Nupen, photo-gallery, 'Allegro Molto': an Allegro Films compilation.   Ⓕⓞⓞ

Christopher Nupen's 1967 film profile of Jacqueline du Pré is a television classic. The updating, which he made in 1981 when multiple sclerosis had tragically put an end to her career, intensifies its emotional impact.The wonder is that the film contains so many key comments about the great cellist and the nature of her artistry. Still only 22 at the time of the original interview, du Pré gives a most endearing account of first hearing a cello on the radio and asking for whatever it was that made 'that noise'. She remembers her first cello – far too big for a four-year-old – and how her mother (also interviewed) wrote little pieces for her to play. Du Pré even plays one of the pieces, and we see her mother's drawings in the manuscript.

William Pleeth her teacher remembers how the little girl's playing was magnetic, phrasing naturally and imaginatively without being told, while John Barbirolli remembers the audition for the Suggia Gift three years later, when after a couple of minutes listening he turned to his colleague, the great viola player William Primrose and said (in his gravelly voice): 'This is IT!' All this is extraordinarily vivid, as is Daniel Barenboim's description of his first meeting with du Pré at pianist Fou Ts'Ong's house, when 'instead of saying "good evening" we played Brahms'.

The half-hour of the 1967 profile is packed with such illuminating details, leading to a performance of the Elgar Concerto, with Barenboim conducting the New Philharmonia, a performance with a warmth and intensity to match that of the classic 1965 EMI recording that's so long been a favourite.

Nupen's 1981 updating in colour comes as a 10-minute introduction to the main black-and-white film. The most illuminating sequence is with Moray Welsh, whom du Pré coaches in the Elgar Concerto. Her minute analysis of the work confounds the assumption that her talent was simply a spontaneous one.

The Ghost offers a performance of Beethoven's *Ghost* Trio, recorded in 1970 in the atmospheric setting of St John's, Smith Square in London. It vividly conveys the rapport between du Pré, Barenboim and their violinist friend Pinchas Zukerman.

Remembering Jacqueline du Pré – a film by Christopher Nupen
Includes performances of **Beethoven** Cello Sonata No 3. Piano Trio No 5, 'Ghost' Brahms Cello Sonata No 2 **Elgar** Cello Concerto **Schubert** Piano Quintet, 'Trout' Jacqueline du Pré vc with **Zubin Mehta, Daniel Barenboim, William Pleeth, Sir John Barbirolli and Pinchas Zukerman**
EMI 🎦 599728-9 (56' · 4:3 · PCM mono & stereo · 0)   Ⓕ

Originally shown on television in January 1995 to celebrate the 50th anniversary of Jacqueline du Pré's birth, this is the third Christopher Nupen film of the cellist to appear on DVD in quick succession. There's a fair degree of overlap between them, notably in the performances of the Elgar Cello Concerto and Beethoven's

Ghost Trio, each given complete in the earlier films. None of the works listed above is heard complete, but excerpts from each vividly illustrate the exuberance typical of du Pré.

Using some of the same interviews as before, generally from different sections, Nupen has built up a portrait that reflects the joy which surrounded du Pré. Most moving and illuminating of all is the extended section devoted to her association with William Pleeth, who was one of the first to identify her unique gift. Crowning his interview is a hilarious sequence of clips of her playing Offenbach duets with him. Hilarious, too, is the backstage scene, when before their performance of Schubert's *Trout* Quintet, du Pré, Barenboim, Perlman, Zukerman and Mehta played each other's instruments. Thanks to Nupen we can now share their fun, while lamenting the tragedy of du Pré's career.

Glen Gould   *piano*

The Alchemist – A film by Bruno Monsaingeon[a]
Bach English Suite No 1 in A, BWV806 – Toccata; Bourée. Partita No 6 in E minor, BWV830 **Berg** Piano Sonata, Op 1 **Byrd** Pavan and Gaillard No 6 **G Gould** So you want to write a Fugue? (excerpt) **Gibbons** Pavan and Galliard in A minor, 'Lord Salisbury' **Schoenberg** Suite, Op 25 – Intermezzo **Scriabin** Two Pieces, Op 57 **Wagner** Die Meistersinger von Nürnberg – Prelude (excerpt arr Gould) **Webern** Variations, Op 27

The Piano Revealed on Film: Trials with Glenn Gould[b]
Glenn Gould pf Film directors [a]**François-Louis Ribadeau**, [b]**Michel Hirvy**
EMI Classic Archive 🎦 490127-9 (157' · 4:3 Black & White · 2.0 mono · 0) Filmed in [a]1974, [b]1950s. Notes included   Ⓕ**OO**

Bruno Monsaingeon's film *Glenn Gould, The Alchemist*, divided between performance and discussion, unwittingly suggests a journey into narcissism. Here, once more, are those familiar arguments concerning Gould's dislike of public performance, of a hedonistic life-style, of passing references to Orlando Gibbons as his favourite composer, of his love of the Romantics (he means Bizet and Sibelius) and of how Chopin simply 'goes in one ear and out the other'. Even the simplest questions prompt a torrent of impenetrable verbiage, contradiction and parenthesis which he clearly sees as the height of intellectual clarity; a relentless playing to the gallery. His insistence, too, that great music is in serious need of technological help for its survival ('maybe we could cut back to 7 here, insert 3 there, create a *crescendo* here, a *decrescendo* there' etc) often leads to freeze-dried results that have little connection with the human spirit in all its richness, fullness and variety. Gould remains hermetically sealed within his own brilliance. The filming is outstanding, Gould's hyperactivity provides its own fascinating visual commentary.

Leonid Kogan   *violin*

Bach Partita No 2 in D minor – Sarabande[a]
Beethoven Violin Concerto in D, Op 61[b] **Brahms**
Hungarian Dance No 17 in F sharp minor (arr
Heifetz)[c] **Debussy** Beau soir (arr Heifetz)[d] **Falla** Suite
populaire espagnole (arr Kochánski)[e] **Handel** Violin
Sonata No 9 in E, HWV373[f] **Leclair** Sonata No 3 for 2
Violins in C, Op 3[g] **Paganini** Cantabile (arr Kinsky/
Rothschild)[h] **Shostakovich** Preludes, Op 34 (arr
Tsiganov)[i] – No 10 in C sharp minor; No 15 in D flat;
No 16 in B flat minor; No 24 in D minor
Leonid Kogan, [g]**Elizaveta Gilels-Kogan** *vns*
[dfi]**Andrei Mytnik,** [ceh]**Naum Walter** *pfs* [b]**ORTF
National Orchestra / Louis Froment**
EMI/IMG Artists **DVD** 492834-9 (96' · 4:3 Black &
White · mono · 0) Recorded live [dfi]1962, [g]1963,
[abi]1966, [ceh]1968   Ⓕ**O**

EMI's Classic Archive series offers vivid portraits of great musicians of the 20th century
thanks to archive films patiently collected from a
variety of sources, mainly BBC Television in
London and ORTF in Paris. The Kogan DVD
impresses for having as its centrepiece his
superb, concentrated reading of the Beethoven
Violin Concerto, matching in intensity the
readings we already know on CD, even though
the mono sound from ORTF is on the dry side.
The tender simplicity of the coda in the first
movement leads to one of the most dedicated
readings of the slow movement you will meet,
with the lovely third theme bringing a breathtaking *pianissimo*, and with the finale light and
dancing.
   The other shorter items all demonstrate the
flawless intonation and tonal control which
always marked Kogan's playing. Specially valuable is the Sonata for two violins by Leclair, with
Kogan's wife, Elisaveta, a perfectly matched
partner. Even though Kogan's grim look of
thunder as he plays isn't always reassuring, this
makes a fine visual reminder of an artist overshadowed to an unfair degree by his 16-years-
older Soviet colleague, David Oistrakh.

Wanda Landowska   *harpsichord*

Uncommon Visionary   Ⓗ
Includes performances of **Bach** Goldberg Variations,
BWV988 (audio only)[a]. Harpsichord Concerto in D
BWV1054 – Allegro[b]. Concerto in the Italian style,
'Italian Concerto', BWV971 – (Allegro – excerpt)[b]
Bach/Vivaldi Organ Concerto in D, BWV972/RV230[b]
Francisque Pavane and Bransles[b]
Wanda Landowska *hpd*
Video Artists International **DVD** VAIDVD4246 (57' · 4:3
b/w · mono · 0) Recorded [a]in Paris, November 1933;
[b]at Wanda Landowska's home in Lakewood,
Connecticut, 1953.   Ⓕ

This is an intricate mosaic evoking the trials,
tribulations and above all the triumphs of one of
the greatest, most innovative musicians of the
20th century. First and foremost there is the
playing, the complete extant footage filmed in

Lakewood, Connecticut, in 1953, followed by
her calling-card, Bach's *Goldberg Variations*
recorded in Paris in 1933.
   Even in old age her performances blazed with
the sort of conviction demonstrated by very few
artists, a mirror of her tireless fight to get a then
seemingly redundant instrument recognised as
the only suitable medium for early music and for
Bach in particular. She wished to share her joy in
music-making with her audience ('the hearts of
my audience are my acoustic') and, by her own
candid admission, surmount every obstacle in
her path and achieve every ambition ('I long to
be famous'). even in her childhood in Poland she
shied away from the eternal Chopin, announcing 'I will play what I want to play.'
   Watching as well as hearing Landowska is an
unforgettable experience; her intensity, wit and
perhaps above all her steel-fingered mastery are
revealed in every intimate camera shot. VAI's
sound is impressive and its portrait of 'an old
Jewess, neither French, Polish or American,
who loves music' (Landowska) is a superb mirror of an artist for whom music was the ultimate
reflection of experience, a refuge in trouble, a
provider of solace in grief, as well as an instiga-
tor of human warmth, spontaneity and happiness.

David Oistrakh   *violin*

Beethoven Romance No 1. Violin Sonata No 9,   Ⓗ
'Kreutzer' (first movement) – in rehearsal **Brahms**
Violin Concerto **Kreisler** Liebesleid **Lalo** Symphonie
espagnole – Intermezzo **Locatelli** Caprice in D, 'Il
laborinto armonico' **Sibelius** Violin Concerto
Tchaikovsky Violin Concerto
David Oistrakh *vn* **Frida Bauer, Vladimir Yampolsky**
pfs **Moscow Philharmonic Orchestra; Moscow
Radio Symphony Orchestra / Gennady
Rozhdestvensky**
EMI Classic Archive **DVD** DVB5996859 (131' · 4:3 b/w ·
PCM mono · 0) Recorded 1937-68   Ⓕ

The svelte figure and film-star good looks evident in some grainy footage shot in 1937 make
David Oistrakh almost unrecognisable from the
later podgy musical icon familiar to all. The art-
deco setting, the moody lighting and the anonymous pianist banished to the back of the stage
provide an *echt* period setting for *Liebesleid*. The
Intermezzo from Lalo's *Symphonie espagnole* was
filmed 15 years later, the year Stalin and
Prokofiev died.
   The remainder of the programme comes from
the 1960s and is the compelling reason for
investing in this DVD: three of the greatest concertos in the repertoire played with all the mastery and maturity of Oistrakh at the height of his
powers. The unflashy demeanour, his warm,
silky tone and the palette of colours achieved
with such economical means make for a richly
enjoyable and rewarding experience. The
Brahms, Tchaikovsky and Sibelius concertos are
similar in conception to his DG recordings from
that period, though 14 years on from his 1952

recording of the Brahms, the slow movement is taken at a broader tempo. Oistrakh's encore after the Tchaikovsky is a rarity – Locatelli's Caprice Op 3 No 23 orchestrated (and conducted) by Rozhdestvensky. The bonus, filmed in Japan in 1967, is of a rehearsal of the first movement of the *Kreutzer* Sonata. Single camera, extreme close-up on Oistrakh for the duration. The poor pianist, Frida Bauer, might as well be a backing track.

Sviatoslav Richter   *piano*

Richter – The Enigma
A documentary film by **Bruno Monsaingeon**
Warner Music Vision/NVC Arts *DVD* 3984-23029-2
(154' · Regions 2-6)   Ⓕ**OO**

Is Richter really an enigma? This epic documentary was originally titled 'Richter l'insoumis', meaning anything from 'irrepressible' to 'indomitable'. Constructed around interviews with Richter, his wife, and fellow luminaries such as Glenn Gould and Rubinstein, it reveals him as both – the precocious genius who never practised scales and chords, but instead launched into Chopin Etudes, and who lists his three masters as his father, his mentor Neuhaus and Wagner. And in his last years Monsaingeon's camera captures, not the grim scowl and prognathous jaw, but an urbane egotist whose deceptively naive charm must have helped him sail through life under the Soviet regime he despised, surviving to shed gentle vitriol on contemporaries. Prokofiev patronised him as 'fit for Rachmaninov'; Richter played at his funeral – 'Rachmaninov!' he adds, with a lethal twinkle. Among other victims are Oistrakh and Karajan.

Against this anecdotal ambience, though, are set some 50 performance extracts which capture the electrifying reality of Richter's playing – his vast repertoire, including Berg's *Kammerkonzert*, and the penetrating, expressive intensity which offsets his virtuoso eloquence and massive dynamics. It isn't too fanciful to see him possessed and shaped by the score, especially in his native repertoire. Even those who aren't primarily piano aficionados can hardly fail to respond. We even glimpse him happily playing Liszt – man and music – in a cameo film role.

Unlike videotape, DVD allows each excerpt to be accessed swiftly via its 'chapter', and its image quality enhances even elderly material. The worst flaw of this fascinating montage is that, though skilfully edited, it leaves one desperate to hear every single piece complete.

Mstislav Rostropovich   *cello*

Mussorgsky Songs and Dances of Death[a] **Prokofiev** Symphony-Concerto in E minor, Op 125[b]
Shostakovich Cello Concerto No 1 in E flat, Op 107[c]
Mstislav Rostropovich [bc]*vc*/[e]*pf* [a]Galina Vishnevskaya *sop* [c]London Symphony Orchestra / Charles Groves; [b]Monte Carlo National Opera

Orchestra / **Okko Kamu** *Video directors* [a]**Gérard Herzog,** [b]**Denise Billon,** [c]**Walter Todds**
EMI/IMG Artists *DVD* 490120-9 (85' · 4:3 [c]Black & White · 1.0 · 0) Recorded [c]1961[ab], 1970   Ⓕ

When he came to know Shostakovich personally in the 1950s Rostropovich wanted to ask him for a cello concerto. Fortunately he never did: the composer's wife later told him that only if he didn't ask or mention his wish might Shostakovich produce something out of the musical hat. She was right, and in 1959 the great cellist's restraint was rewarded. Here is a performance from two years later that Rostropovich gave of the First Concerto in London. The Prokofiev Symphony-Concerto, which reputedly inspired Shostakovich's Concerto, is an altogether mellower lyrical work but has an extraordinary *Scherzo* which Rostropovich plays with such staggering virtuosity that the audience breaks into applause at the end of the movement. Throughout both works the camera frequently focuses closely on the solo cello, which makes Rostropovich's playing enormously involving, intensely so in the Prokofiev, where the live communication is even more marked. It's good to have colour here, which always seems to add an extra degree of vividness. For a bonus, Galina Vishnevskaya joins her husband (at the piano) in a splendidly characterised performance of Mussorgsky's dark song cycle. But it's for the sheer presence of this remarkable cello playing that this DVD is indispensable.

Beethoven Cello Sonatas[a] **Mendelssohn** Variations sérieuses, Op 54[b]
[a]Mstislav Rostropovich *vc* [ab]Sviatoslav Richter *pf*
EMI / IMG Artists *DVD* 492848-9 (129' · 4:3 Black & White · 5.1 · 0) Recorded [a]1964, [b]1966   Ⓕ**O**

Even duos as celebrated as Casals and Horszowski or Piatigorsky and Solomon, hardly achieved such flawless unanimity as Rostropovich and Richter do in both the letter and spirit of Beethoven's Cello Sonatas.

Rostropovich and Richter play, quite simply, as one, taking us and their lucky audience on a journey that's a marvel of sustained mastery and eloquence. Hear their hushed magic at the start of the First Sonata's development (truly *dolce* and *piano*) or their knockabout sense of fun in the final Rondo and you'll be made aware that nothing can quell their joy in recreation, in every aspect of Beethoven's sensitivity and exuberance. Throughout, textures are kept meticulously clean, rhythms as spine-tingling as they're buoyant, and this despite often precipitate tempos that could so easily throw lesser players.

The two last sonatas where Beethoven, always the intrepid visionary and explorer, steps into the unknown, are given with a matchless sense of their verve and sobriety and never more so than in the closing fugue (a near relative of the fugue from the *Hammerklavier* piano sonata) of Op 102. As a substantial bonus, EMI adds a 1966 Moscow performance of Mendelssohn's

Variations sérieuses where Richter's thunder and serenity would surely have taken the composer's urbane nature by surprise.

The recital is well recorded. Highly recommended as a vital reminder of two great artists.

Various Artists   *violin*

The Art of Violin – A film by Bruno Monsaingeon
Includes excerpts from performances by Ivry Gitlis, Mischa Elman, Zino Francescatti, George Enescu, Boris Goldstein, Ida Haendel, Josef Hassid, Jascha Heifetz, Fritz Kreisler, Leonid Kogan, Laurent Korcia, Alexander Markov, Yehudi Menuhin, Nathan Milstein, Ginette Neveu, David Oistrakh, Michael Rabin, Ruggiero Ricci, Isaac Stern, Henryk Szeryng, Joseph Szigeti, Jacques Thibaud, Eugène Ysaÿe
NVC DVD 8573-85801-2 (113' · Region 0)   ⓕ ⊙⊙

The best of Bruno Monsaingeon's video productions marry a film maker's technical expertise with a musician's instinct, and in the context of The Art of Violin both qualities register more or less from the start. Within minutes, Itzhak Perlman is telling us that most of the 'old-world' violinists 'sounded different' from each other. No sooner has he spoken than Monsaingeon provides the evidence. He splices us from a 1958 David Oistrakh film of Mendelssohn's Concerto to Isaac Stern in 1957, Christian Ferras in 1963, Fritz Kreisler in 1927 (a charming shot of silent film with the 1935 commercial recording as its soundtrack) and Nathan Milstein in 1966. Then there's Yehudi Menuhin in 1979 and 1947 (under Dorati), Arthur Grumiaux in 1961, Jascha Heifetz in 1959 (the RCA recording with overlaid film footage) and, perhaps most interesting of all, Mischa Elman in London in 1962. And yes, they do all sound different – very different.

But what's the technical mechanism that turns these interpretative differences into sound? The interview evidence is as detailed as one could wish given the breadth of Monsaingeon's targeted audience. The principal commentators are Perlman, Ivry Gitlis, Ida Haendel, Menuhin and Hilary Hahn, all of them inspired to frequent eloquence and unflagging enthusiasm.

There are in effect two films. The first, 'The Devil's Instrument', contains some of the most interesting archive footage; the second, 'Transcending the Violin', veers more in the direction of specific instruments and overall musicianship. Menuhin stresses the self-destructive properties of soulless virtuosity and it's appropriate that the closing footage should give us the last section of Bach's Chaconne as played by Menuhin at Gstaad in 1972 – quite marvellously too. Earlier on, he offers an extraordinarily beautiful account of 'Erbarme dich' from Bach's St Matthew Passion, recorded in Hollywood in 1947.

Before Menuhin's Bach we experience the piercing gaze and musical intensity of Ginette Neveu as she burns the closing pages of Chaus-son's Poème onto our memories. We see Szigeti dispatch Schubert's The Bee framed by apposite commentary from Haendel, Perlman and Gitlis. Elman's preoccupation with sound for sound's sake comes in for some stick, though the evidence is ravishing and his own claims that the new generation owes a certain debt to the old, is both honest and justified.

A brief prodigy section gives us the 12-year-old Ruggiero Ricci playing part of Vieuxtemps' Fifth Concerto – amazing stuff – and the long-forgotten Boris Goldstein performing Kreisler.

We see rare silent film of Ysaÿe and valuable sound film of Jacques Thibaud, Leonid Kogan and Henryk Szeryng. And there are the surprises. For example, Perlman's attitude to Szeryng (and to a lesser extent Hilary Hahn's), which is guardedly negative. Both view Szeryng as a beautiful player who's lacking in character. Perlman puts it on the line. 'He sounds like everybody,' he says. 'If I'm listening, and I don't know who it is…I think, oh, it must be Szeryng'. Still, it's doubtful there's a better stereo version of Schumann's Violin Concerto than Szeryng's. Nathan Milstein is seen and heard, cool as ever, in Bach and Paganini. Gitlis challenges the myth of Heifetz's coldness by asking us to close our eyes as we listen, while Perlman compares Heifetz's beautiful sound in concert with his more aggressive, close-up recordings. We also see snippets of a 'staged' Heifetz recital, which has long circulated in private hands and where a bunch of college kids race through the campus shouting 'Hey guys, Heifetz is giving a free concert!'

Violin lovers will be in seventh heaven, but what's perhaps more important is that non-specialists should enjoy the experience just as much. The Art of Violin is utterly unmissable.

Titans of the Keyboard
Beethoven Piano Sonata No 3 in C minor, Op 2 No 3[a] **Brahms** Intermezzo in E minor, Op 116 No 5[b] **Prokofiev** Piano Sonata No 2 in D minor, Op 14[b] **Ravel** Jeux d'eau[b]. Miroirs – Alborada del gracioso[b] [a]**Arturo Benedetti Michelangeli**, [b]**Sviatoslav Richter** pfs
Video Artists International DVD VAIDVD4213 (65' · 4:3 · 1.0 · 0) Recorded for television by the Canadian Broadcasting Corporation [b]1964, [a]1970,   ⓕ

Heaven for piano-buffs. Here is Michelangeli on top form in one of Beethoven's grandest early sonatas, his magnificent technique displayed in breathtaking close-up. What marvellous preparation and address for each phrase; what fabulous transfer of weight through the knuckles and wrists; what amazingly economical body language, and yet what stunning effect when the noble bearing occasionally allows itself a fraction more freedom.

Richter is altogether more uptight. Hunched over the keyboard and prone to lurching from the left shoulder or jutting his jaw, he's nevertheless just as able to channel the essence of the music through his mind to his fingers. His

Brahms is gravely austere, his Prokofiev grimly determined. His rattle through *Jeux d'eau* may be hard to warm to, but his razor-sharp 'Alborada' is harder to resist. The slow movement of Richter's Prokofiev is shot initially from floor-level, memorably capturing his facial intensity.

Only five-and-a-half years separate these two Canadian telecasts. Yet there's a world of difference between the black-and-white picture and blistery sound-quality for Richter and the rich colour and bell-like tonal clarity accorded to Michelangeli. There's even an apparently unrepairable 10-second electronic glitch in the first movement of the Prokofiev, to which the DVD insert candidly alerts us.

Although it's certainly not true that this is 'the only extant visual document of Michelangeli playing Beethoven', that doesn't make this DVD any less inspiring. Pure heaven.

CHOIRS

King's College Choir

The Story of King's College Choir
A visual and musical journey around King's College Chapel. Includes works by **Allegri, Bach, Dupré, Goss, Howells, Ley, R Newman, Parsons, Porter** and **Radcliffe**
King's College Choir, Cambridge / **Philip Ledger** with **John Butt** org Video director **Robert Chesterman**
Regis DVD RDVD101 (60' · 4:3 · PCM stereo · 0) Filmed in 1983   Ⓑ

A film which has confidence in the value of its subject and the taste of its viewers. There are no catch-penny gimmicks, no patronising diversions. The camera ranges freely, and sometimes one might like it to stay longer with one of its many objects of beauty and interest; but the filming is always pleasing, relevant and illuminating. The commentary relies much on quoted passages of verse or prose and is uniformly well spoken. The daily routine of the choristers and choral scholars is informative, with intelligent boys and men, telling us what they think of it. The Dean and the director of music both present themselves as men of good sense and ample learning. And the principal subject of the film, the choral music sung at chapel services, involves a fine selection, some with organ accompaniment, some *a cappella*, illustrating the quality of the choir and the special experience of hearing it in that priceless setting.

Bainton And I saw a new heaven **W Davies** God be in my head **Gardiner** Evening Hymn **W Harris** Bring us, O Lord God. Faire is the Heaven **Howells** Like as the hart **Ireland** Greater love hath no man **Naylor** Vox dicentis: clama **Parry** I was glad **Stanford** Beati quorum via, Op 38 No 3. Gloria in excelsis, Op 10

Vaughan Williams Five Mystical Songs – Antiphon **C Wood** Hail, gladdening light
King's College Choir, Cambridge / **Stephen Cleobury** with **Daniel Hyde** and **Ashley Grote** org Video director **David Kremer**
BBC Opus Arte DVD OA0834D (92' · 16:9 · 2.0 & DTS 5.1 · 0) Includes notes, texts and documentary, 'The King's Choristers'   Ⓕ

They're all here, these Sunday-best anthems of the Stanford-to-Howells era, the years of plenty we may think of them as far as English church music is concerned if nothing else. The sequence of *Hail, gladdening light, Greater love hath no man* and *I was glad* is rich fare for a start. Some surprises on the way include EW Naylor's *Vox dicentis*, an impressively resourceful, well-sustained piece written for King's when the composer was organist at Emmanuel. That's followed by William Harris's *Faire is the heaven* (lovely example of quiet expertise and restrained opulence), with Vaughan Williams' antiphon 'Let all the world' to finish. This isn't the period and style of music most associated with the famous choir, but they command nowadays an ample body of tone and supplement this with the refinement which comes with their long tradition in the mastery of Tudor polyphony.

It might be questioned whether there's a film to be made out of this; but the visual element is a genuine enrichment, and the beauty of the candlelit chapel is a presence that accompanies the music. The video direction is wonderfully precise and plays its own set of intricate variations on the themes of choir and chapel. For those who want more, there's a 30-minute documentary which looks at a chorister's life at King's.

Carols from King's
Anonymous Gloria in excelsis Deo **Bach** Christmas Oratorio, BWV248 – Und es waren Hirten **Berlioz** L'enfance du Christ, Op 25 – The Shepherds' Farewell **Gruber** Silent Night. **Traditional** The Angel and the Shepherds. Angels from the realms of glory. Coventry Shepherd's Carol. God rest ye merry gentlemen. Hail, Blessed Virgin Mary!. Hark! the herald angels sing. I wonder as I wander. In dulci jubilo. In the bleak mid-winter. The Three Kings. O come, all ye faithful. O little town of Bethlehem. Once in Royal David's City. Quem pastores laudavere. Quittez, pasteurs. Riu, riu, chiu. Sing lullaby. Small wonder the star. The Sussex Carol. Up! good Christen folk. A virgin most pure. While shepherds watched their flocks by night
King's College Choir, Cambridge / **Boris Ord, Stephen Cleobury**
BBC Opus Arte Media DVD OA0815D (146' · 4:3 & 16:9 · 2.0 · 0) Live recordings from carol services in 1954 & 2000. Notes and texts included   Ⓕ●

Central to the formulation of this DVD is the awareness of tradition. First you watch the service in its present-day form, but, whereas on radio you had to confine your attentions to words and music, here on film the chapel itself is a presence. Stephen Cleobury, present director of King's, is filmed in company with his predecessors, Sir David Willcocks and Sir Philip Ledger, both of whom refer back a further generation to Boris Ord. And he's seen, in the second part, conducting the first televised service, in 1954, stored in the BBC's archives and never released until now, a little crackly in its mono sound and a little fuzzy in its black-and-white, but specific in atmosphere and rich in its store of time and place.

The service, filmed in 2000, shows very well how traditions survive – they move with the times just enough. So: the choir is still composed of trebles and male choral scholars, but at least half of the lessons are read by women. *Once in Royal David's City* still opens the service, but several of the once-regular carols have gone to make room for new ones such as the cheerfully syncopated Spanish carol. The Lessons have proved mutable too: the Bible is still allowed, but so are poems. The Bidding Prayer survives but in curtailed and rather sanitised form. There's no chanted prayer from the altar. The musical standards are surely as high as ever.

The Tallis Scholars

Live in Rome
Allegri Miserere mei **Palestrina** Alma redemptoris mater. Magnificat I toni. Missa Papae Marcelli. Motets, Book 3 – Surge illuminare Jerusalem. Nunc dimittis. Stabat mater
The Tallis Scholars / Peter Phillips
Gimell **DVD** GIMDP903 (82' · 4:3 · PCM stereo & 5.1 · 0). Recorded live at the Basilica of Santa Maria Maggiore, Rome. Includes audio bonus 'Tallis Scholars sing Palestrina'   Ⓕ❍

Few concerts can have been as successfully filmed as this one in the church of Santa Maria Maggiore, where Palestrina was both a chorister and chapelmaster. But this film, appearing on DVD 10 years after its video release, goes well beyond using the church as an atmospheric backdrop; the space, with its stunning fifth-century mosaics, gold-laid ceiling and wealth of paintings and sculpture, becomes a kind of visual trope for the music.

Traditionally conceived long shots and close-ups of the performers and audience (including a row of scarlet-capped cardinals) establish the context, but then the camera becomes, as it were, a roving eye, focusing on details in the iconography of the mosaics, the painting, the sculpture, to complement and enhance the meaning of the texts. It sounds an obvious idea when described in this bald manner, yet it's extraordinarily effective, adding an extra dimension to experiencing Palestrina's music, and reinforcing its message in a natural and refreshingly undidactic manner.

The performances by The Tallis Scholars are equally ravishing: the pacing is measured to accommodate a rich acoustic; the sound is clear and direct; intonation and ensemble are pretty much flawless: a veritable feast for ear and eye.

SINGERS

Cecilia Bartoli   *mezzo-soprano*

Mozart Al desio di chi t'adora, K577[a]. Bella mia fiamma…Resta, o cara, K528[a]. Vado, ma dove? oh Dei!, K583[a]. Voi avete un cor fedele, K217[a]. Le nozze di Figaro – Un moto di gioia, K579[a]
[a]**Cecilia Bartoli** *mez* **Vienna Concentus Musicus / Nikolaus Harnoncourt** *Video director* **Brian Large**
BBC/Opus Arte **DVD** OA0820D (112' · 16:9 · 2.0, 5.1 & DTS 5.1 · 0)   Ⓕ

No doubt this concert, recorded at Graz's elegant Stefaniensaal, is aimed primarily at Bartoli-philes, who will not be disappointed; it's predictably impressive, if a shade short. Mozart's so-called concert arias are formidable pieces, some actually alternatives for his own and other operas, but others, in particular *Bella mia fiamma*, created to challenge ambitious singers such as Josepha Duschek. Bartoli copes with characteristic aplomb, tossing off bravura trills and alarming roulades just effortlessly enough not to be infuriating. The advantage of video, though, is that we can actually see the feeling with which she infuses even the most conventional sentiments, as vivid as her stage interpretations – though with her characteristically earthy twinkle never far off.

What's more, though, this is one of the best-recorded concerts, not just in its excellent picture and first-rate surround-sound, but in its video direction. Shooting in a lower, mellower light than usual, Brian Large captures the platform drama in vividly immediate close-up, without Karajan-style excesses. Thoroughly recommended.

Viva Vivaldi
Di due rai languir costante[a]. L'Olimpiade – Tra la follie…Siam navi all'onde algenti[a]. Tito Manlio – Non ti lusinghi la crudeltade[ab]. Ottone in Villa – Gelosia, tu già rendi l'alma mia[a]. Concerto for Sopranino Recorder and Strings in C, RV443[e]. Gloria in D, RV589 – Domine Deus, Agnus Dei[ac]. Juditha Triumphans, RV645 – Armatae face[a]. Zeffiretti, che sussurrate[acd]. Concerto for Lute and Two Violins, RV93[cde]. Farnace – Gelido in ogni vena[a]. Bajazet – Anch'il mar par che sommerga[a]. La fida ninfa – Dite, oimè[ae]. Griselda – Agitata da due venti[a]. Il giustino – Sventurata Navicella[a]
[a]**Cecilia Bartoli** *mez* with [b]**Maria Grazia d'Alessio** *ob* [c]**Enrico Onofri**, [d]**Marco Bianchi** *vns* [e]**Luca Pianca** *lte* **Il Giardino Armonico / Giovanni Antonini** *rec Video director* **Brian Large**
Arthaus Musik **DVD** 100 228 (106' · 16:9 · 2.0 · 0)   Ⓕ❍

This recital is typical of Bartoli's present form: the voice, in prime condition, can do just about anything its owner requires, both in terms of emotional projection and vocal pyrotechnics. As her present mission seems to be to convince us that Vivaldi was a great composer of operas, she here sings a very wide range of his arias with consummate ease of execution. Whether languishing in a piece from *Tito Manlio*, finding the tragic depths of the eponymous hero's big scena from *Farnace*, delighting in the fireworks of a jealous outburst from *Ottone in Villa* or – perhaps best of all – singing with lyrical beauty in the 'Domine Deus' from the composer's *Gloria*, Bartoli involves herself entirely with the mood in hand. Occasionally, the extent of her dynamic range seems exaggerated, as does her penchant for going into overdrive when executing fast divisions evinced in aspiration. You somtimes feel that a little less would mean so much more. But that's perhaps a downside to be borne for the sheer exciting exuberance of such an upfront performer. The widescreen picture is perfect, the sound perspective excellent.

Teresa Berganza   *mezzo-soprano*

Arias and songs by **Donizetti, Falla, Guridi, Montsalvatge, Mozart, Obradors, Rossini, Schubert, J Strauss II, R Strauss, Wolf Teresa Berganza** *mez* **Christa Ludwig** *mez* **Julius Patzak** *ten* **Dietrich Fischer-Dieskau** *bar* **Hans Hotter** *bass-bar* **Felix Lavilla, Gerald Moore** *pfs* **ORTF National Orchestra / Eugen Jochum; ORTF Philharmonic Orchestra / Serge Baudo** EMI/IMG Artists **DVD** 490118-9 (82' · 4:3 Black & White · 1.0 · 0) Texts included Recorded 1959-67 ⓕ**OO**

What television channel today would dare to put out a regular live programme in which singer and accompanist give an unadorned Lieder recital? Yet in the late 1950s and early 60s that was just what Gerald Moore did for the BBC. This DVD, although mostly devoted to Teresa Berganza, has as a bonus Moore accompanying Dietrich Fischer-Dieskau, Hans Hotter, Julius Patzak and Christa Ludwig. The programme opens with Berganza in 1960, aged 25, singing Falla's *Siete canciones populares españolas*. She nearly always included at least some of these in her recitals. Here, and throughout, she's in pristine voice.

At the Aix Festival a few years later, she's grown up. In white silk strapless evening gown, she's become a confident diva. Although she was always classified as a mezzo, in the first of the Montsalvatge songs, her voice is poised in the soprano register. The quality of the film is fuzzy and the camerawork less accomplished. However, this is Berganza very much as one remembers her. She had a subtle sense of comedy and pathos, and is in magnificent form in this Aix concert: the security of line, tone and her use of restrained gestures are admirable throughout.

Sadly, the picture quality of the first Paris orchestral concert is variable, hazy in long-shot, not so bad in close up. The simplicity and sweetness of her expression in the first part of *Cenerentola*'s big scene is lovely, then the final rondo brings a triumphant grin. It really is an advantage to *see* and hear Berganza: she lives each part, each poem.

Maria Callas   *soprano*

Maria Callas: A Documentary by John Ardoin Franco Zefirelli *narr* Bel Canto ▪▪ BCS0194 (117' · ADD) Recorded 1978. Includes bonus documentary, featuring Ardoin, Gobbi, Rescigno and Scotto Ⓜ**O**

The film begins with a newsreel of Callas's funeral in Paris, and it isn't immediately apparent that it's to be more than an anthology of pious platitudes, oral and visual, assembled and marketed in the emotional floodtide following her then-recent death. Zefirelli is stationed in the auditorium of La Scala, where he can look toward the stage which 'still seems to reverberate with the sound of her voice'. Then we see Callas herself – but not herself, for this is her persona as gracious and glamorous purveyor of artistic truth. Then the witnesses arrive, starting with Menotti, who recalls an association with fear and, in her voice, 'something bitter'. This is more interesting, but instead of pursuing it the film moves on. From Rescigno comes 'a supremely dedicated performer', from Caballé 'Thank you, Maria, for coming to us,' and from Zefirelli 'She literally changed the face of opera.'

Yet in spite of the patchwork method and flaccid generalisations, the film does succeed in what were presumably its primary aims – to show the fascination of the woman and the artist, the interaction of the one with the other, and, in doing so, to move its audience with the strange mixture of glorious public achievement and deep personal unfulfilment. Stranger still, perhaps, is the stirring of so many conflicting reactions. In the midst of such insistent testimony, the film-footage of Callas 'in action' inevitably tests the claims. Does it truly support them? Is that filmed 'Vissi d'arte', for instance, really the work of a great operatic actress? Often it rather strengthens the view that with Callas, as with all great opera singers, most of the acting is done with the voice. And yet at the end we're left with her singing 'Ah, non credea mirarti' from *La sonnambula*, where the voice becomes frail and unsteady while the face is transfigured, infinitely touching. No: it isn't a film to be missed, and the bonus footage sheds interesting light on its making, especially from the late John Ardoin, clearly one of its prime movers.

Bizet Carmen[a] – Prelude; L'amour est un oiseau rebelle (Habanera); Séguedille; Act 3, Entr'acte **Puccini** Tosca[b] – Act 2 **Verdi** Don Carlo – Tu che le vanità[a] **Maria Callas** *sop* with [b]**Renato Cioni,** [b]**Robert Bowman** *tens* [b]**Tito Gobbi** *bar* **Dennis Wicks** *bass* **Royal Opera House Orchestra, Covent Garden /** [a]**Georges Prêtre,** [b]**Carlo Felice Cillario** EMI **DVD** DVA4 92851-9 (70' · 4:3 · 1.0 · 0) Notes included Recorded live at the Royal Opera House, Covent Garden [a]4 November 1962, [b]9 February 1964 ⓕ**OO**

Because of her transcendent reputation as a

singing actress, everything that survives of Callas's stage performances on film is precious, even though the sound recordings, along with the most vivid of contemporary reviews, tell what really needs to be known.

The two televised Golden Hour programmes seen here are justly famous, the special feature of their present reissue being the finer quality of sound reproduction as heard on DVD. The concert came at a time of acknowledged vocal difficulties: Callas's appearances were becoming rare and she hadn't sung in public for five months. She's in trouble with high notes in the *Don Carlo* aria but much in that's impressive, and her voice is happily placed in the *Carmen*.

Tosca's Act 2 is something of a rough-house at the best of times, and the climax of 'Vissi d'arte' is clearly under strain. Her partnership with Gobbi is exciting none the less, though he, too, is somewhat past his vocal prime. But he's superb – he's clearly acting not for the camera but the audience. Cioni is good, too. And all the subsidiary and silent others – that creepy old official hobbling on his stick towards the torture-chamber, the baleful bruiser, and the bespectacled Spoletta looking like an Alan Bennett character who has strayed into a world of horrors.

Régine Crespin   *soprano*

Arias and songs by **Berlioz, Brahms, Duparc, Fauré, Poulenc, Ravel, Roussel, Schubert, Schumann**
Régine Crespin, Denise Duval sops **Christian Ivaldi, Francis Poulenc, Janine Reiss** pfs **ORTF Philharmonic Orchestra / ªJean-Claude Hartemann**
EMI/IMG Artists 📀 492846-9 (68' · 4:3 Black & White · 1.0 · 0) Recorded live 1959-72   Ⓕ**OOO**

 Lucky French television viewers in the 1960s, who were treated to concerts such as those featured on this DVD. Régine Crespin was an actress of great subtlety, and clearly understood exactly how to use face, eyes and hands for the camera. The photography is pretty basic. In the opening three Berlioz items, with the ORTF Philharmonie under Jean-Claude Hartemann, there are only two angles: first a wide-shot from above, showing the orchestra with Crespin at the conductor's left, then a close-up of her face.

Crespin recorded 'D'amour l'ardente flamme' from *La damnation de Faust* several times, but it's wonderful to be able to watch her negotiate this aria, the tessitura of which exactly suited her voice. Then, in Dido's 'Adieu, fière cité', we have a souvenir of Crespin in a role that she made very much her own, but which, alas, she never recorded complete.

Crespin had a wonderful sense of fun, which can be seen in Roussel's 'Coeur en péril' and in 'Les gars qui vont à la fête' from Poulenc's *Chansons villageoises*. Poulenc nicknamed her 'Crespinette', and she remained his ideal Mme

Lidoine in *Dialogues des Carmélites*. Poulenc's female interpreter par excellence, though, was Denise Duval, and the DVD offers as a 'Bonus' a wonderful chance to see Poulenc accompanying her in extracts from the three operas of his she created. First comes a passage from *Carmélites*, 'Oh! Mon père, cessons ce jeu, par pitié!' – the last moments of the first scene, in which Blanche decides to take the veil. This is followed by a much longer extract from *La voix humaine*, which had been given its première just three months before this Salle Gaveau concert. It's the third item, though, that makes this a must for any admirer of Poulenc. Duval sings the scene from Act 1 of *Les mamelles de Tirésias*, and Poulenc accompanies her, while singing the role of Le Mari himself. This is sheer joy to watch, and confirms what a great artist Duval was, an actress and singer in the greatest tradition of the Paris theatre. The quality of the film is so-so, but the sound is excellent; the personalities of the performers are incomparable.

Kathleen Ferrier   *contralto*

An Ordinary Diva
BBC documentary based on Ferrier's diary and letters. Includes contributions from Dame Janet Baker, Sir John and Lady Barbirolli, Benjamin Britten and Sir George Christie
Narrated by **Robert Lindsay; Vivien Parry; Patricia Routledge** spkr; *Film director* **Suzanne Phillips**
Decca ② (📀 + 1 CD) 074 3067DX2 (58' · NTSC · 16:9 · PCM mono/stereo · 0). Extra features include picture gallery, Kathleen Ferrier's Decca discography, record covers and recording cards. Includes 77-min bonus CD of Ferrier's best-known recordings   Ⓕ

This much-praised profile is very welcome on DVD. Among the most telling contributions are those of Britten and Winifred Ferrier, the singer's sister. Even more perceptive and illuminating are Evelyn Barbirolli – Ferrier was a particular favourite and friend of Sir John's – and Janet Baker. There are interesting contributions from Christopher Fifield, editor of the Ferrier letters, and a little-known soprano who worked with Ferrier early in her career.

The music has been well chosen, with telling moments from Ferrier's assumption of the title role in Britten's *Rape of Lucretia*, recorded in Holland (a set still not officially available), and several from more famous interpretations, although inevitably some are too short to make much impression. The small amount of dramatisation has been imaginatively done.

There are faults and omissions. Poor use is made of the Canadian party at which Ferrier, presumably a trifle inebriated, let her hair down. Her marvellous parody of *The Floral Dance* is hardly heard at all, and – as in some other cases – the party snippets are not flagged. Directors can be reluctant to give this sort of information, but it should have been included here. So should identification of her accompanists other than

Bruno Walter. The worst error, however, is the use of Patricia Routledge to read the letters. Her actressy voice is nothing like Ferrier's and jars every time it is heard.

Of the DVD 'extras', only the discography is invaluable. The bonus CD includes the well-known tracks you might expect to be chosen, but Decca includes some carelessly prepared material, with distortion and/or over-loading. Still, as a whole, the project has been lovingly thought through.

Angela Gheorghiu   *soprano*

Live from Covent Garden
Bellini Norma – Casta Diva...Ah! bello a me ritorna **Brediceanu** Le seceris – Câte flori pe deal în sus **Charpentier** Louise – Depuis le jour **Cilea** Adriana Lecouvreur – Ecco: respiro appena; Io son l'umile ancella **Handel** Rinaldo, HWV7a – Lascia ch'io pianga **Loewe** My Fair Lady – I could have danced all night **Massenet** Manon – Allons! Il le faut pour lui-même...Adieu, notre petite table **Mozart** Le nozze di Figaro, K492 – Porgi, amor **Puccini** Gianni Schicchi – O mio babbino caro. Madama Butterfly – Un bel dì vedremo. Turandot – Tu, che di gel sei cinta **Angela Gheorghiu** *sop* **Royal Opera House Orchestra, Covent Garden / Ion Marin** *Video director* **Dominic Best**
EMI **DVD** DVB4 92695-9 (72' · 16:9 · 2.0, 5.0 & DTS 5.0 · 0) Includes interview with Angela Gheorghiu and photo gallery. Notes, texts and translations included Soundtrack from CDC5 57264-2   Ⓕ

Here's proof, if proof were still needed, that Gheorghiu is visually and aurally the most accomplished and involving soprano of the day. In a wide-ranging programme from the Royal Opera House, Covent Garden in 2001 she deploys her glorious voice with the utmost care for stylistic veracity, emotional commitment and communication with her audience by means of facial expression and gesture, so that each character is brought vividly before us without the need for any stage trappings.

The Handel and Mozart will not be for purists who would prefer smaller voices and quicker tempos, but the diva's singing of both arias is heartfelt and poised at speeds that, for her, are perfectly judged.

Manon's Farewell is even more poignantly sung than in Georghiu's complete recording of the role on CD. If 'Depuis le jour' isn't quite as effortless as it should be, one is consoled by the breadth of phrase. The recital proper finds its appropriate climax in a 'Casta diva' to equal versions by the great sopranos of the past: the expression in the aria is inward and intimate, as it should be, the cabaletta determined in accent, and words, as with Callas, are given their full due.

A main feature lasting 56 minutes may seem like short measure but in this case quality is all. This is a wonderful adumbration of an artist at the height of her powers.

Marilyn Horne   *mezzo-soprano*

A Portrait
Video director **Nigel Wattis**
ArtHaus Musik **DVD** 100 218 (52' · 4:3 · 2.0 · 2, 5)   Ⓕ

This DVD comprises a *South Bank Show* feature on the celebrated singer, shown in 1994, year of her 60th birthday, though some reference books give her date of birth as 1929, which would have made her 65 at the time of the programme. However that may be, this is a model of what a portrait of a famous singer should be. Done with the full co-operation of Horne herself, it relates her life story in just enough detail from her fascinating start, making bootleg recordings of popular songs, through her leap to fame when she dubbed for Dorothy Dandridge in *Carmen Jones*, through to her triumphs on stage in Handel, Rossini and so much else. There are tantalisingly short snatches of Horne in several of her major successes, to convey something of the singer's genius to those who never heard her on stage. Her own evidence is supported by that of, among others, Sutherland, her former husband and mentor, the conductor Henry Lewis (the difficulties she faced back in 1960 in marrying a black man aren't shirked), Samuel Ramey and several others. There are many touching moments such as, for example, Horne and her two sisters reunited in singing a close-harmony song; she and Sutherland, seated, intoning *Chatanooga Choo-Choo*. But the most important aspect of the film is the impression of an utterly sincere, warm-hearted and compelling artist recalling her exploits with disarming frankness and a sense of humour. The only pity is that the feature isn't longer.

Kiri Te Kanawa   *soprano*

A Portrait
Edited and narrated by **Melvyn Bragg**
Film director **Nigel Wattis**
ArtHaus Musik **DVD** 100 226 (157' · 4:3 · 2.0 · 2, 5)
Includes highlights from three concert performances
    Ⓕ

The heart of this portrait, and of Te Kanawa's professional work, is in the exacting, detailed rehearsals of *Capriccio* with her coach and the *Four Last Songs* with Sir Georg Solti. Above all, the film involves a fresh realisation of the importance of a sound basic technique. Sister Mary Leo, who so remorselessly kept the exercises going, working at the centre of the voice and the evenness of its production from note to note, is seen only briefly but the effect of her teaching is felt throughout. So too, incidentally, is the other teacher, to whom the film is dedicated: Vera Rozsa. The fidgety TV style in which a 40-second span of anything, aural or visual, is reckoned to be enough, is compensated for later in continuous filming of concerts in Wellington and Greenwich, and in scenes from *Arabella* and *Capriccio*. Like Dame Kiri's persistence with Mozart and Strauss, it's very worth while.

Elisabeth Schwarzkopf *soprano*

A Self-Portrait
Dame Elisabeth Schwarzkopf *sop/narr* with various
artists *Video director* **Gérald Caillat**
EMI ᴅᴠᴅ 492852-9 (57' · 4:3 · 1.0 · 0)   Ⓕ●

This documentary, made for television in 1995,
is subtitled 'A Self-Portrait', so one assumes that
Schwarzkopf herself had at least some say in
which items were chosen. Towards the end she
explains that now she prefers to be heard and not
seen, so although there are many film and television clips from the late 1930s through to the 80s,
the 'present' is evoked by her voice on the
soundtrack, and some discreet shots of flowers
in her garden. 'Addio del passato' from *La traviata* is the first thing one hears, the mood is established, nostalgia mixed with the characteristic
Schwarzkopf no-nonsense professionalism.

Even now film-makers have yet to find a really
convincing way of showing singers in action that
doesn't sometimes overwhelm the screen. Since
she made only one film of a complete opera (the
famous Salzburg *Der Rosenkavalier*), it's interesting to see some early television extracts, showing her as the Countess in *Figaro*, Donna Elvira
in *Don Giovanni* and the Marschallin. You're
conscious of the attempt to match the lips to the
soundtrack, and of her efforts to scale down her
facial gestures for the close-ups. She wasn't a
film star, though, but a real creature of the theatre. About 20 minutes into the film there's a
moment that should bring a thrill of recognition
to those who saw her perform. She's accompanied by Gerald Moore in a black-and-white live
broadcast from around 1960, singing one of her
folksong encores about the girl with three loves.
There's the communication, the charm, the
beauty – the mixture of reticence and individuality that made every Schwarzkopf recital an
extraordinary event.

Bryn Terfel *bass-baritone*

Bernstein Candide – Overture **Gwynn Williams** My
little Welsh home **Leigh** Man of La Mancha – The
Impossible Dream **Loewe** Camelot – How to handle
a woman **Mozart** Le nozze di Figaro – Overture; Non
più andrai. Die Zauberflöte – Der Vogelfänger bin ich
ja **Rodgers** State Fair – It might as well be spring
C-M Schönberg Les Misérables – There out in the
darkness **Traditional** Suo Gan **Verdi** Falstaff – Ehi!
Paggio!...L'onore! Ladri! **Wagner** Tannhäuser – Wie
Todesahnung Dämmrung deckt die Lande ... O du
mein holder Abendstern. Die Walküre – Leb wohl;
Ride of the Valkyries
Bryn Terfel *bass-bar* **Netherlands Radio
Philharmonic Orchestra / Edo de Waart** *Video
director* **Rob van den Berg**
DG ᴅᴠᴅ 073 047-9GH (140' · NTSC · 16:9 · 2.0, 5.1 &
DTS 5.1 · 0) Includes interviews, documentary and
promotional videos   Ⓕ

There's a devil-may-care bonhomie here that
could only mean one singer. This concert makes
a fine memento of Terfel's recent celebrity
appearances and his larger-than-life personality
in general. The first half of the concert concentrated on Wagner. In Wolfram's 'O du mein
holder Abendstern' it's good to hear him risking
as wide a range of colours live as he has in the
recording studio. Wotan's Farewell from *Die
Walküre* is also nicely varied, sung with a well-
studied sense of line and breadth, but not really
inside the character. Having looked unexpectedly formal in the first half, Terfel relaxes after
the interval for his comic arias by Mozart and
Verdi, followed by a winning selection of songs
from the shows. Nobody can touch him today
for inspirational entertainment value, whether
he's pretending to play Papageno's flute across
his fingers or getting the words of *Man of La
Mancha* to send a tingle down your back. His last
encore, a lullaby, is breathtakingly beautiful.

THE INDEXES

INDEX OF COUPLINGS

Goss, John
Praise my soul, the King of Heaven   1201, 1347
These are they which follow the Lamb   1199

Gould, Glenn
So you want to write a Fugue?   1343

Gounod, Charles
Au printemps   412, 1241
Ave Maria   1218, 1234, 1247
Barcarola   1216
Cinq Mars (excs)   1232
Faust (excs)   611, 1216, 1219, 1223, 1224, 1234,
   1235, 1237, 1242, 1250, 1251, 1255, 1256, 1341
Marche funèbre d'une marionette   1167
Mireille (excs)   611, 1216, 1256
Où voulez-vous aller?   1255
Philémon et Baucis (excs)   1216
Polyeucte (excs)   611
(La) Reine de Saba (excs)   611, 1217
Roméo et Juliette (excs)   611, 1216, 1219, 1222,
   1232, 1250, 1252, 1256
Sapho (excs)   1232
Sérénade   412, 1216, 1256
(Le) Soir   1238
Vierge d'Athénes   1233

Gowers, Patrick
(An) Occasional Trumpet Voluntary   1183

Grainger, Percy
Bold William Taylor - BFMS43   1214
Brigg Fair - BFMS7   1214
Tribute to Foster   1340

Granados, Enrique
Canciones amatorias (excs)   1208
Cuentos de la juventud (excs)   9, 1179
Danzas españolas - Op 37 (excs)   9, 418, 542, 1179,
   1189
Tonadillas al estilo antiguo (excs)   9, 1179, 1208,
   1209
Valses poeticos   9, 418, 1160, 1179

Grandi, Alessandro
O intemerata   1277
O quam tu pulchra es   1277

Grant, Bert
Arrah Go on I'm Gonna Go back to Oregon   389

Grant, David
Psalm 23   1202

Gratiani, Bonifatio
Dominus illuminatio mea   1283

Grechaninov, Alexandr Tikhonovich
Dobrinya Nikitich   1255, 1256
I wish I were with you   1255
Lullaby - Op 1/5   1255
My Native Land   1233
(The) Seven Days of the Passion (excs)   1200
She was yours   1255, 1256

Greene, Maurice
Magnificat & Nunc dimittis in C   1201
O God of my righteousness   1210
Orpheus with his lute   1230
Praise the Lord, O my soul   1210

Greiter, Matthias
Von Eyren   1287

Grieg, Edvard
Lyric Pieces, Book 3 - Op 43 (excs)   1177, 1187
Lyric Pieces, Book 8 - Op 65 (excs)   1177
Lyric Pieces, Book 10 - Op 71 (excs)   1170
Melodies of the Heart - Op 5 (excs)   1241, 1242,
   1248
Norway - Op 58 (excs)   1248
Norwegian peasant dances - Op 72 (excs)   415
Peer Gynt (excs)   951, 1214, 1222, 1241, 1252
Piano Concerto   421, 422, 1177
Songs - Op 18 (excs)   1242
Songs - Opp 21 & 25 (excs)   951
Songs - Op 26 (excs)   1210
Songs - Op 33 (excs)   951, 1242
Songs - Op 39 (excs)   951
Songs - Op 49 (excs)   1242
Songs & Ballads - Op 9 (excs)   1242

Griffes, Charles
Auf geheimen Waldespfade   1241
(The) White Peacock   1166

Grimace
Se Zephirus, Phebus et leur lignie   1275

Grofé, Ferde
Grand Canyon Suite   388

Grosvenor
I carry you in my pocket   1239

Gruber, Ludwig
Mei Muaterl war a Weanerin   1232

Gruenberg, Louis
Jazz Masks   1192

Guagni-Benvenuti
Guardami!   1236

Guami, Gioseffo
Canzon sopra la Battaglia   1281

Guarnieri, Mozart Camargo
Sái arnê   1248

Guerrero, Francisco
Ave Maria   648
Ave virgo sanctissima   1283, 1285
Beatus es et bene tibi   1278
Cancións   647
Dexó la venda, el arco   1208
Dulcissima Maria   648
Duo Seraphim   1285
Huyd, huyd   1272
Lauda, Jerusalem   1278
Maria Magdalene   570
Niño Dios, d'amor herido   1272
O Doctor optime   647
Pange lingua   1278
Prado verde y florido   1272
Si tus penas no pruevo   1272
Todo quanto pudo dar   1272

Guerrero, Pedro
Dì, perra mora   1282

Guerrero, Jacinto
(El) Huésped del Sevillano (excs)   1232

Guest, Douglas
For the Fallen   1207

Guglielmo Ebreo da Pesaro
Collinetto   1280

Guillaume le Rouge
Se je fayz dueil   1175

Guilmant, Alexandre
Marche funèbre et chant séraphique   1197
Sonata No 7 in F (excs)   1183

Guridi, Jesús
Canciones castellanas (excs)   1208, 1209, 1349
(El) Caserío (excs)   1232
La meiga (excs)   1232
Triptico del Buen Pastor   1197

Gurney, Ivor
I will go with my father a-ploughing   1214
Sleep   1214, 1252

Gwynn Williams, WS
My little Welsh home   1352

Hahn, Reynaldo
A Chloris   1226
Brummell (excs)   1225
Chansons grises (excs)   1224
Ciboulette (excs)   1225
Dernier voeu   1216
D'une prison   1233
(L')Heure exquise   1216
Mozart (excs)   1225
O mon bel inconnu! (excs)   1225

Halévy, Fromental
(La) Juive   1221, 1255, 1256

Halffter, Cristóbal
Panxoliña   1208

Halffter, Ernesto
Dos Canciones   1208

INDEX TO ARTISTS

Beke, RO von *vc* 1255
Bekova, Eleonora *pf* 608
Bekova Sisters 419
Belcea Quartet 208, 223, 305, 869
Bell, Joshua *vn* 76, 195, 541, 614, 835
Bell, Sebastian *fl* 137, 408
Bell, Stephen *cond* 1160
— *hn* 650, 669
Bell'Arte Antiqua 1257
Bellezza, Vincenzo *cond* 760
Bellocq, Eric *gtr/lte/theo* 1276
Belohlávek, Jiří *cond* 340, 341, 349, 606, 1160, 1303
Benacková, Marta *mez* 349
Benda, Christian *cond* 604
Benda, Sebastian *pf* 604
Bender, Philippe *cond* 893
Benedetti-Michelangeli, Arturo *pf* 289
Benelli, Ugo *ten* 635
Benjamin, George *cond* 137, 138, 462
— *elec* 137
Bennett, Alan *clpf/sngr* 262
Bennett, William *fl* 37
Benoit, Jean-Christoph *bar* 736
Benson, Clifford *pf* 205, 965
Benson-Guy, Elizabeth *sop* 1343
Bentzon, Johan *fl* 1242
Benzi, Roberto *cond* 600, 857
Berberian, Cathy *mez* 145
Berbié, Jane *mez* 1249
Berezovsky, Boris *pf* 77, 214, 618, 619, 746, 975
(Alban) Berg Quartet 141, 207, 626, 866, 869
Berg, Nathan *bar* 447, 674
Berganza, Teresa *sop* 367, 1349
Bergen Philharmonic Orchestra 1050, 1177
Berglund, Paavo *cond* 653, 943
Bergonzi, Carlo *ten* 1249, 1251
Bergset, Arve Moen *hard* 1053
Berio, Luciano *cond* 144, 145
Berkes, Kálmán *cl* 86
Berki, Sándor *bn* 112
Berlin Academy of Ancient Music 400, 402, 449, 531, 817, 844, 1037, 1041
Berlin Baroque Soloists 65, 1036
Berlin Cathedral Choir 858
Berlin Children's Choir 711
Berlin Deutsche Oper Chorus 104, 253, 311, 487, 686, 710, 711, 755, 1121, 1123, 1240
Berlin Deutsche Oper Orchestra 686, 710, 711, 985, 1240
Berlin Deutsches Symphony Orchestra 3, 1118, 1148, 1294, 1300
Berlin Opera Chorus & Orchestra 1119, 1333
Berlin Philharmonic Orchestra 32, 81, 84, 88, 98, 103, 104, 105, 107, 193, 194, 195, 197, 200, 201, 239, 242, 246, 247, 303, 311, 329, 337, 338, 342, 379, 399, 423, 487, 505, 562, 585, 592, 594, 595, 596, 597, 631, 663, 665, 676, 689, 694, 741, 742, 744, 745, 755, 774, 791, 855, 862, 896, 898, 906, 928, 941, 972, 973, 975, 976, 1019, 1022, 1023, 1067, 1068, 1071, 1077, 1104, 1117, 1123, 1130, 1145, 1159, 1162, 1187, 1341
Berlin Philharmonic Orchestra Academy 558
Berlin Radio Children's Choir 494
Berlin Radio Chorus 201, 494, 553, 562, 564, 585, 694, 791, 1077

Berlin Radio Ensemble 1146
Berlin Radio Symphony Orchestra 81, 379, 494, 553, 564, 598, 753, 774, 961, 976
Berlin RIAS Chamber Choir 65, 215, 487, 531, 682, 735, 817, 878, 1041
Berlin RIAS Symphony Orchestra 682
Berlin Scharoun Ensemble 878
Berlin Staatskapelle 103, 253, 1119, 1121, 1129, 1250, 1298
Berlin State Opera Chorus & Orchestra 1128, 1129, 1130
Berlin Symphony Orchestra 393, 598, 599, 858, 1242
Berman, Lazar *pf* 567
Bern, Jeni *sop* 485
Bernard, Anthony *cond* 1255
Bernardini, Alfredo *cond* 1104, 1106
— *ob* 1097, 1104
Bernays, John *bass* 71
Berne, Harry van *ten* 72
Bernhardt, Louise *cont* 586
Bernold, Philippe *fl* 306
Bernstein, Leonard *cond* 78, 136, 160, 161, 274, 388, 516, 563, 590, 593, 594, 927, 994, 1341
— *pf* 78, 388
Béroff, Michel *pf* 631
Berry, Walter *bar/bbar* 105, 248, 487, 978
Bertagnolli, Gemma *sop* 447, 1101, 1235
Bertin, Pascal *alto* 268
Bertotti, Lavinia *sop* 966
Best, Jonathan *bass* 509, 770, 1061
Best, Matthew *cond* 129, 152, 160, 248, 273, 378, 509, 954, 1033, 1061, 1062, 1095
Bettendorf, Emmy *sop* 1250
Beynon, Catherine *hp* 840
Beynon, Emily *fl* 616
Bezaly, Sharon *fl* 1007
Beznosiuk, Lisa *fl* 1105
Beznosiuk, Pavlo *vn* 166
Bianchi, Marco *vn* 1348
Bibl, Rudolf *cond* 968
Biccire, Patrizia *sop* 818
Bicket, Harry *cond* 1218, 1225
— *org* 378
Bickley, Susan *mez* 70, 74, 138, 181, 378, 430, 446, 447, 827, 996
Bihlmaier, Hans Norbert *cond* 979
Bilgram, Hedwig *hpd/org* 1161
Billy, Bertrand de *cond* 1336
Binchois Consort 251, 328, 1269
Binelli, Daniel *band* 729
Biondi, Fabio *va/vn* 603, 1104, 1105, 1110, 1113
Biret, Idil *pf* 189, 212, 991
Birkeland, Øystein *vc* 220
Birmingham Contemporary Music Group 6, 162
Biryukova, Natalia *mez* 934
Bisengaliev, Marat *vn* 361
Björling, Jussi *ten* 132
Bjørn-Larsen, Jens *tuba* 499
Blachly, Alexander *bar/cond* 1288
Black, George *gtr* 416
Black, Neil *ob* 650
Black, Nigel *hn* 898
Blackwell, Harolyn *sop* 213
Blake, Peter *hn* 898
Blake, Richard *fl* 137
Blankestijn, Marieke *vn* 465, 1097
Blas-Net *pf* 36
Blasi, Angela Maria *sop* 672, 676

Blaze, Robin *alto/ctnr* 60, 61, 62, 260, 407, 440, 447, 766, 1109, 1110, 1270, 1295
Blech, Harry *cond* 1247
Blech, Leo *cond* 1128, 1228
Bloch, Thomas *onde* 631
Blochwitz, Hans-Peter *ten* 906, 1150
Blomstedt, Herbert *cond* 697, 699
Blume, Norbert *vad* 493
Blythe, Stephanie *cont* 214, 1214
Bockelmann, Rudolf *bbar* 1128
Boer, Michele de *sop* 1108
Boettcher, Wilfried *cond* 677, 1179
Boffard, Florent *pf* 86, 145, 188
Bogdanovich, Aleksandr *ten* 1256
Böhm, Karl *cond* 100, 110, 134, 243, 658, 663, 665, 686, 862, 976, 981, 987, 1130
Bohuss, Irena *sop* 1255
Bolcom, William *pf* 183
Bolister, Ruth *ob* 1160
Bollen, Ria *cont* 605
Bologna Teatro Comunale Chorus & Orchestra 323, 817
Bolshoi Theatre Chorus & Orchestra 694
Bolton, Ivor *cond* 679, 1305
Bond, Danny *bn* 468
Bond, Jonathon *treb* 334
Bonde-Hansen, Henriette *sop* 316, 317, 569
Bonell, Carlos *gtr* 367
Boni, Marco *cond* 824
Bonifacio, Tina *hp* 1249
Bonn Beethovenhalle Orchestra 725
Bonneau, Jacqueline *pf* 1248
Bonner, Tessa *sop* 68, 392, 766, 770
Bonney, Barbara *sop* 68, 486, 629, 699, 767, 879, 906, 978, 1214
Bonynge, Richard *cond* 1, 137, 312, 323, 528, 551, 610, 708, 823, 1228, 1249, 1251, 1325, 1332
Booth, Juliet *sop* 248
Booth, Webster *ten* 1255
Boothby, Richard *vc* 295
Borchers, Christel *cont* 242
Bordeaux Opera Chorus 612
Bordeaux-Aquitaine National Orchestra 335, 612
Borg, Kim *bass* 248
Borgioli, Dino *ten* 1236
Bori, Lucrezia *sop* 1243, 1244
Bork, Hanneke van *sop* 588
Borodin Quartet 931, 1031
Borodin Trio 961
Borodina, Olga *mez* 780
Borowski, Daniel *bass* 817
Borst, Danielle *sop* 331
Bosini, Gemma *sop* 1224
Boskovsky, Willi *cond* 967
Bostock, Douglas *cond* 23
Boston Baroque 33, 404
Boston Pops Orchestra 388, 709
Boston Symphony Orchestra 103, 140, 335, 369, 562, 563, 611, 773, 792, 838, 940, 1135, 1159, 1165, 1341
Bostridge, Ian *ten* 228, 430, 879, 880, 886, 888, 908, 911, 1057, 1214, 1324
Bosworth, Nicholas *pf* 635
Botha, Johan *ten* 349
Botstein, Leon *cond* 400, 1004
Bott, Catherine *sop* 437, 452, 699, 770, 966, 1276
Bottone, Bonaventura *ten* 187
Boughton, William *cond* 377, 852
Boulanger, François *cond* 736

Boulez, Pierre *cond* 81, 89, 142, 168, 188, 189, 190, 303, 557, 586, 590, 599, 631, 634, 790, 791, 795, 855, 856, 858, 859, 860, 994, 1144, 1145, 1301, 1324, 1340

Boult, Adrian *cond* 91, 175, 194, 353, 356, 357, 360, 363, 501, 503, 827, 864, 925, 1057, 1065, 1158, 1350

Bourdon, Rosario *cond* 1233, 1242, 1243, 1244
— *pf* 1224

Bourgue, Maurice *ob* 336

Bournemouth Sinfonietta 25, 651, 831, 835, 962

Bournemouth Symphony Chorus 160, 315, 316, 962, 1132

Bournemouth Symphony Orchestra 160, 315, 316, 358, 562, 798, 893, 952, 953, 1023, 1043, 1044, 1132

Bovino, Maria *sop* 635

Bowen, John *ten* 628, 644, 1061

Bowen, Kenneth *ten* 1057

Bowen, Maurice *bass* 1251

Bowers-Broadbent, Christopher *org* 722, 1015

Bowes, Thomas *vn* 853

Bowman, James *alto* 71, 419, 443, 444, 446, 726, 765, 766, 767, 769, 914, 1013, 1111

Bowman, Robin *pf* 230

Bowyer, Kevin *org* 8, 52, 53

Boyce, Bruce *bar* 316

Boyd, Douglas *ob* 31, 465, 653, 1097

Boyd, James *va* 191, 361

Boysen, Thomas *gtr/theo* 602

Brabbins, Martyn *cond* 74, 168, 170, 177, 190, 291, 420, 493, 496, 498, 541, 578, 580, 837, 962

Bradbury, Colin *cl* 17, 1144

Bradbury, John *cl* 23

Brafield, Mark *org* 317

Brahim-Djelloul, Amel *sop* 575

Brailowsky, Alexander *pf* 289

Brain, Aubrey *hn* 205

Brain, Dennis *hn* 112, 201, 228, 651, 972, 1136, 1174

(Dennis) Brain Wind Ensemble 1174

Brain, Leonard *ob* 651

Braithwaite, Warwick *cond* 1247, 1255

Braley, Frank *pf* 625, 839, 868

(The) Brandenburg Consort 432, 452, 1113

Brandis Quartet 892

Bratislava Children's Choir 523

Bratislava Radio Symphony Orchestra 532, 757

Braucher, Ernest *va* 1104

Brautigam, Ronald *pf* 384, 493, 905, 931

Bream, Julian *gtr* 9, 809, 1178, 1179

Breda Sacraments Choir 72

Bremen Baroque Orchestra 72

Brendel, Adrian *vc* 119

Brendel, Alfred *pf* 97, 101, 119, 122, 125, 127, 128, 478, 655, 656, 671, 677, 867, 873, 874, 889, 1179, 1342

Brett, Charles *alto* 68

Brewer, Christine *sop* 183, 595, 978

Brewer, Michael *cond* 1202

Brezina, Jaroslav *ten* 1155

Briggs, David *org* 1180

Briggs, Stephen *ten* 1251

Brindisi Quartet 668

Britten, Benjamin *cond* 71, 218, 221, 222, 223, 226, 228, 230, 231, 233, 234, 337, 656, 657, 1136
— *pf* 215, 223, 224, 228, 230, 232, 1136

Britten Sinfonia 228, 614, 650, 652, 971, 1189

Britten Singers 227

Brno Janácek Opera Chorus & Orchestra 351

Brno State Philharmonic Orchestra 350

Broadbent, Peter *cond* 79, 463, 719

Broadway Chorus & Orchestra 161

Bröcheler, John *bass* 600

Brodsky Quartet 224

Bronder, Peter *ten* 107

Brook, Matthew *bar* 1063, 1327

(The) Brook Street Band 1257

Brooklyn Boys' Choir 586

Brooks, Gerard *org* 393, 1197

Brouwer, Leo *cond* 809

Brown, Donna *sop* 152, 483, 485, 1069

Brown, Ian *pf* 93, 498, 514, 734, 839, 1137, 1171

Brown, Iona *cond* 665, 856

Brown, Jonathan *bass* 766, 1279
— *cond* 407

Brown, Nils *ten* 770, 1108

Brown, Rachel *fl* 549

Brown, Timothy *cond* 832, 1002, 1200

Brua, Claire *mez/sop* 156, 412

Brueggergosman, Measha *sop* 183

Brüggen, Frans *cond* 102, 468, 782, 1037
— *rec* 1037

Brummelstroete, Wilke te *cont* 62

Bruns, Peter *vc* 178

Brunt, Andrew *treb* 334

Brussels Théâtre de la Monnaie Chorus & Orchestra 612, 1330

Brutscher, Markus *ten* 71

Bruun, Mogens *va* 1242

(Gavin) Bryars Ensemble 249

Brymer, Jack *cl* 650

Bryn-Julson, Phyllis *sop* 189, 560

BT Scottish Ensemble 1017

Bucharest Philharmonic Choir & Orchestra 364

Buchbinder, Rudolf *pf* 129

Büchsel, Walter *fl* 492

Budapest Camerata 322

Budapest Children's Choir Magnificat 535

Budapest Festival Orchestra 82, 83, 342, 345, 535, 563, 1187

Budapest Symphony Orchestra 274

Budd, Jeremy *treb* 1204

Buenos Aires Coral Lírico 730

Buet, Alain *bar/ten* 235, 269, 409

Buffalo Philharmonic Orchestra 427

Bukhtoyarov, Dmitri *bass* 1255

Bulgarian Male Chorus, Sofia 1323

Bullock, Susan *sop* 17, 495

Bumbry, Grace *mez* 1251

Burchell, David *org* 1048

Burgess, Russell *cond* 232
— *ten* 71

Burgess, Sally *mez* 316

Burnside, Iain *pf* 295, 860

Burrowes, Connor *treb* 444, 765

Burrowes, Edward *treb* 440

Burrowes, Norma *sop* 1057

Burrowes, Patrick *treb* 192

Burtt, Timothy *treb* 440

Busbridge, Judith *va* 828

Busch, Adolf *vn* 205

Busch, Christine *vn* 1096

Busch, Fritz *cond* 1341

Busch Quartet 205

Bush, Alan *pf* 250

Busher, Andrew *ten* 484, 1206

Busoni, Ferruccio *pf* 289

Buswell, James *vn* 7, 77, 731

Butler, Verity *cl* 1166

Butt, John *cond* 1347
— *org* 361, 1347

Butt, Yondani *cond* 535

Butterfield, Peter *ten* 483, 484

Buwalda, Sytse *alto* 56, 66

Bychkov, Semyon *cond* 974

Byers, Alan *ten* 348

Byng, George W *cond* 1249

Byram-Wigfield, Timothy *org* 1132, 1197

(William) Byrd Ensemble 440

Cachemaille, Gilles *bar* 105, 152, 336

Caen, Maîtrise de 235

Calcara, Tad *cl* 1167

Callas, Maria *sop* 1215

Calleja, Joseph *ten* 1215

Calnan, Patricia *vn* 321

Calvé, Emma *sop* 1216, 1238

Calzi, Nelson *fp* 816

Cambreling, Frédérique *hp* 145, 188, 636

Cambreling, Sylvain *cond* 543, 1298, 1330

Cambridge King's College Choir (Mens' Voices) 1202

Cambridge Singers 139, 372, 832, 1198, 1199

Cambridge University Musical Society Chorus 363

Camden, Anthony *ob* 12

Camerata Academica 659

Camerata Singers 586

Cameron, John *bar* 1057

Cámpa, Adela Gonzáles *cast* 1191

Campanini, Cleofonte *pf* 1252

Campbell, Colin *bar* 333, 765

Campbell, David *cl* 176

Canadian String Quartet 1343

Cannes Regional Orchestra 893

Canonici, Luca *ten* 1069

Cantamen 387

Cantate Domino Chorus 529

Cantate Youth Choir 995

Cantelli, Guido *cond* 201, 304

Cantilena 1057

Cantus Cölln 640, 815, 914

Canzona (La) 179

Canzonetta 17

Capella Augustina 486

Capella Brugensis 823

(La) Capella Ducale 712

(La) Capella Reial Instrumental & Vocal Ensemble 1271

Capilla Flamenca 1271

Cappella Amsterdam 557

Cappella de' Turchini 266

Capriccio Stravagante 256, 448, 1272

Capricorn 1203

Capuana, Franco *cond* 1251

Capuçon, Gautier *vc* 839, 868

Capuçon, Renaud *vn* 839, 868, 894

(The) Cardinall's Musick 257, 258, 259, 375, 718, 1091

Cardon, Stéphane *cond* 736

Carewe, Mary *sop* 6, 24

Cariven, Marcel *cond* 736

Carlsson, Roger *perc* 721

Davis, Richard *fl* 369
Davislim, Steve *ten* 107, 978
Dawson, Anne *sop* 1062
Dawson, Herbert *org* 1249
Dawson, Lynne *sop* 187, 442, 444, 456, 673, 765, 827, 885, 886, 1061
De Cogan, Dara *vn* 222
De Labyrintho 526
Dearden, Ian *taop* 170
Dearnley, Christopher *org* 1196
Deas, Kevin *bass* 1054
Debussy, Claude *pf* 309
Dechorgnat, Patrick *pf* 654
Dedyukhin, Alexander *pf* 1159
Deeva, Anna *va* 783
Defontaine, Martial *ten* 187
Degout, Stéphane *bar* 214
Del Mar, Norman *cond* 155, 196, 232, 250, 314, 827, 928, 962
Delaigue, Renaud *bass* 644
Deliau, Vincent *bar* 156
Deller, Alfred *alto* 1255
Delmé Quartet 349, 953
Delogu, Gaetano *cond* 1303
Delunsch, Mireille *sop* 154, 1054
Demertzis, Georgios *vn* 955
Demeyere, Ewald *hpd* 823
Demidenko, Nikolai *pf* 565, 617, 915, 1295
Demus, Jörg *pf* 572, 887, 890
Denize, Nadine *mez* 595
Denk, Jeremy *pf* 1171
Denley, Catherine *mez* 160, 333, 442, 444, 886, 1109, 1111
Dent, Susan *hn* 897
Deppe, François *vc* 462
Dermota, Anton *ten* 675
Dervaux, Pierre *cond* 736
Derwinger, Love *pf* 950
Desborough School Choir 334
Desenclos, Frédéric *cond* 329
— *org* 329
Desjardins, Christophe *va* 145
Desormière, Roger *cond* 309
Dessay, Natalie *sop* 611, 677, 678
Dessì, Daniella *sop* 817
Destinn, Emmy *sop* 1234
Detroit Symphony Orchestra 294, 1031, 1033
Deubner, Maacha *sop* 529
Deutsch, Helmut *pf* 217, 891
Deutsche Kammerakademie Neuss 551
Deutsche Kammerphilharmonie, Bremen 894
Devine, Steven *hpd* 1327
Devoyon, Pascal *pf* 271, 370, 835, 840
Di Donato, Joyce *mez* 452, 1109
Diaconescu, Florin *ten* 364
Diaz, Raul *hn* 1036
Dickerson, Bernard *ten* 1057
Dickey, Bruce *cond* 383
Dickinson, Meriel *cont* 1057
Didur, Adam *bass* 1255
Dieleman, Marianne *cont* 588
Dieltiens, Roel *vc* 625, 1096
Diener, Melanie *sop* 859
Ding, Lucy *cond* 409
Dinkin, Alvin *va* 856
Dippel, Andreas *ten* 1216
Diry, Roland *cl* 803
Divertimenti 508
Dixon, Alistair *cond* 1008, 1010
Dixon, Peter *vc* 369, 1167
Djupsjöbacka, Gustav *pf* 583
Dobber, Andrzej *bar* 408
Dobozy, Borbála *hpd* 1098

Dobroven, Issay *cond* 618, 694, 1247
Dohnányi, Christoph von *cond* 195, 1296
Dolton, Geoffrey *bar* 635
Domingo, Plácido *cond* 367, 754, 810, 1332
— *ten* 810, 1118
Dominguez, Rosa *sop* 263
Domus 347, 369, 370
Donath, Helen *sop* 627
Donatis, Fiorenza de *vn* 1104
Donato, Vincenzo Di *ten* 642
Donohoe, Peter *pf* 175, 176, 570, 796, 992, 1136, 1137, 1161
Donose, Ruxandra *mez* 349
Dorati, Antál *cond* 294, 338, 467, 1029
Dordolo, Luca *ten* 642
Dorey, Sue *vc* 139
Doufexis, Stella *mez* 374, 911
Doulce Mémoire 1273
Doumenge, Pierre *vc* 828
Douse, Stephen *ten* 317
Dowd, Ronald *ten* 150, 151
Downer, Jane *rec* 437
Downes, Edward *cond* 358, 1067, 1248, 1332
Dowson, Stephen *bbar* 1251
D'Oyly Carte Opera Chorus & Orchestra 999, 1000
Drahos, Béla *fl* 1097
Drake, Julius *pf* 879, 880, 908, 950, 1214, 1217, 1324
Dresden Instrumental-Concert 489
Dresden Körnerscher Sing-Verein 489
Dresden Kreuzchor 1200
Dresden State Opera Chorus 1124, 1126
Dreyfus, Huguette *hpd* 336
Driscoll, Loren *ten* 988
Drottningholm Court Theatre Chorus & Orchestra 400, 403, 1214
Drummond, David *cond* 302
Drury, David *org* 918
Drury Byrne, Aisling *vc* 579
Du Brassus Choir 708
Du Pré, Jacqueline *vc* 118, 364, 895, 1158, 1342, 1343
Dubois, Cyrille *treb* 235
Dubow, Marilyn *vn* 298
Duchâble, François-René *pf* 236
(René) Duclos Choir 841, 1215
Dufour, Mathieu *fl* 306
Dufourcet, Marie-Bernadette *org* 1049
Duftschmid, Lorenz *vion* 1281
Dugardin, Steve *alto* 179
Dukel, Franciska *mez* 255
Dukes, Philip *va* 137, 138, 963, 1007, 1169
Dumay, Augustin *vn* 209, 210, 306, 659, 670, 894
Dumestre, Vincent *bqtr* 182
— *cond* 1288
Dun, Tan *cond* 1326
Dune, Catherine *sop* 429
Dunn, Susan *sop* 599, 858
Dunn, Vivian *cond* 1001
Duquesnoy, Jean-François *hn* 734
Durrant, Benjamin *treb* 146
Durvesh, Aref *tabl* 1189
Dussek, Michael *pf* 75, 76, 94, 554, 828, 829
Dussek, Rachel *pf* 829
Düsseldorf Musikverein Chorus 599, 858

Dutch Radio Philharmonic Orchestra 1352
Duthoit, Marie-Louise *sop* 270
Dutilleux, Henri *pf* 336
Dutoit, Charles *cond* 82, 157, 275, 367, 501, 505, 545, 714, 729, 741, 838, 839, 1019, 1027
Duval, Pierre *ten* 1249
Duven, Richard *vc* 867
Dyadkova, Larissa *mez* 1220
Eadie, Noel *sop* 1128
Eaglen, Jane *sop* 1340
Eames, Emma *sop* 1238
Early Music Consort of London 1273
Easley, Lydia *mez* 1215
East Anglian Choirs 218
East Suffolk Children's Orchestra 232
Easton, Florence *sop* 1128
Ebbinge, Ku *ob* 468
Ebony Band 806
Ebrahim, Omar *bar* 560
Echániz, José *pf* 1244
Economou, Nicholas *pf* 1019
Edelmann, Otto *bass* 110
Eder, György *vc* 1098
Edgar-Wilson, Richard *ten* 192, 966
Edinburgh Festival Chorus 628, 683
Edison, Noel *cond* 1061
Edwardes, Claire *perc* 169
Edwards, Gavin *hn* 897
Edwards, Jack *spkr* 192
Edwards, John Owen *cond* 162
Edwards, Sian *cond* 1030
Egarr, Richard *hpd* 39, 48, 49, 166, 296, 385, 437, 438, 718, 799
Egener, Minnie *mez* 1222
Eguchi, Akira *pf* 371
Ehlert, Sibylle *sop* 560
Ehnes, James *vn* 1171
Ehrhardt, Werner *cond* 1149
Ehrling, Sixten *cond* 163
Eichelberger, Freddy *hpd* 1273
Eikaas, Anne-Margrethe *sop* 423
Ejsing, Mette *cont* 701
El-Tour, Anna *sop* 1255
Elder, Mark *cond* 137, 252, 501
Elgar, Edward *cond* 355, 360
— *pf* 360
Elgar Chamber Orchestra 1160
Elkins, Margreta *mez* 1249
Ellerhein Girls' Choir 448
Ellett, Charlotte *sop* 798
Elliott, Paul *ten* 262, 766
Elliott, Rachel *sop* 1327
Ellis, Gregory *vn* 294
Ellis, Osian *hp* 380
Elmo, Cloe *mez* 1070
Elms, Roderick *pf* 5
Elora Festival Singers 1061
Ely Cathedral Choir 1201
Elyma Ensemble 1049
Elysian Singers of London 317
Emerson Quartet 84, 205, 205, 346, 476, 517, 932
Emilia Romagna 'Toscanini' Symphony Orchestra 395
Emmanuel Music Orchestra 65
Emperor Quartet 581, 1137
Endellion Quartet 6
Endo, Yoshiko *pf* 798
Endrödy, Sandor *hn* 878
Engel, Karl *pf* 215, 1151
Engel, Norman *tpt* 770
Engerer, Brigitte *pf* 214, 893
Engeset, Bjarte *cond* 1053
English, Gerald *ten* 711

Foster, Lawrence *cond* 621, 849, 1162

Fouchécourt, Jean-Paul *ten* 235, 374, 1276

Foulkes, Carolyn *sop* 462

Four Nations Ensemble 263

Fournier, Pierre *vc* 35, 338

Fousek, Josef *perc* 997

Fowke, Philip *pf* 5, 314

Fowler, Bruce *ten* 817

Fox, Jacqueline *spkr* 482

Fradkin, Frederic *vn* 1241

Francesch, Homero *pf* 994

Francis, Alun *cond* 377, 727

Franck, Mikko *cond* 945

Frank, Pamela *vn* 277, 659

Frankfurt Radio Symphony Orchestra 19, 492, 740, 1144

Frasca, Dominic *egtr* 802

Fredman, Myer *cond* 91

Fredriksson, Karl-Magnus *bar* 12

Freiburg Baroque Orchestra 64, 466, 487

Freire, Nelson *pf* 774

Frémaux, Louis *cond* 610

French Army Chorus 412

French National Orchestra 156, 174, 310, 750

French National Radio Symphony Orchestra 171, 173, 634, 694, 837, 1215

French New Philharmonic Orchestra 736

French Radio Choir/Chorus 173, 174, 611, 736, 750

French Radio Philharmonic Orchestra 611, 1156

French String Trio 368

Fretwork 50, 138, 249, 260, 1017, 1258

Freund, Pia *sop* 789

Fricsay, Ferenc *cond* 81, 682

Frideswide Consort 258

Fried, Miriam *vn* 937

Friedman, Ignaz *pf* 289, 1182

Friedrich, Reinhold *tpt* 492

Friend, Lionel *cond* 797

Friends of Sibelius 948

Fries, Dorothee *sop* 1041

Frimmer, Monika *sop* 59, 73

Frith, Benjamin *pf* 361, 375, 376, 622, 627, 633, 903

Frizza, Riccardo *cond* 1220

Froeliger, Philippe *ten* 54

Fröhlich, Christian *cond* 961

Fromm, Nancy Wait *sop* 697

Fröst, Martin *cl* 20, 499

Frühbeck de Burgos, Rafael *cond* 367, 368, 421, 1208, 1333

Fry, Howard *bar* 1128

(Tristan) Fry Percussion Ensemble 996

Fryatt, John *ten* 992

Fuchs, Marta *sop* 1152

Fuge, Katharine *sop* 62

Fugère, Lucien *bar* 1238

Fukacová, Michaela *vc* 997

Fulgoni, Sara *mez* 628

Fullbrook, Charles *bell* 139, 1014

Fuller, Andrew *vc* 75, 554

Fuller, Louisa *vn* 504

Fullington, Andrea *voc* 262

Furtwängler, Wilhelm *cond* 103, 110, 200, 1117, 1341

Gabarain, Marina de *mez* 367

Gabriel, Alain *ten* 156

Gabriel Quartet 429

Gabrieli Consort 67, 70, 446, 447, 647, 738, 1091, 1277, 1278

Gabrieli Players 67, 70, 446, 447, 647, 738, 1277, 1278

Gabrieli Quartet 205, 650

Gächinger Kantorei, Stuttgart 73

Gadd, Charmian *vn* 607

Gadulanka, Jadwiga *sop* 1003

Gaetani, Jan de *mez* 494

Gage, Irwin *pf* 350, 882, 883

Galbraith, Paul *gtr* 41

Galimir Quartet 140

Gallardo-Domâs, Cristina *sop* 1222

Gallego, Francisco Rubio *cort* 1092

Gallén, Ricardo *gtr* 809, 811

Galli, Emanuela *sop* 966

Galli-Curci, Amelita *sop* 1222, 1243, 1244

Galliera, Alceo *cond* 1215

Gallimaufry Ensemble 169

Gallois, Pascal *bn* 145

Gallois, Patrick *fl* 698, 786, 1006

Galloway, Jennifer *ob* 21

Galstian, Juliette *mez* 447

Galvez Vallejo, Daniel *ten* 153

Galway, James *fl* 37

Gamba, Rumon *cond* 5, 17, 21, 22, 23, 24, 138, 798, 1060

Gambill, Robert *ten* 550

Gandini, Gerardo *pf* 730

Gandolfi, Alfredo *bar* 1236

Garbarek, Jan *sax* 1175, 1282

Garde Républicaine Soloists Ensemble 736

Gardelli, Lamberto *cond* 274, 1079, 1081, 1251

Garden, Mary *sop* 309

Gardiner, John Eliot *cond* 62, 68, 105, 130, 131, 134, 147, 149, 152, 213, 267, 353, 404, 406, 441, 444, 480, 483, 484, 485, 486, 552, 645, 674, 680, 681, 683, 685, 809, 897, 996, 1069, 1285, 1298, 1302, 1312

Gardino, Jolanda *mez* 1256

Garmo, Tilly de *sop* 1128

Garrett, Lesley *sop* 1223

Garrido, Gabriel *cond* 1049

Garrison, Jon *ten* 1004, 1046

Gasciarrino, Michel *hn* 878

Gastinel, Anne *vc* 536

Gáti, Istvan *bar* 64

Gatti, Daniele *cond* 1026

Gatti, Enrico *cond* 966

Gaudier Ensemble 346, 661, 865

Gauntlett, Ambrose *vada* 1210

Gauvin, Karina *sop* 79

Gavazzeni, Gianandrea *cond* 322, 1074, 1251, 1321

Gaver, Elizabeth *vn* 1291

Gävle Symphony Orchestra 12

Gavoty, Bernard *org* 837

Gavrilov, Andrei *pf* 1162, 1295

Gawriloff, Saschko *vn* 557, 559

Gaylor, Robert *pf* 1236

Geidt, James *treb* 146

Gélinas, Johanne-Valérie *fl* 1093

Gellhorn, Peter *cond* 999, 1001

Gelmetti, Gianluigi *cond* 1323

Geneva Grand Theatre Chorus 253, 822

Gens, Véronique *sop* 155, 264, 448, 679, 770

Genz, Christoph *ten* 27, 677

Genz, Stephan *bar* 27, 129, 217, 372, 599, 677, 907, 1151

Georg, Mechthild *cont* 1041

George, Donald *ten* 627

George, Michael *bar/bass* 192, 442, 444, 446, 449, 673, 765, 766, 767, 769, 884, 885, 886, 962, 1109, 1154

George Enescu Philharmonic Orchestra 365

Georgiadis, John *cond* 12

Georgian, Karine *vc* 205, 514

Gérard, Jean-Claude *fl* 368, 1208

Gerecz, Arpad *vn* 667

Gerecz, Arpad *cond* 32

Gergiev, Valery *cond* 185, 690, 692, 695, 745, 748, 749, 750, 806, 808, 916, 992, 1034, 1314, 1327

Gerhaher, Christian *bar* 888, 910

Gerhardt, Alban *vc* 218

Gerhardt, Charles *cond* 1117

Gerhardt, Elena *mez* 1152

Geringas, David *vc* 336, 1052

Gershwin, George *pf* 389

Gerzso, Andrew *elec* 188

Getchell, Robert *ten* 56

Ghelardini, Francesco *ctnr* 642

Ghent Collegium Vocale 64

Gheorghiu, Angela *sop* 753, 1068, 1071, 1223

Gheorghiu, Valentin *pf* 365

Ghiaurov, Nicolai *bass* 1251

Ghiglia, Oscar *gtr* 1208

Ghione, Franco *cond* 1086, 1215, 1241

Giacometti, Paolo *pf* 339

Giannini, Dusolina *sop* 1224

(Il) Giardino Armonico Ensemble 164, 1100, 1101, 1103, 1106, 1348

Gibbons, Jack *pf* 14, 389

(Orlando) Gibbons Viol Ensemble 259

Gibbs, John *bar* 1249

Gibbs, Robert *vn* 5, 92, 93

Gibson, Rodney *ten* 1071

Gibson, Alexander *cond* 313

Gielen, Michael *cond* 82, 241, 265, 1155, 1179

Giesa, Susanne *pf* 887

Gieseking, Walter *pf* 112, 289, 306, 308, 677, 1246

Gigli, Beniamino *ten* 1224, 1242

Gilbert, Kenneth *hpd* 44

Gilchrist, James *ten* 61, 62, 70, 71, 415, 441, 488, 512, 1015

Gilels, Elena *pf* 658

Gilels, Emil *pf* 99, 126, 193, 207, 425, 658, 836

Giles, Andrew *alto* 348

Gilfry, Rodney *bar* 213, 485

Gilibert, Gabrielle *mez* 1216

Gill, Tim *vc* 830

Giménez, Raúl *ten* 817

Gimse, Håvard *pf* 1053

Ginn, Michael *treb* 441

Ginster, Ria *sop* 1152

Giordano, Laura *sop* 816

Girdwood, Julia *ob* 12

Gispert, Enrique *cond* 1208

Giulini, Carlo Maria *cond* 67, 100, 101, 155, 225, 240, 246, 247, 276, 368, 680, 1067, 1075, 1088, 1340

(Philip) Glass Ensemble 397, 398

Gledhill, Rachel *vib* 856

Gleizes, Mireille *pf* 721

Glemser, Bernd *pf* 277, 544, 906

Glennie, Evelyn *perc* 583

Glodeanu, Mira *vn* 448

Gluck, Alma *sop* 1224

Glyndebourne Festival Chorus 389, 684, 820, 999, 1000, 1001, 1308, 1309, 1310, 1311, 1314, 1327, 1350

Glyndebourne Festival Orchestra 684, 1309

Godowsky, Leopold *pf* 289

Harris, Michael *org* 1197
Harrison, Beatrice *vc* 355
Harrison, Julius *cond* 1255
Hartelius, Malin *sop* 62
Härtelová, Lydie *hp* 349
Hartenstein, István *bn* 1098
Hartley, Jacqueline *vn* 1043
Hartmann, Arno *org* 877
Hartmann-Claverie, Valerie *onde* 634
Hartog, Bernhard *vn* 1031
Hartwig, Hildegard *cont* 107, 111
Harvey, Peter *bass* 62, 67, 70, 129, 181, 255, 446, 488, 766, 770
Haskin, Howard *ten* 1146
Haslam, David *cond* 375, 376
Hasson, Maurice *vn* 200
Haugland, Aage *bass* 701
Haugsand, Ketil *hpd* 45
Hauk, Franz *org* 801
Haukås, Jan-Inge *db* 277
Hauke, Ernst *cond* 1250
Hauptmann, Cornelius *bass* 68, 674
Hauts-de-Seine Maîtrise 1082
Haverinen, Margareta *sop* 929
Hayes, Oliver *treb* 529
Hayward, Marie *sop* 1057
Heger, Robert *cond* 1128, 1152
Hegyi, Ildikó *vn* 112
Heifetz, Jascha *vn* 103, 195, 538, 937, 1135, 1162, 1341
Heilmann, Uwe *ten* 672
Helbich, Wolfgang *cond* 72
Heller, Marsha *ob* 298
Hellmann, Claudia *mez* 248
Helm, Karl *bass* 242
Helsingborg Symphony Orchestra 221
(East) Helsinki Music Insitute Choir 842
Helsinki Philharmonic Orchestra 630, 786, 787, 842, 937, 938, 939, 941, 943
Helsinki University Chorus 948
Hemmi, Tomoko *pf* 543
Hemsley, Thomas *bar* 215
Henck, Herbert *pf* 638
Henderson, Andrew *org* 1002
Henderson, Roy *bar* 1163, 1227
Hendl, Walter *cond* 538, 1162
Hendry, Linn *pf* 852, 853
Heneghan & Lawson Virtual Orchestra 805
Hengelbrock, Thomas *cond* 439, 573, 574
Henke, Waldemar *ten* 1128
Hennis, Tim *bass* 1229
Henry, Didier *bar* 429
Henry, Michel *ob* 1097
Henry's Eight 407, 1279, 1280
Henschel, Dietrich *bar/bass* 62, 69, 487
Henschel, Jane *cont* 595
Henschel Quartet 626, 654
Herbers, Werner *cond* 806
Herbert, Victor *cond* 1224
Herford, Henry *bar* 177
Hering, Jörg *ten* 480, 485, 877
Heringman, Jacob *gtr/viol* 527
— *lte* 527, 1214, 1259
Hermann, Roland *bar* 107, 111
Hernandez, Cesar *ten* 1070
Herreweghe, Philippe *cond* 64, 65, 154, 372, 548, 766
Herrick, Christopher *org* 50, 51, 52, 53, 54, 1183
Herrmann, Anke *sop* 1112
Hesch, Wilhelm *bass* 1238

Hespèrion XXI 765, 1219, 1260, 1280, 1281, 1282
Hess, Cliff *pf* 389
Hess, Myra *pf* 204
Hessian Radio Orchestra, Frankfurt 306
Het National Childrens Choir 555
Hetzel, Gerhart *vn* 866
Heward, Leslie *pf* 1227
Heward, Leslie *cond* 1252
Hewitt, Angela *pf* 42, 44, 45, 46, 47, 48, 632, 793, 1295
Heyerick, Simon *vn* 1276
Heynis, Aafje *cont* 588
Hickox, Richard *cond* 16, 17, 21, 22, 68, 130, 146, 218, 225, 227, 230, 232, 233, 315, 316, 352, 353, 362, 364, 377, 400, 414, 415, 481, 482, 503, 507, 512, 514, 629, 769, 805, 826, 827, 964, 998, 1043, 1044, 1057, 1058, 1061, 1062, 1063, 1064, 1065, 1066, 1115, 1139, 1300, 1306, 1327
(Richard) Hickox Singers 1058
Hicks, Malcolm *org* 428, 1058
Hida, Yoshie *sop* 62, 70
Higginbottom, Edward *cond* 71, 1048, 1203
Highgate School Choir 223, 226
Hilander, Esko *vn* 730
Hill, David *cond* 227, 258, 695, 964, 965, 1091, 1132
— *org* 965
Hill, Jenny *sop* 67, 71
Hill, Kate *fl* 650, 652, 1160
Hill, Martyn *ten* 225, 227, 335, 417, 441, 509, 859, 886, 962, 996, 1046, 1062, 1327
Hill, Peter *pf* 141, 633
Hill Smith, Marilyn *sop* 492
Hilliard Ensemble 249, 527, 579, 580, 727, 1145, 1175, 1282, 1283
Hillier, Paul *bass* 262, 722, 1283
— *cond* 262, 527, 579, 704, 722, 727, 803
Hilton, Janet *cl* 667
Hind, Rolf *pf* 3
Hindemith, Paul *cond* 972
Hindmarsh, Martin *ten* 1060
Hines, Jerome *bass* 107
Hinz, Helle *sop* 906
Hiolski, Andrzej *bar* 1003
Hirsch, Rebecca *vn* 222, 797, 1203
Hirvonen, Anssi *ten* 950
Hirzel, Franziska *sop* 725
His Majestys Sagbutts & Cornetts 383, 428
Hlavenková, Anna *sop* 1155
Hockings, David *perc* 408
Hodges, Nicolas *pf* 3, 169
Hodgson, Alfreda *cont* 71, 363, 601, 1057
Hoel, Lena *sop* 12
Hoelscher, Ulf *vn* 961
Hoeprich, Eric *bsbn/cl* 661
Hoffman, Gary *vc* 271
Hoffren, Taito *sngr* 949
Hofmann, Josef *pf* 289
Hogwood, Christopher *clav* 49
Hogwood, Christopher *cond* 65, 384, 443, 456, 487, 673, 679, 726, 769, 1214
Hohenfeld, Linda *sop* 183
Hoitenga, Camilla *fl* 833
Holbrooke, Joseph *cond* 1255
Holl, Robert *bass* 104, 105, 131, 878
Höll, Hartmut *pf* 1142
Holland boys choir 56
Hölle, Matthias *bass* 242

Holliger, Heinz *cond* 497, 537, 538
— *ob* 32
Hollingworth, Robert *cond* 382, 1327
Holloway, John *vn* 164, 165, 166, 851
Hollreiser, Heinrich *cond* 1124
Hollweg, Ilse *sop* 426
Hollweg, Werner *ten* 487, 599
Hollywood Quartet 493, 856
Holman, Peter *cond* 1264
— *hpd* 192
Holmes, James *cond* 1223, 1337
Holmes, Ralph *vn* 314, 315
Holst, Imogen *cond* 218
Holst Singers 419, 856, 1016
Holten, Bo *cond* 316, 317
Holton, Ruth *sop* 56, 71, 444
Holzmair, Wolfgang *bar* 910
Holzman, Adam *gtr* 959
Homer, Louise *cont* 1216, 1224
Honda-Rosenberg, Latica *vn* 550
Honeyman, Ian *ten* 269
Hong Kong Philharmonic Orchestra 252
Höngen, Elisabeth *cont* 110
Honma, Tamami *pf* 616, 799
Honoré, Philippe *vn* 93
Hoog, Viola de *vc* 857
Hooten, Florence *vc* 514
Hope, Daniel *vn* 361, 378, 852, 1169
Hopf, Hans *ten* 110
Hopkins, Louise *vc* 6
Hoppe, Esther *vn* 839
Hörberg, Alf *bsbn/cl* 661
Horenstein, Jascha *cond* 590, 601
Horne, Marilyn *mez* 1249, 1325
Horowitz, Vladimir *pf* 289, 775, 1184, 1185
Horsley, Colin *pf* 651
Horst, Claar ter *pf* 907
Horváth, Béla *ob* 1098
Hosford, Richard *cl* 209, 734, 839
Host, Frantisek *vc* 997
Hotter, Hans *bbar* 110, 889, 1150, 1227, 1336, 1349
Hough, Stephen *pf* 208, 282, 381, 510, 511, 621, 638, 772, 836, 849, 873, 911, 974, 1185
Houssart, Robert *org* 301
Hovhaness, Alan *cond* 505
Howard, Jason *bar* 187
Howard, Kathleen *mez* 1236
Howard, Leslie *pf* 567, 568, 569
Howarth, Judith *sop* 129, 362, 1061, 1173
Howell, Gwynne *bass* 71, 152, 248, 362, 1062, 1138
Høyer, Per *bar* 546
Høyer Hansen, Helle *sop* 316
Hu, Nai-Yuan *vn* 237
Huang, Frank *vn* 1170
Hubeau, Jean *pf* 370
Huber, Gerold *pf* 888, 910
Huberman, Bronislaw *vn* 103
Huddersfield Choral Society 362, 445, 1138
Hudez, Karl *pf* 1247
Hudson, Paul *bass* 994
Huelgas-Ensemble 813
Huggett, Monica *vn* 165, 166
Hugh, Tim *vc* 25, 174, 180, 197, 222, 496, 501, 852, 853, 1015, 1133
Hughes, David *ten* 1067
Hughes, Peter *sax* 291
Hughes, Owain Arwel *cond* 499, 500
Huguet, Josefina *sop* 1238
Hula, Pavel *vn* 607

Hulse, Eileen *sop* 400, 856
Hulse, Gareth *ob* 93, 137, 734, 839
Humburg, Will *cond* 818, 1078
Hungarian Quintet 1179
Hungarian Radio Choir/Chorus 64, 83, 132, 274, 753, 818
Hungarian State Choir 563
Hungarian State Opera Chorus & Orchestra 753, 1070, 1078
Hungarian State Orchestra 88, 320
Hunt, Gordon *ob* 499
Hunt, Lorraine *sop* 369, 1306
Hunt Lieberson, Lorraine *mez* 3, 65
Hünteler, Konrad *fl* 26
Hurford, Peter *org* 53, 838
Hüsch, Gerhard *bar* 1152
Huttenlocher, Philippe *bar* 877, 966
Huybrechts, François *cond* 523
Hyde, Philippa *sop* 192
Hye-Knudsen, Johan *cond* 1242, 1243
Hynninen, Jorma *bar* 595, 842, 950
I Fagiolini 260, 382, 1275
I Fiamminghi 529
Iceland Symphony Orchestra 12, 553, 554, 943, 944, 945, 954
Ictus 462, 802
Ijichi, Hiroyuki *bass* 878
Ile de France Vittoria Regional Choir 299
Illing, Rosamund *sop* 610
Ilosfalvy, Róbert *ten* 348
Im, Sunhae *sop* 486
Imai, Nobuko *va* 193, 899, 1062
Immer Trumpet Consort (Friedemann) 1041
Immerseel, Jos van *cond* 255, 666
Immler, Christian M *bar* 1176
Inanga, Glen *pf* 498
Ingham, Nick *cond* 397
Innsbruck Trumpet Consort 164
International Piano Quartet 996
Invernizzi, Roberta *sop* 642
(L')Inviti 1132
Ireland, John *pf* 514
Ireland, Robin *va* 669
Ireland National Symphony Orchestra 21, 196, 240, 368, 698, 777
Irish National Symphony Orchestra 22
Isaac, Eduardo *gtr* 729
Isbin, Sharon *gtr* 1010, 1175
Isepp, Martin *hpd/pf* 879, 1210, 1214
Ishay, Roglit *pf* 178
Isokoski, Soile *sop* 595, 908, 976
Israel Philharmonic Orchestra 627
Isserlis, Rachel *vn* 508, 571
Isserlis, Steven *vc* 208, 353, 370, 465, 627, 835, 894, 974, 1013
Istomin, Eugene *pf* 100
Italian Baroque Orchestra 386
Italian Broadcasting Authority Chorus & Orchestra 1078
Ito, Kanako *vn* 93
Ivashkin, Alexander *vc* 428, 607, 746
Iven, Christiane *cont* 72
Ivogün, Maria *sop* 1228
Ivy, Claude *pf* 1227
Izquierdo, Ernest Martínez *cond* 387
Izuha, Mari *pf* 1142
Jaatinen, Jussi *ob* 788
Jablonski, Peter *pf* 267
Jackson, Francis *pf* 1249
Jackson, Garfield *va* 92, 1060
Jackson, Laurence *vn* 176, 219
Jackson, Richard *bar* 885
Jacob, Ariane *cels* 306

Jacob, Ariane *pf* 306
Jacob, Francis *org* 54
Jacob, Irène *spkr* 306
Jacobs, René *alto* 68, 844
— *cond* 179, 263, 454, 487, 531, 644, 645, 646, 686, 767, 846, 1041
Jacoby, Josephine *mez* 1252
Jaho, Ermonela *sop* 1220
Jairo *voc* 730
Jakobsson, Anna-Lisa *mez* 944
James, Cecil *bn* 112, 651
Janál, Roman *bar* 1303
Jandó, Jenö *pf* 86, 479, 536, 568, 868
Janes, Paul *pf* 414
Janezic, Ronald *bn* 267
Janowitz, Gundula *sop* 105, 487, 677, 710, 882, 976
Janowski, Marek *cond* 494, 923, 976, 1126
Jansen, Hans Hermann *ten* 66
Jansen, Rudolf *pf* 1150
Jansons, Mariss *cond* 594, 742, 807, 926, 928, 1024, 1025, 1026
Janssen, Herbert *bar* 1152
Jarrige, Béatrice *alto* 770
Järvi, Neeme *cond* 342, 448, 505, 534, 606, 721, 743, 747, 799, 922, 924, 944, 947, 1031, 1033, 1050, 1134, 1135, 1214
Järvi, Paavo *cond* 721, 790, 991, 1177
Jena Philharmonic Orchestra 459
Jenkins, Neil *ten* 766
Jennings, Gloria *cont* 1057
Jennings, Graeme *vn* 319
Jensen, Folmer *pf* 1242
Jensen, Gert Henning *ten* 976
Jerie, Marek *vc* 997
Jerusalem, Siegfried *ten* 858
Jezierski, Stefan *bn* 215
Jo, Sumi *sop* 968, 1228, 1229
Joachim Trio 840
Jochens, Wilfried *ten* 74, 1040
Jochum, Eugen *cond* 193, 239, 248, 710, 1227, 1349
Jodelet, Florent *perc* 839
Johann Strauss Orchestra of Vienna 967
Johannesberg Philharmonic Orchestra 291
Johannsen, Kay *org* 50, 52
Johnson, Emma *cl* 299, 1173
Johnson, Graham *pf* 228, 349, 374, 411, 430, 736, 840, 879, 881, 883, 884, 885, 886, 888, 907, 909, 910, 911, 912, 1150, 1240
Johnson, James *bar* 1155
Johnston, James *ten* 445
Johnston, Jennifer *cont* 302
Johnston, Rachel *vc* 428
Johnstone, James *hpd/virg* 1047
Joly, Simon *cond* 76
(Simon) Joly Chorale 859, 996
Jones, Aled *bar* 443
Jones, Della *mez* 107, 416, 503, 509, 635, 827, 1230
Jones, Joela *pf* 634
Jones, Karen *fl* 832
Jones, Martin *pf* 229, 377, 540, 1173
Jones, Max *treb* 1015
Jones, Parry *ten* 359
Jones, Susan Hemington *sop* 446
Joppich, Godehard *cond* 1291
Jordan, Irene *sop* 988
Jordan, Armin *cond* 737, 974, 1156, 1229, 1233
Josefowicz, Leila *vn* 3
Joshua, Rosemary *sop* 985
Josífko, Tomás *db* 997

Journet, Marcel *bass* 1216, 1222, 1252
Joy, Geneviève *pf* 336
Joyful Company of Singers 79, 463, 503, 719
Juan, Santiago *vn* 366
Juda, Iris *vn* 93
Judd, Roger *org* 720, 1061
Judd, James *cond* 159, 218, 292, 919
Juilliard Ensemble 145
Juilliard Quartet 731, 1144
Junge Deutsche Philharmonie 84
Junghänel, Konrad *theo* 1266
Junghänel, Konrad *cond* 640, 815, 914
Jürgensen, Nicola *cl* 815
Jurowski, Michail *cond* 553
Jussila, Kari *org* 787
Jyväskylä Sinfonia 789
Kabalevsky, Dimitry *cond* 1159
Kaidanov, KE *bass* 1255
Kaiserslautern Radio Orchestra 1
Kajanus, Robert *cond* 941
Kakhidze, Jansug *cond* 529
Kakuska, Thomas *va* 208
Kaler, Ilya *vn* 196, 714, 901
Kalish, Gilbert *pf* 1253
Kaljuste, Tınu *cond* 722, 723, 853, 1052
Kallisch, Cornelia *cont* 628
Kalter, Sabine *cont* 1250
Kam, Sharon *cl* 879, 1141
Kamionsky, Oskar *bar* 1255
Kamp, Harry van der *bass* 480, 485, 877, 1040
Kamp, Harry van der *cond* 251
Kampen, Christopher van *vc* 93, 534, 953, 1189
Kamu, Okko *cond* 221, 842, 937, 1345
Kaneko, Yoko *pf* 429
Kang, Dong-Suk *vn* 947, 1133
Kang, Hae-Sun *vn* 188
Kang, Juliette *vn* 896
Kanga, Skaila *hp* 93
Kangas, Timo *va* 702
Kangas, Juha *cond* 702, 937, 1055
Kanka, Michal *vc* 607
Kantiléna Children's Chorus 350
Kantorei Saarlouis 751
Kapel van de Lage Landen 251
Karajan, Herbert von *cond* 104, 105, 107, 112, 200, 239, 245, 248, 303, 311, 337, 423, 487, 505, 513, 556, 594, 595, 596, 651, 744, 745, 755, 757, 762, 855, 928, 941, 970, 972, 973, 975, 976, 980, 983, 1022, 1023, 1067, 1077, 1088, 1089, 1104, 1117, 1118, 1123, 1132, 1159, 1162, 1232, 1251, 1317, 1341
Karamazov, Edin *fl* 1245
Karamazov, Edin *gtr* 1245
Karamazov, Edin *lte* 1245
Karczykowski, Ryszard *ten* 924
Karnéus, Katarina *mez* 950, 1176
Károlyi, Katalin *mez* 557
Kars, Jean-Rodolphe *pf* 313
Karttunen, Anssi *vc* 560, 833, 1326
Karttunen, Petteri *pf* 730
Kasarova, Vesselina *mez* 1229, 1298
Kashkashian, Kim *va* 82, 493
Kasík, Martin *pf* 1303
Kaspszyk, Jacek *cond* 726, 738, 1006
Kastorsky, Vladimir Ivanovich *bass* 1255, 1256
Kataeva, Irina *pf* 560
Katchen, Julius *pf* 210, 1186
Katims, Milton *va* 204, 865

Kreisler Quartet 541
Kreizberg, Yakov *cond* 533
Kremer, Gidon *vn* 1, 102, 121, 207, 222, 529, 833, 851, 901, 1162
Kremerata Musica 730
Kriikku, Kari *cl* 299, 1114, 1141
Krips, Josef *cond* 1247
Kristufek, Jaroslav *vn* 997
Krivine, Emmanuel *cond* 533, 937
Kronos Quartet 2, 802, 1168
Kroumata Percussion Ensemble 8
Kruszewski, Adam *bar* 725
Kryger, Urszula *mez* 1005
Ksica, James *org* 349
Kubánek, Libor *perc* 997
Kubelík, Rafael *cond* 338, 342, 344, 345, 461, 520, 586, 588, 729, 897, 957, 997, 1121, 1122
Kuchar, Theodore *va* 607
Kuchar, Theodore *cond* 7, 690, 731
Kuebler, David *ten* 711
Kuhn, Gustav *cond* 906, 983
Kühn Chorus 350
Kühn Mixed Choir 351, 1303, 1304
Kuijken, Barthold *cond* 27
— *fl* 297, 437, 1040, 1260
Kuijken, Sigiswald *cond* 27, 66, 68, 677, 680
— *vn* 63, 756
Kuijken, Wieland *vada* 437, 1040
Kulka, Konstanty Andrzej *vn* 493, 1003
Künne, Thomas *ten* 878
Kunz, Erich *bar* 1232
Kunzel, Erich *cond* 810, 967
Kuopio Symphony Orchestra 730, 937
Kupfer, Jochen *bar* 62, 887
Kupiec, Ewa *pf* 86
Kurtág, György *cels/pf* 543
Kurtág, Márta *pf* 543
Kusnjer, Iván *bar* 606, 1303
Kussmaul, Rainer *dire* 65, 1036
— *vn* 622
Kuusisto, Jaakko *vn* 937
Kuusisto, Pekka *vn* 938
Kuznetsov, Fyodor *bass* 934
Kuznetsova, Ludmila *mez* 399, 934
Kuznetsova, Maria *sop* 1255
Kvapil, Radoslav *pf* 520, 703
Kwella, Patrizia *sop* 68, 441
Kynaston, Nicolas *org* 150, 151
Laarhoven, Paulina Van *vada* 1264
Labbette, Dora *sop* 1163
Labé, Thomas *pf* 460
Labelle, Dominique *sop* 844
Labinsky, Andrei *ten* 1255, 1256
Lacey, William *cond* 407
Laethem, Katelijne van *sop* 66
Lagger, Peter *bass* 605
Lagrange, Michèle *sop* 153
Lahti Chamber Choir 949
Lahti Opera Chorus 950
Lahti Symphony Orchestra 8, 936, 939, 941, 942, 944, 945, 948, 949, 950
Laitinen, Heikki *sngr* 949
Lajarrige, Christine *pf* 735
Lallouette, Olivier *bass* 235
Lamaña, José María *cond* 1208
Lambert, Constant *cond* 175, 1165
Lamminmäki, Juhani *cond* 937
Lamon, Jeanne *vn* 434, 436
Lamy, Hervé *ten* 235, 575
Lancelot, James *org* 719
Lanchbery, John *cond* 490, 546
Landauer, Bernhard *alto* 72
Landowska, Wanda *hpd* 1344

Lane, Carys *sop* 1058, 1206, 1327
Lane, Jennifer *mez* 859, 996
Lane, Piers *pf* 315, 361, 416, 916, 917, 1056
Lang, Ellen *mez* 298
Lang, Lang *pf* 1020
Lang, Petra *mez* 817
Lang, Rosemarie *mez* 585
Langford, Gordon *pf* 492
Langlamet, Marie-Pierre *hp* 215, 839
Langrée, Louis *cond* 155, 678
Langridge, Philip *ten* 225, 352, 504, 885, 886, 1061
Lapinski, Zdzislaw *vc* 1003
Lapitino, Francis *hp* 1216, 1224
Laporte, Christophe *alto* 644
Laredo, Jaime *va* 204, 668
Laredo, Jaime *vn* 207
Larmore, Jennifer *mez* 367
Larrocha, Alicia de *pf* 10, 367, 418, 1208
Larsson, Anna *cont* 304
Larsson, Lisa *sop* 58
Laske, Thomas *bar* 71
Latchem, Malcolm *vn* 619
Latham, Catherine *ob* 11
Latham-König, Jan *cond* 1134, 1316
Laubenthal, Rudolf *ten* 1128
Laudibus 1202
Laukka, Raimo *bar* 944, 948, 949
Laurel, Eduard *pf* 1171
Laurence, Elisabeth *mez* 189
Laurens, Guillemette *mez* 1272
Laurenti, Mario *bar* 1236
Lauri-Volpi, Giacomo *ten* 1242
Lausanne Chamber Orchestra 596, 608, 822, 877
Lausanne Choral Union 605
Lausanne Opera Chorus 575
Lausanne Pro Arte Choir 708
Lausanne Vocal Ensemble 877
(La) Lauzeta, Children Choir of Toulouse 172
Lavender, John *pf* 415, 416
Lavilla, Felix *pf* 1349
Lavoisier, Annie *hp* 462
Lawrence-King, Andrew *hp* 385, 390, 1048, 1258, 1259, 1261, 1264, 1279, 1283, 1284
— *hpd* 1048
— *org* 1048, 1279, 1283
Lawson, Peter *pf* 5
Layton, Stephen *cond* 227, 419, 430, 722, 724, 831, 832, 856, 884, 885, 886, 911, 1015, 1016, 1139, 1214
Lazarev, Alexander *cond* 617, 915
Lazareva, Tatyana *pf* 746
Lazic, Dejan *pf* 277, 1195
Le Blanc, Suzie *sop* 914, 1292
Le Brocq, Mark *ten* 440
Le Monnier, David *ten* 442
Le Roux, François *bar* 331, 725, 840
Le Sage, Eric *pf* 1173
Lea, Tobias *va* 878
Lea-Cox, Graham *cond* 192
Leaper, Adrian *cond* 419, 532, 698, 963, 1093
Leblanc, Suzie *sop* 255, 451
Lebrun, Eric *org* 9
Lederlin, Antoine *vc* 429
Ledger, Philip *cond* 363, 1347
— *org* 1347
— *pf* 720
Lee, Yoon K *cond* 26
Leeds Festival Chorus 495
Leeds Philharmonic Chorus 964
Leeson-Williams, Nigel *bbar* 963

Leeuw, Reinbert de *cond* 18, 168, 557
— *pf* 843
Lefebvre, Philippe *org* 733
Lehmann, Lilli *sop* 1238
Lehmann, Lotte *sop* 1233, 1250
Lehner, Karl Heinz *bass* 878
Lehtinen, Markus *cond* 789
Lehtipuu, Topi *ten* 480, 484, 789
Lehto, Petri *ten* 949
Leider, Frida *sop* 1128
Leiferkus, Sergei *bar* 780, 781
Leighton Smith, Laurence *cond* 697
Leipzig Gewandhaus Orchestra 977, 1141, 1309
Leipzig Quartet 114, 205, 206, 867
Leipzig Radio Chorus 627, 1124, 1126, 1143
Leipzig Symphony Orchestra 1187
Leisner, Emmi *cont* 1128
Leister, Karl *cl* 205, 800
Leith Hill Festival Singers 962
Leitner, Franz *ten* 878
Leitner, Ferdinand *cond* 461
Lejeune, Matthieu *vc* 429
Leleux, François *ob* 734
Lemaire, Bertrand *cond* 525
Lemalu, Jonathan *bass* 446
Lemieux, Marie-Nicole *cont* 216
Lemnitz, Tiana *sop* 1152
Lemper, Ute *sop* 1146
Lenaerts, Thibaut *ctnr* 269
Lenehan, John *pf* 177, 515, 1172, 1188
Leningrad Philharmonic Orchestra 927, 1025, 1159
Leonard, Sarah *sop* 1054
Leonhardt, Gustav *hpd* 1037, 1261
Leonhardt, Carl *cond* 1214
Leonskaja, Elisabeth *pf* 671, 931, 9341
Leopold String Trio 669
Leopold Trio 118, 119
Lepore, Carlo *bass* 966
Leppard, Raymond *cond* 91, 658, 1310
(Les) Eléments 172, 1114
(Les) Veilleurs de Nuit 165
Lesne, Gérard *alto* 179, 259, 270, 966, 1110, 1285
Lessing, Kolja *vn* 13
Lester, Richard *vc* 181, 209
Lesueur, Max *va* 667
Letzbor, Gunar *vn* 163
Leusink, Pieter Jan *cond* 56
Leveaux, Ursula *bn* 734, 839
Levi, Erik *pf* 1176
Levi, Yoel *cond* 691, 826
Levine, James *pf* 866, 1211
Levine, Joanna *viol* 765
Levine, James *cond* 99, 140, 329, 395, 609, 758, 774, 1079, 1080, 1083, 1134, 1221, 1251, 1334, 1335
Levionnois, Eric *vc* 634
Levy, Mark *viol* 1275
Lewis, Keith *ten* 107, 111
Lewis, Paul *pf* 566, 669
Lewis, Richard *ten* 151, 1067, 1255
Lewis, Anthony *cond* 769
Liceu Grand Theatre Symphony Orchestra 1336
Lidiard, Pamela *pf* 1217
Lidström, Mats *vc* 528
Lieberfeld, Dan *pf* 1241
Lieberson, Lorraine hunt *mez* 1294
Liège Philharmonic Orchestra 1049
Lifschitz, Konstantin *pf* 1176
Ligeti, Andras *cond* 563

Nuti, Giampaolo *pf* 856
Nyman, Michael *cond* 703
(Michael) Nyman Band 703
Oborin, Lev *pf* 121
Ochman, Wieslaw *ten* 248, 345
Ockenden, Rebecca *sop* 318
Ockert, Christian *db* 867
Octors, Georges-Elie *cond* 462
Oddone, Graciela *sop* 844
Odense Symphony Orchestra 393
O'Dette, Paul *chit/gtr* 1284
— *lte* 326, 327, 1262
Odinius, Lothar *ten* 1072
O'Donnell, James *cond* 428, 605, 717, 719, 1092
— *org* 227, 605, 1277
O'Duinn, Prionnsías *cond* 5, 622
O'Dwyer, Eamonn *treb* 765
Oelze, Christiane *sop* 560, 711, 1150, 1240
Offers, Maartje *mez* 1128
Ogawa, Noriko *pf* 309, 499, 1007
Ogden, Craig *gtr* 734, 1046, 1137, 1218
Ogdon, John *pf* 252, 562
Ogg, Jacques *hpd* 181
Oistrakh, David *vn* 104, 121, 196, 746, 1344
O'Keefe, Mark *tpt* 921
Oleg, Raphael *vn* 112
Oliver, Robert *bass* 988
Oliveri, Dino *cond* 1249
Ollila, Tuomas *cond* 235, 630, 947
Olmi, Paolo *cond* 1229
Olsen, Frode *bass* 1306
Olszewska, Maria *mez* 1128
O'Mara, Stephen *ten* 859
O'Neal, Christopher *ob* 560
Onofri, Enrico *vn* 1100, 1101, 1348
Oosten, Ben van *org* 332
Oostenrijk, Nienke *sop* 1090
Opera North Chorus 1139, 1251
Opera Restor'd 192
Opéra-Comique Choir & Orchestra 611
Opie, Alan *bar* 1061, 1062
Oppens, Ursula *pf* 265
Oramas, Carlos *gtr* 1093
Oramo, Sakari *cond* 299, 378, 423, 836, 951, 1093, 1114, 1141
Orazio, Francesco d' *vn* 856
Orchestra of the Age of Enlightenment 179, 450, 468, 628, 678, 679, 767, 841, 877, 1105, 1214, 1218, 1225, 1245, 1306
Orchestra of the Eighteenth Century 102, 468, 782
Orchestra of the Golden Age 1038
Orchestra of the Renaissance 648, 1115
Orchestre Révolutionnaire et Romantique 105, 130, 134, 147, 149, 152, 213, 897, 1069, 1298
Ord, Boris *cond* 1347
O'Reilly, Graham *cond* 440
Orfeón Donostiarra 368
Orgonasova, Luba *sop* 105, 817, 1069
Orlando Consort 330, 706, 1287, 1287, 1288
Orlov, Polikarp *bar* 1255
Ormandy, Eugene *cond* 100, 974
Oro, Martín *ctnr* 844
Orpheus Chamber Orchestra 650, 655, 656, 658, 660, 662
Orpheus Quartet 115
Orpheus Singers 183
Orsanic, Vlatka *sop* 1155

ORTF National Orchestra 838, 1349
ORTF Philharmonic Orchestra 1349
Ortiz, Cristina *pf* 838
Ortner, Erwin *cond* 878
Orton, Stephen *vc* 619, 651
Osborne, Steven *pf* 14, 567, 580, 631, 632
Osinska, Eva *pf* 277
Oslo Philharmonic Orchestra 807, 923, 1024, 1025, 1026
Oslo Wind Quintet 700
Osostowicz, Krysia *va/vn* 86, 828, 829, 840
Ossia 802
Ossonce, Jean-Yves *cond* 583, 584
Osten, Sigune von *sop* 724
Osterkorn, Natascha *pf* 1324
Östman, Arnold *cond* 400, 403, 1214
Ostrcil, Otakar *cond* 959
Ostrobothnian Chamber Orchestra 702, 937, 1055
Otaka, Tadaaki *cond* 1007
Otter, Anne Sofie von *mez/sop* 68, 105, 141, 216, 267, 400, 402, 426, 444, 456, 585, 590, 599, 795, 882, 907, 950, 1069, 11521237, 1238
Oue, Eiji *cond* 293
Outakoski, Niiles *vc* 702
Outram, Martin *va* 176, 219
Ovenden, Jeremy *ten* 644
Over, Simon *pf* 178
Owen, Charles *pf* 522
Owen, Thelma *hp* 1199
Owens, Shabda *elec/voc* 262
Oxford Bach Choir 614
Oxford Camerata 392, 706
Oxford Christ Church Cathedral Choir 348, 485, 640, 920
Oxford Girls' Choir 491
Oxford Schola Cantorum 547
Oxley, James *ten* 554
Ozawa, Seiji *cond* 140, 335, 369, 562, 773, 968, 1159, 1325
Paajanen, Mika *hn* 788
Paasikivi, Lilli *mez* 789, 948, 949, 950
Pacht, Nurit *vn* 1176
Pacini, Adolfo *bar* 1224
Padaut, Catherine *sop* 235
Paderewski, Ignace Jan *pf* 289
Padmore, Mark *ten* 62, 64, 67, 70, 130, 416, 446, 481, 482, 765, 766, 769, 770, 1238
Paëvatalu, Guido *bar* 701, 906
Pagano, Caio *pf* 1094
Page, Christopher *cond* 490, 1278, 1279
— *lte* 1278
Page, Neil *cond* 1214
(Les) Pages et les chantres de la Chapelle 575
Pahud, Emmanuel *fl* 532, 668, 839, 1036, 1173, 1176
Palacios, Isabel *dire* 1289
Palladian Ensemble 35, 1263
Palm, Siegfried *vc* 557
Palma, Susan *fl* 650
Palmer, Felicity *sop* 362, 364, 503, 522
Palmer, Gladys *cont* 1128
Palomares, Joaquín *vn* 637
Palombi, Antonello *ten* 753
Palumbo, Massimo *pf* 824
Palviainen, Eero *lte* 603
Pancík, Josef *cond* 349
Pandolfo, Paolo *vada* 602, 1264, 1281

Panenka, Jan *pf* 997
Panina, Antonina *mez* 1255
Panocha Quartet 346
Panula, Jorma *cond* 366
Panzarella, Anna Maria *sop* 674
Pape, René *bass* 1307
Papi, Gennaro *cond* 1241
Pappano, Antonio *cond* 612, 613, 743, 759, 760, 761, 1075, 1118, 1329
— *pf* 743, 759, 1214
Papunen, Margit *sop* 842
Parikian, Manoug *vn* 250
Paris, Orchestre de 151, 837, 1075, 1308, 1329, 1341
Paris, Orchestre de, Chamber Ensemble 14, 449, 1214, 1229
Paris, Orchestre de, Chorus 151
Paris Conservatoire Orchestra 736, 836, 1208, 1248, 1249
Paris Conservatoire Soloists 736
Paris, Maîtrise de, Children's Choir 1294
Paris Opéra Chorus & Orchestra 142, 736, 841, 1215, 1249, 1321
Paris Opéra-Bastille Chorus & Orchestra 841, 935, 1082
Paris Opéra-Comique Chorus & Orchestra 312, 708, 736
Parker, Patricia *mez* 994
Parker-Smith, Jane *org* 522
Parkin, Eric *pf* 78, 314, 418, 515, 615, 1134
Parkman, Stefan *cond* 12, 801, 976
(The) Parley of Instruments 20, 440, 764, 1246
Parodi, Giovanni Battista *bar* 1215
Parrott, Andrew *cond* 390, 443, 641, 766
Parry, David *cond* 323, 325, 413, 556, 609, 635, 712, 713, 756, 762, 764, 818, 985, 1221, 1230, 1235
Parry, Wilfrid *pf* 1174
Parsons, Brian *ten* 1071
Parsons, Geoffrey *pf* 629, 879, 1012, 1152, 1210
(Adrian) Partington Singers 1065
Partridge, Ian *ten* 94, 158, 769, 1057
Pasero, Tancredi *bass* 1256
Pashley, Anne *sop* 1067
Pasiecznik, Olga *sop* 577
Pasternack, Josef *cond* 1222, 1224, 1233, 1244, 1252
Pászthy, Júlia *sop* 64
Pásztory-Bartók, Ditta *pf* 88
Pataky, Koloman von *ten* 132
Patanè, Franco *cond* 1320
Paton, Iain *ten* 770
Patras, Karel *hp* 304
Patti, Adelina *sop* 1238
Patzak, Julius *ten* 591, 889, 1349
Pauk, György *vn* 86
Paul, Reginald *pf* 1249
Paulik, Anton *cond* 1232
Pavarotti, Luciano *ten* 1068, 1249, 1325
Pavlovski, Nina *sop* 546
Pavlutskaya, Natalia *vc* 428
Pay, Antony *bscl* 1225
Payne, Sally Bruce *mez* 483
Pays de Loire, Maîtrise des 525, 527
Pazmany, Tibor *org* 540
Pearce, Colman *cond* 963
Pearlman, Martin *cond* 33, 404
Pears, Peter *spkr* 228, 1136
— *ten* 67, 71, 215, 222, 223, 225, 226, 228, 230, 1136
Pearson, Justin *vc* 137
Pecková, Dagmar *mez* 350

Rosekrans, Charles *cond* 1255
Rosen, Charles *pf* 1144
Rosen, Max *vn* 1241
Rosenberger, Carol *pf* 459
Rosenfeld, Jayn *fl* 298
Rosenthal, Manuel *cond* 709
Roskilde Cathedral Boys' Choir & Congregation 738
Rössel-Majdan, Hilde *mez* 105
Rossi, Cristiano *vn* 1102
Rössl-Majdan, Hilde *mez* 248, 589
Rost, Andrea *sop* 585
Rostropovich, Mstislav *cond* 221, 399, 742, 750, 922, 925, 929, 935, 1324
— *pf* 1345
— *vc* 104, 209, 222, 224, 337, 1022, 1159, 1345
Rosvaenge, Helge *ten* 1070, 1152
Roth, Detlef *bar* 107
Rothbauer, Martina *vada* 1264
Rothman, George *cond* 830
Rothwell, Evelyn *ob* 1338
Rotterdam Chamber Orchestra 811
Rotterdam Philharmonic Orchestra 748
Rousset, Christophe *cond* 451, 575, 605, 684, 781, 1213, 1214
— *hpd* 783
Rowicki, Witold *cond* 741
Rowland-Jones, Simon *va* 346
Royal Aarhus Academy of Music Symphony Orchestra 23
Royal Academy of Music Chamber Ensemble 169
Royal Albert Hall Orchestra 355, 360
Royal Ballet Sinfonia 5, 158, 616, 999
Royal Consort 255
Royal Danish Opera Choir 831
Royal Danish Orchestra 831
Royal Liverpool Philharmonic Orchestra 107, 218, 291, 313, 376, 506, 703, 952, 999, 1030, 1056, 1167
Royal Liverpool Philharmonic Choir 1056
Royal Military School of Music Band, Kneller Hall 1074
Royal Northern College of Music Wind Orchestra 415
Royal Opera House Chorus, Covent Garden 135, 223, 233, 234, 313, 323, 756, 761, 762, 1064, 1074, 1080, 1087, 1129, 1130, 1223, 1249, 1250, 1296, 1325, 1332
Royal Opera House Orchestra, Covent Garden 1, 135, 154, 175, 223, 233, 234, 323, 490, 524, 613, 756, 761, 762, 1064, 1075, 1080, 1087, 1118, 1223, 1248, 1249, 1250, 1251, 1296, 1325, 1332
Royal Philharmonic Chorus 151
Royal Philharmonic Concert Orchestra 1223
Royal Philharmonic Orchestra 75, 149, 150, 151, 158, 171, 196, 203, 252, 264, 276, 314, 315, 318, 353, 426, 635, 804, 820, 839, 862, 864, 928, 941, 952, 1026, 1056, 1079, 1135, 1158, 1163, 1164, 1248, 1255, 1341
Royal Scottish National Orchestra 77, 79, 90, 91, 175, 240, 241, 245, 314, 342, 376, 501, 534, 699, 743, 747, 787, 796, 922, 924, 1053
Royal Scottish Orchestra Chorus 747
Royal Stockholm Philharmonic Choir 12

Royal Stockholm Philharmonic Orchestra 203, 930, 1242
Royal Swedish Opera Orchestra 143
Royal Welsh College of Music & Drama Chamber Choir 352
Rozario, Patricia *sop* 503, 885, 886, 1014, 1015, 1016, 1017, 1327
Rozhdestvensky, Gennady *cond* 509, 546, 547, 701, 930, 1013, 1019, 1028, 1035, 1159, 1344
RTBF Symphony Orchestra 926
RTE Concert Orchestra 5
RTE Philharmonic Choir 963
RTE Sinfonietta 158, 622
Rubens, Sibylla *sop* 58, 72, 73
Rubinsky, Sonia *pf* 1063, 1095
Rubinstein, Artur *pf* 276, 280, 283, 284, 285, 288, 289
Rudner, Ola *cond* 830
Rudy, Mikhail *pf* 928, 1174
Ruhrseitz, Kurt *pf* 1242
Rumsey, Shirley *lte* 1278
Rundel, Peter *cond* 803, 1051
Rundell, Clark *cond* 415
Rupp, Franz *pf* 541
Russell, David *gtr* 810
Russell, Lucy *vn* 26
Russell, Lynda *sop* 604
Russell Davies, Dennis *cond* 261, 396, 397, 505, 529, 1052, 1337
Russian National Orchestra 533, 650, 777, 1022, 1024, 1026, 1027, 1028
Russian Philharmonic Orchestra 238
Russian State Symphonic Cappella 186, 399
Russian State Symphony Orchestra 399, 934, 1011, 1027
Russill, Patrick *org* 257, 259
Ruth, Peter *harc* 183
Rutherford, Christian *hn* 1036
Rutherford, James *bbar* 373
Rutter, John *cond* 139, 372, 832, 1198, 1199
Ruud, Ole Kristian *cond* 824, 1053
Ruzicka, Peter *cond* 489
Rydén, Susanne *sop* 844
Rydl, Kurt *bass* 724
Rysanek, Leonie *sop* 248
Saarbrücken Radio Symphony Orchestra 247, 727
Saarenpää, Leena *pf* 949
Saarikettu, Kaija *vn* 702
Sabajno, Carlo *cond* 1224
Sabata, Victor de *cond* 1081, 1215
Sabbatini, Giuseppe *ten* 151, 817
Sacher, Paul *cond* 1161
Sachs, Joel *cond/pf/zrb* 298
Sadler's Wells Opera Chorus 1255
Sadler's Wells Orchestra 1000
Sado, Yutaka *cond* 1234
Sagasser, Robert *vada* 1264
St Anthony Singers 769
St Christopher Chamber Orchestra 616
St Clement Danes School Choir 711
St George's Chapel Choir, Windsor Castle 720
St John, Scott *vn* 715
St John's College Choir, Cambridge 146, 223, 228, 334, 509, 554, 829, 964, 1015, 1138
St John's Smith Square Orchestra 411
St Louis Symphony Orchestra 292, 1149
St Luke's Chorus 4
St Luke's Orchestra 1, 4, 79, 1228

St Paul's Cathedral Choir 152, 225, 440, 503, 1061, 1203, 1204, 1327
St Paul's Cathedral Orchestra 77
Saint Paul Chamber Orchestra 77
St Petersburg Chamber Choir 780
St Petersburg Chamber Ensemble 636
St Petersburg Kirov Orchestra 992
St Thomas Church, Fifth Avenue, Choir 1207
St Willibrord & Pius X Children's Choir 588
Sainte-Cécile Academie 440
Sakari, Petri *cond* 12, 943, 944, 945
Saks, Gidon *bass* 456
Saksala, Janne *db* 839
Sakurada, Makoto *ten* 59, 60, 62, 70
Salaman, Clare *vn* 255
Salmon, Jane *vc* 828
Salmon, Philip *ten* 509, 1061
Salo, Per *org* 522, 546
Salomaa, Petteri *bar/bass* 107, 770, 789, 929
Salonen, Esa-Pekka *cond* 3, 560, 697, 833, 937
Salpeter, Max *vn* 1174
Salzburg Chamber Philharmonic Orchestra 26
Salzburg Festival Chamber Choir 1089
Salzburg Mozarteum Camerata Academica 660, 661
Samaltanos, Nikolaos *pf* 956
Sammarco, Mario *bar* 1234
Sammons, Albert *vn* 355, 514
Sampson, Carolyn *sop* 64, 441, 488, 1109
San Francisco Girl's Chorus 517, 991
San Francisco Opera Ballet 1309
San Francisco Opera Chorus & Orchestra 739, 1236, 1309, 1317, 1318
San Francisco Symphony Chorus 517, 991
San Francisco Symphony Orchestra 293, 517, 593, 697, 699, 772, 991, 1187
San Sebastian People's Choral Society 1298
Sánchez, Miguel *voc* 1268
Sanderling, Kurt *cond* 197, 598
Sanderling, Michael *vc* 892
Sandmann, Marcus *bass* 72
Santa Cecilia Academy Chorus & Orchestra 756, 1251
Santana, Lee *chit/gtr/lte* 1264
Santi, Nello *cond* 1249, 1322
Santini, Gabriele *cond* 760, 1085
Santley, Charles *bar* 1238
Saram, Rohan de *vc* 319
Saraste, Jukka-Pekka *cond* 335, 583, 698, 699, 833, 950
Sarfaty, Regina *cont* 988
Sargent, Malcolm *cond* 196, 355, 362, 445, 999, 1000, 1001, 1158, 1162, 1255, 1350
Saroglou, Dimitris *pf* 429
Sarragosse, Jean-Claude *bass* 268
Sauer, Emil von *pf* 289
Saunders, Antony *pf* 79
Savall, Arianna *dhp* 1265
Savall, Jordi *cond* 167, 433, 574, 603, 1260, 1271
— *dire* 108, 1282
— *vada* 39, 509, 603, 1219, 1260, 1265, 1280, 1281
Savchuck, Yevhen *cond* 780
Savitzky, Leonid *bass* 1229

Singphoniker 1291
Sinopoli, Giuseppe *cond* 244, 349, 690, 863, 977, 985, 1129, 1155, 1254
Sirenko, Vladimir *cond* 951
Sitkovetsky, Dimitry *cond* 159
— *vn* 1002
Sivelöv, Niklas *pf* 366
(The) Sixteen 254, 736, 769, 920, 1017, 1018, 1292
Sjöberg, Gitta-Maria *sop* 547
Sjøgren, Kim *vn* 697
Skampa Quartet 1303
Skidmore, Jeffrey *cond* 724, 1111, 1274
Skovhus, Bo *bar* 701
Skrowaczewski, Stanislaw *cond* 247
Slaars, Laurent *bar* 318, 447
Slatford, Rodney *db* 1074
Slatkin, Felix *cond* 1159
Slatkin, Leonard *cond* 80, 183, 292, 1149, 1159
Slattery, Michael *ten* 844
Slobodyanik, Alex *pf* 279
Slovak Folk Ensemble Chorus 82
Slovak Philharmonic Chorus 528, 694, 757, 1314
Slovak Philharmonic Male Chorus 532
Slovak Radio Symphony Orchestra 1, 528, 804
Slovak State Philharmonic Orchestra, Kosice 1027
Sluchin, Benny *tbn* 145
Slutsky, Boris *pf* 901
Smart, Alison *sop* 462
Smetana Quartet 521
Smirnov, Dmitri *ten* 1255
Smirnov, Yuri *hpd/pf/prpf* 851
Smissen, Robert *va* 619, 651
Smith, Angus *ten* 446, 447
Smith, Brinton *vc* 371
Smith, Brooks *pf* 1162
Smith, Carol *mez* 611
Smith, Craig *cond* 65
Smith, Jennifer *sop* 374, 441, 992
Smith, Kevin *alto* 766
Smythe, Russell *bar* 635
Soames, Benjamin *spkr* 994
Sobinov, Leonid *ten* 1255
Sobotka, Iwona *sop* 1005
Sodero, Cesare *cond* 1083
Söderström, Elisabeth *sop* 924, 946
Soffel, Doris *cont/mez* 242, 461
Sohn, Christine *vn* 799
Sokolov, Grigory *pf* 286
Sokolova, Liubov *mez* 748, 934
Sol, Tom *bass* 71
Sólbergsson, Björn Steinar *org* 553
(Les) Solistes Romands 32
(I) Solisti Veneti 822
Sollek-Avella, Kirsten *alto* 62
Söllscher, Göran *gtr* 866, 1006
Solomon *pf* 124, 126, 175, 211, 289, 654
Solomon, Ashley *fl* 26, 38
Solti, Georg *cond* 82, 83, 184, 513, 586, 595, 864, 972, 982, 985, 1044, 1070, 1087, 1124, 1125, 1220, 1251, 1336
Sonatori de la Gioiosa Marca 1213
Sonnentheil, Jürgen *cond* 1154
Sonnerie 165, 668, 1106
Sonntag, Ulrike *sop* 494
Soriano, Gonzalo *pf* 368, 1208
Soroka, Solomia *vn* 607
Sorrel Quartet 224
Sotgiù, Antonia *voc* 818

Sotin, Hans *bass* 588, 595
Souquet, Marie-Bénénedicte *sop* 156
Soustrot, Marc *cond* 725
South German Radio Chorus 1323
South West German Chamber Orchestra 1037
South West German Radio Symphony Orchestra 198, 241, 265, 461, 497, 543, 1155, 1179
Southern Philharmonic Orchestra 1350
Southern Voices 316
Souzay, Gérard *bar* 1248
Spadoni, Giocomo *cond* 1234
Spägele, Mona *sop* 72
Spagnoli, Pietro *bar* 642
Spalding, Albert *vn* 1236
Spang-Hanssen, Ulrik *org* 23
Spanish National Orchestra 368
Spanish National Youth Orchestra 366
Spanjaard, Ed *cond* 319
Spányi, Miklós *fp/hpd* 25
Sparf, Nils-Erik *va/vn* 216, 267, 948
Speculum Musicae 830
Speiser, Elisabeth *sop* 605
Spence, Patricia *mez* 635
Spence, Toby *ten* 177, 498, 885, 1340
Spencer, Robert *lte* 1210
Spering, Andreas *cond* 486
Spicer, Paul *cond* 227, 378, 503, 555, 1046, 1140
Spicer, Susanna *sop* 484
Spinosi, Jean-Christophe *cond* 1114
Spogis, Raimonds *bass* 270
Spoleto Festival Choir & Orchestra 629
Spoliansky, Mischa *pf* 1250
Spooner, Joseph *vc* 250
Springuel, France *va* 529, 721
Spurr, Phyllis *pf* 1350
Staatskapelle Dresden 150, 197, 244, 896, 974, 976, 977, 980, 1124, 1126, 1143, 1341
Stabile, Mariano *bar* 1256
Stabrawa, Daniel *vn* 32
Stade, Frederica von *mez* 264, 585, 590
Stader, Maria *sop* 248, 682
Stadlmair, Hans *cond* 1161
Stafford, Ashley *alto* 440
Staier, Andreas *hpd* 1191
— *pf/fp* 206, 290, 376, 466, 622, 655, 871, 874, 878, 883, 890
Stam, Caroline *sop* 72
Standage, Simon *cond* 433, 449, 549, 1037, 1105
— *vn* 11, 33, 433, 436, 549, 1036
Staples, Andrew *ten* 302
Starker, János *vc* 338, 505
Starobin, David *cond* 830
Statham, Heathcote *org* 1196
Stavanger Symphony Orchestra 1053
Steele-Perkins, Crispian *tpt* 68, 554
Steen, Jac van *cond* 353, 354
Steen-Nøkleberg, Einar *pf* 424, 425
Stefanelli, Massimiliano *cond* 1328
Stefano, Giuseppe di *ten* 1249
Stefanowicz, Artur *alto* 641
Steffl, Martina *mez* 878
Stein, Horst *cond* 946
Steinberg, Mark *vn* 298
Steinberg, Pinchas *cond* 1254
Steinberg, William *cond* 103, 586
Stene, Randi *mez* 522, 976
Stenz, Markus *cond* 6, 408, 1308
Stepán, Pavel *pf* 521, 997

Stepanovich, Dmitri *bass* 748
Stephen, Pamela Helen *mez* 130, 227, 373, 481, 482, 964
Stern, Eric *cond/pf* 1253
Stern, Isaac *vn* 100, 204, 207, 668, 865, 1144
Sternberg, Jonathan *cond* 1179
Stiedry, Fritz *cond* 1350
Stifelman, Leslie *pf* 1253
Stignani, Ebe *mez* 731
Stilgoe, Richard *spkr* 1136
Sting *spkr* 743, 746
Stirling, Stephen *hn* 209, 963
Stokowski, Leopold *cond* 586, 1029, 1341
Stoll, George *cond/pf* 1234
Stoltzman, Richard *cl* 697
Stolze, Gerhard *ten* 710
Stone, Frederick *pf* 1350
Stone, William *bar* 494
Storey, Martin *vc* 93
Storgårds, John *cond/vn* 1055
Stott, Kathryn *pf* 369, 371, 703, 730, 1135
Stötzel, Ulrich *cond* 1041
Stoyanova, Krassimira *sop* 817
Straka, Peter *ten* 242
Strasbourg Philharmonic Orchestra 1316
Stratas, Teresa *sop* 1146
Strauss, Richard *cond* 1341
Stravinsky, Igor *cond* 988, 989, 1338
Streit, Kurt *ten* 675
Strijk, Marjon *sop* 56
Stringer, Mark *cond* 187
Strosser, Emmanuel *pf* 734, 736
Stryncl, Marek *cond* 1155
Stubbs, Stephen *cond/lte* 38, 451
Studer, Cheryl *sop* 585, 977, 1068
Studt, Richard *cond* 25
Sturrock, Kathron *pf* 177
Stuttgart Bach Collegium 73, 628
Stuttgart Chamber Orchestra 396
Stuttgart Choristers 1
Stuttgart Gächinger Kantorei 569, 628
Stuttgart Philharmonic Orchestra 1341
Stuttgart Radio Symphony Orchestra 184, 204, 397, 537, 538, 569, 1001, 1300, 1323, 1340
Stuttgart State Opera Chorus & Orchestra 1320, 1338
Stuttgart Vocal Ensemble 543
Stutzmann, Nathalie *cont* 674, 1110
Suart, Richard *bass* 769
Sudbin, Yevgeny *pf* 848
Suddaby, Elsie *sop* 315, 1128, 1249
Sugawara, Yukiko *pf* 543
Suisse Romande Orchestra 153, 184, 367, 504, 605, 708, 737, 946, 974, 1218, 1233, 1249, 1251
Suisse Romande Radio Chorus 708
Suk, Josef *vn* 340, 622, 997
Suk Quartet 997
Suk Trio 997
Sulzen, Donald *pf* 815
Summereder, Roman *org* 913
Summerhayes, Adam *va/vn* 250
Summerhayes, Catherine *pf* 250
Summerly, Jeremy *cond* 392, 547, 706
Summers, Hilary *cont* 190, 488, 1109
Summers, Jonathan *bar* 1057, 1220
Sumsion, Herbert *org* 1196
Suovanen, Gabriel *bar* 583
Susskind, Walter *cond* 338, 1247
Süssman, Gunilla *pf* 1053

Tuckwell, Barry *hn* 223, 534, 816
Tuma, Jaroslav *org* 1303
Tunkkari, Reijo *vn* 702
Tunnicliffe, Richard *vada* 166
— *vc* 1107
Tureck, Rosalyn *pf* 43
Turin RAI Chorus & Orchestra 733
Türk, Gerd *ten* 58, 59, 60, 61, 62, 70, 72, 73, 263, 1295
Turku Philharmonic Orchestra 366
Turner, John *rec* 797, 1217
Tusa, Andrew *ten* 766
Twentieth Century Classics Ensemble 856
Twentieth Century Consort 614
Tyson, Robin *alto* 62, 259
Uchida, Mitsuko *pf* 307, 658, 671, 855, 872, 873, 875
Uehara, Ayako *pf* 1032
Ukraine National Symphony Orchestra 7, 80, 690, 731, 951
Ulanowsky, Paul *pf* 1233
Ulivieri, Nicola *bass* 1220
Ullén, Fredrik *pf* 1192
Ullmann, Marcus *ten* 73
Ulster Orchestra 159, 637, 796
Underwood, Giles *bass* 407, 485, 1327
Ungureanu, Mihai *pf* 728
Unwin, Nicholas *pf* 1045
Uppingham School Choir 1214
Upshaw, Dawn *sop* 3, 79, 264, 408, 833, 857, 1253, 1294, 1306
Urano, Chiyuki *bar/bass* 61, 70, 1295
Uria-Monzon, Béatrice *mez* 153
Urmana, Violeta *mez* 599, 1118
USSR State Symphony Orchestra 337, 1159
Vainstein, Dina *pf* 1170
Vajda, József *bn* 112
Valade, Pierre-André *cond* 168
Valdés, Maximiano *cond* 809, 811
Válek, Jiří *fl* 997
Válek, Vladimír *cond* 891
Välimäki, Aki *tpt* 788
Valo, Jari *vn* 937
Van Bockstal, Piet *ob* 462
Van Bos, Coenraad *pf* 1152, 1242
Van Dam, George *vn* 462
Van Dam, José *bbar* 129, 152, 1104
Van der Gucht, Jan *ten* 313
Van Doeselaar, Leo *org* 493
Van Evera, Emily *sop* 443, 766
Van Reisen, Margriet *cont* 1090
Van Veldhoven, Jos *cond* 72
Vanbrugh Quartet 181, 294, 320, 617, 963, 1016
Vancouver Festival Orchestra 1341
Vancouver Symphony Orchestra 896, 1338
Vänskä, Osmo *cond* 8, 109, 842, 936, 939, 941, 942, 944, 945, 948, 949, 950
Varady, Julia *sop* 753, 979, 1033, 1072, 1118, 1254
Varcoe, Stephen *bar/bass* 68, 130, 227, 372, 374, 416, 430, 441, 444, 481, 482, 512, 856, 885, 914, 964, 965
Varcol, Liviu *ob* 492
Varèse, Edgard *elec* 1054
Varga, Gilbert *cond* 544
Varsi, Dinorah *pf* 212
Varsov Chamber Choir 738
Vartolo, Sergio *hpd/org* 382
Vasari Singers 333
Vassilakis, Dimitri *pf* 188
Vaughan, Elizabeth *mez* 985
Vaughan, Johnny *org* 146

Vauquet, André *va* 974
Väyrynen, Mika *acco* 730
Végh, Sándor *cond* 660, 661
Végh Quartet 116
Vele, Ludek *bass* 349
Vellard, Dominique *cond* 167
Vellinger Quartet 361
(La) Venexiana 390, 514, 604, 642, 643
Vengerov, Maxim *vn* 221, 339, 399, 742, 922, 1171, 1193
Venice Baroque Orchestra 1099, 1102
Venice La Fenice Chorus & Orchestra 818
Verbruggen, Marion *fl/rec* 438
Vermillion, Iris *mez* 569, 906
Vernizzi, Fulvio *cond* 0
Verona Arena Chorus & Orchestra 1319
Versalle, Richard *ten* 595
Verschuren, Wouter *bn* 1097
Verzier, Alix *vc* 129
Vesna Children's Choir 748
Vester, Frans *fl* 1037
Viala, Jean-Luc *ten* 152
Victor Orchestra 1216, 1233, 1234, 1242, 1244, 1252
Victoria State Orchestra 546, 978
Vieaux, Jason *gtr* 1193
Vienna Boys' Choir 69, 143, 513, 585, 590, 694, 877, 982, 1314
Vienna Chamber Orchestra 678, 1030, 1179
Vienna Chorus 877
Vienna Concentus Musicus 432, 644, 672, 675, 676, 1348
Vienna Concert-Verein 878
Vienna Octet 111, 865
Vienna Philharmonic Orchestra 97, 100, 103, 109, 110, 141, 143, 200, 202, 203, 241, 243, 244, 245, 246, 247, 248, 267, 341, 513, 523, 524, 552, 585, 590, 591, 593, 596, 597, 599, 658, 675, 685, 690, 757, 762, 817, 864, 926, 967, 968, 972, 978, 982, 984, 985, 986, 987, 1022, 1089, 1117, 1118, 1121, 1124, 1125, 1144, 1155, 1214, 1232, 1237, 1247, 1251, 1308, 1325, 1336, 1340, 1341, 1350
Vienna Piano Trio 477, 933
Vienna Pro Musica Orchestra 1179
Vienna Radio Symphony Orchestra 396, 397, 529, 1052, 1147, 1148, 1337
Vienna Singverein 105, 248, 590, 595, 1104
Vienna State Opera Chorus 143, 523, 524, 585, 591, 595, 685, 694, 757, 762, 982, 984, 985, 987, 1081, 1089, 1121, 1125, 1144, 1237, 1297, 1314, 1326, 1333
Vienna State Opera Concert Choir 675, 817, 1308, 1337
Vienna State Opera Orchestra 694, 1081, 1128, 1179, 1297, 1314, 1326, 1333
Vienna Symphony Orchestra 100, 240, 677, 970, 987, 1019
Vienna Volksoper Orchestra 968, 1179, 1232
Vienna Wind Soloists 865
Vienna Youth Choir 595
Vignoles, Roger *pf* 129, 217, 350, 426, 430, 599, 908, 978, 1140, 1151, 1238
Viitasalo, Marita *pf* 908
Vilaprinyó, Jordi *pf* 493
Viljakainen, Raili *sop* 950
Villars, Jon *ten* 595

Villazón, Rolando *ten* 611, 1254
Viñas, Francisco *ten* 1238
Vinikour, Jory *hpd* 1238
Viotti, Marcello *cond* 753, 1254
Virtanen, Otto *bn* 788
(I) Virtuosi Italiani 824
Vishnevskaya, Galina *sop* 223, 226, 1345
Visse, Dominique *cond* 249, 1274
Vlach Quartet 347
Vlachova, Jana *vn* 539
Vladar, Wolfgang *hn* 878
Vogler Quartet 626, 800
Voigt, Deborah *sop* 1118, 1155
(Les) Voix Humaines 834, 1292
Volmer, Arvo *cond* 1050
Volodos, Arcadi *pf* 774, 872, 1194
Voorhees, Donald *cond* 538
Vorster, Len *pf* 158
Votto, Antonino *cond* 325, 732, 733, 1074, 1249
Vronsky, Vitya *pf* 1057
Vybíralová, Ludmila *vn* 997
Vyvyan, Jennifer *sop* 223
Waart, Edo de *cond* 4, 32, 353, 772, 918, 1187, 1352
Wagemans, Michel *pf* 637
Wagner, Jan *cond* 393
Wakamatsu, Natsumi *vn* 32
Wakeford, Lucy *hp* 75, 650
Walker, Ella *pf* 1255
Walker, Kim *bn* 74
Walker, Nellie *cont* 1128
Walker, Norman *bass* 362, 445, 1255
Walker, Sarah *mez* 107, 314, 1046, 1062
Walker, Timothy *gtr* 300
Wallace, John *tpt* 169, 734, 1051
Wallace Collection 832, 1139, 1201
Wallenstein, Alfred *cond* 338, 538
Wallfisch, Elizabeth *vn* 295, 1107
Wallfisch, Raphael *vc* 184, 313, 376, 380, 1030
Wallin, Ulf *vn* 800
Walmsley-Clark, Penelope *sop* 137, 462
Walt, Deon van der *ten* 676, 906
Walter, Bruno *cond* 202, 586, 591, 597, 675, 1079, 1341, 1350
— *pf* 1350
Walton, Bernard *cl* 112
Walton, Sam *perc* 169
Walton, William *cond* 1135, 1138
Wand, Günter *cond* 107, 111, 242, 246, 247
Wandsworth School Boys' Choir 71, 150, 151, 225, 230, 232, 590, 763, 1249
Wang, Jian *vc* 195, 209, 670, 894
Ward, David *bass* 1067
Ward, Jeremy *bn* 28
Ward, Nicholas *cond* 469, 496, 663, 664, 810, 994, 1037
Warren-Green, Christopher *vn* 535
Warsaw Boys' Choir 725
Warsaw National Philharmonic Chorus 724
Warsaw National Philharmonic Orchestra 725, 741
Warsaw Philharmonic Choir 725
Warsaw Philharmonic Orchestra 697
Wass, Ashley *pf* 94
Waterman, David *vc* 370
Waters, Rodney *pf* 517
Waters, Stephen *cl* 651
Waters, Susannah *sop* 770
Watkin, David *vc* 385, 1105
Watkin, Toby *ten* 407